Where Countries Come to Play

FENN

M&S

Conceived and Edited by Andrew Podnieks
Contributing Editor: Birger Nordmark

Supervising Editor: Szymon Szemberg
Editorial Staff: Martin Merk, Adam Steiss
Editorial Contributors: Kristina Koch, Luzia Baldauf, Nicole Bosshardt, Dave Fitzpatrick, Konstantin Komissarov, Stephanie Kallai

Design by Kathryn Zante

First Edition 2010

Published by Fenn/McClelland & Stewart, a division of Random House of Canada Limited, for the IIHF

International Ice Hockey Federation
Brandschenkestrasse 50
Postfach, 8027 Zurich
Switzerland

Main telephone +41.44.562 22 00
www.IIHF.com
e-mail: office@iihf.com or media@iihf.com



Library and Archives Canada Cataloguing in Publication

IIHF 2013 guide and record book / International Ice Hockey Federation

ISBN 978-0-7710-4574-5

1. International Ice Hockey Federation. 2. International Ice Hockey Federation – Statistics. 3. Hockey – Statistics. 4. Hockey – Records. I. International Ice Hockey Federation

GV847.I54 2013 796.962'66 C2012-900976-8

Published simultaneously in the United States of America by
Fenn/McClelland & Stewart, a division of Random House of Canada Limited
P.O. Box 1030, Plattsburgh, New York 12901

Library of Congress Control Number: 2012932355

Printed and bound in the United States of America

Fenn/McClelland & Stewart,
a division of Random House of Canada Limited
One Toronto Street
Toronto, Ontario
M5C 2V6
www.mcclelland.com

1 2 3 4 5 16 15 14 13 12

Special Thanks to: Todd Anderson, Peter Andersson, Lucas Aykroyd, Pavel Barta, Stoian Batchvarov, Reto Bertolotti, Miragh Bitove, Carina Bitzer, Darren Boyko, Marc Branchu, Andre Brin, Craig Cameron, Craig Campbell, Jan Casteels, Michael Chambers, Marek Chlupaty, Sandra Dombrowski, Andy Ecker, Jacqueline Egloff, Benny Ercolani, Balint Fekti, Anders Feltenmark, Dave Fischer, Michael Fischer, Patrick Francheterre, Thomas Freyer, Marius Gliga, Sergej Gontcharov, Emma Grace, Peter Graf, Alison Haas, Martin Harris, Pekka Hellsten, Patrick Houda, Pentti Isotalo, Jarmo Jalarvo, Steffen Karas, David Keon, Jr., Kristina Koch, Kristiina Koivuniemi, Konstantin Komissarov, Igor Kuperman, Francois Larochelle, Jason LaRose, Kathrin Lehman, Kimmo Leinonen, Constance Leshchenko, Joeri Loonen, Kelly Masse, Gord Miller, Stefan Mueller, Kevin Muench, Bob Nadin, Dorthe Nohr, Wilma Olijhoek, Dag Olsson, Risto Pakarinen, Steve Poirier, Phil Pritchard, Antonini Puma, Peter Regos, Jennifer Robins, Paul Romanuk, John Sanful, Dzmitry Sapun, Raimo Seppanen, Istvan Spiller, Harald Springfeld, Dr. Andrej Stare, Barbara Stecher, Monika Svaczynova, Toshi Takahashi, Sho Tomita, Martin Urban, Lasse Vanhanen, Janice Wasilew, Izak Westgate, Frank Wilson, Christian Yngve, Julie Young, Yaraslau Zauharodni

Every effort has been made to ensure the information in this book is as accurate and complete as possible. Please direct any comments about this publication to media@iihf.com.

# Contents

# SCHEDULES

## 2012-13 Events

### 2013 IIHF Ice Hockey World Championship, Men
### Stockholm (Sweden) & Helsinki (Finland), 3-19 May 2013

| Division | Venue | Dates |
|---|---|---|
| **Division I** Group A | Budapest (Hungary) | 14-20 April 2013 |

Participants: Italy, Kazakhstan, Hungary, Japan, Great Britain, Korea

| Division | Venue | Dates |
|---|---|---|
| **Division I** Group B | Donetsk (Ukraine) | 14-20 April 2013 |

Participants: Ukraine, Poland, Netherlands, Romania, Lithuania, Estonia

| Division | Venue | Dates |
|---|---|---|
| **Division II** Group A | Zagreb (Croatia) | 14-20 April 2013 |

Participants: Australia, Spain, Croatia, Iceland, Serbia, Belgium

| Division | Venue | Dates |
|---|---|---|
| **Division II** Group B | Izmit (Turkey) | 21-27 April 2013 |

Participants: New Zealand, China, Bulgaria, Mexico, Israel, Turkey

| Division | Venue | Dates |
|---|---|---|
| **Division III** | Cape Town (South Africa) | 15-21 April 2013 |

Participants: South Africa, DPR Korea, Luxembourg, Ireland, two qualifiers

| Division | Venue | Dates |
|---|---|---|
| **Division III** Qualification | Abu Dhabi (United Arab Emirates) | 14-17 October 2012 |

Participants: Greece, Mongolia, United Arab Emirates, Georgia

### 2013 IIHF Ice Hockey U20 World Championship
### Ufa (Russia), 26 December 2012 - 5 January 2013

| Division | Venue | Dates |
|---|---|---|
| **Division I** Group A | Amiens (France) | 9-15 December 2012 |

Participants: Denmark, Belarus, Norway, Slovenia, Austria, France

| Division | Venue | Dates |
|---|---|---|
| **Division I** Group B | Donetsk (Ukraine) | 10-16 December 2012 |

Participants: Great Britain, Kazakhstan, Italy, Poland, Croatia, Ukraine

| Division | Venue | Dates |
|---|---|---|
| **Division II** Group A | Brasov (Romania) | 9-15 December 2012 |

Participants: Japan, Lithuania, Hungary, Spain, Netherlands, Romania

| Division | Venue | Dates |
|---|---|---|
| **Division II** Group B | Novi Sad (Serbia) | 12-18 January 2013 |

Participants: Korea, Estonia, Serbia, Belgium, Australia, Iceland

| Division | Venue | Dates |
|---|---|---|
| **Division III** | Sofia (Bulgaria) | 14-20 January 2013 |

Participants: Mexico, China, New Zealand, Bulgaria, Turkey, United Arab Emirates

### 2013 IIHF Ice Hockey U18 World Championship
### Sochi (Russia), 18-28 April 2013

| Division | Venue | Dates |
|---|---|---|
| **Division I** Group A | Asiago (Italy) | 7-13 April 2013 |

Participants: Denmark, Norway, Italy, France, Slovenia, Belarus

| Division | Venue | Dates |
|---|---|---|
| **Division I** Group B | Tychy (Poland) | 14-20 April 2013 |

Participants: Japan, Kazakhstan, Austria, Ukraine, Poland, Korea

| Division | Venue | Dates |
|---|---|---|
| **Division II** Group A | Tallinn (Estonia) | 1-7 April 2013 |

Participants: Hungary, Romania, Lithuania, Great Britain, Croatia, Estonia

| Division | Venue | Dates |
|---|---|---|
| **Division II** Group B | Belgrade (Serbia) | 9-15 March 2013 |

Participants: Netherlands, Serbia, Spain, Iceland, Australia, Belgium

| Division | Venue | Dates |
|---|---|---|
| **Division III** Group A | Taipei City (Chinese Taipei) | 11-17 March 2013 |

Participants: China, New Zealand, Mexico, Bulgaria, Chinese Taipei

| Division | Venue | Dates |
|---|---|---|
| **Division III** Group B | Izmit (Turkey) | 6-9 February 2013 |

Participants: Turkey, South Africa, Israel, Ireland

### 2013 IIHF Ice Hockey Women's World Championship
### Ottawa (Canada), 2-9 April 2013

| Division | Venue | Dates |
|---|---|---|
| **Division I** Group A | Stavanger (Norway) | 7-13 April 2013 |

Participants: Slovakia, Norway, Japan, Austria, Latvia, Denmark

| Division | Venue | Dates |
|---|---|---|
| **Division I** Group B | Strasbourg (France) | 7-13 April 2013 |

Participants: Kazakhstan, China, France, Great Britain, Netherlands, DPR Korea

| Division | Venue | Dates |
|---|---|---|
| **Division II** Group A | Auckland (New Zealand) | 8-14 April 2013 |

Participants: Italy, Hungary, Australia, New Zealand, Slovenia, Poland

| Division | Venue | Dates |
|---|---|---|
| **Division II** Group B | Puigcerda (Spain) | March/April 2013 |

Participants: Croatia, Spain, Korea, Iceland, Belgium, South Africa

| Division | Venue | Dates |
|---|---|---|
| **Division II** Group B Qualification | Izmir (Turkey) | 9-12 December 2012 |

Participants: Bulgaria, Ireland, Turkey

### 2013 IIHF Ice Hockey U18 Women's World Championship
### Vierumaki region (Finland), 29 December 2012 - 5 January 2013

| Division | Venue | Dates |
|---|---|---|
| **Division I** | Romanshorn (Switzerland) | 2-8 January 2013 |

Participants: Switzerland, Austria, Japan, Norway + two qualifiers

| Division | Venue | Dates |
|---|---|---|
| **Division I** Qualification | Dumfries (Great Britain) | 27 October - 1 Nov 2012 |

Participants: Great Britain, Slovakia, China, Italy, France, Kazakhstan

### Olympic Qualification, Men, Sochi 2014

Participants: Nations ranked 1-9 according to the 2012 IIHF Men's World Ranking plus three qualifiers.

**SEEDING**
**Group A**: Russia (1), Slovakia (6), USA (7), Qualifier 3
**Group B**: Finland (2), Canada (5), Norway (8), Qualifier 2
**Group C**: Czech Republic (3), Sweden (4), Switzerland (9), Qualifier 1

**Final Olympic Qualification (3 tournaments, 7-10 February 2013)**
Nations ranked 10-18 plus the three winners from the Olympic Pre-Qualification.
**Group D** in Bietigheim-Bissingen, Germany: Germany (10), Austria (15), Italy (16), Qualifier 3
**Group E** in Riga, Latvia: Latvia (11), France (14), Kazakhstan (17), Qualifier 2
**Group F** in Vojens, Denmark: Denmark (12), Belarus (13), Slovenia (18), Qualifier 1

**Olympic Pre-Qualification (3 tournaments, 9-11 November 2012)**
Nations ranked 19-27 plus qualifiers from any preliminary qualification if required.
**Group G** in Budapest, Hungary: Hungary (19), Netherlands (24), Lithuania (25), Qualifier
**Group H** in Kyiv, Ukraine: Ukraine (20), Poland (23), Estonia (26), Spain (29)
**Group J** in Nikko, Japan: Great Britain (21), Japan (22), Romania (27), Korea (28)

**Olympic Preliminary Qualification (1 tournament, 17-19 September 2012)**
**Group K** in Zagreb, Croatia: Croatia (30), Serbia (31), Mexico (32), Israel (33)

### Olympic Qualification, Women, Sochi 2014

Participants: Nations ranked 1-6 according to the 2012 IIHF Women's World Ranking plus two qualifiers.

**SEEDING**
**Group A**: Canada (1), USA (2), Finland (3), Switzerland (4)
**Group B**: Sweden (5), Russia (6) + two qualifiers

**Final Olympic Qualification (2 tournaments, 7-10 February 2013)**
Nations ranked 7-12 plus the two winners from the Olympic Pre-Qualification.
**Group C** in Poprad, Slovakia: Slovakia (7), Norway (10), Japan (11), Qualifier 2
**Group D** in Weiden, Germany: Germany (8), Kazakhstan (9), Czech Republic (12), Qualifier 1

**Olympic Pre-Qualification (2 tournaments, 8-11 November 2012)**
Nations ranked 13-18 plus qualifiers from any preliminary qualification if required.
**Group E** in Shanghai, China: China (13), France (16), Great Britain (17), Qualifier 2
**Group F** in Valmiera, Latvia: Latvia (14), Austria (15), Italy (18), Qualifier 1

**Olympic Preliminary Qualification (2 tournaments)**
**Group G** in Barceona, Spain: Denmark (19), Croatia (22), Hungary (23), Spain (26).
12-14 October 2012
**Group H** in Jastrzebie-Zdroj, Poland: Slovenia (20), Netherlands (21), Korea (24), Poland (25).
27-30 September 2012

## European Women's Champions Cup

**First Round, October 2012**

**Group A**: Bolzano Eagles (ITA, host), HC Neuilly sur Marne (FRA), KHL Gric (CRO), Valladolid Panteras (ESP). Dates: 5-7 October.

**Group B**: Pantera Minsk (BLR, host), Aisulu Almaty (KAZ), SC Miercurea Ciuc (ROU), Milenyum Ankara (TUR). Dates: 19-21 October.

**Group C**: Vaļerenga Oslo (NOR), Laima Riga (LAT), Hvidovre (DEN), MODO Ornskoldsvik (SWE, host). Dates: 20-22 October.

**Group D**: Slavia Prague (CZE), Sabres Vienna (AUT, host), Polonia Bytom (POL), HK Poprad (SVK). Dates: 19-21 October.

**Second Round, 7-9 December 2012**

**Group E**: ZSC Lions Zurich (SUI, host), ESC Planegg (GER), Winner Group A, Winner Group C

**Group F**: Karpat Oulu (FIN, host), Tornado Moscow Region (RUS), Winner Group B, Winner Group D

**Final Tournament, 22-24 February 2013**

The top two teams of each second-round group advance to the final tournament.
Host to be determined.

## Continental Cup

**First Round, 28-30 September 2012**

**Group A** in Miercurea Ciuc, Romania: HSC Csikszereda (ROU), Vitez Belgrade (SRB), Baskent Yildizlari Ankara (TUR), Maccabi Metulla (ISR)

**Second Round, 19-21 October 2012:**

**Group B** in Landshut, Germany: Landshut Cannibals (GER), Belfast Giants (GBR), Eaters Geleen (NED), Winner Group A

**Group C** in Vaasa, Finland: Liepajas Metalurgs (LAT), Miskolc Polar Bears (HUN), Vaasan Sport (FIN), Beibarys Atyrau (KAZ)

**Third Round, 23-25 November 2012:**

**Group D** in Bolzano, Italy: Bolzano Foxes (ITA), Herning Blue Fox (DEN), Toros Neftekamsk (RUS), Winner Group B

**Group E** in Stavanger, Norway: Metallurg Zhlobin (BLR), Stavanger Oilers (NOR), KH Sanok (POL), Winner Group C

**Super Final, 11-13 January 2013:**

Group F in Donetsk, Ukraine: Rouen Dragons (FRA), Donbass Donetsk (UKR), Winner Group D, Winner Group E

# Assigned Tournaments

**OLYMPIC WINTER GAMES**

- 2014 RUSSIA, Sochi 7 – 23 February 2014
- 2018 KOREA, PyeongChang 9-25 February 2018

**YOUTH OLYMPIC WINTER GAMES**

- 2016 NORWAY, Lillehammer, 26 February – 6 March 2016

**WORLD CHAMPIONSHIP**

- 2014 BELARUS, Minsk 9 – 12 May 2014
- 2015 CZECH REPUBLIC, Prague & Ostrava 1 – 17 May 2015
- 2016 RUSSIA, Moscow & St. Petersburg 29 April – 15 May 2016
- 2017 APPLICANTS: LATVIA (Riga), DENMARK (Copenhagen, Herning), FRANCE, GERMANY

**U20 WORLD CHAMPIONSHIP**

- 2014 SWEDEN, Malmo 26 December 2013 – 5 January 2014
- 2015 CANADA, TBA
- 2016 FINLAND, TBA
- 2017 CANADA, TBA
- 2018 UNITED STATES, TBA
- 2019 CANADA, TBA
- 2020 CZECH REPUBLIC, TBA
- 2021 CANADA, TBA

**U18 WORLD CHAMPIONSHIP, MEN**

- 2014 FINLAND, TBA
- 2015 SWITZERLAND, TBA
- 2016 UNITED STATES, TBA
- 2017 SLOVAKIA, TBA

**WOMEN'S WORLD CHAMPIONSHIP**

- 2015 SWEDEN, TBA
- 2016 CANADA, TBA
- 2017 UNITED STATES, TBA
- 2019 FINLAND, TBA
- 2020 CANADA, TBA

**IIHF CONGRESSES**

- 2012 General JAPAN, Tokyo 24-30 September 2012
- 2013 Annual SWEDEN, Stockholm 16-19 May 2012
- 2013 Semi-Annual PORTUGAL, Cascais 19-21 September 2013

*The Bolshoi Ice Dome will be home to Ice Hockey at the 2014 Olympic Winter Games in Sochi, Russia. Photo: IIHF.*

*Although Canada didn't make it to the gold-medal game for the first time in more than a decade, the U20 team won a medal (bronze) for the 14th straight year. Photo: Andy Devlin / HHOF-IIHF Images.*

# 2013 Women's World Championship
## Canada vs United States Guide & Record Book

## Medals History

| | 1990 WW | 1992 WW | 1994 WW | 1997 WW | 1998 OG | 1998 OG | 1999 WW | 2000 WW | 2001 WW | 2002 WW | 2004 WW | 2004 WW | 2005 WW | 2007 WW | 2007 WW | 2008 WW | 2008 WW | 2009 WW | 2009 WW | 2010 OG | 2011 WW | 2012 WW |
|---|---|---|---|---|---|---|---|---|---|---|---|---|---|---|---|---|---|---|---|---|---|---|
| CAN | G | G | G | G | L | S | G | G | G | G | L | G | S | W | G | L | S | W | S | G | S | G |
| USA | S | S | S | S | W | G | S | S | S | S | W | S | G | L | S | W | G | L | G | S | G | S |

WW=Women's World Championship
OG=Olympic Winter Games
W=Win

## Game Records

| | |
|---|---|
| 1-goal games | CAN 7, USA 3 |
| 2-goal games | CAN 3, USA 3 |
| 3-goal games | CAN 2, USA 2 |
| 4-goal games | CAN |
| 7-goal game | USA |
| 8-goal game | CAN |

## Overtime Heroes

1997 Nancy Drolet, CAN
2000 Nancy Drolet, CAN
2011 Hilary Knight, USA
2012 Caroline Ouellette, CAN

## Shootout Heroes

2005 Angela Ruggiero, USA

## Team Records

**MOST GOALS IN A GAME, CAN**
8 April 26, 1992 (WW)

**MOST GOALS IN A GAME, USA**
9 April 7, 2012 (WW)

**MOST GOALS IN A PERIOD, CAN**
3 1st period, April 26, 1992 (WW)
3rd period, April 26, 1992 (WW)
2nd period, April 17, 1994 (WW)
3rd period, April 17, 1994 (WW)
3rd period, February 14, 1998 (OG-W)
2nd period, April 7, 2007 (WW)
2nd period, April 10, 2007 (WW)

**MOST GOALS IN A PERIOD, USA**
6 3rd period, February 14, 1998 (OG-W)

**MOST GOALS, BOTH TEAMS, GAME**
11 USA 7-CAN 4, February 14, 1998 (OG-W)
11 USA 9-CAN 2, April 7, 2012 (WW)

**MOST GOALS, BOTH TEAMS, PERIOD**
9 USA 6-CAN 3, 3rd period, February 14, 1998

**LONGEST WINNING STREAK, CAN**
4 games 1990-1997 & 1999-2002

**LONGEST WINNING STREAK, USA**
2 games 1998 & 2008-2009

## Player Records

**MOST GAMES, CAREER**
20 Jayna Hefford, CAN
20 Hayley Wickenheiser, CAN
19 Jenny Potter, USA
18 Angela Ruggiero, USA
17 Caroline Ouellette, CAN
16 Jennifer Botterill, CAN

**MOST POINTS, CAREER**
16 Hayley Wickenheiser, CAN (6+10)
15 Jayna Hefford, CAN (7+8)
12 Natalie Darwitz, USA (6+6)
12 Nancy Drolet, CAN (7+5)
11 Danielle Goyette, CAN (6+5)
10 Jenny Potter, USA (6+4)

**MOST GOALS, CAREER**
7 Nancy Drolet, CAN
7 Jayna Hefford, CAN
6 Jennifer Botterill, CAN
6 Natalie Darwitz, USA
6 Danielle Goyette, CAN
6 Jenny Potter, USA
6 Hayley Wickenheiser, CAN

**MOST ASSISTS, CAREER**
10 Hayley Wickenheiser, CAN
8 Jayna Hefford, CAN
6 Natalie Darwitz, USA
6 Geraldine Heaney, CAN
5 Julie Chu, USA
5 Nancy Drolet, CAN
5 Danielle Goyette, CAN
5 Cammi Granato, USA

**MOST PENALTY MINUTES, CAREER**
48 Angela Ruggiero, USA
28 Gillian Apps, CAN
26 Jayna Hefford, CAN

**MOST POINTS, GAME**
6 Monique Lamoureux-Kolls, USA, 2012 prel (3+3)
4 Danielle Goyette, CAN, 1992 gold (1+3)
4 France St. Louis, CAN, 1990 gold (2+2)
4 Hayley Wickenheiser, CAN, 2007 qual (2+2)

**MOST GOALS, GAME**
3 Nancy Drolet, CAN, 1992 gold
3 Nancy Drolet, CAN, 1997 gold
3 Monique Lamoureux-Kolls, USA, 2012 prel

**MOST ASSISTS, GAME**
3 Danielle Goyette, CAN, 1992 gold
3 Monique Lamoureux-Kolls, USA, 2012 prel
3 Kelli Stack, USA, 2012 prel

**MOST PENALTY MINUTES, GAME**
14 Angela Ruggiero, USA, 1998 prel
12 Kelly Bechard, CAN, 2007 qual
12 Angela Ruggiero, USA, 2000 gold

## Goalie Records

**SHUTOUTS**
Chanda Gunn, USA, 2005 gold
Manon Rheaume, CAN, 1992 gold
Kim St. Pierre, CAN, 2004 gold
Shannon Szabados, CAN, 2010 gold

**MOST MINUTES PLAYED, CAREER**
419:43 Kim St. Pierre, CAN
377:38 Jessie Vetter, USA
311:05 Charline Labonte, CAN
252:02 Erin Whitten, USA

**MOST WINS, CAREER**
4 Kim St. Pierre, CAN
4 Jessie Vetter, USA
2 Charline Labonte, CAN
2 Manon Rheaume, CAN
2 Sami Jo Small, CAN

**MOST LOSSES, CAREER**
4 Erin Whitten, USA
3 Charline Labonte, CAN
3 Kim St. Pierre, CAN
2 Sara Decosta, USA
2 Chanda Gunn, USA
2 Jessie Vetter, USA

*Team USA players gather in the crease prior to the 2012 gold-medal game. Photo: Andre Ringuette / HHOF-IIHF Images.*

# Players' Register (CAN vs. USA only)

| | | G | A | P | Pim | Medal |
|---|---|---|---|---|---|---|
| **Meghan Agosta** | | | | | | |
| CAN | 2007 WW prel | 0 | 0 | 0 | 0 | — |
| | 2007 WW gold | 0 | 0 | 0 | 2 | G |
| | 2008 WW qual | 0 | 0 | 0 | 0 | — |
| | 2008 WW gold | 0 | 0 | 0 | 4 | S |
| | 2009 WW qual | 0 | 0 | 0 | 2 | — |
| | 2009 WW gold | 0 | 0 | 0 | 0 | S |
| | 2010 OG-W gold | 0 | 1 | 1 | 0 | G |
| | 2011 WW gold | 0 | 0 | 0 | 0 | S |
| | 2012 WW prel | 0 | 0 | 0 | 2 | — |
| | 2012 WW gold | 1 | 2 | 3 | 0 | G |
| **Michelle Amidon** | | | | | | |
| USA | 1992 WW gold | 0 | 0 | 0 | 2 | S |
| **Dana Antal** | | | | | | |
| CAN | 2001 WW gold | 1 | 0 | 1 | 0 | G |
| | 2002 OG-W gold | 0 | 0 | 0 | 0 | G |
| | 2004 WW prel | 0 | 0 | 0 | 0 | — |
| | 2004 WW gold | 0 | 0 | 0 | 0 | G |
| **Lauren Apollo** | | | | | | |
| USA | 1990 WW gold | 0 | 0 | 0 | 2 | S |
| | 1992 WW gold | 0 | 0 | 0 | 2 | S |
| **Gillian Apps** | | | | | | |
| CAN | 2004 WW prel | 0 | 0 | 0 | 0 | — |
| | 2004 WW gold | 0 | 0 | 0 | 4 | G |
| | 2005 WW gold | 0 | 0 | 0 | 2 | S |
| | 2007 WW prel | 1 | 1 | 2 | 4 | — |
| | 2007 WW gold | 0 | 0 | 0 | 2 | G |
| | 2008 WW qual | 0 | 0 | 0 | 2 | — |
| | 2008 WW gold | 0 | 0 | 0 | 4 | S |
| | 2009 WW qual | 0 | 0 | 0 | 2 | — |
| | 2009 WW gold | 0 | 0 | 0 | 0 | S |
| | 2010 OG-W gold | 0 | 0 | 0 | 0 | G |
| | 2011 WW gold | 1 | 0 | 1 | 0 | S |
| | 2012 WW prel | 0 | 0 | 0 | 4 | — |
| | 2012 WW gold | 0 | 0 | 0 | 4 | G |
| **Chris Bailey** | | | | | | |
| USA | 1994 WW gold | 0 | 0 | 0 | 2 | S |
| | 1997 WW gold | 0 | 0 | 0 | 0 | S |
| | 1998 OG-W prel | 0 | 0 | 0 | 2 | — |
| | 1998 OG-W gold | 0 | 0 | 0 | 0 | G |
| | 1999 WW gold | 0 | 0 | 0 | 2 | S |
| | 2000 WW gold | 0 | 0 | 0 | 0 | S |
| | 2001 WW gold | 0 | 0 | 0 | 2 | S |
| | 2002 OG-W gold | 0 | 0 | 0 | 0 | S |
| **Laurie Baker** | | | | | | |
| USA | 1997 WW gold | 0 | 1 | 1 | 0 | S |
| | 1998 OG-W prel | 2 | 0 | 2 | 2 | — |
| | 1998 OG-W gold | 0 | 0 | 0 | 0 | G |
| | 2000 WW gold | 0 | 0 | 0 | 2 | S |
| | 2002 OG-W gold | 0 | 0 | 0 | 2 | S |
| **Beth Beagan** | | | | | | |
| USA | 1990 WW gold | 0 | 0 | 0 | 0 | S |
| | 1992 WW gold | 0 | 0 | 0 | 2 | S |
| | 1994 WW gold | 0 | 0 | 0 | 0 | S |
| **Kelly Bechard** | | | | | | |
| CAN | 2000 WW gold | 0 | 0 | 0 | 0 | G |
| | 2001 WW gold | 0 | 1 | 1 | 0 | G |
| | 2002 OG-W gold | 0 | 0 | 0 | 2 | G |
| | 2004 WW prel | 0 | 0 | 0 | 0 | — |
| | 2004 WW gold | 0 | 0 | 0 | 0 | G |
| | 2005 WW gold | 0 | 0 | 0 | 0 | S |
| | 2007 WW qual | 1 | 0 | 1 | 12 | — |
| | 2007 WW gold | 0 | 0 | 0 | 0 | G |
| | 2008 WW qual | 1 | 0 | 1 | 0 | — |
| | 2008 WW gold | 0 | 0 | 0 | 0 | S |
| **Kacey Bellamy** | | | | | | |
| USA | 2008 WW qual | 0 | 0 | 0 | 4 | — |
| | 2008 WW gold | 0 | 2 | 2 | 2 | G |
| | 2009 WW qual | 0 | 0 | 0 | 2 | — |
| | 2009 WW gold | 0 | 0 | 0 | 0 | G |
| | 2010 OG-W gold | 0 | 0 | 0 | 0 | S |
| | 2011 WW gold | 0 | 0 | 0 | 0 | G |
| | 2012 WW prel | 0 | 0 | 0 | 2 | — |
| | 2012 WW gold | 0 | 0 | 0 | 2 | S |
| **Vicki Bendus** | | | | | | |
| CAN | 2012 WW prel | 0 | 0 | 0 | 0 | — |
| | 2012 WW gold | 0 | 0 | 0 | 0 | G |
| **Amanda Benoit** | | | | | | |
| CAN | 1999 WW gold | 0 | 0 | 0 | 0 | G |
| | 2000 WW gold | 0 | 0 | 0 | 0 | G |
| **Courtney Birchard** | | | | | | |
| CAN | 2012 WW prel | 0 | 0 | 0 | 0 | — |
| | 2012 WW gold | 0 | 0 | 0 | 0 | G |
| **Alana Blahoski** | | | | | | |
| USA | 1997 WW gold | 1 | 1 | 2 | 0 | S |
| | 1998 OG-W prel | 0 | 0 | 0 | 0 | — |
| | 1998 OG-W gold | 0 | 0 | 0 | 0 | G |
| | 1999 WW gold | 0 | 0 | 0 | 0 | S |
| | 2000 WW gold | 0 | 0 | 0 | 0 | S |
| | 2001 WW gold | 0 | 1 | 1 | 0 | S |
| **Tessa Bonhomme** | | | | | | |
| CAN | 2007 WW qual | 0 | 0 | 0 | 2 | — |
| | 2007 WW gold | 0 | 0 | 0 | 0 | G |
| | 2009 WW qual | 0 | 0 | 0 | 0 | — |
| | 2009 WW gold | 0 | 0 | 0 | 0 | S |
| | 2010 OG-W gold | 0 | 0 | 0 | 0 | G |
| | 2011 WW gold | 0 | 0 | 0 | 0 | S |
| | 2012 WW prel | 0 | 0 | 0 | 2 | — |
| | 2012 WW gold | 0 | 0 | 0 | 0 | G |
| **Jennifer Botterill** | | | | | | |
| CAN | 1998 OG-W prel | 0 | 0 | 0 | 0 | — |
| | 1998 OG-W gold | 0 | 0 | 0 | 0 | S |
| | 1999 WW gold | 0 | 0 | 0 | 0 | G |
| | 2000 WW gold | 0 | 1 | 1 | 0 | G |
| | 2001 WW gold | 1 | 0 | 1 | 0 | G |
| | 2002 OG-W gold | 0 | 0 | 0 | 4 | G |
| | 2004 WW prel | 1 | 0 | 1 | 0 | — |
| | 2004 WW gold | 0 | 0 | 0 | 0 | G |
| | 2005 WW gold | 0 | 0 | 0 | 0 | S |
| | 2007 WW qual | 0 | 1 | 1 | 0 | — |
| | 2007 WW gold | 1 | 0 | 1 | 2 | G |
| | 2008 WW qual | 0 | 0 | 0 | 2 | — |
| | 2008 WW gold | 1 | 0 | 1 | 2 | S |
| | 2009 WW qual | 1 | 0 | 1 | 2 | — |
| | 2009 WW gold | 1 | 0 | 1 | 0 | S |
| | 2010 OG-W gold | 0 | 1 | 1 | 0 | G |
| **Stephanie Boyd** | | | | | | |
| USA | 1994 WW gold | 0 | 0 | 0 | 0 | S |
| **Megan Bozek** | | | | | | |
| USA | 2012 WW prel | 0 | 1 | 1 | 0 | — |
| | 2012 WW gold | 0 | 1 | 1 | 0 | S |
| **Bailey Bram** | | | | | | |
| CAN | 2012 WW prel | 0 | 0 | 0 | 0 | — |
| | 2012 WW gold | 0 | 0 | 0 | 0 | G |
| **Hannah Brandt** | | | | | | |
| USA | 2012 WW prel | 0 | 0 | 0 | 0 | — |
| | 2012 WW gold | 0 | 0 | 0 | 0 | S |
| **Correne Bredin** | | | | | | |
| CAN | 2001 WW gold | 0 | 0 | 0 | 2 | G |
| | 2005 WW gold | 0 | 0 | 0 | 0 | S |
| **Therese Brisson** | | | | | | |
| CAN | 1994 WW gold | 0 | 0 | 0 | 0 | G |
| | 1997 WW gold | 0 | 0 | 0 | 0 | G |
| | 1998 OG-M prel | 1 | 1 | 2 | 4 | — |
| | 1998 OG-W gold | 0 | 0 | 0 | 0 | S |
| | 1999 WW gold | 0 | 0 | 0 | 2 | G |
| | 2000 WW gold | 0 | 0 | 0 | 0 | G |
| | 2001 WW gold | 0 | 1 | 1 | 0 | G |
| | 2002 OG-W gold | 0 | 1 | 1 | 2 | G |
| | 2004 WW prel | 0 | 0 | 0 | 2 | — |
| | 2004 WW gold | 0 | 1 | 1 | 0 | G |
| **Winny Brodt** | | | | | | |
| USA | 2000 WW gold | 0 | 0 | 0 | 0 | S |
| | 2001 WW gold | 0 | 0 | 0 | 0 | S |
| **Lisa Brown (-Miller)** | | | | | | |
| USA | 1990 WW gold | 0 | 0 | 0 | 0 | S |
| | 1992 WW gold | 0 | 0 | 0 | 0 | S |
| | 1994 WW gold | 0 | 0 | 0 | 0 | S |
| | 1997 WW gold | 0 | 0 | 0 | 0 | S |
| | 1998 OG-W prel | 1 | 0 | 1 | 0 | — |
| | 1998 OG-W gold | 0 | 0 | 0 | 0 | S |
| **Karyn Bye** | | | | | | |
| USA | 1992 WW gold | 0 | 0 | 0 | 0 | S |
| | 1994 WW gold | 1 | 1 | 2 | 0 | S |
| | 1997 WW gold | 0 | 0 | 0 | 2 | S |
| | 1998 OG-W prel | 0 | 0 | 0 | 2 | — |
| | 1998 OG-W gold | 0 | 0 | 0 | 0 | G |
| | 1999 WW gold | 0 | 0 | 0 | 0 | S |
| | 2000 WW gold | 1 | 0 | 1 | 0 | S |
| | 2001 WW gold | 0 | 1 | 1 | 2 | S |
| | 2002 OG-W gold | 1 | 0 | 1 | 0 | S |
| **Caitlin Cahow** | | | | | | |
| USA | 2007 WW qual | 0 | 0 | 0 | 0 | — |
| | 2007 WW gold | 0 | 0 | 0 | 0 | S |
| | 2008 WW qual | 1 | 0 | 1 | 0 | — |
| | 2008 WW gold | 0 | 1 | 1 | 0 | G |
| | 2009 WW qual | 0 | 0 | 0 | 0 | — |
| | 2009 WW gold | 2 | 0 | 2 | 0 | G |
| | 2010 OG-W gold | 0 | 0 | 0 | 2 | S |
| | 2011 WW gold | 0 | 0 | 0 | 2 | G |
| **Shirley Cameron** | | | | | | |
| CAN | 1990 WW gold | 0 | 0 | 0 | 0 | G |
| **Cassie Campbell** | | | | | | |
| CAN | 1994 WW gold | 0 | 1 | 1 | 0 | G |
| | 1997 WW gold | 0 | 2 | 2 | 4 | G |
| | 1998 OG-W prel | 0 | 0 | 0 | 2 | — |
| | 1998 OG-W gold | 0 | 0 | 0 | 2 | S |
| | 1999 WW gold | 0 | 0 | 0 | 0 | G |
| | 2000 WW gold | 0 | 1 | 1 | 0 | G |
| | 2001 WW gold | 0 | 0 | 0 | 0 | G |
| | 2002 OG-W gold | 0 | 0 | 0 | 0 | G |
| | 2004 WW prel | 0 | 0 | 0 | 0 | — |
| | 2004 WW gold | 0 | 0 | 0 | 0 | G |
| | 2005 WW gold | 0 | 0 | 0 | 0 | S |
| **Tina Cardinale** | | | | | | |
| USA | 1990 WW gold | 0 | 0 | 0 | 2 | S |
| | 1992 WW gold | 0 | 0 | 0 | 0 | S |
| **Heidi Chalupnik** | | | | | | |
| USA | 1990 WW gold | 0 | 0 | 0 | 0 | S |
| **Isabelle Chartrand** | | | | | | |
| CAN | 2001 WW gold | 0 | 1 | 1 | 0 | G |
| | 2002 OG-W gold | 0 | 0 | 0 | 2 | G |
| **Lisa Chesson** | | | | | | |
| USA | 2009 WW qual | 0 | 0 | 0 | 0 | — |
| | 2009 WW gold | 0 | 0 | 0 | 0 | G |
| | 2010 OG-W gold | 0 | 0 | 0 | 2 | S |
| | 2012 WW prel | 0 | 0 | 0 | 0 | — |
| | 2012 WW gold | 0 | 0 | 0 | 0 | S |
| **Julie Chu** | | | | | | |
| USA | 2001 WW gold | 0 | 0 | 0 | 0 | S |
| | 2002 OG-W gold | 0 | 0 | 0 | 0 | S |
| | 2004 WW prel | 0 | 0 | 0 | 0 | — |
| | 2004 WW gold | 0 | 0 | 0 | 0 | S |
| | 2005 WW gold | 0 | 0 | 0 | 0 | G |
| | 2007 WW qual | 0 | 0 | 0 | 0 | — |
| | 2007 WW gold | 0 | 0 | 0 | 0 | S |
| | 2008 WW qual | 0 | 2 | 2 | 0 | — |
| | 2008 WW gold | 0 | 2 | 2 | 2 | G |
| | 2009 WW qual | 0 | 0 | 0 | 0 | — |
| | 2009 WW gold | 0 | 1 | 1 | 0 | G |
| | 2010 OG-W gold | 0 | 0 | 0 | 0 | S |
| | 2011 WW gold | 0 | 0 | 0 | 0 | G |
| | 2012 WW prel | 1 | 0 | 1 | 0 | — |
| | 2012 WW gold | 0 | 0 | 0 | 0 | S |

| | | | | | | | |
|---|---|---|---|---|---|---|---|
| **Amy Coelho** | | | | | | | |
| USA | 1999 WW gold | 0 | 0 | 0 | 0 | S | |
| **Delaney Collins** | | | | | | | |
| CAN | 2000 WW gold | 0 | 1 | 1 | 0 | G | |
| | 2004 WW prel | 0 | 0 | 0 | 2 | — | |
| | 2004 WW gold | 1 | 0 | 1 | 2 | G | |
| | 2005 WW gold | 0 | 0 | 0 | 2 | S | |
| | 2007 WW qual | 0 | 1 | 1 | 0 | — | |
| | 2007 WW gold | 0 | 1 | 1 | 0 | G | |
| | 2008 WW qual | 0 | 0 | 0 | 2 | — | |
| | 2008 WW gold | 0 | 0 | 0 | 2 | S | |
| **Colleen Coyne** | | | | | | | |
| USA | 1992 WW gold | 0 | 0 | 0 | 0 | S | |
| | 1994 WW gold | 0 | 1 | 1 | 2 | S | |
| | 1997 WW gold | 0 | 0 | 0 | 0 | S | |
| | 1998 OG-W prel | 0 | 0 | 0 | 0 | — | |
| | 1998 OG-W gold | 0 | 0 | 0 | 2 | G | |
| **Kendall Coyne** | | | | | | | |
| USA | 2011 WW gold | 0 | 0 | 0 | 0 | G | |
| | 2012 WW prel | 0 | 0 | 0 | 0 | — | |
| | 2012 WW gold | 1 | 0 | 1 | 0 | S | |
| **Cindy Curley** | | | | | | | |
| USA | 1990 WW gold | 1 | 0 | 1 | 0 | S | |
| | 1992 WW gold | 0 | 0 | 0 | 0 | S | |
| | 1994 WW gold | 0 | 0 | 0 | 0 | S | |
| **Natalie Darwitz** | | | | | | | |
| USA | 1999 WW gold | 0 | 0 | 0 | 0 | S | |
| | 2000 WW gold | 0 | 0 | 0 | 2 | S | |
| | 2001 WW gold | 0 | 0 | 0 | 2 | S | |
| | 2002 OG-W gold | 0 | 0 | 0 | 0 | S | |
| | 2004 WW prel | 1 | 2 | 3 | 0 | — | |
| | 2004 WW gold | 0 | 0 | 0 | 0 | S | |
| | 2005 WW gold | 0 | 0 | 0 | 2 | G | |
| | 2007 WW qual | 1 | 1 | 2 | 2 | — | |
| | 2007 WW gold | 0 | 1 | 1 | 2 | S | |
| | 2008 WW qual | 2 | 1 | 3 | 0 | — | |
| | 2008 WW gold | 2 | 0 | 2 | 0 | G | |
| | 2009 WW qual | 0 | 0 | 0 | 0 | — | |
| | 2009 WW gold | 0 | 1 | 1 | 0 | G | |
| | 2010 OG-W gold | 0 | 0 | 0 | 0 | S | |
| **Shawna Davidson** | | | | | | | |
| USA | 1990 WW gold | 1 | 0 | 1 | 0 | S | |
| | 1992 WW gold | 0 | 0 | 0 | 0 | S | |
| | 1994 WW gold | 0 | 0 | 0 | 0 | S | |
| **Brianna Decker** | | | | | | | |
| USA | 2011 WW gold | 0 | 0 | 0 | 0 | G | |
| | 2012 WW prel | 0 | 1 | 1 | 0 | — | |
| | 2012 WW gold | 1 | 1 | 2 | 2 | S | |
| **Sara Decosta** | | | | | | | |
| USA | 1998 OG-W prel | 30:36 | W | 3 | — | | |
| | 2000 WW gold | 66:50 | L | 3 | S | | |
| | 2002 OG-W gold | 59:00 | L | 3 | S | | |
| **Jillian Dempsey** | | | | | | | |
| USA | 2012 WW prel | 0 | 0 | 0 | 0 | — | |
| | 2012 WW gold | 0 | 0 | 0 | 0 | S | |
| **Maria Dennis** | | | | | | | |
| USA | 1990 WW gold | 0 | 0 | 0 | 0 | S | |
| **Judy Diduck** | | | | | | | |
| CAN | 1990 WW gold | 1 | 0 | 1 | 0 | G | |
| | 1992 WW gold | 0 | 1 | 1 | 0 | G | |
| | 1994 WW gold | 0 | 0 | 0 | 0 | G | |
| | 1997 WW gold | 0 | 1 | 1 | 0 | G | |
| | 1998 OG-W prel | 0 | 0 | 0 | 4 | — | |
| | 1998 OG-W gold | 0 | 0 | 0 | 0 | S | |
| **Michelle Difronzo** | | | | | | | |
| USA | 1994 WW gold | 0 | 0 | 0 | 2 | S | |
| **Rachael Drazan** | | | | | | | |
| USA | 2008 WW qual | 0 | 1 | 1 | 2 | — | |
| | 2008 WW gold | 0 | 0 | 0 | 2 | G | |
| **Pam Dreyer** | | | | | | | |
| USA | 2004 WW prel | 60:00 | W | 1 | — | | |
| | 2004 WW gold | 58:39 | L | 2 | S | | |
| **Nancy Drolet** | | | | | | | |
| CAN | 1992 WW gold | 3 | 0 | 3 | 0 | G | |
| | 1994 WW gold | 0 | 2 | 2 | 0 | G | |
| | 1997 WW gold | 3 | 0 | 3 | 2 | G | |
| | 1998 OG-W prel | 0 | 0 | 0 | 0 | — | |
| | 1998 OG-W gold | 0 | 0 | 0 | 2 | S | |
| | 1999 WW gold | 0 | 2 | 2 | 0 | G | |
| | 2000 WW gold | 1 | 0 | 1 | 0 | G | |
| | 2001 WW gold | 0 | 1 | 1 | 2 | G | |
| **Meghan Duggan** | | | | | | | |
| USA | 2007 WW qual | 0 | 1 | 1 | 0 | — | |
| | 2007 WW gold | 0 | 0 | 0 | 0 | S | |
| | 2008 WW qual | 1 | 0 | 1 | 0 | — | |
| | 2008 WW gold | 0 | 1 | 1 | 2 | G | |
| | 2009 WW qual | 0 | 0 | 0 | 2 | — | |
| | 2009 WW gold | 1 | 0 | 1 | 0 | G | |
| | 2010 OG-W gold | 0 | 0 | 0 | 0 | S | |
| | 2011 WW gold | 0 | 0 | 0 | 0 | G | |
| **Tricia Dunn** | | | | | | | |
| USA | 1997 WW gold | 0 | 0 | 0 | 0 | S | |
| | 1998 OG-W prel | 1 | 0 | 1 | 2 | — | |
| | 1998 OG-W gold | 0 | 0 | 0 | 0 | G | |
| | 1999 WW gold | 0 | 0 | 0 | 2 | S | |
| | 2000 WW gold | 1 | 0 | 1 | 0 | S | |
| | 2001 WW gold | 0 | 0 | 0 | 0 | S | |
| | 2002 OG-W gold | 0 | 0 | 0 | 0 | S | |
| | 2004 WW prel | 1 | 1 | 2 | 0 | — | |
| | 2004 WW gold | 0 | 0 | 0 | 0 | S | |
| **Lori Dupuis** | | | | | | | |
| CAN | 1997 WW gold | 0 | 0 | 0 | 0 | G | |
| | 1998 OG-W prel | 2 | 1 | 3 | 2 | — | |
| | 1998 OG-W gold | 0 | 0 | 0 | 0 | S | |
| | 1999 WW gold | 0 | 0 | 0 | 2 | G | |
| | 2000 WW gold | 0 | 0 | 0 | 0 | G | |
| | 2002 OG-W gold | 0 | 0 | 0 | 2 | G | |
| **Kelly Dyer** | | | | | | | |
| USA | 1990 WW gold | 60:00 | L | 5 | S | | |
| **Molly Engstrom** | | | | | | | |
| USA | 2004 WW prel | 0 | 0 | 0 | 0 | — | |
| | 2004 WW gold | 0 | 0 | 0 | 0 | S | |
| | 2005 WW gold | 0 | 0 | 0 | 0 | G | |
| | 2007 WW qual | 0 | 0 | 0 | 0 | — | |
| | 2007 WW gold | 0 | 0 | 0 | 0 | S | |
| | 2008 WW qual | 0 | 0 | 0 | 0 | — | |
| | 2009 WW qual | 0 | 0 | 0 | 2 | — | |
| | 2009 WW gold | 0 | 0 | 0 | 0 | G | |
| | 2010 OG-W gold | 0 | 0 | 0 | 0 | S | |
| | 2011 WW gold | 0 | 0 | 0 | 0 | G | |
| **Kimberly Eisenreid** | | | | | | | |
| USA | 1990 WW gold | 0 | 0 | 0 | 0 | S | |
| **Sam Faber** | | | | | | | |
| USA | 2008 WW qual | 0 | 0 | 0 | 2 | — | |
| | 2008 WW gold | 0 | 0 | 0 | 0 | G | |
| **Rebecca Fahey** | | | | | | | |
| CAN | 1997 WW gold | 0 | 0 | 0 | 2 | G | |
| **Gillian Ferrari** | | | | | | | |
| CAN | 2004 WW prel | 0 | 0 | 0 | 6 | — | |
| | 2004 WW gold | 0 | 0 | 0 | 0 | G | |
| | 2007 WW qual | 0 | 0 | 0 | 0 | — | |
| | 2007 WW gold | 0 | 0 | 0 | 0 | G | |
| | 2008 WW qual | 0 | 0 | 0 | 0 | — | |
| | 2008 WW gold | 0 | 0 | 0 | 0 | S | |
| | 2009 WW qual | 0 | 0 | 0 | 2 | — | |
| | 2009 WW gold | 0 | 0 | 0 | 0 | S | |
| **Brandy Fisher** | | | | | | | |
| USA | 1999 WW gold | 0 | 0 | 0 | 0 | S | |
| | 2000 WW gold | 0 | 1 | 1 | 0 | S | |
| **Laura Fortino** | | | | | | | |
| CAN | 2012 WW prel | 0 | 0 | 0 | 4 | — | |
| | 2012 WW gold | 0 | 0 | 0 | 0 | G | |
| **Heather Ginzel** | | | | | | | |
| CAN | 1990 WW gold | 0 | 0 | 0 | 0 | G | |
| | 1992 WW gold | 0 | 0 | 0 | 0 | G | |
| **Merianne Gmak** | | | | | | | |
| CAN | 1994 WW gold | 0 | 1 | 1 | 2 | G | |
| **Danielle Goyette** | | | | | | | |
| CAN | 1992 WW gold | 1 | 3 | 4 | 0 | G | |
| | 1994 WW gold | 2 | 0 | 2 | 0 | G | |
| | 1997 WW gold | 0 | 0 | 0 | 0 | G | |
| | 1998 OG-W prel | 0 | 0 | 0 | 2 | — | |
| | 1998 OG-W gold | 1 | 0 | 1 | 2 | S | |
| | 1999 WW gold | 1 | 0 | 1 | 0 | G | |
| | 2000 WW gold | 0 | 0 | 0 | 0 | G | |
| | 2001 WW gold | 0 | 0 | 0 | 0 | G | |
| | 2002 OG-W gold | 0 | 1 | 1 | 0 | G | |
| | 2004 WW prel | 0 | 0 | 0 | 0 | — | |
| | 2004 WW gold | 0 | 1 | 1 | 0 | G | |
| | 2005 WW gold | 0 | 0 | 0 | 0 | S | |
| | 2007 WW qual | 0 | 0 | 0 | 0 | — | |
| | 2007 WW gold | 1 | 0 | 1 | 0 | G | |
| **Cammi Granato** | | | | | | | |
| USA | 1990 WW gold | 0 | 0 | 0 | 2 | S | |
| | 1992 WW gold | 0 | 0 | 0 | 0 | S | |
| | 1994 WW gold | 1 | 1 | 2 | 0 | S | |
| | 1997 WW gold | 0 | 2 | 2 | 2 | S | |
| | 1998 OG-W prel | 2 | 1 | 3 | 0 | — | |
| | 1998 OG-W gold | 0 | 0 | 0 | 0 | G | |
| | 1999 WW gold | 0 | 0 | 0 | 0 | S | |
| | 2000 WW gold | 0 | 0 | 0 | 0 | S | |
| | 2001 WW gold | 0 | 0 | 0 | 0 | S | |
| | 2002 OG-W gold | 0 | 1 | 1 | 0 | S | |
| | 2004 WW gold | 0 | 0 | 0 | 0 | S | |
| | 2005 WW gold | 0 | 0 | 0 | 0 | G | |
| **Chanda Gunn** | | | | | | | |
| USA | 2005 WW gold | 80:00 | W | 0 | G | | |
| | 2007 WW gold | 60:00 | L | 5 | S | | |
| **Jamie Hagerman** | | | | | | | |
| USA | 2005 WW gold | 0 | 0 | 0 | 0 | G | |
| **Tiffany Hagge** | | | | | | | |
| USA | 2007 WW qual | 0 | 0 | 0 | 0 | — | |
| | 2007 WW gold | 0 | 0 | 0 | 0 | S | |
| **Kelli Halcisak** | | | | | | | |
| USA | 2004 WW prel | 0 | 0 | 0 | 0 | — | |
| | 2004 WW gold | 0 | 0 | 0 | 0 | S | |
| | 2007 WW qual | 0 | 0 | 0 | 0 | — | |
| | 2007 WW gold | 0 | 0 | 0 | 0 | S | |
| **Kim Haman** | | | | | | | |
| USA | 1992 WW gold | 0 | 0 | 0 | 0 | S | |
| **Catherine Hanson** | | | | | | | |
| USA | 1999 WW gold | 0 | 0 | 0 | 0 | S | |
| **Geraldine Heaney** | | | | | | | |
| CAN | 1990 WW gold | 1 | 1 | 2 | 2 | G | |
| | 1992 WW gold | 0 | 1 | 1 | 2 | G | |
| | 1994 WW gold | 0 | 2 | 2 | 4 | G | |
| | 1997 WW gold | 0 | 1 | 1 | 0 | G | |
| | 1998 OG-W prel | 0 | 0 | 0 | 2 | — | |
| | 1998 OG-W gold | 0 | 1 | 1 | 0 | S | |
| | 1999 WW gold | 1 | 0 | 1 | 0 | G | |
| | 2000 WW gold | 0 | 0 | 0 | 2 | G | |
| | 2001 WW gold | 0 | 0 | 0 | 0 | G | |
| | 2002 OG-W gold | 0 | 0 | 0 | 0 | G | |
| **Jayna Hefford** | | | | | | | |
| CAN | 1997 WW gold | 0 | 1 | 1 | 0 | G | |
| | 1998 OG-W prel | 1 | 0 | 1 | 2 | — | |
| | 1998 OG-W gold | 0 | 0 | 0 | 0 | S | |
| | 1999 WW gold | 0 | 1 | 1 | 0 | G | |
| | 2000 WW gold | 2 | 0 | 2 | 4 | G | |
| | 2001 WW gold | 0 | 0 | 0 | 2 | G | |
| | 2002 OG-W gold | 1 | 0 | 1 | 0 | G | |

| | | | | | | |
|---|---|---|---|---|---|---|
| | 2004 WW prel | 0 | 0 | 0 | 0 | — |
| | 2004 WW gold | 0 | 0 | 0 | 0 | G |
| | 2005 WW gold | 0 | 0 | 0 | 0 | S |
| | 2007 WW qual | 0 | 0 | 0 | 0 | — |
| | 2007 WW gold | 1 | 0 | 1 | 2 | G |
| | 2008 WW qual | 1 | 0 | 1 | 0 | — |
| | 2008 WW gold | 0 | 0 | 0 | 6 | S |
| | 2009 WW qual | 0 | 2 | 2 | 0 | — |
| | 2009 WW gold | 0 | 1 | 1 | 0 | S |
| | 2010 OG-W gold | 0 | 0 | 0 | 6 | G |
| | 2011 WW gold | 0 | 1 | 1 | 0 | S |
| | 2012 WW prel | 0 | 1 | 1 | 0 | — |
| | 2012 WW gold | 1 | 1 | 2 | 4 | G |

**Annamarie Holmes**

| | | | | | | |
|---|---|---|---|---|---|---|
| USA | 2001 WW gold | 0 | 1 | 1 | 0 | S |

**Sarah Hood**

| | | | | | | |
|---|---|---|---|---|---|---|
| USA | 1999 WW gold | 0 | 0 | 0 | 0 | S |

**Andria Hunter**

| | | | | | | |
|---|---|---|---|---|---|---|
| CAN | 1992 WW gold | 1 | 2 | 3 | 0 | G |
| | 1994 WW gold | 0 | 0 | 0 | 0 | G |

**Teresa Hutchinson**

| | | | | | | |
|---|---|---|---|---|---|---|
| CAN | 1990 WW gold | 0 | 0 | 0 | 0 | G |

**Kim Insalaco**

| | | | | | | |
|---|---|---|---|---|---|---|
| USA | 2004 WW prel | 0 | 0 | 0 | 2 | — |
| | 2004 WW gold | 0 | 0 | 0 | 2 | S |
| | 2005 WW gold | 0 | 0 | 0 | 0 | G |

**Haley Irwin**

| | | | | | | |
|---|---|---|---|---|---|---|
| CAN | 2009 WW qual | 0 | 0 | 0 | 0 | — |
| | 2009 WW gold | 0 | 0 | 0 | 0 | S |
| | 2010 OG-W gold | 0 | 0 | 0 | 0 | G |
| | 2011 WW gold | 0 | 0 | 0 | 2 | S |
| | 2012 WW prel | 0 | 0 | 0 | 0 | — |

**Kathy Issel**

| | | | | | | |
|---|---|---|---|---|---|---|
| USA | 1992 WW gold | 0 | 0 | 0 | 0 | S |

**Angela James**

| | | | | | | |
|---|---|---|---|---|---|---|
| CAN | 1990 WW gold | 0 | 1 | 1 | 2 | G |
| | 1992 WW gold | 2 | 0 | 2 | 0 | G |
| | 1994 WW gold | 2 | 0 | 2 | 0 | G |
| | 1997 WW gold | 1 | 0 | 1 | 0 | G |

**Brianne Jenner**

| | | | | | | |
|---|---|---|---|---|---|---|
| CAN | 2012 WW prel | 0 | 0 | 0 | 0 | — |
| | 2012 WW gold | 0 | 0 | 0 | 0 | G |

**Rebecca Johnston**

| | | | | | | |
|---|---|---|---|---|---|---|
| CAN | 2008 WW qual | 0 | 0 | 0 | 0 | — |
| | 2008 WW gold | 0 | 0 | 0 | 0 | S |
| | 2009 WW qual | 0 | 0 | 0 | 0 | — |
| | 2009 WW gold | 0 | 0 | 0 | 0 | S |
| | 2010 OG-W gold | 0 | 0 | 0 | 0 | G |
| | 2011 WW gold | 1 | 0 | 1 | 0 | S |
| | 2012 WW prel | 0 | 1 | 1 | 0 | — |
| | 2012 WW gold | 0 | 0 | 0 | 0 | G |

**Kathleen Kauth**

| | | | | | | |
|---|---|---|---|---|---|---|
| USA | 2004 WW prel | 0 | 0 | 0 | 0 | — |
| | 2004 WW gold | 0 | 0 | 0 | 0 | S |
| | 2005 WW gold | 0 | 0 | 0 | 0 | G |

**Becky Kellar**

| | | | | | | |
|---|---|---|---|---|---|---|
| CAN | 1998 OG-W prel | 0 | 0 | 0 | 0 | — |
| | 1998 OG-W gold | 0 | 0 | 0 | 0 | S |
| | 1999 WW gold | 0 | 0 | 0 | 2 | G |
| | 2000 WW gold | 0 | 0 | 0 | 0 | G |
| | 2001 WW gold | 0 | 0 | 0 | 2 | G |
| | 2002 OG-W gold | 0 | 1 | 1 | 4 | G |
| | 2004 WW prel | 0 | 0 | 0 | 0 | — |
| | 2004 WW gold | 0 | 0 | 0 | 0 | G |
| | 2005 WW gold | 0 | 0 | 0 | 0 | S |
| | 2008 WW qual | 0 | 1 | 1 | 0 | — |
| | 2008 WW gold | 0 | 1 | 1 | 0 | S |
| | 2009 WW qual | 0 | 0 | 0 | 0 | — |
| | 2009 WW gold | 0 | 0 | 0 | 2 | S |
| | 2010 OG-W gold | 0 | 0 | 0 | 2 | G |

**Courtney Kennedy**

| | | | | | | |
|---|---|---|---|---|---|---|
| USA | 2002 OG-W gold | 0 | 0 | 0 | 4 | S |
| | 2005 WW gold | 0 | 0 | 0 | 0 | G |

**Amanda Kessel**

| | | | | | | |
|---|---|---|---|---|---|---|
| USA | 2012 WW prel | 0 | 0 | 0 | 0 | — |
| | 2012 WW gold | 0 | 1 | 1 | 0 | S |

**Andrea Kilbourne**

| | | | | | | |
|---|---|---|---|---|---|---|
| USA | 2002 OG-W gold | 0 | 0 | 0 | 0 | S |
| | 2004 WW prel | 0 | 0 | 0 | 2 | — |
| | 2004 WW gold | 0 | 0 | 0 | 2 | S |

**Katie King**

| | | | | | | |
|---|---|---|---|---|---|---|
| USA | 1997 WW gold | 1 | 1 | 2 | 0 | S |
| | 1998 OG-W prel | 0 | 1 | 1 | 0 | — |
| | 1998 OG-W gold | 0 | 0 | 0 | 0 | G |
| | 1999 WW gold | 0 | 1 | 1 | 0 | S |
| | 2000 WW gold | 0 | 0 | 0 | 0 | S |
| | 2001 WW gold | 0 | 0 | 0 | 0 | S |
| | 2002 OG-W gold | 1 | 0 | 1 | 0 | S |
| | 2004 WW prel | 0 | 0 | 0 | 0 | — |
| | 2004 WW gold | 0 | 0 | 0 | 2 | S |
| | 2005 WW gold | 0 | 0 | 0 | 0 | G |

**Kristin King**

| | | | | | | |
|---|---|---|---|---|---|---|
| USA | 2004 WW prel | 0 | 0 | 0 | 0 | — |
| | 2004 WW gold | 0 | 0 | 0 | 0 | S |
| | 2005 WW gold | 0 | 0 | 0 | 2 | G |
| | 2007 WW qual | 0 | 1 | 1 | 0 | — |
| | 2007 WW gold | 0 | 0 | 0 | 2 | S |

**Gina Kingsbury**

| | | | | | | |
|---|---|---|---|---|---|---|
| CAN | 2001 WW gold | 0 | 0 | 0 | 0 | G |
| | 2004 WW prel | 0 | 0 | 0 | 0 | — |
| | 2004 WW gold | 0 | 0 | 0 | 0 | G |
| | 2005 WW gold | 0 | 0 | 0 | 0 | S |
| | 2007 WW qual | 0 | 0 | 0 | 0 | — |
| | 2007 WW gold | 0 | 0 | 0 | 0 | G |
| | 2008 WW qual | 0 | 1 | 1 | 0 | — |
| | 2008 WW gold | 0 | 1 | 1 | 0 | S |
| | 2009 WW qual | 0 | 0 | 0 | 0 | — |
| | 2009 WW gold | 0 | 0 | 0 | 0 | S |
| | 2010 OG-W gold | 0 | 0 | 0 | 2 | G |

**Hilary Knight**

| | | | | | | |
|---|---|---|---|---|---|---|
| USA | 2007 WW qual | 0 | 0 | 0 | 0 | — |
| | 2007 WW gold | 0 | 0 | 0 | 2 | S |
| | 2008 WW qual | 0 | 0 | 0 | 0 | — |
| | 2008 WW gold | 0 | 0 | 0 | 0 | G |
| | 2009 WW qual | 0 | 0 | 0 | 0 | — |
| | 2009 WW gold | 1 | 1 | 2 | 0 | G |
| | 2010 OG-W gold | 0 | 0 | 0 | 0 | S |
| | 2011 WW gold | 1 | 1 | 2 | 0 | G |
| | 2012 WW prel | 2 | 1 | 3 | 0 | — |
| | 2012 WW gold | 0 | 0 | 0 | 0 | S |

**Jessica Koizumi**

| | | | | | | |
|---|---|---|---|---|---|---|
| USA | 2008 WW qual | 0 | 0 | 0 | 0 | — |
| | 2008 WW gold | 0 | 0 | 0 | 0 | G |

**Charline Labonte**

| | | | | | |
|---|---|---|---|---|---|
| CAN | 2007 WW qual | 70:00 | W | 4 | — |
| | 2008 WW qual | 59:07 | L | 3 | — |
| | 2008 WW gold | 19:22 | nd | 0 | S |
| | 2009 WW qual | 59:58 | W | 1 | — |
| | 2009 WW gold | 59:06 | L | 3 | S |
| | 2012 WW prel | 43:32 | L | 7 | — |

**Jocelyne Lamoureux**

| | | | | | | |
|---|---|---|---|---|---|---|
| USA | 2009 WW qual | 0 | 1 | 1 | 2 | — |
| | 2009 WW gold | 0 | 1 | 1 | 0 | G |
| | 2010 OG-W gold | 0 | 0 | 0 | 0 | S |
| | 2011 WW gold | 1 | 0 | 1 | 2 | G |
| | 2012 WW prel | 2 | 1 | 3 | 0 | — |
| | 2012 WW gold | 0 | 0 | 0 | 4 | S |

**Monique Lamoureux (-Kolls)**

| | | | | | | |
|---|---|---|---|---|---|---|
| USA | 2009 WW qual | 1 | 0 | 1 | 4 | — |
| | 2009 WW gold | 0 | 0 | 0 | 0 | G |
| | 2010 OG-W gold | 0 | 0 | 0 | 0 | S |
| | 2011 WW gold | 0 | 1 | 1 | 2 | G |
| | 2012 WW prel | 3 | 3 | 6 | 0 | — |
| | 2012 WW gold | 0 | 0 | 0 | 2 | S |

**Mai-Lan Le**

| | | | | | | |
|---|---|---|---|---|---|---|
| CAN | 1999 WW gold | 0 | 0 | 0 | 0 | G |

**Jocelyne Larocque**

| | | | | | | |
|---|---|---|---|---|---|---|
| CAN | 2011 WW gold | 0 | 0 | 0 | 2 | S |
| | 2012 WW prel | 0 | 0 | 0 | 2 | — |
| | 2012 WW gold | 0 | 0 | 0 | 2 | G |

**Erika Lawler**

| | | | | | | |
|---|---|---|---|---|---|---|
| USA | 2007 WW qual | 0 | 1 | 1 | 0 | — |
| | 2007 WW gold | 0 | 1 | 1 | 0 | S |
| | 2008 WW qual | 0 | 1 | 1 | 0 | — |
| | 2008 WW gold | 0 | 0 | 0 | 2 | G |
| | 2009 WW qual | 0 | 0 | 0 | 0 | — |
| | 2009 WW gold | 0 | 0 | 0 | 0 | G |
| | 2010 OG-W gold | 0 | 0 | 0 | 0 | S |
| | 2012 WW prel | 0 | 0 | 0 | 0 | — |
| | 2012 WW gold | 0 | 0 | 0 | 0 | S |

**Laura Leslie**

| | | | | | | |
|---|---|---|---|---|---|---|
| CAN | 1994 WW gold | 0 | 0 | 0 | 0 | G |

**Luce Letendre**

| | | | | | | |
|---|---|---|---|---|---|---|
| CAN | 1997 WW gold | 0 | 0 | 0 | 0 | G |

**Shelley Looney**

| | | | | | | |
|---|---|---|---|---|---|---|
| USA | 1992 WW gold | 0 | 0 | 0 | 0 | S |
| | 1994 WW gold | 0 | 0 | 0 | 0 | S |
| | 1997 WW gold | 0 | 0 | 0 | 0 | S |
| | 1998 OG-W prel | 0 | 0 | 0 | 0 | — |
| | 1998 OG-W gold | 1 | 0 | 1 | 0 | G |
| | 1999 WW gold | 0 | 0 | 0 | 0 | S |
| | 2000 WW gold | 0 | 0 | 0 | 0 | S |
| | 2001 WW gold | 0 | 0 | 0 | 0 | S |
| | 2002 OG-W gold | 0 | 0 | 0 | 2 | S |
| | 2005 WW gold | 0 | 0 | 0 | 0 | G |

**Nicki Luongo**

| | | | | | | |
|---|---|---|---|---|---|---|
| USA | 2000 WW gold | 0 | 0 | 0 | 0 | S |
| | 2001 WW gold | 0 | 0 | 0 | 0 | S |

**Carla MacLeod**

| | | | | | | |
|---|---|---|---|---|---|---|
| CAN | 2005 WW gold | 0 | 0 | 0 | 0 | S |
| | 2007 WW qual | 0 | 0 | 0 | 0 | — |
| | 2007 WW gold | 0 | 1 | 1 | 0 | G |
| | 2008 WW qual | 0 | 1 | 1 | 0 | — |
| | 2008 WW gold | 0 | 0 | 0 | 2 | S |
| | 2009 WW qual | 0 | 0 | 0 | 0 | — |
| | 2009 WW gold | 0 | 0 | 0 | 0 | S |
| | 2010 OG-W gold | 0 | 0 | 0 | 0 | G |

**Gigi Marvin**

| | | | | | | |
|---|---|---|---|---|---|---|
| USA | 2007 WW qual | 1 | 0 | 1 | 2 | — |
| | 2007 WW gold | 0 | 0 | 0 | 2 | S |
| | 2008 WW qual | 0 | 1 | 1 | 0 | — |
| | 2008 WW gold | 0 | 0 | 0 | 6 | G |
| | 2009 WW qual | 0 | 0 | 0 | 0 | — |
| | 2009 WW gold | 0 | 1 | 1 | 0 | G |
| | 2010 OG-W gold | 0 | 0 | 0 | 0 | S |
| | 2011 WW gold | 0 | 0 | 0 | 0 | G |
| | 2012 WW prel | 0 | 2 | 2 | 0 | — |
| | 2012 WW gold | 2 | 0 | 2 | 2 | S |

**Katie McCormack**

| | | | | | | |
|---|---|---|---|---|---|---|
| CAN | 1998 OG-W prel | 0 | 0 | 0 | 0 | — |
| | 1998 OG-W gold | 0 | 0 | 0 | 0 | S |

**Dawn McGuire**

| | | | | | | |
|---|---|---|---|---|---|---|
| CAN | 1990 WW gold | 0 | 1 | 1 | 0 | G |
| | 1992 WW gold | 0 | 0 | 0 | 0 | G |

**Sue Merz**

| | | | | | | |
|---|---|---|---|---|---|---|
| USA | 1990 WW gold | 0 | 0 | 0 | 0 | S |
| | 1992 WW gold | 0 | 0 | 0 | 0 | S |
| | 1994 WW gold | 0 | 0 | 0 | 0 | S |
| | 1998 OG-W prel | 0 | 0 | 0 | 2 | — |
| | 1998 OG-W gold | 0 | 1 | 1 | 0 | G |
| | 1999 WW gold | 0 | 0 | 0 | 0 | S |
| | 2000 WW gold | 0 | 0 | 0 | 0 | S |
| | 2001 WW gold | 0 | 0 | 0 | 0 | S |
| | 2002 OG-W gold | 0 | 0 | 0 | 0 | S |

**Diane Michaud**

| | | | | | | |
|---|---|---|---|---|---|---|
| CAN | 1990 WW gold | 0 | 0 | 0 | 0 | G |
| | 1992 WW gold | 0 | 0 | 0 | 2 | G |

**Meaghan Mikkelson**

| | | | | | | |
|---|---|---|---|---|---|---|
| CAN | 2008 WW qual | 0 | 0 | 0 | 0 | — |
| | 2008 WW gold | 0 | 0 | 0 | 0 | S |
| | 2009 WW qual | 0 | 0 | 0 | 2 | — |
| | 2009 WW gold | 0 | 0 | 0 | 0 | S |
| | 2010 OG-W gold | 0 | 0 | 0 | 0 | G |
| | 2011 WW gold | 0 | 0 | 0 | 0 | S |
| | 2012 WW prel | 0 | 0 | 0 | 0 | — |
| | 2012 WW gold | 0 | 0 | 0 | 0 | G |

**A.J. Mleczko**

| | | | | | | |
|---|---|---|---|---|---|---|
| USA | 1997 WW gold | 0 | 0 | 0 | 0 | S |
| | 1998 OG-W prel | 0 | 2 | 2 | 2 | — |
| | 1998 OG-W gold | 0 | 0 | 0 | 0 | G |
| | 2000 WW gold | 0 | 0 | 0 | 0 | S |
| | 2001 WW gold | 1 | 0 | 1 | 0 | S |
| | 2002 OG-W gold | 0 | 0 | 0 | 0 | S |

**France Montour**

| | | | | | | |
|---|---|---|---|---|---|---|
| CAN | 1990 WW gold | 0 | 0 | 0 | 0 | G |
| | 1992 WW gold | 0 | 1 | 1 | 2 | G |

**Tara Mounsey**

| | | | | | | |
|---|---|---|---|---|---|---|
| USA | 1997 WW gold | 0 | 1 | 1 | 2 | S |
| | 1998 OG-W prel | 0 | 1 | 1 | 0 | — |
| | 1998 OG-W gold | 0 | 0 | 0 | 4 | G |
| | 1999 WW gold | 0 | 0 | 0 | 0 | S |
| | 2002 OG-W gold | 0 | 2 | 2 | 0 | S |

**Vicky Movsessian**

| | | | | | | |
|---|---|---|---|---|---|---|
| USA | 1994 WW gold | 0 | 0 | 0 | 0 | S |
| | 1997 WW gold | 0 | 0 | 0 | 2 | S |
| | 1998 OG-W prel | 0 | 0 | 0 | 4 | — |
| | 1998 OG-W gold | 0 | 0 | 0 | 2 | G |

**Karen Nystrom**

| | | | | | | |
|---|---|---|---|---|---|---|
| CAN | 1990 WW gold | 0 | 0 | 0 | 0 | G |
| | 1994 WW gold | 0 | 0 | 0 | 0 | G |
| | 1997 WW gold | 0 | 0 | 0 | 0 | G |
| | 1998 OG-W gold | 0 | 0 | 0 | 0 | S |

**Kelly O'Leary**

| | | | | | | |
|---|---|---|---|---|---|---|
| USA | 1990 WW gold | 0 | 0 | 0 | 0 | S |
| | 1992 WW gold | 0 | 0 | 0 | 2 | S |
| | 1994 WW gold | 0 | 0 | 0 | 4 | S |
| | 1997 WW gold | 0 | 0 | 0 | 2 | S |

**Stephanie O'Sullivan**

| | | | | | | |
|---|---|---|---|---|---|---|
| USA | 1994 WW gold | 1 | 1 | 2 | 2 | S |
| | 1997 WW gold | 1 | 0 | 1 | 0 | S |
| | 1999 WW gold | 0 | 0 | 0 | 0 | S |
| | 2000 WW gold | 0 | 0 | 0 | 0 | S |

**Caroline Ouellette**

| | | | | | | |
|---|---|---|---|---|---|---|
| CAN | 1999 WW gold | 1 | 0 | 1 | 0 | G |
| | 2000 WW gold | 0 | 0 | 0 | 0 | G |
| | 2001 WW gold | 0 | 0 | 0 | 0 | G |
| | 2002 OG-W gold | 1 | 0 | 1 | 4 | G |
| | 2004 WW prel | 0 | 0 | 0 | 0 | — |
| | 2004 WW gold | 0 | 0 | 0 | 0 | G |
| | 2005 WW gold | 0 | 0 | 0 | 0 | S |
| | 2007 WW qual | 0 | 0 | 0 | 0 | — |
| | 2007 WW gold | 0 | 2 | 2 | 0 | G |
| | 2008 WW qual | 0 | 0 | 0 | 2 | — |
| | 2008 WW gold | 0 | 1 | 1 | 0 | S |
| | 2009 WW qual | 1 | 0 | 1 | 2 | — |
| | 2009 WW gold | 0 | 1 | 1 | 0 | S |
| | 2010 OG-W gold | 0 | 0 | 0 | 0 | G |
| | 2011 WW gold | 0 | 0 | 0 | 0 | S |
| | 2012 WW prel | 0 | 1 | 1 | 0 | — |
| | 2012 WW gold | 2 | 1 | 3 | 0 | G |

**Kelley Owen**

| | | | | | | |
|---|---|---|---|---|---|---|
| USA | 1990 WW gold | 0 | 0 | 0 | 2 | S |

**Margot Page (-Verlaan)**

| | | | | | | |
|---|---|---|---|---|---|---|
| CAN | 1990 WW gold | 0 | 0 | 0 | 0 | G |
| | 1992 WW gold | 1 | 1 | 2 | 0 | G |
| | 1994 WW gold | 0 | 0 | 0 | 0 | G |

**Judy Parish**

| | | | | | | |
|---|---|---|---|---|---|---|
| USA | 1990 WW gold | 0 | 0 | 0 | 0 | S |

**Sarah Parsons**

| | | | | | | |
|---|---|---|---|---|---|---|
| USA | 2005 WW gold | 0 | 0 | 0 | 0 | G |
| | 2007 WW qual | 0 | 0 | 0 | 0 | — |
| | 2007 WW gold | 0 | 0 | 0 | 0 | S |
| | 2008 WW qual | 0 | 0 | 0 | 4 | — |
| | 2008 WW gold | 0 | 0 | 0 | 2 | G |

**Yvonne Percy**

| | | | | | | |
|---|---|---|---|---|---|---|
| USA | 1990 WW gold | 0 | 0 | 0 | 0 | S |

**Cathy Phillips**

| | | | | | |
|---|---|---|---|---|---|
| CAN | 1990 WW gold | 60:00 | W | 2 | G |

**Michelle Picard**

| | | | | | | |
|---|---|---|---|---|---|---|
| USA | 2012 WW prel | 0 | 0 | 0 | 0 | — |
| | 2012 WW gold | 0 | 0 | 0 | 0 | S |

**Nathalie Picard**

| | | | | | | |
|---|---|---|---|---|---|---|
| CAN | 1992 WW gold | 0 | 0 | 0 | 4 | G |
| | 1994 WW gold | 0 | 0 | 0 | 0 | G |

**Cherie Piper**

| | | | | | | |
|---|---|---|---|---|---|---|
| CAN | 2002 OG-W gold | 0 | 1 | 1 | 0 | G |
| | 2004 WW prel | 0 | 0 | 0 | 0 | — |
| | 2004 WW gold | 0 | 0 | 0 | 2 | G |
| | 2005 WW gold | 0 | 0 | 0 | 0 | S |
| | 2008 WW qual | 0 | 0 | 0 | 0 | — |
| | 2008 WW gold | 0 | 0 | 0 | 0 | S |
| | 2010 OG-W gold | 0 | 0 | 0 | 0 | G |
| | 2011 WW gold | 0 | 1 | 1 | 0 | S |

**Jenny Potter**

| | | | | | | |
|---|---|---|---|---|---|---|
| USA | 1998 OG-W prel | 1 | 0 | 1 | 0 | — |
| | 1998 OG-W gold | 0 | 0 | 0 | 0 | G |
| | 1999 WW gold | 1 | 0 | 1 | 0 | S |
| | 2000 WW gold | 0 | 0 | 0 | 0 | S |
| | 2001 WW gold | 0 | 0 | 0 | 2 | S |
| | 2002 OG-W gold | 0 | 1 | 1 | 0 | S |
| | 2004 WW prel | 0 | 0 | 0 | 2 | — |
| | 2004 WW gold | 0 | 0 | 0 | 0 | S |
| | 2005 WW gold | 0 | 0 | 0 | 0 | G |
| | 2007 WW qual | 1 | 0 | 1 | 6 | — |
| | 2007 WW gold | 0 | 0 | 0 | 0 | S |
| | 2008 WW qual | 0 | 1 | 1 | 2 | — |
| | 2008 WW gold | 2 | 0 | 2 | 0 | G |
| | 2009 WW qual | 0 | 0 | 0 | 0 | — |
| | 2009 WW gold | 0 | 1 | 1 | 0 | G |
| | 2010 OG-W gold | 0 | 0 | 0 | 2 | S |
| | 2011 WW gold | 1 | 0 | 1 | 0 | G |
| | 2012 WW prel | 0 | 1 | 1 | 0 | — |
| | 2012 WW gold | 0 | 0 | 0 | 0 | S |

**Marie-Philip Poulin (-Nadeau)**

| | | | | | | |
|---|---|---|---|---|---|---|
| CAN | 2009 WW qual | 0 | 0 | 0 | 0 | — |
| | 2009 WW gold | 0 | 0 | 0 | 0 | S |
| | 2010 OG-W gold | 2 | 0 | 2 | 0 | G |
| | 2011 WW gold | 0 | 0 | 0 | 0 | S |
| | 2012 WW prel | 1 | 0 | 1 | 0 | — |
| | 2012 WW gold | 0 | 0 | 0 | 4 | G |

**Cheryl Pounder**

| | | | | | | |
|---|---|---|---|---|---|---|
| CAN | 1994 WW gold | 0 | 0 | 0 | 0 | G |
| | 1999 WW gold | 0 | 0 | 0 | 0 | G |
| | 2000 WW gold | 0 | 0 | 0 | 0 | G |
| | 2001 WW gold | 0 | 0 | 0 | 0 | G |
| | 2002 OG-W gold | 0 | 0 | 0 | 0 | G |
| | 2004 WW prel | 0 | 1 | 1 | 0 | — |
| | 2004 WW gold | 0 | 0 | 0 | 0 | G |
| | 2005 WW gold | 0 | 0 | 0 | 2 | S |
| | 2007 WW qual | 0 | 0 | 0 | 2 | — |
| | 2007 WW gold | 0 | 0 | 0 | 0 | G |

**Josephine Pucci**

| | | | | | | |
|---|---|---|---|---|---|---|
| USA | 2011 WW gold | 0 | 0 | 0 | 2 | G |
| | 2012 WW prel | 1 | 0 | 1 | 2 | — |
| | 2012 WW gold | 0 | 0 | 0 | 0 | S |

**Kim Ratushny**

| | | | | | | |
|---|---|---|---|---|---|---|
| CAN | 1990 WW gold | 0 | 0 | 0 | 0 | G |

**Lesley Reddon**

| | | | | | |
|---|---|---|---|---|---|
| CAN | 1997 WW gold | 72:59 | W | 3 | G |
| | 1998 OG-W prel | 59:41 | L | 6 | — |

**Helen Resor**

| | | | | | | |
|---|---|---|---|---|---|---|
| USA | 2005 WW gold | 0 | 0 | 0 | 2 | G |
| | 2007 WW qual | 0 | 0 | 0 | 0 | — |
| | 2007 WW gold | 0 | 0 | 0 | 2 | S |
| | 2009 WW qual | 0 | 0 | 0 | 2 | — |
| | 2009 WW gold | 0 | 0 | 0 | 0 | G |

**Manon Rheaume**

| | | | | | |
|---|---|---|---|---|---|
| CAN | 1992 WW gold | 60:00 | W | 0 | G |
| | 1994 WW gold | 60:00 | W | 3 | G |
| | 1998 OG-W gold | 59:14 | L | 2 | S |

**Brenda Richard**

| | | | | | | |
|---|---|---|---|---|---|---|
| CAN | 1990 WW gold | 0 | 0 | 0 | 2 | G |

**Nathalie Rivard**

| | | | | | | |
|---|---|---|---|---|---|---|
| CAN | 1992 WW gold | 0 | 0 | 0 | 0 | G |
| | 1999 WW gold | 0 | 0 | 0 | 0 | G |
| | 2000 WW gold | 0 | 0 | 0 | 0 | G |

**Jane Robinson**

| | | | | | | |
|---|---|---|---|---|---|---|
| CAN | 1994 WW gold | 0 | 1 | 1 | 0 | G |

**Lauriane Rougeau**

| | | | | | | |
|---|---|---|---|---|---|---|
| CAN | 2012 WW prel | 0 | 0 | 0 | 0 | — |
| | 2012 WW gold | 0 | 0 | 0 | 2 | G |

**Angela Ruggiero**

| | | | | | | |
|---|---|---|---|---|---|---|
| USA | 1997 WW gold | 0 | 0 | 0 | 4 | S |
| | 1998 OG-W prel | 0 | 0 | 0 | 14 | — |
| | 1998 OG-W gold | 0 | 0 | 0 | 0 | G |
| | 1999 WW gold | 0 | 0 | 0 | 2 | S |
| | 2000 WW gold | 0 | 0 | 0 | 12 | S |
| | 2001 WW gold | 0 | 0 | 0 | 0 | S |
| | 2002 OG-W gold | 0 | 0 | 0 | 0 | S |
| | 2004 WW prel | 0 | 0 | 0 | 0 | — |
| | 2004 WW gold | 0 | 0 | 0 | 2 | S |
| | 2005 WW gold | 1 | 0 | 1 | 0 | G |
| | 2007 WW qual | 0 | 0 | 0 | 6 | — |
| | 2007 WW gold | 0 | 0 | 0 | 0 | S |
| | 2008 WW qual | 0 | 0 | 0 | 0 | — |
| | 2008 WW gold | 0 | 1 | 1 | 2 | G |
| | 2009 WW qual | 0 | 0 | 0 | 4 | — |
| | 2009 WW gold | 0 | 0 | 0 | 0 | G |
| | 2010 OG-W gold | 0 | 0 | 0 | 2 | S |
| | 2011 WW gold | 0 | 1 | 1 | 0 | G |

**Julie Sasner**

| | | | | | | |
|---|---|---|---|---|---|---|
| USA | 1990 WW gold | 0 | 0 | 0 | 0 | S |

**Molly Schaus**

| | | | | | |
|---|---|---|---|---|---|
| USA | 2009 WW qual | 59:22 | L | 2 | — |
| | 2012 WW prel | 60:00 | W | 2 | — |
| | 2012 WW gold | 61:50 | L | 5 | S |

**Sue Scherer**

| | | | | | | |
|---|---|---|---|---|---|---|
| CAN | 1990 WW gold | 0 | 1 | 1 | 0 | G |
| | 1992 WW gold | 0 | 0 | 0 | 0 | G |

**Anne Schleper**

| | | | | | | |
|---|---|---|---|---|---|---|
| USA | 2011 WW gold | 0 | 0 | 0 | 0 | G |
| | 2012 WW prel | 0 | 0 | 0 | 0 | — |
| | 2012 WW gold | 0 | 1 | 1 | 0 | S |

**Jen Scoullis**

| | | | | | | |
|---|---|---|---|---|---|---|
| USA | 2011 WW gold | 0 | 0 | 0 | 0 | G |

**Laura Schuler**

| | | | | | | |
|---|---|---|---|---|---|---|
| CAN | 1990 WW gold | 0 | 0 | 0 | 0 | G |
| | 1992 WW gold | 0 | 0 | 0 | 0 | G |
| | 1997 WW gold | 0 | 0 | 0 | 2 | G |
| | 1998 OG-W prel | 0 | 0 | 0 | 0 | — |
| | 1998 OG-W gold | 0 | 0 | 0 | 0 | S |

**Tammy Shewchuk**

| | | | | | | |
|---|---|---|---|---|---|---|
| CAN | 2000 WW gold | 0 | 0 | 0 | 0 | G |
| | 2001 WW gold | 1 | 0 | 1 | 0 | G |
| | 2002 OG-W gold | 0 | 0 | 0 | 0 | G |

| Bobbi Jo Slusar | | | | | | |
|---|---|---|---|---|---|---|
| CAN | 2011 WW gold | 0 | 0 | 0 | 2 | S |

| Sami Jo Small | | | | | | |
|---|---|---|---|---|---|---|
| CAN | 1999 WW gold | 60:00 | W | 1 | G | |
| | 2000 WW gold | 66:50 | W | 2 | G | |

| Fiona Smith | | | | | | |
|---|---|---|---|---|---|---|
| CAN | 1997 WW gold | 0 | 0 | 0 | 0 | G |
| | 1998 OG-W gold | 0 | 0 | 0 | 0 | S |
| | 1999 WW gold | 0 | 0 | 0 | 0 | G |

| Jeanine Sobek | | | | | | |
|---|---|---|---|---|---|---|
| USA | 1990 WW gold | 0 | 0 | 0 | 2 | S |
| | 1992 WW gold | 0 | 0 | 0 | 0 | S |
| | 1994 WW gold | 0 | 0 | 0 | 2 | S |

| Colleen Sostorics | | | | | | |
|---|---|---|---|---|---|---|
| CAN | 2001 WW gold | 0 | 0 | 0 | 0 | G |
| | 2002 OG-W gold | 0 | 0 | 0 | 2 | G |
| | 2004 WW prel | 0 | 0 | 0 | 0 | — |
| | 2004 WW gold | 0 | 0 | 0 | 0 | G |
| | 2005 WW gold | 0 | 0 | 0 | 0 | S |
| | 2007 WW qual | 0 | 0 | 0 | 0 | — |
| | 2007 WW gold | 0 | 1 | 1 | 0 | G |
| | 2008 WW qual | 0 | 0 | 0 | 2 | — |
| | 2008 WW gold | 0 | 1 | 1 | 4 | S |
| | 2009 WW qual | 0 | 0 | 0 | 2 | — |
| | 2009 WW gold | 0 | 0 | 0 | 0 | S |
| | 2010 OG-W gold | 0 | 0 | 0 | 0 | G |

| Natalie Spooner | | | | | | |
|---|---|---|---|---|---|---|
| CAN | 2011 WW gold | 0 | 1 | 1 | 0 | S |
| | 2012 WW prel | 1 | 0 | 1 | 0 | — |
| | 2012 WW gold | 0 | 0 | 0 | 2 | G |

| Kelli Stack | | | | | | |
|---|---|---|---|---|---|---|
| USA | 2008 WW qual | 0 | 0 | 0 | 2 | — |
| | 2008 WW gold | 0 | 0 | 0 | 0 | G |
| | 2009 WW qual | 0 | 0 | 0 | 2 | — |
| | 2009 WW gold | 0 | 0 | 0 | 0 | G |
| | 2010 OG-W gold | 0 | 0 | 0 | 0 | S |
| | 2011 WW gold | 0 | 0 | 0 | 0 | G |
| | 2012 WW prel | 0 | 3 | 3 | 0 | — |
| | 2012 WW gold | 0 | 0 | 0 | 2 | S |

| Kelley Steadman | | | | | | |
|---|---|---|---|---|---|---|
| USA | 2011 WW gold | 0 | 0 | 0 | 0 | G |

| Kelly Stephens | | | | | | |
|---|---|---|---|---|---|---|
| USA | 2004 WW prel | 0 | 0 | 0 | 2 | — |
| | 2004 WW gold | 0 | 0 | 0 | 0 | S |
| | 2005 WW gold | 0 | 0 | 0 | 0 | G |

| France St. Louis | | | | | | |
|---|---|---|---|---|---|---|
| CAN | 1990 WW gold | 2 | 2 | 4 | 2 | G |
| | 1992 WW gold | 0 | 0 | 0 | 2 | G |
| | 1994 WW gold | 1 | 1 | 2 | 0 | G |
| | 1997 WW gold | 0 | 0 | 0 | 0 | G |
| | 1998 OG-W prel | 0 | 0 | 0 | 0 | — |
| | 1998 OG-W gold | 0 | 0 | 0 | 0 | S |
| | 1999 WW gold | 0 | 0 | 0 | 0 | G |

| Kim St. Pierre | | | | | | |
|---|---|---|---|---|---|---|
| CAN | 2001 WW gold | 60:00 | W | 2 | G | |
| | 2002 OG-W gold | 60:00 | W | 2 | G | |
| | 2004 WW prel | 59:43 | L | 3 | — | |
| | 2004 WW gold | 60:00 | W | 0 | G | |
| | 2005 WW gold | 80:00 | L | 1 | S | |
| | 2007 WW gold | 60:00 | W | 1 | G | |
| | 2008 WW gold | 40:00 | L | 4 | S | |

| Sharon Stridsen | | | | | | |
|---|---|---|---|---|---|---|
| USA | 1990 WW gold | 0 | 0 | 0 | 0 | S |

| Vicky Sunohara | | | | | | |
|---|---|---|---|---|---|---|
| CAN | 1990 WW gold | 0 | 1 | 1 | 0 | G |
| | 1997 WW gold | 0 | 0 | 0 | 2 | G |
| | 1998 OG-W prel | 0 | 1 | 1 | 0 | — |
| | 1998 OG-W gold | 0 | 0 | 0 | 0 | S |
| | 1999 WW gold | 0 | 0 | 0 | 0 | G |
| | 2000 WW gold | 0 | 0 | 0 | 0 | G |
| | 2001 WW gold | 0 | 1 | 1 | 0 | G |
| | 2002 OG-W gold | 0 | 0 | 0 | 2 | G |
| | 2004 WW prel | 0 | 0 | 0 | 0 | — |
| | 2004 WW gold | 0 | 0 | 0 | 0 | G |
| | 2005 WW gold | 0 | 0 | 0 | 0 | S |
| | 2007 WW qual | 0 | 0 | 0 | 0 | — |
| | 2007 WW gold | 0 | 1 | 1 | 2 | G |

| Shannon Szabados | | | | | | |
|---|---|---|---|---|---|---|
| CAN | 2010 OG-W gold | 60:00 | W | 0 | G | |
| | 2011 WW gold | 67:48 | L | 3 | S | |
| | 2012 WW prel | 16:28 | nd | 2 | — | |
| | 2012 WW gold | 61:50 | W | 4 | G | |

| Karen Thatcher | | | | | | |
|---|---|---|---|---|---|---|
| USA | 2008 WW qual | 0 | 0 | 0 | 2 | — |
| | 2008 WW gold | 0 | 0 | 0 | 0 | G |
| | 2009 WW qual | 0 | 0 | 0 | 0 | — |
| | 2009 WW gold | 0 | 0 | 0 | 0 | G |
| | 2010 OG-W gold | 0 | 0 | 0 | 0 | S |

| Sarah Tueting | | | | | | |
|---|---|---|---|---|---|---|
| USA | 1998 OG-W prel | 29:24 | nd | 1 | — | |
| | 1998 OG-W gold | 60:00 | W | 1 | G | |
| | 2001 WW gold | 58:49 | L | 3 | S* | |

*2 pims in 2001 WW gold

| Gretchen Ulion | | | | | | |
|---|---|---|---|---|---|---|
| USA | 1994 WW gold | 0 | 0 | 0 | 0 | S |
| | 1997 WW gold | 0 | 0 | 0 | 0 | S |
| | 1998 OG-W prel | 0 | 1 | 1 | 0 | — |
| | 1998 OG-W gold | 1 | 1 | 2 | 0 | G |

| Sarah Vaillancourt | | | | | | |
|---|---|---|---|---|---|---|
| CAN | 2005 WW gold | 0 | 0 | 0 | 0 | S |
| | 2007 WW qual | 1 | 0 | 1 | 0 | — |
| | 2007 WW gold | 1 | 1 | 2 | 2 | G |
| | 2008 WW qual | 0 | 0 | 0 | 6 | — |
| | 2008 WW gold | 1 | 0 | 1 | 0 | S |
| | 2009 WW qual | 0 | 0 | 0 | 0 | — |
| | 2009 WW gold | 0 | 0 | 0 | 2 | S |
| | 2010 OG-W gold | 0 | 0 | 0 | 0 | G |
| | 2011 WW gold | 0 | 0 | 0 | 0 | S |

| Julianne Vasichek | | | | | | |
|---|---|---|---|---|---|---|
| USA | 2004 WW prel | 0 | 0 | 0 | 2 | — |
| | 2004 WW gold | 0 | 0 | 0 | 2 | S |

| Jessie Vetter | | | | | | |
|---|---|---|---|---|---|---|
| USA | 2007 WW qual | 70:00 | L | 5 | — | |
| | 2008 WW qual | 60:00 | W | 2 | — | |
| | 2008 WW gold | 60:00 | W | 3 | G | |
| | 2009 WW gold | 60:00 | W | 1 | G | |
| | 2010 OG-W gold | 59:50 | L | 2 | S | |
| | 2011 WW gold | 67:48 | W | 2 | G | |

| Jennifer Wakefield | | | | | | |
|---|---|---|---|---|---|---|
| CAN | 2011 WW gold | 0 | 1 | 1 | 2 | S |
| | 2012 WW prel | 0 | 0 | 0 | 0 | — |
| | 2012 WW gold | 0 | 0 | 0 | 4 | G |

| Lyndsay Wall | | | | | | |
|---|---|---|---|---|---|---|
| USA | 2002 OG-W gold | 0 | 0 | 0 | 2 | S |
| | 2005 WW gold | 0 | 0 | 0 | 0 | G |

| Catherine Ward | | | | | | |
|---|---|---|---|---|---|---|
| CAN | 2009 WW qual | 0 | 0 | 0 | 0 | — |
| | 2009 WW gold | 0 | 0 | 0 | 0 | S |
| | 2010 OG-W gold | 0 | 0 | 0 | 2 | G |
| | 2011 WW gold | 0 | 0 | 0 | 0 | S |
| | 2012 WW prel | 0 | 0 | 0 | 0 | — |
| | 2012 WW gold | 0 | 0 | 0 | 0 | G |

| Taylor Wasylk | | | | | | |
|---|---|---|---|---|---|---|
| USA | 2012 WW prel | 0 | 0 | 0 | 0 | — |

| Tara Watchorn | | | | | | |
|---|---|---|---|---|---|---|
| CAN | 2011 WW gold | 0 | 0 | 0 | 0 | S |

| Katie Weatherston | | | | | | |
|---|---|---|---|---|---|---|
| CAN | 2007 WW qual | 0 | 1 | 1 | 0 | — |
| | 2007 WW gold | 0 | 0 | 0 | 0 | G |
| | 2008 WW qual | 0 | 0 | 0 | 2 | — |
| | 2008 WW gold | 1 | 0 | 1 | 0 | S |

| Kerry Weiland | | | | | | |
|---|---|---|---|---|---|---|
| USA | 2004 WW prel | 0 | 0 | 0 | 0 | — |
| | 2004 WW gold | 0 | 0 | 0 | 2 | S |
| | 2007 WW qual | 0 | 0 | 0 | 0 | — |
| | 2007 WW gold | 0 | 0 | 0 | 0 | S |
| | 2008 WW qual | 0 | 0 | 0 | 0 | — |
| | 2008 WW gold | 0 | 0 | 0 | 2 | G |
| | 2009 WW qual | 0 | 0 | 0 | 0 | — |
| | 2009 WW gold | 0 | 0 | 0 | 0 | G |
| | 2010 OG-W gold | 0 | 0 | 0 | 0 | S |

| Ellen Weinberg | | | | | | |
|---|---|---|---|---|---|---|
| USA | 1992 WW gold | 0 | 0 | 0 | 2 | S |

| Krissy Wendell | | | | | | |
|---|---|---|---|---|---|---|
| USA | 1999 WW gold | 0 | 0 | 0 | 0 | S |
| | 2000 WW gold | 0 | 1 | 1 | 0 | S |
| | 2001 WW gold | 0 | 1 | 1 | 0 | S |
| | 2002 OG-W gold | 0 | 0 | 0 | 2 | S |
| | 2004 WW prel | 1 | 0 | 1 | 0 | — |
| | 2005 WW gold | 0 | 0 | 0 | 0 | G |
| | 2007 WW qual | 1 | 1 | 2 | 0 | — |
| | 2007 WW gold | 1 | 0 | 1 | 4 | S |

| Erin Whitten | | | | | | |
|---|---|---|---|---|---|---|
| USA | 1992 WW gold | 60:00 | L | 8 | S | |
| | 1994 WW gold | 60:00 | L | 6 | S | |
| | 1997 WW gold | 72:59 | L | 4 | S | |
| | 1999 WW gold | 59:03 | L | 3 | S | |

| Sandra Whyte | | | | | | |
|---|---|---|---|---|---|---|
| USA | 1992 WW gold | 0 | 0 | 0 | 0 | S |
| | 1994 WW gold | 0 | 0 | 0 | 0 | S |
| | 1997 WW gold | 0 | 0 | 0 | 0 | S |
| | 1998 OG-W prel | 0 | 0 | 0 | 0 | — |
| | 1998 OG-W gold | 1 | 2 | 3 | 0 | G |

| Hayley Wickenheiser | | | | | | |
|---|---|---|---|---|---|---|
| CAN | 1994 WW gold | 0 | 1 | 1 | 0 | G |
| | 1997 WW gold | 0 | 2 | 2 | 4 | G |
| | 1998 OG-W prel | 0 | 1 | 1 | 0 | — |
| | 1998 OG-W gold | 0 | 1 | 1 | 0 | S |
| | 1999 WW gold | 0 | 1 | 1 | 0 | G |
| | 2000 WW gold | 0 | 0 | 0 | 0 | G |
| | 2002 OG-W gold | 1 | 0 | 1 | 2 | G |
| | 2004 WW prel | 0 | 0 | 0 | 0 | — |
| | 2004 WW gold | 1 | 0 | 1 | 0 | G |
| | 2005 WW gold | 0 | 0 | 0 | 0 | S |
| | 2007 WW qual | 2 | 2 | 4 | 0 | — |
| | 2007 WW gold | 1 | 0 | 1 | 0 | G |
| | 2008 WW qual | 0 | 0 | 0 | 0 | — |
| | 2008 WW gold | 0 | 0 | 0 | 2 | S |
| | 2009 WW qual | 0 | 0 | 0 | 0 | — |
| | 2009 WW gold | 0 | 0 | 0 | 0 | S |
| | 2010 OG-W gold | 0 | 0 | 0 | 0 | G |
| | 2011 WW gold | 0 | 0 | 0 | 2 | S |
| | 2012 WW prel | 0 | 1 | 1 | 0 | — |
| | 2012 WW gold | 1 | 1 | 2 | 0 | G |

| Stacy Wilson | | | | | | |
|---|---|---|---|---|---|---|
| CAN | 1990 WW gold | 0 | 0 | 0 | 0 | G |
| | 1992 WW gold | 0 | 0 | 0 | 0 | G |
| | 1994 WW gold | 1 | 0 | 1 | 0 | G |
| | 1997 WW gold | 0 | 1 | 1 | 0 | G |
| | 1998 OG-W prel | 0 | 1 | 1 | 0 | — |
| | 1998 OG-W gold | 0 | 0 | 0 | 0 | S |

| Susana Yuen | | | | | | |
|---|---|---|---|---|---|---|
| CAN | 1990 WW gold | 1 | 0 | 1 | 0 | G |

| Carisa Zaban | | | | | | |
|---|---|---|---|---|---|---|
| USA | 2001 WW gold | 1 | 0 | 1 | 0 | S |

| Jinelle Zaugg (-Siergiej) | | | | | | |
|---|---|---|---|---|---|---|
| USA | 2007 WW qual | 0 | 1 | 1 | 0 | — |
| | 2007 WW gold | 0 | 0 | 0 | 0 | S |
| | 2010 OG-W gold | 0 | 0 | 0 | 2 | S |

# THE IIHF

## IIHF Presidents

Louis Magnus (FRA)—1908-1912 & 1914
Henri van den Bulcke (BEL)—1912-14 & 1914-20
Major Bethune Minet "Peter" Patton (GBR)—1914
Max Sillig (SUI)—1920-22
Paul Loicq (BEL)—1922-47
Dr. Fritz Kraatz (SUI)—1947-48 & 1951-54
George Hardy (CAN)—1948-51
Walter Brown (USA)—1954-57
John "Bunny" Ahearne (GBR)—1957-60 & 1963-66 & 1969-75
Robert Lebel (CAN)—1960-63
Thayer Tutt (USA)—1966-69
Dr. Gunther Sabetzki (GER)—1975-94
Dr. René Fasel (SUI)—1994-present

## IIHF Life Members

Walter Bush, Jr.
Dr. Hans Dobida
Jan-Ake Edvinsson
Kai Hietarinta
Yuri Korolev
Philippe Jacques Lacarriere
Gyorgy Pasztor
Gordon Renwick
Alexander Steblin

## IIHF Honourary Member

Oscar Frei (SUI)

## IIHF Staff

**GENERAL SECRETARIAT**

| | |
|---|---|
| Horst Lichtner | General Secretary |
| Nicole Bosshardt | Assistant to the General Secretary |

**ADMINISTRATION AND FINANCE DEPARTMENT**

| | |
|---|---|
| Gion Veraguth | Director of Finance and Administration |
| Iris Hanni | Administration and Legal Manager |
| Ashley Ehlert | Legal Manager |
| Kristina Koch | Executive Assistant to the President |
| Simona Richiger | Receptionist, IT & Administration |
| Slavko Bartulovic | Facility Caretaker |
| Ruth Kunzle | Finance Coordinator |
| Adrian Oggier | Finance Coordinator |

**MARKETING AND COMMUNICATIONS DEPARTMENT**

| | |
|---|---|
| Christian Hofstetter | Marketing Director |
| Tim Broadbent | Marketing Manager |
| Kira Ebel | Marketing and Communications Assistant |
| Szymon Szemberg | Communications Director |
| Martin Merk | Website Manager |
| Adam Steiss | Communications Manager |

**EVENT DEPARTMENT**

| | |
|---|---|
| Hannes Ederer | Deputy General Secretary / Event Director |
| Cornelia Ljungberg | Event Development Director |
| Eslie Dall'Oglio | Event Manager |
| Eric Trinkler | Event Assistant |
| Rob van Rijswijk | Director Club Competitions |
| Luzia Baldauf | Manager Club Competitions |

**SPORT DEPARTMENT**

| | |
|---|---|
| Dave Fitzpatrick | Sport Director |
| Konstantin Komissarov | Officiating Manager |
| Darryl Easson | Sport Development Manager |
| Andy Ecker | Sport Administration Manager |
| Tanya Foley | Women's Program Manager |
| Aku Nieminen | Coordinator Sport Administration |

**IT DEPARTMENT**

| | |
|---|---|
| Martin Zoellner | IT Director |
| Konstantin Gasilin | IT Developer |
| Marcis Grasis | IT Assistant |

**OFF-SITE CONSULTANTS**

| | |
|---|---|
| Harald Springfeld | Asian Sport Development Manager |
| Adam Sollitt | Research and Audit Coordinator |
| Darren Boyko | Hockey Hall of Fame |

## IIHF Council

(appointed May 24, 2008—term runs 2008-2012)

**IIHF COUNCIL**

René Fasel, President (SUI)
Christer Englund (SWE)
Horst Lichtner, General Secretary (GER)
Shoichi Tomita, Vice President (JPN)
Kalervo Kummola, Vice President (FIN)
Murray Costello, Vice President (CAN)
Ernest Aljancic (SLO)
Frank Gonzalez (ESP)
Beate Grupp (GER)
Alexander Medvedev (RUS)
Frederick Meredith (GBR)
Tony Rossi (USA)
Monique Scheier-Schneider (LUX)
Juraj Siroky (SVK)

*Murray Costello (CAN) and Shoichi Tomita (JPN) are retiring from their duties with the IIHF after long and distinguished careers. Photo (left): Dave Sandford. Photo (right): Matthew Manor.*

# Tournament Structure

Starting in 2011-12, the IIHF tournament structure will feature a radical overhaul of structure between the top level and the divisions below. What will be in place for the men's World Championship will be used by all events, but the change is most dramatic for the men's Worlds.

Previously the last two teams after a World Championship (15th and 16th) were relegated to Division I, groups A and B. That is, Division I, Group A and Division I, Group B were considered equal or parallel events. No longer will this be the case. The last two teams will now both be relegated to Division I, Group A, and this group will feature the six highest ranked teams after the top level. Group B will be UNDER Group A in terms of ranking. The last team from Group A will be demoted to Group B, and the same continues down. The last team from Group B is demoted to Division II, Group A, and so on. This structure will be in place for all IIHF events.

The rationale is simple. IIHF studies have indicated the top and bottom teams of various groups are not as competitive as they should be. By tightening the groups to create a fairer balance between the best and worst, games should all be more competitive, and this can only increase quality of entertainment for fans and contribute to greater development by the lower nations.

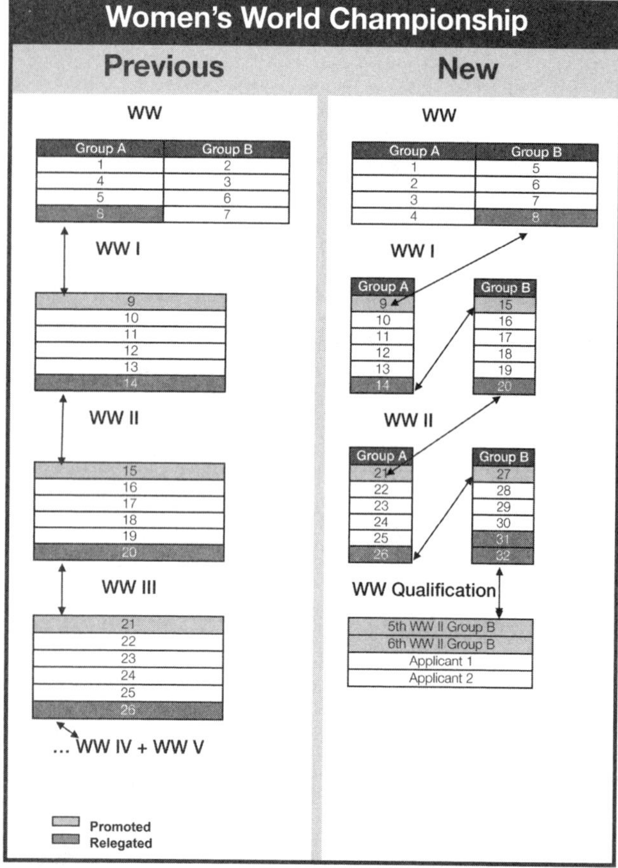


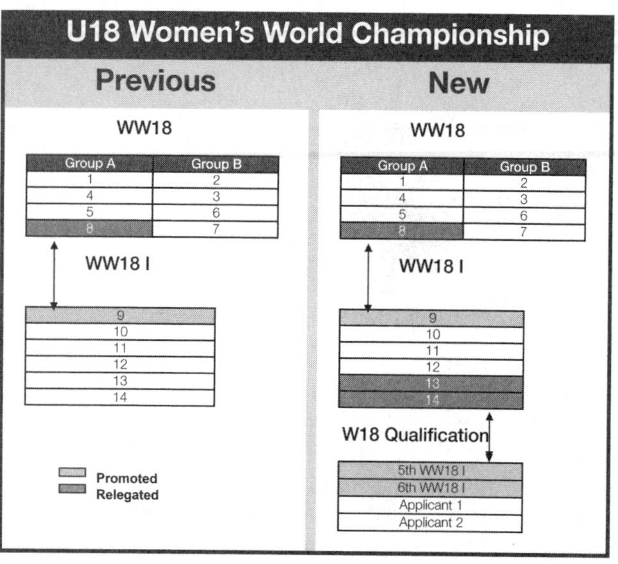


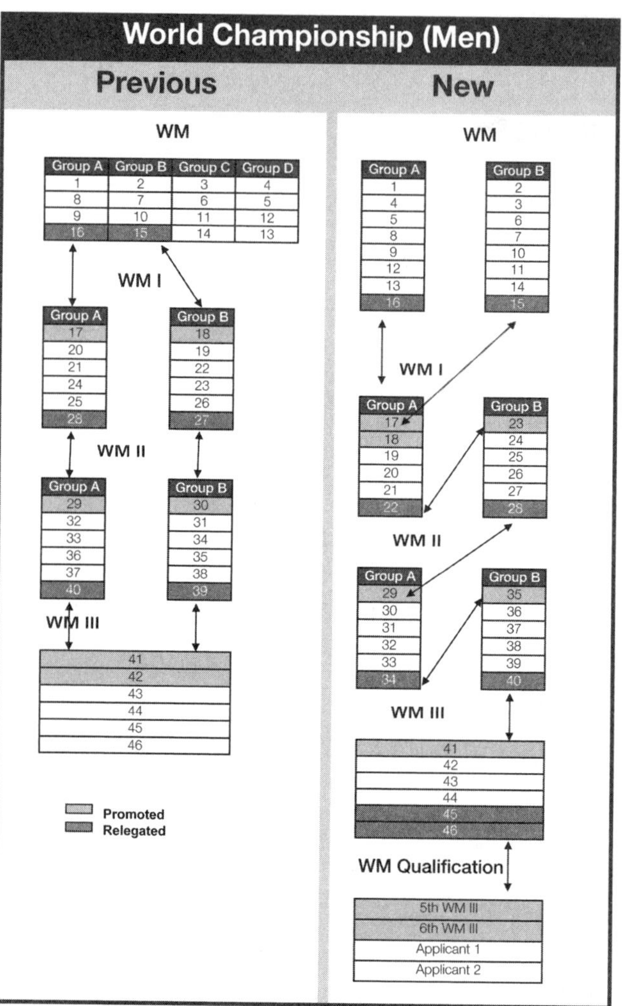


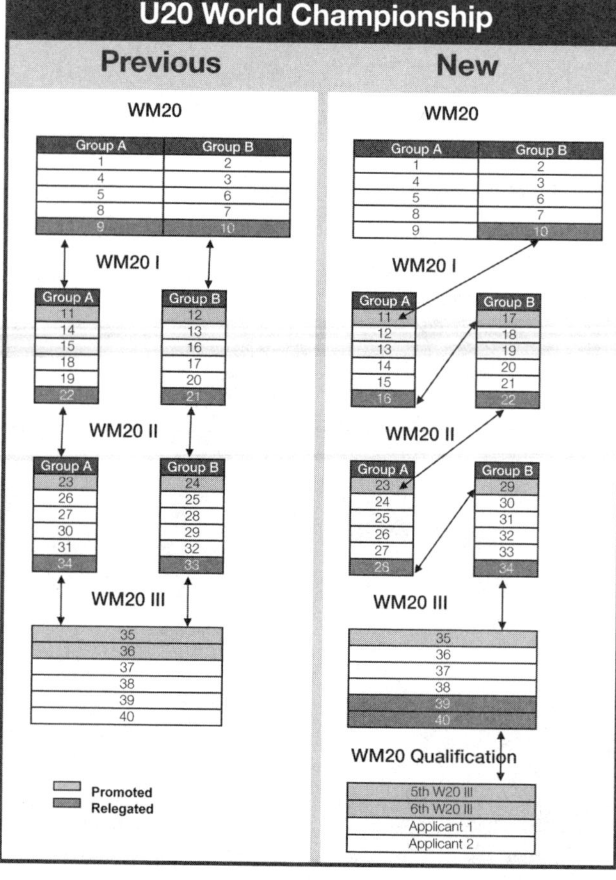

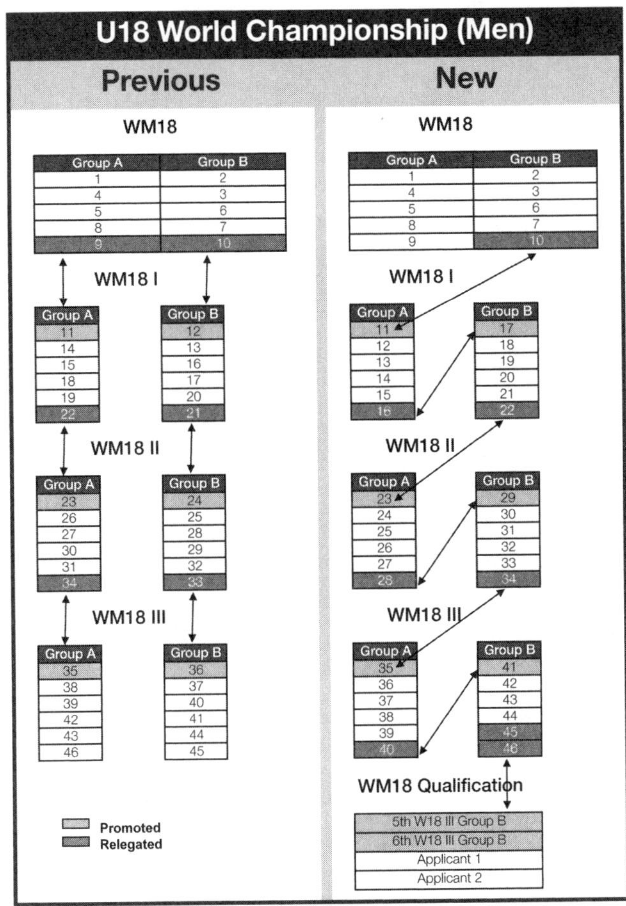


# Tournament Formats for 2012-13

**WM**

Since 2012 the World Championship has revised the group structure for the 16 particioating nations. They now are divided into two Preliminary Round groups of eight teams, using the IIHF World Ranking for seeding. Each team plays seven round-robin games in the Preliminary Round instead of the previous three, but the Qualifying Round has been eliminated. The top four teams in each Preliminary Round group advance to the quarter-finals. The teams that finish last in each group are relegated to Division I. Teams placed 5-8 are eliminated from further competition because the Relegation Round has also been eliminated.

**WM20** No change in format.

**WM18** The bye to the semi-finals for first-place finishers in the Preliminary Round has been eliminated, so the top-four teams in each group advance to a four-game quarter-finals elimination round.

**WW** No change in format.

**WW18** No change in format.

# Current World Championship Tournament Regulations

**TIE BREAKING SYSTEM FOR IIHF CHAPMIONSHIPS**

The tie-breaking system for two teams with the same number of points in a standing will be the game between the two teams, the winner of the game taking precedence.

Due to the fact that the three-point system does not allow a game to end in a tie, then the following tie breaking procedure is applicable when three or more teams are tied in points in a Championship standing.

Should three or more teams be tied on points, then a tie breaking formula will be applied as follows, creating a sub-group amongst the tied teams. This process will continue until only two or none of the teams remain tied. In the case of two tied teams remaining, the game between the two would then be the determining tie-breaker as the game could not end as a tie. In the case of none of the teams being tied, the criteria specified in the respective step applies.

Step 1: Taking into consideration the games between each of the tied teams, a sub-group is created applying the points awarded in the direct games amongst the tied teams from which the teams are then ranked accordingly.

Step 2: Should three or more teams still remain tied in points then the better goal difference in the direct games amongst the tied teams will be decisive.

Step 3: Should three or more teams still remain tied in points and goal difference then the highest number of goals scored by these teams in their direct games will be decisive

Step 4: Should three or more teams still remain tied in points, goal difference and goals scored then the results between each of the three teams and the closest best-ranked team outside the sub-group will be applied. In this case the tied team with the best result (1. points, 2. goal difference, 3. more goals scored) against the closest best ranked-team will take precedence

Step 5: Should the teams still remain tied, then the results between each of the three teams and the next highest best-ranked team outside the sub-group will be applied.

Step 6: Should the teams still remain tied after these five steps have been exercised then Sport considerations will be applied and the teams will be ranked by their positions coming into the Championship (seeding).

**MEDAL ROUND OVERTIME PROCEDURE**

- In case of a tie at the end of regulation in a quarter-final, semi-final, and bronze medal game, there will be a 10-minute, sudden-death overtime period, following a three-minute intermission. The teams will defend the same goals as in the third period. The team, which scores first is the winner.
- In the gold medal game there will be a 20-minute sudden-death overtime, following a full intermission during which the ice will be resurfaced. The teams will change ends. The team which scores first is the winner.
- All sudden death overtime periods are played four skaters on four.
- If no goal is scored during the sudden-death overtime, there will be a game winning shot (GWS) competition (shootout).

**RULES FOR THE FOUR-ON-FOUR OVERTIME PROCEDURE**

1. If a team is penalized in overtime, the teams will play 4-on-3. Coincidental penalties do not affect the on-ice strength when assessed in overtime.
2. In overtime, if a team is penalized such that a two-man advantage is called for, then the offending team will remain at three (3) skaters while the non-offending team will be permitted a fifth skater. At the first stoppage of play after the two-man advantage is no longer in effect, the numerical strength of the team will revert back to either a 4-on-4 or a 4-on-3 situation, as appropriate.
3. If there is a man advantage which carries over from regulation to overtime, the above criteria will be applied at the start of the overtime. If at the end of the regulation, the teams are 5-on-4, overtime begins at 4-on-3.
4. When regulation time ends with a 5-on-3, teams will begin the overtime with 5-on-3. At the end of penalties, due to continuous action, player strength may get to 5-on-5 or 5-on-4. At the first stoppage, player strength must be adjusted to 4-on-4 or 4-on-3.
5. If at the end of regulation time teams are 3-on-3, overtime starts 3-on-3. Once player strength reaches 5-on-4 or 5-on-5, at the next stoppage player strength is adjusted to 4-on-3 or 4-on-4, as appropriate.
6. If at the end of regulation, teams are 4-on-4 with a player or players in the box serving non-coincidental penalties, overtime starts 4-on-4 and players exit the penalty box as normal to 5-on-4 or 5-on-5. At the first stoppage of play, teams are adjusted to 4-on-3 or 4-on-4, as appropriate.

# IIHF Eligibility Regulations

To play in any IIHF World Championship, the Olympic ice hockey tournament, and the qualifications to these competitions, players must fulfill the following qualification requirements:

1. Each player must be under the jurisdiction of an IIHF member national association
2. Each player must be a citizen of the country he represents.

**ACQUIRING A NEW NATIONAL ELIGIBILITY (THE "TWO-YEAR" CASE)**

When a player has changed his citizenship or has acquired another citizenship and wants to participate for the first time in an IIHF competition representing his new country he must:

a) Prove that he has participated for at least two consecutive years in the national competitions of his new country during which period he has neither transferred to another country nor played ice hockey within any other country

b) Have an international transfer card (ITC) that shows the transfer to the national competition of his new country and which was approved and dated at least two years before the start of the IIHF competition in which he wishes to participate.

**CHANGE OF NATIONAL ELIGIBILITY (THE "FOUR-YEAR" CASE)**

A player who has previously participated in IIHF competition can switch national eligibility (but only once in a player's life) if:

a) He is a citizen of the new country of his choice

b) He has participated for at least four consecutive years in the national competitions of his new country, during which period he has neither transferred to another country nor played ice hockey within any other country and has not played for his previous country in an IIHF competition during this four-year period

c) He has an international transfer card (ITC) that shows the transfer to the national competition of his new country and which was approved and dated at least four years before the start of the IIHF competition in which he wishes to participate

The eligibility criteria above, as defined in Bylaw 204 of the IIHF Statues and Bylaws, were adopted by the 2003 IIHF General Congress. Any earlier eligibility regulations, which differ from the ones above, cannot be invoked for any current eligibility issues.

# Tournament Eligibility—Age

| | |
|---|---|
| WM 20 | Players must be born January 1, 1993 or later |
| WM18 & WW18 | Players must be born January 1, 1995 or later |

# Player Entry Protocol

Teams submit the names of the participating players at the first Championship Directorate on the first day of the tournament. The maximum number of players allowed on a Team Registration Form at the beginning of the event is 20 skaters and 3 goalies. The minimum is 15 skaters and 2 goalies.

At the first Directorate meeting on the day of the start of a tournament, the teams must name at least the minimum number of 15 skaters and 2 goalkeepers. The players entered must be present at the championship venue by the time of the Directorate meeting.

The remaining players up to the allowed maximum of 22 + 3 (for World Championship, top level) must be submitted for players' control two hours before any of the following championship games. During a game, a team may enter (dress) 20 skaters and 2 goalkeepers on the Official Game Sheet, with the emergency goalkeeper standing by if a goalie entered to the Official Game Sheet is unable to play.

# Major Rule Changes, 2010-14

- After a penalty has been called, the ensuing faceoff will be in the defending zone of the penalized team.
- No line change allowed after a team ices the puck.
- Faceoffs can be executed only on existing dots.
- The imaginary zone where players (including goalkeepers) can be changed on the fly is limited by the length of the respective player bench plus 1.5 metres from the boards.
- A goalkeeper cannot play with a broken stick.
- If a penalty shot is awarded, the fouled player must take the shot.
- If a player loses his helmet during game action, the player must go to the bench. He is no longer allowed to put it back on and continue playing.
- When there is a delayed penalty called against a team already playing shorthanded – and a goal is scored during the delayed penalty – the first penalty is terminated, but the delayed penalty is assessed.
- The time on the clock for all regulation and all overtime periods counts down to zero.
- A player who delivers a check or blow with any part of the body or equipment to the head and neck area of an opposing player or if the player drives or forces the head of an opposing player into the boards, the player shall be assessed at least a minor and an automatic misconduct penalty (2+10).
- The lacrosse move—whereby the puck is picked up on the blade of the stick and 'whipped' into the net—shall be permitted provided the puck is not raised above the height of the shoulders at any time and, when released, is not carried higher than the height of the crossbar.
- Elbow pads must have a soft protective outer covering of sponge rubber or similar material of at least 1.27 cm (half an inch) thickness.

# IIHF Referees and Linesmen, 2012-13

*for career overview see Officials' Register starting on page 579.
*subject to IIHF Council and Congress approval. Substitutions possible in case of injury.

**WORLD CHAMPIONSHIP (MEN)**

| Referees | Linesmen |
|---|---|
| Baluska, Vladimir SVK | Arm, Roger SUI |
| Brueggemann, Lars GER | Blumel, Petr CZE |
| Bulanov, Vyacheslav RUS | Carlson, Chris CAN |
| Croft, Ian USA | Dahmen, Jimmy SWE |
| Frano, Martin CZE | Dedioulia, Ivan BLR |
| Jerabek, Antonin CZE | Dehaen, Pierre FRA |
| Johansson, Morgan SWE | Kack, Johannes SWE |
| Kaval, Keith USA | Kilian, Jon NOR |
| Kirk, Matt CAN | Morrison, Johnathan USA |
| Olenin, Konstantin RUS | Schrader, Andre GER |
| Piechaczek, Daniel GER | Schulz, Sirko GER |
| Rantala, Aleksi FIN | Shelyanin, Sergei RUS |
| Reiber, Brent SUI | Suominen, Sakari FIN |
| Ronn, Jyri FIN | Valach, Miroslav SVK |
| Vinnerborg, Marcus SWE | Wilmot, Jesse CAN |
| Zalaski, Derek CAN | Woodworth, Christopher USA |

**U20 WORLD CHAMPIONSHIP**

| Referees | Linesmen |
|---|---|
| Dumas, Harry USA | Dussureault, Francois CAN |
| Gofman, Roman RUS | George, Tommy USA |
| Hodek, Pavel CZE | Haster, Tobias SWE |
| Jablukov, Georg GER | Jucers, Raivis LAT |
| Kulakov, Sergei RUS | Kaderli, Roman SUI |
| Kurmann, Danny SUI | Puolakka, Masi FIN |
| Levonen, Jari FIN | Raming, Stanislav RUS |
| Massy, Didier SUI | Semjonov, Anton EST |
| Nord, Mikael SWE | Sivov, Dmitry RUS |
| Patafie, Steve USA | Stano, Peter SVK |
| Sjoqvist, Mikael SWE | |
| Smith, Pat CAN | |

**U18 WORLD CHAMPIONSHIP (MEN)**

| Referees | Linesmen |
|---|---|
| Bjork, Tobias SWE | Kaliada, Vasili BLR |
| Brill, Marcus GER | Kosaka, Kenji JPN |
| Dremelj, Igor SLO | Leermakers, Joep NED |
| Gebei, Péter HUN | McIntyre, Fraser USA |
| Grumsen, Jacob DEN | Metalnikov, Eduard RUS |
| Hradil, Rene CZE | Nieminen, Pasi FIN |
| Koch, Andreas SUI | Pihlblad, Henrik SWE |
| Leppaalho, Jari FIN | Smura, Mariusz POL |
| Mayer, Timothy USA | Tosenovjan, Rudolf CZE |
| Mullner, Robert SVK | Traub, Matt CAN |
| Papp, Steve CAN | |
| Romasko, Evgeniy RUS | |

**WOMEN'S WORLD CHAMPIONSHIP**

| Referees | Linesmen |
|---|---|
| Bordeleau, Melanie CAN | Bjorkman, Therese SWE |
| Hertrich, Nicole GER | Caughey, Denise CAN |
| Hove, Aina NOR | Connolly, Kate USA |
| Langley, Kristine USA | Gagnon, Stephanie CAN |
| Picavet, Marie FRA | Johnson, Laura USA |
| Tottman, Joy GBR | Kudelova, Michaela SVK |
| | Novotna, Ilona CZE |
| | Svobodova, Zuzana CZE |
| | Tauriainen, Johanna FIN |

**U18 WOMEN'S WORLD CHAMPIONSHIP**

| Referees | Linesmen |
|---|---|
| Ariano-Lortie, Gabrielle CAN | Girard, Charlotte FRA |
| Eskola, Anna Maria SUI | Hueffner, Lisa GER |
| Glenn, Jerilyn USA | Loretan, Evelyne SUI |
| Hengst, Debby NED | Partanen, Jonna FIN |
| Ketonen, Kaisa FIN | Silhavikova, Viera SVK |
| Nakayama, Miyuki JPN | Steinberg, Olga RUS |
| | Stratton, Vanessa CAN |
| | Visala, Jenni FIN |
| | Weissman, Andrea USA |

## Sponsors and Partners

Reebok

SHER-WOOD

## IIHF Member Nations, Chronological Date of Membership

**LEVELS OF MEMBERSHIP**

There are three kinds of members within the IIHF's 70-member national associations.

FULL MEMBERS participate annually in IIHF tournaments and have independent national associations specifically for hockey.

ASSOCIATE MEMBERS may or may not take part in IIHF tournaments but do not have independent national associations.

AFFILIATE MEMBERS participate only in IIHF Inline events. All nations below are full members unless noted. Only full members have voting rights at the IIHF Congresses.

| | |
|---|---|
| October 20, 1908 | France |
| November 15, 1908 | Bohemia (later became Czechoslovakia) |
| November 19, 1908 | Great Britain |
| November 23, 1908 | Switzerland |
| December 8, 1908 | Belgium |
| September 19, 1909 | Germany (expelled 1920, rejoined January 11, 1926; expelled April 27, 1946; re-admitted March 10, 1951 as West Germany) |
| February 17, 1911 | Oxford Canadians (defunct April 26, 1920 when Canada admitted), Russia (abandoned September 25, 1911) |
| March 18, 1912 | Austria (expelled 1920, re-admitted January 24, 1924, expelled 1939; re-admitted April 27, 1946) |
| March 23, 1912 | Sweden (expelled 1925, re-admitted January 11, 1926), Luxembourg |
| April 26, 1920 | Canada (replaced Oxford Canadians), USA (expelled 1928, re-admitted January 26, 1930) |
| March 10, 1923 | Spain |
| January 24, 1924 | Italy, Romania |
| January 11, 1926 | Poland |
| January 24, 1927 | Hungary |
| February 10, 1928 | Finland |
| January 26, 1930 | Japan (expelled April 27, 1946; re-admitted March 10, 1951) |
| February 22, 1931 | Latvia (membership expired April 27, 1946) |
| February 1933 | Newfoundland (expelled 1936) |
| January 20, 1935 | Netherlands, Norway |
| February 17, 1935 | Estonia (membership expired April 27, 1946) |
| February 25, 1937 | South Africa |
| February 11, 1938 | Australia (re-admitted September 17, 1950) |
| February 19, 1938 | Lithuania (membership expired April 27, 1946) |
| 1939 | Yugoslavia |
| April 27, 1946 | Denmark |
| April 1, 1952 | Soviet Union |
| June 9, 1954 | German Democratic Republic (East Germany; withdrawn August 31, 1990) |
| July 10, 1957 | China |
| July 25, 1960 | Bulgaria, Korea (South Korea) |
| August 8, 1963 | DPR Korea (North Korea) |
| May 2, 1977 | New Zealand |
| April 30, 1983 | Hong Kong |
| September 30, 1983 | Chinese Taipei |
| June 26, 1984 | Brazil (expulsed May 31, 1998; given Associate Member status May 31, 1998) |
| April 30, 1985 | Mexico, Kuwait (expulsed May 6, 1992) |
| April 29, 1987 | Greece (Associate Member) |
| April 27, 1989 | India, Thailand |
| May 1, 1991 | Israel, Turkey |
| May 6, 1992 | Azerbaijan, Belarus, Croatia, Estonia, Iceland, Kazakhstan, Latvia, Lithuania, Slovenia, Ukraine, Russia (replacing Soviet Union) |
| April 28, 1993 | Slovakia, Czech Republic (replaced Czechoslovakia) |
| May 4, 1995 | Andorra (Associate Member) |
| May 2, 1996 | Singapore (provisional, Associate Member) |
| September 26, 1996 | Ireland |
| May 31, 1998 | Argentina (Affiliate Member; made Associate Member on March 14, 2010), Namibia (Affiliate Member) |
| May 13, 1999 | Mongolia (Associate Member), Portugal (Associate Member) |
| September 22, 1999 | Armenia (Associate Member—suspended May 11, 2007, for two years; re-instated 2009; suspended again indefinitely as of May 22, 2010), Chile (Affiliate Member) |
| May 10, 2001 | Bosnia and Herzegovina, United Arab Emirates (Associate Member) |
| October 4, 2001 | Liechtenstein (Associate Member), Macedonia (Associate Member) |
| 2004 | Serbia and Montenegro (formerly Yugoslavia) |
| May 12, 2005 | Macau (Associate Member) |
| September 28, 2006 | Malaysia, Serbia (formerly Serbia and Montenegro) |
| May 22, 2008 | Moldova |
| May 8, 2009 | Kuwait (re-admitted), Georgia |
| May 22, 2010 | Morocco |
| May 14, 2011 | Kyrgyzstan (Associate Member) |
| May 18, 2012 | Jamaica, Qatar |

# IIHF Congresses

### GENERAL CONGRESS

The General Congress is the IIHF's highest legislative body and makes decisions about the rules of the game, the statutes, and bylaws. The General Congress, which is made up of representatives from all IIHF member associations, elects the president and the council.

With some exceptions, the General Congress is held every fourth year. The General Congress was held for the first time in 1975. Prior to that, the federation elected the president and the council at the Annual Congress that usually was held in conjunction with the IIHF World Championship.

The General Congress meets ever four years. It is organized by the IIHF office in co-operation with the hosting member national association.

Notice of all regular Congresses will be given by the IIHF office not later than two months before such Congress together with the agenda. Relevant documents will be sent out at least one month before the Congress.

### ANNUAL CONGRESS

The Annual Congress meets every year during the IIHF World Championship or where applicable at the time of the General Congress. It is organized by the IIHF office in co-operation with the hosting member national association.

Notice of all regular Congresses will be given by the IIHF office not later than two months before such Congress together with the agenda. Relevant documents will be sent out at least one month before the Congress.

### SEMI-ANNUAL CONGRESS

The Semi-Annual Congress meets every year in the autumn. It is organized by the IIHF office in co-operation with the hosting member national association of the upcoming World Championship.

Notice of all regular Congresses will be given by the IIHF office not later than two months before such Congress together with the agenda. Relevant documents will be sent out at least one month before the Congress.

### EXTRAORDINARY CONGRESS

The Extraordinary Congress meets within three months following the request for such meetings. An Extraordinary Congress shall be called only upon request of one third of the member national associations in good standing or by Council. The items on the agenda shall be limited to those specified at the time the Extraordinary Congress is requested.

### DATES OF CONGRESS

* extraordinary congress as well as annual
+ annual and semi-annual congresses combined

| | | |
|---|---|---|
| 1st Annual | May 15-16, 1908 | Paris, France |
| 2nd Annual | January 23-24, 1909 | Chamonix, France |
| 3rd Annual | January 9, 1910 | Montreux, Switzerland |
| 4th Annual | February 16-17, 1911 | Berlin, Germany |
| 5th Annual | March 22-23, 1912 | Brussels, Belgium |
| 6th Annual | February 22-23, 1913 | St. Moritz, Switzerland |
| 7th Annual* | February 25-26, 1914 | Berlin, Germany |
| 8th Annual | April 26, 1920 | Antwerp, Belgium |
| 9th Annual | February 15, 1922 | St. Moritz, Switzerland |
| 10th Annual | March 8-10, 1923 | Antwerp, Belgium |
| 11th Annual | January 24, 1924 | Chamonix, France |
| 12th Annual | January 6-7, 1925 | Prague, Czechoslovakia |
| 13th Annual | January 11, 1926 | Davos, Switzerland |
| 14th Annual | January 24, 1927 | Vienna, Austria |
| 15th Annual | February 10, 1928 | St. Moritz, Switzerland |
| 16th Annual | January 27-29, 1929 | Budapest, Hungary |
| 17th Annual | January 26, 1930 | Chamonix, France |
| 18th Annual | February 7-8, 1931 | Krynica, Poland |
| 19th Annual | March 13-15, 1932 | Berlin, Germany |
| 20th Annual | February 17-21, 1933 | Prague, Czechoslovakia |
| 21st Annual | February 3-11, 1934 | Milan, Italy |
| 22nd Annual | January 18-20, 1935 | Davos, Switzerland |
| 23rd Annual | February 5-6, 1936 | Garmisch-Partenkirchen, Germany |
| 24th Annual | February 17-25, 1937 | London, Great Britain |
| 25th Annual | February 10-25, 1938 | Prague, Czechoslovakia |
| 26th Annual | February 2-12 & March 5, 1939 | Zurich, Switzerland |
| 27th Annual | April 27-28, 1946 | Brussels, Belgium |
| 28th Congress | September 1, 1946 | Zurich, Switzerland |
| 29th Annual | February 14-23, 1947 | Prague, Czechoslovakia |
| 30th Congress | September 6-7, 1947 | Zurich, Switzerland |
| 31st Congress | January 28-February 8, 1948 | St. Moritz, Switzerland |
| 32nd Annual | July 23-25, 1948 | Zurich, Switzerland |
| 33rd Annual | February 11-20, 1949 | Stockholm, Sweden |
| 1st Bi-Annual | March 13-22, 1950 | London, Great Britain |
| 34th Annual | September 18-19, 1950 | Paris, France |
| 2nd Bi-Annual | March 9-17, 1951 | Paris, France |
| 35th Annual | August 25-28, 1951 | Opatija, Yugoslavia |
| 36th Annual | February 14-25, 1952 | Oslo, Norway |
| 37th Annual | March 7-15, 1953 | Zurich, Switzerland |
| 3rd Bi-Annual | February 26-March 7, 1954 | Stockholm, Sweden |
| 38th Annual | August 26-28, 1954 | Stresa, Italy |
| 39th Annual | February 27-March 5, 1955 | Dusseldorf, West Germany |
| 40th Annual | January 25-February 5, 1956 | Cortina d'Ampezzo, Italy |
| 4th Bi-Annual | February 24-March 5, 1957 | Moscow, Soviet Union |
| 41st Annual | July 10-14, 1957 | Vienna, Austria |
| 42nd Annual | February 27-March 9, 1958 | Oslo, Norway |
| 43rd Annual | March 4-15, 1959 | Prague, Czechoslovakia |
| 5th Bi-Annual | February 18-28, 1960 | Squaw Valley, United States |
| 44th Annual | July 25-30, 1960 | Rimini, Italy |
| 45th Annual | March 6-10, 1961 | Geneva, Switzerland |
| 46th Annual | March 7-13, 1962 | Colorado Springs, United States |
| 6th Bi-Annual | March 6-17, 1963 | Stockholm, Sweden |
| 47th Annual | August 8-14, 1963 | Montana, Switzerland |
| 48th Annual | January 27-February 9, 1964 | Innsbruck, Austria |
| 49th Annual | March 2-14, 1965 | Tampere, Finland |
| 7th Bi-Annual | March 2-13, 1966 | Ljubljana, Yugoslavia |
| 50th Annual | August 30-September 4, 1966 | Portschach, Austria |
| 51st Annual | March 18-29, 1967 | Vienna, Austria |
| 52nd Annual | February 5-18, 1968 | Grenoble, France |
| 53rd Annual | March 15-30, 1969 | Stockholm, Sweden |
| 54th Annual | July 5-12, 1969 | Crans-sur-Sierre, Switzerland |
| 55th Annual | March 13-29, 1970 | Stockholm, Sweden |
| 56th Annual | March 18-April 1, 1971 | Berne/Geneva, Switzerland |
| 57th Annual | April 6-22, 1972 | Prague, Czechoslovakia |
| 8th Bi-Annual | June 28-July 4, 1972 | Mamaia, Romania |
| 58th Annual | March 30-April 15, 1973 | Moscow, Soviet Union |
| 59th Annual | April 6-19, 1974 | Helsinki, Finland |
| 60th Annual* | September 13-14, 1974 | Fussen, West Germany |
| 61st Annual | July 18-26, 1975 | Gstaad, Switzerland |
| 62nd Annual | April 2-19, 1975 | Munich, West Germany |
| 9th Bi-Annual | April 7-25, 1976 | Katowice, Poland |
| 63rd Annual | October 29-30, 1976 | Paris, France |
| 64th Annual | May 2-4, 1977 | Vienna, Austria |
| 65th Annual | October 15-16, 1977 | Prague, Czechoslovakia |
| 66th Annual | July 1-7, 1978 | Sirmione, Italy |
| 67th Annual | October 27-28, 1978 | Vienna, Austria |
| 68th Annual | April 22-26, 1979 | Moscow, Soviet Union |
| 69th Annual | September 21-22, 1979 | The Hague, Netherlands |
| 70th Annual*+ | June 26-27, 1980 | Stennungsund, Sweden |
| 71st Annual | April 23-25, 1981 | Gothenburg, Sweden |
| 72nd Semi-Annual | October 29-31, 1981 | Graz, Austria |
| 73rd Annual | April 26-28, 1982 | Helsinki, Finland |
| 74th General | June 14-19, 1982 | Nice, France |
| 75th Semi-Annual | September 24-25, 1982 | Fussen, West Germany |
| 76th Annual | April 29-30, 1983 | Munich, West Germany |
| 77th Semi-Annual | September 29-October 1, 1983 | Interlaken, Switzerland |
| 78th Annual+ | June 26-30, 1984 | Portschach, Austria |
| 79th Annual | April 27-30, 1985 | Prague, Czechoslovakia |
| 80th Semi-Annual | September 6-7, 1985 | St. Julian's, Malta |
| 81st Annual | April 22-25, 1986 | Moscow, Soviet Union |
| 82nd Semi-Annual/General | June 7-11, 1986 | Colorado Springs, United States |
| 83rd Annual | April 27-29, 1987 | Vienna, Austria |
| 84th Semi-Annual | October 1-3, 1987 | Biarritz, Spain |
| 85th Annual+ | September 6-9, 1988 | Palma de Mallorca, Spain |
| 86th Annual | April 26-27, 1989 | Stockholm, Sweden |
| 87th Semi-Annual | September 15-16, 1989 | Zurich, Switzerland |
| 88th Semi-Annual | April 28-May 1, 1990 | Berne, Switzerland |
| 89th General | June 11-16, 1990 | Saint Vincent, Italy |
| 90th Semi-Annual | September 5-7, 1990 | Alghero, Italy |
| 91st Annual | April 30-May 3, 1991 | Turku, Finland |
| 92nd Semi-Annual | September 27-28, 1991 | Paris, France |
| 93rd Annual | May 6-9, 1992 | Prague, Czechoslovakia |
| 94th Semi-Annual | September 4-5, 1992 | Berlin, Germany |
| 95th Annual | April 28-May 1, 1993 | Munich, Germany |
| 96th Semi-Annual | September 23-25, 1993 | Portoroz, Slovenia |
| 97th Annual | May 4-8, 1994 | Milan, Italy |
| 98th General | June 7-11, 1994 | Venice, Italy |
| 99th Semi-Annual | September 29-October 1, 1994 | London, Great Britain |
| 100th Annual | May 3-6, 1995 | Stockholm, Sweden |
| 101st Semi-Annual | September 29-October 1, 1995 | Budapest, Hungary |
| 102nd Annual | May 1-3, 1996 | Vienna, Austria |
| 103rd Semi-Annual | September 26-28, 1996 | Cannes, France |
| 104th Annual | May 10-14, 1997 | Helsinki, Finland |
| 105th Semi-Annual | September 25-27, 1997 | Vilamoura, Portugal |
| 106th General-Annual | June 1-6, 1998 | Lausanne, Switzerland |
| 107th Semi-Annual | October 1-3, 1998 | Toronto, Canada |
| 108th Annual | May 13-16, 1999 | Lillehammer, Norway |
| 109th Semi-Annual | September 22-26, 1999 | Ft. Lauderdale, United States |
| 110th Annual | May 11-14, 2000 | St. Petersburg, Russia |
| 111th Semi-Annual | September 7-9, 2000 | Palma de Mallorca, Spain |
| 112th Annual | May 10-12, 2001 | Hanover, Germany |
| 113th Semi-Annual | October 4-6, 2001 | Malmo, Sweden |
| 114th Annual | May 8-11, 2002 | Gothenburg, Sweden |

| | | |
|---|---|---|
| 115th Semi-Annual | September 12-14, 2002 | Taormina, Italy |
| 116th General-Annual | June 1-8, 2003 | Marbella, Spain |
| 117th Semi-Annual | September 18-20, 2003 | Hersonissos, Greece |
| 118th Annual | May 6-8, 2004 | Prague, Czech Republic |
| 119th Semi-Annual | September 30-October 2, 2004 | Belek, Turkey |
| 120th Annual | May 12-14, 2005 | Vienna, Austria |
| 121st Semi-Annual | September 15-17, 2005 | Vilamoura, Portugal |
| 122nd Annual | May 17-19, 2006 | Riga, Latvia |
| 123rd Semi-Annual | September 28-30, 2006 | Athens, Greece |
| 124th Annual | May 31, 2007 | Moscow, Russia |
| 125th Semi-Annual | September 20-22, 2007 | Vancouver, Canada |
| 126th Annual | May 22-24, 2008 | Montreal, Canada |
| 127th Semi-Annual | September 25-27, 2008 | Montreux, Switzerland |
| 128th Annual | May 7-9, 2009 | Berne, Switzerland |
| 129th Semi-Annual | September 17-19, 2009 | La Marsa, Tunisia |
| 130th Annual | May 20-23, 2010 | Cologne, Germany |
| 131st Semi-Annual | September 16-18, 2010 | Portoroz, Slovenia |
| 132nd Annual | May 12-14, 2011 | Bratislava, Slovakia |
| 133rd Semi-Annual | September 22-24, 2011 | Istanbul, Turkey |
| 134th Annual | May 17-20, 2012 | Helsinki, Finland |
| 135th General-Semi | September 24-30, 2012 | Tokyo, Japan |

# Triple Gold Club

These 25 players and one coach form the unique group that has won the IIHF World Championship, the Olympic Ice Hockey tournament, and the Stanley Cup. Being given credit with one of these honours requires the player to have participated in at least one game of the event. Players are entered chronologically by date when the final championship of the triple has been achieved. If two or more players complete their triple on the same date, priority is given to the player who was the first to win one of the three titles. If two or more players have identical accomplishments, priority is given to the player who completes the triple at the younger age.

*Boston Bruins forward Patrice Bergeron is the most recent member of the Triple Gold Club. Here he is with the Stanley Cup and his Olympic gold medal in the summer of 2011 during his day with the Cup. Photo: Hockey Hall of Fame.*

*Legend: OG=Olympic Games; SC=Stanley Cup; WM=World (Men's) Championship*

1. **Tomas Jonsson** (b. Falun, Sweden, April 12, 1960)
SC 1982, 1983 (New York Islanders)
WM 1991 (Sweden)
OG-M 1994 (Sweden)
**TGC member as of February 27, 1994, Olympic final win vs. Canada**

2. **Mats Naslund** (b. Timra, Sweden, October 31, 1959)
SC 1986 (Montreal Canadiens)
WM 1991 (Sweden)
OG-M 1994 (Sweden)
**TGC member as of February 27, 1994, Olympic final win vs. Canada**

3. **Hakan Loob** (b. Roma, Sweden, July 3, 1960)
WM 1987, 1991 (Sweden)
SC 1989 (Calgary Flames)
OG-M 1994 (Sweden)
**TGC member as of February 27, 1994, Olympic final win vs. Canada**

4. **Valeri Kamenski** (b. Voskresensk, Soviet Union (Russia), April 18, 1966)
WM 1986, 1989, 1990 (Soviet Union)
OG-M 1988 (Soviet Union)
SC 1996 (Colorado Avalanche)
**TGC member as of June 10, 1996, Stanley Cup win vs. Florida**

5. **Alexei Gusarov** (b. Leningrad (St. Petersburg), Soviet Union (Russia), July 8, 1964)
WM 1986, 1989, 1990 (Soviet Union)
OG-M 1988 (Soviet Union)
SC 1996 (Colorado Avalanche)
**TGC member as of June 10, 1996, Stanley Cup win vs. Florida**

6. **Peter Forsberg** (b. Ornskoldsvik, Sweden, July 20, 1973)
WM 1992, 1998 (Sweden)
OG-M 1994, 2006 (Sweden)
SC 1996, 2001 (Colorado Avalanche)
**TGC member as of June 10, 1996, Stanley Cup win vs. Florida**

7. **Vyacheslav Fetisov** (b. Moscow, Soviet Union (Russia), April 20, 1958)
WM 1978, 1981, 1982, 1983, 1986, 1989, 1990 (Soviet Union)
OG-M 1984, 1988 (Soviet Union)
SC 1997, 1998 (Detroit Red Wings)
**TGC member as of June 7, 1997, Stanley Cup win vs. Philadelphia**

8. **Igor Larionov** (b. Voskresensk, Soviet Union (Russia), December 3, 1960)
WM 1982, 1983, 1986, 1989 (Soviet Union)
OG-M 1984, 1988 (Soviet Union)
SC 1997, 1998, 2002 (Detroit Red Wings)
**TGC member as of June 7, 1997, Stanley Cup win vs. Philadelphia**

9. **Alexander Mogilny** (b. Khabarovsk, Soviet Union (Russia), February 18, 1969)
OG-M 1988 (Soviet Union)
WM 1989 (Soviet Union)
SC 2000 (New Jersey Devils)
**TGC member as of June 10, 2000, Stanley Cup win vs. Dallas**

10. **Vladimir Malakhov** (b. Yekaterinburg, Soviet Union (Russia), August 30, 1968)
WM 1990 (Soviet Union)
OG-M 1992 (Russia)
SC 2000 (New Jersey Devils)
**TGC member as of June 10, 2000, Stanley Cup win vs. Dallas**

11. **Rob Blake** (b. Simcoe, Ontario, Canada, December 10, 1969)
WM 1994, 1997 (Canada)
SC 2001 (Colorado Avalanche)
OG-M 2002 (Canada)
**TGC member as of February 24, 2002, Olympic final win vs. United States**

12. **Joe Sakic** (b. Burnaby, British Columbia, Canada, July 7, 1969)
WM 1994 (Canada)
SC 1996, 2001 (Colorado Avalanche)
OG-M 2002 (Canada)
**TGC member as of February 24, 2002, Olympic final win vs. United States**

13. **Brendan Shanahan** (b. Mimico, Ontario, Canada, January 23, 1969)
WM 1994 (Canada)
SC 1997, 1998, 2002 (Detroit Red Wings)
OG-M 2002 (Canada)
**TGC member as of February 24, 2002, Olympic final win vs. United States**

14. **Scott Niedermayer** (b. Edmonton, Alberta, Canada, August 31, 1973)
SC 1995, 2000, 2003 (New Jersey Devils), 2007 (Anaheim Ducks)
OG-M 2002, 2010 (Canada)
WM 2004 (Canada)
**TGC member as of May 9, 2004, World Championship final win vs. Sweden**

15. **Jaromir Jagr** (b. Kladno, Czechoslovakia (Czech Republic), February 15, 1972)
SC 1991, 1992 (Pittsburgh Penguins)
OG-M 1998 (Czech Republic)
WM 2005, 2010 (Czech Republic)
**TGC member as of May 15, 2005, World Championship final win vs. Canada**

16. **Jiri Slegr** (b. Jihlava, Czechoslovakia (Czech Republic), May 30, 1971)
OG-M 1998 (Czech Republic)
SC 2002 (Detroit Red Wings)
WM 2005 (Czech Republic)
**TGC member as of May 15, 2005, World Championship final win vs. Canada**

**17. Nicklas Lidstrom** (b. Avesta, Sweden, April 28, 1970)
WM 1991 (Sweden)
SC 1997, 1998, 2002, 2008 (Detroit Red Wings)
OG-M 2006 (Sweden)
**TGC member as of February 26, 2006, Olympic final win vs. Finland**

**18. Fredrik Modin** (b. Sundsvall, Sweden, October 8, 1974)
WM 1998 (Sweden)
SC 2004 (Tampa Bay Lightning)
OG-M 2006 (Sweden)
**TGC member as of February 26, 2006, Olympic final win vs. Finland**

**19. Chris Pronger** (b. Dryden, Ontario, Canada, October 10, 1974)
WM 1997 (Canada)
OG-M 2002, 2010 (Canada)
SC 2007 (Anaheim Ducks)
**TGC member as of June 6, 2007, Stanley Cup win vs. Ottawa**

**20. Niklas Kronwall** (b. Jarfalla, Sweden, January 12, 1981)
OG-M 2006 (Sweden)
WM 2006 (Sweden)
SC 2008 (Detroit Red Wings)
**TGC member as of June 4, 2008, Stanley Cup win vs. Pittsburgh**

**21. Henrik Zetterberg** (b. Njurunda, Sweden, October 9, 1980)
OG-M 2006 (Sweden)
WM 2006 (Sweden)
SC 2008 (Detroit Red Wings)
**TGC member as of June 4, 2008, Stanley Cup win vs. Pittsburgh**

**22. Mikael Samuelsson** (b. Mariefred, Sweden, December 23, 1976)
OG-M 2006 (Sweden)
WM 2006 (Sweden)
SC 2008 (Detroit Red Wings)
**TGC member as of June 4, 2008, Stanley Cup win vs. Pittsburgh**

**23. Eric Staal** (b. Thunder Bay, Ontario, Canada, October 29, 1984)
SC 2006 (Carolina Hurricanes)
WM 2007 (Canada)
OG-M 2010 (Canada)
**TGC member as of February 28, 2010, Olympic final win vs. United States**

**24. Jonathan Toews** (b. Winnipeg, Manitoba, Canada, April 29, 1988)
WM 2007 (Canada)
OG-M 2010 (Canada)
SC 2010 (Chicago Blackhawks)
**TGC member as of June 9, 2010, Stanley Cup win vs. Philadelphia**

**25. Patrice Bergeron** (b. Ancienne-Lorette, Quebec, Canada, July 24, 1985)
WM 2004 (Canada)
OG-M 2010 (Canada)
SC 2011 (Boston)
**TGC member as of June 15, 2011, Stanley Cup win vs. Vancouver**

**TRIPLE GOLD CLUB COACHES**
**1. Mike Babcock** (b. Saskatoon, Saskatchewan, Canada, April 29, 1963)
WM 2004 (Canada)
SC 2008 (Detroit Red Wings)
OG-M 2010 (Canada)
**TGC member as of February 28, 2010, Olympic final win vs. United States**

*Mike Babcock (right, seen here with Steve Yzerman) is the only coach who has Triple Gold Club credentials. Photo: Jeff Vinnick.*

# Triple Gold for IIHF Events

| Name | NAT | U20 | WM | OG-M |
|---|---|---|---|---|
| Bergeron, Patrice | CAN | 2005 | 2004 | 2010 |
| Byakin, Ilya | URS | 1983 | 1989, 1990, 1993 | 1988 |
| Chernykh, Alexander | URS | 1983, 1984 | 1989 | 1988 |
| Crosby, Sidney | CAN | 2005 | | 2010 |
| Davydov, Yevgeni | URS | 1986 | 1990 | 1992 |
| Doughty, Drew | CAN | 2008 | | 2010 |
| Getzlaf, Ryan | CAN | 2005 | | 2010 |
| Iginla, Jarome | CAN | 1996 | 1997 | 2002, 2010 |
| Jovanovski, Ed | CAN | 1995 | | 2002 |
| Kariya, Paul | CAN | 1993 | 1994 | 2002 |
| Kasatonov, Alexei | URS | 1978, 1979 | 1981, 1982, 1983, 1986, 1989 | 1984, 1988 |
| Khmylyov, Yuri | URS | 1984 | 1986, 1987 | 1992 |
| Kozhevnikov, Alexander | URS | 1978 | 1982 | 1984, 1988 |
| Kravchuk, Igor | URS | 1986 | 1990 | 1988, 1992 |
| Krutov, Vladimir | URS | 1979, 1980 | 1981, 1982, 1983, 1986, 1989 | 1984, 1988 |
| Makarov, Sergei | URS | 1977, 1978 | 1978, 1979, 1981, 1982, 1983, 1986, 1989, 1990 | 1984, 1988 |
| Mylnikov, Sergei | URS | 1977, 1978 | 1986, 1989, 1990 | 1988 |
| Perry, Corey | CAN | 2005 | | 2010 |
| Richards, Mike | CAN | 2005 | | 2010 |
| Seabrook, Brent | CAN | 2005 | | 2010 |
| Smyth, Ryan | CAN | 1995 | 2003, 2004 | 2002 |
| Starikov, Sergei | URS | 1977, 1978 | 1979, 1983, 1986 | 1984, 1988 |
| Svetlov, Sergei | URS | 1980 | 1986 | 1988 |
| Thornton, Joe | CAN | 1997 | | 2010 |
| Weber, Shea | CAN | 2005 | 2007 | 2010 |
| Yushkevich, Dmitri | RUS | 1989 | 1993 | 1992 |

# IIHF Junior Double Gold

| Name | NAT | U18 | U20 |
|---|---|---|---|
| Beauchemin, Rejean | CAN | 2003 | 2005 |
| Belle, Shawn | CAN | 2003 | 2005 |
| Booth, David | USA | 2002 | 2004 |
| Campbell, Jack | USA | 2009, 2010 | 2010 |
| Carle, Matt | USA | 2002 | 2004 |
| Carter, Jeff | CAN | 2003 | 2005 |
| Chistov, Stanislav | RUS | 2001 | 2002 |
| Coburn, Braydon | CAN | 2003 | 2005 |
| Colliton, Jeremy | CAN | 2003 | 2005 |
| d'Amigo, Jerry | USA | 2009 | 2010 |
| Dixin Stephen | CAN | 2003 | 2005 |
| Eaves, Patrick | USA | 2002 | 2004 |
| Eberle, Jordan | CAN | 2008 | 2009 |
| Ellis, Ryan | CAN | 2008 | 2009 |
| Fowler, Cam | USA | 2009 | 2010 |
| Getzlaf, Ryan*# | CAN | 2003 | 2005 |
| Grebeshkov, Denis** | RUS | 2001 | 2002, 2003 |
| Grigorenko, Igor | RUS | 2001 | 2002 |
| Hodgson, Cody | CAN | 2008 | 2009 |
| Kaigorodov, Alexei | RUS | 2001 | 2003 |
| Kesler, Ryan | USA | 2002 | 2004 |
| Korsunov, Vladimir | RUS | 2001 | 2002 |
| Medvedev, Andrei | RUS | 2001 | 2002, 2003 |
| Moore, Greg | USA | 2002 | 2004 |
| Morin, Jeremy | USA | 2009 | 2010 |
| Myers, Tyler | CAN | 2008 | 2009 |
| O'Sullivan, Patrick | USA | 2002 | 2004 |
| Parise, Zach | USA | 2002 | 2004 |
| Perezhogin, Alexander** | RUS | 2001 | 2002, 2003 |
| Polushin, Alexander | RUS | 2001 | 2002, 2003 |
| Potter, Corey | USA | 2002 | 2004 |
| Ramage, John | USA | 2009 | 2010 |
| Seabrook, Brent*# | CAN | 2003 | 2005 |
| Sterling, Brett | USA | 2002 | 2004 |
| Stewart, Anthony | CAN | 2003 | 2005 |
| Stuart, Mark | USA | 2002 | 2004 |
| Suter, Ryan | USA | 2002 | 2004 |
| Taratukhin, Andrei | RUS | 2001 | 2002, 2003 |
| Teubert, Colten | CAN | 2008 | 2009 |
| Trubachyov, Yuri | RUS | 2001 | 2002, 2003 |
| Tyutin, Fyodor** | RUS | 2001 | 2002, 2003 |
| Werner, Steve | USA | 2002 | 2004 |
| Wisniewski, James | USA | 2002 | 2004 |
| Zucker, Jason | USA | 2009, 2010 | 2010 |

* also won Stanley Cup
**also won World Championship
#also won Olympic gold

# Triple Gold Club Candidates for 2013

| PLAYER | NAT | OLYMPICS | WORLD CHAMPIONSHIP | STANLEY CUP | 2012-13 TEAM |
|---|---|---|---|---|---|
| Boyle, Dan | CAN | OG 2010 CAN | | SC 2004 TB | SJ-NHL |
| Brodeur, Martin | CAN | OG 2002-10 CAN | | SC 1995-2000-03 NJ | NJ-NHL |
| Crosby, Sidney | CAN | OG 2010 CAN | | SC 2009 PIT | PIT-NHL |
| Doughty, Drew | CAN | OG 2010 CAN | | SC 2012 LA | LA-NHL |
| Gagne, Simon | CAN | OG 2002 CAN | | SC 2012 LA | LA-NHL |
| Getzlaf, Ryan | CAN | OG 2010 CAN | | SC 2007 ANA | ANA-NHL |
| Hejduk, Milan | CZE | OG 1998 CZE | | SC 2001 COL | COL-NHL |
| Holmstrom, Tomas | SWE | OG 2006 SWE | | SC 1997-98-2002-08 DET | DET-NHL |
| Keith, Duncan | CAN | OG 2010 CAN | | SC 2010 CHI | CHI-NHL |
| Kovalyov, Alexei | RUS | OG 1992 RUS | | SC 1994 NYR | Myt-KHL |
| Pahlsson, Samuel | SWE | OG 2006 SWE | | SC 2007 ANA | VAN-NHL |
| Perry, Corey | CAN | OG 2010 CAN | | SC 2007 ANA | ANA-NHL |
| Richards, Mike | CAN | OG 2010 CAN | | SC 2012 LA | LA-NHL |
| Seabrook, Brent | CAN | OG 2010 CAN | | SC 2010 CHI | CHI-NHL |
| Brewer, Eric | CAN | OG 2002 CAN | WM 2003-04-07 CAN | | TB-NHL |
| Hannula, Mika | SWE | OG 2006 SWE | WM 2006 SWE | | Esp-FIN |
| Havelid, Niclas | SWE | OG 2006 SWE | WM 1998 SWE | | Link-SWE |
| Heatley, Dany | CAN | OG 2010 CAN | WM 2003-04 CAN | | MIN-NHL |
| Iginla, Jarome | CAN | OG 2002-10 CAN | WM 1997 CAN | | CAL-NHL |
| Luongo, Roberto | CAN | OG 2010 CAN | WM 2003-04 CAN | | VAN-NHL |
| Marleau, Patrick | CAN | OG 2010 CAN | WM 2003 CAN | | SJ-NHL |
| Morrow, Brenden | CAN | OG 2010 CAN | WM 2004 CAN | | DAL-NHL |
| Nash, Rick | CAN | OG 2010 CAN | WM 2007 CAN | | NYR-NHL |
| Ohlund, Mattias | SWE | OG 2006 SWE | WM 1998 SWE | | TB-NHL |
| Patera, Pavel | CZE | OG 1998 CZE | WM 1996-99-2000-01 CZE | | Kla-CZE |
| Prochazka, Libor | CZE | OG 1998 CZE | WM 1999 CZE | | Kla-CZE |
| Prochazka, Martin | CZE | OG 1998 CZE | WM 1996-99-2000-01 CZE | | Kla-CZE |
| Rucinsky, Martin | CZE | OG 1998 CZE | WM 1999-2001-05 CZE | | Lit-CZE |
| Smyth, Ryan | CAN | OG 2002 CAN | WM 2003-04 CAN | | EDM-NHL |
| Spacek, Jaroslav | CZE | OG 1998 CZE | WM 1999-2001-05 CZE | | CAR-NHL |
| Straka, Martin | CZE | OG 1998 CZE | WM 2005 CZE | | Plz-CZE |
| Weber, Shea | CAN | OG 2010 CAN | WM 2007 CAN | | NAS-NHL |

*Corey Perry is one of ten Canadians who is a World Championship gold medal away from being a TGC member.*
*Photo: Jeff Vinnick / HHOF-IIHF Images.*

# IIHF Hall of Fame Honour Roll

(name, nationality, year inducted)
+ denotes Referee;
* denotes Builder;
all others are Players

**MILESTONE AWARD**
(awarded periodically to a team that has made a significant contribution to the development of international hockey)

**2012 INAUGURAL INDUCTEES**
Team Canada 1972
Team Soviet Union 1972

**INDIVIDUAL INDUCTEES**
Quido Adamec (CZE), 2005+
John "Bunny" Ahearne (GBR), 1997*
Veniamin Alexandrov (RUS), 2007
Ernest Aljancic, Sr. (SLO), 2002
Helmuts Balderis (LAT), 1998
Rudi Ball (GER), 2004
Father David Bauer (CAN), 1997*
Art Berglund (USA), 2008*
Curt Berglund (SWE), 2003*
Sven Bergqvist (SWE), 1999
Lars Bjorn (SWE), 1998
Vsevolod Bobrov (RUS), 1997
Roger Bourbonnais (CAN), 1999
Vladimir Bouzek (CZE), 2007
Philippe Bozon (FRA), 2008
Herb Brooks (USA), 1999*
Walter Brown (USA), 1997*
Vlastimil Bubnik (CZE), 1997
Mike Buckna (CAN), 2004*
Ludek Bukac (CZE), 2007*
Pavel Bure (RUS), 2012
Walter Bush, Jr. (USA), 2009*
Karen Bye (-Dietz) (USA), 2011
Enrico Calcaterra (ITA), 1999*
Ferdinand "Pic" Cattini (SUI), 1998
Hans Cattini (SUI), 1998
Josef Cerny (CZE), 2007
Arkadi Chernyshev (RUS), 1999*
Bill Christian (USA), 1998
Bill Cleary (USA), 1997
Gerry Cosby (USA), 1997
Jim Craig (USA), 1999
Mike Curran (USA), 1999
Ove Dahlberg (SWE), 2004+
Vitali Davydov (RUS), 2004
Igor Dmitriev (RUS), 2007*
Hans Dobida (AUT), 2007*
Jaroslav Drobny (CZE), 1997
Vladimir Dzurilla (SVK), 1998
Rudolf Eklow (SWE), 1999*
Carl Erhardt (GBR), 1998
Rickard Fagerlund (SWE), 2010*
Vyacheslav Fetisov (RUS), 2005
Anatoli Firsov (RUS), 1998
Jozef Golonka (SVK), 1998
Cammi Granato (USA), 2008
Wayne Gretzky (CAN), 2000
Arne Grunander (SWE), 1997*
Henryk Gruth (POL), 2006
Bengt-Ake Gustafsson (SWE), 2003
Karel Gut (CZE), 1998
Geraldine Heaney (CAN), 2008
Anders Hedberg (SWE), 1997
Dieter Hegen (GER), 2010
Raimo Helminen (FIN), 2012
Heinz Henschel (GER), 2003*
William Hewitt (CAN), 1998*
Rudi Hiti (SLO), 2009
Ivan Hlinka (CZE), 2002
Jiri Holecek (CZE), 1998
Jiri Holik (CZE), 1999
Derek Holmes (CAN), 1999*
Leif Holmqvist (SWE), 1999
Ladislav Horsky (SVK), 2004*
Phil Housley (USA), 2012
Fran Huck (CAN), 1999
Jorgen Hviid (DEN), 2005*
Arturs Irbe (LAT), 2010
Gustav Jaenecke (GER), 1998
Angela James (CAN), 2008
Tore Johannessen (NOR), 1999*
Sven "Tumba" Johansson (SWE), 1997
Mark Johnson (USA), 1999
Marshall Johnston (CAN), 1998
Tomas Jonsson (SWE), 2000
Gordon Juckes (CAN), 1997*
Timo Jutila (FIN), 2003
Yuri Karandin (RUS), 2004+
Alexei Kasatonov (RUS), 2009
Tsutomu Kawabuchi (JPN), 2004*
Matti Keinonen (FIN), 2002
Valeri Kharlamov (RUS), 1998
Anatoli Khorozov (UKR), 2006*
Udo Kiessling (GER), 2000
Dave King (CAN), 2001*
Jakob Kolliker (SUI), 2007
Josef Kompalla (GER), 2003+
Viktor Konovalenko (RUS), 2007
Vladimir Kostka (CZE), 1997*
Vladimir Krutov (RUS), 2010
Erich Kuhnhackl (GER), 1997
Jari Kurri (FIN), 2000
Viktor Kuzkin (RUS), 2005
Jacques Lacarriere (FRA), 1998
Igor Larionov (RUS), 2008
Bob Lebel (CAN), 1997*
Mario Lemieux (CAN), 2008
Harry Lindblad (FIN), 1999*
Vic Lindquist (CAN), 1997
Paul Loicq (BEL), 1997*
Konstantin Loktev (RUS), 2007
Hakan Loob (SWE), 1998
Tord Lundstrom (SWE), 2011
Cesar Luthi (SUI), 1998*
Oldrich Machac (CZE), 1999
Barry MacKenzie (CAN), 1999
Louis Magnus (FRA), 1997*
Sergei Makarov (RUS), 2001
Josef Malecek (CZE), 2003
Alexander Maltsev (RUS), 1999
Pekka Marjamaki (FIN), 1998
Seth Martin (CAN), 1997
Vladimir Martinec (CZE), 2001
John Mayasich (USA), 1997
Boris Mayorov (RUS), 1999
Jack McCartan (USA), 1998
Jack McLeod (CAN), 1999
Boris Mikhailov (RUS), 2000
Bohumil Modry (CZE), 2011
Andy Murray (CAN), 2012
Lou Nanne (USA), 2004
Mats Naslund (SWE), 2005
Vaclav Nedomansky (CZE), 1997
Riikka Nieminen (-Valila) (FIN), 2010
Kent Nilsson (SWE), 2006
Nils "Nisse" Nilsson (SWE), 2002
Milan Novy (CZE), 2012
Kalevi Numminen (FIN), 2011*
Lasse Oksanen (FIN), 1999
Terry O'Malley (CAN), 1998
Eduard Pana (ROU), 1998
Gyorgy Pasztor (HUN), 2001*
Peter Patton (GBR), 2002*
Esa Peltonen (FIN), 2007
Vladimir Petrov (RUS), 2006
Ronald Pettersson (SWE), 2004
Frantisek Pospisil (CZE), 1999
Josef Puschnig (AUT), 1999
Alexander Ragulin (RUS), 1997
Hans Rampf (GER), 2001
Gordon Renwick (CAN), 2002*
Bob Ridder (USA), 1998*
Jack Riley (USA), 1998*
Thomas Rundqvist (SWE), 2007
Dr. Gunther Sabetzki (GER), 1997*
Borje Salming (SWE), 1998
Laszlo Schell (HUN), 2009+
Alois Schloder (GER), 2005
Harry Sinden (CAN), 1997
Nikolai Sologubov (RUS), 2004
Andrei Starovoitov (RUS), 1997+
Vyacheslav Starshinov (RUS), 2007
Jan Starsi (SVK), 1999*
Peter Stastny (SVK), 2000
Ulf Sterner (SWE), 2001
Roland Stoltz (SWE), 1999
Arne Stromberg (SWE), 1998*
Goran Stubb (FIN), 2000*
Miroslav Subrt (CZE), 2004*
Jan Suchy (CZE), 2009
Anatoli Tarasov (RUS), 1997*
Frantisek Tikal (CZE), 2004
Viktor Tikhonov (RUS), 1998*
Shoichi Tomita (JPN), 2006*
Richard "Bibi" Torriani (SUI), 1997
Vladislav Tretiak (RUS), 1997
Ladislav Trojak (SVK), 2011
Hal Trumble (USA), 1999*
Yoshiaki Tsutsumi (JPN), 1999*
Doru Tureanu (ROU), 2011
Thayer Tutt (USA), 2002*
Xaver Unsinn (GER), 1998*
Jorma Valtonen (FIN), 1999
Valeri Vasilyev (RUS), 1998
Juhani Wahlsten (FIN), 2006
Walter Wasservogel (AUT), 1997*
Harry Watson (CAN), 1998
Unto Wiitala (FIN), 2003+
Alexander Yakushev (RUS), 2003
Urpo Ylonen (FIN), 1997
Vladimir Yurzinov (RUS), 2002*
Vladimir Zabrodsky (CZE), 1997
Joachim Ziesche (GER), 1999

**PAUL LOICQ AWARD**
(outstanding service to IIHF)

| | | |
|---|---|---|
| Wolf-Dieter Montag | GER | 1998 |
| Roman Neumayer | GER | 1999 |
| Vsevolod Kukushkin | RUS | 2000 |
| Isao Kataoka | JPN | 2001 |
| Pat Marsh | GBR | 2002 |
| George Nagobads | USA | 2003 |
| Aggie Kukulowicz | CAN | 2004 |
| Rita Hrbacek | AUT | 2005 |
| Bo Tovland | SWE | 2006 |
| Bob Nadin | CAN | 2007 |
| Juraj Okolicany | SVK | 2008 |
| Harald Griebel | GER | 2009 |
| Lou Vairo | USA | 2010 |
| Yuri Korolev | RUS | 2011 |
| Kent Angus | CAN | 2012 |

# LIHG-IIHF History

(Ligue Internationale de Hockey sur Glace—International Ice Hockey Federation)

The change in usage from LIHG to IIHF was gradual and not precipitated by one particular decision at any one meeting. LIHG was used at the time of the organization's founding on May 15, 1908, because the founder, Louis Magnus, was French, and in the ensuing years many of the presidents and top officials from Belgium and Switzerland also spoke French.

The LIHG formally adopted "International Ice Hockey Federation" as the English translation of LIHG on September 1, 1946. Still, it was many years before that abbreviation took hold.

The last time the LIHG logo appeared on the cover of the organization's minutes books occurred at the 1954 Annual Congress in Stresa, Austria. This also marks the last time the title page was in French only. At the next Congress, the 39th edition in Dusseldorf, West Germany, the title page was in French and English and the LIHG logo was absent. In 1963, the cover for the Congress minutes was in English only.

The last time the contents of the Congress minutes were bilingual was at the 7th Bi-Annual Congress in Ljubljana, Yugoslavia, in March 1966. At the next Congress, the 50th Annual Congress, the text was in English only and there was no reference at all to LIHG.

Later, the Congress minutes became bilingual again, but the second language to complement English was now German. This is currently how the minutes are kept and the IIHF's history recorded.

**OFFICIAL IIHF LANGUAGES**

| | |
|---|---|
| 1908-47 | French only |
| 1948-66 | French & English |
| 1967-76 | English only |
| 1977-2002 | English & German |
| 2003-present | English only |

**IIHF OFFICES**

| | |
|---|---|
| 1977-84 | Prinz Eugen Strasse 12A, Vienna, Austria |
| 1984-91 | Bellevuestrasse 8, Vienna, Austria |
| 1991-96 | Todistrasse 23, Zurich, Switzerland |
| 1996-2002 | Parkring 11, Zurich, Switzerland |
| 2002-present | Brandschenkestrasse 50, Zurich, Switzerland |

**LIHG/IIHF LOGOS THROUGH THE YEARS**

# Important Developments in International Hockey

## Origins

**1873**—James Creighton devises informal rules for a new winter game in Montreal, a game which later became known as ice hockey.

**March 3, 1875**—The first true hockey game is played. The pre-announced indoor game between two named teams, officiated by a referee and using a puck, is played at Montreal's Victoria Skating Rink. Goal posts are six feet wide and the game lasts 60 minutes. The rink's dimensions are approximately 200' x 85', the standard by which all future North American rinks are built. A plaque to honour this game is dedicated at the Bell Centre, across the street from the arena's original location, in 2008.

**January 31, 1877**—McGill University in Montreal forms the first organized hockey team. On February 27, the *Montreal Gazette* publishes the first rules – seven in all – for hockey:

1. *The game shall be commenced, and renewed by a Bully from the center of the ground. Goals shall be changed after each game.*
2. *When a player hits the puck, any one of the same side who at such moment of hitting is nearer to the opponents' goal line is out of play, and may not touch the ball himself, or in any way whatever prevent any other player from doing so, until the ball has been played. A player must always be on his own side of the ball.*
3. *The puck may be stopped, but not carried or knocked on by any part of the body. No player shall raise his stick above his shoulder. Charging from behind, tripping, collaring, kicking or shinning shall not be allowed.*
4. *When the puck is hit behind the goal line by the attacking side, it shall be brought out straight 15 yards, and started again by a Bully; but, if hit behind by any one of the side whose goal line it is, a player of the opposite side shall hit it out from within one yard of the nearest corner, no player of the attacking side at that time shall be within 20 yards of the goal line, and the defenders, with the exception of the goal-keeper, must be behind their goal line.*
5. *When the ball goes off side, a player of the opposite side to that which hit it out shall roll it out from the point on the boundary line at which it went off at right angles with the boundary line, and shall not play it until it has been played by another player, every player being then behind the ball.*
6. *On the infringement of any of the above rules, the ball shall be brought back and a bully shall take place.*
7. *All disputes shall be settled by the Umpires, or in the event of their disagreement, by the referee.*

**December 26, 1894**—The North Avenue Rink, the first artificial arena in the United States, opens. The rink dimensions are 250' x 55'.

## Teams and Players

**1883-1920**: 7 players—Teams in Canada standardize the size of rosters and names of position. Each side now has seven men, and their positions are called left wing, right wing, centre, rover, point, cover point, and goalie.

**1920**: 6 players—During Congress at the 1920 Olympics, the IIHF decides to eliminate the rover, reducing teams to six men a side. The positions are now called goalie, defencemen (two), left wing, right wing, centre (forwards).

**2003**: 6 players for regulation, 5 for overtime (goalie, two defencemen, two forwards).

## Length of Games

| | |
|---|---|
| 1920 | 2 x 20 |
| 1924 | 3 x 20 |
| 1928 | 3 x 15 (finals 3 x 20) |
| 1930-31 | 3 x 15 |
| 1932-39 | 3 x 15 (all games—10:00 mandatory OT (i.e., no sudden death) to a maximum of three overtimes if tied after regulation or 10:00 OT or 20:00 OT) |
| 1947-91 | 3 x 20 |
| 1992-2002 | 3 x 20 (10:00 sudden death OT for all playoff elimination games + game-winning shots (five shots)) |
| 1997 | 3 x 20 (10:00 sudden death OT for all playoff elimination games + game-winning shots (five shots); 20:00 OT for Gold Medal Game) |
| 2003 | 3 x 20 (10:00 sudden death OT for quarter-finals, semi-finals, bronze medal game; 20:00 sudden death OT for gold medal game—all OT played 4-on-4 + shootout (five shots)) |
| 2007-present | 3 x 20 (5:00 sudden death OT + shootout (three shots) for games prior to playoff elimination round; 10:00 sudden death OT + shootout (three shots) for quarter-finals, semi-finals, bronze medal game; 20:00 sudden death OT for gold medal game + shootout (three shots)—all OT games throughout tournament played 4-on-4) |

## Size of Rosters

1920—6 + 1
1924—7 + 1
1928-1936—8 + 1
1937-1939—9 + 1
1947-1948—11 + 1
1949-1952—12 + 2
1953-1963—13 + 2
1964-1966—14 + 2
1967-1972—15 + 2
1973-1975—17 + 2
1976-1990—18 + 2
1991-present—20 + 2

## IIHF Business

**1921**—The first LIHG European Championships after the First World War is contested. Only Sweden and Czechoslovakia take part in the Stockholm event, which the Swedes win, 7-4.

**1930**—The first official World Championship outside the Olympics takes place in Chamonix, Berlin, and Vienna. The event will be held annually in all non-Olympic years.

**February 26, 1933**—The United States becomes the first country other than Canada to win World Championship or Olympic gold.

**1939-47**—There are no World Championships or Olympics played during the Second World War.

**March 9-17, 1951**—At the Semi-Annual Congress in Paris, the IIHF decides not to participate in the Olympics after a rift with the IOC.

**August 25-28, 1951**—At the Annual Congress in Romania, the IIHF makes full reconciliation with the IOC and agrees to participate in the Olympics the following year in Oslo, Norway.

**1957**—Canada and the United States boycott the World Championship to protest the Soviet Union's occupation of Hungary. This World Championship is the last played on natural ice.

**March 5, 1957**—IIHF President Bunny Ahearne proposes three groups—A, B, and C Pool—with promotion and relegation among the three.

**August 26, 1961**—The Hockey Hall of Fame opens in Toronto.

**1962**—Iron Curtain countries do not participate in the World Championship, played in Colorado Springs and Denver, to protest the United States' refusal to grant entry to the East German team.

**July 12, 1969**—Doping controls are introduced to international play.

**1969**—The age of a "junior" player is fixed at a maximum of 20 years old.

**1969**—The IIHF mandates that all World Championship Pool A events be held in venues with indoor arenas.

**January 4, 1970**—Canada withdraws entirely from international hockey after a disagreement with the IIHF over the amateur rule. Sweden hosts the World Championship, initially allocated to Canada (Montreal and Winnipeg). The World Championship in Stockholm is the first where helmets are mandatory for skaters.

**1977**—The IIHF introduces the World U20 (Junior) Championship as an annual event to replace the invitational event that had taken place the previous three years.

**1978**—After holding World Championships in Olympics years twice in the 1970s (1972, 1976), the IIHF decides it will no longer hold its own event in an Olympic year. This decision is in place only for 1984 and 1988.

**September 22, 1979**—The IIHF introduces a tournament for the Thayer Tutt Trophy to be played every four years by top teams not in the Olympics.

**1992**—The IIHF introduces a playoff/elimination system with quarter-finals, semi-finals, and finals. To that end, overtime and game-winning shots become decisive.

**July 21, 1992**—The IOC announces that women's hockey will be a medal sport at the 1998 Olympics in Nagano, Japan.

**1995**—IIHF introduces In-Line Hockey as part of its annual events.

**1997**—The IIHF establishes a Hall of Fame for the purposes on honouring the greatest players of international hockey.

**1999**—The IIHF introduces the World U18 Championship for men.

**September 18, 2003**—IIHF Congress approves the introduction of a World Ranking System and nominates the first two women to its Council, Beate Grupp (GER) and Doris Hogne (SWE).

**2008**—The IIHF introduces the World Women's U18 Championship.

**2008**—IIHF Congress votes to allow Canada to host the World U20 (Junior) Championship at least once every three years.

## National Championships, Tournaments, Trophies

**1982**—Lord Stanley, governor-general of Canada, donates a trophy called the Dominion Challenge Cup to be awarded annually to the best amateur hockey team in Canada.

**1893**—The first games for the Stanley Cup are played, Montreal AAA being the winners.

**1908**—The Allan Cup is donated by Sir Montagu Allan to the best senior amateur team in the country, replacing the Stanley Cup which had become a trophy competed for by professional teams.

**1919**—The Memorial Cup is introduced in Canada to pay tribute to the country's war heroes. The winner is considered the finest junior team in the country.

**April 23-29, 1920**—The Summer Olympic Games in Antwerp, Belgium hosts the first international ice hockey tournament with North American participation. Canada (Winnipeg Falcons) wins gold and the United States silver.

**March 8-10, 1923**—The first Spengler Cup is played.

**January 24, 1927**—The Fair Play Cup is adopted by the LIHG at the 14th Congress, awarded to the least penalized team in a sanctioned tournament.

**1981**—The Hobey Baker Award is inaugurated, given annually to the best men's player in NCAA (U.S. College) hockey.

**1998**—The Patty Kazmaier Award is inaugurated, given annually to the best women's player in NCAA (U.S. College) hockey.

**2009**—The Clarkson Cup is first competed for by the best professional women's teams in Canada and the United States and won by the Montreal Stars.

## Organizations

**1896**—The U.S. Amateur Hockey League is founded in New York City.

**1896**—The first bandy club is formed in Sweden.

**1899**—The first hockey game is played in Finland.

**1904**—The International Professional Hockey League (IPHL) is formed, comprised of teams from Ontario and Michigan, the first fully pro league.

**May 15, 1908**—The Ligue Internationale de Hockey sur Glace (LIHG—later IIHF), is founded in Paris, France. France, Belgium, Switzerland, Great Britain and Bohemia (later Czechoslovakia) are the founding members. The first LIHG-organized games are played in Berlin, Germany on November 3-5, 1908.

**1910**—The National Hockey Association is formed and standardizes games to three periods of 20 minutes. It is replaced by the National Hockey League in 1917.

**January 10-12, 1910**—The first LIHG European Championships take place in the Swiss winter resort of Les Avants. Great Britain wins the tournament.

**February 17, 1911**—The Oxford Canadians are admitted to the LIHG (IIHF) as members.

**February 24, 1914**—The Canadian Amateur Hockey Association, precursor to Hockey Canada, is created.

**1916**—The Swiss National League is founded.

**1917**—The National Hockey League is formed consisting of four teams—Montreal Canadiens, Toronto Arenas, Ottawa Senators, and Montreal Wanderers.

**1946**—Hockey is played in the Soviet Union for the first time.

## IIHF-NHL Relations

**1938**—Montreal Canadiens and Detroit Red Wings play a series of exhibition games in Europe, the first NHL games overseas.

**1947**—The Boston Bruins put Czechoslovakian star Jaroslav Drobny on their reserve list, the first European-trained player so chosen.

**1957**—Swedish star Sven "Tumba" Johansson attends the training camp of the Boston Bruins; the Moscow Selects tour Canada, the first games by Soviets against senior and junior clubs in Canada.

**January 27, 1965**—Sweden's Ulf Sterner becomes the first European-trained player to appear in an NHL game, playing for the New York Rangers. The Rangers beat Boston, 5-2.

**September 24, 1968**—The NHL adopts its first rules regarding transfers of European players to North America.

**1969**—Tommi Salmelainen of Finland is drafted 66th overall at the Amateur Draft, the first European selected.

**July 5, 1969**—Clarence Campbell, president of the NHL, becomes the first major NHL representative to speak at the IIHF Congress.

**1972-73**—Thommie Bergman becomes the first European to play a full season in the NHL.

**September 2-28, 1972**—The Soviet Union takes on a fully professional Team Canada in the eight-game "Summit Series." Canada's Paul Henderson wins the series for Canada with just 34 seconds remaining in Game 8 in Moscow.

**1973**—Swedish defenseman Borje Salming becomes the first European-trained player to achieve star status in the NHL, playing for Toronto.

**April 11, 1974**—Detroit Red Wings owner Bruce Norris, who used the London (England) Lions as a farm team, and NHL president John Zeigler speak and answer questions at the IIHF Congress.

**1974**—Vaclav Nedomansky and Richard Farda of Czechoslovakia are the first two players to defect.

**December 31, 1975**—CSKA Moscow and the Montreal Canadiens play to an historic 3-3 tie at the Montreal Forum on New Year's Eve, one of the finest hockey games ever played.

**1975**—Viktor Khatulev is the first Soviet player drafted into the NHL when Philadelphia uses the 160th selection overall to name him.

**August 1976**—The inaugural "open" international hockey tournament – Canada Cup – is staged. Darryl Sittler's overtime goal in game two of the best-of-three finals against Czechoslovakia in Montreal wins the cup for Canada. It is the first international tournament officiated by one referee and two linesmen (as opposed to the two-referee system).

**May 1977**—The IIHF and WHA agreed that the WHA will pay European club teams when it signs a player.

**February 11, 1979**—The Soviet Union shocks the NHL All-Star Team in the Challenge Cup by winning the third and decisive game 6-0 at New York's Madison Square Garden.

**1980**—Anders Kallur and Stefan Persson of the New York Islanders become the first Europeans to win the Stanley Cup and have their names stamped on the historic trophy; Peter Stastny becomes the first player to defect to play in the NHL, leaving Czechoslovakia to play for the Quebec Nordiques. His brothers, Anton and Marian, join him later.

**1983**—Legendary Soviet goalie Vladislav Tretiak is selected by Montreal in the NHL's Entry Draft, though he is never allowed to join the team. Tretiak retires following the next season as the most successful player in the history of international hockey.

**1985-86**—Finland's Jari Kurri is the first European to lead the NHL in goalscoring (68).

**June 11, 1986**—The first formal player transfer agreement is signed between the NHL and IIHF on behalf of Sweden, Finland, Czechoslovakia, and West Germany.

**1989**—Alexander Mogilny becomes the first Soviet hockey defector as he leaves the team immediately following the gold-medal victory at the World Championship in Stockholm to play in the NHL.

**September 1989**—Calgary Flames and Washington Capitals conduct their training camps in the Soviet Union, playing a series of exhibition games as well.

**March 29, 1989**—Sergei Priakhin is the first Soviet player to be formally allowed to play in the NHL, joining Calgary and making his debut two nights later, March 31.

**June 17, 1989**—Mats Sundin of Sweden is the first European to be selected first overall at the NHL Entry Draft when Quebec uses the selection.

**September 16, 1994**—The IIHF and NHL agree to have NHL players participate in the 1998 Olympic Winter Games.

**1994-95**—Jaromir Jagr of the Pittsburgh Penguins becomes the first European to win the Art Ross Trophy.

**1997**—The NHL opens its regular season in Japan as the Vancouver Canucks and Mighty Ducks of Anaheim play two games in Tokyo.

**February 7-22, 1998**—For the first time since its founding in 1917, the National Hockey League takes a break to allow its players to participate in the Olympic Winter Games. The Czech Republic wins its first Olympic gold in Nagano, Japan. Women's hockey makes its debut on the Olympic program and the United States wins the historic gold medal, defeating arch-rival Canada, 3-1.

**May 22, 2000**—Finland's Alpo Suhonen becomes the first European to be named head coach of an NHL team when he is hired by Chicago. One month later, Ivan Hlinka of the Czech Republic is made coach of Pittsburgh. Neither lasts the season.

**July 15, 2007**—The NHL and IIHF mutually agree to terminate the Player Transfer Agreement.

**September 1, 2008**—The first Victoria Cup is played, providing the first meaningful competition between an NHL club team and a European champion team.

**May 20, 2010**—Swedish referee Marcus Vinnerborg becomes the first European referee to sign with the NHL.

## Rules of Play

**March 14, 1911**—The LIHG adopts "Canadian rules" for all levels of play.

**1920**—The LIHG adopts Canadian rules for all World Championship and Olympic games.

**February 21, 1933**—The IIHF, following Canadian rules, eliminates offside within each of the three zones of play.

**1936**—The three zones of the hockey rink are introduced. Players must carry the puck to another zone, not pass it. Body-checking is allowed only in the defensive zone. Rink size is changed to 60m x 30m.

**September 1, 1946**—The red line at centre ice and the modern offside rule are introduced. Body-checking is allowed only in the defensive half of the ice.

**February 20, 1949**—The IIHF adds a second referee for games (no linesmen).

**1969**—Body-checking is allowed in all three zones in international hockey, a rule change that paves way for future confrontations between "amateurs" and "professionals."

**1971**—Czechoslovakia's Marcel Sakac, Sweden's Leif Holmqvist and Christer Abrahamsson, and United States's Carl Wetzel are the last goaltenders to play without a face mask in the World Championship.

**February 1972**—Team USA becomes the first national squad to wear name bars on their sweaters at the Olympics in Sapporo. Masks for goalies are now mandatory.

**1977**—For the first time the World Championship is officiated by one referee and two linesmen.

**September 22, 1979**—The IIHF mandates the use of visors for all games starting in 1981; the IIHF introduces a tournament for the Thayer Tutt Trophy to be competed every four years by top teams not in the Olympics.

**1980**—The IIHF and IOC introduce shootouts for placement games but none is needed until 1988 when France and Norway go to game-winning shots to decide 11th place.

**1992**—The IIHF bans body-checking from women's hockey.

**1994**—The Lillehammer Olympics mark the introduction of video review. Teams are also now allowed one, 30-second timeout each game.

**1997**—IIHF Congress decides to take away the red line for the purpose of allowing the two-line pass, the most important rule change in international hockey since 1969. The new rule is implemented for the first time at the 1999 World Championship in Norway.

**2006**—IIHF Congress eliminates tie games by introducing overtime and shootouts to games during all rounds of play at all tournaments. The three-point system is simultaneously introduced, giving a team that wins in regulation time three points, while giving a win in overtime or shootout winner two points and a loser in overtime or a shootout one point. New standards for smaller goalie equipment (notably blocker, glove, and pads) are established for the upcoming 2006-07 season.

## The Goal Crease

**1936-37**—A large semi-circle approximately five metres in diameter extending about three metres in front of the goal line.

**1947-70**—A small rectangle with outside lines 30 cm from each post extending 1.25 metres in front of the goal line.

**1971-78**—A semi-circle starting at either end approximately 30 cm from each post and curving around the goal to a maximum distance of 1.25 metres in front of the goal line.

**1979-92**—A return to the rectangular crease from 1947-70.

**1993-94**—A hybrid of the two previous creases; a rectangle with outside lines 30 cm from each post extending 1.25 metres in front of the goal line, and outside this rectangle the semi-circle starting approximately 30 cm outside each outside line and arcing around the rectangle such that the arc touches the top corners of the rectangle farthest from the goal. The total width along the goal line from one end of the outside arc to the other is 3.66 metres.

**1995-present**—A semi-circle only, the inner rectangle having been removed, and the remaining semi-circle now painted blue.

## International Timeline

**1897**—Canadian champion skater George Meagher travels to Paris, France and brings hockey equipment with him. He oversees a series of friendly games between Paris' Palais de Glace Club and bandy clubs from London and Glasgow.

**1900**—The goal net is introduced in Canada.

**1902**—The first true ice hockey games in Europe are played at the Princes' Skating Club in Knightsbridge, England.

**March 4, 1905**—Two international games between Belgium and France are played in Brussels. Ice hockey games, with no unified set of rules, are also played in Switzerland that year; hockey is played in Bohemia (Czechoslovakia) for the first time.

**1947**—Czechoslovakia becomes the first non-North American team to win the IIHF World Championship.

**November 8, 1948**—The entire Czechoslovakian national team dies in a plane crash, harming the nation's development after winning World Championship gold in 1947 and tying Canada en route to a silver medal at the 1948 Olympics.

**1951**—The entire Czechoslovakian team is arrested and charged with treason as it is about to board a plane to travel to London for the World Championship. The Czechs withdraw from the event, and most players are later given stiff prison sentences without any proof from the authorities of the charges.

**February 25, 1952**—Canada (Edmonton Mercurys) wins its sixth Olympic gold in seven events. It is Canada's last Olympic hockey gold medal for 50 years.

**March 15, 1953**—Sweden wins the IIHF World Championship for the first time, but only three teams finish the event held in Zurich and Basel, Switzerland.

**1954**—The Soviet Union enters the IIHF World Championship for the first time and strikes gold in Stockholm, Sweden.

**February 4, 1956**—The Soviet Union wins its first Olympic gold, in Cortina d'Ampezzo, Italy.

**March 5, 1957**—The largest hockey crowd to date, more than 50,000 spectators at Moscow's Lenin Stadium, watches Sweden win World Championship gold after a 4-4-tie against the Soviet Union.

**February 28, 1960**—The United States wins its first Olympic gold, at Squaw Valley, California, becoming the first host nation to win.

**March 12, 1961**—The Trail Smoke Eaters' World Championship gold by Canada in Geneva, Switzerland, is the nation's last for 33 years. It is also the final time a World Championship game is played outdoors. Games in Lausanne are played on an outdoor swimming pool.

**March 17, 1963**—The Soviet Union begins its streak of nine consecutive IIHF World Championship gold medals.

**1964**—Father David Bauer's National Team starts representing Canada in international play.

**February 17, 1968**—The Soviet Union wins its third Olympic gold, in Grenoble, France.

**April 22, 1972**—Czechoslovakia wins its first World Championship gold in 23 years and ends the Soviet Union's streak of nine consecutive world titles. This is the first year where there is both an Olympics and World Championship tournament.

**1977**—Canada re-enters the World Championship with a professional squad in Vienna, Austria, after a seven-year absence. Czechoslovakia becomes the first country other than Canada and the Soviet Union to win two consecutive World Championship gold medals.

**February 22, 1980**—The biggest upset in international hockey history: A collegian Team USA defeats the Soviet Union 4-3 at Lake Placid en route to a gold medal. The Soviet's silver breaks what would have been a streak of eight consecutive Olympic gold medals by Soviet Union/Russia.

**April 24, 1981**—The Soviet Union beats Sweden 13-1 in the most lopsided World Championship game to decide the gold medal and four months later defeats Team Canada 8-1 in the one-game Canada Cup final in Montreal, arguably the most crushing defeat in Canada's international hockey history.

**February 19, 1984**—The Soviet Union sweeps through the Sarajevo Olympics undefeated, claiming its sixth Olympic gold.

**1984**—Canada makes up for its 1981 defeat by winning this year's Canada Cup. Mike Bossy's dramatic overtime goal in the semi-final inflicts on the Soviets their first loss since Lake Placid 1980.

**May 3, 1987**—Sweden wins its first World Championship gold in 25 years, in Vienna, Austria.

**1987**—Canada wins the fourth Canada Cup after a three-game series against the Soviet Union where all games end with the same score, 6-5. Canada's Mario Lemieux and Wayne Gretzky dominate the series.

**February 28, 1988**—The Soviet Union wins its seventh and last Olympic hockey gold, in Calgary, Canada; NHLers play at the Olympics for the first time as seven players join Team Canada. Finland wins silver, its first Olympic medal.

**March 1990**—The first IIHF-sanctioned World Women's Championship takes place in Ottawa, Canada. Body-checking is still permitted in the game.

**May 10, 1992**—Sweden wins consecutive World Championship gold medals for the first time.

**February 23, 1992**—The Commonwealth of Independent States (CIS) – the former Soviet Union and the future Russia – wins Olympic gold in Albertville, France.

**May 2, 1993**—Russia wins its first World Championship gold, but it also marks the end of the Soviet Union/Russian dominance after 39 years.

**February 27, 1994**—Sweden wins its first Olympic gold, in Lillehammer, Norway, after Peter Forsberg's daring shootout goal against Canada, a goal so famous that it eventually becomes a postage stamp in Sweden.

**May 8, 1994**—Canada wins its first World Championship in 33 years, in Milan, Italy, becoming the first team to win gold in a shootout. Luc Robitaille is the shootout hero in the final against Finland.

**May 7, 1995**—Finland becomes the seventh nation to win the IIHF World Championship gold as it defeats arch-rival Sweden in Stockholm. The tournament features no NHLers as a lockout forced a late start and finish to the season.

**1996**—USA wins the inaugural World Cup of Hockey, which replaces the Canada Cup. It's the USA's biggest international success since the 1980 Olympic "Miracle on Ice."

**May 16, 1999**—Jan Hlavac becomes the first player to decide a World Championship gold medal game in overtime as Czechs defeat Finland in Lillehammer, Norway.

**May 13, 2001**—The Czech Republic becomes the first nation other than Canada and the Soviet Union to win three consecutive World Championships.

**February 24, 2002**—Canada ends a 50-year drought by winning Olympic gold in Salt Lake City. The country strikes a double as Canada's women also win.

**May 11, 2002**—Slovakia becomes the eighth nation to win the World Championship, in Gothenburg, Sweden.

**May 9, 2004**—Canada wins consecutive World Championship titles for the first time since 1959. The Canadians defeat Sweden in both 2003 and 2004.

**2006**—Sweden becomes the first country in international hockey history to win Olympic gold and the World Championship in the same year, capturing the titles in Turin and Riga, respectively. The Swedish women also make history by defeating the United States in a shootout in the semi-finals, earning a silver medal and marking the first time a women's final features a matchup other than Canada-United States.

**2006**—Canada's Sidney Crosby, at 18 years of age, becomes the youngest player ever to lead the World Championship in scoring.

**2007**—The World Championship in Moscow is the first IIHF's flagship event where a regulation-time win is awarded with three points.

**2008**—Canada hosts its first World Championship to mark the centenary of the IIHF. Quebec City (also celebrating its 400th anniversary) and Halifax host the 56 games and 16 countries.

**May 18, 2008**—Russia defeats Canada 5-4 in overtime of the gold-medal game to win World Championship gold for the first time since 1993.

**May 7, 2010**—A world record crowd of 77,803 in Gelsenkirchen, Germany watch the home side defeat the United States 2-1 in overtime in the first game of the 2010 World Championship.

# Video Goal Judge System Procedures

The use of the video replay of disputed goals is approved by the IIHF. All available television pictures must be provided and used by the video goal judge. The following are the only situations that are subject to video goal judge review:

1. To determine if the puck has completely crossed the goal line.
2. To determine if the puck entered the net prior to or after the goal frame was dislodged.
3. To determine if the puck entered the net prior to or after expiration of time at the end of a period or the game.
4. To determine if the puck was directed into the net by a hand or kicked into the net by a skate.
5. To determine if a puck deflected into the net off a game official.
6. To determine if the puck was struck with a high stick, above the height of the crossbar, by an attacking player, prior to the puck entering the net.
7. To establish the correct time on the official game clock at the point that the puck completely crossed the goal line, provided that the game time is available on the video goal judge's monitor.

The review can only be requested by the video goal judge or the referee.

**VIDEO GOAL JUDGE PROCEDURE**

- When the referee requests a video review of a disputed goal, he contacts the video goal judge from the scorekeepers' bench using a telephone.
- When the video goal judge requests a review, he will contact the official scorekeeper bench using the telephone during the first stoppage of play.
- If the video review is inconclusive, the video goal judge will report this to the referee who will then make the final decision.
- A team cannot request a video review of any play.
- If the puck enters the net and play is stopped, the referee or the video goal judge asks for a review during this stoppage. If there is no review during this stoppage, the result is final and no review will be permitted later.
- If the puck enters the net and play continues, the review will take place during the first stoppage after the incident. If no review is performed during the first stoppage, then no review will be permitted later.
- When it is indicated that there is to be a video review, all players must go to their respective team benches.
- A video review may be called even though the first stoppage of play signals the end of a period or the end of a game.

# Game Winning Shots Procedure

If, following the completion of regulation time in any IIHF Championship game and the score of such a game is tied, the teams will then play a 4-on-4 overtime period with the team scoring first declared the winner.

If no goal is scored in the overtime period then the IIHF Game Winning Shots Procedure will apply. The following procedure will be utilized:

- Shots will be taken on both ends of the ice unless the referees deem that one end of the ice is in poor enough condition to disadvantage one team, in which case only one end will be used. The longitudinal centre section of the rink will be dry-scraped by the ice-resurfacing machine prior to the Game Winning Shots during the time required to organize the program accordingly.
- The procedure will begin with three different shooters from each team taking alternate shots. The players do not need to be named beforehand. Eligible to participate in the Game Winning Shots will be the four goalkeepers and all players from both teams listed on the official game sheet except any player(s) whose penalty had not been completed when the overtime period ended. This player(s) must remain in the penalty box or in the dressing room. Also, players serving penalties imposed during the Game Winning Shots must remain in the penalty box or in the dressing room until the end of the procedure.
- The Referee will call the two captains to the Referee Crease and flip a coin to determine which team takes the first shot. The winner of the coin toss will have the choice whether his team will shoot first or second.
- The goalkeepers shall defend the same goal as in the overtime period.
- The goalkeepers from each team may be changed after each shot.
- The shots will be taken in accordance with rule 509 of the IIHF Official Rule Book.
- The players of both teams will take the shots alternately until a decisive goal is scored. The remaining shots will not be taken.
- If the result is still tied after three shots by each team, the procedure shall continue with a tie-break shoot-out by one player of each team, with a reversed shooting order. The same player can also be used for each shot by a team in the tie-break shoot-out. The game shall be finished as soon as a duel of two players brings the decisive result.
- The Official Scorekeeper will record all shots taken, indicating the players, goalkeepers, and goals scored, but only the decisive goal will count in the result of the game. It shall be credited to the player who scored and to the goalkeeper concerned.
- If a team declines to participate in the game winning shots procedure the game will be declared as a loss for that team and the other team will be awarded 3 points for a win. If a player declines to take a shot it will be declared "no score" for his team.

# Doping Control

Doping controls were first introduced by the IIHF at the 1969 Congress.

**HOW IT WORKS**

After every game sanctioned by the IIHF, a player from each team is taken directly from the ice to the doping control station by the medical supervisor for that game. The player is not permitted to leave the room until submitting a sample. In IIHF events, IIHF staff handle doping, but in Olympics events it is IOC officials who handle all doping matters. At IIHF events, beer is provided to the athletes (in addition to water and juice), but at the Olympics beer is not provided (alcohol in the blood can result in a positive test at some Olympics events, although not hockey).

In the event of a positive test, the player is automatically suspended for the remainder of the tournament. The goals and points earned by the doped player's teams become invalid unless the opposite result is more favourable for the non-offending team.

**NOTABLE DOPING INFRACTIONS**

**February 8, 1972**—Alois Schloder (FRG) tested positive and was suspended the rest of the tournament. He was allowed to play at the World Championship several weeks later because it was discovered that his doctor has prescribed drugs for an illness and Schloder was found not to be at fault for "doping."

**April 6, 1974**—Ulf Nilsson (SWE) tested positive for ephedrine after his team's 4-1 win over Poland. The score was reversed to Poland 5-Sweden 0.

**April 12, 1974**—Goalie Stig Wetzel (FIN) tested positive for ephedrine after his team's 5-2 win over Czechoslovakia. The score was reversed to Czechoslovakia 5-Finland 0.

**February 10, 1976**—Frantisek Pospisil (TCH) failed a doping test after his team's 7-1 win over Poland. The score was reversed to Poland 1- Czechoslovakia 0.

**February 18, 1988**—Forward Jaroslav Morawiecki (POL) tested positive for testosterone after his team beat France, 6-2. Morawiecki was banned from international competition for 18 months and France was officially awarded a 2–0 win, but not the points in the standings.

**April 18, 1989**—Corey Millen (USA) tested positive after his team's 8-2 loss to Canada. The score was changed to 8-0 as a result.

**May 2, 1994**—Bill Lindsay (USA) tested positive after his team's 7-2 loss to Finland. The score was changed to 7-0 as a result.

**January 21, 2002**—Mattias Ohlund (SWE) tested positive for acetazolomide in out-of-competition testing, but no suspension was handed down because he proved this drug was necessary for recovery from several serious eye operations.

**February 23, 2002**—Vasily Pankov (BLR) tested positive for a drug given him by a team doctor.

**April 30, 2005**—Timofei Filin (BLR) tested positive for nandrolene after his team's 2-1 loss to Slovakia. He was immediately removed from the Belarus team roster and was suspended from international competition for two years.

**May 1, 2005**—Olexander Pobyedonostsev (UKR)—tested positive for nandrolene after his team's 3-2 loss to Sweden. He was immediately removed from the Ukraine team roster and was suspended from international competition for two years.

# IIHF Media Guidelines and Access Policy

**GENERAL GUIDELINES FOR ACCREDITED MEDIA**

The media centre, the press tribune in the arena, the mixed zones, and the media interview rooms are areas for working press only and officials associated with media relations and media services. We respectfully ask you observe the following rules in these working areas:

1. The wearing national team sweaters or significant fan apparel in designated working areas for media is improper. Accredited journalists who do so will be asked either to remove the apparel or leave the area.
2. Excessive cheering and "fan behaviour" in the press tribune and media centre are strictly forbidden. Such conduct is unprofessional and disruptive for working media.
3. Accredited journalists are not allowed to ask players for autographs at any time in any of the above-mentioned designated media working areas.
4. Accredited journalists are not allowed to switch accreditation passes with representatives of other media outlets in order to gain unauthorized access to any part of the arena or for any other purpose.

**Breach of these rules may result in the media accreditation being revoked.**

**GENERAL ACCESS POLICY**

All accredited media have access to cover all team practices, game-day skates, and games. All accredited media have access to the media centre, the media tribune (press box), the mixed-zone area, and the media interview room.

**POST-GAME MIXED ZONE**

Players and assistant coaches will be available in the mixed zone no later than ten (10) minutes after the end of the post-game ceremonies. The general media access period is 30 minutes, starting from the moment the first player arrives. Media officers of the teams will take requests from the media for interviews of players and assistant coaches and will make them available in the mixed zone.

All players are available to the media during the general access period. Up to five players are required to appear in the mixed zone. Media officers are advised that those players for whom the greatest number of requests is made should be available in the mixed zone. If, after a reasonable time, the team's media officer determines that there is no media interest in particular players, they may be excused.

The media officer should inform media whether one of the requested players is selected for doping control. That player will be made available to media upon the conclusion of the doping control procedure.

Rights holders (TV and radio) have first priority to player interviews in the mixed zone area and are allowed to interview players immediately after they have come off the ice.

**POST-GAME PRESS CONFERENCES**

A media conference with both head coaches will take place after each game in the media interview room no later than 15 minutes after the conclusion of the game. Translation to English is mandatory, and translation to other languages will be provided depending on the availability of interpreters. Upon special request, a player can be added to the post game press conference.

**POST-PRACTICE INTERVIEWS**

All interview requests after practices should be forwarded to the team's media officer or team host. Interviews will take place in the mixed zone of either the main rink or the practice facility. The general media access period after non-game day practices is 30 minutes, starting from when the first player arrives. Any player who leaves practice prior to its conclusion will remain available for the general media access period unless alternate arrangements are made by the team's media officer.

Coaching staff and the media officer are entitled to limit game-day interviews to 15 minutes. Interview requests on other occasions during the championship should be addressed to the team's media officer. Players and coaches have the right to decline requests for impromptu interviews in other areas such as the team's hotel.

**GENERAL INFORMATION**

Following a practice or game, players who must remain in the dressing room for medical treatment for any portion of the access period must be available in the mixed zone as soon as possible after the treatment has been completed. When a player's medical treatment takes longer than 30 minutes, the team's media relations officer should make appropriate arrangements for the player to meet the media.

**RIGHTS-HOLDER INTERVIEWS IN THE MIXED ZONE**

All pre-game and post-game interviews, including those during the intermissions by the rights-holders in the mixed zone, must take place in front of the rights-holders interview area or in front of the official IIHF World Championship backdrop area.

**TV & RADIO FLASH INTERVIEWS**

The IIHF recommends that teams participate in flash interviews after the first and second periods if requested by the broadcaster. The maximum time allowed for a flash interview is 60 seconds. The interviews will take place directly behind the player bench area.

# www.IIHF.com

The IIHF re-launched IIHF.com in November 2007. The new IIHF.com became the official website of the IIHF World Championship, replacing IHWC.net. It has all the features that fans and journalists used during the World Championship, in addition to several new and improved functions, and provides more information from the world of hockey than ever before.

As with the rest of the IIHF Championship program, the entire statistics program is under the umbrella of the Hydra System, a statistics system designed by the IIHF specifically for World Championship events. Within the statistics system, users will be able to find schedules, teams, statistics, individual statistics, rosters, upcoming games, standings, and virtually every other type of information about the IIHF World Championship. The easy-to-use navigation at the top of the page will help readers find what they are looking for with a simple click of the mouse.

**IIHF.COM SPECIAL FEATURES**

IIHF.com features top editorial content throughout the 56-game World Championship. In addition to some of the more traditional features such as game recaps and previews, the editorial staff provides:

**Features:** Exclusive IIHF.com background information, player interviews, and Q & A profiles with the great stars of the current World Championship
**Power Rankings:** An irreverent analysis by IIHF.com's editors of each country's performance to date
**Columns:** Subjective and objective editorials from reporters around the world who converge on the World Championship every year
**Blogs:** IIHF.com writers and photographers will illustrate and blog about off-ice action and behind-the-scenes stories

**OFFICAL IIHF.COM CONTENT**

Being the official website also means that IIHF.com is the place to turn to with questions regarding format and rules and other pertinent information fans might be asking during the course of the World Championship.

**Championship Rules:** Tournament format, tiebreak, overtime, and shootout procedures
**IIHF World Ranking:** An up-to-date graph showing the ranking of the top 44 hockey nations
**Event information:** Everything about ticketing, venues, cities, hospitality, accommodation, transportation, and more is available

**IIHF.COM INTERACTIVE**

**Message Boards:** See what fans from around the world are saying about their favourite players and teams—and the players and teams they are not so fond of, either!
**Poll:** A periodic installment created for interactive use for the readers.
**IIHF.com Video:** Check out the TV stations televising World Championship games, the IIHF.com live stream, and game highlights

**PHOTO GALLERY**

Exclusive photographs by IIHF.com staff photographers featuring action images from games at the World Championship

**FACEBOOK/TWITTER**

All stories published on IIHF.com, news alerts, photos and other special features are also available on Facebook and Twitter. Enter the following addresses in your web browser to join thousands of followers:
IIHF.com/Facebook
IIHF.com/Twitter

**IIHF.COM WORLD CHAMPIONSHIP WRITERS**

**Lucas Aykroyd** is a Vancouver writer who has covered every IIHF World Championship and Winter Olympics since 2000, as well as other IIHF tournaments, the NHL, and the WHL.

**Risto Pakarinen** is a freelance writer from Finland, based in Stockholm, Sweden. He contributes to many other international publications.

**Andrew Podnieks** is the editor of the *IIHF Guide & Record Book* and author of some 65 books on hockey (www.andrewpodnieks.com), most recently *Team Canada 1972: The Official 40th Anniversary Celebration of the Summit Series.*

**Paul Romanuk** has been a broadcaster, writer, and producer for 25 years and made his www.IIHF.com debut at the 2011 World Championship in Slovakia.

**John Sanful** is the CEO of Ice Hockey in Harlem and has been a contributor to IIHF.com since 2001 at almost every World Championship.

**2012 WWW.IIHF.COM SUMMARY—WEBSITE AND SOCIAL MEDIA SET RECORDS**

The steady growth of IIHF.com during the IIHF Ice Hockey World Championship continued in 2012. IIHF.com averaged 387,532 visits per day during the event in Helsinki and Stockholm. This represents a more than 50 per-cent growth over last year in Slovakia (258,147) and almost four times more since the redesign of www.IIHF.com in 2007.

The numbers peaked on May 17th when the quarter-finals were played. More than 600,000 visits were registered on that day another IIHF.com record.

During the World Championship period, IIHF.com had 6,588,046 visits compared to 4,584,990 in Slovakia 2011 and 4,065,490 in Germany 2010.

The countries with the most visitors were Finland, Russia, Canada and the United States, but IIHF.com is followed in more than 200 countries each year during the IIHF Ice Hockey World Championship.

Website growth continued with the second-most followed event, the IIHF World Junior Championship. Some 102,485 visits per day were registered during the event in Calgary and Edmonton, an 11 per cent increase over Buffalo 2011.

| Event | Main Venue | Visits/Day | Growth |
|---|---|---|---|
| WM 2012 | Helsinki/Stockholm | 387,532 | +50.1% |
| WM 2011 | Bratislava | 258,147 | +11.7% |
| WM 2010 | Cologne | 231,153 | +25.6% |
| WM 2009 | Berne | 184,103 | +27.2% |
| WM 2008 | Quebec City | 144,760 | +39.9% |
| WM 2007 | Moscow | 103,449 | +28.5% |
| WM 2006 | Riga | 80,508 | |

# World Rankings

## Men

| NOC | 2004 | 2005 | 2006a | 2006b | 2007 | 2008 | 2009 | 2010a | 2010b | 2011 | 2012 |
|---|---|---|---|---|---|---|---|---|---|---|---|
| ARM | 45 | 45 | 45 | 45 | 45 | 48 | 48 | 48 | 49 | | |
| AUS | 35 | 34 | 34 | 34 | 33 | 33 | 31 | 34 | 34 | 34 | 32 |
| AUT | 11 | 13 | 12 | 16 | 17 | 16 | 16 | 14 | 14 | 15 | 15 |
| BLR | 13 | 12 | 13 | 10 | 9 | 9 | 8 | 9 | 10 | 11 | 13 |
| BEL | 33 | 32 | 33 | 35 | 35 | 34 | 33 | 36 | 36 | 35 | 36 |
| BIH | | | 29 | | | 47 | 47 | 47 | 48 | 48 | |
| BUL | 32 | 33 | 30 | 30 | 31 | 32 | 35 | 31 | 31 | 32 | 33 |
| CAN | 1 | 1 | 2 | 3 | 2 | 1 | 2 | 1 | 2 | 4 | 5 |
| CHN | 28 | 28 | 27 | 28 | 27 | 28 | 29 | 35 | 37 | 39 | 38 |
| CRO | 31 | 30 | 28 | 27 | 28 | 26 | 26 | 27 | 26 | 27 | 30 |
| CZE | 4 | 3 | 3 | 2 | 4 | 5 | 6 | 6 | 5 | 5 | 3 |
| DEN | 14 | 14 | 15 | 14 | 12 | 13 | 13 | 13 | 13 | 13 | 12 |
| PRK | 37 | 36 | 36 | 36 | 44 | 44 | 43 | 43 | 43 | 45 | 45 |
| EST | 24 | 24 | 24 | 24 | 23 | 25 | 27 | 26 | 27 | 26 | 26 |
| FIN | 5 | 7 | 5 | 4 | 3 | 4 | 4 | 3 | 4 | 2 | 2 |
| FRA | 18 | 17 | 19 | 19 | 19 | 18 | 14 | 16 | 15 | 14 | 14 |
| GER | 8 | 10 | 10 | 12 | 11 | 10 | 12 | 12 | 9 | 8 | 10 |
| GBR | 25 | 25 | 31 | 31 | 29 | 29 | 25 | 24 | 23 | 21 | 21 |
| GRE | | | | | | 46 | 46 | 46 | 45 | 44 | 44 |
| HUN | 22 | 22 | 22 | 22 | 21 | 20 | 20 | 20 | 20 | 20 | 19 |
| ISL | 39 | 39 | 39 | 40 | 37 | 38 | 37 | 39 | 38 | 36 | 35 |
| IRL | 44 | 44 | 44 | 44 | 43 | 40 | 42 | 42 | 41 | 41 | 42 |
| ISR | 36 | 35 | 35 | 33 | 34 | 35 | 36 | 38 | 39 | 40 | 40 |
| ITA | 19 | 19 | 17 | 17 | 13 | 14 | 15 | 15 | 16 | 17 | 16 |
| JPN | 15 | 20 | 21 | 21 | 22 | 22 | 21 | 21 | 21 | 22 | 22 |
| KAZ | 17 | 15 | 11 | 11 | 16 | 19 | 18 | 19 | 17 | 16 | 17 |
| KOR | 30 | 31 | 32 | 32 | 32 | 31 | 30 | 33 | 33 | 31 | 28 |
| LAT | 10 | 9 | 9 | 9 | 10 | 11 | 10 | 10 | 12 | 12 | 11 |
| LTU | 27 | 27 | 26 | 25 | 25 | 23 | 23 | 23 | 24 | 24 | 25 |
| LUX | 42 | 42 | 42 | 43 | 42 | 43 | 44 | 44 | 44 | 43 | 43 |
| MEX | 41 | 43 | 43 | 39 | 38 | 37 | 38 | 32 | 32 | 33 | 34 |
| MGL | | | | | 46 | 45 | 45 | 45 | 46 | 46 | 46 |
| NED | 23 | 23 | 23 | 23 | 24 | 24 | 24 | 25 | 25 | 25 | 24 |
| NZL | 40 | 38 | 38 | 38 | 39 | 39 | 39 | 40 | 40 | 38 | 37 |
| NOR | 21 | 18 | 18 | 15 | 14 | 12 | 11 | 11 | 11 | 9 | 8 |
| POL | 20 | 21 | 20 | 20 | 20 | 21 | 22 | 22 | 22 | 23 | 23 |
| ROU | 26 | 26 | 25 | 26 | 26 | 27 | 28 | 28 | 28 | 28 | 27 |
| RUS | 7 | 5 | 6 | 5 | 5 | 2 | 1 | 2 | 1 | 1 | 1 |
| SRB | 29 | 29 | | 29 | 30 | 30 | 32 | 29 | 29 | 30 | 31 |
| SVK | 3 | 4 | 4 | 6 | 6 | 8 | 9 | 7 | 8 | 10 | 6 |
| SLO | 16 | 16 | 16 | 18 | 18 | 15 | 17 | 18 | 19 | 18 | 18 |
| RSA | 38 | 40 | 40 | 41 | 41 | 42 | 40 | 41 | 42 | 42 | 41 |
| ESP | 34 | 37 | 37 | 37 | 36 | 36 | 34 | 30 | 30 | 29 | 29 |
| SWE | 2 | 2 | 1 | 1 | 1 | 3 | 3 | 4 | 3 | 3 | 4 |
| SUI | 9 | 8 | 8 | 8 | 8 | 7 | 7 | 8 | 7 | 7 | 9 |
| TUR | 43 | 41 | 41 | 42 | 40 | 41 | 41 | 37 | 35 | 37 | 39 |
| UKR | 12 | 11 | 14 | 13 | 15 | 17 | 19 | 17 | 18 | 19 | 20 |
| UAE | | | | | | | | | 47 | 47 | 47 |
| USA | 6 | 6 | 7 | 7 | 7 | 6 | 5 | 5 | 6 | 6 | 7 |

a=post-Olympic World Ranking, b=post-World Championship World Ranking

## Women

| NOC | 2004 | 2005 | 2006 | 2007 | 2008 | 2009 | 2010 | 2011 | 2012 |
|---|---|---|---|---|---|---|---|---|---|
| AUS | 21 | 22 | 23 | 23 | 22 | 23 | 25 | 24 | 24 |
| AUT | 26 | 25 | 21 | 20 | 19 | 17 | 16 | 15 | 15 |
| BEL | 22 | 23 | 24 | 24 | 24 | 24 | 26 | 26 | 27 |
| BUL | | | | | | | 24 | 23 | 33 |
| CAN | 1 | 1 | 1 | 1 | 1 | 2 | 1 | 2 | 1 |
| CHN | 7 | 7 | 7 | 8 | 8 | 7 | 7 | 9 | 13 |
| CRO | | | | 31 | 30 | 25 | 20 | 20 | 22 |
| CZE | 11 | 11 | 12 | 13 | 12 | 12 | 13 | 14 | 12 |
| DEN | 16 | 14 | 17 | 17 | 18 | 19 | 22 | 21 | 19 |
| PRK | 15 | 16 | 18 | 19 | 20 | 18 | 21 | 32 | 31 |
| EST | | | | 32 | 32 | 32 | 33 | 37 | |
| FIN | 3 | 3 | 4 | 4 | 3 | 3 | 3 | 3 | 3 |
| FRA | 13 | 12 | 14 | 12 | 11 | 13 | 14 | 16 | 16 |
| GER | 6 | 5 | 5 | 5 | 7 | 10 | 11 | 10 | 8 |
| GBR | 20 | 20 | 22 | 22 | 23 | 20 | 18 | 18 | 17 |
| HUN | 23 | 24 | 25 | 25 | 25 | 26 | 27 | 25 | 23 |
| ISL | | 30 | 30 | 30 | 31 | 29 | 29 | 29 | 29 |
| IRL | | | | | | | | 36 | 36 |
| ITA | 17 | 17 | 11 | 14 | 15 | 16 | 17 | 17 | 18 |
| JPN | 10 | 10 | 10 | 10 | 9 | 9 | 9 | 11 | 11 |
| KAZ | 9 | 8 | 9 | 9 | 10 | 8 | 8 | 7 | 9 |
| KOR | 27 | 27 | 26 | 26 | 26 | 27 | 28 | 28 | 26 |
| LAT | 12 | 13 | 13 | 11 | 13 | 14 | 15 | 13 | 14 |
| NED | 19 | 19 | 20 | 21 | 21 | 21 | 23 | 22 | 21 |
| NZL | | 29 | 29 | 29 | 27 | 28 | 30 | 27 | 25 |
| NOR | 14 | 15 | 15 | 15 | 14 | 11 | 12 | 12 | 10 |
| POL | | | | | | | | 34 | 28 |
| ROU | 25 | 26 | 27 | 27 | 29 | 30 | 31 | 30 | 34 |
| RUS | 5 | 6 | 6 | 6 | 6 | 6 | 6 | 5 | 6 |
| SVK | 18 | 18 | 19 | 18 | 17 | 15 | 10 | 8 | 7 |
| SLO | 24 | 21 | 16 | 16 | 16 | 22 | 19 | 19 | 20 |
| RSA | 28 | 28 | 28 | 28 | 28 | 31 | 32 | 31 | 32 |
| ESP | | | | | | | | 35 | 30 |
| SWE | 4 | 4 | 3 | 3 | 4 | 4 | 4 | 4 | 5 |
| SUI | 8 | 9 | 8 | 7 | 5 | 5 | 5 | 6 | 4 |
| TUR | | | | 33 | 33 | 33 | 34 | 33 | 35 |
| USA | 2 | 2 | 2 | 2 | 2 | 1 | 2 | 1 | 2 |

*New Zealand finished 37th in the World Ranking for 2012, one spot better than a year ago. Photo: Bonchuk Andonov.*

# Survey of Players

| FEDERATION | PLAYERS | | | | REFEREES | | RINKS | | PARTICIPATION IN 2012 IIHF CHAMPIONSHIPS | POPULATION* |
|---|---|---|---|---|---|---|---|---|---|---|
| | REGISTERED | SENIOR | UNDER 20 | FEMALE | MALE | FEMALE | INDOOR | OUTDOOR | | |
| Andorra | 56 | 23 | 24 | 9 | 0 | 0 | 1 | 0 | | 85,082 |
| Argentina | 966 | 690 | 130 | 146 | 25 | 4 | 0 | 1 | | 42,192,494 |
| Armenia | 578 | 381 | 197 | 0 | 27 | 0 | 2 | 3 | | 2,970,495 |
| Australia | 3721 | 2217 | 997 | 507 | 268 | 17 | 17 | 0 | WM IB, WM20 IIB, WM18 IIB, WW IIA | 22,015,576 |
| Austria | 11202 | 5897 | 4690 | 615 | 413 | 22 | 45 | 72 | WM IA, WM20 IA, WM18 IB, WW IA, WW18 I | 8,219,743 |
| Belarus | 3937 | 1154 | 2747 | 36 | 128 | 0 | 28 | 3 | WM, WM20 IA, WM18 IB | 9,542,883 |
| Belgium | 1490 | 670 | 736 | 84 | 31 | 4 | 17 | 0 | WM IIB, WM20 IIB, WM18 IIIA, WW IIB | 10,438,353 |
| Bosnia & Herzegovina | 208 | 42 | 162 | 4 | 5 | 0 | 0 | 0 | | 4,622,292 |
| Bulgaria | 330 | 100 | 203 | 27 | 30 | 3 | 3 | 5 | WM IIB, WM20 III, WM18 IIIA | 7,037,935 |
| Canada | 617107 | 74626 | 455806 | 86675 | 31572 | 1834 | 2486 | 5000 | WM, WM20, WM18, WW, WW18 | 34,300,083 |
| China | 610 | 118 | 308 | 184 | 63 | 32 | 46 | 43 | WM IIB, WM20 III, WM18 IIB, WW IB, WW18 IQ | 1,343,239,923 |
| Chinese Taipei | 848 | 142 | 630 | 76 | 84 | 8 | 4 | 0 | WM18 IIIA | 23,113,901 |
| Croatia | 536 | 114 | 379 | 43 | 12 | 1 | 2 | 4 | WM IIA, WM20 IB, WM18 IIA, WW IIA | 4,480,043 |
| Czech Republic | 95094 | 58654 | 34113 | 2327 | 1532 | 71 | 148 | 21 | WM, WM20, WM18, WW IA, WW18 | 10,177,300 |
| Denmark | 4405 | 1764 | 2245 | 396 | 100 | 3 | 25 | 0 | WM, WM20, WM18, WW IB | 5,543,453 |
| DPR Korea | 1575 | 640 | 420 | 515 | 20 | 0 | 3 | 12 | WM III, WM20 III*, WW IIA | 24,589,122 |
| Estonia | 1510 | 442 | 976 | 92 | 142 | 12 | 6 | 15 | WM IIA, WM20 IIB, WM18 IIB | 1,274,709 |
| Finland | 56626 | 16752 | 35929 | 3945 | 1709 | 51 | 246 | 30 | WM, WM20, WM18, WW, WW18 | 5,262,930 |
| FYR Macedonia | 82 | 45 | 37 | 0 | 0 | 0 | 1 | 4 | | 2,082,370 |
| France | 17381 | 6400 | 9767 | 1214 | 123 | 6 | 124 | 5 | WM, WM20 IB, WM18 IA, WW IB, WW18 IQ | 65,630,692 |
| Georgia | 266 | 77 | 189 | 0 | 4 | 0 | 4 | 1 | | 4,570,934 |
| Germany | 27068 | 8042 | 16561 | 2465 | 184 | 13 | 198 | 45 | WM, WM20 IA, WM18, WW, WW18 | 81,305,856 |
| Great Britain | 5119 | 1484 | 2897 | 738 | 285 | 27 | 46 | 0 | WM IA, WM20 IA, WM18 IIA, WW IB, WW18 I | 63,047,162 |
| Greece | 713 | 463 | 153 | 97 | 4 | 2 | 0 | 0 | WM III | 10,767,827 |
| Hong Kong | 496 | 62 | 371 | 63 | 9 | 0 | 4 | 0 | | 7,153,519 |
| Hungary | 3320 | 218 | 2713 | 389 | 75 | 6 | 18 | 18 | WM IA, WM20 IIA, WM18 IB, WW IIA, WW18 I | 9,958,453 |
| Iceland | 587 | 58 | 441 | 88 | 22 | 3 | 3 | 0 | WM IIA, WM20 III, WM18 IIB, WW IIB | 313,183 |
| India | 724 | 400 | 285 | 39 | 10 | 0 | 1 | 8 | | 1,205,073,612 |
| Ireland | 297 | 189 | 70 | 38 | 14 | 4 | 1 | 0 | WM III | 4,722,028 |
| Israel | 653 | 270 | 374 | 9 | 5 | 0 | 2 | 0 | WM IIB | 7,590,758 |
| Italy | 6774 | 1720 | 4571 | 483 | 139 | 5 | 45 | 24 | WM, WM20 IB, WM18 IA, WW IB, WW18 IQ | 61,261,254 |
| Japan | 19975 | 9999 | 7256 | 2720 | 928 | 94 | 99 | 25 | WM IA, WM20 IB, WM18 IA, WW IA, WW18 I | 127,368,088 |
| Kazakhstan | 4067 | 483 | 3491 | 93 | 41 | 7 | 17 | 56 | WM, WM20 IB, WM18 IB, WW IA, WW18 IQ | 17,522,010 |
| Korea | 1636 | 93 | 1365 | 178 | 55 | 9 | 43 | 4 | WM IB, WM20 IIA, WM18 IIA, WW IIB | 48,860,500 |
| Kuwait | 320 | 84 | 122 | 114 | 1 | 1 | 2 | 0 | | 2,646,314 |
| Kyrgyzstan | 330 | 228 | 102 | 0 | 6 | 0 | 2 | 4 | | 5,496,737 |
| Latvia | 3979 | 2348 | 1515 | 116 | 185 | 28 | 16 | 0 | WM, WM20, WM18, WW IA | 2,191,580 |
| Liechtenstein | 80 | 70 | 10 | 0 | 0 | 0 | 0 | 0 | | 36,713 |
| Lithuania | 547 | 137 | 410 | 0 | 19 | 1 | 6 | 0 | WM IB, WM20 IIA, WM18 IIA | 3,525,761 |
| Luxembourg | 392 | 130 | 235 | 27 | 26 | 8 | 3 | 1 | WM III | 509,074 |
| Macau | 106 | 28 | 63 | 15 | 0 | 0 | 1 | 0 | | 578,025 |
| Malaysia | 184 | 91 | 72 | 21 | 1 | 0 | 1 | 0 | | 29,179,952 |
| Mexico | 1568 | 327 | 1139 | 102 | 18 | 2 | 20 | 0 | WM IIB, WM20 IIB, WM18 IIIA | 114,975,406 |
| Mongolia | 1001 | 477 | 524 | 0 | 8 | 0 | 0 | 12 | WM III | 3,179,997 |
| Morocco | 137 | 71 | 52 | 14 | 3 | 0 | 2 | 0 | | 32,309,239 |
| Namibia | 438 | 104 | 215 | 119 | 47 | 10 | 3 | 2 | | 2,165,828 |
| Netherlands | 2842 | 1468 | 1156 | 218 | 52 | 5 | 26 | 4 | WM IB, WM20 IIA, WM18 IIA, WW IB | 16,730,632 |
| New Zealand | 1193 | 593 | 437 | 163 | 60 | 6 | 6 | 3 | WM IIA, WM20 III, WM18 IIIA, WW IIA | 4,327,944 |
| Norway | 6893 | 2130 | 4212 | 551 | 164 | 14 | 41 | 3 | WM, WM20 IA, WM18 IA, WW IA, WW18 I | 4,707,270 |
| Poland | 2575 | 713 | 1494 | 368 | 76 | 3 | 35 | 6 | WM IB, WM20 IB, WM18 IB, WW IIB | 38,415,284 |
| Portugal | 116 | 48 | 50 | 18 | 5 | 2 | 1 | 0 | | 10,781,459 |
| Romania | 1093 | 151 | 872 | 70 | 51 | 5 | 5 | 15 | WM IB, WM20 IIB, WM18 IIA | 21,848,504 |
| Russia | 64326 | 2606 | 61220 | 500 | 230 | 5 | 346 | 2000 | WM, WM20, WM18, WW, WW18 | 138,082,178 |
| Serbia | 564 | 147 | 414 | 3 | 21 | 2 | 4 | 1 | WM IIA, WM20 IIB, WM18 IIB | 7,276,604 |
| Singapore | 414 | 285 | 97 | 32 | 15 | 1 | 2 | 0 | | 5,353,494 |
| Slovakia | 9034 | 2041 | 6576 | 417 | 327 | 16 | 47 | 21 | WM, WM20, WM18 IA, WW, WW18 I | 5,483,088 |
| Slovenia | 924 | 148 | 707 | 69 | 46 | 4 | 7 | 1 | WM IA, WM20 IA, WM18 IA, WW IIA | 1,996,617 |
| South Africa | 466 | 171 | 235 | 60 | 8 | 2 | 5 | 0 | WM IIB, WM18 IIIA, WW IIB | 48,810,427 |
| Spain | 854 | 236 | 530 | 88 | 30 | 1 | 18 | 0 | WM IIA, WM20 IIA, WM18 IIB, WW IIB | 47,042,984 |
| Sweden | 69921 | 13084 | 53334 | 3503 | 2420 | 41 | 342 | 136 | WM, WM20, WM18, WW, WW18 | 9,103,788 |
| Switzerland | 26166 | 11219 | 13775 | 1172 | 1079 | 43 | 158 | 29 | WM, WM20, WM18, WW, WW18 | 7,655,628 |
| Thailand | 114 | 43 | 62 | 9 | 15 | 3 | 3 | 0 | | 67,091,089 |
| Turkey | 790 | 310 | 320 | 160 | 80 | 30 | 8 | 3 | WM III, WM20 III | 79,749,461 |
| Ukraine | 4003 | 607 | 3384 | 12 | 74 | 0 | 25 | 0 | WM IA, WM20 IIA, WM18 IB | 44,854,065 |
| United Arab Emirates | 371 | 118 | 186 | 67 | 12 | 0 | 4 | 0 | | 5,314,317 |
| United States | 511178 | 139033 | 305453 | 66692 | 23693 | 1263 | 2000 | 0 | WM, WM20, WM18, WW, WW18 | 313,847,465 |

**LEGEND:**
(all tournaments from the 2011-2012 season)

| | |
|---|---|
| WM | IIHF World Championship |
| WM I | IIHF World Championship Division I |
| WM II | IIHF World Championship Division II |
| WM III | IIHF World Championship Division III |
| WM20 | IIHF World U20 Championship |
| WM20 I | IIHF World U20 Championship Division I |
| WM20 II | IIHF World U20 Championship Division II |
| WM20 III | IIHF World U20 Championship Division III |
| WM18 | IIHF World U18 Championship |
| WM18 I | IIHF World U18 Championship Division I |
| WM18 II | IIHF World U18 Championship Division II |
| WM18 III | IIHF World U18 Championship Division III |
| WW | IIHF World Women's Championship |
| WW I | IIHF World Women's Championship Division I |
| WW II | IIHF World Women's Championship Division II |
| WW III | IIHF World Women's Championship Division III |
| WW IV | IIHF World Women's Championshipp Division IV |
| WW V | IIHF World Women's Championship Division V |
| WW18 | IIHF World Women's U18 Championship |
| WW18 I | IIHF World Women's U18 Championship Division I |

*denotes team withdrawal
Source of population numbers: 2012 CIA World Factbook

# Quick Summary of 2011-12 Season Participation By Nation

(G, S, B used only for top level)

**AUS**
2012 WM-I-B....... 6th
2012 WM20-II-B.... 5th
2012 WM18-II-B.... 5th
2012 WW-II-A...... 3rd

**AUT**
2012 WM-I-A....... 2nd
2012 WM20-I-A..... 5th
2012 WM18-I-B..... 3rd
2012 WW-I-A....... 4th
2012 WW18-I...... 2nd

**BEL**
2012 WM-II-B...... 1st
2012 WM20-II-B.... 4th
2012 WM18-III...... 1st
2012 WW-II-B...... 5th

**BLR**
2012 WM.......... 14th
2012 WM20-I-A..... 2nd
2012 WM18-I-B..... 1st

**BUL**
2012 WM-II-B...... 3rd
2012 WM20-III...... 4th
2012 WM18-III...... 4th

**CAN**
2012 WM.......... 5th
2012 WM20........ B
2012 WM18........ B
2012 WW.......... G
2012 WW18........ G

**CHN**
2012 WM-II-B...... 2nd
2012 WM20-III...... 2nd
2012 WM18-II-B.... 6th
2012 WW-I-B....... 2nd

**CRO**
2012 WM-II-A...... 3rd
2012 WM20-I-B..... 5th
2012 WM18-II-A.... 5th
2012 WW-II-A...... 6th

**CZE**
2012 WM.......... B
2012 WM20........ 5th
2012 WM18........ 8th
2012 WW-I-A....... 1st
2012 WW18........ 6th

**DEN**
2012 WM.......... 13th
2012 WM20........ 10th
2012 WM18........ 10th
2012 WW-I-B....... 1st

**ESP**
2012 WM-II-A...... 2nd
2012 WM20-II-A.... 4th
2012 WM18-II-B.... 3rd
2012 WW-II-B...... 2nd

**EST**
2012 WM-II-A...... 1st
2012 WM20-II-B.... 2nd
2012 WM18-II-B.... 1st

**FIN**
2012 WM.......... 4th
2012 WM20........ 4th
2012 WM18........ 4th
2012 WW.......... 4th
2012 WW18........ 5th

**FRA**
2012 WM.......... 9th
2012 WM20-I-B..... 1st
2012 WM18-I-A..... 4th
2012 WW-I-B....... 3rd

**GBR**
2012 WM-I-A....... 5th
2012 WM20-I-A..... 6th
2012 WM18-II-A.... 4th
2012 WW-I-B....... 4th
2012 WW18-I...... 5th

**GER**
2012 WM.......... 12th
2012 WM20-I-A..... 1st
2012 WM18........ 6th
2012 WW.......... 7th
2012 WW18........ 4th

**GRE**
2012 WM-III........ 5th

**HUN**
2012 WM-I-A....... 3rd
2012 WM20-II-A.... 3rd
2012 WM18-I-B..... 6th
2012 WW-II-A...... 2nd
2012 WW18-I...... 1st

**IRL**
2012 WM-III........ 4th

**ISL**
2012 WM-II-A...... 4th
2012 WM20-III...... 1st
2012 WM18-II-B.... 4th
2012 WW-II-B...... 4th

**ISR**
2012 WM-II-B...... 5th

**ITA**
2012 WM.......... 15th
2012 WM20-I-B..... 3rd
2012 WM18-I-A..... 3rd
2012 WW-I-B....... 6th

**JPN**
2012 WM-I-A....... 4th
2012 WM20-I-B..... 6th
2012 WW18-I-A..... 6th
2012 WW-I-A....... 3rd
2012 WW18-I...... 3rd

**KAZ**
2012 WM.......... 16th
2012 WM20-I-B..... 2nd
2012 WM18-I-B..... 2nd
2012 WW-I-A....... 6th

**KOR**
2012 WM-I-B....... 1st
2012 WM20-II-A.... 6th
2012 WM18-II-A.... 1st
2012 WW-II-B...... 3rd

**LAT**
2012 WM.......... 10th
2012 WM20........ 9th
2012 WM18........ 9th
2012 WW-I-A....... 5th

**LTU**
2012 WM-I-B....... 5th
2012 WM20-II-A.... 2nd
2012 WM18-II-A.... 3rd

**LUX**
2012 WM-III........ 3rd

**MEX**
2012 WM-II-B...... 4th
2012 WM20-II-B.... 6th
2012 WM18-III...... 3rd

**MGL**
2012 WM-III........ 6th

**NED**
2012 WM-I-B....... 3rd
2012 WM20-II-A.... 5th
2012 WM18-II-A.... 6th
2012 WW-I-B....... 5th

**NOR**
2012 WM.......... 8th
2012 WM20-I-A..... 3rd
2012 WM18-I-A..... 2nd
2012 WW-I-A....... 2nd
2012 WW18-I...... 4th

**NZL**
2012 WM-II-A...... 6th
2012 WM20-III...... 3rd
2012 WM18-III...... 2nd
2012 WW-II-A...... 4th

**POL**
2012 WM-I-B....... 2nd
2012 WM20-I-B..... 4th
2012 WM18-I-B..... 5th
2012 WW-II-B...... 1st

**PRK**
2012 WM-III........ 2nd
2012 WW-II-A...... 1st

**ROU**
2012 WM-I-B....... 4th
2012 WM20-II-B.... 1st
2012 WM18-II-A.... 2nd

**RSA**
2012 WM-II-B...... 6th
2012 WM18-III...... 6th
2012 WW-II-B...... 6th

**RUS**
2012 WM.......... G
2012 WM20........ S
2012 WM18........ 5th
2012 WW.......... 6th
2012 WW18........ 7th

**SLO**
2012 WM-I-A....... 1st
2012 WM20-I-A..... 4th
2012 WM18-I-A..... 5th
2012 WW-II-A...... 5th

**SRB**
2012 WM-II-A...... 5th
2012 WM20-II-B.... 3rd
2012 WM18-II-B.... 2nd

**SVK**
2012 WM.......... S
2012 WM20........ 6th
2012 WM18-I-A..... 1st
2012 WW.......... 8th
2012 WW18-I...... 6th

**SWE**
2012 WM.......... 6th
2012 WM20........ G
2012 WM18........ S
2012 WW.......... 5th
2012 WW18........ S

**SUI**
2012 WM.......... 11th
2012 WM20........ 8th
2012 WM18........ 7th
2012 WW.......... B
2012 WW18........ 8th

**TPE**
2012 WM18-III...... 5th

**TUR**
2012 WM-III........ 1st
2012 WM20-III...... 5th

**UKR**
2012 WM-I-A....... 6th
2012 WM20-II-A.... 1st
2012 WM18-I-B..... 4th

**USA**
2012 WM.......... 7th
2012 WM20........ 7th
2012 WM18........ G
2012 WW.......... S
2012 WW18........ S

# All Medallists Year-by-Year

**OLYMPICS, MEN**

| Year | Gold | Silver | Bronze | Main Venue |
|---|---|---|---|---|
| 1920 | Canada | United States | Czechoslovakia | Antwerp |
| 1924 | Canada | United States | Great Britain | Chamonix |
| 1928 | Canada | Sweden | Switzerland | St. Moritz |
| 1932 | Canada | United States | Germany | Lake Placid |
| 1936 | Great Britain | Canada | United States | Garmisch-Partenkirchen |
| 1948 | Canada | Czechoslovakia | Switzerland | St. Moritz |
| 1952 | Canada | United States | Sweden | Oslo |
| 1956 | Soviet Union | United States | Canada | Cortina d'Ampezzo |
| 1960 | United States | Canada | Soviet Union | Squaw Valley |
| 1964 | Soviet Union | Sweden | Czechoslovakia | Innsbruck |
| 1968 | Soviet Union | Czechoslovakia | Canada | Grenoble |
| 1972 | Soviet Union | United States | Czechoslovakia | Sapporo |
| 1976 | Soviet Union | Czechoslovakia | West Germany | Innsbruck |
| 1980 | United States | Soviet Union | Sweden | Lake Placid |
| 1984 | Soviet Union | Czechoslovakia | Sweden | Sarajevo |
| 1988 | Soviet Union | Finland | Sweden | Calgary |
| 1992 | Russia | Canada | Czechoslovakia | Albertville |
| 1994 | Sweden | Canada | Finland | Lillehammer |
| 1998 | Czech Republic | Russia | Finland | Nagano |
| 2002 | Canada | United States | Russia | Salt Lake City |
| 2006 | Sweden | Finland | Czech Republic | Turin |
| 2010 | Canada | United States | Finland | Vancouver |

*the 1920 Olympic ice hockey tournament was part of the summer Olympics
*all Olympics between 1920 and 1968 also counted as World Championships

**WORLD CHAMPIONSHIP (INDEPENDENT OF THE OLYMPICS)**

| Year | Gold | Silver | Bronze | Main Venue(s) |
|---|---|---|---|---|
| 1930 | Canada | Germany | Switzerland | Chamonix, Vienna, Berlin |
| 1931 | Canada | United States | Austria | Krynica |
| 1933 | United States | Canada | Czechoslovakia | Prague |
| 1934 | Canada | United States | Germany | Milan |
| 1935 | Canada | Switzerland | Great Britain | Davos |
| 1937 | Canada | Great Britain | Switzerland | London |
| 1938 | Canada | Great Britain | Czechoslovakia | Prague |
| 1939 | Canada | United States | Switzerland | Zurich, Basel |
| *1940-46* | | *No championships (World War II)* | | |
| 1947 | Czechoslovakia | Sweden | Austria | Prague |
| 1949 | Czechoslovakia | Canada | United States | Stockholm |
| 1950 | Canada | United States | Switzerland | London |
| 1951 | Canada | Sweden | Switzerland | Paris |
| 1953 | Sweden | West Germany | Switzerland | Zurich, Basel |
| 1954 | Soviet Union | Canada | Sweden | Stockholm |
| 1955 | Canada | Soviet Union | Czechoslovakia | Krefeld, Dortmund, Cologne, Dusseldorf |
| 1957 | Sweden | Soviet Union | Czechoslovakia | Moscow |
| 1958 | Canada | Soviet Union | Sweden | Oslo |
| 1959 | Canada | Soviet Union | Czechoslovakia | Prague, Bratislava |
| 1961 | Canada | Czechoslovakia | Soviet Union | Geneva, Lausanne |
| 1962 | Sweden | Canada | United States | Colorado Springs, Denver |
| 1963 | Soviet Union | Sweden | Czechoslovakia | Stockholm |
| 1965 | Soviet Union | Czechoslovakia | Sweden | Tampere |
| 1966 | Soviet Union | Czechoslovakia | Canada | Ljubljana |
| 1967 | Soviet Union | Sweden | Canada | Vienna |
| 1969 | Soviet Union | Sweden | Czechoslovakia | Stockholm |
| 1970 | Soviet Union | Sweden | Czechoslovakia | Stockholm |
| 1971 | Soviet Union | Czechoslovakia | Sweden | Berne, Geneva |
| 1972 | Czechoslovakia | Soviet Union | Sweden | Prague |
| 1973 | Soviet Union | Sweden | Czechoslovakia | Moscow |
| 1974 | Soviet Union | Czechoslovakia | Sweden | Helsinki |
| 1975 | Soviet Union | Czechoslovakia | Sweden | Munich, Dusseldorf |
| 1976 | Czechoslovakia | Soviet Union | Sweden | Katowice |
| 1977 | Czechoslovakia | Sweden | Soviet Union | Vienna |
| 1978 | Soviet Union | Czechoslovakia | Canada | Prague |
| 1979 | Soviet Union | Czechoslovakia | Sweden | Moscow |
| 1981 | Soviet Union | Sweden | Czechoslovakia | Gothenburg, Stockholm |
| 1982 | Soviet Union | Czechoslovakia | Canada | Helsinki, Tampere |
| 1983 | Soviet Union | Czechoslovakia | Canada | Munich, Dusseldorf, Dortmund |
| 1985 | Czechoslovakia | Canada | Soviet Union | Prague |
| 1986 | Soviet Union | Sweden | Canada | Moscow |
| 1987 | Sweden | Soviet Union | Czechoslovakia | Vienna |
| 1989 | Soviet Union | Canada | Czechoslovakia | Stockholm, Sodertalje |
| 1990 | Soviet Union | Sweden | Czechoslovakia | Berne, Fribourg |
| 1991 | Sweden | Canada | Soviet Union | Turku, Helsinki, Tampere |
| 1992 | Sweden | Finland | Czechoslovakia | Prague, Bratislava |
| 1993 | Russia | Sweden | Czech Republic | Munich, Dortmund |
| 1994 | Canada | Finland | Sweden | Milan, Bolzano, Canazei |
| 1995 | Finland | Sweden | Canada | Stockholm, Gavle |
| 1996 | Czech Republic | Canada | United States | Vienna |
| 1997 | Canada | Sweden | Czech Republic | Helsinki, Turku, Tampere |
| 1998 | Sweden | Finland | Czech Republic | Zurich, Basel |

| 1999 | Czech Republic | Finland | Sweden | Lillehammer, Oslo, Hamar |
|---|---|---|---|---|
| 2000 | Czech Republic | Slovakia | Finland | St. Petersburg |
| 2001 | Czech Republic | Finland | Sweden | Hanover, Cologne, Nuremburg |
| 2002 | Slovakia | Russia | Sweden | Gothenburg, Karlstad, Jonkoping |
| 2003 | Canada | Sweden | Slovakia | Helsinki, Turku, Tampere |
| 2004 | Canada | Sweden | United States | Prague, Ostrava |
| 2005 | Czech Republic | Canada | Russia | Vienna, Innsbruck |
| 2006 | Sweden | Czech Republic | Finland | Riga |
| 2007 | Canada | Finland | Russia | Moscow, Mytishi |
| 2008 | Russia | Canada | Finland | Quebec City, Halifax |
| 2009 | Russia | Canada | Sweden | Berne, Kloten |
| 2010 | Czech Republic | Russia | Sweden | Cologne, Mannheim |
| 2011 | Finland | Sweden | Czech Republic | Bratislava, Kosice |
| 2012 | Russia | Slovakia | Czech Republic | Helsinki, Stockholm |

*in the Olympic years 1980, 1984, and 1988, no IIHF World Championships were staged

**U20 WORLD CHAMPIONSHIP**

| Year | Gold | Silver | Bronze | Main Venue(s) |
|---|---|---|---|---|
| 1977 | Soviet Union | Canada | Czechoslovakia | Zvolen, Banska Bystrica |
| 1978 | Soviet Union | Sweden | Canada | Montreal, Quebec City |
| 1979 | Soviet Union | Czechoslovakia | Sweden | Karlsrad, Karlskoga |
| 1980 | Soviet Union | Finland | Sweden | Helsinki, Vantaa |
| 1981 | Sweden | Finland | Soviet Union | Landsberg |
| 1982 | Canada | Czechoslovakia | Finland | Bloomington |
| 1983 | Soviet Union | Czechoslovakia | Canada | Leningrad (St. Petersburg) |
| 1984 | Soviet Union | Finland | Czechoslovakia | Norrkoping, Nykoping |
| 1985 | Canada | Czechoslovakia | Soviet Union | Vantaa, Helsinki |
| 1986 | Soviet Union | Canada | United States | Hamilton |
| 1987 | Finland | Czechoslovakia | Sweden | Trencin, Piestany |
| 1988 | Canada | Soviet Union | Finland | Moscow |
| 1989 | Soviet Union | Sweden | Czechoslovakia | Anchorage, Fire Lake |
| 1990 | Canada | Soviet Union | Czechoslovakia | Helsinki, Turku |
| 1991 | Canada | Soviet Union | Czechoslovakia | Regina, Saskatoon |
| 1992 | Russia | Sweden | United States | Fussen, Kaufbeuren |
| 1993 | Canada | Sweden | Czech/Slovak Rep. | Gavle |
| 1994 | Canada | Sweden | Russia | Ostrava, Frydek-Mistek |
| 1995 | Canada | Russia | Sweden | Red Deer |
| 1996 | Canada | Sweden | Russia | Boston, Chestnut Hill |
| 1997 | Canada | United States | Russia | Geneva, Morges |
| 1998 | Finland | Russia | Switzerland | Helsinki, Hameenlinna |
| 1999 | Russia | Canada | Slovakia | Winnipeg |
| 2000 | Czech Republic | Russia | Canada | Skelleftea, Umea |
| 2001 | Czech Republic | Finland | Canada | Moscow, Podolsk |
| 2002 | Russia | Canada | Finland | Pardubice, Hradec Kralove |
| 2003 | Russia | Canada | Finland | Halifax, Sydney |
| 2004 | United States | Canada | Finland | Helsinki, Hameenlinna |
| 2005 | Canada | Russia | Czech Republic | Grand Forks, Thief River Falls |
| 2006 | Canada | Russia | Finland | Vancouver, Kamloops |
| 2007 | Canada | Russia | United States | Leksand, Mora |
| 2008 | Canada | Sweden | Russia | Pardubice, Liberec |
| 2009 | Canada | Sweden | Russia | Ottawa |
| 2010 | United States | Canada | Sweden | Saskatoon, Regina |
| 2011 | Russia | Canada | United States | Buffalo, Niagara |
| 2012 | Sweden | Russia | Canada | Calgary, Edmonton |

**U18 WORLD CHAMPIONSHIP (MEN)**

| Year | Gold | Silver | Bronze | Main Venue(s) |
|---|---|---|---|---|
| 1999 | Finland | Sweden | Slovakia | Fussen, Kaufbeuren |
| 2000 | Finland | Russia | Sweden | Kloten, Weinfelden |
| 2001 | Russia | Switzerland | Finland | Heinola, Helsinki, Lahti |
| 2002 | United States | Russia | Czech Republic | Piestany, Trnava |
| 2003 | Canada | Slovakia | Russia | Yaroslavl |
| 2004 | Russia | United States | Czech Republic | Minsk |
| 2005 | United States | Canada | Sweden | Ceske Budejovice, Plzen |
| 2006 | United States | Finland | Czech Republic | Anglehom, Hamstad |
| 2007 | Russia | United States | Sweden | Tampere, Rauma |
| 2008 | Canada | Russia | United States | Kazan |
| 2009 | United States | Russia | Finland | Fargo, Moorhead |
| 2010 | United States | Sweden | Finland | Minsk, Bobruisk |
| 2011 | United States | Sweden | Russia | Crimmitschau, Dresden |
| 2012 | United States | Sweden | Canada | Brno, Znojmo |

**OLYMPICS, WOMEN**

| Year | Gold | Silver | Bronze | Main Venue(s) |
|---|---|---|---|---|
| 1998 | United States | Canada | Finland | Nagano |
| 2002 | Canada | United States | Sweden | Salt Lake City |
| 2006 | Canada | Sweden | United States | Turin |
| 2010 | Canada | United States | Finland | Vancouver |

**WOMEN'S WORLD CHAMPIONSHIP**

| Year | Gold | Silver | Bronze | Main Venue(s) |
|---|---|---|---|---|
| 1990 | Canada | United States | Finland | Ottawa |
| 1992 | Canada | United States | Finland | Tampere |
| 1994 | Canada | United States | Finland | Lake Placid |

| 1997 | Canada | United States | Finland | Kitchener |
|---|---|---|---|---|
| 1999 | Canada | United States | Finland | Espoo |
| 2000 | Canada | United States | Finland | Mississauga |
| 2001 | Canada | United States | Russia | Minneapolis |
| 2004 | Canada | United States | Finland | Halifax |
| 2005 | United States | Canada | Sweden | Linkoping, Norrkoping |
| 2007 | Canada | United States | Sweden | Winnipeg, Selkirk |
| 2008 | United States | Canada | Finland | Harbin |
| 2009 | United States | Canada | Finland | Hameenlinna |
| 2011 | United States | Canada | Finland | Zurich, Winterthur |
| 2012 | Canada | United States | Switzerland | Burlington |

**U18 WOMEN'S WORLD CHAMPIONSHIP**

| Year | Gold | Silver | Bronze | Main Venue |
|---|---|---|---|---|
| 2008 | United States | Canada | Czech Republic | Calgary |
| 2009 | United States | Canada | Finland | Fussen |
| 2010 | Canada | United States | Sweden | Chicago |
| 2011 | United States | Canada | Finland | Stockholm |
| 2012 | Canada | United States | Sweden | Zlin, Prerov |

*Slovakia's Zdeno Chara donned a Pavol Demitra sweater after the gold-medal game of the 2012 World Championships in honour of a friend and teammate who perished in the Yaroslavl plane crash the previous September. Photo: Jeff Vinnick / HHOF-IIHF Images.*

# Overview of Placings

**OLYMPIC GAMES, MEN**

| | 1920 | 1924 | 1928 | 1932 | 1936 | 1948 | 1952 | 1956 | 1960 | 1964 | 1968 | 1972 | 1976 | 1980 | 1984 | 1988 | 1992 | 1994 | 1998 | 2002 | 2006 | 2010 | |
|---|---|---|---|---|---|---|---|---|---|---|---|---|---|---|---|---|---|---|---|---|---|---|---|
| AUS | | | | | | | | | 9 | | | | | | | | | | | | | | AUS |
| AUT | | | | | 7 | 8 | 11 | 10 | | 13 | 13 | | 8 | | 10 | 9 | | 12 | 14 | 12 | 15 | 13 | AUT |
| BEL | 7 | 7 | 8 | | 13 | | 14 | 13 | | | | | | | | | | | | | | | BEL |
| BLR | | | | | | | | | | | | | | | | | | | 7 | 4 | 13 | 9 | BLR |
| BUL | | | | | | | | | | | | | 12 | | | | | | 28 | 29 | 29 | 31 | BUL |
| CAN | **G** | **G** | **G** | **G** | **S** | **G** | **G** | **B** | **S** | 4 | **B** | | | 6 | 4 | 4 | **S** | **S** | 4 | **G** | 7 | **G** | CAN |
| CHN | | | | | | | | | | | | | | | | | | | 21 | 30 | 27 | | CHN |
| CRO | | | | | | | | | | | | | | | | | | | 33 | | 28 | 26 | CRO |
| CZE | | | | | | | | | | | | | | | | | **B** | 5 | **G** | 7 | **B** | 7 | CZE |
| DEN | | | | | | | | | | | | | | | | | | | 24 | 15 | 17 | 15 | DEN |
| ESP | | | | | | | | | | | | | | | | | | | | | | 30 | ESP |
| EST | | | | | | | | | | | | | | | | | | | 27 | 21 | 25 | 23 | EST |
| FIN | | | | | | | 7 | | 7 | 6 | 5 | 5 | 4 | 4 | 6 | **S** | 7 | **B** | **B** | 6 | **S** | **B** | FIN |
| FRA | 6 | 5 | 6 | | 9 | | 15 | | | | 14 | | | | | 11 | 8 | 10 | 11 | 14 | 16 | 20 | FRA |
| GBR | | **B** | 4 | | **G** | 6 | 10 | | | | | | | | | | | 16 | 19 | 23 | | 25 | GBR |
| GDR | | | | | | | | 11 | | | 8 | | | | | | | | | | | | GDR |
| GER | | | 9 | **B** | 5 | | 8 | 6 | 6 | 7 | 7 | 7 | **B** | 10 | 5 | 5 | 6 | 7 | 9 | 8 | 10 | 11 | GER |
| HUN | | | 11 | | 7 | | | | | 16 | | | | | | | | | 23 | 25 | 22 | 21 | HUN |
| ISR | | | | | | | | | | | | | | | | | | | 32 | | | | ISR |
| ITA | | | | | 9 | 9 | 12 | 7 | | 15 | | | | | 9 | | 12 | 9 | 12 | 17 | 11 | 17 | ITA |
| JPN | | | | | 9 | | | | 8 | 11 | 10 | 9 | 9 | 12 | | | | 15 | 13 | 20 | 21 | 18 | JPN |
| KAZ | | | | | | | | | | | | | | | | | | | 8 | 18 | 9 | 16 | KAZ |
| KOR | | | | | | | | | | | | | | | | | | | 25 | | | | KOR |
| LAT | | | | | 13 | | | | | | | | | | | | | 13 | 20 | 9 | 12 | 12 | LAT |
| LTU | | | | | | | | | | | | | | | | | | | 31 | 26 | 26 | 22 | LTU |
| MEX | | | | | | | | | | | | | | | | | | | | | | 32 | MEX |
| NED | | | | | | | 13 | | | | | | | 9 | | | | | 29 | 24 | 23 | 27 | NED |
| NOR | | | | | | | 9 | 12 | | 10 | 11 | 8 | | 11 | 12 | 12 | 9 | 11 | 16 | 16 | 14 | 10 | NOR |
| POL | | | 10 | 4 | 9 | 7 | 6 | 8 | | 9 | | 6 | 6 | 7 | 8 | 10 | 11 | 14 | 18 | 19 | 20 | 24 | POL |
| ROU | | | | | | | | | | 12 | 12 | | 7 | 8 | | | | | 22 | 27 | 24 | 29 | ROU |
| RUS | | | | | | | | | | | | | | | | | **G** | 4 | **S** | **B** | 4 | 6 | RUS |
| SRB | | | | | | | | | | | | | | | | | | | 30 | | 30 | 28 | SRB |
| SLO | | | | | | | | | | | | | | | | | | | 26 | 22 | 18 | 19 | SLO |
| SUI | 5 | 7 | **B** | | 13 | **B** | 5 | 9 | | 8 | | 10 | 11 | | | 8 | 10 | | 15 | 11 | 6 | 8 | SUI |
| SVK | | | | | | | | | | | | | | | | | | 6 | 10 | 13 | 5 | 4 | SVK |
| SWE | 4 | 4 | **S** | | 5 | 5 | **B** | 4 | 5 | **S** | 4 | 4 | | **B** | **B** | **B** | 5 | **G** | 5 | 5 | **G** | 5 | SWE |
| TCH | **B** | 5 | 7 | | 4 | **S** | 4 | 5 | 4 | **B** | **S** | **B** | **S** | 5 | **S** | 6 | B | | | | | | TCH |
| TUR | | | | | | | | | | | | | | | | | | | | | | 33 | TUR |
| UKR | | | | | | | | | | | | | | | | | | | 17 | 10 | 19 | 14 | UKR |
| URS | | | | | | | | **G** | **B** | **G** | **G** | **G** | **G** | **S** | **G** | **G** | | | | | | | URS |
| USA | **S** | **S** | | **S** | **B** | 4 | **S** | **S** | **G** | 5 | 6 | **S** | 5 | **G** | 7 | 7 | 4 | 8 | 6 | **S** | 8 | **S** | USA |
| YUG | | | | | | | | | | 14 | 9 | 11 | 10 | | 11 | | | | | | | | YUG |
| | **1920** | **1924** | **1928** | **1932** | **1936** | **1948** | **1952** | **1956** | **1960** | **1964** | **1968** | **1972** | **1976** | **1980** | **1984** | **1988** | **1992** | **1994** | **1998** | **2002** | **2006** | **2010** | |

*The Vancouver Olympics were the most successful hockey tournaments played as virtually every seat for every men's and women's game was sold out well in advance of the Opening Ceremonies. Photo: Jeff Vinnick.*

**WORLD CHAMPIONSHIP (MEN), 1930-1976**

| | 1930 | 1931 | 1933 | 1934 | 1935 | 1937 | 1938 | 1939 | 1947 | 1949 | 1950 | 1951 | 1953 | 1954 | 1955 | 1957 | 1958 | 1959 | 1961 | 1962 | 1963 | 1965 | 1966 | 1967 | 1969 | 1970 | 1971 | 1972 | 1973 | 1974 | 1975 | 1976 | |
|---|---|---|---|---|---|---|---|---|---|---|---|---|---|---|---|---|---|---|---|---|---|---|---|---|---|---|---|---|---|---|---|---|---|
| ARM | | | | | | | | | | | | | | | | | | | | | | | | | | | | | | | | | ARM |
| AUS | | | | | | | | | | | | | | | | | | | | 13 | | | | | | | | | | 21 | | | AUS |
| AUT | 4 | **B** | 4 | 7 | 6 | | 10 | | **B** | 6 | | 11 | 6 | | 11 | 7 | | 15 | 14 | 10 | 16 | 13 | 13 | 14 | 13 | 15 | 13 | 14 | 12 | 14 | 17 | 17 | AUT |
| BEL | 12 | | 12 | 12 | 14 | | | 11 | 8 | 9 | 7 | 12 | | | 14 | | | | 20 | | 21 | | | | | 21 | 22 | | | | 21 | | BEL |
| BLR | | | | | | | | | | | | | | | | | | | | | | | | | | | | | | | | | BLR |
| BUL | | | | | | | | | | | | | | | | | | | | | 19 | | | 18 | 19 | 14 | 19 | 17 | 18 | 17 | 16 | 16 | BUL |
| CAN | **G** | **G** | **S** | **G** | **G** | **G** | **G** | **G** | | **S** | **G** | **G** | | **S** | **G** | | **G** | **G** | **G** | **S** | 4 | 4 | **B** | **B** | 4 | | | | | | | | CAN |
| CHN | | | | | | | | | | | | | | | | | | | | | | | | | | | | 18 | 19 | 20 | | | CHN |
| CRO | | | | | | | | | | | | | | | | | | | | | | | | | | | | | | | | | CRO |
| CZE | | | | | | | | | | | | | | | | | | | | | | | | | | | | | | | | | CZE |
| DEN | | | | | | | | | | 10 | | | | | | | | | | 14 | 18 | | 18 | 19 | 20 | 19 | 20 | 20 | 21 | | 20 | 20 | DEN |
| ESP | | | | | | | | | | | | | | | | | | | | | | | | | | | | | | | | | ESP |
| EST | | | | | | | | | | | | | | | | | | | | | | | | | | | | | | | | | EST |
| FIN | | | | | | | | 13 | | 7 | | 7 | | 6 | 9 | 4 | 6 | 6 | 7 | 4 | 5 | 7 | 7 | 6 | 5 | 4 | 4 | 4 | 4 | 4 | 4 | 5 | FIN |
| FRA | 7 | 9 | | 11 | 7 | 7 | | | | | 9 | 9 | 8 | | | | | | 16 | 11 | 14 | | | 20 | | 18 | 16 | | 20 | 19 | 19 | 19 | FRA |
| GBR | 10 | 8 | | 8 | **B** | **S** | **S** | 8 | | | 4 | 5 | 5 | | | | | | 10 | 8 | 15 | 14 | 16 | | | | 18 | | 22 | | | 21 | GBR |
| GDR | | | | | | | | | | | | | | | | 5 | | 9 | 5 | | 6 | 5 | 5 | 7 | 7 | 5 | 9 | 9 | 7 | 6 | 7 | 8 | GDR |
| GER | **S** | | 5 | **B** | 9 | 4 | 4 | 5 | | | | | **S** | 5 | 6 | | | 7 | 8 | 6 | 7 | 11 | 9 | 8 | 10 | 8 | 5 | 5 | 6 | 9 | 8 | 6 | GER |
| GRE | | | | | | | | | | | | | | | | | | | | | | | | | | | | | | | | | GRE |
| HGK | | | | | | | | | | | | | | | | | | | | | | | | | | | | | | | | | HGK |
| HUN | 6 | 7 | 7 | 6 | 11 | 5 | 7 | 7 | | | | | | | | | | 14 | | | 17 | 12 | 15 | 16 | 17 | 17 | 17 | 16 | 17 | 18 | 18 | 18 | HUN |
| IRL | | | | | | | | | | | | | | | | | | | | | | | | | | | | | | | | | IRL |
| ISL | | | | | | | | | | | | | | | | | | | | | | | | | | | | | | | | | ISL |
| ISR | | | | | | | | | | | | | | | | | | | | | | | | | | | | | | | | | ISR |
| ITA | 11 | | 11 | 9 | 8 | | | 9 | | | | 8 | 4 | | 10 | | | 10 | 12 | | | | 17 | 13 | 14 | 16 | 14 | 15 | 14 | 16 | 13 | 15 | ITA |
| JPN | 8 | | | | | | | | | | | | | | | 8 | | | | 9 | | | | 17 | 15 | 11 | 12 | 11 | 11 | 10 | 12 | 10 | JPN |
| KAZ | | | | | | | | | | | | | | | | | | | | | | | | | | | | | | | | | KAZ |
| KOR | | | | | | | | | | | | | | | | | | | | | | | | | | | | | | | | | KOR |
| LAT | | | 10 | | 13 | | 10 | 10 | | | | | | | | | | | | | | | | | | | | | | | | | LAT |
| LTU | | | | | | | 10 | | | | | | | | | | | | | | | | | | | | | | | | | | LTU |
| LUX | | | | | | | | | | | | | | | | | | | | | | | | | | | | | | | | | LUX |
| MEX | | | | | | | | | | | | | | | | | | | | | | | | | | | | | | | | | MEX |
| NED | | | | | 14 | | | 11 | | | 8 | 10 | 7 | | 12 | | | | 18 | 12 | 20 | | | 21 | 18 | 20 | 21 | 19 | 16 | 11 | 14 | 14 | NED |
| NOR | | | | | | 9 | 13 | | | 8 | 6 | 4 | | 8 | | | 7 | 8 | 9 | 5 | 9 | 8 | 12 | 11 | 11 | 9 | 10 | 13 | 15 | 13 | 15 | 11 | NOR |
| NZL | | | | | | | | | | | | | | | | | | | | | | | | | | | | | | | | | NZL |
| POL | 5 | 4 | 8 | | 10 | 8 | 7 | 6 | 6 | | | | | | 7 | 6 | 8 | 11 | 13 | | 12 | 9 | 8 | 9 | 8 | 6 | 8 | 7 | 5 | 5 | 5 | 7 | POL |
| PRK | | | | | | | | | | | | | | | | | | | | | | | | | | | | | | 22 | | | PRK |
| ROU | | 10 | 9 | 10 | 11 | 9 | 13 | | 7 | | | | | | | | | 13 | 15 | | 11 | | 10 | 10 | 12 | 13 | 15 | 10 | 10 | 12 | 11 | 9 | ROU |
| RSA | | | | | | | | | | | | | | | | | | | 19 | | | | 19 | | | | | | | | | | RSA |
| RUS | | | | | | | | | | | | | | | | | | | | | | | | | | | | | | | | | RUS |
| SRB | | | | | | | | | | | | | | | | | | | | | | | | | | | | | | | | | SRB |
| SLO | | | | | | | | | | | | | | | | | | | | | | | | | | | | | | | | | SLO |
| SUI | **B** | | 6 | 4 | **S** | **B** | 6 | **B** | 4 | 5 | **B** | **B** | **B** | 7 | 8 | | | 12 | 11 | 7 | 10 | 10 | 14 | 15 | 16 | 12 | 7 | 6 | 13 | 15 | 9 | 12 | SUI |
| SVK | | | | | | | | | | | | | | | | | | | | | | | | | | | | | | | | | SVK |
| SWE | | 6 | | | 5 | 9 | 5 | | **S** | 4 | 5 | **S** | **G** | **B** | 5 | **G** | **B** | 5 | 4 | **G** | **S** | **B** | 4 | **S** | **S** | **S** | **B** | **B** | **S** | **B** | **B** | **B** | SWE |
| TCH | 9 | 5 | **B** | 5 | 4 | 6 | **B** | 4 | **G** | **G** | | | DNF | 4 | **B** | **B** | 4 | **B** | **S** | | **B** | **S** | **S** | 4 | **B** | **B** | **S** | **G** | **B** | **S** | **S** | **G** | TCH |
| TPE | | | | | | | | | | | | | | | | | | | | | | | | | | | | | | | | | TPE |
| TUR | | | | | | | | | | | | | | | | | | | | | | | | | | | | | | | | | TUR |
| UKR | | | | | | | | | | | | | | | | | | | | | | | | | | | | | | | | | UKR |
| URS | | | | | | | | | | | | | | **G** | **S** | **S** | **S** | **S** | **B** | | **G** | **G** | **G** | **G** | **G** | **G** | **G** | **S** | **G** | **G** | **G** | **S** | URS |
| USA | | **S** | **G** | **S** | | | 7 | **S** | 5 | **B** | **S** | 6 | | | 4 | | 5 | 4 | 6 | **B** | 8 | 6 | 6 | 5 | 6 | 7 | 6 | 8 | 8 | 7 | 6 | 4 | USA |
| YUG | | | | | | | | 13 | | | | 13 | | | 13 | | | | 17 | | 13 | 15 | 11 | 12 | 9 | 10 | 11 | 12 | 9 | 8 | 10 | 13 | YUG |
| | **1930** | **1931** | **1933** | **1934** | **1935** | **1937** | **1938** | **1939** | **1947** | **1949** | **1950** | **1951** | **1953** | **1954** | **1955** | **1957** | **1958** | **1959** | **1961** | **1962** | **1963** | **1965** | **1966** | **1967** | **1969** | **1970** | **1971** | **1972** | **1973** | **1974** | **1975** | **1976** | |

*United States' Andy Roach scores the game-winning goal in a shootout against Czech Republic's Tomas Vokoun in the 2004 World Championship quarter-final. Photo: HHOF-IIHF Images.*

**WORLD CHAMPIONSHIP (MEN), 1977-2012**

| | 1977 | 1978 | 1979 | 1981 | 1982 | 1983 | 1985 | 1986 | 1987 | 1989 | 1990 | 1991 | 1992 | 1993 | 1994 | 1995 | 1996 | 1997 | 1998 | 1999 | 2000 | 2001 | 2002 | 2003 | 2004 | 2005 | 2006 | 2007 | 2008 | 2009 | 2010 | 2011 | 2012 | |
|---|---|---|---|---|---|---|---|---|---|---|---|---|---|---|---|---|---|---|---|---|---|---|---|---|---|---|---|---|---|---|---|---|---|---|
| ARM | | | | | | | | | | | | | | | | | | | | | | | | | 45 | 45 | 43 | | 48 | | 48 | | | ARM |
| AUS | | | 26 | | | | | 26 | 25 | 24 | 27 | | 23 | 27 | 33 | 36 | 36 | 34 | 34 | 34 | 36 | 33 | 36 | 36 | 33 | 31 | 33 | 31 | 30 | 27 | 32 | 30 | 28 | AUS |
| AUT | 17 | 18 | 15 | 17 | 10 | 11 | 12 | 14 | 11 | 14 | 11 | 13 | 13 | 9 | 8 | 11 | 12 | 16 | 15 | 10 | 13 | 11 | 12 | 10 | 11 | 16 | 18 | 15 | 17 | 14 | 17 | 15 | 18 | AUT |
| BEL | 24 | 24 | | | | | | | 24 | 25 | 24 | 25 | 25 | 28 | 32 | 34 | 32 | 36 | 36 | 35 | 35 | 37 | 31 | 30 | 28 | 36 | 34 | 32 | 31 | 32 | 33 | 35 | 35 | BEL |
| BIH | | | | | | | | | | | | | | | | | | | | | | | | | | | | | 47 | | | | | BIH |
| BLR | | | | | | | | | | | | | | | 22 | 21 | 15 | 13 | 8 | 9 | 9 | 14 | 17 | 14 | 18 | 10 | 6 | 11 | 9 | 8 | 10 | 14 | 14 | BLR |
| BUL | 20 | 21 | 22 | 22 | 22 | 22 | 22 | 19 | 23 | 21 | 22 | 20 | 17 | 20 | 27 | 29 | 34 | 35 | 33 | 31 | 33 | 35 | 35 | 34 | 36 | 35 | 32 | 38 | 38 | 36 | 35 | 38 | 37 | BUL |
| CAN | 4 | **B** | 4 | 4 | **B** | **B** | **S** | **B** | 4 | **S** | 4 | **S** | 8 | 4 | **G** | **B** | **S** | **G** | 6 | 4 | 4 | 5 | 6 | **G** | **G** | **S** | 4 | **G** | **S** | **S** | 7 | 5 | 5 | CAN |
| CHN | | 20 | 17 | 18 | 15 | 19 | 19 | 18 | 16 | 19 | 19 | 18 | 19 | 19 | 20 | 25 | 27 | 27 | 28 | 28 | 26 | 26 | 28 | 32 | 30 | 28 | 30 | 28 | 32 | 34 | 38 | 36 | 36 | CHN |
| CRO | | | | | | | | | | | | | | | 31 | 30 | 28 | 29 | 29 | 29 | 27 | 24 | 26 | 27 | 32 | 29 | 27 | 29 | 26 | 26 | 28 | 31 | 31 | CRO |
| CZE | | | | | | | | | | | | | | **B** | 7 | 4 | **G** | **B** | **B** | **G** | **G** | **G** | 5 | 4 | 5 | **G** | **S** | 7 | 5 | 6 | **G** | **B** | **B** | CZE |
| DEN | 19 | 19 | 16 | 20 | 19 | 20 | 21 | 21 | 18 | 16 | 18 | 17 | 16 | 16 | 17 | 17 | 18 | 20 | 20 | 17 | 21 | 22 | 18 | 11 | 12 | 14 | 13 | 10 | 12 | 13 | 8 | 11 | 13 | DEN |
| ESP | 23 | 23 | 23 | | 23 | 23 | 24 | 24 | | 28 | 28 | | 27 | 30 | 29 | 32 | 31 | 31 | 32 | 32 | 31 | 31 | 33 | 33 | 35 | 37 | 37 | 33 | 34 | 33 | 30 | 26 | 30 | ESP |
| EST | | | | | | | | | | | | | | | 28 | 24 | 25 | 23 | 19 | 22 | 22 | 27 | 29 | 22 | 23 | 23 | 24 | 23 | 27 | 31 | 29 | 27 | 29 | EST |
| FIN | 5 | 7 | 5 | 6 | 5 | 7 | 5 | 4 | 5 | 5 | 6 | 5 | **S** | 7 | **S** | **G** | 5 | 5 | **S** | **S** | **B** | **S** | 4 | 5 | 6 | 7 | **B** | **S** | **B** | 5 | 6 | **G** | 4 | FIN |
| FRA | 21 | 22 | 21 | 21 | 21 | 21 | 17 | 12 | 12 | 11 | 12 | 11 | 11 | 10 | 10 | 8 | 11 | 10 | 13 | 15 | 15 | 20 | 19 | 18 | 16 | 20 | 20 | 18 | 14 | 12 | 14 | 12 | 9 | FRA |
| GBR | 22 | | 24 | 24 | | | | | | 27 | 26 | 21 | 21 | 13 | 12 | 19 | 16 | 18 | 22 | 18 | 19 | 19 | 23 | 25 | 25 | 25 | 26 | 24 | 23 | 22 | 23 | 20 | 21 | GBR |
| GDR | 9 | 8 | 10 | 12 | 9 | 6 | 8 | 11 | 13 | 13 | 13 | | | | | | | | | | | | | | | | | | | | | | | GDR |
| GER | 7 | 5 | 6 | 7 | 6 | 5 | 7 | 7 | 6 | 7 | 7 | 8 | 6 | 5 | 9 | 10 | 8 | 11 | 11 | 20 | 17 | 8 | 8 | 6 | 9 | 15 | 17 | 9 | 10 | 15 | 4 | 7 | 12 | GER |
| GRE | | | | | | | | | | | | | 29 | | | 38 | | | 40 | 39 | | | | | | | | | 45 | 44 | 43 | 45 | 45 | GRE |
| HGK | | | | | | | | | 28 | | | | | | | | | | | | | | | | | | | | | | | | | HGK |
| HUN | 14 | 13 | 17 | 19 | 20 | 18 | 16 | 22 | 21 | 20 | 23 | 22 | 24 | 25 | 26 | 26 | 24 | 26 | 25 | 24 | 25 | 23 | 20 | 21 | 24 | 21 | 23 | 19 | 18 | 16 | 20 | 19 | 19 | HUN |
| IRL | | | | | | | | | | | | | | | | | | | | | | | | | 44 | 44 | 44 | 41 | 40 | 45 | 41 | 40 | 44 | IRL |
| ISL | | | | | | | | | | | | | | | | | | | | 40 | 38 | 38 | 38 | 39 | 41 | 39 | 41 | 36 | 37 | 35 | 34 | 34 | 32 | ISL |
| ISR | | | | | | | | | | | | | 30 | 31 | 34 | 35 | 35 | 33 | 35 | 33 | 34 | 32 | 34 | 37 | 38 | 30 | 28 | 34 | 36 | 38 | 39 | 41 | 39 | ISR |
| ITA | 18 | 15 | 20 | 9 | 7 | 8 | 11 | 10 | 14 | 10 | 10 | 9 | 9 | 8 | 6 | 7 | 7 | 8 | 10 | 13 | 12 | 12 | 15 | 23 | 19 | 18 | 14 | 12 | 16 | 18 | 15 | 18 | 15 | ITA |
| JPN | 11 | 10 | 14 | 16 | 17 | 13 | 13 | 16 | 17 | 15 | 15 | 16 | 15 | 17 | 16 | 18 | 20 | 24 | 14 | 16 | 16 | 16 | 16 | 16 | 15 | 24 | 22 | 22 | 21 | 21 | 21 | 28 | 20 | JPN |
| KAZ | | | | | | | | | | | | | | 23 | 24 | 22 | 21 | 14 | 16 | 19 | 18 | 21 | 21 | 17 | 13 | 12 | 15 | 21 | 20 | 17 | 16 | 17 | 16 | KAZ |
| KOR | | | 25 | | 24 | | | 25 | 26 | 23 | 25 | 24 | 26 | 29 | 30 | 33 | 33 | 30 | 31 | 30 | 29 | 30 | 27 | 29 | 27 | 33 | 31 | 30 | 28 | 29 | 25 | 22 | 23 | KOR |
| LAT | | | | | | | | | | | | | | 21 | 14 | 14 | 13 | 7 | 9 | 11 | 8 | 13 | 11 | 9 | 7 | 9 | 10 | 13 | 11 | 7 | 11 | 13 | 10 | LAT |
| LTU | | | | | | | | | | | | | | | | 31 | 29 | 28 | 27 | 27 | 28 | 28 | 30 | 28 | 29 | 26 | 19 | 26 | 24 | 24 | 26 | 25 | 27 | LTU |
| LUX | | | | | | | | | | | | | 31 | | | | | | | | 41 | | 40 | 42 | 39 | 43 | 45 | 42 | 43 | 43 | 45 | 44 | 43 | LUX |
| MEX | | | | | | | | | | | | | | | | | | | | | 40 | 40 | 42 | 40 | 43 | 41 | 38 | 37 | 35 | 37 | 37 | 37 | 38 | MEX |
| MGL | | | | | | | | | | | | | | | | | | | | | | | | | | | | | 46 | 46 | 47 | 46 | 46 | MGL |
| NED | 16 | 17 | 9 | 8 | 16 | 17 | 14 | 13 | 15 | 17 | 16 | 15 | 14 | 15 | 18 | 16 | 19 | 19 | 24 | 25 | 24 | 25 | 24 | 24 | 22 | 22 | 25 | 25 | 25 | 25 | 24 | 24 | 25 | NED |
| NOR | 12 | 14 | 12 | 14 | 12 | 12 | 15 | 17 | 10 | 9 | 8 | 10 | 10 | 11 | 11 | 9 | 9 | 12 | 21 | 12 | 10 | 15 | 22 | 20 | 20 | 17 | 11 | 14 | 8 | 11 | 9 | 6 | 8 | NOR |
| NZL | | | | | | | | | 27 | 29 | | | | | | 39 | | | 38 | 37 | 39 | 39 | 43 | 41 | 37 | 38 | 39 | 40 | 39 | 41 | 36 | 32 | 34 | NZL |
| POL | 10 | 9 | 8 | 10 | 11 | 10 | 9 | 8 | 9 | 8 | 14 | 12 | 12 | 14 | 15 | 15 | 17 | 17 | 23 | 23 | 20 | 18 | 14 | 19 | 21 | 19 | 21 | 20 | 22 | 23 | 22 | 23 | 24 | POL |
| PRK | | | | 23 | | 24 | 23 | 23 | 22 | 22 | 21 | 23 | 22 | 26 | | | | | | | | | 41 | 35 | 34 | 34 | 36 | | 41 | 39 | 42 | 39 | 42 | PRK |
| ROU | 8 | 12 | 11 | 13 | 13 | 15 | 20 | 20 | 19 | 26 | 20 | 19 | 18 | 18 | 19 | 20 | 26 | 25 | 26 | 26 | 30 | 29 | 25 | 26 | 26 | 27 | 29 | 27 | 29 | 28 | 31 | 29 | 26 | ROU |
| RSA | | | | | | | | | | | | | 28 | 32 | 35 | 37 | | | 37 | 36 | 37 | 36 | 37 | 38 | 40 | 42 | 40 | 43 | 42 | 40 | 44 | 42 | 40 | RSA |
| RUS | | | | | | | | | | | | | 5 | **G** | 5 | 5 | 4 | 4 | 5 | 5 | 11 | 6 | **S** | 7 | 10 | **B** | 5 | **B** | **G** | **G** | **S** | 4 | **G** | RUS |
| SLO | | | | | | | | | | | | | | 24 | 25 | 27 | 23 | 22 | 18 | 21 | 23 | 17 | 13 | 15 | 17 | 13 | 16 | 17 | 15 | 19 | 18 | 16 | 17 | SLO |
| SRB | | | | | | | | | | | | | | | | | | | | | | | | 31 | 31 | 32 | 35 | 35 | 33 | 30 | 27 | 33 | 33 | SRB |
| SUI | 13 | 11 | 13 | 11 | 14 | 14 | 10 | 9 | 8 | 12 | 9 | 7 | 4 | 12 | 13 | 12 | 14 | 15 | 4 | 8 | 6 | 9 | 10 | 8 | 8 | 8 | 9 | 8 | 7 | 9 | 5 | 9 | 11 | SUI |
| SVK | | | | | | | | | | | | | | | 21 | 13 | 10 | 9 | 7 | 7 | **S** | 7 | **G** | **B** | 4 | 5 | 8 | 6 | 13 | 10 | 12 | 10 | **S** | SVK |
| SWE | **S** | 4 | **B** | **S** | 4 | 4 | 6 | **S** | **G** | 4 | **S** | **G** | **G** | **S** | **B** | **S** | 6 | **S** | **G** | **B** | 7 | **B** | **B** | **S** | **S** | 4 | **G** | 4 | 4 | **B** | **B** | **S** | 6 | SWE |
| TCH | **G** | **S** | **S** | **B** | **S** | **S** | **G** | 5 | **B** | **B** | **B** | 6 | **B** | | | | | | | | | | | | | | | | | | | | | TCH |
| TPE | | | | | | | | | | | | | | | | | | | | | | | | | | | | | | | | | | TPE |
| TUR | | | | | | | | | | | | | 32 | | | | | | 39 | 38 | 42 | | 39 | 43 | 42 | 40 | 42 | 39 | 44 | 42 | 40 | 43 | 41 | TUR |
| UAE | | | | | | | | | | | | | | | | | | | | | | | | | | | | | | | 46 | | | UAE |
| UKR | | | | | | | | | | | | | | 22 | 23 | 23 | 22 | 21 | 17 | 14 | 14 | 10 | 9 | 12 | 14 | 11 | 12 | 16 | 19 | 20 | 19 | 21 | 22 | UKR |
| URS | **B** | **G** | **G** | **G** | **G** | **G** | **B** | **G** | **S** | **G** | **G** | **B** | | | | | | | | | | | | | | | | | | | | | | URS |
| USA | 6 | 6 | 7 | 5 | 8 | 9 | 4 | 6 | 7 | 6 | 5 | 4 | 7 | 6 | 4 | 6 | **B** | 6 | 12 | 6 | 5 | 4 | 7 | 13 | **B** | 6 | 7 | 5 | 6 | 4 | 13 | 8 | 7 | USA |
| YUG | 15 | 16 | 19 | 15 | 18 | 16 | 18 | 15 | 20 | 18 | 17 | 14 | 20 | | | 28 | 30 | 32 | 30 | | 32 | 34 | 32 | | | | | | | | | | | YUG |
| | **1977** | **1978** | **1979** | **1981** | **1982** | **1983** | **1985** | **1986** | **1987** | **1989** | **1990** | **1991** | **1992** | **1993** | **1994** | **1995** | **1996** | **1997** | **1998** | **1999** | **2000** | **2001** | **2002** | **2003** | **2004** | **2005** | **2006** | **2007** | **2008** | **2009** | **2010** | **2011** | **2012** | |

**U20 WORLD CHAMPIONSHIP, 1977-2000**

| | 1977 | 1978 | 1979 | 1980 | 1981 | 1982 | 1983 | 1984 | 1985 | 1986 | 1987 | 1988 | 1989 | 1990 | 1991 | 1992 | 1993 | 1994 | 1995 | 1996 | 1997 | 1998 | 1999 | 2000 | |
|---|---|---|---|---|---|---|---|---|---|---|---|---|---|---|---|---|---|---|---|---|---|---|---|---|---|
| ARM | | | | | | | | | | | | | | | | | | | | | | | | | ARM |
| AUS | | | | | | | 20 | 23 | | | 22 | | | | | | | | | | | | | 33 | AUS |
| AUT | | | 13 | 9 | 8 | 10 | 12 | 10 | 12 | 11 | 12 | 16 | 17 | 14 | 15 | 15 | 12 | 14 | 14 | 18 | 23 | 22 | 22 | 19 | AUT |
| BEL | | | 16 | | | | | 21 | 19 | 22 | | 24 | | | | | | | | | | | | | BEL |
| BLR | | | | | | | | | | | | | | | | | 29 | 26 | 20 | 22 | 19 | 18 | 10 | 11 | BLR |
| BUL | | | | | | | 18 | 18 | 17 | 16 | 20 | 19 | 21 | 20 | 22 | 24 | 20 | 24 | | 31 | 32 | 32 | 33 | 34 | BUL |
| CAN | **S** | **B** | 5 | 5 | 7 | **G** | **B** | 4 | **G** | **S** | DQ | **G** | 4 | **G** | **G** | 6 | **G** | **G** | **G** | **G** | **G** | 8 | **S** | **B** | CAN |
| CHN | | | | | | | | | | 20 | | | | | | | | | | | | | | | CHN |
| CRO | | | | | | | | | | | | | | | | | 30 | 28 | 29 | 27 | 25 | 23 | 26 | 27 | CRO |
| CZE | | | | | | | | | | | | | | | | | | 5 | 6 | 4 | 4 | 4 | 7 | **G** | CZE |
| DEN | | | 12 | 13 | 13 | 12 | 15 | 16 | | 18 | 18 | 17 | 15 | 12 | 16 | 18 | 18 | 19 | 19 | 21 | 21 | 19 | 13 | 18 | DEN |
| ESP | | | | | | | | 20 | 21 | | 21 | 21 | | | | 20 | 23 | 23 | 21 | 26 | 30 | 30 | 30 | 30 | ESP |
| EST | | | | | | | | | | | | | | | | | 28 | 29 | 27 | 28 | 27 | 24 | 23 | 24 | EST |
| FIN | 4 | 6 | 4 | **S** | **S** | **B** | 6 | **S** | 4 | 6 | **G** | **B** | 6 | 4 | 5 | 4 | 5 | 4 | 4 | 6 | 5 | **G** | 5 | 7 | FIN |
| FRA | | | 10 | 15 | 16 | 13 | 13 | 14 | 16 | 17 | 13 | 13 | 14 | 13 | 11 | 12 | 13 | 11 | 12 | 17 | 13 | 16 | 17 | 13 | FRA |
| GBR | | | | | | | | 22 | 20 | 19 | 19 | 20 | 20 | 22 | 20 | 19 | 21 | 20 | 24 | 23 | 22 | 25 | 25 | 21 | GBR |
| GER | 6 | 7 | 7 | 6 | 5 | 7 | 7 | 7 | 7 | 8 | 9 | 7 | 8 | 10 | 9 | 7 | 7 | 7 | 7 | 8 | 9 | 10 | 14 | 12 | GER |
| GRE | | | | | | | | | | | | | | | 24 | | 32 | | | | | | | | GRE |
| HUN | | | | 16 | | | 19 | 19 | 18 | 21 | | 22 | | 23 | 23 | 21 | 19 | 21 | 18 | 14 | 17 | 15 | 18 | 22 | HUN |
| IRL | | | | | | | | | | | | | | | | | | | | | | | | | IRL |
| ISL | | | | | | | | | | | | | | | | | | | | | | | 34 | 35 | ISL |
| ISR | | | | | | | | | | | | | | | | | | | | | 31 | | | | ISR |
| ITA | | | 15 | 14 | 15 | 14 | 16 | 17 | 14 | 15 | 16 | 18 | 18 | 19 | 18 | 17 | 11 | 13 | 16 | 15 | 18 | 20 | 19 | 16 | ITA |
| JPN | | | | | | 11 | 10 | 11 | 11 | 13 | 11 | 12 | 12 | 11 | 12 | 9 | 8 | 15 | 15 | 16 | 16 | | 20 | 23 | JPN |
| KAZ | | | | | | | | | | | | | | | | | 27 | 25 | 25 | 19 | 11 | 7 | 6 | 8 | KAZ |
| KOR | | | | | | | | | | | | | | 21 | 21 | 22 | 24 | | | | | | | | KOR |
| LAT | | | | | | | | | | | | | | | | | 25 | 18 | 17 | 12 | 12 | 14 | 15 | 17 | LAT |
| LTU | | | | | | | | | | | | | | | | | 31 | | 28 | 30 | 28 | 27 | 24 | 25 | LTU |
| LUX | | | | | | | | | | | | | | | | | | | | | | | | | LUX |
| MEX | | | | | | | | | | | | | | | | | | | | | 34 | 31 | 31 | 31 | MEX |
| NED | | | 14 | 12 | 12 | 15 | 14 | 13 | 10 | 14 | 15 | 15 | 16 | 17 | 14 | 14 | 16 | 22 | 23 | 25 | 26 | 28 | 28 | 29 | NED |
| NOR | | | 8 | 11 | 10 | 9 | 8 | 12 | 13 | 10 | 10 | 9 | 7 | 6 | 8 | 11 | 10 | 10 | 13 | 13 | 14 | 17 | 16 | 14 | NOR |
| NZL | | | | | | | | | | | | | | | | | | | | | | | | | NZL |
| POL | 8 | | 11 | 10 | 11 | | 11 | 9 | 8 | 9 | 5 | 8 | 9 | 8 | 10 | 10 | 14 | 12 | 11 | 11 | 10 | 13 | 12 | 15 | POL |
| PRK | | | | | | | | | | | | 23 | 19 | 18 | 17 | 16 | 22 | | | | | | | | PRK |
| ROU | | | | | | | 17 | 15 | 15 | 12 | 14 | 10 | 11 | 15 | 13 | 13 | 15 | 16 | 22 | 24 | 24 | 26 | 29 | 28 | ROU |
| RSA | | | | | | | | | | | | | | | | | | | | 32 | 33 | 33 | 32 | 32 | RSA |
| RUS | | | | | | | | | | | | | | | | **G** | 6 | **B** | **S** | **B** | **B** | **S** | **G** | **S** | RUS |
| SLO | | | | | | | | | | | | | | | | | 26 | 27 | 26 | 20 | 20 | 21 | 21 | 20 | SLO |
| SRB | | | | | 14 | 16 | | | | | 17 | 14 | 13 | 16 | 19 | 23 | | | 30 | 29 | 29 | 29 | 27 | 26 | SRB |
| SUI | | 8 | 9 | 8 | 9 | 8 | 9 | 8 | 9 | 7 | 6 | 11 | 10 | 9 | 7 | 8 | 9 | 8 | 9 | 9 | 7 | **B** | 9 | 6 | SUI |
| SVK | | | | | | | | | | | | | | | | | | 17 | 10 | 7 | 6 | 9 | **B** | 9 | SVK |
| SWE | 5 | **S** | **B** | **B** | **G** | 5 | 4 | 5 | 5 | 4 | **B** | 5 | **S** | 5 | 6 | **S** | **S** | **S** | **B** | **S** | 8 | 6 | 4 | 5 | SWE |
| TCH | **B** | 4 | **S** | 4 | 4 | **S** | **S** | **B** | **S** | 5 | **S** | 4 | **B** | **B** | **B** | 5 | **B** | | | | | | | | TCH |
| TPE | | | | | | | | | | | | | | | | | | | | | | | | | TPE |
| TUR | | | | | | | | | | | | | | | | | | | | | | 34 | 35 | | TUR |
| UKR | | | | | | | | | | | | | | | | | 17 | 9 | 8 | 10 | 15 | 12 | 11 | 10 | UKR |
| URS | **G** | **G** | **G** | **G** | **B** | 4 | **G** | **G** | **B** | **G** | DQ | **S** | **G** | **S** | **S** | | | | | | | | | | URS |
| USA | 7 | 5 | 6 | 7 | 6 | 6 | 5 | 6 | 6 | **B** | 4 | 6 | 5 | 7 | 4 | **B** | 4 | 6 | 5 | 5 | **S** | 5 | 8 | 4 | USA |
| | **1977** | **1978** | **1979** | **1980** | **1981** | **1982** | **1983** | **1984** | **1985** | **1986** | **1987** | **1988** | **1989** | **1990** | **1991** | **1992** | **1993** | **1994** | **1995** | **1996** | **1997** | **1998** | **1999** | **2000** | |

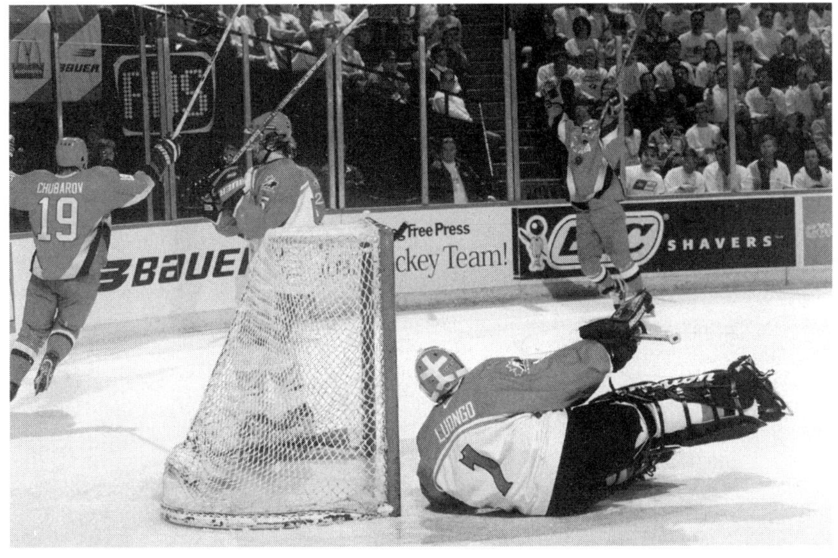


*Artem Chubarov scores the winning goal in overtime against Roberto Luongo in the 1999 World Junior gold medal game.*
*Photo: IIHF.*

**U20 WORLD CHAMPIONSHIP, 2001-2012**

| | 2001 | 2002 | 2003 | 2004 | 2005 | 2006 | 2007 | 2008 | 2009 | 2010 | 2011 | 2012 | |
|---|---|---|---|---|---|---|---|---|---|---|---|---|---|
| ARM | | | | | | 39 | 38 | 37 | | | | | ARM |
| AUS | 34 | | 38 | 35 | 32 | 32 | 34 | 38 | | 35 | 32 | 33 | AUS |
| AUT | 15 | 12 | 11 | 9 | 16 | 20 | 15 | 12 | 12 | 10 | 15 | 15 | AUT |
| BEL | | | 36 | 32 | 33 | | 36 | 30 | 29 | 30 | 30 | 32 | BEL |
| BLR | 9 | 9 | 10 | 11 | 10 | 12 | 10 | 14 | 13 | 14 | 14 | 12 | BLR |
| BUL | 31 | 34 | 34 | 39 | 40 | 38 | 40 | 41 | | 41 | 40 | 38 | BUL |
| CAN | **B** | **S** | **S** | **S** | **G** | **G** | **G** | **G** | **G** | **S** | **S** | **B** | CAN |
| CHN | | | | 36 | 29 | 31 | 35 | 34 | 34 | 31 | 34 | 36 | CHN |
| CRO | 24 | 22 | 22 | 29 | 28 | 27 | 27 | 28 | 23 | 22 | 19 | 21 | CRO |
| CZE | **G** | 7 | 6 | 4 | **B** | 6 | 5 | 5 | 6 | 7 | 7 | 5 | CZE |
| DEN | 22 | 20 | 19 | 13 | 15 | 14 | 11 | 10 | 14 | 13 | 12 | 10 | DEN |
| ESP | | 28 | 30 | 28 | 30 | 30 | 29 | 29 | 31 | 27 | 28 | 26 | ESP |
| EST | 28 | 27 | 23 | 20 | 22 | 24 | 22 | 24 | 22 | 32 | 31 | 30 | EST |
| FIN | **S** | **B** | **B** | **B** | 5 | **B** | 6 | 6 | 7 | 5 | 6 | 4 | FIN |
| FRA | 11 | 10 | 17 | 15 | 18 | 17 | 17 | 19 | 15 | 19 | 24 | 17 | FRA |
| GBR | 23 | 23 | 25 | 24 | 21 | 23 | 16 | 22 | 26 | 24 | 16 | 16 | GBR |
| GER | 12 | 11 | 9 | 12 | 9 | 11 | 9 | 11 | 9 | 11 | 10 | 11 | GER |
| GRE | | | | | | | | | | | | | GRE |
| HUN | 25 | 24 | 24 | 22 | 23 | 21 | 23 | 17 | 21 | 25 | 25 | 25 | HUN |
| IRL | 37 | | | | | | | | | | | | IRL |
| ISL | 35 | 32 | 31 | 34 | 37 | 36 | 31 | 33 | | 36 | 33 | 35 | ISL |
| ISR | | | | | | | | | | | | | ISR |
| ITA | 17 | 18 | 20 | 17 | 20 | 16 | 21 | 23 | 17 | 15 | 17 | 19 | ITA |
| JPN | 20 | 19 | 13 | 21 | 24 | 22 | 28 | 26 | 24 | 21 | 20 | 22 | JPN |
| KAZ | 10 | 15 | 14 | 19 | 13 | 13 | 14 | 8 | 10 | 17 | 18 | 18 | KAZ |
| KOR | | | 35 | 25 | 25 | 28 | 30 | 27 | 27 | 29 | 27 | 28 | KOR |
| LAT | 18 | 21 | 18 | 18 | 12 | 9 | 12 | 13 | 8 | 9 | 11 | 9 | LAT |
| LTU | 21 | 26 | 29 | 31 | 34 | 35 | 24 | 21 | 25 | 23 | 21 | 24 | LTU |
| LUX | 36 | | 39 | | | | | | | | | | LUX |
| MEX | 33 | 33 | 33 | 37 | 35 | 33 | 33 | 32 | 30 | 34 | 35 | 34 | MEX |
| NED | 27 | 25 | 26 | 27 | 27 | 25 | 25 | 25 | 28 | 26 | 26 | 27 | NED |
| NOR | 14 | 13 | 16 | 14 | 11 | 10 | 19 | 16 | 16 | 12 | 9 | 13 | NOR |
| NZL | | | | 40 | 36 | 34 | 37 | 35 | | 38 | 39 | 37 | NZL |
| POL | 16 | 17 | 21 | 23 | 17 | 18 | 18 | 18 | 20 | 20 | 23 | 20 | POL |
| PRK | | | | | | | | | | 37 | 37 | | PRK |
| ROU | 29 | 30 | 27 | 26 | 26 | 26 | 26 | 31 | 33 | 28 | 29 | 29 | ROU |
| RSA | 32 | 31 | 32 | 33 | 38 | | | 39 | | | | | RSA |
| RUS | 7 | **G** | **G** | 5 | **S** | **S** | **S** | **B** | **B** | 6 | **G** | **S** | RUS |
| SLO | 19 | 16 | 15 | 16 | 14 | 15 | 20 | 15 | 18 | 16 | 13 | 14 | SLO |
| SRB | 30 | 29 | 28 | 30 | 31 | 29 | 32 | 36 | 32 | 33 | 36 | 31 | SRB |
| SUI | 6 | 4 | 7 | 8 | 8 | 7 | 7 | 9 | 11 | 4 | 5 | 8 | SUI |
| SVK | 8 | 8 | 5 | 6 | 7 | 8 | 8 | 7 | 4 | 8 | 8 | 6 | SVK |
| SWE | 4 | 6 | 8 | 7 | 6 | 5 | 4 | **S** | **S** | **B** | 4 | **G** | SWE |
| TCH | | | | | | | | | | | | | TCH |
| TPE | | | | | | | | | | 39 | 41 | | TPE |
| TUR | | | 37 | 38 | 39 | 37 | 39 | 40 | | 40 | 38 | 39 | TUR |
| UKR | 13 | 14 | 12 | 10 | 19 | 19 | 13 | 20 | 19 | 18 | 22 | 23 | UKR |
| URS | | | | | | | | | | | | | URS |
| USA | 5 | 5 | 4 | **G** | 4 | 4 | **B** | 4 | 5 | **G** | **B** | 7 | USA |
| | **2001** | **2002** | **2003** | **2004** | **2005** | **2006** | **2007** | **2008** | **2009** | **2010** | **2011** | **2012** | |

**U18 WORLD CHAMPIONSHIP (MEN)**

| | 1999 | 2000 | 2001 | 2002 | 2003 | 2004 | 2005 | 2006 | 2007 | 2008 | 2009 | 2010 | 2011 | 2012 | |
|---|---|---|---|---|---|---|---|---|---|---|---|---|---|---|---|
| ARM | | | | | | | 42 | | | 43 | | | | | ARM |
| AUS | | | | | 35 | 34 | 35 | 28 | 31 | 32 | 35 | 34 | 35 | 33 | AUS |
| AUT | 12 | 12 | 12 | 15 | 19 | 15 | 19 | 19 | 20 | 15 | 15 | 21 | 23 | 19 | AUT |
| BEL | | | 31 | 31 | 30 | 33 | 36 | 31 | 30 | 29 | 28 | 33 | 33 | 35 | BEL |
| BIH | | | | | 40 | 41 | 41 | | | | | | | | BIH |
| BLR | 11 | 10 | 11 | 5 | 8 | 9 | 11 | 9 | 12 | 9 | 11 | 10 | 17 | 17 | BLR |
| BUL | | | 32 | 34 | 34 | 38 | 40 | 39 | 41 | 40 | 42 | 42 | 39 | 38 | BUL |
| CAN | | | | 6 | **G** | 4 | **S** | 4 | 4 | **G** | 4 | 7 | 4 | **B** | CAN |
| CHN | | | | | 39 | | | | 36 | | 33 | 35 | 31 | 34 | CHN |
| CRO | | | 24 | 26 | 28 | 28 | 28 | 29 | 27 | 27 | 30 | 27 | 27 | 27 | CRO |
| CZE | 5 | 6 | 4 | **B** | 6 | **B** | 4 | **B** | 9 | 11 | 6 | 6 | 8 | 8 | CZE |
| DEN | 14 | 15 | 17 | 18 | 11 | 8 | 10 | 13 | 11 | 10 | 14 | 13 | 11 | 10 | DEN |
| ESP | | | 29 | 30 | 31 | 30 | 30 | 33 | 35 | 31 | 32 | 28 | 29 | 31 | ESP |
| EST | | | 22 | 23 | 25 | 25 | 26 | 27 | 28 | 28 | 26 | 31 | 30 | 29 | EST |
| FIN | **G** | **G** | **B** | 4 | 7 | 7 | 7 | **S** | 7 | 6 | **B** | **B** | 5 | 4 | FIN |
| FRA | 16 | 18 | 20 | 20 | 17 | 19 | 18 | 18 | 21 | 23 | 18 | 16 | 15 | 14 | FRA |
| GBR | 18 | | 23 | 22 | 22 | 24 | 21 | 23 | 22 | 25 | 23 | 19 | 20 | 26 | GBR |
| GER | 9 | 7 | 5 | 10 | 13 | 11 | 8 | 8 | 8 | 5 | 10 | 11 | 6 | 6 | GER |
| HUN | 17 | | 25 | 25 | 26 | 26 | 24 | 21 | 25 | 24 | 16 | 14 | 18 | 22 | HUN |
| IRL | | | | | | | | | | | 40 | 43 | 43 | | IRL |
| ISL | | | 36 | | 36 | 32 | 32 | 34 | 37 | 36 | 36 | 32 | 36 | 32 | ISL |
| ISR | | | 34 | | 41 | 39 | 37 | 36 | 32 | 33 | | 41 | 41 | | ISR |
| ITA | 15 | 16 | 16 | 17 | 16 | 17 | 22 | 24 | 17 | 16 | 21 | 24 | 14 | 13 | ITA |
| JPN | | 14 | 13 | 19 | 20 | 13 | 20 | 16 | 13 | 21 | 19 | 15 | 22 | 16 | JPN |
| KAZ | | | 15 | 13 | 10 | 18 | 14 | 15 | 15 | 14 | 17 | 18 | 16 | 18 | KAZ |
| KOR | | | | 28 | 23 | 21 | 23 | 22 | 26 | 26 | 24 | 20 | 21 | 23 | KOR |
| LAT | | 13 | 14 | 16 | 18 | 16 | 15 | 11 | 10 | 13 | 12 | 9 | 12 | 9 | LAT |
| LTU | | | 26 | 33 | 32 | 29 | 25 | 25 | 24 | 17 | 20 | 22 | 28 | 25 | LTU |
| MEX | | | | | 37 | 35 | 29 | 30 | 34 | 35 | 34 | 37 | 37 | 37 | MEX |
| MGL | | | | | | | | | | 42 | 43 | 44 | 44 | | MGL |
| NED | | | 27 | 24 | 27 | 27 | 27 | 26 | 23 | 22 | 29 | 29 | 26 | 28 | NED |
| NOR | 10 | 11 | 9 | 11 | 12 | 10 | 12 | 10 | 16 | 12 | 9 | 12 | 9 | 12 | NOR |
| NZL | | | | | 42 | 37 | 38 | 38 | 38 | 38 | 37 | 36 | 34 | 36 | NZL |
| POL | 13 | 17 | 21 | 21 | 14 | 20 | 17 | 17 | 18 | 18 | 13 | 17 | 19 | 21 | POL |
| PRK | | | 18 | | | | | | | | | | | | PRK |
| ROU | | | 28 | 27 | 24 | 22 | 33 | 35 | 29 | 30 | 27 | 26 | 25 | 24 | ROU |
| RSA | | | 30 | 32 | 33 | 36 | 34 | 37 | 39 | 41 | 41 | 40 | 40 | 40 | RSA |
| RUS | 6 | **S** | **G** | **S** | **B** | **G** | 5 | 5 | **G** | **S** | **S** | 4 | **B** | 5 | RUS |
| SLO | | | 19 | 14 | 15 | 14 | 13 | 14 | 14 | 20 | 25 | 23 | 13 | 15 | SLO |
| SRB | | | 33 | 29 | 29 | 31 | 31 | 32 | 33 | 34 | 31 | 30 | 32 | 30 | SRB |
| SUI | 4 | 4 | **S** | 7 | 9 | 12 | 9 | 12 | 6 | 8 | 8 | 5 | 7 | 7 | SUI |
| SVK | **B** | 5 | 8 | 8 | **S** | 6 | 6 | 7 | 5 | 7 | 7 | 8 | 10 | 11 | SVK |
| SWE | **S** | **B** | 7 | 9 | 5 | 5 | **B** | 6 | **B** | 4 | 5 | **S** | **S** | **S** | SWE |
| TPE | | | | | | | | | | 37 | 39 | 39 | 38 | 39 | TPE |
| TUR | | | 35 | 35 | 38 | 40 | 39 | 40 | 40 | 39 | 38 | 38 | 42 | | TUR |
| UKR | 8 | 9 | 10 | 12 | 21 | 23 | 16 | 20 | 19 | 19 | 22 | 25 | 24 | 20 | UKR |
| USA | 7 | 8 | 6 | **G** | 4 | **S** | **G** | **G** | **S** | **B** | **G** | **G** | **G** | **G** | USA |
| | **1999** | **2000** | **2001** | **2002** | **2003** | **2004** | **2005** | **2006** | **2007** | **2008** | **2009** | **2010** | **2011** | **2012** | |

*(left-right) Vladimir Dzurilla, Reggie Leach, Josef Augusta, and Bobby Clarke at the 1976 Canada Cup. Czechoslovakia vs. Canada at the Montreal Forum. Photo: HHOF.*

**IIHF-NHL INVITATIONALS**

| | 1972 SS | 1976 CC | 1981 CC | 1984 CC | 1987 CC | 1991 CC | 1996 WCH | 2004 WCH | |
|---|---|---|---|---|---|---|---|---|---|
| CAN | **1** | **1** | 2 | **1** | **1** | **1** | 2 | **1** | CAN |
| CZE | | | | | | | 8 | 3 | CZE |
| FIN | | 6 | 6 | | 6 | 3 | 5 | 2 | FIN |
| GER | | | | 5 | | | 6 | 8 | GER |
| RUS | | | | | | | 4 | 6 | RUS |
| TCH | | 2 | 3 | 6 | 4 | 6 | | | TCH |
| SVK | | | | | | | 7 | 7 | SVK |
| SWE | | 4 | 5 | 2 | 3 | 4 | 3 | 5 | SWE |
| URS | 2 | 3 | **1** | 3 | 2 | 5 | | | URS |
| USA | | 5 | 4 | 4 | 5 | 2 | **1** | 4 | USA |
| | **1972 SS** | **1976 CC** | **1981 CC** | **1984 CC** | **1987 CC** | **1991 CC** | **1996 WCH** | **2004 WCH** | |

**OLYMPIC GAMES, WOMEN**

| | 1998 | 2002 | 2006 | 2010 | |
|---|---|---|---|---|---|
| CAN | **S** | **G** | **G** | **G** | CAN |
| CHN | 4 | 7 | 10 | 7 | CHN |
| CZE | | | 14 | | CZE |
| FIN | **B** | 4 | 4 | **B** | FIN |
| FRA | | | 13 | | FRA |
| GER | | 6 | 5 | | GER |
| ITA | | | 8 | | ITA |
| JPN | 6 | 10 | 11 | | JPN |
| KAZ | | 8 | 9 | | KAZ |
| KOR | | | 27 | | KOR |
| LAT | | | 12 | | LAT |
| NOR | | | 15 | | NOR |
| RSA | | 23 | 26 | | RSA |
| RUS | | 5 | 6 | 6 | RUS |
| SLO | | | 16 | | SLO |
| SUI | | 9 | 7 | 5 | SUI |
| SVK | | 17 | 17 | 8 | SVK |
| SWE | 5 | **B** | **S** | 4 | SWE |
| USA | **G** | **S** | **B** | **S** | USA |
| | **1998** | **2002** | **2006** | **2010** | |

**WOMEN'S WORLD CHAMPIONSHIP**

| | 1990 | 1992 | 1994 | 1997 | 1999 | 2000 | 2001 | 2003 | 2004 | 2005 | 2007 | 2008 | 2009 | 2011 | 2012 | |
|---|---|---|---|---|---|---|---|---|---|---|---|---|---|---|---|---|
| AUS | | | | | | | 22 | 21 | 20 | 25 | 22 | 21 | | 22 | 23 | AUS |
| AUT | | | | | | | | | 22 | 19 | 19 | 16 | 13 | 12 | 12 | AUT |
| BEL | | | | | | | | 23 | 25 | 23 | 24 | 25 | | 26 | 31 | BEL |
| BUL | | | | | | | | | | | | | | 34 | | BUL |
| CAN | **G** | **G** | **G** | **G** | **G** | **G** | **G** | | **G** | **S** | **G** | **S** | **S** | **S** | **G** | CAN |
| CHN | | 5 | 4 | 4 | 5 | 6 | 6 | | 7 | 6 | 6 | 8 | 9 | 13 | 16 | CHN |
| CRO | | | | | | | | | | | 28 | 24 | | 25 | 26 | CRO |
| CZE | | | | | 12 | 15 | 11 | 11 | 11 | 11 | 14 | 12 | 14 | 15 | 9 | CZE |
| DEN | | 7 | | | 14 | 12 | 16 | 16 | 16 | 13 | 15 | 17 | 20 | 17 | 15 | DEN |
| ESP | | | | | | | | | | | | | | 33 | 28 | ESP |
| EST | | | | | | | | | | | 31 | 31 | | | | EST |
| FIN | **B** | **B** | **B** | **B** | **B** | **B** | 4 | | **B** | 4 | 4 | **B** | **B** | **B** | 4 | FIN |
| FRA | | | | | 11 | 13 | 13 | 12 | 13 | 12 | 12 | 13 | 15 | 16 | 17 | FRA |
| GBR | | | | | | | 18 | 20 | 21 | 22 | 23 | 22 | 18 | 19 | 18 | GBR |
| GER | 7 | | 8 | | 7 | 7 | 5 | | 6 | 5 | 8 | 9 | 11 | 9 | 7 | GER |
| HUN | | | | | | | 21 | 24 | 24 | 24 | 25 | 26 | | 23 | 22 | HUN |
| IRL | | | | | | | | | | | | | | 36 | | IRL |
| ISL | | | | | | | | | | 30 | 32 | 28 | | 29 | 30 | ISL |
| ITA | | | | | | 16 | | 18 | 17 | 16 | 17 | 19 | 19 | 18 | 20 | ITA |
| JPN | 8 | | | | 9 | 8 | 10 | 9 | 9 | 10 | 10 | 7 | 8 | 14 | 11 | JPN |
| KAZ | | | | | | 9 | 8 | 10 | 10 | 7 | 9 | 10 | 6 | 8 | 14 | KAZ |
| KOR | | | | | | | | | | 27 | 26 | 27 | | 28 | 29 | KOR |
| LAT | | | | | 13 | 14 | 14 | 13 | 12 | 14 | 11 | 15 | 16 | 11 | 13 | LAT |
| NED | | | | | 16 | | 20 | 19 | 19 | 20 | 20 | 20 | 21 | 21 | 19 | NED |
| NOR | 6 | 6 | 6 | 8 | 10 | 11 | 15 | 15 | 14 | 15 | 13 | 14 | 12 | 10 | 10 | NOR |
| NZL | | | | | | | | | | 28 | 30 | 29 | | 27 | 24 | NZL |
| POL | | | | | | | | | | | | | | 32 | 27 | POL |
| PRK | | | | | | | 12 | 14 | 15 | 18 | 18 | 18 | 17 | 20 | 21 | PRK |
| ROU | | | | | | | | 26 | 26 | 29 | 29 | 30 | | 30 | | ROU |
| RSA | | | | | | | | | 25 | | 27 | 32 | | 31 | 32 | RSA |
| RUS | | | | 6 | 6 | 5 | **B** | | 5 | 8 | 7 | 6 | 5 | 4 | 6 | RUS |
| SLO | | | | | | | | 22 | 23 | 21 | 21 | 23 | | 24 | 25 | SLO |
| SUI | 5 | 8 | 7 | 7 | 8 | 10 | 9 | | 8 | 9 | 5 | 4 | 7 | 6 | **B** | SUI |
| SVK | | | | | | 15 | | | 17 | 18 | 16 | 11 | 10 | 7 | 8 | SVK |
| SWE | 4 | 4 | 5 | 5 | 4 | 4 | 7 | | 4 | **B** | **B** | 5 | 4 | 5 | 5 | SWE |
| TUR | | | | | | | | | | | 33 | 33 | | 35 | | TUR |
| USA | **S** | **S** | **S** | **S** | **S** | **S** | **S** | | **S** | **G** | **S** | **G** | **G** | **G** | **S** | USA |
| | **1990** | **1992** | **1994** | **1997** | **1999** | **2000** | **2001** | **2003** | **2004** | **2005** | **2007** | **2008** | **2009** | **2011** | **2012** | |

**U18 WOMEN'S WORLD CHAMPIONSHIP**

| | 2008 | 2009 | 2010 | 2011 | 2012 | |
|---|---|---|---|---|---|---|
| AUT | | 12 | 12 | 11 | 10 | AUT |
| CAN | **S** | **S** | **G** | **S** | **G** | CAN |
| CHN | | | | | 15 | CHN |
| CZE | **B** | 4 | 7 | 4 | 6 | CZE |
| FIN | 6 | 5 | 5 | **B** | 5 | FIN |
| FRA | | 10 | 10 | 13 | 17 | FRA |
| GBR | | | | | 13 | GBR |
| GER | 5 | 6 | 4 | 6 | 4 | GER |
| HUN | | | | | 9 | HUN |
| ITA | | | | | 16 | ITA |
| JPN | | 9 | 6 | 8 | 11 | JPN |
| KAZ | | | 14 | 14 | 18 | KAZ |
| NOR | | 13 | 13 | 12 | 12 | NOR |
| RUS | 8 | 7 | 8 | 9 | 7 | RUS |
| SUI | 7 | 8 | 9 | 7 | 8 | SUI |
| SVK | | 11 | 11 | 10 | 14 | SVK |
| SWE | 4 | **B** | **B** | 5 | **B** | SWE |
| USA | **G** | **G** | **S** | **G** | **S** | USA |
| | **2008** | **2009** | **2010** | **2011** | **2012** | |

*Canada won its second gold medal at the U18 World Championship for women in 2012. Photo: Jana Chytilova / HHOF-IIHF Images.*

*Daniel Alfredsson warms up prior to his final game with Tre Kronor at the 2012 World Championship in Stockholm, May 17, 2012. Photo: Andre Ringuette / HHOF-IIHF Images.*

# SUMMARY INFORMATION

## Guide to Abbreviations

**NATIONS**

| | | | | | | | | | |
|---|---|---|---|---|---|---|---|---|---|
| AND | Andorra | DEN | Denmark | ISR | Israel | MKD | FYR Macedonia | SRB | Serbia |
| ARG | Argentina | EST | Estonia | ITA | Italy | MGL | Mongolia | SUI | Switzerland |
| ARM | Armenia | ESP | Spain | JAM | Jamaica | MOR | Morocco | SVK | Slovakia |
| AUS | Australia | FIN | Finland | JPN | Japan | NAM | Namibia | SWE | Sweden |
| AUT | Austria | FRA | France | KAZ | Kazakhstan | NED | Netherlands | TCH | Czechoslovakia |
| AZE | Azerbaijan | FRG | West Germany | KGZ | Kyrgyzstan | NOR | Norway | THA | Thailand |
| BEL | Belgium | GBR | Great Britain | KOR | Korea | NZL | New Zealand | TPE | Chinese Taipei |
| BIH | Bosnia and Herzegovina | GDR | East Germany | KUW | Kuwait | POL | Poland | TUR | Turkey |
| BLR | Belarus | GEO | Georgia | LAT | Latvia | POR | Portugal | UAE | United Arab Emirates |
| BRA | Brazil | GER | Germany | LIE | Liechtenstein | PRK | North Korea | UKR | Ukraine |
| BUL | Bulgaria | GRE | Greece | LTU | Lithuania | QAT | Qatar | URS | Soviet Union |
| CAN | Canada | HKG | Hong Kong | LUX | Luxembourg | ROU | Romania | USA | United States |
| CHI | Chile | HUN | Hungary | MAC | Macau | RSA | South Africa | YUG | Yugoslavia |
| CHN | China | IND | India | MAS | Malaysia | RUS | Russia | | |
| CRO | Croatia | IRL | Ireland | MDA | Moldova | SIN | Singapore | | |
| CZE | Czech Republic | ISL | Iceland | MEX | Mexico | SLO | Slovenia | | |

**TOURNAMENTS**

| | |
|---|---|
| OG-M | Olympics, Men (1920-present) |
| OG-W | Olympics, Women (1998-present) |
| WM | World Championship (Men) (1930-present) |
| WW | Women's World Championship (1990-present) |
| WM20 | U20 World Championship (1977-present) |
| WM18 | U18 World Championship (Men) (1999-present) |
| WW18 | U18 Women's World Championship (2008-present) |
| CC | Canada Cup (1976-1991) |
| WCH | World Cup of Hockey (1996 and 2004) |
| SS | 1972 Summit Series |

**STATISTICS**

| | |
|---|---|
| A | assists |
| G | goals |
| GA | goals against, team |
| GAA | goals against average, goalie |
| GF | goals for, team |
| GP | games played |
| GWS | game winning shots/shootout |
| L | loss |
| Mins | minutes played, goalie |
| OTL | overtime loss |
| OTW | overtime win |
| P | points (team, in standings; player, in scoring table) |
| Pim | penalties in minutes |
| SO | shutout, goalie |
| T | tie |
| W | win |

## All-Time IIHF Hosting History—Top Level

| Nation | OG | WM | WW | WM20 | WM18 | WW18 | Total |
|---|---|---|---|---|---|---|---|
| CAN | 2 | 1 | 5 | 10 | 0 | 1 | 19 |
| SWE | 0 | **10 | 1 | 5 | 1 | 1 | 18 |
| FIN | 0 | **7 | 3 | 5 | 2 | 0 | 17 |
| CZE (a) | 0 | 9 | 0 | 5 | 2 | 1 | 17 |
| USA | 4 | 1 | 3 | 5 | 1 | 1 | 15 |
| SUI | 2 | 8 | 1 | 1 | 1 | 0 | 13 |
| GER (b)* | 1 | 7 | 0 | 2 | 2 | 1 | 13 |
| RUS (c) | 0 | 6 | 0 | 3 | 2 | 0 | 11 |
| AUT* | 2 | 6 | 0 | 0 | 0 | 0 | 8 |
| FRA* | 3 | 2 | 0 | 0 | 0 | 0 | 5 |
| ITA | 2 | 2 | 0 | 0 | 0 | 0 | 4 |
| NOR | 2 | 2 | 0 | 0 | 0 | 0 | 4 |
| JPN | 2 | 0 | 0 | 0 | 0 | 0 | 2 |
| YUG | 1 | 1 | 0 | 0 | 0 | 0 | 2 |
| GBR | 0 | 2 | 0 | 0 | 0 | 0 | 2 |
| POL | 0 | 2 | 0 | 0 | 0 | 0 | 2 |
| BLR | 0 | 0 | 0 | 0 | 2 | 0 | 2 |
| SVK | 0 | 1 | 0 | 0 | 1 | 0 | 2 |
| BEL | 1 | 0 | 0 | 0 | 0 | 0 | 1 |
| LAT | 0 | 1 | 0 | 0 | 0 | 0 | 1 |
| CHN | 0 | 0 | 1 | 0 | 0 | 0 | 1 |

*co-hosts Chamonix, Vienna, Berlin in 1930
**co-hosts in 2012
(a) includes TCH
(b) includes FRG & GDR
(c) includes URS

**BY YEAR/EVENT**

**Canada**
19 (1978 WM20, 1986 WM20, 1988 OG, 1990 WW, 1991 WM20, 1995 WM20, 1997 WW, 1999 WM20, 2000 WW, 2003 WM20, 2004 WW, 2006 WM20, 2007 WW, 2008 WW U18, 2008 WM, 2009 WM20, 2010 WM20, 2010 OG, 2012 WM20)

**Sweden**
18 (1949 WM, 1954 WM, 1963 WM, 1969 WM, 1970 WM, 1979 WM20, 1981 WM, 1984 WM20, 1989 WM, 1993 WM20, 1995 WM, 2000 WM20, 2002 WM, 2005 WW, 2006 WM18, 2007 WM20, 2011 WW18, 2012 WM)

**Finland**
17 (1965 WM, 1974 WM, 1980 WM20, 1982 WM, 1985 WM20, 1990 WM20, 1991 WM, 1992 WW, 1997 WM, 1998 WM20, 1999 WW, 2001 WM18, 2003 WM, 2004 WM20, 2007 WM18, 2009 WW, 2012 WM)

**Czech Republic**
17 (1933 WM, 1938 WM, 1947 WM, 1959 WM, 1972 WM, 1977 WM20, 1978 WM, 1985 WM, 1987 WM20, 1992 WM, 1994 WM20, 2002 WM20, 2004 WM, 2005 WM18, 2008 WM20, 2012 WM18, 2012 WW18)

**United States**
15 (1932 OG-WM, 1960 OG-WM, 1962 WM, 1980 OG, 1982 WM20, 1989 WM20, 1994 WW, 1996 WM20, 2001 WW, 2002 OG, 2005 WM20, 2009 WM18, 2010 WW18, 2011 WM20, 2012 WW)

**Switzerland**
13 (1928 OG-WM, 1935 WM, 1939 WM, 1948 OG-WM, 1953 WM, 1961 WM, 1971 WM, 1990 WM, 1997 WM20, 1998 WM, 2000 WM18, 2009 WM, 2011 WW)

**Germany**
13 (1930 WM*, 1936OG-WM, 1955 WM, 1975 WM, 1981 WM20, 1983 WM, 1992 WM20, 1993 WM, 1999 WM18, 2001 WM, 2009 WW18, 2010 WM, 2011 WM18)
*co-hosts Chamonix, Vienna, Berlin

**Russia**
11 (1957 WM, 1973 WM, 1979 WM, 1983 WM20, 1986 WM, 1988 WM20, 2000 WM, 2001 WM20, 2003 WM18, 2007 WM, 2008 WM18)

**Austria**
8 (1930 WM*, 1964OG-WM, 1967 WM, 1976 OG, 1977 WM, 1987 WM, 1996 WM, 2005 WM)
*co-hosts Chamonix, Vienna, Berlin

**France**
5 (1924 OG-WM, 1930 WM*, 1951 WM, 1968 OG-WM, 1992 OG)
*co-hosts Chamonix, Vienna, Berlin

**Italy** 4 (1934 WM, 1956 OG-WM, 1994 WM, 2006 OG)
**Norway** 4 (1952 OG-WM, 1958 WM, 1994 OG, 1999 WM)
**Japan** 2 (1972 OG, 1998 OG)
**Yugoslavia** 2 (1966 WM, 1984 OG)
**Great Britain** 2 (1937 WM, 1950 WM)
**Poland** 2 (1931 WM, 1976 WM)
**Belarus** 2 (2004 WM18, 2010 WM18)
**Slovakia** 2 (2002 WM18, 2011 WM)
**Belgium** 1 (1920 OG-WM)
**Latvia** 1 (2006 WM)
**China** 1 (2008 WW)

| City (Country) | Total | Breakdown |
|---|---|---|
| Albertville (FRA) | 46 | 46 (1992 OG-M) |
| Amherst (USA) | 7 | 7 (1996 WM20) |
| Anchorage (USA) | 21 | 21 (1989 WM20) |
| Angelholm (SWE) | 17 | 17 (2006 WM18) |
| Antwerp (BEL) | 10 | 10 (1920 OG-M) |
| Augsburg (FRG) | 3 | 3 (1981 WM20) |
| Banska Bystrica (TCH) | 14 | 14 (1977 WM20) |
| Basel (SUI) | 47 | 25 (1939 WM), 3 (1953 WM), 19 (1998 WM) |
| Berlin (GER) | 2 | 2 (1930 WM) |
| Berne (SUI) | 79 | 15 (1971 WM), 34 (1990 WM), 32 (2009 WM) |
| Bloomington (USA) | 9 | 9 (1982 WM20) |
| Bobruisk (BLR) | 14 | 14 (2010 WM18) |
| Bollnas (SWE) | 2 | 2 (1993 WM20) |
| Bolzano (ITA) | 16 | 16 (1994 WM) |
| Boston (USA) | 10 | 10 (1996 WM20) |
| Brainerd (USA) | 1 | 1 (1982 WM20) |
| Brandon (CAN) | 8 | 1 (1982 WM20), 7 (1999 WM20) |
| Brantford (CAN) | 2 | 2 (1986 WM20) |
| Bratislava (TCH/SVK) | 53 | 6 (1959 WM), 15 (1992 WM), 32 (2011 WM) |
| Breclav (CZE) | 4 | 4 (2012 WM18) |
| Brno (TCH) | 18 | 6 (1959 WM), 12 (2012 WM18) |
| Buffalo (USA) | 22 | 1 (1984 CC), 21 (2011 WM20) |
| Burlington (USA) | 21 | 21 (2012 WW) |
| Burnsville (USA) | 1 | 1 (1982 WM20) |
| Calgary (CAN) | 94 | 6 (1984 CC), 2 (1987 CC), 42 (1988 OG-M), 3 (1995 WM20), 20 (2008 WW18), 21 (2012 WM20) |
| Camrose (CAN) | 1 | 1 (1995 WM20) |
| Ceske Budejovice (CZE) | 14 | 14 (2005 WM18) |
| Chamonix (FRA) | 25 | 16 (1924 OG-M), 9 (1930 WM) |
| Chestnut Hill (USA) | 2 | 2 (1996 WM20) |
| Chicago (USA) | 23 | 2 (1991 CC), 21 (2010 WW18) |
| Chicoutimi (CAN) | 3 | 3 (1978 WM20) |
| Cologne (FRG/GER) | 52 | 11 (1955 WM), 11 (2001 WM), 1 (2004 WCH), 29 (2010 WM) |
| Colorado Springs (USA) | 16 | 16 (1962 WM) |
| Cornwall (CAN) | 6 | 6 (1978 WM20) |
| Cortina D'Ampezzo (ITA) | 33 | 33 (1956 OG-M) |
| Crimmitschau (GER) | 17 | 17 (2011 WM18) |
| Davos (SUI) | 50 | 50 (1935 WM) |
| Denver (USA) | 12 | 12 (1962 WM) |
| Detroit (USA) | 1 | 1 (1991 CC) |
| Dortmund (FRG/GER) | 34 | 3 (1955 WM), 16 (1983 WM), 15 (1993 WM) |
| Dresden (GER) | 14 | 14 (2011 WM18) |
| Duluth (USA) | 4 | 4 (1982 WM20) |
| Dundas (CAN) | 1 | 1 (1986 WM20) |
| Dusseldorf (FRG/GER) | 33 | 12 (1955 WM), 15 (1975 WM), 6 (1983 WM) |
| Edmonton (CAN) | 23 | 5 (1981 CC), 5 (1984 CC), 3 (1995 WM20), 10 (2012 WM20) |
| Espoo (FIN) | 21 | 1 (1985 WM20), 20 (1999 WW) |
| Falun (SWE) | 3 | 3 (1993 WM20) |
| Fargo (USA) | 17 | 17 (2009 WM18) |
| Fire Lake (USA) | 7 | 7 (1989 WM20) |
| Fribourg (SUI) | 6 | 6 (1990 WM) |
| Frydek-Mistek (CZE) | 14 | 14 (1994 WM20) |
| Fussen (FRG/GER) | 66 | 5 (1981 WM20), 21 (1992 WM20), 20 (1999 WM18), 20 (2009 WW18) |
| Garmisch-Partenkirchen (GER) | 38 | 37 (1936 OG-M), 1 (1996 WCH) |
| Gavle (SWE) | 31 | 15 (1993 WM20), 16 (1995 WM) |
| Gelsenkirchen (GER) | 1 | 1 (2010 WM) |
| Geneva (SUI) | 44 | 13 (1961 WM), 15 (1971 WM), 16 (1997 WM20) |
| Georgetown (CAN) | 1 | 1 (1986 WM20) |
| Gothenburg (SWE) | 31 | 6 (1981 WM), 25 (2002 WM) |
| Grand Forks (USA) | 22 | 22 (2005 WM20) |
| Grand Rapids (USA) | 1 | 1 (1982 WM20) |
| Grenoble (FRA) | 43 | 43 (1968 OG-M) |
| Guelph (CAN) | 1 | 1 (1986 WM20) |
| Halifax (CAN) | 68 | 1 (1984 CC), 1 (1987 CC), 21 (2003 WM20), 20 (2004 WW), 25 (2008 WM) |
| Halmstad (SWE) | 14 | 14 (2006 WM18) |
| Hamar (NOR) | 20 | 20 (1999 WM) |
| Hameenlinna (FIN) | 48 | 15 (1998 WM20), 13 (2004 WM20), 20 (2009 WW) |
| Hamilton (CAN) | 20 | 9 (1986 WM20), 7 (1987 CC), 4 (1991 CC) |
| Hanover (GER) | 31 | 31 (2001 WM) |
| Harbin (CHN) | 20 | 20 (2008 WW) |
| Hartford (USA) | 2 | 2 (1987 CC) |
| Heinola (FIN) | 15 | 15 (2001 WM18) |
| Helsinki (FIN) | 216 | 30 (1974 WM), 12 (1980 WM20), 20 (1982 WM), 10 (1985 WM20), 12 (1990 WM20), 8 (1991 WM), 2 (1996 WCH), 28 (1997 WM), 19 (1998 WM20), 4 (2001 WM18), 25 (2003 WM), 18 (2004 WM20), 3 (2004 WCH), 34 (2012 WM) |
| Hofors (SWE) | 2 | 2 (1993 WM20) |
| Hradec Kralove (CZE) | 17 | 17 (2002 WM20) |
| Hudiksvall (SWE) | 1 | 1 (1993 WM20) |
| Hull (CAN) | 4 | 4 (1978 WM20) |
| Humboldt (CAN) | 1 | 1 (1991 WM20) |
| Innisfail (CAN) | 1 | 1 (1995 WM20) |
| Innsbruck (AUT) | 114 | 56 (1964 OG-M), 30 (1976 OG-M), 28 (2005 WM) |
| International Falls (USA) | 1 | 1 (1982 WM20) |
| Jonkoping (SWE) | 18 | 18 (2002 WM) |
| Kamloops (CAN) | 5 | 5 (2006 WM20) |
| Karlskoga (SWE) | 11 | 11 (1979 WM20) |
| Karlstad (SWE) | 24 | 11 (1979 WM20), 13 (2002 WM) |
| Katowice (POL) | 40 | 40 (1976 WM) |
| Kaufbeuren (FRG/GER) | 24 | 4 (1981 WM20), 7 (1992 WM20), 13 (1999 WM18) |
| Kauniainen (FIN) | 5 | 5 (1990 WM20) |
| Kazan (RUS) | 31 | 31 (2008 WM18) |
| Kelowna (CAN) | 5 | 5 (2006 WM20) |
| Kempten (FRG) | 1 | 1 (1981 WM20) |
| Kenora (CAN) | 1 | 1 (1982 WM20) |
| Kerava (FIN) | 4 | 4 (1990 WM20) |
| Kindersley (CAN) | 1 | 1 (1991 WM20) |
| Kitchener (CAN) | 22 | 2 (1986 WM20), 20 (1997 WW) |
| Kladno (TCH) | 5 | 5 (1959 WM) |
| Kloten (SUI) | 41 | 17 (2000 WM18), 24 (2010 WM) |
| Kolin (TCH) | 5 | 5 (1959 WM) |
| Kosice (SVK) | 24 | 24 (2011 WM) |
| Krefeld (FRG) | 10 | 10 (1955 WM) |
| Krynica (POL) | 29 | 29 (1931 WM) |
| Lacombe (CAN) | 1 | 1 (1995 WM20) |
| Lahti (FIN) | 12 | 12 (2001 WM18) |
| Lake Placid (USA) | 67 | 12 (1932 OG-M), 35 (1980 OG-M), 20 (1994 WW) |
| Landsberg (FRG) | 5 | 5 (1981 WM20) |
| Lausanne (SUI) | 14 | 14 (1961 WM) |
| Leduc (CAN) | 1 | 1 (1995 WM20) |
| Leksand (SWE) | 15 | 15 (2007 WM20) |
| Liberec (CZE) | 14 | 14 (2008 WM20) |
| Lillehammer (NOR) | 57 | 46 (1994 OG-M), 11 (1999 WM) |
| Linkoping (SWE) | 10 | 10 (2005 WW) |
| Ljubljana (YUG) | 28 | 28 (1966 WM) |
| London (CAN) | 3 | 1 (1984 CC), 2 (1986 WM20) |
| London (GBR) | 64 | 37 (1937 WM), 27 (1950 WM) |
| Mankato (USA) | 1 | 1 (1982 WM20) |
| Mannheim (GER) | 26 | 26 (2010 WM) |
| Marlborough (USA) | 8 | 8 (1996 WM20) |
| Milan (ITA) | 41 | 33, (1934 WM), 8 (1994 WM) |
| Minneapolis (USA) | 21 | 1 (1982 WM20), 20 (2001 WW) |
| Minsk (BLR) | 48 | 31 (2004 WM18), 17 (2010 WM18) |
| Mississauga (CAN) | 20 | 20 (2000 WW) |
| Mlada Boleslav (TCH) | 5 | 5 (1959 WM) |
| Montreal (CAN) | 36 | 1 (1972 SS), 7 (1976 CC), 7 (1978 WM20), 6 (1981 CC), 3 (1984 CC), 3 (1987 CC), 3 (1991 CC), 4 (1996 WCH), 2 (2004 WCH) |
| Moorhead (USA) | 14 | 14 (2009 WM18) |
| Moose Jaw (CAN) | 1 | 1 (1991 WM20) |
| Mora (SWE) | 16 | 16 (2007 WM20) |
| Morden (CAN) | 2 | 2 (1999 WM20) |
| Morges (SUI) | 15 | 15 (1997 WM20) |
| Moscow (URS/RUS) | 224 | 28 (1957 WM), 4 (1972 SS), 30 (1973 WM), 32 (1979 WM), 40 (1986 WM), 28 (1988 WM20), 30 (2001 WM20), 32 (2007 WM) |
| Munich (FRG/GER) | 59 | 15 (1975 WM), 18 (1983 WM), 26 (1993 WM) |
| Mytishi (RUS) | 24 | 24 (2007 WM) |
| Nagano (JPN) | 52 | 35 (1998 OG-M), 17 (1998 OG-W) |
| Newmarket (CAN) | 1 | 1 (1986 WM20) |
| New Ulm (USA) | 1 | 1 (1982 WM20) |
| New York (USA) | 2 | 2 (1996 WCH) |
| Niagara (USA) | 10 | 10 (2011 WM20) |
| Niagara Falls (CAN) | 1 | 1 (1986 WM20) |
| Nitra (TCH) | 7 | 7 (1987 WM20) |
| Norrkoping (SWE) | 24 | 14 (1984 WM20), 10 (2005 WW) |
| North Battleford (CAN) | 1 | 1 (1991 WM20) |
| Nuremberg (GER) | 14 | 14 (2001 WM) |
| Nykoping (SWE) | 14 | 14 (1984 WM20) |
| Nynashamn (SWE) | 1 | 1 (1949 WM) |
| Oakville (CAN) | 1 | 1 (1986 WM20) |
| Oberstdorf (FRG) | 2 | 2 (1981 WM20) |
| Orillia (CAN) | 1 | 1 (1986 WM20) |
| Oshawa (CAN) | 2 | 2 (1986 WM20) |
| Oslo (NOR) | 83 | 37 (1952 OG-M), 28 (1958 WM), 18 (1999 WM) |
| Ostrava (TCH/CZE) | 42 | 6 (1959 WM), 14 (1994 WM20), 22 (2004 WM) |
| Ottawa (CAN) | 57 | 1 (1976 CC), 2 (1981 CC), 20 (1990 WW), (1996 WCH), 31 (2009 WM20) |
| Pardubice (CZE) | 35 | 18 (2002 WM20), 17 (2008 WM20) |
| Paris (FRA) | 21 | 21 (1951 WM) |
| Philadelphia (USA) | 4 | 1 (1976 CC), 3 (1996 WCH) |
| Piestany (TCH/SVK) | 31 | 7 (1987 WM20), 24 (2002 WM18) |

| | | |
|---|---|---|
| Pittsburgh (USA) | 1 | 1 (1991 CC) |
| Plzen (CZE) | 17 | 17 (2005 WM18) |
| Podolsk (RUS) | 4 | 4 (2001 WM20) |
| Ponoka (CAN) | 1 | 1 (1995 WM20) |
| Portage La Prairie (CAN) | 3 | 3 (1999 WM20) |
| Prague (TCH/CZE) | 286 | 33 (1933 WM), 40 (1938 WM), 28 (1947 WM), 15 (1959 WM), 30 (1972 WM), 40 (1978 WM), 40 (1985 WM), 24 (1992 WM), 1 (1996 WCH), 34 (2004 WM), 1 (2004 WCH) |
| Prerov (CZE) | 10 | 10 (2012 WW18) |
| Prince Albert (CAN) | 2 | 2 (1991 WM20) |
| Quebec City (CAN) | 36 | 36 1 (1976 CC), 5 (1978 WM20), 1 (1991 CC), 29 (2008 WM) |
| Rauma (FIN) | 14 | 14 (2007 WM18) |
| Red Deer (CAN) | 11 | 11 (1995 WM20) |
| Regina (CAN) | 19 | 2 (1987 CC), 7 (1991 WM20), 10 (2010 WM20) |
| Riga (LAT) | 56 | 56 (2006 WM) |
| Rochester (USA) | 1 | 1 (1982 WM20) |
| Rocky Mountain House (CAN) | 1 | 1 (1995 WM20) |
| Rosetown (CAN) | 1 | 1 (1991 WM20) |
| Salt Lake City (USA) | 55 | 35 (2002 OG-M), 20 (2002 OG-W) |
| Sapporo (JPN) | 25 | 25 (1972 OG-M) |
| Sarajevo (YUG) | 36 | 36 (1984 OG-M) |
| Saskatoon (CAN) | 36 | 13 (1991 WM20), 2 (1991 CC), 21 (2010 WM20) |
| Selkirk (CAN) | 7 | 4 (1999 WM20), 3 (2007 WW) |
| Sherwood Park (CAN) | 1 | 1 (1995 WM20) |
| Skelleftea (SWE) | 16 | 16 (2000 WM20) |
| Skutskar (SWE) | 1 | 1 (1993 WM20) |
| Springfield (USA) | 2 | 2 (1996 WM20) |
| Spruce Grove (CAN) | 1 | 1 (1995 WM20) |
| Squaw Valley (USA) | 30 | 30 (1960 OG-M) |
| St. Catharines (CAN) | 1 | 1 (1986 WM20) |
| St. Cloud (USA) | 1 | 1 (1982 WM20) |
| Stettler (CAN) | 2 | 2 (1995 WM20) |
| St. Moritz (SUI) | 54 | 18 (1928 OG-M), 36 (1948 OG-M) |
| Stockholm (SWE) | 293 | 30 (1949 WM), 28 (1954 WM), 28 (1963 WM), 30 (1969 WM), 30 (1970 WM), 26 (1981 WM), 40 (1989 WM), 24 (1995 WM), 2 (1996 WCH), 3 (2004 WCH), 22 (2011 WW18), 30 (2012 WM) |
| St. Paul (USA) | 4 | 4 (2004 WCH) |
| St. Petersburg URS/(RUS) | 84 | 28 (1983 WM20—Leningrad), 56 (2000 WM) |
| Stratford (CAN) | 1 | 1 (1986 WM20) |
| Sydney (CAN) | 13 | 3 (1987 CC), 10 (2003 WM20) |
| Tampere (FIN) | 107 | 28 (1965 WM), 14 (1982 WM), 6 (1991 WM), 20 (1992 WW), 9 (1997 WM), 13 (2003 WM), 17 (2007 WM18) |
| Teulon (CAN) | 1 | 1 (1999 WM20) |
| Thief River Falls (USA) | 9 | 9 (2005 WM20) |
| Topolcany (TCH) | 7 | 7 (1987 WM20) |
| Toronto (CAN) | 18 | 1 (1972 SS), 5 (1976 CC), 2 (1986 WM20), 5 (1991 CC), 5 (2004 WCH) |
| Trencin (TCH) | 7 | 7 (1987 WM20) |
| Trnava (SVK) | 24 | 24 (2002 WM18) |
| Turin (ITA) | 58 | 38 (2006 OG-M), 20 (2006 OG-W) |
| Turku (FIN) | 78 | 12 (1985 WM20), 7 (1990 WM20), 26 (1991 WM), 15 (1997 WM), 18 (2003 WM) |
| Umea (SWE) | 19 | 19 (2000 WM20) |
| Uppsala (SWE) | 4 | 4 (1993 WM20) |
| Val di Fassa (ITA) | 15 | 15 (1994 WM) |
| Vancouver (CAN) | 75 | 1 (1972 SS), 2 (1984 CC), 1 (1996 WCH), 21 (2006 WM20), 30 (2010 OG-M), 20 (2010 OG-W) |
| Vantaa (FIN) | 13 | 8 (1980 WM20), 5 (1985 WM20) |
| Vienna (AUT) | 177 | 1 (1930 WM), 28 (1967 WM), 40 (1977 WM), 40 (1987 WM), 40 (1996 WM), 28 (2005 WM) |
| Virginia (USA) | 1 | 1 (1982 WM20) |
| Weinfelden (SUI) | 14 | 14 (2000 WM18) |
| Wetaskiwin (CAN) | 1 | 1 (1995 WM20) |
| Winnipeg (CAN) | 41 | 1 (1972 SS), 1 (1976 CC), 5 (1981 CC), 3 (1982 WM20), 14 (1999 WM20), 17 (2007 WW) |
| Winterthur (SUI) | 10 | 10 (2011 WW) |
| Worcester (USA) | 2 | 2 (1996 WM20) |
| Yaroslavl (RUS) | 31 | 31 (2003 WM18) |
| Yorkton (CAN) | 1 | 1 (1991 WM20) |
| Zlin (CZE) | 12 | 12 (2012 WW18) |
| Znojmo (CZE) | 15 | 15 (2012 WM18) |
| Zurich (SUI) | 67 | 23 (1939 WM), 3 (1953 WM), 30 (1998 WM), 11 (2011 WW) |
| Zvolen (TCH) | 14 | 14 (1977 WM20) |

# Event Attendance

**OLYMPICS, MEN**

| Year | Host City | GP | Attendance | Average |
|---|---|---|---|---|
| 1920 | Antwerp | 10 | 6,946 | 695 |
| 1924 | Chamonix | 16 | 24,177 | 1,511 |
| 1928 | St. Moritz | 18 | n/a | n/a |
| 1932 | Lake Placid | 12 | n/a | n/a |
| 1936 | Garmisch-Partenkirchen | 37 | n/a | n/a |
| 1948 | St. Moritz | 36 | n/a | n/a |
| 1952 | Oslo | 37 | n/a | n/a |
| 1956 | Cortina d'Ampezzo | 33 | 122,230 | 3,704 |
| 1960 | Squaw Valley | 30 | n/a | n/a |
| 1964 | Innsbruck | 28 | 199,450 | 7,123 |
| 1968 | Grenoble | 28 | n/a | n/a |
| 1972 | Sapporo | 15 | n/a | n/a |
| 1976 | Innsbruck | 15 | 85,000 | 5,160 |
| 1980 | Lake Placid | 35 | 144,700 | 4,134 |
| 1984 | Sarajevo | 36 | n/a | n/a |
| 1988 | Calgary | 42 | n/a | n/a |
| 1992 | Albertville | 46 | 237,370 | 5,160 |
| 1994 | Lillehammer | 46 | 334,373 | 7,269 |
| 1998 | Nagano | 35 | 282,535 | 8,072 |
| 2002 | Salt Lake City | 35 | 268,139 | 7,661 |
| 2006 | Turin | 38 | 236,013 | 6,211 |
| 2010 | Vancouver | 30 | **491,444** | **16,381** |

**WORLD CHAMPIONSHIP (MEN)**

| Year | Host City | GP | Attendance | Average |
|---|---|---|---|---|
| 1930 | Chamonix/Various | 12 | n/a | n/a |
| 1931 | Krynica | 29 | n/a | n/a |
| 1933 | Prague | 33 | n/a | n/a |
| 1934 | Milan | 33 | n/a | n/a |
| 1935 | Davos | 50 | n/a | n/a |
| 1937 | London | 37 | n/a | n/a |
| 1938 | Prague | 40 | n/a | n/a |
| 1939 | Zurich, Basel | 48 | 299,600 | 6,242 |
| *1940-1946 No championships (Second World War)* | | | | |
| 1947 | Prague | 28 | n/a | n/a |
| 1949 | Stockholm | 31 | n/a | n/a |
| 1950 | London | 27 | 127,700 | 4,730 |
| 1951 | Paris | 21 | n/a | n/a |
| 1953 | Zurich, Basel | 6 | 53,000 | 8,833 |
| 1954 | Stockholm | 28 | 148,399 | 5,300 |
| 1955 | Krefeld/Various | 36 | 153,300 | 4,258 |
| 1957 | Moscow | 28 | 223,700 | 7,989 |
| 1958 | Oslo | 28 | 73,786 | 2,653 |
| 1959 | Prague/Various | 48 | 406,601 | 8,471 |
| 1961 | Geneva, Lausanne | 27 | 141,300 | 5,233 |
| 1962 | Colorado Springs, Denver | 28 | 70,702 | 2,525 |
| 1963 | Stockholm | 28 | 216,056 | 7,716 |
| 1965 | Tampere | 28 | 178,968 | 6,392 |
| 1966 | Ljubljana | 28 | 147,492 | 5,268 |
| 1967 | Vienna | 28 | 172,800 | 6,171 |
| 1969 | Stockholm | 30 | 196,769 | 6,559 |
| 1970 | Stockholm | 30 | 154,485 | 5,150 |
| 1971 | Berne, Geneva | 30 | 190,251 | 6,342 |
| 1972 | Prague | 30 | 285,564 | 9,519 |
| 1973 | Moscow | 30 | 331,500 | 11,050 |
| 1974 | Helsinki | 30 | 192,856 | 6,429 |
| 1975 | Munich, Dusseldorf | 30 | 169,000 | 5,633 |
| 1976 | Katowice | 40 | 219,000 | 5,475 |
| 1977 | Vienna | 40 | 171,900 | 4,298 |
| 1978 | Prague | 40 | 362,642 | 9,066 |
| 1979 | Moscow | 32 | 354,500 | **11,078** |
| 1981 | Gothenburg, Stockholm | 32 | 171,675 | 5,365 |
| 1982 | Helsinki, Tampere | 34 | 193,224 | 5,683 |
| 1983 | Munich/Various | 40 | 189,555 | 4,739 |
| 1985 | Prague | 40 | 411,659 | 10,291 |
| 1986 | Moscow | 40 | 375,820 | 9,396 |
| 1987 | Vienna | 40 | 205,401 | 5,135 |
| 1989 | Stockholm, Sodertalje | 40 | 388,563 | 9,714 |
| 1990 | Berne, Fribourg | 40 | 250,309 | 6,258 |
| 1991 | Turku, Helsinki, Tampere | 40 | 310,627 | 7,766 |
| 1992 | Prague, Bratislava | 39 | 249,748 | 6,404 |
| 1993 | Munich, Dortmund | 41 | 226,379 | 5,521 |
| 1994 | Milan, Bolzano, Canazei | 39 | 154,210 | 3,954 |
| 1995 | Stockholm, Gavle | 40 | 326,571 | 8,164 |
| 1996 | Vienna | 40 | 186,830 | 4,671 |
| 1997 | Helsinki, Turku, Tampere | 52 | 526,172 | 10,119 |
| 1998 | Zurich, Basel | 49 | 220,641 | 4,503 |
| 1999 | Lillehammer/Various | 49 | 180,394 | 3,682 |
| 2000 | St. Petersburg | 56 | 318,449 | 5,687 |
| 2001 | Hanover/Cologne | 56 | 407,542 | 7,278 |
| 2002 | Gothenburg/Various | 56 | 305,541 | 5,456 |
| 2003 | Helsinki/Various | 56 | 454,693 | 8,120 |
| 2004 | Prague, Ostrava | 56 | **552,097** | 9,859 |
| 2005 | Vienna, Innsbruck | 56 | 323,974 | 5,785 |
| 2006 | Riga | 56 | 331,626 | 5,922 |
| 2007 | Moscow, Mytishi | 56 | 342,708 | 6,120 |
| 2008 | Quebec City, Halifax | 54 | 477,040 | 8,834 |
| 2009 | Berne, Kloten | 56 | 379,044 | 6,768 |
| 2010 | Cologne/Mannheim | 56 | 548,768 | 9,799 |
| 2011 | Bratislava, Kosice | 56 | 406,804 | 7,264 |
| 2012 | Helsinki, Stockholm | 64 | 451,054 | 7,047 |

**IIHF-NHL INVITATIONALS**

| Event | GP | Attendance | Average |
|---|---|---|---|
| 1972 SS Various | 8 | 120,673 | 15,084 |
| 1976 CC Various | 17 | 244,925 | 14,407 |
| 1981 CC Various | 18 | n/a | n/a |
| 1984 CC Various | 19 | 158,193 | 8,326 |
| 1987 CC Various | 20 | 188,652 | 9,433 |
| 1991 CC Various | 19 | 222,971 | 11,735 |
| 1996 WCH Various | 19 | 279,310 | 14,701 |
| 2004 WCH Various | 19 | 303,249 | 15,960 |

**U20 WORLD CHAMPIONSHIP**

| Year | Host City | GP | Attendance | Average |
|---|---|---|---|---|
| 1977 | Banska Bystrica, Zvolen | 28 | 53,172 | 1,899 |
| 1978 | Montreal, Quebec | 25 | 41,681 | 1,667 |
| 1979 | Karlstad, Karlskoga | 22 | n/a | n/a |
| 1980 | Helsinki/Various | 20 | 60,784 | 3,039 |
| 1981 | Landsberg/Various | 20 | n/a | n/a |
| 1982 | Bloomington/Various | 28 | 86,941 | 3,105 |
| 1983 | Leningrad | 28 | n/a | n/a |
| 1984 | Norrkoping, Nykoping | 28 | 32,384 | 1,157 |
| 1985 | Helsinki/Various | 28 | 61,023 | 2,179 |
| 1986 | Hamilton/Various | 28 | 154,172 | 5,506 |
| 1987 | Topolcany/Various | 28 | n/a | n/a |
| 1988 | Moscow | 28 | 46,220 | 1,651 |
| 1989 | Anchorage, Fire Lake | 28 | 45,934 | 1,641 |
| 1990 | Helsinki/Various | 28 | n/a | n/a |
| 1991 | Saskatoon/Various | 28 | 137,067 | 4,895 |
| 1992 | Fussen, Kaufbeuren | 28 | 55,750 | 1,991 |
| 1993 | Gavle/Various | 28 | 36,397 | 1,300 |
| 1994 | Ostrava, Frydek-Mistek | 28 | 58,143 | 2,077 |
| 1995 | Red Deer/Various | 28 | n/a | n/a |

| | | | | |
|---|---|---|---|---|
| 1996 | Boston/Various | 31 | n/a | n/a |
| 1997 | Geneva, Morges | 31 | 31,336 | 1,011 |
| 1998 | Helsinki, Hameenlinna | 34 | 139,680 | 4,108 |
| 1999 | Winnipeg/Various | 31 | 173,453 | 5,595 |
| 2000 | Skelleftea, Umea | 34 | 41,693 | 1,226 |
| 2001 | Moscow, Podolsk | 34 | 84,100 | 2,474 |
| 2002 | Pardubice, Hradec Kralove | 34 | 111,128 | 3,268 |
| 2003 | Halifax, Sydney | 31 | 242,173 | 7,812 |
| 2004 | Helsinki, Hameenlinna | 31 | 116,556 | 3,760 |
| 2005 | Grand Forks, Thief River Falls | 31 | 193,256 | 6,234 |
| 2006 | Vancouver/Various | 31 | 325,138 | 10,488 |
| 2007 | Leksand, Mora | 31 | 63,493 | 2,048 |
| 2008 | Pardubice, Liberec | 31 | 103,179 | 3,328 |
| 2009 | Ottawa | 31 | **453,282** | **14,622** |
| 2010 | Saskatoon, Regina | 31 | 301,944 | 9,740 |
| 2011 | Buffalo, Niagara | 31 | 331,297 | 10,687 |
| 2012 | Calgary, Edmonton | 31 | 444,718 | 14,345 |

**U18 WORLD CHAMPIONSHIP (MEN)**

| | | | | |
|---|---|---|---|---|
| 1999 | Fussen/Kaufbeuren | 33 | 15,491 | 469 |
| 2000 | Kloten,Weinfelden | 31 | 33,988 | 1,096 |
| 2001 | Heinola/Various | 33 | 26,594 | 806 |
| 2002 | Piestany, Trnava | 48 | 93,914 | 1,957 |
| 2003 | Yaroslavl | 31 | 90,150 | 1,908 |
| 2004 | Minsk | 31 | 76,650 | 2,473 |
| 2005 | Ceske Budejovice, Plzen | 32 | 71,936 | 2,248 |
| 2006 | Angelhom, Halmstad | 30 | 11,798 | 393 |
| 2007 | Tampere, Rauma | 31 | 53,312 | 1,720 |
| 2008 | Kazan | 31 | 66,839 | 2,156 |
| 2009 | Fargo, Moorhead | 31 | 44,779 | 1,444 |
| 2010 | Minsk | 31 | **115,340** | **3,721** |
| 2011 | Crimmitschau, Dresden | 31 | 47,289 | 1,525 |
| 2012 | Brno, Znojmo | 31 | 26,228 | 846 |

**OLYMPICS, WOMEN**

| | | | | |
|---|---|---|---|---|
| 1998 | Nagano | 17 | 81,707 | 4,806 |
| 2002 | Salt Lake City | 20 | 129,435 | 6,472 |
| 2006 | Turin | 20 | 91,609 | 4,580 |
| 2010 | Vancouver | 20 | **162,419** | **8,121** |

**WOMEN'S WORLD CHAMPIONSHIP**

| | | | | |
|---|---|---|---|---|
| 1990 | Ottawa | 20 | n/a | n/a |
| 1992 | Tampere | 20 | 18,540 | 927 |
| 1994 | Lake Placid | 20 | n/a | n/a |
| 1997 | Kitchener | 20 | 60,418 | 3,021 |
| 1999 | Espoo | 20 | 25,234 | 1,262 |
| 2000 | Mississauga | 20 | 57,444 | 2,872 |
| 2001 | Minneapolis | 20 | 21,847 | 1,092 |
| 2004 | Halifax | 20 | 89,461 | 4,473 |
| 2005 | Linkoping, Norrkoping | 20 | 21,436 | 1,072 |
| 2007 | Winnipeg, Selkirk | 20 | **119,231** | **5,962** |
| 2008 | Harbin | 20 | 26,067 | 1,303 |
| 2009 | Hameenlinna | 20 | 28,980 | 1,449 |
| 2011 | Zurich, Winterthur | 21 | 28,437 | 1,354 |
| 2012 | Burlington | 21 | 28,605 | 1,362 |

**U18 WOMEN'S WORLD CHAMPIONSHIP**

| | | | | |
|---|---|---|---|---|
| 2008 | Calgary | 20 | 9,872 | 494 |
| 2009 | Fussen | 20 | 4,810 | 241 |
| 2010 | Chicago | 21 | 4,270 | 203 |
| 2011 | Stockholm | 22 | 3,317 | 150 |
| 2012 | Prerov, Zlin | 22 | **17,480** | **794** |

# Goals Per Game

**OLYMPICS, MEN**

| Year | Teams | Games | Goals | Avg/Game |
|---|---|---|---|---|
| 1920 | 7 | 10 | 99 | 9.90 |
| 1924 | 8 | 16 | 277 | 17.3 |
| 1928 | 11 | 18 | 98 | 5.44 |
| 1932 | 4 | 12 | 69 | 5.75 |
| 1936 | 15 | 37 | 165 | 4.46 |
| 1948 | 8 | 36 | 482 | 13.39 |
| 1952 | 9 | 37 | 335 | 9.05 |
| 1956 | 10 | 33 | 262 | 7.94 |
| 1960 | 9 | 30 | 334 | 11.13 |
| 1964 | 16 | 56 | 469 | 8.38 |
| 1968 | 14 | 43 | 316 | 7.35 |
| 1972 | 11 | 25 | 190 | 7.60 |
| 1976 | 12 | 30 | 254 | 8.47 |
| 1980 | 12 | 35 | 308 | 8.80 |
| 1984 | 12 | 36 | 297 | 8.25 |
| 1988 | 12 | 42 | 310 | 7.38 |
| 1992 | 12 | 46 | 316 | 6.87 |
| 1994 | 12 | 46 | 308 | 6.70 |
| 1998 | 14 | 35 | 210 | 6.00 |
| 2002 | 14 | 35 | 213 | 6.09 |
| 2006 | 12 | 38 | 206 | 5.42 |
| 2010 | 12 | 30 | 180 | 6.00 |

**WORLD CHAMPIONSHIP (MEN)**

| Year | Teams | Games | Goals | Avg/Game |
|---|---|---|---|---|
| 1930 | 12 | 12 | 50 | 4.17 |
| 1931 | 10 | 29 | 119 | 4.10 |
| 1933 | 12 | 33 | 115 | 3.48 |
| 1934 | 12 | 33 | 127 | 3.85 |
| 1935 | 15 | 50 | 254 | 5.08 |
| 1937 | 11 | 39 | 224 | 5.74 |
| 1938 | 14 | 40 | 159 | 3.98 |
| 1939 | 14 | 48 | 267 | 5.56 |
| 1947 | 8 | 28 | 337 | 12.04 |
| 1949 | 10 | 31 | 360 | 11.61 |
| 1950 | 9 | 27 | 302 | 11.19 |
| 1951 | 7 | 21 | 180 | 8.57 |
| 1953 | 4 | 6 | 64 | 10.67 |
| 1954 | 8 | 28 | 222 | 7.93 |
| 1955 | 9 | 36 | 319 | 8.86 |
| 1957 | 8 | 28 | 300 | 10.71 |
| 1958 | 8 | 28 | 257 | 9.18 |
| 1959 | 15 | 48 | 397 | 8.27 |
| 1961 | 8 | 28 | 236 | 8.43 |
| 1962 | 8 | 28 | 310 | 11.07 |
| 1963 | 8 | 28 | 256 | 9.14 |
| 1965 | 8 | 28 | 221 | 7.89 |
| 1966 | 8 | 28 | 205 | 7.32 |
| 1967 | 8 | 28 | 205 | 7.32 |
| 1969 | 6 | 30 | 219 | 7.30 |
| 1970 | 6 | 30 | 222 | 7.40 |
| 1971 | 6 | 30 | 234 | 7.80 |
| 1972 | 6 | 30 | 288 | 9.60 |
| 1973 | 6 | 30 | 258 | 8.60 |
| 1974 | 6 | 30 | 236 | 7.87 |
| 1975 | 6 | 30 | 272 | 9.07 |
| 1976 | 8 | 40 | 289 | 7.23 |
| 1977 | 8 | 40 | 338 | 8.45 |
| 1978 | 8 | 40 | 322 | 8.05 |
| 1979 | 8 | 32 | 263 | 8.22 |
| 1981 | 8 | 32 | 288 | 9.00 |
| 1982 | 8 | 34 | 249 | 7.32 |
| 1983 | 8 | 40 | 259 | 6.48 |
| 1985 | 8 | 40 | 305 | 7.63 |
| 1986 | 8 | 40 | 296 | 7.40 |
| 1987 | 8 | 40 | 282 | 7.05 |
| 1989 | 8 | 40 | 282 | 7.05 |
| 1990 | 8 | 40 | 276 | 6.90 |
| 1991 | 8 | 40 | 272 | 6.80 |
| 1992 | 12 | 39 | 242 | 6.21 |
| 1993 | 12 | 41 | 235 | 5.73 |
| 1994 | 12 | 39 | 267 | 6.85 |
| 1995 | 12 | 40 | 229 | 5.73 |
| 1996 | 12 | 40 | 249 | 6.23 |
| 1997 | 12 | 52 | 302 | 5.81 |
| 1998 | 16 | 49 | 276 | 5.63 |
| 1999 | 16 | 49 | 302 | 6.16 |
| 2000 | 16 | 56 | 327 | 5.84 |
| 2001 | 16 | 56 | 318 | 5.68 |
| 2002 | 16 | 56 | 340 | 6.07 |
| 2003 | 16 | 56 | 349 | 6.23 |
| 2004 | 16 | 56 | 286 | 5.11 |
| 2005 | 16 | 56 | 289 | 5.16 |
| 2006 | 16 | 56 | 329 | 5.88 |
| 2007 | 16 | 56 | 361 | 6.45 |
| 2008 | 16 | 54 | 357 | 6.61 |
| 2009 | 16 | 56 | 323 | 5.77 |
| 2010 | 16 | 56 | 277 | 4.95 |
| 2011 | 16 | 56 | 325 | 5.80 |
| 2012 | 16 | 64 | 376 | 5.88 |

**IIHF-NHL INVITATIONALS**

| Year | Teams | Games | Goals | Avg/Game |
|---|---|---|---|---|
| 1972 SS | 2 | 8 | 63 | 7.88 |
| 1976 CC | 6 | 17 | 125 | 7.35 |
| 1981 CC | 6 | 18 | 128 | 7.11 |
| 1984 CC | 6 | 19 | 138 | 7.26 |
| 1987 CC | 6 | 18 | 125 | 6.94 |
| 1991 CC | 6 | 19 | 113 | 5.95 |
| 1996 WCH | 8 | 19 | 140 | 7.37 |
| 2004 WCH | 8 | 19 | 104 | 5.47 |

**U20 WORLD CHAMPIONSHIP**

| Year | Teams | Games | Goals | Avg/Game |
|---|---|---|---|---|
| 1977 | 8 | 28 | 251 | 8.96 |
| 1978 | 8 | 25 | 248 | 9.92 |
| 1979 | 8 | 22 | 171 | 7.77 |
| 1980 | 8 | 20 | 178 | 8.90 |
| 1981 | 8 | 20 | 207 | 10.35 |
| 1982 | 8 | 28 | 282 | 10.07 |
| 1983 | 8 | 28 | 257 | 9.18 |
| 1984 | 8 | 28 | 271 | 9.68 |
| 1985 | 8 | 28 | 230 | 8.21 |
| 1986 | 8 | 28 | 246 | 8.79 |
| 1987 | 8 | 27 | 272 | 10.07 |
| 1988 | 8 | 28 | 247 | 8.82 |
| 1989 | 8 | 28 | 254 | 9.07 |
| 1990 | 8 | 28 | 261 | 9.32 |
| 1991 | 8 | 28 | 253 | 9.04 |
| 1992 | 8 | 28 | 214 | 7.64 |
| 1993 | 8 | 28 | 242 | 8.64 |
| 1994 | 8 | 28 | 195 | 6.94 |
| 1995 | 8 | 28 | 249 | 8.89 |
| 1996 | 10 | 31 | 218 | 7.03 |
| 1997 | 10 | 31 | 204 | 6.58 |
| 1998 | 10 | 34 | 219 | 7.06 |
| 1999 | 10 | 31 | 225 | 7.26 |
| 2000 | 10 | 35 | 218 | 6.23 |
| 2001 | 10 | 34 | 205 | 6.03 |
| 2002 | 10 | 34 | 201 | 5.91 |
| 2003 | 10 | 31 | 187 | 6.03 |
| 2004 | 10 | 31 | 190 | 6.13 |
| 2005 | 10 | 31 | 205 | 6.61 |
| 2006 | 10 | 31 | 195 | 6.29 |
| 2007 | 10 | 31 | 173 | 5.58 |
| 2008 | 10 | 31 | 197 | 6.35 |
| 2009 | 10 | 31 | 241 | 7.77 |
| 2010 | 10 | 31 | 266 | 8.58 |
| 2011 | 10 | 31 | 201 | 6.48 |
| 2012 | 10 | 31 | 230 | 7.42 |

# Single Game Attendance Records

| Event | Attendance | Host | Venue, City | Game, Date |
|---|---|---|---|---|
| OG-M | 17,799 | Canada | Canada Hockey Place, Vancouver | CAN-SVK, February 26, 2010 |
| WM | 77,803 (out) | Germany | Veltins Arena, Gelsenkirchen | USA-GER, May 7, 2010 |
| | 19,132 (in) | Germany | Lanxess Arena, Cologne | RUS-CZE, May 23, 2010 |
| WM20 | 20,380 | Canada | Scotiabank Place, Ottawa | CAN-SWE, January 5, 2009 |
| WM18 | 12,820 | Belarus | Minsk Palace, Minsk | USA-SWE, April 23, 2010 |
| OG-W | 16,805 | Canada | Canada Hockey Place, Vancouver | CAN-USA, February 25, 2010 |
| WW | 15,003 | Canada | MTS Centre, Winnipeg | CAN-USA, April 7, 2007 |
| | 15,003 | Canada | MTS Centre, Winnipeg | CAN-USA, April 10, 2007 |
| WW18 | 3,250 | Czech Rep. | Zimni Stadion, Prerov | FIN-CZE, January 6, 2012 |

**U18 WORLD CHAMPIONSHIP (MEN)**

| Year | Teams | Games | Goals | Avg/Game |
|---|---|---|---|---|
| 1999 | 10 | 33 | 200 | 6.06 |
| 2000 | 10 | 31 | 216 | 6.97 |
| 2001 | 10 | 31 | 239 | 7.71 |
| 2002 | 12 | 48 | 328 | 6.83 |
| 2003 | 10 | 31 | 225 | 7.26 |
| 2004 | 10 | 31 | 186 | 6.00 |
| 2005 | 10 | 31 | 181 | 5.84 |
| 2006 | 10 | 31 | 183 | 5.90 |
| 2007 | 10 | 31 | 210 | 6.77 |
| 2008 | 10 | 31 | 221 | 7.13 |
| 2009 | 10 | 31 | 252 | 8.13 |
| 2010 | 10 | 31 | 219 | 7.06 |
| 2011 | 10 | 31 | 216 | 6.97 |
| 2012 | 10 | 31 | 209 | 6.74 |

**OLYMPICS, WOMEN**

| Year | Teams | Games | Goals | Avg/Game |
|---|---|---|---|---|
| 1998 | 6 | 17 | 119 | 7.00 |
| 2002 | 8 | 20 | 127 | 6.35 |
| 2006 | 8 | 20 | 136 | 6.80 |
| 2010 | 8 | 20 | 146 | 7.30 |

**WOMEN'S WORLD CHAMPIONSHIP**

| Year | Teams | Games | Goals | Avg/Game |
|---|---|---|---|---|
| 1990 | 8 | 20 | 237 | 11.85 |
| 1992 | 8 | 20 | 163 | 8.15 |
| 1994 | 8 | 20 | 185 | 9.25 |
| 1997 | 8 | 20 | 129 | 6.45 |
| 1999 | 8 | 20 | 138 | 6.90 |
| 2000 | 8 | 20 | 148 | 7.40 |
| 2001 | 8 | 20 | 143 | 7.15 |
| 2004 | 9 | 20 | 129 | 6.45 |
| 2005 | 8 | 20 | 121 | 6.05 |
| 2007 | 9 | 20 | 118 | 5.90 |
| 2008 | 9 | 20 | 117 | 5.85 |
| 2009 | 9 | 20 | 140 | 7.00 |
| 2011 | 8 | 21 | 129 | 6.14 |
| 2012 | 8 | 21 | 141 | 6.71 |

**U18 WOMEN'S WORLD CHAMPIONSHIP**

| Year | Teams | Games | Goals | Avg/Game |
|---|---|---|---|---|
| 2008 | 8 | 20 | 168 | 8.40 |
| 2009 | 8 | 20 | 172 | 8.60 |
| 2010 | 8 | 21 | 154 | 7.33 |
| 2011 | 8 | 22 | 138 | 6.27 |
| 2012 | 8 | 22 | 145 | 6.59 |

# Number of Competing Nations

**OLYMPICS, MEN**

| | | |
|---|---|---|
| 1920 OG-M | 7 nations | |
| 1924 OG-M | 8 nations | |
| 1928 OG-M | 11 nations | |
| 1932 OG-M | 4 nations | |
| 1936 OG-M | 15 nations | |
| 1948 OG-M | 9 nations | |
| 1952 OG-WM | 15 nations | 9 Olympics, 6 B pool |
| 1956 OG-WM | 13 nations | 10 Olympics, 3 B pool |
| 1960 OG-M | 9 nations | |
| 1964 OG-WM | 16 nations | 8 Olympics, 8 B pool |
| 1968 OG-WM | 14 nations | 8 Olympics, 6 B pool |
| 1972 OG-M | 11 nations | |
| 1976 OG-M | 12 nations | |
| 1980 OG-M | 12 nations | |
| 1984 OG-M | 11 nations | |
| 1988 OG-M | 12 nations | |
| 1992 OG-M | 12 nations | |
| 1994 OG-M | 12 nations | |
| 1998 OG-M | 14 nations | |
| 2002 OG-M | 14 nations | |
| 2006 OG-M | 12 nations | |
| 2010 OG-M | 12 nations | |

**WORLD CHAMPIONSHIP (MEN)**

| | | |
|---|---|---|
| 1930 WM | 12 nations | |
| 1931 WM | 10 nations | |
| 1933 WM | 12 nations | |
| 1934 WM | 12 nations | |
| 1935 WM | 15 nations | |
| 1937 WM | 11 nations | |
| 1938 WM | 14 nations | |
| 1939 WM | 14 nations | |
| 1947 WM | 8 nations | |
| 1949 WM | 10 nations | |
| 1950 WM | 9 nations | |
| 1951 WM | 13 nations | 7 A pool, 6 B pool |
| 1953 WM | 9 nations | 4 A pool, 5 B pool |
| 1954 WM | 8 nations | |
| 1955 WM | 14 nations | 9 A pool, 5 B pool |
| 1957 WM | 8 nations | |
| 1958 WM | 8 nations | |
| 1959 WM | 15 nations | |
| 1961 WM | 20 nations | 8 A pool, 6 B pool, 6 C pool |
| 1962 WM | 14 nations | 8 A pool, 6 B pool |
| 1963 WM | 21 nations | 8 A pool, 7 B pool, 6 C pool |
| 1965 WM | 15 nations | 8 A pool, 7 B pool |
| 1966 WM | 19 nations | 8 A pool, 8 B pool, 3 C pool |
| 1967 WM | 21 nations | 8 A pool, 8 B pool, 5 C pool |
| 1969 WM | 20 nations | 6 A pool, 8 B pool, 6 C pool |
| 1970 WM | 21 nations | 6 A pool, 8 B pool, 7 C pool |
| 1971 WM | 22 nations | 6 A pool, 8 B pool, 8 C pool |
| 1972 WM | 20 nations | 6 A pool, 7 B pool, 7 C pool |
| 1973 WM | 22 nations | 6 A pool, 8 B pool, 8 C pool |
| 1974 WM | 22 nations | 6 A pool, 8 B pool, 8 C pool |
| 1975 WM | 21 nations | 6 A pool, 8 B pool, 7 C pool |
| 1976 WM | 21 nations | 8 A pool, 8 B pool, 5 C pool |
| 1977 WM | 24 nations | 8 A pool, 9 B pool, 7 C pool |
| 1978 WM | 24 nations | 8 A pool, 8 B pool, 8 C pool |
| 1979 WM | 26 nations | 8 A pool, 10 B pool, 8 C pool |
| 1981 WM | 24 nations | 8 A pool, 8 B pool, 8 C pool |
| 1982 WM | 24 nations | 8 A pool, 8 B pool, 8 C pool |
| 1983 WM | 24 nations | 8 A pool, 8 B pool, 8 C pool |
| 1985 WM | 24 nations | 8 A pool, 8 B pool, 8 C pool |
| 1986 WM | 26 nations | 8 A pool, 8 B pool, 10 C pool |
| 1987 WM | 28 nations | 8 A pool, 8 B pool, 8 C pool, 4 D pool |
| 1989 WM | 29 nations | 8 A pool, 8 B pool, 8 C pool, 5 D pool |
| 1990 WM | 28 nations | 8 A pool, 8 B pool, 9 C pool, 3 D pool |
| 1991 WM | 25 nations | 8 A pool, 8 B pool, 9 C pool |
| 1992 WM | 32 nations | 12 A pool, 8 B pool, 12 C pool |
| 1993 WM | 32 nations | 12 A pool, 8 B pool, 12 C pool |
| 1994 WM | 35 nations | 12 A pool, 8 B pool, 15 C pool |
| 1995 WM | 39 nations | 12 A pool, 8 B pool, 19 C pool |
| 1996 WM | 36 nations | 12 A pool, 8 B pool, 8 C pool, 8 D pool |
| 1997 WM | 36 nations | 12 A pool, 8 B pool, 8 C pool, 8 D pool |
| 1998 WM | 40 nations | 16 A pool, 8 B pool, 8 C pool, 8 D pool |
| 1999 WM | 40 nations | 16 A pool, 8 B pool, 7 C pool, 9 D pool |
| 2000 WM | 42 nations | 16 A pool, 8 B pool, 9 C pool, 9 D pool |
| 2001 WM | 40 nations | 16 Top Pool, 6 Division IA, 6 Division IB, 6 Division IIA, 6 Division IIB |
| 2002 WM | 43 nations | 16 Top Pool, 6 Division IA, 6 Division IB, 6 Division IIA, 6 Division IIB, 3 Division IIQ |
| 2003 WM | 43 nations | 16 Top Pool, 6 Division IA, 6 Division IB, 6 Division IIA, 6 Division IIB, 3 Division III |
| 2004 WM | 45 nations | 16 Top Pool, 6 Division IA, 6 Division IB, 6 Division IIA, 6 Division IIB, 5 Division III |
| 2005 WM | 45 nations | 16 Top Pool, 6 Division IA, 6 Division IB, 6 Division IIA, 6 Division IIB, 5 Division III |
| 2006 WM | 45 nations | 16 Top Pool, 6 Division IA, 6 Division IB, 6 Division IIA, 6 Division IIB, 5 Division III |
| 2007 WM | 45 nations | 16 Top Pool, 6 Division IA, 6 Division IB, 6 Division IIA, 6 Division IIB, 5 Division III |
| 2008 WM | 45 nations | 16 Top Pool, 6 Division IA, 6 Division IB, 6 Division IIA, 6 Division IIB, 5 Division III |
| 2009 WM | 45 nations | 16 Top Pool, 6 Division IA, 6 Division IB, 6 Division IIA, 6 Division IIB, 6 Division III |
| 2010 WM | 48 nations | 16 Top Pool, 6 Division IA, 6 Division IB, 6 Division IIA, 6 Division IIB, 8 Division III |
| 2011 WM | 45 nations | 16 Top Pool, 5 Division IA, 6 Division IB, 6 Division IIA 6 Division IIB, 6 Division III |
| 2012 WM | 46 nations | 16 Top Pool, 6 Division IA, 6 Division IB, 6 Division IIA, 6 Division IIB, 6 Division III |

**U20 WORLD CHAMPIONSHIP**

| | | |
|---|---|---|
| 1977 WM20 | 8 nations | |
| 1978 WM20 | 8 nations | |
| 1979 WM20 | 16 nations | 8 A pool, 8 B pool |
| 1980 WM20 | 16 nations | 8 A pool, 8 B pool |
| 1981 WM20 | 16 nations | 8 A pool, 8 B pool |
| 1982 WM20 | 16 nations | 8 A pool, 8 B pool |
| 1983 WM20 | 20 nations | 8 A pool, 8 B pool, 4 C Pool |
| 1984 WM20 | 24 nations | 8 A pool, 8 B pool, 8 C Pool |
| 1985 WM20 | 22 nations | 8 A pool, 8 B pool, 6 C Pool |
| 1986 WM20 | 22 nations | 8 A pool, 8 B pool, 6 C Pool |
| 1987 WM20 | 22 nations | 8 A pool, 8 B pool, 6 C Pool |
| 1988 WM20 | 24 nations | 8 A pool, 8 B pool, 8 C Pool |
| 1989 WM20 | 21 nations | 8 A pool, 8 B pool, 5 C Pool |
| 1990 WM20 | 23 nations | 8 A pool, 8 B pool, 7 C Pool |
| 1991 WM20 | 24 nations | 8 A pool, 8 B pool, 8 C Pool |
| 1992 WM20 | 25 nations | 8 A pool, 8 B pool, 9 C Pool |
| 1993 WM20 | 24 nations | 8 A pool, 8 B pool, 8 C Pool |
| 1994 WM20 | 24 nations | 8 A pool, 8 B pool, 8 C Pool |
| 1995 WM20 | 33 nations | 8 A pool, 8 B pool, 8 C Pool, Group I, 6 C Pool, Group II, 3 C Pool Qualification |
| 1996 WM20 | 32 nations | 10 A Pool, 8 B Pool, 8 C Pool, 6 D Pool |
| 1997 WM20 | 34 nations | 10 A Pool, 8 B Pool, 8 C Pool, 8 D Pool |
| 1998 WM20 | 34 nations | 10 A Pool, 8 B Pool, 8 C Pool, 8 D Pool |
| 1999 WM20 | 35 nations | 10 A Pool, 8 B Pool, 8 C Pool, 9 D Pool |
| 2000 WM20 | 35 nations | 10 A Pool, 8 B Pool, 8 C Pool, 9 D Pool |
| 2001 WM20 | 37 nations | 10 Top Pool, 8 Division I, 8 Division II, 8 Division III, 3 Division III Qualification |
| 2002 WM20 | 34 nations | 10 Top Pool, 8 Division I, 8 Division II, 8 Division III |
| 2003 WM20 | 39 nations | 10 Top Pool, 6 Division IA, 6 Division IB, 6 Division IIA, 6 Division IIB, 5 Division III |
| 2004 WM20 | 40 nations | 10 Top Pool, 6 Division IA, 6 Division IB, 6 Division IIA, 6 Division IIB, 6 Division III |
| 2005 WM20 | 40 nations | 10 Top Pool, 6 Division IA, 6 Division IB, 6 Division IIA, 6 Division IIB, 6 Division III |
| 2006 WM20 | 40 nations | 10 Top Pool, 6 Division IA, 6 Division IB, 6 Division IIA, 6 Division IIB, 6 Division III |
| 2007 WM20 | 40 nations | 10 Top Pool, 6 Division IA, 6 Division IB, 6 Division IIA, 6 Division IIB, 6 Division III |
| 2008 WM20 | 41 nations | 10 Top Pool, 6 Division IA, 6 Division IB, 6 Division IIA, 6 Division IIB, 7 Division III |
| 2009 WM20 | 34 nations | 10 Top Pool, 6 Division IA, 6 Division IB, 6 Division IIA, 6 Division IIB |
| 2010 WM20 | 38 nations | 10 Top Pool, 6 Division IA, 6 Division IB, 6 Division IIA, 6 Division IIB, 4 Division III |
| 2011 WM20 | 41 nations | 10 Top Pool, 6 Division IA, 6 Division IB, 6 Division IIA, 6 Division IIB, 7 Division III |
| 2012 WM20 | 39 nations | 10 Top Pool, 6 Division IA, 6 Division IB, 6 Division IIA, 6 Division IIB, 5 Division III |

**U18 WORLD CHAMPIONSHIP (MEN)**

| | | |
|---|---|---|
| 1999 WM18 | 18 nations | 10 A Pool, 8 B Pool |
| 2000 WM18 | 18 nations | 10 A Pool, 8 B Pool |
| 2001 WM18 | 36 nations | 10 Top Pool, 8 Division I, 8 Division II, 8 Division III, 2 Division III Qualification |

| | | |
|---|---|---|
| 2002 WM18 | 35 nations | 10 Top Pool, 7 Division I, 8 Division II, 8 Division III |
| 2003 WM18 | 42 nations | 10 Top Pool, 6 Division IA, 6 Division IB, 6 Division IIA, 6 Division IIB, 4 Division IIIA, 4 Division IIIB |
| 2004 WM18 | 41 nations | 10 Top Pool, 6 Division IA, 6 Division IB, 6 Division IIA, 6 Division IIB, 7 Division III |
| 2005 WM18 | 43 nations | 10 Top Pool, 6 Division IA, 6 Division IB, 6 Division IIA, 6 Division IIB, 6 Division III, 3 Division III Qualification |
| 2006 WM18 | 40 nations | 10 Top Pool, 6 Division IA, 6 Division IB, 6 Division IIA, 6 Division IIB, 6 Division III |
| 2007 WM18 | 42 nations | 10 Top Pool, 6 Division IA, 6 Division IB, 6 Division IIA, 6 Division IIB, 6 Division III, 2 Division III Qualification |
| 2008 WM18 | 44 nations | 10 Top Pool, 6 Division IA, 6 Division IB, 6 Division IIA, 6 Division IIB, 5 Division IIIA, 5 Division IIIB |
| 2009 WM18 | 43 nations | 10 Top Pool, 6 Division IA, 6 Division IB, 6 Division IIA, 6 Division IIB, 5 Division IIIA, 4 Division IIIB |
| 2010 WM18 | 44 nations | 10 Top Pool, 6 Division IA, 6 Division IB, 6 Division IIA, 6 Division IIB, 5 Division IIIA, 5 Division IIIB |
| 2011 WM18 | 42 nations | 10 Top Pool, 5 Division IA, 6 Division IB, 6 Division IIA, 6 Division IIB, 4 Division IIIA, 5 Division IIIB |
| 2012 WM18 | 40 nations | 10 Top Pool, 6 Division IA, 6 Division IB, 6 Division IIA, 6 Division IIB, 6 Division III |

**OLYMPICS, WOMEN**

| | |
|---|---|
| 1998 OG-W | 6 nations |
| 2002 OG-W | 8 nations |
| 2006 OG-W | 8 nations |
| 2010 OG-W | 8 nations |

**WOMEN'S WORLD CHAMPIONSHIP**

| | | |
|---|---|---|
| 1990 WW | 8 nations | |
| 1992 WW | 8 nations | |
| 1994 WW | 8 nations | |
| 1997 WW | 8 nations | |
| 1999 WW | 21 nations | 8 A Pool, 8 B Pool, 5 Qualifying |
| 2000 WW | 24 nations | 8 A Pool, 8 B Pool, 8 Qualifying |
| 2001 WW | 26 nations | 8 A Pool, 8 B Pool, 10 Qualifying |
| 2003 WW | 26 nations | 8 Top Pool, 6 Division I, 6 Division II, 6 Division III |
| 2004 WW | 27 nations | 9 Top Pool, 6 Division I, 6 Division II, 6 Division III |
| 2005 WW | 30 nations | 8 Top Pool, 6 Division I, 6 Division II, 6 Division III, 4 Division IV |
| 2007 WW | 33 nations | 9 Top Pool, 6 Division I, 6 Division II, 6 Division III, 6 Division IV |
| 2008 WW | 33 nations | 9 Top Pool, 6 Division I, 6 Division II, 6 Division III, 6 Division IV |
| 2009 WW | 21 nations | 9 Top Pool, 6 Division I, 6 Division II |
| 2011 WW | 35 nations | 8 Top Pool, 5 Division I, 6 Division II, 6 Division III, 5 Division IV, 5 Division V |
| 2012 WW | 32 nations | 8 Top Pool, 6 Division IA, 6 Division IB, 6 Division IIA, 6 Division IIB |

**U18 WOMEN'S WORLD CHAMPIONSHIP**

| | | |
|---|---|---|
| 2008 WW18 | 8 nations | |
| 2009 WW18 | 13 nations | 8 Top Pool, 5 Division I |
| 2010 WW18 | 14 nations | 8 Top Pool, 6 Division I |
| 2011 WW18 | 14 nations | 8 Top Pool, 6 Division I |
| 2012 WW18 | 20 nations | 8 Top Pool, 6 Division I, 6 Division I Qualification |

# All-Time Medal Standings

**OLYMPICS, MEN, 1920-2010**

| | G | S | B | Total |
|---|---|---|---|---|
| Canada | 8 | 4 | 2 | 14 |
| United States | 2 | 8 | 1 | 11 |
| Soviet Union | 7 | 1 | 1 | 9 |
| Sweden | 2 | 2 | 4 | 8 |
| Czechoslovakia | 0 | 4 | 4 | 8 |
| Finland | 0 | 2 | 3 | 5 |
| Russia | 1 | 1 | 1 | 3 |
| Czech Republic | 1 | 0 | 1 | 2 |
| Great Britain | 1 | 0 | 1 | 2 |
| Switzerland | 0 | 0 | 2 | 2 |
| Germany | 0 | 0 | 1 | 1 |
| West Germany | 0 | 0 | 1 | 1 |

**WORLD CHAMPIONSHIP (MEN), (EXCLUDING OLYMPICS), 1930-2012**

| | G | S | B | Total |
|---|---|---|---|---|
| Sweden | 8 | 17 | 15 | 40 |
| Canada | 18 | 11 | 7 | 36 |
| Soviet Union | 19 | 7 | 4 | 30 |
| Czechoslovakia | 6 | 10 | 14 | 30 |
| Czech Republic | 6 | 1 | 5 | 12 |
| Finland | 2 | 6 | 3 | 11 |
| United States | 1 | 4 | 4 | 9 |
| Russia | 4 | 2 | 2 | 8 |
| Switzerland | 0 | 1 | 6 | 7 |
| Slovakia | 1 | 2 | 1 | 4 |
| Great Britain | 0 | 2 | 1 | 3 |
| Germany | 0 | 1 | 1 | 2 |
| Austria | 0 | 0 | 2 | 2 |
| West Germany | 0 | 1 | 0 | 1 |

**WORLD CHAMPIONSHIP (MEN), 1920-2012**
(including Olympics which counted as WM results 1920-1968)

| | G | S | B | Total |
|---|---|---|---|---|
| Canada | 24 | 13 | 9 | 46 |
| Sweden | 8 | 18 | 17 | 43 |
| Soviet Union | 22 | 7 | 5 | 34 |
| Czechoslovakia | 6 | 12 | 16 | 34 |
| United States | 2 | 10 | 5 | 17 |
| Czech Republic | 6 | 1 | 5 | 12 |
| Finland | 2 | 6 | 4 | 12 |
| Switzerland | 0 | 1 | 8 | 9 |
| Russia | 4 | 2 | 2 | 8 |
| Great Britain | 1 | 2 | 2 | 5 |
| Slovakia | 1 | 2 | 1 | 4 |
| Germany | 0 | 1 | 2 | 3 |
| Austria | 0 | 0 | 2 | 2 |
| West Germany | 0 | 1 | 0 | 1 |

**U20 WORLD CHAMPIONSHIP, 1977-2012**

| | G | S | B | Total |
|---|---|---|---|---|
| Canada | 15 | 8 | 5 | 28 |
| Russia | 4 | 7 | 5 | 16 |
| Sweden | 2 | 8 | 5 | 15 |
| Soviet Union* | 9 | 3 | 2 | 14 |
| Finland | 2 | 4 | 6 | 12 |
| Czechoslovakia** | 0 | 5 | 6 | 11 |
| United States | 2 | 1 | 4 | 7 |
| Czech Republic | 2 | 0 | 1 | 3 |
| Slovakia | 0 | 0 | 1 | 1 |
| Switzerland | 0 | 0 | 1 | 1 |

*includes CIS in 1992
**includes Czech & Slovak Republics in 1993

**U18 WORLD CHAMPIONSHIP (MEN), 1999-2012**

| | G | S | B | Total |
|---|---|---|---|---|
| United States | 7 | 2 | 1 | 10 |
| Russia | 3 | 4 | 2 | 9 |
| Sweden | 0 | 4 | 3 | 7 |
| Finland | 2 | 1 | 3 | 6 |
| Canada | 2 | 1 | 1 | 4 |
| Czech Republic | 0 | 0 | 3 | 3 |
| Slovakia | 0 | 1 | 1 | 2 |
| Switzerland | 0 | 1 | 0 | 1 |

**OLYMPICS, WOMEN, 1998-2010**

| | G | S | B | Total |
|---|---|---|---|---|
| Canada | 3 | 1 | 0 | 4 |
| United States | 1 | 2 | 1 | 4 |
| Sweden | 0 | 1 | 1 | 2 |
| Finland | 0 | 0 | 2 | 2 |

**WOMEN'S WORLD CHAMPIONSHIP, 1990-2012**

| | G | S | B | Total |
|---|---|---|---|---|
| Canada | 10 | 4 | 0 | 14 |
| United States | 4 | 10 | 0 | 14 |
| Finland | 0 | 0 | 10 | 10 |
| Sweden | 0 | 0 | 2 | 2 |
| Russia | 0 | 0 | 1 | 1 |
| Switzerland | 0 | 0 | 1 | 1 |

**U18 WOMEN'S WORLD CHAMPIONSHIP, 2008-2012**

| | G | S | B | Total |
|---|---|---|---|---|
| United States | 3 | 2 | 0 | 5 |
| Canada | 2 | 3 | 0 | 5 |
| Sweden | 0 | 0 | 3 | 3 |
| Czech Republic | 0 | 0 | 1 | 1 |
| Finland | 0 | 0 | 1 | 1 |

# Most National Team Games*

| | |
|---|---|
| 1. Raimo Helminen, FIN | 331 |
| 2. Udo Kiessling, GER | 320 |
| 3. Jiri Holik, TCH | 319 |
| 4. Alexander Maltsev, URS | 316 |
| 5. Sergei Makarov, URS | 315 |
| 5. Dietmar Peters, GDR | 315 |
| 7. Vyacheslav Fetisov, URS | 314 |
| 8. Alexei Kasatonov, URS | 299 |
| 9. Denis Perez, FRA | 297 |
| 10. Dieter Frenzel, GDR | 296 |
| 11. Oldrich Machac, TCH | 293 |
| 12. Henryk Gruth, POL | 292 |
| 13. Dieter Hegen, GER | 290 |
| 14. Vladimir Martinec, TCH | 289 |
| 15. Vladislav Tretiak**, URS | 288 |
| 16. Valeri Kharlamov, URS | 287 |
| 17. Jorgen Jonsson, SWE | 285 |
| 18. Boris Mikhailov, URS | 282 |
| 19. Lasse Oksanen, FIN | 282 |
| 19. Valeri Vasilyev, URS | 282 |
| 21. Vasili Pervukhin, URS | 280 |
| 22. Esa Peltonen, FIN | 277 |
| 23. Vladimir Petrov, URS | 276 |
| 23. Vladimir Lutchenko, URS | 276 |
| 25. Antoine Richer, FRA | 274 |
| 26. Roland Peters, GDR | 273 |
| 27. Jonas Bergqvist, SWE | 272 |
| 28. Frank Braun, GDR | 270 |
| 29. Thomas Rundqvist, SWE | 267 |
| 30. Matthias Seger, SUI | 263 |

*Includes all official senior national team games versus other national teams.
**Goalie

# Most Valuable Player, Directorate Awards, All-Star Teams

## IIHF Centennial All-Star Team

(announced May 18, 2008, in honour of the IIHF's 100th anniversary)

| | |
|---|---|
| Goal | Vladislav Tretiak (RUS) |
| Defence | Vyacheslav Fetisov (RUS), Borje Salming (SWE) |
| Forward | Valeri Kharlamov (RUS), Sergei Makarov (RUS) |
| Centre | Wayne Gretzky (CAN) |

*Wayne Gretzky was named to the IIHF's Centennial team in 2008. Photo: Paul Bereswill / HHOF.*

## Most Valuable Player

| MEN | OG-M | WM | WM20 | WM18 |
|---|---|---|---|---|
| 1999 | | Teemu Selanne, F (FIN) | | |
| 2000 | | Martin Prohazka, F (CZE) | | |
| 2001 | | David Moravec, F (CZE) | | |
| 2002 | Joe Sakic, F (CAN) | Miroslav Satan, F (SVK) | | |
| 2003 | | Mats Sundin, F (SWE) | | |
| 2004 | | Dany Heatley, F (CAN) | Zach Parise, F (USA) | |
| 2005 | | Joe Thornton, F (CAN) | Patrice Bergeron, F (CAN) | |
| 2006 | Antero Niittymaki, GK (FIN) | Niklas Kronwall, D (SWE) | Yevgeni Malkin, F (RUS) | |
| 2007 | | Rick Nash, F (CAN) | Carey Price, GK (CAN) | |
| 2008 | | Dany Heatley, F (CAN) | Steve Mason, GK (CAN) | Jake Allen, GK (CAN) |
| 2009 | | Ilya Kovalchuk, F (RUS) | John Tavares, F (CAN) | not awarded |
| 2010 | Ryan Miller, GK (USA) | Dennis Endras, GK (GER) | Jordan Eberle, F (CAN) | not awarded |
| 2011 | | Viktor Fasth, GK (SWE) | Brayden Schenn, F (CAN) | not awarded |
| 2012 | | Yevgeni Malkin, F (RUS) | Yevgeni Kuznetsov, F (RUS) | not awarded |

| WOMEN | OG-W | WW | WW18 |
|---|---|---|---|
| 2001 | | Jennifer Botterill, F (CAN) | |
| 2002 | Hayley Wickenheiser, F (CAN) | | |
| 2003 | | no tournament | |
| 2004 | | Jennifer Botterill, F (CAN) | |
| 2005 | | Krissy Wendell, F (USA) | |
| 2006 | Hayley Wickenheiser, F (CAN) | | |
| 2007 | | Hayley Wickenheiser, F (CAN) | |
| 2008 | | Noora Raty, GK (FIN) | |
| 2009 | | Carla MacLeod, D (CAN) | |
| 2010 | Meghan Agosta, F (CAN) | | Jessica Campbell, F (CAN) |
| 2011 | | Zuzana Tomcikova, GK (SVK) | not awarded |
| 2012 | | not awarded | not awarded |

## Directorate Awards/All-Star Teams

| Directorate<br>All-Star Team | Best Goalie<br>Goal | Best Defenceman<br>Defence | Best Forward<br>Forward |
|---|---|---|---|
| 1956 OG-M | Willard Ikola (USA) | Nikolai Sologubov (URS) | Jack MacKenzie (CAN) |
| 1960 OG-M | Jack McCartan (USA) | Nikolai Sologubov (USA) | Nils "Nisse" Nilsson (SWE) |
| 1964 OG-M | Seth Martin (CAN) | Frantisek Tikal (TCH) | Eduard Ivanov (URS) |
| | Seth Martin (CAN) | Alexander Ragulin (URS), Rod Seiling (CAN) | Roger Bourbonnais (CAN), Josef Cerny (TCH), Viktor Yakushev (URS) |
| 1968 OG-M | Ken Broderick (CAN) | Josef Horesovsky (TCH) | Anatoli Firsov (URS) |
| | Ken Broderick (CAN) | Jan Suchy (TCH), Lennart Svedberg (SWE) | Anatoli Firsov (URS), Fran Huck (CAN), Frantisek Sevcik (TCH) |
| 1972-88 OG-M | No Selections | | |
| 1992 OG-M | Not Awarded | | |
| | Roy Leblanc (USA) | Igor Kravchuk (RUS), Dmitri Mironov (RUS) | Vyacheslav Bykov (RUS), Eric Lindros (CAN), Hakan Loob (SWE) |
| 1994 OG-M | Not Awarded | | |
| 1998 OG-M | Dominik Hasek (CZE) | Rob Blake (CAN) | Pavel Bure (RUS) |
| | Not Awarded | | |
| 2002 OG-M | Nikolai Khabibulin (RUS) | Chris Chelios (USA) | Joe Sakic (CAN) |
| | Mike Richter (USA) | Chris Chelios (USA), Brian Leetch (USA) | John LeClair (USA), Joe Sakic (CAN), Mats Sundin (SWE) |
| 2006 OG-M | Antero Niittymaki (FIN) | Kenny Jonsson (SWE) | Teemu Selanne (FIN) |
| | Antero Niittymaki (FIN) | Nicklas Lidstrom (SWE), Kimmo Timonen (FIN) | Saku Koivu (FIN), Teemu Selanne (FIN), Alexander Ovechkin (RUS) |
| 2010 OG-M | Ryan Miller (USA) | Brian Rafalski (USA) | Jonathan Toews (CAN) |
| | Ryan Miller (USA) | Brian Rafalski (USA), Shea Weber (CAN) | Pavol Demitra (SVK), Zach Parise (USA), Jonathan Toews (CAN) |

| Directorate<br>All-Star Team | Best Goalie<br>Goal | Best Defenceman<br>Defence | Best Forward<br>Forward |
|---|---|---|---|
| 1954 WM | Don Lockhart (CAN) | Lars Bjorn (SWE) | Vsevelod Bobrov (URS) |
| | Not Awarded | | |
| 1955 WM | Don Rigazio (USA) | Karel Gut (TCH) | Bill Warwick (CAN) |
| | Not Awarded | | |
| 1957 WM | Karel Straka (TCH) | Nikolai Sologubov (URS) | Sven Tumba Johansson (SWE) |
| | Not Awarded | | |
| 1958 WM | Vladimir Nadrchal (TCH) | Ivan Tregubov (URS) | Charlie Burns (CAN) |
| | Not Awarded | | |
| 1959 WM | Nikolai Puchkov (URS) | J-P Lamirande (CAN) | Bill Cleary (USA) |
| | Not Awarded | | |
| 1961 WM | Seth Martin (CAN) | Ivan Tregubov (URS) | Vlastimil Bubnik (TCH) |
| | Seth Martin (CAN) | Darryl Sly (CAN), Harry Smith (CAN) | Mike Legace (CAN), Boris Mayorov (URS), Miroslav Vlach (TCH) |
| 1962 WM | Lennart Haggroth (SWE) | John Mayasich (USA) | Sven Tumba Johansson (SWE) |
| | Lennart Haggroth (SWE) | Jack Douglas (CAN), Harry Smith (CAN) | Jack McLeod (CAN), Nils "Nisse" Nilsson (SWE), Ulf Sterner (SWE) |
| 1963 WM | Seth Martin (CAN) | Roland Stoltz (SWE) | Miroslav Vlach (TCH) |
| | Kjell Svensson (SWE) | Alexander Ragulin (URS), Harry Smith (CAN) | Hans Mild (SWE), Addie Tambellini (CAN), Miroslav Vlach (TCH) |
| 1965 WM | Vladimir Dzurilla (TCH) | Frantisek Tikal (TCH) | Vyacheslav Starshinov (URS) |
| | Vladimir Dzurilla (TCH) | Alexander Ragulin (URS), Frantisek Tikal (TCH) | Alexander Almetov (URS), Jaroslav Jirik (TCH), Konstantin Loktev (URS) |
| 1966 WM | Seth Martin (CAN) | Alexander Ragulin (URS) | Konstantin Loktev (URS) |
| | Seth Martin (CAN) | Gary Begg (CAN), Alexander Ragulin (URS) | Veniamin Alexandrov (URS), Fran Huck (CAN), Konstantin Loktev (URS) |

| | | | |
|---|---|---|---|
| 1967 WM | Carl Wetzel (USA) | Vitali Davydov (URS) | Anatoli Firsov (URS) |
| | Carl Wetzel (USA) | Carl Brewer (CAN), Alexander Ragulin (URS) | Veniamin Alexandrov (URS), Alexander Almetov (URS), Anatoli Firsov (URS) |
| 1969 WM | Leif Holmqvist (SWE) | Jan Suchy (TCH) | Ulf Sterner (SWE) |
| | Vladimir Dzurilla (TCH) | Jan Suchy (TCH), Lennart Svedberg (SWE) | Anatoli Firsov (URS), Vaclav Nedomansky (TCH), Ulf Sterner (SWE) |
| 1970 WM | Urpo Ylonen (FIN) | Lennart Svedberg (SWE) | Alexander Maltsev (URS) |
| | Viktor Konovalenko (URS) | Jan Suchy (TCH), Lennart Svedberg (SWE) | Anatoli Firsov (URS), Alexander Maltsev (URS), Vaclav Nedomansky (TCH) |
| 1971 WM | Jiri Holecek (TCH) | Jan Suchy (TCH) | Anatoli Firsov (URS) |
| | Jiri Holecek (TCH) | Ilpo Koskela (FIN), Jan Suchy (TCH) | Valeri Kharlamov (URS), Alexander Maltsev (URS), Vladimir Vikulov (URS) |
| 1972 WM | Jorma Valtonen (FIN) | Frantisek Pospisil (TCH) | Alexander Maltsev (URS) |
| | Jiri Holecek (TCH) | Oldrich Machac (TCH), Frantisek Pospisil (TCH) | Valeri Kharlamov (URS), Alexander Maltsev (URS), Vladimir Vikulov (URS) |
| 1973 WM | Jiri Holecek (TCH) | Valeri Vasilyev (URS) | Boris Mikhailov (URS) |
| | Jiri Holecek (TCH) | Alexander Gusev (URS), Borje Salming (SWE) | Valeri Kharlamov (URS), Boris Mikhailov (URS), Vladimir Petrov (URS) |
| 1974 WM | Vladislav Tretiak (URS) | Lars-Erik Sjoberg (SWE) | Vaclav Nedomansky (TCH |
| | Curt Larsson (SWE) | Lars-Erik Sjoberg (SWE), Valeri Vasilyev (URS) | Vladimir Martinec (TCH), Vaclav Nedomansky (TCH), Alexander Yakushev (URS) |
| 1975 WM | Jiri Holecek (TCH) | Pekka Marjamaki (FIN) | Alexander Yakushev (URS) |
| | Vladislav Tretiak (URS) | Pekka Marjamaki (FIN), Valeri Vasilyev (URS) | Vladimir Martinec (TCH), Vladimir Petrov (URS), Alexander Yakushev (URS) |
| 1976 WM | Jiri Holecek (TCH) | Frantisek Pospisil (TCH) | Vladimir Martinec (TCH) |
| | Jiri Holecek (TCH) | Frantisek Pospisil (TCH), Mats Waltin (SWE) | Valeri Kharlamov (URS), Vladimir Martinec (TCH), Milan Novy (TCH) |
| 1977 WM | Goran Hogosta (SWE) | Valeri Vasilyev (URS) | Helmuts Balderis (URS) |
| | Goran Hogosta (SWE) | Frantisek Pospisil (TCH), Valeri Vasilyev (URS) | Helmuts Balderis (URS), Vladimir Martinec (TCH), Vladimir Petrov (URS) |
| 1978 WM | Jiri Holecek (TCH) | Vyacheslav Fetisov (URS) | Marcel Dionne (CAN) |
| | Jiri Holecek (TCH) | Jiri Bubla (TCH), Vyacheslav Fetisov (URS) | Ivan Hlinka (TCH), Sergei Kapustin (URS), Alexander Maltsev (URS) |
| 1979 WM | Vladislav Tretiak (URS) | Valeri Vasilyev (URS) | Wilf Paiement (CAN) |
| | Vladislav Tretiak (URS) | Jiri Bubla (TCH), Valeri Vasilyev (URS) | Sergei Makarov (URS), Boris Mikhailov (URS), Vladimir Petrov (URS) |
| 1981 WM | Peter Lindmark (SWE) | Larry Robinson (CAN) | Alexander Maltsev (URS) |
| | Peter Lindmark (SWE) | Larry Robinson (CAN), Valeri Vasilyev (URS) | Sergei Kapustin (URS), Alexander Maltsev (URS), Sergei Makarov (URS) |
| 1982 WM | Jiri Kralik (TCH) | Vyacheslav Fetisov (URS) | Viktor Shalimov (URS) |
| | Jiri Kralik (TCH) | Vyacheslav Fetisov (URS), Alexei Kasatonov (URS) | Bill Barber (CAN), Wayne Gretzky (CAN), Sergei Makarov (URS) |
| 1983 WM | Vladislav Tretiak (URS) | Alexei Kasatonov (URS) | Jiri Lala (TCH) |
| | Vladislav Tretiak (URS) | Vyacheslav Fetisov (URS), Alexei Kasatonov (URS) | Vladimir Krutov (URS), Igor Larionov (URS), Sergei Makarov (URS) |
| 1985 WM | Jiri Kralik (TCH) | Vyacheslav Fetisov (URS) | Sergei Makarov (URS) |
| | Jiri Kralik (TCH) | Vyacheslav Fetisov (URS), Alexei Kasatonov (URS) | Vladimir Krutov (URS), Sergei Makarov (URS), Vladimir Ruzicka (TCH) |
| 1986 WM | Peter Lindmark (SWE) | Vyacheslav Fetisov (URS) | Vladimir Krutov (URS) |
| | Peter Lindmark (SWE) | Vyacheslav Fetisov (URS), Alexei Kasatonov (URS) | Vladimir Krutov (URS), Igor Larionov (URS), Sergei Makarov (URS) |
| 1987 WM | Dominik Hasek (TCH) | Craig Hartsburg (CAN) | Vladimir Krutov (URS) |
| | Dominik Hasek (TCH) | Vyacheslav Fetisov (URS), Udo Kiessling (FRG) | Vladimir Krutov (URS), Sergei Makarov (URS), Gerd Truntschka (FRG) |
| 1989 WM | Dominik Hasek (TCH) | Vyacheslav Fetisov (URS) | Brian Bellows (CAN) |
| | Dominik Hasek (TCH) | Anders Eldebrink (SWE), Vyacheslav Fetisov (URS) | Vyacheslav Bykov (URS), Sergei Makarov (URS), Steve Yzerman (CAN) |
| 1990 WM | Arturs Irbe (URS) | Mikhail Tatarinov (URS) | Steve Yzerman (CAN) |
| | Dominik Hasek (TCH) | Vyacheslav Fetisov (URS), Mikhail Tatarinov (URS) | Andrei Khomutov (URS), Robert Reichel (TCH), Steve Yzerman (CAN) |
| 1991 WM | Markus Ketterer (FIN) | Jamie Macoun (CAN) | Valeri Kamenski (URS) |
| | Sean Burke (CAN) | Vyacheslav Fetisov (URS), Alexei Kasatonov (URS) | Valeri Kamenski (URS), Jari Kurri (FIN), Thomas Rundqvist (SWE) |
| 1992 WM | Tommy Soderstrom (SWE) | Robert Svehla (TCH) | Mats Sundin (SWE) |
| | Markus Ketterer (FIN) | Timo Jutila (FIN), Frantisek Musil (TCH) | Petr Hrbek (TCH), Mats Sundin (SWE), Jarkko Varvio (FIN) |
| 1993 WM | Petr Briza (CZE) | Ilya Byakin (RUS) | Eric Lindros (CAN) |
| | Petr Briza (CZE) | Ilya Byakin (RUS), Dave Manson (CAN) | Ulf Dahlen (SWE), Eric Lindros (CAN), Mikael Renberg (SWE) |
| 1994 WM | Bill Ranford (CAN) | Magnus Svensson (SWE) | Paul Kariya (CAN) |
| | Bill Ranford (CAN) | Timo Jutila (FIN), Magnus Svensson (SWE) | Paul Kariya (CAN), Saku Koivu (FIN), Jari Kurri (FIN) |
| 1995 WM | Jarmo Myllys (FIN) | Christer Olsson (SWE) | Saku Koivu (FIN) |
| | Jarmo Myllys (FIN) | Timo Jutila (FIN), Tommy Sjodin (SWE) | Saku Koivu (FIN), Jere Lehtinen (FIN), Ville Peltonen (FIN) |
| 1996 WM | Roman Turek (CZE) | Alexei Zhitnik (RUS) | Yanic Perreault (CAN) |
| | Roman Turek (CZE) | Michal Sykora (CZE), Alexei Zhitnik (RUS) | Paul Kariya (CAN), Robert Reichel (CZE), Otakar Vejvoda (CZE) |
| 1997 WM | Tommy Salo (SWE) | Rob Blake (CAN) | Mikael Nylander (SWE) |
| | Tommy Salo (SWE) | Rob Blake (CAN), Teppo Numminen (FIN) | Mikael Nylander (SWE), Martin Prochazka (CZE), Vladimir Vujtek (CZE) |
| 1998 WM | Ari Sulander (FIN) | Frantisek Kucera (CZE) | Peter Forsberg (SWE) |
| | Tommy Salo (SWE) | Jere Karalahti (FIN), Frantisek Kucera (CZE) | Peter Forsberg (SWE), Ville Peltonen (FIN), Mats Sundin (SWE) |
| 1999 WM | Tommy Salo (SWE) | Frantisek Kucera (CZE) | Saku Koivu (FIN) |
| | Tommy Salo (SWE) | Jere Karalahti (FIN), Pavel Kubina (CZE) | Saku Koivu (FIN), Martin Rucinsky (CZE), Teemu Selanne (FIN) |
| 2000 WM | Roman Cechmanek (CZE) | Petteri Nummelin (FIN) | Miroslav Satan (SVK) |
| | Roman Cechmanek (CZE) | Petteri Nummelin (FIN), Michal Sykora (CZE) | Jiri Dopita (CZE), Miroslav Satan (SVK), Tomas Vlasak (CZE) |
| 2001 WM | Milan Hnilicka (CZE) | Kim Johnsson (SWE) | Sami Kapanen (FIN) |
| | Milan Hnilicka (CZE) | Kim Johnsson (SWE), Petteri Nummelin (FIN) | Sami Kapanen (FIN), Robert Reichel (CZE), Martin Rucinsky (CZE) |
| 2002 WM | Maxim Sokolov (RUS) | Daniel Tjarnqvist (SWE) | Niklas Hagman (FIN) |
| | Maxim Sokolov (RUS) | Richard Lintner (SVK), Thomas Rhodin (SWE) | Peter Bondra (SVK), Niklas Hagman (FIN), Miroslav Satan (SVK) |
| 2003 WM | Sean Burke (CAN) | Jay Bouwmeester (CAN) | Mats Sundin (SWE) |
| | Sean Burke (CAN) | Jay Bouwmeester (CAN), Lubomir Visnovsky (SVK) | Peter Forsberg (SWE), Dany Heatley (CAN), Mats Sundin (SWE) |
| 2004 WM | Ty Conklin (USA) | Dick Tarnstrom (SWE) | Dany Heatley (CAN) |
| | Henrik Lundqvist (SWE) | Zdeno Chara (SVK), Dick Tarnstrom (SWE) | Dany Heatley (CAN), Jaromir Jagr (CZE), Ville Peltonen (FIN) |
| 2005 WM | Tomas Vokoun (CZE) | Wade Redden (CAN) | Alexei Kovalyov (RUS) |
| | Tomas Vokoun (CZE) | Niklas Kronwall (SWE), Marek Zidlicky (CZE) | Jaromir Jagr (CZE), Rick Nash (CAN), Joe Thornton (CAN) |
| 2006 WM | Johan Holmqvist (SWE) | Niklas Kronwall (SWE) | Sidney Crosby (CAN) |
| | Andrei Mezin (BLR) | Niklas Kronwall (SWE), Timo Nummelin (FIN) | Sidney Crosby (CAN), Alexander Ovechkin (RUS), David Vyborny (CZE) |
| 2007 WM | Kari Lehtonen (FIN) | Andrei Markov (RUS) | Alexei Morozov (RUS) |
| | Kari Lehtonen (FIN) | Andrei Markov (RUS), Petteri Nummelin (FIN) | Yevgeni Malkin (RUS), Alexei Morozov (RUS), Rick Nash (CAN) |
| 2008 WM | Yevgeni Nabokov (RUS) | Brent Burns (CAN) | Dany Heatley (CAN) |
| | Yevgeni Nabokov (RUS) | Mike Green (CAN), Tomas Kaberle (CZE) | Dany Heatley (CAN), Rick Nash (CAN), Alexander Ovechkin (RUS) |
| 2009 WM | Andrei Mezin (BLR) | Shea Weber (CAN) | Ilya Kovalchuk (RUS) |
| | Andrei Mezin (BLR) | Kenny Jonsson (SWE), Shea Weber (CAN) | Ilya Kovalchuk (RUS), Steve Stamkos (CAN), Martin St. Louis (CAN) |
| 2010 WM | Dennis Endras (GER) | Petteri Nummelin (FIN) | Pavel Datsyuk (RUS) |
| | Dennis Endras (GER) | Petteri Nummelin (FIN), Christian Ehrhoff (GER) | Pavel Datsyuk (RUS),Yevgeni Malkin (RUS), Magnus Paajarvi-Svensson (SWE) |
| 2011 WM | Viktor Fasth (SWE) | Alex Pietrangelo (CAN) | Jaromir Jagr (CZE) |
| | Viktor Fasth (SWE) | David Petrasek (SWE), Marek Zidlicky (CZE) | Patrik Berglund (SWE), Jarkko Immonen (FIN), Jaromir Jagr (CZE) |
| 2012 WM | Jan Laco (SVK) | Zdeno Chara (SVK) | Yevgeni Malkin (RUS) |
| | Jan Laco (SVK) | Zdeno Chara (SVK), Ilya Nikulin (RUS) | Yevgeni Malkin (RUS), Patrick Thoresen (NOR), Henrik Zetterberg (SWE) |

| Directorate | Best Goalie | Best Defenceman | Best Forward |
|---|---|---|---|
| All-Star Team | Goal | Defence | Forward |
| 1977 WM20 | Jan Hrabak (TCH) | Vyacheslav Fetisov (URS) | Dale McCourt (CAN) |
| | Alexander Tyzhnykh (URS) | Risto Siltanen (FIN), Lubomir Oslizlo (TCH) | Dale McCourt (CAN), Bengt-Ake Gustafsson (SWE), Igor Romashin (URS) |
| 1978 WM20 | Alexander Tyzhnykh (URS) | Vyacheslav Fetisov (URS) | Wayne Gretzky (CAN) |
| | Alexander Tyzhnykh (URS) | Risto Siltanen (FIN), Vyacheslav Fetisov (URS) | Wayne Gretzky (CAN), Mats Naslund (SWE), Anton Stastny (TCH) |
| 1979 WM20 | Pelle Lindbergh (SWE) | Alexei Kasatonov (URS) | Vladimir Krutov (URS) |
| | Pelle Lindbergh (SWE) | Ivan Cerny (TCH), Alexei Kasatonov (URS) | Anatoli Tarasov (URS), Thomas Steen (SWE), Vladimir Krutov (URS) |
| 1980 WM20 | Jari Paavola (FIN) | Reijo Ruotsalainen (FIN) | Vladimir Krutov (URS) |
| | Jari Paavola (FIN) | Reijo Ruotsalainen (FIN), Tomas Jonsson (SWE) | Hakan Loob (SWE), Igor Larionov (URS), Vladimir Krutov (URS) |
| 1981 WM20 | Lars Eriksson (SWE) | Miloslav Horava (TCH) | Patrik Sundstrom (SWE) |
| | Lars Eriksson (SWE) | Miloslav Horava (TCH), Hakan Nordin (SWE) | Ari Lahteenmaki (FIN), Patrik Sundstrom (SWE), Jan Erixon (SWE) |
| 1982 WM20 | Mike Moffat (CAN) | Gord Kluzak (CAN) | Petri Skriko (FIN) |
| | Mike Moffat (CAN) | Gord Kluzak (CAN), Ilya Byakin (URS) | Mike Moller (CAN), Petri Skriko (FIN), Vladimir Ruzicka (TCH) |
| 1983 WM20 | Dominik Hasek (TCH) | Ilya Byakin (URS) | Tomas Sandstrom (SWE) |
| | Matti Rautiainen (FIN) | Ilya Byakin (URS), Simo Saarinen (FIN) | Tomas Sandstrom (SWE), Vladimir Ruzicka (TCH), German Volgin (URS) |
| 1984 WM20 | Alan Perry (USA) | Alexei Gusarov (URS) | Raimo Helminen (FIN) |
| | Yevgeni Belosheikin (URS) | Alexei Gusarov (URS), Frantisek Musil (TCH) | Petr Rosol (TCH), Raimo Helminen (FIN), Nikolai Borshevski (URS) |
| 1985 WM20 | Craig Billington (CAN) | Vesa Salo (FIN) | Michal Pivonka (TCH) |
| | Timo Lehkonen (FIN) | Bobby Dollas (CAN), Mikhail Tatarinov (URS) | Mikko Makela (FIN), Michal Pivonka (TCH), Esa Tikkanen (FIN) |
| 1986 WM20 | Yevgeni Belosheikin (URS) | Mikhail Tatarinov (URS) | Jim Sandlak (CAN) |
| | Yevgeni Belosheikin (URS) | Sylvain Cote (CAN), Mikhail Tatarinov (URS) | Shayne Corson (CAN), Igor Vyazmikin (URS), Michal Pivonka (TCH) |
| 1987 WM20 | Markus Ketterer (FIN) | Calle Johansson (SWE) | Robert Kron (TCH) |
| | Sam Lindstahl (SWE) | Jiri Latal (TCH), Brian Leetch (USA) | Ulf Dahlen (SWE), Juraj Jurik (TCH), Scott Young (USA) |
| 1988 WM20 | Jimmy Waite (CAN) | Teppo Numminen (FIN) | Alexander Mogilny (URS) |
| | Jimmy Waite (CAN) | Greg Hawgood (CAN), Teppo Numminen (FIN) | Theo Fleury (CAN), Alexander Mogilny (URS), Petr Hrbek (TCH) |
| 1989 WM20 | Alexei Ivashkin (URS) | Rickard Persson (SWE) | Pavel Bure (URS) |
| | Alexei Ivashkin (URS) | Rickard Persson (SWE), Milan Tichy (TCH) | Niklas Eriksson (SWE), Pavel Bure (URS), Jeremy Roenick (USA) |
| 1990 WM20 | Stephane Fiset (CAN) | Alexander Godynyuk (URS) | Robert Reichel (TCH) |
| | Stephane Fiset (CAN) | Alexander Godynyuk (URS), Jiri Slegr (TCH) | Dave Chyzowski (CAN), Jaromir Jagr (TCH), Robert Reichel (TCH) |
| 1991 WM20 | Pauli Jaks (SUI) | Jiri Slegr (TCH) | Eric Lindros (CAN) |
| | Pauli Jaks (SUI) | Dmitri Yushkevich (URS), Scott Lachance (USA) | Mike Craig (CAN), Eric Lindros (CAN), Martin Rucinsky (TCH) |
| 1992 WM20 | Mike Dunham (USA) | Darius Kasparaitis (RUS) | Michael Nylander (SWE) |
| | Mike Dunham (USA) | Scott Niedermayer (CAN), Janne Gronvall (FIN) | Alexei Kovalyov (RUS), Michael Nylander (SWE), Peter Ferraro (USA) |
| 1993 WM20 | Manny Legace (CAN) | Janne Gronvall (FIN) | Peter Forsberg (SWE) |
| | Manny Legace (CAN) | Brent Tully (CAN), Kenny Jonsson (SWE) | Paul Kariya (CAN), Markus Naslund (SWE), Peter Forsberg (SWE) |
| 1994 WM20 | Jamie Storr (CAN) | Kenny Jonsson (SWE) | Niklas Sundstrom (SWE) |
| | Yevgeni Ryabchikov (RUS) | Kenny Jonsson (SWE), Kimmo Timonen (FIN) | Niklas Sundstrom (SWE), Valeri Bure (RUS), David Vyborny (CZE) |
| 1995 WM20 | Yevgeni Tarasov (RUS) | Bryan McCabe (CAN) | Marty Murray (CAN) |
| | Igor Karpenko (UKR) | Bryan McCabe (CAN), Anders Eriksson (SWE) | Jason Allison (CAN), Eric Daze (CAN), Marty Murray (CAN) |
| 1996 WM20 | Jose Theodore (CAN) | Mattias Ohlund (SWE) | Jarome Iginla (CAN) |
| | Jose Theodore (CAN) | Nolan Baumgartner (CAN), Mattias Ohlund (SWE) | Jarome Iginla (CAN), Johan Davidsson (SWE), Alexei Morozov (RUS) |
| 1997 WM20 | Marc Denis (CAN) | Joe Corvo (USA) | Alexei Morozov (RUS) |
| | Brian Boucher (USA) | Chris Phillips (CAN), Mark Streit (SUI) | Christian Dube (CAN), Sergei Samsonov (RUS), Mike York (USA) |
| 1998 WM20 | David Aebischer (SUI) | Pavel Skrbek (CZE) | Olli Jokinen (FIN) |
| | David Aebischer (SUI) | Pierre Hedin (SWE), Andrei Markov (RUS) | Olli Jokinen (FIN), Eero Somervuori (FIN), Maxim Balmochnykh (RUS) |
| 1999 WM20 | Roberto Luongo (CAN) | Vitali Vishnevski (RUS) | Maxim Afinogenov (RUS) |
| | Roberto Luongo (CAN) | Brian Campbell (CAN), Vitali Vishnevski (RUS) | Daniel Tkaczuk (CAN), Brian Gionta (USA), Maxim Balmochnykh (RUS) |
| 2000 WM20 | Rick DiPietro (USA) | Alexander Ryazantsev (RUS) | Milan Kraft (CZE) |
| | Rick DiPietro (USA) | Mathieu Biron (CAN), Alexander Ryazantsev (RUS) | Milan Kraft (CZE), Yevgeni Muratov (RUS), Alexei Tereshenko (RUS) |
| 2001 WM20 | Tomas Duba (CZE) | Rostislav Klesla (CZE) | Pavel Brendl (CZE) |
| | Ari Ahonen (FIN) | Rostislav Klesla (CZE), Tuukka Mantyla (FIN) | Jani Rita (FIN), Pavel Brendl (CZE), Jason Spezza (CAN) |
| 2002 WM20 | Kari Lehtonen (FIN) | Igor Knyazev (RUS) | Mike Cammalleri (CAN) |
| | Pascal Leclaire (CAN) | Igor Knyazev (RUS), Jay Bouwmeester (CAN) | Mike Cammalleri (CAN), Stanislav Chistov (RUS), Marek Svatos (SVK) |
| 2003 WM20 | Marc-Andre Fleury (CAN) | Joni Pitkanen (FIN) | Igor Grigorenko (RUS) |
| | Marc-Andre Fleury (CAN) | Carlo Colaiacovo (CAN), Joni Pitkanen (FIN) | Igor Grigorenko (RUS), Yuri Trubachyov (RUS), Scottie Upshall (CAN) |
| 2004 WM20 | Al Montoya (USA) | Sami Lepisto (FIN) | Zach Parise (USA) |
| | Al Montoya (USA) | Dion Phaneuf (CAN), Sami Lepisto (FIN) | Jeff Carter (CAN), Zach Parise (USA), Valtteri Filppula (FIN) |
| 2005 WM20 | Marek Schwarz (CZE) | Dion Phaneuf (CAN) | Alexander Ovechkin (RUS) |
| | Marek Schwarz (CZE) | Dion Phaneuf (CAN), Ryan Suter (USA) | Patrice Bergeron (CAN), Jeff Carter (CAN), Alexander Ovechkin (RUS) |
| 2006 WM20 | Tuukka Rask (FIN) | Marc Staal (CAN) | Yevgeni Malkin (RUS) |
| | Tuukka Rask (FIN) | Luc Bourdon (CAN), Jack Johnson (USA) | Steve Downie (CAN), Yevgeni Malkin (RUS), Lauri Tukonen (FIN) |
| 2007 WM20 | Carey Price (CAN) | Erik Johnson (USA) | Alexei Cherepanov (RUS) |
| | Carey Price (CAN) | Erik Johnson (USA), Kris Letang (CAN) | Jonathan Toews (CAN), Alexei Cherepanov (RUS), Patrick Kane (USA) |
| 2008 WM20 | Steve Mason (CAN) | Drew Doughty (CAN) | Viktor Tikhonov (RUS) |
| | Steve Mason (CAN) | Drew Doughty (CAN), Victor Hedman (SWE) | Patrik Berglund (SWE), Viktor Tikhonov (RUS), James van Riemsdyk (USA) |
| 2009 WM20 | Jacob Markstrom (SWE) | Erik Karlsson (SWE) | John Tavares (CAN) |
| | Jaroslav Janus (SVK) | Erik Karlsson (SWE), P.K. Subban (CAN) | Nikita Filatov (RUS), Cody Hodgson (CAN), John Tavares (CAN) |
| 2010 WM20 | Benjamin Conz (SUI) | Alex Pietrangelo (CAN) | Jordan Eberle (CAN) |
| | Benjamin Conz (SUI) | John Carlson (USA), Alex Pietrangelo (CAN) | Jordan Eberle (CAN), Nino Niederreiter (SUI), Derek Stepan (USA) |
| 2011 WM20 | Jack Campbell (USA) | Ryan Ellis (CAN) | Brayden Schenn (CAN) |
| | Jack Campbell (USA) | Ryan Ellis (CAN), Dmitri Orlov (RUS) | Ryan Johansen (CAN), Yevgeni Kuznetsov (RUS), Brayden Schenn (CAN) |
| 2012 WM20 | Petr Mrazek (CZE) | Brandon Gormley (CAN) | Yevgeni Kuznetsov (RUS) |
| | Petr Mrazek (CZE) | Brandon Gormley (CAN), Oscar Klefbom (SWE) | Max Friberg (SWE), Mikael Granlund (FIN), Yevgeni Kuznetsov (RUS) |

| Directorate<br>All-Star Team | Best Goalie<br>Goal | Best Defenceman<br>Defence | Best Forward<br>Forward |
|---|---|---|---|
| 2002 WM18 | Lukas Mensator (CZE) | Ryan Suter (USA) | Nikolai Zherdev (RUS) |
| | Lukas Mensator (CZE) | Konstantin Korneyev (RUS), Richard Stehlik (SVK) | Alexander Ovechkin (RUS), Jiri Hudler (CZE), Nikolai Zherdev (RUS) |
| 2003 WM18 | Jaroslav Halak (SVK) | Brent Seabrook (CAN) | Alexander Ovechkin (RUS) |
| | Jaroslav Halak (SVK) | Brent Seabrook (CAN), Lukas Pulpan (CZE) | Anthony Stewart (CAN), Tim Hensick (USA), Alexander Ovechkin (RUS) |
| 2004-06 WM18 | Not Awarded | | |
| 2007 WM18 | Josh Unice (USA) | Kevin Shattenkirk (USA) | James van Riemsdyk (USA) |
| | Josh Unice (USA) | Victor Hedman (SWE), Kevin Shattenkirk (USA) | Alexei Cherepanov (RUS), Steve Stamkos (CAN), James van Riemsdyk (USA) |
| 2008 WM18 | Jake Allen (CAN) | Erik Karlsson (SWE) | Kirill Petrov (RUS) |
| | Jake Allen (CAN) | Vyacheslav Voinov (RUS), Victor Hedman (SWE) | Kirill Petrov (RUS), Mattias Tedenby (SWE), Nikita Filatov (RUS) |
| 2009 WM18 | Igor Bobkov (RUS) | Cam Fowler (USA) | Toni Rajala (FIN) |
| | Jack Campbell (USA) | Tim Erixon (SWE), Cam Fowler (USA) | Toni Rajala (FIN), Jerry D'Amigo (USA), Vladimir Tarasenko (RUS) |
| 2010 WM18 | Jack Campbell (USA) | Adam Larsson (SWE) | Teemu Pulkkinen (FIN) |
| | Jack Campbell (USA) | Adam Clendening (USA), Adam Larsson (SWE) | Johan Larsson (SWE), Yevgeni Kuznetsov (RUS), Teemu Pulkkinen (FIN) |
| 2011 WM18 | John Gibson (USA) | Ryan Murphy (CAN) | Nikita Kucherov (RUS) |
| | Not Awarded | | |
| 2012 WM18 | Collin Olson (USA) | Matt Dumba (CAN) | Filip Forsberg (SWE) |
| | Not Awarded | | |

| Directorate<br>All-Star Team | Best Goalie<br>Goal | Best Defenceman<br>Defence | Best Forward<br>Forward |
|---|---|---|---|
| 2002 OG-W | Kim St. Pierre (CAN) | Angela Ruggiero (USA) | Hayley Wickenheiser (CAN) |
| | Kim St. Pierre (CAN) | Tara Mounsey (USA), Angela Ruggiero (USA) | Hayley Wickenheiser (CAN), Natalie Darwitz (USA), Cammi Granato (USA) |
| 2006 OG-W | Kim Martin (SWE) | Angela Ruggiero (USA) | Hayley Wickenheiser (CAN) |
| | Kim Martin (SWE) | Carla MacLeod (CAN), Angela Ruggiero (USA) | Hayley Wickenheiser (CAN), Gillian Apps (CAN), Maria Rooth (SWE) |
| 2010 OG-W | Shannon Szabados (CAN) | Molly Engstrom (USA) | Meghan Agosta (CAN) |
| | Shannon Szabados (CAN) | Molly Engstrom (USA), Angela Ruggiero (USA) | Meghan Agosta (CAN), Jenny Potter (USA), Marie-Philip Poulin (CAN) |

| Directorate<br>All-Star Team | Best Goalie<br>Goal | Best Defenceman<br>Defence | Best Forward<br>Forward |
|---|---|---|---|
| 1992 WW | Annica Ahlen (SWE) | Geraldine Heaney (CAN) | Cammi Granato (USA) |
| | Manon Rheaume (CAN) | Geraldine Heaney (CAN), Ellen Weinberg (USA) | Angela James (CAN), Riikka Nieminen (FIN), Cammi Granato (USA) |
| 1994 WW | Erin Whitten (USA) | Geraldine Heaney (CAN) | Riikka Nieminen (FIN) |
| | Manon Rheaume (CAN) | Kelly O'Leary (USA), Therese Brisson (CAN) | Danielle Goyette (CAN), Riikka Nieminen (FIN), Karyn Bye (USA) |
| 1997 WW | Not Awarded | | |
| | Patricia Sautter (SUI) | Kelly O'Leary (USA), Cassie Campbell (CAN) | Hayley Wickenheiser (CAN), Riikka Nieminen (FIN), Cammi Granato (USA) |
| 1999 WW | Sami Jo Small (CAN) | Kirsi Hanninen (FIN) | Jenny Schmidgall (-Potter) (USA) |
| | Sami Jo Small (CAN) | Kirsi Hanninen (FIN), Sue Merz (USA) | Hayley Wickenheiser (CAN), Jayna Hefford (CAN), Jenny Schmidgall (USA) |
| 2000 WW | Sami Jo Small (CAN) | Angela Ruggiero (USA) | Katja Riipi (FIN) |
| | Not Awarded | | |
| 2001 WW | Kim St. Pierre (CAN) | Karyn Bye (USA) | Jennifer Botterill (CAN) |
| | Not Awarded | | |
| 2004 WW | Kim St. Pierre (CAN) | Angela Ruggiero (USA) | Jayna Hefford (CAN) |
| | Pam Dreyer (USA) | Gunilla Andersson (SWE), Angela Ruggiero (USA) | Jayna Hefford (CAN), Jennifer Botterill (CAN), Natalie Darwitz (USA) |
| 2005 WW | Chanda Gunn (USA) | Angela Ruggiero (USA) | Jayna Hefford (CAN) |
| | Natalya Trunova (KAZ) | Cheryl Pounder (CAN), Angela Ruggiero (USA) | Hayley Wickenheiser (CAN), Maria Rooth (SWE), Krissy Wendell (USA) |
| 2007 WW | Noora Raty (FIN) | Molly Engstrom (USA) | Hayley Wickenheiser (CAN) |
| | Kim St. Pierre (CAN) | Delaney Collins (CAN), Angela Ruggiero (USA) | Natalie Darwitz (USA), Krissy Wendell (USA), Hayley Wickenheiser (CAN) |
| 2008 WW | Noora Raty (FIN) | Angela Ruggiero (USA) | Natalie Darwitz (USA) |
| | Noora Raty (FIN) | Emma Laaksonen (FIN), Julie Chu (USA) | Hayley Wickenheiser (CAN), Jayna Hefford (CAN), Natalie Darwitz (USA) |
| 2009 WW | Charline Labonte (CAN) | Jenni Hiirikoski (FIN) | Hayley Wickenheiser (CAN) |
| | Jessie Vetter (USA) | Carla MacLeod (CAN), Angela Ruggiero (USA) | Michelle Karvinen (FIN), Julie Chu (USA), Natalie Darwitz (USA) |
| 2011 WW | Noora Raty (FIN) | Meaghan Mikkelson (CAN) | Monique Lamoureux-Kolls (USA) |
| | Zuzana Tomcikova (SVK) | Caitlin Cahow (USA), Meaghan Mikkelson (CAN) | Michelle Karvinen (FIN), Hilary Knight (USA), Hayley Wickenheiser (CAN) |
| 2012 WW | Florence Schelling (SUI) | Jenni Hiirikoski (FIN) | Kelli Stack (USA) |
| | Not Awarded | | |

| Directorate<br>All-Star Team | Best Goalie<br>Goal | Best Defenceman<br>Defence | Best Forward<br>Forward |
|---|---|---|---|
| 2008 WW18 | Alyssa Grogan (USA) | Lauriane Rougeau (CAN) | Marie-Philip Poulin (CAN) |
| | Not Awarded | | |
| 2009 WW18 | Alex Rigsby (USA) | Alev Kelter (USA) | Amanda Kessel (USA) |
| | Not Awarded | | |
| 2010 WW18 | Alex Rigsby (USA) | Brigette Lacquette (CAN) | Kendall Coyne (USA) |
| | Not Awarded | | |
| 2011 WW18 | Isabella Portnoj (FIN) | Milica McMillen (USA) | Alex Carpenter (USA) |
| | Not Awarded | | |
| 2012 WW18 | Franziska Albl (GER) | Erin Ambrose (CAN) | Alex Carpenter (USA) |
| | Not Awarded | | |

# Youngest/Oldest

**YOUNGEST PLAYERS, OLYMPICS, MEN**

| | |
|---|---|
| Mark Howe (USA) | 16 years, 8 months, 8 days |
| Franz Berry (SUI) | 17 years, 2 months, 7 days |
| Jack Kirrane (USA) | 17 years, 5 months, 10 days |
| Ed Olczyk (USA) | 17 years, 5 months, 22 days |
| Alfred Huber (AUT) | 17 years, 9 months, 16 days |
| Al Iafrate (USA) | 17 years, 11 months, 14 days |
| Kirk Muller (CAN) | 17 years, 11 months, 31 days |

**OLDEST PLAYERS, OLYMPICS, MEN**

| | |
|---|---|
| Max Sillig (SUI) | 46 years, 5 months, 5 days |
| Alfred Steinke (GER) | 45 years, 1 month, 18 days |
| Chris Chelios (USA) | 44 years, 28 days |
| Michal Antuszewicz (POL) | 42 years, 4 months, 16 days |
| Matyas Farkas (HUN) | 42 years, 5 months, 30 days |
| Jan Lichnowski (TCH) | 42 years, 6 months, 4 days |
| Igor Larionov (RUS) | 41 years, 2 months, 20 days |
| Alfred Hoffmann (FRG) | 41 years, 1 month, 10 days |
| Dominik Hasek (CZE) | 41 years, 17 days |

**YOUNGEST PLAYERS, WORLD CHAMPIONSHIP (MEN)**

| | |
|---|---|
| Sandor Miklos (HUN) | 15 years, 10 months, 27 days |
| Serge Renault (FRA) | 16 years, 3 months, 3 days |
| Pic Cattini (SUI | 16 years, 4 months, 22 days |
| Georges Pootmans (BEL) | 16 years, 8 months, 15 days |
| Luigi Venosta (ITA) | 16 years, 9 months, 3 days |
| Alfred Huber (AUT) | 16 years, 10 months, 3 days |

**OLDEST PLAYERS, WORLD CHAMPIONSHIP (MEN)**

| | |
|---|---|
| Fernand Carez (BEL) | 43 years, 3 months, 22 days |
| Yuri Shundrov (UKR) | 42 years, 11 months, 0 days |
| Albert Geromini (SUI) | 42 years, 10 months, 0 days |
| Jesper Duus (DEN) | 42 years, 5 months, 16 days |
| Konstantin Shafranov (KAZ) | 41 years, 8 months, 7 days |
| Alexander Koreshkov (KAZ) | 41 years, 6 months, 20 days |
| Matyas Farkas (HUN) | 41 years, 5 months, 12 days |
| Petr Nedved (CZE) | 41 years, 5 months, 11 days |

**YOUNGEST PLAYERS, U20 WORLD CHAMPIONSHIP**

| | |
|---|---|
| Viktor Alexandrov (KAZ) | 14 years, 11 months, 28 days |
| Konstantin Zakharov (BLR) | 15 years, 7 months, 24 days |
| Vitali Arystov (BLR) | 15 years, 10 months, 20 days |
| Andrei Kostitsyn (BLR) | 15 years, 10 months, 23 days |

**YOUNGEST PLAYERS, U18 WORLD CHAMPIONSHIP (MEN)**

| | |
|---|---|
| Pavlo Borysenko (UKR) | 14 years, 10 months, 7 days |
| Konstantin Zakharov (BLR) | 14 years, 10 months, 14 days |
| Andrei Kostitsyn (BLR) | 15 years, 2 months, 13 days |
| Yegor Yegorov (UKR) | 15 years, 2 months, 22 days |
| Valentyn Lays (UKR) | 15 years, 3 months, 4 days |
| Mikkel Bodker (DEN) | 15 years, 3 months, 30 days |
| John Tavares (CAN) | 15 years, 6 months, 23 days |

**YOUNGEST PLAYERS, OLYMPICS, WOMEN**

| | |
|---|---|
| Kim Martin (SWE) | 15 years, 1 month, 8 days |
| Valentina Bettarini (ITA) | 15 years, 7 months, 13 days |
| Katharina Sparer (ITA) | 15 years, 11 months, 20 days |
| Jenni Asserholt (SWE) | 15 years, 11 months, 22 days |

**OLDEST PLAYERS, OLYMPICS, WOMEN**

| | |
|---|---|
| Danielle Goyette (CAN) | 40 years, 21 days |
| France St. Louis (CAN) | 39 years, 4 months |
| Kristina Bergstrand (SWE) | 38 years, 4 months, 17 days |
| Zhanna Shchelchkova (RUS) | 37 years even |

**YOUNGEST PLAYERS, WOMEN'S WORLD CHAMPIONSHIP**

| | |
|---|---|
| Iris Holzer (SUI) | 14 years, 15 days |
| Nicole Walder (SUI) | 14 years, 3 months, 26 days |
| Daniela Diaz (SUI) | 14 years, 9 months, 15 days |
| Kristina Soderstrom (NOR) | 14 years, 10 months, 6 days |
| Natascha Schaffrik (GER) | 14 years, 10 months, 13 days |
| Ramona Fuhrer (SUI) | 14 years, 11 months, 29 days |

**OLDEST PLAYERS, WOMEN'S WORLD CHAMPIONSHIP**

| | |
|---|---|
| Danielle Goyette (CAN) | 41 years, 2 months, 11 days |
| France St. Louis (CAN) | 40 years, 4 months, 25 days |
| Kristina Bergstrand (SWE) | 38 years, 4 months, 17 days |
| Anne Haanpaa (FIN) | 37 years, 10 months, 12 days |
| Shirley Cameron (CAN) | 37 years, 7 months, 13 days |
| Therese Brisson (CAN) | 37 years, 5 months, 1 day |

**YOUNGEST PLAYERS, U18 WOMEN'S WORLD CHAMPIONSHIP**

| | |
|---|---|
| Michelle Lowenhielm (SWE) | 15 years, 5 days |
| Sandra Thalmann (SUI) | 15 years, 21 days |

# Game-Winning Shots (Shootouts)/Overtime

**OLYMPICS, MEN**

| Year | OT/ GWS | Round | Date | Final Score | Extra Time | Winning Goal (GWS score) |
|---|---|---|---|---|---|---|
| 1988 | GWS | 11th/12th | Feb 23, 1988 | FRA 8-NOR 6 | 10:00 | Derek Haas (2-0)* |
| 1992 | GWS | QF | Feb 18, 1992 | CAN 4-GER 3 | 10:00 | Eric Lindros (3-2) |
| 1994 | GWS | CONS | Feb 22, 1994 | FRA 5-AUT 4 | 10:00 | Serge Poudrier (4-1) |
| 1994 | GWS | GOLD | Feb 27, 1994 | SWE 3-CAN 2 | 10:00 | Peter Forsberg (3-2) |
| 1998 | GWS | SF | Feb 20, 1998 | CZE 2-CAN 1 | 10:00 | Robert Reichel (1-0) |
| 2010 | GWS | PRE | Feb 18, 2010 | CAN 3-SUI 2 | 5:00 | Sidney Crosby (1-0) |
| 2010 | GWS | PRE | Feb 18, 2010 | SVK 2-RUS 1 | 5:00 | Pavol Demitra (2-1) |
| 2010 | GWS | QUAL | Feb 23, 2010 | SUI 3-BLR 2 | 10:00 | Romano Lemm (2-1) |

**WORLD CHAMPIONSHIP, MEN**

| Year | OT/ GWS | Round | Date | Final Score | Extra Time | Winning Goal (GWS score) |
|---|---|---|---|---|---|---|
| 1992 | GWS | SF | May 9, 1992 | FIN 3-CZE 2 | 10:00 | Jarkko Varvio (2-0) |
| 1994 | GWS | GOLD | May 8, 1994 | CAN 2-FIN 1 | 10:00 | Luc Robitaille (3-2) |
| 1996 | GWS | SF | May 3, 1996 | CAN 3-RUS 2 | 10:00 | Yanic Perreault (3-2) |
| 1999 | GWS | SF | May 13, 1999 | CZE 7-CAN 4* | 10:00 | Jaroslav Spacek (4-3) |
| | | | *best-of-two + shootout/CZE used two goalies | | | |
| 2001 | GWS | SF | May 12, 2001 | CZE 3-SWE 2 | 10:00 | Viktor Ujcik (2-1) |
| 2002 | GWS | SF | May 9, 2002 | RUS 3-FIN 2 | 10:00 | Valeri Karpov (2-0) |
| 2002 | GWS | SF | May 9, 2002 | SVK 3-SWE 2 | 10:00 | Zigmund Palffy (2-0) |
| 2004 | GWS | QF | May 5, 2004 | USA 3-CZE 2 | 10:00 | Andy Roach (1-0) |
| 2004 | GWS | BRONZE | May 9, 2004 | USA 1-SVK 0 | 10:00 | Andy Roach (4-2) |
| 2005 | GWS | QF | May 12, 2005 | CZE 3-USA 2 | 10:00 | Martin Rucinsky (1-0) |
| 2005 | GWS | QF | May 12, 2005 | RUS 4-FIN 3 | 10:00 | Maxim Afinogenov (3-2) |
| 2007 | GWS | QF | May 10, 2007 | FIN 5-USA 4 | 10:00 | Jere Lehtinen (1-0) |
| 2010 | GWS | REL | May 18, 2010 | USA 3-ITA 2 | 5:00 | T.J. Oshie (2-1) |
| 2010 | GWS | QF | May 20, 2010 | CZE 2-FIN 1 | 10:00 | Jan Marek (2-1) |
| 2010 | GWS | SF | May 22, 2010 | CZE 3-SWE 2 | 10:00 | Jan Marek (2-1) |
| 2011 | GWS | PRE | Apr 30, 2011 | NOR 5-SWE 4 | 5:00 | Per-Age Skroder (2-0) |
| 2011 | GWS | PRE | May 2, 2011 | FIN 3-LAT 2 | 5:00 | Jarkko Imonen (2-0) |
| 2011 | GWS | PRE | May 3, 2011 | GER 3-SLO 2 | 5:00 | Frank Hordler (2-1) |
| 2011 | GWS | PRE | May 4, 2011 | DEN 3-LAT 2 | 5:00 | Mads Christensen (1-0) |
| 2011 | GWS | QUAL | May 6, 2011 | FIN 5-GER 4 | 5:00 | Mikko Koivu (3-2) |
| 2011 | GWS | QUAL | May 6, 2011 | CAN 4-USA 3 | 5:00 | Jordan Eberle (2-0) |
| 2011 | GWS | QUAL | May 7, 2011 | DEN 4-GER 3 | 5:00 | Mikkel Bodker (2-1) |
| 2011 | GWS | QUAL | May 9, 2011 | FIN 3-RUS 2 | 5:00 | Jarkko Imonen (2-0) |
| 2012 | GWS | PRE | May 7, 2012 | CZE 4-NOR 3 | 5:00 | Ales Hemsky (1-0) |

**WORLD U20 (JUNIOR) CHAMPIONSHIP**

| Year | OT/ GWS | Round | Date | Final Score | Extra Time | Winning Goal (GWS score) |
|---|---|---|---|---|---|---|
| 1997 | GWS | QF | Jan 1, 1997 | CZE 3-FIN 2 | 10:00 | Radek Matejovski (3-1) |
| 1998 | GWS | QF | Dec 31, 1997 | SUI 2-SWE 1 | 10:00 | Bjorn Christen (1-0) |
| 1998 | GWS | BRONZE | Jan 3, 1998 | SUI 4-CZE 3 | 10:00 | Sandro Rizzi (2-0) |
| 2000 | GWS | REL | Jan 4, 2000 | SVK 1-UKR 0 | 10:00 | Miroslav Zalesak (1-0) |
| 2000 | GWS | BRONZE | Jan 4, 2000 | CAN 4-USA 3 | 10:00 | Brandon Reid (1-0) |
| 2000 | GWS | GOLD | Jan 4, 2000 | CZE 1-RUS 0* | 10:00 | Libor Pivko (2-0) |
| | | | *RUS used two goalies | | | |
| 2001 | GWS | 7th/8th | Jan 5, 2001 | RUS 4-SVK 3 | 10:00 | Andrei Shefer (3-1) |
| 2002 | GWS | QF | Jan 1, 2002 | SUI 3-SVK 2 | 10:00 | Sven Helfenstein (1-0) |
| 2002 | GWS | REL | Jan 3, 2002 | BLR 1-FRA 0 | 10:00 | Dmitri Mialeshka (4-3) |
| 2007 | GWS | SF | Jan 3, 2007 | CAN 2-USA 1 | 10:00 | Jonathan Toews (5-4) |
| 2009 | GWS | PRE | Dec 31, 2008 | SVK 3-FIN 2 | 5:00 | Tomas Tatar (2-1) |
| 2009 | GWS | SF | Jan 3, 2009 | CAN 6-RUS 5 | 10:00 | Jordan Eberle (2-0) |
| 2010 | GWS | PRE | Dec 31, 2009 | CAN 5-USA 4 | 5:00 | Brandon Kozum (3-2) |
| 2011 | GWS | PRE | Dec 31, 2010 | SWE 6-CAN 5 | 5:00 | Oscar Lindberg (2-0) |
| 2011 | GWS | SF | Jan 3, 2011 | RUS 4-SWE 3 | 10:00 | Denis Golubev (1-0) |
| 2011 | GWS | 5th/6th | Jan 4, 2011 | SUI 3-FIN 2 | 5:00 | Yannick Herren (1-0) |
| 2012 | GWS | PRE | Dec 28, 2011 | SWE 4-SUI 3 | 5:00 | Sebastian Collberg (2-0) |
| 2012 | GWS | SF | Jan 3, 2012 | SWE 3-FIN 2 | 10:00 | Max Friberg (2-1) |

**WORLD U18 CHAMPIONSHIP, MEN**

| Year | OT/ GWS | Round | Date | Final Score | Extra Time | Winning Goal (GWS score) |
|---|---|---|---|---|---|---|
| 2000 | GWS | 5th/6th | Apr 24, 2000 | SVK 4-CZE 3 | 10:00 | Marek Svatos (1-0) |
| 2001 | GWS | QF | Apr 19, 2001 | CZE 5-USA 4 | 10:00 | Jan Rehard (3-2) |
| 2003 | GWS | SF | Apr 20, 2003 | SVK 2-RUS 1 | 10:00 | Stefan Ruzicka (3-1) |
| 2007 | GWS | PRE | Apr 11, 2007 | SWE 2-FIN 1 | 5:00 | Michael Backlund (1-0) |
| 2007 | GWS | PRE | Apr 14, 2007 | CZE 3-SVK 2 | 5:00 | Roman Szturk (1-0) |
| 2007 | GWS | PRE | Apr 15, 2007 | CAN 3-USA 2 | 5:00 | Zack Boychuk (2-1) |
| 2007 | GWS | SF | Apr 20, 2007 | USA 4-CAN 3 | 10:00 | James van Riemsdyk (1-0) |
| 2009 | GWS | REL | Apr 17, 2009 | GER 5-SVK 4 | 5:00 | Thomas Brandl (1-0) |
| 2009 | GWS | BRONZE | Apr 19, 2009 | FIN 5-CAN 4 | 10:00 | Tony Rajala (2-0) |
| 2010 | GWS | PRE | Apr 18, 2010 | FIN 4-CZE 3 | 5:00 | Teemu Pulkkinen (3-1) |
| 2010 | GWS | REL | Apr 22, 2010 | LAT 5-BLR 4 | 5:00 | Davis Straupe (3-1) |
| 2011 | GWS | PRE | Apr 16, 2011 | RUS 5-GER 4 | 5:00 | Nikita Kucherov (2-1) |

**OLYMPICS, WOMEN**

| Year | OT/ GWS | Round | Date | Final Score | Extra Time | Winning Goal (GWS score) |
|---|---|---|---|---|---|---|
| 2006 | GWS | SF | Feb 17, 2006 | SWE 3-USA 2 | 10:00 | Pernilla Winberg (2-0) |
| 2006 | GWS | 5th/6th | Feb 20, 2006 | GER 1-RUS 0 | 10:00 | Maritta Becker (2-0) |
| 2010 | GWS | 5th/6th | Feb 22, 2010 | SUI 2-RUS 1 | 10:00 | Stephanie Marty (2-1) |

**WORLD WOMEN'S CHAMPIONSHIP**

| Year | OT/ GWS | Round | Date | Final Score | Extra Time | Winning Goal (GWS score) |
|---|---|---|---|---|---|---|
| 1992 | GWS | PLACE | Apr 24, 1992 | CHN 2-SUI 1 | 10:00 | Yan Lu (2-0) |
| 1992 | GWS | BRONZE | Apr 26, 1992 | FIN 5-SWE 4 | 10:00 | Riikka Nieminen (2-1) |
| 2005 | GWS | 7th/8th | Apr 9, 2005 | KAZ 2-RUS 1 | 10:00 | Olga Potapova (1-0) |
| 2005 | GWS | GOLD | Apr 9, 2005 | USA 1-CAN 0 | 20:00 | Angela Ruggiero (3-1) |
| 2007 | GWS | QUAL | Apr 7, 2007 | CAN 5-USA 4 | 10:00 | Hayley Wickenheiser (1-0) |
| 2008 | GWS | QUAL | Apr 8, 2008 | KAZ 4-SWE 3 | 5:00 | Kathrin Lehmann (1-0) |
| 2009 | GWS | PRE | Apr 5, 2009 | KAZ 2-SUI 1 | 5:00 | Alena Fux (1-0) |
| 2009 | GWS | REL | Apr 8, 2009 | SUI 5-CHN 4 | 5:00 | Nicole Bullo (2-0) |

| | | | | | | |
|---|---|---|---|---|---|---|
| 2011 | GWS | 5th/6th | Apr 24, 2011 | SWE 3-SUI 2 | 10:00 | Elin Holmlov (2-1) |
| 2011 | GWS | REL | Apr 24, 2011 | SVK 2-KAZ 1 | 5:00 | Martina Velickova (1-0) |
| 2012 | GWS | REL | Apr 11, 2012 | GER 2-SVK 1 | 5:00 | Manuela Anwander (2-1) |

**WORLD WOMEN'S U18 CHAMPIONSHIP**

| | | | | | | |
|---|---|---|---|---|---|---|
| 2009 | GWS | PRE | Jan 5, 2009 | FIN 2-CZE 1 | 5:00 | Susanna Tapani (1-0) |
| 2009 | GWS | 5th/6th | Jan 9, 2009 | GER 2-SUI 1 | 5:00 | Manuela Anwander (1-0) |
| 2009 | GWS | 7th/8th | Jan 10, 2009 | RUS 3-SUI 2 | 5:00 | Olga Sosina (1-0) |

**OLYMPICS, MEN**

| | | | | | | |
|---|---|---|---|---|---|---|
| 1994 | OT | QF | Feb 23, 1994 | CAN 3-CZE 2 | 5:54 | Paul Kariya |
| 1994 | OT | QF | Feb 23, 1994 | RUS 3-SVK 2 | 8:39 | Alexander Vinogradov |
| 2010 | OT | PRE | Feb 20, 2010 | SUI 5-NOR 4 | 6:28 | Romano Lemm |
| 2010 | OT | QUAL | Feb 23, 2010 | CZE 3-LAT 2 | 5:10 | David Krejci |
| 2010 | OT | GOLD | Feb 28, 2010 | CAN 3-USA 2 | 7:40 | Sidney Crosby |

**WORLD CHAMPIONSHIP, MEN**

| | | | | | | |
|---|---|---|---|---|---|---|
| 1993 | OT | SF | Apr 30, 1993 | SWE 3-CZE 2 | 8:38 | Thomas Rundqvist |
| 1995 | OT | SF | May 5, 1995 | SWE 3-CAN 2 | 8:17 | Daniel Alfredsson |
| 1996 | OT | BRONZE | May 4, 1996 | USA 4-RUS 3 | 4:48 | Brian Rolston |
| 1999 | OT | SF | May 13, 1999 | FIN 3-SWE 1/SWE 2-FIN 0* | 6:25 | Marko Tuomainen |
| | | | | | | *best of two + OT/GWS |
| 1999 | OT | GOLD | May 15, 1999 | CZE 3-FIN 1/FIN 4-CZE 0* | 16:32 | Jan Hlavac |
| | | | | | | *best of two + OT/GWS |
| 2001 | OT | QF | May 10, 2001 | USA 4-CAN 3 | 0:32 | Darby Hendrickson |
| 2001 | OT | QF | May 10, 2001 | SWE 4-RUS 3 | 6:03 | Kim Johnsson |
| 2001 | OT | GOLD | May 13, 2001 | CZE 3-FIN 2 | 10:38 | David Moravec |
| 2003 | OT | QF | May 7, 2003 | CAN 3-GER 2 | 0:37 | Eric Brewer |
| 2003 | OT | GOLD | May 11, 2003 | CAN 3-SWE 2 | 13:49 | Anson Carter |
| 2004 | OT | QF | May 6, 2004 | CAN 5-FIN 4 | 5:33 | Dany Heatley |
| 2005 | OT | SF | May 14, 2005 | CZE 3-SWE 2 | 4:43 | Radek Dvorak |
| 2006 | OT | QF | May 18, 2006 | CZE 4-RUS 3 | 7:58 | Zbynek Irgl |
| 2007 | OT | SF | May 12, 2007 | FIN 2-RUS 1 | 5:40 | Mikko Koivu |
| 2008 | OT | QF | May 14, 2008 | SWE 3-CZE 2 | 3:15 | Mattias Weinhandl |
| 2008 | OT | QF | May 14, 2008 | FIN 3-USA 2 | 3:59 | Sami Lepisto |
| 2008 | OT | GOLD | May 18, 2008 | RUS 5-CAN 4 | 2:42 | Ilya Kovalchuk |
| 2011 | OT | PRE | Apr 29, 2011 | SUI 1-FRA 0 | 1:46 | Julien Vauclair |
| 2011 | OT | PRE | May 3, 2011 | CAN 4-SUI 3 | 4:14 | Alex Pietrangelo |
| 2011 | OT | PRE | May 3, 2011 | FRA 2-BLR 1 | 0:46 | Kevin Hecquefeuille |
| 2012 | OT | PRE | May 5, 2012 | USA 5-CAN 4 | 1:47 | Jack Johnson |
| 2012 | OT | PRE | May 6, 2012 | ITA 4-DEN 3 | 0:52 | Giulio Scandella |
| 2012 | OT | PRE | May 11, 2012 | USA 3-KAZ 2 | 4:38 | Justin Faulk |

**IIHF-NHL INVITATIONALS**

| Year | Event | OT/ GWS | Round | Date | Final Score | Extra Time | Winning Goal (GWS score) |
|---|---|---|---|---|---|---|---|
| 1976 | CC | OT | #2 Finals | Sept 15, 1976 | CAN 5-TCH 4 | 11.33 | Darryl Sittler |
| 1984 | CC | OT | SF | Sept 13, 1984 | CAN 3-URS 2 | 12.29 | Mike Bossy |
| 1987 | CC | OT | #1 Finals | Sept 11, 1987 | URS 6-CAN 5 | 5:33 | Alexander Semak |
| 1987 | CC | OT | #2 Finals | Sept 13, 1987 | CAN 6-URS 5 | 30-07 | Mario Lemieux |
| 1996 | WCH | OT | SF | Sept 7, 1996 | CAN 3-SWE 2 | 39-47 | Theo Fleury |
| 1996 | WCH | OT | #1 Finals | Sept 10, 1996 | CAN 4-USA 3 | 10:37 | Steve Yzerman |
| 2004 | WCH | OT | SF | Sept 11, 2004 | CAN 4-CZE 3 | 3:45 | Vincent Lecavalier |

**WORLD U20 (JUNIOR) CHAMPIONSHIP**

| | | | | | | |
|---|---|---|---|---|---|---|
| 1996 | OT | 5th/6th | Jan 4, 1996 | USA 8-FIN 7 | 3:02 | Jeremiah McCarthy |
| 1998 | OT | QF | Dec 31, 1997 | RUS 2-CAN 1 | 9:21 | Maxim Afinogenov |
| 1998 | OT | GOLD | Jan 3, 1998 | FIN 2-RUS 1 | 13:41 | Niklas Hagman |
| 1999 | OT | QF | Jan 2, 1999 | RUS 3-FIN 2 | 7:33 | Denis Arkhipov |
| 1999 | OT | GOLD | Jan 5, 1999 | RUS 3-CAN 2 | 5:13 | Artyom Chubarov |
| 2001 | OT | BRONZE | Jan 5, 2001 | CAN 2-SWE 1 | 0:37 | Raffi Torres |
| 2002 | OT | SF | Jan 2, 2002 | RUS 2-FIN 1 | 1:44 | Sergei Soin |
| 2005 | OT | BRONZE | Jan 4, 2005 | CZE 3-USA 2 | 2:38 | Petr Vrana |
| 2007 | OT | PRE | Dec 26, 2006 | GER 2-USA 1 | 1:51 | Marcel Muller |
| 2007 | OT | PRE | Dec 31, 2006 | USA 3-SWE 2 | 3:16 | Jack Johnson |
| 2009 | OT | 5th/6th | Jan 4, 2009 | USA 3-CZE 2 | 2:49 | James van Riemsdyk |
| 2010 | OT | QF | Jan 2, 2010 | SUI 3-RUS 2 | 9:46 | Nino Niederreiter |
| 2010 | OT | GOLD | Jan 5, 2010 | USA 6-CAN 5 | 4:21 | John Carlson |
| 2011 | OT | PRE | Dec 26, 2010 | USA 3-FIN 2 | 3:08 | Nick Bjugstad |
| 2011 | OT | PRE | Dec 27, 2010 | SVK 2-GER 1 | 3:39 | Marek Hrivik |
| 2011 | OT | QF | Jan 2, 2011 | RUS 4-FIN 3 | 6:44 | Yevgeni Kuznetsov |
| 2012 | OT | PRE | Dec 31, 2011 | SWE 4-RUS 3 | 2:44 | Joakim Nordstrom |
| 2012 | OT | REL | Jan 2, 2012 | SUI 4-DEN 3 | 3:27 | Tanner Richard |
| 2012 | OT | QF | Jan 2, 2012 | RUS 2-CZE 1 | 1:30 | Grigori Zheldakov |
| 2012 | OT | REL | Jan 4, 2012 | LAT 2-DEN 1 | 1:43 | Nikita Jevpalovs |
| 2012 | OT | GOLD | Jan 5, 2012 | SWE 1-RUS 0 | 10:09 | Mika Zibanejad |

**WORLD U18 CHAMPIONSHIP, MEN**

| | | | | | | |
|---|---|---|---|---|---|---|
| 2003 | OT | SF | Apr 20, 2003 | CAN 2-USA 1 | 3:38 | Alexandre Bolduc |
| 2003 | OT | 5th/6th | Apr 21, 2003 | SWE 3-CZE 2 | 8:20 | Linus Videll |
| 2005 | OT | SF | Apr 22, 2005 | CAN 3-CZE 2 | 5:29 | Guillaume Latendresse |
| 2006 | OT | SF | Apr 20, 2006 | FIN 3-CAN 2 | 1:22 | Jan-Mikael Jarvinen |
| 2006 | OT | SF | Apr 20, 2006 | USA 4-CZE 3 | 6:50 | Patrick Kane |
| 2007 | OT | QF | Apr 19, 2007 | RUS 4-SUI 3 | 6:37 | Nikita Filatov |
| 2009 | OT | PRE | Apr 13, 2009 | CAN 4-CZE 3 | 1:23 | Brett Connolly |
| 2011 | OT | SF | Apr 23, 2011 | USA 5-CAN 4 | 4:22 | Tyler Biggs |
| 2011 | OT | GOLD | Apr 24, 2011 | USA 4-SWE 3 | 6:06 | Connor Murphy |
| 2012 | OT | REL | Apr 19, 2012 | DEN 4-LAT 3 | 4:04 | Kristoffer Lauridsen |
| 2012 | OT | BRONZE | Apr 22, 2012 | CAN 5-FIN 4 | 2:05 | Hunter Shinkaruk |

**OLYMPICS, WOMEN**

| | | | | | | |
|---|---|---|---|---|---|---|
| 2002 | OT | 7th/8th | Feb 19, 2002 | CHN 2-KAZ 1 | 1:39 | Hongmei Liu |
| 2010 | OT | BRONZE | Feb 25, 2010 | FIN 3-SWE 2 | 2:33 | Karoliina Rantamaki |

**WORLD WOMEN'S CHAMPIONSHIP**

| | | | | | | |
|---|---|---|---|---|---|---|
| 1992 | OT | 7th/8th | Apr 26, 1992 | DEN 4-SUI 3 | 6:05 | Jannie Hadsen |
| 1997 | OT | GOLD | Apr 6, 1997 | CAN 4-USA 3 | 12:59 | Nancy Drolet |
| 2000 | OT | GOLD | Apr 9, 2000 | CAN 3-USA 2 | 6:50 | Nancy Drolet |
| 2007 | OT | PRE | Apr 5, 2007 | FIN 1-SWE 0 | 1:32 | Saija Sirvio |
| 2008 | OT | PRE | Apr 6, 2008 | FIN 3-SWE 2 | 3:00 | Mari Pehkonen |
| 2008 | OT | QUAL | Apr 8, 2008 | FIN 1-USA 0 | 3:42 | Heidi Pelttari |
| 2011 | OT | PRE | Apr 17, 2011 | SUI 2-FIN 1 | 1:50 | Stefanie Marty |
| 2011 | OT | QF | Apr 22, 2011 | RUS 5-SUI 4 | 2:58 | Tatyana Burina |
| 2011 | OT | BRONZE | Apr 25, 2011 | FIN 3-RUS 2 | 2:49 | Karoliina Rantamaki |
| 2011 | OT | GOLD | Apr 25, 2011 | USA 3-CAN 2 | 7:48 | Hilary Knight |
| 2012 | OT | PRE | Apr 8, 2012 | SWE 2-GER 1 | 0:24 | Elin Holmlov |
| 2012 | OT | 5th/6th | Apr 13, 2012 | SWE 2-RUS 1 | 0:34 | Elin Holmlov |
| 2012 | OT | GOLD | Apr 14, 2012 | CAN 5-USA 4 | 1:50 | Caroline Ouellette |

**WORLD WOMEN'S U18 CHAMPIONSHIP**

| | | | | | | |
|---|---|---|---|---|---|---|
| 2009 | OT | GOLD | Jan 10, 2009 | USA 3-CAN 2 | 6:47 | Kendall Coyne |
| 2010 | OT | QF | Mar 31, 2010 | GER 2-FIN 1 | 6:21 | Manuela Anwander |
| 2010 | OT | GOLD | Apr 3, 2010 | CAN 5-USA 4 | 3:10 | Jessica Campbell |
| 2011 | OT | QF | Jan 5, 2011 | FIN 3-SWE 2 | 1:46 | Sanna Valkama |
| 2012 | OT | QF | Jan 4, 2012 | SWE 2-FIN 1 | 7:27 | Matildah Andersson |
| 2012 | OT | REL | Jan 7, 2012 | RUS 3-SUI 2 | 1:44 | Valeria Pavlova |

## Game-Winning Shots (Shootouts) Summary

| | OG-M | WM | IIHF-NHL | WM20 | WM18 | OG-W | WW | WW18 | Total |
|---|---|---|---|---|---|---|---|---|---|
| FIN (14) | 0-0 | 5-4 | 0-0 | 0-3 | 1-0 | 0-0 | 1-0 | 0-0 | 7-7 |
| CZE (13) | 1-0 | 6-2 | 0-0 | 2-1 | 1-0 | 0-0 | 0-0 | 0-0 | 10-3 |
| CAN (13) | 1-2 | 3-1 | 0-0 | 3-1 | 0-2 | 0-0 | 0-0 | 0-0 | 7-6 |
| SWE (13) | 1-0 | 0-4 | 0-0 | 3-2 | 0-0 | 1-0 | 1-1 | 0-0 | 6-7 |
| USA (11) | 0-0 | 2-3 | 0-0 | 0-2 | 1-1 | 0-1 | 1-0 | 0-0 | 4-7 |
| RUS (9) | 0-0 | 2-2 | 0-0 | 1-2 | 1-1 | 0-0 | 0-0 | 0-0 | 4-5 |
| SUI (6) | 0-0 | 0-0 | 0-0 | 3-2 | 0-0 | 0-0 | 0-1 | 0-0 | 3-3 |
| GER (6) | 0-1 | 1-2 | 0-0 | 0-0 | 0-1 | 0-0 | 1-0 | 0-0 | 2-4 |
| SVK (5) | 0-0 | 1-1 | 0-0 | 0-1 | 1-0 | 0-0 | 1-1 | 0-0 | 3-2 |
| DEN (2) | 0-0 | 2-0 | 0-0 | 0-0 | 0-0 | 0-0 | 0-0 | 0-0 | 2-0 |
| NOR (2) | 0-0 | 1-1 | 0-0 | 0-0 | 0-0 | 0-0 | 0-0 | 0-0 | 1-1 |
| LAT (2) | 0-0 | 0-2 | 0-0 | 0-0 | 0-0 | 0-0 | 0-0 | 0-0 | 0-2 |
| KAZ (1) | 0-0 | 0-1 | 0-0 | 0-0 | 0-0 | 0-0 | 0-0 | 0-0 | 0-1 |
| SLO (1) | 0-0 | 0-1 | 0-0 | 0-0 | 0-0 | 0-0 | 0-0 | 0-0 | 0-1 |

## Overtime Summary

| | OG-M | WM | IIHF-NHL | WM20 | WM18 | OG-W | WW | WW18 | Total |
|---|---|---|---|---|---|---|---|---|---|
| CAN (32) | 2-0 | 4-4 | 6-1 | 1-3 | 3-2 | 0-0 | 3-1 | 1-1 | 20-12 |
| RUS (22) | 1-0 | 1-4 | 1-2 | 5-3 | 1-0 | 0-0 | 1-2 | 1-0 | 11-11 |
| USA (21) | 0-1 | 4-1 | 0-1 | 2-1 | 3-1 | 0-0 | 1-4 | 1-1 | 11-10 |
| SWE (18) | 0-0 | 4-3 | 0-1 | 2-1 | 1-0 | 0-1 | 2-0 | 1-1 | 10-8 |
| FIN (18) | 0-0 | 3-3 | 0-0 | 0-3 | 1-1 | 1-0 | 2-1 | 1-2 | 8-10 |
| CZE (14) | 0-1 | 4-2 | 0-2 | 1-1 | 0-3 | 0-0 | 0-0 | 0-0 | 5-9 |
| SUI (8) | 0-0 | 1-1 | 0-0 | 2-0 | 1-1 | 0-0 | 1-1 | 0-1 | 4-4 |
| GER (4) | 0-0 | 0-1 | 0-0 | 0-1 | 0-0 | 0-0 | 0-1 | 1-0 | 1-3 |
| DEN (3) | 0-0 | 0-1 | 0-0 | 0-2 | 1-0 | 0-0 | 0-0 | 0-0 | 1-2 |
| FRA (2) | 0-0 | 1-1 | 0-0 | 0-0 | 0-0 | 0-0 | 0-0 | 0-0 | 1-1 |
| LAT (2) | 0-0 | 0-0 | 0-0 | 1-0 | 0-1 | 0-0 | 0-0 | 0-0 | 1-1 |
| SVK (2) | 0-1 | 0-0 | 0-0 | 1-0 | 0-0 | 0-0 | 0-0 | 0-0 | 1-1 |
| ITA (1) | 0-0 | 1-0 | 0-0 | 0-0 | 0-0 | 0-0 | 0-0 | 0-0 | 1-0 |
| BLR (1) | 0-0 | 0-1 | 0-0 | 0-0 | 0-0 | 0-0 | 0-0 | 0-0 | 0-1 |
| KAZ (1) | 0-0 | 0-1 | 0-0 | 0-0 | 0-0 | 0-0 | 0-0 | 0-0 | 0-1 |

# Biggest Comebacks/Worst Blown Leads

### OLYMPICS, MEN

**4 goals—France 8-Norway 6**
**February 23, 1988**
France led 5-1 at 14:37 of 2nd but Norway tied game 6-6 in 3rd before losing in a shootout (the first ever shootout—France was awarded goals for both its shootout goals)

**3 goals—France 7-Belgium 5**
**January 31, 1924**
Belgium led 3-0 in 1st but France tied the game before the end of the period and went on to win, 7-5

**3 goals—Switzerland 4-Austria 4**
**February 11, 1928**
Austria led 4-1 at 8:00 of 1st but Switzerland scored a goal in each period to tie game, 4-4

**3 goals—Czechoslovakia 8-Switzerland 3**
**February 22, 1952**
Switzerland led 3-0 at 9:00 of 2nd but Czechoslovakia scored 8 goals to win, 8-3

**3 goals—Sweden 5-Czechoslovakia 3**
**February 25, 1952**
Czechoslovakia led 3-0 at 4:00 of 2nd but Sweden scored 5 goals to win, 5-3

**3 goals—Sweden 6-Switzerland 5**
**January 28, 1956**
Switzerland led 3-0 at 13:00 of 1st but Sweden scored the next 3 goals and went on to win, 6-5

**3 goals—Japan 6-Finland, 6**
**February 23, 1960**
Finland led 6-3 at 1:57 of 3rd but Japan scored 3 goals later in 3rd to tie game, 6-6

**3 goals—Canada 6-Sweden 5**
**February 27, 1960**
Sweden led 3-0 and 4-2 in 1st but Canada scored 4 of 5 goals in 3rd to win, 6-5

**3 goals—Japan 5-Romania 4**
**February 12, 1968**
Japan led 3-0 at 14:54 of 1st but Romania scored 3 goals in 2nd to tie, 3-3, ultimately losing, 5-4

**3 goals—Japan 7-Germany 6**
**February 12, 1972**
Japan led 3-0 at 10:09 of 1st but Germany scored 3 goals in 2nd to tie game, ultimately losing, 7-6

**3 goals—Japan 4-Yugoslavia 3**
**February 11, 1976**
Japan led 3-0 at 14:17 of 2nd but Yugoslavia scored 3 goals to tie game, ultimately losing, 4-3

**3 goals—Japan 7-Bulgaria 5**
**February 13, 1976**
Japan led 3-0 at 10:08 of 1st but Bulgaria scored 3 goals later in 1st to tie, ultimately losing, 7-5

**3 goals—Netherlands 3-Japan 3**
**February 16, 1980**
Japan led 3-0 at 18:01 of 1st but Netherlands scored one goal in each period to tie game, 3-3

**3 goals—Czechoslovakia 7-United States 5**
**February 15, 1988**
United States led 4-1 at 5:15 of 2nd but Czechoslovakia scored 3 goals to tie, 4-4, en route to 7-5 win

**3 goals—Sweden 3-United States 3**
**February 17, 1992**
United States led 3-0 at 2:42 of 3rd but Sweden scored 3 goals to tie game, 3-3

**3 goals—Slovakia 6-Germany 5**
**February 24, 1994**
Germany led 3-0 at 19:32 of 1st but Slovakia scored 3 goals in 2nd to tie game en route to 6-5 overtime win

**3 goals—Latvia 6-Slovakia 6**
**February 10, 2002**
Slovakia led 6-3 at 18:20 of second but Latvia scored once in 2nd and twice in 3rd to tie game, 6-6

### WORLD CHAMPIONSHIP (MEN)

**4 goals—Canada 11-East Germany 5**
**March 9, 1963**
East Germany led 4-0 at 4:40 of 1st but Canada scored 3 goals later in 1st and one goal in 2nd to tie game, 4-4, en route to 11-5 win

**4 goals—Canada 6-Finland 5**
**April 19, 1990**
Finland led 4-0 at 12:37 of 2nd but Canada scored 3 goals later in 2nd & 3 goals in 3rd en route to 6-5 win

**4 goals—Sweden 6-Finland 5**
**May 7, 2003**
Finland led 5-1 at 6:44 of 2nd but Sweden scored 3 goals later in 2nd & 2 goals in 3rd to win, 6-5

### U20 WORLD CHAMPIONSHIP (MEN)

**4 goals—Soviet Union 5-Finland 5**
**January 3, 1990**
Finland led 4-0 at 14:55 of 2nd but Soviets scored 5 goals in 2nd & 3rd and Finland rallied to tie, 5-5

**3 goals—United States 5-Sweden 5**
**December 28, 1979**
Sweden led 3-0 at 11:00 of 1st but United States scored 3 goals in 2nd to tie game which ended 5-5

**3 goals—Canada 7-Czechoslovakia 7**
**January 1, 1983**
Czechoslovakia led 6-3 at 9:51 of 2nd but Canada scored 3 goals later in 2nd to tie game which ended 7-7

**3 goals—United States 6-West Germany 5**
**January 4, 1983**
West Germany led 4-1 and 5-2 in 3rd period but United States scored 4 goals later in 3rd to win, 6-5

**3 goals—Finland 5-United States 5**
**December 26, 1988**
United States led 4-1 at 12:32 of 1st and at end of 2nd but Finland scored 4 goals in 3rd and game ended 5-5

**3 goals—Norway 6-United States 5**
**January 2, 1990**
United States led 3-0 and 4-1 but Norway scored only 3 goals of 3rd and won, 6-5

**3 goals—Sweden 6-Finland 4**
**January 4, 1992**
Finland led 4-1 at 7:57 of 2nd but Sweden scored one goal in 2nd & 4 goals in 3rd to win, 6-4

**3 goals—Russia 3-Canada 3**
**December 29, 1993**
Canada led 3-0 at 5:14 of 3rd but Russia scored 3 goals to tie, 3-3

**3 goals—Finland 3-Sweden 3**
**December 1, 1995**
Sweden led 3-0 at 10:55 of 2nd but Finland scored once later in 2nd & twice in 3rd to tie game, 3-3

**3 goals—Czech Republic 4-Slovakia 4**
**December 29, 1995**
Slovakia led 3-0 and 4-1 but Czech Republic scored 3 goals in 3rd to tie game, 4-4

**3 goals—United States 8-Finland 7**
**January 4, 1996**
Finland led 4-1 at 5:08 of 2nd but United States scored 4 goals to take 5-4 lead in 2nd en route to 8-7 overtime win

**3 goals—United States 5-Switzerland 4**
**January 3, 1999**
Switzerland led 4-1 at 12:51 of 1st but United States scored final 4 goals to win, 5-4

**3 goals—Russia 4-Slovakia 3**
**January 5, 2001**
Russia led 3-0 at 6:07 of 2nd but Slovakia scored one goal later in 2nd and two goals in 3rd to tie game, 3-3, ultimately losing 4-3 in shootout

**3 goals—Finland 5-Sweden 4**
**December 30, 2004**
Sweden led 3-0 and 4-1 but Finland scored 4 goals in 3rd to win, 5-4

**3 goals—Canada 7-United States 4**
**December 31, 2008**
United States led 3-0 at 12:35 of 1st but Canada tied game later in 1st en route to 7-4 win

**3 goals—Finland 4-Czech Republic 3**
**December 27, 2009**
Czech Republic led 3-0 at 7:53 of 2nd but Finland scored one goal later in 2nd & 3 goals in 3rd to win, 4-3

**3 goals—Russia 5-Canada 3**
**January 5, 2011**
Canada led 3-0 at 6:27 of 2nd but Russia scored 5 goals in 3rd to win, 5-3

### U18 WORLD CHAMPIONSHIP (MEN)

**3 goals—Belarus 3-United States 3**
**April 12, 2003**
United States led 3-0 at 15:58 of 2nd but Belarus scored 3 goals in 3rd to tie game, 3-3

**3 goals—Czech Republic 3-Canada 3**
**April 14, 2003**
Canada led 3-0 at 18:28 of 1st but Czech Republic scored one goal in 2nd and two goals in 3rd to tie game, 3-3

**3 goals—Norway 6-Belarus 6**
**April 20, 2006**
Belarus led 3-0 at 5:47 of 1st, 5-2 at 19:52 of 2nd, and 6-3 at 5:37 of 3rd but Norway scored 3 goals in final 5 minutes to tie game, 6-6

**3 goals—United States 4-Czech Republic 3**
**April 20, 2006**
United States led 3-0 at 18:47 of 1st but Czechs tied game 3-3, ultimately losing 4-3 in overtime

**3 goals—Canada 4-Czech Republic 3**
**April 13, 2009**
Czech Republic led 3-0 at 16:44 of 2nd but Canada scored 3 goals in 3rd and won 4-3 in overtime

**3 goals—Finland 5-Canada 4**
**April 19, 2009**
Canada led 4-1 at 15:58 of 2nd but Finland scored one goal later in 2nd, 2 goals in 3rd, and again in overtime to win, 5-4

**3 goals—Russia 5-Germany 4**
**April 16, 2011**
Russia led 3-0 at 12:01 of 1st but Germany tied game with 3 goals in 2nd, ultimately losing 5-4 in a shootout

**3 goals—United States 5-Canada 4**
**April 23, 2011**
United States led 4-1 at 7:16 of 3rd but Canada scored 3 goals to tie game 4-4, ultimately losing, 5-4, in overtime

### OLYMPICS, WOMEN

**3 goals—United States 7-Canada 4**
**February 14, 1998**
Canada led 4-1 at 5:53 of 3rd but United States scored 6 goals later in 3rd to win, 7-4

**3 goals—Germany 5-China 5**
**February 16, 2002**
China led 5-2 at end of 2nd but Germany scored 3 goals in 3rd to tie game 5-5

### WOMEN'S WORLD CHAMPIONSHIP

**3 goals—China 4-Sweden 4**
**April 12, 1994**
Sweden led 4-1 at 12:33 of 2nd but China scored 3 goals in 3rd to tie game, 4-4

**3 goals—Switzerland 5-China 4**
**April 8, 2009**
China led 4-1 at 6:26 of 2nd but Switzerland scored 3 goals in 3rd and won, 5-4, in shootout

**3 goals—Russia 5-Switzerland 4**
**April 22, 2011**
Switzerland led 3-0 at 13:33 of 2nd but Russia tied game 3-3 en route to 5-4 win in overtime

### U18 WOMEN'S WORLD CHAMPIONSHIP

**3 goals—Switzerland 4-Finland 3**
**January 7, 2009**
Finland led 3-0 at 7:51 of 2nd but Switzerland scored 4 goals later in 2nd to win, 4-3

# Longest Shootouts

**LONGEST IIHF SHOOTOUT**
January 3, 2002 . . . . . . . . . . . . . . . . 26 shots (13 each)
Belarus 1-France 0 (best-of-two tie)

**LONGEST WOMEN'S SHOOTOUT (EXHIBITION)**
October 12, 2003 . . . . . . . . . . . . . . . 22 shots (11 each)
United States 2-Canada 1

**LONGEST NHL SHOOTOUT**
November 26, 2005 . . . . . . . . . . . . . 30 shots (15 each)
NY Rangers 3-Washington Capitals 2

**LONGEST EUROPEAN LEAGUE SHOOTOUT**
November 21, 2010 . . . . . . . . . . . . . 42 shots (21 each)
Straubing Tigers 5-EHC Munchen 4

# Game-Winning Goals in Gold Medal Games

**OLYMPICS, MEN**

| Year | Scorer | Venue | Result |
|---|---|---|---|
| 1920 | Chris Fridfinnson | Antwerp | Canada 12-Sweden 1 |
| 1992 | Igor Boldin | Albertville | Russia 3-Canada 1 |
| 1994 | Peter Forsberg | Lillehammer | Sweden 3-Canada 2 (SO) |
| 1998 | Petr Svoboda | Nagano | Czech Republic 1-Russia 0 |
| 2002 | Joe Sakic | Salt Lake | Canada 5-United States 2 |
| 2006 | Nicklas Lidstrom | Turin | Sweden 3-Finland 2 |
| 2010 | Sidney Crosby | Vancouver | Canada 3-United States 2 (OT) |

**WORLD CHAMPIONSHIP (MEN)**

| | | | |
|---|---|---|---|
| 1930 | Alex Park | Berlin | Canada 6-Germany 1 |
| 1933 | John Garrison | Prague | United States 2-Canada 1 (OT) |
| 1934 | Jim Dewey | Milan | Canada 2-United States 1 |
| 1935 | Norm Yellowlees | Davos | Canada 4-Switzerland 2 |
| 1938 | Pat McReavy | Prague | Canada 3-Great Britain 1 |
| 1992 | Roger Hansson | Prague | Sweden 5-Finland 2 |
| 1993 | Andrei Nikolishin | Munich | Russia 3-Sweden 1 |
| 1994 | Luc Robitaille | Milan | Canada 2-Finland 1 (SO) |
| 1995 | Ville Peltonen | Stockholm | Finland 4-Sweden 1 |
| 1996 | Martin Prochazka | Vienna | Czech Republic 4-Canada 2 |
| 1997 | Owen Nolan | Helsinki | Canada 2-Sweden 1 (best-of-three) |
| 1998 | Johan Tornberg | Zurich | Sweden 1-Finland 0 (game one, best-of-two; game two 0-0) |
| 1999 | Jan Hlavac | | 16:32 OT, best-of-two tie-break (game one Czech Republic 3-Finland 1; game two Finland 4-Czech Republic 0) |
| 2000 | Jan Tomajko | St. Petersburg | Czech Republic 5-Slovakia 3 |
| 2001 | David Moravec | Hanover | Czech Republic 3-Finland 2 (OT) |
| 2002 | Peter Bondra | Gothenburg | Slovakia 4-Russia 3 |
| 2003 | Anson Carter | Helsinki | Canada 3-Sweden 2 (OT) |
| 2004 | Jay Bouwmeester | Prague | Canada 5-Sweden 3 |
| 2005 | Vaclav Prospal | Vienna | Czech Republic 3-Canada 0 |
| 2006 | Jesper Mattsson | Riga | Sweden 4-Czech Republic 0 |
| 2007 | Colby Armstrong | Moscow | Canada 4-Finland 2 |
| 2008 | Ilya Kovalchuk | Quebec City | Russia 5-Canada 4 (OT) |
| 2009 | Alexander Radulov | Berne | Russia 2-Canada 1 |
| 2010 | Tomas Rolinek | Cologne | Czech Republic 2-Russia 1 |
| 2011 | Petteri Nokelainen | Bratislava | Finland 6-Sweden 1 |
| 2012 | Alexei Tereshenko | Helsinki | Russia 6-Slovakia 2 |

**U20 WORLD CHAMPIONSHIP**

| | | | |
|---|---|---|---|
| 1978 | Vyacheslav Fetisov | Montreal | Soviet Union 5-Sweden 2 |
| 1996 | Daymond Langkow | Chestnut Hill | Canada 4-Sweden 1 |
| 1997 | Boyd Devereaux | Geneva | Canada 2-United States 0 |
| 1998 | Niklas Hagman | Helsinki | Finland 2-Russia 1 |
| 1999 | Artyom Chubarov | Winnipeg | Russia 3-Canada 2 (OT) |
| 2000 | Milan Kraft | Skelleftea | Czech Republic 1-Russia 0 (SO) |
| 2001 | Vaclav Nedorost | Moscow | Czech Republic 2-Finland 1 |
| 2002 | Anton Volchenkov | Pardubice | Russia 5-Canada 4 |
| 2003 | Yuri Trubachyov | Halifax | Russia 3-Canada 2 |
| 2004 | Patrick O'Sullivan | Helsinki | United States 4-Canada 3 |
| 2005 | Danny Syvret | Grand Forks | Canada 6-Russia 1 |
| 2006 | Steve Downie | Vancouver | Canada 5-Russia 0 |
| 2007 | Jonathan Toews | Leksand | Canada 4-Russia 2 |
| 2008 | Matt Halischuk | Pardubice | Canada 3-Sweden 2 (OT) |
| 2009 | Angelo Esposito | Ottawa | Canada 5-Sweden 1 |
| 2010 | John Carlson | Saskatoon | United States 6-Canada 5 (OT) |
| 2011 | Artemi Panarin | Buffalo | Russia 5-Canada 3 |
| 2012 | Mika Zibanejad | Calgary | Sweden 1-Russia 0 (OT) |

**U18 WORLD CHAMPIONSHIP (MEN)**

| | | | |
|---|---|---|---|
| 2000 | Markus Seikola | Kloten | Finland 3-Russia 1 |
| 2001 | Timofei Shishkanov | Helsinki | Russia 6-Switzerland 2 |
| 2003 | Anthony Stewart | Yaroslavl | Canada 3-Slovakia 0 |
| 2004 | Dmitri Shitikov | Minsk | Russia 3-United States 2 |
| 2005 | Jason Lawrence | Plzen | United States 5-Canada 1 |
| 2006 | Chris Summers | Angelholm | United States 3-Finland 1 |
| 2007 | Yegor Averin | Tampere | Russia 6-United States 5 |
| 2008 | Nicolas Deschamps | Kazan | Canada 8-Russia 0 |
| 2009 | Cam Fowler | Fargo | United States 5-Russia 0 |
| 2010 | Justin Faulk | Minsk | United States 3-Sweden 1 |
| 2011 | Connor Murphy | Crimmitschau | United States 4-Sweden 3 (OT) |
| 2012 | Tom Dipauli | Brno | United States 7-Sweden 0 |

**OLYMPICS, WOMEN**

| | | | |
|---|---|---|---|
| 1998 | Shelley Looney | Nagano | United States 3-Canada 1 |
| 2002 | Jayna Hefford | Salt Lake | Canada 3-United States 2 |
| 2006 | Caroline Ouellette | Turin | Canada 4-Sweden 1 |
| 2010 | Marie-Philip Poulin | Vancouver | Canada 2-United States 0 |

**WOMEN'S WORLD CHAMPIONSHIP**

| | | | |
|---|---|---|---|
| 1990 | Geraldine Heaney | Ottawa | Canada 5-United States 2 |
| 1992 | Danielle Goyette | Tampere | Canada 8-United States 0 |
| 1994 | Danielle Goyette | Lake Placid | Canada 6-United States 3 |
| 1997 | Nancy Drolet | Kitchener | Canada 4-United States 3 (OT) |
| 1999 | Danielle Goyette | Espoo | Canada 3-United States 1 |
| 2000 | Nancy Drolet | Mississauga | Canada 3-United States 2 (OT) |
| 2001 | Jennifer Botterill | Minneapolis | Canada 3-United States 2 |
| 2004 | Hayley Wickenheiser | Halifax | Canada 2-United States 0 |
| 2005 | Krissy Wendell | Linkoping | United States 1-Canada 0 (SO) |
| 2007 | Jayna Hefford | Winnipeg | Canada 5-United States 1 |
| 2008 | Natalie Darwitz | Harbin | United States 4-Canada 3 |
| 2009 | Meghan Duggan | Hameenlinna | United States 4-Canada 1 |
| 2011 | Hilary Knight | Zurich | United States 3-Canada 2 (OT) |
| 2012 | Caroline Ouellette | Burlington | Canada 5-United States 4 (OT) |

**U18 WOMEN'S WORLD CHAMPIONSHIP**

| | | | |
|---|---|---|---|
| 2008 | Kendall Coyne | Calgary | United States 5-Canada 2 |
| 2009 | Kendall Coyne | Fussen | United States 3-Canada 2 |
| 2010 | Jessica Campbell | Chicago | Canada 5-United States 4 (OT) |
| 2011 | Layla Marvin | Stockholm | United States 5-Canada 2 |
| 2012 | Alexia Crossley | Zlin | Canada 3-United States 0 |

# Players Who Appeared in the U20 World Championship, World Championship, and/or Olympic Games in the Same Year

Note: players who appeared in all three tournaments in the same year are denoted in bold

| Player | NAT | Year | WM20 Finish | WM Finish | OG Finish |
|---|---|---|---|---|---|
| David Aebischer | SUI | 1998 | B | 4th | — |
| Maxim Afinogenov | RUS | 1999 | G | 5th | — |
| Peter Andersson | SWE | 1982 | 5th | 4th | — |
| Nikolai Antropov | KAZ | 1998 | 7th | 6th | DNP |
| Nicklas Backstrom | SWE | 2006 | 5th | G | DNP |
| Nicklas Backstorm | SWE | 2007 | 4th | 4th | — |
| Patrik Bartschi | SUI | 2003 | 7th | 8th | — |
| Yevgeni Belosheikin | URS | 1986 | G | G | — |
| Jiri Bicek | SVK | 1997 | 6th | 9th | — |
| Severin Blindenbacher | SUI | 2003 | 7th | 8th | — |
| Jonas Brodin | SWE | 2012 | G | 6th | — |
| Ilya Bryzgalov | RUS | 2000 | S | 11th | — |
| Pavel Bure | URS | 1990 | S | G | — |
| Valeri Bure | RUS | 1994 | 5th | DNP | |
| Zdenko Ciger | TCH | 1989 | B | B | — |
| Flavien Conne | SUI | 2000 | 6th | 6th | — |
| Russ Courtnall | CAN | 1984 | 4th | — | 4th |
| J.J. Daigneault | CAN | 1984 | 4th | — | 4th |
| Kaspars Daugavins | LAT | 2007 | 9th | 10th | — |
| Rick DiPietro | USA | 2001 | 5th | 4th | — |
| Clark Donatelli | USA | 1985 | 6th | 4th | — |
| Mike Dunham | USA | 1992 | B | 7th | DNP |
| Jordan Eberle | CAN | 2010 | S | 7th | — |
| Oliver Ekman-Larsson | SWE | 2010 | B | B | — |
| Bernd Engelbrecht | FRG | 1978 | 7th | 5th | — |
| Thomas Eriksson | SWE | 1979 | B | B | — |
| Tim Erixon | SWE | 2011 | 4th | 5th | — |
| Vyacheslav Fetisov | URS | 1977 | G | B | — |
| Pat Flatley | CAN | 1983 | B | B | — |
| Peter Forsberg | SWE | 1992 | S | G | DNP |
| Peter Forsberg | SWE | 1993 | S | S | — |
| Beat Forster | SUI | 2003 | 7th | 8th | — |
| Georg Franz | FRG | 1985 | 7th | 7th | — |
| Miroslav Frycer | TCH | 1979 | S | S | — |
| Dave Gagner | CAN | 1984 | 4th | — | 4th |
| Guntis Galvins | LAT | 2006 | 9th | 10th | DNP |
| Patrick Geering | SUI | 2010 | 4th | 5th | — |
| Beat Gerber | SUI | 2002 | 4th | 10th | DNP |
| Sascha Goc | GER | 1998 | 10th | 11th | DNP |
| Philip Gogulla | GER | 2007 | 9th | 9th | — |
| Erich Goldmann | GER | 1996 | 8th | 8th | — |
| Mikael Granlund | FIN | 2012 | 4th | 4th | — |
| Igor Grigorenko | RUS | 2003 | G | 7th | — |
| Dominik Hasek | TCH | 1983 | S | S | — |
| Martin Havlat | CZE | 2000 | G | G | — |
| Jochen Hecht | GER | 1996 | 8th | 8th | — |

| | | | | | |
|---|---|---|---|---|---|
| Jochen Hecht | GER | 1997 | 9th | 11th | — |
| Dieter Hegen | FRG | 1982 | 7th | 6th | — |
| Raimo Helminen | FIN | 1984 | S | — | 6th |
| Uli Hiemer | FRG | 1981 | 5th | 7th | — |
| Uli Hiemer | FRG | 1982 | 7th | 6th | — |
| Robert Holik | TCH | 1990 | B | B | — |
| Jonas Holos | NOR | 2006 | 10th | 11th | — |
| Miloslav Horava | TCH | 1981 | 4th | B | — |
| Patric Hornqvist | SWE | 2007 | 4th | 4th | — |
| Marian Hossa | SVK | 1997 | 6th | 9th | — |
| Phil Housley | USA | 1992 | 6th | 8th | DNP |
| Jiri Hudler | CZE | 2003 | 6th | 4th | — |
| Jaromir Jagr | TCH | 1990 | B | B | — |
| Erik Johnson | USA | 2007 | B | 5th | — |
| Jack Johnson | USA | 2007 | B | 5th | — |
| Olli Jokinen | FIN | 1997 | 5th | 5th | — |
| **Kenny Jonsson** | **SWE** | **1994** | **S** | **B** | **G** |
| Tomas Jonsson | SWE | 1979 | B | B | — |
| Tomas Jonsson | SWE | 1980 | B | — | B |
| Roman Josi | SUI | 2010 | 4th | 5th | — |
| Alexei Kaigorodov | RUS | 2003 | G | 7th | — |
| Valeri Kamenski | URS | 1986 | G | G | — |
| Vadim Karaha | BLR | 2003 | 10th | 14th | — |
| Paul Kariya | CAN | 1993 | G | 4th | — |
| **Darius Kasparaitis** | **RUS** | **1992** | **G** | **5th** | **G** |
| Phil Kessel | USA | 2006 | 4th | 7th | DNP |
| Andrei Khomutov | URS | 1981 | B | G | — |
| Trevor Kidd | CAN | 1992 | 6th | 8th | DNP |
| Saku Koivu | FIN | 1993 | 5th | 7th | — |
| **Saku Koivu** | **FIN** | **1994** | **4th** | **S** | **B** |
| Konstantin Koltsov | BLR | 1999 | 10th | 9th | — |
| Konstantin Koltsov | BLR | 2001 | 9th | 14th | — |
| Vladimir Konstantinov | URS | 1986 | G | G | — |
| Andrei Kostitsyn | BLR | 2003 | 9th | 14th | — |
| **Alexei Kovalyov** | **RUS** | **1992** | **G** | **5th** | **G** |
| Vyacheslav Kozlov | URS | 1991 | S | B | — |
| Ondrej Kratena | CZE | 1997 | 4th | B | — |
| Chris Kreider | USA | 2011 | B | 8th | — |
| Harold Kreis | FRG | 1979 | 7th | 6th | — |
| Roman Krivomazov | KAZ | 1998 | 7th | 16th | DNP |
| Vladimir Krutov | URS | 1980 | G | — | S |
| Nikolai Kulyomin | RUS | 2006 | S | 5th | DNP |
| Jari Kurri | FIN | 1980 | S | — | 4th |
| Yevgeni Kuznetsov | RUS | 2012 | S | G | — |
| Scott Lachance | USA | 1992 | B | DNP | 4th |
| Johan Larsson | SWE | 2012 | G | 6th | — |
| Brian Leetch | USA | 1987 | 4th | 7th | — |
| David Legwand | USA | 1999 | 9th | 6th | — |
| Jere Lehtinen | FIN | 1992 | 4th | S | DNP |
| Mikko Lehtonen | FIN | 2006 | B | B | DNP |
| Pelle Lindbergh | SWE | 1979 | B | B | — |
| Eric Lindros | CAN | 1992 | 6th | DNP | S |
| Sergei Makarov | URS | 1978 | G | G | — |
| Mikko Makela | FIN | 1985 | 4th | 5th | — |
| Jarmo Makitalo | FIN | 1980 | S | — | 4th |
| Yevgeni Malkin | RUS | 2005 | S | B | — |
| Yevgeni Malkin | RUS | 2006 | S | DNP | 4th |
| Jakob Markstrom | SWE | 2010 | B | B | — |
| Andrej Meszaros | SVK | 2004 | 6th | 4th | — |
| Milan Michalek | CZE | 2003 | 6th | 4th | — |
| Alexander Mogilny | URS | 1988 | S | — | G |
| Alexander Mogilny | URS | 1989 | G | G | — |
| Alexei Morozov | RUS | 1997 | B | 4th | — |
| Petr Mrazek | CZE | 2012 | 5th | B | — |
| Kirk Muller | CAN | 1984 | 4th | — | 4th |
| Ryan Murray | CAN | 2012 | B | 5th | — |
| Frantisek Musil | TCH | 1983 | S | S | — |
| Markus Naslund | SWE | 1993 | S | S | — |
| Mats Naslund | SWE | 1979 | B | B | — |
| Nino Niederreiter | SUI | 2010 | 4th | 5th | — |
| Janne Niinimaa | FIN | 1995 | 4th | G | — |
| Teppo Numminen | FIN | 1988 | B | — | S |
| Mikael Nylander | SWE | 1992 | S | G | DNP |
| Janne Ojanen | FIN | 1987 | G | 5th | — |
| Janne Ojanen | FIN | 1988 | B | — | S |
| Fredrik Olausson | SWE | 1986 | 5th | S | — |
| Alexander Ovechkin | RUS | 2004 | 5th | 10th | — |
| Alexander Ovechkin | RUS | 2005 | S | B | — |
| Magnus Paajarvi-Svensson | SWE | 2010 | B | B | — |
| Richard Panik | SVK | 2010 | 8th | 12th | — |
| James Patrick | CAN | 1983 | B | B | — |
| Michal Pivonka | TCH | 1985 | S | G | — |
| Michal Pivonka | TCH | 1986 | 4th | 5th | — |
| Robert Reichel | TCH | 1990 | B | B | — |
| Mike Richter | USA | 1986 | B | 6th | — |
| Michel Riesen | SUI | 1998 | B | 4th | — |
| Kevin Romy | SUI | 2005 | 8th | 8th | — |
| Reijo Ruotsalainen | FIN | 1978 | 6th | 7th | — |
| Reijo Ruotsalainen | FIN | 1979 | 4th | 5th | — |
| Vladimir Ruzicka | TCH | 1983 | S | S | — |
| Tommy Samuelsson | SWE | 1980 | B | — | B |
| Tomas Sandstrom | SWE | 1984 | 5th | — | B |
| Luca Sbisa | SUI | 2010 | 4th | — | 8th |
| Daniel Sedin | SWE | 1999 | 4th | B | — |
| Daniel Sedin | SWE | 2000 | 5th | 7th | — |
| Henrik Sedin | SWE | 1999 | 4th | B | — |
| Henrik Sedin | SWE | 2000 | 5th | 7th | — |
| Jukka Seppo | FIN | 1987 | G | 5th | — |
| Gord Sherven | CAN | 1983 | B | B | — |
| Risto Siltanen | FIN | 1977 | 4th | 5th | — |
| Risto Siltanen | FIN | 1978 | 6th | 7th | — |
| Ville Siren | FIN | 1984 | S | — | 6th |
| Jiri Slegr | TCH | 1991 | B | 6th | — |
| Anton Stastny | TCH | 1979 | S | S | — |
| Mats Sundin | SWE | 1990 | 5th | S | — |
| Patrik Sundstrom | SWE | 1981 | G | S | — |
| Ryan Suter | USA | 2005 | 4th | 6th | — |
| Vladimir Tarasenko | RUS | 2011 | G | 4th | — |
| Tomas Tatar | SVK | 2010 | 8th | 12th | — |
| Esa Tikkanen | FIN | 1985 | 4th | 5th | — |
| Keith Tkachuk | USA | 1992 | B | DNP | 4th |
| Jonathan Toews | CAN | 2007 | G | G | — |
| Andrei Troshinski | KAZ | 1998 | 7th | 16th | DNP |
| Alexey Ugarov | BLR | 2005 | 10th | 10th | — |
| Stefan Ustorf | GER | 1992 | 7th | 6th | DNP |
| Stefan Ustorf | GER | 1994 | 7th | DNP | 7th |
| Thomas Vanek | AUT | 2004 | 9th | 11th | — |
| Jarkko Varvio | FIN | 1992 | 4th | S | — |
| Sami Vatanen | FIN | 2010 | 5th | 6th | — |
| Vitali Vishnevski | RUS | 1999 | G | 5th | — |
| Lubomir Visnovsky | SVK | 1996 | 7th | 10th | — |
| Anton Volchenkov | RUS | 2002 | G | S | DNP |
| Markus Wieland | GER | 1995 | 8th | 9th | — |
| Alexei Yashin | RUS | 1993 | 6th | G | — |
| Scott Young | USA | 1987 | 4th | 7th | — |
| **Alexei Zhitnik** | **RUS** | **1992** | **G** | **5th** | **G** |

## Players Who Appeared in the World Championship (Men) Before Playing in the U20 World Championship

| Player | NAT | WM Debut (Finish) | WM20 Debut (Finish) |
|---|---|---|---|
| Oskars Bartulis | LAT | 2005 (9th) | 2006 (9th) |
| **Patrice Bergeron** | **CAN** | **2004 (G)** | **2005 (G)** |
| Guntis Galvins | LAT | 2005 (9th) | 2006 (9th) |
| Henryk Gruth | POL | 1975 (5th) | 1977 (8th) |
| Henryk Gruth | POL | 1976 (7th) | 1977 (8th) |
| Per Gustafsson | SWE | 1996 (6th) | 1997 (8th) |
| Teppo Numminen | FIN | 1987 (5th) | 1988 (B) |
| Alexander Syomin | RUS | 2003 (7th) | 2004 (5th) |

## Players Who Appeared in the WW18 and WW/OG-W in the Same Year

| Player | NAT | Year | WW18 Finish | WW Finish | OG-W Finish |
|---|---|---|---|---|---|
| Yekaterina Ananina | RUS | 2009 | 7th | 5th | — |
| Manuela Anwander | GER | 2008 | 5th | 9th | — |
| Camille Balanche | SUI | 2008 | 7th | 4th | — |
| Lyudmila Belyakova | RUS | 2012 | 7th | 6th | — |
| Laura Benz | SUI | 2009 | 8th | 7th | — |
| Sara Benz | SUI | 2009 | 8th | 7th | — |
| Inna Dyubanok | RUS | 2008 | 8th | 6th | — |
| Yevgeniya Dyupina | RUS | 2012 | 7th | 6th | — |
| Tina Enstrom | SWE | 2008 | 4th | 5th | — |
| Tina Enstrom | SWE | 2009 | B | 4th | — |
| Angelina Goncharenko | RUS | 2012 | 7th | 6th | — |
| Linnea Hedin | SWE | 2012 | B | 5th | — |

| | | | | | |
|---|---|---|---|---|---|
| Isabelle Jordansson | SWE | 2008 | 4th | 5th | — |
| Isabelle Jordansson | SWE | 2009 | B | 4th | — |
| Anna Kilponen | FIN | 2012 | 5th | 4th | — |
| Rahel Michielin | SUI | 2008 | 7th | 4th | — |
| Margarita Monakhova | RUS | 2012 | 7th | 6th | — |
| Klara Myren | SWE | 2008 | 4th | 5th | — |
| Klara Myren | SWE | 2009 | B | 4th | — |
| Emma Nordin | SWE | 2008 | 4th | 5th | — |
| Emma Nordin | SWE | 2009 | B | 4th | — |
| Cecilia Ostberg | SWE | 2008 | 4th | 5th | — |
| Cecilia Ostberg | SWE | 2009 | B | 4th | — |
| Valeria Pavlova | RUS | 2012 | 7th | 6th | — |
| Marie-Philip Poulin | CAN | 2009 | S | S | — |
| Isabella Portnoj | FIN | 2012 | 5th | 4th | — |
| Anna Prugova | RUS | 2010 | 8th | — | 6th |
| Anni Rantanen | FIN | 2012 | 5th | 4th | — |
| Olga Sosina | RUS | 2009 | 7th | 5th | |
| Olga Sosina | RUS | 2010 | 8th | — | 6th |
| Kerstin Spielberger | GER | 2012 | 4th | 7th | — |
| Laura Stalder | SUI | 2011 | 7th | 6th | — |
| Phoebe Stanz | SUI | 2011 | 7th | 6th | — |
| Phoebe Stanz | SUI | 2012 | 8th | B | — |
| Anja Stiefel | SUI | 2008 | 7th | 4th | — |
| Jenny Tamas | GER | 2008 | 5th | 9th | — |
| Susanna Tapani | FIN | 2011 | B | B | — |
| Sandra Thalmann | SUI | 2009 | 8th | 7th | — |
| Alexandra Vafina | RUS | 2008 | 8th | 6th | — |
| Saana Valkama | FIN | 2012 | 5th | 4th | — |
| Sabrina Zollinger | SUI | 2009 | 8th | 7th | — |
| Sabrina Zollinger | SUI | 2011 | 7th | 6th | — |

# Players Who Appeared in the Women's World Championship or Olympics Before the U18 Women's World Championship

| Player | NAT | OG-W/WW Debut (Finish) | WW18 Debut (Finish) |
|---|---|---|---|
| Tina Enstrom | SWE | WW 2007 (B) | 2008 (4th) |
| Chiho Osawa | JPN | WW 2009 (8th) | 2010 (6th) |
| Carina Spuhler | GER | WW 2007 (8th) | 2008 (5th) |
| Jenny Tamas | GER | OG-W 2006 (5th) | 2008 (5th) |
| Jenny Tamas | GER | WW 2007 (8th) | 2008 (5th) |

*Germany's Jenny Tamas (dark sweater) played at both the World Championships and Olympics before playing at the U18. Photo: Phillip MacCallum / HHOF-IIHF Images*

# Modern Outdoor Games

| Date | Dubbed | League | Host City | Venue | Att | Score |
|---|---|---|---|---|---|---|
| March 5, 1957 | none | IIHF WM | Moscow | Lenin Stadium | 55,000 | Soviet Union 4-Sweden 4 |
| November 8, 1962 | none | SEL | Gothenburg | Ullevi Stadium | 23,192 | Frolunda 3-Djurgarden 2 |
| September 28, 1991 | none | NHL | Las Vegas | Caesar's Palace | 13,000 | Los Angeles Kings 5-New York Rangers 2 |
| October 6, 2001 | Cold War | NCAA | East Lansing | Spartan Stadium | 74,554 | Michigan State University 3-University of Michigan 3 |
| November 22, 2003 | Heritage Classic | NHL | Edmonton | Commonwealth Stadium | 57,167 | Montreal 4-Edmonton 3 |
| February 11, 2006 | Frozen Tundra Classic | NCAA | Green Bay | Lambeau Field | 40,890 | Ohio State 2-Wisconsin 4 |
| January 14, 2007 | Tatzen Derby | SUI | Berne | Stade de Suisse | 30,076 | Langnau 2-Bern 5 |
| January 1, 2008 | Winter Classic 1 | NHL | Buffalo | Ralph Wilson Stadium | 71,217 | Pittsburgh 2-Buffalo 1 (SO) |
| January 10, 2008 | All-Star Game | KHL | Moscow | Red Square | 3,000 | Team Jagr 7-Team Yashin 6 |
| January 1, 2009 | Winter Classic 2 | NHL | Chicago | Wrigley Field | 40,818 | Detroit 6-Chicago 4 |
| December 28, 2009 | Rekordmatchen | SEL | Gothenburg | Ullevi Stadium | 31,144 | Frolunda 4-Farjestad 1 |
| January 1, 2010 | Winter Classic 3 | NHL | Boston | Fenway Park | 38,112 | Boston 2-Philadelphia 1 |
| January 8, 2010 | Frozen Fenway | NCAA | Boston | Fenway Park | 6,889 | New Hampshire 5-Northeastern 3 (women) |
| January 8, 2010 | Frozen Fenway | NCAA | Boston | Fenway Park | 38,472 | Boston University 3-Boston College 2 |
| January 9, 2010 | none | AUT | Klagenfurt | Sportpark | 30,500 | Klagenfurt 1-Villach 3 |
| February 6, 2010 | Camp Randall Hockey Classic | NCAA | Madison | Camp Randall Stadium | 8,263 | Wisconsin 6-Bemidji State 1 (women) |
| February 6, 2010 | Camp Randall Hockey Classic | NCAA | Madison | Camp Randall Stadium | 55,031 | Wisconsin 3-Michigan 2 |
| February 20, 2010 | Mirabito Outdoor Classic | AHL | Syracuse | New York State Fairgrounds | 21,502 | Syracuse 2-Binghamton 1 |
| April 8, 2010 | Frozen Four Semi-Finals 1 | NCAA | Detroit | Ford Field | 34,954 | Wisconsin 8-Rochester 1 |
| April 8, 2010 | Frozen Four Semi-Finals 2 | NCAA | Detroit | Ford Field | 34,954 | Boston College 7-Miami (Ohio) 1 |
| April 10, 2010 | Frozen Four Final | NCAA | Detroit | Ford Field | 37,592 | Boston College 5-Wisconsin 0 |
| May 7, 2010 | none | IIHF WM | Gelsenkirchen | Veltins Arena | 77,803 | Germany 2-United States 1 (OT) |
| December 11, 2010 | The Big Chill at the Big House | NCAA | Ann Arbour | Michigan Stadium | 104,173 | Michigan 5-Michigan State 0 |
| December 26, 2010 | none | SEL | Karlstad | Lofbergs Lila Utomhusarena | 15,274 | Farjestad 5-Frolunda 2 |
| January 1, 2011 | Winter Classic 4 | NHL | Pittsburgh | Heinz Field | 68,111 | Washington 3 at Pittsburgh 1 |
| January 9, 2011 | none | IIHF WM20-III | Mexico City | Zocalo Square | 3,000 | Mexico 8-Bulgaria 0 |
| February 5, 2011 | Talviklassikko | FIN | Helsinki | Olympic Stadium | 36,644 | HIFK 4-Jokerit 3 |
| February 20, 2011 | Heritage Classic 2 | NHL | Calgary | McMahon Stadium | 41,022 | Calgary 4-Montreal 0 |
| December 10, 2011 | Utomhusmatchen | SEL | Jonkoping | Elmia | 18,884 | Linkoping 1-HV71 Jonkoping 0 (OT) |
| January 2, 2012 | Winter Classic 5 | NHL | Philadelphia | Citizens Bank Park | 46,967 | New York Rangers 3-Philadelphia Flyers 2 |
| September 14, 2012 | Ice Fever MMXII | EBEL | Pula | Pula Arena | 7,022 | Medvescak Zagreb 2-Olimpija Ljubljana 3 |
| September 16, 2012 | Ice Fever MMXII | EBEL | Pula | Pula Arena | 7,130 | Medvescak Zagreb 4-Vienna Capitals 1 |

# THE NATIONS

## Andorra (AND)

Andorra has been an Associate Member in the IIHF since joining 16 years ago.

### Joined IIHF: May 4, 1995 (Associate Member)

Webiste: www.faeg.org
E-mail: faeg@faeg.org

Federació Andorrana d'Esports de Gel
Ctra. General,
Edif. Perecaus
1a planta - despatx 5 100 Canillo, Andorra

Phone: +376 85 2666 • Fax: +376 85 2667

**Top Level Host History** none

## Argentina (ARG)

The women's ice hockey national team played its first exhibition games at a camp in Mexico in 2012. Photo: Ulises Gutierrez Bonilla.

### Joined IIHF: May 31, 1998 (Associate Member)

Website: http://www.aahhl.com.ar
E-mail: rh_iannicelli@hotmail.com

Asociación Argentina de Hockey
sobre Hielo y En Línea
Ruben Hector Iannicelli
Hualfin 1083
Capital Federal (1424)
Argentina

Phone: +54 11 4432 1212 • Fax: +54 11 4854 1060

**Top Level Host History** none

## Armenia (ARM)

Armenia captured first place at the U20, Division III-B, in 2008. Photo: Serbian Ice Hockey Association.

### Joined IIHF: September 22, 1999 (Associate Member)

Website: www.icehockeyarmenia.com
Email: aihf@arminco.com

Ice Hockey Federation of Armenia
Av. Avetisyan str.1 apt.12
375033 Yerevan
Republic of Armenia

Phone: +374 9999 2351/+374 9140 2351

**World Ranking**

**MEN**
2012 no rank
2011 no rank
2010........49
2009........48
2008........48
2007........45
2006........45
2005........45
2004........45

**Top Level Host History** none

**World Championship (Men)**

| Year Event | GP | W | T | L | GF | GA | Place | Coach | Captain |
|---|---|---|---|---|---|---|---|---|---|
| 2004 WM-III | 4 | 0 | 0 | 4 | 2 | 73 | 5th | Gagik Vardanyan | Samuel Zakharyan |
| 2005 WM-III | 4 | 0 | 0 | 4 | 5 | 142 | 5th | Gagik Vardanyan | Samuel Zakharyan |
| 2006 WM-III | 4 | 2 | 0 | 2 | 23 | 19 | 3rd | Doug Decesare | Raffi Kajberouni |

# Australia (AUS)

Australian U18 national team goalkeeper Rhett Kelly makes a stick save against Serbia. Photo: Filip Bakic.

## Joined IIHF: February 11, 1938

Website: www.iha.org.au
E-mail: iha@iha.org.au

Ice Hockey Australia
23 Dickerson Way
Redwood Park
South Australia 5097
Australia

Phone: +61 8 8251 1734 • Fax: +61 8 8251 5156

**World Ranking**

| MEN | | WOMEN | |
|---|---|---|---|
| 2012 | 32 | 2012 | 24 |
| 2011 | 34 | 2011 | 24 |
| 2010 | 34 | 2010 | 25 |
| 2009 | 31 | 2009 | 23 |
| 2008 | 33 | 2008 | 22 |
| 2007 | 33 | 2007 | 23 |
| 2006 | 34 | 2006 | 23 |
| 2005 | 34 | 2005 | 22 |
| 2004 | 35 | 2004 | 21 |

**Top Level Host History** none

**Olympics, Men**
(bold=top level)

| Year Event | GP | W | T | L | GF | GA | Place | Coach | Captain |
|---|---|---|---|---|---|---|---|---|---|
| **1960 OG-M** | **6** | **0** | **0** | **6** | **10** | **87** | **9th** | **Bud McEachern** | **Ben Acton** |

**World Championship (Men)**

| Year Event | GP | W | T | | L | GF | GA | Place | Coach | Captain |
|---|---|---|---|---|---|---|---|---|---|---|
| Year Event | GP | W | OTW | OTL | L | GF | GA | Place | Coach | Captain |
| 1962 WM-B | 5 | 1 | 0 | | 4 | 13 | 51 | 5th | Ken Kennedy/Bud McEachern | Ken Wellman |
| 1974 WM-C | 7 | 1 | 0 | | 6 | 13 | 74 | 7th | Luke Elgin | Charles Grandy |
| 1979 WM-C | 7 | 0 | 1 | | 6 | 13 | 53 | 8th | Dan Reynolds | Charles Grandy |
| 1986 WM-C | 5 | 0 | 1 | | 4 | 16 | 42 | 10th | David Fehily/Charles Naish | *unknown* |
| 1987 WM-D | 6 | 5 | 1 | | 0 | 177 | 6 | 1st | Dan Reynolds | Alexander Gardner |
| 1989 WM-C | 7 | 0 | 0 | | 7 | 14 | 58 | 8th | Dan Reynolds | Scott Davidson |
| 1990 WM-D | 4 | 0 | 2 | | 2 | 10 | 34 | 2nd | Ryan Switzer | Glen Foll |
| 1992-WM-C-A | 5 | 2 | 1 | | 2 | 24 | 26 | 3rd | Ryan Switzer | Glen Foll |
| 1993 WM-C | 5 | 2 | 0 | | 3 | 19 | 51 | 7th | Ryan Switzer | Glen Foll |
| 1994 WM-C-B | 5 | 2 | 0 | | 3 | 20 | 16 | 6th | Ryan Switzer | *unknown* |
| 1995 WM-C-2 | 6 | 3 | 0 | | 3 | 31 | 31 | 7th | Dan Reynolds | Glen Foll |
| 1996 WM-D | 5 | 0 | 0 | | 5 | 14 | 43 | 8th | Mark Bowles | Howard Jones |
| 1997 WM-D | 5 | 1 | 1 | | 3 | 20 | 25 | 6th | Mark Bowles | Glen Foll |
| 1998 WM-D | 5 | 3 | 1 | | 1 | 35 | 15 | 2nd | Kelly Lovering | Glen Foll |
| 1999 WM-D | 4 | 2 | 0 | | 2 | 29 | 9 | 3rd | Kelly Lovering | Glen Foll |
| 2000 WM-D | 4 | 2 | 0 | | 2 | 23 | 16 | 3rd | Kelly Lovering | Glen Foll |
| 2001 WM-II-A | 5 | 3 | 0 | | 2 | 40 | 23 | 3rd | Kelly Lovering | Glen Foll |
| 2002 WM-II-A | 5 | 2 | 0 | | 3 | 32 | 39 | 4th | John Botterill | Glen Foll |
| 2003 WM-II-A | 5 | 2 | 0 | | 3 | 25 | 26 | 4th | Jari Gronstrand | Glen Foll |
| 2004 WM-II-A | 5 | 3 | 1 | | 1 | 40 | 18 | 3rd | Rob Barnes | Glen Foll |
| 2005 WM-II-A | 5 | 4 | 0 | | 1 | 34 | 5 | 2nd | Rob Barnes | Glen Foll |
| 2006 WM-II-B | 5 | 3 | 1 | | 1 | 27 | 14 | 3rd | Robert Champagne | Glen Foll |
| 2007 WM-II-B | 4 | 3 | 0 | 0 | 1 | 25 | 11 | 2nd | Steve McKenna | Tony Wilson |
| 2008 WM-II-B | 5 | 5 | 0 | 0 | 0 | 20 | 6 | 1st | Steve McKenna | Tony Wilson |
| 2009 WM-I-A | 5 | 0 | 0 | 0 | 5 | 7 | 40 | 6th | Steve McKenna | Robert Starke |
| 2010 WM-II-A | 5 | 4 | 0 | 0 | 1 | 31 | 15 | 2nd | Alain Shank | Greg Oddy |
| 2011 WM-II-A | 5 | 5 | 0 | 0 | 0 | 27 | 6 | 1st | Vladimir Rubes | Greg Oddy |
| 2012 WM-I-B | 5 | 0 | 0 | 0 | 5 | 14 | 27 | 6th | Vladimir Rubes | Greg Oddy |

**U20 World Championship**

| Year Event | GP | W | T | | L | GF | GA | Place | Coach | Captain |
|---|---|---|---|---|---|---|---|---|---|---|
| Year Event | GP | W | OTW | OTL | L | GF | GA | Place | Coach | Captain |
| 1983 WM20-C | 6 | 0 | 0 | | 6 | 12 | 41 | 4th | Glen Williamson | *unknown* |
| 1984 WM20-C | 4 | 0 | 0 | | 4 | 14 | 36 | 7th | Scott Davidson | John Rice |
| 1987 WM20-C | 5 | 0 | 0 | | 5 | 5 | 56 | 6th | Gerry Skuta | Radomir Benicky |
| 2000 WM20-D | 4 | 2 | 0 | | 2 | 21 | 29 | 7th | John Botterill | Greg Oddy |
| 2001 WM20-III | 4 | 0 | 1 | | 3 | 10 | 39 | 8th | Brad Hunt | Mark Rummukainen |
| 2003 WM20-III | 4 | 1 | 0 | | 3 | 8 | 25 | 4th | Stewart Hicks | Brinn Lupton |
| 2004 WM20-III | 5 | 5 | 0 | | 0 | 42 | 13 | 1st | Graham Homann | James Keane |
| 2005 WM20-II-B | 5 | 1 | 0 | | 4 | 16 | 40 | 5th | Graham Homann | Joshua Harding |
| 2006 WM20-II-A | 5 | 1 | 0 | | 4 | 17 | 37 | 5th | Graham Homann | Aubyn Martin |
| 2007 WM20-II-A | 5 | 0 | 0 | 0 | 5 | 11 | 32 | 6th | Graham Homann | Todd Stephenson |
| 2008 WM20-III | 6 | 3 | 0 | 0 | 3 | 44 | 23 | 4th | Simon Holmes | Michael Beaton |
| 2010 WM20-III | 4 | 3 | 1 | 0 | 0 | 23 | 6 | 1st | Simon Holmes | Troy Robertson |
| 2011 WM20-II-B | 5 | 1 | 0 | 0 | 4 | 21 | 39 | 5th | Stephen Laforet | Eric Sewell |
| 2012 WM20-II-B | 5 | 1 | 0 | 0 | 4 | 12 | 36 | 5th | Ryan O'Handley | Hamish Powell |

### U18 World Championship (Men)

| Year Event | GP | W | T | | L | GF | GA | Place | Coach | Captain |
|---|---|---|---|---|---|---|---|---|---|---|
| Year Event | GP | W | OTW | OTL | L | GF | GA | Place | Coach | Captain |
| 2003 WM18-III-A | 3 | 3 | 0 | | 0 | 28 | 6 | 1st | Vladimir Ruben | Lliam Webster |
| 2004 WM18-II-B | 5 | 0 | 1 | | 4 | 5 | 42 | 6th | Vladimir Rubes | Tristan Stoakes |
| 2005 WM18-III | 5 | 5 | 0 | | 0 | 46 | 6 | 1st | Vladimir Rubes | Todd Stephenson |
| 2006 WM18-II-B | 5 | 2 | 0 | | 3 | 13 | 30 | 3rd | Vladimir Rubes | Todd Stephenson |
| 2007 WM18-II-B | 5 | 0 | 2 | 0 | 3 | 13 | 25 | 5th | Robert Starke | Andrew Belic |
| 2008 WM18-II-A | 5 | 0 | 0 | 0 | 5 | 8 | 33 | 6th | Pier-Alexandre Martin | Sean Greer |
| 2009 WM18-III-A | 4 | 4 | 0 | 0 | 0 | 63 | 3 | 1st | Pier-Alexandre Martin | Seph Renner |
| 2010 WM18-II-B | 5 | 0 | 0 | 1 | 4 | 7 | 37 | 6th | Pier-Alexandre Martin | Marcus Wong |
| 2011 WM18-III-A | 5 | 5 | 0 | 0 | 0 | 47 | 5 | 1st | Pier-Alexandre Martin | Marcus Wong |
| 2012 WM18-II-B | 5 | 1 | 0 | 1 | 3 | 8 | 20 | 5th | Pier Martin | Cameron Todd |

### Women's World Championship

| Year Event | GP | W | T | | L | GF | GA | Place | Coach | Captain |
|---|---|---|---|---|---|---|---|---|---|---|
| Year Event | GP | W | OTW | OTL | L | GF | GA | Place | Coach | Captain |
| 2003 WW-III | 5 | 4 | 1 | | 0 | 34 | 7 | 1st | Kathy Berg | Stephanie Boxall |
| 2004 WW-II | 5 | 1 | 0 | | 4 | 6 | 32 | 5th | Kathy Berg | Stephanie Boxall |
| 2005 WW-III | 5 | 1 | 1 | | 3 | 15 | 18 | 5th | Kathy Berg | *unknown* |
| 2007 WW-III | 5 | 4 | 1 | 0 | 0 | 41 | 9 | 1st | Rocky Padjen | Candice Mitchell |
| 2008 WW-II | 5 | 0 | 0 | 0 | 5 | 5 | 39 | 6th | Rocky Padjen | Kaylee White |
| 2011 WW-III | 5 | 4 | 0 | 1 | 0 | 22 | 9 | 2nd | Rocky Padjen | Kaylee White |
| 2012 WW-II-A | 5 | 3 | 0 | 0 | 2 | 11 | 12 | 3rd | Rockey Padjen | Shona Green |

### U18 Women's World Championship

| Year Event | GP | W | T | | L | GF | GA | Place | Coach | Captain |
|---|---|---|---|---|---|---|---|---|---|---|
| Year Event | GP | W | OTW | OTL | L | GF | GA | Place | Coach | Captain |
| 2009 WW18-I | 4 | 1 | 0 | 0 | 3 | 8 | 13 | 4th | Miroslav Berek | Janine Weber |
| 2010 WW18-I | 5 | 2 | 0 | 0 | 3 | 16 | 14 | 4th | Christian Dolinar | Anna Schneider |

# Austria (AUT)

*Daniel Welsner from Austria celebrates the nation's promotion to the top division after a victory against Hungary. Photo: Samo Vidic.*

## Joined IIHF: March 18, 1912

(expelled 1920, re-admitted January 24, 1924, expelled 1939; re-admitted April 27, 1946)

Website: www.eishockey.at
E-mail: info@eishockey.at

Österreichischer Eishockeyverband (ÖEHV)
Attemsgasse 7/D, 1. OG
A-1220 Wien

Phone: +43 0 1 20 200 200 • Fax: +43 0 1 20 200 2050

**World Ranking**

| MEN | | WOMEN | |
|---|---|---|---|
| 2012 | 15 | 2012 | 15 |
| 2011 | 15 | 2011 | 15 |
| 2010 | 14 | 2010 | 16 |
| 2009 | 16 | 2009 | 17 |
| 2008 | 16 | 2008 | 19 |
| 2007 | 17 | 2007 | 20 |
| 2006 | 16 | 2006 | 21 |
| 2005 | 13 | 2005 | 25 |
| 2004 | 11 | 2004 | 26 |

### Top Level Host History

Olympics: 1964 (Innsbruck); 1976 (Innsbruck)
World Championship (Men): 1930 (Vienna); 1977 (Vienna); 1987 (Vienna); 1996 (Vienna); 2005 (Vienna, Innsbruck)

### Olympics, Men

(bold=top level)

| Year Event | GP | W | T | L | GF | GA | Place | Coach | Captain |
|---|---|---|---|---|---|---|---|---|---|
| **1928 OG-M** | **2** | **0** | **2** | **0** | **4** | **4** | **7th** | **Edgar Dietrichstein** | **Ulrich Lederer** |
| **1936 OG-M** | **6** | **2** | **0** | **4** | **12** | **11** | **7th** | **Rem Manners** | ***unknown*** |
| **1948 OG-M** | **8** | **1** | **0** | **7** | **33** | **77** | **8th** | ***unknown*** | ***unknown*** |
| **1956 OG-M** | **6** | **0** | **1** | **5** | **11** | **51** | **10th** | **Udo Hohlfeld** | ***unknown*** |
| **1964 OG-M** | **7** | **3** | **1** | **3** | **24** | **28** | **13th** | **Zdenek Ujcik** | **Walter Znenahlik** |
| **1968 OG-M** | **5** | **1** | **0** | **4** | **12** | **27** | **13th** | **Jiri Hanzl** | **Dieter Kalt** |
| **1976 OG-M** | **5** | **3** | **0** | **2** | **18** | **14** | **8th** | **Yuri Baulin** | **Josef Puschnig** |
| **1984 OG-M** | **5** | **1** | **0** | **4** | **13** | **37** | **11th** | **Rudolf Killias** | **Rudolf Konig** |
| **1988 OG-M** | **6** | **1** | **1** | **4** | **15** | **31** | **9th** | **Ludek Bukac** | **Kurt Harand** |
| **1994 OG-M** | **7** | **1** | **0** | **6** | **18** | **36** | **12th** | **Ken Tyler** | **Manfred Muhr** |
| **1998 OG-M** | **4** | **0** | **2** | **2** | **12** | **16** | **14th** | **Ron Kennedy** | **Herbert Hohenberger** |
| **2002 OG-M** | **4** | **1** | **0** | **3** | **8** | **13** | **12th** | **Ron Kennedy** | **Martin Ulrich** |

### World Championship (Men)

(bold=top level)

| Year Event | GP | W | T | | L | GF | GA | Place | Coach | Captain |
|---|---|---|---|---|---|---|---|---|---|---|
| Year Event | GP | W | OTW | OTL | L | GF | GA | Place | Coach | Captain |
| **1930 WM** | **3** | **2** | **0** | | **1** | **5** | **3** | **4th** | **Blake Watson** | **Walter Bruck** |
| **1931 WM** | **8** | **4** | **0** | | **4** | **14** | **16** | **B** | **Hans Weinberger** | ***unknown*** |
| **1933 WM** | **8** | **4** | **0** | | **4** | **14** | **13** | **4th** | **Hans Weinberger** | ***unknown*** |
| **1934 WM** | **7** | **3** | **1** | | **3** | **9** | **11** | **7th** | **Hans Weinberger** | ***unknown*** |
| **1935 WM** | **8** | **4** | **1** | | **3** | **18** | **14** | **6th** | **Hans Weinberger** | ***unknown*** |

| | | | | | | | | | | |
|---|---|---|---|---|---|---|---|---|---|---|
| **1938 WM** | **3** | **0** | **1** | | **2** | **1** | **5** | **10th** | **Hans Weinberger** | ***unknown*** |
| **1947 WM** | **7** | **5** | **0** | | **2** | **49** | **32** | **B** | ***unknown*** | **Franz Csongei** |
| **1949 WM** | **7** | **1** | **0** | | **6** | **30** | **60** | **6th** | ***unknown*** | ***unknown*** |
| 1951 WM-B | 5 | 1 | 0 | | 4 | 16 | 25 | 5th | Kurt Wollinger | Rudolf Wurmbrand |
| 1953 WM-B | 5 | 2 | 0 | | 3 | 20 | 24 | 3rd | Cam Miller | unknown |
| 1955 WM-B | 4 | 3 | 0 | | 1 | 15 | 9 | 2nd | Udo Hohlfeld | *unknown* |
| **1957 WM** | **7** | **0** | **1** | | **6** | **8** | **61** | **7th** | **Udo Hohlfeld** | **Franz Potucek** |
| 1961 WM-B | 5 | 1 | 0 | | 4 | 10 | 35 | 6th | Bohumil Rejda | *unknown* |
| 1962 WM-B | 5 | 4 | 0 | | 1 | 49 | 9 | 2nd | Ernst Gassler | *unknown* |
| 1963 WM-C | 5 | 5 | 0 | | 0 | 62 | 7 | 1st | Zdenek Ujcik | Walter Znenahlik |
| 1965 WM-B | 6 | 2 | 0 | | 4 | 21 | 28 | 5th | Zdenek Ujcik | Walter Znenahlik |
| 1966 WM-B | 7 | 3 | 0 | | 4 | 25 | 30 | 5th | Jiri Hanzl | Walter Znenahlik |
| 1967 WM-B | 7 | 2 | 1 | | 4 | 23 | 34 | 6th | Jiri Hanzl | Walter Znenahlik |
| 1969 WM-B | 7 | 1 | 1 | | 5 | 15 | 39 | 7th | Josef Koller/ Frantisek Tikal | Dieter Kalt |
| 1970 WM-C | 6 | 5 | 1 | | 0 | 37 | 12 | 1st | Josef Koller/ Frantisek Tikal | Walter Znenahlik |
| 1971 WM-B | 7 | 1 | 0 | | 6 | 17 | 34 | 7th | Frantisek Tikal | *unknown* |
| 1972 WM-C | 6 | 5 | 1 | | 0 | 21 | 12 | 1st | Rudolf Novak | Dieter Kalt |
| 1973 WM-B | 7 | 2 | 0 | | 5 | 21 | 44 | 5th | Rudolf Novak/David Bauer | Josef Puschnig |
| 1974 WM-B | 7 | 0 | 1 | | 6 | 12 | 42 | 8th | Franz Moser/Yuri Baulin | Josef Puschnig |
| 1975 WM-C | 6 | 3 | 1 | | 2 | 32 | 16 | 3rd | Yuri Baulin | Gerhard Hausner |
| 1976 WM-C | 4 | 4 | 0 | | 0 | 38 | 9 | 1st | Yuri Baulin | *unknown* |
| 1977 WM-B | 8 | 0 | 0 | | 8 | 19 | 47 | 9th | Yuri Baulin | Walter Schneider |
| 1978 WM-C | 7 | 5 | 1 | | 1 | 65 | 31 | 2nd | Walter Znenahlik | Herbert Mortl |
| 1979 WM-B | 6 | 2 | 1 | | 3 | 19 | 30 | 7th | Dieter Kalt | *unknown* |
| 1981 WM-C | 7 | 7 | 0 | | 0 | 43 | 5 | 1st | Rudolf Killias | *unknown* |
| 1982 WM-B | 7 | 4 | 1 | | 2 | 33 | 26 | 2nd | Rudolf Killias | Rudolf Konig |
| 1983 WM-B | 7 | 3 | 4 | | 0 | 41 | 27 | 3rd | Rudolf Killias | *unknown* |
| 1985 WM-B | 7 | 3 | 0 | | 4 | 18 | 24 | 4th | Rudolf Killias | Rudolf Konig |
| 1986 WM-B | 7 | 3 | 0 | | 4 | 24 | 27 | 6th | Rudolf Killias | Kurt Harand |
| 1987 WM-B | 7 | 5 | 0 | | 2 | 41 | 27 | 3rd | Ludek Bukac | Kurt Harand |
| 1989 WM-B | 7 | 2 | 0 | | 5 | 25 | 32 | 6th | Ludek Bukac | Thomas Cijan |
| 1990 WM-B | 7 | 4 | 2 | | 1 | 30 | 14 | 3rd | Ludek Bukac | Thomas Cijan |
| 1991 WM-B | 7 | 3 | 1 | | 3 | 21 | 18 | 5th | Ludek Bukac | Thomas Cijan |
| 1992 WM-B | 7 | 7 | 0 | | 0 | 73 | 4 | 1st | Ken Tyler | Friedrich Ganster |
| **1993 WM** | **6** | **1** | **1** | | **4** | **10** | **24** | **9th** | **Ken Tyler** | **Manfred Muhr** |
| **1994 WM** | **6** | **1** | **1** | | **4** | **15** | **25** | **8th** | **Ron Kennedy** | **Manfred Muhr** |
| **1995 WM** | **7** | **1** | **1** | | **5** | **17** | **31** | **11th** | **Ken Tyler** | **Manfred Muhr** |
| **1996 WM** | **7** | **1** | **0** | | **6** | **9** | **31** | **12th** | **Ken Tyler** | **Manfred Muhr (1)** |
| 1997 WM-B | 7 | 2 | 3 | | 2 | 22 | 22 | 4th | Ron Kennedy | Manfred Muhr |
| **1998 WM** | **3** | **0** | **0** | | **3** | **3** | **15** | **15th** | **Ron Kennedy** | **Andreas Pusnik (2)** |
| **1999 WM** | **6** | **3** | **0** | | **3** | **16** | **19** | **10th** | **Ron Kennedy** | **Andreas Pusnik (3)** |
| **2000 WM** | **6** | **2** | **2** | | **2** | **14** | **16** | **13th** | **Ron Kennedy** | **Mario Schaden (4)** |
| **2001 WM** | **6** | **2** | **0** | | **4** | **7** | **25** | **11th** | **Ron Kennedy** | **Mario Schaden** |
| **2002 WM** | **6** | **1** | **0** | | **5** | **17** | **26** | **12th** | **Ron Kennedy** | **Martin Ulrich** |
| **2003 WM** | **6** | **2** | **0** | | **4** | **15** | **29** | **10th** | **Herbert Pock** | **Dieter Kalt (5)** |
| **2004 WM** | **6** | **1** | **2** | | **3** | **15** | **16** | **11th** | **Herbert Pock** | **Dieter Kalt (6)** |
| **2005 WM** | **6** | **0** | **1** | | **5** | **10** | **29** | **16th** | **Herbert Pock** | **Dieter Kalt** |
| 2006 WM-I-B | 5 | 5 | 0 | | 0 | 27 | 9 | 1st | Jim Boni | Dieter Kalt |
| **2007 WM** | **6** | **1** | **0** | **1** | **4** | **16** | **29** | **15th** | **Jim Boni** | **Dieter Kalt** |
| 2008 WM-I-A | 5 | 5 | 0 | 0 | 0 | 34 | 12 | 1st | Lars Bergstrom | Dieter Kalt |
| **2009 WM** | **6** | **2** | **0** | **0** | **4** | **11** | **20** | **14th** | **Lars Bergstrom** | **Gerhard Unterluggauer** |
| 2010 WM-I-A | 5 | 5 | 0 | 0 | 0 | 28 | 5 | 1st | Bill Gilligan | Gerhard Unterluggauer |
| **2011 WM** | **6** | **1** | **0** | **0** | **5** | **7** | **26** | **15th** | **Bill Gilligan** | **Gerhard Unterluggauer** |
| 2012 WM-I-A | 5 | 3 | 0 | 1 | 1 | 24 | 16 | 2nd | Manny Viveiros | Thomas Koch |

(1) Martin Ulrich captain vs. Canada (Apr. 23)
(2) Herbert Hohenberger captain vs. Italy (May 3)
(3) Herbert Hohenberger captain vs. Czech Republic (May 1)
(4) Gerald Ressmann captain vs. Italy (May 4)
(5) Herbert Hohenberger captain vs. Czech Republic (Apr. 28)
(6) Martin Ulrich captain vs. Czech Republic (Apr. 30) and Germany (May 1)

### U20 World Championship

(bold=top level)

| Year Event | GP | W | T | | L | GF | GA | Place | Coach | Captain |
|---|---|---|---|---|---|---|---|---|---|---|
| Year Event | GP | W | OTW | OTL | L | GF | GA | Place | Coach | Captain |
| 1979 WM20-B | 4 | 2 | 0 | | 2 | 17 | 20 | 5th | Paul Samonig | Johan Sulzer |
| 1980 WM20-B | 4 | 4 | 0 | | 0 | 33 | 9 | 1st | Hermann Knoll | Gert Kompajn |
| **1981 WM20** | **5** | **0** | **0** | | **5** | **9** | **67** | **8th** | **Hermann Knoll** | **Robert Kasan** |
| 1982 WM20-B | 4 | 3 | 0 | | 1 | 21 | 13 | 2nd | Paul Samonig | Christian Heinrich |
| 1983 WM20-B | 5 | 2 | 0 | | 3 | 23 | 25 | 4th | Paul Samonig | Martin Platzer |
| 1984 WM20-B | 5 | 4 | 0 | | 1 | 22 | 17 | 2nd | Rudolf Killias | Harald Tammer |
| 1985 WM20-B | 7 | 3 | 1 | | 3 | 30 | 53 | 4th | Harry Konig | *unknown* |
| 1986 WM20-B | 7 | 5 | 0 | | 2 | 42 | 35 | 3rd | Bill Gilliagn | Manfred Muhr |
| 1987 WM20-B | 5 | 1 | 1 | | 3 | 14 | 36 | 4th | Hermann Knoll | *unknown* |
| 1988 WM20-B | 7 | 0 | 1 | | 6 | 26 | 42 | 8th | Ludek Bukac | *unknown* |
| 1989 WM20-C | 4 | 3 | 1 | | 0 | 21 | 14 | 1st | Bernhard Stricker | Gerald Ressmann |
| 1990 WM20-B | 7 | 2 | 1 | | 4 | 20 | 43 | 6th | Bill Gilligan | *unknown* |
| 1991 WM20-B | 7 | 1 | 0 | | 6 | 13 | 48 | 7th | Max Moser | Mario Bellina |
| 1992 WM20-B | 7 | 2 | 0 | | 5 | 16 | 29 | 7th | Franz Kotnauer | Ewald Seebacher |
| 1993 WM20-B | 7 | 4 | 0 | | 3 | 26 | 23 | 4th | Herbert Pock | Dieter Kalt |
| 1994 WM20-B | 7 | 1 | 3 | | 3 | 21 | 27 | 6th | Chris Reynolds | Dieter Kalt |
| 1995 WM20-B | 7 | 2 | 1 | | 4 | 20 | 31 | 6th | Helmut Keckeis | Christoph Brandner |
| 1996 WM20-B | 5 | 0 | 0 | | 5 | 10 | 35 | 8th | Helmut Keckeis | Bjorn Kraiger |
| 1997 WM20-C | 4 | 2 | 0 | | 2 | 9 | 13 | 5th | Kurt Harand | Robert Lukas |

| Year Event | GP | W | T | OTW | OTL | L | GF | GA | Place | Coach | Captain |
|---|---|---|---|---|---|---|---|---|---|---|---|
| 1998 WM20-C | 4 | 2 | 1 | | | 1 | 20 | 10 | 4th | Greg Holst | Raimund Divis |
| 1999 WM20-C | 4 | 2 | 0 | | | 2 | 17 | 17 | 4th | Greg Holst | Philipp Lukas |
| 2000 WM20-C | 4 | 4 | 0 | | | 0 | 37 | 7 | 1st | Greg Holst | Gregor Hager |
| 2001 WM20-I | 5 | 2 | 2 | | | 1 | 19 | 18 | 5th | Greg Holst | Gregor Hager |
| 2002 WM20-I | 5 | 3 | 1 | | | 1 | 19 | 13 | 2nd | Greg Holst | Oliver Setzinger |
| 2003 WM20-I-B | 5 | 5 | 0 | | | 0 | 35 | 9 | 1st | Greg Holst | Phillippe-Michael Horsky |
| **2004 WM20** | **6** | **0** | **1** | | | **5** | **5** | **32** | **9th** | **Peter Schramm** | **Thomas Vanek** |
| 2005 WM20-I-A | 5 | 3 | 0 | | | 2 | 12 | 16 | 3rd | Greg Holst | Christopher Ibounig |
| 2006 WM20-I-B | 5 | 0 | 2 | | | 3 | 5 | 16 | 5th | Dieter Werfring | Matthias Schwab |
| 2007 WM20-I-B | 5 | 3 | | 0 | 1 | 1 | 18 | 15 | 2nd | Dieter Werfring | Rafael Rotter |
| 2008 WM20-I-A | 5 | 4 | | 0 | 0 | 1 | 36 | 11 | 2nd | Dieter Werfring | Michael Raffl |
| 2009 WM20-I-B | 5 | 4 | | 0 | 1 | 0 | 28 | 9 | 1st | Dieter Werfring | Raphael Herburger |
| **2010 WM20** | **6** | **0** | | **0** | **0** | **6** | **13** | **39** | **10th** | **Dieter Werfring** | **Dominique Heinrich** |
| 2011 WM20-I-B | 5 | 3 | | 1 | 0 | 1 | 24 | 13 | 3rd | Dieter Werfring | Marco Brucker |
| 2012 WM20-I-A | 5 | 1 | | 0 | 1 | 3 | 11 | 26 | 5th | Christian Weber | Markus Pock |

**U18 World Championship (Men)**

| Year Event | GP | W | T | | L | GF | GA | Place | Coach | Captain |
|---|---|---|---|---|---|---|---|---|---|---|
| Year Event | GP | W | OTW | OTL | L | GF | GA | Place | Coach | Captain |
| 1999 WM18-B | 5 | 2 | 2 | | 1 | 28 | 12 | 2nd | Greg Holst | Gregor Hager |
| 2000 WM18-B | 5 | 3 | 1 | | 1 | 21 | 13 | 2nd | Greg Holst | Michael Pollross |
| 2001 WM18-I | 5 | 2 | 3 | | 0 | 17 | 12 | 2nd | Greg Holst | Oliver Setzinger |
| 2002 WM18-I | 4 | 2 | 0 | | 2 | 10 | 11 | 3rd | Greg Holst | Stefan Pittl |
| 2003 WM18-I-B | 5 | 1 | 1 | | 3 | 15 | 18 | 5th | Herbert Haiszan | Phillip Kink |
| 2004 WM18-I-A | 5 | 3 | 0 | | 2 | 21 | 18 | 3rd | Peter Raffl | Mario Altmann |
| 2005 WM18-I-A | 5 | 2 | 0 | | 3 | 15 | 25 | 5th | Greg Holst | Rafael Rotter |
| 2006 WM18-I-A | 5 | 1 | 1 | | 3 | 22 | 26 | 5th | Peter Raffl | Wilhelm Lanz |
| 2007 WM18-I-A | 5 | 1 | 0 | 1 | 3 | 14 | 21 | 5th | Peter Raffl | Michael Schiechl |
| 2008 WM18-I-B | 5 | 2 | 1 | 0 | 2 | 11 | 6 | 3rd | Tom Pokel | Patrick Maier |
| 2009 WM18-I-B | 5 | 2 | 2 | 0 | 1 | 21 | 20 | 3rd | Kurt Harand | Nikolaus Hartl |
| 2010 WM18-I-A | 5 | 0 | 0 | 1 | 4 | 12 | 25 | 6th | Martin Ulrich | Markus Pock |
| 2011 WM18-II-A | 5 | 5 | 0 | 0 | 0 | 56 | 3 | 1st | Mike Shea | Patrick Obrist |
| 2012 WM18-I-B | 5 | 2 | 1 | 0 | 2 | 21 | 21 | 3rd | Jason O'Leary | Christoph Duller |

**Women's World Championship**

| Year Event | GP | W | T | | L | GF | GA | Place | Coach | Captain |
|---|---|---|---|---|---|---|---|---|---|---|
| Year Event | GP | W | OTW | OTL | L | GF | GA | Place | Coach | Captain |
| 2004 WW-III | 5 | 5 | 0 | | 0 | 35 | 4 | 1st | Timo Sutinen | *unknown* |
| 2005 WW-II | 5 | 1 | 0 | | 4 | 10 | 24 | 5th | Timo Sutinen | *unknown* |
| 2007 WW-II | 5 | 2 | 0 | 0 | 3 | 17 | 11 | 4th | Timo Sutinen | Cacillia Reichel |
| 2008 WW-II | 5 | 5 | 0 | 0 | 0 | 22 | 10 | 1st | Timo Sutinen | Katharina Janach |
| 2009 WW-I | 5 | 2 | 0 | 1 | 2 | 16 | 16 | 4th | Miroslav Berek | Katharina Janach |
| 2011 WW-I | 4 | 1 | 0 | 0 | 3 | 6 | 12 | 4th | Miroslav Berek | Kerstin Oberhuber |
| 2012 WW-I-A | 5 | 2 | 0 | 0 | 3 | 16 | 18 | 4th | Christian Yngve | Denise Altmann |

**U18 Women's World Championship**

| Year Event | GP | W | OTW | OTL | L | GF | GA | Place | Coach | Captain |
|---|---|---|---|---|---|---|---|---|---|---|
| 2009 WW18-I | 4 | 1 | 0 | 0 | 3 | 8 | 13 | 4th | Miroslav Berek | Janine Weber |
| 2010 WW18-I | 5 | 2 | 0 | 0 | 3 | 16 | 14 | 4th | Christian Dolinar | Anna Schneider |
| 2011 WW18-I | 5 | 3 | 0 | 0 | 2 | 19 | 14 | 3rd | Jorma Siitarinen | Charlotte Wittich |
| 2012 WW18-I | 5 | 3 | 1 | 0 | 1 | 16 | 9 | 2nd | Christian Yngve | Tamara Graschner |

# Azerbaijan (AZE)

## Joined IIHF: May 6, 1992

Website: n/a
E-mail: n/a

Ice Hockey Federation of the Republic of Azerbaijan
Litemiy pereulok 2
370603 Baku
Azerbaijan

Phone: +994 1 294 4000 • Fax: +7 892 298 535

**Top Level Host History** none

# Belarus (BLR)

The Belarusian U18 national team celebrates promotion to Division I, Group A. Photo: Viktor David Koppan.

## Joined IIHF: May 6, 1992

Website: www.hockey.by
E-mail: BIHA@Hockey.by

Belarusian Ice Hockey Association
Pobeditelei Avenue, 20/3
220020 Minsk
Belarus

Phone: +375 172 54 5819/+375 172 50 2593 (intl. dep.)
Fax: +375 172 54 58 42

**World Ranking**

**MEN**
2012........13
2011........11
2010........10
2009........8
2008........9
2007........9
2006........10
2005........12
2004........13

### Top Level Host History

World Championship (Men): 2014 (Minsk)
U18 World Championship (Men): 2004 (Minsk), 2012 (Minsk, Bobruisk)

### Olympics, Men

(bold=top level)

| Year Event | GP | W | T | | | L | GF | GA | Place | Coach | Captain |
|---|---|---|---|---|---|---|---|---|---|---|---|
| Year Event | GP | W | | OTW | OTL | L | GF | GA | Place | Coach | Captain |
| **1998 OG-M** | **7** | **2** | **1** | | | **4** | **19** | **23** | **7th** | **Anatoli Varivonchik** | **Alexander Andrievsky (1)** |
| **2002 OG-M** | **9** | **3** | **0** | | | **6** | **18** | **42** | **4th** | **Vladimir Krikunov** | **Alexander Andrievsky** |
| **2010 OG-M** | **4** | **1** | | **0** | **0** | **3** | **10** | **15** | **9th** | **Mikhail Zakharov** | **Ruslan Salei** |

(1) Ruslan Salei captain vs. United States (Feb. 14)

### World Championship (Men)

(bold=top level)

| Year Event | GP | W | T | | | L | GF | GA | Place | Coach | Captain |
|---|---|---|---|---|---|---|---|---|---|---|---|
| Year Event | GP | W | | OTW | OTL | L | GF | GA | Place | Coach | Captain |
| 1994 WM-C | 6 | 5 | 0 | | | 1 | 35 | 11 | 2nd | Andrei Sidorenko | Edward Zankovets |
| 1995 WM-C | 4 | 4 | 0 | | | 0 | 16 | 7 | 1st | Andrei Sidorenko | Edward Zankovets |
| 1996 WM-B | 7 | 5 | 0 | | | 2 | 29 | 18 | 3rd | Andrei Sidorenko | Edward Zankovets |
| 1997 WM-B | 7 | 7 | 0 | | | 0 | 48 | 21 | 1st | Anatoli Varivonchik | Alexander Andrievsky |
| **1998 WM** | **6** | **2** | **0** | | | **4** | **17** | **23** | **8th** | **Anatoli Varivonchik** | **Alexander Andrievsky** |
| **1999 WM** | **6** | **4** | **1** | | | **1** | **16** | **10** | **9th** | **Anatoli Varivonchik** | **Alexander Andrievsky** |
| **2000 WM** | **6** | **3** | **0** | | | **3** | **16** | **20** | **9th** | **Anatoli Varivonchik** | **Alexander Andrievsky (1)** |
| **2001 WM** | **6** | **3** | **1** | | | **2** | **14** | **15** | **14th** | **Anatoli Varivonchik** | **Alexander Andrievsky** |
| 2002 WM-I-A | 5 | 5 | 0 | | | 0 | 45 | 10 | 1st | Valeri Voronin | Oleg Khmyl |
| **2003 WM** | **6** | **2** | **0** | | | **4** | **10** | **17** | **14th** | **Vladimir Krikunov** | **Oleg Khmyl** |
| 2004 WM-I-A | 5 | 5 | 0 | | | 0 | 34 | 9 | 1st | Mikhail Zakharov | Vladimir Tsyplakov |
| **2005 WM** | **6** | **2** | **0** | | | **4** | **9** | **11** | **10th** | **Glen Hanlon** | **Vladimir Tsyplakov** |
| **2006 WM** | **7** | **4** | **0** | | | **3** | **23** | **14** | **6th** | **Glen Hanlon** | **Oleg Antonenko** |
| **2007 WM** | **6** | **1** | | **0** | **0** | **5** | **19** | **31** | **11th** | **Curt Fraser** | **Oleg Antonenko** |
| **2008 WM** | **6** | **1** | | **0** | **3** | **2** | **16** | **19** | **9th** | **Curt Fraser** | **Oleg Antonenko** |
| **2009 WM** | **7** | **1** | | **3** | **0** | **3** | **14** | **18** | **8th** | **Glen Hanlon** | **Konstantin Koltsov** |
| **2010 WM** | **6** | **2** | | **1** | **0** | **3** | **12** | **13** | **10th** | **Eduard Zankovets** | **Ruslan Salei** |
| **2011 WM** | **6** | **2** | | **0** | **1** | **3** | **20** | **19** | **14th** | **Eduard Zankovets** | **Mikhail Grabovski** |
| **2012 WM** | **7** | **1** | | **0** | **0** | **6** | **11** | **23** | **14th** | **Kari Heikkila** | **Vladimir Denisov** |

(1) Vladimir Tsyplakov captain vs. United States (May 5) and Russia (May 7); Andrei Kovalev captain vs. Switzerland (May 9)

### U20 World Championship

(bold=top level)

| Year Event | GP | W | T | | | L | GF | GA | Place | Coach | Captain |
|---|---|---|---|---|---|---|---|---|---|---|---|
| Year Event | GP | W | | OTW | OTL | L | GF | GA | Place | Coach | Captain |
| 1995 WM20-C-1 | 4 | 2 | 0 | | | 2 | 15 | 12 | 4th | Yuri Peregudov | Vladimir Khailak |
| 1996 WM20-C | 4 | 2 | 0 | | | 2 | 27 | 16 | 4th | Andrei Sidorenko | Alexei Verbitsky |
| 1997 WM20-C | 4 | 4 | 0 | | | 0 | 34 | 4 | 1st | Vladimir Melenchuk | Alexei Kalyuzny |
| 1998 WM20-B | 6 | 4 | 1 | | | 1 | 22 | 11 | 1st | Vladimir Melenchuk | Sergei Stakhovich |
| **1999 WM20** | **6** | **0** | **1** | | | **5** | **13** | **38** | **10th** | **Mikhail Zakharov** | **Alexander Poliukh (1)** |
| 2000 WM20-B | 5 | 4 | 1 | | | 0 | 20 | 10 | 1st | Vladimir Melenchuk | Aliaksei Krutsikau |
| **2001 WM20** | **6** | **1** | **1** | | | **4** | **12** | **36** | **9th** | **Vladimir Melenchuk** | **Konstantin Koltsov** |
| **2002 WM20** | **6** | **1** | **0** | | | **5** | **10** | **31** | **9th** | **Vladimir Melenchuk** | **Andrei Bashko (2)** |
| **2003 WM20** | **6** | **0** | **0** | | | **6** | **10** | **37** | **10th** | **Vladimir Melenchuk** | **Alexander Kulakov (3)** |
| 2004 WM20-I-B | 5 | 5 | 0 | | | 0 | 34 | 11 | 1st | Mikhail Zakharov | Konstantin Zakharov |
| **2005 WM20** | **6** | **1** | **0** | | | **5** | **13** | **28** | **10th** | **Mikhail Zakharov** | **Alexei Ugarov** |
| 2006 WM20-I-B | 5 | 4 | 1 | | | 0 | 24 | 6 | 1st | Eduard Zankavets | Alexei Savin |
| **2007 WM20** | **6** | **2** | | **0** | **0** | **4** | **10** | **25** | **10th** | **Eduard Zankovets** | **Roman Magdeyev** |
| 2008 WM20-I-B | 5 | 4 | | 0 | 0 | 1 | 21 | 8 | 2nd | Andrei Rasolko | Dmitri Shumski |
| 2009 WM20-I-A | 5 | 4 | | 0 | 0 | 1 | 39 | 7 | 2nd | Andrei Gusov | Pavel Razvodovski |
| 2010 WM20-I-B | 5 | 3 | | 0 | 2 | 0 | 30 | 12 | 2nd | Vasili Spiridonov | Sergei Drozd |

| Year Event | GP | W | OTW | OTL | L | GF | GA | Place | Coach | Captain |
|---|---|---|---|---|---|---|---|---|---|---|
| 2011 WM20-I-A | 5 | 4 | 0 | 0 | 1 | 18 | 9 | 2nd | Oleg Mikulchik | Mikhail Khoromando |
| 2012 WM20-I-A | 5 | 3 | 0 | 1 | 1 | 21 | 10 | 2nd | Vladimir Zablotski | Yevgeni Leonov |

(1) Yevgeni Krivomaz captain Jan. 3 vs. CZE & Jan. 4 vs. USA
(2) Maxim Shymansky captain Dec. 29 vs. USA
(3) Andrei Karshunov captain Dec. 29 vs. RUS

### U18 World Championship (Men)

(bold=top level)

| Year Event | GP | W | T | | L | GF | GA | Place | Coach | Captain |
|---|---|---|---|---|---|---|---|---|---|---|
| Year Event | GP | W | OTW | OTL | L | GF | GA | Place | Coach | Captain |
| 1999 WM18-B | 5 | 3 | 2 | | 0 | 28 | 11 | 1st | Barys Kosarev | Andrei Tsikhan |
| **2000 WM18** | **6** | **0** | **0** | | **6** | **7** | **63** | **10th** | **Barys Kosarev** | **Andrei Bashko** |
| 2001 WM18-I | 5 | 4 | 1 | | 0 | 34 | 15 | 1st | Mikhail Zakharov | Vitali Klimiankov |
| **2002 WM18** | **8** | **3** | **0** | | **5** | **20** | **40** | **5th** | **Mikhail Zakharov** | **Konstantin Zakharov** |
| **2003 WM18** | **6** | **2** | **1** | | **3** | **27** | **37** | **8th** | **Mikhail Zakharov** | **Konstantin Zakharov** |
| **2004 WM18** | **6** | **1** | **0** | | **5** | **9** | **32** | **9th** | **Vladimir Sinitsyn** | **Sergei Kolosov (1)** |
| 2005 WM18-I-A | 5 | 4 | 0 | | 1 | 23 | 10 | 1st | Vasili Pankov | Alexander Kitarov |
| **2006 WM18** | **6** | **1** | **1** | | **4** | **12** | **36** | **9th** | **Vasili Pankov** | **Dmitri Shumski** |
| 2007 WM18-I-A | 5 | 4 | 1 | 0 | 0 | 37 | 11 | 1st | Andrei Gusov | Dmitri Korobov |
| **2008 WM18** | **6** | **1** | **0** | **0** | **5** | **16** | **27** | **9th** | **Vladimir Tsyplakov** | **Sergei Sheleg** |
| 2009 WM18-I-A | 5 | 4 | 1 | 0 | 0 | 23 | 6 | 1st | Sergei Pushkov | Nikolai Suslo |
| **2010 WM18** | **6** | **0** | **0** | **1** | **5** | **11** | **38** | **10th** | **Vladimir Safonov** | **Stanislav Lopachuk** |
| 2011 WM18-I-B | 5 | 2 | 0 | 1 | 2 | 25 | 13 | 4th | Eduard Valiullin | Pavel Kazakevich |
| 2012 WM18-I-B | 5 | 5 | 0 | 0 | 0 | 28 | 9 | 1st | Mikhail Vasiliev | Valeri Kubrakov |

(1) also Alexei Shagov

# Belgium (BEL)

*Belgium's men's national team is promoted to Division II Group A for 2013. Photo: Bonchuk Andonov.*

## Joined IIHF: December 8, 1908

Website: www.rbihf.be
Email: belgium@rbihf.be

Royal Belgian Ice Hockey Federation
Boomgaardsstraat 22
2600 Berchem
Belgium

Phone: +32 16 53 78 94 • Fax: +32 16 53 78 94

**World Ranking**

| MEN | | WOMEN | |
|---|---|---|---|
| 2012 | 36 | 2012 | 27 |
| 2011 | 35 | 2011 | 26 |
| 2010 | 36 | 2010 | 26 |
| 2009 | 33 | 2009 | 24 |
| 2008 | 34 | 2008 | 24 |
| 2007 | 35 | 2007 | 24 |
| 2006 | 35 | 2006 | 24 |
| 2005 | 32 | 2005 | 23 |
| 2004 | 33 | 2004 | 22 |

### Top Level Host History

Olympics: 1920 (Antwerp)

### Olympics, Men

(bold=top level)

| Year Event | GP | W | T | L | GF | GA | Place | Coach | Captain |
|---|---|---|---|---|---|---|---|---|---|
| **1920 OG-M** | **1** | **0** | **0** | **1** | **0** | **8** | **7th** | **Paul Loicq** | **Paul Loicq** |
| **1924 OG-M** | **3** | **0** | **0** | **3** | **8** | **45** | **7th** | **Andre Poplimont** | **Andre Poplimont** |
| **1928 OG-M** | **3** | **2** | **0** | **1** | **9** | **10** | **7th** | **Jean de Craene** | **Pierre van Reysschoot** |
| **1936 OG-M** | **3** | **0** | **0** | **3** | **4** | **20** | **13th** | **Bert Forsyth** | **Pierre van Reysschoot** |

### World Championship (Men)

(bold=top level)

| Year Event | GP | W | T | | L | GF | GA | Place | Coach | Captain |
|---|---|---|---|---|---|---|---|---|---|---|
| Year Event | GP | W | OTW | OTL | L | GF | GA | Place | Coach | Captain |
| **1930 WM** | **1** | **0** | **0** | | **1** | **1** | **4** | **10th** | **Pierre Van Reysschoot** | **Pierre van Reysschoot** |
| **1933 WM** | **3** | **0** | **0** | | **3** | **2** | **10** | **12th** | **Pierre Van Reysschoot** | **Pierre van Reysschoot** |
| **1934 WM** | **4** | **1** | **0** | | **3** | **5** | **26** | **12th** | **Pierre Van Reysschoot** | **Pierre van Reysschoot** |
| **1935 WM** | **5** | **0** | **0** | | **5** | **5** | **48** | **14th** | **Pierre Van Reysschoot** | **Pierre van Reysschoot** |
| **1939 WM** | **4** | **0** | **1** | | **3** | **6** | **19** | **11th** | **Paul De Weerdt** | **Pierre van Reysschoot** |
| **1947 WM** | **7** | **0** | **0** | | **7** | **15** | **104** | **8th** | **Carlos van den Driessche** | **Pierre van Reysschoot (1)** |
| **1949 WM** | **6** | **1** | **0** | | **5** | **13** | **66** | **9th** | **Gusty de Backer** | **Leon van Eeckhout** |
| **1950 WM** | **4** | **2** | **0** | | **2** | **14** | **60** | **7th** | **Jacques Contzen** | **Leon van Eeckhout** |
| 1951 WM-B | 5 | 1 | 0 | | 4 | 20 | 27 | 4th | Wilf Cook | Leon van Eeckhout |
| 1955 WM-B | 4 | 0 | 0 | | 4 | 8 | 44 | 5th | Jef Lekens | Jacques Moris |
| 1961 WM-C | 5 | 0 | 0 | | 5 | 9 | 56 | 6th | Jef Lekens | Jacques Moris |
| 1963 WM-C | 5 | 0 | 0 | | 5 | 8 | 83 | 6th | Jef Lekens | Piet Briels |
| 1970 WM-C | 6 | 0 | 0 | | 6 | 9 | 63 | 7th | Vaclav Pipa | Willy Vinken |
| 1971 WM-C | 7 | 0 | 0 | | 7 | 6 | 139 | 8th | Vaclav Pipa | Alberic Braas |
| 1975 WM-C | 6 | 0 | 0 | | 6 | 5 | 111 | 7th | Brian Bird | Henry "Bob" Moris |
| 1977 WM-C | 6 | 1 | 0 | | 5 | 24 | 89 | 6th | Bud Laidler | Karoly Orosz |

| | | | | | | | | | | |
|---|---|---|---|---|---|---|---|---|---|---|
| 1978 WM-C | 7 | 0 | 0 | | 7 | 13 | 101 | 8th | Peter Hubregtse | Alain Zwikel |
| 1987 WM-C | 7 | 0 | 0 | | 7 | 8 | 97 | 8th | Alain Zwikel | Patrick Hartmeyer |
| 1989 WM-D | 4 | 3 | 0 | | 1 | 35 | 9 | 1st | Dirk Laenen | Jos Lejeune |
| 1990 WM-C | 8 | 1 | 0 | | 7 | 16 | 67 | 8th | Dirk Laenen | Jos Lejeune |
| 1991 WM-C | 8 | 0 | 0 | | 8 | 11 | 101 | 9th | Angelo Dana | Bart Roels |
| 1992 WM-C | 5 | 2 | 0 | | 3 | 17 | 24 | 5th | Henry "Bob" Moris | Mike Pellegrims |
| 1993 WM-C | 5 | 2 | 0 | | 3 | 19 | 74 | 8th | Bill Morgan | Aldo van den Aker |
| 1994 WM-C-B | 5 | 3 | 0 | | 2 | 25 | 21 | 5th | Henry "Bob" Moris | Bob Moris, Jr. |
| 1995 WM-C-2 | 6 | 2 | 1 | | 3 | 30 | 27 | 5th | Henry "Bob" Moris | Bob Moris. Jr. |
| 1996 WM-D | 5 | 2 | 0 | | 3 | 13 | 24 | 4th | Josef Lejeune | Tim Vos |
| 1997 WM-D | 5 | 3 | 0 | | 2 | 14 | 14 | 8th | Josef Lejeune | Tim Vos |
| 1998 WM-D | 5 | 3 | 0 | | 2 | 28 | 15 | 4th | Zlatko Hrelja | Tim Vos |
| 1999 WM-D | 4 | 3 | 0 | | 1 | 32 | 9 | 4th | Zlatko Hrelja | Tim Vos |
| 2000 WM-D | 4 | 3 | 1 | | 0 | 23 | 5 | 2nd | Jan van Beveren | Tim Vos |
| 2001 WM-II-B | 5 | 1 | 1 | | 3 | 23 | 20 | 5th | Jan van Beveren | Gil Paelinck |
| 2002 WM-II-A | 5 | 4 | 0 | | 1 | 37 | 11 | 2nd | Josef Lejeune | Tim Vos |
| 2003 WM-II-B | 5 | 4 | 0 | | 1 | 29 | 8 | 1st | Josef Lejeune | Tim Vos |
| 2004 WM-I-A | 5 | 0 | 0 | | 5 | 7 | 44 | 6th | Josef Lejeune | Tim Vos |
| 2005 WM-II-B | 5 | 2 | 0 | | 3 | 13 | 19 | 4th | Bill Morgan | Joris Peussens |
| 2006 WM-II-A | 5 | 2 | 2 | | 1 | 19 | 10 | 3rd | Gil Paelinck | Tim Vos |
| 2007 WM-II-A | 5 | 4 | 0 | 0 | 1 | 25 | 18 | 2nd | Gil Paelinck | Tim Vos |
| 2008 WM-II-A | 5 | 3 | 1 | 0 | 1 | 29 | 14 | 2nd | Gil Paelinck | Tim Vos |
| 2009 WM-II-B | 5 | 4 | 0 | 0 | 1 | 31 | 11 | 2nd | Gil Paelinck | Tim Vos |
| 2010 WM-II-A | 5 | 3 | 0 | 0 | 2 | 26 | 18 | 3rd | Josef Lejeune | Tim Vos |
| 2011 WM-II-A | 5 | 3 | 0 | 0 | 2 | 19 | 14 | 4th | Josef Lejeune | Vincent Morgan |
| 2012 WM-II-B | 5 | 5 | 0 | 0 | 0 | 49 | 11 | 1st | Jozef Lejeune | Vincent Morgan |

(1) Jef Lekens captain vs. Switzerland (Feb. 19) and Czechoslovakia (Feb. 21)

### U20 World Championship

| Year Event | GP | W | T | | L | GF | GA | Place | Coach | Captain |
|---|---|---|---|---|---|---|---|---|---|---|
| Year Event | GP | W | OTW | OTL | L | GF | GA | Place | Coach | Captain |
| 1979 WM20-B | 4 | 0 | 0 | | 4 | 9 | 59 | 8th | Louis Chiasson | Christian Cuvelier |
| 1984 WM20-C | 5 | 3 | 0 | | 2 | 26 | 18 | 5th | Dirk Laenen | Jan Sys |
| 1985 WM20-C | 4 | 2 | 0 | | 2 | 27 | 22 | 3rd | Dirk Laenen | Bob Moris |
| 1986 WM20-C | 5 | 0 | 1 | | 4 | 14 | 34 | 6th | *unknown* | Bob Moris |
| 1988 WM20-C | 7 | 0 | 0 | | 7 | 8 | 34 | 8th | Rene Labonte | Mike Pellegrims |
| 2003 WM20-III | 4 | 3 | 0 | | 1 | 32 | 10 | 2nd | Jan van Beveren | Sven van Buren |
| 2004 WM20-II-A | 5 | 1 | 0 | | 4 | 16 | 31 | 5th | Jan van Beveren | Kristof van Looy |
| 2005 WM20-II-B | 5 | 0 | 0 | | 5 | 12 | 41 | 6th | Gil Paelinck | Vincent Morgan |
| 2007 WM20-III | 5 | 4 | 0 | 1 | 0 | 38 | 12 | 2nd | Eddy de Clerck | Xavier Claes |
| 2008 WM20-II-A | 5 | 1 | 1 | 0 | 3 | 12 | 21 | 4th | Dominique van de Locht | Ben Vercammen |
| 2009 WM20-II-A | 5 | 2 | 0 | 0 | 3 | 17 | 32 | 4th | Dominique van de Locht | Matti Agemans |
| 2010 WM20-II-B | 5 | 1 | 1 | 0 | 3 | 15 | 24 | 4th | Dominique van de Locht | Bryan Kolodziejczyk |
| 2011 WM20-II-A | 5 | 1 | 1 | 0 | 3 | 17 | 34 | 4th | Dominique van de Locht | Bryan Kolodziejczyk |
| 2012 WM20-II-B | 5 | 1 | 1 | 0 | 3 | 17 | 23 | 4th | Domin van der Locht | Maxime Pellegrims |

### U18 World Championship (Men)

| Year Event | GP | W | T | | L | GF | GA | Place | Coach | Captain |
|---|---|---|---|---|---|---|---|---|---|---|
| Year Event | GP | W | OTW | OTL | L | GF | GA | Place | Coach | Captain |
| 2001 WM18-III | 4 | 2 | 0 | | 2 | 19 | 12 | 5th | Domin Van De Locht | Geert Vermeulen |
| 2002 WM18-III | 4 | 2 | 0 | | 2 | 15 | 26 | 4th | Domin Van De Locht | Kenny de Ceulaer |
| 2003 WM18-II-A | 5 | 2 | 1 | | 2 | 20 | 32 | 4th | Domin Van De Locht | Vincent Morgan |
| 2004 WM18-II-A | 5 | 0 | 1 | | 4 | 12 | 49 | 6th | Domin Van De Locht | Kjell Cazaerck |
| 2005 WM18-III | 5 | 4 | 0 | | 1 | 34 | 8 | 2nd | Gert Peeters | Xavier Claes |
| 2006 WM18-II-A | 5 | 1 | 1 | | 3 | 12 | 23 | 4th | Gert Peeters | Wesley Oben |
| 2007 WM18-II-A | 5 | 2 | 0 | 0 | 3 | 17 | 37 | 4th | Philippe Cools | Michael Distate |
| 2008 WM18-II-A | 5 | 2 | 1 | 0 | 2 | 14 | 30 | 4th | Danny Gyesbreghs | Bryan Kolodziejczyk |
| 2009 WM18-II-B | 5 | 1 | 2 | 1 | 1 | 23 | 19 | 3rd | Danny Gyesbreghs | Bryan Kolodziejczyk |
| 2010 WM18-II-B | 5 | 0 | 1 | 0 | 4 | 7 | 41 | 5th | Danny Gyesbreghs | Lorenzo Maas |
| 2011 WM18-II-B | 5 | 0 | 0 | 0 | 5 | 8 | 53 | 6th | Philippe Cools | Maxime Pellegrims |
| 2012 WM18-III | 5 | 5 | 0 | 0 | 0 | 48 | 12 | 1st | Philippe Cools | Ben Dolfyn |

### Women's World Championship

| Year Event | GP | W | T | | L | GF | GA | Place | Coach | Captain |
|---|---|---|---|---|---|---|---|---|---|---|
| Year Event | GP | W | OTW | OTL | L | GF | GA | Place | Coach | Captain |
| 2003 WW-III | 5 | 2 | 1 | | 2 | 10 | 12 | 3rd | Guy van Gelder | Nadine Leirs |
| 2004 WW-III | 5 | 2 | 0 | | 3 | 13 | 19 | 4th | Guy van Gelder | Nadine Leirs |
| 2005 WW-III | 5 | 2 | 1 | | 2 | 7 | 20 | 3rd | Guy van Gelder | *unknown* |
| 2007 WW-III | 5 | 3 | 0 | 0 | 2 | 22 | 18 | 3rd | Rob Baeck | Nadine Leirs |
| 2008 WW-III | 5 | 2 | 0 | 0 | 3 | 12 | 16 | 4th | Rob Baeck | Sara Verpoest |
| 2011 WW-III | 5 | 0 | 0 | 0 | 5 | 3 | 40 | 6th | Patrick Frere | Leen de Decker |
| 2012 WW-II-B | 5 | 1 | 0 | 0 | 4 | 7 | 12 | 5th | Patrick Frere | Sara Mommen |

# Bosnia and Herzegovina (BIH)

Bosnia played Greece at the 2008 IIHF World Championship (Men) Division III Qualification in Sarajevo, Bosnia & Herzegovina. Photo: Aleksandar Kordic.

## Joined IIHF: May 10, 2001

Website: www.shlbih.com.ba
E-mail: shlbih@bih.net.ba

Bosnia and Herzegovina Ice Hockey Federation
Aleja Lipa 57
71000 Sarajevo
Bosnia and Herzegovina

Phone: +387 33 715 600 • Fax: +387 33 715 601

**World Ranking**

**MEN**
2012 no rank
2011........48
2010........48
2009........47
2008........47

**Top Level Host History**
Olympics: 1984 (Sarajevo, YUG)

**U18 World Championship (Men)**

| Year Event | GP | W | T | L | GF | GA | Place | Coach | Captain |
|---|---|---|---|---|---|---|---|---|---|
| 2003 WM18-III-B | 3 | 1 | 0 | 2 | 8 | 19 | 3rd | Nikola Dujmovic | Admir Pilav |
| 2004 WM18-III-B | 6 | 0 | 0 | 6 | 7 | 54 | 7th | Dragan Krajic | Admir Pilav |

# Brazil (BRA)

## Joined IIHF: June 26, 1984 (Associate Member)

Website: www.cbdg.com.br
E-mail: mail@cbdg.org.br

Confederacao Brasileira de Desportos no Gelo
Av. Atlantica, 4240 / Lj. 232
Copacabana Rio de Janeiro, RJ
CEP: 22070-002
Brazil

Phone: +55 21 7739 2793 (Brazil) • +1 781 659 3367 (International) • Fax: +1 781 659 7363

**Top Level Host History** none

Brazil versus Japan at the 2010 IIHF In-Line Hockey World Championship Division I. Photo: Matic Klansek Velej.

# Bulgaria (BUL)

*Bulgaria's men's team listens to the national anthem on home ice in Sofia. Photo: Bonchuk Andonov.*

## Joined IIHF: July 25, 1960

Website: www.bghockey.com
E-mail: bihf@mail.com

Bulgarian Ice Hockey Federation
75 Vassil Levski Blvd.
1040 Sofia
Bulgaria

Phone: +359 2 980 28 80/+359 2 930 06 10
Fax: +359 2 981 57 28/+359 2 980 28 80

**World Ranking**

| MEN | | WOMEN | |
|---|---|---|---|
| 2012 | 33 | 2012 | 33 |
| 2011 | 32 | 2011 | 23 |
| 2010 | 31 | 2010 | 24 |
| 2009 | 35 | | |
| 2008 | 32 | | |
| 2007 | 31 | | |
| 2006 | 30 | | |
| 2005 | 33 | | |
| 2004 | 32 | | |

**Top Level Host History** none

**Olympics, Men**
(bold=top level)

| Year Event | GP | W | T | L | GF | GA | Place | Coach | Captain |
|---|---|---|---|---|---|---|---|---|---|
| **1976 OG-M** | **5** | **0** | **0** | **5** | **19** | **38** | **12th** | **Pantelei Pantev** | **Ilia Batchvarov** |

**World Championship (Men)**

| Year Event | GP | W | T | | L | GF | GA | Place | Coach | Captain |
|---|---|---|---|---|---|---|---|---|---|---|
| Year Event | GP | W | OTW | OTL | L | GF | GA | Place | Coach | Captain |
| 1963 WM-C | 5 | 1 | 1 | | 3 | 19 | 22 | 4th | Pantelei Pantev | Georgi Strassimirov |
| 1967 WM-C | 4 | 2 | 0 | | 2 | 17 | 17 | 3rd | Pantelei Pantev | Stefan Chomakov |
| 1969 WM-C | 5 | 2 | 0 | | 3 | 19 | 28 | 5th | Pantelei Pantev | Pancho Mikhailov |
| 1970 WM-B | 7 | 0 | 0 | | 7 | 10 | 67 | 8th | Pantelei Pantev | Pancho Mikhailov (1) |
| 1971 WM-C | 7 | 2 | 1 | | 4 | 37 | 32 | 5th | Pantelei Pantev | Ilia Bachvarov |
| 1972 WM-C | 6 | 3 | 0 | | 3 | 20 | 19 | 4th | Pantelei Pantev | Ilia Bachvarov |
| 1973 WM-C | 7 | 3 | 1 | | 3 | 29 | 28 | 4th | Veniamin Alexandrov | Ilia Bachvarov |
| 1974 WM-C | 7 | 4 | 1 | | 2 | 39 | 18 | 3rd | Pantelei Pantev | Ilia Bachvarov |
| 1975 WM-C | 6 | 4 | 1 | | 1 | 40 | 17 | 2nd | Pantelei Pantev | Ilia Bachvarov |
| 1976 WM-B | 7 | 0 | 0 | | 7 | 23 | 47 | 8th | Pantelei Pantev | *unknown* |
| 1977 WM-C | 6 | 4 | 0 | | 2 | 47 | 25 | 3rd | Pantelei Pantev | Georgi Iliev |
| 1978 WM-C | 7 | 3 | 1 | | 3 | 27 | 30 | 5th | Pantelei Pantev | Georgi Iliev |
| 1979 WM-C | 7 | 4 | 0 | | 3 | 35 | 28 | 4th | Pantelei Pantev | Krum Christov |
| 1981 WM-C | 7 | 3 | 0 | | 4 | 22 | 32 | 6th | Ewald Grabovskis | Milcho Nenov |
| 1982 WM-C | 7 | 2 | 1 | | 4 | 29 | 30 | 6th | Pancho Mikhailov | Georgi Iliev |
| 1983 WM-C | 7 | 1 | 1 | | 5 | 20 | 36 | 6th | Georgi Strassimirov/Ilia Bachvarov | Malin Atanasov |
| 1985 WM-C | 7 | 2 | 0 | | 5 | 27 | 45 | 6th | Pantelei Pantev | Pejo Ralenkov |
| 1986 WM-C | 6 | 4 | 0 | | 2 | 21 | 30 | 3rd | Nikolai Yankov | Pavel Georgiev |
| 1987 WM-C | 7 | 1 | 1 | | 5 | 21 | 40 | 7th | Andrei Zabunov | Valentin Dimov |
| 1989 WM-C | 7 | 3 | 1 | | 3 | 35 | 35 | 5th | Vladimir Kiselev | Valentin Dimov |
| 1990 WM-C | 8 | 4 | 0 | | 4 | 31 | 38 | 6th | Nikolai Yankov | Boris Mihaylov |
| 1991 WM-C | 8 | 4 | 1 | | 3 | 35 | 26 | 4th | Nikolai Yankov | Ventzislav Venev |
| 1992 WM-B | 7 | 3 | 0 | | 4 | 14 | 38 | 5th | Nikolai Yankov | Ventzislav Venev |
| 1993 WM-B | 7 | 0 | 0 | | 7 | 9 | 58 | 8th | Nikolai Yankov | Ventzislav Venev |
| 1994 WM-C | 6 | 0 | 0 | | 6 | 3 | 115 | 7th | Nikolai Yankov | Istalian Zarev |
| 1995 WM-C-1 | 4 | 0 | 0 | | 4 | 4 | 32 | 9th | Nikolai Yankov | Istalian Zarev |
| 1996 WM-D | 5 | 2 | 0 | | 3 | 16 | 16 | 6th | Borislav Tachev | Boris Mihaylov |
| 1997 WM-D | 5 | 2 | 2 | | 1 | 17 | 15 | 7th | Georgi Milanov | Boris Mihaylov |
| 1998 WM-D | 5 | 4 | 1 | | 0 | 50 | 7 | 1st | Andrei Zabunov | Boris Mihaylov |
| 1999 WM-C | 4 | 0 | 0 | | 4 | 7 | 35 | 7th | Andrei Zabunov | Boris Mihaylov |
| 2000 WM-C | 4 | 0 | 1 | | 3 | 7 | 28 | 9th | Nikolai Yankov | Boris Mihaylov |
| 2001 WM-II-B | 5 | 2 | 0 | | 3 | 21 | 25 | 4th | Nikolai Yankov | Boris Mihaylov |
| 2002 WM-II-B | 5 | 2 | 0 | | 3 | 30 | 29 | 4th | Nikolai Yankov | Boris Mihaylov |
| 2003 WM-II-B | 5 | 2 | 1 | | 2 | 15 | 10 | 3rd | Georgi Milanov | Boris Mihaylov |
| 2004 WM-II-B | 5 | 2 | 0 | | 3 | 20 | 30 | 4th | Georgi Milanov | Ivaylo Velev |
| 2005 WM-II-A | 5 | 2 | 0 | | 3 | 22 | 26 | 4th | Georgi Milanov | Ivaylo Velev |
| 2006 WM-II-A | 5 | 3 | 1 | | 1 | 25 | 17 | 2nd | Kirill Hodulov | Zlatko Zinoviev |
| 2007 WM-II-A | 5 | 1 | 0 | 0 | 4 | 10 | 32 | 5th | Kirill Hodulov | Zlatko Zinoviev |
| 2008 WM-II-A | 5 | 1 | 0 | 1 | 3 | 14 | 44 | 5th | Georgi Milanov | Rosen Stefanov |
| 2009 WM-II-B | 5 | 2 | 0 | 0 | 3 | 30 | 33 | 4th | Georgi Milanov | Rosen Stefanov |
| 2010 WM-II-A | 5 | 2 | 0 | 0 | 3 | 28 | 31 | 4th | Georgi Milanov | Rosen Stefanov |
| 2011 WM-II-B | 5 | 1 | 0 | 0 | 4 | 17 | 42 | 5th | Georgi Milanov | Georgi Mladenov |
| 2012 WM-II-B | 5 | 2 | 1 | 0 | 2 | 21 | 28 | 3rd | Georgi Milanov | Vasily Vasilev |

(1) Ioutscho Iontschev captain Mar. 5 vs. ROM

### U20 World Championship

| Year Event | GP | W | T | | L | GF | GA | Place | Coach | Captain |
|---|---|---|---|---|---|---|---|---|---|---|
| Year Event | GP | W | OTW | OTL | L | GF | GA | Place | Coach | Captain |
| 1983 WM20-C | 6 | 3 | 0 | | 3 | 16 | 18 | 2nd | Andrei Zabunov | *unknown* |
| 1984 WM20-C | 5 | 3 | 1 | | 1 | 24 | 12 | 2nd | Pancho Mikhailov | Valentin Dimov |
| 1985 WM20-C | 4 | 4 | 0 | | 0 | 23 | 16 | 1st | Nikolai Nikolov | Pawel Georgiev |
| 1986 WM20-B | 7 | 0 | 0 | | 7 | 9 | 62 | 8th | Atanas Dmitrov | Latschesar Zonevski |
| 1987 WM20-C | 5 | 2 | 0 | | 3 | 21 | 23 | 4th | Pancho Mikhailov | *unknown* |
| 1988 WM20-C | 7 | 5 | 0 | | 2 | 39 | 16 | 3rd | Pancho Mikhailov | Ivaylo Velev |
| 1989 WM20-C | 4 | 0 | 1 | | 3 | 12 | 20 | 5th | Nikolai Mikhailov | Georgi Dimitrov |
| 1990 WM20-C | 6 | 3 | 1 | | 2 | 25 | 31 | 4th | Nikolai Mikhailov | *unknown* |
| 1991 WM20-C | 7 | 2 | 0 | | 5 | 34 | 48 | 6th | Nikolai Mikhailov | Anton Bratanov |
| 1992 WM20-C | 3 | 0 | 1 | | 2 | 2 | 21 | 8th | Nikolai Mikhailov | Iovko Terziev |
| 1993 WM20-C | 4 | 1 | 1 | | 2 | 16 | 32 | 4th | Nikolai Mikhailov | *unknown* |
| 1994 WM20-C | 4 | 0 | 0 | | 4 | 10 | 45 | 8th | *unknown* | *unknown* |
| 1996 WM20-D | 3 | 1 | 0 | | 2 | 14 | 35 | 5th | *unknown* | *unknown* |
| 1997 WM20-D | 4 | 1 | 0 | | 3 | 12 | 27 | 6th | Nikolai Mikhailov | Atanas Masliankov |
| 1998 WM20-D | 4 | 1 | 0 | | 3 | 21 | 35 | 6th | Andrei Zabunov | Atanas Masliankov |
| 1999 WM20-D | 4 | 2 | 0 | | 2 | 25 | 37 | 7th | Vladimir Polupanov | Vasko Polizoev |
| 2000 WM20-D | 4 | 1 | 0 | | 3 | 11 | 43 | 8th | Nikolai Mikhailov | Simeon Radkov |
| 2001 WM20-III | 4 | 2 | 0 | | 2 | 8 | 16 | 5th | Nikolai Mikhailov | Martin Kostadinov |
| 2002 WM20-III | 4 | 0 | 0 | | 4 | 7 | 48 | 8th | George Milanov | Rossen Hristov |
| 2003 WM20-II-A | 5 | 0 | 0 | | 5 | 5 | 68 | 6th | George Milanov | Pavlin Moldovanov |
| 2004 WM20-III | 5 | 1 | 0 | | 4 | 13 | 34 | 5th | George Milanov | Pav Moldovanov |
| 2005 WM20-III | 5 | 0 | 0 | | 5 | 10 | 39 | 6th | Rouslan Hristov | Velko Geshakov |
| 2006 WM20-III | 4 | 1 | 0 | | 3 | 26 | 32 | 4th | Rouslan Hristov | Velko Geshakov |
| 2007 WM20-III | 5 | 0 | 0 | 0 | 5 | 13 | 45 | 6th | Atanas Dimitrov | Petar Hadzitonev |
| 2008 WM20-III | 6 | 0 | 0 | 0 | 6 | 10 | 84 | 7th | Atanas Todorov | Ivan Velev |
| 2010 WM20-III | 3 | 0 | 0 | 0 | 3 | 9 | 24 | 7th | Martin Milanov | Rosen Asenov |
| 2011 WM20-III | 6 | 0 | 1 | 0 | 5 | 13 | 52 | 6th | Kirill Hodulov | Petar Mihov |
| 2012 WM20-III | 4 | 1 | 0 | 0 | 3 | 7 | 19 | 4th | Martin Milanov | Kristian Radovanov |

### U18 World Championship (Men)

| Year Event | GP | W | T | | L | GF | GA | Place | Coach | Captain |
|---|---|---|---|---|---|---|---|---|---|---|
| Year Event | GP | W | OTW | OTL | L | GF | GA | Place | Coach | Captain |
| 2001 WM18-III | 4 | 1 | 0 | | 3 | 8 | 38 | 6th | Nikolai Mihailov | Borislav Blagoev |
| 2002 WM18-III | 4 | 1 | 0 | | 3 | 8 | 25 | 4th | Ivo Nikolov | Pavlin Moldovanov |
| 2003 WM18-II-A | 5 | 0 | 0 | | 5 | 2 | 80 | 6th | Ivo Nikolov | Milo Nenov |
| 2004 WM18-III-B | 6 | 3 | 0 | | 3 | 22 | 22 | 4th | Atanas Dimitrov | Velko Geshakov |
| 2005 WM18-III | 5 | 0 | 0 | | 5 | 6 | 53 | 6th | Atanas Dimitrov | Martin Boyadjiev |
| 2006 WM18-III | 5 | 1 | 1 | | 3 | 10 | 41 | 5th | Atanas Dimitrov | Ivan Velev |
| 2008 WM18-III-B | 4 | 1 | 0 | 0 | 3 | 27 | 35 | 4th | Atanas Dimitrov | Rosen Asenov |
| 2009 WM18-III-B | 3 | 0 | 0 | 0 | 3 | 8 | 24 | 4th | Kirill Hodulov | Petar Mihov |
| 2010 WM18-III-A | 4 | 1 | 0 | 1 | 2 | 24 | 22 | 4th | Martin Milanov | Stefan Georgiev |
| 2011 WM18-III-A | 5 | 3 | 0 | 0 | 2 | 25 | 19 | 3rd | Kirill Hodulov | Ivan Hodulov |
| 2012 WM18-III | 5 | 2 | 0 | 0 | 3 | 27 | 23 | 4th | Martin Milanov | Martin Nikolov |

### Women's World Championship

| Year Event | GP | W | OTW | OTL | L | GF | GA | Place | Coach | Captain |
|---|---|---|---|---|---|---|---|---|---|---|
| 2011 WW-V | 4 | 2 | 0 | 0 | 2 | 5 | 27 | 3rd | Atanas Dimitrov | Tina Lisichkova |

*Veteran Bulgarian goalie Konstantin Mihaylov makes a save. Photo: Bonchuk Andonov.*

# Canada (CAN)

Hayley Wickenheiser hoists the trophy as Canada wins the 2012 IIHF Ice Hockey Women's World Championship. Photo: Dave Sandford / HHOF-IIHF Images.

## Joined IIHF: April 26, 1920

Website: www.hockeycanada.ca
E-mail: terb@hockeycanada.ca

Hockey Canada
155 Olympic Road SW
Suite 201
Calgary, Alberta T3B 5R5
Canada

Phone: +1 403 777 3636 • Fax: +1 403 777 3635

**World Ranking**

| MEN | | WOMEN | |
|---|---|---|---|
| 2012 | 5 | 2012 | 1 |
| 2011 | 4 | 2011 | 2 |
| 2010 | 2 | 2010 | 1 |
| 2009 | 2 | 2009 | 2 |
| 2008 | 1 | 2008 | 1 |
| 2007 | 2 | 2007 | 1 |
| 2006 | 3 | 2006 | 1 |
| 2005 | 1 | 2005 | 1 |
| 2004 | 1 | 2004 | 1 |

### Top Level Host History

Olympics: 1988 (Calgary); 2010 (Vancouver)
World Championship (Men): 2008 (Quebec City, Halifax)
U20 World Championship: 1978 (Montreal, Quebec City), 1986 (Hamilton), 1991 (Saskatoon), 1995 (Red Deer), 1999 (Winnipeg), 2003 (Halifax, Sydney), 2006 (Vancouver, Kelowna, Kamloops), 2009 (Ottawa), 2010 (Saskatoon, Regina), 2012 (Calgary, Edmonton)
Women's World Championship: 1990 (Ottawa), 1997 (Kitchener), 2000 (Mississauga), 2004 (Halifax), 2007 (Winnipeg, Selkirk), 2013 (TBA)
U18 Women's World Championship: 2008 (Calgary)

### Olympics, Men

(bold=top level)

| Year Event | GP | W | T | | L | GF | GA | Place | Coach | Captain |
|---|---|---|---|---|---|---|---|---|---|---|
| Year Event | GP | W | OTW | OTL | L | GF | GA | Place | Coach | Captain |
| 1920 OG-M | 3 | 3 | 0 | | 0 | 29 | 1 | G | Fred "Steamer" Maxwell | Gordon Sigurjonsson |
| 1924 OG-M | 5 | 5 | 0 | | 0 | 110 | 3 | G | Frank Rankin | Dunc Munro |
| 1928 OG-M | 3 | 3 | 0 | | 0 | 38 | 0 | G | Conn Smythe | "Red" Porter |
| 1932 OG-M | 6 | 5 | 1 | | 0 | 32 | 4 | G | Jack Hughes | William Cockburn |
| 1936 OG-M | 8 | 7 | 0 | | 1 | 54 | 7 | S | Al Pudas | Herman Murray |
| 1948 OG-M | 8 | 7 | 1 | | 0 | 69 | 5 | G | Frank Boucher | George Mara |
| 1952 OG-M | 8 | 7 | 1 | | 0 | 71 | 14 | G | Lou Holmes | Billy Dawe |
| 1956 OG-M | 8 | 6 | 0 | | 2 | 53 | 12 | B | Bobby Bauer | Jack MacKenzie |
| 1960 OG-M | 7 | 6 | 0 | | 1 | 55 | 15 | S | Bobby Bauer | Harry Sinden |
| 1964 OG-M | 7 | 5 | 0 | | 2 | 32 | 17 | 4th | Father David Bauer | Hank Akervall |
| 1968 OG-M | 7 | 5 | 0 | | 2 | 28 | 15 | B | Jackie McLeod | Marshall Johnston |
| 1980 OG-M | 6 | 3 | 0 | | 3 | 29 | 18 | 6th | Lorne Davis** | Randy Gregg |
| 1984 OG-M | 7 | 4 | 0 | | 3 | 24 | 16 | 4th | Dave King | Dave Tippett |
| 1988 OG-M | 8 | 5 | 1 | | 2 | 31 | 21 | 4th | Dave King | Trent Yawney |
| 1992 OG-M | 8 | 6 | 0 | | 2 | 37 | 17 | S | Dave King | Brad Schlegel |
| 1994 OG-M | 8 | 5 | 1 | | 2 | 27 | 19 | S | Tom Renney | Fabian Joseph |
| 1998 OG-M | 6 | 4 | 0 | | 2 | 19 | 9 | 4th | Marc Crawford | Eric Lindros |
| 2002 OG-M | 6 | 4 | 1 | | 1 | 22 | 14 | G | Pat Quinn | Mario Lemieux (1) |
| 2006 OG-M | 6 | 3 | 0 | | 3 | 15 | 11 | 7th | Pat Quinn | Joe Sakic |
| 2010 OG-M | 7 | 4 | 2 | 0 | 1 | 35 | 16 | G | Mike Babcock | Scott Niedermayer |

** co-coach with Clare Drake, Tom Watt
(1) Joe Sakic captain vs. Germany (Feb. 17)

NOTE: Club teams represented Canada from 1920-1960 as follows: 1920—Winnipeg Falcons, 1924—Toronto Granites, 1928—University of Toronto Grads, 1932—The Winnipegs, 1936—Port Arthur Bearcats, 1948—RCAF Flyers, 1952—Edmonton Mercurys, 1956—Kitchener-Waterloo Dutchmen, 1960—Kitchener-Waterloo Dutchmen

### World Championship (Men)

(bold=top level)

| Year Event | GP | W | T | | L | GF | GA | Place | Coach | Captain |
|---|---|---|---|---|---|---|---|---|---|---|
| Year Event | GP | W | OTW | OTL | L | GF | GA | Place | Coach | Captain |
| 1930 WM | 1 | 1 | 0 | | 0 | 6 | 1 | G | Les Allen | Howard Armstrong |
| 1931 WM | 6 | 5 | 1 | | 0 | 24 | 0 | G | Blake Watson | Gord MacKenzie |
| 1933 WM | 5 | 4 | 0 | | 1 | 17 | 3 | S | Harold Ballard | Marty Nugent |
| 1934 WM | 4 | 4 | 0 | | 0 | 19 | 2 | G | Johnny Walker | Harold "Hobb" Wilson |
| 1935 WM | 7 | 7 | 0 | | 0 | 44 | 7 | G | Scotty Oliver | Vic Lindquist |
| 1937 WM | 9 | 9 | 0 | | 0 | 60 | 4 | G | John Achtzener | Bill Burnett |
| 1938 WM | 7 | 6 | 1 | | 0 | 17 | 6 | G | Max Silverman | Roy Heximer |
| 1939 WM | 8 | 8 | 0 | | 0 | 42 | 1 | G | Elmer Piper | *unknown* |
| 1949 WM | 7 | 4 | 2 | | 1 | 74 | 10 | S | Max Silverman | *unknown* |
| 1950 WM | 7 | 7 | 0 | | 0 | 88 | 5 | G | Jimmy Graham | Marsh Darling |
| 1951 WM | 6 | 6 | 0 | | 0 | 62 | 6 | G | Dick Gray | Hec Negrello |
| 1954 WM | 7 | 6 | 0 | | 1 | 59 | 12 | S | Greg Currie | Tom Campbell |
| 1955 WM | 8 | 8 | 0 | | 0 | 66 | 6 | G | Grant Warwick | George McAvoy |
| 1958 WM | 7 | 7 | 0 | | 0 | 82 | 6 | G | Sid Smith | Harry Sinden |
| 1959 WM | 8 | 7 | 0 | | 1 | 60 | 9 | G | Ike Hildebrand | Floyd Crawford |
| 1961 WM | 7 | 6 | 1 | | 0 | 45 | 11 | G | Bobby Kromm | Hal Jones |
| 1962 WM | 7 | 6 | 0 | | 1 | 58 | 12 | S | Lloyd Roubell | *unknown* |
| 1963 WM | 7 | 4 | 1 | | 2 | 46 | 23 | 4th | Bobby Kromm | Hal Jones |
| 1965 WM | 7 | 4 | 0 | | 3 | 28 | 21 | 4th | Father David Bauer | *unknown* |
| 1966 WM | 7 | 5 | 0 | | 2 | 33 | 10 | B | Jackie McLeod | Terry O'Malley |

| | | | | | | | | | | |
|---|---|---|---|---|---|---|---|---|---|---|
| 1967 WM | 7 | 4 | 1 | | 2 | 28 | 15 | B | Jackie McLeod | Roger Bourbonnais |
| 1969 WM | 10 | 4 | 0 | | 6 | 26 | 31 | 4th | Jackie McLeod | Gary Begg |
| 1977 WM | 10 | 6 | 1 | | 3 | 47 | 35 | 4th | Johnny Wilson | Phil Esposito |
| 1978 WM | 10 | 5 | 0 | | 5 | 38 | 36 | B | Harry Howell | Marcel Dionne |
| 1979 WM | 8 | 3 | 0 | | 5 | 31 | 43 | 4th | Marshall Johnston | Guy Charron (1) |
| 1981 WM | 8 | 2 | 1 | | 5 | 28 | 34 | 4th | Don Cherry | Lanny McDonald |
| 1982 WM | 10 | 5 | 2 | | 3 | 46 | 30 | B | Marshall Johnston | Bill Barber (2) |
| 1983 WM | 10 | 6 | 0 | | 4 | 35 | 30 | B | Dave King | Darryl Sittler (3) |
| 1985 WM | 10 | 6 | 1 | | 3 | 42 | 31 | S | Doug Carpenter | Dave Taylor |
| 1986 WM | 10 | 4 | 0 | | 6 | 37 | 38 | B | Pat Quinn | Marcel Dionne |
| 1987 WM | 10 | 3 | 2 | | 5 | 27 | 30 | 4th | Dave King | Mike Foligno |
| 1989 WM | 10 | 7 | 0 | | 3 | 57 | 29 | S | Dave King | Dale Hawerchuk |
| 1990 WM | 10 | 6 | 1 | | 3 | 43 | 32 | 4th | Dave King | Paul Coffey |
| 1991 WM | 10 | 5 | 3 | | 2 | 39 | 30 | S | Dave King | Doug Lidster |
| 1992 WM | 6 | 2 | 1 | | 3 | 18 | 22 | 8th | Dave King | Glenn Anderson |
| 1993 WM | 8 | 6 | 0 | | 2 | 41 | 17 | 4th | Mike Keenan | Adam Graves |
| 1994 WM | 8 | 8 | 0 | | 0 | 35 | 10 | G | George Kingston | Luc Robitaille |
| 1995 WM | 8 | 4 | 1 | | 3 | 27 | 21 | B | Tom Renney | Brian Tutt |
| 1996 WM | 8 | 4 | 1 | | 3 | 25 | 22 | S | Tom Renney | Steve Thomas |
| 1997 WM | 11 | 7 | 1 | | 3 | 36 | 22 | G | Andy Murray | Dean Evason |
| 1998 WM | 6 | 3 | 2 | | 1 | 22 | 17 | 6th | Andy Murray | Keith Primeau |
| 1999 WM | 9 | 6 | 0 | | 3 | 34 | 23 | 4th | Mike Johnston | Rob Blake |
| 2000 WM | 9 | 5 | 0 | | 4 | 32 | 17 | 4th | Tom Renney | Mike Sillinger |
| 2001 WM | 7 | 4 | 1 | | 2 | 27 | 15 | 5th | Wayne Fleming | Ryan Smyth (4) |
| 2002 WM | 7 | 5 | 0 | | 2 | 20 | 13 | 6th | Wayne Fleming | Ryan Smyth |
| 2003 WM | 9 | 8 | 1 | | 0 | 35 | 14 | G | Andy Murray | Ryan Smyth |
| 2004 WM | 9 | 7 | 1 | | 1 | 30 | 18 | G | Mike Babcock | Ryan Smyth |
| 2005 WM | 9 | 6 | 1 | | 2 | 35 | 24 | S | Marc Habscheid | Ryan Smyth |
| 2006 WM | 9 | 6 | 0 | | 3 | 41 | 24 | 4th | Marc Habscheid | Brendan Shanahan |
| 2007 WM | 9 | 8 | 1 | 0 | 0 | 41 | 21 | G | Andy Murray | Shane Doan |
| 2008 WM | 9 | 8 | 0 | 1 | 0 | 52 | 21 | S | Ken Hitchcock | Shane Doan |
| 2009 WM | 9 | 7 | 0 | 1 | 1 | 43 | 15 | S | Lindy Ruff | Shane Doan |
| 2010 WM | 7 | 3 | 0 | 0 | 4 | 29 | 18 | 7th | Craig MacTavish | Ray Whitney (5) |
| 2011 WM | 7 | 4 | 2 | 0 | 1 | 28 | 14 | 5th | Ken Hitchcock | Rick Nash |
| 2012 WM | 8 | 6 | 0 | 1 | 1 | 38 | 19 | 5th | Brent Sutter | Ryan Getzlaf |

(1) Wilf Paiement captain vs. Soviet Union (Apr. 25) and Sweden (Apr. 27)
(2) Bobby Clarke captain vs. Finland (Apr. 15); Darryl Sittler captain vs. Czechoslovakia (Apr. 16); Bob Gainey captain vs. West Germany (Apr. 19); Craig Hartsburg captain vs. Italy (Apr. 21); Bobby Smith captain vs. United States (Apr. 22)
(3) Marcel Dionne captain vs. Finland (Apr. 22), West Germany (Apr. 24), Czechoslovakia (Apr. 28), and Soviet Union (May 2)
(4) Michael Peca captain vs. Norway (April 28), Italy (Apr. 30), and Russia (May 2)
(5) Ryan Smyth captain vs. ITA (May 8), no captain vs. LAT (May 10)

NOTE: Club teams represented Canada from 1930-1963 as follows: 1930—Toronto CCM, 1931—Manitoba Grads, 1933—Toronto Sea Fleas, 1934—Saskatoon Quakers, 1935—Winnipeg Monarchs, 1937—Kimberley Dynamiters, 1938—Sudbury Wolves, 1939—Trail Smoke Eaters, 1949—Sudbury Wolves, 1950—Edmonton Mercurys, 1951—Lethbridge Maple Leafs, 1954—East York Lyndhursts, 1955—Penticton Vees, 1958—Whitby Dunlops, 1959—Belleville McFarlands, 1961—Trail Smoke Eaters, 1962—Galt Terriers, 1963—Trail Smoke Eaters

## IIHF-NHL Invitationals

(bold=top level)

| Year Event | GP | W | T | L | GF | GA | Place | Coach | Captain |
|---|---|---|---|---|---|---|---|---|---|
| 1972 SS | 8 | 4 | 1 | 3 | 31 | 32 | 1st | Harry Sinden | no captain |
| 1976 CC | 7 | 6 | 0 | 1 | 33 | 10 | 1st | Scotty Bowman | Bobby Clarke |
| 1981 CC | 7 | 5 | 1 | 1 | 37 | 22 | 2nd | Scotty Bowman | Denis Potvin |
| 1984 CC | 8 | 5 | 1 | 2 | 37 | 27 | 1st | Glen Sather | Wayne Gretzky (1) |
| 1987 CC | 8 | 5 | 2 | 1 | 36 | 29 | 1st | Mike Keenan | Wayne Gretzky |
| 1991 CC | 8 | 6 | 2 | 0 | 33 | 14 | 1st | Mike Keenan | Wayne Gretzky |
| 1996 WCH | 8 | 5 | 0 | 3 | 26 | 26 | 2nd | Glen Sather | Wayne Gretzky |
| 2004 WCH | 6 | 6 | 0 | 0 | 22 | 9 | 1st | Pat Quinn | Mario Lemieux |

(1) also Larry Robinson

## U20 World Championship

(bold=top level)

| Year Event | GP | W | T | L | GF | GA | Place | Coach | Captain |
|---|---|---|---|---|---|---|---|---|---|
| Year Event | GP | W | OTW OTL | L | GF | GA | Place | Coach | Captain |
| 1977 WM20 | 7 | 5 | 1 | 1 | 50 | 20 | S | Bert Templeton | Dale McCourt |
| 1978 WM20 | 6 | 4 | 0 | 2 | 36 | 18 | B | Ernie McLean | Ryan Walter |
| 1979 WM20 | 5 | 3 | 0 | 2 | 23 | 10 | 5th | Ernie McLean | John Paul Kelly |
| 1980 WM20 | 5 | 3 | 0 | 2 | 25 | 18 | 5th | Mike Keenan | Rick Lanz/Dave Fenyves |
| 1981 WM20 | 5 | 1 | 1 | 3 | 26 | 25 | 7th | Bob Kilger | Marc Crawford |
| 1982 WM20 | 7 | 6 | 1 | 0 | 45 | 14 | G | Dave King | Troy Murray |
| 1983 WM20 | 7 | 4 | 1 | 2 | 39 | 24 | B | Dave King | James Patrick |
| 1984 WM20 | 7 | 4 | 1 | 2 | 39 | 17 | 4th | Brian Kilrea | Russ Courtnall |
| 1985 WM20 | 7 | 5 | 2 | 0 | 44 | 14 | G | Terry Simpson | Dan Hodgson |
| 1986 WM20 | 7 | 5 | 0 | 2 | 54 | 21 | S | Terry Simpson | Jim Sandlak |
| 1987 WM20 | 6 | 4 | 1 | 1 | 41 | 23 | DQ | Bert Templeton | Steve Chiasson |
| 1988 WM20 | 7 | 6 | 1 | 0 | 37 | 16 | G | Dave Chambers | Theo Fleury |
| 1989 WM20 | 7 | 4 | 1 | 2 | 31 | 23 | 4th | Tom Webster | Eric Desjardins |
| 1990 WM20 | 7 | 5 | 1 | 1 | 36 | 18 | G | Guy Charron | Mike Ricci (1) |
| 1991 WM20 | 7 | 5 | 1 | 1 | 40 | 18 | G | Dick Todd | Steve Rice |
| 1992 WM20 | 7 | 2 | 2 | 3 | 21 | 30 | 6th | Rick Cornacchia | Eric Lindros |
| 1993 WM20 | 7 | 6 | 0 | 1 | 37 | 17 | G | Perry Pearn | Martin Lapointe |
| 1994 WM20 | 7 | 6 | 1 | 0 | 39 | 20 | G | Jos Canale | Brent Tully |
| 1995 WM20 | 7 | 7 | 0 | 0 | 49 | 22 | G | Don Hay | Todd Harvey |
| 1996 WM20 | 6 | 6 | 0 | 0 | 27 | 8 | G | Marcel Comeau | Nolan Baumgartner |
| 1997 WM20 | 7 | 5 | 2 | 0 | 27 | 13 | G | Mike Babcock | Brad Larsen |

| | | | | | | | | | | |
|---|---|---|---|---|---|---|---|---|---|---|
| 1998 WM20 | 7 | 2 | 0 | | 5 | 13 | 18 | 8th | Real Paiement | Cory Sarich/Jesse Wallin |
| 1999 WM20 | 7 | 4 | 1 | | 2 | 30 | 15 | S | Tom Renney | Mike Van Ryn |
| 2000 WM20 | 7 | 4 | 2 | | 1 | 23 | 14 | B | Claude Julien | Manny Malhotra |
| 2001 WM20 | 7 | 4 | 1 | | 2 | 26 | 16 | B | Stan Butler | Steve McCarthy |
| 2002 WM20 | 7 | 5 | 0 | | 2 | 40 | 14 | S | Stan Butler | Jarret Stoll |
| 2003 WM20 | 6 | 5 | 0 | | 1 | 26 | 11 | S | Marc Habscheid | Scottie Upshall |
| 2004 WM20 | 6 | 5 | 0 | | 1 | 35 | 9 | S | Mario Durocher | Daniel Paille |
| 2005 WM20 | 6 | 6 | 0 | | 0 | 41 | 7 | G | Brent Sutter | Michael Richards |
| 2006 WM20 | 6 | 6 | 0 | | 0 | 25 | 6 | G | Brent Sutter | Kyle Chipchura |
| 2007 WM20 | 6 | 5 | 1 | 0 | 0 | 20 | 7 | G | Craig Hartsburg | Kris Letang |
| 2008 WM20 | 7 | 5 | 1 | 0 | 1 | 23 | 10 | G | Craig Hartsburg | Karl Alzner |
| 2009 WM20 | 6 | 5 | 1 | 0 | 0 | 46 | 12 | G | Pat Quinn | Tom Hickey |
| 2010 WM20 | 6 | 4 | 1 | 1 | 0 | 46 | 13 | S | Willie Desjardins | Patrice Cormier |
| 2011 WM20 | 7 | 5 | 0 | 1 | 1 | 39 | 19 | S | Dave Cameron | Ryan Ellis |
| 2012 WM20 | 6 | 5 | 0 | 0 | 1 | 35 | 11 | B | Don Hay | Jaden Schwartz |

(1) also Dave Chyzowski, Dan Ratushny

NOTE: Club teams represented Canada as follows: 1977—Hamilton Fincups, 1979—New Westminster Bruins, 1980—Peterborough Petes, 1981—Cornwall Royals

## U18 World Championship (Men)

(bold=top level)

| Year Event | GP | W | T | | L | GF | GA | Place | Coach | Captain |
|---|---|---|---|---|---|---|---|---|---|---|
| Year Event | GP | W | OTW | OTL | L | GF | GA | Place | Coach | Captain |
| 2002 WM18 | 8 | 3 | 0 | | 5 | 28 | 35 | 6th | Mike Pelino | Andre Benoit |
| 2003 WM18 | 7 | 5 | 1 | | 1 | 32 | 12 | G | Mike Kelly | Braydon Coburn |
| 2004 WM18 | 7 | 4 | 0 | | 3 | 22 | 14 | 4th | Dean Chynoweth | John Lammers |
| 2005 WM18 | 6 | 4 | 0 | | 2 | 28 | 14 | S | Shawn Camp | Ryan Parent |
| 2006 WM18 | 7 | 3 | 1 | | 3 | 19 | 13 | 4th | Greg Gilbert | Ty Wishart |
| 2007 WM18 | 6 | 3 | 1 | 1 | 1 | 30 | 20 | 4th | Trent Yawney | Angelo Esposito |
| 2008 WM18 | 7 | 6 | 0 | 0 | 1 | 34 | 10 | G | Pat Quinn | Cody Hodgson |
| 2009 WM18 | 6 | 3 | 1 | 1 | 1 | 32 | 15 | 4th | Mike Johnston | Ryan O'Reilly |
| 2010 WM18 | 6 | 3 | 0 | 0 | 3 | 25 | 19 | 7th | Guy Carbonneau | Erik Gudbranson |
| 2011 WM18 | 7 | 4 | 0 | 1 | 2 | 29 | 22 | 4th | Mike Williamson | Ryan Murray |
| 2012 WM18 | 7 | 3 | 1 | 0 | 3 | 27 | 20 | B | Jesse Wallin | Matt Dumba |

## Olympics, Women

(bold=top level)

| Year Event | GP | W | T | | L | GF | GA | Place | Coach | Captain |
|---|---|---|---|---|---|---|---|---|---|---|
| Year Event | GP | W | OTW | OTL | L | GF | GA | Place | Coach | Captain |
| 1998 OG-W | 6 | 4 | 0 | | 2 | 29 | 15 | S | Shannon Miller | Stacy Wilson |
| 2002 OG-W | 5 | 5 | 0 | | 0 | 35 | 5 | G | Daniele Sauvageau | Cassie Campbell |
| 2006 OG-W | 5 | 5 | 0 | | 0 | 46 | 2 | G | Melody Davidson | Cassie Campbell |
| 2010 OG-W | 5 | 5 | 0 | 0 | 0 | 48 | 2 | G | Melody Davidson | Hayley Wickenheiser |

## Women's World Championship

(bold=top level)

| Year Event | GP | W | T | | L | GF | GA | Place | Coach | Captain |
|---|---|---|---|---|---|---|---|---|---|---|
| Year Event | GP | W | OTW | OTL | L | GF | GA | Place | Coach | Captain |
| 1990 WW | 5 | 5 | 0 | | 0 | 61 | 8 | G | Dave McMaster | Sue Scherer |
| 1992 WW | 5 | 5 | 0 | | 0 | 38 | 3 | G | Rick Polutnik | France St. Louis |
| 1994 WW | 5 | 5 | 0 | | 0 | 37 | 7 | G | Les Lawton | France St. Louis |
| 1997 WW | 5 | 5 | 0 | | 0 | 28 | 6 | G | Shannon Miller | Stacy Wilson |
| 1999 WW | 5 | 5 | 0 | | 0 | 31 | 2 | G | Daniele Sauvageau | Therese Brisson |
| 2000 WW | 5 | 5 | 0 | | 0 | 27 | 5 | G | Melody Davidson | Therese Brisson |
| 2001 WW | 5 | 5 | 0 | | 0 | 40 | 3 | G | Daniele Sauvageau | Therese Brisson |
| 2004 WW | 5 | 4 | 0 | | 1 | 34 | 4 | G | Karen Hughes | Cassie Campbell |
| 2005 WW | 5 | 4 | 0 | | 1 | 38 | 1 | S | Melody Davidson | Cassie Campbell |
| 2007 WW | 5 | 4 | 1 | 0 | 0 | 32 | 5 | G | Melody Davidson | Hayley Wickenheiser |
| 2008 WW | 5 | 3 | 0 | 0 | 2 | 28 | 11 | S | Peter Smith | Hayley Wickenheiser |
| 2009 WW | 5 | 4 | 0 | 0 | 1 | 31 | 6 | S | Melody Davidson | Hayley Wickenheiser |
| 2011 WW | 5 | 4 | 0 | 1 | 0 | 27 | 4 | S | Ryan Walter | Hayley Wickenheiser |
| 2012 WW | 5 | 3 | 1 | 0 | 1 | 29 | 17 | G | Dan Church | Hayley Wickenheiser |

## U18 Women's World Championship

(bold=top level)

| Year Event | GP | W | OTW | OTL | L | GF | GA | Place | Coach | Captain |
|---|---|---|---|---|---|---|---|---|---|---|
| 2008 WW18 | 5 | 4 | 0 | 0 | 1 | 47 | 9 | S | Melody Davidson | Laurianne Rougeau |
| 2009 WW18 | 5 | 4 | 0 | 1 | 0 | 43 | 5 | S | Stephanie White | Brianne Jenner |
| 2010 WW18 | 5 | 4 | 1 | 0 | 0 | 44 | 7 | G | Dan Church | Jessica Campbell |
| 2011 WW18 | 5 | 4 | 0 | 0 | 1 | 31 | 8 | S | Sarah Hodges | Sarah Edney |
| 2012 WW18 | 5 | 5 | 0 | 0 | 0 | 36 | 1 | G | Pierre Alain | Erin Ambrose |

# Chile (CHI)

Locals enjoy a little pleasure skating at one of the few skating rinks in Chile.

**Joined IIHF: September 22, 1999 (Affiliate Member)**

Website: n/a
E-mail: Nick72@operamail.com

Asociacion Nacional de Hockey en Hielo y en Linea
Cali# 715—Parad. 20 La Florida
Santiago, Chile

Phone: +56 2 211 64 53 • Fax: +56 2 341 36 12

**Top Level Host History** none

# China (CHN)

Cheng Zhang captained the Chinese U18 national team in 2012. Photo: Filip Bakic.

**Joined IIHF: July 25, 1963**

Website: n/a
E-mail: hockey.china@yahoo.com.cn

Chinese Ice Hockey Association
56 Zhongguancun South Street
Haidian District
100044 Beijing
China

Phone: +86 8831 8351 • Fax: +86 10 883 18 354

**World Ranking**

| MEN | | WOMEN | |
|---|---|---|---|
| 2012 | 38 | 2012 | 13 |
| 2011 | 39 | 2011 | 9 |
| 2010 | 37 | 2010 | 7 |
| 2009 | 29 | 2009 | 7 |
| 2008 | 28 | 2008 | 8 |
| 2007 | 27 | 2007 | 8 |
| 2006 | 28 | 2006 | 7 |
| 2005 | 28 | 2005 | 7 |
| 2004 | 28 | 2004 | 7 |

**Top Level Host History**
Women's World Championship: 2008 (Harbin)

**World Championship (Men)**

| Year Event | GP | W | T | | L | GF | GA | Place | Coach | Captain |
|---|---|---|---|---|---|---|---|---|---|---|
| Year Event | GP | W | OTW | OTL | L | GF | GA | Place | Coach | Captain |
| 1972 WM-C | 6 | 2 | 2 | | 2 | 19 | 20 | 3rd | *unknown* | Pen-fa Huang |
| 1973 WM-C | 7 | 2 | 2 | | 3 | 21 | 28 | 5th | Wan Chi Li | Pen-fa Huang |
| 1974 WM-C | 7 | 1 | 1 | | 5 | 15 | 38 | 6th | *unknown* | Yu-Lin Yen |
| 1978 WM-C | 7 | 4 | 0 | | 3 | 47 | 30 | 4th | Wan Chi Li/Chung Liang Cheng | Yung Ke Yang |
| 1979 WM-B | 4 | 0 | 0 | | 4 | 8 | 31 | 9th | Wan Chi Li | *unknown* |
| 1981 WM-C | 7 | 6 | 0 | | 1 | 46 | 14 | 2nd | Wan Chi Li | *unknown* |
| 1982 WM-B | 7 | 2 | 1 | | 4 | 32 | 47 | 7th | Wan Chi Li | Youke Yang |
| 1983 WM-C | 7 | 4 | 1 | | 2 | 28 | 23 | 3rd | Wan Chi Li | Youke Yang |
| 1985 WM-C | 7 | 5 | 1 | | 1 | 45 | 22 | 3rd | Zheng Ping | S Zhimin |
| 1986 WM-C | 6 | 4 | 2 | | 0 | 42 | 10 | 2nd | Zheng Wang/H Jing | *unknown* |
| 1987 WM-B | 7 | 0 | 0 | | 7 | 14 | 60 | 8th | Zheng Wang | Anfu Wang |
| 1989 WM-C | 7 | 4 | 1 | | 2 | 31 | 29 | 3rd | Keqiang Wu | Anfu Wang |
| 1990 WM-C | 8 | 4 | 1 | | 3 | 34 | 29 | 3rd | Wenhung Li | Anfu Wang |
| 1991 WM-C | 8 | 6 | 1 | | 1 | 44 | 24 | 2nd | Zhongliang Chen | Anfu Wang |
| 1992 WM-B | 7 | 1 | 1 | | 5 | 15 | 50 | 7th | Keqiang Wu | Yujie Tian |
| 1993 WM-B | 7 | 1 | 0 | | 6 | 12 | 79 | 7th | Baocai Wang | Ling Yuan Wei |
| 1994 WM-B | 7 | 0 | 0 | | 7 | 11 | 98 | 8th | Baocai Wang | Ling Yuan Wei |
| 1995 WM-C-1 | 4 | 2 | 0 | | 2 | 13 | 26 | 5th | Baocai Wang | Ling Yuan Wei |
| 1996 WM-C | 7 | 1 | 0 | | 6 | 17 | 68 | 7th | Baocai Wang | Hongqun Gao |
| 1997 WM-C | 5 | 1 | 0 | | 4 | 16 | 34 | 7th | Jingang Wang | Hiaofang Guan |
| 1998 WM-C | 5 | 2 | 0 | | 3 | 21 | 25 | 4th | Jingang Wang | Lei Yu |
| 1999 WM-C | 5 | 2 | 1 | | 2 | 16 | 26 | 4th | Jingang Wang | Guofeng Wu |
| 2000 WM-C | 4 | 3 | 0 | | 1 | 25 | 5 | 2nd | Jingang Wang | Guofeng Wu |
| 2001 WM-I-B | 5 | 1 | 0 | | 4 | 8 | 39 | 5th | Jingang Wang | Guofeng Wu |
| 2002 WM-I-B | 5 | 0 | 0 | | 5 | 7 | 43 | 6th | Guocheng Wang | Guanghua Chen |
| 2003 WM-II-B | 5 | 4 | 0 | | 1 | 19 | 13 | 2nd | Guocheng Wang | Guofeng Wu |
| 2004 WM-II-A | 5 | 4 | 0 | | 1 | 39 | 13 | 1st | Guocheng Wang | *unknown* |
| 2005 WM-I-A | 5 | 0 | 0 | | 5 | 5 | 61 | 6th | Guocheng Wang | Dahai Wang |
| 2006 WM-II-B | 5 | 4 | 1 | | 0 | 34 | 11 | 1st | Shuqing Xiang | Dahai Wang |
| 2007 WM-I-A | 5 | 0 | 0 | 0 | 5 | 8 | 45 | 6th | Shuqing Xiang | Kai Yin |
| 2008 WM-II-B | 5 | 2 | 2 | 0 | 1 | 21 | 14 | 2nd | Benyu Wang | Dahai Wang |
| 2009 WM-II-A | 5 | 2 | 1 | 0 | 2 | 21 | 29 | 3rd | Benyu Wang | Qingyuan Meng |

| 2010 WM-II-B | 5 | 1 | | 0 | 0 | 4 | 12 | 26 | 5th | Andrei Kovalev | Dahai Wang |
|---|---|---|---|---|---|---|---|---|---|---|---|
| 2011 WM-II-B | 5 | 2 | | 0 | 0 | 3 | 26 | 25 | 4th | Yevgeni Levedev | Weiyang Zhang |
| 2012 WM-II-B | 5 | 3 | | 0 | 0 | 2 | 28 | 21 | 2nd | Keisuke Araki | Weiyang Zhang |

**U20 World Championship**

| Year Event | GP | W | T | | | L | GF | GA | Place | Coach | Captain |
|---|---|---|---|---|---|---|---|---|---|---|---|
| Year Event | GP | W | | OTW | OTL | L | GF | GA | Place | Coach | Captain |
| 1986 WM20-C | 5 | 2 | 0 | | | 3 | 23 | 27 | 4th | *unknown* | Z Zhang |
| 2004 WM20-III | 5 | 4 | 0 | | | 1 | 41 | 10 | 2nd | Jiuming Liu | Zhinan Cui |
| 2005 WM20-II-A | 5 | 3 | 0 | | | 2 | 16 | 14 | 4th | Jiuming Liu | Zhinan Cui |
| 2006 WM20-II-B | 5 | 1 | 0 | | | 4 | 12 | 31 | 6th | Xiaodong Li | Wang Zhi Quiang |
| 2007 WM20-III | 5 | 4 | | 1 | 0 | 0 | 37 | 12 | 1st | Jiuming Liu | Longtan Liu |
| 2008 WM20-II-B | 5 | 0 | | 0 | 0 | 5 | 8 | 49 | 6th | Xiaodong Li | Longtan Liu |
| 2009 WM20-II-B | 5 | 0 | | 0 | 0 | 5 | 9 | 40 | 6th | Xiaobo Guan | Ling Chen |
| 2010 WM20-II-A | 5 | 1 | | 0 | 0 | 4 | 8 | 48 | 5th | Xiaobo Guan | Tianyu Hu |
| 2011 WM20-II-B | 5 | 0 | | 0 | 0 | 5 | 10 | 66 | 6th | Xiaobo Guan | Wei Lu |
| 2012 WM20-III | 4 | 3 | | 0 | 0 | 1 | 26 | 10 | 2nd | Xiaobo Guan | Jin Chen |

**U18 World Championship (Men)**

| Year Event | GP | W | T | | | L | GF | GA | Place | Coach | Captain |
|---|---|---|---|---|---|---|---|---|---|---|---|
| Year Event | GP | W | | OTW | OTL | L | GF | GA | Place | Coach | Captain |
| 2003 WM18-III-A | 3 | 1 | 0 | | | 2 | 11 | 12 | 3rd | Jiuming Liu | Yandi Li |
| 2007 WM18-III | 5 | 4 | | 0 | 0 | 1 | 46 | 16 | 2nd | Xiaobo Guan | Chongwei Wang |
| 2008 WM18-II-A | 5 | 1 | | 0 | 0 | 4 | 14 | 52 | 5th | Xiaobo Guan | Ling Chen |
| 2009 WM18-II-B | 5 | 0 | | 0 | 0 | 5 | 9 | 49 | 6th | Jianye Wang | Ling Chen |
| 2010 WM18-III-A | 4 | 4 | | 0 | 0 | 0 | 53 | 11 | 1st | Wencai Hou | Xiaofeng Zhu |
| 2011 WM18-II-B | 5 | 1 | | 0 | 0 | 4 | 13 | 47 | 5th | Yuqiang Pan | Tianxiang Xia |
| 2012 WM18-II-B | 5 | 0 | | 1 | 1 | 3 | 18 | 30 | 6th | Wencai Hou | Cheng Zhang |

**Olympics, Women**
(bold=top level)

| Year Event | GP | W | T | | | L | GF | GA | Place | Coach | Captain |
|---|---|---|---|---|---|---|---|---|---|---|---|
| Year Event | GP | W | | OTW | OTL | L | GF | GA | Place | Coach | Captain |
| **1998 OG-W** | **6** | **2** | **0** | | | **4** | **11** | **19** | **4th** | **Zhinan Zhang** | **Hong Dang** |
| **2002 OG-W** | **5** | **1** | **1** | | | **3** | **9** | **26** | **7th** | **Naifeng Yao** | **Hongmei Liu** |
| **2010 OG-W** | **5** | **1** | | **0** | **0** | **4** | **6** | **23** | **7th** | **Hannu Saintula** | **Linuo Wang** |

**Women's World Championship**
(bold=top level)

| Year Event | GP | W | T | | | L | GF | GA | Place | Coach | Captain |
|---|---|---|---|---|---|---|---|---|---|---|---|
| Year Event | GP | W | | OTW | OTL | L | GF | GA | Place | Coach | Captain |
| **1992 WW** | **5** | **3** | **0** | | | **2** | **11** | **18** | **5th** | **Wang Guocheng** | **Xiaojuan Ma** |
| **1994 WW** | **5** | **1** | **1** | | | **3** | **17** | **34** | **4th** | **Zhinan Zhang** | **Hong Dang** |
| **1997 WW** | **5** | **2** | **0** | | | **3** | **18** | **21** | **4th** | **Zhinan Zhang** | **Hong Dang** |
| **1999 WW** | **5** | **3** | **0** | | | **2** | **11** | **14** | **5th** | **Zhinan Zhang** | **Hongmei Liu** |
| **2000 WW** | **5** | **2** | **1** | | | **2** | **8** | **13** | **6th** | **Zhinan Zhang** | **Hongmei Liu** |
| **2001 WW** | **5** | **1** | **1** | | | **3** | **10** | **22** | **6th** | **Naifeng Yao** | **Hongmei Liu** |
| **2004 WW** | **4** | **2** | **0** | | | **2** | **13** | **20** | **7th** | **Jan Votruba** | **Xuan Li** |
| **2005 WW** | **5** | **1** | **1** | | | **3** | **9** | **19** | **6th** | **Paul Strople** | **Zinuo Wang** |
| **2007 WW** | **4** | **1** | | **0** | **0** | **3** | **11** | **26** | **6th** | **Jorma Siitarinen** | **Linuo Wang** |
| **2008 WW** | **4** | **1** | | **0** | **0** | **3** | **8** | **21** | **8th** | **Steve Carlyle** | **Linuo Wang** |
| **2009 WW** | **4** | **0** | | **0** | **1** | **3** | **7** | **26** | **9th** | **Paul Strople** | **Linuo Wang** |
| 2011 WW-I | 4 | 1 | | 0 | 0 | 3 | 8 | 16 | 5th | Hannu Saintula | Rui Sun |
| 2012 WW-I-B | 5 | 4 | | 0 | 0 | 1 | 21 | 8 | 2nd | Mikhail Chekanov | Baiwei Yu |

*China played in Division I, Group B at the Women's World Championship in 2012, finishing in second place and remaining in that division for 2013. Photo: Colin Lawson.*

# Chinese Taipei (TPE)

*Chinese Taipei players celebrate a goal at the 2012 IIHF Ice Hockey U18 World Championship Division III. Photo: Bonchuk Andonov.*

## Joined IIHF: September 30, 1983

Website: www.cihl.com.tw
E-mail: tpe@hockey-hotline.com

Chinese Taipei Ice Hockey Federation
20, Chu Lun St.
Room 610, 6 Fl.
10489 Taipei
Taiwan ROC

Phone: +886 2 8771 1451 • Fax: +886 2 227 82 778

**Top Level Host History** none

**U20 World Championship**

| Year Event | GP | W | OTW | OTL | L | GF | GA | Place | Coach | Captain |
|---|---|---|---|---|---|---|---|---|---|---|
| 2010 WM20-III | 4 | 2 | 0 | 0 | 2 | 18 | 25 | 5th | Kristof Kovago | Yu-Lun Liu |
| 2011 WM20-III | 6 | 0 | 0 | 1 | 5 | 16 | 47 | 7th | Kristof Kovago | Fa-Ben Lu |

**U18 World Championship (Men)**

| Year Event | GP | W | OTW | OTL | L | GF | GA | Place | Coach | Captain |
|---|---|---|---|---|---|---|---|---|---|---|
| 2008 WM18-III-A | 4 | 3 | 0 | 0 | 1 | 31 | 23 | 2nd | Kristof Kovago | *unknown* |
| 2009 WM18-III-A | 4 | 2 | 0 | 0 | 2 | 28 | 14 | 3rd | Kristof Kovago | Yen Lin Shen |
| 2010 WM18-III-A | 4 | 2 | 0 | 0 | 2 | 30 | 18 | 3rd | Kristof Kovago | Yun-Pu Lee |
| 2011 WM18-III-A | 5 | 2 | 0 | 0 | 3 | 20 | 22 | 2nd | Kristof Kovago | Po-Yun Hsiao |
| 2012 WM18-III | 5 | 1 | 0 | 0 | 4 | 19 | 26 | 5th | Kristof Kovago | Po-Yun Hsiao |

# Croatia (CRO)

*Club team Medvescak Zagreb wrote history when it hosted Olimpija Ljubljana in the 2,000-year-old amphitheatre of Pula for a game of the EBEL league on September 14, 2012. Photo: Martin Merk.*

## Joined IIHF: May 6, 1992

(Croatia and Slovenia split from Yugoslavia (joined IIHF in 1939) on June 25, 1991; Yugoslavia became Serbia & Montenegro in 2004; became Serbia on September 28, 2006 after Serbia and Montenegro split and only Serbia maintained IIHF membership status) For Yugoslavia see Slovenia.

Website: www.hshl.hr
E-mail: hshl@zg.t-com.hr

Croatian Ice Hockey Association
Trg Kresimira Cosica 11
10000 Zagreb
Croatia

Phone: +385 1 304 26 50 • Fax: +385 1 304 26 49

**World Ranking**

| MEN | | WOMEN | |
|---|---|---|---|
| 2012 | 30 | 2012 | 22 |
| 2011 | 27 | 2011 | 20 |
| 2010 | 26 | 2010 | 20 |
| 2009 | 26 | 2009 | 25 |
| 2008 | 26 | 2008 | 30 |
| 2007 | 28 | 2007 | 31 |
| 2006 | 27 | | |
| 2005 | 30 | | |
| 2004 | 31 | | |

**Top Level Host History** none

**World Championship (Men)**

| Year Event | GP | W | T | | L | GF | GA | Place | Coach | Captain |
|---|---|---|---|---|---|---|---|---|---|---|
| Year Event | GP | W | OTW | OTL | L | GF | GA | Place | Coach | Captain |
| 1994 WM-C-B | 5 | 2 | 0 | | 3 | 8 | 21 | 4th | Vlado Kucera | unknown |
| 1995 WM-C-2 | 6 | 5 | 1 | | 0 | 50 | 17 | 1st | Vlado Kucera | Dubravko Orlic |
| 1996 WM-C | 7 | 0 | 0 | | 7 | 11 | 71 | 8th | Svato Kosik | Dubravko Orlic |
| 1997 WM-D | 5 | 3 | 1 | | 1 | 16 | 9 | 1st | Ivo Ratej | Igor Zajec |
| 1998 WM-C | 5 | 1 | 2 | | 2 | 11 | 15 | 5th | Vlado Kucera | Damir Gojanovic |
| 1999 WM-C | 4 | 1 | 1 | | 2 | 20 | 18 | 5th | Vlado Kucera | Damir Gojanovic |
| 2000 WM-C | 4 | 1 | 1 | | 2 | 18 | 22 | 3rd | *unknown* | Damir Gojanovic |
| 2001 WM-I-B | 5 | 1 | 1 | | 3 | 17 | 45 | 4th | Svato Kosik | Damir Gojanovic |
| 2002 WM-I-A | 5 | 1 | 0 | | 4 | 6 | 32 | 5th | Vlado Kucera | Damir Gojanovic |
| 2003 WM-I-B | 5 | 1 | 0 | | 4 | 10 | 35 | 6th | Ivano Zanatta | Damir Gojanovic |
| 2004 WM-II-A | 5 | 4 | 0 | | 1 | 32 | 6 | 2nd | Svato Kosik | Mato Mladjenovic |
| 2005 WM-II-A | 5 | 5 | 0 | | 0 | 46 | 6 | 1st | Zdenek Vojta | Damir Gojanovic |
| 2006 WM-I-B | 5 | 0 | 0 | | 5 | 11 | 35 | 6th | Bruno Bregant | Mato Mladjenovic |
| 2007 WM-II-A | 5 | 5 | 0 | 0 | 0 | 58 | 10 | 1st | Rudolf Ulicny | Damir Gojanovic |
| 2008 WM-I-B | 5 | 0 | 1 | 0 | 4 | 5 | 15 | 5th | Pavel Kavcic | Ivan Glavota |
| 2009 WM-I-A | 5 | 1 | 0 | 0 | 4 | 11 | 25 | 5th | Pavel Kavcic | Kresimir Svigir |

| | | | | | | | | | | |
|---|---|---|---|---|---|---|---|---|---|---|
| 2010 WM-I-B | 5 | 0 | 0 | 0 | 5 | 4 | 33 | 6th | Pavel Kavcic | Marko Lovrencic |
| 2011 WM-II-B | 5 | 4 | 0 | 0 | 1 | 53 | 10 | 2nd | Bruno Bregant | Marko Lovrencic |
| 2012 WM-II-A | 5 | 3 | 0 | 0 | 2 | 27 | 13 | 3rd | Michael Shea | Mario Novak |

**U20 World Championship**

| Year Event | GP | W | T | | | L | GF | GA | Place | Coach | Captain |
|---|---|---|---|---|---|---|---|---|---|---|---|
| Year Event | GP | W | | OTW | OTL | L | GF | GA | Place | Coach | Captain |
| 1995 WM20-C-2 | 5 | 0 | 3 | | | 2 | 10 | 21 | 5th | Bruno Bregant | Goran Jelinek |
| 1996 WM20-D | 3 | 3 | 0 | | | 0 | 22 | 4 | 1st | Bruno Bregant | *unknown* |
| 1997 WM20-C | 4 | 1 | 0 | | | 3 | 5 | 25 | 7th | Zvonko Ostric | Igor Grosic |
| 1998 WM20-C | 4 | 2 | 0 | | | 2 | 9 | 16 | 5th | Bruno Bregant | Igor Jacmenjak |
| 1999 WM20-C | 4 | 0 | 1 | | | 3 | 10 | 22 | 8th | Bruno Bregant | Dalibor Franjkovic |
| 2000 WM20-D | 4 | 4 | 0 | | | 0 | 47 | 10 | 1st | Stanislav Nevesely | Marco Sertic |
| 2001 WM20-II | 4 | 0 | 1 | | | 3 | 13 | 28 | 6th | Miroslav Cerny | Sasa Belic |
| 2002 WM20-II | 4 | 1 | 1 | | | 2 | 15 | 24 | 4th | Vlado Kucera | Marko Lovrencic |
| 2003 WM20-I-A | 5 | 0 | 0 | | | 5 | 6 | 42 | 6th | Jan Potkonicky | Marko Ljubic |
| 2004 WM20-II-B | 5 | 2 | 0 | | | 3 | 18 | 18 | 3rd | Bruno Bregant | Tomislav Grozaj |
| 2005 WM20-II-B | 5 | 3 | 0 | | | 2 | 27 | 21 | 3rd | Milan Canky | *unknown* |
| 2006 WM20-II-B | 5 | 3 | 0 | | | 2 | 22 | 15 | 2nd | Bruno Bregant | Marko Tadic |
| 2007 WM20-II-A | 5 | 3 | | 0 | 1 | 1 | 23 | 16 | 3rd | Bruno Bregant | Janko Kucera |
| 2008 WM20-II-B | 5 | 3 | | 0 | 0 | 2 | 24 | 19 | 3rd | Bruno Bregant | Mario Sertic |
| 2009 WM20-II-B | 5 | 5 | | 0 | 0 | 0 | 34 | 15 | 1st | Danijel Kolombo | Niksa Trstenjak |
| 2010 WM20-I-B | 5 | 1 | | 0 | 0 | 4 | 14 | 51 | 5th | Danijel Kolombo | Niksa Trstenjak |
| 2011 WM20-I-B | 5 | 1 | | 0 | 1 | 3 | 16 | 35 | 5th | Danijel Kolombo | Borna Rendulic |
| 2012 WM20-I-B | 5 | 2 | | 0 | 0 | 3 | 12 | 25 | 5th | Danijel Kolombo | Nikola Senzel |

**U18 World Championship (Men)**

| Year Event | GP | W | T | | | L | GF | GA | Place | Coach | Captain |
|---|---|---|---|---|---|---|---|---|---|---|---|
| Year Event | GP | W | | OTW | OTL | L | GF | GA | Place | Coach | Captain |
| 2001 WM18-II | 4 | 1 | 0 | | | 3 | 12 | 32 | 6th | Bruno Bregant | Mario Novak |
| 2002 WM18-II | 5 | 1 | 0 | | | 4 | 14 | 39 | 7th | Bruno Bregant | Marco Ljubik |
| 2003 WM18-II-A | 5 | 2 | 1 | | | 2 | 38 | 20 | 3rd | Bruno Bregant | Kresimir Radovic |
| 2004 WM18-II-B | 5 | 3 | 0 | | | 2 | 17 | 14 | 3rd | Bruno Bregant | David Iveziqm |
| 2005 WM18-II-B | 5 | 2 | 1 | | | 2 | 17 | 18 | 3rd | Bruno Bregant | Jankov Kucera |
| 2006 WM18-II-B | 5 | 2 | 0 | | | 3 | 22 | 23 | 4th | Milan Canky | Mario Certic |
| 2007 WM18-II-B | 5 | 2 | | 0 | 2 | 1 | 24 | 19 | 3rd | Ludek Konopik | Lovro Siseta |
| 2008 WM18-II-A | 5 | 3 | | 0 | 0 | 2 | 32 | 24 | 3rd | Bruno Bregant | Niksa Trstenjak |
| 2009 WM18-II-A | 5 | 2 | | 0 | 0 | 3 | 23 | 27 | 4th | Danijel Kolombo | Dominik Kanaet |
| 2010 WM18-II-A | 5 | 1 | | 3 | 0 | 1 | 20 | 16 | 3rd | Enio Sacilotto | Igor Lazic |
| 2011 WM18-II-A | 5 | 3 | | 0 | 1 | 1 | 28 | 9 | 3rd | Danijel Kolombo | Ivo Kaleb |
| 2012 WM18-II-A | 5 | 1 | | 0 | 1 | 3 | 8 | 23 | 5th | Danijel Kolombo | Marko Sakic |

**Women's World Championship**

| Year Event | GP | W | OTW | OTL | L | GF | GA | Place | Coach | Captain |
|---|---|---|---|---|---|---|---|---|---|---|
| 2007 WW-IV | 5 | 5 | 0 | 0 | 0 | 41 | 6 | 1st | Genadij Gorbacev | Diana Kruselj Posavec |
| 2008 WW-III | 5 | 2 | 0 | 1 | 2 | 12 | 20 | 3rd | Genadij Gorbacev | Diana Kruselj Posavec |
| 2011 WW-III | 5 | 1 | 0 | 0 | 4 | 5 | 29 | 5th | Dusko Janjatovic | Diana Kruselj Posavec |
| 2012 WW-II-A | 5 | 0 | 0 | 1 | 4 | 4 | 27 | 6th | Marijo Budja | Diana Kruselj-Posavec |

*The Croatian U18 national team celebrates a goal against Korea. Photo: Patrick Nijdam.*

# Czech Republic (CZE)

*Jakub Kovar of the Czech Republic makes a save on Norway's Patrick Thoresen during a preliminary-round shootout at the 2012 IIHF World Championship. Photo: Andre Ringuette / HHOF-IIHF Images.*

**Joined IIHF: Bohemia, later Czechoslovakia, joined November 15, 1908; Czech Republic & Slovakia replaced Czechoslovakia on April 28, 1993**

Website: www.czehockey.cz
E-mail: office@czehockey.cz

Czech Ice Hockey Association
Prvniho pluku 621/8a
186 00 Prague 8
Czech Republic

Phone: +420 2 2 489 1470 • Fax: +420 2 3 333 6096

**World Ranking**

| MEN | | WOMEN | |
|---|---|---|---|
| 2012 | 3 | 2012 | 12 |
| 2011 | 5 | 2011 | 14 |
| 2010 | 5 | 2010 | 13 |
| 2009 | 6 | 2009 | 12 |
| 2008 | 5 | 2008 | 12 |
| 2007 | 4 | 2007 | 13 |
| 2006 | 2 | 2006 | 12 |
| 2005 | 3 | 2005 | 11 |
| 2004 | 4 | 2004 | 11 |

### Top Level Host History

World Championship (Men): 1933 (Prague), 1938 (Prague), 1947 (Prague), 1959 (Prague), 1972 (Prague), 1978 (Prague), 1985 (Prague), 1992 (Prague), 2004 (Prague, Ostrava), 2015 (Prague, Ostrava)
U20 World Championship: 1977 (Zvolen, Banska Bystrica), 1987 (Trencin, Topolcany), 1994 (Ostrava, Frydek-Mistek), 2002 (Pardubice, Hradec Kralove), 2008 (Pardubice, Liberec)
U18 World Championship (Men): 2005 (Ceske Budejovice, Plzen), 2012 (Brno, Znojmo, Breclav)
U18 Women's World Championship: 2012 (Zlin, Prerov)

### Czechoslovakia—Olympics, Men

(bold=top level)

| Year Event | GP | W | T | L | GF | GA | Place | Coach | Captain |
|---|---|---|---|---|---|---|---|---|---|
| **1920 OG-M** | **3** | **1** | **0** | **2** | **1** | **31** | **B** | **Adolf Dusek** | **Josef Sroubek** |
| **1924 OG-M** | **3** | **1** | **0** | **2** | **14** | **41** | **5th** | **Jaroslav Rezac** | **Josef Sroubek** |
| **1928 OG-M** | **2** | **1** | **0** | **1** | **3** | **5** | **6th** | **Frantisek Lorenz** | **Josef Sroubek** |
| **1936 OG-M** | **8** | **5** | **0** | **3** | **16** | **16** | **4th** | **Antonin Porges** | **Josef Malecek** |
| **1948 OG-M** | **8** | **7** | **1** | **0** | **80** | **18** | **S** | **Mike Buckna** | **Vladimir Zabrodsky** |
| **1952 OG-M** | **9** | **6** | **0** | **3** | **50** | **23** | **4th** | **Jiri Tozicka/Josef Herman** | **Karel Gut** |
| **1956 OG-M** | **7** | **3** | **0** | **4** | **32** | **36** | **5th** | **Vladimir Bouzek** | **Karel Gut** |
| **1960 OG-M** | **7** | **3** | **0** | **4** | **44** | **31** | **4th** | **Eduard Farda** | **Karel Gut** |
| **1964 OG-M** | **7** | **5** | **0** | **2** | **38** | **19** | **B** | **Jiri Anton** | **Vlastimil Bubnik** |
| **1968 OG-M** | **7** | **5** | **1** | **1** | **33** | **17** | **S** | **Vladimir Kostka/Jaroslav Pitner** | **Jozef Golonka** |
| **1972 OG-M** | **5** | **3** | **0** | **2** | **26** | **13** | **B** | **Vladimir Kostka/Jaroslav Pitner** | **Josef Cerny** |
| **1976 OG-M** | **5** | **3** | **0** | **2** | **24** | **10** | **S** | **Karel Gut/Jan Starsi** | **Frantisek Pospisil** |
| **1980 OG-M** | **6** | **4** | **0** | **2** | **40** | **17** | **5th** | **Karel Gut/Ludek Bukac** | **Bohuslav Ebermann** |
| **1984 OG-M** | **7** | **6** | **0** | **1** | **40** | **9** | **S** | **Vladimir Kostka** | **Frantisek Cernik** |
| **1988 OG-M** | **8** | **4** | **0** | **4** | **33** | **28** | **6th** | **Jan Starsi/Frantisek Pospisil** | **Dusan Pasek** |
| **1992 OG-M** | **8** | **6** | **0** | **2** | **36** | **21** | **B** | **Ivan Hlinka/Jaroslav Walter** | **Tomas Jelinek** |

### Czech Republic—Olympics, Men

(bold=top level)

| Year Event | GP | W | T | | L | GF | GA | Place | Coach | Captain |
|---|---|---|---|---|---|---|---|---|---|---|
| Year Event | GP | W | OTW | OTL | L | GF | GA | Place | Coach | Captain |
| **1994 OG-M** | **8** | **5** | **0** | | **3** | **30** | **18** | **5th** | **Ivan Hlinka** | **Otakar Janecky** |
| **1998 OG-M** | **6** | **5** | **0** | | **1** | **19** | **6** | **G** | **Ivan Hlinka/Slavomir Lener** | **Vladimir Ruzicka** |
| **2002 OG-M** | **4** | **1** | **1** | | **2** | **12** | **8** | **7th** | **Josef Augusta** | **Jaromir Jagr** |
| **2006 OG-M** | **8** | **4** | **0** | | **4** | **23** | **20** | **B** | **Alois Hadamczik** | **Robert Lang** |
| **2010 OG-M** | **5** | **2** | **1** | **0** | **2** | **13** | **11** | **7th** | **Vladimir Ruzicka** | **Patrik Elias** |

### Czechoslovakia—World Championship (Men)

(bold=top level)

| Year Event | GP | W | T | L | GF | GA | Place | Coach | Captain |
|---|---|---|---|---|---|---|---|---|---|
| **1930 WM** | **1** | **0** | **0** | **1** | **1** | **3** | **6th** | ***unknown*** | ***unknown*** |
| **1931 WM** | **7** | **3** | **1** | **3** | **10** | **7** | **5th** | ***unknown*** | ***unknown*** |
| **1933 WM** | **8** | **6** | **0** | **2** | **17** | **12** | **B** | ***unknown*** | ***unknown*** |
| **1934 WM** | **6** | **3** | **0** | **3** | **7** | **4** | **5th** | **Howie Grant** | ***unknown*** |
| **1935 WM** | **8** | **5** | **0** | **3** | **37** | **13** | **4th** | ***unknown*** | ***unknown*** |
| **1937 WM** | **8** | **4** | **2** | **2** | **22** | **9** | **6th** | ***unknown*** | **Josef Malecek** |
| **1938 WM** | **7** | **4** | **1** | **2** | **9** | **6** | **B** | **Mike Buckna** | **Josef Malecek** |
| **1939 WM** | **10** | **3** | **2** | **5** | **37** | **11** | **4th** | **Mike Buckna** | **Josef Malecek** |
| **1947 WM** | **7** | **6** | **0** | **1** | **85** | **10** | **G** | **Mike Buckna** | **Frantisek Pacalt (1)** |
| **1949 WM** | **7** | **5** | **0** | **2** | **42** | **12** | **G** | **Antonin Vodicka** | **Vladimir Zabrodsky** |
| **1954 WM** | **7** | **4** | **0** | **3** | **41** | **21** | **4th** | **Vladimir Bouzek/Jiri Anton** | **Karel Gut** |
| **1955 WM** | **8** | **5** | **1** | **2** | **63** | **22** | **B** | **Vladimir Bouzek** | **Karel Gut** |
| **1957 WM** | **7** | **5** | **1** | **1** | **66** | **9** | **B** | **Vladimir Kostka/Bohumil Rejda** | **Karel Gut** |
| **1958 WM** | **7** | **3** | **2** | **2** | **21** | **21** | **4th** | **Bohumil Rejda** | **Karel Gut** |
| **1959 WM** | **8** | **5** | **0** | **3** | **46** | **22** | **B** | **Vlastimil Sykora** | **Karel Gut** |
| **1961 WM** | **7** | **6** | **1** | **0** | **33** | **9** | **S** | **Vladimir Kostka/Jiri Andrst** | **Vlastimil Bubnik** |
| **1963 WM** | **7** | **5** | **1** | **1** | **41** | **16** | **B** | **Jiri Anton** | **Vlastimil Bubnik** |
| **1965 WM** | **7** | **6** | **0** | **1** | **43** | **10** | **S** | **Vladimir Bouzek/Vladimir Kostka** | **Frantisek Tikal** |
| **1966 WM** | **7** | **6** | **0** | **1** | **32** | **15** | **S** | **Vladimir Bouzek/Vladimir Kostka** | **Frantisek Tikal** |
| **1967 WM** | **7** | **3** | **2** | **2** | **29** | **18** | **4th** | **Jaroslav Pitner/Vladimir Kostka** | **Frantisek Tikal** |
| **1969 WM** | **10** | **8** | **0** | **2** | **40** | **20** | **B** | **Jaroslav Pitner/Vladimir Kostka** | **Jozef Golonka** |
| **1970 WM** | **10** | **5** | **1** | **4** | **47** | **30** | **B** | **Jaroslav Pitner/Vladimir Kostka** | **Josef Cerny** |

| 1971 WM | 10 | 7 | 1 | 2 | 44 | 20 | S | Jaroslav Pitner/Vladimir Kostka | Josef Cerny |
|---|---|---|---|---|---|---|---|---|---|
| 1972 WM | 10 | 9 | 1 | 0 | 72 | 16 | G | Jaroslav Pitner/Vladimir Kostka | Frantisek Pospisil |
| 1973 WM | 10 | 6 | 1 | 3 | 48 | 20 | B | Jaroslav Pitner/Vladimir Kostka | Frantisek Pospisil |
| 1974 WM | 10 | 7 | 0 | 3 | 57 | 20 | S | Karel Gut/Jan Starsi | Frantisek Pospisil |
| 1975 WM | 10 | 8 | 0 | 2 | 55 | 19 | S | Karel Gut/Jan Starsi | Frantisek Pospisil |
| 1976 WM | 10 | 9 | 1 | 0 | 67 | 14 | G | Karel Gut/Jan Starsi | Frantisek Pospisil |
| 1977 WM | 10 | 7 | 1 | 2 | 54 | 32 | G | Karel Gut/Jan Starsi | Frantisek Pospisil |
| 1978 WM | 10 | 9 | 0 | 1 | 54 | 21 | S | Karel Gut | Ivan Hlinka |
| 1979 WM | 8 | 4 | 2 | 2 | 32 | 32 | S | Karel Gut/Jan Starsi | Ivan Hlinka |
| 1981 WM | 8 | 4 | 2 | 2 | 37 | 26 | B | Ludek Bukac | Milan Novy |
| 1982 WM | 10 | 5 | 2 | 3 | 38 | 20 | S | Ludek Bukac | Milan Novy |
| 1983 WM | 10 | 6 | 2 | 2 | 40 | 21 | S | Ludek Bukac | Frantisek Cernik |
| 1985 WM | 10 | 7 | 1 | 2 | 48 | 22 | G | Ludek Bukac | Darius Rusnak |
| 1986 WM | 10 | 5 | 1 | 4 | 38 | 21 | 5th | Jan Starsi | Darius Rusnak (2) |
| 1987 WM | 10 | 6 | 2 | 2 | 32 | 24 | B | Jan Starsi | Dusan Pasek |
| 1989 WM | 10 | 4 | 2 | 2 | 38 | 21 | B | Pavel Wohl | Vladimir Ruzicka |
| 1990 WM | 10 | 5 | 1 | 4 | 36 | 30 | B | Pavel Wohl | Jiri Dolezal |
| 1991 WM | 10 | 4 | 0 | 6 | 28 | 27 | 6th | Stanislav Nevesely | Bedrich Scerban |
| 1992 WM | 8 | 6 | 0 | 2 | 33 | 13 | B | Ivan Hlinka | Tomas Jelinek |

(1) Vladimir Zabrodsky captain vs. Sweden (Feb. 22) and United States (Feb. 23)
(2) Vladimir Ruzicka captain vs. West Germany (Apr. 25)

### Czech Republic—World Championship (Men)

(bold=top level)

| Year Event | GP | W | T | | L | GF | GA | Place | Coach | Captain |
|---|---|---|---|---|---|---|---|---|---|---|
| Year Event | GP | W | OTW | OTL | L | GF | GA | Place | Coach | Captain |
| 1993 WM | 8 | 6 | 1 | | 1 | 33 | 10 | B | Ivan Hlinka | Otakar Janecky |
| 1994 WM | 6 | 1 | 2 | | 3 | 17 | 20 | 7th | Stanislav Nevesely | Otakar Janecky |
| 1995 WM | 8 | 4 | 0 | | 4 | 17 | 16 | 4th | Ludek Bukac | Jiri Kucera |
| 1996 WM | 8 | 7 | 1 | | 0 | 42 | 15 | G | Ludek Bukac | Robert Reichel |
| 1997 WM | 9 | 6 | 0 | | 3 | 30 | 20 | B | Ivan Hlinka/Slavomir Lener | Robert Reichel |
| 1998 WM | 9 | 6 | 2 | | 1 | 33 | 14 | B | Ivan Hlinka/Slavomir Lener | Robert Reichel (1) |
| 1999 WM | 10 | 7 | 0 | | 3 | 45 | 24 | G | Ivan Hlinka | Pavel Patera |
| 2000 WM | 9 | 8 | 0 | | 1 | 41 | 19 | G | Josef Augusta | Robert Reichel |
| 2001 WM | 9 | 8 | 1 | | 0 | 37 | 13 | G | Josef Augusta | Robert Reichel |
| 2002 WM | 7 | 6 | 0 | | 1 | 31 | 17 | 5th | Josef Augusta | Jaromir Jagr |
| 2003 WM | 9 | 6 | 1 | | 2 | 36 | 21 | 4th | Slavomir Lener | Robert Reichel |
| 2004 WM | 7 | 6 | 0 | | 1 | 28 | 8 | 5th | Slavomir Lener | Martin Straka |
| 2005 WM | 9 | 8 | 0 | | 1 | 26 | 9 | G | Vladimir Ruzicka | David Vyborny |
| 2006 WM | 9 | 5 | 2 | | 2 | 26 | 24 | S | Alois Hadamczik | David Vyborny |
| 2007 WM | 7 | 3 | 0 | 1 | 3 | 23 | 19 | 7th | Alois Hadamczik | David Vyborny |
| 2008 WM | 7 | 3 | 1 | 2 | 1 | 29 | 19 | 5th | Alois Hadamczik | Tomas Kaberle |
| 2009 WM | 7 | 4 | 0 | 0 | 3 | 26 | 14 | 6th | Vladimir Ruzicka | Marek Zidlicky |
| 2010 WM | 9 | 5 | 2 | 0 | 2 | 25 | 16 | G | Vladimir Ruzicka | Tomas Rolinek |
| 2011 WM | 9 | 8 | 0 | 0 | 1 | 36 | 18 | B | Alois Hadamczik | Tomas Rolinek |
| 2012 WM | 10 | 6 | 1 | 0 | 3 | 32 | 19 | B | Alois Hadamczik | Tomas Plekanec |

(1) Pavel Patera captain vs. Switzerland (May 15)

### IIHF-NHL Invitationals

(bold=top level)

| Year Event | GP | W | T | L | GF | GA | Place | Coach | Captain |
|---|---|---|---|---|---|---|---|---|---|
| 1976 CC | 7 | 3 | 1 | 3 | 23 | 20 | 2nd | Karel Gut/Jan Starsi | Frantisek Pospisil |
| 1981 CC | 6 | 2 | 2 | 2 | 22 | 17 | 3rd | Ludek Bukac | Milan Novy |
| 1984 CC | 5 | 0 | 1 | 4 | 10 | 21 | 6th | Ludek Bukac | *unknown* |
| 1987 CC | 5 | 2 | 1 | 2 | 12 | 15 | 4th | Jan Starsi | Dusan Pasek |
| 1991 CC | 5 | 1 | 0 | 4 | 11 | 18 | 6th | Stanislav Nevesely | Richard Smehlik |
| 1996 WCH | 3 | 0 | 0 | 3 | 4 | 17 | 8th | Ludek Bukac | Jaromir Jagr |
| 2004 WCH | 5 | 2 | 0 | 3 | 19 | 15 | 3rd | Vladimir Ruzicka | Robert Reichel |

### Czechoslovakia—U20 World Championship

(bold=top level)

| Year Event | GP | W | T | L | GF | GA | Place | Coach | Captain |
|---|---|---|---|---|---|---|---|---|---|
| 1977 WM20 | 7 | 4 | 1 | 2 | 32 | 17 | B | Ladislav Horsky | Jindrich Kokrment |
| 1978 WM20 | 6 | 2 | 0 | 4 | 21 | 32 | 4th | Ladislav Horsky | Ladislav Svozil |
| 1979 WM20 | 6 | 3 | 2 | 1 | 19 | 23 | S | Ladislav Horsky | Frantisek Cerny |
| 1980 WM20 | 5 | 2 | 0 | 3 | 28 | 27 | 4th | Jozef Golonka | Dusan Pasek |
| 1981 WM20 | 5 | 1 | 3 | 1 | 34 | 21 | 4th | Jozef Golonka | Jiri Dudacek (1) |
| 1982 WM20 | 7 | 5 | 1 | 1 | 44 | 17 | S | Frantisek Pospisil | *unknown* |
| 1983 WM20 | 7 | 5 | 1 | 1 | 43 | 22 | S | Frantisek Pospisil | Antonin Stavjana |
| 1984 WM20 | 7 | 5 | 0 | 2 | 51 | 24 | B | Frantisek Pospisil | *unknown* |
| 1985 WM20 | 7 | 5 | 2 | 0 | 32 | 13 | S | Frantisek Pospisil | Michal Pivonka |
| 1986 WM20 | 7 | 4 | 0 | 3 | 30 | 20 | 4th | Jiri Justra/Julius Cernicky | Michal Pivonka |
| 1987 WM20 | 7 | 5 | 0 | 2 | 36 | 23 | S | Jiri Justra | Ladislav Lubina |
| 1988 WM20 | 7 | 3 | 1 | 3 | 36 | 23 | 4th | Zdenek Uher | *unknown* |
| 1989 WM20 | 7 | 4 | 1 | 2 | 36 | 19 | B | Josef Vimmer | Zdeno Ciger |
| 1990 WM20 | 7 | 5 | 0 | 2 | 51 | 17 | B | Josef Vimmer | Robert Reichel |
| 1991 WM20 | 7 | 5 | 0 | 2 | 44 | 19 | B | Josef Vimmer | *unknown* |
| 1992 WM20 | 7 | 3 | 0 | 4 | 28 | 24 | 5th | Bedrich Brunclik | Roman Meluzin |
| 1993 WM20* | 7 | 4 | 1 | 2 | 38 | 27 | B | Jan Sterbak | Jan Vopat |

* played as Czech/Slovak Republics
(1) Eduard Uvira captain Dec. 28 vs. AUT

### Czech Republic—U20 World Championship

(bold=top level)

| Year Event | GP | W | T | | | L | GF | GA | Place | Coach | Captain |
|---|---|---|---|---|---|---|---|---|---|---|---|
| Year Event | GP | W | | OTW | OTL | L | GF | GA | Place | Coach | Captain |
| **1994 WM20** | 7 | 3 | 0 | | | 4 | 31 | 29 | 5th | Vladimir Vujtek | David Vyborny |
| **1995 WM20** | 7 | 3 | 0 | | | 4 | 43 | 26 | 6th | Jaroslav Jagr | Frantisek Ptacek |
| **1996 WM20** | 6 | 2 | 2 | | | 2 | 18 | 22 | 4th | Slavomir Lener | Robert Jindrich |
| **1997 WM20** | 7 | 2 | 2 | | | 3 | 19 | 19 | 4th | Vladimir Martinec | Jiri Burger |
| **1998 WM20** | 7 | 3 | 1 | | | 3 | 24 | 22 | 4th | Vladimir Martinec | Tomas Kaberle |
| **1999 WM20** | 6 | 3 | 0 | | | 3 | 26 | 18 | 7th | Vladimir Martinec | Petr Vala |
| **2000 WM20** | 7 | 5 | 2 | | | 0 | 23 | 11 | G | Jaroslav Holik | Milan Kraft |
| **2001 WM20** | 7 | 7 | 0 | | | 0 | 27 | 8 | G | Jaroslav Holik | Michal Sivek (1) |
| **2002 WM20** | 7 | 2 | 0 | | | 5 | 21 | 16 | 7th | Jaroslav Holik | Libor Ustrnul |
| **2003 WM20** | 6 | 2 | 1 | | | 3 | 11 | 13 | 6th | Jaroslav Holik | Lukas Chmelir |
| **2004 WM20** | 7 | 3 | 0 | | | 4 | 20 | 20 | 4th | Alois Hadamczik | Jiri Hudler |
| **2005 WM20** | 7 | 5 | 0 | | | 2 | 23 | 14 | B | Alois Hadamczik | Petr Vrana |
| **2006 WM20** | 6 | 2 | 0 | | | 4 | 16 | 19 | 6th | Radim Rulik | Ladislav Smid |
| **2007 WM20** | 6 | 3 | | 0 | 0 | 3 | 17 | 19 | 5th | Vladimir Bednar | Jakub Kindl |
| **2008 WM20** | 6 | 3 | | 0 | 0 | 3 | 18 | 16 | 5th | Miloslav Horava | Michal Frolik |
| **2009 WM20** | 6 | 2 | | 0 | 1 | 3 | 23 | 22 | 6th | Marek Sykora | David Stich |
| **2010 WM20** | 6 | 3 | | 0 | 0 | 3 | 28 | 24 | 7th | Jaromir Sindel | Michal Jordan |
| **2011 WM20** | 6 | 3 | | 0 | 0 | 3 | 18 | 25 | 7th | Miroslav Prerost | Jakub Jerabek |
| **2012 WM20** | 6 | 3 | | 0 | 1 | 2 | 18 | 15 | 5th | Miroslav Prerost | Tomas Nosek |

(1) Rostislav Klesla captain Dec. 29 vs. USA

### U18 World Championship (Men)

(bold=top level)

| Year Event | GP | W | T | | | L | GF | GA | Place | Coach | Captain |
|---|---|---|---|---|---|---|---|---|---|---|---|
| Year Event | GP | W | | OTW | OTL | L | GF | GA | Place | Coach | Captain |
| **1999 WM18** | 7 | 3 | 1 | | | 3 | 22 | 14 | 5th | Petr Misek | Michal Sivek |
| **2000 WM18** | 6 | 2 | 0 | | | 4 | 18 | 19 | 6th | Stanislav Berger | Vaclav Nedorost |
| **2001 WM18** | 7 | 3 | 0 | | | 4 | 22 | 28 | 4th | Jiri Kalous | Jiri Novotny |
| **2002 WM18** | 8 | 7 | 0 | | | 1 | 35 | 15 | B | Bretislav Kopriva | Jiri Hudler |
| **2003 WM18** | 6 | 2 | 1 | | | 3 | 17 | 16 | 6th | Karel Najman | Vojtech Polak |
| **2004 WM18** | 7 | 3 | 3 | | | 1 | 20 | 9 | B | Jaromir Sindel | Jakub Sindel |
| **2005 WM18** | 7 | 4 | 0 | | | 3 | 25 | 14 | 4th | Bretislav Kopriva | Jakub Vojta |
| **2006 WM18** | 7 | 4 | 0 | | | 3 | 19 | 16 | B | Martin Pesout | *unknown* |
| **2007 WM18** | 6 | 2 | | 1 | 0 | 3 | 16 | 18 | 9th | Martin Pesout | Vladimir Ruzicka |
| 2008 WM18-I-A | 5 | 5 | | 0 | 0 | 0 | 36 | 5 | 1st | Marek Sykora | *unknown* |
| **2009 WM18** | 6 | 1 | | 0 | 1 | 4 | 16 | 27 | 6th | Marek Sykora | Michal Poletin |
| **2010 WM18** | 6 | 2 | | 0 | 1 | 3 | 18 | 27 | 6th | Jiri Kopecky | Bohumil Jank |
| **2011 WM18** | 6 | 3 | | 0 | 0 | 3 | 14 | 20 | 8th | Jiri Solc | Marek Hrbas |
| **2012 WM18** | 6 | 2 | | 0 | 0 | 4 | 21 | 29 | 8th | Jiri Veber | Petr Sidlik |

### Women's World Championship

| Year Event | GP | W | T | | | L | GF | GA | Place | Coach | Captain |
|---|---|---|---|---|---|---|---|---|---|---|---|
| Year Event | GP | W | | OTW | OTL | L | GF | GA | Place | Coach | Captain |
| 1999 WW-B | 5 | 2 | 1 | | | 2 | 19 | 11 | 4th | Milan Koks | Hana Fidrmucova |
| 2000 WW-B | 5 | 1 | 1 | | | 3 | 13 | 12 | 7th | Milan Koks | Hana Fidrmucova |
| 2001 WW-I | 4 | 2 | 1 | | | 1 | 12 | 9 | 3rd | Jan Fidrmuc | *unknown* |
| 2003 WW-I | 5 | 3 | 0 | | | 2 | 15 | 22 | 3rd | Jan Fidrmuc | Draha Fialova |
| 2004 WW-I | 5 | 3 | 1 | | | 1 | 19 | 11 | 2nd | Jan Fidrmuc | Draha Fialova |
| 2005 WW-I | 5 | 2 | 1 | | | 2 | 13 | 9 | 3rd | Jan Fidrmuc | Draha Fialova |
| 2007 WW-I | 5 | 1 | | 1 | 0 | 3 | 12 | 16 | 5th | Jan Fidrmuc | Petra Zibarova |
| 2008 WW-I | 5 | 2 | | 1 | 0 | 2 | 12 | 11 | 3rd | Jan Fidrmuc | Eva Holesova |
| 2009 WW-I | 5 | 2 | | 0 | 0 | 3 | 17 | 18 | 5th | Karel Manhart | Alena Polenska |
| 2011 WW-II | 5 | 5 | | 0 | 0 | 0 | 23 | 2 | 1st | Karel Manhart | Alena Polenska |
| 2012 WW-I-A | 5 | 4 | | 0 | 0 | 1 | 19 | 8 | 1st | Karel Manhart | Alena Polenska |

### U18 Women's World Championship

(bold=top level)

| Year Event | GP | W | OTW | OTL | L | GF | GA | Place | Coach | Captain |
|---|---|---|---|---|---|---|---|---|---|---|
| **2008 WW18** | 5 | 3 | 0 | 0 | 2 | 14 | 26 | B | Tomas Vytisk | Tereza Stastna |
| **2009 WW18** | 5 | 1 | 0 | 1 | 3 | 9 | 45 | 4th | Tomas Vytisk | Katerina Mrazova |
| **2010 WW18** | 5 | 3 | 0 | 0 | 2 | 14 | 24 | 7th | Tomas Vytisk | Barbora Pekarkova |
| **2011 WW18** | 6 | 2 | 0 | 0 | 4 | 10 | 33 | 4th | Tomas Vytisk | Jana Fialova |
| **2012 WW18** | 5 | 1 | 0 | 0 | 4 | 8 | 24 | 6th | Tomas Vytisk | Marketa Vytiskova |

# Denmark (DEN)

Denmark maintained its top-pool participation for the eleventh straight year.
Photo: Andre Ringuette / HHOF-IIHF Images.

**Joined IIHF: April 27, 1946**

Website: www.ishockey.dk
E-mail: ishockey@ishockey.dk

Danmarks Ishockey Union
Fodboldens Hus
DBU Allé 1
DK-2605 Brøndby
Denmark

Phone: +45 4326 5464 • Fax: +45 4326 5460

**World Ranking**

| MEN | | WOMEN | |
|---|---|---|---|
| 2012 | 12 | 2012 | 19 |
| 2011 | 13 | 2011 | 21 |
| 2010 | 13 | 2010 | 22 |
| 2009 | 13 | 2009 | 19 |
| 2008 | 13 | 2008 | 18 |
| 2007 | 12 | 2007 | 17 |
| 2006 | 14 | 2006 | 17 |
| 2005 | 14 | 2005 | 14 |
| 2004 | 14 | 2004 | 16 |

**Top Level Host History** none

## World Championship (Men)

(bold=top level)

| Year Event | GP | W | T | OTW | OTL | L | GF | GA | Place | Coach | Captain |
|---|---|---|---|---|---|---|---|---|---|---|---|
| **1949 WM** | **5** | **0** | **0** | | | **5** | **4** | **90** | **10th** | **(1)** | **Jesper Hviid** |
| 1962 WM-B | 5 | 0 | 0 | | | 5 | 9 | 42 | 6th | Freddy Bond | Bjarne Carlsen |
| 1963 WM-C | 5 | 3 | 0 | | | 2 | 22 | 31 | 3rd | Ake Wilhelmsson | Guddi Hojbye |
| 1966 WM-C | 4 | 2 | 0 | | | 2 | 21 | 21 | 2nd | Ake Wilhelmsson | Guddi Hojbye |
| 1967 WM-C | 4 | 2 | 0 | | | 2 | 19 | 24 | 2nd | Ake Wilhelmsson | Michael Gautier |
| 1969 WM-C | 5 | 0 | 0 | | | 5 | 7 | 32 | 6th | Olle Stenar | Keld Bjerrum |
| 1970 WM-C | 6 | 1 | 1 | | | 4 | 20 | 22 | 5th | Olle Stenar | Sven Andersson |
| 1971 WM-C | 7 | 2 | 0 | | | 5 | 33 | 26 | 7th | Olle Stenar | Sven Andersson |
| 1972 WM-C | 6 | 1 | 0 | | | 5 | 11 | 33 | 6th | Lasse Lilja | Sven Andersson |
| 1973 WM-C | 7 | 0 | 2 | | | 5 | 22 | 58 | 7th | Kai Lassen | Henrik Fabricius |
| 1975 WM-C | 6 | 1 | 1 | | | 4 | 31 | 33 | 6th | Kai Lassen | Per Holten Moller |
| 1976 WM-C | 4 | 1 | 0 | | | 3 | 16 | 24 | 4th | Dan Hober | Per Holten Moller |
| 1977 WM-C | 6 | 5 | 1 | | | 0 | 61 | 15 | 2nd | Richard David | Nis Petersen |
| 1978 WM-C | 7 | 4 | 1 | | | 2 | 56 | 25 | 3th | Richard David | Per Holten Moller |
| 1979 WM-B | 6 | 1 | 0 | | | 5 | 13 | 32 | 8th | Richard David/Niels Nornberg | Per Holten Moller |
| 1981 WM-C | 7 | 3 | 1 | | | 3 | 36 | 27 | 4th | Jiri Justra | unknown |
| 1982 WM-C | 7 | 4 | 1 | | | 2 | 35 | 20 | 3rd | Pavel Zabojnik | Olaf Eller |
| 1983 WM-C | 7 | 4 | 0 | | | 3 | 24 | 26 | 4th | Pavel Zabojnik | Olaf Eller |
| 1985 WM-C | 7 | 3 | 0 | | | 4 | 16 | 23 | 5th | Bjorn Kinding | Olaf Eller |
| 1986 WM-C | 6 | 4 | 0 | | | 2 | 32 | 18 | 5th | Dana Barbin/Frank Barth | *unknown* |
| 1987 WM-C | 7 | 5 | 1 | | | 1 | 47 | 23 | 2nd | Dana Barbin/Frank Barth | Olaf Eller |
| 1989 WM-B | 7 | 0 | 0 | | | 7 | 9 | 44 | 8th | Richard David | Jesper Hille |
| 1990 WM-C | 8 | 7 | 0 | | | 1 | 55 | 14 | 2nd | Per Holten-Moller | Fredrik Akesson |
| 1991 WM-C | 8 | 7 | 1 | | | 0 | 71 | 13 | 1st | Per Holten-Moller | Fredrik Akesson |
| 1992 WM-B | 7 | 4 | 0 | | | 3 | 23 | 24 | 4th | Per Holten-Moller | Fredrik Akesson |
| 1993 WM-B | 7 | 4 | 0 | | | 3 | 38 | 24 | 4th | Per Holten-Moller | Fredrik Akesson |
| 1994 WM-B | 7 | 3 | 0 | | | 4 | 31 | 27 | 5th | Per Holten-Moller | Soren True |
| 1995 WM-B | 7 | 3 | 0 | | | 4 | 30 | 28 | 5th | Dan Hober | Soren True |
| 1996 WM-B | 7 | 1 | 1 | | | 5 | 14 | 32 | 6th | Dan Hober | Soren True |
| 1997 WM-B | 7 | 0 | 0 | | | 7 | 19 | 44 | 8th | Jim Brithen | Lars Oxholm |
| 1998 WM-B | 7 | 2 | 3 | | | 2 | 18 | 24 | 4th | Jim Brithen | Lars Oxholm |
| 1999 WM-B | 7 | 6 | 1 | | | 0 | 30 | 12 | 1st | Jim Brithen | Jesper Damgaard |
| 2000 WM-B | 7 | 2 | 2 | | | 3 | 22 | 19 | 5th | Jim Brithen | Jesper Damgaard |
| 2001 WM-I-A | 5 | 3 | 0 | | | 2 | 23 | 14 | 3rd | Jim Brithen | Jesper Damgaard |
| 2002 WM-I-B | 5 | 5 | 0 | | | 0 | 40 | 10 | 1st | Mikael Lundstrom | Jesper Damgaard |
| **2003 WM** | **6** | **1** | **1** | | | **4** | **13** | **27** | **11th** | **Mikael Lundstrom** | **Jesper Damgaard** |
| **2004 WM** | **6** | **1** | **0** | | | **5** | **10** | **36** | **12th** | **Mikael Lundstrom** | **Jesper Damgaard** |
| **2005 WM** | **6** | **2** | **0** | | | **4** | **12** | **20** | **14th** | **Mikael Lundstrom** | **Jesper Damgaard** |
| **2006 WM** | **6** | **2** | **1** | | | **3** | **17** | **19** | **13th** | **Mikael Lundstrom** | **Bo Nordby-Andersen** |
| **2007 WM** | **6** | **2** | | **0** | **0** | **4** | **15** | **29** | **10th** | **Mike Sirant** | **Jesper Damgaard** |
| **2008 WM** | **6** | **1** | | **1** | **0** | **4** | **15** | **28** | **12th** | **Mike Sirant** | **Jesper Damgaard** |
| **2009 WM** | **6** | **3** | | **0** | **1** | **2** | **18** | **19** | **13th** | **Per Backman** | **Jesper Damgaard** |
| **2010 WM** | **7** | **2** | | **1** | **0** | **4** | **17** | **17** | **8th** | **Per Backman** | **Jesper Damgaard** |
| **2011 WM** | **6** | **0** | | **2** | **0** | **4** | **12** | **24** | **11th** | **Per Backman** | **Morten Green** |
| **2012 WM** | **7** | **1** | | **0** | **1** | **5** | **13** | **23** | **13th** | **Per Backman** | **Morten Green** |

(1) Team had no formal coach but travelled with three team leaders—A.E. Nielsen, Helge Lund Christiansen, Henry Bloch

## U20 World Championship

(bold=top level)

| Year Event | GP | W | T | OTW | OTL | L | GF | GA | Place | Coach | Captain |
|---|---|---|---|---|---|---|---|---|---|---|---|
| 1979 WM20-B | 4 | 2 | 0 | | | 2 | 13 | 14 | 4th | Guido Radaelli | Keld Pedersen |
| 1980 WM20-B | 4 | 2 | 0 | | | 2 | 18 | 19 | 5th | Dusan Bosko | Olaf Eller |
| 1981 WM20-B | 5 | 3 | 0 | | | 2 | 22 | 22 | 5th | Benny Burakowski | Karsten Vestergaard |
| 1982 WM20-B | 4 | 2 | 0 | | | 2 | 22 | 18 | 4th | Benny Burakowski | Erik Andersen |
| 1983 WM20-B | 5 | 1 | 1 | | | 3 | 17 | 41 | 7th | Benny Burakowski | *unknown* |

| | | | | | | | | | | | |
|---|---|---|---|---|---|---|---|---|---|---|---|
| 1984 WM20-B | 5 | 0 | 0 | | | 5 | 9 | 29 | 8th | Bjorn Kinding | Jesper Hille |
| 1986 WM20-C | 5 | 3 | 2 | | | 0 | 28 | 16 | 2nd | Frits Nielsen | Per Steffensen |
| 1987 WM20-C | 5 | 4 | 0 | | | 1 | 44 | 24 | 2nd | Frits Nielsen | Per Steffensen |
| 1988 WM20-C | 7 | 7 | 0 | | | 0 | 59 | 11 | 1st | Frits Nielsen | Jan Kristensen |
| 1989 WM20-B | 7 | 1 | 1 | | | 5 | 25 | 42 | 7th | Frits Nielsen | Henrik Poul Pedersen |
| 1990 WM20-B | 7 | 2 | 2 | | | 3 | 26 | 31 | 4th | Carsten Nielsen | Thomas Kjogs |
| 1991 WM20-B | 7 | 1 | 0 | | | 6 | 22 | 45 | 8th | Carsetn Nilesen | Thomas Kjogs |
| 1992 WM20-C | 4 | 3 | 0 | | | 1 | 30 | 9 | 2nd | Carsten Nielsen | Peter Green |
| 1993 WM20-C | 4 | 2 | 1 | | | 1 | 26 | 18 | 2nd | Carsten Nielsen | *unknown* |
| 1994 WM20-C | 4 | 3 | 0 | | | 1 | 15 | 31 | 3rd | *unknown* | *unknown* |
| 1995 WM20-C-1 | 4 | 3 | 0 | | | 1 | 18 | 13 | 3rd | Stig Nielsen | Jesper Damgaard |
| 1996 WM20-C | 4 | 3 | 0 | | | 1 | 23 | 9 | 3rd | Adam Wozninski | Jesper Molby |
| 1997 WM20-C | 4 | 3 | 0 | | | 1 | 32 | 12 | 3rd | Adam Wozninski | Lasse Degn |
| 1998 WM20-C | 4 | 4 | 0 | | | 0 | 32 | 12 | 1st | Carsten Nielsen | Bo Nordby Andersen |
| 1999 WM20-B | 6 | 3 | 1 | | | 2 | 18 | 18 | 3rd | Niklas Frissel | Bo Nordby Andersen |
| 2000 WM20-B | 5 | 1 | 0 | | | 4 | 17 | 25 | 8th | Per Svensson | Lars Pedersen |
| 2001 WM20-II | 4 | 2 | 0 | | | 2 | 26 | 18 | 4th | Jiri Justra | Kasper Degn |
| 2002 WM20-II | 4 | 3 | 0 | | | 1 | 32 | 14 | 2nd | Stefan Bergkvist | Kasper Degn |
| 2003 WM20-I-B | 5 | 1 | 1 | | | 3 | 18 | 19 | 5th | Stefan Bergkvist | Frans Nielsen |
| 2004 WM20-I-A | 5 | 3 | 1 | | | 1 | 23 | 16 | 2nd | Stefan Bergkvist | Frans Schmidt Nielsen |
| 2005 WM20-I-B | 5 | 3 | 0 | | | 2 | 22 | 13 | 3rd | Stefan Bergkvist | Peter Regin |
| 2006 WM20-I-A | 5 | 3 | 1 | | | 1 | 20 | 17 | 2nd | Stefan Bergkvist | Peter Regin |
| 2007 WM20-I-A | 5 | 4 | | 0 | 0 | 1 | 23 | 11 | 1st | Ken Babey | Mads Christensen |
| **2008 WM20** | **6** | **0** | | **0** | **0** | **6** | **12** | **34** | **10th** | **Ken Babey** | **Nichlas Hardt** |
| 2009 WM20-I-B | 5 | 4 | | 0 | 0 | 1 | 16 | 13 | 2nd | Olaf Eller | Sune Hjulmand |
| 2010 WM20-I-A | 5 | 4 | | 0 | 0 | 1 | 21 | 9 | 2nd | Olaf Eller | Rasmus Nielsen |
| 2011 WM20-I-B | 5 | 4 | | 0 | 0 | 1 | 35 | 14 | 1st | Todd Bjorkstrand | Jesper Jensen |
| **2012 WM20** | **6** | **0** | | **0** | **2** | **4** | **10** | **44** | **10th** | **Todd Bjorkstrand** | **Jannik Christensen** |

### U18 World Championship (Men)

(bold=top level)

| Year Event | GP | W | T | | | L | GF | GA | Place | Coach | Captain |
|---|---|---|---|---|---|---|---|---|---|---|---|
| Year Event | GP | W | | OTW | OTL | L | GF | GA | Place | Coach | Captain |
| 1999 WM18-B | 5 | 2 | 1 | | | 2 | 23 | 22 | 4th | Leif Thomsen | Casper Degn |
| 2000 WM18-B | 5 | 2 | 0 | | | 3 | 22 | 24 | 5th | Niels Laursen | Casper Degn |
| 2001 WM18-I | 5 | 1 | 0 | | | 4 | 19 | 33 | 7th | Jan Otto Sorensen | Mikkel Nilesen |
| 2002 WM18-I | 4 | 2 | 0 | | | 2 | 12 | 13 | 6th | Henrik Christiansen | Mads Christensen |
| 2003 WM18-I-A | 5 | 4 | 1 | | | 0 | 31 | 12 | 1st | Leif Thomsen | David Petersson |
| **2004 WM18** | **6** | **2** | **0** | | | **4** | **16** | **18** | **8th** | **Leif Thomsen** | **Michael Eskesen** |
| **2005 WM18** | **6** | **0** | **0** | | | **6** | **8** | **30** | **10th** | **Leif Thomsen** | **Frederik Hentze** |
| 2006 WM18-I-B | 5 | 4 | 0 | | | 1 | 24 | 12 | 2nd | Leif Thomsen | Morten Poulsen |
| 2007 WM18-I-B | 5 | 5 | | 0 | 0 | 0 | 22 | 6 | 1st | Flemming Green | Frederik Storm |
| **2008 WM18** | **6** | **0** | | **0** | **0** | **6** | **7** | **35** | **10th** | **Flemming Green** | **Simon Dalsgaard** |
| 2009 WM18-I-B | 5 | 3 | | 0 | 0 | 1 | 15 | 7 | 2nd | Erik Petersen | Christian Nordentoft |
| 2010 WM18-I-A | 5 | 4 | | 0 | 0 | 1 | 34 | 14 | 2nd | Erik Petersen | Mads Aagaard |
| 2011 WM18-I-B | 5 | 4 | | 0 | 0 | 1 | 31 | 10 | 1st | Morten Hagen | Jonas Sass |
| **2012 WM18** | **6** | **0** | | **1** | **0** | **5** | **11** | **28** | **10th** | **Morten Hagen** | **Kristoffer Lauridsen** |

### Women's World Championship

(bold=top level)

| Year Event | GP | W | T | | | L | GF | GA | Place | Coach | Captain |
|---|---|---|---|---|---|---|---|---|---|---|---|
| Year Event | GP | W | | OTW | OTL | L | GF | GA | Place | Coach | Captain |
| **1992 WW** | **5** | **1** | **0** | | | **4** | **7** | **24** | **7th** | **Dion Christiansen** | **Katja Moesgaard** |
| 1999 WW-B | 5 | 2 | 0 | | | 3 | 17 | 17 | 6th | Bjorne Christiansen | Dorthe Schaffer |
| 2000 WW-B | 5 | 1 | 1 | | | 3 | 8 | 12 | 4th | Craig Chapman | Dorthe Schaffer |
| 2001 WW-I | 4 | 1 | 0 | | | 3 | 12 | 11 | 8th` | Bjorne Christiansen | *unknown* |
| 2003 WW-II | 5 | 3 | 1 | | | 1 | 16 | 13 | 2nd | Ed Maggiacomo | Bettina Johnsen |
| 2004 WW-II | 5 | 4 | 1 | | | 0 | 24 | 7 | 1st | Ed Maggiacomo | Bettina Johnsen |
| 2005 WW-I | 5 | 1 | 0 | | | 4 | 15 | 31 | 5th | Ed Maggiacomo | Marie Henriksen |
| 2007 WW-I | 5 | 0 | | 1 | 0 | 4 | 5 | 17 | 6th | Laura MacKenzie | Marie Henriksen |
| 2008 WW-II | 5 | 4 | | 0 | 0 | 1 | 25 | 7 | 2nd | Soren Gjerding | Dorthe Schaffer |
| 2009 WW-II | 5 | 0 | | 1 | 2 | 2 | 10 | 17 | 5th | Denis Larsen | Josephine Svendsen |
| 2011 WW-II | 5 | 3 | | 0 | 0 | 2 | 17 | 12 | 3rd | Denis Larsen | Marie Henriksen |
| 2012 WW-I-B | 5 | 4 | | 0 | 0 | 1 | 31 | 6 | 1st | Denis Larsen | Marie Henriksen |

# DPR Korea (North Korea—PRK)

The women's national team from DPR Korea celebrates a successful comeback and gains promotion to Division I, Group B. Photo: Denis Zelnik.

**Joined IIHF: August 8, 1963**
Website: n/a
E-mail: noc-kp@co.chesin.com

Ice Hockey Association of the DPR Korea
Kumsongdong 2
Mangyongdae District
P.O. Box 56
Pyongyang
DPR Korea

Phone: +850 2 181 11 ex. 8164 • Fax: +850 2 381 4410/4403

**World Ranking**

| MEN | | WOMEN | |
|---|---|---|---|
| 2012 | 45 | 2012 | 31 |
| 2011 | 45 | 2011 | 32 |
| 2010 | 43 | 2010 | 21 |
| 2009 | 43 | 2009 | 18 |
| 2008 | 44 | 2008 | 20 |
| 2007 | 44 | 2007 | 19 |
| 2006 | 36 | 2006 | 18 |
| 2005 | 36 | 2005 | 16 |
| 2004 | 37 | 2004 | 15 |

**Top Level Host History** none

**World Championship (Men)**

| Year Event | GP | W | T | | L | GF | GA | Place | Coach | Captain |
|---|---|---|---|---|---|---|---|---|---|---|
| Year Event | GP | W | OTW | OTL | L | GF | GA | Place | Coach | Captain |
| 1974 WM-C | 7 | 1 | 0 | | 6 | 12 | 64 | 8th | *unknown* | Jung Guil Jung |
| 1981 WM-C | 7 | 1 | 0 | | 6 | 18 | 66 | 7th | Nam Gil U/Pak Dok Song | *unknown* |
| 1983 WM-C | 7 | 1 | 0 | | 6 | 15 | 72 | 8th | Nam Gil U | Kim Chol Ho |
| 1985 WM-C | 7 | 1 | 0 | | 6 | 18 | 56 | 7th | C Chang Jun/C In Mun | O Gun Ung |
| 1986 WM-C | 6 | 1 | 1 | | 4 | 14 | 27 | 7th | Nam Gil U | *unknown* |
| 1987 WM-C | 7 | 2 | 0 | | 5 | 13 | 45 | 6th | Yong Song Mun | Song Jun Chu |
| 1989 WM-C | 7 | 2 | 0 | | 5 | 26 | 40 | 6th | Yong Song Mun | Song Jun Chu |
| 1990 WM-C | 8 | 4 | 0 | | 4 | 27 | 35 | 5th | Pak Dok Song | Song Jun Chu |
| 1991 WM-C | 8 | 2 | 1 | | 5 | 29 | 35 | 7th | Song Ik Kim | Won Son Ri |
| 1992 WM-C-A | 5 | 3 | 0 | | 2 | 25 | 28 | 2nd | Song Ik Kim | Won Son Ri |
| 1993 WM-C | 5 | 3 | 0 | | 2 | 30 | 26 | 6th | Chang Jun Jo | Won Son Ri |
| 2003 WM-II-B | 5 | 2 | 1 | | 2 | 16 | 13 | 4th | Chang Dok Pak | Pong Chol Yun |
| 2004 WM-II-B | 5 | 3 | 0 | | 2 | 22 | 20 | 3rd | Chang Dok Pak | Pong Chol Yun |
| 2005 WM-II-B | 5 | 2 | 1 | | 2 | 14 | 17 | 3rd | Chang Dok Pak | Kwang Chol Ho |
| 2006 WM-II-B | 5 | 2 | 0 | | 3 | 10 | 24 | 4th | Chang Dok Pak | Jong Uk Han |
| 2008 WM-III | 5 | 5 | 0 | 0 | 0 | 40 | 6 | 1st | Chang Dok Pak | Chung Song Song |
| 2009 WM-II-A | 5 | 0 | 0 | 0 | 5 | 11 | 40 | 6th | Chang Dok Pak | Myong Jin Jang |
| 2010 WM-III-B | 4 | 3 | 0 | 0 | 1 | 37 | 13 | 1st | *unknown* | *unknown* |
| 2011 WM-II-A | 5 | 0 | 0 | 0 | 5 | 0 | 25 | 6th | all games forfeited | |
| 2012 WM-III | 5 | 4 | 0 | 0 | 1 | 27 | 8 | 2nd | Chang Dok Pak | Chol Min Ri |

**U20 World Championship**

| Year Event | GP | W | T | | L | GF | GA | Place | Coach | Captain |
|---|---|---|---|---|---|---|---|---|---|---|
| Year Event | GP | W | OTW | OTL | L | GF | GA | Place | Coach | Captain |
| 1988 WM20-C | 7 | 1 | 2 | | 4 | 20 | 29 | 7th | Chol Ho Kim | In Kang |
| 1989 WM20-C | 4 | 2 | 0 | | 2 | 17 | 20 | 3rd | Chol Ho KIm | Guk Chan Son |
| 1990 WM20-C | 6 | 4 | 1 | | 1 | 27 | 14 | 2nd | Ubg Ryol Choe | *unknown* |
| 1991 WM20-C | 7 | 6 | 0 | | 1 | 50 | 18 | 1st | Chol Hyong Nam | Ho Chol Rim |
| 1992 WM20-B | 7 | 0 | 0 | | 7 | 13 | 54 | 8th | Chol Hyong Nam | Jae Guk Kim |
| 1993 WM20-C | 4 | 0 | 2 | | 2 | 11 | 28 | 6th | Chol Hyong Nam | Han Ung Gil |
| 2010 WM20-III | 5 | 2 | 1 | 1 | 1 | 27 | 22 | 3rd | Chol Ho Pak | Nam Hyok Kim |
| 2011 WM20-III | 6 | 4 | 0 | 0 | 2 | 37 | 22 | 3rd | Ki Chol Hong | Chol Hyok An |

**U18 World Championship (Men)**

| Year Event | GP | W | T | L | GF | GA | Place | Coach | Captain |
|---|---|---|---|---|---|---|---|---|---|
| 2001 WM18-I | 5 | 0 | 0 | 5 | 12 | 42 | 8th | Chang Dok Pak | Myong Hyok Yun |

**Women's World Championship**

| Year Event | GP | W | T | | L | GF | GA | Place | Coach | Captain |
|---|---|---|---|---|---|---|---|---|---|---|
| Year Event | GP | W | OTW | OTL | L | GF | GA | Place | Coach | Captain |
| 2001 WW-I | 4 | 1 | 1 | | 2 | 12 | 17 | 4th | Won Son Ri | *unknown* |
| 2003 WW-I | 5 | 0 | 0 | | 5 | 10 | 24 | 6th | Won Son Ri | Kum Sil Kwak |
| 2004 WW-I | 5 | 0 | 0 | | 5 | 5 | 29 | 6th | Won Son Ri | Kum Sil Kwak |
| 2005 WW-II | 5 | 2 | 0 | | 3 | 12 | 15 | 4th | Won Son Ri | *unknown* |
| 2007 WW-II | 5 | 3 | 0 | 1 | 1 | 22 | 7 | 3rd | Won Son Ri | Yong Sun Ri |
| 2008 WW-II | 5 | 3 | 0 | 0 | 2 | 21 | 10 | 3rd | Won Son Ri | In Hwa Kim |
| 2009 WW-II | 5 | 3 | 1 | 0 | 1 | 15 | 13 | 2nd | Won Son Ri | Sun Im Kim |
| 2011 WW-II | 5 | 0 | 0 | 0 | 5 | 5 | 25 | 6th | all games forfeited | |
| 2012 WW-II-A | 5 | 5 | 0 | 0 | 0 | 33 | 7 | 1st | Ki Chol Thae | Sok Hwa Kim |

# Estonia (EST)

*The Estonian U18 national team goalie makes a glove save against Iceland's Falur Gudnason. Photo: Filip Bakic.*

## Joined IIHF: February 17, 1935

(membership expired on April 27, 1946; re-joined as an independent nation on May 6, 1992)

Website: www.icehockey.ee
E-mail: ejhl@sport.ee

Estonian Ice Hockey Association
Pirita tee 12
10127 Tallinn
Estonia

Phone: +372 639 86 89 • Fax: +372 639 86 49

**World Ranking**

| MEN | WOMEN |
|---|---|
| 2012........26 | 2012 no rank |
| 2011........26 | 2011........37 |
| 2010........27 | 2010........33 |
| 2009........27 | 2009........32 |
| 2008........25 | 2008........32 |
| 2007........23 | 2007........32 |
| 2006........24 | |
| 2005........24 | |
| 2004........24 | |

**Top Level Host History** none

### World Championship (Men)

| Year Event | GP | W | T | | L | GF | GA | Place | Coach | Captain |
|---|---|---|---|---|---|---|---|---|---|---|
| Year Event | GP | W | OTW | OTL | L | GF | GA | Place | Coach | Captain |
| 1994 WM-C-B | 5 | 5 | 0 | | 0 | 66 | 1 | 1st | Alexander Romantsov | unknown |
| 1995 WM-C | 4 | 3 | 0 | | 1 | 22 | 16 | 4th | Alexander Romantsov | Vjatseslav Kulpin |
| 1996 WM-C | 7 | 3 | 1 | | 3 | 36 | 29 | 5th | Alexander Romantsov | Mihail Korsunov |
| 1997 WM-C | 5 | 1 | 3 | | 1 | 22 | 17 | 3rd | Alexander Romantsov | Olle Sildre |
| 1998 WM-B | 7 | 3 | 1 | | 3 | 15 | 19 | 3rd | Alexander Romantsov | Eduard Valiullin |
| 1999 WM-B | 7 | 2 | 1 | | 4 | 17 | 25 | 6th | Alexander Romantsov | Eduard Valiullin |
| 2000 WM-B | 7 | 3 | 0 | | 4 | 19 | 27 | 6th | Alexander Romantsov | Eduard Valiullin |
| 2001 WM-I-B | 5 | 0 | 1 | | 4 | 13 | 39 | 6th | Alexander Romantsov | Igor Ossipenkov |
| 2002 WM-II-A | 5 | 5 | 0 | | 0 | 74 | 7 | 1st | Vesa Surenkin | Oleg Puzanov |
| 2003 WM-I-B | 5 | 2 | 0 | | 3 | 12 | 20 | 3rd | Vesa Surenkin | Mikhail Kozlov |
| 2004 WM-I-B | 5 | 2 | 1 | | 2 | 26 | 23 | 4th | Yuri Tsepilov | Mikhail Kozlov |
| 2005 WM-I-B | 5 | 1 | 3 | | 1 | 16 | 15 | 4th | Yuri Tsepilov | Mikhail Kozlov |
| 2006 WM-I-B | 5 | 2 | 0 | | 3 | 19 | 21 | 4th | Yuri Tsepilov | Mikhail Kozlov |
| 2007 WM-I-A | 5 | 1 | 1 | 2 | 1 | 16 | 17 | 4th | Jorma Raisanen | Eduard Valiullin |
| 2008 WM-I-B | 5 | 0 | 0 | 1 | 4 | 9 | 21 | 6th | Rais Davletkildejev | Alexander Petrov |
| 2009 WM-II-A | 5 | 4 | 0 | 1 | 0 | 68 | 12 | 2nd | Rais Davletkildejev | Maxim Ivanov |
| 2010 WM-II-B | 5 | 5 | 0 | 0 | 0 | 62 | 5 | 1st | Ismo Lehkonen | Dmitri Suur |
| 2011 WM-I-B | 5 | 0 | 0 | 0 | 5 | 8 | 30 | 6th | Dmitrij Medvedev | Dmitri Suur |
| 2012 WM-II-A | 5 | 5 | 0 | 0 | 0 | 39 | 11 | 1st | Dmitri Medvedev | Dmitri Rodin |

### U20 World Championship

| Year Event | GP | W | T | | L | GF | GA | Place | Coach | Captain |
|---|---|---|---|---|---|---|---|---|---|---|
| Year Event | GP | W | OTW | OTL | L | GF | GA | Place | Coach | Captain |
| 1995 WM20-C2 | 5 | 2 | 2 | | 1 | 24 | 25 | 3rd | Vyacheslav Baranov | Dmitri Rodin |
| 1996 WM20-D | 3 | 2 | 0 | | 1 | 24 | 5 | 2nd | Rais Davletkildejev | *unknown* |
| 1997 WM20-D | 4 | 4 | 0 | | 0 | 46 | 11 | 1st | Rais Davletkildejev | Sergei Tulzakov |
| 1998 WM20-C | 4 | 1 | 0 | | 3 | 7 | 23 | 6th | Alexander Sljapnikov | Lauri Lahesalu |
| 1999 WM20-C | 4 | 2 | 1 | | 1 | 13 | 11 | 5th | Igor Hlobostin | Lauri Lahesalu |
| 2000 WM20-C | 4 | 0 | 1 | | 3 | 11 | 28 | 6th | Alexander Romantsov | Alexei Sustov |
| 2001 WM20-II | 4 | 0 | 0 | | 4 | 6 | 15 | 8th | Alexander Romantsov | Kirill Kolpakov |
| 2002 WM20-III | 4 | 4 | 0 | | 0 | 65 | 5 | 1st | Sergei Konosev | Kirill Kolpakov |
| 2003 WM20-II-A | 5 | 5 | 0 | | 0 | 62 | 8 | 1st | Sergei Konosev | Roman Razumovski |
| 2004 WM20-I-B | 5 | 1 | 0 | | 4 | 9 | 33 | 5th | Vladimir Tsiprovski | Sergei Svanov |
| 2005 WM20-I-B | 5 | 0 | 0 | | 5 | 6 | 41 | 6th | Vladimir Tsiprovski | Vassili Titarenko |
| 2006 WM20-II-B | 5 | 5 | 0 | | 0 | 46 | 8 | 1st | Juri Tsepilov | Anton Nekrasov |
| 2007 WM20-I-A | 5 | 0 | 0 | 0 | 5 | 5 | 25 | 6th | Rais Davletkildejev | Alexander Ossipov |
| 2008 WM20-II-B | 5 | 4 | 1 | 0 | 0 | 35 | 8 | 1st | Jorma Raisanen | Anton Jastrebov |
| 2009 WM20-I-A | 5 | 0 | 0 | 0 | 5 | 6 | 76 | 6th | Olle Sildre | Kaspar Karik |
| 2010 WM20-II-B | 5 | 0 | 0 | 3 | 2 | 15 | 24 | 5th | Sergei Konosev | Roman Andrejev |
| 2011 WM20-II-A | 5 | 1 | 0 | 0 | 4 | 16 | 29 | 5th | Simo Vehvilainen | Robert Rooba |
| 2012 WM20-II-B | 5 | 4 | 0 | 0 | 1 | 51 | 14 | 2nd | Juri Rooba | Robert Rooba |

### U18 World Championship (Men)

| Year Event | GP | W | T | | L | GF | GA | Place | Coach | Captain |
|---|---|---|---|---|---|---|---|---|---|---|
| Year Event | GP | W | OTW | OTL | L | GF | GA | Place | Coach | Captain |
| 2001 WM18-II | 4 | 2 | 1 | | 1 | 18 | 12 | 4th | Sergei Konosev | Alexei Perov |
| 2002 WM18-II | 5 | 2 | 0 | | 3 | 15 | 33 | 4th | Vladimir Tsiprovski | Pjetr Nikonov |
| 2003 WM18-II-A | 5 | 4 | 0 | | 1 | 49 | 8 | 2nd | Vladimir Tsiprovski | Alexander Kliznetsov |
| 2004 WM18-II-B | 5 | 4 | 0 | | 1 | 35 | 6 | 2nd | Rais Davletkildejev | Rene Lilloveer |
| 2005 WM18-II-A | 5 | 4 | 0 | | 1 | 25 | 17 | 2nd | Rais Davletkildajev | Ilya Urusev |
| 2006 WM18-II-A | 5 | 2 | 1 | | 2 | 13 | 20 | 3rd | Alexander Romantsov | Maxim Brandis |
| 2007 WM18-II-A | 5 | 2 | 1 | 0 | 2 | 21 | 23 | 3rd | Igor Ossipenkov | Andrei Lukin |
| 2008 WM18-II-B | 5 | 3 | 0 | 0 | 2 | 20 | 14 | 3rd | Hannu Jarvenpaa | Artjom Abramov |
| 2009 WM18-II-B | 5 | 3 | 1 | 0 | 1 | 22 | 14 | 2nd | Juri Rooba | Artur Fedoruk |
| 2010 WM18-II-A | 5 | 1 | 0 | 1 | 3 | 17 | 32 | 5th | Juri Rooba | Artur Fedoruk |
| 2011 WM18-II-A | 5 | 2 | 0 | 0 | 3 | 33 | 25 | 4th | Aleksei Bogdanov | Artjom Gornostajev |
| 2012 WM18-II-B | 5 | 4 | 1 | 0 | 0 | 32 | 17 | 1st | Aleksandr Sljapnikov | Pavel Kulakov |

### Women's World Championship

| Year Event | GP | W | OTW | OTL | L | GF | GA | Place | Coach | Captain |
|---|---|---|---|---|---|---|---|---|---|---|
| 2007 WW-IV | 5 | 1 | 1 | 0 | 3 | 21 | 30 | 4th | Sari Keisa | Kadri Reitalu |
| 2008 WW-IV | 5 | 2 | 0 | 0 | 3 | 11 | 17 | 4th | Veiko Suvaoja | Diana Kaareste |

# Finland (FIN)

*Finnish players applaud their fans after a game at the 2012 IIHF Ice Hockey World Championship in Helsinki. Photo: Jeff Vinnick / HHOF-IIHF Images.*

## Joined IIHF: February 10, 1928

Website: www.finhockey.fi
E-mail: office@finhockey.fi

The Finnish Ice Hockey Association
Mäkelänkatu 91
00610 Helsinki
Finland

Phone: +358 9 756 750 • Fax: +358 9 756 755 75

**World Ranking**

| MEN | | WOMEN | |
|---|---|---|---|
| 2012 | 2 | 2012 | 3 |
| 2011 | 2 | 2011 | 3 |
| 2010 | 4 | 2010 | 3 |
| 2009 | 4 | 2009 | 3 |
| 2008 | 4 | 2008 | 3 |
| 2007 | 3 | 2007 | 4 |
| 2006 | 4 | 2006 | 4 |
| 2005 | 7 | 2005 | 3 |
| 2004 | 5 | 2004 | 3 |

### Top Level Host History

World Championship (Men): 1965 (Tampere); 1974 (Helsinki); 1982 (Helsinki, Tampere); 1991 (Turku, Helsinki, Tampere); 1997 (Helsinki, Turku, Tampere); 2003 (Helsinki, Turku, Tampere), 2012 (Helsinki, with Stockholm), 2013 (Helsinki, with Stockholm)

U20 World Championship: 1980 (Helsinki, Vantaa); 1985 (Helsinki, Vantaa, Turku, Espoo); 1990 (Turku, Kerava, Helsinki, Kauniainen); 1998 (Helsinki, Hameenlinna); 2004 (Helsinki, Hameenlinna)

U18 World Championship (Men): 2001 (Heinola, Helsinki, Lahti), 2007 (Tampere, Rauma)

Women's World Championship: 1992 (Tampere); 1999 (Espoo, Vantaa), 2009 (Hameenlinna)

### Olympics, Men

(bold=top level)

| Year Event | GP | W | T | | | L | GF | GA | Place | Coach | Captain |
|---|---|---|---|---|---|---|---|---|---|---|---|
| Year Event | GP | W | | OTW | OTL | L | GF | GA | Place | Coach | Captain |
| **1952 OG-M** | **8** | **2** | **0** | | | **6** | **21** | **60** | **7th** | **Risto Lindroos** | **Aarne Honkavaara** |
| **1960 OG-M** | **6** | **3** | **1** | | | **2** | **55** | **23** | **7th** | **Joe Wirkkunen/Aarne Honkavaara** | **Yrjo Hakala** |
| **1964 OG-M** | **7** | **2** | **0** | | | **5** | **10** | **31** | **6th** | **Joe Wirkkunen/Aarne Honkavaara** | **Raimo Kilpio** |
| **1968 OG-M** | **7** | **3** | **1** | | | **3** | **17** | **23** | **5th** | **Gustav Bubnik** | **Matti Reunamaki** |
| **1972 OG-M** | **5** | **2** | **0** | | | **3** | **14** | **24** | **5th** | **Seppo Liitsola/Rauli Virtanen** | **Lasse Oksanen** |
| **1976 OG-M** | **5** | **2** | **0** | | | **3** | **19** | **18** | **4th** | **Seppo Liitsola** | **Seppo Lindstrom** |
| **1980 OG-M** | **7** | **3** | **1** | | | **3** | **31** | **25** | **4th** | **Kalevi Numminen** | **Tapio Levo (1)** |
| **1984 OG-M** | **6** | **2** | **1** | | | **3** | **31** | **26** | **6th** | **Alpo Suhonen/Reino Ruotsalainen** | **Anssi Melametsa** |
| **1988 OG-M** | **8** | **5** | **1** | | | **2** | **34** | **14** | **S** | **Pentti Matikainen/Hannu Jortikka** | **Timo Blomqvist** |
| **1992 OG-M** | **8** | **4** | **1** | | | **3** | **29** | **21** | **7th** | **Pentti Matikainen** | **Pekka Tuomisto** |
| **1994 OG-M** | **8** | **7** | **0** | | | **1** | **38** | **10** | **B** | **Curt Lindstrom/Hannu Aravirta** | **Timo Jutila** |
| **1998 OG-M** | **6** | **3** | **0** | | | **3** | **20** | **19** | **B** | **Hannu Aravirta** | **Saku Koivu** |
| **2002 OG-M** | **4** | **2** | **0** | | | **2** | **12** | **10** | **6th** | **Hannu Aravirta** | **Teemu Selanne** |
| **2006 OG-M** | **8** | **7** | **0** | | | **1** | **29** | **8** | **S** | **Erkka Westerlund** | **Saku Koivu** |
| **2010 OG-M** | **6** | **4** | | **0** | **0** | **2** | **18** | **13** | **B** | **Jukka Jalonen** | **Saku Koivu** |

(1) Jukka Porvari captain vs. Netherlands (Feb. 20), Sweden (Feb. 22), United States (Feb. 24)

### World Championship (Men)

(bold=top level)

| Year Event | GP | W | T | | | L | GF | GA | Place | Coach | Captain |
|---|---|---|---|---|---|---|---|---|---|---|---|
| Year Event | GP | W | | OTW | OTL | L | GF | GA | Place | Coach | Captain |
| **1939 WM** | **5** | **0** | **0** | | | **5** | **5** | **25** | **13th** | **Erkki Saarinen** | **Risto Tiitola** |
| **1949 WM** | **5** | **3** | **0** | | | **2** | **32** | **36** | **7th** | **Henry Kvist** | **Keijo Kuusela** |
| **1951 WM** | **6** | **1** | **0** | | | **5** | **15** | **37** | **7th** | **Risto Lindroos** | **Keijo Kuusela** |
| **1954 WM** | **7** | **1** | **1** | | | **5** | **12** | **52** | **6th** | **Risto Lindroos** | **Matti Rintakoski** |
| **1955 WM** | **8** | **1** | **0** | | | **7** | **16** | **72** | **9th** | **Aarne Honkavaara** | **Matti Rintakoski** |
| **1957 WM** | **7** | **4** | **0** | | | **3** | **28** | **33** | **4th** | **Aarne Honkavaara** | **Yrjo Hakala** |
| **1958 WM** | **7** | **1** | **1** | | | **5** | **9** | **51** | **6th** | **Aarne Honkavaara** | **Yrjo Hakala** |
| **1959 WM** | **8** | **1** | **1** | | | **6** | **20** | **44** | **6th** | **Aarne Honkavaara** | **Yrjo Hakala** |
| **1961 WM** | **7** | **1** | **1** | | | **5** | **19** | **43** | **7th** | **Derek Holmes** | **Erkki Koiso** |
| **1962 WM** | **7** | **3** | **0** | | | **4** | **32** | **42** | **4th** | **Joe Wirkkunen** | **Teppo Rastio** |
| **1963 WM** | **7** | **1** | **1** | | | **5** | **20** | **35** | **5th** | **Joe Wirkkunen/Aarne Honkavaara** | **Esko Luostarinen (1)** |
| **1965 WM** | **7** | **1** | **1** | | | **5** | **14** | **27** | **7th** | **Joe Wirkkunen/Aarne Honkavaara** | **Raimo Kilpio** |
| **1966 WM** | **7** | **2** | **0** | | | **5** | **18** | **43** | **7th** | **Joe Wirkkunen/Aarne Honkavaara** | **Lalli Partinen** |
| **1967 WM** | **7** | **2** | **1** | | | **4** | **14** | **24** | **6th** | **Gustav Bubnik** | **Matti Reunamaki** |
| **1969 WM** | **10** | **2** | **0** | | | **8** | **26** | **52** | **5th** | **Gustav Bubnik/Seppo Liitsola** | **Juhani Wahlsten** |
| **1970 WM** | **10** | **5** | **0** | | | **5** | **31** | **40** | **4th** | **Seppo Liitsola** | **Lasse Oksanen** |
| **1971 WM** | **10** | **4** | **1** | | | **5** | **31** | **42** | **4th** | **Seppo Liitsola/Rauli Virtanen** | **Lasse Oksanen** |
| **1972 WM** | **10** | **4** | **0** | | | **6** | **47** | **48** | **4th** | **Seppo Liitsola/Rauli Virtanen** | **Lasse Oksanen** |
| **1973 WM** | **10** | **3** | **1** | | | **6** | **24** | **39** | **4th** | **Len Lunde** | **Veli-Pekka Ketola** |

| | | | | | | | | | | | |
|---|---|---|---|---|---|---|---|---|---|---|---|
| 1974 WM | 10 | 4 | 2 | | | 4 | 34 | 39 | 4th | Kalevi Numminen/Raimo Maattanen | Veli-Pekka Ketola |
| 1975 WM | 10 | 5 | 0 | | | 5 | 36 | 34 | 4th | Seppo Liitsola | Seppo Lindstrom |
| 1976 WM | 10 | 2 | 4 | | | 4 | 35 | 41 | 5th | Seppo Liitsola/Lasse Heikkila | Lasse Oksanen (2) |
| 1977 WM | 10 | 5 | 0 | | | 5 | 45 | 43 | 5th | Lasse Heikkila | Pertti Koivulahti |
| 1978 WM | 10 | 2 | 2 | | | 6 | 37 | 44 | 7th | Kalevi Numminen | Seppo Repo |
| 1979 WM | 8 | 4 | 1 | | | 3 | 27 | 27 | 5th | Kalevi Numminen | Juhani Tamminen |
| 1981 WM | 8 | 3 | 2 | | | 3 | 37 | 32 | 6th | Kalevi Numminen | Juhani Tamminen |
| 1982 WM | 7 | 3 | 1 | | | 3 | 21 | 31 | 5th | Kalevi Numminen | Juhani Tamminen |
| 1983 WM | 10 | 2 | 2 | | | 6 | 30 | 40 | 7th | Alpo Suhonen | Pekka Rautakallio |
| 1985 WM | 10 | 4 | 2 | | | 4 | 39 | 33 | 5th | Alpo Suhonen | Anssi Melametsa |
| 1986 WM | 10 | 4 | 3 | | | 3 | 35 | 34 | 4th | Rauno Korpi | Kari Makkonen |
| 1987 WM | 10 | 5 | 1 | | | 4 | 32 | 34 | 5th | Rauno Korpi | Pekka Jarvela |
| 1989 WM | 10 | 5 | 1 | | | 4 | 35 | 27 | 5th | Pentti Matikainen | Timo Blomqvist |
| 1990 WM | 10 | 2 | 2 | | | 7 | 29 | 32 | 6th | Pentti Matikainen | Arto Ruotanen |
| 1991 WM | 10 | 6 | 1 | | | 3 | 35 | 21 | 5th | Pentti Matikainen | Hannu Virta (3) |
| 1992 WM | 8 | 7 | 0 | | | 1 | 41 | 18 | S | Pentti Matikainen | Pekka Tuomisto |
| 1993 WM | 6 | 2 | 1 | | | 3 | 8 | 12 | 7th | Pentti Matikainen | Timo Jutila |
| 1994 WM | 8 | 6 | 1 | | | 1 | 48 | 11 | S | Curt Lindstrom | Timo Jutila |
| 1995 WM | 8 | 6 | 1 | | | 1 | 34 | 15 | G | Curt Lindstrom | Timo Jutila |
| 1996 WM | 6 | 2 | 2 | | | 2 | 24 | 18 | 5th | Curt Lindstrom | Timo Jutila |
| 1997 WM | 8 | 5 | 0 | | | 3 | 29 | 15 | 5th | Curt Lindstrom | Timo Jutila |
| 1998 WM | 10 | 4 | 3 | | | 3 | 26 | 14 | S | Hannu Aravirta | Ville Peltonen |
| 1999 WM | 10 | 7 | 1 | | | 2 | 32 | 18 | S | Hannu Aravirta | Saku Koivu (4) |
| 2000 WM | 9 | 5 | 2 | | | 2 | 30 | 23 | B | Hannu Aravirta | Ville Peltonen |
| 2001 WM | 9 | 7 | 0 | | | 2 | 40 | 17 | S | Hannu Aravirta | Petteri Nummelin |
| 2002 WM | 9 | 6 | 0 | | | 3 | 28 | 15 | 4th | Hannu Aravirta | Petteri Nummelin (5) |
| 2003 WM | 7 | 3 | 1 | | | 3 | 35 | 16 | 5th | Hannu Aravirta | Saku Koivu |
| 2004 WM | 7 | 4 | 1 | | | 2 | 26 | 14 | 6th | Raimo Summanen | Olli Jokinen (6) |
| 2005 WM | 7 | 2 | 3 | | | 2 | 17 | 18 | 7th | Erkka Westerlund | Ville Peltonen (7) |
| 2006 WM | 9 | 6 | 1 | | | 2 | 31 | 13 | B | Erkka Westerlund | Ville Peltonen |
| 2007 WM | 9 | 4 | | 2 | 0 | 3 | 29 | 17 | S | Erkka Westerlund | Ville Peltonen |
| 2008 WM | 9 | 5 | | 2 | 0 | 2 | 26 | 20 | B | Doug Shedden | Ville Peltonen |
| 2009 WM | 7 | 3 | | 2 | 1 | 1 | 23 | 13 | 5th | Jukka Jalonen | Sami Kapanen |
| 2010 WM | 7 | 4 | | 0 | 1 | 2 | 13 | 15 | 6th | Jukka Jalonen | Sami Kapanen |
| 2011 WM | 9 | 5 | | 3 | 0 | 1 | 32 | 14 | G | Jukka Jalonen | Mikko Koivu |
| 2012 WM | 10 | 6 | | 0 | 0 | 4 | 28 | 25 | 4th | Jukka Jalonen | Mikko Koivu |

1) Raimo Kilpio captain vs. Soviet Union (Mar. 7)
(2) Esa Peltonen captain vs. West Germany (Apr. 10)
(3) Jari Kurri captain vs. Germany (Apr. 29), Switzerland (May 1), and Czechoslovakia (May 3)
(4) Teemu Selanne captain vs. Czech Republic (May 16)
(5) Raimo Helminen captain vs. Russia (May 9) and Sweden (May 10)
(6) Jere Karalahti captain vs. Sweden (Apr. 30)
(7) Olli Jokinen captain vs. CAN (May 8)

### IIHF-NHL Invitationals

(bold=top level)

| Year Event | GP | W | T | L | GF | GA | Place | Coach | Captain |
|---|---|---|---|---|---|---|---|---|---|
| 1976 CC | 5 | 1 | 0 | 4 | 16 | 42 | 6th | Lasse Heikkila | Veli-Pekka Ketola |
| 1981 CC | 5 | 0 | 1 | 4 | 6 | 31 | 6th | Kalevi Numminen | Veli-Pekka Ketola |
| 1987 CC | 5 | 0 | 0 | 5 | 9 | 23 | 6th | Rauno Korpi | Jari Kurri |
| 1991 CC | 6 | 2 | 1 | 3 | 13 | 20 | 3rd | Pentti Matikainen | Petri Skriko |
| 1996 WCH | 4 | 2 | 0 | 2 | 17 | 16 | 5th | Curt Lindstrom | Jari Kurri |
| 2004 WCH | 6 | 4 | 1 | 1 | 17 | 9 | 2nd | Raimo Summanen | Saku Koivu |

### U20 World Championship

(bold=top level)

| Year Event | GP | W | T | | L | GF | GA | Place | Coach | Captain |
|---|---|---|---|---|---|---|---|---|---|---|
| Year Event | GP | W | OTW | OTL | L | GF | GA | Place | Coach | Captain |
| 1977 WM20 | 7 | 4 | 0 | | 3 | 35 | 29 | 4th | Matti Vaisanen | Matti Forss |
| 1978 WM20 | 6 | 3 | 1 | | 2 | 45 | 25 | 6th | Matti Vaisanen | Risto Siltanen |
| 1979 WM20 | 6 | 2 | 0 | | 4 | 20 | 19 | 4th | Matti Reunamaki | Harri Tuohimaa |
| 1980 WM20 | 5 | 4 | 0 | | 1 | 29 | 8 | S | Olli Hietanen/Rauno Korpi | Kari Jalonen |
| 1981 WM20 | 5 | 3 | 1 | | 1 | 29 | 18 | S | Olli Hietanen | Tony Arima |
| 1982 WM20 | 7 | 5 | 0 | | 2 | 47 | 29 | B | Alpo Suhonen/Jorma Thusberg | Heikki Leime |
| 1983 WM20 | 7 | 3 | 0 | | 4 | 35 | 29 | 6th | Juhani Wahlsten | Simo Saarinen |
| 1984 WM20 | 7 | 6 | 0 | | 1 | 44 | 21 | S | Pentti Matikainen | Ville Siren |
| 1985 WM20 | 7 | 4 | 2 | | 1 | 42 | 20 | 4th | Pentti Matikainen | Mikko Makela |
| 1986 WM20 | 7 | 3 | 0 | | 4 | 31 | 23 | 6th | Hannu Jortikka | Ville Kentala |
| 1987 WM20 | 7 | 5 | 1 | | 1 | 45 | 23 | G | Hannu Jortikka | Janne Ojanen |
| 1988 WM20 | 7 | 5 | 1 | | 1 | 36 | 20 | B | Hannu Jortikka | Janne Ojanen |
| 1989 WM20 | 7 | 2 | 1 | | 4 | 29 | 37 | 6th | Erkka Westerlund | Petri Aaltonen |
| 1990 WM20 | 7 | 4 | 1 | | 2 | 32 | 21 | 4th | Hannu Jortikka | Mika Valila |
| 1991 WM20 | 7 | 3 | 1 | | 3 | 35 | 30 | 5th | Samu Kuitunen | Vesa Viitakoski |
| 1992 WM20 | 7 | 3 | 1 | | 3 | 21 | 21 | 4th | Jarmo Tolvanen | Jarkko Varvio |
| 1993 WM20 | 7 | 3 | 1 | | 3 | 31 | 20 | 5th | Jarmo Tolvanen | Janne Gronvall |
| 1994 WM20 | 7 | 4 | 0 | | 3 | 27 | 24 | 4th | Esko Nokelainen | Jukka Tiilikainen |
| 1995 WM20 | 7 | 3 | 1 | | 3 | 29 | 26 | 4th | Harri Rindell | Janne Niinimaa |
| 1996 WM20 | 6 | 2 | 0 | | 4 | 23 | 24 | 6th | Harri Rindell | Martti Jarventie (1) |
| 1997 WM20 | 6 | 4 | 0 | | 2 | 25 | 16 | 5th | Hannu Jortikka | Tommi Kallio |
| 1998 WM20 | 7 | 6 | 1 | | 0 | 35 | 13 | G | Hannu Kapanen | Pasi Petrilainen |
| 1999 WM20 | 6 | 3 | 0 | | 3 | 25 | 20 | 5th | Jukka Rautakorpi | Olli Ahonen |
| 2000 WM20 | 7 | 2 | 1 | | 4 | 19 | 19 | 7th | Hannu Kapanen | Riku Hahl |
| 2001 WM20 | 7 | 5 | 1 | | 1 | 22 | 10 | S | Kari Jalonen | Ville Hamalainen |
| 2002 WM20 | 7 | 5 | 0 | | 2 | 23 | 9 | B | Erkka Westerlund | Mikko Koivu |

| Year Event | GP | W | T | OTW | OTL | L | GF | GA | Place | Coach | Captain |
|---|---|---|---|---|---|---|---|---|---|---|---|
| 2003 WM20 | 7 | 4 | 1 | | | 2 | 22 | 15 | B | Erkka Westerlund | Tuomo Ruutu |
| 2004 WM20 | 7 | 5 | 0 | | | 2 | 26 | 12 | B | Hannu Aravirta | Joni Toykkala |
| 2005 WM20 | 6 | 3 | 0 | | | 3 | 14 | 21 | 5th | Risto Dufva | Arsi Piispanen |
| 2006 WM20 | 7 | 4 | 0 | | | 3 | 24 | 19 | B | Hannu Aravirta | Petteri Wirtanen |
| 2007 WM20 | 6 | 2 | | 0 | 0 | 4 | 18 | 23 | 6th | Jarmo Tolvanen | Leo Komarov |
| 2008 WM20 | 6 | 1 | | 1 | 0 | 4 | 19 | 24 | 6th | Jukka Rautakorpi | Nico Aaltonen |
| 2009 WM20 | 6 | 3 | | 0 | 1 | 2 | 20 | 14 | 7th | Jukka Rautakorpi | Tomi Sallinen |
| 2010 WM20 | 6 | 3 | | 0 | 0 | 3 | 21 | 22 | 5th | Hannu Jortikka | Jyri Niemi |
| 2011 WM20 | 6 | 3 | | 0 | 3 | 0 | 22 | 11 | 6th | Lauri Marjamaki | Sami Vatanen |
| 2012 WM20 | 7 | 4 | | 0 | 1 | 2 | 29 | 22 | 4th | Raimo Helminen | Mikael Granlund |

(1) Arto Kuki captain Dec. 26 vs. SUI

### U18 World Championship (Men)

(bold=top level)

| Year Event | GP | W | T | | | L | GF | GA | Place | Coach | Captain |
|---|---|---|---|---|---|---|---|---|---|---|---|
| Year Event | GP | W | | OTW | OTL | L | GF | GA | Place | Coach | Captain |
| 1999 WM18 | 7 | 5 | 1 | | | 1 | 27 | 14 | G | Jouko Lukkarila | Tuukka Mantyla |
| 2000 WM18 | 7 | 6 | 0 | | | 1 | 29 | 12 | G | Timo Tuomi | Harri Suutarinen |
| 2001 WM18 | 6 | 5 | 0 | | | 1 | 21 | 8 | B | Pekka Hamalainen | Mikko Koivu |
| 2002 WM18 | 8 | 5 | 0 | | | 3 | 30 | 16 | 4th | Jukka-Pekka Annala | Joni Toykkala |
| 2003 WM18 | 6 | 2 | 2 | | | 2 | 21 | 21 | 7th | Mika Saarinen | Ville Mantymaa |
| 2004 WM18 | 6 | 3 | 2 | | | 1 | 23 | 11 | 7th | Harri Ahola | Petteri Wirtanen |
| 2005 WM18 | 6 | 3 | 0 | | | 3 | 13 | 17 | 7th | Juha Pajouja | Jesse Joensuu |
| 2006 WM18 | 6 | 4 | 1 | | | 1 | 16 | 12 | S | Rauli Urama | Jan Mikael Juutilainen |
| 2007 WM18 | 6 | 3 | | 0 | 1 | 2 | 16 | 16 | 7th | Harri Laurila | Tomi Sallinen |
| 2008 WM18 | 6 | 2 | | 0 | 0 | 4 | 19 | 21 | 6th | Jukka-Pekka Annala | Joonas Rask |
| 2009 WM18 | 6 | 3 | | 1 | 0 | 2 | 32 | 17 | B | Mika Marttila | Sami Vatanen |
| 2010 WM18 | 6 | 4 | | 1 | 0 | 1 | 26 | 17 | B | Sakari Pietila | Teemu Rautiainen |
| 2011 WM18 | 6 | 3 | | 0 | 0 | 3 | 24 | 20 | 5th | Jukka Rautakorpi | Markus Granlund |
| 2012 WM18 | 7 | 4 | | 0 | 1 | 2 | 30 | 21 | 4th | Jussi Tapola | Mikko Vainonen |

### Olympics, Women

(bold=top level)

| Year Event | GP | W | T | | | L | GF | GA | Place | Coach | Captain |
|---|---|---|---|---|---|---|---|---|---|---|---|
| Year Event | GP | W | | OTW | OTL | L | GF | GA | Place | Coach | Captain |
| 1998 OG-W | 6 | 4 | 0 | | | 2 | 31 | 11 | B | Rauno Korpi | Marianne Ihalainen |
| 2002 OG-W | 5 | 2 | 0 | | | 3 | 11 | 15 | 4th | Jouko Lukkarila | Sari Fisk |
| 2006 OG-W | 5 | 2 | 0 | | | 3 | 10 | 17 | 4th | Hannu Saintula | Sari Fisk |
| 2010 OG-W | 5 | 2 | | 1 | 0 | 2 | 10 | 15 | B | Pekka Hamalainen | Emma Laaksonen |

### Women's World Championship

(bold=top level)

| Year Event | GP | W | T | | | L | GF | GA | Place | Coach | Captain |
|---|---|---|---|---|---|---|---|---|---|---|---|
| Year Event | GP | W | | OTW | OTL | L | GF | GA | Place | Coach | Captain |
| 1990 WW | 5 | 3 | 0 | | | 2 | 35 | 15 | B | Jouko Oystila | Anne Haanpaa |
| 1992 WW | 5 | 3 | 0 | | | 2 | 34 | 19 | B | Jouko Oystila | Marianne Ihalainen |
| 1994 WW | 5 | 3 | 0 | | | 2 | 40 | 8 | B | Jorma Valtonen | Marianne Ihalainen |
| 1997 WW | 5 | 3 | 1 | | | 1 | 22 | 5 | B | Rauno Korpi | Marianne Ihalainen |
| 1999 WW | 5 | 3 | 0 | | | 2 | 25 | 6 | B | Kari Savolainen | Katja Lehto |
| 2000 WW | 5 | 3 | 0 | | | 2 | 23 | 10 | B | Hannu Saintula | Marianne Ihalainen |
| 2001 WW | 5 | 2 | 0 | | | 3 | 13 | 27 | 4th | Jouko Lukkarila | Sari Fisk |
| 2004 WW | 5 | 4 | 1 | | | 0 | 12 | 5 | B | Hannu Saintula | Sari Fisk |
| 2005 WW | 5 | 2 | 0 | | | 3 | 13 | 18 | 4th | Hannu Saintula | Sari Fisk |
| 2007 WW | 5 | 1 | | 1 | 0 | 3 | 5 | 10 | 4 | Hannu Saintula | Emma Laaksonen |
| 2008 WW | 5 | 2 | | 2 | 0 | 1 | 16 | 8 | B | Hannu Saintula | Emma Laaksonen |
| 2009 WW | 5 | 3 | | 0 | 0 | 2 | 17 | 19 | B | Hannu Saintula | Emma Laaksonen |
| 2011 WW | 6 | 2 | | 1 | 1 | 2 | 15 | 14 | B | Pekka Hamalainen | Karoliina Rantamaki |
| 2012 WW | 6 | 2 | | 0 | 0 | 4 | 12 | 30 | 4th | Pekka Hamalainen | Jenni Hiirikoski |

### U18 Women's World Championship

(bold=top level)

| Year Event | GP | W | OTW | OTL | L | GF | GA | Place | Coach | Captain |
|---|---|---|---|---|---|---|---|---|---|---|
| 2008 WW18 | 5 | 1 | 0 | 0 | 4 | 13 | 32 | 6th | Seppo Karjalainen | Tea Villila |
| 2009 WW18 | 5 | 1 | 2 | 0 | 2 | 9 | 13 | 5th | Pekka Hamalainen | Tea Villila |
| 2010 WW18 | 5 | 2 | 0 | 1 | 2 | 11 | 12 | 5th | Harri Laurila | Milla Heikkinen |
| 2011 WW18 | 6 | 2 | 1 | 0 | 3 | 11 | 16 | B | Juuso Toivola | Isa Rahunen |
| 2012 WW18 | 5 | 2 | 0 | 1 | 2 | 12 | 17 | 5th | Juuso Toivola | Anna Kilponen |

# France (FRA)

France's Stéphane da Costa, Alexandre Gaudreau Rouleau, and Damien Fleury celebrate a goal in their win against Switzerland at the 2012 World Championship. Photo: Jeff Vinnick / HHOF-IIHF Images.

## Joined IIHF: October 20, 1908

Website: www.hockeyfrance.com
E-mail: e.ropert@ffhg.eu

Federation Française de Hockey sur Glace
36 bis, rue Roger Salengro
92 130 Issy Les Moulineaux
France

Phone: +33 1 41 33 0340 • Fax: +33 1 41 33 0344

**World Ranking**

| MEN | | WOMEN | |
|---|---|---|---|
| 2012 | 14 | 2012 | 16 |
| 2011 | 14 | 2011 | 16 |
| 2010 | 15 | 2010 | 14 |
| 2009 | 14 | 2009 | 13 |
| 2008 | 18 | 2008 | 11 |
| 2007 | 19 | 2007 | 12 |
| 2006 | 19 | 2006 | 14 |
| 2005 | 17 | 2005 | 12 |
| 2004 | 18 | 2004 | 13 |

### Top Level Host History

Olympics: 1924 (Chamonix); 1968 (Grenoble); 1992 (Albertville)
World Championship (Men): 1930 (Chamonix); 1951 (Paris)

### Olympics, Men

(bold=top level)

| Year Event | GP | W | T | L | GF | GA | Place | Coach | Captain |
|---|---|---|---|---|---|---|---|---|---|
| **1920 OG-M** | **1** | **0** | **0** | **1** | **0** | **4** | **6th** | **Joseph Garon** | **Alfred de Rauch** |
| **1924 OG-M** | **3** | **1** | **0** | **2** | **9** | **42** | **5th** | **Robert Lacroix** | **Alfred de Rauch** |
| **1928 OG-M** | **3** | **2** | **0** | **1** | **6** | **5** | **5th** | ***unknown*** | **Alfred de Rauch** |
| **1936 OG-M** | **3** | **1** | **0** | **2** | **4** | **7** | **9th** | ***unknown*** | **Jacques Lacarriere** |
| **1968 OG-M** | **5** | **0** | **0** | **5** | **9** | **32** | **14th** | **Pete LaLiberte** | **Claude Blanchard** |
| **1988 OG-M** | **6** | **2** | **0** | **4** | **18** | **47** | **11th** | **Kjell Larsson** | **Andre Peloffy** |
| **1992 OG-M** | **8** | **2** | **0** | **6** | **20** | **35** | **8th** | **Kjell Larsson** | **Antoine Richer** |
| **1994 OG-M** | **7** | **1** | **1** | **5** | **18** | **34** | **10th** | **Kjell Larsson** | **Antoine Richer (1)** |
| **1998 OG-M** | **4** | **2** | **0** | **2** | **10** | **9** | **11th** | **Herb Brooks** | **Jean-Philippe Lemoine** |
| **2002 OG-M** | **4** | **0** | **1** | **3** | **7** | **17** | **14th** | **Heikki Leime** | **Arnaud Briand (2)** |

(1) Denis Perez captain vs. Slovakia (Feb. 21)
(2) Philippe Bozon captain vs. Slovakia (Feb. 14)

### World Championship (Men)

(bold=top level)

| Year Event | GP | W | T | L | GF | GA | Place | Coach | Captain |
|---|---|---|---|---|---|---|---|---|---|
| Year Event | GP | W | OTW OTL | L | GF | GA | Place | Coach | Captain |
| **1930 WM** | **2** | **1** | **0** | **1** | **5** | **3** | **6th** | ***unknown*** | **Albert Hassler** |
| **1931 WM** | **5** | **1** | **0** | **4** | **9** | **15** | **9th** | ***unknown*** | **Albert Hassler** |
| **1934 WM** | **5** | **1** | **0** | **4** | **4** | **19** | **11th** | ***unknown*** | **Albert Hassler** |
| **1935 WM** | **7** | **2** | **1** | **4** | **9** | **16** | **7th** | ***unknown*** | **Albert Hassler** |
| **1937 WM** | **9** | **2** | **0** | **7** | **12** | **54** | **7th** | ***unknown*** | **Jacques Lacarriere** |
| **1950 WM** | **4** | **0** | **0** | **4** | **3** | **31** | **9th** | **Louis Bourdereau** | **Jacques de Mezieres** |
| 1951 WM-B | 5 | 4 | 0 | 1 | 35 | 15 | 2nd | Jacques Perreault | Paul Revoyaz |
| 1953 WM-B | 5 | 0 | 0 | 5 | 10 | 36 | 5th | Jacques Perreault | Paul Revoyaz |
| 1961 WM-C | 5 | 4 | 0 | 1 | 34 | 16 | 2nd | Paul-Emile Provost | *unknown* |
| 1962 WM-B | 5 | 3 | 0 | 2 | 35 | 25 | 3rd | Pete Laliberte | *unknown* |
| 1963 WM-B | 6 | 1 | 0 | 5 | 14 | 38 | 6th | Pete Laliberte/Raynald Lacroix | Calixte Pianfetti |
| 1967 WM-C | 4 | 1 | 0 | 3 | 18 | 21 | 4th | Pierre Lacoste | Philippe Lacarriere |
| 1970 WM-C | 6 | 4 | 0 | 2 | 29 | 15 | 3rd | Pete Laliberte | Gerard Faucomprez |
| 1971 WM-C | 7 | 6 | 0 | 1 | 49 | 20 | 2nd | Pete Laliberte | Gilbert Itzicsohn |
| 1973 WM-C | 7 | 3 | 0 | 4 | 23 | 29 | 6th | Pete Laliberte | Jean-Claude Guennelon |
| 1974 WM-C | 7 | 4 | 0 | 3 | 37 | 25 | 5th | Pete Laliberte | Joel Godeau |
| 1975 WM-C | 6 | 2 | 2 | 2 | 32 | 22 | 5th | Pete Laliberte | Gilbert Itzicsohn |
| 1976 WM-C | 4 | 2 | 0 | 2 | 14 | 18 | 3rd | Pete Laliberte | Jean Vassieux |
| 1977 WM-C | 6 | 3 | 0 | 3 | 37 | 24 | 4th | Pete Laliberte | Jean Vassieux |
| 1978 WM-C | 7 | 3 | 0 | 4 | 46 | 39 | 6th | Pete Laliberte | Jean Vassieux |
| 1979 WM-C | 7 | 5 | 0 | 2 | 59 | 27 | 3rd | Zdenek Blaha | Jean Vassieux |
| 1981 WM-C | 7 | 3 | 0 | 4 | 48 | 36 | 5th | Pete Laliberte | Andre Peloffy |
| 1982 WM-C | 7 | 4 | 0 | 3 | 47 | 30 | 4th | Jacques Tremblay | Jean Le Blond |
| 1983 WM-C | 7 | 3 | 1 | 3 | 41 | 25 | 5th | Jacques Tremblay | Jean Le Blond |
| 1985 WM-C | 7 | 6 | 1 | 0 | 54 | 13 | 1st | Patrick Francheterre/Paul Lang | Andre Peloffy |
| 1986 WM-B | 7 | 3 | 0 | 4 | 22 | 25 | 4th | Patrick Francheterre/Paul Lang | Andre Peloffy |
| 1987 WM-B | 7 | 4 | 1 | 2 | 37 | 26 | 4th | Kjell Larsson | Andre Peloffy |
| 1989 WM-B | 7 | 4 | 2 | 1 | 29 | 18 | 3rd | Kjell Larsson | Antoine Richer |
| 1990 WM-B | 7 | 4 | 1 | 2 | 19 | 20 | 4th | Kjell Larsson | Antoine Richer |
| 1991 WM-B | 7 | 5 | 0 | 2 | 28 | 18 | 3rd | Kjell Larsson | Antoine Richer |
| **1992 WM** | **6** | **1** | **0** | **5** | **11** | **23** | **11th** | **Kjell Larsson** | **Antoine Richer** |
| **1993 WM** | **6** | **1** | **0** | **5** | **13** | **25** | **10th** | **Jean-Claude Sozzi** | **Antoine Richer** |
| **1994 WM** | **5** | **1** | **0** | **4** | **8** | **25** | **10th** | **Kjell Larsson** | **Denis Perez** |
| **1995 WM** | **6** | **3** | **0** | **3** | **14** | **16** | **8th** | **Juhani Tamminen** | **Antoine Richer** |
| **1996 WM** | **7** | **2** | **0** | **5** | **24** | **32** | **11th** | **Juhani Tamminen** | **Antoine Richer** |
| **1997 WM** | **8** | **2** | **0** | **6** | **20** | **43** | **10th** | **Dany Dube** | **Jean-Philippe Lemoine (1)** |
| **1998 WM** | **3** | **1** | **0** | **2** | **5** | **12** | **13th** | **Herb Brooks** | **Jean-Philippe Lemoine** |

| Year Event | GP | W | T | OTW | OTL | L | GF | GA | Place | Coach | Captain |
|---|---|---|---|---|---|---|---|---|---|---|---|
| **1999 WM** | **3** | **0** | **0** | | | **3** | **6** | **18** | **15th** | **Mikael Lundstrom** | **Jean-Philippe Lemoine** |
| **2000 WM** | **6** | **2** | **1** | | | **3** | **19** | **21** | **15th** | **Stephane Sabourin** | **Arnaud Briand** |
| 2001 WM-I-A | 5 | 3 | 1 | | | 1 | 20 | 10 | 2nd | Heikki Leime | Denis Perez |
| 2002 WM-I-A | 5 | 4 | 0 | | | 1 | 27 | 6 | 2nd | Heikki Leime | Arnaud Briand |
| 2003 WM-I-B | 5 | 4 | 1 | | | 0 | 21 | 5 | 1st | Heikki Leime | Arnaud Briand |
| **2004 WM** | **6** | **0** | **1** | | | **5** | **4** | **28** | **16th** | **Heikki Leime** | **Arnaud Briand** |
| 2005 WM-I-B | 5 | 3 | 1 | | | 1 | 16 | 9 | 2nd | Dave Henderson | Laurent Meunier (2) |
| 2006 WM-I-A | 5 | 3 | 1 | | | 1 | 17 | 9 | 2nd | Dave Henderson | Laurent Meunier |
| 2007 WM I-A | 5 | 4 | | 0 | 1 | 0 | 24 | 7 | 1st | Dave Henderson | Laurent Meunier |
| **2008 WM** | **5** | **2** | | **0** | **0** | **3** | **11** | **22** | **14th** | **Dave Henderson** | **Laurent Meunier** |
| **2009 WM** | **6** | **1** | | **0** | **0** | **5** | **10** | **28** | **12th** | **Dave Henderson** | **Laurent Meunier** |
| **2010 WM** | **6** | **2** | | **0** | **0** | **4** | **12** | **22** | **14th** | **Dave Henderson** | **Laurent Meunier** |
| **2011 WM** | **6** | **0** | | **1** | **1** | **4** | **7** | **23** | **12th** | **Dave Henderson** | **Laurent Meunier** |
| **2012 WM** | **7** | **3** | | **0** | **0** | **4** | **21** | **32** | **9th** | **Dave Henderson** | **Laurent Meunier** |

(1) Philippe Bozon captain vs. Latvia (May 8)
(2) Jean-Francois Bonnard captain Apr. 18 vs. EST

### U20 World Championship

(bold=top level)

| Year Event | GP | W | T | | | L | GF | GA | Place | Coach | Captain |
|---|---|---|---|---|---|---|---|---|---|---|---|
| **Year Event** | **GP** | **W** | | **OTW** | **OTL** | **L** | **GF** | **GA** | **Place** | **Coach** | **Captain** |
| 1979 WM20-B | 4 | 3 | 0 | | | 1 | 26 | 13 | 2nd | Pete Laliberte | Jean-Paul Collard |
| 1980 WM20-B | 4 | 1 | 0 | | | 3 | 19 | 31 | 7th | Pete Laliberte | Aram Kevorkian |
| 1981 WM20-B | 5 | 0 | 1 | | | 4 | 20 | 35 | 8th | Thierry Monier | Jean Stinco |
| 1982 WM20-B | 4 | 2 | 0 | | | 2 | 18 | 16 | 5th | Thierry Monier/Alain Bozon | Jean-Christophe Lerondeau |
| 1983 WM20-B | 5 | 2 | 1 | | | 2 | 32 | 21 | 5th | Thierry Monier/Alain Bozon | Christophe Ville |
| 1984 WM20-B | 5 | 2 | 0 | | | 3 | 28 | 25 | 6th | Alain Vinard | Laurent Lecomte |
| 1985 WM20-B | 7 | 1 | 1 | | | 5 | 19 | 42 | 8th | Alain Vinard/Alain Bozon | *unknown* |
| 1986 WM20-C | 5 | 4 | 1 | | | 0 | 51 | 13 | 1st | Alain Bozon/Daniel Grando | *unknown* |
| 1987 WM20-B | 5 | 3 | 1 | | | 1 | 21 | 16 | 5th | Alain Bozon/Daniel Grando | *unknown* |
| 1988 WM20-B | 7 | 4 | 0 | | | 3 | 31 | 36 | 5th | Alain Bozon/Daniel Grando | *unknown* |
| 1989 WM20-B | 7 | 1 | 1 | | | 5 | 23 | 31 | 6th | Alain Bozon | *unknown* |
| 1990 WM20-B | 7 | 3 | 0 | | | 4 | 39 | 30 | 5th | Daniel Grando | Bruno Maynard |
| 1991 WM20-B | 7 | 4 | 2 | | | 1 | 42 | 19 | 3rd | Thierry Monier | Bruno Maynard |
| 1992 WM20-B | 7 | 5 | 0 | | | 2 | 31 | 15 | 4th | Jean-Claude Sozzi | Stephane Arcangeloni |
| 1993 WM20-B | 7 | 3 | 0 | | | 4 | 26 | 30 | 5th | Thierry Monier | Fabrice Huot-Marchand |
| 1994 WM20-B | 7 | 3 | 1 | | | 3 | 23 | 23 | 3rd | Thierry Monier | Anthony Mortas |
| 1995 WM20-B | 7 | 4 | 0 | | | 3 | 24 | 15 | 4th | Thierry Monier | Greg Dubois |
| 1996 WM20-B | 5 | 3 | 0 | | | 2 | 18 | 14 | 7th | Marc Djelloul | Mathieu Guidoux |
| 1997 WM20-B | 7 | 4 | 2 | | | 1 | 22 | 16 | 3rd | Marc Djelloul | *unknown* |
| 1998 WM20-B | 6 | 1 | 1 | | | 4 | 20 | 29 | 6th | Marc Djelloul | Vincent Bachet |
| 1999 WM20-B | 5 | 3 | 0 | | | 2 | 22 | 16 | 7th | Marc Djelloul | Laurent Meunier |
| 2000 WM20-B | 5 | 2 | 1 | | | 2 | 15 | 21 | 3rd | Dave Henderson | Sebastien Dermigny |
| 2001 WM20-I | 5 | 3 | 0 | | | 2 | 9 | 15 | 1st | Dave Henderson | Sebastien Dermigny |
| **2002 WM20** | **6** | **1** | **0** | | | **5** | **6** | **42** | **10th** | **Dave Henderson** | **Wilfried Molmy** |
| 2003 WM20-I-A | 5 | 2 | 0 | | | 3 | 17 | 13 | 4th | Dave Henderson | Ghislain Folcke |
| 2004 WM20-I-B | 5 | 3 | 0 | | | 2 | 22 | 16 | 3rd | Dave Henderson | Xavier Lasalle |
| 2005 WM20-I-A | 5 | 2 | 0 | | | 3 | 18 | 19 | 4th | Christer Eriksson | Pierre-Edouard Bellemare |
| 2006 WM20-I-A | 5 | 1 | 2 | | | 2 | 8 | 7 | 4th | Dany Gelinas | Geoffrey Paillet |
| 2007 WM20-I-B | 5 | 2 | | 0 | 1 | 2 | 15 | 17 | 4th | Patrick Rolland | Pierre Bennett |
| 2008 WM20-I-B | 5 | 1 | | 0 | 0 | 4 | 14 | 29 | 5th | Patrick Rolland | Romain Orset |
| 2009 WM20-I-A | 5 | 3 | | 0 | 0 | 2 | 33 | 17 | 3rd | Patrick Rolland | Antoine Roussel |
| 2010 WM20-I-A | 5 | 1 | | 0 | 0 | 4 | 9 | 16 | 6th | Philippe Bozon | Jason Crossman |
| 2011 WM20-II-A | 5 | 5 | | 0 | 0 | 0 | 49 | 5 | 1st | Lionel Charrier | Robin Gaborit |
| 2012 WM20-I-B | 5 | 4 | | 0 | 0 | 1 | 19 | 6 | 1st | Lionel Charrier | Anthony Rech |

### U18 World Championship (Men)

| Year Event | GP | W | T | | | L | GF | GA | Place | Coach | Captain |
|---|---|---|---|---|---|---|---|---|---|---|---|
| **Year Event** | **GP** | **W** | | **OTW** | **OTL** | **L** | **GF** | **GA** | **Place** | **Coach** | **Captain** |
| 1999 WM18-B | 5 | 3 | 1 | | | 1 | 24 | 12 | 6th | Marc Peythieu | Sebastien Dermigny |
| 2000 WM18-B | 5 | 0 | 0 | | | 5 | 12 | 25 | 8th | Marc Peythieu | Geoffroy Bessard du Parc |
| 2001 WM18-II | 4 | 2 | 1 | | | 1 | 23 | 9 | 2nd | Marc Peythieu | Elie Marcos |
| 2002 WM18-II | 5 | 5 | 0 | | | 0 | 73 | 2 | 1st | Marc Peythieu | Geffroy Thibault |
| 2003 WM18-I-B | 5 | 2 | 0 | | | 3 | 20 | 17 | 4th | Bernard Combe | Pierre-Eduard Bellemare |
| 2004 WM18-I-B | 5 | 1 | 1 | | | 3 | 14 | 13 | 5th | James Tibbets | Johann Morant |
| 2005 WM18-I-A | 5 | 2 | 0 | | | 3 | 11 | 14 | 4th | Lionel Charrier | Quentin Pepy |
| 2006 WM18-I-A | 5 | 1 | 2 | | | 2 | 20 | 26 | 4th | Lionel Charrier | Julien Correia |
| 2007 WM18-I-A | 5 | 0 | | 1 | 0 | 4 | 13 | 40 | 6th | Lionel Charrier | Remy Rimann |
| 2008 WM18-II-A | 5 | 5 | | 0 | 0 | 0 | 53 | 4 | 1st | Lionel Charrier | Timotey Perez |
| 2009 WM18-I-B | 5 | 1 | | 1 | 1 | 2 | 15 | 17 | 4th | Lionel Charrier | Victor Barbero |
| 2010 WM18-I-A | 5 | 3 | | 0 | 0 | 2 | 21 | 21 | 4th | Lionel Charrier | Romain Gutierrez |
| 2011 WM18-I-B | 5 | 2 | | 1 | 0 | 2 | 19 | 11 | 3rd | Sebastien Roujon | Marius Serer |
| 2012 WM18-I-A | 5 | 1 | | 1 | 0 | 3 | 12 | 19 | 4th | Sebastien Roujon | Nicolas Leclerc |

### Women's World Championship

| Year Event | GP | W | T | | | L | GF | GA | Place | Coach | Captain |
|---|---|---|---|---|---|---|---|---|---|---|---|
| **Year Event** | **GP** | **W** | | **OTW** | **OTL** | **L** | **GF** | **GA** | **Place** | **Coach** | **Captain** |
| 1999 WW-B | 5 | 3 | 1 | | | 1 | 21 | 10 | 3rd | Patrick Adin | Gwenola Personne |
| 2000 WW-B | 5 | 2 | 2 | | | 1 | 16 | 13 | 5th | James Tibbetts | Christine Duchamp |
| 2001 WW-I | 4 | 2 | 1 | | | 1 | 9 | 9 | 5th | Stephane Sabourin | *unknown* |
| 2003 WW-I | 5 | 2 | 1 | | | 2 | 9 | 9 | 4th | Christer Eriksson | Christine Duchamp |
| 2004 WW-I | 5 | 1 | 2 | | | 2 | 14 | 13 | 4th | Renaud Jacquin | Christine Duchamp |
| 2005 WW-I | 5 | 2 | 1 | | | 2 | 18 | 19 | 4th | Renuad Jacquin | Christine Duchamp |
| 2007 WW-I | 5 | 1 | | 1 | 2 | 1 | 10 | 17 | 3rd | Christine Duchamp | Laetitia Philippon |

| | | | | | | | | | | |
|---|---|---|---|---|---|---|---|---|---|---|
| 2008 WW-I | 5 | 2 | 0 | 0 | 3 | 7 | 12 | 4th | Christine Duchamp | Deborah Iszraelewicz |
| 2009 WW-I | 5 | 0 | 0 | 0 | 5 | 10 | 24 | 6th | Christine Duchamp | Marion Allemoz |
| 2011 WW-II | 5 | 4 | 0 | 0 | 1 | 13 | 5 | 2nd | Christine Duchamp | Marion Allemoz |
| 2012 WW-I-B | 5 | 4 | 0 | 0 | 1 | 22 | 9 | 3rd | Christine Duchamp | Marion Allemoz |

**U18 Women's World Championship**

| Year Event | GP | W | OTW | OTL | L | GF | GA | Place | Coach | Captain |
|---|---|---|---|---|---|---|---|---|---|---|
| 2009 WW18-I | 4 | 2 | 1 | 0 | 1 | 9 | 7 | 2nd | Nolwenn Rousselle | Athena Locatelli |
| 2010 WW18-I | 5 | 4 | 0 | 0 | 1 | 16 | 15 | 2nd | Nolwenn Rousselle | Betty Jouanny |
| 2011 WW18-I | 5 | 1 | 0 | 0 | 4 | 5 | 25 | 5th | Nolwenn Rousselle | Morgane Rihet |

*France's Yohann Auvitu gets a high five from teammates during the 2012 IIHF World Championship. Photo: Jeff Vinnick / HHOF-IIHF Images.*

# FYR Macedonia (MKD)

*FYR Macedonia competed in the InLine Hockey Qualification for the second straight time in 2012. Photo: Tzveti Krasteva.*

**Joined IIHF: October 4, 2001 (Associate Member)**

E-mail: macedoniahockey@yahoo.com

SSFM Macedonian Ice Hockey Federation
Sports Hall K K Rabotnicki
City Park Post Box 5
1000 Skopje
Macedonia

Phone: +389 2 3220 750
Fax: +389 2 3220 750

**Top Level Host History** none

# Georgia (GEO)

*Georgia and Armenia played an exhibition game in Yerevan, Armenia, in 2010. Photo: GIHF.*

**Joined IIHF: May 8, 2009 (Associate Member)**

Website: n/a
E-mail: sandro@una.ge

2 Dolidze Street
0171 Tbilisi
Georgia

Phone: +995 77 44 99 88

**Top Level Host History** none

# Germany (GER)/East Germany (GDR)/West Germany (FRG)

Germany's Jessica Ujcik is surrounded by her teammates as the players celebrate a win over the Czech Republic at the 2012 IIHF Ice Hockey U18 World Women's Championship. Photo: Phillip MacCallum / HHOF-IIHF Images.

### Germany (GER) joined IIHF: September 19, 1909

(expelled 1920, rejoined January 11, 1926; expelled April 27, 1946; resumed play as Germany on October 3, 1990)

### East Germany (GDR) joined IIHF: June 9, 1954

(membership withdrawn on August 31, 1990)

### West Germany (FRG) joined IIHF: March 10, 1951

(ceased independant membership after reunification with East Germany)

Website: www.deb-online.de
E-mail: info@deb-online.de

Deutscher Eishockey Bund
Betzenweg 34
D-81247 München
Germany

Phone: +49 89 81 82 0 • Fax: +49 89 81 82 36

**World Ranking**

| MEN | | WOMEN | |
|---|---|---|---|
| 2012 | 10 | 2012 | 8 |
| 2011 | 8 | 2011 | 10 |
| 2010 | 9 | 2010 | 11 |
| 2009 | 12 | 2009 | 10 |
| 2008 | 10 | 2008 | 7 |
| 2007 | 11 | 2007 | 5 |
| 2006 | 12 | 2006 | 5 |
| 2005 | 10 | 2005 | 5 |
| 2004 | 8 | 2004 | 6 |

**Top Level Host History**

Olympics: 1936 (Garmisch-Partenkirchen)
World Championship (Men): 1930 (Berlin), 1975 (Munich, Dusseldorf), 1983 (Munich, Dusseldorf, Dortmund), 1993 (Munich, Dortmund), 1995 (Dusseldorf, Dortmund, Krefeld, Cologne), 2001 (Hanover, Cologne, Nuremberg), 2010 (Cologne, Mannheim, Gelsenkirchen)
U20 World Championship: 1981 (Landsberg, Augsburg, Fussen, Kaufbeuren, Kempten, Oberstdorf), 1992 (Fussen, Kaufbeuren)
U18 World Championship (Men): 1999 (Fussen, Kaufbeuren), 2011 (Crimmitschau, Dresden)
U18 Women's World Championship: 2009 (Fussen)

**Olympics, Men**

(bold=top level)

| Year Event | GP | W | T | | L | GF | GA | Place | Coach | Captain |
|---|---|---|---|---|---|---|---|---|---|---|
| Year Event | GP | W | OTW | OTL | L | GF | GA | Place | Coach | Captain |
| 1928 OG-M | 2 | 0 | 1 | | 1 | 0 | 1 | 10th | Erich Romer | Walter Sachs |
| 1932 OG-M | 6 | 2 | 0 | | 4 | 7 | 26 | B | Erich Romer | Gustav Jaenecke |
| 1936 OG-M | 6 | 3 | 1 | | 2 | 10 | 9 | 5th | Val Hoffinger | Rudi Ball |
| 1952 OG-M^ | 8 | 1 | 1 | | 6 | 21 | 53 | 8th | Joe Aitken | *unknown* |
| 1956 OG-M^ | 8 | 1 | 2 | | 5 | 15 | 41 | 6th | Frank Trottier | *unknown* |
| 1960 OG-M^ | 7 | 1 | 0 | | 6 | 9 | 54 | 6th | Karl Wild | *unknown* |
| 1964 OG-M^ | 7 | 2 | 0 | | 5 | 13 | 49 | 7th | Xaver Unsinn** | *unknown* |
| 1968 OG-M* | 7 | 0 | 0 | | 7 | 13 | 48 | 8th | Rudi Schmieder | Joachim Ziesche |
| 1968 OG-M^ | 7 | 1 | 0 | | 6 | 13 | 39 | 7th | Ed Riegle | Heinz Bader |
| 1972 OG-M^ | 4 | 3 | 0 | | 1 | 22 | 10 | 7th | Gerhard Kiessling | Alois Schloder |
| 1976 OG-M^ | 5 | 2 | 0 | | 3 | 21 | 24 | B | Xaver Unsinn | *unknown* |
| 1980 OG-M^ | 5 | 1 | 0 | | 4 | 21 | 30 | 10th | Hans Rampf | Rainer Philipp |
| 1984 OG-M^ | 6 | 4 | 1 | | 1 | 34 | 21 | 5th | Xaver Unsinn | Erich Kuhnhackl |
| 1988 OG-M^ | 8 | 4 | 0 | | 4 | 22 | 31 | 5th | Xaver Unsinn | *unknown* |
| 1992 OG-M | 8 | 3 | 0 | | 5 | 22 | 24 | 6th | Ludek Bukac | Gerd Truntschka (1) |
| 1994 OG-M | 8 | 4 | 0 | | 4 | 20 | 26 | 7th | Ludek Bukac/Franz Reindl | Uli Hiemer (2) |
| 1998 OG-M | 4 | 3 | 0 | | 1 | 11 | 11 | 9th | George Kingston | Dieter Hegen (3) |
| 2002 OG-M | 7 | 3 | 0 | | 4 | 15 | 26 | 8th | Hans Zach | Jurgen Rumrich |
| 2006 OG-M | 5 | 0 | 2 | | 3 | 7 | 16 | 10th | Uwe Krupp | Stefan Ustorf |
| 2010 OG-M | 4 | 0 | 0 | 0 | 4 | 5 | 20 | 11th | Uwe Krupp | Marco Sturm |

*East Germany
^West Germany
**co-coach with Markus Egen & Engelbert Holdereid
(1) Udo Kiessling captain vs. Sweden (Feb. 22)
(2) Richard Amann captain vs. Slovakia (Feb. 24) and United States (Feb. 26)
(3) Uwe Krupp captain vs. France (Feb. 10)

**World Championship (Men)**

(bold=top level)

| Year Event | GP | W | T | | L | GF | GA | Place | Coach | Captain |
|---|---|---|---|---|---|---|---|---|---|---|
| Year Event | GP | W | OTW | OTL | L | GF | GA | Place | Coach | Captain |
| 1930 WM | 5 | 4 | 0 | | 1 | 15 | 11 | S | Erich Romer | Erich Romer |
| 1933 WM | 6 | 3 | 1 | | 2 | 13 | 8 | 5th | Erich Romer | *unknown* |
| 1934 WM | 8 | 5 | 0 | | 3 | 10 | 14 | B | Erich Romer | Erich Romer |
| 1935 WM | 7 | 4 | 0 | | 3 | 18 | 9 | 9th | Val Hoffinger | *unknown* |
| 1937 WM | 9 | 3 | 1 | | 5 | 13 | 32 | 4th | Bobby Bell | *unknown* |
| 1938 WM | 8 | 3 | 0 | | 5 | 12 | 9 | 4th | Bobby Bell | Gustav Jaenecke |
| 1939 WM | 8 | 4 | 2 | | 2 | 24 | 17 | 5th | Bobby Bell | Gustav Jaenecke |
| 1953 WM^ | 4 | 1 | 0 | | 3 | 17 | 26 | S | Bruno Leinweber | *unknown* |
| 1954 WM^ | 7 | 2 | 1 | | 4 | 22 | 32 | 5th | Bruno Leinweber | *unknown* |
| 1955 WM^ | 8 | 2 | 0 | | 6 | 28 | 43 | 6th | Frank Trottier | *unknown* |
| 1957 WM* | 7 | 3 | 0 | | 4 | 23 | 48 | 5th | Gerhard Kiessling | *unknown* |
| 1959 WM^ | 8 | 5 | 1 | | 2 | 41 | 22 | 7th | Gerhard Kiessling | *unknown* |
| 1959 WM* | 8 | 3 | 0 | | 5 | 26 | 42 | 9th | Rudi Schmieder | *unknown* |
| 1961 WM* | 7 | 2 | 0 | | 5 | 21 | 33 | 5th | Rudi Schmieder | *unknown* |

| | | | | | | | | | | |
|---|---|---|---|---|---|---|---|---|---|---|
| **1961 WM^** | 7 | 0 | 2 | | 5 | 10 | 50 | 8th | Markus Egen | *unknown* |
| **1962 WM^** | 7 | 2 | 0 | | 5 | 27 | 36 | 6th | Vic Heyliger | *unknown* |
| **1963 WM*** | 7 | 1 | 1 | | 5 | 16 | 43 | 6th | Rudi Schmieder | Joachim Zeische |
| **1963 WM^** | 7 | 1 | 1 | | 5 | 18 | 56 | 7th | Vic Heyliger | Ernst Trautwein |
| **1965 WM*** | 7 | 3 | 0 | | 4 | 18 | 33 | 5th | Rudi Schmieder | *unknown* |
| 1965 WM-B^ | 6 | 3 | 2 | | 1 | 30 | 20 | 3rd | Marcus Egen | unknown |
| **1966 WM*** | 7 | 3 | 0 | | 4 | 12 | 30 | 5th | Rudi Schmieder | *unknown* |
| 1966 WM-B^ | 7 | 7 | 0 | | 0 | 34 | 12 | 1st | Ed Reigle | *unknown* |
| **1967 WM*** | 7 | 1 | 1 | | 5 | 14 | 38 | 7th | Rudi Schmieder | Joachim Zeische |
| **1967 WM^** | 7 | 0 | 1 | | 6 | 11 | 56 | 8th | Ed Reigle | Leonhard Waitl |
| 1969 WM-B* | 7 | 7 | 0 | | 0 | 62 | 13 | 1st | Rudi Schmieder | Heinz Bader |
| 1969 WM-B^ | 7 | 4 | 0 | | 3 | 28 | 16 | 4th | Vladimir Bouzek | Joachim Ziesche |
| **1970 WM*** | 10 | 2 | 1 | | 7 | 20 | 50 | 5th | Rudi Schmieder | Joachim Ziesche |
| 1970 WM-B^ | 7 | 6 | 0 | | 1 | 34 | 13 | 2nd | Vladimir Bouzek | Ernst Kopf |
| **1971 WM^** | 10 | 2 | 0 | | 8 | 22 | 62 | 5th | Gerhard Kiessling | *unknown* |
| 1971 WM-B* | 7 | 5 | 0 | | 2 | 49 | 24 | 3rd | Klaus Hirche/Joachim Ziesche | *unknown* |
| **1972 WM^** | 10 | 2 | 0 | | 8 | 23 | 76 | 5th | Gerhard Kiessling | Alois Schloder |
| 1972 WM-B* | 6 | 4 | 0 | | 2 | 31 | 18 | 3rd | Joachim Ziesche | Rudiger Noack |
| **1973 WM^** | 10 | 1 | 0 | | 9 | 19 | 82 | 6th | Gerhard Kiessling | Alois Schloder |
| 1973 WM-B* | 7 | 7 | 0 | | 0 | 56 | 21 | 1st | Joachim Ziesche | Rudiger Noack |
| **1974 WM*** | 10 | 1 | 1 | | 8 | 21 | 71 | 6th | Joachim Ziesche/Klaus Hirche | *unknown* |
| 1974 WM-B^ | 7 | 5 | 0 | | 2 | 34 | 28 | 3rd | Gerhard Kiessling | Alois Schloder |
| 1975 WM-B* | 7 | 6 | 0 | | 1 | 41 | 18 | 1st | Klaus Hirche/ Joachim Ziesche | Rudiger Noack |
| 1975 WM-B^ | 7 | 6 | 0 | | 1 | 34 | 17 | 2nd | Xaver Unsinn | Alois Schloder |
| **1976 WM*** | 10 | 2 | 1 | | 7 | 19 | 52 | 8th | Joachim Ziesche/Klaus Hirche | Rudiger Noack |
| **1976 WM^** | 10 | 3 | 2 | | 5 | 26 | 41 | 6th | Xaver Unsinn | Alois Schloder |
| **1977 WM^** | 10 | 2 | 1 | | 7 | 23 | 58 | 7th | Hans Rampf | Alois Schloder |
| 1977 WM-B* | 8 | 8 | 0 | | 0 | 57 | 16 | 1st | Wolfgang Nickel | Rudiger Noack |
| **1978 WM^** | 10 | 3 | 3 | | 4 | 35 | 43 | 5th | Hans Rampf | Alois Schloder |
| **1978 WM*** | 10 | 1 | 3 | | 6 | 20 | 57 | 8th | Gunther Schischefski | Peter Slapke |
| **1979 WM^** | 8 | 3 | 1 | | 4 | 32 | 31 | 6th | Hans Rampf | Rainer Philipp |
| 1979 WM-B* | 6 | 5 | 0 | | 1 | 42 | 12 | 2nd | Gunter Schischefski | *unknown* |
| **1981 WM^** | 8 | 3 | 1 | | 4 | 44 | 40 | 7th | Hans Rampf | Rainer Philipp |
| 1981 WM-B* | 7 | 4 | 1 | | 2 | 37 | 25 | 4th | Joachim Ziesche | Gerhard Muller |
| **1982 WM^** | 7 | 2 | 1 | | 4 | 19 | 30 | 6th | Xaver Unsinn | Erich Kuhnhackl |
| 1982 WM-B* | 7 | 6 | 1 | | 0 | 48 | 25 | 1st | Joachim Ziesche | Dieter Frenzel |
| **1983 WM*** | 10 | 5 | 1 | | 4 | 31 | 34 | 5th | Joachim Ziesche | Dieter Frenzel |
| **1983 WM^** | 10 | 3 | 0 | | 7 | 29 | 40 | 6th | Xaver Unsinn | Erich Kuhnhackl |
| **1985 WM^** | 10 | 3 | 1 | | 6 | 28 | 41 | 7th | Xaver Unsinn | Dieter Frenzel |
| **1985 WM*** | 10 | 0 | 2 | | 8 | 16 | 64 | 8th | Joachim Ziesche | *unknown* |
| **1986 WM^** | 10 | 2 | 1 | | 7 | 23 | 52 | 7th | Xaver Unsinn | Udo Kiessling |
| 1986 WM-B* | 7 | 4 | 0 | | 3 | 25 | 21 | 3rd | Joachim Ziesche | Dieter Frenzel |
| **1987 WM^** | 10 | 4 | 1 | | 5 | 31 | 37 | 6th | Xaver Unsinn | Udo Kiessling |
| 1987 WM-B* | 7 | 2 | 2 | | 3 | 25 | 31 | 5th | Joachim Ziesche | Dieter Frenzel |
| **1989 WM^** | 10 | 1 | 2 | | 7 | 22 | 41 | 7th | Xaver Unsinn/Erich Kuhnhackl | Udo Kiessling |
| 1989 WM-B* | 7 | 3 | 0 | | 4 | 22 | 29 | 5th | Rudi Ortmann | Dieter Frenzel |
| **1990 WM^** | 10 | 1 | 1 | | 8 | 19 | 42 | 7th | Xaver Unsinn | Udo Kiessling |
| 1990 WM-B* | 7 | 2 | 2 | | 3 | 22 | 19 | 5th | Rudiger Noack | Ralf Hantschke |
| **1991 WM** | 10 | 0 | 2 | | 8 | 19 | 51 | 8th | Ladislav Olejnik | Udo Kiessling |
| **1992 WM** | 6 | 4 | 0 | | 2 | 31 | 17 | 6th | Ludek Bukac | Gerd Truntschka |
| **1993 WM** | 6 | 4 | 0 | | 2 | 21 | 17 | 5th | Franz Reindl | Gerd Truntschka |
| **1994 WM** | 5 | 1 | 1 | | 3 | 9 | 14 | 9th | Ludek Bukac | Jorg Mayr |
| **1995 WM** | 5 | 1 | 0 | | 4 | 11 | 20 | 9th | George Kingston | Uli Hiemer |
| **1996 WM** | 6 | 2 | 0 | | 4 | 13 | 17 | 8th | George Kingston | Dieter Hegen |
| **1997 WM** | 8 | 2 | 0 | | 6 | 10 | 30 | 11th | George Kingston | Dieter Hegen |
| **1998 WM** | 6 | 1 | 2 | | 3 | 13 | 23 | 11th | George Kingston | Dieter Hegen |
| 1999 WM-B | 7 | 5 | 0 | | 2 | 19 | 17 | 4th | Hans Zach | Jurgen Rumrich |
| 2000 WM-B | 7 | 6 | 0 | | 1 | 30 | 15 | 1st | Hans Zach | Jurgen Rumrich |
| **2001 WM** | 7 | 1 | 2 | | 4 | 11 | 18 | 8th | Hans Zach | Jurgen Rumrich |
| **2002 WM** | 7 | 3 | 1 | | 3 | 25 | 22 | 8th | Hans Zach | Jurgen Rumrich |
| **2003 WM** | 7 | 3 | 1 | | 3 | 18 | 18 | 6th | Hans Zach | Jan Benda (1) |
| **2004 WM** | 6 | 2 | 1 | | 3 | 10 | 16 | 9th | Hans Zach | Stefan Ustorf |
| **2005 WM** | 6 | 1 | 1 | | 4 | 15 | 15 | 15th | Greg Poss | Jan Benda |
| 2006 WM-I-A | 5 | 5 | 0 | | 0 | 34 | 4 | 1st | Uwe Krupp | Stefan Ustorf |
| **2007 WM** | 6 | 3 | 0 | 0 | 3 | 16 | 19 | 9th | Uwe Krupp | Petr Fical |
| **2008 WM** | 6 | 2 | 0 | 0 | 4 | 17 | 29 | 10th | Uwe Krupp | Marco Sturm |
| **2009 WM** | 6 | 1 | 0 | 1 | 4 | 6 | 15 | 15th | Uwe Krupp | Andreas Renz |
| **2010 WM** | 9 | 3 | 1 | 1 | 4 | 13 | 14 | 4th | Uwe Krupp | Marcel Goc |
| **2011 WM** | 7 | 2 | 1 | 2 | 2 | 20 | 24 | 7th | Uwe Krupp | Michael Wolf |
| **2012 WM** | 7 | 2 | 0 | 0 | 5 | 14 | 31 | 12th | Jakob Kolliker | Marcel Goc |

*East Germany
^West Germany
(1) Tobias Abstreiter captain vs. Czech Republic (May 4)

### IIHF-NHL Invitationals

(bold=top level)

| Year Event | GP | W | T | L | GF | GA | Place | Coach | Captain |
|---|---|---|---|---|---|---|---|---|---|
| **1984 CC** | **5** | **0** | **1** | **4** | **13** | **29** | **5th** | **Xaver Unsinn** | ***unknown*** |
| **1996 WCH** | **4** | **1** | **0** | **3** | **12** | **19** | **6th** | **George Kingston** | **Dieter Hegen** |
| **2004 WCH** | **4** | **0** | **0** | **4** | **5** | **17** | **8th** | **Franz Reindl** | **Marco Sturm** |

### U20 World Championship

(bold=top level)

| Year Event | GP | W | T | | | L | GF | GA | Place | Coach | Captain |
|---|---|---|---|---|---|---|---|---|---|---|---|
| Year Event | GP | W | | OTW | OTL | L | GF | GA | Place | Coach | Captain |
| **1977 WM20^** | **7** | **2** | **0** | | | **5** | **18** | **33** | **6th** | **Hans Rampf** | **Dieter Medicus** |
| **1978 WM20^** | **6** | **1** | **0** | | | **5** | **20** | **33** | **7th** | **Helmut Perkuhn** | **Harry Pflugl (1)** |
| **1979 WM20^** | **5** | **1** | **0** | | | **4** | **17** | **26** | **7th** | **Ladislav Olejnik** | ***unknown*** |
| **1980 WM20^** | **5** | **2** | **0** | | | **3** | **15** | **28** | **6th** | **Ladislav Olejnik** | **Michael Eggerbauer** |
| **1981 WM20^** | **5** | **3** | **0** | | | **2** | **29** | **24** | **5th** | **Helmut Perkuhn** | **Georg Holzmann** |
| **1982 WM20^** | **7** | **1** | **0** | | | **6** | **19** | **56** | **7th** | **Hans Rampf** | ***unknown*** |
| **1983 WM20^** | **7** | **1** | **0** | | | **6** | **14** | **46** | **7th** | **Hans Rampf** | **Andreas Niederberger** |
| **1984 WM20^** | **7** | **1** | **0** | | | **6** | **12** | **54** | **7th** | **Hans Rampf** | ***unknown*** |
| **1985 WM20^** | **7** | **0** | **1** | | | **6** | **9** | **44** | **7th** | **Hans Rampf** | **Uwe Krupp** |
| **1986 WM20^** | **7** | **0** | **0** | | | **7** | **9** | **65** | **8th** | **Hans Rampf** | **Andreas Volland** |
| 1987 WM20-B^ | 5 | 4 | 1 | | | 0 | 48 | 11 | 1st | Hans Rampf | *unknown* |
| **1988 WM20^** | **7** | **1** | **0** | | | **6** | **18** | **47** | **7th** | **Hans Rampf** | ***unknown*** |
| **1989 WM20^** | **7** | **0** | **0** | | | **7** | **13** | **66** | **8th** | **Hans Rampf** | **Thomas Brandl (2)** |
| 1990 WM20-B^ | 7 | 6 | 0 | | | 1 | 35 | 12 | 2nd | Hans Rampf | Jorg Mayr |
| 1991 WM20-B | 7 | 6 | 1 | | | 0 | 49 | 15 | 1st | Hans Rampf | Christoph Sander. |
| **1992 WM20** | **7** | **1** | **0** | | | **6** | **15** | **40** | **7th** | **Hans Rampf** | **Josef Lehner** |
| **1993 WM20** | **7** | **1** | **0** | | | **6** | **16** | **37** | **7th** | **Erich Kuhnhackl** | **Rafael Jedamzik** |
| **1994 WM20** | **7** | **1** | **0** | | | **6** | **10** | **26** | **7th** | **Erich Kuhnhackl** | **Rafael Jedamzik** |
| **1995 WM20** | **7** | **1** | **0** | | | **6** | **17** | **55** | **7th** | **Erich Kuhnhackl** | **Alexander Serikow** |
| **1996 WM20** | **6** | **1** | **2** | | | **3** | **19** | **27** | **8th** | **Erich Kuhnhackl** | **Jochen Hecht** |
| **1997 WM20** | **6** | **1** | **0** | | | **5** | **14** | **34** | **9th** | **Erich Kuhnhackl** | **Andreas Renz** |
| **1998 WM20** | **6** | **0** | **0** | | | **6** | **4** | **41** | **10th** | **Jim Setters** | **Markus Pottinger** |
| 1999 WM20-B | 6 | 2 | 0 | | | 4 | 19 | 14 | 4th | Jim Setters | *unknown* |
| 2000 WM20-B | 5 | 4 | 0 | | | 1 | 15 | 7 | 2nd | Ernst Hofner | Lasse Kopitz |
| 2001 WM20-I | 5 | 4 | 0 | | | 1 | 14 | 6 | 2nd | Ernst Hofner | Dennis Seidenberg |
| 2002 WM20-I | 5 | 5 | 0 | | | 0 | 26 | 6 | 1st | Ernst Hofner | Christian Ehrhoff |
| **2003 WM20** | **6** | **1** | **0** | | | **5** | **9** | **24** | **9th** | **Ernst Hofner** | **Marcel Goc** |
| 2004 WM20-I-A | 5 | 3 | 2 | | | 0 | 29 | 10 | 1st | Ernst Hofner | Alexander Sulzer |
| **2005 WM20** | **6** | **1** | **0** | | | **5** | **5** | **32** | **9th** | **Ernst Hofner** | **Markus Kink** |
| 2006 WM20-I-A | 5 | 5 | 0 | | | 0 | 20 | 2 | 1st | Ernst Hofner | Moritz Muller |
| **2007 WM20** | **6** | **1** | | **1** | **0** | **4** | **12** | **17** | **9th** | **Ernst Hofner** | **Florian Ondruschka** |
| **2009 WM20** | **6** | **1** | | **0** | **0** | **5** | **14** | **29** | **9th** | **Ernst Hofner** | **Gerrit Fauser** |
| 2008 WM20-I-A | 5 | 5 | | 0 | 0 | 0 | 42 | 6 | 1st | Ernst Hofner | Christopher Fischer |
| 2010 WM20-I-A | 5 | 5 | | 0 | 0 | 0 | 27 | 3 | 1st | Ernst Hofner | Benedikt Bruckner |
| **2011 WM20** | **6** | **0** | | **0** | **1** | **4** | **8** | **21** | **10th** | **Ernst Hofner** | **Laurin Braun** |
| 2012 WM20-I-A | 5 | 5 | | 0 | 0 | 0 | 34 | 9 | 1st | Ernst Hofner | Konrad Abeltshauser |

^West Germany

(1) Gerd Truntshka captain Dec. 23 vs. CAN

(2) Stefan Sinner captain Jan. 4 vs. NOR

### U18 World Championship (Men)

(bold=top level)

| Year Event | GP | W | T | | | L | GF | GA | Place | Coach | Captain |
|---|---|---|---|---|---|---|---|---|---|---|---|
| Year Event | GP | W | | OTW | OTL | L | GF | GA | Place | Coach | Captain |
| **1999 WM18** | **6** | **1** | **0** | | | **5** | **6** | **24** | **9th** | **Franz Fritzmeier** | **Svend Wiele** |
| **2000 WM18** | **6** | **2** | **1** | | | **3** | **21** | **16** | **7th** | **Jim Setters** | **Christoph Schubert** |
| **2001 WM18** | **6** | **3** | **1** | | | **2** | **13** | **20** | **5th** | **Jim Setters** | **Marcel Goc** |
| **2002 WM18** | **8** | **1** | **1** | | | **6** | **13** | **39** | **10th** | **Jim Setters** | **Felix Petermann** |
| 2003 WM18-I-A | 5 | 4 | 0 | | | 1 | 34 | 8 | 2nd | Jim Setters | Raphael Kapzan |
| 2004 WM18-I-B | 5 | 5 | 0 | | | 0 | 38 | 12 | 1st | Jim Setters | Anton Saal |
| **2005 WM18** | **6** | **2** | **0** | | | **4** | **14** | **22** | **8th** | **Jim Setters** | **Florian Ondruschka** |
| **2006 WM18** | **6** | **1** | **1** | | | **4** | **15** | **27** | **8th** | **Jim Setters** | **Maximillian Brandl** |
| **2007 WM18** | **6** | **2** | | **0** | **0** | **4** | **17** | **28** | **8th** | **Jim Setters** | **Steven Rupprich** |
| **2008 WM18** | **6** | **2** | | **1** | **0** | **3** | **18** | **26** | **5th** | **Jim Setters** | **Daniel Weiss** |
| **2009 WM18** | **6** | **1** | | **1** | **0** | **4** | **20** | **36** | **10th** | **Jim Setters** | **Marc El-Sayed** |
| 2010 WM18-I-B | 5 | 5 | | 0 | 0 | 0 | 51 | 2 | 1st | Jim Setters | Achim Moosberger |
| **2011 WM18** | **6** | **1** | | **0** | **1** | **4** | **14** | **27** | **6th** | **Jim Setters** | **Stephan Kronthaler** |
| **2012 WM18** | **6** | **2** | | **0** | **0** | **4** | **16** | **29** | **6th** | **Jim Setters** | **Kai Herpich** |

### Olympics, Women

(bold=top level)

| Year Event | GP | W | T | L | GF | GA | Place | Coach | Captain |
|---|---|---|---|---|---|---|---|---|---|
| **2002 OG-W** | **5** | **1** | **1** | **3** | **10** | **23** | **6th** | **Rainer Nittel** | **Christina Oswald** |
| **2006 OG-W** | **5** | **3** | **0** | **2** | **8** | **11** | **5th** | **Peter Kathan** | **Christina Fellner** |

### Women's World Championship

(bold=top level)

| Year Event | GP | W | T | | | L | GF | GA | Place | Coach | Captain |
|---|---|---|---|---|---|---|---|---|---|---|---|
| Year Event | GP | W | | OTW | OTL | L | GF | GA | Place | Coach | Captain |
| **1990 WW** | **5** | **2** | **0** | | | **3** | **16** | **33** | **7th** | **Pierre Delisle** | **Cornelia Ostrowski** |
| **1994 WW** | **5** | **0** | **0** | | | **5** | **6** | **46** | **8th** | **Hanspeter Amend** | **Stefanie Putz** |
| **1999 WW** | **5** | **2** | **0** | | | **3** | **10** | **32** | **7th** | **Rainer Nittel** | **Christina Oswald** |
| **2000 WW** | **5** | **1** | **0** | | | **4** | **7** | **32** | **7th** | **Rainer Nittel** | **Christina Oswald** |
| **2001 WW** | **5** | **2** | **1** | | | **2** | **9** | **20** | **6th** | **Rainer Nittel** | **Christina Oswald** |
| **2004 WW** | **4** | **1** | **0** | | | **3** | **6** | **23** | **6th** | **Peter Kathan** | **Christina Oswald** |
| **2005 WW** | **5** | **2** | **1** | | | **2** | **9** | **16** | **5th** | **Peter Kathan** | **Sabrina Kruck** |
| **2007 WW** | **4** | **1** | | **0** | **0** | **3** | **4** | **13** | **8th** | **Peter Kathan** | **Christina Fellner** |
| **2008 WW** | **4** | **1** | | **0** | **0** | **3** | **5** | **16** | **9th** | **Peter Kathan** | **Susanne Fellner** |

| Year Event | GP | W | OTW | OTL | L | GF | GA | Place | Coach | Captain |
|---|---|---|---|---|---|---|---|---|---|---|
| 2009 WW-I | 5 | 4 | 0 | 0 | 1 | 20 | 13 | 2nd | Peter Kathan | Maritta Becker |
| 2011 WW-I | 4 | 4 | 0 | 0 | 0 | 12 | 2 | 1st | Peter Kathan | Susann Gotz |
| **2012 WW** | **5** | **2** | **1** | **1** | **1** | **11** | **10** | **7th** | **Peter Kathan** | **Susann Gotz** |

**U18 Women's World Championship**
(bold=top level)

| Year Event | GP | W | OTW | OTL | L | GF | GA | Place | Coach | Captain |
|---|---|---|---|---|---|---|---|---|---|---|
| **2008 WW18** | **5** | **3** | **0** | **0** | **2** | **13** | **17** | **5th** | **Peter Kathan** | **Jenny Tamas** |
| **2009 WW18** | **5** | **0** | **1** | **0** | **4** | **6** | **27** | **6th** | **Werner Schneider** | **Jessica Geml** |
| **2010 WW18** | **6** | **1** | **1** | **0** | **4** | **12** | **39** | **4th** | **Peter Kathan** | **Manuela Anwander** |
| **2011 WW18** | **5** | **2** | **0** | **0** | **3** | **7** | **15** | **6th** | **Werner Schneider** | **Tanja Eisenschmid** |
| **2012 WW18** | **6** | **2** | **0** | **0** | **4** | **10** | **22** | **4th** | **Maritta Becker** | **Anna-Maria Fiegert** |

# Great Britain (GBR)

*Goalkeeper Stephen Murphy helped Great Britain remain in the Division I, Group A for 2013. Photo: Samo Vidic.*

**Joined IIHF: November 19, 1908**

Website: www.icehockeyuk.co.uk
E-mail: general.secretary@icehockeyuk.co.uk

Ice Hockey UK
3 Ocean House
Clarence Road
Cardiff
CF10 5FR
United Kingdom

Phone: +44 7713 5905 06 • Fax: +44 1708 775 241

**World Ranking**

| MEN | | WOMEN | |
|---|---|---|---|
| 2012 | 21 | 2012 | 17 |
| 2011 | 21 | 2011 | 18 |
| 2010 | 23 | 2010 | 18 |
| 2009 | 25 | 2009 | 20 |
| 2008 | 29 | 2008 | 23 |
| 2007 | 29 | 2007 | 22 |
| 2006 | 31 | 2006 | 22 |
| 2005 | 25 | 2005 | 20 |
| 2004 | 25 | 2004 | 20 |

**Top Level Host History**
World Championship (Men): 1937 (London); 1950 (London)

**Olympics, Men**
(bold=top level)

| Year Event | GP | W | T | L | GF | GA | Place | Coach | Captain |
|---|---|---|---|---|---|---|---|---|---|
| **1924 OG-M** | **5** | **3** | **0** | **2** | **40** | **38** | **B** | **George Elliott** | **Colin Carruthers** |
| **1928 OG-M** | **6** | **2** | **0** | **4** | **11** | **27** | **4th** | ***unknown*** | **G.R. Cuthbert** |
| **1936 OG-M** | **7** | **5** | **2** | **0** | **17** | **3** | **G** | **Percy Nicklin** | **Carl Erhardt** |
| **1948 OG-M** | **8** | **3** | **0** | **5** | **39** | **47** | **6th** | **Carl Erhardt** | **Archie Stinchcombe** |

**World Championship (Men)**
(bold=top level)

| Year Event | GP | W | T | | L | GF | GA | Place | Coach | Captain |
|---|---|---|---|---|---|---|---|---|---|---|
| Year Event | GP | W | OTW | OTL | L | GF | GA | Place | Coach | Captain |
| **1930 WM** | **1** | **0** | **0** | | **1** | **2** | **4** | **10th** | ***unknown*** | **William Home** |
| **1931 WM** | **4** | **2** | **0** | | **2** | **14** | **5** | **8th** | ***unknown*** | **Clarence Wedgewood** |
| **1934 WM** | **6** | **4** | **0** | | **2** | **12** | **7** | **8th** | **John Magwood** | **Carl Erhardt** |
| **1935 WM** | **7** | **4** | **0** | | **3** | **14** | **14** | **B** | **Bunny Ahearne** | **Carl Erhardt** |
| **1937 WM** | **9** | **8** | **0** | | **1** | **50** | **3** | **S** | **Percy Nicklin** | **Gordon Dailley** |
| **1938 WM** | **8** | **6** | **1** | | **1** | **27** | **8** | **S** | **Percy Nicklin** | **Gordon Dailley** |
| **1939 WM** | **5** | **2** | **0** | | **3** | **4** | **8** | **8th** | **Percy Nicklin** | **Gordon Dailley** |
| **1950 WM** | **7** | **4** | **0** | | **3** | **25** | **32** | **4th** | **Lou Bates** | **Ken Nicholson** |
| **1951 WM** | **6** | **1** | **1** | | **4** | **18** | **42** | **5th** | **J.B. Mowat** | **Ken Nicholson** |
| 1953 WM-B | 5 | 4 | 0 | | 1 | 24 | 11 | 2nd | John Murray | *unknown* |
| 1961 WM-B | 5 | 3 | 2 | | 0 | 21 | 11 | 2nd | Sam Covan | *unknown* |
| **1962 WM** | **7** | **1** | **0** | | **6** | **19** | **73** | **8th** | **John Murray** | **Billy Brennan** |
| 1963 WM-B | 6 | 0 | 0 | | 6 | 8 | 47 | 7th | Malcolm Beaton | Bert Smith |
| 1965 WM-B | 6 | 1 | 1 | | 4 | 24 | 41 | 6th | John Milne | Billy Brennan |
| 1966 WM-B | 7 | 0 | 1 | | 6 | 15 | 45 | 8th | John Milne | Billy Brennan |
| 1971 WM-C | 7 | 3 | 1 | | 3 | 47 | 39 | 4th | Johnny Carlyle | Robert Stevenson |
| 1973 WM-C | 7 | 0 | 1 | | 6 | 18 | 60 | 8th | Johnny Carlyle | Terry Matthews |
| 1976 WM-C | 4 | 0 | 0 | | 4 | 6 | 44 | 5th | George Beach | *unknown* |
| 1977 WM-C | 6 | 1 | 0 | | 5 | 17 | 47 | 7th | Terry Matthews | Les Lovell |
| 1979 WM-C | 7 | 2 | 0 | | 5 | 23 | 68 | 5th | Joe McIntosh | Alistair Brennan |
| 1981 WM-C | 7 | 0 | 0 | | 7 | 11 | 60 | 8th | Alex Dampier | *unknown* |
| 1989 WM-D | 4 | 1 | 1 | | 2 | 19 | 16 | 3rd | Terry Matthews | Stephen Cooper |
| 1990 WM-D | 4 | 4 | 0 | | 0 | 57 | 7 | 1st | Alex Dampier | Chris Kelland |
| 1991 WM-C | 8 | 4 | 1 | | 3 | 45 | 25 | 5th | Alex Dampier | Chris Kelland |
| 1992 WM-C | 5 | 5 | 0 | | 0 | 62 | 10 | 1st | Alex Dampier | Chris Kelland |
| 1993 WM-B | 7 | 7 | 0 | | 0 | 50 | 13 | 1st | Alex Dampier | Chris Kelland |
| **1994 WM** | **6** | **0** | **0** | | **6** | **9** | **49** | **12th** | **Alex Dampier** | **Chris Kelland** |
| 1995 WM-B | 7 | 2 | 0 | | 5 | 19 | 35 | 7th | George Peternousek | Shannon Hope |
| 1996 WM-B | 7 | 4 | 1 | | 2 | 29 | 23 | 4th | Peter Woods | Shannon Hope |
| 1997 WM-B | 7 | 2 | 1 | | 4 | 28 | 22 | 6th | Peter Woods | Shannon Hope |
| 1998 WM-B | 7 | 3 | 0 | | 4 | 32 | 27 | 6th | Peter Woods | Shannon Hope |
| 1999 WM-B | 7 | 5 | 1 | | 1 | 24 | 16 | 2nd | Peter Woods | Steve Moria |

| | | | | | | | | | | |
|---|---|---|---|---|---|---|---|---|---|---|
| 2000 WM-B | 7 | 4 | 1 | | 2 | 31 | 23 | 3rd | Peter Woods | Steve Moria |
| 2001 WM-I-B | 5 | 4 | 1 | | 0 | 42 | 9 | 2nd | Chris McSorley | David Longstaff |
| 2002 WM-I-B | 5 | 2 | 0 | | 3 | 18 | 16 | 4th | Chris McSorley | David Longstaff |
| 2003 WM-I-B | 5 | 1 | 1 | | 3 | 16 | 14 | 5th | Chris McSorley | David Longstaff |
| 2004 WM-I-A | 5 | 1 | 1 | | 3 | 18 | 18 | 5th | Chris McSorley | Steve Thornton |
| 2005 WM-I-A | 5 | 2 | 0 | | 3 | 19 | 15 | 4th | Rick Strachan | Kevin Phillips |
| 2006 WM-I-A | 5 | 1 | 0 | | 4 | 17 | 17 | 5th | Rick Strachan | Jonathan Weaver |
| 2007 WM-I-B | 5 | 2 | 0 | 0 | 3 | 14 | 15 | 4th | Paul Thompson | Jonathan Weaver |
| 2008 WM-I-A | 5 | 2 | 0 | 1 | 2 | 19 | 17 | 4th | Paul Thompson | Jonathan Weaver |
| 2009 WM-I-B | 5 | 2 | 1 | 0 | 2 | 17 | 12 | 3rd | Paul Thompson | Jonathan Weaver |
| 2010 WM-I-B | 5 | 2 | 0 | 1 | 2 | 10 | 10 | 4th | Paul Thompson | Jonathan Weaver |
| 2011 WM-I-B | 5 | 4 | 0 | 0 | 1 | 21 | 9 | 2nd | Paul Thompson | Jonathan Weaver |
| 2012 WM-I-A | 5 | 1 | 1 | 0 | 3 | 14 | 22 | 5th | Tony Hand/Doug Christiansen | Jonathan Phillips |

### U20 World Championship

| Year Event | GP | W | T | | L | GF | GA | Place | Coach | Captain |
|---|---|---|---|---|---|---|---|---|---|---|
| **Year Event** | **GP** | **W** | **OTW** | **OTL** | **L** | **GF** | **GA** | **Place** | **Coach** | **Captain** |
| 1984 WM20-C | 4 | 1 | 0 | | 3 | 16 | 33 | 6th | Alex Dampier | Peter Lee |
| 1985 WM20-C | 4 | 1 | 0 | | 3 | 9 | 29 | 4th | Robert Petrie | Stephen Johnson |
| 1986 WM20-C | 5 | 3 | 0 | | 2 | 20 | 31 | 3rd | *unknown* | *unknown* |
| 1987 WM20-C | 5 | 3 | 0 | | 2 | 25 | 21 | 3rd | Alex Dampier | *unknown* |
| 1988 WM20-C | 7 | 3 | 1 | | 3 | 21 | 27 | 4th | Alex Dampier | Ian Cooper |
| 1989 WM20-C | 4 | 0 | 2 | | 2 | 15 | 19 | 4th | Alex Dampier | Tony Johnson |
| 1990 WM20-C | 6 | 2 | 0 | | 4 | 17 | 31 | 6th | Mike O'Connor | *unknown* |
| 1991 WM20-C | 7 | 4 | 0 | | 3 | 45 | 20 | 4th | Mike Sirant | Robert Wilkinson |
| 1992 WM20-C | 4 | 1 | 0 | | 3 | 22 | 19 | 3rd | Mike Sirant | Graham Waghorn |
| 1993 WM20-C | 4 | 2 | 1 | | 1 | 19 | 14 | 5th | Peter Woods | David Longstaff |
| 1994 WM20-C | 4 | 2 | 0 | | 2 | 21 | 28 | 4th | *unknown* | *unknown* |
| 1995 WM20-C-1 | 4 | 0 | 0 | | 4 | 9 | 22 | 8th | Iain Finlayson | Ashley Tait |
| 1996 WM20-C | 4 | 2 | 0 | | 2 | 17 | 16 | 5th | Peter Johnson | Andy Port |
| 1997 WM20-C | 4 | 2 | 0 | | 2 | 17 | 14 | 4th | Peter Johnson | Jonathan Weaver |
| 1998 WM20-C | 4 | 1 | 0 | | 3 | 10 | 19 | 7th | Peter Johnson | Lee Brathwaite |
| 1999 WM20-C | 4 | 1 | 1 | | 2 | 9 | 15 | 7th | Troy Walkington | Ian Defty |
| 2000 WM20-C | 4 | 2 | 2 | | 0 | 16 | 9 | 3rd | Troy Walkington | Joe Baird |
| 2001 WM20-II | 4 | 2 | 0 | | 2 | 13 | 19 | 5th | Erskine Douglas | Dave Clarke |
| 2002 WM20-II | 4 | 2 | 0 | | 2 | 16 | 23 | 5th | Kevin King | John Phillips |
| 2003 WM20-II-A | 5 | 4 | 0 | | 1 | 64 | 7 | 2nd | Kevin King | Dan Meyers |
| 2004 WM20-II-B | 5 | 5 | 0 | | 0 | 38 | 5 | 1st | Roger Hunt | Paddy Ward |
| 2005 WM20-I-A | 5 | 0 | 0 | | 5 | 8 | 29 | 6th | Roger Hunt | Mark Richardson |
| 2006 WM20-II-A | 5 | 5 | 0 | | 0 | 53 | 3 | 1st | Peter Russell | Kevin Phillips |
| 2007 WM20-I-B | 5 | 3 | 0 | 0 | 2 | 15 | 13 | 3rd | Mike Urquhart | Shaun Thompson |
| 2008 WM20-I-B | 5 | 0 | 0 | 1 | 4 | 8 | 30 | 6th | Peter Russell | Matthew Towe |
| 2009 WM20-II-B | 5 | 4 | 0 | 0 | 1 | 29 | 10 | 2nd | Peter Russell | Mark Garside |
| 2010 WM20-II-A | 5 | 3 | 2 | 0 | 0 | 51 | 11 | 1st | Peter Russell | Stephen Lee |
| 2011 WM20-I-A | 5 | 3 | 0 | 0 | 2 | 12 | 10 | 3rd | Peter Russell | Robert Farmer |
| 2012 WM20-I-A | 5 | 0 | 0 | 0 | 5 | 6 | 37 | 6th | Joel Poirier | Daniel Scott |

### U18 World Championship (Men)

| Year Event | GP | W | T | | L | GF | GA | Place | Coach | Captain |
|---|---|---|---|---|---|---|---|---|---|---|
| **Year Event** | **GP** | **W** | **OTW** | **OTL** | **L** | **GF** | **GA** | **Place** | **Coach** | **Captain** |
| 1999 WM18-B | 5 | 0 | 0 | | 5 | 9 | 31 | 8th | Daryl Easson | David Clark |
| 2001 WM18-II | 4 | 2 | 0 | | 2 | 15 | 22 | 5th | Allan Anderson | Paul Moran |
| 2002 WM18-II | 5 | 3 | 0 | | 2 | 26 | 23 | 3rd | Allan Anderson | Patrick Ward |
| 2003 WM18-I-A | 5 | 0 | 0 | | 5 | 8 | 45 | 6th | Allan Anderson | Adam Brittle |
| 2004 WM18-II-B | 5 | 5 | 0 | | 0 | 30 | 6 | 1st | Mike Urquhart | Matthew Towe |
| 2005 WM18-I-A | 5 | 1 | 0 | | 4 | 10 | 23 | 6th | Mike Urquhart | Thomas Carlon |
| 2006 WM18-II-B | 5 | 5 | 0 | | 0 | 40 | 5 | 1st | Mick Mishner | Matthew Towe |
| 2007 WM18-I-B | 5 | 0 | 0 | 0 | 5 | 10 | 26 | 6th | Mick Mishner | Thomas Mills |
| 2008 WM18-II-B | 5 | 4 | 0 | 0 | 1 | 27 | 11 | 2nd | Jonathan Rowbotham | Stephen Lee |
| 2009 WM18-II-B | 5 | 5 | 0 | 0 | 0 | 46 | 11 | 1st | Jonathan Rowbotham | John Connolly |
| 2010 WM18-I-B | 5 | 1 | 1 | 0 | 3 | 13 | 24 | 5th | Jonathan Rowbotham | Daniel Scott |
| 2011 WM18-I-A | 4 | 0 | 0 | 0 | 4 | 12 | 25 | 5th | Mark Beggs | James Griffin |
| 2012 WM18-II-A | 5 | 1 | 1 | 0 | 3 | 18 | 17 | 4th | Mark Beggs | David Clements |

### Women's World Championship

| Year Event | GP | W | T | | L | GF | GA | Place | Coach | Captain |
|---|---|---|---|---|---|---|---|---|---|---|
| **Year Event** | **GP** | **W** | **OTW** | **OTL** | **L** | **GF** | **GA** | **Place** | **Coach** | **Captain** |
| 2004 WW-II | 5 | 0 | 0 | | 5 | 6 | 29 | 6th | Reggie Wilcox | Fiona King |
| 2005 WW-III | 5 | 4 | 0 | | 1 | 42 | 6 | 2nd | Reggie Wilcox | *unknown* |
| 2007 WW-III | 5 | 4 | 0 | 1 | 0 | 57 | 8 | 2nd | Richard Wilcox | Fiona King |
| 2008 WW-III | 5 | 4 | 1 | 0 | 0 | 29 | 7 | 1st | Reggie Wilcox | Angela Taylor |
| 2009 WW-II | 5 | 3 | 0 | 0 | 2 | 11 | 11 | 3rd | Reggie Wilcox | Angela Taylor |
| 2011 WW-II | 5 | 1 | 0 | 0 | 4 | 10 | 21 | 5th | Reggie Wilcox | Emily Turner |
| 2012 WW-I-B | 5 | 1 | 0 | 0 | 4 | 10 | 17 | 4th | Simon Manning | Angela Taylor |

### U18 Women's World Championship

(bold=top level)

| Year Event | GP | W | OTW | OTL | L | GF | GA | Place | Coach | Captain |
|---|---|---|---|---|---|---|---|---|---|---|
| 2012 WW18-I | 5 | 1 | 0 | 0 | 4 | 10 | 14 | 5th | Sean Alderson | Katherine Gale |

# Greece (GRE)

*Greece had its only team entered in the men's category at Division III level in Turkey. Photo: TIHF.*

## Joined IIHF: April 29, 1987 (Associate Member)

Website: www.icehockey.gr
E-mail: hisf@otenet.gr

Hellenic Ice Sports Federation
52, Akakion Str.
15125 Polydroso Amarousiou
Greece

Phone: +30 210 684 93 24 • Fax: +30 210 685 82 81

**World Ranking**

**MEN**
2012........44
2011........44
2010........45
2009........46
2008........46

**Top Level Host History**
none

**World Championship (Men)**

| Year Event | GP | W | T | | | L | GF | GA | Place | Coach | Captain |
|---|---|---|---|---|---|---|---|---|---|---|---|
| Year Event | GP | W | | OTW | OTL | L | GF | GA | Place | Coach | Captain |
| 1992 WM-C-B | 5 | 3 | 0 | | | 2 | 36 | 31 | 3rd | Mirel Dumitrache | Giorgios Adamidis |
| 1995 WM-C-2 | 5 | 1 | 1 | | | 3 | 19 | 63 | 9th | Mirel Dumitrache | Giorgios Adamidis |
| 1998 WM-D | 5 | 1 | 0 | | | 4 | 15 | 53 | 8th | Mirel Dumitrache | Dimitrios Kalyvas |
| 1999 WM-D | 4 | 1 | 0 | | | 3 | 10 | 18 | 8th | Mirel Dumitrache | Dimitrios Kalyvas |
| 2008 WM-III | 5 | 1 | | 0 | 1 | 3 | 17 | 28 | 5th | Panagiotis Efkarpidis | Dimitrios Kalyvas |
| 2009 WM-III | 5 | 2 | | 0 | 1 | 2 | 18 | 21 | 4th | Panagiotis Efkarpidis | Dimitrios Kalyvas |
| 2010 WM-III-A | 3 | 2 | | 0 | 0 | 1 | 10 | 5 | 2nd | Igor Apostolidis | Dimitrios Kalyvas |
| 2011 WM-III | 5 | 1 | | 0 | 0 | 4 | 7 | 79 | 5th | Mirel Dumitrache | Georgios Adamidis |
| 2012 WM-III | 5 | 1 | | 0 | 0 | 4 | 9 | 22 | 5th | Igor Apostolidis | Dimitrios Kalyvas |

**U20 World Championship**

| Year Event | GP | W | T | L | GF | GA | Place | Coach | Captain |
|---|---|---|---|---|---|---|---|---|---|
| 1991 WM20-C | 7 | 0 | 0 | 7 | 4 | 158 | 8th | Mirel Dumitrache | Vaskios Karpetas |

# Hong Kong (HKG)

*Hong Kong competed in the 2012 IIHF U18 Challenge Cup of Asia in Abu Dhabi. Photo: Fatima Al Ali.*

## Joined IIHF: April 30, 1983

Website: www.hkiha.org
Email: hkiha@hkolympic.org

Hong Kong Ice Hockey Association
Room 1023, Olympic House
1 Stadium Path
So Kon Po
Causeway Bay
Hong Kong, China

Phone: +852 25 04 81 89 • Fax: +852 25 04 81 91

**Top Level Host History** none

**World Championship (Men)**

| Year Event | GP | W | T | L | GF | GA | Place | Coach | Captain |
|---|---|---|---|---|---|---|---|---|---|
| 1987 WM-D | 6 | 0 | 0 | 6 | 1 | 185 | 4th | Chun Hei Siu | Chung Ting |

# Hungary (HUN)

*The Hungarian U18 women's national team players celebrate promotion to the top division. Photo: Julian Andre Stavnesvik.*

**Joined IIHF: January 24, 1927**

Website: www.icehockey.hu
E-mail: info@icehockey.hu

Hungarian Ice Hockey Federation
Magyar Sport Haza
Istvanmezei ut 1-3
1146 Budapest
Hungary

Phone: +36 1 460 68 63 • Fax: +36 1 460 68 64

**World Ranking**

| MEN | | WOMEN | |
|---|---|---|---|
| 2012 | 19 | 2012 | 23 |
| 2011 | 20 | 2011 | 25 |
| 2010 | 20 | 2010 | 27 |
| 2009 | 20 | 2009 | 26 |
| 2008 | 20 | 2008 | 25 |
| 2007 | 21 | 2007 | 25 |
| 2006 | 22 | 2006 | 25 |
| 2005 | 22 | 2005 | 24 |
| 2004 | 22 | 2004 | 23 |

**Top Level Host History** none

### Olympics, Men

(bold=top level)

| Year Event | GP | W | T | L | GF | GA | Place | Coach | Captain |
|---|---|---|---|---|---|---|---|---|---|
| **1928 OG-M** | **3** | **0** | **0** | **3** | **2** | **6** | **11th** | **Phil Taylor** | **Geza Lator** |
| **1936 OG-M** | **6** | **2** | **0** | **4** | **16** | **27** | **7th** | **Geza Lator** | ***unknown*** |
| **1964 OG-M** | **7** | **0** | **0** | **7** | **14** | **39** | **16th** | **Vladimir Kominek** | **Jozsef Baban** |

### World Championship (Men)

(bold=top level)

| Year Event | GP | W | T | | | L | GF | GA | Place | Coach | Captain |
|---|---|---|---|---|---|---|---|---|---|---|---|
| Year Event | GP | W | | OTW | OTL | L | GF | GA | Place | Coach | Captain |
| **1930 WM** | **2** | **1** | **0** | | | **1** | **3** | **4** | **6th** | **Frigyes Minder** | **Geza Lator** |
| **1931 WM** | **4** | **3** | **0** | | | **1** | **14** | **6** | **7th** | **Frigyes Minder** | ***unknown*** |
| **1933 WM** | **6** | **1** | **1** | | | **4** | **5** | **10** | **7th** | **Frigyes Minder** | ***unknown*** |
| **1934 WM** | **6** | **1** | **1** | | | **4** | **2** | **4** | **6th** | **John Dewar** | ***unknown*** |
| **1935 WM** | **5** | **2** | **2** | | | **1** | **14** | **6** | **11th** | **Geza Lator** | ***unknown*** |
| **1937 WM** | **9** | **3** | **2** | | | **4** | **18** | **24** | **5th** | **Geza Lator** | ***unknown*** |
| **1938 WM** | **6** | **2** | **1** | | | **3** | **14** | **8** | **7th** | **Geza Lator** | ***unknown*** |
| **1939 WM** | **7** | **1** | **0** | | | **6** | **15** | **24** | **7th** | **Edward Trottier** | ***unknown*** |
| 1963 WM-C | 5 | 4 | 0 | | | 1 | 57 | 12 | 2nd | Vladimir Kominek | Jozsef Baban |
| 1965 WM-B | 6 | 2 | 1 | | | 3 | 19 | 24 | 4th | Laszlo Rajkai | unknown |
| 1966 WM-B | 7 | 1 | 0 | | | 6 | 19 | 30 | 7th | Laszlo Rajkai | *unknown* |
| 1967 WM-B | 7 | 0 | 2 | | | 5 | 27 | 40 | 8th | Laszlo Rajkai | Gyorgy Raffa |
| 1969 WM-C | 5 | 3 | 0 | | | 2 | 26 | 22 | 3rd | Laszlo Rajkai | Viktor Zsitva |
| 1970 WM-C | 6 | 4 | 0 | | | 2 | 38 | 15 | 4th | Laszlo Jakabhazy | Viktor Zsitva |
| 1971 WM-C | 7 | 5 | 1 | | | 1 | 58 | 27 | 3rd | Laszlo Jakabhazy | Zoltan Horvath |
| 1972 WM-C | 6 | 2 | 2 | | | 2 | 31 | 24 | 5th | Laszlo Jakabhazy | Peter Bikar |
| 1973 WM-C | 7 | 5 | 0 | | | 2 | 44 | 24 | 3rd | Andrei Chaplinsky | Peter Bikar |
| 1974 WM-C | 7 | 3 | 3 | | | 1 | 38 | 22 | 4th | Gabor Boroczi/ Laszlo Jakabhazy | Peter Bikar |
| 1975 WM-C | 6 | 3 | 1 | | | 2 | 44 | 21 | 4th | Gabor Boroczi/ Laszlo Jakabhazy | Andras Meszoly |
| 1976 WM-C | 4 | 3 | 0 | | | 1 | 30 | 9 | 2nd | Gabor Boroczi | Andras Meszoly |
| 1977 WM-B | 8 | 3 | 0 | | | 5 | 27 | 46 | 6th | Gabor Boroczi | Andras Meszoly |
| 1978 WM-B | 7 | 3 | 0 | | | 4 | 21 | 36 | 5th | Gabor Boroczi | Andras Meszoly |
| 1979 WM-B | 4 | 0 | 0 | | | 4 | 10 | 25 | 10th | Laszlo Rajkai | *unknown* |
| 1981 WM-C | 7 | 4 | 1 | | | 2 | 38 | 22 | 3rd | Laszlo Jakabhazy | *unknown* |
| 1982 WM-C | 7 | 4 | 0 | | | 3 | 43 | 29 | 5th | Vitali Davydov | Andras Meszoly |
| 1983 WM-C | 7 | 5 | 0 | | | 2 | 50 | 25 | 2nd | Gabor Boroczi | Antal Palla |
| 1985 WM-B | 7 | 0 | 0 | | | 7 | 17 | 54 | 8th | Gabor Boroczi | Antal Palla |
| 1986 WM-C | 6 | 2 | 1 | | | 3 | 30 | 28 | 6th | Gabor Boroczi | Csaba Kovacs |
| 1987 WM-C | 7 | 3 | 0 | | | 4 | 33 | 28 | 5th | Gabor Boroczi | Csaba Kovacs |
| 1989 WM-C | 7 | 3 | 1 | | | 3 | 32 | 30 | 4th | Gabor Boroczi | Csaba Kovacs |
| 1990 WM-C | 8 | 2 | 1 | | | 5 | 33 | 28 | 7th | Gabor Boroczi | Istvan Terjek |
| 1991 WM-C | 8 | 3 | 1 | | | 4 | 37 | 32 | 6th | Deszo Szeles | Istvan Terjek |
| 1992 WM-C-A | 5 | 2 | 0 | | | 3 | 18 | 33 | 4th | Deszo Szeles | Tibor Kiss |
| 1993 WM-C | 5 | 3 | 0 | | | 2 | 36 | 31 | 5th | Deszo Szeles | Tibor Kiss |
| 1994 WM-C | 6 | 1 | 0 | | | 5 | 14 | 47 | 6th | Deszo Szeles | Tibor Kiss |
| 1995 WM-C | 4 | 1 | 0 | | | 3 | 15 | 20 | 6th | Arpad Kercso | Janos Ancsin |
| 1996 WM-C | 7 | 3 | 1 | | | 3 | 34 | 25 | 4th | Arpad Kercso | Janos Ancin |
| 1997 WM-C | 5 | 2 | 1 | | | 2 | 18 | 16 | 6th | Antal Palla | Janos Ancsin |
| 1998 WM-C | 5 | 5 | 0 | | | 0 | 36 | 4 | 1st | Arpad Kercso | Janos Ancsin |
| 1999 WM-B | 7 | 0 | 0 | | | 7 | 10 | 33 | 8th | Antal Palla | Tamas Dobos |
| 2000 WM-C | 5 | 5 | 0 | | | 0 | 32 | 9 | 1st | Dezso Szeles | Tamas Dobos |
| 2001 WM-I-A | 5 | 3 | 0 | | | 2 | 19 | 15 | 4th | Arpad Kercso | Balazs Kangyal |
| 2002 WM-I-B | 5 | 4 | 0 | | | 1 | 19 | 9 | 2nd | Jan Jasko | Balazs Kangyal |
| 2003 WM-I-A | 5 | 2 | 1 | | | 2 | 14 | 13 | 3rd | Jan Jasko | Balazs Kangyal |
| 2004 WM-I-A | 5 | 2 | 1 | | | 2 | 20 | 24 | 4th | Dusan Kapusta | Balazs Kangyal |
| 2005 WM-I-A | 5 | 2 | 2 | | | 1 | 15 | 6 | 3rd | Pat Cortina | Balazs Kangyal |
| 2006 WM-I-A | 5 | 2 | 1 | | | 2 | 20 | 18 | 4th | Pat Cortina | Balazs Kangyal |
| 2007 WM-I-B | 5 | 3 | | 1 | 0 | 1 | 20 | 13 | 2nd | Pat Cortina | Balazs Kangyal |

| | | | | | | | | | | |
|---|---|---|---|---|---|---|---|---|---|---|
| 2008 WM-I-B | 5 | 5 | 0 | 0 | 0 | 22 | 7 | 1st | Pat Cortina | Balazs Kangyal |
| **2009 WM** | **6** | **0** | **0** | **0** | **6** | **6** | **29** | **16th** | **Pat Cortina** | **Balazs Kangyal** |
| 2010 WM-I-B | 5 | 4 | 0 | 0 | 1 | 21 | 6 | 2nd | Ted Sator | Viktor Szelig |
| 2011 WM-I-A | 4 | 3 | 0 | 1 | 0 | 29 | 11 | 2nd | Ted Sator | Viktor Szelig |
| 2012 WM-I-A | 5 | 2 | 0 | 0 | 3 | 15 | 18 | 3rd | Kevin Primeau | Viktor Szelig |

### U20 World Championship

| Year Event | GP | W | T | | L | GF | GA | Place | Coach | Captain |
|---|---|---|---|---|---|---|---|---|---|---|
| Year Event | GP | W | OTW | OTL | L | GF | GA | Place | Coach | Captain |
| 1980 WM20-B | 4 | 0 | 0 | | 4 | 11 | 55 | 8th | Laszlo Rajkai/Lajos Tichy | Denzso Szabo |
| 1983 WM20-C | 6 | 3 | 0 | | 3 | 21 | 30 | 3rd | Gyorgy Rozgonyi | *unknown* |
| 1984 WM20-C | 5 | 3 | 1 | | 1 | 34 | 18 | 3rd | Gyorgy Rozgonyi | Gabor Hudac |
| 1985 WM20-C | 4 | 3 | 0 | | 1 | 25 | 10 | 2nd | Gyorgy Rozgonyi | Laszlo Ancsin |
| 1986 WM20-C | 5 | 1 | 0 | | 4 | 16 | 31 | 5th | *unknown* | *unknown* |
| 1988 WM20-C | 7 | 2 | 0 | | 5 | 14 | 28 | 6th | Laszlo Rajkai | Erno Paraizs |
| 1990 WM20-C | 6 | 0 | 0 | | 6 | 19 | 46 | 7th | Attila Szabo | *unknown* |
| 1991 WM20-C | 7 | 1 | 0 | | 6 | 28 | 46 | 7th | Attila Szabo | Miklos Keszthelyi |
| 1992 WM20-C | 4 | 2 | 0 | | 2 | 16 | 18 | 5th | Arpad Kercso | Sandor Rancz |
| 1993 WM20-C | 4 | 2 | 1 | | 1 | 30 | 19 | 3rd | Ocskay Spibor | Istvan Kaltenecker |
| 1994 WM20-C | 4 | 2 | 0 | | 2 | 26 | 18 | 5th | *unknown* | *unknown* |
| 1995 WM20-C-1 | 4 | 3 | 0 | | 1 | 24 | 8 | 2nd | Arpad Kercso | Kristof Kovago |
| 1996 WM20-B | 6 | 3 | 0 | | 3 | 24 | 20 | 4th | Arpad Kercso | Kristof Kovago |
| 1997 WM20-B | 7 | 1 | 0 | | 6 | 14 | 44 | 7th | Antal Palla | *unknown* |
| 1998 WM20-B | 6 | 1 | 2 | | 3 | 11 | 29 | 5th | Antal Palla | Barna Czvikovski |
| 1999 WM20-B | 5 | 1 | 0 | | 4 | 5 | 24 | 8th | Antal Palla | Barna Czvikovski |
| 2000 WM20-C | 4 | 2 | 0 | | 2 | 16 | 25 | 4th | Tibor Kiss | Tamas Groschl |
| 2001 WM20-II | 4 | 1 | 1 | | 2 | 15 | 30 | 7th | Tibor Kiss | Csaba Janosi |
| 2002 WM20-II | 4 | 1 | 1 | | 2 | 11 | 19 | 6th | Albert Fekete | Borbas Gergely |
| 2003 WM20-II-B | 5 | 5 | 0 | | 0 | 47 | 14 | 1st | Ignac Biro | Arnold Feil |
| 2004 WM20-I-A | 5 | 0 | 0 | | 5 | 8 | 46 | 6th | Ignac Biro | *unknown* |
| 2005 WM20-II-B | 5 | 5 | 0 | | 0 | 41 | 10 | 1st | Dusan Kapusta | Patrik Szjabert |
| 2006 WM20-I-B | 5 | 0 | 2 | | 3 | 6 | 20 | 6th | Vladimir Matejov | Viktor Papp |
| 2007 WM20-II-A | 5 | 5 | 0 | 0 | 0 | 52 | 12 | 1st | Gyorgy Pek | Peter Erdelyi |
| 2008 WM20-I-B | 5 | 2 | 0 | 0 | 3 | 17 | 21 | 4th | Gyorgy Pek | Peter Erdelyi |
| 2009 WM20-I-B | 5 | 0 | 0 | 1 | 4 | 11 | 28 | 6th | Gyorgy Pek | Gergo Nagy |
| 2010 WM20-II-A | 5 | 4 | 0 | 1 | 0 | 66 | 8 | 2nd | Pat MacCallum | Attila Orban |
| 2011 WM20-II-B | 5 | 4 | 0 | 0 | 1 | 50 | 16 | 2nd | Robert Dever | Attila Pavuk |
| 2012 WM20-II-A | 5 | 2 | 1 | 0 | 2 | 24 | 15 | 3rd | Eric Thurston | Tamas Erdelyi |

### U18 World Championship (Men)

| Year Event | GP | W | T | | L | GF | GA | Place | Coach | Captain |
|---|---|---|---|---|---|---|---|---|---|---|
| Year Event | GP | W | OTW | OTL | L | GF | GA | Place | Coach | Captain |
| 1999 WM18-B | 5 | 1 | 0 | | 4 | 11 | 41 | 7th | Tibor Kiss | Janosi Csaba |
| 2001 WM18-II | 4 | 1 | 0 | | 3 | 18 | 31 | 7th | Tibor Kiss | Zoltan Revak |
| 2002 WM18-II | 5 | 2 | 0 | | 3 | 16 | 19 | 6th | Tibor Kiss | Gabor Krisztu |
| 2003 WM18-II-B | 5 | 3 | 1 | | 1 | 27 | 12 | 2nd | Vladimir Matejov | Viktor Papp |
| 2004 WM18-II-A | 5 | 3 | 1 | | 1 | 41 | 18 | 2nd | Vladimir Matejov | Viktor Papp |
| 2005 WM18-II-B | 5 | 5 | 0 | | 0 | 40 | 8 | 1st | Eduard Giblak | Andras Benk |
| 2006 WM18-I-A | 5 | 0 | 1 | | 4 | 14 | 24 | 6th | Dusan Kapusta | David Jobb |
| 2007 WM18-II-A | 5 | 4 | 0 | 0 | 1 | 48 | 7 | 2nd | Eduard Giblak | Balazs Somogyi |
| 2008 WM18-II-B | 5 | 4 | 0 | 0 | 1 | 37 | 12 | 1st | Gyorgy Pek | Patrik Popovics |
| 2009 WM18-I-A | 5 | 3 | 0 | 0 | 1 | 19 | 18 | 3rd | Laszlo Ancsin | Balazs Somogyi |
| 2010 WM18-I-B | 5 | 3 | 0 | 1 | 1 | 19 | 17 | 2nd | Robert Dever | Janos Hari |
| 2011 WM18-I-A | 4 | 1 | 0 | 1 | 2 | 10 | 16 | 4th | Kevin Primeau | Benjamin Nemes |
| 2012 WM18-I-B | 5 | 0 | 0 | 2 | 3 | 13 | 20 | 6th | Eric Thurston | Gergely Korbuly |

### Women's World Championship

| Year Event | GP | W | T | | L | GF | GA | Place | Coach | Captain |
|---|---|---|---|---|---|---|---|---|---|---|
| Year Event | GP | W | OTW | OTL | L | GF | GA | Place | Coach | Captain |
| 2003 WW-III | 5 | 1 | 1 | | 3 | 5 | 14 | 4th | Tibor Balogh | Edit Daranyi |
| 2004 WW-III | 5 | 3 | 0 | | 2 | 15 | 20 | 3rd | Tibor Balogh | *unknown* |
| 2005 WW-III | 5 | 2 | 0 | | 3 | 16 | 14 | 4th | Tibor Balogh | *unknown* |
| 2007 WW-III | 5 | 2 | 0 | 0 | 3 | 22 | 19 | 4th | Laszlo Pindak | Edit Daranyi |
| 2008 WW-III | 5 | 1 | 0 | 0 | 4 | 4 | 20 | 5th | Andras Kis | Gyongyi Szlaby |
| 2011 WW-III | 5 | 2 | 1 | 0 | 2 | 27 | 11 | 3rd | Csaba Gomori | Gyongyi Szlaby |
| 2012 WW-II-A | 5 | 4 | 0 | 0 | 1 | 26 | 6 | 2nd | Csaba Gomori | Gyongyi Szlaby |

### U18 Women's World Championship

(bold=top level)

| Year Event | GP | W | OTW | OTL | L | GF | GA | Place | Coach | Captain |
|---|---|---|---|---|---|---|---|---|---|---|
| 2012 WW18-I | 5 | 4 | 1 | 0 | 0 | 24 | 10 | 1st | Csaba Gomori | Franciska Kiss-Simon |

# Iceland (ISL)

*Orri Blondal skates with the puck as Iceland hosts the 2012 IIHF Ice Hockey World Championship Division II Group A in Reykjavik. Photo: Kristjan Maack.*

## Joined IIHF: May 6, 1992

Website: www.ihi.is
E-mail: ihi@ihi.is

Ice Hockey Iceland
Sport Center Laugardal
Engjavegi 6
104 Reykjavik
Iceland

Phone: +354 514 4075 • Fax: +354 514 4079

**World Ranking**

| MEN | | WOMEN | |
|---|---|---|---|
| 2012 | 35 | 2012 | 29 |
| 2011 | 36 | 2011 | 29 |
| 2010 | 38 | 2010 | 29 |
| 2009 | 37 | 2009 | 29 |
| 2008 | 38 | 2008 | 31 |
| 2007 | 37 | 2007 | 30 |
| 2006 | 40 | 2006 | 30 |
| 2005 | 39 | 2005 | 30 |
| 2004 | 39 | | |

**Top Level Host History** none

**World Championship (Men)**

| Year Event | GP | W | T | | | L | GF | GA | Place | Coach | Captain |
|---|---|---|---|---|---|---|---|---|---|---|---|
| Year Event | GP | W | | OTW | OTL | L | GF | GA | Place | Coach | Captain |
| 1999 WM-D | 4 | 1 | 0 | | | 3 | 9 | 35 | 9th | Jan Stolpe | Kristjan Oskarsson |
| 2000 WM-D | 4 | 2 | 0 | | | 2 | 22 | 18 | 5th | Thomas Billgren | Heidar Agustsson |
| 2001 WM-II-A | 5 | 1 | 0 | | | 4 | 11 | 34 | 5th | Thomas Billgren | Ingvar Jonsson |
| 2002 WM-II-B | 5 | 1 | 0 | | | 4 | 14 | 44 | 5th | Boris Mindel | Ingvar Jonsson |
| 2003 WM-II-B | 5 | 0 | 0 | | | 5 | 4 | 31 | 6th | Peter Bolin | Sigurdsson Sigurdur |
| 2004 WM-III | 4 | 3 | 1 | | | 0 | 46 | 8 | 1st | Peter Bolin | Ingvar Jonsson |
| 2005 WM-II-B | 5 | 1 | 0 | | | 4 | 12 | 26 | 6th | Stanislav Berger | Ingvar Jonsson |
| 2006 WM-III | 4 | 4 | 0 | | | 0 | 27 | 6 | 1st | Ed Maggiacomo | Ingvar Jonsson |
| 2007 WM-II-B | 4 | 1 | | 0 | 0 | 3 | 9 | 29 | 4th | Ed Maggiacomo | Ingvar Jonsson |
| 2008 WM-II-B | 5 | 1 | | 0 | 1 | 3 | 17 | 21 | 5th | Sveinn Bjornsson | Ingvar Jonsson |
| 2009 WM-II-A | 5 | 2 | | 0 | 1 | 2 | 11 | 30 | 4th | Richard Tahtinen | Ingvar Jonsson |
| 2010 WM-II-B | 5 | 3 | | 0 | 0 | 2 | 16 | 18 | 3rd | Richard Tahtinen | Ingvar Jonsson |
| 2011 WM-II-B | 5 | 3 | | 0 | 0 | 2 | 24 | 18 | 3rd | Olaf Eller | Ingvar Jonsson |
| 2012 WM-II-A | 5 | 2 | | 0 | 0 | 3 | 12 | 19 | 4th | Olaf Eller | Ingvar Jonsson |

**U20 World Championship**

| Year Event | GP | W | T | | | L | GF | GA | Place | Coach | Captain |
|---|---|---|---|---|---|---|---|---|---|---|---|
| Year Event | GP | W | | OTW | OTL | L | GF | GA | Place | Coach | Captain |
| 1999 WM20-D | 4 | 1 | 1 | | | 2 | 24 | 29 | 8th | Jan Stolpe | Ingvor Jonsson |
| 2000 WM20-D | 4 | 0 | 0 | | | 4 | 9 | 37 | 9th | Jan Stolpe | Ingvar Jonsson |
| 2002 WM20-III | 4 | 1 | 0 | | | 3 | 10 | 36 | 6th | Jan Stolpe | Stefan Hrafnsson |
| 2003 WM20-II-B | 5 | 1 | 1 | | | 3 | 19 | 43 | 5th | Sergei Zak | Stefan Hrafnsson |
| 2004 WM20-II-A | 5 | 0 | 0 | | | 5 | 10 | 80 | 6th | Jan Kobezda | Jon Hallgrimsson |
| 2005 WM20-III | 5 | 3 | 0 | | | 2 | 30 | 19 | 3rd | Owe Holmberg | Jon Hallgrimsson |
| 2006 WM20-III | 4 | 3 | 0 | | | 1 | 79 | 6 | 2nd | Edward Maggiacomo | Jon Hallgrimsson |
| 2007 WM20-II-A | 5 | 1 | | 0 | 0 | 4 | 13 | 35 | 5th | Edward Maggiacomo | Birkir Arnason |
| 2008 WM20-II-A | 5 | 0 | | 0 | 0 | 5 | 7 | 47 | 6th | Jukka Isoantilla | Thorsteinn Bjornsson |
| 2010 WM20-III | 5 | 4 | | 0 | 0 | 1 | 30 | 9 | 2nd | Josh Gribben | Andri Mikaelsson |
| 2011 WM20-II-A | 5 | 1 | | 0 | 0 | 4 | 10 | 23 | 6th | Josh Gribben | Robert Palsson |
| 2012 WM20-III | 4 | 4 | | 0 | 0 | 0 | 30 | 2 | 1st | Josh Gribben | Olafur Bjornsson |

**U18 World Championship (Men)**

| Year Event | GP | W | T | | | L | GF | GA | Place | Coach | Captain |
|---|---|---|---|---|---|---|---|---|---|---|---|
| Year Event | GP | W | | OTW | OTL | L | GF | GA | Place | Coach | Captain |
| 2003 WM18-III-B | 3 | 3 | 0 | | | 0 | 19 | 4 | 1st | Patrick Flynn | Ragnar Oskarsson |
| 2004 WM18-II-A | 5 | 1 | 0 | | | 4 | 14 | 57 | 5th | Sergei Zak | Jon Ingi Hallgrimsson |
| 2005 WM18-II-B | 5 | 1 | 0 | | | 4 | 19 | 29 | 5th | Sergei Zak | Bikir Arnason |
| 2006 WM18-II-B | 5 | 0 | 0 | | | 5 | 7 | 40 | 6th | Edward Maggiacomo | Ulfar Jon Andresson |
| 2007 WM18-III | 5 | 3 | | 0 | 0 | 2 | 41 | 17 | 3rd | Sergei Zak | Thorsteinn Bjornsson |
| 2008 WM18-III-B | 4 | 3 | | 0 | 0 | 1 | 48 | 7 | 2nd | Sergei Zak | Sigurdur Arnason |
| 2009 WM18-III-B | 3 | 3 | | 0 | 0 | 0 | 48 | 1 | 1st | Sergei Zak | Egill Thormodsson |
| 2010 WM18-II-A | 5 | 1 | | 0 | 0 | 4 | 12 | 44 | 6th | Sergei Zak | Gunnar Sigurdsson |
| 2011 WM18-III-B | 4 | 3 | | 1 | 0 | 0 | 52 | 5 | 1st | Sergei Zak | Ingolfur Eliasson |
| 2012 WM18-II-B | 5 | 2 | | 0 | 1 | 2 | 23 | 23 | 4th | Sergei Zak | Steindor Ingason |

**Women's World Championship**
(bold=top level)

| Year Event | GP | W | T | | | L | GF | GA | Place | Coach | Captain |
|---|---|---|---|---|---|---|---|---|---|---|---|
| Year Event | GP | W | | OTW | OTL | L | GF | GA | Place | Coach | Captain |
| 2005 WW-IV | 3 | 0 | 1 | | | 2 | 6 | 14 | 4th | Sveinn Bjornsson | *unknown* |
| 2007 WW-IV | 5 | 1 | | 0 | 1 | 3 | 17 | 23 | 5th | Sarah Shantz Smiley | Hanna Heimisdottir |
| 2008 WW-IV | 5 | 5 | | 0 | 0 | 0 | 30 | 5 | 1st | Sarah Shantz Smiley | Hanna Heimisdottir |
| 2011 WW-IV | 4 | 2 | | 0 | 0 | 2 | 10 | 10 | 3rd | Sarah Smiley | Hanna Heimisdottir |
| 2012 WW-II-B | 5 | 2 | | 0 | 1 | 2 | 11 | 15 | 4th | Richard Tahtinen | Anna Agustsdottir |

# India (IND)

India challenges Macau at the 2012 IIHF Challenge Cup of Asia in Dehradun, India. Photo: IHAI.

### Joined IIHF: April 27, 1989

Website: www.icehockeyindia.com
E-mail: info@icehockeyindia.com / akshay@himalayanadventure.com

Ice Hockey Association of India
D-502, Som Vihar Apartments
Sangam Road, R.K. Puram
New Delhi 11002
India

Phone: +91 11 233 400 33 • Fax: +91 11 237 420 13

# Ireland (IRL)

Ireland had its only team entered in the men's category at Division III level in Turkey. Photo: TIHF.

### Joined IIHF: September 26, 1996

Website: www.iiha.org
E-mail: info@iiha.org

Irish Ice Hockey Association
Sport HQ,
13 Joyce Way,
Parkwest Business Park,
Dublin 12
Ireland

Phone: +353 1 625 1157 • Fax: +353 1 686 5213

**World Ranking**

| MEN | WOMEN |
|---|---|
| 2012........42 | 2012........36 |
| 2011........41 | 2011........36 |
| 2010........41 | |
| 2009........42 | |
| 2008........40 | |
| 2007........43 | |
| 2006........44 | |
| 2005........44 | |
| 2004........44 | |

**Top Level Host History** none

**World Championship (Men)**

| Year Event | GP | W | T | | | L | GF | GA | Place | Coach | Captain |
|---|---|---|---|---|---|---|---|---|---|---|---|
| Year Event | GP | W | | OTW | OTL | L | GF | GA | Place | Coach | Captain |
| 2004 WM-III | 4 | 1 | 0 | | | 3 | 23 | 23 | 4th | Greg Fitzgerald | Mark Bowes |
| 2005 WM-III | 4 | 1 | 0 | | | 3 | 32 | 20 | 4th | James Graves | David Morrison |
| 2006 WM-III | 4 | 1 | 1 | | | 2 | 5 | 17 | 4th | James Tibbetts | David Morrison |
| 2007 WM-III | 4 | 2 | | 1 | 0 | 1 | 20 | 8 | 2nd | James Tibbetts | David Morrison |
| 2008 WM-II-A | 5 | 0 | | 0 | 0 | 5 | 8 | 57 | 6th | James Tibbetts | David Morrison |
| 2009 WM-III | 5 | 1 | | 0 | 0 | 4 | 12 | 31 | 5th | James Tibbetts | Mark Morrison |
| 2010 WM-III-A | 3 | 3 | | 0 | 0 | 0 | 17 | 7 | 1st | James Tibbetts | Mark Morrison |
| 2011 WM-II-B | 5 | 0 | | 0 | 0 | 5 | 4 | 68 | 6th | James Tibbetts | Mark Morrison |
| 2012 WM-III | 5 | 2 | | 0 | 0 | 3 | 18 | 24 | 4th | Kenneth Redmond | Stephen Hamill |

**U18 World Championship (Men)**

| Year Event | GP | W | OTW | OTL | L | GF | GA | Place | Coach | Captain |
|---|---|---|---|---|---|---|---|---|---|---|
| 2009 WM18-III-B | 3 | 1 | 0 | 0 | 2 | 9 | 39 | 3rd | Sean Dooley | Stephen Balmer |
| 2010 WM18-III-B | 4 | 0 | 0 | 0 | 4 | 6 | 26 | 5th | Sean Dooley | Philip Catherwood |
| 2011 WM18-III-B | 4 | 0 | 0 | 0 | 4 | 3 | 59 | 5th | Kenneth Redmond | Rian Larkin |

# Israel (ISR)

*Israel celebrates a win at the 2012 IIHF Ice Hockey World Championship Division II, Group B. Photo: Bonchuk Andonov.*

**Joined IIHF: May 1, 1991**

Website: www.israhockey.co.il
E-mail: israhockey@gmail.com

Ice Hockey Federation of Israel
Kikar Hill 3
Appartment 4
Tel-Aviv 62492
Israel

Phone: +972 3 60 40 722 • Fax: +972 3 544 56 32

**World Ranking**

**MEN**
2012........40
2011........40
2010........39
2009........36
2008........35
2007........34
2006........33
2005........35
2004........36

**Top Level Host History** none

**World Championship (Men)**

| Year Event | GP | W | T | | L | GF | GA | Place | Coach | Captain |
|---|---|---|---|---|---|---|---|---|---|---|
| Year Event | GP | W | OTW | OTL | L | GF | GA | Place | Coach | Captain |
| 1992 WM-C | 5 | 1 | 1 | | 3 | 22 | 42 | 4th | Gideon Lee | *unknown* |
| 1993 WM-C | 5 | 0 | 0 | | 5 | 8 | 91 | 11th | Gideon Lee | Uzi Lee |
| 1994 WM-C-B | 5 | 1 | 0 | | 4 | 15 | 31 | 7th | Lev Genin | *unknown* |
| 1995 WM-C-2 | 6 | 3 | 0 | | 3 | 31 | 22 | 6th | Semion Yakubovich | Evgeni Feldman |
| 1996 WM-D | 5 | 1 | 1 | | 3 | 10 | 20 | 7th | Nikolaj Epshtein | Evgeni Feldman |
| 1997 WM-D | 5 | 2 | 0 | | 3 | 18 | 25 | 5th | Nikolaj Epshtein | Evgeni Feldman |
| 1998 WM-D | 5 | 3 | 0 | | 2 | 34 | 16 | 3rd | Lev Sudat | Sergei Belo |
| 1999 WM-D | 4 | 3 | 1 | | 0 | 22 | 5 | 2nd | Sergei Martin | Sergei Belo |
| 2000 WM-D | 4 | 3 | 1 | | 0 | 31 | 7 | 1st | Sergei Martin | Sergei Belo |
| 2001 WM-II-B | 5 | 4 | 0 | | 1 | 21 | 11 | 2nd | Boris Mindel | Sergei Belo |
| 2002 WM-II-A | 5 | 3 | 0 | | 2 | 14 | 22 | 3rd | Boris Mindel | Sergei Belo |
| 2003 WM-II-B | 5 | 1 | 2 | | 2 | 11 | 19 | 5th | Boris Mindel | Sergei Belo |
| 2004 WM-II-A | 5 | 0 | 1 | | 4 | 3 | 28 | 5th | Boris Mindel | Sergei Belo |
| 2005 WM-II-B | 5 | 4 | 1 | | 0 | 21 | 11 | 1st | Jean Perron | Sergei Belo |
| 2006 WM-I-A | 5 | 0 | 0 | | 5 | 3 | 47 | 6th | Jean Perron | Sergei Belo |
| 2007 WM-II-B | 4 | 2 | 0 | 0 | 2 | 11 | 11 | 3rd | Jean Perron | Sergei Belo |
| 2008 WM-II-A | 5 | 1 | 1 | 0 | 3 | 16 | 28 | 4th | Jean Perron | Sergei Belo |
| 2009 WM-II-A | 5 | 1 | 0 | 0 | 4 | 9 | 38 | 5th | Jean Perron | Sergei Belo |
| 2010 WM-II-B | 5 | 0 | 0 | 0 | 5 | 11 | 55 | 6th | Boris Mindel | Sergei Belo |
| 2011 WM-III | 5 | 4 | 1 | 0 | 0 | 57 | 9 | 1st | Sergei Belo | Avishai Geller |
| 2012 WM-II-B | 5 | 1 | 1 | 1 | 2 | 19 | 22 | 5th | Jean Perron | Avishai Geller |

**U20 World Championship**

| Year Event | GP | W | T | L | GF | GA | Place | Coach | Captain |
|---|---|---|---|---|---|---|---|---|---|
| 1997 WM20-D | 4 | 2 | 0 | 2 | 20 | 26 | 5th | Sergei Martin | Ran Oz |

**U18 World Championship (Men)**

| Year Event | GP | W | T | | L | GF | GA | Place | Coach | Captain |
|---|---|---|---|---|---|---|---|---|---|---|
| Year Event | GP | W | OTW | OTL | L | GF | GA | Place | Coach | Captain |
| 2001 WM18-III | 4 | 0 | 0 | | 4 | 11 | 25 | 8th | Semion Yacurovitch | Hof Eden |
| 2003 WM18-III-B | 3 | 1 | 0 | | 2 | 5 | 14 | 4th | Edward Ravniaga | Raviv Bull |
| 2004 WM18-III-B | 6 | 2 | 0 | | 4 | 15 | 28 | 5th | Edward Ravniaga | Raviv Bull |
| 2005 WM18-III | 5 | 3 | 0 | | 2 | 36 | 15 | 3rd | Jean Perron | Raviv Bull |
| 2006 WM18-III | 5 | 3 | 1 | | 1 | 42 | 26 | 2nd | Jean Perron | Michael Horwitz |
| 2007 WM18-II-A | 5 | 1 | 0 | 0 | 4 | 11 | 36 | 5th | Jean Perron | George Pisha |
| 2008 WM18-II-B | 5 | 0 | 0 | 0 | 5 | 11 | 68 | 6th | Dusan Kralik | George Pisha |
| 2010 WM18-III-B | 4 | 1 | 0 | 1 | 2 | 21 | 16 | 4th | Edward Ravniaga | Kai Malachi |
| 2011 WM18-III-B | 4 | 1 | 0 | 0 | 3 | 17 | 24 | 4th | Boris Mindel | Daniel Golodnizky |

# Italy (ITA)

*Italy earned promotion to the top pool of the World Championship for 2012 but was demoted to Division I, Group A for 2013.*
*Photo: Andre Ringuette / HHOF-IIHF Images.*

**Joined IIHF: January 24, 1924**

Website: www.fisg.it
E-mail: hockey@fisg.it

Federazione Italiana
Sport Ghiaccio
Via G.B. Piranesi, 46
20137 Milano, Italy

Phone: +39 02 70 1413 ext. 22 or 31 • Fax: +39 02 70 141 380

| World Ranking | |
|---|---|
| **MEN** | **WOMEN** |
| 2012........16 | 2012........18 |
| 2011........17 | 2011........17 |
| 2010........16 | 2010........17 |
| 2009........15 | 2009........16 |
| 2008........14 | 2008........15 |
| 2007........13 | 2007........14 |
| 2006........17 | 2006........11 |
| 2005........19 | 2005........17 |
| 2004........19 | 2004........17 |

**Top Level Host History**
Olympics: 1956 (Cortina d'Ampezzo); 2006 (Turin)
World Championship (Men): 1934 (Milan); 1994 (Milan, Bolzano, Canazei)

**Olympics, Men**
(bold=top level)

| Year Event | GP | W | T | L | GF | GA | Place | Coach | Captain |
|---|---|---|---|---|---|---|---|---|---|
| **1936 OG-M** | **3** | **1** | **0** | **2** | **2** | **5** | **9th** | **Giampiero Medri** | ***unknown*** |
| **1948 OG-M** | **8** | **0** | **0** | **8** | **24** | **156** | **9th** | **Othmar Delnon** | ***unknown*** |
| **1956 OG-M** | **6** | **3** | **2** | **1** | **26** | **14** | **7th** | **Richard "Bibi" Torriani** | **Mario Bedogni** |
| **1964 OG-M** | **7** | **2** | **0** | **5** | **24** | **42** | **15th** | **Slavomir Barton** | **Gianfranco Darin** |
| **1984 OG-M** | **5** | **2** | **0** | **3** | **15** | **21** | **9th** | **Ron Ivany** | **Adolf Insam** |
| **1992 OG-M** | **7** | **1** | **0** | **6** | **22** | **33** | **12th** | **Gene Ubriaco** | **Robert Oberrauch** |
| **1994 OG-M** | **7** | **3** | **0** | **4** | **24** | **36** | **9th** | **Bryan Lefley** | **Robert Oberrauch** |
| **1998 OG-M** | **4** | **1** | **0** | **3** | **12** | **16** | **12th** | **Adolf Insam** | **Robert Oberrauch** |
| **2006 OG-M** | **5** | **0** | **2** | **3** | **9** | **23** | **11th** | **Michel Goulet** | **Giuseppe Busillo** |

**World Championship (Men)**
(bold=top level)

| Year Event | GP | W | T | L | GF | GA | Place | Coach | Captain |
|---|---|---|---|---|---|---|---|---|---|
| Year Event | GP | W | OTW OTL | L | GF | GA | Place | Coach | Captain |
| **1930 WM** | **1** | **0** | **0** | **1** | **0** | **2** | **10th** | **Enrico Bombilla** | ***unknown*** |
| **1933 WM** | **4** | **1** | **0** | **3** | **3** | **8** | **11th** | ***unknown*** | ***unknown*** |
| **1934 WM** | **7** | **2** | **2** | **3** | **9** | **12** | **9th** | **Giorgio Baroni** | **Francesco Roncarelli** |
| **1935 WM** | **7** | **1** | **3** | **3** | **7** | **19** | **8th** | **Giuseppe Crivelli** | **Decio Trovati** |
| **1939 WM** | **6** | **4** | **1** | **1** | **11** | **10** | **9th** | ***unknown*** | **Augusto Gerosa** |
| 1951 WM-B | 5 | 5 | 0 | 0 | 27 | 8 | 1st | Luigi Bestagini/Franco Rossi | Dino Innocenti |
| 1953 WM-B | 5 | 5 | 0 | 0 | 26 | 10 | 1st | Pete Bessone | Aldo Federici |
| 1955 WM-B | 4 | 4 | 0 | 0 | 50 | 4 | 1st | Bibi Torriani | Aldo Federici |
| **1959 WM** | **8** | **3** | **1** | **4** | **27** | **39** | **10th** | **Bill Cupolo** | ***unknown*** |
| 1961 WM-B | 5 | 2 | 1 | 2 | 19 | 20 | 4th | Aldo Federici | Giancarlo Agazzi |
| 1966 WM-C | 4 | 4 | 0 | 0 | 54 | 8 | 1st | Brian Whittal | Gianfranco Da Rin |
| 1967 WM-B | 7 | 2 | 1 | 4 | 23 | 31 | 5th | Brian Whittal | Gianfranco Da Rin |
| 1969 WM-B | 7 | 0 | 0 | 7 | 10 | 41 | 8th | Robert Robetin | Gianfranco Da Rin |
| 1970 WM-C | 6 | 4 | 1 | 1 | 27 | 14 | 2nd | Brian Whittal | Giulio Verocai |
| 1971 WM-B | 7 | 0 | 2 | 5 | 12 | 43 | 8th | Brian Whittal | Gianfranco Da Rin |
| 1972 WM-C | 6 | 4 | 1 | 1 | 31 | 13 | 2nd | Ernesto Crotti | Giulio Verocai |
| 1973 WM-B | 7 | 0 | 0 | 7 | 18 | 54 | 8th | Ernesto Crotti/Robert Robetin | Alberto Da Rin (1) |
| 1974 WM-C | 7 | 5 | 1 | 1 | 42 | 14 | 2nd | Aldo Federici | Gianfranco Da Rin |
| 1975 WM-B | 7 | 2 | 0 | 5 | 22 | 40 | 7th | Aldo Federici | Gianfranco Da Rin |
| 1976 WM-B | 7 | 2 | 1 | 4 | 23 | 41 | 7th | Aldo Federici | unknown |
| 1977 WM-C | 6 | 5 | 1 | 0 | 64 | 6 | 1st | Billy Harris | Alberto Da Rin |
| 1978 WM-B | 7 | 1 | 1 | 5 | 32 | 41 | 7th | Billy Harris | Alberto Da Rin |
| 1979 WM-C | 7 | 6 | 0 | 1 | 64 | 17 | 2nd | Alberto Da Rin | Manuel de Toni |
| 1981 WM-B | 7 | 6 | 1 | 0 | 38 | 18 | 1st | Dave Chambers | Adolf Insam |
| **1982 WM** | **7** | **1** | **1** | **5** | **20** | **44** | **7th** | **Dave Chambers** | **Michael Mair** |
| **1983 WM** | **10** | **1** | **1** | **8** | **16** | **56** | **8th** | **Dave Chambers** | **Michael Mair** |
| 1985 WM-B | 7 | 5 | 0 | 2 | 29 | 22 | 3rd | Ron Ivany | Michael Mair |
| 1986 WM-B | 7 | 4 | 0 | 3 | 21 | 18 | 2nd | Mike Kelly/Alberto Da Rin | Lodovico Migliore |
| 1987 WM-B | 7 | 2 | 1 | 4 | 28 | 30 | 6th | Dave Chambers | Lodovico Migliore |
| 1989 WM-B | 7 | 5 | 1 | 1 | 37 | 16 | 2nd | Ron Ivany | Erwin Kostner |
| 1990 WM-B | 7 | 5 | 1 | 1 | 41 | 18 | 2nd | Barry Smith | Erwin Kostner |
| 1991 WM-B | 7 | 7 | 0 | 0 | 49 | 10 | 1st | Gene Ubriaco | Erwin Kostner |
| **1992 WM** | **5** | **1** | **1** | **3** | **10** | **18** | **9th** | **Bryan Lefley** | **Robert Oberrauch** |
| **1993 WM** | **6** | **1** | **2** | **3** | **9** | **28** | **8th** | **Bryan Lefley** | **Robert Oberrauch** |
| **1994 WM** | **6** | **3** | **0** | **3** | **19** | **22** | **6th** | **Bryan Lefley** | **Robert Oberrauch** |
| **1995 WM** | **6** | **3** | **1** | **2** | **14** | **18** | **7th** | **Bryan Lefley** | **Robert Oberrauch** |
| **1996 WM** | **6** | **2** | **1** | **3** | **22** | **31** | **7th** | **Bryan Lefley** | **Robert Oberrauch** |
| **1997 WM** | **8** | **3** | **1** | **4** | **28** | **28** | **8th** | **Bryan Lefley** | **Martin Pavlu** |
| **1998 WM** | **6** | **2** | **2** | **2** | **17** | **13** | **10th** | **Adolf Insam** | **Robert Oberrauch** |
| **1999 WM** | **3** | **0** | **0** | **3** | **8** | **17** | **13th** | **Adolf Insam** | **Gates Orlando** |

| Year Event | GP | W | T | | L | GF | GA | Place | Coach | Captain |
|---|---|---|---|---|---|---|---|---|---|---|
| **2000 WM** | **6** | **1** | **1** | | **4** | **8** | **28** | **12th** | **Adolf Insam** | **Bruno Zarillo** |
| **2001 WM** | **6** | **1** | **1** | | **4** | **9** | **34** | **12th** | **Pat Cortina** | **Bruno Zarillo** |
| **2002 WM** | **6** | **1** | **0** | | **5** | **10** | **25** | **15th** | **Pat Cortina** | **Lucio Topatigh** |
| 2003 WM-I-B | 5 | 2 | 0 | | 3 | 16 | 11 | 4th | Pat Cortina | Roland Ramoser |
| 2004 WM-I-B | 5 | 4 | 0 | | 1 | 26 | 7 | 2nd | Michel Goulet | Giuseppe Busillo |
| 2005 WM-I-B | 5 | 4 | 1 | | 0 | 17 | 3 | 1st | Michel Goulet | Giuseppe Busillo |
| **2006 WM** | **6** | **1** | **1** | | **4** | **9** | **21** | **14th** | **Michel Goulet** | **Giuseppe Busillo** |
| **2007 WM** | **6** | **0** | **1** | **0** | **5** | **8** | **23** | **12th** | **Michel Goulet** | **Mario Chittaroni** |
| **2008 WM** | **5** | **0** | **0** | **0** | **5** | **11** | **29** | **16th** | **Michel Goulet** | **Mario Chittaroni** |
| 2009 WM-I-B | 5 | 5 | 0 | 0 | 0 | 26 | 4 | 1st | Rick Cornacchia | Roland Ramoser |
| **2010 WM** | **6** | **1** | **0** | **1** | **4** | **8** | **19** | **15th** | **Rick Cornacchia** | **Roland Ramoser** |
| 2011 WM-I-A | 4 | 3 | 1 | 0 | 0 | 15 | 5 | 1st | Rick Cornacchia | Manuel de Toni |
| **2012 WM** | **7** | **0** | **1** | **0** | **6** | **6** | **31** | **15th** | **Rick Cornacchia** | **Manuel de Toni** |

(1)Giulio Verocai captain Mar. 22 vs. SUI, Mar. 23 vs. AUT, Mar. 25 vs. ROM

### U20 World Championship

| Year Event | GP | W | T | | L | GF | GA | Place | Coach | Captain |
|---|---|---|---|---|---|---|---|---|---|---|
| Year Event | GP | W | OTW | OTL | L | GF | GA | Place | Coach | Captain |
| 1979 WM20-B | 4 | 1 | 0 | | 3 | 22 | 21 | 7th | Dusan Bosko | Paolo di Bassio |
| 1980 WM20-B | 4 | 1 | 0 | | 3 | 12 | 20 | 6th | Werner Holzner | Paolo di Bassio |
| 1981 WM20-B | 5 | 1 | 1 | | 3 | 17 | 33 | 7th | Jaroslaw Pavlu | Gabriele Rossi |
| 1982 WM20-B | 4 | 0 | 1 | | 3 | 8 | 19 | 6th | Edmund Rabanser | Antonio Polazzon |
| 1983 WM20-B | 5 | 0 | 1 | | 4 | 18 | 38 | 8th | Edmund Rabanser | Andrea Gios |
| 1984 WM20-C | 5 | 4 | 1 | | 0 | 41 | 14 | 1st | Jiri Vrba | Franco dell'Osta |
| 1985 WM20-B | 7 | 2 | 0 | | 5 | 14 | 28 | 6th | Gianfranco Da Rin | Robert Oberrauch |
| 1986 WM20-B | 7 | 1 | 1 | | 5 | 26 | 40 | 7th | Ron Ivany | Ilario Riva |
| 1987 WM20-B | 5 | 0 | 1 | | 4 | 14 | 35 | 8th | Slavomir Barton | *unknown* |
| 1988 WM20-C | 7 | 6 | 0 | | 1 | 27 | 17 | 2nd | Hans Schultz | Luca Origoni |
| 1989 WM20-C | 4 | 2 | 2 | | 0 | 22 | 14 | 2nd | Edmondo Rabanser | Riky Tessari |
| 1990 WM20-C | 6 | 4 | 0 | | 2 | 35 | 10 | 3rd | Edmondo Rabanser | *unknown* |
| 1991 WM20-C | 7 | 6 | 0 | | 1 | 57 | 11 | 2nd | Fabio Pollini | Boris Meneghetti |
| 1992 WM20-C | 3 | 3 | 0 | | 0 | 17 | 6 | 1st | Adolf Insam | Marcus Brunner |
| 1993 WM20-B | 7 | 4 | 1 | | 2 | 23 | 18 | 3rd | Miroslav Berek | Armando Chelodi |
| 1994 WM20-B | 7 | 2 | 1 | | 4 | 20 | 22 | 5th | Adolf Insam | Federico Zancanella |
| 1995 WM20-B | 7 | 1 | 0 | | 6 | 16 | 37 | 8th | Michael Mair | Luca Rigoni |
| 1996 WM20-B | 6 | 2 | 0 | | 4 | 13 | 27 | 5th | Pat Cortina | Christian Timpone |
| 1997 WM20-B | 7 | 0 | 0 | | 7 | 12 | 46 | 8th | Bob Manno | *unknown* |
| 1998 WM20-C | 4 | 2 | 1 | | 1 | 24 | 12 | 2nd | Massimo Da Rin | Daniele Veggiato |
| 1999 WM20-C | 4 | 3 | 0 | | 1 | 10 | 6 | 1st | Adolf Insam | Manuel de Toni |
| 2000 WM20-B | 5 | 1 | 2 | | 2 | 6 | 10 | 6th | Adolf Insam | Stefan Zisser |
| 2001 WM20-I | 5 | 0 | 2 | | 3 | 11 | 17 | 7th | Adolf Insam | Alessandro Rotolo |
| 2002 WM20-I | 5 | 0 | 2 | | 3 | 14 | 28 | 8th | Adolf Insam | Christian Borgatello |
| 2003 WM20-I-A | 5 | 1 | 0 | | 4 | 11 | 16 | 5th | Massimo Da Rin | Paolo Bustreo |
| 2004 WM20-I-B | 5 | 3 | 0 | | 2 | 15 | 18 | 4th | Massimo Da Rin | Luca Scardoni |
| 2005 WM20-I-A | 5 | 1 | 0 | | 4 | 11 | 16 | 5th | Erwin Kostner | Claudio Mantese |
| 2006 WM20-I-B | 5 | 2 | 1 | | 2 | 14 | 15 | 3rd | Erwin Kostner | Andreas Lutz |
| 2007 WM20-I-B | 5 | 1 | 0 | 0 | 4 | 8 | 17 | 6th | Erwin Kostner | Armin Hofer |
| 2008 WM20-II-A | 5 | 5 | 0 | 0 | 0 | 37 | 8 | 1st | Fabio Polloni | Ivan Demetz |
| 2009 WM20-I-B | 5 | 2 | 1 | 0 | 2 | 14 | 10 | 4th | Michel Goulet | Anton Bernard |
| 2010 WM20-I-B | 5 | 2 | 1 | 0 | 2 | 8 | 8 | 3rd | Fabio Polloni | Marian Zelger |
| 2011 WM20-I-A | 5 | 2 | 0 | 0 | 3 | 13 | 8 | 4th | Fabio Polloni | Jan Waldner |
| 2012 WM20-I-B | 5 | 2 | 1 | 0 | 2 | 14 | 9 | 3rd | Fabio Polloni | Jan Waldner |

### U18 World Championship (Men)

| Year Event | GP | W | T | | L | GF | GA | Place | Coach | Captain |
|---|---|---|---|---|---|---|---|---|---|---|
| Year Event | GP | W | OTW | OTL | L | GF | GA | Place | Coach | Captain |
| 1999 WM18-B | 5 | 3 | 1 | | 1 | 22 | 13 | 5th | Massimo Da Rin | Alessandro Rotolo |
| 2000 WM18-B | 5 | 2 | 1 | | 2 | 15 | 19 | 6th | Massimo Da Rin | Christian Borgatello |
| 2001 WM18-I | 5 | 2 | 1 | | 2 | 14 | 22 | 6th | Massimo Da Rin | Paolo Bustreo |
| 2002 WM18-I | 4 | 1 | 0 | | 3 | 9 | 15 | 5th | Massimo Da Rin | Lorenz Daccordo |
| 2003 WM18-I-B | 5 | 2 | 1 | | 2 | 15 | 13 | 3rd | Erwin Kostner | Claudio Mantese |
| 2004 WM18-I-B | 5 | 2 | 1 | | 2 | 14 | 16 | 3rd | Erwin Kostner | Andreas Lutz |
| 2005 WM18-I-B | 5 | 0 | 2 | | 3 | 14 | 17 | 6th | Erwin Kostner | Luca Zandonella |
| 2006 WM18-II-A | 5 | 5 | 0 | | 0 | 35 | 2 | 1st | Massimo Da Rin | Ivan Demetz |
| 2007 WM18-I-A | 5 | 2 | 0 | 1 | 2 | 19 | 20 | 4th | Stefan Mair | Florian Wieser |
| 2008 WM18-I-B | 5 | 2 | 0 | 1 | 2 | 17 | 10 | 4th | Stefan Mair | Simon Kostner |
| 2009 WM18-I-B | 5 | 0 | 0 | 2 | 3 | 8 | 20 | 6th | Michel Goulet | Jan Waldner |
| 2010 WM18-II-A | 5 | 5 | 0 | 0 | 0 | 55 | 3 | 1st | Robert Chizzali | Daniel Rizzi |
| 2011 WM18-I-A | 4 | 3 | 0 | 0 | 1 | 16 | 9 | 2nd | Robert Chizzali | Alex Trivellato |
| 2012 WM18-I-A | 5 | 1 | 1 | 2 | 1 | 17 | 20 | 3rd | Robert Chizzali | Peter Hochkofler |

### Olympics, Women

(bold=top level)

| Year Event | GP | W | T | L | GF | GA | Place | Coach | Captain |
|---|---|---|---|---|---|---|---|---|---|
| **2006 OG-W** | **5** | **0** | **0** | **5** | **3** | **48** | **8th** | **Markus Sparer** | **Evelyn Bazzanella** |

### Women's World Championship

| Year Event | GP | W | T | | L | GF | GA | Place | Coach | Captain |
|---|---|---|---|---|---|---|---|---|---|---|
| Year Event | GP | W | OTW | OTL | L | GF | GA | Place | Coach | Captain |
| 2000 WW-B | 5 | 0 | 0 | | 5 | 4 | 29 | 8th | Markus Sparer | Evelyn Bazzanella |
| 2003 WW-II | 5 | 2 | 0 | | 3 | 13 | 21 | 4th | Markus Sparer | Evelyn Bazzanella |
| 2004 WW-II | 5 | 4 | 0 | | 1 | 24 | 7 | 2nd | Markus Sparer | Evelyn Bazzanella |
| 2005 WW-II | 5 | 4 | 0 | | 1 | 21 | 7 | 2nd | Markus Sparer | unknown |
| 2007 WW-II | 5 | 2 | 2 | 0 | 1 | 14 | 15 | 2nd | Herbert Frisch | Evelyn Bazzanella |

| | | | | | | | | | | |
|---|---|---|---|---|---|---|---|---|---|---|
| 2008 WW-II | 5 | 1 | 1 | 0 | 3 | 15 | 17 | 4th | Marco Liberatore | Evelyn Bazzanella |
| 2009 WW-II | 5 | 1 | 1 | 0 | 3 | 15 | 18 | 4th | Marco Liberatore | Linda de Rocco |
| 2011 WW-II | 5 | 2 | 0 | 0 | 3 | 11 | 9 | 4th | Marco Liberatore | Linda de Rocco |
| 2012 WW-I-B | 5 | 1 | 0 | 0 | 4 | 5 | 22 | 6th | Marco Liberatore | Linda de Rocco |

# Jamaica (JAM)

*Jamaica was admitted as new member at the 2012 IIHF Annual Congress in Helsinki. Photo: Jeff Vinnick / HHOF-IIHF Images.*

## Joined IIHF: May 18, 2012 (Associate Member)

Website: www.joiht.org
E-mail: JOIHT@joiht.org

Jamaican Olympic Ice Hockey Federation
c/o Lenford Salmon
5 Central Avenue, Kingston 5
Jamaica

Phone: +1 720 810 3204

**Top Level Host History** none

# Japan (JPN)

*Japan celebrates a goal as the Asians upset Austria in the 2012 IIHF Ice Hockey World Championship Division I, Group A. Photo: Samo Vidic.*

## Joined IIHF: January 26, 1930

(expelled April 27, 1946; re-admitted March 10, 1951)

Website: www.jihf.or.jp
E-mail: jihf@jihf.or.jp

Japan Ice Hockey Federation
Kishi Memorial Hall
1-1-1 Jin'nan
Shibuya-ku
Tokyo 150-8050
Japan

Phone: +81 3 34 81 24 04 • Fax: +81 3 34 81 24 07

**World Ranking**

| MEN | | WOMEN | |
|---|---|---|---|
| 2012 | 22 | 2012 | 11 |
| 2011 | 22 | 2011 | 11 |
| 2010 | 21 | 2010 | 9 |
| 2009 | 21 | 2009 | 9 |
| 2008 | 22 | 2008 | 9 |
| 2007 | 22 | 2007 | 10 |
| 2006 | 21 | 2006 | 10 |
| 2005 | 20 | 2005 | 10 |
| 2004 | 15 | 2004 | 10 |

**Top Level Host History**
Olympics: 1972 (Sapporo), 1998 (Nagano)

**Olympics, Men**
(bold=top level)

| Year Event | GP | W | T | L | GF | GA | Place | Coach | Captain |
|---|---|---|---|---|---|---|---|---|---|
| **1936 OG-M** | **2** | **0** | **0** | **2** | **0** | **5** | **9th** | **Shunichi Tezuka** | **Toshihiko Shoji** |
| **1960 OG-M** | **6** | **2** | **1** | **3** | **33** | **60** | **8th** | **Hiroki Onikura** | **Yoshihiro Miyazaki** |
| **1964 OG-M** | **7** | **4** | **1** | **2** | **35** | **31** | **11th** | **Nijuro Hoshino** | ***unknown*** |
| **1968 OG-M** | **5** | **4** | **0** | **1** | **27** | **12** | **10th** | **Yuji Kaneda/Tadao Nakajima** | **Mamoru Takashima** |
| **1972 OG-M** | **4** | **2** | **1** | **1** | **17** | **16** | **9th** | **Masami Tanabu** | **Koji Iwamoto** |
| **1976 OG-M** | **5** | **3** | **0** | **2** | **20** | **18** | **9th** | **Yoshihiro Miyazaki** | **Osamu Wakabayashi** |
| **1980 OG-M** | **5** | **0** | **1** | **4** | **7** | **36** | **12th** | **Hitoshi Wakabayashi** | **Osamu Wakabayashi** |
| **1998 OG-M** | **4** | **1** | **1** | **2** | **9** | **13** | **13th** | **Bjorn Kinding** | **Toshiyuki Sakai** |

**World Championship (Men)**
(bold=top level)

| Year Event | GP | W | T | | L | GF | GA | Place | Coach | Captain |
|---|---|---|---|---|---|---|---|---|---|---|
| Year Event | GP | W | OTW | OTL | L | GF | GA | Place | Coach | Captain |
| **1930 WM** | **1** | **0** | **0** | | **1** | **0** | **5** | **6th** | **Seiji Yamaguchi** | **Kiyoshi Kitagawa** |
| **1957 WM** | **7** | **0** | **1** | | **6** | **11** | **84** | **8th** | **Kiyoteru Nishiura** | ***unknown*** |
| 1962 WM-B | 5 | 5 | 0 | | 0 | 63 | 16 | 1st | Tsutomu Kawabuchi | Kuso Kaneda |
| 1967 WM-C | 4 | 4 | 0 | | 0 | 46 | 8 | 1st | Isao Ono/K Fujiwara | Takanori Suzuki |
| 1969 WM-C | 5 | 4 | 0 | | 1 | 36 | 10 | 1st | *unknown* | Kenji Toriyabe |
| 1970 WM-B | 7 | 3 | 1 | | 3 | 31 | 33 | 5th | *unknown* | Koji Iwamoto |
| 1971 WM-B | 7 | 2 | 1 | | 4 | 33 | 40 | 6th | *unknown* | *unknown* |
| 1972 WM-B | 6 | 1 | 1 | | 4 | 20 | 49 | 5th | *unknown* | Yasushin Tanaka |
| 1973 WM-B | 7 | 2 | 0 | | 5 | 23 | 28 | 6th | Junji Masukawa | Takao Hikigi |
| 1974 WM-B | 7 | 4 | 0 | | 3 | 31 | 31 | 4th | Masami Tanabe | Takao Hikigi |

| Year Event | GP | W | T | OTW | OTL | L | GF | GA | Place | Coach | Captain |
|---|---|---|---|---|---|---|---|---|---|---|---|
| 1975 WM-B | 7 | 2 | 2 | | | 3 | 21 | 23 | 6th | Father David Bauer | Takao Hikigi |
| 1976 WM-B | 7 | 5 | 0 | | | 2 | 34 | 17 | 2nd | *unknown* | *unknown* |
| 1977 WM-B | 8 | 5 | 1 | | | 2 | 30 | 21 | 3rd | Kazuhiko Hirota | Osamu Wakabayashi |
| 1978 WM-B | 7 | 5 | 1 | | | 1 | 26 | 17 | 2nd | Hitoshi Wakabayashi | Tsutomu Hanzawa |
| 1979 WM-B | 6 | 3 | 0 | | | 3 | 34 | 23 | 6th | Hitoshi Wakabayashi | *unknown* |
| 1981 WM-B | 7 | 1 | 0 | | | 6 | 18 | 38 | 8th | Toshimitsu Ohtsubo | Yoshio Hoshino |
| 1982 WM-C | 7 | 7 | 0 | | | 0 | 70 | 14 | 1st | Osamu Wakabayashi | Tsutomu Hanzawa |
| 1983 WM-B | 7 | 2 | 2 | | | 3 | 23 | 31 | 5th | Kiyoteru Nishiura | *unknown* |
| 1985 WM-B | 7 | 3 | 0 | | | 4 | 31 | 36 | 5th | Junji Masukawa | Katsutoshi Kawamura |
| 1986 WM-B | 7 | 2 | 0 | | | 5 | 15 | 26 | 8th | Hirohisha Kobori/I Hanzawa | Yoshio Hoshino |
| 1987 WM-C | 7 | 5 | 1 | | | 1 | 61 | 13 | 1st | Junji Masukawa | Koji Wakasa |
| 1989 WM-B | 7 | 2 | 0 | | | 5 | 20 | 34 | 7th | Yoshio Hoshino | Fumihiko Kajikawa |
| 1990 WM-B | 7 | 0 | 1 | | | 6 | 13 | 41 | 7th | Yoshio Hoshino | Fumihiko Kajikawa |
| 1991 WM-B | 7 | 0 | 1 | | | 6 | 9 | 34 | 8th | Yoshio Hoshino | Kunio Takagi |
| 1992 WM-B | 7 | 4 | 0 | | | 3 | 30 | 24 | 3rd | Hitoshi Wakabayashi | Fumihiko Kajikawa |
| 1993 WM-B | 7 | 3 | 0 | | | 4 | 34 | 31 | 5th | Hitoshi Wakabayashi | Motoki Ebina |
| 1994 WM-B | 7 | 3 | 1 | | | 3 | 37 | 38 | 4th | Sadaki Homma | Shuji Momoi |
| 1995 WM-B | 7 | 2 | 0 | | | 5 | 26 | 45 | 6th | Mikio Matsuda | Toshiyuki Sakai |
| 1996 WM-B | 7 | 0 | 3 | | | 4 | 14 | 30 | 8th | Dave King | Kunio Takagi |
| 1997 WM-C | 5 | 2 | 2 | | | 1 | 14 | 9 | 4th | Bjorn Kinding | Masaki Shirono |
| **1998 WM** | **3** | **0** | **0** | | | **3** | **7** | **19** | **14th** | **Masaru Seino** | **Toshiyuki Sakai** |
| **1999 WM** | **3** | **0** | **0** | | | **3** | **5** | **23** | **16th** | **Steve Tsujiura** | **Yoshikazu Kabayama** |
| **2000 WM** | **6** | **0** | **0** | | | **6** | **8** | **37** | **16th** | **Steve Tsujiura** | **Yoshikazu Kabayama** |
| **2001 WM** | **6** | **0** | **1** | | | **5** | **12** | **34** | **16th** | **Steve Tsujiura** | **Ryan Kuwabara** |
| **2002 WM** | **6** | **0** | **0** | | | **6** | **13** | **34** | **16th** | **Steve Tsujiura** | **Yoshikazu Kabayama** |
| **2003 WM** | **6** | **0** | **1** | | | **5** | **11** | **34** | **16th** | **Timo Tuomi** | **Yoshikazu Kabayama** |
| **2004 WM** | **6** | **0** | **2** | | | **4** | **12** | **24** | **15th** | **Mark Mahon** | **Kunihiko Sakurai** |
| 2005 WM-I-A | 5 | 2 | 0 | | | 3 | 14 | 14 | 5th | Mark Mahon | Takahito Suzuki |
| 2006 WM-I-A | 5 | 3 | 0 | | | 2 | 18 | 14 | 3rd | Mark Mahon | Takahito Suzuki |
| 2007 WM-I-B | 5 | 1 | | 1 | 1 | 2 | 19 | 22 | 3rd | Mark Mahon | Takahito Suzuki |
| 2008 WM-I-B | 5 | 3 | | 0 | 1 | 1 | 19 | 10 | 3rd | Mark Mahon | Takahito Suzuki |
| 2009 WM-I-A | 5 | 3 | | 0 | 0 | 2 | 21 | 8 | 3rd | Mark Mahon | Takahito Suzuki |
| 2010 WM-I-A | 5 | 3 | | 0 | 0 | 2 | 17 | 7 | 3rd | Mark Mahon | Takahito Suzuki |
| 2012 WM-I-A | 5 | 1 | | 1 | 1 | 2 | 13 | 14 | 4th | Mark Mahon | Jun Tonosaki |

**U20 World Championship**

(bold=top level)

| Year Event | GP | W | T | | L | GF | GA | Place | Coach | Captain |
|---|---|---|---|---|---|---|---|---|---|---|
| **Year Event** | **GP** | **W** | **OTW** | **OTL** | **L** | **GF** | **GA** | **Place** | **Coach** | **Captain** |
| 1982 WM20-B | 4 | 3 | 0 | | 1 | 22 | 12 | 3rd | Koji Iwamoto/Takeshi Akiba | Fumihiko Kajikawa |
| 1983 WM20-B | 5 | 3 | 0 | | 2 | 29 | 16 | 2nd | Koji Iwamoto | Kunio Takagi |
| 1984 WM20-B | 5 | 2 | 2 | | 1 | 30 | 21 | 3rd | Masaru Seino | Motoki Ebina |
| 1985 WM20-B | 7 | 4 | 1 | | 2 | 34 | 23 | 3rd | Masaru Seino/Yoshiaki Kyoya | *unknown* |
| 1986 WM20-B | 7 | 3 | 0 | | 4 | 35 | 31 | 5th | Masaru Seino/Yoshiaki Kyoya | Fumihiro Takahashi |
| 1987 WM20-B | 5 | 3 | 0 | | 2 | 28 | 24 | 3rd | Koji Iwamoto | *unknown* |
| 1988 WM20-B | 7 | 3 | 2 | | 2 | 34 | 27 | 4th | Koji Iwamoto | *unknown* |
| 1989 WM20-B | 7 | 4 | 0 | | 3 | 32 | 34 | 4th | Masaru Seino | Takayuki Kobori |
| 1990 WM20-B | 7 | 4 | 1 | | 2 | 38 | 33 | 3rd | Hirohisha Kobori | *unknown* |
| 1991 WM20-B | 7 | 4 | 1 | | 2 | 34 | 22 | 4th | Hirohisha Kobori | Takeshi Yamanaka |
| 1992 WM20-B | 7 | 5 | 0 | | 2 | 32 | 18 | 1st | Mikihito Tanaka | Kunihiko Sakurai |
| **1993 WM20** | **7** | **0** | **0** | | **7** | **9** | **83** | **8th** | **Masaru Seino** | **Mitsuaki Nitta** |
| 1994 WM20-B | 7 | 2 | 0 | | 5 | 19 | 27 | 7th | Masaru Seino | Shinichi Itabashi |
| 1995 WM20-B | 7 | 1 | 1 | | 5 | 17 | 44 | 7th | Ryo Yamada | Gen Ishioka |
| 1996 WM20-B | 6 | 1 | 0 | | 5 | 13 | 31 | 6th | Wally Kozak/Keiji Takahashi | Yoshifumi Fujisawa |
| 1997 WM20-B | 7 | 2 | 2 | | 3 | 24 | 17 | 6th | Ryo Yamada | *unknown* |
| 1998 WM20-B | 6 | 1 | 1 | | 4 | 21 | 34 | 8th | Ryo Yamada | Junichi Takahashi |
| 1999 WM20-C | 4 | 3 | 0 | | 1 | 16 | 5 | 2nd | Ryo Yamada | Daisuke Haratake |
| 2000 WM20-C | 4 | 2 | 1 | | 1 | 20 | 10 | 5th | Koji Aizawa | Tomohiri Sonoda |
| 2001 WM20-II | 4 | 3 | 0 | | 1 | 29 | 8 | 2nd | Koji Aizawa | Takeshi Saito |
| 2002 WM20-II | 4 | 4 | 0 | | 0 | 30 | 8 | 1st | Koji Aizawa | Masahito Nishiwaki |
| 2003 WM20-I-A | 5 | 4 | 0 | | 1 | 24 | 10 | 2nd | Kenji Nobuta | Hiroshi Sato |
| 2004 WM20-I-B | 5 | 0 | 0 | | 5 | 9 | 22 | 6th | Norio Suzuki | Jun Tonosaki |
| 2005 WM20-II-A | 5 | 4 | 1 | | 0 | 32 | 4 | 1st | Norio Suzuki | Katsuya Ogawa |
| 2006 WM20-I-A | 5 | 0 | 0 | | 5 | 10 | 29 | 6th | Norio Suzuki | Shinya Yanadori |
| 2007 WM20-II-B | 5 | 2 | 2 | 0 | 1 | 31 | 14 | 3rd | Norio Suzuki | Shuhei Kuji |
| 2008 WM20-II-A | 5 | 4 | 0 | 0 | 1 | 37 | 7 | 2nd | Yuji Iwamoto | Teruyuki Tsuchiya |
| 2009 WM20-II-A | 5 | 4 | 0 | 0 | 1 | 45 | 11 | 1st | Yuji Iwamoto | Kazumasa Sasaki |
| 2010 WM20-I-A | 5 | 1 | 0 | 0 | 4 | 9 | 26 | 5th | Yuji Iwamoto | Mitsuyoshi Konno |
| 2011 WM20-I-A | 5 | 1 | 0 | 0 | 4 | 9 | 15 | 5th | Mark Mahon | Mei Ushu |
| 2012 WM20-I-B | 5 | 0 | 1 | 0 | 4 | 9 | 20 | 6th | Nobuo Yamanaka | Kotaro Yamada |

**U18 World Championship (Men)**

| Year Event | GP | W | T | | L | GF | GA | Place | Coach | Captain |
|---|---|---|---|---|---|---|---|---|---|---|
| **Year Event** | **GP** | **W** | **OTW** | **OTL** | **L** | **GF** | **GA** | **Place** | **Coach** | **Captain** |
| 2000 WM18-B | 5 | 2 | 1 | | 2 | 13 | 15 | 4th | Kazutoshi Kawamura | Masahito Nishiwaki |
| 2001 WM18-I | 5 | 3 | 1 | | 1 | 25 | 12 | 3rd | Kenji Nobuta | Hiroshi Sato |
| 2002 WM18-I | 4 | 1 | 2 | | 1 | 14 | 15 | 7th | Kenji Nobuta | Bin Ishioka |
| 2003 WM18-I-A | 5 | 1 | 1 | | 3 | 15 | 19 | 5th | Norio Suzuki | Yusuke Miyakoshi |
| 2004 WM18-I-B | 5 | 4 | 0 | | 1 | 14 | 14 | 2nd | Hiroaki Sasaki | Reo Amano |
| 2005 WM18-I-B | 5 | 1 | 1 | | 3 | 12 | 17 | 5th | Hiroaki Sasaki | Shuhei Kuji |
| 2006 WM18-I-B | 5 | 2 | 1 | | 2 | 19 | 16 | 3rd | Hiroaki Sasaki | Takuya Koizumi |
| 2007 WM18-I-B | 5 | 3 | 1 | 0 | 1 | 22 | 13 | 2nd | Hiroaki Sasaki | Yuhei Shinohara |

| Year Event | GP | W | OTW | OTL | L | GF | GA | Place | Coach | Captain |
|---|---|---|---|---|---|---|---|---|---|---|
| 2008 WM18-I-B | 5 | 1 | 0 | 0 | 4 | 12 | 26 | 5th | Kazuya Akamatsu | Junki Takei |
| 2009 WM18-I-B | 5 | 0 | 2 | 1 | 2 | 13 | 16 | 5th | Kazuya Akamatsu | Takuto Gorai |
| 2010 WM18-I-A | 5 | 3 | 0 | 0 | 2 | 27 | 25 | 3rd | Kazuya Akamatsu | Kotaro Yamada |
| 2012 WW18-I-A | 5 | 1 | 0 | 1 | 3 | 14 | 21 | 6th | Kazuya Akamatsu | Yoshiya Yokoyama |

**Olympics, Women**
(bold=top level)

| Year Event | GP | W | T | L | GF | GA | Place | Coach | Captain |
|---|---|---|---|---|---|---|---|---|---|
| **1998 OG-W** | **5** | **0** | **0** | **5** | **2** | **45** | **6th** | **Toru Itabashi** | **Maiko Obikawa** |

**Women's World Championship**
(bold=top level)

| Year Event | GP | W | T | | | L | GF | GA | Place | Coach | Captain |
|---|---|---|---|---|---|---|---|---|---|---|---|
| Year Event | GP | W | | OTW | OTL | L | GF | GA | Place | Coach | Captain |
| **1990 WW** | **5** | **0** | **0** | | | **5** | **11** | **47** | **8th** | **Norio Fukada** | **Tamami Nishida** |
| 1999 WW-B | 5 | 5 | 0 | | | 0 | 25 | 4 | 1st | Takayuki Hatanda | Maiko Obikawa |
| **2000 WW** | **5** | **0** | **0** | | | **5** | **6** | **33** | **8th** | **Takayuki Hattanda** | **Akiko Hatanaka** |
| 2001 WW-I | 4 | 1 | 2 | | | 1 | 11 | 10 | 2nd | Takayuki Hatanda | *unknown* |
| 2003 WW-I | 5 | 5 | 0 | | | 0 | 23 | 6 | 1st | Masayuki Takahashi | Yuki Togawa |
| **2004 WW** | **4** | **0** | **0** | | | **4** | **4** | **18** | **9th** | **Kenji Nobuta** | **Masako Sato** |
| 2005 WW-I | 5 | 4 | 0 | | | 1 | 18 | 8 | 2nd | Kenji Nobuta | Yuki Togawa |
| 2007 WW-I | 5 | 5 | | 0 | 0 | 0 | 25 | 5 | 1st | Kohichi Satoh | Yoko Kondo |
| **2008 WW** | **4** | **1** | | **0** | **0** | **3** | **5** | **14** | **7th** | **Yuji Iizuka** | **Chiaki Yamanaka** |
| **2009 WW** | **4** | **1** | | **0** | **0** | **3** | **5** | **15** | **8th** | **Yuji Iizuka** | **Chiaki Yamanaka** |
| 2012 WW-I-A | 5 | 3 | | 0 | 0 | 2 | 15 | 10 | 3rd | Yuji Iizuka | Yuka Hirano |

**U18 Women's World Championship**
(bold=top level)

| Year Event | GP | W | OTW | OTL | L | GF | GA | Place | Coach | Captain |
|---|---|---|---|---|---|---|---|---|---|---|
| 2009 WW18-I | 4 | 4 | 0 | 0 | 0 | 18 | 5 | 1st | Yuji Iizuka | Nachi Fujimoto |
| **2010 WW18** | **5** | **1** | **0** | **0** | **4** | **9** | **23** | **6th** | **Yuji Iizuka** | **Chiho Osawa** |
| **2011 WW18** | **6** | **1** | **0** | **0** | **5** | **9** | **23** | **8th** | **Yuji Iizuka** | **Shiori Koike** |
| 2012 WW18-I | 5 | 3 | 0 | 2 | 0 | 14 | 7 | 3rd | Yoshifumi Fujisawa | Seika Yuyama |

# Kazakhstan (KAZ)

*The Kazakh U18 national team's bench. Photo: Viktor David Koppan.*

## Joined IIHF: May 6, 1992

Website: www.icehockey.kz
E-mail: office@icehockey.kz

Kazakhstan Ice Hockey Federation
12/1 D. Konayeva Str., office 508
010000 Astana
Republic of Kazakhstan

Phone: +7 7172 605041/42/43 • Fax: +7 7172 605044

**World Ranking**

| MEN | | WOMEN | |
|---|---|---|---|
| 2012 | 17 | 2012 | 9 |
| 2011 | 16 | 2011 | 7 |
| 2010 | 17 | 2010 | 8 |
| 2009 | 18 | 2009 | 8 |
| 2008 | 19 | 2008 | 10 |
| 2007 | 16 | 2007 | 9 |
| 2006 | 11 | 2006 | 9 |
| 2005 | 15 | 2005 | 8 |
| 2004 | 17 | 2004 | 9 |

**Top Level Host History** none

**Olympics, Men**
(bold=top level)

| Year Event | GP | W | T | L | GF | GA | Place | Coach | Captain |
|---|---|---|---|---|---|---|---|---|---|
| **1998 OG-M** | **7** | **2** | **1** | **4** | **21** | **40** | **8th** | **Boris Alexandrov** | ***unknown*** |
| **2006 OG-M** | **5** | **1** | **0** | **4** | **9** | **16** | **9th** | **Nikolai Myshagin** | **Alexander Koreshkov** |

**World Championship (Men)**
(bold=top level)

| Year Event | GP | W | T | | | L | GF | GA | Place | Coach | Captain |
|---|---|---|---|---|---|---|---|---|---|---|---|
| Year Event | GP | W | | OTW | OTL | L | GF | GA | Place | Coach | Captain |
| 1993 WM-C | 7 | 5 | 0 | | | 2 | 85 | 12 | 3rd | Valeri Kiritchenko | Igor Zemlyanoi |
| 1994 WM-C-A | 6 | 3 | 2 | | | 1 | 52 | 12 | 4th | Aleksandrs Golts | Igor Zemlyanoi |
| 1995 WM-C-1 | 4 | 2 | 1 | | | 1 | 23 | 5 | 2nd | Vladimir Koptsov | Igor Zemlyanoi |
| 1996 WM-C | 7 | 6 | 0 | | | 1 | 51 | 10 | 1st | Boris Alexandrov | Sergei Mogilnikov |
| 1997 WM-B | 7 | 5 | 1 | | | 1 | 31 | 21 | 2nd | Boris Alexandrov | Igor Dorokhin |
| **1998 WM** | **3** | **0** | **0** | | | **3** | **6** | **19** | **16th** | **Boris Alexandrov** | **Yerlan Sagymbayev** |
| 1999 WM-B | 7 | 5 | 0 | | | 2 | 25 | 11 | 3rd | Boris Alexandrov | Pavel Kamentsev |
| 2000 WM-B | 7 | 5 | 0 | | | 2 | 30 | 22 | 2nd | Boris Alexandrov | Yuri Karatyev |
| 2001 WM-I-B | 5 | 3 | 0 | | | 2 | 35 | 21 | 3rd | Boris Alexandrov | Konstantin Shafranov |
| 2002 WM-I-A | 5 | 3 | 0 | | | 2 | 30 | 14 | 3rd | Boris Alexandrov | Anatoli Filatov |
| 2003 WM-I-A | 5 | 5 | 0 | | | 0 | 34 | 9 | 1st | Nikolai Myshyagin | Oleg Kovalenko |

| | | | | | | | | | | |
|---|---|---|---|---|---|---|---|---|---|---|
| **2004 WM** | **6** | **2** | **1** | | **3** | **15** | **19** | **13th** | **Nikolai Myshyagin** | **Alexei Troshinsky** |
| **2005 WM** | **6** | **1** | **0** | | **5** | **5** | **12** | **12th** | **Nikolai Myshyagin** | **Andrey Sokolov** |
| **2006 WM** | **6** | **1** | **0** | | **5** | **11** | **29** | **15th** | **Nikolai Myshyagin** | **Alexander Koreshkov** |
| 2007 WM-I-A | 5 | 3 | 0 | 0 | 2 | 22 | 11 | 3rd | Sergei Drozdov | Alexander Koreshkov |
| 2008 WM-I-A | 5 | 3 | 1 | 0 | 1 | 21 | 12 | 2ns | Yerlan Sagymbayev | Artyom Argokov |
| 2009 WM-I-A | 5 | 5 | 0 | 0 | 0 | 29 | 6 | 1st | Andrei Shayanov | Alexander Koreshkov |
| **2010 WM** | **6** | **0** | **0** | **0** | **6** | **8** | **31** | **16th** | **Andrei Shayanov** | **Alexander Koreshkov** |
| 2011 WM-I-B | 5 | 4 | 1 | 0 | 0 | 21 | 6 | 1st | Andrei Khomutov | Vitali Novopashin |
| **2012 WM** | **7** | **0** | **0** | **1** | **6** | **11** | **33** | **16th** | **Andrei Shayanov** | **Dmitri Upper** |

### U20 World Championship

(bold=top level)

| Year Event | GP | W | T | | L | GF | GA | Place | Coach | Captain |
|---|---|---|---|---|---|---|---|---|---|---|
| Year Event | GP | W | OTW | OTL | L | GF | GA | Place | Coach | Captain |
| 1995 WM20-C-2 | 5 | 3 | 2 | | 0 | 47 | 10 | 1st | A Melnikov | Dmitri Dudarev |
| 1996 WM20-C | 4 | 4 | 0 | | 0 | 31 | 16 | 1st | Vladimir Belayev | Dmitri Dudarev |
| 1997 WM20-B | 7 | 6 | 1 | | 0 | 39 | 15 | 1st | *unknown* | *unknown* |
| **1998 WM20** | **7** | **2** | **0** | | **5** | **16** | **51** | **7th** | **Vladimir Belyayev** | **Vitali Novopashin** |
| **1999 WM20** | **6** | **1** | **1** | | **4** | **12** | **38** | **6th** | **Vasili Vasilchenko** | **Nikolai Antropov** |
| **2000 WM20** | **7** | **1** | **0** | | **6** | **13** | **61** | **8th** | **Vasili Vasilchenko** | **Rustam Yessirenkov** |
| **2001 WM20** | **6** | **0** | **1** | | **5** | **11** | **43** | **10th** | **Sergey Starygin** | **Roman Kozlov** |
| 2002 WM20-I | 5 | 3 | 0 | | 2 | 35 | 19 | 5th | Alexander Buzik | Alexander Semenov |
| 2003 WM20-I-A | 5 | 3 | 1 | | 1 | 25 | 12 | 3rd | Valeri Kirichenko | Mikhail Zlobin |
| 2004 WM20-I-A | 5 | 1 | 1 | | 3 | 16 | 19 | 5th | Sergei Kislitsyn | Alexei Vyatkin |
| 2005 WM20-I-A | 5 | 4 | 0 | | 1 | 29 | 15 | 2nd | Vladimir Belayev | Dmitri Shakhov |
| 2006 WM20-I-B | 5 | 4 | 0 | | 1 | 21 | 8 | 2nd | Yerlan Sagymbayev | Roman Starchenko |
| 2007 WM20-I-B | 5 | 3 | 1 | 0 | 1 | 14 | 9 | 1st | Oleg Bolyakin | Yevgeni Gasnikov |
| **2008 WM20** | **6** | **2** | **0** | **0** | **4** | **14** | **27** | **8th** | **Oleg Bolyakin** | **Yevgeni Gasnikov** |
| **2009 WM20** | **6** | **0** | **0** | **0** | **6** | **4** | **60** | **10th** | **Oleg Bolyakin** | **Nikita Ivanov** |
| 2010 WM20-I-B | 5 | 2 | 0 | 0 | 3 | 20 | 16 | 4th | Valeri Kirichenko | Konstantin Savenkov |
| 2011 WM20-I-B | 5 | 2 | 0 | 0 | 3 | 19 | 24 | 4th | Alexander Shimin | Valentin Milyukov |
| 2012 WM20-I-B | 5 | 3 | 0 | 1 | 1 | 9 | 7 | 2nd | Yerlan Sagymbayev | Vyacheslav Borisov |

### U18 World Championship (Men)

(bold=top level)

| Year Event | GP | W | T | | L | GF | GA | Place | Coach | Captain |
|---|---|---|---|---|---|---|---|---|---|---|
| Year Event | GP | W | OTW | OTL | L | GF | GA | Place | Coach | Captain |
| 2001 WM18-I | 5 | 3 | 1 | | 1 | 32 | 14 | 5th | Vladimir Belyayev | Maxim Semenov |
| 2002 WM18-I | 4 | 4 | 0 | | 0 | 21 | 5 | 1st | Sergei Mogilnikov | Dmitri Larionov |
| **2003 WM18** | **6** | **0** | **0** | | **6** | **16** | **44** | **10th** | **Vladimir Belyayev** | **Dmitri Shakov** |
| 2004 WM18-I-B | 5 | 1 | 1 | | 3 | 12 | 19 | 4th | Anatoli Melikhov | Rustam Kusainov |
| 2005 WM18-I-A | 5 | 3 | 0 | | 2 | 19 | 14 | 3rd | Sergei Starygin | Yevgeni Tumashov |
| 2006 WM18-I-A | 5 | 2 | 1 | | 2 | 25 | 20 | 3rd | Sergei Starygin | Yevgeni Gasnikov |
| 2007 WM18-I-A | 5 | 2 | 1 | 0 | 2 | 24 | 18 | 3rd | Vladimir Belyayev | Nikita Ivanov |
| 2008 WM18-I-A | 5 | 3 | 0 | 0 | 2 | 19 | 13 | 2nd | Vladimir Belyayev | *unknown* |
| 2009 WM18-I-A | 5 | 2 | 1 | 0 | 2 | 16 | 21 | 4th | Vladimir Belyayev | Viktor Ivashin |
| 2010 WM18-I-B | 5 | 2 | 0 | 0 | 3 | 9 | 16 | 4th | Pavel Makerov | Vladimir Grebenshchikov |
| 2011 WM18-I-A | 4 | 1 | 1 | 0 | 2 | 12 | 19 | 3rd | Vasili Vasilchenko | Vyacheslav Borisov |
| 2012 WM18-I-B | 5 | 3 | 1 | 0 | 1 | 27 | 16 | 2nd | Vasili Vasilchenko | Askhat Baubekov |

### Olympics, Women

(bold=top level)

| Year Event | GP | W | T | L | GF | GA | Place | Coach | Captain |
|---|---|---|---|---|---|---|---|---|---|
| **2002 OG-W** | **5** | **0** | **0** | **5** | **2** | **24** | **8th** | **Alexander Maltsev** | **Olga Kryukova** |

### Women's World Championship

(bold=top level)

| Year Event | GP | W | T | | L | GF | GA | Place | Coach | Captain |
|---|---|---|---|---|---|---|---|---|---|---|
| Year Event | GP | W | OTW | OTL | L | GF | GA | Place | Coach | Captain |
| 2000 WW-B | 5 | 5 | 0 | | 0 | 13 | 4 | 1st | Alexander Maltsev | Olga Kryukova |
| **2001 WW** | **5** | **0** | **0** | | **5** | **5** | **29** | **8th** | **Alexander Maltsev** | **Olga Kryukova** |
| 2003 WW-I | 5 | 3 | 1 | | 1 | 20 | 7 | 2nd | Sergei Solovyev | Svetlana Maltseva |
| 2004 WW-I | 5 | 4 | 1 | | 0 | 15 | 4 | 1st | Sergei Solovyev | Svetlana Maltseva |
| **2005 WW** | **5** | **1** | **1** | | **3** | **5** | **24** | **7th** | **Alexander Maltsev** | **Olga Kryukova** |
| **2007 WW** | **4** | **0** | **0** | **0** | **4** | **0** | **26** | **9th** | **Natalya Skobelkina** | **Olga Potapova** |
| 2008 WW-I | 5 | 4 | 0 | 0 | 1 | 14 | 8 | 1st | Sergei Solovyev | Olga Kryukova |
| **2009 WW** | **4** | **0** | **1** | **0** | **3** | **4** | **26** | **6th** | **Alexander Maltsev** | **Natalya Yakovchuk** |
| **2011 WW** | **5** | **0** | **0** | **1** | **4** | **5** | **21** | **8th** | **Alexander Maltsev** | **Viktoria Sazonova** |
| 2012 WW-I-A | 5 | 0 | 0 | 2 | 3 | 7 | 19 | 6th | Alexander Maltsev | Viktoria Sazonova |

### U18 Women's World Championship

| Year Event | GP | W | OTW | OTL | L | GF | GA | Place | Coach | Captain |
|---|---|---|---|---|---|---|---|---|---|---|
| 2010 WW18-I | 5 | 0 | 0 | 0 | 5 | 9 | 46 | 6th | Alexander Sidorenko | Natalia Karpeyeva |
| 2011 WW18-I | 5 | 0 | 0 | 0 | 5 | 8 | 48 | 6th | Alexander Sidorenko | Natalia Karpeyeva |

# Korea (KOR)

*The Koreans celebrate the tournament win at the 2012 IIHF Ice Hockey U18 World Championship Division II, Group A. Photo: Nicolien Sijtsema.*

**Joined IIHF: July 25, 1963**

Website: www.kiha.or.kr
E-mail: icehockey@sports.or.kr

Korea Ice Hockey Association
902 Olympic Center
88 Oryun-Dong
138-749 Songpa-Ku, Seoul
Korea

Phone: +82 2 425 7001/7002 • Fax: +82 2 420 41 60

| World Ranking | |
|---|---|
| MEN | WOMEN |
| 2012........28 | 2012........26 |
| 2011........31 | 2011........28 |
| 2010........33 | 2010........28 |
| 2009........30 | 2009........27 |
| 2008........31 | 2008........26 |
| 2007........32 | 2007........26 |
| 2006........32 | 2006........26 |
| 2005........31 | 2005........27 |
| 2004........30 | 2004........27 |

**Top Level Host History** none

**World Championship (Men)**

| Year Event | GP | W | T | | L | GF | GA | Place | Coach | Captain |
|---|---|---|---|---|---|---|---|---|---|---|
| Year Event | GP | W | OTW | OTL | L | GF | GA | Place | Coach | Captain |
| 1979 WM-C | 7 | 1 | 1 | | 5 | 16 | 67 | 7th | Man Young Kim | Yung Suk Choi |
| 1982 WM-C | 7 | 0 | 0 | | 7 | 13 | 127 | 8th | Yoong Kook Park | Sung Soo Kim |
| 1986 WM-C | 5 | 1 | 1 | | 3 | 14 | 45 | 9th | Yoong Kook Park | *unknown* |
| 1987 WM-D | 6 | 4 | 1 | | 1 | 130 | 16 | 2nd | Jong Kuk Park | Won Sik Choi |
| 1989 WM-C | 7 | 1 | 1 | | 5 | 27 | 46 | 7th | Sea Il Kim | Won Sik Choi |
| 1990 WM-C | 8 | 1 | 0 | | 7 | 22 | 57 | 9th | Sea Il Kim | Ki Young Song |
| 1991 WM-C | 8 | 1 | 0 | | 7 | 19 | 64 | 8th | Sea Il Kim | Kang Soo Lee |
| 1992 WM-C-A | 5 | 0 | 1 | | 4 | 18 | 43 | 6th | Sea Il Kim | Dong Ho Lee |
| 1993 WM-C | 6 | 2 | 0 | | 4 | 23 | 63 | 9th | Chul Ho Kim | Kyoung Woon Park |
| 1994 WM-C-B | 5 | 3 | 1 | | 1 | 13 | 17 | 3rd | Chang Jin Kim | *unknown* |
| 1995 WM-C-2 | 6 | 3 | 0 | | 3 | 44 | 19 | 4th | Chang Jin Kim | Eui-Sik Shim |
| 1996 WM-D | 5 | 2 | 2 | | 1 | 24 | 17 | 5th | Sea Il Kim | Won Noh Jun |
| 1997 WM-D | 5 | 4 | 0 | | 1 | 19 | 9 | 2nd | Kim Jean Hyun | Eui-Sik Shim |
| 1998 WM-C | 5 | 1 | 0 | | 4 | 4 | 18 | 7th | Sea Il Kim | Eui-Sik Shim |
| 1999 WM-C | 4 | 1 | 2 | | 1 | 18 | 22 | 6th | Sea Il Kim | Eui-Sik Shim |
| 2000 WM-C | 4 | 2 | 0 | | 2 | 19 | 23 | 5th | Sea Il Kim | Eui-Sik Shim |
| 2001 WM-II-A | 5 | 5 | 0 | | 0 | 42 | 5 | 1st | Sam Duk Kim | Eui-Sik Shim |
| 2002 WM-I-A | 5 | 0 | 0 | | 5 | 7 | 42 | 6th | Jei Hyun Lee | Woo-Sam Shin |
| 2003 WM-II-A | 5 | 5 | 0 | | 0 | 50 | 10 | 1st | Sam Deuk Kim | Sung Kim Yoon |
| 2004 WM-I-B | 5 | 0 | 0 | | 5 | 7 | 42 | 6th | Sun Wook Byun | Chang Bum Kim |
| 2005 WM-II-A | 5 | 3 | 0 | | 2 | 26 | 9 | 3rd | Jei Hyun Lee | Jin Hong Park |
| 2006 WM-II-B | 5 | 4 | 0 | | 1 | 35 | 12 | 2nd | Jei Hyun Lee | Jong Moon Jang |
| 2007 WM-II-B | 4 | 4 | 0 | 0 | 0 | 33 | 9 | 1st | Sun Wook Byun | Sung Min Park |
| 2008 WM-I-A | 5 | 0 | 0 | 1 | 4 | 8 | 27 | 6th | Sun Wook Byun | Myung Woo Lee |
| 2009 WM-II-B | 5 | 5 | 0 | 0 | 0 | 48 | 10 | 1st | Hee Woo Kim | Sung Min Park |
| 2010 WM-I-B | 5 | 1 | 0 | 0 | 4 | 13 | 21 | 5th | Hee Woo Kim | Woo Jae Kim |
| 2011 WM-I-A | 4 | 1 | 0 | 1 | 2 | 11 | 18 | 3rd | Hee Woo Kim | Woo Jae Kim |
| 2012 WM-I-B | 5 | 4 | 1 | 0 | 0 | 24 | 10 | 1st | Sun Wook Byun | Donghwan Kim |

**U20 World Championship**

| Year Event | GP | W | T | | L | GF | GA | Place | Coach | Captain |
|---|---|---|---|---|---|---|---|---|---|---|
| Year Event | GP | W | OTW | OTL | L | GF | GA | Place | Coach | Captain |
| 1990 WM20-C | 6 | 2 | 0 | | 4 | 25 | 39 | 5th | Hong Yeol Yoo | *unknown* |
| 1991 WM20-C | 7 | 3 | 1 | | 3 | 55 | 28 | 5th | Hong Yeol Yoo | Woo Sam Shin |
| 1992 WM20-C | 3 | 0 | 0 | | 3 | 8 | 18 | 6th | Sung Ku Kim | Jung Hwan Hong |
| 1993 WM20-C | 4 | 0 | 1 | | 3 | 12 | 34 | 8th | Hong Yeol Yoo | *unknown* |
| 2003 WM20-III | 4 | 4 | 0 | | 0 | 37 | 5 | 1st | Sung Yub Joon | Kwun Jae Lee |
| 2004 WM20-II-B | 5 | 4 | 0 | | 1 | 45 | 7 | 2nd | Hee Sang Moon | Sang Hyun Kwon |
| 2005 WM20-II-B | 5 | 4 | 0 | | 1 | 46 | 12 | 2nd | Hyungjun Cho | Yong Jung Lee |
| 2006 WM20-II-B | 5 | 2 | 1 | | 2 | 20 | 15 | 3rd | Sung Yub Yoon | Lee Hyun Jun |
| 2007 WM20-II-B | 5 | 1 | 0 | 1 | 3 | 13 | 18 | 4th | Hee-Sang Moon | Bum Jin Kim |
| 2008 WM20-II-A | 5 | 3 | 0 | 0 | 2 | 18 | 11 | 3rd | Sung Yub Yoon | Don Ku Lee |
| 2009 WM20-II-A | 5 | 2 | 2 | 0 | 1 | 19 | 18 | 3rd | Sung Yub Yoon | Sang Hyuk Yoon |
| 2010 WM20-II-A | 5 | 2 | 0 | 0 | 3 | 20 | 18 | 4th | Hyung Jun Cho | Yeon Jun Chung |
| 2011 WM20-II-B | 5 | 3 | 0 | 0 | 2 | 27 | 30 | 3rd | Hyung Jun Cho | Jiho Song |
| 2012 WM20-II-A | 5 | 0 | 0 | 2 | 3 | 9 | 18 | 6th | Hyung Jun Cho | Jae Woo Kim |

**U18 World Championship (Men)**

| Year Event | GP | W | T | | L | GF | GA | Place | Coach | Captain |
|---|---|---|---|---|---|---|---|---|---|---|
| Year Event | GP | W | OTW | OTL | L | GF | GA | Place | Coach | Captain |
| 2002 WM18-III | 4 | 4 | 0 | | 0 | 47 | 2 | 1st | Yoon Young Choi | Sang Hyun Kwon |
| 2003 WM18-II-A | 5 | 5 | 0 | | 0 | 56 | 12 | 1st | Yoon Young Choi | Yun Ho Kwak |
| 2004 WM18-I-B | 5 | 0 | 1 | | 4 | 8 | 26 | 6th | Sung Ku Kim | Ki Hoon Han |
| 2005 WM18-II-A | 5 | 5 | 0 | | 0 | 51 | 7 | 1st | Sung Ku Kim | Min Ho Cho |
| 2006 WM18-I-B | 5 | 0 | 1 | | 4 | 11 | 23 | 6th | Hwan Sung Lee | Dong Yeon Kim |
| 2007 WM18-II-B | 5 | 3 | 1 | 0 | 1 | 27 | 14 | 2nd | Jae Hyuk Lee | Sang Hyuk Yoon |

| | | | | | | | | | | |
|---|---|---|---|---|---|---|---|---|---|---|
| 2008 WM18-II-A | 5 | 3 | 1 | 0 | 1 | 31 | 9 | 2nd | Yoon Young Choi | Yeon Jun Chung |
| 2009 WM18-II-A | 5 | 5 | 0 | 0 | 0 | 30 | 4 | 1st | Yoon Young Choi | Ji Man Yoon |
| 2010 WM18-I-A | 5 | 0 | 1 | 0 | 4 | 18 | 45 | 5th | Jong Hoy Heo | Ye Ju Jun |
| 2011 WM18-I-B | 5 | 0 | 0 | 0 | 5 | 11 | 48 | 6th | Jong Hoy Heo | Sang Hoon Shin |
| 2012 WM18-II-A | 5 | 3 | 1 | 1 | 0 | 17 | 14 | 1st | Yoon Young Choi | Dong Gun Lee |

**Women's World Championship**

| Year Event | GP | W | T | | L | GF | GA | Place | Coach | Captain |
|---|---|---|---|---|---|---|---|---|---|---|
| Year Event | GP | W | OTW | OTL | L | GF | GA | Place | Coach | Captain |
| 2004 WW-III | 5 | 0 | 0 | | 5 | 7 | 30 | 6th | Seung Han Sheen | *unknown* |
| 2005 WW-IV | 3 | 3 | 0 | | 0 | 15 | 5 | 1st | Seung Han Sheen | Young Hwangbo |
| 2007 WW-III | 5 | 1 | 0 | 0 | 4 | 12 | 27 | 5th | Ick Hee Kim | Kyou Sun Lee |
| 2008 WW-III | 5 | 0 | 1 | 0 | 4 | 7 | 22 | 6th | Ick Hee Kim | Young Hwangbo |
| 2011 WW-IV | 4 | 3 | 0 | 0 | 1 | 15 | 6 | 2nd | Young Gon Kim | Bo Young Choi |
| 2012 WW-II-B | 5 | 2 | 1 | 1 | 1 | 16 | 8 | 3rd | Young Oh Kim | Bo Young Choi |

# Kuwait (KUW)

*Kuwait attempts to score against host India at the 2012 IIHF Challenge Cup of Asia. Photo: IHAI.*

**Joined IIHF: April 30, 1985 (Associate Member)**
(expulsed May 6, 1992; readmitted May 8, 2009)

Website: n/a
Email: Kuwait_icehockey@hotmail.com

Kuwait Ice Hockey Association
Kuwait Olympic Committee
Post Box 795 Safat
13008 Kuwait

Phone: + 965 600 009 59 • Fax: +965 2487 4539

**Top Level Host History** none

# Kyrgyzstan (KGZ)

*Kyrgyzstan won the Premier Division of the 2011 Asian Winter Games in Astana, Kazakhstan. Photo: KIHF.*

**Joined IIHF: May 14, 2011**
Website: www.kihf.kg
E-mail: world@kihf.kg

Ice Hockey Federation of the Kyrgyz Republic
Toktonalieva str., 8a
720021 Bishkek
Kyrgyzstan

Phone: +7 777 216 50 28
Fax: +7 705 452 58 09 (interpreter)/+7 7272 93 66 86

**Top Level Host History** none

# Latvia (LAT)

Latvia finished in 10th place at the 2012 World Championship in Helsinki/Stockholm, remaining in the top division for the 17th straight season. Photo: Andre Ringuette / HHOF-IIHF Images.

## Joined IIHF: February 22, 1931

(membership expired April 27, 1946; played under Soviet Union, 1947-91; received independent status again May 6, 1992)

Website: www.lhf.lv
E-mail: lhf@lhf.lv

Latvian Ice Hockey Federation
Raunas iela 23
LV 1039 Riga
Latvia

Phone: +371 6756 5614/6756 3921 • Fax: +371 6756 5015

**World Ranking**

| MEN | | WOMEN | |
|---|---|---|---|
| 2012 | 11 | 2012 | 14 |
| 2011 | 12 | 2011 | 13 |
| 2010 | 12 | 2010 | 15 |
| 2009 | 10 | 2009 | 14 |
| 2008 | 11 | 2008 | 13 |
| 2007 | 10 | 2007 | 11 |
| 2006 | 9 | 2006 | 13 |
| 2005 | 9 | 2005 | 13 |
| 2004 | 10 | 2004 | 12 |

### Top Level Host History

World Championship (Men): 2006 (Riga)

### Olympics, Men

(bold=top level)

| Year Event | GP | W | T | OTW | OTL | L | GF | GA | Place | Coach | Captain |
|---|---|---|---|---|---|---|---|---|---|---|---|
| **1936 OG-M** | 3 | 0 | 0 | | | 3 | 3 | 27 | 13th | *unknown* | Leonids Vedejs |
| **2002 OG-M** | 4 | 2 | 1 | | | 1 | 20 | 14 | 9th | Curt Lindstrom | Harijs Vitolins |
| **2006 OG-M** | 5 | 0 | 1 | | | 4 | 11 | 29 | 12th | Leonids Beresnevs | Karlis Skrastins |
| **2010 OG-M** | 4 | 0 | | 0 | 1 | 3 | 6 | 22 | 12th | Olegs Znaroks | Karlis Skrastins |

### World Championship (Men)

(bold=top level)

| Year Event | GP | W | T | OTW | OTL | L | GF | GA | Place | Coach | Captain |
|---|---|---|---|---|---|---|---|---|---|---|---|
| **1933 WM** | 4 | 1 | 0 | | | 3 | 3 | 9 | 10th | *unknown* | Indrikis Reinbahs |
| **1935 WM** | 5 | 1 | 0 | | | 4 | 11 | 25 | 13th | *unknown* | Leonids Vedejs |
| **1938 WM** | 4 | 1 | 0 | | | 3 | 4 | 8 | 10th | *unknown* | Leonids Vedejs |
| **1939 WM** | 6 | 3 | 0 | | | 3 | 16 | 24 | 10th | Larry March | Leonids Vedejs |
| 1993 WM-C | 7 | 6 | 1 | | | 0 | 101 | 9 | 2nd | Helmuts Balderis | Konstantins Grigorjevs |
| 1994 WM-B | 7 | 6 | 0 | | | 1 | 61 | 9 | 2nd | Helmuts Balderis | *unknown* |
| 1995 WM-B | 7 | 6 | 0 | | | 1 | 65 | 16 | 2nd | Ewald Grabovskis | Aleksanders Beliavskis |
| 1996 WM-B | 7 | 6 | 1 | | | 0 | 41 | 16 | 1st | Leonids Beresnevs | Andrejs Maticins |
| **1997 WM** | 8 | 4 | 2 | | | 2 | 37 | 23 | 7th | Leonids Beresnevs | Olegs Znaroks |
| **1998 WM** | 6 | 3 | 1 | | | 2 | 21 | 18 | 9th | Leonids Beresnevs | Olegs Znaroks (1) |
| **1999 WM** | 6 | 2 | 0 | | | 4 | 24 | 22 | 11th | Leonids Beresnevs | Olegs Znaroks |
| **2000 WM** | 7 | 3 | 1 | | | 3 | 15 | 17 | 8th | Haralds Vasiljevs | Harijs Vitolins |
| **2001 WM** | 6 | 3 | 1 | | | 2 | 19 | 13 | 13th | Haralds Vasiljevs | Harijs Vitolins |
| **2002 WM** | 6 | 1 | 0 | | | 5 | 14 | 20 | 11th | Curt Lindstrom | Harijs Vitolins |
| **2003 WM** | 6 | 3 | 0 | | | 3 | 14 | 16 | 9th | Curt Lindstrom | Vjaceslavs Fanduls |
| **2004 WM** | 7 | 2 | 2 | | | 3 | 12 | 14 | 7th | Curt Lindstrom | Vjaceslavs Fanduls |
| **2005 WM** | 6 | 2 | 1 | | | 3 | 12 | 19 | 9th | Leonids Beresnevs | Karlis Skrastins |
| **2006 WM** | 6 | 2 | 1 | | | 3 | 12 | 24 | 10th | Pyotr Vorobyov | Aleksandrs Semjenovs |
| **2007 WM** | 6 | 2 | | 0 | 1 | 3 | 20 | 22 | 13th | Olegs Znaroks | Rodrigo Lavins |
| **2008 WM** | 6 | 2 | | 0 | 0 | 4 | 11 | 19 | 11th | Olegs Znaroks | Rodrigo Lavins |
| **2009 WM** | 7 | 3 | | 1 | 0 | 3 | 19 | 18 | 7th | Olegs Znaroks | Karlis Skrastins |
| **2010 WM** | 6 | 2 | | 0 | 0 | 4 | 15 | 18 | 11th | Olegs Znaroks | Herberts Vasiljevs |
| **2011 WM** | 6 | 2 | | 0 | 2 | 2 | 18 | 19 | 13th | Olegs Znaroks | Herberts Vasiljevs |
| **2012 WM** | 7 | 2 | | 0 | 0 | 5 | 11 | 19 | 10th | Ted Nolan | Janis Sprukts |

(1) Harijs Vitolins captain vs. Kazakhstan (May 6)

### U20 World Championship

(bold=top level)

| Year Event | GP | W | T | OTW | OTL | L | GF | GA | Place | Coach | Captain |
|---|---|---|---|---|---|---|---|---|---|---|---|
| 1994 WM20-C | 4 | 3 | 0 | | | 1 | 57 | 9 | 2nd | *unknown* | *unknown* |
| 1995 WM20-C1 | 4 | 4 | 0 | | | 0 | 34 | 8 | 1st | Juris Reps | Aleksandrs Nizivijs |
| 1996 WM20-B | 6 | 5 | 0 | | | 1 | 27 | 20 | 2nd | Leonids Beresnevs | Aleksandrs Nizivijs |
| 1997 WM20-B | 7 | 5 | 1 | | | 1 | 28 | 19 | 2nd | Leonids Beresnevs | *unknown* |
| 1998 WM20-B | 6 | 3 | 0 | | | 3 | 20 | 20 | 4th | Aleksandrs Cicurskis | Vitalijs Galuzo |
| 1999 WM20-B | 6 | 2 | 0 | | | 4 | 12 | 17 | 5th | Leonids Beresnevs | Arvids Rekis |
| 2000 WM20-B | 5 | 1 | 0 | | | 4 | 8 | 14 | 7th | Sergejs Iveyenko | Aleksejs Sirokovs |
| 2001 WM20I | 5 | 1 | 1 | | | 3 | 16 | 24 | 8th | Leonids Beresnevs | Aleksejs Sirokovs |
| 2002 WM20-II | 4 | 3 | 0 | | | 1 | 32 | 7 | 3rd | Leonids Beresnevs | Janis Sprukts |
| 2003 WM20-I-B | 5 | 1 | 1 | | | 3 | 13 | 21 | 4th | Mihails Beskasnovs | Aigars Berzins |
| 2004 WM20-I-A | 5 | 2 | 2 | | | 1 | 35 | 19 | 4th | Mihails Beskasnovs | Aleksandrs Jerofejevs |
| 2005 WM20-I-B | 5 | 4 | 1 | | | 0 | 28 | 12 | 1st | Olegs Znaroks | Lauris Darzins |
| **2006 WM20** | 6 | 1 | 0 | | | 5 | 14 | 30 | 9th | Olegs Znaroks | Martins Karsums |
| 2007 WM20-I-A | 5 | 4 | | 0 | 0 | 1 | 29 | 13 | 2nd | Leonids Beresnevs | Oskars Bartulis |
| 2008 WM20-I-B | 5 | 4 | | 0 | 0 | 1 | 28 | 9 | 1st | Andrejs Maticins | Oskars Cibulskis |

| Year Event | GP | W | T | | L | GF | GA | Place | Coach | Captain |
|---|---|---|---|---|---|---|---|---|---|---|
| **2009 WM20** | **6** | **2** | **0** | **0** | **4** | **19** | **28** | **8th** | **Andrejs Maticins** | **Janis Straupe** |
| **2010 WM20** | **6** | **1** | **0** | **0** | **5** | **17** | **57** | **9th** | **Andrejs Maticins** | **Roberts Bukarts** |
| 2011 WM20-I-A | 5 | 5 | 0 | 0 | 0 | 21 | 3 | 1st | Leonids Beresnevs | Juris Upitis |
| **2012 WM20** | **6** | **0** | **1** | **0** | **5** | **12** | **44** | **9th** | **Eriks Miluns** | **Kristians Pelss** |

### U18 World Championship (Men)

(bold=top level)

| Year Event | GP | W | T | | L | GF | GA | Place | Coach | Captain |
|---|---|---|---|---|---|---|---|---|---|---|
| Year Event | GP | W | OTW | OTL | L | GF | GA | Place | Coach | Captain |
| 2000 WM18-B | 5 | 2 | 2 | | 1 | 19 | 17 | 3rd | Gints Bisenieks | Janis Sprukts |
| 2001 WM18-I | 5 | 1 | 1 | | 3 | 18 | 21 | 4th | Maris Baldonieks | Aigars Berzins |
| 2002 WM18-I | 5 | 1 | 1 | | 3 | 10 | 16 | 4th | Anatolijs Jemeljanenko | Jurijs Galajevs |
| 2003 WM18-I-A | 5 | 1 | 2 | | 2 | 14 | 15 | 4th | Aleksandrs Klinisovs | Raimonds Danilics |
| 2004 WM18-I-A | 5 | 2 | 1 | | 2 | 27 | 17 | 4th | Olegs Znaroks | Oskars Bartulis |
| 2005 WM18-I-B | 5 | 3 | 0 | | 2 | 14 | 13 | 2nd | Vjaceslavs Nazarovs | Toms Hartmanis |
| 2006 WM18-I-B | 5 | 5 | 0 | | 0 | 27 | 7 | 1st | Aleksandrs Klinisovs | Arturs Ozolins |
| **2007 U18** | **6** | **0** | **0** | **0** | **6** | **10** | **36** | **10th** | **Aleksandrs Klinisovs** | **Vitalijs Pavlovs** |
| 2008 WM18-I-B | 5 | 4 | 0 | 0 | 1 | 21 | 2 | 2nd | Vjaceslavs Nazarovs | Raimonds Vilkoits |
| 2009 WM18-I-B | 5 | 4 | 0 | 0 | 1 | 18 | 10 | 1st | Aleksandrs Klinisovs | Ralfs Freibergs |
| **2010 U18** | **6** | **0** | **1** | **0** | **5** | **15** | **34** | **9th** | **Leonids Beresnevs** | **Kristers Freibergs** |
| 2011 WM18-I-A | 4 | 4 | 0 | 0 | 0 | 21 | 2 | 1st | Eriks Miluns | Kristaps Nimanis |
| **2012 WM18** | **6** | **2** | **0** | **1** | **3** | **18** | **26** | **9th** | **Leonids Tambijevs** | **Nikita Jevpalovs** |

### Women's World Championship

| Year Event | GP | W | T | | L | GF | GA | Place | Coach | Captain |
|---|---|---|---|---|---|---|---|---|---|---|
| Year Event | GP | W | OTW | OTL | L | GF | GA | Place | Coach | Captain |
| 1999 WW-B | 5 | 3 | 0 | | 2 | 18 | 13 | 5th | Vjaceslavs Nazarovs | Baiba Liepina |
| 2000 WW-B | 5 | 1 | 1 | | 2 | 7 | 13 | 6th | Vjaceslavs Nazarovs | Baiba Liepina |
| 2001 WW-I | 4 | 1 | 1 | | 2 | 7 | 10 | 6th | Vjaceslavs Nazarovs | *unknown* |
| 2003 WW-I | 5 | 1 | 0 | | 4 | 7 | 16 | 5th | Andrejs Zakis | Baiba Liepina |
| 2004 WW-I | 5 | 3 | 1 | | 1 | 18 | 15 | 3rd | Andrejs Zakis | Laila Stolte |
| 2005 WW-I | 5 | 0 | 0 | | 5 | 12 | 31 | 6th | Andrejs Zakis | Laila Stolte |
| 2007 WW-I | 5 | 3 | 0 | 0 | 1 | 13 | 9 | 2nd | Andrejs Zakis | Laila Stolte |
| 2008 WW-I | 5 | 1 | 0 | 1 | 3 | 9 | 12 | 6th | Andrejs Zakis | Laila Stolte |
| 2009 WW-II | 5 | 5 | 0 | 0 | 0 | 25 | 4 | 1st | Girts Udris | Iveta Koka |
| 2011 WW-I | 4 | 1 | 0 | 0 | 3 | 5 | 7 | 3rd | Girts Udris | Iveta Koka |
| 2012 WW-I-A | 5 | 1 | 1 | 0 | 3 | 5 | 20 | 5th | Andreja Zakis | Aija Apsite |

# Liechtenstein (LIE)

*Liechtenstein plays one of its only two international games against Luxembourg in Widnau, Switzerland, in 2007. Luxembourg won 4-2. Photo: Christian Hausler / hockeyfans.ch.*

**Joined IIHF: October 4, 2001 (Associate Member)**

Website: www.leiv.li
E-mail: info@leiv.li

Liechtensteiner Eishockey Verband
Martin Rudisuhli
Hof 52
9487 Gamprin-Bendern
Liechtenstein

Phone: +423 777 81 71 • Fax: +423 373 81 73

**Top Level Host History** none

# Lithuania (LTU)

*The Lithuanian U18 national team players listen to their national anthem. Photo: Nicolien Sijtsema.*

## Joined IIHF: February 19, 1938

(membership expired April 27, 1946; re-joined as an independent nation on May 6, 1992)

Website: www.ledas.lt
E-mail: llrf@llrf.lt

Lithuanian Ice Hockey Federation
Zemaites str. 6
LT-09601 Vilnius
Lithuania

Phone: +370 52 33 45 87 • Fax: +370 52 33 45 87

| World Ranking | |
|---|---|
| **MEN** | |
| 2012 | 25 |
| 2011 | 24 |
| 2010 | 24 |
| 2009 | 23 |
| 2008 | 23 |
| 2007 | 25 |
| 2006 | 25 |
| 2005 | 27 |
| 2004 | 27 |

**Top Level Host History** none

### World Championship (Men)

(bold=top level)

| Year Event | GP | W | T | | L | GF | GA | Place | Coach | Captain |
|---|---|---|---|---|---|---|---|---|---|---|
| Year Event | GP | W | OTW | OTL | L | GF | GA | Place | Coach | Captain |
| **1938 WM** | **4** | **0** | **1** | | **3** | **3** | **33** | **10th** | ***unknown*** | ***unknown*** |
| 1995 WM-C | 6 | 5 | 1 | | 0 | 48 | 13 | 2nd | Viktor Senin | Rolandas Bucys |
| 1996 WM-D | 5 | 5 | 0 | | 0 | 33 | 4 | 1st | Viktor Senin | Rolandas Bucys |
| 1997 WM-C | 5 | 0 | 0 | | 5 | 11 | 32 | 8th | Viktor Senin | Rolandas Bucys |
| 1998 WM-C | 5 | 3 | 0 | | 2 | 13 | 29 | 3rd | Viktor Senin | Rolandas Bucys |
| 1999 WM-C | 4 | 0 | 2 | | 2 | 11 | 19 | 3rd | Viktor Senin | Vladas Skadauskas |
| 2000 WM-C | 4 | 2 | 1 | | 1 | 23 | 16 | 4th | Viktor Senin | Vladas Skadauskas |
| 2001 WM-I-A | 5 | 0 | 0 | | 5 | 10 | 36 | 6th | Viktor Senin | Sarunas Kuliesius |
| 2002 WM-II-B | 5 | 5 | 0 | | 0 | 71 | 6 | 1st | Dmitri Medvedev | Dmitrijus Bernatavicius |
| 2003 WM-I-A | 5 | 0 | 1 | | 4 | 7 | 30 | 6th | Dmitri Medvedev | Rolandas Aliukonis |
| 2004 WM-II-B | 5 | 5 | 0 | | 0 | 70 | 7 | 1st | Dmitri Medvedev | Dmitrijus Bernatavicius |
| 2005 WM-I-B | 5 | 1 | 2 | | 2 | 16 | 17 | 5th | Dmitri Medvedev | Dainius Zubrus |
| 2006 WM-I-B | 5 | 3 | 1 | | 1 | 24 | 14 | 2nd | Dmitri Medvedev | Dainius Bauba |
| 2007 WM-I-B | 5 | 2 | 0 | 0 | 3 | 13 | 20 | 5th | Dmitri Medvedev | Dainius Bauba |
| 2008 WM-I-B | 5 | 2 | 0 | 0 | 3 | 9 | 21 | 4th | Dmitri Medvedev | Martynas Slikas |
| 2009 WM-I-A | 5 | 2 | 0 | 0 | 3 | 20 | 23 | 4th | Dmitri Medvedev | Dmitrijus Bernatavicius |
| 2010 WM-I-A | 5 | 1 | 0 | 0 | 4 | 19 | 33 | 5th | Rimantas Sidaravicius | Sarunas Kuliesius |
| 2011 WM-I-B | 5 | 1 | 0 | 0 | 4 | 9 | 24 | 5th | Sergej Borisov | Dalius Vaiciukevicius |
| 2012 WM-I-B | 5 | 1 | 0 | 0 | 4 | 9 | 27 | 5th | Sergei Borisov | Arturas Katulis |

### U20 World Championship

| Year Event | GP | W | T | | L | GF | GA | Place | Coach | Captain |
|---|---|---|---|---|---|---|---|---|---|---|
| Year Event | GP | W | OTW | OTL | L | GF | GA | Place | Coach | Captain |
| 1995 WM20-C2 | 5 | 2 | 0 | | 3 | 29 | 30 | 4th | Vytautas Slikas | Egidijus Bauba |
| 1996 WM20-D | 3 | 1 | 0 | | 2 | 25 | 12 | 4th | *unknown* | *unknown* |
| 1997 WM20-D | 4 | 3 | 0 | | 1 | 49 | 12 | 2nd | Viktor Senin | Egidijus Bauba |
| 1998 WM20-D | 4 | 4 | 0 | | 0 | 39 | 5 | 1st | Viktor Senin | Egidijus Bauba |
| 1999 WM20-C | 4 | 0 | 1 | | 3 | 11 | 18 | 6th | Rimantas Sidaravicius | Rolandas Aliukonis |
| 2000 WM20-C | 4 | 1 | 0 | | 3 | 11 | 16 | 7th | Vytautas Slikas | Rolandas Aliukonis |
| 2001 WM20-II | 4 | 3 | 0 | | 1 | 16 | 14 | 3rd | Rimantas Sidaravicius | Arturas Katulis |
| 2002 WM20-II | 4 | 0 | 0 | | 4 | 11 | 33 | 8th | Rimantas Sidaravicius | Douydas Kulevicius |
| 2003 WM20-II-A | 5 | 2 | 0 | | 3 | 21 | 31 | 4th | Gintaras Armanavicius | Tomas Lauksedis |
| 2004 WM20-II-B | 5 | 2 | 0 | | 3 | 12 | 25 | 5th | Rimantas Sidaravicius | Simas Sakaitis |
| 2005 WM20-II-A | 5 | 0 | 0 | | 5 | 5 | 35 | 6th | Rimantas Sidaravicius | Algimantas Visockas |
| 2006 WM20-III | 4 | 4 | 0 | | 0 | 81 | 3 | 1st | Rimantas Sidaravicius | Donatas Kumeliauskas |
| 2007 WM20-II-B | 5 | 4 | 1 | 0 | 0 | 30 | 7 | 1st | Rimantas Sidaravicius | Algimantas Visockas |
| 2008 WM20-I-A | 5 | 0 | 1 | 0 | 4 | 8 | 39 | 6th | Rimantas Sidaravicius | Paulius Tamkevicius |
| 2009 WM20-II-A | 5 | 4 | 0 | 0 | 1 | 35 | 9 | 2nd | Rimantas Sidaravicius | Karolis Nekrasevicius |
| 2010 WM20-II-B | 5 | 5 | 0 | 0 | 0 | 34 | 12 | 1st | Rimantas Sidaravicius | Tadas Kumeliauskas |
| 2011 WM20-I-B | 5 | 0 | 0 | 0 | 5 | 10 | 35 | 6th | Rimantas Sidaravicius | Nerijus Alisauskas |
| 2012 WM20-II-A | 5 | 3 | 0 | 2 | 0 | 19 | 11 | 2nd | Andrejus Jadkauskas | Aivaras Bendzius |

### U18 World Championship (Men)

| Year Event | GP | W | T | | L | GF | GA | Place | Coach | Captain |
|---|---|---|---|---|---|---|---|---|---|---|
| Year Event | GP | W | OTW | OTL | L | GF | GA | Place | Coach | Captain |
| 2001 WM18-II | 4 | 0 | 0 | | 4 | 6 | 33 | 8th | Sergei Krumkac | Andrius Poskus |
| 2002 WM18-III | 4 | 1 | 0 | | 3 | 14 | 23 | 6th | Girantas Armanavicius | Donatas Kumeliauskas |
| 2003 WM18-II-B | 5 | 1 | 0 | | 4 | 15 | 29 | 5th | Rimantas Sidaravicius | Petras Nauseda |
| 2004 WM18-II-B | 5 | 1 | 1 | | 3 | 10 | 15 | 4th | Rimantas Sidaravicius | Algimantas Visockas |
| 2005 WM18-II-B | 5 | 4 | 0 | | 1 | 31 | 19 | 2nd | Rimantas Sidaravicius | Donatas Kumeliauskas |
| 2006 WM18-II-B | 5 | 4 | 0 | | 1 | 39 | 12 | 2nd | Rimantas Sidaravicius | Paulius Tamkevicius |
| 2007 WM18-II-B | 5 | 5 | 0 | 0 | 0 | 32 | 9 | 1st | Gracijus Girdauskas | Arnoldas Bosas |

| 2008 WM18-I-A | 5 | 2 | 0 | 0 | 3 | 13 | 26 | 3rd | Gracijus Girdauskas | *unknown* |
|---|---|---|---|---|---|---|---|---|---|---|
| 2009 WM18-I-A | 5 | 1 | 0 | 1 | 3 | 13 | 16 | 5th | Rimantas Sidaravicius | Nerijus Aliauskas |
| 2010 WM18-I-B | 5 | 0 | 0 | 0 | 5 | 6 | 39 | 6th | Daugirdas Gricius | Pijus Rulevicius |
| 2011 WM18-II-B | 5 | 3 | 0 | 0 | 2 | 44 | 15 | 3rd | Andrejus Jadkauskas | Aivaras Bendzius |
| 2012 WM18-II-A | 5 | 3 | 1 | 0 | 1 | 22 | 11 | 3rd | Andrejus Jadkauskas | Daniel Bogdziul |

# Luxembourg (LUX)

Luxembourg missed promotion at the 2012 IIHF Ice Hockey World Championship Division III in Turkey. Photo: TIHF.

## Joined IIHF: March 23, 1912

Website: www.icehockey.lu
E-mail: amscheier@pt.lu

Fédération Luxembourgeoise de Hockey sur Glace
1, rue Christophe Plantin
BP 1632
1016 Luxembourg
Luxembourg

Phone: +352 621 177 185 • Fax: +352 40 22 28

**World Ranking**

**MEN**
2012........43
2001........43
2010........44
2009........44
2008........43
2007........42
2006........43
2005........42
2004........42

**Top Level Host History** none

**World Championship (Men)**

| Year Event | GP | W | T | | | L | GF | GA | Place | Coach | Captain |
|---|---|---|---|---|---|---|---|---|---|---|---|
| Year Event | GP | W | | OTW | OTL | L | GF | GA | Place | Coach | Captain |
| 1992 WM-C | 5 | 1 | 1 | | | 3 | 20 | 73 | 5th | Timo Tikkinen | *unknown* |
| 2000-WM-D | 4 | 1 | 0 | | | 3 | 9 | 23 | 8th | Robert Beran | Alain Schneider |
| 2002 WM-II-B | 5 | 0 | 0 | | | 5 | 2 | 68 | 6th | Carlo Welter | Benny Welter |
| 2003 WM-III | 2 | 1 | 0 | | | 1 | 7 | 10 | 2nd | Hakan Gronlund | Benny Welter |
| 2004 WM-II-A | 5 | 0 | 1 | | | 4 | 5 | 70 | 6th | Hakan Gronlund | Benny Welter |
| 2005 WM-III | 4 | 2 | 0 | | | 2 | 49 | 16 | 3rd | Hakan Gronlund | Ronny Scheier |
| 2006 WM-III | 4 | 0 | 0 | | | 4 | 11 | 26 | 5th | Hakan Gronlund | Ronny Scheier |
| 2007 WM-III | 4 | 2 | | 0 | 1 | 1 | 21 | 15 | 3rd | Hakan Gronlund | Ronny Scheier |
| 2008 WM-III | 5 | 1 | | 2 | 0 | 2 | 22 | 13 | 3rd | Hakan Gronlund | Ronny Scheier |
| 2009 WM-III | 5 | 3 | | 0 | 0 | 2 | 26 | 18 | 3rd | Marian Gallo | Ronny Scheier |
| 2010 WM-III-A | 3 | 1 | | 0 | 0 | 2 | 8 | 10 | 3rd | Joakim Eriksson | Ronny Scheier |
| 2011 WM-III | 5 | 2 | | 0 | 0 | 3 | 33 | 22 | 4th | Yves Barthels | Ronny Scheier |
| 2012 WM-III | 5 | 3 | | 0 | 0 | 2 | 20 | 15 | 3rd | Marian Gallo | Ronny Scheier |

**U20 World Championship**

| Year Event | GP | W | T | L | GF | GA | Place | Coach | Captain |
|---|---|---|---|---|---|---|---|---|---|
| 2003 WM20-III | 4 | 0 | 0 | 4 | 1 | 48 | 5th | Robert Beran | Georges Scheier |

# Macau (MAC)

Macau's Chon Kong Leong tries to score against India. Photo: IHAI.

## Joined IIHF: May 12, 2005 (Associate Member)

Website: www.moisf.org
Email: fbap@macau.ctm.net

Macau Ice Sports Federation
Praca De Luis De Camoes
Future Bright Amusement Park
Lai Hou Garden, No 6-8 R/C
Macau

Phone: +853 668 56 16/+853 953 399 • Fax: +853 950 211

**Top Level Host History** none

# Malaysia (MAS)

*Malaysian forward Tack Hoong Jeremy Chee skates with the puck. Photo: IHAI.*

**Joined IIHF: September 28, 2006 (Associate Member)**

Website: www.malaysiaicehockey.com
E-mail: susan@malaysiaicehockey.com

Malaysia Ice Hockey Federation
17 Jalan USJ 5/1E
UEP Subang Jaya
47610 Petaling Jaya Selanger
Malaysia

Phone: +603 7804 5678 • Fax: +603 7805 4680

**Top Level Host History** none

# Mexico (MEX)

*Mexican goalie Alfonso del Alba tries to save the puck against Belgium's Bryan Kolodziejczyk. Photo: Bonchuk Andonov.*

**Joined IIHF: April 30, 1985**

Website: www.hockeymexico.com
E-mail: contacto@hockeymexico.com

Federacion Deportiva de Mexico de Hockey sobre Hielo, A.C.
Transmisiones 16
Lomas San Angel Inn
Alvaro Obregon
01790 Mexico, D.F.
Mexico

Phone: +52-55-95-59-17 / +52-59-13-65-60 • Fax: +52-15-20-07-64

| World Ranking | |
|---|---|
| **MEN** | |
| 2012 | 34 |
| 2011 | 33 |
| 2010 | 32 |
| 2009 | 38 |
| 2008 | 37 |
| 2007 | 38 |
| 2006 | 39 |
| 2005 | 43 |
| 2004 | 41 |

**Top Level Host History** none

**World Championship (Men)**

| Year Event | GP | W | T | | | L | GF | GA | Place | Coach | Captain |
|---|---|---|---|---|---|---|---|---|---|---|---|
| Year Event | GP | W | | OTW | OTL | L | GF | GA | Place | Coach | Captain |
| 2000 WM-D | 4 | 2 | 0 | | | 2 | 16 | 17 | 7th | Michel Charron | Juan Pablo Roberts |
| 2001 WM-II-B | 5 | 0 | 0 | | | 5 | 4 | 66 | 6th | Joaquin de la Garma | Federico Obregon |
| 2003 WM-II-A | 5 | 0 | 0 | | | 5 | 5 | 70 | 6th | Joaquin de la Garma | Juan Pablo Roberts |
| 2004 WM-III | 4 | 2 | 1 | | | 1 | 29 | 8 | 3rd | Joaquin de la Garma | Juan Pablo Roberts |
| 2005 WM-III | 4 | 4 | 0 | | | 0 | 60 | 3 | 1st | Joaquin de la Garma | Juan Pablo Roberts |
| 2006 WM-II-B | 5 | 1 | 0 | | | 4 | 9 | 35 | 5th | Joaquin de la Garma | Manuel Sierra |
| 2007 WM-II-B | 4 | 0 | | 0 | 0 | 4 | 6 | 24 | 5th | Joaquin de la Garma | Fernando Ugarte |
| 2008 WM-II-B | 5 | 2 | | 0 | 0 | 3 | 14 | 20 | 4th | Joaquin de la Garma | Fernando Ugarte |
| 2009 WM-II-B | 5 | 1 | | 0 | 0 | 4 | 11 | 33 | 5th | Diego de la Garma | Fernando Ugarte |
| 2010 WM-II-A | 5 | 1 | | 0 | 0 | 4 | 17 | 21 | 5th | Joaquin de la Garma | Fernando Ugarte |
| 2011 WM-II-A | 5 | 1 | | 0 | 0 | 4 | 8 | 31 | 5th | Joaquin de la Garma | Fernando Ugarte |
| 2012 WM-II-B | 5 | 2 | | 0 | 1 | 2 | 17 | 24 | 4th | Diego de la Garma | Fernando Ugarte |

**U20 World Championship**

| Year Event | GP | W | T | | | L | GF | GA | Place | Coach | Captain |
|---|---|---|---|---|---|---|---|---|---|---|---|
| Year Event | GP | W | | OTW | OTL | L | GF | GA | Place | Coach | Captain |
| 1997 WM20-D | 4 | 0 | 0 | | | 4 | 8 | 45 | 8th | Daniel Gendron | Juan Pablo Roberts |
| 1998 WM20-D | 4 | 2 | 0 | | | 2 | 9 | 32 | 5th | Daniel Gendron | Juan Pablo Roberts |
| 1999 WM20-D | 4 | 2 | 0 | | | 2 | 40 | 13 | 5th | Michel Charron | Juan Pablo Roberts |
| 2000 WM20-D | 4 | 2 | 0 | | | 2 | 13 | 24 | 5th | Michel Charron | Carlos Potts |
| 2001 WM20-III | 4 | 1 | 0 | | | 3 | 8 | 24 | 7th | Roy Reid | Roberto Delano |
| 2002 WM20-III | 4 | 1 | 0 | | | 3 | 17 | 34 | 7th | Joaquin de la Garma | Fernando Ugarte |
| 2003 WM20-II-B | 5 | 0 | 0 | | | 5 | 4 | 25 | 6th | Joaquin de la Garma | Fernando Ugarte |
| 2004 WM20-III | 5 | 3 | 0 | | | 2 | 25 | 16 | 3rd | Diego de la Garma | Alex Cervantes |
| 2005 WM20-III | 5 | 5 | 0 | | | 0 | 37 | 6 | 1st | Joaquin de la Garma | Adrian Cervantes |
| 2006 WM20-II-B | 5 | 1 | 0 | | | 4 | 11 | 40 | 5th | Diego de la Garma | Alejandro Rosette |
| 2007 WM20-II-B | 5 | 1 | | 0 | 0 | 4 | 7 | 37 | 5th | Joaquin de la Garma | Alejandro Rosette |
| 2008 WM20-II-B | 5 | 1 | | 0 | 0 | 4 | 8 | 27 | 5th | Joaquin de la Garma | Luis de la Vega |
| 2009 WM20-II-B | 5 | 2 | | 0 | 0 | 3 | 11 | 27 | 4th | Diego de la Garma | Pablo Ehlers |
| 2010 WM20-II-A | 5 | 0 | | 0 | 0 | 5 | 4 | 77 | 6th | Diego de la Garma | Alan Smithers |
| 2011 WM20-III | 6 | 6 | | 0 | 0 | 0 | 39 | 9 | 1st | Diego de la Garma | Manuel Escandon |
| 2012 WM20-II-B | 5 | 0 | | 0 | 1 | 4 | 5 | 39 | 6th | Diego de la Garma | Oscar Flores |

U18 World Championship (Men)

| Year Event | GP | W | T<br>OTW | <br>OTL | L | GF | GA | Place | Coach | Captain |
|---|---|---|---|---|---|---|---|---|---|---|
| 2003 WM18-III-A | 3 | 2 | 0 | | 1 | 12 | 12 | 2nd | Joaquin de la Garma | Adrian Cervantes |
| 2004 WM18-III-B | 6 | 6 | 0 | | 0 | 41 | 4 | 1st | Joaquin de la Garma | Eduardo Glennie |
| 2005 WM18-II-B | 5 | 2 | 0 | | 3 | 15 | 26 | 4th | Joaquin de la Garma | Cristofer Kelo |
| 2006 WM18-II-B | 5 | 2 | 0 | | 3 | 10 | 21 | 5th | Joaquin de la Garma | Luis de la Vega |
| 2007 WM18-II-A | 5 | 0 | 0 | 1 | 4 | 9 | 33 | 6th | Joaquin de la Garma | Ander Barberena |
| 2008 WM18-III-A | 4 | 4 | 0 | 0 | 0 | 32 | 2 | 1st | Diego de la Garma | *unknown* |
| 2009 WM18-II-A | 5 | 0 | 0 | 0 | 5 | 3 | 50 | 6th | Diego de la Garma | Manuel Escandon |
| 2010 WM18-III-B | 4 | 3 | 0 | 0 | 1 | 15 | 11 | 2nd | Diego de la Garma | Christian Smithers |
| 2011 WM18-III-B | 4 | 3 | 0 | 1 | 0 | 30 | 8 | 2nd | Diego de la Garma | Francisco Padilla |
| 2012 WM18-III | 5 | 3 | 0 | 0 | 2 | 24 | 15 | 3rd | Diego de la Garma | Miguel Colas |

# Moldova (MDA)

*The Platina Chisinau team from Moldova's capital plays games in neighbouring Romania. Photo: Henrik Manninen.*

### Joined IIHF: May 22, 2008 (Associate Member)

Website: www.nihf.md
Email: nihfrm@yahoo.com

National Ice Hockey Federation of Moldova
Str. Pushkin, 24, 4th floor, of. 67
MD-2012 Chisinau
Republic of Moldova

Phone: +373 22 220332 • Fax: +373 22 234898

**Top Level Host History** none

# Mongolia (MGL)

*Mongolia competed in the 2012 IIHF Ice Hockey World Championship Division III in Turkey. Photo: TIHF.*

### Joined IIHF: May 13, 1999

Website: n/a
E-mail: sganjargal@yahoo.com

Mongolian Ice Hockey Federation
11 Khoroolol, Bldg Nr. 33
Erdenet City
213900 Orhon Aimag
Mongolia

Phone: +976 13 527 15 11 • Fax: +976 13 527 18 66

**World Ranking**

**MEN**
2012........46
2011........46
2010........46
2009........45
2008........45
2007........46

**Top Level Host History** none

World Championship (Men)

| Year Event | GP | W | OTW | OTL | L | GF | GA | Place | Coach | Captain |
|---|---|---|---|---|---|---|---|---|---|---|
| 2007 WM-III | 4 | 0 | 0 | 0 | 4 | 3 | 45 | 5th | Otgonbayar Munkhnasan | Purevdavaa Choijiljav |
| 2008 WM-III | 5 | 0 | 0 | 0 | 5 | 11 | 59 | 6th | Shinebayar Enkhbayar | Altangerel Ichinnorov |
| 2010 WM-III-B | 4 | 0 | 0 | 0 | 4 | 5 | 57 | 3rd | *unknown* | *unknown* |
| 2011 WM-III | 5 | 0 | 0 | 0 | 5 | 0 | 25 | 6th | all games forfeited | |
| 2012 WM-III | 5 | 0 | 0 | 0 | 5 | 8 | 39 | 6th | Shinebayar Enkhbayar | Mishigsuren Namjil |

U18 World Championship (Men)

| Year Event | GP | W | OTW | OTL | L | GF | GA | Place | Coach | Captain |
|---|---|---|---|---|---|---|---|---|---|---|
| 2008 WM18-III-A | 4 | 0 | 0 | 0 | 4 | 7 | 64 | 5th | Boldbaatar Shirnen | *unknown* |
| 2009 WM18-III-A | 4 | 0 | 0 | 0 | 4 | 4 | 81 | 5th | Boldbaatar Shirnen | Ankhnaran Narangerel |
| 2010 WM18-III-A | 4 | 0 | 0 | 0 | 4 | 2 | 78 | 5th | Boldbaatar Shirnen/Tserenbaljir Baatarkhuu | *unknown* |

# Morocco (MAR)

The Moroccan national team which participated in the 2008 Arab Cup poses for a photo at the Mega Mall ice rink in Rabat, their only rink. Photo: ANMHG.

**Joined IIHF: May 22, 2010 (Associate Member)**
Website: www.moroccanicehockey.com
E-mail: khalid.mrini@gmail.com

Association National Marocaine de Hockey sur Glace (ANMHG)
576, Avenue Allal El Fassi Secteur 5
Hay Salam
11000 Salé
Morocco

Phone: +212 66 25 48792

**Top Level Host History** none

# Namibia (NAM)

Namibia during InLine game action during qualification for 2010 IIHF InLine Hockey World Championship Division I. Photo: NIIHA.

**Joined IIHF: May 31, 1998 (Affiliate Member)**
Website: www.niiha.com
E-mail: secretary@niiha.com

Namibia Ice and InLine Hockey Association
PO Box 90464
Klein Windhoek
Windhoek
Namibia

Phone: +264 81 250 4869 • Fax: +264 8863 8881

**Top Level Host History** none

# Netherlands (NED)

The Netherlands battles Romania at the 2012 IIHF Ice Hockey World Championship Division I Group B. Photo: Mirek Ring.

**Joined IIHF: January 20, 1935**
Website: www.nijb.nl
E-mail: info@nijb.nl

Ice Hockey Association of The Netherlands
P.O. Box 292
2700 AG Zoetermeer
The Netherlands

Phone: +31 79 330 50 50 • Fax: +31 79 330 50 51

**World Ranking**

| MEN | | WOMEN | |
|---|---|---|---|
| 2012 | 24 | 2012 | 21 |
| 2011 | 25 | 2011 | 22 |
| 2010 | 25 | 2010 | 23 |
| 2009 | 24 | 2009 | 21 |
| 2008 | 24 | 2008 | 21 |
| 2007 | 24 | 2007 | 21 |
| 2006 | 23 | 2006 | 20 |
| 2005 | 23 | 2005 | 19 |
| 2004 | 23 | 2004 | 19 |

**Top Level Host History** none

**Olympics, Men**
(bold=top level)

| Year Event | GP | W | T | L | GF | GA | Place | Coach | Captain |
|---|---|---|---|---|---|---|---|---|---|
| **1980 OG-M** | **5** | **1** | **1** | **3** | **16** | **43** | **9th** | **Hans Westberg** | **Larrie van Wieren** |

**World Championship (Men)**
(bold=top level)

| Year Event | GP | W | T | | L | GF | GA | Place | Coach | Captain |
|---|---|---|---|---|---|---|---|---|---|---|
| Year Event | GP | W | OTW | OTL | L | GF | GA | Place | Coach | Captain |
| **1935 WM** | **6** | **0** | **0** | | **6** | **0** | **34** | **14th** | **Hans Weinberg** | **Frits van der Vlugt** |
| **1939 WM** | **4** | **1** | **0** | | **3** | **3** | **20** | **11th** | ***unknown*** | ***unknown*** |
| **1950 WM** | **4** | **1** | **0** | | **3** | **7** | **33** | **8th** | **Andy Andreola** | ***unknown*** |

| | | | | | | | | | | |
|---|---|---|---|---|---|---|---|---|---|---|
| 1951 WM-B | 5 | 3 | 0 | | 2 | 17 | 16 | 3rd | *unknown* | Johan von Rehde van der Kloot |
| 1953 WM-B | 5 | 1 | 0 | | 4 | 20 | 30 | 4th | Ed Zukiwsky | *unknown* |
| 1955 WM-B | 4 | 2 | 0 | | 2 | 18 | 20 | 3rd | *unknown* | *unknown* |
| 1961 WM-C | 5 | 2 | 0 | | 3 | 18 | 36 | 4th | *unknown* | *unknown* |
| 1962 WM-B | 5 | 2 | 0 | | 3 | 20 | 46 | 4th | Eduard Hopman | *unknown* |
| 1963 WM-C | 5 | 1 | 1 | | 3 | 21 | 34 | 5th | Frans Franken | Arie Klein |
| 1967 WM-C | 4 | 0 | 1 | | 3 | 20 | 50 | 5th | *unknown* | Arie Klein |
| 1969 WM-C | 5 | 2 | 0 | | 3 | 12 | 40 | 4th | Bob Naylor | Arie Klein |
| 1970 WM-C | 6 | 1 | 1 | | 4 | 16 | 35 | 6th | *unknown* | Wil van Dommelen |
| 1971 WM-C | 7 | 2 | 0 | | 5 | 32 | 38 | 6th | *unknown* | Wil van Dommelen |
| 1972 WM-C | 6 | 1 | 0 | | 5 | 13 | 25 | 7th | Wayne Hunter | Hans Christiaans |
| 1973 WM-C | 7 | 5 | 0 | | 2 | 52 | 21 | 2nd | Wayne Hunter | Hans Christiaans |
| 1974 WM-B | 7 | 2 | 1 | | 4 | 33 | 37 | 5th | Bob Jastremski | Hans Christiaans |
| 1975 WM-B | 7 | 0 | 1 | | 6 | 11 | 36 | 8th | Bob Jastremski | Hans Christiaans |
| 1976 WM-B | 7 | 3 | 0 | | 4 | 22 | 30 | 6th | Bob Jastremski | Hans Christiaans |
| 1977 WM-B | 8 | 1 | 2 | | 5 | 23 | 39 | 8th | Hal Laycoe | Hans Christiaans |
| 1978 WM-C | 7 | 6 | 1 | | 0 | 74 | 17 | 1st | Hans Westberg | Larry von Wieren |
| 1979 WM-B | 6 | 6 | 0 | | 0 | 36 | 13 | 1st | Hans Westberg | *unknown* |
| **1981 WM** | **8** | **0** | **0** | | **8** | **24** | **69** | **8th** | **Gustav Bubnik** | **Larry van Wieren** |
| 1982 WM-B | 7 | 2 | 0 | | 5 | 22 | 27 | 8th | Gustav Bubnik | *unknown* |
| 1983 WM-C | 7 | 7 | 0 | | 0 | 78 | 11 | 1st | Cliff Stewart | Ron Berteling |
| 1985 WM-B | 7 | 3 | 0 | | 5 | 36 | 25 | 6th | Claes-Goran Wallin | Ron Berteling |
| 1986 WM-B | 7 | 3 | 0 | | 4 | 25 | 32 | 5th | Cliff Stewart | Ron Berteling |
| 1987 WM-B | 7 | 1 | 1 | | 5 | 30 | 37 | 7th | Lou Vairo | Ron Berteling |
| 1989 WM-C | 7 | 7 | 0 | | 0 | 48 | 15 | 1st | Larry van Wieren | Ron Berteling |
| 1990 WM-B | 7 | 0 | 1 | | 6 | 14 | 43 | 8th | Larry van Wieren | Ron Berteling |
| 1991 WM-B | 7 | 1 | 0 | | 6 | 9 | 40 | 7th | Larry van Wieren | Ron Berteling |
| 1992 WM-B | 7 | 5 | 1 | | 1 | 53 | 16 | 2nd | Larry van Wieren | Ron Berteling |
| 1993 WM-B | 7 | 5 | 0 | | 2 | 47 | 20 | 3rd | Larry van Wieren | Ron Berteling |
| 1994 WM-B | 7 | 2 | 1 | | 4 | 23 | 33 | 6th | Larry van Wieren | Frank Versteeg |
| 1995 WM-B | 7 | 3 | 0 | | 4 | 20 | 38 | 4th | Doug Mason | Frank Versteeg |
| 1996 WM-B | 7 | 1 | 1 | | 5 | 12 | 37 | 7th | Doug Mason | Tommie Hartogs |
| 1997 WM-B | 7 | 2 | 1 | | 4 | 21 | 38 | 7th | Doug Mason | Tommie Hartogs |
| 1998 WM-B | 7 | 0 | 0 | | 7 | 12 | 40 | 8th | Doug Mason | Michael Smithurst |
| 1999 WM-C | 5 | 5 | 0 | | 0 | 43 | 3 | 1st | Doug Mason | Tommie Hartogs |
| 2000 WM-B | 7 | 0 | 2 | | 5 | 13 | 33 | 8th | Doug Mason | Tommie Hartogs |
| 2001 WM-I-A | 5 | 1 | 1 | | 3 | 10 | 25 | 5th | Brian de Bruyn | Tommie Hartogs |
| 2002 WM-I-A | 5 | 2 | 0 | | 3 | 19 | 30 | 4th | Manfred Wolf | Tommie Hartogs |
| 2003 WM-I-A | 5 | 1 | 1 | | 3 | 17 | 22 | 4th | Theo van Gerwen | Tommie Hartogs |
| 2004 WM-I-A | 5 | 2 | 1 | | 2 | 21 | 22 | 3rd | Martin Trommelen | Tommie Hartogs |
| 2005 WM-I-B | 5 | 1 | 3 | | 1 | 13 | 11 | 3rd | Doug Mason | Tommie Hartogs |
| 2006 WM-I-B | 5 | 1 | 1 | | 3 | 13 | 24 | 5th | Doug Mason | Tommie Hartogs |
| 2007 WM-I-A | 5 | 1 | 1 | 1 | 2 | 20 | 19 | 5th | Tommie Hartogs | Kevin Bruijsten |
| 2008 WM-I-A | 5 | 0 | 1 | 0 | 4 | 15 | 30 | 5th | Tommie Hartogs | Simon de Wit |
| 2009 WM-I-B | 5 | 1 | 0 | 0 | 4 | 9 | 16 | 5th | Tommie Hartogs | Bob Teunissen |
| 2010 WM-I-A | 5 | 1 | 1 | 0 | 3 | 11 | 19 | 4th | Tommie Hartogs | Bob Teunissen |
| 2011 WM-I-A | 4 | 1 | 0 | 0 | 3 | 16 | 18 | 4th | Tommie Hartogs | Bob Teunissen |
| 2012 WM-I-B | 5 | 3 | 0 | 1 | 1 | 21 | 13 | 3rd | Larry Suarez | Marcel Kars |

**U20 World Championship**

| Year Event | GP | W | T | | L | GF | GA | Place | Coach | Captain |
|---|---|---|---|---|---|---|---|---|---|---|
| Year Event | GP | W | OTW | OTL | L | GF | GA | Place | Coach | Captain |
| 1979 WM20-B | 4 | 1 | 0 | | 3 | 16 | 23 | 6th | G Staettle | Carry Bekink |
| 1980 WM20-B | 4 | 2 | 0 | | 2 | 19 | 16 | 4th | Eddie Gosselin | Maarten Burgers |
| 1981 WM20-B | 5 | 2 | 0 | | 3 | 10 | 28 | 4th | Eddie Gosselin | Stanley Peter |
| 1982 WM20-B | 4 | 1 | 1 | | 2 | 12 | 19 | 7th | Dummy Smit | Peter-Paul van Rooy |
| 1983 WM20-B | 5 | 2 | 1 | | 2 | 29 | 34 | 6th | George Peternousek | Bert Hille |
| 1984 WM20-B | 5 | 3 | 1 | | 1 | 22 | 20 | 5th | George Peternousek | Henk Maas |
| 1985 WM20-B | 7 | 5 | 1 | | 1 | 47 | 14 | 2nd | Alex Andjelic | Roel Bannenberg |
| 1986 WM20-B | 7 | 3 | 0 | | 4 | 30 | 43 | 6th | Doug Mason | Eric Noorman |
| 1987 WM20-B | 5 | 1 | 1 | | 3 | 25 | 30 | 7th | Eddy Gosselin | *unknown* |
| 1988 WM20-B | 7 | 0 | 3 | | 4 | 20 | 35 | 7th | Jan Janssen | *unknown* |
| 1989 WM20-B | 7 | 0 | 0 | | 7 | 17 | 48 | 8th | Jan Janssen | *unknown* |
| 1990 WM20-C | 6 | 5 | 0 | | 1 | 40 | 17 | 1st | Doug Mason | *unknown* |
| 1991 WM20-B | 7 | 1 | 1 | | 5 | 16 | 43 | 6th | Doug Mason | Wille von Megen |
| 1992 WM20-B | 7 | 2 | 0 | | 5 | 14 | 38 | 6th | Danny Cuomo | Christian Eimers |
| 1993 WM20-B | 7 | 1 | 0 | | 6 | 10 | 46 | 8th | Danny Cuomo | Stefan Collard |
| 1994 WM20-C | 4 | 1 | 0 | | 3 | 7 | 33 | 6th | *unknown* | *unknown* |
| 1995 WM20-C1 | 4 | 1 | 0 | | 3 | 10 | 25 | 7th | John Griffith | Rene Kronenburg |
| 1996 WM20-C | 4 | 1 | 0 | | 3 | 10 | 21 | 7th | Bert Hille | Rody Jacobs |
| 1997 WM20-C | 4 | 0 | 0 | | 4 | 10 | 37 | 8th | Doug Mason | Robert Delcliseur |
| 1998 WM20-D | 4 | 3 | 0 | | 1 | 61 | 10 | 2nd | Bert Hille | Maarten Loos |
| 1999 WM20-D | 4 | 3 | 0 | | 1 | 51 | 9 | 2nd | Bert Hille | Patrick van Eldonk |
| 2000 WM20-D | 4 | 2 | 0 | | 2 | 30 | 12 | 3rd | Rob Serviss | Bas de Haan |
| 2001 WM20-III | 4 | 4 | 0 | | 0 | 36 | 4 | 1st | Dennis van Rijswijk | Bob Teunissen |
| 2002 WM20-II | 4 | 1 | 0 | | 3 | 13 | 32 | 7th | Dennis van Rijswijk | Andri Solomonson |
| 2003 WM20-II-B | 5 | 4 | 0 | | 1 | 34 | 13 | 2nd | Dennis van Rijswijk | Andri Salomonson |
| 2004 WM20-II-A | 5 | 3 | 0 | | 2 | 32 | 19 | 3rd | Risto Mollen | Robert Maas |
| 2005 WM20-II-A | 5 | 3 | 0 | | 2 | 29 | 14 | 3rd | Rob Serviss | Mark Donders |
| 2006 WM20-II-A | 5 | 3 | 1 | | 1 | 38 | 8 | 2nd | Rob Serviss | Sander Dijkstra |
| 2007 WM20-II-B | 5 | 3 | 0 | 2 | 0 | 30 | 13 | 2nd | Rob Serviss | Kevin Bruijsten |
| 2008 WM20-II-B | 5 | 4 | 0 | 1 | 0 | 36 | 5 | 2nd | Rob Serviss | Ivy van den Heuvel |
| 2009 WM20-II-B | 5 | 3 | 0 | 0 | 2 | 28 | 12 | 3rd | Tommie Hartogs | Reinier Staats |
| 2010 WM20-II-B | 5 | 4 | 0 | 0 | 1 | 26 | 19 | 2nd | Tommie Hartogs | Jurryt Smid |

| Year Event | GP | W | T | OTW | OTL | L | GF | GA | Place | Coach | Captain |
|---|---|---|---|---|---|---|---|---|---|---|---|
| 2011 WM20-II-A | 5 | 3 | | 0 | 1 | 1 | 19 | 16 | 2nd | Rob Serviss | Levi Houkes |
| 2012 WM20-II-A | 5 | 1 | | 1 | 0 | 3 | 9 | 23 | 5th | Leo van den Thillart | Mickey Bastings |

**U18 World Championship (Men)**

| Year Event | GP | W | T | OTW | OTL | L | GF | GA | Place | Coach | Captain |
|---|---|---|---|---|---|---|---|---|---|---|---|
| 2001 WM18-III | 4 | 4 | 0 | | | 0 | 39 | 6 | 1st | Jorma Mantere | Bert van den Braak |
| 2002 WM18-II | 5 | 3 | 0 | | | 2 | 13 | 23 | 5th | Henry Stoer | Erwin Ophelders |
| 2003 WM18-II-B | 5 | 3 | 0 | | | 2 | 22 | 17 | 3rd | Henry Stoer | Mark Donders |
| 2004 WM18-II-A | 5 | 3 | 1 | | | 1 | 41 | 24 | 3rd | Henry Stoer | Bart van Roosmalen |
| 2005 WM18-II-A | 5 | 3 | 0 | | | 2 | 30 | 15 | 3rd | Johannes Stoer | Jeffrey Schiedon |
| 2006 WM18-II-A | 5 | 4 | 0 | | | 1 | 28 | 8 | 2nd | Jan Bruijsten | Diederick Hagemeijer |
| 2007 WM18-II-A | 5 | 5 | | 0 | 0 | 0 | 39 | 9 | 1st | Alexander Jacobs | Bram van Uden |
| 2008 WM18-I-B | 5 | 0 | | 0 | 0 | 5 | 4 | 33 | 6th | Alexander Jacobs | Reinier Staats |
| 2009 WM18-II-B | 5 | 2 | | 0 | 1 | 2 | 34 | 22 | 4th | Wil Zwarthoed | Calvin Pohlman |
| 2010 WM18-II-B | 5 | 2 | | 0 | 1 | 2 | 14 | 27 | 4th | Wil Zwarthoed | Dax van de Velden |
| 2011 WM18-II-B | 5 | 3 | | 1 | 0 | 1 | 19 | 11 | 2nd | Robb Serviss | Tony Ras |
| 2012 WM18-II-A | 5 | 0 | | 0 | 1 | 4 | 16 | 26 | 6th | Robb Serviss | Tony Ras |

**Women's World Championship**

| Year Event | GP | W | T | OTW | OTL | L | GF | GA | Place | Coach | Captain |
|---|---|---|---|---|---|---|---|---|---|---|---|
| 1999 WW-B | 5 | 0 | 0 | | | 5 | 11 | 39 | 8th | Ferry Lorincz | Marion Pepels |
| 2003 WW-II | 5 | 1 | 1 | | | 3 | 8 | 18 | 5th | Richard de Wilde | Marion Pepels |
| 2004 WW-II | 5 | 2 | 0 | | | 3 | 8 | 14 | 4th | Richard de Wilde | Marion Pepels |
| 2005 WW-II | 5 | 0 | 0 | | | 5 | 6 | 26 | 6th | Richard de Wilde | *unknown* |
| 2007 WW-II | 5 | 0 | | 1 | 1 | 3 | 6 | 23 | 5th | Willem van de Kraak | Maaike Hoogewoning |
| 2008 WW-II | 5 | 1 | | 0 | 1 | 3 | 10 | 15 | 5th | Willem van de Kraak | Maaike Hoogewoning |
| 2009 WW-II | 5 | 0 | | 0 | 1 | 4 | 4 | 17 | 6th | Willem van de Kraak | Jose Schipper |
| 2011 WW-III | 5 | 4 | | 1 | 0 | 0 | 33 | 4 | 1st | Willem van de Kraak | Maritza van Leeuwen |
| 2012 WW-I-B | 5 | 1 | | 0 | 0 | 4 | 7 | 34 | 5th | Willem van de Kraak | Maritza van Leeuwen |

# New Zealand (NZL)

*New Zealand celebrates a goal at the 2012 IIHF Ice Hockey World Championship Division II, Group A. Photo: Kristjan Maack.*

## Joined IIHF: May 2, 1977

Website: www.nzicehockey.co.nz
E-mail: president@nzicehockey.co.nz

New Zealand Ice Hockey Federation
64 Epsom Ave
Epsom
Auckland 1023
New Zealand

Phone: +64 9 638 8503

**World Ranking**

| MEN | WOMEN |
|---|---|
| 2012........37 | 2012........25 |
| 2011........38 | 2011........27 |
| 2010........40 | 2010........30 |
| 2009........39 | 2009........28 |
| 2008........39 | 2008........27 |
| 2007........39 | 2007........29 |
| 2006........38 | 2006........29 |
| 2005........38 | 2005........29 |
| 2004........40 | |

**Top Level Host History** none

**World Championship (Men)**

| Year Event | GP | W | T | OTW | OTL | L | GF | GA | Place | Coach | Captain |
|---|---|---|---|---|---|---|---|---|---|---|---|
| 1987 WM-D | 6 | 2 | 0 | | | 4 | 42 | 143 | 3rd | Brian Lewthwaithe | Norm Hawker |
| 1989 WM-D | 4 | 0 | 0 | | | 4 | 3 | 96 | 5th | Brian Lewthwaithe | Ray Bates |
| 1995 WM-C | 5 | 0 | 0 | | | 5 | 14 | 63 | 10th | Mark Bowles | Darren Blong |
| 1998 WM-D | 5 | 1 | 0 | | | 4 | 15 | 39 | 6th | Rod Philpot | Darren Blong |
| 1999 WM-D | 4 | 1 | 0 | | | 3 | 7 | 39 | 6th | Rod Philpot | Darren Blong |
| 2000 WM-D | 4 | 1 | 0 | | | 3 | 9 | 24 | 6th | Rod Philpot | Darren Blong |
| 2001 WM-II-A | 5 | 0 | 0 | | | 5 | 12 | 56 | 6th | Dave le Comte | Rene Aish |
| 2003 WM-III | 2 | 2 | 0 | | | 0 | 14 | 3 | 1st | Dave le Comte | Darren Blong |
| 2004 WM-II-B | 5 | 1 | 0 | | | 4 | 13 | 61 | 5th | Dave le Comte | Simon Glass |
| 2005 WM-II-A | 5 | 1 | 0 | | | 4 | 14 | 31 | 5th | Dave le Comte | Simon Glass |
| 2006 WM-II-B | 5 | 0 | 0 | | | 5 | 6 | 26 | 6th | Dave le Comte | Simon Glass |
| 2007 WM-III | 4 | 4 | | 0 | 0 | 0 | 29 | 6 | 1st | Jeff Bonazzo | Simon Glass |
| 2008 WM-II-B | 5 | 0 | | 0 | 0 | 5 | 11 | 23 | 6th | Jeff Bonazzo | Simon Glass |
| 2009 WM-III | 5 | 4 | | 1 | 0 | 0 | 32 | 7 | 1st | Jeff Bonazzo | Corey Down |
| 2010 WM-II-B | 5 | 2 | | 0 | 0 | 3 | 9 | 39 | 4th | Jeff Bonazzo | Corey Down |
| 2011 WM-II-A | 5 | 3 | | 0 | 0 | 2 | 19 | 8 | 2nd | Jeff Bonazzo | Corey Down |
| 2012 WM-II-A | 5 | 0 | | 0 | 0 | 5 | 5 | 59 | 6th | Andreas Kaisser | Berton Haines |

**U20 World Championship**

| Year Event | GP | W | T | OTW | OTL | L | GF | GA | Place | Coach | Captain |
|---|---|---|---|---|---|---|---|---|---|---|---|
| 2004 WM20-III | 5 | 1 | 0 | | | 4 | 10 | 30 | 6th | Steve Jackson | Tim Faull |
| 2005 WM20-III | 5 | 3 | 1 | | | 1 | 28 | 15 | 2nd | Anatoliy Khorozov | Tom Cuddy |

| Year Event | GP | W | T (OTW) | T (OTL) | L | GF | GA | Place | Coach | Captain |
|---|---|---|---|---|---|---|---|---|---|---|
| 2006 WM20-II-A | 5 | 0 | 0 | | 5 | 2 | 64 | 6th | Anatoliy Khorozov | Lukas Birgel |
| 2007 WM20-III | 5 | 2 | 1 | 0 | 2 | 22 | 18 | 3rd | Dmitri Gunchenko | Joshua Hay |
| 2008 WM20-III | 6 | 6 | 0 | 0 | 0 | 66 | 15 | 1st | Dmitri Gunchenko | Joshua Hay |
| 2010 WM20-III | 4 | 1 | 0 | 1 | 2 | 11 | 16 | 4th | George Pilgrim | Samuel Bonifcae |
| 2011 WM20-III | 6 | 2 | 0 | 0 | 4 | 17 | 43 | 5th | George Pilgrim | Michael Attwell |
| 2012 WM20-III | 4 | 2 | 0 | 0 | 2 | 19 | 14 | 3rd | Stephen Reid | Mitchell Frear |

### U18 World Championship (Men)

| Year Event | GP | W | T | | L | GF | GA | Place | Coach | Captain |
|---|---|---|---|---|---|---|---|---|---|---|
| Year Event | GP | W | OTW | OTL | L | GF | GA | Place | Coach | Captain |
| 2003 WM18-III-A | 3 | 0 | 0 | | 3 | 2 | 23 | 4th | Steve Jackson | Brent Soper |
| 2004 WM18-III-B | 6 | 4 | 1 | | 1 | 28 | 6 | 3rd | Eugene van Aalst | Richard de Vere |
| 2005 WM18-III | 5 | 2 | 0 | | 3 | 22 | 17 | 4th | Eugene van Aalst | Damian Watson |
| 2006 WM18-III | 5 | 1 | 3 | | 1 | 28 | 26 | 4th | Dmitri Gunchenko | James Gaffikin |
| 2007 WM18-III | 5 | 2 | 0 | 0 | 3 | 30 | 25 | 4th | Dmitri Gunchenko | Dale Harrop |
| 2008 WM18-III-A | 4 | 2 | 0 | 0 | 2 | 45 | 18 | 3rd | George Pilgrim | *unknown* |
| 2009 WM18-III-A | 4 | 3 | 0 | 0 | 1 | 28 | 12 | 2nd | George Pilgrim | Jordan Challis |
| 2010 WM18-III-B | 4 | 4 | 0 | 0 | 0 | 26 | 16 | 1st | Jonathan Albright | Regan Wilson |
| 2011 WM18-II-A | 5 | 0 | 0 | 0 | 5 | 1 | 58 | 6th | Jonathan Albright | Mitchell Frear |
| 2012 WM18-III | 5 | 4 | 0 | 0 | 1 | 33 | 13 | 2nd | Jonathan Albright | Thomas Richards |

### Women's World Championship

| Year Event | GP | W | T | | L | GF | GA | Place | Coach | Captain |
|---|---|---|---|---|---|---|---|---|---|---|
| Year Event | GP | W | OTW | OTL | L | GF | GA | Place | Coach | Captain |
| 2005 WW-IV | 3 | 1 | 1 | | 1 | 9 | 9 | 2nd | Mark Symons | Alyx Anderson |
| 2007 WW-IV | 5 | 3 | 0 | 0 | 2 | 45 | 9 | 3rd | Mark Symons | Alyx Anderson |
| 2008 WW-IV | 5 | 4 | 0 | 0 | 1 | 37 | 9 | 2nd | Mark Symons | Sheree Haslemore |
| 2011 WW-IV | 4 | 4 | 0 | 0 | 0 | 20 | 6 | 1st | Corey Down | Casey Redman |
| 2012 WW-II-A | 5 | 2 | 0 | 0 | 3 | 12 | 23 | 4th | Corey Down | Tara Tissink |

# Norway (NOR)

Norway celebrates its 12-4 win against Germany at the 2012 IIHF Ice Hockey World Championship. Photo: Andre Ringuette / HHOF-IIHF Images.

## Joined IIHF: January 20, 1935

Website: www.hockey.no
E-mail: hockey@hockey.no

Norwegian Ice Hockey Association
Sognsvn. 75 J
Service Box 1 U.S.
0840 Oslo
Norway

Phone: +47 2102 9000/9630 • Fax: +47 2102 9631

**World Ranking**

| MEN | | WOMEN | |
|---|---|---|---|
| 2012 | 8 | 2012 | 10 |
| 2011 | 9 | 2011 | 12 |
| 2010 | 11 | 2010 | 12 |
| 2009 | 11 | 2009 | 11 |
| 2008 | 12 | 2008 | 14 |
| 2007 | 14 | 2007 | 15 |
| 2006 | 15 | 2006 | 15 |
| 2005 | 18 | 2005 | 15 |
| 2004 | 21 | 2004 | 14 |

### Top Level Host History

Olympics: 1952 (Oslo); 1994 (Lillehammer)
World Championship (Men): 1958 (Oslo); 1999 (Lillehammer, Oslo, Hamar)

### Olympics, Men

(bold=top level)

| Year Event | GP | W | T | | L | GF | GA | Place | Coach | Captain |
|---|---|---|---|---|---|---|---|---|---|---|
| Year Event | GP | W | OTW | OTL | L | GF | GA | Place | Coach | Captain |
| **1952 OG-M** | **8** | **0** | **0** | | **8** | **15** | **46** | **9th** | **Bud McEachern** | **Roar Bakke** |
| **1964 OG-M** | **7** | **5** | **0** | | **2** | **40** | **19** | **10th** | **Rolf Kirkvaag** | **Olav Dalsoren** |
| **1968 OG-M** | **5** | **3** | **0** | | **2** | **15** | **15** | **11th** | **Egil Bjerklund** | **Olav Dalsoren** |
| **1972 OG-M** | **4** | **3** | **0** | | **1** | **16** | **14** | **8th** | **Ake Brask** | **Terje Steen** |
| **1980 OG-M** | **5** | **0** | **1** | | **4** | **9** | **36** | **11th** | **Ronald Pettersson** | **Rune Molberg** |
| **1984 OG-M** | **5** | **0** | **1** | | **4** | **15** | **43** | **10th** | **Hans Westberg** | **Geir Myhre** |
| **1988 OG-M** | **6** | **0** | **1** | | **5** | **17** | **40** | **12th** | **Lennart Ahlberg** | **Age Ellingsen** |
| **1992 OG-M** | **7** | **2** | **0** | | **5** | **17** | **43** | **9th** | **Bengt Ohlson** | **Petter Salsten** |
| **1994 OG-M** | **7** | **1** | **0** | | **6** | **11** | **26** | **11th** | **Bengt Ohlson** | **Petter Salsten** |
| **2010 OG-M** | **4** | **0** | **0** | **1** | **3** | **8** | **23** | **10th** | **Roy Johansen** | **Tommy Jakobsen** |

### World Championship (Men)

(bold=top level)

| Year Event | GP | W | T | | L | GF | GA | Place | Coach | Captain |
|---|---|---|---|---|---|---|---|---|---|---|
| Year Event | GP | W | OTW | OTL | L | GF | GA | Place | Coach | Captain |
| **1937 WM** | **2** | **0** | **0** | | **2** | **2** | **20** | **9th** | **Ivar Lytkis** | **Johann Narvestad** |
| **1938 WM** | **4** | **0** | **0** | | **4** | **2** | **26** | **13th** | ***unknown*** | **Johann Narvestad** |
| **1949 WM** | **6** | **3** | **0** | | **3** | **26** | **27** | **8th** | **Trygve Holter** | **Johnny Larntvedt** |
| **1950 WM** | **7** | **1** | **0** | | **6** | **26** | **47** | **6th** | **Johan Narvestad** | **Johnny Larntvedt** |

| | | | | | | | | | | | |
|---|---|---|---|---|---|---|---|---|---|---|---|
| **1951 WM** | **6** | **2** | **0** | | | **4** | **10** | **27** | **4th** | **Bud McEachern** | **Johnny Larntvedt** |
| **1954 WM** | **7** | **1** | **0** | | | **6** | **6** | **43** | **8th** | **Carsten Christensen** | **Roar Bakke** |
| **1958 WM** | **7** | **1** | **0** | | | **6** | **12** | **44** | **7th** | **Johnny Larntvedt** | **Roar Bakke** |
| **1959 WM** | **8** | **4** | **1** | | | **3** | **30** | **46** | **8th** | **Johnny Larntvedt** | **Roar Bakke** |
| 1961 WM-B | 5 | 4 | 0 | | | 1 | 27 | 9 | 1st | *unknown* | *unknown* |
| **1962 WM** | **7** | **3** | **0** | | | **4** | **32** | **54** | **5th** | **Johan Narvestad** | **Roar Bakke** |
| 1963 WM-B | 6 | 5 | 0 | | | 1 | 35 | 15 | 1st | Knut Kristiansen | Egil Bjerklund |
| **1965 WM** | **7** | **0** | **0** | | | **7** | **12** | **56** | **8th** | **Ake Brask/Gunnar Kroge** | **Egil Bjerklund** |
| 1966 WM-B | 7 | 4 | 0 | | | 3 | 28 | 17 | 4th | Gunnar Kroge | *unknown* |
| 1967 WM-B | 7 | 5 | 0 | | | 2 | 35 | 21 | 3rd | Egil Bjerklund | Olav Dalsoren |
| 1969 WM-B | 7 | 2 | 2 | | | 3 | 26 | 35 | 5th | Ludek Brabnik | Georg Smefjell (1) |
| 1970 WM-B | 7 | 3 | 2 | | | 2 | 26 | 28 | 3rd | Ludek Brabnik | Olav Dalsoren (2) |
| 1971 WM-B | 7 | 4 | 0 | | | 3 | 37 | 32 | 4th | Ludek Brabnik | *unknown* |
| 1972 WM-B | 6 | 0 | 1 | | | 5 | 15 | 41 | 7th | Ake Brask | Terje Steen |
| 1973 WM-C | 7 | 7 | 0 | | | 0 | 53 | 14 | 1st | Ake Brask | Jan Kinder |
| 1974 WM-B | 7 | 1 | 1 | | | 5 | 18 | 31 | 7th | Ake Brask | Birger Jansen |
| 1975 WM-C | 6 | 4 | 2 | | | 0 | 44 | 8 | 1st | Egil Bjerklund | Thor Martinsen |
| 1976 WM-B | 7 | 4 | 0 | | | 3 | 29 | 21 | 3rd | Lennart Skordaker | Thor Martinsen |
| 1977 WM-B | 8 | 4 | 2 | | | 2 | 30 | 30 | 4th | Lennart Skordaker | Thor Martinsen |
| 1978 WM-B | 7 | 2 | 1 | | | 4 | 29 | 34 | 6th | Ronald Pettersson | Roar Ovstedal |
| 1979 WM-B | 6 | 3 | 0 | | | 3 | 20 | 25 | 4th | Ronald Pettersson | *unknown* |
| 1981 WM-B | 7 | 2 | 0 | | | 5 | 21 | 39 | 6th | Ronald Pettersson | Rune Molberg |
| 1982 WM-B | 7 | 3 | 0 | | | 4 | 24 | 43 | 4th | Arne Stromberg | Rune Molberg |
| 1983 WM-B | 7 | 4 | 0 | | | 3 | 29 | 28 | 4th | Hans Westberg | *unknown* |
| 1985 WM-B | 7 | 2 | 0 | | | 5 | 28 | 38 | 7th | Barry Smith | Orjan Lovdal |
| 1986 WM-C | 6 | 5 | 1 | | | 0 | 55 | 11 | 1st | Lennart Ahlberg | *unknown* |
| 1987 WM-B | 7 | 5 | 1 | | | 1 | 33 | 25 | 2nd | Lennart Ahlberg | Age Ellingsen |
| 1989 WM-B | 7 | 5 | 1 | | | 1 | 28 | 16 | 1st | Lennart Ahlberg | Age Ellingsen |
| **1990 WM** | **10** | **1** | **1** | | | **8** | **21** | **61** | **8th** | **George Kingston** | **Age Ellingsen (3)** |
| 1991 WM-B | 7 | 5 | 0 | | | 2 | 26 | 13 | 2nd | George Kingston | Petter Salsten |
| **1992 WM** | **5** | **1** | **0** | | | **4** | **8** | **16** | **10th** | **Bengt Ohlson** | **Petter Salsten** |
| **1993 WM** | **7** | **2** | **0** | | | **5** | **13** | **25** | **11th** | **Bengt Ohlson** | **Petter Salsten** |
| **1994 WM** | **6** | **1** | **2** | | | **3** | **14** | **23** | **11th** | **Bengt Ohlson** | **Petter Salsten** |
| **1995 WM** | **5** | **1** | **0** | | | **4** | **9** | **18** | **10th** | **Geir Myhre** | **Petter Salsten** |
| **1996 WM** | **5** | **1** | **2** | | | **2** | **6** | **11** | **9th** | **Geir Myhre** | **Petter Salsten** |
| **1997 WM** | **8** | **0** | **1** | | | **7** | **13** | **32** | **12th** | **Brent McEwen** | **Ole Eskild Dahlstrom** |
| 1998 WM-B | 7 | 3 | 0 | | | 4 | 21 | 19 | 5th | Leif Boork | Dave Livingston |
| **1999 WM** | **6** | **1** | **0** | | | **5** | **10** | **26** | **12th** | **Leif Boork** | **Ole Eskild Dahlstrom (4)** |
| **2000 WM** | **6** | **2** | **1** | | | **3** | **19** | **24** | **10th** | **Leif Boork** | **Trond Magnussen** |
| **2001 WM** | **6** | **0** | **2** | | | **4** | **9** | **22** | **15th** | **Leif Boork** | **Svein Enok Norstebo (5)** |
| 2002 WM-I-B | 5 | 3 | 0 | | | 2 | 26 | 11 | 3rd | Roy Johansen | Atle Olsen |
| 2003 WM-I-B | 5 | 4 | 0 | | | 1 | 19 | 9 | 2nd | Roy Johansen | Trond Magnussen |
| 2004 WM-I-A | 5 | 3 | 1 | | | 1 | 31 | 14 | 2nd | Roy Johansen | Trond Magnussen |
| 2005 WM-I-A | 5 | 4 | 1 | | | 0 | 43 | 8 | 1st | Roy Johansen | Tommy Jaokbsen |
| **2006 WM** | **6** | **1** | **0** | | | **5** | **11** | **23** | **11th** | **Roy Johansen** | **Tommy Jakobsen** |
| **2007 WM** | **6** | **1** | | **1** | **0** | **4** | **17** | **21** | **14th** | **Roy Johansen** | **Tommy Jakobsen** |
| **2008 WM** | **7** | **1** | | **0** | **1** | **5** | **11** | **33** | **8th** | **Roy Johansen** | **Tommy Jakobsen** |
| **2009 WM** | **6** | **0** | | **1** | **2** | **3** | **12** | **25** | **11th** | **Roy Johansen** | **Tommy Jakobsen** |
| **2010 WM** | **6** | **3** | | **0** | **0** | **3** | **14** | **27** | **9th** | **Roy Johansen** | **Tommy Jakobsen (6)** |
| **2011 WM** | **7** | **3** | | **1** | **0** | **3** | **23** | **19** | **6th** | **Roy Johansen** | **Ole-Kristian Tollefsen** |
| **2012 WM** | **8** | **4** | | **0** | **1** | **3** | **35** | **24** | **8th** | **Roy Johansen** | **Ole-Kristian Tollefsen** |

(1) Bjorn Elvenes captain Feb. 28 vs. AUT; Thor Martinsen captain Mar. 8 vs. YUG & Mar. 9 vs. ITA
(2) Georg Smefjell captain Mar. 1 vs. YUG
(3) Orjan Lovdal captain vs. Finland (Apr. 22); Petter Salsten captain vs. West Germany (Apr. 25)
(4) Trond Magnussen captain vs. Latvia (May 10)
(5) Trond Magnussen captain vs. Belarus (May 5) and Latvia (May 7)
(6) Anders Bastiansen captain vs. LAT (May 16), Patrick Thoresen captain vs. SUI (May 17)

### U20 World Championship

(bold=top level)

| Year Event | GP | W | T | | L | GF | GA | Place | Coach | Captain |
|---|---|---|---|---|---|---|---|---|---|---|
| Year Event | GP | W | OTW | OTL | L | GF | GA | Place | Coach | Captain |
| **1979 WM20** | **5** | **0** | **0** | | **5** | **6** | **46** | **8th** | **Egil Bjerklund** | **Knut Andresen** |
| 1980 WM20-B | 4 | 3 | 0 | | 1 | 28 | 10 | 3rd | Sverre Hogh | Bjorn Kolsrud |
| 1981 WM20-B | 5 | 3 | 2 | | 0 | 32 | 18 | 2nd | Rolff Kirkvaag | Harald Bastiansen |
| 1982 WM20-B | 4 | 4 | 0 | | 0 | 18 | 8 | 1st | Lars Backman | Bjorn Johansen |
| **1983 WM20** | **7** | **0** | **0** | | **7** | **13** | **69** | **8th** | **Bernie Lynch** | **Rune Gulliksen** |
| 1984 WM20-B | 5 | 2 | 0 | | 3 | 29 | 21 | 4th | Tore Falch-Nilsen | Erik Nerell |
| 1985 WM20-B | 7 | 2 | 1 | | 4 | 23 | 28 | 5th | Lennart Ahlberg | *unknown* |
| 1986 WM20-B | 7 | 5 | 1 | | 1 | 54 | 18 | 2nd | Jon Haukeland | Ole Petter Nykaas |
| 1987 WM20-B | 5 | 3 | 1 | | 1 | 38 | 25 | 2nd | Rune Molberg | *unknown* |
| 1988 WM20-B | 7 | 5 | 0 | | 2 | 38 | 18 | 1st | Bjorn Mathisrud | *unknown* |
| **1989 WM20** | **7** | **1** | **0** | | **6** | **14** | **56** | **7th** | **Tor Johan Haga** | **Ole Eskild Dahlstrom** |
| **1990 WM20** | **7** | **2** | **0** | | **5** | **25** | **51** | **6th** | **George Kingston** | **Ole Eskild Dahlstrom** |
| **1991 WM20** | **7** | **0** | **0** | | **7** | **8** | **75** | **8th** | **George Kingston** | **Espen Knutsen** |
| 1992 WM20-B | 7 | 5 | 0 | | 2 | 45 | 17 | 3rd | Geir Myhre | Svein Enok Norstebo |
| 1993 WM20-B | 7 | 6 | 0 | | 1 | 49 | 11 | 2nd | Geir Myhre | Trond Magnussen |
| 1994 WM20-B | 7 | 5 | 1 | | 1 | 28 | 15 | 2nd | Audun Larssen | Anders Myrvold |
| 1995 WM20-B | 7 | 3 | 1 | | 3 | 27 | 26 | 5th | Audun Larssen | Anders Myrvold |
| 1996 WM20-B | 6 | 3 | 0 | | 3 | 18 | 16 | 3rd | Audun Larssen | Martin Knold |
| 1997 WM20-B | 7 | 2 | 3 | | 2 | 33 | 23 | 4th | Matti Heikkila | *unknown* |
| 1998 WM20-B | 6 | 3 | 0 | | 3 | 21 | 22 | 7th | Morten Sethereng | Jarle Naesset |
| 1999 WM20-B | 6 | 2 | 0 | | 4 | 17 | 25 | 6th | Arne Billkvan | Snore Hallem |
| 2000 WM20-B | 5 | 2 | 0 | | 3 | 18 | 14 | 4th | Petter Thoresen | Ole Kirkebye |

| 2001 WM20-I | 5 | 2 | 1 | | | 2 | 17 | 12 | 4th | Petter Thoresen | Ola Johannessen |
|---|---|---|---|---|---|---|---|---|---|---|---|
| 2002 WM20-I | 5 | 3 | 0 | | | 2 | 20 | 14 | 3rd | Orjan Lovdal | Patrick Thoresen |
| 2003 WM20-I-B | 5 | 2 | 1 | | | 2 | 17 | 16 | 3rd | Orjan Lovdal | Ole-Kristian Tollefsen |
| 2004 WM20-I-B | 5 | 3 | 0 | | | 2 | 21 | 10 | 2nd | Orjan Lovdal | Ole-Kristian Tollefsen |
| 2005 WM20-I-A | 5 | 5 | 0 | | | 0 | 29 | 12 | 1st | Petter Thoresen | Havard Boe |
| **2006 WM20** | **6** | **0** | **0** | | | **6** | **6** | **34** | **10th** | **Petter Thoresen** | **Martin Roymark** |
| 2007 WM20-I-B | 5 | 1 | | 1 | 0 | 3 | 15 | 14 | 5th | Rune Guliksen | Mats Aasen |
| 2008 WM20-I-A | 5 | 3 | | 0 | 0 | 2 | 19 | 16 | 3rd | Rune Guliksen | Mats Froshaug |
| 2009 WM20-I-B | 5 | 2 | | 1 | 0 | 2 | 14 | 17 | 3rd | Knut Jorgen Stubdal | Scott Winkler |
| 2010 WM20-I-B | 5 | 4 | | 1 | 0 | 0 | 33 | 8 | 1st | Geir Hoff | Jonas Djupvik Lovlie |
| **2011 WM20** | **6** | **1** | | **0** | **0** | **5** | **7** | **33** | **9th** | **Geir Hoff** | **Andreas Stene** |
| 2012 WM20-I-A | 5 | 3 | | 0 | 0 | 2 | 19 | 13 | 3rd | Orjan Lovdahl | Michael Haga |

## U18 World Championship (Men)

(bold=top level)

| Year Event | GP | W | T | | | L | GF | GA | Place | Coach | Captain |
|---|---|---|---|---|---|---|---|---|---|---|---|
| Year Event | GP | W | | OTW | OTL | L | GF | GA | Place | Coach | Captain |
| **1999 WM18** | **6** | **0** | **0** | | | **6** | **8** | **42** | **10th** | **Morten Sethereng** | **Lars Peder Nagel** |
| 2000 WM18-B | 5 | 4 | 0 | | | 1 | 27 | 12 | 1st | Orjan Lovdal | Patrick Thoresen |
| **2001 WM18** | **6** | **1** | **2** | | | **3** | **17** | **29** | **9th** | **Orjan Lovdal** | **Patrick Thoresen** |
| **2002 WM18** | **8** | **1** | **1** | | | **6** | **19** | **38** | **11th** | **Morten Sethereng** | **Ole-Kristian Tollefsen** |
| 2003 WM18-I-B | 5 | 4 | 1 | | | 0 | 22 | 13 | 1st | Arne Billkvam | Havard Boe |
| **2004 WM18** | **6** | **0** | **0** | | | **6** | **13** | **43** | **10th** | **Arne Billkvam** | **Mathis Olimb** |
| 2005 WM18-I-B | 5 | 4 | 0 | | | 1 | 18 | 10 | 1st | Orjan Lovdal | Jonas Holos |
| **2006 WM18** | **6** | **0** | **2** | | | **4** | **15** | **29** | **10th** | **Orjan Lovdal** | **Mats Froshaug** |
| 2007 WM18-I-B | 5 | 2 | | 0 | 2 | 1 | 22 | 19 | 3rd | Orjan Lovdal | Ken Olimb |
| 2008 WM18-I-B | 5 | 5 | | 0 | 0 | 0 | 15 | 3 | 1st | Orjan Lovdal | Daniel Sorvik |
| **2009 WM18** | **6** | **1** | | **0** | **0** | **5** | **12** | **40** | **9th** | **Orjan Lovdal** | **Andreas Stene** |
| 2010 WM18-I-A | 5 | 4 | | 0 | 0 | 1 | 33 | 15 | 1st | Orjan Lovdal | Michael Haga |
| **2011 WM18** | **6** | **1** | | **0** | **0** | **5** | **13** | **29** | **9th** | **Orjan Lovdal** | **Magnus Hoff** |
| 2012 WM18-I-A | 5 | 3 | | 0 | 0 | 2 | 22 | 20 | 2nd | Robert Jonsson | Endre Medby |

## Women's World Championship

(bold=top level)

| Year Event | GP | W | T | | | L | GF | GA | Place | Coach | Captain |
|---|---|---|---|---|---|---|---|---|---|---|---|
| Year Event | GP | W | | OTW | OTL | L | GF | GA | Place | Coach | Captain |
| **1990 WW** | **5** | **1** | **0** | | | **4** | **16** | **45** | **6th** | **Harald Haugen** | **Anne Eriksen Moseby (1)** |
| **1992 WW** | **5** | **2** | **0** | | | **3** | **11** | **23** | **6th** | **Harald Haugen** | **Inger Lise Fagernes** |
| **1994 WW** | **5** | **1** | **0** | | | **4** | **12** | **33** | **6th** | **Harald Haugen** | **Nina Johansen** |
| **1997 WW** | **5** | **0** | **1** | | | **4** | **3** | **22** | **8th** | **Torbjorn Orskaug** | **Inger Lise Fagernes** |
| 1999 WW-B | 5 | 2 | 0 | | | 3 | 9 | 17 | 2nd | Morten Haglund/Christin Smerud | Aina Hove |
| 2000 WW-B | 5 | 4 | 1 | | | 0 | 20 | 6 | 3rd | Sverre Hogemark | Marianne Dahlstrom |
| 2001 WW-I | 4 | 1 | 0 | | | 3 | 6 | 18 | 7th | Trond Roed | *unknown* |
| 2003 WW-II | 5 | 4 | 1 | | | 0 | 24 | 9 | 1st | Trond Roed | Hege Ask |
| 2004 WW-I | 5 | 1 | 1 | | | 3 | 18 | 17 | 5th | Trond Roed | Hege Ask |
| 2005 WW-II | 5 | 4 | 0 | | | 1 | 21 | 6 | 1st | Jan Petter Nagel | *unknown* |
| 2007 WW-I | 5 | 2 | | 0 | 0 | 3 | 8 | 9 | 4th | Jan Petter Nagel | Trine Martens |
| 2008 WW-I | 5 | 1 | | 0 | 1 | 3 | 11 | 13 | 5th | George Kingston | Trine Martens |
| 2009 WW-I | 5 | 2 | | 1 | 0 | 2 | 18 | 18 | 3rd | George Kingston | Ingrid Renli |
| 2011 WW-I | 4 | 3 | | 0 | 0 | 1 | 13 | 7 | 2nd | Sten Gunnar Jorgensen | Line Bialik |
| 2012 WW-I-A | 5 | 3 | | 1 | 0 | 1 | 20 | 7 | 2nd | Sten Gunnar Jorgensen | Line Bialik Oien |

(1) Nina Johansen captain vs. Switzerland (Mar. 25)

## U18 Women's World Championship

| Year Event | GP | W | OTW | OTL | L | GF | GA | Place | Coach Captain | |
|---|---|---|---|---|---|---|---|---|---|---|
| 2009 WW18-I | 4 | 0 | 0 | 0 | 4 | 9 | 16 | 5th | Birger Aaserud | Celine Strandrud |
| 2010 WW18-I | 5 | 1 | 0 | 0 | 4 | 14 | 27 | 5th | Birger Aaserud | Andrea Dalen |
| 2011 WW18-I | 5 | 2 | 0 | 0 | 3 | 16 | 11 | 4th | Birger Aaserud | Ingrid Morset |
| 2012 WW18-I | 5 | 2 | 0 | 0 | 3 | 13 | 13 | 4th | Laura Rollins | Victoria Lovdal |

# Poland (POL)

The Polish women's national team remains undefeated in IIHF play and earned promotion to the Division II, Group A. Photo: KIHA.

**Joined IIHF: January 11, 1926**

Website: www.pzhl.org.pl
E-mail: pzhl@pzhl.org.pl

Polish Ice Hockey Federation
M. Konopnickiej Street 3, Apt. 2
00-491 Warszawa
Poland

Phone: +48 22 628 80 63/64 • Fax: +48 22 629 37 54

**World Ranking**

| MEN | WOMEN |
|---|---|
| 2012........23 | 2012........28 |
| 2011........23 | 2011........34 |
| 2010........22 | |
| 2009........22 | |
| 2008........21 | |
| 2007........20 | |
| 2006........20 | |
| 2005........21 | |
| 2004........20 | |

### Top Level Host History

World Championship (Men): 1931 (Krynica); 1976 (Katowice)

### Olympics, Men

(bold=top level)

| Year Event | GP | W | T | L | GF | GA | Place | Coach | Captain |
|---|---|---|---|---|---|---|---|---|---|
| **1928 OG-M** | 2 | 0 | 1 | 1 | 4 | 5 | 9th | Tadeusz Adamowski | Tadeusz Adamowski |
| **1932 OG-M** | 6 | 0 | 0 | 6 | 3 | 34 | 4th | Tadeusz Sachs | *unknown* |
| **1936 OG-M** | 3 | 1 | 0 | 2 | 11 | 12 | 9th | Alexander Tupalski/Lucjan Kulej | *unknown* |
| **1948 OG-M** | 8 | 2 | 0 | 6 | 29 | 97 | 7th | Zbigniew Kasprzak | *unknown* |
| **1952 OG-M** | 8 | 2 | 1 | 5 | 21 | 56 | 6th | Mieczyslaw Kasprzycki | *unknown* |
| **1956 OG-M** | 5 | 2 | 0 | 3 | 15 | 22 | 8th | Mieczyslaw Palus/Wladyslaw Wiro-Kiro | Jozef Kurek |
| **1964 OG-M** | 7 | 6 | 0 | 1 | 40 | 13 | 9th | Gary Hughes | Jozef Kurek |
| **1972 OG-M** | 5 | 0 | 0 | 5 | 9 | 39 | 6th | Anatoli Yegorov/Mieczyslaw Chmura | Ludwik Czachowski (1) |
| **1976 OG-M** | 5 | 1 | 0 | 4 | 9 | 44 | 6th | Josef Kurek | Robert Goralczyk |
| **1980 OG-M** | 5 | 2 | 0 | 3 | 15 | 23 | 7th | Czeslaw Borowicz | Stefan Chowaniec |
| **1984 OG-M** | 6 | 1 | 0 | 5 | 20 | 44 | 8th | Emil Nikodemowicz | Henryk Gruth |
| **1988 OG-M** | 6 | 0 | 1 | 5 | 5 | 16 | 10th | Leszek Lejczyk | Henryk Gruth |
| **1992 OG-M** | 7 | 1 | 0 | 6 | 10 | 38 | 11th | Leszek Lejczyk | Henryk Gruth |

(1) Marian Feter captain Feb. 5 vs. TCH

### World Championship (Men)

(bold=top level)

| Year Event | GP | W | T | | L | GF | GA | Place | Coach | Captain |
|---|---|---|---|---|---|---|---|---|---|---|
| Year Event | GP | W | OTW | OTL | L | GF | GA | Place | Coach | Captain |
| **1930 WM** | 3 | 1 | 0 | | 2 | 6 | 6 | 5th | Tadeusz Adamowski | Alexander Tupalski |
| **1931 WM** | 7 | 2 | 1 | | 4 | 6 | 11 | 4th | Harold Farlow | *unknown* |
| **1933 WM** | 6 | 1 | 1 | | 4 | 3 | 11 | 7th | Tadeusz Sachs | *unknown* |
| **1935 WM** | 6 | 2 | 2 | | 2 | 20 | 13 | 10th | Tadeusz Sachs | *unknown* |
| **1937 WM** | 9 | 3 | 0 | | 6 | 16 | 32 | 8th | Tadeusz Sachs | *unknown* |
| **1938 WM** | 6 | 3 | 0 | | 3 | 16 | 16 | 7th | Przemyslaw Warminski | *unknown* |
| **1939 WM** | 7 | 3 | 0 | | 4 | 17 | 19 | 6th | Zenon Paruszewski | Andrzej Wolkowski |
| **1947 WM** | 7 | 2 | 0 | | 5 | 27 | 40 | 6th | Waclaw Kuchar | Kazimierz Sokolowski |
| **1955 WM** | 8 | 2 | 0 | | 6 | 19 | 59 | 7th | Witalis Ludwiczak/Kazimierz Osmanski | *unknown* |
| **1957 WM** | 7 | 2 | 0 | | 5 | 25 | 45 | 6th | Antonin Haukvic | *unknown* |
| **1958 WM** | 7 | 0 | 1 | | 6 | 14 | 65 | 8th | Andrzej Wolkowski/Wladyslaw Wiro-Kiro | *unknown* |
| **1959 WM** | 8 | 1 | 0 | | 7 | 15 | 50 | 11th | Alfred Gansiniec | Janusz Zawadski |
| 1961 WM-B | 5 | 1 | 0 | | 4 | 13 | 17 | 5th | Stefan Csorich | *unknown* |
| 1963 WM-B | 6 | 4 | 0 | | 2 | 52 | 13 | 4th | Gary Hughes | Stanislaw Olczyk (1) |
| 1965 WM-B | 6 | 5 | 1 | | 0 | 35 | 15 | 1st | Marian Jezak | *unknown* |
| **1966 WM** | 7 | 0 | 0 | | 7 | 11 | 44 | 8th | Zdzislaw Maselko | Jozef Kurek |
| 1967 WM-B | 7 | 5 | 2 | | 0 | 32 | 13 | 1st | Zdzislaw Maselko | Andrzej Zurawski |
| 1969 WM-B | 7 | 6 | 0 | | 1 | 31 | 13 | 2nd | Zdzislaw Maselko/Emil Nikodemowicz | Andrzej Fonfara |
| **1970 WM** | 10 | 0 | 1 | | 9 | 11 | 70 | 6th | Anatoli Yegorov | Andrzej Fonfara |
| 1971 WM-B | 7 | 5 | 1 | | 1 | 36 | 19 | 2nd | Mieczyslaw Chmura/Anatoli Yegorov | *unknown* |
| 1972 WM-B | 6 | 6 | 0 | | 0 | 41 | 12 | 1st | Mieczyslaw Chmura/Anatoli Yegorov | Ludwik Czachowski |
| **1973 WM** | 10 | 1 | 1 | | 8 | 14 | 76 | 5th | Anatoli Yegorov | *unknown* |
| **1974 WM** | 10 | 1 | 2 | | 7 | 22 | 64 | 5th | Anatoli Yegorov | *unknown* |
| **1975 WM** | 10 | 2 | 0 | | 8 | 18 | 78 | 5th | Anatoli Yegorov | Leszek Tokarz |
| **1976 WM** | 10 | 3 | 2 | | 5 | 32 | 47 | 7th | *unknown* | Robert Goralczyk |
| 1977 WM-B | 8 | 6 | 0 | | 2 | 39 | 22 | 2nd | Jozef Kurek | Walenty Zietara |
| 1978 WM-B | 7 | 6 | 1 | | 0 | 51 | 19 | 1st | Jozef Kurek | Leszek Tokarz |
| **1979 WM** | 8 | 0 | 2 | | 6 | 20 | 42 | 8th | Slavomir Barton | Robert Goralczyk |
| 1981 WM-B | 7 | 5 | 1 | | 1 | 49 | 25 | 2nd | Czeslaw Borowicz | Jerzy Potz |
| 1982 WM-B | 7 | 4 | 1 | | 2 | 42 | 23 | 3rd | Czeslaw Borowicz | Jerzy Potz |
| 1983 WM-B | 7 | 5 | 1 | | 1 | 43 | 19 | 2nd | Jan Wycisk | *unknown* |
| 1985 WM-B | 7 | 6 | 1 | | 0 | 37 | 13 | 1st | Leszek Lejczyk | Henryk Gruth |
| **1986 WM** | 10 | 1 | 1 | | 8 | 26 | 63 | 8th | Leszek Lejczyk | Andrzej Zabawa |
| 1987 WM-B | 7 | 6 | 0 | | 1 | 39 | 11 | 1st | Leszek Lejczyk/Jerzy Mruk | Henryk Gruth |
| **1989 WM** | 10 | 1 | 0 | | 9 | 12 | 76 | 8th | Leszek Lejczyk | Henryk Gruth |
| 1990 WM-B | 7 | 2 | 2 | | 3 | 25 | 25 | 6th | Emil Nikodemowicz | Krystian Sikorski |
| 1991 WM-B | 7 | 4 | 0 | | 3 | 24 | 15 | 4th | Leszek Lejczyk | Henryk Gruth |

| **1992 WM** | **6** | **0** | **0** | | **6** | **9** | **44** | **12th** | **Leszek Lejczyk** | **Henryk Gruth** |
|---|---|---|---|---|---|---|---|---|---|---|
| 1993 WM-B | 7 | 6 | 0 | | 1 | 71 | 12 | 2nd | Ewald Grabovskis | Henryk Gruth |
| 1994 WM-B | 7 | 5 | 1 | | 1 | 45 | 21 | 3rd | Ewald Grabovskis | Andrzej Schubert |
| 1995 WM-B | 7 | 4 | 0 | | 3 | 29 | 30 | 3rd | Vladimir Safonov | Waldemar Klisiak |
| 1996 WM-B | 7 | 1 | 2 | | 4 | 18 | 27 | 5th | Vladimir Safonov | Wojciech Tkacz |
| 1997 WM-B | 7 | 2 | 2 | | 3 | 19 | 24 | 5th | Andrzej Tkacz | Wojciech Tkacz |
| 1998 WM-B | 7 | 2 | 1 | | 4 | 21 | 28 | 7th | Jan Eysselt | Sebastian Gonera |
| 1999 WM-B | 7 | 1 | 0 | | 6 | 15 | 23 | 7th | Ludek Bukac | Sebastian Gonera |
| 2000 WM-B | 7 | 4 | 1 | | 2 | 28 | 19 | 4th | Wiktor Pysz | Waldemar Klisiak |
| 2001 WM-I-A | 5 | 4 | 0 | | 1 | 27 | 9 | 1st | Wiktor Pysz | Waldemar Klisiak |
| **2002 WM** | **6** | **2** | **0** | | **4** | **12** | **25** | **14th** | **Wiktor Pysz** | **Waldemar Klisiak** |
| 2003 WM-I-A | 5 | 4 | 0 | | 1 | 24 | 9 | 2nd | Wiktor Pysz | Jacek Plachta |
| 2004 WM-I-B | 5 | 2 | 1 | | 2 | 25 | 14 | 3rd | Wiktor Pysz | Jacek Zamojski |
| 2005 WM-I-A | 5 | 3 | 1 | | 1 | 16 | 8 | 2nd | Andrei Sidorenko | Jacek Plachta |
| 2006 WM-I-B | 5 | 3 | 0 | | 2 | 19 | 10 | 3rd | Rudolf Rohacek | Michal Garbocz |
| 2007 WM-I-A | 5 | 2 | 2 | 0 | 1 | 22 | 13 | 2nd | Rudolf Rohacek | Jacek Plachta |
| 2008 WM-I-A | 5 | 2 | 1 | 1 | 1 | 18 | 17 | 3rd | Rudolf Rohacek | Leszek Laszkiewicz |
| 2009 WM-I-B | 5 | 2 | 0 | 2 | 1 | 14 | 9 | 4th | Peter Ekroth | Leszek Laszkiewicz |
| 2010 WM-I-B | 5 | 3 | 0 | 0 | 2 | 15 | 12 | 3rd | Wiktor Pysz | Leszek Laszkiewicz |
| 2011 WM-I-B | 5 | 2 | 0 | 0 | 3 | 18 | 15 | 4th | Wiktor Pysz | Leszek Laszkiewicz |
| 2012 WM-I-B | 5 | 4 | 0 | 0 | 1 | 31 | 7 | 2nd | Wiktor Pysz | Marcin Kolusz |

(1) Jozef Kurek captain March 16 vs. YUG

## U20 World Championship

(bold=top level)

| Year Event | GP | W | T | | L | GF | GA | Place | Coach | Captain |
|---|---|---|---|---|---|---|---|---|---|---|
| Year Event | GP | W | OTW | OTL | L | GF | GA | Place | Coach | Captain |
| **1977 WM20** | **7** | **0** | **1** | | **6** | **12** | **58** | **8th** | **Sylwester Wilczek/Augustyn Skorski** | **Witold Pulka** |
| 1979 WM20-B | 4 | 3 | 0 | | 1 | 43 | 17 | 3rd | Zenon Hajduga | Jerzy Kotyla |
| 1980 WM20-B | 4 | 3 | 0 | | 1 | 30 | 10 | 2nd | Zenon Hajduga | Zbigniew Ksiazkiewicz |
| 1981 WM20-B | 5 | 3 | 0 | | 2 | 34 | 15 | 3rd | Stanislaw Michalski | Wladyslaw Klich |
| 1983 WM20-B | 5 | 4 | 0 | | 1 | 29 | 17 | 3rd | Tadeusz Bujar | Jakub Batkiewicz |
| 1984 WM20-B | 5 | 4 | 1 | | 0 | 29 | 18 | 1st | Tadeusz Bujar | Jaroslaw Morawiecki |
| **1985 WM20** | **7** | **0** | **1** | | **6** | **10** | **59** | **8th** | **Tadeusz Bujar** | **Marek Stebnicki** |
| 1986 WM20-B | 7 | 6 | 0 | | 1 | 46 | 17 | 1st | Tadeusz Japol | Mariusz Puzio |
| **1987 WM20** | **7** | **1** | **0** | | **6** | **21** | **80** | **5th** | **Jerzy Malez** | **Krzysztof Ruchala** |
| **1988 WM20** | **7** | **1** | **0** | | **6** | **12** | **53** | **8th** | **Andrzej Szczepaniec** | ***unknown*** |
| 1989 WM20-B | 7 | 7 | 0 | | 0 | 49 | 20 | 1st | Andrzej Szczepaniec | Wojciech Tkacz |
| **1990 WM20** | **7** | **0** | **0** | | **7** | **7** | **65** | **8th** | **Leszek Lejczyk** | **Leszek Trybus** |
| 1991 WM20-B | 7 | 6 | 0 | | 1 | 53 | 17 | 2nd | Eugeniusz Imiolczyk | Arkadiusz Sikora |
| 1992 WM20-B | 7 | 5 | 0 | | 2 | 42 | 19 | 2nd | Stanislav Malkov | Artur Malicki |
| 1993 WM20-B | 7 | 1 | 1 | | 5 | 17 | 28 | 6th | Emil Nikodemowicz | Tomasz Franczak |
| 1994 WM20-B | 7 | 3 | 0 | | 4 | 15 | 26 | 4th | Jerzy Mruk | Ireneusz Jarosz |
| 1995 WM20-B | 7 | 4 | 1 | | 2 | 26 | 22 | 3rd | Jerzy Mruk | Dariusz Lyszczarczyk |
| 1996 WM20-B | 6 | 6 | 0 | | 0 | 47 | 7 | 1st | Vladimir Safonov | Dariusz Zabawa |
| **1997 WM20** | **6** | **0** | **0** | | **6** | **7** | **46** | **10th** | **Vladimir Safonov** | **Mariusz Trzopek** |
| 1998 WM20-B | 6 | 4 | 0 | | 2 | 29 | 17 | 3rd | Jerzy Pawlowski | Adam Borzecki |
| 1999 WM20-B | 6 | 3 | 2 | | 1 | 20 | 16 | 2nd | Vladimir Safonov | Damian Slabon |
| 2000 WM20-B | 5 | 2 | 2 | | 1 | 17 | 15 | 5th | Vladimir Safonov | Bart Piotrowski |
| 2001 WM20-I | 5 | 2 | 0 | | 3 | 21 | 22 | 6th | Jerzy Pawlowski | Lukasz Sokol |
| 2002 WM20-I | 5 | 1 | 1 | | 3 | 16 | 26 | 7th | Wincenty Kawa | Lukasz Zachariasz |
| 2003 WM20-I-B | 5 | 1 | 0 | | 4 | 12 | 31 | 6th | Miloslav Pavelka | Patryk Noworyta |
| 2004 WM20-II-A | 5 | 5 | 0 | | 0 | 59 | 4 | 1st | Tomasz Rutkowski | Bartosz Dabkowski |
| 2005 WM20-I-B | 5 | 2 | 2 | | 1 | 15 | 13 | 4th | Jan Eysselt | Bartosz Dabrowski |
| 2006 WM20-I-B | 5 | 1 | 2 | | 2 | 9 | 14 | 4th | Jan Eysselt | Maciej Urbanowicz |
| 2007 WM20-I-A | 5 | 2 | 0 | 0 | 3 | 14 | 21 | 4th | Milan Skokan | Tomasz Landowski |
| 2008 WM20-I-A | 5 | 1 | 0 | 1 | 3 | 7 | 24 | 4th | Tomasz Rutkowski | Patryk Wajda |
| 2009 WM20-I-A | 5 | 1 | 0 | 0 | 4 | 7 | 23 | 5th | Tomasz Rutkowski | Tomasz Cieslicki |
| 2010 WM20-I-B | 5 | 1 | 0 | 0 | 4 | 12 | 22 | 6th | Mieczyslaw Nahunko | Kasper Bryniczka |
| 2011 WM20-II-B | 5 | 5 | 0 | 0 | 0 | 61 | 10 | 1st | Jaroslaw Morawiecki | Jakub Wanacki |
| 2012 WM20-I-B | 5 | 2 | 0 | 1 | 2 | 16 | 12 | 4th | Jaroslaw Morawiecki | Bartosz Ciura |

## U18 World Championship (Men)

| Year Event | GP | W | T | | L | GF | GA | Place | Coach | Captain |
|---|---|---|---|---|---|---|---|---|---|---|
| Year Event | GP | W | OTW | OTL | L | GF | GA | Place | Coach | Captain |
| 1999 WM18-B | 5 | 3 | 1 | | 1 | 19 | 16 | 3rd | Andrzej Tkacz | Lukasz Ziober |
| 2000 WM18-B | 5 | 2 | 1 | | 2 | 20 | 24 | 7th | Andrzej Tkacz | Marius Jakubik |
| 2001 WM18-II | 4 | 3 | 0 | | 1 | 28 | 13 | 3rd | Wincenty Kawa | Tobias Bernat |
| 2002 WM18-II | 5 | 4 | 0 | | 1 | 36 | 17 | 2nd | Jerzy Pawlowski | Artur Gwizdz |
| 2003 WM18-I-B | 5 | 3 | 1 | | 1 | 11 | 14 | 2nd | Tomasz Rutkowski | Bartosz Dabkoski |
| 2004 WM18-I-A | 5 | 0 | 1 | | 4 | 12 | 20 | 5th | Andrzej Tkacz | Jaroslaw Rzeszutko |
| 2005 WM18-I-B | 5 | 2 | 1 | | 2 | 15 | 20 | 4th | Milan Skokan | Rafal Noworyta |
| 2006 WM18-I-B | 5 | 2 | 0 | | 3 | 16 | 15 | 4th | Milan Skokan | Mateusz Pawlak |
| 2007 WM18-I-B | 5 | 2 | 0 | 0 | 3 | 16 | 26 | 4th | Tomasz Rutkowski | Kamil Kapica |
| 2008 WM18-I-A | 5 | 2 | 0 | 0 | 3 | 7 | 18 | 4th | Mariusz Kieca | *unknown* |
| 2009 WM18-I-A | 5 | 2 | 2 | 0 | 1 | 25 | 13 | 2nd | Mariusz Kieca | Wladyslaw Bryniczka |
| 2010 WM18-I-B | 5 | 3 | 0 | 0 | 2 | 21 | 21 | 3rd | Andrzej Masewicz | Mateusz Michalski |
| 2011 WM18-I-B | 5 | 2 | 0 | 0 | 3 | 12 | 20 | 5th | Andrzej Masewicz | Filip Starzynski |
| 2012 WM18-I-B | 5 | 0 | 1 | 1 | 3 | 13 | 30 | 5th | Andrzej Masewicz | Noureddine Bettahar |

## Women's World Championship

| Year Event | GP | W | OTW | OTL | L | GF | GA | Place | Coach | Captain |
|---|---|---|---|---|---|---|---|---|---|---|
| 2011 WW-V | 4 | 3 | 1 | 0 | 0 | 61 | 4 | 1st | Marek Kozyra | Aleksandra Berecka |
| 2012 WW-II-B | 5 | 4 | 1 | 0 | 0 | 38 | 6 | 1st | Marek Kozyra | Magdalena Szynal |

# Portugal (POR)

*Portugal didn't participate in any IIHF competition in 2011 but remains an Associate Member. Photo: FPDG.*

**Joined IIHF: May 13, 1999 (Associate Member)**

Website: www.fp-dg.com
E-mail: moxpt@hotmail.com

Federacao Portuguesa de Desportos no Gelo
R. Rogerio Paulo, n° 48, 4° A
Tercena
2730-194 Barcarena
Portugal

Phone: +351 210 15 4682 • Fax: n/a

**Top Level Host History** none

# Qatar (QAT)

*The first Qatar ice hockey championship was played in the 2010/2011 season at the Villagio Ice Rink in Doha. Photo: QIHF.*

**Joined IIHF: May 18, 2012**

Website: n/a
E-mail: tareks@olympic.qa

Qatar Ice Hockey Federation
PO Box 7494
Olympic Tower
Doha
Qatar

Phone: +974 449 447 00 • Fax: +974 449 447 33

**Top Level Host History** none

# Romania (ROU)

*The Romanian U20 national team celebrates a goal. Photo: Tonu Stoltsen.*

**Joined IIHF: January 24, 1924**

*ROM replaced by ROU in 2006

Website: www.rohockey.ro
E-mail: office@rohockey.ro

Romanian Ice Hockey Federation
Bdul. Basarabia 35-37
Patinoarul Mihai Flamaropol
Codul postal 022103, Sectorul 2
Bucuresti
Romania

Phone: +40 21 324 68 71 • Fax: +40 21 324 77 13

**World Ranking**

| MEN | | WOMEN | |
|---|---|---|---|
| 2012 | 27 | 2012 | 34 |
| 2011 | 28 | 2011 | 30 |
| 2010 | 28 | 2010 | 31 |
| 2009 | 28 | 2009 | 30 |
| 2008 | 27 | 2008 | 29 |
| 2007 | 26 | 2007 | 27 |
| 2006 | 26 | 2006 | 27 |
| 2005 | 26 | 2005 | 26 |
| 2004 | 26 | 2004 | 25 |

**Top Level Host History** none

**Olympics, Men**
(bold=top level)

| Year Event | GP | W | T | L | GF | GA | Place | Coach | Captain |
|---|---|---|---|---|---|---|---|---|---|
| 1964 OG-M | 7 | 3 | 1 | 3 | 31 | 28 | 12th | Mihai Flamaropol | Zoltan Czaka |
| 1968 OG-M | 5 | 2 | 0 | 3 | 22 | 23 | 12th | Mihai Flamoropol/Constantin Tico | Zoltan Czaka |
| 1976 OG-M | 5 | 4 | 0 | 1 | 23 | 15 | 7th | Stefan Ionescu/Ion Tiron | Dezideriu Varga |
| 1980 OG-M | 5 | 1 | 1 | 3 | 13 | 29 | 8th | Stefan Ionescu/Ion Tiron | Doru Tureanu |

**World Championship (Men)**
(bold=top level)

| Year Event | GP | W | T | L | GF | GA | Place | Coach | Captain |
|---|---|---|---|---|---|---|---|---|---|
| Year Event | GP | W | OTW OTL | L | GF | GA | Place | Coach | Captain |
| 1931 WM | 5 | 0 | 0 | 5 | 2 | 49 | 10th | *unknown* | Constantin Cantacuzino |

| **1933 WM** | **5** | **2** | **0** | | **3** | **5** | **19** | **9th** | **Walter Sell** | **Constantin Cantacuzino** |
|---|---|---|---|---|---|---|---|---|---|---|
| **1934 WM** | **6** | **1** | **0** | | **5** | **8** | **21** | **10th** | ***unknown*** | **Constantin Cantacuzino** |
| **1935 WM** | **6** | **3** | **0** | | **3** | **14** | **12** | **11th** | **Dumitru Danielopol** | **Constantin Cantacuzino** |
| **1937 WM** | **3** | **0** | **0** | | **3** | **3** | **19** | **9th** | **Francis Quinn** | **Paul Anastasiu+** |
| **1938 WM** | **4** | **0** | **0** | | **4** | **2** | **15** | **13th** | ***unknown*** | ***unknown*** |
| **1947 WM** | **7** | **1** | **0** | | **6** | **17** | **88** | **7th** | ***unknown*** | **Eduard Pana (1)** |
| 1961 WM-C | 5 | 5 | 0 | | 0 | 69 | 5 | 1st | Mihai Flamaropol | Zoltan Czaka |
| 1963 WM-B | 6 | 4 | 1 | | 1 | 29 | 17 | 3rd | Mihai Flamaropol | Zoltan Czaka |
| 1966 WM-B | 7 | 5 | 1 | | 1 | 29 | 16 | 2nd | Mihai Flamaropol | Zoltan Czaka |
| 1967 WM-B | 7 | 5 | 2 | | 0 | 34 | 18 | 2nd | Ion Tiron | Zoltan Czaka |
| 1969 WM-B | 7 | 2 | 1 | | 4 | 24 | 36 | 6th | Mihai Flamaropol/Ion Tiron | Dezideriu Varga (2) |
| 1970 WM-B | 7 | 2 | 0 | | 5 | 21 | 38 | 7th | Ion Tiron | Dezideriu Varga |
| 1971 WM-C | 7 | 6 | 1 | | 0 | 70 | 11 | 1st | Zoltan Czaka | Dezideriu Varga |
| 1972 WM-B | 6 | 3 | 0 | | 3 | 25 | 26 | 4th | Zoltan Czaka | Dezideriu Varga |
| 1973 WM-B | 7 | 4 | 1 | | 2 | 24 | 20 | 4th | Mihai Flamaropol/Ion Tiron | Dezideriu Varga (3) |
| 1974 WM-B | 7 | 2 | 1 | | 4 | 30 | 29 | 6th | Victor Suvalov | Dezideriu Varga |
| 1975 WM-B | 7 | 2 | 2 | | 3 | 26 | 26 | 5th | Mihai Flamaropol | Dezideriu Varga |
| 1976 WM-B | 7 | 5 | 1 | | 1 | 40 | 23 | 1st | Stefan Ionescu | Eduard Pana |
| **1977 WM** | **10** | **1** | **0** | | **9** | **20** | **84** | **8th** | **Stefan Ionescu** | **Dezideriu Varga** |
| 1978 WM-B | 7 | 3 | 1 | | 3 | 41 | 29 | 4th | Stefan Ionescu | Doru Tureanu |
| 1979 WM-B | 6 | 3 | 1 | | 2 | 27 | 21 | 3rd | Stefan Ionescu | Doru Tureanu |
| 1981 WM-B | 7 | 2 | 0 | | 5 | 25 | 30 | 5th | Eduard Pana | Doru Morosanu |
| 1982 WM-B | 7 | 2 | 1 | | 4 | 27 | 30 | 5th | Eduard Pana | Doru Morosanu |
| 1983 WM-B | 7 | 1 | 1 | | 5 | 20 | 48 | 7th | Eduard Pana | Doru Tureanu |
| 1985 WM-C | 7 | 4 | 0 | | 3 | 51 | 29 | 4th | Ion Gheorghiu/Eduard Pana | Doru Tureanu |
| 1986 WM-C | 6 | 3 | 0 | | 3 | 33 | 20 | 4th | Alexandru Calamar/Ion Tiron | Doru Tureanu |
| 1987 WM-C | 7 | 5 | 1 | | 1 | 48 | 22 | 3rd | Alexandru Calamar | Alexandru Halauca |
| 1989 WM-D | 4 | 2 | 1 | | 1 | 69 | 7 | 2nd | Ion Gheorghiu | Alexandru Halauca |
| 1990 WM-C | 8 | 4 | 1 | | 3 | 36 | 27 | 4th | Ion Gheorghiu | Alexandru Halauca |
| 1991 WM-C | 8 | 6 | 0 | | 2 | 51 | 22 | 3rd | Florian Gheorghe | Cornel Chirita |
| 1992 WM-B | 7 | 1 | 3 | | 3 | 13 | 26 | 6th | Florian Gheorghe | Cornel Chirita |
| 1993 WM-B | 7 | 2 | 0 | | 5 | 20 | 44 | 6th | Anton Crisan | Alexandru Halauca |
| 1994 WM-B | 7 | 1 | 0 | | 6 | 18 | 43 | 7th | Anton Crisan | Alexandru Halauca |
| 1995 WM-B | 7 | 1 | 0 | | 6 | 15 | 57 | 8th | Anton Crisan | Marius Gliga |
| 1996 WM-C | 7 | 3 | 0 | | 4 | 32 | 27 | 6th | Florian Gheorghe | Marius Gliga |
| 1997 WM-C | 5 | 3 | 0 | | 2 | 15 | 20 | 5th | Florian Gheorghe | Marius Gliga |
| 1998 WM-C | 5 | 4 | 0 | | 1 | 31 | 13 | 2nd | Florian Gheorghe | Marius Gliga |
| 1999 WM-C | 4 | 3 | 0 | | 1 | 24 | 16 | 2nd | Ion Ionita | Marius Gliga |
| 2000 WM-C | 4 | 1 | 2 | | 1 | 21 | 14 | 6th | Ion Ionita | Marius Gliga |
| 2001 WM-II-B | 5 | 5 | 0 | | 0 | 46 | 4 | 1st | Florian Gheorghe | Daniel Herlea |
| 2002 WM-I-B | 5 | 1 | 0 | | 4 | 10 | 31 | 5th | Marius Gliga | Catalin Geru |
| 2003 WM-I-A | 5 | 1 | 1 | | 3 | 13 | 26 | 5th | Daniel Herlea | Nutu Andrei |
| 2004 WM-I-B | 5 | 1 | 0 | | 4 | 9 | 35 | 5th | Daniel Herlea | Cristian Daia |
| 2005 WM-I-B | 5 | 0 | 0 | | 5 | 7 | 30 | 6th | Daniel Herlea | Catalin Geru |
| 2006 WM-II-A | 5 | 5 | 0 | | 0 | 59 | 9 | 1st | Daniel Herlea | Ioan Timaru |
| 2007 WM-I-B | 5 | 0 | 0 | 1 | 4 | 12 | 32 | 6th | Daniel Herlea | Ervin Moldovan |
| 2008 WM-II-A | 5 | 5 | 0 | 0 | 0 | 65 | 2 | 1st | Dusan Kapusta | Ioan Timaru |
| 2009 WM-I-B | 5 | 0 | 0 | 0 | 5 | 1 | 38 | 6th | Tom Skinner | Catalin Geru |
| 2010 WM-II-B | 5 | 4 | 0 | 0 | 1 | 47 | 14 | 2nd | Tom Skinner | Szabolcs Szocs |
| 2011 WM-II-B | 5 | 5 | 0 | 0 | 0 | 47 | 8 | 1st | Tom Skinner | Szabolcs Papp |
| 2012 WM-I-B | 5 | 2 | 0 | 0 | 3 | 13 | 28 | 4th | Tom Skinner | Szabolcs Szocs |

(1) Robert Sadowski captain vs. Switzerland (Feb. 17)
(2) Eduard Pana captain Mar. 3 vs. GDR & Mar. 9 vs. AUT
(3) Eduard Pana captain Mar. 27 vs. GDR
+also Constantin Cantacuzino

**U20 World Championship**

| Year Event | GP | W | T | | L | GF | GA | Place | Coach | Captain |
|---|---|---|---|---|---|---|---|---|---|---|
| Year Event | GP | W | OTW | OTL | L | GF | GA | Place | Coach | Captain |
| 1983 WM20-C | 6 | 6 | 0 | | 0 | 49 | 9 | 1st | Ion Tiron | *unknown* |
| 1984 WM20-B | 5 | 1 | 0 | | 4 | 15 | 33 | 7th | Ioan Ganga | Gergely Lukacs |
| 1985 WM20-B | 7 | 1 | 1 | | 5 | 27 | 42 | 7th | Ioan Basa | unknown |
| 1986 WM20-B | 7 | 3 | 2 | | 2 | 32 | 28 | 4th | Ioan Basa | Paul Burada |
| 1987 WM20-B | 5 | 2 | 0 | | 3 | 25 | 36 | 6th | Ioan Basa/Florian Gheorghe | *unknown* |
| 1988 WM20-B | 7 | 5 | 0 | | 2 | 24 | 27 | 2nd | Ioan Basa/Florian Gheorghe | *unknown* |
| 1989 WM20-B | 7 | 4 | 0 | | 3 | 32 | 31 | 3rd | Florian Gheorghe | Danut-Gigi Popovici |
| 1990 WM20-B | 7 | 2 | 1 | | 4 | 27 | 39 | 7th | Ioan Basa/Florian Gheorghe | Zsolt Antal |
| 1991 WM20-B | 7 | 2 | 1 | | 4 | 23 | 43 | 5th | Ioan Basa | Valentin Toader |
| 1992 WM20-B | 7 | 4 | 0 | | 3 | 23 | 26 | 5th | Jon Jonita/Dumitru Jordan | Valentin Toader |
| 1993 WM20-B | 7 | 1 | 1 | | 5 | 16 | 37 | 7th | Ioan Ionita | Tiberius Cutov |
| 1994 WM20-B | 7 | 1 | 2 | | 4 | 21 | 32 | 8th | Ioan Ionita | Roberto Cazacu |
| 1995 WM20-C-1 | 4 | 1 | 0 | | 3 | 8 | 20 | 6th | Ioan Basa | Jozsef Adorjan |
| 1996 WM20-C | 4 | 1 | 0 | | 3 | 12 | 29 | 6th | Csaba Basilides | Lehel Gergely |
| 1997 WM20-C | 4 | 1 | 0 | | 3 | 9 | 21 | 6th | Elod Antal | Robert Mihai Rusu |
| 1998 WM20-C | 4 | 0 | 0 | | 4 | 12 | 31 | 8th | Zsombor Antal | Ervin Moldovan |
| 1999 WM20-D | 4 | 2 | 0 | | 2 | 33 | 11 | 3rd | Remus Bianu | Attila Tanko Szabolcs |
| 2000 WM20-D | 4 | 3 | 0 | | 1 | 33 | 13 | 2nd | Emerich Mezei | Szabolcs Szolcs |
| 2001 WM20-III | 4 | 3 | 0 | | 1 | 31 | 10 | 3rd | George Justinian | Attila Goga |
| 2002 WM20-III | 4 | 2 | 0 | | 2 | 22 | 14 | 4th | George Justinian | Tibor Basilidesz |
| 2003 WM20-II-A | 5 | 3 | 0 | | 2 | 34 | 26 | 3rd | George Justinian | Robert Peter |
| 2004 WM20-II-A | 5 | 3 | 1 | | 1 | 44 | 16 | 2nd | George Justinian | Andrei Justinian |
| 2005 WM20-II-A | 5 | 3 | 1 | | 1 | 23 | 13 | 2nd | Tamas Gyorgypal | Tivadar Petres |
| 2006 WM20-II-A | 5 | 3 | 1 | | 1 | 31 | 11 | 3rd | Tamas Gyorgypal | Szabolcs Molnar |
| 2007 WM20-II-A | 5 | 3 | 1 | 0 | 1 | 23 | 13 | 2nd | George Justinian | Attila Kanya |

| | | | | | | | | | | |
|---|---|---|---|---|---|---|---|---|---|---|
| 2008 WM20-II-A | 5 | 1 | 0 | 1 | 3 | 13 | 30 | 5th | Nelu Alexe | Otto Biro |
| 2009 WM20-II-A | 5 | 0 | 0 | 2 | 3 | 9 | 32 | 6th | Nelu Alexe | Ciprian Tapu |
| 2010 WM20-II-B | 5 | 2 | 1 | 0 | 2 | 21 | 21 | 3rd | Elod Antal | Vlad Botos |
| 2011 WM20-II-B | 5 | 2 | 0 | 0 | 3 | 16 | 24 | 4th | Elod Antal | Tamas Biro |
| 2012 WM20-II-B | 5 | 5 | 0 | 0 | 0 | 44 | 9 | 1st | Otto Keresztes | Roberto Gliga |

**U18 World Championship (Men)**

| Year Event | GP | W | T | | L | GF | GA | Place | Coach | Captain |
|---|---|---|---|---|---|---|---|---|---|---|
| Year Event | GP | W | OTW | OTL | L | GF | GA | Place | Coach | Captain |
| 2001 WM18-III | 4 | 3 | 0 | | 1 | 19 | 6 | 2nd | George Justinian | Robert Peter |
| 2002 WM18-II | 5 | 0 | 0 | | 5 | 6 | 43 | 8th | George Justinian | Andrei Justinian (1) |
| 2003 WM18-II-B | 5 | 5 | 0 | | 0 | 33 | 10 | 1st | George Justinian | Cosmin Flueros |
| 2004 WM18-I-A | 5 | 0 | 1 | | 4 | 5 | 42 | 6th | George Justinian | Szabolcs Molnar (2) |
| 2005 WM18-II-B | 5 | 0 | 1 | | 4 | 8 | 30 | 6th | George Justinian | Cornel Moraru (3) |
| 2006 WM18-III | 5 | 5 | 0 | | 0 | 68 | 3 | 1st | George Justinian | Otto Biro (4) |
| 2007 WM18-II-B | 5 | 2 | 0 | 0 | 3 | 15 | 25 | 4th | George Justinian | Zsolt Balint |
| 2008 WM18-II-B | 5 | 2 | 0 | 0 | 3 | 32 | 21 | 4th | Elod Antal | Vlad Botos |
| 2009 WM1 8-II-A | 5 | 3 | 0 | 0 | 2 | 23 | 20 | 3rd | Elod Antal | Tamas Biro |
| 2010 WM18-II-A | 5 | 3 | 0 | 1 | 1 | 22 | 23 | 2nd | Gabor Prakab | Roberto Gliga |
| 2011 WM18-II-A | 5 | 3 | 1 | 0 | 1 | 26 | 12 | 2nd | Otto Keresztes | Roberto Gliga |
| 2012 WM18-II-A | 5 | 4 | 0 | 0 | 1 | 25 | 15 | 2nd | Otto Keresztes | Daniel Tranca |

(1) Andrei Justinian captain Mar. 22 vs. FRA; Istvan Antal captain Mar. 24 vs. GBR; Daniel Jipa captain Mar. 26 vs. CRO; Gabor Antal captain Mar. 28 vs. NED; Mikhail Georgescu captain Mar. 29 vs. HUN
(2) Szabolcs Molnar captain Mar. 27 vs. SUI; Zsolt Molnar captain Mar. 28 vs. SLO; Botond Szocs captain Mar. 30 vs. LAT; Ede Mihaly captain Mar. 31 vs. POL; Istvan Veress captain Apr. 2 vs. AUT
(3) Cornel Moraru captain Mar. 21 vs. MEX; Alexandru Munteanu captain Mar. 22 vs. LTU; Endre Peter captain Mar. 24 vs. ISL; Tibor Sara captain Mar. 25 vs. CRO & Mar. 27 vs. HUN
(4) Otto Biro captain Mar. 13 vs. BUL; Zsolt Kopacz captain Mar. 14 vs. NZL; Attila Balint captain Mar. 16 vs. TUR; Zoltan Szogyor captain Mar. 17 vs. ISR; Csanad Virag captain Mar. 19 vs. RSA

**Women's World Championship**

| Year Event | GP | W | T | | L | GF | GA | Place | Coach | Captain |
|---|---|---|---|---|---|---|---|---|---|---|
| Year Event | GP | W | OTW | OTL | L | GF | GA | Place | Coach | Captain |
| 2003 WW-III | 5 | 1 | 0 | | 4 | 11 | 23 | 6th | Gheorge Tabacaru | Ibolya Sandor |
| 2004 WW-III | 5 | 1 | 0 | | 4 | 4 | 21 | 5th | Gheorge Tabacaru | *unknown* |
| 2005 WW-IV | 3 | 1 | 0 | | 2 | 3 | 5 | 3rd | Gheorge Tabacaru | Ibolya Sandor |
| 2007 WW-IV | 5 | 4 | 0 | 0 | 1 | 44 | 12 | 2nd | Gheorge Tabacaru | Ibolya Sandor |
| 2008 WW-IV | 5 | 2 | 0 | 1 | 2 | 25 | 16 | 3rd | Istvan Antal | Ibolya Sandor |
| 2011 WW-IV | 4 | 1 | 0 | 0 | 3 | 9 | 15 | 4th | Per Larsson | Kinga Koncsag |

# Russia (RUS)

*The Russian national team celebrates after winning the gold medal at the 2012 IIHF Ice Hockey World Championship. Photo: Jeff Vinnick / HHOF-IIHF Images.*

**Joined IIHF: Soviet Union joined April 1, 1952; Russia replaced Soviet Union on May 6, 1992**

Website: www.fhr.ru
E-mail: sokolova@fhr.ru

Ice Hockey Federation of Russia
Luzhnetskaia Naberezhnaia 8
119991 Moscow
Russia

Phone: +7 495 637 02 77 • Fax: +7 495 637 02 22

**World Ranking**

| MEN | | WOMEN | |
|---|---|---|---|
| 2012 | 1 | 2012 | 6 |
| 2011 | 1 | 2011 | 5 |
| 2010 | 1 | 2010 | 6 |
| 2009 | 1 | 2009 | 6 |
| 2008 | 2 | 2008 | 6 |
| 2007 | 5 | 2007 | 6 |
| 2006 | 5 | 2006 | 6 |
| 2005 | 5 | 2005 | 6 |
| 2004 | 7 | 2004 | 5 |

**Top Level Host History**

Olympics: 2014 (Sochi)
World Championship (Men): 1957 (Moscow), 1973 (Moscow), 1979 (Moscow), 1986 (Moscow), 2000 (St. Petersburg); 2007 (Moscow, Mytischi)
U20 World Championship: 1983 (Leningrad), 1988 (Moscow), 2001 (Moscow, Podolsk), 2013 (Ufa)
U18 World Championship (Men): 2003 (Yaroslavl), 2008 (Kazan), 2013 (Sochi)

**Soviet Union—Olympics, Men**
(bold=top level)

| Year Event | GP | W | T | L | GF | GA | Place | Coach | Captain |
|---|---|---|---|---|---|---|---|---|---|
| **1956 OG-M** | **7** | **7** | **0** | **0** | **40** | **9** | **G** | **Arkadi Chernyshev** | **Vsevelod Bobrov** |
| **1960 OG-M** | **7** | **4** | **1** | **2** | **40** | **23** | **B** | **Anatoli Tarasov** | **Nikolai Sologubov** |
| **1964 OG-M** | **7** | **7** | **0** | **0** | **54** | **10** | **G** | **Anatoli Tarasov/Arkadi Chernyshev** | **Boris Mayorov** |
| **1968 OG-M** | **7** | **6** | **0** | **1** | **48** | **10** | **G** | **Anatoli Tarasov/Arkadi Chernyshev** | **Boris Mayorov** |
| **1972 OG-M** | **5** | **4** | **1** | **0** | **33** | **13** | **G** | **Anatoli Tarasov/Arkadi Chernyshev** | **Viktor Kuzkin** |
| **1976 OG-M** | **5** | **5** | **0** | **0** | **40** | **11** | **G** | **Boris Kulagin** | **Boris Mikhailov** |
| **1980 OG-M** | **7** | **6** | **0** | **1** | **63** | **17** | **S** | **Viktor Tikhonov** | **Boris Mikhailov** |
| **1984 OG-M** | **7** | **7** | **0** | **0** | **48** | **5** | **G** | **Viktor Tikhonov** | **Vyacheslav Fetisov** |
| **1988 OG-M** | **8** | **7** | **0** | **1** | **45** | **13** | **G** | **Viktor Tikhonov** | **Vyacheslav Fetisov** |

### Russia—Olympics, Men
(bold=top level)

| Year Event | GP | W | T | OTW | OTL | L | GF | GA | Place | Coach | Captain |
|---|---|---|---|---|---|---|---|---|---|---|---|
| 1992 OG-M | 8 | 7 | 0 | | | 1 | 46 | 14 | G | Viktor Tikhonov | Vyacheslav Bykov |
| 1994 OG-M | 8 | 4 | 0 | | | 4 | 26 | 24 | 4th | Viktor Tikhonov | Alexander Smirnov |
| 1998 OG-M | 6 | 5 | 0 | | | 1 | 26 | 12 | S | Vladimir Yurzinov | Pavel Bure |
| 2002 OG-M | 6 | 3 | 1 | | | 2 | 19 | 14 | B | Vyacheslav Fetisov | Igor Larionov |
| 2006 OG-M | 8 | 5 | 0 | | | 3 | 25 | 18 | 4th | Vladimir Krikunov | Alexei Kovalev |
| 2010 OG-M | 4 | 2 | | 0 | 1 | 1 | 16 | 13 | 6th | Vyacheslav Bykov | Alexei Morozov |

### Soviet Union—World Championship (Men)
(bold=top level)

| Year Event | GP | W | T | L | GF | GA | Place | Coach | Captain |
|---|---|---|---|---|---|---|---|---|---|
| 1954 WM | 7 | 6 | 1 | 0 | 37 | 10 | G | Arkadi Chernyshev | *unknown* |
| 1955 WM | 8 | 7 | 0 | 1 | 39 | 13 | S | Arkadi Chernyshev | Vsevelod Bobrov |
| 1957 WM | 7 | 5 | 2 | 0 | 77 | 9 | S | Arkadi Chernyshev | Vsevelod Bobrov |
| 1958 WM | 7 | 5 | 1 | 1 | 44 | 15 | S | Anatoli Tarasov | *unknown* |
| 1959 WM | 8 | 7 | 0 | 1 | 44 | 15 | S | Anatoli Tarasov | Nikolai Sologubov |
| 1961 WM | 7 | 5 | 0 | 2 | 51 | 20 | B | Arkadi Chernyshev | Nikolai Sologubov |
| 1963 WM | 7 | 6 | 0 | 1 | 50 | 9 | G | Arkadi Chernyshev/Anatoli Tarasov | Boris Mayorov |
| 1965 WM | 7 | 7 | 0 | 0 | 51 | 13 | G | Arkadi Chernyshev/Anatoli Tarasov | Boris Mayorov |
| 1966 WM | 7 | 6 | 1 | 0 | 55 | 7 | G | Arkadi Chernyshev/Anatoli Tarasov | Viktor Kuzkin |
| 1967 WM | 7 | 7 | 0 | 0 | 58 | 9 | G | Arkadi Chernyshev/Anatoli Tarasov | Boris Mayorov |
| 1969 WM | 10 | 8 | 0 | 2 | 59 | 23 | G | Arkadi Chernyshev/Anatoli Tarasov | Vyacheslav Starshinov |
| 1970 WM | 10 | 9 | 0 | 1 | 68 | 11 | G | Arkadi Chernyshev/Anatoli Tarasov | Vyacheslav Starshinov |
| 1971 WM | 10 | 8 | 1 | 1 | 77 | 24 | G | Arkadi Chernyshev/Anatoli Tarasov | Vyacheslav Starshinov |
| 1972 WM | 10 | 7 | 2 | 1 | 78 | 19 | S | Vsevolod Bobrov | Viktor Kuzkin (1) |
| 1973 WM | 10 | 10 | 0 | 0 | 100 | 18 | G | Vsevolod Bobrov | Boris Mikhailov |
| 1974 WM | 10 | 9 | 0 | 1 | 64 | 18 | G | Vsevolod Bobrov | Boris Mikhailov |
| 1975 WM | 10 | 10 | 0 | 0 | 90 | 23 | G | Boris Kulagin | Boris Mikhailov (2) |
| 1976 WM | 10 | 6 | 1 | 3 | 50 | 23 | S | Boris Kulagin | Boris Mikhailov |
| 1977 WM | 10 | 7 | 0 | 3 | 77 | 24 | B | Boris Kulagin | Boris Mikhailov |
| 1978 WM | 10 | 9 | 0 | 1 | 61 | 26 | G | Viktor Tikhonov | Boris Mikhailov |
| 1979 WM | 8 | 8 | 0 | 0 | 61 | 14 | G | Viktor Tikhonov | Boris Mikhailov |
| 1981 WM | 8 | 6 | 2 | 0 | 55 | 14 | G | Viktor Tikhonov | Valeri Vasiliev |
| 1982 WM | 10 | 9 | 1 | 0 | 58 | 20 | G | Viktor Tikhonov | Valeri Vasiliev |
| 1983 WM | 10 | 9 | 1 | 0 | 53 | 7 | G | Viktor Tikhonov | Vyacheslav Fetisov |
| 1985 WM | 10 | 8 | 0 | 2 | 64 | 16 | B | Viktor Tikhonov | Vyacheslav Fetisov |
| 1986 WM | 10 | 10 | 0 | 0 | 50 | 15 | G | Viktor Tikhonov | Vyacheslav Fetisov |
| 1987 WM | 10 | 8 | 2 | 0 | 52 | 15 | S | Viktor Tikhonov | Vyacheslav Fetisov |
| 1989 WM | 10 | 10 | 0 | 0 | 47 | 16 | G | Viktor Tikhonov | Vyacheslav Fetisov |
| 1990 WM | 10 | 8 | 1 | 1 | 53 | 13 | G | Viktor Tikhonov | Vyacheslav Bykov |
| 1991 WM | 10 | 7 | 2 | 1 | 51 | 25 | B | Viktor Tikhonov | Vladimir Konstantinov |

(1) Alexander Ragulin captain vs. Switzerland (Apr. 10)
(2) Vladimir Shadrin captain vs. Poland (Apr. 15)

### Russia—World Championship (Men)
(bold=top level)

| Year Event | GP | W | T | OTW | OTL | L | GF | GA | Place | Coach | Captain |
|---|---|---|---|---|---|---|---|---|---|---|---|
| 1992 WM | 6 | 4 | 1 | | | 1 | 23 | 12 | 5th | Viktor Tikhonov | Vitali Prokhorov |
| 1993 WM | 8 | 5 | 1 | | | 2 | 30 | 18 | G | Boris Mikhailov | Vyacheslav Bykov |
| 1994 WM | 6 | 4 | 0 | | | 2 | 31 | 10 | 5th | Boris Mikhailov | Ilya Biakin |
| 1995 WM | 6 | 5 | 0 | | | 1 | 26 | 12 | 5th | Boris Mikhailov | Vyacheslav Bykov |
| 1996 WM | 8 | 6 | 0 | | | 2 | 33 | 17 | 4th | Vladimir Vasiliev | Alexei Yashin |
| 1997 WM | 9 | 4 | 2 | | | 3 | 28 | 24 | 4th | Igor Dmitriev | Sergei Bautin (1) |
| 1998 WM | 6 | 4 | 1 | | | 1 | 29 | 18 | 5th | Vladimir Yurzinov | Vitali Prokhorov |
| 1999 WM | 6 | 2 | 3 | | | 1 | 18 | 13 | 5th | Alexander Yakushev | Alexei Yashin |
| 2000 WM | 6 | 2 | 0 | | | 4 | 16 | 13 | 11th | Alexander Yakushev | Pavel Bure |
| 2001 WM | 7 | 4 | 0 | | | 3 | 23 | 15 | 6th | Boris Mikhailov | Alexei Yashin |
| 2002 WM | 9 | 4 | 1 | | | 4 | 30 | 23 | S | Boris Mikhailov | Andrei Kovalenko |
| 2003 WM | 7 | 3 | 0 | | | 4 | 19 | 19 | 7th | Vladimir Plyushev | Sergei Gusev |
| 2004 WM | 6 | 2 | 0 | | | 4 | 16 | 15 | 10th | Viktor Tikhonov | Oleg Tverdovsky |
| 2005 WM | 9 | 6 | 2 | | | 1 | 30 | 20 | B | Vladimir Krikunov | Alexei Kovalev |
| 2006 WM | 7 | 5 | 1 | | | 1 | 35 | 16 | 5th | Vladimir Krikunov | Maxim Sushinsky |
| 2007 WM | 9 | 8 | | 0 | 1 | 0 | 43 | 14 | B | Vyacheslav Bykov | Petr Schastlivy |
| 2008 WM | 9 | 6 | | 3 | 0 | 0 | 43 | 18 | G | Vyacheslav Bykov | Maxim Sushinsky |
| 2009 WM | 9 | 8 | | 1 | 0 | 0 | 41 | 17 | G | Vyacheslav Bykov | Alexei Morozov |
| 2010 WM | 9 | 8 | | 0 | 0 | 1 | 32 | 11 | S | Vyacheslav Bykov | Ilya Kovalchuk |
| 2011 WM | 9 | 4 | | 0 | 1 | 4 | 24 | 29 | 4th | Vyacheslav Bykov | Alexei Morozov |
| 2012 WM | 10 | 10 | | 0 | 0 | 0 | 44 | 14 | G | Zinetula Bilyaletdinov | Ilya Nikulin |

(1) Sergei Fokin captain vs. Slovakia (Apr. 27)

### Soviet Union/Russia—IIHF-NHL Invitationals
(bold=top level)

| Year Event | GP | W | T | L | GF | GA | Place | Coach | Captain |
|---|---|---|---|---|---|---|---|---|---|
| 1972 SS | 8 | 3 | 1 | 4 | 32 | 31 | 2nd | Vsevelod Bobrov | Viktor Kuzkin (1) |
| 1976 CC | 5 | 2 | 1 | 2 | 23 | 14 | 3rd | Viktor Tikhonov | Alexander Maltsev |
| 1981 CC | 7 | 5 | 1 | 1 | 32 | 15 | 1st | Viktor Tikhonov | Valeri Vasiliev |
| 1984 CC | 6 | 5 | 0 | 1 | 24 | 10 | 3rd | Viktor Tikhonov | *unknown* |
| 1987 CC | 8 | 4 | 1 | 3 | 38 | 30 | 2nd | Viktor Tikhonov | Vyacheslav Fetisov |

| | | | | | | | | | |
|---|---|---|---|---|---|---|---|---|---|
| 1991 CC | 5 | 1 | 1 | 3 | 14 | 14 | 5th | Viktor Tikhonov | Igor Kravchuk |
| 1996 WCH | 5 | 2 | 0 | 3 | 19 | 19 | 4th | Boris Mikhailov | Vyacheslav Fetisov |
| 2004 WCH | 4 | 2 | 0 | 2 | 11 | 11 | 6th | Zinetula Bilyaletdinov | Alexei Yashin |

(1) Alexander Ragulin captain for Game 6, September 24

### Soviet Union—U20 World Championship

(bold=top level)

| Year Event | GP | W | T | L | GF | GA | Place | Coach | Captain |
|---|---|---|---|---|---|---|---|---|---|
| 1977 WM20 | 7 | 7 | 0 | 0 | 51 | 19 | G | Vitali Davydov | Valeri Yefstifeyev |
| 1978 WM20 | 7 | 6 | 0 | 1 | 50 | 16 | G | Vitali Davydov | Sergei Starikov |
| 1979 WM20 | 6 | 5 | 1 | 0 | 46 | 11 | G | Vitali Davydov | Alexander Gerasimov |
| 1980 WM20 | 5 | 5 | 0 | 0 | 24 | 9 | G | Yuri Morozov | Vladimir Shashov (1) |
| 1981 WM20 | 5 | 3 | 0 | 2 | 36 | 14 | B | Yuri Morozov | Anatoli Semenov |
| 1982 WM20 | 7 | 4 | 0 | 3 | 42 | 25 | 4th | Igor Tuzik | *unknown* |
| 1983 WM20 | 7 | 7 | 0 | 0 | 50 | 15 | G | Anatoli Kostriukov | Ilya Biakin |
| 1984 WM20 | 7 | 6 | 1 | 0 | 50 | 17 | G | Igor Dmitriev | *unknown* |
| 1985 WM20 | 7 | 5 | 0 | 2 | 38 | 17 | B | Vladimir Kiselev | Alexander Chernykh |
| 1986 WM20 | 7 | 7 | 0 | 0 | 42 | 14 | G | Vladimir Vasiliev | Pavel Torgayev |
| 1987 WM20 | 6 | 2 | 1 | 3 | 27 | 20 | DQ | Vladimir Vasiliev | Vladimir Konstantinov |
| 1988 WM20 | 7 | 6 | 0 | 1 | 44 | 18 | S | Anatoli Kostriukov | *unknown* |
| 1989 WM20 | 7 | 6 | 0 | 1 | 51 | 14 | G | Robert Cherenkov | Alexander Mogilny |
| 1990 WM20 | 7 | 5 | 1 | 1 | 50 | 23 | S | Robert Cherenkov | Sergei Zubov |
| 1991 WM20 | 7 | 5 | 1 | 1 | 44 | 15 | S | Robert Cherenkov | Pavel Bure |

(1) Vladimir Golovkov captain Dec. 30 vs. FIN & Jan. 1 vs. TCH

### Russia—U20 World Championship

(bold=top level)

| Year Event | GP | W | T | | L | GF | GA | Place | Coach | Captain |
|---|---|---|---|---|---|---|---|---|---|---|
| Year Event | GP | W | OTW | OTL | L | GF | GA | Place | Coach | Captain |
| 1992 WM20 | 7 | 6 | 0 | | 1 | 39 | 13 | G | Pyotr Vorobyov | Alexander Kuzminski |
| 1993 WM20 | 7 | 2 | 2 | | 3 | 26 | 20 | 6th | Yuri Moiseyev | Nikolai Syomin |
| 1994 WM20 | 7 | 5 | 1 | | 1 | 23 | 17 | B | Gennadi Tsygurov | Maxim Tsvetkov |
| 1995 WM20 | 7 | 5 | 0 | | 2 | 36 | 24 | S | Igor Dmitriev | Nikolai Zavarukhin |
| 1996 WM20 | 7 | 4 | 1 | | 2 | 32 | 19 | B | Igor Dmitriev | Igor Meliakov |
| 1997 WM20 | 6 | 4 | 1 | | 1 | 26 | 9 | B | Pyotr Vorobyov | Alexei Vasiliev |
| 1998 WM20 | 7 | 5 | 1 | | 1 | 30 | 10 | S | Pyotr Vorobyov | Sergei Shikanov |
| 1999 WM20 | 7 | 6 | 0 | | 1 | 34 | 10 | G | Gennadi Tsygurov | Roman Lyashenko |
| 2000 WM20 | 7 | 6 | 0 | | 1 | 37 | 7 | S | Pyotr Vorobyov | Alexander Zevakhin (1) |
| 2001 WM20 | 7 | 3 | 1 | | 3 | 27 | 17 | 7th | Pyotr Vorobyov | Yevgeni Muratov |
| 2002 WM20 | 7 | 5 | 0 | | 2 | 25 | 14 | G | Vladimir Plyushev | Anton Volchenkov |
| 2003 WM20 | 6 | 6 | 0 | | 0 | 28 | 10 | G | Rafael Ishmatov | Yuri Trubachev |
| 2004 WM20 | 6 | 3 | 1 | | 2 | 17 | 16 | 5th | Rafael Ishmatov | Alexander Ovechkin |
| 2005 WM20 | 6 | 4 | 0 | | 2 | 29 | 17 | S | Valeri Bragin | Alexander Ovechkin |
| 2006 WM20 | 6 | 5 | 0 | | 1 | 26 | 12 | S | Sergei Mikhalev | Yevgeni Malkin |
| 2007 WM20 | 6 | 5 | 0 | 0 | 1 | 26 | 9 | S | Yevgeni Popikhin | Vyacheslav Buravchikov |
| 2008 WM20 | 7 | 5 | 0 | 1 | 1 | 27 | 19 | B | Sergei Nemchinov | Yevgeni Kurbatov |
| 2009 WM20 | 7 | 5 | 0 | 1 | 1 | 32 | 18 | B | Sergei Nemchinov | Nikita Filatov |
| 2010 WM20 | 6 | 3 | 0 | 1 | 2 | 19 | 15 | 6th | Vladimir Plyushev | Nikita Filatov |
| 2011 WM20 | 7 | 3 | 2 | 0 | 2 | 32 | 22 | G | Valeri Bragin | Vladimir Tarasenko |
| 2012 WM20 | 7 | 4 | 1 | 2 | 0 | 31 | 12 | S | Valeri Bragin | Yevgeni Kuznetsov |

(1) Alexei Tereshenko captain Jan. 3 vs. CAN & Jan. 4 vs. CZE

### U18 World Championship (Men)

(bold=top level)

| Year Event | GP | W | T | | L | GF | GA | Place | Coach | Captain |
|---|---|---|---|---|---|---|---|---|---|---|
| Year Event | GP | W | OTW | OTL | L | GF | GA | Place | Coach | Captain |
| 1999 WM18 | 7 | 3 | 0 | | 4 | 19 | 20 | 6th | Valentin Gureyev | Kirill Safronov |
| 2000 WM18 | 6 | 5 | 0 | | 1 | 38 | 8 | S | Andrei Piatanov | Alexander Tatarinov |
| 2001 WM18 | 6 | 5 | 0 | | 1 | 43 | 16 | G | Vladimir Plyushev | Igor Knayazev |
| 2002 WM18 | 8 | 7 | 0 | | 1 | 50 | 16 | S | Ravil Iskhakov | Maxim Sheyvey |
| 2003 WM18 | 6 | 5 | 0 | | 1 | 34 | 13 | B | Vladimir Kryuchkov | Andrei Pervyshin |
| 2004 WM18 | 6 | 4 | 2 | | 0 | 24 | 13 | G | Valeri Bragin | Evgeni Malkin |
| 2005 WM18 | 6 | 4 | 0 | | 2 | 25 | 19 | 5th | Mihail Slipchenko | Andrei Zubarev |
| 2006 WM18 | 6 | 4 | 0 | | 2 | 27 | 15 | 5th | Fedor Kanareykin | Yuri Alexandrov |
| 2007 WM18 | 7 | 5 | 1 | 0 | 1 | 31 | 24 | G | Miskhat Fakhrutdinov | Vitali Karamnov |
| 2008 WM18 | 6 | 5 | 0 | 0 | 1 | 29 | 18 | S | Alexander Biryukov | Nikita Filatov |
| 2009 WM18 | 7 | 5 | 0 | 0 | 2 | 33 | 21 | S | Vladimir Plyushev | Sergei Chvanov |
| 2010 WM18 | 7 | 4 | 0 | 0 | 3 | 26 | 18 | 4th | Mikhail Vasiliev | Yevgeni Kuznetsov |
| 2011 WM18 | 7 | 4 | 1 | 0 | 2 | 36 | 22 | B | Yuri Rumyantsev | Albert Yarullin |
| 2012 WM18 | 6 | 3 | 0 | 0 | 3 | 20 | 12 | 5th | Andrei Parfyonov | Anton Slepyshev |

### Olympics, Women

(bold=top level)

| Year Event | GP | W | T | | L | GF | GA | Place | Coach | Captain |
|---|---|---|---|---|---|---|---|---|---|---|
| Year Event | GP | W | OTW | OTL | L | GF | GA | Place | Coach | Captain |
| 2002 OG-W | 5 | 3 | 0 | | 2 | 15 | 12 | 5th | Vyacheslav Dolgushin | Zhanna Shchelchkova |
| 2006 OG-W | 5 | 2 | 0 | | 3 | 12 | 19 | 6th | Alexei Kalintsev | Zhanna Shchelchkova |
| 2010 OG-W | 5 | 2 | 0 | 1 | 2 | 8 | 23 | 6th | Valentin Gureyev | Yekaterina Smolentseva |

### Women's World Championship

(bold=top level)

| Year Event | GP | W | T | | L | GF | GA | Place | Coach | Captain |
|---|---|---|---|---|---|---|---|---|---|---|
| Year Event | GP | W | OTW | OTL | L | GF | GA | Place | Coach | Captain |
| 1997 WW | 5 | 1 | 1 | | 3 | 9 | 22 | 6th | Valentin Yegorov | Yulia Voronina |

| | | | | | | | | | | | |
|---|---|---|---|---|---|---|---|---|---|---|---|
| **1999 WW** | 5 | 1 | 0 | | | 4 | 11 | 26 | 6th | Jakov Kamenetski | Zhanna Shchelchkova |
| **2000 WW** | 5 | 3 | 0 | | | 2 | 20 | 28 | 5th | Oleg Galiamin | Zhanna Shchelchkova |
| **2001 WW** | 5 | 3 | 0 | | | 2 | 15 | 14 | B | Vyacheslav Dolgushin | Zhanna Shchelchkova |
| **2004 WW** | 4 | 2 | 0 | | | 2 | 7 | 13 | 5th | Viktor Krutov | Zhanna Shchelchkova |
| **2005 WW** | 5 | 0 | 1 | | | 4 | 5 | 21 | 8th | Viktor Krutov | Zhanna Shchelchkova |
| **2007 WW** | 4 | 2 | | 0 | 0 | 2 | 13 | 8 | 7th | Vladimir Kucherenko | Yekaterina Smolentseva |
| **2008 WW** | 4 | 1 | | 0 | 0 | 3 | 8 | 16 | 6th | Vladimir Kucherenko | Yekaterina Smolentseva |
| **2009 WW** | 4 | 2 | | 0 | 0 | 2 | 12 | 19 | 5th | Valentin Gureyev | Yekaterina Smolentseva |
| **2011 WW** | 6 | 1 | | 1 | 1 | 3 | 14 | 33 | 4th | Valentin Gureyev | Olga Permyakova |
| **2012 WW** | 5 | 0 | | 0 | 1 | 4 | 8 | 35 | 6th | Valentin Gureyev | Olga Permyakova |

**U18 Women's World Championship**
(bold=top level)

| Year Event | GP | W | OTW | OTL | L | GF | GA | Place | Coach | Captain |
|---|---|---|---|---|---|---|---|---|---|---|
| **2008 WW18** | 5 | 0 | 0 | 0 | 5 | 4 | 37 | 8th | Alexander Viryasov | Yulia Vasyukova |
| **2009 WW18** | 5 | 1 | 1 | 1 | 2 | 10 | 29 | 7th | Yuri Rychkov | Yekaterina Solovyeva |
| **2010 WW18** | 5 | 0 | 0 | 0 | 5 | 6 | 21 | 8th | Yuri Rychkov | Olga Sosina |
| 2011 WW18-I | 5 | 5 | 0 | 0 | 0 | 44 | 2 | 1st | Alexander Ulyankin | Valeria Pavlova |
| **2012 WW18** | 6 | 1 | 1 | 0 | 4 | 12 | 25 | 7th | Alexander Ulyankin | Valeria Pavlova |

# Serbia (SRB)

*Nikola Kerezovic was named best player of the Serbian U18 national team. Photo: Filip Bakic.*

## Joined IIHF: September 28, 2006

(Croatia and Slovenia split from Yugoslavia (joined IIHF in 1939) on June 25, 1991; Yugoslavia became Serbia & Montenegro in 2004; became Serbia on September 28, 2006 after Serbia and Montenegro split and only Serbia maintained IIHF membership status)

Website: n/a
E-mail: office@hockeyserbia.com

Serbian Ice Hockey Association
Carli Caplina 39
(Hala "Pionir")
11000 Belgrade
Serbia

Phone: +381 11 3292 449 • Fax: +381 11 2764 976

**World Ranking**

**MEN**
2012........31
2011........30
2010........29
2009........32
2008........30
2007........30
2006........29
2005........29
2004........29

**Top Level Host History** none

**Yugoslavia—Olympics, Men**
(bold=top level)

| Year Event | GP | W | T | L | GF | GA | Place | Coach | Captain |
|---|---|---|---|---|---|---|---|---|---|
| **1964 OG-M** | 7 | 3 | 1 | 3 | 29 | 37 | 14th | Vaclav Bubnik | *unknown* |
| **1968 OG-M** | 5 | 5 | 0 | 0 | 33 | 9 | 9th | Oldrich Mlcoh | Viktor Ravnik |
| **1972 OG-M** | 4 | 0 | 1 | 3 | 9 | 17 | 11th | Vladimir Kluc | Viktor Ravnik |
| **1976 OG-M** | 5 | 3 | 0 | 2 | 22 | 19 | 10th | Premsyl Hajny | *unknown* |
| **1984 OG-M** | 5 | 1 | 0 | 4 | 8 | 37 | 11th | Stefan Seme | Mustafa Besic |

**Yugoslavia—World Championship (Men)**
(bold=top level)

| Year Event | GP | W | T | L | GF | GA | Place | Coach | Captain |
|---|---|---|---|---|---|---|---|---|---|
| **1939 WM** | 5 | 0 | 1 | 4 | 3 | 60 | 13th | Viktor Vodisek | Tone Pogacnik |
| 1951 WM-B | 5 | 1 | 0 | 4 | 13 | 37 | 6th | Karel Pavletic | Ludvik Zitnik |
| 1955 WM-B | 4 | 1 | 0 | 3 | 9 | 23 | 4th | Ludvik Zitnik | Ernest Aljancic |
| 1961 WM-C | 5 | 3 | 0 | 2 | 34 | 22 | 3rd | Jovan Tomic | Cene Valentar |
| 1963 WM-B | 6 | 2 | 0 | 4 | 23 | 49 | 5th | Jovan Tomic | Dusan Brun |
| 1965 WM-B | 6 | 0 | 2 | 4 | 16 | 29 | 7th | Vaclav Bubnik | Viktor Ravnik |
| 1966 WM-B | 7 | 4 | 2 | 1 | 25 | 23 | 3rd | Vaclav Bubnik | Miran Krmelj |
| 1967 WM-B | 7 | 2 | 3 | 2 | 29 | 31 | 4th | Vaclav Bubnik | Ivo Rataj |
| 1969 WM-B | 7 | 3 | 2 | 2 | 17 | 20 | 3rd | Oldrich Mlcoh | Viktor Ravnik |
| 1970 WM-B | 7 | 3 | 1 | 3 | 30 | 23 | 4th | Ciril Klinar | Ivo Rataj |
| 1971 WM-B | 7 | 2 | 1 | 4 | 25 | 34 | 5th | Ciril Klinar | Viktor Ravnik |
| 1972 WM-B | 6 | 1 | 0 | 5 | 25 | 28 | 6th | Vladimir Kluc | Viktor Ravnik |
| 1973 WM-B | 7 | 4 | 2 | 1 | 36 | 22 | 3rd | Anton Franzot | Viktor Tisler |
| 1974 WM-B | 7 | 4 | 2 | 1 | 41 | 27 | 2nd | Vladimir Kluc | Roman Smolej |
| 1975 WM-B | 7 | 3 | 1 | 3 | 30 | 23 | 4th | Premsyl Hajny | Viktor Tisler |
| 1976 WM-B | 7 | 4 | 0 | 3 | 37 | 26 | 5th | Premsyl Hajny | Viktor Tislar |
| 1977 WM-B | 8 | 2 | 1 | 5 | 30 | 36 | 7th | Marjan Jelovcan | Renaud Boris |
| 1978 WM-B | 7 | 1 | 0 | 6 | 14 | 48 | 8th | Edvard Hafner/Boris Svetlin | Roman Smolej |
| 1979 WM-C | 7 | 7 | 0 | 0 | 83 | 10 | 1st | Boris Svetlin | Edvard Hafner |
| 1981 WM-B | 7 | 1 | 1 | 5 | 23 | 44 | 7th | Jure Benzia | Edvard Hafner |
| 1982 WM-C | 7 | 5 | 0 | 2 | 59 | 22 | 2nd | Janex Petac/Jure Benzia | Mustafa Besic |
| 1983 WM-B | 7 | 0 | 1 | 6 | 18 | 50 | 8th | Ladislav Pejcha | Gorazd Hiti |
| 1985 WM-C | 7 | 6 | 0 | 1 | 36 | 13 | 2nd | Stefan Seme | Petar Klemenc |
| 1986 WM-B | 7 | 3 | 0 | 4 | 24 | 25 | 7th | Dusan Ilic | Mustafa Besic |
| 1987 WM-C | 7 | 3 | 4 | 0 | 60 | 23 | 4th | Dusan Ilic/Ciril Klinar | Edo Hafner |

| Year Event | GP | W | T | L | GF | GA | Place | Coach | Captain |
|---|---|---|---|---|---|---|---|---|---|
| 1989 WM-C | 7 | 6 | 0 | 1 | 55 | 15 | 2ns | Stefan Seme | Mustafa Besic |
| 1990 WM-C | 8 | 7 | 1 | 0 | 57 | 16 | 1st | Anatoli Kostryukov | Zvone Suvak |
| 1991 WM-B | 7 | 2 | 0 | 5 | 18 | 36 | 6th | Anatoli Kostryukov | Zvone Suvak |
| 1992 WM-B | 7 | 0 | 1 | 6 | 7 | 46 | 8th | Vjestica Mildrad | Nenad Ilic |
| 1995 WM-C-I | 4 | 1 | 0 | 3 | 13 | 31 | 8th | Rasid Semsedinovic | Goran Radovic |
| 1996 WM-D | 5 | 4 | 0 | 1 | 20 | 10 | 2nd | Milorad Vjestica | Kolja Lazarevic |
| 1997 WM-D | 5 | 2 | 2 | 1 | 18 | 13 | 4th | Vojin Koljensic | Kolja Lazarevic |
| 1998 WM-C | 5 | 1 | 1 | 2 | 10 | 13 | 6th | Dusan Ilic | Igor Kosovic |
| 2000 WM-C | 4 | 0 | 2 | 2 | 4 | 22 | 8th | Dusan Dundjerovic | Mirko Karaica |
| 2001 WM-II-B | 5 | 2 | 1 | 2 | 24 | 13 | 3rd | Aleksandar Andjelic | Goran Radovic |
| 2002 WM-II-B | 5 | 4 | 0 | 1 | 34 | 10 | 2nd | Aleksandar Andjelic | Goran Radovic |

**Serbia & Montenegro—World Championship (Men)**

| Year Event | GP | W | T | L | GF | GA | Place | Coach | Captain |
|---|---|---|---|---|---|---|---|---|---|
| 2003 WM-II-A | 5 | 4 | 0 | 11 | 46 | 11 | 2nd | Aleksandar Andjelic | Ivan Prokic |
| 2004 WM-II-B | 5 | 4 | 0 | 1 | 55 | 23 | 2nd | Marko Zidjarevic | Ivan Prokic |
| 2005 WM-II-B | 5 | 4 | 0 | 1 | 30 | 10 | 2nd | Nenad Ilic | Ivan Prokic |
| 2006 WM-II-A | 5 | 2 | 1 | 2 | 23 | 23 | 4th | Vitali Stain | Ivan Prokic |

**Serbia—World Championship (Men)**

| Year Event | GP | W | OTW | OTL | L | GF | GA | Place | Coach | Captain |
|---|---|---|---|---|---|---|---|---|---|---|
| 2007 WM-II-A | 5 | 2 | 0 | 0 | 3 | 18 | 16 | 4th | Andrei Brodnik | Nenad Milinkovic |
| 2008 WM-II-A | 5 | 3 | 0 | 1 | 1 | 32 | 19 | 3rd | Adam Shell | Aleksandr Kosic |
| 2009 WM-II-A | 5 | 4 | 1 | 0 | 0 | 40 | 11 | 1st | Dave Hyrsky | Aleksandr Kosic |
| 2010 WM-I-A | 5 | 0 | 0 | 1 | 4 | 8 | 46 | 6th | Mark Pederson | Aleksandr Kosic |
| 2011 WM-II-A | 5 | 3 | 0 | 0 | 2 | 22 | 11 | 3rd | Pavle Kavcic | Marko Kovacevic |
| 2012 WM-II-A | 5 | 1 | 0 | 0 | 4 | 27 | 20 | 5th | Pavel Kavcic | Marko Kovacevic |

**Yugoslavia—U20 World Championship**

| Year Event | GP | W | T | L | GF | GA | Place | Coach | Captain |
|---|---|---|---|---|---|---|---|---|---|
| 1981 WM20-B | 5 | 1 | 1 | 3 | 20 | 27 | 6th | Rudi Hiti | Pajic Murajica |
| 1982 WM20-B | 4 | 0 | 0 | 4 | 12 | 28 | 8th | Janez Albreht | Bojan Kelih |
| 1987 WM20-C | 5 | 5 | 0 | 0 | 56 | 12 | 1st | Bogdan Jakobic | Andrej Jovanovic |
| 1988 WM20-B | 7 | 3 | 1 | 3 | 37 | 36 | 6th | Ciril Vister | *unknown* |
| 1989 WM20-B | 7 | 4 | 0 | 3 | 42 | 40 | 5th | Vojin Koljensic | Andrej Brodnik |
| 1990 WM20-B | 7 | 0 | 1 | 6 | 24 | 55 | 8th | Aci Ferjanic | Andrej Brodnik |
| 1991 WM20-C | 7 | 5 | 1 | 1 | 77 | 21 | 3rd | Bostjan Lesnjak | Roman Vrscaj |
| 1992 WM20-C | 3 | 1 | 1 | 1 | 11 | 16 | 7th | Rasid Semsedinovic | Aleksandr Kosic |
| 1995 WM20-C-2 | 5 | 0 | 1 | 4 | 13 | 62 | 6th | Aleksandr Yermakov | Ivan Prokic |
| 1996 WM20-D | 3 | 2 | 0 | 1 | 15 | 9 | 3rd | Rasid Semsedinovic | *unknown* |
| 1997 WM20-D | 4 | 3 | 0 | 1 | 26 | 13 | 3rd | Rasid Semsedinovic | Jovica Rus |
| 1998 WM20-D | 4 | 3 | 0 | 1 | 32 | 7 | 3rd | Milorad Vjestica | *unknown* |
| 1999 WM20-D | 4 | 4 | 0 | 0 | 30 | 4 | 1st | Rasid Semsedinovic | Dejan Pavicevic |
| 2000 WM20-C | 4 | 0 | 1 | 3 | 8 | 25 | 8th | Rasid Semsedinovic | Csaba Prokec |
| 2001 WM20-III | 4 | 2 | 0 | 2 | 23 | 14 | 4th | Rasid Semsedinovic | Nemanja Nikolic |
| 2002 WM20-III | 4 | 3 | 0 | 1 | 27 | 12 | 3rd | Alex Andjelic | Igor Molnar |
| 2003 WM20-IIB | 5 | 3 | 0 | 2 | 27 | 22 | 3rd | Igor Kosovic | Boris Gabric |

**Serbia & Montenegro—U20 World Championship**

| Year Event | GP | W | T | L | GF | GA | Place | Coach | Captain |
|---|---|---|---|---|---|---|---|---|---|
| 2004 WM20-IIB | 5 | 2 | 0 | 3 | 15 | 21 | 4th | Nenad Milinkovic | Bojan Jankovic |
| 2005 WM20-IIA | 5 | 1 | 0 | 4 | 11 | 36 | 5th | Dusan Rudan | Dejan Pajic |
| 2006 WM20-IIB | 5 | 2 | 1 | 2 | 14 | 16 | 4th | Rasid Semsedinovic | Nenad Rakovic |

**Serbia—U20 World Championship**

| Year Event | GP | W | OTW | OTL | L | GF | GA | Place | Coach | Captain |
|---|---|---|---|---|---|---|---|---|---|---|
| 2007 WM20-IIB | 5 | 1 | 0 | 0 | 4 | 12 | 34 | 6th | Rasid Semsedinovic | Nikola Dunda |
| 2008 WM20-III | 6 | 5 | 0 | 0 | 1 | 55 | 7 | 2nd | Mike Brewer | Milos Babic |
| 2009 WM20-IIA | 5 | 0 | 1 | 1 | 3 | 10 | 33 | 5th | Gorazd Hiti | Oliver Varga |
| 2010 WM20-IIB | 5 | 0 | 1 | 0 | 4 | 17 | 28 | 6th | Fred Perowne | Stefan Ilic |
| 2011 WM20-III | 6 | 5 | 0 | 0 | 1 | 56 | 8 | 2nd | Dusan Rudan | Mihajlo Korac |
| 2012 WM20-II-B | 5 | 3 | 0 | 0 | 2 | 18 | 26 | 3rd | Jovica Rus | Aleksa Lukovic |

**Yugoslavia—U18 World Championship (Men)**

| Year Event | GP | W | T | L | GF | GA | Place | Coach | Captain |
|---|---|---|---|---|---|---|---|---|---|
| 2001 WM18-III | 4 | 1 | 0 | 3 | 11 | 15 | 7th | Dusan Rudan | Dejan Bugarski |
| 2002 WM18-III | 4 | 3 | 0 | 1 | 43 | 16 | 2nd | Dave Hyrsky | Nebojsa Banovic |
| 2003 WM18-II-B | 5 | 2 | 1 | 2 | 14 | 19 | 4th | Dusan Rudan | Marko Kovacevic |

**Serbia & Montenegro—U18 World Championship (Men)**

| Year Event | GP | W | T | L | GF | GA | Place | Coach | Captain |
|---|---|---|---|---|---|---|---|---|---|
| 2004 WM18-II-B | 5 | 1 | 0 | 4 | 12 | 26 | 5th | Dusan Rudan | Marko Savic |
| 2005 WM18-II-A | 5 | 1 | 0 | 4 | 21 | 20 | 5th | Dusan Rudan | Marko Sretovic |
| 2006 WM18-II-A | 5 | 1 | 0 | 4 | 15 | 26 | 5th | Rasid Semsedinovic | Marko Milovanovic |

**Serbia—U18 World Championship (Men)**

| Year Event | GP | W | OTW | OTL | L | GF | GA | Place | Coach | Captain |
|---|---|---|---|---|---|---|---|---|---|---|
| 2007 WM18-II-B | 5 | 0 | 0 | 1 | 4 | 10 | 29 | 6th | Vitali Stain | Dragan Komazec |
| 2008 WM18-III-B | 4 | 4 | 0 | 0 | 0 | 45 | 0 | 1st | Michael Brewer | Stefan Ilic |
| 2009 WM18-II-B | 5 | 1 | 0 | 1 | 3 | 16 | 35 | 5th | Aleksandar Protic | Aleksa Despotovic |
| 2010 WM18-II-A | 5 | 1 | 0 | 1 | 3 | 11 | 19 | 4th | Fred Perowne | Mihajlo Korac |
| 2011 WM18-II-A | 5 | 1 | 0 | 0 | 4 | 6 | 43 | 5th | Nenad Ilic | Dimitrije Filipovic |
| 2012 WM18-II-B | 5 | 3 | 0 | 0 | 2 | 22 | 16 | 2nd | Aleksandar Andjelic | Nikola Kerezovic |

# Singapore (SIN)

Singapore participated in the 2010 IIHF Challenge Cup of Asia in Taipei City, Chinese Taipei. Photo: Fion Hsu.

**Joined IIHF: May 2, 1996 (Associate Member)**
Website: www.singaporeicehockey.com
E-mail: hockeysingapore@gmail.com

Singapore Ice Hockey Association
5 Mount Faber Road
Blk 5 #01-12 The Pearl
Singapore 099197
Singapore

Phone: +65 - 9680-2025

**Top Level Host History** none

# Slovakia (SVK)

The Slovak national team stands for their nation anthem after defeating Canada in the quarter-finals of the 2012 IIHF Ice Hockey World Championship. Photo: Jeff Vinnick / HHOF-IIHF Images.

**Joined IIHF: Bohemia, later Czechoslovakia, joined November 15, 1908; Czech Republic & Slovakia replaced Czechoslovakia on April 28, 1993**
Website: www.hockeyslovakia.sk
E-mail: international@szlh.sk

Slovensky Zvaz Ladoveho Hokeja
Trnavska cesta 27/B
831 04 Bratislava
Slovakia

Phone: +421 232 340 901 • Fax: +421 232 340 921

| World Ranking | | | |
|---|---|---|---|
| MEN | | WOMEN | |
| 2012 | 6 | 2012 | 7 |
| 2011 | 10 | 2011 | 8 |
| 2010 | 8 | 2010 | 10 |
| 2009 | 9 | 2009 | 15 |
| 2008 | 8 | 2008 | 17 |
| 2007 | 6 | 2007 | 18 |
| 2006 | 6 | 2006 | 19 |
| 2005 | 4 | 2005 | 18 |
| 2004 | 3 | 2004 | 18 |

**Top Level Host History**
World Championship (Men): 2011 (Bratislava, Kosice)
U18 World Championship (Men): 2002 (Trnava, Piestany)

**Olympics, Men**
(bold=top level)

| Year Event | GP | W | T | | L | GF | GA | Place | Coach | Captain |
|---|---|---|---|---|---|---|---|---|---|---|
| Year Event | GP | W | OTW | OTL | L | GF | GA | Place | Coach | Captain |
| **1994 OG-M** | **8** | **4** | **2** | | **2** | **35** | **29** | **6th** | **Julius Supler** | **Peter Stastny** |
| **1998 OG-M** | **4** | **1** | **1** | | **2** | **11** | **13** | **10th** | **Frantisek Hossa** | **Zdeno Ciger** |
| **2002 OG-M** | **4** | **1** | **1** | | **2** | **15** | **13** | **13th** | **Jan Filc** | **Robert Petrovicky (1)** |
| **2006 OG-M** | **6** | **5** | **0** | | **1** | **19** | **11** | **5th** | **Frantisek Hossa** | **Pavol Demitra** |
| **2010 OG-M** | **7** | **3** | **1** | **0** | **3** | **22** | **18** | **4th** | **Jan Filc** | **Zdeno Chara** |

(1) Pavol Demitra captain vs. Latvia (Feb. 10)

**World Championship (Men)**
(bold=top level)

| Year Event | GP | W | T | | L | GF | GA | Place | Coach | Captain |
|---|---|---|---|---|---|---|---|---|---|---|
| Year Event | GP | W | OTW | OTL | L | GF | GA | Place | Coach | Captain |
| 1994 WM-C | 6 | 4 | 2 | | 0 | 43 | 3 | 1st | Julius Supler | Miroslav Marcinko |
| 1995 WM-B | 7 | 7 | 0 | | 0 | 60 | 15 | 1st | Julius Supler | Peter Stastny |
| **1996 WM** | **5** | **1** | **1** | | **3** | **13** | **16** | **10th** | **Julius Supler** | **Oto Hascak** |
| **1997 WM** | **8** | **3** | **1** | | **4** | **20** | **23** | **9th** | **Jozef Golonka** | **Zdeno Ciger** |
| **1998 WM** | **6** | **2** | **2** | | **2** | **11** | **12** | **7th** | **Jan Sterbak** | **Zdeno Ciger** |
| **1999 WM** | **6** | **2** | **1** | | **3** | **22** | **21** | **7th** | **Jan Sterbak** | **Zdeno Ciger** |
| **2000 WM** | **9** | **5** | **1** | | **3** | **34** | **22** | **S** | **Jan Filc** | **Miroslav Satan** |
| **2001 WM** | **7** | **3** | **0** | | **4** | **20** | **18** | **7th** | **Jan Filc** | **Zdeno Chara** |
| **2002 WM** | **9** | **8** | **0** | | **1** | **37** | **22** | **G** | **Jan Filc** | **Miroslav Satan (1)** |
| **2003 WM** | **9** | **7** | **1** | | **1** | **45** | **17** | **B** | **Frantisek Hossa** | **Miroslav Satan** |
| **2004 WM** | **9** | **5** | **2** | | **2** | **24** | **9** | **4th** | **Frantisek Hossa** | **Miroslav Satan** |
| **2005 WM** | **7** | **4** | **1** | | **2** | **24** | **17** | **5th** | **Frantisek Hossa** | **Miroslav Satan** |
| **2006 WM** | **7** | **3** | **1** | | **3** | **26** | **14** | **8th** | **Frantisek Hossa** | **Marian Hossa** |
| **2007 WM** | **7** | **4** | **0** | **0** | **3** | **25** | **22** | **6th** | **Julius Supler** | **Miroslav Satan** |

| | | | | | | | | | | |
|---|---|---|---|---|---|---|---|---|---|---|
| **2008 WM** | **5** | **2** | **1** | **0** | **2** | **18** | **12** | **13th** | **Julius Supler** | **Robert Petrovicky** |
| **2009 WM** | **6** | **1** | **1** | **2** | **2** | **12** | **24** | **10th** | **Jan Filc** | **Lubos Bartecko** |
| **2010 WM** | **6** | **2** | **0** | **0** | **4** | **13** | **19** | **12th** | **Glen Hanlon** | **Richard Lintner** |
| **2011 WM** | **6** | **2** | **0** | **0** | **4** | **16** | **15** | **10th** | **Glen Hanlon** | **Pavol Demitra** |
| **2012 WM** | **10** | **7** | **0** | **0** | **3** | **30** | **23** | **S** | **Vladimir Vujtek** | **Zdeno Chara** |

(1) Lubomir Bartecko captain vs. Russia (May 6)

### IIHF-NHL Invitationals

(bold=top level)

| Year Event | GP | W | T | L | GF | GA | Place | Coach | Captain |
|---|---|---|---|---|---|---|---|---|---|
| **1996 WCH** | **3** | **0** | **0** | **3** | **9** | **19** | **7th** | **Jozef Golonka** | **Peter Bondra** |
| **2004 WCH** | **4** | **0** | **0** | **4** | **5** | **18** | **7th** | **Jan Filc** | **Miroslav Satan** |

### U20 World Championship

(bold=top level)

| Year Event | GP | W | T | | L | GF | GA | Place | Coach | Captain |
|---|---|---|---|---|---|---|---|---|---|---|
| Year Event | GP | W | OTW | OTL | L | GF | GA | Place | Coach | Captain |
| 1994 WM20-C | 4 | 4 | 0 | | 0 | 55 | 3 | 1st | *unknown* | *unknown* |
| 1995 WM20-B | 7 | 5 | 0 | | 2 | 33 | 16 | 2nd | Dusan Ziska | Radoslav Kropak |
| **1996 WM20** | **6** | **2** | **3** | | **1** | **24** | **23** | **7th** | **Julius Supler** | **Lubomir Visnovsky** |
| **1997 WM20** | **6** | **2** | **0** | | **4** | **23** | **26** | **6th** | **Frantisek Hossa** | **Richard Lintner** |
| **1998 WM20** | **6** | **3** | **0** | | **3** | **26** | **18** | **9th** | **Dusan Ziska** | **Marian Cisar** |
| **1999 WM20** | **6** | **4** | **1** | | **1** | **17** | **14** | **B** | **Jan Filc** | **Ladislav Nagy** |
| **2000 WM20** | **6** | **1** | **1** | | **4** | **11** | **15** | **9th** | **Dusan Ziska** | **Miroslav Zalesak** |
| **2001 WM20** | **7** | **1** | **0** | | **6** | **16** | **25** | **8th** | **Jan Selvek** | **Rene Vydareny** |
| **2002 WM20** | **7** | **2** | **2** | | **3** | **20** | **19** | **8th** | **Julius Supler** | **Frantisek Skladany** |
| **2003 WM20** | **6** | **3** | **0** | | **3** | **17** | **14** | **5th** | **Robert Spisak** | **Ivan Kolozvary** |
| **2004 WM20** | **6** | **2** | **1** | | **3** | **13** | **14** | **6th** | **Jozef Fruhauf** | **Richard Stehlik** |
| **2005 WM20** | **6** | **4** | **0** | | **2** | **15** | **13** | **7th** | **Dusan Gregor** | **Andrej Meszaros** |
| **2006 WM20** | **6** | **2** | **1** | | **3** | **19** | **27** | **8th** | **Branislav Sajban** | **Andrej Sekera** |
| **2007 WM20** | **6** | **1** | **0** | **0** | **5** | **16** | **21** | **8th** | **Jan Jasko** | **David Buc** |
| **2008 WM20** | **6** | **3** | **0** | **0** | **3** | **22** | **16** | **7th** | **Stefan Mikes** | **Erik Caladi** |
| **2009 WM20** | **7** | **2** | **1** | **0** | **4** | **22** | **28** | **4th** | **Stefan Mikes** | **Marek Mertel** |
| **2010 WM20** | **6** | **2** | **0** | **0** | **4** | **19** | **29** | **8th** | **Stefan Mikes** | **Jakub Gasparovic** |
| **2011 WM20** | **6** | **1** | **1** | **0** | **4** | **14** | **24** | **8th** | **Stefan Mikes** | **Richard Panik** |
| **2012 WM20** | **6** | **2** | **0** | **0** | **4** | **18** | **30** | **6th** | **Ernest Bokros** | **Tomas Matousek** |

### U18 World Championship (Men)

(bold=top level)

| Year Event | GP | W | T | | L | GF | GA | Place | Coach | Captain |
|---|---|---|---|---|---|---|---|---|---|---|
| Year Event | GP | W | OTW | OTL | L | GF | GA | Place | Coach | Captain |
| **1999 WM18** | **7** | **5** | **0** | | **2** | **26** | **17** | **B** | **Miroslav Kimijan** | **Rene Vydareny** |
| **2000 WM18** | **6** | **3** | **0** | | **3** | **16** | **16** | **5th** | **Miroslav Kimijan** | **Marian Gaborik** |
| **2001 WM18** | **6** | **1** | **1** | | **4** | **19** | **24** | **8th** | **Jan Simcik** | **Tomas Slovak** |
| **2002 WM18** | **8** | **3** | **0** | | **5** | **18** | **25** | **8th** | **Igor Toth** | **Richard Stehlik** |
| **2003 WM18** | **7** | **5** | **0** | | **2** | **22** | **14** | **S** | **Jindrich Novotny** | **Andrej Meszaros** |
| **2004 WM18** | **6** | **1** | **3** | | **2** | **18** | **15** | **6th** | **Jindrich Novotny** | **Andrej Sekera** |
| **2005 WM18** | **6** | **2** | **0** | | **4** | **11** | **19** | **6th** | **Jozef Cepan** | **Marek Bartanus** |
| **2006 WM18** | **6** | **2** | **0** | | **4** | **13** | **19** | **7th** | **Jozef Fruhauf** | **Erik Caladi** |
| **2007 WM18** | **6** | **3** | **0** | **1** | **2** | **15** | **18** | **5th** | **Tibor Danis** | **Milan Kytnar** |
| **2008 WM18** | **6** | **3** | **0** | **1** | **2** | **22** | **22** | **7th** | **Jozef Cepan** | **Adam Lapsansky** |
| **2009 WM18** | **6** | **2** | **0** | **1** | **3** | **15** | **35** | **7th** | **Peter Bohunicky** | **Andrej Stastny** |
| **2010 WM18** | **6** | **2** | **0** | **0** | **4** | **17** | **20** | **8th** | **Andrej Vyboh** | **Martin Marincin** |
| **2011 WM18** | **6** | **1** | **0** | **0** | **5** | **14** | **29** | **10th** | **Jozef Fruhauf** | **Peter Ceresnak** |
| 2012 WM18-I-A | 5 | 5 | 0 | 0 | 0 | 30 | 6 | 1st | Ernest Bokros | Milan Kolena |

### Olympics, Women

(bold=top level)

| Year Event | GP | W | OTW | OTL | L | GF | GA | Place | Coach | Captain |
|---|---|---|---|---|---|---|---|---|---|---|
| **2010 OG-W** | **5** | **0** | **0** | **0** | **5** | **7** | **36** | **8th** | **Miroslav Karafiat** | **Iveta Karafiatova** |

### Women's World Championship

(bold=top level)

| Year Event | GP | W | T | | L | GF | GA | Place | Coach | Captain |
|---|---|---|---|---|---|---|---|---|---|---|
| Year Event | GP | W | OTW | OTL | L | GF | GA | Place | Coach | Captain |
| 1999 WW-B | 5 | 2 | 0 | | 3 | 14 | 23 | 7th | Jaroslav Hrabcak | Slavka Kollarova |
| 2003 WW-II | 5 | 2 | 2 | | 1 | 23 | 7 | 3rd | Jan Kis | Martina Kisova |
| 2004 WW-II | 5 | 3 | 1 | | 1 | 28 | 7 | 3rd | Jan Kis | Gabriela Sabolova |
| 2005 WW-II | 5 | 4 | 0 | | 1 | 16 | 8 | 3rd | Miroslav Karafiat | *unknown* |
| 2007 WW-II | 5 | 5 | 0 | 0 | 0 | 25 | 3 | 1st | Miroslav Karafiat | Zuzana Moravcikova |
| 2008 WW-I | 5 | 3 | 1 | 0 | 1 | 14 | 11 | 2nd | Miroslav Karafiat | Zuzana Moravcikova |
| 2009 WW-I | 5 | 4 | 0 | 0 | 1 | 22 | 14 | 1st | Miroslav Karafiat | Zuzana Moravcikova |
| **2011 WW** | **5** | **1** | **1** | **0** | **3** | **4** | **13** | **7th** | **Miroslav Karafiat** | **Iveta Karafiatova** |
| **2012 WW** | **5** | **1** | **0** | **1** | **3** | **8** | **14** | **8th** | **Miroslav Karafiat** | **Jana Kapustova** |

### U18 Women's World Championship

(bold=top level)

| Year Event | GP | W | OTW | OTL | L | GF | GA | Place | Coach | Captain |
|---|---|---|---|---|---|---|---|---|---|---|
| 2009 WW18-I | 4 | 2 | 0 | 1 | 1 | 11 | 14 | 3rd | Miroslav Karafiat | Nicol Cupkova |
| 2010 WW18-I | 5 | 3 | 0 | 0 | 2 | 17 | 9 | 3rd | Igor Andrejkovic | Nicol Cupkova |
| 2011 WW18-I | 5 | 4 | 0 | 0 | 1 | 19 | 11 | 2nd | Stanislav Kubus | Alica Mihalicova |
| 2012 WW18-I | 5 | 0 | 0 | 0 | 5 | 5 | 29 | 6th | Stanislav Kubus | Denisa Lalikova |

# Slovenia (SLO)

*Slovenian goalie Robert Kristan and his teammate celebrate promotion to the top division. Photo: Samo Vidic.*

## Joined IIHF: May 6, 1992

(Croatia and Slovenia split from Yugoslavia (joined IIHF in 1939) on June 25, 1991; Yugoslavia became Serbia & Montenegro in 2004; became Serbia on September 28, 2006 after Serbia and Montenegro split and only Serbia maintained IIHF membership status)

Website: www.hokejska-zveza.si
E-mail: hzs@hokejska-zveza.si

Ice Hockey Federation of Slovenia
Celovska 25
1000 Ljubljana
Slovenia

Phone: +386 1 430 64 80 • Fax: +386 1 231 31 21

**World Ranking**

| MEN | | WOMEN | |
|---|---|---|---|
| 2012 | 18 | 2012 | 20 |
| 2011 | 18 | 2011 | 19 |
| 2010 | 19 | 2010 | 19 |
| 2009 | 17 | 2009 | 22 |
| 2008 | 15 | 2008 | 16 |
| 2007 | 18 | 2007 | 16 |
| 2006 | 18 | 2006 | 16 |
| 2005 | 16 | 2005 | 21 |
| 2004 | 16 | 2004 | 24 |

### Top Level Host History

Olympics: 1984 (Sarajevo, YUG)
World Championship (Men): 1966 (Ljubljana, YUG)

### World Championship (Men)

(bold=top level)

| Year Event | GP | W | T | | L | GF | GA | Place | Coach | Captain |
|---|---|---|---|---|---|---|---|---|---|---|
| Year Event | GP | W | OTW | OTL | L | GF | GA | Place | Coach | Captain |
| 1993 WM-C | 7 | 5 | 0 | | 2 | 78 | 16 | 4th | Rudi Hiti | Dragutin Mlinarec |
| 1994 WM-C | 6 | 2 | 0 | | 4 | 26 | 27 | 5th | Rudi Hiti | Dragutin Mlinarec |
| 1995 WM-C-1 | 4 | 2 | 0 | | 2 | 28 | 15 | 7th | Rudi Hiti | Nik Zupancic |
| 1996 WM-C | 7 | 5 | 0 | | 2 | 41 | 19 | 3rd | Vladimir Krikunov | Nik Zupancic |
| 1997 WM-C | 5 | 3 | 1 | | 1 | 25 | 8 | 2nd | Pavle Kavcic | Tomaz Vnuk |
| 1998 WM-B | 7 | 5 | 1 | | 1 | 28 | 15 | 2nd | Pavle Kavcic | Bojan Zajc |
| 1999 WM-B | 7 | 2 | 1 | | 4 | 14 | 17 | 5th | Pavle Kavcic | Bojan Zajc |
| 2000 WM-B | 7 | 0 | 2 | | 5 | 16 | 31 | 7th | Rudi Hiti | Bojan Zajc |
| 2001 WM-I-B | 5 | 4 | 1 | | 0 | 44 | 6 | 1st | Matjaz Sekelj | Tomaz Vnuk |
| **2002 WM** | **6** | **3** | **0** | | **3** | **18** | **26** | **13th** | **Matjaz Sekelj** | **Tomaz Vnuk** |
| **2003 WM** | **6** | **0** | **1** | | **5** | **12** | **37** | **15th** | **Matjaz Sekelj** | **Tomaz Vnuk** |
| 2004 WM-I-B | 5 | 5 | 0 | | 0 | 33 | 5 | 1st | Kari Savolainen | Tomaz Vnuk |
| **2005 WM** | **6** | **2** | **0** | | **4** | **12** | **32** | **13th** | **Kari Savolainen** | **Robert Ciglenecki** |
| **2006 WM** | **6** | **0** | **2** | | **4** | **14** | **26** | **16th** | **Frantisek Vyborny** | **Dejan Varl** |
| 2007 WM-I-B | 5 | 5 | 0 | 0 | 0 | 29 | 5 | 1st | Ted Sator | Marcel Rodman |
| **2008 WM** | **5** | **0** | **0** | **1** | **4** | **6** | **22** | **15th** | **Mats Waltin** | **Marcel Rodman** |
| 2009 WM-I-A | 5 | 4 | 0 | 0 | 1 | 21 | 7 | 2nd | John Harrington | Tomaz Razingar |
| 2010 WM-I-B | 5 | 4 | 1 | 0 | 0 | 29 | 10 | 1st | John Harrington | Tomaz Razingar |
| **2011 WM** | **6** | **1** | **0** | **1** | **4** | **15** | **24** | **16th** | **Matjaz Kopitar** | **Tomaz Razingar** |
| 2012 WM-I-A | 5 | 5 | 0 | 0 | 0 | 17 | 9 | 1st | Matjaz Kopitar | Tomaz Razingar |

### U20 World Championship

| Year Event | GP | W | T | | L | GF | GA | Place | Coach | Captain |
|---|---|---|---|---|---|---|---|---|---|---|
| Year Event | GP | W | OTW | OTL | L | GF | GA | Place | Coach | Captain |
| 1995 WM20-C-2 | 5 | 3 | 2 | | 0 | 40 | 15 | 2nd | Vladimir Krikunov | M Poljanshek |
| 1996 WM20-C | 4 | 3 | 0 | | 1 | 27 | 11 | 2nd | Vladimir Krikunov | Grega Krajnc |
| 1997 WM20-C | 4 | 3 | 0 | | 1 | 24 | 14 | 2nd | Frantisek Vyborny | Miha Rebolj |
| 1998 WM20-C | 4 | 3 | 0 | | 1 | 19 | 10 | 3rd | Frantisek Vyborny | Tomaz Razingar |
| 1999 WM20-C | 4 | 3 | 0 | | 1 | 19 | 11 | 3rd | Edvard Hafner | Tomaz Razingar |
| 2000 WM20-C | 4 | 2 | 1 | | 1 | 14 | 13 | 2nd | Branko Terglav | Edo Terglav |
| 2001 WM20-II | 4 | 4 | 0 | | 0 | 21 | 7 | 1st | Gorazd Hiti | Davor Durakovic |
| 2002 WM20-I | 5 | 1 | 1 | | 3 | 17 | 27 | 6th | Gorazd Hiti | Damjan Dervaric |
| 2003 WM20-I-B | 5 | 3 | 1 | | 1 | 15 | 14 | 2nd | Gorazd Hiti | Martin Markoja |
| 2004 WM20-I-A | 5 | 3 | 0 | | 2 | 18 | 19 | 3rd | Gorazd Hiti | Andrej Hebar |
| 2005 WM20-I-B | 5 | 3 | 0 | | 2 | 28 | 12 | 2nd | Gorazd Drinovec | Ziga Pavlin |
| 2006 WM20-I-A | 5 | 3 | 0 | | 2 | 17 | 8 | 3rd | Gorazd Drinovec | Anze Ahacic |
| 2007 WM20-I-A | 5 | 1 | 0 | 0 | 4 | 12 | 19 | 5th | Jozef Petho | Klemen Zbontar |
| 2008 WM20-I-B | 5 | 3 | 1 | 0 | 1 | 17 | 8 | 3rd | Valerij Sahraj | Luka Tosic |
| 2009 WM20-I-A | 5 | 2 | 0 | 0 | 3 | 31 | 17 | 4th | Andrej Brodnik | Ziga Pance |
| 2010 WM20-I-A | 5 | 2 | 1 | 0 | 2 | 8 | 12 | 3rd | Joseph-Dany Gelinas | Blaz Gregorc |
| 2011 WM20-I-B | 5 | 4 | 0 | 0 | 1 | 31 | 14 | 2nd | Gorazd Drinovec | Eric Pance |
| 2012 WM20-I-A | 5 | 1 | 2 | 0 | 2 | 16 | 12 | 4th | Gorazd Drinovec | Gasper Kopitar |

### U18 World Championship (Men)

| Year Event | GP | W | T | | L | GF | GA | Place | Coach | Captain |
|---|---|---|---|---|---|---|---|---|---|---|
| Year Event | GP | W | OTW | OTL | L | GF | GA | Place | Coach | Captain |
| 2001 WM18-II | 4 | 4 | 0 | | 0 | 36 | 4 | 1st | Gorazd Hiti | Martin Markoja |
| 2002 WM18-I | 5 | 3 | 1 | | 1 | 16 | 13 | 2nd | Gorazd Hiti | Andrej Hebar |
| 2003 WM18-I-A | 5 | 3 | 0 | | 2 | 24 | 27 | 3rd | Gorazd Hiti | Anze Gogala |
| 2004 WM18-I-A | 5 | 3 | 1 | | 1 | 20 | 13 | 2nd | Gorazd Drinovec | Anze Ahacic |
| 2005 WM18-I-A | 5 | 3 | 0 | | 2 | 22 | 14 | 2nd | Jan Vidner | Matevs Benedik |
| 2006 WM18-I-A | 5 | 4 | 0 | | 1 | 19 | 12 | 2nd | Valerij Sahraj | Klemen Sodrznik |
| 2007 WM18-I-A | 5 | 3 | 0 | 1 | 1 | 23 | 20 | 2nd | Igor Beribak | Anze Ropret |
| 2008 WM18-I-A | 5 | 1 | 0 | 0 | 4 | 15 | 24 | 6th | Mitja Kern | *unknown* |

| 2009 WM18-II-A | 5 | 4 | 0 | 0 | 1 | 42 | 5 | 2nd | Iztok Petelin | Gregor Rezek |
|---|---|---|---|---|---|---|---|---|---|---|
| 2010 WM18-II-B | 5 | 5 | 0 | 0 | 0 | 63 | 4 | 1st | Dany Gelinas | Gal Koren |
| 2011 WM18-I-B | 5 | 4 | 0 | 0 | 1 | 18 | 14 | 2nd | Bojan Zajc | Miha Pesjak |
| 2012 WM18-I-A | 5 | 1 | 1 | 0 | 3 | 12 | 21 | 5th | Valerij Sahraj | Jurij Repe |

**Women's World Championship**

| Year Event | GP | W | T | | L | GF | GA | Place | Coach | Captain |
|---|---|---|---|---|---|---|---|---|---|---|
| Year Event | GP | W | OTW | OTL | L | GF | GA | Place | Coach | Captain |
| 2003 WW-III | 5 | 3 | 2 | | 0 | 20 | 8 | 2nd | Andrej Verlic | Jasmina Rosar |
| 2004 WW-III | 5 | 4 | 0 | | 1 | 28 | 8 | 2nd | Andrej Verlic | *unknown* |
| 2005 WW-III | 5 | 5 | 0 | | 0 | 41 | 8 | 1st | Andrej Verlic | Jasmina Rosar |
| 2007 WW-II | 5 | 0 | 0 | 1 | 4 | 5 | 30 | 6th | Andrej Verlic | Jasmina Rosar |
| 2008 WW-III | 5 | 4 | 0 | 1 | 0 | 27 | 6 | 2nd | Andrej Verlic | Jasmina Rosar |
| 2011 WW-III | 5 | 2 | 0 | 1 | 2 | 19 | 16 | 4th | Andrej Verlic | Barbara Kavcic |
| 2012 WW-II-A | 5 | 0 | 1 | 0 | 4 | 7 | 18 | 5th | Gorazd Rekelj | Metka Manfreda |

# South Africa (RSA)

*The South African women's national team players shake hands with the Polish players. Photo: KIHA.*

## Joined IIHF: February 25, 1937

Website: www.saicehockey.org.za
E-mail: elsabe.stockhoff@bmw.co.za

South African Ice Hockey Association
PO Box 34474
Erasmia
0023
South Africa

Phone: +27 12 522 2494 • Fax: +27 86 501 1780

**World Ranking**

| MEN | | WOMEN | |
|---|---|---|---|
| 2012 | 41 | 2012 | 32 |
| 2011 | 42 | 2011 | 31 |
| 2010 | 42 | 2010 | 32 |
| 2009 | 40 | 2009 | 31 |
| 2008 | 42 | 2008 | 28 |
| 2007 | 41 | 2007 | 28 |
| 2006 | 41 | 2006 | 28 |
| 2005 | 40 | 2005 | 28 |
| 2004 | 38 | 2004 | 28 |

**Top Level Host History** none

**World Championship (Men)**

| Year Event | GP | W | T | | L | GF | GA | Place | Coach | Captain |
|---|---|---|---|---|---|---|---|---|---|---|
| Year Event | GP | W | OTW | OTL | L | GF | GA | Place | Coach | Captain |
| 1961 WM-C | 5 | 1 | 0 | | 4 | 18 | 47 | 5th | Tommy Durling | *unknown* |
| 1966 WM-C | 4 | 0 | 0 | | 4 | 4 | 50 | 3rd | Cobie Grobler/Gunther Wodak | Edmund Lucas |
| 1992 WM-C-2 | 5 | 4 | 0 | | 1 | 55 | 18 | 2nd | Denis Anderson | *unknown* |
| 1993 WM-C | 5 | 0 | 0 | | 5 | 8 | 100 | 12th | Edward Lawrence | Andy Milne |
| 1994 WM-C-2 | 5 | 0 | 0 | | 5 | 8 | 62 | 8th | Jim Fuyarchuk | *unknown* |
| 1995 WM-C-2 | 6 | 1 | 0 | | 5 | 14 | 49 | 8th | Ted Lawrence | Alan Verwey |
| 1998 WM-D | 5 | 3 | 0 | | 2 | 32 | 20 | 5th | Ted Lawrence | Alan Verwey |
| 1999 WM-D | 4 | 2 | 0 | | 2 | 24 | 14 | 5th | Igor Zajec | Alan Verwey |
| 2000 WM-D | 4 | 3 | 0 | | 1 | 26 | 19 | 4th | Ted Lawrence | Alan Verwey |
| 2001 WM-II-A | 5 | 2 | 0 | | 3 | 17 | 48 | 4th | Ted Lawrence | Dan van Hemert |
| 2002 WM-II-A | 5 | 1 | 0 | | 4 | 13 | 37 | 5th | Ted Lawrence | Dan van Hemert |
| 2003 WM-II-A | 5 | 1 | 0 | | 4 | 19 | 32 | 5th | Igor Zajec | Stephen Perry |
| 2004 WM-II-B | 5 | 0 | 0 | | 5 | 9 | 48 | 6th | Kristof Kovago | Andrew Boushy |
| 2005 WM-III | 4 | 3 | 0 | | 1 | 47 | 12 | 2nd | Kristof Kovago | Andrew Boushy |
| 2006 WM-II-A | 5 | 0 | 0 | | 5 | 12 | 59 | 6th | Ted Lawrence | Mike Edwards |
| 2007 WM-III | 4 | 1 | 0 | 0 | 3 | 17 | 16 | 4th | Michael Agrette | Macky Reinecke |
| 2008 WM-III | 5 | 4 | 0 | 0 | 1 | 29 | 16 | 2nd | Ronnie Wood | Andre Marais |
| 2009 WM-II-B | 5 | 0 | 0 | 0 | 5 | 8 | 54 | 6th | Ronnie Wood | Andre Marais |
| 2010 WM-III-B | 4 | 2 | 0 | 0 | 2 | 25 | 17 | 2nd | *unknown* | *unknown* |
| 2011 WM-III | 5 | 4 | 0 | 1 | 0 | 43 | 9 | 2nd | Ronnie Wood | Joaquim Valadas |
| 2012 WM-II-B | 5 | 0 | 0 | 0 | 5 | 4 | 32 | 6th | Ronald Wood | Andre Marais |

**U20 World Championship**

| Year Event | GP | W | T | | L | GF | GA | Place | Coach | Captain |
|---|---|---|---|---|---|---|---|---|---|---|
| Year Event | GP | W | OTW | OTL | L | GF | GA | Place | Coach | Captain |
| 1996 WM20-D | 3 | 0 | 0 | | 3 | 3 | 38 | 6th | Ashley Marsh | *unknown* |
| 1997 WM20-D | 4 | 1 | 0 | | 3 | 8 | 37 | 7th | Andrew Boushy | Greg Quinn |
| 1998 WM20-D | 4 | 1 | 0 | | 3 | 15 | 26 | 7th | Alan Verwey | Michael Edwards |
| 1999 WM20-D | 4 | 1 | 0 | | 3 | 13 | 22 | 6th | Igor Zajec | Gareth Reinecke |
| 2000 WM20-D | 4 | 1 | 0 | | 3 | 18 | 23 | 6th | Ronnie Wood | Philip Woolf |
| 2001 WM20-III | 4 | 0 | 1 | | 3 | 12 | 32 | 6th | Ronnie Wood | Andre Marais |
| 2002 WM20-III | 4 | 2 | 0 | | 2 | 12 | 13 | 5th | Igor Zajec | Chris Jeavons |
| 2003 WM20-II-A | 5 | 1 | 0 | | 4 | 12 | 58 | 5th | Igor Zajec | Renier Bredenhann |

| | | | | | | | | | | | |
|---|---|---|---|---|---|---|---|---|---|---|---|
| 2004 WM20-II-B | 5 | 0 | 0 | | | 5 | 4 | 56 | 6th | Kristof Kovago | Ryan Marsh |
| 2005 WM20-III | 5 | 2 | 1 | | | 2 | 15 | 24 | 4th | Kristof Kovago | Ryan Marsh |
| 2008 WM20-III | 6 | 2 | | 0 | 0 | 4 | 26 | 52 | 5th | Ronnie Wood | Chris Reeves |

**U18 World Championship (Men)**

| Year Event | GP | W | T | | | L | GF | GA | Place | Coach | Captain |
|---|---|---|---|---|---|---|---|---|---|---|---|
| Year Event | GP | W | | OTW | OTL | L | GF | GA | Place | Coach | Captain |
| 2001 WM18-III | 4 | 2 | 0 | | | 2 | 8 | 23 | 4th | Igor Zajec | David Watson |
| 2002 WM18-III | 4 | 2 | 1 | | | 1 | 16 | 28 | 5th | Kieran Edge | Burton Matthews |
| 2003 WM18-II-B | 5 | 0 | 0 | | | 5 | 9 | 33 | 6th | Igor Zajec | Burton Matthews |
| 2004 WM18-III-B | 6 | 4 | 1 | | | 1 | 40 | 11 | 2nd | Kristof Kovago | Matthew Comforth |
| 2005 WM18-II-A | 5 | 0 | 0 | | | 5 | 8 | 62 | 6th | Kristof Kovago | Jan Ashworth |
| 2006 WM18-III | 5 | 2 | 1 | | | 2 | 25 | 22 | 3rd | Alan Verwey | Grant van Eeckhoven |
| 2007 WM18-III | 5 | 1 | | 0 | 0 | 4 | 11 | 53 | 5th | Alan Verwey | Charles Strydom |
| 2008 WM18-III-A | 4 | 1 | | 0 | 0 | 3 | 18 | 26 | 4th | Lawrence Mngoma | *unknown* |
| 2009 WM18-III-A | 4 | 1 | | 0 | 0 | 3 | 19 | 32 | 4th | Ronald Wood | Bernhardt Gouws |
| 2010 WM18-III-B | 4 | 1 | | 1 | 0 | 2 | 15 | 14 | 3rd | Andre Marais | Cai Nebe |
| 2011 WM18-III-B | 4 | 2 | | 0 | 0 | 2 | 19 | 25 | 3rd | Andre Marais | Uthman Samaai |
| 2012 WM18-III | 5 | 0 | | 0 | 0 | 5 | 6 | 68 | 6th | Alan Verwey | Jacques Botha |

**Women's World Championship**

| Year Event | GP | W | T | | | L | GF | GA | Place | Coach | Captain |
|---|---|---|---|---|---|---|---|---|---|---|---|
| Year Event | GP | W | | OTW | OTL | L | GF | GA | Place | Coach | Captain |
| 2003 WW-III | 5 | 1 | 1 | | | 3 | 7 | 23 | 5th | Kristof Kovago | Nadia Kemp |
| 2005 WW-III | 5 | 0 | 0 | | | 5 | 6 | 61 | 6th | Alan Verwey | *unknown* |
| 2007 WW-III | 5 | 0 | | 0 | 0 | 5 | 4 | 77 | 6th | Adele Kohlmeyer | Sabrina Bundock |
| 2008 WW-IV | 5 | 1 | | 1 | 0 | 3 | 15 | 24 | 5th | Adele Kohlmeyer | Sabrina Bundock |
| 2011 WW-IV | 4 | 0 | | 0 | 0 | 4 | 4 | 21 | 5th | Kieren Edge | Nadine Sheffield |
| 2012 WW-II-B | 5 | 0 | | 0 | 0 | 5 | 4 | 52 | 6th | Nickolas Beukes | Nadine Sheffield |

# Spain (ESP)

*Spanish forward Desiderio Perez skates with the puck in a 2012 IIHF Ice Hockey World Championship Division I, Group A game against Croatia.*
*Photo: Kristjan Maack.*

## Joined IIHF: March 10, 1923

Website: www.fedhielo.com
E-mail: Secretaria.Hockeyhielo@fedhielo.com

Federacion Espanola Deportes De Hielo
C/ Tuset 28, 2° 1a
08006 Barcelona
Spain

Phone: +34 93 3683 761 • Fax: +34 93 3683 759

**World Ranking**

| MEN | | WOMEN | |
|---|---|---|---|
| 2012 | 29 | 2012 | 30 |
| 2011 | 29 | 2011 | 35 |
| 2010 | 30 | | |
| 2009 | 34 | | |
| 2008 | 36 | | |
| 2007 | 36 | | |
| 2006 | 37 | | |
| 2005 | 37 | | |
| 2004 | 34 | | |

**Top Level Host History** none

**World Championship (Men)**

| Year Event | GP | W | T | | | L | GF | GA | Place | Coach | Captain |
|---|---|---|---|---|---|---|---|---|---|---|---|
| Year Event | GP | W | | OTW | OTL | L | GF | GA | Place | Coach | Captain |
| 1977 WM-C | 6 | 1 | 0 | | | 5 | 17 | 61 | 5th | Tony Waldman | Frank Gonzales |
| 1978 WM-C | 7 | 1 | 0 | | | 6 | 26 | 81 | 7th | Jan Mitosinka | Frank Gonzales |
| 1979 WM-C | 7 | 2 | 0 | | | 5 | 25 | 48 | 6th | Jan Mitosinka | Frank Gonzales |
| 1982 WM-C | 7 | 1 | 0 | | | 6 | 26 | 50 | 7th | Jan Mitosinka | Frank Gonzales |
| 1983 WM-C | 7 | 1 | 1 | | | 5 | 17 | 55 | 7th | Louis Chabot | Antonio Capillas |
| 1985 WM-C | 7 | 0 | 0 | | | 7 | 9 | 55 | 8th | Carlos Gordovil | Antonio Capillas |
| 1986 WM-C | 6 | 1 | 1 | | | 4 | 19 | 47 | 8th | Carlos Gordovil | Antonio Capillas |
| 1989 WM-D | 4 | 1 | 0 | | | 3 | 29 | 27 | 4th | Jose Arbues | Antonio Capillas |
| 1990 WM-D | 4 | 0 | 2 | | | 2 | 11 | 37 | 3rd | Jacques Delorme | Luis Marcelino |
| 1992 WM-C-2 | 5 | 5 | 0 | | | 0 | 114 | 5 | 1st | Carlos Gordovil | *unknown* |
| 1993 WM-C | 6 | 1 | 0 | | | 5 | 21 | 46 | 10th | Carlos Gordovil | Miguel Baldris |
| 1994 WM-C-2 | 5 | 3 | 1 | | | 1 | 30 | 16 | 2nd | Antonio Capillas | *unknown* |
| 1995 WM-C-2 | 6 | 4 | 0 | | | 2 | 42 | 19 | 3rd | Antonio Capillas | Miguel Baldris |
| 1996 WM-D | 5 | 2 | 1 | | | 2 | 22 | 18 | 3rd | Antonio Capillas | Miguel Baldris |
| 1997 WM-D | 5 | 2 | 0 | | | 3 | 21 | 19 | 3rd | Antonio Capillas | Inaki Salegui |
| 1998 WM-C | 5 | 0 | 2 | | | 3 | 5 | 21 | 8th | Antonio Capillas | Miguel Baldris |
| 1999 WM-D | 4 | 3 | 1 | | | 0 | 38 | 7 | 1st | Antonio Capillas | Miguel Baldris |
| 2000 WM-C | 4 | 1 | 1 | | | 2 | 11 | 21 | 7th | Antonio Capillas | Miguel Baldris |

| Year Event | GP | W | T | OTW | OTL | L | GF | GA | Place | Coach | Captain |
|---|---|---|---|---|---|---|---|---|---|---|---|
| 2001 WM-II-A | 5 | 4 | 0 | | | 1 | 52 | 8 | 2nd | Antonio Capillas | Miguel Baldris |
| 2002 WM-II-B | 5 | 3 | 0 | | | 2 | 28 | 22 | 3rd | Antonio Capillas | Miguel Baldris |
| 2003 WM-II-A | 5 | 3 | 0 | | | 2 | 27 | 23 | 3rd | Inaki Bolea | Inaki Salegui |
| 2004 WM-II-A | 5 | 2 | 1 | | | 2 | 29 | 13 | 4th | Miguel Baldris | Inaki Salegui |
| 2005 WM-II-B | 5 | 1 | 0 | | | 4 | 8 | 15 | 5th | Antonio Capillas | Miguel Baldris |
| 2006 WM-II-A | 5 | 1 | 0 | | | 4 | 10 | 30 | 5th | Carlos Gordovil | Inaki Salegui |
| 2007 WM-II-A | 5 | 3 | | 0 | 0 | 2 | 25 | 17 | 3rd | Carlos Gordovil | Inaki Salegui |
| 2008 WM-II-B | 5 | 3 | | 0 | 1 | 1 | 20 | 19 | 3rd | Carlos Gordovil | Inaki Salegui |
| 2009 WM-II-B | 5 | 3 | | 0 | 0 | 2 | 28 | 15 | 3rd | Carlos Gordovil | Salvador Barnola |
| 2010 WM-II-A | 5 | 5 | | 0 | 0 | 0 | 35 | 7 | 1st | Carlos Gordovil | Salvador Barnola |
| 2011 WM-I-A | 4 | 0 | | 1 | 0 | 3 | 6 | 25 | 5th | Antoine Lucien Basile | Salvador Barnola |
| 2012 WM-II-A | 5 | 4 | | 0 | 0 | 1 | 21 | 9 | 2nd | Luciano Basile | Salvador Barnola |

## U20 World Championship

| Year Event | GP | W | T | | | L | GF | GA | Place | Coach | Captain |
|---|---|---|---|---|---|---|---|---|---|---|---|
| **Year Event** | **GP** | **W** | | **OTW** | **OTL** | **L** | **GF** | **GA** | **Place** | **Coach** | **Captain** |
| 1984 WM20-C | 5 | 2 | 1 | | | 2 | 21 | 29 | 4th | Carlos Gordovil | Alberto Platz |
| 1985 WM20-C | 4 | 0 | 0 | | | 4 | 15 | 22 | 5th | Carlos Gordovil | Alberto Platz |
| 1987 WM20-C | 5 | 1 | 0 | | | 4 | 19 | 34 | 5th | Jose Arbues | *unknown* |
| 1988 WM20-C | 7 | 2 | 1 | | | 4 | 19 | 45 | 5th | Jose Arbues | Ara Ara Javier |
| 1992 WM20-C | 4 | 3 | 0 | | | 1 | 19 | 18 | 4th | Carlos Gordovil | Jordi Lucarini |
| 1993 WM20-C | 4 | 1 | 1 | | | 2 | 17 | 26 | 7th | Jose Arbues | Alain Iturralde |
| 1994 WM20-C | 4 | 1 | 0 | | | 3 | 7 | 31 | 7th | *unknown* | *unknown* |
| 1995 WM20-C-1 | 4 | 2 | 0 | | | 2 | 9 | 19 | 5th | Antonio Capillas | Javier Cuadrado |
| 1996 WM20-C | 4 | 0 | 0 | | | 4 | 5 | 34 | 8th | Antonio Capillas | Jorge Calvo |
| 1997 WM20-D | 4 | 2 | 0 | | | 2 | 18 | 16 | 4th | Antonio Capillas | Jordi Bernet |
| 1998 WM20-D | 4 | 2 | 0 | | | 2 | 18 | 18 | 4th | Antonio Capillas | Aitor Armino |
| 1999 WM20-D | 4 | 2 | 1 | | | 1 | 16 | 15 | 4th | Antonio Capillas | Aitor Armino |
| 2000 WM20-D | 4 | 3 | 0 | | | 1 | 24 | 15 | 4th | Antonio Capillas | Lopaz Guillarmo |
| 2001 WM20-III | 4 | 3 | 0 | | | 1 | 21 | 10 | 2nd | Enrique Perez | Jon Martin |
| 2002 WM20-III | 4 | 3 | 0 | | | 1 | 21 | 19 | 2nd | Antonio Capillas | Igor Martin |
| 2003 WM20-II-B | 5 | 1 | 1 | | | 3 | 12 | 26 | 4th | Peter Oppitz | Gorka Echevarria |
| 2004 WM20-II-A | 5 | 2 | 1 | | | 2 | 21 | 32 | 4th | Antonio Capillas | Ivan Gracio |
| 2005 WM20-II-B | 5 | 2 | 0 | | | 3 | 14 | 32 | 4th | Antonio Capillas | Marc Bosom |
| 2006 WM20-II-A | 5 | 2 | 0 | | | 3 | 15 | 33 | 4th | Antonio Capillas | Desiderio Perez |
| 2007 WM20-II-A | 5 | 2 | | 0 | 0 | 3 | 16 | 30 | 4th | Carlos Gordovil | Pablo Munoz |
| 2008 WM20-II-B | 5 | 2 | | 0 | 0 | 3 | 24 | 27 | 4th | Carlos Gordovil | Adrian Betran |
| 2009 WM20-II-B | 5 | 1 | | 0 | 0 | 4 | 12 | 19 | 5th | Carlos Gordovil | Adrian Betran |
| 2010 WM20-II-A | 5 | 3 | | 0 | 1 | 1 | 30 | 17 | 3rd | Lars Lisspers | Adrian Betran |
| 2011 WM20-II-A | 5 | 3 | | 0 | 0 | 2 | 12 | 16 | 3rd | Malte Steen | Erik Michelena |
| 2012 WM20-II-A | 5 | 2 | | 0 | 0 | 3 | 14 | 22 | 4th | Lars Lisspers | Pol Gonzalez |

## U18 World Championship (Men)

| Year Event | GP | W | T | | | L | GF | GA | Place | Coach | Captain |
|---|---|---|---|---|---|---|---|---|---|---|---|
| **Year Event** | **GP** | **W** | | **OTW** | **OTL** | **L** | **GF** | **GA** | **Place** | **Coach** | **Captain** |
| 2001 WM18-III | 4 | 3 | 0 | | | 1 | 27 | 17 | 3rd | Antonio Capillas | Ivan Gracia |
| 2002 WM18-III | 4 | 2 | 1 | | | 1 | 34 | 16 | 3rd | Antonio Capillas | Ivan Garcia |
| 2003 WM18-II-A | 5 | 1 | 0 | | | 4 | 23 | 36 | 5th | Toni Vera | Diego Coscojuela |
| 2004 WM18-II-A | 5 | 1 | 1 | | | 3 | 21 | 36 | 4th | Ramon Baron | Desiderio Perez |
| 2005 WM18-II-A | 5 | 2 | 0 | | | 3 | 16 | 30 | 4th | Ramon Baron | Aitor Torres |
| 2006 WM18-II-A | 5 | 1 | 0 | | | 4 | 8 | 32 | 6th | Antonio Capillas | Marc Ribas |
| 2007 WM18-III | 5 | 5 | | 0 | 0 | 0 | 54 | 9 | 1st | Carlos Gordovil | Inigo Gorrochategui |
| 2008 WM18-II-B | 5 | 2 | | 0 | 0 | 3 | 20 | 21 | 5th | Andr Svitac | Adrian Betran |
| 2009 WM18-II-A | 5 | 1 | | 0 | 0 | 4 | 12 | 27 | 5th | Lars Lisspers | Alex Vea |
| 2010 WM18-II-B | 5 | 2 | | 1 | 0 | 2 | 17 | 22 | 3rd | Lars Lisspers | Pol Gonzalez |
| 2011 WM18-II-B | 5 | 2 | | 0 | 1 | 2 | 19 | 21 | 4th | Malte Steen | Pablo Puyuelo |
| 2012 WM18-II-B | 5 | 2 | | 1 | 0 | 2 | 21 | 18 | 3rd | Jose Antonio Rivero | Alejandro Carbonell |

## Women's World Championship

| Year Event | GP | W | OTW | OTL | L | GF | GA | Place | Coach | Captain |
|---|---|---|---|---|---|---|---|---|---|---|
| 2011 WW-V | 4 | 3 | 0 | 1 | 0 | 32 | 5 | 2nd | Sylvain Humeau | Maria Gurrea |
| 2012 WW-II-B | 5 | 4 | 0 | 0 | 1 | 22 | 5 | 2nd | Sylvain Humeau | Maria Gurrea |

# Sweden (SWE)

The Swedish U20 national team players celebrate their first World Junior gold in 31 years. Photo: Andy Devlin / HHOF-IIHF Images.

## Joined IIHF: March 23, 1912

Website: www.swehockey.se
E-mail: info@swehockey.se

Swedish Ice Hockey Association
Box 5204
Tjurhornsgrand 6
12116 Johanneshov
Sweden

Phone: +46 8 449 04 00 • Fax: +46 8 910 035

**World Ranking**

| MEN | WOMEN |
|---|---|
| 2012........4 | 2012........5 |
| 2011........3 | 2011........4 |
| 2010........3 | 2010........4 |
| 2009........3 | 2009........4 |
| 2008........3 | 2008........4 |
| 2007........1 | 2007........3 |
| 2006........1 | 2006........3 |
| 2005........2 | 2005........4 |
| 2004........2 | 2004........4 |

### Top Level Host History

World Championship (Men): 1949 (Stockholm), 1954 (Stockholm), 1963 (Stockholm), 1969 (Stockholm), 1970 (Stockholm), 1981 (Gothenburg, Stockholm), 1989 (Stockholm, Sodertalje), 1995 (Stockholm, Gavle), 2002 (Gothenburg, Karlstad, Jonkoping), 2012 (Stockholm, with Finland), 2013 (Stockholm, with Finland)
U20 World Championship: 1979 (Karlstad, Karlskoga), 1984 (Norrkoping, Nykoping), 1993 (Gavle, Falun, Bollnas, Uppsala, Hofors, Hudiksvall), 2000 (Skelleftea, Umea), 2007 (Leksand, Mora)
U18 World Championship (Men): 2006 (Angelholm, Halmstad)
Women's World Championship: 2005 (Linkoping, Norrkoping)
U18 Women's World Championship: 2011 (Stockholm)

### Olympics, Men

(bold=top level)

| Year Event | GP | W | T | | L | GF | GA | Place | Coach | Captain |
|---|---|---|---|---|---|---|---|---|---|---|
| Year Event | GP | W | OTW | OTL | L | GF | GA | Place | Coach | Captain |
| **1920 OG-M** | **6** | **3** | **0** | | **3** | **17** | **20** | **4th** | **Raoul Le Mat** | **Einar Lindqvist** |
| **1924 OG-M** | **5** | **2** | **0** | | **3** | **21** | **49** | **4th** | **Ruben Rundqvist/Erik Gustafsson** | **Birger Holmqvist** |
| **1928 OG-M** | **5** | **3** | **1** | | **1** | **12** | **14** | **S** | **Viking Harbom/Sten Mellgren** | **Carl Abrahamsson** |
| **1936 OG-M** | **5** | **2** | **0** | | **3** | **5** | **7** | **5th** | **Vic Lindquist** | **Herman Carlson** |
| **1948 OG-M** | **8** | **4** | **0** | | **4** | **55** | **28** | **5th** | **Sven Bergqvist** | **Ake Andersson** |
| **1952 OG-M** | **9** | **7** | **0** | | **2** | **53** | **22** | **B** | **Folke Jansson/Herman Carlson** | **Eric Johansson** |
| **1956 OG-M** | **7** | **2** | **1** | | **4** | **17** | **27** | **4th** | **Folke Jansson** | **Holger Nurmela/Lars Bjorn** |
| **1960 OG-M** | **7** | **2** | **1** | | **4** | **40** | **24** | **5th** | **Ed Reigle** | **Lars Bjorn** |
| **1964 OG-M** | **7** | **5** | **0** | | **2** | **47** | **16** | **S** | **Arne Stromberg** | **Sven "Tumba" Johansson** |
| **1968 OG-M** | **7** | **4** | **1** | | **2** | **23** | **18** | **4th** | **Arne Stromberg** | **Carl Oberg** |
| **1972 OG-M** | **5** | **2** | **1** | | **2** | **17** | **13** | **4th** | **Billy Harris** | **Bert-Ola Nordlander** |
| **1980 OG-M** | **7** | **4** | **2** | | **1** | **31** | **19** | **B** | **Tommy Sandlin** | **Mats Waltin** |
| **1984 OG-M** | **7** | **3** | **1** | | **3** | **26** | **17** | **B** | **Anders Parmstrom** | **Hakan Eriksson** |
| **1988 OG-M** | **8** | **4** | **3** | | **1** | **33** | **21** | **B** | **Tommy Sandlin** | **Thomas Rundqvist** |
| **1992 OG-M** | **8** | **5** | **2** | | **1** | **30** | **19** | **5th** | **Conny Evensson** | **Thomas Rundqvist** |
| **1994 OG-M** | **8** | **6** | **1** | | **1** | **33** | **18** | **G** | **Curt Lundmark** | **Charles Berglund (1)** |
| **1998 OG-M** | **4** | **2** | **0** | | **2** | **12** | **9** | **5th** | **Kent Forsberg** | **Calle Johansson** |
| **2002 OG-M** | **4** | **3** | **0** | | **1** | **17** | **8** | **5th** | **Hardy Nilsson** | **Mats Sundin** |
| **2006 OG-M** | **8** | **6** | **0** | | **2** | **31** | **19** | **G** | **Bengt-Ake Gustafsson** | **Mats Sundin** |
| **2010 OG-M** | **4** | **3** | **0** | **0** | **1** | **12** | **6** | **5th** | **Bengt-Ake Gustafsson** | **Nicklas Lidstrom** |

(1) Tomas Jonsson captain vs. Germany (Feb. 23), Russia (Feb. 25), and Canada (Feb. 27)

### World Championship (Men)

(bold=top level)

| Year Event | GP | W | T | | L | GF | GA | Place | Coach | Captain |
|---|---|---|---|---|---|---|---|---|---|---|
| Year Event | GP | W | OTW | OTL | L | GF | GA | Place | Coach | Captain |
| **1931 WM** | **6** | **2** | **1** | | **3** | **4** | **7** | **6th** | **Viking Harbom** | ***unknown*** |
| **1935 WM** | **8** | **4** | **1** | | **3** | **19** | **16** | **5th** | **Carl Abrahamsson/Viking Harbom** | ***unknown*** |
| **1937 WM** | **3** | **0** | **0** | | **3** | **1** | **14** | **9th** | **Carl Abrahamsson** | ***unknown*** |
| **1938 WM** | **6** | **2** | **2** | | **2** | **8** | **7** | **5th** | **Viking Harbom** | ***unknown*** |
| **1947 WM** | **7** | **5** | **1** | | **1** | **55** | **15** | **S** | **Sten Ahner** | **Ake Andersson** |
| **1949 WM** | **7** | **4** | **1** | | **2** | **42** | **15** | **4th** | **Sven Bergqvist** | **Ake Andersson** |
| **1950 WM** | **7** | **3** | **0** | | **4** | **33** | **19** | **5th** | **Frank Trottier** | **Ake Andersson** |
| **1951 WM** | **6** | **4** | **1** | | **1** | **33** | **14** | **S** | **Folke Jansson/Herman Carlson** | **Ake Andersson** |
| **1953 WM** | **4** | **4** | **0** | | **0** | **38** | **11** | **G** | **Folke Jansson** | **Ake Andersson** |
| **1954 WM** | **7** | **5** | **1** | | **1** | **30** | **18** | **B** | **Folke Jansson/Herman Carlson** | **Ake Andersson** |
| **1955 WM** | **8** | **4** | **1** | | **3** | **40** | **16** | **5th** | **Herman Carlson** | ***unknown*** |
| **1957 WM** | **7** | **6** | **1** | | **0** | **62** | **11** | **G** | **Folke Jansson** | **Lars Bjorn** |
| **1958 WM** | **7** | **5** | **0** | | **2** | **46** | **22** | **B** | **Ed Reigle** | **Hans Svedberg** |
| **1959 WM** | **8** | **3** | **1** | | **4** | **27** | **26** | **5th** | **Ed Reigle** | **Lars Bjorn** |
| **1961 WM** | **7** | **4** | **0** | | **3** | **33** | **27** | **4th** | **Arne Stromberg** | **Lars Bjorn** |
| **1962 WM** | **7** | **7** | **0** | | **0** | **67** | **10** | **G** | **Arne Stromberg** | **Ronald Pettersson** |
| **1963 WM** | **7** | **6** | **0** | | **1** | **44** | **10** | **S** | **Arne Stromberg** | **Ronald Pettersson (1)** |
| **1965 WM** | **7** | **4** | **1** | | **2** | **33** | **17** | **B** | **Arne Stromberg** | **Sven "Tumba" Johansson** |
| **1966 WM** | **7** | **3** | **1** | | **3** | **26** | **17** | **4th** | **Arne Stromberg** | **Sven "Tumba" Johansson (2)** |
| **1967 WM** | **7** | **4** | **1** | | **2** | **31** | **22** | **S** | **Arne Stromberg** | **Roland Stoltz** |
| **1969 WM** | **10** | **8** | **0** | | **2** | **45** | **19** | **S** | **Arne Stromberg** | **Ulf Sterner** |
| **1970 WM** | **10** | **7** | **1** | | **2** | **45** | **21** | **S** | **Arne Stromberg** | **Ulf Sterner** |
| **1971 WM** | **10** | **5** | **1** | | **4** | **29** | **33** | **B** | **Arne Stromberg** | ***unknown*** |

| Year Event | GP | W | T | OTW | OTL | L | GF | GA | Place | Coach | Captain |
|---|---|---|---|---|---|---|---|---|---|---|---|
| 1972 WM | 10 | 5 | 1 | | | 4 | 49 | 33 | B | Billy Harris | Tord Lundstrom (3) |
| 1973 WM | 10 | 7 | 1 | | | 2 | 53 | 23 | S | Kjell Svensson | Arne Karlsson |
| 1974 WM | 10 | 5 | 1 | | | 4 | 38 | 24 | B | Kjell Svensson | *unknown* |
| 1975 WM | 10 | 5 | 0 | | | 5 | 51 | 34 | B | Ronald Pettersson | Tord Lundstrom |
| 1976 WM | 10 | 6 | 0 | | | 4 | 36 | 29 | B | Hans Lindberg | Stig Salming (4) |
| 1977 WM | 10 | 7 | 0 | | | 3 | 43 | 19 | S | Hans Lindberg | Mats Ahlberg |
| 1978 WM | 10 | 4 | 0 | | | 6 | 39 | 37 | 4th | Hans Lindberg | Mats Ahlberg |
| 1979 WM | 8 | 3 | 1 | | | 4 | 33 | 46 | B | Tommy Sandlin | Mats Waltin (5) |
| 1981 WM | 8 | 5 | 1 | | | 2 | 24 | 30 | S | Bengt Ohlson | Mats Waltin |
| 1982 WM | 10 | 3 | 3 | | | 4 | 26 | 35 | 4th | Anders Parmstrom | Goran Lindblom |
| 1983 WM | 10 | 4 | 1 | | | 5 | 25 | 31 | 4th | Anders Parmstrom | Thomas Eriksson |
| 1985 WM | 10 | 4 | 0 | | | 6 | 37 | 40 | 6th | Leif Boork | Per-Erik Eklund |
| 1986 WM | 10 | 6 | 2 | | | 2 | 46 | 30 | S | Curt Lindstrom | Anders Eldebrink (6) |
| 1987 WM | 10 | 5 | 2 | | | 3 | 44 | 22 | G | Tommy Sandlin | Bengt-Ake Gustafsson |
| 1989 WM | 10 | 4 | 2 | | | 4 | 34 | 32 | 4th | Tommy Sandlin | Thomas Rundqvist (7) |
| 1990 WM | 10 | 7 | 1 | | | 2 | 40 | 23 | S | Tommy Sandlin | Thomas Rundqvist |
| 1991 WM | 10 | 5 | 5 | | | 0 | 43 | 29 | G | Conny Evensson | Thomas Rundqvist |
| 1992 WM | 8 | 4 | 2 | | | 2 | 25 | 15 | G | Conny Evensson | Tommy Sjodin |
| 1993 WM | 8 | 5 | 0 | | | 3 | 27 | 22 | S | Curt Lundmark | Thomas Rundqvist |
| 1994 WM | 8 | 5 | 1 | | | 2 | 36 | 21 | B | Curt Lundmark | Charles Berglund |
| 1995 WM | 8 | 5 | 1 | | | 2 | 28 | 15 | S | Curt Lundmark | Charles Berglund |
| 1996 WM | 6 | 2 | 2 | | | 2 | 16 | 15 | 6th | Kent Forsberg | Jonas Bergqvist |
| 1997 WM | 11 | 7 | 1 | | | 3 | 32 | 21 | S | Kent Forsberg | Stefan Nilsson |
| 1998 WM | 10 | 9 | 1 | | | 0 | 38 | 9 | G | Kent Forsberg | Mats Sundin |
| 1999 WM | 9 | 7 | 0 | | | 2 | 26 | 15 | B | Sune Bergman/Stephan Lundh | Nichlas Falk |
| 2000 WM | 7 | 3 | 1 | | | 3 | 24 | 15 | 7th | Hardy Nilsson/Stephan Lundh | Jorgen Jonsson (8) |
| 2001 WM | 9 | 6 | 1 | | | 2 | 39 | 18 | B | Hardy Nilsson | Jorgen Jonsson |
| 2002 WM | 9 | 7 | 0 | | | 2 | 40 | 17 | B | Hardy Nilsson | Jorgen Jonsson |
| 2003 WM | 9 | 7 | 0 | | | 2 | 34 | 19 | S | Hardy Nilsson | Jorgen Jonsson |
| 2004 WM | 9 | 6 | 2 | | | 1 | 27 | 14 | S | Hardy Nilsson | Jorgen Jonsson |
| 2005 WM | 9 | 6 | 0 | | | 3 | 37 | 23 | 4th | Bengt-Ake Gustafsson | Jorgen Jonsson |
| 2006 WM | 9 | 6 | 2 | | | 1 | 36 | 19 | G | Bengt-Ake Gustafsson | Kenny Jonsson |
| 2007 WM | 9 | 6 | | 0 | 0 | 3 | 38 | 20 | 4th | Bengt-Ake Gustafsson | Kenny Jonsson |
| 2008 WM | 9 | 4 | | 1 | 0 | 4 | 39 | 27 | 4th | Bengt-Ake Gustafsson | Kenny Jonsson |
| 2009 WM | 9 | 5 | | 1 | 2 | 1 | 38 | 25 | B | Bengt-Ake Gustafsson | Kenny Jonsson |
| 2010 WM | 9 | 7 | | 0 | 1 | 1 | 30 | 15 | B | Bengt-Ake Gustafsson | Magnus Johansson |
| 2011 WM | 9 | 6 | | 0 | 1 | 2 | 32 | 20 | S | Par Marts | Rickard Wallin |
| 2012 WM | 8 | 6 | | 0 | 0 | 2 | 32 | 19 | 6th | Par Marts | Daniel Alfredsson |

(1) Nils Nilsson captain vs. United States (Mar. 12)
(2) Ronald Pettersson captain vs. Czechoslovakia (Mar. 11) and Canada (Mar. 13)
(3) Lars-Goran Nilsson captain vs. East Germany (Apr. 11)
(4) Dan Soderstrom captain vs. Poland (Apr. 19), Soviet Union (Apr. 21), and United States (Apr. 25)
(5) Mats Naslund captain vs. Soviet Union (Apr. 17)
(6) Hakan Sodergren captain vs. West Germany (Apr. 18), Poland (Apr. 19), Finland (Apr. 21), Canada (Apr. 26), and Soviet Union (Apr. 28)
(7) Anders Eldebrink captain vs. West Germany (Apr. 18)
(8) Peter Andersson captain vs. Belarus (May 4)

### IIHF-NHL Invitationals

(bold=top level)

| Year Event | GP | W | T | L | GF | GA | Place | Coach | Captain |
|---|---|---|---|---|---|---|---|---|---|
| 1976 CC | 5 | 2 | 1 | 2 | 16 | 18 | 4th | Hans Lindberg | Lars-Erik Sjoberg |
| 1981 CC | 5 | 1 | 0 | 4 | 13 | 20 | 5th | Anders Parmstrom | Anders Hedberg |
| 1984 CC | 8 | 4 | 0 | 4 | 31 | 29 | 2nd | Leif Boork | Thomas Gradin |
| 1987 CC | 5 | 3 | 0 | 2 | 17 | 14 | 3rd | Tommy Sandlin | Bengt-Ake Gustafsson |
| 1991 CC | 6 | 2 | 0 | 4 | 13 | 21 | 4th | Conny Evensson | Thomas Rundqvist |
| 1996 WCH | 4 | 3 | 0 | 1 | 16 | 6 | 3rd | Kent Forsberg | Mats Sundin |
| 2004 WCH | 4 | 2 | 1 | 1 | 14 | 15 | 5th | Hardy Nilsson | Mats Sundin |

### U20 World Championship

(bold=top level)

| Year Event | GP | W | T | | L | GF | GA | Place | Coach | Captain |
|---|---|---|---|---|---|---|---|---|---|---|
| Year Event | GP | W | OTW | OTL | L | GF | GA | Place | Coach | Captain |
| 1977 WM20 | 7 | 3 | 0 | | 4 | 28 | 30 | 5th | Lennart Johansson | Hans Sarkijarvi |
| 1978 WM20 | 7 | 4 | 1 | | 2 | 28 | 24 | S | Bengt Ohlson | Bengt-Ake Gustafsson |
| 1979 WM20 | 6 | 4 | 1 | | 1 | 19 | 13 | B | Bengt Ohlson | Tommy Samuelsson |
| 1980 WM20 | 5 | 2 | 1 | | 2 | 23 | 15 | B | Bengt Ohlson | *unknown* |
| 1981 WM20 | 5 | 4 | 1 | | 0 | 25 | 11 | G | Kjell Damberg | Hakan Nordin |
| 1982 WM20 | 7 | 4 | 0 | | 3 | 42 | 26 | 5th | Kjell Larsson | *unknown* |
| 1983 WM20 | 7 | 4 | 0 | | 3 | 35 | 23 | 4th | Conny Evensson | Per-Erik Eklund |
| 1984 WM20 | 7 | 3 | 0 | | 4 | 27 | 28 | 5th | Conny Evensson | *unknown* |
| 1985 WM20 | 7 | 3 | 0 | | 4 | 32 | 26 | 5th | Kjell Larsson | Lars Bystrom (1) |
| 1986 WM20 | 7 | 4 | 0 | | 3 | 26 | 23 | 5th | Ingvar Carlsson | Ulf Dahlen |
| 1987 WM20 | 7 | 4 | 1 | | 2 | 45 | 11 | B | Lars-Gunnar Jansson | Ulf Dahlen |
| 1988 WM20 | 7 | 3 | 1 | | 3 | 36 | 24 | 5th | Clas-Goran Wallin | *unknown* |
| 1989 WM20 | 7 | 6 | 0 | | 1 | 39 | 14 | S | Clas-Goran Wallin | Jan Bergman |
| 1990 WM20 | 7 | 4 | 1 | | 2 | 38 | 29 | 5th | Curt Lundmark | Joacim Esbjors |
| 1991 WM20 | 7 | 3 | 0 | | 4 | 32 | 29 | 6th | Bengt Ohlson | *unknown* |
| 1992 WM20 | 7 | 5 | 1 | | 1 | 41 | 24 | S | Tommy Tomth | Mikael Renberg |
| 1993 WM20 | 7 | 6 | 0 | | 1 | 53 | 15 | S | Tommy Tomth | Markus Naslund |
| 1994 WM20 | 7 | 6 | 0 | | 1 | 35 | 16 | S | Tommy Tomth | Kenny Jonsson |
| 1995 WM20 | 7 | 4 | 1 | | 2 | 35 | 21 | B | Tommy Tomth | Jesper Mattsson |
| 1996 WM20 | 7 | 4 | 1 | | 2 | 26 | 13 | S | Harald Luckner | Johan Davidsson |
| 1997 WM20 | 6 | 2 | 1 | | 3 | 20 | 18 | 8th | Harald Luckner | Henrik Andersson |
| 1998 WM20 | 7 | 3 | 0 | | 4 | 25 | 13 | 6th | Harald Luckner | Johan Forsander |

| | | | | | | | | | | |
|---|---|---|---|---|---|---|---|---|---|---|
| 1999 WM20 | 6 | 4 | 0 | | 2 | 30 | 22 | 4th | Mats Hallin | Henrik Tallinder (2) |
| 2000 WM20 | 7 | 5 | 0 | | 2 | 45 | 17 | 5th | Lars Molin | Christian Berglund |
| 2001 WM20 | 7 | 3 | 0 | | 4 | 17 | 13 | 4th | Bo Lennartsson | Niklas Kronwall (3) |
| 2002 WM20 | 7 | 3 | 2 | | 2 | 18 | 15 | 6th | Bo Lennartsson | Joel Lundqvist |
| 2003 WM20 | 6 | 2 | 0 | | 4 | 20 | 25 | 8th | Peo Larsson | Alexander Steen |
| 2004 WM20 | 6 | 3 | 0 | | 3 | 21 | 13 | 7th | Torgny Bendelin | Alexander Steen |
| 2005 WM20 | 6 | 2 | 0 | | 4 | 19 | 25 | 6th | Torgny Bendelin | Nicklas Grossmann |
| 2006 WM20 | 6 | 4 | 0 | | 2 | 23 | 11 | 5th | Torgny Bendelin | Sebastian Karlsson |
| 2007 WM20 | 7 | 3 | 0 | 1 | 3 | 19 | 16 | 4th | Torgny Bendelin | Nicklas Backstrom |
| 2008 WM20 | 6 | 4 | 1 | 1 | 0 | 26 | 13 | S | Par Marts | Patrik Berglund |
| 2009 WM20 | 6 | 5 | 0 | 0 | 1 | 27 | 11 | S | Par Marts | Oscar Moller |
| 2010 WM20 | 6 | 5 | 0 | 0 | 1 | 41 | 15 | B | Par Marts | Marcus Johansson |
| 2011 WM20 | 6 | 3 | 1 | 1 | 1 | 26 | 17 | 4th | Roger Ronnberg | Anton Lander |
| 2012 WM20 | 6 | 2 | 4 | 0 | 0 | 30 | 13 | G | Roger Ronnberg | Johan Larsson |

(1) Stefan Jonsson captain Dec. 23 vs. CAN
(2) Niklas Persson captain Dec. 30 vs. BLR
(3) Fredrik Sundin captain Dec. 26 vs. CZE & Dec. 31 vs. USA

### U18 World Championship (Men)

(bold=top level)

| Year Event | GP | W | T | | L | GF | GA | Place | Coach | Captain |
|---|---|---|---|---|---|---|---|---|---|---|
| Year Event | GP | W | OTW | OTL | L | GF | GA | Place | Coach | Captain |
| 1999 WM18 | 7 | 4 | 2 | | 1 | 30 | 14 | S | Lars Erik Lundstrom | *unknown* |
| 2000 WM18 | 6 | 5 | 0 | | 1 | 30 | 10 | B | Lars Lisspers | Johan Eneqvist |
| 2001 WM18 | 6 | 4 | 0 | | 2 | 24 | 15 | 7th | Kjell-Rune Milton | Yared Hagos |
| 2002 WM18 | 8 | 4 | 0 | | 4 | 26 | 23 | 9th | Johan Schillgard | Alexander Steen |
| 2003 WM18 | 6 | 2 | 1 | | 3 | 19 | 23 | 5th | Peter Johansson | Ola Svanberg |
| 2004 WM18 | 6 | 3 | 0 | | 3 | 14 | 21 | 5th | Tomas Thelin | Sebastian Karlsson |
| 2005 WM18 | 7 | 5 | 0 | | 2 | 20 | 17 | B | Mikael Tisell | Alexander Ribbenstrand (1) |
| 2006 WM18 | 6 | 3 | 0 | | 3 | 17 | 16 | 6th | Mikael Tisell | Tony Lagerstrom |
| 2007 WM18 | 6 | 3 | 1 | 0 | 2 | 22 | 15 | B | Lars Lindgren | Oscar Moller |
| 2008 WM18 | 6 | 4 | 0 | 0 | 2 | 28 | 18 | 4th | Stephan Lundh | Victor Hedman |
| 2009 WM18 | 6 | 4 | 0 | 0 | 2 | 30 | 14 | 5th | Stephan Lundh | Anton Lander |
| 2010 WM18 | 6 | 5 | 0 | 0 | 1 | 30 | 12 | S | Stephan Lundh | Johan Larsson |
| 2011 WM18 | 6 | 4 | 0 | 1 | 1 | 26 | 13 | S | Rikard Gronborg | Oscar Klefbom |
| 2012 WM18 | 6 | 5 | 0 | 0 | 1 | 27 | 14 | S | Rikard Gronborg | Filip Forsberg |

(1) also Robin Lindqvist

### Olympics, Women

(bold=top level)

| Year Event | GP | W | T | | L | GF | GA | Place | Coach | Captain |
|---|---|---|---|---|---|---|---|---|---|---|
| Year Event | GP | W | OTW | OTL | L | GF | GA | Place | Coach | Captain |
| 1998 OG-W | 5 | 1 | 0 | | 4 | 10 | 21 | 5th | Bengt Ohlson | Susanne Ceder (1) |
| 2002 OG-W | 5 | 3 | 0 | | 2 | 12 | 18 | B | Christian Yngve | Erika Holst |
| 2006 OG-W | 5 | 3 | 0 | | 2 | 19 | 15 | S | Peter Elander | Erika Holst |
| 2010 OG-W | 5 | 2 | 0 | 1 | 2 | 13 | 27 | 4th | Peter Elander | Erika Holst |

(1) Asa Elfving captain vs. Finland (Feb. 8, 1998)

### Women's World Championship

(bold=top level)

| Year Event | GP | W | T | | L | GF | GA | Place | Coach | Captain |
|---|---|---|---|---|---|---|---|---|---|---|
| Year Event | GP | W | OTW | OTL | L | GF | GA | Place | Coach | Captain |
| 1990 WW | 5 | 2 | 0 | | 3 | 25 | 35 | 4th | Christian Yngve | Kristina Bergstrand |
| 1992 WW | 5 | 2 | 0 | | 3 | 19 | 20 | 4th | Christian Yngve | Lisa Plahn |
| 1994 WW | 5 | 3 | 1 | | 1 | 22 | 17 | 5th | Christian Yngve | Lisa Plahn |
| 1997 WW | 5 | 2 | 1 | | 2 | 12 | 19 | 5th | Bengt Ohlson | Asa Elfving |
| 1999 WW | 5 | 2 | 0 | | 3 | 13 | 24 | 4th | Christian Yngve | Therese Sjolander |
| 2000 WW | 5 | 1 | 1 | | 3 | 13 | 19 | 4th | Christian Yngve | Ylva Lindberg |
| 2001 WW | 5 | 2 | 0 | | 3 | 8 | 24 | 5th | Christian Yngve | Ylva Lindberg |
| 2004 WW | 5 | 1 | 1 | | 3 | 15 | 23 | 4th | Peter Elander | Erika Holst |
| 2005 WW | 5 | 3 | 0 | | 2 | 14 | 18 | B | Peter Elander | Erika Holst |
| 2007 WW | 5 | 4 | 0 | 1 | 0 | 20 | 5 | B | Peter Elander | Erika Holst |
| 2008 WW | 4 | 2 | 0 | 2 | 0 | 13 | 8 | 5th | Peter Elander | Erika Holst |
| 2009 WW | 5 | 3 | 0 | 0 | 2 | 24 | 12 | 4th | Peter Elander | Erika Holst |
| 2011 WW | 5 | 2 | 1 | 0 | 2 | 15 | 17 | 5th | Niclas Hogberg | Erika Holst |
| 2012 WW | 5 | 1 | 2 | 0 | 2 | 12 | 8 | 5th | Niclas Hogberg | Erika Holst |

### U18 Women's World Championship

(bold=top level)

| Year Event | GP | W | OTW | OTL | L | GF | GA | Place | Coach | Captain |
|---|---|---|---|---|---|---|---|---|---|---|
| 2008 WW18 | 5 | 2 | 0 | 0 | 3 | 23 | 18 | 4th | Niclas Hogberg | Emma Nordin |
| 2009 WW18 | 5 | 3 | 0 | 0 | 2 | 26 | 18 | B | Niclas Hogberg | Erika Grahm |
| 2010 WW18 | 6 | 4 | 0 | 0 | 2 | 18 | 22 | B | Niclas Hogberg | Josefine Holmgren |
| 2011 WW18 | 5 | 3 | 0 | 1 | 1 | 9 | 16 | 5th | Henrik Cedergren | Josefine Holmgren |
| 2012 WW18 | 6 | 3 | 1 | 0 | 2 | 16 | 19 | B | Henrik Cedergren | Cajsa Lillback |

# Switzerland (SUI)

Switzerland celebrates a goal during the bronze-medal win at the 2012 IIHF Ice Hockey Women's World Championship.
Photo: Andre Ringuette / HHOF-IIHF Images.

## Joined IIHF: November 23, 1908

Website: www.swiss-icehockey.ch
E-mail: info@swiss-icehockey.ch

Swiss Ice Hockey
P.O. Box
Hagenholzstrasse 81
8050 Zürich
Switzerland

Phone: +41 44 306 50 50 • Fax: +41 44 306 50 51

| World Ranking | |
|---|---|
| **MEN** | **WOMEN** |
| 2012........9 | 2012........4 |
| 2011........7 | 2011........6 |
| 2010........7 | 2010........5 |
| 2009........7 | 2009........5 |
| 2008........7 | 2008........5 |
| 2007........8 | 2007........7 |
| 2006........8 | 2006........8 |
| 2005........8 | 2005........9 |
| 2004........9 | 2004........8 |

### Top Level Host History

Olympics: 1928 (St. Moritz); 1948 (St. Moritz)
World Championship (Men): 1935 (Davos), 1939 (Zurich, Basel), 1953 (Zurich, Basel), 1961 (Geneva, Lausanne), 1971 (Berne, Geneva), 1990 (Berne, Fribourg), 1998 (Zurich, Basel), 2009 (Berne, Zurich-Kloten)
U20 World Championship: 1997 (Geneva, Morges)
U18 World Championship (Men): 2000 (Kloten, Weinfelden)
Women's World Championship: 2011 (Zurich, Winterthur)

### Olympics, Men

(bold=top level)

| Year Event | GP | W | T | | L | GF | GA | Place | Coach | Captain |
|---|---|---|---|---|---|---|---|---|---|---|
| Year Event | GP | W | OTW | OTL | L | GF | GA | Place | Coach | Captain |
| **1920 OG-M** | **2** | **0** | **0** | | **2** | **0** | **33** | **5th** | **Max Sillig** | **Max Sillig** |
| **1924 OG-M** | **3** | **0** | **0** | | **3** | **2** | **53** | **7th** | **Paul Muller** | **Wilhelm de Siebenthal** |
| **1928 OG-M** | **5** | **2** | **1** | | **2** | **9** | **21** | **B** | **Bobby Bell** | **Louis Dufour** |
| **1936 OG-M** | **3** | **1** | **0** | | **2** | **1** | **5** | **13th** | **Ulrich von Sury** | **Richard "Bibi" Torriani** |
| **1948 OG-M** | **8** | **6** | **0** | | **2** | **67** | **21** | **B** | **Wyn Cook** | **Richard "Bibi" Torriani** |
| **1952 OG-M** | **8** | **4** | **0** | | **4** | **40** | **40** | **5th** | **Richard "Bibi" Torriani** | **Uli Poltera** |
| **1956 OG-M** | **5** | **1** | **0** | | **4** | **20** | **34** | **9th** | **Heimlich Boller** | **Emil Handschin** |
| **1964 OG-M** | **7** | **0** | **0** | | **7** | **9** | **57** | **8th** | **Herve Lalonde** | **Elwin Friedrich** |
| **1972 OG-M** | **4** | **0** | **2** | | **2** | **9** | **16** | **10th** | **Gaston Pelletier/Derek Holmes** | **Rene Huguenin** |
| **1976 OG-M** | **5** | **2** | **0** | | **3** | **24** | **22** | **11th** | **Rudolf Killias** | **Charly Henzen** |
| **1988 OG-M** | **6** | **3** | **0** | | **3** | **23** | **18** | **8th** | **Simon Schenk** | **Jakob Kolliker** |
| **1992 OG-M** | **7** | **2** | **0** | | **5** | **22** | **32** | **10th** | **Juhani Tamminen** | **Jorg Eberle** |
| **2002 OG-M** | **4** | **2** | **1** | | **1** | **11** | **10** | **11th** | **Ralph Krueger** | **Mark Streit** |
| **2006 OG-M** | **6** | **2** | **2** | | **2** | **12** | **18** | **6th** | **Ralph Krueger** | **Mark Streit** |
| **2010 OG-M** | **5** | **1** | **1** | **1** | **2** | **11** | **14** | **8th** | **Ralph Krueger** | **Mark Streit** |

### World Championship (Men)

(bold=top level)

| Year Event | GP | W | T | | L | GF | GA | Place | Coach | Captain |
|---|---|---|---|---|---|---|---|---|---|---|
| Year Event | GP | W | OTW | OTL | L | GF | GA | Place | Coach | Captain |
| **1930 WM** | **3** | **2** | **0** | | **1** | **6** | **4** | **B** | **Bobby Bell** | **Heini Meng** |
| **1933 WM** | **6** | **3** | **1** | | **2** | **10** | **11** | **5th** | **Mezzi Andreossi** | **Richard "Bibi" Torriani** |
| **1934 WM** | **7** | **5** | **0** | | **2** | **36** | **7** | **4th** | **Charles Fasel** | **Richard "Bibi" Torriani** |
| **1935 WM** | **8** | **5** | **2** | | **1** | **24** | **8** | **S** | **Charles Fasel** | **Richard "Bibi" Torriani** |
| **1937 WM** | **8** | **4** | **1** | | **3** | **27** | **13** | **B** | **Ulrich von Sury** | **Richard "Bibi" Torriani** |
| **1938 WM** | **7** | **5** | **0** | | **2** | **34** | **7** | **6th** | **Ulrich von Sury** | **Richard "Bibi" Torriani** |
| **1939 WM** | **10** | **7** | **1** | | **2** | **51** | **13** | **B** | **Ulrich von Sury** | **Richard "Bibi" Torriani** |
| **1947 WM** | **7** | **4** | **1** | | **2** | **47** | **22** | **4th** | **Richard "Bibi" Torriani** | **Othmar Delnon (1)** |
| **1949 WM** | **8** | **4** | **1** | | **3** | **48** | **32** | **5th** | **Richard "Bibi" Torriani** | **Uli Poltera** |
| **1950 WM** | **7** | **4** | **0** | | **3** | **57** | **46** | **B** | **Richard "Bibi" Torriani** | **Uli Poltera** |
| **1951 WM** | **6** | **4** | **1** | | **1** | **28** | **12** | **B** | **Richard "Bibi" Torriani** | **Fredy Bieler** |
| **1953 WM** | **4** | **1** | **0** | | **3** | **9** | **27** | **B** | **Frank Sullivan** | **Uli Poltera** |
| **1954 WM** | **7** | **0** | **2** | | **5** | **15** | **34** | **7th** | **Heinrich Boller** | **Uli Poltera** |
| **1955 WM** | **8** | **1** | **0** | | **7** | **15** | **59** | **8th** | **Heinrich Boller** | **Emil Handschin** |
| **1959 WM** | **8** | **1** | **1** | | **6** | **16** | **57** | **12th** | **Andre Girard** | **Otto Schlapfer** |
| 1961 WM-B | 5 | 2 | 1 | | 2 | 17 | 15 | 3rd | Beat Ruedi | *unknown* |
| **1962 WM** | **7** | **1** | **0** | | **6** | **21** | **60** | **7th** | **Beat Ruedi** | **Elwin Friedrich** |
| 1963 WM-B | 6 | 4 | 1 | | 1 | 28 | 10 | 2nd | Herve Lalonde | Elwin Friedrich |
| 1965 WM-B | 6 | 4 | 1 | | 1 | 27 | 15 | 2nd | Andre Girard | *unknown* |
| 1966 WM-B | 7 | 2 | 0 | | 5 | 24 | 26 | 6th | Andre Girard | *unknown* |
| 1967 WM-B | 7 | 1 | 1 | | 5 | 22 | 37 | 7th | Rastislav Jancuska | Peter Luthi |
| 1969 WM-C | 5 | 4 | 0 | | 1 | 41 | 9 | 2nd | Gaston Pelletier | Rene Huguenin |
| 1970 WM-B | 7 | 2 | 0 | | 5 | 22 | 31 | 6th | Gaston Pelletier | Rene Huguenin |
| 1971 WM-B | 7 | 6 | 1 | | 0 | 31 | 14 | 1st | Gaston Pelletier | *unknown* |
| **1972 WM** | **10** | **1** | **0** | | **9** | **19** | **96** | **6th** | **Gaston Pelletier** | **Rene Huguenin** |
| 1973 WM-B | 7 | 2 | 0 | | 5 | 26 | 44 | 7th | Stu Robertson | Gaston Furrer |
| 1974 WM-C | 7 | 6 | 0 | | 1 | 63 | 4 | 1st | Rudolf Killias | Charly Henzen |
| 1975 WM-B | 7 | 4 | 0 | | 3 | 31 | 33 | 3rd | Rudolf Killias | Charly Henzen |
| 1976 WM-B | 7 | 4 | 0 | | 3 | 25 | 28 | 4th | Rudolf Killias | Charly Henzen |
| 1977 WM-B | 8 | 4 | 0 | | 4 | 35 | 33 | 5th | Rudolf Killias | Aldo Zenhausern |
| 1978 WM-B | 7 | 4 | 1 | | 2 | 42 | 32 | 3rd | Jaroslav Jirik | Aldo Zenhausern |

| Year Event | GP | W | T (OTW) | OTL | L | GF | GA | Place | Coach | Captain |
|---|---|---|---|---|---|---|---|---|---|---|
| 1979 WM-B | 6 | 4 | 0 | | 2 | 23 | 20 | 5th | Jaroslav Jirik | *unknown* |
| 1981 WM-B | 7 | 4 | 2 | | 1 | 28 | 20 | 3rd | Lasse Lilja | Jakob Kolliker |
| 1982 WM-B | 7 | 1 | 3 | | 3 | 20 | 27 | 6th | Lasse Lilja | Jakob Kolliker |
| 1983 WM-B | 7 | 1 | 2 | | 4 | 25 | 35 | 6th | Bengt Ohlsson | *unknown* |
| 1985 WM-B | 7 | 5 | 1 | | 1 | 29 | 13 | 2nd | Bengt Ohlsson | Lorenzo Schmid |
| 1986 WM-B | 7 | 6 | 0 | | 1 | 38 | 20 | 1st | Simon Schenk | Jakob Kolliker |
| **1987 WM** | **10** | **0** | **0** | | **10** | **26** | **71** | **8th** | **Simon Schenk** | **Jakob Kolliker** |
| 1989 WM-B | 7 | 5 | 0 | | 2 | 40 | 21 | 4th | Simon Schenk | Fausto Mazzoleni |
| 1990 WM-B | 7 | 5 | 2 | | 0 | 30 | 14 | 1st | Simon Schenk | Fausto Mazzoleni |
| **1991 WM** | **10** | **2** | **1** | | **7** | **22** | **38** | **7th** | **Hans Lindberg** | **Jorg Eberle** |
| **1992 WM** | **8** | **3** | **2** | | **3** | **18** | **21** | **4th** | **Bill Gilligan** | **Jorg Eberle** |
| **1993 WM** | **7** | **2** | **0** | | **5** | **14** | **22** | **12th** | **Bill Gilligan** | **Jorg Eberle (2)** |
| 1994 WM-B | 7 | 6 | 1 | | 0 | 52 | 9 | 1st | Hans Lindberg | Jorg Eberle |
| **1995 WM** | **7** | **0** | **1** | | **6** | **14** | **32** | **12th** | **Mats Waltin** | **Roberto Triulzi** |
| 1996 WM-B | 7 | 5 | 1 | | 1 | 37 | 13 | 2nd | Simon Schenk | Felix Hollenstein |
| 1997 WM-B | 7 | 3 | 2 | | 2 | 26 | 22 | 3rd | Simon Schenk | Andre Rotheli |
| **1998 WM** | **9** | **2** | **1** | | **6** | **18** | **31** | **4th** | **Ralph Krueger** | **Martin Rauch** |
| **1999 WM** | **6** | **2** | **0** | | **4** | **15** | **25** | **8th** | **Ralph Krueger** | **Patrick Sutter** |
| **2000 WM** | **7** | **2** | **2** | | **3** | **19** | **21** | **6th** | **Ralph Krueger** | **Reto von Arx** |
| **2001 WM** | **6** | **2** | **0** | | **4** | **18** | **17** | **9th** | **Ralph Krueger** | **J-J Aeschlimann** |
| **2002 WM** | **6** | **2** | **0** | | **4** | **13** | **19** | **10th** | **Ralph Krueger** | **Mark Streit** |
| **2003 WM** | **7** | **3** | **0** | | **4** | **16** | **19** | **8th** | **Ralph Krueger** | **Mark Streit** |
| **2004 WM** | **7** | **2** | **2** | | **3** | **15** | **14** | **8th** | **Ralph Krueger** | **Mark Streit** |
| **2005 WM** | **7** | **3** | **1** | | **3** | **15** | **13** | **8th** | **Ralph Krueger** | **Mark Streit** |
| **2006 WM** | **6** | **2** | **2** | | **2** | **15** | **16** | **9th** | **Ralph Krueger** | **Mark Streit** |
| **2007 WM** | **7** | **3** | **0** | **0** | **4** | **12** | **22** | **8th** | **Ralph Krueger** | **Mark Streit** |
| **2008 WM** | **7** | **4** | **0** | **0** | **3** | **20** | **22** | **7th** | **Ralph Krueger** | **Sandy Jeannin** |
| **2009 WM** | **6** | **1** | **2** | **0** | **3** | **12** | **15** | **9th** | **Ralph Krueger** | **Mark Streit** |
| **2010 WM** | **7** | **4** | **0** | **0** | **3** | **15** | **13** | **5th** | **Sean Simpson** | **Mathias Seger** |
| **2011 WM** | **6** | **2** | **1** | **1** | **2** | **15** | **13** | **9th** | **Sean Simpson** | **Mathias Seger** |
| **2012 WM** | **7** | **2** | **0** | **0** | **5** | **16** | **21** | **11th** | **Sean Simpson** | **Mark Streit** |

(1) Heinrich Boller captain vs. Romania (Feb. 17)
(2) Felix Hollenstein captain vs. Italy (Apr. 20)

## U20 World Championship

(bold=top level)

| Year Event | GP | W | T | | L | GF | GA | Place | Coach | Captain |
|---|---|---|---|---|---|---|---|---|---|---|
| Year Event | GP | W | OTW | OTL | L | GF | GA | Place | Coach | Captain |
| **1978 WM20** | **6** | **0** | **0** | | **6** | **7** | **70** | **8th** | **Robert Stephen** | **Daniel Dubois** |
| 1979 WM20-B | 4 | 4 | 0 | | 0 | 32 | 11 | 1st | Gerhard Staeli | Henri Loher |
| **1980 WM20** | **5** | **0** | **0** | | **5** | **13** | **47** | **8th** | **Georges Rochat** | **Peter Schlagenhauf** |
| 1981 WM20-B | 5 | 4 | 1 | | 0 | 34 | 10 | 1st | Georges Rochat | Pius Kuonen |
| **1982 WM20** | **7** | **0** | **0** | | **7** | **15** | **81** | **8th** | **Jack Holmes** | ***unknown*** |
| 1983 WM20-B | 5 | 4 | 0 | | 1 | 29 | 14 | 1st | Werner Meier/Andres Kuenzi | Urs Burkart |
| **1984 WM20** | **7** | **0** | **0** | | **7** | **16** | **72** | **8th** | **Res Kunzi** | ***unknown*** |
| 1985 WM20-B | 7 | 7 | 0 | | 0 | 58 | 22 | 1st | *unknown* | *unknown* |
| **1986 WM20** | **7** | **1** | **0** | | **6** | **19** | **54** | **7th** | **Rolf Altorfer** | **Manuele Celio** |
| **1987 WM20** | **7** | **0** | **0** | | **7** | **15** | **62** | **6th** | **Rolf Altorfer** | **Bruno Vollmer** |
| 1988 WM20-B | 7 | 4 | 1 | | 2 | 34 | 23 | 3rd | Andres Kuenzi | *unknown* |
| 1989 WM20-B | 7 | 6 | 0 | | 1 | 45 | 19 | 2nd | Andres Kuenzi | Joel Aeschlimann |
| 1990 WM20-B | 7 | 6 | 0 | | 1 | 48 | 14 | 1st | Bruno Zenhausern | *unknown* |
| **1991 WM20** | **7** | **1** | **0** | | **6** | **5** | **48** | **7th** | **Bruno Zenhausern** | **Didier Princi** |
| **1992 WM20** | **7** | **1** | **0** | | **6** | **19** | **40** | **8th** | **Juhani Tamminen** | **Noel Guyaz** |
| 1993 WM20-B | 7 | 6 | 1 | | 0 | 39 | 13 | 1st | John Slettvoll | Bjorn Schneider |
| **1994 WM20** | **7** | **0** | **1** | | **6** | **10** | **30** | **8th** | **Arno del Curto** | **Jakub Horak** |
| 1995 WM20-B | 7 | 5 | 2 | | 0 | 40 | 12 | 1st | Arno del Curto | Marco Kloti |
| **1996 WM20** | **6** | **1** | **1** | | **4** | **16** | **24** | **9th** | **Arno del Curto** | **Sandy Jeannin** |
| **1997 WM20** | **6** | **3** | **1** | | **2** | **20** | **14** | **7th** | **Ueli Schwarz** | **Mathias Seger** |
| **1998 WM20** | **7** | **4** | **1** | | **2** | **21** | **14** | **B** | **Bill Gilligan** | **Laurent Muller (1)** |
| **1999 WM20** | **6** | **1** | **0** | | **5** | **13** | **27** | **9th** | **John Slettvoll** | **Michel Riesen** |
| **2000 WM20** | **7** | **3** | **0** | | **4** | **23** | **31** | **6th** | **Jakob Kolliker** | **Bjorn Christen** |
| **2001 WM20** | **7** | **2** | **1** | | **4** | **18** | **25** | **6th** | **Jakob Kolliker** | **Paolo Duca** |
| **2002 WM20** | **7** | **3** | **0** | | **4** | **16** | **21** | **4th** | **Jakob Kolliker** | **Andreas Camenzind** |
| **2003 WM20** | **6** | **3** | **0** | | **3** | **21** | **20** | **7th** | **Jakob Kolliker** | **Severin Blindenbacher** |
| **2004 WM20** | **6** | **2** | **0** | | **4** | **23** | **17** | **8th** | **Jakob Kolliker** | **Patrik Bartschi** |
| **2005 WM20** | **6** | **2** | **0** | | **4** | **19** | **20** | **8th** | **Jakob Kolliker** | **Victor Stancescu** |
| **2006 WM20** | **6** | **2** | **2** | | **2** | **16** | **15** | **7th** | **Jakob Kolliker** | **Raphael Diaz** |
| **2007 WM20** | **6** | **3** | **0** | **0** | **3** | **13** | **19** | **7th** | **Jakob Kolliker** | **Dario Burgler** |
| **2008 WM20** | **6** | **1** | **0** | **1** | **4** | **16** | **22** | **9th** | **Jakob Kolliker** | **Yannick Weber** |
| 2009 WM20-I-A | 5 | 5 | 0 | 0 | 0 | 31 | 7 | 1st | Jakob Kolliker | Pascal Berger |
| **2010 WM20** | **7** | **2** | **1** | **0** | **4** | **19** | **34** | **4th** | **Jakob Kolliker** | **Luca Sbisa** |
| **2011 WM20** | **6** | **2** | **1** | **0** | **3** | **15** | **19** | **5th** | **Richard Jost** | **Nino Niederreiter** |
| **2012 WM20** | **6** | **1** | **1** | **1** | **3** | **17** | **21** | **8th** | **Manuele Celio** | **Dario Trutmann** |

**(1) Michel Riesen captain Dec. 30 vs. USA**

## U18 World Championship (Men)

(bold=top level)

| Year Event | GP | W | T | | L | GF | GA | Place | Coach | Captain |
|---|---|---|---|---|---|---|---|---|---|---|
| Year Event | GP | W | OTW | OTL | L | GF | GA | Place | Coach | Captain |
| **1999 WM18** | **7** | **5** | **0** | | **2** | **23** | **14** | **4th** | **Alfred Bohren** | **Sebastien Reuille** |
| **2000 WM18** | **7** | **4** | **0** | | **3** | **23** | **23** | **4th** | **Beat Lautenschlager** | **Duri Camichel** |
| **2001 WM18** | **7** | **4** | **0** | | **3** | **25** | **19** | **S** | **Charly Oppliger** | **Andres Ambuhl** |
| **2002 WM18** | **8** | **5** | **0** | | **3** | **33** | **25** | **7th** | **Roger Bader** | **Romano Lemm** |
| **2003 WM18** | **6** | **1** | **1** | | **4** | **22** | **30** | **9th** | **Roger Bader** | **Philippe Furrer** |

| Year Event | GP | W | T / OTW | OTL | L | GF | GA | Place | Coach | Captain |
|---|---|---|---|---|---|---|---|---|---|---|
| 2004 WM18-I-A | 5 | 5 | 0 | | 0 | 35 | 10 | 1st | Charly Oppliger | Simon Bachmann |
| **2005 WM18** | 6 | 1 | 0 | | 5 | 8 | 20 | 9th | Alfred Bohren | Janik Steinmann |
| 2006 WM18-I-A | 5 | 4 | 1 | | 0 | 18 | 10 | 1st | Roger Bader | Arnaud Jacquemet |
| **2007 WM18** | 6 | 2 | 0 | 1 | 3 | 15 | 15 | 6th | Felix Hollenstein | Etienne Froidevaux |
| **2008 WM18** | 6 | 2 | 0 | 0 | 4 | 17 | 25 | 8th | Alfred Bohren | Alain Berger |
| **2009 WM18** | 6 | 2 | 0 | 0 | 4 | 20 | 35 | 8th | Manuele Celio | Reto Schappi |
| **2010 WM18** | 6 | 3 | 0 | 0 | 3 | 18 | 27 | 5th | Manuele Celio | Dario Trutmann |
| **2011 WM18** | 6 | 3 | 0 | 0 | 3 | 16 | 19 | 7th | Manuele Celio | Jan Neuenschwander |
| **2012 WM18** | 6 | 2 | 0 | 0 | 4 | 12 | 26 | 7th | Alfred Bohren | Samuel Kreis |

### Olympics, Women

(bold=top level)

| Year Event | GP | W | T | | L | GF | GA | Place | Coach | Captain |
|---|---|---|---|---|---|---|---|---|---|---|
| Year Event | GP | W | OTW | OTL | L | GF | GA | Place | Coach | Captain |
| **2006 OL-W** | 5 | 1 | 0 | | 4 | 14 | 18 | 7th | Rene Kammerer | Tina Schumacher |
| **2010 OG-W** | 5 | 2 | 1 | 0 | 2 | 14 | 16 | 5th | Rene Kammerer | Kathrin Lehmann |

### Women's World Championship

(bold=top level)

| Year Event | GP | W | T | | L | GF | GA | Place | Coach | Captain |
|---|---|---|---|---|---|---|---|---|---|---|
| Year Event | GP | W | OTW | OTL | L | GF | GA | Place | Coach | Captain |
| **1990 WW** | 5 | 3 | 0 | | 2 | 23 | 39 | 5th | Hansjorg Egli | Kim Urech |
| **1992 WW** | 5 | 0 | 0 | | 5 | 6 | 40 | 8th | Roger Maier | Claudia Blattler |
| **1994 WW** | 5 | 2 | 0 | | 3 | 10 | 30 | 7th | Francois Ceretti | Ruth Kunzle |
| **1997 WW** | 5 | 1 | 1 | | 3 | 8 | 27 | 7th | France Montour | Jeanette Marty |
| **1999 WW** | 5 | 0 | 0 | | 5 | 6 | 28 | 8th | Edi Grubauer | Ruth Kunzle |
| 2000 WW-B | 5 | 3 | 1 | | 1 | 16 | 6 | 2nd | Diane Michaud | Jeanette Marty |
| 2001 WW-I | 4 | 4 | 0 | | 0 | 18 | 3 | 1st | Francois Ceretti | *unknown* |
| **2004 WW** | 4 | 1 | 0 | | 3 | 9 | 17 | 8th | Diane Michaud | Tina Schumacher |
| 2005 WW-I | 5 | 5 | 0 | | 0 | 29 | 7 | 1st | Rene Kammerer | Ramona Fuhrer |
| **2007 WW** | 4 | 2 | 0 | 0 | 2 | 6 | 14 | 5th | Rene Kammerer | Kathrin Lehmann |
| **2008 WW** | 5 | 2 | 1 | 0 | 2 | 11 | 15 | 4th | Rene Kammerer | Kathrin Lehmann |
| **2009 WW** | 4 | 1 | 1 | 1 | 1 | 12 | 14 | 7th | Rene Kammerer | Kathrin Lehmann |
| **2011 WW** | 5 | 1 | 1 | 2 | 1 | 14 | 22 | 6th | Rene Kammerer | Kathrin Lehmann |
| **2012 WW** | 6 | 4 | 0 | 0 | 2 | 18 | 20 | B | Rene Kammerer | Kathrin Lehmann |

### U18 Women's World Championship

(bold=top level)

| Year Event | GP | W | OTW | OTL | L | GF | GA | Place | Coach | Captain |
|---|---|---|---|---|---|---|---|---|---|---|
| **2008 WW18** | 5 | 2 | 0 | 0 | 3 | 13 | 25 | 7th | Jorg Toggwiler | Anja Stiefel |
| **2009 WW18** | 5 | 1 | 0 | 2 | 2 | 11 | 31 | 8th | Jorg Toggwiler | Laura Benz |
| 2010 WW18-I | 5 | 5 | 0 | 0 | 0 | 44 | 5 | 1st | Dominik Schaer | Sarah Forster |
| **2011 WW18** | 6 | 2 | 0 | 0 | 4 | 14 | 23 | 7th | Dominik Schaer | Sarah Forster |
| **2012 WW18** | 6 | 2 | 0 | 1 | 3 | 16 | 32 | 8th | Dominik Schar | Phoebe Stanz |

# Thailand (THA)

*Thailand's men's team won the 2012 IIHF U18 Challenge Cup of Asia with the help of female goalkeeper Wasunun Angkulpattanasuk. Photo: Fatima Al Ali.*

### Joined IIHF: April 27, 1989

Website: www.thailandicehockey.com
E-mail: ihat2002@hotmail.com

Ice Hockey Association of Thailand
Room 238, Zone W, Rajamangala National Stadium
The Sports Authority of Thailand
2088 Ramkhamhaeng Road
Hua Mak Bangkapi Bangkok 10240
Thailand

Phone: +66 2 369 1517/+66 2 369 2510 • Fax: +66 2 369 1517

**Top Level Host History** none

# Turkey (TUR)

*Turkey won the 2012 IIHF Ice Hockey World Championship Division III on home ice in Erzurum. Photo: TIHF.*

## Joined IIHF: May 1, 1991

Website: www.tbhf.org.tr
E-mail: info@tbhf.org.tr

Turkish Ice Hockey Federation
Yukari Bahcelievler Mah. 70. Sokak No 5/1
B.Evler / Cankaya
06490 Ankara
Turkey

Phone: +90 312 215 7000 • Fax: +90 312 215 7003

**World Ranking**

| MEN | | WOMEN | |
|---|---|---|---|
| 2012 | 39 | 2012 | 35 |
| 2011 | 37 | 2011 | 33 |
| 2010 | 35 | 2010 | 34 |
| 2009 | 41 | 2009 | 33 |
| 2008 | 41 | 2008 | 33 |
| 2007 | 40 | 2007 | 33 |
| 2006 | 42 | | |
| 2005 | 41 | | |
| 2004 | 43 | | |

**Top Level Host History** none

### World Championship (Men)

| Year Event | GP | W | T | OTW | OTL | L | GF | GA | Place | Coach | Captain |
|---|---|---|---|---|---|---|---|---|---|---|---|
| 1992 WM-C | 5 | 0 | 0 | | | 5 | 11 | 89 | 6th | Rino Ouellette | *unknown* |
| 1998 WM-D | 5 | 1 | 0 | | | 4 | 12 | 56 | 7th | Stoian Batchvarov | Deniz Ince |
| 1999 WM-D | 4 | 1 | 0 | | | 3 | 7 | 42 | 7th | Colin Dodunski | Onur Polatoglu |
| 2000 WM-D | 4 | 0 | 0 | | | 4 | 7 | 37 | 9th | Stoian Batchvarov | Deniz Ince |
| 2002 WM-II-A | 5 | 0 | 0 | | | 5 | 3 | 57 | 6th | Oleg Zak | Deniz Ince |
| 2003 WM-III | 2 | 0 | 0 | | | 2 | 4 | 12 | 3rd | Oleg Zak | Deniz Ince |
| 2004 WM-III | 4 | 3 | 0 | | | 1 | 26 | 14 | 2nd | Oleg Zak | Cengiz Ciplak |
| 2005 WM-II-A | 5 | 0 | 0 | | | 5 | 5 | 70 | 6th | Oleg Zak | Cengiz Ciplak |
| 2006 WM-III | 4 | 2 | 1 | | | 1 | 18 | 16 | 2nd | Serhat Enyuce | Gokturk Tasdemir |
| 2007 WM-II-A | 5 | 0 | | 0 | 0 | 5 | 15 | 58 | 6th | Clive Tolley | Cengiz Ciplak |
| 2008 WM-III | 5 | 2 | | 0 | 1 | 2 | 27 | 24 | 4th | James MacEachern | Deniz Ince |
| 2009 WM-III | 5 | 4 | | 0 | 0 | 1 | 28 | 14 | 2nd | Andrei Brodnik | Gokturk Tasdemir |
| 2010 WM-II-A | 5 | 0 | | 0 | 0 | 5 | 8 | 53 | 6th | Matjaz Mahkovec | Deniz Ince |
| 2011 WM-III | 5 | 3 | | 0 | 0 | 2 | 29 | 25 | 3rd | Tarik Gocmen | Deniz Ince |
| 2012 WM-III | 5 | 5 | | 0 | 0 | 0 | 33 | 7 | 1st | Tuncay Kilic | Emrah Ozmen |

### U20 World Championship

| Year Event | GP | W | T | OTW | OTL | L | GF | GA | Place | Coach | Captain |
|---|---|---|---|---|---|---|---|---|---|---|---|
| 1998 WM20-D | 4 | 0 | 0 | | | 4 | 5 | 67 | 8th | Tahsin Kaya | Serhat Altinci |
| 1999 WM20-D | 4 | 0 | 0 | | | 4 | 1 | 93 | 9th | Ertug Gurhan | Kuntay Oget |
| 2003 WM20-III | 4 | 2 | 0 | | | 2 | 26 | 16 | 3rd | Oleg Zak | Cengiz Giplak |
| 2004 WM20-III | 5 | 1 | 0 | | | 4 | 10 | 38 | 4th | Oleg Zak | Galip Hamarat |
| 2005 WM20-III | 5 | 1 | 0 | | | 4 | 10 | 27 | 5th | Oleg Zak | Can Karabey |
| 2006 WM20-III | 4 | 2 | 0 | | | 2 | 35 | 40 | 3rd | Serhat Enyuce | Mustafa Yapicilar |
| 2007 WM20-III | 5 | 1 | | 0 | 0 | 4 | 9 | 31 | 5th | Clive Tolley | Gurkan Cetinkaya |
| 2008 WM20-III | 6 | 1 | | 0 | 0 | 5 | 18 | 62 | 6th | James MacEachern | Yavuz Karakoc |
| 2010 WM20-III | 5 | 1 | | 0 | 0 | 4 | 20 | 36 | 6th | Matjaz Mahkovic | Batin Kosemen |
| 2011 WM20-III | 6 | 3 | | 0 | 0 | 3 | 36 | 33 | 4th | Tarik Gocmen | Serkan Gumus |
| 2012 WM20-III | 4 | 0 | | 0 | 0 | 4 | 1 | 38 | 5th | Oktay Yavuzarslan | Kerem Islam |

### U18 World Championship (Men)

| Year Event | GP | W | T | OTW | OTL | L | GF | GA | Place | Coach | Captain |
|---|---|---|---|---|---|---|---|---|---|---|---|
| 2002 WM18-III | 4 | 0 | 0 | | | 4 | 6 | 47 | 8th | Oleg Zak | Utku Gaalip Hamarat |
| 2003 WM18-III-B | 3 | 1 | 0 | | | 2 | 16 | 11 | 2nd | Oleg Zak | Can Karabey |
| 2004 WM18-III-B | 6 | 1 | 0 | | | 5 | 12 | 40 | 6th | Kilic Tunkay | Sercan Yapicilar |
| 2005 WM18-III | 5 | 1 | 0 | | | 4 | 6 | 51 | 5th | Oleg Zak | Can Karabey |
| 2006 WM18-III | 5 | 0 | 0 | | | 5 | 8 | 63 | 6th | Tuncay Kilic | Mert Tahmazoglu |
| 2007 WM18-III | 5 | 0 | | 0 | 0 | 5 | 6 | 68 | 6th | Clive Tolley | Serkan Kocakara |
| 2008 WM18-III-B | 4 | 2 | | 0 | 0 | 2 | 34 | 26 | 3rd | James MacEachern | Batin Kosemen |
| 2009 WM18-III-B | 3 | 2 | | 0 | 0 | 1 | 25 | 26 | 2nd | William Schneider | Batin Kosemen |
| 2010 WM18-III-A | 4 | 2 | | 1 | 0 | 1 | 33 | 13 | 2nd | Matjaz Mahkovic | Serkan Gumus |
| 2011 WM18-III-A | 5 | 0 | | 0 | 0 | 5 | 7 | 53 | 4th | Serhat Enyuce | Taha Aksoy |

### Women's World Championship

| Year Event | GP | W | OTW | OTL | L | GF | GA | Place | Coach | Captain |
|---|---|---|---|---|---|---|---|---|---|---|
| 2007 WW-IV | 5 | 0 | 0 | 0 | 5 | 3 | 91 | 6th | Clive Tolley | Sinem Dogu |
| 2008 WW-IV | 5 | 0 | 0 | 0 | 5 | 3 | 50 | 6th | James MacEachern | Elif Ulas |
| 2011 WW-V | 4 | 1 | 0 | 0 | 3 | 4 | 23 | 4th | Tarik Gocmen | Elif Ulas |

# Ukraine (UKR)

*Ukraine's Kostyantyn Kasyanchuk shoots on the Japanese net. Photo: Samo Vidic.*

## Joined IIHF: May 6, 1992

Website: www.fhu.com.ua
E-mail: office@fhu.com.ua

Ice Hockey Federation of Ukraine
46 Melnikova Street
041 19 Kyiv
Ukraine

Phone: +38 044 484 6807 • Fax: +38 044 484 0273

| World Ranking | |
|---|---|
| **MEN** | |
| 2012 | 20 |
| 2011 | 19 |
| 2010 | 18 |
| 2009 | 19 |
| 2008 | 17 |
| 2007 | 15 |
| 2006 | 13 |
| 2005 | 11 |
| 2004 | 12 |

**Top Level Host History** none

### Olympics, Men
(bold=top level)

| Year Event | GP | W | T | L | GF | GA | Place | Coach | Captain |
|---|---|---|---|---|---|---|---|---|---|
| **2002 OG-M** | **4** | **2** | **0** | **2** | **11** | **14** | **10th** | **Anatoli Bogdanov** | **Valeri Shiryayev** |

### World Championship (Men)
(bold=top level)

| Year Event | GP | W | T | | L | GF | GA | Place | Coach | Captain |
|---|---|---|---|---|---|---|---|---|---|---|
| Year Event | GP | W | OTW | OTL | L | GF | GA | Place | Coach | Captain |
| 1993 WM-C | 7 | 5 | 1 | | 1 | 105 | 14 | 2nd | Alexander Fadeyev | Anatoli Stepanichev |
| 1994 WM-C-A | 6 | 3 | 2 | | 1 | 49 | 7 | 3rd | Alexander Fadeyev | Petr Malkov |
| 1995 WM-C | 4 | 2 | 1 | | 1 | 27 | 9 | 3rd | Anatoli Bogdanov | Vitali Litvinenko |
| 1996 WM-C | 7 | 6 | 0 | | 1 | 40 | 13 | 2nd | Olexander Seukand | Anatoli Stepanichev |
| 1997 WM-C | 5 | 4 | 1 | | 0 | 21 | 6 | 1st | Vasili Fadeyev | Valentin Oletski |
| 1998 WM-B | 7 | 7 | 0 | | 0 | 38 | 13 | 1st | Anatoli Bogdanov | Valeri Shiryayev |
| **1999 WM** | **3** | **0** | **0** | | **3** | **3** | **13** | **14th** | **Anatoli Bogdanov** | **Olexander Savitsky** |
| **2000 WM** | **6** | **2** | **0** | | **4** | **15** | **21** | **14th** | **Anatoli Bogdanov** | **Olexander Savitsky** |
| **2001 WM** | **6** | **2** | **0** | | **4** | **11** | **23** | **10th** | **Anatoli Bogdanov** | **Valeri Shiryayev** |
| **2002 WM** | **6** | **2** | **1** | | **3** | **13** | **20** | **9th** | **Anatoli Bogdanov** | **Valeri Shiryayev** |
| **2003 WM** | **6** | **1** | **0** | | **5** | **13** | **32** | **12th** | **Anatoli Bogdanov** | **Valeri Shiryayev** |
| **2004 WM** | **6** | **1** | **2** | | **3** | **12** | **20** | **14th** | **Olexander Seukand** | **Valeri Shiryayev** |
| **2005 WM** | **6** | **1** | **1** | | **4** | **7** | **14** | **11th** | **Olexander Seukand** | **Sergiy Klimentyev** |
| **2006 WM** | **6** | **1** | **0** | | **5** | **8** | **31** | **12th** | **Olexander Seukand** | **Sergiy Klimentyev** |
| **2007 WM** | **6** | **1** | **0** | **0** | **5** | **11** | **32** | **16th** | **Olexander Seukand** | **Yuri Gunko** |
| 2008 WM-I-B | 5 | 3 | 1 | 0 | 1 | 18 | 8 | 2nd | Vladimir Golubovich | Yuri Gunko |
| 2009 WM-I-B | 5 | 3 | 1 | 0 | 1 | 18 | 6 | 2nd | Olexander Seukand | Sergiy Klimentyev |
| 2010 WM-I-A | 5 | 4 | 0 | 0 | 1 | 39 | 12 | 2nd | Mikhail Zakharov | Vadym Shakhraychuk |
| 2011 WM-I-B | 5 | 3 | 0 | 1 | 1 | 19 | 12 | 3rd | Dave Lewis | Andri Sryubko |
| 2012 WM-I-A | 5 | 0 | 1 | 1 | 3 | 12 | 16 | 6th | Anatoli Khomenko | Sergiy Klimentyev |

### U20 World Championship
(bold=top level)

| Year Event | GP | W | T | | L | GF | GA | Place | Coach | Captain |
|---|---|---|---|---|---|---|---|---|---|---|
| Year Event | GP | W | OTW | OTL | L | GF | GA | Place | Coach | Captain |
| 1993 WM20-C | 4 | 4 | 0 | | 0 | 46 | 6 | 1st | Viktor Chibiryev | Dmitri Pidgurski |
| 1994 WM20-B | 7 | 7 | 0 | | 0 | 35 | 10 | 1st | Vladimir Osipchuk | Nikolai Maiko |
| **1995 WM20** | **7** | **1** | **0** | | **6** | **12** | **42** | **8th** | **Viktor Chibiryev** | **Oleksi Bernatsky** |
| **1996 WM20** | **6** | **1** | **0** | | **5** | **12** | **31** | **10th** | **Viktor Chibiryev** | **Roman Salnikov** |
| 1997 WM20-B | 7 | 3 | 1 | | 3 | 26 | 18 | 5th | Viktor Chibiryev | *unknown* |
| 1998 WM20-B | 6 | 4 | 1 | | 1 | 31 | 13 | 2nd | Viktor Chibiryev | Sergiy Sadiy |
| 1999 WM20-B | 6 | 5 | 1 | | 0 | 30 | 13 | 1st | Olexander Kulikov | Dmytro Tsyrul |
| **2000 WM20** | **6** | **0** | **0** | | **6** | **10** | **28** | **10th** | **Olexander Kulikov** | **Denis Isayenko** |
| 2001 WM20-I | 5 | 3 | 0 | | 2 | 15 | 9 | 3rd | Olexander Kulikov | Olexander Pobyedonostsev |
| 2002 WM20-I | 5 | 1 | 1 | | 3 | 9 | 23 | 4th | Olexander Kulikov | Vasyl Gorbenko |
| 2003 WM20-I-A | 5 | 4 | 1 | | 0 | 18 | 8 | 1st | Sergiy Lubnin | Olexander Skorokhod |
| **2004 WM20** | **6** | **0** | **1** | | **5** | **3** | **49** | **10th** | **Sergiy Lubnin** | **Sergei Chernenko** |
| 2005 WM20-I-B | 5 | 1 | 1 | | 3 | 11 | 19 | 5th | Vladimir Yelovikov | Viktor Andrushenko |
| 2006 WM20-I-A | 5 | 1 | 1 | | 3 | 10 | 22 | 5th | Ivan Pravylov | Yegor Yegorov |
| 2007 WM20-I-A | 5 | 4 | 0 | 0 | 1 | 15 | 9 | 3rd | Ivan Pravylov | Yegor Yegorov |
| 2008 WM20-I-A | 5 | 0 | 1 | 1 | 3 | 10 | 26 | 5th | Sergiy Lubnin | Dmytro Nimenko |
| 2009 WM20-I-B | 5 | 1 | 0 | 0 | 4 | 10 | 16 | 5th | Sergiy Lubnin | Dmytro Siryy |
| 2010 WM20-I-A | 5 | 1 | 0 | 1 | 3 | 15 | 23 | 4th | Olexander Savytsky | Maxim Kvitchenko |
| 2011 WM20-I-A | 5 | 0 | 0 | 0 | 5 | 4 | 32 | 6th | Olexander Savytsky | Volodymyr Romanenko |
| 2012 WM20-II-A | 5 | 3 | 2 | 0 | 0 | 24 | 10 | 1st | Alexander Godynyuk | Danil Korzh |

**U18 World Championship (Men)**
(bold=top level)

| Year Event | GP | W | T | OTW | OTL | L | GF | GA | Place | Coach | Captain |
|---|---|---|---|---|---|---|---|---|---|---|---|
| Year Event | GP | W | | OTW | OTL | L | GF | GA | Place | Coach | Captain |
| **1999 WM18** | **6** | **2** | **0** | | | **4** | **11** | **26** | **8th** | **Sergiy Lubnin** | **Vitali Donika** |
| **2000 WM18** | **6** | **1** | **1** | | | **4** | **14** | **33** | **9th** | **Sergiy Lubnin** | **Vitali Donika** |
| **2001 WM18** | **6** | **0** | **0** | | | **6** | **9** | **48** | **10th** | **Sergiy Lubnin** | **Olexander Skorokhod** |
| **2002 WM18** | **8** | **1** | **0** | | | **7** | **10** | **46** | **12th** | **Anatoli Donika** | **Sergei Chernenko** |
| 2003 WM18-I-B | 5 | 1 | 0 | | | 4 | 16 | 24 | 6th | Anatoliy Stepanyshchev | Victor Andrushenko |
| 2004 WM18-II-A | 5 | 5 | 0 | | | 0 | 62 | 7 | 1st | Ivan Pravylov | Danylo Guryev |
| 2005 WM18-I-B | 5 | 3 | 0 | | | 2 | 16 | 12 | 3rd | Ivan Pravylov | Yegor Yegorov |
| 2006 WM18-I-B | 5 | 1 | 0 | | | 4 | 7 | 31 | 5th | Viktor Chibirev | Dmitro Nimenko |
| 2007 WM18-I-B | 5 | 1 | | 1 | 0 | 3 | 15 | 17 | 5th | Ramil Yuldashev | Dmitri Siry |
| 2008 WM18-I-A | 5 | 2 | | 0 | 0 | 3 | 8 | 12 | 5th | Ramil Yuldashev | *unknown* |
| 2009 WM18-I-A | 5 | 0 | | 0 | 0 | 5 | 7 | 29 | 6th | Ramil Yuldashev | Vladimir Romanenko |
| 2010 WM18-II-B | 5 | 4 | | 0 | 0 | 1 | 26 | 3 | 2nd | Alexander Godynyuk | Danil Korzh |
| 2011 WM18-II-B | 5 | 5 | | 0 | 0 | 0 | 51 | 7 | 1st | Alexander Godynyuk | Vsevelod Tolstushko |
| 2012 WM18-I-B | 5 | 1 | | 1 | 1 | 2 | 20 | 26 | 4th | Alexander Godynyuk | Maxym Martyshko |

*Ukraine's Artem Bondaryev flies through the air against Great Britain. Photo: Samo Vidic.*

# United Arab Emirates (UAE)

*The United Arab Emirates players celebrate their 2012 IIHF Challenge Cup of Asia triumph. Photo: IHAI.*

**Joined IIHF: May 10, 2001 (Associate Member)**
Website: www.uaeihf.ae
E-mail: uaeiha@gmail.com

UAE Ice Hockey Association
P.O. Box 111025
Abu Dhabi
United Arab Emirates

Phone: +971 2 444 6178 • Fax: +971 2 444 6279

**World Ranking**

**MEN**
2012........47
2011........47
2010........47

**Top Level Host History** none

**World Championship (Men)**

| Year Event | GP | W | OTW | OTL | L | GF | GA | Place | Coach | Captain |
|---|---|---|---|---|---|---|---|---|---|---|
| 2010 WM-III-A | 3 | 0 | 0 | 0 | 3 | 5 | 18 | 4th | Teemu Taruvuori | Juma al Dhaheri |

# United States (USA)

*Team USA celebrates after winning the 2012 IIHF Ice Hockey U18 World Championship. Photo: Phillip MacCallum / HHOF-IIHF Images.*

**Joined IIHF: April 26, 1920**
Website: www.usahockey.com
E-mail: usah@usahockey.org

USA Hockey
1775 Bob Johnson Drive
Colorado Springs, CO 80906
USA

Phone: +1 719 576 8724 • Fax: +1 719 538 1160

**World Ranking**

| MEN | WOMEN |
|---|---|
| 2012........7 | 2012........2 |
| 2011........6 | 2011........1 |
| 2010........6 | 2010........2 |
| 2009........5 | 2009........1 |
| 2008........6 | 2008........2 |
| 2007........7 | 2007........2 |
| 2006........7 | 2006........2 |
| 2005........6 | 2005........2 |
| 2004........6 | 2004........2 |

### Top Level Host History

Olympics: 1932 (Lake Placid); 1960 (Squaw Valley); 1980 (Lake Placid); 2002 (Salt Lake City)
World Championship (Men): 1962 (Colorado Springs, Denver)
U20 World Championship: 1982 (Duluth, Grand Rapids, Brainerd, Virginia, Bloomington, International Falls, St. Cloud, Burnsville, New Ulm, Minneapolis, Rochester, Mankato); 1989 (Anchorage, Fire Lake); 1996 (Worcester, Marlborough, Amherst, Boston, Springfield); 2005 (Grand Forks, Thief River Falls), 2011 (Buffalo, Niagara)
U18 World Championship (Men): 2009 (Fargo, Moorhead)
Women's World Championship: 1994 (Lake Placid); 2001 (Rochester, Minneapolis, Blaine, St. Cloud, Plymouth, Fridley), 2012 (Burlington)
U18 Women's World Championship: 2010 (Chicago)

### Olympics, Men

(bold=top level)

| Year Event | GP | W | T | | L | GF | GA | Place | Coach | Captain |
|---|---|---|---|---|---|---|---|---|---|---|
| Year Event | GP | W | OTW | OTL | L | GF | GA | Place | Coach | Captain |
| 1920 OG-M | 4 | 3 | 0 | | 1 | 52 | 2 | S | Cornelius Fellowes | Joe McCormick (1) |
| 1924 OG-M | 5 | 4 | 0 | | 1 | 73 | 6 | S | William Haddock | Irving Small |
| 1932 OG-M | 6 | 4 | 1 | | 1 | 27 | 5 | S | Alfred Winsor | John Chase |
| 1936 OG-M | 8 | 5 | 1 | | 2 | 10 | 4 | B | Bert Prettyman | Jack Garrison |
| 1948 OG-M | 8 | 5 | 0 | | 3 | 86 | 33 | 4th | John Garrison | Goodwin Harding |
| 1952 OG-M | 8 | 6 | 1 | | 1 | 43 | 21 | S | John Pleban | Al Van |
| 1956 OG-M | 7 | 5 | 0 | | 2 | 33 | 16 | S | John Mariucci | Gene Campbell |
| 1960 OG-M | 7 | 7 | 0 | | 0 | 48 | 17 | G | Jack Riley | Jack Kirrane |
| 1964 OG-M | 7 | 2 | 0 | | 5 | 29 | 33 | 5th | Ed Jeremiah | Herb Brooks/Bill Reichert |
| 1968 OG-M | 7 | 2 | 1 | | 4 | 23 | 28 | 6th | Murray Williamson | Lou Nanne |
| 1972 OG-M | 5 | 3 | 0 | | 2 | 18 | 15 | S | Murray Williamson | Tim Sheehy (2) |
| 1976 OG-M | 5 | 2 | 0 | | 3 | 15 | 21 | 5th | Bob Johnson | John Taft |
| 1980 OG-M | 7 | 6 | 1 | | 0 | 33 | 15 | G | Herb Brooks | Mike Eruzione |
| 1984 OG-M | 6 | 2 | 2 | | 2 | 23 | 21 | 7th | Lou Vairo | Phil Verchota |
| 1988 OG-M | 6 | 3 | 0 | | 3 | 35 | 31 | 7th | Dave Peterson | Brian Leetch |
| 1992 OG-M | 8 | 5 | 1 | | 2 | 25 | 19 | 4th | Dave Peterson | Clark Donatelli |
| 1994 OG-M | 8 | 1 | 3 | | 4 | 28 | 32 | 8th | Tim Taylor | Peter Laviolette |
| 1998 OG-M | 4 | 1 | 0 | | 3 | 9 | 14 | 6th | Ron Wilson | Chris Chelios |
| 2002 OG-M | 6 | 4 | 1 | | 1 | 26 | 10 | S | Herb Brooks | Chris Chelios |
| 2006 OG-M | 6 | 1 | 1 | | 4 | 16 | 17 | 8th | Peter Laviolette | Chris Chelios |
| 2010 OG-M | 6 | 5 | 0 | 1 | 0 | 24 | 9 | S | Ron Wilson | Jamie Langenbrunner |

(1) Frank "Red" Synott captain for game of April 27, 1920 vs. SWE
(2) Keith Christiansen captain vs. Switzerland (Feb. 4), Czechoslovakia (Feb. 7), and Finland (Feb. 10)

NOTE: Between 1920 and 1952 Teams represented the United States as follows: 1920—USAHA players from St. Paul, Pittsburgh, and Boston, 1924—USAHA players from St. Paul, Pittsburgh, and Boston, 1932—AAU all-star team, 1936—AAU all-star team, 1952—United States Ice Hockey Committee all-star team

### World Championship (Men)

(bold=top level)

| Year Event | GP | W | T | | L | GF | GA | Place | Coach | Captain |
|---|---|---|---|---|---|---|---|---|---|---|
| Year Event | GP | W | OTW | OTL | L | GF | GA | Place | Coach | Captain |
| 1931 WM | 6 | 5 | 0 | | 1 | 22 | 3 | S | Walter Brown | *unknown* |
| 1933 WM | 5 | 5 | 0 | | 0 | 23 | 1 | G | Walter Brown | Ben Langmaid |
| 1934 WM | 4 | 3 | 0 | | 1 | 6 | 2 | S | Walter Brown | *unknown* |
| 1938 WM | 6 | 3 | 1 | | 2 | 10 | 5 | 7th | John Hutchinson | *unknown* |
| 1939 WM | 9 | 7 | 0 | | 2 | 25 | 8 | S | John Hutchinson | *unknown* |
| 1947 WM | 7 | 4 | 0 | | 3 | 42 | 26 | 5th | Herb Ralby | Hec Rousseau |
| 1949 WM | 8 | 6 | 0 | | 2 | 59 | 22 | B | Jack Riley | Jack Riley |
| 1950 WM | 7 | 5 | 0 | | 2 | 49 | 29 | S | John Pleban | Al Van |
| 1951 WM | 6 | 1 | 1 | | 4 | 14 | 42 | 6th | Larry Charest | Ray Marcotte |
| 1955 WM | 8 | 4 | 2 | | 2 | 33 | 29 | 4th | Al Yurkewicz | Ruben Bjorkman |
| 1958 WM | 7 | 3 | 1 | | 3 | 29 | 33 | 5th | Cal Marvin | *unknown* |
| 1959 WM | 8 | 5 | 0 | | 3 | 45 | 25 | 4th | Marsh Ryman | Bill Cleary |
| 1961 WM | 7 | 1 | 1 | | 5 | 24 | 43 | 6th | John Pleban | *unknown* |
| 1962 WM | 7 | 5 | 0 | | 2 | 54 | 23 | B | John Pleban | *unknown* |
| 1963 WM | 7 | 1 | 1 | | 5 | 21 | 64 | 8th | Harry Cleverly | Frank Silka |
| 1965 WM | 7 | 2 | 0 | | 5 | 22 | 44 | 6th | Ken Yackel | *unknown* |
| 1966 WM | 7 | 2 | 0 | | 5 | 18 | 39 | 6th | Vic Heyliger | John Mayasich |

| | | | | | | | | | | |
|---|---|---|---|---|---|---|---|---|---|---|
| **1967 WM** | **7** | **3** | **1** | | **3** | **20** | **23** | **5th** | **Murray Williamson** | **Bob Curry (1)** |
| **1969 WM** | **10** | **0** | **0** | | **10** | **23** | **74** | **6th** | **John Mayasich** | ***unknown*** |
| 1970 WM-B | 7 | 7 | 0 | | 0 | 70 | 11 | 1st | Murray Williamson | Don Ross |
| **1971 WM** | **10** | **2** | **0** | | **8** | **31** | **53** | **6th** | **Murray Williamson** | ***unknown*** |
| 1972 WM-B | 6 | 5 | 0 | | 1 | 39 | 22 | 2nd | John Kelley | Robbie Ftorek (2) |
| 1973 WM-B | 7 | 5 | 1 | | 1 | 52 | 23 | 2nd | Lou Vairo | Charlie Brown |
| 1974 WM-B | 7 | 7 | 0 | | 0 | 40 | 14 | 1st | Bob Johnson/Len Lilyholm | Len Lilyholm |
| **1975 WM** | **10** | **0** | **0** | | **10** | **22** | **84** | **6th** | **Bob Johnson** | **Herb Boxer** |
| **1976 WM** | **10** | **3** | **1** | | **6** | **24** | **42** | **4th** | **John Mariucci/Glenn Gostick** | **Lou Nanne** |
| **1977 WM** | **10** | **3** | **1** | | **6** | **29** | **43** | **6th** | **John Mariucci** | **Lou Nanne** |
| **1978 WM** | **10** | **2** | **2** | | **6** | **38** | **58** | **6th** | **John Mariucci** | **Curt Bennett** |
| **1979 WM** | **8** | **2** | **3** | | **3** | **27** | **28** | **7th** | **Herb Brooks** | **Craig Patrick** |
| **1981 WM** | **8** | **4** | **1** | | **3** | **39** | **43** | **5th** | **Bob Johnson** | **Bill Baker** |
| **1982 WM** | **7** | **0** | **1** | | **6** | **21** | **39** | **8th** | **Bill Selman/Mike Smith** | **Rod Langway (3)** |
| 1983 WM-B | 7 | 6 | 1 | | 0 | 53 | 14 | 1st | Lou Vairo | *unknown* |
| **1985 WM** | **10** | **4** | **1** | | **5** | **31** | **58** | **4th** | **Dave Peterson** | ***unknown*** |
| **1986 WM** | **10** | **4** | **0** | | **6** | **41** | **43** | **6th** | **Dave Peterson** | **Mark Johnson** |
| **1987 WM** | **10** | **4** | **0** | | **6** | **38** | **49** | **7th** | **Dave Peterson** | **Mark Johnson** |
| **1989 WM** | **10** | **4** | **1** | | **5** | **37** | **40** | **6th** | **Tim Taylor** | **Pat LaFontaine** |
| **1990 WM** | **10** | **6** | **0** | | **4** | **35** | **43** | **5th** | **Tim Taylor** | **Jim Johnson** |
| **1991 WM** | **10** | **3** | **2** | | **5** | **35** | **51** | **4th** | **Tim Taylor** | **Moe Mantha** |
| **1992 WM** | **6** | **2** | **1** | | **3** | **15** | **23** | **7th** | **Tim Taylor** | **Gary Suter** |
| **1993 WM** | **6** | **2** | **2** | | **2** | **16** | **15** | **6th** | **Tim Taylor** | **Ed Olczyk** |
| **1994 WM** | **8** | **4** | **0** | | **4** | **24** | **35** | **4th** | **Ron Wilson** | **Craig Wolanin** |
| **1995 WM** | **6** | **3** | **2** | | **1** | **18** | **15** | **6th** | **Jeff Sauer** | **Tom O'Regan** |
| **1996 WM** | **8** | **5** | **0** | | **3** | **22** | **24** | **B** | **Ron Wilson** | **Kevin Stevens** |
| **1997 WM** | **8** | **4** | **1** | | **3** | **19** | **21** | **6th** | **Jeff Jackson** | **Ted Donato** |
| **1998 WM** | **6** | **1** | **1** | | **4** | **10** | **19** | **12th** | **Jeff Jackson** | **Eric Weinrich** |
| **1999 WM** | **6** | **3** | **0** | | **3** | **22** | **15** | **6th** | **Terry Murray** | **Kelly Miller** |
| **2000 WM** | **7** | **4** | **2** | | **1** | **17** | **13** | **5th** | **Lou Vairo** | **Phil Housley** |
| **2001 WM** | **9** | **4** | **1** | | **4** | **22** | **21** | **4th** | **Lou Vairo** | **Phil Housley** |
| **2002 WM** | **7** | **3** | **1** | | **3** | **19** | **16** | **7th** | **Lou Vairo** | **Steve Konowalchuk** |
| **2003 WM** | **6** | **3** | **0** | | **3** | **23** | **14** | **13th** | **Lou Vairo** | **Kevin Miller** |
| **2004 WM** | **9** | **5** | **1** | | **3** | **30** | **21** | **B** | **Peter Laviolette** | **Chris Drury** |
| **2005 WM** | **7** | **3** | **2** | | **2** | **23** | **13** | **6th** | **Peter Laviolette** | **Mike Modano** |
| **2006 WM** | **7** | **4** | **0** | | **3** | **14** | **16** | **7th** | **Mike Eaves** | **Richard Park** |
| **2007 WM** | **7** | **4** | **0** | **1** | **2** | **28** | **20** | **5th** | **Mike Sullivan** | **Chris Clark** |
| **2008 WM** | **7** | **4** | **0** | **1** | **2** | **32** | **17** | **6th** | **John Tortorella** | **Jeff Halpern** |
| **2009 WM** | **9** | **4** | **0** | **2** | **3** | **32** | **28** | **4th** | **Ron Wilson** | **Dustin Brown** |
| **2010 WM** | **6** | **2** | **1** | **2** | **1** | **21** | **9** | **13th** | **Scott Gordon** | **Jack Johnson** |
| **2011 WM** | **7** | **3** | **0** | **1** | **3** | **20** | **24** | **8th** | **Scott Gordon** | **Mark Stuart** |
| **2012 WM** | **8** | **4** | **2** | **0** | **2** | **34** | **20** | **7th** | **Scott Gordon** | **Jack Johnson** |

(1) Herb Brooks captain vs. East Germany (Mar. 25)
(2) Tim Sheehy captain vs. Norway (Mar. 30)
(3) Joe Micheletti captain vs. Sweden (Apr. 15)

NOTE: Between 1931 and 1955 club teams represented the United States as follows: 1931—Boston Olympics, 1933—Boston Olympics, 1938—AAU all-star team, 1939—AAU all-star team, 1947—AHAUS all-star team, 1949—AHAUS all-star team, 1950—AHAUS all-star team, 1951—Bates Hockey Club (Lewiston, Maine), 1955—AHAUS all-star team

### IIHF-NHL Invitationals

(bold=top level)

| Year Event | GP | W | T | L | GF | GA | Place | Coach | Captain |
|---|---|---|---|---|---|---|---|---|---|
| **1976 CC** | **5** | **1** | **1** | **3** | **14** | **21** | **5th** | **Bob Pulford** | **Bill Nyrop** |
| **1981 CC** | **6** | **2** | **1** | **3** | **18** | **23** | **4th** | **Bob Johnson** | **Robbie Ftorek** |
| **1984 CC** | **6** | **3** | **1** | **2** | **23** | **22** | **4th** | **Bob Johnson** | **Rod Langway** |
| **1987 CC** | **5** | **2** | **0** | **3** | **13** | **14** | **5th** | **Bob Johnson** | **Rod Langway** |
| **1991 CC** | **8** | **5** | **0** | **3** | **29** | **26** | **2nd** | **Bob Johnson** | **Joel Otto** |
| **1996 WCH** | **7** | **6** | **0** | **1** | **37** | **18** | **1st** | **Ron Wilson** | **Brian Leetch** |
| **2004 WCH** | **5** | **2** | **0** | **3** | **11** | **10** | **4th** | **Ron Wilson** | **Chris Chelios** |

### U20 World Championship

(bold=top level)

| Year Event | GP | W | T | | L | GF | GA | Place | Coach | Captain |
|---|---|---|---|---|---|---|---|---|---|---|
| Year Event | GP | W | OTW | OTL | L | GF | GA | Place | Coach | Captain |
| **1977 WM20** | **7** | **1** | **1** | | **5** | **25** | **45** | **7th** | **Marshall Johnston** | **Doug Olson** |
| **1978 WM20** | **6** | **4** | **0** | | **2** | **41** | **30** | **5th** | **Len Lilyholm** | **Don Waddell** |
| **1979 WM20** | **5** | **2** | **0** | | **3** | **21** | **23** | **6th** | **Lou Vairo** | **Steve Ulseth** |
| **1980 WM20** | **5** | **1** | **1** | | **3** | **21** | **26** | **7th** | **Lou Vairo** | **Bryan Erickson (1)** |
| **1981 WM20** | **5** | **2** | **0** | | **3** | **19** | **27** | **6th** | **Lou Vairo** | **David Jensen (2)** |
| **1982 WM20** | **7** | **2** | **0** | | **5** | **28** | **34** | **6th** | **Lou Vairo** | ***unknown*** |
| **1983 WM20** | **7** | **3** | **0** | | **4** | **28** | **29** | **5th** | **Bill Hasler** | **Kelly Miller** |
| **1984 WM20** | **7** | **2** | **0** | | **5** | **32** | **38** | **6th** | **John Perpich** | ***unknown*** |
| **1985 WM20** | **7** | **2** | **0** | | **5** | **23** | **37** | **6th** | **Doug Woog** | **Brian Johnson (3)** |
| **1986 WM20** | **7** | **4** | **0** | | **3** | **35** | **26** | **B** | **Dave Peterson** | **Steve Leach** |
| **1987 WM20** | **7** | **4** | **0** | | **3** | **42** | **30** | **4th** | **Dave Peterson** | **Scott Young** |
| **1988 WM20** | **7** | **1** | **0** | | **6** | **28** | **46** | **6th** | **Terry Christensen** | ***unknown*** |
| **1989 WM20** | **7** | **3** | **1** | | **3** | **41** | **25** | **5th** | **Steve Cedorchuk** | **Adam Burt** |
| **1990 WM20** | **7** | **1** | **0** | | **6** | **22** | **37** | **7th** | **Steve Cedorchuk** | **Barry Richter** |
| **1991 WM20** | **7** | **4** | **1** | | **2** | **45** | **19** | **4th** | **Kevin Constantine** | **Ted Drury** |
| **1992 WM20** | **7** | **5** | **0** | | **2** | **30** | **22** | **B** | **Walt Kyle** | **Keith Tkachuk** |
| **1993 WM20** | **7** | **4** | **0** | | **3** | **32** | **23** | **4th** | **Walt Kyle** | **Brent Bilodeau** |
| **1994 WM20** | **7** | **1** | **1** | | **5** | **20** | **33** | **6th** | **Dean Blais** | **John Emmons (4)** |
| **1995 WM20** | **7** | **3** | **0** | | **4** | **28** | **33** | **5th** | **Jeff Jackson** | **Adam Deadmarsh** |
| **1996 WM20** | **6** | **3** | **0** | | **3** | **21** | **27** | **5th** | **Jack Parker** | **Bryan Berard** |

| | | | | | | | | | | |
|---|---|---|---|---|---|---|---|---|---|---|
| **1997 WM20** | 6 | 4 | 1 | | 1 | 23 | 9 | S | Jeff Jackson | Marty Reasoner |
| **1998 WM20** | 7 | 4 | 0 | | 3 | 25 | 19 | 5th | Jeff Jackson | Mike York (5) |
| **1999 WM20** | 6 | 3 | 0 | | 3 | 25 | 23 | 8th | Jeff Jackson | Paul Mara |
| **2000 WM20** | 7 | 2 | 2 | | 3 | 14 | 15 | 4th | Jeff Jackson | Adam Hall |
| **2001 WM20** | 7 | 5 | 0 | | 2 | 29 | 12 | 5th | Keith Allain | Connor Dunlop |
| **2002 WM20** | 7 | 4 | 2 | | 1 | 22 | 20 | 5th | Keith Allain | R.J. Umberger |
| **2003 WM20** | 7 | 4 | 0 | | 3 | 23 | 18 | 4th | Lou Vairo | Eric Nystrom |
| **2004 WM20** | 6 | 6 | 0 | | 0 | 27 | 8 | G | Mike Eaves | Mark Stuart |
| **2005 WM20** | 7 | 3 | 0 | | 4 | 27 | 28 | 4th | Scott Sandelin | Gary Suter |
| **2006 WM20** | 7 | 3 | 1 | | 3 | 26 | 22 | 4th | Walt Kyle | Kevin Porter |
| **2007 WM20** | 7 | 3 | 1 | 2 | 1 | 22 | 17 | B | Ron Rolston | Taylor Chorney |
| **2008 WM20** | 6 | 4 | 0 | 0 | 2 | 20 | 16 | 4th | John Hynes | Brian Strait |
| **2009 WM20** | 6 | 3 | 1 | 0 | 2 | 34 | 19 | 5th | Ron Rolston | Jonathon Blum |
| **2010 WM20** | 7 | 5 | 1 | 1 | 0 | 43 | 18 | G | Dean Blais | Derek Stepan |
| **2011 WM20** | 6 | 4 | 1 | 0 | 1 | 20 | 10 | B | Keith Allain | John Ramage |
| **2012 WM20** | 6 | 3 | 0 | 0 | 3 | 30 | 18 | 7th | Dean Blais | Jason Zucker |

(1) Bob Brooke captain Jan. 1 vs. CAN
(2) Gregg Moore captain Dec. 27 vs. FIN & Dec. 28 vs. SWE
(3) Jay Octeau captain Dec. 28 vs. CAN, Dec. 29 vs. FRG, Dec. 31 vs. POL; Clark Donatelli captain Jan. 1 vs. SWE
(4) Ryan Sittler captain Dec. 26 vs. FIN; David Wilkie captain Dec. 27 vs. SUI
(5) Chris Hajt captain Dec. 26 vs. KAZ, Dec. 31 vs. CZE, Jan. 3 vs. SWE

### U18 World Championship (Men)

(bold=top level)

| Year Event | GP | W | T | | L | GF | GA | Place | Coach | Captain |
|---|---|---|---|---|---|---|---|---|---|---|
| Year Event | GP | W | OTW | OTL | L | GF | GA | Place | Coach | Captain |
| **1999 WM18** | 6 | 3 | 0 | | 3 | 28 | 15 | 7th | Jeff Jackson | Connor Dunlop |
| **2000 WM18** | 6 | 2 | 0 | | 4 | 20 | 16 | 8th | Jeff Jackson | Jonathan Waibel |
| **2001 WM18** | 6 | 3 | 0 | | 3 | 28 | 14 | 6th | Mike Eaves | Brian McConnell |
| **2002 WM18** | 8 | 7 | 0 | | 1 | 46 | 10 | G | Mike Eaves | Mark Stuart |
| **2003 WM18** | 6 | 3 | 1 | | 2 | 15 | 15 | 4th | Moe Mantha | Ryan Suter |
| **2004 WM18** | 6 | 5 | 0 | | 1 | 27 | 10 | S | John Hynes | Nate Hagemo |
| **2005 WM18** | 6 | 6 | 0 | | 0 | 28 | 8 | G | Ron Rolston | Jim Fraser |
| **2006 WM18** | 6 | 6 | 0 | | 0 | 37 | 7 | G | John Hynes | James van Riemsdyk |
| **2007 WM18** | 7 | 3 | 1 | 1 | 2 | 38 | 20 | S | Ron Rolston | Kevin Shattenkirk |
| **2008 WM18** | 7 | 5 | 0 | 0 | 2 | 31 | 19 | B | John Hynes | David Warsofsky |
| **2009 WM18** | 7 | 6 | 0 | 0 | 1 | 42 | 12 | G | Ron Rolston | William Wrenn |
| **2010 WM18** | 7 | 6 | 0 | 0 | 1 | 33 | 7 | G | Kurt Kleinendorst | Jarred Tinordi |
| **2011 WM18** | 6 | 4 | 2 | 0 | 0 | 30 | 15 | G | Ron Rolston | Robbie Russo |
| **2012 WM18** | 6 | 6 | 0 | 0 | 0 | 27 | 4 | G | Danton Cole | Seth Jones |

### Olympics, Women

(bold=top level)

| Year Event | GP | W | T | | L | GF | GA | Place | Coach | Captain |
|---|---|---|---|---|---|---|---|---|---|---|
| Year Event | GP | W | OTW | OTL | L | GF | GA | Place | Coach | Captain |
| **1998 OG-W** | 6 | 6 | 0 | | 0 | 36 | 8 | G | Ben Smith | Cammi Granato |
| **2002 OG-W** | 5 | 4 | 0 | | 1 | 33 | 4 | S | Ben Smith | Cammi Granato |
| **2006 OG-W** | 5 | 4 | 0 | | 1 | 24 | 6 | B | Ben Smith | Krissy Wendell |
| **2010 OG-W** | 5 | 4 | 0 | 0 | 1 | 40 | 4 | S | Mark Johnson | Natalie Darwitz |

### Women's World Championship

(bold=top level)

| Year Event | GP | W | T | | L | GF | GA | Place | Coach | Captain |
|---|---|---|---|---|---|---|---|---|---|---|
| Year Event | GP | W | OTW | OTL | L | GF | GA | Place | Coach | Captain |
| **1990 WW** | 5 | 4 | 0 | | 1 | 50 | 15 | S | Don MacLeod | Tina Cardinale |
| **1992 WW** | 5 | 4 | 0 | | 1 | 37 | 16 | S | Russ McCurdy | Cindy Curley |
| **1994 WW** | 5 | 4 | 0 | | 1 | 41 | 10 | S | Karen Kay | Cindy Curley |
| **1997 WW** | 5 | 3 | 1 | | 1 | 29 | 7 | S | Ben Smith | Cammi Granato |
| **1999 WW** | 5 | 4 | 0 | | 1 | 31 | 6 | S | Ben Smith | Cammi Granato |
| **2000 WW** | 5 | 4 | 0 | | 1 | 44 | 8 | S | Ben Smith | Cammi Granato |
| **2001 WW** | 5 | 4 | 0 | | 1 | 43 | 4 | S | Ben Smith | Cammi Granato |
| **2004 WW** | 5 | 4 | 0 | | 1 | 29 | 6 | S | Ben Smith | Cammi Granato |
| **2005 WW** | 5 | 5 | 0 | | 0 | 28 | 4 | G | Ben Smith | Cammi Granato |
| **2007 WW** | 5 | 3 | 0 | 1 | 1 | 27 | 11 | S | Mark Johnson | Krissy Wendell |
| **2008 WW** | 5 | 4 | 0 | 1 | 0 | 23 | 8 | G | Jackie Barto | Sarah Erickson |
| **2009 WW** | 5 | 4 | 0 | 0 | 1 | 28 | 3 | G | Mark Johnson | Natalie Darwitz |
| **2011 WW** | 5 | 4 | 1 | 0 | 0 | 35 | 5 | G | Katey Stone | Jenny Potter |
| **2012 WW** | 5 | 4 | 0 | 1 | 0 | 43 | 7 | S | Katey Stone | Julie Chu |

### U18 Women's World Championship

(bold=top level)

| Year Event | GP | W | OTW | OTL | L | GF | GA | Place | Coach | Captain |
|---|---|---|---|---|---|---|---|---|---|---|
| **2008 WW18** | 5 | 5 | 0 | 0 | 0 | 41 | 4 | G | Katey Stone | Sarah Erickson |
| **2009 WW18** | 5 | 4 | 1 | 0 | 0 | 58 | 4 | G | Mark Johnson | Alev Kelter |
| **2010 WW18** | 5 | 4 | 0 | 1 | 0 | 40 | 6 | S | Katie King | Brittany Ammerman |
| **2011 WW18** | 5 | 5 | 0 | 0 | 0 | 47 | 4 | G | Jodi McKenna | Michelle Picard |
| **2012 WW18** | 5 | 4 | 0 | 0 | 1 | 35 | 5 | S | Heather Linstad | Alex Carpenter |

*Team USA's Seth Jones hoists the championship trophy after his team beat Sweden to claim the U18 men's championship in 2012. Photo: Phillip MacCallum / HHOF-IIHF Images.*

# TOURNAMENT RESULTS OLYMPICS, MEN

## GAMES OF THE VIIth OLYMPIAD
**April 23-September 12, 1920**
**(Winter Olympics held April 23–29, 1920)**
**Antwerp, Belgium**

### Final Placing

| | |
|---|---|
| Gold ........Canada | 5th .........Switzerland |
| Silver ......United States | 6th .........France |
| Bronze ....Czechoslovakia | 7th .........Belgium |
| 4th..........Sweden | |

### Tournament Format
The Bergvall system of elimination was employed, that being a unique knockout format between the nations in the first round. Those who won went on to compete for the gold medal; those who lost games to the champion—Canada—played another knockout series for the silver; and those who lost games to the silver medalists—the United States—went on to play for the bronze. France received a bye in the first playdown and thus qualified right away for the gold medal round.

### GOLD MEDAL ROUND

| | | |
|---|---|---|
| April 23 | Sweden 8 | Belgium 0 |
| April 24 | United States 29 | Switzerland 0 |
| April 24 | Canada 15 | Czechoslovakia 0 |
| April 25 | Sweden 4 | France 0 |
| April 25 | Canada 2 | United States 0 |
| April 26 | Canada 12 | Sweden 1 |

### SILVER MEDAL ROUND

| | | |
|---|---|---|
| April 27 | United States 7 | Sweden 0 |
| April 28 | United States 16 | Czechoslovakia 0 |

### BRONZE MEDAL ROUND

| | | |
|---|---|---|
| April 28 | Sweden 4 | Switzerland 0 |
| April 29 | Czechoslovakia 1 | Sweden 0 |

### Rosters
**Belgium** (Paul Loicq, coach) GK—Francois Vergult—Maurice Deprez, Paul Goeminne, Jean-Maurice Goossens, Paul Loicq, Philippe von Volcksom, Gaston van Volxem

**Canada** (Winnipeg Falcons—Fred "Steamer" Maxwell, coach) GK—Wally Byron—Bobby Benson, Konnie Johannesson, Frank Fredrickson, Chris Fridfinnson, Mike Goodman, Slim Halderson, Allan "Huck" Woodman

**Czechoslovakia** (Adolf Dusek, coach) GK—Jan Peka, Karel Walzer—Karel Hartmann, Josef Loos, Jan Palous, Karel Pesek-Kada, Josef Sroubek, Otakar Vindys

**France** (Joseph Garon, coach) GK—Jacques Gaittet—Jean Chaland, Pierre Charpentier, Henri Couttet, Georges Dary, Leon Quaglia, Alfred de Rauch

**Sweden** (Raoul Le Mat, coach) GK—Seth Howander, Albin Jansson—Wilhelm Arwe, Erik Burman, Georg Johansson, Einar Lindqvist, Einar Lundell, Hansjacob Mattsson, Nils Molander, David Safwenberg, Einar Svensson

**Switzerland** (Max Sillig, coach) GK—Rene Savoie—Rodolphe Cuendet, Louis Dufour, Max Holsbauer, Marius Jaccard, Bruno Leuzinger, Paul Lob, Max Sillig

**United States** (Cornelius Fellowes, coach) GK—Ray Bonney, Cy Weidenborner—Tony Conroy, Herb Drury, Ed Fitzgerald, George Geran, Frank Goheen, Joe McCormick, Larry McCormick, Frank Synott, Leon Tuck

## 1st OLYMPIC WINTER GAMES
**January 25-February 5, 1924**
**Chamonix, France**

### Final Placing

| | |
|---|---|
| Gold ........Canada | 4th .........Sweden |
| Silver ......United States | 5th .........Czechoslovakia, France |
| Bronze ....Great Britain | 7th .........Belgium, Switzerland |

### Tournament Format
Eight nations were divided into two groups of four teams and played a round-robin series within each group. The top two teams advanced to the finals. Preliminary round games between teams that advanced to the finals were carried over. The preliminary games consisted of three 15-minute periods, but the finals were three 20-minute periods, and all were played at the Stade Olympique du Mont Blanc.

### Results & Standings
**GROUP A**

| | GP | W | T | L | GF | GA | P |
|---|---|---|---|---|---|---|---|
| Canada | 3 | 3 | 0 | 0 | 85 | 0 | 6 |
| Sweden | 3 | 2 | 0 | 1 | 18 | 25 | 4 |
| Czechoslovakia | 3 | 1 | 0 | 2 | 14 | 41 | 2 |
| Switzerland | 3 | 0 | 0 | 3 | 2 | 53 | 0 |

| | | |
|---|---|---|
| January 28 | Sweden 9 | Switzerland 0 |
| January 28 | Canada 30 | Czechoslovakia 0 |
| January 29 | Canada 22 | Sweden 0 |
| January 30 | Canada 33 | Switzerland 0 |
| January 31 | Sweden 9 | Czechoslovakia 3 |
| February 1 | Czechoslovakia 11 | Switzerland 2 |

**GROUP B**

| | GP | W | T | L | GF | GA | P |
|---|---|---|---|---|---|---|---|
| United States | 3 | 3 | 0 | 0 | 52 | 0 | 6 |
| Great Britain | 3 | 2 | 0 | 1 | 34 | 16 | 4 |
| France | 3 | 1 | 0 | 2 | 9 | 42 | 2 |
| Belgium | 3 | 0 | 0 | 3 | 8 | 45 | 0 |

| | | |
|---|---|---|
| January 28 | United States 19 | Belgium 0 |
| January 29 | Great Britain 15 | France 2 |
| January 30 | Great Britain 19 | Belgium 3 |
| January 30 | United States 22 | France 0 |
| January 31 | United States 11 | Great Britain 0 |
| January 31 | France 7 | Belgium 5 |

**MEDAL ROUND**

| | GP | W | T | L | GF | GA | P |
|---|---|---|---|---|---|---|---|
| Canada | 3 | 3 | 0 | 0 | 47 | 3 | 6 |
| United States | 3 | 2 | 0 | 1 | 32 | 6 | 4 |
| Great Britain | 3 | 1 | 0 | 2 | 6 | 33 | 2 |
| Sweden | 3 | 0 | 0 | 3 | 3 | 46 | 0 |

| | | |
|---|---|---|
| February 1 | Canada 19 | Great Britain 2 |
| February 1 | United States 20 | Sweden 0 |
| February 3 | Great Britain 4 | Sweden 3 |
| February 3 | Canada 6 | United States 1 |

### Rosters
**Belgium** (Andre Poplimont, coach) GK—Paul van den Broeck, Victor Verschueren—Louis de Ridder, Francois Franck, Charles van den Driessche, Willy Kreitz, Henri Louette, Andre Poplimont, Louis de Ridder, Ferdinand Rudolph, Gaston van Volxem

**Canada** (Toronto Granites—Frank Rankin, coach) GK—Jack Cameron, Ernie Collett—Dunc Munro, Beattie Ramsay, Hooley Smith, Cyril "Sig" Slater, Harry Watson, Bert McCaffery, Harold McMunn

**Czechoslovakia** (Jaroslav Rezak, coach) GK—Jaroslav Stransky, Jaroslav Rezac—Jan Palous, Otakar Vindys, Josef Sroubek, Josef Malecek, Vilem Loos, Miroslav Fleischmann, Jaroslav Fleischmann, Jaroslav Pusbauer, Jaroslav Jirkovsky, Jan Krasl

**France** (Robert Lacroix, coach) GK—Maurice del Valle, Charles Lavaivre—Andre Charlet, Pierre Charpentier, Jacques Chaudron, Raoul Couvert, Albert Hassler, Joseph Monard, Calixte Payot, Leon Quaglia, Alfred de Rauch, Philippe Payot, Henri Couttet

**Great Britain** (George Elliott, coach) GK—William Anderson, Lorne Carr-Harris—Colin Carruthers, Eric Carruthers, George "Guy" Clarkson, Cuthbert Ross Cuthbert, George Holmes, Hamilton Jukes, Edward Pitblado, Blaine Sexton

**Sweden** (Ruben Rundqvist/Erik Gustafsson, coaches) GK—Carl Josefsson, Einar Ohlsson—Helge Johansson, Ruben Allinger, Wilhelm Arwe, Erik Burman, Birger Holmqvist, Gustaf Johansson, Ernst Karlberg, Nils Molander

**Switzerland** (Paul Muller, coach) GK—Emil Filiol, Rene Savoie—Fred Auckenthaler, Marius Jaccard, Emile Jaquet, Bruno Leuzinger, Ernest Mottier, Paul Muller, Wilhelm de Siebenthal, Donald Unger, Andre Verdeil

**United States** (William Haddock, coach) GK—Alphonse "Frenchy" Lacroix, Art Langley—Clarence "Taffy" Abel, Herb Drury, John Lyons, Justin McCarthy, Williard Rice, Irving Small, Frank Synott, George Geran

## 2nd OLYMPIC WINTER GAMES
## February 11-20, 1928
## St. Moritz, Switzerland

**Final Placing**

Gold ........Canada
Silver ......Sweden
Bronze ....Switzerland
4th ..........Great Britain
5th ..........France
6th .........Czechoslovakia
7th .........Belgium, Austria
9th .........Poland
10th .......Germany
11th .......Hungary

**Tournament Format**

All ten European teams were placed in three divisions to play round-robin preliminary matches. One team from each division moved on to the medal round. Because of the team's universally acknowledged superiority, Canada received a bye directly into the medal round, which again was set up as a round-robin schedule for the four finalists.

**Results & Standings**

**GROUP A**

| | GP | W | T | L | GF | GA | P |
|---|---|---|---|---|---|---|---|
| Great Britain | 3 | 2 | 0 | 1 | 10 | 6 | 4 |
| France | 3 | 2 | 0 | 1 | 6 | 5 | 4 |
| Belgium | 3 | 2 | 0 | 1 | 9 | 10 | 4 |
| Hungary | 3 | 0 | 0 | 3 | 2 | 6 | 0 |

| | | |
|---|---|---|
| February 11 | Great Britain 7 | Belgium 3 |
| February 11 | France 2 | Hungary 0 |
| February 12 | Belgium 3 | Hungary 2 |
| February 12 | France 3 | Great Britain 2 |
| February 16 | Great Britain 1 | Hungary 0 |
| February 16 | Belgium 3 | France 1 |

**GROUP B**

| | GP | W | T | L | GF | GA | P |
|---|---|---|---|---|---|---|---|
| Sweden | 2 | 1 | 1 | 0 | 5 | 2 | 3 |
| Czechoslovakia | 2 | 1 | 0 | 1 | 3 | 5 | 2 |
| Poland | 2 | 0 | 1 | 1 | 4 | 5 | 1 |

| | | |
|---|---|---|
| February 11 | Sweden 3 | Czechoslovakia 0 |
| February 12 | Sweden 2 | Poland 2 |
| February 13 | Czechoslovakia 3 | Poland 2 |

**GROUP C**

| | GP | W | T | L | GF | GA | P |
|---|---|---|---|---|---|---|---|
| Switzerland | 2 | 1 | 1 | 0 | 5 | 4 | 3 |
| Austria | 2 | 0 | 2 | 0 | 4 | 4 | 2 |
| Germany | 2 | 0 | 1 | 1 | 0 | 1 | 1 |

| | | |
|---|---|---|
| February 11 | Austria 4 | Switzerland 4 |
| February 12 | Germany 0 | Austria 0 |
| February 16 | Switzerland 1 | Germany 0 |

**MEDAL ROUND**

| | GP | W | T | L | GF | GA | P |
|---|---|---|---|---|---|---|---|
| Canada | 3 | 3 | 0 | 0 | 38 | 0 | 6 |
| Sweden | 3 | 2 | 0 | 1 | 7 | 12 | 4 |
| Switzerland | 3 | 1 | 0 | 2 | 4 | 17 | 2 |
| Great Britain | 3 | 0 | 0 | 3 | 1 | 21 | 0 |

| | | |
|---|---|---|
| February 17 | Canada 11 | Sweden 0 |
| February 17 | Switzerland 4 | Great Britain 0 |
| February 18 | Canada 14 | Great Britain 0 |
| February 18 | Sweden 4 | Switzerland 0 |
| February 19 | Canada 13 | Switzerland 0 |
| February 19 | Sweden 3 | Great Britain 1 |

**Rosters**

**Austria** (Edgar Dietrichstein, coach) GK—Hermann Weiss, Hans Kail—Herbert Bruck, Walter Bruck, Jacques Dietrichstein, Hans Ertl, Josef Gobel, Herbert Klang, Uli Lederer, Walter Sell, Reginald Spevak

**Belgium** (Jean de Craene, coach) GK—Hector Chotteau—Andre Bautier, Roger Bureau, Albert Collon, Francois Frank, David Meyer, Marc-Paul Pelzer, Jacques van Reysschoot, Pierre van Reysschoot, Jean van de Wouwer

**Canada** (University of Toronto Graduates—Conn Smythe, coach) GK—Norbert "Stuffy" Mueller, Joe Sullivan—Frank Fisher, Rogers "Rod" Plaxton, John "Red" Porter, Ross Taylor, Dr. Lou Hudson, Dave Trottier, Hugh Plaxton, Charlie Delahey, Bert Plaxton, Grant Gordon, Frank Sullivan

**Czechoslovakia** (Frantisek Lorenz, coach) GK—Jan Peka—Wolfgang Dorasil, Karel Hromadka, Jan Krasl, Jan Lichnovski, Josef Malecek, Jiri Pusbauer, Bohumil Stiegenhofer, Josef Sroubek, Jiri Tozicka

**France** GK—Philippe Lefebure, Robert George—Andre Charlet, Raoul Couvert, Albert Hassler, Francois Mautin, Calixte Payot, Philippe Payot, Leon Quaglia, Alfred de Rauch, Gerard Simond

**Germany** (Erich Romer, coach) GK—Alfred Steinke—Gustav Jaenecke, Wolfgang Kittel, Franz Kreisel, Fritz Rammelmayr, Erich Romer, Walter Sachs, Hans Schmid, Martin Schrottle, Marquardt Slevogt

**Great Britain** GK—John Rogers, William Speechley—Wilbert Brown, Colin Carruthers, Eric Carruthers, Cuthbert Ross Cuthbert, Bernard Fawcett, Harold Greenwood, Neville Melland, Blaine Sexton, Victor Tait, Charles Wyld

**Hungary** (Phil Taylor, coach) GK—Tibor Heinrich, Bela Ordody—Miklos Barcza, Frigyes Barna, Matyas Farkas, Peter Krempels, Istvan Krepuska, Geza Lator, Sandor Minder, Josef de Revay, Bela Weiner

**Poland** (Tadeusz Adamowski, coach) GK—Jozef Stogowski—Tadeusz Adamowski, Alexander Kowalski, Wlodzimierz Krygier, Lucjan Kulej, Alexander Sluczanowski, Karol Szenajch, Alexander Tupalski, Kazimierz Zebrowski

**Sweden** (Viking Harbom/Sten Mellgren, coaches) GK—Nils Johansson, Curt Sucksdorff—Carl Abrahamsson, Emil Bergman, Birger Holmqvist, Gustaf "Lulle" Johansson, Helge Johansson, Ernst Karlberg, Erik Larsson, Bertil Linde, Sigfrid Oberg, Wilhelm Petersen

**Switzerland** (Bobby Bell, coach) GK—Charles Fasel, Arnold Martignoni—Murezzan Andreossi, Robert Breiter, Louis Dufour, Albert Geromini, Fritz Kraatz, Heini Meng, Anton Morosani, Luzius Ruedi, Richard "Bibi" Torriani

## 3rd OLYMPIC WINTER GAMES
## February 4–13, 1932
## Lake Placid, United States

**Final Placing**

Gold ........Canada
Silver ......United States
Bronze....Germany
4th .........Poland

**Tournament Format**

Teams received two points for a win and one for a tie. With just four teams entered — Canada, Germany, Poland, United States — each team played a double round-robin, two games against each opponent. Each game consisted of three, 15-minute periods. A two-referee system was used and all hockey matches were officiated by the same two men, Lou Marsh of Canada and Don Sands of the United States.

**Results & Standings**

| | GP | W | T | L | GF | GA | P |
|---|---|---|---|---|---|---|---|
| Canada | 6 | 5 | 1 | 0 | 32 | 4 | 11 |
| United States | 6 | 4 | 1 | 1 | 27 | 5 | 9 |
| Germany | 6 | 2 | 0 | 4 | 7 | 26 | 4 |
| Poland | 6 | 0 | 0 | 6 | 3 | 34 | 0 |

| | | |
|---|---|---|
| February 4 | Canada 2 | United States 1 (10:00 OT—Vic Lindquist) |
| February 4 | Germany 2 | Poland 1 |
| February 5 | United States 4 | Poland 1 |
| February 6 | Canada 4 | Germany 1 |
| February 7 | Canada 9 | Poland 0 |
| February 7 | United States 7 | Germany 0 |
| February 8 | United States 5 | Poland 0 |
| February 8 | Canada 5 | Germany 0 |
| February 9 | Canada 10 | Poland 0 |
| February 10 | United States 8 | Germany 0 |
| February 13 | Germany 4 | Poland 1 |
| February 13 | Canada 2 | United States 2 (30:00 OT) |

**Rosters**

**Canada** (The Winnipegs—Jack Hughes, coach) GK—William Cockburn, Stanley Wagner—Roy Hinkel, Hugh Sutherland, George Garbutt, Walter Monson, Harold "Hack" Simpson, Bert Duncanson, Romeo Rivers, Alston "Stoney" Wise, Clifford Crowley, Vic Lindquist, Norm Malloy, Ken Moore

**Germany** (Erich Romer, coach) GK—Walter Leinweber—Rudi Ball, Alfred Heinrich, Erich Herker, Gustav Jaenecke, Werner Korff, Erich Romer, Martin Schrottle, Marquardt Slevogt, Georg Strobl

**Poland** (Tadeusz Sachs, coach) GK—Jozef Stogowski—Adam Kowalski, Alexander Kowalski, Wlodzimierz Krygier, Witalis Ludwiczak, Czeslaw Marchewczyk, Kazimierz Materski, Albert Mauer, Roman Sabinski, Kazimierz Sokolowski

**United States** (Alfred Winsor, coach) GK—Frank Farrell—Osborn Anderson, John Bent, John Chase, John Cookman, Doug Everett, Joe Fitzgerald, John Garrison, Gerald Hallock, Bob Livingston, Francis Nelson, Winthrop Palmer, Gordon Smith, Ted Frazier

## 4th OLYMPIC WINTER GAMES
## February 6–16, 1936
## Garmisch-Partenkirchen, Germany

**Final Placing**

| | | | |
|---|---|---|---|
| Gold | Great Britain | 5th | Germany, Sweden |
| Silver | Canada | 7th | Austria, Hungary |
| Bronze | United States | 9th | Italy, France, Japan, Poland |
| 4th | Czechoslovakia | 13th | Belgium, Latvia, Switzerland |

**Tournament Format**

The 15 entries were divided into four divisions (three of four teams, one of three teams) and played a round-robin series within each division. The top two countries then advanced to a semi-final round and the top two from that advanced to the finals. Any ties in the groupings would be decided by total number of goals scored in the Games. Games consisted of three 15-minute periods and each team could dress only ten players. Three substitutes per game were allowed.

An extremely important, complex rule for the final round stated that any team that had beaten another in a previous round did not have to play against that same team in the finals. Instead, they were automatically given two points for the earlier win (the one win, therefore, counted two points in both the semi-final and final rounds for Britain at these Olympics). Thus, Canada's loss to Great Britain in the semi-finals virtually assured them of losing the gold medal, for they couldn't play the English in the final round to avenge the earlier defeat.

**Results & Standings**

**ROUND ONE**

**GROUP A**

| | GP | W | T | L | GF | GA | P |
|---|---|---|---|---|---|---|---|
| Canada | 3 | 3 | 0 | 0 | 24 | 3 | 6 |
| Austria | 3 | 2 | 0 | 1 | 11 | 7 | 4 |
| Poland | 3 | 1 | 0 | 2 | 11 | 12 | 2 |
| Latvia | 3 | 0 | 0 | 3 | 3 | 27 | 0 |

| | | |
|---|---|---|
| February 6 | Canada 8 | Poland 1 |
| February 7 | Canada 11 | Latvia 0 |
| February 7 | Austria 2 | Poland 1 |
| February 8 | Poland 9 | Latvia 2 |
| February 8 | Canada 5 | Austria 2 |
| February 9 | Austria 7 | Latvia 1 |

**GROUP B**

| | GP | W | T | L | GF | GA | P |
|---|---|---|---|---|---|---|---|
| Germany | 3 | 2 | 0 | 1 | 5 | 1 | 4 |
| United States | 3 | 2 | 0 | 1 | 5 | 2 | 4 |
| Italy | 3 | 1 | 0 | 2 | 2 | 5 | 2 |
| Switzerland | 3 | 1 | 0 | 2 | 1 | 5 | 2 |

| | | |
|---|---|---|
| February 6 | United States 1 | Germany 0 |
| February 7 | United States 3 | Switzerland 0 |
| February 7 | Germany 3 | Italy 0 |
| February 8 | Italy 2 | United States 1 (20:00 OT—Gianni Scotti) |
| February 8 | Germany 2 | Switzerland 0 |
| February 9 | Switzerland 1 | Italy 0 |

**GROUP C**

| | GP | W | T | L | GF | GA | P |
|---|---|---|---|---|---|---|---|
| Czechoslovakia | 3 | 3 | 0 | 0 | 10 | 0 | 6 |
| Hungary | 3 | 2 | 0 | 1 | 14 | 5 | 4 |
| France | 3 | 1 | 0 | 2 | 4 | 7 | 2 |
| Belgium | 3 | 0 | 0 | 3 | 4 | 20 | 0 |

| | | |
|---|---|---|
| February 6 | Hungary 11 | Belgium 2 |
| February 7 | Czechoslovakia 5 | Belgium 0 |
| February 7 | Hungary 3 | France 0 |
| February 8 | Czechoslovakia 3 | Hungary 0 |
| February 8 | France 4 | Belgium 2 (20:00 OT—1st OT Marcel Couttet (FRA), Pierre van Reysschoot (BEL); 2nd OT Michel Delesalle (FRA), Jean-Pierre Hagnauer (FRA)) |
| February 9 | Czechoslovakia 2 | France 0 |

**GROUP D**

| | GP | W | T | L | GF | GA | P |
|---|---|---|---|---|---|---|---|
| Great Britain | 2 | 2 | 0 | 0 | 4 | 0 | 4 |
| Sweden | 2 | 1 | 0 | 1 | 2 | 1 | 2 |
| Japan | 2 | 0 | 0 | 2 | 0 | 5 | 0 |

| | | |
|---|---|---|
| February 6 | Sweden 2 | Japan 0 |
| February 7 | Great Britain 1 | Sweden 0 |
| February 8 | Great Britain 3 | Japan 0 |

**ROUND TWO**

**GROUP A**

| | GP | W | T | L | GF | GA | P |
|---|---|---|---|---|---|---|---|
| Great Britain | 3 | 2 | 1 | 0 | 8 | 3 | 5 |
| Canada | 3 | 2 | 0 | 1 | 22 | 4 | 4 |
| Germany | 3 | 1 | 1 | 1 | 5 | 8 | 3 |
| Hungary | 3 | 0 | 0 | 3 | 2 | 22 | 0 |

| | | |
|---|---|---|
| February 11 | Germany 2 | Hungary 1 |
| February 11 | Great Britain 2 | Canada 1 |
| February 12 | Canada 15 | Hungary 0 |
| February 12 | Great Britain 1 | Germany 1 (30:00 OT—no scoring) |
| February 13 | Great Britain 5 | Hungary 1 |
| February 13 | Canada 6 | Germany 2 |

**GROUP B**

| | GP | W | T | L | GF | GA | P |
|---|---|---|---|---|---|---|---|
| United States | 3 | 3 | 0 | 0 | 5 | 1 | 6 |
| Czechoslovakia | 3 | 2 | 0 | 1 | 6 | 4 | 4 |
| Sweden | 3 | 1 | 0 | 2 | 3 | 6 | 2 |
| Austria | 3 | 0 | 0 | 3 | 1 | 4 | 0 |

| | | |
|---|---|---|
| February 11 | Sweden 1 | Austria 0 |
| February 11 | United States 2 | Czechoslovakia 0 |
| February 12 | Czechoslovakia 4 | Sweden 1 |
| February 12 | United States 1 | Austria 0 |
| February 13 | Czechoslovakia 2 | Austria 1 |
| February 13 | United States 2 | Sweden 1 |

**MEDAL ROUND**

| | GP | W | T | L | GF | GA | P |
|---|---|---|---|---|---|---|---|
| Great Britain | 3 | 2 | 1 | 0 | 7 | 1 | 5 |
| Canada | 3 | 2 | 0 | 1 | 9 | 2 | 4 |
| United States | 3 | 1 | 1 | 1 | 2 | 1 | 3 |
| Czechoslovakia | 3 | 0 | 0 | 3 | 0 | 14 | 0 |

| | | |
|---|---|---|
| February 14 | Great Britain 5 | Czechoslovakia 0 |
| February 15 | Canada 7 | Czechoslovakia 0 |
| February 15 | Great Britain 0 | United States 0 (30:00 OT) |
| February 16 | Canada 1 | United States 0 |

**Rosters**

**Austria** (Hans Weinberger, coach) GK—Hermann Weiss—Franz Csongei, Fritz Demmer, Josef Gobel, Lambert Neumaier, Oskar Nowak, Franz Schussler, Emil Seidler, Willibald Stanek, Hans Tatzer, Hans Trauttenberg, Rudolf Vojta

**Belgium** (Bert Forsyth, coach) GK—Robert Baudinne—Walter Bastenie, Roger Bureau, Fernand Carez, Louis de Ridder, Willy Kreitz, Jef Lekens, Georges Pootmans, Carlos van den Driessche, Pierre van Reysschoot

**Canada** (Port Arthur Bear Cats—Al Pudas, coach) GK—Francis "Dinty" Moore, Arthur "Jakie" Nash—Walter "Pud" Kitchen, Ray Milton, Herman Murray, Hugh Farquharson, Alex Sinclair, Maxwell "Bill" Deacon, Ralph St. Germain, Dave Neville, Bill Thomson, Ken Farmer, Jim Haggarty

**Czechoslovakia** (Antonin Porges, coach) GK—Josef Bohac, Jan Peka—Alois Cetkovsky, Karel Hromadka, Drahos Jirotka, Zdenek Jirotka, Jan Kosek, Oldrich Kucera, Josef Malecek, Jaroslav Pusbauer, Jiri Tozicka, Ladislav Trojak, Walter Ulrich

**France** GK—Jacques Morisson, Michel Paccard—Philippe Boyard, Pierre Claret, Marcel Couttet, Michel Delesalle, Jean-Pierre Hagnauer, Albert Hassler, Jacques Lacarriere, Pierre Lorin, Guy Volpert

**Germany** (Bobby Hoffinger, coach) GK—Wilhelm Egginger—Joachim Albrecht von Bethmann-Hollweg, Rudi Ball, Werner George, Gustav Jaenecke, Karl Kogel, Alois Kuhn, Phillip Schenk, Herbert Schibukat, Georg Strobl, Paul Trautmann, Anton Wiedemann

**Great Britain** (Percy Nicklin, coach) GK—Jimmy Foster—Alex Archer, Jim Borland, Edgar Brenchley, Jimmy Chappell, Johnny Coward, Gordon Dailley, Gerry Davey, Carl Erhardt, Jack Kilpatrick, Archie Stinchcombe, Bob Wyman

**Hungary** (Geza Lator, coach) GK—Ferenc Monostori-Marx, Istvan Hircsak—Miklos Barcza, Matyas Farkas, Andras Gergely, Laszlo Gergely, Bela Haray, Frigyes Helmeczi, Zoltan Jeney, Sandor Magyar, Sandor Miklos, Laszlo Rona, Ferenc Szamosi-Stoics, Sandor Mindor

**Italy** GK—Augusto Gerosa—Gianmario Baroni, Ignazio Dionisi, Mario Maiocchi, Camillo Mussi, Franco Rossi, Gianni Scotti, Decio Trovati, Luigi Zucchini, Mario Zucchini

**Japan** (Shunichi Tezuka, coach) GK—Teiji Honma—Kenichi Furuya, Masahiro Hayama, Susumu Hirano, Tatsuo Ichikawa, Shinkichi Kamei, Kozue Kinoshita, Masatutsu Kitazawa, Toshihiko Shoji

**Latvia** GK—Herberts Kuskis, Roberts Lapainis—Alexejs Auzins, Roberts Blukis, Janis Bebris, Arvids Jurgens, Karlis Paegle, Arvids Petersons, Adolfs Petrovskis, Janis Rozitis, Leonids Vedejs

**Poland** (Alexander Tupalski/Lucjan Kulej, coaches) GK—Henryk Przezdziecki—Mieczyslaw Kasprzycki, Adam Kowalski, Wladyslaw Krol, Witalis Ludwiczak, Czeslaw Marchewczyk, Kazimierz Sokolowski, Roman Stupnicki, Andrzej Wolkowski, Edmund Zielinski

**Sweden** (Vic Lindquist, coach) GK—Herman Carlson, Wilhelm Larsson—Stig Andersson, Sven Bergqvist, Ruben Carlsson, Holger Engberg, Ake Ericson, Lennart Hellman, Torsten Johncke, Yngve Liljeberg, Bertil Lundell, Bertil Norberg, Wilhelm Petersen

**Switzerland** (Ulrich von Sury, coach) GK—Arnold Hirtz, Albert Kunzler—Ferdinand "Pic" Cattini, Hans Cattini, Otto Heller, Ernst Hug, Charles Kessler, Herbert Kessler, Adolf Martignoni, Thomas Pleisch, Oscar Schmidt, Richard "Bibi" Torriani

**United States** (Bert Prettyman, coach) GK—Tom Moone—Jack Garrison, Fred Kammer, Phil LaBatte, John Lax, Eldridge Ross, Paul Rowe, Frank Shaughnessy, Gord Smith, Frank Spain, Frank Stubbs

## 5th OLYMPIC WINTER GAMES
## January 30–February 8, 1948
## St. Moritz, Switzerland

### Final Placing

Gold ........Canada
Silver ......Czechoslovakia
Bronze ....Switzerland
4th..........United States
5th..........Sweden
6th .........Great Britain
7th .........Poland
8th .........Austria
9th .........Italy

### Tournament Format

With nine teams entered, all were placed together with a simple round-robin format used as a schedule. Teams received two points for a win, one for a tie. In the final game, an overtime period would be played, but no overtime would be played throughout the balance of the round-robin. Teams could take 15 players to the Olympics, but only 12 (including a spare goalie) could dress for any one game. For the first time, all games now consisted of three 20-minute periods. In the case of a tie in the standings after the round-robin, goal average would decide the final positions. This meant dividing the goals scored by goals against. For instance, Canada scored 69 and gave up 5 for a figure of 13.8. The Czechs, by comparison, scored 80 but surrendered 18 for an average of just 4.3. That is how Canada won the gold in St. Moritz.

### Results & Standings

| | GP | W | T | L | GF | GA | P |
|---|---|---|---|---|---|---|---|
| Canada | 8 | 7 | 1 | 0 | 69 | 5 | 15 |
| Czechoslovakia | 8 | 7 | 1 | 0 | 80 | 18 | 15 |
| Switzerland | 8 | 6 | 0 | 2 | 67 | 21 | 12 |
| United States | 8 | 5 | 0 | 3 | 86 | 33 | 10 |
| Sweden | 8 | 4 | 0 | 4 | 55 | 28 | 8 |
| Great Britain | 8 | 3 | 0 | 5 | 39 | 47 | 6 |
| Poland | 8 | 2 | 0 | 6 | 29 | 97 | 4 |
| Austria | 8 | 1 | 0 | 7 | 33 | 77 | 2 |
| Italy | 8 | 0 | 0 | 8 | 24 | 156 | 0 |

| | | |
|---|---|---|
| January 30 | Canada 3 | Sweden 1 |
| January 30 | Czechoslovakia 22 | Italy 3 |
| January 30 | Poland 7 | Austria 5 |
| January 30 | Switzerland 5 | United States 4 |
| January 31 | Czechoslovakia 6 | Sweden 3 |
| January 31 | Great Britain 5 | Austria 4 |
| January 31 | Switzerland 16 | Italy 0 |
| January 31 | United States 23 | Poland 4 |
| February 1 | Canada 3 | Great Britain 0 |
| February 1 | Czechoslovakia 13 | Poland 1 |
| February 1 | Switzerland 11 | Austria 2 |
| February 1 | United States 31 | Italy 1 |
| February 2 | Canada 15 | Poland 0 |
| February 2 | Czechoslovakia 11 | Great Britain 4 |
| February 2 | Sweden 7 | Austria 2 |
| February 3 | Canada 21 | Italy 1 |
| February 3 | United States 5 | Sweden 2 |
| February 4 | Switzerland 12 | Great Britain 3 |
| February 4 | Czechoslovakia 17 | Austria 3 |
| February 4 | Poland 13 | Italy 7 |
| February 5 | Canada 12 | United States 3 |
| February 5 | Switzerland 8 | Sweden 2 |
| February 5 | Austria 16 | Italy 5 |
| February 5 | Great Britain 8 | Poland 2 |
| February 6 | Canada 0 | Czechoslovakia 0 |
| February 6 | Switzerland 14 | Poland 0 |
| February 6 | Sweden 4 | Great Britain 2 |
| February 6 | United States 13 | Austria 2 |
| February 7 | Canada 12 | Austria 0 |
| February 7 | Czechoslovakia 7 | Switzerland 1 |
| February 7 | Sweden 23 | Italy 0 |
| February 7 | United States 4 | Great Britain 3 |
| February 8 | Canada 3 | Switzerland 0 |
| February 8 | Great Britain 14 | Italy 7 |
| February 8 | Sweden 13 | Poland 2 |
| February 8 | Czechoslovakia 4 | United States 3 |

### Rosters

**Austria** GK—Jorg Reichel, Alfred Huber—Albert Bohm, Franz Csongei, Fritz Demmer, Egon Engel, Walter Feistritzer, Gustav Gross, Adolf Hafner, Julius Juhn, Oskar Nowak, Johann "Hans" Schneider, Willibald Stanek, Herbert Ulrich, Fritz Walter, Helfried Winger, Rudolf Wurmbrandt

**Canada** (Royal Canadian Air Force (RCAF) Flyers—Frank Boucher, coach) GK—Murray Dowey—Frank Dunster, Andre Laperriere, Louis Lecompte, Orval Gravelle, Patrick "Patsy" Guzzo, Wally Halder, Ted Hibberd, George Mara, Ab Renaud, Reg Schroeter, Irving Taylor, Hubert Brooks, Roy Forbes, Andy Gilpin, Ross King, Pete Leichnitz

**Czechoslovakia** (Mike Buckna, coach) GK—Zdenek Jarkovsky, Bohumil Modry—Vladimir Bouzek, Gustav Bubnik, Jaroslav Drobny, Premsyl Hajny, Vladimir Kobranov, Stanislav Konopasek, Miloslav Pokorny, Vaclav Rozinak, Miroslav Slama, Karel Stibor, Vilibald Stovik, Ladislav Trojak, Josef Trousilek, Oldrich Zabrodsky, Vladimir Zabrodsky

**Great Britain** (Carl Erhardt, coach) GK—Stan Simon—George Baillie, Lennie Baker, Jimmy Chappell, Gerry Davey, Fred Dunkelman, Art Green, Frank Green, Frank Jardine, John Murray, John Oxley, Bert Smith, Archie Stinchcombe, Tom "Tuck" Syme

**Italy** (Othmar Delnon, coach) GK—Gianantonio Zopegni, Constanzo Mangini—Claudio Apollonio, Giancarlo Bassi, Mario Bedogni, Luigi Bestagini, Giancarlo Buchetti, Carlo Bulgheroni, Ignazio Dionisi, Arnaldo Fabris, Vincenzo Fardella, Aldo Federici, Umberto Gerli, Dino Innocenti, Dino Menardi, Otto Rauth, Franco Rossi

**Poland** (Zbigniew Kasprzak, coach) GK—Henryk Przezdziecki, Jan Maciejko—Henryk Bromowicz, Mieczyslaw Burda, Stefan Csorich, Tadeusz Dolewski, Alfred Gansiniec, Tomaz Jasinski, Mieczyslaw Kasprzycki, Boleslaw Kolasa, Adam Kowalski, Eugeniusz Lewacki, Czeslaw Marchewczyk, Mieczyslaw Palus, Hilary Skarzynski, Maksymilian Wiecek, Ernest Ziaja

**Sweden** (Sven Bergqvist, coach) GK—Kurt Svanberg, Arne Johansson—Ake Andersson, Stig Andersson, Stig Carlsson, Ake Ericson, Rolf Ericson, Svante Granlund, Rune Johansson, Gunnar Landelius, Claes Lindstrom, Lars Ljungman, Holger Nurmela, Bror Petterson, Rolf Pettersson, Sven Thunman

**Switzerland** (Wyn Cook, coach) GK—Hans Banninger, Reto Perl—Alfred Bieler, Heinrich Boller, Ferdinand Cattini, Hans Cattini, Hans Durst, Walter Durst, Emil Handschin, Heini Lohrer, Werner Lohrer, Gebi Poltera, Ulrich Poltera, Beat Ruedi, Otto Schubiger, Richard Torriani, Hans-Martin Trepp

**United States** (John Garrison, coach) GK—Goodwin Harding—Bob Baker, Bob Boeser, Bruce Cunliffe, Jack Garrity, Don Geary, Herb Vaningen, Jack Kirrane, Bruce Mather, Al Opsahl, Fred Pearson, Stan Priddy, Jack Riley, Ralph Warburton

## 6th OLYMPIC WINTER GAMES
## February 15–25, 1952
## Oslo, Norway

### Final Placing

Gold ........Canada
Silver ......United States
Bronze ....Sweden
4th..........Czechoslovakia
5th..........Switzerland
6th .........Poland
7th .........Finland
8th .........Germany
9th .........Norway

### Tournament Format

All nine countries were placed in a single division, and the schedule was again a simple round-robin format, each nation playing all others once. There was no overtime in the event of a tie after 60 minutes of regulation play. If two teams were tied in the standings and a medal were at stake, they would play an extra playoff game. In case of a tie between three teams, the team with the better goal differential (goals allowed subtracted from goals scored) would be given the better placing in the final standings.

### Results & Standings

| | GP | W | T | L | GF | GA | PTS |
|---|---|---|---|---|---|---|---|
| Canada | 8 | 7 | 1 | 0 | 71 | 14 | 15 |
| United States | 8 | 6 | 1 | 1 | 43 | 21 | 13 |
| Sweden* | 8 | 6 | 0 | 2 | 48 | 19 | 12 |
| Czechoslovakia* | 8 | 6 | 0 | 2 | 47 | 18 | 12 |
| Switzerland | 8 | 4 | 0 | 4 | 40 | 40 | 8 |
| Poland | 8 | 2 | 1 | 5 | 21 | 56 | 5 |
| Finland | 8 | 2 | 0 | 6 | 21 | 60 | 4 |
| Germany | 8 | 1 | 1 | 6 | 21 | 53 | 3 |
| Norway | 8 | 0 | 0 | 8 | 15 | 46 | 0 |

*Because of identical point totals and goal differential, Sweden and Czechoslovakia played an extra game on February 25 to determine third place (the winner was also considered European champion).

| | | |
|---|---|---|
| February 15 | United States 3 | Norway 2 |
| February 15 | Sweden 9 | Finland 2 |
| February 15 | Czechoslovakia 8 | Poland 2 |
| February 15 | Canada 15 | Germany 1 |
| February 16 | Switzerland 12 | Finland 0 |
| February 16 | Czechoslovakia 6 | Norway 0 |
| February 16 | United States 8 | Germany 2 |
| February 16 | Sweden 17 | Poland 1 |
| February 17 | Sweden 4 | Norway 2 |
| February 17 | Switzerland 6 | Poland 3 |
| February 17 | Canada 13 | Finland 3 |
| February 17 | Czechoslovakia 6 | Germany 1 |
| February 18 | United States 8 | Finland 2 |
| February 18 | Canada 11 | Poland 0 |
| February 18 | Switzerland 7 | Norway 2 |
| February 18 | Sweden 7 | Germany 3 |
| February 19 | Canada 4 | Czechoslovakia 1 |
| February 19 | United States 8 | Switzerland 2 |
| February 20 | Poland 4 | Germany 4 |
| February 20 | Finland 5 | Norway 2 |
| February 21 | Sweden 4 | United States 2 |
| February 21 | Canada 11 | Switzerland 2 |
| February 21 | Czechoslovakia 11 | Finland 2 |
| February 21 | Germany 6 | Norway 2 |
| February 22 | Finland 5 | Germany 1 |
| February 22 | Czechoslovakia 8 | Switzerland 3 |
| February 22 | United States 5 | Poland 3 |
| February 22 | Canada 3 | Sweden 2 |
| February 23 | Sweden 5 | Switzerland 2 |
| February 23 | Canada 11 | Norway 2 |
| February 23 | Poland 4 | Finland 2 |
| February 23 | United States 6 | Czechoslovakia 3 |
| February 24 | Czechoslovakia 4 | Sweden 0 |
| February 24 | Switzerland 6 | Germany 3 |
| February 24 | Canada 3 | United States 3 |
| February 25 | Poland 4 | Norway 3 |
| February 25 | Sweden 5 | Czechoslovakia 3 |

**Rosters**

**Canada** (Edmonton Mercurys—Lou Holmes, coach) GK—Ralph Hansch, Eric Patterson—John Davies, Don Gauf, Bob Meyers, Tom Pollock, Al Purvis, George Abel, Billy Dawe, Bruce Dickson, Billy Gibson, David Miller, Gordie Robertson, Louis Secco, Frank "Sully" Sullivan, Robert Watt

**Czechoslovakia** (Jiri Tozicka/Josef Herman, coaches) GK—Jan Richter, Josef Zahorsky—Slavomir Barton, Miloslav Blazek, Vaclav Bubnik, Vlastimil Bubnik, Miloslav Charouzd, Bronislav Danda, Karel Gut, Vlastimil Hajsman, Jan Lidral, Miroslav Novy, Miloslav Osmera, Zdenek Pycha, Miloslav Rejman, Oldrich Sedlak, Jiri Sekyra

**Finland** (Risto Lindroos, coach) GK—Pekka Myllyla, Unto Wiitala—Yrjo Hakala, Aarne Honkavaara, Erkki Hytonen, Pentti Isotalo, Matti Karumaa, Ossi Kauppi, Keijo Kuusela, Kauko Makinen, Christian Rapp, Esko Rekomaa, Matti Rintakoski, Eero Saari, Eero Salisma, Lauri Silvan, Jukka Vuolio

**Germany** (Joe Aitken, coach) GK—Alfred Hoffmann, Hans Wackers—Karl Bierschel, Markus Egen, Karl Enzler, Georg Guggemos, Engelbert Holdereid, Walter Kremershof, Ludwig Kuhn, Dieter Niess, Hans Georg Pescher, Fritz Poitsch, Herbert Schibukat, Xaver Unsinn, Karl Wild

**Norway** (Bud McEachern, coach) GK—Arthur Kristiansen, Per Dahl—Jan Erik Adolfsen, Arne Berg, Egil Bjerklund, Bjorn Gulbrandsen (I), Bjorn Gulbrandsen (II), Finn Gundersen, Gunnar Kroge, Johnny Larntvet, Annar Pedersen, Roar Pedersen, Ragnar Rygel, Leif Solheim, Oivind Solheim, Roy Strandem, Per Voigt

**Poland** (Mieczyslaw Kasprzycki, coach) GK—Jan Hampel, Stanislav Szlendak—Michal Antuszewicz, Henryk Bromowicz, Kazimierz Chodakowski, Stefan Csorich, Rudolf Czech, Alfred Gansiniec, Jan Hampel, Marian Jezak, Eugeniusz Lewacki, Roman Penczek, Hilary Skarzynski, Tadeusz Swicarz, Zdzislaw Trojanowski, Antoni Wrobel, Alfred Wrobel

**Sweden** (Folke Jansson/Herman Carlson, coaches) GK—Lars Svensson, Thord Flodqvist—Gote Almqvist, Ake Andersson, Hans Andersson, Stig "Tvilling" Andersson, Lars Bjorn, Gote Blomqvist, Erik Johansson, Gosta Johansson, Rune Johansson, Sven "Tumba" Johansson, Ake Lassas, Holger Nurmela, Hans Oberg, Lars Pettersson, Sven Thunman

**Switzerland** (Richard "Bibi" Torriani, coach) GK—Hans Banninger, Paul Wyss—Gian Bazzi, Francois Blank, Bixio Celio, Reto Delnon, Walter Durst, Milo Golaz, Emil Handschin, Paul Hofer, Willy Pfister, Gebi Poltera, Uli Poltera, Otto Schlapfer, Otto Schubiger, Alfred Streun, Hans-Martin Trepp

**United States** (John Pleban, coach) GK—Dick Desmond, Don Whiston—Ruben Bjorkman, Len Ceglarski, Joe Czarnota, Andre Gambucci, Cliff Harrison, Gerry Kilmartin, Jack Mulhern, John Noah, Arnold Oss, Bob Rompre, Jim Sedin, Al Van, Ken Yackel

## 7th OLYMPIC WINTER GAMES
## January 26–February 4, 1956
## Cortina D'Ampezzo, Italy

**Final Placing**

| | |
|---|---|
| Gold ........Soviet Union | 6th .........Germany |
| Silver ......United States | 7th .........Italy |
| Bronze ....Canada | 8th .........Poland |
| 4th..........Sweden | 9th .........Switzerland |
| 5th..........Czechoslovakia | 10th .......Austria |

**Tournament Format**

Ten teams were divided into three groups, each playing a round-robin schedule within that group. The top two teams from each section then advanced to a six-team finals round. The team with the most points among the six (two points for a win, one for a tie) won the gold, with goal differential being the deciding factor in the event of a tie. If still tied, goals against average would be the last method to decide the winner. Tie games after 60 minutes of play would not be decided by overtime.

**Results & Standings**

**GROUP A**

| | GP | W | T | L | GF | GA | P |
|---|---|---|---|---|---|---|---|
| Canada | 3 | 3 | 0 | 0 | 30 | 1 | 6 |
| Germany | 3 | 1 | 1 | 1 | 9 | 6 | 3 |
| Italy | 3 | 0 | 2 | 1 | 5 | 7 | 2 |
| Austria | 3 | 0 | 1 | 2 | 2 | 32 | 1 |

| | | |
|---|---|---|
| January 26 | Italy 2 | Austria 2 |
| January 26 | Canada 4 | Germany 0 |
| January 27 | Canada 23 | Austria 0 |
| January 27 | Italy 2 | Germany 2 |
| January 28 | Canada 3 | Italy 1 |
| January 29 | Germany 7 | Austria 0 |

**GROUP B**

| | GP | W | T | L | GF | GA | P |
|---|---|---|---|---|---|---|---|
| Czechoslovakia | 2 | 2 | 0 | 0 | 12 | 6 | 4 |
| United States | 2 | 1 | 0 | 1 | 7 | 4 | 2 |
| Poland | 2 | 0 | 0 | 2 | 3 | 12 | 0 |

| | | |
|---|---|---|
| January 27 | Czechoslovakia 4 | United States 3 |
| January 28 | United States 4 | Poland 0 |
| January 29 | Czechoslovakia 8 | Poland 3 |

**GROUP C**

| | GP | W | T | L | GF | GA | P |
|---|---|---|---|---|---|---|---|
| Soviet Union | 2 | 2 | 0 | 0 | 15 | 4 | 4 |
| Sweden | 2 | 1 | 0 | 1 | 7 | 10 | 2 |
| Switzerland | 2 | 0 | 0 | 2 | 8 | 16 | 0 |

| | | |
|---|---|---|
| January 27 | Soviet Union 5 | Sweden 1 |
| January 28 | Sweden 6 | Switzerland 5 |
| January 29 | Soviet Union 10 | Switzerland 3 |

**CONSOLATION ROUND**

| | GP | W | T | L | GF | GA | P |
|---|---|---|---|---|---|---|---|
| Italy | 3 | 3 | 0 | 0 | 21 | 7 | 6 |
| Poland | 3 | 2 | 0 | 1 | 12 | 10 | 4 |
| Switzerland | 3 | 1 | 0 | 2 | 12 | 18 | 2 |
| Austria | 3 | 0 | 0 | 3 | 9 | 19 | 0 |

| | | |
|---|---|---|
| January 31 | Switzerland 7 | Austria 4 |
| February 1 | Italy 8 | Austria 2 |
| February 1 | Poland 6 | Switzerland 2 |
| February 2 | Italy 8 | Switzerland 3 |
| February 2 | Poland 4 | Austria 3 |
| February 3 | Italy 5 | Poland 2 |

**MEDAL ROUND**

| | GP | W | T | L | GF | GA | P |
|---|---|---|---|---|---|---|---|
| Soviet Union | 5 | 5 | 0 | 0 | 25 | 5 | 10 |
| United States | 5 | 4 | 0 | 1 | 26 | 12 | 8 |
| Canada | 5 | 3 | 0 | 2 | 23 | 11 | 6 |
| Sweden | 5 | 1 | 1 | 3 | 10 | 17 | 3 |
| Czechoslovakia | 5 | 1 | 0 | 4 | 20 | 30 | 2 |
| Germany | 5 | 0 | 1 | 4 | 6 | 35 | 1 |

| | | |
|---|---|---|
| January 30 | United States 7 | Germany 2 |
| January 30 | Soviet Union 4 | Sweden 1 |
| January 30 | Canada 6 | Czechoslovakia 3 |
| January 31 | Sweden 5 | Czechoslovakia 0 |
| January 31 | Soviet Union 8 | Germany 0 |
| January 31 | United States 4 | Canada 1 |
| February 2 | Canada 10 | Germany 0 |
| February 2 | United States 6 | Sweden 1 |
| February 2 | Soviet Union 7 | Czechoslovakia 4 |

| | | |
|---|---|---|
| February 3 | Canada 6 | Sweden 2 |
| February 3 | Czechoslovakia 9 | Germany 3 |
| February 3 | Soviet Union 4 | United States 0 |
| February 4 | Sweden 1 | Germany 1 |
| February 4 | United States 9 | Czechoslovakia 4 |
| February 4 | Soviet Union 2 | Canada 0 |

**Rosters**

**Austria** (Udo Hohlfeld, coach) GK—Alfred Puls, Robert Nusser—Adolf Hafner, Wolfgang Jochl, Hermann Knoll, Kurt Kurz, Hans Mossmer, Franz Potucek, Hans Scarsini, Wilhelm Schmid, Max Singewald, Fritz Spielmann, Gerhard Springer, Konrad Staudinger, Hans Wagner, Walter Znenahlik, Hans Zollner

**Canada** (Kitchener-Waterloo Dutchmen—Bobby Bauer, coach) GK—Denis Brodeur, Keith Woodall—Art Hurst, Byrle Klinck, Howie Lee, Jack MacKenzie, Floyd Martin, Billy Colvin, Ken Laufman, Bob White, Charlie Brooker, Jim Logan, Don Rope, Gerry Theberge, Buddy Horne, Paul Knox, George Scholes

**Czechoslovakia** (Vladimir Bouzek, coach) GK—Jan Vodicka, Jan Jendek—Stanislav Bacilek, Slavomir Barton, Vaclav Bubnik, Vlastimil Bubnik, Jaromir Bunter, Otto Cimrman, Bronislav Danda, Karel Gut, Jan Kasper, Miroslav Kluc, Zdenek Navrat, Vaclav Pantucek, Bohumil Prosek, Frantisek Vanek, Vladimir Zabrodsky

**Germany** (Frank Trottier, coach) GK—Ulrich Jansen, Alfred Hoffmann—Paul Ambros, Martin Beck, Toni Biersack, Karl Bierschel, Markus Egen, Arthur Endres, Bruno Guttowski, Hans Huber, Gunther Jochems, Rainer Kossmann, Rudolf Pittrich, Hans Rampf, Kurt Sepp, Ernst Trautwein, Martin Zach

**Italy** (Richard "Bibi" Torriani, coach) GK—Vittoria Bolla, Giuliano Ferraris—Giancarlo Agazzi, Rino Alberton, Mario Bedogni, Giampiero Branduardi, Ernesto Crotti, Gianfranco Da Rin, Aldo Federici, Giovanni Furlani, Francesco Machietto, Aldo Maniacco, Carlo Montemurro, Giulio Oberhammer, Bernardo Tomei, Carmine Tucci

**Poland** (Mieczyslaw Palus/Wladyslaw Wiro-Kiro, coaches) GK—Wladyslaw Pabisz, Edward Koczab—Henryk Bromowicz, Kazimierz Bryniarski, Mieczyslaw Chmura, Kazimierz Chodakowski, Rudolf Czech, Bronislaw Gosztyla, Marian Herda, Szymon Janiczko, Josef Kurek, Zdzislaw Nowak, Stanislaw Olczyk, Hilary Skarzynski, Adolf Wrobel, Alfred Wrobel, Janusz Zawadzki

**Soviet Union** (Arkady Chernyshev, coach) GK—Nikolai Puchkov, Grigori Mkrtychan—Yevgeni Babich, Vsevolod Bobrov, Nikolai Khlystov, Alexei Guryshev, Yuri Krylov, Alfred Kuchevski, Valentin Kuzin, Viktor Nikiforov, Yuri Pantyukhov, Viktor Shuvalov, Genrikh Sidorenkov, Nikolai Sologubov, Ivan Tregubov, Dmitri Ukolov, Alexander Uvarov

**Sweden** (Folke Jansson, coach) GK—Yngve Casslind, Lars Svensson—Stig Andersson-Tvilling, Hans Andersson-Tvilling, Lars Bjorn, Sigurd Broms, Stig Carlsson, Sven "Tumba" Johansson, Vilgot Larsson, Ake Lassas, Lars-Eric Lundvall, Ove Malmberg, Nils Nilsson, Holger Nurmela, Hans Oberg, Ronald Pettersson, Bert Zetterberg

**Switzerland** (Hanggi Boller, coach) GK—Martin Riesen, Christian Conrad—Sepp Weingartner, Kurt Peter, Georg Riesch, Milo Golaz, Ruedi Keller, Ratus Frei, Paul Hofer, Hans Ott, Bernard Bagnoud, Emil Handschin, Fritz Naef, Walter Keller, Hans Pappa, Otto Schlapfer, Franz Berry

**United States** (John Mariucci, coach) GK—Don Rigazio, Willard Ikola—Wendell Anderson, Wellington Burnett, Gene Campbell, Gord Christian, Bill Cleary, Dick Dougherty, John Matchefts, John Mayasich, Dan McKinnon, Dick Meredith, Weldon Olson, John Petroske, Ken Purpur, Dick Rodenhiser, Ed Sampson

## 8th OLYMPIC WINTER GAMES
## February 19–28, 1960
## Squaw Valley, United States

**Final Placing**

Gold........United States
Silver......Canada
Bronze....Soviet Union
4th..........Czechoslovakia
5th..........Sweden
6th.........Germany
7th.........Finland
8th.........Japan
9th.........Australia

**Tournament Format**

The format remained unchanged from the one used in Cortina d'Ampezzo in 1956. The nine competing countries were divided into three pools of three teams, each pool playing round-robin games with the others in their division. The top two teams from each pool then advanced to a six-team finals round-robin, the gold medal going to the team with the most points (two for a win, one for a tie). In the event of a tie in the standings, goal differential would decide the winner.

**Results & Standings**

**GROUP A**

| | GP | W | T | L | GF | GA | P |
|---|---|---|---|---|---|---|---|
| Canada | 2 | 2 | 0 | 0 | 24 | 3 | 4 |
| Sweden | 2 | 1 | 0 | 1 | 21 | 5 | 2 |
| Japan | 2 | 0 | 0 | 2 | 1 | 38 | 0 |

| | | |
|---|---|---|
| February 19 | Canada 5 | Sweden 2 |
| February 20 | Canada 19 | Japan 1 |
| February 21 | Sweden 19 | Japan 0 |

**GROUP B**

| | GP | W | T | L | GF | GA | P |
|---|---|---|---|---|---|---|---|
| Soviet Union | 2 | 2 | 0 | 0 | 16 | 4 | 4 |
| Germany | 2 | 1 | 0 | 1 | 4 | 9 | 2 |
| Finland | 2 | 0 | 0 | 2 | 5 | 12 | 0 |

| | | |
|---|---|---|
| February 19 | Soviet Union 8 | Germany 0 |
| February 20 | Soviet Union 8 | Finland 4 |
| February 21 | Germany 4 | Finland 1 |

**GROUP C**

| | GP | W | T | L | GF | GA | P |
|---|---|---|---|---|---|---|---|
| United States | 2 | 2 | 0 | 0 | 19 | 6 | 4 |
| Czechoslovakia | 2 | 1 | 0 | 1 | 23 | 8 | 2 |
| Australia | 2 | 0 | 0 | 2 | 2 | 30 | 0 |

| | | |
|---|---|---|
| February 19 | United States 7 | Czechoslovakia 5 |
| February 20 | Czechoslovakia 18 | Australia 1 |
| February 21 | United States 12 | Australia 1 |

**CONSOLATION ROUND**

| | GP | W | T | L | GF | GA | P |
|---|---|---|---|---|---|---|---|
| Finland | 4 | 3 | 1 | 0 | 50 | 11 | 7 |
| Japan | 4 | 2 | 1 | 1 | 32 | 22 | 5 |
| Australia | 4 | 0 | 0 | 4 | 8 | 57 | 0 |

| | | |
|---|---|---|
| February 22 | Finland 14 | Australia 1 |
| February 23 | Finland 6 | Japan 6 |
| February 24 | Japan 13 | Australia 2 |
| February 25 | Finland 19 | Australia 2 |
| February 26 | Finland 11 | Japan 2 |
| February 27 | Japan 11 | Australia 3 |

**MEDAL ROUND**

| | GP | W | T | L | GF | GA | P |
|---|---|---|---|---|---|---|---|
| United States | 5 | 5 | 0 | 0 | 29 | 11 | 10 |
| Canada | 5 | 4 | 0 | 1 | 31 | 12 | 8 |
| Soviet Union | 5 | 2 | 1 | 2 | 24 | 19 | 5 |
| Czechoslovakia | 5 | 2 | 0 | 3 | 21 | 23 | 4 |
| Sweden | 5 | 1 | 1 | 3 | 19 | 19 | 3 |
| Germany | 5 | 0 | 0 | 5 | 5 | 45 | 0 |

| | | |
|---|---|---|
| February 22 | Soviet Union 8 | Czechoslovakia 5 |
| February 22 | United States 6 | Sweden 3 |
| February 22 | Canada 12 | Germany 0 |
| February 24 | United States 9 | Germany 1 |
| February 24 | Sweden 2 | Soviet Union 2 |
| February 24 | Canada 4 | Czechoslovakia 0 |
| February 25 | Soviet Union 7 | Germany 1 |
| February 25 | Czechoslovakia 3 | Sweden 1 |
| February 25 | United States 2 | Canada 1 |
| February 27 | Czechoslovakia 9 | Germany 1 |
| February 27 | United States 3 | Soviet Union 2 |
| February 27 | Canada 6 | Sweden 5 |
| February 28 | United States 9 | Czechoslovakia 4 |
| February 28 | Sweden 8 | Germany 2 |
| February 28 | Canada 8 | Soviet Union 5 |

**Rosters**

**Australia** (Bud McEachern, coach) GK—Noel McLoughlin, Robert Reid—Benjamin Acton, Ronald Amess, David Cunningham, Noel Derrick, Victor Ekberg, Bassel Hansen, Clive Hitch, Russell Jones, Allan Nicholas, Peter Parrott, Kenneth Pawsey, John Thomas, Zdenek Tikal, Ivo Vesely, Ken Wellman

**Canada** (Kitchener–Waterloo Dutchmen—Bobby Bauer, coach) GK—Don Head, Harold "Boat" Hurley—Moe Benoit, Jack Douglas, Harry Sinden, Darryl Sly, Bob Attersley, Jim Connelly, Fred Etcher, Bob Forhan, Ken Laufman, Floyd "Butch" Martin, Bob McKnight, Cliff Pennington, Don Rope, Bobby Rousseau, George Samolenko

**Czechoslovakia** (Eduard Farda, coach) GK—Vladimir Dvoracek, Vladimir Nadrchal—Vlastimil Bubnik, Josef Cerny, Bronislav Danda, Jozef Golonka, Karel Gut, Jaroslav Jirik, Jan Kasper, Frantisek Maslan, Vaclav Pantucek, Rudolf Potsch, Jan Starsi, Frantisek Tikal, Frantisek Vanek, Miroslav Vlach, Jaroslav Volf

**Finland** (Joe Wirkkunen/Aarne Honkavaara, coaches) GK—Juhani Lahtinen, Esko Niemi—Yrjo Hakala, Raimo Kilpio, Erkki Koiso, Matti Lampainen, Esko Luostarinen, Pertti Nieminen, Veijo Numminen, Heino Pulli, Kalevi Rassa, Teppo Rastio, Jouni Seistamo, Seppo Vainio, Juhani Wahlsten, Jorma Salmi, Vaito Soini

**Germany** (Karl Wild, coach) GK—Michael Hobelsberger, Uli Jansen—Paul Ambros, Georg Eberl, Markus Egen, Ernst Eggerbauer, Hans Huber, Hans Rampf, Josef Reif, Otto Schneitberger, Siegfried Schubert, Horst Schuldes, Kurt Sepp, Ernst Trautwein, Xaver Unsinn, Leonhard Waitl

**Japan** (Hiroki Onikura, coach) GK—Shoichi Tomita, Toshiei Honma—Chikashi Akazawa, Shinichi Honma, Hidenori Inatsu, Atsuo Irie, Joji Iwaoka, Takashi Kakihara, Yoshihiro Miyazaki, Masao Murano, Isao Ono, Akiyoshi Segawa, Shigeru Shimada, Kunito Takagi, Mamoru Takashima, Mashyoshi Tanabu, Toshihiko Yamada

**Soviet Union** (Anatoli Tarasov, coach) GK—Nikolai Puchkov, Yevgeni Yerkin—Veniamin Alexandrov, Alexander Almetov, Yuri Baulin, Mikhail Bychkov, Vladimir Grebennikov, Yevgeni Grosev, Nikolai Karpov, Alfred Kuchevski, Konstantin Loktev, Stanislav Petukhov, Viktor Pryazhnikov, Genrikh Sidorenkov, Nikolai Sologubov, Yuri Tsytsynov, Viktor Yakushev

**Sweden** (Ed Reigle, coach) GK—Kjell Svensson, Bengt Lindqvist—Anders Andersson, Lars Bjorn, Gert Blome, Sigurd Broms, Einar Granath, Sven "Tumba" Johansson, Lars-Eric Lundvall, Nils Nilsson, Bert-Ola Nordlander, Carl-Goran Oberg, Ronald Pettersson, Ulf Sterner, Roland Stoltz, Hans Svedberg, Sune Wretling

**United States** (Jack Riley, coach) GK—Jack McCartan, Larry Palmer—Roger Christian, Bill Christian, Bob Cleary, Bill Cleary, Gene Grazia, Paul Johnson, Jack Kirrane, John Mayasich, Bob McVey, Dick Meredith, Weldon Olson, Edwyn "Bob" Owen, Rodney Paavola, Dick Rodenhiser, Tommy Williams

## 9th OLYMPIC WINTER GAMES
## January 29–February 9, 1964
## Innsbruck, Austria

### Final Placing

| | | | |
|---|---|---|---|
| Gold | Soviet Union | 9th | Poland |
| Silver | Sweden | 10th | Norway |
| Bronze | Czechoslovakia | 11th | Japan |
| 4th | Canada | 12th | Romania |
| 5th | United States | 13th | Austria |
| 6th | Finland | 14th | Yugoslavia |
| 7th | Germany | 15th | Italy |
| 8th | Switzerland | 16th | Hungary |

### Qualifying Round Results
(winners advance to A Pool/medal group; loser to B Pool/consolation round)

| | | |
|---|---|---|
| January 27 | Canada 14 | Yugoslavia 1 |
| January 27 | Czechoslovakia 17 | Japan 2 |
| January 27 | Switzerland 5 | Norway 1 |
| January 27 | Sweden 12 | Italy 2 |
| January 27 | Germany 2 | Poland 1 |
| January 27 | Finland 8 | Austria 2 |
| January 27 | Soviet Union 19 | Hungary 1 |
| January 27 | United States 7 | Romania 2 |

### Tournament Format
A simple round-robin format was used, the winner being decided by points (two for a win, one for a tie, as always). In the event of a tie in the standings, the team with the better goal differential (goals allowed subtracted from goals scored) would finish ahead. If this calculation did not yield a winner, head-to-head wins would be decisive followed by goal average (goals scored divided by goals allowed).

### Results & Standings
**A POOL/MEDAL ROUND**

| | GP | W | T | L | GF | GA | P |
|---|---|---|---|---|---|---|---|
| Soviet Union | 7 | 7 | 0 | 0 | 54 | 10 | 14 |
| Sweden | 7 | 5 | 0 | 2 | 47 | 16 | 10 |
| Czechoslovakia | 7 | 5 | 0 | 2 | 38 | 19 | 10 |
| Canada | 7 | 5 | 0 | 2 | 32 | 17 | 10 |
| United States | 7 | 2 | 0 | 5 | 29 | 33 | 4 |
| Finland | 7 | 2 | 0 | 5 | 10 | 31 | 4 |
| Germany | 7 | 2 | 0 | 5 | 13 | 49 | 4 |
| Switzerland | 7 | 0 | 0 | 7 | 9 | 57 | 0 |

| | | |
|---|---|---|
| January 29 | Soviet Union 5 | United States 1 |
| January 29 | Czechoslovakia 11 | Germany 1 |
| January 29 | Canada 8 | Switzerland 0 |
| January 30 | Finland 4 | Switzerland 0 |
| January 30 | Canada 3 | Sweden 1 |
| January 31 | United States 8 | Germany 0 |
| January 31 | Soviet Union 7 | Czechoslovakia 5 |
| February 1 | Czechoslovakia 4 | Finland 0 |
| February 1 | Soviet Union 15 | Switzerland 0 |
| February 1 | Sweden 7 | United States 4 |
| February 2 | Canada 4 | Germany 2 |
| February 2 | Sweden 7 | Finland 0 |
| February 3 | Canada 8 | United States 6 |
| February 4 | Soviet Union 10 | Finland 0 |
| February 4 | Czechoslovakia 5 | Switzerland 1 |
| February 4 | Sweden 10 | Germany 2 |
| February 5 | Canada 6 | Finland 2 |
| February 5 | Soviet Union 10 | Germany 0 |
| February 5 | Sweden 12 | Switzerland 0 |
| February 5 | Czechoslovakia 7 | United States 1 |
| February 7 | Germany 6 | Switzerland 5 |
| February 7 | Finland 3 | United States 2 |
| February 7 | Soviet Union 4 | Sweden 2 |
| February 7 | Czechoslovakia 3 | Canada 1 |
| February 8 | Germany 2 | Finland 1 |
| February 8 | United States 7 | Switzerland 3 |
| February 8 | Soviet Union 3 | Canada 2 |
| February 8 | Sweden 8 | Czechoslovakia 3 |

**B POOL/CONSOLATION ROUND**

| | GP | W | T | L | GF | GA | P |
|---|---|---|---|---|---|---|---|
| Poland | 7 | 6 | 0 | 1 | 40 | 13 | 12 |
| Norway | 7 | 5 | 0 | 2 | 40 | 19 | 10 |
| Japan | 7 | 4 | 1 | 2 | 35 | 31 | 9 |
| Romania | 7 | 3 | 1 | 3 | 31 | 28 | 7 |
| Austria | 7 | 3 | 1 | 3 | 24 | 28 | 7 |
| Yugoslavia | 7 | 3 | 1 | 3 | 29 | 37 | 7 |
| Italy | 7 | 2 | 0 | 5 | 24 | 42 | 4 |
| Hungary | 7 | 0 | 0 | 7 | 14 | 39 | 0 |

| | | |
|---|---|---|
| January 30 | Poland 6 | Romania 1 |
| January 30 | Italy 6 | Hungary 4 |
| January 30 | Austria 6 | Yugoslavia 2 |
| January 30 | Japan 6 | Norway 3 |
| January 31 | Poland 6 | Norway 2 |
| January 31 | Japan 6 | Romania 4 |
| February 1 | Austria 3 | Hungary 0 |
| February 1 | Yugoslavia 5 | Italy 3 |
| February 2 | Norway 9 | Italy 2 |
| February 2 | Romania 5 | Yugoslavia 5 |
| February 3 | Poland 6 | Hungary 2 |
| February 3 | Austria 5 | Japan 5 |
| February 4 | Yugoslavia 6 | Japan 4 |
| February 5 | Poland 7 | Italy 0 |
| February 5 | Romania 5 | Austria 2 |
| February 5 | Norway 6 | Hungary 1 |
| February 6 | Austria 5 | Italy 3 |
| February 6 | Yugoslavia 4 | Hungary 2 |
| February 6 | Japan 4 | Poland 3 |
| February 6 | Norway 4 | Romania 2 |
| February 7 | Norway 8 | Austria 2 |
| February 7 | Poland 9 | Yugoslavia 3 |
| February 7 | Romania 6 | Italy 2 |
| February 7 | Japan 6 | Hungary 2 |
| February 8 | Poland 5 | Austria 1 |
| February 8 | Romania 8 | Hungary 3 |
| February 8 | Italy 8 | Japan 6 |
| February 8 | Norway 8 | Yugoslavia 4 |

### Rosters
**Austria** (Zdenek Ujcik, coach) GK—Alfred Puls, Friedrich Turek—Adolf Bachura, Horst Kakl, Dieter Kalt, Christian Kirchberger, Hermann Knoll, Eduard Mossmer, Tassilo Neuwirth, Josef Puschnig, Erich Romauch, Fritz Spielmann, Adelbert St. John, Gustav Tischer, Fritz Wechselberger, Erich Winkler, Walter Znenahlik

**Canada** (Father David Bauer, coach) GK—Ken Broderick, Seth Martin—Hank Akervall, Barry MacKenzie, Terry O'Malley, Rod Seiling, Gary Begg, Gary Dineen, George Swarbrick, Roger Bourbonnais, Terry Clancy, Brian Conacher, Ray Cadieux, Paul Conlin, Bob Forhan, Marshall Johnston

**Czechoslovakia** (Jiri Anton, coach) GK—Vladimir Nadrchal, Vladimir Dzurilla—Vlastimil Bubnik, Josef Cerny, Jiri Dolana, Jozef Golonka, Frantisek Gregor, Jiri Holik, Jaroslav Jirik, Jan Klapac, Rudolf Potsch, Stanislav Pryl, Ladislav Smid, Stanislav Sventek, Frantisek Tikal, Miroslav Vlach, Jaroslav Walter

**Finland** (Joe Wirkkunen/Aarne Honkavaara, coaches) GK—Juhani Latinen, Urpo Ylonen—Esko Kaonpaa, Raimo Kilpio, Rauno Lehtio, Esko Luostarinen, Ilka Masikammen, Seppo Nikkila, Kalevi Numminen, Lasse Oksanen, Jorma Peltonen, Heino Pulli, Matti Reunamaki, Jauni Seistamo, Jorma Suokko, Juhani Wahlsten, Jarmo Wasama

**Germany** (Xaver Unsinn, Markus Egen, Engelbert Holdereid, co-coaches) GK—Michael Hobelsberger, Ulrich Jansen—Paul Ambros, Bernd Herzig, Ernst Kopf, Albert Loibl, Josef Reif, Otto Schneitberger, Georg Scholz, Siegfried Schubert, Horst Schuldes, Peter Schwimmbeck, Kurt Sepp, Ernst Trautwein, Sylvester Wackerle, Leonhard Waitl, Helmut Zanghellini

**Hungary** (Vladimir Kominek, coach) GK—Matyas Vedres, Gyorgy Losonczi—Joszef Baban, Arnad Bankuti, Janos Beszteri, Peter Bikar, Gabor Boroczi, Laszlo Jakabhazi, Joszef Kertesz, Lajos Koutny, Ferenc Lorincz, Karoly Orosz, Gyorgy Raffa, Gyorgy Rozgonyi, Bela Schwalm, Janos Ziegler, Viktor Zsitva

**Italy** (Aldo Federici, coach) GK—Vittorio Bolla, Roberto Gamper—Giancarlo Agazzi, Isidoro Alvera, Heini Bacher, Enrico Benedetti, Gianfranco Branduardi, Bruno Frison, Bruno Ghedina, Ivo Ghezze, Francesco Machhietto, Giovanni Mastel, Giulio Oberhammer, Edmondo Rabanser, Alberto da Rin, Giafranco da Rin, Giulio Verocai

**Japan** (Nijuro Hoshino, coach) GK—Toshiei Honma, Katsuyi Morishima—Shinochi Honma, Atsuo Irie, Koji Iwamoto, Isao Kawabuchi, Kimio Kazahari, Kimihisa Kudo, Hiroyuki Matsuura, Nakano Minoru, Jiro Ogawa, Isao Ono, Masahiro Sato, Shigeru Shimada, Manoru Takashima, Masami Tanabu

**Norway** (Rolf Kirkvaag, coach) GK—Kare Ostensen, Oystein Mellerud—Egil Bjerklund, Olav Dalsoren, Bjorn Elvenes, Erik Fjeldstad, Tor Gundersen, Jan-Erik Hansen, Svein Hansen, Einar Larsen, Thor Lundby, Thor Martinsen, Franz Olafsen, Per Olsen, Christian Petersen, Rodney Riise, Georg Smefjell, Ragnar Sobye, Jan-Roar Thoresen

**Poland** (Gary Hughes, coach) GK—Jozef Wisniewski, Wladyslaw Pabisz—Andrzej Fonfara, Bronislaw Gosztyla, Henrik Handy, Tadeusz Kilanowicz, Jozef Kurek, Gerd Langner, Jozef Manowski, Jerzy Ogorczyk, Stanislaw Olczyk, Hubert Sitko, Augustyn Skorski, Jozef Stefaniak, Andrzej Szal, Sylwester Wilczek, Andrzej Zurawski

**Romania** (Mihai Flamaropol, coach) GK—Anton Crisan, Josif Safian—Nicolae Andrei, Anton Biro, Zoltan Czaka, Ioan Ferenczi, Iulian Florescu, Andrei Ianovici, Stefan Ionescu, Alexandru Calamar, Dan Mihailescu, Adalbert Nagy, Eduard Pana, Geza Szabo, Gyula Szabo, Ion Tiriac, Dezideriu Varga

**Soviet Union** (Anatoli Tarasov/Arkadi Chernyshev, coaches) GK—Viktor Konovalenko, Boris Zaitsev—Veniamin Alexandrov, Alexander Almetov, Vitali Davydov, Anatoli Firsov, Eduard Ivanov, Viktor Kuzkin, Konstantin Loktev, Boris Mayorov, Yevgeni Mayorov, Stanislav Petukhov, Alexander Ragulin, Vyacheslav Starshinov, Leonid Volkov, Viktor Yakushev, Oleg Zaitsev

**Sweden** (Arne Stromberg, coach) GK—Kjell Svensson, Lennart Haggroth—Anders Andersson, Gert Blome, Lennart Johansson, Nils Johansson, Sven "Tumba" Johansson, Lars-Eric Lundvall, Eilert Maatta, Hans Mild, Nils Nilsson, Bert-Ola Nordlander, Carl Oberg, Uno Ohrlund, Ronald Pettersson, Ulf Sterner, Roland Stoltz

**Switzerland** (Herve Lalonde, coach) GK—Gerald Rigolet, Rene Keiner—Franz Berry, Roger Chappot, Rolf Diethelm, Elvin Friedrich, Gaston Furrer, Oskar Jenny, Pio Parolini, Kurt Pfammatter, Max Ruegg, Walter Salzmann, Peter Stammbach, Herold Truffer, Peter Wespi, Otto Wittwer, Jurg Zimmermann

**United States** (Ed Jeremiah, coach) GK—Tom Yurkovich, Pat Rupp—Dave Brooks, Herb Brooks, Bill Christian, Roger Christian, Paul Coppo, Daniel Dilworth, Dates Fryberger, Paul Johnson, Tom Martin, Jim McCoy, Wayne Meredith, Bill Reichart, Don Ross, Gary Schmalzbauer, Jim Thomas, Jim Westby

**Yugoslavia** (Vaclav Bubnik, coach) GK—Anton Gale, Rasid Semsedinovic—Alexander Andjelic, Bogo Jan, Miroljub Djordjevic, Albin Felc, Mirko Holbus, Ivo Jan, Marjan Kristan, Igor Radin, Ivo Rataj, Viktor Ravnik, Boris Renaud, Franc Smolej, Viktor Tisler, Vinko Valentar

## 10th OLYMPIC WINTER GAMES
## February 6–17, 1968
## Grenoble, France

### Final Placing

| | | | |
|---|---|---|---|
| Gold | Soviet Union | 8th | East Germany |
| Silver | Czechoslovakia | 9th | Yugoslavia |
| Bronze | Canada | 10th | Japan |
| 4th | Sweden | 11th | Norway |
| 5th | Finland | 12th | Romania |
| 6th | United States | 13th | Austria |
| 7th | West Germany | 14th | France |

### Qualifying Round Results
(winners advance to A Pool/medal group; losers to B Pool)

| | | |
|---|---|---|
| February 4 | East Germany 3 | Norway 1 |
| February 4 | West Germany 7 | Romania 0 |
| February 4 | Finland 11 | Yugoslavia 0 |

### Tournament Format
The top eight teams were grouped into a medal round section, each playing a round-robin schedule. The top team in the standings (two points for a win, one for a tie) would win the gold medal. In the event of a two-way tie, the winner of the head-to-head game would get the gold. If there were a tie between more than two teams, goal differential (goals against subtracted from goals scored) would be the deciding factor.

### A POOL/MEDAL ROUND

| | GP | W | T | L | GF | GA | P |
|---|---|---|---|---|---|---|---|
| Soviet Union | 7 | 6 | 0 | 1 | 48 | 10 | 12 |
| Czechoslovakia | 7 | 5 | 1 | 1 | 33 | 17 | 11 |
| Canada | 7 | 5 | 0 | 2 | 28 | 15 | 10 |
| Sweden | 7 | 4 | 1 | 2 | 23 | 18 | 9 |
| Finland | 7 | 3 | 1 | 3 | 17 | 23 | 7 |
| United States | 7 | 2 | 1 | 4 | 23 | 28 | 5 |
| West Germany | 7 | 1 | 0 | 6 | 13 | 39 | 2 |
| East Germany | 7 | 0 | 0 | 7 | 13 | 48 | 0 |

| | | |
|---|---|---|
| February 6 | Czechoslovakia 5 | United States 1 |
| February 6 | Soviet Union 8 | Finland 0 |
| February 6 | Canada 6 | West Germany 1 |
| February 7 | Sweden 4 | United States 3 |
| February 7 | Soviet Union 9 | East Germany 0 |
| February 8 | Czechoslovakia 5 | West Germany 1 |
| February 8 | Finland 5 | Canada 2 |
| February 9 | Sweden 5 | West Germany 4 |
| February 9 | Soviet Union 10 | United States 2 |
| February 9 | Canada 11 | East Germany 0 |
| February 10 | Czechoslovakia 4 | Finland 3 |
| February 10 | Sweden 5 | East Germany 2 |
| February 11 | Canada 3 | United States 2 |
| February 11 | Soviet Union 9 | West Germany 1 |
| February 12 | Czechoslovakia 10 | East Germany 3 |
| February 12 | Sweden 5 | Finland 1 |
| February 12 | United States 8 | West Germany 1 |
| February 13 | Soviet Union 3 | Sweden 2 |
| February 13 | Canada 3 | Czechoslovakia 2 |
| February 14 | Finland 3 | East Germany 2 |
| February 15 | United States 6 | East Germany 4 |
| February 15 | Canada 3 | Sweden 0 |
| February 15 | Czechoslovakia 5 | Soviet Union 4 |
| February 16 | Finland 4 | West Germany 1 |
| February 17 | West Germany 4 | East Germany 2 |
| February 17 | Finland 1 | United States 1 |
| February 17 | Czechoslovakia 2 | Sweden 2 |
| February 17 | Soviet Union 5 | Canada 0 |

### B POOL/CONSOLATION ROUND

| | GP | W | T | L | GF | GA | P |
|---|---|---|---|---|---|---|---|
| Yugoslavia | 5 | 5 | 0 | 0 | 33 | 9 | 10 |
| Japan | 5 | 4 | 0 | 1 | 27 | 12 | 8 |
| Norway | 5 | 3 | 0 | 2 | 15 | 15 | 6 |
| Romania | 5 | 2 | 0 | 3 | 22 | 23 | 4 |
| Austria | 5 | 1 | 0 | 4 | 12 | 27 | 2 |
| France | 5 | 0 | 0 | 5 | 9 | 32 | 0 |

| | | |
|---|---|---|
| February 7 | Yugoslavia 5 | Japan 1 |
| February 7 | Romania 3 | Austria 2 |
| February 8 | Norway 4 | France 1 |
| February 9 | Romania 7 | France 3 |
| February 9 | Yugoslavia 6 | Austria 0 |
| February 10 | Japan 4 | Norway 0 |
| February 11 | Austria 5 | France 2 |
| February 12 | Japan 5 | Romania 4 |
| February 12 | Norway 5 | Austria 4 |
| February 13 | Yugoslavia 10 | France 1 |
| February 14 | Norway 4 | Romania 3 |
| February 15 | Japan 11 | Austria 1 |
| February 16 | Yugoslavia 9 | Romania 5 |
| February 17 | Japan 6 | France 2 |
| February 17 | Yugoslavia 3 | Norway 2 |

### Rosters
**Austria** (Jiri Hanzl, coach) GK—Franz Schilcher, Karl Pregl—Gunter Burkhart, Adalbert St. John, Hermann Erhart, Gerhard Felfernig, Gerhard Hausner, Dieter Kalt, Klaus Kirchbaumer, Heinz Knoflach, Walter Konig, Josef Mossmer, Josef Puschnig, Paul Samonig, Gerd Schager, Heinz Schupp, Josef Schwitzer, Klaus Weingartner

**Canada** (Jackie McLeod, coach) GK—Ken Broderick, Wayne Stephenson—Paul Conlin, Brian Glennie, Ted Hargreaves, Marshall Johnston, Barry MacKenzie, Terry O'Malley, Roger Bourbonnais, Ray Cadieux, Gary Dineen, Fran Huck, Billy MacMillan, Steve Monteith, Morris Mott, Danny O'Shea, Gerry Pinder, Herb Pinder

**Czechoslovakia** (Vladimir Kostka/Jaroslav Pitner, coaches) GK—Vladimir Dzurilla, Vladimir Nadrchal—Josef Cerny, Jozef Golonka, Jan Havel, Petr Hejma, Jiri Holik, Josef Horesovsky, Jan Hrbaty, Jaroslav Jirik, Jan Klapac, Jiri Kochta, Oldrich Machac, Karel Masopust, Vaclav Nedomansky, Frantisek Pospisil, Frantisek Sevcik, Jan Suchy

**East Germany** (Rudi Schmieder, coach) GK—Klaus Hirche, Dieter Purschel—Manfred Buder, Lothar Fuchs, Bernd Hiller, Bernd Karrenbauer, Dieter Kratzsch, Hartmut Nickel, Rudiger Noack, Ulrich Noack, Helmut Novy, Dietmar Peters, Wolfgang Plotka, Bernd Poindl, Peter Prusa, Wilfried Sock, Dieter Vogt, Joachim Ziesche

**Finland** (Gustav Bubnik, coach) GK—Urpo Ylonen, Pentti Koskela—Matti Harju, Kari Johansson, Matti Keinonen, Veli-Pekka Ketola, Ilpo Koskela, Pekka Kuusisto, Pekka Leimu, Seppo Lindstrom, Lasse Oksanen, Lalli Partinen, Esa Peltonen, Jorma Peltonen, Juha Rantasila, Matti Reunamaki, Paavo Tirkkonen, Juhani Wahlsten

**France** (Pete LaLiberte, coach) GK—Jean-Claude Sozzi, Bernard Deschamps—Claude Blanchard, Rene Blanchard, Bernard Cabanis, Michel Caux, Gerard Faucomprez, Patrick Francheterre, Joel Gauvin, Joel Godeau, Daniel Grando, Gilbert Itzigsohn, Philippe Lacarriere, Gilbert Lepre, Charles Liberman, Alain Mazza, Patrice Pourtanel, Olivier Prechac

**Japan** (Yuji Kaneda/Tadao Nakajima, coaches) GK—Toshimito Ohtsubo, Katsuyi Morishima—Takeshi Akiba, Nobuhiro Araki, Isao Asai, Yutaka Ebina, Takao Hikigi, Toru Itabashi, Hisashi Kasa, Minoru Ito, Koji Iwamoto, Takaaki Kaneiri, Kimihisa Kudo, Kazuo Matsuda, Toru Okajima, Michihiro Sato, Mamoru Takashima, Kenji Toriyabe

**Norway** (Egil Bjerklund, coach) GK—Kare Ostensen, Harald Brathen—Svein Hansen, Trygve Bergeid, Steinar Bjolbakk, Olav Dalsoren, Tor Gundersen, Svein Haagensen, Bjorn Johansen, Thor Martinsen, Arne Mikkelsen, Per Skjerwen-Olsen, Christian Petersen, Rodney Riise, Georg Smefjell, Terje Steen, Odd Syversen, Terje Thoen

**Romania** (Mihai Flamoropol/Constantin Tico, coaches) GK—Constantin Dumitras, Mihai Stoiculescu—Ion Basa, Vasile Boldescu, Zoltan Czaka, Iulian Florescu, Zoltan Fagarasi, Ion Ghiorghiu, Stefan Ionescu, Alexandru Calamar, Aurel Mois, Eduard Pana, Razvan Schiau, Valentin Stefanov, Geza Szabo, Gyula Szabo, Stefan Texe, Dezideriu Varga

**Soviet Union** (Anatoli Tarasov/Arkadi Chernyshev, coaches) GK—Viktor Konovalenko, Viktor Zinger—Veniamin Alexandrov, Viktor Blinov, Vitali Davydov, Anatoli Firsov, Anatoli Ionov, Viktor Kuzkin, Boris Mayorov, Yevgeni Mishakov, Yuri Moiseyev, Viktor Polupanov, Alexander Ragulin, Igor Romishevski, Vyacheslav Starshinov, Vladimir Vikulov, Oleg Zaitsev, Yevgeni Zimin

**Sweden** (Arne Stromberg, coach) GK—Hans Dahllof, Leif Holmqvist—Folke Bengtsson, Arne Carlsson, Svante Granholm, Henric Hedlund, Leif Henriksson, Nils Johansson, Tord Lundstrom, Lars-Goran Nilsson, Carl-Goran Oberg, Roger Olsson, Bjorn Palmqvist, Lars-Erik Sjoberg, Roland Stoltz, Lennart Svedberg, Hakan Wickberg

**United States** (Murray Williamson, coach) GK—Jim Logue, Pat Rupp—Herb Brooks, John Cunniff, John Dale, Craig Falkman, Paul Hurley, Tom Hurley, Len Lilyholm, John Morrison, Lou Nanne, Bob Paradise, Larry Pleau, Bruce Riutta, Don Ross, Larry Stordahl, Doug Volmar, Rob Gaudreau

**West Germany** (Ed Riegle, coach) GK—Gunther Knauss, Josef Schramm—Heinz Bader, Lorenz Funk, Manfred Gmeiner, Gustav Hanig, Ernst Kopf, Bernd Kuhn, Peter Lax, Horst Meindl, Josef Reif, Hans Schichtl, Alois Schloder, Rudolf Thanner, Leonhard Waitl, Heinz Weisenbach, Josef Volk

**Yugoslavia** (Oldrich Mlcoh, coach) GK—Anton Gale, Rudolf Knez—Slavko Beravs, Albin Felc, Miroslav Gojanovic, Rudi Hiti, Ivo Jan, Bogo Jan, Lado Jug, Ciril Klinar, Janez Mlakar, Ivo Rataj, Viktor Ravnik, Rado Razinger, Boris Renaud, Franc Smolej, Roman Smolej, Viktor Tisler

## 11th OLYMPIC WINTER GAMES
## February 5-13, 1972
## Sapporo, Japan

**Final Placing**

| | | | |
|---|---|---|---|
| Gold | Soviet Union | 7th | West Germany |
| Silver | United States | 8th | Norway |
| Bronze | Czechoslovakia | 9th | Japan |
| 4th | Sweden | 10th | Switzerland |
| 5th | Finland | 11th | Yugoslavia |
| 6th | Poland | | |

**Qualifying Round Results**
(winners advance to A Pool/medal round; losers to B Pool/consolation round)

| | | |
|---|---|---|
| February 3 | Czechoslovakia 8 | Japan 2 |
| February 3 | Sweden 8 | Yugoslavia 1 |
| February 4 | United States 5 | Switzerland 3 |
| February 4 | Poland 4 | Germany 0 |
| February 4 | Finland 13 | Norway 1 |

*because only eleven teams participated, the top-ranked Soviet Union received a bye directly to A Pool

**Tournament Format**
The six teams were grouped into one section, each playing a round-robin schedule. The top team in the standings (two points for a win, one for a tie) would win the gold medal. In the event of a two-way tie, the winner of the head-to-head game would get the gold. If there were a tie between more than two teams, goal differential (goals against subtracted from goals scored) would be the deciding factor.

**A POOL/MEDAL ROUND**

| | GP | W | T | L | GF | GA | P |
|---|---|---|---|---|---|---|---|
| Soviet Union | 5 | 4 | 1 | 0 | 33 | 13 | 9 |
| United States | 5 | 3 | 0 | 2 | 18 | 15 | 6 |
| Czechoslovakia | 5 | 3 | 0 | 2 | 26 | 13 | 6 |
| Sweden | 5 | 2 | 1 | 2 | 17 | 13 | 5 |
| Finland | 5 | 2 | 0 | 3 | 14 | 24 | 4 |
| Poland | 5 | 0 | 0 | 5 | 9 | 39 | 0 |

| | | |
|---|---|---|
| February 5 | Sweden 5 | United States 1 |
| February 5 | Czechoslovakia 14 | Poland 1 |
| February 5 | Soviet Union 9 | Finland 3 |
| February 7 | Sweden 3 | Soviet Union 3 |
| February 7 | United States 5 | Czechoslovakia 1 |
| February 7 | Finland 5 | Poland 1 |
| February 8 | Czechoslovakia 7 | Finland 1 |
| February 9 | Sweden 5 | Poland 3 |
| February 9 | Soviet Union 7 | United States 2 |
| February 10 | Soviet Union 9 | Poland 3 |
| February 10 | Czechoslovakia 2 | Sweden 1 |
| February 10 | United States 4 | Finland 1 |
| February 12 | United States 6 | Poland 1 |
| February 13 | Finland 4 | Sweden 3 |
| February 13 | Soviet Union 5 | Czechoslovakia 2 |

**B POOL/CONSOLATION ROUND**

| | GP | W | T | L | GF | GA | P |
|---|---|---|---|---|---|---|---|
| West Germany | 4 | 3 | 0 | 1 | 22 | 10 | 6 |
| Norway | 4 | 3 | 0 | 1 | 16 | 14 | 6 |
| Japan | 4 | 2 | 1 | 1 | 17 | 16 | 5 |
| Switzerland | 4 | 0 | 2 | 2 | 9 | 16 | 2 |
| Yugoslavia | 4 | 0 | 1 | 3 | 9 | 17 | 1 |

| | | |
|---|---|---|
| February 6 | Norway 5 | Yugoslavia 2 |
| February 6 | West Germany 5 | Switzerland 0 |
| February 7 | West Germany 6 | Yugoslavia 2 |
| February 7 | Japan 3 | Switzerland 3 |
| February 9 | Japan 3 | Yugoslavia 2 |
| February 9 | West Germany 5 | Norway 1 |
| February 10 | Norway 5 | Japan 4 |
| February 10 | Switzerland 3 | Yugoslavia 3 |
| February 12 | Norway 5 | Switzerland 3 |
| February 12 | Japan 7 | West Germany 6 |

**Rosters**

**Czechoslovakia** (Vladimir Kostka/Jaroslav Pitner, coaches) GK—Vladimir Dzurilla, Jiri Holecek—Karel Vohralik, Josef Horesovsky, Oldrich Machac, Vladimir Bednar, Rudolf Tajcnar, Josef Cerny, Jiri Holik, Frantisek Pospisil, Bohuslav Stastny, Richard Farda, Ivan Hlinka, Jiri Kochta, Vaclav Nedomansky, Vladimir Martinec, Eduard Novak, Jaroslav Holik

**Finland** (Seppo Liitsola/Rauli Virtanen, coaches) GK—Jorma Valtonen, Stig Wetzell—Ilpo Koskela, Seppo Lindstrom, Heikki Riihrainta, Heikki Jarn, Juha Rantasila, Pekka Marjamaki, Lauri Mononen, Veli-Pekka Ketola, Matti Murto, Seppo Repo, Harri Linnonmaa, Juhani Tamminen, Lasse Oksanen, Esa Peltonen, Timo Turunen, Jorma Vehmanen, Matti Keinonen, Jorma Peltonen

**Japan** (Masami Tanabu, coach) GK—Toshimito Ohtsubo, Minoru Misawa—Koji Iwamoto, Takao Hikigi, Yoshio Hoshino, Osamu Wakabayashi, Toru Okajima, Minoru Ito, Fumio Yamazaki, Tasushin Tanaka, Hori Hiroshi, Iwao Nakayama, Takeshi Akiba, Takeshi Tsuburai, Teruyasu Honma, Hideaki Kurokawa, Isao Kakihara, Tsutomu Hanzawa, Hideo Suzuki

**Norway** (Ake Brask, coach) GK—Kare Ostensen—Arne Mikkelsen, Svein Hagensen, Steinar Bjolbakk, Bjorn Andressen, Tom Roymark, Roy Jansen, Terje Thon, Oyvind Berg, Jan Kinder, Svein Hansen, Terje Steen, Birger Jansen, Thor Martinsen, Morten Sethering, Bjorn Johansen, Thom Kristensen

**Poland** (Anatoli Yegorov/Mieczyslaw Chmura, coaches) GK—Valery Kosyl, Andrzej Tkacz—Jerzy Potz, Stanislaw Fryzlewicz, Ludwik Czachowski, Andrzej Szczepaniec, Adam Kopczynski, Marian Feter, Stefan Chowaniec, Tadeusz Kacik, Feliks Goralczyk, Wieslaw Tokarz, Leszek Tokarz, Jozef Slowakiewicz, Walenty Zietara, Tadeusz Obloj, Jozef Batkiewicz, Krzysztof Bialynicki, Robert Goralczyk

**Soviet Union** (Anatoli Tarasov/Arkadi Chernyshev, coaches) GK—Vladislav Tretiak, Alexander Pashkov—Vitali Davydov, Vladimir Lutchenko, Alexander Ragulin, Viktor Kuzkin, Gennadi Tsygankov, Valeri Vasilyev, Valeri Kharlamov, Yuri Blinov, Vladimir Petrov, Anatoli Firsov, Alexander Maltsev, Vladimir Shadrin, Boris Mikhailov, Vladimir Vikulov, Alexander Yakushev, Igor Romishevski, Yevgeni Mishakov, Yevgeni Zimin

**Sweden** (Billy Harris, coach) GK—Leif Holmqvist, Christer Abrahamsson—Stig Ostling, Lars-Erik Sjoberg, Kenneth Ekman, Thommie Bergman, Bert-Ola Nordlander, Thommy Abrahamsson, Stig-Goran Johansson, Bjorn Palmqvist, Hans Lindberg, Tord Lundstrom, Mats Lindh, Hakan Pettersson, Hakan Wickberg, Lars-Goran Nilsson, Inge Hammarstrom, Kjell Rune Milton, Mats Ahlberg, Hans Hansson

**Switzerland** (Gaston Pelletier/Derek Holmes, coaches) GK—Gerald Rigolet, Alfio Molina—Michel Turler, Francis Reinhard, Jacques Pousaz, Marcel Sgualdo, Peter Lehmann, Gaston Furrer, Charles, Henzen, Peter Aeschlimann, Rene Berra, Heinz Jenni, Hans Keller, Paul Probst, Gerard Dubi, Toni Neininger, Guy Dubois, Rene Huguenin

**West Germany** (Gerhard Kiessling, coach) GK—Toni Kehle, Rainer Makatsch—Erich Kuhnhackl, Rudolf Thanner, Anton Hofherr, Josef Volk, Alois Schloder, Johann Eimansberger, Hans Rothkirch, Otto Schneitberger, Georg Kink, Werner Modes, Paul Langner, Karl-Heinz Egger, Rainer Philipp, Bernd Kuhn, Lorenz Funk, Martin Wild, Heiko Antons, Reinhold Bauer

**United States** (Murray Williamson, coach) GK—Mike Curran, Tim Regan, Pat Sears—Charlie Brown, Tom Mellor, Frank Sanders, Jim McElmury, Dick McGlynn, Wally Olds, Kevin Ahearn, Stu Irving, Mark Howe, Henry Boucha, Keith Christiansen, Robbie Ftorek, Ron Naslund, Craig Sarner, Tim Sheehy, Larry Bader

**Yugoslavia** (Vladimir Kluc, coach) GK—Anton Gale, Rudolf Knez—Gorazd Hiti, Ivo Jan, Viktor Tisler, Boris Renaud, Bogo Jan, Viktor Ravnik, Ivo Rataj, Dragomir Savic, Franci Zbontar, Rudi Hiti, Janez Puterle, Albin Felc, Roman Smolej, Silvo Poljansek, Slavko Beravs, Bojan Kumar, Stefan Seme, Bozidar Beravs

## 12th OLYMPIC WINTER GAMES
## February 6-14, 1976
## Innsbruck, Austria

**Final Placing**

| | |
|---|---|
| Gold ........Soviet Union | 7th .........Romania |
| Silver ......Czechoslovakia | 8th .........Austria |
| Bronze ....West Germany | 9th .........Japan |
| 4th ..........Finland | 10th .......Yugoslavia |
| 5th ..........United States | 11th .......Switzerland |
| 6th ..........Poland | 12th .......Bulgaria |

**Qualifying Round Results**
(winners advanced to A Pool/medal round; losers went to B Pool/consolation round)

| | |
|---|---|
| Soviet Union 16 | Austria 3 |
| Czechoslovakia 14 | Bulgaria 1 |
| West Germany 5 | Switzerland 1 |
| Poland 7 | Romania 4 |
| Finland 11 | Japan 2 |
| United States 8 | Yugoslavia 4 |

**Tournament Format**
The six teams were grouped into a medal round section, each playing a round-robin schedule. The top team in the standings (two points for a win, one for a tie) would win the gold medal. In the event of a two-way tie, the winner of the head-to-head game would get the gold. If there were a tie between more than two teams, goal differential (goals against subtracted from goals scored) would be the deciding factor.

**A POOL/MEDAL ROUND**

| | GP | W | T | L | GF | GA | P |
|---|---|---|---|---|---|---|---|
| Soviet Union | 5 | 5 | 0 | 0 | 40 | 11 | 10 |
| Czechoslovakia | 5 | 3 | 0 | 2 | 24 | 10 | 6 |
| West Germany | 5 | 2 | 0 | 3 | 21 | 24 | 4 |
| Finland | 5 | 2 | 0 | 3 | 19 | 18 | 4 |
| United States | 5 | 2 | 0 | 3 | 15 | 21 | 4 |
| Poland | 5 | 1 | 0 | 4 | 9 | 44 | 2 |

| | | |
|---|---|---|
| February 6 | West Germany 7 | Poland 4 |
| February 6 | Soviet Union 6 | United States 2 |
| February 6 | Czechoslovakia 2 | Finland 1 |
| February 8 | Soviet Union 16 | Poland 1 |
| February 8 | Finland 5 | West Germany 3 |
| February 8 | Czechoslovakia 5 | United States 0 |
| February 10 | United States 5 | Finland 4 |
| February 10 | Poland 1 | Czechoslovakia 0* |
| February 10 | Soviet Union 7 | West Germany 3 |
| February 12 | United States 7 | Poland 2 |
| February 12 | Czechoslovakia 7 | West Germany 4 |
| February 12 | Soviet Union 7 | Finland 2 |
| February 14 | West Germany 4 | United States 1 |
| February 14 | Finland 7 | Poland 1 |
| February 14 | Soviet Union 4 | Czechoslovakia 3 |

*Czechoslovakia won the game 7-1 but a doping violation by Frantisek Pospisil caused the result to be reversed

**B POOL/CONSOLATION ROUND**

| | GP | W | T | L | GF | GA | P |
|---|---|---|---|---|---|---|---|
| Romania | 5 | 4 | 0 | 1 | 23 | 15 | 8 |
| Austria | 5 | 3 | 0 | 2 | 18 | 14 | 6 |
| Japan | 5 | 3 | 0 | 2 | 20 | 18 | 6 |
| Yugoslavia | 5 | 3 | 0 | 2 | 22 | 19 | 6 |
| Switzerland | 5 | 2 | 0 | 3 | 24 | 22 | 4 |
| Bulgaria | 5 | 0 | 0 | 5 | 19 | 38 | 0 |

| | | |
|---|---|---|
| February 5 | Yugoslavia 6 | Switzerland 4 |
| February 5 | Romania 3 | Japan 1 |
| February 5 | Austria 6 | Bulgaria 2 |
| February 7 | Yugoslavia 4 | Romania 3 |
| February 7 | Switzerland 8 | Bulgaria 3 |
| February 7 | Austria 3 | Japan 2 |
| February 9 | Yugoslavia 8 | Bulgaria 5 |
| February 9 | Japan 6 | Switzerland 4 |
| February 9 | Romania 4 | Austria 3 |
| February 11 | Romania 9 | Bulgaria 4 |
| February 11 | Japan 4 | Yugoslavia 3 |
| February 11 | Switzerland 5 | Austria 3 |
| February 13 | Japan 7 | Bulgaria 5 |
| February 13 | Romania 4 | Switzerland 3 |
| February 13 | Austria 3 | Yugoslavia 1 |

**Rosters**

**Austria** (Yuri Baulin, coach) GK—Franz Schilcher—Franz Voves, Herbert Pock, Herbert Mortl, Rudolf Konig, Max Moser, Josef Puschnig, Michael Herzog, Gunther Oberhuber, Josef Schwitzer, Alexander Sadjina, Peter Zini, Othmar Russ, Gerhard Hausner, Johann Schuller, Walter Schneider, Josef Kriechbaum

**Bulgaria** (Pantelei Pantev, coach) GK—Atanas Iliev, Petar Radev—Kirill Gerasimov, Miltcho Nenov, Bojidar Mintchev, Ivan Penelov, Ivailo Kalev, Dimo Krastinov, Iliya Batchvarov, Lubomir Lyubomirov, Marin Batchvarov, Nikolai Mikhailov, Ivan Atanasov, Malin Atanasov, Nikolai Petrov, Ivan Markovski, Gheorghi Iliev, Dimitre Lazarov

**Czechoslovakia** (Karel Gut/Jan Starsi, coaches) GK—Jiri Holecek, Jiri Crha—Oldrich Machac, Milan Chalupa, Frantisek Pospisil, Miroslav Dvorak, Milan Kajkl, Jiri Bubla, Milan Novy, Vladimir Martinec, Jiri Novak, Bohuslav Stastny, Jiri Holik, Ivan Hlinka, Eduard Novak, Jaroslav Pouzar, Bohuslav Ebermann, Josef Augusta

**Finland** (Seppo Liitsola, coach) GK—Antti Leppanen, Urpo Ylonen—Reijo Laksola, Timo Nummelin, Seppo Lindstrom, Hannu Haapalainen, Pekka Marjamaki, Timo Saari, Seppo Ahokainen, Henry Leppa, Esa Peltonen, Tapio Koskinen, Matti Murto, Pertti Koivulahti, Matti Hagman, Hannu Kapanen, Jorma Vehmanen, Matti Rautiainen

**Germany** (Xaver Unsinn, coach) GK—Anton Kehle, Erich Weishaupt—Rudolf Thanner, Josef Volk, Udo Kiessling, Stefan Metz, Klaus Auhuber, Ignaz Berndaner, Rainer Philipp, Lorenz Funk, Wolfgang Boos, Ernst Kopf, Ferenc Vozar, Walter Koberle, Erich Kuhnhackl, Alois Schloder, Martin Hinterstocker, Franz Reindl

**Japan** (Yoshihiro Miyazaki, coach) GK—Minoru Misawa, Toshimitsu Ohtsubo—Hideo Sakurai, Yasushin Tanaka, Osamu Wakabayashi, Hideo Urabe, Minoru Ito, Takeshi Azuma, Tsutomu Hanzawa, Yoshio Hoshino, Iwao Nakayama, Kiyoshi Esashika, Sadaki Honma, Takeshi Akiba, Hitoshi Nakamura, Hiroshi Hori, Koji Wakasa, Yoshiaki Kyoya

**Poland** (Jozef Kurek, coach) GK—Andrzej Tkacz, Walery Kosyl—Andrzej Slowakiewicz, Andrzej Iskrzycki, Robert Goralczyk, Kordian Jajszczok, Jerzy Potz, Marek Marcinczak, Stefan Chowaniec, Wieslaw Jobczyk, Tadeusz Obloj, Karol Zurek, Leszek Kokoszka, Walenty Zietara, Andrzej Zabawa, Henryk Pytel, Mieczyslaw Jaskierski, Marian Kajzerek

**Romania** (Stefan Ionescu/Ion Tiron, coaches) GK—Valerian Netedu, Vasile Morar—Doru Tureanu, Eduard Pana, Marian Pisaru, Marian Costea, Dumitru Axinte, Elod Antal, George Justinian, Ioan Gheorghiu, Tiberiu Miklos, Dezideriu Varga, Vasile Hutanu, Ion Ionita, Alexandru Halauca, Sandor Gall, Doru Morosan, Nicolae Visan

**Soviet Union** (Boris Kulagin, coach) GK—Alexander Sidelnikov, Vladislav Tretiak—Alexander Gusev, Vladimir Lutchenko, Sergei Babinov, Yuri Lyapkin, Valeri Vasilyev, Gennadi Tsygankov, Sergei Kapustin, Viktor Shalimov, Alexander Maltsev, Boris Mikhailov, Alexander Yakushev, Vladimir Petrov, Valeri Kharlamov, Vladimir Shadrin, Viktor Zhluktov, Boris Alexandrov

**Switzerland** (Rudolf Killias, coach) GK—Andre Jorns, Alfio Molina—Toni Neininger, Nando Mathieu, Rolf Tschiemer, Walter Durst, Renzo Holzer, Jurg Berger, Daniel Widmer, Guy Dubois, Bernhard Neininger, Ernst Luthi, Jakob Kolliker, Aldo Zenhausern, Andreas Meyer, Ueli Hoffmann, Charles Henzen, Georg Mattli

**United States** (Bob Johnson, coach) GK—Jim Warden, Blane Comstock—John Taft, Gary Ross, Paul Jensen, Bob Lundeen, Dick Lamby, Jeff Hymanson, Steve Sertich, Bob Miller, Steve Jensen, Steve Alley, Bob Harris, Bill "Buzz" Schneider, Ted Thorndike, Bob Dobek, Doug Ross, Dan Bolduc

**Yugoslavia** (Premsyl Hajny, coach) GK—Janez Albreht—Franci Zbontar, Eduard Hafner, Roman Smolej, Gorazd Hiti, Janez Puterle, Ignac Kavec, Miroslav Gojanovic, Silvo Poljansek, Marjan Zbontar, Tomaz Lepsa, Miroslav Lap, Karel Savic, Bogdan Jakopic, Bozidar Beravs, Bojan Kumar, Ivan Scap, Janez Petac

## 13th OLYMPIC WINTER GAMES
## February 13–24, 1980
## Lake Placid, United States

**Final Placing**

| | |
|---|---|
| Gold ........United States | 7th .........Poland |
| Silver ......Soviet Union | 8th .........Romania |
| Bronze ....Sweden | 9th .........Netherlands |
| 4th ..........Finland | 10th .......West Germany |
| 5th ..........Czechoslovakia | 11th .......Norway |
| 6th ..........Canada | 12th .......Japan |

**Tournament Format**
Twelve teams were divided into two groups and played a round-robin schedule within each division. The top two teams from each then advanced to a four-team, medal-round round-robin. Results carried over from earlier rounds. In case of a tie in the standings, the winner of the head-to-head meeting would be awarded the superior position.

**Results & Standings**

**RED DIVISION**

| | GP | W | T | L | GF | GA | P |
|---|---|---|---|---|---|---|---|
| Soviet Union | 5 | 5 | 0 | 0 | 51 | 11 | 10 |
| Finland | 5 | 3 | 0 | 2 | 26 | 18 | 6 |
| Canada | 5 | 3 | 0 | 2 | 28 | 12 | 6 |
| Poland | 5 | 2 | 0 | 3 | 15 | 23 | 4 |
| Netherlands | 5 | 1 | 1 | 3 | 16 | 43 | 3 |
| Japan | 5 | 0 | 1 | 4 | 7 | 36 | 1 |

| | | |
|---|---|---|
| February 12 | Canada 10 | Netherlands 1 |
| February 12 | Poland 5 | Finland 4 |
| February 12 | Soviet Union 16 | Japan 0 |
| February 14 | Soviet Union 17 | Netherlands 4 |
| February 14 | Canada 5 | Poland 1 |
| February 14 | Finland 6 | Japan 3 |
| February 16 | Netherlands 3 | Japan 3 |
| February 16 | Soviet Union 8 | Poland 1 |
| February 16 | Finland 4 | Canada 3 |
| February 18 | Canada 6 | Japan 0 |
| February 18 | Netherlands 5 | Poland 3 |
| February 18 | Soviet Union 4 | Finland 2 |
| February 20 | Poland 5 | Japan 1 |
| February 20 | Soviet Union 6 | Canada 4 |
| February 20 | Finland 10 | Netherlands 3 |

**BLUE DIVISION**

| | GP | W | T | L | GF | GA | P |
|---|---|---|---|---|---|---|---|
| Sweden | 5 | 4 | 1 | 0 | 26 | 7 | 9 |
| United States | 5 | 4 | 1 | 0 | 25 | 10 | 9 |
| Czechoslovakia | 5 | 3 | 0 | 2 | 34 | 16 | 6 |
| Romania | 5 | 1 | 1 | 3 | 13 | 29 | 3 |
| West Germany | 5 | 1 | 0 | 4 | 21 | 30 | 2 |
| Norway | 5 | 0 | 1 | 4 | 9 | 36 | 1 |

| | | |
|---|---|---|
| February 12 | Czechoslovakia 11 | Norway 0 |
| February 12 | Romania 6 | West Germany 4 |
| February 12 | Sweden 2 | United States 2 |
| February 14 | Sweden 8 | Romania 0 |
| February 14 | West Germany 10 | Norway 4 |
| February 14 | United States 7 | Czechoslovakia 3 |
| February 16 | United States 5 | Norway 1 |
| February 16 | Czechoslovakia 7 | Romania 2 |
| February 16 | Sweden 5 | West Germany 2 |
| February 18 | Sweden 7 | Norway 1 |
| February 18 | Czechoslovakia 11 | West Germany 3 |
| February 18 | United States 7 | Romania 2 |
| February 20 | Norway 3 | Romania 3 |
| February 20 | Sweden 4 | Czechoslovakia 2 |
| February 20 | United States 4 | West Germany 2 |

**5TH-PLACE GAME**

| | | |
|---|---|---|
| February 22 | Czechoslovakia 6 | Canada 1 |

**MEDAL ROUND**

| | GP | W | T | L | GF | GA | P |
|---|---|---|---|---|---|---|---|
| United States | 3 | 2 | 1 | 0 | 10 | 7 | 5 |
| Soviet Union | 3 | 2 | 0 | 1 | 16 | 8 | 4 |
| Sweden | 3 | 0 | 2 | 1 | 7 | 14 | 2 |
| Finland | 3 | 0 | 1 | 2 | 7 | 11 | 1 |

| | | |
|---|---|---|
| February 22 | United States 4 | Soviet Union 3 |
| February 22 | Finland 3 | Sweden 3 |
| February 24 | United States 4 | Finland 2 |
| February 24 | Soviet Union 9 | Sweden 2 |

**Rosters**

**Canada** (Lorne Davis/Clare Drake/Tom Watt, co-coaches) GK—Bob Dupuis, Paul Pageau—Warren Anderson, Joe Grant, Randy Gregg, Terry O'Malley, Brad Pirie, Don Spring, Tim Watters, Glenn Anderson, Ken Berry, Dan D'Alvise, Ron Davidson, John Devaney, Dave Hindmarch, Paul MacLean, Kevin Maxwell, Jim Nill, Kevin Primeau, Stelio Zupancich

**Czechoslovakia** (Karel Gut/Ludek Bukac, coaches) GK—Jiri Kralik, Karel Lang—Jiri Bubla, Milan Chalupa, Vitezslav Duris, Miroslav Dvorak, Bohuslav Ebermann, Miroslav Frycer, Karel Holy, Frantisek Kaberle, Arnold Kadlec, Vincent Lukac, Jan Neliba, Jiri Novak, Milan Novy, Jaroslav Pouzar, Anton Stastny, Marian Stastny, Peter Stastny, Vladimir Martinec

**Finland** (Kalevi Numminen, coach) GK—Antero Kivela, Jorma Valtonen—Kari Eloranta, Hannu Haapalainen, Markku Hakulinen, Markku Kiimalainen, Jukka Koskilahti, Hannu Koskinen, Jari Kurri, Mikko Leinonen, Reijo Leppanen, Tapio Levo, Lasse Litma, Jarmo Makitalo, Esa Peltonen, Jukka Porvari, Olli Saarinen, Seppo Suoraniemi, Timo Susi, Ismo Villa

**Japan** (Hitoshi Wakabayashi, coach) GK—Takeshi Iwamoto, Minoru Misawa—Takeshi Azuma, Tadamitsu Fujii, Tsutomu Hanzawa, Yoshiaki Honda, Sadaki Honma, Hiroshi Hori, Yoshio Hoshino, Mikio Hosoi, Norio Ito, Katsuyoshi Kawamura, Mikio Matsuda, Satoru Misawa, Hitoshi Nakamura, Iwao Nakayama, Hideo Sakurai, Hideo Urabe, Koji Wakasa, Osama Wakabayashi

**Netherlands** (Hans Westberg, coach) GK—Ted Lenssen, John de Bruyn—Ron Berteling, Klaas van de Broek, Brian de Bruyn, Dick de Cloe, Rick van Gog, Corky de Graauw, Jack de Heer, Harry van Heumen, Henk Hille, Chuck Huizinga, Jan Janssen, William Klooster, Patrick Kolijn, Leo Koopmans, George Peternousek, Al Pluymers, Frank van Soldt, Larrie van Wieren

**Norway** (Ronald Pettersson, coach) GK—Jim Marthinsen, Tore Waalberg—Trond Abrahamsen, Knut Andresen, Knut Fjeldsgaard, Stephen Foyn, Oystein Jarlsbo, Morten Johansen, Vidar Johansen, Oivind Losamoen, Haakon Lundenes, Thor Martinsen, Rune Molberg, Geir Myhre, Nils Nilsen, Tore Falk Nilsen, Erik Pedersen, Tom Roymark, Morten Sethereng, Petter Thoresen

**Poland** (Czeslaw Borowicz, coach) GK—Pawel Lukaszka, Henryk Wojtynek—Stefan Chowaniec, Bogdan Dziubinski, Henryk Gruth, Leszek Jachna, Andrzej Janczy, Henryk Janiszewski, Wieslaw Jobczyk, Stanislaw Klocek, Leszek Kokoszka, Andrzej Malysiak, Marek Marcinczak, Tadeusz Obloj, Jerzy Potz, Henryk Pytel, Dariusz Sikora, Ludwik Synowiec, Andrzej Ujwary, Andrzej Zabawa

**Romania** (Stefan Ionescu/Ion Tiron, coaches) GK—Gheorghe Hutan, Valerian Netedu—Elod Antal, Istvan Antal, Dumitru Axinte, Ion Berdila, Traian Cazacu, Marian Costea, Sandor Gall, Alexandru Halauca, George Justinian, Doru Morosan, Bela Nagy, Zoltan Nagy, Constantin Nistor, Adrian Olenici, Marian Pisaru, Mihai Popescu, Laszlo Solyom, Doru Tureanu

**Soviet Union** (Viktor Tikhonov, coach) GK—Vladislav Tretiak, Vladimir Myshkin—Helmuts Balderis, Zinetula Bilyaletdinov, Vyacheslav Fetisov, Alexander Golikov, Vladimir Golikov, Alexei Kasatonov, Valeri Kharlamov, Vladimir Krutov, Yuri Lebedev, Sergei Makarov, Alexander Maltsev, Boris Mikhailov, Vasili Pervukhin, Vladimir Petrov, Alexander Skvortsov, Sergei Starikov, Valeri Vasilyev, Viktor Zhluktov

**Sweden** (Tommy Sandlin, coach) GK—Pelle Lindbergh, William Lofqvist—Mats Ahlberg, Sture Andersson, Bo Berglund, Hakan Eriksson, Jan Eriksson, Thomas Eriksson, Leif Holmgren, Tomas Jonsson, Harald Luckner, Bengt Lundholm, Per Lundqvist, Lars Mohlin, Mats Naslund, Lennart Norberg, Tommy Samuelsson, Dan Soderstrom, Mats Waltin, Ulf Weinstock

**United States** (Herb Brooks, coach) GK—Jim Craig, Steve Janaszak—Bill Baker, Neal Broten, Dave Christian, Steve Christoff, Mike Eruzione, John Harrington, Mark Johnson, Rob McClanahan, Ken Morrow, Jack O'Callahan, Mark Pavelich, Mike Ramsey, Bill "Buzz" Schneider, Dave Silk, Eric Strobel, Bob Suter, Phil Verchota, Mark Wells

**West Germany** (Hans Rampf, coach) GK—Bernhard Engelbrecht, Sigmund Suttner—Klaus Auhuber, Ulrich Egen, Hermann Hinterstocker, Martin Hinterstocker, Ernst Hofner, Udo Kiessling, Horst-Peter Kretschmer, Harald Krull, Marcus Kuhl, Holger Meitinger, Rainer Philipp, Joachim Reil, Franz Reindl, Peter Scharf, Gerd Truntschka, Vladimir Vacatko, Martin Wild, Hans Zach

## 14th OLYMPIC WINTER GAMES
## February 7–19, 1984
## Sarajevo, Yugoslavia

**Final Placing**

| | |
|---|---|
| Gold ........Soviet Union | 7th .........United States |
| Silver ......Czechoslovakia | 8th .........Poland |
| Bronze ....Sweden | 9th .........Italy |
| 4th ..........Canada | 10th .......Norway |
| 5th ..........West Germany | 11th .......Austria, Yugoslavia |
| 6th ..........Finland | |

**Qualifying Results (winner advances to Olympics)**

| | | |
|---|---|---|
| April 9, 1983 | Norway 4 | Netherlands 4 |
| April 10, 1983 | Norway 10 | Netherlands 2 |

**Tournament Format**

The 12 teams were divided into two groups of six, all teams playing a round-robin schedule within each group. The top two teams from each group then advanced to a four country round-robin medal round with the results from the qualifying round between qualifying teams counting in the finals round as well. In the event of a tie in the preliminary round standings, head-to-head results would be the first determining factor. If that game were a tie, then overall goal differential would decide the issue.

**Results & Standings**

**GROUP A**

| | GP | W | T | L | GF | GA | P |
|---|---|---|---|---|---|---|---|
| Soviet Union | 5 | 5 | 0 | 0 | 42 | 5 | 10 |
| Sweden | 5 | 3 | 1 | 1 | 24 | 15 | 7 |
| West Germany | 5 | 3 | 1 | 1 | 27 | 17 | 7 |
| Poland | 5 | 1 | 0 | 4 | 16 | 37 | 2 |
| Italy | 5 | 1 | 0 | 4 | 15 | 21 | 2 |
| Yugoslavia | 5 | 1 | 0 | 4 | 8 | 37 | 2 |

| | | |
|---|---|---|
| February 7 | Sweden 11 | Italy 1 |
| February 7 | Soviet Union 12 | Poland 1 |
| February 7 | West Germany 8 | Yugoslavia 1 |
| February 9 | Soviet Union 5 | Italy 1 |
| February 9 | West Germany 8 | Poland 5 |

| | | |
|---|---|---|
| February 9 | Sweden 11 | Yugoslavia 0 |
| February 11 | Sweden 1 | West Germany 1 |
| February 11 | Soviet Union 9 | Yugoslavia 1 |
| February 11 | Italy 6 | Poland 1 |
| February 13 | Soviet Union 6 | West Germany 1 |
| February 13 | Sweden 10 | Poland 1 |
| February 13 | Yugoslavia 5 | Italy 1 |
| February 15 | Soviet Union 10 | Sweden 1 |
| February 15 | Poland 8 | Yugoslavia 1 |
| February 15 | West Germany 9 | Italy 4 |

**GROUP B**

| | GP | W | T | L | GF | GA | P |
|---|---|---|---|---|---|---|---|
| Czechoslovakia | 5 | 5 | 0 | 0 | 38 | 7 | 10 |
| Canada | 5 | 4 | 0 | 1 | 24 | 10 | 8 |
| Finland | 5 | 2 | 1 | 2 | 27 | 19 | 5 |
| United States | 5 | 1 | 2 | 2 | 16 | 17 | 4 |
| Austria | 5 | 1 | 0 | 4 | 13 | 37 | 2 |
| Norway | 5 | 0 | 1 | 4 | 15 | 43 | 1 |

| | | |
|---|---|---|
| February 7 | Canada 4 | United States 2 |
| February 7 | Finland 4 | Austria 3 |
| February 7 | Czechoslovakia 10 | Norway 4 |
| February 9 | Canada 8 | Austria 1 |
| February 9 | Czechoslovakia 4 | United States 1 |
| February 9 | Finland 16 | Norway 2 |
| February 11 | Czechoslovakia 13 | Austria 0 |
| February 11 | Norway 3 | United States 3 |
| February 11 | Canada 4 | Finland 2 |
| February 13 | Canada 8 | Norway 1 |
| February 13 | Czechoslovakia 7 | Finland 2 |
| February 13 | United States 7 | Austria 3 |
| February 15 | Finland 3 | United States 3 |
| February 15 | Czechoslovakia 4 | Canada 0 |
| February 15 | Austria 6 | Norway 5 |

**5TH-PLACE GAME**

February 17 West Germany 7 Finland 4

**7TH-PLACE GAME**

February 17 United States 7 Poland 4

**MEDAL ROUND**

| | GP | W | T | L | GF | GA | P |
|---|---|---|---|---|---|---|---|
| Soviet Union | 3 | 3 | 0 | 0 | 16 | 1 | 6 |
| Czechoslovakia | 3 | 2 | 0 | 1 | 6 | 2 | 4 |
| Sweden | 3 | 1 | 0 | 2 | 3 | 12 | 2 |
| Canada | 3 | 0 | 0 | 3 | 0 | 10 | 0 |

| | | |
|---|---|---|
| February 17 | Czechoslovakia 2 | Sweden 0 |
| February 17 | Soviet Union 4 | Canada 0 |
| February 19 | Sweden 2 | Canada 0 |
| February 19 | Soviet Union 2 | Czechoslovakia 0 |

**Rosters**

**Austria** (Rudolf Killias, coach) GK—Michael Rudman, Brian Stankiewicz —Thomas Cijan, Leopold Civec, Richard Cunningham, Konrad Dorn, Fritz Ganster, Kurt Harand, Bernie Hutz, Rudolph Koenig, Helmut Koren, Helmut Petrik, Martin Platzer, Herbert Pock, Peter Raffl, Krunoslav Seculic, Giuseppe Mion, Kelly Greenbank

**Canada** (Dave King, coach) GK—Darren Eliot, Mario Gosselin—Warren Anderson, J-J Daigneault, Bruce Driver, Doug Lidster, James Patrick, Craig Redmond, Russ Courtnall, Kevin Dineen, Dave Donnelly, Pat Flatley, Dave Gagner, Vaughn Karpan, Darren Lowe, Kirk Muller, Dave Tippett, Carey Wilson, Robin Bartel, Dan Wood

**Czechoslovakia** (Vladimir Kostka, coach) GK—Jiri Kralik, Jaromir Sindel—Jaroslav Benak, Vladimir Caldr, Frantisek Cernik, Miloslav Horava, Jiri Hrdina, Arnold Kadlec, Jiri Lala, Igor Liba, Vincent Lukac, Dusan Pasek, Darius Rusnak, Vladimir Ruzicka, Radoslav Svoboda, Eduard Uvira, Pavel Richter, Jaroslav Korbela, Vladimir Kyhos

**Finland** (Alpo Suhonen/Reino Ruotsalainen, coaches) GK—Kari Takko, Jorma Valtonen—Raimo Helminen, Risto Jalo, Arto Javanainen, Timo Jutila, Erkki Laine, Marcus Lehto, Pertti Lehtonen, Jarmo Makitalo, Anssi Melametsa, Hannu Oksanen, Arto Ruotanen, Arto Sirvio, Petri Skriko, Raimo Summanen, Harri Tuohimaa

**Italy** (Ron Ivany, coach) GK—Adriano Tancon, Marco Capone—John Bellio, Cary Farelli, Norbert Gasser, Grant Goegan, Adolf Insam, Fabrizio Kasslatter, Erwin Kostner, Michael Mair, Michael Mastrullo, Lodovico Migliore, Thomas Milani, Gino Pasqualloto, Martin Pavlu, Constantine Priondolo, Norbert Prunster, David Tomassoni, Bob DePiero, Gerry Ciarcia

**Norway** (Hans Westberg, coach) GK—Jim Marthinsen, Jorn Goldstein—Trond Abrahamsen, Cato Andersen, Arne Bergseng, Per Arne Christiansen, Age Ellingsen, Stephen Foyn, Oystein Jarslbo, Roy Johansen, Erik Kristiansen, Sven Lien, Oivind Losamoen, Orjan Lovdal, Geir Myhre, Erik Nerell, Bjorn Skaare, Petter Thoresen, Frank Vestreng

**Poland** (Emil Nikodemowicz, coach) GK—Wlodzimierz Olszewski, Gabriel Samolej—Marek Cholewa, Jerzy Christ, Henryk Gruth, Andrzej Hachula, Leszek Jachna, Wieslaw Jobczyk, Stanislaw Klocek, Andrzej Nowak, Jan Piecko, Henryk Pytel, Krystian Sikorski, Jan Stopczyk, Ludwik Synowiec, Robert Szopinski, Andrzej Zabawa, Janusz Adamiec

**Soviet Union** (Viktor Tikhonov, coach) GK—Vladislav Tretiak, Vladimir Myshkin—Zinetula Bilyaletdinov, Sergei Shepelev, Nikolai Drozdetski, Vyacheslav Fetisov, Alexander Gerasimov, Alexei Kasatonov, Andrei Khomutov, Vladimir Kovin, Alexander Kozhevnikov, Vladimir Krutov, Igor Larionov, Sergei Makarov, Vasili Pervukhin, Alexander Skvortsov, Sergei Starikov, Igor Stelnov, Viktor Tyumenev, Mikhail Vasilyev

**Sweden** (Anders Parmstrom, coach) GK—Rolf Ridderwall, Gote Walitalo—Thomas Ahlen, Per-Erik Eklund, Bo Ericson, Hakan Eriksson, Peter Gradin, Mats Hessel, Michael Hjalm, Tommy Morth, Jens Ohling, Thomas Rundquist, Tomas Sandstrom, Hakan Sodergren, Michael Thelven, Mats Waltin, Hakan Nordin

**United States** (Lou Vairo, coach) GK—Bob Mason, Marc Behrend—Corey Millen, Scott Bjugstad, Bob Brooke, Chris Chelios, Mark Fusco, Scott Fusco, Steven Griffith, John Harrington, Al Iafrate, David A. Jensen, David H. Jensen, Pat Lafontaine, Ed Olczyk, Gary Sampson, Phil Verchota, Paul Guay, Mark Kumpel

**West Germany** (Xaver Unsinn, coach) GK—Bernd Engelbrecht, Karl Friesen—Manfred Ahne, Ignaz Berndaner, Dieter Hegen, Uli Hiemer, Ernst Hofner, Udo Kiessling, Harold Kreis, Marcus Kuhl, Erich Kuhnhackl, Joachim Reil, Franz Reindl, Roy Roedger, Helmut Steiger, Gerd Truntschka, Manfred Wolf

**Yugoslavia** (Stefan Seme, coach) GK—Cveto Pretnar, Dominik Lomovsek—Igor Beribak, Mustafa Besic, Dejan Burnik, Marjan Gorenc, Gorazd Hiti, Drago Horvat, Vojko Lajovec, Blaz Lomovsek, Murajca Pajic, Bojan Raspet, Ivan Scap, Matjaz Sekelj, Zvone Suvak, Andrej Vidmar, Igor Peter Klemenc

## 15th OLYMPIC WINTER GAMES
## February 13–28, 1988
## Calgary, Canada

**Final Placing**

| | |
|---|---|
| Gold ........Soviet Union | 7th .........United States |
| Silver ......Finland | 8th .........Switzerland |
| Bronze ....Sweden | 9th .........Austria |
| 4th..........Canada | 10th .......Poland |
| 5th..........West Germany | 11th .......France |
| 6th..........Czechoslovakia | 12th .......Norway |

**Tournament Format**

The 12 teams entered in the Olympics were divided into two groups of six and then played a round-robin schedule within each division. The top three teams in each pool then advanced to a medal round in which all previous results against opponents in the medal round counted. The other teams were placed in another pool to determine 7th–12th place rankings. In the case of a tie in the final standings, goal differential would be the deciding factor.

**Results & Standings**

**GROUP A**

| | GP | W | T | L | GF | GA | P |
|---|---|---|---|---|---|---|---|
| Finland | 5 | 3 | 1 | 1 | 22 | 8 | 7 |
| Sweden | 5 | 2 | 3 | 0 | 23 | 10 | 7 |
| Canada | 5 | 3 | 1 | 1 | 17 | 12 | 7 |
| Switzerland | 5 | 3 | 0 | 2 | 19 | 10 | 6 |
| Poland | 5 | 0 | 1 | 4 | 3 | 13 | 1* |
| France | 5 | 1 | 0 | 4 | 10 | 41 | 0* |

| | | |
|---|---|---|
| February 14 | Sweden 13 | France 2 |
| February 14 | Canada 1 | Poland 0 |
| February 14 | Switzerland 2 | Finland 1 |
| February 16 | Sweden 1 | Poland 1 |
| February 16 | Canada 4 | Switzerland 2 |
| February 16 | Finland 10 | France 1 |
| February 18 | France 2 | Poland 0* |
| February 18 | Sweden 4 | Switzerland 2 |
| February 18 | Finland 3 | Canada 1 |
| February 20 | Finland 3 | Sweden 3 |
| February 20 | Canada 9 | France 5 |
| February 20 | Switzerland 4 | Poland 1 |
| February 22 | Finland 5 | Poland 1 |
| February 22 | Canada 2 | Sweden 2 |
| February 22 | Switzerland 9 | France 0 |

*Poland won the game 6–2 but was stripped of the win after forward Jaroslav Morawiecki tested positive for testosterone. He was banned from international competition for 18 months and France was officially awarded a 2–0 win, but not the points.

GROUP B

| | GP | W | T | L | GF | GA | P |
|---|---|---|---|---|---|---|---|
| Soviet Union | 5 | 5 | 0 | 0 | 32 | 10 | 10 |
| West Germany | 5 | 4 | 0 | 1 | 19 | 12 | 8 |
| Czechoslovakia | 5 | 3 | 0 | 2 | 23 | 14 | 6 |
| United States | 5 | 2 | 0 | 3 | 27 | 27 | 4 |
| Austria | 5 | 0 | 1 | 4 | 12 | 29 | 1 |
| Norway | 5 | 0 | 1 | 4 | 11 | 32 | 1 |

| | | |
|---|---|---|
| February 13 | West Germany 2 | Czechoslovakia 1 |
| February 13 | Soviet Union 5 | Norway 0 |
| February 13 | United States 10 | Austria 6 |
| February 15 | West Germany 7 | Norway 3 |
| February 15 | Soviet Union 8 | Austria 1 |
| February 15 | Czechoslovakia 7 | United States 5 |
| February 17 | West Germany 3 | Austria 1 |
| February 17 | Czechoslovakia 10 | Norway 1 |
| February 17 | Soviet Union 7 | United States 5 |
| February 19 | Czechoslovakia 4 | Austria 0 |
| February 19 | Soviet Union 6 | West Germany 3 |
| February 19 | United States 6 | Norway 3 |
| February 21 | Soviet Union 6 | Czechoslovakia 1 |
| February 21 | Austria 4 | Norway 4 |
| February 21 | West Germany 4 | United States 1 |

11TH-PLACE GAME

February 23 France 8 Norway 6 (10:00 OT/GWS—Derek Haas, Paulin Bordeleau)*

*both goals counted

9TH-PLACE GAME

February 23 Austria 3 Poland 2

7TH-PLACE GAME

February 25 United States 8 Switzerland 4

MEDAL ROUND

| | GP | W | T | L | GF | GA | P |
|---|---|---|---|---|---|---|---|
| Soviet Union | 5 | 4 | 0 | 1 | 25 | 7 | 8 |
| Finland | 5 | 3 | 1 | 1 | 18 | 10 | 7 |
| Sweden | 5 | 2 | 2 | 1 | 15 | 16 | 6 |
| Canada | 5 | 2 | 1 | 2 | 17 | 14 | 5 |
| West Germany | 5 | 1 | 0 | 4 | 8 | 26 | 2 |
| Czechoslovakia | 5 | 1 | 0 | 4 | 12 | 22 | 2 |

| | | |
|---|---|---|
| February 24 | Sweden 6 | Czechoslovakia 2 |
| February 24 | Finland 8 | West Germany 0 |
| February 24 | Soviet Union 5 | Canada 0 |
| February 26 | Canada 8 | West Germany 1 |
| February 26 | Czechoslovakia 5 | Finland 2 |
| February 26 | Soviet Union 7 | Sweden 1 |
| February 27 | Canada 6 | Czechoslovakia 3 |
| February 28 | Sweden 3 | West Germany 2 |
| February 28 | Finland 2 | Soviet Union 1 |

Rosters

**Austria** (Ludek Bukac, coach) GK—Brian Stankiewicz, Andreas Salat, Robert Mack—Thomas Cijan, Konrad Dorn, Kelly Greenbank, Kurt Harand, Bernie Hutz, Werner Kerth, Rudolf Koenig, Gert Kompajn, Gunter Koren, Edward Lebler, Manfred Muhr, Martin Platzer, Herbert Pock, Gerhard Pusnik, Peter Raffl, Robin Sadler, Michael Shea, Johann Sulzer, Silvester Szybisti, Peter Znenahlik

**Canada** (Dave King, coach) GK—Sean Burke, Andy Moog, Rick Kosti—Chris Felix, Randy Gregg, Serge Roy, Tony Stiles, Tim Watters, Trent Yawney, Zarley Zalapski, Ken Berry, Mark Habscheid, Vaughn Karpan, Wally Schreiber, Gord Sherven, Claude Vilgrain, Serge Boisvert, Brian Bradley, Bob Joyce, Merlin Malinowski, Jim Peplinski, Steve Tambellini, Ken Yaremchuk

**Czechoslovakia** (Jan Starsi/Frantisek Pospisil, coaches) GK—Dominik Hasek, Jaromir Sindel, Petr Briza—Jaroslav Benak, Mojmir Bozik, Jiri Dolezal, Otto Hascak, Miloslav Horava, Jiri Hrdina, Jiri Lala, Igor Liba, Dusan Pasek, Radim Radevic, Petr Rosol, Vladimir Ruzicka, Bedrich Scerban, Jiri Sejba, Antonin Stavjana, Rudolf Suchanek, Eduard Uvira, David Volek, Petr Vlk, Rostislav Vlach

**Finland** (Pentti Matikainen/Hannu Jortikka, coaches) GK—Jarmo Myllys, Jukka Tammi, Sakari Lindfors—Timo Blomqvist, Kari Eloranta, Raimo Helminen, Iiro Jarvi, Esa Keskinen, Erkki Laine, Erkki Lehtonen, Jyrki Lumme, Reijo Mikkolainen, Teppo Numminen, Janne Ojanen, Arto Ruotanen, Reijo Ruotsalainen, Simo Saarinen, Kai Suikkanen, Timo Susi, Jari Torkki, Pekka Tuomisto, Jukka Virtanen, Kari Laitinen

**France** (Kjell Larsson, coach) GK—Patrick Foliot, Daniel Maric, Jean-Marc Djian—Peter Almasy, Paulin Bordeleau, Stephane Botteri, Phillippe Bozon, Guy Dupuis, Derek Haas, Michel Leblanc, Jean-Philippe Lemoine, Jean Lerondeau, Stephane Lessard, Francois Ouimet, Franck Pajonkowski, Andre Peloffy, Denis Perez, Christian Pouget, Antoine Richer, Pierre Schmitt, Christophe Ville, Steve Woodburn

**Norway** (Lennart Ahlberg, coach) GK—Jarl Eriksen, Vernon Mott, Tommy Skaarberg—Cato Tom Andersen, Morgan Andersen, Lars Bergseng, Arne Billkvam, Tor Eikeland, Age Ellingsen, Stephen Foyn, Jarle Friis, Rune Gulliksen, Geir Hoff, Roy Johansen, Erik Kristiansen, Truls Kristiansen, Orjan Lovdal, Jorgen Salsten, Petter Salsten, Kim Sogaard, Sigurd Thinn, Petter Thoresen, Frank Vestreng, Marius Voigt

**Poland** (Leszek Lejczyk, coach) GK—Andrzej Hanisz, Gabriel Samolej, Franciszek Kukla—Janusz Adamiec, Zbiginiew Bryjak, Krzysztof Bujar, Marek Cholewa, Jerzy Christ, Miroslaw Copija, Henryk Gruth, Leszek Jachna, Andrzej Kadziolka, Jedrzej Kasperczyk, Piotr Kwasigroch, Jaroslaw Morawiecki, Ireneusz Pacula, Krzysztof Podsialdo, Jerzy Potz, Krystian Sikorski, Roman Steblecki, Marek Stebnicki, Jan Stopczyk, Andrzej Swiatek, Jacek Szopinski, Robert Szopinski, Jacek Zamojski

**Soviet Union** (Viktor Tikhonov, coach) GK—Sergei Mylnikov, Vitali Samoilov, Yevgeni Belosheikin—Ilya Byakin, Vyacheslav Bykov, Alexander Chernykh, Vyacheslav Fetisov, Alexei Gusarov, Valeri Kamenski, Alexei Kasatonov, Andrei Khomutov, Alexander Kozhevnikov, Igor Kravchuk, Vladimir Krutov, Igor Larionov, Andrei Lomakin, Sergei Makarov, Alexander Mogilny, Anatoli Semyonov, Sergei Starikov, Igor Stelnov, Sergei Svetlov, Sergei Yashin

**Sweden** (Tommy Sandlin, coach) GK—Peter Aslin, Anders Bergman, Peter Lindmark—Peter Andersson, Mikael Andersson, Bo Berglund, Jonas Bergqvist, Thom Eklund, Anders Eldebrink, Peter Eriksson, Thomas Eriksson, Michael Hjalm, Lars Ivarsson, Mikael Johansson, Lars Karlsson, Mats Kihlstrom, Lars Molin, Jens Ohling, Lars-Gunnar Pettersson, Thomas Rundqvist, Tommy Samuelsson, Ulf Sandstrom, Hakan Sodergren

**Switzerland** (Simon Schenk, coach) GK—Olivier Anken, Richard Bucher, Renato Tosio—Gaetan Boucher, Patrice Brasey, Urs Burkhart, Manuele Celio, Pietro Cunti, Jorg Eberle, Felix Hollenstein, Peter Jaks, Jakob Kolliker, Andre Kuenzi, Markus Leuenberger, Fredy Luethi, Fausto Mazzoleni, Gil Montandon, Thomas Mueller, Philipp Neuenschwander, Andreas Ritsch, Bruno Rogger, Peter Schlagenhauf, Thomas Vrabec, Roman Waeger, Andreas Zehnder

**United States** (Dave Peterson, coach) GK—Mike Richter, Chris Terreri, John Blue—Al Bourbeau, Greg Brown, Clark Donatelli, Scott Fusco, Guy Gosselin, Tony Granato, Craig Janney, Jim Johannson, Peter Laviolette, Steve Leach, Brian Leetch, Lane MacDonald, Corey Millen, Kevin Miller, Jeff Norton, Todd Okerlund, Dave Snuggerud, Kevin Stevens, Eric Weinrich, Scott Young

**West Germany** (Xaver Unsinn, coach) GK—Helmut de Raaf, Karl Friesen, Josef Schlickenrieder—Christian Brittig, Peter Draisaitl, Ron Fischer, Georg Franz, Dieter Hegen, Georg Holzmann, Udo Kiessling, Horst Kretschmer, Harold Kreis, Dieter Medicus, Andreas Niederberger, Peter Obresa, Joachim Reil, Roy Roedger, Peter Schiller, Manfred Schuster, Helmut Steiger, Bernd Truntschka, Gerd Truntschka, Manfred Wolf

## 16th OLYMPIC WINTER GAMES
## February 8–23, 1992
## Albertville, France

Final Placing

| | |
|---|---|
| Gold ........Russia (Unified Team) | 7th .........Finland |
| Silver ......Canada | 8th .........France |
| Bronze ....Czechoslovakia | 9th .........Norway |
| 4th ..........United States | 10th .......Switzerland |
| 5th ..........Sweden | 11th .......Poland |
| 6th ..........Germany | 12th .......Italy |

Tournament Format

The 12 competing nations were divided into two pools of six teams each and played a round-robin schedule within each group. The top four teams from each then advanced to a playoff round elimination quarter-finals. The top team in group A played the fourth team in group B; the top team in group B played the fourth team in group A; the second team in group A played the third team in group B; and, the second team in group B played the third team in group A. The elimination play-offs (a quarter-finals, semi-finals and finals) represented a new way to bring excitement to the Olympics.

In case of a tie in the standings in the preliminary round, goal differential only in games played between those teams that were tied would be the deciding factor (for example, Canada tied with Unified Team and Czechs but wound up on top). In the elimination playoff round, there would be a 10-minute sudden-death overtime period, then a penalty shot-style shootout after 70 minutes if the game were still tied.

Results & Standings

POOL A

| | GP | W | T | L | GF | GA | P |
|---|---|---|---|---|---|---|---|
| United States | 5 | 4 | 1 | 0 | 18 | 7 | 9 |
| Sweden | 5 | 3 | 2 | 0 | 22 | 11 | 8 |
| Finland | 5 | 3 | 1 | 1 | 22 | 11 | 7 |
| Germany | 5 | 2 | 0 | 3 | 11 | 12 | 4 |
| Italy | 5 | 1 | 0 | 4 | 18 | 24 | 2 |
| Poland | 5 | 0 | 0 | 5 | 4 | 30 | 0 |

| | | |
|---|---|---|
| February 9 | Sweden 7 | Poland 2 |
| February 9 | Finland 5 | Germany 1 |
| February 9 | United States 6 | Italy 3 |
| February 11 | Finland 9 | Poland 1 |
| February 11 | United States 2 | Germany 0 |
| February 11 | Sweden 7 | Italy 3 |
| February 13 | Italy 7 | Poland 1 |
| February 13 | United States 4 | Finland 1 |
| February 13 | Sweden 3 | Germany 1 |

| | | |
|---|---|---|
| February 15 | Germany 5 | Italy 2 |
| February 15 | Sweden 2 | Finland 2 |
| February 15 | United States 3 | Poland 0 |
| February 17 | Germany 4 | Poland 0 |
| February 17 | Finland 5 | Italy 3 |
| February 17 | Sweden 3 | United States 3 |

**POOL B**

| | GP | W | T | L | GF | GA | P |
|---|---|---|---|---|---|---|---|
| Canada | 5 | 4 | 0 | 1 | 28 | 9 | 8 |
| Russia* | 5 | 4 | 0 | 1 | 32 | 10 | 8 |
| Czechoslovakia | 5 | 4 | 0 | 1 | 25 | 15 | 8 |
| France | 5 | 2 | 0 | 3 | 14 | 22 | 4 |
| Switzerland | 5 | 1 | 0 | 4 | 13 | 25 | 2 |
| Norway | 5 | 0 | 0 | 5 | 7 | 38 | 0 |

*called Unified Team during Olympics; name changed after to reflect the roster

| | | |
|---|---|---|
| February 8 | Canada 3 | France 2 |
| February 8 | Czechoslovakia 10 | Norway 1 |
| February 8 | Russia 8 | Switzerland 1 |
| February 10 | Russia 8 | Norway 1 |
| February 10 | Czechoslovakia 6 | France 4 |
| February 10 | Canada 6 | Switzerland 1 |
| February 12 | Canada 10 | Norway 0 |
| February 12 | France 4 | Switzerland 3 |
| February 12 | Czechoslovakia 4 | Russia 3 |
| February 14 | Russia 8 | France 0 |
| February 14 | Switzerland 6 | Norway 3 |
| February 14 | Canada 5 | Czechoslovakia 1 |
| February 16 | France 4 | Norway 2 |
| February 16 | Czechoslovakia 4 | Switzerland 2 |
| February 16 | Russia 5 | Canada 4 |

**CONSOLATION ROUND**

| | | |
|---|---|---|
| February 18 | Norway 5 | Italy 3 |
| February 19 | Switzerland 7 | Poland 2 |

**11TH-PLACE GAME**

| | | |
|---|---|---|
| February 20 | Poland 4 | Italy 1 |

**9TH-PLACE GAME**

| | | |
|---|---|---|
| February 21 | Norway 5 | Switzerland 2 |

**PLACEMENT GAMES**

| | | |
|---|---|---|
| February 20 | Germany 5 | France 4 |
| February 20 | Sweden 3 | Finland 2 |

**7TH-PLACE GAME**

| | | |
|---|---|---|
| February 22 | Finland 4 | France 1 |

**5TH-PLACE GAME**

| | | |
|---|---|---|
| February 22 | Sweden 4 | Germany 3 |

**PLAYOFFS**
**QUARTER-FINALS**

| | | |
|---|---|---|
| February 18 | Canada 4 | Germany 3 (10:00 OT/GWS—Eric Lindros) |
| February 18 | United States 4 | France 1 |
| February 19 | Russia 6 | Finland 1 |
| February 19 | Czechoslovakia 3 | Sweden 1 |

**SEMI-FINALS**

| | | |
|---|---|---|
| February 21 | Russia 5 | United States 2 |
| February 21 | Canada 4 | Czechoslovakia 2 |

**BRONZE MEDAL GAME**

| | | |
|---|---|---|
| February 22 | Czechoslovakia 6 | United States 1 |

**GOLD MEDAL GAME**

| | | |
|---|---|---|
| February 23 | Russia 3 | Canada 1 |

**Rosters**

**Canada** (Dave King, coach) GK—Sean Burke, Trevor Kidd, Sam St. Laurent—Kevin Dahl, Curt Giles, Gord Hynes, Adrien Plavsic, Dan Ratushny, Brad Schlegel, Brian Tutt, Jason Woolley, Dave Archibald, Todd Brost, Dave Hannan, Fabian Joseph, Joe Juneau, Patrick Lebeau, Chris Lindberg, Eric Lindros, Kent Manderville, Wally Schreiber, Randy Smith, Dave Tippett

**Czechoslovakia** (Ivan Hlinka/Jaroslav Walter, coaches) GK—Petr Briza, Oldrich Svoboda, Jaromir Dragan—Patrick Augusta, Leo Gudas, Miloslav Horova, Petr Hrbek, Otakar Janecky, Tomas Jelinek, Drahomir Kadlec, Kamil Kastak, Robert Lang, Igor Liba, Ladislav Lubina, Frantisek Prochazka, Petr Rosol, Bedrich Scerban, Jiri Slegr, Richard Smehlik, Robert Svehla, Radek Toupal, Peter Veselovsky, Richard Zemlicka

**Finland** (Pentti Matikainen, coach) GK—Markus Ketterer, Jukka Tammi, Sakari Lindfors—Timo Blomqvist, Kari Eloranta, Raimo Helminen, Hannu Jarvenpaa, Timo Jutila, Janne Laukkanen, Harri Laurila, Jari Lindroos, Mikko Makela, Mika Nieminen, Timo Peltomaa, Arto Ruotanen, Timo Saarikoski, Simo Saarinen, Keijo Sailynoja, Teemu Selanne, Ville-Jussi Siren, Petri Skriko, Raimo Summanen, Pekka Tuomisto

**France** (Kjell Larsson, coach) GK—Jean-Marc Djian, Petri Ylonen, Fabrice Lhenry—Peter Almasy, Michael Babin, Stephane Barin, Stephane Botteri, Phillippe Bozon, Arnaud Briand, Yves Crettenand, Patrick Dunn, Gerald Guennelon, Benoit Laporte, Michel Leblanc, Jean-Philippe Lemoine, Pascal Margerit, Denis Perez, Serge Poudrier, Christian Pouget, Pierre Pousse, Antoine Richer, Bruno Saunier, Christophe Ville

**Germany** (Ludek Bukac, coach) GK—Helmut de Raaf, Karl Friesen, Josef Heiss—Richard Amann, Thomas Brandl, Andreas Brockmann, Peter Draisaitl, Ronald Fischer, Dieter Hegen, Michael Heidt, Uli Hiemer, Raimond Hilger, Georg Holzmann, Axel Kammerer, Udo Kiessling, Ernst Kopf, Jorg Mayr, Andreas Niederberger, Jurgen Rumrich, Michael Rumrich, Michael Schmidt, Bernd Truntschka, Gerd Truntschka

**Italy** (Gene Ubriaco, coach) GK—David Delfino, Diego Riva, Michael Zanier—Michael de Angelis, Jimmy Camazzola, Anthony Circelli, Georg Comploi, Giuseppe Foglietta, Robert Ginnetti, Emilio Iovio, Bob Manno, Giovanni Marchetti, Rick Morocco, Frank Nigro, Robert Oberrauch, Santino Pellegrino, Marco Scapinello, Martino Soracreppa, William Stewart, Lucio Topatigh, John Vecchiarelli, Ivano Zanatta, Bruno Zarrillo

**Norway** (Bengt Ohlson, coach) GK—Steve Allman, Jim Marthinsen, Robert Schistad—Morgan Andersen, Arne Billkvam, Ole-Eskild Dahlstrom, Jan Fagerli, Jarle Friis, Martin Friis, Rune Gulliksen, Carl Gunnar Gundersen, Geir Hoff, Tommy Jakobsen, Tom Johansen, Jon Karlstad, Erik Kristiansen, Orjan Lovdal, Oystein Olsen, Eirik Paulsen, Marius Rath, Petter Salsten, Kim Sogaard, Petter Thoresen

**Poland** (Leszek Lejczyk, coach) GK—Marek Batkiewicz, Mariusz Kieca, Gabriel Samolej—Janusz Adamiec, Krzysztof Bujar, Marek Cholewa, Mariusz Czerkawski, Dariusz Garbocz, Henryk Gruth, Janusz Hajnos, Kazimierz Jurek, Andrzej Kadziolka, Waldemar Klisiak, Krzysztof Kuzniecow, Dariusz Platek, Mariusz Puzio, Jerzy Sobera, Rafal Sroka, Andrzej Swistak, Robert Szopinski, Miroslaw Tomasik, Wojciech Tkacz, Slawomir Wieloch

**Russia** (Unified Team—Viktor Tikhonov, coach) GK—Andrei Trefilov, Mikhail Shtalenkov, Nikolai Khabibulin—Sergei Bautin, Igor Boldin, Nikolai Borshevski, Vyacheslav Butsayev, Vyacheslav Bykov, Yevgeni Davydov, Darius Kasparaitis, Yuri Khmylyov, Andrei Khomutov, Andrei Kovalenko, Alexei Kovalyov, Igor Kravchuk, Vladimir Malakhov, Dmitri Mironov, Sergei Petrenko, Vitali Prokhorov, Dmitri Yushkevich, Alexei Zhamnov, Alexei Zhitnik, Sergei Zubov

**Sweden** (Conny Evensson, coach) GK—Roger Nordstrom, Tommy Soderstrom, Fredrik Andersson—Peter Andersson (I), Peter Andersson (II), Charles Berglund, Patrik Carnback, Lars Edstrom, Patrik Erickson, Bengt-Ake Gustafsson, Mikael Johansson, Kenneth Kennholt, Patric Kjellberg, Petri Liimatainen, Hakan Loob, Mats Naslund, Peter Ottosson, Thomas Rundqvist, Daniel Rydmark, Borje Salming, Tommy Sjodin, Fredrik Stillman, Jan Viktorsson

**Switzerland** (Juhani Tamminen, coach) GK—Reto Pavoni, Renato Tosio, Christophe Wahl—Samuel Balmer, Sandro Bertaggia, Patrice Brasey, Mario Brodmann, Andreas Beutler, Manuele Celio, Jorg Eberle, Keith Fair, Doug Honegger, Patrick Howald, Peter Jaks, Dino Kessler, Andre Kuenzi, Sven Leuenberger, Fredy Luethi, Gil Montandon, Andre Rotheli, Mario Rottaris, Andreas Ton, Thomas Vrabec

**United States** (Dave Peterson, coach) GK—Scott Gordon, Ray LeBlanc, Mike Dunham—Greg Brown, Clark Donatelli, Ted Donato, Ted Drury, David Emma, Guy Gosselin, Bret Hedican, Steve Heinze, Sean Hill, Jim Johannson, Scott Lachance, Moe Mantha, Shawn McEachern, Marty McInnis, Joe Sacco, Tim Sweeney, Keith Tkachuk, David Tretowicz, Carl Young, Scott Young

## 17th OLYMPIC WINTER GAMES
## February 13–27, 1994
## Lillehammer, Norway

**Final Placing**

| | |
|---|---|
| Gold ........Sweden | 7th .........Germany |
| Silver ......Canada | 8th .........United States |
| Bronze ....Finland | 9th .........Italy |
| 4th ..........Russia | 10th .......France |
| 5th ..........Czech Republic | 11th .......Norway |
| 6th ..........Slovakia | 12th .......Austria |

**Tournament Format**

The format was the same as that for the 1992 Olympics: the 12 competing nations were divided into two pools of six teams each and played a round-robin tournament within each group. The top four teams from each group then advanced to a playoff elimination round.

In the case of a tie in the standings in the preliminary round, goal differential in games played only between those teams that were tied would be the deciding factor (in group B, for instance, Canada was given second place over Sweden because it had beaten the Swedes 3–2. In group A, with six points each, Germany, Czech Republic, and Russia were tied, but their ranking reflected the goal differentials (4–3 for Germany, 4–4 Czech Republic, and 6–7 for Russia). In the elimination round, a ten-minute overtime period would be followed by a shootout until a winner was decided.

**Results & Standings**

**POOL A**

| | GP | W | T | L | GF | GA | P |
|---|---|---|---|---|---|---|---|
| Finland | 5 | 5 | 0 | 0 | 25 | 4 | 10 |
| Germany | 5 | 3 | 0 | 2 | 11 | 14 | 6 |
| Czech Republic | 5 | 3 | 0 | 2 | 16 | 11 | 6 |
| Russia | 5 | 3 | 0 | 2 | 20 | 14 | 6 |
| Austria | 5 | 1 | 0 | 4 | 13 | 28 | 2 |
| Norway | 5 | 0 | 0 | 5 | 5 | 19 | 0 |

| | | |
|---|---|---|
| February 12 | Finland 3 | Czech Republic 1 |
| February 12 | Russia 5 | Norway 1 |
| February 12 | Germany 4 | Austria 3 |
| February 14 | Germany 2 | Norway 1 |
| February 14 | Czech Republic 7 | Austria 3 |
| February 14 | Finland 5 | Russia 0 |
| February 16 | Russia 9 | Austria 1 |
| February 16 | Czech Republic 1 | Germany 0 |
| February 16 | Finland 4 | Norway 0 |
| February 18 | Germany 4 | Russia 2 |
| February 18 | Finland 6 | Austria 2 |
| February 18 | Czech Republic 4 | Norway 1 |
| February 20 | Russia 4 | Czech Republic 3 |
| February 20 | Finland 7 | Germany 1 |
| February 20 | Austria 4 | Norway 2 |

**POOL B**

| | GP | W | T | L | GF | GA | P |
|---|---|---|---|---|---|---|---|
| Slovakia | 5 | 3 | 2 | 0 | 26 | 14 | 8 |
| Canada | 5 | 3 | 1 | 1 | 17 | 11 | 7 |
| Sweden | 5 | 3 | 1 | 1 | 23 | 13 | 7 |
| United States | 5 | 1 | 3 | 1 | 21 | 17 | 5 |
| Italy | 5 | 1 | 0 | 4 | 15 | 31 | 2 |
| France | 5 | 0 | 1 | 4 | 11 | 27 | 1 |

| | | |
|---|---|---|
| February 13 | Sweden 4 | Slovakia 4 |
| February 13 | Canada 7 | Italy 2 |
| February 13 | France 4 | United States 4 |
| February 15 | Sweden 4 | Italy 1 |
| February 15 | Slovakia 3 | United States 3 |
| February 15 | Canada 3 | France 1 |
| February 17 | Slovakia 10 | Italy 4 |
| February 17 | Sweden 7 | France 1 |
| February 17 | Canada 3 | United States 3 |
| February 19 | Slovakia 3 | Canada 1 |
| February 19 | Italy 7 | France 3 |
| February 19 | Sweden 6 | United States 4 |
| February 21 | Canada 3 | Sweden 2 |
| February 21 | Slovakia 6 | France 2 |
| February 21 | United States 7 | Italy 1 |

**CONSOLATION ROUND**

| | | |
|---|---|---|
| February 22 | France 5 | Austria 4 (10:00 OT/GWS—Serge Poudrier) |
| February 22 | Italy 6 | Norway 3 |

**11TH-PLACE GAME**

February 24 Norway 3 Austria 1

**9TH-PLACE GAME**

February 24 Italy 3 France 2

**PLACEMENT GAMES**

| | | |
|---|---|---|
| February 24 | Czech Republic 5 | United States 3 |
| February 24 | Slovakia 6 | Germany 5 (Oto Hascak 1:38 OT) |

**7TH-PLACE GAME**

February 26 Germany 4 United States 3

**5TH-PLACE GAME**

February 26 Czech Republic 7 Slovakia 1

**PLAYOFFS**

**QUARTER-FINALS**

| | | |
|---|---|---|
| February 23 | Canada 3 | Czech Republic 2 (Paul Kariya 5:54 OT) |
| February 23 | Finland 6 | United States 1 |
| February 23 | Sweden 3 | Germany 0 |
| February 23 | Russia 3 | Slovakia 2 (Alexander Vinogradov 8:39 OT) |

**SEMI-FINALS**

| | | |
|---|---|---|
| February 25 | Canada 5 | Finland 3 |
| February 25 | Sweden 4 | Russia 3 |

**BRONZE MEDAL GAMES**

February 26 Finland 4 Russia 0

**GOLD MEDAL GAME**

February 27 Sweden 3 Canada 2 (10:00 OT/GWS—Peter Forsberg)

**Rosters**

**Austria** (Ken Tyler, coach) GK—Michael Puschacher, Claus Dalpiaz, Brian Stankiewicz—James Burton, Marty Dallman, Rob Doyle, Michael Guntner, Karl Heinzle, Herbert Hohenberger, Dieter Kalt, Werner Kerth, Martin Krainz, Wolfgang Kromp, Gunther Lanzinger, Englebert Linder, Manfred Muhr, Richard Nasheim, Andreas Puschnik, Gerhard Puschnik, Gerald Ressman, Michael Shea, Ken Strong, Martin Ulrich

**Canada** (Tom Renney, coach) GK—Corey Hirsch, Manny Legace, Alain Roy—Mark Astley, Adrian Aucoin, David Harlock, Ken Lovsin, Derek Mayer, Brad Schlegel, Chris Therien, Brad Werenka, Greg Johnson, Petr Nedved, Greg Parks, Todd Warriner, Fabian Joseph, Paul Kariya, Jean-Yves Roy, Wally Schreiber, Todd Hlushko, Chris Kontos, Dwayne Norris, Brian Savage

**Czech Republic** (Ivan Hlinka, coach) GK—Petr Briza, Roman Turek, Jaroslav Kames—Jan Alinc, Jiri Dolezal, Pavel Geffert, Roman Horak, Miroslav Horava, Petr Hrbek, Martin Hostak, Otakar Janecky, Drahomir Kadlec, Tomas Kapusta, Kamil Kastak, Jiri Kucera, Bedrich Scerban, Tomas Srsen, Antonin Stavjana, Radek Toupal, Jrir Veber, Jan Vopat, Jiri Vykoukal, Richard Zemlicka

**Finland** (Curt Lindstrom/Hannu Aravirta, coaches) GK—Jarmo Myllys, Jukka Tammi, Pasi Kuivalainen—Mika Alatalo, Vesa Hamalainen, Raimo Helminen, Timo Jutila, Sami Kapanen, Esa Keskinen, Marko Kiprusoff, Saku Koivu, Janne Laukkanen, Tero Lehtera, Jere Lehtinen, Mikko Makela, Mika Nieminen, Janne Ojanen, Marko Palo, Ville Peltonen, Pasi Sormunen, Mika Stromberg, Petri Varis, Hannu Virta

**France** (Kjell Larsson, coach) GK—Michel Valliere, Petri Ylonen, Fabrice Lhenry—Benjamin Agnel, Stephane Arcangeloni, Stephane Barin, Stephane Botteri, Arnaud Briand, Sylvain Girard, Gerard Guennelon, Benoit Laporte, Eric Lemarque, Pierrick Maia, Christophe Moyon, Franck Pajonkowski, Denis Perez, Serge Poudrier, Pierre Pousse, Antoine Richer, Bruno Saunier, Franck Saunier, Stephane Ville, Steven Woodburn

**Germany** (Ludek Bukac/Franz Reindl, coaches) GK—Helmut de Raaf, Klaus Merk, Josef Heiss—Richard Amann, Jan Benda, Thomas Brandl, Benoit Doucet, Georg Franz, Jorg Handrick, Dieter Hegen, Uli Hiemer, Raimund Hilger, Torsten Kienass, Wolfgang Kummer, Mirko Ludemann, Jorg Mayr, Jayson Meyer, Andreas Niederberger, Michael Rumrich, Alexander Serikow, Leo Stefan, Bernhard Truntschka, Stefan Ustorf

**Italy** (Bryan Lefley, coach) GK—Bruno Campese, David Delfino, Mike Rosati—Michael de Angelis, Patrick Brugnoli, Jimmy Camazzola, Anthony Circelli, Luigi da Corte, Stefan Figliuzzi, Philip de Gaetano, Alexander Gschliesser, Leo Insam, Emilio Iovio, Maurizio Mansi, Robert Oberrauch, Gates Orlando, Martin Pavlu, Roland Ramoser, Vezio Sacratini, Bill Stewart, Lino de Toni, Lucio Topatigh, Bruno Zarrillo

**Norway** (Bengt Ohlson, coach) GK—Jim Marthinsen, Robert Schistad, Steve Allman—Cato Tom Andersen, Lars Andersen, Morgan Andersen, Vegar Barlie, Arne Billkvam, Svenn Bjornstad, Ole-Eskild Dahlstrom, Jan Roar Fagerli, Morten Finstad, Geir Hoff, Tommy Jakobsen, Roy Johansen, Tom Johansen, Espen Knutsen, Erik Kristiansen, Trond Magnussen, Svein Norstebo, Marius Rath, Petter Salsten, Petter Thoresen

**Russia** (Viktor Tikhonov, coach) GK—Sergei Abramov, Andrei Zuyev, Valeri Ivanikov—Sergei Berezin, Vyacheslav Bezukladnikov, Oleg Shargorodski, Sergei Shendelev, Oleg Davydov, Dmitri Denisov, Georgi Yevtyukhin, Ravil Gusmanov, Igor Ivanov, Valeri Karpov, Alexei Kudashov, Andrei Nikolishin, Alexander Smirnov, Sergei Sorokin, Andrei Tarasenko, Vladimir Tarasov, Sergei Tertyshny, Pavel Torgayev, Igor Varitski, Alexander Vinogradov, Igor Kravchuk

**Slovakia** (Julius Supler, coach) GK—Jaromir Dragan, Eduard Hartmann, Miroslav Michalek—Jergus Baca, Vladimir Buril, Jozef Dano, Oto Hascak, Branislav Janos, Lubomir Kolnik, Roman Kontsek, Miroslav Marcinko, Stanislav Medrik, Zigmund Palffy, Robert Petrovicky, Vlastimil Plavucha, Dusan Pohorelec, Rene Pucher, Miroslav Satan, Lubomil Sekeras, Marian Smerciak, Peter Stastny, Robert Svehla, Jan Varholik

**Sweden** (Curt Lundmark, coach) GK—Tommy Salo, Hakan Algotsson, Mikael Sundlov—Jonas Bergqvist, Charles Berglund, Andreas Dackell, Christian Due-Boje, Niklas Eriksson, Peter Forsberg, Roger Hansson, Roger Johansson, Jorgen Jonsson, Kenny Jonsson, Tomas Jonsson, Patrik Juhlin, Patric Kjellberg, Hakan Loob, Mats Naslund, Stefan Ornskog, Leif Rohlin, Daniel Rydmark, Fredrik Stillman, Magnus Svensson

**United States** (Tim Taylor, coach) GK—Garth Snow, Mike Dunham, Jonathon Hillebrandt—Mark Beaufait, Jim Campbell, Pete Ciavaglia, Ted Crowley, Ted Drury, Pete Ferraro, Brett Hauer, Darby Hendrickson, Chris Imes, Craig Johnson, Peter Laviolette, Jeff Lazaro, John Lilley, Todd Marchant, Matt Martin, Travis Richards, Barry Richter, Dave Roberts, Brian Rolston, David Sacco

## 18th OLYMPIC WINTER GAMES
## February 7–22, 1998
## Nagano, Japan

### Final Placing

| | |
|---|---|
| Gold........Czech Republic | 8th.........Kazakhstan |
| Silver......Russia | 9th.........Germany |
| Bronze....Finland | 10th.......Slovakia |
| 4th.........Canada | 11th.......France |
| 5th.........Sweden | 12th.......Italy |
| 6th.........United States | 13th.......Japan |
| 7th.........Belarus | 14th.......Austria |

### Qualification

The top six teams from A Pool after the 1995 World Championship automatically qualified for the final round of the 1998 Olympics (Finland, Sweden, Canada, Czech Republic, Russia, United States). The seventh and eighth place teams after the 1995 World Championship (France and Italy), the host nation (Japan), and the top five teams from the qualification tournaments (Germany, Austria, Slovakia, Belarus, Kazakhstan) qualified for the preliminary round of the 1998 Olympics.

### Tournament Format

To allow for NHL participation, the tournament was divided into three distinct stages. The preliminary stage featured the eight lowest ranking teams to qualify for the Olympics. These eight were divided into two groups of four teams each and played a round robin series of games within each group. The top team from each then advanced to the main draw which featured the "big six" of Canada, Russia, Czech Republic, Sweden, Finland, and United States. Again, the eight teams were put into two groups of four and played a round robin within each.

To ensure quality, this stage did not eliminate any teams. Instead, it allowed the players traveling halfway around the world from the NHL a chance to acclimatize to the time difference and play three games with new teammates. The positions of the teams then determined the quarter-finals matchups. The top team in one group played the fourth team in the other, and second place played third place in crossover games as well. This led to semi-finals and finals to determine medal winners.

### Results & Standings

#### PRELIMINARY ROUND

#### GROUP A

| | GP | W | T | L | GF | GA | P |
|---|---|---|---|---|---|---|---|
| Kazakhstan | 3 | 2 | 1 | 0 | 14 | 11 | 5 |
| Slovakia | 3 | 1 | 1 | 1 | 9 | 9 | 3 |
| Italy | 3 | 1 | 0 | 2 | 11 | 11 | 2 |
| Austria | 3 | 0 | 2 | 1 | 9 | 12 | 2 |

| | | |
|---|---|---|
| February 7 | Kazakhstan 5 | Italy 3 |
| February 7 | Austria 2 | Slovakia 2 |
| February 8 | Austria 5 | Kazakhstan 5 |
| February 8 | Slovakia 4 | Italy 3 |
| February 10 | Kazakhstan 4 | Slovakia 3 |
| February 10 | Italy 5 | Austria 2 |

#### GROUP B

| | GP | W | T | L | GF | GA | P |
|---|---|---|---|---|---|---|---|
| Belarus | 3 | 2 | 1 | 0 | 14 | 4 | 5 |
| Germany | 3 | 2 | 0 | 1 | 7 | 9 | 4 |
| France | 3 | 1 | 0 | 2 | 5 | 8 | 2 |
| Japan | 3 | 0 | 1 | 2 | 5 | 10 | 1 |

| | | |
|---|---|---|
| February 7 | Germany 3 | Japan 1 |
| February 7 | Belarus 4 | France 0 |
| February 9 | Belarus 8 | Germany 2 |
| February 9 | France 5 | Japan 2 |
| February 10 | Belarus 2 | Japan 2 |
| February 10 | Germany 2 | France 0 |

#### FINAL ROUND

#### GROUP C

| | GP | W | T | L | GF | GA | P |
|---|---|---|---|---|---|---|---|
| Russia | 3 | 3 | 0 | 0 | 15 | 6 | 6 |
| Czech Republic | 3 | 2 | 0 | 1 | 12 | 4 | 4 |
| Finland | 3 | 1 | 0 | 2 | 11 | 9 | 2 |
| Kazakhstan | 3 | 0 | 0 | 3 | 6 | 25 | 0 |

| | | |
|---|---|---|
| February 13 | Czech Republic 3 | Finland 0 |
| February 13 | Russia 9 | Kazakhstan 2 |
| February 15 | Russia 4 | Finland 3 |
| February 15 | Czech Republic 8 | Kazakhstan 2 |
| February 16 | Finland 8 | Kazakhstan 2 |
| February 16 | Russia 2 | Czech Republic 1 |

#### GROUP D

| | GP | W | T | L | GF | GA | P |
|---|---|---|---|---|---|---|---|
| Canada | 3 | 3 | 0 | 0 | 12 | 3 | 6 |
| Sweden | 3 | 2 | 0 | 1 | 11 | 7 | 4 |
| United States | 3 | 1 | 0 | 2 | 8 | 10 | 2 |
| Belarus | 3 | 0 | 0 | 3 | 4 | 15 | 0 |

| | | |
|---|---|---|
| February 13 | Sweden 4 | United States 2 |
| February 13 | Canada 5 | Belarus 0 |
| February 14 | United States 5 | Belarus 2 |
| February 14 | Canada 3 | Sweden 2 |
| February 16 | Canada 4 | United States 1 |
| February 16 | Sweden 5 | Belarus 2 |

#### PLACEMENT GAMES

#### 9TH-PLACE GAME

| | | |
|---|---|---|
| February 12 | Germany 4 | Slovakia 2 |

#### 11TH-PLACE GAME

| | | |
|---|---|---|
| February 12 | France 5 | Italy 1 |

#### 13TH-PLACE GAME

| | | |
|---|---|---|
| February 12 | Japan 4 | Austria 3 |

#### PLAYOFFS

#### QUARTER-FINALS

| | | |
|---|---|---|
| February 18 | Czech Republic 4 | United States 1 |
| February 18 | Russia 4 | Belarus 1 |
| February 18 | Canada 4 | Kazakhstan 1 |
| February 18 | Finland 2 | Sweden 1 |

#### SEMI-FINALS

| | | |
|---|---|---|
| February 20 | Czech Republic 2 | Canada 1 (10:00 OT/GWS—Robert Reichel) |
| February 20 | Russia 7 | Finland 4 |

#### BRONZE MEDAL GAME

| | | |
|---|---|---|
| February 21 | Finland 3 | Canada 2 |

#### GOLD MEDAL GAME

| | | |
|---|---|---|
| February 22 | Czech Republic 1 | Russia 0 |

### Rosters

**Austria** (Ron Kennedy, coach) GK—Claus Dalpiaz, Reinhard Divis, Michael Puschacher—Dominic Lavoie, Tommy Searle, Andreas Puschnig, Herbert Hohenberger, Martin Ulrich, Gerhard Unterluggauer, Mario Schaden, Simon Wheeldon, Christian Perthaler, Wolfgang Kromp, Dieter Kalt, Gerald Ressmann, Dick Nasheim, Gerhard Puschnik, Christoph Brandner, Patrick Pilloni, Martin Hohenberger, Engelbert Linder, Normand Krumpschmid, Michael Lampert

**Belarus** (Anatoli Varivonchik, coach) GK—Andrei Mezin, Alexander Shumidub, Leonid Grishukevich—Andrei Skabelka, Alexander Galchenyuk, Ruslan Salei, Oleg Romanov, Igor Matushkin, Vadim Bekbulatov, Oleg Khmyl, Andrei Kovalyov, Viktor Karachun, Sergei Yerkovich, Alexei Lozhkin, Alexei Kalyuzhny, Sergei Stas, Alexander Andrievski, Alexander Alexeyev, Vladimir Tsyplakov, Yevgeni Roshin, Vasili Pankov, Eduard Zankovets, Alexander Zhurik

**Canada** (Marc Crawford, coach) GK—Patrick Roy, Martin Brodeur, Curtis Joseph—Rob Blake, Ray Bourque, Eric Desjardins, Adam Foote, Al MacInnis, Chris Pronger, Scott Stevens, Rod Brind'Amour, Shayne Corson, Theo Fleury, Wayne Gretzky, Trevor Linden, Eric Lindros, Joe Nieuwendyk, Keith Primeau, Mark Recchi, Joe Sakic, Brendan Shanahan, Steve Yzerman, Rob Zamuner

**Czech Republic** (Ivan Hlinka/Slavomir Lener, coaches) GK—Dominik Hasek, Milan Hnilicka, Roman Cechmanek—Jiri Slegr, Frantisek Kucera, Jiri Dopita, Roman Hamrlik, Richard Smehlik, Jaroslav Spacek, Petr Svoboda, Martin Rucinsky, Jaromir Jagr, Martin Straka, Robert Reichel, Robert Lang, Pavel Patera, Martin Prochazka, Josef Beranek, Vladimir Ruzicka, David Moravec, Milan Hejduk, Jan Caloun, Libor Prochazka

**Finland** (Hannu Aravirta, coach) GK—Jarmo Myllys, Ari Sulander, Jukka Tammi—Janne Laukkanen, Saku Koivu, Teppo Numminen, Janne Niinimaa, Jere Lehtinen, Jyrki Lumme, Jari Kurri, Aki-Petteri Berg, Teemu Selanne, Raimo Helminen, Kimmo Timonen, Esa Tikkanen, Juha Ylonen, Ville Peltonen, Sami Kapanen, Juha Lind, Kimmo Rintanen, Mikka Nieminen, Antti Tormanen, Tuomas Gronman

**France** (Herb Brooks, coach) GK—Francois Gravel, Cristobal Huet, Fabrice Lhenry—Serge Poudrier, Philippe Bozon, Denis Perez, Jean-Philippe Lemoine, Christian Pouget, Stephane Barin, Serge Djelloul, Robert Ouellet, Jonathan Zwikel, Anthony Mortas, Arnaud Briand, Karl Dewolf, Jean-Christophe Filippin, Gregory Dubois, Richard Aimonetto, Pierre Allard, Maurice Rozenthal, Francois Rozenthal, Laurent Gras, Roger Dube

**Germany** (George Kingston, coach) GK—Josef Heiss, Olaf Kolzig, Klaus Merk—Mirko Ludemann, Peter Draisaitl, Erich Goldmann, Jan Benda, Uwe Krupp, Markus Wieland, Daniel Kunce, Mark MacKay, Brad Bergen, Reemt Pyka, Jochen Molling, Jochen Hecht, Benoit Doucet, Stefan Ustorf, Thomas Brandl, Andreas Lupzig, Dieter Hegen, Lars Bruggemann, Jurgen Rumrich, Marco Sturm

**Italy** (Adolf Insam, coach) GK—Mario Brunetta, David Delfino, Mike Rosati—Chad Biafore, Larry Rucchin, Stefan Figliuzzi, Gates Orlando, Chris Bartolone, Bob Nardella, Bruno Zarrillo, Dino Felicetti, Michael de Angelis, Roland Ramoser, Leo Insam, Lucio Topatigh, Maurizio Mansi, Guiseppe Busillo, Martin Pavlu, Mario Chitarroni, Robert Oberrauch, Patrick Brugnoli, Stefano Margoni, Markus Brunner

**Japan** (Bjorn Kinding, coach) GK—Dusty Imoo, Shinichi Iwasaki, Jiro Nihei—Takeshi Yamanaka, Shin Yahata, Kiyoshi Fujita, Takayuki Kobori, Matthew Kabayama, Hiroyuki Miura, Akihito Sugisawa, Ryan Kuwabara, Kunihiko Sakurai, Tatsuki Katayama, Toshiyuki Sakai, Tsutsumi Otomo, Yutaka Kawaguchi, Takayuki Miura, Atsuo Kudoh, Yuji Iga, Chris Yule, Steven Tsujiura, Hiroshi Matsuura, Makoto Kawahiro

**Kazakhstan** (Boris Alexandrov, coach) GK—Alexander Shimin, Vitali Yeremeyev—Andrei Sokolov, Vadim Glovatski, Vladimir Antipin, Alexander Koreshkov, Konstantin Shafranov, Igor Zemlyanoy, Dmitri Dudarev, Igor Nikitin, Igor Dorokhin, Alexei Troshinski, Andrei Savenkov, Pavel Kamentsev, Mikhail Borodulin, Vitali Tregubov, Yevgeni Koreshkov, Andrei Pchelyakov, Yerlan Sagymbayev, Vladimir Zavyalov, Oleg Kryazhev, Petr Devyatkin

**Russia** (Vladimir Yurzinov, coach) GK—Oleg Shevtsov, Mikhail Shtalenkov, Andrei Trefilov—Pavel Bure, Sergei Fyodorov, Dmitri Mironov, Alexei Yashin, Alexei Zhamnov, Darius Kasparaitis, Alexei Zhitnik, Igor Kravchuk, Valeri Zelepukin, Andrei Kovalenko, German Titov, Valeri Kamenski, Boris Mironov, Dmitri Yushkevich, Valeri Bure, Alexei Morozov, Sergei Nemchinov, Sergei Gonchar, Alexei Gusarov, Sergei Krivokrasov

**Slovakia** (Jan Sterbak, coach) GK—Igor Murin, Pavol Rybar, Miroslav Simonovic—Lubomir Sekeras, Stanislav Jasecko, Ivan Droppa, Vlastimil Plavucha, Robert Petrovicky, Jan Varholik, Jozef Dano, Lubomir Visnovsky, Roman Kontsek, Branislav Janos, Zdeno Ciger, Robert Svehla, Karol Rusznyak, Miroslav Mosnar, Roman Stantien, Jan Pardavy, Lubomir Kolnik, Peter Bondra, Oto Hascak, Peter Pucher

**Sweden** (Kent Forsberg, coach) GK—Johan Hedberg, Tommy Salo, Tommy Soderstrom—Mattias Norstrom, Nicklas Lidstrom, Niklas Sundstrom, Daniel Alfredsson, Mikael Andersson, Calle Johansson, Peter Forsberg, Mats Sundin, Mattias Ohlund, Mikael Renberg, Ulf Samuelsson, Ulf Dahlen, Patric Kjellberg, Mats Lindgren, Michael Nylander, Marcus Ragnarsson, Tommy Albelin, Tomas Sandstrom, Jorgen Jonsson, Andreas Johansson

**United States** (Ron Wilson, coach) GK—Guy Hebert, Mike Richter, John Vanbiesbrouck—Chris Chelios, Brian Leetch, Mike Modano, Bill Guerin, Gary Suter, Brett Hull, Derian Hatcher, Pat Lafontaine, Kevin Hatcher, Jeremy Roenick, John LeClair, Keith Tkachuk, Doug Weight, Mathieu Schneider, Jamie Langenbrunner, Adam Deadmarsh, Tony Amonte, Joel Otto, Keith Carney, Bryan Berard

## 19th OLYMPIC WINTER GAMES
## February 11-21, 2002
## Salt Lake City, United States

**Final Placing**

| | | | |
|---|---|---|---|
| Gold | Canada | 8th | Germany |
| Silver | United States | 9th | Latvia |
| Bronze | Russia | 10th | Ukraine |
| 4th | Belarus | 11th | Switzerland |
| 5th | Sweden | 12th | Austria |
| 6th | Finland | 13th | Slovakia |
| 7th | Czech Republic | 14th | France |

**Tournament Format**

To allow for NHL participation, the tournament was divided into three distinct stages. The preliminary stage featured the eight lowest ranking teams to qualify for the Olympics. These eight were divided into two groups of four teams each and played a round robin series of games within each group. The top team from each then advanced to the main draw which featured the "big six" of Canada, Russia, Czech Republic, Sweden, Finland, and United States. Again, the eight teams were put into two groups of four and played a round robin within each.

To ensure quality, this stage did not eliminate any teams. Instead, it allowed the players a chance to play three games with new teammates. The positions of the teams then determined the quarter-finals matchups. The top team in one group played the fourth team in the other, and second place played third place in crossover games as well. This led to semi-finals and finals to determine medal winners.

**Results & Standings**

**PRELIMINARY ROUND**

**GROUP A**

| | GP | W | T | L | GF | GA | P |
|---|---|---|---|---|---|---|---|
| Germany | 3 | 3 | 0 | 0 | 10 | 3 | 6 |
| Latvia | 3 | 1 | 1 | 1 | 11 | 12 | 3 |
| Austria | 3 | 1 | 0 | 2 | 7 | 9 | 2 |
| Slovakia | 3 | 0 | 1 | 2 | 8 | 12 | 1 |

| | | |
|---|---|---|
| February 9 | Germany 3 | Slovakia 0 |
| February 9 | Latvia 4 | Austria 2 |
| February 10 | Germany 3 | Austria 2 |
| February 10 | Latvia 6 | Slovakia 6 |
| February 12 | Austria 3 | Slovakia 2 |
| February 12 | Germany 4 | Latvia 1 |

**GROUP B**

| | GP | W | T | L | GF | GA | P |
|---|---|---|---|---|---|---|---|
| Belarus | 3 | 2 | 1 | 0 | 5 | 3 | 4 |
| Ukraine | 3 | 2 | 0 | 1 | 9 | 5 | 4 |
| Switzerland | 3 | 1 | 1 | 1 | 7 | 9 | 3 |
| France | 3 | 0 | 1 | 2 | 6 | 10 | 1 |

| | | |
|---|---|---|
| February 9 | Belarus 1 | Ukraine 0 |
| February 9 | France 3 | Switzerland 3 |
| February 11 | Ukraine 5 | Switzerland 2 |
| February 11 | Belarus 3 | France 1 |
| February 13 | Switzerland 2 | Belarus 1 |
| February 13 | Ukraine 4 | France 2 |

**FINAL ROUND**

**GROUP C**

| | GP | W | T | L | GF | GA | P |
|---|---|---|---|---|---|---|---|
| Sweden | 3 | 3 | 0 | 0 | 14 | 4 | 6 |
| Czech Republic | 3 | 1 | 1 | 1 | 12 | 7 | 3 |
| Canada | 3 | 1 | 1 | 1 | 8 | 10 | 3 |
| Germany | 3 | 0 | 0 | 3 | 5 | 18 | 0 |

| | | |
|---|---|---|
| February 15 | Sweden 5 | Canada 2 |
| February 15 | Czech Republic 8 | Germany 2 |
| February 17 | Sweden 2 | Czech Republic 1 |
| February 17 | Canada 3 | Germany 2 |
| February 18 | Canada 3 | Czech Republic 3 |
| February 18 | Sweden 7 | Germany 1 |

**GROUP D**

| | GP | W | T | L | GF | GA | P |
|---|---|---|---|---|---|---|---|
| United States | 3 | 2 | 1 | 0 | 16 | 3 | 5 |
| Finland | 3 | 2 | 0 | 1 | 11 | 8 | 4 |
| Russia | 3 | 1 | 1 | 1 | 9 | 9 | 3 |
| Belarus | 3 | 0 | 0 | 3 | 6 | 22 | 0 |

| | | |
|---|---|---|
| February 15 | Russia 6 | Belarus 4 |
| February 15 | United States 6 | Finland 0 |
| February 16 | Finland 8 | Belarus 1 |
| February 16 | Russia 2 | United States 2 |
| February 18 | United States 8 | Belarus 1 |
| February 18 | Finland 3 | Russia 1 |

**13TH-PLACE GAME**

February 14 Slovakia 7 France 1

**11TH-PLACE GAME**

February 14 Switzerland 4 Austria 1

**9TH-PLACE GAME**

February 14 Latvia 9 Ukraine 2

**PLAYOFFS**

**QUARTER-FINALS**

| | | |
|---|---|---|
| February 20 | Belarus 4 | Sweden 3 |
| February 20 | Russia 1 | Czech Republic 0 |
| February 20 | United States 5 | Germany 0 |
| February 20 | Canada 2 | Finland 1 |

**SEMI-FINALS**

| | | |
|---|---|---|
| February 22 | Canada 7 | Belarus 1 |
| February 22 | United States 3 | Russia 2 |

**BRONZE MEDAL GAME**

February 23 Russia 7 Belarus 2

**GOLD MEDAL GAME**

February 24 Canada 5 United States 2

**Rosters**

**Austria** (Ron Kennedy, coach) GK—Claus Dalpiaz, Reinhard Divis, Michael Suttnig—Gerhard Unterluggauer, Joseph Lavoie, Tommy Searle, Christoph Brandner, Gerald Ressmann, Matthias Trattnig, Robert Lukas, Oliver Setzinger, Thomas Pock, Kent Salfi, Mario Schaden, Martin Hohenberger, Gunther Lanzinger, Simon Wheeldon, Wolfgang Kromp, Christian Perthaler, Andre Lakos, Martin Ulrich, Dieter Kalt, Peter Kasper

**Belarus** (Vladimir Krikunov, coach) GK—Leonid Fatikov, Andrei Mezin, Sergei Shabanov—Oleg Khmyl, Alexander Makritski, Oleg Romanov, Igor Matushkin, Alexander Andrievski, Vadim Bekbulatov, Andrei Kovalyov, Vasili Pankov, Andrei Skabelka, Alexei Kalyuzhny, Oleg Antonenko, Eduard Zankovets, Oleg Mikulchik, Ruslan Salei, Dmitri Dudik, Sergei Stas, Alexander Zhurik, Konstantin Koltsov, Vladimir Tsyplakov, Vladimir Kopat, Dmitri Pankov, Andrei Rasolko

**Canada** (Pat Quinn, coach) GK—Curtis Joseph, Martin Brodeur, Ed Belfour—Rob Blake, Eric Brewer, Adam Foote, Ed Jovanovski, Al MacInnis, Scott Niedermayer, Chris Pronger, Theo Fleury, Simon Gagne, Jarome Iginla, Paul Kariya, Mario Lemieux, Eric Lindros, Joe Nieuwendyk, Owen Nolan, Michael Peca, Joe Sakic, Brendan Shanahan, Ryan Smyth, Steve Yzerman

**Czech Republic** (Josef Augusta, coach) GK—Roman Cechmanek, Dominik Hasek, Milan Hnilicka—Roman Hamrlik, Jaroslav Spacek, Martin Havlat, Pavel Patera, Pavel Kubina, Tomas Kaberle, Petr Cajanek, Petr Sykora, Radek Dvorak, Robert Lang, Robert Reichel, Milan Hejduk, Patrik Elias, Martin Ruchinsky, Michal Sykora, Jiri Dopita, Jan Hrdina, Martin Skoula, Richard Smehlik, Jaromir Jagr

**Finland** (Hannu Aravirta, coach) GK—Jani Hurme, Jussi Markkanen, Pasi Nurminen—Kimmo Timonen, Sami Salo, Ossi Vaananen, Aki-Petteri Berg, Teemu Selanne, Ville Nieminen, Olli Jokinen, Raimo Helminen, Niklas Hagman, Tomi Kallio, Jyrki Lumme, Mikko Eloranta, Sami Kapanen, Jere Lehtinen, Teppo Numminen, Juha Ylonen, Jarkko Ruutu, Antti Aalto, Juha Lind, Janne Niinimaa

**France** (Heikki Leime, coach) GK—Cristobal Huet, Fabrice Lhenry, Patrick Rolland—Allan Carriou, Vincent Bachet, Benoit Bachelet, Stephane Barin, Arnaud Briand, Maurice Rozenthal, Laurent Meunier, Francois Rozenthal, Philippe Bozon, Karl Dewolf, Yorick Treille, Guillaume Besse, Jean-Francois Bonnard, Jonathan Zwikel, Anthony Mortas, Denis Perez, Richard Aimonetto, Benoit Pourtanel, Baptiste Amar, Laurent Gras

**Germany** (Hans Zach, coach) GK—Christian Kunast, Robert Muller, Marc Seliger—Jorg Mayr, Christian Ehrhoff, Mirko Ludemann, Christoph Schubert, Wayne Hynes, Jochen Hecht, Andreas Loth, Marco Sturm, Jurgen Rumrich, Stefan Ustorf, Martin Reichel, Daniel Kreutzer, Tobias Abstreiter, Andreas Renz, Erich Goldmann, Daniel Kunce, Leonard Soccio, Klaus Kathan, Andreas Morczinietz, Mark MacKay, Jan Benda, Dennis Seidenberg

**Latvia** (Curt Lindstrom, coach) GK—Arturs Irbe, Edgars Masalskis, Sergejs Naumovs—Rodrigo Lavins, Viktors Ignatjevs, Igors Bondarevs, Karlis Skrastins, Vyacheslavs Fanduls, Aleksandrs Belavskis, Sergejs Senins, Aleksandrs Macijevskis, Grigorijs Pantelejevs, Leonids Tambijevs, Kaspars Astasenko, Aleksanrds Nizivijs, Sandis Ozolinsh, Harijs Vitolins, Aleksandrs Kercs, Olegs Sorokins, Atvars Tribuncovs, Aleksanrds Semjonovs, Andrejs Maticins, Aigars Cipruss

**Russia** (Vyacheslav Fetisov, coach) GK—Ilya Bryzgalov, Nikolai Khabibulin, Yegor Podomatski—Boris Mironov, Daniil Markov, Oleg Tverdovski, Igor Larionov, Pavel Bure, Darius Kasparaitis, Oleg Kvasha, Alexei Zhamnov, Sergei Samsonov, Valeri Bure, Vladimir Malakhov, Pavel Datsyuk, Alexei Kovalyov, Igor Kravchuk, Andrei Nikolishin, Sergei Gonchar, Maxim Afinogenov, Ilya Kovalchuk, Alexei Yashin, Sergei Fyodorov

**Slovakia** (Jan Flic, coach) GK—Jan Lasak, Pavol Rybar, Rastislav Stana—Peter Smrek, Jaroslav Obsut, Dusan Milo, Jozef Stumpel, Lubomir Visnovsky, Mrioslav Satan, Rastislav Pavlikovsky, Ivan Majesky, Lubos Bartecko, Jan Pardavy, Michal Handzus, Richard Kapus, Zigmund Palffy, Pavol Demitra, Robert Petrovicky, Richard Lintner, Richard Sechny, Richard Pavlikovsky, Jaroslav Torok, Marian Hossa

**Sweden** (Hardy Nilsson, coach) GK—Johan Hedberg, Tommy Salo, Mikael Tellqvist—Mattias Ohlund, Kim Johnsson, Fredrik Olausson, Nicklas Lidstrom, Marcus Ragnarsson, Daniel Alfredsson, Per-Johan Axelsson, Mats Sundin, Mattias Norstrom, Mathias Johansson, Mikael Renberg, Magnus Arvedson, Ulf Dahlen, Niklas Sundstrom, Kenny Jonsson, Henrik Zetterberg, Jorgen Jonsson, Markus Naslund, Michael Nylander, Tomas Holmstrom

**Switzerland** (Ralph Krueger, coach) GK—David Aebischer, Martin Gerber, Lars Weibel—Julien Vauclair, Flavien Conne, Patrick Sutter, Mark Streit, Martin Hohener, Martin Steinegger, Patric della Rossa, Reto von Arx, Gian-Marco Crameri, Andre Rotheli, Jean-Jacques Aeschlimann, Patrick Fischer, Olivier Keller, Edgar Salis, Martin Pluss, Marcel Jenni, Mathias Seger, Ivo Ruthemann, Sandy Jeannin, Bjorn Christen

**Ukraine** (Anatoliy Bogdanov, coach) GK—Olexander Fedorov, Igor Karpenko, Kostyantyn Simchuk—Yuriy Gunko, Sergiy Klimentyev, Andri Sryubko, Vasyl Bobrovnikov, Dmitri Khristich, Vadym Slivchenko, Vadim Shakraychuk, Ruslan Fedotenko, Dmitri Tolkunov, Valeri Shiryayev, Vitaliy Lytvynenko, Igor Chibirev, Sergi Varlamov, Valentyn Oletsky, Roman Salnikov, Vladyslav Serov, Bogdan Savenko, Olexi Ponikarovski, Vyacheslav Timchenko, Vyacheslav Zavalnyuk

**United States** (Herb Brooks, coach) GK—Tom Barrasso, Mike Dunham, Mike Richter—Brian Leetch, Brian Rafalski, Tom Poti, Phil Housley, Keith Tkachuk, Mike Modano, John LeClair, Tony Amonte, Brian Rolston, Bill Guerin, Brett Hull, Chris Drury, Gary Suter, Chris Chelios, Adam Deadmarsh, Aaron Miller, Doug Weight, Scott Young, Mike York, Jeremy Roenick

## 20th OLYMPIC WINTER GAMES
## February 15-26, 2006
## Turin, Italy

**Final Placing**

| | | | |
|---|---|---|---|
| Gold | Sweden | 7th | Canada |
| Silver | Finland | 8th | United States |
| Bronze | Czech Republic | 9th | Kazakhstan |
| 4th | Russia | 10th | Germany |
| 5th | Slovakia | 11th | Italy |
| 6th | Switzerland | 12th | Latvia |

**Qualification**
The top nine teams after the 2008 World Championship automatically qualified for Vancouver in 2010. The remaining three teams (Germany, Latvia, Norway) won their groups in final qualification games.

**Tournament Format**
For the third year of NHL participation the format changed slightly. Gone was the first round of games and instead all 12 nations started playing at the same time. Two groups of six teams played a round robin within each group, the top four from each advancing to a quarter-finals playoffs of crossover elimination games.

**Results & Standings**
**GROUP A**

| | GP | W | T | L | GF | GA | P |
|---|---|---|---|---|---|---|---|
| Finland | 5 | 5 | 0 | 0 | 19 | 2 | 10 |
| Switzerland | 5 | 2 | 2 | 1 | 10 | 12 | 6 |
| Canada | 5 | 3 | 0 | 2 | 15 | 9 | 6 |
| Czech Republic | 5 | 2 | 0 | 3 | 14 | 12 | 4 |
| Germany | 5 | 0 | 2 | 3 | 7 | 16 | 2 |
| Italy | 5 | 0 | 2 | 3 | 9 | 23 | 2 |

| | | |
|---|---|---|
| February 15 | Canada 7 | Italy 2 |
| February 15 | Finland 5 | Switzerland 0 |
| February 15 | Czech Republic 4 | Germany 1 |
| February 16 | Finland 6 | Italy 0 |
| February 16 | Switzerland 3 | Czech Republic 2 |
| February 16 | Canada 5 | Germany 1 |
| February 18 | Italy 3 | Germany 3 |
| February 18 | Switzerland 2 | Canada 0 |
| February 18 | Finland 4 | Czech Republic 2 |
| February 19 | Germany 2 | Switzerland 2 |
| February 19 | Czech Republic 4 | Italy 1 |
| February 19 | Finland 2 | Canada 0 |
| February 21 | Italy 3 | Switzerland 3 |
| February 21 | Finland 2 | Germany 0 |
| February 21 | Canada 3 | Czech Republic 2 |

**GROUP B**

| | GP | W | T | L | GF | GA | P |
|---|---|---|---|---|---|---|---|
| Slovakia | 5 | 5 | 0 | 0 | 18 | 8 | 10 |
| Russia | 5 | 4 | 0 | 1 | 23 | 11 | 8 |
| Sweden | 5 | 3 | 0 | 2 | 15 | 12 | 6 |
| United States | 5 | 1 | 1 | 3 | 13 | 13 | 3 |
| Kazakhstan | 5 | 1 | 0 | 4 | 9 | 16 | 2 |
| Latvia | 5 | 0 | 1 | 4 | 11 | 29 | 1 |

| | | |
|---|---|---|
| February 15 | Sweden 7 | Kazakhstan 2 |
| February 15 | Slovakia 5 | Russia 3 |
| February 15 | Latvia 3 | United States 3 |
| February 16 | Russia 5 | Sweden 0 |
| February 16 | Slovakia 6 | Latvia 3 |
| February 16 | United States 4 | Kazakhstan 1 |
| February 18 | Russia 1 | Kazakhstan 0 |
| February 18 | Sweden 6 | Latvia 1 |
| February 18 | Slovakia 2 | United States 1 |
| February 19 | Russia 9 | Latvia 2 |
| February 19 | Slovakia 2 | Kazakhstan 1 |
| February 19 | Sweden 2 | United States 1 |
| February 21 | Kazakhstan 5 | Latvia 2 |
| February 21 | Slovakia 3 | Sweden 0 |
| February 21 | Russia 5 | United States 4 |

**PLAYOFFS**
**QUARTER-FINALS**

| | | |
|---|---|---|
| February 22 | Sweden 6 | Switzerland 2 |
| February 22 | Finland 4 | United States 3 |
| February 22 | Russia 2 | Canada 0 |
| February 22 | Czech Republic 3 | Slovakia 1 |

**SEMI-FINALS**

| | | |
|---|---|---|
| February 24 | Sweden 7 | Czech Republic 3 |
| February 24 | Finland 4 | Russia 0 |

**BRONZE MEDAL GAME**

| | | |
|---|---|---|
| February 25 | Czech Republic 3 | Russia 0 |

**GOLD MEDAL GAME**

| | | |
|---|---|---|
| February 26 | Sweden 3 | Finland 2 |

**Rosters**
**Canada** (Pat Quinn, coach) GK—Martin Brodeur, Roberto Luongo, Marty Turco—Rob Blake, Jay Bouwmeester, Adam Foote, Bryan McCabe, Chris Pronger, Wade Redden, Robyn Regehr, Todd Bertuzzi, Shane Doan, Kris Draper, Simon Gagne, Dany Heatley, Jarome Iginla, Vincent Lecavalier, Rick Nash, Brad Richards, Joe Sakic, Ryan Smyth, Martin St. Louis, Joe Thornton

**Czech Republic** (Alois Hadamczik, coach) GK—Dominik Hasek, Milan Hnilicka, Dusan Salficky, Tomas Vokoun—Marek Zidlicky, Jaroslav Spacek, Marek Malik, David Vyborny, Frantisek Kaberle, Pavel Kubina, Tomas Kaberle, Petr Cajanek, Filip Kuba, Robert Lang, Ales Kotalik, Milan Hejduk, Martin Rucinsky, Martin Straka, Jan Bulis, Vaclav Prospal, Patrik Elias, Jaromir Jagr, Ales Hemsky, Rostislav Olesz, Martin Erat

**Finland** (Erkka Westerlund, coach) GK— Fredrik Norrena, Antero Niittymaki, Niklas Backstrom—Petteri Nummelin, Kimmo Timonen, Lasse Kukkonen, Sami Salo, Aki-Petteri Berg, Teemu Selanne, Ville Nieminen, Saku Koivu, Olli Jokinen, Niklas Hagman, Ville Peltonen, Mikko Koivu, Antti Laaksonen, Jukka Hentunen, Jere Lehtinen, Teppo Numminen, Toni Lydman, Jussi Jokinen, Jarkko Ruutu, Niko Kapanen, Antti-Jussi Niemi

**Germany** (Uwe Krupp, coach) GK— Olaf Kolzig, Robert Muller, Thomas Greiss—Robert Leask, Sascha Goc, Christian Ehrhof, Sven Felski, Christoph Schubert, Stefan Schauer, Stefan Ustorf, Daniel Kreutzer, Alexander Barta, Andreas Renz, Tomas Martinec, Eduard Lewandowski, Florian Busch, Klaus Kathan, Alexander Sulzer, Sebastian Furchner, Marcel Goc, Lasse Kopitz, Petr Fical, Tino Boos, Dennis Seidenberg

**Italy** (Michel Goulet, coach) GK— Jason Muzatti, Gunther Hell, Rene Baur—Stefan Zisser, Carter Trevisani, Michele Strazzabosco, Bob Nardella, Florian Ramoser, Giorgio de Bettin, Giulio Scandella, Andre Signoretti, Carlo Lorenzi, John Parco, Tony Iob, Nicola Fontanive, Joe Busillo, Stefano Margoni, Mario Chitarroni, Armin Helfer, Lucio Topatigh, Manuel de Toni, Tony Tuzzolino, Jason Cirone, Christian Borgatello, Luca Ansoldi

**Kazakhstan** (Nikolai Myshagin, coach) GK— Vitali Yeremeyev, Vitali Kolesnik, Kirill Zinoviev—Alexei Vasilchenko, Vladimir Antipin, Oleg Kovalenko, Yevgeni Blokhin, Alexander Koreshkov, Konstantin Shafranov, Yevgeni Koreshkov, Dmitri Dudarev, Andrei Ogorodnikov, Andrei Pchelyakov, Andrei Samokhvalov, Andrei Savenkov, Denis Shemelin, Sergei Alexandrov, Dmitri Upper, Yevgeni Pupkov, Alexei Koledayev, Andrei Troshinski, Artyom Argokov, Fyodor Polischuk, Nikolai Antropov

**Latvia** (Leonid Beresnevs, coach) GK— Arturs Irbe, Edgars Masalskis, Sergejs Naumovs—Rodrigo Lavins, Arvids Rekis, Agris Saviels, Karlis Skrastins, Sandis Ozolins, Girts Ankipans, Vladimirs Mamonvs, Herberts Vasiljevs, Grigorijs Pantelejevs, Leonids Tambijevs, Maris Ziedins, Aleksandrs Nizivijs, Georgijs Pujacs, Armands Berzins, Atvars Tribuncovs, Mikelis Redlihs, Krisjanis Redlihs, Aleksandrs Semjonovs, Aigars Cipruss, Martins Cipulis

**Russia** (Vladimir Krikunov, coach) GK— Ilya Bryzgalov, Yevgeni Nabokov, Maxim Sokolov—Sergei Zhukov, Vitali Vishnevski, Anton Volchenkov, Alexander Ovechkin, Darius Kasparaitis, Pavel Datsyuk, Yevgeni Malkin, Alexander Kharitonov, Andrei Taratukhin, Ivan Nepryayev, Alexander Frolov, Viktor Kozlov, Alexei Kovalyov, Danil Markov, Maxim Sushinski, Fyodor Tyutin, Andrei Markov, Sergei Gonchar, Maxim Afinogenov, Ilya Kovalchuk, Alexei Yashin, Alexander Korolyuk

**Slovakia** (Frantisek Hossa, coach) GK— Peter Budaj, Jan Lasak, Karol Krizan—Zdeno Chara, Radoslav Suchy, Martin Strbak, Marian Gaborik, Peter Bondra, Andrej Meszaros, Jozef Stumpel, Lubomir Visnovsky, Miroslav Satan, Richard Zednik, Richard Kapus, Lubos Bartecko, Ronald Petrovicky, Ivan Majesky, Pavol Demitra, Marek Svatos, Tomas Surovy, Milan Jurcina, Marian Hossa, Marcel Hossa

**Sweden** (Bengt-Ake Gustafsson, coach) GK— Stefan Liv, Henrik Lundqvist, Mikael Tellqvist—Mattias Ohlund, Nicklas Lidstrom, Niklas Kronwall, Christian Backman, Daniel Alfredsson, Daniel Sedin, Mats Sundin, Niclas Havelid, Henrik Sedin, Peter Forsberg, Per-Johan Axelsson, Ronnie Sundin, Samuel Pahlsson, Kenny Jonsson, Fredrik Modin, Daniel Tjarnqvist, Mikael Samuelsson, Henrik Zetterberg, Mika Hannula, Jorgen Jonsson, Tomas Holmstrom

**Switzerland** (Ralph Krueger, coach) GK— David Aebischer, Martin Gerber, Marco Buhrer—Julien Vauclair, Flavien Conne, Severin Blindenbacher, Mark Streit, Andres Ambuhl, Patric Della Rossa, Paul di Pietro, Patrick Fischer, Olivier Keller, Thierry Paterlini, Martin Pluss, Beat Forster, Marcel Jenni, Mathias Seger, Ivo Ruthemann, Steve Hirschi, Sandy Jeannin, Thomas Ziegler, Goran Bezina, Romano Lemm, Adrian Wichser

**United States** (Peter Laviolette, coach) GK— Rick DiPietro, Robert Esche, John Grahame—Derian Hatcher, Jordan Leopold, Bret Hedican, Keith Tkachuk, Mike Modano, Scott Gomez, Brian Rolston, Bill Guerin, Brian Gionta, Chris Drury, Mike Knuble, Craig Conroy, Mathieu Schneider, Chris Chelios, Erik Cole, John-Michael Liles, Brian Rafalski, Mark Parrish, Doug Weight, Jason Blake

## 21st OLYMPIC WINTER GAMES
## February 12-28, 2010
## Vancouver, Canada

### Final Placing

| | |
|---|---|
| Gold........Canada | 7th .........Czech Republic |
| Silver ......United States | 8th .........Switzerland |
| Bronze ....Finland | 9th .........Belarus |
| 4th..........Slovakia | 10th .......Norway |
| 5th..........Sweden | 11th .......Germany |
| 6th..........Russia | 12th .......Latvia |

### Tournament Format

All 12 teams were placed in three groups of four teams each and played a round robin series of games within each group. The teams were then placed in one standings, the top four teams receiving byes to the quarter-finals. Teams 5 through 12 played a qualification round, the winners also advancing to the quarter-finals, the losers being eliminated. The team ranked 5 played the team ranked 12, the team ranked 6 played the team ranked 11, and so on. Once the quarter-finals were set, the rest of the tournament was an elimination series of games until the semi-finals. Those winners played for the gold medal, and the losers played for bronze.

### Results & Standings

**GROUP A**

| | GP | W | OTW | OTL | L | GF | GA | P |
|---|---|---|---|---|---|---|---|---|
| United States | 3 | 3 | 0 | 0 | 0 | 14 | 5 | 9 |
| Canada | 3 | 1 | 1 | 0 | 1 | 14 | 7 | 5 |
| Switzerland | 3 | 0 | 1 | 1 | 1 | 8 | 10 | 3 |
| Norway | 3 | 0 | 0 | 1 | 2 | 5 | 19 | 1 |

| | | |
|---|---|---|
| February 16 | United States 3 | Switzerland 1 |
| February 16 | Canada 8 | Norway 0 |
| February 18 | United States 6 | Norway 1 |
| February 18 | Canada 3 | Switzerland 2 (5:00 OT/GWS—Sidney Crosby) |
| February 20 | Switzerland 5 | Norway 4 (Romano Lemm 2:28 OT) |
| February 21 | United States 5 | Canada 3 |

**GROUP B**

| | GP | W | OTW | OTL | L | GF | GA | P |
|---|---|---|---|---|---|---|---|---|
| Russia | 3 | 2 | 0 | 1 | 0 | 13 | 6 | 7 |
| Czech Republic | 3 | 2 | 0 | 0 | 1 | 10 | 7 | 6 |
| Slovakia | 3 | 1 | 1 | 0 | 1 | 9 | 4 | 5 |
| Latvia | 3 | 0 | 0 | 0 | 3 | 4 | 19 | 0 |

| | | |
|---|---|---|
| February 16 | Russia 8 | Latvia 2 |
| February 17 | Czech Republic 3 | Slovakia 1 |
| February 18 | Slovakia 2 | Russia 1 (5:00 OT/GWS—Pavol Demitra) |
| February 19 | Czech Republic 5 | Latvia 2 |
| February 20 | Slovakia 6 | Latvia 0 |
| February 21 | Russia 4 | Czech Republic 2 |

**GROUP C**

| | GP | W | OTW | OTL | L | GF | GA | P |
|---|---|---|---|---|---|---|---|---|
| Sweden | 3 | 3 | 0 | 0 | 0 | 9 | 2 | 9 |
| Finland | 3 | 2 | 0 | 0 | 1 | 10 | 4 | 6 |
| Belarus | 3 | 1 | 0 | 0 | 2 | 8 | 12 | 3 |
| Germany | 3 | 0 | 0 | 0 | 3 | 3 | 12 | 0 |

| | | |
|---|---|---|
| February 17 | Finland 5 | Belarus 1 |
| February 17 | Sweden 2 | Germany 0 |
| February 19 | Sweden 4 | Belarus 2 |
| February 19 | Finland 5 | Germany 0 |
| February 20 | Belarus 5 | Germany 3 |
| February 21 | Sweden 3 | Finland 0 |

**PLAYOFFS**

**QUALIFICATION**

| | | |
|---|---|---|
| February 23 | Switzerland 3 | Belarus 2 (10:00 OT/GWS—Romano Lemm) |
| February 23 | Canada 8 | Germany 2 |
| February 23 | Czech Republic 3 | Latvia 2 (David Krejci 5:10 OT) |
| February 23 | Slovakia 4 | Norway 3 |

**QUARTER-FINALS**

| | | |
|---|---|---|
| February 24 | United States 2 | Switzerland 0 |
| February 24 | Canada 7 | Russia 3 |
| February 24 | Finland 2 | Czech Republic 0 |
| February 24 | Slovakia 4 | Sweden 3 |

**SEMI-FINALS**

| | | |
|---|---|---|
| February 26 | United States 6 | Finland 1 |
| February 26 | Canada 3 | Slovakia 2 |

**BRONZE MEDAL GAME**

| | | |
|---|---|---|
| February 27 | Finland 5 | Slovakia 3 |

**GOLD MEDAL GAME**

| | | |
|---|---|---|
| February 28 | Canada 3 | United States 2 (Sidney Crosby 7:40 OT) |

### Rosters

**Belarus** (Mikhail Zakharov, coach) GK— Vitali Koval, Andrei Mezin, Maxim Maliutin—Sergei Kostitsyn, Alexei Kalyuzhny, Nikolai Stasenko, Dmitri Meleshko, Alexei Ugarov, Konstantin Koltsov, Konstantin Zakharov, Ruslan Salei, Sergei Demagin, Viktor Kostyuchenok, Alexander Ryadinski, Alexander Kulakov, Alexander Makritski, Andrei Karev, Andrei Mikhalyov, Andrei Stas, Oleg Antonenko, Vladimir Denisov, Sergei Kolosov, Sergei Zadelenov

**Canada** (Mike Babcock, coach) GK— Martin Brodeur, Roberto Luongo, Marc-Andre Fleury—Jonathan Toews, Jarome Iginla, Sidney Crosby, Dany Heatley, Ryan Getzlaf, Shea Weber, Eric Staal, Dan Boyle, Duncan Keith, Corey Perry, Rick Nash, Mike Richards, Patrick Marleau, Chris Pronger, Brenden Morrow, Scott Niedermayer, Joe Thornton, Drew Doughty, Patrice Bergeron, Brent Seabrook

**Czech Republic** (Vladimir Ruzicka, coach) GK— Tomas Vokoun, Ondrej Pavelec, Jakub Stepanek—Marek Zidlicky, Patrik Elias, Jaromir Jagr, David Krejci, Tomas Plekanec, Tomas Fleischmann, Tomas Kaberle, Milan Michalek, Miroslav Blatak, Roman Cervenka, Martin Havlat, Tomas Rolinek, Martin Erat, Filip Kuba, Petr Cajanek, Jan Hejda, Roman Polak, Zbynek Michalek, Pavel Kubina, Josef Vasicek

**Finland** (Jukka Jalonen, coach) GK— Niklas Backstrom, Miikka Kiprusoff, Antero Niittymaki—Niklas Hagman, Olli Jokinen, Kimmo Timonen, Mikko Koivu, Valtteri Filppula, Jarkko Ruutu, Joni Pitkanen, Sami Salo, Saku Koivu, Janne Niskala, Niko Kapanen, Teemu Selanne, Tuomu Ruutu, Antti Miettinen, Sami Lepisto, Lasse Kukkonen, Ville Peltonen, Toni Lydman, Jarkko Immonen, Jere Lehtinen

**Germany** (Uwe Krupp, coach) GK— Thomas Greiss, Dimitri Patzold, Dennis Endras—Marcel Goc, Marcel Muller, Dennis Seidenberg, John Tripp, Manuel Klinge, Jochen Hecht, Kai Hospelt, Chris Schmidt, Andre Rankel, Marco Sturm, Christian Ehrhoff, Jakub Ficenec, Alexander Sulzer, Sven Butenschon, Sven Felski, Thomas Greilinger, Korbinian Holzer, Travis Mulock, Michael Wolf, Michael Bakos

**Latvia** (Olegs Znaroks, coach) GK— Edgars Masalskis, Ervins Mustukovs, Sergejs Naumovs—Girts Ankipans, Herberts Vasiljevs, Martins Cipulis, Martins Karsums, Aleksandrs Nizivijs, Mikelis Redlihs, Lauris Darzins, Kristaps Sotnieks, Armands Berzins, Georgijs Pujacs, Krisjanis Redlihs, Janis Sprukts, Arvids Rekis, Oskars Bartulis, Kaspars Daugavins, Gints Meija, Aleksejs Sirokovs, Guntis Galvins, Rodrigo Lavins, Karlis Skrastins

**Norway** (Roy Johansen, coach) GK— Pal Grotnes, Andre Lysenstoen, Ruben Smith—Patrick Thoresen, Tore Vikingstad, Mathis Olimb, Anders Bastiansen, Mads Hansen, Marius Holtet, Tommy Jakobsen, Jonas Holos, Ole Kristian Tollefsen, Alexander Bonsaksen, Lars Erik Spets, Mats Trygg, Jonas Andersen, Kristian Forsberg, Juha Kaunismaki, Martin Laumann Ylven, Lars Erik Lund, Martin Roymark, Per-Age Skroder

**Russia** (Vyacheslav Bykov, coach) GK— Yevgeni Nabokov, Ilya Bryzgalov, Semyon Varlamov—Yevgeni Malkin, Alexander Ovechkin, Sergei Fyodorov, Pavel Datsyuk, Ilya Kovalchuk, Danis Zaripov, Alexei Morozov, Alexander Radulov, Maxim Afinogenov, Dmitri Kalinin, Alexander Syomin, Fyodor Tyutin, Andrei Markov, Sergei Zinoviev, Sergei Gonchar, Viktor Kozlov, Denis Grebeshkov, Ilya Nikulin, Anton Volchenkov, Konstantin Korneyev

**Slovakia** (Jan Filc, coach) GK— Jaroslav Halak, Peter Budaj (did not play), Rastislav Stana—Pavol Demitra, Marian Hossa, Michal Handzus, Richard Zednik, Marian Gaborik, Jozef Stumpel, Lubomir Visnovsky, Zigmund Palffy, Zdeno Chara, Miroslav Satan, Tomas Kopecky, Ivan Baranka, Andrej Sekera, Martin Strbak, Lubos Bartecko, Marcel Hossa, Martin Cibak, Branko Radivojevic, Andrej Meszaros, Milan Jurcina

**Sweden** (Bengt-Ake Gustafsson, coach) GK— Henrik Lundqvist, Jonas Gustavsson, Stefan Liv—Nicklas Backstrom, Loui Eriksson, Daniel Alfredsson, Daniel Sedin, Johan Franzen, Tobias Enstrom, Magnus Johansson, Henrik Sedin, Mattias Weinhandl, Patric Hornqvist, Mattias Ohlund, Henrik Zetterberg, Peter Forsberg, Samuel Pahlsson, Fredrik Modin, Johnny Oduya, Henrik Tallinder, Niklas Kronwall, Nicklas Lidstrom, Douglas Murray

**Switzerland** (Ralph Krueger, coach) GK— Jonas Hiller, Tobias Stephan, Ronnie Rueger—Roman Wick, Hnat Domenichelli, Martin Pluss, Mark Streit, Romano Lemm, Julien Sprunger, Raffaele Sannitz, Severin Blindenbacher, Mathias Seger, Ivo Ruthemann, Patrick von Gunten, Thierry Paterlini, Philippe Furrer, Sandy Jeannin, Thibaut Monnet, Yannick Weber, Rafael Diaz, Andres Ambuhl, Thomas Deruns, Luca Sbisa

**United States** (Ron Wilson, coach) GK— Ryan Miller, Tim Thomas, Jonathan Quick—Brian Rafalski, Zach Parise, Ryan Malone, Patrick Kane, Jamie Langenbrunner, Ryan Suter, David Backes, Paul Stastny, Joe Pavelski, Ryan Kesler, Chris Drury, Bobby Ryan, Phil Kessel, Erik Johnson, Ryan Callahan, Jack Johnson, Dustin Brown, Tim Gleason, Brooks Orpik, Ryan Whitney

*Sidney Crosby's golden goal at 7:40 of overtime gave Canada Olympic gold in 2010. Photo: Matthew Manor / HHOF-IIHF Images.*

# WORLD CHAMPIONSHIP (MEN)

## 4th WORLD CHAMPIONSHIP (MEN)
**January 29-February 10, 1930**
**Chamonix, France/Berlin, Germany/Vienna, Austria**

(the IIHF counts the 1920, 1924, and 1928 Olympics as the 1st, 2nd, and 3rd World Championship)

**Final Placing**

Gold........Canada
Silver......Germany
Bronze....Switzerland
4th.........Austria
5th.........Poland
6th.........Czechoslovakia, France, Hungary, Japan
10th.......Belgium, Great Britain, Italy

**Tournament Format**

A knockout system was used. Winners advanced, losers were eliminated. Canada was given one place in the finals, and the other countries played for the other spot in the gold medal game.

**Results & Standings**

**FIRST ROUND (CHAMONIX)**

(Poland, Japan, Austria, Switzerland, Czechoslovakia given bye to second round)

| | | |
|---|---|---|
| January 31 | Hungary 2 | Italy 0 |
| January 31 | Germany 4 | Great Britain 2 |
| January 31 | France 4 | Belgium 1 |

**SECOND ROUND (CHAMONIX)**

| | | |
|---|---|---|
| February 1 | Germany 4 | Hungary 1 |
| February 1 | Poland 5 | Japan 0 |
| February 1 | Austria 2 | France 1 |
| February 1 | Switzerland 3 | Czechoslovakia 1 |

**THIRD ROUND (CHAMONIX)**

| | | |
|---|---|---|
| February 2 | Germany 4 | Poland 1 |
| February 2 | Switzerland 2 | Austria 1 |

**FOURTH ROUND (BERLIN)**

| | | |
|---|---|---|
| February 9 | Germany 2 | Switzerland 1 |

**4TH PLACE GAME (VIENNA)**

| | | |
|---|---|---|
| February 5 | Austria 2 | Poland 0 |

**GOLD MEDAL GAME (BERLIN)**

| | | |
|---|---|---|
| February 10 | Canada 6 | Germany 1 |

**Rosters**

**Austria** (Blake Watson, coach) GK—Fritz Lichtschein, Hermann Weiss—Walter Bruck, Friedrich Demmer, Hans Ertl, Karl Kirchberger, Ulrich Lederer, Walter Sell, Hans Tatzer, Hans Trauttenberg, Jacques Dietriechstein

**Belgium** (Pierre van Reysschoot, coach) GK—Hector Chotteau—Jacques van Reysschoot, Willy Kreitz, Jean Van de Wouwer, Albert Collon, Louis De Ridder, Jef Lekens, Jean de Craene, Jules Lecomte, David Meyer, Marco Peltzer, Willy Van Rompaey

**Canada** (Toronto CCM—Les Allen, coach) GK—Percy Timpson—Joe Griffin, Willie Adams, Howard Armstrong, Bert Clayton, Gordon Grant, Alex Park, Fred Radke, Don Hutchinson

**Czechoslovakia** GK—Jan Peka, Jaroslav Pospisil—Jaroslav Pusbauer, Wolfgang Dorasil, Josef Kral, Jiri Tozicka, Josef Malecek, Karel Hromadka, Tomas Svihovec, Bohumil Steigenhofer, Jan Krasl, Wilhelm Heinz

**France** GK—Jacques Morrisson, Philippe Lefebure—Armand Charlet, Raoul Couvert, Marcial Couvert, Jean-Pierre Hagnauer, Albert Hassler, Jacques Lacarriere, Charles Muntz, Leon Quaglia, Gerard Simond, Michel Tournier

**Germany** (Erich Romer, playing coach) GK—Walter Leinweber—Erich Romer, Franz Kreisel, Alfred Heinrich, Gustav Jaenecke, Gunther Kummetz, Erich Herker, Rudi Ball, Martin Schrottle, Marquardt Slevogt

**Great Britain** GK—William Speechley, John Rogers—Blaine Sexton, Frank de Marwicz, Neville Melland, William Home, Eric Carruthers, RD Mulholland, Norman Grace

**Hungary** (Frigyes Minder, coach) GK—Tibor Heinrich, Istvan Benyovits—Bela Weiner, Geza Lator, Frigyes Barna, Dejan Bikar, Miklos Barcza, Peter Krempels, Zoltan Jeney, Zoltan Rajnai, Sandor Minder, Laszlo Blazejovsky, Istvan Krepuska

**Italy** (Enrico Bombilla, coach) GK—Enrico Calcaterra, Augusto Gerosa—Franco Roncarrelli, Guido Botturi, Decio Trovati, Gianni Scotti, Gian Mario Baroni, Gigi Venosta, Gino de Mazzeri, Giovanni Iskaki, Emilio Zardini, Camillo Mussi

**Japan** (Seiji Yamaguchi, coach) GK—Toshio Takahashi—Kiku Inaba, Kiyoshi Ohga, Kiyoshi, Kitagawa, Seichi Hayashi, Toshihiko Shoji, Towohiko Nishiuchi, S Hirano, Y Kinoshita

**Poland** (Tadeusz Adamowski, coach) GK—Jozef Stogowski, Tadeusz Sachs—Kazimierz Sokolowski, Alexander Kowalski, Lucjan Kulej, Alexander Tupalski, Tadeusz Adamowski, Wlodzimierz Krygier, Roman Sabinski, Karol Szenajch, Czeslaw Marchewczyk, Karol Weissberg

**Switzerland** (Bobby Bell, coach) GK—Albert Kunzler, Emil Eberle—Albert Geromini, Carletto Mai, Heini Meng, Richard "Bibi" Torriani, Conrad Torriani, Fritz Fuchs, Fritz Kraatz, Beat Ruedi, Albert Rudolf

## 5th WORLD CHAMPIONSHIP (MEN)
**February 1-8, 1931**
**Krynica, Poland**

**Final Placing**

Gold........Canada
Silver......United States
Bronze....Austria
4th.........Poland
5th.........Czechoslovakia
6th.........Sweden
7th.........Hungary
8th.........Great Britain
9th.........France
10th.......Romania

**Tournament Format**

Round robin in which each team played each other once, the top three in the standings winning gold, silver, and bronze.

**Results & Standings**

**FIRST QUALIFICATION ROUND (WINNERS TO ROUND TWO; LOSERS TO CONSOLATION)**

| | | |
|---|---|---|
| February 1 | Austria 1 | Great Britain 0 (Herbert Bruck OT) |
| February 1 | Czechoslovakia 4 | Hungary 1 |

**SECOND QUALIFICATION ROUND**

| | | |
|---|---|---|
| February 1 | Canada 9 | France 0 |
| February 1 | United States 15 | Romania 0 |
| February 2 | Czechoslovakia 4 | Poland 1 |
| February 2 | Sweden 3 | Austria 1 |

**THIRD QUALIFICATION ROUND (ROUND TWO LOSERS; WINNERS GO TO MEDAL GROUP)**

| | | |
|---|---|---|
| February 3 | Austria 7 | Romania 0 |
| February 3 | Poland 2 | France 1 (Alexander Tupalski OT) |

**MEDAL GROUP**

| | GP | W | T | L | GF | GA | P |
|---|---|---|---|---|---|---|---|
| Canada | 5 | 4 | 1 | 0 | 15 | 0 | 9 |
| United States | 5 | 4 | 0 | 1 | 7 | 3 | 8 |
| Austria | 5 | 2 | 0 | 3 | 5 | 13 | 4 |
| Poland | 5 | 1 | 1 | 3 | 3 | 6 | 3 |
| Czechoslovakia | 5 | 1 | 1 | 3 | 2 | 5 | 3 |
| Sweden | 5 | 1 | 1 | 3 | 1 | 6 | 3 |

| | | |
|---|---|---|
| February 4 | Canada 2 | Czechoslovakia 0 |
| February 4 | Poland 2 | Sweden 0 |
| February 4 | United States 2 | Austria 1 |
| February 5 | Canada 3 | Poland 0 |
| February 5 | Czechoslovakia 2 | Austria 1 |
| February 5 | United States 3 | Sweden 0 |
| February 6 | Canada 0 | Sweden 0 |
| February 6 | Austria 2 | Poland 1 |
| February 6 | United States 1 | Czechoslovakia 0 |
| February 7 | Canada 8 | Austria 0 |
| February 7 | United States 1 | Poland 0 |
| February 7 | Sweden 1 | Czechoslovakia 0 |
| February 8 | Canada 2 | United States 0 |
| February 8 | Austria 1 | Sweden 0 |
| February 8 | Czechoslovakia 0 | Poland 0 |

**CONSOLATION ROUND**

| | GP | W | T | L | GF | GA | P |
|---|---|---|---|---|---|---|---|
| Hungary | 3 | 3 | 0 | 0 | 13 | 2 | 6 |
| Great Britain | 3 | 2 | 0 | 1 | 14 | 4 | 4 |
| France | 3 | 1 | 0 | 2 | 8 | 4 | 2 |
| Romania | 3 | 0 | 0 | 3 | 2 | 27 | 0 |

| | | |
|---|---|---|
| February 3 | Hungary 3 | Great Britain 1 |
| February 4 | France 7 | Romania 1 |
| February 5 | Hungary 9 | Romania 1 |
| February 5 | Great Britain 2 | France 1 |
| February 6 | Great Britain 11 | Romania 0 |
| February 7 | Hungary 1 | France 0 |

**Rosters**

**Austria** (Hans Weinberger, coach) GK—Hermann Weiss, Bruno Kahane—Jacques Dietriechstein, Hans Trauttenberg, Herbert Bruck, Hans Tatzer, Friedrich Demmer, Karl Kirchberger, Josef Gobel, Ulrich Lederer, Walter Sell, Anton Emhardt

**Canada** (Manitoba Grads—Blake Watson, playing coach) GK—Art Puttee—George Hill, Gord MacKenzie, Sammy McCallum, Ward McVey, Frank Morris, Jack Pidcock, Guy Williamson, Blake Watson, George Garbutt

**Czechoslovakia** GK—Jan Peka, Jaroslav Rezac—Jaroslav Pusbauer, Zbynek Petrs, Wolfgang Dorasil, Josef Kral, Jiri Tozicka, Josef Malecek, Karel Hromadka, Bohumil Steigenhofer, Tomas Svihovec, Wilhelm Heinz

**France** GK—Philippe Lefebure, Jacques Morrisson—Marcial Couvert, Raoul Couvert, Armand Charlet, Leon Quaglia, Albert Hassler, Jean-Pierre Hagnauer, Jacques Lacarriere, Charles Muntz, Francois Mautin, Charles Michaelis, Auguste Mollard, Michel Tournier, Gerard Simond

**Great Britain** GK—Herbert Little, David Turnbull—Brian Carr-Harris, John Magwood, Carl Erhardt, Norman Grace, Neville Melland, Keith Thompson, HW Bushell, HG Parker, Clarence Wedgewood

**Hungary** (Frigyes Minder, coach) GK—Ferenc Monostori-Marx, Istvan Benyovits—Frigyes Barna, Istvan Bethlen, Dejan Bikar, Zoltan Jeney, Geza Lator, Sandor Miklos, Sandor Minder, Bela Weiner, Laszlo Blazejovsky

**Poland** (Harold Farlow, coach) GK—Jozef Stogowski, Tadeusz Sachs—Kazimierz Sokolowski, Wlodzimierz Krygier, Tadeusz Adamowski, Alexander Kowalski, Alexander Tupalski, Roman Sabinski, Kazimierz Materski, Jozef Godlewski, Karol Szenajch, Jan Hemmerling, Lucjan Kulej

**Romania** GK—Dumitru Danieleopol, Ion Doczi—Riri Aslan, Serban Grant, Petre Grant, Constantin Cantacuzino, Alexandru Botez, Nicu Polizu, Dan Bratianu, Henry Frischlander, Josef Jerecinsky

**Sweden** (Viking Harbom, coach) GK—Carl Abrahamsson, Curt Sucksdorff—Emil Bergman, Tage Broberg, Thore Andersson-Dettner, Gustaf Johansson, Bertil Linde, Erik Lindgren, Sigfrid Oberg, Robert Pettersson, Emil Rundqvist

**United States** (Boston Olympics-Walter Brown, coach) GK—Edward Frazier—Ty Andersen, Ed Dagnino, Robert Elliot, Francis Nelson, Charles Ramsey, Larry Sanford, Dwight Shefler, Richard Thayer, Gordon Smith

## 7th WORLD CHAMPIONSHIP (MEN)
## 18-26 February, 1933
## Prague, Czechoslovakia

(the IIHF considers the 1932 Olympics to be the 6th World Championship)

**Final Placing**

| | | | |
|---|---|---|---|
| Gold | United States | 7th | Hungary, Poland |
| Silver | Canada | 9th | Romania |
| Bronze | Czechoslovakia | 10th | Latvia |
| 4th | Austria | 11th | Italy |
| 5th | Germany, Switzerland | 12th | Belgium |

**Tournament Format**

In a preliminary round, ten nations were split into three groups, playing a round robin within each group. The top two nations from each group advanced to a semi-finals round, the other teams being relegated to a placement series. One semi-finals group had Canada, the other the USA. The top two from each of these groups advanced to a semi-finals series, the winners to play for the gold medal, the losers for bronze.

**Results & Standings**

Qualifying (1st place from Group A & C and 2nd place from Group B join USA in Group D; 1st place from Group B and 2nd place from Group A & C join Canada in Group E)

**GROUP A**

| | GP | W | T | L | GF | GA | P |
|---|---|---|---|---|---|---|---|
| Czechoslovakia | 3 | 3 | 0 | 0 | 13 | 2 | 6 |
| Austria | 3 | 2 | 0 | 1 | 11 | 3 | 4 |
| Italy | 3 | 1 | 0 | 2 | 3 | 6 | 2 |
| Romania | 3 | 0 | 0 | 3 | 1 | 17 | 0 |

| | | |
|---|---|---|
| February 18 | Czechoslovakia 8 | Romania 0 |
| February 18 | Austria 3 | Italy 0 |
| February 19 | Czechoslovakia 2 | Austria 1 |
| February 19 | Italy 2 | Romania 0 |
| February 20 | Austria 7 | Romania 1 |
| February 20 | Czechoslovakia 3 | Italy 1 |

**GROUP B**

| | GP | W | T | L | GF | GA | P |
|---|---|---|---|---|---|---|---|
| Germany | 2 | 2 | 0 | 0 | 8 | 0 | 4 |
| Poland | 2 | 1 | 0 | 1 | 1 | 2 | 2 |
| Belgium | 2 | 0 | 0 | 2 | 0 | 7 | 0 |

| | | |
|---|---|---|
| February 18 | Germany 6 | Belgium 0 |
| February 19 | Germany 2 | Poland 0 |
| February 20 | Poland 1 | Belgium 0 |

**GROUP C**

| | GP | W | T | L | GF | GA | P |
|---|---|---|---|---|---|---|---|
| Switzerland | 2 | 2 | 0 | 0 | 6 | 1 | 4 |
| Hungary | 2 | 1 | 0 | 1 | 3 | 1 | 2 |
| Latvia | 2 | 0 | 0 | 2 | 1 | 8 | 0 |

| | | |
|---|---|---|
| February 18 | Switzerland 5 | Latvia 1 |
| February 19 | Switzerland 1 | Hungary 0 |
| February 20 | Hungary 3 | Latvia 0 |

**SEMI-FINAL GROUP D (UNITED STATES GIVEN BYE TO THIS GROUP)**

| | GP | W | T | L | GF | GA | P |
|---|---|---|---|---|---|---|---|
| United States | 3 | 3 | 0 | 0 | 17 | 0 | 6 |
| Czechoslovakia | 3 | 2 | 0 | 1 | 2 | 6 | 4 |
| Switzerland | 3 | 1 | 0 | 2 | 3 | 9 | 2 |
| Poland | 3 | 0 | 0 | 3 | 1 | 8 | 0 |

| | | |
|---|---|---|
| February 21 | Czechoslovakia 1 | Poland 0 |
| February 21 | United States 7 | Switzerland 0 |
| February 22 | United States 4 | Poland 0 |
| February 22 | Czechoslovakia 1 | Switzerland 0 |
| February 23 | Switzerland 3 | Poland 1 |
| February 23 | United States 6 | Czechoslovakia 0 |

**SEMI-FINAL GROUP E (CANADA GIVEN BYE TO THIS GROUP)**

| | GP | W | T | L | GF | GA | P |
|---|---|---|---|---|---|---|---|
| Canada | 3 | 3 | 0 | 0 | 12 | 1 | 6 |
| Austria | 3 | 2 | 0 | 1 | 3 | 4 | 4 |
| Germany | 3 | 1 | 0 | 2 | 4 | 7 | 2 |
| Hungary | 3 | 0 | 0 | 3 | 1 | 8 | 0 |

| | | |
|---|---|---|
| February 21 | Canada 5 | Germany 0 |
| February 21 | Austria 1 | Hungary 0 |
| February 22 | Germany 4 | Hungary 0 |
| February 22 | Canada 4 | Austria 0 |
| February 23 | Canada 3 | Hungary 1 |
| February 23 | Austria 2 | Germany 0 |

**9TH-12TH PLACEMENT GAMES**

| | | |
|---|---|---|
| February 24 | Latvia 2 | Italy 0 |
| February 24 | Romania 3 | Belgium 2 |
| February 25 | Romania 1 | Latvia 0 |
| | Italy-Belgium (Belgium declined to play) | |

**5TH-PLACE GAME**

February 24 Germany 1 Switzerland 1

**7TH-PLACE GAME**

February 24 Poland 1 Hungary 1

**SEMI-FINALS**

| | | |
|---|---|---|
| February 24 | Canada 4 | Czechoslovakia 0 |
| February 24 | United States 4 | Austria 0 |

**BRONZE MEDAL GAME**

February 26 Czechoslovakia 2 Austria 0

**GOLD MEDAL GAME**

February 26 United States 2 Canada 1 (Garrison 10:00 OT)

**Rosters**

**Austria** (Hans Weinberger, coach) GK—Otto Amenth, Herman Weiss—Jacques Dietriechstein, Hans Trauttenberg, Hans Tatzer, Hans Ertl, Friedrich Demmer, Karl Kirchberger, Josef Gobel, Karl Rammer, Franz Csongei, Herbert Bruck, Lambert Neumaier

**Belgium** (Pierre van Reysschoot, coach) GK—Hector Chotteau, Johnny Williams—Francois Franck, Louis de Ridder, Jef Lekens, Pierre van Reysschoot, Willy Kreitz, Jean de Beukelaar, Jean van den Wouwer, Willy Van Rompaey, Charles van Riel, G van Riel

**Canada** (Toronto National Sea Fleas—Harold Ballard, coach) GK—Stuffy Mueller, Ron Geddes—Cliff Chisholm, Frank Collins, John Hern, Kenny Kane, Scotty McAlpine, Clare McIntyre, Marty Nugent, Al Huggins, Tim Kerr

**Czechoslovakia** GK—Jan Peka, Jan Vorel—Zbynek Petrs, Jaroslav Pusbauer, Wolfgang Dorasil, Jiri Tozicka, Josef Malecek, Karel Hromadka, Alois Cetkovsky, Tomas Svihovec, Oldrich Kucera, Jan Michalek, Jan Mattern

**Germany** (Erich Romer, playing coach) GK—Wilhelm Egginger, Gerhard Ball—Erich Romer, Martin Schrottle, Gustav Jaenecke, Rudi Ball, Horst Orbanowski, Anton Wiedemann, Georg Strobl, Hans Lang, Werner Korff, Hans Schutte

**Hungary** (Frigyes Minder, coach) GK—Istvan Hircsak, Ferenc Monostori-Marx—Istvan Bethlen, Bela Weiner, Zoltan Jeney, Sandor Miklos, Sandor Minder, Andras Gergely, Gyorgy Margo, Laszlo Blazejovsky, Ferenc Stoics, Pal Bliesener

**Italy** GK—Augusto Gerosa, Enrico Calcaterra—Decio Trovati, Giovanni Baroni, Ignazio Dionisi, Luigi Venosta, Francesco de Zanna, Tino de Mazzeri, Camillo Mussi, Gianpiero Medri

**Latvia** GK—Herberts Kuskis, Peteris Skuja—Leonids Vedejs, Indrikis Reinbahs, Herberts Keslers, Eriks Petersons, Arvids Jurgens, Adolfs Petrovskis, Roberts Blukis, Johans Skadins, Arvids Petersons

**Poland** (Tadeusz Sachs, coach) GK—Jozef Stogowski, Jozef Sznajder—Witalis Ludwiczak, Kazimierz Sokolowski, Roman Sabinski, Andrzej Wolkowski, Karol Szenajch, Tadeusz Adamowski, Kazimierz Materski, Marian Piechota, Czeslaw Godlewski, Ryszard Werner

**Romania** (Walter Sell, coach) GK—Mircea Ratiu, Ion Doczi—Serban Grant, Nicu Polizu, Gheorghe Buia, Iuliu Rabinovici, Constantin Cantacuzino, Hans Brackl, Alexandru Botez, Paul Anastasiu, Lajos Vakar, Petre Grant, L Tucker

**Switzerland** (Mezzi Andreossi, coach) GK—Arnold Hirtz, Emil Eberle—Oscar Schmidt, Ernst Hug, Adolf Martignoni, Hans Cattini, Richard "Bibi" Torriani, Ferdinand "Pic" Cattini, Herbert Kessler, Otto Heller, Karl Kessler, Thomas Pleisch, Albert Kunzler

**United States** (Boston Olympics-Walter Brown, coach) GK—Gerry Cosby—John Garrison, Ben Langmaid, Winthrop Palmer, Frank Holland, Larry Sanford, Channing Hilliard, Stewart Iglehart, Sherman Forbes, Jim Breckenridge

## 8th WORLD CHAMPIONSHIP (MEN)
## February 3-11, 1934
## Milan, Italy

**Final Placing**

| | |
|---|---|
| Gold ........Canada | 7th .........Austria |
| Silver ......United States | 8th .........Great Britain |
| Bronze ....Germany | 9th .........Italy |
| 4th..........Switzerland | 10th .......Romania |
| 5th..........Czechoslovakia | 11th .......France |
| 6th..........Hungary | 12th .......Belgium |

**Tournament Format**

Ten teams were divided into three groups to play a round robin within each group. The bottom three teams were eliminated, the top seven moved on to a semi-fimals round robin. The first-place teams from that series move on to semi-finals, and the three 2nd-place teams play a round robin, the winner of the group becoming the fourth team of the semis.

**Results & Standings**

**GROUP A**

| | GP | W | T | L | GF | GA | P |
|---|---|---|---|---|---|---|---|
| Switzerland | 3 | 3 | 0 | 0 | 30 | 3 | 6 |
| France | 3 | 1 | 0 | 2 | 4 | 6 | 2 |
| Romania | 3 | 1 | 0 | 2 | 6 | 13 | 2 |
| Belgium | 3 | 1 | 0 | 2 | 5 | 23 | 2 |

| | | |
|---|---|---|
| February 3 | Switzerland 20 | Belgium 1 |
| February 3 | France 4 | Romania 1 |
| February 4 | Switzerland 3 | France 0 |
| February 4 | Romania 3 | Belgium 2 |
| February 5 | Switzerland 7 | Romania 2 |
| February 5 | Belgium 2 | France 0 |

**GROUP B**

| | GP | W | T | L | GF | GA | P |
|---|---|---|---|---|---|---|---|
| Hungary | 2 | 1 | 0 | 1 | 2 | 1 | 2 |
| Czechoslovakia | 2 | 1 | 0 | 1 | 2 | 2 | 2 |
| Great Britain | 2 | 1 | 0 | 1 | 2 | 3 | 2 |

| | | |
|---|---|---|
| February 3 | Hungary 2 | Great Britain 0 |
| February 4 | Great Britain 2 | Czechoslovakia 1 |
| February 5 | Czechoslovakia 1 | Hungary 0 |

**GROUP C**

| | GP | W | T | L | GF | GA | P |
|---|---|---|---|---|---|---|---|
| Austria | 2 | 1 | 0 | 1 | 2 | 2 | 2 |
| Italy | 2 | 1 | 0 | 1 | 3 | 3 | 2 |
| Germany | 2 | 1 | 0 | 1 | 4 | 4 | 2 |

| | | |
|---|---|---|
| February 3 | Austria 2 | Germany 1 |
| February 4 | Germany 3 | Italy 2 |
| February 5 | Italy 1 | Austria 0 |

**SEMI-FINALS**

(1st place teams move on to semi-finals; three 2nd-place teams play a round robin, the winner of the group becoming the fourth team of the semis)

**SEMI-FINALS GROUP A**

| | GP | W | T | L | GF | GA | P |
|---|---|---|---|---|---|---|---|
| United States | 2 | 2 | 0 | 0 | 2 | 0 | 4 |
| Czechoslovakia | 2 | 1 | 0 | 1 | 4 | 1 | 2 |
| Austria | 2 | 0 | 0 | 2 | 0 | 5 | 0 |

| | | |
|---|---|---|
| February 6 | United States 1 | Czechoslovakia 0 |
| February 7 | Czechoslovakia 4 | Austria 0 |
| February 8 | United States 1 | Austria 0 |

**SEMI-FINALS GROUP B**

| | GP | W | T | L | GF | GA | P |
|---|---|---|---|---|---|---|---|
| Switzerland | 2 | 2 | 0 | 0 | 4 | 0 | 4 |
| Hungary | 2 | 0 | 1 | 1 | 0 | 1 | 1 |
| Italy | 2 | 0 | 1 | 1 | 0 | 3 | 1 |

| | | |
|---|---|---|
| February 6 | Hungary 0 | Italy 0 (30:00 OT) |
| February 7 | Switzerland 1 | Hungary 0 |
| February 8 | Switzerland 3 | Italy 0 |

**SEMI-FINALS GROUP C**

| | GP | W | T | L | GF | GA | P |
|---|---|---|---|---|---|---|---|
| Canada | 2 | 2 | 0 | 0 | 15 | 0 | 4 |
| Germany | 2 | 1 | 0 | 1 | 4 | 6 | 2 |
| France | 2 | 0 | 0 | 2 | 0 | 13 | 0 |

| | | |
|---|---|---|
| February 6 | Canada 9 | France 0 |
| February 7 | Canada 6 | Germany 0 |
| February 8 | Germany 4 | France 0 |

**SEMI-FINALS QUALIFYING GROUP (ALL 2ND-PLACE TEAMS FROM SEMI-FINALS GROUPS A, B, C)**

| | GP | W | T | L | GF | GA | P |
|---|---|---|---|---|---|---|---|
| Germany | 2 | 2 | 0 | 0 | 1 | 0 | 4 |
| Czechoslovakia | 2 | 1 | 0 | 1 | 1 | 1 | 2 |
| Hungary | 2 | 0 | 0 | 2 | 0 | 1 | 0 |

(Hungary withdrew, forfeiting both games which were officially recorded as 1-0 wins for Germany and Czechoslovakia, respectively)

| | | |
|---|---|---|
| February 9 | Germany 1 | Czechoslovakia 0 (Werner George OT) |
| February 10 | Czechoslovakia 1 | Hungary 0 |

**CONSOLATION ROUND**

| | GP | W | T | L | GF | GA | P |
|---|---|---|---|---|---|---|---|
| Austria | 3 | 2 | 1 | 0 | 7 | 4 | 5 |
| Great Britain | 3 | 2 | 0 | 1 | 7 | 4 | 4 |
| Italy | 3 | 1 | 1 | 1 | 6 | 6 | 3 |
| Romania | 3 | 0 | 0 | 3 | 2 | 8 | 0 |

**QUALIFICATION FOR CONSOLATION ROUND**

| | | |
|---|---|---|
| February 6 | Great Britain 3 | Belgium 0 |

**CONSOLATION ROUND RESULTS**

| | | |
|---|---|---|
| February 9 | Austria 2 | Great Britain 1 |
| February 9 | Italy 3 | Romania 0 |
| February 10 | Austria 3 | Romania 1 |
| February 10 | Great Britain 4 | Italy 1 |
| February 11 | Austria 2 | Italy 2 |
| February 11 | Great Britain 2 | Romania 1 |

**SEMI-FINALS**

| | | |
|---|---|---|
| February 10 | Canada 2 | Switzerland 1 (Cliff Lake OT) |
| February 10 | United States 3 | Germany 0 |

**BRONZE MEDAL GAME**

| | | |
|---|---|---|
| February 11 | Germany 2 | Switzerland 1 (20:00 OT—2nd OT: Lang (GER) 5:00) |

**GOLD MEDAL GAME**

| | | |
|---|---|---|
| February 11 | Canada 2 | United States 1 |

**Rosters**

**Austria** (Hans Weinberger, coach) GK—Otto Amenth, Karl Oerdoegh—Jacques Dietriechstein, Franz Schussler, Franz Csongei, Friedrich Demmer, Josef Gobel, Oskar Nowak, Karl Rammer, Hans Stertin, Hans Tatzer, Karl Kirchberger, Willibald Stanek, Reinhold Egger

**Belgium** (Pierre van Reysschoot, coach) GK—Rene Laloux—Francois Franck, Louis Franck, Louis de Ridder, Jean Barbanson, Carlos Van Den Driessche, Pierre van Reysschoot, Willy Kreitz, Georges Pootmans, Marco Peltzer, Emile Duvivier, Jean de Beukelaer, Henri Matthyssen

**Canada** (Saskatoon Quakers—Johnny Walker, coach) GK—Cooney Woods—Les Bird, Tommy Dewar, Jim Dewey, Cliff Lake, Elmer Piper, Ab Rogers, Bert Scharfe, Ron Silver, Ray Watkins, Ab Welsh, Harold "Hobb" Wilson

**Czechoslovakia** (Howie Grant, coach) GK—Jan Peka, Antonin Houba—Jaroslav Pusbauer, Wolfgang Dorasil, Jiri Tozicka, Tomas Svihovec, Josef Malecek, Karel Hromadka, Oldrich Kucera, Alois Cetkovsky, Jan Michalek, Zdenek Jirotka

**France** GK—Jean Despas, Michel Paccard—Jacques Lacarriere, Andre Bossoney, Jean-Pierre Hagnauer, Marcel Claret, Martial Couvert, Leon Quaglia, Albert Hassler, Gerard Simond, Pierre Savoye, Pierre Perreau, Jacques Bottenheim

**Germany** (Erich Romer, playing coach) GK—Walter Leinweber, Theo Kaufmann—Erich Romer, Johann Albrecht von Bethmann-Hollweg, Roman Kessler, Gustav Jaenecke, Horst Orbanowski, Werner George, Georg Strobl, Hans Lang, Alois Kuhn, Werner Korff

**Great Britain** (John Magwood, coach) GK—Vic Gardner—Carl Erhardt, Harry Mayes, Jim Borland, Gerry Davey, Neville Melland, Peter Fair, Keith Thompson, Ted Jackson, Ivor Nesbitt, Fred de Marwicz

**Hungary** (John Dewar, coach) GK—Istvan Hircsak, Gyorgy Kramer-Katay— Matyas Farkas, Miklos Barcza, Istvan Bethlen, Sandor Miklos, Ferenc Erdi, Bela Haray, Gyorgy Margo, Andras Gergely, Zoltan Jeney, Ferenc Stoics, Laszlo Blazejovsky

**Italy** (Giorgio Baroni, coach) GK—Augusto Gerosa, Enrico Calcaterra—Gianmario Baroni, Francesco Roncarelli, Franco Rossi, Decio Trovati, Tino de Mazzeri, Ignazio Dionisi, Camillo Mussi, Gianpiero Medri, Gianni Scotti, Luigi Venosta, Mario Zucchini, Aldo Marazza

**Romania** GK—Mircea Ratiu, Arthur Vogel—Gheorghe Buia, Nicu Polizu, Radu Reineck, Constantin Cantacuzino, Alexandru Botez, Paul Anastasiu, Petre Grant, Constantin Tico, Iuliu Rabinovici, Franz Bratoscu, Lajos Vakar, Dan Bratianu, Ion Petrovici

**Switzerland** (Charles Fasel, coach) GK—Emil Eberle, Arnold Hirtz—Ernst Hug, Oscar Schmidt, Albert Geromini, Charles Kessler, Hans Cattini, Ferdinand "Pic" Cattini, Richard "Bibi" Torriani, Peter Muller, Thomas Pleisch, Conrad Torriani

**United States** (Walter Brown, coach) GK—Clem Harnedy—Art Smith, Ed Keating, Walt Bender, Frank Stubbs, Dick Maley, Bob Jeremiah, Fred Macdonell, Bob Nilon, Pete Bessone

## 9th WORLD CHAMPIONSHIP (MEN)
**January 19-27, 1935**
**Davos, Switzerland**

**Final Placing**

Gold........Canada
Silver......Switzerland
Bronze....Great Britain
4th..........Czechoslovakia
5th..........Sweden
6th..........Austria
7th..........France
8th.........Italy
9th.........Germany
10th.......Poland
11th.......Hungary, Romania
13th.......Latvia
14th.......Belgium, Netherlands

**Tournament Format**

Teams played round robin within their group, the top two from each of the four groups advancing to a semi-finals grouping. Another round robin within each group then took place, and the top two from each played a cross-over semi-finals game, the winners going on to the gold medal game, the losers playing for the bronze.

**Results & Standings**

**GROUP A**

| | GP | W | T | L | GF | GA | P |
|---|---|---|---|---|---|---|---|
| Switzerland | 3 | 2 | 1 | 0 | 11 | 2 | 5 |
| Sweden | 3 | 2 | 0 | 1 | 10 | 6 | 4 |
| Hungary | 3 | 1 | 1 | 1 | 7 | 4 | 3 |
| Netherlands | 3 | 0 | 0 | 3 | 0 | 16 | 0 |

| | | |
|---|---|---|
| January 19 | Switzerland 6 | Sweden 1 |
| January 19 | Hungary 6 | Netherlands 0 |
| January 20 | Switzerland 1 | Hungary 1 |
| January 20 | Sweden 6 | Netherlands 0 |
| January 21 | Switzerland 4 | Netherlands 0 |
| January 21 | Sweden 3 | Hungary 0 |

**Group B**

| | GP | W | T | L | GF | GA | P |
|---|---|---|---|---|---|---|---|
| France | 3 | 2 | 1 | 0 | 6 | 4 | 5 |
| Italy | 3 | 1 | 2 | 0 | 4 | 2 | 4 |
| Poland | 3 | 1 | 1 | 1 | 6 | 5 | 3 |
| Germany | 3 | 0 | 0 | 3 | 2 | 7 | 0 |

| | | |
|---|---|---|
| January 19 | France 3 | Poland 2 |
| January 19 | Italy 2 | Germany 0 |
| January 20 | Italy 1 | France 1 |
| January 20 | Poland 3 | Germany 1 |
| January 21 | Poland 1 | Italy 1 |
| January 21 | France 2 | Germany 1 |

**GROUP C**

| | GP | W | T | L | GF | GA | P |
|---|---|---|---|---|---|---|---|
| Czechoslovakia | 3 | 3 | 0 | 0 | 28 | 3 | 6 |
| Austria | 3 | 2 | 0 | 1 | 9 | 4 | 4 |
| Romania | 3 | 1 | 0 | 2 | 5 | 7 | 2 |
| Belgium | 3 | 0 | 0 | 3 | 2 | 30 | 0 |

| | | |
|---|---|---|
| January 19 | Czechoslovakia 2 | Austria 1 |
| January 19 | Romania 2 | Belgium 1 |
| January 20 | Austria 6 | Belgium 1 |
| January 20 | Czechoslovakia 4 | Romania 2 |
| January 21 | Austria 2 | Romania 1 |
| January 21 | Czechoslovakia 22 | Belgium 0 |

**GROUP D**

| | GP | W | T | L | GF | GA | P |
|---|---|---|---|---|---|---|---|
| Canada | 2 | 2 | 0 | 0 | 18 | 2 | 4 |
| Great Britain | 2 | 1 | 0 | 1 | 7 | 5 | 2 |
| Latvia | 2 | 0 | 0 | 2 | 1 | 19 | 0 |

| | | |
|---|---|---|
| January 19 | Canada 4 | Great Britain 2 |
| January 20 | Canada 14 | Latvia 0 |
| January 21 | Great Britain 5 | Latvia 1 |

**SEMI-FINAL GROUP A**

| | GP | W | T | L | GF | GA | P |
|---|---|---|---|---|---|---|---|
| Canada | 3 | 3 | 0 | 0 | 16 | 3 | 6 |
| Czechoslovakia | 3 | 2 | 0 | 1 | 8 | 4 | 4 |
| Sweden | 3 | 0 | 1 | 2 | 4 | 8 | 1 |
| Italy | 3 | 0 | 1 | 2 | 2 | 15 | 1 |

| | | |
|---|---|---|
| January 22 | Canada 5 | Sweden 2 |
| January 22 | Czechoslovakia 5 | Italy 1 |
| January 23 | Canada 9 | Italy 0 |
| January 23 | Czechoslovakia 2 | Sweden 1 (Josef Malecek 4:00 OT) |
| January 24 | Canada 2 | Czechoslovakia 1 |
| January 24 | Sweden 1 | Italy 1 |

**SEMI-FINAL GROUP B**

| | GP | W | T | L | GF | GA | P |
|---|---|---|---|---|---|---|---|
| Switzerland | 3 | 2 | 1 | 0 | 7 | 2 | 5 |
| Great Britain | 3 | 2 | 0 | 1 | 5 | 2 | 4 |
| Austria | 3 | 1 | 1 | 1 | 6 | 6 | 3 |
| France | 3 | 0 | 0 | 3 | 2 | 10 | 0 |

| | | |
|---|---|---|
| January 22 | Switzerland 1 | Austria 1 (30:00 OT—no scoring) |
| January 22 | Great Britain 1 | France 0 |
| January 23 | Great Britain 4 | Austria 1 |
| January 23 | Switzerland 5 | France 1 |
| January 24 | Austria 4 | France 1 |
| January 24 | Switzerland 1 | Great Britain 0 |

**9-15 PLACEMENT GROUP A**

| | GP | W | T | L | GF | GA | P |
|---|---|---|---|---|---|---|---|
| Germany | 3 | 3 | 0 | 0 | 11 | 1 | 6 |
| Romania | 3 | 2 | 0 | 1 | 9 | 5 | 4 |
| Latvia | 3 | 1 | 0 | 2 | 10 | 6 | 2 |
| Netherlands | 3 | 0 | 0 | 3 | 0 | 18 | 0 |

| | | |
|---|---|---|
| January 22 | Germany 5 | Netherlands 0 |
| January 23 | Romania 3 | Latvia 2 |
| January 24 | Romania 6 | Netherlands 0 |
| January 24 | Germany 3 | Latvia 1 |
| January 25 | Germany 3 | Romania 0 |
| January 25 | Latvia 7 | Netherlands 0 |

**9-15 PLACEMENT GROUP B**

| | GP | W | T | L | GF | GA | P |
|---|---|---|---|---|---|---|---|
| Poland | 2 | 1 | 1 | 0 | 13 | 3 | 3 |
| Hungary | 2 | 1 | 1 | 0 | 7 | 2 | 3 |
| Belgium | 2 | 0 | 0 | 2 | 3 | 18 | 0 |

| | | |
|---|---|---|
| January 22 | Poland 12 | Belgium 2 |
| January 23 | Hungary 6 | Belgium 1 |
| January 25 | Poland 1 | Hungary 1 |

**5TH-8TH PLACE GAMES**

| | | |
|---|---|---|
| January 26 | Sweden 2 | France 1 |
| January 26 | Austria 2 | Italy 1 |

**5TH-PLACE GAME**

| | | |
|---|---|---|
| January 27 | Sweden 3 | Austria 1 |

**9TH-PLACE GAME**

| | | |
|---|---|---|
| January 27 | Germany 5 | Poland 1 |

**SEMI-FINALS**

| | | |
|---|---|---|
| January 26 | Canada 6 | Great Britain 0 |
| January 26 | Switzerland 4 | Czechoslovakia 0 |

**BRONZE MEDAL GAME**

| | | |
|---|---|---|
| January 27 | Great Britain 2 | Czechoslovakia 1 |

**GOLD MEDAL GAME**

| | | |
|---|---|---|
| January 27 | Canada 4 | Switzerland 2 |

**Rosters**

**Austria** (Hans Weinberger, coach) GK—Karl Oerdoegh, Herman Weiss—Hans Trauttenberg, Franz Schussler, Hans Tatzer, Oskar Nowak, Friedrich Demmer, Karl Kirchberger, Josef Gobel, Hans Schneider, Willibald Stanek, Rudolf Vojta, Emil Seidler

**Belgium** (Pierre van Reysschoot, coach) GK—Georges Brohee—Carlos van den Driessche, Jean Barbanson, Pierre van Reysschoot, Willy Kreitz, Georges Pootmans, Marco Peltzer, Percy Lippit, Francois Franck

**Canada** (Winnipeg Monarchs—Scotty Oliver, coach) GK—Art Rice-Jones—Archie Creighton, Roy Hinkel, Albert Lemay, Tony Lemay, Vic Lindquist, Romeo Rivers, Cam Shewan, Norm Yellowlees, Joe Rivers

**Czehoslovakia** GK—Jan Peka, Josef Bohac—Karel Hromadka, Jaroslav Pusbauer, Jiri Tozicka, Josef Malecek, Oldrich Kucera, Alois Cetkovsky, Jan Michalek, Jaroslav Cisar, Zdenek Jirotka, Frantisek Pergl, Drahos Jirotka

**France** GK—Jacques Morrisson, Michel Paccard—Pierre Claret, Pierre Lorin, Jean-Pierre Hagnauer, Miguel Delesalle, Jacques Lacarriere, Leon Quaglia, Albert Hassler, Pierre Savoie, Guy Volpert

**Germany** (Erich Romer, playing coach) GK—Wilhelm Egginger, Walter Leinweber—Martin Schrottle, Gustav Jaenecke, Hans Lang, Georg Strobl, Werner Korff, Alois Kuhn, Horst Orbanowski, Philipp Schenk, Karl Kogel, Herbert Schibukat, Erich Romer

**Great Britain** (John "Bunny" Ahearne, coach) GK—Ronnie Milne, Gordon Dailley, Carl Erhardt, Bob Wyman, Gordon Johnson, Gerry Davey, Pete Stevenson, Ernie Ramus, Ted Jackson

**Hungary** (Geza Lator, coach) GK—Istvan Hircsak, Gyorgy Kramer-Katay—Miklos Barcza, Matyas Farkas, Sandor Miklos, Laszlo Gergely, Andras Gergely, Zoltan Jeney, Ferenc Stoics, Laszlo Blazejovsky

**Italy** (Giuseppe Crivelli, coach) GK—Enrico Calcaterra, Augusto Gerosa—Decio Trovati, Franco Rossi, Ignazio Dionisi, Mario Zucchini, Gianni Scotti, Tino de Mazzeri, Camillo Mussi, Mario Maiocchi, Franco Carlassare, Gianmario Baroni

**Latvia** GK—Roberts Lapainis, Herberts Kuskis—Edgar Klavs, Karlis Paegle, Leonids Vedejs, Arvids Jurgens, Adolfs Petrovskis, Arnolds Peterssons, Andrejs Jessens, Aleksejs Auzins, Roberts Blukis

**Netherlands** (Hans Weinberg, coach) GK—Jan Gerritsen II, Sjoerd van Marle—Fritz van der Vlugt, Bob van der Stok, Hans Gerritsen I, Huib de Pon, Zeger Reyers, Felix de Jong, Chris van de Madele, Hans Maas, Dirk Jan Koeleman, Hans van der Flier

**Poland** (Tadeusz Sachs, coach) GK—Jozef Stogowski, Henryk Przezdziecki—Kazimierz Sokolowski, Witalis Ludwiczak, Czeslaw Marchewczyk, Andrzej Wolkowski, Adam Kowalski, Franciszek Glowacki, Roman Stupnicki, Edward Zielinski, Wladyslaw Lemiszko

**Romania** (Dumitru Danielopol, coach) GK—Emil Maesciuc, Dumitru Danielopol—Arthur Vogel, Alexandru Botez, Lajos Vakar, Constantin Tico, Constantin Cantacuzino, Paul Anastasiu, Ladislaus Dietrich, Antonin Panenka, Iuliu Rabinovici, Wilhelm Suc, Gheorghe Buia

**Sweden** (Carl Abrahamsson/Viking Harbom, coaches) GK—Wilhelm Larsson, Bengt Liedstrand—Bertil Lundell, Sven Bergqvist, Torsten Johncke, Gustav Johansson, Sigfrid Oberg, Ynge Liljeberg, Evert Low, Lennart Hellman, Borje Abelstedt, Olle Andersson

**Switzerland** (Charles Fasel, coach) GK—Albert Kunzler, Arnold Hirtz—Ernst Hug, Hirsch Badrutt, Richard "Bibi" Torriani, Hans Cattini, Ferdinand "Pic" Cattini, Thomas Pleisch, Peter Muller, Charles Kessler

## 11th WORLD CHAMPIONSHIP (MEN)
## February 17-27, 1937
## London, Great Britain

(the IIHF considers the 1936 Olympics to be the 10th World Championship)

**Final Placing**

Gold ........Canada
Silver ......Great Britain
Bronze ....Switzerland
4th ..........Germany
5th ..........Hungary
6th .........Czechoslovakia
7th .........France
8th .........Poland
9th .........Norway, Romania, Sweden

**Tournament Format**

Three groups played a round-robin within each group, the top three teams in Groups A and B and the top two teams in Group C advancing to a semi-finals round, the bottom four teams being relegated to a placement division of round-robin games. The top two teams from each group of the semi-finals then advanced to a finals round robin group, the top three from that winning gold, silver, and bronze.

**Results & Standings**

**GROUP A**

| | GP | W | T | L | GF | GA | P |
|---|---|---|---|---|---|---|---|
| Great Britain | 3 | 3 | 0 | 0 | 24 | 0 | 6 |
| Germany | 3 | 1 | 1 | 1 | 6 | 10 | 3 |
| Hungary | 3 | 1 | 1 | 1 | 6 | 10 | 3 |
| Romania | 3 | 0 | 0 | 3 | 3 | 19 | 0 |

| | | |
|---|---|---|
| February 17 | Great Britain 6 | Germany 0 |
| February 17 | Hungary 4 | Romania 1 |
| February 18 | Great Britain 7 | Hungary 0 |
| February 18 | Germany 4 | Romania 2 |
| February 19 | Great Britain 11 | Romania 0 |
| February 19 | Germany 2 | Hungary 2 (30:00 OT—2nd OT: Horst Orbanowski (GER), Sandor Miklos (HUN)) |

**GROUP B**

| | GP | W | T | L | GF | GA | P |
|---|---|---|---|---|---|---|---|
| Canada | 3 | 3 | 0 | 0 | 29 | 2 | 6 |
| Poland | 3 | 2 | 0 | 1 | 12 | 9 | 4 |
| France | 3 | 1 | 0 | 2 | 3 | 20 | 2 |
| Sweden | 3 | 0 | 0 | 3 | 1 | 14 | 0 |

| | | |
|---|---|---|
| February 17 | Canada 12 | France 0 |
| February 17 | Poland 3 | Sweden 0 |
| February 18 | Canada 8 | Poland 2 |
| February 18 | France 2 | Sweden 1 |
| February 19 | Canada 9 | Sweden 0 |
| February 19 | Poland 7 | France 1 |

**GROUP C**

| | GP | W | T | L | GF | GA | P |
|---|---|---|---|---|---|---|---|
| Switzerland | 2 | 1 | 1 | 0 | 15 | 4 | 3 |
| Czechoslovakia | 2 | 1 | 1 | 0 | 9 | 2 | 3 |
| Norway | 2 | 0 | 0 | 2 | 2 | 20 | 0 |

| | | |
|---|---|---|
| February 17 | Czechoslovakia 7 | Norway 0 |
| February 18 | Switzerland 13 | Norway 2 |
| February 19 | Czechoslovakia 2 | Switzerland 2 |

**SEMI-FINALS GROUP A**

| | GP | W | T | L | GF | GA | P |
|---|---|---|---|---|---|---|---|
| Canada | 3 | 3 | 0 | 0 | 21 | 1 | 6 |
| Germany | 3 | 2 | 0 | 1 | 7 | 6 | 4 |
| Czechoslovakia | 3 | 1 | 0 | 2 | 9 | 6 | 2 |
| France | 3 | 0 | 0 | 3 | 2 | 26 | 0 |

| | | |
|---|---|---|
| February 20 | Canada 3 | Czechoslovakia 0 |
| February 20 | Germany 5 | France 0 |
| February 22 | Canada 5 | Germany 0 |
| February 22 | Czechoslovakia 8 | France 1 |
| February 23 | Canada 13 | France 1 |
| February 23 | Germany 2 | Czechoslovakia 1 (30:000T—Karl Kogel) |

**SEMI-FINALS GROUP B**

| | GP | W | T | L | GF | GA | P |
|---|---|---|---|---|---|---|---|
| Great Britain | 3 | 3 | 0 | 0 | 19 | 0 | 6 |
| Switzerland | 3 | 2 | 0 | 1 | 5 | 5 | 4 |
| Poland | 3 | 1 | 0 | 2 | 4 | 12 | 2 |
| Hungary | 3 | 0 | 0 | 3 | 2 | 13 | 0 |

| | | |
|---|---|---|
| February 20 | Great Britain 3 | Switzerland 0 |
| February 20 | Poland 4 | Hungary 0 |
| February 21 | Great Britain 11 | Poland 0 |
| February 22 | Switzerland 4 | Hungary 2 |
| February 23 | Great Britain 5 | Hungary 0 |
| February 23 | Switzerland 1 | Poland 0 |

**5-8 PLACEMENT GROUP**

| | GP | W | T | L | GF | GA | P |
|---|---|---|---|---|---|---|---|
| Hungary | 3 | 2 | 1 | 0 | 10 | 1 | 5 |
| Czechoslovakia | 3 | 2 | 1 | 0 | 4 | 1 | 5 |
| France | 3 | 1 | 0 | 2 | 7 | 8 | 2 |
| Poland | 3 | 0 | 0 | 3 | 0 | 11 | 0 |

| | | |
|---|---|---|
| February 25 | Czechoslovakia 1 | Poland 0 |
| February 25 | Hungary 5 | France 1 |
| February 26 | Czechoslovakia 3 | France 1 |
| February 26 | Hungary 5 | Poland 0 (forfeit) |
| February 27 | Hungary 0 | Czechoslovakia 0 |
| February 27 | France 5 | Poland 0 (forfeit) |

**FINALS GROUP**

| | GP | W | T | L | GF | GA | P |
|---|---|---|---|---|---|---|---|
| Canada | 3 | 3 | 0 | 0 | 10 | 1 | 6 |
| Great Britain | 3 | 2 | 0 | 1 | 7 | 3 | 4 |
| Switzerland | 3 | 1 | 0 | 2 | 7 | 4 | 2 |
| Germany | 3 | 0 | 0 | 3 | 0 | 16 | 0 |

| | | |
|---|---|---|
| February 25 | Canada 5 | Germany 0 |
| February 25 | Great Britain 2 | Switzerland 0 (Chirp Brenchley & Gerry Davey 20:00 OT) |
| February 26 | Canada 3 | Great Britain 0 |
| February 26 | Switzerland 6 | Germany 0 |
| February 27 | Canada 2 | Switzerland 1 (George Goble OT) |
| February 27 | Great Britain 5 | Germany 0 |

**Rosters**

**Canada** (Kimberley Dynamiters—John Achtzener, coach) GK—Ken Campbell—Fred Botterill, Fred Burnett, George Goble, Doug Keiver, James Kemp, Paul Kozak, Ralph Redding, Harry Robertson, George Wilson, Thomas Almack

**Czechoslovakia** GK—Bohumil Modry, Antonin Houba—Jan Kosek, Jan Michalek, Vilibald Stovik, Oldrich Kucera, Josef Malecek, Ladislav Trojak, Jaroslav Cisar, Alois Cetkovsky, Frantisek Pergl, Drahos Jirotka, Zdenek Jirotka, Frantisek Pacalt

**France** GK—Michel Paccard, Gerard Lambert—Pierre Lorin, Jacques Lacarriere, Pierre Claret, Martin Payot, Albert Hassler, Paul Revoyaz, Philippe Boyard, Miguel de Mezieres, Roger Ete, Serge Renaud, Charles Bertrand, Marcel Couttet

**Germany** (Bobby Bell, coach) GK—Wilhelm Egginger, Theo Kaufmann—Rolf Haffner, Horst Orbanowski, Rudi Ball, Philipp Schenk, Hans Lang, Karl Kogel, Herbert Schibukat, Gunther Kelch, Walter Schmiedinger, Karl Wild, Gustav Jaenecke, Roman Kessler

**Great Britain** (Percy Nicklin, coach) GK—Jimmy Foster, Ronnie Milne—Gordon Dailley, Carl Erhardt, Paul McPhail, Jimmy Anderson, Alex Archer, Archie Stinchcombe, Gerry Davey, Edgar "Chirp" Brenchley, Jimmy Chappell, Jimmy Kelly, Norm McQuade, Johnny Coward

**Hungary** (Geza Lator, coach) GK—Istvan Hirscak, Mihaly Apor—Laszlo Rona, Miklos Barcza, Pal Bekesi, Sandor Miklos, Andras Gergely, Laszlo Gergely, Bela Haray, Ferenc Szamosi, Zoltan Jeney, Robert Lonyai, Gyorgy Margo, Sandor Minder

**Norway** (Ivar Lytkis, coach) GK—Karl Agheim Andersen, Ernst Henriksen—Johan Narvestad, Hans Jensen, Eugen Martinsen, Kolbjorn Fjeldstad, Bjarne By, Eugen Skalleberg, Gustav Edvardsen, Tryggve Holten, Per Dahl, Ole Brodahl, Knut Bogh, Carsten Cristiansen, Sverre Kristiansen

**Poland** (Tadeusz Sachs, coach) GK—Jozef Stogowski, Henryk Przedziecki—Kazimierz Sokolowski, Witalis Ludwiczak, Zbigniew Kasprzak, Andrzej Wolkowski, Adam Kowalski, Czeslaw Marchewczyk, Roman Stupnicki, Mieczyslaw Kasprzycki, Mieczyslaw Burda, Rajmund Przedpelski, Jozef Kulig, Edward Zielinski

**Romania** (Frank Quinn, coach) GK—Emil Maesciuc, Pal Sprencz—Paul Anastasiu, Gheorghe Buia, Ladislau Engster, Robert Sadowsky, Antonin Panenka, Wilhelm Suc, Ludovic Vacar, Alexandru Botez, Eduard Pana, Laszlo Biro, Jules Radian, Constantin Cantacuzino, Ion Petrovici

**Sweden** (Carl Abrahamsson, coach) GK—Bengt Liedstrand, Kurt Svanberg—Axel Nilsson, Bertil Lundell, Erik Persson, Olle Andersson, Bertil Norberg, Ruben Carlsson, Holger Engberg, Ake Ericson, Yngve Liljeberg, Wilhelm Petersen

**Switzerland** (Ulrich von Sury, coach) GK—Arnold Hirtz, Albert Kunzler—Albert Geromini, Franz Geromini, Hirsch Badrutt, Ferdinand "Pic" Cattini, Hans Cattini, Herbert Kessler, Charles Kessler, Heini Lohrer, Richard "Bibi" Torriani, Beat Ruedi, Max Keller, Jurg Bachtold

## 12th WORLD CHAMPIONSHIP (MEN)
### February 11-20, 1938
### Prague, Czechoslovakia

**Final Placing**

Gold ........Canada
Silver ......Great Britain
Bronze ....Czechoslovakia
4th..........Germany
5th..........Sweden
6th .........Switzerland
7th .........Hungary, Poland, United States
10th .......Austria, Latvia, Lithuania
13th .......Norway, Romania

**Tournament Format**

Fourteen teams were divided into three groups, playing a round robin within each. The top three teams from each group advanced to a semi-finals round robin in which the nine teams were divided into three groups of three teams each. The top team from each advanced to a semi-finals elimination, the fourth team coming from second place in Group C.

**Results & Standings**

**GROUP A**

| | GP | W | T | L | GF | GA | P |
|---|---|---|---|---|---|---|---|
| Switzerland | 4 | 4 | 0 | 0 | 31 | 2 | 8 |
| Poland | 4 | 3 | 0 | 1 | 15 | 8 | 6 |
| Hungary | 4 | 2 | 0 | 2 | 13 | 6 | 4 |
| Lithuania | 4 | 1 | 0 | 3 | 3 | 33 | 2 |
| Romania | 4 | 0 | 0 | 4 | 2 | 15 | 0 |

| | | |
|---|---|---|
| February 11 | Switzerland 1 | Hungary 0 |
| February 11 | Lithuania 1 | Romania 0 |
| February 12 | Switzerland 8 | Romania 1 |
| February 12 | Poland 8 | Lithuania 1 |
| February 13 | Poland 3 | Romania 0 |
| February 13 | Hungary 10 | Lithuania 1 |
| February 14 | Switzerland 15 | Lithuania 0 |
| February 14 | Poland 3 | Hungary 0 |
| February 15 | Hungary 3 | Romania 1 |
| February 15 | Switzerland 7 | Poland 1 |

**GROUP B**

| | GP | W | T | L | GF | GA | P |
|---|---|---|---|---|---|---|---|
| Great Britain | 4 | 3 | 1 | 0 | 15 | 2 | 7 |
| United States | 4 | 3 | 1 | 0 | 10 | 2 | 7 |
| Germany | 4 | 2 | 0 | 2 | 9 | 2 | 4 |
| Latvia | 4 | 1 | 0 | 3 | 4 | 8 | 2 |
| Norway | 4 | 0 | 0 | 4 | 2 | 26 | 0 |

| | | |
|---|---|---|
| February 11 | Great Britain 1 | Germany 0 |
| February 11 | Latvia 3 | Norway 1 |
| February 12 | United States 1 | Latvia 0 |
| February 12 | Great Britain 8 | Norway 0 |
| February 13 | United States 7 | Norway 1 |
| February 13 | Germany 1 | Latvia 0 |
| February 14 | Great Britain 5 | Latvia 1 |
| February 14 | United States 1 | Germany 0 |
| February 15 | Great Britain 1 | United States 1 |
| February 15 | Germany 8 | Norway 0 |

**GROUP C**

| | GP | W | T | L | GF | GA | P |
|---|---|---|---|---|---|---|---|
| Canada | 3 | 3 | 0 | 0 | 9 | 2 | 6 |
| Czechoslovakia | 3 | 1 | 1 | 1 | 1 | 3 | 3 |
| Sweden | 3 | 0 | 2 | 1 | 3 | 4 | 2 |
| Austria | 3 | 0 | 1 | 2 | 1 | 5 | 1 |

| | | |
|---|---|---|
| February 12 | Canada 3 | Sweden 2 |
| February 12 | Czechoslovakia 1 | Austria 0 |
| February 13 | Sweden 0 | Czechoslovakia 0 (30:00 OT) |
| February 13 | Canada 3 | Austria 0 |
| February 15 | Canada 3 | Czechoslovakia 0 |
| February 15 | Austria 1 | Sweden 1 |

**SEMI-FINALS GROUP A**

| | GP | W | T | L | GF | GA | P |
|---|---|---|---|---|---|---|---|
| Great Britain | 2 | 2 | 0 | 0 | 10 | 3 | 4 |
| Sweden | 2 | 1 | 0 | 1 | 3 | 3 | 2 |
| Poland | 2 | 0 | 0 | 2 | 1 | 8 | 0 |

| | | |
|---|---|---|
| February 16 | Sweden 1 | Poland 0 |
| February 17 | Great Britain 3 | Sweden 2 |
| February 18 | Great Britain 7 | Poland 1 |

**SEMI-FINALS GROUP B**

| | GP | W | T | L | GF | GA | P |
|---|---|---|---|---|---|---|---|
| Czechoslovakia | 2 | 2 | 0 | 0 | 5 | 2 | 4 |
| Switzerland | 2 | 1 | 0 | 1 | 3 | 3 | 2 |
| United States | 2 | 0 | 0 | 2 | 0 | 3 | 0 |

| | | |
|---|---|---|
| February 16 | Czechoslovakia 2 | United States 0 |
| February 17 | Switzerland 1 | United States 0 |
| February 18 | Czechoslovakia 3 | Switzerland 2 (20:00 OT—Ladislav Trojak) |

**SEMI-FINALS GROUP C**

| | GP | W | T | L | GF | GA | P |
|---|---|---|---|---|---|---|---|
| Canada | 2 | 1 | 1 | 0 | 4 | 3 | 3 |
| Germany | 2 | 1 | 0 | 1 | 3 | 3 | 2 |
| Hungary | 2 | 0 | 1 | 1 | 1 | 2 | 1 |

| | | |
|---|---|---|
| February 16 | Canada 3 | Germany 2 (OT—Johnny Godfrey) |
| February 17 | Germany 1 | Hungary 0 |
| February 18 | Canada 1 | Hungary 1 |

**5TH-PLACE GAME**

| | | |
|---|---|---|
| February 18 | Sweden 2 | Switzerland 0 |

**SEMI-FINALS**

| | | |
|---|---|---|
| February 19 | Canada 1 | Germany 0 |
| February 19 | Great Britain 1 | Czechoslovakia 0 |

**BRONZE MEDAL GAME**

| | | |
|---|---|---|
| February 20 | Czechoslovakia 3 | Germany 0 |

**GOLD MEDAL GAME**

| | | |
|---|---|---|
| February 20 | Canada 3 | Great Britain 1 |

**Rosters**

**Austria** (Hans Weinberger, coach) GK—Josef Wurm, Robert Nusser—Franz Csongei, Rudolf Vojta, Karl Kirchberger, Oskar Nowak, Friedrich Demmer, Max Schneider, Hans Stertin, Hans Tatzer, Franz Zehetmeyer, Walter Feistritzer

**Canada** (Sudbury Wolves—Max Silverman, coach) GK—John Coulter, Mel Albright—Percy Allen, Gordie Bruce, Reg Chipman, Johnny Godfrey, Roy Heximer, Jack Marshall, Pat McReavy, Buster Portland, Jimmy Russell, Glen Sutherland

**Czechoslovakia** (Mike Buckna, coach) GK—Bohumil Modry, Antonin Houba—Jan Michalek, Oldrich Kucera, Josef Malecek, Frantisek Pergl, Ladislav Trojak, Zdenek Jirotka, Drahos Jirotka, Jaroslav Cisar, Alois Cetkovsky, Frantisek Pacalt, Jaroslav Pusbauer, Jan Kosek

**Germany** (Bobby Bell, coach) GK—Wilhelm Egginger, Alfred Hoffmann—Gustav Jaenecke, Rudi Ball, Philipp Schenk, Hans Lang, Herbert Schibukat, Roman Kessler, Walter Schmiedinger, Karl Wild, Rudolf Tobien, Georg Strobl, Ludwig Kuhn, Anton Wiedemann

**Great Britain** (Percy Nicklin, coach) GK—Jimmy Foster, Reg Merrifield—Gordon Dailley, Alex Archer, Archie Stinchcombe, Jimmy Kelly, Gerry Davey, Jimmy Chappell, Ronnie Wilson, Pete Woozley, Bob Wyman, Pete Halford, Art Ridley

**Hungary** (Frank Stapleford/Geza Lator, coaches) GK—Istvan Hircsak, Laszlo Gati-Grozdics—Laszlo Rona, Pal Bekesi, Zoltan Jeney, Gyorgy Margo, Ferenc Szamosi, Bela Haray, Sandor Miklos, Miklos Barcza, Istvan Hubay-Hruby, Bela Erdodi, Jeno Palfalvi, Frigyes Helmeczy

**Latvia** GK—Roberts Lapainis, Herberts Kuskis—Leonids Vedejs, Karlis Paegle, Arvids Petersons, Adolfs Petrovskis, Edgars Klavs, Karlis Zilpauss, Ludvigs Putnins, Roberts Blukis, Aleksejs Auzins

**Lithuania** GK—A Macius, — Gudaitis—Antanas Kuzmickas, Bronius Kuzmickas, Juozas Klimas, Vytautas Ilgunas, Juozas Grigalauskas, E Bacinskas, — Jocius, Vladas Karalius, Vladas Matulevicius, A Hofmanas, V Dornas

**Norway** GK—Ernst Henriksen, Hans Fjeld—Hans Jensen, Johan Narvestad, Rudolf Eisenhardt, Jonny Larsen, Per Dahl, Knut Bogh, Kaare Hansen, Eugen Skalleberg, Per Linnes, Ottar Buran

**Poland** (Przemyslaw Warminski, coach) GK—Jozef Stogowski, Kazimierz Tarlowski—Zbigniew Kasprzak, Witalis Ludwiczak, Andrzej Wolkowski, Czeslaw Marchewczyk, Mieczyslaw Burda, Adam Kowalski, Rajmund Przedpelski, Edward Zielinski, Wladyslaw Krol, Alfred Andrzejewski, Wladyslaw Michalik, Herbert Urson

**Romania** GK—Gheorghe Flueras, Emil Maesciuc—Paul Anastasiu, Robert Sadowsky, Laszlo Biro, Antonin Panenka, Alexandru Botez, Wilhelm Suc, Alexandru Hugaru, Constantin Tico, Radu Tanase, Alexandru Teodorescu, Stefan Tomovici

**Sweden** (Viking Harbom, coach) GK—Arne Johansson, Kurt Svanberg—Sven Bergqvist, Axel Nilsson, Holger Engberg, Olle Andersson, Stig Andersson, Ake Andersson, Ake Ericson, Karl Forsstrom, Lennart Hellman, Folke Jansson, Ragnar Johansson

**Switzerland** (Ulrich von Sury, coach) GK—Arnold Hirtz, Albert Kunzler—Ferdinand "Pic" Cattini, Franz Geromini, Albert Geromini, Richard "Bibi" Torriani, Hans Cattini, Charlie Kessler, Heini Lohrer, Herbert Kessler, Hirsch Badrutt, Otto Heller

**United States** (John Hutchinson, coach) GK—Gerry Cosby—Allan Van, Spencer Wagnild, Art Bogue, George Quirk, Larry Charest, Ralph Dondi, Hugh Young, Ray Lemieux, John Hutchinson

## 13th WORLD CHAMPIONSHIP (MEN)
## February 3-12, 1939
## Basel/Zurich, Switzerland

**Final Placing**

| | |
|---|---|
| Gold........Canada | 7th.........Hungary |
| Silver......United States | 8th.........Great Britain |
| Bronze....Switzerland | 9th.........Italy |
| 4th..........Czechoslovakia | 10th.......Latvia |
| 5th..........Germany | 11th.......Belgium, Netherlands |
| 6th..........Poland | 13th.......Finland, Yugoslavia |

**Tournament Format**

The 14 teams were divided into four groups of either three teams or four. The top two teams from each group advanced to a semi-finals series of two groups of four teams each, again playing a round robin series. The top two teams from each of these groups advanced to a finals grouping of round robin play, the top three teams winning gold, silver, and bronze, while the bottom two from each were placed in another round robin group to play for placement.

**Results & Standings**

**GROUP A (BASEL)**

| | GP | W | T | L | GF | GA | P |
|---|---|---|---|---|---|---|---|
| United States | 3 | 3 | 0 | 0 | 13 | 0 | 6 |
| Germany | 3 | 1 | 1 | 1 | 12 | 5 | 3 |
| Italy | 3 | 1 | 1 | 1 | 5 | 7 | 3 |
| Finland | 3 | 0 | 0 | 3 | 3 | 21 | 0 |

| | | |
|---|---|---|
| February 3 | Germany 12 | Finland 1 |
| February 3 | United States 5 | Italy 0 |
| February 4 | Italy 5 | Finland 2 |
| February 4 | United States 4 | Germany 0 |
| February 5 | Germany 4 | Italy 4 (30:00 OT)* |
| February 5 | United States 4 | Finland 0 |
| February 6 | Germany 0 | Italy 0* |

*after a tie in the first game which went to three overtime periods, these teams played again the next night, also to a tie. A coin toss resulted in Germany being placed ahead of Italy in the standings and advancing to the semi-finals.

**GROUP B (ZURICH)**

| | GP | W | T | L | GF | GA | P |
|---|---|---|---|---|---|---|---|
| Switzerland | 3 | 3 | 0 | 0 | 36 | 0 | 6 |
| Czechoslovakia | 3 | 2 | 0 | 1 | 33 | 1 | 4 |
| Latvia | 3 | 1 | 0 | 2 | 6 | 21 | 2 |
| Yugoslavia | 3 | 0 | 0 | 3 | 0 | 53 | 0 |

| | | |
|---|---|---|
| February 3 | Czechoslovakia 24 | Yugoslavia 0 |
| February 3 | Switzerland 12 | Latvia 0 |
| February 4 | Switzerland 23 | Yugoslavia 0 |
| February 4 | Czechoslovakia 9 | Latvia 0 |
| February 5 | Latvia 6 | Yugoslavia 0 |
| February 5 | Switzerland 1 | Czechoslovakia 0 |

**GROUP C (BASEL)**

| | GP | W | T | L | GF | GA | P |
|---|---|---|---|---|---|---|---|
| Canada | 2 | 2 | 0 | 0 | 12 | 0 | 4 |
| Poland | 2 | 1 | 0 | 1 | 9 | 4 | 2 |
| Netherlands | 2 | 0 | 0 | 2 | 0 | 17 | 0 |

| | | |
|---|---|---|
| February 3 | Canada 8 | Netherlands 0 |
| February 4 | Poland 9 | Netherlands 0 |
| February 5 | Canada 4 | Poland 0 |

**GROUP D (ZURICH)**

| | GP | W | T | L | GF | GA | P |
|---|---|---|---|---|---|---|---|
| Great Britain | 2 | 2 | 0 | 0 | 4 | 1 | 4 |
| Hungary | 2 | 1 | 0 | 1 | 8 | 2 | 2 |
| Belgium | 2 | 0 | 0 | 2 | 2 | 11 | 0 |

| | | |
|---|---|---|
| February 3 | Hungary 8 | Belgium 1 |
| February 4 | Great Britain 3 | Belgium 1 |
| February 5 | Great Britain 1 | Hungary 0 |

**SEMI-FINALS (ZURICH)**

| | GP | W | T | L | GF | GA | P |
|---|---|---|---|---|---|---|---|
| Canada | 3 | 3 | 0 | 0 | 15 | 1 | 6 |
| Czechoslovakia | 3 | 1 | 1 | 1 | 4 | 3 | 3 |
| Germany | 3 | 1 | 1 | 1 | 2 | 10 | 3 |
| Great Britain | 3 | 0 | 0 | 3 | 0 | 7 | 0 |

| | | |
|---|---|---|
| February 7 | Germany 1 | Czechoslovakia 1 (30:00 OT—no scoring) |
| February 7 | Canada 4 | Great Britain 0 |
| February 8 | Canada 2 | Czechoslovakia 1 |
| February 8 | Germany 1 | Great Britain 0 |
| February 9 | Canada 9 | Germany 0 |
| February 9 | Czechoslovakia 2 | Great Britain 0 |

**SEMI-FINALS (BASEL)**

| | GP | W | T | L | GF | GA | P |
|---|---|---|---|---|---|---|---|
| Switzerland | 3 | 3 | 0 | 0 | 12 | 4 | 6 |
| United States | 3 | 2 | 0 | 1 | 9 | 3 | 4 |
| Poland | 3 | 1 | 0 | 2 | 5 | 11 | 2 |
| Hungary | 3 | 0 | 0 | 3 | 5 | 13 | 0 |

| | | |
|---|---|---|
| February 7 | United States 3 | Hungary 0 |
| February 7 | Switzerland 4 | Poland 0 |
| February 8 | Poland 5 | Hungary 3 |

| | | |
|---|---|---|
| February 8 | Switzerland 3 | United States 2 |
| February 9 | United States 4 | Poland 0 |
| February 9 | Switzerland 5 | Hungary 2 |

**5-9 PLACEMENT GROUP**

| | GP | W | T | L | GF | GA | P |
|---|---|---|---|---|---|---|---|
| Germany | 2 | 2 | 0 | 0 | 10 | 2 | 4 |
| Poland | 2 | 1 | 0 | 1 | 3 | 4 | 2 |
| Hungary | 2 | 0 | 0 | 2 | 2 | 9 | 0 |
| Great Britain | withdrew | | | | | | |

| | | | |
|---|---|---|---|
| February 10 | Basel | Poland 3 | Hungary 0 |
| February 11 | Zurich | Germany 6 | Hungary 2 |
| February 12 | Basel | Germany 4 | Poland 0 |

**9-14 PLACEMENT GROUP A (BASEL)**

| | GP | W | T | L | GF | GA | P |
|---|---|---|---|---|---|---|---|
| Italy | 2 | 2 | 0 | 0 | 4 | 2 | 4 |
| Netherlands | 2 | 1 | 0 | 1 | 3 | 3 | 2 |
| Finland | 2 | 0 | 0 | 2 | 2 | 4 | 0 |

| | | |
|---|---|---|
| February 6 | Netherlands 2 | Finland 1 |
| February 7 | Italy 2 | Netherlands 1 |
| February 8 | Italy 2 | Finland 1 |

**9-14 PLACEMENT GROUP B (ZURICH)**

| | GP | W | T | L | GF | GA | P |
|---|---|---|---|---|---|---|---|
| Latvia | 2 | 2 | 0 | 0 | 9 | 1 | 4 |
| Belgium | 2 | 0 | 1 | 1 | 4 | 8 | 1 |
| Yugoslavia | 2 | 0 | 1 | 1 | 3 | 7 | 1 |

| | | |
|---|---|---|
| February 6 | Latvia 5 | Belgium 1 |
| February 7 | Belgium 3 | Yugoslavia 3 |
| February 8 | Latvia 4 | Yugoslavia 0 |

**9TH-PLACE GAME**

February 9 Basel Italy 2 Latvia 1

**FINALS GROUP**

| | GP | W | T | L | GF | GA | P |
|---|---|---|---|---|---|---|---|
| Canada | 3 | 3 | 0 | 0 | 15 | 0 | 6 |
| United States | 3 | 2 | 0 | 1 | 3 | 5 | 4 |
| Switzerland | 3 | 0 | 1 | 2 | 1 | 9 | 1 |
| Czechoslovakia | 3 | 0 | 1 | 2 | 0 | 5 | 1 |

| | | | |
|---|---|---|---|
| February 10 | Basel | Canada 7 | Switzerland 0 |
| February 10 | Zurich | United States 1 | Czechoslovakia 0 |
| | | (20:00 OT—George Quirk) | |
| February 11 | Basel | Canada 4 | Czechoslovakia 0 |
| February 11 | Zurich | United States 2 | Switzerland 1 |
| February 12 | Basel | Canada 4 | United States 0 |
| February 12 | Zurich | Switzerland 0 | Czechoslovakia 0 (30:00 OT) |

**BRONZE MEDAL/EUROPEAN CHAMPIONS GAME**

March 5 Basel Switzerland 2 Czechoslovakia 0

**Rosters**

**Belgium** (Paul De Weerdt, coach) GK—Henri Heirman, Rene Boulanger—Roger Bureau, Fernand Carez, Jef Lekens, Andre Leempoels, Pierre van Reysschoot, Georges Pootmans, Leon van Eeckhout, Jimmy Graeffe, Johny Hartog, Percy Lippit, Paul Van den Busche, Rene Lamode

**Canada** (Trail Smoke Eaters—Elmer Piper, coach) GK—Duke Scodellaro, Buck Buchanan—Joe Benoit, Mickey Brennan, Ab Cronie, Bunny Dame, Jim Haight, Benny Hayes, Tom Johnston, Dick Kowcinak, John McCreedy, Jim Morris, Mel Snowden

**Czechoslovakia** (Mike Buckna, coach) GK—Bohumil Modry, Jiri Hertl—Frantisek Pacalt, Ladislav Trojak, Josef Malecek, Oldrich Kucera, Jaroslav Cisar, Frantisek Pergl, Viktor Lonsmin, Jan Michalik, Alois Cetkovsky, Oldrich Hurych, Jaroslav Drobny, Vilibald Stovik, Josef Trousilek

**Finland** (Erkki Saarinen, coach) GK—Lars Blom, Teuvo Castren—Kalevi Sutinen, Seppo Jaakkola, Erik Hedman, Henry Lindahl, Edmund Sjoberg, Olof Nyholm, Holger Granstrom, Pentti Lappalainen, Kalevi Ihalainen, Romeo Mikalunas, Erkki Rintala, Risto Tiitola, Klaus Hagstrom

**Germany** (Bobby Bell, coach) GK—Wilhelm Egginger, Alfred Hoffmann—Rudolf Tobien, Gustav Jaenecke, Karl Wild, Franz Csongei, Walter Feistritzer, Oscar Nowak, Friedrich Demmer, Ludwig Kuhn, Walter Schmiedinger, Philipp Schenk, Karl Kogel, Gunther Kelch, Herbert Schibukat

**Great Britain** (Percy Nicklin, coach) GK—Jimmy Foster, Stan Simon—Bob Wyman, Gordon Dailley, Joe Collins, Jimmy Kelly, Tommy McInroy, Billy Fullerton, Pete Halford, Pip Perrin, Art Ridley, Tommy Grace, Art Green

**Hungary** (Edward Trottier, coach) GK—Istvan Hircsak, Laszlo Gati-Grozdics—Pal Bekesi, Jeno Palfalvi, Miklos Barcza, Zoltan Jeney, Sandor Miklos, Laszlo Rona, Frigyes Helmeczy, Bela Haray, Bela Gosztonyi, Ferenc Szamosi, Andras Gergely, Gyorgy Margo

**Italy** GK—Augusto Gerosa, Roberto Gandini—Tino de Mazzeri, Franco Rossi, Franco Carlassare, Antonio Prete, Ignazio Dionisi, Otto Rauth, Dino Innocenti, Ontario Venturi, Leo Gasparini, Egidio Bruciamonti, Egidio D'Appollonio, Giorgio Pellegrini, Luigi Venosta

**Latvia** (Larry March, coach) GK—Herberts Kuskis, Roberts Lapainis—Leonids Vedejs, Karlis Paegle, Roberts Blukis, Ludvigs Putnins, Arvids Petersons, Edgars Klavs, Karlis Zilpauss, Karlis Muske, Eriks Koneckis, Harijs Vitolins

**Netherlands** GK—Jan Gerritsen, Joost van Os—Henk Taconis, Ko Klotz, Rein Everwijn, Felix de Jong, Huib du Pon, Martin Lammers, Thijs Cohen-Tervaert, Jan Suurbeek, Dick Benjamins, Hans Smalhout, Hans Gerritsen

**Poland** (Zenon Paruszewski, coach) GK—Jan Maciejko, Witold Muszinski—Wladyslaw Michalik, Mieczyslaw Kasprzycki, Czeslaw Marchewczyk, Andrzej Wolkowski, Adam Kowalski, Henryk Jarecki, Mieczyslaw Burda, Herbert Urson, Alfred Andrzejewski, Rajmund Przedpelski, Ryszard Werner, Zygmunt Czyzewski

**Switzerland** (Ulrich von Sury, coach) GK—Hugo Muller, Albert Kunzler—Franz Geromini, Hans Trauffer, Albert Geromini, Richard "Bibi" Torriani, Hans Cattini, Ferdinand "Pic" Cattini, Charlie Kessler, Herbert Kessler, Hirsch Badrutt, Reto Delnon, Rudolf Mathys, Heini Lohrer, Beat Ruedi

**United States** (John Hutchinson, coach) GK—Ed Maki—Allan Van, Spencer Wagnild, Thomas Leaky, George Quirk, Art Bogue, Leonard Saari, Ed Nicholson, Ralph Dondi, Richard Maley

**Yugoslavia** (Viktor Vodisek, coach) GK—Ivan Rihar—Tone Pogocnik, Ludvik Zitnik, Zvonko Stipetic, Otokar Gregoric, Karel Pavletic, Jule Kacic, Joze Gogola, Milan Lombar, Mirko Erzen, Miljan Popovic, Jovan Tomic

## 14th WORLD CHAMPIONSHIP (MEN)
## February 15-23, 1947
## Prague, Czechoslovakia

**Final Placing**

| | |
|---|---|
| Gold ........Czechoslovakia | 5th .........United States |
| Silver .......Sweden | 6th .........Poland |
| Bronze ....Austria | 7th .........Romania |
| 4th .........Switzerland | 8th .........Belgium |

**Tournament Format**

All eight teams played a single round robin, placings being determined by final standings in one group, the top three positions winning medals.

**Results & Standings**

| | GP | W | T | L | GF | GA | Pts |
|---|---|---|---|---|---|---|---|
| Czechoslovakia | 7 | 6 | 0 | 1 | 85 | 10 | 12 |
| Sweden | 7 | 5 | 1 | 1 | 55 | 15 | 11 |
| Austria | 7 | 5 | 0 | 2 | 49 | 32 | 10 |
| Switzerland | 7 | 4 | 1 | 2 | 47 | 22 | 9 |
| United States | 7 | 4 | 0 | 3 | 42 | 26 | 8 |
| Poland | 7 | 2 | 0 | 5 | 27 | 40 | 4 |
| Romania | 7 | 1 | 0 | 6 | 17 | 88 | 2 |
| Belgium | 7 | 0 | 0 | 7 | 15 | 104 | 0 |

| | | |
|---|---|---|
| February 15 | Austria 10 | Poland 2 |
| February 15 | Czechoslovakia 23 | Romania 1 |
| February 15 | Sweden 4 | Switzerland 4 |
| February 16 | Sweden 24 | Belgium 1 |
| February 16 | Poland 6 | Romania 0 |
| February 16 | United States 4 | Switzerland 3 |
| February 17 | Austria 14 | Belgium 5 |
| February 17 | Switzerland 13 | Romania 3 |
| February 17 | Sweden 4 | United States 1 |
| February 18 | Czechoslovakia 13 | Austria 5 |
| February 18 | United States 13 | Belgium 2 |
| February 18 | Sweden 5 | Poland 3 |
| February 18 | Austria 6 | United States 5 |
| February 19 | Sweden 15 | Romania 3 |
| February 19 | Czechoslovakia 12 | Poland 0 |
| February 19 | Switzerland 12 | Belgium 2 |
| February 20 | United States 15 | Romania 3 |
| February 20 | Poland 11 | Belgium 1 |
| February 20 | Czechoslovakia 6 | Switzerland 1 |
| February 21 | Austria 12 | Romania 1 |
| February 21 | United States 3 | Poland 2 |
| February 21 | Czechoslovakia 24 | Belgium 0 |
| February 22 | Romania 6 | Belgium 4 |
| February 22 | Switzerland 5 | Austria 0 |
| February 22 | Sweden 2 | Czechoslovakia 1 |
| February 23 | Switzerland 9 | Poland 3 |
| February 23 | Austria 2 | Sweden 1 |
| February 23 | Czechoslovakia 6 | United States 1 |

**Rosters**

**Austria** GK—Josef Wurm, Alfred Huber—Felix Egger, Franz Csongei, Egon Engel, Friedrich Demmer, Franz Zehetmeyer, Oskar Nowak , Walter Feistritzer, Johann Schneider, Fritz Walter, Rudolph Wurmbrand, Helfried Winger, Willibald Stanek, Gerhard Springer, Adolf Hafner

**Belgium** (Carlos Van den Driessche, coach) GK—Milo Jahn, Henri Heirman, Bob van der Heyden—Pierre van Reysschoot, Jef Lekens, Jacques Mullenders, Charel Laurencin, Johny Haneveer, Johny Hartog, Georges Hartmeyer, Hubert Anciaux, Raymond Lombard, Jules Dupre, Percy Lippit, Leon van Eeckhout, Bob van der Heyden

**Czechoslovakia** (Mike Buckna, coach) GK—Bohumil Modry, Zdenek Jarkovsky—Frantisek Pacalt, Miroslav Slama, Josef Trousilek, Vilibald Stovik, Ladislav Trojak, Vladimir Zabrodsky, Stanislav Konopasek, Josef Kus, Jaroslav Drobny, Karel Stibor, Miroslav Pokorny, Vaclav Rozinak, Miroslav Bouzek

**Poland** (Waclaw Kuchar, coach) GK—Henryk Makutynowicz, Jan Maciejko—Kazimierz Sokolowski, Mieczyslaw Kasprzycki, Henryk Bromer, Zygmunt Czyzewski, Tomasz Jasinski, Mieczyslaw Palus, Stefan Csorich, Andrzej Wolkowski, Hilary Skarzynski, Alfred Gansiniec, Ernest Ziaja, Tadeusz Dolewski, Boleslaw Kolasa

**Romania** GK—Dorin Dron, Gheorghe Flueiras—Paul Anastasiu, Robert Sadowski, Radu Tanase, Florin Popescu, Mihai Flamaropol, Hans Dlugos, Eduard Pana, Gabor Incze, Lajos Incze, Stefan Tomovici, Ion Racovica, Ferenc Fenke, Gaetan Amirovici, Antonin Panenka, Andrei Barbulescu, Dede Cosman

**Sweden** (Sten Ahner, coach) GK—Arne Johansson, Charles Larsson—Gunnar Landelius, Rune Johansson, Ake Olsson, Hans Hjelm, Rolf Pettersson, Ake Andersson, Holger Nurmela, Rolf Eriksson, Lars Ljungman, Bror Pettersson, Erik Johansson, Birger Nilsson, Sigge Bostrom

**Switzerland** (Richard "Bibi" Torriani, coach) GK—Hans Banninger, Reto Perl—Heinrich Boller, Alfred Lack, Emil Handschin, Otto Schubiger, Hans-Martin Trepp, Ulrich Poltera, Gebhart Poltera, Hugo Delnon, Othmar Delnon, Reto Delnon, Heinz Hinterkircher, Pons Verges

**United States** (Herb Ralby, coach) GK—John Meoli, Robert McCabe, Gus Galipeau, Norm Walker, Allan Van, Jim Fletcher, Bob Verrier, Hec Rousseau, Perley Grant, Gerry Kilmartin, Robert Heavern, Ed Cahoon, Ross McIntyre, Lowell Booten, Tom Dugan

## 16th WORLD CHAMPIONSHIP (MEN)
## February 12-20, 1949
## Stockholm, Sweden

(the IIHF considers the 1948 Olympics to be the 15th World Championship)

**Final Placing**

| | | | |
|---|---|---|---|
| Gold | Czechoslovakia | 6th | Austria |
| Silver | Canada | 7th | Finland |
| Bronze | United States | 8th | Norway |
| 4th | Sweden | 9th | Belgium |
| 5th | Switzerland | 10th | Denmark |

**Tournament Format**

Ten teams were divided into three pools, playing a round robin within each. The top two from each group advanced to a finals group of round robin play, the final standings from that pool determining final positions. The last four teams that did not qualify for this medals group played a round robin for placement.

**Results & Standings**

**GROUP A**

| | GP | W | T | L | GF | GA | P |
|---|---|---|---|---|---|---|---|
| Canada | 2 | 2 | 0 | 0 | 54 | 0 | 4 |
| Austria | 2 | 1 | 0 | 1 | 25 | 8 | 2 |
| Denmark | 2 | 0 | 0 | 2 | 1 | 72 | 0 |

| | | |
|---|---|---|
| February 12 | Canada 47 | Denmark 0 |
| February 13 | Canada 7 | Austria 0 |
| February 14 | Austria 25 | Denmark 1 |

**GROUP B**

| | GP | W | T | L | GF | GA | P |
|---|---|---|---|---|---|---|---|
| Sweden | 2 | 2 | 0 | 0 | 16 | 3 | 4 |
| Czechoslovakia | 2 | 1 | 0 | 1 | 21 | 6 | 2 |
| Finland | 2 | 0 | 0 | 2 | 3 | 31 | 0 |

| | | |
|---|---|---|
| February 12 | Sweden 12 | Finland 1 |
| February 13 | Sweden 4 | Czechoslovakia 2 |
| February 14 | Czechoslovakia 19 | Finland 2 |

**GROUP C**

| | GP | W | T | L | GF | GA | P |
|---|---|---|---|---|---|---|---|
| United States | 3 | 3 | 0 | 0 | 36 | 6 | 6 |
| Switzerland | 3 | 2 | 0 | 1 | 30 | 15 | 4 |
| Norway | 3 | 1 | 0 | 2 | 4 | 19 | 2 |
| Belgium | 3 | 0 | 0 | 3 | 2 | 32 | 0 |

| | | |
|---|---|---|
| February 12 | United States 12 | Switzerland 5 |
| February 12 | Norway 2 | Belgium 0 |
| February 13 | United States 12 | Norway 1 |
| February 13 | Switzerland 18 | Belgium 2 |
| February 14 | United States 12 | Belgium 0 |
| February 14 | Switzerland 7 | Norway 1 |

**7-10 PLACEMENT GROUP**

| | GP | W | T | L | GF | GA | P |
|---|---|---|---|---|---|---|---|
| Finland | 3 | 3 | 0 | 0 | 29 | 5 | 6 |
| Norway | 3 | 2 | 0 | 1 | 22 | 8 | 4 |
| Belgium | 3 | 1 | 0 | 2 | 11 | 34 | 2 |
| Denmark | 3 | 0 | 0 | 3 | 3 | 18 | 0 |

| | | |
|---|---|---|
| February 17 | Belgium 8 | Denmark 3 |
| February 17 | Finland 7 | Norway 3 |
| February 18 | Norway 5 | Denmark 0 (forfeit) |
| February 18 | Finland 17 | Belgium 2 |
| February 19 | Finland 5 | Denmark 0 (forfeit) |
| February 19 | Norway 14 | Belgium 1 |

**FINALS GROUP**

| | GP | W | T | L | GF | GA | P |
|---|---|---|---|---|---|---|---|
| Czechoslovakia | 5 | 4 | 0 | 1 | 21 | 6 | 8 |
| Canada | 5 | 2 | 2 | 1 | 20 | 10 | 6 |
| United States | 5 | 3 | 0 | 2 | 23 | 16 | 6 |
| Sweden | 5 | 2 | 1 | 2 | 26 | 12 | 5 |
| Switzerland | 5 | 2 | 1 | 2 | 18 | 17 | 5 |
| Austria | 5 | 0 | 0 | 5 | 5 | 52 | 0 |

| | | |
|---|---|---|
| February 15 | Czechoslovakia 3 | Canada 2 |
| February 15 | Switzerland 5 | United States 4 |
| February 15 | Sweden 18 | Austria 0 |
| February 16 | Canada 2 | Sweden 2 |
| February 16 | Czechoslovakia 7 | Austria 1 |
| February 17 | Canada 7 | United States 2 |
| February 17 | Sweden 3 | Switzerland 1 |
| February 18 | Canada 8 | Austria 2 |
| February 18 | United States 6 | Sweden 3 |
| February 18 | Czechoslovakia 8 | Switzerland 1 |
| February 19 | Switzerland 10 | Austria 1 |
| February 19 | United States 2 | Czechoslovakia 0 |
| February 20 | Canada 1 | Switzerland 1 |
| February 20 | Czechoslovakia 3 | Sweden 0 |
| February 20 | United States 9 | Austria 1 |

**Rosters**

**Austria** GK—Alfred Huber, Jorg Reichl—Rudolf Wurmbrand, Franz Potucek, Willibald Stanek, Friedrich Penitz, Fritz Walter, Hans Wagner, Hermann Springer, Rudolf Vojta, Albert Bohm, Friedrich Demmer, Wilhelm Schmid, Hans Schneider, Walter Feistritzer

**Belgium** (Gusty de Backer, coach) GK—Henri Heirman—Tony Delrez, Constant Delarge, Fernand Carez, Roland Dumont, Hubert Anciaux, Raymond Lombard, Leon van Eeckhout, Coco Berry, Jules Dupre, Louis Beck, Percy Lippit, Georges Hartmeyer, Jimmy Graeffe

**Canada** (Sudbury Wolves—Max Silverman, coach) GK—Al Picard, Bob Mills—Don Stanley, Emil Gagne, Herb Kewley, Joe Tergesen, Barney Hillson, Ray Bauer, Jim Russell, Don Munroe, John Kovich, Bill Dimoch, Bud Hashey, Joe de Bastiani, Tom Russell

**Czechoslovakia** (Antonin Vodicka, coach) GK—Bohumil Modry, Josef Jirka—Premysl Hajny, Oldrich Nemec, Jiri Vacovsky, Josef Trousilek, Stanislav Konopasek, Gustav Bubnik, Rudolf Macelis, Josef Mizera, Zdenek Picha, Vladimir Zabrodsky, Vaclav Rozinak, Miroslav Bouzek, Vladimir Kobranov, Miroslav Marek

**Denmark** GK—Flemming Jensen, Leif Jonsen—Borge Hamann, Svend Malver, Dan Danry, Jorgen Hviid, Erik Hviid, Knud Lebech, Erik Halberg, Frede Sorensen, Poul Nielsen, Ole Nielsen, Leif Ammentorp, Sven Christensen

**Finland** (Henry Kvist, coach) GK—Unto Wiitala, Juhani Linkosuo—Teuvo Hellen, Matti Rintakoski, Ossi Kauppi, Tuomo Pohjavirta, Eero Salisma, Keijo Kuusela, Matti Karumaa, Kalle Havulinna, Aarne Honkavaara, Lotfi Nasibullen, Rauni Laine, Nils Nummelin, Esko Tie, Paul Vainjarvi

**Norway** (Trygve Holter, coach) GK—Per Dahl, Arthur Kristiansen—Johnny Larntvedt, Bjorn Kristiansen, Kjell Hauger, Gunnar Kroge, Roar Pedersen, Ragnar Rygel, Bjorn Gulbrandsen, Odd Hansen, Oivind Solheim, Per Voigt, Roy Sorensen, Per Moe, Leif Solheim

**Sweden** (Sven Bergqvist, coach) GK—Arne Johansson, Kurt Svanberg—Ake Andersson, Rune Johansson, Sven Thunman, Ake Olsson, Ake Lassas, Bengt Larsson, Gosta Johansson, Holger Nurmela, Hans Oberg, Stig Carlsson, Erik Johansson, Ake Engqvist, Stig Jonsson, Rolf Eriksson

**Switzerland** (Richard "Bibi" Torriani, coach) GK—Hans Banninger, Reto Perl—Heinrich Boller, Heinz Hinterkircher, Hans Cattini, Ferdinand "Pic" Cattini, Emil Handschin, Hans-Martin Trepp, Ulrich Poltera, Gebhart Poltera, Freddy Bieler, Othmar Delnon, Reto Delnon, Hugo Delnon, Heini Lohrer, Ernst Harter, Otto Schubiger

**United States** (Jack Riley, coach) GK—Richard Bittner, Al Yurkewicz—Jack Riley, Bruce Mather, Gerry Kilmartin, Norm Walker, William Thayer, Allan Van, Dan Crowley, Pat Finnigan, Charles Holt, Arthur Crouse, Prince Johnson, Buzz Johnson, John Kelly

## 17th WORLD CHAMPIONSHIP (MEN)
## February 13-22, 1950
## London, Great Britain

**Final Placing**

Gold ........Canada
Silver ......United States
Bronze ....Switzerland
4th..........Great Britain
5th..........Sweden
6th .........Norway
7th .........Belgium
8th .........Netherlands
9th .........France

**Tournament Format**

Nine teams were divided into three pools, playing a round robin within each. The top two from each group advanced to a finals group of round robin play, the final standings from that pool determining final positions. The last three teams that did not qualify for this medals group played a round robin for placement.

**Results & Standings**

**GROUP A**

| | GP | W | T | L | GF | GA | P |
|---|---|---|---|---|---|---|---|
| Canada | 2 | 2 | 0 | 0 | 46 | 2 | 4 |
| Switzerland | 2 | 1 | 0 | 1 | 26 | 16 | 2 |
| Belgium | 2 | 0 | 0 | 2 | 3 | 57 | 0 |

| | | |
|---|---|---|
| March 13 | Switzerland 24 | Belgium 3 |
| March 14 | Canada 13 | Switzerland 2 |
| March 15 | Canada 33 | Belgium 0 |

**GROUP B**

| | GP | W | T | L | GF | GA | P |
|---|---|---|---|---|---|---|---|
| Sweden | 2 | 2 | 0 | 0 | 18 | 3 | 4 |
| United States | 2 | 1 | 0 | 1 | 20 | 9 | 2 |
| Netherlands | 2 | 0 | 0 | 2 | 1 | 27 | 0 |

| | | |
|---|---|---|
| March 13 | Sweden 8 | United States 3 |
| March 14 | Sweden 10 | Netherlands 0 |
| March 15 | United States 17 | Netherlands 1 |

**GROUP C**

| | GP | W | T | L | GF | GA | P |
|---|---|---|---|---|---|---|---|
| Great Britain | 2 | 2 | 0 | 0 | 11 | 0 | 4 |
| Norway | 2 | 1 | 0 | 1 | 11 | 2 | 2 |
| France | 2 | 0 | 0 | 2 | 0 | 20 | 0 |

| | | |
|---|---|---|
| March 14 | Great Britain 9 | France 0 |
| March 14 | Norway 11 | France 0 |
| March 15 | Great Britain 2 | Norway 0 |

**RELEGATION ROUND**

| | GP | W | T | L | GF | GA | P |
|---|---|---|---|---|---|---|---|
| Belgium | 2 | 2 | 0 | 0 | 11 | 3 | 4 |
| Netherlands | 2 | 1 | 0 | 1 | 6 | 6 | 2 |
| France | 2 | 0 | 0 | 2 | 3 | 11 | 0 |

| | | |
|---|---|---|
| March 20 | Belgium 7 | France 1 |
| March 21 | Netherlands 4 | France 2 |
| March 22 | Belgium 4 | Netherlands 2 |

**FINALS GROUP**

| | GP | W | T | L | GF | GA | P |
|---|---|---|---|---|---|---|---|
| Canada | 5 | 5 | 0 | 0 | 42 | 3 | 10 |
| United States | 5 | 4 | 0 | 1 | 29 | 20 | 8 |
| Switzerland | 5 | 3 | 0 | 2 | 31 | 30 | 6 |
| Great Britain | 5 | 2 | 0 | 3 | 14 | 32 | 4 |
| Sweden | 5 | 1 | 0 | 4 | 15 | 16 | 2 |
| Norway | 5 | 0 | 0 | 5 | 15 | 45 | 0 |

| | | |
|---|---|---|
| March 17 | United States 4 | Sweden 2 |
| March 17 | Great Britain 4 | Norway 3 |
| March 17 | Canada 11 | Switzerland 1 |
| March 18 | Canada 5 | United States 0 |
| March 18 | Switzerland 12 | Norway 4 |
| March 18 | Great Britain 5 | Sweden 4 |
| March 20 | Switzerland 3 | Sweden 2 |
| March 20 | Canada 11 | Norway 1 |
| March 20 | United States 3 | Great Britain 2 |
| March 21 | Sweden 6 | Norway 1 |
| March 21 | Canada 12 | Great Britain 0 |
| March 21 | United States 10 | Switzerland 5 |
| March 22 | United States 12 | Norway 6 |
| March 22 | Canada 3 | Sweden 1 |
| March 22 | Switzerland 10 | Great Britain 3 |

**Rosters**

**Belgium** (Jacques Contzen, coach) GK—Henri Heirman, Jacques Heylen—Percy Lippit, Roland Dumont, Jimmy Graeffe, Jef Lekens, Leon van Eeckhout, Robert Waldschmitt, Andre Elsen, Andre Waldschmitt, Albert Dupre, Gentil Noterman, Hubert Anciaux, Jacques Moris, Luc Verstrepen, Georges Hartmeyer

**Canada** (Edmonton Mercurys—Jimmy Graham, coach) GK—Jack Manson, Wilbur Delaney—Leo Lucchini, Hassie Young, Ab Newsome, Billy Dawe, Harry Allen, Doug Macauley, Don Stanley, Robert Watt, Marsh Darling, Al Purvis, Jack Davies, Jim Kilburn, Pete Wright, Don Gauf, Robert David

**France** (Louis Bourdereau, coach) GK—Rolland Willaume, Bruno Ranzoni—Hubert Nivet, Jean Lacorne, Pierre Luis, Serge Renault, Jean Pepin, Jacques Heylliard, Claude Risler, Michel Le Bas, Guy Volpert, Francois Charlet, Marcel Claret, Jacques de Mezieres, Marcel Carrier, Michel Mrozek, Andre Longuet

**Great Britain** (Lou Bates, coach) GK—Harold Smith, Stan Christie—Tom "Tuck" Syme, Tiny Syme, Bill Sneddon, Lawson Neil , Ray Hammond, Ken Nicholson, John Quales, Bert Smith, Ian Forbes, Johnny Carlyle, John Rolland, John Murray, Roy Harnett, Pete Ravenscroft, Dave McCrae

**Netherlands** (Andy Andreola, coach) GK—Jan van der Heyden, Joost van Os—Kappie Taconis, Arie Klein, Frans Vaal, Jacques Feenstra, J. Rhede van der Kloot, Piet Bierensbroodspot, Dolf Overakker, Piet van Heeswijk, Rijk Loek, Cor Schwencke, Dick Groenteman, Nico Kremers, Alfons de Laat, Theo Dietz, Rolf van der Baumen, Jan Dinger

**Norway** (Johan Narvestad, coach) GK—Per Dahl, Lorang Wifladt—Johnny Larntvedt, Carl Rasmussen, Gunnar Kroge, Odd Hansen, Annar Pettersen, Bjorn Gulbrandsen, Ragnar Rygel, Roar Pedersen, Per Voigt, Oivind Solheim, Leif Solheim, Per Moe, Per-Erik Adolfsen, Ragnar Edvardsen

**Sweden** (Frank Trottier, coach) GK—Arne Johansson, Lars Svensson—Ake Andersson, Rune Johansson, Sven Thunman, Borje Lofgren, Ake Lassas, Gosta Johansson, Holger Nurmela, Rolf Pettersson, Stig Carlsson, Gote Blomqvist, Erik Johansson, Hans Oberg, Stig Jonsson, Hans Adrian, Rolf Eriksson

**Switzerland** (Richard "Bibi" Torriani, coach) GK—Hans Banninger, Martin Riesen—Hanggi Boller, Othmar Delnon, Hans Heierling, Milo Golaz, Silvio Rossi, Hans Trepp, Ulrich Poltera, Willi Pfister, Fredy Bieler, Walter Durst, Reto Delnon, Fredy Streun, Gebhart Poltera, Emil Handschin, Ernst Harter

**United States** (John Pleban, coach) GK—Dick Desmond, Bernie Burke—Al Van, Bob Frick, John Gallagher, Bob Graiziger, Jim Pleban, Jim Troumbly, Buzz Johnson, Prince Johnson, Bruce Gardner, John McIntyre, Bob Rompre, Sam Poling

## 18th WORLD CHAMPIONSHIP (MEN)
## March 9-17, 1951
## Paris, France

**Final Placing**

Gold ........Canada
Silver .....Sweden
Bronze ....Switzerland
4th..........Norway
5th .........Great Britain
6th .........United States
7th .........Finland

**Tournament Format**

A round robin format was used, each of the seven teams playing once against all other nations, the top three placings winning gold, silver, and bronze.

**Results & Standings**

| | GP | W | T | L | GF | GA | P |
|---|---|---|---|---|---|---|---|
| Canada | 6 | 6 | 0 | 0 | 62 | 6 | 12 |
| Sweden | 6 | 4 | 1 | 1 | 33 | 14 | 9 |
| Switzerland | 6 | 4 | 1 | 1 | 28 | 12 | 9 |
| Norway | 6 | 2 | 0 | 4 | 10 | 27 | 4 |
| Great Britain | 6 | 1 | 1 | 4 | 18 | 42 | 3 |
| United States | 6 | 1 | 1 | 4 | 14 | 42 | 3 |
| Finland | 6 | 1 | 0 | 5 | 15 | 37 | 2 |

| | | |
|---|---|---|
| March 9 | Norway 3 | United States 0 |
| March 10 | Sweden 5 | Great Britain 1 |
| March 10 | Switzerland 8 | Norway 1 |
| March 10 | Canada 11 | Finland 1 |
| March 11 | Canada 8 | Norway 0 |
| March 11 | Sweden 8 | United States 0 |
| March 12 | United States 5 | Finland 4 |
| March 12 | Switzerland 7 | Great Britain 1 |
| March 13 | Sweden 5 | Norway 2 |
| March 13 | Switzerland 4 | Finland 1 |
| March 13 | Canada 17 | Great Britain 1 |
| March 14 | Switzerland 3 | Sweden 3 |
| March 15 | Norway 4 | Great Britain 3 |
| March 15 | Sweden 11 | Finland 3 |
| March 15 | Canada 16 | United States 2 |
| March 16 | Finland 3 | Norway 0 |

| | | |
|---|---|---|
| March 16 | Great Britain 6 | United States 6 |
| March 16 | Canada 5 | Switzerland 1 |
| March 17 | Switzerland 5 | United States 1 |
| March 17 | Great Britain 6 | Finland 3 |
| March 17 | Canada 5 | Sweden 1 |

**Rosters**

**Canada** (Lethbridge Maple Leafs—Dick Gray, coach) GK—Mallie Hughes, Carl Sorokoski—Jim "Shorty" Malacko, Don Vogan, Walter "Whitey" Rimstad, Bill Gibson, Don MacLean, Hector Negrello, Stan Obodiac, Tom Wood, Bill Chandler, Andrew "Nap" Milroy, Denny Flanagan, Bill Flick, Mickey Roth, Dick Gray

**Finland** (Risto Lindroos, coach) GK—Unto Wiitala, Matti Naapuri—Pentti Isotalo, Jukka Wuolio, Ossi Kauppi, Matti Rintakoski, Kauko Makinen, Matti Karumaa, Keijo Kuusela, Esko Tie, Kalle Havulinna, Aarne Honkavaara, Yrjo Hakala, Lotfi Nasibullen, Eero Saari, Teuvo Takala, Christian Rapp

**Great Britain** (J.B. Mowat, coach) GK—Stan Christie, Harold Smith—Jim Mitchell, Lawson Neil, Georges Watt, Doug Wilson, Roy Shepherd, John Carlyle, William Crawford, Ian Forbes, David MacCrae, Ken Nicholson, Tom Paton, John Quales, John Rolland, Bert Smith

**Norway** (Bud McEachern, coach) GK—Per Dahl, Arthur Kristiansen—Johnny Larntvedt, Roar Pedersen, Gunnar Kroge, Per Hagfors, Bjorn Gulbrandsen, Ragnar Rygel, Per Voigt, Leif Solheim, Finn Gundersen, Jan-Erik Adolfsen, Annar Petersen, Arne Berg, Odd Hansen

**Sweden** (Folke Jansson/Herman Carlson, coaches) GK—Arne Johansson, Lars Svensson—Ake Andersson, Rune Johansson, Sven Thunman, Borje Lofgren, Bengt Larsson, Gosta Johansson, Lars Pettersson, Stig Tvilling Andersson, Hans Tvilling Andersson, Yngve Karlsson, Ake Lassas, Stig Carlsson, Erik Johansson, Rolf Eriksson

**Switzerland** (Richard "Bibi" Torriani, coach) GK—Hans Banninger, Jean Ayer—Emil Handschin, Hans Heierling, Walter Durst, Otto Schlapfer, Milo Golaz, Gian Bazzi, Gebhart Poltera, Ulrich Poltera, Fredy Bieler, Hans-Martin Trepp, Reto Delnon, Otto Schubiger, Will Pfister, Walter Guggenbuhl, Andre Favre

**United States** (Bates Hockey Club—Laurier Charest, playing coach) GK—Hank Brodeur—Leon Lafrance, Jim Fife, Hank Martineau, Norm Parent, Chuck Poirier, Larry Berube, Ray Marcotte, Albert Moreau, Laurier Charest, Amede Beland, George Morin, Pete Theriault, Bob Dubois, Gaston Lauze

## 20th WORLD CHAMPIONSHIP (MEN)
## March 6-15, 1953
## Zurich/Basel, Switzerland

(the IIHF considers the 1952 Olympics to be the 19th World Championship)

**Final Placing**

Gold ........Sweden
Silver ......West Germany
Bronze....Switzerland
4th .........Czechoslovakia

**Tournament Format**

Each team was supposed to play every other twice, in a double round robin, but when the Czechs withdrew the tournament became a four-game series for each nation. All Czech results were not counted, though the scores are listed below.

**Results & Standings**

| | GP | W | T | L | GF | GA | P |
|---|---|---|---|---|---|---|---|
| Sweden | 4 | 4 | 0 | 0 | 38 | 11 | 8 |
| West Germany | 4 | 1 | 0 | 3 | 17 | 26 | 2 |
| Switzerland | 4 | 1 | 0 | 3 | 9 | 27 | 2 |
| Czechoslovakia* | 4 | 3 | 0 | 1 | 32 | 15 | 6 |

*Czechoslovakia withdrew after playing only four games because of the death of President Klement Gottwald. As a result, the official standings omit all results involving the Czechs.

| | | | |
|---|---|---|---|
| March 7 | Zurich | Sweden 9 | Switzerland 2 |
| March 7 | Basel | Czechoslovakia 11 | West Germany 2 |
| March 8 | Basel | Czechoslovakia 9 | Switzerland 4 |
| March 8 | Basel | Sweden 8 | West Germany 6 |
| March 10 | Zurich | Switzerland 3 | West Germany 2 |
| March 10 | Basel | Sweden 5 | Czechoslovakia 3 |
| March 12 | Zurich | Czechoslovakia 9 | West Germany 4 |
| March 12 | Zurich | Sweden 9 | Switzerland 1 |
| March 13 | Basel | Sweden 12 | West Germany 2 |
| March 15 | Basel | West Germany 7 | Switzerland 3 |

**Rosters**

**Czechoslovakia** (unofficial participation) GK—Jan Richter, Josef Zahorsky—Karel Gut, Jan Lidral, Miroslav Osmera, Miroslav Novy, Slavomir Barton, Miroslav Rejman, Jiri Sekyra, Vlastimil Bubnik, Bronislav Danda, Miroslav Charouzd, Oldrich Seiml, Miroslav Kluc, Milan Vidlak, Karel Bilek, Stanislav Bacilek

**Sweden** (Folke Jansson, coach) GK—Thord Flodqvist, Hans Isaksson—Rune Johansson, Sven Thunman, Ake Andersson, Lars Bjorn, Sigurd Broms, Sven "Tumba" Johansson, Gosta Johansson, Erik Johansson, Hans Tvilling Andersson, Stig Tvilling Andersson, Stig Carlsson, Rolf Pettersson, Hans Oberg, Gote Blomqvist, Gota Almqvist

**Switzerland** (Frank Sullivan, coach) GK—Hans Banninger, Martin Riesen—Emil Handschin, Rudi Keller, Silvio Rossi, Armin Schutz, Ulrich Poltera, Gebhart Poltera, Hans-Martin Trepp, Walter Durst, Otto Schlapfer, Otto Schubiger, Gian Bazzi, Michel Wehrli, Francis Blank, Oscar Mudry

**West Germany** (Bruno Leinweber, coach) GK—Ulrich Jansen, Alfred Hoffmann—Martin Beck, Toni Biersack, Karl Bierschel, Bruno Guttowski, Kurt Sepp, Xaver Unsinn, Georg Guggemos, Markus Egen, Fritz Poitsch, Karl Enzler, Hans Rampf, Otto Brandenburg, Walter Kremershof, Dieter Niess

## 21st WORLD CHAMPIONSHIP (MEN)
## February 26-March 7, 1954
## Stockholm, Sweden

**Final Placing**

Gold ........Soviet Union
Silver ......Canada
Bronze ....Sweden
4th ..........Czechoslovakia
5th .........West Germany
6th .........Finland
7th .........Switzerland
8th .........Norway

**Tournament Format**

Eight teams played each opponent once, placing determined by final standings.

**Results & Standings**

| | GP | W | T | L | GF | GA | P |
|---|---|---|---|---|---|---|---|
| Soviet Union | 7 | 6 | 1 | 0 | 37 | 10 | 13 |
| Canada | 7 | 6 | 0 | 1 | 59 | 12 | 12 |
| Sweden | 7 | 5 | 1 | 1 | 30 | 18 | 11 |
| Czechoslovakia | 7 | 4 | 0 | 3 | 41 | 21 | 8 |
| West Germany | 7 | 2 | 1 | 4 | 22 | 32 | 5 |
| Finland | 7 | 1 | 1 | 5 | 12 | 52 | 3 |
| Switzerland | 7 | 0 | 2 | 5 | 15 | 34 | 2 |
| Norway | 7 | 1 | 0 | 6 | 6 | 43 | 2 |

| | | |
|---|---|---|
| February 26 | Czechoslovakia 7 | Switzerland 1 |
| February 26 | Sweden 10 | Norway 1 |
| February 26 | Soviet Union 7 | Finland 1 |
| February 27 | Canada 8 | Switzerland 1 |
| February 27 | Czechoslovakia 9 | West Germany 4 |
| February 27 | Soviet Union 7 | Norway 0 |
| February 28 | Canada 8 | Norway 0 |
| February 28 | Sweden 5 | Finland 3 |
| February 28 | Switzerland 3 | West Germany 3 |
| March 1 | Canada 8 | Sweden 0 |
| March 1 | Czechoslovakia 12 | Finland 1 |
| March 1 | Soviet Union 6 | West Germany 2 |
| March 2 | Finland 2 | Norway 0 |
| March 2 | Soviet Union 5 | Czechoslovakia 2 |
| March 2 | Sweden 6 | Switzerland 3 |
| March 3 | Canada 8 | West Germany 1 |
| March 3 | Czechoslovakia 7 | Norway 1 |
| March 3 | Soviet Union 4 | Switzerland 2 |
| March 4 | Canada 20 | Finland 1 |
| March 4 | Norway 3 | Switzerland 2 |
| March 4 | Sweden 4 | West Germany 0 |
| March 5 | Canada 5 | Czechoslovakia 2 |
| March 5 | Sweden 1 | Soviet Union 1 |
| March 5 | West Germany 5 | Finland 1 |
| March 6 | Switzerland 3 | Finland 3 |
| March 6 | Sweden 4 | Czechoslovakia 2 |
| March 7 | Soviet Union 7 | Canada 2 |
| March 7 | West Germany 7 | Norway 1 |

**Rosters**

**Canada** (East York Lyndhursts—Greg Currie, coach) GK—Don Lockhart, Gavin Lindsay—Benny Chapman, John Scott, Bill Shill, John Petro, Moe Galland, George Sayliss, Harold Fiskari, Norm Gray, Vic Sluce, Eric Unger, Tom Jamieson, Russ Robertson, Earl Clements, Tom Campbell, Bob Kennedy

**Czechoslovakia** (Vladimir Bouzek/Jiri Anton, coaches) GK—Jiri Kolouch, Jan Richter—Karel Gut, Vaclav Bubnik, Miroslav Novy, Stanislav Bacilek, Vlastimil Bubnik, Miroslav Osmera, Bronislav Danda, Miroslav Charouzd, Miroslav Rejman, Vaclav Pantucek, Jiri Sekyra, Vlastimil Hajsman, Vladimir Zabrodsky, Miroslav Pospisil, Milan Vidlak

**Finland** (Risto Lindroos, coach) GK—Unto Wiitala, Esko Niemi—Ossi Kauppi, Matti Rintakoski, Matti Lampainen, Yrjo Hakala, Teuvo Takala, Christian Rapp, Lauri Silvan, Erkki Hytonen, Esko Rekomaa, Teppo Rastio, Panu Ignatius, Rainer Lindstrom, Aarno Hiekkaranta, Raino Rautanen, Olli Knuutinen

**Norway** (Carsten Christensen, coach) GK—Arthur Kristiansen, Kurt Kristiansen—Roar Bakke, Knut Blomberg, Per Voigt, Arne Berg, Leif Solheim, Oivind Solheim, Egil Bjerklund, Jan-Erik Adolfsen, Ragnar Rygel, Bjorn Gulbrandsen II, Bjorn Gulbrandsen I, Svein Adolfsen, Finn Gundersen, Kjell Kristensen

**Soviet Union** (Arkadi Chernyshev, coach) GK—Grigori Mkrtychan, Nikolai Puchkov—Alexander Vinogradov, Genrikh Sidorenkov, Dmitri Ukolov, Alfred Kuchevski, Yevgeni Babich, Viktor Shuvalov, Vsevolod Bobrov, Valentin Kuzin, Alexander Uvarov, Yuri Krylov, Nikolai Khlystov, Alexei Guryshev, Mikhail Bychkov, Alexander Komarov, Pavel Zhiburtovich

**Sweden** (Folke Jansson/Herman Carlson, coaches) GK—Hans Isaksson, Thord Flodqvist—Ake Andersson, Gote Almqvist, Sven Thunman, Lars Bjorn, Gote Blomqvist, Stig Carlsson, Erik Johansson, Holger Nurmela, Sven "Tumba" Johansson, Hans Oberg, Stig Tvilling Andersson, Hans Tvilling Andersson, Gosta Johansson, Ake Lassas, Rolf Pettersson

**Switzerland** (Hanggi Boller, coach) GK—Jean Ayer, Martin Riesen—Walter Keller, Emil Handschin, Bixio Celio, Gebhart Poltera, Ulrich Poltera, Francis Blank, Otto Schlapfer, Rudolf Keller, Paul Zimmermann, Hans Ott, Paul Hofer, Werner Stauffer, Jean-Pierre Ubersax, Michel Wehrli, Ladislav Ott

**West Germany** (Bruno Leinweber, coach) GK—Ulrich Jansen, Richard Worschhauser—Toni Biersack, Bruno Guttowski, Martin Beck, Xaver Unsinn, Markus Egen, Hans Huber, Fritz Poitsch, Gunther Jochems, Kurt Sepp, Hans Rampf, Karl Enzler, Ernst Eggerbauer, Rudolf Weide, Jakob Probst, Fritz Kleber

## 22nd WORLD CHAMPIONSHIP (MEN)
## February 25-March 6, 1955
## Dusseldorf/Dortmund/Krefeld/Cologne, West Germany

**Final Placing**

Gold ........Canada
Silver ......Soviet Union
Bronze ....Czechoslovakia
4th..........United States
5th..........Sweden
6th .........West Germany
7th .........Poland
8th .........Switzerland
9th .........Finland

**Tournament Format**

Each team played every opponent once, placing determined by final standings.

**Results & Standings**

| | GP | W | T | L | GF | GA | P |
|---|---|---|---|---|---|---|---|
| Canada | 8 | 8 | 0 | 0 | 66 | 6 | 16 |
| Soviet Union | 8 | 7 | 0 | 1 | 39 | 13 | 14 |
| Czechoslovakia | 8 | 5 | 1 | 2 | 63 | 22 | 11 |
| United States | 8 | 4 | 2 | 2 | 33 | 29 | 10 |
| Sweden | 8 | 4 | 1 | 3 | 40 | 16 | 9 |
| West Germany | 8 | 2 | 0 | 6 | 28 | 43 | 4 |
| Poland | 8 | 2 | 0 | 6 | 19 | 59 | 4 |
| Switzerland | 8 | 1 | 0 | 7 | 15 | 59 | 2 |
| Finland | 8 | 1 | 0 | 7 | 16 | 72 | 2 |

| | | | |
|---|---|---|---|
| February 25 | Krefeld | Sweden 5 | West Germany 4 |
| February 25 | Dortmund | Canada 12 | United States 1 |
| February 25 | Dusseldorf | Soviet Union 10 | Finland 2 |
| February 25 | Cologne | Czechoslovakia 7 | Switzerland 0 |
| February 26 | Krefeld | Poland 5 | West Germany 4 |
| February 26 | Cologne | United States 8 | Finland 1 |
| February 26 | Dusseldorf | Canada 5 | Czechoslovakia 3 |
| February 26 | Dortmund | Soviet Union 2 | Sweden 1 |
| February 27 | Dortmund | United States 6 | West Germany 3 |
| February 27 | Dusseldorf | Sweden 10 | Switzerland 0 |
| February 27 | Krefeld | Soviet Union 4 | Czechoslovakia 0 |
| February 27 | Cologne | Canada 8 | Poland 0 |
| February 28 | Cologne | Soviet Union 8 | Poland 2 |
| February 28 | Dusseldorf | Canada 12 | Finland 0 |
| February 28 | Krefeld | United States 7 | Switzerland 3 |
| March 1 | Cologne | Czechoslovakia 6 | Sweden 5 |
| March 1 | Krefeld | West Germany 7 | Finland 1 |
| March 1 | Dusseldorf | Switzerland 4 | Poland 2 |
| March 2 | Dusseldorf | Czechoslovakia 8 | West Germany 0 |
| March 2 | Dusseldorf | Sweden 9 | Finland 0 |
| March 2 | Krefeld | Soviet Union 3 | United States 0 |
| March 2 | Cologne | Canada 11 | Switzerland 1 |
| March 3 | Dusseldorf | Soviet Union 5 | West Germany 1 |
| March 3 | Cologne | Poland 6 | Finland 3 |
| March 3 | Cologne | Czechoslovakia 4 | United States 4 |
| March 3 | Krefeld | Canada 3 | Sweden 0 |
| March 4 | Dusseldorf | United States 6 | Poland 2 |
| March 4 | Cologne | Canada 10 | West Germany 1 |
| March 4 | Krefeld | Soviet Union 7 | Switzerland 2 |
| March 5 | Dusseldorf | United States 1 | Sweden 1 |
| March 5 | Krefeld | Czechoslovakia 17 | Poland 2 |
| March 5 | Cologne | Finland 7 | Switzerland 2 |
| March 6 | Krefeld | Canada 5 | Soviet Union 0 |
| March 6 | Dusseldorf | Czechoslovakia 18 | Finland 2 |
| March 6 | Cologne | Sweden 9 | Poland 0 |
| March 6 | Dusseldorf | West Germany 8 | Switzerland 3 |

**Rosters**

**Canada** (Penticton Vees—Grant Warwick, coach) GK—Ivan McLelland, Don Moog—George McAvoy, Hal Tarala, Kevin Conway, Jack McDonald, Doug Kilburn, Dick Warwick, Bill Warwick, Jim Fairburn, Jack McIntyre, Grant Warwick, Mike Shebaga, Bernie Bathgate, Don Berry, Jim Middleton, Jack Taggart

**Czechoslovakia** (Vladimir Bouzek, coach) GK—Jan Jendek, Jiri Hanzl—Karel Gut, Stanislav Bacilek, Vaclav Bubnik, Jan Lidral, Vlastimil Bubnik, Slavomir Barton, Bronislav Danda, Vlastimil Hajsman, Oldrich Sedlak, Vaclav Pantucek, Miroslav Rejman, Vladimir Zabrodsky, Milan Vidlak, Jiri Sekyra, Jan Kasper

**Finland** (Aarne Honkavaara, coach) GK—Unto Wiitala, Esko Niemi—Matti Rintakoski, Matti Lampainen, Esko Tie, Yrjo Hakala, Seppo Liitsola, Matti Sundelin, Lenni Lainesalo, Rainer Lindstrom, Teppo Rastio, Erkki Hytonen, Esko Rekomaa, Aarno Hiekkaranta, Teuvo Takala, Christian Rapp, Panu Ignatius

**Poland** (Witalis Ludwiczak/Kazimierz Osmanski, coaches) GK—Edward Koczab, Ryszard Forys—Kazimierz Chodakowski, Stanislaw Olczyk, Henryk Bromowicz, Wiktor Gburek, Roman Penczek, Jozef Kurek, Zdzislaw Nowak, Szymon Janiczko, Alfred Gansiniec, Eugeniusz Lewacki, Stefan Csorich, Alfred Wrobel, Marian Jezak, Adolf Wrobel, Kazimierz Bryniarski, Bronislaw Gostyla

**Soviet Union** (Arkadi Chernyshev, coach) GK—Nikolai Puchkov, Grigori Mkrtychan—Nikolai Sologubov, Alfred Kuchevski, Ivan Tregubov, Pavel Zhiburtovich, Dmitri Ukolov, Yevgeni Babich, Viktor Shuvalov, Vsevolod Bobrov, Valenin Kuzin, Alexander Uvarov, Yuri Krylov, Nikolai Khlystov, Alexei Guryshev, Mikhail Bychkov, Alexander Komarov

**Sweden** (Herman Carlson, coach) GK—Lars Svensson, Yngve Johansson—Sven Thunman, Lars Bjorn, Vilgot Larsson, Ake Lassas, Sigurd Broms, Sven Johansson, Hans Oberg, Stig Tvilling Andersson, Hans Tvilling Andersson, Gosta Johansson, Rolf Pettersson, Stig Carlsson, Erik Johansson, Lars-Eric Lundvall, Ronald Pettersson

**Switzerland** (Hanggi Boller, coach) GK—Jean Ayer, Martin Riesen—Paul Hofer, Emil Handschin, Ruedi Keller, Milo Golaz, Raymond Cattin, Otto Schlapfer, Otto Schubiger, Francis Blank, Reto Delnon, Paul Zimmermann, Hans Ott, Hans Morger, Urs Frei, Fritz Naef, Felix Dietiker

**United States** (Albert Yurkewicz, coach) GK—Don Rigazio, Henry Bothfeld—John Grocott, John Matchefts, Walt Greely, Dick Doherty, Gene Campbell, Arnie Bauer, Ed Robson, John Titus, Ruben Bjorkman, Gordon Christian, John Gilbert, Wendell Anderson, Richard Rodenhiser

**West Germany** (Frank Trottier, coach) GK—Ulrich Jansen, Karl Fischer—Karl Bierschel, Bruno Guttowski, Martin Beck, Ernst Eggerbauer, Hans Huber, Kurt Sepp, Hans-Georg Pescher, Markus Egen, Rainer Kossmann, Gunther Jochems, Walter Kremershof, Rudolf Weide, Ulrich Eckstein, Ernst Trautwein, Rudolf Pittrich

## 24th WORLD CHAMPIONSHIP (MEN)
## February 24-March 5, 1957
## Moscow, Soviet Union

(the IIHF considers the 1956 Olympics to be the 23th World Championship)

**Final Placing**

Gold ........Sweden
Silver ......Soviet Union
Bronze ....Czechoslovakia
4th..........Finland
5th .........East Germany
6th .........Poland
7th .........Austria
8th .........Japan

**Tournament Format**

Each team played every opponent once, placing determined by final standings.

**Results & Standings**

| | GP | W | T | L | GF | GA | P |
|---|---|---|---|---|---|---|---|
| Sweden | 7 | 6 | 1 | 0 | 62 | 11 | 13 |
| Soviet Union | 7 | 5 | 2 | 0 | 77 | 9 | 12 |
| Czechoslovakia | 7 | 5 | 1 | 1 | 66 | 9 | 11 |
| Finland | 7 | 4 | 0 | 3 | 28 | 33 | 8 |
| East Germany | 7 | 3 | 0 | 4 | 23 | 48 | 6 |
| Poland | 7 | 2 | 0 | 5 | 25 | 45 | 4 |
| Austria | 7 | 0 | 1 | 6 | 8 | 61 | 1 |
| Japan | 7 | 0 | 1 | 6 | 11 | 84 | 1 |

| | | |
|---|---|---|
| February 24 | Sweden 11 | East Germany 1 |
| February 24 | Soviet Union 16 | Japan 0 |
| February 24 | Finland 5 | Poland 3 |
| February 24 | Czechoslovakia 9 | Austria 0 |
| February 25 | Czechoslovakia 15 | East Germany 1 |
| February 25 | Soviet Union 11 | Finland 1 |
| February 25 | Sweden 8 | Poland 3 |
| February 26 | Japan 3 | Austria 3 |
| February 27 | Finland 5 | East Germany 3 |
| February 27 | Sweden 2 | Czechoslovakia 0 |
| February 27 | Poland 8 | Japan 3 |
| February 27 | Soviet Union 22 | Austria 1 |
| February 28 | Soviet Union 10 | Poland 1 |
| February 28 | Czechoslovakia 3 | Finland 0 |
| March 1 | Sweden 10 | Austria 0 |
| March 1 | East Germany 9 | Japan 2 |
| March 2 | Finland 9 | Austria 2 |
| March 2 | Soviet Union 2 | Czechoslovakia 2 |
| March 2 | East Germany 6 | Poland 2 |
| March 2 | Sweden 18 | Japan 0 |
| March 3 | Poland 5 | Austria 1 |

| | | |
|---|---|---|
| March 4 | Sweden 9 | Finland 3 |
| March 4 | Soviet Union 12 | East Germany 0 |
| March 4 | Czechoslovakia 25 | Japan 1 |
| March 5 | East Germany 3 | Austria 1 |
| March 5 | Finland 5 | Japan 2 |
| March 5 | Czechoslovakia 12 | Poland 3 |
| March 5 | Sweden 4 | Soviet Union 4 |

**Rosters**

**Austria** (Udo Hohlfeld, coach) GK—Wolfgang Gerl , Robert Nusser—Franz Potuczek , Rudolf Wurmbrand , Hermann Knoll , Adolf Bachura, Gustav Tischer, Herbert Foderl, Hans Zollner, Wolfgang Jochl, Konrad Staudinger, Rudolf Monitzer, Walter Znenahlik, Hans Wagner, Otmar Steiner, Gerhard Springer, Kurt Kurz

**Czechoslovakia** (Vladimir Kostka/Bohumil Rejda, coaches) GK—Jiri Kulicek, Karel Straka—Karel Gut, Frantisek Tikal, Stanislav Sventek, Stanislav Bacilek, Jan Kasper, Slavomir Barton, Ladislav Grabovsky, Miroslav Sasek, Vaclav Pantucek, Miloslav Pokorny, Bohumil Prosek, Vaclav Vilem, Frantisek Vanek, Miloslav Vins, Miroslav Vlach

**East Germany** (Gerhard Kiessling, coach) GK—Hans Mack, Gunther Katzur—Heinz Kuczera, Gunther Schischefski, Werner Heinicke, Helmut Senftleben, Lothar Zoller, Erich Novy, Hans Frenzel, Wolfgang Nickel, Wolfgang Blumel, Kurt Sturmer, Werner Kunstler, Kurt Jablonski, Joachim Rudert, Manfred Buder, Herbert Honig

**Finland** (Aarne Honkavaara, coach) GK—Unto Wiitala, Esko Niemi—Matti Lampainen, Olli Knuutinen, Erkki Koiso, Aki Salonen, Mauno Nurmi, Risto Aaltonen, Yrjo Hakala, Reimo Kilpio, Voitto Soini, Jorma Salmi, Matti Sundelin, Esko Luostarinen, Pertti Nieminen, Teppo Rastio, Erkki Hytonen

**Japan** (Kiyoteru Nishiura, coach) GK—Yasumoto Takagi, Toshio Sato—Naruhiro Miyazaki, Takeshi Kikuchi, Yuso Kanedo, Akiyoshi Segawa, Shinichi Honma, Isao Ono, Kazuo Watanabe, Masasi Sato, Teno Sakurai, Tereu Sakurai, Toshiniko Yamada, Toshihito Emori, Ahira Mohji, Jun Fujimori, Tsukasa Kawanishi

**Poland** (Antonin Haukvic, coach) GK—Wladyslaw Pabisz, Jozef Waclaw—Kazimierz Chodakowski, Stefan Csorich, Stanislaw Olczyk, Mieczyslaw Chmura, Janusz Zawadzki, Bronislaw Gosztyla, Rudolf Czech, Jozef Kurek, Sylwester Wilczek, Zdzislaw Nowak, Roman Pawelczyk, Szymon Janiczko, Stanislaw Jonczyk, Werner Kadow, Stanislaw Rozanski

**Soviet Union** (Arkadi Chernyshev, coach) GK—Nikolai Puchkov, Yevgeni Yerkin—Nikolai Sologubov, Ivan Tregubov, Genrikh Sidorenkov, Pavel Zhiburtovich, Vitali Kostarev, Vsevolod Bobrov, Yevgeni Babich, Alexander Uvarov, Nikolai Khlystov, Alexei Guryshev, Yuri Pantyukhov, Konstantin Loktev, Veniamin Alexandrov, Alexander Cherepanov, Vladimir Grebennikov

**Sweden** (Folke Jansson, coach) GK—Thord Flodqvist, Yngve Casslind—Roland Stoltz, Lars Bjorn, Hans Svedberg, Vilgot Larsson, Anders Andersson, Eilert Maattaa, Sven Johansson, Erling Lindstrom, Ronald Pettersson, Nisse Nilsson, Lar-Eric Lundvall, Sigurd Broms, Hans Ericsson, Hans Oberg, Walter Ahlen

## 25th WORLD CHAMPIONSHIP (MEN)
## February 25-March 9, 1958
## Oslo, Norway

**Final Placing**

| | |
|---|---|
| Gold ........Canada | 5th .........United States |
| Silver ......Soviet Union | 6th .........Finland |
| Bronze ....Sweden | 7th .........Norway |
| 4th..........Czechoslovakia | 8th .........Poland |

**Tournament Format**

Each team played every opponent once, placing determined by final standings.

**Results & Standings**

| | GP | W | T | L | GF | GA | P |
|---|---|---|---|---|---|---|---|
| Canada | 7 | 7 | 0 | 0 | 82 | 6 | 14 |
| Soviet Union | 7 | 5 | 1 | 1 | 44 | 15 | 11 |
| Sweden | 7 | 5 | 0 | 2 | 46 | 22 | 10 |
| Czechoslovakia | 7 | 3 | 2 | 2 | 21 | 21 | 8 |
| United States | 7 | 3 | 1 | 3 | 29 | 33 | 7 |
| Finland | 7 | 1 | 1 | 5 | 9 | 51 | 3 |
| Norway | 7 | 1 | 0 | 6 | 12 | 44 | 2 |
| Poland | 7 | 0 | 1 | 6 | 14 | 65 | 1 |

| | | |
|---|---|---|
| February 28 | United States 12 | Poland 4 |
| February 28 | Sweden 9 | Norway 0 |
| February 28 | Czechoslovakia 5 | Finland 1 |
| March 1 | Canada 14 | Poland 1 |
| March 1 | Sweden 5 | Finland 2 |
| March 1 | Soviet Union 10 | Norway 2 |
| March 2 | Canada 12 | Norway 0 |
| March 2 | Soviet Union 10 | Finland 0 |
| March 3 | Canada 24 | Finland 0 |
| March 3 | Czechoslovakia 7 | Poland 1 |
| March 3 | United States 6 | Norway 1 |
| March 4 | Sweden 8 | United States 3 |
| March 4 | Czechoslovakia 4 | Soviet Union 4 |
| March 5 | Finland 2 | Poland 2 |
| March 6 | Canada 10 | Sweden 2 |
| March 6 | Soviet Union 10 | Poland 1 |
| March 6 | Czechoslovakia 2 | United States 2 |
| March 6 | Finland 2 | Norway 1 |
| March 7 | Canada 6 | Czechoslovakia 0 |
| March 7 | Sweden 12 | Poland 2 |
| March 7 | Soviet Union 4 | United States 1 |
| March 8 | Canada 12 | United States 1 |
| March 8 | Soviet Union 4 | Sweden 3 |
| March 8 | Czechoslovakia 2 | Norway 0 |
| March 9 | Canada 4 | Soviet Union 2 |
| March 9 | Sweden 7 | Czechoslovakia 1 |
| March 9 | Norway 8 | Poland 3 |
| March 9 | United States 4 | Finland 2 |

**Rosters**

**Canada** (Whitby Dunlops—Sid Smith, coach) GK—Roy Edwards, John Henderson—Sid Smith, Harry Sinden, Sandy Air, Bob Attersley, Connie Broden, Bus Gagnon, George Gosselin, Jean-Paul Lamirande, Gord Myles, Ted O'Connor, Tom O'Connor, George Samolenko, Alf Treen, John McKenzie, Charlie Burns

**Czechoslovakia** (Bohumil Rejda, coach) GK—Vladimir Nadrchal, Jiri Kulicek—Karel Gut, Frantisek Tikal, Jan Kasper, Stanislav Sventek, Stanislav Bacilek, Jan Starsi, Slavomir Barton, Vaclav Pantucek, Miroslav Sasek, Frantisek Schwach, Miroslav Vlach, Jaroslav Volf, Vaclav Frolich, Jaroslav Jirik, Frantisek Vanek

**Finland** (Aarne Honkavaara, coach) GK—Esko Niemi, Juhani Lahtinen—Matti Lampainen, Erkki Koiso, Mauno Nurmi, Pasi Vuorinen, Heino Pulli, Jorma Salmi, Raimo Kilpio, Teppo Rastio, Yrjo Hakala, Erkki Hytonen, Esko Luostarinen, Voitto Soini, Eino Pollari, Kari Aro, Pertti Nieminen

**Norway** (Johnny Larntvedt, coach) GK—Lorang Wifladt, Frank Steinbo—Roar Bakke, Per Brattas, Egil Bjerklund, Tor Gundersen, Per Voigt, Georg Smefjell, Ragnar Nielsen, Annar Petersen, Willy Walbye, Christian Petersen, Terje Hellerud, Olav Dalsoren, Einar Bruno Larsen, Henrik Petersen, Per Skjerwen Olsen

**Poland** (Andrzej Wolkowski/Wladyslaw Wiro-Kiro, coaches) GK—Edward Koczab, Jozef Waclaw—Kazimierz Chodakowski, Stanislaw Olczyk, Henryk Regula, Marian Zawada, Augustyn Skorski, Jozef Kurek, Rudolf Czech, Bronislaw Gosztyla, Marian Pawelczyk, Sylwester Wilczek, Jerzy Ogorczyk, Karol Burek, Kazimierz Bryniarski, Kazimierz Malysiak, Stanislaw Jonczyk

**Soviet Union** (Anatoli Tarasov, coach) GK—Nikolai Puchkov, Yevgeni Yerkin—Nikolai Sologubov, Ivan Tregubov, Dmitri Ukolov, Genrik Sidorenkov, Alexei Guryshev, Konstantin Loktev, Alexander Cherepanov, Veniamin Alexandrov, Yuri Krylov, Nikolai Khlystov, Yuri Pantyukhov, Yuri Kopylov, Vladimir Elizarov, Alfred Kuchevski, Valentin Bystrov

**Sweden** (Ed Reigle, coach) GK—Thord Flodqvist, Rune Gudmundsson—Lars Bjorn, Roland Stoltz, Hans Svedberg, Vilgot Larsson, Sigurd Broms, Sven "Tumba" Johansson, Carl-Goran Oberg, Ronald Pettersson, Nisse Nilsson, Lars-Eric Lundvall, Hans Oberg, Gosta Westerlund, Erling Lindstrom, Gert Blome, Karl-Soren Hedlund

**United States** (Cal Marvin, coach) GK—Willard Ikola, Don Rigazio—John Mayasich, Dan McKinnon, Ed Zifcak, Roger Christian, Bill Christian, Gord Christian, Weldon Olsen, Ed Kirrane, Ed Miller, Paul Johnson, Larry Lawman, Oscar Mahle, Jack Petroske, Dick Meredith

## 26th WORLD CHAMPIONSHIP (MEN)
## March 9-15, 1959
## Bratislava/Brno/Ostrava/Kolin/Mlada Boleslav/Kladno/Prague, Czechoslovakia

**Final Placing**

| | |
|---|---|
| Gold ........Canada | 7th .........West Germany |
| Silver ......Soviet Union | 8th .........Norway |
| Bronze ....Czechoslovakia | 9 th .........East Germany |
| 4th..........United States | 10th .......Italy |
| 5th..........Sweden | 11th .......Poland |
| 6th..........Finland | 12th .......Switzerland |

**Tournament Format**

Twelve teams were divided into three groups of four teams each to play a round robin series within each group. The top two teams from each group advanced to a finals group to play for medals in a round robin series, the bottom six played in another round robin series for placement.

**Results & Standings**

**GROUP A (BRATISLAVA)**

| | GP | W | T | L | GF | GA | P |
|---|---|---|---|---|---|---|---|
| Canada | 3 | 3 | 0 | 0 | 39 | 2 | 6 |
| Czechoslovakia | 3 | 2 | 0 | 1 | 24 | 8 | 4 |
| Switzerland | 3 | 1 | 0 | 2 | 8 | 35 | 2 |
| Poland | 3 | 0 | 0 | 3 | 4 | 30 | 0 |

| | | |
|---|---|---|
| March 5 | Czechoslovakia 9 | Switzerland 0 |
| March 5 | Canada 9 | Poland 0 |
| March 6 | Canada 23 | Switzerland 0 |

| | | |
|---|---|---|
| March 6 | Czechoslovakia 13 | Poland 1 |
| March 7 | Switzerland 8 | Poland 3 |
| March 7 | Canada 7 | Czechoslovakia 2 |

**GROUP B (BRNO)**

| | GP | W | T | L | GF | GA | P |
|---|---|---|---|---|---|---|---|
| Soviet Union | 3 | 3 | 0 | 0 | 24 | 5 | 6 |
| United States | 3 | 2 | 0 | 1 | 22 | 10 | 4 |
| Norway | 3 | 1 | 0 | 2 | 10 | 26 | 2 |
| East Germany | 3 | 0 | 0 | 3 | 6 | 21 | 0 |

| | | |
|---|---|---|
| March 5 | Soviet Union 6 | East Germany 1 |
| March 5 | United States 10 | Norway 3 |
| March 6 | United States 9 | East Germany 2 |
| March 6 | Soviet Union 13 | Norway 1 |
| March 7 | Norway 6 | East Germany 3 |
| March 7 | Soviet Union 5 | United States 3 |

**GROUP C (OSTRAVA)**

| | GP | W | T | L | GF | GA | P |
|---|---|---|---|---|---|---|---|
| Sweden | 3 | 2 | 1 | 0 | 21 | 8 | 5 |
| Finland | 3 | 1 | 1 | 1 | 13 | 12 | 3 |
| West Germany | 3 | 1 | 0 | 2 | 11 | 13 | 2 |
| Italy | 3 | 1 | 0 | 2 | 7 | 22 | 2 |

| | | |
|---|---|---|
| March 5 | Sweden 11 | Italy 0 |
| March 5 | Finland 5 | West Germany 3 |
| March 6 | West Germany 7 | Italy 2 |
| March 6 | Sweden 4 | Finland 4 |
| March 7 | Sweden 6 | West Germany 1 |
| March 7 | Italy 5 | Finland 4 |

**7-12 PLACEMENT GROUP**

| | GP | W | T | L | GF | GA | P |
|---|---|---|---|---|---|---|---|
| West Germany | 5 | 4 | 1 | 0 | 30 | 9 | 9 |
| Norway | 5 | 3 | 1 | 1 | 20 | 20 | 7 |
| East Germany | 5 | 3 | 0 | 2 | 20 | 21 | 6 |
| Italy | 5 | 2 | 1 | 2 | 20 | 17 | 5 |
| Poland | 5 | 1 | 0 | 4 | 11 | 20 | 2 |
| Switzerland | 5 | 0 | 1 | 4 | 8 | 22 | 1 |

| | | | |
|---|---|---|---|
| March 9 | Kolin | West Germany 2 | Italy 2 |
| March 9 | Mlada Boleslav | Norway 4 | Switzerland 4 |
| March 9 | Kladno | East Germany 5 | Poland 1 |
| March 10 | Kladno | Norway 4 | Italy 3 |
| March 10 | Kolin | East Germany 6 | Switzerland 2 |
| March 10 | Mlada Boleslav | West Germany 5 | Poland 3 |
| March 11 | Mlada Boleslav | Italy 4 | Switzerland 1 |
| March 11 | Kladno | West Germany 8 | East Germany 0 |
| March 11 | Kolin | Norway 4 | Poland 3 |
| March 13 | Kolin | Poland 2 | Switzerland 1 |
| March 13 | Mlada Boleslav | West Germany 9 | Norway 4 |
| March 13 | Kladno | East Germany 8 | Italy 6 |
| March 14 | Mlada Boleslav | Italy 5 | Poland 2 |
| March 14 | Kladno | West Germany 6 | Switzerland 0 |
| March 14 | Kolin | Norway 4 | East Germany 1 |

**MEDAL ROUND (PRAGUE)**

| | GP | W | T | L | GF | GA | P |
|---|---|---|---|---|---|---|---|
| Canada | 5 | 4 | 0 | 1 | 21 | 5 | 8 |
| Soviet Union | 5 | 4 | 0 | 1 | 20 | 10 | 8 |
| Czechoslovakia | 5 | 3 | 0 | 2 | 22 | 14 | 6 |
| United States | 5 | 3 | 0 | 2 | 23 | 15 | 6 |
| Sweden | 5 | 1 | 0 | 4 | 6 | 21 | 2 |
| Finland | 5 | 0 | 0 | 5 | 7 | 32 | 0 |

| | | |
|---|---|---|
| March 9 | Canada 6 | Finland 0 |
| March 9 | Soviet Union 5 | United States 1 |
| March 9 | Czechoslovakia 4 | Sweden 1 |
| March 10 | Czechoslovakia 8 | Finland 2 |
| March 10 | United States 7 | Sweden 1 |
| March 11 | United States 10 | Finland 3 |
| March 11 | Canada 3 | Soviet Union 1 |
| March 12 | Canada 5 | Sweden 0 |
| March 12 | Soviet Union 4 | Czechoslovakia 3 |
| March 13 | Sweden 2 | Finland 1 |
| March 13 | United States 4 | Czechoslovakia 2 |
| March 14 | Soviet Union 6 | Finland 1 |
| March 14 | Canada 4 | United States 1 |
| March 15 | Soviet Union 4 | Sweden 2 |
| March 15 | Czechoslovakia 5 | Canada 3 |

**Rosters**

**Canada** (Belleville McFarlands—Ike Hildebrand, playing coach) GK—Gordon Bell, Marv Edwards—Jean-Paul Lamirande, Floyd Crawford, Al Dewsbury, Moe Benoit, Dave Jones, Paul Payette, John McLellan, Wayne Brown, Lou Smrke, Red Berenson, Denis Boucher, George Gosselin, Ike Hildebrand, Pete Conacher, Bart Bradley

**Czechoslovakia** (Vlastimil Sykora, coach) GK—Jiri Kulicek, Vladimir Nadrchal—Karel Gut, Frantisek Tikal, Jan Kasper, Rudolf Potsch, Stanislav Bacilek, Bohumil Prosek, Miroslav Vlach, Jan Starsi, Frantisek Vanek, Josef Cerny, Karol Fako, Jozef Golonka, Miroslav Rys, Jaroslav Jirik, Jaroslav Volf

**East Germany** (Rudi Schmieder, coach) GK—Walter Kindermann, Gunther Katzur—Horst Heinze, Heinz Kuczera, Dieter Greiner, Gunther Heinicke, Werner Heinicke, Erich Novy, Werner Kunstler, Kurt Sturmer, Joachim Ziesche, Hans Frenzel, Gerhard Klugel, Joachim Franke, Joachim Rudert, Manfred Buder, Wolfgang Blumel

**Finland** (Aarne Honkavaara, coach) GK—Esko Niemi, Juhani Lahtinen—Matti Haapaniemi, Kalevi Numminen, Matti Lampainen, Erkki Koiso, Jorma Salmi, Raimo Kilpio, Teppo Rastio, Yrjo Hakala, Esko Luostarinen, Jouni Seistamo, Heino Pulli, Pertti Nieminen, Juhani Wahlsten, Aaro Nurminen, Unto Nevalainen

**Italy** (Bill Cupolo, coach) GK—Giuliano Ferraris, Vittorio Bolla—Gianfranco Darin, Carmine Tucci, Giuseppe Zandegiacomo, Enrico Bacher, Igino Larese-Fece, Alberto Darin, Giancarlo Agazzi, Gianpiero Branduardi, Alfredo Coletti, Ernesto Crotti, Bruno Frison, Giovanni Furlani, Giulio Oberhammer, Bernardo Tomei, Giorgio Zerbetto

**Norway** (Johnny Larntvedt, coach) GK—Knut Nygaard, Lorang Wifladt—Roar Bakke, Egil Bjerklund, Tor Gundersen, Henrik Petersen, Henrik Bruun, Terje Hellerud, Olav Dalsoren, Einar-Bruno Larsen, Per Skjerwen, Georg Smefjell, Christian Petersen, Oddvar Midsatter, Per Moe, Willy Walbye, Roy Sorensen

**Poland** (Alfred Gansiniec, coach) GK—Wladyslaw Pabisz, Jozef Goralczyk—Kazimierz Chodakowski, Stanislaw Olczyk, Henryk Regula, Marian Zawada, Bronislaw Gosztyla, Janusz Zawadski, Jozef Kurek, Zbigniew Skotnicki, Szymon Janiczko, Kazimierz Malysiak, Sylwester Wilczek, Jerzy Ogorczyk, Augustyn Skorski, Andrzej Fonfara, Marian Jezak

**Soviet Union** (Anatoli Tarasov, coach) GK—Nikolai Puchkov, Yevgeni Yerkin—Nikolai Sologubov, Yuri Baulin, Konstantin Loktev, Veniamin Alexandrov, Yuri Pantyukhov, Yuri Krylov, Viktor Pryaznikov, Igor Dekonski, Nikolai Snetkov, Yevgeni Grosev, Viktor Yakushev, Alexei Guryshev, Ivan Tregubov, Dmitri Ukolov, Genrikh Sidorenkov

**Sweden** (Ed Reigle, coach) GK—Yngve Johansson, Per Agne Karlstrom—Roland Stoltz, Lars Bjorn, Hans Svedberg, Vilgot Larsson, Sigurd Broms, Hans Mild, Erling Lindstrom, Roland Pettersson, Anders Andersson, Lars-Eric Lundvall, Goran Lysen, Gosta Westerlund, Carl Oberg, Bertil Karlsson, Curt Thulin

**Switzerland** (Andre Girard, coach) GK—Rene Kiener, Jean Ayer—Bruno Gerber, Kurt Nobs, Josef Weingartner, Emil Handschin, Hans-Martin Sprecher, Otto Schlapfer, Georg Riesch, Bernard Bagnoud, Franz Berry, Peter Stammbach, Hans Pappa, Michael Wehrli, Roger Chappot

**United States** (Marsh Ryman, coach) GK—Jack McCartan, Don Cooper—John Newkirk, Rodney Paavola, James Westby, Robert Owen, Weldon Olsen, Bob Cleary, Gene Grazia, Dick Burg, Tom Williams, Paul Johnson, Bob Turk, Bill Cleary, Robert Dupuis, Richard Meredith

**West Germany** (Gerhard Kiessling, coach) GK—Ulrich Jansen, Hans Obermann—Paul Ambros, Ernst Eggerbauer, Hans Huber, Hans Rampf, Leonhard Waitl, Max Pfefferle, Markus Egen, Horst Schuldes, Georg Eberl, Jakob Probst, Alois Mayer, Kurt Sepp, Xaver Unsinn, Ernst Trautwein, Siegfried Schubert

## 28th WORLD CHAMPIONSHIP (MEN)
**March 1-12, 1961**
**Geneva/Lausanne, Switzerland**

(the IIHF considers the 1960 Olympics to be the 27th World Championship)

**Final Placing**

| | |
|---|---|
| Gold ........Canada | 5th .........East Germany |
| Silver .......Czechoslovakia | 6th .........United States |
| Bronze ....Soviet Union | 7th .........Finland |
| 4th..........Sweden | 8th .........West Germany |

**Tournament Format**

Each team played every opponent once, placing determined by final standings.

**Results & Standings**

| | GP | W | T | L | GF | GA | P |
|---|---|---|---|---|---|---|---|
| Canada | 7 | 6 | 1 | 0 | 45 | 11 | 13 |
| Czechoslovakia | 7 | 6 | 1 | 0 | 33 | 9 | 13 |
| Soviet Union | 7 | 5 | 0 | 2 | 51 | 20 | 10 |
| Sweden | 7 | 4 | 0 | 3 | 33 | 27 | 8 |
| East Germany | 7 | 2 | 0 | 5 | 21 | 33 | 4 |
| United States | 7 | 1 | 1 | 5 | 24 | 43 | 3 |
| Finland | 7 | 1 | 1 | 5 | 19 | 43 | 3 |
| West Germany | 7 | 0 | 2 | 5 | 10 | 50 | 2 |

| | | | |
|---|---|---|---|
| March 2 | Lausanne | Czechoslovakia 6 | Finland 0 |
| March 2 | Geneva | Canada 6 | Sweden 1 |
| March 2 | Lausanne | Soviet Union 13 | United States 2 |
| March 4 | Geneva | Finland 6 | East Germany 4 |
| March 4 | Lausanne | Canada 9 | West Germany 1 |
| March 4 | Lausanne | Soviet Union 6 | Sweden 2 |
| March 5 | Geneva | Czechoslovakia 4 | United States 1 |
| March 5 | Geneva | Canada 7 | United States 4 |
| March 5 | Lausanne | Soviet Union 7 | Finland 3 |
| March 5 | Geneva | Czechoslovakia 6 | West Germany 0 |
| March 5 | Lausanne | Sweden 3 | East Germany 2 |
| March 7 | Geneva | Sweden 6 | Finland 4 |
| March 7 | Lausanne | United States 4 | West Germany 4 |
| March 7 | Lausanne | Canada 5 | East Germany 2 |
| March 7 | Geneva | Czechoslovakia 6 | Soviet Union 4 |
| March 8 | Lausanne | East Germany 6 | United States 5 |
| March 8 | Geneva | Sweden 12 | West Germany 1 |
| March 9 | Geneva | Finland 3 | West Germany 3 |
| March 9 | Geneva | Soviet Union 9 | East Germany 1 |
| March 9 | Lausanne | Canada 1 | Czechoslovakia 1 |
| March 11 | Geneva | Czechoslovakia 5 | East Germany 1 |
| March 11 | Lausanne | Soviet Union 11 | West Germany 1 |
| March 11 | Lausanne | Canada 12 | Finland 1 |
| March 11 | Geneva | Sweden 7 | United States 3 |
| March 12 | Geneva | East Germany 5 | West Germany 0 (forfeit) |
| March 12 | Lausanne | Czechoslovakia 5 | Sweden 2 |
| March 12 | Lausanne | United States 5 | Finland 2 |
| March 12 | Geneva | Canada 5 | Soviet Union 1 |

**Rosters**

**Canada** (Trail Smoke Eaters—Bobby Kromm, coach) GK—Seth Martin, Claude Cyr—George Ferguson, Hal Jones, Pinoke McIntyre, Walt Peacosh, Darryl Sly, Jackie McLeod, Don Fletcher, Harry Smith, Cal Hockley, Addy Tambellini, Dave Rusnell, Ed Christofoli, Norm Lenardon, Mike Lagace, Bobby Kromm

**Czechoslovakia** (Vladimir Kostka/Jiri Andrst, coaches) GK—Josef Mikolas, Vladimir Nadrchal—Rudolf Potsch, Jan Kasper, Frantisek Gregor, Stanislav Sventek, Jaromir Bunter, Bohumil Prosek, Vaclav Pantucek, Vlastimil Bubnik, Miroslav Vlach, Frantisek Vanek, Jan Starsi, Josef Cerny, Jiri Dolana, Ludek Bukac, Zdenek Kepak

**East Germany** (Rudi Schmieder, coach) GK—Peter Kolbe, Klaus Hirche—Heinz Kuczera, Horst Heinze, Dieter Voigt, Heinz Schildan, Gunther Heinicke, Joachim Franke, Manfred Buder, Erich Novy, Bernd Hiller, Dieter Kratzsch, Karl Szengel, Joachim Ziesche, Harald Grimm, Bernd Poindl, Gerhard Klugel

**Finland** (Derek Holmes, coach) GK—Juhani Lahtinen, Isto Virtanen—Matti Haapaniemi, Kalevi Numminen, Jorma Suokko, Erkki Koiso, Mauno Nurmi, Anssi Salonen, Raimo Kilpio, Teppo Rastio, Pertti Nieminen, Jouni Seistamo, Timo Ahlquist, Pentti Hytiainen, Jorma Rikala, Seppo Vainio, Esko Luostarinen

**Soviet Union** (Arkadi Chernyshev, coach) GK—Viktor Konovalenko, Vladimir Chinov—Nikolai Sologubov, Ivan Tregubov, Genrikh Sidorenkov, Alexander Ragulin, Vladimir Brezhnev, Konstantin Loktev, Veniamin Alexandrov, Alexander Almetov, Nikolai Snetkov, Viktor Yakushev, Viktor Tsyplakov, Yevgeni Mayorov, Vyacheslav Starshinov, Vladimir Yurzinov, Boris Mayorov

**Sweden** (Arne Stromberg, coach) GK—Kjell Svensson, Tommy Bjorkman—Roland Stoltz, Lars Bjorn, Gert Blome, Bert-Ola Nordlander, Hans Svedberg, Per-Olof Hardin, Anders Andersson, Ulf Sterner, Sigurd Broms, Sven "Tumba" Johansson, Carl-Goran Oberg, Ronald Pettersson, Hans Mild, Ake Rydberg, Gosta Sandberg

**United States** (John Pleban, coach) GK—Tom Yurkovich, Larry Palmer—Tom Riley, Dale Noreen, Jim Westby, Marv Jorde, John Mayasich, Bob Turk, Herb Brooks, Dick Burg, Sam Grafstrom, David Rovick, David Frank, Jack Poole, Jack Williams, Paul Johnson, Dan Dilworth

**West Germany** (Markus Egen, coach) GK—Wilhelm Edelmann, Harry Lindner—Paul Ambros, Leonhard Waitl, Hans Rampf, Walter Riedel, Josef Reif, Bernd Herzig, Horst Schuldes, Georg Scholz, Kurt Sepp, Ernst Trautwein, Georg Eberl, Helmut Zanghellini, Siegfried Schubert, Remigius Wellen, Otto Schneitberger

## 29th WORLD CHAMPIONSHIP (MEN)
## March 8-18, 1962
## Colorado Springs/Denver, United States

**Final Placing**

| | |
|---|---|
| Gold ........Sweden | 5th .........Norway |
| Silver ......Canada | 6th .........West Germany |
| Bronze ....United States | 7th .........Switzerland |
| 4th..........Finland | 8th .........Great Britain |

**Tournament Format**

Each team played every opponent once, placing determined by final standings.

**Results & Standings**

| | GP | W | T | L | GF | GA | P |
|---|---|---|---|---|---|---|---|
| Sweden | 7 | 7 | 0 | 0 | 67 | 10 | 14 |
| Canada | 7 | 6 | 0 | 1 | 58 | 12 | 12 |
| United States | 7 | 5 | 0 | 2 | 54 | 23 | 10 |
| Finland | 7 | 3 | 0 | 4 | 32 | 42 | 6 |
| Norway | 7 | 3 | 0 | 4 | 32 | 54 | 6 |
| West Germany | 7 | 2 | 0 | 5 | 27 | 36 | 4 |
| Switzerland | 7 | 1 | 0 | 6 | 21 | 60 | 2 |
| Great Britain | 7 | 1 | 0 | 6 | 19 | 73 | 2 |

| | | | |
|---|---|---|---|
| March 8 | Denver | Canada 8 | Finland 1 |
| March 8 | Colorado Springs | United States 14 | Norway 2 |
| March 8 | Colorado Springs | Switzerland 6 | Great Britain 3 |
| March 9 | Colorado Springs | Great Britain 7 | Finland 5 |
| March 9 | Colorado Springs | Sweden 17 | Switzerland 2 |
| March 9 | Denver | Norway 6 | West Germany 4 |
| March 10 | Colorado Springs | Sweden 2 | United States 1 |
| March 10 | Denver | Canada 8 | West Germany 0 |
| March 11 | Colorado Springs | Canada 7 | Switzerland 2 |
| March 11 | Denver | Norway 12 | Great Britain 2 |
| March 11 | Denver | United States 6 | Finland 3 |
| March 12 | Colorado Springs | Norway 7 | Switzerland 5 |
| March 12 | Colorado Springs | West Germany 9 | Great Britain 0 |
| March 12 | Denver | Sweden 12 | Finland 2 |
| March 13 | Colorado Springs | Sweden 5 | Canada 3 |
| March 13 | Denver | United States 8 | West Germany 4 |
| March 13 | Denver | Canada 14 | Norway 1 |
| March 14 | Colorado Springs | Finland 7 | Switzerland 4 |
| March 14 | Colorado Springs | West Germany 7 | Switzerland 1 |
| March 14 | Colorado Springs | United States 12 | Great Britain 5 |
| March 15 | Colorado Springs | Finland 9 | West Germany 3 |
| March 15 | Denver | Sweden 17 | Great Britain 0 |
| March 16 | Denver | United States 12 | Switzerland 1 |
| March 16 | Colorado Springs | Sweden 10 | Norway 2 |
| March 17 | Colorado Springs | Canada 12 | Great Britain 2 |
| March 17 | Denver | Finland 5 | Norway 2 |
| March 17 | Denver | Sweden 4 | West Germany 0 |
| March 18 | Colorado Springs | Canada 6 | United States 1 |

**Rosters**

**Canada** (Galt Terriers—Lloyd Roubell, coach) GK—Harold "Boat" Hurley, John Sofiak—Ted Maki, Jack Douglas, Harry Smith, Bill Mitchell, Bill Wylie, Bob McKnight, Floyd Martin, Tod Sloan, Joe Malo, Bobby Brown, Joe Hogan, Bob Mader, Jackie McLeod, Don Rope, Bobby Robertson, John Sofiak

**Finland** (Viljo Wirkkunen, coach) GK—Juhani Lahtinen, Risto Kaitala—Jorma Suokko, Kalevi Numminen, Mauno Nurmi, Jarmo Wasama, Matti Lampainen, Teppo Rastio, Kari Aro, Juhani Wahlsten, Jouni Seistamo, Heino Pulli, Pentti Hytiainen, Seppo Nikkila, Rauno Lehtio, Pertti Nieminen, Matti Keinonen

**Great Britain** (John Murray, coach) GK—Ray Partridge, Derek Metcalfe—Roy Shepherd, Gerald "Red" Devereaux, Joe Brown, John Cook, John Milne, Billy Brennan, Tom Imrie, Ian Forbes, Terry Matthews, Sam McDonald, Rupert Fresher, Bert Smith, Dave Lammin, Harry Pearson, Tony Whitehead, John Murray

**Norway** (Johan Narvestad, coach) GK—Knut Nygaard, Oystein Mellerud—Roar Bakke, Henrik Petersen, Tor Gundersen, Svein Hansen, Bjorn Elvenes, Terje Hellerud, Einar-Bruno Larsen, Per Voigt, Olav Dalsoren, Georg Smefjell, Per Moe, Per Skjerwen Olsen, Christian Petersen, Jan-Erik Hansen, Trond Ekmo, Trygve Bergeid

**Sweden** (Arne Stromberg, coach) GK—Kjell Svensson, Lennart Haggroth—Gert Blome, Bertil Karlsson, Roland Stoltz, Bert-Ola Nordlander, Nils Johansson, Ronald Pettersson, Nisse Nilsson, Lars-Eric Lundvall, Eilert Maatta, Anders Andersson, Ulf Sterner, Per-Olov Hardin, Uno Ohrlund, Leif Andersson, Sven "Tumba" Johansson

**Switzerland** (Beat Ruedi, coach) GK—Rene Kiener, Werner Bassani—Kurt Peter, Elwin Friedrich, Bruno Gerber, Kurt Nobs, Andres Kunzi, Roland Bernasconi, Roger Chappot, Fritz Naef, Herold Truffer, Gian Bazzi, Oskar Jenny, Pio Parolini, Gerhard Diethelm, Peter Stammbach, Jurg Zimmermann

**United States** (John Pleban, coach) GK—Mike Larson, Jim Logue—Brian MacKay, Gord Tottle, John Mayasich, Tom Martin, Roger Christian, Roger Roberge, Don Hall, Reg Meserve, Paul Coppo, Bill Daley, Oscar Mahle, Herb Brooks, Ken Johannson, John Poole, Bill Christian

**West Germany** (Vic Heyliger, coach)—Harry Lindner, Wilhelm Edelmann—Hans Rampf, Leonhard Waitl, Otto Schneitberger, Walter Riedl, Heinz Bader, Georg Eberl, Josef Reif, Siegfried Schubert, Ernst Kopf, Manfred Gmeiner, Rudolf Pittrich, Dieter Lang, Ernst Trautwein, Paul Ambros, Helmuth Zanghellini

## 30th WORLD CHAMPIONSHIP (MEN)
**March 7-17, 1963**
**Stockholm, Sweden**

### Final Placing

| | |
|---|---|
| Gold ........Soviet Union | 5th .........Finland |
| Silver ......Sweden | 6th .........East Germany |
| Bronze ....Czechoslovakia | 7th .........West Germany |
| 4th .........Canada | 8th .........United States |

### Tournament Format
Each team played every opponent once, placing determined by final standings.

### Results & Standings

| | GP | W | T | L | GF | GA | P |
|---|---|---|---|---|---|---|---|
| Soviet Union | 7 | 6 | 0 | 1 | 50 | 9 | 12 |
| Sweden | 7 | 6 | 0 | 1 | 44 | 10 | 12 |
| Czechoslovakia | 7 | 5 | 1 | 1 | 41 | 16 | 11 |
| Canada | 7 | 4 | 1 | 2 | 46 | 23 | 9 |
| Finland | 7 | 1 | 1 | 5 | 20 | 35 | 3 |
| East Germany | 7 | 1 | 1 | 5 | 16 | 43 | 3 |
| West Germany | 7 | 1 | 1 | 5 | 18 | 56 | 3 |
| United States | 7 | 1 | 1 | 5 | 21 | 64 | 3 |

| | | |
|---|---|---|
| March 7 | Soviet Union 6 | Finland 1 |
| March 7 | Czechoslovakia 10 | West Germany 1 |
| March 7 | Sweden 5 | East Germany 1 |
| March 8 | Canada 6 | West Germany 0 |
| March 8 | Sweden 2 | Soviet Union 1 |
| March 8 | Finland 11 | United States 3 |
| March 9 | Canada 11 | East Germany 5 |
| March 9 | Czechoslovakia 10 | United States 1 |
| March 10 | Czechoslovakia 8 | East Germany 3 |
| March 10 | Sweden 4 | Finland 0 |
| March 10 | Soviet Union 15 | West Germany 3 |
| March 11 | Canada 10 | United States 4 |
| March 11 | Finland 4 | West Germany 4 |
| March 12 | Canada 4 | Czechoslovakia 4 |
| March 12 | Soviet Union 12 | East Germany 0 |
| March 12 | Sweden 17 | United States 2 |
| March 13 | East Germany 1 | Finland 0 |
| March 13 | Sweden 10 | West Germany 2 |
| March 14 | Canada 12 | Finland 2 |
| March 14 | Soviet Union 3 | Czechoslovakia 1 |
| March 14 | United States 8 | West Germany 4 |
| March 15 | Sweden 4 | Canada 1 |
| March 15 | Soviet Union 9 | United States 0 |
| March 15 | Czechoslovakia 5 | Finland 2 |
| March 16 | West Germany 4 | East Germany 3 |
| March 16 | Soviet Union 4 | Canada 2 |
| March 17 | Czechoslovakia 3 | Sweden 2 |
| March 17 | United States 3 | East Germany 3 |

### Rosters
**Canada** (Trail Smoke Eaters—Bobby Kromm, coach) GK—Seth Martin—Don Fletcher, Harry Smith, Ed Pollesol, Addy Tambellini, Gerry Penner, Howie Penner, Pinoke McIntyre, Harold Jones, Walt Peacosh, Howie Hornby, George Ferguson, Jackie McLeod, Bob McKnight, Norm Lenardon, Ted Maki, Bob Forhan

**Czechoslovakia** (Jiri Anton, coach) GK—Vladimir Dzurilla, Josef Mikolas—Frantisek Tikal, Rudolf Potsch, Stanislav Sventek, Jan Kasper, Frantisek Gregor, Jiri Dolana, Jaroslav Jirik, Miroslav Vlach, Frantisek Vanek, Josef Cerny, Jaroslav Walter, Jan Starsi, Vlastimil Bubnik, Ludek Bukac, Stanislav Pryl

**East Germany** (Rudi Schmieder, coach) GK—Peter Kolbe, Klaus Hirche—Heinz Kuczera, Heinz Schildan, Wolfgang Plotka, Horst Heinze, Manfred Buder, Joachim Franke, Erich Novy, Bernd Hiller, Joachim Ziesche, Gerhard Klugel, Rainer Tudyka, Bernd Poindl, Helmut Novy, Dieter Kratzsch, Werner Engelmann, Josef Schmutzler

**Finland** (Joe Wirkkunen/Aarne Honkavaara, coaches) GK—Juhani Lahtinen, Urpo Ylonen—Matti Keinonen, Raimo Kilpio, Seppo Nikkila, Heino Pulli, Kalevi Numminen, Matti Reunamaki, Pentti Hytiainen, Jarmo Wasama, Jouni Seistamo, Matti Lampainen, Esko Luostarinen, Rauno Lehtio, Jorma Suokko, Ilkka Mesikammen, Pentti Rautalin

**Soviet Union** (Arkadi Chernyshev/Anatoli Tarasov, coaches) GK—Viktor Konovalenko, Boris Zaitsev—Eduard Ivanov, Alexander Ragulin, Viktor Kuzkin, Vitali Davydov, Nikolai Sologubov, Vladimir Yurzinov, Vyacheslav Starshinov, Alexander Almetov, Veniamin Alexandrov, Boris Mayorov, Stanislav Petukhov, Yuri Volkov, Viktor Yakushev, Yevgeni Mayorov, Yuri Paramoshkin

**Sweden** (Arne Stromberg, coach) GK—Kjell Svensson, Lennart Haggroth—Roland Stoltz, Nils Johansson, Bert-Ola Nordlander, Gert Blome, Bertil Karlsson, Sven "Tumba" Johansson, Ulf Sterner, Carl-Goran Oberg, Uno Ohrlund, Hans Mild, Ronald Pettersson, Eilert Maatta, Nils Nilsson, Lars-Eric Lundvall, Per-Olof Hardin

**United States** (Harry Cleverly, coach) GK—Ronald Chisholm, Charles Driscoll—Russell McCurdy, Frank Silka, John Warchol, Glen Marien, Tom Morse, Jack Kirrane, David Rovick, Gerald Westby, Donald Norqual, Tom Mustonen, John Poole, Marshall Tschida, Robert Quinn, Charles McCarthy, Ron Famiglietti, Bill Daley

**West Germany** (Vic Heyliger, coach) GK—Michael Hobelsberger, Heinz Ohlber—Paul Ambros, Hans-Jorg Nagel, Sylvester Wackerle, Hans Rampf, Peter Lax, Kurt Sepp, Ernst Trautwein, Helmuth Zanghellini, Georg Scholz, Ernst Kopf, Siegfried Schubert, Manfred Gmeiner, Heinz Bader, Peter Rohde, Josef Reif

## 32nd WORLD CHAMPIONSHIP (MEN)
**March 3-14, 1965**
**Tampere, Finland**

(the IIHF considers the 1964 Olympics to be the 31st World Championship)

### Final Placing

| | |
|---|---|
| Gold ........Soviet Union | 5th .........East Germany |
| Silver ......Czechoslovakia | 6th .........United States |
| Bronze ....Sweden | 7th .........Finland |
| 4th .........Canada | 8th .........Norway* |

*demoted to B Pool for 1966

### Tournament Format
Each team played every opponent once, placing determined by final standings.

### Results & Standings

| | GP | W | T | L | GF | GA | P |
|---|---|---|---|---|---|---|---|
| Soviet Union | 7 | 7 | 0 | 0 | 51 | 13 | 14 |
| Czechoslovakia | 7 | 6 | 0 | 1 | 43 | 10 | 12 |
| Sweden | 7 | 4 | 1 | 2 | 33 | 17 | 9 |
| Canada | 7 | 4 | 0 | 3 | 28 | 21 | 8 |
| East Germany | 7 | 3 | 0 | 4 | 18 | 33 | 6 |
| United States | 7 | 2 | 0 | 5 | 22 | 44 | 4 |
| Finland | 7 | 1 | 1 | 5 | 14 | 27 | 3 |
| Norway | 7 | 0 | 0 | 7 | 12 | 56 | 0 |

| | | |
|---|---|---|
| March 4 | Czechoslovakia 5 | East Germany 1 |
| March 4 | Sweden 5 | United States 2 |
| March 4 | Soviet Union 8 | Finland 4 |
| March 5 | Soviet Union 14 | Norway 2 |
| March 5 | Sweden 5 | East Germany 1 |
| March 5 | Canada 4 | Finland 0 |
| March 6 | Canada 6 | Norway 0 |
| March 6 | Czechoslovakia 12 | United States 0 |
| March 7 | Soviet Union 8 | East Germany 0 |
| March 7 | Finland 2 | Sweden 2 |
| March 8 | Czechoslovakia 9 | Norway 2 |
| March 8 | Canada 5 | United States 2 |
| March 9 | East Germany 7 | United States 4 |
| March 9 | Finland 4 | Norway 1 |
| March 10 | Canada 8 | East Germany 1 |
| March 10 | Soviet Union 5 | Sweden 3 |
| March 10 | Czechoslovakia 5 | Finland 2 |
| March 11 | Soviet Union 9 | United States 2 |
| March 11 | Sweden 10 | Norway 0 |
| March 11 | Czechoslovakia 8 | Canada 0 |
| March 12 | East Germany 5 | Norway 1 |
| March 12 | United States 4 | Finland 0 |
| March 13 | Sweden 6 | Canada 4 |
| March 13 | Soviet Union 3 | Czechoslovakia 1 |
| March 13 | East Germany 3 | Finland 2 |
| March 14 | United States 8 | Norway 6 |
| March 14 | Czechoslovakia 3 | Sweden 2 |
| March 14 | Soviet Union 4 | Canada 1 |

### Rosters
**Canada** (Gordon Simpson/Father David Bauer, coaches) GK—Ken Broderick, Don Collins—Gary Dineen, Bob Forhan, Gary Aldcorn, Al Johnson, Reg Abbott, Brian Conacher, Barry MacKenzie, Terry O'Malley, Bill Johnson, Fred Dunsmore, Gary Begg, Grant Moore, Jim MacKenzie, Roger Bourbonnais, Paul Conlin

**Czechoslovakia** (Vladimir Bouzek/Vladimir Kostka, coaches) GK—Vladimir Nadrchal, Vladimir Dzurilla—Rudolf Potsch, Josef Cerny, Vaclav Nedomansky, Stanislav Pryl, Jaroslav Jirik, Frantisek Sevcik, Jozef Golonka, Jiri Holik, Jaroslav Holik, Jan Klapac, Jan Suchy, Frantisek Tikal, Jaromir Meixner, Zdenek Kepak, Josef Capla

**East Germany** (Rudi Schmeider, coach) GK—Peter Kolbe, Klaus Hirche—Ulrich Noack, Wilfried Sock, Heinz Schildan, Wolfgang Plotka, Manfred Buder, Rainer Tudyka, Bernd Hiller, Joachim Ziesche, Bernd Poindl, Helmut Novy, Dieter Kratzsch, Erich Novy, Bernd Karrenbauer, Rudiger Noack, Joachim Franke

**Finland** (Joe Wirkkunen/Aarne Honkavaara, coaches) GK—Juhani Lahtinen, Urpo Ylonen—Jarmo Wasama, Pentti Lindgren, Kalevi Numminen, Ilkka Mesikammen, Lalli Partinen, Raimo Kilpio, Juhani Wahlsten, Matti Reunamaki, Heino Pulli, Matti Keinonen, Seppo Nikkila, Reijo Hakanen, Lasse Oksanen, Jaakko Honkanen, Pentti Rautalin

**Norway** (Ake Brask/Gunnar Kroge, coaches) GK—Kare Ostensen, Thore Nilsen—Egil Bjerklund, Odd Syversen, Thor Martinsen, Jan-Roar Thoresen, Jan-Erik Hansen, Christian Petersen, Georg Smefjell, Terje Thoen, Bjorn Elvenes, Bjorn Johansen, Arne Mikkelsen, Svein Hagensen, Steinar Bjolbakk, Ragnar Sobye, Arild Hammer

**Soviet Union** (Arkadi Chernyshev/Anatoli Tarasov, coaches) GK—Viktor Konovalenko, Viktor Zinger—Viktor Kuzkin, Eduard Ivanov, Vitali Davydov, Alexander Ragulin, Vladimir Brezhnev, Konstantin Loktev, Veniamin Alexandrov, Alexander Almetov, Boris Mayorov, Vyacheslav Starshinov, Anatoli Ionov, Leonid Volkov, Viktor Yakushev, Anatoli Firsov, Yuri Volkov

**Sweden** (Arne Stromberg, coach) GK—Kjell Svensson, Leif Holmqvist—Gert Blome, Nils Johansson, Roland Stoltz, Lennart Svedberg, Ronald Pettersson, Nisse Nilsson, Lars-Ake Sivertsson, Carl-Goran Oberg, Anders Andersson, Tord Lundstrom, Eilert Maatta, Hakan Wickberg, Uno Ohrlund, Sven "Tumba" Johansson, Bert-Ola Nordlander

**United States** (Ken Yackel, coach) GK—Tom Haugh, Ted Marks—Larry Alm, Larry Johnson, Bernard Nielsen, Herb Brooks, Bill Christian, Roger Christian, Paul Coppo, Myron Grafstrom, John Marsh, Tom Roe, Larry Smith, Dan Storsteen, Tim Taylor, Bob Lund, Sam Grafstrom

## 33rd WORLD CHAMPIONSHIP (MEN)
## March 3-14, 1966
## Ljubljana, Yugoslavia

### Final Placing

Gold ........Soviet Union
Silver ......Czechoslovakia
Bronze ....Canada
4th..........Sweden
5th .........East Germany
6th .........United States
7th .........Finland
8th .........Poland^*
^promoted from B Pool in 1965
*demoted to B Pool for 1967

### Tournament Format

Each team played every opponent once, placing determined by final standings.

### Results & Standings

| | GP | W | T | L | GF | GA | P |
|---|---|---|---|---|---|---|---|
| Soviet Union | 7 | 6 | 1 | 0 | 55 | 7 | 13 |
| Czechoslovakia | 7 | 6 | 0 | 1 | 32 | 15 | 12 |
| Canada | 7 | 5 | 0 | 2 | 33 | 10 | 10 |
| Sweden | 7 | 3 | 1 | 3 | 26 | 17 | 7 |
| East Germany | 7 | 3 | 0 | 4 | 12 | 30 | 6 |
| United States | 7 | 2 | 0 | 5 | 18 | 39 | 4 |
| Finland | 7 | 2 | 0 | 5 | 18 | 43 | 4 |
| Poland | 7 | 0 | 0 | 7 | 11 | 44 | 0 |

| | | |
|---|---|---|
| March 3 | Soviet Union 8 | Poland 1 |
| March 3 | Czechoslovakia 6 | East Germany 0 |
| March 3 | Sweden 5 | Finland 1 |
| March 3 | Canada 7 | United States 2 |
| March 5 | Canada 6 | Poland 0 |
| March 5 | Czechoslovakia 8 | Finland 1 |
| March 5 | East Germany 4 | Sweden 1 |
| March 5 | Soviet Union 11 | United States 0 |
| March 6 | Czechoslovakia 6 | Poland 1 |
| March 6 | Canada 9 | Finland 1 |
| March 6 | Sweden 6 | United States 1 |
| March 6 | Soviet Union 10 | East Germany 0 |
| March 8 | Sweden 8 | Poland 2 |
| March 8 | Soviet Union 13 | Finland 2 |
| March 8 | Czechoslovakia 7 | United States 4 |
| March 8 | Canada 6 | East Germany 0 |
| March 9 | East Germany 4 | Poland 0 |
| March 9 | Finland 4 | United States 1 |
| March 10 | Czechoslovakia 2 | Canada 1 |
| March 10 | Soviet Union 3 | Sweden 3 |
| March 11 | Finland 6 | Poland 3 |
| March 11 | United States 4 | East Germany 0 |
| March 11 | Czechoslovakia 2 | Sweden 1 |
| March 11 | Soviet Union 3 | Canada 0 |
| March 12 | United States 6 | Poland 4 |
| March 12 | East Germany 4 | Finland 3 |
| March 13 | Canada 4 | Sweden 2 |
| March 13 | Soviet Union 7 | Czechoslovakia 1 |

### Rosters

**Canada** (Jackie McLeod, coach) GK—Ken Broderick, Seth Martin—George Faulkner, Fran Huck, Roger Bourbonnais, Marshall Johnston, Ray Cadieux, Jackie McLeod, Billy MacMillan, Gary Begg, Barry MacKenzie, Morris Mott, Paul Conlin, Lorne Davis, Harvey Schmidt, Terry O'Malley, Rick McCann

**Czechoslovakia** (Vladimir Bouzek/Vladimir Kostka, coaches) GK—Vladimir Dzurilla, Jiri Holecek—Rudolf Potsch, Jaromir Meixner, Frantisek Tikal, Jan Suchy, Ladislav Smid, Josef Cerny, Vaclav Nedomansky, Jiri Holik, Jaroslav Jirik, Jan Klapac, Jozef Golonka, Stanislav Pryl, Frantisek Sevcik, Milan Koks, Jaroslav Holik

**East Germany** (Rudi Schmider, coach) GK—Peter Kolbe, Klaus Hirche—Bernd Karrenbauer, Rudiger Noack, Bernd Poindl, Joachim Ziesche, Joachim Franke, Reiner Tudyka, Dieter Kratzsch, Erhard Braun, Wolfgang Plotka, Dieter Voigt, Manfred Buder, Heinz Schildan, Erich Novy, Lothar Fuchs, Helmut Novy

**Finland** (Joe Wirkkunen/Aarne Honkavaara, coaches) GK—Risto Kaitala, Juhani Lahtinen—Reijo Hakanen, Lasse Oksansen, Jorma Peltonen, Matti Keinonen, Raimo Kilpio, Matti Reunamaki, Esa Isaksson, Juhani Jylha, Jorma Vehmanen, Lalli Partinen, Juha Rantasila, Ilkka Mesikammen, Kalevi Numminen, Erkki Mononen, Antti Heikkila

**Poland** (Zdzislaw Maselko, coach) GK—Walery Kosyl, Jozef Wisniewski—Tadeusz Kilanowicz, Jozef Stefaniak, Andrzej Zurawski, Andrzej Fonfara, Karol Fonfara, Bronislaw Gosztyla, Andrzej Szal, Wlodzimierz Komorski, Piotr Szlapa, Henryk Regula, Robert Goralczyk, Marian Zawada, Jozef Kurek, Sylwester Wilczek, Krzysztof Bialynicki-Birula

**Soviet Union** (Arkadi Chernyshev/Anatoli Tarasov, coaches) GK—Viktor Konovalenko, Viktor Zinger—Alexander Ragulin, Vladimir Brezhnev, Vitali Davydov, Oleg Zaitsev, Konstantin Loktev, Alexander Almetov, Veniamin Alexandrov, Vyacheslav Starshinov, Boris Mayorov, Viktor Yakushev, Vladimir Vikulov, Viktor Polupanov, Anatoli Firsov, Anatoli Ionov, Viktor Kuzkin

**Sweden** (Arne Stromberg, coach) GK—Leif Holmqvist, Ingemar Caris—Lars Bylund, Nils Johansson, Roland Stoltz, Lennart Svedberg, Ulf Torstensson, Nisse Nilsson, Bjorn Palmqvist, Ronald Pettersson, Folke Bengtsson, Ulf Sterner, Hans Lindberg, Tord Lundstrom, Sven "Tumba" Johansson, Lars-Ake Sivertsson, Lars-Goran Nilsson

**United States** (Vic Heyliger, coach) GK—Rod Blackburn, Tom Yurkovich—Emery Ruelle, Len Lilyholm, Ken Johannson, Ron Naslund, Marshall Tschida, Larry Stordahl, Richard Roberge, Lyle Porter, Roger Maisonneuve, Don Ross, Jim Stordahl, John Mayasich, Bob Currie, Brad Teal, Henry Therrien

## 34th WORLD CHAMPIONSHIP (MEN)
## March 18-29, 1967
## Vienna, Austria

### Final Placing

Gold ........Soviet Union
Silver ......Sweden
Bronze ....Canada
4th..........Czechoslovakia
5th .........United States
6th .........Finland
7th .........East Germany
8th .........West Germany^*
^promoted from B Pool in 1966
*demoted to B Pool for 1968

### Tournament Format

Each team played every opponent once, placing determined by final standings.

### Results & Standings

| | GP | W | T | L | GF | GA | P |
|---|---|---|---|---|---|---|---|
| Soviet Union | 7 | 7 | 0 | 0 | 58 | 9 | 14 |
| Sweden | 7 | 4 | 1 | 2 | 31 | 22 | 9 |
| Canada | 7 | 4 | 1 | 2 | 28 | 15 | 9 |
| Czechoslovakia | 7 | 3 | 2 | 2 | 29 | 18 | 8 |
| United States | 7 | 3 | 1 | 3 | 20 | 23 | 7 |
| Finland | 7 | 2 | 1 | 4 | 14 | 24 | 5 |
| East Germany | 7 | 1 | 1 | 5 | 14 | 38 | 3 |
| West Germany | 7 | 0 | 1 | 6 | 11 | 56 | 1 |

| | | |
|---|---|---|
| March 18 | Soviet Union 8 | Finland 2 |
| March 18 | Czechoslovakia 6 | West Germany 2 |
| March 18 | United States 4 | Sweden 3 |
| March 18 | Canada 6 | East Germany 3 |
| March 19 | Soviet Union 7 | United States 2 |
| March 19 | Canada 5 | Finland 1 |
| March 20 | Czechoslovakia 6 | East Germany 0 |
| March 20 | Sweden 3 | West Germany 1 |
| March 21 | Soviet Union 12 | East Germany 0 |
| March 21 | Sweden 5 | Finland 1 |
| March 21 | Canada 13 | West Germany 1 |
| March 21 | Czechoslovakia 8 | United States 3 |
| March 23 | Finland 3 | Czechoslovakia 1 |
| March 23 | Sweden 8 | East Germany 2 |
| March 23 | Soviet Union 16 | West Germany 1 |
| March 23 | Canada 2 | United States 1 |
| March 25 | Canada 1 | Czechoslovakia 1 |
| March 25 | United States 0 | East Germany 0 |
| March 25 | West Germany 2 | Finland 2 |
| March 25 | Soviet Union 9 | Sweden 1 |
| March 26 | United States 2 | Finland 0 |
| March 26 | East Germany 8 | West Germany 1 |
| March 27 | Czechoslovakia 5 | Sweden 5 |

| | | |
|---|---|---|
| March 27 | Soviet Union 2 | Canada 1 |
| March 28 | Finland 5 | East Germany 1 |
| March 28 | United States 8 | West Germany 3 |
| March 29 | Sweden 6 | Canada 0 |
| March 29 | Soviet Union 4 | Czechoslovakia 2 |

**Rosters**

**Canada** (Jackie McLeod, coach) GK—Seth Martin, Wayne Stephenson—Fran Huck, Addy Tambellini, Carl Brewer, Morris Mott, Billy MacMillan, Roger Bourbonnais, Ted Hargreaves, Gary Dineen, Marshall Johnston, Jean Cusson, Jack Bownass, Terry O'Malley, Paul Conlin, Gary Begg, Barry MacKenzie, Ray Cadieux

**Czechoslovakia** (Jaroslav Pitner/Vladimir Kostka, coaches) GK—Vladimir Nadrchal, Jiri Holecek—Jan Suchy, Frantisek Tikal, Oldrich Machac, Frantisek Pospisil, Jan Havel, Jozef Golonka, Jiri Kochta, Stanislav Pryl, Jaroslav Holik, Jiri Holik, Ivan Grandtner, Vaclav Nedomansky, Josef Cerny, Ladislav Smid, Jaroslav Jirik, Jan Hrbaty

**East Germany** (Rudi Schmieder, coach) GK—Peter Kolbe, Klaus Hirche—Wolfgang Plotka, Dieter Voigt, Manfred Buder, Erich Novy, Bernd Hiller, Joachim Ziesche, Bernd Karrenbauer, Dieter Kratzsch, Lothar Fuchs, Peter Prusa, Rudiger Noack , Bernd Poindl, Joachim Franke, Jurgen Schmutzler, Rainer Tudyka, Erhard Braun

**Finland** (Gustav Bubnik, coach) GK—Juhani Lahtinen, Urpo Ylonen—Kalevi Numminen, Pekka Marjamaki, Pekka Kuusisto, Raimo Maattanen, Matti Reunamaki, Raimo Kilpio, Matti Keinonen, Jorma Vehmanen, Juhani Wahlsten, Esa Peltonen, Lasse Oksanen, Jorma Peltonen, Reijo Hakanen, Ilkka Mesikammen, Kari Johansson, Matti Harju

**Soviet Union** (Arkadi Chernyshev/Anatoli Tarasov, coaches) GK—Viktor Konovalenko, Viktor Zinger—Alexander Ragulin, Eduard Ivanov, Viktor Kuzkin, Vitali Davydov, Viktor Yakushev, Alexander Almetov, Veniamin Alexandrov, Viktor Yaroslavtsev, Vyacheslav Starshinov, Boris Mayorov, Vladimir Vikulov, Viktor Polupanov, Anatoli Firsov, Valeri Nikitin, Oleg Zaitsev, Alexander Yakushev

**Sweden** (Arne Stromberg, coach) GK—Leif Holmquist, Kjell Svensson—Gert Blome, Arne Carlsson, Roland Stoltz, Nils Johansson, Ronald Pettersson, Nisse Nilsson, Carl Oberg, Stig Johansson, Ulf Sterner, Bjorn Palmqvist, Hans Lindberg, Leif Henriksson, Lars-Goran Nilsson, Eilert Maatta, Bert-Ola Nordlander, Folke Bengtsson

**United States** (Murray Williamson, coach) GK—Carl Wetzel, Tom Haugh—Bob Curry, Marty Howe, Don Ross, Herb Brooks, Craig Falkman, Marshall Tschida, Len Lilyholm, Ron Naslund, Terry Casey, John Cunniff, Tom Hurley, Gerry Melynchuk, Doug Woog, Dave Metzen, Art Miller

**West Germany** (Ed Reigle, coach) GK—Heinz Schmengler, Gunther Knauss—Horst Roes, Leonhard Waitl, Heinz Bader, Rudolf Thanner, Peter Lax, Kurt Schloder, Josef Reif, Lorenz Funk, Horst Ludwig, Alois Schloder, Bernd Kuhn, Heinz Weisenbach, Willi Leitner, Gustav Hanig, Horst Meindl, Walter Riedl, Helmut Klotz

## 36th WORLD CHAMPIONSHIP (MEN)
## March 15-30, 1969
## Stockholm, Sweden

(the IIHF considers the 1968 Olympics to be the 35th World Championship)

**Final Placing**

Gold ........Soviet Union
Silver ......Sweden
Bronze ....Czechoslovakia
4th .........Canada
5th .........Finland
6th .........United States*

*demoted to B Pool for 1970

**Tournament Format**

Each team played every other twice, in a double round robin, the final standings determining placing.

**Results & Standings**

| | GP | W | T | L | GF | GA | P |
|---|---|---|---|---|---|---|---|
| Soviet Union | 10 | 8 | 0 | 2 | 59 | 23 | 16 |
| Sweden | 10 | 8 | 0 | 2 | 45 | 19 | 16 |
| Czechoslovakia | 10 | 8 | 0 | 2 | 40 | 20 | 16 |
| Canada | 10 | 4 | 0 | 6 | 26 | 31 | 8 |
| Finland | 10 | 2 | 0 | 8 | 26 | 52 | 4 |
| United States | 10 | 0 | 0 | 10 | 23 | 74 | 0 |

| | | |
|---|---|---|
| March 15 | Czechoslovakia 6 | Canada 1 |
| March 15 | Sweden 6 | Finland 3 |
| March 15 | Soviet Union 17 | United States 2 |
| March 16 | Canada 5 | Finland 1 |
| March 16 | Soviet Union 4 | Sweden 2 |
| March 16 | Czechoslovakia 8 | United States 3 |
| March 18 | Czechoslovakia 7 | Finland 4 |
| March 18 | Sweden 8 | United States 2 |
| March 18 | Soviet Union 7 | Canada 1 |
| March 19 | Soviet Union 6 | Finland 1 |
| March 19 | Sweden 2 | Czechoslovakia 0 |
| March 20 | Canada 5 | United States 0 |
| March 21 | Sweden 5 | Canada 1 |
| March 21 | Czechoslovakia 2 | Soviet Union 0 |
| March 22 | Finland 4 | United States 3 |
| March 23 | Soviet Union 8 | United States 4 |
| March 23 | Sweden 5 | Finland 0 |
| March 23 | Czechoslovakia 3 | Canada 2 |
| March 24 | Soviet Union 3 | Sweden 2 |
| March 25 | Czechoslovakia 4 | Finland 2 |
| March 25 | Canada 1 | United States 0 |
| March 26 | Soviet Union 7 | Finland 3 |
| March 26 | Czechoslovakia 6 | United States 2 |
| March 27 | Sweden 4 | Canada 2 |
| March 28 | Czechoslovakia 4 | Soviet Union 3 |
| March 29 | Canada 6 | Finland 1 |
| March 29 | Sweden 10 | United States 4 |
| March 30 | Finland 7 | United States 3 |
| March 30 | Sweden 1 | Czechoslovakia 0 |
| March 30 | Soviet Union 4 | Canada 2 |

**Rosters**

**Canada** (Jackie McLeod, coach) GK—Wayne Stephenson, Steve Rexe, Ken Dryden—Terry Caffery, Bill Heindl, Fran Huck, Gerry Pinder, Steve King, Morris Mott, Richie Bayes, Roger Bourbonnais, Gary Begg, Ken Stephenson, Terry O'Malley, Ted Hargreaves, Ab DeMarco, Chuck Lefley, Kevin O'Shea, Jack Bownass, Bob Murdoch

**Czechoslovakia** (Jaroslav Pitner/Vladimir Kostka, coaches) GK—Vladimir Dzurilla, Miroslav Lacky—Oldrich Machac, Jan Suchy, Josef Horesovsky, Frantisek Pospisil, Vladimir Bednar, Jan Klapac, Josef Augusta, Frantisek Sevcik, Jozef Golonka, Jaroslav Jirik, Jan Havel, Jaroslav Holik, Jiri Holik, Jan Hrbaty, Vaclav Nedomansky, Josef Cerny, Richard Farda

**Finland** (Gustav Bubnik/Seppo Liitsola, coaches) GK—Urpo Ylonen, Lasse Kiili—Seppo Lindstrom, Juha Rantasila, Lalli Partinen, Pekka Marjamaki, Ilpo Koskela, Esa Isaksson, Lasse Oksanen, Juhani Wahlsten, Matti Keinonen, Esa Peltonen, Jorma Peltonen, Pekka Leimu, Matti Harju, Veli-Pekka Ketola, Lauri Mononen, Kari Johansson, Juhani Jylha

**Soviet Union** (Arkadi Chernyshev/Anatoli Tarasov, coaches) GK—Viktor Zinger, Viktor Puchkov—Alexander Ragulin, Vitali Davydov, Viktor Kuzkin, Vladimir Yurzinov, Igor Romishevski, Vladimir Lutchenko, Yevgeni Paladiev, Valeri Kharlamov, Anatoli Firsov, Yevgeni Zimin, Vyacheslav Starshinov, Boris Mikhailov, Yevgeni Mishakov, Vladimir Petrov, Alexander Yakushev, Alexander Maltsev, Vladimir Vikulov

**Sweden** (Arne Stromberg, coach) GK—Leif Holmqvist, Gunnar Backman—Kjell-Rune Milton, Arne Carlsson, Lennart Svedberg, Bert-Ola Nordlander, Nils Johansson, Lars-Erik Sjoberg, Hakan Nygren, Stefan Karlsson, Tord Lundstrom, Stig-Goran Johansson, Ulf Sterner, Lars-Goran Nilsson, Leif Henriksson, Roger Olsson, Bjorn Palmqvist, Dick Yderstrom, Mats Hysing

**United States** (John Mayasich, coach) GK—Mike Curran, John Lothrop—Bob Paradise, Bruce Riutta, Carl Lackey, James Branch, John Mayasich, Bill Reichart, Paul Coppo, Keith Christiansen, Larry Stordahl, Jerry Lackey, Tim Sheehy, Larry Skime, Gary Gambucci, Pete Markle, Ron Nasland, Larry Pleau

## 37th WORLD CHAMPIONSHIP (MEN)
## March 14-30, 1970
## Stockholm, Sweden

**Final Placing**

Gold ........Soviet Union
Silver ......Sweden
Bronze ....Czechoslovakia
4th .........Finland
5th .........East Germany^*
6th .........Poland^*

^promoted from B Pool in 1969
*demoted to B Pool for 1971

**Tournament Format**

Each team played every other twice, in a double round robin, the final standings determining placing.

**Results & Standings**

| | GP | W | T | L | GF | GA | P |
|---|---|---|---|---|---|---|---|
| Soviet Union | 10 | 9 | 0 | 1 | 68 | 11 | 18 |
| Sweden | 10 | 7 | 1 | 2 | 45 | 21 | 15 |
| Czechoslovakia | 10 | 5 | 1 | 4 | 47 | 30 | 11 |
| Finland | 10 | 5 | 0 | 5 | 31 | 40 | 10 |
| East Germany | 10 | 2 | 1 | 7 | 20 | 50 | 5 |
| Poland | 10 | 0 | 1 | 9 | 11 | 70 | 1 |

| | | |
|---|---|---|
| March 14 | Soviet Union 2 | Finland 1 |
| March 14 | Sweden 6 | East Germany 1 |
| March 14 | Czechoslovakia 6 | Poland 3 |
| March 15 | Soviet Union 12 | East Germany 1 |
| March 15 | Finland 9 | Poland 1 |
| March 15 | Sweden 5 | Czechoslovakia 4 |
| March 17 | Soviet Union 7 | Poland 0 |
| March 17 | Czechoslovakia 4 | East Germany 1 |
| March 17 | Finland 3 | Sweden 1 |
| March 18 | Soviet Union 3 | Czechoslovakia 1 |
| March 19 | Finland 1 | East Germany 0 |

| | | |
|---|---|---|
| March 19 | Sweden 11 | Poland 0 |
| March 20 | Czechoslovakia 9 | Finland 1 |
| March 20 | Sweden 4 | Soviet Union 2 |
| March 21 | Poland 2 | East Germany 2 |
| March 22 | Czechoslovakia 10 | Poland 2 |
| March 22 | Sweden 6 | East Germany 2 |
| March 22 | Soviet Union 16 | Finland 1 |
| March 24 | Finland 4 | Poland 0 |
| March 24 | Soviet Union 7 | East Germany 1 |
| March 24 | Sweden 2 | Czechoslovakia 2 |
| March 25 | Soviet Union 11 | Poland 0 |
| March 25 | Czechoslovakia 7 | East Germany 3 |
| March 26 | Sweden 4 | Finland 3 |
| March 27 | Soviet Union 5 | Czechoslovakia 1 |
| March 28 | East Germany 4 | Finland 3 |
| March 28 | Sweden 5 | Poland 1 |
| March 30 | East Germany 5 | Poland 2 |
| March 30 | Finland 5 | Czechoslovakia 3 |
| March 30 | Soviet Union 3 | Sweden 1 |

**Rosters**

**Czechoslovakia** (Jaroslav Pitner/Vladimir Kostka, coaches) GK—Vladimir Dzurilla, Miroslav Lacky—Jan Suchy, Josef Horesovsky, Frantisek Pospisil, Oldrich Machac, Lubomir Ujvary, Vladimir Bednar, Ivan Hlinka, Jaroslav Holik, Jiri Holik, Vaclav Nedomansky, Jiri Kochta, Richard Farda, Josef Cerny, Vladimir Martinec, Jan Hrbaty, Stanislav Pryl, Frantisek Sevcik

**East Germany** (Rudi Schmieler, coach) GK—Klaus Hirche, Dieter Purschel—Dietmar Peters, Erich Braun, Wolfgang Plotka, Peter Slapke, Bernd Karrenbauer, Dieter Dewitz, Rudiger Noack, Hartmut Nickel, Joachim Ziesche, Winfried Rohrbach, Rainer Patschinski, Bernd Hiller, Lothar Fuchs, Rainhard Karger, Dieter Rohl, Helmut Novy, Rolf Bielas, Peter Prusa

**Finland** (Seppo Liitsola, coaches) GK—Urpo Ylonen, Jorma Valtonen—Seppo Lindstrom, Ilpo Koskela, Juha Rantasila, Heikki Riihiranta, Pekka Marjamaki, Lalli Partinen, Pekka Leimu, Jorma Peltonen, Lasse Oksanen, Jorma Vehmanen, Veli-Pekka Ketola, Matti Keinonen, Vaino Kolkka, Matti Murto, Lauri Mononen, Esa Peltonen, Juhani Tamminen, Harri Linnonmaa

**Poland** (Anatoli Yegorov, coach) GK—Walery Kosyl, Andrzej Tkacz—Andrzej Slowakiewicz, Stanislaw Fryzlewicz, Ludwik Czachowski, Robert Goralczyk, Marian Feter, Stanislaw Szewczyk, Walenty Zietara, Jozef Stefaniak, Tadeusz Kacik, Czeslaw Ruchala, Marian Kajzerek, Krzysztof Bialynicki-Birula, Tadeusz Obloj, Tadeusz Malicki, Feliks Goralczyk, Bogdan Migacz, Mieczysylaw Jaskierski, Wlodzimierz Komorski

**Soviet Union** (Arkadi Chernyshev/Anatoli Tarasov, coach) GK—Viktor Konovalenko, Vladislav Tretiak—Vitali Davydov, Valeri Vasilyev, Alexander Ragulin, Vladimir Lutchenko, Igor Romishevski, Yevgeni Paladiev, Valeri Nikitin, Valeri Kharlamov, Vladimir Petrov, Boris Mikhailov, Anatoli Firsov, Viktor Polupanov, Vladimir Vikulov, Vyacheslav Starshinov, Alexander Maltsev, Yevgeni Mishakov, Alexander Yakushev, Vladimir Shadrin

**Sweden** (Arne Stromberg, coach) GK—Leif Holmqvist, Gunnar Backman—Arne Carlsson, Lennart Svedberg, Nils Johansson, Kjell-Rune Milton, Lars-Erik Sjoberg, Thommy Abrahamsson, Anders Hagstrom, Stefan Karlsson, Hakan Wickberg, Tord Lundstrom, Stig-Goran Johansson, Ulf Sterner, Lars-Goran Nilsson, Roger Olsson, Bjorn Palmqvist, Anders Hedberg, Anders Nordin, Hans Lindberg

## 38th WORLD CHAMPIONSHIP (MEN)
## March 19-April 3, 1971
## Berne/Geneva, Switzerland

**Final Placing**

| | |
|---|---|
| Gold ........Soviet Union | 4th .........Finland |
| Silver ......Czechoslovakia | 5th .........West Germany^ |
| Bronze ....Sweden | 6th .........United States^* |

^promoted from B Pool in 1970
*demoted to B Pool for 1972

**Tournament Format**

Each team played every other twice, in a double round robin, the final standings determining placing.

**Results & Standings**

| | GP | W | T | L | GF | GA | P |
|---|---|---|---|---|---|---|---|
| Soviet Union | 10 | 8 | 1 | 1 | 77 | 24 | 17 |
| Czechoslovakia | 10 | 7 | 1 | 2 | 44 | 20 | 15 |
| Sweden | 10 | 5 | 1 | 4 | 29 | 33 | 11 |
| Finland | 10 | 4 | 1 | 5 | 31 | 42 | 9 |
| West Germany | 10 | 2 | 0 | 8 | 22 | 62 | 4 |
| United States | 10 | 2 | 0 | 8 | 31 | 53 | 4 |

| | | | |
|---|---|---|---|
| March 19 | Berne | Soviet Union 11 | West Germany 2 |
| March 19 | Berne | United States 5 | Czechoslovakia 1 |
| March 20 | Berne | Finland 4 | West Germany 3 |
| March 20 | Berne | Sweden 4 | United States 2 |
| March 21 | Berne | Sweden 6 | Czechoslovakia 5 |
| March 21 | Berne | Soviet Union 8 | Finland 1 |
| March 22 | Berne | Czechoslovakia 9 | West Germany 1 |
| March 22 | Berne | Soviet Union 10 | United States 2 |
| March 23 | Berne | Sweden 7 | West Germany 2 |
| March 23 | Berne | Finland 7 | United States 4 |
| March 24 | Berne | Sweden 1 | Finland 1 |
| March 24 | Berne | Czechoslovakia 3 | Soviet Union 3 |
| March 25 | Berne | West Germany 7 | United States 2 |
| March 26 | Berne | Czechoslovakia 5 | Finland 0 |
| March 26 | Berne | Soviet Union 8 | Sweden 0 |
| March 27 | Geneva | Czechoslovakia 5 | United States 0 |
| March 27 | Geneva | Soviet Union 12 | West Germany 1 |
| March 28 | Geneva | Finland 7 | West Germany 2 |
| March 28 | Geneva | Sweden 4 | United States 3 |
| March 29 | Geneva | Soviet Union 10 | Finland 1 |
| March 29 | Geneva | Czechoslovakia 3 | Sweden 1 |
| March 30 | Geneva | Czechoslovakia 4 | West Germany 0 |
| March 30 | Geneva | Soviet Union 7 | United States 5 |
| March 31 | Geneva | West Germany 2 | Sweden 1 |
| March 31 | Geneva | Finland 7 | United States 3 |
| April 1 | Geneva | Sweden 2 | Finland 1 |
| April 1 | Geneva | Czechoslovakia 5 | Soviet Union 2 |
| April 2 | Geneva | United States 5 | West Germany 1 |
| April 3 | Geneva | Czechoslovakia 4 | Finland 2 |
| April 3 | Geneva | Soviet Union 6 | Sweden 3 |

**Rosters**

**Czechoslovakia** (Jaroslav Pitner/Vladimir Kostka, coaches) GK—Marcel Sakac, Jiri Holecek—Josef Horesovsky, Oldrich Machac, Rudolf Tajcnar, Frantisek Panchartek, Frantisek Pospisil, Jan Suchy, Jiri Bubla, Jiri Kochta, Jan Havel, Vladimir Martinec, Richard Farda, Bohuslav Stastny, Vaclav Nedomansky, Josef Cerny, Bedrich Brunclik, Eduard Novak, Jiri Holik, Ivan Hlinka

**Finland** (Seppo Liitsola/Rauli Virtanen, coaches) GK—Jorma Valtonen, Urpo Ylonen—Ilpo Koskela, Seppo Lindstrom, Hannu Luojola, Pekka Marjamaki, Jouko Oystyla, Heikki Jarn, Esa Isaksson, Veli-Pekka Ketola, Harri Linnonmaa, Erkki Mononen, Lauri Mononen, Matti Murto, Lasse Oksanen, Esa Peltonen, Seppo Repo, Tommi Salmelainen, Juhani Tamminen, Jorma Vehmanen

**Soviet Union** (Arkadi Chernyshev/Anatoli Tarasov, coaches) GK—Viktor Konovalenko, Vladislav Tretiak—Vitali Davydov, Vladimir Lutchenko, Viktor Kuzkin, Alexander Ragulin, Igor Romishevski, Gennadi Tsygankov, Yuri Lyapkin, Vyacheslav Starshinov, Yevgeni Zimin, Alexander Maltsev, Anatoli Firsov, Yevgeni Mishakov, Boris Mikhailov, Alexander Martinyuk, Vladimir Petrov, Valeri Kharlamov, Vladimir Vikulov, Vladimir Shadrin

**Sweden** (Arne Stromberg, coach) GK—Leif Holmqvist, Christer Abrahamsson, William Lofqvist—Arne Carlsson, Lennart Svedberg, Bert-Ola Nordlander, Tommy Abrahamsson, Thommie Bergman, Kjell-Rune Milton, Gunnar Andersson, Stefan Karlsson, Hakan Wickberg, Tord Lundstrom, Stig-Goran Johansson, Ulf Sterner, Lars-Goran Nilsson, Hakan Nygren, Bjorn Palmqvist, Inge Hammarstrom, Hakan Pettersson, Hans Lindberg

**United States** (Murray Williamson, coach) GK—Mike Curran, Carl Wetzel, Dick Tomasoni—Jim McElmury, Bruce Riutta, Tom Mellor, Don Ross, George Konik, Dick McGlynn, Gary Gambucci, Keith Christiansen, Len Lilyholm, Henry Boucha, Craig Patrick, Pete Fichuk, Dick Toomey, Paul Schilling, Bob Lindberg, Craig Falkman, Tim Sheehy, Kevin Ahearn

**West Germany** (Gerhard Kiessling, coach) GK—Josef Schramm, Toni Kehle—Rudolf Thanner, Josef Volk, Hans Schichtl, Erwin Riedmeier, Werner Modes, Paul Langner, Johann Eimansberger, Karl-Heinz Egger, Klaus Ego, Anton Hofherr, Otto Schneitberger, Heinz Weisenbach, Alois Schloder, Gustav Hanig, Rainer Philipp, Bernd Kuhn, Franz Hofherr, Lorenz Funk

## 39th WORLD CHAMPIONSHIP (MEN)
## April 7-22, 1972
## Prague, Czechoslovakia

**Final Placing**

| | |
|---|---|
| Gold ........Czechoslovakia | 4th .........Finland |
| Silver ......Soviet Union | 5th .........West Germany |
| Bronze ....Sweden | 6th .........Switzerland^* |

^promoted from B Pool in 1971
*demoted to B Pool for 1973

**Tournament Format**

Each team played every other twice, in a double round robin, the final standings determining placing.

**Results & Standings**

| | GP | W | T | L | GF | GA | P |
|---|---|---|---|---|---|---|---|
| Czechoslovakia | 10 | 9 | 1 | 0 | 72 | 16 | 19 |
| Soviet Union | 10 | 7 | 2 | 1 | 78 | 19 | 16 |
| Sweden | 10 | 5 | 1 | 4 | 49 | 33 | 11 |
| Finland | 10 | 4 | 0 | 6 | 47 | 48 | 8 |
| West Germany | 10 | 2 | 0 | 8 | 23 | 76 | 4 |
| Switzerland | 10 | 1 | 0 | 9 | 19 | 96 | 2 |

| | | |
|---|---|---|
| April 7 | Czechoslovakia 19 | Switzerland 1 |
| April 7 | Soviet Union 11 | West Germany 2 |
| April 8 | Sweden 12 | Switzerland 1 |

| | | |
|---|---|---|
| April 8 | Finland 8 | West Germany 5 |
| April 9 | Czechoslovakia 4 | Sweden 1 |
| April 9 | Soviet Union 10 | Finland 2 |
| April 10 | Czechoslovakia 8 | West Germany 1 |
| April 10 | Soviet Union 10 | Switzerland 2 |
| April 11 | Sweden 10 | West Germany 0 |
| April 11 | Switzerland 3 | Finland 2 |
| April 12 | Czechoslovakia 3 | Soviet Union 3 |
| April 12 | Sweden 2 | Finland 1 |
| April 13 | West Germany 6 | Switzerland 3 |
| April 14 | Czechoslovakia 5 | Finland 3 |
| April 14 | Soviet Union 11 | Sweden 2 |
| April 15 | Czechoslovakia 12 | Switzerland 2 |
| April 15 | Soviet Union 7 | West Germany 0 |
| April 16 | Sweden 8 | Switzerland 5 |
| April 16 | Finland 13 | West Germany 3 |
| April 17 | Czechoslovakia 2 | Sweden 0 |
| April 17 | Soviet Union 7 | Finland 2 |
| April 18 | Czechoslovakia 8 | West Germany 1 |
| April 18 | Soviet Union 14 | Switzerland 0 |
| April 19 | Sweden 7 | West Germany 1 |
| April 19 | Finland 9 | Switzerland 1 |
| April 20 | Czechoslovakia 3 | Soviet Union 2 |
| April 20 | Finland 5 | Sweden 4 |
| April 21 | West Germany 4 | Switzerland 1 |
| April 22 | Sweden 3 | Soviet Union 3 |
| April 22 | Czechoslovakia 8 | Finland 2 |

**Rosters**

**Czechoslovakia** (Jaroslav Pitner/Vladimir Kostka, coaches) GK—Vladimir Dzurilla, Jiri Holecek—Josef Horesovsky, Frantisek Pospisil, Oldrich Machac, Rudolf Tajcnar, Vladimir Bednar, Jiri Bubla, Ivan Hlinka, Jaroslav Holik, Jiri Holik, Vaclav Nedomansky, Jiri Kochta, Richard Farda, Vladimir Martinec, Jan Klapac, Bohuslav Stastny, Julius Haas, Josef Palecek, Milan Kuzela

**Finland** (Seppo Liitsola/Rauli Virtanen, coaches) GK—Jorma Valtonen, Stig Wetzell—Pekka Marjamaki, Timo Nummelin, Juha Rantasila, Pekka Rautakallio, Heikki Riihiranta, Pertti Valkepaa, Jouko Oystila, Timo Turunen, Seppo Repo, Lauri Mononen, Esa Peltonen, Lasse Oksanen, Veli-Pekka Ketola, Juhani Tamminen, Harri Linnonmaa, Matti Keinonen, Matti Murto, Seppo Ahokainen

**Soviet Union** (Vsevolod Bobrov, coach) GK—Vladislav Tretiak, Vladimir Shepovalov—Gennadi Tsygankov, Valeri Vasilyev, Alexander Ragulin, Viktor Kuzkin, Vladimir Lutchenko, Igor Romishevski, Alexander Gusev, Valeri Kharlamov, Vladimir Petrov, Boris Mikhailov, Yuri Blinov, Vyacheslav Solodukhin, Vladimir Vikulov, Vladimir Shadrin, Alexander Maltsev, Yevgeni Mishakov, Alexander Yakushev, Vyacheslav Anisin

**Sweden** (Billy Harris, coach) GK—Leif Holmqvist, Christer Abrahamsson, Curt Larsson—Thommie Bergman, Bjorn Johansson, Borje Salming, Carl-Johan Sundqvist, Lars-Erik Sjoberg, Thommy Abrahamsson, Stig Ostling, Stefan Karlsson, Hakan Wickberg, Tord Lundström, Stig-Goran Johansson, Inge Hammarstrom, Lars-Goran Nilsson, Mats Lindh, Bjorn Palmqvist, Anders Hedberg, Hakan Pettersson, Stig Larsson

**Switzerland** (Gaston Pelletier, coach) GK—Alfio Molina, Gerald Rigolet—Gaston Furrer, Charles Henzen, Rene Huguenin, Peter Aeschlimann, Marcel Sgualdo, Francis Reinhard, Michel Turler, Gerard Dubi, Ueli Luthi, Paul Probst, Hans Keller, Toni Neininger, Walter Durst, Heinz Jenni, Guy Dubois, Roger Chappot, Rene Berra, Bruno Wittwer

**West Germany** (Gerhard Kiessling, coach) GK—Toni Kehle, Rainer Makatsch, Franz Funk—Josef Volk, Rudolf Thanner, Paul Langner, Hans Schichtl, Harald Kadow, Otto Schneitberger, Michael Eibl, Alois Schloder, Gustav Hanig, Bernd Kuhn, Johann Eimansberger, Lorenz Funk, Hans Rothkirch, Karl-Heinz Egger, Rainer Philipp, Anton Pohl, Anton Hofherr, Reinhold Bauer

## 40th WORLD CHAMPIONSHIP (MEN)
## March 31-April 15, 1973
## Moscow, Soviet Union

**Final Placing**

Gold ........Soviet Union
Silver ......Sweden
Bronze ....Czechoslovakia
4th .........Finland
5th .........Poland^
6th .........West Germany*

^promoted from B Pool in 1972
*demoted to B Pool for 1974

**Tournament Format**

Each team played every other twice, in a double round robin, the final standings determining placing.

**Results & Standings**

| | GP | W | T | L | GF | GA | P |
|---|---|---|---|---|---|---|---|
| Soviet Union | 10 | 10 | 0 | 0 | 100 | 18 | 20 |
| Sweden | 10 | 7 | 1 | 2 | 53 | 23 | 15 |
| Czechoslovakia | 10 | 6 | 1 | 3 | 48 | 20 | 13 |
| Finland | 10 | 3 | 1 | 6 | 24 | 39 | 7 |
| Poland | 10 | 1 | 1 | 8 | 14 | 76 | 3 |
| West Germany | 10 | 1 | 0 | 9 | 19 | 82 | 2 |

| | | |
|---|---|---|
| March 31 | Czechoslovakia 14 | Poland 1 |
| March 31 | Soviet Union 17 | West Germany 1 |
| April 1 | Finland 8 | West Germany 3 |
| April 1 | Sweden 11 | Poland 2 |
| April 2 | Sweden 2 | Czechoslovakia 0 |
| April 2 | Soviet Union 8 | Finland 2 |
| April 3 | Czechoslovakia 4 | West Germany 2 |
| April 3 | Soviet Union 9 | Poland 3 |
| April 4 | Finland 5 | Poland 0 |
| April 4 | Sweden 8 | West Germany 2 |
| April 5 | Sweden 3 | Finland 2 |
| April 5 | Soviet Union 3 | Czechoslovakia 2 |
| April 6 | West Germany 4 | Poland 2 |
| April 7 | Soviet Union 6 | Sweden 1 |
| April 7 | Czechoslovakia 4 | Finland 2 |
| April 8 | Czechoslovakia 4 | Poland 1 |
| April 8 | Soviet Union 18 | West Germany 2 |
| April 9 | Sweden 7 | Poland 0 |
| April 9 | Finland 2 | West Germany 1 |
| April 10 | Soviet Union 9 | Finland 1 |
| April 10 | Sweden 3 | Czechoslovakia 3 |
| April 11 | Soviet Union 20 | Poland 0 |
| April 11 | Czechoslovakia 7 | West Germany 2 |
| April 12 | Sweden 12 | West Germany 1 |
| April 12 | Finland 1 | Poland 1 |
| April 13 | Sweden 2 | Finland 1 |
| April 13 | Soviet Union 4 | Czechoslovakia 2 |
| April 14 | Poland 4 | West Germany 1 |
| April 15 | Czechoslovakia 8 | Finland 0 |
| April 15 | Soviet Union 6 | Sweden 4 |

**Rosters**

**Czechoslovakia** (Jaroslav Pitner/Vladimir Kostka, coaches) GK—Jiri Holecek, Jiri Crha—Oldrich Machac, Frantisek Pospisil, Jiri Bubla, Josef Horesovsky, Milan Kuzela, Karel Vohralik, Petr Adamik, Jiri Holik, Jaroslav Holik, Jan Klapac, Vaclav Nedomansky, Jiri Kochta, Josef Palecek, Vladimir Martinec, Jiri Novak, Bohuslav Stastny, Ivan Hlinka, Richard Farda

**Finland** (Len Lunde/Heimo Huotari, coaches) GK—Jorma Valtonen, Antti Leppanen—Jouko Oystila, Heikki Riihiranta, Ilpo Koskela, Seppo Lindstrom, Lalli Partinen, Pekka Kuusisto, Pekka Rautakallio, Lauri Mononen, Veli-Pekka Ketola, Seppo Repo, Seppo Ahokainen, Timo Sutinen, Henry Leppa, Esa Peltonen, Timo Turunen, Juhanni Tamminen, Jorma Vehmanen, Matti Keinonen

**Poland** (Anatoli Jegorow, coach) GK—Walery Kosyl, Wojciech Wojtynek—Jerzy Potz, Adam Kopczynski, Ludwig Czachowski, Andrzej Szczepaniec, Tadeusz Obloj, Tadeusz Kacik, Jozef Slowakiewicz, Walenty Zietara, Krzysztof Bialynicki-Birula, Mieczyslaw Jaskierski, Jan Szeja, Andrzej Slowakiewicz, Stanislaw Fryzlewicz, Stefan Chowaniec, Wieslaw Tokarz, Leszek Tokarz, Robert Goralczyk, Jozef Batkiewicz

**Soviet Union** (Vsevolod Bobrov, coach) GK—Vladislav Tretiak, Alexander Sidelnikov—Gennadi Tsygankov, Valeri Vasilyev, Alexander Ragulin, Yevgeni Paladiev, Vladimir Lutchenko, Yuri Lyapkin, Alexander Gusev, Valeri Kharlamov, Vladimir Petrov, Boris Mikhailov, Alexander Bodunov, Yuri Lebedev, Alexander Volchkov, Vladimir Shadrin, Alexander Maltsev, Alexander Martinyuk, Alexander Yakushev, Vyacheslav Anisin

**Sweden** (Kjell Svensson, coach) GK—Christer Abrahamsson, William Lofqvist, Curt Larsson—Roland Bond, Arne Carlsson, Borje Salming, Thommy Abrahamsson, Lars-Erik Sjoberg, Karl-Johan Sundqvist, Bjorn Johansson, Hakan Wickberg, Tord Lundstrom, Stefan Karlsson, Ulf Sterner, Mats Ahlberg, Ulf Nilsson, Dick Yderstrom, Inge Hammarstrom, Anders Hedberg, Dan Soderstrom, Kjell-Arne Vickstrom

**West Germany** (Gerhard Kiessling, coach) GK—Toni Kehle, Robert Merkle—Paul Langner, Rudolf Thanner, Eric Weide, Josef Volk, Helmut Keller, Ignaz Berndaner, Udo Kiessling, Bernd Kuhn, Lorenz Funk, Alois Schloder, Rainer Philipp, Erich Kuhnhackl, Reinhold Bauer, Martin Hinterstocker, Karl-Heinz Egger, Johan Eimansberger, Josef Wunsch

## 41st WORLD CHAMPIONSHIP (MEN)
## April 5-20, 1974
## Helsinki, Finland

**Final Placing**

Gold ........Soviet Union
Silver ......Czechoslovakia
Bronze ....Sweden
4th .........Finland
5th .........Poland
6th .........East Germany^*

^promoted from B Pool in 1973
*demoted to B Pool for 1975

**Tournament Format**

Each team played every other twice, in a double round robin, the final standings determining placing.

**Results & Standings**

| | GP | W | T | L | GF | GA | P |
|---|---|---|---|---|---|---|---|
| Soviet Union | 10 | 9 | 0 | 1 | 64 | 18 | 18 |
| Czechoslovakia | 10 | 7 | 0 | 3 | 57 | 20 | 14 |
| Sweden | 10 | 5 | 1 | 4 | 38 | 24 | 11 |
| Finland | 10 | 4 | 2 | 4 | 34 | 39 | 10 |
| Poland | 10 | 1 | 2 | 7 | 22 | 64 | 4 |
| East Germany | 10 | 1 | 1 | 8 | 21 | 71 | 3 |

| | | |
|---|---|---|
| April 5 | Czechoslovakia 8 | Poland 0 |
| April 5 | Soviet Union 5 | East Germany 0 |
| April 6 | Poland 5 | Sweden 0* |
| April 6 | Finland 7 | East Germany 3 |
| April 7 | Czechoslovakia 3 | Sweden 2 |
| April 7 | Soviet Union 7 | Finland 1 |
| April 8 | Czechoslovakia 8 | East Germany 0 |
| April 8 | Soviet Union 8 | Poland 3 |
| April 9 | Sweden 10 | East Germany 1 |
| April 9 | Finland 2 | Poland 2 |
| April 10 | Czechoslovakia 7 | Soviet Union 2 |
| April 10 | Sweden 3 | Finland 3 |
| April 11 | East Germany 5 | Poland 3 |
| April 12 | Czechoslovakia 5 | Finland 0** |
| April 12 | Soviet Union 3 | Sweden 1 |
| April 13 | Czechoslovakia 12 | Poland 3 |
| April 13 | Soviet Union 10 | East Germany 3 |
| April 14 | Sweden 3 | Poland 1 |
| April 14 | Finland 7 | East Germany 1 |
| April 15 | Sweden 3 | Czechoslovakia 0 |
| April 15 | Soviet Union 6 | Finland 1 |
| April 16 | Czechoslovakia 9 | East Germany 2 |
| April 16 | Soviet Union 17 | Poland 0 |
| April 17 | Sweden 9 | East Germany 3 |
| April 17 | Finland 6 | Poland 2 |
| April 18 | Soviet Union 3 | Czechoslovakia 1 |
| April 18 | Sweden 6 | Finland 2 |
| April 19 | East Germany 3 | Poland 3 |
| April 20 | Soviet Union 3 | Sweden 1 |
| April 20 | Finland 5 | Czechoslovakia 4 |

*score was Sweden 4-Poland 1, but overturned to 5-0 for Poland after Ulf Nilsson (SWE) tested positive for efedrin

**score was Finland 5-Czechoslovakia 2 but overturned to 5-0 for Czechoslovakia after Stig Wetzell (FIN) failed post-game doping test

**Rosters**

**Czechoslovakia** (Karel Gut/Jan Starsi, coaches) GK—Jiri Crha, Jiri Holecek—Oldrich Machac, Jiri Neubauer, Frantisek Pospisil, Jiri Kochta, Miroslav Dvorak, Vladimir Martinec, Richard Farda, Bohuslav Stastny, Vaclav Nedomansky, Josef Palecek, Jan Suchy, Milan Kuzela, Jiri Bubla, Jiri Holik, Ivan Hlinka, Vladimir Veith, Bohuslav Ebermann, Josef Augusta

**East Germany** (Joachim Ziesche/Klaus Hirche, coaches) GK—Joachim Hurbanek, Wolfgang Fischer—Dietmar Peters, Dieter Huschto, Hartwig Schur, Frank Braun, Dieter Frenzel, Bernd Karrenbauer, Gerhard Muller, Hartmut Nickel, Rainer Patschinski, Joachim Stasche, Rudiger Noack, Ralf Thomas, Reinhard Karger, Dieter Simon, Peter Slapke, Rolf Bielas, Bernd Engelmann, Peter Prusa

**Finland** (Kalevi Numminen/Raimo Maatanen, coaches) GK—Stig Wetzell, Jorma Valtonen, Antti Leppanen—Juha Rantasila, Seppo Lindstrom, Jouko Oystila, Heikki Riihiranta, Timo Saari, Pekka Marjamaki, Seppo Suoraniemi, Seppo Ahokainen, Henry Leppa, Esa Peltonen, Veli-Pekka Ketola, Harri Linnonmaa, Juhani Tamminen, Matti Murto, Lasse Oksanen, Jorma Peltonen, Seppo Repo, Timo Sutinen

**Poland** (Anatoli Yegorov, coach) GK—Walery Kosyl, Andrzej Tkacz—Henryk Janiszewski, Ludwik Czachowski, Andrzej Slowakiewicz, Robert Goralczyk, Stanislaw Fryzlewicz, Jan Piecko, Jozef Slowakiewicz, Leszek Tokarz, Walenty Zietara, Wieslaw Tokarz, Tadeusz Obloj, Tadeusz Kacik, Stefan Chowaniec, Mieczyslaw Jaskierski, Karol Zurek, Jerzy Potz, Adam Kopczynski, Jan Szeja

**Soviet Union** (Vsevolod Bobrov, coach) GK—Alexander Sidelnikov, Vladislav Tretiak—Alexander Gusev, Vladimir Lutchenko, Yuri Lyapkin, Yuri Shatalov, Valeri Vasilyev, Gennadi Tsygankov, Sergei Kapustin, Alexander Maltsev, Yuri Lebedev, Viktor Kuznetsov, Boris Mikhailov, Alexander Yakushev, Vladimir Petrov, Valeri Kharlamov, Vladimir Shadrin, Vyacheslav Anisin, Vladimir Repnyev, Alexander Bodunov

**Sweden** (Kjell Svensson, coach) GK—Christer Abrahamsson, Curt Larsson—Karl-Johan Sundqvist, Arne Carlsson, Kjell-Rune Milton, Gunnar Andersson, Thommy Abrahamsson, Lars-Erik Sjoberg, Bjorn Johansson, Hakan Wickberg, Sitg-Goran Johansson, Stefan Karlsson, Lars-Goran Nilsson, Mats Ahlberg, Ulf Nilsson, Willy Lindstrom, Anders Hedberg, Dan Labraaten, Per-Olov Brasar, Dan Soderstrom, Hakan Pettersson

## 42nd WORLD CHAMPIONSHIP (MEN)
## April 3-19, 1975
## Munich/Dusseldorf, West Germany

**Final Placing**

| | |
|---|---|
| Gold ........Soviet Union | 4th .........Finland |
| Silver ......Czechoslovakia | 5th .........Poland |
| Bronze ....Sweden | 6th .........United States^ |

^promoted from B Pool in 1974

~no team demoted for 1976 as World Championship expanded to eight teams

**Tournament Format**

Each team played every other twice, in a double round robin, the final standings determining placing.

**Results & Standings**

| | GP | W | T | L | GF | GA | P |
|---|---|---|---|---|---|---|---|
| Soviet Union | 10 | 10 | 0 | 0 | 90 | 23 | 20 |
| Czechoslovakia | 10 | 8 | 0 | 2 | 55 | 19 | 16 |
| Sweden | 10 | 5 | 0 | 5 | 51 | 34 | 10 |
| Finland | 10 | 5 | 0 | 5 | 36 | 34 | 10 |
| Poland | 10 | 2 | 0 | 8 | 18 | 78 | 4 |
| United States | 10 | 0 | 0 | 10 | 22 | 84 | 0 |

| | | | |
|---|---|---|---|
| April 3 | Munich | Czechoslovakia 5 | Poland 0 |
| April 3 | Munich | Soviet Union 10 | United States 5 |
| April 4 | Munich | Sweden 10 | Poland 0 |
| April 4 | Munich | Finland 7 | United States 4 |
| April 5 | Munich | Czechoslovakia 5 | Sweden 2 |
| April 5 | Munich | Soviet Union 8 | Finland 4 |
| April 6 | Munich | Czechoslovakia 8 | United States 3 |
| April 6 | Munich | Soviet Union 13 | Poland 2 |
| April 7 | Munich | Sweden 7 | United States 0 |
| April 7 | Munich | Finland 5 | Poland 2 |
| April 8 | Munich | Soviet Union 5 | Czechoslovakia 2 |
| April 8 | Munich | Sweden 1 | Finland 0 |
| April 9 | Munich | Poland 5 | United States 3 |
| April 10 | Munich | Czechoslovakia 6 | Finland 2 |
| April 10 | Munich | Soviet Union 4 | Sweden 1 |
| April 12 | Dusseldorf | Czechoslovakia 8 | Poland 2 |
| April 12 | Dusseldorf | Soviet Union 13 | United States 1 |
| April 13 | Dusseldorf | Sweden 13 | Poland 0 |
| April 13 | Dusseldorf | Finland 9 | United States 1 |
| April 14 | Dusseldorf | Czechoslovakia 7 | Sweden 0 |
| April 14 | Dusseldorf | Soviet Union 5 | Finland 2 |
| April 15 | Dusseldorf | Czechoslovakia 8 | United States 0 |
| April 15 | Dusseldorf | Soviet Union 15 | Poland 1 |
| April 16 | Dusseldorf | Sweden 12 | United States 3 |
| April 16 | Dusseldorf | Finland 4 | Poland 1 |
| April 17 | Dusseldorf | Soviet Union 4 | Czechoslovakia 1 |
| April 17 | Dusseldorf | Finland 2 | Sweden 1 |
| April 18 | Dusseldorf | Poland 5 | United States 2 |
| April 19 | Dusseldorf | Czechoslovakia 5 | Finland 1 |
| April 19 | Dusseldorf | Soviet Union 13 | Sweden 4 |

**Rosters**

**Czechoslovakia** (Karel Gut/Jan Starsi, coaches) GK—Jiri Holecek, Jiri Crha—Vladimir Kostka, Oldrich Machac, Frantisek Pospisil, Miroslav Dvorak, Frantisek Kaberle, Milan Kajkl, Jiri Bubla, Milan Novy, Jiri Kochta, Vladimir Martinec, Jiri Novak, Bohuslav Stastny, Marian Stastny, Jiri Holik, Ivan Hlinka, Eduard Novak, Bohuslav Ebermann, Josef Augusta

**Finland** (Seppo Liitsola, coach) GK—Antti Leppanen, Jorma Valtonen—Pekka Rautakallio, Seppo Lindstrom, Rejo Laksola, Jouko Oystila, Timo Nummelin, Pekka Marjamaki, Timo Saari, Matti Hagman, Henry Leppa, Lasse Oksanen, Juhani Tamminen, Lauri Mononen, Harri Linnonmaa, Jorma Peltonen, Seppo Repo, Jorma Vehmanen, Matti Murto, Oiva Oijennus

**Poland** (Anatoli Yegorov, coach) GK—Andrzej Tkacz, Tadeusz Slowakiewicz—Andrzej Slowakiewicz, Andrzej Iskrzycki, Henryk Gruth, Marian Feter, Jerzy Potz, Adam Kopczynski, Marek Marcinczak, Jan Piecko, Tadeusz Obloj, Karol Zurek, Jozef Matkiewicz, Walenty Zietara, Andrzej Rybski, Andrzej Zabawa, Stefan Chowaniec, Mieczyslaw Jaskierski, Leszek Tokarz, Jan Szeja

**Soviet Union** (Boris Kulagin, coach) GK—Vladislav Tretiak, Viktor Krivolapov—Vladimir Lutchenko, Yuri Fyodorov, Yuri Lyapkin, Valeri Vasilyev, Gennadi Tsygankov, Yuri Churin, Alexander Filippov, Sergei Kapustin, Viktor Shalimov, Alexander Maltsev, Yuri Lebedev, Boris Mikhailov, Alexander Yakushev, Vladimir Petrov, Valeri Kharlamov, Vladimir Vikulov, Vladimir Shadrin, Vyacheslav Anisin

**Sweden** (Ronald Pettersson, coach) GK—Leif Holmqvist, Goran Hogosta—Stig Ostling, Kjell-Rune Milton, Ulf Weinstock, Mats Waltin, Stig Salming, Karl-Johan Sundqvist, Bjorn Johansson, Mats Lindh, Hakan Pettersson, Mats Ahlberg, Tord Lundstrom, Willy Lindstrom, Dan Labraaten, Per-Olov Brasar, Dan Soderstrom, Hans Jax, Kjell-Arne Vikstrom, Finn Lundstrom

**United States** (Bob Johnson, coach) GK—Jim Warden, Blane Comstock—Ron Wilson, John Taft, John Cunniff, Jack Brownschidle, Pete Brown, Steve Sertich, Bob Lundeen, Steve Jensen, Steve Alley, Herb Boxer, Bill "Buzz" Schneider, Mike Polich, Tom Ross, Clark Hamilton, Richie Smith, Jim Warner, Mike Eruzione, Jeff Rotsch

## 43rd WORLD CHAMPIONSHIP (MEN)
## April 8-25, 1976
## Katowice, Poland

**Final Placing**

| | | | |
|---|---|---|---|
| Gold | Czechoslovakia | 5th | Finland |
| Silver | Soviet Union | 6th | West Germany |
| Bronze | Sweden | 7th | Poland* |
| 4th | United States | 8th | East Germany* |

*demoted to B Pool for 1977

**Tournament Format**

Eight teams played each other in a single round robin series, the top four going on to a final series of round robin games for medals, the bottom four to another group playing round robin for placement. Preliminary round scores carried over.

**Results & Standings**

| | GP | W | T | L | GF | GA | P |
|---|---|---|---|---|---|---|---|
| Czechoslovakia | 7 | 7 | 0 | 0 | 54 | 7 | 14 |
| Soviet Union | 7 | 5 | 0 | 2 | 37 | 15 | 10 |
| Sweden | 7 | 4 | 0 | 3 | 22 | 18 | 8 |
| United States | 7 | 3 | 1 | 3 | 19 | 23 | 7 |
| Poland | 7 | 2 | 1 | 4 | 21 | 36 | 5 |
| West Germany | 7 | 2 | 0 | 5 | 19 | 35 | 4 |
| Finland | 7 | 1 | 2 | 4 | 17 | 29 | 4 |
| East Germany | 7 | 2 | 0 | 5 | 11 | 37 | 4 |

| | | |
|---|---|---|
| April 8 | Sweden 4 | West Germany 1 |
| April 8 | Czechoslovakia 10 | East Germany 0 |
| April 8 | Finland 3 | United States 3 |
| April 8 | Poland 6 | Soviet Union 4 |
| April 9 | Czechoslovakia 12 | Poland 0 |
| April 9 | Soviet Union 4 | East Germany 0 |
| April 10 | Finland 5 | West Germany 2 |
| April 10 | United States 2 | Sweden 0 |
| April 11 | Poland 6 | East Germany 4 |
| April 11 | Soviet Union 8 | Finland 1 |
| April 11 | Czechoslovakia 3 | Sweden 1 |
| April 12 | West Germany 5 | Poland 3 |
| April 12 | East Germany 2 | United States 1 |
| April 13 | Czechoslovakia 7 | Finland 1 |
| April 13 | Soviet Union 6 | Sweden 1 |
| April 14 | United States 4 | Poland 2 |
| April 14 | West Germany 7 | East Germany 1 |
| April 15 | Sweden 4 | Finland 3 |
| April 15 | Czechoslovakia 10 | United States 2 |
| April 15 | Soviet Union 8 | West Germany 2 |
| April 17 | Sweden 8 | East Germany 2 |
| April 17 | Poland 3 | Finland 3 |
| April 17 | Czechoslovakia 3 | Soviet Union 2 |
| April 18 | United States 5 | West Germany 1 |
| April 18 | East Germany 2 | Finland 1 |
| April 19 | Czechoslovakia 9 | West Germany 1 |
| April 19 | Sweden 4 | Poland 1 |
| April 19 | Soviet Union 5 | United States 2 |

**RELEGATION ROUND**

| | GP | W | T | L | GF | GA | P |
|---|---|---|---|---|---|---|---|
| Finland | 10 | 2 | 4 | 4 | 35 | 41 | 8 |
| West Germany | 10 | 3 | 2 | 5 | 26 | 41 | 8 |
| Poland | 10 | 3 | 2 | 5 | 32 | 47 | 8 |
| East Germany | 10 | 2 | 1 | 7 | 19 | 52 | 5 |

| | | |
|---|---|---|
| April 20 | Poland 5 | East Germany 4 |
| April 20 | Finland 4 | West Germany 4 |
| April 22 | Finland 5 | Poland 5 |
| April 22 | West Germany 1 | East Germany 1 |
| April 24 | Finland 9 | East Germany 3 |
| April 24 | West Germany 2 | Poland 1 |

**MEDAL ROUND**

| | GP | W | T | L | GF | GA | P |
|---|---|---|---|---|---|---|---|
| Czechoslovakia | 10 | 9 | 1 | 0 | 67 | 14 | 19 |
| Soviet Union | 10 | 6 | 1 | 3 | 50 | 23 | 13 |
| Sweden | 10 | 6 | 0 | 4 | 36 | 29 | 12 |
| United States | 10 | 3 | 1 | 6 | 24 | 42 | 7 |

| | | |
|---|---|---|
| April 21 | Czechoslovakia 5 | United States 1 |
| April 21 | Sweden 4 | Soviet Union 3 |
| April 23 | Czechoslovakia 5 | Sweden 3 |
| April 23 | Soviet Union 7 | United States 1 |
| April 25 | Sweden 7 | United States 3 |
| April 25 | Czechoslovakia 3 | Soviet Union 3 |

**Rosters**

**Czechoslovakia** (Jan Starsi/Karel Gut, coaches) GK—Jiri Holecek, Vladimir Dzurilla—Vladimir Martinec, Jiri Novak, Milan Novy, Ivan Hlinka, Peter Stastny, Jiri Holik, Bohuslav Stastny, Jiri Bubla, Frantisek Cernik, Marian Stastny, Jaroslav Pouzar, Milan Chalupa, Frantisek Pospisil, Eduard Novak, Oldrich Machac, Frantisek Kaberle, Milan Kajkl, Miroslav Dvorak

**East Germany** (Joachim Ziesche/Klaus Hirche, coaches) GK—Wolfgang Kraske, Roland Herzig—Reiner Patschinski, Joachim Stasche, Peter Slapke, Roland Peters, Ralf Thomas, Rolf Bielas, Frank Braun, Rienhardt Fengler, Jurgen Franke, Gerhard Muller, Jurgen Brieitschuh, Dieter Franzel, Dietmar Peters, Dieter Simon, Rudiger Noack, Harald Felber, Detlef Mark, Heinz Pohland

**Finland** (Seppo Liitsola/Lasse Heikkila, coaches) GK—Jorma Valtonen, Marcus Mattsson—Tapio Koskinen, Matti Hagman, Esa Peltonen, Jouni Rinne, Hannu Kapanen, Henry Leppa, Kari Makkonen, Matti Murto, Timo Nummelin, Timo Saari, Tapio Flinck, Tapio Levo, Jorma Vehmanen, Lasse Oksanen, Ari Kankaanpera, Seppo Suoraniemi, Timo Sutinen, Jouni Peltonen

**Poland** (Jozef Kurek/Emil Nikodemowicz, coaches) GK—Andrzej Tkacz, Henryk Wojtynek—Mieczyslaw Jaskierski, Walenty Zietara, Wieslaw Jobczyk, Leszek Kokoszka, Andrzej Zabawa, Robert Goralczyk, Stefan Chowaniec, Henryk Gruth, Marek Marcinczak, Karol Zurek, Jozef Stefaniak, Jerzy Potz, Ryszard Nowinski, Stanislaw Szewczyk, Andrzej Szczepaniec, Kordian Jajszczok, Zdzislaw Wlodarczyk, Henryk Pytel

**Soviet Union** (Boris Kulagin, coach) GK—Vladislav Tretiak, Alexander Sidelnikov—Valeri Kharlamov, Boris Mikhailov, Viktor Zhluktov, Helmuts Balderis, Viktor Shalimov, Alexander Yakushev, Valeri Vasilyev, Yuri Lyapkin, Alexander Maltsev, Alexander Golikov, Vladimir Shadrin, Sergei Kapustin, Sergei Korotkov, Vladimir Lutchenko, Vladimir Golikov, Gennadi Tsygankov, Sergei Babinov, Alexander Filippov

**Sweden** (Ronald Pettersson, coach) GK—William Lofqvist, Goran Hogosta—Roland Eriksson, Hans Jax, Lars-Gunnar Lundberg, Dan Labraaten, Mats Ahlberg, Dan Soderstrom, Roland Bond, Bjorn Johansson, Lars-Erik Ericsson, Mats Waltin, Stig Salming, Lars-Erik Esbjors, Martin Karlsson, Bengt Lundholm, Jan-Olov Svensson, Stig Ostling, Lars Oberg, Per-Olov Brasar

**United States** (John Mariucci/Glenn Gostick, coaches) GK—Mike Curran, Pete LoPresti—Steve Jensen, Gary Gambucci, Bill Klatt, Jim Warner, Tom Younghans, Mike Antonovich, Lou Nanne, Mike Eaves, Bill "Buzz" Schneider, Craig Sarner, Brad Morrow, Gary Ross, Dave Langevin, Jeff Hymanson, Bob Lundeen Mike Eruzione, Pat Phippen

**West Germany** (Xaver Unsinn, coach) GK—Erich Weishaupt, Toni Kehle—Reiner Philipp, Alois Schloder, Erich Kuhnhackl, Walter Koberle, Lorenz Funk, Ignaz Berndaner, Ernst Kopf, Hermann Hinterstocker, Josef Volk, Vladimir Vacatko, Horst-Peter Kretschmer, Hans Zach, Udo Kiessling, Franz Reindl, Werner Klatt, Rudolf Thanner, Wolfgang Boos, Klaus Mangold

## 44th WORLD CHAMPIONSHIP (MEN)
## April 21-May 8, 1977
## Vienna, Austria

**Final Placing**

| | | | |
|---|---|---|---|
| Gold | Czechoslovakia | 5th | Finland |
| Silver | Sweden | 6th | United States |
| Bronze | Soviet Union | 7th | West Germany |
| 4th | Canada | 8th | Romania^* |

^promoted from B Pool in 1976
*demoted to B Pool for 1978

**Tournament Format**

Each team played every other once, after which the top four played another round robin to determine medal winners, the bottom four playing in a classification/relegation group. All scores carried forward from the first round robin to the second.

**Results & Standings**

**PRELIMINARY ROUND**

| | GP | W | T | L | GF | GA | P |
|---|---|---|---|---|---|---|---|
| Sweden | 7 | 6 | 0 | 1 | 39 | 9 | 12 |
| Soviet Union | 7 | 6 | 0 | 1 | 65 | 16 | 12 |
| Czechoslovakia | 7 | 5 | 1 | 1 | 46 | 20 | 11 |
| Canada | 7 | 4 | 1 | 2 | 31 | 25 | 9 |
| Finland | 7 | 3 | 0 | 4 | 22 | 37 | 6 |
| United States | 7 | 1 | 1 | 5 | 18 | 35 | 3 |
| West Germany | 7 | 1 | 1 | 5 | 17 | 45 | 3 |
| Romania | 7 | 0 | 0 | 7 | 12 | 63 | 0 |

| | | |
|---|---|---|
| April 21 | Sweden 8 | Romania 1 |
| April 21 | Soviet Union 10 | West Germany 0 |
| April 21 | Czechoslovakia 11 | Finland 3 |
| April 21 | Canada 4 | United States 1 |
| April 22 | United States 7 | Romania 2 |

| | | |
|---|---|---|
| April 22 | Soviet Union 11 | Finland 6 |
| April 22 | Czechoslovakia 9 | West Germany 3 |
| April 22 | Sweden 4 | Canada 2 |
| April 24 | Czechoslovakia 13 | Romania 1 |
| April 24 | Sweden 5 | Finland 1 |
| April 24 | West Germany 3 | United States 3 |
| April 24 | Soviet Union 11 | Canada 1 |
| April 25 | Sweden 7 | West Germany 1 |
| April 25 | Soviet Union 18 | Romania 1 |
| April 26 | Finland 3 | United States 2 |
| April 26 | Canada 3 | Czechoslovakia 3 |
| April 27 | West Germany 6 | Romania 3 |
| April 27 | Canada 5 | Finland 1 |
| April 28 | Sweden 9 | United States 0 |
| April 28 | Soviet Union 6 | Czechoslovakia 1 |
| April 29 | Finland 4 | Romania 2 |
| April 29 | Canada 9 | West Germany 3 |
| April 30 | Czechoslovakia 3 | Sweden 1 |
| April 30 | Soviet Union 8 | United States 2 |
| May 1 | Canada 7 | Romania 2 |
| May 1 | Finland 4 | West Germany 1 |
| May 2 | Czechoslovakia 6 | United States 3 |
| May 2 | Sweden 5 | Soviet Union 1 |

**RELEGATION ROUND**

| | GP | W | T | L | GF | GA | P |
|---|---|---|---|---|---|---|---|
| Finland | 10 | 5 | 0 | 5 | 45 | 43 | 10 |
| United States | 10 | 3 | 1 | 6 | 29 | 43 | 7 |
| West Germany | 10 | 2 | 1 | 7 | 23 | 58 | 5 |
| Romania | 10 | 1 | 0 | 9 | 20 | 84 | 2 |

| | | |
|---|---|---|
| May 3 | Finland 14 | Romania 1 |
| May 3 | United States 4 | West Germany 1 |
| May 5 | Finland 7 | West Germany 2 |
| May 5 | Romania 5 | United States 4 |
| May 7 | West Germany 3 | Romania 2 |
| May 7 | United States 3 | Finland 2 |

**MEDAL ROUND**

| | GP | W | T | L | GF | GA | P |
|---|---|---|---|---|---|---|---|
| Czechoslovakia | 10 | 7 | 1 | 2 | 54 | 32 | 15 |
| Sweden | 10 | 7 | 0 | 3 | 43 | 19 | 14 |
| Soviet Union | 10 | 7 | 0 | 3 | 77 | 24 | 14 |
| Canada | 10 | 6 | 1 | 3 | 47 | 35 | 13 |

| | | |
|---|---|---|
| May 4 | Czechoslovakia 4 | Soviet Union 3 |
| May 4 | Canada 7 | Sweden 0 |
| May 6 | Czechoslovakia 2 | Sweden 1 |
| May 6 | Soviet Union 8 | Canada 1 |
| May 8 | Canada 8 | Czechoslovakia 2 |
| May 8 | Sweden 3 | Soviet Union 1 |

**Rosters**

**Canada** (Johnny Wilson, coach) GK—Jim Rutherford, Tony Esposito—Rick Hampton, Greg Smith, Carol Vadnais, Dennis Kearns, Dallas Smith, Phil Russell, Rod Gilbert, Ron Ellis, Wilf Paiement, Walt McKechnie, Wayne Merrick, Ralph Klassen, Guy Charron, Pierre Larouche, Jean Pronovost, Al MacAdam, Eric Vail, Phil Esposito

**Czechoslovakia** (Jan Starsi/Karel Gut, coaches) GK—Vladimir Dzurilla, Jiri Holecek—Oldrich Machac, Milan Chalupa, Frantisek Pospisil, Miroslav Dvorak, Frantisek Kaberle, Milan Kajkl, Jiri Bubla, Milan Novy, Vladimir Martinec, Jiri Novak, Vincent Lukac, Marian Stastny, Jiri Holik, Ivan Hlinka, Eduard Novak, Jaroslav Pouzar, Bohuslav Ebermann, Peter Stastny

**Finland** (Lasse Heikkila, coach) GK—Urpo Ylonen, Jorma Valtonen—Timo Nummelin, Risto Siltanen, Hannu Haapalainen, Pekka Marjamaki, Seppo Suoraniemi, Pekka Rautakallio, Kari Makkonen, Esa Peltonen, Lasse Oksanen, Jukka Alkula, Martti Jarkko, Seppo Ahokainen, Jukka Porvari, Antero Lehtonen, Timo Sutinen, Pertti Koivulahti, Veli-Matti Ruisma, Seppo Lindstrom

**Romania** (Stefan Ionescu, coach) GK—Valerian Netedu, Gheorghe Hutan—Florea Zginca, Ion Ionita, Dezideriu Varga, Sandor Gall, Antal Eloed, Doru Morosan, George Justinian, Doru Tureanu, Dumitru Axinte, Constantin Dumitru, Marian Costea, Tibor Miklos, Constantin Nistor, Ion Gheorghiu, Eduard Pana, Laszlo Solyom, Adrian Olenici, Marian Pisaru

**Soviet Union** (Boris Kulagin, coach) GK—Alexander Sidelnikov, Vladislav Tretiak—Alexander Gusev, Vladimir Lutchenko, Sergei Babinov, Valeri Vasilyev, Gennadi Tsygankov, Vasili Pervukhin, Vyacheslav Fetisov, Sergei Kapustin, Viktor Shalimov, Alexander Maltsev, Boris Mikhailov, Alexander Yakushev, Vladimir Petrov, Valeri Kharlamov, Vladimir Shadrin, Viktor Zhluktov, Alexander Golikov, Helmuts Balderis

**Sweden** (Hans Lindberg, coach) GK—Goran Hogosta, Hardy Astrom—Jan-Erik Silfverberg, Ulf Weinstock, Mats Waltin, Stefan Persson, Stig Salming, Lars Zetterstrom, Lars Lindgren, Martin Karlsson, Roland Eriksson, Lars-Eric Ericsson, Rolf Edberg, Mats Ahlberg, Bengt Lundholm, Lars-Gunnar Lundberg, Nils-Olov Olsson, Per-Olov Brasar, Kent-Erik Andersson, Hans Jax

**United States** (John Mariucci, coach) GK—Mike Curran, Dave Reece—Jim McElmury, Wally Olds, Joe Micheletti, Bob Paradise, Lou Nanne, Russ Anderson, Bill "Buzz" Schneider, Dave Hynes, Bob Miller, Warren Williams, Tom Younghans, Mark Heaslip, Tom Rowe, Dave Debol, Warren Miller, Tom Vannelli, Mike Antonovich, Bob Krieger

**West Germany** (Hans Rampf, coach) GK—Toni Kehle, Siegmund Suttner—Josef Volk, Udo Kiessling, Klaus Auhuber, Peter Scharf, Ignaz Berndaner, Werner Klatt, Horst-Peter Kretschmer, Walter Stadler, Rainer Philipp, Lorenz Funk, Franz Reindl, Karel Slezak, Walter Koberle, Erich Kuhnhackl, Alois Schloder, Hans Zach, Hermann Hinterstocker, Vladimir Vacatko

## 45th WORLD CHAMPIONSHIP (MEN)
## April 25-May 8, 1978
## Prague, Czechoslovakia

**Final Placing**

| | |
|---|---|
| Gold ........Soviet Union | 5th .........West Germany |
| Silver ......Czechoslovakia | 6th .........United States |
| Bronze ....Canada | 7th .........Finland |
| 4th..........Sweden | 8th .........East Germany^* |

^promoted from B Pool in 1977
*demoted to B Pool for 1979

**Tournament Format**

Each team played every other once, after which the top four played another round robin to determine medal winners, the bottom four playing in a classification/relegation group. All scores carried forward from the first round robin to the second.

**Results & Standings**

**PRELIMINARY ROUND**

| | GP | W | T | L | GF | GA | P |
|---|---|---|---|---|---|---|---|
| Czechoslovakia | 7 | 7 | 0 | 0 | 44 | 15 | 14 |
| Soviet Union | 7 | 6 | 0 | 1 | 46 | 23 | 12 |
| Canada | 7 | 4 | 0 | 3 | 32 | 26 | 8 |
| Sweden | 7 | 4 | 0 | 3 | 35 | 21 | 8 |
| West Germany | 7 | 2 | 1 | 4 | 23 | 35 | 5 |
| United States | 7 | 1 | 1 | 5 | 25 | 42 | 3 |
| Finland | 7 | 1 | 1 | 5 | 23 | 34 | 3 |
| East Germany | 7 | 1 | 1 | 5 | 13 | 45 | 3 |

| | | |
|---|---|---|
| April 26 | Sweden 6 | East Germany 2 |
| April 26 | Soviet Union 9 | United States 5 |
| April 26 | Czechoslovakia 8 | West Germany 0 |
| April 27 | Finland 6 | Canada 4 |
| April 27 | Soviet Union 7 | East Germany 4 |
| April 27 | Sweden 5 | United States 1 |
| April 28 | Czechoslovakia 6 | Finland 4 |
| April 28 | Canada 6 | West Germany 2 |
| April 29 | Czechoslovakia 8 | East Germany 2 |
| April 29 | Sweden 10 | West Germany 1 |
| April 30 | Soviet Union 6 | Finland 3 |
| April 30 | Canada 7 | United States 2 |
| May 1 | Soviet Union 10 | West Germany 2 |
| May 1 | Canada 6 | East Germany 2 |
| May 2 | Czechoslovakia 8 | United States 3 |
| May 2 | Sweden 6 | Finland 1 |
| May 3 | East Germany 7 | United States 4 |
| May 3 | West Germany 4 | Finland 3 |
| May 4 | Soviet Union 6 | Sweden 1 |
| May 4 | Czechoslovakia 5 | Canada 0 |
| May 5 | West Germany 5 | Finland 3 |
| May 5 | United States 7 | West Germany 3 |
| May 6 | Czechoslovakia 6 | Soviet Union 4 |
| May 6 | Canada 7 | Sweden 5 |
| May 7 | East Germany 1 | West Germany 1 |
| May 7 | Finland 3 | United States 3 |
| May 8 | Czechoslovakia 3 | Sweden 2 |
| May 8 | Soviet Union 4 | Canada 2 |

**RELEGATION ROUND**

| | GP | W | T | L | GF | GA | P |
|---|---|---|---|---|---|---|---|
| West Germany | 10 | 3 | 3 | 4 | 35 | 43 | 9 |
| United States | 10 | 2 | 2 | 6 | 38 | 58 | 6 |
| Finland | 10 | 2 | 2 | 6 | 37 | 44 | 6 |
| East Germany | 10 | 1 | 3 | 6 | 20 | 57 | 5 |

| | | |
|---|---|---|
| May 9 | Finland 4 | East Germany 4 |
| May 9 | United States 5 | West Germany 5 |
| May 11 | West Germany 0 | East Germany 0 |
| May 11 | United States 4 | Finland 3 |
| May 13 | Finland 7 | West Germany 2 |
| May 13 | East Germany 8 | United States 4 |

**MEDAL ROUND**

| | GP | W | T | L | GF | GA | P |
|---|---|---|---|---|---|---|---|
| Soviet Union | 10 | 9 | 0 | 1 | 61 | 26 | 18 |
| Czechoslovakia | 10 | 9 | 0 | 1 | 54 | 21 | 18 |
| Canada | 10 | 5 | 0 | 5 | 38 | 36 | 10 |
| Sweden | 10 | 4 | 0 | 6 | 39 | 37 | 8 |

| | | |
|---|---|---|
| May 10 | Soviet Union 5 | Canada 1 |
| May 10 | Czechoslovakia 6 | Sweden 1 |
| May 12 | Soviet Union 7 | Sweden 1 |
| May 12 | Czechoslovakia 3 | Canada 2 |
| May 14 | Canada 3 | Sweden 2 |
| May 14 | Soviet Union 3 | Czechoslovakia 1 |

**Rosters**

**Canada** (Harry Howell, coach) GK—Dennis Herron, Dan Bouchard—Dennis Kearns, Brad Maxwell, Robert Picard, Rick Hampton, David Shand, Pat Ribble, Dennis Maruk, Garry Unger, Tom Lysiak, Pat Hickey, Don Lever, Guy Charron, Marcel Dionne, Mike Murphy, Wilf Paiement, Jean Pronovost, Glen Sharpley, Bob MacMillan

**Czechoslovakia** (Karel Gut, coach) GK—Jiri Holecek, Jiri Crha—Jiri Bubla, Milan Kajkl, Oldrich Machac, Miroslav Dvorak, Milan Chalupa, Frantisek Kaberle, Jan Zajicek, Vladimir Martinec, Jiri Novak, Jaroslav Pouzar, Pavel Richter, Ivan Hlinka, Bohuslav Ebermann, Marian Stastny, Peter Stastny, Frantisek Cernik, Milan Novy, Josef Augusta

**East Germany** (Gunther Schischefski, coach) GK—Wolfgang Kraske, Roland Herzig—Frank Braun, Dieter Simon, Dietmar Peters, Joachim Lempio, Dieter Frenzel, Klaus Schroder, Joachim Stasche, Rainer Patschinski, Rolf Bielas, Peter Slapke, Eckhard Scholz, Friedhelm Bogelsack, Gerhard Muller, Roland Peters, Jurgen Franke, Reinhard Fengler, Wolfgang Unterdorfel, Frank Proske

**Finland** (Kalevi Numminen, coach) GK—Antero Kivela, Urpo Ylonen—Pekka Rautakallio, Timo Nummelin, Risto Siltanen, Pekka Marjamaki, Tapio Levo, Lasse Litma, Reijo Ruotsalainen, Seppo Ahokainen, Esa Peltonen, Martti Jarkko, Juhani Tamminen, Mikko Leinonen, Matti Hagman, Seppo Repo, Kari Makkonen, Jukka Porvari, Matti Rautiainen, Pertti Koivulahti

**Soviet Union** (Viktor Tikhonov, coach) GK—Vladislav Tretiak, Alexander Pashkov—Vyacheslav Fetisov, Vladimir Lutchenko, Vasili Pervukhin, Valeri Vasilyev, Gennadi Tsygankov, Zinetula Bilyaletdinov, Yuri Fyodorov, Boris Mikhailov, Vladimir Petrov, Valeri Kharlamov, Helmuts Balderis, Viktor Zhluktov, Sergei Kapustin, Alexander Golikov, Alexander Maltsev, Vladimir Golikov, Yuri Lebedev, Sergei Makarov

**Sweden** (Hans Lindberg, coach) GK—Goran Hogosta, Hardy Astrom—Stig Ostling, Ulf Weinstock, Mats Waltin, Goran Lindblom, Stig Salming, Lars Zetterstrom, Lars Lindgren, Leif Holmgren, Roland Eriksson, Rolf Edberg, Mats Ahlberg, Bengt Lundholm, Lars-Gunnar Lundberg, Lennart Norberg, Nils-Olov Olsson, Per-Olov Brasar, Kent-Erik Andersson, Thomas Gradin

**United States** (John Mariucci, coach) GK—Pete LoPresti, Jim Warden—Don Jackson, Dick Lamby, Craig Norwich, Glenn Patrick, Mike Fidler, Tom Younghans, Mark Johnson, Harvey Bennett, Steve Jensen, Jim Warner, Curt Bennett, Mike Eaves, Dave Debol, Patrick Westrum, Ken Morrow, Steve Alley, Bob Collyard, William Gilligan

**West Germany** (Hans Rampf, coach) GK—Erich Weishaupt, Bernd Engelbrecht—Ignaz Berndaner, Robert Murray, Peter Scharf, Udo Kiessling, Klaus Auhuber, Horst-Peter Kretschmer, Alois Schloder, Erich Kuhnhackl, Rainer Philipp, Martin Hinterstocker, Martin Wild, Franz Reindl, Walter Koberle, Lorenz Funk, Vladimir Vacatko, Hermann Hinterstocker, Hans Zach, Marcus Kuhl

## 46th WORLD CHAMPIONSHIP (MEN)
## April 14-27, 1979
## Moscow, Soviet Union

**Final Placing**

| | |
|---|---|
| Gold ........Soviet Union | 5th .........Finland |
| Silver ......Czechoslovakia | 6th .........West Germany |
| Bronze ....Sweden | 7th .........United States |
| 4th..........Canada | 8th .........Poland^* |

^promoted from B Pool in 1978
*demoted to B Pool for 1980

**Tournament Format**

Eight teams were divided into two groups of four teams each, playing a round robin within each group. The top two nations from each group advanced to a finals round robin group to play for medals, the bottom four went to a placement pool where they played a round robin as well. Games between teams from round robin within each group carried over.

**Results & Standings**

**GROUP A**

| | GP | W | T | L | GF | GA | P |
|---|---|---|---|---|---|---|---|
| Soviet Union | 3 | 3 | 0 | 0 | 19 | 5 | 6 |
| Sweden | 3 | 2 | 0 | 1 | 16 | 17 | 4 |
| West Germany | 3 | 0 | 1 | 2 | 8 | 13 | 1 |
| Poland | 3 | 0 | 1 | 2 | 8 | 16 | 1 |

| | | |
|---|---|---|
| April 14 | Sweden 7 | West Germany 3 |
| April 14 | Soviet Union 7 | Poland 0 |
| April 15 | Soviet Union 3 | West Germany 2 |
| April 15 | Sweden 6 | Poland 5 |
| April 17 | West Germany 3 | Poland 3 |
| April 17 | Soviet Union 9 | Sweden 3 |

**GROUP B**

| | GP | W | T | L | GF | GA | P |
|---|---|---|---|---|---|---|---|
| Czechoslovakia | 3 | 2 | 1 | 0 | 11 | 3 | 5 |
| Canada | 3 | 2 | 0 | 1 | 12 | 11 | 4 |
| United States | 3 | 0 | 2 | 1 | 6 | 9 | 2 |
| Finland | 3 | 0 | 1 | 2 | 5 | 11 | 1 |

| | | |
|---|---|---|
| April 14 | Czechoslovakia 5 | Finland 0 |
| April 14 | Canada 6 | United States 3 |
| April 15 | Czechoslovakia 4 | Canada 1 |
| April 16 | United States 1 | Finland 1 |
| April 17 | Canada 5 | Finland 4 |
| April 17 | Czechoslovakia 2 | United States 2 |

**CONSOLATION ROUND**

| | GP | W | T | L | GF | GA | P |
|---|---|---|---|---|---|---|---|
| Finland | 6 | 4 | 1 | 1 | 23 | 17 | 9 |
| West Germany | 6 | 3 | 1 | 2 | 27 | 21 | 7 |
| United States | 6 | 2 | 2 | 2 | 22 | 20 | 6 |
| Poland | 6 | 0 | 2 | 4 | 15 | 29 | 2 |

| | | |
|---|---|---|
| April 18 | Poland 5 | United States 5 |
| April 18 | Finland 5 | West Germany 2 |
| April 20 | Finland 4 | Poland 3 |
| April 20 | West Germany 6 | United States 3 |
| April 22 | United States 6 | Finland 2 |
| April 22 | West Germany 8 | Poland 1 |
| April 24 | United States 5 | Poland 1 |
| April 24 | Finland 7 | West Germany 3 |
| April 26 | Finland 4 | Poland 2 |
| April 26 | West Germany 5 | United States 2 |

**FINALS GROUP**

| | GP | W | T | L | GF | GA | P |
|---|---|---|---|---|---|---|---|
| Soviet Union | 6 | 6 | 0 | 0 | 51 | 12 | 12 |
| Czechoslovakia | 6 | 3 | 1 | 2 | 25 | 30 | 7 |
| Sweden | 6 | 1 | 1 | 4 | 20 | 38 | 3 |
| Canada | 6 | 1 | 0 | 5 | 20 | 36 | 2 |

| | | |
|---|---|---|
| April 19 | Czechoslovakia 3 | Sweden 3 |
| April 19 | Soviet Union 5 | Canada 2 |
| April 21 | Sweden 5 | Canada 3 |
| April 21 | Soviet Union 11 | Czechoslovakia 1 |
| April 23 | Czechoslovakia 10 | Canada 6 |
| April 23 | Soviet Union 11 | Sweden 3 |
| April 25 | Czechoslovakia 6 | Sweden 3 |
| April 25 | Soviet Union 9 | Canada 2 |
| April 27 | Canada 6 | Sweden 3 |
| April 27 | Soviet Union 6 | Czechoslovakia 1 |

**Rosters**

**Canada** (Marshall Johnston, coach) GK—Jim Rutherford, Ed Staniowski—Brad Marsh, Rick Green, Trevor Johansen, Brad Maxwell, Dave Shand, Greg Smith, Robert Picard, Garry Unger, Wayne Babych, Wilf Paiement, Dale McCourt, Bobby Smith, Ryan Walter, Nick Libett, Guy Charron, Paul Woods, Marcel Dionne, Dennis Maruk, Al MacAdam, Steve Payne

**Czechoslovakia** (Karel Gut/Jan Starsi, coaches) GK—Jiri Kralik, Marcel Sakac—Milan Figala, Vitezslav Duris, Milan Chalupa, Jozef Bukovinsky, Milan Kuzela, Miroslav Dvorak, Frantisek Kaberle, Jiri Bubla, Milan Novy, Vladimir Martinec, Jiri Novak, Ladislav Svozil, Miroslav Frycer, Marian Stastny, Anton Stastny, Ivan Hlinka, Libor Havlicek, Jaroslav Pouzar, Bohuslav Ebermann, Peter Stastny

**Finland** (Kalevi Numminen, coach) GK—Antero Kivela, Jorma Valtonen—Pekka Rautakallio, Timo Nummelin, Pertti Valkeapaa, Reijo Ruotsalainen, Hannu Haapalainen, Pekka Marjamaki, Kari Eloranta, Lasse Litma, Tapio Koskinen, Antero Lehtonen, Jouni Rinne, Mikko Leinonen, Juhani Tamminen, Jukka Koskilahti, Veli-Matti Ruisma, Seppo Repo, Seppo Ahokainen, Matti Rautiainen, Jukka Porvari, Pertti Koivulahti

**Poland** (Slavomir Barton, coach) GK—Henryk Wojtynek, Henryk Buk—Andrzej Slowakiewicz, Andrzej Iskrzycki, Henryk Januszewski, Henryk Gruth, Andrzej Janczi, Jerzy Potz, Andrzej Chowaniec, Marek Marcinczak, Stefan Chowaniec, Wieslaw Jobczyk, Tadeusz Obloj, Walenty Zientara, Leszek Kokoszka, Jan Szeja, Andrzej Zabawa, Henryk Pytel, Mieczyslaw Jaskierski, Wojciech Tkacz, Andrzej Malysiak, Jan Piecko

**Soviet Union** (Viktor Tikhonov, coach) GK—Vladislav Tretiak, Vladimir Myshkin—Valeri Vasilyev, Vasili Pervukhin, Zinetula Bilyaletdinov, Vladimir Lutchenko, Sergei Babinov, Gennadi Tsygankov, Irek Gimayev, Sergei Starikov, Boris Mikhailov, Vladimir Petrov, Valeri Kharlamov, Viktor Zhluktov, Sergei Kapustin, Helmuts Balderis, Alexander Golikov, Vladimir Golikov, Sergei Makarov, Alexander Yakushev, Alexander Skvortsov, Yuri Lebedev

**Sweden** (Tommy Sandlin, coach) GK—Pelle Lindbergh, Sune Odling—Tomas Jonsson, Sture Andersson, Ulf Weinstock, Leif Svensson, Mats Waltin, Thomas Eriksson, Tord Nanzen, Roger Lindstrom, Per Lundqvist, Rolf Edberg, Bengt-Ake Gustafsson, Mats Naslund, Lennart Norberg, Bengt Lundholm, Leif Holmgren, Lars-Eric Ericsson, Dan Labraaten, Inge Hammarstrom, Hakan Eriksson, Peter Wallin

**United States** (Herb Brooks, coach) GK—Jim Warden, Jim Craig—Jack Brownschidle, Don Jackson, Les Auge, Jim Korn, Bill Baker, Wally Olds, Jack O'Callahan, Rob McClanahan, Mark Johnson, Steve Christoff, Bob Collyard, Phil Verchota, Dan Bolduc, Craig Patrick, Craig Sarner, Curt Bennett, Eric Strobel, Joe Mullen, Ralph Cox

**West Germany** (Hans Rampf, coach) GK—Siegmund Suttner, Erich Weishaupt—Udo Kiessling, Ignaz Berndaner, Robert Murray, Klaus Auhuber, Harald Krull, Peter Scharf, Harold Kreis, Rainer Philipp, Hermann Hinterstocker, Marcus Kuhl, Hans Zach, Uli Egen, Hubert Muller, Gerd Truntschka, Holger Meitinger, Lorenz Funk, Franz Reindl, Martin Hinterstocker, Vladimir Vacatko, Dieter Medicus

## 47th WORLD CHAMPIONSHIP (MEN)
## April 12-26, 1981
## Gothenburg/Stockholm, Sweden

**Final Placing**

| | | | |
|---|---|---|---|
| Gold | Soviet Union | 5th | United States |
| Silver | Sweden | 6th | Finland |
| Bronze | Czechoslovakia | 7th | West Germany |
| 4th | Canada | 8th | Netherlands^* |

^promoted from B Pool in 1979
*demoted to B Pool for 1982

**Tournament Format**

Eight teams were divided into two groups of four teams each, playing a round robin within each group. The top two nations from each group advanced to a finals round robin group to play for medals, the bottom four went to a placement pool where they played a round robin as well. Games between teams from round robin within each group carried over.

**Results & Standings**

**GROUP A (STOCKHOLM)**

| | GP | W | T | L | GF | GA | P |
|---|---|---|---|---|---|---|---|
| Soviet Union | 3 | 3 | 0 | 0 | 25 | 4 | 6 |
| Canada | 3 | 2 | 0 | 1 | 14 | 12 | 4 |
| Finland | 3 | 1 | 0 | 2 | 16 | 14 | 2 |
| Netherlands | 3 | 0 | 0 | 3 | 5 | 30 | 0 |

| | | |
|---|---|---|
| April 12 | Canada 4 | Finland 3 |
| April 12 | Soviet Union 10 | Netherlands 1 |
| April 13 | Canada 8 | Netherlands 1 |
| April 13 | Soviet Union 7 | Finland 1 |
| April 15 | Soviet Union 8 | Canada 2 |
| April 15 | Finland 12 | Netherlands 3 |

**GROUP B (GOTHENBURG)**

| | GP | W | T | L | GF | GA | P |
|---|---|---|---|---|---|---|---|
| Czechoslovakia | 3 | 2 | 1 | 0 | 20 | 7 | 5 |
| Sweden | 3 | 2 | 1 | 0 | 11 | 7 | 5 |
| United States | 3 | 1 | 0 | 2 | 14 | 21 | 2 |
| West Germany | 3 | 0 | 0 | 3 | 10 | 20 | 0 |

| | | |
|---|---|---|
| April 12 | Czechoslovakia 11 | United States 2 |
| April 12 | Sweden 4 | West Germany 2 |
| April 14 | Czechoslovakia 6 | West Germany 2 |
| April 14 | Sweden 4 | United States 2 |
| April 15 | Sweden 3 | Czechoslovakia 3 |
| April 15 | United States 10 | West Germany 6 |

**CONSOLATION ROUND (STOCKHOLM)**

| | GP | W | T | L | GF | GA | P |
|---|---|---|---|---|---|---|---|
| United States | 6 | 4 | 1 | 1 | 35 | 28 | 9 |
| Finland | 6 | 3 | 2 | 1 | 33 | 21 | 8 |
| West Germany | 6 | 3 | 1 | 2 | 40 | 30 | 7 |
| Netherlands | 6 | 0 | 0 | 6 | 22 | 51 | 0 |

| | | |
|---|---|---|
| April 17 | United States 7 | Netherlands 6 |
| April 17 | Finland 6 | West Germany 3 |
| April 19 | West Germany 9 | Netherlands 2 |
| April 19 | United States 6 | Finland 4 |
| April 21 | West Germany 6 | United States 2 |
| April 21 | Finland 4 | Netherlands 2 |
| April 23 | United States 7 | Netherlands 3 |
| April 23 | West Germany 4 | Finland 4 |
| April 25 | West Germany 12 | Netherlands 6 |
| April 25 | United States 3 | Finland 3 |

**FINAL ROUND (STOCKHOLM)**

| | GP | W | T | L | GF | GA | P |
|---|---|---|---|---|---|---|---|
| Soviet Union | 6 | 4 | 2 | 0 | 38 | 12 | 10 |
| Sweden | 6 | 3 | 1 | 2 | 16 | 26 | 7 |
| Czechoslovakia | 6 | 2 | 2 | 2 | 20 | 22 | 6 |
| Canada | 6 | 0 | 1 | 5 | 16 | 30 | 1 |

| | | |
|---|---|---|
| April 18 | Czechoslovakia 7 | Canada 4 |
| April 18 | Soviet Union 4 | Sweden 1 |
| April 20 | Sweden 3 | Canada 1 |
| April 20 | Soviet Union 8 | Czechoslovakia 3 |
| April 22 | Sweden 4 | Czechoslovakia 2 |
| April 22 | Canada 4 | Soviet Union 4 |
| April 24 | Czechoslovakia 4 | Canada 2 |
| April 24 | Soviet Union 13 | Sweden 1 |
| April 26 | Sweden 4 | Canada 3 |
| April 26 | Czechoslovakia 1 | Soviet Union 1 |

**Rosters**

**Canada** (Don Cherry, coach) GK—Phil Myre, John Garrett—Barry Long, Rob Ramage, Rick Green, Willie Huber, Lanny McDonald, Dale McCourt, Mike Gartner, Morris Lukowich, Steve Tambellini, John Ogrodnick, Mike Rogers, Ryan Walter, Guy Lafleur, Dennis Maruk, Larry Robinson, Lucien Deblois, Dave Babych, Norm Barnes, Mike Foligno, Pat Boutette

**Czechoslovakia** (Ludek Bukac, coach) GK—Karel Lang, Jaromir Sindel—Jan Neliba, Miloslav Horava, Norbert Kral, Milan Novy, Jaroslav Pouzar, Milan Chalupa, Miroslav Dvorak, Jiri Lala, Jindrich Kokrment, Pavel Richter, Arnold Kadlec, Petr Misek, Miroslav Frycer, Ivan Hlinka, Frantisek Cernik, Vladimir Martinec, Darius Rusnak, Bohuslav Ebermann, Stanislav Hajdusek, Jaroslav Korbela

**Finland** (Kalevi Numminen, coach) GK—Hannu Lassila, Hannu Kamppuri—Lasse Litma, Reijo Ruotsalainen, Seppo Suoraniemi, Kari Eloranta, Juha Tuohimaa, Pertti Lehtonen, Tapio Levo, Timo Nummelin, Markku Kiimalainen, Mikko Leinonen, Jorma Sevon, Seppo Ahokainen, Pertti Koivulahti, Jukka Porvari, Pekka Arbelius, Kari Jalonen, Ilkka Sinisalo, Antero Lehtonen, Hannu Koskinen, Juhani Tamminen

**Netherlands** (Gustav Bubnik, coach) GK—Ted Lenssen, John de Bruyn—Allen Pluymers, Rick van Gog, Leo Koopmans, Corky de Graauw, Tjakko de Vos, George Peternousek, Henk Hille, Jack de Heer, Larrie van Wieren, Jan Janssen, William Klooster, Fred Homburg, Brian de Bruyn, Ron Berteling, Mike Kouwenhoven, Tony Collard, Mari Saris, Harrie van Heumen, Henk Krikke, Chuck Huizinga

**Soviet Union** (Viktor Tikhonov, coach) GK—Vladimir Myshkin, Vladislav Tretiak—Sergei Babinov, Valeri Vasilyev, Alexei Kasatonov, Zinetula Bilyaletdinov, Vyacheslav Fetisov, Vasili Pervukhin, Nikolai Makarov, Sergei Makarov, Andrei Khomutov, Nikolai Drozdetski, Viktor Shalimov, Alexander Maltsev, Sergei Kapustin, Vladimir Krutov, Yuri Lebedev, Vladimir Petrov, Viktor Zhluktov, Sergei Shepelev, Vladimir Golikov, Alexander Skvortsov

**Sweden** (Bengt Ohlsson, coach) GK—Peter Lindmark, Christer Abrahamsson, Reino Sundberg—Mats Waltin, Anders Eldebrink, Dan Soderstrom, Roland Eriksson, Anders Hakansson, Stig Ostling, Tomas Jonsson, Mats Naslund, Thomas Steen, Bengt-Ake Gustafsson, Goran Lindblom, Peter Helander, Inge Hammarstrom, Lars Molin, Roland Stoltz, Lennart Norberg, Patrik Sundstrom, Tommy Samuelsson, Ulf Isaksson, Harald Luckner

**United States** (Bob Johnson, coach) GK—Greg Moffett, Ed Walsh—Craig Norwich, Bill Baker, John Harrington, Mark Pavelich, Phil Verchota, Reed Larson, Alan Hangsleben, Dave Debol, Dave Christian, Bobby Miller, Ron Wilson, Jim Korn, Warren Miller, Bobby Sheehan, Steve Ulseth, Aaron Broten, Wally Olds, Bob Suter, Craig Homola, Mark Johnson

**West Germany** (Hans Rampf, coach) GK—Karl-Heinz Friesen, Bernd Engelbrecht—Horst-Peter Kretschmer, Joachim Reil, Rainer Philipp, Erich Kuhnhackl, Marcus Kuhl, Peter Gailer, Robet Murray, Holger Meitinger, Ernst Hofner, Peter Schiller, Peter Scharf, Harold Kreis, Vladimir Vacatko, Manfred Wolf, Ralph Krueger, Jorg Hiemer, Uli Egen, Jochen Morz, Uli Hiemer

## 48th WORLD CHAMPIONSHIP (MEN)
## April 15-29, 1982
## Helsinki/Tampere, Finland

**Final Placing**

| | | | |
|---|---|---|---|
| Gold | Soviet Union | 5th | Finland |
| Silver | Czechoslovakia | 6th | West Germany |
| Bronze | Canada | 7th | Italy^ |
| 4th | Sweden | 8th | United States* |

^promoted from B Pool in 1981
*demoted to B Pool for 1983

**Tournament Format**

Each team played every other once, after which the top four played another round robin to determine medal winners, the bottom four playing in a classification/relegation group. All scores carried forward from the first round robin to the second.

**Results & Standings**
**PRELIMINARY ROUND**

| | GP | W | T | L | GF | GA | P |
|---|---|---|---|---|---|---|---|
| Soviet Union | 7 | 7 | 0 | 0 | 48 | 16 | 14 |
| Czechoslovakia | 7 | 4 | 1 | 2 | 33 | 14 | 9 |
| Sweden | 7 | 3 | 3 | 1 | 24 | 22 | 9 |
| Canada | 7 | 3 | 2 | 2 | 32 | 22 | 8 |
| Finland | 7 | 3 | 1 | 3 | 21 | 31 | 7 |
| West Germany | 7 | 2 | 1 | 4 | 19 | 30 | 5 |
| Italy | 7 | 1 | 1 | 5 | 20 | 44 | 3 |
| United States | 7 | 0 | 1 | 6 | 21 | 39 | 1 |

| | | | |
|---|---|---|---|
| April 15 | Tampere | Soviet Union 9 | Italy 2 |
| April 15 | Helsinki | West Germany 4 | Czechoslovakia 2 |
| April 15 | Tampere | Sweden 4 | United States 2 |
| April 15 | Helsinki | Canada 9 | Finland 2 |
| April 16 | Tampere | Italy 7 | United States 5 |
| April 16 | Helsinki | Czechoslovakia 6 | Canada 2 |
| April 16 | Tampere | Soviet Union 7 | Sweden 3 |
| April 16 | Helsinki | Finland 4 | West Germany 3 |
| April 18 | Tampere | Soviet Union 5 | Czechoslovakia 3 |
| April 18 | Helsinki | West Germany 5 | Italy 2 |
| April 18 | Tampere | Finland 4 | United States 2 |
| April 18 | Helsinki | Sweden 3 | Canada 3 |
| April 19 | Tampere | Czechoslovakia 6 | United States 0 |
| April 19 | Helsinki | Sweden 5 | Italy 2 |
| April 19 | Tampere | Soviet Union 8 | Finland 1 |
| April 19 | Helsinki | Canada 7 | West Germany 1 |
| April 21 | Tampere | Czechoslovakia 3 | Finland 0 |
| April 21 | Helsinki | Soviet Union 8 | United States 4 |
| April 21 | Tampere | Canada 3 | Italy 3 |
| April 21 | Helsinki | Sweden 3 | West Germany 1 |
| April 22 | Tampere | Soviet Union 7 | West Germany 0 |
| April 22 | Helsinki | Finland 7 | Italy 3 |
| April 22 | Tampere | Canada 5 | United States 3 |
| April 22 | Helsinki | Sweden 3 | Czechoslovakia 3 |
| April 24 | Tampere | West Germany 5 | United States 5 |
| April 24 | Helsinki | Czechoslovakia 10 | Italy 0 |
| April 24 | Tampere | Soviet Union 4 | Canada 3 |
| April 24 | Helsinki | Finland 3 | Sweden 3 |

**MEDAL ROUND (HELSINKI)**

| | GP | W | T | L | GF | GA | P |
|---|---|---|---|---|---|---|---|
| Soviet Union | 10 | 9 | 1 | 0 | 58 | 20 | 19 |
| Czechoslovakia | 10 | 5 | 2 | 3 | 38 | 20 | 12 |
| Canada | 10 | 5 | 2 | 3 | 46 | 30 | 12 |
| Sweden | 10 | 3 | 3 | 4 | 26 | 35 | 9 |

| | | |
|---|---|---|
| April 25 | Soviet Union 6 | Canada 4 |
| April 25 | Czechoslovakia 3 | Sweden 2 |
| April 27 | Canada 4 | Czechoslovakia 2 |
| April 27 | Soviet Union 4 | Sweden 0 |
| April 29 | Canada 6 | Sweden 0 |
| April 29 | Soviet Union 0 | Czechoslovakia 0 |

**Rosters**

**Canada** (Marshall Johnston/Red Berenson, coaches) GK—Greg Millen, Gilles Meloche—Paul Reinhart, Craig Hartsburg, Darryl Sittler, Bobby Clarke, Brian Propp, Curt Giles, Kevin Lowe, Mark Napier, Wayne Gretzky, Bill Barber, John Van Boxmeer, Rick Green, Mike Gartner, Dale Hawerchuk, Ryan Walter, Rick Vaive, Bobby Smith, Bob Gainey, Brad Maxwell, Dino Ciccarelli

**Czechoslovakia** (Ludek Bukac, coach) GK—Jiri Kralik, Karel Lang—Arnold Kadlec, Miloslav Horava, Jaroslav Korbela, Milan Novy, Pavel Richter, Eduard Uvira, Radoslav Svoboda, Jiri Lala, Jindrich Kokrment, Frantisek Cernik, Milan Chalupa, Miroslav Dvorak, Jiri Hrdina, Dusan Pasek, Jaroslav Pouzar, Vincent Lukac, Darius Rusnak, Igor Liba, Peter Ihnacak, Antonin Planovsky

**Finland** (Kalevi Numminen, coach) GK—Hannu Kamppuri, Hannu Lassila—Pertti Lehtonen, Raimo Hirvonen, Ilkka Sinisalo, Kari Jalonen, Jari Kurri, Tapio Levo, Hannu Helander, Arto Javanainen, Matti Forss, Kari Makkonen, Timo Nummelin, Juhani Tamminen, Juha Nurmi, Seppo Ahokainen, Pertti Valkeapaa, Pertti Koivulahti, Reijo Leppanen, Seppo Repo, Hannu Haapalainen, Pekka Arbelius

**Italy** (Dave Chambers, coach) GK—Jim Corsi, Nick Sanza—Dave Tomassoni, John Bellio, Cary Farelli, Rick Bragnalo, Bob Manno, Gerry Ciarcia, Guido Tenisi, Tom Milani, Patrick Dell'Jannone, Bob De Piero, Mike Mastrullo, Mike Amodeo, Constant Priondolo, Grant Goegan, Emilio Iovio, Michael Mair, Albert Di Fazio, Martin Pavlu, Gino Pasqualotto, Adolf Insam

**Soviet Union** (Viktor Tikhonov, coach) GK—Vladislav Tretiak, Vladimir Myshkin—Alexei Kasatonov, Vyacheslav Fetisov, Sergei Makarov, Igor Larionov, Vladimir Krutov, Sergei Babinov, Valeri Vasilyev, Viktor Shalimov, Sergei Shepelev, Sergei Kapustin, Zinetula Bilyaletdinov, Vasili Pervukhin, Vladimir Golikov, Alexander Kozhevnikov, Viktor Tyumenev, Nikolai Drozdetski, Viktor Zhluktov, Andrei Khomutov, Vladimir Zubkov, Irek Gimayev

**Sweden** (Anders Parmstrom, coach) GK—Peter Lindmark, Gote Walitalo—Goran Lindblom, Mats Thelin, Peter Sundstrom, Patrik Sundstrom, Ulf Isaksson, Peter Andersson, Peter Helander, Mats Naslund, Ove Olsson, Jan Erixon, Thomas Eriksson, Tommy Samuelsson, Hakan Loob, Thomas Rundqvist, Mats Ulander, Jan Eriksson, Tommy Morth, Tommy Sjalin, Roger Hagglund, Hasse Sjoo

**United States** (Bill Selman/Mike Smith, coaches) GK—Steve Janaszak, Glenn Resch—Moe Mantha, Rod Langway, Bryan Erickson, Mark Johnson, Mike Antonovich, Tom Hirsch, Gordie Roberts, Tom Gorence, Bob Miller, Buzz Schneider, Mike Ramsey, Phil Housley, John Harrington, Gary De Grio, Kurt Kleinendorst, Aaron Broten, Paul Miller, Peter Johnson, Joe Micheletti, Scot Kleinendorst

**West Germany** (Xaver Unsinn, coach) GK—Karl-Heinz Friesen, Bernd Engelbrecht—Udo Kiessling, Horst-Peter Kretschmer, Erich Kuhnhackl, Helmut Steiger, Roy Roedger, Joachim Reil, Ignaz Berndaner, Franz Reindl, Ernst Hofner, Holger Meitinger, Peter Gailer, Harold Kreis, Peter Schiller, Manfred Wolf, Gerd Truntschka, Jochen Morz, Dieter Hegen, Uli Egen, Marcus Kuhl

## 49th WORLD CHAMPIONSHIP (MEN)
## April 16-May 2, 1983
## Munich/Dortmund/Dusseldorf, West Germany

**Final Placing**

| | |
|---|---|
| Gold ........Soviet Union | 5th .........East Germany^ |
| Silver ......Czechoslovakia | 6th .........West Germany |
| Bronze ....Canada | 7th .........Finland |
| 4th..........Sweden | 8th .........Italy* |

^promoted from B Pool in 1982
*demoted to B Pool for 1984

**Tournament Format**

All teams played every other once in a preliminary round robin. The top four advanced to a medal group to play a round robin; the lower four also played a round robin to determine which teams qualified for the 1984 Olympics.

**Results & Standings**
**PRELIMINARY ROUND**

| | GP | W | T | L | GF | GA | P |
|---|---|---|---|---|---|---|---|
| Soviet Union | 7 | 7 | 0 | 0 | 40 | 4 | 14 |
| Canada | 7 | 5 | 0 | 2 | 26 | 16 | 10 |
| Czechoslovakia | 7 | 4 | 1 | 2 | 30 | 15 | 9 |
| Sweden | 7 | 4 | 1 | 2 | 23 | 20 | 9 |
| West Germany | 7 | 3 | 1 | 3 | 17 | 23 | 7 |
| East Germany | 7 | 2 | 0 | 5 | 19 | 28 | 4 |
| Finland | 7 | 1 | 1 | 5 | 20 | 28 | 3 |
| Italy | 7 | 0 | 0 | 7 | 5 | 46 | 0 |

| | | | |
|---|---|---|---|
| April 16 | Dortmund | Soviet Union 3 | East Germany 0 |
| April 16 | Dusseldorf | Czechoslovakia 4 | Finland 2 |
| April 16 | Dortmund | Sweden 5 | West Germany 1 |
| April 16 | Dusseldorf | Canada 6 | Italy 0 |
| April 17 | Dortmund | Czechoslovakia 6 | East Germany 1 |
| April 17 | Dortmund | Sweden 3 | Canada 2 |
| April 17 | Dusseldorf | West Germany 4 | Italy 0 |
| April 17 | Dusseldorf | Soviet Union 3 | Finland 0 |
| April 19 | Dortmund | East Germany 3 | Italy 1 |
| April 19 | Dusseldorf | Czechoslovakia 4 | Sweden 1 |
| April 19 | Dortmund | Soviet Union 8 | Canada 2 |
| April 19 | Dusseldorf | West Germany 4 | Finland 3 |
| April 20 | Dortmund | Sweden 5 | East Germany 4 |
| April 20 | Dortmund | Soviet Union 6 | West Germany 0 |
| April 21 | Dortmund | Finland 6 | Italy 2 |
| April 21 | Dortmund | Canada 3 | Czechoslovakia 1 |
| April 22 | Dortmund | Canada 5 | Finland 1 |
| April 22 | Dortmund | West Germany 4 | East Germany 3 |
| April 23 | Dortmund | Soviet Union 5 | Czechoslovakia 1 |
| April 23 | Dortmund | Sweden 5 | Italy 1 |
| April 24 | Dortmund | Finland 4 | Sweden 4 |
| April 24 | Munich | Canada 5 | East Germany 2 |
| April 24 | Dortmund | Soviet Union 11 | Italy 1 |
| April 24 | Munich | West Germany 3 | Czechoslovakia 3 |
| April 25 | Munich | Canada 3 | West Germany 1 |
| April 25 | Munich | East Germany 6 | Finland 4 |
| April 26 | Munich | Czechoslovakia 11 | Italy 0 |
| April 26 | Munich | Soviet Union 4 | Sweden 0 |

**RELEGATION ROUND (MUNICH)**

| | GP | W | T | L | GF | GA | P |
|---|---|---|---|---|---|---|---|
| East Germany | 10 | 5 | 1 | 4 | 31 | 34 | 11 |
| West Germany | 10 | 3 | 0 | 7 | 29 | 40 | 6 |
| Finland | 10 | 2 | 2 | 6 | 30 | 40 | 6 |
| Italy | 10 | 1 | 1 | 8 | 16 | 56 | 3 |

| | | |
|---|---|---|
| April 27 | West Germany 5 | Italy 4 |
| April 27 | East Germany 6 | Finland 2 |
| April 29 | Finland 4 | West Germany 2 |
| April 29 | Italy 3 | East Germany 1 |

| | | |
|---|---|---|
| May 1 | Italy 4 | Finland 4 |
| May 1 | West Germany 7 | East Germany 3 |

**MEDAL ROUND (MUNICH)**

| | GP | W | T | L | GF | GA | P |
|---|---|---|---|---|---|---|---|
| Soviet Union | 3 | 2 | 1 | 0 | 13 | 3 | 5 |
| Czechoslovakia | 3 | 2 | 1 | 0 | 10 | 6 | 5 |
| Canada | 3 | 1 | 0 | 2 | 9 | 14 | 2 |
| Sweden | 3 | 0 | 0 | 3 | 2 | 11 | 0 |

| | | |
|---|---|---|
| April 28 | Soviet Union 4 | Sweden 0 |
| April 28 | Czechoslovakia 5 | Canada 4 |
| April 30 | Canada 3 | Sweden 1 |
| April 30 | Soviet Union 1 | Czechoslovakia 1 |
| May 2 | Czechoslovakia 4 | Sweden 1 |
| May 2 | Soviet Union 8 | Canada 2 |

**Rosters**

**Canada** (Dave King, coach) GK—Rick Wamsley, Mike Veisor—Marcel Dionne, Michel Goulet, Brian Propp, Dennis Maruk, Paul Reinhart, Bob Gainey, Mike Gartner, Charlie Simmer, Dave Taylor, Darryl Sittler, John Anderson, Gord Sherven, Craig Hartsburg, Doug Halward, Brian Engblom, James Patrick, Rick Lanz, Scott Stevens, Pat Flatley, Tim Watters

**Czechoslovakia** (Ludek Bukac, coach) GK—Jiri Kralik, Dominik Hasek—Jiri Lala, Igor Liba, Darius Rusnak, Vincent Lukac, Vladimir Caldr, Dusan Pasek, Ladislav Svozil, Pavel Richter, Jaroslav Benak, Vladimir Ruzicka, Frantisek Cernik, Milan Chalupa, Oldrich Valek, Radoslav Svoboda, Miroslav Dvorak, Arnold Kadlec, Jiri Hrdina, Frantisek Musil, Frantisek Cerny, Eduard Uvira

**East Germany** (Joachim Ziesche, coach) GK—Rene Bielke, Ingolf Spantig—Dieter Frenzel, Thomas Graul, Harald Kuhnke, Andreas Ludwig, Frank Proske, Detlef Radant, Roland Peters, Fred Bartell, Dieter Simon, Dietmar Peters, Eckhard Scholz, Dieter Kinzel, Friedhelm Bogelsack, Gerhard Muller, Frank Braun, Stefan Steinbock, Reinhard Fengler, Guido Hiller, Joachim Lempio, Klaus Schroder

**Finland** (Alpo Suhonen, coach) GK—Hannu Kamppuri, Kari Takko—Anssi Melametsa, Pekka Rautakallio, Matti Hagman, Petri Skriko, Tony Arima, Tapio Levo, Kari Jalonen, Hannu Helander, Pertti Lehtonen, Arto Javanainen, Risto Jalo, Raimo Summanen, Kari Makkonen, Lasse Litma, Ilkka Sinisalo, Matti Kaario, Arto Sirvio, Risto Siltanen, Juha Nurmi, Timo Susi

**Italy** (Dave Chambers, coach) GK—Jim Corsi, Nick Sanza—Constant Priondolo, Albert Di Fazio, Bob De Piero, Bob Manno, Patrick Dell'Jannone, Grant Goegan, Rick Bragnalo, Tom Milani, Mike Amodeo, John Bellio, Adolf Insam, Erwin Kostner, Dave Tomassoni, Michael Mair, Guido Tenisi, Gerry Ciarcia, Lodovico Migliore, Mike Mastrullo, Martin Pavlu

**Soviet Union** (Viktor Tikhonov, coach) GK—Vladislav Tretiak, Vladimir Myshkin—Sergei Makarov, Vladimir Krutov, Igor Larionov, Alexei Kasatonov, Vyacheslav Fetisov, Helmuts Balderis, Viktor Zhluktov, Sergei Kapustin, Mikhail Vasilyev, Alexander Skvortsov, Sergei Shepelev, Vyacheslav Bykov, Sergei Starikov, Andrei Khomutov, Alexander Maltsev, Vladimir Zubkov, Zinetula Bilyaletdinov, Irek Gimayev, Sergei Babinov, Vasili Pervukhin

**Sweden** (Anders Parmstrom, coach) GK—Pelle Lindbergh, Gote Walitalo—Bengt-Ake Gustafsson, Mats Naslund, Peter Sundstrom, Jan Erixon, Kent Johansson, Bo Ericson, Roland Eriksson, Thomas Rundqvist, Leif Holmgren, Peter Loob, Tommy Morth, Mats Thelin, Roger Hagglund, Jorgen Pettersson, Peter Andersson, Tom Eklund, Mats Waltin, Hakan Sodergren, Thomas Eriksson, Tommy Samuelsson

**West Germany** (Xaver Unsinn, coach) GK—Erich Weishaupt, Karl-Heinz Friesen—Erich Kuhnhackl, Helmut Steiger, Gerd Truntschka, Harold Kreis, Franz Reindl, Michael Betz, Marcus Kuhl, Ernst Hofner, Dieter Hegen, Peter Scharf, Uli Hiemer, Manfred Wolf, Ignaz Berndaner, Peter Schiller, Holger Meitinger, Udo Kiessling, Dieter Medicus, Rainer Lutz, Roy Roedger, Thomas Gandorfer, Rene Bielke, Ingolf Spantig

## 50th WORLD CHAMPIONSHIP (MEN)
## April 17-May 3, 1985
## Prague, Czechoslovakia

**Final Placing**

Gold ........Czechoslovakia
Silver ......Canada
Bronze ....Soviet Union
4th..........United States^
5th .........Finland
6th .........Sweden
7th .........West Germany
8th .........East Germany*

^promoted from B Pool in 1984
*demoted to B Pool for 1986

**Tournament Format**

All teams played one game against every other. The top four advanced to a medal group to play a round robin; the lower four also played a round robin to determine which team was demoted for next year's World Championship.

**Results & Standings**

**PRELIMINARY ROUND**

| | GP | W | T | L | GF | GA | P |
|---|---|---|---|---|---|---|---|
| Soviet Union | 7 | 7 | 0 | 0 | 52 | 8 | 14 |
| United States | 7 | 4 | 1 | 2 | 24 | 34 | 9 |
| Canada | 7 | 4 | 1 | 2 | 33 | 23 | 9 |
| Czechoslovakia | 7 | 4 | 1 | 2 | 30 | 16 | 9 |
| Finland | 7 | 2 | 2 | 3 | 23 | 25 | 6 |
| Sweden | 7 | 2 | 0 | 5 | 24 | 30 | 4 |
| West Germany | 7 | 1 | 1 | 5 | 17 | 31 | 3 |
| East Germany | 7 | 0 | 2 | 5 | 11 | 47 | 2 |

| | | |
|---|---|---|
| April 17 | Canada 9 | East Germany 1 |
| April 17 | Soviet Union 11 | United States 1 |
| April 17 | Sweden 3 | West Germany 2 |
| April 17 | Czechoslovakia 5 | Finland 0 |
| April 18 | Canada 5 | West Germany 0 |
| April 18 | Soviet Union 5 | Finland 1 |
| April 18 | United States 4 | Sweden 3 |
| April 18 | Czechoslovakia 6 | East Germany 1 |
| April 20 | United States 4 | Canada 3 |
| April 20 | Finland 5 | Sweden 0 |
| April 20 | Czechoslovakia 6 | West Germany 1 |
| April 20 | Soviet Union 6 | East Germany 0 |
| April 21 | Canada 5 | Finland 2 |
| April 21 | Sweden 11 | East Germany 0 |
| April 21 | Soviet Union 10 | West Germany 2 |
| April 21 | United States 3 | Czechoslovakia 1 |
| April 23 | Canada 4 | Czechoslovakia 4 |
| April 23 | Finland 4 | East Germany 4 |
| April 23 | United States 4 | West Germany 3 |
| April 23 | Soviet Union 6 | Sweden 2 |
| April 24 | East Germany 5 | United States 5 |
| April 24 | Finland 3 | West Germany 3 |
| April 25 | Soviet Union 9 | Canada 1 |
| April 25 | Czechoslovakia 7 | Sweden 2 |
| April 26 | West Germany 6 | East Germany 0 |
| April 26 | Finland 8 | United States 3 |
| April 27 | Canada 6 | Sweden 3 |
| April 27 | Soviet Union 5 | Czechoslovakia 1 |

**RELEGATION ROUND**

| | GP | W | T | L | GF | GA | P |
|---|---|---|---|---|---|---|---|
| Finland | 10 | 4 | 2 | 4 | 39 | 33 | 10 |
| Sweden | 10 | 4 | 0 | 6 | 37 | 40 | 8 |
| West Germany | 10 | 3 | 1 | 6 | 28 | 41 | 7 |
| East Germany | 10 | 0 | 2 | 8 | 16 | 64 | 2 |

| | | |
|---|---|---|
| April 28 | Finland 6 | East Germany 2 |
| April 28 | Sweden 5 | West Germany 2 |
| April 30 | Sweden 7 | East Germany 2 |
| April 30 | West Germany 5 | Finland 4 |
| May 2 | West Germany 4 | East Germany 1 |
| May 2 | Finland 6 | Sweden 1 |

**MEDAL ROUND**

| | GP | W | T | L | GF | GA | P |
|---|---|---|---|---|---|---|---|
| Czechoslovakia | 3 | 3 | 0 | 0 | 18 | 6 | 6 |
| Canada | 3 | 2 | 0 | 1 | 9 | 8 | 4 |
| Soviet Union | 3 | 1 | 0 | 2 | 12 | 8 | 2 |
| United States | 3 | 0 | 0 | 3 | 7 | 24 | 0 |

| | | |
|---|---|---|
| April 29 | Canada 3 | United States 2 |
| April 29 | Czechoslovakia 2 | Soviet Union 1 |
| May 1 | Canada 3 | Soviet Union 1 |
| May 1 | Czechoslovakia 11 | United States 2 |
| May 3 | Czechoslovakia 5 | Canada 3 |
| May 3 | Soviet Union 10 | United States 3 |

**Rosters**

**Canada** (Doug Carpenter, coach) GK—Steve Weeks, Rick Wamsley, Pat Riggin—Kirk Muller, Doug Halward, Kevin Dineen, Ron Francis, Stan Smyl, John Anderson, Tony Tanti, Doug Lidster, Steve Konroyd, Don Maloney, Mario Lemieux, Jamie Macoun, Grant Ledyard, Dave Taylor, Bernie Nicholls, Steve Yzerman, Rick Vaive, Larry Murphy, Scott Stevens, Brian McLelland

**Czechoslovakia** (Ludek Bukac, coach) GK—Jiri Kralik, Jaromir Sindel—Arnold Kadlec, Eduard Uvira, Miroslav Horava, Antonin Stavjana, Jaroslav Benak, Radoslav Svoboda, Frantisek Musil, Vincent Lukac, Darius Rusnak, Igor Liba, Petr Rosol, Vladimir Ruzicka, Pavel Richter, Jiri Lala, Dusan Pasek, Jiri Hrdina, Oldrich Valek, Michal Pivonka, Jiri Sejba, Vladimir Kames

**East Germany** (Joachim Ziesche, coach) GK—Rene Bielke, Egon Schmeisser—Joachim Lempio, Thomas Graul, Reinhard Fengler, Dieter Frenzel, Detlef Mark, Gerd Vogel, Uwe Geisert, Friedhelm Bogelsack, Roland Peters, Mario Naster, Detlef Radant, Harald Kuhnke, Frank Proske, Ralf Hantschke, Andreas Ludwig, Andreas Gebauer, Eckhard Scholz, Rolf Nitz, Harald Bolke, Dietmar Peters

**Finland** (Alpo Suhonen, coach) GK—Kari Takko, Jukka Tammi—Jouko Narvanmaa, Markus Lehto, Reijo Ruotsalainen, Arto Ruotanen, Ville Siren, Risto Jalo, Petri Skriko, Hannu Jarvenpaa, Pekka Jarvela, Christian Ruuttu, Harri Tuohimaa, Kari Makkonen, Anssi Melametsa, Mikko Makela, Pekka Arbelius, Raimo Helminen, Esa Tikkanen, Juha Huikari, Timo Blomqvist, Kari Suoraniemi

**Soviet Union** (Viktor Tikhonov, coach) GK—Vladimir Myshkin, Sergei Mylnikov—Vyacheslav Fetisov, Alexei Kasatonov, Alexei Gusarov, Vasili Pervukhin, Zinetula Bilyaletdinov, Sergei Starikov, Irek Gimayev, Sergei Makarov, Igor Larionov, Vladimir Krutov, Nikolai Drozdetski, Andrei Khomutov, Mikhail Vasilyev, Vyacheslav Bykov, Sergei Svetlov, Sergei Yashin, Mikhail Varnakov, Viktor Tyumenev, Alexander Skvortsov, Vladimir Kovin

**Sweden** (Leif Boork, coach) GK—Rolf Ridderwall, Peter Lindmark—Anders Eldebrink, Tommy Abelin, Michael Thelven, Bo Ericson, Mats Waltin, Jens Ohling, Per-Erik Eklund, Peter Gradin, Lars-Gunnar Pettersson, Mikael Hjalm, Kent Johansson, Lars Molin, Dan Labraaten, Hakan Sodergren, Ulf Samuelsson, Matti Pauna, Hans Sarkijarvi, Tomas Sandstrom, Mats Kihlstrom, Kent Nilsson

**United States** (David Peterson, coach) GK—John Vanbiesbrouck, Chris Terreri—Mark Fusco, Gary Haight, Jim Johnson, Moe Mantha, Gary Suter, Tim Thomas, Bob Brooke, Mark Johnson, Aaron Broten, Clark Donatelli, Dan Dorion, Tony Granato, Corey Millen, Kelly Miller, Paul Fenton, Joel Otto, Bob Miller, Mike O'Connell, Neil Sheehy, Tom Fergus

**West Germany** (Xaver Unsinn, coach) GK—Karl Friesen, Helmut De Raaf—Udo Kiessling, Uli Hiemer, Harold Kreis, Peter Scharf, Rainer Blum, Erich Kuhnhackl, Michael Betz, Franz Reindl, Ernst Hofner, Roy Roedger, Manfred Wolf, Marcus Kuhl, Manfred Ahne, Dieter Hegen, Axel Kammerer, Markus Berwanger, Georg Franz, Andreas Niederberger, Manfred Schuster, Horst Heckelsmuller

## 51st WORLD CHAMPIONSHIP (MEN)
## April 12-28, 1986
## Moscow, Soviet Union

**Final Placing**

Gold ........Soviet Union
Silver .....Sweden
Bronze ....Canada
4th..........Finland
5th .........Czechoslovakia
6th .........United States
7th .........West Germany
8th .........Poland^*

^promoted from B Pool in 1985
*demoted to B Pool for 1987

**Tournament Format**

Each team played every other in a preliminary round robin. The top four teams advanced to a medal round, playing another round robin to determine medal winners. The lower four teams played another round robin, and the preliminary round scores carried over to the standings to determine which team would be relegated for the 1987 World Championship.

**Results & Standings**

**PRELIMINARY ROUND**

| | GP | W | T | L | GF | GA | P |
|---|---|---|---|---|---|---|---|
| Soviet Union | 7 | 7 | 0 | 0 | 32 | 9 | 14 |
| Sweden | 7 | 5 | 1 | 1 | 34 | 18 | 11 |
| Finland | 7 | 4 | 2 | 1 | 28 | 18 | 10 |
| Canada | 7 | 3 | 0 | 4 | 24 | 22 | 6 |
| Czechoslovakia | 7 | 2 | 1 | 4 | 17 | 17 | 5 |
| United States | 7 | 2 | 0 | 5 | 27 | 28 | 4 |
| West Germany | 7 | 2 | 0 | 5 | 17 | 39 | 4 |
| Poland | 7 | 1 | 0 | 6 | 15 | 43 | 2 |

| | | |
|---|---|---|
| April 12 | Finland 5 | United States 4 |
| April 12 | Canada 8 | West Germany 3 |
| April 12 | Soviet Union 4 | Sweden 2 |
| April 12 | Poland 2 | Czechoslovakia 1 |
| April 13 | West Germany 4 | Czechoslovakia 3 |
| April 13 | United States 7 | Poland 2 |
| April 13 | Soviet Union 4 | Finland 1 |
| April 13 | Sweden 4 | Canada 1 |
| April 15 | Sweden 3 | Czechoslovakia 2 |
| April 15 | United States 9 | West Germany 2 |
| April 15 | Soviet Union 7 | Poland 2 |
| April 15 | Finland 3 | Canada 2 |
| April 16 | Canada 8 | Poland 3 |
| April 16 | Czechoslovakia 1 | Finland 1 |
| April 16 | Soviet Union 4 | West Germany 1 |
| April 16 | Sweden 5 | United States 2 |
| April 18 | Czechoslovakia 5 | United States 2 |
| April 18 | Finland 4 | Poland 2 |
| April 18 | Soviet Union 4 | Canada 0 |
| April 18 | Sweden 4 | West Germany 2 |
| April 19 | Sweden 12 | Poland 3 |
| April 19 | Finland 10 | West Germany 1 |
| April 20 | Soviet Union 4 | Czechoslovakia 2 |
| April 20 | Canada 4 | United States 2 |
| April 21 | West Germany 4 | Poland 1 |
| April 21 | Sweden 4 | Finland 4 |
| April 22 | Czechoslovakia 3 | Canada 1 |
| April 22 | Soviet Union 5 | United States 1 |

**RELEGATION ROUND**

| | GP | W | T | L | GF | GA | P |
|---|---|---|---|---|---|---|---|
| Czechoslovakia | 10 | 5 | 1 | 4 | 38 | 21 | 11 |
| United States | 10 | 4 | 0 | 6 | 41 | 43 | 8 |
| West Germany | 10 | 2 | 1 | 7 | 23 | 52 | 5 |
| Poland | 10 | 1 | 1 | 8 | 26 | 63 | 3 |

| | | |
|---|---|---|
| April 23 | Czechoslovakia 8 | Poland 1 |
| April 23 | United States 5 | West Germany 0 |
| April 25 | United States 7 | Poland 5 |
| April 25 | Czechoslovakia 3 | West Germany 1 |
| April 27 | Czechoslovakia 10 | United States 2 |
| April 27 | West Germany 5 | Poland 5 |

**FINAL ROUND**

| | GP | W | T | L | GF | GA | P |
|---|---|---|---|---|---|---|---|
| Soviet Union | 3 | 3 | 0 | 0 | 18 | 6 | 6 |
| Sweden | 3 | 1 | 1 | 1 | 12 | 12 | 3 |
| Canada | 3 | 1 | 0 | 2 | 13 | 16 | 2 |
| Finland | 3 | 0 | 1 | 2 | 7 | 16 | 1 |

| | | |
|---|---|---|
| April 24 | Soviet Union 7 | Canada 4 |
| April 24 | Sweden 4 | Finland 4 |
| April 26 | Sweden 6 | Canada 5 |
| April 26 | Soviet Union 8 | Finland 0 |
| April 28 | Canada 4 | Finland 3 |
| April 28 | Soviet Union 3 | Sweden 2 |

**Rosters**

**Canada** (Pat Quinn, coach) GK—Kelly Hrudey, Jacques Cloutier—Craig Redmond, Mark Hardy, Grant Ledyard, Jay Wells, Phil Russell, Ken Daneyko, Denis Potvin, Dale Hawerchuk, Marcel Dionne, Dave Taylor, Jim Fox, Phil Sykes, Mike Foligno, Brent Sutter, Dave Andreychuk, Mike Bullard, Kirk Muller, Greg Adams, Toni Tanti

**Czechoslovakia** (Jan Starsi, coach) GK—Dominik Hasek, Jaromir Sindel—Peter Slanina, Frantisek Prochazka, Frantisek Musil, Arnold Kadlec, Jaroslav Benak, Antonin Stavjana, Mojmir Bozik, Petr Rosol, Igor Liba, Vladimir Ruzicka, Darius Rusnak, Vladimir Caldr, Jiri Lala, Dusan Pasek, Jiri Sejba, Milan Stas, Jiri Hrdina, Jan Vodila, Vladimir Svitek, Michal Pivonka

**Finland** (Rauno Korpi, coach) GK—Hannu Kamppuri, Jukka Tammi—Jouko Narvanmaa, Harri Nikander, Arto Ruotanen, Kari Suoraniemi, Jari Gronstrand, Kari Eloranta, Pekka Laksola, Jukka Virtanen, Timo Susi, Kari Jalonen, Kai Suikkanen, Hannu Jarvenpaa, Tommi Pohja, Christian Ruuttu, Erkki Lehtonen, Kari Makkonen, Hannu Oksanen, Jukka Vilander, Pekka Arbelius, Ari Vuori

**Poland** (Leszek Lejczyk, coach) GK—Franciszek Kukla, Andrzej Hanisz—Andrzej Ujwary, Henryk Gruth, Robert Szopinski, Andrzej Swiatek, Ludwik Synowiec, Marek Cholewa, Andrzej Kadziolka, Jan Stopczyk, Henryk Pytel, Krystian Sikorski, Jaroslaw Morawiecki, Bogdan Pawlik, Andrzej Zabawa, Roman Steblecki, Leszek Jachna, Jerzy Christ, Piotr Kwasigoroch, Marek Stebnicki, Janusz Wielgus, Krzysztof Podsiadlo

**Soviet Union** (Viktor Tikhonov, coach) GK—Sergei Mylnikov, Yevgeni Belosheikin—Vyacheslav Fetisov, Alexei Gusarov, Igor Stelnov, Vasili Pervukhin, Alexei Kasatonov, Sergei Starikov, Zinetula Bilyaletdinov, Vladimir Krutov, Igor Larionov, Andrei Khomutov, Sergei Svetlov, Mikhail Varnakov, Sergei Makarov, Sergei Yashin, Vladimir Konstantinov, Vyacheslav Bykov, Viktor Tyumenev, Sergei Ageikin, Valeri Kamenski, Yuri Khmylyov

**Sweden** (Curt Lindstrom, coach) GK—Peter Lindmark, Ake Lilljebjorn, Peter Aslin—Anders Eldebrink, Tommy Albelin, Mats Kihlstrom, Tommy Samuelsson, Fredrik Olausson, Thomas Steen, Robert Nordmark, Tomas Jonsson, Per-Erik Eklund, Thom Eklund, Thomas Rundqvist, Matti Pauna, Michael Hjalm, Jonas Bergqvist, Lars-Gunnar Pettersson, Dan Labraaten, Hakan Sodergren, Staffan Lundh, Anders Carlsson, Kenneth Andersson

**United States** (Dave Peterson, coach) GK—Chris Terreri, Tom Barrasso, Mike Richter—Jim Sprenger, Guy Gosselin, Richie Dunn, Scott Sandelin, Phil Housley, Jim Johnson, David H. Jensen, Peter McNab, Ed Olczyk, Mark Johnson, Tony Granato, Brian Williams, Brett Hull, Aaron Broten, Clark Donatelli, Bryan Erickson, John Carter, Doug Brown, Alfie Turcotte, Randy Wood

**West Germany** (Xaver Unsinn, coach) GK—Erich Weishaupt, Helmut De Raaf—Udo Kiessling, Uwe Krupp, Horst-Peter Kretschmer, Andreas Niederberger, Rainer Blum, Manfred Schuster, Peter Scharf, Dieter Hegen, Gerd Truntschka, Helmut Steiger, Georg Holzmann, Roy Roedger, Axel Kammerer, Manfred Ahne, Georg Fritz, Peter Schiller, Ralph Krueger, Georg Franz, Ernst Hofner, Franz Reindl

## 52nd WORLD CHAMPIONSHIP (MEN)
## April 17-May 3, 1987
## Vienna, Austria

**Final Placing**

Gold .......Sweden
Silver ......Soviet Union
Bronze ....Czechoslovakia
4th..........Canada
5th .........Finland
6th .........West Germany
7th .........United States
8th .........Switzerland^*

^promoted from B Pool in 1986
*demoted to B Pool for 1988

**Tournament Format**
Each team played every other in a preliminary round robin. The top four teams advanced to a medal round, playing another round robin to determine medal winners. The lower four teams played another round robin, and the preliminary round scores carried over to the standings to determine which team would be relegated for the 1988 World Championship.

**Results & Standings**
**PRELIMINARY ROUND**

| | GP | W | T | L | GF | GA | P |
|---|---|---|---|---|---|---|---|
| Soviet Union | 7 | 7 | 0 | 0 | 48 | 12 | 14 |
| Czechoslovakia | 7 | 5 | 1 | 1 | 24 | 17 | 11 |
| Sweden | 7 | 4 | 0 | 3 | 30 | 17 | 8 |
| Canada | 7 | 3 | 1 | 3 | 25 | 17 | 7 |
| West Germany | 7 | 3 | 0 | 4 | 18 | 28 | 6 |
| Finland | 7 | 3 | 0 | 4 | 17 | 24 | 6 |
| United States | 7 | 2 | 0 | 5 | 21 | 36 | 4 |
| Switzerland | 7 | 0 | 0 | 7 | 17 | 49 | 0 |

| | | |
|---|---|---|
| April 17 | Soviet Union 13 | Switzerland 5 |
| April 17 | Sweden 3 | West Germany 0 |
| April 17 | Czechoslovakia 5 | Finland 2 |
| April 17 | Canada 3 | United States 1 |
| April 18 | Finland 3 | Switzerland 2 |
| April 18 | Sweden 6 | United States 2 |
| April 18 | Soviet Union 7 | West Germany 0 |
| April 18 | Canada 1 | Czechoslovakia 1 |
| April 20 | West Germany 3 | Finland 1 |
| April 20 | Soviet Union 11 | United States 2 |
| April 20 | Canada 6 | Switzerland 1 |
| April 20 | Czechoslovakia 3 | Sweden 2 |
| April 21 | West Germany 5 | Canada 3 |
| April 21 | Sweden 12 | Switzerland 1 |
| April 21 | Finland 5 | United States 2 |
| April 21 | Soviet Union 6 | Czechoslovakia 1 |
| April 23 | Soviet Union 4 | Finland 0 |
| April 23 | United States 6 | West Germany 4 |
| April 23 | Czechoslovakia 5 | Switzerland 2 |
| April 23 | Sweden 4 | Canada 3 |
| April 24 | Finland 4 | Sweden 1 |
| April 24 | Soviet Union 3 | Canada 2 |
| April 25 | United States 6 | Switzerland 3 |
| April 25 | Czechoslovakia 5 | West Germany 2 |
| April 26 | Canada 7 | Finland 2 |
| April 26 | Soviet Union 4 | Sweden 2 |
| April 27 | West Germany 4 | Switzerland 3 |
| April 27 | Czechoslovakia 4 | United States 2 |

**RELEGATION ROUND**

| | GP | W | T | L | GF | GA | P |
|---|---|---|---|---|---|---|---|
| Finland | 10 | 5 | 1 | 4 | 32 | 34 | 11 |
| West Germany | 10 | 4 | 1 | 5 | 31 | 37 | 9 |
| United States | 10 | 4 | 0 | 6 | 36 | 49 | 8 |
| Switzerland | 10 | 0 | 0 | 10 | 26 | 71 | 0 |

| | | |
|---|---|---|
| April 28 | West Germany 8 | Switzerland 1 |
| April 28 | Finland 6 | United States 4 |
| April 30 | Finland 7 | Switzerland 4 |
| April 30 | United States 6 | West Germany 3 |
| May 2 | United States 7 | Switzerland 4 |
| May 2 | West Germany 2 | Finland 2 |

**MEDAL ROUND**

| | GP | W | T | L | GF | GA | P |
|---|---|---|---|---|---|---|---|
| Sweden | 3 | 1 | 2 | 0 | 14 | 5 | 4 |
| Soviet Union | 3 | 1 | 2 | 0 | 4 | 3 | 4 |
| Czechoslovakia | 3 | 1 | 1 | 1 | 8 | 7 | 3 |
| Canada | 3 | 0 | 1 | 2 | 2 | 13 | 1 |

| | | |
|---|---|---|
| April 29 | Canada 0 | Soviet Union 0 |
| April 29 | Czechoslovakia 3 | Sweden 3 |
| May 1 | Czechoslovakia 4 | Canada 2 |
| May 1 | Sweden 2 | Soviet Union 2 |
| May 3 | Sweden 9 | Canada 0 |
| May 3 | Soviet Union 2 | Czechoslovakia 1 |

**Rosters**
**Canada** (Dave King, coach) GK—Sean Burke, Bob Froese, Pat Riggin—Bruce Driver, Doug Bodger, Craig Hartsburg, Bob Rouse, Scott Stevens, Barry Pederson, Tony Tanti, Dan Quinn, Kevin Dineen, Keith Acton, Troy Murray, Mike Foligno, Larry Murphy, Dino Ciccarelli, Al Secord, Dirk Graham, James Patrick, Brian Bellows, Zarley Zalapski, Kirk Muller

**Czechoslovakia** (Jan Starsi, coach) GK—Dominik Hasek, Jaromir Sindel, Karel Lang—Miloslav Horava, Drahomir Kadlec, Ludek Cajka, Bedrich Scerban, Jaroslav Benak, Petr Rosol, Igor Liba, Jiri Kucera, Jiri Dolezal, Antonin Stavjana, Vladimir Ruzicka, David Volek, Petr Vlk, Dusan Pasek, Jiri Sejba, Libor Dolana, Jiri Hrdina, Frantisek Cerny, Rostislav Vlach, Mojmir Bozik

**Finland** (Rauno Korpi, coach) GK—Hannu Kamppuri, Jarmo Myllys, Jukka Tammi—Teppo Numminen, Pekka Laksola, Jarmo Kuusisto, Arto Ruotanen, Timo Jutila, Janne Ojanen, Petri Skriko, Timo Susi, Kari Jalonen, Risto Jalo, Risto Kurkinen, Iiro Jarvi, Jukka Virtanen, Pekka Jarvela, Christian Ruuttu, Jukka Seppo, Hannu Virta, Raimo Summanen, Jari Torkki, Reijo Mikkolainen

**Soviet Union** (Viktor Tikhonov, coach) GK—Sergei Mylnikov, Yevgeni Belosheikin, Vitali Samoilov—Vyacheslav Fetisov, Alexei Gusarov, Igor Stelnov, Vasili Pervukhin, Alexei Kasatonov, Yuri Khmylyov, Vladimir Krutov, Igor Larionov, Sergei Starikov, Valeri Kamenski, Zinetula Bilyaletdinov, Andrei Khomutov, Sergei Svetlov, Alexander Semak, Mikhail Varnakov, Sergei Pryakhin, Mikhail Vasilyev, Sergei Makarov, Vyacheslav Bykov, Anatoli Semyonov

**Sweden** (Tommy Sandlin, coach) GK—Peter Lindmark, Ake Lilljebjorn, Anders Bergman—Anders Eldebrink, Tommy Albelin, Thom Eklund, Mats Kihlstrom, Lars Karlsson, Thomas Rundquist, Matti Pauna, Hakan Loob, Mikael Andersson, Magnus Svensson, Bengt-Ake Gustafsson, Peter Sundstrom, Jonas Bergqvist, Peter Andersson, Robert Nordmark, Lars-Gunnar Pettersson, Hakan Sodergren, Lars Molin, Tomas Sandstrom, Anders Carlsson

**Switzerland** (Simon Schenk, coach) GK—Richard Bucher, Renato Tosio, Oliver Anken—Fausto Mazzoleni, Andreas Ritsch, Marco Mueller, Eduard Rauch, Sandro Bertaggia, Gil Montandon, Pietro Cunti, Thomas Muller, Jakob Kolliker, Gaetan Boucher, Bruno Rogger, Alfred Luthi, Reto Dekumbis, Jorg Eberle, Roman Wager, Peter Schlagenhauf, Manuele Celio, Peter Jaks, Thomas Vrabec, Patrice Brasey

**United States** (Dave Peterson, coach) GK—John Vanbiesbrouck, Chris Terreri, Mike Richter—Brian Leetch, Ron Wilson, Jim Johnson, Gordie Roberts, Brian Lawton, Bob Carpenter, Bryan Erickson, Mark Johnson, Bob Brooke, Jimmy Carson, Aaron Broten, Ed Olczyk, Clark Donatelli, Kevin Stevens, Lane MacDonald, Craig Janney, Tony Granato, Tom Kurvers, Craig Wolanin

**West Germany** (Xaver Unsinn, coach) GK—Helmut De Raaf, Karl Friesen, Josef Schlickenrieder—Harold Kreis, Udo Kiessling, Manfred Schuster, Dieter Medicus, Daniel Held, Manfred Wolf, Markus Kuhl, Horst-Peter Kretschmer, Georg Holzmann, Gerd Truntschka, Joachim Reil, Andreas Niederberger, Axel Kammerer, Roy Roedger, Dieter Hegen, Helmut Steiger, Manfred Ahne, Georg Franz, Ernst Hofner

## 53rd WORLD CHAMPIONSHIP (MEN)
## April 15-May 1, 1989
## Stockholm/Sodertalje, Sweden

**Final Placing**

| | |
|---|---|
| Gold ........Soviet Union | 5th .........Finland |
| Silver .....Canada | 6th .........United States |
| Bronze ....Czechoslovakia | 7th .........West Germany |
| 4th ..........Sweden | 8th .........Poland^* |

^promoted from B Pool in 1987
*demoted to B Pool for 1990

**Tournament Format**
Each team played every other in a preliminary round robin. The top four teams advanced to a medal round, playing another round robin to determine medal winners. The lower four teams played another round robin, and the preliminary round scores carried over to the final standings to determine which team would be relegated for the 1989 World Championship.

**Results & Standings**
**PRELIMINARY ROUND**

| | GP | W | T | L | GF | GA | P |
|---|---|---|---|---|---|---|---|
| Soviet Union | 7 | 7 | 0 | 0 | 36 | 12 | 14 |
| Sweden | 7 | 4 | 2 | 1 | 29 | 20 | 10 |
| Canada | 7 | 5 | 0 | 2 | 45 | 18 | 10 |
| Czechoslovakia | 7 | 3 | 2 | 2 | 33 | 15 | 8 |
| Finland | 7 | 2 | 1 | 4 | 22 | 25 | 5 |
| United States | 7 | 2 | 1 | 4 | 20 | 29 | 5 |
| Poland | 7 | 1 | 0 | 6 | 10 | 59 | 2 |
| West Germany | 7 | 0 | 2 | 5 | 17 | 34 | 2 |

| | | | |
|---|---|---|---|
| April 15 | Stockholm | Czechoslovakia 3 | West Germany 3 |
| April 15 | Stockholm | Soviet Union 4 | United States 2 |
| April 15 | Sodertalje | Canada 6 | Finland 4 |
| April 15 | Stockholm | Sweden 5 | Poland 1 |
| April 16 | Sodertalje | Czechoslovakia 3 | Finland 1 |
| April 16 | Stockholm | Sweden 4 | United States 2 |
| April 16 | Stockholm | Canada 11 | Poland 0 |
| April 16 | Sodertalje | Soviet Union 5 | West Germany 1 |
| April 18 | Stockholm | Canada 8 | United States 0 |
| April 18 | Stockholm | Czechoslovakia 15 | Poland 0 |
| April 18 | Sodertalje | Soviet Union 4 | Finland 1 |
| April 18 | Stockholm | Sweden 3 | West Germany 3 |
| April 19 | Stockholm | Soviet Union 12 | Poland 1 |
| April 19 | Stockholm | Canada 8 | West Germany 2 |
| April 19 | Sodertalje | Czechoslovakia 5 | United States 0 |

| | | | |
|---|---|---|---|
| April 19 | Stockholm | Sweden 6 | Finland 3 |
| April 21 | Stockholm | Finland 7 | Poland 2 |
| April 21 | Stockholm | Soviet Union 4 | Czechoslovakia 2 |
| April 21 | Sodertalje | United States 7 | West Germany 4 |
| April 21 | Stockholm | Sweden 6 | Canada 5 |
| April 22 | Stockholm | Czechoslovakia 3 | Sweden 3 |
| April 22 | Stockholm | Soviet Union 4 | Canada 3 |
| April 23 | Stockholm | United States 3 | Finland 3 |
| April 23 | Stockholm | Poland 5 | West Germany 3 |
| April 24 | Stockholm | Canada 4 | Czechoslovakia 2 |
| April 24 | Stockholm | Soviet Union 3 | Sweden 2 |
| April 25 | Stockholm | United States 6 | Poland 1 |
| April 25 | Stockholm | Finland 3 | West Germany 1 |

**RELEGATION ROUND**

| | GP | W | T | L | GF | GA | P |
|---|---|---|---|---|---|---|---|
| Finland | 10 | 5 | 1 | 4 | 35 | 27 | 11 |
| United States | 10 | 4 | 1 | 5 | 37 | 40 | 9 |
| West Germany | 10 | 1 | 2 | 7 | 22 | 41 | 4 |
| Poland | 10 | 1 | 0 | 9 | 12 | 76 | 2 |

| | | |
|---|---|---|
| April 26 | Finland 3 | West Germany 0 |
| April 26 | United States 11 | Poland 2 |
| April 28 | United States 4 | West Germany 3 |
| April 28 | Finland 4 | Poland 0 |
| April 30 | West Germany 2 | Poland 0 |
| April 30 | Finland 6 | United States 2 |

**MEDAL ROUND**

| | GP | W | T | L | GF | GA | P |
|---|---|---|---|---|---|---|---|
| Soviet Union | 3 | 3 | 0 | 0 | 11 | 4 | 6 |
| Canada | 3 | 2 | 0 | 1 | 12 | 11 | 4 |
| Czechoslovakia | 3 | 1 | 0 | 2 | 5 | 6 | 2 |
| Sweden | 3 | 0 | 0 | 3 | 5 | 12 | 0 |

| | | |
|---|---|---|
| April 27 | Soviet Union 1 | Czechoslovakia 0 |
| April 27 | Canada 5 | Sweden 3 |
| April 29 | Czechoslovakia 2 | Sweden 1 |
| April 29 | Soviet Union 5 | Canada 3 |
| May 1 | Canada 4 | Czechoslovakia 3 |
| May 1 | Soviet Union 5 | Sweden 1 |

**Rosters**

**Canada** (Dave King, coach) GK—Sean Burke, Peter Sidorkiewicz, Grant Fuhr—Dave Ellett, Ken Daneyko, James Patrick, Brent Ashton, Randy Carlyle, Kirk Muller, Dale Hawerchuk, Kevin Dineen, John McLean, Pat Verbeek, Gerard Gallant, Glenn Anderson, Steve Yzerman, Andrew McBain, Mark Messier, Brian Bellows, Dave Babych, Scott Stevens, Ray Ferraro, Mario Marois

**Czechoslovakia** (Pavel Wohl, coach) GK—Dominik Hasek, Jaromir Sindel, Peter Briza—Leo Gudas, Frantisek Kucera, Drahomir Kadlec, Jiri Latal, Bedrich Scerban, Frantisek Prochazka, Otakar Janecky, Jiri Kucera, Jiri Dolezal, Antonin Stavjana, Vladimir Ruzicka, Jergus Baca, Robert Kron, Zdeno Ciger, Oldrich Valek, Jiri Sejba, Tomas Jelinek, Otto Hascak, Rostislav Vlach, Vladimir Svitek

**Finland** (Pentti Matikainen, coach) GK—Jukka Tammi, Sakari Lindfors, Markus Ketterer—Timo Blomquist, Pertti Lehtonen, Jarmo Kuusisto, Simo Saarinen, Jouko Narvanmaa, Kari Eloranta, Timo Susi, Esa Tikkanen, Kari Jalonen, Pauli Jarvinen, Hannu Jarvenpaa, Jari Kurri, Jukka Vilander, Ari Vuori, Hannu Virta, Reijo Mikkolainen, Esa Keskinen, Reijo Ruotsalainen, Iiro Jarvi, Jukka Seppo

**Poland** (Leszek Lejczyk, coach) GK—Andrzej Hanisz, Dariusz Wieczorek, Gabriel Samolej—Andrzej Kadziolka, Jan Stopczyk, Henryk Gruth, Robert Szopinski, Krzysztof Bujar, Miroslaw Copija, Piotr Zdunek, Janusz Adamiec, Marian Drasyk, Jacek Szopinski, Roman Steblecki, Ludwik Czapka, Jerzy Christ, Zbigniew Bryjak, Piotr Kwasigroch, Marek Teodorczak, Marek Stebnicki, Janusz Syposz, Krzysztof Podsiadlo, Jerzy Potz

**Soviet Union** (Viktor Tikhonov, coach) GK—Sergei Mylnikov, Arturs Irbe, Vladimir Myshkin—Vyacheslav Fetisov, Svyatoslav Khalizov, Alexei Gusarov, Ilya Byakin, Alexei Kasatonov, Yuri Khmylyov, Vladimir Krutov, Alexander Mogilny, Igor Larionov, Sergei Nemchinov, Valeri Kamenski, Valeri Shiryayev, Andrei Khomutov, Dmitri Kvartalnov, Alexander Chernykh, Vladimir Konstantinov, Sergei Makarov, Sergei Yashin, Vyacheslav Bykov, Sergei Fyodorov

**Sweden** (Tommy Sandlin, coach) GK—Peter Lindmark, Peter Aslin, Rolf Ridderwall—Anders Eldebrink, Tommy Albelin, Fredrik Olausson, Mats Kihlstrom, Tommy Samuelsson, Thomas Rundqvist, Kent Nilsson, Jens Ohling, Johan Stromwall, Peter Eriksson, Jonas Bergqvist, Peter Andersson, Bo Berglund, Borje Salming, Hakan Sodergren, Anders Carlsson, Thomas Steen, Thomas Eriksson, Tomas Sandstrom, Ulf Dahlen

**United States** (Tim Taylor, coach) GK—Rob Stauber, John Vanbiesbrouck, Cleon Daskalakis—Brian Leetch, Greg Brown, Jeff Norton, Tom Kurvers, Phil Housley, Jack O'Callahan, Tom O'Regan, Ed Olczyk, Randy Wood, Tom Fitzgerald, Paul Fenton, Pat Lafontaine, Kelly Miller, Brian Mullen, Scott Young, Tom Chorske, Dave Snuggerud, Doug Brown, Dave Christian, Corey Millen

**West Germany** (Xaver Unsinn/Erich Kuhnhackl, coaches) GK—Josef Schlickenrieder, Karl Friesen, Matthias Hoppe—Andreas Pokorny, Harold Kreis, Udo Kiessling, Bernd Wagner, Ron Fischer, Harald Birk, Peter Obresa, Markus Berwanger, Georg Holzmann, Gerd Truntschka, Michael Schmidt, Andreas Niederberger, Peter Draisaitl, Axel Kammerer, Roy Roedger, Dieter Hegen, Helmut Steiger, Uli Hiemer, Manfred Ahne, Georg Franz

## 54th WORLD CHAMPIONSHIP (MEN)
**April 16-May 2, 1990**
**Berne/Fribourg, Switzerland**

**Final Placing**

| | |
|---|---|
| Gold ........Soviet Union | 5th .........United States |
| Silver ......Sweden | 6th .........Finland |
| Bronze ....Czechoslovakia | 7th .........West Germany |
| 4th ..........Canada | 8th .........Norway^* |

^promoted from B Pool in 1989
*demoted to B Pool for 1991

**Tournament Format**

Each team played every other in a preliminary round robin. The top four teams advanced to a medal round, playing another round robin to determine medal winners. The lower four teams played another round robin, and the preliminary round scores carried over to the final standings to determine which team would be relegated for the 1991 World Championship.

**Results & Standings**

**PRELIMINARY ROUND**

| | GP | W | T | L | GF | GA | P |
|---|---|---|---|---|---|---|---|
| Canada | 7 | 6 | 1 | 0 | 36 | 16 | 13 |
| Sweden | 7 | 6 | 0 | 1 | 29 | 11 | 12 |
| Soviet Union | 7 | 5 | 1 | 1 | 38 | 12 | 11 |
| Czechoslovakia | 7 | 4 | 0 | 3 | 28 | 18 | 8 |
| United States | 7 | 3 | 0 | 4 | 23 | 37 | 6 |
| Finland | 7 | 1 | 1 | 5 | 18 | 27 | 3 |
| Norway | 7 | 1 | 1 | 5 | 19 | 45 | 3 |
| West Germany | 7 | 0 | 0 | 7 | 11 | 36 | 0 |

| | | | |
|---|---|---|---|
| April 16 | Berne | Soviet Union 9 | Norway 1 |
| April 16 | Fribourg | Canada 5 | West Germany 1 |
| April 16 | Berne | Sweden 4 | Finland 2 |
| April 16 | Fribourg | Czechoslovakia 7 | United States 1 |
| April 17 | Berne | Soviet Union 5 | West Germany 2 |
| April 17 | Berne | Canada 6 | United States 3 |
| April 17 | Fribourg | Sweden 4 | Norway 3 |
| April 17 | Berne | Czechoslovakia 4 | Finland 2 |
| April 19 | Berne | Czechoslovakia 9 | Norway 1 |
| April 19 | Berne | Canada 6 | Finland 5 |
| April 19 | Fribourg | Soviet Union 10 | United States 1 |
| April 19 | Berne | Sweden 6 | West Germany 0 |
| April 20 | Berne | Canada 8 | Norway 0 |
| April 20 | Berne | Sweden 6 | United States 1 |
| April 20 | Fribourg | Czechoslovakia 3 | West Germany 0 |
| April 20 | Berne | Soviet Union 6 | Finland 1 |
| April 22 | Berne | United States 6 | West Germany 3 |
| April 22 | Berne | Sweden 3 | Soviet Union 1 |
| April 22 | Fribourg | Norway 3 | Finland 3 |
| April 22 | Berne | Canada 5 | Czechoslovakia 3 |
| April 23 | Berne | United States 9 | Norway 4 |
| April 23 | Berne | Finland 4 | West Germany 2 |
| April 24 | Berne | Canada 3 | Sweden 1 |
| April 24 | Berne | Soviet Union 4 | Czechoslovakia 1 |
| April 25 | Berne | Norway 7 | West Germany 3 |
| April 25 | Berne | United States 2 | Finland 1 |
| April 26 | Berne | Sweden 5 | Czechoslovakia 1 |
| April 26 | Berne | Soviet Union 3 | Canada 3 |

**RELEGATION ROUND (BERNE)**

| | GP | W | T | L | GF | GA | P |
|---|---|---|---|---|---|---|---|
| United States | 10 | 6 | 0 | 4 | 35 | 43 | 12 |
| Finland | 10 | 2 | 2 | 7 | 24 | 32 | 6 |
| West Germany | 10 | 1 | 1 | 8 | 19 | 42 | 3 |
| Norway | 10 | 1 | 1 | 8 | 21 | 61 | 3 |

| | | |
|---|---|---|
| April 27 | Finland 8 | Norway 1 |
| April 27 | United States 5 | West Germany 3 |
| April 29 | Finland 1 | West Germany 1 |
| April 29 | United States 4 | Norway 1 |
| May 1 | United States 3 | Finland 2 |
| May 1 | West Germany 4 | Norway 0 |

**MEDAL ROUND (BERNE)**

| | GP | W | T | L | GF | GA | P |
|---|---|---|---|---|---|---|---|
| Soviet Union | 3 | 3 | 0 | 0 | 15 | 1 | 6 |
| Sweden | 3 | 1 | 1 | 1 | 11 | 12 | 3 |
| Czechoslovakia | 3 | 1 | 1 | 1 | 8 | 12 | 3 |
| Canada | 3 | 0 | 0 | 3 | 7 | 16 | 0 |

| | | |
|---|---|---|
| April 28 | Czechoslovakia 3 | Canada 2 |
| April 28 | Soviet Union 3 | Sweden 0 |
| April 30 | Sweden 5 | Czechoslovakia 5 |
| April 30 | Soviet Union 7 | Canada 1 |
| May 2 | Soviet Union 5 | Czechoslovakia 0 |
| May 2 | Sweden 6 | Canada 4 |

**Rosters**

**Canada** (Dave King, coach) GK—Kirk McLean, Ken Wregget, Bob Essensa—Al MacInnis, Doug Lidster, Curtis Leschyshyn, Rick Green, Greg Adams, Shawn Burr, Ron Sutter, Joe Nieuwendyk, Murray Craven, Mark Recchi, Steve Yzerman, Rick Tocchet, Brian Bellows, Michel Petit, Keith Acton, Theo Fleury, Doug Gilmour, John Cullen, Jamie Macoun, Paul Coffey

**Czechoslovakia** (Pavel Wohl, coach) GK—Petr Briza, Dominik Hasek, Eduard Hartmann—Leo Gudas, Mojmir Bozik, Drahomir Kadlec, Bedrich Scerban, Frantisek Prochazka, Martin Hostak, Jiri Kucera, Jiri Dolezal, Antonin Stavjana, Robert Reichel, Jergus Baca, Robert Kron, Zdeno Ciger, Robert Holik, Jaromir Jagr, Libor Dolana, Tomas Jelinek, Ladislav Lubina, Otto Hascak, Jiri Hrdina

**Finland** (Pentti Matikainen, coach) GK—Sakari Lindfors, Jukka Tammi—Kai Rautio, Jyrki Lumme, Jarmo Kuusisto, Arto Ruotanen, Simo Saarinen, Pekka Laksola, Heikki Leime, Juha Jarvenpaa, Risto Jalo, Pauli Jarvinen, Pekka Arbelius, Jukka Vilander, Christian Ruuttu, Ari Vuori, Hannu Henrikkson, Reijo Mikkolainen, Raimo Summanen, Esa Keskinen, Raimo Helminen, Pekka Tirkkoknen

**Norway** (George Kingston, coach) GK—Jim Marthinsen, Steve Allman, Torbjorn Orskaug—Torbjorn Orskaug, Petter Salsten, Jorgen Salsten, Age Ellingsen, Morgan Andersen, Jan-Roar Fagerli, Rune Gulliksen, Geir Hoff, Orjan Lovdal, Carl-Gunnar Gundersen, Kim Sogaard, Lars Bergseng, Knut Walbye, Ole Eskild Dahlstrom, Arne Billkvam, Erik Kristiansen, Per Christian Knold, Stephen Foyn, Morten Finstad, Cato Tom Andersen, Tor-Helge Eikeland

**Soviet Union** (Viktor Tikhonov, coach) GK—Arturs Irbe, Vladimir Myshkin, Sergei Mylnikov—Vyacheslav Fetisov, Igor Kravchuk, Vladimir Malakhov, Alexei Gusarov, Ilya Byakin, Mikhail Tatarinov, Pavel Bure, Yevgeni Davydov, Sergei Nemchinov, Valeri Kamenski, Andrei Khomutov, Vladimir Konstantinov, Alexander Semak, Sergei Pryakhin, Viktor Tyumenev, Sergei Makarov, Vyacheslav Bykov, Dmitri Khristich, Sergei Fyodorov, Yuri Leonov

**Sweden** (Tommy Sandlin, coach) GK—Rolf Ridderwall, Peter Aslin, Fredrik Andersson—Anders Eldebrink, Tomas Jonsson, Par Djoos, Ulf Samuelsson, Tommy Samuelsson, Magnus Svensson, Thomas Rundqvist, Kent Nilsson, Per-Erik Eklund, Hakan Loob, Johan Stromwall, Patrik Erickson, Peter Andersson, Johan Garpenlov, Magnus Roupe, Anders Carlsson, Mikael Johansson, Anders Huss, Thomas Eriksson, Mats Sundin

**United States** (Tim Taylor, coach) GK—John Blue, Jon Casey, Billy Pye—William Pye, Guy Gosselin, Chris Dahlquist, Greg Brown, Neal Broten, Jim Johnson, Danton Cole, Tom O'Regan, Kip Miller, Paul Ranheim, Bobby Reynolds, Edmund Galiani, Mark Johnson, John Fritsche, Steve MacSwain, Joe Sacco, Joel Otto, Mike Modano, Dan Keczmer, Jeff Norton, Kevin Stevens

**West Germany** (Xaver Unsinn, coach) GK—Klaus Merk, Josef Heiss, Helmut De Raaf—Andreas Pokorny, Harold Kreis, Udo Kiessling, Uwe Krupp, Harald Birk, Thomas Brandl, Christian Brittig, Bernd Truntschka, Raimund Hilger, Georg Holzmann, Gerd Truntschka, Michael Schmidt, Andreas Niederberger, Peter Draisaitl, Axel Kammerer, Andreas Lupzig, Dieter Hegen, Helmut Steiger, Uli Hiemer, Dieter Willmann

## 55th WORLD CHAMPIONSHIP (MEN)
## April 14-May 5, 1991
## Turku/Helsinki/Tampere, Finland

**Final Placing**

| | |
|---|---|
| Gold ........Sweden | 5th .........Finland |
| Silver ......Canada | 6th .........Czechoslovakia |
| Bronze ....Soviet Union | 7th .........Switzerland^ |
| 4th..........United States | 8th .........Germany |

^promoted from B Pool in 1990
~no team demoted as World Championship expanded to 12 teams for 1992

**Tournament Format**

Each team played every other in a preliminary round robin. The top four teams advanced to a medal round, playing another round robin to determine medal winners. The lower four teams played another round robin, and the preliminary round scores carried over to the final standings to determine which team would be relegated for the 1991 World Championship.

**Results & Standings**

**PRELIMINARY ROUND**

| | GP | W | T | L | GF | GA | P |
|---|---|---|---|---|---|---|---|
| Soviet Union | 7 | 6 | 1 | 0 | 41 | 16 | 13 |
| Sweden | 7 | 3 | 4 | 0 | 30 | 21 | 10 |
| Canada | 7 | 4 | 1 | 2 | 24 | 20 | 9 |
| United States | 7 | 3 | 2 | 2 | 23 | 28 | 8 |
| Finland | 7 | 3 | 1 | 3 | 22 | 15 | 7 |
| Czechoslovakia | 7 | 3 | 0 | 4 | 19 | 19 | 6 |
| Switzerland | 7 | 1 | 0 | 6 | 13 | 26 | 2 |
| Germany | 7 | 0 | 1 | 6 | 13 | 40 | 1 |

| | | | |
|---|---|---|---|
| April 19 | Helsinki | Canada 4 | United States 3 |
| April 19 | Turku | Finland 2 | Czechoslovakia 0 |
| April 19 | Turku | Soviet Union 3 | Switzerland 1 |
| April 19 | Helsinki | Sweden 8 | Germany 1 |
| April 20 | Turku | Canada 3 | Switzerland 0 |
| April 20 | Helsinki | Finland 4 | Sweden 4 |
| April 20 | Turku | Soviet Union 7 | Germany 3 |
| April 20 | Helsinki | United States 4 | Czechoslovakia 1 |
| April 22 | Turku | Canada 3 | Germany 2 |
| April 22 | Turku | Czechoslovakia 4 | Switzerland 1 |
| April 22 | Helsinki | Soviet Union 3 | Finland 0 |
| April 22 | Helsinki | Sweden 4 | United States 4 |
| April 23 | Helsinki | Canada 5 | Finland 3 |
| April 23 | Turku | Czechoslovakia 7 | Germany 1 |
| April 23 | Turku | Sweden 4 | Switzerland 3 |
| April 23 | Helsinki | Soviet Union 12 | United States 2 |
| April 25 | Turku | Soviet Union 5 | Canada 3 |
| April 25 | Turku | Sweden 2 | Czechoslovakia 1 |
| April 25 | Tampere | United States 4 | Switzerland 2 |
| April 25 | Tampere | Finland 6 | Germany 0 |
| April 26 | Turku | Canada 3 | Sweden 3 |
| April 26 | Tampere | United States 4 | Germany 4 |
| April 26 | Turku | Soviet Union 6 | Czechoslovakia 2 |
| April 26 | Tampere | Finland 6 | Switzerland 1 |
| April 28 | Tampere | Czechoslovakia 4 | Canada 3 |
| April 28 | Turku | United States 2 | Finland 1 |
| April 28 | Turku | Soviet Union 5 | Sweden 5 |
| April 28 | Tampere | Switzerland 5 | Germany 2 |

**RELEGATION ROUND (HELSINKI)**

| | GP | W | T | L | GF | GA | P |
|---|---|---|---|---|---|---|---|
| Finland | 10 | 6 | 1 | 3 | 35 | 21 | 13 |
| Czechoslovakia | 10 | 4 | 0 | 6 | 28 | 27 | 8 |
| Switzerland | 10 | 2 | 1 | 7 | 22 | 38 | 5 |
| Germany | 10 | 0 | 2 | 8 | 19 | 51 | 2 |

| | | |
|---|---|---|
| April 29 | Finland 4 | Germany 2 |
| April 29 | Switzerland 4 | Czechoslovakia 3 |
| May 1 | Czechoslovakia 4 | Germany 1 |
| May 1 | Finland 6 | Switzerland 2 |
| May 3 | Finland 3 | Czechoslovakia 2 |
| May 3 | Switzerland 3 | Germany 3 |

**MEDAL ROUND (TURKU)**

| | GP | W | T | L | GF | GA | P |
|---|---|---|---|---|---|---|---|
| Sweden | 3 | 2 | 1 | 0 | 13 | 8 | 5 |
| Canada | 3 | 1 | 2 | 0 | 15 | 10 | 4 |
| Soviet Union | 3 | 1 | 1 | 1 | 10 | 9 | 3 |
| United States | 3 | 0 | 0 | 3 | 12 | 23 | 0 |

| | | |
|---|---|---|
| April 30 | Canada 3 | Sweden 3 |
| April 30 | Soviet Union 6 | United States 4 |
| May 2 | Canada 3 | Soviet Union 3 |
| May 2 | Sweden 8 | United States 4 |
| May 4 | Canada 9 | United States 4 |
| May 4 | Sweden 2 | Soviet Union 1 |

**Rosters**

**Canada** (Dave King, coach) GK—Sean Burke, Mike Vernon, Craig Billington—Joe Sakic, Theo Fleury, Steve Thomas, Steve Larmer, Geoff Courtnall, Trent Yawney, Jamie Macoun, Trevor Linden, Cliff Ronning, Doug Lidster, Steve Konroyd, Russ Courtnall, Murray Craven, Steve Bozek, Rob Blake, Ric Nattress, Dave Archibald, Brad Schlegel, Randy Smith, Yves Racine

**Czechoslovakia** (Stanislav Nevesely, coach) GK—Petr Briza, Oldrich Svoboda, Milan Hnilicka—Petr Rosol, Jiri Dolezal, Robert Holik, Robert Reichel, David Volek, Josef Beranek, Jiri Slegr, Richard Zemlicka, Lubomir Kolnik, Richard Smehlik, Bedrich Scerban, Frantisek Musil, Radek Toupal, Josef Reznicek, Leo Gudas, Ladislav Lubina, Stanislav Medrik, Jiri Kucera, Petr Vlk, Libor Dolana

**Finland** (Pentti Matikainen, coach) GK—Kari Takko, Markus Ketterer, Sakari Lindfors—Jari Kurri, Temmu Selanne, Mika Nieminen, Christian Ruuttu, Esa Keskinen, Jyrki Lumme, Ville Siren, Hannu Jarvenpaa, Teppo Numminen, Pekka Tirkonen, Risto Kurkinen, Raimo Summanen, Timo Peltomaa, Hannu Virta, Hannu Henriksson, Timo Jutila, Arto Ruotanen, Teppo Kivela, Pauli Jarvinen, Pekka Tuomisto

**Germany** (Ladislav Olejnik, coach) GK—Klaus Merk, Helmut De Raaf, Josef Heiss—Thomas Brandl, Dieter Hegen, Bernd Truntschka, Raimund Hilger, Gunter Oswald, Andreas Pokorny, Ernst Kopf, Peter Draisaitl, Andreas Niederberger, Bernd Wagner, Axel Kammerer, Markus Berwanger, Thomas Werner, Michael Rumrich, Udo Kiessling, Michael Schmidt, Mario Naster, Jorg Mayr, Marco Rentzsch, Jan Schertz

**Soviet Union** (Viktor Tikhonov, coach) GK—Andrei Trefilov, Vladimir Myshkin, Alexei Marin—Valeri Kamenski, Pavel Bure, Alexander Semak, Sergei Makarov, Alexei Zhamnov, Vyacheslav Bykov, Vyacheslav Kozlov, Dmitri Mironov, Andrei Lomakin, Alexei Kasatonov, Vyacheslav Butsayev, Sergei Nemchinov, Alexei Gusarov, Vyacheslav Fetisov, Igor Kravchuk, Valeri Zelepukin, Ilya Byakin, Vladimir Konstantinov, Dmitri Kvartalnov, Vladimir Malakhov

**Sweden** (Conny Evensson, coach) GK—Rolf Ridderwall, Tommy Soderstrom, Peter Lindmark—Mats Sundin, Thomas Rundqvist, Mikael Johansson, Hakan Loob, Mats Naslund, Jonas Bergqvist, Nicklas Lidstrom, Kenneth Kennholt, Bengt-Ake Gustafsson, Johan Garpenlov, Kjell Samuelsson, Per-Erik Eklund, Thomas Jonsson, Fredrik Stillmann, Charles Berglund, Calle Johansson, Jan Viktorsson, Anders Carlsson, Peter Anderson, Patrick Erickson

**Switzerland** (Hans Lindberg, coach) GK—Renato Tosio, Reto Pavoni, Christophe Wahl—Andreas Ton, Gil Montandon, Jorg Eberle, Thomas Vrabec, Fredy Luthi, Sandro Bertaggia, Patrick Howald, Roberto Triulzi, Martin Rauch, Peter Jaks, Andre Rotheli, Manuele Celio, Samuel Balmer, Raymond Walder, Sven Leuenberger, Christian Weber, Andreas Beutler, Didier Massy, Rick Tschumi, Doug Honegger

**United States** (Tim Taylor, coach) GK—John Vanbiesbrouck, Scott Gordon, Damian Rhodes—Jeremy Roenick, Danton Cole, Todd Krygier, Brian Mullen, Kevin Miller, Tony Amonte, Shawn McEachern, Craig Wolanin, Tom Pederson, Eric Weinrich, Dave Tretowicz, Dave Williams, David Emma, Tom Fitzgerald, Joe Sacco, Mike McNeill, David Maley, Doug Brown, Guy Gosselin, Moe Mantha

## 56th WORLD CHAMPIONSHIP (MEN)
## April 28-May 10, 1992
## Prague/Bratislava, Czechoslovakia

### Final Placing

| | | | |
|---|---|---|---|
| Gold | Sweden | 7th | United States |
| Silver | Finland | 8th | Canada |
| Bronze | Czechoslovakia | 9th | Italy |
| 4th | Switzerland | 10th | Norway |
| 5th | Russia | 11th | France |
| 6th | Germany | 12th | Poland* |

*demoted to B Pool for 1993

### Tournament Format

For the first time, a full playoff format was used. Teams played round-robin series within each of two groups, the top four advancing to one-game elimination quarter-finals games. The bottom teams in each group played to see which would be relegated for the following year. The quarter-finals winners advanced to a semi-finals, and those winners to a gold-medal game. The semis losers played for the bronze medal.

### Results & Standings

#### GROUP A

| | GP | W | T | L | GF | GA | P |
|---|---|---|---|---|---|---|---|
| Finland | 5 | 5 | 0 | 0 | 32 | 8 | 10 |
| Germany | 5 | 4 | 0 | 1 | 30 | 14 | 8 |
| United States | 5 | 2 | 1 | 2 | 14 | 15 | 5 |
| Sweden | 5 | 1 | 2 | 2 | 14 | 12 | 4 |
| Italy | 5 | 1 | 1 | 3 | 10 | 18 | 3 |
| Poland | 5 | 0 | 0 | 5 | 8 | 41 | 0 |

| | | | |
|---|---|---|---|
| April 28 | Prague | Finland 6 | Germany 3 |
| April 28 | Prague | Sweden 7 | Poland 0 |
| April 28 | Prague | United States 1 | Italy 0 |
| April 29 | Prague | Finland 11 | Poland 2 |
| April 29 | Prague | Germany 5 | United States 3 |
| April 29 | Prague | Sweden 0 | Italy 0 |
| May 1 | Prague | Italy 7 | Poland 5 |
| May 1 | Prague | Germany 5 | Sweden 2 |
| May 1 | Prague | Finland 6 | United States 1 |
| May 3 | Bratislava | Finland 3 | Sweden 1 |
| May 3 | Bratislava | Germany 6 | Italy 2 |
| May 3 | Bratislava | United States 5 | Poland 0 |
| May 4 | Bratislava | Finland 6 | Italy 1 |
| May 4 | Bratislava | Germany 11 | Poland 1 |
| May 4 | Bratislava | Sweden 4 | United States 4 |

#### GROUP B

| | GP | W | T | L | GF | GA | P |
|---|---|---|---|---|---|---|---|
| Russia | 5 | 4 | 1 | 0 | 23 | 10 | 9 |
| Czechoslovakia | 5 | 4 | 0 | 1 | 18 | 7 | 8 |
| Switzerland | 5 | 2 | 2 | 1 | 12 | 11 | 6 |
| Canada | 5 | 2 | 1 | 2 | 15 | 18 | 5 |
| Norway | 5 | 1 | 0 | 4 | 8 | 16 | 2 |
| France | 5 | 0 | 0 | 5 | 8 | 22 | 0 |

| | | | |
|---|---|---|---|
| April 28 | Bratislava | Canada 4 | France 3 |
| April 28 | Bratislava | Switzerland 2 | Russia 2 |
| April 28 | Bratislava | Czechoslovakia 6 | Norway 1 |
| April 30 | Bratislava | Canada 1 | Switzerland 1 |
| April 30 | Bratislava | Czechoslovakia 3 | France 0 |
| April 30 | Bratislava | Russia 3 | Norway 2 |
| May 1 | Bratislava | Switzerland 6 | France 5 |
| May 1 | Bratislava | Canada 4 | Norway 3 |
| May 1 | Bratislava | Russia 4 | Czechoslovakia 2 |
| May 3 | Prague | Russia 8 | France 0 |
| May 3 | Prague | Switzerland 3 | Norway 1 |
| May 3 | Prague | Czechoslovakia 5 | Canada 2 |
| May 4 | Prague | Norway 1 | France 0 |
| May 4 | Prague | Russia 6 | Canada 4 |
| May 4 | Prague | Czechoslovakia 2 | Switzerland 0 |

#### PLAYOFF RELEGATION (PRAGUE)

| | | |
|---|---|---|
| May 6 | France 3 | Poland 1 |

#### PLAYOFFS (PRAGUE)

#### QUARTER-FINALS

| | | |
|---|---|---|
| May 6 | Finland 4 | Canada 3 |
| May 6 | Sweden 2 | Russia 0 |
| May 7 | Switzerland 3 | Germany 1 |
| May 7 | Czechoslovakia 8 | United States 1 |

#### SEMI-FINALS

| | | |
|---|---|---|
| May 9 | Finland 3 | Czechoslovakia 2 (10:00 OT/GWS—Jarkko Varvio) |
| May 9 | Sweden 4 | Switzerland 1 |

#### BRONZE MEDAL GAME

| | | |
|---|---|---|
| May 10 | Czechoslovakia 5 | Switzerland 2 |

#### GOLD MEDAL GAME

| | | |
|---|---|---|
| May 10 | Sweden 5 | Finland 2 |

### Rosters

**Canada** (Dave King, coach) GK—Trevor Kidd, Ron Hextall, Rick Tabaracci—Garth Butcher, Brian Tutt, Jason Woolley, Kerry Huffman, Brad Schlegel, Derek King, Sylvain Cote, Glenn Anderson, Chris Lindberg, Keith Acton, Marc Habscheid, Rod Brind'Amour, Trent Yawney, Pat Falloon, Ray Ferraro, Nelson Emerson, Randy Smith, Todd Gill, Bob Bassen, Steve Thomas

**Czechoslovakia** (Ivan Hlinka, coach) GK—Petr Briza, Oldrich Svoboda—Leo Gudas, Frantisek Musil, Drahomir Kadlec, Bedrich Scerban, Richard Smehlik, Frantisek Prochazka, Robert Svehla, Petr Rosol, Robert Lang, Kamil Kastak, Richard Zemlicka, Ladislav Lubina, Peter Veselovsky, Petr Hrbek, Otakar Janecky, Patrik Augusta, Robert Reichel, Jiri Jonak, Tomas Jelinek, Igor Liba

**Finland** (Pentti Matikainen, coach) GK—Markus Ketterer, Sakari Lindfors, Ari-Pekka Siekkinen—Erik Hamalainen, Timo Jutila, Arto Ruotanen, Waltteri Immonen, Kai Rautio, Vesa Viitakoski, Janne Laukkanen, Jere Lehtinen, Hannu Jarvenpaa, Keijo Sailynoja, Pekka Tuomisto, Christian Ruuttu, Timo Saarikoski, Juha Riihijarvi, Rauli Raitanen, Timo Peltomaa, Jarkko Varvio, Mika Nieminen, Mikko Makela, Harri Laurila

**France** (Kjell Larsson, coach) GK—Petri Ylonen, Michel Valliere, Jean-Marc Dijan—Peter Almasy, Steve Woodburn, Lionel Orsolini, Stephane Barin, Patrick Dunn, Pierre Pousse, Michael Babin, Philippe Bozon, Benoit Laporte, Jean-Philippe Lemoine, Yannick Goicoechea, Serge Poudrier, Stephane Botteri, Michel Leblanc, Christophe Ville, Bruno Saunier, Gerald Guennelon, Denis Perez, Antoine Richer, Christian Pouget

**Germany** (Ludek Bukac, coach) GK—Helmut De Raaf, Josef Heiss, Rene Bielke—Jorg Mayr, Stefan Ustorf, Ernst Kopf, Ron Fischer, Peter Draisaitl, Bernd Truntschka, Raimond Hilger, Georg Holzmann, Gerd Truntschka, Michael Schmidt, Andreas Niederberger, Richard Amann, Wolfgang Kummer, Georg Franz, Dieter Hegen, Michael Heidt, Uli Hiemer, Michael Rumrich, Jurgen Rumrich, Andreas Brockmann

**Italy** (Brian Lefley, coach) GK—Roberto Romano, Dave Delfino—Robert Oberrauch, Jimmy Camazzola, Bill Stewart, Emilio Iovio, Robert Ginnetti, Maurizio Mansi, Ivano Zanatta, Santino Pellegrino, Mario Simioni, Bruno Zarrillo, Gates Orlando, Stefan Figliuzzi, Georg Comploi, Carmine Vani, Giovanni Marchetti, Mario Chitarroni, Anthony Circelli, Lucio Topatigh, Michael De Angelis, Frank Lattuca

**Norway** (Bengt Ohlson, coach) GK—Robert Schistad, Jim Marthinsen, Steve Allman—Petter Salsten, Age Ellingsen, Jon-Magne Karlstad, Tommy Jakobsen, Geir Hoff, Roy Johansen, Carl Gundersen, Kim Sogaard, Svein-Enok Norstebo, Jarle Friis, Trond Magnussen, Ole Eskild Dahlstrom, Arne Billkvam, Erik Kristiansen, Knut Walbye, Petter Thoresen, Cato Tom Andersen, Bjorn Bekkerud, Olsen Oystein, Jan-Roar Fagerli

**Poland** (Leszek Lejczyk, coach) GK—Marek Batkiewicz, Mariusz Kieca, Andrzej Hanisz—Andrzej Kadziolka, Dariusz Garbocz, Sebastian Gonera, Henryk Gruth, Boguslaw Maj, Zbigniew Koziel, Krzysztof Kuzniecow, Wojciech Matczak, Janusz Adamiec, Wojciech Tkacz, Roman Steblicki, Krzysztof Bujar, Marek Koszowski, Kazimierz Jurek, Mariusz Czerkawski, Ireneusz Pacula, Zbigniew Bryjak, Andrzej Swistak, Dariusz Czerwiec

**Russia** (Viktor Tikhonov, coach) GK—Andrei Trefilov, Mikhail Shtalenkov, Maxim Mikhailovski—Dmitri Yushkevich, Vladimir Malakhov, Dmitri Mironov, Darius Kasparaitis, Sergei Bautin, Igor Boldin, Sergei Petrenko, Igor Korolyov, Ilya Byakin, Alexei Kovalyov, Alexei Tkachuk, Sergei Zubov, Nikolai Dorshevski, Vyacheslav Butsayev, Alexei Zhitnik, Vitali Prokhorov, Alexei Zhamnov, Yuri Khmylyov, Andrei Kovalenko, Alexander Barkov

**Sweden** (Conny Evensson, coach) GK—Tommy Soderstrom, Peter Aslin, Hakan Algotsson—Petri Liimatainen, Fredrik Stillman, Arto Blomsten, Tommy Sjodin, Kenneth Kennholt, Peter Ottosson, Mats Sundin, Roger Hansson, Patrik Carnback, Michael Nylander, Daniel Rydmark, Jan Larsson, Johan Garpenlov, Peter Forsberg, Joacim Esbjors, Calle Johansson, Anders Huss, Patric Kjellberg, Lars Karlsson, Mikael Andersson

**Switzerland** (Bill Gilligan, coach) GK—Reto Pavoni, Renato Tosio, Patrick Schopf—Dino Kessler, Sandro Bertaggia, Christian Weber, Luigi Riva, Patrick Howald, Felix Hollenstein, Roberto Triulzi, Mario Brodmann, Sven Leuenberger, Patrick Sutter, Andy Ton, Misko Antisin, Keith Fair, Fredy Luthi, Gil Montandon, Jorg Eberle, Manuele Celio, Samuel Balmer, Mario Rottaris, Doug Honegger

**United States** (Tim Taylor, coach) GK—Ray LeBlanc, Mike Dunham, John Blue—Ken Klee, Barry Richter, Todd Copeland, Chris Winnes, Dave Williams, Todd Harkins, John Byce, Tom Bissett, Joe Sacco, Neil Sheehy, Todd Krygier, David Jensen, Mike Boback, Dennis Vaske, Gary Suter, Jim Johannson, Mark Osiecki, Andy Brickley, Derek Plante, Paul Ranheim

## 57th WORLD CHAMPIONSHIP (MEN)
## April 18-May 2, 1993
## Munich/Dortmund, Germany

**Final Placing**

| | | | |
|---|---|---|---|
| Gold | Russia | 7th | Finland |
| Silver | Sweden | 8th | Italy |
| Bronze | Czech Republic | 9th | Austria^ |
| 4th | Canada | 10th | France |
| 5th | Germany | 11th | Norway |
| 6th | United States | 12th | Switzerland* |

^promoted from B Pool in 1992
*demoted to B Pool for 1994

**Tournament Format**
The World Championship expanded from ten teams to 12. Teams played round-robin series within each of two groups, the top four from each advancing to the playoff elimination round. The bottom two teams in each group played to see which would be relegated for the following year. The semis losers played for the bronze medal.

**Results & Standings**
**GROUP A (DORTMUND)**

| | GP | W | T | L | GF | GA | P |
|---|---|---|---|---|---|---|---|
| Czech Republic | 5 | 4 | 1 | 0 | 17 | 4 | 9 |
| Germany | 5 | 4 | 0 | 1 | 20 | 12 | 8 |
| United States | 5 | 2 | 2 | 1 | 14 | 10 | 6 |
| Finland | 5 | 2 | 1 | 2 | 7 | 7 | 5 |
| Norway | 5 | 1 | 0 | 4 | 6 | 17 | 2 |
| France | 5 | 0 | 0 | 5 | 10 | 24 | 0 |

| | | |
|---|---|---|
| April 18 | Germany 6 | Norway 0 |
| April 18 | Czech Republic 1 | United States 1 |
| April 19 | Finland 2 | France 0 |
| April 20 | Czech Republic 5 | Germany 0 |
| April 20 | Finland 1 | United States 1 |
| April 21 | Germany 5 | France 3 |
| April 21 | Czech Republic 2 | Norway 0 |
| April 22 | Finland 2 | Norway 0 |
| April 22 | United States 6 | France 1 |
| April 23 | Germany 3 | Finland 1 |
| April 24 | Czech Republic 6 | France 2 |
| April 24 | United States 3 | Norway 1 |
| April 25 | Germany 6 | United States 3 |
| April 25 | Czech Republic 3 | Finland 1 |
| April 26 | Norway 5 | France 4 |

**GROUP B (MUNICH)**

| | GP | W | T | L | GF | GA | P |
|---|---|---|---|---|---|---|---|
| Canada | 5 | 5 | 0 | 0 | 31 | 4 | 10 |
| Sweden | 5 | 3 | 0 | 2 | 17 | 14 | 6 |
| Russia | 5 | 2 | 1 | 2 | 15 | 12 | 5 |
| Italy | 5 | 1 | 2 | 2 | 8 | 20 | 4 |
| Switzerland | 5 | 2 | 0 | 3 | 11 | 14 | 4 |
| Austria | 5 | 0 | 1 | 4 | 4 | 22 | 1 |

| | | |
|---|---|---|
| April 18 | Italy 2 | Russia 2 |
| April 18 | Sweden 1 | Austria 0 |
| April 19 | Canada 2 | Switzerland 0 |
| April 19 | Russia 4 | Austria 2 |
| April 20 | Canada 4 | Sweden 1 |
| April 20 | Italy 1 | Switzerland 0 |
| April 21 | Sweden 6 | Italy 2 |
| April 22 | Canada 11 | Austria 0 |
| April 22 | Russia 6 | Switzerland 0 |
| April 23 | Switzerland 5 | Austria 1 |
| April 24 | Canada 11 | Italy 2 |
| April 24 | Sweden 5 | Russia 2 |
| April 25 | Canada 3 | Russia 1 |
| April 25 | Switzerland 6 | Sweden 4 |
| April 26 | Austria 1 | Italy 1 |

**RELEGATION GAMES (MUNICH)**

| | | |
|---|---|---|
| April 29 | France 3 | Switzerland 1 |
| April 29 | Austria 6 | Norway 2 |
| May 1 | Norway 5 | Switzerland 2 |

**PLAYOFFS (MUNICH)**
**QUARTER-FINALS**

| | | |
|---|---|---|
| April 27 | Sweden 5 | United States 2 |
| April 27 | Russia 5 | Germany 1 |
| April 28 | Canada 5 | Finland 1 |
| April 28 | Czech Republic 8 | Italy 1 |

**SEMI-FINALS**

| | | |
|---|---|---|
| April 30 | Sweden 4 | Czech Republic 3 (Thomas Rundqvist 8:38 OT) |
| April 30 | Russia 7 | Canada 4 |

**BRONZE MEDAL GAME**

| | | |
|---|---|---|
| May 1 | Czech Republic 5 | Canada 1 |

**GOLD MEDAL GAME**

| | | |
|---|---|---|
| May 2 | Russia 3 | Sweden 1 |

**Rosters**
**Austria** (Ken Tyler, coach) GK—Brian Stankiewicz, Claus Dalpiaz, Michael Puschacher—Martin Ulrich, Martin Krainz, Karl Heinzle, James Burton, Andreas Puschnig, Wayne Groulx, Richard Nasheim, Marty Dallman, Manfred Huehr, Gerhard Puschnik, Engelbert Linder, Michael Guntner, Gunther Lanzinger, Christian Perthaler, Dieter Kalt, Michael Shea, Werner Kerth, Wolfgang Kromp, Rob Doyle, Herbert Hohenberger

**Canada** (Mike Keenan, coach) GK—Ron Tugnutt, Bill Ranford—Garry Galley, Derek Mayer, Norm Maciver, Terry Carkner, Mark Recchi, Shayne Corson, Geoff Sanderson, Kevin Dineen, Dave Gagner, Kelly Buchberger, Rod Brind'Amour, Brian Benning, Paul Kariya, Mike Gartner, Dave Manson, Geoff Smith, Adam Graves, Eric Lindros, Greg Johnson, Brian Savage

**Czech Republic** (Ivan Hlinka, coach) GK—Petr Briza, Roman Turek, Zdenik Orct—Leo Gudas, Milos Holan, Drahomir Kadlec, Bedrich Scerban, Antonin Stavjana, Miloslav Horava, Ales Flasar, Petr Rosol, Kamil Kastak, Richard Zemlicka, Jiri Kucera, Jan Caloun, Petr Hrbek, Tomas Kapusta, Otakar Janecky, Roman Horak, Martin Hostak, Radek Toupal, Jiri Dolezal, Josef Beranek

**Finland** (Pentti Matikainen, coach) GK—Markus Ketterer, Sakari Lindfors, Ari Sulander—Mikko Haapakoski, Erik Hamalainen, Timo Jutila, Vesa Viitakoski, Janne Laukkanen, Saku Koivu, Jari Korpisalo, Mika Alatalo, Keijo Sailynoja, Marko Palo, Timo Saarikoski, Juha Riihijarvi, Kari Harila, Jarkko Varvio, Mika Nieminen, Ville Siren, Esa Tikkanen, Timo Peltomaa, Waltteri Immonen, Juha Ylonen

**France** (Jean-Claude Sozzi, coach) GK—Michel Valliere, Petri Ylonen, Christophe Renard—Peter Almasy, Bruno Maynart, Steven Woodburn, Stephane Barin, Arnaud Briand, Patrick Dunn, Pierre Pousse, Michael Babin, Benoit Laporte, Jean-Phillippe Lemoine, Pierrick Maia, Stephane Botteri, Michel Leblanc, Christophe Ville, Bruno Saunier, Denis Perez, Antoine Richer, Christian Pouget, Joseph Poudrier, Frank Pajonkowski

**Germany** (Franz Reindl, coach) GK—Helmut De Raaf, Klaus Merk, Josef Heiss—Torsten Kienass, Jorg Mayr, Thomas Brandl, Ernst Kopf, Andreas Volland, Bernd Truntschka, Raimund Hilger, Benoit Doucet, Gerd Truntschka, Greg Thomson, Andreas Niederberger, Richard Amann, Wolfgang Kummer, Georg Franz, Dieter Hegen, Stefan Ustorf, Uli Hiemer, Michael Rumrich, Karsten Mende, Jason Meyer

**Italy** (Bryan Lefley, coach) GK—Diego Riva, David Delfino, Bruno Campese—Robert Oberrauch, Raphael Di Fiore, William Stewart, Mark Michael Cupolo, Emilio Iovio, Maurizio Mansi, Ivano Zanatta, Bruno Zarrillo, Gates Orlando, John Vecchiarelli, Georg Comploi, Carmine Vani, Giovanni Marchetti, Mario Chitarroni, Anthony Circelli, Pierangelo Cibien, Lucio Topatigh, Martin Pavlu, Michael De Angelis, Maurizio Bortolussi

**Norway** (Bengt Ohlson, coach) GK—Robert Schistad, Jim Marthinsen, Svein Arnesen—Petter Salsten, Jon-Magne Karlstad, Tommy Jakobsen, Tom-Erik Olsen, Geir Hoff, Carl-Gunnar Gundersen, Kim Sogaard, Svein-Enok Norstebo, Ole Eskild Dahlstrom, Arne Billkvam, Erik Kristiansen, Trond Magnussen, Petter Thoresen, Morten Finstad, Cato Tom Andersen, Pal Kristiansen, Bjorn Freddy Bekkerud, Roy Johansen, Marius Rath, Per-Christian Knold

**Russia** (Boris Mikhailov, coach) GK—Andrei Zuyev, Maxim Mikhailovski, Andrei Trefilov—Alexander Karpovtsev, Sergei Sorokin, Alexander Smirnov, Ilya Byakin, Dmitri Frolov, Igor Varitski, Sergei Petrenko, German Titov, Andrei Khomutov, Yan Kaminski, Alexei Yashin, Sergei Pushkov, Sergei Shendelev, Andrei Nikolishin, Valeri Karpov, Konstantin Astrakhantsev, Vyacheslav Bykov, Andrei Sapozhnikov, Dmitri Yushkevich, Vyacheslav Butsayev

**Sweden** (Curt Lundmark, coach) GK—Michael Sundlov, Tommy Soderstrom, Peter Aslin—Peter Popovic, Stefan Nilsson, Patrik Juhlin, Arto Blomsten, Kenneth Kennholt, Thomas Rundqvist, Fredrik Stillman, Jonas Bergqvist, Markus Naslund, Jan Larsson, Peter Forsberg, Charles Berglund, Roger Akerstrom, Mikael Renberg, Stefan Larsson, Mikael Andersson, Michael Nylander, Peter Andersson, Ulf Dahlen, Hakan Ahlund

**Switzerland** (Bill Gilligan, coach) GK—Reto Pavoni, Renato Tosio, Patrick Schopf—Martin Steinegger, Sandro Bertaggia, Patrick Howald, Felix Hollenstein, Roberto Triulzi, Martin Rauch, Bruno Erni, Sven Leuenberger, Andy Ton, Fredy Luthi, Gil Montandon, Jorg Eberle, Roman Wager, Rick Tschumi, Samuel Balmer, Christian Weber, Misko Antisin, Manuele Celio, Thomas Vrabec, Patrick Sutter

**United States** (Tim Taylor, coach) GK—Mike Dunham, Pat Jablonski, Mike Richter—Bob Beers, Eric Weinrich, Brett Hauer, Adam Burt, Ian Moran, Darren Turcotte, Mike Modano, Travis Richards, Barry Richter, Ed Olczyk, Craig Johnson, Doug Weight, Ted Drury, Jeff Lazaro, David Sacco, Shjon Podein, Derek Plante, Rob Gaudreau, Derian Hatcher, Tony Amonte

## 58th WORLD CHAMPIONSHIP (MEN)
## April 25-May 8, 1994
## Bolzano/Milan/Canazei, Italy

### Final Placing

| | | | |
|---|---|---|---|
| Gold | Canada | 7th | Czech Republic |
| Silver | Finland | 8th | Austria |
| Bronze | Sweden | 9th | Germany |
| 4th | United States | 10th | France |
| 5th | Russia | 11th | Norway |
| 6th | Italy | 12th | Great Britain^* |

^promoted from B Pool in 1993
*demoted to B Pool for 1995

### Tournament Format

The World Championship expanded from ten teams to 12. Teams played round-robin series within each of two groups, the top four from each advancing to the playoff elimination round. The bottom two teams in each group played to see which would be relegated for the following year. The semis losers played for the bronze medal.

### Results & Standings

**GROUP A (BOLZANO)**

| | GP | W | T | L | GF | GA | P |
|---|---|---|---|---|---|---|---|
| Canada | 5 | 5 | 0 | 0 | 24 | 7 | 10 |
| Russia | 5 | 4 | 0 | 1 | 30 | 7 | 8 |
| Italy | 5 | 3 | 0 | 2 | 17 | 15 | 6 |
| Austria | 5 | 1 | 1 | 3 | 15 | 15 | 3 |
| Germany | 5 | 1 | 1 | 3 | 9 | 14 | 3 |
| Great Britain | 5 | 0 | 0 | 5 | 7 | 44 | 0 |

| | | |
|---|---|---|
| April 25 | Canada 4 | Italy 1 |
| April 25 | Austria 2 | Germany 2 |
| April 26 | Russia 12 | Great Britain 3 |
| April 26 | Canada 6 | Austria 1 |
| April 27 | Germany 4 | Great Britain 0 |
| April 27 | Russia 7 | Italy 0 |
| April 28 | Canada 3 | Germany 2 |
| April 29 | Russia 4 | Austria 1 |
| April 29 | Italy 10 | Great Britain 2 |
| April 30 | Russia 6 | Germany 0 |
| April 30 | Canada 8 | Great Britain 2 |
| May 1 | Italy 3 | Austria 1 |
| May 2 | Italy 3 | Germany 1 |
| May 2 | Canada 3 | Russia 1 |
| May 3 | Austria 10 | Great Britain 0 |

**GROUP B (CANAZEI)**

| | GP | W | T | L | GF | GA | P |
|---|---|---|---|---|---|---|---|
| Finland | 5 | 4 | 1 | 0 | 29 | 11 | 9 |
| Sweden | 5 | 3 | 1 | 1 | 22 | 11 | 7 |
| United States | 5 | 3 | 0 | 2 | 21 | 19 | 6 |
| Czech Republic | 5 | 1 | 2 | 2 | 15 | 17 | 4 |
| France | 5 | 1 | 0 | 4 | 8 | 25 | 2 |
| Norway | 5 | 0 | 2 | 3 | 9 | 21 | 2 |

| | | |
|---|---|---|
| April 25 | Finland 4 | Czech Republic 4 |
| April 25 | United States 5 | France 1 |
| April 25 | Sweden 3 | Norway 3 |
| April 26 | Czech Republic 5 | France 2 |
| April 27 | United States 7 | Norway 2 |
| April 27 | Finland 5 | Sweden 3 |
| April 28 | United States 5 | Czech Republic 3 |
| April 28 | Sweden 6 | France 0 |
| April 29 | Finland 5 | Norway 1 |
| April 30 | Finland 8 | France 1 |
| April 30 | Norway 2 | Czech Republic 2 |
| April 30 | Sweden 6 | United States 2 |
| May 2 | France 4 | Norway 1 |
| May 2* | Finland 7 | United States 0 |
| May 2 | Sweden 4 | Czech Republic 1 |

*game score was 7-2 but because USA forward Bill Lindsay tested positive for efedrin, a banned substance, his team had all its goals taken away and the score was officially made 7-0

**11TH-PLACE GAME**

| | | | |
|---|---|---|---|
| May 6 | Bolzano | Norway 5 | Great Britain 2 |

**PLAYOFFS (MILAN)**

**QUARTER-FINALS**

| | | |
|---|---|---|
| May 4 | United States 3 | Russia 1 |
| May 4 | Sweden 7 | Italy 2 |
| May 5 | Canada 3 | Czech Republic 2 |
| May 5 | Finland 10 | Austria 0 |

**SEMI-FINALS**

| | | |
|---|---|---|
| May 7 | Canada 6 | Sweden 0 |
| May 7 | Finland 8 | United States 0 |

**BRONZE MEDAL GAME**

| | | |
|---|---|---|
| May 8 | Sweden 7 | United States 2 |

**GOLD MEDAL GAME**

| | | |
|---|---|---|
| May 8 | Canada 2 | Finland 1 (10:00 OT/GWS—Luc Robitaille) |

### Rosters

**Austria** (Ken Tyler, coach) GK—Michael Puschacher, Claus Dalpiaz, Michael Suttnig—Michael Guntner, Martin Ulrich, James Burton, Engelbert Linder, Herbert Hohenberger, Robin Doyle, Michael Shea, Wolfgang Strauss, Gerhard Unterluggauer, Werner Kerth, Dieter Kalt, Andreas Puschnig, Patrick Pilloni, Manfred Muhr, Ken Strong, Gunther Lanzinger, Wolfgang Kromp, Gerald Rauchenwald, Richard Nasheim, Gerhard Puschnik

**Canada** (George Kingston, coach) GK—Bill Ranford, Stephane Fiset, Jamie Storr—Joe Sakic, Darryl Sydor, Geoff Sanderson, Luc Robitaille, Luke Richardson, Mike Ricci, Yves Racine, Paul Kariya, Nelson Emerson, Bobby Dollas, Shayne Corson, Kelly Buchberger, Rod Brind'Amour, Rob Blake, Marc Bergevin, Jason Arnott, Pat Verbeek, Brendan Shanahan, Steve Duchesne, Steve Thomas

**Czech Republic** (Ivan Hlinka, coach) GK—Petr Briza, Roman Turek, Radek Biegl—Milos Holan, Drahomir Kadlec, Bedrich Scerban, Roman Hamrlik, Frantisek Kucera, Stanislav Meciar, Kamil Kastak, Richard Zemlicka, Jiri Kucera, Jiri Dopita, Tomas Srsen, Otakar Janecky, Roman Horak, Martin Rucinsky, Jiri Dolezal, Josef Beranek, Petr Tejkl, Martin Straka, Jaromir Jagr, Frantisek Musil

**Finland** (Curt Lindstrom, coach) GK—Jukka Tammi, Jarmo Myllys, Pasi Kuivalainen—Jere Lehtinen, Ville Peltonen, Mika Alatalo, Erik Hamalainen, Sami Kapanen, Mikko Makela, Timo Jutila, Mika Stromberg, Janne Ojanen, Janne Laukkanen, Mika Nieminen, Marko Palo, Raimo Helminen, Marko Kiprusoff, Hannu Virta, Jari Kurri, Saku Koivu, Esa Keskinen, Waltteri Immonen, Christian Ruuttu

**France** (Kjell Larsson, coach) GK— Petri Ylonen, Michel Valliere, Fabrice Lhenry—Roger Dube, Eric Lemarque, Franck Pajonkowski, Patrick Dunn, Pierre Pousse, Michel Leblanc, Benoit Laporte, Lionel Orsolini, Christophe Ville, Christophe Moyon, Denis Perez, Serge Poudrier, Stephane Barin, Philippe Bozon, Gerald Guennelon, Jean-Philippe Lemoine, Michael Babin, Arnaud Briand, Pierrick Maia, Steve Woodburn

**Germany** (Ludek Bukac, coach) GK—Klaus Merk, Joseph Heiss, Marc Seliger—Richard Boehm, Martin Reichel, Gregory Evtushevski, Jorg Handrick, Thomas Schinko, Michael Rumrich, Thomas Brandl, Leo Stefan, Tobias Abstreiter, Ernst Kopf, Wolfgang Kummer, Mirko Ludemann, Peter Gulda, Michael Bresagk, Jayson Meyer, Jorg Mayr, Andreas Niederberger, Torsten Kienass, Raimund Hilger, Jan Benda

**Great Britain** (Alex Dampier, coach) GK—Martin McKay, Moray Hanson, John McCrone—Matthew Cote, Michael O'Conner, Brian Mason, Doug McEwen, Stephen Cooper, Christopher Kelland, Andre Malo, Frank Morris, Shannon Hope, Kevin Conway, Patrick Scott, Tim Cranston, Tony Hand, Nicholas Chinn, Ian Cooper, Terry Kurtenbach, Scott Morrison, David Longstaff, Richard Fera, Richard Brebant

**Italy** (Bryan Lefley, coach) GK—Mike Rosati, David Delfino, Bruno Campese—Christ-Paul Bartolone, Paul Beraldo, Patrick Brugnoli, Mario Chitarroni, Anthony Circelli, Georg Comploi, Luigi Da Corte, Michael De Angelis, Philip De Gaetano, Lino De Toni, Stefan Figliuzzi, Emilio Iovio, Giovanni Marchetti, Robert Oberrauch, Gates Orlando, Martin Pavlu, Vezio Sacratini, Lucio Topatigh, Bruno Zarrillo, Roland Ramoser

**Norway** (Bengt Ohlson, coach) GK—Robert Schistad, Steve Allman, Jim Marthinsen—Petter Salsten, Carl Andersen-Boe, Tommy Jakobsen, Anders Myrvold, Vegar Barlie, Jan-Roar Fagerli, Svein-Enok Norstebo, Per-Christian Knold, Ole Eskild Dahlstrom, Erik Kristiansen, Trond Magnussen, Petter Thoresen, Morten Finstad, Sjur Nilsen, Jorgen Salsten, Tom Johansen, Oystein Olsen, Marius Rath, Espen Knutsen, Geir Hoff

**Russia** (Boris Mikhailov, coach) GK—Valeri Ivannikov, Mikhail Shtalenkov, Albert Shirgaziev—Sergei Berezin, Vyacheslav Bezukladnikov, Andrei Kovalenko, Yuri Tsyplakov, Andrei Nikolishin, Valeri Bure, Alexei Yashin, Anatoli Yemelin, Valeri Kamenski, Eduard Gorbachyov, Igor Fedulov, Igor Ulanov, Sergei Shendelev, Dmitri Frolov, Ilya Byakin, Alexander Smirnov, Alexei Zhitnik, Dmitri Yushkevich, Sergei Sorokin, Vyacheslav Kozlov

**Sweden** (Curt Lundmark, coach) GK—Roger Nordstrom, Tommy Salo, Johan Hedberg—Mikael Andersson, Peter Andersson, Charles Berglund, Jonas Bergqvist, Patrik Carnback, Roger Hansson, Mikael Johansson, Roger Johansson, Patrik Juhlin, Kenny Jonsson, Jan Larsson, Tommy Sjodin, Fredrik Stillman, Mats Sundin, Magnus Svensson, Stefan Ornskog, Andreas Dackell, Jorgen Jonsson, Tomas Forslund, Nicklas Lidstrom

**United States** (Ron Wilson, coach) GK—Guy Hebert, Les Kuntar, David Littman—Bob Beers, Shawn Chambers, Sean Hill, Don McSween, Pat Neaton, Barry Richter, Craig Wolanin, Phil Bourque, Pete Ciavaglia, Danton Cole, Jeff Lazaro, John Lilley, Bill Lindsay, Shjon Podein, Joe Sacco, Tim Sweeney, Doug Weight, Scott Young, Craig Janney

## 59th WORLD CHAMPIONSHIP (MEN)
## April 23-May 7, 1995
## Stockholm/Gavle, Sweden

**Final Placing**

Gold........Finland
Silver......Sweden
Bronze....Canada
4th.........Czech Republic
5th.........Russia
6th.........United States
7th.........Italy
8th.........France
9th.........Germany
10th.......Norway
11th.......Austria
12th.......Switzerland^*

^promoted from B Pool in 1994
*demoted to B Pool for 1996

**Tournament Format**

The World Championship expanded from ten teams to 12. Teams played round-robin series within each of two groups, the top four from each advancing to the playoff elimination round. The bottom two teams in each group played to see which would be relegated for the following year. The semis losers played for the bronze medal.

**Results & Standings**

**GROUP A (GAVLE)**

| | GP | W | T | L | GF | GA | P |
|---|---|---|---|---|---|---|---|
| Russia | 5 | 5 | 0 | 0 | 26 | 10 | 10 |
| Italy | 5 | 3 | 1 | 1 | 14 | 11 | 7 |
| France | 5 | 3 | 0 | 2 | 14 | 11 | 6 |
| Canada | 5 | 2 | 1 | 2 | 17 | 16 | 5 |
| Germany | 5 | 1 | 0 | 4 | 11 | 20 | 2 |
| Switzerland | 5 | 0 | 0 | 5 | 10 | 24 | 0 |

| | | |
|---|---|---|
| April 23 | France 4 | Germany 0 |
| April 23 | Russia 4 | Italy 2 |
| April 24 | Italy 2 | Germany 1 |
| April 24 | Canada 5 | Switzerland 3 |
| April 25 | France 4 | Canada 1 |
| April 25 | Russia 8 | Switzerland 0 |
| April 26 | Russia 3 | France 1 |
| April 27 | Canada 5 | Germany 2 |
| April 27 | Italy 3 | Switzerland 2 |
| April 28 | Russia 6 | Germany 3 |
| April 28 | France 3 | Switzerland 2 |
| April 29 | Canada 2 | Italy 2 |
| April 30 | Germany 5 | Switzerland 3 |
| April 30 | Russia 5 | Canada 4 |
| May 1 | Italy 5 | France 2 |

**GROUP B (STOCKHOLM)**

| | GP | W | T | L | GF | GA | P |
|---|---|---|---|---|---|---|---|
| United States | 5 | 3 | 2 | 0 | 17 | 11 | 8 |
| Finland | 5 | 3 | 1 | 1 | 22 | 14 | 7 |
| Sweden | 5 | 3 | 1 | 1 | 17 | 9 | 7 |
| Czech Republic | 5 | 3 | 0 | 2 | 14 | 9 | 6 |
| Norway | 5 | 1 | 0 | 4 | 9 | 18 | 2 |
| Austria | 5 | 0 | 0 | 5 | 9 | 27 | 0 |

| | | |
|---|---|---|
| April 23 | Sweden 5 | Norway 0 |
| April 23 | Czech Republic 3 | Finland 0 |
| April 24 | United States 5 | Austria 2 |
| April 25 | United States 2 | Norway 1 |
| April 25 | Finland 6 | Sweden 3 |
| April 26 | Czech Republic 5 | Austria 2 |
| April 26 | Finland 5 | Norway 2 |
| April 27 | United States 4 | Czech Republic 2 |
| April 27 | Sweden 5 | Austria 0 |
| April 28 | United States 2 | Sweden 2 |
| April 29 | Finland 7 | Austria 2 |
| April 29 | Czech Republic 3 | Norway 1 |
| April 30 | United States 4 | Finland 4 |
| April 30 | Sweden 2 | Czech Republic 1 |
| May 1 | Norway 5 | Austria 3 |

**RELEGATION GAMES (BEST-OF-TWO)**

| | | | |
|---|---|---|---|
| May 2 | Gavle | Austria 4 | Switzerland 0 |
| May 3 | Stockholm | Switzerland 4 | Austria 4 |

**PLAYOFFS (STOCKHOLM)**

**QUARTER-FINALS**

| | | |
|---|---|---|
| May 2 | Sweden 7 | Italy 0 |
| May 2 | Finland 5 | France 0 |
| May 3 | Czech Republic 2 | Russia 0 |
| May 3 | Canada 4 | United States 1 |

**SEMI-FINALS**

| | | |
|---|---|---|
| May 5 | Sweden 3 | Canada 2 (Daniel Alfredsson 8:17 OT) |
| May 5 | Finland 3 | Czech Republic 0 |

**BRONZE MEDAL GAME**

| | | |
|---|---|---|
| May 6 | Canada 4 | Czech Republic 1 |

**GOLD MEDAL GAME**

| | | |
|---|---|---|
| May 7 | Finland 4 | Sweden 1 |

**Rosters**

**Austria** (Ken Tyler, coach) GK—Michael Suttnig, Michael Puschacher, Claus Dalpiaz—Karl Heinzle, James Burton, Gerhard Unterluggauer, Engelbert Linder, Michael Shea, Herbert Hohenberger, Michael Guntner, Martin Ulrich, Andreas Puschnig, Gerald Rauchenwald, Gerald Ressmann, Gerhard Puschnik, Manfred Muhr, Richard Nasheim, Patrick Pilloni, Ken Strong, Werner Kerth, Rob Doyle, Helmut Karel, Dieter Kalt

**Canada** (Tom Renney, coach) GK—Corey Hirsch, Andrew Verner, Dwayne Roloson—Len Esau, Brian Tutt, Jamie Heward, Greg Andrusak, Dale DeGray, Peter Allen, Brad Schlegel, Todd Hlushko, Iain Fraser, Ralph Intranuovo, Luciano Borsato, Brandon Convery, Andrew McKim, Mark Freer, Rick Chernomaz, Chris Govedaris, Chris Bright, Jean-Francois Jomphe, Mike Maneluk, Tom Tilley

**Czech Republic** (Ludek Bukac, coach) GK—Petr Briza, Roman Turek, Roman Cechmanek—Frantisek Kaberle, Jiri Vykoukal, Bedrich Scerban, Antonin Stavjana, Ivan Vlcek, Petr Kuchyna, Jan Vopat, Pavel Patera, Martin Hostak, Richard Zemlicka, Jiri Kucera, Jiri Dopita, Tomas Srsen, Radek Belohlav, Martin Prochazka, Roman Horak, Otakar Vejvoda, Pavel Janku, Pavel Geffert, Roman Meluzin

**Finland** (Curt Lindstrom, coach) GK—Ari Sulander, Jarmo Myllys, Jukka Tammi—Marko Kiprusoff, Petteri Nummelin, Erik Hamalainen, Timo Jutila, Janne Niinimaa, Hannu Virta, Mika Stromberg, Janne Ojanen, Esa Keskinen, Saku Koivu, Marko Palo, Raimo Helminen, Antti Tormanen, Ville Peltonen, Jere Lehtinen, Juha Ylonen, Sami Kapanen, Tero Lehtera, Mika Nieminen, Raimo Summanen

**France** (Juhani Tamminen, coach) GK—Petri Ylonen, Antoine Mindjimba, Michel Valliere—Jean-Marc Soghomonian, Serge Djelloul, Steve Woodburn, Terrence Zytynsky, Jean-Philippe Lemoine, Denis Perez, Serge Poudrier, Lionel Orsolini, Stephane Barin, Pierre Pousse, Philippe Bozon, Andre Vittenberg, Eric Lemarque, Franck Pajonkowski, Christophe Ville, Michel Galarneau, Antoine Richer, Christian Pouget, Roger Dube, Patrick Dunn

**Germany** (George Kingston, coach) GK—Klaus Merk, Josef Heiss, Marc Seliger—Michael Bresagk, Torsten Kienass, Mirko Ludemann, Andreas Niederberger, Uli Hiemer, Daniel Nowak, Markus Wieland, Jayson Meyer, Thomas Brandl, Reemt Pyka, Georg Holzmann, Leo Stefan, Raimund Hilger, Benoit Doucet, Andreas Lupzig, Sven Zywitza, Georg Franz, Gunther Oswald, Martin Reichel, Alexander Serikow

**Italy** (Bryan Lefley, coach) GK—Bruno Campese, Mario Brunetta, Mike Rosati—Robert Oberrauch, Leo Insam, Georg Comploi, Giovanni Marchetti, Anthony Circelli, Christopher Bartolone, Robert Nardella, Michael De Angelis, Armando Chelodi, John Massara, Lino De Toni, Roland Ramoser, Maurizio Mansi, Bruno Zarrillo, Gates Orlando, Mario Chitarroni, Giuseppe Busillo, Lucio Topatigh, Martin Pavlu, Stefano Figliuzzi

**Norway** (Geir Myhre, coach) GK—Robert Schistad, Jim Marthinsen, Mattis Haakensen—Petter Salsten, Rene Hansen, Tommy Jakobsen, Johnny Nilsen, Svein Enok Norstebo, Carl Boe-Andersen, Oystein Olsen, Henrik Aaby, Geir Hoff, Orjan Lovdal, Trond Magnussen, Petter Thoresen, Eirik Paulsen, Erik Tveten, Bjorn Anders Dahl, Rune Fjeldstad, Tom Johansen, Sjur Nilsen, Marius Rath, Espen Knutsen

**Russia** (Boris Mikhailov, coach) GK—Alexei Cherviakov, Sergei Abramov, Andrei Zuyev—Sergei Sorokin, Yevgeni Gribko, Alexander Smirnov, Sergei Fokin, Dmitri Krasotkin, Andrei Skopintsev, Sergei Shendelev, Dmitri Frolov, Sergei Berezin, Alexei Salomatin, Ravil Yakubov, Igor Fedulov, Andrei Tarasenko, Andrei Khomutov, Stanislav Romanov, Alexander Prokopiev, Vladimir Vorobyov, Pavel Torgayev, Vyacheslav Bykov, Oleg Belov

**Sweden** (Curt Lundmark, coach) GK—Thomas Ostlund, Roger Nordstrom, Boo Ahl—Tomas Jonsson, Marcus Ragnarsson, Leif Rohlin, Fredrik Stillman, Christer Olsson, Robert Nordmark, Tommy Sjodin, Erik Huusko, Stefan Nilsson, Per-Erik Eklund, Andreas Johansson, Roger Hansson, Andreas Dackell, Stefan Ornskog, Jonas Bergqvist, Charles Berglund, Daniel Alfredsson, Mikael Johansson, Tomas Forslund, Jonas Johnsson

**Switzerland** (Mats Waltin, coach) GK—Reto Pavoni, Renato Tosio, Lars Weibel—Martin Birch, Andreas Zehnder, Sandro Bertaggia, Martin Bruderer, Samuel Balmer, Marco Bayer, Patrick Howald, Felix Hollenstein, Roberto Triulzi, Theo Wittmann, Bruno Erni, Jean-Jacques Aeschlimann, Andy Ton, Roman Wager, Thomas Heldner, Harry Rogenmoser, Marcel Jenni, Vjeran Ivankovic, Christian Weber, Martin Steinegger

**United States** (Jeff Sauer, coach) GK—Pat Jablonski, Tim Thomas, Ray LeBlanc—Keith Aldridge, Chris Imes, Brett Hauer, Jason McBain, Brian Rafalski, Tom O'Regan, Paul Stanton, Pat Neaton, Craig Charron, Brad Jones, Jacques Joubert, Mike Knuble, Joe Frederick, Cal McGowan, Jon Morris, Chris O'Sullivan, Mike Pomichter, Todd Harkins, Jim Spencer, Tim Bergland

## 60th WORLD CHAMPIONSHIP (MEN)
**April 21-May 5, 1996**
**Vienna, Austria**

### Final Placing

| | | | |
|---|---|---|---|
| Gold | Czech Republic | 7th | Italy |
| Silver | Canada | 8th | Germany |
| Bronze | United States | 9th | Norway |
| 4th | Russia | 10th | Slovakia^ |
| 5th | Finland | 11th | France |
| 6th | Sweden | 12th | Austria* |

^promoted from B Pool in 1995
*demoted to B Pool for 1997

### Tournament Format
The World Championship expanded from ten teams to 12. Teams played round-robin series within each of two groups, the top four from each advancing to the playoff elimination round. The bottom two teams in each group played to see which would be relegated for the following year. The semis losers played for the bronze medal.

### Results & Standings
**GROUP A**

| | GP | W | T | L | GF | GA | P |
|---|---|---|---|---|---|---|---|
| Russia | 5 | 5 | 0 | 0 | 23 | 8 | 10 |
| United States | 5 | 3 | 0 | 2 | 15 | 14 | 6 |
| Canada | 5 | 2 | 1 | 2 | 17 | 15 | 5 |
| Germany | 5 | 2 | 0 | 3 | 12 | 11 | 4 |
| Slovakia | 5 | 1 | 1 | 3 | 13 | 16 | 3 |
| Austria | 5 | 1 | 0 | 4 | 3 | 19 | 2 |

| | | |
|---|---|---|
| April 21 | Canada 3 | Slovakia 3 |
| April 21 | Russia 2 | Germany 1 |
| April 22 | United States 5 | Austria 1 |
| April 22 | Russia 6 | Slovakia 2 |
| April 23 | United States 4 | Germany 2 |
| April 23 | Canada 4 | Austria 0 |
| April 24 | Germany 5 | Canada 1 |
| April 25 | Austria 2 | Slovakia 1 |
| April 25 | Russia 3 | United States 1 |
| April 26 | Germany 3 | Austria 0 |
| April 26 | Russia 6 | Canada 4 |
| April 27 | United States 4 | Slovakia 3 |
| April 28 | Russia 6 | Austria 0 |
| April 28 | Canada 5 | United States 1 |
| April 29 | Slovakia 4 | Germany 1 |

**GROUP B**

| | GP | W | T | L | GF | GA | P |
|---|---|---|---|---|---|---|---|
| Czech Republic | 5 | 4 | 1 | 0 | 27 | 12 | 9 |
| Finland | 5 | 2 | 2 | 1 | 23 | 15 | 6 |
| Sweden | 5 | 2 | 2 | 1 | 14 | 12 | 6 |
| Italy | 5 | 2 | 1 | 2 | 20 | 26 | 5 |
| Norway | 5 | 1 | 2 | 2 | 6 | 11 | 4 |
| France | 5 | 0 | 0 | 5 | 12 | 26 | 0 |

| | | |
|---|---|---|
| April 21 | Czech Republic 3 | Sweden 1 |
| April 21 | Finland 1 | Norway 1 |
| April 22 | Italy 6 | France 5 |
| April 23 | Italy 4 | Norway 0 |
| April 23 | Czech Republic 4 | Finland 2 |
| April 24 | Sweden 2 | France 1 |
| April 24 | Czech Republic 2 | Norway 2 |
| April 25 | Finland 6 | France 3 |
| April 25 | Italy 3 | Sweden 3 |
| April 26 | Finland 9 | Italy 2 |
| April 27 | Czech Republic 9 | France 2 |
| April 27 | Sweden 3 | Norway 0 |
| April 28 | Czech Republic 9 | Italy 5 |
| April 28 | Finland 5 | Sweden 5 |
| April 29 | Norway 3 | France 1 |

**RELEGATION GAMES (BEST-OF-TWO)**

| | | |
|---|---|---|
| May 1 | France 6 | Austria 3 |
| May 2 | France 6 | Austria 3 |

**PLAYOFFS**
**QUARTER-FINALS**

| | | |
|---|---|---|
| April 30 | United States 3 | Sweden 2 |
| April 30 | Canada 3 | Finland 1 |
| May 1 | Russia 5 | Italy 2 |
| May 1 | Czech Republic 6 | Germany 1 |

**SEMI-FINALS**

| | | |
|---|---|---|
| May 3 | Czech Republic 5 | United States 0 |
| May 3 | Canada 3 | Russia 2 (10:00 OT/GWS—Yanic Perreault) |

**BRONZE MEDAL GAME**

| | | |
|---|---|---|
| May 4 | United States 4 | Russia 3 (Brian Rolston 4:48 OT) |

**GOLD MEDAL GAME**

| | | |
|---|---|---|
| May 5 | Czech Republic 4 | Canada 2 |

### Rosters
**Austria** (Ken Tyler, coach) GK—Claus Dalpiaz, Michael Puschacher, Reinhard Divis—Martin Krainz, Karl Heinzle, Rob Doyle, Konrad Dorn, Gerald Ressmann, Gerhard Puschnik, Manfred Muhr, Engelbert Linder, Richard Nasheim, Gunter Lanzinger, Arthur Marczell, Mario Schaden, Michael Shea, Werner Kerth, Peter Kasper, Kraig Nienhuis, Herbert Hohenberger, Thomas Cijan, Martin Ulrich, Dieter Kalt

**Canada** (Tom Renney, coach) GK—Martin Brodeur, Curtis Joseph, Andrew Verner—Glen Wesley, Doug Bodger, Derek Mayer, Paul Kariya, Brad May, Jeff Friesen, Kelly Buchberger, David Matsos, Ray Ferraro, Andrew Cassels, Luke Richardson, Darryl Sydor, Steve Duchesne, Steve Thomas, Garry Galley, Dean McAmmond, Travis Green, Jason Dawe, Yanic Perreault, Jean-Francois Jomphe

**Czech Republic** (Ludek Bukac, coach) GK—Roman Turek, Roman Cechmanek, Petr Franek—Stanislav Neckar, Jiri Vykoukal, Drahomir Kadlec, Antonin Stavjana, Pavel Patera, Viktor Ujcik, Frantisek Kaberle, David Vyborny, Jiri Kucera, Jiri Dopita, Jiri Veber, Radek Bonk, Radek Belohlav, Martin Prochazka, Robert Lang, Robert Kysela, Otakar Vejvoda, Robert Reichel, Roman Meluzin, Michal Sykora

**Finland** (Curt Lindstrom, coach) GK—Jarmo Myllys, Markus Ketterer, Ari Sulander—Petteri Nummelin, Jyrki Lumme, Timo Jutila, Janne Niinimaa, Teppo Numminen, Janne Ojanen, Esa Keskinen, Esa Tikkanen, Raimo Helminen, Ville Peltonen, Juha Ylonen, Christian Ruuttu, Hannu Virta, Sami Kapanen, Mika Stromberg, Kai Nurminen, Juha Riihijarvi, Kimmo Timonen, Mika Nieminen, Teemu Selanne

**France** (Juhani Tamminen, coach) GK—Michel Valliere, Petri Ylonen, Antoine Mindjimba—Serge Djelloul, Steve Woodburn, Stephane Barin, Arnaud Briand, Maurice Rozenthal, Pierre Pousse, Terrence Zytynsky, Philippe Bozon, Francois Rozenthal, Jean-Philippe Lemoine, Michel Breistroff, Robert Ouellet, Franck Pajonkowski, Christophe Ville, Denis Perez, Antoine Richer, Christian Pouget, Serge Poudrier, Roger Dube, Patrick Dunn

**Germany** (George Kingston, coach) GK—Klaus Merk, Josef Heiss, Christian Kunast—Torsten Kienass, Rochus Schneider, Mirko Ludemann, Leo Stefan, Benoit Doucet, Peter Draisaitl, Bernd Kuhnhauser, Jurgen Rumrich, Dieter Hegen, Michael Heidt, Daniel Nowak, Jochen Hecht, Erich Goldmann, Markus Wieland, Jayson Meyer, Martin Reichel, Jan Schertz, Mark MacKay, Brad Bergen, Jan Benda

**Italy** (Bryan Lefley, coach) GK—David Delfino, Mike Rosati, Bruno Campese—Robert Oberrauch, Leo Insam, Robert Nardella, John Massara, Lino De Toni, Roland Ramoser, Maurizio Mansi, Bruno Zarrillo, Gates Orlando, Patrick Brugnoli, Georg Comploi, Giovanni Marchetti, Mario Chitarroni, Larry Rucchin, Lucio Topatigh, Martin Pavlu, Christopher Bartolone, Scott Beattie, Michael De Angelis, Stefan Figliuzzi

**Norway** (Geir Myhre, coach) GK—Robert Schistad, Jim Marthinsen, Mattis Haakensen—Petter Salsten, Tommy Jakobsen, Per-Christian Knold, Tom-Erik Olsen, Geir Hoff, Bjorn-Anders Dahl, Orjan Lovdal, Lars-Hakon Andersen, Svein Enok Norstebo, Henrik Aaby, Ole Eskild Dahlstrom, Sjur Nilsen, Trond Magnussen, Cato Tom Andersen, Erik Tveten, Mattis Haakensen, Michael Smithurst, Rene Hansen, Oystein Olsen, Atle Olsen, Espen Knutsen

**Russia** (Vladimir Vasiliev, coach) GK—Andrei Trefilov, Mikhail Shtalenkov, Maxim Mikhailovski—Dmitri Yerofeyev, Alexei Zhitnik, Sergei Fokin, Alexander Smirnov, Andrei Skopintsev, Vladimir Vorobyov, Andrei Nikolishin, Darius Kasparaitis, Vitali Karamnov, Dmitri Kvartalnov, Alexei Yashin, Sergei Brylin, Roman Oksiuta, Alexander Prokopiev, Valeri Karpov, Viktor Kozlov, Oleg Tverdovski, Sergei Berezin, Andrei Potaichuk, Boris Mironov

**Slovakia** (Julius Supler, coach) GK—Igor Murin, Jaromir Dragan, Martin Klempa—Lubomir Visnovsky, Stanislav Jasecko, Lubomir Sekeras, Zdeno Ciger, Rene Pucher, Stanislav Medrik, Oto Hascak, Lubomir Kolnik, Pavol Demitra, Zigmund Palffy, Vlastimil Plavucha, Jozef Dano, Robert Petrovicky, Miroslav Satan, Lubomir Rybovic, Jan Varholik, Slavomir Vorobel, Branislav Janos, Marian Smerciak

**Sweden** (Kent Forsberg, coach) GK—Boo Ahl, Thomas Ostlund, Mikael Sandberg—Hans Jonsson, Kenny Jonsson, Tomas Forslund, Andreas Dackell, Anders Huusko, Roger Johansson, Tommy Sjodin, Tomas Holmstrom, Jan Larsson, Per Gustafsson, Niklas Andersson, Jonas Bergqvist, Daniel Alfredsson, Fredrik Modin, Per-Erik Eklund, Michael Nylander, Mattias Norstrom, Andreas Karlsson, Ronnie Sundin, Markus Naslund

**United States** (Ron Wilson, coach) GK—Parris Duffus, John Grahame, Tim Thomas—Paul Stanton, Mike Crowley, Keith Aldridge, Brian Bonin, Chris Luongo, Scott Lachance, Tom O'Regan, Mike Lalor, Brian Rolston, Joe Sacco, Tom Pederson, Bobby Reynolds, Tom Chorske, Marty McInnis, Chris Tancill, Dan Plante, Craig Johnson, Kevin Stevens, Derek Plante, Darby Hendrickson

## 61st WORLD CHAMPIONSHIP (MEN)
## April 26-May 14, 1997
## Helsinki/Tampere/Turku, Finland

**Final Placing**

| | | | |
|---|---|---|---|
| Gold | Canada | 7th | Latvia^ |
| Silver | Sweden | 8th | Italy |
| Bronze | Czech Republic | 9th | Slovakia |
| 4th | Russia | 10th | France |
| 5th | Finland | 11th | Germany |
| 6th | United States | 12th | Norway* |

^promoted from B Pool in 1996
*demoted to B Pool for 1998

**Tournament Format**

Teams played round-robin series within each of two groups, the top three advancing to a medal round round robin with scores between teams in that group carrying over from the preliminary round. The bottom three teams in each group played in another round robin to see which would be relegated for the following year. The top two teams of the medal round played for the gold medal in a best two-of-three while the third and fourth place teams played one game for the bronze medal.

**Results & Standings**

**GROUP A (HELSINKI)**

| | GP | W | T | L | GF | GA | P |
|---|---|---|---|---|---|---|---|
| Czech Republic | 5 | 4 | 0 | 1 | 18 | 9 | 8 |
| Finland | 5 | 4 | 0 | 1 | 25 | 9 | 8 |
| Russia | 5 | 3 | 1 | 1 | 19 | 16 | 7 |
| Slovakia | 5 | 1 | 1 | 3 | 10 | 14 | 3 |
| France | 5 | 1 | 0 | 4 | 13 | 26 | 2 |
| Germany | 5 | 1 | 0 | 4 | 4 | 15 | 2 |

| | | |
|---|---|---|
| April 26 | Czech Republic 2 | Germany 1 |
| April 26 | Finland 6 | France 1 |
| April 27 | Slovakia 2 | Russia 2 |
| April 27 | Czech Republic 2 | Finland 1 |
| April 28 | Russia 5 | Germany 1 |
| April 28 | Slovakia 5 | France 3 |
| April 29 | Finland 6 | Germany 0 |
| April 30 | Russia 5 | France 4 |
| April 30 | Czech Republic 3 | Slovakia 1 |
| May 1 | Russia 3 | Czech Republic 2 |
| May 2 | France 2 | Germany 1 |
| May 2 | Finland 5 | Slovakia 2 |
| May 3 | Czech Republic 9 | France 3 |
| May 3 | Germany 1 | Slovakia 0 |
| May 3 | Finland 7 | Russia 4 |

**GROUP B (TURKU)**

| | GP | W | T | L | GF | GA | P |
|---|---|---|---|---|---|---|---|
| Sweden | 5 | 4 | 1 | 0 | 20 | 8 | 9 |
| Canada | 5 | 3 | 1 | 1 | 23 | 11 | 7 |
| United States | 5 | 3 | 0 | 2 | 14 | 15 | 6 |
| Latvia | 5 | 1 | 2 | 2 | 18 | 17 | 4 |
| Italy | 5 | 1 | 1 | 3 | 12 | 21 | 3 |
| Norway | 5 | 0 | 1 | 4 | 7 | 22 | 1 |

| | | |
|---|---|---|
| April 26 | Canada 7 | Norway 0 |
| April 26 | Sweden 5 | Italy 3 |
| April 27 | United States 5 | Latvia 4 |
| April 27 | Sweden 7 | Canada 2 |
| April 28 | Italy 5 | Latvia 4 |
| April 28 | United States 3 | Norway 1 |
| April 29 | Sweden 4 | Norway 1 |
| April 30 | Canada 3 | Latvia 3 |
| April 30 | United States 4 | Italy 2 |
| May 1 | Canada 5 | United States 1 |
| May 2 | Norway 2 | Italy 2 |
| May 2 | Sweden 1 | Latvia 1 |
| May 3 | Canada 6 | Italy 0 |
| May 3 | Sweden 3 | United States 1 |
| May 3 | Latvia 6 | Norway 3 |

**RELEGATION ROUND (TAMPERE)**

| | GP | W | T | L | GF | GA | P |
|---|---|---|---|---|---|---|---|
| Latvia | 5 | 4 | 0 | 1 | 29 | 14 | 8 |
| Italy | 5 | 3 | 1 | 1 | 23 | 13 | 7 |
| Slovakia | 5 | 3 | 0 | 2 | 15 | 13 | 6 |
| France | 5 | 2 | 0 | 3 | 12 | 23 | 4 |
| Germany | 5 | 2 | 0 | 3 | 8 | 17 | 4 |
| Norway | 5 | 0 | 1 | 4 | 11 | 18 | 1 |

| | | |
|---|---|---|
| May 5 | Slovakia 2 | Norway 1 |
| May 6 | Latvia 8 | Germany 0 |
| May 7 | France 4 | Norway 3 |
| May 7 | Italy 5 | Germany 2 |
| May 8 | Slovakia 4 | Italy 3 |
| May 8 | Latvia 6 | France 2 |
| May 9 | Germany 4 | Norway 2 |
| May 10 | Latvia 5 | Slovakia 4 |
| May 10 | Italy 8 | France 1 |

**FINAL ROUND (HELSINKI)**

| | GP | W | T | L | GF | GA | P |
|---|---|---|---|---|---|---|---|
| Sweden | 5 | 4 | 0 | 1 | 17 | 9 | 8 |
| Canada | 5 | 3 | 0 | 2 | 13 | 14 | 6 |
| Russia | 5 | 2 | 1 | 2 | 13 | 13 | 5 |
| Czech Republic | 5 | 2 | 0 | 3 | 12 | 12 | 4 |
| Finland | 5 | 2 | 0 | 3 | 12 | 12 | 4 |
| United States | 5 | 1 | 1 | 3 | 7 | 14 | 3 |

| | | |
|---|---|---|
| May 5 | United States 4 | Czech Republic 3 |
| May 5 | Russia 4 | Sweden 1 |
| May 6 | Canada 1 | Finland 0 |
| May 6 | Russia 1 | United States 1 |
| May 7 | Czech Republic 5 | Canada 3 |
| May 7 | Sweden 5 | Finland 2 |
| May 8 | Sweden 1 | Czech Republic 0 |
| May 9 | Canada 2 | Russia 1 |
| May 9 | Finland 2 | United States 0 |

**BRONZE MEDAL GAME (HELSINKI)**

| | | |
|---|---|---|
| May 10 | Czech Republic 4 | Russia 3 |

**GOLD MEDAL GAMES (BEST-OF-THREE, HELSINKI)**

| | | |
|---|---|---|
| May 11 | Sweden 3 | Canada 2 |
| May 13 | Canada 3 | Sweden 1 |
| May 14 | Canada 2 | Sweden 1 |

**Rosters**

**Canada** (Andy Murray, coach) GK—Sean Burke, Rick Tabaracci, Eric Fichaud—Travis Green, Owen Nolan, Jeff Friesen, Rob Zamuner, Anson Carter, Keith Primeau, Mark Recchi, Geoff Sanderson, Dean Evason, Jarome Iginla, Chris Gratton, Rob Blake, Don Sweeney, Bob Errey, Steve Chiasson, Cory Cross, Chris Pronger, Bryan McCabe, Shean Donovan, Joel Bouchard

**Czech Republic** (Ivan Hlinka & Slavomir Lener, coaches) GK—Milan Hnilicka, Roman Cechmanek, Martin Prusek—Martin Prochazka, Vladimir Vujtek, Pavel Patera, Robert Reichel, Jiri Dopita, Vlastimil Kroupa, David Vyborny, Frantisek Kaberle, Libor Prochazka, Rostislav Vlach, Viktor Ujcik, Jiri Vykoukal, Robert Lang, Jiri Slegr, Richard Zemlicka, Roman Simicek, David Moravec, Ladislav Benysek, Ondrej Kratena, Jiri Veber

**Finland** (Curt Lindstrom, coach) GK—Ari Sulander, Jarmo Myllys, Jani Hurme—Mika Nieminen, Olli Jokinen, Mika Stromberg, Janne Ojanen, Raimo Helminen, Petri Varis, Ville Peltonen, Saku Koivu, Teppo Numminen, Timo Jutila, Kai Nurminen, Hannu Virta, Jyrki Lumme, Antti Aalto, Marko Jantunen, Juha Lind, Antti Tormanen, Jarkko Varvio, Marko Kiprusoff, Petteri Nummelin

**France** (Dany Dube, coach) GK—Cristobal Huet, Francois Gravel, Fabrice Lhenry—Roger Dube, Christian Pouget, Philippe Bozon, Arnaud Briand, Joseph Ouellet, Pierre Allard, Stephane Barin, Karl Dewolf, Serge Djelloul, Jean-Marc Soghomonian, Maurice Rozenthal, Laurent Lecomte, Jonathan Zwikel, Steve Woodburn, Jean-Christophe Filippin, Anthony Mortas, Laurent Gras, Denis Perez, Guillaume Besse, Jean-Philippe Lemoine

**Germany** (George Kingston, coach) GK—Olaf Kolzig, Josef Heiss, Marc Seliger—Peter Draisaitl, Mirko Ludemann, Brad Bergen, Jochen Hecht, Marco Sturm, Daniel Nowak, Andreas Lupzig, Jan Benda, Reemt Pyka, Jurgen Rumrich, Markus Wieland, Martin Reichel, Torsten Kienass, Leo Stefan, Erich Goldmann, Daniel Kunce, Jochen Molling, Mark MacKay, Dieter Hegen, Alexander Serikow

**Italy** (Bryan Lefley, coach) GK—Mike Rosati, David Delfino, Andrea Carpano—Bruno Zarrillo, Gates Orlando, Maurizio Mansi, Mario Chitarroni, Robert Nardella, Roland Ramoser, Lucio Topatigh, Christopher Bartolone, Dino Felicetti, Anthony Iob, Giuseppe Busillo, Michael De Angelis, Markus Brunner, Leo Insam, Armando Chelodi, Martin Pavlu, Georg Comploi, Chad Biafore, Larry Rucchin, Giovanni Marchetti

**Latvia** (Leonids Beresnevs, coach) GK—Arturs Irbe, Peteris Skudra, Juris Klodans—Olegs Znaroks, Harijs Vitolins, Aleksandrs Kercs, Sergejs Cudinovs, Aleksandrs Belavskis, Sergejs Zoltoks, Igors Pavlovs, Leonids Tambijevs, Andrejs Maticins, Aigars Cipruss, Rodrigo Lavins, Aleksandrs Semjonovs, Andrejs Ignatovics, Igors Bondarevs, Normunds Sejejs, Karlis Skrastins, Sergejs Boldavesko, Sergejs Senins, Aleksandrs Macijevskis, Arturs Kupaks, Arvids Petersons

**Norway** (Brent McEwen, coach) GK—Steve Allman, Robert Schistad, Oyvind Sorli—Ole Eskild Dahlstrom, Espen Knutsen, Atle Olsen, Rune Fjeldstad, Svein Enok Norstebo, Trond Magnussen, Oystein Olsen, Per Age Skroder, Sjur Nilsen, Michael Smithurst, Mats Trygg, Erik Tveten, Tore Vikingstad, Tommy Jakobsen, Per Christian Knold, Carl Boe-Andersen, Marius Trygg, Jan Roar Fagerli, Pal Johnsen, Morten Fjeld

**Russia** (Igor Dmitriev, coach) GK—Sergei Fadeyev, Maxim Mikhailovski, Alexei Yegorov—Alexander Prokopiev, Alexander Barkov, Alexei Morozov, Oleg Belov, Alexander Korolyuk, Sergei Petrenko, Vyacheslav Butsayev, Anatoli Fedotov, Alexei Yashin, Alexei Chupin, Mikhail Sarmatin, Denis Afinogenov, Dmitri Krasotkin, Dmitri Yerofeyev, Sergei Fokin, Sergei Bautin, Andrei Skopintsev, Andrei Nikolishin, Vadim Yepantchintsev, Marat Davydov

**Slovakia** (Jozef Golonka, coach) GK—Jaromir Dragan, Eduard Hartmann, Pavol Rybar—Roman Konstek, Zdeno Ciger, Jan Pardavy, Lubomir Kolnik, Branislav Janos, Jozef Stumpel, Lubomir Sekeras, Roman Stantien, Marian Hossa, Vladimir Vlk, Jergus Baca, Ivan Droppa, Jozef Dano, Jiri Bicek, Daniel Babka, Lubomir Visnovsky, Robert Pukalovic, Peter Pucher, Stanislav Medrik, Vlastimil Plavucha

**Sweden** (Kent Forsberg, coach) GK—Johan Hedberg, Tommy Salo, Mikael Sandberg—Tommy Albelin, Roger Johansson, Mattias Norstrom, Marcus Ragnarsson, Ronnie Sundin, Magnus Svensson, Mattias Ohlund, Niklas Andersson, Magnus Arvedson, Anders Carlsson, Per Eklund, Nichlas Falk, Jonas Hoglund, Jorgen Jonsson, Johan Lindbom, Stefan Nilsson, Michael Nylander, Per Svartvadet, Niklas Sundblad, Marcus Thuresson

**United States** (Jeff Jackson, coach) GK—Chris Terreri, John Blue, Tom Askey—Ted Donato, Chris Tancill, Donald Brashear, Bret Hedican, Marty McInnis, Eric Weinrich, Mike Sullivan, Paul Ranheim, Dan Plante, Todd Krygier, Scott Lachance, Jon Rohloff, Bryan Berard, Chris Marinucci, Bob Beers, Ken Klee, Chris Drury, Darby Hendrickson, Matt Martin, Jim Campbell

## 62nd WORLD CHAMPIONSHIP (MEN)
## May 1-17, 1998
## Zurich/Basel, Switzerland

### Final Placing

Gold ........Sweden
Silver ......Finland
Bronze ....Czech Republic
4th..........Switzerland^
5th..........Russia
6th..........Canada
7th..........Slovakia
8th..........Belarus^
9th .........Latvia
10th .......Italy
11th .......Germany*
12th .......United States
13th .......France
14th .......Japan+
15th .......Austria^
16th .......Kazakhstan^*

+Far East qualifier
^promoted from B Pool in 1997
*demoted to B Pool for 1999

### Tournament Format

For the first time, there were 16 teams in the tournament, divided into four groups of four teams each for the Preliminary Round. The top two from each group advanced to a Qualification Round which made them eligible for medals. The third place teams were put in another group for placement, and the bottom four were placed according to record, the last two being demoted. In the next round, the top two from each group advanced to a semi-finals round, the winners playing for gold, the losers for bronze.

### Results & Standings

**GROUP A (BASEL)**

| | GP | W | T | L | GF | GA | P |
|---|---|---|---|---|---|---|---|
| Czech Republic | 3 | 3 | 0 | 0 | 20 | 5 | 6 |
| Belarus | 3 | 2 | 0 | 1 | 12 | 10 | 4 |
| Germany | 3 | 1 | 0 | 2 | 8 | 13 | 2 |
| Japan | 3 | 0 | 0 | 3 | 7 | 19 | 0 |

| | | |
|---|---|---|
| May 1 | Czech Republic 8 | Japan 2 |
| May 1 | Belarus 4 | Germany 2 |
| May 3 | Czech Republic 4 | Belarus 2 |
| May 3 | Germany 5 | Japan 1 |
| May 5 | Belarus 6 | Japan 4 |
| May 5 | Czech Republic 8 | Germany 1 |

**GROUP B (ZURICH)**

| | GP | W | T | L | GF | GA | P |
|---|---|---|---|---|---|---|---|
| Canada | 3 | 2 | 1 | 0 | 12 | 5 | 5 |
| Slovakia | 3 | 2 | 1 | 0 | 9 | 4 | 5 |
| Italy | 3 | 1 | 0 | 2 | 8 | 8 | 2 |
| Austria | 3 | 0 | 0 | 3 | 3 | 15 | 0 |

| | | |
|---|---|---|
| May 1 | Canada 5 | Austria 1 |
| May 1 | Slovakia 2 | Italy 1 |
| May 3 | Canada 2 | Slovakia 2 |
| May 3 | Italy 5 | Austria 1 |
| May 5 | Canada 5 | Italy 2 |
| May 5 | Slovakia 5 | Austria 1 |

**GROUP C (ZURICH)**

| | GP | W | T | L | GF | GA | P |
|---|---|---|---|---|---|---|---|
| Sweden | 3 | 3 | 0 | 0 | 16 | 4 | 6 |
| Switzerland | 3 | 1 | 0 | 2 | 9 | 10 | 2 |
| United States | 3 | 1 | 0 | 2 | 7 | 11 | 2 |
| France | 3 | 1 | 0 | 2 | 5 | 12 | 2 |

| | | |
|---|---|---|
| May 2 | United States 5 | Switzerland 1 |
| May 2 | Sweden 6 | France 1 |
| May 4 | France 3 | United States 1 |
| May 4 | Sweden 4 | Switzerland 2 |
| May 6 | Sweden 6 | United States 1 |
| May 6 | Switzerland 5 | France 1 |

**GROUP D (BASEL)**

| | GP | W | T | L | GF | GA | P |
|---|---|---|---|---|---|---|---|
| Russia | 3 | 3 | 0 | 0 | 19 | 11 | 6 |
| Finland | 3 | 2 | 0 | 1 | 12 | 4 | 4 |
| Latvia | 3 | 1 | 0 | 2 | 12 | 15 | 2 |
| Kazakhstan | 3 | 0 | 0 | 3 | 6 | 19 | 0 |

| | | |
|---|---|---|
| May 2 | Russia 8 | Kazakhstan 4 |
| May 2 | Finland 6 | Latvia 0 |
| May 4 | Russia 7 | Latvia 5 |
| May 4 | Finland 4 | Kazakhstan 0 |
| May 6 | Latvia 7 | Kazakhstan 2 |
| May 6 | Russia 4 | Finland 2 |

**QUALIFYING ROUND**
**GROUP E (ZURICH)**

| | GP | W | T | L | GF | GA | P |
|---|---|---|---|---|---|---|---|
| Sweden | 3 | 3 | 0 | 0 | 16 | 2 | 6 |
| Finland | 3 | 1 | 1 | 1 | 8 | 6 | 3 |
| Canada | 3 | 1 | 1 | 1 | 10 | 12 | 3 |
| Belarus | 3 | 0 | 0 | 3 | 5 | 13 | 0 |

| | | |
|---|---|---|
| May 7 | Canada 6 | Belarus 2 |
| May 7 | Sweden 1 | Finland 0 |
| May 9 | Canada 3 | Finland 3 |
| May 9 | Sweden 2 | Belarus 1 |
| May 10 | Sweden 7 | Canada 1 |
| May 10 | Finland 5 | Belarus 2 |

**GROUP F (BASEL)**

| | GP | W | T | L | GF | GA | P |
|---|---|---|---|---|---|---|---|
| CzechRepublic | 3 | 2 | 1 | 0 | 6 | 3 | 5 |
| Switzerland | 3 | 1 | 1 | 1 | 6 | 6 | 3 |
| Russia | 3 | 1 | 1 | 1 | 10 | 7 | 3 |
| Slovakia | 3 | 0 | 1 | 2 | 2 | 8 | 1 |

| | | |
|---|---|---|
| May 7 | Czech Republic 1 | Slovakia 0 |
| May 7 | Switzerland 4 | Russia 2 |
| May 9 | Czech Republic 3 | Switzerland 1 |
| May 9 | Russia 6 | Slovakia 1 |
| May 10 | Czech Republic 2 | Russia 2 |
| May 10 | Switzerland 1 | Slovakia 1 |

**PLACEMENT ROUND**
**GROUP G**

| | GP | W | T | L | GF | GA | P |
|---|---|---|---|---|---|---|---|
| Latvia | 3 | 2 | 1 | 0 | 9 | 3 | 5 |
| Italy | 3 | 1 | 2 | 0 | 9 | 5 | 4 |
| Germany | 3 | 0 | 2 | 1 | 5 | 10 | 2 |
| United States | 3 | 0 | 1 | 2 | 3 | 8 | 1 |

| | | | |
|---|---|---|---|
| May 8 | Zurich | Germany 1 | United States 1 |
| May 8 | Zurich | Italy 1 | Latvia 1 |
| May 10 | Zurich | Italy 4 | United States 0 |
| May 10 | Basel | Latvia 5 | Germany 0 |
| May 11 | Zurich | Italy 4 | Germany 4 |
| May 11 | Zurich | Latvia 3 | United States 2 |

**PLAYOFFS (ZURICH)**
**SEMI-FINALS (BEST-OF-TWO)**

| | | |
|---|---|---|
| May 12 | Sweden 4 | Switzerland 1 |
| May 14 | Sweden 7 | Switzerland 2 |
| May 12 | Finland 4 | Czech Republic 1 |
| May 14 | Finland 2 | Czech Republic 2 |

**BRONZE MEDAL GAME**

| | | |
|---|---|---|
| May 15 | Czech Republic 4 | Switzerland 0 |

**GOLD MEDAL GAMES (BEST-OF-TWO)**

| | | |
|---|---|---|
| May 16 | Sweden 1 | Finland 0 |
| May 17 | Sweden 0 | Finland 0 |

**Rosters**

**Austria** (Ron Kennedy, coach) GK—Claus Dalpiaz, Reinhard Divis, Michael Suttnig—Dieter Kalt, Andreas Puschnig, Simon Wheeldon, Gerhard Unterluggauer, Christoph Brandner, Tom Searle, Gunter Lanzinger, Normand Krumpschmid, Wolfgang Kromp, Mario Schaden, Patrick Pilloni, Herbert Hohenberger, Engelbert Linder, Christian Perthaler, Martin Ulrich, Richard Nasheim, Michael Guntner, Gerhard Puschnik, Michael Lampert, Gerald Ressmann

**Belarus** (Anatoli Varivonchik, coach) GK—Alexander Gavrilenok, Andrei Mezin, Alexander Shumidub—Oleg Romanov, Vadim Bekbulatov, Igor Matushkin, Alexei Kalyuzhny, Vasili Pankov, Dmitri Pankov, Alexander Andrievski, Andrei Skabelka, Sergei Stas, Sergei Shitkovski, Alexei Lozhkin, Ruslan Salei, Sergei Yerkovich, Oleg Mikulchik, Andrei Kovalyov, Viktor Karachun, Oleg Antonenko, Alexander Galchenyuk, Oleg Khmyl

**Canada** (Andy Murray, coach) GK—Jeff Hackett, Felix Potvin, Christian Bronsard—Ray Whitney, Eric Daze, Trevor Linden, Keith Primeau, Nelson Emerson, Ed Jovanovski, Steve Rucchin, Bryan McCabe, Glen Murray, Todd Bertuzzi, Travis Green, Rob Zamuner, Cory Cross, Gord Murphy, Chris Gratton, Martin Gelinas, Rob Blake, James Patrick, Mickey John Elick

**Czech Republic** (Ivan Hlinka, coach) GK—Milan Hnilicka, Roman Cechmanek, Martin Prusek—Radek Belohlav, Pavel Patera, Martin Prochazka, David Vyborny, Ladislav Lubina, Frantisek Kucera, Jiri Dopita, Marian Kacir, Jan Hlavac, Frantisek Kaberle, Robert Reichel, David Moravec, Josef Beranek, Jiri Vykoukal, Petr Sykora, Libor Prochazka, Patrik Elias, Robert Kantor, Jiri Veber, Jiri Slegr, Vaclav Burda, Milan Hejduk

**Finland** (Hannu Aravirta, coach) GK—Ari Sulander, Jarmo Myllys, Vesa Toskala—Raimo Helminen, Ville Peltonen, Kimmo Timonen, Sami Kapanen, Jere Karalahti, Antti Tormanen, Juha Ikonen, Marko Kiprusoff, Mika Alatalo, Mikko Eloranta, Kimmo Rintanen, Jarkko Ruutu, Joni Lius, Olli Jokinen, Marko Tuomainen, Toni Lydman, Janne Laukkannen, Petteri Nummelin, Antti-Jussi Niemi, Toni Makiaho, Kaj Linna

**France** (Herb Brooks, coach) GK—Francois Gravel, Cristobal Huet, Fabrice Lhenry—Philippe Bozon, Stanislas Solaux, Jean-Christophe Filippin, Jonathan Zwikel, Stephane Barin, Richard Aimonetto, Stephane Gachet, Francois Rozenthal, Maurice Rozenthal, Pierre Allard, Anthony Mortas, Arnaud Briand, Steve Woodburn, Laurent Gras, Roger Dube, Bob Ouellet, Denis Perez, Gerald Guennelon, Karl Dewolf, Jean-Philippe Lemoine

**Germany** (George Kingston, coach) GK—Marc Seliger, Josef Heiss, Kai Fischer—Dieter Hegen, Peter Draisaitl, Mark MacKay, Andreas Lupzig, Sascha Goc, Jurgen Rumrich, Jochen Hecht, Stefan Mayer, Sven Felski, Daniel Nowak, Florian Keller, Klaus Micheller, Leo Stefan, Christopher Straube, Christoph Sandner, Rainer Zerwesz, Reemt Pyka, Lars Brueggemann, Michael Bresagk, Erich Goldmann

**Italy** (Adolf Insam, coach) GK—Mario Brunetta, Mike Rosati, Andrea Carpano—Lucio Topatigh, Maurizio Mansi, Gates Orlando, Mario Chitarroni, Leo Insam, Bruno Zarrillo, Roland Ramoser, Anthony Iob, Armando Chelodi, Robert Oberrauch, Michele Strazzabosco, Giuseppe Busillo, Chris Bartolone, Giovanni Marchetti, Michael De Angelis, Stefano Margoni, Markus Brunner, Alexander Gschliesser, Larry Rucchin, Chad Biafore

**Japan** (Masaru Seino, coach) GK—Shinichi Iwasaki, Jiro Nihei, Dusty Imoo—Shin Yahata, Toshiyuki Sakai, Takeshi Yamanaka, Ryan Kuwabara, Yoshikazu Kabayama, Yasunori Iwata, Tatsuki Katayama, Daniel Daikawa, Hiroshi Matsuura, Takayuki Kobori, Kiyoshi Fujita, Hiroyuki Miura, Hideji Tsuchida, Junji Sakata, Yutaka Kawaguchi, Takayuki Miura, Masaki Shirono, Akihito Sugisawa, Fumitaka Miyauchi, Tsutsumi Otomo

**Kazakhstan** (Boris Alexandrov, coach) GK—Vitali Yeremeyev, Roman Krivomazov, Alexander Shimin—Andrei Pchelyakov, Vadim Glovatski, Alexander Koreshkov, Pavel Kamentsev, Mikhail Borodulin, Oleg Kryazhev, Yevgeni Koreshkov, Andrei Raiski, Dmitri Dudarev, Nikolai Antropov, Andrei Sokolov, Viktor Bystryantsev, Igor Zemlyanoy, Yerlan Sagymbayev, Vladimir Antipin, Andrei Troshinski, Vitali Tregubov, Alexei Troshinski, Igor Nikitin, Konstantin Shafranov

**Latvia** (Leonids Beresnevs, coach) GK—Arturs Irbe, Juris Klodans, Juris Klodans—Olegs Znaroks, Harijs Vitolins, Aleksandrs Kercs, Leonids Tambijevs, Sandis Ozolins, Aleksandrs Nizivijs, Sergejs Cudinovs, Aigars Cipruss, Andrejs Ignatovics, Aleksandrs Belavskis, Herberts Vasiljevs, Aleksandrs Semjonovs, Normunds Sejejs, Juris Opulskis, Igors Bondarevs, Karlis Skrastins, Rodrigo Lavins, Andrejs Maticins, Igors Pavlovs, Atvars Tribuncovs

**Russia** (Vladimir Yurzinov, coach) GK—Yegor Podomatski, Oleg Shevtsov, Maxim Sokolov—Viktor Kozlov, Sergei Berezin, Alexei Kovalyov, Oleg Petrov, Sergei Petrenko, Dmitri Yushkevich, Dmitri Yerofeyev, Alexei Kudashov, Andrei Nazarov, Alexei Morozov, Mikhail Sarmatin, Oleg Belov, Alexei Chupin, Andrei Skopintsev, Vitali Prokhorov, Sergei Nemchinov, Marat Davydov, Sergei Fokin, Daniil Markov, Sergei Zhukov

**Slovakia** (Jan Sterbak, coach) GK—Miroslav Simonovic, Pavol Rybar, Pavol Rybar—Jozef Dano, Branislav Janos, Jan Pardavy, Jozef Stumpel, Robert Svehla, Peter Bartos, Jozef Voskar, Zdeno Ciger, Richard Kapus, Roman Stantien, Radoslav Kropac, Lubomir Visnovsky, Robert Pukalovic, Jergus Baca, Stanislav Jasecko, Peter Pucher, Igor Rataj, Rene Pucher, Ivan Droppa, Lubomir Sekeras

**Sweden** (Kent Forsberg, coach) GK—Johan Hedberg, Tommy Salo, Magnus Eriksson—Peter Forsberg, Mats Sundin, Mikael Renberg, Mikael Johansson, Ulf Dahlen, Fredrik Modin, Patric Kjellberg, Niklas Sundstrom, Jorgen Jonsson, Mattias Ohlund, Christer Olsson, Johan Tornberg, Jonas Bergqvist, Anders Huusko, Peter Nordstrom, Niclas Havelid, Nichlas Falk, Kim Johnsson, Hans Jonsson, Jan Mertzig, Tommy Westlund, Mattias Norstrom

**Switzerland** (Ralph Krueger, coach) GK—Reto Pavoni, David Aebischer, Ronnie Rueger—Marcel Jenni, Gian-Marco Crameri, Reto Von Arx, Patrik Sutter, Martin Steinegger, Patrick Fischer, Petr Jaks, Michel Zeiter, Misko Antisin, Claudio Micheli, Edgar Salis, Mathias Seger, Ivo Ruthemann, Michel Riesen, Martin Pluss, Dino Kessler, Mark Streit, Franz Steffen, Olivier Keller, Mattia Baldi, Sandy Jeannin, Martin Rauch

**United States** (Jeff Jackson, coach) GK—Mike Dunham, Tim Thomas, Garth Snow—Chris Luongo, Bryan Smolinski, Matt Cullen, Chris Drury, Tom Chorske, Bates Battaglia, Al Iafrate, Eric Weinrich, Darby Hendrickson, Mike Crowley, Ted Drury, Kevin Miller, Greg Brown, Paul Stanton, Dan Trebil, Kevin Dean, Mark Parrish, Adam Burt, Shjon Podein, Donald Brashear

## 63rd WORLD CHAMPIONSHIP (MEN)
## May 1-16, 1999
## Oslo/Hamar/Lillehammer, Norway

**Final Placing**

| | |
|---|---|
| Gold ........Czech Republic | 9th .........Belarus |
| Silver ......Finland | 10th .......Austria |
| Bronze ....Sweden | 11th .......Latvia |
| 4th ..........Canada | 12th .......Norway^ |
| 5th ..........Russia | 13th .......Italy |
| 6th ..........United States | 14th .......Ukraine^ |
| 7th ..........Slovakia | 15th .......France |
| 8th ..........Switzerland | 16th .......Japan+ |

+Far East qualifier
^promoted from B Pool in 1998
*no demotions for 2000

**Tournament Format**

There were 16 teams in the tournament, divided into four groups of four teams each for the Preliminary Round. The top two from each group advanced to a Qualification Round which made them eligible for medals. The third place teams were put in another group for placement, and the bottom four were placed in a relegation pool, the last two being demoted. In the next round, the top two from each group advanced to a semi-finals round (best-of-two), the winners playing for gold in a best-of-two format, the losers for bronze.

**Results & Standings**

**GROUP A (HAMAR)**

| | GP | W | T | L | GF | GA | P |
|---|---|---|---|---|---|---|---|
| Canada | 3 | 3 | 0 | 0 | 12 | 6 | 6 |
| Slovakia | 3 | 2 | 0 | 1 | 17 | 9 | 4 |
| Norway | 3 | 1 | 0 | 2 | 9 | 14 | 2 |
| Italy | 3 | 0 | 0 | 3 | 8 | 17 | 0 |

| | | |
|---|---|---|
| May 1 | Canada 3 | Slovakia 2 |
| May 1 | Norway 5 | Italy 2 |
| May 3 | Canada 4 | Norway 2 |
| May 3 | Slovakia 7 | Italy 4 |
| May 5 | Canada 5 | Italy 2 |
| May 5 | Slovakia 8 | Norway 2 |

**GROUP B (OSLO)**

| | GP | W | T | L | GF | GA | P |
|---|---|---|---|---|---|---|---|
| Sweden | 3 | 3 | 0 | 0 | 14 | 5 | 6 |
| Switzerland | 3 | 2 | 0 | 1 | 12 | 9 | 4 |
| Latvia | 3 | 1 | 0 | 2 | 14 | 14 | 2 |
| France | 3 | 0 | 0 | 3 | 6 | 18 | 0 |

| | | |
|---|---|---|
| May 2 | Switzerland 5 | Latvia 3 |
| May 2 | Sweden 4 | France 1 |
| May 4 | Sweden 6 | Switzerland 1 |
| May 4 | Latvia 8 | France 5 |
| May 6 | Switzerland 6 | France 0 |
| May 6 | Sweden 4 | Latvia 3 |

**GROUP C (OSLO)**

| | GP | W | T | L | GF | GA | P |
|---|---|---|---|---|---|---|---|
| Czech Republic | 3 | 3 | 0 | 0 | 23 | 5 | 6 |
| United States | 3 | 2 | 0 | 1 | 15 | 7 | 4 |
| Austria | 3 | 1 | 0 | 2 | 6 | 14 | 2 |
| Japan | 3 | 0 | 0 | 3 | 5 | 23 | 0 |

| | | |
|---|---|---|
| May 1 | United States 7 | Japan 1 |
| May 1 | Czech Republic 7 | Austria 0 |
| May 3 | Czech Republic 12 | Japan 2 |
| May 3 | United States 5 | Austria 2 |
| May 5 | Czech Republic 4 | United States 3 |
| May 5 | Austria 4 | Japan 2 |

GROUP D (HAMAR)

| | GP | W | T | L | GF | GA | P |
|---|---|---|---|---|---|---|---|
| Finland | 3 | 2 | 1 | 0 | 10 | 5 | 5 |
| Russia | 3 | 1 | 2 | 0 | 9 | 6 | 4 |
| Belarus | 3 | 1 | 1 | 1 | 9 | 7 | 3 |
| Ukraine | 3 | 0 | 0 | 3 | 3 | 13 | 0 |

| | | |
|---|---|---|
| May 2 | Belarus 2 | Russia 2 |
| May 2 | Finland 3 | Ukraine 1 |
| May 4 | Russia 4 | Ukraine 1 |
| May 4 | Finland 4 | Belarus 1 |
| May 6 | Belarus 6 | Ukraine 1 |
| May 6 | Finland 3 | Russia 3 |

QUALIFYING ROUND
GROUP G

| | GP | W | T | L | GF | GA | P |
|---|---|---|---|---|---|---|---|
| Belarus | 3 | 3 | 0 | 0 | 7 | 3 | 6 |
| Austria | 3 | 2 | 0 | 1 | 10 | 5 | 4 |
| Latvia | 3 | 1 | 0 | 2 | 10 | 8 | 2 |
| Norway | 3 | 0 | 0 | 3 | 1 | 12 | 0 |

| | | | |
|---|---|---|---|
| May 8 | Hamar | Austria 5 | Latvia 2 |
| May 8 | Hamar | Belarus 2 | Norway 0 |
| May 10 | Lillehammer | Belarus 3 | Austria 2 |
| May 10 | Lillehammer | Latvia 7 | Norway 1 |
| May 11 | Lillehammer | Belarus 2 | Latvia 1 |
| May 11 | Lillehammer | Austria 3 | Norway 0 |

FINAL ROUND
GROUP E (HAMAR)

| | GP | W | T | L | GF | GA | P |
|---|---|---|---|---|---|---|---|
| Finland | 3 | 3 | 0 | 0 | 13 | 6 | 6 |
| Canada | 3 | 2 | 0 | 1 | 14 | 7 | 4 |
| United States | 3 | 1 | 0 | 2 | 7 | 8 | 2 |
| Switzerland | 3 | 0 | 0 | 3 | 3 | 16 | 0 |

| | | |
|---|---|---|
| May 7 | Canada 8 | Switzerland 2 |
| May 7 | Finland 4 | United States 3 |
| May 9 | Canada 4 | United States 1 |
| May 9 | Finland 5 | Switzerland 1 |
| May 10 | Finland 4 | Canada 2 |
| May 10 | United States 3 | Switzerland 0 |

GROUP F (OSLO)

| | GP | W | T | L | GF | GA | P |
|---|---|---|---|---|---|---|---|
| Czech Republic | 3 | 2 | 0 | 1 | 11 | 8 | 4 |
| Sweden | 3 | 2 | 0 | 1 | 6 | 4 | 4 |
| Russia | 3 | 1 | 1 | 1 | 9 | 7 | 3 |
| Slovakia | 3 | 0 | 1 | 2 | 5 | 12 | 1 |

| | | |
|---|---|---|
| May 7 | Russia 6 | Czech Republic 1 |
| May 7 | Sweden 2 | Slovakia 1 |
| May 9 | Sweden 4 | Russia 1 |
| May 9 | Czech Republic 8 | Slovakia 2 |
| May 10 | Slovakia 2 | Russia 2 |
| May 10 | Czech Republic 2 | Sweden 0 |

PLAYOFFS (LILLEHAMMER)
SEMI-FINALS (BEST-OF-TWO PLUS 10:00 OT & GWS)

| | | | |
|---|---|---|---|
| May 12 | Game 1 | Canada 2 | Czech Republic 1 |
| May 13 | Game 2 | Czech Republic 6 | Canada 4 |

~Czech Republic won game two, 5-4, to force overtime to determine series winner. No goal was scored, resulting in a shootout. GWS—Jaroslav Spacek (CZE).

| | | | |
|---|---|---|---|
| May 12 | Game 1 | Finland 3 | Sweden 1 |
| May 13 | Game 2 | Sweden 2 | Finland 1 |

~Sweden won game two, 2-0, to force overtime to determine series winner. Marko Tuomainen (FIN) 6:25 OT.

BRONZE MEDAL GAME

| | | |
|---|---|---|
| May 15 | Sweden 3 | Canada 2 |

GOLD MEDAL GAMES (BEST-OF-TWO PLUS 10:00 OT & GWS)

| | | | |
|---|---|---|---|
| May 15 | Game 1 | Czech Republic 3 | Finland 1 |
| May 16 | Game 2 | Finland 4 | Czech Republic 1 |

~Finland won game two, 4-0, to force overtime to determine a series winner. Jan Hlavac (CZE) 16:32 OT.

Rosters

**Austria** (Ron Kennedy, coach) GK—Reinhard Divis, Claus Dalpiaz, Michael Suttnig—Andreas Puschnig, Christoph Brandner, Gerald Ressmann, Richard Nasheim, Dieter Kalt, Matthias Trattnig, Dominic Lavoie, Normand Krumpschmid, Christian Perthaler, Christoph Konig, Martin Ulrich, Tom Searle, Raymond Podloski, Gerhard Unterluggauer, Mario Schaden, Herbert Hohenberger, Gunther Lanzinger, Michael Guntner, Peter Kasper, Andre Lakos

**Belarus** (Anatoli Varivonchik, coach) GK—Andrei Mezin, Leonid Fatikov, Sergei Shabanov—Andrei Kovalyov, Vladimir Tsyplakov, Viktor Karachun, Oleg Antonenko, Vasili Pankov, Oleg Khmyl, Alexander Andrievski, Dmitri Pankov, Alexei Kalyuzhny, Andrei Skabelka, Vadim Bekbulatov, Oleg Leontiev, Oleg Romanov, Alexander Galchenyuk, Yuri Krivokhizha, Igor Matushkin, Konstantin Koltsov, Alexander Zhurik, Vladimir Kopat, Oleg Mikulchik

**Canada** (Mike Johnston, coach) GK—Ron Tugnutt, Rick Tabaracci, Fred Brathwaite—Cory Stillman, Rob Blake, Scott Thornton, Adam Graves, Ray Whitney, Stephane Quintal, Scott Walker, Brian Savage, Jeff Friesen, Claude Lapointe, Bryan McCabe, Derek Morris, Rob Niedermayer, Wade Redden, Sean O'Donnell, Patrick Marleau, Ryan Smyth, Doug Bodger, Eric Daze, Chris Szysky, Shane Doan

**Czech Republic** (Ivan Hlinka, coach) GK—Milan Hnilicka, Roman Cechmanek, Martin Prusek—Jan Hlavac, Martin Rucinsky, Viktor Ujcik, David Vyborny, Radek Dvorak, Pavel Kubina, Pavel Patera, Roman Simicek, Jan Caloun, Libor Prochazka, Frantisek Kaberle, Martin Prochazka, Petr Sykora, Jaroslav Spacek, Frantisek Kucera, Tomas Vlasak, Jiri Vykoukal, Tomas Kucharcik, Ladislav Benysek, Roman Meluzin, David Moravec

**France** (Mikael Lundstrom, coach) GK—Cristobal Huet, Francois Gravel, Fabrice Lhenry—Arnaud Briand, Bob Ouellet, Serge Poudrier, Pierre Allard, Philippe Bozon, Denis Perez, Stephane Barin, Maurice Rozenthal, Richard Aimonetto, Franck Guillemard, Laurent Meunier, Francois Rozenthal, Karl Dewolf, Anthony Mortas, Benoit Bachelet, Gregory Dubois, Jean-Christophe Filippin, Gerald Guennelon, Christian Pouget, Jean-Philippe Lemoine

**Finland** (Hannu Aravirta, coach) GK—Miikka Kiprusoff, Ari Sulander, Vesa Toskala—Saku Koivu, Teemu Selanne, Jere Karalahti, Marko Tuomainen, Juha Lind, Ville Peltonen, Marko Kiprusoff, Kimmo Timonen, Olli Jokinen, Raimo Helminen, Kari Martikainen, Tomi Kallio, Mikko Eloranta, Kimmo Rintanen, Toni Sihvonen, Antti-Jussi Niemi, Toni Lydman, Petteri Nummelin, Antti Tormanen, Aki Berg

**Italy** (Adolf Insam, coach) GK—Andrea Carpano, Jim Mazzoli, Bruno Campese—Chris Bartolone, Lucio Topatigh, Giuseppe Busillo, Mario Chitarroni, Maurizio Mansi, Georg Comploi, Roland Ramoser, Michael de Angelis, Gates Orlando, Dino Felicetti, Armando Chelodi, Giuseppe Ciccarello, Stefano Margoni, Michele Strazzabosco, Chad Biafore, Manuel de Toni, Larry Rucchin, Lino de Toni, Carlo Lorenzi, Giovanni Marchetti

**Japan** (Steve Tsujiura, coach) GK—Shinichi Iwasaki, Dusty Imoo, Masahito Haruna—Takahito Suzuki, Takeshi Yamanaka, Shin Yahata, Toshiyuki Sakai, Yujiro Nakajimaya, Junji Sakata, Yasunori Iwata, Chris Yule, Daniel Daikawa, Yoshikazu Kabayama, Tatsuki Katayama, Akihito Sugisawa, Akihito Isojima, Masaki Shirono, Hiroshi Matsuura, Hiroyuki Murakami, Kunio Tagaki, Masakazu Sato, Takayuki Kobori, Yutaka Kawaguchi

**Latvia** (Leonids Beresnevs, coach) GK—Arturs Irbe, Andrejs Zinkovs, Juris Klodans—Aigars Cipruss, Vjaceslavs Fanduls, Aleksandrs Belavskis, Andrejs Maticins, Sergejs Zoltoks, Leonids Tambijevs, Aleksandrs Nizivijs, Aleksandrs Semjonovs, Aleksandrs Kercs, Sergejs Cudinovs, Karlis Skrastins, Andrejs Ignatovics, Harijs Vitolins, Mareks Jass, Atvars Tribuncovs, Normunds Sejejs, Olegs Znaroks, Artis Abols, Rodrigo Lavins, Mihails Bogdanovs

**Norway** (Leif Boork, coach) GK—Robert Schistad, Oivind Sorli, Bjorge Josefsen—Lars-Hakon Andersen, Per Age Skroder, Tore Vikingstad, Mats Trygg, Ole Eskild Dahlstrom, Svein Enok Norstebo, Trond Magnussen, Tommy Jakobsen, Andre Hansen-Manskow, Sjur Nilsen, Martin Knold, Marius Trygg, Anders Myrvold, Henrik Aaby, Morten Fjeld, Pal Jonsen, Carl Boe-Andersen, Geir Svendsberget, Ketil Wold, Bard Sorlie

**Russia** (Alexander Yakushev, coach) GK—Yegor Podomatski, Andrei Tsarev, Alexei Volkov—Alexei Yashin, Sergei Petrenko, Ravil Gusmanov, Andrei Markov, Maxim Afinogenov, Maxim Sushinski, Alexander Prokopiev, Sergei Tertyshny, Sergei Bautin, Oleg Petrov, Alexei Kudashov, Vitali Vishnevski, Alexander Barkov, Valeri Karpov, Dmitri Subotin, Alexander Khavanov, Andrei Yakhanov, Artur Oktyabryov, Mikhail Sarmatin, Dmitri Bykov

**Slovakia** (Jan Sterbak, coach) GK—Miroslav Simonovic, Igor Murin, Rastislav Rovnianek—Zigmund Palffy, Marian Hossa, Jozef Dano, Zdeno Ciger, Lubomir Kolnik, Lubomir Sekeras, Richard Kapus, Ivan Droppa, Lubomir Visnovsky, Jan Pardavy, Zdeno Chara, Peter Pucher, Peter Bartos, Stanislav Jasecko, Daniel Babka, Richard Sechny, Radoslav Hecl, Rene Pucher, Vladimir Vlk, Jan Lipiansky

**Sweden** (Sune Bergman/Stefan Lundh, coaches) GK—Tommy Salo, Petter Ronnqvist, Johan Hedberg—Markus Naslund, Daniel Alfredsson, Niklas Sundstrom, Michael Nylander, Per Djoos, Jorgen Jonsson, Samuel Pahlsson, Christer Olsson, Anders Eriksson, Thomas Johansson, Jan Larsson, Jan Huokko, Nichlas Falk, Daniel S

**Switzerland** (Ralph Krueger, coach) GK—Reto Pavoni, David Aebischer, Pauli Jaks—Mark Streit, Patrick Fischer, Reto Von Arx, Patrik Sutter, Gian-Marco Crameri, Marcel Jenni, Mathias Seger, Ivo Ruthemann, Michel Zeiter, Patric Della Rossa, Mattia Baldi, Martin Pluss, Laurent Muller, Philippe Marquis, Sandro Rizzi, Geoffrey Vauclair, Benjamin Winkler, Sandy Jeannin, Olivier Keller, Martin Steinegger

**Ukraine** (Anatoli Bogdanov, coach) GK—Yuriy Shundrov, Olexander Vyukhin, Olexander Vasylyev—Sergiy Klimentyev, Vitaliy Lytvynenko, Oleg Synkov, Olexander Savitsky, Vasyl Bobrovnikov, Alexander Godynyuk, Viktor Goncharenko, Kostyantyn Kasyanchuk, Valentyn Oletskiy, Vadym Slivchenko, Anatoli Stepanyshev, Dmytro Markovsky, Konstyantyn Butsenko, Artyom Ostrushko, Roman Salnikov, Yuriy Gunko, Danil Didkovski, Valeri Shirayev, Vadim Shakhraychuk, Vyacheslav Zavalnyuk

**United States** (Terry Murray, coach) GK—Parris Duffus, Tim Thomas, Chris Rogles—Ted Donato, Matt Cullen, Bryan Smolinski, David Emma, Trent Klatt, Tom Bisset, Mike Mottau, Eric Weinrich, Craig Johnson, Barry Richter, Dan Keczmer, Tom Chorske, Darby Hendrickson, David Legwand, Chris Tamer, Kelly Miller, Bret Hedican, Jay Pandolfo, Scott Lachance, Mike Knuble

## 64th WORLD CHAMPIONSHIP (MEN)
## April 29-May 14, 2000
## St. Petersburg, Russia

**Final Placing**

| | | | |
|---|---|---|---|
| Gold | Czech Republic | 9th | Belarus |
| Silver | Slovakia | 10th | Norway |
| Bronze | Finland | 11th | Russia |
| 4th | Canada | 12th | Italy |
| 5th | United States | 13th | Austria |
| 6th | Switzerland | 14th | Ukraine |
| 7th | Sweden | 15th | France* |
| 8th | Latvia | 16th | Japan* |

^no teams promoted from B Pool in 1999
*demoted to Division I for 2001

**Tournament Format**

There were 16 teams in the tournament, divided into four groups of four teams each for the Preliminary Round. The top two from each group advanced to a Qualification Round which made them eligible for medals. The third place teams were put in another group for placement, and the bottom four were placed in a relegation pool, the last two being demoted. In the next round, the top two from each group advanced to a semi-finals round, the winners playing for gold, the losers for bronze.

**Results & Standings**

**GROUP A**

| | GP | W | T | L | GF | GA | P |
|---|---|---|---|---|---|---|---|
| Sweden | 3 | 3 | 0 | 0 | 17 | 3 | 6 |
| Latvia | 3 | 2 | 0 | 1 | 9 | 7 | 4 |
| Belarus | 3 | 1 | 0 | 2 | 10 | 16 | 2 |
| Ukraine | 3 | 0 | 0 | 3 | 6 | 16 | 0 |

| | | |
|---|---|---|
| April 30 | Belarus 7 | Ukraine 3 |
| April 30 | Sweden 3 | Latvia 1 |
| May 2 | Latvia 6 | Belarus 3 |
| May 2 | Sweden 7 | Ukraine 2 |
| May 4 | Latvia 2 | Ukraine 1 |
| May 4 | Sweden 7 | Belarus 0 |

**GROUP B**

| | GP | W | T | L | GF | GA | P |
|---|---|---|---|---|---|---|---|
| Slovakia | 3 | 2 | 1 | 0 | 10 | 4 | 5 |
| Finland | 3 | 1 | 2 | 0 | 11 | 5 | 4 |
| Italy | 3 | 1 | 0 | 2 | 5 | 12 | 2 |
| Austria | 3 | 0 | 1 | 2 | 3 | 8 | 1 |

| | | |
|---|---|---|
| April 30 | Finland 6 | Italy 0 |
| April 30 | Slovakia 2 | Austria 0 |
| May 2 | Slovakia 6 | Italy 2 |
| May 2 | Finland 3 | Austria 3 |
| May 4 | Italy 3 | Austria 0 |
| May 4 | Slovakia 2 | Finland 2 |

**GROUP C**

| | GP | W | T | L | GF | GA | P |
|---|---|---|---|---|---|---|---|
| Czech Republic | 3 | 3 | 0 | 0 | 12 | 4 | 6 |
| Norway | 3 | 2 | 0 | 1 | 13 | 7 | 4 |
| Canada | 3 | 1 | 0 | 2 | 10 | 6 | 2 |
| Japan | 3 | 0 | 0 | 3 | 3 | 21 | 0 |

| | | |
|---|---|---|
| April 29 | Canada 6 | Japan 0 |
| April 29 | Czech Republic 4 | Norway 0 |
| May 1 | Norway 4 | Canada 3 |
| May 1 | Czech Republic 6 | Japan 3 |
| May 3 | Czech Republic 2 | Canada 1 |
| May 3 | Norway 9 | Japan 0 |

**GROUP D**

| | GP | W | T | L | GF | GA | P |
|---|---|---|---|---|---|---|---|
| United States | 3 | 2 | 1 | 0 | 9 | 5 | 5 |
| Switzerland | 3 | 1 | 1 | 1 | 8 | 9 | 3 |
| Russia | 3 | 1 | 0 | 2 | 10 | 7 | 2 |
| France | 3 | 1 | 0 | 2 | 7 | 13 | 2 |

| | | |
|---|---|---|
| April 29 | Switzerland 3 | United States 3 |
| April 29 | Russia 8 | France 1 |
| May 1 | France 4 | Switzerland 2 |
| May 1 | United States 3 | Russia 0 |
| May 3 | Switzerland 3 | Russia 2 |
| May 3 | United States 3 | France 2 |

**RELEGATION ROUND**

**GROUP G**

| | GP | W | T | L | GF | GA | P |
|---|---|---|---|---|---|---|---|
| Austria | 3 | 2 | 1 | 0 | 11 | 8 | 5 |
| Ukraine | 3 | 2 | 0 | 1 | 9 | 5 | 4 |
| France | 3 | 1 | 1 | 1 | 12 | 8 | 3 |
| Japan | 3 | 0 | 0 | 3 | 5 | 16 | 0 |

| | | |
|---|---|---|
| May 6 | France 3 | Austria 3 |
| May 6 | Ukraine 4 | Japan 0 |
| May 7 | Ukraine 3 | France 2 |
| May 7 | Austria 5 | Japan 3 |
| May 9 | France 7 | Japan 2 |
| May 9 | Austria 3 | Ukraine 2 |

**QUALIFYING ROUND**

**GROUP E**

| | GP | W | T | L | GF | GA | P |
|---|---|---|---|---|---|---|---|
| United States | 5 | 3 | 2 | 0 | 13 | 7 | 8 |
| Switzerland | 5 | 2 | 2 | 1 | 14 | 12 | 6 |
| Sweden | 5 | 2 | 1 | 2 | 16 | 11 | 5 |
| Latvia | 5 | 2 | 1 | 2 | 12 | 13 | 5 |
| Belarus | 5 | 2 | 0 | 3 | 9 | 17 | 4 |
| Russia | 5 | 1 | 0 | 4 | 8 | 12 | 2 |

| | | |
|---|---|---|
| May 5 | Latvia 3 | Russia 2 |
| May 5 | United States 1 | Belarus 0 |
| May 6 | Sweden 1 | Switzerland 1 |
| May 7 | Belarus 1 | Russia 0 |
| May 7 | Latvia 1 | United States 1 |
| May 8 | Switzerland 4 | Latvia 1 |
| May 8 | United States 5 | Sweden 3 |
| May 9 | Belarus 5 | Switzerland 3 |
| May 9 | Russia 4 | Sweden 2 |

**GROUP F**

| | GP | W | T | L | GF | GA | P |
|---|---|---|---|---|---|---|---|
| Czech Republic | 5 | 4 | 0 | 1 | 25 | 11 | 8 |
| Finland | 5 | 3 | 1 | 1 | 22 | 15 | 7 |
| Canada | 5 | 3 | 0 | 2 | 19 | 10 | 6 |
| Slovakia | 5 | 2 | 1 | 2 | 22 | 15 | 5 |
| Norway | 5 | 1 | 1 | 3 | 10 | 24 | 3 |
| Italy | 5 | 0 | 1 | 4 | 5 | 28 | 1 |

| | | |
|---|---|---|
| May 5 | Canada 5 | Finland 1 |
| May 5 | Czech Republic 9 | Italy 2 |
| May 6 | Slovakia 9 | Norway 1 |
| May 7 | Canada 6 | Italy 0 |
| May 7 | Finland 6 | Czech Republic 4 |
| May 8 | Finland 7 | Norway 4 |
| May 8 | Czech Republic 6 | Slovakia 2 |
| May 9 | Norway 1 | Italy 1 |
| May 9 | Canada 4 | Slovakia 3 |

**PLAYOFFS**

**QUARTER-FINALS**

| | | |
|---|---|---|
| May 11 | Canada 5 | Switzerland 3 |
| May 11 | Finland 2 | Sweden 1 |
| May 11 | Czech Republic 3 | Latvia 1 |
| May 11 | Slovakia 4 | United States 1 |

**SEMI-FINALS**

| | | |
|---|---|---|
| May 12 | Czech Republic 2 | Canada 1 |
| May 12 | Slovakia 3 | Finland 1 |

**BRONZE MEDAL GAME**

| | | |
|---|---|---|
| May 14 | Finland 2 | Canada 1 |

**GOLD MEDAL GAME**

| | | |
|---|---|---|
| May 14 | Czech Republic 5 | Slovakia 3 |

**Rosters**

**Austria** (Ron Kennedy, coach) GK—Reinhard Divis, Claus Dalpiaz, Michael Suttnig—Christoph Brandner, Dieter Kalt, Simon Wheeldon, Tom Searle, Gerhard Unterluggauer, Martin Hohenberger, Matthias Trattnig, Martin Ulrich, Herbert Hohenberger, Arthur Marczell, Gerald Ressmann, Dominic Lavoie, Peter Kasper, Wolfgang Kromp, Christian Perthaler, Gregor Baumgartner, Mario Schaden, Philipp Lukas, Andre Lakos, Gunther Lanzinger

**Belarus** (Anatoli Varivonchik, coach) GK—Andrei Mezin, Leonid Fatikov, Sergei Shabanov—Vladimir Tsyplakov, Andrei Kovalyov, Sergei Stas, Alexander Andrievski, Alexei Kalyuzhny, Andrei Skabelka, Viktor Karachun, Oleg Khmyl, Vitali Valui, Vasili Pankov, Dmitri Starostenko, Yuri Krivokhizha, Oleg Romanov, Dmitri Pankov, Igor Matushkin, Ruslan Salei, Dmitri Dudik, Alexander Makritski, Vladimir Kopat, Alexander Galchenyuk

**Canada** (Tom Renney, coach) GK—Jose Theodore, Fred Brathwaite, Jamie Ram—Todd Bertuzzi, Ryan Smyth, Brad Isbister, Adrian Aucoin, Steve Sullivan, Curtis Brown, Brendan Morrison, Mike Sillinger, Mike Johnson, Ed Jovanovski, Yannick Tremblay, Jeff Finley, Trevor Letowski, Peter Schaefer, Jamal Mayers, Patrick Traverse, Kris Draper, Martin Lapointe, Chris Phillips, Robyn Regehr, Dean McAmmond, Larry Murphy, Peter Allen

**Czech Republic** (Josef Augusta, coach) GK—Roman Cechmanek, Dusan Salficky, Vladimir Hudacek—Jiri Dopita, David Vyborny, Tomas Vlasak, Michal Sykora, Vaclav Prospal, Vaclav Varada, Frantisek Kaberle, Robert Reichel, Martin Prochazka, Frantisek Kucera, Petr Cajanek, Petr Buzek, Martin Havlat, Martin Stepanek, Jan Tomajko, Pavel Patera, Martin Spanhel, Michal Bros, Ladislav Benysek, Radek Martinek

**Finland** (Hannu Aravirta, coach) GK—Pasi Nurminen, Ari Sulander, Vesa Toskala—Niko Kapanen, Juha Lind, Tomi Kallio, Kimmo Rintanen, Jukka Hentunen, Petteri Nummelin, Jyrki Lumme, Marko Tuomainen, Raimo Helminen, Olli Jokinen, Ville Peltonen, Janne Niinimaa, Esa Tikkanen, Tony Virta, Jere Karalahti, Aki Berg, Toni Lydman, Toni Sihvonen, Antti Aalto, Antti-Jussi Niemi

**France** (Stephane Sabourin, coach) GK—Cristobal Huet, Fabrice Lhenry, Patrick Rolland—Arnaud Briand, Maurice Rozenthal, Laurent Meunier, Benoit Bachelet, Jonathan Zwikel, Stephane Barin, Philippe Bozon, Francois Rozenthal, Richard Aimonetto, Denis Perez, Vincent Bachet, Yorick Treille, Pierre Allard, Gregory Dubois, Baptiste Amar, Anthony Mortas, Bob Ouellet, Jean-Marc Soghomonian, Jean-Christophe Filippin, Karl Dewolf

**Italy** (Adolf Insam, coach) GK—Andrea Carpano, Mike Rosati, Gunther Hell—Bruno Zarrillo, Mario Chitarroni, Dino Felicetti, Vezio Sacratini, Lucio Topatigh, Maurizio Mansi, Lino de Toni, Stephan Zisser, Armando Chelodi, Michele Strazzabosco, Giuseppe Busillo, Ingemar Gruber, Manuel de Toni, Stefano Margoni, Roland Ramoser, Carlo Lorenzi, Leo Insam, Armin Helfer, Georg Comploi, Chris Bartolone

**Japan** (Steve Tsujiura, coach) GK—Dusty Imoo, Shinichi Iwasaki, Masahito Haruna—Ryan Kuwabara, Yasunori Iwata, Tomohito Kobayashi, Chris Yule, Kiyoshi Fujita, Yoshikazu Kabayama, Akihito Isojima, Takayuki Kobori, Yutaka Kawaguchi, Yutaka Ono, Takahito Suzuki, Hideji Tsuchida, Yosuke Kon, Taro Nihei, Masakazu Sato, Fumitaka Miyauchi, Tatsuki Katayama, Kengo Ito, Makoto Kawashima, Hiroyuki Miura

**Latvia** (Haralds Vasiljevs, coach) GK—Arturs Irbe, Sergejs Naumovs—Aleksandrs Belavskis, Aleksandrs Nisivijs, Juris Opulskis, Aleksandrs Semjonovs, Leonids Tambijevs, Aleksandrs Kercs, Rodrigo Lavins, Karlis Skrastins, Vjaceslavs Fanduls, Gregorijs Pantelejevs, Harijs Vitolins, Andrejs Maticins, Normunds Sejejs, Herberts Vasiljevs, Aigars Cipruss, Sergejs Senins, Janis Sprukts, Artis Abols, Igors Bondarevs, Atvars Tribuncovs, Viktors Ignatjevs

**Norway** (Leif Boork, coach) GK—Robert Schistad, Vidar Wold, Bjorge Josefsen—Trond Magnussen, Per Age Skroder, Tore Vikingstad, Martin Knold, Mats Trygg, Ole Eskild Dahlstrom, Marius Trygg, Morten Fjeld, Tommy Jakobsen, Joakim Saether, Sjur Nilsen, Svein Enok Norstebo, Pal Johnsen, Stig Vesterheim, Anders Fredriksen, Mads Hansen, Martin Sellgren, Johnny Nilsen, Geir Svendsberget, Ketil Wold

**Russia** (Alexander Yakushev, coach) GK—Yegor Podomatski, Ilya Bryzgalov—Pavel Bure, Alexander Kharitonov, Maxim Sushinski, Alexander Prokopiev, Viktor Kozlov, Alexei Yashin, Oleg Petrov, Alexander Khavanov, Andrei Markov, Sergei Gonchar, Maxim Afinogenov, Alexei Zhamnov, Alexei Zhitnik, Alexei Kudashov, Andrei Nikolishin, Igor Kravchuk, Maxim Galanov, Andrei Kovalenko, Dmitri Mironov, Valeri Kamenski

**Slovakia** (Jan Filc, coach) GK—Jan Lasak, Pavol Rybar, Miroslav Lipkovsky—Miroslav Satan, Jan Pardavy, Vlastimil Plavucha, Lubomir Sekeras, Richard Kapus, Lubomir Visnovsky, Lubos Bartecko, Michal Handzus, Radoslav Suchy, Peter Bartos, Miroslav Hlinka, Michal Hreus, Peter Pucher, Lubomir Hurtaj, Lubomir Vaic, Martin Strbak, Ivan Droppa, Peter Podhradsky, Ronald Petrovicky, Stanislav Jasecko, Zdeno Chara

**Sweden** (Hardy Nilsson/Stephan Lundh, coaches) GK—Tommy Salo, Mikael Tellqvist, Andreas Hadelov—Bjorn Nord, Michael Nylander, Kristian Huselius, Daniel Sedin, Henrik Sedin, Fredrik Modin, Per-Johan Axelsson, Peter Andersson, Peter Nordstrom, Kristian Gahn, Jonas Ronnqvist, Fredrik Lindquist, Daniel Tjarnqvist, Jorgen Jonsson, Mikael Hakansson, Rikard Franzen, Mattias Norstrom, Samuel Pahlsson, Ricard Persson, Mikael Magnusson

**Switzerland** (Ralph Krueger, coach) GK—Reto Pavoni, Martin Gerber, Pauli Jaks—Gian-Marco Crameri, Patrick Fischer, Marcel Jenni, Thomas Ziegler, Patrik Sutter, Ivo Ruthemann, Reto von Arx, Edgar Salis, Olivier Keller, Michel Riesen, Alain Demuth, Flavien Conne, Claudio Micheli, Mark Streit, Patric Della Rossa, Jean-Jacques Aeschlimann, Julien Vauclair, Martin Steinegger, Rolf Ziegler, Michel Zeiter, Mathias Seger

**Ukraine** (Anatoli Bogdanov, coach) GK—Igor Karpenko, Yevgeni Brul, Vadym Seliverstov—Vitaliy Lytvynenko, Olexander Matvichuk, Sergi Varlamov, Vadim Shakhraychuk, Borys Protsenko, Olexander Savitsky, Konstantin Kalmikov, Dmitri Yakushyn, Gennady Razin, Vasyl Bobrovnikov, Vyacheslav Zavalnyuk, Valentyn Oletskiy, Sergiy Klimentyev, Oleksiy Lazarenko, Oleg Polkovnikov, Andri Voyush, Olexander Yakovenko, Ruslan Bezshasny, Bogdan Savenko, Artyom Ostrushko

**United States** (Lou Vairo, coach) GK—Robert Esche, Damian Rhodes, Karl Goehring—Phil Housley, Mike Peluso, Steve Konowalchuk, Brian Gionta, Chris Tancill, Steve Heinze, David Legwand, Jeff Nielsen, Jason Blake, Jeff Halpern, Derek Plante, Sean Haggerty, Darby Hendrickson, Eric Weinrich, Chris Luongo, Mike Mottau, Chris O'Sullivan, Eric Boguniecki, Ben Clymer, Hal Gill

## 65th WORLD CHAMPIONSHIP (MEN)
## April 28-May 13, 2001
## Hanover/Cologne/Nuremberg, Germany

**Final Placing**

Gold ........Czech Republic
Silver ......Finland
Bronze ....Sweden
4th ..........United States
5th ..........Canada
6th ..........Russia
7th ..........Slovakia
8th ..........Germany^
9th ........Switzerland
10th .......Ukraine
11th .......Austria
12th .......Italy
13th .......Latvia
14th .......Belarus*
15th .......Norway*
16th .......Japan+

+Far East qualifier
^promoted from B Pool in 2000
*demoted to Division I for 2002

**Tournament Format**

There were 16 teams in the tournament, divided into four groups of four teams each for the Preliminary Round. The top two from each group advanced to a Qualification Round which made them eligible for medals. The third place teams were put in another group for placement, and the bottom four were placed in a relegation pool, the last two being demoted. In the next round, the top two from each group advanced to a semi-finals round, the winners playing for gold, the losers for bronze.

**Results & Standings**

**GROUP A**

| | GP | W | T | L | GF | GA | P |
|---|---|---|---|---|---|---|---|
| Czech Republic | 3 | 2 | 1 | 0 | 10 | 4 | 5 |
| Germany | 3 | 1 | 1 | 1 | 5 | 5 | 3 |
| Switzerland | 3 | 1 | 0 | 2 | 7 | 8 | 2 |
| Belarus | 3 | 1 | 0 | 2 | 5 | 10 | 2 |

| | | | |
|---|---|---|---|
| April 28 | Cologne | Germany 3 | Switzerland 1 |
| April 28 | Nuremburg | Czech Republic 5 | Belarus 1 |
| April 29 | Cologne | Germany 2 | Czech Republic 2 |
| April 30 | Cologne | Switzerland 5 | Belarus 2 |
| May 1 | Nuremburg | Czech Republic 3 | Switzerland 1 |
| May 2 | Hanover | Belarus 2 | Germany 0 |

**GROUP B (NUREMBURG)**

| | GP | W | T | L | GF | GA | P |
|---|---|---|---|---|---|---|---|
| Finland | 3 | 3 | 0 | 0 | 18 | 3 | 6 |
| Slovakia | 3 | 2 | 0 | 1 | 15 | 9 | 4 |
| Austria | 3 | 1 | 0 | 2 | 4 | 12 | 2 |
| Japan | 3 | 0 | 0 | 3 | 6 | 19 | 0 |

| | | |
|---|---|---|
| April 28 | Finland 5 | Austria 1 |
| April 29 | Slovakia 8 | Japan 4 |
| April 30 | Slovakia 5 | Austria 0 |
| April 30 | Finland 8 | Japan 0 |
| May 2 | Austria 3 | Japan 2 |
| May 2 | Finland 5 | Slovakia 2 |

**GROUP C (COLOGNE)**

| | GP | W | T | L | GF | GA | P |
|---|---|---|---|---|---|---|---|
| Sweden | 3 | 2 | 1 | 0 | 12 | 4 | 5 |
| United States | 3 | 1 | 1 | 1 | 8 | 7 | 3 |
| Ukraine | 3 | 1 | 0 | 2 | 7 | 13 | 2 |
| Latvia | 3 | 1 | 0 | 2 | 6 | 9 | 2 |

| | | |
|---|---|---|
| April 28 | United States 6 | Ukraine 3 |
| April 29 | Sweden 5 | Latvia 2 |
| April 30 | Latvia 2 | United States 0 |
| May 1 | Sweden 5 | Ukraine 0 |
| May 2 | Ukraine 4 | Latvia 2 |
| May 2 | Sweden 2 | United States 2 |

**GROUP D (HANOVER)**

| | GP | W | T | L | GF | GA | P |
|---|---|---|---|---|---|---|---|
| Canada | 3 | 3 | 0 | 0 | 13 | 2 | 6 |
| Russia | 3 | 2 | 0 | 1 | 12 | 5 | 4 |
| Italy | 3 | 0 | 1 | 2 | 5 | 14 | 1 |
| Norway | 3 | 0 | 1 | 2 | 4 | 13 | 1 |

| | | |
|---|---|---|
| April 28 | Canada 5 | Norway 0 |
| April 28 | Russia 7 | Italy 0 |
| April 29 | Russia 4 | Norway 0 |
| April 30 | Canada 3 | Italy 1 |
| May 1 | Italy 1 | Norway 1 |
| May 2 | Canada 5 | Russia 1 |

**RELEGATION ROUND**
**GROUP G (NUREMBURG)**

| | GP | W | L | T | GF | GA | P |
|---|---|---|---|---|---|---|---|
| Latvia | 3 | 2 | 1 | 0 | 13 | 4 | 5 |
| Belarus | 3 | 2 | 1 | 0 | 9 | 5 | 5 |
| Norway | 3 | 0 | 1 | 2 | 5 | 9 | 1 |
| Japan | 3 | 0 | 1 | 2 | 6 | 15 | 1 |

| | | |
|---|---|---|
| May 4 | Latvia 2 | Belarus 2 |
| May 4 | Norway 3 | Japan 3 |
| May 5 | Belarus 3 | Norway 2 |
| May 5 | Latvia 8 | Japan 2 |
| May 7 | Belarus 4 | Japan 1 |
| May 7 | Latvia 3 | Norway 0 |

**QUALIFYING ROUND**
**GROUP E (HANOVER)**

| | GP | W | T | L | GF | GA | P |
|---|---|---|---|---|---|---|---|
| Czech Republic | 5 | 4 | 1 | 0 | 24 | 8 | 9 |
| Canada | 5 | 3 | 1 | 1 | 19 | 11 | 7 |
| Russia | 5 | 3 | 0 | 2 | 16 | 11 | 6 |
| Germany | 5 | 1 | 2 | 2 | 10 | 12 | 4 |
| Switzerland | 5 | 1 | 0 | 4 | 13 | 15 | 2 |
| Italy | 5 | 1 | 0 | 4 | 5 | 30 | 2 |

| | | |
|---|---|---|
| May 4 | Canada 6 | Switzerland 2 |
| May 4 | Italy 3 | Germany 1 |
| May 5 | Czech Republic 4 | Russia 3 |
| May 5 | Canada 3 | Germany 3 |
| May 6 | Russia 2 | Switzerland 1 |
| May 6 | Czech Republic 11 | Italy 0 |
| May 7 | Switzerland 8 | Italy 1 |
| May 8 | Russia 3 | Germany 1 |
| May 8 | Czech Republic 4 | Canada 2 |

**GROUP F (HANOVER)**

| | GP | W | T | L | GF | GA | P |
|---|---|---|---|---|---|---|---|
| Finland | 5 | 4 | 0 | 1 | 23 | 12 | 8 |
| Sweden | 5 | 3 | 1 | 1 | 25 | 8 | 7 |
| United States | 5 | 3 | 1 | 1 | 15 | 10 | 7 |
| Slovakia | 5 | 2 | 0 | 3 | 12 | 12 | 4 |
| Ukraine | 5 | 1 | 0 | 4 | 7 | 21 | 2 |
| Austria | 5 | 1 | 0 | 4 | 4 | 23 | 2 |

| | | |
|---|---|---|
| May 4 | Slovakia 3 | Ukraine 1 |
| May 4 | Sweden 11 | Austria 0 |
| May 5 | United States 4 | Finland 1 |
| May 5 | Sweden 3 | Slovakia 1 |
| May 6 | Austria 3 | United States 0 |
| May 6 | Finland 7 | Ukraine 1 |
| May 7 | Ukraine 2 | Austria 0 |
| May 8 | United States 3 | Slovakia 1 |
| May 8 | Finland 5 | Sweden 4 |

**PLAYOFFS**
**QUARTER-FINALS**

| | | | |
|---|---|---|---|
| May 10 | Hanover | United States 4 (Darby Hendrickson 0:32 OT) | Canada 3 |
| May 10 | Hanover | Czech Republic 2 | Slovakia 0 |
| May 10 | Cologne | Finland 4 | Germany 1 |
| May 10 | Cologne | Sweden 4 | Russia 3 (Kim Johnsson 6:03 OT) |

**SEMI-FINALS**

| | | | |
|---|---|---|---|
| May 12 | Hanover | Czech Republic 3 (10:00 OT/GWS—Viktor Ujcik) | Sweden 2 |
| May 12 | Hanover | Finland 3 | United States 1 |

**BRONZE MEDAL GAME**

| | | | |
|---|---|---|---|
| May 13 | Hanover | Sweden 3 | United States 2 |

**GOLD MEDAL GAME**

| | | | |
|---|---|---|---|
| May 13 | Hanover | Czech Republic 3 (David Moravec 10:38 OT) | Finland 2 |

**Rosters**

**Austria** (Ron Kennedy, coach) GK—Reinhard Divis, Claus Dalpiaz, Michael Suttnig—Christoph Brandner, Dieter Kalt, Simon Wheeldon, Tom Searle, Gerhard Unterluggauer, Matthias Trattnig, Martin Ulrich, Herbert Hohenberger, Gerald Ressmann, Joseph Lavoie, Peter Kasper, Wolfgang Kromp, Christian Perthaler, Mario Schaden, Philipp Lukas, Gunther Lanzinger, Andreas Pusnik, Patrick Pilloni, Oliver Setzinger, Heimo Lindner

**Belarus** (Anatoli Varivonchik, coach) GK—Andrei Mezin, Leonid Fatikov, Sergei Shabanov—Andrei Kovalyov, Sergei Stas, Alexander Andrievski, Alexei Kalyuzhny, Andrei Skabelka, Viktor Karachun, Oleg Khmyl, Vitali Valui, Vasili Pankov, Dmitri Starostenko, Oleg Romanov, Dmitri Pankov, Ruslan Salei, Vladimir Kopat, Alexander Galchenyuk, Oleg Antonenko, Sergei Yerkovich, Alexander Zhurik, Oleg Mikulchik, Konstantin Koltsov

**Canada** (Wayne Fleming, coach) GK—Roberto Luongo, Fred Brathwaite, Jean-Sebastien Giguere—Brad Richards, Scott Walker, Brad Isbister, Vincent Lecavalier, Ryan Smyth, Patrick Marleau, Michael Peca, Rem Murray, Jeff Friesen, Wes Walz, Kris Draper, Steve Sullivan, Wade Redden, Joe Thornton, Brad Stuart, Derek Morris, Kyle McLaren, Eric Brewer, Jason Smith, Daniel Marois, Stephane Robidas, Kirk Muller, Brenden Morrow

**Czech Republic** (Josef Augusta, coach) GK—Milan Hnilicka, Dusan Salficky, Vladimir Hudacek—Jiri Dopita, David Vyborny, Tomas Vlasak, Frantisek Kaberle, Robert Reichel, Martin Prochazka, Petr Cajanek, Jan Tomajko, Pavel Patera, Radek Martinek, Radek Dvorak, Viktor Ujcik, David Moravec, Martin Rucinsky, Pavel Kubina, Jaroslav Spacek, Filip Kuba, Jaroslav Hlinka, Martin Richter, Karel Pilar

**Finland** (Hannu Aravirta, coach) GK—Pasi Nurminen, Miikka Kiprusoff, Jarmo Myllys—Juha Ylonen, Petteri Nummelin, Sami Kapanen, Sami Salo, Tony Virta, Timo Parssinen, Antti Laaksonen, Raimo Helminen, Tomi Kallio, Niko Kapanen, Toni Sihvonen, Kimmo Timonen, Jukka Hentunen, Juha Lind, Kimmo Rintanen, Marko Kiprusoff, Ossi Vaananen, Jarkko Ruutu, Antti-Jussi Niemi, Aki-Petteri Berg, Janne Gronvall

**Germany** (Hans Zach, coach) GK—Christian Kunast, Robert Muller, Leonardo Conti—Marco Sturm, Daniel Kreutzer, Thomas Daffner, Klaus Kathan, Wayne Hynes, Tobias Abstreiter, Andreas Loth, Mirko Ludemann, Dennis Seidenberg, Jan Benda, Leonard Soccio, Sven Felski, Christoph Schubert, Mark MacKay, Thomas Greilinger, Heiko Smazal, Jorg Mayr, Jochen Molling, Jurgen Rumrich, Marcel Goc, Erich Goldmann, Andreas Renz

**Italy** (Pat Cortina, coach) GK—Mike Rosati, Andrea Carpano, Gunther Hell—Michael de Angelis, Vezio Sacratini, Chris Bartolone, Mario Chitarroni, Lino de Toni, Dino Felicetti, Anthony Iob, Bruno Zarrillo, Scott Beattie, Giuseppe Busillo, Maurizio Mansi, Leo Insam, Roland Ramoser, Stefano Margoni, Manuel de Toni, Armando Chelodi, Carlo Lorenzi, Larry Rucchin, Michele Strazzabosco, Armin Helfer

**Japan** (Steve Tsujiura, coach) GK—Jiro Nihei, Shinichi Iwasaki, Yutaka Fukifuji—Ryan Kuwabara, Yasunori Iwata, Chris Yule, Kiyoshi Fujita, Akihito Isojima, Yutaka Kawaguchi, Takahito Suzuki, Taro Nihei, Fumitaka Miyauchi, Tatsuki Katayama, Kengo Ito, Makoto Kawashima, Hiroyuki Miura, Makoto Kawahira, Masaki Shirono, Shin Yahata, Daniel Daikawa, Tomohiko Uchiyama, Junji Sakata, Hiroyuki Murakami

**Latvia** (Haralds Vasiljevs, coach) GK—Arturs Irbe, Sergejs Naumovs—Juris Opulskis, Aleksandrs Semjonovs, Leonids Tambijevs, Aleksandrs Kercs, Karlis Skrastins, Vjaceslavs Fanduls, Gregorijs Pantelejevs, Harijs Vitolins, Normunds Sejejs, Aigars Cipruss, Artis Abols, Atvars Tribuncovs, Viktors Ignatjevs, Sergejs Zoltoks, Sandis Ozolins, Kaspars Astasenko, Arturs Kupaks, Aleksandrs Belavskis, Aleksandrs Macijevskis, Olegs Sorokins

**Norway** (Leif Boork, coach) GK—Bjorge Josefsen, Jonas Norgren, Vidar Wold—Tore Vikingstad, Martin Knold, Mats Trygg, Marius Trygg, Morten Fjeld, Svein Enok Norstebo, Pal Johnsen, Stig Vesterheim, Anders Fredriksen, Mads Hansen, Martin Sellgren, Johnny Nilsen, Geir Svendsberget, Ketil Wold, Morten Ask, Tommy Martinsen, Bard Sorlie, Trond Magnussen, Kjell Nygard, Jan Morten Dahl

**Russia** (Boris Mikhailov, coach) GK—Maxim Sokolov, Mikhail Shtalenkov, Denis Khlopotnov—Ravil Gusmanov, Andrei Razin, Alexei Yashin, Alexander Golts, Oleg Tverdovski, Pavel Datsyuk, Anton But, Valeri Karpov, Alexander Prokopiev, Yuri Kuznetsov, Alexander Zhdan, Vitali Vishnevski, Alexander Kharitonov, Alexander Kuvaldin, Alexander Korolyuk, Andrei Yevstafiev, Dmitri Krasotkin, Sergei Zhukov, Denis Arkhipov, Oleg Orekhovski, Yevgeni Petroshinin

**Slovakia** (Jan Filc, coach) GK—Jan Lasak, Pavol Rybar, Rastislav Stana—Lubomir Sekeras, Peter Bartos, Miroslav Hlinka, Peter Pucher, Martin Strbak, Ivan Droppa, Robert Petrovicky, Vladimir Orszagh, Richard Zednik, Marian Gaborik, Ladislav Nagy, Marian Hossa, Zdeno Ciger, Richard Lintner, Richard Pavlikovsky, Zdeno Chara, Jan Pardavy, Andrej Nedorost, Radovan Somik, Branislav Mezei

**Sweden** (Hardy Nilsson, coach) GK—Tommy Salo, Mikael Tellqvist, Andreas Hadelov—Per-Johan Axelsson, Kristofer Ottosson, Kim Johnsson, Daniel Alfredsson, Mikael Renberg, Daniel Tjarnqvist, Andreas Johansson, Fredrik Modin, Kristian Huselius, Jorgen Jonsson, Mattias Ohlund, Andreas Salomonsson, Henrik Zetterberg, Leif Rohlin, Mathias Johansson, Daniel Sedin, Bjorn Nord, Henrik Sedin, Christer Olsson, Mats Sundin, Jimmie Olvestad, Peter Andersson

**Switzerland** (Ralph Krueger, coach) GK—Martin Gerber, Lars Weibel, Marco Kuhrer—Martin Pluss, Michel Riesen, Gian-Marco Crameri, Marc Reichert, Marcel Jenni, Mark Streit, Mathias Seger, Jean-Jacques Aeschlimann, Flavien Conne, Martin Steinegger, Patric Della Rossa, Alain Demuth, Edgar Salis, Julien Vauclair, Thomas Ziegler, Sandy Jeannin, Patrik Sutter, Goran Bezina, Michel Zeiter, Olivier Keller

**Ukraine** (Anatoli Bogdanov, coach) GK—Igor Karpenko, Kostyantyn Simchuk, Vadym Seliverstov—Vitaliy Lytvynenko, Olexander Matvichuk, Vadim Shakhraychuk, Borys Protsenko, Olexander Savitsky, Vasyl Bobrovnikov, Vyacheslav Zavalnyuk, Valentyn Oletskiy, Sergiy Klimentyev, Oleksiy Lazarenko, Oleg Polkovnikov, Bogdan Savenko, Artyom Ostrushko, Vadym Slivchenko, Dmitri Khristich, Valeri Shirayev, Kostyantyn Kasyanchuk, Roman Salnikov, Andri Sryubko, Vitaliy Liutkevych

**United States** (Lou Vairo, coach) GK—Robert Esche, Rick DiPietro, Ryan Miller—Tim Connolly, Darby Hendrickson, David Legwand, Bret Hedican, Jim Campbell, Doug Brown, David Tanabe, Mike Knuble, Brian Gionta, Mark Eaton, Landon Wilson, Jeff Halpern, Ryan Kraft, Craig Darby, Derek Plante, Eric Weinrich, Mark Parrish, Phil Housley, Hal Gill, Deron Quint

**66th WORLD CHAMPIONSHIP (MEN)**
**April 26-May 11, 2002**
**Gothenburg/Karlstad/Jonkoping, Sweden**

**Final Placing**

| | |
|---|---|
| Gold ........Slovakia | 9th .........Ukraine |
| Silver ......Russia | 10th .......Switzerland |
| Bronze ....Sweden | 11th .......Latvia |
| 4th ..........Finland | 12th .......Austria |
| 5th ..........Czech Republic | 13th .......Slovenia^ |
| 6th ..........Canada | 14th .......Poland^* |
| 7th ..........United States | 15th .......Italy* |
| 8th ..........Germany | 16th .......Japan+ |

+Far East qualifier
^promoted from Division I in 2001
*demoted to Division I for 2003

**Tournament Format**
There were 16 teams in the tournament, divided into four groups of four teams each for the Preliminary Round. The top two from each group advanced to a Qualification Round which made them eligible for medals. The third place teams were put in another group for placement, and the bottom four were placed in a relegation pool, the last two being demoted. In the next round, the top two from each group advanced to a semi-finals round, the winners playing for gold, the losers for bronze.

**Results & Standings**
**GROUP A (JONKOPING)**

| | GP | W | T | L | GF | GA | P |
|---|---|---|---|---|---|---|---|
| Czech Republic | 3 | 3 | 0 | 0 | 17 | 8 | 6 |
| Germany | 3 | 2 | 0 | 1 | 17 | 9 | 4 |
| Switzerland | 3 | 1 | 0 | 2 | 5 | 9 | 2 |
| Japan | 3 | 0 | 0 | 3 | 6 | 19 | 0 |

| | | |
|---|---|---|
| April 26 | Germany 9 | Japan 2 |
| April 26 | Czech Republic 5 | Switzerland 0 |
| April 28 | Germany 3 | Switzerland 0 |
| April 28 | Czech Republic 5 | Japan 3 |
| April 29 | Switzerland 5 | Japan 1 |
| April 29 | Czech Republic 7 | Germany 5 |

**GROUP B**

| | GP | W | T | L | GF | GA | P |
|---|---|---|---|---|---|---|---|
| Finland | 3 | 3 | 0 | 0 | 14 | 1 | 6 |
| Slovakia | 3 | 2 | 0 | 1 | 13 | 7 | 4 |
| Ukraine | 3 | 1 | 0 | 2 | 7 | 8 | 2 |
| Poland | 3 | 0 | 0 | 3 | 0 | 18 | 0 |

| | | | |
|---|---|---|---|
| April 27 | Gothenburg | Slovakia 7 | Poland 0 |
| April 27 | Gothenburg | Finland 3 | Ukraine 0 |
| April 29 | Gothenburg | Slovakia 5 | Ukraine 4 |
| April 29 | Gothenburg | Finland 8 | Poland 0 |
| April 30 | Gothenburg | Finland 3 | Slovakia 1 |
| April 30 | Jonkoping | Ukraine 3 | Poland 0 |

**GROUP C**

| | GP | W | T | L | GF | GA | P |
|---|---|---|---|---|---|---|---|
| Sweden | 3 | 3 | 0 | 0 | 15 | 5 | 6 |
| Russia | 3 | 2 | 0 | 1 | 14 | 6 | 4 |
| Austria | 3 | 1 | 0 | 2 | 11 | 14 | 2 |
| Slovenia | 3 | 0 | 0 | 3 | 6 | 21 | 0 |

| | | | |
|---|---|---|---|
| April 26 | Gothenburg | Russia 8 | Slovenia 1 |
| April 26 | Gothenburg | Sweden 5 | Austria 3 |
| April 28 | Gothenburg | Russia 6 | Austria 3 |
| April 28 | Gothenburg | Sweden 8 | Slovenia 2 |
| April 30 | Jonkoping | Austria 5 | Slovenia 3 |
| April 30 | Gothenburg | Sweden 2 | Russia 0 |

**GROUP D (KARLSTAD)**

| | GP | W | T | L | GF | GA | P |
|---|---|---|---|---|---|---|---|
| Canada | 3 | 3 | 0 | 0 | 11 | 2 | 6 |
| United States | 3 | 2 | 0 | 1 | 9 | 6 | 4 |
| Latvia | 3 | 1 | 0 | 2 | 7 | 8 | 2 |
| Italy | 3 | 0 | 0 | 3 | 3 | 14 | 0 |

| | | |
|---|---|---|
| April 27 | United States 5 | Italy 2 |
| April 27 | Canada 4 | Latvia 1 |
| April 29 | Canada 5 | Italy 0 |
| April 29 | United States 3 | Latvia 2 |
| April 30 | Latvia 4 | Italy 1 |
| April 30 | Canada 2 | United States 1 |

**QUALIFICATION ROUND**
**GROUP E**

| | GP | W | T | L | GF | GA | P |
|---|---|---|---|---|---|---|---|
| Czech Republic | 5 | 5 | 0 | 0 | 25 | 11 | 10 |
| Canada | 5 | 4 | 0 | 1 | 13 | 10 | 8 |
| United States | 5 | 2 | 1 | 2 | 13 | 11 | 5 |
| Germany | 5 | 2 | 1 | 2 | 14 | 14 | 5 |
| Switzerland | 5 | 1 | 0 | 4 | 8 | 18 | 2 |
| Latvia | 5 | 0 | 0 | 5 | 10 | 19 | 0 |

| | | | |
|---|---|---|---|
| May 2 | Karlstad | Canada 3 | Germany 1 |
| May 2 | Karlstad | United States 3 | Switzerland 0 |
| May 2 | Jonkoping | Czech Republic 3 | Latvia 1 |
| May 3 | Karlstad | Canada 3 | Switzerland 2 |
| May 3 | Karlstad | Germany 3 | Latvia 2 |
| May 4 | Jonkoping | Czech Republic 5 | United States 4 |
| May 5 | Jonkoping | Czech Republic 5 | Canada 1 |
| May 5 | Karlstad | Switzerland 6 | Latvia 4 |
| May 5 | Karlstad | Germany 2 | United States 2 |

**GROUP F (GOTHENBURG)**

| | GP | W | T | L | GF | GA | P |
|---|---|---|---|---|---|---|---|
| Sweden | 5 | 4 | 0 | 1 | 19 | 7 | 8 |
| Finland | 5 | 4 | 0 | 1 | 12 | 6 | 8 |
| Slovakia | 5 | 4 | 0 | 1 | 20 | 15 | 8 |
| Russia | 5 | 1 | 1 | 3 | 13 | 15 | 3 |
| Ukraine | 5 | 1 | 1 | 3 | 10 | 20 | 3 |
| Austria | 5 | 0 | 0 | 5 | 12 | 23 | 0 |

| | | |
|---|---|---|
| May 2 | Finland 3 | Austria 1 |
| May 2 | Slovakia 2 | Sweden 1 |
| May 3 | Russia 3 | Ukraine 3 |
| May 3 | Slovakia 6 | Austria 3 |
| May 4 | Sweden 7 | Ukraine 0 |
| May 4 | Finland 1 | Russia 0 |
| May 5 | Sweden 4 | Finland 2 |
| May 6 | Ukraine 3 | Austria 2 |
| May 6 | Slovakia 6 | Russia 4 |

**RELEGATION ROUND**
**GROUP G (JONKOPING)**

| | GP | W | T | L | GF | GA | P |
|---|---|---|---|---|---|---|---|
| Slovenia | 3 | 3 | 0 | 0 | 12 | 5 | 6 |
| Poland | 3 | 2 | 0 | 1 | 12 | 7 | 4 |
| Italy | 3 | 1 | 0 | 2 | 7 | 11 | 2 |
| Japan | 3 | 0 | 0 | 3 | 7 | 15 | 0 |

| | | |
|---|---|---|
| May 2 | Slovenia 4 | Japan 3 |
| May 2 | Poland 5 | Italy 1 |
| May 3 | Slovenia 4 | Poland 2 |
| May 3 | Italy 6 | Japan 2 |
| May 5 | Slovenia 4 | Italy 0 |
| May 5 | Poland 5 | Japan 2 |

**PLAYOFFS**
**QUARTER-FINALS**

| | | | |
|---|---|---|---|
| May 7 | Karlstad | Slovakia 3 | Canada 2 |
| May 7 | Gothenburg | Sweden 6 | Germany 2 |
| May 7 | Jonkoping | Russia 3 | Czech Republic 1 |
| May 7 | Gothenburg | Finland 3 | United States 1 |

**SEMI-FINALS**

| | | | |
|---|---|---|---|
| May 9 | Gothenburg | Russia 3 | Finland 2 |
| | | (10:00 OT/GWS—Valeri Karpov) | |
| May 9 | Gothenburg | Slovakia 3 | Sweden 2 |
| | | (10:00 OT/GWS—Ziggy Palffy) | |

**BRONZE MEDAL GAME**

| | | | |
|---|---|---|---|
| May 10 | Gothenburg | Sweden 5 | Finland 3 |

**GOLD MEDAL GAME**

| | | | |
|---|---|---|---|
| May 11 | Gothenburg | Slovakia 4 | Russia 3 |

**Rosters**
**Austria** (Ron Kennedy, coach) GK—Michael Suttnig, Claus Dalpiaz, Gert Prohaska—Dieter Kalt, Christoph Brandner, Joseph Lavoie, Oliver Setzinger, Andre Lakos, Philipp Lukas, Gerhard Unterluggauer, Herbert Hohenberger, Robert Lukas, Thomas Pock, Matthias Trattnig, Roland Kaspitz, Martin Ulrich, Kent Salfi, Christoph Konig, Christian Sintschnig, Mario Schaden, Christian Perthaler, Mark Szucs, Martin Hohenberger

**Canada** (Wayne Fleming, coach) GK—Marty Turco, Jean-Sebastien Giguere, Jamie Storr—Andy McDonald, Eric Brewer, Ryan Smyth, Dany Heatley, Ray Whitney, Daniel Cleary, Mike Comrie, Justin Williams, Jamie Wright, James Patrick, Tyler Wright, Steve Staios, Brad Schlegel, Richard Matvichuk, Dan McGillis, Brenden Morrow, Peter Schaefer, Darryl Sydor, Kyle Calder, Brad Ference, Manny Malhotra

**Czech Republic** (Josef Augusta, coach) GK—Milan Hnilicka, Jiri Trvaj, Dusan Salficky—Jaromir Jagr, Martin Prochazka, Pavel Kubina, Tomas Vlasak, Jaroslav Hlinka, Petr Cajanek, Pavel Patera, Viktor Ujcik, David Vyborny, Jan Hrdina, David Moravec, Rostislav Klesla, Jaroslav Spacek, Michal Sykora, Filip Kuba, Michal Bros, Frantisek Kaberle, Zdenek Sedlak, Ondrej Kratena, Martin Richter

**Finland** (Hannu Aravirta, coach) GK—Jussi Markkanen, Fredrik Norrena, Kari Lehtonen—Timo Parssinen, Niklas Hagman, Antti Miettinen, Tomi Kallio, Jere Karalahti, Kimmo Rintanen, Janne Ojanen, Janne Niinimaa, Niko Kapanen, Tom Koivisto, Kimmo Timonen, Marko Tuulola, Vesa Viitakoski, Olli Jokinen, Toni Lydman, Raimo Helminen, Petteri Nummelin, Antti Aalto, Juha Lind, Lasse Pirjeta

**Germany** (Hans Zach, coach) GK—Marc Seliger, Robert Muller, Markus Janka—Leonard Soccio, Christian Ehrhoff, Stefan Ustorf, Jan Benda, Wayne Hynes, Klaus Kathan, Andreas Morczinietz, Boris Blank, Andreas Loth, Dennis Seidenberg, Daniel Kreutzer, Jurgen Rumrich, Tobias Abstreiter, Martin Reichel, Erich Goldmann, Christoph Schubert, Jochen Molling, Eduard Lewandowski, David Sulkovsky, Tomas Martinec, Patrick Koppchen, Andreas Renz

**Italy** (Pat Cortina, coach) GK—Andrea Carpano, Mike Rosati, Mario Brunetta—Christian Timpone, Vezio Sacratini, Maurizio Mansi, Roland Ramoser, Carlo Lorenzi, Manuel de Toni, Stefano Margoni, Armin Helfer, Giuseppe Busillo, Christian Borgatello, Ingemar Gruber, Lucio Topatigh, Armando Chelodi, Lino de Toni, Georgio de Bettin, Michele Strazzabosco, Giustino Peca, Ruggero Rossi de Mio, Stefan Zisser, Chris Bartolone

**Japan** (Steve Tsujiura, coach) GK—Naoya Kikuchi, Jiro Nihei, Yutaka Fukifuji—Kiyoshi Fujita, Chris Yule, Takahito Suzuki, Takayuki Kobori, Taro Nihei, Yoshikazu Kabayama, Masatushi Ito, Toshiyuki Sakai, Ryan Kuwabara, Yasunori Iwata, Kengo Ito, Yutaka Kawaguchi, Shin Yahata, Makoto Kawashima, Tomohito Kobayashi, Yuichi Sasaki, Robert Miwa, Koichi Yamazaki, Joel Oshiro, Yosuke Kon

**Latvia** (Curt Lindstrom, coach) GK—Sergejs Naumovs, Edgars Masalskis—Aleksandrs Belavskis, Sergejs Zoltoks, Sandis Ozolins, Aigars Cipruss, Gregorijs Pantelejevs, Rodrigo Lavins, Vjaceslavs Fanduls, Olegs Sorokins, Aleksandrs Nizivijs, Leonids Tambijevs, Harijs Vitolins, Aleksandrs Kercs, Aleksandrs Semjonovs, Aleksandrs Macijevskis, Krisjanis Redlihs, Igors Bondarevs, Viktors Blinovs, Viktors Ignatjevs, Artis Abols, Atvars Tribuncovs

**Poland** (Wiktor Pysz, coach) GK—Tomasz Jaworski, Tomasz Wawrzkiewicz, Krzysztof Zborowski—Jacek Plachta, Mariusz Czerkawski, Sebastian Gonera, Krzysztof Oliwa, Waldemar Klisiak, Jaroslav Rozanski, Leszek Laszkiewicz, Adrian Parzyszek, Krzysztof Smielowski, Tomasz Demkowicz, Sebastian Labuz, Mariusz Justka, Patryk Pysz, Artur Slusarczyk, Damian Slabon, Piotr Gil, Lukasz Sokol, Michal Garbocz, Tomasz Mieszkowski, Mariusz Duleba

**Russia** (Boris Mikhailov, coach) GK—Yegor Podomatski, Maxim Sokolov, Viktor Chistov—Maxim Sushinski, Alexander Prokopiev, Valeri Karpov, Ivan Tkachenko, Alexei Koznev, Dmitri Zatonski, Dmitri Bykov, Andrei Kovalenko, Ravil Gusmanov, Maxim Afinogenov, Sergei Zhukov, Vladimir Antipov, Vyacheslav Butsayev, Dmitri Ryabikin, Roman Lyashenko, Dmitri Kalinin, Alexander Guskov, Alexander Savchenkov, Sergei Gusev, Anton Volchenkov, Alexander Yudin, Sergei Vyshedkevich

**Slovakia** (Jan Filc, coach) GK—Jan Lasak, Rastislav Stana, Miroslav Simonovic—Miroslav Satan, Peter Bondra, Richard Lintner, Zigmund Palffy, Rastislav Pavlikovsky, Dusan Milo, Michal Handzus, Vladimir Orszagh, Lubomir Bartecko, Ladislav Nagy, Robert Tomik, Lubomir Visnovsky, Radovan Somik, Robert Petrovicky, Miroslav Hlinka, Peter Pucher, Martin Strbak, Ladislav Cierny, Jozef Stumpel, Jergus Baca, Radoslav Hecl, Marek Uram, Peter Smrek

**Slovenia** (Matjaz Sekelj, coach) GK—Stan Reddick, Gaber Glavic, Robert Kristan—Marcel Rodman, Tomaz Vnuk, Dejan Kontrec, Tomaz Razingar, Nik Zupancic, Ivo Jan, Valerij Sahraj, Andrej Brodnik, Toni Tislar, Peter Rozic, Gregor Poloncic, Igor Beribak, Elvis Beslagic, Robert Ciglenecki, Miha Rebolj, Luka Zagar, Jaka Avgustincic, Gregor Krajnc, Bojan Zajc, Edo Terglav

**Sweden** (Hardy Nilsson, coach) GK—Tommy Salo, Stefan Liv, Rolf Wanhainen—Kristian Huselius, Ulf Dahlen, Mattias Weinhandl, Michael Nylander, Henrik Zetterberg, Per-Johan Axelsson, Thomas Rhodin, Niklas Andersson, Daniel Tjarnqvist, Jonas Johnson, Ronnie Sundin, Jorgen Jonsson, Andreas Johansson, Pierre Hedin, Markus Naslund, Mathias Johansson, Thomas Johansson, Niklas Falk, Johan Davidsson, Magnus Johansson, Kim Johnsson

**Switzerland** (Ralph Krueger, coach) GK—Martin Gerber, Lars Weibel, Marco Kuhrer—Jean-Jacques Aeschlimann, Sandy Jeannin, Martin Pluss, Mark Streit, Adrian Wichser, Martin Steinegger, Julien Vauclair, Ivo Ruthemann, Gian-Marco Crameri, Marc Reichert, Thierry Paterlini, Steve Hirschi, Mattia Baldi, Bjorn Christen, Martin Hohener, Thomas Ziegler, Patrick Fischer, Beat Gerber, Flavien Conne, Mathias Seger

**Ukraine** (Anatoli Bogdanov, coach) GK—Kostyantyn Simchuk, Igor Karpenko, Alexander Fedorov—Vadim Shakhraychuk, Borys Protsenko, Sergiy Klimentyev, Dmytro Tsyrul, Bogdan Savenko, Dmitri Khristich, Roman Salnikov, Valeri Shirayev, Olexander Zinevich, Vasyl Bobrovnikov, Kostyantyn Kasyanchuk, Dmitri Tolkunov, Vyacheslav Timchenko, Sergiy Kharchenko, Olexander Matvichuk, Dmytro Markovsky, Yuriy Gunko, Valentyn Oletskiy, Artyom Ostrushko, Vyacheslav Zavalnyuk

**United States** (Lou Vairo, coach) GK—Ryan Miller, Dieter Kochan, Gregg Naumenko—Richard Park, Dan LaCouture, Ted Donato, Derek Plante, Joe Sacco, Steve Konowalchuk, Andy Hilbert, Mark Mowers, Mark Eaton, Mark Murphy, Chris Clark, Eric Weinrich, Derian Hatcher, Chris Tamer, Erik Rasmussen, Todd Rohloff, Jordan Leopold, Marty Reasoner, Chris O'Sullivan, Josh De Wolf

## 67th WORLD CHAMPIONSHIP (MEN)
## April 27-May 11, 2003
## Helsinki/Tampere/Turku, Finland

**Final Placing**

| | | | |
|---|---|---|---|
| Gold | Canada | 9th | Latvia |
| Silver | Sweden | 10th | Austria |
| Bronze | Slovakia | 11th | Denmark^ |
| 4th | Czech Republic | 12th | Ukraine |
| 5th | Finland | 13th | United States |
| 6th | Germany | 14th | Belarus^* |
| 7th | Russia | 15th | Slovenia* |
| 8th | Switzerland | 16th | Japan+ |

+Far East qualifier
^promoted from Division I in 2002
*demoted to Division I for 2004

**Tournament Format**

There were 16 teams in the tournament, divided into four groups of four teams each for the Preliminary Round. The top two from each group advanced to a Qualification Round which made them eligible for medals. The third place teams were put in another group for placement, and the bottom four were placed in a relegation pool, the last two being demoted. In the next round, the top two from each group advanced to a semi-finals round, the winners playing for gold, the losers for bronze.

**Results & Standings**

**GROUP A (HELSINKI)**

| | GP | W | T | L | GF | GA | P |
|---|---|---|---|---|---|---|---|
| Slovakia | 3 | 3 | 0 | 0 | 22 | 5 | 6 |
| Germany | 3 | 2 | 0 | 1 | 9 | 8 | 4 |
| Ukraine | 3 | 1 | 0 | 2 | 9 | 13 | 2 |
| Japan | 3 | 0 | 0 | 3 | 6 | 20 | 0 |

| | | |
|---|---|---|
| April 27 | Germany 5 | Japan 4 |
| April 27 | Slovakia 9 | Ukraine 3 |
| April 28 | Slovakia 10 | Japan 1 |
| April 29 | Germany 3 | Ukraine 1 |
| April 30 | Slovakia 3 | Germany 1 |
| April 30 | Ukraine 5 | Japan 1 |

**GROUP B (TAMPERE)**

| | GP | W | T | L | GF | GA | P |
|---|---|---|---|---|---|---|---|
| Russia | 3 | 3 | 0 | 0 | 14 | 5 | 6 |
| Switzerland | 3 | 2 | 0 | 1 | 9 | 7 | 4 |
| Denmark | 3 | 1 | 0 | 2 | 8 | 14 | 2 |
| United States | 3 | 0 | 0 | 3 | 4 | 9 | 0 |

| | | |
|---|---|---|
| April 26 | Denmark 5 | United States 2 |
| April 26 | Russia 5 | Switzerland 2 |
| April 27 | Switzerland 1 | United States 0 |
| April 27 | Russia 6 | Denmark 1 |
| April 29 | Switzerland 6 | Denmark 2 |
| April 29 | Russia 3 | United States 2 |

**GROUP C (TURKU)**

| | GP | W | T | L | GF | GA | P |
|---|---|---|---|---|---|---|---|
| Canada | 3 | 3 | 0 | 0 | 12 | 2 | 6 |
| Sweden | 3 | 2 | 0 | 1 | 6 | 5 | 4 |
| Latvia | 3 | 1 | 0 | 2 | 6 | 9 | 2 |
| Belarus | 3 | 0 | 0 | 3 | 1 | 9 | 0 |

| | | |
|---|---|---|
| April 26 | Canada 3 | Belarus 0 |
| April 26 | Sweden 3 | Latvia 1 |
| April 27 | Canada 6 | Latvia 1 |
| April 27 | Sweden 2 | Belarus 1 |
| April 29 | Latvia 4 | Belarus 0 |
| April 29 | Canada 3 | Sweden 1 |

**GROUP D**

| | GP | W | T | L | GF | GA | P |
|---|---|---|---|---|---|---|---|
| Czech Republic | 3 | 3 | 0 | 0 | 15 | 4 | 6 |
| Finland | 3 | 2 | 0 | 1 | 18 | 3 | 4 |
| Austria | 3 | 1 | 0 | 2 | 8 | 15 | 2 |
| Slovenia | 3 | 0 | 0 | 3 | 4 | 23 | 0 |

| | | | |
|---|---|---|---|
| April 26 | Helsinki | Czech Republic 5 | Slovenia 2 |
| April 26 | Helsinki | Finland 5 | Austria 1 |
| April 28 | Tampere | Finland 12 | Slovenia 0 |
| April 28 | Helsinki | Czech Republic 8 | Austria 1 |
| April 29 | Helsinki | Austria 6 | Slovenia 2 |
| April 30 | Turku | Czech Republic 2 | Finland 1 |

**RELEGATION ROUND**
**GROUP G (TAMPERE)**

| | GP | W | T | L | GF | GA | P |
|---|---|---|---|---|---|---|---|
| United States | 3 | 3 | 0 | 0 | 19 | 5 | 6 |
| Belarus | 3 | 2 | 0 | 1 | 9 | 8 | 4 |
| Slovenia | 3 | 0 | 1 | 2 | 8 | 14 | 1 |
| Japan | 3 | 0 | 1 | 2 | 5 | 14 | 1 |

| | | |
|---|---|---|
| May 2 | United States 7 | Slovenia 2 |
| May 2 | Belarus 3 | Japan 1 |
| May 3 | Japan 3 | Slovenia 3 |
| May 3 | United States 4 | Belarus 2 |
| May 5 | Belarus 4 | Slovenia 3 |
| May 5 | United States 8 | Japan 1 |

**QUALIFICATION ROUND**
**GROUP E (HELSINKI)**

| | GP | W | T | L | GF | GA | P |
|---|---|---|---|---|---|---|---|
| Slovakia | 5 | 4 | 1 | 0 | 27 | 9 | 9 |
| Czech Republic | 5 | 4 | 1 | 0 | 22 | 7 | 9 |
| Finland | 5 | 2 | 1 | 2 | 18 | 10 | 5 |
| Germany | 5 | 2 | 1 | 2 | 11 | 11 | 5 |
| Austria | 5 | 1 | 0 | 4 | 9 | 27 | 2 |
| Ukraine | 5 | 0 | 0 | 5 | 8 | 31 | 0 |

| | | |
|---|---|---|
| May 2 | Slovakia 5 | Finland 1 |
| May 2 | Czech Republic 5 | Ukraine 2 |
| May 3 | Germany 5 | Austria 1 |
| May 3 | Finland 9 | Ukraine 0 |
| May 4 | Slovakia 7 | Austria 1 |
| May 4 | Czech Republic 4 | Germany 0 |
| May 5 | Slovakia 3 | Czech Republic 3 |
| May 6 | Austria 5 | Ukraine 2 |
| May 6 | Finland 2 | Germany 2 |

**GROUP F (TURKU)**

| | GP | W | T | L | GF | GA | P |
|---|---|---|---|---|---|---|---|
| Canada | 5 | 4 | 1 | 0 | 18 | 6 | 9 |
| Sweden | 5 | 4 | 0 | 1 | 20 | 9 | 8 |
| Russia | 5 | 2 | 0 | 3 | 16 | 14 | 4 |
| Switzerland | 5 | 2 | 0 | 3 | 14 | 16 | 4 |
| Latvia | 5 | 2 | 0 | 3 | 10 | 16 | 4 |
| Denmark | 5 | 0 | 1 | 4 | 8 | 25 | 1 |

| | | |
|---|---|---|
| May 2 | Canada 2 | Denmark 2 |
| May 2 | Sweden 4 | Russia 2 |
| May 3 | Switzerland 4 | Latvia 2 |
| May 3 | Sweden 7 | Denmark 1 |
| May 4 | Latvia 2 | Russia 1 |
| May 4 | Canada 2 | Switzerland 0 |
| May 5 | Canada 5 | Russia 2 |
| May 6 | Latvia 4 | Denmark 2 |
| May 6 | Sweden 5 | Switzerland 2 |

**PLAYOFFS**
**QUARTER-FINALS**

| | | | |
|---|---|---|---|
| May 7 | Turku | Canada 3 (Eric Brewer 0:37 OT) | Germany 2 |
| May 7 | Helsinki | Slovakia 3 | Switzerland 1 |
| May 7 | Turku | Czech Republic 3 | Russia 0 |
| May 7 | Helsinki | Sweden 6 | Finland 5 |

**SEMI-FINALS**

| | | | |
|---|---|---|---|
| May 9 | Helsinki | Canada 8 | Czech Republic 4 |
| May 9 | Helsinki | Sweden 4 | Slovakia 1 |

**BRONZE MEDAL GAME**

| | | | |
|---|---|---|---|
| May 10 | Helsinki | Slovakia 4 | Czech Republic 2 |

**GOLD MEDAL GAME**

| | | | |
|---|---|---|---|
| May 11 | Helsinki | Canada 3 | Sweden 2 (Anson Carter 13:49 OT) |

**Rosters**

**Austria** (Herbert Pock, coach) GK—Claus Dalpiaz, Michael Suttnig, Gert Prohaska—Raimund Divis, Martin Hohenberger, Daniel Welser, Philipp Lukas, Andre Lakos, Christoph Brandner, Rob Doyle, Robert Lukas, Dieter Kalt, Thomas Pock, Mark Szucs, Gerhard Unterluggauer, Oliver Setzinger, Christian Perthaler, Matthias Trattnig, Herbert Hohenberger, Kent Salfi, Thomas Koch, Peter Kasper, Philippe Lakos

**Belarus** (Vladimir Krikunov, coach) GK—Sergei Shabanov, Andrei Mezin, Leonid Grishukevich—Vladimir Tsyplakov, Dmitri Pankov, Alexei Kalyuzhny, Sergei Zadelenov, Alexander Makritski, Alexander Ryadinsky, Andrei Kostitsyn, Andrei Rasolko, Alexei Strakhov, Yaroslav Chuprys, Andrei Kovalyov, Alexander Alexeyev, Yevgeni Yesaulov, Oleg Khmyl, Vadim Karaga, Dmitri Starostenko, Vladimir Kopat, Gennadi Savilov, Sergei Stas, Vadim Bekbulatov, Sergei Yerkovich, Alexander Zhurik

**Canada** (Andy Murray, coach) GK—Sean Burke, Roberto Luongo, Martin Biron—Daniel Briere, Dany Heatley, Shawn Horcoff, Jay Bouwmeester, Shane Doan, Steve Reinprecht, Mike Comrie, Mathieu Dandenault, Ryan Smyth, Kirk Maltby, Patrick Marleau, Anson Carter, Cory Cross, Eric Brewer, Steve Staios, Kris Draper, Kyle Calder, Craig Rivet, Krys Kolanos, Jamie Heward

**Czech Republic** (Slavomir Lener, coach) GK—Tomas Vokoun, Roman Malek, Jiri Trvaj—Martin Straka, Robert Reichel, Petr Kadlec, Tomas Kaberle, Milan Hejduk, Jan Hlavac, Radim Vrbata, Jiri Hudler, Jaroslav Spacek, David Vyborny, Radek Duda, Jaroslav Hlinka, Jaroslav Modry, Josef Vasicek, Pavel Trnka, Jaroslav Balastik, Michal Sup, Pavel Kolarik, Jindrich Kotrla, Martin Richter, Milan Michalek, Jan Hejda

**Denmark** (Mikael Lundstrom, coach) GK—Jan Jensen, Peter Hirsch, Michael Madsen—Ronny Larsen, Kim Staal, Soren True, Lars Molgaard, Frederik Akesson, Jens Nielsen, Morten Green, Mike Grey, Lasse Degn, Daniel Jensen, Jesper Damgaard, Bo Nordby-Andersen, Mads True, Jesper Duus, Daniel Nielsen, Thor Dresler, Nicolas Monberg, Andreas Andreasen, Frans Nielsen, Thomas Johnsen

**Finland** (Hannu Aravirta, coach) GK—Jani Hurme, Pasi Nurminen, Kari Lehtonen—Teemu Selanne, Saku Koivu, Kimmo Rintanen, Ville Peltonen, Kimmo Timonen, Tomi Kallio, Esa Pirnes, Petteri Nummelin, Aki-Petteri Berg, Ossi Vaananen, Toni Lydman, Niklas Hagman, Olli Jokinen, Janne Niinimaa, Mikko Eloranta, Lasse Pirjeta, Marko Kiprusoff, Antti Miettinen, Tommi Santala, Sami Helenius, Tony Virta, Juha Ylonen

**Germany** (Hans Zach, coach) GK—Oliver Jonas, Robert Muller, Alexander Jung—Leonard Soccio, Mirko Ludemann, Andreas Morczinietz, Daniel Kreutzer, Jan Benda, Marcel Goc, Tino Boos, Eduard Lewandowski, Sven Felski, Martin Reichel, Tobias Abstreiter, Stephan Retzer, Klaus Kathan, Sascha Goc, Boris Blank, Lasse Kopitz, Tomas Martinec, Daniel Kunce, Jochen Molling, Christian Hommel, Andreas Renz, Christian Ehrhoff

**Japan** (Timo Tuomi, coach) GK—Jiro Nihei, Masahito Haruna, Naoya Kikuchi—Chris Yule, Masatoshi Ito, Makoto Kawashima, Joel Oshiro, Ryan Kuwabara, Takahito Suzuki, Kunihiko Sakurai, Daisuke Obara, Kengo Ito, Tetsuya Saito, Koichi Yamazaki, Shuji Masuko, Yoshikazu Kabayama, Tomohito Kobayashi, Fumitaka Miyauchi, Yosuke Kon, Keiji Sasaki, Yutaka Kawaguchi, Daniel Daikawa, Tomohiko Uchiyama, Nobuhiro Sugawara, Takeshi Saito

**Latvia** (Curt Lindstrom, coach) GK—Arturs Irbe, Sergejs Naumovs, Edgars Masalskis—Karlis Skrastins, Gregorijs Pantelejevs, Olegs Sorokins, Aleksandrs Kercs, Vjaceslavs Fanduls, Vadims Romanovskis, Sergejs Cubars, Leonids Tambijevs, Aigars Cipruss, Janis Sprukts, Rodrigo Lavins, Aleksejs Sirokovs, Girts Ankipans, Aleksandrs Semjonovs, Vents Feldmanis, Aleksandrs Macijevskis, Krisjanis Redlihs, Arvids Rekis, Aleksandrs Nizivijs, Atvars Tribuncovs

**Russia** (Vladimir Plyushev, coach) GK—Yegor Podomatski, Maxim Sokolov, Andrei Tsarev—Alexander Frolov, Pavel Datsyuk, Ilya Kovalchuk, Vladimir Antipov, Oleg Saprykin, Alexander Suglobov, Denis Arkhipov, Igor Grigorenko, Sergei Gusev, Sergei Soin, Sergei Zinoviev, Dmitri Kalinin, Vitali Proshkin, Alexander Khavanov, Dmitri Yerofeyev, Alexei Kaigorodov, Alexander Zhdan, Alexander Syomin, Ivan Novoseltsev, Alexander Guskov, Vasili Turkovski, Sergei Vyshedkevich

**Slovakia** (Frantisek Hossa, coach) GK—Pavol Rybar, Jan Lasak, Rastislav Stana—Zigmund Palffy, Jozef Stumpel, Lubomir Visnovsky, Miroslav Satan, Richard Zednik, Ladislav Nagy, Martin Strbak, Peter Bondra, Miroslav Hlinka, Richard Kapus, Pavol Demitra, Richard Lintner, Branko Radivojevic, Vladimir Orszagh, Radoslav Suchy, Robert Svehla, Lubomir Vaic, Dusan Milo, Ladislav Cierny, Zdeno Ciger, Peter Sejna, Ivan Majesky

**Slovenia** (Matjaz Sekelj, coach) GK—Gaber Glavic, Robert Kristan, Klemen Mohoric—Tomaz Vnuk, Ivo Jan, Tomaz Razingar, Dejan Kontrec, Marcel Rodman, Gregor Por, Damjan Dervaric, Ales Krajnc, Jurij Golicic, Elvis Beslagic, Andrej Brodnik, Boris Pretnar, Anze Terlikar, Mitja Sivic, Peter Rozic, Luka Zagar, Jaca Avgustincic, Robert Ciglenecki, Bojan Zajc, Edo Terglav, Miha Rebolj, Gregor Polончic

**Sweden** (Hardy Nilsson, coach) GK—Mikael Tellqvist, Tommy Salo, Henrik Lundqvist—Mats Sundin, Peter Forsberg, Peter Nordstrom, Per-Johan Axelsson, Henrik Zetterberg, Jorgen Jonsson, Niklas Andersson, Mikael Renberg, Jonas Hoglund, Dick Tarnstrom, Ronnie Sundin, Daniel Tjarnqvist, Mattias Norstrom, Mika Hannula, Mathias Tjarnqvist, Thomas Rhodin, Johan Davidsson, Marcus Nilson, Per Gustafsson, Niklas Kronwall, Mathias Johansson, Magnus Johansson

**Switzerland** (Ralph Krueger, coach) GK—Marco Buhrer, Lars Weibel, Tobias Stephan—Martin Pluss, Patrick Fischer, Mathias Seger, Mark Streit, Beat Forster, Goran Bezina, Adrian Wichser, Thierry Paterlini, Luca Cereda, Olivier Keller, Patrik Bartschi, Bjorn Christen, Flavien Conne, Jean-Jacques Aeschlimann, Valentin Wirz, Severin Blindenbacher, Sandy Jeannin, Patrick Fischer, Marcel Jenni, Patrick Della Rossa, Lukas Gerber, Martin Steinegger

**Ukraine** (Anatoli Bogdanov, coach) GK—Igor Karpenko, Kostyantyn Simchuk, Vadim Seliverstov—Borys Protsenko, Vadim Shakhraychuk, Ruslan Bezshasny, Vitaliy Lytvynenko, Valeri Shirayev, Sergiy Kharchenko, Roman Salnikov, Sergiy Klimentyev, Olexander Zinevich, Vasyl Bobrovnikov, Vyacheslav Zavalnyuk, Kostyantyn Kasyanchuk, Sergi Varlamov, Artyom Hnidenko, Dmitri Khristich, Artyom Ostruchko, Bogdan Savenko, Andri Nikolayev, Andri Sryubko, Yuriy Gunko, Vyacheslav Timchenko

**United States** (Lou Vairo, coach) GK—Damian Rhodes, Ryan Miller, Chris Rogles—John Pohl, Kelly Fairchild, Peter Ferraro, Adam Hall, Ted Drury, Craig Johnson, Marty Reasoner, Jordan Leopold, Matt Cullen, Brett Hauer, Phil Housley, Brad Defauw, Kevin Miller, Chris Ferraro, Jim Fahey, Mike Mottau, Francis Bouillon, Joe Corvo, John Gruden, Niko Dimitrakos

## 68th WORLD CHAMPIONSHIP (MEN)
## April 24-May 9, 2004
## Prague/Ostrava, Czech Republic

**Final Placing**

| | |
|---|---|
| Gold ........Canada | 9th .........Germany |
| Silver ......Sweden | 10th .......Russia |
| Bronze ....United States | 11th .......Austria |
| 4th..........Slovakia | 12th .......Denmark |
| 5th..........Czech Republic | 13th .......Kazakhstan^ |
| 6th..........Finland | 14th .......Ukraine |
| 7th..........Latvia | 15th .......Japan+* |
| 8th..........Switzerland | 16th .......France^* |

+Far East qualifier (final year of exemption)
^promoted from Division I in 2003
*demoted to Division I for 2005

**Tournament Format**

Teams were divided into four groups of four teams each for the Preliminary Round. The top three teams from each group advanced to the Qualification Round. The bottom four were placed in a relegation pool, with the last two being relegated. In the Qualifying Round, the top four from advanced to a cross-over quarter-final.

**Results & Standings**

**GROUP A (PRAGUE)**

| | GP | W | T | L | GF | GA | P |
|---|---|---|---|---|---|---|---|
| Czech Republic | 3 | 3 | 0 | 0 | 15 | 2 | 6 |
| Latvia | 3 | 1 | 1 | 1 | 5 | 5 | 3 |
| Germany | 3 | 1 | 1 | 1 | 6 | 8 | 3 |
| Kazakhstan | 3 | 0 | 0 | 3 | 3 | 14 | 0 |

| | | |
|---|---|---|
| April 24 | Czech Republic 3 | Latvia 1 |
| April 24 | Germany 4 | Kazakhstan 2 |
| April 26 | Germany 1 | Latvia 1 |
| April 26 | Czech Republic 7 | Kazakhstan 0 |
| April 27 | Latvia 3 | Kazakhstan 1 |
| April 28 | Czech Republic 5 | Germany 1 |

**GROUP B (OSTRAVA)**

| | GP | W | T | L | GF | GA | P |
|---|---|---|---|---|---|---|---|
| Slovakia | 3 | 2 | 1 | 0 | 10 | 5 | 5 |
| **Finland** | 3 | 2 | 0 | 1 | 11 | 8 | 4 |
| United States | 3 | 1 | 1 | 1 | 12 | 8 | 3 |
| Ukraine | 3 | 0 | 0 | 3 | 2 | 14 | 0 |

| | | |
|---|---|---|
| April 24 | Slovakia 2 | Ukraine 0 |
| April 24 | Finland 4 | United States 2 |
| April 26 | Finland 5 | Ukraine 1 |
| April 26 | Slovakia 3 | United States 3 |
| April 28 | United States 7 | Ukraine 1 |
| April 28 | Slovakia 5 | Finland 2 |

**GROUP C (OSTRAVA)**

| | GP | W | T | L | GF | GA | P |
|---|---|---|---|---|---|---|---|
| Sweden | 3 | 3 | 0 | 0 | 13 | 4 | 6 |
| Russia | 3 | 2 | 0 | 1 | 14 | 6 | 4 |
| Denmark | 3 | 1 | 0 | 2 | 7 | 14 | 2 |
| Japan | 3 | 0 | 0 | 3 | 5 | 15 | 0 |

| | | |
|---|---|---|
| April 24 | Sweden 5 | Denmark 1 |
| April 25 | Russia 6 | Denmark 2 |
| April 25 | Sweden 5 | Japan 1 |
| April 27 | Denmark 4 | Japan 3 |
| April 27 | Sweden 3 | Russia 2 |
| April 28 | Russia 6 | Japan 1 |

**GROUP D (PRAGUE)**

| | GP | W | T | L | GF | GA | P |
|---|---|---|---|---|---|---|---|
| Canada | 3 | 2 | 1 | 0 | 8 | 3 | 5 |
| Austria | 3 | 1 | 2 | 0 | 12 | 6 | 4 |
| Switzerland | 3 | 1 | 1 | 1 | 11 | 7 | 3 |
| France | 3 | 0 | 0 | 3 | 0 | 15 | 0 |

| | | |
|---|---|---|
| April 24 | Austria 6 | France 0 |
| April 25 | Switzerland 6 | France 0 |
| April 25 | Canada 2 | Austria 2 |
| April 27 | Canada 3 | France 0 |
| April 27 | Austria 4 | Switzerland 4 |
| April 28 | Canada 3 | Switzerland 1 |

**RELEGATION ROUND**

| | GP | W | T | L | GF | GA | P |
|---|---|---|---|---|---|---|---|
| Kazakhstan | 3 | 2 | 1 | 0 | 12 | 5 | 5 |
| Ukraine | 3 | 1 | 2 | 0 | 10 | 6 | 4 |
| Japan | 3 | 0 | 2 | 1 | 7 | 9 | 2 |
| France | 3 | 0 | 1 | 2 | 4 | 13 | 1 |

| | | | |
|---|---|---|---|
| April 30 | Prague | Kazakhstan 5 | France 0 |
| April 30 | Ostrava | Ukraine 2 | Japan 2 |
| May 1 | Prague | Kazakhstan 5 | Japan 3 |
| May 2 | Prague | Ukraine 6 | France 2 |
| May 3 | Prague | Ukraine 2 | Kazakhstan 2 |
| May 4 | Prague | France 2 | Japan 2 |

**QUALIFYING ROUND**
**GROUP E (PRAGUE)**

| | GP | W | T | L | GF | GA | P |
|---|---|---|---|---|---|---|---|
| Czech Republic | 5 | 5 | 0 | 0 | 19 | 5 | 10 |
| Canada | 5 | 3 | 1 | 1 | 15 | 10 | 7 |
| Latvia | 5 | 1 | 2 | 2 | 8 | 9 | 4 |
| Switzerland | 5 | 1 | 2 | 2 | 8 | 11 | 4 |
| Germany | 5 | 1 | 1 | 3 | 6 | 14 | 3 |
| Austria | 5 | 0 | 2 | 3 | 9 | 16 | 2 |

| | | |
|---|---|---|
| April 30 | Canada 2 | Latvia 0 |
| April 30 | Czech Republic 2 | Austria 0 |
| May 1 | Latvia 1 | Switzerland 1 |
| May 1 | Germany 3 | Austria 1 |
| May 2 | Czech Republic 3 | Switzerland 1 |
| May 2 | Canada 6 | Germany 1 |
| May 3 | Latvia 5 | Austria 2 |
| May 3 | Czech Republic 6 | Canada 2 |
| May 4 | Switzerland 1 | Germany 0 |

**GROUP F (OSTRAVA)**

| | GP | W | T | L | GF | GA | P |
|---|---|---|---|---|---|---|---|
| Slovakia | 5 | 3 | 2 | 0 | 18 | 5 | 8 |
| Sweden | 5 | 3 | 2 | 0 | 12 | 5 | 8 |
| Finland | 5 | 3 | 1 | 1 | 17 | 8 | 7 |
| United States | 5 | 2 | 1 | 2 | 17 | 15 | 5 |
| Russia | 5 | 1 | 0 | 4 | 10 | 14 | 2 |
| Denmark | 5 | 0 | 0 | 5 | 6 | 33 | 0 |

| | | |
|---|---|---|
| April 30 | Sweden 1 | Finland 1 |
| April 30 | Slovakia 2 | Russia 0 |
| May 1 | Finland 6 | Denmark 0 |
| May 1 | United States 3 | Russia 2 |
| May 2 | Slovakia 8 | Denmark 0 |
| May 2 | Sweden 3 | United States 1 |
| May 3 | Finland 4 | Russia 0 |
| May 3 | Slovakia 0 | Sweden 0 |
| May 4 | United States 8 | Denmark 3 |

**PLAYOFFS (PRAGUE)**
**QUARTER-FINALS**

| | | |
|---|---|---|
| May 5 | Sweden 4 | Latvia 1 |
| May 5 | United States 3 | Czech Republic 2 (10:00 OT/GWS—Andy Roach) |
| May 6 | Canada 5 | Finland 4 (Dany Heatley 5:33 OT) |
| May 6 | Slovakia 3 | Switzerland 1 |

**SEMI-FINALS**

| | | |
|---|---|---|
| May 8 | Canada 2 | Slovakia 1 |
| May 8 | Sweden 3 | United States 2 |

**BRONZE MEDAL GAME**

| | | |
|---|---|---|
| May 9 | United States 1 | Slovakia 0 (10:00 OT/GWS—Andy Roach) |

**GOLD MEDAL GAME**

| | | |
|---|---|---|
| May 9 | Canada 5 | Sweden 3 |

**Rosters**

**Austria** (Herbert Pock, coach) GK—Reinhard Divis, Bernd Bruckler, Claus Dalpiaz—Sven Klimbacher, Andre Lakos, Philippe Lakos, Robert Lukas, Thomas Pock, Johannes Reichel, Martin Ulrich, Gerhard Unterluggauer, Raimund Divis, Christoph Harand, Phillippe Horsky, Dieter Kalt, Thomas Koch, Phillip Lukas, Roland Kaspitz, Markus Peitner, Oliver Setzinger, Mark Szucs, Matthias Trattnig, Daniel Welser, David Schuller, Oliver Setzinger, Thomas Vanek

**Canada** (Mike Babcock, coach) GK—Roberto Luongo, J.S. Giguere, Marc Denis—Jay Bouwmeester, Eric Brewer, Jamie Heward, Willie Mitchell, Derek Morris, Scott Niedermayer, Nick Schultz, Steve Staios, Patrice Bergeron, Daniel Briere, Matt Cooke, J-P Dumont, Jeff Friesen, Dany Heatley, Shawn Horcoff, Brendan Morrison, Brenden Morrow, Glen Murray, Rob Niedermayer, Jeff Shantz, Ryan Smyth, Justin Williams

**Czech Republic** (Slavomir Lener, coach) GK—Tomas Vokoun, Roman Cechmanek—Roman Hamrlik, Jan Hejda, Frantisek Kaberle, Jan Novak, Martin Skoula, Jiri Slegr, Jaroslav Spacek, Josef Beranek, Jiri Dopita,Radek Dvorak, Martin Havlat, Jan Hlavac, Jaroslav Hlinka, Jaromir Jagr, Milan Kraft, Vaclav Prospal, Petr Prucha, Martin Rucinsky, Martin Straka, Michal Sup, David Vyborny

**Denmark** (Mikael Lundstrom, coach) GK—Peter Hirsch, Jan Jensen, Michael Madsen—Andreas Andreasen, Morten Dahlmann, Jesper Damgaard, Jesper Duus, Dan Jensen, Thomas Johnsen, Daniel Nielsen, Christian Schioldan, Bo Nordby Andersen, Bent Christensen, Kasper Degn, Thor Dresler, Morten Green, Mike Grey, Ronny Larsen, Nicolas Monberg, Frans Nielsen, Jens Nielsen, Michael Smidt, Kim Staal, Alexander Sundberg, Mads True

**Finland** (Raimo Summanen, coach) GK—Mika Noronen, Fredrik Norrena, Jussi Markkanen—Jere Karalahti, Tuukka Mantyla, Antti-Jussi Niemi, Janne Niinimaa, Petteri Nummelin, Sami Salo, Toni Soderholm, Niklas Hagman, Jukka Hentunen, Tomi Kallio, Niko Kapanen, Olli Jokinen, Antti Laaksonen, Timo Parssinen, Ville Peltonen, Lasse Pirjeta, Esa Pirnes, Kimmo Rintanen, Jarkko Ruutu, Tony Virta, Jari Viuhkola

**France** (Heikki Leime, coach) GK—Cristobal Huet, Fabrice Lhenry, Patrick Rolland—Baptiste Amar, Vincent Bachet, Allan Carriou, Karl Dewolf, Nicolas Favarin, Christian Pouget, Nicolas Pousset, Lilian Prunet, Benoit Bachelet, P-E Bellemare, Sebastien Bordeleau, Arnaud Briand, Brice Chauvel, Olivier Coqueux, Xavier Daramy, David Dostal, Laurent Gras, Anthony Mortas, Francois Rozenthal, Maurice Rozenthal, Jonathan Zwikel

**Germany** (Hans Zach, coach) GK—Olaf Kolzig, Robert Muller, Oliver Jonas—Jan Benda, Erich Goldmann, Daniel Kunce, Robert Leask, Mirko Ludemann, Jochen Molling, Andreas Renz, Stephan Retzer, Heiko Smazal, Tobias Abstreiter, Boris Blank,Tino Boos,Thomas Greilinger, Jochen Hecht, Klaus Kathan, Daniel Kreutzer, Eduard Lewandowski, Tomas Martinec, Andreas Morczinietz, Martin Reichel, Christoph Ullmann, Stefan Ustorf

**Japan** (Mark Mahon,coach) GK—Yutaka Fukufuji, Jiro Nihei, Junji Ogino—Kengo Ito, Makoto Kawashima, Takavuki Kobori, Fumitaka Miyauchi, Hirovuki Miura, Joel Oshiro, Nobuhiro Sugawara, Junichi Takahashi, Chris Bright, Kivoshi Fujita, Yasunori Iwata, Tomohito Kobayashi, Yosuke Kon, Masatushi Ito, Yasunori Iwata, Shuji Matsuko, Robert Miwa, Daisuke Obara, Takeshi Saito, Kunihiko Sakurai, Hiroshi Sato, Takahito Suzuki, Chris Yule

**Kazakhstan** (Nikolai Myshyagin, coach) GK—Vitali Yeremeyev, Vitali Kolesnik, Sergei Tambulov—Vladimir Antipin, Artyom Argokov, Oleg Kovalenko, Yevgeni Kuzmin, Yevgeni Mazunin, Sergei Nevstruyev, Andrei Savenkov, Denis Shemelin, Alexei Troshinski, Sergei Alexandrov, Dmitri Dudarev, Anatoli Filatov, Anton Komissarov, Alexander Koreshkov, Yevgeni Koreshkov, Roman Kozlov, Fyodor Polischuk, Vadim Rifel, Andrei Samokhvalov, Andrei Troshinski, Dmitri Upper, Rustam Yesirkenov

**Latvia** (Curt Lindstrom, coach) GK—Arturs Irbe, Sergejs Naumovs, Edgars Masalskis—Viktors Ignatjevs, Krisjanis Redlihs, Arvids Rekis, Agris Saviels, Normunds Sejejs, Olegs Sorokins, Atvars Tribuncovs, Aigars Cipruss, Vjaceslavs Fanduls, Aleksandrs Kercs, Aleksandrs Macijevskis, Aleksandrs Nizivijs, Juris Ozols, Grigorijs Pantelejevs, Vadims Romanovskis, Aleksandrs Semjonovs, Alekseis Sirokovs, Leonids Tambijevs, Herberts Vasiljevs, Sergejs Zoltoks

**Russia** (Viktor Tikhonov, coach) GK—Maxim Sokolov, Yegor Podomatski, Alexander Fomichev—Dmitri Bykov, Alexander Guskov, Dmitri Kalinin, Maxim Kondratiev, Vitali Proshkin, Andrei Skopintsev, Vasili Turkovski, Oleg Tverdovski, Dmitri Yushkevich, Maxim Afinogenov, Vladimir Antipov, Andrei Bashkirov, Vyacheslav Butsayev, Ilya Kovalchuk, Alexei Morozov, Alexander Ovechkin, Nikolai Pronin, Alexander Prokopiev, Alexander Skugarev, Maxim Sushinski, Alexei Yashin, Valeri Zelepukin

**Slovakia** (Frantisek Hossa, coach) GK—Jan Lasak, Karol Krizan, Rastislav Stana—Zdeno Chara, Ladislav Cierny, Dominik Granak, Richard Lintner, Ivan Majesky, Andrei Meszaros, Branislav Mezei, Martin Strbak, Lubos Bartecko, Pavol Demitra, Marian Gaborik, Marian Hossa, Richard Kapus, Juraj Kolnik, Roman Kukumberg, Vladimir Orszagh, Rastislav Pavlikovsky, Ronald Petrovicky, Miroslav Satan, Juraj Stefanka, Jozef Stumpel

**Sweden** (Hardy Nilsson, coach) GK—Henrik Lundqvist, Stefan Liv, Daniel Henriksson—Christian Backman, Per Hallberg, Niclas Havelid, Nicklas Lidstrom, Ronnie Sundin, Dick Tarnstrom, Daniel Tjarnqvist, Daniel Alfredsson, Niklas Andersson, Per-Johan Axelsson, Johan Davidsson, Peter Forsberg, Jonathan Hedstrom, Jonas Hoglund, Andreas Johansson, Jorgen Jonsson, Magnus Kahnberg, Michael Nylander, Samuel Pahlsson, Andreas Salomonsson, Fredrik Sjostrom, Matthias Tjarnqvist

**Switzerland** (Ralph Krueger, coach) GK—Martin Gerber, Marco Buhrer, Ronnie Rueger—Goran Bezina, Beat Forster, Steve Hirschi, Olivier Keller, Reto Kobach, Mathias Seger, Martin Steinegger, Mark Streit, Julien Vauclair, Andres Ambuhl, Luca Cereda, Patric Della Rossa, Patrick Fischer, Sandy Jeannin, Marcel Jenni, Thierry Paterlini, Martin Pluss, Marc Reichert, Ivo Ruthemann, Adrian Wichser, Valentin Wirz, Thomas Ziegler

**Ukraine** (Olexander Seukand, coach) GK—Kostyantyn Simchuk, Igor Karpenko, Yevgeni Brul—Yuriy Gunko, Denys Isayenko, Artyom Ostrushko, Gennadi Razin, Olexander Savitsky, Valeri Shiryayev, Andri Sryubko, Dmitri Tolkunov, Vyacheslav Zavalnyuk, Vasyl Bobrovnikov, Artyom Gnidenko, Sergiy Karchenko, Kostiantyn Kasyanchuk, Vitaliy Lytvynenko, Olexander Matvichuk, Roman Salnikov, Vitali Semenchenko, Vadim Shakhraychuk, Vladyslav Serov, Oleg Timchenko, Dmytro Tsyrul, Sergi Varlamov

**United States** (Peter Laviolette, coach) GK—Ty Conklin, Mike Dunham, Alex Westlund—Keith Ballard, Hal Gill, Brett Hauer, Jeff Jillson, Paul Mara, Aaron Miller, Andy Roach, Blake Sloan, Eric Weinrich, Bates Battaglia, Dustin Brown, Matt Cullen, Chris Drury, Mike Grier, Adam Hall, Jeff Halpern, Jeff Hamilton, Andy Hilbert, Ryan Malone, Richard Park, Erik Westrum

## 69th WORLD CHAMPIONSHIP (MEN)
## April 30-May 15, 2005
## Vienna/Innsbruck, Austria

**Final Placing**

| | | | |
|---|---|---|---|
| Gold | Czech Republic | 9th | Latvia |
| Silver | Canada | 10th | Belarus^ |
| Bronze | Russia | 11th | Ukraine |
| 4th | Sweden | 12th | Kazakhstan |
| 5th | Slovakia | 13th | Slovenia^ |
| 6th | United States | 14th | Denmark |
| 7th | Finland | 15th | Germany* |
| 8th | Switzerland | 16th | Austria* |

^promoted from Division I in 2004
*demoted to Division I for 2006

**Tournament Format**

Teams were divided into four groups of four teams each for the Preliminary Round. The top three teams from each group advanced to the Qualification Round. The bottom four were placed in a relegation pool, with the last two being relegated. In the Qualifying Round, the top four from advanced to a cross-over quarter-final.

**Results & Standings**

**GROUP A (VIENNA)**

| | GP | W | T | L | GF | GA | P |
|---|---|---|---|---|---|---|---|
| Slovakia | 3 | 2 | 1 | 0 | 13 | 5 | 5 |
| Russia | 3 | 2 | 1 | 0 | 9 | 5 | 5 |
| Belarus | 3 | 1 | 0 | 2 | 6 | 4 | 2 |
| Austria | 3 | 0 | 0 | 3 | 3 | 17 | 0 |

| | | |
|---|---|---|
| April 30 | Russia 4 | Austria 2 |
| April 30 | Slovakia 2 | Belarus 1 |
| May 2 | Slovakia 3 | Russia 3 |
| May 2 | Belarus 5 | Austria 0 |
| May 4 | Russia 2 | Belarus 0 |
| May 4 | Slovakia 8 | Austria 1 |

**GROUP B (INNSBRUCK)**

| | GP | W | T | L | GF | GA | P |
|---|---|---|---|---|---|---|---|
| Canada | 3 | 3 | 0 | 0 | 17 | 5 | 6 |
| United States | 3 | 2 | 0 | 1 | 11 | 4 | 4 |
| Latvia | 3 | 1 | 0 | 2 | 8 | 10 | 2 |
| Slovenia | 3 | 0 | 0 | 3 | 1 | 18 | 0 |

| | | |
|---|---|---|
| April 30 | Canada 6 | Latvia 4 |
| May 1 | United States 7 | Slovenia 0 |
| May 3 | Canada 8 | Slovenia 0 |
| May 3 | United States 3 | Latvia 1 |
| May 5 | Latvia 3 | Slovenia 1 |
| May 5 | Canada 3 | United States 1 |

**GROUP C (INNSBRUCK)**

| | GP | W | T | L | GF | GA | P |
|---|---|---|---|---|---|---|---|
| Sweden | 3 | 3 | 0 | 0 | 15 | 3 | 6 |
| Finland | 3 | 2 | 0 | 1 | 7 | 7 | 4 |
| Ukraine | 3 | 1 | 0 | 2 | 5 | 8 | 2 |
| Denmark | 3 | 0 | 0 | 3 | 2 | 11 | 0 |

| | | |
|---|---|---|
| April 30 | Finland 2 | Denmark 1 |
| May 1 | Sweden 3 | Ukraine 2 |
| May 2 | Finland 4 | Ukraine 1 |
| May 2 | Sweden 7 | Denmark 0 |
| May 4 | Ukraine 2 | Denmark 1 |
| May 4 | Sweden 5 | Finland 1 |

**GROUP D (VIENNA)**

| | GP | W | T | L | GF | GA | P |
|---|---|---|---|---|---|---|---|
| Czech Republic | 3 | 3 | 0 | 0 | 6 | 1 | 6 |
| Switzerland | 3 | 2 | 0 | 1 | 8 | 5 | 4 |
| Kazakhstan | 3 | 1 | 0 | 2 | 3 | 4 | 2 |
| Germany | 3 | 0 | 0 | 3 | 2 | 9 | 0 |

| | | |
|---|---|---|
| May 1 | Czech Republic 3 | Switzerland 1 |
| May 1 | Kazakhstan 2 | Germany 1 |
| May 3 | Switzerland 2 | Kazakhstan 1 |
| May 3 | Czech Republic 2 | Germany 0 |
| May 5 | Czech Republic 1 | Kazakhstan 0 |
| May 5 | Switzerland 5 | Germany 1 |

**RELEGATION ROUND**

| | GP | W | T | L | GF | GA | P |
|---|---|---|---|---|---|---|---|
| Slovenia | 3 | 2 | 0 | 1 | 11 | 14 | 4 |
| Denmark | 3 | 2 | 0 | 1 | 10 | 9 | 4 |
| Germany | 3 | 1 | 1 | 1 | 13 | 6 | 3 |
| Austria | 3 | 0 | 1 | 2 | 7 | 12 | 1 |

| | | | |
|---|---|---|---|
| May 6 | Vienna | Germany 2 | Austria 2 |
| May 6 | Innsbruck | Slovenia 4 | Denmark 3 |
| May 8 | Innsbruck | Denmark 4 | Austria 3 |
| May 9 | Innsbruck | Germany 9 | Slovenia 1 |
| May 10 | Innsbruck | Denmark 3 | Germany 2 |
| May 11 | Innsbruck | Slovenia 6 | Austria 2 |

**QUALIFYING ROUND**
**GROUP E (VIENNA)**

| | GP | W | T | L | GF | GA | P |
|---|---|---|---|---|---|---|---|
| Russia | 5 | 3 | 2 | 0 | 13 | 8 | 8 |
| Czech Republic | 5 | 4 | 0 | 1 | 15 | 5 | 8 |
| Slovakia | 5 | 3 | 1 | 1 | 12 | 11 | 7 |
| Switzerland | 5 | 2 | 1 | 2 | 9 | 10 | 5 |
| Belarus | 5 | 1 | 0 | 4 | 4 | 11 | 2 |
| Kazakhstan | 5 | 0 | 0 | 5 | 3 | 11 | 0 |

| | | |
|---|---|---|
| May 6 | Russia 3 | Switzerland 3 |
| May 7 | Belarus 2 | Kazakhstan 0 |
| May 7 | Czech Republic 5 | Slovakia 1 |
| May 8 | Slovakia 3 | Switzerland 1 |
| May 8 | Russia 2 | Czech Republic 1 |
| May 9 | Russia 3 | Kazakhstan 1 |
| May 9 | Switzerland 2 | Belarus 0 |
| May 10 | Slovakia 3 | Kazakhstan 1 |
| May 10 | Czech Republic 5 | Belarus 1 |

**GROUP F (INNSBRUCK)**

| | GP | W | T | L | GF | GA | P |
|---|---|---|---|---|---|---|---|
| Sweden | 5 | 4 | 0 | 1 | 23 | 13 | 8 |
| Canada | 5 | 3 | 1 | 1 | 18 | 14 | 7 |
| United States | 5 | 2 | 2 | 1 | 14 | 10 | 6 |
| Finland | 5 | 1 | 3 | 1 | 12 | 13 | 5 |
| Latvia | 5 | 1 | 1 | 3 | 9 | 18 | 3 |
| Ukraine | 5 | 0 | 1 | 4 | 5 | 13 | 1 |

| | | |
|---|---|---|
| May 6 | United States 4 | Finland 4 |
| May 7 | Latvia 3 | Ukraine 0 |
| May 7 | Sweden 5 | Canada 4 |
| May 8 | Canada 3 | Finland 3 |
| May 8 | United States 5 | Sweden 1 |
| May 9 | United States 1 | Ukraine 1 |
| May 9 | Finland 0 | Latvia 0 |
| May 10 | Canada 2 | Ukraine 1 |
| May 10 | Sweden 9 | Latvia 1 |

**PLAYOFFS**
**QUARTER-FINALS**

| | | | |
|---|---|---|---|
| May 12 | Vienna | Czech Republic 3 | United States 2 |
| | (10:00 OT/GWS—Martin Rucinsky) | | |
| May 12 | Innsbruck | Canada 5 | Slovakia 4 |
| May 12 | Vienna | Russia 4 | Finland 3 |
| | (10:00 OT/GWS—Maxim Afinogenov) | | |
| May 12 | Innsbruck | Sweden 2 | Switzerland 1 |

**SEMI-FINALS**

| | | | |
|---|---|---|---|
| May 14 | Vienna | Canada 4 | Russia 3 |
| May 14 | Vienna | Czech Republic 3 | Sweden 2 (Radek Dvorak 4:43 OT) |

**BRONZE MEDAL GAME**

| | | | |
|---|---|---|---|
| May 15 | Vienna | Russia 6 | Sweden 3 |

**GOLD MEDAL GAME**

| | | | |
|---|---|---|---|
| May 15 | Vienna | Czech Republic 3 | Canada 0 |

**Rosters**

**Austria** (Herbert Poeck, coach) GK—Bernd Brueckler, Patrick Machreich, Jurgen Penker—Gerhard Unterluggauer, Emanuel Viveiros, Sven Klimbacher, Philippe Lakos, Andre Lakos, Mike Stewart, Martin Ulrich, Robert Lukas, Roland Kaspitz, Oliver Setzinger, Daniel Welser, Dieter Kalt, Matthias Trattnig, Raimund Divis, Markus Peintner, Thomas Pock, Christoph Harand, Patrick Harand, Philippe Horsky, Gerald Ressmann, Mario Schaden, David Schuller

**Belarus** (Glen Hanlon, coach) GK—Andrei Mezin, Sergei Shabanov, Stepan Goryachevskikh—Alexander Makritski, Alexander Ryadinski, Sergei Yerkovich, Andrei Bashko, Oleg Mikulchik, Alexander Zhurik, Vladimir Kopat, Vladimir Svito, Konstantin Koltsov, Mikhail Grabovski, Vladimir Tsyplakov, Sergei Zadelenov, Andrei Skabelka, Dmitri Dudik, Andrei Kostitsyn, Alexei Krutikov, Alexei Strakhov, Alexei Ugarov, Andrei Mikhalyov, Dmitri Meleshko, Timofei Filin (DQ), Alexei Savin

**Canada** (Marc Habscheid, coach) GK—Martin Brodeur, Roberto Luongo, Marty Turco—Chris Phillips, Jamie Heward, Wade Redden, Scott Hannan, Dan Boyle, Robyn Regehr, Sheldon Souray, Ed Jovanovski, Joe Thornton, Rick Nash, Simon Gagne, Dany Heatley, Patrick Marleau, Shane Doan, Brendan Morrison, Ryan Smyth, Kirk Maltby, Kris Draper, Mike Fisher, Brenden Morrow, Scott Walker

**Czech Republic** (Vladimir Ruzicka, coach) GK—Tomas Vokoun, Milan Hnilicka, Adam Svoboda—Jiri Fischer, Jaroslav Spacek, Marek Zidlicky, Petr Kubina, Tomas Kaberle, Frantisek Kaberle, Jan Hejda, Jiri Slegr, Jaromir Jagr, Vaclav Prospal, Martin Rucinsky, Martin Straka, Petr Cajanek, David Vyborny, Petr Sykora, Jan Hlavac, Ales Hemsky, Radek Dvorak, Josef Vasicek, Vaclav Varada, Radim Vrbata, Petr Prucha

**Denmark** (Mikael Lundstrom, coach GK—Peter Hirsch, Michael Madsen, Simon Nielsen—Jesper Damgaard, Mads Christensen, Christian Schioldan, Andreas Andreasen, Frederik Akesson, Mads Moller, Morten Dahlmann, Thomas Johnsen, Morten Green, Kasper Degn, Frans Nielsen, Peter Regin, Mike Grey, Bo Nordby Andersen, Lasse Degn, Christoffer Kjaergaard, Michael Smidt, Nicolas Monberg, Mads True, Jannik Hansen, Thor Dresler, Kim Staal

**Finland** (Erkka Westerlund, coach) GK—Niklas Backstrom, Fredrik Norrena, Pasi Nurminen—Petteri Nummelin, Lasse Kukkonen, Kimmo Timonen, Ossi Vaananen, Antti-Jussi Niemi, Jere Karalahti, Toni Soderholm, Olli Jokinen, Niko Kapanen, Timo Parssinen, Jukka Hentunen, Tomi Kallio, Ville Peltonen, Niklas Hagman, Jani Rita, Petri Pakaslahti, Jarkko Ruutu, Jussi Jokinen, Mikko Eloranta, Riku Hahl, Pekka Saravo, Jari Viuhkola

**Germany** (Greg Poss, coach) GK—Robert Muller, Oliver Jonas, Alexander Jung—Nico Pyka, Christian Ehrhoff, Stefan Schauer, Christoph Schubert, Michael Bakos, Andreas Renz, Alexander Sulzer, Stephan Retzer, Lasse Kopitz, Jochen Hecht, Jan Benda, Sebastian Furchner, Eduard Lewandowski, Tino Boos, Marcel Goc, Tomas Martinec, Alexander Barta, Klaus Kathan, Daniel Kreutzer, Sven Felski, Petr Fical, Andreas Morczinietz

**Kazakhstan** (Nikolai Myshyagin, coach) GK—Vitali Kolesnik, Sergei Ogoreshnikov, Sergei Tambulov—Alexei Koledayev, Yevgeni Mazunin, Vitali Novopashin, Alexei Litvinenko, Alexei Vasilchenko, Yevgeni Blokhin, Andrei Sokolov, Vladimir Antipin, Oleg Kovalenko, Artyom Argokov, Dmitri Upper, Dmitri Dudarev, Yevgeni Koreshkov, Andrei Ogorodnikov, Alexander Koreshkov, Roman Kozlov, Andrei Pchelyakov, Andrei Troshinski, Sergei Alexandrov, Anton Komissarov, Fyodor Polischuk, Konstantin Shafranov

**Latvia** (Leonids Beresnevs, coach) GK—Arturs Irbe, Edgars Masalskis, Martins Raitums—Rodrigo Lavins, Agris Saviels, Karlis Skrastins, Guntis Galvins, Oskars Bartulis, Alekseis Sirokovs, Atvars Tribuncovs, Viktors Ignatjevs, Leonids Tambijevs, Girts Ankipans, Aleksandrs Semjonovs, Janis Sprukts, Martins Cipulis, Aleksandrs Nizivijs, Grigorijs Pantelejevs, Maris Ziedins, Aigars Cipruss, Aleksandrs Macijevskis, Krisjanis Redlihs, Herberts Vasiljevs

**Russia** (Vladimir Krikunov, coach) GK—Maxim Sokolov, Sergei Zvyagin, Alexander Yeryomenko—Sergei Gusev, Alexander Karpovtsev, Denis Denisov, Vitali Proshkin, Sergei Vyshedkevich, Alexander Ryazantsev, Dmitri Kalinin, Andrei Markov, Alexander Ovechkin, Pavel Datsyuk, Alexei Kovalyov, Ilya Kovalchuk, Maxim Afinogenov, Yevgeni Malkin, Alexander Syomin, Alexei Yashin, Sergei Zinoviev, Alexander Kharitonov, Viktor Kozlov, Ivan Nepryayev, Vladimir Antipov, Fedor Fyodorov

**Slovenia** (Kari Savolainen, coach) GK—Gaber Glavic, Robert Kristan, Andrei Hocevar—Bojan Zajc, Robert Ciglenecki, Mitia Robar, Blaz Klinar, Dejan Varl, Samian Dervaric, Mitia Sotlar, Miha Rebolj, Dejan Kontrec, Ivo Jan, Edo Terglav, Tomaz Razingar, Marcel Rodman, Jurii Golicic, Anze Kopitar, Peter Rozic, Luka Zagar, Jaka Avgustincic, Mitia Sivic, David Rodman, Tomo Hafner, Boris Pretnar

**Slovakia** (Frantisek Hossa, coach) GK: Jan Lasak, Rastislav Stana, Karol Krizan—Martin Strbak, Zdeno Chara, Radoslav Suchy, Rene Vydareny, Lubomir Visnovsky, Jaroslav Obsut, Ivan Majesky, Richard Lintner, Dominik Granak, Zigmund Palffy, Marian Hossa, Pavol Demitra, Jozef Stumpel, Marian Gaborik, Miroslav Satan, Michal Handzus, Peter Pucher, Richard Zednik, Lubos Bartecko, Vladimir Orszagh, Juraj Stefanka, Marcel Hossa

**Sweden** (Bengt-Ake Gustafsson, coach) GK—Henrik Lundqvist, Johan Holmqvist, Stefan Liv—Sanny Lindstrom, Magnus Johansson, Christian Backman, Niklas Kronwall, Mattias Norstrom, Ronnie Sundin, Thomas Rhodin, Kenny Jonsson, Daniel Sedin, Daniel Alfredsson, Jonathan Hedstrom, Samuel Pahlsson, Jonas Hoglund, Henrik Sedin, Henrik Zetterberg, Jorgen Jonsson, Peter Nordstrom, Mikael Samuelsson, Magnus Kahnberg, Per-Johan Axelsson, Johan Franzen, Mattias Weinhandl

**Switzerland** (Ralph Krueger, coach) GK—Martin Gerber, David Aebischer, Marco Buhrer—Julien Vauclair, Severin Blindenbacher, Mark Streit, Cyrill Geyer, Olivier Keller, Beat Forster, Goran Bezina, Mathias Seger, Martin Pluss, Patrick Fischer, Ivo Ruthemann, Romano Lemm, Paul DiPietro, Adrian Wichser, Sandy Jeannin, Thomas Ziegler, Flavien Conne, Patric Della Rossa, Thierry Paterlini, Kevin Romy, Andres Ambuhl, Patrik Bartschi

**Ukraine** (Olexander Seukand, coach) GK—Kostyantyn Simchuk, Olexander Fedorov, Vadym Seliverstov—Yuriy Gunko, Sergiy Klimentyev, Vyacheslav Timchenko, Dmitri Tolkunov, Andri Sryubko, Oleg Timchenko, Vitaliy Lyutkevych, Olexander Pobyedonostsev, Vyacheslav Zavalnyuk, Denys Isayenko, Bogdan Savenko, Vasyl Bobrovnikov, Sergi Varlamov, Kostiantyn Kasyanchuk, Vitali Semenchenko, Vadim Shakhraychuk, Vitaliy Lytvynenko, Olexander Matvichuk, Roman Salnikov, Dmytro Tsyrul, Artyom Gnidenko

**United States** (Peter Laviolette, coach ) GK—Rick DiPietro, Ty Conklin, Tim Thomas—Jordan Leopold, Brett Hauer, Aaron Miller, Andy Roach, John-Michael Liles, Paul Martin, Ryan Suter, Hal Gill, Mike Knuble, Erik Cole, Doug Weight, Mark Parrish, Mike Modano, Brian Gionta, Yan Stastny, Zach Parise, Adam Hall, Jeff Halpern, Richard Park, David Legwand, Mike York, Kevyn Adams

## 70th WORLD CHAMPIONSHIP (MEN)
**May 5-21, 2006**
**Riga, Latvia**

### Final Placing
Gold........Sweden
Silver......Czech Republic
Bronze....Finland
4th..........Canada
5th..........Russia
6th..........Belarus
7th..........United States
8th..........Slovakia
9th.........Switzerland
10th.......Latvia
11th.......Norway^
12th.......Ukraine
13th.......Denmark
14th.......Italy^
15th.......Kazakhstan*
16th.......Slovenia*
^promoted from Division I in 2005
*demoted to Division I for 2007

### Tournament Format
Teams were divided into four groups of four teams each for the Preliminary Round. The top three teams from each group advanced to the Qualification Round. The bottom four were placed in a relegation pool, with the last two being relegated. In the Qualifying Round, the top four from advanced to a cross-over quarter-final.

### Results & Standings
**PRELIMINARY ROUND**
**GROUP A**

| | GP | W | L | T | GF | GA | P |
|---|---|---|---|---|---|---|---|
| Finland | 3 | 2 | 0 | 1 | 13 | 6 | 5 |
| Czech Republic | 3 | 1 | 0 | 2 | 9 | 8 | 4 |
| Latvia | 3 | 1 | 1 | 1 | 6 | 7 | 3 |
| Slovenia | 3 | 0 | 3 | 0 | 8 | 15 | 0 |

| | | |
|---|---|---|
| May 5 | Finland 5 | Slovenia 3 |
| May 5 | Latvia 1 | Czech Republic 1 |
| May 7 | Czech Republic 5 | Slovenia 4 |
| May 7 | Finland 5 | Latvia 0 |
| May 9 | Latvia 5 | Slovenia 1 |
| May 9 | Finland 3 | Czech Republic 3 |

**GROUP B**

| | GP | W | L | T | GF | GA | P |
|---|---|---|---|---|---|---|---|
| Sweden | 3 | 2 | 0 | 1 | 12 | 6 | 5 |
| Switzerland | 3 | 2 | 0 | 1 | 9 | 6 | 5 |
| Ukraine | 3 | 1 | 2 | 0 | 7 | 8 | 2 |
| Italy | 3 | 0 | 3 | 0 | 3 | 11 | 0 |

| | | |
|---|---|---|
| May 6 | Switzerland 3 | Italy 1 |
| May 6 | Sweden 4 | Ukraine 2 |
| May 8 | Switzerland 2 | Ukraine 1 |
| May 8 | Sweden 4 | Italy 0 |
| May 10 | Ukraine 4 | Italy 2 |
| May 10 | Sweden 4 | Switzerland 4 |

**Group C**

| | GP | W | L | T | GF | GA | P |
|---|---|---|---|---|---|---|---|
| Russia | 3 | 3 | 0 | 0 | 17 | 6 | 6 |
| Belarus | 3 | 2 | 1 | 0 | 11 | 5 | 4 |
| Slovakia | 3 | 1 | 2 | 0 | 10 | 6 | 2 |
| Kazakhstan | 3 | 0 | 3 | 0 | 2 | 23 | 0 |

| | | |
|---|---|---|
| May 6 | Belarus 2 | Slovakia 1 |
| May 6 | Russia 10 | Kazakhstan 1 |
| May 8 | Russia 3 | Belarus 2 |
| May 8 | Slovakia 6 | Kazakhstan 0 |
| May 10 | Russia 4 | Slovakia 3 |
| May 10 | Belarus 7 | Kazakhstan 1 |

**GROUP D**

| | GP | W | L | T | GF | GA | P |
|---|---|---|---|---|---|---|---|
| Canada | 3 | 3 | 0 | 0 | 14 | 5 | 6 |
| United States | 3 | 2 | 1 | 0 | 7 | 3 | 4 |
| Norway | 3 | 1 | 2 | 0 | 8 | 13 | 2 |
| Denmark | 3 | 0 | 3 | 0 | 6 | 14 | 0 |

| | | |
|---|---|---|
| May 5 | United States 3 | Norway 1 |
| May 5 | Canada 5 | Denmark 3 |
| May 7 | United States 3 | Denmark 0 |
| May 7 | Canada 7 | Norway 1 |
| May 9 | Norway 6 | Denmark 3 |
| May 9 | Canada 2 | United States 1 |

**QUALIFYING ROUND**
**GROUP E**

| | GP | W | L | T | GF | GA | P |
|---|---|---|---|---|---|---|---|
| Canada | 5 | 4 | 1 | 0 | 28 | 10 | 8 |
| Finland | 5 | 3 | 1 | 1 | 17 | 7 | 7 |
| United States | 5 | 3 | 2 | 0 | 11 | 10 | 6 |
| Czech Republic | 5 | 2 | 1 | 2 | 14 | 12 | 6 |
| Latvia | 5 | 1 | 3 | 1 | 7 | 23 | 3 |
| Norway | 5 | 0 | 5 | 0 | 5 | 20 | 0 |

| | | |
|---|---|---|
| May 11 | Canada 11 | Latvia 0 |
| May 12 | Czech Republic 3 | Norway 1 |
| May 12 | Finland 4 | United States 0 |
| May 13 | United States 4 | Latvia 2 |
| May 14 | Finland 3 | Norway 0 |
| May 14 | Czech Republic 6 | Canada 4 |
| May 15 | Canada 4 | Finland 2 |
| May 16 | United States 3 | Czech Republic 1 |
| May 16 | Latvia 4 | Norway 2 |

**GROUP F**

| | GP | W | L | T | GF | GA | P |
|---|---|---|---|---|---|---|---|
| Russia | 5 | 4 | 0 | 1 | 22 | 11 | 9 |
| Sweden | 5 | 2 | 1 | 2 | 17 | 15 | 6 |
| Belarus | 5 | 3 | 2 | 0 | 16 | 10 | 6 |
| Slovakia | 5 | 2 | 2 | 1 | 19 | 10 | 5 |
| Switzerland | 5 | 1 | 2 | 2 | 12 | 15 | 4 |
| Ukraine | 5 | 0 | 5 | 0 | 4 | 29 | 0 |

| | | |
|---|---|---|
| May 11 | Russia 6 | Ukraine 0 |
| May 12 | Switzerland 2 | Slovakia 2 |
| May 12 | Sweden 4 | Belarus 1 |
| May 13 | Belarus 9 | Ukraine 1 |
| May 14 | Russia 6 | Switzerland 3 |
| May 14 | Slovakia 5 | Sweden 2 |
| May 15 | Sweden 3 | Russia 3 |
| May 16 | Belarus 2 | Switzerland 1 |
| May 16 | Slovakia 8 | Ukraine 0 |

**RELEGATION ROUND**

| | GP | W | L | T | GF | GA | P |
|---|---|---|---|---|---|---|---|
| Denmark | 3 | 2 | 0 | 1 | 11 | 5 | 5 |
| Italy | 3 | 1 | 1 | 1 | 6 | 10 | 3 |
| Kazakhstan | 3 | 1 | 2 | 0 | 9 | 6 | 2 |
| Slovenia | 3 | 0 | 1 | 2 | 6 | 11 | 2 |

| | | |
|---|---|---|
| May 12 | Slovenia 3 | Denmark 3 |
| May 12 | Italy 3 | Kazakhstan 2 |
| May 13 | Kazakhstan 5 | Slovenia 0 |
| May 13 | Denmark 5 | Italy 0 |
| May 15 | Slovenia 3 | Italy 3 |
| May 15 | Denmark 3 | Kazakhstan 2 |

**PLAYOFFS**
**QUARTER-FINALS**

| | | |
|---|---|---|
| May 17 | Sweden 6 | United States 0 |
| May 17 | Canada 4 | Slovakia 1 |
| May 18 | Czech Republic 4 | Russia 3 (Zbynek Irgl 7:58 OT) |
| May 18 | Finland 4 | Belarus 0 |

**SEMI-FINALS**

| | | |
|---|---|---|
| May 20 | Czech Republic 3 | Finland 1 |
| May 20 | Sweden 5 | Canada 4 |

**BRONZE MEDAL GAME**

| | | |
|---|---|---|
| May 21 | Finland 5 | Canada 0 |

**GOLD MEDAL GAME**

| | | |
|---|---|---|
| May 21 | Sweden 4 | Czech Republic 0 |

### Rosters
**Belarus** (Glen Hanlon, coach) GK—Andrei Mezin, Sergei Shabanov, Stepan Goryachevskikh—Vladimir Denisov, Sergei Yerkovich, Vladimir Kopat, Viktor Kostyuchenok, Alexander Makritski, Alexander Ryadinsky, Vladimir Svito, Alexander Zhurik, Oleg Antonenko, Yaroslav Chupris, Dmitri Dudik, Yevgeni Yesaulov, Mikhail Grabovski, Andrei Kostitsyn, Sergei Kukushkin, Yevgeni Kurilin, Andrei Mikhalyov, Dmitri Meleshko, Alexei Savin, Andrei Skabelka, Alexei Ugarov, Sergei Zadelenov

**Canada** (Marc Habscheid, coach) GK—Alex Auld, Marc Denis, Chris Mason—Trevor Daley, Micki DuPont, Dan Hamhuis, Stephane Robidas, Brent Seabrook, Nick Schultz, Brad Stuart, Patrice Bergeron, Brad Boyes, Kyle Calder, Mike Cammalleri, Jeff Carter, Mike Comrie, Sidney Crosby, Scott Hartnell, Glen Metropolit, Matt Pettinger, Mike Richards, Stacey Roest, Brendan Shanahan, Jason Williams

**Czech Republic** (Alois Hadamczik, coach) GK—Milan Hnilicka, Tomas Popperle, Adam Svoboda—Miroslav Blatak, Jan Hejda, Tomas Kaberle, Lukas Krajicek, Zdenek Kutlak, Zbynek Michalek, Martin Richter, Martin Skoula, Jaroslav Balastik, Jaroslav Bednar, Jan Bulis, Martin Erat, Zbynek Irgl, Jan Hlavac, Jaroslav Hlinka, Petr Hubacek, Tomas Plekanec, Ivo Prorok, Tomas Rolinek, Patrik Stefan, Petr Tenkrat, David Vyborny

**Denmark** (Mikael Lundstrom, coach) GK—Peter Hirsch, Michael Madsen, Patrick Galbraith—Andreas Andreasen, Mads Bodker, Morten Dahlmann, Jesper Damgaard, Thomas Johnsen, Daniel Nielsen, Rasmus Pander, Christian Schioldan, Kasper Degn, Morten Green, Jannik Hansen, Christoffer Kjargaard, Morten Madsen, Frans Nielsen, Jens Nielsen, Bo Nordby Andersen, Martin Pyndt, Peter Regin, Thomas Reinert, Michael Smidt, Kim Staal

**Finland** (Erkka Westerlund, coach) GK—Niklas Backstrom, Antero Niittymaki, Fredrik Norrena—Aki-Petteri Berg, Lasse Kukkonen, Mikko Lehtonen, Mikko Luoma, Tuukka Mantyla, Petteri Nummelin, Pekka Saravo, Sean Bergenheim, Riku Hahl, Jukka Hentunen, Jussi Jokinen, Olli Jokinen, Tomi Kallio, Mikko Koivu, Antti Miettinen, Ville Peltonen, Esa Pirnes, Jani Rita, Jarkko Ruutu, Tuomo Ruutu, Tommi Santala, Jari Viuhkola

**Italy** (Michel Goulet, coach) GK—Rene Baur, Jason Muzzatti, Thomas Tragust—Christian Borgatello, Alexander Egger, Armin Helfer, Carlo Lorenzi, Florian Ramoser, Michele Strazzabosco, Carter Trevisani, Luca Ansoldi, Giuseppe Busillo, Enrico Chelodi, Jason Cirone, Giorgio de Bettin, Paolo Bustreo, Manuel deToni, Luca Felicetti, Nicola Fontanive, Anthony Iob, Stefano Margoni, Andrea Molteni, John Parco, Roland Ramoser, Luca Rigoni

**Kazakhstan** (Nikolai Myshyagin, coach) GK—Roman Medvedev, Sergei Ogoreshnikov, Sergei Tambulov—Artyom Argokov, Yevgeni Blokhin, Alexei Koledayev, Oleg Kovalenko, Yevgeni Mazunin, Yevgeni Pupkov, Andrei Savenkov, Maxim Belayev, Alexander Koreshkov, Yevgeni Koreshkov, Vadim Krasnoslabotsev, Alexei Litvinenko, Andrei Ogorodnikov, Andrei Pchelyakov, Vadim Rifel, Andrei Samokhvalov, Konstantin Shafranov, Andrei Spiridonov, Roman Starchenko, Andrei Troshinski, Nikolai Zarzhitski, Talgat Zhailauov

**Latvia** (Pyotr Vorobyov, coach) GK—Edgars Masalskis, Sergejs Naumovs, Martins Raitums—Kaspars Astasenko, Guntis Galvins, Maris Jass, Alexandrs Jerofejevs, Georgijs Pujacs, Arvids Rekis, Agris Saviels, Atvars Tribuncovs, Viktors Blinovs, Martins Cipulis, Lauris Darzins, Kaspars Daugavins, Aleksandrs Nizivijs, Grigorijs Pantelejevs, Mikelis Redlihs, Aleksandrs Semjonovs, Aleksejs Sirokovs, Janis Sprukts, Leonids Tambijevs, Herberts Vasiljevs

**Norway** (Roy Johansen, coach) GK—Pal Grotnes, Mathias Gundersen, Jonas Norgren—Jonas Holos, Tommy Jakobsen, Lars Erik Lund, Anders Myrvold, Johnny Nielsen, Erik Ryman, Mats Trygg, Jonas Andersen, Morten Ask, Anders Bastiansen, Mads Hansen, Marius Holtet, Tommy Marthinsen, Lars Peder Nagel, Kjell Richard Nygard, Per-Age Skroder, Lars Erik Spets, Patrick Thoresen, Marius Trygg, Tore Vikingstad

**Russia** (Vladimir Krikunov, coach) GK—Alexander Fomichev, Maxim Sokolov, Sergei Zvyagin—Vitali Atyushov, Dmitri Bykov, Vadim Khomitski, Kirill Koltsov, Andrei Kruchinin, Denis Kulyash, Georgi Misharin, Ilya Nikulin, Sergei Zhukov, Denis Arkhipov, Konstantin Gorovikov, Igor Grigorenko, Alexander Kharitonov, Nikolai Kulyomin, Yevgeni Malkin, Sergei Mozyakin, Alexei Mikhnov, Alexander Ovechkin, Alexander Syomin, Maxim Sushinski, Igor Yemeleyev, Danis Zaripov

**Slovenia** (Frantysek Vyborny, coach) GK—Gaber Glavic, Andrej Hocevar, Robert Kristan—Robert Ciglenecki, Bostjan Groznik, Tomo Hafner, Ales Kranjc, Jakob Milovanovic, Mitja Robar, David Rodman, Marcel Rodman, Mitja Soltar, Uros Vidmar, Jaka Avgustincic, Jurij Golicic, Andrej Hebar, Dejan Kontrec, Anze Kopitar, Egon Muric, Rok Pajic, Tomaz Razingar, Mitja Sivic, Anze Terlikar, Dejan Varl, Luka Zagar

**Slovakia** (Frantisek Hossa, coach) GK—Karol Krizan, Jan Lasak, Rastislav Stana—Dominik Granak, Tomas Harant, Stanislav Hudec, Milan Jurcina, Andrej Meszaros, Dusan Milo, Richard Stehlik, Martin Strbak, Rene Vydareny, Milan Bartovic, Martin Cibak, Ivan Ciernik, Marcel Hossa, Marian Hossa, Michal Hudec, Richard Kapus, Andrej Kollar, Miroslav Kovacik, Rastislav Pavlikovsky, Tomas Surovy, Lubomir Vaic, Miroslav Zalesak

**Sweden** (Bengt-Ake Gustafsson, coach) GK—Daniel Henriksson, Johan Holmqvist, Stefan Liv—Per Hallberg, Andreas Holmqvist, Magnus Johansson, Kenny Jonsson, Niklas Kronwall, Ronnie Sundin, Mattias Timander, Nicklas Backstrom, Fredrik Emvall, Johan Franzen, Mika Hannula, Mathias Johansson, Jorgen Jonsson, Andreas Karlsson, Joel Lundqvist, Tony Martensson, Jesper Mattsson, Bjorn Melin, Jonas Nordquist, Michael Nylander, Mikael Samuelsson, Henrik Zetterberg

**Switzerland** (Ralph Krueger, coach) GK—David Aebischer, Marco Buhrer, Jonas Hiller—Goran Bezina, Severin Blindenbacher, Beat Forster, Beat Gerber, Timo Helbling, Mathias Seger, Martin Steinegger, Mark Streit, Julien Vauclair, Andres Ambuhl, Patric Della Rossa, Alain Demuth, Thomas Deruns, Sandy Jeannin, Romano Lemm, Thierry Paterlini, Martin Pluss, Marc Reichert, Kevin Romy, Ivo Ruthemann, Raffaele Sannitz, Valentin Wirtz

**Ukraine** (Olexander Seukand, coach) GK—Olexander Fedorov, Igor Karpenko, Konstyantyn Simchuk—Yuriy Gunko, Denys Isayenko, Sergiy Klimentyev, Yuriy Navarenko, Artyom Ostrushko, Vasyl Polonitski, Andri Sryubko, Vyacheslav Zavalnyuk, Olexander Bobkin, Vasyl Bobrovnikov, Vitaliy Donika, Yuriy Dyachenko, Kostyantyn Kasyanchuk, Vitaliy Lytvynenko, Olexander Materukhin, Andri Mikhnov, Valentyn Oletskiy, Borys Protsenko, Roman Salnikov, Vitali Semenchenko, Oleg Shafarenko, Vadim Shakhraychuk

**United States** (Mike Eaves, coach) GK—Craig Anderson, Jason Bacashihua, David McKee—Andrew Alberts, Joe Corvo, Hal Gill, Mike Komisarek, Freddy Meyer, Brooks Orpik, Ryan Suter, Dustin Brown, Mark Cullen, Adam Hall, Andy Hilbert, Ryan Kesler, Phil Kessel, Ryan Malone, Patrick O'Sullivan, Richard Park, Marty Reasoner, James Slater, Drew Stafford, Yan Stastny, R.J. Umberger

## 71st WORLD CHAMPIONSHIP (MEN)
## April 24–May 10, 2007
## Moscow/Mytischi, Russia

**Final Placing**

Gold ........Canada
Silver ......Finland
Bronze ....Russia
4th ..........Sweden
5th ..........United States
6th ..........Slovakia
7th ..........Czech Republic
8th ..........Switzerland
9th .........Germany^
10th .......Denmark
11th .......Belarus
12th .......Italy
13th .......Latvia
14th .......Norway
15th .......Austria^*
16th .......Ukraine*

^promoted from Division I in 2006
*demoted to Division I for 2008

**Tournament Format**

Teams were divided into four groups of four teams each for the Preliminary Round. The top three teams from each group advanced to the Qualification Round. The bottom four were placed in a relegation pool, with the last two being relegated. In the Qualifying Round, the top four from advanced to a cross-over quarter-final. This was the first year of the three-point system (three points for a regulation win, two points for an overtime or shootout win, and one point for an overtime or shootout loss).

**Results & Standings**

**GROUP A (MOSCOW)**

| | GP | W | OTW | OTL | L | GF | GA | P |
|---|---|---|---|---|---|---|---|---|
| Sweden | 3 | 3 | 0 | 0 | 0 | 21 | 3 | 9 |
| Switzerland | 3 | 2 | 0 | 0 | 1 | 4 | 8 | 6 |
| Italy | 3 | 0 | 1 | 0 | 2 | 6 | 12 | 2 |
| Latvia | 3 | 0 | 0 | 1 | 2 | 6 | 14 | 1 |

| | | |
|---|---|---|
| April 28 | Switzerland 2 | Latvia 1 |
| April 28 | Sweden 7 | Italy 1 |
| April 30 | Switzerland 2 | Italy 1 |
| April 30 | Sweden 8 | Latvia 2 |
| May 2 | Italy 4 | Latvia 3 (Jason Cirone 4:10 OT) |
| May 2 | Sweden 6 | Switzerland 0 |

**GROUP B (MYTISCHI)**

| | GP | W | OTW | OTL | L | GF | GA | P |
|---|---|---|---|---|---|---|---|---|
| Czech Republic | 3 | 3 | 0 | 0 | 0 | 18 | 6 | 9 |
| United States | 3 | 2 | 0 | 0 | 1 | 14 | 7 | 6 |
| Belarus | 3 | 1 | 0 | 0 | 2 | 8 | 15 | 3 |
| Austria | 3 | 0 | 0 | 0 | 3 | 5 | 17 | 0 |

| | | |
|---|---|---|
| April 27 | United States 6 | Austria 2 |
| April 27 | Czech Republic 8 | Belarus 2 |
| April 29 | Czech Republic 6 | Austria 1 |
| April 29 | United States 5 | Belarus 1 |
| May 1 | Belarus 5 | Austria 2 |
| May 1 | Czech Republic 4 | United States 3 |

**GROUP C (MYTISCHI)**

| | GP | W | OTW | OTL | L | GF | GA | P |
|---|---|---|---|---|---|---|---|---|
| Canada | 3 | 3 | 0 | 0 | 0 | 12 | 8 | 9 |
| Slovakia | 3 | 2 | 0 | 0 | 1 | 12 | 6 | 6 |
| Germany | 3 | 1 | 0 | 0 | 2 | 8 | 11 | 3 |
| Norway | 3 | 0 | 0 | 0 | 3 | 5 | 12 | 0 |

| | | |
|---|---|---|
| April 28 | Canada 3 | Germany 2 |
| April 28 | Slovakia 3 | Norway 0 |
| April 30 | Slovakia 5 | Germany 1 |
| April 30 | Canada 4 | Norway 2 |
| May 2 | Germany 5 | Norway 3 |
| May 2 | Canada 5 | Slovakia 4 |

**GROUP D (MOSCOW)**

| | GP | W | OTW | OTL | L | GF | GA | P |
|---|---|---|---|---|---|---|---|---|
| Russia | 3 | 3 | 0 | 0 | 0 | 22 | 6 | 9 |
| Finland | 3 | 2 | 0 | 0 | 1 | 15 | 7 | 6 |
| Denmark | 3 | 1 | 0 | 0 | 2 | 7 | 18 | 3 |
| Ukraine | 3 | 0 | 0 | 0 | 3 | 4 | 17 | 0 |

| | | |
|---|---|---|
| April 27 | Finland 5 | Ukraine 0 |
| April 27 | Russia 9 | Denmark 1 |
| April 29 | Finland 6 | Denmark 2 |
| April 29 | Russia 8 | Ukraine 1 |
| May 1 | Denmark 4 | Ukraine 3 |
| May 1 | Russia 5 | Finland 4 |

**QUALIFYING ROUND**
**GROUP E (MOSCOW)**

| | GP | W | OTW | OTL | L | GF | GA | P |
|---|---|---|---|---|---|---|---|---|
| Russia | 5 | 5 | 0 | 0 | 0 | 27 | 10 | 15 |
| Sweden | 5 | 4 | 0 | 0 | 1 | 21 | 7 | 12 |
| Finland | 5 | 3 | 0 | 0 | 2 | 15 | 8 | 9 |
| Switzerland | 5 | 2 | 0 | 0 | 3 | 9 | 16 | 6 |
| Denmark | 5 | 1 | 0 | 0 | 4 | 11 | 26 | 3 |
| Italy | 5 | 0 | 0 | 0 | 5 | 4 | 20 | 0 |

| | | |
|---|---|---|
| May 3 | Finland 2 | Switzerland 0 |
| May 3 | Sweden 5 | Denmark 2 |
| May 4 | Russia 3 | Italy 0 |
| May 5 | Switzerland 4 | Denmark 1 |
| May 5 | Finland 3 | Italy 0 |
| May 6 | Russia 6 | Switzerland 3 |
| May 6 | Sweden 1 | Finland 0 |
| May 7 | Denmark 5 | Italy 2 |
| May 7 | Russia 4 | Sweden 2 |

**GROUP F**

| | GP | W | OTW | OTL | L | GF | GA | P |
|---|---|---|---|---|---|---|---|---|
| Canada | 5 | 4 | 1 | 0 | 0 | 24 | 15 | 14 |
| United States | 5 | 3 | 0 | 0 | 2 | 18 | 13 | 9 |
| Slovakia | 5 | 3 | 0 | 0 | 2 | 18 | 15 | 9 |
| Czech Republic | 5 | 2 | 0 | 1 | 2 | 17 | 14 | 7 |
| Germany | 5 | 2 | 0 | 0 | 3 | 11 | 16 | 6 |
| Belarus | 5 | 0 | 0 | 0 | 5 | 14 | 29 | 0 |

| | | | |
|---|---|---|---|
| May 3 | Mytischi | United States 4 | Slovakia 2 |
| May 3 | Mytischi | Germany 2 | Czech Republic 0 |
| May 4 | Moscow | Canada 6 | Belarus 3 |
| May 5 | Mytischi | United States 3 | Germany 0 |
| May 5 | Mytischi | Slovakia 3 | Czech Republic 2 |
| May 6 | Mytischi | Slovakia 4 | Belarus 3 |
| May 6 | Mytischi | Canada 4 (Eric Staal 0:23 OT) | Czech Republic 3 |
| May 7 | Mytischi | Germany 6 | Belarus 5 |
| May 7 | Mytischi | Canada 6 | United States 3 |

**RELEGATION ROUND**
**GROUP G**

| | GP | W | OTW | OTL | L | GF | GA | P |
|---|---|---|---|---|---|---|---|---|
| Latvia | 3 | 2 | 0 | 0 | 1 | 14 | 8 | 6 |
| Norway | 3 | 1 | 1 | 0 | 1 | 12 | 9 | 5 |
| Austria | 3 | 1 | 0 | 1 | 1 | 11 | 12 | 4 |
| Ukraine | 3 | 1 | 0 | 0 | 2 | 7 | 15 | 3 |

| | | | |
|---|---|---|---|
| May 4 | Mytischi | Norway 3 | Austria 2 (Morten Ask 2:22 OT) |
| May 4 | Mytischi | Latvia 5 | Ukraine 0 |
| May 6 | Moscow | Latvia 5 | Austria 1 |
| May 6 | Mytischi | Ukraine 3 | Norway 2 |
| May 7 | Moscow | Austria 8 | Ukraine 4 |
| May 7 | Mytischi | Norway 7 | Latvia 4 |

**PLAYOFFS (MOSCOW)**
**QUARTER-FINALS**

| | | |
|---|---|---|
| May 9 | Russia 4 | Czech Republic 0 |
| May 9 | Sweden 7 | Slovakia 4 |
| May 10 | Canada 5 | Switzerland 1 |
| May 10 | Finland 5 | United States 4 (10:00 OT/GWS—Jere Lehtinen) |

**SEMI-FINALS**

| | | |
|---|---|---|
| May 12 | Finland 2 | Russia 1 (Mikko Koivu 5:40 OT) |
| May 12 | Canada 4 | Sweden 1 |

**BRONZE MEDAL GAME**

| | | |
|---|---|---|
| May 13 | Russia 3 | Sweden 1 |

**GOLD MEDAL GAME**

| | | |
|---|---|---|
| May 13 | Canada 4 | Finland 2 |

**Rosters**

**Austria** (Jim Boni, coach) GK—Bernd Brueckler, Reinhard Divis, Patrick Machreich—Andre Lakos, Robert Lukas, Mike Stewart, Thomas Pfeffer, Jeremy Drebek, Gerhard Unterluggauer, Philippe Lakos, Jamie Mattie, Martin Ulrich, Thomas Koch, Oliver Setzinger, Raimund Divis, Philipp Lukas, Markus Peintner, Daniel Welser, Dieter Kalt, Gregor Baumgartner, David Schuller, Matthias Trattnig, Patrick Harand, Marco Pewal

**Belarus** (Curt Fraser, coach) GK—Stepan Goryachevskikh, Andrei Mezin, Sergei Shabanov—Alexander Ryadinsky, Oleg Leontiev, Viktor Kostyuchenok, Andrei Glebov, Vladimir Denisov, Alexander Makritski, Alexander Zhurik, Sergei Yerkovich, Oleg Antonenko, Dmitri Dudik, Konstantin Koltsov, Dmitri Meleshko, Sergei Zadelenov, Alexei Ugarov, Alexander Kulakov, Yevgeni Kurilin, Sergei Kukushkin, Alexander Borovkov, Alexei Strakhov, Artyom Volkov, Sergei Demagin, Andrei Mikhalyov

**Canada** (Andy Murray, coach) GK—Chris Mason, Dwayne Roloson, Cam Ward—Dion Phaneuf, Cory Murphy, Eric Brewer, Dan Hamhuis, Shea Weber, Barret Jackman, Mike Commodore, Nick Schultz, Matthew Lombardi, Rick Nash, Shane Doan, Eric Staal, Mike Cammalleri, Jonathan Toews, Jason Chimera, Jamal Mayers, Jay McClement, Justin Williams, Colby Armstrong, Jordan Staal

**Czech Republic** (Alois Hadamczik, coach) GK—Roman Cechmanek, Marek Pinc, Adam Svoboda—Marek Zidlicky, Michal Barinka, Petr Caslava, Zbynek Michalek, Rostislav Klesla, Radek Hamr, Ladislav Smid, Jan Platil, Tomas Plekanec, Jaroslav Hlinka, Jan Marek, Rostislav Olesz, Petr Sykora, David Vyborny, Zbynek Irgl, Petr Cajanek, Jaroslav Bednar, Petr Tenkrat, Petr Hubacek, Jaroslav Balastik, Jiri Novotny, Tomas Rolinek

**Denmark** (Mike Sirant, coach) GK—Peter Hirsch, Michael Madsen, Simon Nielsen—Jesper Damgaard, Rasmus Pander, Daniel Nielsen, Andreas Andreasen, Mads Boedker, Stefan Lassen, Mads Moeller; Peter Regin, Kim Staal, Jens Nielsen, Frans Nielsen, Mads Christensen, Christoffer Kjaergaard, Kirill Starkov, Rasmus Olsen, Bo Nordby Tranholm, Morten Green, Thor Dresler, Morten Madsen, Michael Smidt, Alexander Sundberg

**Finland** (Erkka Westerlund, coach) GK—Kari Lehtonen, Fredrik Norrena, Sinuhe Wallinheimo—Petteri Nummelin, Pekka Saravo, Tuukka Mantyla, Aki-Petteri Berg, Lasse Kukkonen, Jukka-Pekka Laamanen, Toni Soderholm, Ville Koistinen, Ville Peltonen, Petri Kontiola, Niko Kapanen, Tuomo Ruutu, Jukka Hentunen, Jere Lehtinen, Mikko Koivu, Sean Bergenheim, Tomi Kallio, Kari Viuhkola, Antti Miettinen, Timo Parssinen, Mika Pyorala, Jarkko Ruutu

**Germany** (Uwe Krupp, coach) GK—Oliver Jonas, Dimitrij Kotschnew, Dimitri Patzold—Robert Dietrich, Martin Ancicka, Michael Bakos, Tobias Draxinger, Frank Hordler, Sebastian Osterloh, Alexander Sulzer, Robin Bretibach, Felix Petermann, Michael Wolf, Michael Hacker, Philip Gogulla, Sven Felski, John Tripp, Alexander Barta, Daniel Kreutzer, Florian Busch, Christoph Ullmann, Petr Fical, Andre Rankel, Alexander Polaczek, Yannic Seidenberg

**Italy** (Michel Goulet, coach) GK—Andrea Carpano, Guenther Hell, Jason Muzzatti—Luca Ansoldi, Christian Borgatello, Carlo Lorenzi, Andre Signoretti, Michele Strazzabosco, Armin Helfer, Florian Ramoser, Carter Trevisani, Jason Cirone, Giorgio de Bettin, Roland Ramoser, Stefano Margoni, Giulio Scandella, Mario Chitarroni, Manuel de Toni, Flavio Faggioni, John Parco, Luca Rigoni, Patrice Lefebvre, Jonathan Pittis, Paolo Bustreo

**Latvia** (Oleg Znaroks, coach) GK—Edgars Masalskis, Sergejs Naumovs, Martins Raitums—Olegs Sorokins, Rodrigo Lavins, Guntis Galvins, Aleksandrs Jerofejevs, Agris Saviels, Atvars Tribuncovs, Georgijs Pujacs, Arvids Rekis, Kaspars Daugavins, Lauris Darzins, Herberts Vasiljevs, Martins Cipulis, Mikelis Redlihs, Armands Berzins, Aleksandrs Semjonovs, Leonids Tambijevs, Grigorijs Pantelejevs, Janis Sprukts, Aleksejs Sirokovs, Aleksandrs Nizivijs, Aleksandrs Macijevskis, Guntis Dzerins

**Norway** (Roy Johansen, coach) GK—Pal Grotnes, Mathias Gundersen, Halvor Harstad-Evjen—Mats Trygg, Lars Erik Lund, Tommy Jakobsen, Mathias Livf, Jonas Holos, Erik Ryman, Cato Orbaek, Morten Ask, Anders Bastiansen, Patrick Thoresen, Mads Hansen, Jonas Andersen, Lars Erik Spets, Mathis Olimb, Marius Trygg, Kristian Forsberg, Alexander Nervik, Kjell Richard Nygard, Knut Spets, Steffen Thoresen

**Russia** (Vyacheslav Bykov, coach) GK—Alexander Yeryomenko, Vasili Koshechkin, Konstantin Barulin—Andrei Markov, Sergei Gonchar, Alexei Yemelin, Denis Grebeshkov, Vitali Atyushov, Ilya Nikulin, Vitali Proshkin, Maxim Kondratiev, Konstantin Korneyev, Alexei Morozov, Sergei Zinoviev, Danis Zaripov, Alexander Frolov, Yevgeni Malkin, Ilya Kovalchuk, Pyotr Schastlivy, Nikolai Kulyomin, Alexander Ovechkin, Ivan Nepryayev, Alexander Radulov, Alexander Kharitonov, Sergei Brylin

**Slovakia** (Julius Supler, coach) GK—Jaroslav Halak, Karol Krizan, Branislav Konrad—Peter Podhradsky, Zdeno Chara, Milan Jurcina, Richard Stehlik, Martin Strbak, Tomas Starosta, Dominik Granak, Marian Gaborik, Richard Kapus, Miroslav Satan, Marian Hossa, Marek Uram, Pavol Demitra, Branko Radivojevic, Roman Kukumberg, Radovan Somik, Miroslav Kovacik, Tomas Surovy, Tomas Harant, Tibor Melicharek, Ivan Ciernik, Andrej Podkonicky

**Sweden** (Bengt-Ake Gustafsson, coach) GK—Johan Backlund, Erik Ersberg, Daniel Henriksson—Dick Tarnstrom, Johan Akerman, Per Hallberg, Magnus Johansson, Anton Stralman, Tobias Enstrom, Kenny Jonsson, Jan Sandstrom, Johan Davidsson, Tony Martensson, Jorgen Jonsson, Fredrik Bremberg, Patric Hornqvist, Nicklas Backstrom, Jonathan Hedstrom, Fredrik Warg, Alexander Steen, Martin Thornberg, Fredrik Emvall, Rickard Wallin, Mattias Mansson, Magnus Kahnberg

**Switzerland** (Ralph Krueger, coach) GK—David Aebischer, Jonas Hiller, Daniel Manzato—Mark Streit, Goran Bezina, Severin Blindenbacher, Beat Forster, Beat Gerber, Julien Vauclair, Steve Hirschi, Paul di Pietro, Adrian Wichser, Romano Lemm, Marc Reichert, Julien Sprunger, Sandy Jeannin, Thibaut Monnet, Ivo Ruthemann, Duri Camichel, Andres Ambuhl, Patric Della Rossa,Valentin Wirz, Martin Steinegger, Thierry Paterlini, Raffaele Sannitz

**Ukraine** (Olexander Seukand, coach) GK—Olexander Fyodorov, Igor Karpenko, Vadym Seliverstov—Vitaliy Lyutkevych, Yuriy Navarenko, Vyacheslav Zavalnyuk, Sergiy Klimentyev, Olexander Materukhin, Denys Isayenko, Yurij Gunko, Andri Sryubko, Olexander Pobyedonostsev, Vyacheslav Timchenko, Dmytro Tsyrul, Roman Salnikov, Olexander Matvichuk, Olexander Bobkin, Valentyn Oletskiy, Oleg Shafarenko, Oleg Blagoi, Vasyl Bobrovnikov, Artyom Gnidenko, Sergiy Kharchenko, Vitali Semenchenko, Vitaliy Donika

**United States** (Mike Sullivan, coach) GK—Jason Bacashihua, John Grahame, Cory Schneider—Andrew Hutchinson, Ryan Suter, Keith Ballard, Matt Greene, Erik Johnson, Jack Johnson, Andrew Alberts, Brian Pothier, Lee Stempniak, Paul Stastny, Phil Kessel, Brandon Bochenski, Erik Cole, Tyler Arnason, Chris Clark, Chad Larose, Tobias Petersen, David Backes, Adam Hall, Nate Davis, Zach Parise, Ryan Callahan

## 72nd WORLD CHAMPIONSHIP (MEN)
## May 2-18, 2008
## Halifax/Quebec City, Canada

### Final Placing

| | |
|---|---|
| Gold ........Russia | 9th ........Belarus |
| Silver ......Canada | 10th .......Germany |
| Bronze ....Finland | 11th .......Latvia |
| 4th ..........Sweden | 12th .......Denmark |
| 5th ..........Czech Republic | 13th .......Slovakia |
| 6th ..........United States | 14th .......France^ |
| 7th ..........Switzerland | 15th .......Slovenia^* |
| 8th ..........Norway | 16th .......Italy* |

^promoted from Division I in 2007
*demoted to Division I for 2009

### Tournament Format

Teams were divided into four groups of four teams each for the Preliminary Round. The top three teams from each group advanced to the Qualification Round. The bottom four were placed in a relegation pool, with the last two being relegated. In the Qualifying Round, the top four from advanced to a cross-over quarter-final.

### Results & Standings
### PRELIMINARY ROUND
#### GROUP A (QUEBEC CITY)

| | GP | W | OTW | OTL | L | GF | GA | P |
|---|---|---|---|---|---|---|---|---|
| Switzerland | 3 | 3 | 0 | 0 | 0 | 10 | 4 | 9 |
| Sweden | 3 | 2 | 0 | 0 | 1 | 17 | 9 | 6 |
| Belarus | 3 | 1 | 0 | 0 | 2 | 9 | 9 | 3 |
| France | 3 | 0 | 0 | 0 | 3 | 2 | 16 | 0 |

| | | |
|---|---|---|
| May 3 | Sweden 6 | Belarus 5 |
| May 3 | Switzerland 4 | France 1 |
| May 5 | Switzerland 2 | Belarus 1 |
| May 5 | Sweden 9 | France 0 |
| May 7 | Switzerland 4 | Sweden 2 |
| May 7 | Belarus 3 | France 1 |

#### GROUP B (HALIFAX)

| | GP | W | OTW | OTL | L | GF | GA | P |
|---|---|---|---|---|---|---|---|---|
| Canada | 3 | 3 | 0 | 0 | 0 | 17 | 5 | 9 |
| United States | 3 | 2 | 0 | 0 | 1 | 13 | 6 | 6 |
| Latvia | 3 | 1 | 0 | 0 | 2 | 3 | 11 | 3 |
| Slovenia | 3 | 0 | 0 | 0 | 3 | 2 | 13 | 0 |

| | | |
|---|---|---|
| May 2 | Canada 5 | Slovenia 1 |
| May 2 | United States 4 | Latvia 0 |
| May 4 | Canada 7 | Latvia 0 |
| May 4 | United States 5 | Slovenia 1 |
| May 6 | Canada 5 | United States 4 |
| May 6 | Latvia 3 | Slovenia 0 |

#### GROUP C (HALIFAX)

| | GP | W | OTW | OTL | L | GF | GA | P |
|---|---|---|---|---|---|---|---|---|
| Finland | 3 | 2 | 1 | 0 | 0 | 11 | 5 | 8 |
| Norway | 3 | 1 | 0 | 1 | 1 | 6 | 10 | 4 |
| Germany | 3 | 1 | 0 | 0 | 2 | 7 | 10 | 3 |
| Slovakia | 3 | 1 | 0 | 0 | 2 | 9 | 8 | 3 |

| | | |
|---|---|---|
| May 3 | Finland 5 | Germany 1 |
| May 3 | Slovakia 5 | Norway 1 |
| May 5 | Finland 3 | Norway 2 (Tuomu Ruutu 1:27 OT) |
| May 5 | Germany 4 | Slovakia 2 |
| May 7 | Finland 3 | Slovakia 2 |
| May 7 | Norway 3 | Germany 2 |

#### GROUP D (QUEBEC CITY)

| | GP | W | OTW | OTL | L | GF | GA | P |
|---|---|---|---|---|---|---|---|---|
| Russia | 3 | 2 | 1 | 0 | 0 | 16 | 6 | 8 |
| Czech Republic | 3 | 2 | 0 | 1 | 0 | 16 | 9 | 7 |
| Denmark | 3 | 1 | 0 | 0 | 2 | 9 | 11 | 3 |
| Italy | 3 | 0 | 0 | 0 | 3 | 5 | 20 | 0 |

| | | |
|---|---|---|
| May 2 | Czech Republic 5 | Denmark 2 |
| May 2 | Russia 7 | Italy 1 |
| May 4 | Russia 5 | Czech Republic 4 (Alexei Morozov 3:10 OT) |
| May 4 | Denmark 6 | Italy 2 |
| May 6 | Russia 4 | Denmark 1 |
| May 6 | Czech Republic 7 | Italy 2 |

### QUALIFICATION ROUND
#### GROUP E (QUEBEC CITY)

| | GP | W | OTW | OTL | L | GF | GA | P |
|---|---|---|---|---|---|---|---|---|
| Russia | 5 | 3 | 2 | 0 | 0 | 21 | 13 | 13 |
| Czech Republic | 5 | 2 | 1 | 1 | 1 | 20 | 14 | 9 |
| Sweden | 5 | 3 | 0 | 0 | 2 | 23 | 16 | 9 |
| Switzerland | 5 | 3 | 0 | 0 | 2 | 16 | 15 | 9 |
| Belarus | 5 | 0 | 0 | 3 | 2 | 13 | 18 | 3 |
| Denmark | 5 | 0 | 1 | 0 | 4 | 9 | 26 | 2 |

| | | |
|---|---|---|
| May 8 | Sweden 8 | Denmark 1 |
| May 8 | Czech Republic 5 | Switzerland 0 |
| May 9 | Russia 4 | Belarus 3 (5:00 OT/GWS—Alexei Morozov) |
| May 10 | Czech Republic 3 | Belarus 2 (5:00 OT/GWS—Ales Kotalik) |
| May 10 | Russia 3 | Sweden 2 |
| May 11 | Switzerland 7 | Denmark 2 |
| May 11 | Sweden 5 | Czech Republic 3 |
| May 12 | Russia 5 | Switzerland 3 |
| May 12 | Denmark 3 | Belarus 2 (Peter Regin 2:11 OT) |

#### GROUP F (HALIFAX)

| | GP | W | OTW | OTL | L | GF | GA | P |
|---|---|---|---|---|---|---|---|---|
| Canada | 5 | 5 | 0 | 0 | 0 | 30 | 9 | 15 |
| Finland | 5 | 3 | 1 | 0 | 1 | 16 | 12 | 11 |
| United States | 5 | 3 | 0 | 0 | 2 | 25 | 13 | 9 |
| Norway | 5 | 1 | 0 | 1 | 3 | 8 | 20 | 4 |
| Germany | 5 | 1 | 0 | 0 | 4 | 13 | 27 | 3 |
| Latvia | 5 | 1 | 0 | 0 | 4 | 8 | 19 | 3 |

| | | |
|---|---|---|
| May 8 | Canada 2 | Norway 1 |
| May 8 | United States 6 | Germany 4 |
| May 9 | Finland 2 | Latvia 1 |
| May 10 | Canada 10 | Germany 1 |
| May 11 | Latvia 4 | Norway 1 |
| May 11 | Finland 3 | United States 2 |
| May 12 | United States 9 | Norway 1 |
| May 12 | Canada 6 | Finland 3 |
| May 12 | Germany 5 | Latvia 3 |

### RELEGATION ROUND (QUEBEC CITY)
#### GROUP H

| | GP | W | OTW | OTL | L | GF | GA | P |
|---|---|---|---|---|---|---|---|---|
| France | 2 | 2 | 0 | 0 | 0 | 9 | 6 | 6 |
| Italy | 2 | 0 | 0 | 0 | 2 | 6 | 9 | 0 |

| | | |
|---|---|---|
| May 9 | France 3 | Italy 2 |
| May 10 | France 6 | Italy 4 |

### RELEGATION ROUND (HALIFAX)
#### GROUP H

| | GP | W | OTW | OTL | L | GF | GA | P |
|---|---|---|---|---|---|---|---|---|
| Slovakia | 2 | 1 | 1 | 0 | 0 | 9 | 4 | 4 |
| Slovenia | 2 | 0 | 0 | 1 | 1 | 4 | 9 | 1 |

| | | |
|---|---|---|
| May 9 | Slovakia 5 | Slovenia 1 |
| May 10 | Slovakia 4 | Slovenia 3 (5:00 OT/GWS—Lubomir Visnovsky) |

### PLAYOFFS
#### QUARTER-FINALS

| | | | |
|---|---|---|---|
| May 14 | Quebec City | Sweden 3 (Mattias Weinhandl 3:15 OT) | Czech Republic 2 |
| May 14 | Quebec City | Russia 6 | Switzerland 0 |
| May 14 | Halifax | Canada 8 | Norway 2 |
| May 14 | Halifax | Finland 3 (Sami Lepsito 3:59 OT) | United States 2 |

#### SEMI-FINALS

| | | | |
|---|---|---|---|
| May 16 | Quebec City | Russia 4 | Finland 0 |
| May 16 | Quebec City | Canada 5 | Sweden 4 |

#### BRONZE MEDAL GAME

| | | | |
|---|---|---|---|
| May 17 | Quebec City | Finland 4 | Sweden 0 |

#### GOLD MEDAL GAME

| | | | |
|---|---|---|---|
| May 18 | Quebec City | Russia 5 | Canada 4 (Ilya Kovalchuk 2:42 OT) |

### Rosters

**Belarus** (Curt Fraser, coach) GK—Vitali Koval, Stepan Goryachevskikh, Dmitri Milchakov—Alexei Ugarov, Alexei Kalyuzhny, Andrei Kostitsyn, Dmitri Meleshko, Konstantin Koltsov, Viktor Kostyuchenok, Sergei Zadelenov, Vladimir Denisov, Mikhail Grabovski, Yaroslav Chuprys, Dmitri Dudik, Andrei Mikhalyov, Ruslan Salei, Alexander Zhurik, Sergei Kostitsyn, Alexander Kulakov, Sergei Kolosov, Andrei Bashko, Yevgeni Kurilin, Oleg Antonenko, Alexander Makritski

**Canada** (Ken Hitchcock, coach) GK—Cam Ward, Pascal LeClaire, Mathieu Garon—Dany Heatley, Ryan Getzlaf, Rick Nash, Mike Green, Derek Roy, Martin St. Louis, Brent Burns, Eric Staal, Chris Kunitz, Shane Doan, Jamal Mayers, Jonathan Toews, Patrick Sharp, Jason Spezza, Dan Hamhuis, Jason Chimera, Duncan Keith, Ed Jovanovski, Jay Bouwmeester, Steve Staios, Sam Gagner, Marc Giordano

**Czech Republic** (Alois Hadamczik, coach) GK—Milan Hnilicka, Marek Pinc, Adam Svoboda—Tomas Kaberle, Patrik Elias, Ales Kotalik, Radim Vrbata, Martin Erat, Tomas Fleischmann, Marek Zidlicky, Jaroslav Hlinka, Tomas Rolinek, Zbynek Irgl, Filip Kuba, Martin Hanzal, Tomas Plekanec, Jiri Novotny, Jan Hejda, Ladislav Kohn, Jakub Klepis, Petr Caslava, Zbynek Michalek, David Krejcl, Michal Rozsival, Vaclav Skuhravy

**Denmark** (Mike Sirant, coach) GK—Patrick Galbraith, Peter Hirsch, Simon Nielsen—Kim Staal, Morten Green, Jannik Hansen, Peter Regin, Daniel Nielsen, Kasper Degn, Jesper Damgaard, Stefan Lassen, Morten Madsen, Lars Eller, Andreas Andreasen, Morten Dahlmann, Christoffer Kjargaard, Thor Dresler, Mads Bodker, Nichlas Hardt, Bo Nordby Tranholm, Kim Lykkeskov, Mads Christensen, Mads Christensen, Rasmus Olsen, Mads Schaarup

**Finland** (Doug Shedden, coach) GK—Niklas Backstrom, Petri Vehanen, Kari Ramo—Mikko Koivu, Antti Pihlstrom, Teemu Selanne, Niko Kapanen, Tuomo Ruutu, Olli Jokinen, Janne Niskala, Jussi Jokinen, Ville Peltonen, Hannes Hyvonen, Saku Koivu, Ville Koistinen, Ossi Vaananen, Antti-Jussi Niemi, Riku Hahl, Mikko Jokela, Mika Pyorala, Mikko Luoma, Anssi Salmela, Sami Lepisto, Sean Bergenheim, Esa Pirnes

**France** (Dave Henderson, coach) GK—Cristobal Huet, Fabrice Lhenry, Eddy Ferhi—Sebastien Bordeleau, Baptiste Amar, Julien Desrosiers, Yorick Treille, Jonathan Zwikel, Olivier Coqueux, Vincent Bachet, Simon Lacroix, Francois Rozenthal, Sacha Treille, Pierre Bellemare, Nicolas Besch, Jean F. Bonnard, Laurent Gras, Kevin Hecquefeuille, Anthoine Lussier, Benoit Quessandier, Luc Tardif, Laurent Meunier, Damien Raux, Mathieu Mille, Teddy Trabichet

**Germany** (Uwe Krupp, coach) GK—Robert Muller, Dimitri Patzold, Dmitri Kotschnew—Christopher Schmidt, Florian Busch, Michael Hackert, Philip Gogulla, Christoph Ullmann, Marco Sturm, Christoph Schubert, Yannic Seidenberg, Stefan Ustorf, Michael Wolf, Michael Bakos, Andreas Renz, Frank Hordler, Sven Felski, Jason Holland, John Tripp, Petr Fical, Sebastian Osterloh, Dennis Seidenberg, Marcel Goc, Andre Reiss, Andre Rankel

**Italy** (Fabio Polloni, coach) GK—Guenther Hell, Thomas Tragust, Adam Russo—Jason Cirone, Nicola Fontanive, Pat Iannone, Andre Signoretti, Jonathan Pittis, Luca Ansoldi, Armin Helfer, Giulio Scandella, Christian Borgatello, Paolo Bustreo, Mario Chitarroni, Giorgio de Bettin, Michele Strazzabosco, Manuel de Toni, Armin Hofer, Stefano Margoni, Roland Ramoser, Carter Trevisani, Andreas Lutz, Carlo Lorenzi, John Parco, Marco Insam

**Latvia** (Olegs Znaroks, coach) GK—Edgars Masalskis, Sergejs Naumovs, Dmitrijs Zabotinskis—Lauris Darzins, Herberts Vasiljevs, Martins Cipulis, Martins Karsums, Mikelis Redlihs, Aleksejs Sirokovs, Aleksandrs Nizivijs, Rodrigo Lavins, Janis Sprukts, Armands Berzins, Georgijs Pujacs, Kaspars Daugavins, Guntis Galvins, Raitis Ivanans, Aleksandrs Jerofejevs, Krisjanis Redlihs, Arvids Rekis, Agris Saviel, Juris Stals, Jekabs Redlihs, Aleksandrs Macijevski, Viktors Slinov

**Norway** (Roy Johansen, coach) GK—Pal Grotnes, Andre Lysenstoen, Ruben Smith—Anders Bastiansen, Morten Ask, Mats Trygg, Mads Hansen, Mathis Olimb, Marius Holtet, Lars Erik Spets, Mats Zuccarello Aasen, Jonas Holos, Martin Roymark, Per-Age Skroder, Tommy Jakobsen, Henrik Odegaard, Kristian Forsberg, Mats Froshaug, Kjell Richard Nygard, Anders Myrvold, Juha Kaunismaki, Erik Ryman, Eirik Skadsdammen, Matthias Holmstedt

**Russia** (Vyacheslav Bykov, coach) GK—Yevgeni Nabokov, Mikhail Biryukov, Alexander Yeryomenko—Alexander Syomin, Alexander Ovechkin, Sergei Fyodorov, Ilya Kovalchuk, Alexei Morozov, Danis Zaripov, Maxim Afinogenov, Alexei Tereshenko, Konstantin Korneyev, Sergei Zinoviev, Denis Grebeshkov, Maxim Sushinski, Konstantin Gorovikov, Dmitri Kalinin, Vitali Proshkin, Alexander Radulov, Andrei Markov, Daniil Markov, Ilya Nikulin, Dmitri Vorobyov, Sergei Mozyakin, Fyodor Tyutin

**Slovakia** (Julius Supler, coach) GK—Jan Lasak, Peter Budaj, Karol Krizan—Lubomir Visnovsky, Robert Petrovicky, Juraj Kolnik, Marcel Hossa, Ivan Ciernik, Andrej Podkonicky, Peter Fabus, Andrej Kollar, Miroslav Kovacik, Tibor Melicharek, Peter Podhradsky, Dominik Granak, Peter Huzevka, Andrej Sekera, Frantisek Skladany, Ivan Majeski, Branislav Mezei, Tomas Starosta, Martin Strbak, Radovan Somik, Juraj Mikus, Rene Vydareny

**Slovenia** (Mats Waltin, coach) GK—Robert Kristan, Andrej Hocevar, Gaber Glavic—Anze Kopitar, Tomaz Razingar, Mitja Robar, David Rodman, Marjan Manfreda, Damjan Dervaric, Ales Kranjc, Jakob Milovanovic, Marcel Rodman, Jurij Golicic, Tomo Hafner, Andrej Hebar, Ales Music, Rok Pajic, Miha Rebolj, Andrej Tavzelj, Dejan Varl, Uros Vidmar, Egon Muric, Gregor Poloncic, Boris Pretnar, Anze Terlikar

**Sweden** (Bengt-Ake Gustafsson, coach) GK—Henrik Lundqvist, Stefan Liv, Mikael Tellqvist—Mattias Weinhandl, Tony Martensson, Anton Stralman, Nicklas Backstrom, Fredrik Warg, Marcus Nilson, Kenny Jonsson, Robert Nilsson, Nils Ekman, Patric Hornqvist, Rickard Wallin, Per Ledin, Niclas Wallin, Karl Fabricius, Alexander Edler, Magnus Johansson, Daniel Fernholm, Jonas Frogen, Johan Andersson, Michael Holmqvist, Douglas Murray, Daniel Widing

**Switzerland** (Ralph Krueger, coach) GK—Martin Gerber, Jonas Hiller, Ronnie Rueger—Julien Sprunger, Andres Ambuhl, Beat Forster, Raffaele Sannitz, Paul DiPietro, Thierry Paterlini, Patrik Bartschi, Thibaut Monet, Severin Blindenbacher, Thomas Deruns, Philippe Furrer, Sandy Jeannin, Julien Vauclair, Roman Wick, Goran Bezina, Romano Lemm, Marc Reichert, Raphael Diaz, Thomas Ziegler, Beat Gerber, Mathias Seger, Peter Guggisberg

**United States** (Mike Sullivan, coach) GK—Robert Esche, Tim Thomas, Craig Anderson—Phil Kessel, Patrick Kane, Dustin Brown, Zach Parise, Paul Martin, Patrick O'Sullivan, Jason Pominville, Tom Gilbert, Drew Stafford, Peter Mueller, Brandon Dubinsky, James Wisniewski, Adam Burish, Lee Stempniak, Keith Ballard, David Booth, David Backes, Tim Gleason, Jeff Halpern, Jordan Leopold, Matt Greene, Mark Stuart

## 73rd WORLD CHAMPIONSHIP (MEN)
## April 24-May 10, 2009
## Kloten/Berne, Switzerland

**Final Placing**

| | |
|---|---|
| Gold ........Russia | 9th .........Switzerland |
| Silver ......Canada | 10th .......Slovakia |
| Bronze ....Sweden | 11th .......Norway |
| 4th..........United States | 12th .......France |
| 5th..........Finland | 13th .......Denmark |
| 6th..........Czech Republic | 14th .......Austria^* |
| 7th..........Latvia | 15th .......Germany+ |
| 8th..........Belarus | 16th .......Hungary^* |

+host for the next World Championship (2010) cannot be relegated
^promoted from Division I in 2008
*demoted to Division I for 2010

**Tournament Format**
Teams were divided into four groups of four teams each for the Preliminary Round. The top three teams from each group advanced to the Qualification Round. The bottom four were placed in a relegation pool, with the last two being relegated. In the Qualifying Round, the top four from advanced to a cross-over quarter-final.

**Results & Standings**
**PRELIMINARY ROUND**
**GROUP A (KLOTEN)**

| | GP | W | OTW | OTL | L | GF | GA | P |
|---|---|---|---|---|---|---|---|---|
| Canada | 3 | 3 | 0 | 0 | 0 | 22 | 4 | 9 |
| Belarus | 3 | 1 | 1 | 0 | 1 | 6 | 8 | 5 |
| Slovakia | 3 | 1 | 0 | 1 | 1 | 8 | 12 | 4 |
| Hungary | 3 | 0 | 0 | 0 | 3 | 4 | 16 | 0 |

| | | |
|---|---|---|
| April 24 | Canada 6 | Belarus 1 |
| April 24 | Slovakia 4 | Hungary 3 |
| April 26 | Belarus 2 | Slovakia 1 (5:00 OT/GWS—Oleg Antonenko) |
| April 26 | Canada 9 | Hungary 0 |
| April 28 | Belarus 3 | Hungary 1 |
| April 28 | Canada 7 | Slovakia 3 |

**GROUP B (BERNE)**

| | GP | W | OTW | OTL | L | GF | GA | P |
|---|---|---|---|---|---|---|---|---|
| Russia | 3 | 3 | 0 | 0 | 0 | 16 | 4 | 9 |
| Switzerland | 3 | 1 | 1 | 0 | 1 | 6 | 6 | 5 |
| France | 3 | 1 | 0 | 0 | 2 | 4 | 9 | 3 |
| Germany | 3 | 0 | 0 | 1 | 2 | 3 | 10 | 1 |

| | | |
|---|---|---|
| April 24 | Russia 5 | Germany 0 |
| April 24 | Switzerland 1 | France 0 |
| April 26 | Switzerland 3 | Germany 2 (Mark Streit 1:18 OT) |
| April 26 | Russia 7 | France 2 |
| April 28 | Russia 4 | Switzerland 2 |
| April 28 | France 2 | Germany 1 |

**GROUP C (BERNE)**

| | GP | W | OTW | OTL | L | GF | GA | P |
|---|---|---|---|---|---|---|---|---|
| United States | 3 | 2 | 0 | 1 | 0 | 15 | 9 | 7 |
| Sweden | 3 | 1 | 1 | 1 | 0 | 15 | 9 | 6 |
| Latvia | 3 | 1 | 1 | 0 | 1 | 7 | 6 | 5 |
| Austria | 3 | 0 | 0 | 0 | 3 | 2 | 15 | 0 |

| | | |
|---|---|---|
| April 25 | United States 4 | Latvia 2 |
| April 25 | Sweden 7 | Austria 1 |
| April 27 | United States 6 | Austria 1 |
| April 27 | Latvia 3 | Sweden 2 (5:00 OT/GWS—Aleksandrs Nizivijs) |
| April 29 | Latvia 2 | Austria 0 |
| April 29 | Sweden 6 | United States 5 (Kristian Huselius 1:59 OT) |

**GROUP D (KLOTEN)**

| | GP | W | OTW | OTL | L | GF | GA | P |
|---|---|---|---|---|---|---|---|---|
| Finland | 3 | 3 | 0 | 0 | 0 | 14 | 4 | 9 |
| Czech Republic | 3 | 2 | 0 | 0 | 1 | 13 | 6 | 6 |
| Norway | 3 | 0 | 1 | 0 | 2 | 7 | 14 | 2 |
| Denmark | 3 | 0 | 0 | 1 | 2 | 5 | 15 | 1 |

| | | |
|---|---|---|
| April 25 | Finland 5 | Norway 0 |
| April 25 | Czech Republic 5 | Denmark 0 |
| April 27 | Czech Republic 5 | Norway 2 |
| April 27 | Finland 5 | Denmark 1 |

| | | |
|---|---|---|
| April 29 | Norway 5 | Denmark 4 (Tommy Jakobsen 1:06 OT) |
| April 29 | Finland 4 | Czech Republic 3 |

**QUALIFICATION ROUND**
**GROUP E (BERNE)**

| | GP | W | OTW | OTL | L | GF | GA | P |
|---|---|---|---|---|---|---|---|---|
| Russia | 5 | 4 | 1 | 0 | 0 | 27 | 11 | 14 |
| Sweden | 5 | 2 | 1 | 2 | 0 | 23 | 18 | 10 |
| United States | 5 | 2 | 0 | 2 | 1 | 19 | 18 | 8 |
| Latvia | 5 | 1 | 2 | 0 | 2 | 15 | 14 | 7 |
| Switzerland | 5 | 1 | 1 | 1 | 2 | 9 | 13 | 6 |
| France | 5 | 0 | 0 | 0 | 5 | 8 | 27 | 0 |

| | | |
|---|---|---|
| April 30 | Russia 6 | Sweden 5 (Dmitri Kalinen 4:04 OT) |
| April 30 | Latvia 2 | Switzerland 1 (5:00 OT/GWS—Aleksandrs Nizivijs) |
| May 1 | United States 6 | France 2 |
| May 2 | Latvia 7 | France 1 |
| May 2 | Russia 4 | United States 1 |
| May 3 | Sweden 4 | Switzerland 1 |
| May 3 | Russia 6 | Latvia 1 |
| May 4 | Sweden 6 | France 3 |
| May 4 | Switzerland 4 | United States 3 (Roman Wick 0:13 OT) |

**GROUP F (KLOTEN)**

| | GP | W | OTW | OTL | L | GF | GA | P |
|---|---|---|---|---|---|---|---|---|
| Canada | 5 | 4 | 0 | 1 | 0 | 26 | 10 | 13 |
| Finland | 5 | 2 | 2 | 1 | 0 | 16 | 9 | 11 |
| Czech Republic | 5 | 3 | 0 | 0 | 2 | 20 | 11 | 9 |
| Belarus | 5 | 0 | 3 | 0 | 2 | 8 | 13 | 6 |
| Slovakia | 5 | 0 | 1 | 2 | 2 | 8 | 21 | 4 |
| Norway | 5 | 0 | 0 | 2 | 3 | 7 | 21 | 2 |

| | | |
|---|---|---|
| April 30 | Belarus 3 | Norway 2 (Ruslan Salei 4:35 OT) |
| April 30 | Canada 5 | Czech Republic 1 |
| May 1 | Finland 2 | Slovakia 1 (Sami Kapanen 3:39 OT) |
| May 2 | Czech Republic 8 | Slovakia 0 |
| May 2 | Belarus 2 | Finland 1 (5:00 OT/GWS—Oleg Antonenko) |
| May 3 | Canada 5 | Norway 1 |
| May 3 | Czech Republic 3 | Belarus 0 |
| May 4 | Slovakia 3 | Norway 2 (Ladislav Nagy 2:07 OT) |
| May 4 | Finland 4 | Canada 3 (5:00 OT/GWS—Hannes Hyvonen) |

**RELEGATION ROUND**
**GROUP G**

| | GP | W | OTW | OTL | L | GF | GA | P |
|---|---|---|---|---|---|---|---|---|
| Denmark | 3 | 3 | 0 | 0 | 0 | 13 | 4 | 9 |
| Austria | 3 | 2 | 0 | 0 | 1 | 9 | 5 | 6 |
| Germany | 3 | 1 | 0 | 0 | 2 | 3 | 5 | 3 |
| Hungary | 3 | 0 | 0 | 0 | 3 | 2 | 13 | 0 |

| | | | |
|---|---|---|---|
| May 1 | Berne | Denmark 3 | Germany 1 |
| May 1 | Kloten | Austria 6 | Hungary 0 |
| May 3 | Berne | Austria 1 | Germany 0 |
| May 3 | Kloten | Denmark 5 | Hungary 1 |
| May 4 | Berne | Germany 2 | Hungary 1 |
| May 4 | Kloten | Denmark 5 | Austria 2 |

**PLAYOFFS (BERNE)**
**QUARTER-FINALS**

| | | |
|---|---|---|
| May 6 | Russia 4 | Belarus 3 |
| May 6 | United States 3 | Finland 2 |
| May 7 | Canada 4 | Latvia 2 |
| May 7 | Sweden 3 | Czech Republic 1 |

**SEMI-FINALS**

| | | |
|---|---|---|
| May 8 | Russia 3 | United States 2 |
| May 8 | Canada 3 | Sweden 1 |

**BRONZE MEDAL GAME**

| | | |
|---|---|---|
| May 10 | Sweden 4 | United States 2 |

**GOLD MEDAL GAME**

| | | |
|---|---|---|
| May 10 | Russia 2 | Canada 1 |

**Rosters**

**Austria** (Lars Bergstrom, coach) GK—Jurgen Penker, Bernd Bruckler, Bernhard Starkbaum—Gerhard Unterluggauer, Roland Kaspitz, Philippe Lakos, Michael Raffl, Andreas Nodl, Paul Schellander, Thomas Koch, Matthias Trattnig, Darcy Werenka, Thomas Vanek, Jeremy Rebek, Andre Lakos, Markus Peintner, Andreas Kristler, Martin Oraze, Mario Altmann, David Schuller, Harald Ofner, Robert Lukas, Christoph Harand, Gregor Baumgartner, Oliver Setzinger

**Belarus** (Glen Hanlon, coach) GK—Vitali Koval, Andrei Mezin, Igor Brikun—Ivan Usenko, Alexander Makritski, Alexander Ryadinski, Vladimir Denisov, Andrei Mikhalyov, Oleg Antonenko, Alexander Kulakov, Yevgeni Kovyrshin, Mikhail Stefanovich, Alexei Ugarov, Dmitri Meleshko, Andrei Stas, Ruslan Salei, Konstantin Koltsov, Andrei Bashko, Viktor Kostyuchenok, Sergei Demagin, Yaroslav Chuprys, Alexei Kalyuzhny, Mikhail Grabovski, Andrei Antonov, Dmitri Korobov

**Canada** (Lindy Ruff, coach) GK—Dwayne Roloson, Chris Mason, Josh Harding—Dan Hamhuis, Drew Doughty, Chris Phillips, Luke Schenn, Shea Weber, Ian White, Scottie Upshall, Derek Roy, Shawn Horcoff, Mike Fisher, Dany Heatley, Travis Zajac, Steve Stamkos, Matt Lombardi, Shane Doan, Colby Armstrong, Martin St. Louis, James Neal, Joel Kwiatkowski, Marc-Edouard Vlasic, Braydon Coburn, Jason Spezza

**Czech Republic** (Vladimir Ruzicka, coach) GK—Martin Prusek, Jakub Stepanek, Lukas Mensator—Marek Zidlicky, Roman Polak, Ondrej Nemec, Roman Cervenka, Michal Barinka, Ales Kotalik, Tomas Plekanec, Jan Marek, Petr Cajanek, Jaroslav Hlinka, Milan Michalek, Jakub Klepis, Karel Rachunek, Zbynek Irgl, Patrik Elias, Petr Caslava, Miroslav Blatak, Tomas Rolinek, Josef Vasicek, Jaromir Jagr, Ales Hemsky, Rostislav Olesz

**Denmark** (Per Backman, coach) GK—Patrick Galbraith, Sebastian Dahm, Frederik Andersen—Philip Hersby, Philip Larsen, Mads Bodker, Daniel Nielsen, Jesper Damgaard, Kasper Degn, Rasmus Olsen, Morten Green, Kim Lykkeskov, Mads Christensen, Kim Staal, Thor Dresler, Alexander Sundberg, Kasper Pedersen, Mads Christensen, Morten Madsen, Julian Jakobsen, Nichlas Hardt, Jesper Jensen, Mikkel Bodker, Peter Regin

**Finland** (Jukka Jalonen, coach) GK—Kari Ramo, Pekka Rinne, Juuso Riksman—Petteri Nummelin, Ville Koistinen, Lasse Kukkonen, Topi Jaakola, Hannes Hyvonen, Niklas Hagman, Antti Miettinen, Janne Niskala, Tommi Santala, Sami Kapanen, Jarkko Immonen, Anssi Salmela, Kalle Kerman, Mikko Lehtonen, Mika Pyorala, Niko Kapanen, Leo Komarov, Janne Niinimaa, Tuomas Pihlman, Juha-Pekka Hytonen, Jarkko Ruutu, Ville Vahalahti

**France** (Dave Henderson, coach) GK—Eddy Ferhi, Fabrice Lhenry, Henri Corentin Buysse—Vincent Bachet, Yorick Treille, Laurent Meunier, Francois Rozenthal, Jonathan Zwikel, Stepahne da Costa, Benoit Quessandier, Luc Tardif, Damien Raux, Cyril Papa, Anthoine Lussier, Baptiste Amar, Laurent Gras, Mathieu Mille, Thomas Roussel, Pierre Edouard Bellemare, Antonin Manavian, Kevin Igier, Gary Leveque, Sacha Treille, Kevin Hecquefeuille, Damien Fleury

**Germany** (Uwe Krupp, coach) GK—Dimitri Patzold, Dimitrij Kotschnew, Dennis Endras—Sven Butenschon, Chris Schmidt, Sebastian Osterloh, Sven Felski, Christoph Schubert, Travis Mulock, Michael Wolf, Jochen Hecht, Kai Hospelt, Michael Bakos, Andre Rankel, Daniel Kreutzer, Alexander Barta, Andreas Renz, Michael Hackert, Yannic Seidenberg, Christoph Ullmann, Frank Hordler, Patrick Hager, Nicolai Goc, Phillip Gogulla, Moritz Muller

**Hungary** (Pat Cortina, coach) GK—Zoltan Hetenyi, Levente Szuper, Krisztian Budai—Csaba Kovacs, Andras Horvath, Viktor Szelig, Viktor Tokaji, Andras Benk, Balazs Ladanyi, Csaba Janosi, Rastislav Ondrejcik, Gergely Majoross, Daniel Koger, Janos Vas, Roger Holeczy, Krisztian Palkovics, Balazs Kangyal, Bence Svasznek, Marton Vas, Tamas Sille, Omar Ennaffati, Imre Peterdi, Artyom Vaszjunyin, Daniel Fekete, Gergo Nagy

**Latvia** (Olegs Znaroks, coach) GK—Edgars Masalskis, Sergejs Naumovs, Dmitrijs Zabotinskis—Rodrigo Lavins, Oskars Bartulis, Janis Sprukts, Karlis Skrastins, Martins Karsums, Lauris Darzins, Kristaps Sotnieks, Herberts Vasiljevs, Guntis Galvins, Guntis Dzerins, Aleksandrs Jerofejevs, Aleksejs Sirokovs, Aleksandrs Nizivijs, Georgijs Pujacs, Mikelis Redlihs, Armands Berzins, Olegs Sorokins, Krisjanis Redlihs, Roberts Jekimovs, Aigars Cipruss, Martins Cipulis, Girts Ankipans

**Norway** (Roy Johansen, coach) GK—Pal Grotnes, Andre Lysenstoen, Ruben Smith—Juha Kaunismaki, Jonas Holos, Tommy Jakobsen, Mads Hansen, Marius Holtet, Lars Erik Spets, Peter Lorentzen, Per-Age Skroder, Anders Bastiansen, Morten Ask, Martin Roymark, Mats Trygg, Kristian Forsberg, Tore Vikingstad, Martin Laumann-Ylven, Lars Erik Lund, Patrick Thoresen, Alexander Bonsaksen, Mats Zuccarello-Aasen, Anders Myrvold

**Russia** (Vyacheslav Bykov, coach) GK—Alexander Yeryomenko, Ilya Bryzgalov, Vasili Kosechkin—Vitali Vishnevski, Ilya Nikulin, Anton Volchenkov, Dmitri Kalinin, Sergei Mozyakin, Nikolai Zherdev, Alexander Perezhogin, Anton Kuryanov, Konstantin Gorovikov, Konstantin Korneyev, Alexei Tereshenko, Alexander Frolov, Danis Zaripov, Vitali Atyushov, Denis Grebeshkov, Sergei Zinoviev, Vitali Proshkin, Alexander Radulov, Oleg Tverdovski, Ilya Kovalchuk, Oleg Saprykin, Alexei Morozov

**Slovakia** (Jan Filc, coach) GK—Jan Lasak, Rastislav Stana, Jaroslav Halak—Jiri Bicek, Peter Smrek, Ivan Baranka, Milan Bartovic, Ivan Svarny, Stefan Ruzicka, Dominik Granak, Michal Macho, Rastislav Pavlikovsky, Juraj Stefanka, Lubos Bartecko, Michal Handzus, Ladislav Nagy, Peter Olvecky, Rene Vydareny,Tomas Surovy, Jaroslav Obsut, Andrej Sekera, Boris Valabik, Juraj Mikus, Marcel Hossa, Branko Radivojevic

**Sweden** (Begt-Ake Gustafsson, coach) GK—Stefan Liv, Johan Holmqvist, Jonas Gustavsson—Nicklas Grossman, Johan Akerman, Magnus Johansson, Johnny Oduya, Tony Martensson, Martin Thornberg, Carl Gunnarsson, Patrik Berglund, Rickard Wallin, Johan Andersson, Joel Lundqvist, Loui Eriksson, Niklas Persson, Linus Omark, Johan Harju, Marcus Nilson,Dick Tarnstrom,Kenny Jonsson, Anton Stralman, Tobias Enstrom, Kristian Huselius, Mattias Weinhandl

**Switzerland** (Ralph Krueger, coach) GK—Martin Gerber, Ronnie Rueger—Severin Blindenbacher, Mark Streit, Andres Ambuhl, Felicien Du Bois, Roman Wick, Thomas Deruns, Thierry Paterlini, Thibaut Monnet, Martin Pluss, Mathias Seger, Ivo Ruthemann, Sandy Jeannin, Thomas Ziegler, Raffaele Sannitz, Ryan Gardner, Philippe Furrer, Goran Bezina, Romano Lemm, Yannick Weber, Julien Sprunger, Kevin Romy, Roman Josi

**United States** (Ron Wilson, coach) GK—Robert Esche, Al Montoya, Scott Clemmensen—Keith Ballard, Jack Johnson, Zach Bogosian, Matt Niskanen, Ron Hainsey, Peter Harrold, Joe Pavelski, Kyle Okposo, Patrick O'Sullivan, John-Michael Liles, Nick Foligno, Chris Higgins, Ryan Suter, Drew Stafford, Lee Stempniak, Dustin Brown, Ryan Shannon, Colin Wilson, David Backes, Colin Stuart, Jason Blake, T.J. Oshie

## 74th WORLD CHAMPIONSHIP (MEN)
## May 7-23, 2010
## Gelsenkirchen/Mannheim/Cologne, Germany

### Final Placing

| | |
|---|---|
| Gold ........Czech Republic | 9th .........Norway |
| Silver ......Russia | 10th .......Belarus |
| Bronze ....Sweden | 11th .......Latvia |
| 4th ..........Germany | 12th .......Slovakia |
| 5th ..........Switzerland | 13th .......United States |
| 6th ..........Finland | 14th .......France |
| 7th ..........Canada | 15th .......Italy^* |
| 8th ..........Denmark | 16th .......Kazakhstan^* |

^promoted from Division I in 2009
*demoted to Division I for 2011

### Tournament Format

Teams were divided into four groups of four teams each for the Preliminary Round. The top three teams from each group advanced to the Qualification Round. The bottom four were placed in a relegation pool, with the last two being relegated. In the Qualifying Round, the top four from advanced to a cross-over quarter-final.

### Results & Standings
### PRELIMINARY ROUND
### GROUP A (COLOGNE)

| | GP | W | OTW | OTL | L | GF | GA | P |
|---|---|---|---|---|---|---|---|---|
| Russia | 3 | 3 | 0 | 0 | 0 | 10 | 3 | 9 |
| Slovakia | 3 | 2 | 0 | 0 | 1 | 10 | 6 | 6 |
| Belarus | 3 | 1 | 0 | 0 | 2 | 8 | 9 | 3 |
| Kazakhstan | 3 | 0 | 0 | 0 | 3 | 4 | 14 | 0 |

| | | |
|---|---|---|
| May 9 | Belarus 5 | Kazakhstan 2 |
| May 9 | Russia 3 | Slovakia 1 |
| May 11 | Russia 4 | Kazakhstan 1 |
| May 11 | Slovakia 4 | Belarus 2 |
| May 13 | Russia 3 | Belarus 1 |
| May 13 | Slovakia 5 | Kazakhstan 1 |

### GROUP B (MANNHEIM)

| | GP | W | OTW | OTL | L | GF | GA | P |
|---|---|---|---|---|---|---|---|---|
| Switzerland | 3 | 3 | 0 | 0 | 0 | 10 | 2 | 9 |
| Canada | 3 | 2 | 0 | 0 | 1 | 12 | 6 | 6 |
| Latvia | 3 | 1 | 0 | 0 | 2 | 7 | 11 | 3 |
| Italy | 3 | 0 | 0 | 0 | 3 | 3 | 13 | 0 |

| | | |
|---|---|---|
| May 8 | Canada 5 | Italy 1 |
| May 8 | Switzerland 3 | Latvia 1 |
| May 10 | Switzerland 3 | Italy 0 |
| May 10 | Canada 6 | Latvia 1 |
| May 12 | Latvia 5 | Italy 2 |
| May 12 | Switzerland 4 | Canada 1 |

### GROUP C (MANNHEIM)

| | GP | W | OTW | OTL | L | GF | GA | P |
|---|---|---|---|---|---|---|---|---|
| Sweden | 3 | 2 | 0 | 0 | 1 | 9 | 6 | 6 |
| Czech Republic | 3 | 2 | 0 | 0 | 1 | 10 | 6 | 6 |
| Norway | 3 | 2 | 0 | 0 | 1 | 10 | 8 | 6 |
| France | 3 | 0 | 0 | 0 | 3 | 5 | 14 | 0 |

| | | |
|---|---|---|
| May 9 | Czech Republic 6 | France 2 |
| May 9 | Sweden 5 | Norway 2 |
| May 11 | Norway 3 | Czech Republic 2 |
| May 11 | Sweden 3 | France 2 |
| May 13 | Norway 5 | France 1 |
| May 13 | Czech Republic 2 | Sweden 1 |

### GROUP D

| | GP | W | OTW | OTL | L | GF | GA | P |
|---|---|---|---|---|---|---|---|---|
| Finland | 3 | 2 | 0 | 0 | 1 | 5 | 6 | 6 |
| Germany | 3 | 1 | 1 | 0 | 1 | 5 | 3 | 5 |
| Denmark | 3 | 1 | 1 | 0 | 1 | 7 | 5 | 5 |
| United States | 3 | 0 | 0 | 2 | 1 | 4 | 7 | 2 |

| | | | |
|---|---|---|---|
| May 7 | Gelsenkirchen | Germany 2 (Felix Schutz 0:21 OT)* | United States 1 |
| May 8 | Cologne | Denmark 4 | Finland 1 |
| May 10 | Cologne | Denmark 2 (Stefan Lassen 2:04 OT) | United States 1 |
| May 10 | Cologne | Finland 1 | Germany 0 |
| May 12 | Cologne | Germany 3 | Denmark 1 |
| May 12 | Cologne | Finland 3 | United States 2 |

*played before a world record crowd of 77,803 at Veltins Arena

### RELEGATION ROUND

| | GP | W | OTW | OTL | L | GF | GA | P |
|---|---|---|---|---|---|---|---|---|
| United States | 3 | 2 | 1 | 0 | 0 | 17 | 2 | 8 |
| France | 3 | 2 | 0 | 0 | 1 | 7 | 8 | 6 |
| Italy | 3 | 1 | 0 | 1 | 1 | 5 | 6 | 4 |
| Kazakhstan | 3 | 0 | 0 | 0 | 3 | 4 | 17 | 0 |

| | | | |
|---|---|---|---|
| May 15 | Cologne | United States 10 | Kazakhstan 0 |
| May 15 | Mannheim | France 2 | Italy 1 |
| May 16 | Cologne | United States 4 | France 0 |
| May 16 | Mannheim | Italy 2 | Kazakhstan 1 |
| May 18 | Cologne | United States 3 | Italy 2 (5:00 OT/GWS—T.J. Oshie) |
| May 18 | Mannheim | France 5 | Kazakhstan 3 |

### QUALIFYING ROUND
### GROUP E (COLOGNE)

| | GP | W | OTW | OTL | L | GF | GA | P |
|---|---|---|---|---|---|---|---|---|
| Russia | 5 | 5 | 0 | 0 | 0 | 20 | 5 | 15 |
| Finland | 5 | 3 | 0 | 0 | 2 | 9 | 11 | 9 |
| Germany | 5 | 2 | 0 | 1 | 2 | 8 | 8 | 7 |
| Denmark | 5 | 2 | 0 | 0 | 3 | 13 | 12 | 6 |
| Belarus | 5 | 1 | 1 | 0 | 3 | 7 | 11 | 5 |
| Slovakia | 5 | 1 | 0 | 0 | 4 | 8 | 18 | 3 |

| | | |
|---|---|---|
| May 14 | Denmark 6 | Slovakia 0 |
| May 14 | Finland 2 | Belarus 0 |
| May 15 | Russia 3 | Germany 2 |
| May 16 | Russia 6 | Denmark 1 |
| May 16 | Belarus 2 | Germany 1 (Alexei Kalyuzhny 4:45 OT) |
| May 17 | Finland 5 | Slovakia 2 |
| May 17 | Belarus 2 | Denmark 1 |
| May 18 | Germany 2 | Slovakia 1 |
| May 18 | Russia 5 | Finland 0 |

### GROUP F (MANNHEIM)

| | GP | W | OTW | OTL | L | GF | GA | P |
|---|---|---|---|---|---|---|---|---|
| Sweden | 5 | 4 | 0 | 0 | 1 | 18 | 7 | 12 |
| Switzerland | 5 | 3 | 0 | 0 | 2 | 12 | 12 | 9 |
| Czech Republic | 5 | 3 | 0 | 0 | 2 | 12 | 10 | 9 |
| Canada | 5 | 2 | 0 | 0 | 3 | 22 | 12 | 6 |
| Norway | 5 | 2 | 0 | 0 | 3 | 9 | 26 | 6 |
| Latvia | 5 | 1 | 0 | 0 | 4 | 10 | 16 | 3 |

| | | |
|---|---|---|
| May 14 | Canada 12 | Norway 1 |
| May 14 | Sweden 4 | Latvia 2 |
| May 15 | Switzerland 3 | Czech Republic 2 |
| May 16 | Latvia 5 | Norway 0 |
| May 16 | Sweden 3 | Canada 1 |
| May 17 | Norway 3 | Switzerland 2 |
| May 17 | Czech Republic 3 | Latvia 1 |
| May 18 | Czech Republic 3 | Canada 2 |
| May 18 | Sweden 5 | Switzerland 0 |

### PLAYOFFS
### QUARTER-FINALS

| | | | |
|---|---|---|---|
| May 20 | Cologne | Czech Republic 2 (10:00 OT/GWS—Jan Marek) | Finland 1 |
| May 20 | Mannheim | Sweden 4 | Denmark 2 |
| May 20 | Cologne | Russia 5 | Canada 2 |
| May 20 | Mannheim | Germany 1 | Switzerland 0 |

### SEMI-FINALS

| | | | |
|---|---|---|---|
| May 22 | Cologne | Czech Republic 3 (10:00 OT/GWS—Jan Marek) | Sweden 2 |
| May 22 | Cologne | Russia 2 | Germany 1 |

### BRONZE MEDAL GAME

| | | | |
|---|---|---|---|
| May 23 | Cologne | Sweden 3 | Germany 1 |

### GOLD MEDAL GAME

| | | | |
|---|---|---|---|
| May 23 | Cologne | Czech Republic 2 | Russia 1 |

### Rosters

**Belarus** (Eduard Zankovets, coach) GK—Vitali Koval, Sergei Shabanov, Andrei Mezin—Alexander Makritski, Nikolai Stasenko, Vladimir Denisov, Andrei Mikhalyov, Alexander Kulakov, Sergei Drozd, Mikhail Stefanovich, Alexei Ugarov, Dmitri Meleshko, Ruslan Salei, Sergei Kolosov, Andrei Stas, Viktor Kostyuchenok, Alexander Ryadinski, Sergei Demagin, Yaroslav Chuprys, Alexei Kalyuzhny, Artyom Senkevich, Mikhail Grabovski, Yevgeni Kovyrshin, Kirill Gotovets

**Canada** (Craig MacTavish, coach) GK—Devan Dubnyk, Chris Mason, Chad Johnson—Kris Russell, Michael del Zotto, Marc Giordano, Brent Burns, Steve Downie, Corey Perry, Mason Raymond, Ray Whitney, Jordan Eberle, Rene Bourque, Marc Staal, Evander Kane, John Tavares, Brooks Laich, Francois Beauchemin, Kyle Cumiskey, Steve Ott, Rich Peverley, Tyler Myers, Steve Stamkos, Matt Duchene, Ryan Smyth

**Czech Republic** (Vladimir Ruzicka, coach) GK—Tomas Vokoun, Ondrej Pavelec, Jakub Stepanek—Michal Rozsival, Karel Rachunek, Filip Novak, Tomas Mojzis, Michal Barinka, Roman Cervenka, Petr Hubacek, Jiri Novotny, Petr Vampola, Jan Marek, Jakub Klepis, Lukas Kaspar, Petr Gregorek, Martin Ruzicka, Petr Caslava, Petr Koukal, Miroslav Blatak, Tomas Rolinek, Ondrej Nemec, Jaromir Jagr, Marek Kvapil, Jakub Voracek

**Denmark** (Per Backman, coach) GK—Peter Hirsch, Patrick Galbraith, Frederik Andersen—Philip Larsen, Mads Bodker, Daniel Nielsen, Stefan Lassen, Jesper Damgaard, Kasper Degn, Alexander Sundberg, Morten Green, Kim Staal, Thor Dresler, Jesper Jensen, Kim Lykkeskov, Mads Christensen, Morten Madsen, Julian Jakobsen, Jesper Duus, Nichlas Hardt, Frans Nielsen, Mads Christensen, Lars Eller, Peter Regin

**Finland** (Jukka Jalonen, coach) GK—Pekka Rinne, Petri Vehanen, Iiro Tarkki—Petteri Nummelin, Lasse Kukkonen, Topi Jaakola, Mikko Maenpaa, Juuso Hietanen, Juha-Pekka Hytonen, Antti Miettinen, Janne Niskala, Tommi Santala, Riku Hahl, Sami Kapanen, Jarkko Immonen, Petri Kontiola, Lauri Korpikoski, Jussi Jokinen, Antti Pihlstrom, Pasi Puistola, Sami Vatanen, Oskar Osala, Juhamatti Aaltonen, Jori Lehtera, Leo Komarov

**France** (Dave Henderson, coach) GK—Fabrice Lhenry, Eddy Ferhi, Florian Hardy—Vincent Bachet, Yorick Treille, Kevin Igier, Laurent Meunier, Luc Tardif, Stephane da Costa, Benoit Quessandier, Yohann Auvitu, Loic Lamperier, Brian Henderson, Anthoine Lussier, Baptiste Amar, Laurent Gras, Thomas Roussel, Pierre-Edouard Bellemare, Antonin Manavian, Nicolas Besch, Sacha Treille, Teddy da Costa, Erwan Pain, Damien Raux, Kevin Hecquefeuille

**Germany** (Uwe Krupp, coach) GK—Dennis Endras, Robert Zepp, Dimitri Kotschnew—Justin Krueger, Korbinian Holzer, Sven Butenschon, Christian Ehrhoff, Sven Felski, Michael Wolf, Kai Hospelt, Robert Dietrich, John Tripp, Andre Rankel, Marcel Muller, Daniel Kreutzer, Alexander Barta, Christoph Ullmann, Frank Hordler, Patrick Hager, Alexander Sulzer, Felix Schutz, Marcel Goc, Nikolai Goc, Philip Gogulla, Constantin Braun

**Italy** (Rick Cornacchia, coach) GK—Thomas Tragust, Dan Bellissimo, Adam Russo—Stefan Zisser, Max Oberrauch, Trevor Johnson, Michele Strazzabosco, Armin Hofer, John Parco, Giorgio de Bettin, Giulio Scandella, Roland Ramoser, Patrick Iannone, Alexander Egger, Matthew de Marchi, Stefano Margoni, Stefano Marchetti, Armin Helfer, Michael Souza, Manuel de Toni, Jonathan Pittis, Nicholas Plastino, Christian Borgatello, Luca Ansoldi, Nicola Fontanive

**Kazakhstan** (Andrei Shayanov, coach) GK—Vitali Yeremeyev, Alexei Kuznetsov, Pavel Zhitkov—Roman Savchenko, Anton Kazantsev, Alexei Litvinenko, Maxim Semenov, Talgat Zhailauov, Vladimir Antipin, Georgi Petrov, Alexander Koreshkov, Dmitri Dudarev, Andrei Spiridonov, Konstantin Shafranov, Ilya Solarev, Yevgeni Bumagin, Alexei Vasilchenko, Andrei Gavrilin, Yevgeni Fadeyev, Roman Starchenko, Alexander Shin, Alexei Koledayev, Alexei Vorontsov, Vadim Krasnoslabotsev, Yevgeni Rymarev

**Latvia** (Olegs Znaroks, coach) GK—Edgars Masalskis, Martins Raitums, Edgars Lusins—Arvids Rekis, Janis Sprukts, Juris Stals, Martins Karsums, Lauris Darzins, Kristaps Sotneiks, Herberts Vasiljevs, Guntis Galvins, Janis Andersons, Aleksandrs Jerofejevs, Kaspars Daugavins, Aleksandrs Nizivijs, Kaspars Saulietis, Maris Jass, Andris Dzerins, Mikelis Redlihs, Jekabs Redlihs, Sergejs Pecura, Arturs Kulda, Martins Cipulis, Georgijs Pujacs, Gints Meija

**Norway** (Roy Johansen, coach) GK—Pal Grotnes, Andre Lysenstoen, Ruben Smith—Juha Kaunismaki, Jonas Holos, Tommy Jakobsen, Marius Holtet, Lars-Erik Spets, Peter Lorentzen, Knut-Henrik Spets, Anders Bastiansen, Martin Roymark, Andreas Martinsen, Kristian Forsberg, Martin Laumann-Ylven, Lars Lokken-Ostli, Henrik Solberg, Ken-Andre Olimb, Patrick Thoresen, Brede Csiszar, Mathis Olimb, Alexander Bonsaksen, Mats Zuccarello-Aasen, Anders Fredriksen, Ole-Kristian Tollefsen

**Russia** (Vyacheslav Bykov, coach) GK—Semyon Varlamov, Alexander Yeryomenko, Vasili Koshechkin—Ilya Nikulin, Dmitri Kalinin, Alexander Ovechkin, Sergei Mozyakin, Yevgeni Malkin, Pavel Datsyuk, Konstantin Korneyev, Alexei Tereshenko, Alexander Frolov, Vitali Atyushov, Alexander Syomin, Sergei Fyodorov, Maxim Sushinski, Denis Grebeshkov, Nikolai Kulyomin, Artyom Anisimov, Dmitri Kulikov, Viktor Kozlov, Sergei Gonchar, Maxim Afinogenov, Ilya Kovalchuk, Alexei Yemelin

**Slovakia** (Glen Hanlon, coach) GK—Rastislav Stana, Peter Budaj, Peter Hamerlik—Ivan Majesky, Andrej Podkonicky, Dominik Granak, Roman Kukumberg, Michal Macho, Miroslav Satan, Tomas Starosta, Miroslav Zalesak, Marek Zagrapan, Vladimir Dravecky, Ivan Ciernik, Richard Panik, Marek Svatos, Richard Lintner, Peter Fruhauf, Andrej Sekera, Vladimir Mihalik, Milan Bartovic, Tomas Bulik, Tomas Tatar, Stanislav Gron

**Sweden** (Bengt-Ake Gustafsson, coach) GK—Jonas Gustavsson, Jacob Markstrom, Anders Lindback—Oliver Ekman-Larsson, Christian Backman, Magnus Johansson, Sanny Lindstrom, Tony Martensson, Carl Gunnarsson, Fredrik Pettersson, Andreas Engqvist, Jimmie Ericsson, Niklas Persson, Linus Omark, Johan Harju, Marcus Nilson, Rickard Wallin, Jonathan Ericsson, Mikael Backlund, Erik Karlsson, Jonas Andersson, Victor Hedman, Mattias Weinhandl, Magnus Paajarvi-Svensson, Michael Nylander

**Switzerland** (Sean Simpson, coach) GK—Martin Gerber, Tobias Stephan, Daniel Manzato—Julien Vauclair, Patrick Geering, Timo Helbling, Paul Savary, Andres Ambuhl, Felicien du Bois, Thomas Deruns, Nino Niederreiter, Thibaut Monnet, Martin Pluss, Marcel Jenni, Mathias Seger, Ivo Ruthemann, Steve Hirschi, Bjorn Christen, Morris Trachsler, Paolo Duca, Goran Bezina, Romano Lemm, Kevin Romy, Roman Josi, Damien Brunner

**United States** (Scott Gordon, coach) GK—Scott Clemmensen, Ben Bishop, David Leggio—Matt Greene, Jack Johnson, Andy Greene, Tim Kennedy, Ryan Potulny, Brandon Dubinsky, T.J. Galiardi, Chris Kreider, Christian Hanson, Kyle Okposo, Ryan Carter, Eric Nystrom, David Moss, Jack Hillen, Mike Lundin, Taylor Chorney, Nick Foligno, T.J. Oshie, Keith Yandle, Matt Gilroy

## 75th WORLD CHAMPIONSHIP (MEN)
## April 29-May 15, 2011
## Bratislava/Kosice, Slovakia

**Final Placing**

| | | | |
|---|---|---|---|
| Gold | Finland | 9th | Switzerland |
| Silver | Sweden | 10th | Slovakia |
| Bronze | Czech Republic | 11th | Denmark |
| 4th | Russia | 12th | France |
| 5th | Canada | 13th | Latvia |
| 6th | Norway | 14th | Belarus |
| 7th | Germany | 15th | Austria+ |
| 8th | United States | 16th | Slovenia+ |

+promoted from Division I in 2010/demoted to Division I for 2012

**Tournament Format**

Teams were divided into four groups of four teams each for the Preliminary Round. The top three teams from each group advanced to the Qualifying Round. The bottom four were placed in a relegation pool, with the last two being relegated. In the Qualifying Round, the top four from each group of six advanced to a cross-over quarter-final.

**Results & Standings**

**PRELIMINARY ROUND**

**GROUP A (BRATISLAVA)**

| | GP | W | OTW | OTL | L | GF | GA | P |
|---|---|---|---|---|---|---|---|---|
| Germany | 3 | 2 | 1 | 0 | 0 | 9 | 5 | 8 |
| Russia | 3 | 2 | 0 | 0 | 1 | 10 | 9 | 6 |
| Slovakia | 3 | 1 | 0 | 0 | 2 | 9 | 9 | 3 |
| Slovenia | 3 | 0 | 0 | 1 | 2 | 7 | 12 | 1 |

| | | |
|---|---|---|
| April 29 | Germany 2 | Russia 0 |
| April 29 | Slovakia 3 | Slovenia 1 |
| May 1 | Russia 6 | Slovenia 4 |
| May 1 | Germany 4 | Slovakia 3 |
| May 3 | Germany 3 | Slovenia 2 (5:00 OT/GWS—Frank Hordler) |
| May 3 | Russia 4 | Slovakia 3 |

**GROUP B (KOSICE)**

| | GP | W | OTW | OTL | L | GF | GA | P |
|---|---|---|---|---|---|---|---|---|
| Canada | 3 | 2 | 1 | 0 | 0 | 17 | 5 | 8 |
| Switzerland | 3 | 1 | 1 | 1 | 0 | 8 | 5 | 6 |
| France | 3 | 0 | 1 | 1 | 1 | 3 | 11 | 3 |
| Belarus | 3 | 0 | 0 | 1 | 2 | 3 | 10 | 1 |

| | | |
|---|---|---|
| April 29 | Switzerland 1 | France 0 (Julien Vauclair 1:46 OT) |
| April 29 | Canada 4 | Belarus 1 |
| May 1 | Canada 9 | France 1 |
| May 1 | Switzerland 4 | Belarus 1 |
| May 3 | Canada 4 | Switzerland 3 (Alex Pietrangelo 4:14 OT) |
| May 3 | France 2 | Belarus 1 (Kevin Hecquefeuille 0:46 OT) |

**GROUP C (KOSICE)**

| | GP | W | OTW | OTL | L | GF | GA | P |
|---|---|---|---|---|---|---|---|---|
| Sweden | 3 | 2 | 0 | 1 | 0 | 13 | 7 | 7 |
| United States | 3 | 2 | 0 | 0 | 1 | 11 | 9 | 6 |
| Norway | 3 | 1 | 1 | 0 | 1 | 12 | 8 | 5 |
| Austria | 3 | 0 | 0 | 0 | 3 | 1 | 13 | 0 |

| | | |
|---|---|---|
| April 30 | United States 5 | Austria 1 |
| April 30 | Norway 5 | Sweden 4 (5:00 OT/GWS—Per-Age Skroder) |
| May 2 | United States 4 | Norway 2 |
| May 2 | Sweden 3 | Austria 0 |
| May 4 | Norway 5 | Austria 0 |
| May 4 | Sweden 6 | United States 2 |

**GROUP D (BRATISLAVA)**

| | GP | W | OTW | OTL | L | GF | GA | P |
|---|---|---|---|---|---|---|---|---|
| Czech Republic | 3 | 3 | 0 | 0 | 0 | 12 | 3 | 9 |
| Finland | 3 | 1 | 1 | 0 | 1 | 9 | 5 | 5 |
| Denmark | 3 | 0 | 1 | 0 | 2 | 4 | 13 | 2 |
| Latvia | 3 | 0 | 0 | 2 | 1 | 6 | 10 | 2 |

| | | |
|---|---|---|
| April 30 | Finland 5 | Denmark 1 |
| April 30 | Czech Republic 4 | Latvia 2 |
| May 2 | Czech Republic 6 | Denmark 0 |
| May 2 | Finland 3 | Latvia 2 (5:00 OT/GWS—Jarkko Immonen) |
| May 4 | Denmark 3 | Latvia 2 (5:00 OT/GWS—Mads Christensen) |
| May 4 | Czech Republic 2 | Finland 1 |

**QUALIFYING ROUND**
**GROUP E (BRATISLAVA)**

| | GP | W | OTW | OTL | L | GF | GA | P |
|---|---|---|---|---|---|---|---|---|
| Czech Republic | 5 | 5 | 0 | 0 | 0 | 19 | 7 | 15 |
| Finland | 5 | 2 | 2 | 0 | 1 | 16 | 10 | 10 |
| Germany | 5 | 2 | 0 | 2 | 1 | 15 | 17 | 8 |
| Russia | 5 | 2 | 0 | 1 | 2 | 12 | 14 | 7 |
| Slovakia | 5 | 1 | 0 | 0 | 4 | 13 | 14 | 3 |
| Denmark | 5 | 0 | 1 | 0 | 4 | 9 | 22 | 2 |

| | | |
|---|---|---|
| May 5 | Russia 4 | Denmark 3 |
| May 6 | Finland 5 | Germany 4 (5:00 OT/GWS—Mikko Koivu) |
| May 6 | Czech Republic 3 | Slovakia 2 |
| May 7 | Denmark 4 | Germany 3 (5:00 OT/GWS—Mikkel Bodker) |
| May 7 | Finland 2 | Slovakia 1 |
| May 8 | Czech Republic 3 | Russia 2 |
| May 9 | Slovakia 4 | Denmark 1 |
| May 9 | Finland 3 | Russia 2 (5:00 OT/GWS—Jarkko Immonen) |
| May 9 | Czech Republic 5 | Germany 2 |

**GROUP F (KOSICE)**

| | GP | W | OTW | OTL | L | GF | GA | P |
|---|---|---|---|---|---|---|---|---|
| Canada | 5 | 3 | 2 | 0 | 0 | 23 | 11 | 13 |
| Sweden | 5 | 3 | 0 | 1 | 1 | 18 | 10 | 10 |
| Norway | 5 | 2 | 1 | 0 | 2 | 17 | 15 | 8 |
| United States | 5 | 2 | 0 | 1 | 2 | 15 | 19 | 7 |
| Switzerland | 5 | 1 | 1 | 1 | 2 | 11 | 12 | 6 |
| France | 5 | 0 | 0 | 1 | 4 | 5 | 22 | 1 |

| | | |
|---|---|---|
| May 5 | Norway 3 | Switzerland 2 |
| May 6 | Canada 4 | United States 3 (5:00 OT/GWS—Jordan Eberle) |
| May 6 | Sweden 4 | France 0 |
| May 7 | Canada 3 | Norway 2 |
| May 7 | United States 3 | France 2 |
| May 8 | Sweden 2 | Switzerland 0 |
| May 9 | Norway 5 | France 2 |
| May 9 | Switzerland 5 | United States 3 |
| May 9 | Canada 3 | Sweden 2 |

**RELEGATION ROUND**
**GROUP G**

| | GP | W | OTW | OTL | L | GF | GA | P |
|---|---|---|---|---|---|---|---|---|
| Latvia | 3 | 2 | 0 | 0 | 1 | 12 | 9 | 6 |
| Belarus | 3 | 2 | 0 | 0 | 1 | 17 | 9 | 6 |
| Austria | 3 | 1 | 0 | 0 | 2 | 6 | 13 | 3 |
| Slovenia | 3 | 1 | 0 | 0 | 2 | 8 | 12 | 3 |

| | | | |
|---|---|---|---|
| May 5 | Bratislava | Slovenia 5 | Latvia 2 |
| May 5 | Kosice | Belarus 7 | Austria 2 |
| May 7 | Bratislava | Austria 3 | Slovenia 2 |
| May 7 | Kosice | Latvia 6 | Belarus 3 |
| May 8 | Bratislava | Belarus 7 | Slovenia 1 |
| May 8 | Kosice | Latvia 4 | Austria 1 |

**PLAYOFFS (BRATISLAVA)**
**QUARTER-FINALS**

| | | |
|---|---|---|
| May 11 | Czech Republic 4 | United States 0 |
| May 11 | Sweden 5 | Germany 2 |
| May 12 | Finland 4 | Norway 1 |
| May 12 | Russia 2 | Canada 1 |

**SEMI-FINALS**

| | | |
|---|---|---|
| May 13 | Sweden 5 | Czech Republic 2 |
| May 13 | Finland 3 | Russia 0 |

**BRONZE MEDAL GAME**

| | | |
|---|---|---|
| May 15 | Czech Republic 7 | Russia 4 |

**GOLD MEDAL GAME**

| | | |
|---|---|---|
| May 15 | Finland 6 | Sweden 1 |

**Rosters**

**Austria** (Bill Gilligan, coach) GK—Jurgen Penker, Rene Swette, Fabian Weinhandl—Gerhard Unterluggauer, Thomas Raffl, Rafael Rotter, Roland Kaspitz, Philippe Lakos, Michael Raffl, Michael Schiechl, Manuel Latusa, Patrick Harand, Johannes Reichel, Thomas Koch, Philipp Lukas, Daniel Welser, Darcy Werenka, Martin Schumnig, Markus Peintner, Marco Pewal, Mario Altmann, Matthias Trattnig, Robert Lukas, Thomas Hundertpfund, Oliver Setzinger

**Belarus** (Eduard Zankovets, coach) GK—Sergei Shabanov, Andrei Mezin, Dmitri Milchakov—Nikolai Stasenko, Vladimir Denisov, Andrei Mikhalyov, Alexander Kulakov, Sergei Drozd, Artyom Demkov, Alexei Ugarov, Dmitri Meleshko, Oleg Goroshko, Andrei Kostitsyn, Sergei Kolosov, Andrei Stas, Viktor Kostyuchenok, Alexander Ryadinski, Sergei Demagin, Andrei Stepanov, Alexander Kitarov, Alexander Pavlovich, Mikhail Grabovski, Yevgeni Kovyrshin, Dmitri Korobov, Kirill Gotovets

**Canada** (Ken Hitchcock, coach) GK—James Reimer, Jonathan Bernier, Devan Dubnyk—John Tavares, Jason Spezza, Jeff Skinner, James Neal, Rick Nash, Alex Pietrangelo, Jordan Eberle, Brent Burns, Chris Stewart, Travis Zajac, Dion Phaneuf, Marc-Andre Gragnani, Evander Kane, Mario Scalzo, Cal Clutterbuck, Luke Schenn, Matt Duchene, Andrew Ladd, Marc Methot, Carlo Colaiacovo, Antoine Vermette

**Czech Republic** (Alois Hadamczik, coach) GK—Jakub Kovar, Ondrej Pavelec, Jakub Stepanek—Zbynek Michalek, Marek Zidlicky, Karel Rachunek, Radek Martinek, Milan Michalek, Roman Cervenka, Petr Hubacek, Jiri Novotny, Petr Vampola, Jan Marek, Michael Frolik, Martin Havlat, Lukas Krajicek, Patrik Elias, Petr Caslava, Martin Skoula, Tomas Rolinek, Ondrej Nemec, Jaromir Jagr, Petr Prucha, Tomas Plekanec, Jakub Voracek

**Denmark** (Per Backman, coach) GK—Patrick Galbraith, Frederik Andersen, Simon Nielsen—Mads Bodker, Daniel Nielsen, Stefan Lassen, Frederik Storm, Kasper Degn, Morten Green, Kirill Starkov, Kasper Jensen, Kim Staal, Thor Dresler, Michael Eskesen, Morten Madsen, Julian Jakobsen, Morten Poulsen, Jesper Jensen, Jesper B Jensen, Nichlas Hardt, Mads Christensen, Philip Hersby, Mikkel Bodker

**Finland** (Jukka Jalonen, coach) GK—Petri Vehanen, Niko Hovinen, Teemu Lassila—Ossi Vaananen, Lasse Kukkonen, Topi Jaakola, Mikko Koivu, Tuomo Ruutu, Sami Lepisto, Jyrki Valivaara, Janne Pesonen, Janne Niskala, Jani Lajunen, Jarkko Immonen, Anssi Salmela, Petteri Nokelainen, Mika Pyorala, Niko Kapanen, Antti Pihlstrom, Pasi Puistola, Janne Lahti, Juhamatti Aaltonen, Jesse Joensuu, Mikael Granlund, Leo Komarov

**France** (Dave Henderson, coach) GK—Ronan Quemener, Cristobal Huet, Fabrice Lhenry—Vincent Bachet, Damien Fleury, Laurent Meunier, Luc Tardif, Stephane da Costa, Jeremie Romand, Yohann Auvitu, Loic Lamperier, Maxime Moisand, Jonathan Janil, Brian Henderson, Nicolas Arrossamena, Julien Desrosiers, Laurent Gras, Thomas Roussel, Pierre Edouard Bellemare, Nicolas Besch, Sacha Treille, Teddy da Costa, Damien Raux, Kevin Hecquefeuille, Teddy Trabichet

**Germany** (Uwe Krupp, coach) GK—Jochen Reimer, Dimitri Patzold, Dennis Endras—Denis Reul, Justin Krueger, Korbinian Holzer, Michael Wolf, Kai Hospelt, Robert Dietrich, John Tripp, Andre Rankel, Marcel Muller, Daniel Kreutzer, Kevin Lavallee, Frank Mauer, Alexander Barta, Patrick Reimer, Thomas Geilinger, Christoph Ullmann, Frank Hordler, Felix Schutz, Marcus Kink, Nicolai Goc, Philip Gogulla, Constantin Braun

**Latvia** (Olegs Znaroks, coach) GK—Maris Jucers, Martins Raitums, Edgars Masalskis—Arvids Rekis, Janis Andersons, Juris Stals, Roberts Bukarts, Lauris Darzins, Kristaps Sotnieks, Herberts Vasiljevs, Ronalds Kenins, Aleksandrs Nizivijs, Kaspars Saulietis, Armands Berzins, Andris Dzerins, Mikelis Redlihs, Jekabs Redlihs, Krisjanis Redlihs, Sergejs Pecura, Arturs Kulda, Oskars Cibulskis, Martins Cipulis, Girts Ankipans, Georgijs Pujacs, Gints Meija

**Norway** (Roy Johansen, coach) GK—Lars Haugen, Pal Grotnes, Robert Hestmann—Erik Follestad Johansen, Eerikki Koivu, Jonas Holos, Mads Hansen, Marius Holtet, Lars Erik Spets, Peter Lorentzen, Tommy Kristiansen, Per-Age Skroder, Anders Bastiansen, Morten Ask, Martin Roymark, Andreas Martinsen, Kristian Forsberg, Martin Laumann Ylven, Lars Ostli, Ken Andre Olimb, Brede Csiszar, Mathis Olimb, Alexander Bonsaksen, Anders Fredriksen, Ole-Kristian Tollefsen

**Russia** (Vyacheslav Bykov, coach) GK—Yevgeni Nabokov, Vasili Koshechkin, Konstantin Barulin—Ilya Nikulin, Dmitri Kalinin, Alexander Ovechkin, Konstantin Gorovikov, Konstantin Korneyev, Alexei Tereshenko, Danis Zaripov, Vitali Atyushov, Denis Grebeshkov, Nikolai Kulyomin, Sergei Zinoviev, Dmitri Kulikov, Nikolai Belov, Alexander Radulov, Yevgeni Artyukhin, Fyodor Tyutin, Alexei Kaigorodov, Maxim Afinogenov, Ilya Kovalchuk, Alexei Yemelin, Vladimir Tarasenko, Alexei Morozov

**Slovakia** (Glen Hanlon, coach) GK—Peter Hamerlik, Jan Lasak, Jaroslav Halak—Michal Sersen, Ivan Baranka, Martin Cibak, Marian Gaborik, Stefan Ruzicka, Jozef Stumpel, Ivan Majesky, Lubomir Visnovsky, Miroslav Satan, Richard Zednik, Lubos Bartecko, Michal Handzus, Ladislav Nagy, Peter Podhradsky, Pavol Demitra, Tomas Surovy, Dominik Granak, Milan Jurcina, Martin Strbak, Marian Hossa, Marcel Hossa, Branko Radivojevic

**Slovenia** (Matjaz Kopitar, coach) GK—Andrej Hocevar, Robert Kristan, Matija Pintaric—Andrej Tavzelj, Ziga Jeglic, Tomaz Razingar, Mitka Sivic, David Rodman, Matej Hocevar, Blaz Gregorc, Ziga Pavlin, Gregory Kuznik, Ziga Pance, Klemen Pretnar, Marcel Rodman, Damjan Dervaric, Rok Ticar, Jaka Ankerst, Ales Kranjc, Mitja Robar, Robert Sabolic, Bostjan Golicic, Rok Pajic, Andrej Hebar, Sabahudin Kovacevic

**Sweden** (Par Marts, coach) GK—Viktor Fasth, Anders Nilsson, Erik Ersberg—Nicklas Grossman, Oliver Ekman Larsson, Daniel Fernholm, David Rundblad, Andreas Jamtin, Mattias Tedenby, Martin Thornberg, Carl Gunnarsson, Mattias Sjogren, Patrik Berglund, Loui Eriksson, David Petrasek, Niklas Persson, Staffan Kronwall, Robert Nilsson, Marcus Kruger, Jakob Silfverberg, Jimmie Ericsson, Tim Erixon, Rickard Wallin, Mikael Backlund, Magnus Paajarvi

**Switzerland** (Sean Simpson, coach) GK—Tobias Stephan, Leonardo Genoni, Daniel Manzato—Beat Gerber, Julien Vauclair, Andres Ambuhl, Felicien du Bois, Raphael Diaz, John Gobbi, Victor Stancescu, Thibaut Monnet, Martin Pluss, Mathias Seger, Ivo Ruthemann, Daniel Rubin, Morris Trachsler, Matthias Bieber, Luca Sbisa, Ryan Gardner, Philippe Furrer, Goran Bezina, Romano Lemm, Kevin Lotscher, Simon Moser, Julien Sprunger

**United States** (Scott Gordon, coach) GK—Jack Campbell, Ty Conklin, Al Montoya—Ryan McDonagh, Jack Johnson, Clay Wilson, Mark Stuart, Cam Fowler, Mike Komisarek, Derek Stepan, Kevin Shattenkirk, Craig Smith, James van Riemsdyk, Blake Wheeler, Mike Brown, Chris Kreider, Jack Skille, Andy Miele, Yan Stastny, Tim Stapleton, Chris Porter, Nick Palmieri, Ryan Shannon, Paul Gaustad, Mark Fayne

## 76th WORLD CHAMPIONSHIP
## Helsinki, Finland/Stockholm, Sweden
## May 4-20, 2012

**Final Placing**

Gold ........Russia
Silver ......Slovakia
Bronze ....Czech Republic
4th ..........Finland
5th ..........Canada
6th ..........Sweden
7th ..........United States
8th ..........Norway
9th .........France
10th .......Latvia
11th .......Switzerland
12th .......Germany
13th .......Denmark
14th .......Belarus
15th .......Italy^+
16th .......Kazakhstan^+

^promoted from Division I in 2011
+demoted to Division I for 2013

**Tournament Format**

A new format was adopted at the same time as a new hosting structure was used. Finland and Sweden acted as co-hosts through to the quarter-finals, after which the remaining games (semi-finals, medal games) were played only in Helsinki. The 16 teams were divided into two groups of eight, and each group played a round robin. The last team in each group was demoted to Division I and only the top four from each group advanced to the playoffs. The bottom four teams didn't play again, the relegation round series having been abolished. The top team played the fourth-place team within each group for the quarter-finals, and the semi-finals saw teams cross over.

**Results & Standings**

**GROUP H (HELSINKI)**

| | GP | W | OTW | OTL | L | GF | GA | P |
|---|---|---|---|---|---|---|---|---|
| Canada | 7 | 6 | 0 | 1 | 0 | 35 | 15 | 19 |
| United States | 7 | 4 | 2 | 0 | 1 | 32 | 17 | 16 |
| Finland | 7 | 5 | 0 | 0 | 2 | 21 | 14 | 15 |
| Slovakia | 7 | 5 | 0 | 0 | 2 | 21 | 13 | 15 |
| France | 7 | 3 | 0 | 0 | 4 | 21 | 32 | 9 |
| Switzerland | 7 | 2 | 0 | 0 | 5 | 16 | 21 | 6 |
| Belarus | 7 | 1 | 0 | 0 | 6 | 11 | 23 | 3 |
| Kazakhstan | 7 | 0 | 0 | 1 | 6 | 11 | 33 | 1 |

| | | |
|---|---|---|
| May 4 | United States 7 | France 2 |
| May 4 | Canada 3 | Slovakia 2 |
| May 4 | Finland 1 | Belarus 0 |
| May 5 | Switzerland 5 | Kazakhstan 1 |
| May 5 | United States 5 | Canada 4 (Jack Johnson 1:47 OT) |
| May 6 | France 6 | Kazakhstan 3 |
| May 6 | Finland 1 | Slovakia 0 |
| May 6 | Switzerland 3 | Belarus 2 |
| May 7 | Canada 7 | France 2 |
| May 7 | Slovakia 4 | United States 2 |
| May 8 | Belarus 3 | Kazakhstan 2 |
| May 8 | Finland 5 | Switzerland 2 |
| May 9 | Slovakia 4 | Kazakhstan 2 |
| May 9 | Canada 3 | Switzerland 2 |
| May 10 | United States 5 | Belarus 3 |
| May 10 | Finland 7 | France 1 |
| May 11 | United States 3 | Kazakhstan 2 (Justin Faulk 4:38 OT) |
| May 11 | Canada 5 | Finland 3 |
| May 12 | Slovakia 5 | Belarus 1 |
| May 12 | France 4 | Switzerland 2 |
| May 12 | Canada 8 | Kazakhstan 0 |
| May 13 | United States 5 | Finland 0 |
| May 13 | Slovakia 1 | Switzerland 0 |
| May 14 | France 2 | Belarus 1 |
| May 14 | Finland 4 | Kazakhstan 1 |
| May 15 | Canada 5 | Belarus 1 |
| May 15 | Slovakia 5 | France 4 |
| May 15 | United States 5 | Switzerland 2 |

**GROUP S (STOCKHOLM)**

| | GP | W | OTW | OTL | L | GF | GA | P |
|---|---|---|---|---|---|---|---|---|
| Russia | 7 | 7 | 0 | 0 | 0 | 27 | 8 | 21 |
| Sweden | 7 | 6 | 0 | 0 | 1 | 29 | 15 | 18 |
| Czech Republic | 7 | 4 | 1 | 0 | 2 | 24 | 11 | 14 |
| Norway | 7 | 4 | 0 | 1 | 2 | 33 | 19 | 13 |
| Latvia | 7 | 2 | 0 | 0 | 5 | 11 | 19 | 6 |
| Germany | 7 | 2 | 0 | 0 | 5 | 14 | 31 | 6 |
| Denmark | 7 | 1 | 0 | 1 | 5 | 13 | 23 | 4 |
| Italy | 7 | 0 | 1 | 0 | 6 | 6 | 31 | 2 |

| | | |
|---|---|---|
| May 4 | Germany 3 | Italy 0 |
| May 4 | Czech Republic 2 | Denmark 0 |
| May 4 | Sweden 3 | Norway 1 |
| May 5 | Russia 5 | Latvia 2 |
| May 5 | Sweden 4 | Czech Republic 1 |
| May 6 | Italy 4 | Denmark 3 (Giulio Scandella 0:52 OT) |
| May 6 | Russia 4 | Norway 2 |
| May 6 | Latvia 3 | Germany 2 |
| May 7 | Czech Republic 4 | Norway 3 (5:00 OT/Ales Hemsky GWS) |
| May 7 | Sweden 6 | Denmark 4 |
| May 8 | Latvia 5 | Italy 0 |
| May 8 | Russia 2 | Germany 0 |
| May 9 | Norway 6 | Italy 2 |
| May 9 | Sweden 5 | Germany 2 |
| May 10 | Russia 3 | Denmark 1 |
| May 10 | Czech Republic 3 | Latvia 1 |
| May 11 | Czech Republic 6 | Italy 0 |
| May 11 | Russia 7 | Sweden 3 |
| May 12 | Norway 3 | Latvia 0 |
| May 12 | Germany 2 | Denmark 1 |
| May 12 | Sweden 4 | Italy 0 |
| May 13 | Russia 2 | Czech Republic 0 |
| May 13 | Norway 12 | Germany 4 |
| May 14 | Denmark 2 | Latvia 0 |
| May 14 | Russia 4 | Italy 0 |
| May 15 | Norway 6 | Denmark 2 |
| May 15 | Czech Republic 8 | Germany 1 |
| May 15 | Sweden 4 | Latvia 0 |

**PLAYOFFS**

**QUARTER-FINALS**

| | | | |
|---|---|---|---|
| May 17 | Helsinki | Slovakia 4 | Canada 3 |
| May 17 | Stockholm | Russia 5 | Norway 2 |
| May 17 | Helsinki | Finland 3 | United States 2 |
| May 17 | Stockholm | Czech Republic 4 | Sweden 3 |

**SEMI-FINALS**

| | | | |
|---|---|---|---|
| May 19 | Helsinki | Russia 6 | Finland 2 |
| May 19 | Helsinki | Slovakia 3 | Czech Republic 1 |

**BRONZE MEDAL GAME**

| | | | |
|---|---|---|---|
| May 20 | Helsinki | Czech Republic 3 | Finland 2 |

**GOLD MEDAL GAME**

| | | | |
|---|---|---|---|
| May 20 | Helsinki | Russia 6 | Slovakia 2 |

**Rosters**

**Belarus** (Kari Heikkila, coach) GK: Vitali Koval, Andrei Mezin, Dmitri Milchakov—Nikolai Stasenko, Vladimor Denisov, Andrei Kolosov, Andrei Mikhalyov, Alexander Kulakov, Sergei Drozd, Andrei Stepanov, Alexei Ugarov, Dmitri Meleshko, Oleg Goroshko, Andrei Kostitsyn, Andrei Stas, Konstantin Koltsov, Viktor Kostyuchyonok, Alexei Kalyuzhny, Sergei Kostitsyn, Alexander Kitarov, Pavel Chernaok, Mikhail Grabovski, Yevgeni Kovyrshin, Dmitri Korobov, Roman Graborenko

**Canada** (Brent Sutter, coach) GK: Cam Ward, Devan Dubnyk, Matt Hackett—Duncan Keith, Dion Phaneuf, Jay Bouwmeester, Luke Schenn, Kris Russell, Evander Kane, Corey Perry, Jordan Eberle, Ryan Getzlaf, Andrew Ladd, John Tavares, Kyle Quincey, Jamie Benn, Teddy Purcell, Ryan Murray, Marc Methot, Ryan O'Reilly, Alexandre Burrows, Marc-Edouard Vlasic, Jeff Skinner, Patrick Sharp, Ryan Nugent-Hopkins

**Czech Republic** (Alois Hadamczik, coach) GK: Jakub Kovar, Petr Mrazek, Jakub Stepanek—Tomas Mojzis, Milan Michalek, Martin Erat, Jiri Novotny, Tomas Plekanec, Lukas Kaspar, Ondrej Nemec, Lukas Krajicek, Jakub Krejcik, Petr Caslava, Petr Koukal, Miroslav Blatak, David Krejci, Petr Tenkrat, Michael Frolik, Petr Prucha, Zdenek Kutlak, Michal Vondrka, Ales Hemsky, Jakub Nakladal, Jakub Petruzalek, Petr Nedved

**Denmark** (Per Backman, coach) GK: Frederik Andersen, Simon Nielsen, Patrick Galbraith—Philip Larsen, Mads Bodker, Daniel Nielsen, Stefan Lassen, Frederik Storm, Bjarke Moller, Morten Green, Kirill Starkov, Kasper Jensen, Kim Lykkeskov, Michael Eskesen, Morten Madsen, Julian Jakobsen, Jannik Hansen, Morten Poulsen, Jesper Jensen, Jesper B. Jensen, Nichlas Hardt, Frans Nielsen, Lars Eller, Philip Hersby

**Finland** (Jukka Jalonen, coach) GK: Kari Lehtonen, Petri Vehanen, Karri Ramo—Ossi Vaananen, Lasse Kukkonen, Topi Jaakola, Mikko Maenpaa, Mikko Koivu, Jani Tuppurainen, Jesse Joensuu, Tuomas Kiiskinen, Janne Pesonen, Janne Niskala, Jarkko Immonen, Petri Kontiola, Anssi Salmela, Jussi Jokinen, Mika Pyorala, Juuso Hietanen, Niko Kapanen, Antti Pihlstrom, Valtteri Filppula, Joonas Jarvinen, Mikael Granlund, Leo Komarov

**France** (Dave Henderson, coach) GK: Cristobal Huet, Fabrice Lhenry, Florian Hardy—Vincent Bachet, Antonin Manavian, Yorick Treille, Damien Fleury, Laurent Meunier, Stephane da Costa, Yohann Auvitu, Loic Lamperier, Maxime Moisand, Brian Henderson, Julien Desrosiers, Charles Bertrand, Baptiste Amar, Damien Raux, Alexandre Rouleau, Pierre-Edouard Bellemare, Antoine Roussel, Anthony Guttig, Nicolas Besch, Sacha Treille, Teddy da Costa, Kevin Hecquefeuille

**Germany** (Jakob Kolliker, coach) GK: Dennis Endras, Dimitri Kotschnew, Dimitri Patzold—Denis Reul, Justin Krueger, Florian Ondruschka, Christopher Fischer, Christoph Schubert, Marcus Kink, Kai Hospelt, Evan Kaufmann, John Tripp, Andre Rankel, Kevin Lavallee, Alexander Barta, Patrick Reimer, Thomas Greilinger, Christoph Ullmann, Felix Schutz, Marcel Goc, Sebastian Furchner, Nikolai Goc, Sinan Akdag, Daniel Pietta, Philip Gogulla

**Italy** (Rick Cornacchia, coach) GK: Daniel Bellissimo, Thomas Tragust, Andreas Bernard—Diego Iori, Roland Hofer, Marco Insam, Derek Edwardson, Giulio Scandella, Nicola Fontanive, Luca Felicetti, Daniel Tudin, Alexander Egger, Anton Bernard, Matt de Marchi, Stefano Marchetti, Trevor Johnson, Armin Helfer, Thomas Larkin, Manuel de Toni, Patrick Iannone, Nicholas Plastino, Christain Borgatello, Luca Ansoldi, Vincent Rocco, Robert Sirianni

**Kazakhstan** (Andrei Shayanov, coach) GK: Vitali Yeremeyev, Vitali Kolesnik, Alexei Ivanov—Roman Savchenko, Vitali Novopashin, Andrei Korabeinikov, Alexei Litvinenko, Talgat Zhailauov, Denis Shemelin, Fyodor Polishuk, Dmitri Dudarev, Andrei Spiridonov, Konstantin Savenkov, Yevgeni Bumagin, Dmitri Upper, Yevgeni Fadeyev, Roman Starchenko, Alexei Vorontsov, Alexei Troshinski, Vadim Krasnoslobodtsev, Vladislav Kolesnikov, Sergei Yakovenko, Konstantin Pushkaryov, Konstantin Romanov, Yevgeni Rymarev

**Latvia** (Ted Nolan, coach) GK: Edgars Masalskis, Maris Jucers, Ervins Mustukovs—Rodrigo Lavins, Janis Andersons, Janis Sprukts, Oskars Bartulis, Roberts Bukarts, Kristaps Sotnieks, Andris Dzerins, Guntis Galvins, Ronalds Kenins, Kaspars Daugavins, Aleksejs Sirokovs, Kaspars Saulietis, Armands Berzins, Mikelis Redlihs, Krisjanis Redlihs, Oskars Cibulskis, Martins Cipulis, Juris Stals, Miks Indrasis, Georgijs Pujacs, Gints Meija, Koba Jass

**Norway** (Roy Johansen, coach) GK: Lars Haugen, Lars Volden, Pal Grotnes—Juha Kaunismaki, Jonas Holos, Mads Hansen, Marius Holtet, Lars Erik Spets, Tommy Kristiansen, Per-Age Skroder, Anders Bastiansen, Morten Ask, Martin Roymark, Mats Trygg, Andreas Martinsen, Kristian Forsberg, Lars Lokken-Ostli, Henrik Solberg, Ken Andre Olimb, Patrick Thoresen, Mathis Olimb, Alexander Bonsaksen, Mats Rosseli-Olsen, Ole-Kristian Tollefsen

**Russia** (Zinetula Bilyaletdinov, coach) GK: Semyon Varlamov, Konstantin Barulin, Mikhail Biryukov—Ilya Nikulin, Denis Denisov, Dmitri Kalinin, Alexander Ovechkin, Yevgeni Malkin, Nikita Nikitin, Pavel Datsyuk, Alexander Svitov, Denis Kokarev, Alexander Popov, Alexei Tereshenko, Alexander Syomin, Alexander Perezhogin, Nikolai Kulyomin, Yevgeni Biryukov, Sergei Shirokov, Alexei Yemelin, Yevgeni Ryasenski, Yevgeni Ketov, Yevgeni Medvedev, Yevgeni Kuznetsov, Nikolai Zherdev

**Slovakia** (Vladimir Vujtek, coach) GK: Jan Laco, Peter Hamerlik, Julius Hudacek—Michal Sersen, Ivan Baranka, Miroslav Satan, Tomas Starosta, Libor Hudacek, Rene Vydareny, Marek Hovorka, Michal Handzus, Zdeno Chara, Tomas Surovy, Andrej Sekera, Dominik Granak, Mario Bliznak, Milan Bartovic, Juraj Mikus, Kristian Kudroc, Marcel Hossa, Tomas Kopecky, Marcel Hascak, Tomas Tatar, Michel Miklik, Branko Radivojevic

**Sweden** (Par Marts, coach) GK: Viktor Fasth, Jhonas Enroth, Cristopher Nilstorp—Staffan Kronwall, Niklas Kronwall, Johan Larsson, Daniel Alfredsson, Fredrik Pettersson, Calle Jarnkrok, Nicklas Backstrom, Joel Lundqvist, Loui Eriksson, Niklas Persson, Viktor Stalberg, Patric Hornqvist, Jonas Brodin, Marcus Kruger, Jakob Silfverberg, Henrik Zetterberg, Niklas Hjalmarsson, Jonathan Ericsson, Erik Karlsson, Victor Hedman, Gabriel Landeskog, Johan Franzen

**Switzerland** (Sean Simpson, coach) GK: Reto Berra, Tobias Stephan, Lukas Flueler—Severin Blindenbacher, Mark Streit, Andres Ambuhl, Benjamin Pluss, Felicien du Bois, Roman Wick, Nino Niederreiter, Thibaut Monnet, Mathias Seger, Ivo Ruthemann, Daniel Rubin, Morris Trachsler, Luca Sbisa, Matthias Bieber, Philippe Furrer, Goran Bezina, Denis Hollenstein, Patrick von Gunten, Simon Moser, Kevin Romy, Roman Josi, Damien Brunner

**United States** (Scott Gordon, coach) GK: Jimmy Howard, Richard Backman, John Curry—Jeff Petry, Jack Johnson, Cam Fowler, Alex Goligoski, Bobby Ryan, Ryan Lasch, Cam Atkinson, Joey Crabb, Justin Abdelkader, Jim Slater, Justin Brown, Kyle Okposo, J.T. Brown, Craig Smith, Paul Stastny, Justin Faulk, Chris Butler, Patrick Dwyer, Nate Thompson, Kyle Palmieri, Max Pacioretty

*Yevgeni Malkin receives the MVP award after his dominating performance led to gold for Russia at the 2012 World Championship.*
*Photo: Andre Ringuette / HHOF-IIHF Images.*

# IIHF-NHL INVITATIONALS

## 1972 Summit Series
## September 2-28, 1972
## Montreal/Toronto/Winnipeg/Vancouver, Canada & Moscow, Soviet Union

**Results & Standings**

| | GP | W | T | L | GF | GA | P |
|---|---|---|---|---|---|---|---|
| Canada | 8 | 4 | 1 | 3 | 31 | 32 | 9 |
| Soviet Union | 8 | 3 | 1 | 4 | 32 | 31 | 7 |

| | | | |
|---|---|---|---|
| Game 1—September 2 | Montreal | Soviet Union 7 | Canada 3 |
| Game 2—September 4 | Toronto | Canada 4 | Soviet Union 1 |
| Game 3—September 6 | Winnipeg | Canada 4 | Soviet Union 4 |
| Game 4—September 8 | Vancouver | Soviet Union 5 | Canada 3 |
| Game 5—September 22 | Moscow | Soviet Union 5 | Canada 4 |
| Game 6—September 24 | Moscow | Canada 3 | Soviet Union 2 |
| Game 7—September 26 | Moscow | Canada 4 | Soviet Union 3 |
| Game 8—September 28 | Moscow | Canada 6 | Soviet Union 5 |

**Rosters**

**Canada** (Harry Sinden, coach) GK—Ken Dryden, Tony Esposito, Ed Johnston—Phil Esposito, Paul Henderson, Bobby Clarke, Yvan Cournoyer, Brad Park, Dennis Hull, J.P. Parise, Rod Gilbert, Jean Ratelle, Gary Bergman, Ron Ellis, Gilbert Perreault, Bill Goldsworthy, Frank Mahovlich, Pete Mahovlich, Bill White, Wayne Cashman, Serge Savard, Stan Mikita, "Red" Berenson, Guy Lapointe, Mickey Redmond, Don Awrey, Vic Hadfield, Rod Seiling, Pat Stapleton, Bobby Orr, Jocelyn Guevremont, Brian Glennie, Dale Tallon, Marcel Dionne, Rick Martin

**Soviet Union** (Vsevolod Bobrov, coach) GK—Vladislav Tretiak, Alexander Sidelnikov, Viktor Zinger, Alexander Pashkov—Alexander Yakushev, Vladimir Shadrin, Valeri Kharlamov, Vladimir Petrov, Yuri Liapkin, Boris Mikhailov, Alexander Maltsev, Vyacheslav Anisin, Vladimir Lutchenko, Yevgeni Zimin, Yuri Blinov, Vladimir Vikulov, Valeri Vasilyev, Gennadi Tsygankov, Yuri Lebedev, Alexander Bodunov, Alexander Gusev, Alexander Ragulin, Viktor Kuzkin, Alexander Martinyuk, Vyacheslav Solodukhin, Vyacheslav Starshinov, Yuri Shatalov, Alexander Volchkov, Yevgeni Paladiev, Yevgeni Mishakov

## 1976 Canada Cup
## September 2-15, 1976
## Montreal, Toronto, Ottawa, Quebec City, Winnipeg, Philadelphia

**Results & Standings**

| | GP | W | T | L | GF | GA | P |
|---|---|---|---|---|---|---|---|
| Canada | 5 | 4 | 0 | 1 | 22 | 6 | 8 |
| Czechoslovakia | 5 | 3 | 1 | 1 | 19 | 9 | 7 |
| Soviet Union | 5 | 2 | 1 | 2 | 23 | 14 | 5 |
| Sweden | 5 | 2 | 1 | 2 | 16 | 18 | 5 |
| United States | 5 | 1 | 1 | 3 | 14 | 21 | 3 |
| Finland | 5 | 1 | 0 | 4 | 16 | 42 | 2 |

| | | | |
|---|---|---|---|
| September 2 | Ottawa | Canada 11 | Finland 2 |
| September 3 | Toronto | Sweden 5 | United States 2 |
| September 3 | Montreal | Czechoslovakia 5 | Soviet Union 3 |
| September 5 | Montreal | Canada 4 | United States 2 |
| September 5 | Montreal | Soviet Union 3 | Sweden 3 |
| September 5 | Toronto | Czechoslovakia 8 | Finland 0 |
| September 7 | Toronto | Canada 4 | Sweden 0 |
| September 7 | Montreal | Soviet Union 11 | Finland 3 |
| September 7 | Philadelphia | Czechoslovakia 4 | United States 4 |
| September 9 | Montreal | Czechoslovakia 1 | Canada 0 |
| September 9 | Winnipeg | Finland 8 | Sweden 6 |
| September 9 | Philadelphia | Soviet Union 5 | United States 0 |
| September 11 | Toronto | Canada 3 | Soviet Union 1 |
| September 11 | Quebec City | Sweden 2 | Czechoslovakia 1 |
| September 11 | Montreal | United States 6 | Finland 3 |

**FINALS (BEST TWO-OF-THREE)**

| | | | |
|---|---|---|---|
| September 13 | Toronto | Canada 6 | Czechoslovakia 0 |
| September 15 | Montreal | Canada 5 (Darryl Sittler 11:33 OT) | Czechoslovakia 4 |

**Rosters**

**Canada** (Scotty Bowman, coach) GK—Rogie Vachon, Glenn "Chico" Resch, Gerry Cheevers—Bobby Orr, Denis Potvin, Bobby Hull, Gilbert Perreault, Phil Esposito, Darryl Sittler, Marcel Dionne, Guy Lafleur, Rick Martin, Pete Mahovlich, Guy Lapointe, Steve Shutt, Bobby Clarke, Serge Savard, Bob Gainey, Bill Barber, Reggie Leach, Lanny McDonald, Danny Gare, Jim Watson, Larry Robinson

**Czechoslovakia** (Karel Gut/Jan Starsi, coaches) GK—Vladimir Dzurilla, Jiri Holecek, Pavol Svitana—Milan Novy, Vladimir Martinec, Jiri Bubla, Josef Augusta, Marian Stastny, Ivan Hlinka, Peter Statsny, Oldrich Machac, Jiri Holik, Jaroslav Pouzar, Frantisek Pospisil, Bohuslav Stastny, Milan Chalupa, Jiri Novak, Bohuslav Ebermann, Milan Kajkl, Miroslav Dvorak, Frantisek Cernik, Frantisek Kaberle

**Finland** (Lasse Heikkila, coach) GK—Antti Lepanen, Markus Mattsson, Jorma Valtonen—Matti Hagman, Kari Makkonen, Pekka Rautakallio, Pertti Koivulahti, Lasse Oksanen, Juhani Tamminen, Tapio Levo, Seppo Repo, Tapio Koskinen, Heikki Riihiranta, Matti Rautiainen, Harri Linnonmaa, Hannu Kapanen, Esa Peltonen, Timo Nummelin, Jouni Peltonen, Lasse Litma, Jouni Rinne, Timo Saari, Jorma Vehmanen, Tapio Flinck, Veli-Pekka Ketola

**Soviet Union** (Viktor Tikhonov, coach) GK—Vladislav Tretiak, Viktor Zinger, Mikhail Vasilenok—Viktor Zhluktov, Vladimir Vikulov, Alexander Maltsev, Sergei Kapustin, Boris Alexandrov, Helmuts Balderis, Alexander Gusev, Vladimir Repnev, Valeri Vasilyev, Vladimir Kovin, Alexander Skvortsov, Viktor Shalimov, Alexander Golikov, Alexander Kulikov, Vladimir Lutchenko, Sergei Babinov, Valeri Belousov, Zinetula Bilyaletdinov, Vladimir Lebedev, Vladimir Krikunov

**Sweden** (Hans Lindberg, coach) GK—Goran Hogosta, Hardy Astrom, William Lofqvist—Borje Salming, Anders Hedberg, Roland Eriksson, Tord Lundstrom, Lars-Erik Ericsson, Inge Hammarstrom, Bjorn Johansson, Lars-Erik Sjoberg, Mats Ahlberg, Juha Widing, Ulf Nilsson, Thommie Bergman, Mats Waltin, Stig Salming, Dan Labraaten, Per-Olov Brasar, Kjell-Arne Vikstrom, Stig Ostling, Willy Lindstrom, Lars-Erik Esbjors, Lars-Goran Nilsson

**United States** (Bob Pulford, coach) GK—Mike Curran, Pete LoPresti, Cap Raeder—Robbie Ftorek, Dean Talafous, Craig Patrick, Mike Milbury, Warren Williams, Curt Bennett, Fred Ahern, Alan Hangsleben, Bill Nyrop, Mike Polich, Harvey Bennett, Lou Nanne, Steve Jensen, Joe Noris, Gerry O'Flaherty, Lee Fogolin, Dan Bolduc, Doug Palazzari, Mike Christie, Rick Chartraw, Gary Sargent

## 1981 Canada Cup
## September 1-13, 1981
## Edmonton/Winnipeg/Montreal/Ottawa, Canada

**Results & Standings**

| | GP | W | T | L | GF | GA | P |
|---|---|---|---|---|---|---|---|
| Canada | 5 | 4 | 1 | 0 | 32 | 13 | 9 |
| Soviet Union | 5 | 3 | 1 | 1 | 20 | 13 | 7 |
| Czechoslovakia | 5 | 2 | 2 | 1 | 21 | 13 | 6 |
| United States | 5 | 2 | 1 | 2 | 17 | 19 | 5 |
| Sweden | 5 | 1 | 0 | 4 | 13 | 20 | 2 |
| Finland | 5 | 0 | 1 | 4 | 6 | 31 | 1 |

| | | | |
|---|---|---|---|
| September 1 | Edmonton | Canada 9 | Finland 0 |
| September 1 | Edmonton | United States 3 | Sweden 1 |
| September 1 | Winnipeg | Czechoslovakia 1 | Soviet Union 1 |
| September 3 | Edmonton | Canada 8 | United States 3 |
| September 3 | Edmonton | Czechoslovakia 7 | Finland 1 |
| September 3 | Winnipeg | Soviet Union 6 | Sweden 3 |
| September 5 | Winnipeg | Canada 4 | Czechoslovakia 4 |
| September 5 | Winnipeg | Sweden 5 | Finland 0 |
| September 5 | Edmonton | Soviet Union 4 | United States 1 |
| September 7 | Montreal | Canada 4 | Sweden 3 |
| September 7 | Winnipeg | Soviet Union 6 | Finland 1 |
| September 7 | Montreal | United States 6 | Czechoslovakia 2 |
| September 9 | Montreal | Canada 7 | Soviet Union 3 |
| September 9 | Ottawa | Czechoslovakia 7 | Sweden 1 |
| September 9 | Montreal | Finland 4 | United States 4 |

**SEMI-FINALS**

| | | | |
|---|---|---|---|
| September 11 | Montreal | Canada 4 | United States 1 |
| September 11 | Ottawa | Soviet Union 4 | Czechoslovakia 1 |

**FINALS**

| | | | |
|---|---|---|---|
| September 13 | Montreal | Soviet Union 8 | Canada 1 |

**Rosters**

**Canada** (Scotty Bowman, coach) GK—Mike Liut, Don Edwards—Wayne Gretzky, Mike Bossy, Bryan Trottier, Guy Lafleur, Gilbert Perreault, Clark Gillies, Denis Potvin, Danny Gare, Marcel Dionne, Butch Goring, Ray Bourque, Bob Gainey, Rick Middleton, Ron Duguay, Brian Engblom, Ken Linseman, Craig Hartsburg, Larry Robinson, Paul Reinhart, Barry Beck

**Czechoslovakia** (Ludek Bukac, coach) GK—Jiri Kralik, Karel Lang—Jiri Dudacek, Jiri Lala, Jindrich Kokrment, Darius Rusnak, Pavel Richter, Arnold Kadlec, Milan Novy, Radoslav Svoboda, Miroslav Dvorak, Norbert Kral, Miloslav Horava, Jaroslav Pouzar, Milan Chalupa, Lubomir Penicka, Dusan Pasek, Stanislav Hajdusek, Jaroslav Korbela, Jan Neliba, Oldrich Valek, Frantisek Cernik

**Finland** (Kalevi Numminen, coach) GK—Markus Mattsson, Hannu Lassila—Matti Hagman, Risto Siltanen, Ilkka Sinisalo, Arto Javanainen, Jukka Porvari, Markku Kimalainen, Tapio Levo, Pekka Rautakallio, Reijo Ruotsalainen, Kari Jalonen, Mikko Leinonen, Jari Kurri, Jorma Sevon, Juha Huikari, Timo Nummelin, Raimo Hirvonen, Juha Tuohimaa, Kari Makkonen, Veli-Pekka Ketola, Pekka Arbelius

**Soviet Union** (Viktor Tikhonov, coach) GK—Vladislav Tretiak, Vladimir Myshkin—Alexei Kasatonov, Sergei Makarov, Sergei Shepelev, Vladimir Krutov, Vyacheslav Fetisov, Igor Larionov, Sergei Kapustin, Nikolai Drozdetski, Viktor Shalimov, Vladimir Golikov, Viktor Zhluktov, Alexander Maltsev, Vasili Pervukhin, Sergei Babinov, Alexander Skvortsov, Vladimir Zubkov, Irek Gimayev, Valeri Vasiliev, Zinetula Bilyaletdinov, Andrei Khomutov

**Sweden** (Anders Parmstrom, coach) GK—Peter Lindmark, Pelle Lindbergh—Anders Hedberg, Anders Kallur, Lars Molin, Ulf Nilsson, Thomas Gradin, Anders Hakansson, Kent Nilsson, Peter Helander, Borje Salming, Patrik Sundstrom, Bengt Lundholm, Tomas Jonsson, Kent-Erik Andersson, Lars Lindgren, Jan Erixon, Ulf Isaksson, Thomas Eriksson, Thomas Steen, Mats Waltin, Jorgen Pettersson, Stefan Persson

**United States** (Bob Johnson, coach) GK—Tony Esposito, Steve Baker—Mike Eaves, Steve Christoff, Neal Broten, Dean Talafous, Mike O'Connell, Richie Dunn, Mark Johnson, Mark Howe, Warren Miller, Reed Larson, Tom Gorence, Dave Christian, Dave Langevin, Rod Langway, Bob Miller, Bill Baker, Tom Younghans, Robbie Ftorek, Ken Morrow, Rob McClanahan

## 1984 Canada Cup
## September 1-18, 1984
## Calgary, Edmonton, Halifax, Montreal, London, Vancouver, Buffalo

**Results & Standings**

| | GP | W | T | L | GF | GA | P |
|---|---|---|---|---|---|---|---|
| Soviet Union | 5 | 5 | 0 | 0 | 22 | 7 | 10 |
| United States | 5 | 3 | 1 | 1 | 21 | 13 | 7 |
| Sweden | 5 | 3 | 0 | 2 | 15 | 16 | 6 |
| Canada | 5 | 2 | 1 | 2 | 23 | 18 | 5 |
| West Germany | 5 | 0 | 1 | 4 | 13 | 29 | 1 |
| Czechoslovakia | 5 | 0 | 1 | 4 | 10 | 21 | 1 |

| | | | |
|---|---|---|---|
| September 1 | Montreal | Canada 7 | West Germany 2 |
| September 1 | Halifax | United States 7 | Sweden 1 |
| September 2 | Montreal | Soviet Union 3 | Czechoslovakia 0 |
| September 3 | Montreal | Canada 4 | United States 4 |
| September 4 | London | Czechoslovakia 4 | West Germany 4 |
| September 4 | Calgary | Soviet Union 3 | Sweden 2 |
| September 6 | Vancouver | Sweden 4 | Canada 2 |
| September 6 | Edmonton | Soviet Union 8 | West Germany 1 |
| September 6 | Buffalo | United States 3 | Czechoslovakia 2 |
| September 8 | Calgary | Canada 7 | Czechoslovakia 2 |
| September 8 | Calgary | Sweden 4 | West Germany 2 |
| September 8 | Edmonton | Soviet Union 2 | United States 1 |
| September 10 | Edmonton | Soviet Union 6 | Canada 3 |
| September 10 | Vancouver | Sweden 4 | Czechoslovakia 2 |
| September 10 | Calgary | United States 6 | West Germany 4 |

**SEMI-FINALS**

| | | | |
|---|---|---|---|
| September 12 | Edmonton | Sweden 9 | United States 2 |
| September 13 | Calgary | Canada 3<br>(Mike Bossy 12:29 OT) | Soviet Union 2 |

**FINALS (BEST-OF-THREE)**

| | | | |
|---|---|---|---|
| September 16 | Calgary | Canada 5 | Sweden 2 |
| September 18 | Edmonton | Canada 6 | Sweden 5 |

**Rosters**

**Canada** (Glen Sather, coach) GK—Pete Peeters, Rejean Lemelin, Grant Fuhr—Charlie Huddy, Kevin Lowe, Ray Bourque, Larry Robinson, Randy Gregg, Doug Wilson, Paul Coffey, Steve Yzerman, Glenn Anderson, Brent Sutter, Mark Messier, Bob Bourne, Michel Goulet, Rick Middleton, Mike Gartner, Mike Bossy, Brian Bellows, Peter Stastny, John Tonelli, Wayne Gretzky

**Czechoslovakia** (Ludek Bukac, coach) GK—Dominik Hasek, Jaromir Sindel—Miloslav Horava, Frantisek Musil, Eduard Uvira, Arnold Kadlec, Jaroslav Benak, Radoslav Svoboda, Antonin Stavjana, Petr Rosol, Igor Liba, Petr Klima, Jiri Dudacek, Vladimir Ruzicka, Vladimir Caldr, Jiri Lala, Dusan Pasek, Ladislav Svozil, Vladimir Kames, Jiri Hrdina, Jaroslav Korbela, Vincent Lukac

**Soviet Union** (Viktor Tikhonov, coach) GK—Vladimir Myshkin, Alexander Tyzhnykh—Vladimir Zubkov, Igor Stelnov, Vasili Pervukhin, Alexei Kasatonov, Alexei Gusarov, Sergei Starikov, Zinetula Bilyaletdinov, Vladimir Krutov, Igor Larionov, Sergei Svetlov, Irek Gimayev, Mikhail Varnakov, Sergei Shepelev, Sergei Makarov, Sergei Yashin, Alexander Skvortsov, Mikhail Vasilyev, Alexander Kozhevnikov, Anatoli Semyonov, Vladimir Kovin

**Sweden** (Leif Boork, coach) GK—Peter Lindmark, Gote Walitalo—Mats Thelin, Anders Eldebrink, Jan Lindholm, Michael Thelven, Bo Ericson, Thomas Ahlen, Peter Andersson, Thomas Eriksson, Hakan Loob, Kent Nilsson, Bengt-Ake Gustafsson, Patrik Sundstrom, Peter Sundstrom, Thomas Steen, Anders Hakansson, Thomas Gradin, Per-Erik Eklund, Mats Naslund, Tomas Sandstrom, Jan Claesson

**United States** (Bob Johnson, coach) GK—Tom Barrasso, Glenn "Chico" Resch—Mark Fusco, Mike Ramsey, Phil Housley, Rod Langway, Gordie Roberts, Chris Chelios, Tom Hirsch, Neal Broten, Bobby Carpenter, Ed Olczyk, Mark Johnson, Bob Brooke, Joe Mullen, Bryan Trottier, Brian Mullen, Aaron Broten, Bryan Erickson, David A. Jensen, Brian Lawton, Dave Christian

**West Germany** (Xaver Unsinn, coach) GK—Karl Friesen, Bernd Engelbrecht—Andreas Niederberger, Udo Kiessling, Rainer Blum, Joachim Reil, Peter Scharf, Dieter Medicus, Ignaz Berndaner, Uli Hiemer, Peter Schiller, Ernst Hofner, Franz Reindl, Manfred Wolf, Peter Obresa, Marcus Kuhl, Holger Meitinger, Gerd Truntschka, Roy Roedger, Dieter Hegen, Helmut Steiger, Michael Betz

## 1987 Canada Cup
## August 28-September 15, 1987
## Hamilton, Calgary, Regina, Halifax, Sydney, Hartford

**Results & Standings**

| | GP | W | T | L | GF | GA | P |
|---|---|---|---|---|---|---|---|
| Canada | 5 | 3 | 2 | 0 | 19 | 13 | 8 |
| Soviet Union | 5 | 3 | 1 | 1 | 22 | 13 | 7 |
| Sweden | 5 | 3 | 0 | 2 | 17 | 14 | 6 |
| Czechoslovakia | 5 | 2 | 1 | 2 | 12 | 15 | 5 |
| United States | 5 | 2 | 0 | 3 | 13 | 14 | 4 |
| Finland | 5 | 0 | 0 | 5 | 9 | 23 | 0 |

| | | | |
|---|---|---|---|
| August 28 | Calgary | Canada 4 | Czechoslovakia 4 |
| August 28 | Hartford | United States 4 | Finland 1 |
| August 29 | Calgary | Sweden 5 | Soviet Union 3 |
| August 30 | Hamilton | Canada 4 | Finland 1 |
| August 31 | Regina | Soviet Union 4 | Czechoslovakia 0 |
| August 31 | Hamilton | United States 5 | Sweden 2 |
| September 2 | Halifax | Soviet Union 7 | Finland 4 |
| September 2 | Hamilton | Canada 3 | United States 2 |
| September 2 | Regina | Sweden 4 | Czechoslovakia 0 |
| September 4 | Hartford | Soviet Union 5 | United States 1 |
| September 4 | Sydney | Czechoslovakia 5 | Finland 2 |
| September 4 | Montreal | Canada 5 | Sweden 3 |
| September 6 | Sydney | Sweden 3 | Finland 1 |
| September 6 | Sydney | Czechoslovakia 3 | United States 1 |
| September 6 | Hamilton | Canada 3 | Soviet Union 3 |

**SEMI-FINALS**

| | | | |
|---|---|---|---|
| September 8 | Hamilton | Soviet Union 4 | Sweden 2 |
| September 8 | Montreal | Canada 5 | Czechoslovakia 3 |

**FINALS (BEST-OF-THREE)**

| | | | |
|---|---|---|---|
| September 11 | Montreal | Soviet Union 6<br>(Alexander Semak 5:33 OT) | Canada 5 |
| September 13 | Hamilton | Canada 6<br>(Mario Lemieux 30:07 OT) | Soviet Union 5 |
| September 15 | Hamilton | Canada 6 | Soviet Union 5 |

**Rosters**

**Canada** (Mike Keenan, coach) GK—Grant Fuhr, Ron Hextall, Kelly Hrudey—Wayne Gretzky, Mario Lemieux, Ray Bourque, Larry Murphy, Mark Messier, Dale Hawerchuk, Paul Coffey, Rick Tocchet, Michel Goulet, Brent Sutter, Mike Gartner, Brian Propp, Glenn Anderson, Kevin Dineen, Normand Rochefort, Doug Gilmour, Craig Hartsburg, Claude Lemieux, James Patrick, Doug Crossman

**Czechoslovakia** (Jan Starsi, coach) GK—Dominik Hasek, Karel Lang, Jaromir Sindel—Dusan Pasek, Jaroslav Benak, David Volek, Igor Liba, Ludek Cajka, Jiri Sejba, Miloslav Horava, Jiri Hrdina, Peter Vlk, Vladimir Ruzicka, Mojmir Bozik, Antonin Stavjana, Ladislav Lubina, Rostislav Vlach, Jiri Dolezal, Drahomir Kadlec, Jan Jasko, Jiri Kucera, Bedrich Scerban, Petr Rosol

**Finland** (Rauno Korpi, coach) GK—Jarmo Myllys, Kari Takko, Jukka Tammi—Christian Ruuttu, Raimo Helminen, Raimo Summanen, Mikko Makela, Markku Kyllonen, Jari Kurri, Petri Skriko, Janne Ojanen, Matti Hagman, Jukka Seppo, Hannu Virta, Timo Jutila, Teppo Numminen, Esa Tikkanen, Iiro Jarvi, Ville Siren, Jari Gronstrand, Jouko Narvanmaa, Timo Blomqvist, Reijo Ruotsalainen

**Sweden** (Tommy Sandlin, coach) GK—Peter Lindmark, Anders Bergman, Ake Lilljebjorn—Mikael Andersson, Kent Nilsson, Tommy Albelin, Michael Thelven, Mats Naslund, Anders Eldebrink, Thom Eklund, Bengt-Ake Gustafsson, Thomas Rundqvist, Jonas Bergqvist, Lars Karlsson, Hakan Sodergren, Magnus Roupe, Tomas Jonsson, Lars-Gunnar Pettersson, Peter Andersson, Anders Carlsson, Tommy Samuelsson, Peter Sundstrom, Peter Eriksson

**Soviet Union** (Viktor Tikhonov, coach) GK—Sergei Mylnikov, Yevgeni Belosheikin, Vitali Samoilov—Sergei Makarov, Vladimir Krutov, Vyacheslav Bykov, Andrei Khomutov, Valeri Kamenski, Vyacheslav Fetisov, Anatoli Semyonov, Andrei Lomakin, Igor Stelnov, Alexei Kasatonov, Sergei Svetlov, Igor Kravchuk, Igor Larionov, Alexander Semak, Alexei Gusarov, Vasili Pervukhin, Sergei Pryakhin, Yuri Khmylyov, Anatoli Fedotov, Sergei Nemchinov

**United States** (Bob Johnson, coach) GK—John Vanbiesbrouck, Tom Barrasso, Bob Mason (did not play)—Joe Mullen, Gary Suter, Bobby Carpenter, Pat Lafontaine, Aaron Broten, Chris Chelios, Ed Olczyk, Joel Otto, Chris Nilan, Phil Housley, Mike Ramsey, Rod Langway, Bob Brooke, Curt Fraser, Mark Johnson, Wayne Presley, Corey Millen, Kevin Hatcher, Kelly Miller

## 1991 Canada Cup
## August 31-September 16, 1991
## Hamilton, Montreal, Toronto, Saskatoon, Quebec City, Pittsburgh, Detroit, Chicago

**Results & Standings**

| | GP | W | T | L | GF | GA | P |
|---|---|---|---|---|---|---|---|
| Canada | 5 | 3 | 2 | 0 | 21 | 11 | 8 |
| United States | 5 | 4 | 0 | 1 | 19 | 15 | 8 |
| Finland | 5 | 2 | 1 | 2 | 10 | 13 | 5 |
| Sweden | 5 | 2 | 0 | 3 | 13 | 17 | 4 |
| Soviet Union | 5 | 1 | 1 | 3 | 14 | 14 | 3 |
| Czechoslovakia | 5 | 1 | 0 | 4 | 11 | 18 | 2 |

| | | | |
|---|---|---|---|
| August 31 | Toronto | Canada 2 | Finland 2 |
| August 31 | Saskatoon | Czechoslovakia 5 | Soviet Union 2 |
| August 31 | Pittsburgh | United States 6 | Sweden 3 |
| September 2 | Hamilton | Canada 6 | United States 3 |
| September 2 | Montreal | Sweden 3 | Soviet Union 2 |
| September 2 | Saskatoon | Finland 1 | Czechoslovakia 0 |
| September 5 | Toronto | Canada 4 | Sweden 1 |
| September 5 | Hamilton | Soviet Union 6 | Finland 1 |
| September 5 | Detroit | United States 4 | Czechoslovakia 2 |
| September 7 | Montreal | Canada 6 | Czechoslovakia 2 |
| September 7 | Toronto | Finland 3 | Sweden 1 |
| September 7 | Chicago | United States 2 | Soviet Union 1 |
| September 9 | Quebec City | Canada 3 | Soviet Union 3 |
| September 9 | Toronto | Sweden 5 | Czechoslovakia 2 |
| September 9 | Chicago | United States 4 | Finland 3 |

**SEMI-FINALS**

| | | | |
|---|---|---|---|
| September 11 | Hamilton | United States 7 | Finland 3 |
| September 12 | Toronto | Canada 4 | Sweden 0 |

**FINALS (BEST-OF-THREE)**

| | | | |
|---|---|---|---|
| September 14 | Montreal | Canada 4 | United States 1 |
| September 16 | Hamilton | Canada 4 | United States 2 |

**Rosters**

**Canada** (Mike Keenan, coach) GK—Bill Ranford, Sean Burke, Ed Belfour—Wayne Gretzky, Steve Larmer, Mark Messier, Paul Coffey, Al MacInnis, Eric Lindros, Dale Hawerchuk, Theo Fleury, Shayne Corson, Brent Sutter, Dirk Graham, Luc Robitaille, Eric Desjardins, Rick Tocchet, Brendan Shanahan, Russ Courtnall, Steve Smith, Scott Stevens, Larry Murphy, Mark Tinordi

**Czechoslovakia** (Stanislav Nevesely, coach) GK—Dominik Hasek, Milan Hnilicka, Oldrich Svoboda—Thomas Jelinek, Jergus Baca, Kamil Kastak, Michal Pivonka, Robert Reichel, Richard Zemlicka, Josef Beranek, Martin Rucinsky, Leo Gudas, Jiri Slegr, Richard Smehlik, Jaromir Jagr, Lubomir Kolnik, Zigmund Palffy, Petr Hrbek, Frantisek Kucera, Frantisek Musil, Kamil Prachar, Zdeno Ciger, Robert Kron

**Finland** (Pentti Matikainen, coach) GK—Markus Ketterer, Jukka Tammi—Christian Ruuttu, Petri Skriko, Janne Ojanen, Esa Tikkanen, Janne Laukkanen, Jyrki Lumme, Jari Kurri, Teemu Selanne, Teppo Numminen, Timo Peltomaa, Raimo Summanen, Jarmo Kekalainen, Pekka Tirkkonen, Hannu Jarvenpaa, Ville Siren, Kari Eloranta, Iiro Jarvi, Arto Ruotanen, Timo Jutila, Pasi Huura

**Sweden** (Conny Evensson, coach) GK—Tommy Soderstrom, Rolf Ridderwall, Fredrik Andersson—Mats Sundin, Thomas Rundqvist, Mats Naslund, Thomas Steen, Tomas Sandstrom, Ulf Dahlen, Calle Johansson, Nicklas Lidstrom, Johan Garpenlov, Tomas Forslund, Lars Edstrom, Jonas Bergqvist, Charles Berglund, Niklas Andersson, Mikael Andersson, Kjell Samuelsson, Ulf Samuelsson, Borje Salming, Peter Andersson, Tommy Albelin

**Soviet Union** (Viktor Tikhonov, coach) GK—Andrei Trefilov, Mikhail Shtalenkov, Alexei Maryin—Sergei Fyodorov, Andrei Kovalenko, Alexei Zhamnov, Vitali Prokhorov, Alexander Semak, Vyacheslav Kozlov, Ravil Khaidarov, Vyacheslav Butsayev, Andrei Lomakin, Viktor Gordiyuk, Alexei Gusarov, Alexander Galchenyuk, Dmitri Mironov, Mikhail Tatarinov, Alexei Kasatonov, Alexei Zhitnik, Igor Korolyov, Dmitri Filimonov, Vladimir Malakhov, Igor Kravchuk

**United States** (Bob Johnson, coach) GK—John Vanbiesbrouck, Mike Richter, Pat Jablonski—Brett Hull, Mike Modano, Craig Janney, Jeremy Roenick, Kevin Miller, Joe Mullen, Joel Otto, Chris Chelios, Gary Suter, Pat Lafontaine, Kevin Hatcher, Brian Leetch, Doug Brown, Tony Granato, Ed Olczyk, Craig Wolanin, Randy Wood, Dave Christian, Eric Weinrich, Jim Johnson

## 1996 World Cup of Hockey
## August 26-September 14, 1996
## Canada/Europe/United States

**Results & Standings**

**NORTH AMERICAN POOL**

| | GP | W | T | L | GF | GA | P |
|---|---|---|---|---|---|---|---|
| United States | 3 | 3 | 0 | 0 | 19 | 8 | 6 |
| Canada | 3 | 2 | 0 | 1 | 11 | 10 | 4 |
| Russia | 3 | 1 | 0 | 2 | 12 | 14 | 2 |
| Slovakia | 3 | 0 | 0 | 3 | 9 | 19 | 0 |

| | | | |
|---|---|---|---|
| August 28 | Vancouver | Canada 5 | Russia 3 |
| August 31 | Montreal | Russia 7 | Slovakia 4 |
| August 31 | Philadelphia | United States 5 | Canada 3 |
| September 1 | Ottawa | Canada 3 | Slovakia 2 |
| September 2 | New York | United States 5 | Russia 2 |
| September 3 | New York | United States 9 | Slovakia 3 |

**EUROPEAN POOL**

| | GP | W | T | L | GF | GA | P |
|---|---|---|---|---|---|---|---|
| Sweden | 3 | 3 | 0 | 0 | 14 | 3 | 6 |
| Finland | 3 | 2 | 0 | 1 | 17 | 11 | 4 |
| Germany | 3 | 1 | 0 | 2 | 11 | 15 | 2 |
| Czech Republic | 3 | 0 | 0 | 3 | 4 | 17 | 0 |

| | | | |
|---|---|---|---|
| August 26 | Stockholm | Sweden 6 | Germany 1 |
| August 27 | Helsinki | Finland 7 | Czech Republic 3 |
| August 28 | Helsinki | Finland 8 | Germany 3 |
| August 28 | Prague | Sweden 3 | Czech Republic 0 |
| August 31 | Garmisch | Germany 7 | Czech Republic 1 |
| September 1 | Stockholm | Sweden 5 | Finland 2 |

**QUARTER-FINALS**

| | | | |
|---|---|---|---|
| September 5 | Montreal | Canada 4 | Germany 1 |
| September 6 | Ottawa | Russia 5 | Finland 0 |

**SEMI-FINALS**

| | | | |
|---|---|---|---|
| September 7 | Philadelphia | Canada 3 (Theo Fleury 39:47 OT) | Sweden 2 |
| September 8 | Ottawa | United States 5 | Russia 2 |

**FINALS (BEST-OF-THREE)**

| | | | |
|---|---|---|---|
| September 10 | Philadelphia | Canada 4 (Steve Yzerman 10:37 OT) | United States 3 |
| September 12 | Montreal | United States 5 | Canada 2 |
| September 14 | Montreal | United States 5 | Canada 2 |

**Rosters**

**Canada** (Glen Sather, coach) GK—Martin Brodeur, Curtis Joseph, Bill Ranford—Brendan Shanahan, Theo Fleury, Paul Coffey, Wayne Gretzky, Eric Lindros, Mark Messier, Joe Sakic, Scott Niedermayer, Steve Yzerman, Rod Brind'Amour, Eric Desjardins, Vincent Damphousse, Claude Lemieux, Trevor Linden, Scott Stevens, Sylvain Cote, Rob Blake, Adam Graves, Pat Verbeek, Keith Primeau, Adam Foote, Lyle Odelein

**Czech Republic** (Ludek Bukac, coach) GK—Petr Briza, Roman Turek, Dominik Hasek—Jiri Dopita, Jaromir Jagr, Robert Reichel, Radek Bonk, Petr Sykora, Pavel Patera, Petr Nedved, Jiri Vykoukal, Martin Straka, Jiri Veber, Drahomir Kadlec, Jiri Kucera, Martin Prochazka, Michal Sykora, Frantisek Kaberle, Otakar Vejvoda, Robert Holik, Josef Beranek, Robert Lang, Jiri Slegr, Martin Rucinsky, Roman Hamrlik, Stanislav Neckar

**Finland** (Curt Lindstrom, coach) GK—Jarmo Myllys, Kari Takko, Markus Ketterer—Teemu Selanne, Jere Lehtinen, Juha Ylonen, Saku Koivu, Ville Peltonen, Juha Riihijarvi, Jyrki Lumme, Mika Stromberg, Mika Nieminen, Janne Ojanen, Raimo Helminen, Jari Kurri, Christian Ruuttu, Hannu Virta, Kai Numinen, Marko Kiprusoff, Petteri Nummelin, Teppo Numminen, Janne Niinimaa, Sami Kapanen, Janne Laukkanen

**Germany** (George Kingston, coach) GK—Josef Heiss, Olaf Kolzig, Klaus Merk—Peter Draisaitl, Mark MacKay, Andreas Lupzig, Dieter Hegen, Jan Benda, Thomas Brandl, Stefan Ustorf, Leo Stefan, Benoit Doucet, Jochen Hecht, Jurgen Rumrich, Reemt Pyka, Daniel Nowak, Mirko Ludemann, Erich Goldmann, Mike Heidt, Jayson Meyer, Torsten Kienass, Brad Bergen, Daniel Kunce

**Russia** (Boris Mikhailov, coach) GK—Nikolai Khabibulin, Andrei Trefilov, Mikhail Shtalenkov—Sergei Fyodorov, Alexander Mogilny, Sergei Gonchar, Andrei Nikolishin, Igor Larionov, Alexei Kovalyov, Vyacheslav Kozlov, Sergei Nemchinov, Andrei Kovalenko, Alexei Zhitnik, Dmitri Yushkevich, Vyacheslav Fetisov, Alexei Zhamnov, Alexei Yashin, Darius Kasparaitis, Sergei Berezin, Vladimir Malakhov, Oleg Tverdovski, Sergei Zubov, Alexander Semak, Igor Ulanov, Valeri Bure, Alexander Karpovtsev, Valeri Zelepukin

**Slovakia** (Jozef Golonka, coach) GK—Jaromir Dragan, Roman Mega—Peter Bondra, Zigmund Palffy, Robert Svehla, Slavomir Ilavsky, Vlastimil Plavucha, Jergus Baca, Zdeno Ciger, Lubomir Kolnik, Lubomir Rybovic, Ivan Droppa, Otto Hascak, Jan Varholik, Marian Smerciak, Lubomir Sekeras, Stanislav Medrik, Stanislav Jasecko, Lubomir Visnovsky, Peter Bartos, Matej Buckna, Jozef Stumpel, Miroslav Satan, Pavol Demitra, Richard Zednik

**Sweden** (Kent Forsberg, coach) GK—Tommy Salo, Tommy Soderstrom, Johan Hedberg—Mats Sundin, Calle Johansson, Peter Forsberg, Niklas Sundstrom, Nicklas Lidstrom, Michael Nylander, Ulf Dahlen, Johan Garpenlov, Tommy Albelin, Jonas Bergqvist, Mikael Andersson, Fredrik Nilsson, Mattias Norstrom, Niklas Andersson, Leif Rohlin, Markus Naslund, Kenny Jonsson, Andreas Johansson, Roger Johansson, Peter Popovic, Patrik Juhlin, Daniel Alfredsson

**United States** (Ron Wilson, coach) GK—Mike Richter, Guy Hebert, Jim Carey—John LeClair, Brett Hull, Doug Weight, Keith Tkachuk, Mike Modano, Tony Amonte, Brian Leetch, Pat LaFontaine, Scott Young, Bryan Smolinski, Chris Chelios, Derian Hatcher, Joel Otto, Adam Deadmarsh, Kevin Hatcher, Mathieu Schneider, Gary Suter, Bill Guerin, Phil Housley, Shawn McEachern, Shawn Chambers, Brian Rolston, Steve Konowalchuk

## 2004 World Cup of Hockey
## August 30-September 14, 2004
## Canada/Europe/United States

**Results & Standings**

**EUROPEAN POOL**

| | GP | W | T | L | GF | GA | P |
|---|---|---|---|---|---|---|---|
| Finland | 3 | 2 | 1 | 0 | 11 | 4 | 5 |
| Sweden | 3 | 2 | 1 | 0 | 13 | 9 | 5 |
| Czech Republic | 3 | 1 | 0 | 2 | 10 | 10 | 2 |
| Germany | 3 | 0 | 0 | 3 | 4 | 15 | 0 |

| | | | |
|---|---|---|---|
| August 30 | Helsinki | Finland 4 | Czech Republic 0 |
| August 31 | Stockholm | Sweden 5 | Germany 2 |
| September 1 | Stockholm | Sweden 4 | Czech Republic 3 |
| September 2 | Cologne | Finland 3 | Germany 0 |
| September 3 | Prague | Czech Republic 7 | Germany 2 |
| September 4 | Helsinki | Finland 4 | Sweden 4 (5:00 OT) |

**NORTH AMERICAN POOL**

| | GP | W | T | L | GF | GA | P |
|---|---|---|---|---|---|---|---|
| Canada | 3 | 3 | 0 | 0 | 10 | 3 | 6 |
| Russia | 3 | 2 | 0 | 1 | 9 | 6 | 4 |
| United States | 3 | 1 | 0 | 2 | 5 | 6 | 2 |
| Slovakia | 3 | 0 | 0 | 3 | 4 | 13 | 0 |

| | | | |
|---|---|---|---|
| August 31 | Montreal | Canada 2 | United States 1 |
| September 1 | Montreal | Canada 5 | Slovakia 1 |
| September 2 | St. Paul | Russia 3 | United States 1 |
| September 3 | St. Paul | United States 3 | Slovakia 1 |
| September 4 | Toronto | Canada 3 | Russia 1 |
| September 5 | Toronto | Russia 5 | Slovakia 2 |

**QUARTER-FINALS**

| | | | |
|---|---|---|---|
| September 6 | Helsinki | Finland 2 | Germany 1 |
| September 7 | Stockholm | Czech Republic 6 | Sweden 1 |
| September 7 | St. Paul | United States 5 | Russia 2 |
| September 8 | Toronto | Canada 5 | Slovakia 1 |

**SEMI-FINALS**

| | | | |
|---|---|---|---|
| September 11 | St. Paul | Finland 2 | United States 1 |
| September 12 | Toronto | Canada 4 | Czech Republic 3 |
| | | (Vincent Lecavalier 3:45 OT) | |

**FINALS**

| | | | |
|---|---|---|---|
| September 14 | Toronto | Canada 3 | Finland 2 |

**Rosters**

**Canada** (Pat Quinn, coach) GK—Martin Brodeur, Roberto Luongo, Jose Theodore—Vincent Lecavalier, Joe Sakic, Joe Thornton, Mario Lemieux, Ryan Smyth, Kris Draper, Martin St. Louis, Eric Brewer, Brad Richards, Jarome Iginla, Adam Foote, Scott Niedermayer, Shane Doan, Simon Gagne, Dany Heatley, Scott Hannan, Wade Redden, Robyn Regehr, Brenden Morrow, Jay Bouwmeester, Ed Jovanovski

**Czech Republic** (Vladimir Ruzicka, coach) GK—Tomas Vokoun, Roman Cechmanek, Petr Briza—Martin Havlat, Patrik Elias, Milan Hejduk, Marek Zidlicky, Vaclav Prospal, Martin Straka, Petr Cajanek, Jaromir Jagr, Martin Rucinsky, Roman Hamrlik, Jiri Slegr, Radek Dvorak, Petr Sykora, Jiri Dopita, Tomas Kaberle, Tomas Vlasak, Marek Malik, David Vyborny, Jiri Fischer, Robert Reichel, Martin Skoula, Jaroslav Spacek, Josef Vasicek

**Finland** (Raimo Summanen, coach) GK—Miikka Kiprusoff, Kari Lehtonen, Vesa Toskala—Kimmo Timonen, Saku Koivu, Teemu Selanne, Jere Lehtinen, Olli Jokinen, Tuomo Ruutu, Ville Peltonen, Niko Kapanen, Ossi Vaananen, Toni Lydman, Mikko Eloranta, Jukka Hentunen, Teppo Numminen, Niklas Hagman, Riku Hahl, Sami Salo, Aki-Petteri Berg, Mikko Koivu, Jarkko Ruutu, Janne Niinimaa, Ville Nieminen, Antti Laaksonen

**Germany** (Franz Reindl, coach) GK—Olaf Kolzig, Robert Muller, Oliver Jonas—Marco Sturm, Daniel Kreutzer, Tino Boos, Jochen Hecht, Rob Leask, Eduard Lewandowski, Marcel Goc, Christoph Schubert, Lasse Kopitz, Tobias Abstreiter, Christian Ehrhoff, Sascha Goc, Klaus Kathan, Tomas Martinec, Andreas Renz, Petr Fical, Mirko Ludemann, Dennis Seidenberg, Stefan Ustorf, Martin Reichel, Stephan Retzer

**Russia** (Zinetula Bilyaletdinov, coach) GK—Ilya Bryzgalov, Maxim Sokolov, Alexander Fomichev—Alexei Kovalyov, Dainius Zubrus, Sergei Gonchar, Alexei Yashin, Sergei Samsonov, Alexander Frolov, Dmitri Afanasenkov, Ilya Kovalchuk, Pavel Datsyuk, Viktor Kozlov, Alexander Ovechkin, Darius Kasparaitis, Alexander Khavanov, Maxim Afinogenov, Andrei Markov, Artyom Chubarov, Oleg Kvasha, Andrei Kovalenko, Dmitri Kalinin, Oleg Tverdovski, Vitali Vishnevski, Anton Volchenkov

**Slovakia** (Jan Filc, coach) GK— Rastislav Stana, Jan Lasak, Peter Budaj—Pavol Demitra, Zdeno Chara, Marian Hossa, Ladislav Nagy, Lubos Bartecko, Martin Cibak, Branko Radivojevic, Marian Gaborik, Jozef Stumpel, Miroslav Satan, Martin Strbak, Richard Zednik, Radovan Somik, Vladimir Orszagh, Jaroslav Obsut, Richard Lintner, Radoslav Suchy, Rastislav Pavlikovsky, Branislav Mezei, Lubomir Visnovsky, Miroslav Hlinka, Ladislav Cierny

**Sweden** (Hardy Nilsson, coach) GK—Tommy Salo, Mikael Tellqvist, Henrik Lundqvist—Fredrik Modin, Daniel Alfredsson, Tomas Holmstrom, Mats Sundin, Kim Johnsson, Peter Forsberg, Markus Naslund, Henrik Zetterberg, Marcus Nilson, Nicklas Lidstrom, Mattias Ohlund, Sami Pahlsson, Andreas Johansson, Per-Johan Axelsson, Daniel Tjarnqvist, Jorgen Jonsson, Mattias Norstrom, Marcus Ragnarsson, Dick Tarnstrom

**United States** (Ron Wilson, coach) GK—Robert Esche, Rick DiPietro, Ty Conklin—Keith Tkachuk, Mike Modano, Bill Guerin, Scott Gomez, Brian Rafalski, Doug Weight, Jason Blake, Bryan Smolinski, Chris Chelios, Brian Leetch, Tony Amonte, Paul Martin, Jeff Halpern, Steve Konowalchuk, Aaron Miller, Jamie Langenbrunner, Brett Hull, Chris Drury, Ken Klee, Craig Conroy, John-Michael Liles, Brian Rolston, Eric Weinrich

*Sweden's first Hall of Famer Borje Salming presents Team Canada's captain Mario Lemieux with the 2004 World Cup of Hockey trophy. Photo: HHOF.*

# U20 WORLD CHAMPIONSHIP

## 1st U20 WORLD CHAMPIONSHIP
**December 22, 1976-January 2, 1977**
**Zvolen/Banska Bystrica, Czechoslovakia**

**Final Placing**

| | | | |
|---|---|---|---|
| Gold | Soviet Union | 5th | Sweden |
| Silver | Canada | 6th | West Germany |
| Bronze | Czechoslovakia | 7th | United States |
| 4th | Finland | 8th | Poland* |

*demoted to B Pool for 1978

**Tournament Format**
The eight nations in the tournament were placed in one division and played a single round-robin schedule. Tie games were not decided by overtime, and the top three teams won gold, silver, and bronze. A tie in the standings would be broken by the head-to-head result in the round robin.

**Results & Standings**

| | GP | W | T | L | GF | GA | P |
|---|---|---|---|---|---|---|---|
| Soviet Union | 7 | 7 | 0 | 0 | 51 | 19 | 14 |
| Canada | 7 | 5 | 1 | 1 | 50 | 20 | 11 |
| Czechoslovakia | 7 | 4 | 1 | 2 | 32 | 17 | 9 |
| Finland | 7 | 4 | 0 | 3 | 35 | 29 | 8 |
| Sweden | 7 | 3 | 0 | 4 | 28 | 30 | 6 |
| West Germany | 7 | 2 | 0 | 5 | 18 | 33 | 4 |
| United States | 7 | 1 | 1 | 5 | 25 | 45 | 3 |
| Poland | 7 | 0 | 1 | 6 | 12 | 58 | 1 |

| | | | |
|---|---|---|---|
| December 22 | Banska Bystrica | Finland 6 | United States 3 |
| December 23 | Banska Bystrica | Canada 14 | Poland 0 |
| December 23 | Zvolen | Sweden 5 | Finland 4 |
| December 23 | Banska Bystrica | Soviet Union 4 | Czechoslovakia 0 |
| December 23 | Zvolen | West Germany 4 | United States 3 |
| December 25 | Zvolen | Canada 4 | Czechoslovakia 4 |
| December 25 | Banska Bystrica | Finland 4 | West Germany 1 |
| December 25 | Zvolen | Soviet Union 10 | Poland 1 |
| December 25 | Banska Bystrica | United States 8 | Sweden 5 |
| December 26 | Zvolen | Canada 6 | Finland 4 |
| December 26 | Banska Bystrica | Czechoslovakia 8 | West Germany 2 |
| December 26 | Zvolen | Soviet Union 4 | Sweden 2 |
| December 26 | Banska Bystrica | United States 2 | Poland 2 |
| December 28 | Banska Bystrica | Canada 5 | Sweden 3 |
| December 28 | Banska Bystrica | Soviet Union 2 | West Germany 1 |
| December 28 | Zvolen | Finland 8 | Poland 2 |
| December 28 | Zvolen | Czechoslovakia 5 | United States 2 |
| December 29 | Banska Bystrica | Canada 9 | West Germany 1 |
| December 29 | Zvolen | Sweden 6 | Poland 5 |
| December 30 | Zvolen | Finland 3 | Czechoslovakia 2 |
| December 30 | Banska Bystrica | Soviet Union 15 | United States 5 |
| January 1 | Zvolen | Canada 8 | United States 2 |
| January 1 | Banska Bystrica | Czechoslovakia 9 | Poland 0 |
| January 1 | Zvolen | Sweden 5 | West Germany 0 |
| January 1 | Banska Bystrica | Soviet Union 10 | Finland 6 |
| January 2 | Zvolen | Soviet Union 6 | Canada 4 |
| January 2 | Zvolen | West Germany 9 | Poland 2 |
| January 2 | Banska Bystrica | Czechoslovakia 4 | Sweden 2 |

**Rosters**
**Canada** (Bert Templeton, coach) GK—Al Jensen, Bob Daly—Dale McCourt, John Anderson, Joe Contini, Steve Hazlett, Dave Hunter, Ric Seiling, Dwight Foster, Ron Duguay, Geoff Shaw, Al Secord, Brad Marsh, Willie Huber, Trevor Johansen, Rob Ramage, Mike Keating, Mike Forbes, Mark Plantery, Denis Houle, Craig Hartsburg, Brian Ostrowski

**Czechoslovakia** (Ladislav Horsky, coach) GK—Jan Hrabak, Jiri Cerveny—Jaroslav Korbela, Peter Ihnacak, Jaroslav Hubl, Jindrich Kokrment, Jozef Lukac, Ladislav Svozil, Jiri Hrdina, Jiri Lala, Jiri Otoupalik, Pavel Skalicky, Vladimir Caldr, Lubomir Oslizlo, Alexander Vostry, Vladimir Urban, Jordan Karagavrilidis, Jaroslav Klacl, Frantisek Cerny, Rene Andrejs

**Finland** (Matti Vaisanen, coach) GK—Hannu Kamppuri, Rauli Sohlman—Juha Jyrkkio, Erkki Laine, Matti Forss, Risto Siltanen, Arto Javanainen, Reijo Ruotsalainen, Kari Jarvinen, Tomi Taimio, Jarmo Huhtala, Jouko Kamarainen, Jukka Hirsimaki, Raimo Hirvonen, Harry Nikander, Jukka Peitsoma, Ari Makinen, Pertti Vaelma, Hannu Ihala, Jukka Laukkanen

**Poland** (Sylwester Wilczek/Augustyn Skorski, co-coaches) GK—Stefan Wadas, Andrzej Jarosz—Andrzej Malysiak, Bogdan Dziubinski, Witold Pulka, Miroslaw Sikora, Leszek Minge, Andrzej Swiatek, Tadeusz Rylko, Slawomir Zawadzki, Boleslaw Remlein, Ludwik Synowiec, Zbigniew Tomaszkiewicz, Adam Bernat, Franciszek Bryniarski, Kazimierz Bednarski, Jerzy Gotalski, Dariusz Sikora, Henryk Gruth, Leszek Jachna

**Soviet Union** (Vitali Davydov, coach) GK—Sergei Mylnikov, Alexander Tyzhnykh—Igor Romashin, Alexei Frolikov, Sergei Makarov, Alexander Khabanov, Ivan Avdeyev, Mikhail Tolochko, Vyacheslav Fetisov, Vladimir Shvetsov, Nikolai Narimanov, Irek Gimayev, Valeri Yevstifeyev, Vladimir Zubkov, Sergei Starikov, Konstantin Makartsev, Vasili Payusov, Igor Kapustin, Mikhail Slipchenko, Mikhail Shostak

**Sweden** (Lennart Johansson, coach) GK—Pelle Lindberg, Reino Sundberg—Tore Okvist, Harald Luckner, Hans Sarkijarvi, Torbjorn Andersson, Roger Mikko, Dan Hermansson, Bengt-Ake Gustafsson, Bo Ericson, Mats Naslund, Bjorn Olsson, Lars-Eje Lindstrom, Kent Eriksson, Robin Eriksson, Conny Silfverberg, Leif Carlsson, Rolf Berglund, Karl-Erik Lilja, Lars Nyberg

**United States** (Marshall Johnston, coach) GK—Mike Parker, Carl Bloomberg—Mike MacDougal, Dave Gandini, Paul Miller, Roy Sommer, Bob Bergloff, Mickey Rego, Richie Dunn, Jim Penningrowth, Don Waddell, Doug Olson, Kevin McCloskey, Dave Wilkins, Jeff Brownschidle, Keith Hanson, Terry Houck, Bobby Crawford, Charlie Malloy, Barry Ryan

**West Germany** (Hans Rampf, coach) GK—Matthias Hoppe, Bernd Engelbrecht—Holger Meitinger, Gerd Truntschka, Ernst Hofner, Peter Schiller, Dieter Medicus, Albton Paulus, Horst Heckelsmuller, Verner Lupzig, Harald Krull, Armin Lauer, Josef Klaus, Manfred Schuster, Helmut Barensoi, Andy Groger, Herbert Heinrich, Jorg Hiemer, Peter Eimannsberger, Hans Muhlhausen

## 2nd U20 WORLD CHAMPIONSHIP
**December 22, 1977-January 3, 1978**
**Montreal/Quebec City, Canada**

**Final Placing**

| | | | |
|---|---|---|---|
| Gold | Soviet Union | 5th | United States |
| Silver | Sweden | 6th | Finland |
| Bronze | Canada | 7th | West Germany |
| 4th | Czechoslovakia | 8th | Switzerland^* |

^promoted from B Pool in 1977
*demoted to B Pool for 1979

**Tournament Format**
A round-robin format was used within each division so that each team played three games. The top two teams from each division advanced to a medal round, and the last two teams from each were grouped in a "B" pool. Another series of round-robin was played (no first round results carried over), the top two teams playing a one-game final for gold.

**Results & Standings**
**GOLD DIVISION**

| | GP | W | T | L | GF | GA | P |
|---|---|---|---|---|---|---|---|
| Sweden | 3 | 2 | 1 | 0 | 18 | 8 | 5 |
| Soviet Union | 3 | 2 | 0 | 1 | 31 | 11 | 4 |
| Finland | 3 | 1 | 1 | 1 | 26 | 15 | 3 |
| Switzerland | 3 | 0 | 0 | 3 | 3 | 44 | 0 |

| | | | |
|---|---|---|---|
| December 22 | Cornwall | Soviet Union 18 | Switzerland 1 |
| December 22 | Chicoutimi | Finland 4 | Sweden 4 |
| December 23 | Quebec City | Sweden 6 | Soviet Union 3 |
| December 23 | Chicoutimi | Finland 18 | Switzerland 1 |
| December 26 | Cornwall | Sweden 8 | Switzerland 1 |
| December 26 | Montreal | Soviet Union 10 | Finland 4 |

**BLUE DIVISION**

| | GP | W | T | L | GF | GA | P |
|---|---|---|---|---|---|---|---|
| Canada | 3 | 3 | 0 | 0 | 23 | 6 | 6 |
| Czechoslovakia | 3 | 2 | 0 | 1 | 16 | 18 | 4 |
| United States | 3 | 1 | 0 | 2 | 16 | 18 | 2 |
| West Germany | 3 | 0 | 0 | 3 | 8 | 21 | 0 |

| | | | |
|---|---|---|---|
| December 22 | Montreal | Canada 6 | United States 3 |
| December 22 | Quebec City | Czechoslovakia 5 | West Germany 4 |
| December 23 | Cornwall | Canada 8 | West Germany 0 |
| December 23 | Hull | Czechoslovakia 8 | United States 5 |
| December 25 | Montreal | Canada 9 | Czechoslovakia 3 |
| December 25 | Hull | United States 8 | West Germany 4 |

**CHAMPIONSHIP SERIES**
**A DIVISION**

| | GP | W | T | L | GF | GA | P |
|---|---|---|---|---|---|---|---|
| Soviet Union | 3 | 3 | 0 | 0 | 14 | 3 | 6 |
| Sweden | 3 | 2 | 0 | 1 | 8 | 11 | 4 |
| Canada | 3 | 1 | 0 | 2 | 13 | 12 | 2 |
| Czechoslovakia | 3 | 0 | 0 | 3 | 5 | 14 | 0 |

| | | | |
|---|---|---|---|
| December 28 | Quebec City | Soviet Union 3 | Canada 2 |
| December 28 | Montreal | Sweden 2 | Czechoslovakia 1 |
| December 31 | Montreal | Canada 6 | Czechoslovakia 3 |
| December 31 | Quebec City | Soviet Union 5 | Sweden 0 |
| January 1 | Montreal | Sweden 6 | Canada 5 |
| January 1 | Quebec City | Soviet Union 6 | Czechoslovakia 1 |

**B DIVISION**

| | GP | W | T | L | GF | GA | P |
|---|---|---|---|---|---|---|---|
| United States | 3 | 3 | 0 | 0 | 25 | 12 | 6 |
| Finland | 3 | 2 | 0 | 1 | 19 | 10 | 4 |
| West Germany | 3 | 1 | 0 | 2 | 12 | 12 | 2 |
| Switzerland | 3 | 0 | 0 | 3 | 4 | 26 | 0 |

| | | | |
|---|---|---|---|
| December 28 | Chicoutimi | Finland 4 | West Germany 1 |
| December 28 | Cornwall | United States 11 | Switzerland 1 |
| December 30 | Cornwall | Finland 9 | Switzerland 1 |
| December 30 | Hull | United States 6 | West Germany 5 |
| December 31 | Hull | United States 8 | Finland 6 |
| December 31 | Cornwall | West Germany 6 | Switzerland 2 |

**GOLD MEDAL GAME**

| | | | |
|---|---|---|---|
| January 3 | Montreal | Soviet Union 5 | Sweden 2 |

**Rosters**

**Canada** (Orval Tessier, coach) GK—Tim Bernhardt, Al Jensen—Wayne Gretzky, Wayne Babych, Ryan Walter, Tony McKegney, Mike Gartner, Pat Daley, Craig Hartsburg, Bobby Smith, Steve Tambellini, Rob Ramage, Brad Marsh, Rick Vaive, Rick Paterson, Stan Smyl, Brad McCrimmon, Willie Huber, Brian Young, Curt Fraser

**Czechoslovakia** (Ladislav Horsky, coach) GK—Jan Hrabak, Jaromir Sindel—Anton Stastny, Vladimir Caldr, Vlastimil Vajcner, Frantisek Cerny, Ivan Cerny, Jiri Hrdina, Rene Andrejs, Marian Bezak, Miroslav Frycer, Ladislav Svozil, Ondrej Weissman, Arnold Kadlec, Miroslav Moc, Jan Jasko, Vladimir Urban, Eugen Krajcovic, Darius Rusnak, Pavel Skalicky

**Finland** (Matti Vaisanen, coach) GK—Tuomo Laukkanen, Rauli Sohlman—Jorma Sevon, Rainer Risku, Timo Susi, Arto Javanainen, Ilkka Sinisalo, Kai Suikkanen, Reijo Ruotsalainen, Jari Viitala, Juha Jyrkkio, Tero Kapynen, Antti Heikkila, Harri Tuohimaa, Risto Kankaanpera, Reijo Mansikka, Pekka Laukkanen, Risto Siltanen, Jukka Peitsoma, Jouko Urvikko

**Soviet Union** (Vitali Davydov, coach) GK—Sergei Mylnikov, Alexander Tyzhnykh—Viktor Skurdyuk, Sergei Makarov, Alexander Kozhevnikov, Vyacheslav Ryanov, Vyacheslav Fetisov, Alexander Gerasimov, Alexander Guryev, Nikolai Narimanov, Nikolai Varianov, Sergei Tukmachev, Sergei Starikov, Pavel Yezovski, Alexei Kasatonov, Sergei Paramanov, Anatoli Tarasov, Konstantin Makartsev, Yuri Vozhakov, Vladimir Zubkov

**Sweden** (Bengt Ohlson, coach) GK—Pelle Lindbergh, Goran Henriksson—Mats Naslund, Mats Hallin, Bengt-Ake Gustafsson, Thomas Steen, Dan Hermansson, Conny Silfverberg, Claes-Henrik Silfver, Jan Eriksson, Tomas Jonsson, Anders Wallin, Bo Ericson, Christer Lowdahl, Tommy Samuelsson, Ulf Skoglund, Mikael Andersson, Thomas Karrbrandt, Gunnar Persson, Ulf Zetterstrom

**Switzerland** (Robert Stephen, coach) GK—Roland Scheibli, Roland Gerber—Reto Durst, Didier Mayor, Claude Domeniconi, Pierre Flotirant, Michael Braun, Pierre Houriet, Beat Lautenschlager, Philippe Favrod, Roger Geiger, Gerald Scheurer, Daniel Dubois, Markus Graf, Rolf Leuenberger, Christian Patt, Hanspeter Sagesser, Diego Ulrich, Marcel Wick, Bernhard Wuthrich

**United States** (Len Lilyholm, coach) GK—Paul Joswiak, Carl Bloomberg—Bobby Crawford, Mark Green, Mike McDougal, Kevin Hartzell, Don Waddell, John Liprando, Ed Hospodar, Scott Lecy, Bret Bjerken, Steve Ulseth, Dave Feamster, Terry Jones, Jeff Lundgren, Steve Blue, Bart Larson, Steve Pepper, Jack McKinch, Ron Griffin

**West Germany** (Helmut Perkuhn, coach) GK—Bernd Engelbrecht, Matthias Hoppe—Gerd Truntschka, Helmut Steiger, Martin Muller, Johann Diepold, Thomas Gandorfer, Les Koch, Alexander Gross, Jorg Hiemer, Norbert Kafer, Sepp Klaus, Harry Pflugl, Karl Altmann, Miro Nentwich, Michael Eggerbauer, Peter Eimannsberger, Horst Heckelsmuller, Armin Lauer, Manfred Schuster

## 3rd U20 WORLD CHAMPIONSHIP
## December 27, 1978-January 3, 1979
## Karlstad/Karlskoga, Sweden

**Final Placing**

| | |
|---|---|
| Gold .......Soviet Union | 5th ........Canada |
| Silver .....Czechoslovakia | 6th ........United States |
| Bronze ...Sweden | 7th ........West Germany |
| 4th .........Finland | 8th ........Norway^* |

^promoted from B Pool in 1978
*demoted to B Pool for 1980

**Tournament Format**

A round-robin format was used within each division so that each team played three games. The top two teams from each division advanced to a medal round, and the last two teams from each were grouped in a "B" pool. Another series of round-robin was played (first round results carried over for the consolation round but not the championship round), the top three teams winning medals.

**Results & Standings**

**GOLD DIVISION**

| | GP | W | T | L | GF | GA | P |
|---|---|---|---|---|---|---|---|
| Sweden | 3 | 3 | 0 | 0 | 8 | 3 | 6 |
| Finland | 3 | 2 | 0 | 1 | 11 | 4 | 4 |
| Canada | 3 | 1 | 0 | 2 | 7 | 6 | 2 |
| West Germany | 3 | 0 | 0 | 3 | 5 | 18 | 0 |

| | | | |
|---|---|---|---|
| December 27 | Karlstad | Finland 3 | Canada 1 |
| December 27 | Karlstad | Sweden 5 | West Germany 2 |
| December 28 | Karlstad | Canada 6 | West Germany 2 |
| December 28 | Karlskoga | Sweden 2 | Finland 1 |
| December 30 | Karlskoga | Sweden 1 | Canada 0 |
| December 30 | Karlskoga | Finland 7 | West Germany 1 |

**BLUE DIVISION**

| | GP | W | T | L | GF | GA | P |
|---|---|---|---|---|---|---|---|
| Soviet Union | 3 | 3 | 0 | 0 | 33 | 2 | 6 |
| Czechoslovakia | 3 | 2 | 0 | 1 | 10 | 15 | 4 |
| United States | 3 | 1 | 0 | 2 | 10 | 11 | 2 |
| Norway | 3 | 0 | 0 | 3 | 5 | 30 | 0 |

| | | | |
|---|---|---|---|
| December 27 | Karlskoga | Soviet Union 17 | Norway 0 |
| December 27 | Karlskoga | Czechoslovakia 3 | United States 2 |
| December 28 | Karlstad | Czechoslovakia 6 | Norway 4 |
| December 28 | Karlskoga | Soviet Union 7 | United States 1 |
| December 30 | Karlstad | Soviet Union 9 | Czechoslovakia 1 |
| December 30 | Karlstad | United States 7 | Norway 1 |

**CONSOLATION ROUND**

| | GP | W | T | L | GF | GA | P |
|---|---|---|---|---|---|---|---|
| Canada | 3 | 3 | 0 | 0 | 22 | 6 | 6 |
| United States | 3 | 2 | 0 | 1 | 18 | 13 | 4 |
| West Germany | 3 | 1 | 0 | 2 | 14 | 14 | 2 |
| Norway | 3 | 0 | 0 | 3 | 2 | 23 | 0 |

| | | | |
|---|---|---|---|
| December 31 | Karlstad | Canada 10 | Norway 1 |
| December 31 | Karlskoga | United States 8 | West Germany 6 |
| January 2 | Karlskoga | Canada 6 | United States 3 |
| January 2 | Karlstad | West Germany 6 | Norway 0 |

**CHAMPIONSHIP ROUND**

| | GP | W | T | L | GF | GA | P |
|---|---|---|---|---|---|---|---|
| Soviet Union | 3 | 2 | 1 | 0 | 13 | 9 | 5 |
| Czechoslovakia | 3 | 1 | 2 | 0 | 9 | 8 | 4 |
| Sweden | 3 | 1 | 1 | 1 | 11 | 10 | 3 |
| Finland | 3 | 0 | 0 | 3 | 9 | 15 | 0 |

| | | | |
|---|---|---|---|
| December 31 | Karlstad | Soviet Union 4 | Finland 2 |
| December 31 | Karlskoga | Sweden 1 | Czechoslovakia 1 |
| January 2 | Karlstad | Sweden 5 | Finland 2 |
| January 2 | Karlskoga | Czechoslovakia 2 | Soviet Union 2 |
| January 3 | Karlskoga | Czechoslovakia 6 | Finland 5 |
| January 3 | Karlstad | Soviet Union 7 | Sweden 5 |

**Rosters**

**Canada** (New Westminster Bruins—Ernie McLean, coach) GK—Tom Semenchuk, Rollie Melanson—Randy Irving, Ray Allison, John Ogrodnick, Dave Orleski, Kent Reardon, Terry Kirkham, Brian Propp, Scott MacLeod, Brad McCrimmon, Yvan Joly, Gary Lupul, Larry Melnyk, Errol Rausse, Keith Brown, Bill Hobbins, Bruce Howes, Boris Fistric, John Paul Kelly

**Czechoslovakia** (Ladislav Horsky, coach) GK—Pavol Norovsky, Jan Hrabak—Jan Jasko, Anton Stastny, Darius Rusnak, Ivan Cerny, Frantisek Cerny, Jiri Lala, Dusan Pasek, Jaroslav Horsky, Miroslav Frycer, Ondrej Weissman, Vladimir Jerabek, Arnold Kadlec, Pavel Setikovsky, Peter Slanina, Juraj Bakos, Igor Liba, Antonin Planovsky, Vlastimil Vajcner

**Finland** (Matti Reunamaki, coach) GK—Rauli Sohlman, Jari Paavola—Jarmo Makitalo, Kari Jalonen, Arto Javanainen, Jari Kurri, Harri Tuohimaa, Kai Suikkanen, Jari Jarvinen, Reijo Ruotsalainen, Juha Huikari, Juha Jyrkkio, Timo Susi, Pekka Laukkanen, Timo Blomqvist, Jari Hytti, Jarmo Jamalainen, Jussi Lepisto, Jari Lindgren, Juha Nurmi

**Norway** (Egil Bjerklund, coach) GK—Tommy Skarberg, Frank Stromsnes—Orjan Lovdahl, Harald Bastiansen, Tor Eikeland, Trond Abrahamsen, Knut Andersen, Stephen Foyn, Oysten Jarlsbo, Arne Billkvam, Cato Andersen, Bjorn Bratz, Frode Gaare, Geir Hansen, Tom Huse, Roy Johansen, Knut Johansen, Bjorn Kolsrud, Petter Thoresen, Tor Torp

**Soviet Union** (Vitali Davydov, coach) GK—Vladimir Gerasimov, Dmitri Saprykin— Vladimir Krutov, Anatoli Tarasov, Vyacheslav Ryanov, Alexander Gerasimov, Andrei Andreyev, Alexei Kasatonov, Gennadi Kurdin, Igor Larionov, Nikolai Varianov, Yuri Vozhakov, Anatoli Antipov, Nikolai Maslov, Andrei Sidorenko, Yuri Strakhov, Vladimir Golovkov, Viktor Glushenkov, Sergei Karpov, Valeri Krylov

**Sweden** (Bengt Ohlsson, coach) GK—Pelle Lindbergh, Goran Henriksson (dnp)—Thomas Steen, Hakan Sodergren, Mats Naslund, Conny Silfverberg, Tommy Morth, Sivert Andersson, Thomas Eriksson, Mikael Andersson, Tomas Jonsson, Ove Olsson, Hakan Loob, Bjorn Akerblom, Thomas Karrbrandt, Lars Karlsson, Jan-Ake Danielsson, Jan Remmelg, Tommy Samuelsson, Per Sjolander

**United States** (Lou Vairo, coach) GK—Jim Jetland, Stuart Birenbaum—Aaron Broten, Neal Broten, Dave Christian, Bryan Erickson, Steve Murphy, Jeff Brownschidle, Bobby Crawford, Steve Palazzi, Gary DeGrio, John Liprando, Mike Ramsey, Steve Ulseth, Todd Mishler, Mike LaBianca, Peter Johnson, Jeff Lundgren, Marc Pettygrove, Mike Stone

**West Germany** (Ladislav Olejnik, coach) GK—Gerhard Hegen, Bernhard Kopf—Georg Holzmann, Harry Pflugel, Helmut Steiger, Jurgen Lechl, Klaus Haider, Miro Nentwich, Willi Hofer, Karl Altmann, Michael Eggerbauer, Alexander Gross, Harold Kreiss, Bernhard Seyller, Gunther Stauner, Jurgen Adams, Rainer Blum, Peter Obressa, Joachim Janzon, Michael Tack

## 4th U20 WORLD CHAMPIONSHIP
## December 27, 1979-January 2, 1980
## Helsinki/Vantaa, Finland

**Final Placing**

Gold .......Soviet Union
Silver .....Finland
Bronze ...Sweden
4th .........Czechoslovakia
5th ........Canada
6th ........West Germany
7th ........United States
8th ........Switzerland^*
^promoted from B Pool in 1979
*demoted to B Pool for 1981

**Tournament Format**

Eight countries were placed in two divisions of four teams each. All teams played a round-robin format within each division (three games each). The top two advanced to a four team medal round, the bottom two to a consolation round. Results from the preliminary round between teams that ended up in the same division in the next round were carried over so that no team played twice against any other in the tournament.

**Results & Standings**

**GOLD DIVISION**

| | GP | W | T | L | GF | GA | P |
|---|---|---|---|---|---|---|---|
| Soviet Union | 3 | 3 | 0 | 0 | 16 | 6 | 6 |
| Finland | 3 | 2 | 0 | 1 | 22 | 4 | 4 |
| Canada | 3 | 1 | 0 | 2 | 15 | 15 | 2 |
| Switzerland | 3 | 0 | 0 | 3 | 6 | 34 | 0 |

| | | | |
|---|---|---|---|
| December 27 | Helsinki | Finland 2 | Canada 1 |
| December 27 | Vantaa | Soviet Union 6 | Switzerland 0 |
| December 28 | Vantaa | Soviet Union 8 | Canada 5 |
| December 28 | Helsinki | Finland 19 | Switzerland 1 |
| December 30 | Vantaa | Canada 9 | Switzerland 5 |
| December 30 | Helsinki | Soviet Union 2 | Finland 1 |

**BLUE DIVISION**

| | GP | W | T | L | GF | GA | P |
|---|---|---|---|---|---|---|---|
| Sweden | 3 | 2 | 1 | 0 | 20 | 10 | 5 |
| Czechoslovakia | 3 | 2 | 0 | 1 | 24 | 17 | 4 |
| West Germany | 3 | 1 | 0 | 2 | 10 | 20 | 2 |
| United States | 3 | 0 | 1 | 2 | 10 | 17 | 1 |

| | | | |
|---|---|---|---|
| December 27 | Vantaa | Czechoslovakia 7 | United States 3 |
| December 27 | Vantaa | Sweden 5 | West Germany 1 |
| December 28 | Vantaa | Sweden 5 | United States 5 |
| December 28 | Vantaa | Czechoslovakia 13 | West Germany 4 |
| December 30 | Vantaa | West Germany 5 | United States 2 |
| December 30 | Helsinki | Sweden 10 | Czechoslovakia 4 |

**CONSOLATION ROUND**

| | GP | W | T | L | GF | GA | P |
|---|---|---|---|---|---|---|---|
| Canada | 3 | 3 | 0 | 0 | 19 | 8 | 6 |
| West Germany | 3 | 2 | 0 | 1 | 10 | 10 | 4 |
| United States | 3 | 1 | 0 | 2 | 13 | 14 | 2 |
| Switzerland | 3 | 0 | 0 | 3 | 12 | 22 | 0 |

| | | | |
|---|---|---|---|
| January 1 | Vantaa | Canada 4 | United States 2 |
| January 1 | Vantaa | West Germany 4 | Switzerland 2 |
| January 2 | Helsinki | Canada 6 | West Germany 1 |
| January 2 | Vantaa | United States 9 | Switzerland 5 |

**MEDAL ROUND**

| | GP | W | T | L | GF | GA | P |
|---|---|---|---|---|---|---|---|
| Soviet Union | 3 | 3 | 0 | 0 | 10 | 4 | 6 |
| Finland | 3 | 2 | 0 | 1 | 8 | 6 | 4 |
| Sweden | 3 | 1 | 0 | 2 | 13 | 9 | 2 |
| Czechoslovakia | 3 | 0 | 0 | 3 | 8 | 20 | 0 |

| | | | |
|---|---|---|---|
| January 1 | Helsinki | Finland 3 | Sweden 2 |
| January 1 | Helsinki | Soviet Union 6 | Czechoslovakia 2 |
| January 2 | Vantaa | Finland 4 | Czechoslovakia 2 |
| January 2 | Vantaa | Soviet Union 2 | Sweden 1 |

**Rosters**

**Canada** (Peterborough Petes—Mike Keenan, coach) GK—Rick Laferriere, Terry Wright—Dino Ciccarelli, Jim Fox, Carmine Cirella, Terry Bovair, Dave Beckon, Jim Wiemer, Bill Gardner, Yvan Joly, Andre Hidi, Brad Ryder, Doug Crossman, Sean Simpson, Stuart Smith, Larry Murphy, Mark Reeds, Bill Kitchen, Rick Lanz, Dave Fenyves

**Czechoslovakia** (Jozef Golonka, coach) GK—Ivan Beno, Jiri Hamal—Jan Vodila, Dusan Pasek, Igor Liba, Oldrich Valek, Miroslav Venkrbec, Zdenek Pata, Josef Metlicka, Pavel Setikovsky, Pavel Jiskra, Zdenek Albrecht, Otakar Janecky, Juraj Bakos, Petr Fiala, Miloslav Horava, Eduard Uvira, Jiri Dudacek, Miroslav Majernik, Kamil Kaluzik

**Finland** (Olli Hietanen/Rauno Korpi, co-coaches) GK—Jari Paavola, Ari Timosaari—Jari Kurri, Kari Jalonen, Reijo Ruotsalainen, Ari Lahteenmaki, Pekka Arbelius, Mika Helkearo, Jouni Koutuaniemi, Juha Huikari, Anssi Melametsa, Jarmo Makitalo, Timo Blomqvist, Tony Arima, Jari Jarvinen, Risto Tuomi, Pekka Tuomisto, Jari Munck, Harri Haapaniemi, Kari Suoraniemi

**Soviet Union** (Yuri Morozov, coach) GK—Dmitri Saprykin, Yuri Nikitin—Vladimir Krutov, Igor Larionov, Yevgeni Shastin, Sergei Svetlov, Vladimir Golovkov, Mikhail Panin, Vladimir Shashov, Valeri Mikhailov, Alexander Zybin, Dmitri Yerastov, Ildar Rakhmatulin, Alexei Bevz, Viktor Glushenkov, Igor Panin, Yevgeni Popikhin, Igor Bubenshikov, Andrei Morozov, Igor Morozov

**Sweden** (Bengt Ohlsson, coach) GK—Lars Eriksson, Peter Aslin—Hakan Loob, Thomas Steen, Lars-Gunnar Pettersson, Tomas Jonsson, Peter Elander, Thomas Rundqvist, Hakan Nordin, Tommy Samulesson, Per Nilsson, Matti Pauna, Ove Olsson, Bjorn Akerblom, Patrik Sundstrom, Jan-Ake Danielsson, Lars Karlsson, Torbjorn Mattsson, Anders Backstrom, Roland Nyman

**Switzerland** (Georges Rochat, coach) GK—Kenneth Green, Hansruedi Eberle—Peter Schlagenhauf, Marco Muller, Fausto Mazzoleni, Henry Loher, Marcel Niederer, Pius Kuonen, Andreas Trumpler, Remo Gross, Jakob Gross, Philippe Petey, Peter Baldinger, Andreas Ritsch, Beat Eggiman, Gabriele Guscetti, Mauro Foschi, Ludwig Waidacher, Marcel Meier, Bernhard Wist

**United States** (Lou Vairo, coach) GK—Scott Stolzner, Mark Chiamp—Scott Carlston, Bob Brooke, Mike Lauen, Brian Mullen, Todd Lecy, Bryan Erickson, Win Dahm, Dave Jensen, Venci Sebek, Julian Vanbiesbrouck, Paul Brandrup, Lexi Doner, Jim Gardner, Pat Ethier, John Anderson, Glen Demota, Dan Vlaisavljevich, Barry Mills

**West Germany** (Ladislav Olejnik, coach) GK—Peter Zankl, Jurgen Breuer—Uli Hiemer, Jurgen Lechl, Peter Obressa, Jurgen Adams, Bernhard Seyller, Christoph Augsten, Georg Holzmann, Michael Eggerbauer, Klaus Gotsch, Gerhard Alber, Manfred Ahne, Michael Schmidt, Franco De Nobili, Rainer Blum, Willi Hofer, Anton Maidl, Ralph Hoja, Rainer Lutz

## 5th U20 WORLD CHAMPIONSHIP
## December 27, 1980-January 2, 1981
## Kaufbeuren, West Germany

**Final Placing**

Gold .......Sweden
Silver .....Finland
Bronze ...Soviet Union
4th .........Czechoslovakia
5th ........West Germany
6th ........United States
7th ........Canada
8th ........Austria^*
^promoted from B Pool in 1980
*demoted to B Pool for 1982

**Tournament Format**

The same method was used in 1981 as the previous year. A preliminary round robin was set up in two divisions of four nations each. The top two advanced to a medal round robin, the bottom two to a consolation round. One important factor that came into play this year was a tie in the standings, with goal differential being the deciding factor. In the preliminary round, both Canada and Czechoslovakia had three points, but Canada finished third to the Czechs' second because of a poorer goal differential (the teams had tied 3-3 in the round robin).

**Results & Standings**

**GOLD DIVISION**

| | GP | W | T | L | GF | GA | P |
|---|---|---|---|---|---|---|---|
| Soviet Union | 3 | 3 | 0 | 0 | 31 | 5 | 6 |
| Czechoslovakia | 3 | 1 | 1 | 1 | 25 | 12 | 3 |
| Canada | 3 | 1 | 1 | 1 | 17 | 11 | 3 |
| Austria | 3 | 0 | 0 | 3 | 6 | 51 | 0 |

| | | | |
|---|---|---|---|
| December 27 | Kaufbeuren | Canada 3 | Czechoslovakia 3 |
| December 27 | Augsburg | Soviet Union 19 | Austria 1 |
| December 28 | Landsberg | Soviet Union 7 | Canada 3 |
| December 28 | Fussen | Czechoslovakia 21 | Austria 4 |
| December 30 | Landsberg | Canada 11 | Austria 1 |
| December 30 | Fussen | Soviet Union 5 | Czechoslovakia 1 |

**BLUE DIVISION**

| | GP | W | T | L | GF | GA | P |
|---|---|---|---|---|---|---|---|
| Sweden | 3 | 3 | 0 | 0 | 19 | 6 | 6 |
| Finland | 3 | 2 | 0 | 1 | 17 | 9 | 4 |
| West Germany | 3 | 1 | 0 | 2 | 13 | 17 | 2 |
| United States | 3 | 0 | 0 | 3 | 5 | 22 | 0 |

| | | | |
|---|---|---|---|
| December 27 | Fussen | Sweden 7 | West Germany 3 |
| December 27 | Landsberg | Finland 8 | United States 1 |
| December 28 | Obertsdorf | Finland 8 | West Germany 6 |
| December 28 | Augsburg | Sweden 10 | United States 2 |
| December 30 | Kempten | Sweden 2 | Finland 1 |
| December 30 | Kaufbeuren | West Germany 4 | United States 2 |

**CONSOLATION ROUND**

| | GP | W | T | L | GF | GA | P |
|---|---|---|---|---|---|---|---|
| West Germany | 3 | 3 | 0 | 0 | 20 | 9 | 6 |
| United States | 3 | 2 | 0 | 1 | 16 | 9 | 4 |
| Canada | 3 | 1 | 0 | 2 | 20 | 15 | 2 |
| Austria | 3 | 0 | 0 | 3 | 4 | 27 | 0 |

| | | | |
|---|---|---|---|
| December 31 | Landsberg | United States 7 | Canada 3 |
| December 31 | Fussen | West Germany 9 | Austria 1 |
| January 2 | Kaufbeuren | West Germany 7 | Canada 6 |
| January 2 | Fussen | United States 7 | Austria 2 |

**CHAMPIONSHIP ROUND**

| | GP | W | T | L | GF | GA | P |
|---|---|---|---|---|---|---|---|
| Sweden | 3 | 2 | 1 | 0 | 8 | 6 | 5 |
| Finland | 3 | 1 | 1 | 1 | 13 | 11 | 3 |
| Soviet Union | 3 | 1 | 0 | 2 | 10 | 10 | 2 |
| Czechoslovakia | 3 | 0 | 2 | 1 | 10 | 14 | 2 |

| | | | |
|---|---|---|---|
| December 31 | Kaufbeuren | Finland 6 | Soviet Union 3 |
| December 31 | Oberstdorf | Sweden 3 | Czechoslovakia 3 |
| January 2 | Augsburg | Sweden 3 | Soviet Union 2 |
| January 2 | Landsberg | Finland 6 | Czechoslovakia 6 |

**Rosters**

**Austria** (Hermann Knoll, coach) GK—Andreas Philipp, Arno Cuder—Herbert Keckeis, Gunther Stockhammer, Michael Platzer, Helmut Petrik, Walter Wolf, Ewald Brandstetter, Rudolf Hofer, Konrad Dorn, Dieter Haberl, Wolfgang Kocher, Bernie Hutz, Gunther Koren, Robert Kasan, Michael Salat, Manfred Frosch, Alexander Gruber, Rupert Hopfer, Dietmar Zach

**Canada** (Cornwall Royals—Bob Kilger, coach) GK—Tom Graovac, Corrado Micalef—Dale Hawerchuk, John Kirk, Scott Arniel, Marc Crawford, Fred Boimistruck, Andre Chartrain, Denis Cyr, Jeff Eatough, Guy Fournier, Jean-Marc Gaulin, Fred Arthur, Robert Savard, Eric Calder, Gilbert Delorme, Bill Campbell, Craig Halliday, Doug Gilmour, Roy Russell

**Czechoslovakia** (Jozef Golonka, coach) GK—Jaroslav Linc, Jiri Steklik, Vaclav Furbacher—Vladimir Svitek, Jan Vodila, Rostislav Vlach, Vladimir Ruzicka, Miloslav Horava, Tomas Jelinek, Jaroslav Hauer, Jiri Dudacek, Milan Eberle, Milos Krayzel, Libor Martinek, Miroslav Majernik, Eduard Uvira, Mojmir Bozik, Vaclav Badoucek, Antonin Stavjana, Frantisek Ibermajer, Milan Razym

**Finland** (Olli Hietanen, coach) GK—Kari Takko, Ilmo Uotila—Ari Lahteenmaki, Pekka Jarvela, Petri Skriko, Risto Jalo, Arto Sirvio, Timo Blomqvist, Anssi Melametsa, Tony Arima, Veli-Pekka Kinnunen, Jyrki Seppa, Jouni Koutuaniemi, Sakari Petajaaho, Jari Munck, Timo Jutila, Heikki Leime, Arto Ruatonen, Jarmo Kuusisto, Juha Saarenoja

**Soviet Union** (Yuri Morozov, coach) GK—Yuri Nikitin, Sergei Kostyukhin—Sergei Yashin, Ravil Yudashev, Mikhail Panin, Sergei Odintsov, Sergei Kudashov, Anatoli Semyonov, Sergei Zemchenko, Andrei Khomutov, Sergei Svetlov, Andri Ovchinnikov, Andrei Zemko, Yuri Shipitsin, Igor Strelnov, Mikhail Zakharov, Oleg Kudriavtsev, Vladimir Tyurikov, Alexander Ledovskikh, Sergei Kudyashov

**Sweden** (Kjell Damberg, coach) GK—Lars Eriksson, Peter Aslin—Hakan Nordin, Patrik Sundstrom, Roger Hagglund, Jan Erixon, Jan Ingman, Peter Sundstrom, Jens Ohling, Mikael Thelven, Michael Granstedt, Peter Andersson, Martin Pettersson, Anders Bjorklund, Anders Jonsson, Peter Madach, Peter Nilsson, Robert Nordmark, Ove Pettersson, Dan Nicklasson

**United States** (Lou Vairo, coach) GK—Cleon Daskalakis, Bob O'Connor—Bob Carpenter, Ed Lee, Keith Knight, Jim Chisholm, Steve Griffith, John Johannson, Pat Ethier, Andy Brickley, Gregg Olson, Brian Mullen, Jeff Grade, Dan Fishback, Craig Ludwig, Mark Huglen, Dave Jensen, Mark Fusco, Kelly Miller, Gregg Moore

**West Germany** (Helmut Perkuhn, coach) GK—Helmut De Raaf, Josef Heiss—Dieter Hegen, Klaus Gotsch, Georg Holzmann, Uli Hiemer, Jurgen Adams, Manfred Ahne, Ferdinand Strodl, Robert Sterflinger, Daniel Held, Rainer Lutz, Michael Betz, Christoph Schodl, Christoph Augsten, Klaus Feistl, Franco De Nobili, Franz Juttner, Jens Tosse, Andreas Niederberger

## 6th U20 WORLD CHAMPIONSHIP
## December 22, 1981-January 2, 1982
## United States (some games played in Canada)

**Final Placing**

Gold .......Canada
Silver .....Czechoslovakia
Bronze ...Finland
4th .........Soviet Union
5th ........Sweden
6th ........United States
7th ........West Germany
8th ........Switzerland^*

^promoted from B Pool in 1981
*demoted to B Pool for 1983

**Tournament Format**

All teams were placed in one division and played a round-robin series of games. Tie games would not go into overtime, and ties in the standings were broken first by results between the tied teams (which is how the fourth place Soviets finished ahead of Sweden in the final standings).

**Results & Standings**

| | GP | W | T | L | GF | GA | P |
|---|---|---|---|---|---|---|---|
| Canada | 7 | 6 | 1 | 0 | 45 | 14 | 13 |
| Czechoslovakia | 7 | 5 | 1 | 1 | 44 | 17 | 11 |
| Finland | 7 | 5 | 0 | 2 | 47 | 29 | 10 |
| Soviet Union | 7 | 4 | 0 | 3 | 42 | 25 | 8 |
| Sweden | 7 | 4 | 0 | 3 | 42 | 26 | 8 |
| United States | 7 | 2 | 0 | 5 | 28 | 34 | 4 |
| West Germany | 7 | 1 | 0 | 6 | 19 | 56 | 2 |
| Switzerland | 7 | 0 | 0 | 7 | 15 | 81 | 0 |

| | | | |
|---|---|---|---|
| December 22 | Winnipeg | Canada 5 | Finland 1 |
| December 22 | Kenora | Sweden 17 | Switzerland 0 |
| December 22 | Duluth | Soviet Union 12 | West Germany 3 |
| December 22 | Duluth | Czechoslovakia 6 | United States 4 |
| December 23 | Winnipeg | Canada 3 | Sweden 2 |
| December 23 | Brandon | Finland 14 | Switzerland 2 |
| December 23 | Duluth | United States 8 | West Germany 1 |
| December 23 | Duluth | Czechoslovakia 3 | Soviet Union 2 |
| December 26 | Winnipeg | Canada 7 | Soviet Union 0 |
| December 26 | Grand Rapids | United States 6 | Switzerland 3 |
| December 26 | Brainerd | Sweden 5 | West Germany 1 |
| December 26 | Virginia | Czechoslovakia 5 | Finland 1 |
| December 27 | Bloomington | Canada 5 | United States 4 |
| December 27 | Bloomington | Sweden 6 | Czechoslovakia 4 |
| December 27 | International Falls | Soviet Union 11 | Switzerland 4 |
| December 27 | St. Cloud | Finland 8 | West Germany 4 |
| December 29 | Bloomington | Canada 11 | West Germany 3 |
| December 29 | Bloomington | Czechoslovakia 16 | Switzerland 0 |
| December 29 | Bloomington | Soviet Union 7 | United States 0 |
| December 30 | Burnsville | Finland 9 | Sweden 6 |
| December 31 | New Ulm | Czechoslovakia 7 | West Germany 1 |
| December 31 | Bloomington | Finland 6 | Soviet Union 3 |
| December 31 | Bloomington | Sweden 4 | United States 2 |
| January 1 | Minneapolis | Canada 11 | Switzerland 1 |
| January 2 | Rochester | Canada 3 | Czechoslovakia 3 |
| January 2 | Mankato | West Germany 6 | Switzerland 5 |
| January 2 | Bloomington | Soviet Union 7 | Sweden 2 |
| January 2 | Bloomington | Finland 8 | United States 4 |

**Rosters**

**Canada** (Dave King, coach) GK—Mike Moffat, Frank Caprice—Mike Moller, Marc Habscheid, Scott Arniel, Bruce Eakin, Paul Cyr, Mark Morrison, Troy Murray, Paul Boutillier, Pierre Rioux, Carey Wilson, Todd Strueby, Garth Butcher, Gary Nylund, Dave Morrison, Randy Moller, Moe Lemay, James Patrick, Gord Kluzak

**Czechoslovakia** (Frantisek Pospisil, coach) GK—Vaclav Furbacher, Peter Harazin—Jiri Dudacek, Vladimir Ruzicka, Milan Eberle, Karel Soudek, Rostislav Vlach, Antonin Stavjana, Vladimir Svitek, Kamil Precechtel, Ivan Dornic, Ludvik Kopecky, Petr Rosol, Tomas Jelinek, Peter Kasik, Jaroslav Hauer, Vaclav Badoucek, Frantisek Musil, Pavel Prorok, Mojmir Bozik

**Finland** (Alpo Suhonen/Jorma Thusberg, co-coaches) GK—Kari Takko, Jukka Tammi—Raimo Summanen, Petri Skriko, Risto Jalo, Pekka Jarvela, Markus Lehto, Hannu Jarvenpaa, Hannu Virta, Sakari Petajaaho, Teppo Virta, Timo Jutila, Simo Saarinen, Arto Sirvio, Heikki Leime, Jari Munck, Jose Pekkala, Harri Nystrom, Esa Tommila, Hannu Henriksson

**Soviet Union** (Igor Tuzik, coach) GK—Vitali Samoilov, Andrei Karpin—Anatoli Semyonov, Oleg Starkov, Igor Stelnov, Mikhail Vasilyev, Sergei Kuchin, Sergei Yashin, Yevgeni Roshin, Leonid Trukhno, Yuri Shipitsin, Sergei Odintsov, Vladimir Tyurikov, Yevgeni Belov, Ilya Byakin, Sergei Kudashov, Sergei Pryakhin, Konstantin Kurashev, Svyatoslav Khalizov, Yevgeni Shtepa

**Sweden** (Kjell Larsson, coach) GK—Ake Lilljebjorn, Peter Aslin—Magnus Roupe, Jonas Bergqvist, Peter Andersson, Jens Ohling, Mikael Hjalm, Anders Jonsson, Kjell Dahlin, Martin Linse, Peter Madach, Peter Nilsson, Per-Erik Eklund, Mats Lusth, Robert Nordmark, Jens Johansson, Ulf Samulesson, Anders Wikberg, Ove Pettersson, Lennart Dahlberg

**Switzerland** (Jack Holmes, coach) GK—Ludwig Lemmenmeier, Cedric Lengacher, Renato Tosio—Peter Moser, Jorg Eberle, Pierre Girardin, Eric Jeandupeux, Willy Kohler, Yvan Griga, Roman Waeger, Sergio Soguel, Philippe Giachino, Andreas Beutler, Fredy Bosch, Richard Jost, Patrice Brasey, Urs Burkart, Bruno Hidber, Jurg Marton, Thomas Meyer, Yvan Schwartz

**United States** (Lou Vairo, coach) GK—John Vanbiesbrouck, Jon Casey—Scott Fusco, Kevin Foster, Tom Kurvers, Corey Millen, Kelly Miller, Rick Erdall, Charlie Lundeen, Tom Herzig, Tony Kellin, Mike O'Connor, Mark Maroste, Chris Chelios, Tim Thomas, Dan McFall, Phil Housley, Bill Schafhauser, Dan Gerarden, Chris Guy

**West Germany** (Hans Rampf, coach) GK—Josef Heiss, Thomas Borntrager—Dieter Hegen, Michael Betz, Andreas Niederberger, Klaus Faistl, Uli Hiemer, Peter Stankovic, Franz Kummer, Helmut Patzner, Robert Hammerle, Jens Tosse, Joe Wassereck, Hans-Georg Eder, Franz Juttner, Boris Capla, Robert Sterflinger, Peter Wiegl, Edgar Lill, Alexander Schnoll

### 7th U20 WORLD CHAMPIONSHIP
### December 26, 1982-January 4, 1983
### Leningrad (St. Petersburg), Soviet Union

**Final Placing**

| | |
|---|---|
| Gold .......Soviet Union | 5th ........United States |
| Silver .....Czechoslovakia | 6th ........Finland |
| Bronze ...Canada | 7th ........West Germany |
| 4th .........Sweden | 8th ........Norway^* |

^promoted from B Pool in 1982
*demoted to B Pool for 1984

**Tournament Format**
All eight teams were placed in one division and played a round- robin. In the case of a tie in the standings, the winner of the head-to-head match was placed above the loser. Goal differential would be the next deciding factor if a tie in the standings persisted.

**Results & Standings**

| | GP | W | T | L | GF | GA | P |
|---|---|---|---|---|---|---|---|
| Soviet Union | 7 | 7 | 0 | 0 | 50 | 15 | 14 |
| Czechoslovakia | 7 | 5 | 1 | 1 | 43 | 22 | 11 |
| Canada | 7 | 4 | 1 | 2 | 39 | 24 | 9 |
| Sweden | 7 | 4 | 0 | 3 | 35 | 23 | 8 |
| United States | 7 | 3 | 0 | 4 | 28 | 29 | 6 |
| Finland | 7 | 3 | 0 | 4 | 35 | 29 | 6 |
| West Germany | 7 | 1 | 0 | 6 | 14 | 46 | 2 |
| Norway | 7 | 0 | 0 | 7 | 13 | 69 | 0 |

| | | |
|---|---|---|
| December 26 | Canada 4 | West Germany 0 |
| December 26 | Soviet Union 10 | Norway 1 |
| December 26 | Finland 6 | Sweden 4 |
| December 26 | Czechoslovakia 6 | United States 4 |
| December 27 | Canada 4 | United States 2 |
| December 27 | Soviet Union 4 | Czechoslovakia 3 |
| December 27 | Sweden 4 | West Germany 2 |
| December 27 | Finland 10 | Norway 2 |
| December 29 | Canada 6 | Finland 3 |
| December 29 | Soviet Union 12 | West Germany 2 |
| December 29 | Czechoslovakia 9 | Norway 2 |
| December 29 | Sweden 4 | United States 1 |
| December 30 | Soviet Union 7 | Canada 3 |
| December 30 | Czechoslovakia 4 | Sweden 2 |
| December 30 | West Germany 4 | Norway 2 |
| December 30 | United States 4 | Finland 2 |
| January 1 | Canada 7 | Czechoslovakia 7 |
| January 1 | Finland 9 | West Germany 1 |
| January 1 | Sweden 15 | Norway 3 |
| January 1 | Soviet Union 5 | United States 3 |
| January 2 | Sweden 5 | Canada 2 |
| January 2 | Soviet Union 7 | Finland 2 |
| January 2 | Czechoslovakia 9 | West Germany 0 |
| January 2 | United States 8 | Norway 3 |
| January 4 | Canada 13 | Norway 0 |
| January 4 | Soviet Union 5 | Sweden 1 |
| January 4 | Czechoslovakia 5 | Finland 3 |
| January 4 | United States 6 | West Germany 5 |

**Rosters**
**Canada** (Dave King, coach) GK—Mike Vernon, Mike Sands—Dave Andreychuk, Mario Lemieux, Dale Derkatch, Sylvain Turgeon, Mike Eagles, Mark Morrison, Larry Trader, Paul Boutillier, Steve Yzerman, Pat Flatley, Pat Verbeek, Paul Cyr, Toni Tanti, Gord Sherven, Gary Leeman, Brad Shaw, James Patrick, Joe Cirella

**Czechoslovakia** (Frantisek Pospisil, coach) GK—Dominik Hasek, Vaclav Furbacher—Libor Dolana, Ludvik Kopecky, Milos Hrubes, Vladimir Ruzicka, Jiri Jiroutek, Petr Rosol, Lumir Kotala, Petr Klima, Vladimir Kames, Antonin Stavjana, Frantisek Musil, Kamil Prachar, Jaromir Latal, Milan Cerny, Ernest Hornak, Miroslav Blaha, Roman Bozek, Jiri Jonak

**Finland** (Juhani Wahlsten, coach) GK—Juha Jaaskelainen, Matti Rautiainen—Ville Siren, Hannu Henriksson, Pekka Laksola, Timo Jutila, Simo Saarinen, Raimo Helminen, Esa Tikkanen, Christian Ruuttu, Hannu Jarvenpaa, Jouni Vuorinen, Jouni Kalliokoski, Kari Kanervo, Markku Tiinus, Iiro Jarvi, Mika Lartama, Risto Kurkinen, Keijo Tutti, Jali Wahlsten

**Norway** (Bernie Lynch, coach) GK—Tommi Hansen, Jarl Eriksen, Ingmar Gundersen—Erik Nerell, Truls Kristiansen, Kim Sogaard, Lars Cato Svendsen, Olle Peter Studstrud, Rune Eriksen, Geir Hoff, Paul Ole Wideroe, Rune Gulliksen, Jarl Friis, Jon Fjeld, Lars Bergseng, Paul Thoresen, Karl Erik Ulseth, Christian Arnesen, William Steinsland, Jon Neumann

**Soviet Union** (Anatoli Kostriukov, coach) GK—Sergei Goloshumov, Andrei Karpin—Ilya Byakin, Sergei Nemchinov, Vladimir Tyurikov, Leonid Trukhno, Sergei Pryakhin, Igor Boldin, Yevgeni Shtepa, Oleg Starkov, Alexander Chernykh, Svyatoslav Khalizov, Sergei Gorbunov, Andrei Matytsin, Andrei Martemianov, Valeri Shiryayev, Sergei Kharin, Arkadi Obukhov, German Volgin, Sergei Ageikin

**Sweden** (Conny Evensson, coach) GK—Jacob Gustavsson, Anders Bergman—Jens Johansson, Ulf Samuelsson, Tommy Albelin, Mats Kihlstrom, Jan Karlsson, Peter Andersson, Kjell Dahlin, Per-Erik Eklund, Tomas Sandstrom, Tommy Lehmann, Mikael Hjalm, Jon Lundstrom, Magnus Roupe, Anders Wikberg, Roger Eliasson, Erik Holmberg, Thomas Ljungberg, Per Hedenstrom

**United States** (Bill Hasler, coach) GK—John Vanbiesbrouck, Tom Barrasso—Rick Zombo, Dan McFall, Rick Erdall, Jim Johannson, Kelly Miller, Tony Kellin, Tony Granato, Mark Maroste, Brian Lawton, Tim Thomas, Peter Sawkins, Venci Sebek, Ron Duda, Ernie Vargas, Andy Otto, Scott Harlow, Chris Cichocki, Chris Seychel

**West Germany** (Hans Rampf, coach) GK—Josef Heiss, Rainer Guck—Uwe Krupp, Bernd Wagner, Robert Sterflinger, Franz Ibelherr, Axel Kammerer, Bernd Truntschka, Hans-Georg Eder, Joe Wassereck, Alfred Weiss, Andreas Niederberger, Engelbert Grzesiczek, Florian Aeger, Harald Birk, Georg Franz, Georg Kisslinger, Walter Kirchmaier, Markus Berwanger, Peter Weigl

### 8th U20 WORLD CHAMPIONSHIP
### December 25, 1983-January 3, 1984
### Norrkoping/Nykoping, Sweden

**Final Placing**

| | |
|---|---|
| Gold .......Soviet Union | 5th ........Sweden |
| Silver .....Finland | 6th ........United States |
| Bronze ...Czechoslovakia | 7th ........West Germany |
| 4th .........Canada | 8th ........Switzerland^* |

^promoted from B Pool in 1983
*demoted to B Pool for 1985

**Tournament Format**
All countries were placed in one group and each played every other nation once. First place won gold, second silver, third bronze, and tie-breaks would be decided by results against those teams tied.

**Results & Standings**

| | GP | W | T | L | GF | GA | P |
|---|---|---|---|---|---|---|---|
| Soviet Union | 7 | 6 | 1 | 0 | 50 | 17 | 13 |
| Finland | 7 | 6 | 0 | 1 | 44 | 21 | 12 |
| Czechoslovakia | 7 | 5 | 0 | 2 | 51 | 24 | 10 |
| Canada | 7 | 4 | 1 | 2 | 39 | 17 | 9 |
| Sweden | 7 | 3 | 0 | 4 | 27 | 28 | 6 |
| United States | 7 | 2 | 0 | 5 | 32 | 38 | 4 |
| West Germany | 7 | 1 | 0 | 6 | 12 | 54 | 2 |
| Switzerland | 7 | 0 | 0 | 7 | 16 | 72 | 0 |

| | | | |
|---|---|---|---|
| December 25 | Nykoping | Finland 4 | Canada 2 |
| December 25 | Norrkoping | Soviet Union 14 | Switzerland 2 |
| December 25 | Nykoping | Czechoslovakia 6 | West Germany 1 |
| December 25 | Norrkoping | Sweden 4 | United States 1 |
| December 26 | Nykoping | Canada 5 | United States 2 |
| December 26 | Nykoping | Sweden 5 | Switzerland 2 |
| December 26 | Norrkoping | Soviet Union 9 | West Germany 1 |
| December 26 | Norrkoping | Finland 8 | Czechoslovakia 7 |
| December 28 | Norrkoping | Canada 12 | Switzerland 0 |
| December 28 | Nykoping | Soviet Union 3 | Finland 1 |
| December 28 | Nykoping | Sweden 11 | West Germany 2 |
| December 28 | Norrkoping | Czechoslovakia 10 | United States 1 |
| December 29 | Nykoping | Canada 7 | West Germany 0 |
| December 29 | Nykoping | Czechoslovakia 13 | Switzerland 2 |
| December 29 | Norrkoping | Finland 4 | Sweden 1 |
| December 29 | Norrkoping | Soviet Union 7 | United States 4 |
| December 31 | Norrkoping | Canada 6 | Sweden 2 |
| December 31 | Nykoping | Soviet Union 6 | Czechoslovakia 4 |
| December 31 | Norrkoping | West Germany 4 | Switzerland 3 |
| December 31 | Nykoping | Finland 7 | United States 2 |
| January 2 | Norrkoping | Canada 3 | Soviet Union 3 |
| January 2 | Nykoping | Finland 12 | Switzerland 4 |
| January 2 | Nykoping | Czechoslovakia 5 | Sweden 2 |
| January 2 | Norrkoping | United States 10 | West Germany 2 |
| January 3 | Nykoping | Czechoslovakia 6 | Canada 4 |
| January 3 | Nykoping | Finland 8 | West Germany 2 |
| January 3 | Norrkoping | Soviet Union 8 | Sweden 2 |
| January 3 | Norrkoping | United States 12 | Switzerland 3 |

**Rosters**
**Canada** (Brian Kilrea, coach) GK—Ken Wregget, Allan Bester—Russ Courtnall, Dean Evason, Randy Heath, Gary Leeman, John MacLean, Dave Gagner, Dale Derkatch, Dan Hodgson, Kirk Muller, Lyndon Byers, Sylvain Cote, Mark Paterson, J.J. Daigneault, Brad Shaw, Yves Courteau, Bruce Cassidy, Gerald Diduck, Gary Lacey

**Czechoslovakia** (Frantisek Pospisil, coach) GK—Petr Briza, Ivo Pesat—Petr Rosol, Vladimir Kames, Libor Dolana, Petr Klima, Jiri Jiroutek, Lumir Kotala, Igor Talpas, Ernest Hornak, Stanislav Pavelec, Jozef Petho, Petr Svoboda, Kamil Kastak, Michal Pivonka, Milos Hrubes, Jiri Paska, Frantisek Musil, Martin Strida, Petr Holubar

**Finland** (Pentti Matikainen, coach) GK—Jarmo Myllys, Jarmo Uronen—Raimo Helminen, Esa Keskinen, Esa Tikkanen, Ari Haanpaa, Iiro Jarvi, Jari Torkki, Harri Laurila, Reijo Mikkolainen, Joel Paunio, Ari Suutari, Ville Siren, Pekka Laksola, Mikko Makela, Tommy Pohja, Erik Hamalainen, Christian Ruuttu, Vesa Salo, Janne Karelius

**Soviet Union** (Igor Dmitriev, coach) GK—Yevgeni Belosheikin, Alexei Cherviakov—Alexander Chernykh, Nikolai Borshevski, Igor Vyazmikin, Sergei Nemchinov, Andrei Lomakin, Alexei Gusarov, Yuri Khmylyov, Igor Martynov, Yevgeni Chizhmin, Alexander Smirnov, Igor Boldin, Vasili Kamenev, Alexander Semak, Mikhail Tatarinov, Oleg Mikulchik, Alexander Lysenko, Sergei Shendelev, Sergei Vostrikov

**Sweden** (Conny Evensson, coach) GK—Ulf Nilsson, Jacob Gustavsson—Tommy Lehmann, Tomas Sandstrom, Anders Huss, Ulf Samuelsson, Jon Lundstrom, Tommy Albelin, Roland Westin, Mats Kihlstrom, Mikael Andersson, Henrik Cedergren, Mikael Wikstrom, Jens Johansson, Per Forsberg, Peter Andersson, Lars Bystrom, Jorgen Marklund, Jan Karlsson

**Switzerland** (Res Kunzi, coach) GK—Andreas Jurt, Dino Stecher—Thomas Mueller, Philipp Neuenschwander, Daniel Dubois, Christof Ruefenacht, Jean-Luc Rod, Rene Gehri, Andreas Caduff, Guido Pfosi, Patrick Mueller, Marc Heitzmann, Felix Hollenstein, Bernhard Lauber, Patrice Niederhausen, Markus Bleuer, Andrea Cahenzli, Markus Maef, Martin Rauch, Pascal Speck

**United States** (John Perpich, coach) GK—Brian Jopling, Alan Perry—Alfie Turcotte, Wally Chapman, Jim Johannson, Al Bourbeau, Todd Okerlund, Marty Wiitala, Mike Golden, Tony Granato, Paul Ames, Bob Curtis, Clark Donatelli, Brian Johnson, Steve Leach, Mark LaVarre, Craig Mack, Gary Suter, Kevin Hatcher, Scott Sandelin

**West Germany** (Hans Rampf, coach) GK—Thomas Frolich, Rupert Meister—Peter Draisaitl, Klaus Pillmaier, Udo Schmid, Axel Kammerer, Christian Reuter, Fritz Brunner, Bernd Truntschka, Sven Erhart, Michael Rumrich, Gunther Preuss, Franz Ibelherr, Robert Sterflinger, Frank Gentges, Jorg Hanft, Michael Komma, Bernd Wagner, Alfred Weiss, Tauno Zobel

## 9th U20 WORLD CHAMPIONSHIP
## December 23, 1984-January 1, 1985
## Vantaa/Helsinki, Finland

**Final Placing**

| | | | |
|---|---|---|---|
| Gold | Canada | 5th | Sweden |
| Silver | Czechoslovakia | 6th | United States |
| Bronze | Soviet Union | 7th | West Germany |
| 4th | Finland | 8th | Poland^* |

^promoted from B Pool in 1984
*demoted to B Pool for 1986

**Tournament Format**

All eight teams were placed in one group and a simple round robin schedule was adopted. In the case of a tie in the standings between two teams, the result of the game between those two would be the first tie-breaker and goal differential the second decider. Thus, the Soviets won the bronze despite finishing with the same number of points as fourth place Finland because the Russians won the head-to-head game 6-5.

**Results & Standings**

| | GP | W | T | L | GF | GA | P |
|---|---|---|---|---|---|---|---|
| Canada | 7 | 5 | 2 | 0 | 44 | 14 | 12 |
| Czechoslovakia | 7 | 5 | 2 | 0 | 32 | 13 | 12 |
| Soviet Union | 7 | 5 | 0 | 2 | 38 | 17 | 10 |
| Finland | 7 | 4 | 2 | 1 | 42 | 20 | 10 |
| Sweden | 7 | 3 | 0 | 4 | 32 | 26 | 6 |
| United States | 7 | 2 | 0 | 5 | 23 | 37 | 4 |
| West Germany | 7 | 0 | 1 | 6 | 9 | 44 | 1 |
| Poland | 7 | 0 | 1 | 6 | 10 | 59 | 1 |

| | | | |
|---|---|---|---|
| December 23 | Helsinki | Canada 8 | Sweden 2 |
| December 23 | Vantaa | Soviet Union 10 | Poland 0 |
| December 23 | Turku | Finland 9 | West Germany 0 |
| December 23 | Turku | Czechoslovakia 9 | United States 1 |
| December 25 | Turku | Canada 12 | Poland 1 |
| December 25 | Vantaa | Soviet Union 12 | West Germany 1 |
| December 25 | Helsinki | Czechoslovakia 4 | Sweden 3 |
| December 25 | Turku | Finland 7 | United States 4 |
| December 26 | Helsinki | Canada 6 | West Germany 0 |
| December 26 | Espoo | Czechoslovakia 6 | Poland 2 |
| December 26 | Turku | Finland 5 | Sweden 3 |
| December 26 | Turku | Soviet Union 4 | United States 2 |
| December 28 | Turku | Canada 7 | United States 5 |
| December 28 | Turku | Soviet Union 5 | Sweden 1 |
| December 28 | Vantaa | Czechoslovakia 7 | West Germany 3 |
| December 28 | Helsinki | Finland 11 | Poland 2 |
| December 29 | Turku | Canada 5 | Soviet Union 0 |
| December 29 | Turku | Sweden 11 | Poland 0 |
| December 29 | Helsinki | Czechoslovakia 1 | Finland 1 |
| December 29 | Helsinki | United States 2 | West Germany 1 |
| December 31 | Helsinki | Canada 4 | Finland 4 |
| December 31 | Turku | Sweden 5 | West Germany 1 |
| December 31 | Turku | Czechoslovakia 3 | Soviet Union 1 |
| December 31 | Helsinki | United States 6 | Poland 2 |
| January 1 | Helsinki | Canada 2 | Czechoslovakia 2 |
| January 1 | Vantaa | West Germany 3 | Poland 3 |
| January 1 | Helsinki | Soviet Union 6 | Finland 5 |
| January 1 | Vantaa | Sweden 7 | United States 3 |

**Rosters**

**Canada** (Terry Simpson, coach) GK—Craig Billington, Norm Foster—Adam Creighton, Brian Bradley, Jeff Jackson, Dan Hodgson, Stephane Richer, Wendel Clark, Shayne Corson, Selmar Odelein, Claude Lemieux, Dan Gratton, Yves Beaudoin, Bob Bassen, Greg Johnston, Bobby Dollas, John Miner, Jim Sandlak, Jeff Beukeboom, Brad Berry

**Czechoslovakia** (Frantisek Pospisil, coach) GK—Dominik Hasek, Eduard Hartmann—Michal Pivonka, Robert Kron, Tomas Mares, Ladislav Lubina, Jiri Kucera, Leo Gudas, Jiri Latal, Ales Flasar, Petr Prajzler, Drahomir Kadlec, Tomas Kapusta, Michal Tomek, Vojtech Kucera, Kamil Kastak, Marian Horvath, Jaroslav Sevcik, Stanislav Horansky, Stanislav Medrik

**Finland** (Pentti Matikainen, coach) GK—Jarmo Myllys, Timo Lekhonen—Esa Keskinen, Esa Tikkanen, Mikko Makela, Jari Torkki, Ari Haanpaa, Harri Laurila, Eerik Sjoblom, Timo Norppa, Iiro Jarvi, Vesa Salo, Ari Suutari, Kari-Pekka Friman, Ossi Piitulainen, Erik Hamalainen, Mikko Mustala, Kari Tuiskula, Vesa Ruotsalainen, Arto Taipola

**Poland** (Tadeusz Bujar, coach) GK—Jaroslaw Wajda, Robert Walczewski—Zbigniew Bryjak, Ireneusz Pacula, Mariusz Puzio, Wladyslaw Balakowicz, Marek Stebnicki, Adam Golinski, Miroslaw Tomasik, Ryszard Mroz, Jacek Kurowski, Wlodzimierz Cieslik, Janusz Syposz, Wojciech Musial, Jerzy Matras, Adam Dolinski, Marek Litwin, Roman Szewczyk, Miroslaw Copija, Ludwik Czapka

**Soviet Union** (Vladimir Kiselev, coach) GK—Yevgeni Belosheikin, Oleg Bratash—Sergei Novoselov, Alexander Semak, Ravil Khaidarov, Alexander Chernykh, Sergei Sverzhov, Vladimir Yelovikov, Alexei Grishenko, Valeri Kamenski, Pavel Torgayev, Igor Nikitin, Oleg Posmetyev, Mikhail Tatarinov, Igor Kravchuk, Andrei Vakrushev, Yuri Lynov, Anatoli Fedotov, Igor Rasko, Andrei Popugayev

**Sweden** (Kjell Larsson, coach) GK—Sam Lindstahl, Ulf Nilsson (dnp)—Peter Andersson, Mats Lundstrom, Eddy Eriksson, Reine Karlsson, Leif Carlsson, Lars Bystrom, Mikael Andersson, Tommy Eriksson, Lennart Hermansson, Stefan Nilsson, Fredrik Olausson, Stefan Larsson, Christian Due-Boije, Harri Tiala, Ulf Konradsson, Arto Blomsten, Goran Arnmark, Stefan Jonsson, Peter Berndtsson

**United States** (Doug Woog, coach) GK—Alan Perry, Mike Richter—Craig Janney, Al Bourbeau, Brian Hannon, Clark Donatelli, Greg Dornbach, Scott Young, Jay Octeau, Steve Leach, Bill Kopecky, Eric Weinrich, Scott Schneider, Jeff Rohlicek, Brian Johnson, Doug Wieck, Perry Florio, Chris Biotti, Brian Leetch, David Espe

**West Germany** (Hans Rampf, coach) GK—Rupert Meister, Oliver Weissenberger—Udo Schmid, Thomas Groger, Andreas Volland, Klaus Birk, Raimond Hilger, Andreas Brockmann, Richard Trojan, Jurgen Stortz, Uwe Krupp, Christian Reuter, Peter Romberg, Rene Ledock, Frank Gentges, Toni Krinner, Georg Franz, Thomas Riedel, Josef Wassermann, Michael Flemming

## 10th U20 WORLD CHAMPIONSHIP
## December 26, 1985-January 4, 1986
## Hamilton, Canada

**Final Placing**

| | | | |
|---|---|---|---|
| Gold | Soviet Union | 5th | Sweden |
| Silver | Canada | 6th | Finland |
| Bronze | United States | 7th | Switzerland^ |
| 4th | Czechoslovakia | 8th | West Germany* |

^promoted from B Pool in 1985
*demoted to B Pool for 1987

**Tournament Format**

All eight teams were placed in one group and a simple round robin schedule was adopted. In the case of a tie in the standings between two teams, the result of the game between those two would be the first tie-breaker and goal differential the second decider.

**Results & Standings**

| | GP | W | T | L | GF | GA | P |
|---|---|---|---|---|---|---|---|
| Soviet Union | 7 | 7 | 0 | 0 | 42 | 14 | 14 |
| Canada | 7 | 5 | 0 | 2 | 54 | 21 | 10 |
| United States | 7 | 4 | 0 | 3 | 35 | 26 | 8 |
| Czechoslovakia | 7 | 4 | 0 | 3 | 30 | 20 | 8 |
| Sweden | 7 | 4 | 0 | 3 | 26 | 23 | 8 |
| Finland | 7 | 3 | 0 | 4 | 31 | 23 | 6 |
| Switzerland | 7 | 1 | 0 | 6 | 19 | 54 | 2 |
| West Germany | 7 | 0 | 0 | 7 | 9 | 65 | 0 |

| | | | |
|---|---|---|---|
| December 26 | Hamilton | Canada 12 | Switzerland 1 |
| December 26 | London | Soviet Union 7 | United States 3 |
| December 26 | Orillia | Sweden 2 | Finland 0 |
| December 26 | Newmarket | Czechoslovakia 9 | West Germany 3 |
| December 27 | Kitchener | Canada 18 | West Germany 2 |
| December 27 | St. Catharines | Finland 9 | Switzerland 2 |
| December 27 | Oshawa | Soviet Union 6 | Sweden 1 |
| December 27 | Hamilton | United States 5 | Czechoslovakia 2 |
| December 29 | Hamilton | Canada 5 | United States 2 |

| | | | |
|---|---|---|---|
| December 29 | Guelph | Soviet Union 7 | Switzerland 3 |
| December 29 | Stratford | Sweden 3 | Czechoslovakia 2 |
| December 29 | Toronto | Finland 7 | West Germany 2 |
| December 30 | Hamilton | Canada 9 | Sweden 2 |
| December 30 | Dundas | Czechoslovakia 7 | Switzerland 2 |
| December 30 | Kitchener | Soviet Union 10 | West Germany 0 |
| December 30 | Oshawa | Finland 7 | United States 5 |
| January 1 | Toronto | Canada 6 | Finland 5 |
| January 1 | London | Soviet Union 4 | Czechoslovakia 3 |
| January 1 | Hamilton | United States 4 | West Germany 1 |
| January 1 | Oakville | Sweden 7 | Switzerland 1 |
| January 2 | Hamilton | Soviet Union 4 | Canada 1 |
| January 2 | Brantford | Czechoslovakia 2 | Finland 0 |
| January 2 | Georgetown | Sweden 10 | West Germany 0 |
| January 2 | Niagara Falls | United States 11 | Switzerland 3 |
| January 4 | Hamilton | Czechoslovakia 5 | Canada 3 |
| January 4 | Hamilton | United States 5 | Sweden 1 |
| January 4 | Brantford | Switzerland 7 | West Germany 1 |
| January 4 | Hamilton | Soviet Union 4 | Finland 3 |

**Rosters**

**Canada** (Terry Simpson, coach) GK—Craig Billington, Sean Burke—Shayne Corson, Joe Murphy, Jim Sandlak, Joe Nieuwendyk, Gary Roberts, Scott Mellanby, Al Conroy, Luc Robitaille, Peter Douris, Mike Stapleton, Alain Cote, Derek Laxdal, Sylvain Cote, Jeff Greenlaw, Terry Carkner, Dave Moylan, Emanuel Viveiros, Selmar Odelein

**Czechoslovakia** (Jiri Justra/Julius Cernicky, co-coaches) GK—Oldrich Svoboda, Jaroslav Landsman—Radek Toupal, Michal Pivonka, Jiri Kucera, David Volek, Kamil Kastak, Ladislav Lubina, Robert Kron, Tomas Kapusta, Josef Reznicek, Tomas Srsen, Lubos Pazler, Michal Madl, Stanislav Medrik, Jiri Latal, Roman Lipovsky, Rudolf Zaruba, Richard Kolar, Dusan Kralik, Petr Hodek

**Finland** (Hannu Jortikka, coach) GK—Timo Lehkonen, Sakari Lindfors—Jari Korpisalo, Mikko Laaksonen, Jarmo Kekalainen, Sami Wahlsten, Jouni Kantola, Teppo Kivela, Lasse Nieminen, Pentti Lehtosaari, Timo Iljina, Ville Kentala, Jyrki Lumme, Kimmo Nurro, Kari-Pekka Friman, Antti Tuomenoska, Vesa Ruotsalainen, Mikko Haapakoski, Petri Matikainen, Timo Kulonen

**Soviet Union** (Vladimir Vasiliev, coach) GK—Oleg Bratash, Yevgeni Belosheikin—Valeri Kamenski, Igor Vyazmikin, Alexander Semak, Ravil Khaidarov, Sergei Osipov, Mikhail Tatarinov, Vladimir Konstantinov, Anatoli Fedotov, Sergei Gapeyenko, Yevgeni Davydov, Pavel Torgayev, Yuri Nikonov, Alexander Galchenyuk, Igor Kravchuk, Sergei Selianin, Igor Monayenkov, Igor Nikitin, Andrei Kovalyov

**Sweden** (Ingvar Carlsson, coach) GK—Sam Lindstahl, Hans-Goran Elo—Mats Lundstrom, Mikael Andersson, Ulf Dahlen, Fredrik Olausson, Joakim Persson, Mikael Johansson, Roger Ohman, Par Edlund, Roger Johansson, Robert Burakovsky, Stefan Falk, Calle Johansson, Tony Barthelsson, Christian Due-Boije, Stefan Jansson, Fredrik Stillman, Tomas Bjuhr, Anders Lindstrom

**Switzerland** (Rolf Altorfer, coach) GK—Beat Aebischer, Marius Boesch—Peter Jaks, Manuele Celio, Beat Nuspliger, Roger Thony, Thomas Vrabec, Bruno Vollmer, Raymond Walder, Andre Kunzi, Andreas Schneeberger, Gilles Dubois, Filippo Celio, Thomas Wiedmer, Andreas Fisher, Beat Cattaruzza, Dino Kessler, Jean-Jacques Aeschlimann, Martin Hofacker, Martin Bruderer

**United States** (Dave Peterson, coach) GK—Mike Richter, Alan Perry—Steve Leach, Paul Ranheim, Greg Dornbach, Dan Shea, Lane MacDonald, Jim Carson, Brian Leetch, Scott Paluch, Max Middendorf, David Quinn, Scott Young, Chris Biotti, Mike Wolak, Mike Kelfer, Craig Janney, Greg Brown, Eric Weinrich, Tom Chorske

**West Germany** (Hans Rampf, coach) GK—Michael Schmidt, Klaus Merk—Andreas Volland, Klaus Micheller, Thomas Groger, Toni Krinner, Marco Rentzsch, Thomas Werner, Rudolf Sternkopf, Christian Reuter, Klaus Birk, Richard Trojan, Andreas Lupzig, Josef Wassermann, Dan Nowak, Rene Ledock, Christian Ott, Stefan Steinecker, Andreas Brockmann, Christian Gelzinus

## 11th U20 WORLD CHAMPIONSHIP
## December 26, 1986-January 4, 1987
## Topolcany/Piestany, Czechoslovakia

**Final Placing**

| | |
|---|---|
| Gold .......Finland | 5th ........Poland^ |
| Silver .....Czechoslovakia | 6th ........Switzerland* |
| Bronze ...Sweden | Canada—DQ |
| 4th .........United States | Soviet Union—DQ |

^promoted from B Pool in 1986
*demoted to B Pool for 1988

**Tournament Format**

All eight nations were placed in one group and played a single round-robin schedule. Because of the Canada-Russia brawl, both nations were disqualified from medal contention. Thus, even though Canada had nine points in six games and Sweden had nine points in seven games, Sweden was awarded the bronze.

**Results & Standings**

| | GP | W | T | L | GF | GA | P |
|---|---|---|---|---|---|---|---|
| Finland | 7 | 5 | 1 | 1 | 45 | 23 | 11 |
| Czechoslovakia | 7 | 5 | 0 | 2 | 36 | 23 | 10 |
| Sweden | 7 | 4 | 1 | 2 | 45 | 11 | 9 |
| United States | 7 | 4 | 0 | 3 | 42 | 30 | 8 |
| Poland | 7 | 1 | 0 | 6 | 21 | 80 | 2 |
| Switzerland | 7 | 0 | 0 | 7 | 15 | 62 | 0 |
| Canada | 6 | 4 | 1 | 1 | 41 | 23 | DQ |
| Soviet Union | 6 | 2 | 1 | 3 | 27 | 20 | DQ |

| | | | |
|---|---|---|---|
| December 26 | Topolcany | Canada 6 | Switzerland 4 |
| December 26 | Trencin | Soviet Union 7 | Poland 3 |
| December 26 | Nitra | Czechoslovakia 4 | Sweden 3 |
| December 26 | Piestany | Finland 4 | United States 1 |
| December 27 | Trencin | Canada 6 | Finland 5 |
| December 27 | Piestany | Soviet Union 8 | Switzerland 0 |
| December 27 | Topolcany | Sweden 15 | Poland 0 |
| December 27 | Nitra | United States 8 | Czechoslovakia 2 |
| December 29 | Nitra | Czechoslovakia 5 | Canada 1 |
| December 29 | Piestany | Sweden 8 | Switzerland 0 |
| December 29 | Topolcany | Finland 5 | Soviet Union 4 |
| December 29 | Trencin | United States 15 | Poland 2 |
| December 30 | Nitra | Canada 18 | Poland 3 |
| December 30 | Piestany | Sweden 5 | Finland 0 |
| December 30 | Trencin | Czechoslovakia 5 | Soviet Union 3 |
| December 30 | Topolcany | United States 12 | Switzerland 6 |
| January 1 | Piestany | Canada 6 | United States 2 |
| January 1 | Nitra | Soviet Union 3 | Sweden 3 |
| January 1 | Trencin | Finland 12 | Switzerland 1 |
| January 1 | Topolcany | Czechoslovakia 9 | Poland 2 |
| January 2 | Trencin | Canada 4 | Sweden 3 |
| January 2 | Piestany | Czechoslovakia 8 | Switzerland 1 |
| January 2 | Nitra | Finland 13 | Poland 3 |
| January 2 | Topolcany | United States 4 | Soviet Union 2 |
| January 4 | Piestany | Canada 4 | Soviet Union 2 |
| (suspended by brawl—statistics from this game not counted) | | | |
| January 4 | Nitra | Finland 5 | Czechoslovakia 3 |
| January 4 | Topolcany | Poland 8 | Switzerland 3 |
| January 4 | Trencin | Sweden 8 | United States 0 |

**Rosters**

**Canada** (Bert Templeton, coach) GK—Shawn Simpson, Jimmy Waite—Pat Elynuik, David Latta, Steve Nemeth, Dave McLlwain, Scott Metcalfe, Brendan Shanahan, Everett Sanipass, Theo Fleury, Steve Chiasson, Greg Hawgood, Pierre Turgeon, Yvon Corriveau, Glen Wesley, Chris Joseph, Stephane Roy, Kerry Huffman, Mike Keane, Luke Richardson

**Czechoslovakia** (Jiri Justra, coach) GK—Oldrich Svoboda, Rudolf Pejchar—Jiri Latal, Frantisek Kucera, Roman Lipovsky, Radomir Brazda, Robert Svoboda, Petr Pavlas, Martin Hostak, Lubos Pazler, Roman Andrys, Robert Kron, Tomas Kapusta, Juraj Jurik, Ales Badal, Lubomir Vaclavicek, Karol Rusznak, Ivan Matulik, Roman Nemcicky, Ladislav Lubina

**Finland** (Hannu Jortikka, coach) GK—Markus Ketterer, Kari Rosenberg—Marko Allen, Mikko Haapakoski, Timo Kulonen, Jukka Marttila, Petri Matikainen, Jari Parviainen, Antti Tuomenoska, Teppo Kivela, Marko Kiuru, Mikko Laaksonen, Jari Laukkanen, Pentti Lehtosaari, Janne Ojanen, Jukka Seppo, Jyrki Silius, Pekka Tirkkonen, Sami Wahlsten, Sami Wikstrom

**Poland** (Jerzy Malez, coach) GK—Wlodzimierz Krauzowicz, Grzegorz Wojakiewicz— Ryszard Bielak, Wlodzimierz Krol, Zbigniew Niedospial, Andrzej Husse, Ryszard Borecki, Jacek Zamojski, Jacek Jankowski, Marek Adamek, Damian Adamus, Janusz Janikowski, Jacek Kubowicz, Jedrzej Kasperczyk, Jerzy Merta, Krzysztof Ruchala, Zbigniew Raszewski, Marek Trybus, Piotr Zdunek, Robert Zymankowski

**Soviet Union** (Vladimir Vasiliev, coach) GK—Valeri Ivannikov, Vadim Privalov— Vladimir Konstantinov, Igor Monayenkov, Vadim Musatov, Andrei Smirnov, Dmitri Tsygurov, Vladimir Malakhov, Alexander Galchenyuk, Yevgeni Davydov, Anton Zagorodny, Valeri Zelepukin, Alexander Kerch, Pavel Kostichkin, Dmitri Medvedev, Sergei Osipov, Valeri Popov, Sergei Shesterikov, Alexander Mogilny, Sergei Fyodorov

**Sweden** (Lars-Gunnar Jansson, coach) GK—Sam Lindstahl, Johan Borg—Calle Johansson, Niklas Gallstedt, Jonas Heed, Roger Akerstrom, Orjan Lindmark, Rickard Franzen, Roger Johansson, Tomas Sjogren, Ulf Dahlen, Hakan Ahlund, Johan Garpenlov, Bo Svanberg, Ulf Sandstrom, Par Edlund, Anders Gozzi, Roger Ohman, Roger Hansson, Tomaz Ericsson

**Switzerland** (Rolf Altorfer, coach) GK—Beat Aebischer, Reto Pavoni—Daniel Buenzli, Marco Dazzi, Christian Hofstetter, Andre Kuenzi, Luigi Riva, Peter Meier, Martin Lang, Romeo Mattioni, Olivier Hoffmann, Raymond Walder, Bruno Vollmer, Laurent Stehlin, Peter Baertschi, Jean-Jacques Aeschlimann, Ruben Fontana, Toni Nyffenegger, Achim Pleschberger, Roger Thoeni

**United States** (Dave Peterson, coach) GK—Pat Jablonski, Robb Stauber—Brian Leetch, Adam Burt, Greg Brown, Todd Copeland, Chris Biotti, Mike Posma, Dave Capuano, Tom Fitzgerald, Darren Turcotte, Mike Kelfer, Lee Davidson, Ed Krayer, Bob Corkum, Scott Young, Mike Hartman, Bobby Reynolds, Mike Wolak, Marty Nanne

## 12th U20 WORLD CHAMPIONSHIP
## December 26, 1987-January 4, 1988
## Moscow, Soviet Union

**Final Placing**

| | | | |
|---|---|---|---|
| Gold | .......Canada | 5th | ........Sweden |
| Silver | .....Soviet Union | 6th | ........United States |
| Bronze | ...Finland | 7th | ........West Germany^ |
| 4th | .........Czechoslovakia | 8th | ........Poland* |

^promoted from B Pool in 1987
*demoted to B Pool for 1989

**Tournament Format**
All eight teams were placed in one group and a simple round robin schedule was adopted. In the case of a tie in the standings between two teams, the result of the game between those two would be the first tie-breaker and goal differential the second decider.

**Results & Standings**

| | GP | W | T | L | GF | GA | P |
|---|---|---|---|---|---|---|---|
| Canada | 7 | 6 | 1 | 0 | 37 | 16 | 13 |
| Soviet Union | 7 | 6 | 0 | 1 | 44 | 18 | 12 |
| Finland | 7 | 5 | 1 | 1 | 36 | 20 | 11 |
| Czechoslovakia | 7 | 3 | 1 | 3 | 36 | 23 | 7 |
| Sweden | 7 | 3 | 1 | 3 | 36 | 24 | 7 |
| United States | 7 | 1 | 0 | 6 | 28 | 46 | 2 |
| West Germany | 7 | 1 | 0 | 6 | 18 | 47 | 2 |
| Poland | 7 | 1 | 0 | 6 | 12 | 53 | 2 |

| | | |
|---|---|---|
| December 26 | Canada 4 | Sweden 2 |
| December 26 | Soviet Union 6 | Czechoslovakia 4 |
| December 26 | Finland 6 | West Germany 0 |
| December 26 | Poland 4 | United States 3 |
| December 28 | Canada 4 | Czechoslovakia 2 |
| December 28 | Sweden 13 | Poland 0 |
| December 28 | Soviet Union 6 | Finland 2 |
| December 28 | United States 6 | West Germany 4 |
| December 29 | Canada 4 | Finland 4 |
| December 29 | Sweden 5 | West Germany 1 |
| December 29 | Czechoslovakia 6 | Poland 1 |
| December 29 | Soviet Union 7 | United States 3 |
| December 31 | Canada 5 | United States 4 |
| December 31 | Czechoslovakia 7 | West Germany 4 |
| December 31 | Soviet Union 4 | Sweden 2 |
| December 31 | Finland 9 | Poland 1 |
| January 1 | Canada 3 | Soviet Union 2 |
| January 1 | West Germany 6 | Poland 3 |
| January 1 | Czechoslovakia 5 | Sweden 5 |
| January 1 | Finland 8 | United States 6 |
| January 3 | Canada 8 | West Germany 1 |
| January 3 | Finland 5 | Sweden 2 |
| January 3 | Soviet Union 7 | Poland 2 |
| January 3 | Czechoslovakia 11 | United States 1 |
| January 4 | Canada 9 | Poland 1 |
| January 4 | Soviet Union 12 | West Germany 2 |
| January 4 | Finland 2 | Czechoslovakia 1 |
| January 4 | Sweden 7 | United States 5 |

**Rosters**
**Canada** (Dave Chambers, coach) GK—Jimmy Waite, Jeff Hackett—Greg Hawgood, Theo Fleury, Rob Brown, Dan Currie, Sheldon Kennedy, Adam Graves, Mark Recchi, Joe Sakic, Jody Hull, Chris Joseph, Marc Laniel, Mark Pederson, Warren Babe, Rob Dimaio, Wayne McBean, Trevor Linden, Scott McCrady, Eric Desjardins

**Czechoslovakia** (Zdenek Uher, coach) GK—Rudolf Pejchar, Roman Svacina—Robert Reichel, Petr Pavlas, Petr Hrbek, Zdeno Ciger, Robert Kisela, Roman Horak, Juraj Jurik, Pavel Gross, Radek Gardon, Frantisek Kucera, Milan Tichy, Josef Zajic, Karel Mimochodek, Pavel Valko, Roman Nemcicky, Ondrej Vosta, Pavel Taborsky, Karel Smid

**Finland** (Hannu Jortikka, coach) GK—Mika Rautio, Ari Hilli—Janne Ojanen, Tero Toivola, Teppo Numminen, Pekka Tirkkonen, Jukka Seppo, Arto Kulmala, Markku Jokinen, Juha Jokiharju, Tero Arkiomaa, Marko Kiuru, Petri Pulkkinen, Timo Peltomaa, Marko Lapinkoski, Vesa Savolainen, Harri Aho, Jukka Marttila, Kari Harila, Mika Tuovinen

**Poland** (Andrzej Szczepaniec, coach) GK—Marek Batkiewicz, Mariusz Kieca—Dariusz Olejowski, Janusz Janikowski, Jedrzej Kasperczyk, Jacek Plachta, Wlodzimierz Krol, Tomasz Zmudzinski, Marek Koszowski, Krzysztof Kuzniecow, Tadeusz Pulawski, Marek Trybus, Slawomir Wieloch, Krzysztof Niedziolka, Andrzej Szlapka, Jacek Zamojski, Zbigniew Niedospial, Czeslaw Niedzwiedz, Janusz Strzempek, Wojciech Tkacz

**Soviet Union** (Anatoli Kostriukov, coach) GK—Alexei Sheblanov, Alexei Ivashkin—Alexander Mogilny, Sergei Fyodorov, Andrei Sidorov, Valeri Zelepukin, Stanislav Panfilenkov, Igor Chibirev, Pavel Kostichkin, Igor Dorofeyev, Ulvis Katlaps, Yuri Krivokhizha, Igor Malykhin, Harijs Vitolins, Dmitri Khristich, Vladimir Aleksushin, Yevgeni Mukhin, Sergei Sorokin, Andrei Rasolko, Sergei Petrenko

**Sweden** (Clas-Goran Wallin, coach) GK—Fredrik Andersson, Patrik Hofbauer—Tomas Sjogren, Ola Rosander, Patrik Carnback, Ricard Persson, Johan Garpenlov, Peter Larsson, Patrik Eriksson, Stefan Nilsson (I), Per Lundell, Stefan Nilsson (III), Leif Rohlin, Per Djoos, Petri Liimatainen, Per Ljusterang, Markus Akerblom, Stefan Nilsson (II), Rickard Franzen, Tomas Forslund

**United States** (Terry Christensen, coach) GK—Damian Rhodes, Jason Glickman—Jeremy Roenick, John LeClair, Mike Modano, Ted Donato, Kip Miller, Darren Turcotte, Lee Davidson, Joe Day, Carl Young, Randy Skarda, Rob Mendel, Mike Sullivan, Steve Scheifele, Mathieu Schneider, Ted Crowley, Kris Miller, Kevin Dean, David Emma

**West Germany** (Hans Rampf, coach) GK—Peter Franke, Markus Flemming—Ernst Kopf, Andreas Lupzig, Thomas Brandl, Thomas Schinko, Andreas Pokorny, Gunther Oswald, Jorg Mayr, Lutz Bongers, Jurgen Trattner, Tobias Abstreiter, Stefan Sinner, Michael Pohl, Alfred Burghard, Heinz Schiffl, Christian Lukes, Frank Hirtreiter, Jurgen Rumrich, Lorenz Funk

## 13th U20 WORLD CHAMPIONSHIP
## December 26, 1988-January 4, 1989
## Anchorage/Fire Lake, United States

**Final Placing**

| | | | |
|---|---|---|---|
| Gold | .......Soviet Union | 5th | ........United States |
| Silver | .....Sweden | 6th | ........Finland |
| Bronze | ...Czechoslovakia | 7th | ........Norway^ |
| 4th | .........Canada | 8th | ........West Germany* |

^promoted from B Pool in 1988
*demoted to B Pool for 1990

**Tournament Format**
All eight countries were placed in a single division and played a round-robin schedule. The first factor in breaking a tie between two nations was the result of the head-to-head game in the round-robin (which is how the Soviets beat Sweden for the gold). The second determining factor was goals differential (goals against subtracted from goals for), which is how the Czechs beat Canada for the bronze.

**Results & Standings**

| | GP | W | T | L | GF | GA | P |
|---|---|---|---|---|---|---|---|
| Soviet Union | 7 | 6 | 0 | 1 | 51 | 14 | 12 |
| Sweden | 7 | 6 | 0 | 1 | 39 | 14 | 12 |
| Czechoslovakia | 7 | 4 | 1 | 2 | 36 | 19 | 9 |
| Canada | 7 | 4 | 1 | 2 | 31 | 23 | 9 |
| United States | 7 | 3 | 1 | 3 | 41 | 25 | 7 |
| Finland | 7 | 2 | 1 | 4 | 29 | 37 | 5 |
| Norway | 7 | 1 | 0 | 6 | 14 | 56 | 2 |
| West Germany | 7 | 0 | 0 | 7 | 13 | 66 | 0 |

| | | | |
|---|---|---|---|
| December 26 | Fire Lake | Canada 7 | Norway 1 |
| December 26 | Anchorage | Sweden 5 | Czechoslovakia 3 |
| December 26 | Anchorage | Soviet Union 15 | West Germany 0 |
| December 26 | Anchorage | Finland 5 | United States 5 |
| December 27 | Anchorage | Czechoslovakia 7 | Norway 1 |
| December 27 | Anchorage | Soviet Union 4 | United States 2 |
| December 28 | Anchorage | Canada 7 | West Germany 4 |
| December 28 | Anchorage | Sweden 6 | Finland 2 |
| December 29 | Anchorage | Canada 5 | United States 1 |
| December 29 | Anchorage | Soviet Union 3 | Sweden 2 |
| December 29 | Fire Lake | Finland 9 | Norway 3 |
| December 29 | Fire Lake | Czechoslovakia 11 | West Germany 1 |
| December 30 | Anchorage | Soviet Union 10 | Norway 0 |
| December 30 | Anchorage | United States 5 | Czechoslovakia 1 |
| December 31 | Anchorage | Sweden 5 | Canada 4 |
| December 31 | Anchorage | Finland 5 | West Germany 3 |
| January 1 | Anchorage | Canada 2 | Czechoslovakia 2 |
| January 1 | Fire Lake | Soviet Union 9 | Finland 3 |
| January 1 | Fire Lake | Sweden 9 | Norway 1 |
| January 1 | Anchorage | United States 15 | West Germany 3 |
| January 2 | Anchorage | Czechoslovakia 5 | Soviet Union 3 |
| January 2 | Anchorage | United States 12 | Norway 4 |
| January 3 | Anchorage | Canada 4 | Finland 3 |
| January 3 | Anchorage | Sweden 9 | West Germany 0 |
| January 4 | Anchorage | Soviet Union 7 | Canada 2 |
| January 4 | Fire Lake | Norway 4 | West Germany 2 |
| January 4 | Fire Lake | Czechoslovakia 7 | Finland 2 |
| January 4 | Anchorage | Sweden 3 | United States 1 |

**Rosters**
**Canada** (Tom Webster, coach) GK—Stephane Fiset, Gus Morschauser—Rob Cimetta, Reginald Savage, Mike Ricci, Sheldon Kennedy, Andrew Cassels, Rod Brind'Amour, Eric Desjardins, Jamie Leach, Darrin Shannon, Corey Foster, Dan Lambert, Darcy Loewen, Martin Gelinas, Rob Murphy, John McIntyre, Geoff Smith, Steve Veilleux, Yves Racine

**Czechoslovakia** (Josef Vimmer, coach) GK—Roman Turek, Jaroslav Kames—Josef Beranek, Roman Kontsek, Robert Holik, Robert Reichel, Zdeno Ciger, Lubos Rob, Martin Maskarinec, Milan Tichy, Petr Hrbek, Jiri Cihlar, Radek Gardon, Jan Varholik, Martin Bakula, Vladimir Buril, Jiri Vykoukal, Peter Zubek, Pavol Zubek, Roman Veber

**Finland** (Erkka Westerlund, coach) GK—Henry Eskelinen, Timo Maki (dnp)—Petri Aaltonen, Teemu Selanne, Timo Saarikoski, Veli-Pekka Kautonen, Petro Koivunen, Marko Lapinkoski, Marko Kiuru, Mika Alatalo, Mika Stromberg, Keijo Sailynoja, Mika Valila, Karri Kivi, Sami Nuutinen, Teemu Sillanpaa, Janne Leppanen, Juha Lampinen, Jouko Myrra, Rauli Raitanen, Juha Virenius

**Norway** (Tor Johan Haga, coach) GK—Mattis Haakensen, Remo Martinsen—Ole Eskild Dahlstrom, Marius Rath, Tom Erik Olsen, Klas Forfang, Bjornar Sorensen, Jan Erik Smithurst, Stig Johansen, Espen Knutsen, Glenn Asland, Pal Kristiansen, Tommy Jakobsen, Magnus Christoffersen, Christian Olsvik, Rune Kraft, Bjorn Berg Larsen, Magne Nordnes, Oystein Olsen, Kent Inge Kristiansen

**Soviet Union** (Robert Cherenkov, coach) GK—Maxim Mikhailovski, Alexei Ivashkin— Pavel Bure, Alexander Mogilny, Sergei Fyodorov, Andrei Sidorov, Roman Oksiuta, Dmitri Khristich, Viktor Gordiyuk, Sergei Gomolyako, Stanislav Ranfilenkov, Sergei Zubov, Igor Malykhin, Igor Ivanov, Alexander Yudin, Sergei Sorokin, Dmitri Yushkevich, Vladimir Tsyplakov, Alexander Godynyuk, Boris Bykovsky

**Sweden** (Clas-Goran Wallin, coach) GK—Tommy Soderstrom, Jonas Karlsson—Patrik Erickson, Niklas Eriksson, Markus Akerblom, Ola Rosander, Ricard Persson, Patric Kjellberg, Stefan Claesson, Daniel Rydmark, Torbjorn Lindberg, Mattias Svedberg, Stefan Elvenes, Magnus Jansson, Niklas Andersson, Peter Hammarstrom, Stefan Ornskog, Jan Bergman, Petri Liimatainen, Pierre Johnsson

**United States** (Steve Cedorchuk, coach) GK—Jason Glickman, Mark Richards—Jeremy Roenick, Mike Modano, John LeClair, Tom Pederson, David Emma, Adam Burt, Mike Lappin, Pete Ciavaglia, Rodger Sykes, Joe Sacco, Neil Carnes, Tony Amonte, Steve Heinze, Bill Guerin, Ted Crowley, Tom Dion, Barry Richter, Shaun Kane

**West Germany** (Hans Rampf, coach) GK—Bernd Zimmer, Reinhard Haider, Christian Frutel—Lorenz Funk, Gunther Oswald, Stefan Sinner, Rolf Hammer, Wolfgang Kummer, Thomas Brandl, Tobias Abstreiter, Jorg Mayr, Reemt Pyka, Roland Timoschuk, Jurgen Schulz, Andreas Ott, Michael Raubal, Christian Curth, Christian Lukes, Peter Hejma, Raphael Kruger, Stefan Urban

## 14th U20 WORLD CHAMPIONSHIP
## December 26, 1989-January 4, 1990
## Helsinki/Turku, Finland

**Final Placing**

| | | | |
|---|---|---|---|
| Gold | Canada | 5th | Sweden |
| Silver | Soviet Union | 6th | Norway |
| Bronze | Czechoslovakia | 7th | United States |
| 4th | Finland | 8th | Poland^* |

^promoted from B Pool in 1989
*demoted to B Pool for 1991

**Tournament Format**
All eight teams played a simple round-robin in one division. A tie in the standings between two teams was broken first by the result of the game between the two (which is how Canada beat the Soviet Union for gold, and also why Finland was placed above Sweden in the final table). In case of a tie still, goals differential would decide the placings.

**Results & Standings**

| | GP | W | T | L | GF | GA | P |
|---|---|---|---|---|---|---|---|
| Canada | 7 | 5 | 1 | 1 | 36 | 18 | 11 |
| Soviet Union | 7 | 5 | 1 | 1 | 50 | 23 | 11 |
| Czechoslovakia | 7 | 5 | 0 | 2 | 51 | 17 | 10 |
| Finland | 7 | 4 | 1 | 2 | 32 | 21 | 9 |
| Sweden | 7 | 4 | 1 | 2 | 38 | 29 | 9 |
| Norway | 7 | 2 | 0 | 5 | 25 | 51 | 4 |
| United States | 7 | 1 | 0 | 6 | 22 | 37 | 2 |
| Poland | 7 | 0 | 0 | 7 | 7 | 65 | 0 |

| | | | |
|---|---|---|---|
| December 26 | Turku | Canada 3 | United States 2 |
| December 26 | Kerava | Soviet Union 11 | Poland 0 |
| December 26 | Kauniainen | Sweden 4 | Norway 3 |
| December 26 | Helsinki | Czechoslovakia 7 | Finland 1 |
| December 27 | Kauniainen | Soviet Union 12 | Norway 2 |
| December 27 | Helsinki | Czechoslovakia 7 | United States 1 |
| December 28 | Kauniainen | Canada 12 | Poland 0 |
| December 28 | Turku | Finland 5 | Sweden 2 |
| December 29 | Kerava | Canada 6 | Norway 3 |
| December 29 | Turku | Soviet Union 3 | Finland 2 |
| December 29 | Kauniainen | Czechoslovakia 11 | Poland 1 |
| December 29 | Helsinki | Sweden 6 | United States 5 |
| December 30 | Kauniainen | Czechoslovakia 13 | Norway 2 |
| December 30 | Helsinki | Soviet Union 7 | United States 3 |
| December 31 | Helsinki | Canada 3 | Finland 3 |
| December 31 | Turku | Sweden 14 | Poland 0 |
| January 1 | Helsinki | Canada 6 | Soviet Union 4 |
| January 1 | Turku | Czechoslovakia 7 | Sweden 2 |
| January 1 | Helsinki | Finland 8 | Norway 2 |
| January 1 | Kerava | United States 3 | Poland 2 |
| January 2 | Helsinki | Soviet Union 8 | Czechoslovakia 5 |
| January 2 | Kerava | Norway 6 | United States 5 |
| January 3 | Helsinki | Sweden 5 | Canada 4 |
| January 3 | Helsinki | Finland 7 | Poland 1 |
| January 4 | Turku | Canada 2 | Czechoslovakia 1 |
| January 4 | Helsinki | Soviet Union 5 | Sweden 5 |
| January 4 | Turku | Norway 7 | Poland 3 |
| January 4 | Helsinki | Finland 6 | United States 3 |

**Rosters**

**Canada** (Guy Charron, coach) GK—Stephane Fiset, Trevor Kidd—Dave Chyzowski, Mike Needham, Stu Barnes, Dwayne Norris, Wes Walz, Eric Lindros, Kevin Haller, Patrice Brisebois, Dan Ratushny, Mike Ricci, Mike Craig, Kent Manderville, Steve Rice, Scott Pellerin, Kris Draper, Adrien Plavsic, Jason Herter, Stewart Malgunas

**Czechoslovakia** (Josef Vimmer, coach) GK—Roman Turek, Robert Horyna—Robert Reichel, Jaromir Jagr, Robert Holik, Pavol Zubek, Martin Prochazka, Jiri Slegr, Jiri Vykoukal, Lubos Rob, Petr Kuchyna, Jiri Malinsky, Ladislav Karabin, Petr Bares, Jan Varholik, Milos Holan, Miroslav Mach, Peter Zubek, Richard Smehlik, Marian Uharcek

**Finland** (Hannu Jortikka, coach) GK—Pasi Raty, Henry Eskelinen—Mika Valila, Vesa Viitakoski, Keijo Sailynoja, Harri Suvanto, Veli-Pekka Kautonen, Jonas Hemming, Petro Koivunen, Rauli Raitanen, Mika Stromberg, Mika Alatalo, Petri Aaltonen, Sami Nuutinen, Janne Kekalainen, Toni Porkka, Janne Laukkanen, Tommi Pullola, Karri Kivi, Teemu Sillanpaa

**Norway** (George Kingston, coach) GK—Lasse Syversen, Mattis Haakensen—Espen Knutsen, Marius Rath, Ole Eskild Dahlstrom, Stig Johansen, Henrik Buskoven, Trond Magnussen, Tom-Erik Olsen, Vegar Barlie, Pal Kristiansen, Tommie Eriksen, Rene Hansen, Jan Tore Ronningen, Svein Enok Norstebo, Tommy Jakobsen, Peter Samuelsen, Per Martinsen, Bjornar Sorensen, Geir Dalene

**Poland** (Leszek Lejczyk, coach) GK—Wojciech Baca, Dariusz Karamuz—Leszek Trybus, Slawomir Furca, Andrzej Secemski, Dariusz Garbocz, Adam Fras, Mariusz Czerkawski, Janusz Misterka, Rafal Sroka, Wojciech Winiarski, Wojciech Sosinski, Ryszard Tyrala, Maciej Pachucki, Jerzy Sobera, Piotr Matlakiewicz, Jacek Kuc, Maciej Funiok, Piotr Sadlocha, Jacek Szlapka

**Soviet Union** (Robert Cherenkov, coach) GK—Sergei Tkachenko, Sergei Poliakov—Andrei Kovalenko, Vyacheslav Kozlov, Pavel Bure, Roman Oksiuta, Viktor Gordiyuk, Alexei Zhamnov, Vyacheslav Butsayev, Sergei Martinyuk, Andrei Potaichuk, Alexander Godynyuk, Igor Ivanov, Sergei Zubov, Dmitri Yushkevich, Alexei Kudashov, Yan Kaminski, Sergei Tertyshny, Yevgeni Namestnikov, Alexander Karpovtsev

**Sweden** (Curt Lundmark, coach) GK—Joakim Persson, Jonas Leven—Patric Englund, Daniel Rydmark, Mats Sundin, Mattias Olsson, Niklas Brannstrom, Nicklas Lidstrom, Niklas Andersson, Patrik Ross, Torbjorn Lindberg, Henrik Nilsson, Joacim Esbjors, Marcus Thuresson, Fredrik Nilsson, Patrik Juhlin, Osmo Soutokorva, Henrik Andersson, Pelle Svensson, Henrik Bjorkman

**United States** (Steve Cedorchuk, coach) GK-Chuck Hughes, Jeff Stolp—Tony Amonte, Bryan Smolinski, Ted Crowley, Barry Richter, Rob Gaudreau, Jeff Blaeser, Mike Boback, Ted Drury, Keith Carney, Sean Hill, Marc Beran, Shaun Kane, Jim Larkin, Jason Zent, Doug Zmolek, Cory Laylin, Brian Bruininks, Bill Guerin

## 15th U20 WORLD CHAMPIONSHIP
## December 26, 1990-January 4, 1991
## Saskatoon, Canada

**Final Placing**

| | | | |
|---|---|---|---|
| Gold | Canada | 5th | Finland |
| Silver | Soviet Union | 6th | Sweden |
| Bronze | Czechoslovakia | 7th | Switzerland^ |
| 4th | United States | 8th | Norway* |

^promoted from B Pool in 1990
*demoted to B Pool for 1992

**Tournament Format**
As was the standard, the eight teams were pooled in one division to play a round-robin tournament. In case of a tie in the standings, head-to-head results were the deciding factor. This came into play on the last day of the championships when Canada and the Soviet Union were tied for first and set to play each other.

**Results & Standings**

| | GP | W | T | L | GF | GA | P |
|---|---|---|---|---|---|---|---|
| Canada | 7 | 5 | 1 | 1 | 40 | 18 | 11 |
| Soviet Union | 7 | 5 | 1 | 1 | 44 | 15 | 11 |
| Czechoslovakia | 7 | 5 | 0 | 2 | 44 | 19 | 10 |
| United States | 7 | 4 | 1 | 2 | 45 | 19 | 9 |
| Finland | 7 | 3 | 1 | 3 | 35 | 30 | 7 |
| Sweden | 7 | 3 | 0 | 4 | 32 | 29 | 6 |
| Switzerland | 7 | 1 | 0 | 6 | 5 | 48 | 2 |
| Norway | 7 | 0 | 0 | 7 | 8 | 75 | 0 |

| | | | |
|---|---|---|---|
| December 26 | Saskatoon | Canada 6 | Switzerland 0 |
| December 26 | Rosetown | Czechoslovakia 11 | Norway 3 |
| December 26 | Saskatoon | Finland 8 | Sweden 5 |
| December 26 | Prince Albert | Soviet Union 4 | United States 2 |
| December 27 | Saskatoon | Canada 4 | United States 4 |
| December 27 | Regina | Sweden 4 | Czechoslovakia 3 |
| December 28 | Moose Jaw | Finland 7 | Switzerland 1 |
| December 28 | Saskatoon | Soviet Union 13 | Norway 0 |
| December 29 | Regina | Canada 10 | Norway 1 |

| | | | |
|---|---|---|---|
| December 29 | Saskatoon | Soviet Union 5 | Sweden 1 |
| December 29 | Kindersley | Czechoslovakia 10 | Switzerland 0 |
| December 29 | North Battleford | United States 6 | Finland 3 |
| December 30 | Regina | Canada 7 | Sweden 4 |
| December 30 | Saskatoon | Czechoslovakia 5 | United States 1 |
| December 31 | Saskatoon | Finland 10 | Norway 2 |
| December 31 | Yorkton | Soviet Union 10 | Switzerland 1 |
| January 1 | Saskatoon | Canada 5 | Finland 1 |
| January 1 | Regina | United States 19 | Norway 1 |
| January 1 | Saskatoon | Sweden 6 | Switzerland 1 |
| January 1 | Regina | Soviet Union 5 | Czechoslovakia 3 |
| January 2 | Saskatoon | Czechoslovakia 6 | Canada 5 |
| January 2 | Humboldt | United States 5 | Sweden 2 |
| January 3 | Regina | Soviet Union 5 | Finland 5 |
| January 3 | Saskatoon | Switzerland 2 | Norway 1 |
| January 4 | Saskatoon | Canada 3 | Soviet Union 2 |
| January 4 | Prince Albert | Sweden 10 | Norway 0 |
| January 4 | Saskatoon | Czechoslovakia 6 | Finland 1 |
| January 4 | Regina | United States 8 | Switzerland 0 |

**Rosters**

**Canada** (Dick Todd, coach) GK—Trevor Kidd, Felix Potvin—Eric Lindros, Mike Craig, Patrice Brisebois, Kent Manderville, Pierre Sevigny, Mike Sillinger, Greg Johnson, Pat Falloon, Steve Rice, Scott Thornton, Kris Draper, Jason Marshall, Chris Snell, John Slaney, Dale Craigwell, Karl Dykhuis, Martin Lapointe, David Harlock, Brad May, Scott Niedermayer

**Czechoslovakia** (Josef Vimmer, coach) GK—Milan Hnilicka, Roman Cechmanek—Martin Rucinsky, Zigmund Palffy, Jiri Slegr, Martin Madovy, Branislav Janos, Jozef Stumpel, Jaromir Kverka, Marian Uharcek, Martin Straka, Martin Prochazka, Jiri Kuntos, Roman Meluzin, Jaroslav Brabec, Martin Hamrlik, Jiri Malinsky, Tomas Mikolasek, Milos Holan, Jaroslav Modry, Ivan Droppa

**Finland** (Samu Kuitunen, coach) GK—Pasi Kuivalainen, Mikael Granlund—Marko Jantunen, Vesa Viitakoski, Tommi Pullola, Jarkko Varvio, Petteri Koskimaki, Mika Alatalo, Niko Marttila, Kim Ahlroos, Tommy Kiviaho, Tero Lehtera, Jere Lehtinen, Juha Ylonen, Toni Koivunen, Teemu Sillanpaa, Petri Kalteva, Sami Nuutinen, Mika Yli-Maenpaa, Erik Kakko, Janne Gronvall, Tommi Gronlund

**Norway** (George Kingston, coach) GK—Morten Kristoffersen, Oyvind Sorli, Kim Kristiansen—Per Odvar Walbye, Erik Tveten, Kim Fagerhoi, Espen Knutsen, Peter Samuelsen, Michael Smithurst, Jo Espen Leibnitz, Arve Jansen, Rune Fjeldstad, Thomas Johansson, Terje Haukali, Christian Kjelsberg, Robert Sundt, Jarle Gundersen, Karl Andersen, Svein Enok Norstebo, Anders Larsen, Jan Tore Ronningen, Eivind Olsen, Vegar Barlie

**Soviet Union** (Robert Cherenkov, coach) GK—Sergei Tkachenko, Sergei Zvyagin—Pavel Bure, Vyacheslav Kozlov, Alexei Kudashov, Mikhail Volkov, Oleg Petrov, Dmitri Yushkevich, Konstantin Korotkov, Sergei Zolotov, Darius Kasparaitis, Sergei Berezin, Valeri Karpov, Sergejs Zoltoks, Sandis Ozolins, Yegor Bashkatov, Boris Mironov, Alexei Zhitnik, Dmitri Motkov, Yan Kaminski, Yevgeni Namestnikov, Sergei Martinyuk

**Sweden** (Bengt Ohlsson, coach) GK—Tommy Salo, Rolf Wanhainen—Mikael Nylander, Niklas Andersson, Kristian Gahn, Mattias Olsson, Marcus Thuresson, Anders Huusko, Ove Molin, Henrik Bjorkman, Erik Huusko, Erik Andersson, Nichlas Falk, Stefan Ketola, Fredrik Nilsson, Stefan Nyman, Thomas Carlsson, Peter Jacobsson, Thomas Rhodin, Bjorn Ahlstrom, Jorgen Eriksson, Peter Ekelund

**Switzerland** (Bruno Zenhausern, coach) GK—Pauli Jaks, Nando Wieser, Martin Buehler—Marco Fischer, Harry Derungs, Raoul Baumgartner, Bjorn Schneider, Daniel Meier, Noel Guyaz, Marco Bayer, Bernhard Schumperli, Axel Heim, Nicola Celio, Andy Rufener, Didier Princi, Olivier Keller, Simon Hochuli, Rene Ackermann, Arthur Camenzind, Marco Ferrari, Andy Krapf, Daniel Sigg, Thomas Burillo

**United States** (Kevin Constantine, coach) GK—Mike Heinke, Mike Dunham—Doug Weight, Trent Klatt, Ted Drury, Keith Tkachuk, Bill Lindsay, Chris Gotziaman, Jim Storm, Pat Neaton, Brian Rolston, Mike Doers, Scott Lachance, Derek Plante, Ken Klee, Aaron Miller, Chris Imes, Craig Johnson, Ian Moran, Bryan Ganz, Tony Burns, Brent Brekke

## 16th U20 WORLD CHAMPIONSHIP
## December 26, 1991-January 4, 1992
## Fussen/Kaufbeuren, Germany

**Final Placing**

| | |
|---|---|
| Gold .......Russia (CIS**) | 5th ........Czechoslovakia |
| Silver .....Sweden | 6th ........Canada |
| Bronze ...United States | 7th ........Germany^ |
| 4th .........Finland | 8th ........Switzerland* |

**started tournament as Soviet Union, and changed name to Commonweath of Independant States on January 1, 1992

^promoted from B Pool in 1991

*demoted to B Pool for 1993

**Tournament Format**

A simple round-robin formula was used with all nations being grouped into one division. Ties would be decided first by head-to-head meetings, then goals differential, and then goals ratio (goals for divided by goals allowed).

**Results & Standings**

| | GP | W | T | L | GF | GA | P |
|---|---|---|---|---|---|---|---|
| Russia | 7 | 6 | 0 | 1 | 39 | 13 | 12 |
| Sweden | 7 | 5 | 1 | 1 | 41 | 24 | 11 |
| United States | 7 | 5 | 0 | 2 | 30 | 22 | 10 |
| Finland | 7 | 3 | 1 | 3 | 21 | 21 | 7 |
| Czechoslovakia | 7 | 3 | 0 | 4 | 28 | 24 | 6 |
| Canada | 7 | 2 | 2 | 3 | 21 | 30 | 6 |
| Germany | 7 | 1 | 0 | 6 | 15 | 40 | 2 |
| Switzerland | 7 | 1 | 0 | 6 | 19 | 40 | 2 |

| | | | |
|---|---|---|---|
| December 26 | Fussen | Canada 5 | Germany 4 |
| December 26 | Fussen | Sweden 8 | Czechoslovakia 4 |
| December 26 | Kaufbeuren | Russia 10 | Switzerland 2 |
| December 26 | Fussen | United States 5 | Finland 1 |
| December 27 | Fussen | Canada 6 | Switzerland 4 |
| December 27 | Kaufbeuren | Finland 4 | Czechoslovakia 1 |
| December 27 | Fussen | Russia 4 | Sweden 3 |
| December 27 | Fussen | United States 6 | Germany 2 |
| December 29 | Kaufbeuren | Canada 2 | Sweden 2 |
| December 29 | Fussen | Russia 4 | Finland 1 |
| December 29 | Fussen | Czechoslovakia 8 | Germany 2 |
| December 29 | Fussen | United States 5 | Switzerland 1 |
| December 30 | Fussen | Canada 2 | Finland 2 |
| December 30 | Fussen | Switzerland 4 | Czechoslovakia 2 |
| December 30 | Fussen | Russia 7 | Germany 0 |
| December 30 | Kaufbeuren | Sweden 8 | United States 6 |
| January 1 | Fussen | United States 5 | Canada 3 |
| January 1 | Fussen | Sweden 4 | Switzerland 3 |
| January 1 | Kaufbeuren | Finland 2 | Germany 0 |
| January 1 | Fussen | Czechoslovakia 5 | Russia 2 |
| January 2 | Fussen | Czechoslovakia 6 | Canada 1 |
| January 2 | Fussen | Finland 7 | Switzerland 3 |
| January 2 | Fussen | Sweden 10 | Germany 1 |
| January 2 | Kaufbeuren | Russia 5 | United States 0 |
| January 4 | Fussen | Russia 7 | Canada 2 |
| January 4 | Fussen | Sweden 6 | Finland 4 |
| January 4 | Kaufbeuren | Germany 6 | Switzerland 2 |
| January 4 | Fussen | United States 3 | Czechoslovakia 2 |

**Rosters**

**Canada** (Rick Cornacchia, coach) GK—Trevor Kidd, Mike Fountain (dnp)—Eric Lindros, Kimbi Daniels, Martin Lapointe, Darryl Sydor, Steve Junker, Patrick Poulin, John Slaney, Brad Bombardir, Jeff Nelson, Paul Kariya, Turner Stevenson, Tyler Wright, Jassen Cullimore, Ryan Hughes, Scott Niedermayer, Karl Dykhuis, Andy Schneider, Chad Penney, Richard Matvichuk, David St. Pierre

**Czechoslovakia** (Bedrich Brunclik, coach) GK—Milan Hnilicka, Igor Murin—Jan Caloun, Robert Petrovicky, Martin Straka, Viktor Ujcik, Zigmund Palffy, Milan Nedoma, Patrik Rimmel, Roman Hamrlik, Ivan Droppa, Jiri Zelenka, Patrik Luza, Martin Prochazka, Frantisek Kaberle, Roman Meluzin, Jan Vopat, Michal Chromco, Jan Alinc, Marek Zadina, Tomas Chlubna, Miroslav Skovira

**Finland** (Jarmo Tolvanen, coach) GK—Ilpo Kauhanen, Pasi Kuivalainen—Jarkko Varvio, Juha Ylonen, Sami Kapanen, Marko Tuomainen, Marko Kiprusoff, Janne Gronvall, Mikko Luovi, Tero Lehtera, Petri Gunther, Jere Lehtinen, Tuomas Gronman, Tony Virta, Petteri Nummelin, Jukka Ollila, Janne Nikko, Sakari Palsola, Janne Niinimaa, Jussi Kiuru, Jarno Miikkulainen, Pasi Maattanen

**Germany** (Hans Rampf, coach) GK—Marc Seliger, Thomas Wilhelm—Jens Schwabe, Hans-Jorg Mayer, Henrik Holscher, Till Feser, Ronny Martin, Thomas Schubert, Stefan Ustorf, Heiko-Michael Smazal, Josef Lehner, Timo Gschwill, Andreas Naumann, Steffen Ziesche, Mirko Ludemann, Andreas Loth, Christian Althoff, Oliver Mayer, Frank Hohenadl, Robert Hock, Markus Kehle, Peter Hartung

**Russia** (Pyotr Vorobyov, coach) GK—Nikolai Khabibulin, Ildar Mukhometov—Alexei Kovalyov, Denis Metlyuk, Alexander Cherbayev, Konstantin Korotkov, Alexei Yashin, Sergei Krivokrasov, Sergejs Zoltoks, Sandis Ozolins, Darius Kasparaitis, Boris Mironov, Mikhail Volkov, Alexander Sverzhov, Andrei Nikolishin, Alexander Kuzminski, Alexei Zhitnik, Denis Vinokurov, Ravil Gusmanov, Artyom Kopot, Alexei Troshinski, Vladislav Bulyin

**Sweden** (Tommy Tomth, coach) GK—Rolf Wanhainen, Magnus Lindqvist—Mikael Nylander, Peter Forsberg, Markus Naslund, Mikael Renberg, Kristian Gahn, Bjorn Nord, Fredrik Jax, Jonas Hoglund, Niklas Sundblad, Stefan Klockare, Stefan Ketola, Andreas Johansson, Jakob Karlsson, Greger Artursson, Roger Kyro, Mattias Norstrom, Calle Carlsson, Johan Norgren, Jens Hemstrom, Patrik Ekholm

**Switzerland** (Juhani Tamminen, coach) GK—Pauli Jaks, Lars Weibel—Nicola Celio, Marc Weber, Gaetan Voisard, Bernhard Schumperli, Laurent Bucher, Michael Blaha, Bjorn Schneider, Marco Bayer, Daniel Meier, Sasha Ochsner, Tiziano Gianini, Claude Luthi, Noel Guyaz, Mathias Holzer, Gilles Guyaz, Martin Steinegger, Ivan Gazzaroli, Gerd Zenhausern, Michael Diener, Christian Hofstetter

**United States** (Walt Kyle, coach) GK—Mike Dunham, Corwin Saurdiff—Peter Ferraro, Chris Ferraro, John Lilley, Keith Tkachuk, Pat Peake, Brian Rolston, Jim Campbell, Scott Lachance, Steve Konowalchuk, Brian Holzinger, Rich Brennan, Chris Imes, Brian Rafalski, Brent Bilodeau, Ryan Sittler, Brian Mueller, Todd Hall, Marty Schriner, Chris Tucker, Mike Prendergast

### 17th U20 WORLD CHAMPIONSHIP
### December 26, 1992-January 4, 1993
### Gavle, Sweden

**Final Placing**

Gold .......Canada
Silver .....Sweden
Bronze ...Czech/Slovak Republics
4th .........United States
5th ........Finland
6th ........Russia
7th ........Germany
8th ........Japan^*
^promoted from B Pool in 1992
*demoted to B Pool for 1994

**Tournament Format**

No change in the structure was made from last year. Eight teams, one round-robin of play. Ties in the standings were broken by head-to-head results. Thus, Canada's win over Sweden gave it the gold medal.

**Results & Standings**

| | GP | W | T | L | GF | GA | P |
|---|---|---|---|---|---|---|---|
| Canada | 7 | 6 | 0 | 1 | 37 | 17 | 12 |
| Sweden | 7 | 6 | 0 | 1 | 53 | 15 | 12 |
| Czech/Slovak | 7 | 4 | 1 | 2 | 38 | 27 | 9 |
| United States | 7 | 4 | 0 | 3 | 32 | 23 | 8 |
| Finland | 7 | 3 | 1 | 3 | 31 | 20 | 7 |
| Russia | 7 | 2 | 2 | 3 | 26 | 20 | 6 |
| Germany | 7 | 1 | 0 | 6 | 16 | 37 | 2 |
| Japan | 7 | 0 | 0 | 7 | 9 | 83 | 0 |

| | | | |
|---|---|---|---|
| December 26 | Gavle | Canada 3 | United States 0 |
| December 26 | Falun | Russia 16 | Japan 0 |
| December 26 | Bollnas | Finland 5 | Czech/Slovak 2 |
| December 26 | Gavle | Sweden 4 | Germany 2 |
| December 27 | Gavle | Canada 5 | Sweden 4 |
| December 27 | Falun | Russia 4 | Germany 0 |
| December 27 | Gavle | Finland 7 | Japan 0 |
| December 27 | Uppsala | Czech/Slovak 6 | United States 5 |
| December 29 | Gavle | Canada 9 | Russia 1 |
| December 29 | Hofors | Finland 11 | Germany 0 |
| December 29 | Gavle | Sweden 7 | Czech/Slovak 2 |
| December 29 | Falun | United States 12 | Japan 2 |
| December 30 | Uppsala | Canada 3 | Finland 2 |
| December 30 | Gavle | Czech/Slovak 1 | Russia 1 |
| December 30 | Gavle | Sweden 20 | Japan 1 |
| December 30 | Bollnas | United States 4 | Germany 3 |
| January 1 | Gavle | Canada 5 | Germany 2 |
| January 1 | Skutskar | Czech/Slovak 14 | Japan 2 |
| January 1 | Gavle | Finland 1 | Russia 1 |
| January 1 | Uppsala | Sweden 4 | United States 2 |
| January 2 | Hudkisvall | Canada 8 | Japan 1 |
| January 2 | Gavle | Sweden 9 | Finland 2 |
| January 2 | Uppsala | Czech/Slovak 6 | Germany 3 |
| January 2 | Gavle | United States 4 | Russia 2 |
| January 4 | Gavle | Czech/Slovak 7 | Canada 4 |
| January 4 | Hofors | Germany 6 | Japan 3 |
| January 4 | Gavle | Sweden 5 | Russia 1 |
| January 4 | Gavle | United States 5 | Finland 3 |

**Rosters**

**Canada** (Perry Pearn, coach) GK—Manny Legace, Philippe DeRouville—Martin Lapointe, Paul Kariya, Martin Gendron, Jason Dawe, Tyler Wright, Ralph Intranuovo, Jeff Shantz, Alexandre Daigle, Jeff Bes, Nathan Lafayette, Mike Rathje, Chris Gratton, Jason Smith, Chris Pronger, Brent Tully, Rob Niedermayer, Darcy Werenka, Dean McAmmond, Adrian Aucoin, Joel Bouchard

**Czech/Slovak Republics** (Jan Sterbak, coach) GK—Pavel Malac, Igor Murin, Jiri Kucera (dnp)—David Vyborny, Jan Vopat, Pavol Demitra, Michal Cerny, Petr Ton, Kamil Kolacek, Patrik Krisak, Richard Kapus, Pavel Rajnoha, Tomas Nemcicky, Pavel Kowalczyk, Stanislav Neckar, Roman Kadera, Radim Bicanek, Ondrej Steiner, Vaclav Burda, Zdenek Touzimsky, Frantisek Kaberle, Miroslav Skovira, Tomas Klimt

**Finland** (Jarmo Tolvanen, coach) GK—Markus Hatinen, Ilpo Kauhanen, Kimmo Vesa (dnp)— Jere Lehtinen, Ville Peltonen, Saku Koivu, Kimmo Rintanen, Mikko Luovi, Kalle Sahlstedt, Sami Kapanen, Janne Gronvall, Tuomas Gronman, Jonni Vauhkonen, Antti Laaksonen, Kimmo Timonen, Pasi Saarela, Jussi Kiuru, Timo Hirvonen, Tom Koivisto, Janne Nikko, Jarkko Glad, Sami Helenius, Jukka Ollila

**Germany** (Erich Kuhnhackl, coach) GK—Marc Pethke, Marc Seliger, Thomas Wilhelm (dnp)—Andre Grein, Robert Hock, Fabian Brannstrom, Alexander Serikow, Sven Felski, Rafael Jedamzik, Ralf Dobrzynski, Moritz Schmidt, Heiko-Michael Smazal, Markus Kempf, Norbert Zabel, Mike Losch, Matthias Mosebach, Thomas Knobloch, Stefan Mann, Michael Maass, Mirko Ludemann, James Dreseler, Jochen Molling, Michael Schmitz

**Japan** (Masaru Seino, coach) GK—Tomohiro Baba, Kenichi Hiraiwa, Daisuke Murakami (dnp)—Daisuke Sasoya, Akira Ihara, Mitsuaki Nitta, Taiji Susumago, Tsutsumi Otomo, Hiroyuki Miura, Hideji Tsuchida, Yutaka Kawaguchi, Shinichi Itabashi, Yuichi Sasaki, Yuji Iizuka, Shiro Ishiguro, Gen Ishioka, Naoto Ohno, Akihito Isojima, Shinjiro Tsuji, Junji Sakata, Hironori Kawashima, Hideyuki Sano, Yutaka Ebata

**Russia** (Yuri Moiseyev, coach) GK—Nikolai Khabibulin, Alexei Poliakov—Igor Alexandrov, Vitali Tomilin, Sergei Brylin, Vadim Sharifianov, Sergei Klimovich, Alexander Guliavtsev, Alexander Cherbayev, Viktor Kozlov, Oleg Belov, Andrei Yakhanov, Stanislav Shalnov, Igor Ivanov, Sergei Marchkov, Pavel Yevstegneyev, Sergei Gonchar, Maxim Galanov, Alexei Yashin, Nikolai Syomin, Artur Oktyabryov, Nikolai Tsulygin

**Sweden** (Tommy Tomth, coach) GK—Petter Ronnqvist, Johan Mansson, Henrik Espe (dnp)—Peter Forsberg, Markus Naslund, Niklas Sundstrom, Fredrik Lindquist, Reine Rauhala, Daniel Johansson, Andreas Johansson, Kenny Jonsson, Magnus Wernblom, Mikael Magnusson, Hans Jonsson, Mats Lindgren, Andreas Salomonsson, Niklas Sundblad, Johan Tornberg, Clas Eriksson, Mikael Hakansson, Edvin Frylen, Roger Rosen, Niclas Havelid

**United States** (Walt Kyle, coach) GK—Jim Carey, Jeff Callinan, Aaron Israel (dnp)—Pat Peake, Peter Ferraro, Chris Ferraro, Brian Rolston, Jim Campbell, Ryan Sittler, Todd Marchant, Pat Mikesch, Brian Rafalski, Adam Bartell, Todd Hall, David Wilkie, Mike Pomichter, Brent Bilodeau, Brady Kramer, Dan Brierley, Mark Strobel, John Emmons, Liam Garvey, Adam Deadmarsh

### 18th U20 WORLD CHAMPIONSHIP
### December 26, 1993-January 4, 1994
### Ostrava/Frydek-Mistek, Czech Republic

**Final Placing**

Gold .......Canada
Silver .....Sweden
Bronze ...Russia
4th .........Finland
5th ........Czech Republic
6th ........United States
7th ........Germany
8th ........Switzerland^*
^promoted from B Pool in 1993
*demoted to B Pool for 1995

**Tournament Format**

Eight teams were, as usual, grouped in one division to play a single round-robin. Head-to-head results and then goal differential were the first two methods used to determine placings in the standings in case of a tie.

**Results & Standings**

| | GP | W | T | L | GF | GA | P |
|---|---|---|---|---|---|---|---|
| Canada | 7 | 6 | 1 | 0 | 39 | 20 | 13 |
| Sweden | 7 | 6 | 0 | 1 | 35 | 16 | 12 |
| Russia | 7 | 5 | 1 | 1 | 23 | 17 | 11 |
| Finland | 7 | 4 | 0 | 3 | 27 | 24 | 8 |
| Czech Republic | 7 | 3 | 0 | 4 | 31 | 29 | 6 |
| United States | 7 | 1 | 1 | 5 | 20 | 33 | 3 |
| Germany | 7 | 1 | 0 | 6 | 10 | 26 | 2 |
| Switzerland | 7 | 0 | 1 | 6 | 10 | 30 | 1 |

| | | | |
|---|---|---|---|
| December 26 | Frydek-Mistek | Canada 5 | Switzerland 1 |
| December 26 | Ostrava | Sweden 4 | Germany 1 |
| December 26 | Ostrava | Russia 5 | Czech Republic 1 |
| December 26 | Frydek-Mistek | Finland 5 | United States 2 |
| December 27 | Ostrava | Canada 5 | Germany 2 |
| December 27 | Ostrava | Sweden 3 | Russia 0 |
| December 27 | Frydek-Mistek | Finland 7 | Czech Republic 3 |
| December 27 | Frydek-Mistek | Switzerland 1 | United States 1 |
| December 29 | Frydek-Mistek | Canada 3 | Russia 3 |
| December 29 | Frydek-Mistek | Czech Republic 6 | Switzerland 0 |
| December 29 | Ostrava | Sweden 6 | Finland 2 |
| December 29 | Ostrava | United States 7 | Germany 2 |
| December 30 | Ostrava | Canada 6 | Finland 3 |
| December 30 | Ostrava | Czech Republic 6 | Germany 2 |
| December 30 | Frydek-Mistek | Sweden 6 | Switzerland 2 |
| December 30 | Frydek-Mistek | Russia 4 | United States 3 |
| January 1 | Frydek-Mistek | Canada 8 | United States 3 |
| January 1 | Ostrava | Finland 4 | Switzerland 2 |
| January 1 | Frydek-Mistek | Sweden 6 | Czech Republic 4 |
| January 1 | Ostrava | Russia 1 | Germany 0 |
| January 2 | Ostrava | Canada 6 | Czech Republic 4 |
| January 2 | Frydek-Mistek | Finland 2 | Germany 0 |
| January 2 | Frydek-Mistek | Russia 5 | Switzerland 3 |
| January 2 | Ostrava | Sweden 6 | United States 1 |
| January 4 | Ostrava | Canada 6 | Sweden 4 |
| January 4 | Ostrava | Germany 3 | Switzerland 1 |
| January 4 | Frydek-Mistek | Russia 5 | Finland 4 |
| January 4 | Frydek-Mistek | Czech Republic 7 | United States 3 |

**Rosters**

**Canada** (Jos Canale, coach) GK—Jamie Storr, Manny Fernandez—Martin Gendron, Yanick Dube, Rick Girard, Jason Allison, Todd Harvey, Aaron Gavey, Anson Carter, Nick Stajduhar, Michael Peca, Marty Murray, Drew Bannister, Curtis Bowen, Jeff Friesen, Jason Botterill, Brandon Convery, Brent Tully, Joel Bouchard, Chris Armstrong, Bryan McCabe, Brendan Witt

**Czech Republic** (Vladimir Vujtek, coach) GK—Robert Slavik, Jaroslav Miklenda, Petr Franek—Petr Sykora, Zdenek Nedved, David Vyborny, Marek Malik, Pavel Kowalczyk, Josef Marha, Tomas Vlasak, Ladislav Prokupek, Milan Navratil, Tomas Blazek, Jaroslav Spacek, Zdenek Sedlak, Vaclav Prospal, Pavel Zubicek, Lukas Smital, Vyacheslav Skuta, Pavel Rajnoha, Ondrej Steiner, Radim Tesarik, Libor Prochazka

**Finland** (Esko Nokelainen, coach) GK—Petri Engman, Jussi Markkanen—Saku Koivu, Juha Lind, Kimmo Timonen, Tommi Miettinen, Jere Karalahti, Jukka Tiilikainen, Tuomas Gronman, Niko Mikkola, Teemu Kohvakka, Jonni Vauhkonen, Veli-Pekka Nutikka, Antti Aalto, Jani Hassinen, Mikko Turunen, Tom Koivisto, Jari Kauppila, Janne Nikko, Janne Niinimaa, Tommi Hamalainen, Jussi Tarvainen

**Germany** (Erich Kuhnhackl, coach) GK—Marc Seliger, Carsten Gossmann (dnp)—Stefan Ustorf, Alexander Serikow, Sven Felski, Mike Losch, Markus Krawinkel, Rudolf Gorgenlander, Marco Eltner, Stefan Mann, Thomas Knobloch, Andreas Schneider, Fabian Brannstrom, Markus Wieland, Christian Gegenfurtner, Erich Goldmann, Jochen Hecht, Rafael Jedamzik, Daniel Korber, Sven Valenti, Stephan Retzer, Patrick Solf

**Russia** (Gennadi Tsygurov, coach) GK—Yevgeni Ryabchikov, Denis Kuzmenko (dnp)—Valeri Bure, Maxim Sushinski, Oleg Tverdovski, Sergei Brylin, Alexander Kharlamov, Sergei Kondrashkin, Vadim Sharifianov, Nikolai Tsulygin, Yevgeni Babariko, Nikolai Zavarukhin, Ilya Stashenkov, Alexander Osadchi, Maxim Tsvetkov, Dmitri Podlegayev, Alexei Chikalin, Pavel Desiatkov, Maxim Smelnitski, Vasili Turkovski, Maxim Bets, Konstantin Kuzmichev

**Sweden** (Tommy Tomth, coach) GK—Peter Olsson, Jonas Forsberg (dnp)—Niklas Sundstrom, Mats Lindgren, Kenny Jonsson, Daniel Johansson, Dick Tarnstrom, Peter Strom, Johan Davidsson, Anders Soderberg, Fredrik Modin, Roger Rosen, Mathias Johansson, Anders Eriksson, Per Svartvadet, Mikael Hakansson, Peter Gerhardsson, Mattias Ohlund, Joakim Lundberg, Mattias Timander, Johan Hagman, Edvin Frylen

**Switzerland** (Arno del Curto, coach) GK—Lars Weibel, Claudio Bayer—Michel Zeiter, Patric Della Rossa, Thierry Paterlini, Pascal Sommer, Patrick Looser, Stefano Togni, Robin Bauer, Jakub Horak, Marco Kloti, Patrick Fischer, Reto Germann, Marcel Jenni, Vjeran Ivankovic, Daniel Giger, Marco Schellenberg, Jorg Reber, Jerry Zuurmond, Bruno Habisreutinger, Matthias Keller, Sven Dick

**United States** (Dean Blais, coach) GK—Aaron Ellis, Toby Kvalevog—Kevyn Adams, John Emmons, Richard Park, Bob Lachance, Kevin Hilton, David Wilkie, Jason Karmanos, Chris O'Sullivan, Jamie Langenbrunner, John Varga, Jason McBain, Deron Quint, Andy Brink, Jon Coleman, Ashlin Halfnight, Blake Sloan, Jay Pandolfo, Adam Deadmarsh, Jason Bonsignore, Ryan Sittler

## 19th U20 WORLD CHAMPIONSHIP
## December 26, 1994-January 4, 1995
## Red Deer, Canada

**Final Placing**

| | |
|---|---|
| Gold .......Canada | 5th ........United States |
| Silver .....Russia | 6th ........Czech Republic |
| Bronze ...Sweden | 7th ........Germany |
| 4th .........Finland | 8th ........Ukraine^ |

^promoted from B Pool in 1990

~no team demoted as World Junior (WM20) Championship expanded to 10 teams for 1996

**Tournament Format**

Eight teams played a round-robin within one large grouping. In the case of a tie, results of the head-to-head match was the first deciding factor, then goal differential, then goals quotient (goals for divided by goals against).

**Results & Standings**

| | GP | W | T | L | GF | GA | P |
|---|---|---|---|---|---|---|---|
| Canada | 7 | 7 | 0 | 0 | 49 | 22 | 14 |
| Russia | 7 | 5 | 0 | 2 | 36 | 24 | 10 |
| Sweden | 7 | 4 | 1 | 2 | 35 | 21 | 9 |
| Finland | 7 | 3 | 1 | 3 | 29 | 26 | 7 |
| United States | 7 | 3 | 0 | 4 | 28 | 33 | 6 |
| Czech Republic | 7 | 3 | 0 | 4 | 43 | 26 | 6 |
| Germany | 7 | 1 | 0 | 6 | 17 | 55 | 2 |
| Ukraine | 7 | 1 | 0 | 6 | 12 | 42 | 2 |

| | | | |
|---|---|---|---|
| December 26 | Red Deer | Canada 7 | Ukraine 1 |
| December 26 | Leduc | Sweden 10 | Germany 2 |
| December 26 | Spruce Grove | Czech Republic 3 | Finland 0 |
| December 26 | Innisfail | United States 4 | Russia 3 |
| December 27 | Red Deer | Canada 9 | Germany 1 |
| December 27 | Stettler | Russia 4 | Czech Republic 3 |
| December 27 | Rocky Mountain House | Finland 6 | Ukraine 2 |
| December 27 | Red Deer | Sweden 4 | United States 2 |
| December 29 | Red Deer | Canada 8 | United States 3 |
| December 29 | Red Deer | Sweden 4 | Czech Republic 3 |
| December 29 | Edmonton | Russia 4 | Ukraine 2 |
| December 29 | Wetaskiwin | Finland 7 | Germany 1 |
| December 30 | Calgary | Canada 7 | Czech Republic 5 |
| December 30 | Sherwood Park | Sweden 7 | Ukraine 1 |
| December 30 | Lacombe | Russia 8 | Germany 1 |
| December 30 | Red Deer | Finland 7 | United States 5 |
| January 1 | Edmonton | Canada 6 | Finland 4 |
| January 1 | Calgary | Russia 6 | Sweden 4 |
| January 1 | Red Deer | Czech Republic 10 | Ukraine 1 |
| January 1 | Edmonton | United States 5 | Germany 3 |
| January 2 | Red Deer | Canada 8 | Russia 5 |
| January 2 | Calgary | Sweden 3 | Finland 3 |
| January 2 | Red Deer | Czech Republic 14 | Germany 3 |
| January 2 | Camrose | Ukraine 3 | United States 2 |
| January 4 | Red Deer | Canada 4 | Sweden 3 |
| January 4 | Red Deer | Russia 6 | Finland 2 |
| January 4 | Stettler | Germany 6 | Ukraine 2 |
| January 4 | Ponoka | United States 7 | Czech Republic 5 |

**Rosters**

**Canada** (Don Hay, coach) GK—Jamie Storr, Dan Cloutier—Marty Murray, Jason Allison, Bryan McCabe, Eric Daze, Alexandre Daigle, Jeff Friesen, Ryan Smyth, Todd Harvey, Jamie Rivers, Jeff O'Neill, Wade Redden, Larry Courville, Denis Pederson, Darcy Tucker, Jason Botterill, Ed Jovanovski, Lee Sorochan, Nolan Baumgartner, Shean Donovan, Chad Allan

**Czech Republic** (Jaroslav Jagr, coach) GK—Michal Marik, Pavel Nestak—Vaclav Varada, Josef Marha, Vaclav Prospal, Jaroslav Kudrna, Zdenek Nedved, Petr Cajanek, Tomas Blazek, Marek Malik, Vlastimil Kroupa, Jan Hlavac, Petr Buzek, Milan Hejduk, Ladislav Kohn, Jan Hrdina, Marek Zidlicky, Frantisek Ptacek, Angel Nikolov, Miroslav Guren, Pavel Trnka, Petr Sykora

**Finland** (Harri Rindell, coach) GK—Jussi Markkanen, Miikka Kiprusoff—Kimmo Timonen, Veli-Pekka Nutikka, Tommi Miettinen, Jere Karalahti, Antti Aalto, Janne Niinimaa, Jussi Tarvainen, Timo Salonen, Niko Haittunen, Tommi Rajamaki, Tommi Sova, Martti Jarventie, Tommi Hamalainen, Petri Kokko, Mikko Helisten, Miika Elomo, Jani Hassinen, Toni Makiaho, Miska Kangasniemi, Juha Vuorivirta

**Germany** (Erich Kuhnhackl, coach) GK—Oliver Hausler, Stephan Lahn, Kai Fischer—Alexander Serikow, Jochen Hecht, Sven Valenti, Stefan Mann, Martin Williams, Stephan Retzer, Erich Goldmann, Markus Wieland, Lars Bruggemann, Florian Keller, Tino Boos, Hubert Buchwieser, Florian Schneider, Thorsten Fendt, Stefan Tillert, Andreas Renz, Matthias Sanger, Marco Eltner, Marco Sturm, Eric Dylla

**Russia** (Igor Dmitriev, coach) GK—Yevgeni Tarasov, Denis Kuzmenko, Dmitri Tsarev— Alexander Korolyuk, Vadim Sharifianov, Igor Meliakov, Valentin Morozov, Vitali Yachmenev, Sergei Vyshedkevich, Nikolai Zavarukhin, Ruslan Batyrshin, Alexander Kharlamov, Vadim Yepanchintsev, Sergei Gusev, Dmitri Klevakhin, Pavel Boichenko, Vladimir Chebaturkin, Anvar Gatyatulin, Ilya Vorobyov, Ramil Saifullin, Mikhail Okhotnikov, Artyom Anisimov, Alexander Boikov

**Sweden** (Tommy Tomth, coach) GK—Jonas Forsberg, Henrik Smangs—Anders Eriksson, Anders Soderberg, Niklas Sundstrom, Per Svartvadet, Johan Davidsson, Johan Finnstrom, Per-Johan Axelsson, Peter Strom, Jesper Mattsson, Fredrik Johansson, Jonas Andersson-Junkka, Dick Tarnstrom, Andreas Karlsson, Mathias Pihlstrom, Daniel Back, Mattias Ohlund, Daniel Tjarnqvist, Peter Nylander, Anders Burstrom, Kristoffer Ottosson

**Ukraine** (Viktor Chibiryev, coach) GK—Igor Karpenko, Olexander Feodorov—Oleksiy Lazarenko, Andri Kuzminsky, Igor Yankovich, Sergiy Chubenko, Boris Chursin, Roman Salnikov, Olexander Mukhanov, Oleg Tsirkunov, Sergiy Kartchenko, Sergiy Karnaukh, Oleksiy Bernatsky, Vitaliy Tretyakov, Igor Drifan, Vladislav Shevchenko, Yuriy Lyaskovsky, Dmitri Mozheiko, Andri Kurilko, Olexander Govorun, Denis Lobanovsky, Danil Didkovsky

**United States** (Jeff Jackson, coach) GK—John Grahame, Doug Bonner—Adam Deadmarsh, Richard Park, Sean Haggerty, Shawn Bates, Deron Quint, Bates Battaglia, Landon Wilson, Jason Bonsignore, Mike Crowley, Kevin Hilton, Jamie Langenbrunner, Rory Fitzpatrick, Ashlin Halfnight, Mike Grier, Chris Kelleher, Reg Berg, Dan Tompkins, Bryan Berard, Brian Lafleur, Jeff Mitchell

## 20th U20 WORLD CHAMPIONSHIP
## December 26, 1995-January 4, 1996
## Boston, United States

**Final Placing**

| | |
|---|---|
| Gold .......Canada | 6th ........Finland |
| Silver .....Sweden | 7th ........Slovakia^ |
| Bronze ...Russia | 8th ........Germany |
| 4th .........Czech Republic | 9th ........Switzerland^ |
| 5th .........United States | 10th ......Ukraine* |

^promoted from B Pool in 1995

*demoted to B Pool for 1997

**Tournament Format**

The World Junior championships changed radically for the first time for these 1996 games as ten nations were now competing instead of eight. As a result, two divisions of five teams each were created and a dynamic playoff showdown replaced the more staid round-robin format. The preliminary round still consisted of four round-robin games, with the top team in each division earning spots to the semi-finals.

The second and third place team from each division had a one game playoff to earn the other two spots, the second in one division playing the third in the other and vice versa. The semi-finals winners then played for the gold medal, and the semis losers played for the bronze. Ties in the preliminary round would be broken, as always, first by head-to-head results and then goals differential.

In addition, there was a full round-robin in the relegation round between the four teams that did not advance to the playoffs. Previous results between those nations counted, and the team that finished last (fourth) was demoted to the 'B' pool for next year's tournament.

**Results & Standings**
**PRELIMINARY ROUND**
**GROUP A**

| | GP | W | T | L | GF | GA | P |
|---|---|---|---|---|---|---|---|
| Canada | 4 | 4 | 0 | 0 | 19 | 4 | 8 |
| United States | 4 | 2 | 0 | 2 | 13 | 17 | 4 |
| Finland | 4 | 2 | 0 | 2 | 14 | 10 | 4 |
| Switzerland | 4 | 1 | 0 | 3 | 10 | 14 | 2 |
| Ukraine | 4 | 1 | 0 | 3 | 9 | 20 | 2 |

| | | | |
|---|---|---|---|
| December 26 | Worcester | Canada 6 | United States 1 |
| December 26 | Marlborough | Finland 5 | Switzerland 1 |
| December 27 | Amherst | Canada 2 | Switzerland 1 |
| December 27 | Boston | Ukraine 4 | United States 3 |
| December 28 | Boston | Finland 4 | Ukraine 1 |
| December 29 | Boston | Canada 3 | Finland 1 |
| December 29 | Springfield | United States 4 | Switzerland 3 |
| December 30 | Marlborough | Switzerland 5 | Ukraine 3 |
| December 31 | Boston | Canada 8 | Ukraine 1 |
| December 31 | Amherst | United States 5 | Finland 4 |

**GROUP B**

| | GP | W | T | L | GF | GA | P |
|---|---|---|---|---|---|---|---|
| Czech Republic | 4 | 2 | 2 | 0 | 15 | 10 | 6 |
| Russia | 4 | 2 | 1 | 1 | 19 | 12 | 5 |
| Sweden | 4 | 2 | 1 | 1 | 14 | 7 | 5 |
| Slovakia | 4 | 0 | 3 | 1 | 11 | 17 | 3 |
| Germany | 4 | 0 | 1 | 3 | 11 | 24 | 1 |

| | | | |
|---|---|---|---|
| December 26 | Amherst | Czech Republic 5 | Russia 3 |
| December 26 | Worcester | Sweden 6 | Slovakia 0 |
| December 27 | Boston | Slovakia 3 | Russia 3 |
| December 27 | Amherst | Czech Republic 6 | Germany 3 |
| December 28 | Boston | Sweden 6 | Germany 2 |
| December 29 | Boston | Czech Republic 4 | Slovakia 4 |
| December 29 | Springfield | Russia 5 | Sweden 2 |
| December 30 | Marlborough | Germany 4 | Slovakia 4 |
| December 31 | Boston | Czech Republic 0 | Sweden 0 |
| December 31 | Amherst | Russia 8 | Germany 2 |

**RELEGATION ROUND**

| | GP | W | T | L | GF | GA | P |
|---|---|---|---|---|---|---|---|
| Slovakia | 3 | 2 | 1 | 0 | 17 | 10 | 5 |
| Germany | 3 | 1 | 2 | 0 | 12 | 7 | 4 |
| Switzerland | 3 | 1 | 1 | 1 | 11 | 13 | 3 |
| Ukraine | 3 | 0 | 0 | 3 | 6 | 16 | 0 |

| | | | |
|---|---|---|---|
| January 2 | Marlborough | Germany 3 | Switzerland 3 |
| January 2 | Marlborough | Slovakia 6 | Ukraine 3 |
| January 3 | Marlborough | Slovakia 7 | Switzerland 3 |
| January 3 | Marlborough | Germany 5 | Ukraine 0 |

**5TH-PLACE GAME**

| | | | |
|---|---|---|---|
| January 4 | Marlborough | United States 8 (Jeremiah McCarthy 3:02 OT) | Finland 7 |

**PLAYOFFS**
**QUARTER-FINALS**

| | | | |
|---|---|---|---|
| January 1 | Amherst | Sweden 3 | United States 0 |
| January 1 | Amherst | Russia 6 | Finland 2 |

**SEMI-FINALS**

| | | | |
|---|---|---|---|
| January 3 | Boston | Canada 4 | Russia 3 |
| January 3 | Boston | Sweden 8 | Czech Republic 2 |

**BRONZE MEDAL GAME**

| | | | |
|---|---|---|---|
| January 4 | Chestnut Hill | Russia 4 | Czech Republic 1 |

**GOLD MEDAL GAME**

| | | | |
|---|---|---|---|
| January 4 | Chestnut Hill | Canada 4 | Sweden 1 |

**Rosters**

**Canada** (Marcel Comeau, coach) GK—Marc Denis, Jose Theodore—Jarome Iginla, Christian Dube, Daymond Langkow, Hnat Domenichelli, Alyn McCauley, Jason Podollan, Jason Botterill, Robb Gordon, Jason Holland, Mike Watt, Jamie Wright, Nolan Baumgartner, Denis Gauthier, Brad Larsen, Wade Redden, Chad Allan, Curtis Brown, Chris Phillips, Rhett Warrener, Craig Mills

**Czech Republic** (Slavomir, Lener, coach) GK—Ladislav Kudrna, Tomas Vokoun—Miroslav Guren, Robert Jindrich, Pavel Kubina, Jan Nemecek, Ales Pisa, Jiri Polak, Marek Posmyk, Pavel Rosa, Michal Bros, Milan Hejduk, Jan Hlavac, Martin Koudelka, Ondrej Kratena, Marek Melenovsky, Zdenek Skorepa, Jan Tomajko, Vaclav Varada, Marek Vorel, Jan Zurek, Josef Straka

**Finland** (Harri Rindell, coach) GK—Miikka Kiprusoff, Vesa Toskala—Martti Jarventie, Jukka Laamanen, Kimmo Lotvonen, Toni Lydman, Antti-Jussi Niemi, Pasi Petrilainen, Lauri Puolanne, Tommi Rajamaki, Miika Elomo, Tomi Hirvonen, Juho Jokinen, Tomi Kallio, Arto Kuki, Marko Makinen, Mika Puhakka, Teemu Riihijarvi, Timo Salonen, Janne Salpa, Jussi Tarvainen, Juha Vuorivirta

**Germany** (Erich Kuhnhackl, coach) GK—Kai Fischer, David Berge (dnp)—Frank Appel, Lars Bruggemann, Thorsten Fendt, Erich Goldmann, Sebastian Klenner, Andreas Renz, Thomas Vogl, Oliver Bernhardt, Markus Draxler, Jochen Hecht, Klaus Kathan, Florian Keller, Boris Lingemann, Niki Mondt, Andreas Morczinietz, Stephan Retzer, Daniel Schury, Marco Sturm, Martin Kropf, Markus Pottinger

**Russia** (Igor Dmitriev, coach) GK—Alexei Yegorov, Anton Zelenov (did not play)—Ilya Gorokhov, Mikhail Okhotnikov, Yevgeni Petroshinin, Dmitri Ryabikin, Alexei Vasilyev, Sergei Zimakov, Andrei Zyuzin, Vadim Yepanchintsev, Dmitri Klevakhin, Alexei Kolkunov, Alexander Korolyuk, Sergei Luchinkin, Igor Meliakov, Alexei Morozov, Dmitri Nabokov, Andrei Petrakov, Andrei Petrunin, Sergei Samsonov, Ruslan Shafikov, Sergei Shalamai

**Slovakia** (Julius Supler, coach) GK—Stanislav Petrik, Marcel Kuris (did not play)—Miroslav Droppa, Josef Drzik, Juraj Durco, Robert Jurcak, Richard Lintner, Daniel Socha, Radoslav Suchy, Lubomir Visnovsky, Jiri Bicek, Ivan Ciernik, Radovan Somik, Mario Kazda, Vladimir Orszagh, Juraj Stefanka, Robert Tomik, Lubomir Vaic, Rudolf Vercik, Richard Zednik, Michal Handzus, Andrei Podkonicky

**Sweden** (Harald Luckner, coach) GK—Per Ragnar Bergkvist, Magnus Nilsson—Johan Finnstrom, David Halvardsson, David Petrasek, Mattias Ohlund, Kim Johnsson, Per Anton Lundstrom, Daniel Tjarnqvist, Niklas Anger, Anders Burstrom, Johan Davidsson, Nils Ekman, Peter Hogardh, Fredrik Loven, Johan Molin, Fredrik Moller, Markus Nilson, Peter Nylander, Samuel Pahlsson, Kristoffer Ottosson, Patrik Wallenberg

**Switzerland** (Arno del Curto, coach) GK—Paolo Della Bella, Stephane Rosset—Daniel Aegertner, Fabian Guignard, Michael Kress, Philippe Marquis, Dominic Meier, Arne Ramholt, Mathias Seger, Nicolas Steiger, Mark Streit, Mattia Baldi, Andre Baumann, Sandy Jeannin, Laurent Muller, Martin Pluss, Michel Riesen, Sandro Rizzi, Frederic Rothen, Ivo Ruthemann, Reto von Arx, Christian Wohlwend

**Ukraine** (Viktor Chibirev, coach) GK—Igor Karpenko, Valeriy Seredenko—Vladislav Shevchenko, Sergiy Dechevyi, Olexander Mukhanov, Vasyl Polonitsky, Sergi Revenko, Sergi Sady, Dmitriy Tolkunov, Andri Bakunenko, Danil Didkovsky, Ruslan Fedotenko, Yuriy Gorulko, Olexander Yakovenko, Oleg Krikunenko, Oleksiy Lazarenko, Dmitri Mozheiko, Roman Salnikov, Sergiy Chubenko, Andri Voyush, Olexander Zinevich, Nikolai Yaprintsev

**United States** (Jack Parker, coach) GK—Brian Boucher, Marc Magliarditi—Bryan Berard, Chris Bogas, Ben Clymer, Jeff Kealty, Mike McBain, Jeremiah McCarthy, Tom Poti, Reg Berg, Matt Cullen, Chris Drury, Jeff Farkas, Casey Hankinson, Matt Herr, Mark Parrish, Erik Rasmussen, Marty Reasoner, Wyatt Smith, Brian Swanson, Mike Sylvia, Mike York

## 21st U20 WORLD CHAMPIONSHIP
## December 26, 1996-January 4, 1997
## Geneva/Morges, Switzerland

**Final Placing**

| | |
|---|---|
| Gold .......Canada | 6th ........Slovakia |
| Silver .....United States | 7th ........Switzerland |
| Bronze ...Russia | 8th ........Sweden |
| 4th .........Czech Republic | 9th ........Germany |
| 5th .........Finland | 10th .......Poland^* |

^promoted from B Pool in 1996
*demoted to B Pool for 1998

**Tournament Format**
With ten teams in the championships, a new format for the tournament was used (as in '96). Two divisions of five teams were created, and each country played a round-robin series in a preliminary round (four games). The top team from each division advanced to the semi-finals, and the second and third place teams played for the other two spots. The second place team from the one division played the third place team from the other, and vice versa. The two semi-finals winners then went on to play for the gold medal, and the semis losers played for the bronze.

**Results & Standings**
**PRELIMINARY ROUND**
**GROUP A**

| | GP | W | T | L | GF | GA | P |
|---|---|---|---|---|---|---|---|
| United States | 4 | 3 | 1 | 0 | 18 | 5 | 7 |
| Canada | 4 | 2 | 2 | 0 | 15 | 9 | 6 |
| Czech Republic | 4 | 1 | 2 | 1 | 13 | 8 | 4 |
| Switzerland | 4 | 1 | 1 | 2 | 8 | 11 | 3 |
| Germany | 4 | 0 | 0 | 4 | 5 | 26 | 0 |

| | | | |
|---|---|---|---|
| December 26 | Geneva | United States 4 | Switzerland 0 |
| December 26 | Morges | Czech Republic 8 | Germany 2 |
| December 27 | Geneva | Canada 4 | Germany 1 |
| December 27 | Morges | Czech Republic 1 | Switzerland 1 |
| December 28 | Geneva | Canada 4 | United States 4 |
| December 29 | Geneva | Switzerland 6 | Germany 2 |
| December 29 | Geneva | United States 2 | Czech Republic 1 |
| December 30 | Geneva | Canada 4 | Switzerland 1 |
| December 31 | Geneva | Canada 3 | Czech Republic 3 |
| December 31 | Geneva | United States 8 | Germany 0 |

**GROUP B**

| | GP | W | T | L | GF | GA | P |
|---|---|---|---|---|---|---|---|
| Russia | 4 | 3 | 1 | 0 | 20 | 5 | 7 |
| Finland | 4 | 3 | 0 | 1 | 17 | 9 | 6 |
| Slovakia | 4 | 2 | 0 | 2 | 17 | 13 | 4 |
| Sweden | 4 | 1 | 1 | 2 | 10 | 10 | 3 |
| Poland | 4 | 0 | 0 | 4 | 6 | 33 | 0 |

| | | | |
|---|---|---|---|
| December 26 | Geneva | Russia 4 | Slovakia 3 |
| December 26 | Morges | Finland 7 | Poland 0 |
| December 27 | Geneva | Slovakia 4 | Sweden 1 |
| December 27 | Morges | Russia 12 | Poland 0 |
| December 28 | Morges | Finland 4 | Sweden 2 |
| December 29 | Morges | Slovakia 7 | Poland 4 |
| December 29 | Morges | Russia 4 | Finland 2 |
| December 30 | Morges | Sweden 7 | Poland 2 |
| December 31 | Morges | Finland 4 | Slovakia 3 |
| December 31 | Morges | Sweden 0 | Russia 0 |

**RELEGATION ROUND**

| | GP | W | T | L | GF | GA | P |
|---|---|---|---|---|---|---|---|
| Switzerland | 3 | 3 | 0 | 0 | 18 | 5 | 6 |
| Sweden | 3 | 2 | 0 | 1 | 17 | 10 | 4 |
| Germany | 3 | 1 | 0 | 2 | 11 | 14 | 2 |
| Poland | 3 | 0 | 0 | 3 | 3 | 20 | 0 |

| | | | |
|---|---|---|---|
| January 2 | Morges | Switzerland 6 | Poland 1 |
| January 2 | Morges | Sweden 8 | Germany 2 |
| January 3 | Morges | Germany 7 | Poland 0 |
| January 3 | Morges | Switzerland 6 | Sweden 2 |

**5TH-PLACE GAME (MORGES)**

January 3 Finland 6 Slovakia 4

**PLAYOFFS (GENEVA)**

**QUARTER-FINALS**

January 1 Canada 7 Slovakia 2

January 1 Czech Republic 3 Finland 2 (10:00 OT/GWS—Radek Matejovski)

**SEMI-FINALS**

January 3 Canada 3 Russia 2

January 3 United States 5 Czech Republic 2

**BRONZE MEDAL GAME**

January 4 Russia 4 Czech Republic 1

**GOLD MEDAL GAME**

January 4 Canada 2 United States 0

**Rosters**

**Canada** (Mike Babcock, coach) GK—Marc Denis, Martin Biron—Brad Isbister, Christian Dube, Cameron Mann, Daniel Briere, Alyn McCauley, Boyd Devereaux, Peter Schaefer, Joe Thornton, Trevor Letowski, Richard Jackman, Jason Doig, Trent Whitfield, Brad Larsen, Chris Phillips, Hugh Hamilton, Cory Sarich, Jesse Wallin, Jeff Ware, Dwayne Hay, Shane Willis

**Czech Republic** (Vladimir Martinec, coach) GK—Adam Svoboda, Ladislav Kudrna (dnp)—Marek Melenovsky, Ondrej Kratena, Marek Zidlicky, Radek Matejovsky, Jiri Burger, Martin Spanhel, Libor Pavlis, Petr Tenkrat, Michal Horak, Radek Prochazka, Pavel Kriz, David Hruska, Kamil Piros, Ales Pisa, Marek Posmyk, Martin Richter, Petr Kadlec, Jiri Novotny, Martin Streit, Petr Mudroch

**Finland** (Hannu Jortikka, coach) GK—Vesa Toskala, Mika Noronen—Tomi Kallio, Niko Kapanen, Ville Nieminen, Olli Jokinen, Timo Vertala, Eero Somervuori, Toni Lydman, Sami-Ville Salomaa, Tomi Hirvonen, Juha Viinikainen, Santeri Heiskanen, Aki-Petteri Berg, Antti-Jussi Niemi, Esa Pirnes, Sami Salonen, Pekka Kangasalusta, Teemu Riihijarvi, Jarkko Vaananen, Illka Mikkola, Petri Isotalus

**Germany** (Erich Kuhnhackl, coach) GK—David Berge, Kai Fischer—Boris Lingemann, Niki Mondt, Sven Gerike, Klaus Kathan, Thorsten Fendt, Benjamin Hinterstocker, Thomas Dolak, Daniel Kreutzer, Jochen Hecht, Dennis Meyer, Alexander Erdmann, Thorsten Walz, Patrick Senger, Nico Pyka, Markus Pottinger, Christian Schonmoser, Michael Bakos, Sascha Goc, Nils Antons

**Poland** (Wladimir Safonov, coach) GK—Tomasz Wawrzkiewicz, Lukasz Kiedewicz—Sebastian Pajerski, Lukasz Gil, Rafal Twardy, Rafal Piekarski, Rafal Selega, Leszek Laszkiewicz, Bartolomiej Wrobel, Krzysztof Lipkowski, Maciej Radwanski, Damian Slabon, Maciej Baran, Rafal Czychowski, Pawel Zwolinski, Mariusz Trzopek, Piotr Sarnik, Robert Suchomski, Adam Borzecki, Jaroslaw Kuc, Sebastian Labus, Jaroslaw Klys

**Russia** (Pyotr Vorobyov, coach) GK—Denis Khlopotnov, Radmir Faizov—Alexei Morozov, Alexei Kolkunov, Sergei Samsonov, Andrei Petrunin, Alexander Trofimov, Roman Lyashenko, Oleg Kvasha, Vladimir Antipov, Andrei Zyuzin, Rustem Gabdulin, Konstantin Sidulov, Alexander Volchkov, Yuri Butsayev, Dmitri Vlasenkov, Andrei Markov, Ilya Gorokhov, Oleg Orekhovski, Sergei Fedotov, Alexei Vasilyev, Mikhail Donika

**Slovakia** (Frantisek Hossa, coach) GK—Martin Spillar, Stanislav Petrik—Rastislav Pavlikovsky, Lubomir Vaic, Marian Hossa, Michal Handzus, Radovan Somik, Erik Marinov, Richard Lintner, Peter Slamiar, Jiri Bicek, Juraj Durco, Ivan Ciernik, Richard Richnak, Miroslav Droppa, Pavol Rieciciar, Peter Barinka, Martin Tomas, Jozef Potac, Jan Simko, Pavol Pekarik, Peter Bartek

**Sweden** (Harald Luckner, coach) GK—Emanuel Fredriksson, Robert Borgqvist—Niklas Anger, Kristian Huselius, Johan Forsander, Marcus Nilson, Fredrik Loven, Daniel Carlsson, Timmy Pettersson, Henrik Rehnberg, Ragnar Karlsson, Per Hallberg, Per Anton Lundstrom, Linus Fagemo, Henrik Andersson, Peter Wallin, Josef Boumedienne, Patrik Wallenberg, Mikael Burakovsky, Jonas Elofsson, Per Gustafsson, David Engblom

**Switzerland** (Uli Schwarz, coach) GK—David Aebischer, Paolo Della Bella—Michel Riesen, Martin Pluss, Laurent Muller, Sandro Rizzi, Mattia Baldi, Sascha Schneider, Michel Mouther, Benjamin Winkler, Andre Baumann, Mark Streit, Mario Schocher, Mathias Seger, Bjorn Christen, Michel Fah, Rene Stussi, Jan Von Arx, Philipp Portner, Patrik Fischer, Rolf Badertscher, Stefan Grauwiler

**United States** (Jeff Jackson, coach) GK—Robert Esche, Brian Boucher—Mike York, Erik Rasmussen, Mark Parrish, Jerry Young, Marty Reasoner, Tom Poti, Joe Corvo, Jason Sessa, Jeff Farkas, Ben Clymer, Wyatt Smith, Toby Petersen, Dan LaCouture, Chris Hajt, Blake Bellefeuille, Jesse Boulerice, Dan Peters, Paul Mara, Mike McBain, Ben Simon

## 22nd U20 WORLD CHAMPIONSHIP
## December 25, 1997-January 3, 1998
## Helsinki/Hameenlinna, Finland

**Final Placing**

| | |
|---|---|
| Gold .......Finland | 6th ........Sweden |
| Silver .....Russia | 7th ........Kazakhstan^ |
| Bronze ...Switzerland | 8th ........Canada |
| 4th .........Czech Republic | 9th ........Slovakia |
| 5th .........United States | 10th ......Germany* |

^promoted from B Pool in 1997

*demoted to B Pool for 1999

**Tournament Format**

As with the previous year, a shorter round-robin allowed for quick elimination of the weakest two teams while the top eight went on to a playoffs. The two teams that didn't qualify played a two-game total goals series to determine which would be relegated to the 'B' pool for the following year. A ten-minute overtime was used for ties only in the playoffs, after which time a shootout would settle a winner.

**Results & Standings**

**PRELIMINARY ROUND**

**POOL A**

| | GP | W | T | L | GF | GA | P |
|---|---|---|---|---|---|---|---|
| Finland | 4 | 3 | 1 | 0 | 17 | 10 | 7 |
| Czech Republic | 4 | 2 | 1 | 1 | 16 | 12 | 5 |
| Sweden | 4 | 2 | 0 | 2 | 16 | 6 | 4 |
| Canada | 4 | 2 | 0 | 2 | 9 | 7 | 4 |
| Germany | 4 | 0 | 0 | 4 | 1 | 24 | 0 |

| | | | |
|---|---|---|---|
| December 25 | Helsinki | Finland 3 | Canada 2 |
| December 25 | Hameenlinna | Czech Republic 2 | Sweden 1 |
| December 26 | Helsinki | Sweden 4 | Canada 0 |
| December 26 | Hameenlinna | Finland 5 | Germany 0 |
| December 27 | Helsinki | Czech Republic 9 | Germany 1 |
| December 28 | Helsinki | Canada 5 | Czech Republic 0 |
| December 28 | Helsinki | Finland 4 | Sweden 3 |
| December 29 | Helsinki | Sweden 8 | Germany 0 |
| December 30 | Helsinki | Canada 2 | Germany 0 |
| December 30 | Helsinki | Finland 5 | Czech Republic 5 |

**POOL B**

| | GP | W | T | L | GF | GA | P |
|---|---|---|---|---|---|---|---|
| Russia | 4 | 3 | 1 | 0 | 22 | 6 | 7 |
| Switzerland | 4 | 2 | 1 | 1 | 14 | 8 | 5 |
| United States | 4 | 2 | 0 | 2 | 17 | 12 | 4 |
| Slovakia | 4 | 1 | 0 | 3 | 9 | 15 | 2 |
| Kazakhstan | 4 | 1 | 0 | 3 | 8 | 29 | 2 |

| | | | |
|---|---|---|---|
| December 25 | Hameenlinna | Russia 12 | Kazakhstan 1 |
| December 25 | Helsinki | Slovakia 6 | United States 3 |
| December 26 | Helsinki | United States 8 | Kazakhstan 2 |
| December 26 | Hameenlinna | Switzerland 3 | Slovakia 1 |
| December 27 | Helsinki | Switzerland 3 | Russia 3 |
| December 28 | Hameenlinna | Kazakhstan 5 | Slovakia 2 |
| December 28 | Hameenlinna | Russia 3 | United States 2 |
| December 29 | Hameenlinna | Switzerland 7 | Kazakhstan 0 |
| December 30 | Hameenlinna | Russia 4 | Slovakia 0 |
| December 30 | Hameenlinna | United States 4 | Switzerland 1 |

**RELEGATION ROUND (HELSINKI)**

| | | |
|---|---|---|
| January 1 | Slovakia 9 | Germany 0 |
| January 3 | Slovakia 8 | Germany 3 |

~Slovakia wins total goals series 17-3; Germany relegated to 'B' pool for 1999

**PLACEMENT ROUND (HAMEENLINNA)**

| | | |
|---|---|---|
| January 2 | United States 3 | Canada 0 |
| January 2 | Sweden 5 | Kazakhstan 1 |

**5TH-PLACE GAME**

| | | |
|---|---|---|
| January 3 | United States 4 | Sweden 3 |

**7TH-PLACE GAME**

| | | |
|---|---|---|
| January 3 | Kazakhstan 6 | Canada 3 |

**PLAYOFFS**
**QUARTER-FINALS**

| | | | |
|---|---|---|---|
| December 31 | Hameenlinna | Russia 2 (Maxim Afingenov 9:21 OT) | Canada 1 |
| December 31 | Helsinki | Finland 14 | Kazakhstan 1 |
| December 31 | Helsinki | Switzerland 2 (10:00 OT/GWS—Bjorn Christen) | Sweden 1 |
| December 31 | Hameenlinna | Czech Republic 4 | United States 1 |

**SEMI-FINALS**

| | | | |
|---|---|---|---|
| January 1 | Helsinki | Russia 5 | Czech Republic 1 |
| January 1 | Helsinki | Finland 2 | Switzerland 1 |

**BRONZE MEDAL GAME**

| | | | |
|---|---|---|---|
| January 3 | Helsinki | Switzerland 4 (10:00 OT/GWS—Sandro Rizzi) | Czech Republic 3 |

**GOLD MEDAL GAME**

| | | | |
|---|---|---|---|
| January 3 | Helsinki | Finland 2 | Russia 1 (Niklas Hagman 13:41 OT) |

**Rosters**

**Canada** (Real Paiement, coach) GK—Mathieu Garon, Roberto Luongo—Josh Holden, Daniel Tkaczuk, Alex Tanguay, Daniel Corso, Matt Cooke, Vincent Lecavalier, Brett McLean, Matt Bradley, Sean Blanchard, Eric Brewer, Brian Willsie, Jason Ward, Cory Sarich, Brad Ference, Zenith Komarniski, Steve Begin, Mike Van Ryn, Jean-Pierre Dumont, Manny Malhotra, Jesse Wallin

**Czech Republic** (Vladimir Martinec, coach) GK—Vlastimil Lakosil, Adam Svoboda—Pavel Bacho, Radek Duda, Pavel Kabrt, Ales Kotalik, Ivo Novotny, Kamil Piros, Radek Prochazka, Pavel Seliger, Patrik Stefan, Josef Straka, Petr Sykora, Martin Tomasek, Lukas Galvas, Jan Hejda, Tomas Kaberle, Petr Mudroch, Marek Posmyk, Karel Rachunek, Robert Schnabel, Pavel Skrbek

**Finland** (Hannu Kapanen, coach) GK—Niklas Backstrom, Mika Noronen—Olli Ahonen, Johannes Alanen, Toni Dahlman, Teemu Elomo, Niklas Hagman, Olli Jokinen, Kari Kalto, Niko Kapanen, Jyrki Louhi, Timo Seikkula, Eero Somervuori, Tomek Valtonen, Timo Vertala, Timo Ahmaoja, Tomi Kallarsson, Marko Kauppinen, Ilkka Mikkola, Pasi Petrilainen, Pasi Puistola, Ari Vallin

**Germany** (James Setters, coach) GK—Leonardo Conti, Bjorn Leonhardt—Nils Antons, Bjorn Barta, Boris Blank, Thomas Dolak, Robert Francz, Benjamin Hinterstocker, Daniel Kreutzer, Torsten Kunz, Niki Mondt, Andreas Morczinietz, Patrick Senger, David Sulkovski, Michael Bakos, Gordon Borberg, Sascha Goc, Christoph Jahns, Markus Jocher, Andreas Paderhuber, Markus Pottinger, Nicolai Tittus

**Kazakhstan** (Vladimir Belyayev, coach) GK—Roman Krivomazov, Vyacheslav Tregubov—Sergei Alexandrov, Nikolai Antropov, Maxim Belayev, Andrei Gavrilin, Anton Komissarov, Yevgeni Liapunov, Mikhail Medvedev, Alexander Pokladov, Vadim Rifel, Andrei Troshinski, Dmitri Upper, Georgi Xandopulo, Sergei Aksyutenko, Vitali Litvinov, Vladimir Logvin, Vitali Novopashin, Anton Petrov, Denis Shemelin, Andrei Sidorenko, Pavel Yakovlev

**Russia** (Pyotr Vorobyov, coach) GK—Denis Khlopotnov, Dmitri Mylnikov—Maxim Afinogenov, Vladimir Antipov, Denis Arkhipov, Maxim Balmochnykh, Artyom Chubarov, Alexei Krovopuskov, Oleg Kvasha, Roman Lyashenko, Sergei Shikhanov, Denis Shvidki, Dmitri Vlasenkov, Mikhail Chernov, Mikhail Donika, Andrei Markov, Valeri Pokrovski, Vitali Vishnevski, Alexei Tezikov, Andrei Sidiakin, Andrei Kruchinin, Yegor Mikhailov

**Slovakia** (Dusan Ziska, coach) GK—Martin Kucera, Martin Spillar—Karol Bartanus, Marian Cisar, Adrian Daniel, Stanislav Gron, Marian Hossa, Ladislav Nagy, Vladimir Nemec, Andrei Podkonicky, Pavol Rieciciar, Jan Simko, Andrei Szoke, Peter Bartek, Stanislav Fatyka, Peter Gallo, Boris Majesky, Martin Tomas, Marek Topoli, Miroslav Kovacik, Martin Nemcek, Ladislav Harabin

**Sweden** (Harald Luckner, coach) GK—Andreas Andersson, Johan Holmqvist—Kim Cannerheim, Johan Eriksson, Johan Forsander, Mikael Holmqvist, Kristian Huselius, Mattias Karlin, Magnus Nilsson, Marcus Nilson, Niklas Persson, Daniel Sedin, Henrik Sedin, Mikael Simons, Josef Boumedienne, Jonas Elofsson, Per Hallberg, Pierre Hedin, Henrik Petre, Jan Sandstrom, Andreas Westlund, Henrik Tallinder

**Switzerland** (Bill Gilligan, coach) GK—David Aebischer, Marco Buhrer—Alex Chatelain, Bjorn Christen, Flavien Conne, Sven Lindemann, Michel Mouther, Laurent Muller, Marc Reichert, Michel Riesen, Sandro Rizzi, Mario Schocher, Rene Stussi, Adrian Wichser, Thomas Ziegler, Jan von Arx, Ralph Bundi, Patrick Fischer, Julien Vauclair, Marc Werlen, Markus Wuthrich, Alain Reist

**United States** (Jeff Jackson, coach) GK—Robert Esche, Jean-Marc Pelletier—Jesse Boulerice, Kevin Colley, Joe Dusbabek, Jeff Farkas, Brian Gionta, Scott Gomez, Dustin Kuk, David Legwand, Aaron Miskovich, Toby Petersen, Ben Simon, Mike York, Chris Hajt, Kevin Kellett, Jay Leach, Paul Mara, Mike Mottau, Chris St. Croix, Nikos Tselios, Ty Jones

## 23rd U20 WORLD CHAMPIONSHIP
## December 26, 1998-January 5, 1999
## Winnipeg, Canada

**Final Placing**

| | |
|---|---|
| Gold .......Russia | 6th ........Kazakhstan |
| Silver .....Canada | 7th ........Czech Republic |
| Bronze ...Slovakia | 8th ........United States |
| 4th .........Sweden | 9th ........Switzerland |
| 5th .........Finland | 10th ......Belarus^* |

^promoted from B Pool in 1998
*demoted to B Pool for 2000

**Tournament Format**
Two divisions of five teams were created, and each country played a round-robin series in a preliminary round (four games). The top team from each division advanced to the semi-finals, and the second and third place teams played for the other two spots. The second place team from the one division played the third place team from the other, and vice versa. The two semi-finals winners then went on to play for the gold medal, and the semis losers played for the bronze. The bottom four teams were placed in a consolation round pool to determine which two countries remained in the top pool the next year and which two were demoted.

**Results & Standings**
**PRELIMINARY ROUND**
**GROUP A**

| | GP | W | T | L | GF | GA | P |
|---|---|---|---|---|---|---|---|
| Slovakia | 4 | 3 | 1 | 0 | 10 | 7 | 7 |
| Canada | 4 | 2 | 1 | 1 | 10 | 9 | 5 |
| Finland | 4 | 2 | 0 | 2 | 17 | 16 | 4 |
| Czech Republic | 4 | 1 | 0 | 3 | 11 | 12 | 2 |
| United States | 4 | 1 | 0 | 3 | 13 | 17 | 2 |

| | | | |
|---|---|---|---|
| December 26 | Brandon | Slovakia 3 | Czech Republic 2 |
| December 26 | Winnipeg | Finland 6 | United States 3 |
| December 27 | Brandon | Canada 0 | Slovakia 0 |
| December 28 | Winnipeg | Canada 6 | Finland 4 |
| December 28 | Brandon | Czech Republic 6 | United States 3 |
| December 29 | Winnipeg | Slovakia 4 | Finland 3 |
| December 30 | Winnipeg | Canada 2 | Czech Republic 0 |
| December 30 | Selkirk | Slovakia 3 | United States 2 |
| December 31 | Winnipeg | United States 5 | Canada 2 |
| December 31 | Selkirk | Finland 4 | Czech Republic 3 |

**GROUP B**

| | GP | W | T | L | GF | GA | P |
|---|---|---|---|---|---|---|---|
| Sweden | 4 | 4 | 0 | 0 | 25 | 11 | 8 |
| Russia | 4 | 3 | 0 | 1 | 25 | 4 | 6 |
| Kazakhstan | 4 | 1 | 1 | 2 | 9 | 20 | 3 |
| Switzerland | 4 | 1 | 0 | 3 | 5 | 17 | 2 |
| Belarus | 4 | 0 | 1 | 3 | 9 | 21 | 1 |

| | | | |
|---|---|---|---|
| December 26 | Winnipeg | Sweden 4 | Russia 2 |
| December 26 | Selkirk | Switzerland 4 | Belarus 3 |
| December 27 | Portage | Kazakhstan 2 | Belarus 2 |
| December 28 | Winnipeg | Sweden 5 | Switzerland 1 |
| December 28 | Portage | Russia 7 | Kazakhstan 0 |
| December 29 | Brandon | Russia 10 | Belarus 0 |
| December 30 | Brandon | Kazakhstan 3 | Switzerland 0 |
| December 30 | Morden | Sweden 5 | Belarus 4 |
| December 31 | Brandon | Russia 6 | Switzerland 0 |
| December 31 | Teulon | Sweden 11 | Kazakhstan 4 |

**RELEGATION ROUND**

| | GP | W | T | L | GF | GA | P |
|---|---|---|---|---|---|---|---|
| Czech Republic | 3 | 3 | 0 | 0 | 21 | 9 | 6 |
| United States | 3 | 2 | 0 | 1 | 15 | 12 | 4 |
| Switzerland | 3 | 1 | 0 | 2 | 12 | 13 | 2 |
| Belarus | 3 | 0 | 0 | 3 | 7 | 21 | 0 |

| | | | |
|---|---|---|---|
| January 3 | Winnipeg | Czech Republic 10 | Belarus 2 |
| January 3 | Portage | United States 5 | Switzerland 4 |
| January 4 | Morden | Czech Republic 5 | Switzerland 4 |
| January 4 | Selkirk | United States 7 | Belarus 2 |

**5TH-PLACE GAME**

| | | | |
|---|---|---|---|
| January 4 | Brandon | Finland 6 | Kazakhstan 1 |

**PLAYOFFS (WINNIPEG)**
**QUARTER-FINALS**

| | | |
|---|---|---|
| January 2 | Canada 12 | Kazakhstan 2 |
| January 2 | Russia 3 | Finland 2 (Denis Arkhipov 7:33 OT) |

**SEMI-FINALS**

| | | |
|---|---|---|
| January 4 | Canada 6 | Sweden 1 |
| January 4 | Russia 3 | Slovakia 2 |

**BRONZE MEDAL GAME**

| | | |
|---|---|---|
| January 5 | Slovakia 5 | Sweden 4 |

**GOLD MEDAL GAME**

| | | |
|---|---|---|
| January 5 | Russia 3 | Canada 2 (Artyom Chubarov 5:13 OT) |

**Rosters**

**Belarus** (Mikhail Zakharov, coach) GK—Vitali Arystov, Andrei Frolov—Nikolai Vasyukovich, Alexei Andreyev, Vadim Novitski, Denis Grigortsevich, Pavel Bely, Anton Pulver, Yevgeni Kurylin, Viktor Kastsyuchonok, Vasili Rytvinski, Andrei Maroz, Pavel Valchok, Maxim Slysh, Alexander Poliukh, Ilya Bubenshikov, Sergei Paklin, Yevgeni Kryvamaz, Yegor Tsurikov, Andrei Shevelev, Konstantin Koltsov, Andrei Ovsyanikov

**Canada** (Tom Renney, coach) GK—Roberto Luongo, Brian Finley—Brad Ference, Mike Van Ryn, Kyle Calder, Brad Stuart, Rico Fata, Daniel Tkaczuk, Simon Gagne, Brian Campbell, Adam Mair, Harold Druken, Blair Betts, Jason Chimera, Robyn Regehr, Jason Ward, Andrew Ference, Bryan Allen, Tyler Bouck, Brenden Morrow, Brad Leeb, Kent McDonnell

**Czech Republic** (Vladimir Martinec, coach) GK—Vlastimil Lakosil, Filip Sindelar (dnp)—Petr Svoboda, Martin Lamich, Daniel Seman, Petr Caslava, Mario Cartelli, Jan Horacek, Tomas Divisek, Martin Ambruz, Jaroslav Balastik, Lukas Galvas, Petr Mika, Michal Travnicek, Tomas Zizka, Jan Kopecky, Jakub Kraus, Petr Vala, Michal Sivek, Frantisek Mrazek, Vaclav Pletka, Karel Rachunek

**Finland** (Jukka Rautakorpi, coach) GK—Mika Lehto, Mika Noronen—Juha Gustafsson, Ossi Vaananen, Marko Kauppinen, Mikko Jokela, Niklas Hagman, Tommi Santala, Olli Ahonen, Teemu Elomo, Jani Vaananen, Miikka Mannikko, Eero Somervuori, Riku Hahl, Markus Kankaanpera, Tomek Valtonen, Arto Laatikainen, Jani Rita, Teemu Virkkunen, Timo Koskela, Ilkka Mikkola, Marco Tuokko

**Kazakhstan** (Vasili Vasilchenko, coach) GK—Alexander Kolyuzhny, Vitali Kolesnik—Pavel Yakovlev, Vladimir Logvin, Yevgeni Ivanov, Alexei Litvinenko, Roman Rylski, Oleg Yeremeyev, Maxim Belayev, Yevgeni Blokhin, Yevgeni Petrukhin, Nikolai Zarzhitski, Sergei Miroshnichenko, Fyodor Polischuk, Sergei Chebotarevski, Nikolai Antropov, Mikhail Medvedev, Rustam Yesirkenov, Alexei Rodionov, Vadim Rifel, Ivan Tuyembayev

**Russia** (Gennadi Tsygurov, coach) GK—Yuri Gerasimov, Alexei Volkov—Mikhail Donika, Maxim Maslenikov, Dmitri Kokorev, Vitali Vishnevski, Kirill Safronov, Konstantin Gusev, Denis Shvidky, Andrei Nikitenko, Alexander Ryazantsev, Sergei Verenikin, Yuri Dobryshkin, Alexander Zevakhin, Roman Lyashenko, Artyom Chubarov, Piotr Schastlivy, Denis Arkhipov, Artyom Mariams, Dmitri Kirilenko, Maxim Balmochnykh, Maxim Afinogenov

**Slovakia** (Jan Filc, coach) GK—Jan Lasak, Karol Krizan (did not play)—Ladislav Harabin, Branislav Mezei, Miroslav Zalesak, Marek Priechodsky, Peter Smrek, Peter Podhradsky, Tomas Nadasdi, Peter Sejna, Marian Gaborik, Michal Hudec, Zoltan Batovsky, Martin Cakajik, Martin Cibak, Martin Bartek, Martin Hujsa, Lubomir Pistek, Roman Macoszek, Michal Kosik, Juraj Slovak, Istvan Nagy

**Sweden** (Mats Hallin, coach) GK—Andreas Andersson, Johan Asplund—Christian Backman, Sanny Lindstrom, Johan Halvardsson, Karl Helmersson, Henrik Melinder, Viktor Wallin, Daniel Sedin, David Ytfeldt, Gabriel Karlsson, Per Hallin, Mathias Tjarnqvist, Mattias Weinhandl, Christian Berglund, Henrik Sedin, Niklas Persson, Marcus Kristoffersson, Jimmie Olvestad, Henrik Tallinder, Mattias Karlin, Jakob Johansson

**Switzerland** (John Slettvoll, coach) GK—Marco Buhrer, Oliver Wissmann (dnp)—Michel Riesen, Adrian Wichser, Flavien Conne, Alain Demuth, Philipp Folghera, Goran Bezina, Marc Reichert, Julien Vauclair, Jan Cadieux, Luca Cereda, Roland Kaser, David Jobin, Alexis Vacheron, Fabio Beccarelli, Cornel Prinz, Alain Reist, Gregor Thommen, Bjorn Christen, Pascal Muller, Sandro Tschuor

**United States** (Jeff Jackson, coach) GK—Joe Blackburn, Chris Madden—Nikos Tselios, Jordan Leopold, Jeff Jillson, Chris St. Croix, Tim Connolly, David Legwand, Scott Gomez, Matt Doman, Mike Vigilante, Justin Morrison, Adam Hall, Andy Hilbert, Dan Carlson, David Tanabe, Doug Janik, Mike Pandolfo, Brian Gionta, Ryan Murphy, Barrett Heisten, Paul Mara

## 24th U20 WORLD CHAMPIONSHIP
## December 25, 1999-January 4, 2000
## Skelleftea/Umea, Sweden

**Final Placing**

| | |
|---|---|
| Gold .......Czech Republic | 6th ........Switzerland |
| Silver .....Russia | 7th ........Finland |
| Bronze ...Canada | 8th ........Kazakhstan |
| 4th .........United States | 9th ........Slovakia |
| 5th .........Sweden | 10th ......Ukraine^* |

^promoted from B Pool in 1999
*demoted to Division I for 2001

**Tournament Format**

Two divisions of five teams were created, and each country played a round-robin series in a preliminary round (four games). The top four teams advanced to the quarter-finals, first place playing fourth and second playing third in crossover games. The two semi-finals winners then went on to play for the gold medal, and the semis losers played for the bronze.

**Results & Standings**
**PRELIMINARY ROUND**
**GROUP A (SKELLEFTEA)**

| | GP | W | T | L | GF | GA | P |
|---|---|---|---|---|---|---|---|
| Czech Republic | 4 | 2 | 2 | 0 | 12 | 7 | 6 |
| Canada | 4 | 2 | 2 | 0 | 9 | 5 | 6 |
| United States | 4 | 1 | 2 | 1 | 5 | 6 | 4 |
| Finland | 4 | 1 | 1 | 2 | 8 | 9 | 3 |
| Slovakia | 4 | 0 | 1 | 3 | 4 | 11 | 1 |

| | | |
|---|---|---|
| December 25 | Canada 3 | Finland 2 |
| December 25 | Czech Republic 5 | Slovakia 2 |
| December 26 | Slovakia 1 | Finland 1 |
| December 26 | Czech Republic 2 | United States 2 |
| December 28 | Canada 1 | Czech Republic 1 |
| December 28 | United States 1 | Slovakia 0 |
| December 29 | Canada 4 | Slovakia 1 |
| December 29 | Finland 3 | United States 1 |
| December 31 | Canada 1 | United States 1 |
| December 31 | Czech Republic 4 | Finland 2 |

**GROUP B (UMEA)**

| | GP | W | T | L | GF | GA | P |
|---|---|---|---|---|---|---|---|
| Russia | 4 | 4 | 0 | 0 | 30 | 4 | 8 |
| Sweden | 4 | 3 | 0 | 1 | 27 | 8 | 6 |
| Switzerland | 4 | 2 | 0 | 2 | 13 | 16 | 4 |
| Kazakhstan | 4 | 1 | 0 | 3 | 7 | 34 | 2 |
| Ukraine | 4 | 0 | 0 | 4 | 6 | 21 | 0 |

| | | |
|---|---|---|
| December 25 | Switzerland 6 | Ukraine 2 |
| December 25 | Russia 14 | Kazakhstan 1 |
| December 26 | Sweden 7 | Switzerland 1 |
| December 26 | Russia 4 | Ukraine 1 |
| December 28 | Switzerland 5 | Kazakhstan 0 |
| December 28 | Sweden 6 | Ukraine 1 |
| December 29 | Kazakhstan 5 | Ukraine 2 |
| December 29 | Russia 5 | Sweden 1 |
| December 31 | Sweden 13 | Kazakhstan 1 |
| December 31 | Russia 7 | Switzerland 1 |

**PLACEMENT ROUND (UMEA)**

| | | |
|---|---|---|
| January 3 | Switzerland 5 | Finland 2 |
| January 3 | Sweden 12 | Kazakhstan 2 |

**5TH-PLACE GAME**

| | | |
|---|---|---|
| January 4 | Sweden 5 | Switzerland 2 |

**7TH-PLACE GAME**

| | | |
|---|---|---|
| January 4 | Finland 9 | Kazakhstan 1 |

**RELEGATION ROUND (BEST-OF-TWO PLUS OT/GWS)**

| | | | |
|---|---|---|---|
| January 2 | Umea | Ukraine 3 | Slovakia 1 |
| January 4 | Umea | Slovakia 5 | Ukraine 1 |

~Slovakia won game two, 4-1, to force overtime—10:00 OT/GWS—Miroslav Zalesak (SVK)

**PLAYOFFS**
**QUARTER-FINALS**

| | | | |
|---|---|---|---|
| January 1 | Skelleftea | Canada 8 | Switzerland 3 |
| January 1 | Skelleftea | Czech Republic 6 | Kazakhstan 3 |
| January 1 | Umea | United States 5 | Sweden 1 |
| January 1 | Umea | Russia 4 | Finland 0 |

**SEMI-FINALS**

| | | | |
|---|---|---|---|
| January 3 | Skelleftea | Russia 3 | Canada 2 |
| January 3 | Skelleftea | Czech Republic 4 | United States 1 |

**BRONZE MEDAL GAME**

| | | | |
|---|---|---|---|
| January 4 | Skelleftea | Canada 4 | United States 3 |
| | | (10:00 OT/GWS—Brandon Reid) | |

**GOLD MEDAL GAME**

| | | | |
|---|---|---|---|
| January 4 | Skelleftea | Czech Republic 1 | Russia 0 |
| | | (10:00 OT/GWS—Libor Pivko) | |

**Rosters**

**Canada** (Claude Julien, coach) GK—Maxime Ouellet, Brian Finley—Brandon Reid, Jamie Lundmark, Matt Pettinger, Dany Heatley, Michael Ryder, Chris Nielsen, Eric Chouinard, Tyler Bouck, Mark Bell, Brad Richards, Manny Malhotra, Jason Spezza, Steve McCarthy, Mike Ribeiro, Barret Jackman, Kyle Rossiter, Mathieu Biron, Joe Rullier, Jay Bouwmeester, Matt Kinch

**Czech Republic** (Jaroslav Holik, coach) GK—Zdenek Smid, Tomas Duba—Petr Svoboda, David Hajek, Jiri David, Josef Jindra, Zdenek Kutlak, Martin Holy, Tomas Horna, Angel Krstev, Milan Kraft, Martin Havlat, Zbynek Irgl, Vladimir Novak, Vaclav Nedorost, Jan Sochor, Josef Vasicek, Jaroslav Kristek, Michal Sivek, Jaroslav Svoboda, Libor Pivko, Jan Bohac

**Finland** (Hannu Kapanen, coach) GK—Antero Niittymaki, Ari Ahonen—Arto Tukio, Tapio Sammalkangas, Mikko Jokela, Tuukka Mantyla, Ossi Vaananen, Arto Laatikainen, Ville Hamalainen, Teemu Normio, Teemu Laine, Jari Viuhkola, Mikko Kaukokari, Markus Kankaanpera, Jani Vaananen, Tomek Valtonen, Antti Miettinen, Jani Rita, Miika Lindholm, Riku Hahl, Marko Ahosilta, Topi Riutta

**Kazakhstan** (Vasili Vasilchenko, coach) GK—Yevgeni Cherepanov, Alexander Kolyuzhny—Roman Rylski, Yevgeni Ivanov, Vladimir Logvin, Alexei Litvinenko, Pavel Yakovlev, Alexei Vasilchenko, Pavel Serdyukov, Mikhail Yuryev, Yevgeni Tanygin, Sergei Chebotarevski, Yevgeni Petrukhin, Roman Azanov, Alexander Golts, Yevgeni Mazunin, Alexander Krevsun, Vadim Sozinov, Rustam Yesirkenov, Alexei Rodionov, Inar Uteyev, Ivan Tuyembayev

**Russia** (Pyotr Vorobyov, coach) GK—Ilya Bryzgalov, Alexei Volkov—Alexander Lyubimov, Mikhail Balandin, Igor Shadilov, Kirill Safronov, Denis Denisov, Valeri Khlebnikov, Artyom Mariams, Denis Shvidky, Oleg Smirnov, Sergei Zinoviev, Yevgeni Muratov, Alexander Zevakhin, Anton But, Yevgeni Fyodorov, Dmitri Afanasenkov, Alexander Ryazantsev, Andrei Esipov, Yevgeni Lapin, Alexei Tereshenko, Pavel Duma

**Slovakia** (Dusan Ziska, coach) GK—Rastislav Stana, Karol Krizan—Ladislav Harabin, Marek Kolba, Dusan Devecka, Vladimir Urban, Branislav Mezei, Kristian Kudroc, Tomas Starosta, Rene Vydareny, Branko Radivojevic, Jozef Mrina, Lubomir Pistek, Miroslav Zalesak, Marcel Hossa, Martin Cibak, Tomas Kopecky, Marian Gaborik, Roman Kukumberg, Juraj Kolnik, Milan Bartovic, Tomas Surovy

**Sweden** (Lars Molin, coach) GK—Jonas Fransson, Johan Asplund—Peter Messa, Herman Hultgren, Niklas Kronwall, Erik Lewerstrom, Christian Backman, Viktor Wallin, Henrik Zetterberg, Daniel Sedin, Kenneth Bergqvist, Gabriel Karlsson, Per Hallin, Christian Berglund, Henrik Sedin, Bjorn Melin, Magnus Hedlund, Tony Martensson, Jonas Frogren, Jimmie Olvestad, David Nystrom, Rickard Wallin

**Switzerland** (Jakob Kolliker, coach) GK—Simon Zuger, Pasqual Sievert—Timo Helbling, Flavien Conne, Mathias Wust, David Jobin, Reto Kobach, Martin Hohener, Marc Heberlein, Goran Bezina, Fabian Stephan, Luca Cereda, Bjorn Christen, Marc Reichert, Paolo Duca, Marcel Sommer, Stefan Niggli, Loic Burkhalter, Andre Bielmann, Sven Helfenstein, Silvan Lussy, Adrian Wichser

**Ukraine** (Olexander Kulikov, coach) GK—Vadym Seliverstov, Vitaliy Lebed—Denis Isayenko, Yevgeni Pysarenko, Yevgeni Yemelyanenko, Sergiy Mudryi, Olexander Skorokhod, Yevgeni Sydorov, Olexander Pobyedonostsev, Vasyl Gorbenko, Artyom Bondarev, Olexander Khmyl, Andri Butochnov, Oleg Shafarenko, Olexander Panchenko, Artyom Hnidenko, Dmitriy Yudenko, Pavlo Shtefan, Roman Sherbatyuk, Olexander Yanchenko, Denis Zabludovsky, Olexander Materukhin

**United States** (Jeff Jackson, coach) GK—Rick DiPietro, Phillipe Sauve—Ron Hainsey, Brooks Orpik, Jordan Leopold, Pat Aufiero, Jeff Jillson, Willie Levesque, Brad Winchester, Connor Dunlop, Mike Stuart, Brett Henning, Dan Cavanaugh, John Sabo, Adam Hall, Andy Hilbert, David Inman, Doug Janik, Jeff Taffe, Pat Foley, Brett Nowak, Barrett Heisten

## 25th U20 WORLD CHAMPIONSHIP
## December 26, 2000-January 5, 2001
## Moscow/Podolsk, Russia

**Final Placing**

| | |
|---|---|
| Gold .......Czech Republic | 6th ........Switzerland |
| Silver .....Finland | 7th ........Russia |
| Bronze ...Canada | 8th ........Slovakia |
| 4th .........Sweden | 9th ........Belarus^ |
| 5th .........United States | 10th ......Kazakhstan* |

^promoted from B Pool in 2000
*demoted to Division I for 2002

**Tournament Format**

Two divisions of five teams were created, and each country played a round-robin series in a preliminary round (four games). The top four teams advanced to the quarter-finals, first place playing fourth and second playing third in crossover games. The two semi-finals winners then went on to play for the gold medal, and the semis losers played for the bronze.

**Results & Standings**

**PRELIMINARY ROUND**

**GROUP A**

| | GP | W | T | L | GF | GA | P |
|---|---|---|---|---|---|---|---|
| Czech Republic | 4 | 4 | 0 | 0 | 20 | 4 | 8 |
| United States | 4 | 3 | 0 | 1 | 21 | 8 | 6 |
| Sweden | 4 | 2 | 0 | 2 | 13 | 8 | 4 |
| Slovakia | 4 | 1 | 0 | 3 | 10 | 15 | 2 |
| Kazakhstan | 4 | 0 | 0 | 4 | 4 | 33 | 0 |

| | | | |
|---|---|---|---|
| December 26 | Moscow | United States 9 | Kazakhstan 1 |
| December 26 | Moscow | Czech Republic 2 | Sweden 1 |
| December 27 | Moscow | Czech Republic 9 | Kazakhstan 1 |
| December 27 | Moscow | Sweden 3 | Slovakia 1 |
| December 28 | Moscow | United States 7 | Slovakia 2 |
| December 29 | Moscow | Czech Republic 4 | United States 2 |
| December 29 | Podolsk | Sweden 8 | Kazakhstan 2 |
| December 30 | Moscow | Slovakia 7 | Kazakhstan 0 |
| December 31 | Moscow | Czech Republic 5 | Slovakia 0 |
| December 31 | Moscow | United States 3 | Sweden 1 |

**GROUP B**

| | GP | W | T | L | GF | GA | P |
|---|---|---|---|---|---|---|---|
| Finland | 4 | 3 | 1 | 0 | 13 | 5 | 7 |
| Russia | 4 | 2 | 1 | 1 | 19 | 8 | 5 |
| Canada | 4 | 2 | 1 | 1 | 20 | 9 | 5 |
| Switzerland | 4 | 1 | 1 | 2 | 12 | 15 | 3 |
| Belarus | 4 | 0 | 0 | 4 | 2 | 29 | 0 |

| | | | |
|---|---|---|---|
| December 26 | Moscow | Canada 9 | Belarus 0 |
| December 26 | Moscow | Switzerland 3 | Russia 3 |
| December 27 | Moscow | Finland 3 | Switzerland 2 |
| December 27 | Podolsk | Russia 12 | Belarus 1 |
| December 28 | Moscow | Canada 2 | Finland 2 |
| December 29 | Moscow | Russia 3 | Canada 1 |
| December 29 | Moscow | Switzerland 3 | Belarus 1 |
| December 30 | Moscow | Finland 5 | Belarus 0 |
| December 31 | Moscow | Canada 8 | Switzerland 4 |
| December 31 | Moscow | Finland 3 | Russia 1 |

**PLACEMENT ROUND (MOSCOW)**

| | | |
|---|---|---|
| January 3 | Switzerland 3 | Russia 2 |
| January 3 | United States 3 | Slovakia 2 |

**5TH-PLACE GAME**

| | | |
|---|---|---|
| January 5 | United States 4 | Switzerland 0 |

**7TH-PLACE GAME**

| | | |
|---|---|---|
| January 5 | Russia 4 | Slovakia 3 (10:00 OT/GWS—Andrei Sheler) |

**RELEGATION ROUND (BEST-OF-TWO)**

| | | | |
|---|---|---|---|
| January 2 | Podolsk | Belarus 5 | Kazakhstan 2 |
| January 3 | Podolsk | Belarus 5 | Kazakhstan 5 |

**PLAYOFFS (MOSCOW)**

**QUARTER-FINALS**

| | | |
|---|---|---|
| January 2 | Canada 2 | United States 1 |
| January 2 | Czech Republic 4 | Switzerland 3 |
| January 2 | Finland 3 | Slovakia 1 |
| January 2 | Sweden 3 | Russia 2 |

**SEMI-FINALS**

| | | |
|---|---|---|
| January 3 | Finland 5 | Canada 2 |
| January 3 | Czech Republic 1 | Sweden 0 |

**BRONZE MEDAL GAME**

| | | |
|---|---|---|
| January 5 | Canada 2 | Sweden 1 (Raffi Torres 0:37 OT) |

**GOLD MEDAL GAME**

| | | |
|---|---|---|
| January 5 | Czech Republic 2 | Finland 1 |

**Rosters**

**Belarus** (Vladimir Melenchuk, coach) GK—Dmitri Pashelyuk, Vitali Arystov—Valentin Ebert, Andrei Bashko, Ruslan Sharapa, Maxim Shymanski, Andrei Tsikhan, Yaroslav Chuprys, Andrei Maroz, Alexander Kulakov, Mikhail Klimin, Konstantin Nemirka, Dmitri Douben, Artyom Siankevich, Dmitri Mialeshka, Vitali Klimiankov, Konstantin Zakharov, Andrei Kostitsyn, Sergei Paklin, Yevgeni Makarov, Andrei Skrypailiov, Konstantin Koltsov

**Canada** (Stan Butler, coach) GK—Maxime Ouellet, Alexander Auld—Jamie Lundmark, Mike Cammalleri, Jason Spezza, Dany Heatley, Raffi Torres, Mike Zigomanis, Brad Boyes, Brandon Reid, Steve Ott, Derek Mackenzie, Barret Jackman, Steve McCarthy, Jay Bouwmeester, Mark Popovic, Jarret Stoll, Jason Jaspers, Dave Morisset, Dan Hamhuis, Jay Harrison, Nick Schultz

**Czech Republic** (Jaroslav Holik, coach) GK—Tomas Duba, Lukas Cucela—Libor Ustrnul, David Pojkar, Jakub Grof, Jan Vytisk, David Nosek, Jakub Cutta, Patrik Moskal, Ivan Rachunek, Zdenek Blatny, Jan Choteborsky, Tomas Plekanec, Marek Tomica, Rostislav Klesla, Ladislav Vlcek, Vaclav Nedorost, Pavel Brendl, Martin Erat, Lukas Havel, Michal Sivek, Radim Vrbata

**Finland** (Kari Jalonen, coach) GK—Kari Lehtonen, Ari Ahonen—Markku Paukkunen, Harri Tikkanen, Lasse Kukkonen, Janne Niskala, Tuukka Mantyla, Mikko Koivu, Ville Hamalainen, Sami Venalainen, Miro Laitinen, Toni Mustonen, Juha-Pekka Hytonen, Toni Koivisto, Tuomas Pihlman, Tony Salmelainen, Teemu Sainomaa, Olli Malmivaara, Tero Maatta, Jani Rita, Jouni Kulonen, Tuomo Ruutu

**Kazakhstan** (Sergey Starygin, coach) GK—Roman Medvedev, Alexander Kolyuzhny—Alexei Vasilchenko, Yevgeni Fadeyev, Dmitri Babich, Konstantin Vasilyev, Sergei Litvinov, Roman Kozlov, Alexander Semyonov, Anatoli Fokin, Pavel Serdyukov, Roman Azanov, Mikhail Yuryev, Yevgeni Mazunin, Vadim Sozinov, Andrei Ogorodnikov, Yevgeni Tanygin, Pavel Filipenko, Sergei Korobeinikov, Viktor Alexandrov, Andrei Spiridonov, Denis Falfudinov

**Russia** (Pyotr Vorobyov, coach) GK—Andrei Medvedev, Alexei Petrov—Rail Rozakov, Anton Volchenkov, Denis Grebeshkov, Andrei Shefer, Denis Denisov, Pavel Duma, Alexander Seluyanov, Vladislav Korneyev, Ivan Nepryayev, Yevgeni Muratov, Alexander Buturlin, Alexander Svitov, Ilya Kovalchuk, Pavel Vorobyov, Alexander Shagodayev, Yegor Shastin, Stanislav Chistov, Mikhail Yakubov, Artyom Chernov, Alexander Barkunov

**Slovakia** (Jan Selvek, coach) GK—Lubomir Pisar, Peter Budaj—Ladislav Gabris, Tomas Slovak, Alexander Valentin, Peter Szabo, Milan Bartovic, Jozef Balej, Roman Tvrdon, Tomas Starosta, Lukas Hvila, Tomas Surovy, Miroslav Kristin, Martin Drotar, Marcel Hossa, Tomas Kopecky, Tomas Malec, Tomas Skvaridlo, Miroslav Durak, Milan Dubec, Lubos Velebny, Rene Vydareny

**Sweden** (Bo Lennartsson, coach) GK—Henrik Lundqvist, Jimmy Danielsson—Daniel Josefsson, Niklas Kronwall, David Johansson, Andreas Holmqvist, Jonas Nordqvist, Martin Samuelsson, Johan Reineck, Par Backer, Jari Tolsa, Fredrik Sundin, Daniel Ljungkvist, Mattias Wennerberg, Mathias Mansson, Bjorn Melin, Magnus Hedlund, Jonas Andersson, Fredrik Sjostrom, Jonas Lennartsson, Daniel Widing, Tim Eriksson

**Switzerland** (Jakob Kolliker, coach) GK—Pasqual Sievert, Martin Zerzuben—Beat Gerber, Timo Helbling, Severin Blindenbacher, David Jobin, Thibaut Monnet, Steve Hirschi, Marc Heberlein, Fabian Sutter, Beat Forster, Claudio Neff, Fabian Stephan, Patrick Aeberli, Stefan Niggli, Paolo Duca, Andreas Camenzind, Sebastien Reuille, Thomas Nussli, Duri Camichel, Sven Helfenstein, Vitali Lakhmatov

**United States** (Keith Allain, coach) GK—Craig Kowalski, Rick DiPietro—Ron Hainsey, Tim Gleason, Justin Forrest, Mike Komisarek, David Hale, Connor Dunlop, Marc Cavosie, John Sabo, Kris Vernarsky, David Steckel, Damian Surma, Rob Globke, Andy Hilbert, R.J. Umberger, Troy Riddle, Jeff Taffe, Jon Disalvatore, Paul Martin, Freddy Mcycr, Brett Nowak

## 26th U20 WORLD CHAMPIONSHIP
## December 25, 2001-January 4, 2002
## Pardubice/Hradec Kralove, Czech Republic

### Final Placing

| | | | |
|---|---|---|---|
| Gold | Russia | 6th | Sweden |
| Silver | Canada | 7th | Czech Republic |
| Bronze | Finland | 8th | Slovakia |
| 4th | Switzerland | 9th | Belarus |
| 5th | United States | 10th | France^* |

^promoted from Division I in 2001
*demoted to Division I for 2003

### Tournament Format

Two divisions of five teams were created, and each country played a round-robin series in a preliminary round (four games). The top four teams advanced to the quarter-finals, first place playing fourth and second playing third in crossover games. The two semi-finals winners then went on to play for the gold medal, and the semis losers played for the bronze.

### Results & Standings
**PRELIMINARY ROUND**
**GROUP A (PARDUBICE)**

| | GP | W | T | L | GF | GA | P |
|---|---|---|---|---|---|---|---|
| Slovakia | 4 | 2 | 2 | 0 | 14 | 7 | 6 |
| United States | 4 | 2 | 2 | 0 | 14 | 9 | 6 |
| Sweden | 4 | 2 | 2 | 0 | 11 | 5 | 6 |
| Czech Republic | 4 | 1 | 0 | 3 | 11 | 7 | 2 |
| Belarus | 4 | 0 | 0 | 4 | 4 | 26 | 0 |

| | | |
|---|---|---|
| December 25 | Sweden 5 | Belarus 0 |
| December 25 | United States 3 | Czech Republic 1 |
| December 26 | Slovakia 7 | Belarus 1 |
| December 27 | Slovakia 1 | Czech Republic 0 |
| December 27 | Sweden 2 | United States 2 |
| December 28 | Czech Republic 9 | Belarus 1 |
| December 29 | Sweden 2 | Slovakia 2 |
| December 29 | United States 5 | Belarus 2 |
| December 30 | Sweden 2 | Czech Republic 1 |
| December 30 | Slovakia 4 | United States 4 |

**GROUP B (HRADEC KRALOVE)**

| | GP | W | T | L | GF | GA | P |
|---|---|---|---|---|---|---|---|
| Finland | 4 | 3 | 0 | 1 | 14 | 5 | 6 |
| Canada | 4 | 3 | 0 | 1 | 27 | 7 | 6 |
| Russia | 4 | 2 | 0 | 2 | 12 | 8 | 4 |
| Switzerland | 4 | 2 | 0 | 2 | 12 | 10 | 4 |
| France | 4 | 0 | 0 | 4 | 1 | 36 | 0 |

| | | |
|---|---|---|
| December 25 | Canada 15 | France 0 |
| December 25 | Switzerland 3 | Finland 0 |
| December 26 | Russia 5 | France 1 |
| December 27 | Canada 6 | Switzerland 1 |
| December 27 | Finland 2 | Russia 1 |
| December 28 | Finland 8 | France 0 |
| December 29 | Canada 5 | Russia 2 |
| December 29 | Switzerland 8 | France 0 |
| December 30 | Russia 4 | Switzerland 0 |
| December 30 | Finland 4 | Canada 1 |

**RELEGATION ROUND (BEST-OF-TWO)**

| | | | |
|---|---|---|---|
| January 1 | Hradec Kralove | France 3 | Belarus 2 |
| January 3 | Pardubice | Belarus 4 | France 2 |

~Belarus won game two, 3-2 to force overtime—10:00 OT/GWS—Dmitri Mialeshka (BLR)

**PLACEMENT ROUND (HRADEC KRALOVE)**

| | | |
|---|---|---|
| January 2 | Sweden 3 | Slovakia 2 |
| January 2 | United States 4 | Czech Republic 3 |

**5TH-PLACE GAME**

| | | |
|---|---|---|
| January 4 | United States 3 | Sweden 2 |

**7TH-PLACE GAME**

| | | |
|---|---|---|
| January 4 | Czech Republic 6 | Slovakia 2 |

**PLAYOFFS**
**QUARTER-FINALS**

| | | | |
|---|---|---|---|
| January 1 | Hradec Kralove | Canada 5 | Sweden 2 |
| January 1 | Hradec Kralove | Finland 3 | Czech Republic 1 |
| January 1 | Pardubice | Russia 6 | United States 1 |
| January 1 | Pardubice | Switzerland 3 | Slovakia 2 |
| | | (10:00 OT/GWS—Sven Helfenstein) | |

**SEMI-FINALS**

| | | | |
|---|---|---|---|
| January 2 | Pardubice | Canada 4 | Switzerland 0 |
| January 2 | Pardubice | Russia 2 | Finland 1 (Sergei Soin 1:44 OT) |

**BRONZE MEDAL GAME**

| | | | |
|---|---|---|---|
| January 4 | Pardubice | Finland 5 | Switzerland 1 |

**GOLD MEDAL GAME**

| | | | |
|---|---|---|---|
| January 4 | Pardubice | Russia 5 | Canada 4 |

### Rosters

**Belarus** (Vladimir Melenchuk, coach) GK—Sergei Rakovski, Vitali Arystov—Andrei Karshunov, Andrei Bashko, Ruslan Sharapa, Maxim Shymanski, Ilya Yermashkevich, Vasili Harbavy, Alexander Kulakov, Mikhail Klimin, Konstantin Nemirka, Artyom Siankevich, Dmitri Mialeshka, Vitali Klimiankov, Konstantin Zakharov, Andrei Kostitsyn, Yaroslav Maslenikov, Artyom Hlinkin, Konstantin Durnov, Andrei Skrypailov, Stanislav Korabov, Mikhail Grabovski

**Canada** (Stan Butler, coach) GK—Pascal Leclaire, Olivier Michaud—Mike Cammalleri, Brad Boyes, Jared Aulin, Chuck Kobasew, Brian Sutherby, Steve Ott, Scottie Upshall, Garth Murray, Jarret Stoll, Stephen Weiss, Jason Spezza, Rick Nash, Dan Hamhuis, Carlo Colaiacovo, Jay McClement, Nick Schultz, Jay Bouwmeester, Nathan Paetsch, Mark Popovic, Jay Harrison

**Czech Republic** (Jaroslav Holik, coach) GK—Michal Fikrt, Lukas Hronek—Libor Ustrnul, Filip Novak, Jan Hanzlik, Lukas Krajicek, Petr Prucha, Jiri Jakes, Miroslav Blatak, Ales Hemsky, Tomas Plekanec, Lukas Pozivil, Jan Bohac, Jaroslav Sklenar, Frantisek Lukes, Jiri Hudler, Petr Chvojka, Tomas Mojzis, Michal Vondrka, Jiri Novotny, Martin Podlesak, Miloslav Horava

**Finland** (Erkka Westerlund, coach) GK—Kari Lehtonen, Juha Kuokkanen—Topi Jaakola, Joni Pitkanen, Mikko Viitanen, Olli Malmivaara, Jyri Marttinen, Mikko Koivu, Sean Bergenheim, Kim Hirschovits, Jarkko Immonen, Tomi Maki, Mikko Kankaanpera, Tuomo Ruutu, Toni Koivisto, Jussi Jokinen, Tero Maatta, Markus Seikola, Janne Jokila, Pekka Saarenheimo, Joni Yli-Torkko, Tuomas Pihlman

**France** (Dave Henderson, coach) GK—Landry Macrez, Jerome Plumejeau—Mathieu Becuwe, Geoffroy Bessard du Parc, Gael Guilhem, Wilfried Molmy, Elie Marcos, Aram Kevorkian, Ghislain Folcke, Michael Brodin, Simon Petit, Mathieu Jestin, Sebastien Rousselin, Frederic Bastian, Pierre-Yves Albert, Thomas Gueguen, Romain Masson, Michael Bardet, Yannick Maillot, Timo Bayon, Francis Ballet, Julien Thiery

**Russia** (Vladimir Plyushev, coach) GK—Sergei Mylnikov, Andrei Medvedev—Vladimir Sapozhnikov, Vladimir Korsunov, Denis Grebeshkov, Fyodor Tyutin, Maxim Kondratiev, Alexander Suglobov, Sergei Soin, Alexander Frolov, Anton Volchenkov, Yuri Trubachyov, Alexander Svitov, Alexander Polushin, Igor Grigorenko, Andrei Zabolotnev, Stanislav Chistov, Ruslan Zainulin, Alexander Perezhogin, Ivan Nepryayev, Andrei Taratukhin, Igor Knyazev

**Slovakia** (Julius Supler, coach) GK—Peter Budaj, Peter Hamerlik—Stanislav Hudec, Karol Sloboda, Peter Fruhauf, Peter Gajdos, Tomas Jasko, Lubos Velebny, Tomas Oravec, Ivan Kolozvary, Marek Svatos, Miroslav Kristin, Michal Macho, Tomas Malec, Frantisek Skladany, Peter Holecko, Tomas Kopecky, Igor Pohanka, Michal Kolarik, Radovan Sloboda, Richard Stehlik, Milan Jurcina

**Sweden** (Bo Lennartsson, coach) GK—Henrik Lundqvist, Jimmy Danielsson—Per Helmersson, Adam Andersson, Par Backer, Staffan Kronwall, Johan Ejdepalm, Lars Jonsson, Jonas Nordqvist, Martin Samuelsson, Jorgen Sundqvist, Jens Karlsson, Daniel Widing, Gustav Grasberg, Daniel Hermansson, Magnus Hedlund, Yared Hagos, Fredrik Sjostrom, Peter Oberg, Joel Lundqvist, Andreas Jamtin, Tim Eriksson

**Switzerland** (Jakob Kolliker, coach) GK—Tobias Stephan, Matthias Schoder—Beat Gerber, Jurg Dallenbach, Beat Forster, Severin Blindenbacher, Tim Ramholt, Thibaut Monnet, Lukas Baumgartner, Fabian Sutter, Patrik Bartschi, Deny Bartschi, Reto Raffainer, Lukas Gerber, Emanuel Peter, Raffaele Sannitz, Andreas Camenzind, Andres Ambuhl, Thomas Nussli, Rene Back, Sven Helfenstein, Thomas Deruns

**United States** (Keith Allain, coach) GK—Jason Bacashihua, Dwight Labrosse (dnp)—Keith Ballard, Ryan Whitney, Erik Reitz, Mike Komisarek, Ben Eaves, Chad LaRose, Ryan Hollweg, Kris Vernarsky, Brett Lebda, David Steckel, Gregg Johnson, Eric Nystrom, Rob Globke, Jim Slater, Chris Higgins, R.J. Umberger, Dustin Brown, Dwight Helminen, Bryce Lampman, Joe Hope

## 27th U20 WORLD CHAMPIONSHIP
## December 26, 2002-January 5, 2003
## Halifax/Sydney, Canada

### Final Placing

Gold .......Russia
Silver .....Canada
Bronze ...Finland
4th .........United States
5th .........Slovakia
6th ........Czech Republic
7th ........Switzerland
8th ........Sweden
9th ........Germany^*
10th ......Belarus*

^promoted from Division I in 2002
*demoted to Division I for 2004

### Tournament Format

Two divisions of five teams were created, and each country played a round-robin series in a preliminary round (four games). The top team from each division advanced to the semi-finals, and the second and third place teams played for the other two spots. The second place team from the one division played the third place team from the other, and vice versa. The two semi-finals winners then went on to play for the gold medal, and the semis losers played for the bronze.

### Results & Standings

**PRELIMINARY ROUND**

**GROUP A (SYDNEY)**

| | GP | W | T | L | GF | GA | P |
|---|---|---|---|---|---|---|---|
| Russia | 4 | 4 | 0 | 0 | 21 | 7 | 8 |
| United States | 4 | 3 | 0 | 1 | 15 | 9 | 6 |
| Slovakia | 4 | 2 | 0 | 2 | 15 | 8 | 4 |
| Switzerland | 4 | 1 | 0 | 3 | 10 | 15 | 2 |
| Belarus | 4 | 0 | 0 | 4 | 6 | 28 | 0 |

| | | |
|---|---|---|
| December 26 | Switzerland 4 | Belarus 2 |
| December 26 | Russia 5 | United States 1 |
| December 27 | Slovakia 11 | Belarus 1 |
| December 28 | United States 3 | Switzerland 1 |
| December 28 | Russia 4 | Slovakia 0 |
| December 29 | Russia 5 | Belarus 1 |
| December 30 | United States 8 | Belarus 2 |
| December 30 | Slovakia 3 | Switzerland 0 |
| December 31 | United States 3 | Slovakia 1 |
| December 31 | Russia 7 | Switzerland 5 |

**GROUP B (HALIFAX)**

| | GP | W | T | L | GF | GA | P |
|---|---|---|---|---|---|---|---|
| Canada | 4 | 4 | 0 | 0 | 21 | 6 | 8 |
| Finland | 4 | 2 | 1 | 1 | 12 | 9 | 5 |
| Czech Republic | 4 | 2 | 1 | 1 | 8 | 7 | 5 |
| Sweden | 4 | 1 | 0 | 3 | 12 | 16 | 2 |
| Germany | 4 | 0 | 0 | 4 | 3 | 18 | 0 |

| | | |
|---|---|---|
| December 26 | Finland 4 | Germany 0 |
| December 26 | Canada 8 | Sweden 2 |
| December 27 | Czech Republic 3 | Germany 0 |
| December 28 | Canada 4 | Czech Republic 0 |
| December 28 | Finland 3 | Sweden 2 |
| December 29 | Canada 4 | Germany 1 |
| December 30 | Sweden 7 | Germany 2 |
| December 30 | Finland 2 | Czech Republic 2 |
| December 31 | Czech Republic 3 | Sweden 1 |
| December 31 | Canada 5 | Finland 3 |

**RELEGATION ROUND (HALIFAX)**

| | GP | W | T | L | GF | GA | P |
|---|---|---|---|---|---|---|---|
| Switzerland | 3 | 3 | 0 | 0 | 15 | 7 | 6 |
| Sweden | 3 | 2 | 0 | 1 | 15 | 11 | 4 |
| Germany | 3 | 1 | 0 | 2 | 8 | 13 | 2 |
| Belarus | 3 | 0 | 0 | 3 | 6 | 13 | 0 |

| | | |
|---|---|---|
| January 2 | Switzerland 6 | Germany 2 |
| January 3 | Sweden 5 | Belarus 4 |
| January 4 | Switzerland 5 | Sweden 3 |
| January 4 | Germany 4 | Belarus 0 |

**5TH-PLACE GAME**

January 4 Halifax Slovakia 2 Czech Republic 0

**PLAYOFFS (HALIFAX)**

**QUARTER-FINALS**

| | | |
|---|---|---|
| January 2 | United States 4 | Czech Republic 3 |
| January 2 | Finland 6 | Slovakia 0 |

**SEMI-FINALS**

| | | |
|---|---|---|
| January 3 | Canada 3 | United States 2 |
| January 3 | Russia 4 | Finland 1 |

**BRONZE MEDAL GAME**

January 5 Finland 3 United States 2

**GOLD MEDAL GAME**

January 5 Russia 3 Canada 2

### Rosters

**Belarus** (Vladimir Melenchuk, coach) GK—Dmitri Kamovich, Sergei Rakovski—Andrei Karshunov, Anatoli Varyvonchyk, Konstantin Durnov, Vladimir Denisov, Dmitri Parakhonka, Vadim Karaga, Alexander Kulakov, Vasili Harbavy, Artyom Volkov, Alexander Zhydkikh, Pavel Kutsevich, Yevgeni Kashtanov, Sergei Khomka, Konstantin Zakharov, Andrei Kostitsyn, Alexei Yerashov, Mikhail Grabovski, Dmitri Yudzhin, Artyom Hlinkin, Andrei Kazachok

**Canada** (Marc Habscheid, coach) GK—Marc-Andre Fleury, David LeNeveu—Carlo Colaiacovo, Pierre-Alexandre Parenteau, Ian White, Brooks Laich, Scottie Upshall, Pierre-Marc Bouchard, Kyle Wellwood, Joffrey Lupul, Derek Roy, Jay McClement, Jeff Woywitka, Matt Stajan, Gregory Campbell, Jordin Tootoo, Brendan Bell, Steve Eminger, Nathan Paetsch, Alexandre Rouleau, Boyd Gordon, Daniel Paille

**Czech Republic** (Jaroslav Holik, coach) GK—Martin Falter, Lukas Mensator—Ladislav Kolda, Petr Puncochar, Jiri Svoboda, David Turon, Roman Vondracek, Petr Taticek, Jan Holub, Jakub Koreis, Milan Michalek, Zbynek Novak, Petr Domin, Tomas Micka, Lukas Chmelir, Petr Dvorak, Jakub Klepis, Tomas Fleischmann, Jiri Hudler, Jiri Novotny, Martin Toms, Lukas Krajicek

**Finland** (Erkka Westerlund, coach) GK—Tuomas Nissinen, Kari Lehtonen—Jussi Timonen, Topi Jaakola, Joni Pitkanen, Mikko Kalteva, Jesse Niinimaki, Sean Bergenheim, Valtteri Filppula, Matti Aho, Tomi Maki, Tuomo Ruutu, Henrik Juntunen, Matti Naatanen, Teemu Jaaskalainen, Jussi Jokinen, Juho Lehtisalo, Tomi Sykko, Tuomas Mikkonen, Juha Fagerstedt, Tuomas Immonen, Janne Jalasvaara

**Germany** (Ernst Hofner, coach) GK—Dimitri Patzold, Patrick Ehelechner—Daniel Menge, Alexander Sulzer, Marcel Goc, Martin Walter, Felix Petermann, Stefan Schauer, Yannic Seidenberg, David Danner, Robert Bartlick, Alexander Barta, Kai Hospelt, Adrian Grygiel, Benjamin Barz, Martin Hinterstocker, Christoph Ullmann, Josef Menauer, Stefan Wilhelm, Dirk Wrobel, Max Seyller, Marcus Kink

**Russia** (Rafael Ishmatov, coach) GK—Andrei Medvedev, Konstantin Barulin—Konstantin Korneyev, Denis Yezhov, Denis Grebeshkov, Dmitri Pestunov, Fyodor Tyutin, Alexander Ovechkin, Alexei Kaigorodov, Timofei Shishkanov, Kirill Koltsov, Nikolai Zherdev, Yuri Trubachyov, Andrei Taratukhin, Alexander Polushin, Igor Grigorenko, Dmitri Fakhrutdinov, Yevgeni Artyukhin, Maxim Kondratiev, Mikhail Lyubushin, Alexander Perezhogin, Sergei Anshakov

**Slovakia** (Robert Spisak, coach) GK—Imrich Petrik, Jan Chovan, Peter Sevela—Milan Varga, Peter Macek, Milan Jurcina, Richard Stehlik, Dominik Granak, Juraj Sykora, Ivan Kolozvary, Michal Vazan, Anton Zagora, Oliver Maron, Stanislav Valach, Samir Saliji, Rastislav Spirko, Michal Lukac, Karol Sloboda, Igor Pohanka, Rastislav Lipka, Tomas Slovak, Tomas Troliga, Michal Kokavec

**Sweden** (Peo Larsson, coach) GK—Michal Zajkowski, Mathias Fagerstrom—Johan Agu, Patrik Baarnhielm, Joakim Lindstrom, Tobias Enstrom, Jonas Leetma, Mats Hansson, Andreas Falk, Jonas Almtorp, Mattias Beck, Simon Skoog, Adam Andersson, Yared Hagos, Marcus Paulsson, Fredrik Eriksson, Fredrik Sjostrom, Andreas Valdix, Alexander Steen, Andree Persson, Andreas Jamtin, Robert Nilsson

**Switzerland** (Jakob Kolliker, coach) GK—Tobias Stephan, Daniel Manzato—Lukas Baumgartner, Jurg Dallenbach, Alan Tallarini, Severin Blindenbacher, Tim Ramholt, Philippe Furrer, Andreas Ambuhl, Patrik Bartschi, Cyrill Buhler, Gregory Christen, Florian Conz, Emanuel Peter, Kevin Gloor, Roland Gerber, Kevin Romy, Victor Stancescu, Stefan Schnyder, Caryl Neuenschwander, Romano Lemm, Beat Forster

**United States** (Lou Vairo, coach) GK—James Howard, Robert Goepfert—Mark Stuart, Matt Jones, Tim Gleason, Matt Greene, Ryan Suter, Dwight Helminen, Zach Parise, Patrick O'Sullivan, Gino Guyer, Gregg Moore, Brian McConnell, Ryan Kesler, Chris Higgins, Ryan Whitney, James Wisniewski, Eric Nystrom, Ryan Shannon, Dustin Brown, Brett Sterling, Barry Tallackson

## 28th U20 WORLD CHAMPIONSHIP
## December 26, 2003-January 4, 2004
## Helsinki/Hameenlinna, Finland

**Final Placing**

Gold .......United States
Silver .....Canada
Bronze ...Finland
4th .........Czech Republic
5th .........Russia
6th ........Slovakia
7th ........Sweden
8th ........Switzerland
9th ........Austria^*
10th ......Ukraine^*
^promoted from Division I in 2003
*demoted to Division I for 2005

**Tournament Format**

Two divisions of five teams were created, and each country played a round-robin series in a preliminary round (four games). The top team from each division advanced to the semi-finals, and the second and third place teams played for the other two spots. The second place team from the one division played the third place team from the other, and vice versa. The two semi-finals winners then went on to play for the gold medal, and the semis losers played for the bronze.

**Results & Standings**

**PRELIMINARY ROUND**

**GROUP A**

| | GP | W | T | L | GF | GA | P |
|---|---|---|---|---|---|---|---|
| United States | 4 | 4 | 0 | 0 | 21 | 4 | 8 |
| Slovakia | 4 | 2 | 1 | 1 | 9 | 7 | 5 |
| Russia | 4 | 2 | 1 | 1 | 11 | 10 | 5 |
| Sweden | 4 | 1 | 0 | 3 | 13 | 10 | 2 |
| Austria | 4 | 0 | 0 | 4 | 1 | 24 | 0 |

| | | | |
|---|---|---|---|
| December 26 | Hameenlinna | Slovakia 2 | Russia 2 |
| December 26 | Hameenlinna | United States 8 | Austria 0 |
| December 27 | Hameenlinna | Sweden 7 | Austria 0 |
| December 28 | Helsinki | Russia 5 | Sweden 3 |
| December 28 | Hameenlinna | United States 5 | Slovakia 0 |
| December 29 | Hameenlinna | Russia 3 | Austria 1 |
| December 30 | Hameenlinna | Slovakia 6 | Austria 0 |
| December 30 | Hameenlinna | United States 4 | Sweden 3 |
| December 31 | Hameenlinna | United States 4 | Russia 1 |
| December 31 | Hameenlinna | Slovakia 1 | Sweden 0 |

**GROUP B (HELSINKI)**

| | GP | W | T | L | GF | GA | P |
|---|---|---|---|---|---|---|---|
| Canada | 4 | 4 | 0 | 0 | 25 | 4 | 8 |
| Finland | 4 | 3 | 0 | 1 | 19 | 6 | 6 |
| Czech Republic | 4 | 2 | 0 | 2 | 14 | 9 | 4 |
| Switzerland | 4 | 1 | 0 | 3 | 14 | 11 | 2 |
| Ukraine | 4 | 0 | 0 | 4 | 1 | 43 | 0 |

| | | |
|---|---|---|
| December 26 | Czech Republic 8 | Ukraine 0 |
| December 26 | Canada 3 | Finland 0 |
| December 27 | Switzerland 11 | Ukraine 0 |
| December 28 | Finland 3 | Czech Republic 2 |
| December 28 | Canada 7 | Switzerland 2 |
| December 29 | Canada 10 | Ukraine 0 |
| December 30 | Czech Republic 2 | Switzerland 1 |
| December 30 | Finland 14 | Ukraine 1 |
| December 31 | Canada 5 | Czech Republic 2 |
| December 31 | Finland 2 | Switzerland 0 |

**RELEGATION ROUND (HAMEENLINNA)**

| | GP | W | T | L | GF | GA | P |
|---|---|---|---|---|---|---|---|
| Sweden | 3 | 3 | 0 | 0 | 15 | 3 | 6 |
| Switzerland | 3 | 2 | 0 | 1 | 20 | 6 | 4 |
| Austria | 3 | 0 | 1 | 2 | 4 | 15 | 1 |
| Ukraine | 3 | 0 | 1 | 2 | 2 | 17 | 1 |

| | | |
|---|---|---|
| January 2 | Sweden 4 | Ukraine 0 |
| January 2 | Switzerland 6 | Austria 2 |
| January 3 | Austria 2 | Ukraine 2 |
| January 3 | Sweden 4 | Switzerland 3 |

**5TH-PLACE GAME (HELSINKI)**

| | | |
|---|---|---|
| January 4 | Russia 3 | Slovakia 2 |

**PLAYOFFS (HELSINKI)**

**QUARTER-FINALS**

| | | |
|---|---|---|
| January 2 | Czech Republic 4 | Slovakia 2 |
| January 2 | Finland 4 | Russia 3 |

**SEMI-FINALS**

| | | |
|---|---|---|
| January 3 | Canada 7 | Czech Republic 1 |
| January 3 | United States 2 | Finland 1 |

**BRONZE MEDAL GAME**

| | | |
|---|---|---|
| January 5 | Finland 2 | Czech Republic 1 |

**GOLD MEDAL GAME**

| | | |
|---|---|---|
| January 5 | United States 4 | Canada 3 |

**Rosters**

**Austria** (Peter Schramm, coach) GK—Mathais Lange, Thomas Innerwinkler—Stefan Pittl, Martin Dobner, Christoph Quantschnig, Rafael Rotter, Philipp Kink, Yanick Bodemann, Andreas Nodl, Franz Wilfan, Anton Tino Teppert, Philipp Pinter, Manuel Latusa, Patrick Harand, Martin Oraze, Christoph Ibounig, Christoph Rud, Nikolas Petrik, Johannes Kirisits, Victor Lindgren, Thomas Vanek, Matthias Iberer

**Canada** (Mario Durocher, coach) GK—Josh Harding, Marc-Andre Fleury—Derek Meech, Dion Phaneuf, Josh Gorges, Kevin Klein, Tim Brent, Jeff Carter, Anthony Stewart, Ryan Getzlaf, Daniel Paille, Mike Richards, Jeff Tambellini, Jeremy Colliton, Brent Burns, Stephen Dixon, Maxime Talbot, Nigel Dawes, Sidney Crosby, Braydon Coburn, Brent Seabrook, Shawn Belle

**Czech Republic** (Alois Hadamczik, coach) GK—Marek Schwarz, Tomas Popperle—Ondrej Nemec, Martin Vagner, Ctirad Ovcacik, Michal Barinka, Petr Kanko, Marek Chvatal, Tomas Linhart, Ladislav Smid, Karel Hromas, Tomas Fleischmann, Jakub Koreis, Kamil Kreps, Jakub Klepis, Radim Hruska, Jakub Sindel, Jiri Hudler, Rostislav Olesz, Vojtech Polak, Roman Vondracek, Lukas Kaspar

**Finland** (Hannu Aravirta, coach) GK—Mikael Vuorio, Hannu Toivonen—Sami Lepisto, Janne Jalasvaara, Mikko Kalteva, Anssi Salmela, Ville Varakas, Sean Bergenheim, Valtteri Filppula, Arsi Piispanen, Tommi Oksa, Jyri Junnila, Lennart Petrell, Joni Toykkala, Kevin Kantee, Teemu Nurmi, Jarkko Immonen, Oskari Korpikari, Lauri Tukonen, Petri Kontiola, Petteri Nokelainen, Masi Marjamaki

**Russia** (Rafael Ishmatov, coach) GK—Konstantin Barulin, Denis Khudyakov—Denis Yezhov, Konstantin Korneyev, Andrei Spiridonov, Dmitri Kosmachev, Dmitri Pestunov, Alexander Ovechkin, Alexander Syomin, Yevgeni Tunik, Alexei Shkotov, Yevgeni Malkin, Ilya Krikunov, Sergei Gimayev, Mikhail Tyulyapkin, Yuri Yermolin, Grigori Shafigulin, Sergei Karpov, Denis Grot, Alexander Kozhevnikov, Dmitri Kazionov, Sergei Anshakov

**Slovakia** (Jozef Fruhauf, coach) GK—Jaroslav Halak, Jozef Racko—Juraj Liska, Michal Gavalier, Ivan Baranka, Vladislav Balaz, Rastislav Spirko, Tomas Pokrivcak, Tomas Bulik, Stefan Blaho, Branislav Fabry, Andrej Meszaros, Milan Hruska, Pavol Hajduk, Michal Lukac, Stefan Ruzicka, Richard Stehlik, Martin Sagat, Juraj Senko, Tomas Troliga, Karol Biermann, Vladimir Kutny

**Sweden** (Torgny Bendelin, coach) GK—Joakim Lundstrom, Magnus Akerlund—Pierre Johnsson, Henrik Blomqvist, Daniel Sondell, Johan Fransson, Tobias Enstrom, Alexander Tang, Niklas Eckerblom, Robert Nilsson, Fredrik Johansson, Nicklas Danielsson, Sebastian Meijer, Monir Kalgoum, Johannes Salmonsson, Alexander Steen, Patric Blomdahl, Loui Eriksson, Alexander Hult, Johan Bjork, Johan Andersson, Andreas Valdix

**Switzerland** (Jakob Kolliker, coach) GK—Michael Tobler, Daniel Manzato—Lukas Baumgartner, Gianni Ehrensperger, Tim Ramholt, Philippe Seydoux, Martin Stettler, Patrik Bartschi, Yvan Benoit, Lukas Grauwiler, Christoph Roder, Peter Guggisberg, Florian Blatter, Emanuel Peter, Morris Trachsler, Roland Gerber, Kevin Romy, Victor Stancescu, Silvan Anthamatten, Antonio Rizzello, Andri Stoffel, Steivan Hasler

**Ukraine** (Sergiy Lubnin, coach) GK—Yevgeniy Galyuk, Ilia Tarankov, Sergi Gavrylyuk—Igor Kugut, Kyrylo Katrych, Pavlo Akymov, Ivan Nadzon, Oleksiy Lubnin, Olexander Shevchenko, Pavlo Bolshakov, Pavlo Legachev, Sergiy Chernenko, Viktor Andruschenko, Oleksiy Voytsekhivsky, Vitali Kyrychenko, Oleksiy Koval, Yevgeniy Onishenko, Igor Shamansky, Yegor Rufanov, Vadym Gnyazdovsky, Anatoliy Bogdanov, Sergiy Madera

**United States** (Mike Eaves, coach) GK—Al Montoya, Dominic Vicari—Mark Stuart, Corey Potter, Matt Carle, Matt Hunwick, Dan Richmond, Ryan Suter, Patrick Eaves, Jeff Likens, Zach Parise, Patrick O'Sullivan, Brady Murray, Gregg Moore, Jake Dowell, Ryan Kesler, Drew Stafford, James Wisniewski, David Booth, Dan Fristche, Brett Sterling, Steve Werner

## 29th U20 WORLD CHAMPIONSHIP
## December 25, 2004-January 4, 2005
## Grand Forks/Thief River Falls, United States

**Final Placing**

Gold .......Canada
Silver .....Russia
Bronze ...Czech Republic
4th .........United States
5th .........Finland
6th ........Sweden
7th ........Slovakia
8th ........Switzerland
9th ........Germany^*
10th ......Belarus^*

^promoted from Division I in 2004
*demoted to Division I for 2006

**Tournament Format**

Two divisions of five teams were created, and each country played a round-robin series in a preliminary round (four games). The top team from each division advanced to the semi-finals, and the second and third place teams played for the other two spots. The second place team from the one division played the third place team from the other, and vice versa. The two semi-finals winners then went on to play for the gold medal, and the semis losers played for the bronze.

**Results & Standings**

**PRELIMINARY ROUND**

**GROUP A**

| | GP | W | T | L | GF | GA | P |
|---|---|---|---|---|---|---|---|
| Russia | 4 | 3 | 0 | 1 | 21 | 9 | 6 |
| Czech Republic | 4 | 3 | 0 | 1 | 16 | 9 | 6 |
| United States | 4 | 2 | 0 | 2 | 15 | 16 | 4 |
| Switzerland | 4 | 1 | 0 | 3 | 12 | 17 | 2 |
| Belarus | 4 | 1 | 0 | 3 | 9 | 22 | 2 |

| | | | |
|---|---|---|---|
| December 25 | Thief River Falls | Czech Republic 7 | Belarus 2 |
| December 25 | Grand Forks | United States 5 | Russia 4 |
| December 26 | Grand Forks | Switzerland 5 | Belarus 0 |
| December 27 | Thief River Falls | Russia 4 | Czech Republic 1 |
| December 27 | Grand Forks | United States 6 | Switzerland 4 |
| December 28 | Thief River Falls | Russia 7 | Belarus 2 |
| December 29 | Grand Forks | Czech Republic 5 | Switzerland 2 |
| December 29 | Grand Forks | Belarus 5 | United States 3 |
| December 30 | Thief River Falls | Russia 6 | Switzerland 1 |
| December 30 | Grand Forks | Czech Republic 3 | United States 1 |

**GROUP B**

| | GP | W | T | L | GF | GA | P |
|---|---|---|---|---|---|---|---|
| Canada | 4 | 4 | 0 | 0 | 32 | 5 | 8 |
| Sweden | 4 | 2 | 0 | 2 | 14 | 13 | 4 |
| Finland | 4 | 2 | 0 | 2 | 10 | 15 | 4 |
| Slovakia | 4 | 2 | 0 | 2 | 10 | 10 | 4 |
| Germany | 4 | 0 | 0 | 4 | 1 | 24 | 0 |

| | | | |
|---|---|---|---|
| December 25 | Grand Forks | Canada 7 | Slovakia 3 |
| December 25 | Thief River Falls | Finland 4 | Germany 1 |
| December 26 | Thief River Falls | Sweden 6 | Germany 0 |
| December 27 | Grand Forks | Canada 8 | Sweden 1 |
| December 27 | Thief River Falls | Slovakia 2 | Finland 0 |
| December 28 | Grand Forks | Canada 9 | Germany 0 |
| December 29 | Grand Forks | Finland 5 | Sweden 4 |
| December 29 | Thief River Falls | Slovakia 5 | Germany 0 |
| December 30 | Grand Forks | Canada 8 | Finland 1 |
| December 30 | Thief River Falls | Sweden 3 | Slovakia 0 |

**RELEGATION ROUND (GRAND FORKS)**

| | GP | W | T | L | GF | GA | P |
|---|---|---|---|---|---|---|---|
| Slovakia | 3 | 3 | 0 | 0 | 10 | 3 | 6 |
| Switzerland | 3 | 2 | 0 | 1 | 12 | 3 | 4 |
| Germany | 3 | 1 | 0 | 2 | 4 | 13 | 2 |
| Belarus | 3 | 0 | 0 | 3 | 4 | 11 | 0 |

| | | |
|---|---|---|
| January 1 | Switzerland 5 | Germany 0 |
| January 2 | Slovakia 2 | Belarus 1 |
| January 3 | Germany 4 | Belarus 3 |
| January 3 | Slovakia 3 | Switzerland 2 |

**5TH-PLACE GAME (GRAND FORKS)**

| | | |
|---|---|---|
| January 3 | Finland 4 | Sweden 3 |

**PLAYOFFS (GRAND FORKS)**

**QUARTER-FINALS**

| | | |
|---|---|---|
| January 1 | Czech Republic 3 | Finland 0 |
| January 1 | United States 8 | Sweden 2 |

**SEMI-FINALS**

| | | |
|---|---|---|
| January 2 | Canada 3 | Czech Republic 1 |
| January 2 | Russia 7 | United States 2 |

**BRONZE MEDAL GAME**

| | | |
|---|---|---|
| January 4 | Czech Republic 3 | United States 2 (Petr Vrana 2:38 OT) |

**GOLD MEDAL GAME**

| | | |
|---|---|---|
| January 4 | Canada 6 | Russia 1 |

**Rosters**

**Belarus** (Mikhail Zakharov, coach) GK—Dmitri Milchakov, Stepan Goryachevskikh—Andrei Karev, Dmitri Yedeshko, Vadim Sushko, Yevgeni Goranin, Sergei Kolosov, Vadim Karaga, Alexei Savin, Pavel Osmolovski, Roman Blokh, Oleg Frolov, Vyachaslav Shypila, Alexei Ugarov, Alexei Shagov, Konstantin Zakharov, Sergei Kostitsyn, Andrei Kostitsyn, Sergei Giro, Sergei Kukushkin, Alexei Yefiamenko, Artyom Volkov

**Canada** (Brent Sutter, coach) GK—Jeff Glass, Rejean Beauchemin—Patrice Bergeron, Ryan Getzlaf, Jeff Carter, Sidney Crosby, Andrew Ladd, Corey Perry, Nigel Dawes, Dion Phaneuf, Colin Fraser, Mike Richards, Clarke MacArthur, Anthony Stewart, Danny Syvret, Brent Seabrook, Braydon Coburn, Shawn Belle, Cam Barker, Stephen Dixon, Shea Weber, Jeremy Colliton

**Czech Republic** (Alois Hadamczik, coach) GK—Marek Schwarz, Vladislav Koutsky—Martin Lojek, Roman Polak, Martin Tuma, Ladislav Smid, Bedrich Kohler, Lukas Bolf, Ondrej Smach, Zbynek Hrdel, David Krejci, Marek Kvapil, Petr Vrana, Michal Gulasi, Lukas Kaspar, Milan Hluchy, Michal Borovansky, Rostislav Olesz, Michal Polak, Michael Frolik, Jakub Petruzalek, Roman Cervenka

**Finland** (Risto Dufva, coach) GK—Joonas Hallikainen, Tuukka Rask—Anssi Tieranta, Otto Honkaheimo, Risto Korhonen, Ville Mantymaa, Iivo Hokkanen, Petteri Nokelainen, Teemu Nurmi, Mikko Kuukka, Filip Riska, Jesse Joensuu, Arsi Piispanen, Aki Seitsonen, Masi Marjamaki, Kim Nabb, Janne Kolehmainen, Lauri Korpikoski, Juuso Hietanen, Lauri Tukonen, Teemu Laakso, Jussi Makkonen

**Germany** (Ernst Hofner, coach) GK—Thomas Greiss, Youri Ziffzer—Raphael Kapzan, Marco Schutz, Danny Albrecht, Felix Schutz, Benedikt Schopper, Moritz Muller, Steffen Tolzer, Tobias Draxinger, Ulrich Maurer, Fabio Carciola, Marcus Kink, Kai Hospelt, Alexander Janzen, Andre Reiss, Markus Schmidt, Robert Dietrich, Sachar Blank, Andre Rankel, Florian Busch, Jens Baxmann

**Russia** (Valeri Bragin, coach) GK—Andrei Kuznetsov, Anton Khudobin—Anton Belov, Grigori Panin, Dmitri Vorobyov, Yakov Rylov, Alexander Ovechkin, Alexander Galimov, Dmitri Pestunov, Dmitri Megalinski, Georgi Misharin, Yevgeni Malkin, Grigori Shafigulin, Alexei Yemelin, Alexander Nikulin, Alexander Radulov, Mikhail Yunkov, Denis Yezhov, Roman Voloshenko, Enver Lisin, Denis Parshin, Sergei Shirokov

**Slovakia** (Dusan Gregor, coach) GK—Jaroslav Halak, Marek Novotny—Andrej Sekera, Ivan Baranka, Marek Zagrapan, Boris Valabik, Tomas Bulik, Juraj Gracik, Jaroslav Markovic, Branislav Fabry, Andrej Meszaros, Marek Hascak, Ladislav Scurko, Stanislav Lascek, Milan Hruska, Peter Mikus, Stefan Ruzicka, Vladimir Kutny, Richard Jencik, Peter Olvecky, Martin Segla, Juraj Liska

**Sweden** (Torgny Bendelin, coach) GK—Christopher Heino-Lindberg, David Rautio—Elias Granath, Johan Fransson, Anton Stralman, Oscar Hedman, Robert Nilsson, Kalle Olsson, Nicklas Grossmann, Johannes Salmonsson, Per Savilahti-Nagander, Mattias Hellstrom, Nicklas Bergfors, Linus Persson, Linus Videll, David Fredriksson, Ola Svanberg, Loui Eriksson, Daniel Ahsberg, Carl Soderberg, Sebastian Karlsson, Bjorn Svensson

**Switzerland** (Jakob Kolliker, coach) GK—Michael Tobler, Leonardo Genoni—Gianni Ehrensperger, Daniel Schnyder, Philippe Furrer, Fabian Debrunner, Patrick Von Gunten, Yvan Benoit, Stefan Hurlimann, Matthias Bieber, Rafael Diaz, Christian Haldimann, Marco Kaser, Kevin Romy, Victor Stancescu, Clarence Kparghai, Alain Birbaum, Beat Schuler, Julien Sprunger, Roman Wick, Fabian Schnyder, Julian Walker

**United States** (Scott Sandelin, coach) GK—Al Montoya, Cory Schneider—Brian Lee, Jeff Likens, Casey Borer, Ryan Suter, Adam Pineault, Dan Fritsche, Alex Goligoski, T.J. Hensick, Patrick O'Sullivan, Mike Brown, Shawn Weller, Jake Dowell, Robbie Schremp, Nate Hagemo, Drew Stafford, Kevin Porter, Matt Hunwick, Ryan Callahan, Phil Kessel, Chris Bourque

## 30th U20 WORLD CHAMPIONSHIP
## December 26, 2005-January 5, 2006
## Kamloops/Kelowna/Vancouver, Canada

**Final Placing**

Gold .......Canada
Silver .....Russia
Bronze ...Finland
4th .........United States
5th .........Sweden
6th ........Czech Republic
7th ........Switzerland
8th ........Slovakia
9th ........Latvia^*
10th ......Norway^*

^promoted from Division I in 2005
*demoted to Division I for 2007

**Tournament Format**

Two divisions of five teams were created, and each country played a round-robin series in a preliminary round (four games). The top team from each division advanced to the semi-finals, and the second and third place teams played for the other two spots. The second place team from the one division played the third place team from the other, and vice versa. The two semi-finals winners then went on to play for the gold medal, and the semis losers played for the bronze.

**Results & Standings**
**PRELIMINARY ROUND**
**GROUP A (VANCOUVER)**

| | GP | W | T | L | GF | GA | P |
|---|---|---|---|---|---|---|---|
| Canada | 4 | 4 | 0 | 0 | 16 | 6 | 8 |
| United States | 4 | 2 | 1 | 1 | 21 | 12 | 5 |
| Finland | 4 | 2 | 0 | 2 | 19 | 13 | 4 |
| Switzerland | 4 | 1 | 1 | 2 | 8 | 10 | 3 |
| Norway | 4 | 0 | 0 | 4 | 3 | 26 | 0 |

| | | |
|---|---|---|
| December 26 | Canada 5 | Finland 1 |
| December 26 | United States 11 | Norway 2 |
| December 27 | Switzerland 2 | Norway 0 |
| December 28 | Canada 4 | Switzerland 3 |
| December 28 | United States 6 | Finland 5 |
| December 29 | Canada 4 | Norway 0 |
| December 30 | Switzerland 2 | United States 2 |
| December 30 | Finland 9 | Norway 1 |
| December 31 | Canada 3 | United States 2 |
| December 31 | Finland 4 | Switzerland 1 |

**GROUP B**

| | GP | W | T | L | GF | GA | P |
|---|---|---|---|---|---|---|---|
| Russia | 4 | 4 | 0 | 0 | 21 | 6 | 8 |
| Sweden | 4 | 3 | 0 | 1 | 20 | 9 | 6 |
| Czech Republic | 4 | 2 | 0 | 2 | 14 | 14 | 4 |
| Slovakia | 4 | 1 | 0 | 3 | 12 | 21 | 2 |
| Latvia | 4 | 0 | 0 | 4 | 8 | 25 | 0 |

| | | | |
|---|---|---|---|
| December 26 | Kelowna | Russia 5 | Sweden 1 |
| December 26 | Kamloops | Czech Republic 5 | Latvia 1 |
| December 27 | Kelowna | Slovakia 7 | Latvia 4 |
| December 28 | Kelowna | Russia 6 | Slovakia 2 |
| December 28 | Kamloops | Sweden 3 | Czech Republic 2 |
| December 29 | Kamloops | Russia 3 | Latvia 1 |
| December 30 | Kamloops | Sweden 10 | Latvia 2 |
| December 30 | Kelowna | Czech Republic 5 | Slovakia 3 |
| December 31 | Kelowna | Russia7 | Czech Republic 2 |
| December 31 | Kamloops | Sweden 6 | Slovakia 0 |

**RELEGATION ROUND (VANCOUVER)**

| | GP | W | T | L | GF | GA | P |
|---|---|---|---|---|---|---|---|
| Switzerland | 3 | 2 | I | 0 | 10 | 5 | 5 |
| Slovakia | 3 | 2 | 1 | 0 | 14 | 10 | 5 |
| Latvia | 3 | 1 | 0 | 2 | 10 | 12 | 2 |
| Norway | 3 | 0 | 0 | 3 | 3 | 10 | 0 |

| | | |
|---|---|---|
| January 2 | Switzerland 5 | Latvia 2 |
| January 3 | Slovakia 4 | Norway 3 |
| January 4 | Latvia 4 | Norway 0 |
| January 4 | Switzerland 3 | Slovakia 3 |

**5TH-PLACE GAME (VANCOUVER)**
January 4 Sweden 3 Czech Republic 1

**PLAYOFFS (VANCOUVER)**
**QUARTER-FINALS**
January 2 Finland 1 Sweden 0
January 2 United States 2 Czech Republic 1

**SEMI-FINALS**
January 3 Canada 4 Finland 0
January 3 Russia 5 United States 1

**BRONZE MEDAL GAME**
January 5 Finland 4 United States 2

**GOLD MEDAL GAME**
January 5 Canada 5 Russia 0

**Rosters**
**Canada** (Brent Sutter, coach) GK—Justin Pogge, Devan Dubnyk (dnp)—Marc Staal, Ryan Parent, Luc Bourdon, Steve Downie, Andrew Cogliano, Kris Russell, Kristopher Letang, Blake Comeau, Dustin Boyd, Kyle Chipchura, David Bolland, Guillaume Latendresse, Michael Blunden, Daniel Bertram, Ryan O'Marra, Cam Barker, Tom Pyatt, Jonathan Toews, Sasha Pokulok, Benoit Pouliot

**Czech Republic** (Radim Rulik, coach) GK—Marek Schwarz, Radek Fiala—Petr Kalus, Ondrej Smach, Roman Polak, Jiri Tlusty, Ladislav Smid, Jakub Kindl, Vladimir Sobotka, Vaclav Meidl, Jaroslav Mrazek, Tomas Kudelka, Michal Birner, Karel Hromas, Petr Pohl, Jakub Sindel, Zdenek Bahensky, Martin Hanzal, David Krejci, Michal Gulasi, Michael Frolik, Tomas Kana

**Finland** (Hannu Aravirta, coach) GK—Karri Ramo, Tuukka Rask—Matti Koistinen, Risto Korhonen, Timo Seppanen, Erkka Leppanen, Juho Jokinen, Lauri Tukonen, Mikko Alikoski, Janne Kolehmainen, Petteri Wirtanen, Tommi Leinonen, Perttu Lindgren, Leo Komarov, Aki Seitsonen, Jesse Joensuu, Jari Sailio, Mikko Lehtonen, Tomas Sinisalo, Lauri Korpikoski, Teemu Laasko, Henri Heino

**Latvia** (Olegs Znaroks, coach) GK—Kristaps Stigis, Ugis Avotins—Oskars Bartulis, Arturs Kulda, Kristaps Sotnieks, Kriss Grundmanis, Toms Hartmanis, Renars Demiters, Martins Karsums, Edgars Adamovics, Sergejs Pecura, Kaspars Daugavins, Elviss Zelubovskis, Andis Abolins, Edzus Karklins, Kaspars Saulietis, Janis Andersons, Guntis Galvins, Eduards Bullitis, Martins Skuska, Gints Meija, Juriis Klujevskis

**Norway** (Petter Thoresen, coach) GK—Lars Haugen, Ruben Smith—Jonas Nygard, Henrik Borge, Kristian Forsberg, Per Ferdinand Stensund, Martin Hagen, Jonas Holos, Martin Roymark, Stian Hoygard, Mats Aasen, Lars Ostli, Marius Mathisrud, Mathias Trygg, Mathis Olimb, Joakim Jensen, Morten Rolstad, Eirik Grafsronningen, Fredrik Thinn, Alexander Bonsaksen, Dennis Sveum, Niklas Roest

**Russia** (Sergei Mikhalev, coach) GK—Anton Khudobin, Semyon Varlamov—Alexei Yemelin, Nikita Nikitin, Kirill Lyamin, Enver Lisin, Yevgeni Ketov, Sergei Ogorodnikov, Andrei Zubarev, Alexander Aksenenko, Nikolai Kulyomin, Yevgeni Biryukov, Roman Voloshenko, Yevgeni Malkin, Mikhail Yunkov, Vyacheslav Buravchikov, Alexander Radulov, Denis Bodrov, Gennadi Churilov, Nikolai Lemtyugov, Sergei Shirokov

**Slovakia** (Branislav Sajban, coach) GK—Michal Valent, Vladimir Kovac—Andrej Sekera, Michal Korenko, Martin Grundling, Marek Zagrapan, Igor Bacek, Juraj Mikus, Filip Simka, Marek Horsky, Vladimir Mihalek, Stanislav Lascek, Branislav Lemesani, Jozef Wagenhoffer, Ladislav Scurko, Tomas Petruska, David Skokan, Marek Bartanus, Juraj Gracik, Erik Piatak, Boris Valabik, Marcel Ulehla

**Sweden** (Torgny Bendelin, coach) GK—Daniel Larsson, Magnus Akerlund—Niklas Andersson, Sebastian Karlsson, Mattias Hellstrom, Anton Stralman, Tobias Viklund, Oscar Hedman, Alexander Edler, Erik Andersson, Tommy Wargh, Petter Ullman, Anton Axelsson, Oscar Sundh, Nicklas Bergfors, Nicklas Backstrom, Mattias Ritola, Fredrik Pettersson, Jonathan Granstrom, Johannes Salmonsson, Robin Lindqvist, Johan Ryno

**Switzerland** (Jakob Kolliker) GK—Leonardo Genoni, Reto Berra—Yannick Weber, Eric Blum, Patrick Parati, Claudio Berchtold, Alessandro Chiesa, Simon Luthi, Mathias Joggi, Janick Steinmann, Julien Sprunger, Stephan Moser, Matthias Bieber, Raphael Diaz, Dario Burgler, Jeremy Gailland, Nico Spoli-doro, Juraj Simek, Fadri Lemm, Christopher Rivera, Steve Kellenberger, Julian Walker

**United States** (Walt Kyle, coach) GK—Cory Schneider, Jeff Frazee—Taylor Chorney, Jack Johnson, Chris Butler, Erik Johnson, T.J. Oshie, Phil Kessel, Bobby Ryan, Nathan Davis, Kevin Porter, Geoff Paukovich, Matt Niskanen, Blake Wheeler, Robbie Schremp, Nathan Gerbe, Jack Skille, Brian Lee, Mark Mitera, Peter Mueller, Tom Fritschc, Chris Bourque

## 31st U20 WORLD CHAMPIONSHIP
## December 26, 2006-January 5, 2007
## Leksand/Mora, Sweden

**Final Placing**

| | |
|---|---|
| Gold .......Canada | 6th ........Finland |
| Silver .....Russia | 7th ........Switzerland |
| Bronze ...United States | 8th ........Slovakia |
| 4th .........Sweden | 9th ........Germany^* |
| 5th .........Czech Republic | 10th .......Belarus^* |

^promoted from Division I in 2006
*demoted to Division I for 2008

**Tournament Format**
Each team played a round-robin in a preliminary round. The top team from each division advanced to the semifinals, and the second and third place teams played for the other two spots. The second place team from the one division played the third place team from the other, and vice versa. The two semi-finals winners played for gold, and the semis losers played for the bronze.

**Results & Standings**
**PRELIMINARY ROUND**
**GROUP A**

| | GP | W | OTW | OTL | L | GF | GA | P |
|---|---|---|---|---|---|---|---|---|
| Canada | 4 | 4 | 0 | 0 | 0 | 14 | 4 | 12 |
| Sweden | 4 | 2 | 0 | 1 | 1 | 11 | 9 | 7 |
| United States | 4 | 1 | 1 | 1 | 1 | 13 | 11 | 6 |
| Germany | 4 | 1 | 1 | 0 | 2 | 8 | 9 | 5 |
| Slovakia | 4 | 0 | 0 | 0 | 4 | 6 | 19 | 0 |

| | | | |
|---|---|---|---|
| December 26 | Leksand | Germany 2 (Marcel Muller 1:51 OT) | United States 1 |
| December 26 | Leksand | Canada 2 | Sweden 0 |
| December 27 | Leksand | Germany 4 | Slovakia 2 |
| December 27 | Mora | Canada 6 | United States 3 |
| December 28 | Mora | Sweden 6 | Slovakia 3 |
| December 29 | Leksand | Canada 3 | Germany 1 |
| December 30 | Leksand | United States 6 | Slovakia 1 |
| December 30 | Mora | Sweden 3 | Germany 1 |
| December 31 | Leksand | Canada 3 | Slovakia 0 |
| December 31 | Leksand | United States 3 | Sweden 2 (Jack Johnson 3:16 OT) |

**GROUP B**

| | GP | W | OTW | OTL | L | GF | GA | P |
|---|---|---|---|---|---|---|---|---|
| Russia | 4 | 4 | 0 | 0 | 0 | 20 | 3 | 12 |
| Finland | 4 | 2 | 0 | 0 | 2 | 13 | 11 | 6 |
| Czech Republic | 4 | 2 | 0 | 0 | 2 | 10 | 12 | 6 |
| Switzerland | 4 | 1 | 0 | 0 | 3 | 6 | 15 | 3 |
| Belarus | 4 | 1 | 0 | 0 | 3 | 7 | 15 | 3 |

| | | | |
|---|---|---|---|
| December 26 | Mora | Belarus 4 | Finland 3 |
| December 26 | Mora | Russia 3 | Czech Republic 2 |
| December 27 | Mora | Switzerland 4 | Belarus 1 |
| December 28 | Mora | Finland 6 | Czech Republic 2 |
| December 28 | Leksand | Russia 6 | Switzerland 0 |
| December 29 | Mora | Russia 6 | Belarus 1 |
| December 30 | Mora | Finland 4 | Switzerland 0 |
| December 30 | Leksand | Czech Republic 2 | Belarus 1 |
| December 31 | Mora | Russia 5 | Finland 0 |
| December 31 | Mora | Czech Republic 4 | Switzerland 2 |

**RELEGATION ROUND (MORA)**

| | GP | W | OTW | OTL | L | GF | GA | P |
|---|---|---|---|---|---|---|---|---|
| Switzerland | 3 | 3 | 0 | 0 | 0 | 11 | 5 | 9 |
| Slovakia | 3 | 1 | 0 | 0 | 2 | 12 | 6 | 3 |
| Germany | 3 | 1 | 0 | 0 | 2 | 8 | 10 | 3 |
| Belarus | 3 | 1 | 0 | 0 | 2 | 4 | 14 | 3 |

| | | |
|---|---|---|
| January 2 | Switzerland 2 | Slovakia 1 |
| January 3 | Belarus 3 | Germany 1 |
| January 4 | Slovakia 9 | Belarus 0 |
| January 4 | Switzerland 5 | Germany 3 |

**5TH-PLACE GAME (LEKSAND)**

January 4 Czech Republic 6 Finland 2

**PLAYOFFS**

**QUARTER-FINALS**

| | | | |
|---|---|---|---|
| January 2 | Leksand | Sweden 5 | Czech Republic 1 |
| January 2 | Mora | United States 6 | Finland 3 |

**SEMI-FINALS**

| | | | |
|---|---|---|---|
| January 3 | Leksand | Canada 2 (10:00 OT/GWS—Jonathan Toews) | United States 1 |
| January 3 | Leksand | Russia 4 | Sweden 2 |

**BRONZE MEDAL GAME**

January 5 Leksand United States 2 Sweden 1

**GOLD MEDAL GAME**

January 5 Leksand Canada 4 Russia 2

**Rosters**

**Belarus** (Eduard Zankovets, coach) GK—Valeri Pronin, Dmitri Zhuravski—Mikhail Stefanovich, Sergei Kostitsyn, Igor Filin, Alexander Shurko, Alexander Syrei, Nikita Komarov, Andrei Stas, Yuri Ilin, Roman Magdeyev, Alexander Abakunchik, Dmitri Shumski, Pavel Musienko, Nikolai Stasenko, Dmitri Korobov, Igor Shvedov, Alexei Gavrilenok, Georgi Yaskevich, Yegor Korotki, Dmitri Violenti, Igor Voroshilov

**Canada** (Craig Hartsburg, coach) GK—Carey Price, Leland Irving—Jonathan Toews, Kris Russell, Steve Downie, Kristopher Letang, Luc Bourdon, Tom Pyatt, Andrew Cogliano, Darren Helm, Brad Marchand, Bryan Little, Ryan O'Marra, Cody Franson, Karl Alzner, Sam Gagner, James Neal, Ryan Parent, Daniel Bertram, Marc-Andre Cliche, Marc Staal, Kenndal McArdle

**Czech Republic** (Vladimir Bednar, coach) GK—Jakub Kovar, Ondrej Pavelec—Vladimir Sobotka, Michael Frolik, Tomas Svoboda, Tomas Kana, Jakub Kindl, Martin Hanzal, Tomas Kudelka, Jakub Voracek, Jakub Vojta, Jaroslav Barton, Michael Kolarz, Ondrej Pozivil, Jakub Cerny, Daniel Rakos, Jiri Suchy, David Kuchejda, Tomas Pospisil, David Kveton, Michal Repik, Lukas Vantuch

**Finland** (Jarmo Tolvanen, coach) GK—Tuukka Rask, Antti Harma—Mikko Lehtonen, Perttu Lindgren, Oskar Osala, Teemu Laakso, Leo Komarov, Timo Seppanen, Jesse Joensuu, Mikael Kurk, Jonas Enlund, Miika Lahti, Tuomas Huhtanen, Marko Poyhonen, Sami Sandell, Tommi Leinonen, Joni Haverinen, Ville Korhonen, Joonas Lehtivuori, Villi Sopanen, Joonas Jalvanti, Nico Aaltonen

**Germany** (Ernst Hofner, coach) GK—Sebastian Stefaniszin, Timo Pielmeier—Felix Schutz, Philip Gogulla, Christoph Gawlik, Christopher Fischer, Rene Kramer, Constantin Braun, Marcel Muller, Florian Ondruschka, Christopher Giebe, Elia Ostwald, Andre Schietzold, Alexander Weiss, Korbinian Holzer, Stefan Langwieder, Henry Martens, Matthias Potthoff, Christian Wichert, Patrick Buzas, Benedikt Anton Kohl

**Russia** (Yevgeni Popikhin, coach) GK—Semyon Varlamov, Nikita Bespalov—Alexei Cherepanov, Alexander Bumagin, Igor Makarov, Gennadi Churilov, Ilya Zubov, Vyacheslav Buravchikov, Yevgeni Ryasenski, Pavel Valentenko, Artyom Anisimov, Alexander Loginov, Andrei Kiryukhin, Anton Krysanov, Alexander Vasyunov, Andrei Zubarev, Igor Musatov, Vyacheslav Voinov, Vitali Anikeyenko, Anton Glovatski, Alexander Kucheryavenko, Yuri Alexandrov

**Slovakia** (Jan Jasko, coach) GK—Branislav Konrad, Jakub Macek—Juraj Mikus, Tomas Marcinko, David Buc, Ondrej Mikula, Michal Korenko, Marek Bartanus, Tomas Zaborsky, Julius Sinkovic, David Skokan, Martin Grundling, Tomas Brnak ,Jakub Rumpel, Mario Bliznak, Vladimir Mihalik, Matej Kunik, Jakub Drabek, Andrej Themar, Adam Ben, Juraj Valach, Tomas Magusin

**Sweden** (Torgny Bendelin, coach) GK—Jhonas Enroth, Joel Gistedt—Nicklas Backstrom, Linus Omark, Martin Johanssson, Niklas Hjalmarsson, Patric Hornqvist, Andreas Turesson, Patrik Berglund, Magnus Isaksson, Robin Lindqvist, Alexander Sundstrom, Jonas Junland, Patrik Zackrisson, Fredrik Pettersson, Nicklas Bergfors, Jonas Ahnelov, Daniel Rahimi, Alexander Ribbenstrand, Alexander Hellstrom, Andreas Molinder, Patrik Nevalainen

**Switzerland** (Jakob Kolliker, coach) GK—Reto Berra, Lukas Flueler—Juraj Simek, Yannick Weber, Steve Kellenberger, Dario Burgler, Robin Grossmann, Fadri Lemm, Samuel Friedli, Etienne Froidevaux, Marc Welti, Janick Steinmann, Andrei Bykov, Arnaud Jacquemet, Sebastian Schilt, Gregory Sciaroni, Gaetan Augsberger, Antoine Morand, Jerome Bonnet, Roman Josi, Kevin Lotscher, Marco Maurer

**United States** (Ron Rolston, coach) GK—Jeff Frazee, Jeff Zatkoff—Erik Johnson, Patrick Kane, Peter Mueller, Jack Skille, Taylor Chorney, Nathan Gerbe, Jack Johnson, Ryan Stoa, Trevor Lewis, Bill Sweatt, Justin Abdelkader, Mike Carman, James van Riemsdyk, Kyle Okposo, Blake Geoffrion, Brian Lee, Sean Zimmerman, Jim Fraser, Kyle Lawson, Jamie McBain

## 32nd U20 WORLD CHAMPIONSHIP
## December 26, 2007-January 5, 2008
## Pardubice/Liberec, Czech Republic

**Final Placing**

| | |
|---|---|
| Gold .......Canada | 6th ........Finland |
| Silver .....Sweden | 7th ........Slovakia |
| Bronze ...Russia | 8th ........Kazakhstan^ |
| 4th .........United States | 9th ........Switzerland* |
| 5th .........Czech Republic | 10th ......Denmark^* |

^promoted from Division I in 2007
*demoted to Division I for 2009

**Tournament Format**

Two divisions of five teams were made, and each country played a round-robin series in a preliminary round. The top team from each division advanced to the semi-finals, and the second and third place teams played for the other two spots. The second place team from one division played the third place team from the other, and vice versa. The two semi-finals winners then played for the gold medal, and the losers played for bronze.

**Results & Standings**

**GROUP A (PARDUBICE)**

| | GP | W | OTW | OTL | L | GF | GA | P |
|---|---|---|---|---|---|---|---|---|
| Sweden | 4 | 4 | 0 | 0 | 0 | 22 | 9 | 12 |
| Canada | 4 | 3 | 0 | 0 | 1 | 12 | 5 | 9 |
| Czech Republic | 4 | 2 | 0 | 0 | 2 | 12 | 11 | 6 |
| Slovakia | 4 | 1 | 0 | 0 | 3 | 9 | 14 | 3 |
| Denmark | 4 | 0 | 0 | 0 | 4 | 7 | 23 | 0 |

| | | |
|---|---|---|
| December 26 | Sweden 4 | Slovakia 3 |
| December 26 | Canada 3 | Czech Republic 0 |
| December 27 | Canada 2 | Slovakia 0 |
| December 27 | Czech Republic 5 | Denmark 2 |
| December 28 | Sweden 10 | Denmark 1 |
| December 29 | Czech Republic 5 | Slovakia 2 |
| December 29 | Sweden 4 | Canada 3 |
| December 30 | Slovakia 4 | Denmark 3 |
| December 31 | Sweden 4 | Czech Republic 2 |
| December 31 | Canada 4 | Denmark 1 |

**GROUP B (LIBEREC)**

| | GP | W | OTW | OTL | L | GF | GA | P |
|---|---|---|---|---|---|---|---|---|
| United States | 4 | 4 | 0 | 0 | 0 | 17 | 8 | 12 |
| Russia | 4 | 3 | 0 | 0 | 1 | 18 | 14 | 9 |
| Finland | 4 | 1 | 1 | 0 | 2 | 16 | 15 | 5 |
| Kazakhstan | 4 | 1 | 0 | 0 | 3 | 8 | 16 | 3 |
| Switzerland | 4 | 0 | 0 | 1 | 3 | 9 | 15 | 1 |

| | | |
|---|---|---|
| December 26 | United States 5 | Kazakhstan 1 |
| December 26 | Finland 4 | Russia 1 |
| December 27 | Russia 5 | Kazakhstan 4 |
| December 27 | Finland 4 | Switzerland 3 (5:00 OT/GWS—Sakari Salminen) |
| December 28 | United States 4 | Switzerland 2 |
| December 29 | Finland 5 | Kazakhstan 0 |
| December 29 | United States 3 | Russia 2 |
| December 30 | Kazakhstan 3 | Switzerland 1 |
| December 31 | Russia 4 | Switzerland 3 |
| December 31 | United States 5 | Finland 3 |

**RELEGATION ROUND**

| | GP | W | OTW | OTL | L | GF | GA | P |
|---|---|---|---|---|---|---|---|---|
| Slovakia | 3 | 3 | 0 | 0 | 0 | 17 | 5 | 9 |
| Kazakhstan | 3 | 2 | 0 | 0 | 1 | 9 | 12 | 6 |
| Switzerland | 3 | 1 | 0 | 0 | 2 | 8 | 10 | 3 |
| Denmark | 3 | 0 | 0 | 0 | 3 | 8 | 15 | 0 |

| | | | |
|---|---|---|---|
| December 30 | Pardubice | Denmark 3 | Slovakia 4 |
| December 30 | Liberec | Switzerland 1 | Kazakhstan 1 |
| January 2 | Liberec | Slovakia 5 | Switzerland 2 |
| January 2 | Liberec | Kazakhstan 6 | Denmark 3 |
| January 3 | Liberec | Switzerland 5 | Denmark 2 |
| January 3 | Liberec | Slovakia 8 | Kazakhstan 0 |

**5TH-PLACE GAME (PARDUBICE)**

January 3 Czech Republic 5 Finland 1

**PLAYOFFS (PARDUBICE)**
**QUARTER-FINALS**

January 2 Canada 4 Finland 2
January 2 Russia 4 Czech Republic 1

**SEMI-FINALS**

January 4 Sweden 2 Russia 1 (Mikael Backlund 6:18 OT)
January 4 Canada 4 United States 1

**BRONZE MEDAL GAME**

January 5 Russia 4 United States 2

**GOLD MEDAL GAME**

January 5 Canada 3 Sweden 2 (Matt Halischuk 3:36 OT)

**Rosters**

**Canada** (Craig Hartsburg, coach) GK—Jonathan Bernier, Steve Mason—Josh Godfrey, Logan Pyett, Thomas Hickey, Stefan Legein, Drew Doughty, Steven Stamkos, Zac Boychuk, Brandon Sutter, Luke Schenn, Brad Marchand, Colton Gillies, Kyle Turris, John Tavares, Riley Holzapfel, Shawn Matthias, P.K. Subban, Karl Alzner, Claude Giroux, Matt Halischuk, Wayne Simmonds

**Czech Republic** (Miloslav Horava, coach) GK—Michal Neuvirth, Jakub Kovar—Lukas Danecek, Jiri Suchy, Patrik Prokop, Jan Piskacek, Martin Paryzek, Michal Jordan, Daniel Bartek, Martin Latal, Pavel Kubena, Michael Frolik, Antonin Boruta, Jakub Sklenar, David Kveton, Radek Meidl, Jakub Voracek, Zbynek Hamp, Tomas Kundratek, Jiri Ondracek, Jan Semorad, Petr Strpac, Roman Szturc

**Denmark** (Ken Babey, coach) GK—Frederik Andersen, Christian Moeller—Philip Larsen, Oliver Lauridsen, Chris Rasmussen, Emil Bigler, Simon Gronvaldt, Mikkel Bodker, Lasse Holgaard, Mads Lund, Jeppe Henriksen, Nicholas Jensen, Lasse Lassen, Alexander Jensen, Lars Eller, Mathias Pedersen, Morten Poulse, Sune Hjulmand, Nichlas Hardt, John Jensen, Kevin Leder, Sebastian Svendsen

**Finland** (Jukka Rautakorpi, coach) GK—Riku Helenius, Harri Sateri—J.P. Purolinna, Joonas Jarvinen, Miko Malkamaki, Joonas Lehtivuori, Joonas Jalvanti, Mikko Kousa, Ville Lajunen, Juuso Puustinen, Siim Livik, Jarkko Malinen, Eetu Poysti, Max Warn, Harri Pesonen, Tomi Sallinen, Nico Aaltonen, Sakari Salminen, Joonas Kemppainen, Niclas Lucenius, J.M. Juutilainen, Nestori Lahde

**Kazakhstan** (Oleg Bolyakin, coach) GK—Mikhail Smolnikov, Alexander Kurshu, Sergei Rudolf—Roman Savchenko, Alexander Kaznacheyev, Nikita Ivanov, Mikhail Kachulin, Yakov Vorobyov, Alexander Gerasimov, Yevgeni Bolyakin, Dmitri Tikhonov, Konstantin Fast, Rostislav Koreshkov, Yevgeni Rymarev, Yevgeni Gasnikov, Stanislav Vitoshkin, Damir Ramazanov, Eduard Mazula, Kirill Kitsyn, Konstantin Savenkov, Yevgeni Tumashov, Semyon Paramzin

**Russia** (Sergei Nemchinov, coach) GK—Sergei Bobrovski, Stanislav Galimov—Pavel Doronin, Marat Kalimulin, Alexei Cherepanov, Yevgeni Kurbatov, Artyom Gordeyev, Yevgeni Bodrov, Viktor Tikhonov, Artyom Anisimov, Anton Korolyov, Maxim Mamin, Vadim Golubtsov, Dmitri Sayustov, Dmitri Kugryshev, Yakov Seleznev, Nikita Filatov, Yuri Alexandrov, Vyacheslav Voinov, Yevgeni Dadonov, Maxim Chudinov, Mikhail Milekhin

**Switzerland** (Jakob Kolliker, coach) GK—Robert Mayer, Lukas Flueler—Marc Welti, Patrick Geering, Marco Maurer, Lukas Stoop, Dino Wieser, Yannick Weber, Roman Schlagenhauf, Etienne Froidevaux, Denis Hollenstein, Kevin Lotscher, Gianni Donati, Arnaud Jacquemet, Gregory Sciaroni, Andrei Bykov, Luca Sbisa, Aurelio Lemm, Reto Suri, Pascal Berger, Roman Josi, Gaetan Augsburger

**Slovakia** (Stefan Mikes, coach) GK—Julius Hudacek, Tomas Hiadlovsky—Kristian Krajcik, Michal Kozak, Marek Zukal, Tomas Marcinko, Marek Daloga, Marek Biro, Marek Slovak, Jakub Suja, Ivan Rohac, Patrik Lusnak, Milan Jurik, Adam Bena, Erik Caladi, David Skokan, Matej Cesik, Milan Balis, Dalimir Jancovic, Juraj Mikus, Oliver Duris, Julius Sinkovic

**Sweden** (Par Marts, coach) GK—Jhonas Enroth, Stefan Ridderwall—Eric Moe, Johan Motin, Kristofer Berglund, Victor Hedman, Jonathan Carlsson, Oscar Eklund, Niclas Andersen, Mario Kempe, Carl Hagelin, Patrik Berglund, Tobias Forsberg, Patrik Lundh, Joakim Andersson, Magnus Svensson, Mikael Backlund, Robin Figren, Tomas Larsson, Tony Lagerstrom, Oscar Moller, Johan Alcen

**United States** (John Hynes, coach) GK—Jeremy Smith, Joe Palmer—Jamie McBain, Blake Geoffrion, Brian Strait, Kyle Okposo, Rhett Rakhshani, Matt Rust, James van Riemsdyk, Tyler Ruegsegger, Chris Summers, Max Pacioretty, Mike Carman, Bobby Sanguinetti, Bill Sweatt, Ryan Flynn, Kevin Montgomery, Jonathon Blum, Cade Fairchild, Ian Cole, Jordan Schroeder, Colin Wilson

## 33rd U20 WORLD CHAMPIONSHIP
## December 26, 2008-January 5, 2009
## Ottawa, Canada

**Final Placing**

| | |
|---|---|
| Gold .......Canada | 6th ........Czech Republic |
| Silver .....Sweden | 7th ........Finland |
| Bronze ...Russia | 8th ........Latvia^ |
| 4th .........Slovakia | 9th ........Germany^* |
| 5th .........United States | 10th ......Kazakhstan* |

^promoted from Division I in 2008
*demoted to Division I for 2010

**Tournament Format**

There were two divisions of five teams and each played a round-robin series in a preliminary round. The top team from each division advanced to the semi-finals, and the second and third place teams played for the other two spots. The second place team from one division played the third place team from the other, and vice versa. The two semi-finals winners played for gold, and the losers played for bronze.

**Results & Standings**
**PRELIMINARY ROUND**
**GROUP A**

| | GP | W | OTW | OTL | L | GF | GA | P |
|---|---|---|---|---|---|---|---|---|
| Canada | 4 | 4 | 0 | 0 | 0 | 36 | 6 | 12 |
| United States | 4 | 3 | 0 | 0 | 1 | 28 | 12 | 9 |
| Czech Republic | 4 | 2 | 0 | 0 | 2 | 20 | 14 | 6 |
| Germany | 4 | 1 | 0 | 0 | 3 | 12 | 19 | 3 |
| Kazakhstan | 4 | 0 | 0 | 0 | 4 | 2 | 46 | 0 |

| | | |
|---|---|---|
| December 26 | United States 8 | Germany 2 |
| December 26 | Canada 8 | Czech Republic 1 |
| December 27 | Germany 9 | Kazakhstan 0 |
| December 28 | Canada 15 | Kazakhstan 0 |
| December 28 | United States 4 | Czech Republic 3 |
| December 29 | Canada 5 | Germany 1 |
| December 30 | Czech Republic 6 | Germany 0 |
| December 30 | United States 12 | Kazakhstan 0 |
| December 31 | Czech Republic 10 | Kazakhstan 2 |
| December 31 | Canada 7 | United States 4 |

**GROUP B**

| | GP | W | OTW | OTL | L | GF | GA | P |
|---|---|---|---|---|---|---|---|---|
| Sweden | 4 | 4 | 0 | 0 | 0 | 21 | 3 | 12 |
| Russia | 4 | 3 | 0 | 0 | 1 | 17 | 9 | 9 |
| Slovakia | 4 | 1 | 1 | 0 | 2 | 12 | 15 | 5 |
| Finland | 4 | 1 | 0 | 1 | 2 | 10 | 12 | 4 |
| Latvia | 4 | 0 | 0 | 0 | 4 | 5 | 26 | 0 |

| | | |
|---|---|---|
| December 26 | Russia 4 | Latvia 1 |
| December 26 | Sweden 3 | Finland 1 |
| December 27 | Slovakia 7 | Latvia 2 |
| December 28 | Russia 5 | Finland 2 |
| December 28 | Sweden 3 | Slovakia 1 |
| December 29 | Sweden 10 | Latvia 1 |
| December 30 | Russia 8 | Slovakia 1 |
| December 30 | Finland 5 | Latvia 1 |
| December 31 | Sweden 5 | Russia 0 |
| December 31 | Slovakia 3 | Finland 2 (5:00 OT/GWS—Tomas Tatar) |

**RELEGATION ROUND**

| | GP | W | OTW | OTL | L | GF | GA | P |
|---|---|---|---|---|---|---|---|---|
| Finland | 3 | 3 | 0 | 0 | 0 | 15 | 3 | 9 |
| Latvia | 3 | 2 | 0 | 0 | 1 | 15 | 7 | 6 |
| Germany | 3 | 1 | 0 | 0 | 2 | 11 | 10 | 3 |
| Kazakhstan | 3 | 0 | 0 | 0 | 3 | 2 | 23 | 0 |

| | | |
|---|---|---|
| December 27 | Germany 9 | Kazakhstan 0 |
| December 30 | Finland 5 | Latvia 1 |
| January 2 | Latvia 7 | Germany 1 |
| January 3 | Finland 7 | Kazakhstan 1 |
| January 4 | Finland 3 | Germany 1 |
| January 4 | Latvia 7 | Kazakhstan 1 |

**5TH-PLACE GAME**

January 4 United States 3 Czech Republic 2 (James van Riemsdyk 2:49 OT)

**PLAYOFFS**

**QUARTER-FINALS**

| | | |
|---|---|---|
| January 2 | Slovakia 5 | United States 3 |
| January 2 | Russia 5 | Czech Republic 1 |

**SEMI-FINALS**

| | | |
|---|---|---|
| January 3 | Sweden 5 | Slovakia 3 |
| January 3 | Canada 6 | Russia 5 (10:00 OT/GWS—Jordan Eberle) |

**BRONZE MEDAL GAME**

| | | |
|---|---|---|
| January 5 | Russia 5 | Slovakia 2 |

**GOLD MEDAL GAME**

| | | |
|---|---|---|
| January 5 | Canada 5 | Sweden 1 |

**Rosters**

**Canada** (Pat Quinn, coach) GK—Dustin Tokarski, Chet Pickard—Colten Teubert, Tyler Myers, Thomas Hickey, P.K. Subban, Angelo Esposito, Ryan Ellis, Alex Pietrangelo, Zach Boychuk, Brett Sonne, Jordan Eberle, Stefan Della Rovere, Cody Goloubef, Cody Hodgson, John Tavares, Tyler Ennis, Jamie Benn, Chris Di Domenico, Patrice Cormier, Evander Kane, Keith Aulie

**Czech Republic** (Marek Sykora, coach) GK—Dominik Furch, Tomas Vosvrda—Radko Gudas, Jan Piskacek, Milan Doczy, Martin Paryzek, David Stich, Jan Kana, Ondrej Roman, Zdenek Okal, Tomas Knotek, Stepan Novotny, Vladimir Ruzicka, Tomas Kubalik, Michal Jordan, Roman Szturc, Rudolf Cerveny, Radim Valchar, Tomas Kundratek, Jan Eberle, Petr Strapac, Tomas Vincour

**Finland** (Jukka Rautakorpi, coach) GK—Juha Metsola, Harri Sateri—Ari Grondahl, Tommi Kivisto, Ilari Melart, Joonas Jarvinen, Jyri Niemi, Eetu Poysti, Niclas Lucenius, Toni Rajala, Mikael Granlund, Jesse Jyrkkio, Nestori Lahde, Antti Roppo, Tomi Sallinen, Sami Lahteenmaki, Jani Helenius, Veli-Matti Vittasmaki, Joonas Rask, Jani Lajunen, Joonas Nattinen, Teemu Hartikainen

**Germany** (Ernst Hofner, coach) GK—Timo Pielmeier, Philipp Grubauer—Tim Schule, Simon Fischaber, Andre Huebscher, Sinan Akdag, Jerome Flaake, Denis Reul, David Wolf, Armin Wurm, Marco Nowak, Alexander Oblinger, Patrick Pohl, Benedikt Bruckner, Toni Ritter, Gerrit Fauser, Daniel Weiss, Steven Rupprich, Maximilian Forester, Florian Muller, Conor Morrison, Dominik Bielke

**Kazakhstan** (Oleg Bolyakin coach) GK—Maxim Gryaznov, Andrei Yankov—Igor Denisenko, Dmitri Tikhonov, Andrei Korovkin, Igor Netesov, Nikolai Safonov, Vitali Svistunov, Alexander Nurek, Nikita Ivanov, Mikhail Lazorenko, Viktor Ivashin, Alexander Kaznacheyev, Yevgeni Bolyakin, Vyacheslav Fedosenko, Eduard Mazula, Yakov Vorobyov, Leonid Metalnikov, Konstantin Savenkov, Oleg Onichshenko

**Latvia** (Andrejs Maticins, coach) GK—Nauris Enkuzens, Raimonds Ermics—Alberts Ilisko, Gvido Kauss, Aldis Pizans, Martins Gipters, Janis Smits, Roberts Bukarts, Gunars Skvorcovs, Roberts Jekimovs, Koba Jass, Janis Ozolins, Janis Straupe, Kristaps Kuplais, Ronalds Cinks, Vitalijs Pavlovs, Artioms Ogorodnikovs, Lauris Bajaruns, Kriss Grundmanis, Edgars Lipsbergs, Edgars Ulescenko, Ralfs Freibergs

**Russia** (Sergei Nemchinov, coach) GK—Vadim Zhelobnyuk, Danila Alistratov—Igor Golovkov, Dmitri Kulikov, Maxim Goncharov, Mikhail Pashnin, Vasili Tokranov, Dmitri Klopov, Pavel Chernov, Alexander Komaristy, Dinar Khafizullin, Yevgeni Grachyov, Sergei Andronov, Dmitri Kugryshev, Nikita Klyukin, Sergei Korostin, Vyacheslav Voinov, Yevgeni Dadonov, Maxim Chudinov, Nikita Filatov, Alexei Potapov, Kirill Petrov

**Slovakia** (Stefan Mikes, coach) GK—Jaroslav Janus, Zdenko Kotvan—Martin Stajnoch, Michal Siska, Marek Daloga, Juraj Valach, Peter Kopecky, Martin Uhnak, Adam Beznak, Tomas Tatar, Ondrej Rusnak, Matus Vizvary, Marek Hrivik, Jozef Molnar, Jan Brejcak, Radoslav Tybor, Milan Kytnar, Marek Viedensky, Radek Deyl, Tomas Vyletelka, Richard Panik, Marek Mertel

**Sweden** (Par Marts, coach) GK—Jacob Markstrom, Mark Owuya—Sebastian Erixon, Victor Hedman, Erik Karlsson, Nichlas Torp, David Rundblad, Viktor Ekbom, Oscar Moller, Mattias Tedenby, Marcus Johansson, Tim Erixon, Anton Persson, Joakim Andersson, Andre Petersson, Magnus Paajarvi-Svensson, Mikael Backlund, Nicklas Lasu, David Ullstrom, Jacob Josefson, Carl Gustafsson, Simon Hjalmarsson

**United States** (Ron Rolston, coach) GK—Josh Unice, Tom McCollum—Cade Fairchild, Teddy Ruth, Aaron Palushaj, Kevin Shattenkirk, Matt Rust, Tyler Johnson, Mike Hoeffel, Jimmy Hayes, Mitch Wahl, Jim O'Brien, Ryan McDonagh, Danny Kristo, Jordan Schroeder, Blake Kessel, James van Riemsdyk, Jonathon Blum, Eric Tangradi, Drayson Bowman, Ian Cole, Colin Wilson

## 34th U20 WORLD CHAMPIONSHIP
## December 26, 2009-January 5, 2010
## Saskatoon/Regina, Canada

**Final Placing**

| | |
|---|---|
| Gold ........United States | 6th .........Russia |
| Silver ......Canada | 7th .........Czech Republic |
| Bronze ....Sweden | 8th .........Slovakia |
| 4th..........Switzerland^ | 9th .........Latvia* |
| 5th..........Finland | 10th .......Austria^* |

^promoted from Division I in 2009
*demoted to Division I for 2011

**Tournament Format**

There were two divisions of five teams and each played a round-robin series in a preliminary round. The top team from each division advanced to the semi-finals, and the second and third place teams played for the other two spots. The second place team from one division played the third place team from the other, and vice versa. The two semi-finals winners played for gold, and the losers played for bronze.

**Results & Standings**

**PRELIMINARY ROUND**

**GROUP A (SASKATOON)**

| | GP | W | OTW | OTL | L | GF | GA | P |
|---|---|---|---|---|---|---|---|---|
| Canada | 4 | 3 | 1 | 0 | 0 | 35 | 6 | 11 |
| United States | 4 | 3 | 0 | 1 | 0 | 26 | 9 | 10 |
| Switzerland | 4 | 2 | 0 | 0 | 2 | 11 | 15 | 6 |
| Slovakia | 4 | 1 | 0 | 0 | 3 | 14 | 22 | 3 |
| Latvia | 4 | 0 | 0 | 0 | 4 | 9 | 43 | 0 |

| | | |
|---|---|---|
| December 26 | Canada 16 | Latvia 0 |
| December 26 | United States 7 | Slovakia 3 |
| December 27 | United States 3 | Switzerland 0 |
| December 27 | Slovakia 8 | Latvia 3 |
| December 28 | Canada 6 | Switzerland 0 |
| December 29 | United States 12 | Latvia 1 |
| December 29 | Canada 8 | Slovakia 2 |
| December 30 | Switzerland 7 | Latvia 5 |
| December 31 | Switzerland 4 | Slovakia 1 |
| December 31 | Canada 5 | United States 4 (5:00 OT/GWS—Brandon Kozun) |

**GROUP B (REGINA)**

| | GP | W | OTW | OTL | L | GF | GA | P |
|---|---|---|---|---|---|---|---|---|
| Sweden | 4 | 4 | 0 | 0 | 0 | 28 | 6 | 12 |
| Russia | 4 | 3 | 0 | 0 | 1 | 14 | 8 | 9 |
| Finland | 4 | 2 | 0 | 0 | 2 | 15 | 13 | 6 |
| Czech Republic | 4 | 1 | 0 | 0 | 3 | 13 | 20 | 3 |
| Austria | 4 | 0 | 0 | 0 | 4 | 7 | 30 | 0 |

| | | |
|---|---|---|
| December 26 | Sweden 10 | Czech Republic 1 |
| December 26 | Russia 6 | Austria 2 |
| December 27 | Sweden 7 | Austria 3 |
| December 27 | Finland 4 | Czech Republic 3 |
| December 28 | Russia 2 | Finland 0 |
| December 29 | Czech Republic 7 | Austria 1 |
| December 29 | Sweden 4 | Russia 1 |
| December 30 | Finland 10 | Austria 1 |
| December 31 | Sweden 7 | Finland 1 |
| December 31 | Russia 5 | Czech Republic 2 |

**RELEGATION ROUND (SASKATOON)**

| | GP | W | OTW | OTL | L | GF | GA | P |
|---|---|---|---|---|---|---|---|---|
| Czech Republic | 3 | 3 | 0 | 0 | 0 | 22 | 5 | 9 |
| Slovakia | 3 | 2 | 0 | 0 | 1 | 13 | 10 | 6 |
| Latvia | 3 | 1 | 0 | 0 | 2 | 11 | 22 | 3 |
| Austria | 3 | 0 | 0 | 0 | 3 | 7 | 16 | 0 |

| | | |
|---|---|---|
| January 2 | Slovakia 3 | Austria 2 |
| January 3 | Czech Republic 10 | Latvia 2 |
| January 4 | Czech Republic 5 | Slovakia 2 |
| January 4 | Latvia 6 | Austria 4 |

**5TH-PLACE GAME**

| | | | |
|---|---|---|---|
| January 4 | Saskatoon | Finland 4 | Russia 3 |

**PLAYOFFS (SASKATOON)**

**QUARTER-FINALS**

| | | |
|---|---|---|
| January 2 | Switzerland 3 | Russia 2 (Nino Niederreiter 9:46 OT) |
| January 2 | United States 6 | Finland 2 |

**SEMI-FINALS**

| | | |
|---|---|---|
| January 3 | Canada 6 | Switzerland 1 |
| January 3 | United States 5 | Sweden 2 |

**BRONZE MEDAL GAME**

| | | |
|---|---|---|
| January 5 | Sweden 11 | Switzerland 4 |

**GOLD MEDAL GAME**

| | | |
|---|---|---|
| January 5 | United States 6 | Canada 5 (John Carlson 4:21 OT) |

**Rosters**

**Austria** (Dieter Werfring, coach) GK—Lorenz Hirn, Marco Wieser—Andreas Untergaschnigg, Marco Zorec, Alexander Pallestrang, Marcus Unterweger, Stefan Ulmer, Fabian Scholz, Maximilian Oliver Isopp, Kevin Puschnik, Nikolaus Hartl, Fabio Hofer, Konstantin Komarek, Patrick Maier, Markus Pock, Andreas Kristler, Dominique Heinrich, Florian Muhlstein, Peter Schneider, Pascal Kainz, Alexander Korner, Marcel Wolf

**Canada** (Willie Desjardins, coach) GK—Jake Allen, Martin Jones—Jordan Eberle, Taylor Hall, Alex Pietrangelo, Gabriel Bourque, Luke Adam, Brandon McMillan, Nazem Kadri, Brayden Schenn, Ryan Ellis, Brandon Kozun, Stefan Della Rovere, Patrice Cormier, Jordan Caron, Marco Scandella, Travis Hamonic, Adam Henrique, Greg Nemisz, Jared Cowen, Colten Teubert, Calvin de Haan

**Czech Republic** (Jaromir Sindel, coach) GK—Jakub Sedlacek, Pavel Francouz—Radko Gudas, Tomas Voracek, Jakub Jerabek, Andrej Sustr, Jan Kana, Roman Horak, Andrej Nestrasil, Tomas Dolezal, Robert Kousal, Tomas Knotek, Vladimir Roth, Stepan Novotny, Tomas Kubalik, Tomas Vincour, Michal Jordan, Jan Kovar, Michal Poletin, Michal Hlinka, David Ostrizek, Michal Kempny

**Finland** (Hannu Jortikka, coach) GK—Joni Ortio, Petteri Simila—Tommi Kivisto, Teemu Eronen, Kristian Nakyva, Jyri Niemi, Sami Vatanen, Matias Myttynen, Toni Rajala, Aleksi Laakso, Matias Sointu, Pekka Jormakka, Eero Elo, Iiro Pakarinen, Joonas Rask, Jere Sallinen, Jasse Ikonen, Mikael Granlund, Jani Lajunen, Veli-Matti Vittasmaki, Joonas Nattinen, Teemu Hartikainen

**Latvia** (Andrejs Maticins, coach) GK—Janis Kalnins, Raimonds Ermics—Alberts Ilisko, Gvido Kauss, Eriks Sevcenko, Raimonds Vilkoits, Janis Smits, Juris Upitis, Miks Indrasis, Roberts Bukarts, Gunars Skvorcovs, Ronalds Kenins, Arturs Mickevics, Roberts Mazins, Miks Lipsbergs, Ronalds Cinks, Rolands Vigners, Rolands Gritans, Martins Jakovlevs, Karlis Kalvitis, Edgars Ulescenko, Ralfs Freibergs

**Russia** (Vladimir Plyushev coach) GK—Igor Bobkov, Ramis Sadikov—Nikita Zaitsev, Nikita Pivtsakin, Dmitri Kostromitin, Vyacheslav Kulyomin, Alexander Burmistrov, Dmitri Orlov, Vladimir Tarasenko, Maxim Trunyov, Maxim Kitsyn, Ivan Telegin, Piotr Khokhriakov, Yevgeni Kuznetsov, Pavel Dedunov, Kirill Petrov, Yevgeni Timkin, Magomed Gimbatov, Alexander Tarasov, Maxim Chudinov, Nikita Filatov, Anton Klementyev

**Slovakia** (Stefan Mikes, coach) GK—Marek Ciliak, Tomas Halasz—Martin Stajnoch, Henrich Jabornik, Maros Grosaft, Martin Bakos, Matus Rais, Tomas Tatar, Frantisek Gerhat, Libor Hudacek, Samuel Mlynarovic, Peter Hrasko, Radoslav Illo, Jakub Gasparovic, Michael Vandas, Michal Siska, Marek Viedensky, Martin Marincin, Adam Lapsansky, Andrej Stastny, Richard Panik, Ivan Jankovic

**Sweden** (Par Marts, coach) GK—Jacob Markstrom, Anders Nilsson—Lukas Kilstrom, Oliver Ekman-Larsson, Tim Erixon, Adam Larsson, Peter Andersson, David Rundblad, Mattias Tedenby, Jacob Josefson, Marcus Johansson, Dennis Rasmussen, Jakob Silfverberg, Mattias Ekholm, Anton Lander, Carl Klingberg, Anton Rodin, Andre Petersson, Magnus Paajarvi-Svensson, Marcus Kruger, Daniel Brodin, Martin Lundberg

**Switzerland** (Jakob Kolliker, coach) GK—Benjamin Conz, Matthias Mischler—Luca Camperchioli, Nicolas Gay, Patrick Geering, Luca Sbisa, Lukas Stoop, Sven Ryser, Reto Schappi, Tristan Scherwey, Jeffrey Fuglister, Benjamin Antonietti, Tim Weber, Dominik Schlumpf, Ryan McGregor, Mauro Jorg, Nino Niederreiter, Michael Loichat, Pascal Marolf, Roman Josi, Jannik Fischer, Ramon Untersander

**United States** (Dean Blais, coach) GK—Mike Lee, Jack Campbell—John Ramage, Matt Donovan, David Warsofsky, Danny Kristo, Philip McRae, Tyler Johnson, John Carlson, Luke Walker, Jason Zucker, Ryan Bourque, Brian Lashoff, Jordan Schroeder, Chris Kreider, Derek Stepan, A.J. Jenks, Kyle Palmieri, Cam Fowler, Jeremy Morin, Jake Gardiner, Jerry D'Amigo

## 35th U20 WORLD CHAMPIONSHIP
## December 26, 2010-January 5, 2011
## Buffalo/Niagara, United States

**Final Placing**

| | |
|---|---|
| Gold ........Russia | 6th .........Finland |
| Silver ......Canada | 7th .........Czech Republic |
| Bronze ....United States | 8th .........Slovakia |
| 4th..........Sweden | 9th .........Norway^ |
| 5th..........Switzerland | 10th .......Germany^ |

^promoted from Division I in 2010/demoted to Division I for 2012

**Tournament Format**

There were two divisions of five teams and each played a round-robin series in a preliminary round. The top team from each division advanced to the semi-finals, and the second and third place teams played for the other two spots. The second place team from one division played the third place team from the other, and vice versa. The two semi-finals winners played for gold, and the losers played for bronze.

**Results & Standings**

**PRELIMINARY ROUND**

**GROUP A (BUFFALO)**

| | GP | W | OTW | OTL | L | GF | GA | P |
|---|---|---|---|---|---|---|---|---|
| United States | 4 | 3 | 1 | 0 | 0 | 15 | 4 | 11 |
| Finland | 4 | 3 | 0 | 1 | 0 | 17 | 4 | 10 |
| Switzerland | 4 | 2 | 0 | 0 | 2 | 11 | 13 | 6 |
| Slovakia | 4 | 0 | 1 | 0 | 3 | 7 | 19 | 2 |
| Germany | 4 | 0 | 0 | 1 | 3 | 5 | 15 | 1 |

| | | |
|---|---|---|
| December 26 | Switzerland 4 | Germany 3 |
| December 26 | United States 3 | Finland 2 (Nick Bjugstad 3:08 OT) |
| December 27 | Slovakia 2 | Germany 1 (Marek Hrivik 3:39 OT) |
| December 28 | Finland 4 | Switzerland 0 |
| December 28 | United States 6 | Slovakia 1 |
| December 29 | Finland 5 | Germany 1 |
| December 30 | Switzerland 6 | Slovakia 4 |
| December 30 | United States 4 | Germany 0 |
| December 31 | Finland 6 | Slovakia 0 |
| December 31 | United States 2 | Switzerland 1 |

**GROUP B**

| | GP | W | OTW | OTL | L | GF | GA | P |
|---|---|---|---|---|---|---|---|---|
| Sweden | 4 | 3 | 1 | 0 | 0 | 21 | 9 | 11 |
| Canada | 4 | 3 | 0 | 1 | 0 | 28 | 12 | 10 |
| Russia | 4 | 2 | 0 | 0 | 2 | 19 | 13 | 6 |
| Czech Republic | 4 | 1 | 0 | 0 | 3 | 10 | 21 | 3 |
| Norway | 4 | 0 | 0 | 0 | 4 | 4 | 27 | 0 |

| | | | |
|---|---|---|---|
| December 26 | Buffalo | Canada 6 | Russia 3 |
| December 26 | Niagara | Sweden 7 | Norway 1 |
| December 27 | Niagara | Czech Republic 2 | Norway 0 |
| December 28 | Buffalo | Canada 7 | Czech Republic 2 |
| December 28 | Niagara | Sweden 2 | Russia 0 |
| December 29 | Buffalo | Canada 10 | Norway 1 |
| December 30 | Niagara | Sweden 6 | Czech Republic 3 |
| December 30 | Niagara | Russia 8 | Norway 2 |
| December 31 | Buffalo | Sweden 6 (5:00 OT/GWS—Oscar Lindberg) | Canada 5 |
| December 31 | Niagara | Russia 8 | Czech Republic 3 |

**RELEGATION ROUND (NIAGARA)**

| | GP | W | OTW | OTL | L | GF | GA | P |
|---|---|---|---|---|---|---|---|---|
| Czech Republic | 3 | 3 | 0 | 0 | 0 | 10 | 4 | 9 |
| Slovakia | 3 | 1 | 1 | 0 | 1 | 9 | 6 | 5 |
| Norway | 3 | 1 | 0 | 0 | 2 | 3 | 8 | 3 |
| Germany | 3 | 0 | 0 | 1 | 2 | 4 | 8 | 1 |

| | | |
|---|---|---|
| January 2 | Slovakia 5 | Norway 0 |
| January 2 | Czech Republic 3 | Germany 2 |
| January 4 | Norway 3 | Germany 1 |
| January 4 | Czech Republic 5 | Slovakia 2 |

**FIFTH-PLACE GAME**

January 4 Buffalo Switzerland 3 Finland 2 (5:00 OT/GWS—Yannick Herren)

**PLAYOFFS (BUFFALO)**

**QUARTER-FINALS**

| | | |
|---|---|---|
| January 2 | Canada 4 | Switzerland 1 |
| January 2 | Russia 4 | Finland 3 (Yevgeni Kuznetsov 6:44 OT) |

**SEMI-FINALS**

| | | |
|---|---|---|
| January 3 | Russia 4 | Sweden 3 (10:00 OT/GWS—Denis Golubev) |
| January 3 | Canada 4 | United States 1 |

**BRONZE MEDAL GAME**

January 5 United States 4 Sweden 2

**GOLD MEDAL GAME**

January 5 Russia 5 Canada 3

**Rosters**

**Canada** (Dave Cameron, coach) GK—Mark Visentin, Olivier Roy—Jared Cowen, Simon Despres, Dylan Olsen, Erik Gudbranson, Ryan Ellis, Sean Couturier, Jaden Schwartz, Zack Kassian, Brayden Schenn, Casey Cizikas, Quinton Howden, Curtis Hamilton, Marcus Foligno, Ryan Johansen, Louis Leblanc, Cody Eakin, Tyson Barrie, Calvin de Haan, Carter Ashton, Brett Connolly

**Czech Republic** (Miroslav Prerost, coach) GK—Filip Novotny, Marek Mazanec—Oldrich Horak, Martin Frk, Dalibor Reznicek, Michal Hlinka, Petr Senkerik, Tomas Rachunek, Andrej Nestrasil, Jakub Jerabek, Jakub Culek, Martin Planek, Petr Holik, Ondrej Palat, Antonin Honejsek, Petr Straka, Roman Horak, Adam Sedlak, Robin Soudek, David Tuma, Jakub Orsava, Bohumil Jank

**Finland** (Lauri Marjamaki, coach) GK—Sami Aittokallio, Joni Ortio—Jyrki Jokipakka, Tommi Kivisto, Nico Manelius, Teemu Pulkkinen, Rasmus Rissanen, Sami Vatanen, Erik Haula, Miikka Salomaki, Julius Junttila, Olli Maatta, Henri Tuominen, Iiro Pakarinen, Joel Armia, Valtteri Virkkunen, Jesse Virtanen, Teemu Tallberg, Toni Rajala, Joonas Donskoi, Jaakko Turtiainen, Joonas Nattinen

**Germany** (Ernst Hofner, coach) GK—Niklas Treutle, Philipp Grubauer—Peter Lindlbauer, Benjamin Hufner, Konrad Abeltshauser, Dominik Bittner, Corey Mapes, Norman Hauner, Thomas Brandl, Jannik Woidtke, Tom Kuhnhackl, Marcel Noebels, Tobias Rieder, Laurin Braun, Mirko Hofflin, Marcel Ohmann, Marc El-Sayed, Matthias Plachta, Dieter Orendorz, Bernhard Keil, Nickolas Latta, Marius Mochel

**Norway** (Geir Hoff, coach) GK—Steffen Soberg, Lars Volden—Nicolai Bryhnisveen, Tobias Skaarberg, Jens Ulrik Bacher, Kenneth Madso, Adrian Danielsen, Andreas Stene, Magnus Lindahl, Petter Roste Fossen, Rasmus Juell, Sondre Olden, Eirik Borresen, Michael Haga, Nicholas Weberg, Jonas Oppoyen, Mats Rosseli Olsen, Hans Kristian Hollstedt, Joacim Sundelius, Daniel Rokseth, Simen Brekke, Robin Andersen

**Russia** (Valeri Bragin, coach) GK—Dmitri Shikin, Igor Bobkov—Nikita Zaitsev, Nikita Pivtsakin, Maxim Berezin, Georgi Berdyukov, Anton Burdasov, Semyon Valuiski, Dmitri Orlov, Vladimir Tarasenko, Yuri Urychev, Maxim Kitsyn, Danil Sobchenko, Artyom Voronin, Nikita Dvurechenski, Stanislav Bocharov, Sergei Kalinin, Maxim Ignatovich, Yevgeni Kuznetsov, Andrei Sergeyev, Artemi Panarin, Denis Golubev

**Slovakia** (Stefan Mikes, coach) GK—Juraj Holly, Dominik Riecicky—Adam Janosik, Lukas Kozak, Peter Trska, Peter Sisovsky, Juraj Majdan, Oliver Jokel, Tomas Jurco, Peter Hrasko, Andrej Stastny, Dominik Simcak, Dalibor Bortnak, Michael Vandas, Martin Marincin, Tomas Matousek, Andrej Kudrna, Henrich Jabornik, Peter Ceresnak, Marek Hrivik, Richard Panik, Miroslav Preisinger

**Sweden** (Roger Ronnberg, coach) GK—Fredrik Petersson Wentzel, Robin Lehner—Fredrik Styrman, Tim Erixon, Adam Larsson, Klas Dahlbeck, John Klingberg, Johan Larsson, Patrik Nemeth, Johan Sundstrom, Max Friberg, Simon Bertilsson, Anton Lander, Carl Klingberg, Jesper Fasth, Calle Jarnkrok, Sebastian Wannstrom, Gabriel Landeskog, Oscar Lindberg, Rickard Rackell, Jesper Thornberg, Patrick Cehlin

**Switzerland** (Richard Jost, coach) GK—Benjamin Conz, Remo Giovannini—Romain Loeffel, Nicholas Steiner, Luca Camperchioli, Dominik Schlumpf, Reto Schappi, Tristan Scherwey, Gaetan Haas, Gregory Hofmann, Sven Bartschi, Inti Pestoni, Dario Trutmann, Ryan McGregor, Renato Engler, Nino Niederreiter, Benjamin Antonietti, Samuel Walser, Joel Vermin, Yannick Herren, Samuel Guerra, Ramon Untersander

**United States** (Keith Allain, coach) GK—Jack Campbell, Andy Iles—Charlie Coyle, Brian Dumoulin, John Ramage, Nick Leddy, Derek Forbort, Brock Nelson, Jerry D'Amigo, Chris Brown, Jeremy Morin, Jon Merrilal, Drew Shore, Jason Zucker, Ryan Bourque, Patrick Wey, Chris Kreider, Kyle Palmieri, Mitch Callahan, Justin Faulk, Emerson Etem, Nick Bjugstad

## 36th U20 WORLD CHAMPIONSHIP
## December 26, 2011-January 5, 2012
## Calgary/Edmonton, Canada

### Final Placing

| | |
|---|---|
| Gold ........Sweden | 6th .........Slovakia |
| Silver ......Russia | 7th .........United States |
| Bronze ....Canada | 8th .........Switzerland |
| 4th.........Finland | 9th .........Latvia^ |
| 5th.........Czech Republic | 10th .......Denmark^ |

^promoted from Division I in 2011/demoted to Division I for 2013

### Tournament Format

There were two divisions of five teams and each played a round-robin series in a preliminary round. The top team from each division advanced to the semi-finals, and the second and third place teams played for the other two spots. The second place team from one division played the third place team from the other, and vice versa. The two semi-finals winners played for gold, and the losers played for bronze.

### Results & Standings
**PRELIMINARY ROUND**
**GROUP A (CALGARY)**

| | GP | W | OTW | OTL | L | GF | GA | P |
|---|---|---|---|---|---|---|---|---|
| Sweden | 4 | 2 | 2 | 0 | 0 | 26 | 11 | 10 |
| Russia | 4 | 3 | 0 | 1 | 0 | 23 | 5 | 10 |
| Slovakia | 4 | 2 | 0 | 0 | 2 | 11 | 17 | 6 |
| Switzerland | 4 | 1 | 0 | 1 | 2 | 12 | 16 | 4 |
| Latvia | 4 | 0 | 0 | 0 | 4 | 8 | 31 | 0 |

| | | |
|---|---|---|
| December 26 | Sweden 9 | Latvia 4 |
| December 26 | Russia 3 | Switzerland 0 |
| December 27 | Slovakia 3 | Latvia 1 |
| December 28 | Sweden 4 | Switzerland 3 (5:00 OT/GWS—Sebastian Collberg) |
| December 28 | Russia 3 | Slovakia 1 |
| December 29 | Russia 14 | Latvia 0 |
| December 30 | Sweden 9 | Slovakia 1 |
| December 30 | Switzerland 5 | Latvia 3 |
| December 31 | Slovakia 6 | Switzerland 4 |
| December 31 | Sweden 4 | Russia 3 (Joakim Nordstrom 2:44 OT) |

**GROUP B (EDMONTON)**

| | GP | W | OTW | OTL | L | GF | GA | P |
|---|---|---|---|---|---|---|---|---|
| Canada | 4 | 4 | 0 | 0 | 0 | 26 | 5 | 12 |
| Finland | 4 | 3 | 0 | 0 | 1 | 19 | 10 | 9 |
| Czech Republic | 4 | 2 | 0 | 0 | 2 | 12 | 11 | 6 |
| United States | 4 | 1 | 0 | 0 | 3 | 16 | 15 | 3 |
| Denmark | 4 | 0 | 0 | 0 | 4 | 6 | 38 | 0 |

| | | |
|---|---|---|
| December 26 | Canada 8 | Finland 1 |
| December 26 | United States 11 | Denmark 3 |
| December 27 | Czech Republic 7 | Denmark 0 |
| December 28 | Finland 4 | United States 1 |
| December 28 | Canada 5 | Czech Republic 0 |
| December 29 | Canada 10 | Denmark 2 |
| December 30 | Czech Republic 5 | United States 2 |
| December 30 | Finland 10 | Denmark 1 |
| December 31 | Finland 4 | Czech Republic 0 |
| December 31 | Canada 3 | United States 2 |

**RELEGATION ROUND (CALGARY)**

| | GP | W | OTW | OTL | L | GF | GA | P |
|---|---|---|---|---|---|---|---|---|
| United States | 3 | 3 | 0 | 0 | 0 | 25 | 6 | 9 |
| Switzerland | 3 | 1 | 1 | 0 | 1 | 10 | 8 | 5 |
| Latvia | 3 | 0 | 1 | 0 | 2 | 7 | 18 | 2 |
| Denmark | 3 | 0 | 0 | 2 | 1 | 7 | 17 | 2 |

| | | |
|---|---|---|
| January 2 | Switzerland 4 | Denmark 3 (Tanner Richard 3:27 OT) |
| January 3 | United States 12 | Latvia 2 |
| January 4 | Latvia 2 | Denmark 1 (Nikita Jevpalovs 1:43 OT) |
| January 4 | United States 2 | Switzerland 1 |

**FIFTH-PLACE GAME**

| | | | |
|---|---|---|---|
| January 4 | Calgary | Czech Republic 5 | Slovakia 2 |

**PLAYOFFS (CALGARY)**
**QUARTER-FINALS**

| | | |
|---|---|---|
| January 2 | Finland 8 | Slovakia 5 |
| January 2 | Russia 2 | Czech Republic 1 (Grigori Zheldakov 1:30 OT) |

**SEMI-FINALS**

| | | |
|---|---|---|
| January 3 | Sweden 3 | Finland 2 (10:00 OT/GWS—Max Friberg) |
| January 3 | Russia 6 | Canada 5 |

**BRONZE MEDAL GAME**

| | | |
|---|---|---|
| January 5 | Canada 4 | Finland 0 |

**GOLD MEDAL GAME**

| | | |
|---|---|---|
| January 5 | Sweden 1 | Russia 0 (Mika Zibanejad 10:09 OT) |

### Rosters

**Canada** (Don Hay, coach) GK: Mark Visentin, Scott Wedgewood—Jamie Oleksiak, Brandon Gormley, Dougie Hamilton, Mark Pysyk, Scott Harrington, Jaden Schwartz, Michael Bournival, Jonathan Huberdeau, Brendan Gallagher, Freddie Hamilton, Brett Connolly, Tanner Pearson, Mark Stone, Ryan Strome, Mark Scheifele, Boone Jenner, Quinton Howden, Devante Smith-Pelly, Ryan Murray, Nathan Beaulieu

**Czech Republic** (Miroslav Prerost, coach) GK: Petr Mrazek, Libor Kasik, Tomas Kral (DNP)—Jiri Riha, David Musil, Petr Zamorsky, Vojtech Mozik, Daniel Krejci, Marek Hrbas, Jakub Culek, Daniel Pribyl, Radek Faksa, Petr Holik, Tomas Nosek, Tomas Hertl, Dmitrij Jaskin, Petr Straka, Tomas Filippi, Dominik Uher, Jiri Sekac, Tomas Hyka, Bohumil Jank, Lukas Sedlak

**Denmark** (Todd Bjorkstrand, coach) GK: Sebastian Feuk, Dennis Jensen, Christian Larsen—Jannik Christensen, Patrick Madsen, Tobias Hansen, Martin Rahbek, Thomas Spelling, Emil Kristensen, Patrick Bjorkstrand, Oliver Bjorkstrand, Mathais Bau-Hansen, Jonas Sass-Jensen, Nicolai Meyer, Nicklas Jensen, Thomas Sondergaard, Mads Eller, Mark Larsen, Joachim Linnet, Rasmus Bjerrum, Nicki Kisum, Anders Thode, Anders Schultz

**Finland** (Raimo Helminen, coach) GK: Sami Aittokallio, Christopher Gibson, Richard Ullberg—Olli Maata, Simo-Pekka Riikola, Konsta Makinen, Rasmus Ristolainen, Teemu Pulkkinen, Jani Hakanpaa, Miro Hovinen, Alexander Ruuttu, Joel Armia, Markus Granlund, Ville Pokka, Markus Hannikainen, Roope Hamalainen, Miro Aaltonen, Aleksander Barkov, Mikael Granlund, Miikka Salomaki, Joonas Donskoi, Mikael Kuronen, Otto Paajanen

**Latvia** (Eriks Miluns, coach) GK: Kristers Gudlevskis, Elvis Merzlikins, Rihards Cimermanis—Kristaps Nimanis, Nikita Kolesnikovs, Edgars Siksna, Arturs Salija, Pauls Zvirbulis, Kristians Pelss, Kristers Freibergs, Roberts Lipsbergs, Arturs Kuzmenkovs, Vitalijs Hvorostinins, Juris Ziemens, Maris Dilevka, Davis Straupe, Kriss Lipsbergs, Edgars Klavins, Teodors Blugers, Zemgus Girgensons, Toms Andersons, Krists Kalnins, Nikita Jevpalovs

**Russia** (Valeri Bragin, coach) GK: Andrei Vasilevski, Andrei Makarov, Sergei Kostenko—Artyom Sergeyev, Viktor Antipin, Mikhail Naumenkov, Igor Ozhiganov, Nikita Gusev, Nikita Kucherov, Nail Yakupov, Grigori Zheldakov, Danil Apalkov, Pavel Kulikov, Ignat Zemchenko, Mikhail Grigorenko, Yaroslav Kosov, Alexander Khokhlachev, Sergei Barbashev, Ivan Telegin, Zakhar Arzamastsev, Yevgeni Kuznetsov, Ildar Isangulov, Nikita Nesterov

**Slovakia** (Ernest Bokros, coach) GK: Juraj Simboch, Dominik Riecicky, Richard Sabol—Adam Janosik, Peter Bezuska, Peter Trska, Mario Kurali, Michal Toman, Matej Hindos, Michal Cajkovsky, Richard Mraz, Tomas Jurco, Peter Ceresnak, Matej Bene, Marek Tvrdon, Vladimir Dolnik, Martin Daloga, Martin Marincin, Milos Bubela, Martin Gernat, Matus Chovan, Tomas Matousek, Marko Dano

**Sweden** (Roger Ronnberg, coach) GK: Johan Gustafsson, Anton Forsberg, Johan Mattsson—Mattias Backman, Oscar Klefbom, Fredrik Claesson, Petter Granberg, John Klingberg, Johan Larsson, Jeremy Boyce-Rotevall, Patrik Nemeth, Johan Sundstrom, Max Friberg, Sebastian Collberg, Filip Forsberg, William Karlsson, Victor Rask, Joakim Nordstrom, Mika Zibanejad, Ludvig Rensfeldt, Rickard Rackell, Jonas Brodin, Erik Thorell

**Switzerland** (Manuele Celio, coach) GK: Tim Wolf, Lukas Meili, Luca Boltshauser—Cedric Hachler, Phil Baltisberger, Mike Vermeille, Dave Sutter, Christian Marti, Alessio Bertaggia, Gaetan Haas, Lino Martschini, Gregory Hofmann, Dean Kukan, Sven Bartschi, Dario Trutmann, Reto Amstutz, Sven Andrighetto, Cedric Schneuwly, Samuel Walser, Dario Simion, Joel Vermin, Christoph Bertschy, Tanner Richard

**United States** (Dean Blais, coach) GK: Jack Campbell, John Gibson—Austin Czarnik, Charlie Coyle, Derek Forbort, Adam Clendening, Jacob Trouba, Emerson Etem, J.T. Miller, Kevin Gravel, Bill Arnold, Jon Merrill, Jason Zucker, T.J. Tynan, Kyle Rau, Josh Archibald, Brandon Saad, Connor Brickley, Jared Tinordi, Austin Watson, Nick Bjugstad, Stephen Johns

*Mika Zibanejad scored the only goal of the gold-medal game of the 2012 U20 Championship—in overtime no less—to give Sweden its first gold in 31 years. Photo: J.C. Pinheiro / HHOF-IIHF Images.*

# U18 WORLD CHAMPIONSHIP (MEN)

**1st U18 WORLD CHAMPIONSHIP (MEN)**
**April 8-18, 1999**
**Fussen/Kaufbeuren, Germany**

**Final Placing**

| | |
|---|---|
| Gold ........Finland | 6th .........Russia |
| Silver ......Sweden | 7th .........United States |
| Bronze ....Slovakia | 8th .........Ukraine |
| 4th..........Switzerland | 9th .........Germany |
| 5th..........Czech Republic | 10th .......Norway* |

*demoted to B Pool for 2000

**Tournament Format**

The 10 teams were divided into two groups of five and played a round robin within each group. The top three from each group advanced to a playoff round robin, while the bottom two from each group played a relegation round robin. All results from the Preliminary Round carried over.

**Results & Standings**

**GROUP A**

| | GP | W | T | L | GF | GA | P |
|---|---|---|---|---|---|---|---|
| Sweden | 4 | 3 | 1 | 0 | 22 | 8 | 7 |
| Switzerland | 4 | 3 | 0 | 1 | 10 | 6 | 6 |
| Czech Republic | 4 | 2 | 1 | 1 | 16 | 8 | 5 |
| Ukraine | 4 | 1 | 0 | 3 | 8 | 20 | 2 |
| Germany | 4 | 0 | 0 | 4 | 2 | 16 | 0 |

| | | | |
|---|---|---|---|
| April 8 | Fussen | Sweden 3 | Switzerland 0 |
| April 8 | Fussen | Czech Republic 4 | Germany 2 |
| April 9 | Kaufbeuren | Switzerland 4 | Ukraine 1 |
| April 9 | Kaufbeuren | Sweden 5 | Germany 2 |
| April 10 | Fussen | Czech Republic 6 | Ukraine 1 |
| April 11 | Fussen | Czech Republic 4 | Sweden 4 |
| April 11 | Fussen | Switzerland 3 | Germany 0 |
| April 12 | Fussen | Ukraine 4 | Germany 0 |
| April 13 | Kaufbeuren | Switzerland 3 | Czech Republic 2 |
| April 13 | Kaufbeuren | Sweden 10 | Ukraine 2 |

**GROUP B**

| | GP | W | T | L | GF | GA | P |
|---|---|---|---|---|---|---|---|
| Finland | 4 | 4 | 0 | 0 | 21 | 5 | 8 |
| Slovakia | 4 | 3 | 0 | 1 | 18 | 10 | 6 |
| Russia | 4 | 2 | 0 | 2 | 13 | 9 | 4 |
| United States | 4 | 1 | 0 | 3 | 16 | 15 | 2 |
| Norway | 4 | 0 | 0 | 4 | 6 | 35 | 0 |

| | | | |
|---|---|---|---|
| April 8 | Kaufbeuren | Finland 3 | Slovakia 2 |
| April 8 | Kaufbeuren | Russia 2 | United States 1 |
| April 9 | Fussen | Slovakia 7 | Norway 0 |
| April 9 | Fussen | Finland 5 | United States 0 |
| April 10 | Fussen | Russia 8 | Norway 2 |
| April 11 | Kaufbeuren | Slovakia 6 | United States 5 |
| April 11 | Kaufbeuren | Finland 3 | Russia 1 |
| April 12 | Fussen | United States 10 | Norway 2 |
| April 13 | Fussen | Finland 10 | Norway 2 |
| April 13 | Fussen | Slovakia 3 | Russia 2 |

**RELEGATION ROUND**

| | GP | W | T | L | GF | GA | P |
|---|---|---|---|---|---|---|---|
| United States | 3 | 3 | 0 | 0 | 22 | 2 | 6 |
| Ukraine | 3 | 2 | 0 | 1 | 7 | 6 | 4 |
| Germany | 3 | 1 | 0 | 2 | 4 | 12 | 2 |
| Norway | 3 | 0 | 0 | 3 | 4 | 17 | 0 |

| | | | |
|---|---|---|---|
| April 15 | Fussen | United States 6 | Germany 0 |
| April 15 | Kaufbeuren | Ukraine 3 | Norway 0 |
| April 16 | Fussen | Germany 4 | Norway 2 |
| April 16 | Kaufbeuren | United States 6 | Ukraine 0 |

**PLAYOFF ROUND**

| | GP | W | T | L | GF | GA | P |
|---|---|---|---|---|---|---|---|
| Finland | 5 | 3 | 1 | 1 | 12 | 12 | 7 |
| Sweden | 5 | 3 | 2 | 1 | 15 | 10 | 6 |
| Slovakia | 5 | 3 | 0 | 2 | 13 | 12 | 6 |
| Switzerland | 5 | 3 | 0 | 2 | 16 | 13 | 6 |
| Czech Republic | 5 | 1 | 1 | 3 | 12 | 13 | 3 |
| Russia | 5 | 1 | 0 | 4 | 9 | 17 | 2 |

| | | | |
|---|---|---|---|
| April 15 | Fussen | Slovakia 6 | Switzerland 3 |
| April 15 | Kaufbeuren | Russia 3 | Sweden 2 |
| April 16 | Fussen | Finland 3 | Czech Republic 1 |
| April 16 | Fussen | Czech Republic 5 | Russia 2 |
| April 16 | Kaufbeuren | Switzerland 6 | Finland 1 |
| April 16 | Fussen | Sweden 4 | Slovakia 1 |
| April 18 | Kaufbeuren | Slovakia 1 | Czech Republic 0 |
| April 18 | Fussen | Switzerland 4 | Russia 1 |
| April 18 | Fussen | Finland 2 | Sweden 2 |

**Rosters**

**Czech Republic** (Petr Misek, coach) GK—Tomas Duba, Michal Lanicek—Jan Choteborsky, Ondrej Kubes, David Nosek, Filip Novak, David Pojkar, Jan Vytisk, Vaclav Zavoral, Martin Erat, Martin Havlat, Ivan Huml, Ondrej Kavulic,Tomas Kurka, Ondrej Latal, Patrik Moskal, David Nedorost, Michal Pinc, Jiri Polansky, Ivan Rachunek, Michal Sivek, Petr Zajgla

**Finland** (Jouko Lukkarila, coach) GK—Antti Jokela, Ari Ahonen—Arto Tukio, Jaakko Harikkala, Teemu Kesa, Lasse Kukkonen, Petri Tahtisalo, Tukka Mantyla, Juha Alastalo, Mikko Hytia,Antti Aarnio, Miro Laitinen,Tony Salmelainen, Juha-Pekka Hytonen,Ville Hamalainen, Matias Metsaranta, Olli Sillanpaa, Jouni Kulonen, Kasper Kenig, Sami Venalainen, Juhamatti Yli-Junnila

**Germany** (Franz Fritzmeier, coach) GK—Torsten Schmitt, Dimitrij Kotschnew—Robin Breitbach, Anton Prommersberger, Marcel Linke, Christopher Oravec, Svend Wiele, Stefan Schroder, Daniel Hilpert, Dennis Seidenberg, Mario Gschmeidler, Daniel Kowlow, Karl-Josef Stetz, Markus Guggemos, Florian Schnitzer, Markus Schroder, Lukas Slavetinsky, Markus Busch, Nils Watzke, Thomas Greilinger, Rainer Kottstorfer, Christian Ehrhoff

**Norway** (Morten Sethereng, coach) GK—Halvor Haarstad-Evjen, Mats Johansen—Erik Haugon, Ola Johannessen, Svein Melgaard, Petter Skolla, Petter Bart Hansen, Inge Stokvik, Bjarte Bjonnes, Rene Sethreng, Jonas Gabrielsen, Lars Peder Nagel, Karl Johan Sundt, Henrik Knut Spets, Andre Hoibyhagen, Kenneth Bedsvaag, Jonas Andersen, Lasse Fredriksen, Jorgen Gravnaas, Petter Giving, Anders Fredriksen, Leif Jostein Reime

**Russia** (Valentin Gureyev, coach) GK—Yevgeni Konstantinov, Alexei Petrov—Kirill Safronov, Denis Denisov, Stepan Mokhov, Mikhail Bykov, Ilya Nikulin, Rail Rozakov, Vladislav Korneyev, Alexander Buturlin, Maxim Rybin, Maxim Orlov, Dmitri Levinski, Mikhail Kuleshov, Yevgeni Pavlov, Anton Sokolov, Andrei Maximenko, Anton Starovoit, Andrei Shefer, Sergei Soin, Alexei Smirnov, Fedor Fyodorov

**Slovakia** (Miroslav Kimijan, coach) GK—Peter Hamerlik, Ramon Sopko—Stefan Fabian, Tomas Mihalik, Tomas Starosta, Alexander Valentin, Lubos Velebny, Kristian Kudroc, Rene Vydareny, Martin Zajac, Milan Bartovic, Marian Gaborik, Tomas Gron, Marcel Hossa, Lukas Hvila, Kristian Kovac, Daniel Maras, Igor Martak, Tomas Surovy, Peter Szabo, Tomas Skvaridlo, Roman Tvrdon

**Sweden** (Lars-Erik Lundstrom, coach) GK—Magnus Zirath, Kjell Bennemark—Daniel Ljungkvist, Jonas Lennartsson, Magnus Hedlund, David Johansson, Daniel Josefsson, Niklas Kronwall, Daniel Westin, Johan Reineck, Mikael Berg, Tim Eriksson, Jonas Andersson, Martin Samuelsson, Daniel Johansson, Jonas Ferm, Mattias Wennerberg, Fredrik Sundin, Andreas Albinsson, Jonas Nordqvist, Patrik Nilson, Bjorn Melin

**Switzerland** (Alfred Bohren, coach) GK—Pasqual Sievert, Martin Zerzuben—Beat Gerber, Timo Helbling, Steve Hirschi, David Jobin, Marc Huttenmoser-Schefer, Fabian Stephan, Mark Tschudy, Mauro Beccarelli, Andreas Cellar, Paolo Duca, Marc Heberlein, Sven Helfenstein, Gian-Carlo Hendry, Christof Hiltebrand, Thibaut Monnet, Claudio Neff, Stefan Niggli, Sebastien Rueille, Valentin Wirz, Luca Cereda

**Ukraine** (Sergei Lubnin, coach) GK—Vadym Seleverstov, Vyacheslav Krylov—Roman Sherbatyuk, Volodym Chernenko, Yevgeni Yemelyanenko, Olexander Skorokhod, Vitali Kolosov, Olexander Pobyedonostsev, Olexdander Gorbatuk, Kirill Reshetnikov, Yuri Pecherin, Oleg Shafarenko, Andrei Chepurko, Mikhail Kutnyi, Artur Mloian, Olexander Yanchenko, Alex Salaschenko, Vitaliy Donika, Olexander Barsky, Mykola Terlo, Olexander Materukhin, Dmitri Kryvorutski

**United States** (Jeff Jackson, coach) GK—Rob Bonk, Rick DiPietro—Michael Brickley, Joe Cullen, Connor Dunlop, Brian Fahey, Patrick Foley, J.D. Forrest, Ron Hainsey, Paul Harris, Andy Hilbert, Todd Jackson, Freddy Meyer, Brett Nowak, Jason Reimers, John Sabo, Kenny Smith, Jeff Taffe, Jon Waibel, Dan Welch, Brad Winchester, John Wroblewski

## 2nd U18 WORLD CHAMPIONSHIP (MEN)
### April 14-24, 2000
### Kloten/Weinfelden, Switzerland

**Final Placing**

Gold ........Finland
Silver ......Russia
Bronze ....Sweden
4th ..........Switzerland
5th ..........Slovakia
6th .........Czech Republic
7th .........Germany
8th .........United States
9th .........Ukraine
10th .......Belarus^*
^promoted from B Pool in 1999
*demoted to Division I for 2001

**Tournament Format**

The 10 teams were divided into two groups of five and played a round robin within each group. The winner of each group advanced directly to the semi-finals while the second and third place teams played a cross-over quarter-finals. The fourth and fifth place teams in the Preliminary Round went to a Relagation Round, the bottom two teams after this round robin demoted to Division I for 2001.

**Results & Final Standings**

**GROUP A (KLOTEN)**

| | GP | W | T | L | GF | GA | P |
|---|---|---|---|---|---|---|---|
| Sweden | 4 | 4 | 0 | 0 | 21 | 5 | 8 |
| Switzerland | 4 | 3 | 0 | 1 | 18 | 12 | 6 |
| Czech Republic | 4 | 2 | 0 | 2 | 15 | 12 | 4 |
| Germany | 4 | 0 | 1 | 3 | 8 | 15 | 1 |
| Ukraine | 4 | 0 | 1 | 3 | 6 | 24 | 1 |

| | | |
|---|---|---|
| April 14 | Czech Republic 5 | Germany 3 |
| April 14 | Sweden 8 | Switzerland 2 |
| April 15 | Sweden 3 | Germany 0 |
| April 15 | Switzerland 10 | Ukraine 1 |
| April 16 | Czech Republic 6 | Ukraine 0 |
| April 17 | Sweden 6 | Czech Republic 2 |
| April 17 | Switzerland 3 | Germany 1 |
| April 18 | Ukraine 4 | Germany 4 |
| April 19 | Sweden 4 | Ukraine 1 |
| April 19 | Switzerland 3 | Czech Republic 2 |

**GROUP B (WEINFELDEN)**

| | GP | W | T | L | GF | GA | P |
|---|---|---|---|---|---|---|---|
| Russia | 4 | 4 | 0 | 0 | 33 | 4 | 8 |
| Finland | 4 | 3 | 0 | 1 | 19 | 9 | 6 |
| Slovakia | 4 | 2 | 0 | 2 | 12 | 10 | 4 |
| United States | 4 | 1 | 0 | 3 | 13 | 13 | 2 |
| Belarus | 4 | 0 | 0 | 4 | 4 | 45 | 0 |

| | | |
|---|---|---|
| April 14 | Finland 3 | Slovakia 1 |
| April 14 | Russia 5 | United States 1 |
| April 15 | Slovakia 7 | Belarus 1 |
| April 15 | Finland 3 | United States 2 |
| April 16 | Russia 18 | Belarus 1 |
| April 17 | Slovakia 4 | United States 1 |
| April 17 | Russia 5 | Finland 2 |
| April 18 | United States 9 | Belarus 1 |
| April 19 | Finland 11 | Belarus 1 |
| April 19 | Russia 5 | Slovakia 0 |

**RELEGATION ROUND (WEINFELDEN)**

| | GP | W | T | L | GF | GA | P |
|---|---|---|---|---|---|---|---|
| Germany | 3 | 2 | 1 | 0 | 17 | 5 | 5 |
| United States | 3 | 2 | 0 | 1 | 16 | 4 | 4 |
| Ukraine | 3 | 1 | 1 | 1 | 12 | 13 | 3 |
| Belarus | 3 | 0 | 0 | 3 | 4 | 27 | 0 |

| | | |
|---|---|---|
| April 21 | Germany 10 | Belarus 0 |
| April 21 | United States 6 | Ukraine 0 |
| April 22 | Germany 3 | United States 1 |
| April 22 | Ukraine 8 | Belarus 3 |

**5TH-PLACE GAME**

April 24 Weinfelden Slovakia 4 Czech Republic 3
(10:00 OT/GWS—Marek Svatos)

**PLAYOFFS (KLOTEN)**

**QUARTER-FINALS**

| | | |
|---|---|---|
| April 21 | Switzerland 3 | Slovakia 0 |
| April 21 | Finland 3 | Czech Republic 0 |

**SEMI-FINALS**

| | | |
|---|---|---|
| April 22 | Finland 4 | Sweden 2 |
| April 22 | Russia 4 | Switzerland 1 |

**BRONZE MEDAL GAME**

April 24 Sweden 7 Switzerland 1

**GOLD MEDAL GAME**

April 24 Finland 3 Russia 1

**Rosters**

**Belarus** (Borys Kosarev, coach) GK—Vitali Arystov, Yuri Melnikov—Maxim Shymanski, Alexander Sharkevlch, Andrei Skrypailov, Andrei Karshunov, Alexei Khatsko, Dmitri Mialeshka, Artyom Siankevich, Konstantin Zakharov, Konstantin Nemirka, Alexander Kulakov, Vitali Klimiankov, Stanislav Korabov, Viktor Kezik, Mikhail Klimin, Alexander Dubovik, Yuri Badrov, Andrei Kostitsyn, Alexander Yudzhin, Nikolai Vladykin, Andrei Bashko

**Czech Republic** (Stanislav Berger, coach) GK—Martin Barek, Lukas Hronek, Jaroslav Hubl—Ales Cerny, Petr Puncochar, Miroslav Blatak, Petr Chvojka, Jiri Hudler, Martin Frolik, Jan Hanzlik, Tomas Plekanec, Vaclav Nedorost, Ales Pavlas, Stepan Hrebejk, Frantisek Lukes,Tomas Netik, Petr Vampola, Tomas Mojzis, Jan Bohac, Jiri Novotny, Martin Podlesak, Miloslav Horava, Michal Blazek

**Finland** (Timo Tuomi, coach) GK—Kari Lehtonen, Joni Puurula—Tuukka Makela, Matti Kuusisto, Olli Malmivaara, Tero Maatta, Karri Takko, Juho Kuronen, Semir Ben-Amor, Jaakko Hagelberg, Jarkko Immonen, Mikko Koivu, Mikko Kankaanpera, Tuomo Ruutu, Toni Koivisto, Teemu Laine, Tuomas Pihlman, Pekka Saarenheimo, Janne Jokila, Harri Suutarinen, Toni Mustonen, Markus Seikola

**Germany** (James Setters, coach) GK—Benjamin Voigt, Dimitri Patzold—Sebastian Jones, Hardy Gensel, Matthias Frenzel, Christoph Schubert, Harry Kulczynski, Robin Breitbach, Stefan Schauer, Stefan Endrass, Marcel Goc, Daniel Koslow, Jonas Lanier, Kay Kurbanek, Markus Guggemos, Sebastian Furchner, Gert Acker, Bastian Steingross, Christian Urban, Christian Ehrhoff, Christian Retzer, Martin Hinterstocker

**Russia** (Andrei Piatanov, coach) GK—Sergei Mylnikov, Andrei Medvedev—Vladimir Gusev, Anton Volchenkov, Ilya Nikulin, Sergei Soin, Alexander Frolov, Igor Knyazev, Igor Samoylov, Ruslan Zainulin, Mikhail Yakubov, Alexander Svitov, Alexander Tatarinov, Pavel Vorobyov, Vladislav Luchkin, Alexander Seluianov, Artyom Chernov, Alexei Smirnov, Yegor Shastin, Yuri Trubachyov, Ilya Kovalchuk, Andrei Zabolotnev

**Slovakia** (Miroslav Kimijan, coach) GK—Peter Budaj, Peter Hamerlik—Tomas Frolo, Karol Sloboda, Radovan Sloboda, Peter Fruhauf, Tomas Psenka, Jozef Balej, Lukas Bokros, Marian Gaborik, Tomas Malec, Peter Gajdos, Michal Macho, Tomas Kopecky, Frantisek Skladany, Lubos Velebny, Marek Svatos, Stanislav Hudec, Roman Takac, Tomas Oravec, Marek Dubec, Michal Kolarik

**Sweden** (Lars Lisspers, coach) GK—Niklas Holm, Henrik Lundqvist—Mattias Nilsson, Jorgen Sundqvist, Niclas Westlund, Michael Irani, Jens Karlsson, Joel Lundqvist, Tim Eriksson, Daniel Widing, Per Helmersson, Johan Eneqvist, Magnus Hedlund, Peter Oberg, Andreas Jungbeck, Pontus Petterstrom, Martin Samuelsson, Johan Hogglund, Pelle Andersson, Jonas Nordqvist, Lars Jonsson, Daniel Hermansson

**Switzerland** (Beat Lautenschlager, coach) GK—Matthias Schoder, Marco Wegmuller—Beat Gerber, Jurg Dallenbach, Rolf Hildebrand, Marc Gautschi, Thibaut Monnet, Severin Blindenbacher, Thomas Nussli, Fabian Sutter, Paul Savary, Deny Bartschi, Julien Turler, Andreas Camenzind, Beat Schiess-Forster, Patrick Landolt, Cedric Metrailler, Rene Vogler, Duri Camichel, Joel Frohlicher, Rene Back, Sven Helfenstein

**Ukraine** (Sergei Lebnin, coach) GK—Valentyn Chernenko, Ruslan Terchiev—Vasyl Gorbenko, Ruslan Borysenko, Alexander Kubrak, Olexander Skorokhod, Vadym Sabybyn, Taras Bega, Olexander Karaulshuk, Igor Andruschenko, Andrei Sugak, Pavlo Dvoretsky, Sergei Vlasov, Dmitri Kryvorutski, Artyom Bondarev, Yuri Pecherin, Kostya Savchenko, Vyacheslav Dyatlov, Vitaliy Donika, Dmitri Malkov, Vitali Gavrylyuk, Andri Kalitka

**United States** (Jeff Jackson, coach) GK—Travis Weber, Nick Pannoni—Keith Ballard, Mike Komis-arek, Jake Fleming, Jon Waibel, Brady Leisenring, John Snowden, Jim McNamara, David Steckel, Bryan Nathe, Dennis Packard, Cole Bassett, R.J. Umberger, Quinn Fylling, Neil Komadoski, Rob Globke, Kris Bouchard, Ben Eaves, Matt Maglione, Bryan Perez, Joseph Hope

## 3rd U18 WORLD CHAMPIONSHIP (MEN)
### April 12-22, 2001
### Heinola/Helsinki/Lahti, Finland

**Final Placing**

Gold ........Russia
Silver ......Switzerland
Bronze ....Finland
4th ..........Czech Republic
5th ..........Germany
6th .........United States
7th .........Sweden
8th .........Slovakia
9th .........Norway^
10th .......Ukraine
^promoted from B Pool in 2000
~no teams demoted as U18 World Championship expanded to 12 teams for 2002

**Tournament Format**

The 10 teams were divided into two groups of five and played a round robin within each group. The winner of each group advanced directly to the semi-finals while the second and third place teams played a cross-over quarter-finals. The fourth and fifth place teams in the Preliminary Round went to a Relagation Round, the bottom two teams after this round robin demoted to Division I for 2002.

**Results & Standings**
**PRELIMINARY ROUND**
**GROUP A (LAHTI)**

| | GP | W | T | L | GF | GA | P |
|---|---|---|---|---|---|---|---|
| Finland | 4 | 4 | 0 | 0 | 17 | 3 | 8 |
| United States | 4 | 3 | 0 | 1 | 23 | 7 | 6 |
| Switzerland | 4 | 2 | 0 | 2 | 12 | 10 | 4 |
| Slovakia | 4 | 1 | 0 | 3 | 14 | 15 | 2 |
| Ukraine | 4 | 0 | 0 | 4 | 3 | 34 | 0 |

| | | |
|---|---|---|
| April 12 | Switzerland 6 | Ukraine 2 |
| April 12 | Finland 3 | Slovakia 0 |
| April 13 | United States 11 | Ukraine 0 |
| April 14 | Switzerland 5 | Slovakia 2 |
| April 14 | Finland 4 | United States 3 |
| April 15 | Finland 7 | Ukraine 0 |
| April 16 | United States 3 | Switzerland 1 |
| April 16 | Slovakia 10 | Ukraine 1 |
| April 17 | United States 6 | Slovakia 2 |
| April 17 | Finland 3 | Switzerland 0 |

**GROUP B (HEINOLA)**

| | GP | W | T | L | GF | GA | P |
|---|---|---|---|---|---|---|---|
| Russia | 4 | 3 | 0 | 1 | 29 | 11 | 6 |
| Germany | 4 | 2 | 1 | 1 | 10 | 12 | 5 |
| Czech Republic | 4 | 2 | 0 | 2 | 13 | 14 | 4 |
| Sweden | 4 | 2 | 0 | 2 | 10 | 10 | 4 |
| Norway | 4 | 0 | 1 | 3 | 8 | 23 | 1 |

| | | |
|---|---|---|
| April 12 | Russia 8 | Czech Republic 3 |
| April 12 | Sweden 4 | Norway 3 |
| April 13 | Germany 2 | Norway 2 |
| April 14 | Czech Republic 2 | Sweden 1 |
| April 14 | Russia 8 | Germany 3 |
| April 15 | Russia 10 | Norway 1 |
| April 16 | Germany 2 | Sweden 1 |
| April 16 | Czech Republic 7 | Norway 2 |
| April 17 | Sweden 4 | Russia 3 |
| April 17 | Germany 3 | Czech Republic 1 |

**RELEGATION ROUND (HEINOLA)**

| | GP | W | T | L | GF | GA | P |
|---|---|---|---|---|---|---|---|
| Sweden | 3 | 3 | 0 | 0 | 18 | 8 | 6 |
| Slovakia | 3 | 1 | 1 | 1 | 15 | 10 | 3 |
| Norway | 3 | 1 | 1 | 1 | 12 | 10 | 3 |
| Ukraine | 3 | 0 | 0 | 3 | 7 | 24 | 0 |

| | | |
|---|---|---|
| April 19 | Slovakia 4 | Norway 4 |
| April 19 | Sweden 9 | Ukraine 4 |
| April 20 | Sweden 5 | Slovakia 1 |
| April 20 | Norway 5 | Ukraine 2 |

**PLAYOFFS**
**QUARTER-FINALS (LAHTI)**

| | | |
|---|---|---|
| April 19 | Switzerland 7 | Germany 1 |
| April 19 | Czech Republic 5 | United States 4 (10:00 OT/GWS—Jan Rehard) |

**5TH-PLACE GAME (HEINOLA)**

| | | |
|---|---|---|
| April 22 | Germany 2 | United States 1 |

**SEMI-FINALS (HELSINKI)**

| | | |
|---|---|---|
| April 20 | Russia 8 | Czech Republic 3 |
| April 20 | Switzerland 4 | Finland 2 |

**BRONZE MEDAL GAME (HELSINKI)**

| | | |
|---|---|---|
| April 22 | Finland 2 | Czech Republic 1 |

**GOLD MEDAL GAME (HELSINKI)**

| | | |
|---|---|---|
| April 22 | Russia 6 | Switzerland 2 |

**Rosters**

**Czech Republic** (Jiri Kalous, coach) GK—Miroslav Kopriva, Martin Laska—Petr Puncochar, Jan Holub, Jan Platil, Lukas Dobry, Jan Rehor, Daniel Volrab, Martin Soucek, Milan Michalek, Petr Domin, Tomas Micka, Lukas Chmelir, Zbynek Novak, David Turon, Marlan Havel, Petr Kanko, Tomas Plihal, Jiri Novotny, Martin Toms, Frantisek Bakrlik, Ondrej Danicek

**Finland** (Pekka Hamalainen, coach) GK—Kari Lehtonen, Tuomas Nissinen—Juuso Akkanen, Topi Jaakola, Jussi Timonen, Ilkka Tornvall, Mikko Maenpaa, Mikko Koivu, Jussi Jokinen, Juha-Pekka Ketola, Max Kenig, Antti-Jussi Miettinen, Joni Purola, Matti Tahkapaa, Teemu Jaaskelainen, Henrik Juntunen, Tomi Maki, Juha Fagerstedt, Tomi Sykko, Tomi Mustonen, Tommi Jaminki, Sean Bergenheim

**Germany** (James Setters, coach) GK—Christian Kruger, Dimitri Patzold—Felix Petermann, Daniel Menge, Paul Knihs, Marcel Goc, Dirk Wrobel, Marian Rohatsch, Michael Stadele, Stefan Schauer, Yannic Seidenberg, David Danner, Andreas Kleinheinz, Christoph Triller, Adrian Grygiel, Benjamin Barz, Andre Mucke, Christoph Melischko, Thomas Richter, Stephan Gottwald, Martin Hinterstocker, Robert Bartlick

**Norway** (Orjan Lovdal, coach) GK—Per Olsen, Vegard Sagbakken—Alf Buvik, Rune Sundeng, Anders Bartlett, Lars Hammerseng, Peter Lorentzen, Henning Segerblad, Erik Johansen, Rene Boe, Petter Bull, Andre Paulsen, Jorgen Okland, Patrick Thoresen, Marius Holtet, Joachim Tangen, Thomas Tangnes, Bobby Abercrombie, Alexander Simensen, Tom Hammerstad, Ole-Kristian Tollefsen, Kenneth Andersen

**Russia** (Vladimir Plyuschev, coach) GK—Yuri Klyuchnikov, Andrei Medvedev—Igor Knyazev, Vladimir Kornusov, Denis Grebeshkov, Fyodor Tyutin, Viktor Uchevatov, Artyom Ternavski, Anton Babchuk, Alexei Kaigorodov, Yuri Trubachyov, Andrei Taratukhin, Ilya Kovalchuk, Alexander Polushin, Timofei Shishkanov, Igor Grigorenko, Stanislav Chistov, Alexander Golovin, Yevgeni Artyukhin, Alexander Perezhogin, Dmitri Syomin, Kirill Koltsov

**Slovakia** (Jan Simcik, coach) GK—Imrich Petrik, Peter Sevela, Lubomir Misut—Milan Jurcina, Dominik Granak, Peter Svarba, Peter Macek, Tomas Slovak, Rastislav Ocelka, Michal Lukac, Marek Benko, Juraj Matejka, Marek Hornak, Tomas Vodicka, Oliver Maron, Ratislav Lipka, Peter Polcik, Michal Vazan, Matus Luciak, Igor Pohanka, Tomas Jasko, Karol Sloboda, Richard Stehlik

**Sweden** (Kjell-Rune Milton, coach) GK—Kristoffer Olsson, Michal Zajkowski—Robin Jonsson, John Lind, Jonas Living, Eric Nilsson, Simon Skoog, Calle Aslund, Jonas Almtorp, Mattias Beck, Fredrik Eriksson, Gustav Grasberg, Fredrik Hynning, Kristoffer Jobs, Andreas Jamtin, Joakim Lindstrom, Fredrik Vestberg, Yared Hagos, Fredrik Sjostrom, Robert Nilsson, Jonas Leetma, Adam Andersson

**Switzerland** (Charly Oppliger, coach) GK—Thomas Baumle, Daniel Manzato, Tobias Stephan—Jurg Dallenbach, Beat Schiess-Forster, Severin Blindenbacher, Filippo Schenker, Tim Ramholt, Andres Ambuhl, Daniel Boss, Manuel Gossweiler, Marco Gruber, Florian Conz, Lukas Baumgartner, Cyrill Buhler, Raffaele Sannitz, Luca Triulzi, Patrik Bartschi, Marcel Moser, Emanuel Peter, Romano Lemm, Stefan Schnyder, Andreas Kung

**Ukraine** (Sergei Lubnin, coach) GK—Valentyn Chernenko, Olexander Naipak—Dmitro Gashkov, Sergiy Nagruzov, Ruslan Borysenko, Olexander Skorokhod, Yuri Kolesnikov, Oleksiy Lubnin, Olexander Karaulshuk, Igor Andruschenko, Taras Bega, Pavlo Legachev, Olexander Tveritinov, Artyom Bondarev, Olexander Shevchenko, Stanislav Kozhan, Olexi Galyuk, Mykola Ladygin, Igor Shamansky, Sergiy Chernenko, Vitali Gavrylyuk, Igor Zemchenko

**United States** (Mike Eaves, coach) GK—Travis Weber, Dwight LaBrosse—Lee Falardeau, Jesse Lane, Ryan Whitney, Joey Crabb, Derek Smith, Rob Flynn, Brian McConnell, Dwight Helminen, Matt Greene, Matt Gens, Bryan Nathe, Ryan Murphy, Joe Pomaranski, Eric Nystrom, Jason Ryznar, Barry Tallackson, Stephen Gionta, Justin Maiser, Bryan Miller, Dave Spina

## 4th U18 WORLD CHAMPIONSHIP (MEN)
## April 11-21, 2002
## Trnava/Piestany, Slovakia

**Final Placing**

| | |
|---|---|
| Gold ........United States | 7th ........Switzerland |
| Silver ......Russia | 8th ........Slovakia |
| Bronze ....Czech Republic | 9th ........Sweden |
| 4th ..........Finland | 10th .......Germany* |
| 5th ..........Belarus^ | 11th .......Norway* |
| 6th ..........Canada+ | 12th .......Ukraine* |

+granted exemption directly to top pool for inaugural participation
^promoted from Division I in 2001
*demoted to Division I for 2003 (U18 World Championship revetred to 10 teams)

**Tournament Format**

The 12 teams were put into two groups of six and played a round robin series of games within each group. The top three then moved on to a playoff round robin, and the bottom three to a Relegation Round round robin. The bottom two teams were relegated to Division I for 2003. All results from the Preliminary Round carried over.

**Results & Standings**
**GROUP A (TRNAVA)**

| | GP | W | T | L | GF | GA | P |
|---|---|---|---|---|---|---|---|
| Russia | 5 | 5 | 0 | 0 | 34 | 10 | 10 |
| Czech Republic | 5 | 4 | 0 | 1 | 25 | 12 | 8 |
| Canada | 5 | 3 | 0 | 2 | 21 | 17 | 6 |
| Norway | 5 | 1 | 1 | 3 | 13 | 23 | 3 |
| Slovakia | 5 | 1 | 0 | 4 | 10 | 19 | 2 |
| Germany | 5 | 0 | 1 | 4 | 7 | 29 | 1 |

| | | |
|---|---|---|
| April 11 | Norway 2 | Germany 2 |
| April 11 | Czech Republic 5 | Slovakia 1 |
| April 11 | Russia 8 | Canada 4 |
| April 12 | Czech Republic 7 | Norway 4 |
| April 12 | Russia 6 | Slovakia 1 |
| April 12 | Canada 9 | Germany 1 |
| April 14 | Czech Republic 6 | Germany 1 |
| April 14 | Canada 3 | Slovakia 1 |

| | | |
|---|---|---|
| April 14 | Russia 7 | Norway 0 |
| April 15 | Czech Republic 4 | Canada 1 |
| April 15 | Norway 4 | Slovakia 3 |
| April 15 | Russia 8 | Germany 2 |
| April 17 | Canada 4 | Norway 3 |
| April 17 | Russia 5 | Czech Republic 3 |
| April 17 | Slovakia 4 | Germany 1 |

**GROUP B (PIESTANY)**

| | GP | W | T | L | GF | GA | P |
|---|---|---|---|---|---|---|---|
| United States | 5 | 5 | 0 | 0 | 33 | 5 | 10 |
| Finland | 5 | 4 | 0 | 1 | 22 | 7 | 8 |
| Belarus | 5 | 2 | 0 | 3 | 14 | 21 | 4 |
| Sweden | 5 | 2 | 0 | 3 | 16 | 16 | 4 |
| Switzerland | 5 | 2 | 0 | 3 | 18 | 21 | 4 |
| Ukraine | 5 | 0 | 0 | 5 | 4 | 37 | 0 |

| | | |
|---|---|---|
| April 11 | United States 9 | Belarus 0 |
| April 11 | Finland 2 | Sweden 0 |
| April 11 | Switzerland 10 | Ukraine 0 |
| April 12 | Finland 4 | Belarus 3 |
| April 12 | Switzerland 3 | Sweden 2 |
| April 12 | United States 10 | Ukraine 0 |
| April 14 | Sweden 8 | Ukraine 3 |
| April 14 | Belarus 6 | Switzerland 3 |
| April 14 | United States 3 | Finland 2 |
| April 15 | Sweden 4 | Belarus 2 |
| April 15 | Finland 6 | Ukraine 0 |
| April 15 | United States 5 | Switzerland 1 |
| April 17 | Belarus 3 | Ukraine 1 |
| April 17 | United States 6 | Sweden 2 |
| April 17 | Finland 8 | Switzerland 1 |

**RELEGATION ROUND (TRNAVA)**

| | GP | W | T | L | GF | GA | P |
|---|---|---|---|---|---|---|---|
| Switzerland | 5 | 5 | 0 | 0 | 28 | 6 | 10 |
| Slovakia | 5 | 3 | 0 | 2 | 15 | 11 | 6 |
| Sweden | 5 | 3 | 0 | 2 | 20 | 13 | 6 |
| Germany | 5 | 1 | 1 | 3 | 9 | 16 | 3 |
| Norway | 5 | 1 | 1 | 3 | 12 | 20 | 3 |
| Ukraine | 5 | 1 | 0 | 4 | 9 | 27 | 2 |

| | | |
|---|---|---|
| April 18 | Sweden 4 | Germany 0 |
| April 18 | Switzerland 7 | Norway 2 |
| April 18 | Slovakia 3 | Ukraine 0 |
| April 20 | Switzerland 5 | Germany 2 |
| April 20 | Ukraine 5 | Norway 2 |
| April 20 | Slovakia 5 | Sweden 3 |
| April 21 | Germany 4 | Ukraine 1 |
| April 21 | Switzerland 3 | Slovakia 0 |
| April 21 | Sweden 3 | Norway 2 |

**PLAYOFF ROUND (PIESTANY)**

| | GP | W | T | L | GF | GA | P |
|---|---|---|---|---|---|---|---|
| United States | 5 | 4 | 0 | 1 | 25 | 7 | 8 |
| Russia | 5 | 4 | 0 | 1 | 29 | 13 | 8 |
| Czech Republic | 5 | 4 | 0 | 1 | 17 | 9 | 8 |
| Finland | 5 | 2 | 0 | 3 | 14 | 15 | 4 |
| Belarus | 5 | 1 | 0 | 4 | 9 | 32 | 2 |
| Canada | 5 | 0 | 0 | 5 | 12 | 30 | 0 |

| | | |
|---|---|---|
| April 18 | Czech Republic 5 | Belarus 1 |
| April 18 | United States 10 | Canada 3 |
| April 18 | Russia 4 | Finland 3 |
| April 20 | Finland 3 | Canada 1 |
| April 20 | Czech Republic 1 | United States 0 |
| April 20 | Russia 11 | Belarus 0 |
| April 21 | Czech Republic 4 | Finland 2 |
| April 21 | Belarus 5 | Canada 3 |
| April 21 | United States 3 | Russia 1 |

**Rosters**

**Belarus** (Mikhail Zakharov, coach) GK—Alexei Gritsenko, Dmitri Kamovich—Dmitri Grodinski, Dmitri Parakhonka, Konstantin Durnov, Vladimir Denisov, Andrei Kazachok, Viktor Homan, Alexei Yerashov, Timofei Filin, Artyom Volkov, Alexander Zhydkikh, Yevgeni Kashtanov, Alexei Gerlovski, Konstantin Zakharov, Raman Harbakon, Andrei Kostitsyn, Denis Bialotski, Alexei Shaghov, Mikhail Grabovski, Dmitri Yudzhin, Maxim Kazlovich

**Canada** (Mike Pelino, coach) GK—Maxime Daigneault, Tyler Weiman, Josh Harding—Mike Egener, Chris Schlenker, James Sanford, Andre Benoit, Johnny Boychuk, Rosario Ruggeri, Dylan Stanley, Sebastien Courcelles, Adam Henrich, Ben Eager, Brett Trudell, Ryan Keller, Jarrett Lukin, Pierre-Marc Bouchard, Eric Staal, Ryan Card, Brett O'Malley, Jonathan Filewich, Louis-Phillipe Martin, Michael Lambert

**Czech Republic** (Bretislav Kopriva, coach) GK—Lukas Mensator, Lukas Musil—Marek Chvatal, Martin Cizek, Tomas Kolafa, Milan Michalek, Jakub Langhammer, Jiri Hunkes, Tomas Fleischmann, Jan Velich, Roman Bilek, Jakub Koreis, Tomas Csabi, Lukas Pabiska, Jakub Klepis, Ondrej Nemec, Jiri Hudler, Michal Barinka, Jan Kubista, Kamil Kreps, Ctirad Ovcacik, Roman Vondracek

**Finland** (Jukka-Pekka Annala, coach) GK—Tommi Tervo, Hannu Toivonen—Jarno Virkki, Mikko Kalteva, Janne Jalasvaara, Kevin Kantee,Ville Mantymaa, Niko Suoraniemi, Sean Bergenheim, Valtteri Filppula, Teemu Nurmi, Ville Vimpari, Arne Kohler, Janne Tuominen, Joni Toykkala, Jaakko Viljanen, Pasi Salonen, Jarkko Immonen, Joni Lappalainen, Joni Lindlof, Tuukka Pulliainen, Tommi Pelkonen

**Germany** (James Setters, coach) GK—Patrick Ehelechner, Patrick Koslow—Josef Frank, Daniel Pyka, Max Seyller, Florian Eichelkraut, Felix Petermann, Alexander Dotzler, Yannic Seidenberg, Andreas Kruck, Stephan Kreuzmann, Andreas Dorfler, Tobias Worle, Axel Hackert, Thomas Fischer, Raphael Kapzan, Kai Hospelt, Thomas Schenkel, Frank Hordler, Daniel Hatterscheid, Marcus Kink, Matthias Wittmann

**Norway** (Morten Sethereng, coach) GK—Vegard Sagbakken, Joakim Rugdal—Havard Boe, Teddy Midttun, Anders Gjose, Christoffer Hoibye, Espen Lie, Markus Jagersten, Ole-Kristian Tollefsen, Kristoffer Holm, Tom Jacobsen, Lars Erik Spets, Simen Saxrud, Marius Holtet, Joakim Eljar, Steffen Thoresen, Mathis Olimb, Erik Russwurn, Morten Nilsen, Lars Knold, Cato Cocozza, Lars Bjornland

**Russia** (Ravil Iskhakov, coach) GK—Denis Khudyakov, Konstantin Barulin—Konstantin Korneyev, Anton Babchuk, Alexei Stonkus, Dmitri Kostiuk, Alexander Shinin, Alexander Ovechkin, Alexander Syomin, Yevgeni Isakov, Nikolai Zherdev, Denis Grot, Yevgeni Tunik, Igor Ignatushkin, Denis Yezhov, Sergei Anshakov, Ilya Krikunov, Alexei Shkotov, Sergei Shemetov, Dmitri Kazionov, Dmitri Kosmachev

**Slovakia** (Igor Toth, coach) GK—Marek Roznik, Jaroslav Halak—Michal Skoliak, Matus Pavlacka, Martin Nemcok, Andrej Meszaros, Richard Stehlik, Michal Gavalier, Jan Mucha, Daniel Mracka, Rastislav Spirko, Filip Macejka, Stanislav Hajas, Marian Filo, Michal Lukac, Stefan Ruzicka, Tomas Klempa, Pavol Hajduk, Martin Sagat, Tomas Troliga, Samir Saliji, Martin Slovak

**Sweden** (Johan Schillgard, coach) GK—Alexander Blomqvist, Christopher Heino-Lindberg, Joakim Lundstrom—Daniel Sondell, Tomas Skogs, Nicklas Johansson, Henrik Blomqvist, Oscar Brandting, Johan Bjork, Alexander Steen, Niklas Flodin, Dragan Umicevic, Andreas Frisk, Tobias Enstrom, Jonas Johansson, Fredrik Johansson, David Holmqvist, Nicklas Eckerblom, Sebastian Meijer, Bobbie Hagelin, Andreas Valdix, Gustaf Palm, Robert Nilsson

**Switzerland** (Roger Bader, coach) GK—Michael Fluckiger, Tobias Stephan—Lukas Baumgartner, Florian Blatter, Alan Tallarini, Andri Stoffel, Tim Ramholt, Phillipp Rytz, Martin Stettler, Sandro Bruderer, Patrik Bartschi, Florian Conz, Roland Gerber, Lukas Grauwiler, Romano Lemm, Yvan Benoit, Spencer Rezek, Kevin Romy, Victor Stancescu, Caryl Neuenschwander, Christoph Roder, Philippe Furrer

**Ukraine** (Anatoliy Donika, coach) GK—Yevgeni Galyuk, Mikola Voroshnov—Igor Kygyt, Sergiy Nagruzov, Maxim Sydorenko, Konstantin Prymovych, Valentin Lays, Oleksiy Lubnin, Olexander Shevchenko, Olexander Tveritinov, Sergiy Chernenko, Igor Shamansky, Oleksiy Koval, Denis Ryabtsev, Igor Yegorov, Dmitro Naumenko, Viktor Andruschenko, Vitali Verchenko, Roman Lovryk, Pavlo Borysenko, Anatoliy Bogdanov, Vitali Kyrychenko

**United States** (Mike Eaves, coach) GK—Timothy Roth, James Howard—Mark Stuart, Ryan Suter, Matt Carle, David Booth, Tom Sawatske, Patrick Eaves, Gregg Moore, Corey Potter, Noah Babin, Stephen Werner, Zach Parise, Tyler Hirsch, Ryan Kesler, Patrick O'Sullivan, James Wisniewski, Brett Sterling, Ray Ortiz, Evan Shaw, Nate Raduns, Tim Wallace

## 5th U18 WORLD CHAMPIONSHIP (MEN)
## April 12-23 2003
## Yaroslavl, Russia

**Final Placing**

| | |
|---|---|
| Gold ........Canada | 6th .........Czech Republic |
| Silver ......Slovakia | 7th .........Finland |
| Bronze ....Russia | 8th .........Belarus |
| 4th ..........United States | 9th .........Switzerland* |
| 5th ..........Sweden | 10th .......Kazakhstan^* |

^promoted from Division I in 2002
*demoted to Division I for 2004

**Tournament Format**

The 10 teams were divided into two groups of five and played a round robin within each group. The winner of each group advanced directly to the semi-finals while the second and third place teams played a cross-over quarter-finals. The fourth and fifth place teams in the Preliminary Round went to a Relagation Round, the bottom two teams after this round robin demoted to Division I for 2004.

**Results & Standings**
**PRELIMINARY ROUND**
**GROUP A**

| | GP | W | T | L | GF | GA | P |
|---|---|---|---|---|---|---|---|
| United States | 4 | 3 | 1 | 0 | 11 | 7 | 7 |
| Slovakia | 4 | 3 | 0 | 1 | 18 | 9 | 6 |
| Sweden | 4 | 1 | 1 | 2 | 15 | 13 | 3 |
| Finland | 4 | 1 | 1 | 2 | 14 | 15 | 3 |
| Belarus | 4 | 0 | 1 | 3 | 14 | 28 | 1 |

| | | |
|---|---|---|
| April 12 | Sweden 3 | Finland 3 |
| April 12 | Belarus 3 | United States 3 |
| April 13 | Slovakia 4 | Sweden 1 |
| April 14 | Finland 8 | Belarus 6 |
| April 14 | United States 3 | Slovakia 2 |
| April 15 | United States 3 | Sweden 2 |
| April 16 | Slovakia 4 | Finland 3 |
| April 16 | Sweden 9 | Belarus 3 |
| April 17 | United States 2 | Finland 0 |
| April 17 | Slovakia 8 | Belarus 2 |

**GROUP B**

| | GP | W | T | L | GF | GA | P |
|---|---|---|---|---|---|---|---|
| Russia | 4 | 4 | 0 | 0 | 27 | 8 | 8 |
| Canada | 4 | 2 | 1 | 1 | 19 | 10 | 5 |
| Czech Republic | 4 | 2 | 1 | 1 | 14 | 11 | 5 |
| Switzerland | 4 | 1 | 0 | 3 | 17 | 23 | 2 |
| Kazakhstan | 4 | 0 | 0 | 4 | 6 | 31 | 0 |

| | | |
|---|---|---|
| April 12 | Czech Republic 5 | Kazakhstan 3 |
| April 12 | Russia 6 | Canada 3 |
| April 13 | Switzerland 13 | Kazakhstan 2 |
| April 14 | Czech Republic 3 | Canada 3 |
| April 14 | Russia 12 | Switzerland 3 |
| April 15 | Russia 5 | Kazakhstan 0 |
| April 16 | Canada 8 | Kazakhstan 1 |
| April 16 | Czech Republic 4 | Switzerland 1 |
| April 17 | Canada 5 | Switzerland 0 |
| April 17 | Russia 4 | Czech Republic 2 |

**RELEGATION ROUND**

| | GP | W | T | L | GF | GA | P |
|---|---|---|---|---|---|---|---|
| Finland | 3 | 2 | 1 | 0 | 15 | 12 | 5 |
| Belarus | 3 | 2 | 0 | 1 | 19 | 17 | 4 |
| Switzerland | 3 | 1 | 1 | 1 | 18 | 9 | 3 |
| Kazakhstan | 3 | 0 | 0 | 3 | 12 | 26 | 0 |

| | | |
|---|---|---|
| April 19 | Finland 5 | Kazakhstan 4 |
| April 19 | Belarus 5 | Switzerland 3 |
| April 20 | Finland 2 | Switzerland 2 |
| April 20 | Belarus 8 | Kazakhstan 6 |

**5TH-PLACE GAME**

April 21 Sweden 3 Czech Republic 2 (Linus Videll 8:20 OT)

**PLAYOFFS**

**QUARTER-FINALS**

| | | |
|---|---|---|
| April 19 | Slovakia 2 | Czech Republic 1 |
| April 19 | Canada 8 | Sweden 1 |

**SEMI-FINALS**

| | | |
|---|---|---|
| April 20 | Slovakia 2 | Russia 1 (10:00 OT/GWS—Stefan Ruzicka) |
| April 20 | Canada 2 | United States 1 (Alexandre Bolduc 3:38 OT) |

**BRONZE MEDAL GAME**

April 22 Russia 6 United States 3

**GOLD MEDAL GAME**

April 22 Canada 3 Slovakia 0

**Rosters**

**Belarus** (Mikhail Zakharov, coach) GK—Dmitri Milchakov, Alexei Gritsenko—Vadim Sushko, Sergei Giro, Sergei Kolosov, Vadim Karaga, Pavel Badyl, Dmitri Pantsyrev, Yuri Bulhakov, Alexander Karotki, Roman Blokh, Sergei Kukushkin, Konstantin Zakharov, Sergei Rylkov, Andrei Kostitsyn, Sergei Kostitsyn, Alexei Shagov, Dmitri Semyonov, Yevgeni Goranin, Artyom Volkov, Pavel Chernook, Vyacheslav Gusov

**Canada** (Mike Kelly, coach) GK—Ryan Munce, Rejean Beauchemin—Braydon Coburn, Paul Bissonnette, Shawn Belle, Brennan Chapman, Brent Seabrook, Patrick Coulombe, Geoff Platt, Dany Roussin, Alexandre Bolduc, Anthony Stewart, Stephen Dixon, Ryan Getzlaf, Steve Bernier, Jeff Carter, Marc-Antoine Pouliot, Jeremy Colliton, B.J. Crombeen, Jamie Tardif, Dan Carcillo, Mike Green

**Czech Republic** (Karel Najman, coach) GK—Jakub Cech, Marek Schwarz—Ladislav Smid, Petr Horava, Lukas Pulpan, Lukas Bolf, Lukas Spelda, Martin Tuma, Zbynek Hrdel, Milan Hluchy, Karel Hromas, Lukas Kaspar, Kamil Vavra, Ivo Kratena, Jakub Petruzalek, Lukas Vomela, Vaclav Meidl, Vojtech Polak, Petr Machacek, Rostislav Olesz, Michal Polak, Jakub Sindel

**Finland** (Mika Saarinen, coach) GK—Ville Hostikka, Eero Kilpelainen—Otto Honkaheimo, Risto Korhonen, Mikko Kuukka, Olli-Pekka Komulainen, Erkka Leppanen, Niko Vainio, Tero Konttinen, Ville Mantymaa, Juhamatti Aaltonen, Ville Vimpari, Jesse Saarinen, Arsi Piispanen, Pasi Salonen, Tuomas Santavuori, Teemu Nurmi, Valtteri Tenkanen, Matias Keranen, Petteri Nokelainen, Juho Keranen, Miikka Jouhkimainen

**Kazakhstan** (Vladimir Belyayev, coach) GK—Andrei Podoinikov, Sergei Polski—Alexander Cherepanov, Arman Tyuluberdinov, Alexander Shin, Alexander Yevseyev, Roman Dementiev, Alexander Lipin, Artur Kiberlein, Danil Pilyugin, Andrei Fux, Alexander Maznyak, Alexei Yefremov, Doszhan Yesirkenov, Konstantin Pushkaryov, Dmitri Shakhov, Ilya Feoktistov, Talgat Zhailauov, Dmitri Kharko, Eldar Abdulayev, Alexander Skvortsov, Yevgeni Gorban

**Russia** (Vladimir Kryuchkov, coach) GK—Rustam Sidikov, Sergei Goryelov—Denis Yezhov, Dmitri Kosmachev, Anton Belov, Alexander Ovechkin, Andrei Pervyshin, Anton Dubinin, Georgi Misharin, Dmitri Pestunov, Artyom Nosov, Dmitri Chernykh, Yevgeni Malkin, Konstantin Glazachev, Konstantin Makarov, Vitali Anikeyenko, Alexander Naurov, Grigori Shafigulin, Denis Logunov, Alexei Ivanov, Dmitri Petrov, Dmitri Shitikov

**Slovakia** (Jindrich Novotny, coach) GK—Marek Roznik, Jaroslav Halak—Pavol Gurcik, Slavomir Bodnar, Adam Drgon, Marek Zagrapan, Ivan Baranka, Milan Hruska, Ivan Dornic, Michal Sersen, Lukas Mucha, Tomas Bulik, Peter Tabacek, Vladimir Dravecky, Juraj Prokop, Stefan Ruzicka, Ladislav Scurko, Branislav Fabry, Jaroslav Markovic, Andrej Meszaros, Boris Valabik, Stefan Blaho

**Sweden** (Peter Johansson, coach) GK—Christopher Heino-Lindberg, Gustaf Wesslau—Elias Granat, Johan Jonsson, Stefan Erkgards, Gustav Engman, Ola Svanberg, Alexander Tang, Mattias Karlsson, Bobby Williams, Loui Eriksson, Carl Soderberg, Mikael Oberg, Christopher Lindholm, Liam Lindstrom, Linus Videll, Filip Hollstrom, Linus Persson, Kalle Olsson, Adrian Arling, Kristoffer Backstrom, David Fredriksson

**Switzerland** (Roger Bader, coach) GK—Raphael Ducret, Michael Tobler—Alain Birbaum, Philippe Furrer,Thomas Jakob, Simon Luthi, Daniel Schnyder, Philippe Seydoux, Patrick von Gunten, Cedric Botter, Alain Brunold, Gianni Ehrensperger, Peter Guggisberg, Stefan Hurlimann, Antonio Rizzello, Franco Collenberg, Tristan Vauclair, Kevin Romy, Victor Stancescu, Fabian Debrunner, Philipp Wetzel, Roman Wick

**United States** (Moe Mantha, coach) GK—Mike Brown, Chris Holt—Kyle Klubertanz, Kevin Coughlin, Mike Brown, Michael Bartlett, Joshua Sciba, T.J. Hensick, Robbie Earl, Jeff Likens, Matt Cohen, Adam Pineault, Steve Mandes, Jacob Dowell, Dustin Collins, David Robertson, Ryan Suter, Matt Hunwick, Casey Borer, Drew Stafford, Nate Hagemo, Kevin Porter

## 6th U18 WORLD CHAMPIONSHIP (MEN)
## April 18-18, 2004
## Minsk, Belarus

**Final Placing**

| | |
|---|---|
| Gold ........Russia | 6th .........Slovakia |
| Silver ......United States | 7th .........Finland |
| Bronze ....Czech Republic | 8th .........Denmark^ |
| 4th..........Canada | 9th .........Belarus* |
| 5th..........Sweden | 10th .......Norway^* |

^promoted from Division I in 2003
*demoted to Division I for 2005

**Tournament Format**

The 10 teams were divided into two groups of five and played a round robin within each group. The winner of each group advanced directly to the semi-finals while the second and third place teams played a cross-over quarter-finals. The fourth and fifth place teams in the Preliminary Round went to a Relagation Round, the bottom two teams after this round robin demoted to Division I for 2005.

**Results & Standings**

**PRELIMINARY ROUND**

**GROUP A**

| | GP | W | T | L | GF | GA | P |
|---|---|---|---|---|---|---|---|
| United States | 4 | 4 | 0 | 0 | 22 | 5 | 8 |
| Canada | 4 | 3 | 0 | 1 | 15 | 5 | 6 |
| Sweden | 4 | 2 | 0 | 2 | 8 | 12 | 4 |
| Denmark | 4 | 1 | 0 | 3 | 8 | 10 | 2 |
| Belarus | 4 | 0 | 0 | 4 | 3 | 24 | 0 |

| | | |
|---|---|---|
| April 8 | United States 5 | Denmark 2 |
| April 8 | Canada 5 | Sweden 0 |
| April 9 | Denmark 4 | Belarus 1 |
| April 10 | United States 6 | Sweden 2 |
| April 10 | Canada 7 | Belarus 2 |
| April 11 | Canada 2 | Denmark 1 |
| April 12 | Sweden 2 | Denmark 1 |
| April 12 | United States 9 | Belarus 0 |
| April 13 | United States 2 | Canada 1 |
| April 13 | Sweden 4 | Belarus 0 |

**GROUP B**

| | GP | W | T | L | GF | GA | P |
|---|---|---|---|---|---|---|---|
| Russia | 4 | 2 | 2 | 0 | 16 | 9 | 6 |
| Czech Republic | 4 | 1 | 3 | 0 | 10 | 3 | 5 |
| Slovakia | 4 | 1 | 3 | 0 | 13 | 7 | 5 |
| Finland | 4 | 1 | 2 | 1 | 14 | 8 | 4 |
| Norway | 4 | 0 | 0 | 4 | 6 | 32 | 0 |

| | | |
|---|---|---|
| April 8 | Russia 8 | Norway 4 |
| April 8 | Czech Republic 1 | Slovakia 1 |
| April 9 | Finland 9 | Norway 0 |
| April 10 | Russia 1 | Czech Republic 1 |
| April 10 | Slovakia 2 | Finland 2 |
| April 11 | Slovakia 8 | Norway 2 |
| April 12 | Czech Republic 7 | Norway 0 |
| April 12 | Russia 5 | Finland 2 |
| April 13 | Finland 1 | Czech Republic 1 |
| April 13 | Slovakia 2 | Russia 2 |

**RELEGATION ROUND**

| | GP | W | T | L | GF | GA | P |
|---|---|---|---|---|---|---|---|
| Finland | 3 | 3 | 0 | 0 | 18 | 3 | 6 |
| Denmark | 3 | 2 | 0 | 1 | 12 | 9 | 4 |
| Belarus | 3 | 1 | 0 | 2 | 7 | 12 | 2 |
| Norway | 3 | 0 | 0 | 3 | 7 | 20 | 0 |

| | | |
|---|---|---|
| April 15 | Denmark 7 | Norway 4 |
| April 15 | Finland 5 | Belarus 2 |
| April 16 | Finland 4 | Denmark 1 |
| April 16 | Belarus 4 | Norway 3 |

**5TH-PLACE GAME**

April 17 Sweden 5 Slovakia 4

**PLAYOFFS**

**QUARTER-FINALS**

| | | |
|---|---|---|
| April 15 | Canada 3 | Slovakia 1 |
| April 15 | Czech Republic 5 | Sweden 1 |

**SEMI-FINALS**

| | | |
|---|---|---|
| April 16 | United States 3 | Czech Republic 2 |
| April 16 | Russia 5 | Canada 2 |

**BRONZE MEDAL GAME**

April 18 Czech Republic 3 Canada 2

**GOLD MEDAL GAME**

April 18 Russia 3 United States 2

**Rosters**

**Belarus** (Vladimir Sinitsyn, coach) GK—Dmitri Milchakov, Ihar Brikun—Andrei Prakopchyk, Pavel Badyl, Vadim Sushko, Alexander Churko, Sergei Kolosov, Alexander Syrei, Roman Blokh, Sergei Rylkov, Alexander Burmistronak, Sergei Yanovski, Sergei Kostitsyn, Artur Tsyareshka, Dmitri Pantsyrev, Ivan Miadzel, Yevgeni Zhilinski, Vitali Labionak, Dmitri Stelkin, Pavel Chernook, Yevgeni Goranin, Alexei Shagov

**Canada** (Dean Chynoweth, coach) GK—Justin Pogge, Devan Dubnyk—Wes O'Neill, David Schulz, Michael Funk, Andy Rogers, Kyle Wharton, Jonathan Sigalet, Kris Versteeg, John Lammers, Ryan Garlock, Dane Byers, Kyle Chipchura, Jeff Schultz, Evan McGrath, Eric Hunter, Adam Berti, Frederic Cabana, Peter Tsimikalis, Liam Reddox, Jean Michel Rizk, Aaron Gagnon

**Czech Republic** (Jaromir Sindel, coach) GK—Marek Schwarz, Jakub Lev—Adam Lukacovic, Ondrej Smach, Jaroslav Mrazek, Stanislav Balan, Ladislav Smid, Lubomir Stach, Jan Danecek, Michal Birner, Karel Hromas, Vladimir Sobotka, Jakub Sindel, Zdenek Bahensky, Roman Psurny, Tomas Mertl, David Krejci, Roman Polak, Radek Smolenak, Michal Psurny, Michal Gulasi, Michael Frolik

**Denmark** (Leif Thomsen, coach) GK—Simon Nielsen, Sebastian Dahm—Jannik Karvinen, Mads Kjems, Mads Bodker, Frederik Hentze, Michael Eskesen, Kasper Weis, Peter Regin, Christian Olsen, Simon Lorentsen, Mads Christensen, Christian Vaagensoe, Esben Nielsen, Dennis Hojmose, Robin Stilling, Sune Stefani, Mads Schaarup, Morten Madsen, Jannik Hansen, Martin Larsen, Tobias Kisum

**Finland** (Harri Ahola, coach) GK—Karri Ramo, Tuukka Rask—Tuomas Gardstrom, Antti Turunen, Risto Korhonen, Vesa Kulmala, Teemu Laakso, Matti Pinomaki, Jussi Ruohola, Lauri Tukonen, Mikko Alikoski, Joni Finell, Miika Lahti, Petteri Wirtanen, Jari Sailio, Jarmo Jokila, Jesse Joensuu, Antti Jaatinen, Janne Kolehmainen, Miika Tuomainen, Lauri Korpikoski, Petteri Nokelainen

**Norway** (Arne Billkvam, coach) GK—Lars Haugen, Lars Simen Paulgaard—Magnus Kjelstadli, Ole Muhle, Jonas Holos, Jonas Nygard, Kristian Forsberg, Glenn Eliesen, Jesper Hoel, Marius Dischler, Martin Roymark, Lars Ostli, Eirik Grafsronningen, Mats Aasen, Dennis Sveum, Martin Hagen, Mathias Trygg, Lars Paulgaard, Joakim Jensen, Mathis Olimb, Fredrik Thinn, Per Ferdinand Stensund

**Russia** (Valeri Bragin, coach) GK—Anton Khudobin, Ivan Kasutin—Alexei Yemelin, Anton Belov, Kirill Lyamin, Rinat Ibragimov, Nikolai Kulyomin, Sergei Ogorodnikov, Roman Voloshenko, Sergei Karetin, Yevgeni Biryukov, Yevgeni Malkin, Sergei Salnikov, Mikhail Yunkov, Dimitri Shitikov, Alexander Radulov, Alexander Plyushev, Alexander Aksenenko, Enver Lisin, Denis Parshin, Adgur Dzhugelia, Sergei Shirokov

**Slovakia** (Jindrich Novotny, coach) GK—Michal Valent, Juraj Stopka—Lubor Zuzin, Andrej Sekera, Matej Cunik, Peter Huba, Igor Bacek, Richard Lelkes, Lukas Handlovsky, Roman Tomanek, Andrej Direr, Tomas Petruska, Jozef Wagenhoffer, Ladislav Scurko, Marek Zagrapan, Erik Piatak, Filip Simka, Lubomir Chmelo, Juraj Gracik, Boris Valabik, Andrej Piskura, Marcel Ulehla

**Sweden** (Tomas Thelin, coach) GK—Daniel Larsson, Magnus Akerlund—Niklas Andersson, Mattias Hellstrom, Richard Demen-Williaume, Emil Axelsson, Marcus Nyberg, Marcus Niemi, Fredrik Naslund, Jesper Andersson, Tommy Enstrom, Tom Wandell, Tobias Viklund, Fred Wikner, Oscar Sundh, Viktor Lindgren, Niklas Olausson, Sebastian Karlsson, Nicklas Bergfors, Oscar Hedman, Carl Gunnarsson, Martin Gundmundsson

**United States** (John Hynes, coach) GK—Cory Schneider, Jeff Frazee—Jason Desantis, Mike Brennan, Brett Topher Bevis, Zachary Jones, Joe Grimaldi, Nate Hagemo, Kevin Porter, Matt Auffrey, Bryan Lerg, Nathan Davis, Jarod Palmer, Kevin Swallow, Tom Fritsche, Brandon Scero, Jack Skille, Nathan Gerbe, Chad Kolarik, Geoff Paukovich, Phil Kessel, Jack Johnson

## 7th U18 WORLD CHAMPIONSHIP (MEN)
## April 14-24, 2005
## Ceske Budejovice/Plzen, Czech Republic

**Final Placing**

| | |
|---|---|
| Gold ........United States | 6th .........Slovakia |
| Silver ......Canada | 7th .........Finland |
| Bronze ....Sweden | 8th .........Germany^ |
| 4th .........Czech Republic | 9th .........Switzerland^* |
| 5th ..........Russia | 10th .......Denmark* |

^promoted from Division I in 2004
*demoted to Division I for 2006

**Tournament Format**

The 10 teams were divided into two groups of five and played a round robin within each group. The winner of each group advanced directly to the semi-finals while the second and third place teams played a cross-over quarter-finals. The fourth and fifth place teams in the Preliminary Round went to a Relagation Round, the bottom two teams after this round robin demoted to Division I for 2006.

**Results & Standings**

**PRELIMINARY ROUND**

**GROUP A (CESKE BUDEJOVICE)**

| | GP | W | T | L | GF | GA | P |
|---|---|---|---|---|---|---|---|
| Canada | 4 | 3 | 0 | 1 | 24 | 7 | 6 |
| Sweden | 4 | 3 | 0 | 1 | 9 | 6 | 6 |
| Russia | 4 | 3 | 0 | 1 | 19 | 12 | 6 |
| Germany | 4 | 1 | 0 | 3 | 10 | 18 | 2 |
| Denmark | 4 | 0 | 0 | 4 | 4 | 23 | 0 |

| | | |
|---|---|---|
| April 14 | Canada 2 | Germany 1 |
| April 14 | Russia 2 | Sweden 1 |
| April 15 | Germany 3 | Denmark 1 |
| April 16 | Sweden 2 | Canada 1 |
| April 16 | Russia 2 | Denmark 1 |
| April 17 | Russia 12 | Germany 4 |
| April 18 | Canada 15 | Denmark 1 |
| April 18 | Sweden 3 | Germany 2 |
| April 19 | Canada 6 | Russia 3 |
| April 19 | Sweden 3 | Denmark 1 |

**GROUP B (PLZEN)**

| | GP | W | T | L | GF | GA | P |
|---|---|---|---|---|---|---|---|
| United States | 4 | 4 | 0 | 0 | 17 | 5 | 8 |
| Czech Republic | 4 | 3 | 0 | 1 | 16 | 6 | 6 |
| Slovakia | 4 | 2 | 0 | 2 | 6 | 9 | 4 |
| Finland | 4 | 1 | 0 | 3 | 6 | 13 | 2 |
| Switzerland | 4 | 0 | 0 | 4 | 4 | 16 | 0 |

| | | |
|---|---|---|
| April 14 | United States 3 | Slovakia 1 |
| April 14 | Czech Republic 4 | Switzerland 1 |
| April 15 | Finland 3 | Switzerland 1 |
| April 16 | Czech Republic 3 | Slovakia 0 |
| April 16 | United States 3 | Finland 0 |
| April 17 | United States 7 | Switzerland 1 |
| April 18 | Slovakia 2 | Switzerland 1 |
| April 18 | Czech Republic 6 | Finland 1 |
| April 19 | Slovakia 3 | Finland 2 |
| April 19 | United States 4 | Czech Republic 3 |

**RELEGATION ROUND (CESKE BUDEJOVICE)**

| | GP | W | T | L | GF | GA | P |
|---|---|---|---|---|---|---|---|
| Finland | 3 | 3 | 0 | 0 | 10 | 5 | 6 |
| Germany | 3 | 2 | 0 | 1 | 7 | 5 | 4 |
| Switzerland | 3 | 1 | 0 | 2 | 5 | 7 | 2 |
| Denmark | 3 | 0 | 0 | 3 | 5 | 10 | 0 |

| | | |
|---|---|---|
| April 21 | Germany 2 | Switzerland 0 |
| April 21 | Finland 3 | Denmark 2 |
| April 22 | Finland 4 | Germany 2 |
| April 22 | Switzerland 4 | Denmark 2 |

**5TH-PLACE GAME (PLZEN)**

| | | |
|---|---|---|
| April 23 | Russia 5 | Slovakia 2 |

**PLAYOFFS (PLZEN)**
**QUARTER-FINALS**

| | | |
|---|---|---|
| April 21 | Sweden 5 | Slovakia 3 |
| April 21 | Czech Republic 5 | Russia 1 |

**SEMI-FINALS**

| | | |
|---|---|---|
| April 22 | United States 6 | Sweden 2 |
| April 22 | Canada 3 | Czech Republic 2 (Guillaume Latendresse 5:29 OT) |

**BRONZE MEDAL GAME**

| | | |
|---|---|---|
| April 24 | Sweden 4 | Czech Republic 2 |

**GOLD MEDAL GAME**

| | | |
|---|---|---|
| April 24 | United States 5 | Canada 1 |

**Rosters**

**Canada** (Shawn Camp, coach) GK—Carey Price, Pier-Olivier Pelletier—Luc Bourdon, Jean-Philippe Paquet, Brendan Mikkelson, Marc-Andre Gragnani, Kris Letang, Ryan Parent, Adam Hobson, Cody Bass, Cal Clutterbuck, Devin Setoguchi, Paul Kurceba, Guillaume Latendresse, James Neal, Chris Lawrence, Richard Clune, Ryan O'Marra, Colton Yellowhorn, Derick Brassard, Tom Pyatt, Daniel Bertram

**Czech Republic** (Bretislav Kopriva, coach) GK—Ondrej Pavelec, Alexander Salak—Daniel Rakos, Petr Kalus, Jan Kanov, David Ruzicka, Ondrej Pozivil, Ondrej Masek, Tomas Kudelka, Tomas Pospisil, Jiri Tlusty, Michael Frolik, Alexander Hegegy, Vladimir Sobotka, David Kveton, Jakub Cerny, David Kuchejda, Jakub Vojta, Tomas Svoboda, Tomas Kana, Ondrej Fiala, Martin Hanzal

**Denmark** (Leif Thomsen, coach) GK—Sebastian Dahm, Casper Norrild—Patrick Arvidsen, Jonathan Moberg, Mads Bodker, Jesper Nielsen, Frederik Hentze, Joachim Holten Moller, Julian Jakobsen, Christian Olsen, Mads Christensen, Christian Vaagensoe, Mikkel Bodker, Nicholas Phillips, Kasper Jensen, Jesper Jensen, Mads Schaarup, Morten Madsen, Morten Allesoe, Nick Samsoe-Jensen, Alexander Bach, Casper Herlet

**Finland** (Juha Pajouja, coach) GK—Juha Toivonen, Tuukka Rask—Juho Mielonen, Henrik Maunula, Timo Seppanen, Mikael Kurki,Tommi Leinonen, Joni Haverinen, Teemu Ramstedt, Perttu Lindgren, Mikko Lehtonen, Jonas Enlund, Ville Korhonen, Jussi Peltomaa, Oskar Osala, Jesse Joensuu, Miika Lahti, Robert Nyholm, Tommi Huhtala, Joonas Kemppainen, Max Warn, Teemu Laakso

**Germany** (James Setters, coach) GK—Danijel Kovacic, Sebastian Stefaniszin—Max Prommersberger, Andreas Maier, Felix Schutz, Sascha Jocham, Stefan Langwieder, Torsten Ankert, Constantin Braun, Simon Maier, Sandro Schonberger, Korbinian Holzer, Andre Schietzold, Sergej Janzen, Thomas Pielmeier, Florian Pndruschka, Henry Martens, Philip Gogulla, Christian Wichert, Rene Kramer, Maximilian Brandl, Elia Ostwald

**Russia** (Mihail Slipchenko, coach) GK—Semyon Varlamov, Alexander Tryanichev, Ilya Proskuryakov—Igor Nikitin, Andrei Zubarev, Anton Poleshuk, Vitali Anikeyenko, Denis Pakhomov, Vyacheslav Buravchikov, Alexei Sopin, Denis Istomin, Ilya Zubov, Alexander Romanovski, Anton Krysanov, Denis Osipov, Alexander Bumagin, Igor Velichkin, Dmitri Zyuzin, Vyacheslav Trukhno, Igor Antosik, Igor Makarov, Alexander Kucheryavenko, Yegor Zharkov

**Slovakia** (Jozef Cepan) GK—Marek Simko, Vladimir Kovac, Branislav Konrad—Marek Biro, Lukas Bohunicky, Tomas Brnak, Matej Cunik, Tomas Marcinko, Martin Grundling, Jakub Drabek, Peter Hubinsky, Juraj Mikus, Vladimir Mihalik, Richard Rapac, Richard Lelkes, Mario Bliznak, Martin Klucar, David Buc, Marek Bartanus, Martin Domian, Ondrej Otcenas, Michal Hrtus, Michal Klejna

**Sweden** (Mikael Tisell, coach) GK—Mattias Modig, Jhonas Enroth—Christopher From Bjork, Alexander Hellstrom, Niklas Oman, Niklas Hjalmarsson, Alexander Ribbenstrand, Linus Morin, Nicklas Bergfors, Martin Johansson, Robin Lindqvist, Andreas Molinder, Johan Nilsson, Fredrik Pettersson, Mattias Ritola, Patric Hornqvist, Johan Dahlberg, Patrik Zackrisson, Johan Andersson, Nicklas Backstrom, Niclas Andersen, Kim Sunna

**Switzerland** (Alfred Bohren,coach) GK—Leonardo Genoni, Reto Berra—Steven Schoop, Fernando Heynen, Roger Summermatter, Simon Schnyder, Alessandro Chiesa, Yannick Weber, Pascal Zbinden, Nino Fehr, Adrien Lauper, Aurelio Lemm, Fadri Lemm, Dario Burgler, Jeremy Gailland, Steve Kellenberger, Luca Cunti, Juraj Simek, Robin Grossmann, Janik Steinmann, Diego Schwarzenbach, Arnaud Jacquemet

**United States** (Ron Rolston, coach) GK—Joe Palmer, Jeff Frazee—Kyle Lawson, Taylor Chorney, Erik Johnson, Zachary Jones, Brandon Gentile, Phil Kessel, Nathan Gerbe, Chad Rau, Jim Fraser, Dan Collins, Jason Bailey, Mark Mitera, Peter Mueller, Ryan Stoa, Jack Skille, Jason Lawrence, Justin Mercier, Benn Ferriero, Andreas Vlassopoulos, Jack Johnson

## 8th U18 WORLD CHAMPIONSHIP (MEN)
**April 12-22, 2006**
**Angelholm/Halmstad, Sweden**

**Final Placing**

| | |
|---|---|
| Gold........United States | 6th .........Sweden |
| Silver ......Finland | 7th .........Slovakia |
| Bronze ....Czech Republic | 8th .........Germany |
| 4th ..........Canada | 9th .........Belarus^* |
| 5th ..........Russia | 10th .......Norway^* |

^promoted from Division I in 2005
*demoted to Division I for 2007

**Tournament Format**

The 10 teams were divided into two groups of five and played a round robin within each group. The winner of each group advanced directly to the semi-finals while the second and third place teams played a cross-over quarter-finals. The fourth and fifth place teams in the Preliminary Round went to a Relagation Round, the bottom two teams after this round robin demoted to Division I for 2007.

**Results & Standings**
**PRELIMINARY ROUND**
**GROUP A (ANGELHOLM)**

| | GP | W | T | L | GF | GA | P |
|---|---|---|---|---|---|---|---|
| United States | 4 | 4 | 0 | 0 | 30 | 3 | 8 |
| Russia | 4 | 3 | 0 | 1 | 21 | 9 | 6 |
| Czech Republic | 4 | 2 | 0 | 2 | 9 | 11 | 4 |
| Germany | 4 | 1 | 0 | 3 | 12 | 23 | 2 |
| Belarus | 4 | 0 | 0 | 4 | 4 | 30 | 0 |

| | | |
|---|---|---|
| April 12 | Czech Republic 4 | Germany 2 |
| April 12 | United States 4 | Russia 2 |
| April 13 | Russia 8 | Belarus 0 |
| April 13 | United States 9 | Germany 0 |
| April 14 | Czech Republic 5 | Belarus 2 |
| April 15 | Russia 9 | Germany 5 |
| April 15 | United States 5 | Czech Republic 0 |
| April 16 | Germany 5 | Belarus 1 |
| April 17 | Russia 2 | Czech Republic 0 |
| April 17 | United States 12 | Belarus 1 |

**GROUP B (HALMSTAD)**

| | GP | W | T | L | GF | GA | P |
|---|---|---|---|---|---|---|---|
| Finland | 4 | 3 | 1 | 0 | 12 | 7 | 7 |
| Sweden | 4 | 3 | 0 | 1 | 15 | 8 | 6 |
| Canada | 4 | 2 | 1 | 1 | 12 | 5 | 5 |
| Slovakia | 4 | 1 | 0 | 3 | 11 | 16 | 2 |
| Norway | 4 | 0 | 0 | 4 | 7 | 21 | 0 |

| | | |
|---|---|---|
| April 12 | Canada 3 | Slovakia 1 |
| April 12 | Sweden 5 | Norway 2 |
| April 13 | Canada 9 | Norway 2 |
| April 13 | Finland 6 | Slovakia 3 |
| April 14 | Finland 4 | Sweden 3 |
| April 15 | Slovakia 5 | Norway 2 |
| April 15 | Sweden 2 | Canada 0 |
| April 16 | Finland 2 | Norway 1 |
| April 17 | Canada 0 | Finland 0 |
| April 17 | Sweden 5 | Slovakia 2 |

**RELEGATION ROUND (HALMSTAD)**

| | GP | W | T | L | GF | GA | P |
|---|---|---|---|---|---|---|---|
| Slovakia | 3 | 2 | 0 | 1 | 7 | 5 | 4 |
| Germany | 3 | 1 | 1 | 1 | 8 | 5 | 3 |
| Belarus | 3 | 1 | 1 | 1 | 9 | 11 | 3 |
| Norway | 3 | 0 | 2 | 1 | 10 | 13 | 2 |

| | | |
|---|---|---|
| April 19 | Germany 2 | Norway 2 |
| April 19 | Belarus 2 | Slovakia 0 |
| April 20 | Belarus 6 | Norway 6 |
| April 20 | Slovakia 2 | Germany 1 |

**5TH-PLACE GAME**

| | | | |
|---|---|---|---|
| April 21 | Angelholm | Russia 5 | Sweden 2 |

**PLAYOFFS (ANGELHOLM)**
**QUARTER-FINALS**

| | | |
|---|---|---|
| April 19 | Canada 4 | Russia 1 |
| April 19 | Czech Republic 3 | Sweden 0 |

**SEMI-FINALS**

| | | |
|---|---|---|
| April 20 | Finland 3 | Canada 2 (Jan-Mikael Jarvinen 1:22 OT) |
| April 20 | United States 4 | Czech Republic 3 (Patrick Kane 6:50 OT) |

**BRONZE MEDAL GAME**
April 22 Czech Republic 4 Canada 1

**GOLD MEDAL GAME**
April 22 United States 3 Finland 1

**Rosters**

**Belarus** (Vasili Pankov, coach) GK—Vitali Trus, Maxim Laikovski—Sergei Magerov, Dmitri Korobov, Alexander Syrei, Alexander Yeronov, Dmitri Shumski, Fyodor Markevich, Alexander Karatkevich, Vladimir Sachko, Igor Fedotenko, Alexei Golubev, Pavel Razvodovski, Sergei Kozlovich, Igor Voroshilov, Yegor Korotki, Vladimir Mikhailov, Artyom Demkov, Andrei Kolosov, Yevgeni Avdosev, Mikhail Stefanovich, Andrei Stas

**Canada** (Greg Gilbert, coach) GK—Jonathan Bernier, Kris Lazaruk—Matt Corrente, Ty Wishart, Keaton Ellerby, Craig Schira, Stefan Chaput, Jamie McGinn, Ben Maxwell, Matt Beleskey, Brandon Sutter, Ben Shutron, Francois Bouchard, Victor Bartley, Hugo Carpentier, John Tavares, Logan Pyett, Shawn Matthias, Ryan McDonough, Justin Azevedo, Cory Emmerton, Levi Nelson

**Czech Republic** (Martin Pesout, coach) GK—Jakub Kovar, Michal Neuvirth—Bohdan Visnak, Patrik Prokop, Lukas Lang, Jiri Jebavy, David Stich, Antonin Drbohlav, Michal Kazatel, Jiri Tlusty, Martin Latal, Jan Semorad, Pavel Kubena, Ondrej Roman, Vladimir Ruzicka, Jakub Sklenar, Martin Bartos, Jakub Voracek, David Kveton, Martin Kupec, Michael Frolik, David Ruzicka

**Finland** (Rauli Urama, coach) GK—Atte Engren, Riku Helenius—Markus Himanka, Eetu Heikkinen, Miko Malkamaki, Jarkko Nappila, Mikko Kukkonen, Joonas Lehtivuori, Nico Aaltonen, Juuso Puustinen, Ilkka Heikkila, Joonas Kemppainen, Jan-Mikael Juutilainen, Robert Nyholm, Jani Savolainen, Kaarlo Jormakka, Niclas Lucenius, Juhani Jasu, Juuso Antonen, Joonas Jalvanti, Max Warn, Jan-Mikael Jarvinen

**Germany** (James Setters, coach) GK—Timo Pielmeier, Sebastian Staudt—Denis Reul, Benedik Kohl, Florian Kirschbauer, Thorsten Ankert, Bruce Becker, Hans Pienitz, Maximilian Brandl, Adrian Albanese, Elia Ostwald, Marius Garten, Christopher Fischer, Thomas Weiszdorn, Marcel Muller, Constantin Braun, Alexander Oblinger, Patrick Hager, Dominik Quinlan, Frank Mauer, Korbinian Holzer, Michael Endrass

**Norway** (Orjan Lovdal, coach) GK—Andre Lysenstoen, Robert Hestmann—Lars Petter Mengshoel, Patrik Molberg, Marius Hagberg, Henrik Odegaard, Peter Rohn, Benjamin Bakkelund, Henrik Skouen, Daniel Sorvik, Martin Laumann-Ylven, Mats Weberg, Tommy Kristiansen, Ken Olimb, Robin Dahlstrom, Christopher Paulsen, Patrick Andre Bovim, Jo Magnus Hegg, Mats Froshaug, Henrik Heen, Stefan Espeland, Alexander Rindal

**Russia** (Fyodor Kanareykin, coach) GK—Semyon Varlamov, Stanislav Galimov—Yuri Alexandrov, Igor Zubov, Pavel Doronin, Valeri Zhukov, Kirill Tulupov, Mikhail Glukhov, Alexander Ryabev, Andrei Popov, Artyom Anisimov, Ruslan Bashkirov, Mikhail Churlyayev, Maxim Mamin, Vladimir Zharkov, Sergei Zachupeyko, Vadim Golubtsov, Andrei Sobachkin, Alexander Vasyunov, Yevgeni Bodrov, Ilya Kablukov, Anton Glovatski

**Slovakia** (Jozef Fruhauf, coach) GK—Marek Simko, Tomas Hiadlovsky—Ondrej Mikula, Justin Javorek, Marek Slovak, Peter Krsnak, Tomas Marcinko, Juraj Mikus, Ivan Rohac, Branislav Rehus, Adam Bezak, Marek Biro, Milan Jurik, Juraj Valach, Julius Sinkovic, Erik Caladi, Lukas Zeliska, Milan Balis, Rastislav Konecny, Martin Dulak, Jozef Sladok, Lukas Vartovnik

**Sweden** (Mikael Tisell, coach) GK—Stefan Ridderwall, Jhonas Enroth—Eric Moe, Magnus Svanberg, Kristofer Berglund, Mathias Sjoberg, Tomas Larsson, Dennis Persson, Mikael Ahlen, Tony Lagerstrom, Jonas Wallgren, Robin Figren, Kim Johansson, Jimmy Jensen, Patrik Berglund, Joakim Andersson, Mikael Backlund, Patrik Lundh, Mario Kempe, Viktor Sjodin, Niclas Andersen, Fredric Andersson

**United States** (John Hynes, coach) GK—Joe Palmer, Brett Bennett—Cade Fairchild, Nigel Williams, Jamie McBain, Blake Geoffrion, Erik Johnson, Brian Strait, Ryan Hayes, Rhett Rakhshani, Ryan Flynn, Chris Summers, Kevin Montgomery, Trent Palm, Jim O'Brien, Mike Carman, Bill Sweatt, Mike Ratchuk, James van Riemsdyk, Colin Wilson, Patrick Kane, Luke Popko

## 9th U18 WORLD CHAMPIONSHIP (MEN)
## April 11-22, 2007
## Tampere/Rauma, Finland

**Final Placing**

| | |
|---|---|
| Gold ........Russia | 6th .........Switzerland^ |
| Silver ......United States | 7th .........Finland |
| Bronze ....Sweden | 8th .........Germany |
| 4th..........Canada | 9th .........Czech Republic* |
| 5th..........Slovakia | 10th .......Latvia^* |

^promoted from Division I in 2006
*demoted to Division I for 2008

**Tournament Format**
The 10 teams were divided into two groups of five and played a round robin within each group. The winner of each group advanced directly to the semi-finals while the second and third place teams played a cross-over quarter-finals. The fourth and fifth place teams in the Preliminary Round went to a Relagation Round, the bottom two teams after this round robin demoted to Division I for 2008.

**Results & Standings**
**PRELIMINARY ROUND**
**GROUP A (RAUMA)**

| | GP | W | OTW | OTL | L | GF | GA | P |
|---|---|---|---|---|---|---|---|---|
| Canada | 4 | 3 | 1 | 0 | 0 | 24 | 8 | 11 |
| Russia | 4 | 3 | 0 | 0 | 1 | 16 | 12 | 9 |
| United States | 4 | 2 | 0 | 1 | 1 | 22 | 9 | 7 |
| Germany | 4 | 1 | 0 | 0 | 3 | 8 | 21 | 3 |
| Latvia | 4 | 0 | 0 | 0 | 4 | 6 | 26 | 0 |

April 12 Canada 7 Germany 3
April 12 Russia 5 United States 3
April 13 United States 9 Germany 1
April 13 Russia 6 Latvia 3
April 14 Canada 9 Latvia 1
April 15 Russia 3 Germany 1
April 15 Canada 3 United States 2 (5:00 OT/GWS—Zac Boychuk)
April 16 Germany 3 Latvia 2
April 17 United States 8 Latvia 0
April 17 Canada 5 Russia 2

**GROUP B (TAMPERE)**

| | GP | W | OTW | OTL | L | GF | GA | P |
|---|---|---|---|---|---|---|---|---|
| Sweden | 4 | 2 | 1 | 0 | 1 | 10 | 7 | 8 |
| Slovakia | 4 | 2 | 0 | 1 | 1 | 9 | 10 | 7 |
| Switzerland | 4 | 2 | 0 | 0 | 2 | 11 | 7 | 6 |
| Czech Republic | 4 | 1 | 1 | 0 | 2 | 9 | 11 | 5 |
| Finland | 4 | 1 | 0 | 1 | 2 | 6 | 10 | 4 |

April 11 Sweden 2 Finland 1 (5:00 OT/GWS—Mikael Backlund)
April 12 Czech Republic 4 Switzerland 2
April 13 Slovakia 6 Sweden 3
April 13 Switzerland 5 Finland 1
April 14 Czech Republic 3 Slovakia 2 (5:00 OT/GWS—Roman Szturc)
April 15 Sweden 3 Switzerland 0
April 15 Finland 4 Czech Republic 2
April 16 Switzerland 4 Slovakia 0
April 17 Sweden 3 Czech Republic 0
April 17 Slovakia 1 Finland 0

**RELEGATION ROUND (RAUMA)**

| | GP | W | OTW | OTL | L | GF | GA | P |
|---|---|---|---|---|---|---|---|---|
| Finland | 3 | 3 | 0 | 0 | 0 | 14 | 8 | 9 |
| Germany | 3 | 2 | 0 | 0 | 1 | 12 | 9 | 6 |
| Czech Republic | 3 | 1 | 0 | 0 | 2 | 9 | 11 | 3 |
| Latvia | 3 | 0 | 0 | 0 | 3 | 6 | 13 | 0 |

April 19 Czech Republic 4 Latvia 1
April 19 Finland 4 Germany 3
April 20 Germany 6 Czech Republic 3
April 20 Finland 6 Latvia 3

**5TH-PLACE GAME**
April 21 Rauma Slovakia 4 Switzerland 1

**PLAYOFFS (TAMPERE)**
**QUARTER-FINALS**
April 19 Russia 4 Switzerland 3 (Nikita Filatov 6:37 OT)
April 19 United States 7 Slovakia 2

**SEMI-FINALS**
April 20 Russia 5 Sweden 4
April 20 United States 4 Canada 3 (10:00 OT/GWS—James van Riemsdyk)

**BRONZE MEDAL GAME**
April 22 Sweden 8 Canada 3

**GOLD MEDAL GAME**
April 22 Russia 6 United States 5

**Rosters**

**Canada** (Trent Yawney, coach) GK—Trevor Cann, Braden Holtby—Jamie Arniel, Yves Bastien, Zac Boychuk, Logan Couture, Drew Doughty, Eric Doyle, Angelo Esposito, Olivier Fortier, Colton Gillies, Alex Grant, Mark Katic, Dion Knelsen, John Negrin, Yann Sauve, Luke Schenn, Steve Stamkos, Brandon Sutter, Zack Torquato, Kyle Turris, Keven Veilleux

**Czech Republic** (Martin Pesout, coach) GK—Marek Benda, Dominik Furch—Michal Bartosek, Rudolf Cerveny, Jaroslav Hertl, Jiri Jebavy, Michal Jordan, Jakub Kachlik, Tomas Karpov, Tomas Knotek, Tomas Kubalek, Tomas Kundratek, Stepan Novotny, Radim Ostrcil, Ondrej Roman, Vladimir Roth, Vladimir Ruzicka, David Stich, Petr Stoklasa, Roman Szturc, Radim Valchar, Jakub Voracek

**Finland** (Harri Laurila, coach) GK—Juha Metsola, Harri Sateri—Jonas Alatalo, Joonas Jarvinen, Jesse Jyrkkio, Niko Kluuskeri, Lassi Kokkala, Anton Kokkonen, Nestori Lahde, Joni Liljeblad, Niclas Lucenius, Sami Martikainen, Jere Olander, Tomi Pallassalo, Eetu Poysti, Tommi Ranta, Tapio Raty, Antti Roppo, Tomi Sallinen, Janne Tavi, Antti Tyrvainen, Olavi Vauhkonen

**Germany** (James Setters, coach) GK—Timo Pielmeier, Andreas Tanzer—Nicolas Ackermann, Sinan Akdag, Benedikt Bruckner, Martin Buchwieser, Sebastian Eickmann, Gerrit Fauser, Simon Fischhaber, Jerome Flaake, Patrick Geiger, Jens Heyer, Martin Hinterstocker, Andre Huebscher, Alexander Oblinger, Denis Reul, Steven Rupprich, Robert Schopf, Gregor Stein, Soren Sturm, Daniel Weiss, David Wolf

**Latvia** (Aleksandrs Klinisovs, coach) GK—Nauris Enkuzens, Dainis Vasiljevs—Edgars Apelis, Lauris Bajaruns, Ricards Birzins, Roberts Bukarts, Kristaps Buzats, Ronalds Cinks, Sergejs Danilovs, Martins Gipters, Kriss Grundmanis, Alberts Ilisko, Roberts Jekimovs, Gvido Kauss, Edgars Lipsbergs, Janis Ozolins, Karlis Ozols, Vitalijs Pavlovs, Aldis Pizans, Aleksejs Proposins, Karlis Rozkalns, Janis Straupe

**Russia** (Miskhat Fakhrutdinov, coach) GK—Alexander Pechurski, Vadim Zhelobnyuk—Sergei Andronov, Yegor Averin, Alexei Cherepanov, Maxim Chudinov, Mikhail Churlyayev, Yevgeni Dadonov, Nikita Filatov, Maxim Goncharov, Dmitri Kagarlitski, Vitali Karamnov, Nikita Klyukin, Sergei Korostin, Dmitri Kugryshev, Dmitri Kulikov, Andrei Loktionov, Nikolai Lukyanchikov, Kirill Petrov,Yakov Seleznev, Vasili Tokranov, Vyacheslav Voinov

**Slovakia** (Tibor Danis, coach) GK—Jaroslav Janus, Zdenko Kotvan—Martin Baca, Adam Bezak, Marek Daloga, Martin Filo, Peter Galambos, Branislav Horvath, Antonin Hruska, Richard Jancek, Dalimir Jancovic, Michal Kozak, Milan Kytnar, Adam Lapsansky, Matej Misura, Jozef Molnar, Peter Novajovsky, Richard Panik, Peter Rojkovic, Ondrej Rusnak, Martin Stepan, Tomas Striz, Martin Uhnak, Lukas Vartovnik, Matus Vizvari

**Sweden** (Lars Lindgren, coach) GK—Christoffer Bengtsberg, Mark Owuya—Jimmy Andersson, Joakim Andersson, Mikael Backlund, Emil Bejmo, Henrik Bjorklund, Alexander Eriksson, Sebastian Erixon, Johan Erkgards, Carl Gustafsson, Victor Hedman, Jens Hellgren, Simon Hjalmarsson, Marcus Johansson, Oscar Moller, Johan Motin, Robin Olsson, Anton Persson, Andre Petersson, Mattias Tedenby, Nichlas Torp

**Switzerland** (Felix Hollenstein, coach) GK—Damiano Ciaccio, Robert Mayer—Pascal Berger, Elias Bianchi, Yannick Blaser, Tobias Bucher, Luca Cunti, Gianni Donati, Etienne Froidevaux, Patrick Geering, Adam Hasani, Denis Hollenstein, Roman Josi, Desta Kebede, Simon Moser, Yves Muller, Roman Schlagenhauf, Patrick Schommer, Gregory Sciaroni, Lukas Stoop, Reto Suri, Nicolas Villa, Dino Wieser

**United States** (Ron Rolston, coach) GK—Tom McCollum, Josh Unice—John Albert, Ian Cole, Tom Cross, Cade Fairchild, Jimmy Hayes, Ryan Hayes, Ryan McDonagh, Jim O'Brien, Matt Rust, Ted Ruth, Vinny Saponari, Jordan Schroeder, C.J. Severyn, Kevin Shattenkirk, A.J. Sturges, Justin Vaive, James van Riemsdyk, Brennan Vargas, Patrick White, Colin Wilson

## 10th U18 WORLD CHAMPIONSHIP (MEN)
## April 13-23, 2008
## Kazan, Russia

**Final Placing**

Gold........Canada
Silver......Russia
Bronze....United States
4th..........Sweden
5th..........Germany
6th.........Finland
7th.........Slovakia
8th.........Switzerland
9th.........Belarus^*
10th.......Denmark^*

^promoted from Division I in 2007
*demoted to Division I for 2009

**Tournament Format**

The 10 teams were divided into two groups of five and played a round robin within each group. The winner of each group advanced directly to the semi-finals while the second and third place teams played a cross-over quarter-finals. The fourth and fifth place teams in the Preliminary Round went to a Relagation Round, the bottom two teams after this round robin demoted to Division I for 2009.

**Results & Standings**
**PRELIMINARY ROUND**
**GROUP A**

| | GP | W | OTW | OTL | L | GF | GA | P |
|---|---|---|---|---|---|---|---|---|
| Russia | 4 | 4 | 0 | 0 | 0 | 26 | 9 | 12 |
| Canada | 4 | 3 | 0 | 0 | 1 | 21 | 7 | 9 |
| Germany | 4 | 1 | 1 | 0 | 2 | 13 | 19 | 5 |
| Slovakia | 4 | 1 | 0 | 1 | 2 | 13 | 19 | 4 |
| Denmark | 4 | 0 | 0 | 0 | 4 | 4 | 23 | 0 |

| | | |
|---|---|---|
| April 13 | Canada 9 | Germany 2 |
| April 13 | Russia 6 | Slovakia 4 |
| April 14 | Slovakia 5 | Denmark 2 |
| April 14 | Russia 6 | Germany 2 |
| April 15 | Canada 4 | Denmark 1 |
| April 16 | Germany 5 | Slovakia 4 (5:00 OT/GWS—Daniel Weiss) |
| April 16 | Russia 4 | Canada 2 |
| April 17 | Germany 4 | Denmark 0 |
| April 18 | Canada 6 | Slovakia 0 |
| April 18 | Russia 10 | Denmark 1 |

**GROUP B**

| | GP | W | OTW | OTL | L | GF | GA | P |
|---|---|---|---|---|---|---|---|---|
| Sweden | 4 | 4 | 0 | 0 | 0 | 23 | 9 | 12 |
| United States | 4 | 3 | 0 | 0 | 1 | 20 | 12 | 9 |
| Finland | 4 | 2 | 0 | 0 | 2 | 15 | 15 | 6 |
| Switzerland | 4 | 1 | 0 | 0 | 3 | 9 | 21 | 3 |
| Belarus | 4 | 0 | 0 | 0 | 4 | 9 | 19 | 0 |

| | | |
|---|---|---|
| April 13 | Sweden 6 | Belarus 2 |
| April 13 | United States 7 | Switzerland 2 |
| April 14 | United States 5 | Belarus 2 |
| April 14 | Finland 5 | Switzerland 3 |
| April 15 | Sweden 5 | Finland 3 |
| April 16 | Switzerland 4 | Belarus 2 |
| April 16 | Sweden 5 | United States 4 |
| April 17 | Finland 4 | Belarus 3 |
| April 18 | Sweden 7 | Switzerland 0 |
| April 18 | United States 4 | Finland 3 |

**RELEGATION ROUND**

| | GP | W | OTW | OTL | L | GF | GA | P |
|---|---|---|---|---|---|---|---|---|
| Slovakia | 3 | 3 | 0 | 0 | 0 | 14 | 5 | 9 |
| Switzerland | 3 | 2 | 0 | 0 | 1 | 12 | 6 | 6 |
| Belarus | 3 | 1 | 0 | 0 | 2 | 9 | 12 | 3 |
| Denmark | 3 | 0 | 0 | 0 | 3 | 5 | 17 | 0 |

| | | |
|---|---|---|
| April 20 | Slovakia 6 | Belarus 1 |
| April 20 | Switzerland 6 | Denmark 1 |
| April 21 | Belarus 6 | Denmark 2 |
| April 21 | Slovakia 3 | Switzerland 2 |

**5TH-PLACE GAME**

April 22 Germany 4 Finland 3

**PLAYOFFS**
**QUARTER-FINALS**

April 20 Canada 2 Finland 1
April 20 United States 4 Germany 1

**SEMI-FINALS**

April 21 Canada 3 Sweden 2
April 21 Russia 3 United States 1

**BRONZE MEDAL GAME**

April 23 United States 6 Sweden 3

**GOLD MEDAL GAME**

April 23 Canada 8 Russia 0

**Rosters**

**Belarus** (Vladimir Tsyplakov, coach) GK—Alexander Borodulia, Dmitri Volkov—Alexander Obukhovski, Sergei Bogoleisha, Kirill Brykun, Sergei Drozd, Alexander Fomin, Kirill Gotovets, Roman Graborenko, Denis Gribko, Georgi Kachulin, Sergei Korolik, Sergei Markelov, Andrei Pichukha, Igor Revenko, Alexei Sadovik, Yevgeni Solomonov, Sergei Sheleg, Alexander Syomochkin, Igor Stepanov, Nikolai Suslo, Konstantin Zholudev

**Canada** (Pat Quinn, coach) GK—Jake Allen, Chris Carrozzi—Josh Brittain, Tyler Cuma, Nicolas Deschamps, Matt Duchene, Jordan Eberle, Ryan Ellis, Taylor Hall, Travis Hamonic, Cody Hodgson, Jacob Lagace, Tyler Myers, Brandon McMillan, Greg Nemisz, Eric O'Dell, Colby Robak, Maxime Sauve, Marco Scandella, Brayden Schenn, Colten Teubert, Corey Trivino

**Denmark** (Flemming Green, coach) GK—Nikolaj Norbak, Martin Sorensen—Nicklas Carlsen, Kennie Christensen, Rasmus Christensen, Soren Christiansen, Simon Dalsgaard, Simon Gronvaldt, Mikkel Holtenmoeller, Sebastian Jarrov, Alexander Jensen, Jesper Jensen, Kasper Kristensen, Anders Overmark, Markus Lauridsen, Mads Louring, Mads Linke, Jesper Malle, Mark Mieritz, Rasmus Nielsen, Sebastian Svendsen, Mathias Thinnesen

**Finland** (Jukka-Pekka Annala, coach) GK—Joonas Kuusela, Rasmus Rinne—Teemu Eronen, Teemu Hartikainen, Erik Haula, Ville Hietikko, Jasse Ikonen, Pekka Jormakka, Tommi Kivisto, Jani Lajunen, Nico Manelius, Matias Myttynen, Joonas Nattinen, Joona Peranen, Ilmari Pitkanen, Toni Rajala, Joonas Rask, Rasmus Rissanen, Jere Sallinen, Matias Sointu, Sami Vatanen,Veli-Matti Vittasmaki

**Germany** (James Setters, coach) GK—Felix Bruckmann, Philipp Grubauer—Dominik Bielke, Tobias Biersack, Benedikt Bruckner, Bernhard Ebner, Marc El-Sayed, Florian Engel, Jerome Flaake, Maximilian Forster, Steve Hanusch, Maximilian Hofbauer, Tom-Patric Kimmel, Marc Kohl, Marco Muller, Marco Nowak, Patrick Pohl, Philip Riefers, Toni Ritter, Dennis Steinhauer, Florian Strobl, Daniel Weiss

**Russia** (Alexander Birykov, coach) GK—Danila Alistratov, Alexander Pechurski—Igor Biryukov, Pavel Chernov, Maxim Chudinov, Nikita Filatov, Mikhail Fisenko, Igor Golovkov, Yevgeni Grachyov, Azat Kalimulin, Dmitri Kostromitin, Dmitri Kugryshev, Vyacheslav Kulyomin, Dmitri Kulikov, Anton Lazarev, Andrei Loktionov, Dmitri Orlov, Kirill Petrov, Aslan Raisov, Valeri Vasiliev, Vyacheslav Voinov, Artyom Yarchuk

**Slovakia** (Jozef Cepan, coach) GK—Marek Ciliak, Matej Kristin—Martin Dulak, Tomas Hricina, Marek Hrivik, Libor Hudacek, Adam Lapsansky, Marek Lison, Matej Mucka, Richard Panik, Michal Pichnarcik, Valerian Poticny, Miroslav Preisinger, David Puna, Michal Siska, Peter Slimak, Martin Sloboda, Martin Stajnoch, Tomas Stano, Tomas Sykora, Martin Uhnak, Marek Viedensky

**Sweden** (Stephan Lundh, coach) GK—Joacim Eriksson, Jacob Markstrom—Henrik Bjorklund, Dennis Bozic, Mattias Ekholm, Henrik Eriksson, Anton Grundel, Victor Hedman, Marcus Johansson, Jacob Josefson, Erik Karlsson, Anton Lander, Martin Lundberg, Joakim Mattsson, Anton Myllari, Andre Petersson, David Rundblad, Lucas Sandstrom, Jakob Silfverberg, Magnus Paajarvi, Mattias Tedenby, Henrik Thegel

**Switzerland** (Alfred Bohren, coach) GK—Benjamin Conz, Sandro Zurkirchen—Oliver Baur, Alain Berger, Renato Engler, Jannik Fischer, Fabian Ganz, Nicolas Gay, Patrick Geering, Pascal Gemperli, Mauro Jorg, Roman Josi, Marc Kampf, Nicolas Kormann, Romain Loffel, Pascal Marlof, Ryan McGregor, Nino Niederreiter, Sven Ryser, Reto Schappi, Dominik Schlumpf, Lukas Stoop

**United States** (John Hynes, coach) GK—Joe Cannata, Brandon Maxwell—Ryan Bourque, Robbie Czarnik, Justin Florek, Patrick Gaul, Ryan Grimshaw, Ryan Hegarty, Danny Kristo, Sam Lofquist, Sean Lorenz, Colin Moore, Jeremy Morin, Kevin McCarey, Philip McRae, Aaron Ness, Kyle Palmieri, Nick Pryor, Vinny Saponari, Jordan Schroeder, David Warsofsky, David Wohlberg

## 11th U18 WORLD CHAMPIONSHIP (MEN)
## April 9-19, 2009
## Fargo/Moorhead, United States

**Final Placing**

| | | | |
|---|---|---|---|
| Gold | United States | 6th | Czech Republic^ |
| Silver | Russia | 7th | Slovakia |
| Bronze | Finland | 8th | Switzerland |
| 4th | Canada | 9th | Norway^* |
| 5th | Sweden | 10th | Germany* |

^promoted from Division I in 2008
*demoted to Division I for 2010

**Tournament Format**

The 10 teams were divided into two groups of five and played a round robin within each group. The winner of each group advanced directly to the semi-finals while the second and third place teams played a cross-over quarter-finals. The fourth and fifth place teams in the Preliminary Round went to a Relagation Round, the bottom two teams after this round robin demoted to Division I for 2010.

**Results & Standings**
**PRELIMINARY ROUND**
**GROUP A**

| | GP | W | OTW | OTL | L | GF | GA | P |
|---|---|---|---|---|---|---|---|---|
| Canada | 4 | 3 | 1 | 0 | 0 | 27 | 8 | 11 |
| Sweden | 4 | 3 | 0 | 0 | 1 | 25 | 8 | 9 |
| Czech Republic | 4 | 1 | 0 | 1 | 2 | 12 | 17 | 4 |
| Switzerland | 4 | 1 | 0 | 0 | 3 | 11 | 28 | 3 |
| Germany | 4 | 1 | 0 | 0 | 3 | 13 | 27 | 3 |

| | | | |
|---|---|---|---|
| April 9 | Moorhead | Sweden 7 | Czech Republic 0 |
| April 9 | Fargo | Canada 11 | Germany 2 |
| April 10 | Moorhead | Czech Republic 6 | Switzerland 2 |
| April 11 | Moorhead | Sweden 5 | Germany 4 |
| April 11 | Fargo | Canada 8 | Switzerland 1 |
| April 12 | Moorhead | Germany 4 | Czech Republic 3 |
| April 13 | Moorhead | Sweden 11 | Switzerland 0 |
| April 13 | Fargo | Canada 4 (Brett Connolly 1:23 OT) | Czech Republic 3 |
| April 14 | Moorhead | Switzerland 8 | Germany 3 |
| April 14 | Fargo | Canada 4 | Sweden 2 |

**GROUP B**

| | GP | W | OTW | OTL | L | GF | GA | P |
|---|---|---|---|---|---|---|---|---|
| Finland | 4 | 3 | 0 | 0 | 1 | 27 | 9 | 9 |
| United States | 4 | 3 | 0 | 0 | 1 | 29 | 9 | 9 |
| Russia | 4 | 3 | 0 | 0 | 1 | 25 | 15 | 9 |
| Slovakia | 4 | 1 | 0 | 0 | 3 | 7 | 28 | 3 |
| Norway | 4 | 0 | 0 | 0 | 4 | 4 | 31 | 0 |

| | | | |
|---|---|---|---|
| April 9 | Moorhead | Finland 7 | Russia 4 |
| April 9 | Fargo | United States 8 | Norway 0 |
| April 10 | Fargo | Slovakia 5 | Norway 2 |
| April 11 | Moorhead | Russia 7 | Slovakia 2 |
| April 11 | Fargo | United States 4 | Finland 3 |
| April 12 | Fargo | Russia 8 | Norway 1 |
| April 13 | Moorhead | Finland 10 | Norway 1 |
| April 13 | Fargo | United States 12 | Slovakia 0 |
| April 14 | Moorhead | Finland 7 | Slovakia 0 |
| April 14 | Fargo | Russia 6 | United States 5 |

**RELEGATION ROUND (MOORHEAD)**

| | GP | W | OTW | OTL | L | GF | GA | P |
|---|---|---|---|---|---|---|---|---|
| Slovakia | 3 | 2 | 0 | 1 | 0 | 13 | 9 | 7 |
| Switzerland | 3 | 2 | 0 | 0 | 1 | 17 | 10 | 6 |
| Norway | 3 | 1 | 0 | 0 | 2 | 10 | 14 | 3 |
| Germany | 3 | 0 | 1 | 0 | 2 | 10 | 17 | 2 |

| | | |
|---|---|---|
| April 16 | Switzerland 7 | Norway 3 |
| April 17 | Germany 5 | Slovakia 4 (5:00 OT/GWS—Thomas Brandl) |
| April 18 | Slovakia 4 | Switzerland 2 |
| April 18 | Norway 5 | Germany 2 |

**5TH-PLACE GAME**

| | | | |
|---|---|---|---|
| April 18 | Moorhead | Sweden 4 | Czech Republic 2 |

**PLAYOFFS (FARGO)**
**QUARTER-FINALS**

| | | |
|---|---|---|
| April 16 | Russia 4 | Sweden 1 |
| April 16 | United States 6 | Czech Republic 2 |

**SEMI-FINALS**

| | | |
|---|---|---|
| April 17 | Russia 4 | Finland 0 |
| April 17 | United States 2 | Canada 1 |

**BRONZE MEDAL GAME**

| | | |
|---|---|---|
| April 19 | Finland 5 | Canada 4 (10:00 OT/GWS—Toni Rajala) |

**GOLD MEDAL GAME**

| | | |
|---|---|---|
| April 19 | United States 5 | Russia 0 |

**Rosters**

**Canada** (Mike Johnston, coach) GK—Bryce O'Hagan, Michael Zador—Brayden McNabb, Simon Despres, Erik Gudbranson, Stefan Elliott, Brett, Connolly, Ryan O'Reilly, Zack Kassian, Peter Holland, Dylan Olsen, Byron Froese, Garrett Mitchell, Landon Ferraro, John McFarland, Joey Hishon, Cody Eakin, Kyle Clifford, Curtis Hamilton, Calvin de Haan, Ethan Werek, Taylor Doherty

**Czech Republic** (Marek Sykora, coach) GK—Filip Novotny, Petr Mrazek, Marek Mazanec—Adam Polasek, Oldrich Horak, David Musil, Antonin Honejsek, Daniel Krejci, Dan Ruzicka, Petr Straka, Michal Hlinka, Ondrej Palat, Jakub Jerabek, Robin Soudek, Jakub Culek, David Tuma, Michal Poletin, Roman Horak, Jakub Orsava, Radim Herman, Ondrej Dolezal, Andrej Nestrasil

**Finland** (Mika Marttila, coach) GK—Erno Suomalainen, Joni Ortio—Mikael Aaltonen, Joonas Hurri, Tommi Kivisto, Lauri Karmeniemi, Ville Hyvarinen, Rasmus Rissanen, Sami Vatanen, Iiro Pakarinen, Mikael Granlund, Erik Haula, Joni Karjalainen, Jesse Mankinen, Janne Kumpulainen, Jere Laaksonen, Joonas Nattinen, Teemu Pulkkinen, Toni Rajala, Valtteri Virkkunen, Jaakko Turtiainen, Teemu Tallberg

**Germany** (James Setters, coach) GK—Lukas Steinhauer, Dustin Haloschan—Dominik Bittner, Peter Lindbauer, Benjamin Hufner, Konrad Abeltschauser, Dennis Steinhauer, Jan Pietsch, Norman Hauner, Thomas Brandl, Dustin Schumacher, Mirko Hofflin, Tom Kuhnhackl, Marcel Noebels, Jari Pietsch, Laurin Braun, Marcel Ohmann, Marc El-Sayed, Matthias Plachta, Tobias Rieder, Maximilian Waitl, Julian Bogner

**Norway** (Orjan Lovdal, coach) GK—Chris Henrik Nygaard, Lars Volden—Torbjorn Eikeland, Tobias Skaarberg, Nicolai Bryhnisveen, Jens Bacher, Kenneth Madso, Henrik Ljostad, Andreas Stene, Robin Andersen, Tor Fusdahl, Rasmus Juell, Mats Rosseli Olsen, Michael Haga, Sondre Olden, Magnus Lindahl, Simen Brekke, Jonas Oppoyen, Eirik Borresen, Petter Roste Fossen, Hans-Kristian Hollstedt, Jon Rene Kristoffersen

**Russia** (Vladimir Plyushev, coach) GK—Igor Bobkov, Emil Garipov—Nikita Pivtsakin, Stanislav Kalashnikov, Kirill Yuryev, Yevgeni Kuznetsov, Alexander Burmistrov, Sergei Chvanov, Vladimir Tarasenko, Andrei Sergeyev, Andrei Ankudinov, Alexander Karpushkin, Vladimir Malinovski, Pavel Zotov, Kirill Kabanov, Konstantin Bochkaryov, Nikita Zaitsev, Maxim Kitsyn, Nikita Dvurechenski, Danil Gubarev, Stanislav Solovyov, Dmitri Orlov

**Slovakia** (Peter Bohunicky, coach) GK—Juraj Holly, Tomas Pek—Kristian Grman, Michal Imrich, Miroslav Bobocky, Lukas Kozak, Michael Vandas , Adam Janosik, Filip Janosik, Marek Hrivik, Martin Marincin, Juraj Petro, Tomas Daniska, Peter Sisovsky, Juraj Majdan, Dalibor Bortnak, Miroslav Preisinger, Tomas Stano, Tomas Jurco, Jozef Kentos, Andrej Stastny, Henrich Jabornik

**Sweden** (Stephan Lundh, coach) GK—Johan Gustafsson, Robin Lehner—Simon Bertilsson, Niclas Edman, Oliver Ekman Larsson, Fredrik Styrman, Patrick Cehlin, Adam Larsson, Martin Karlsson, Gabriel Landeskog, Anton Lander, Carl Klingberg, Filip Gunnarsson, Peter Andersson, Magnus Paajarvi-Svensson, Jonathan Johansson, William Wallen, Tim Erixon, Calle Jarnkrok, Jacob Josefson, Mattias Lindstrom, Oscar Lindberg

**Switzerland** (Manuele Celio, coach) GK—Benjamin Conz, Leon Sarkis—Mathieu Maret, Romain Loffel, Samuel Erni, Nicholas Steiner, Reto Schappi, Thomas Mettler, Luca Camperchioli, Benjamin Antonietti, Renato Engler, Nino Niederreiter, Ryan McGregor, Reto Schmutz, Nils Berger, Tristan Scherwey, Samuel Walser, Gaetan Haas, Dario Trutmann, Samuel Keller, Sven Bartschi, Matthias Rossi

**United States** (Ron Rolston, coach) GK—Jack Campbell, Adam Murray—Brendan Rempel, Cam Fowler, John Ramage, Jon Merrill, Jason Zucker, Adam Clendening, Jerry D'Amigo, Jeremy Morin, Chris Brown, Kevin Lynch, Drew Shore, John Henrion, Ryan Bourque, Matt Nieto, William Wrenn, David Valek, A.J. Treais, Philip Samuelsson, Kenny Ryan, Nick Mattson

## 12th U18 WORLD CHAMPIONSHIP (MEN)
## April 13-23, 2010
## Minsk/Bobruisk, Belarus

**Final Placing**

Gold........United States
Silver......Sweden
Bronze....Finland
4th..........Russia
5th..........Switzerland
6th.........Czech Republic
7th.........Canada
8th.........Slovakia
9th.........Latvia^*
10th.......Belarus^*
^promoted from Division I in 2009
*demoted to Division I for 2011

**Tournament Format**

The 10 teams were divided into two groups of five and played a round robin within each group. The winner of each group advanced directly to the semi-finals while the second and third place teams played a cross-over quarter-finals. The fourth and fifth place teams in the Preliminary Round went to a Relagation Round, the bottom two teams after this round robin demoted to Division I for 2011.

**Results & Standings**

**PRELIMINARY ROUND**

**GROUP A (BOBRUISK)**

| | GP | W | OTW | OTL | L | GF | GA | P |
|---|---|---|---|---|---|---|---|---|
| Sweden | 4 | 4 | 0 | 0 | 0 | 26 | 8 | 12 |
| United States | 4 | 3 | 0 | 0 | 1 | 19 | 6 | 9 |
| Switzerland | 4 | 2 | 0 | 0 | 2 | 9 | 18 | 6 |
| Canada | 4 | 1 | 0 | 0 | 3 | 16 | 16 | 3 |
| Belarus | 4 | 0 | 0 | 0 | 4 | 6 | 28 | 0 |

| | | |
|---|---|---|
| April 13 | Switzerland 3 | Canada 1 |
| April 13 | Sweden 4 | United States 2 |
| April 14 | United States 5 | Switzerland 1 |
| April 14 | Sweden 7 | Belarus 0 |
| April 15 | Canada 11 | Belarus 3 |
| April 16 | Sweden 10 | Switzerland 2 |
| April 16 | United States 5 | Canada 0 |
| April 17 | Switzerland 3 | Belarus 2 |
| April 18 | Sweden 5 | Canada 4 |
| April 18 | United States 7 | Belarus 1 |

**GROUP B (MINSK)**

| | GP | W | OTW | OTL | L | GF | GA | P |
|---|---|---|---|---|---|---|---|---|
| Finland | 4 | 3 | 1 | 0 | 0 | 21 | 11 | 11 |
| Russia | 4 | 3 | 0 | 0 | 1 | 20 | 7 | 9 |
| Czech Republic | 4 | 2 | 0 | 1 | 1 | 13 | 15 | 7 |
| Slovakia | 4 | 1 | 0 | 0 | 3 | 10 | 15 | 3 |
| Latvia | 4 | 0 | 0 | 0 | 4 | 9 | 25 | 0 |

| | | |
|---|---|---|
| April 13 | Finland 7 | Latvia 2 |
| April 13 | Russia 4 | Czech Republic 1 |
| April 14 | Russia 9 | Latvia 0 |
| April 14 | Czech Republic 4 | Slovakia 3 |
| April 15 | Finland 5 | Slovakia 2 |
| April 16 | Czech Republic 5 | Latvia 4 |
| April 16 | Finland 5 | Russia 4 |
| April 17 | Slovakia 4 | Latvia 3 |
| April 18 | Russia 3 | Slovakia 1 |
| April 18 | Finland 4 | Czech Republic 3 (5:00 OT/GWS—Teemu Pulkkinen) |

**RELEGATION ROUND (BOBRUISK)**

| | GP | W | OTW | OTL | L | GF | GA | P |
|---|---|---|---|---|---|---|---|---|
| Canada | 3 | 3 | 0 | 0 | 0 | 20 | 6 | 9 |
| Slovakia | 3 | 2 | 0 | 0 | 1 | 11 | 8 | 6 |
| Latvia | 3 | 0 | 1 | 0 | 2 | 9 | 13 | 2 |
| Belarus | 3 | 0 | 0 | 1 | 2 | 8 | 21 | 1 |

| | | |
|---|---|---|
| April 20 | Slovakia 5 | Belarus 1 |
| April 21 | Canada 5 | Latvia 1 |
| April 22 | Canada 4 | Slovakia 2 |
| April 22 | Latvia 5 | Belarus 4 (5:00 OT/GWS—Davis Straupe) |

**5TH-PLACE GAME**

| | | | |
|---|---|---|---|
| April 22 | Minsk | Switzerland 6 | Czech Republic 5 |

**PLAYOFFS (MINSK)**

**QUARTER-FINALS**

| | | |
|---|---|---|
| April 20 | United States 6 | Czech Republic 0 |
| April 20 | Russia 4 | Switzerland 3 |

**SEMI-FINALS**

| | | |
|---|---|---|
| April 21 | United States 5 | Finland 0 |
| April 21 | Sweden 3 | Russia 1 |

**BRONZE MEDAL GAME**

| | | |
|---|---|---|
| April 23 | Finland 5 | Russia 1 |

**GOLD MEDAL GAME**

| | | |
|---|---|---|
| April 23 | United States 3 | Sweden 1 |

**Rosters**

**Belarus** (Vladimir Safonov, coach) GK—Yan Shelepnev, Anton Ahres, Sergei Stepanov—Dmitri Lukianenko, Dmitri Zhevlochenko, Nikita Turovets, Denis Dalidovich, Yevgeni Leonov, Pavel Konnov, Stanislav Lopachuk, Artur Gavrus, Yegor Ageyenko, Ruslan Zhurnya, Artur Abmiotka, Yevgeni Samokhin, Maxim Parfeyevets, Alexei Skabelka, Vladislav Lemachko, Igor Karabanov, Nikita Kardashev, Artyom Levsha, Ruslan Andreychikov, Yuri Seryakov

**Canada** (Guy Carbonneau, coach) GK—Calvin Pickard, Kent Simpson—Geoff Schemitsch, Erik Gudbranson, Nathan Chiarlitti, Stephen Silas, Ryan Murray, Brett Connolly, Steven Shipley, Ryan O'Connor, Michael Sgarbossa, Gabriel Desjardins, Max Reinhart, Michael Bournival, Christian Thomas, John McFarland, Jordan Weal, Ryan Spooner, Quinton Howden, Freddie Hamilton, Greg McKegg, Brock Beukeboom

**Czech Republic** (Jiri Kopecky, coach) GK—Libor Kasik, Roman Will—Bohumil Jank, Tomas Valenta, Dusan Zovinec, Filip Pavlik, Patrik Lenoch, Jiri Klimicek, Petr Zamorsky, Filip Hantak, Jiri Sekac, Tomas Filippi, Jakub Herman, David Stach, Dominik Uher, Michal Vachovec, Petr Holik, David Dvoracek, David Koudela, Martin Frk, Jaroslav Vlach, Denis Kindl

**Finland** (Sakari Pietila, coach) GK—Jonathan Iilahti, Christopher Gibson, Sami Aittokallio—Simo-Pekka Riikola, Miro Hovinen, Riku Vakiparta, Miikka Salomaki, Julius Nyqvist, Teemu Pulkkinen, Joonas Donskoi, Petteri Halinen, Roope Hamalainen, Mikael Salmivirta, Micke Asten, Otto Paajanen, Patrik Moisio, Miihkali Teppo, Markus Granlund, Teemu Rautiainen, Jani Hakanpaa, Mikael Granlund, Mika Partanen, Konsta Makinen

**Latvia** (Leonids Beresnevs, coach) GK—Kristers Gudlevskis, Vadims Miscuks—Kriss Lipsbergs, Kristers Freibergs, Arturs Salija, Edgars Siksna, Davis Straupe, Arturs Kuzmenkovs, Raimonds Upenieks, Nikita Kolesnikovs, Kirils Tambijevs, Edgars Klavins, Artjoms Dasutins, Kristians Pelss, Andrejs Smirnovs, Maris Dilevka, Rinalds Rautensilds, Kristaps Nimanis, Juris Ziemins, Zemgus Girgensons, Edgars Kurmis, Vladislav Dudins

**Russia** (Mikhail Vasiliev, coach) GK—Andrei Vasilevski, Sergei Kostenko—Stefan Stepanov, Albert Yarullin, Viktor Antipin, Yefim Gurkin, Vladislav Namestnikov, Roman Berdnikov, Vladislav Kartayev, Grigori Zheldakov, Roman Lyubimov, Danil Apalkov, Pavel Kulikov, Nikita Nesterov, Maxim Shalunov, Yevgeni Grigorenko, Sergei Barbashev, Zakhar Arzamastsev, Yevgeni Kuznetsov, Gleb Zyryanov, Emil Galimov, Dmitri Arkhipov

**Slovakia** (Andrej Vyboh, coach) GK—Dominik Riecicky, Filip Orcik—Miroslav Macejko, Lubor Pokovic, Michal Toman, Boris Krempasky, Denis Mihalik, Bruno Mraz, Michal Murcek, Michal Styk, Marek Tvrdon, Martin Kalinac, Dominik Simcak, Martin Marincin, Viliam Daras, Peter Ceresnak, Juraj Roznik, Peter Trska, Lukas Cingel, Tomas Matousek, Michal Cajkovsky, David Bondra

**Sweden** (Stephan Lundh, coach) GK—Johan Gustafsson, Jonas Gunnarsson—Johan Alm, Victor Berglind, Jonas Brodin, Adam Larsson, Patrick Nemeth, Petter Granberg, Max Friberg, Johan Larsson, Daniel Mannberg, Sebastian Ottosson, Adam Pettersson, Ludvig Rensfeldt, Henri Snall, Victor Rask, Erik Thorell, Mattias Granlund, John Westin, Joachim Nermark, Joakim Nordstrom, Fredrik Claesson

**Switzerland** (Manuele Celio, coach) GK—Lukas Meili, Dennis Saikkonen—Cedric Hachler, Marwin Leu, Sven Andrighetto, Kewin Orellana, Lars Neher, Alban Rexha, Reto Schmutz, Gaetan Haas, Dominic Lammer, Gregory Hofmann, Dean Kukan, Dario Trutmann, Eric Arnold, Kaj Leuenberger, Raphael Kuonen, Lino Martschini, Dave Sutter, Joel Vermin, Sven Bartschi, Samuel Guerra

**United States** (Kurt Kleinendorst, coach) GK—Jack Campbell, Andy Iles—Derek Forbort, Tyler Biggs, Adam Clendening, Luke Moffatt, Bill Arnold, Bryan Rust, Chase Balisy, Austin Watson, Jon Merrill, Jason Zucker, Frankie Simonelli, Austin Czarnik, Matt Nieto, Connor Brickley, Rocco Grimaldi, Brandon Saad, Nick Shore, Jarred Tinordi, Justin Faulk, Stephen Johns

## 13th U18 WORLD CHAMPIONSHIP (MEN)
## April 14-24, 2011
## Crimmitschau/Dresden, Germany

**Final Placing**

Gold........United States
Silver......Sweden
Bronze....Russia
4th..........Canada
5th..........Finland
6th.........Germany+
7th.........Switzerland
8th.........Czech Republic
9th.........Norway+^
10th.......Slovakia^
+promoted from Division I in 2010
^demoted to Division I for 2012

**Tournament Format**
The ten teams were divided into two groups of five and played a round robin within each group. The top two teams advanced to the semi-finals while the second and third place teams played a cross-over quarter-finals. The bottom two teams played a four-team relegation round, the bottom two being demoted to Division I for 2012.

**Results & Standings**
**PRELIMINARY ROUND**
**GROUP A (CRIMMITSCHAU)**

| | GP | W | OTW | OTL | L | GF | GA | P |
|---|---|---|---|---|---|---|---|---|
| United States | 4 | 4 | 0 | 0 | 0 | 21 | 8 | 12 |
| Russia | 4 | 2 | 1 | 0 | 1 | 24 | 13 | 8 |
| Germany | 4 | 1 | 0 | 1 | 2 | 11 | 17 | 4 |
| Switzerland | 4 | 1 | 0 | 0 | 3 | 8 | 16 | 3 |
| Slovakia | 4 | 1 | 0 | 0 | 3 | 9 | 19 | 3 |

| | | |
|---|---|---|
| April 14 | Russia 8 | Slovakia 2 |
| April 14 | United States 2 | Switzerland 1 |
| April 15 | United States 8 | Slovakia 1 |
| April 15 | Germany 4 | Switzerland 1 |
| April 16 | Russia 5 | Germany 4 (5:00 OT/GWS—Nikita Kucherov) |
| April 17 | Switzerland 3 | Slovakia 2 |
| April 17 | United States 4 | Russia 3 |
| April 18 | Slovakia 4 | Germany 0 |
| April 19 | Russia 8 | Switzerland 3 |
| April 19 | United States 7 | Germany 3 |

**GROUP B (DRESDEN)**

| | GP | W | OTW | OTL | L | GF | GA | P |
|---|---|---|---|---|---|---|---|---|
| Sweden | 4 | 3 | 0 | 0 | 1 | 20 | 8 | 9 |
| Canada | 4 | 3 | 0 | 0 | 1 | 17 | 8 | 9 |
| Finland | 4 | 2 | 0 | 0 | 2 | 16 | 15 | 6 |
| Czech Republic | 4 | 2 | 0 | 0 | 2 | 8 | 13 | 6 |
| Norway | 4 | 0 | 0 | 0 | 4 | 6 | 23 | 0 |

| | | |
|---|---|---|
| April 14 | Finland 5 | Norway 2 |
| April 14 | Czech Republic 2 | Sweden 1 |
| April 15 | Sweden 10 | Norway 2 |
| April 15 | Canada 5 | Czech Republic 0 |
| April 16 | Canada 5 | Finland 4 |
| April 17 | Czech Republic 3 | Norway 2 |
| April 17 | Sweden 5 | Finland 2 |
| April 18 | Canada 5 | Norway 0 |
| April 19 | Finland 5 | Czech Republic 3 |
| April 19 | Sweden 4 | Canada 2 |

**RELEGATION ROUND (DRESDEN)**

| | GP | W | OTW | OTL | L | GF | GA | P |
|---|---|---|---|---|---|---|---|---|
| Switzerland | 3 | 3 | 0 | 0 | 0 | 11 | 5 | 9 |
| Czech Republic | 3 | 2 | 0 | 0 | 1 | 9 | 9 | 6 |
| Norway | 3 | 1 | 0 | 0 | 2 | 9 | 9 | 3 |
| Slovakia | 3 | 0 | 0 | 0 | 3 | 7 | 13 | 0 |

| | | |
|---|---|---|
| April 21 | Switzerland 4 | Norway 1 |
| April 21 | Czech Republic 4 | Slovakia 3 |
| April 23 | Norway 6 | Slovakia 2 |
| April 23 | Switzerland 4 | Czech Republic 2 |

**FIFTH-PLACE GAME**
April 23 Crimmitschau Finland 6 Germany 0

**PLAYOFFS (CRIMMITSCHAU)**
**QUARTER-FINALS**
April 21 Russia 5 Finland 2
April 21 Canada 4 Germany 3

**SEMI-FINALS**
April 23 Sweden 3 Russia 1
April 23 United States 5 Canada 4 (Tyler Biggs 4:22 OT)

**BRONZE MEDAL GAME**
April 24 Russia 6 Canada 4

**GOLD MEDAL GAME**
April 24 United States 4 Sweden 3 (Connor Murphy 6:06 OT)

**Rosters**
**Canada** (Mike Williamson, coach) GK—Andrew D'Agostini, Malcolm Subban—Ryan Murphy, Ryan Murray, Mark Scheifele, Nick Cousins, Brett Ritchie, Alan Quine, Mark McNeill, Colin Smith, Eric Locke, Morgan Rielly, Slater Koekkoek, Daniel Catenacci, Brent Andrews, Travis Ewanyk, Austen Brassard, Cody Ceci, Charles Hudon, Scott Harrington, Seth Griffith, Reece Scarlett

**Czech Republic** (Jiri Solc, coach) GK—Jaroslav Pavelka, Matej Machovsky—Tomas Pavelka, Petr Sidlik, Martin Frk, David Musil, Jakub Matai, Tomas Moravec, Lukas Sedlak, Michal Svihalek, Tomas Hyka, Tomas Rousek, Ondrej Hampl, Tomas Hertl, Tomas Kvapil, Stepan Jenik, Antonin Ruzicka, Radek Faksa, Petr Beranek, Dmitrij Jaskin, Matej Beran, Marek Hrbas

**Finland** (Jukka Rautakorpi, coach) GK—Samu Perhonen, Richard Ullberg—Henri Auvinen, Olli Maatta, Ville Pokka, Juho Tommila, Joonas Valkonen, Toni Kallela, Miro Aaltonen, Markus Hannikainen, Ville Jarvelainen, Heikki Liedes, Teuvo Teravainen, Aleksi Rekonen, Kalle Torniainen, Tomi Wilenius, Markus Granlund, Joel Armia, Teemu Henritius, Miikka Salomaki, Petteri Lindbohm, Aleksi Salonen

**Germany** (Jim Setters, coach) GK—Philip Lehr, Marvin Cupper—Henry Haase, Maximilian Faber, Max Meirandres, Stephan Kronthaler, Huba Sekesi, Steven Bar, Leonhard Pfoderl, Oliver Mebus, Lars Grozinger, Daniel Fischbuch, Alexander Ackermann, Dominik Daxlberger, Christian Kretschmann, Dennis Reimer, Tobias Rieder, Frederik Tiffels, Sebastian Uvira, Niklas Solder, Kilian Keller, Nickolas Latta

**Norway** (Orjan Lovdal, coach) GK—Steffen Soberg, Espen Johansen—Martin Bjorsland, Markus Pedersen, Martin Lund, Endre Medby, Andreas Heier, Magnus Hoff, Magnus Fischer, Jorgen Karterud, Sebastian Saves, Markus Soberg, Espen Salo, Sebastian Weberg, Adrian Aslaksen, Jonas Knutsen, Mathais Trettenes, Markus Noteng, Eirik Saltsen, John Nicolay Nasgaard, Iver Haaland, Erlend Lesund

**Russia** (Yuri Rumyantsev, coach) GK—Andrei Vasilevski, Pavel Shegalo—Gennadi Sabinin, Alexei Vasilevski, Andrei Pedan, Konstantin Vorshev, Dmitri Mikhailov, Nikita Nesterov, Nail Yakupov, Roman Konkov, Anton Ivanyuzhenkov, Maxim Shuvalov, Nikita Kucherov, Maxim Shalunov, Anton Slepyshev, Bogdan Yakimov, Albert Yarullin, Anton Saveliev, Mikhail Grigorenko, Sergei Smurov, Alexander Kuvayev, Vladimir Tkachev

**Slovakia** (Jozef Fruhauf, coach) GK—Richard Sabol, Patrik Rybar—Patrik Luza, Karol Korim, Peter Bezuska, Emil Bagin, Andrej Bires, Tomas Nechala, Richard Mraz, Filip Vasko, Bruno Mraz, Dominik Fujerik, Peter Boltun, Juraj Bezuch, Marko Dano, Peter Ceresnak, Tomas Mikus, Denis Hudec, Branislav Rapac, Matej Hindos, Vladimir Dolnik, Martin Gernat

**Sweden** (Rikard Gronborg, coach) GK—Joel Lassinantti, Niklas Lundstrom—Jonas Brodin, Rasmus Bengtsson, Albin Blomkvist, Karl Johansson, Tom Nilsson, Mikael Vikstrand, Gustav Bjorklund, Viktor Arvidsson, Jeremy Boyce Rotevall, Ludwig Blomstrand, Joachim Nermark, William Karlsson, Victor Rask, Oscar Klefbom, David Lilliestrom Karlsson, Mika Zibanejad, Emil Lundberg, Anton Wedin, Linus Froberg, Filip Forsberg

**Switzerland** (Manuele Celio, coach) GK—Luca Boltshauser, Robin Kuonen—Cedric Hachler, Marwin Leu, Yannic Celio, Christian Marti, Tanner Richard, Alessio Bertaggia, Daniele Grassi, Dean Kukan, Julian Schmutz, Lino Martschini, Reto Amstutz, Lukas Balmelli, Silvan Hebeisen, Jan Neuenschwander, Sven Andrighetto, Dario Simion, Luka Hoffmann, Christoph Bertschy, Samuel Guerra, Sami Kreis

**United States** (Ron Rolston, coach) GK—John Gibson, Matt McNeely—Michael Paliotta, Connor Murphy, Barrett Kaib, Robbie Russo, Adam Reid, Blake Pietila, J.T. Miller, Nick Kerdiles, Reid Boucher, Henrik Samuelsson, Zac Larraza, Cole Bardreau, Jake McCabe, Ryan Haggerty, Tyler Biggs, Rocco Grimaldi, Jacob Trouba, Dan Carlson, Travis Boyd, Seth Jones

## 14th WORLD MEN'S U18 CHAMPIONSHIP
## April 12-22, 2012
## Brno/Znojmo/Breclav, Czech Republic

**Final Placing**

| | |
|---|---|
| Gold ........United States | 6th .........Germany |
| Silver ......Sweden | 7th .........Switzerland |
| Bronze ....Canada | 8th .........Czech Republic |
| 4th..........Finland | 9th .........Latvia+^ |
| 5th..........Russia | 10th .......Denmark^ |

+promoted from Division I in 2011
^demoted to Division I for 2013

**Tournament Format**
The ten teams were divided into two groups of five and played a round robin within each group. The top two teams advanced to the semi-finals while the second and third place teams played a cross-over quarter-finals. The bottom two teams played a four-team relegation round, the bottom two being demoted to Division I for 2012.

**Results & Standings**
**PRELIMINARY ROUND**
**GROUP A**

| | GP | W | OTW | OTL | L | GF | GA | P |
|---|---|---|---|---|---|---|---|---|
| United States | 4 | 4 | 0 | 0 | 0 | 18 | 3 | 12 |
| Finland | 4 | 3 | 0 | 0 | 1 | 15 | 9 | 9 |
| Canada | 4 | 2 | 0 | 0 | 2 | 17 | 12 | 6 |
| Czech Republic | 4 | 1 | 0 | 0 | 3 | 12 | 21 | 3 |
| Denmark | 4 | 0 | 0 | 0 | 4 | 6 | 23 | 0 |

| | | | |
|---|---|---|---|
| April 12 | Brno | Canada 6 | Denmark 1 |
| April 12 | Brno | United States 4 | Finland 0 |
| April 13 | Znojmo | Czech Republic 8 | Denmark 4 |
| April 14 | Breclav | United States 5 | Czech Republic 0 |
| April 14 | Breclav | Finland 4 | Canada 2 |

| | | | |
|---|---|---|---|
| April 15 | Brno | United States 4 | Denmark 0 |
| April 16 | Brno | Canada 6 | Czech Republic 2 |
| April 16 | Brno | Finland 5 | Denmark 1 |
| April 17 | Brno | Finland 6 | Czech Republic 2 |
| April 17 | Brno | United States 5 | Canada 3 |

**GROUP B (ZNOJMO)**

| | GP | W | OTW | OTL | L | GF | GA | P |
|---|---|---|---|---|---|---|---|---|
| Sweden | 4 | 4 | 0 | 0 | 0 | 20 | 4 | 12 |
| Russia | 4 | 2 | 0 | 0 | 2 | 14 | 7 | 6 |
| Germany | 4 | 2 | 0 | 0 | 2 | 15 | 17 | 6 |
| Latvia | 4 | 2 | 0 | 0 | 2 | 11 | 15 | 6 |
| Switzerland | 4 | 0 | 0 | 0 | 4 | 6 | 23 | 0 |

| | | |
|---|---|---|
| April 12 | Russia 6 | Latvia 1 |
| April 12 | Sweden 8 | Germany 1 |
| April 13 | Latvia 4 | Switzerland 2 |
| April 14 | Germany 4 | Russia 2 |
| April 14 | Sweden 7 | Switzerland 2 |
| April 15 | Sweden 3 | Latvia 1 |
| April 16 | Latvia 5 | Germany 4 |
| April 16 | Russia 6 | Switzerland 0 |
| April 17 | Sweden 2 | Russia 0 |
| April 17 | Germany 6 | Switzerland 2 |

**RELEGATION ROUND (ZNOJMO)**

| | GP | W | OTW | OTL | L | GF | GA | P |
|---|---|---|---|---|---|---|---|---|
| Switzerland | 3 | 2 | 0 | 0 | 1 | 8 | 7 | 6 |
| Czech Republic | 3 | 2 | 0 | 0 | 1 | 17 | 12 | 6 |
| Latvia | 3 | 1 | 0 | 1 | 1 | 11 | 13 | 4 |
| Denmark | 3 | 0 | 1 | 0 | 2 | 9 | 13 | 2 |

| | | |
|---|---|---|
| April 19 | Switzerland 4 | Czech Republic 2 |
| April 19 | Denmark 4 | Latvia 3 (Kristoffer Lauridsen 4:04 OT) |
| April 20 | Czech Republic 7 | Latvia 4 |
| April 20 | Switzerland 2 | Denmark 1 |

**FIFTH-PLACE GAME**

| | | | |
|---|---|---|---|
| April 21 | Brno | Russia 4 | Germany 1 |

**PLAYOFFS**

**QUARTER-FINALS**

| | | | |
|---|---|---|---|
| April 19 | Breclav | Finland 8 | Germany 0 |
| April 19 | Breclav | Canada 4 | Russia 2 |

**SEMI-FINALS**

| | | | |
|---|---|---|---|
| April 20 | Brno | Sweden 7 | Finland 3 |
| April 20 | Brno | United States 2 | Canada 1 |

**BRONZE MEDAL GAME**

| | | | |
|---|---|---|---|
| April 22 | Brno | Canada 5 | Finland 4 (Hunter Shinkaruk 2:05 OT) |

**GOLD MEDAL GAME**

| | | | |
|---|---|---|---|
| April 22 | Brno | United States 7 | Sweden 0 |

**Rosters**

**Canada** (Jesse Wallin, coach) GK: Matt Murray, Brandon Whitney, Spencer Martin—Darnell Nurse, Ryan Pulock, Damon Severson, Josh Morrissey, Warren Steele, Hunter Shinkaruk, Tony Mantha, Brendan Gaunce, Branden Troock, Kerby Rychel, Scott Kosmachuk, Mike Winther, Felix Girard, Gemel Smith, Troy Bourke, Scott Laughton, Sam Reinhart, Matt Dumba, William Carrier, Adam Pelech

**Czech Republic** (Jiri Weber, coach) GK: Patrik Polivka, Marek Langhammer, Dominik Hrachovina—Jiri Behal, Petr Sidlik, Jan Kostalek, Jakub Houfek, Ronald Knot, Jan Stencel, Patrik Machac, Pavel Sedlacek, Jakub Vrana, Martin Matejcek, Ondrej Slovacek, Adam Chlapik, Matej Zadrazil, Dominik Volek, Eustathios Soumelidis, Martin Prochazka, Dominik Simon, Vojtech Tomecek, Jan Hudecek, Libor Sulak

**Denmark** (Morten Hagen, coach) GK: George Sorensen, Matthias Hansen, Matthias Andersen—Christoffer Lindhoj, Mads Larsen, Rasmus Lyoe, Magnus Povlsen, Bjorn Uldall, Sonny Hertzberg, Marco Illemann, Mads Eller, Yannick Vedel, Oliver Bjorkstrand, Mikkel Aalgaard, Kristoffer Lauridsen, Morten Brodersen, Nikolai Gade, Lasse Korsgaard, Matthias Asperup, Emil Kristensen, Soren Mortensen, Christopher Frederiksen, Nikolaj Zorko

**Finland** (Jussi Tapola, coach) GK: Joonas Korpisalo, Jean Auren, Juuse Saros—Mikko Lehtonen, Atte Makinen, Mikko Vainonen, Rasmus Ristolainen, Joonas Huovinen, Aleksander Barkov, Juuso Ikonen, Samu Markkula, Aleksi Mustonen, Saku Salminen, Esa Lindell, Teuvo Teravainen, Joose Antonen, Ville Pokka, Janne Juutinen, Henri Ikonen, Henrik Haapala, Rasmus Kulmala, Niklas Tikkinen, Artturi Lehkonen

**Germany** (Jim Setters, coach) GK: Marvin Cupper, Patrick Klein—Sebastian Koberger, Dominik Tiffels, Nicolai Quinlan, Andreas Schwarz, Thomas Schmid, Tim Bender, Eric Stephan, Dominik Kahun, Benjamin Zientek, Kai Herpich, Marcel Kurth, Leon Draisaitl, Markus Eisenschmid, Denis Shevyrin, Janik Moser, Lennart Palausch, Sven Ziegler, Raphael Kaefer, Frederik Tiffels, Patrick Klopper

**Latvia** (Leonids Tambijevs, coach) GK: Ivars Punnenovs, Elvis Merzlikins, Nils Grinfogels—Rinalds Rosinskis, Patriks Skuratovs, Martins Freimanis, Matiss Gelazis, Rudolfs Kalvitis, Edmunds Augstkalns, Ricrads Kondrats, Rihards Bukarts, Martins Lavrovs, Arturs Sevcenko, Nikita Jevpalovs, Girts Zemitis, Karlis Ozolins, Nikolajs Jelisejevs, Georgs Golovkovs, Daniels Riekstins, Teodors Blugers, Roberts Lipsbergs, Edgars Kulda, Ilja Makarovs

**Russia** (Andrei Parfyonov, coach) GK: Andrei Vasilevski, Ivan Nalimov, Igor Ustinski—Andrei Mironov, Stanislav Gareyev, Nikita Lisov, Alexei Bereglazov, Kirill Mazlov, Yegor Malenkikh, Anton Slepyshev, Bogdan Yakimov, Alexei Filippov, Sergei Kuptsov, Nikita Zadorov, Danil Zharkov, Vyacheslav Osnovin, Alexander Barabanov, Denis Kamayev, Damir Galin, Arseni Khatsei, Alexander Lebedev, Valeri Nichushkin, Alexander Delnov

**Sweden** (Rikard Gronborg, coach) GK: Oscar Dansk, Marcus Hogberg, Ebbe Sionas—Christian Djoos, Calle Andersson, Linus Arnesson, Jesper Pettersson, Hampus Lindholm, Mattias Nilsson, Ludvig Nilsson, Tobias Tornkvist, Mattias Kalin, Sebastian Collberg, Filip Forsberg, Anton Brehmer, Jacob de la Rose, Gustav Possler, Filip Sandberg, Elias Lindholm, Erik Karlsson, Andre Burakowsky, Alexander Wennberg, Ludwig Bystrom

**Switzerland** (Alfred Bohren, coach) GK: Melvin Nyffeler, Niklas Schlegel—Timon Zuber, Alessandro Lanzarotti, Anthony Rouiller, Lukas Balmelli, Samuel Kreis, Flavio Schmutz, Thomas Studer, Nicola Brandi, Julian Schmutz, Phil Baltisberger, Sandro Zangger, Lukas Sieber, Dario Kummer, Ramon Diem, Riccardo Sartori, Marco Muller, Nico Dunner, Dario Simion, Fabrice Herzog, Xeno Busser

**United States** (Danton Cole, coach) GK: Colin Olson, Jared Rutledge—Seth Jones, Bill Butcher, Matt Grzelcyk, Jacob Trouba, Kyle Osterberg, Pat Sieloff, J.T. Compher, Frank Vatrano, Tom Dipauli, Dan O'Regan, Brady Skjei, Nick Kerdiles, Ryan Hartman, Cam Darcy, Matt Lane, Riley Barber, Connor Carrick, Andrew Copp, Quentin Shore, Tony Louis

*Canada won bronze at the 2012 U18 championship in the Czech Republic. Photo: Jana Chytilova / HHOF-IIHF Images.*

# OLYMPICS, WOMEN

## 18th OLYMPIC WINTER GAMES
**February 7-22, 1998**
**Nagano, Japan**

### Final Placing
Gold .......United States
Silver .....Canada
Bronze ...Finland
4th ........China
5th ........Sweden
6th ........Japan

### Tournament Format
All six teams were placed in one group and played a round-robin series of games. The top two teams played for the gold medal, and the next two teams (3rd and 4th place) played for the bronze medal.

### Results & Standings

| | GP | W | T | L | GF | GA | P |
|---|---|---|---|---|---|---|---|
| United States | 5 | 5 | 0 | 0 | 33 | 7 | 10 |
| Canada | 5 | 4 | 0 | 1 | 28 | 12 | 8 |
| Finland | 5 | 3 | 0 | 2 | 27 | 10 | 6 |
| China | 5 | 2 | 0 | 3 | 10 | 15 | 4 |
| Sweden | 5 | 1 | 0 | 4 | 10 | 21 | 2 |
| Japan | 5 | 0 | 0 | 5 | 2 | 45 | 0 |

| | | |
|---|---|---|
| February 8 | Finland 6 | Sweden 0 |
| February 8 | Canada 13 | Japan 0 |
| February 8 | United States 5 | China 0 |
| February 9 | Finland 11 | Japan 1 |
| February 9 | United States 7 | Sweden 1 |
| February 9 | Canada 2 | China 0 |
| February 11 | Canada 5 | Sweden 3 |
| February 11 | China 6 | Japan 1 |
| February 11 | United States 4 | Finland 2 |
| February 12 | China 3 | Sweden 1 |
| February 12 | United States 10 | Japan 0 |
| February 12 | Canada 4 | Finland 2 |
| February 14 | Sweden 5 | Japan 0 |
| February 14 | Finland 6 | China 1 |
| February 14 | United States 7 | Canada 4 |

### BRONZE MEDAL GAME
February 17 Finland 4 China 1

### GOLD MEDAL GAME
February 17 United States 3 Canada 1

### Rosters
**Canada** (Shannon Miller, coach) GK—Lesley Reddon, Manon Rheaume—France St. Louis, Becky Kellar, Therese Brisson, Jennifer Botterill, Fiona Smith, Lori Dupuis, Kathy McCormack, Danielle Goyette, Jayna Hefford, Stacy Wilson, Nancy Drolet, Judy Diduck, Hayley Wickenheiser, Laura Schuler, Vicky Sunohara, Cassie Campbell, Karen Nystrom, Geraldine Heaney

**China** (Zhinan Zhang, coach) GK—Lina Huo, Hong Guo—Ming Gong, Hongmei Liu, Xuan Li, Hong Dang, Yan Lu, Lan Zhang, Xiuqing Yang, Hong Sang, Jing Chen, Ying Diao, Jing Zhang, Wei Guo, Lei Xu, Lili Guo, Wei Wang, Jinping Ma, Xiaojun Ma, Chunhua Liu

**Finland** (Rauno Korpi coach) GK—Liisa-Maria Sneck, Tuula Puputti—Emma Laaksonen, Katja Lehto, Satu Huotari, Marianne Ihalainen, Sari Fisk, Riikka Nieminen, Maria Selin, Johanna Ikonen, Tiia Reima, Sari Krooks, Kirsi Hanninen, Petra Vaarakallio, Sanna Lankosaari, Marja-Helena Palvila, Marika Lehtimaki, Paivi Salo, Katja Riipi, Karoliina Rantamaki

**Japan** (Toru Itabashi, coach) GK—Yuka Oda, Haruka Watanabe—Yoko Kondo, Rie Sato, Akiko Hatanaka, Chie Sakuma, Maiko Obikawa, Satomi Ono, Naho Yoshimi, Yuiko Satomi, Yuki Togawa, Miharu Araki, Ayumi Sato, Mitsuko Igarashi, Yukari Ohno, Masako Sato, Aki Sudo, Shiho Fujiwara, Aki Tsuchida, Akiko Naka

**Sweden** (Bengt Ohlson, coach) GK—Charlotte Gothesson, Annica Ahlen—Linda Gustafsson, Maria Rooth, Erika Holst, Kristina Bergstrand, Malin Gustafsson, Charlotte Almblad, Asa Elfving, Tina Mansson, Pernilla Burholm, Joa Elfsberg, Anne Ferm, Gunilla Andersson, Ann Louise Edstrand, Therese Sjolander, Pia Morelius, Ylva Lindberg, Susanne Ceder, Asa Lidstrom

**United States** (Ben Smith, coach) GK—Sara DeCosta, Sarah Tueting—Tara Mounsey, Lisa Brown-Miller, Angela Ruggiero, Colleen Coyne, Karyn Bye, Sue Merz, Laurie Baker, Sandra Whyte, A.J. Mleczko, Jenny Schmidgall, Vicki Movsessian, Shelley Looney, Alana Blahoski, Katie King, Cammi Granato, Gretchen Ulion, Chris Bailey, Tricia Dunn

## 19th OLYMPIC WINTER GAMES
**February 9-24, 2002**
**Salt Lake City, United States**

### Final Placing
Gold .......Canada
Silver .....United States
Bronze ...Sweden
4th .........Finland
5th ........Russia
6th ........Germany
7th ........China
8th ........Kazakhstan

### Tournament Format
Eight teams were placed in two groups and played a round-robin series within each group. The top two teams from each advanced to a crossover semi-finals. Those winners played for the gold medal, and the semi-finals losers played for the bronze medal.

### Results & Standings
**GROUP A**

| | GP | W | T | L | GF | GA | P |
|---|---|---|---|---|---|---|---|
| Canada | 3 | 3 | 0 | 0 | 25 | 0 | 6 |
| Sweden | 3 | 2 | 0 | 1 | 10 | 13 | 4 |
| Russia | 3 | 1 | 0 | 2 | 6 | 11 | 2 |
| Kazakhstan | 3 | 0 | 0 | 3 | 1 | 18 | 0 |

| | | |
|---|---|---|
| February 11 | Canada 7 | Kazakhstan 0 |
| February 11 | Sweden 3 | Russia 2 |
| February 13 | Canada 7 | Russia 0 |
| February 13 | Sweden 7 | Kazakhstan 0 |
| February 15 | Russia 4 | Kazakhstan 1 |
| February 16 | Canada 11 | Sweden 0 |

**GROUP B**

| | GP | W | T | L | GF | GA | P |
|---|---|---|---|---|---|---|---|
| United States | 3 | 3 | 0 | 0 | 27 | 1 | 6 |
| Finland | 3 | 2 | 0 | 1 | 7 | 6 | 4 |
| Germany | 3 | 0 | 1 | 2 | 6 | 18 | 1 |
| China | 3 | 0 | 1 | 2 | 6 | 21 | 1 |

| | | |
|---|---|---|
| February 12 | United States 10 | Germany 0 |
| February 12 | Finland 4 | China 0 |
| February 14 | Finland 3 | Germany 1 |
| February 14 | United States 12 | China 1 |
| February 16 | United States 5 | Finland 0 |
| February 16 | Germany 5 | China 5 |

### 5TH-8TH PLACE SEMI-FINALS
February 17 Russia 4 China 1
February 17 Germany 4 Kazakhstan 0

### 5TH-PLACE GAME
February 19 Russia 5 Germany 0

### 7TH-PLACE GAME
February 19 China 2 Kazakhstan 1 (Hongmei Liu 1:39 OT)

### SEMI-FINALS
February 19 Canada 7 Finland 3
February 19 United States 4 Sweden 0

### BRONZE MEDAL GAME
February 21 Sweden 2 Finland 1

### GOLD MEDAL GAME
February 21 Canada 3 United States 2

### Rosters
**Canada** (Daniele Sauvageau, coach) GK—Sami-Jo Small, Kim St. Pierre—Becky Kellar, Colleen Sostorics, Therese Brisson, Jennifer Botterill, Cherie Piper, Lori Dupuis, Cheryl Pounder, Danielle Goyette, Jayna Hefford, Hayley Wickenheiser, Vicky Sunohara, Cassie Campbell, Geraldine Heaney, Caroline Ouellette, Dana Antal, Kelly Bechard, Tammy Shewchuk, Isabelle Chartrand

**China** (Naifeng Yao, coach) GK—Limei Jiang, Hong Guo—Hongmei Liu, Xuan Li, Yan Lu, Xiuqing Yang, Hong Sang, Jing Chen, Jing Zhang, Lei Xu, Xiaojun Ma, Ying Wang, Chunrong Hu, Fengling Jin, Rui Sun, Yanhui Liu, Linuo Wang, Weinan Guan, Qiuwa Dai, Tiantian Shen

**Finland** (Jouko Lukkarila, coach) GK—Minna Halonen, Tuula Puputti—Emma Laaksonen, Sari Fisk, Riikka Nieminen, Tiia Reima, Petra Vaarakallio, Marja-Helena Palvila, Paivi Salo, Katja Riipi, Karoliina Rantamaki, Pirjo Ahonen, Saija Sirvio, Marjo Voutilainen, Terhi Mertanen, Oona Parviainen, Satu Hoikkala, Kirsi Hanninen, Hanne Sikio, Henna Savikuja

**Germany** (Rainer Nittel, coach) GK—Stephanie Wartosch-Kurten, Esther Thyssen—Nina Ziegenhals, Raffi Wolf, Anja Scheytt, Nina Ritter, Franziska Reindl, Christina Oswald, Nina Linde, Michaela Lanzl, Sabrina Kruck, Stephanie Fruhwirt, Sabine Ruckauer, Claudia Grundmann, Jana Schreckenbach, Maren Valenti, Bettina Evers, Sandra Kinza, Julia Wierscher, Maritta Becker

**Kazakhstan** (Alexander Maltsev, coach) GK—Anna Akimbetyeva, Natalya Trunova—Antonida Asonova, Oxsana Taikevich, Tatyana Khlyzova, Lyubov Vafina, Lyubov Alexeyeva, Olga Potapova, Yelena Shtelmaister, Nadezhda Losyeva, Viktoria Adyeva, Dinara Dikambayeva, Olga Konysheva, Olga Kryukova, Natalya Yakovchuk, Viktoria Sazonova, Yekaterina Maltseva, Svetlana Maltseva, Svetlana Vassina, Yulia Solovyeva

**Russia** (Vyacheslav Dolgushin, coach) GK—Irina Gashennikova, Irina Votintseva—Maria Barykina, Kristina Petrovskaya, Alyona Khomich, Yelena Bobrova, Larisa Mishina, Tatyana Sotnikova, Yulia Gladysheva, Olga Permyakova, Yekaterina Smolentseva, Tatyana Tsareva, Svetlana Trefilova, Svetlana Terentieva, Tatyana Burina, Yekaterina Pashkevich, Olga Savenkova, Yelena Bialkovskaya, Oxana Tretiakova, Zhanna Shchelchkova

**Sweden** (Christian Yngve, coach) GK—Kim Martin, Annica Ahlen—Emelie Berggren, Anna Andersson, Maria Rooth, Erika Holst, Anna Vikman, Evelina Samuelsson, Maria Larsson, Kristina Bergstrand, Ann Louise Edstrand, Josefin Pettersson, Charlotte Almblad, Joa Elfsberg, Gunilla Andersson, Nanna Jansson, Therese Sjolander, Ylva Lindberg, Danijela Rundqvist, Ulrica Lindstrom

**United States** (Ben Smith, coach) GK—Sara DeCosta, Sarah Tueting—Tara Mounsey, Courtney Kennedy, Angela Ruggiero, Lyndsay Wall, Karyn Bye, Sue Merz, Laurie Baker, Andrea Kilbourne, A.J. Mleczko, Jenny Potter, Julie Chu, Shelley Looney, Krissy Wendell, Katie King, Cammi Granato, Natalie Darwitz, Chris Bailey, Tricia Dunn

## 20th OLYMPIC WINTER GAMES
## February 10-26, 2006
## Turin, Italy

### Final Placing

Gold .......Canada
Silver .....Sweden
Bronze ...United States
4th .........Finland
5th ........Germany
6th ........Russia
7th ........Switzerland
8th ........Italy

### Tournament Format

Eight teams were placed in two groups and played a round-robin series within each group. The top two teams from each advanced to a crossover semi-finals. Those winners played for the gold medal, and the semi-finals losers played for the bronze medal.

### Results & Standings

**GROUP A**

| | GP | W | T | L | GF | GA | P |
|---|---|---|---|---|---|---|---|
| Canada | 3 | 3 | 0 | 0 | 36 | 1 | 6 |
| Sweden | 3 | 2 | 0 | 1 | 15 | 9 | 4 |
| Russia | 3 | 1 | 0 | 2 | 6 | 16 | 2 |
| Italy | 3 | 0 | 0 | 3 | 1 | 32 | 0 |

February 11 Canada 16 Italy 0
February 11 Sweden 3 Russia 1
February 12 Canada 12 Russia 0
February 13 Sweden 11 Italy 0
February 14 Canada 8 Sweden 1
February 14 Russia 5 Italy 1

**GROUP B**

| | GP | W | T | L | GF | GA | P |
|---|---|---|---|---|---|---|---|
| United States | 3 | 3 | 0 | 0 | 18 | 3 | 6 |
| Finland | 3 | 2 | 0 | 1 | 10 | 7 | 4 |
| Germany | 3 | 1 | 0 | 2 | 2 | 9 | 2 |
| Switzerland | 3 | 0 | 0 | 3 | 1 | 12 | 0 |

February 11 Finland 3 Germany 0
February 11 United States 6 Switzerland 0
February 12 United States 5 Germany 0
February 13 Finland 4 Switzerland 0
February 14 Germany 2 Switzerland 1
February 14 United States 7 Finland 3

**5TH-8TH PLACE SEMI-FINALS**
February 17 Russia 6 Switzerland 2
February 17 Germany 5 Italy 2

**5TH-PLACE GAME**
February 20 Germany 1 Russia 0 (10:00 OT/GWS—Maritta Becker)

**7TH-PLACE GAME**
February 20 Switzerland 11 Italy 0

**SEMI-FINALS**
February 17 Canada 6 Finland 0
February 17 Sweden 3 United States 2 (10:00 OT/GWS—Pernilla Winberg)

**BRONZE MEDAL GAME**
February 20 United States 4 Finland 0

**GOLD MEDAL GAME**
February 20 Canada 4 Sweden 1

### Rosters

**Canada** (Melody Davidson, coach) GK—Charline Labonte, Kim St. Pierre—Hayley Wickenheiser, Cherie Piper, Gillian Apps, Caroline Ouellette, Jayna Hefford, Jennifer Botterill, Danielle Goyette, Sarah Vaillancourt, Katie Weatherston, Cassie Campbell, Meghan Agosta, Cheryl Pounder, Carla MacLeod, Vicky Sunohara, Gina Kingsbury, Colleen Sostorics, Becky Kellar, Gillian Ferrari

**Finland** (Hannu Saintula, coach) GK—Maija Hassinen, Noora Raty—Mari Pehkonen, Heidi Pelttari, Karoliina Rantamaki, Saara Tuominen, Mari Saarinen, Emma Laaksonen, Kati Kovalainen, Marja-Helena Palvila, Satu Hoikkala, Nora Tallus, Saija Sirvio, Terhi Mertanen, Sari Fisk, Hanna Kuoppala, Satu Kiipeli, Oona Parviainen, Satu Tuominen, Eveliina Simila

**Germany** (Peter Kathan, coach) GK—Jennifer Harss, Stephanie Wartosch-Kurten—Maritta Becker, Michaela Lanzl, Nina Ritter, Christina Oswald, Sara Seiler, Nikola Holmes, Jenny Tamas, Denise Soesilo, Stephanie Fruhwirt, Anja Scheytt, Susann Gotz, Claudia Grundmann, Andrea Lanzl, Sabrina Kruck, Franziska Busch, Bettina Evers, Susanne Fellner, Raffi Wolf

**Italy** (Markus Sparer, coach) GK—Debora Montanari, Luana Frasnelli—Maria Michaela Leitner, Sabina Florian, Waltraud Kaser, Evelyn Bazzanella, Valentina Bettarini, Linda de Rocco, Nadia de Nardin, Rebecca Fiorese, Michela Angeloni, Diana da Rugna, Katharina Sparer, Celeste Bissardella, Heidi Caldart, Silvia Carignano, Anna de la Forest, Manuela Friz, Silvia Toffano, Sabrina Viel

**Russia** (Alexei Kalintsev, coach) GK—Irina Gashennikova, Nadezhda Alexandrova—Svetlana Trefilova, Larisa Mishina, Iya Gavrilova, Zhanna Shchelchkova, Yekaterina Smolentseva, Tatyana Burina, Alexandra Kapustina, Yulia Gladysheva, Yekaterina Pashkevich, Maria Barykina, Alyona Khomich, Tatyana Sotnikova, Yelena Bialkovskaya, Yekaterina Smolina, Kristina Petrovskaya, Galina Skiba, Oxana Tretiakova, Olga Permyakova

**Sweden** (Peter Elander, coach) GK—Kim Martin, Cecilia Andersson—Maria Rooth, Gunilla Andersson, Erika Holst, Therese Sjolander, Pernilla Winberg, Nanna Jansson, Ylva Lindberg, Ann Louise Edstrand, Jenni Asserholt, Frida Nevalainen, Emilie O'Konor, Katarina Timglas, Emma Eliasson, Danijela Rundqvist, Joa Elfsberg, Kristina Lundberg, Jenny Lindqvist, Anna Vikman

**Switzerland** (Rene Kammerer, coach) GK—Florence Schelling, Patricia Elsmore-Sautter—Kathrin Lehmann, Laura Ruhnke, Daniela Diaz, Julia Marty, Stephanie Marty, Rachel Rochat, Prisca Mosimann, Tina Schumacher, Christine Meier, Nicole Bullo, Ruth Kunzle, Sandra Cattaneo, Monika Leuenberger, Ramona Fuhrer, Jeanette Marty, Angela Frautschi, Sandrine Ray, Silvia Bruggmann

**United States** (Ben Smith, coach) GK—Pam Dreyer, Chanda Gunn—Jenny Potter, Katie King, Sarah Parsons, Natalie Darwitz, Angela Ruggiero, Julie Chu, Krissy Wendell, Kelly Stephens, Kristin King, Helen Resor, Lyndsay Wall, Tricia Dunn-Luoma, Courtney Kennedy, Jamie Hagerman, Molly Engstrom, Kim Insalaco, Kathleen Kauth, Caitlin Cahow

## 21st OLYMPIC WINTER GAMES
## February 13-25, 2010
## Vancouver, Canada

### Final Placing

Gold ........Canada
Silver ......United States
Bronze ....Finland
4th .........Sweden
5th .........Switzerland
6th .........Russia
7th .........China
8th .........Slovakia

### Tournament Format

Eight teams were placed in two groups and played a round-robin series within each group. The top two teams from each advanced to a crossover semi-finals. Those winners played for the gold medal, and the semi-finals losers played for the bronze medal.

### Results & Standings

**GROUP A**

| | GP | W | OTW | OTL | L | GF | GA | P |
|---|---|---|---|---|---|---|---|---|
| Canada | 3 | 3 | 0 | 0 | 0 | 41 | 2 | 9 |
| Sweden | 3 | 2 | 0 | 0 | 1 | 10 | 15 | 6 |
| Switzerland | 3 | 1 | 0 | 0 | 2 | 6 | 15 | 3 |
| Slovakia | 3 | 0 | 0 | 0 | 3 | 4 | 29 | 0 |

February 13 Sweden 3 Switzerland 0
February 13 Canada 18 Slovakia 0
February 15 Canada 10 Switzerland 1
February 15 Sweden 6 Slovakia 2
February 17 Canada 13 Sweden 1
February 17 Switzerland 5 Slovakia 2

**GROUP B**

| | GP | W | OTW | OTL | L | GF | GA | P |
|---|---|---|---|---|---|---|---|---|
| United States | 3 | 3 | 0 | 0 | 0 | 31 | 1 | 9 |
| Finland | 3 | 2 | 0 | 0 | 1 | 7 | 8 | 6 |
| Russia | 3 | 1 | 0 | 0 | 2 | 3 | 19 | 3 |
| China | 3 | 0 | 0 | 0 | 3 | 3 | 16 | 0 |

February 14 United States 12 China 1
February 14 Finland 5 Russia 1

| | | |
|---|---|---|
| February 16 | United States 13 | Russia 0 |
| February 16 | Finland 2 | China 1 |
| February 18 | United States 6 | Finland 0 |
| February 18 | Russia 2 | China 1 |

**PLACEMENT GAMES**

| | | |
|---|---|---|
| February 20 | Switzerland 6 | China 0 |
| February 20 | Russia 4 | Slovakia 2 |
| February 22 | China 3 | Slovakia 1 |
| February 22 | Switzerland 2 | Russia 1 (10:00 OT/GWS—Stefanie Marty) |

**SEMI-FINALS**

| | | |
|---|---|---|
| February 22 | United States 9 | Sweden 1 |
| February 22 | Canada 5 | Finland 0 |

**BRONZE MEDAL GAME**

| | | |
|---|---|---|
| February 25 | Finland 3 | Sweden 2 (Karoliina Rantamaki 2:33 OT) |

**GOLD MEDAL GAME**

| | | |
|---|---|---|
| February 25 | Canada 2 | United States 0 |

**Rosters**

**Canada** (Melody Davidson, coach) GK—Shannon Szabados, Kim St. Pierre, Charline Labonte—Meghan Agosta, Carla MacLeod, Becky Kellar, Colleen Sostorics, Rebecca Johnston, Cherie Piper, Gillian Apps, Meaghan Mikkelson, Caroline Ouellette, Jayna Hefford, Jennifer Botterill, Catherine Ward, Haley Irwin, Hayley Wickenheiser, Tessa Bonhomme, Sarah Vaillancourt, Gina Kingsbury, Marie-Philip Poulin

**China** (Hannu Saintula, coach) GH—Dandan Jia, Yao Shi, Danni Han—Baiwei Yu, Yue Lou, Zhixin Liu, Mengying Zhang, Ben Zhang, Haijing Huang, Fengling Jin, Rui Sun, Rui Ma, Shanshan Cui, Linuo Wang, Na Jiang, Cui Huo, Liang Tang, Anqi Tan, Fujin Gao, Xueting Qi, Shuang Zhang

**Finland** (Pekka Hamalainen, coach) GK—Noora Raty, Mira Kuisma, Anna Vanhatalo—Emma Laaksonen, Rosa Lindstedt, Mariia Posa, Jenni Hiirikoski, Marjo Voutilainen, Venla Hovi, Annina Rajahuhta, Mari Saarinen, Linda Valimaki, Minnamari Tuominen, Terhi Mertanen, Saija Sirvio, Michelle Karvinen, Saara Tuominen, Nina Tikkinen, Heidi Pelttari, Anne Helin, Karoliina Rantamaki

**Russia** (Valentin Gureyev, coach) GK—Irina Gashennikova, Anna Prugova, Maria Onolbayeva—Alyona Khomich, Olga Sosina, Iya Gavrilova, Alexandra Vafina, Marina Sergina, Kristina Petrovskaya, Olga Permyakova, Yekaterina Smolentseva, Yulia Deulina, Tatyana Burina, Yekaterina Lebedeva, Zoya Polunina, Svetlana Terentieva, Tatyana Sotnikova, Svetlana Tkachyova, Alexandra Kapustina, Yekaterina Ananina, Inna Dyubanok

**Slovakia** (Miroslav Karafiat, coach) GK—Zuzana Tomcikova, Monika Kvakova, Jana Budajova—Nicol Cupkova, Petra Orszaghova, Jana Kapustova, Barbora Bremova, Natalie Babonyova, Petra Bibiakova, Zuzana Moravcikova, Edita Rakova, Maria Herichova, Petra Jurcova, Anna Dzurnakova, Michaela Matejova, Martina Velickova, Janka Culikova, Iveta Karafiatova, Nikoleta Celarova, Nikola Gapova, Petra Pravlikova

**Sweden** (Peter Elander, coach) GK—Sara Grahn, Kim Martin, Valentina Lizana—Elin Holmlov, Frida Nevalainen, Jenni Asserholt, Maria Rooth, Erika Holst, Tina Enstrom, Emilia Andersson, Cecilia Ostberg, Erica Uden-Johansson, Katarina Timglas, Pernilla Winberg, Klara Myren, Emma Eliasson, Gunilla Andersson, Frida Svedin-Thunstrom, Emma Nordin, Danijela Rundqvist, Isabelle Jordansson

**Switzerland** (Rene Kammerer, coach) GK—Florence Schelling, Dominique Slongo, Sophie Anthamatten—Katrin Nabholz, Julia Marty, Darcia Leimgruber, Stefanie Marty, Nicole Bullo, Angela Frautschi, Sara Benz, Christine Meier, Lucrece Nussbaum, Rahel Michielin, Kathrin Lehmann, Laura Benz, Melanie Hafliger, Anja Stiefel, Stefanie Wyss, Claudia Riechsteiner, Sandra Thalmann, Sabrina Zollinger

**United States** (Mark Johnson, coach) GK—Jessie Vetter, Molly Schaus, Brianne McLaughlin—Erika Lawler, Angela Ruggiero, Karen Thatcher, Monique Lamoureux, Caitlin Cahow, Molly Engstrom, Meghan Duggan, Lisa Chesson, Jenny Potter, Julie Chu, Kelli Stack, Jocelyne Lamoureux, Gigi Marvin, Natalie Darwitz, Hilary Knight, Kacey Bellamy, Kerry Weiland, Jinelle Zaugg-Siergiej

*As in 2002, Canada's women won gold at the 2010 Olympics in Vancouver followed soon after by the men. Photo: Matthew Manor / HHOF-IIHF Images.*

# www.imagesonice.net

The website www.imagesonice.net is the official source of photographs by the International Ice Hockey Federation. Operated in alliance with the Hockey Hall of Fame since 2007, the website provides images of all top IIHF events to the world. Newspapers, magazines, and broadcasters can use this site to access photos of every top tournament and every superstar player. In addition, the site provides access to the Hockey Hall of Fame's vast collection of hockey images, the world's largest hockey archive.

IIHF staff photographers are among the most experienced and skilled shooters of game-action hockey and provide high-quality, strobed images in full digital colour. It is their ability to anticipate play and capture the decisive moment that sets them apart from most others in sports photography.

The 2012 World Championship in Helsinki and Stockholm was once again an event which brought out many of the world's finest hockey stars. Here is a sampling of great images from the tournament featuring the best in the game.

*(left) Sweden's Daniel Alfredsson controls play behind the Norway goal.*
*Photo: Andre Ringuette / HHOF-IIHF Images.*

*(bottom) Canada's Jordan Eberle, playing in his third straight World Championship, is closely checked by Switzerland's captain, defenceman Mark Streit.*
*Photo: Jeff Vinnick / HHOF-IIHF Images.*

(top) Zdeno Chara led Slovakia to a silver medal at the 2012 World Championship and then donned a #38 sweater in memory of friend Pavol Demitra who perished in the Yaroslavl plane crash in 2011. Photo: Jeff Vinnick / HHOF-IIHF Images.

(left) Canada's Corey Perry screens Slovakian goalie Peter Hamerlik. Photo: Jeff Vinnick / HHOF-IIHF Images.

(bottom) Miroslav Satan celebrates his go-ahead goal early in the third period of the semi-finals against the Czech Republic. It turned out to be the winner in a 3-1 game. Photo: Jeff Vinnick / HHOF-IIHF Images..

(top) Sweden's Henrik Zetterberg works the puck in behind the Italian net while goalie Daniel Bellissimo gets ready for a shot. Photo: Andre Ringuette / HHOF-IIHF Images.

(bottom) Russia's MVP, Yevgeni Malkin, celebrates gold in style. Photo: Andre Ringuette / HHOF-IIHF Images.

(top) John Tavares of Canada tries to maintain control of the puck while being watched by Slovakian Tomas Tatar. Jeff Vinnick / HHOF-IIHF Images.

(bottom) Alexander Ovechkin joined Team Russia midway through the 2012 World Championship but became an important player in the team's gold-medal victory. Photo: Jeff Vinnick / HHOF-IIHF Images.

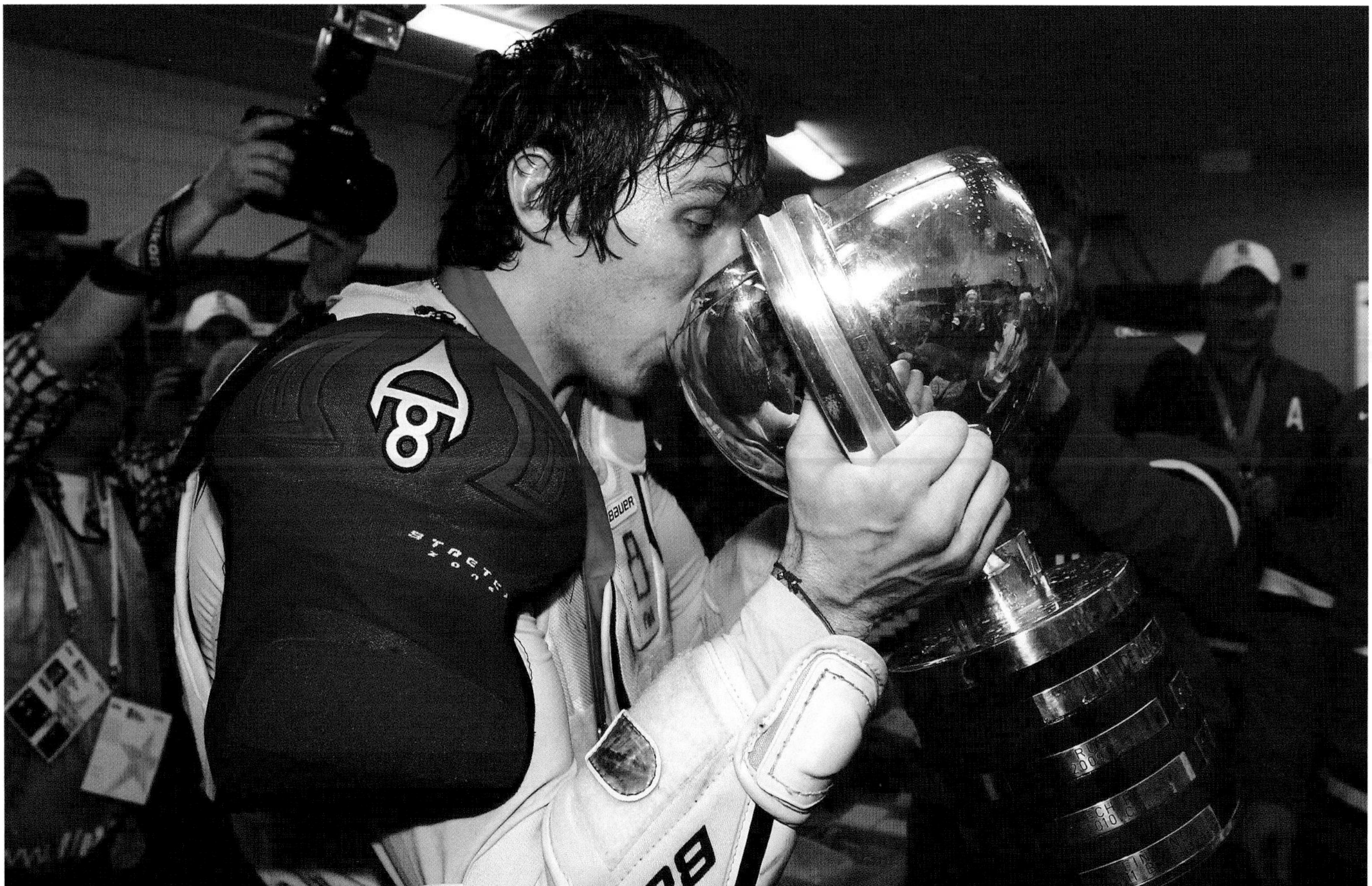

# WOMEN'S WORLD CHAMPIONSHIP

## 1st WOMEN'S WORLD CHAMPIONSHIP
**March 19-25, 1990**
**Ottawa, Canada**

### Final Placing

| | |
|---|---|
| Gold ........Canada | 5th ........Switzerland |
| Silver ......United States | 6th ........Norway |
| Bronze ....Finland | 7th ........West Germany |
| 4th .........Sweden | 8th ........Japan |

### Tournament Format
Eight teams were placed in two groups and played a round-robin series within each group. The top two teams from each advanced to a crossover semi-finals. Those winners played for the gold medal, and the semi-finals losers played for the bronze medal.

### Results & Final Standings
**GROUP A**

| | GP | W | T | L | GF | GA | P |
|---|---|---|---|---|---|---|---|
| Canada | 3 | 3 | 0 | 0 | 50 | 1 | 6 |
| Sweden | 3 | 2 | 0 | 1 | 19 | 19 | 4 |
| West Germany | 3 | 1 | 0 | 2 | 4 | 25 | 2 |
| Japan | 3 | 0 | 0 | 3 | 5 | 33 | 0 |

| | | | |
|---|---|---|---|
| March 19 | Ottawa | Canada 15 | Sweden 1 |
| March 19 | Ottawa | West Germany 4 | Japan 1 |
| March 21 | Gloucester | Canada 17 | West Germany 0 |
| March 21 | Kanata | Sweden 11 | Japan 4 |
| March 22 | Ottawa | Canada 18 | Japan 0 |
| March 22 | Nepean | Sweden 7 | West Germany 0 |

**GROUP B**

| | GP | W | T | L | GF | GA | P |
|---|---|---|---|---|---|---|---|
| United States | 3 | 3 | 0 | 0 | 38 | 7 | 6 |
| Finland | 3 | 2 | 0 | 1 | 24 | 6 | 4 |
| Switzerland | 3 | 1 | 0 | 2 | 11 | 29 | 2 |
| Norway | 3 | 0 | 0 | 3 | 4 | 35 | 0 |

| | | | |
|---|---|---|---|
| March 19 | Kanata | Finland 10 | Norway 1 |
| March 19 | Gloucester | United States 16 | Switzerland 3 |
| March 21 | Ottawa | United States 17 | Norway 0 |
| March 21 | Nepean | Finland 10 | Switzerland 0 |
| March 22 | Ottawa | Switzerland 8 | Norway 3 |
| March 22 | Ottawa | United States 5 | Finland 4 |

**5TH-8TH PLACE SEMI-FINALS**

| | | | |
|---|---|---|---|
| March 24 | Kanata | Switzerland 5 | Japan 4 |
| March 24 | Nepean | Norway 6 | West Germany 3 |

**5TH-PLACE GAME**

| | | | |
|---|---|---|---|
| March 25 | Gloucester | Switzerland 7 | Norway 6 |

**7TH-PLACE GAME**

| | | | |
|---|---|---|---|
| March 25 | Nepean | West Germany 9 | Japan 2 |

**PLAYOFFS (OTTAWA)**
**SEMI-FINALS**

| | | |
|---|---|---|
| March 24 | United States 10 | Sweden 3 |
| March 24 | Canada 6 | Finland 5 |

**BRONZE MEDAL GAME**

| | | |
|---|---|---|
| March 25 | Finland 6 | Sweden 3 |

**GOLD MEDAL GAME**

| | | |
|---|---|---|
| March 25 | Canada 5 | United States 2 |

### Rosters
**Canada** (Dave McMaster, coach) GK—Cathy Phillips, Denise Caron, Michelle Patry—Angela James, Heather Ginzel, Susana Yuen, Shirley Cameron, Stacy Wilson, Vicky Sunohara, France Montour, France St. Louis, Geraldine Heaney, Dawn McGuire, Sue Scherer, Margot Verlaan, Diane Michaud, Laura Schuler, Brenda Richard, Kim Ratushny, Teresa Hutchinson, Judy Diduck

**Finland** (Jouko Oystila, coach) GK—Ritva Ahola, Liisa-Maria Sneck, Kati Ahonen, Leila Tuomiranta—Liisa Karikoski, Riikka Nieminen, Sari Krooks, Anne Haanpaa, Marianne Ihalainen, Leena Majaranta, Tiina Pihala, Tiia Reima, Marika Lehtimaki, Johanna Ikonen, Katri-Helena Luomajoki, Minna Honkanen, Paivi Halonen, Katja Lavonius, Kirsi Hirvonen, Katri Javanainen, Leena Pajunen, Jaana Rautavuoma

**Japan** (Norio Fukada, coach) GK—Tamae Satsu, Kaori Takahashi—Masako Sato, Rie Satoh, Ayako Okada, Chieko Tanaka, Yuko Kurihashi, Shiho Fujiwara, Rika Hasegawa, Michiko Hatakeyama, Yumiko Itoh, Kayoko Miura, Yumiko Tsukamoto, Chihomi Ishii, Hiroko Mabuchi, Misayo Shibata, Sairi Honda, Tamami Nishida, Yoko Suzuki, Yasuko Masuda

**Norway** (Harald Haugen, coach) GK—Kari Berg, Kari Fjellhammer—Inger Lise Fagernes, Gine Marie Moe, Nina Johansen, Hilde Johansen, Christin Smerud, Marit Larssen, Marianne Gomsrud, Camilla Hille, Tonje Larsen, May Olaug Ansnes, Lena Bergersen, Anne Eriksen-Moseby, Jeanette Hansen, Tone Oppegard, Kristina Soderstrom, Christine Wennerberg, Anne Therese Petersen, Eva Stromsborg

**Sweden** (Christian Yngve, coach) GK—Annica Ahlen, Agneta Nilsson—Kristina Bergstrand, Lisa Plahn, Camilla Kempe, Susanne Ceder, Annika Persson, Asa Elfving, Malin Persson, Ann-Sofie Erikson, Linda Gustafsson, Tina Mansson, Tina Bjork, Anette Jarvi, Karin Andersson, Pernilla Hallengren, Helena Nyberg, Pia Morelius, Petra Wikstrom

**Switzerland** (Hansjorg Egli, coach) GK—Tanja Muller, Christiane Bischofberger—Kim Urech, Barbara Wolf, Edith Niederhauser, Regula Stebler, Iris Holzer, Mireille Nothiger, Cornelia Ochsner, Andrea Schweizer, Doris Wyss, Daniela Maag, Leila Zach, Nicole Walder, Nicole Andermatt, Mirjam Baechler, Monika Leuenberger, Cornelia Tanner, Claudia Blattler, Sandra Grutter, Nicole Schumacher

**United States** (Don MacLeod, coach) GK—Mary Jones, Kelly Dyer—Cindy Curley, Tina Cardinale, Cammi Granato, Kelly O'Leary, Kimberly Eisenreid, Beth Beagan, Lisa Brown, Shawna Davidson, Jeanine Sobek, Judy Parish, Heidi Chalupnik, Sharon Stidsen, Lauren Apollo, Sue Merz, Kelley Owen, Maria Dennis, Julie Sasner, Yvonne Percy

**West Germany** (Pierre Delisle, coach) GK—Aurelia Vonderstrass, Karin Berlinghof—Stefanie Putz, Birgit Lisewski, Monika Spring, Christina Oswald, Beate Bart, Sandra Kinza, Elvira Saager, Maren Valenti, Silvia Schneegans, Karin Korn, Karin Obermaier, Kira Berger, Bettina Kirschner, Ines Molitor, Natascha Schaffrik, Claudie Haaf, Cornelia Ostrowski, Claudia Patzold

## 2nd WOMEN'S WORLD CHAMPIONSHIP
**April 20-26, 1992**
**Tampere, Finland**

### Final Placing

| | |
|---|---|
| Gold ........Canada | 5th ........China |
| Silver ......United States | 6th ........Norway |
| Bronze ....Finland | 7th ........Denmark |
| 4th .........Sweden | 8th ........Switzerland |

### Tournament Format
Eight teams were placed in two groups and played a round-robin series within each group. The top two teams from each advanced to a crossover semi-finals. Those winners played for the gold medal, and the semi-finals losers played for the bronze medal.

### Results & Final Standings
**GROUP A**

| | GP | W | T | L | GF | GA | P |
|---|---|---|---|---|---|---|---|
| Canada | 3 | 3 | 0 | 0 | 24 | 1 | 6 |
| Sweden | 3 | 2 | 0 | 1 | 11 | 9 | 4 |
| China | 3 | 1 | 0 | 2 | 7 | 16 | 2 |
| Denmark | 3 | 0 | 0 | 3 | 3 | 19 | 0 |

| | | |
|---|---|---|
| April 20 | Canada 8 | China 0 |
| April 20 | Sweden 4 | Denmark 1 |
| April 21 | Sweden 6 | China 2 |
| April 21 | Canada 10 | Denmark 0 |
| April 23 | China 5 | Denmark 2 |
| April 23 | Canada 6 | Sweden 1 |

**GROUP B**

| | GP | W | T | L | GF | GA | P |
|---|---|---|---|---|---|---|---|
| United States | 3 | 3 | 0 | 0 | 31 | 4 | 6 |
| Finland | 3 | 2 | 0 | 1 | 27 | 9 | 4 |
| Norway | 3 | 1 | 0 | 2 | 8 | 21 | 2 |
| Switzerland | 3 | 0 | 0 | 3 | 2 | 34 | 0 |

| | | |
|---|---|---|
| April 20 | United States 17 | Switzerland 0 |
| April 20 | Finland 11 | Norway 3 |
| April 21 | United States 9 | Norway 1 |
| April 21 | Finland 13 | Switzerland 1 |
| April 23 | Norway 4 | Switzerland 1 |
| April 23 | United States 5 | Finland 3 |

**5TH-8TH PLACE SEMI-FINALS**

| | | |
|---|---|---|
| April 24 | China 2 | Switzerland 1 (10:00 OT/GWS—Yan Lu) |
| April 24 | Norway 2 | Denmark 0 |

**5TH-PLACE GAME**

| | | |
|---|---|---|
| April 26 | China 2 | Norway 1 |

**7TH-PLACE GAME**

| | | |
|---|---|---|
| April 26 | Denmark 4 | Switzerland 3 (Jannie Hadsen 6:05 OT) |

**PLAYOFFS**
**SEMI-FINALS**

| | | |
|---|---|---|
| April 25 | Canada 6 | Finland 2 |
| April 25 | United States 6 | Sweden 4 |

**BRONZE MEDAL GAME**

| | | |
|---|---|---|
| April 26 | Finland 5 | Sweden 4 (10:00 OT/GWS—Riikka Nieminen) |

**GOLD MEDAL GAME**

| | | |
|---|---|---|
| April 26 | Canada 8 | United States 0 |

**Rosters**

**Canada** (Rick Polutnik, coach) GK—Manon Rheaume, Marie-Claude Roy—Dawn McGuire, Diane Michaud, Judy Diduck, Nathalie Rivard, Nathalie Picard, Geraldine Heaney, France St. Louis, France Montour, Angela James, Nancy Drolet, Sue Scherer, Stacy Wilson, Danielle Goyette, Karen Nystrom, Heather Ginzel, Margot Verlaan, Laura Schuler, Andria Hunter

**China** (Wang Guocheng, coach) GK—Lei Wang, Hong Guo—Ming Gong, Xuan Li, Yan Lu, Yan Liang, Jin Chen, Ruolan Feng, Xiaojuan Ma, Hongmei Liu, Hong Dang, Lan Zhang, Yuzhi Chen, Guofeng Gao, Wei Guo, Jingzi Huang, Xiuyan Xin, Caili Zhang, Jinping Ma

**Denmark** (Dion Christiansen, coach) GK—Leila Christensen, Lene Rasmussen—Sussi Hansen, Christina Palsmar, Charlotte Schou-Nielsen, Jeanette Johansen, Susan Gregersen, Lisbeth Boldt, Dorthe Schaeffer, Susanne Jensen, Jannie Madsen, Susanne Hougaard, Anne Mette Nedergaard, Helle Brask, Linda Jensen, Jette Hinrichs, Lene Christensen, Tina Christoffersen, Katja Moesgaard, Maibrit Svendsen, Louise Pedersen, Line Baun Danielsen

**Finland** (Jouko Oystila, coach) GK—Liisa-Maria Sneck, Katariina Ahonen—Katri-Helena Luomajoki, Paivi Halonen, Kirsi Hirvonen, Anne Haanpaa, Leena Pajunen, Satu Huotari, Marika Lehtimaki, Taina Kiljunen, Marianne Ihalainen, Johanna Ikonen, Hanna Teerijoki, Liisa Karikoski, Riikka Nieminen, Katri Niemela, Anne Nurmi, Tiia Reima, Sari Krooks, Susan Reima, Sari Fisk

**Norway** (Harald Haugen, coach) GK—Hege Moe, Linda Brunborg, Kari Fjellhammer—Marit Larssen, Marianne Dahlstrom, Eva Stromsborg, Christin Smerud, Birgitte Lersbryggen, Anne Meisingset, Vibeke Waters, Inger Lise Fagernes, Nina Johansen, Vibeke Laerum, Jeanette Hansen, Tonje Larsen, Camilla Hille, Hege Haugen, Jeanette Giortz, Kristina Soderstrom, Aina Hove, Heidi Flolo

**Sweden** (Christian Yngve, coach) GK—Helen Johansson, Annica Ahlen—Asa Lidstrom, Pia Morelius, Karin Andersson, Linda Gustafsson, Pernilla Burholm, Gunilla Andersson, Maria Hedlund, Annika Eriksson, Lisa Plahn, Pernilla Hallengren, Kristina Bergstrand, Charlotte Almblad, Camilla Kempe, Minna Dunder, Asa Elfving, Tina Mansson, Susanne Ceder, Anne Ferm

**Switzerland** (Roger Maier, coach) GK—Nadine Keller, Monika Vetsch, Claudia Frenzel—Ruth Kunzle, Daniela Maag, Iris Holzer, Brigitte Amhof, Ursula Walther, Monika Leuenberger, Regula Stebler, Mireille Nothiger, Anita Micheli, Edith Niederhauser, Barbara Wolf, Mirjam Baechler, Sandra Cattaneo, Claudia Blattler, Karin Maurer, Jeanette Marty, Edith Enzler

**United States** (Russ McCurdy, coach) GK—Kelly Dyer, Jennifer Hanley, Erin Whitten—Lauren Apollo, Shawna Davidson, Ellen Weinberg, Colleen Coyne, Sandra Whyte, Kelly O'Leary, Lisa Brown, Karyn Bye, Cindy Curley, Kathy Issel, Michele Amidon, Tina Cardinale, Shelley Looney, Wendy Tatarouns, Jeanine Sobek, Sue Merz, Kim Haman, Beth Beagan, Cammi Granato

## 3rd WOMEN'S WORLD CHAMPIONSHIP
**April 11-17, 1994**
**Lake Placid, United States**

**Final Placing**

| | |
|---|---|
| Gold ........Canada | 5th .........Sweden |
| Silver ......United States | 6th .........Norway |
| Bronze ....Finland | 7th .........Switzerland |
| 4th ..........China | 8th .........Germany |

**Tournament Format**

Eight teams were placed in two groups and played a round-robin series within each group. The top two teams from each advanced to a crossover semi-finals. Those winners played for the gold medal, and the semi-finals losers played for the bronze medal.

**Results & Final Standings**
**GROUP A**

| | GP | W | T | L | GF | GA | P |
|---|---|---|---|---|---|---|---|
| Canada | 3 | 3 | 0 | 0 | 27 | 3 | 6 |
| China | 3 | 1 | 1 | 1 | 13 | 12 | 3 |
| Sweden | 3 | 1 | 1 | 1 | 9 | 13 | 3 |
| Norway | 3 | 0 | 0 | 3 | 2 | 23 | 0 |

| | | |
|---|---|---|
| April 11 | Sweden 3 | Norway 1 |
| April 11 | Canada 7 | China 1 |
| April 12 | Sweden 4 | China 4 |
| April 12 | Canada 12 | Norway 0 |
| April 14 | Canada 8 | Sweden 2 |
| April 14 | China 8 | Norway 1 |

**GROUP B**

| | GP | W | T | L | GF | GA | P |
|---|---|---|---|---|---|---|---|
| United States | 3 | 3 | 0 | 0 | 24 | 1 | 6 |
| Finland | 3 | 2 | 0 | 1 | 31 | 3 | 4 |
| Switzerland | 3 | 1 | 0 | 2 | 2 | 20 | 2 |
| Germany | 3 | 0 | 0 | 3 | 2 | 35 | 0 |

| | | |
|---|---|---|
| April 11 | Finland 17 | Germany 1 |
| April 11 | United States 6 | Switzerland 0 |
| April 12 | Finland 13 | Switzerland 0 |
| April 12 | United States 16 | Germany 0 |
| April 14 | Switzerland 2 | Germany 1 |
| April 14 | United States 2 | Finland 1 |

**5TH-8TH PLACE SEMI-FINALS**

| | | |
|---|---|---|
| April 16 | Sweden 7 | Germany 1 |
| April 16 | Norway 7 | Switzerland 4 |

**5TH-PLACE GAME**

| | | |
|---|---|---|
| April 17 | Sweden 6 | Norway 3 |

**7TH-PLACE GAME**

| | | |
|---|---|---|
| April 17 | Switzerland 4 | Germany 3 |

**PLAYOFFS**
**SEMI-FINALS**

| | | |
|---|---|---|
| April 15 | Canada 4 | Finland 1 |
| April 15 | United States 14 | China 3 |

**BRONZE MEDAL GAME**

| | | |
|---|---|---|
| April 17 | Finland 8 | China 1 |

**GOLD MEDAL GAME**

| | | |
|---|---|---|
| April 17 | Canada 6 | United States 3 |

**Rosters**

**Canada** (Lea Lawton, coach) GK—Manon Rheaume, Lesley Reddon—Judy Diduck, Nathalie Picard, Geraldine Heaney, France St. Louis, Angela James, Nancy Drolet, Stacy Wilson, Danielle Goyette, Karen Nystrom, Andria Hunter, Cheryl Pounder, Therese Brisson, Cassie Campbell, Jane Robinson, Margot Page, Laura Leslie, Hayley Wickenheiser, Merianne Gmak

**China** (Zhinan Zhang, coach) GK—Lina Huo, Hong Guo—Ming Gong, Xuan Li, Yan Lu, Hongmei Liu, Hong Dang, Lan Zhang, Wei Guo, Xiuyan Xin, Caili Zhang, Jinping Ma, Hong Sang, Jing Chen, Hongjiao Liu, Ying Diao, Lei Xu, Jianhua Zheng, Wei Wang

**Finland** (Jorma Valtonen, coach) GK—Liisa-Maria Sneck, Katariina Ahonen—Katri-Helena Luomajoki, Paivi Halonen, Kirsi Hirvonen, Anne Haanpaa, Satu Huotari, Marika Lehtimaki, Marianne Ihalainen, Johanna Ikonen, Hanna Teerijoki, Riikka Nieminen, Tiia Reima, Sari Krooks, Susan Reima, Sari Fisk, Kirsi Hanninen, Rose Matilainen, Petra Vaarakallio, Katja Lavonius

**Germany** (Hanspeter Amend, coach) GK—Stephanie Kurten, Aurelia Vonderstrass—Nicole Schmitten, Silvia Hockauf, Simone Schnabel, Ilona Holliday, Silvia Schneegans, Antje Pfau, Natascha Schaffrik, Petra Weber, Birgit Bandelow, Stefanie Putz, Iris Heuben, Andrea Weissbach, Sabine Kurten, Sonja Kuisle, Christina Oswald, Ines Molitor, Maren Valenti, Monika Spring

**Norway** (Harald Haugen, coach) GK—Hege Moe, Linda Brunborg, Kari Fjellhammer—Marit Larssen, Marianne Dahlstrom, Birgitte Lersbryggen, Anne Meisingset, Vibeke Waters, Inger Lise Fagernes, Nina Johansen, Vibeke Laerum, Jeanette Hansen, Tonje Larsen, Camilla Hille, Hege Haugen, Jeanette Giortz, Aina Hove, Heidi Flolo, Hege Ask, Lena Bergersen, Unn Haugen

**Sweden** (Christian Yngve, coach) GK—Lotta Gothessson, Annica Ahlen—Asa Lidstrom, Pia Morelius, Pernilla Burholm, Gunilla Andersson, Annika Eriksson, Lisa Plahn, Kristina Bergstrand, Charlotte Almblad, Camilla Kempe, Asa Elfving, Tina Mansson, Susanne Ceder, Anne Ferm, Ann Sofie Gustafsson, Lena Nilsson, Marie Nordgren, Ylva Lindberg, Ann Louise Edstrand

**Switzerland** (Francois Ceretti, coach) GK—Nadine Keller, Patricia Sautter—Ruth Kunzle, Iris Holzer, Brigitte Amhof, Ursula Walther, Monika Leuenberger, Mireille Nothiger, Edith Niederhauser, Mirjam Baechler, Sandra Cattaneo, Edith Enzler, Carole Laederach, Nicole Andermatt, Prisca Mosimann, Ramona Fuhrer, Doris Wyss, Gillian Jeannottat, Regula Muller

**United States** (Karen Kay, coach) GK—Kelly Dyer, Erin Whitten—Shawna Davidson, Colleen Coyne, Sandra Whyte, Kelly O'Leary, Lisa Brown, Karyn Bye, Cindy Curley, Shelley Looney, Jeanine Sobek, Sue Merz, Beth Beagan, Cammi Granato, Vicki Movsessian, Gretchen Ulion, Shelly DiFronzo, Stephanie Boyd, Chris Bailey, Stephanie O'Sullivan

## 4th WOMEN'S WORLD CHAMPIONSHIP
### March 31-April 6, 1997
### Kitchener, Canada

**Final Placing**

| | | | |
|---|---|---|---|
| Gold | Canada | 5th | Sweden |
| Silver | United States | 6th | Russia |
| Bronze | Finland | 7th | Switzerland |
| 4th | China | 8th | Norway |

**Tournament Format**

Eight teams were placed in two groups and played a round-robin series within each group. The top two teams from each advanced to a crossover semi-finals. Those winners played for the gold medal, and the semi-finals losers played for the bronze medal.

**Results & Final Standings**

**GROUP A**

| | GP | W | T | L | GF | GA | P |
|---|---|---|---|---|---|---|---|
| Canada | 3 | 3 | 0 | 0 | 22 | 2 | 6 |
| China | 3 | 2 | 0 | 1 | 18 | 12 | 4 |
| Russia | 3 | 0 | 1 | 2 | 6 | 18 | 1 |
| Switzerland | 3 | 0 | 1 | 2 | 6 | 20 | 1 |

| | | | |
|---|---|---|---|
| March 31 | Hamilton | China 6 | Russia 2 |
| March 31 | Kitchener | Canada 6 | Switzerland 0 |
| April 1 | Mississauga | China 11 | Switzerland 3 |
| April 1 | Kitchener | Canada 9 | Russia 1 |
| April 3 | North York | Switzerland 3 | Russia 3 |
| April 3 | Kitchener | Canada 7 | China 1 |

**GROUP B**

| | GP | W | T | L | GF | GA | P |
|---|---|---|---|---|---|---|---|
| United States | 3 | 2 | 1 | 0 | 20 | 3 | 5 |
| Finland | 3 | 2 | 1 | 0 | 18 | 3 | 5 |
| Sweden | 3 | 0 | 1 | 2 | 2 | 17 | 1 |
| Norway | 3 | 0 | 1 | 2 | 2 | 19 | 1 |

| | | | |
|---|---|---|---|
| March 31 | Kitchener | United States 7 | Norway 0 |
| March 31 | Brampton | Finland 3 | Sweden 0 |
| April 1 | Kitchener | Sweden 2 | Norway 2 |
| April 1 | Brantford | Finland 3 | United States 3 |
| April 3 | Kitchener | Finland 10 | Norway 0 |
| April 3 | London | United States 10 | Sweden 0 |

**5TH-8TH PLACE SEMI-FINALS**

| | | | |
|---|---|---|---|
| April 4 | Kitchener | Sweden 7 | Switzerland 1 |
| April 4 | Kitchener | Russia 2 | Norway 1 |

**5TH-PLACE GAME**

| | | | |
|---|---|---|---|
| April 6 | Kitchener | Sweden 3 | Russia 1 |

**7TH-PLACE GAME**

| | | | |
|---|---|---|---|
| April 6 | Kitchener | Switzerland 1 | Norway 0 |

**PLAYOFFS (KITCHENER)**
**SEMI-FINALS**

| | | |
|---|---|---|
| April 5 | Canada 2 | Finland 1 |
| April 5 | United States 6 | China 0 |

**BRONZE MEDAL GAME**

| | | |
|---|---|---|
| April 6 | Finland 3 | China 0 |

**GOLD MEDAL GAME**

| | | |
|---|---|---|
| April 6 | Canada 4 | United States 3 (Nancy Drolet 12:59 OT) |

**Rosters**

**Canada** (Shannon Miller, coach) GK—Danielle Dube, Lesley Reddon—Judy Diduck, Geraldine Heaney, France St. Louis, Angela James, Nancy Drolet, Stacy Wilson, Danielle Goyette, Karen Nystrom, Therese Brisson, Cassie Campbell, Hayley Wickenheiser, Rebecca Fahey, Fiona Smith, Lori Dupuis, Jayna Hefford, Luce Letendre, Laura Schuler, Vicky Sunohara

**China** (Zhinan Zhang, coach) GK—Lina Huo, Hong Guo—Ming Gong, Xuan Li, Yan Lu, Hongmei Liu, Hong Dang, Lan Zhang, Wei Guo, Jinping Ma, Hong Sang, Jing Chen, Ying Diao, Lei Xu, Wei Wang, Haiyan Zhang, Lili Guo, Xiaojun Ma, Xiuqing Yang, Jing Zhang

**Finland** (Rauno Korpi, coach) GK—Liisa-Maria Sneck, Tuula Puputti—Katri-Helena Luomajoki, Anne Haanpaa, Marianne Ihalainen, Johanna Ikonen, Riikka Nieminen, Tiia Reima, Sari Krooks, Sari Fisk, Kirsi Hanninen, Petra Vaarakallio, Katja Lehto, Marja-Helena Palvila, Paivi Salo, Kati Kovalainen, Sanna Lankosaari, Tiina Paananen, Karoliina Rantamaki, Katja Riipi

**Norway** (Torbjorn Orskaug, coach) GK—Hege Moe, Erika Wagner—Marianne Dahlstrom, Birgitte Lersbryggen, Inger Lise Fagernes, Nina Johansen, Tonje Larsen, Camilla Hille, Hege Haugen, Jeanette Giortz, Aina Hove, Hege Ask, Unn Haugen, Sissel Bruvik, Christin Smerud, Janne Bergesen, Guro Brandshaug, Trude Myhrvold, Ingvild Oversveen, Kristina Soderstrom

**Russia** (Valentin Yegorov, coach) GK—Irina Gashennikova, Maria Onolbayeva— Yelena Bialkovskaya, Zhanna Shchelchkova, Ludmilla Yurlova, Maria Misropian, Svetlana Nikolayva, Yelena Rodikova, Svetlana Gavrilova, Larisa Mishina, Elena Ossipova, Yekaterina Pashkevich, Yulia Perova, Kristina Petrovskaya, Violetta Simanova, Yekaterina Smolentseva, Svetlana Trefilova, Oxana Tretiakova, Tatyana Tsareva, Yulia Voronina

**Sweden** (Bengt Ohlson, coach) GK—Lotta Gothesson, Annica Ahlen—Asa Lidstrom, Pia Morelius, Pernilla Burholm, Gunilla Andersson, Kristina Bergstrand, Charlotte Almblad, Camilla Kempe, Asa Elfving, Tina Mansson, Anne Ferm, Ann Sofie Gustafsson, Ann Louise Edstrand, Minna Dunder, Malin Persson, Joa Elfsberg, Malin Gustafsson, Erika Holst, Maria Rooth

**Switzerland** (France Montour, coach) GK—Barbara Gfeller, Patricia Sautter—Ruth Kunzle, Iris Holzer, Mireille Nothiger, Edith Niederhauser, Mirjam Baechler, Sandra Cattaneo, Prisca Mosimann, Ramona Fuhrer, Doris Wyss, Gillian Jeannottat, Regula Muller, Christina Marano, Daniela Diaz, Gina Kienle, Kathrin Lehmann, Jeanette Marty, Nicole Walder, Rachel Wild

**United States** (Ben Smith, coach) GK—Sarah Tueting, Erin Whitten—Colleen Coyne, Sandra Whyte, Kelly O'Leary, Lisa Brown-Miller, Karyn Bye, Shelley Looney, Cammi Granato, Vicki Movsessian, Gretchen Ulion, Chris Bailey, Stephanie O'Sullivan, Tara Mounsey, Angela Ruggiero, Laurie Baker, Alana Blahoski, Tricia Dunn, Katie King, A.J. Mleczko

## 5th WOMEN'S WORLD CHAMPIONSHIP
### March 8-14, 1999
### Espoo/Vantaa, Finland

**Final Placing**

| | | | |
|---|---|---|---|
| Gold | Canada | 5th | China |
| Silver | United States | 6th | Russia |
| Bronze | Finland | 7th | Germany |
| 4th | Sweden | 8th | Switzerland* |

*demoted to B pool for 2000

**Tournament Format**

Eight teams were placed in two groups and played a round-robin series within each group. The top two teams from each advanced to a crossover semi-finals. Those winners played for the gold medal, and the semi-finals losers played for the bronze medal.

**Results & Final Standings**

**GROUP A**

| | GP | W | T | L | GF | GA | P |
|---|---|---|---|---|---|---|---|
| United States | 3 | 3 | 0 | 0 | 27 | 2 | 6 |
| Sweden | 3 | 2 | 0 | 1 | 10 | 12 | 4 |
| China | 3 | 1 | 0 | 2 | 4 | 11 | 2 |
| Russia | 3 | 0 | 0 | 3 | 4 | 20 | 0 |

| | | | |
|---|---|---|---|
| March 8 | Espoo | United States 10 | Russia 2 |
| March 8 | Vantaa | Sweden 3 | China 1 |
| March 9 | Vantaa | China 3 | Russia 2 |
| March 9 | Vantaa | United States 11 | Sweden 0 |
| March 11 | Espoo | Sweden 7 | Russia 0 |
| March 11 | Vantaa | United States 6 | China 0 |

**GROUP B**

| | GP | W | T | L | GF | GA | P |
|---|---|---|---|---|---|---|---|
| Canada | 3 | 3 | 0 | 0 | 24 | 0 | 6 |
| Finland | 3 | 2 | 0 | 1 | 16 | 1 | 4 |
| Germany | 3 | 1 | 0 | 2 | 5 | 26 | 2 |
| Switzerland | 3 | 0 | 0 | 3 | 4 | 22 | 0 |

| | | | |
|---|---|---|---|
| March 8 | Vantaa | Canada 10 | Switzerland 0 |
| March 8 | Espoo | Finland 9 | Germany 0 |
| March 9 | Espoo | Canada 13 | Germany 0 |
| March 9 | Espoo | Finland 7 | Switzerland 0 |
| March 11 | Vantaa | Germany 5 | Switzerland 4 |
| March 11 | Espoo | Canada 1 | Finland 0 |

**5TH-8TH PLACE SEMI-FINALS**

| | | | |
|---|---|---|---|
| March 12 | Vantaa | Russia 6 | Germany 2 |
| March 12 | Vantaa | China 3 | Switzerland 2 |

**5TH-PLACE GAME**

| | | | |
|---|---|---|---|
| March 14 | Vantaa | China 4 | Russia 1 |

**7TH-PLACE GAME**

| | | | |
|---|---|---|---|
| March 14 | Vantaa | Germany 3 | Switzerland 0 |

**PLAYOFFS (ESPOO)**
**SEMI-FINALS**

| | | |
|---|---|---|
| March 13 | Canada 4 | Sweden 1 |
| March 13 | United States 3 | Finland 1 |

**BRONZE MEDAL GAME**

| | | |
|---|---|---|
| March 14 | Finland 8 | Sweden 2 |

**GOLD MEDAL GAME**

| March 14 | Canada 3 | United States 1 |
|---|---|---|

**Rosters**

**Canada** (Daniele Sauvageau, coach) GK—Sami Jo Small, Kim St. Pierre—Geraldine Heaney, France St. Louis, Danielle Goyette, Therese Brisson, Cassie Campbell, Hayley Wickenheiser, Fiona Smith, Lori Dupuis, Jayna Hefford, Becky Kellar, Cheryl Pounder, Nathalie Rivard, Mai-Lan Le, Caroline Ouellette, Nancy Drolet, Amanda Benoit, Vicky Sunohara, Jennifer Botterill

**China** (Zhinan Zhang, coach) GK—Lina Huo, Hong Guo—Xuan Li, Yan Lu, Hongmei Liu, Lan Zhang, Hong Sang, Jing Chen, Ying Diao, Lei Xu, Wei Wang, Haiyan Zhang, Lili Guo, Xiaojun Ma, Xiuqing Yang, Jing Zhang, Yanan Li, Chunrong Hu, Rui Sun, Linuo Wang

**Finland** (Kari Savolainen, coach) GK—Minna-Riikka Hurskainen, Tuula Puputti—Katri-Helena Luomajoki, Tiia Reima, Sari Krooks, Sari Fisk, Kirsi Hanninen, Petra Vaarakallio, Katja Lehto, Kati Kovalainen, Sanna Lankosaari, Tiina Paananen, Karoliina Rantamaki, Katja Riipi, Satu Huotari, Paivi Halonen, Pirjo Blomqvist, Maria Selin, Hanne Sikio, Sanna Kanerva

**Germany** (Rainer Nittel, coach) GK—Stephanie Wartosch-Kurten, Esther Thyssen—Anja Merkel, Christina Oswald, Nina Linde, Sabrina Kruck, Sabine Kurten, Sandra Kinza, Sonja Kuisle, Sandra Kurten, Sandra Rumswinkel, Anja Scheytt, Michaela Lanzl, Stephanie Fruhwirt, Claudia Grundmann, Julia Wierscher, Natascha Schaffrik, Bettina Evers, Maritta Becker, Maren Valenti

**Russia** (Jakov Kamenetski, coach) GK—Irina Gashennikova, Irina Votintseva—Zhanna Shchelchkova, Ludmilla Yurlova, Larisa Mishina, Yekaterina Pashkevich, Kristina Petrovskaya, Violetta Simanova, Yekaterina Smolentseva, Svetlana Trefilova, Oxana Tretiakova, Tatyana Tsareva, Alyona Khomich, Viktoria Volobuyeva, Yekaterina Dil, Tatyana Sotnikova, Tatyana Burina, Yelena Rodikova, Olga Savenkova, Svetlana Terentieva

**Sweden** (Christian Yngve, coach) GK—Lotta Gothesson, Hanna Holmberg—Pernilla Burholm, Gunilla Andersson, Charlotte Almblad, Tina Mansson, Ann Louise Edstrand, Joa Elfsberg, Erika Holst, Maria Rooth, Therese Sjolander, Ylva Lindberg, Anna Vikman, Maria Larsson, Jenny Lindqvist, Emilie Lundmark, Josefin Rudberg, Susanne Ceder, Ulrica Lindstrom, Caroline Tornstrom

**Switzerland** (Edi Grubauer, coach) GK—Riita Schaublin, Patricia Sautter—Ruth Kunzle, Mireille Nothiger, Mirjam Baechler, Sandra Cattaneo, Prisca Mosimann, Ramona Fuhrer, Doris Wyss, Gillian Jeannottat, Regula Muller, Christina Marano, Daniela Diaz, Kathrin Lehmann, Jeanette Marty, Nicole Walder, Michelle von Allmen, Monika Leuenberger, Rachel Rochat, Patrizia Chiavi, Sandrine Ray

**United States** (Ben Smith, coach) GK—Laurie Belliveau, Erin Whitten—Karyn Bye, Shelley Looney, Cammi Granato, Chris Bailey, Stephanie O'Sullivan, Tara Mounsey, Angela Ruggiero, Alana Blahoski, Tricia Dunn, Katie King, Amy Coelho, Sue Merz, Catherine Hanson, Brandy Fisher, Jenny Schmidgall, Krissy Wendell, Natalie Darwitz, Sarah Hood

## 6th WOMEN'S WORLD CHAMPIONSHIP
**April 3-9, 2000**
**Mississauga, Canada**

**Final Placing**

Gold ........Canada
Silver ......United States
Bronze ....Finland
4th .........Sweden
5th .........Russia
6th .........China
7th .........Germany
8th .........Japan^*

^promoted from B Pool in 2000
*demoted to Division I for 2001

**Tournament Format**

Eight teams were placed in two groups and played a round-robin series within each group. The top two teams from each advanced to a crossover semi-finals. Those winners played for the gold medal, and the semi-finals losers played for the bronze medal.

**Results & Final Standings**

**GROUP A**

| | GP | W | T | L | GF | GA | P |
|---|---|---|---|---|---|---|---|
| Canada | 3 | 3 | 0 | 0 | 21 | 1 | 6 |
| Sweden | 3 | 1 | 1 | 1 | 11 | 5 | 3 |
| China | 3 | 1 | 1 | 1 | 5 | 9 | 3 |
| Japan | 3 | 0 | 0 | 3 | 0 | 22 | 0 |

| | | | |
|---|---|---|---|
| April 3 | Peterborough | Sweden 1 | China 1 |
| April 3 | Mississauga | Canada 9 | Japan 0 |
| April 4 | Niagara Falls | Sweden 10 | Japan 0 |
| April 4 | Kitchener | Canada 8 | China 1 |
| April 6 | Mississauga | China 3 | Japan 0 |
| April 6 | Mississauga | Canada 4 | Sweden 0 |

**GROUP B**

| | GP | W | T | L | GF | GA | P |
|---|---|---|---|---|---|---|---|
| United States | 3 | 3 | 0 | 0 | 35 | 4 | 6 |
| Finland | 3 | 2 | 0 | 1 | 14 | 6 | 4 |
| Russia | 3 | 1 | 0 | 2 | 8 | 24 | 2 |
| Germany | 3 | 0 | 0 | 3 | 4 | 27 | 0 |

| | | | |
|---|---|---|---|
| April 3 | Mississauga | Finland 7 | Russia 1 |
| April 3 | Barrie | United States 16 | Germany 1 |
| April 4 | Mississauga | Finland 4 | Germany 1 |
| April 4 | Mississauga | United States 15 | Russia 0 |
| April 6 | London | United States 4 | Finland 3 |
| April 6 | Oshawa | Russia 7 | Germany 2 |

**5TH-8TH PLACE SEMI-FINALS**

| | | | |
|---|---|---|---|
| April 8 | Mississauga | China 3 | Germany 0 |
| April 8 | Mississauga | Russia 8 | Japan 4 |

**5TH-PLACE GAME**

| | | | |
|---|---|---|---|
| April 9 | Mississauga | Russia 4 | China 0 |

**7TH-PLACE GAME**

| | | | |
|---|---|---|---|
| April 9 | Mississauga | Germany 3 | Japan 2 |

**PLAYOFFS (MISSISSAUGA)**

**SEMI FINALS**

| | | |
|---|---|---|
| April 8 | Canada 3 | Finland 2 |
| April 8 | United States 7 | Sweden 1 |

**BRONZE MEDAL GAME**

| | | |
|---|---|---|
| April 9 | Finland 7 | Sweden 1 |

**GOLD MEDAL GAME**

| | | |
|---|---|---|
| April 9 | Canada 3 | United States 2 (Nancy Drolet 6:50 OT) |

**Rosters**

**Canada** (Melody Davidson, coach) GK—Sami Jo Small, Kim St. Pierre—Geraldine Heaney, Danielle Goyette, Therese Brisson, Cassie Campbell, Hayley Wickenheiser, Lori Dupuis, Jayna Hefford, Becky Kellar, Cheryl Pounder, Nathalie Rivard, Caroline Ouellette, Nancy Drolet, Amanda Benoit, Vicky Sunohara, Jennifer Botterill, Kelly Bechard, Tammy Shewchuk, Delaney Collins

**China** (Zhinan Zhang, coach) GK—Lina Huo, Hong Guo—Xuan Li, Yan Lu, Hongmei Liu, Hong Sang, Jing Chen, Lei Xu, Wei Wang, Xiaojun Ma, Xiuqing Yang, Jing Zhang, Rui Sun, Linuo Wang, Ying Wang, Lu Sun, Fengling Jin, Yanhui Liu, Chun Feng, Weinan Guan

**Finland** (Hannu Saintula, coach) GK—Johanna Hirvinen, Tuula Puputti—Katri-Helena Luomajoki, Sari Fisk, Kirsi Hanninen, Petra Vaarakallio, Katja Lehto, Kati Kovalainen, Sanna Lankosaari, Karoliina Rantamaki, Katja Riipi, Paivi Halonen, Maria Selin, Hanne Sikio, Emma Laaksonen, Sanna Peura, Vilja Lipsonen, Marianne Ihalainen, Marja-Helena Palvila, Henna Savikuja

**Germany** (Rainer Nittel, coach) GK—Stephanie Wartosch-Kurten, Manuela Hirschbeck—Christina Oswald, Nina Linde, Sabrina Kruck, Sonja Kuisle, Sandra Rumswinkel, Anja Scheytt, Nina Ritter, Michaela Lanzl, Stephanie Fruhwirt, Claudia Grundmann, Nina Gall, Julia Wierscher, Natascha Schaffrik, Bettina Evers, Maritta Becker, Maren Valenti, Raffi Wolf, Nina Ziegenhals

**Japan** (Takayuki Hattanda, coach) GK—Risa Hayashi, Tomoko Fujimoto—Rie Sato, Akiko Hatanaka, Emi Nonaka, Naho Yoshimi, Yuko Osanai, Yoko Kondo, Masako Sato, Akiko Iwase, Mitsuko Igarashi, Hanae Kubo, Aki Sudo, Yuki Togawa, Aki Tsuchida, Akiko Naka, Yoko Tamada, Etsuko Wada, Ayumi Sato, Sayaka Sado

**Russia** (Oleg Galyamin, coach) GK—Irina Gashennikova, Irina Votintseva—Zhanna Shchelchkova, Ludmilla Yurlova, Svetlana Nikolayva, Larisa Mishina, Yekaterina Pashkevich, Kristina Petrovskaya, Violetta Simanova, Yekaterina Smolentseva, Svetlana Trefilova, Oxana Tretiakova, Tatyana Tsareva, Alyona Khomich, Viktoria Volobuyeva, Tatyana Sotnikova, Tatyana Burina, Maria Misropian, Svetlana Terentieva, Olga Savenkova

**Sweden** (Christian Yngve, coach) GK—Lotta Gothesson, Hanna Holmberg—Pernilla Burholm, Gunilla Andersson, Charlotte Almblad, Ann Louise Edstrand, Joa Elfsberg, Erika Holst, Maria Rooth, Therese Sjolander, Ylva Lindberg, Anna Vikman, Jenny Lindqvist, Josefin Rudberg, Susanne Ceder, Ulrica Lindstrom, Elisabet Olofsson, Anna Andersson, Evelina Samuelsson, Kristina Bergstrand

**United States** (Ben Smith, coach) GK—Sara DeCosta, Sarah Tueting—Karyn Bye, Shelley Looney, Cammi Granato, Chris Bailey, Stephanie O'Sullivan, Angela Ruggiero, Alana Blahoski, Tricia Dunn, Katie King, Sue Merz, Brandy Fisher, Jenny Schmidgall, Krissy Wendell, Natalie Darwitz, Nicki Luongo, Laurie Baker, Winny Brodt, A.J. Mleczko

## 7th WOMEN'S WORLD CHAMPIONSHIP
**April 2-8, 2001**
**Minneapolis, United States**

**Final Placing**

Gold ........Canada
Silver ......United States
Bronze ....Russia
4th .........Finland
5th .........Germany
6th .........China
7th .........Sweden
8th .........Kazakhstan^*

^promoted from B Pool in 2000
*demoted to Division I for 2003

**Tournament Format**
Eight teams were placed in two groups and played a round-robin series within each group. The top two teams from each advanced to a crossover semi-finals. Those winners played for the gold medal, and the semi-finals losers played for the bronze medal.

**Results & Final Standings**
**GROUP A**

| | GP | W | T | L | GF | GA | P |
|---|---|---|---|---|---|---|---|
| Canada | 3 | 3 | 0 | 0 | 29 | 1 | 6 |
| Russia | 3 | 2 | 0 | 1 | 12 | 7 | 4 |
| Sweden | 3 | 1 | 0 | 2 | 3 | 17 | 2 |
| Kazakhstan | 3 | 0 | 0 | 3 | 3 | 22 | 0 |

| | | | |
|---|---|---|---|
| April 2 | Rochester | Canada 11 | Kazakhstan 0 |
| April 2 | Rochester | Russia 3 | Sweden 0 |
| April 3 | Rochester | Canada 5 | Russia 1 |
| April 3 | Rochester | Sweden 3 | Kazakhstan 1 |
| April 5 | Minneapolis | Canada 13 | Sweden 0 |
| April 5 | Blaine | Russia 8 | Kazakhstan 2 |

**GROUP B**

| | GP | W | T | L | GF | GA | P |
|---|---|---|---|---|---|---|---|
| United States | 3 | 3 | 0 | 0 | 35 | 0 | 6 |
| Finland | 3 | 2 | 0 | 1 | 12 | 17 | 4 |
| China | 3 | 0 | 1 | 2 | 6 | 20 | 1 |
| Germany | 3 | 0 | 1 | 2 | 2 | 18 | 1 |

| | | | |
|---|---|---|---|
| April 2 | St. Cloud | Finland 7 | China 6 |
| April 2 | St. Cloud | United States 13 | Germany 0 |
| April 3 | St. Cloud | Finland 5 | Germany 2 |
| April 3 | St. Cloud | United States 13 | China 0 |
| April 5 | Plymouth | China 0 | Germany 0 |
| April 5 | Minneapolis | United States 9 | Finland 0 |

**5TH-8TH PLACE SEMI-FINALS**

| | | | |
|---|---|---|---|
| April 6 | Fridley | China 4 | Kazakhstan 1 |
| April 6 | Fridley | Germany 6 | Sweden 2 |

**5TH-PLACE GAME**

| | | | |
|---|---|---|---|
| April 8 | Fridley | Germany 1 | China 0 |

**7TH-PLACE GAME**

| | | | |
|---|---|---|---|
| April 8 | Blaine | Sweden 3 | Kazakhstan 1 |

**PLAYOFFS (MINNEAPOLIS)**
**SEMI FINALS**

| | | |
|---|---|---|
| April 7 | Canada 8 | Finland 0 |
| April 7 | United States 6 | Russia 1 |

**BRONZE MEDAL GAME**

| | | |
|---|---|---|
| April 8 | Russia 2 | Finland 1 |

**GOLD MEDAL GAME**

| | | |
|---|---|---|
| April 8 | Canada 3 | United States 2 |

**Rosters**
**Canada** (Daniele Sauvageau, coach) GK—Sami Jo Small, Kim St. Pierre—Geraldine Heaney, Danielle Goyette, Therese Brisson, Cassie Campbell, Jayna Hefford, Becky Kellar, Cheryl Pounder, Caroline Ouellette, Nancy Drolet, Vicky Sunohara, Jennifer Botterill, Kelly Bechard, Tammy Shewchuk, Colleen Sostorics, Correne Bredin, Dana Antal, Gina Kingsbury, Isabelle Chartrand

**China** (Naifeng Yao, coach) GK—Lina Huo, Hong Guo—Xuan Li, Yan Lu, Hongmei Liu, Hong Sang, Jing Chen, Lei Xu, Wei Wang, Xiaojun Ma, Xiuqing Yang, Jing Zhang, Rui Sun, Linuo Wang, Ying Wang, Fengling Jin, Yanhui Liu, Weinan Guan, Qiuwa Dai, Chunrong Hu

**Finland** (Jouko Lukkarila, coach) GK—Minna Halonen, Tuula Puputti—Sari Fisk, Kati Kovalainen, Karoliina Rantamaki, Katja Riipi, Hanne Sikio, Emma Laaksonen, Sanna Peura, Vilja Lipsonen, Marja-Helena Palvila, Hanna Kuoppala, Satu Kiipeli, Terhi Mertanen, Marjo Voutilainen, Mari Saarinen, Sanna Sainio, Suvi Seppala, Paivi Salo, Saija Sirvio

**Germany** (Rainer Nittel, coach) GK—Stephanie Wartosch-Kurten, Nadine Pfreundschuh—Christina Oswald, Nina Linde, Sonja Kuisle, Anja Scheytt, Nina Ritter, Stephanie Fruhwirt, Claudia Grundmann, Nina Gall, Julia Wierscher, Natascha Schaffrik, Bettina Evers, Maritta Becker, Maren Valenti, Raffi Wolf, Nina Ziegenhals, Jana Schreckenbach, Sandra Kinza, Christine Berndaner

**Kazakhstan** (Alexander Maltsev, coach) GK—Anna Akimbetyeva, Tatyana Khlyzova, Natalya Trunova—Antonida Asonova, Oxana Taikevich, Lyubov Vafina, Lyubov Alexeyeva, Maria Prokopyeva, Olga Potapova, Yelena Shtelmaister, Nadezhda Losyeva, Viktoria Adyeva, Oxana Sokolova, Dinara Dikambayeva, Svetlana Yechtchenko, Olga Konysheva, Olga Kryukova, Natalya Yakovchuk, Viktoria Sazonova, Svetlana Vassina

**Russia** (Vyacheslav Dolgushin, coach) GK—Irina Gashennikova, Irina Votintseva—Zhanna Shchelchkova, Ludmilla Yurlova, Larisa Mishina, Yekaterina Pashkevich, Kristina Petrovskaya, Violetta Simanova, Yekaterina Smolentseva, Svetlana Trefilova, Oxana Tretiakova, Tatyana Tsareva, Alyona Khomich, Tatyana Sotnikova, Tatyana Burina, Maria Misropian, Svetlana Terentieva, Olga Savenkova, Yelena Bobrova, Yulia Gladysheva

**Sweden** (Christian Yngve, coach) GK—Kim Martin, Annica Ahlen—Pernilla Burholm, Gunilla Andersson, Ann Louise Edstrand, Joa Elfsberg, Erika Holst, Maria Rooth, Therese Sjolander, Ylva Lindberg, Jenny Lindqvist, Josefin Rudberg, Ulrica Lindstrom, Anna Andersson, Evelina Samuelsson, Kristina Bergstrand, Maria Larsson, Anna Richaud, Josefin Pettersson, Nanna Jansson

**United States** (Ben Smith, coach) GK—Sara DeCosta, Sarah Tueting—Karyn Bye, Shelley Looney, Cammi Granato, Chris Bailey, Angela Ruggiero, Alana Blahoski, Tricia Dunn, Katie King, Sue Merz, Jenny Schmidgall, Krissy Wendell, Natalie Darwitz, Nicki Luongo, Winny Brodt, A.J. Mleczko, Julie Chu, Annamarie Holmes, Carisa Zaban

## 8th WOMEN'S WORLD CHAMPIONSHIP
## April 3-9, 2003
## Beijing, China

**GROUP A**—Canada, Finland, Germany, Switzerland
**GROUP B**—United States, Russia, China, Sweden

CANCELLED BECAUSE OF SARS

## 8th WOMEN'S WORLD CHAMPIONSHIP
## March 30-April 6, 2004
## Halifax/Dartmouth, Canada

**Final Placing**

| | |
|---|---|
| Gold ........Canada | 6th .........Germany |
| Silver ......United States | 7th .........China |
| Bronze ....Finland | 8th .........Switzerland^* |
| 4th ..........Sweden | 9th .........Japan+* |
| 5th ..........Russia | |

^promoted from Division I in 2001
+promoted from Division I in 2003
*demoted to Division I for 2005

**Tournament Format**
Nine nations took part for the first time. They were divided into three groups of three and played a round-robin series within each. The top team from each group advanced to one group (D); the second-place teams advanced to a second group (E); and, the bottom three advanced to a last group (F). Once again, they played a round-robin series within each new group. The top two teams from group D advanced to the gold-medal game. The third team from this group played the top team from the second-place group (E) for the bronze medal. The last team from the final group (F) was relegated to Division I for the following year.

**Results & Final Standings**
**GROUP A (HALIFAX)**

| | GP | W | T | L | GF | GA | P |
|---|---|---|---|---|---|---|---|
| Canada | 2 | 2 | 0 | 0 | 24 | 0 | 4 |
| Germany | 2 | 1 | 0 | 1 | 4 | 15 | 2 |
| China | 2 | 0 | 0 | 2 | 2 | 15 | 0 |

| | | |
|---|---|---|
| March 30 | Canada 11 | China 0 |
| March 31 | Germany 4 | China 2 |
| April 1 | Canada 13 | Germany 0 |

**GROUP B (HALIFAX)**

| | GP | W | T | L | GF | GA | P |
|---|---|---|---|---|---|---|---|
| United States | 2 | 2 | 0 | 0 | 17 | 1 | 4 |
| Russia | 2 | 1 | 0 | 1 | 2 | 9 | 2 |
| Switzerland | 2 | 0 | 0 | 2 | 2 | 11 | 0 |

| | | |
|---|---|---|
| March 30 | United States 9 | Switzerland 1 |
| March 31 | Russia 2 | Switzerland 1 |
| April 1 | United States 8 | Russia 0 |

**GROUP C (DARTMOUTH)**

| | GP | W | T | L | GF | GA | P |
|---|---|---|---|---|---|---|---|
| Sweden | 2 | 1 | 1 | 0 | 10 | 4 | 3 |
| Finland | 2 | 1 | 1 | 0 | 3 | 2 | 3 |
| Japan | 2 | 0 | 0 | 2 | 2 | 9 | 0 |

| | | |
|---|---|---|
| March 30 | Sweden 8 | Japan 2 |
| March 31 | Finland 1 | Japan 0 |
| April 1 | Sweden 2 | Finland 2 |

**GROUP D (HALIFAX)**

| | GP | W | T | L | GF | GA | P |
|---|---|---|---|---|---|---|---|
| United States | 2 | 2 | 0 | 0 | 12 | 3 | 4 |
| Canada | 2 | 1 | 0 | 1 | 8 | 4 | 2 |
| Sweden | 2 | 0 | 0 | 2 | 3 | 16 | 0 |

| | | |
|---|---|---|
| April 3 | United States 3 | Canada 1 |
| April 4 | Canada 7 | Sweden 1 |
| April 5 | United States 9 | Sweden 2 |

**GROUP E (HALIFAX)**

| | GP | W | T | L | GF | GA | P |
|---|---|---|---|---|---|---|---|
| Finland | 2 | 2 | 0 | 0 | 6 | 1 | 4 |
| Russia | 2 | 1 | 0 | 1 | 5 | 4 | 2 |
| Germany | 2 | 0 | 0 | 2 | 2 | 8 | 0 |

| | | |
|---|---|---|
| April 3 | Russia 4 | Germany 2 |
| April 4 | Finland 4 | Germany 0 |
| April 5 | Finland 2 | Russia 1 |

**GROUP F (DARTMOUTH)**

| | GP | W | T | L | GF | GA | P |
|---|---|---|---|---|---|---|---|
| China | 2 | 2 | 0 | 0 | 11 | 5 | 4 |
| Switzerland | 2 | 1 | 0 | 1 | 7 | 6 | 2 |
| Japan | 2 | 0 | 0 | 2 | 2 | 9 | 0 |

| | | |
|---|---|---|
| April 3 | China 6 | Switzerland 3 |
| April 4 | China 5 | Japan 2 |
| April 5 | Switzerland 4 | Japan 0 |

**BRONZE MEDAL GAME**

| | | | |
|---|---|---|---|
| April 6 | Halifax | Finland 3 | Sweden 2 |

**GOLD MEDAL GAME**

| | | | |
|---|---|---|---|
| April 6 | Halifax | Canada 2 | United States 0 |

**Rosters**

**Canada** (Karen Hughes, coach) GK—Sami Jo Small, Kim St. Pierre—Danielle Goyette, Therese Brisson, Cassie Campbell, Jayna Hefford, Becky Kellar, Cheryl Pounder, Caroline Ouellette, Vicky Sunohara, Jennifer Botterill, Kelly Bechard, Colleen Sostorics, Dana Antal, Gina Kingsbury, Cherie Piper, Gillian Ferrari, Gillian Apps, Hayley Wickenheiser, Delaney Collins

**China** (Jan Votruba, coach) GK—Limei Jiang, Hong Guo—Xuan Li, Yan Lu, Xiaojun Ma, Jing Zhang, Rui Sun, Linuo Wang, Ying Wang, Fengling Jin, Yanhui Liu, Weinan Guan, Qiuwa Dai, Xuefei Li, Xiuli Li, Ben Zhang, Tiantian Shen, Liang Tang, Jinping Ma, Xueting Qi

**Finland** (Hannu Saintula, coach) GK—Minna Halonen, Heidi Wiik—Sari Fisk, Kati Kovalainen, Karoliina Rantamaki, Katja Riipi, Emma Laaksonen, Vilja Lipsonen, Hanna Kuoppala, Terhi Mertanen, Mari Saarinen, Saija Sirvio, Jenni Hiirikoski, Merita Bruun, Satu Tuominen, Satu Hoikkala, Nora Tallus, Eveliina Simila, Saara Tuominen, Henna Savikuja

**Germany** (Peter Kathan, coach) GK—Stephanie Wartosch-Kurten, Viona Harrer—Christina Oswald, Anja Scheytt, Nina Ritter, Stephanie Fruhwirt, Nina Gall, Julia Wierscher, Bettina Evers, Maritta Becker, Raffi Wolf, Nina Ziegenhals, Jana Schreckenbach, Sandra Rumswinkel, Susann Gotz, Denise Soesilo, Sara Seiler, Michaela Lanzl, Sabrina Kruck, Franziska Busch

**Japan** (Kenji Nobuta, coach) GK—Tomoko Fujimoto, Yuka Oda—Haruna Kumano, Masami Akama, Tomoe Yamane, Emi Nonaka, Etsuko Wada, Yoko Kondo, Hanae Kubo, Shoko Nihonyanagi, Yae Kawashima, Masako Sato, Yuki Togawa, Aki Tsuchida, Yuka Hirano, Chiaki Yamanaka, Michiko Ibe, Chiemi Noshita, Kanae Aoki, Haruka Takashima

**Russia** (Viktor Krutov, coach) GK—Irina Gashennikova, Irina Votintseva—Zhanna Shchelchkova, Larisa Mishina, Svetlana Trefilova, Oxana Tretiakova, Alyona Khomich, Tatyana Sotnikova, Svetlana Terentieva, Yulia Gladysheva, Svetlana Kazakova, Viktoria Volobyeva, Marina Borisova, Olga Permyakova, Alexandra Kapustina, Yulia Silyeva, Oxana Lyskova, Iya Gavrilova, Olga Volkova, Yelena Bialkovskaya

**Sweden** (Peter Elander, coach) GK—Kim Martin, Frida Glavhammar—Gunilla Andersson, Ann Louise Edstrand, Erika Holst, Maria Rooth, Therese Sjolander, Ylva Lindberg, Jenny Lindqvist, Josefin Rudberg, Nanna Jansson, Elin Holmlov, Frida Nevalainen, Jenni Asserholt, Anna Vikman, Maria Larsson, Angelica Lorsell, Pernilla Winberg, Kristina Lundberg, Danijela Rundqvist

**Switzerland** (Diane Michaud, coach) GK—Patricia Sautter, Florence Schelling—Melanie Hafliger, Daniela Diaz, Julia Marty, Ruth Kunzle, Nicole Bullo, Mirjam Baechler, Jeanette Marty, Ramona Fuhrer, Christine Meier, Tina Schumacher, Stefanie Marty, Kathrin Lehmann, Sandra Cattaneo, Silvia Bruggmann, Sandrine Ray, Monika Leuenberger, Anita Steinmann, Sabrina Arnet

**United States** (Ben Smith, coach) GK—Chanda Gunn, Pam Dreyer—Shelley Looney, Cammi Granato, Angela Ruggiero, Tricia Dunn, Katie King, Krissy Wendell, Natalie Darwitz, Julie Cahu, Molly Engstrom, Julianne Vasichek, Kelly Stephens, Kerry Weiland, Andrea Kilbourne, Kim Insalaco, Jenny Potter, Kathleen Kauth, Kristin King, Kelli Halcisak

## 9th WOMEN'S WORLD CHAMPIONSHIP
## April 2-9, 2005
## Linkoping/Norrkoping, Sweden

**Final Placing**

| | |
|---|---|
| Gold ........United States | 5th .........Germany |
| Silver ......Canada | 6th .........China |
| Bronze ....Sweden | 7th .........Kazakhstan^ |
| 4th ..........Finland | 8th .........Russia |

^promoted from Division I in 2004
~no teams demoted as World Women's Championship expanded to nine teams for 2007

**Tournament Format**

Eight teams were placed in two groups and played a round-robin series within each group. The top two teams from each advanced to a crossover semi-finals. Those winners played for the gold medal, and the semi-finals losers played for the bronze medal.

**Results & Final Standings**
**GROUP A**

| | GP | W | T | L | GF | GA | P |
|---|---|---|---|---|---|---|---|
| Canada | 3 | 3 | 0 | 0 | 35 | 0 | 6 |
| Sweden | 3 | 2 | 0 | 1 | 8 | 12 | 4 |
| Russia | 3 | 0 | 1 | 2 | 3 | 17 | 1 |
| Kazakhstan | 3 | 0 | 1 | 2 | 3 | 20 | 1 |

| | | | |
|---|---|---|---|
| April 2 | Linkoping | Sweden 3 | Russia 1 |
| April 3 | Linkoping | Canada 13 | Kazakhstan 0 |
| April 4 | Linkoping | Canada 12 | Russia 0 |
| April 4 | Norrkoping | Sweden 5 | Kazakhstan 1 |
| April 6 | Linkoping | Kazakhstan 2 | Russia 2 |
| April 6 | Linkoping | Canada 10 | Sweden 0 |

**GROUP B**

| | GP | W | T | L | GF | GA | P |
|---|---|---|---|---|---|---|---|
| United States | 3 | 3 | 0 | 0 | 23 | 3 | 6 |
| Finland | 3 | 2 | 0 | 1 | 11 | 10 | 4 |
| China | 3 | 0 | 1 | 2 | 6 | 16 | 1 |
| Germany | 3 | 0 | 1 | 2 | 4 | 15 | 1 |

| | | | |
|---|---|---|---|
| April 3 | Norrkoping | United States 8 | China 2 |
| April 3 | Norrkoping | Finland 5 | Germany 1 |
| April 5 | Linkoping | United States 7 | Germany 0 |
| April 5 | Norrkoping | Finland 5 | China 1 |
| April 6 | Norrkoping | China 3 | Germany 3 |
| April 6 | Norrkoping | United States 8 | Finland 1 |

**5TH-8TH PLACE SEMI-FINALS**

| | | | |
|---|---|---|---|
| April 8 | Norrkoping | China 3 | Kazakhstan 0 |
| April 8 | Norrkoping | Germany 2 | Russia 1 |

**5TH-PLACE GAME**

| | | | |
|---|---|---|---|
| April 9 | Norrkoping | Germany 3 | China 0 |

**7TH-PLACE GAME**

| | | | |
|---|---|---|---|
| April 9 | Norrkoping | Kazakhstan 2 | Russia 1 |

(10:00 OT/GWS—Olga Potapova)

**PLAYOFFS (LINKOPING)**
**SEMI-FINALS**

| | | |
|---|---|---|
| April 8 | Canada 3 | Finland 0 |
| April 8 | United States 4 | Sweden 1 |

**BRONZE MEDAL GAME**

| | | |
|---|---|---|
| April 9 | Sweden 5 | Finland 2 |

**GOLD MEDAL GAME**

| | | |
|---|---|---|
| April 9 | United States 1 | Canada 0 (20:00 OT/GWS—Angela Ruggiero) |

**Rosters**

**Canada** (Melody Davidson, coach) GK—Charline Labonte, Kim St. Pierre—Danielle Goyette, Cassie Campbell, Jayna Hefford, Becky Kellar, Cheryl Pounder, Caroline Ouellette, Vicky Sunohara, Jennifer Botterill, Kelly Bechard, Colleen Sostorics, Gina Kingsbury, Cherie Piper, Gillian Apps, Hayley Wickenheiser, Delaney Collins, Carla MacLeod, Correne Bredin, Sarah Vaillancourt

**China** (Paul Strople, coach) GK—Lina Huo, Dandan Jia—Xiaojun Ma, Jing Zhang, Rui Sun, Linuo Wang, Ying Wang, Fengling Jin, Yanhui Liu, Xuefei Li, Xiuli Li, Ben Zhang, Liang Tang, Jinping Ma, Xueting Qi, Ziwei Su, Yue Fu, Anqi Tan, Fujin Gao, Shuang Zhang

**Finland** (Hannu Saintula, coach) GK—Noora Raty, Annakaisa Piiroinen—Sari Fisk, Kati Kovalainen, Karoliina Rantamaki, Katja Riipi, Emma Laaksonen, Vilja Lipsonen, Terhi Mertanen, Mari Saarinen, Saija Sirvio, Jenni Hiirikoski, Saara Tuominen, Satu Hoikkala, Nora Tallus, Eveliina Simila, Heidi Pelttari, Satu Kiipeli, Oona Parviainen, Tiia Reima

**Germany** (Peter Kathan, coach) GK—Stephanie Wartosch-Kurten, Viona Harrer, Jennifer Harss—Christina Oswald, Anja Scheytt, Nina Ritter, Stephanie Fruhwirt, Bettina Evers, Maritta Becker, Raffi Wolf, Nina Ziegenhals, Susann Gotz, Denise Soesilo, Sara Seiler, Michaela Lanzl, Sabrina Kruck, Franziska Busch, Susanne Fellner, Nina Linde, Andrea Lanzl, Claudia Grundmann

**Kazakhstan** (Alexander Maltsev) GK—Yekaterina Ryzhova, Natalya Trunova—Lyubov Alexeyeva, Maria Prokopyeva, Olga Potapova, Tatyana Shtelmaister, Olga Konysheva, Olga Kryukova, Natalya Yakovchuk, Viktoria Sazonova, Svetlana Vassina, Alexandra Babushkina, Galina Zyatkova, Zarina Tukhtieva, Larisa Sviridova, Albina Suprun, Tatyana Korolyova, Maria Atarskaya, Vera Nazyrova, Svetlana Maltseva

**Russia** (Viktor Krutov, coach) GK—Marina Yudina, Maria Onolbayeva —Zhanna Shchelchkova, Svetlana Trefilova, Oxana Tretiakova, Alyona Khomich, Tatyana Sotnikova, Svetlana Terentieva, Yulia Gladysheva, Marina Borisova, Olga Permyakova, Yulia Silyeva, Oxana Lyskova, Iya Gavrilova, Olga Volkova, Viktoria Volobuyeva, Yelena Bialkovskaya, Maria Barykina, Galina Skiba, Tatyana Burina, Yekaterina Dil

**Sweden** (Peter Elander, coach) GK—Kim Martin, Cecilia Andersson—Gunilla Andersson, Ann Louise Edstrand, Erika Holst, Maria Rooth, Therese Sjolander, Ylva Lindberg, Nanna Jansson, Elin Holmlov, Frida Nevalainen, Jenni Asserholt, Anna Vikman, Pernilla Winberg, Kristina Lundberg, Danijela Rundqvist, Evelina Samuelsson, Katarina Timglas, Emilie O'Konor, Emma Eliasson

**United States** (Ben Smith, coach) GK—Chanda Gunn, Megan Van Beusekom—Shelley Looney, Cammi Granato, Angela Ruggiero, Katie King, Krissy Wendell, Natalie Darwitz, Julie Chu, Molly Engstrom, Kelly Stephens, Kim Insalaco, Jenny Potter, Kathleen Kauth, Kristin King, Lyndsay Wall, Courtney Kennedy, Helen Resor, Jamie Hagerman, Sarah Parsons

## 10th WOMEN'S WORLD CHAMPIONSHIP
## April 3-10, 2007
## Winnipeg/Selkirk, Canada

**Final Placing**

Gold ........Canada
Silver ......United States
Bronze ....Sweden
4th.........Finland
5th.........Switzerland^
6th .........China
7th .........Russia
8th .........Germany
9th .........Kazakhstan*

^Promoted from Division I in 2005
*demoted to Division I for 2008

**Tournament Format**

Nine nations were divided into three groups of three and played a round-robin series within each. The top team from each group advanced to one group (D); the second-place teams advanced to a second group (E); and, the bottom three advanced to a last group (F). Once again, they played a round-robin series within each new group. The top two teams from group D advanced to the gold-medal game. The third team from this group played the top team from the second-place group (E) for the bronze medal. The last team from the final group (F) was relegated to Division I for the following year.

For the first time, teams received three points for a regulation time victory. All games tied after 60 minutes went to overtime and, if needed, a shootout. The winner in OT/SO received two points and the loser one point.

**Results & Final Standings**

**GROUP A (SELKIRK)**

| | GP | W | OTW | OTL | L | GF | GA | P |
|---|---|---|---|---|---|---|---|---|
| United States | 2 | 2 | 0 | 0 | 0 | 18 | 1 | 6 |
| China | 2 | 1 | 0 | 0 | 1 | 8 | 9 | 3 |
| Kazakhstan | 2 | 0 | 0 | 0 | 2 | 0 | 16 | 0 |

April 3 United States 9 Kazakhstan 0
April 4 China 7 Kazakhstan 0
April 5 United States 9 China 1

**GROUP B (WINNIPEG)**

| | GP | W | OTW | OTL | L | GF | GA | P |
|---|---|---|---|---|---|---|---|---|
| Canada | 2 | 2 | 0 | 0 | 0 | 17 | 0 | 6 |
| Switzerland | 2 | 1 | 0 | 0 | 1 | 1 | 9 | 3 |
| Germany | 2 | 0 | 0 | 0 | 2 | 0 | 9 | 0 |

April 3 Canada 9 Switzerland 0
April 4 Switzerland 1 Germany 0
April 5 Canada 8 Germany 0

**GROUP C (WINNIPEG)**

| | GP | W | OTW | OTL | L | GF | GA | P |
|---|---|---|---|---|---|---|---|---|
| Finland | 2 | 1 | 1 | 0 | 0 | 5 | 0 | 5 |
| Sweden | 2 | 1 | 0 | 1 | 0 | 3 | 3 | 4 |
| Russia | 2 | 0 | 0 | 0 | 2 | 2 | 7 | 0 |

April 3 Sweden 3 Russia 2
April 4 Finland 4 Russia 0
April 5 Finland 1 Sweden 0 (5:00 OT/GWS)

**GROUP D (WINNIPEG)**

| | GP | W | OTW | OTL | L | GF | GA | P |
|---|---|---|---|---|---|---|---|---|
| Canada | 2 | 1 | 1 | 0 | 0 | 10 | 4 | 5 |
| United States | 2 | 1 | 0 | 1 | 0 | 8 | 5 | 4 |
| Finland | 2 | 0 | 0 | 0 | 2 | 0 | 9 | 0 |

April 7 Canada 5 United States 4 (10:00 OT/GWS—Hayley Wickenheiser)
April 8 United States 4 Finland 0
April 9 Canada 5 Finland 0

**GROUP E (WINNIPEG)**

| | GP | W | OTW | OTL | L | GF | GA | P |
|---|---|---|---|---|---|---|---|---|
| Sweden | 2 | 2 | 0 | 0 | 0 | 16 | 2 | 6 |
| Switzerland | 2 | 1 | 0 | 0 | 1 | 5 | 5 | 3 |
| China | 2 | 0 | 0 | 0 | 2 | 3 | 17 | 0 |

April 7 Switzerland 5 China 1
April 8 Sweden 12 China 2
April 9 Sweden 4 Switzerland 0

**GROUP F (WINNIPEG)**

| | GP | W | OTW | OTL | L | GF | GA | P |
|---|---|---|---|---|---|---|---|---|
| Russia | 2 | 2 | 0 | 0 | 0 | 11 | 1 | 6 |
| Germany | 2 | 1 | 0 | 0 | 1 | 4 | 4 | 3 |
| Kazakhstan | 2 | 0 | 0 | 0 | 2 | 0 | 10 | 0 |

April 7 Germany 3 Kazakhstan 0
April 8 Russia 7 Kazakhstan 0
April 9 Russia 4 Germany 1

**BRONZE MEDAL GAME**

April 10 Winnipeg Sweden 1 Finland 0

**GOLD MEDAL GAME**

April 10 Winnipeg Canada 5 United States 1

**Rosters**

**Canada** (Melody Davidson, coach) GK—Charline Labonte, Kim St. Pierre—Hayley Wickenheiser, Danielle Goyette, Sarah Vaillancourt, Jennifer Botterill, Vicky Sunohara, Kelly Bechard, Katie Weatherston, Gillian Apps, Caroline Ouellette, Meghan Agosta, Delaney Collins, Jayna Hefford, Colleen Sostorics, Gina Kingsbury, Tessa Bonhomme, Carla MacLeod, Gillian Ferrari, Cheryl Pounder

**China** (Jorma Siitarinen, coach) GK— Yao Shi—Rui Sun, Fengling Jin, Hong Sang, Ben Zhang, Ziwei Su, Rui Ma, Liang Tang, Anqi Tan, Linuo Wang, Fujin Gao, Jing Zhang, Shuang Zhang, Yue Fu, Xueting Qi, Shanshan Cui, Xiaolin Ding, Zhenglai Xia, Baiwei Yu

**Finland** (Hannu Saintula, coach) GK—Noora Raty—Mari Pehkonen, Mari Saarinen, Nora Tallus, Saija Sirvio, Kati Kovalainen, Katja Riipi, Jenni Hiirikoski, Karoliina Rantamaki, Emma Laaksonen, Satu Hoikkala, Heidi Pelttari, Mira Jalosuo, Eini Lehtinen, Katariina Soikkanen, Satu Tuominen, Venia Heikkila, Nina Tikkinen, Saara Tuominen

**Germany** (Peter Kathan, coach) GK— Jennifer Harss, Viona Harrer—Sabrina Kruck, Andrea Lanzl, Bettina Evers, Franziska Busch, Carina Spuhler, Maritta Becker, Susanne Fellner, Michaela Lanzl, Denise Soesilo, Claudia Grundmann, Miriam Kresse, Christina Fellner, Susann Gotz, Nikola Holmes, Anja Scheytt, Jenny Tamas, Monika Bittner, Sara Seiler

**Kazakhstan** (Natalya Skobelkina, coach) GK—Daria Obydennova, Yekaterina Ryzhova—Galina Shu, Olga Kryukova, Tatyana Shtelmaister, Viktoria Adyeva, Vera Nazyrova, Zarina Tukhtieva, Svetlana Vassina, Lyubov Ibragimova, Viktoria Sazonova, Albina Suprun, Xenia Yelfimova, Alexandra Babushkina, Alyona Fux, Yevgenia Ivchenko, Tatyana Korolyova, Olga Potapova, Larisa Sviridova

**Russia** (Vladimir Kucherenko, coach) GK—Irina Gashennikova, Maria Onolbayeva—Iya Gavrilova, Yekaterina Smolentseva, Svetlana Terentieva, Tatyana Burina, Svetlana Trefilova, Maria Barykina, Olga Semenets, Olga Permyakova, Alyona Khomich, Kristina Petrovskaya, Galina Skiba, Oxana Tretiakova, Yelena Bialkovskaya, Yekaterina Smolina, Alexandra Kapustina, Natalia Puzikova, Yelena Bobrova, Yekaterina Lebedeva

**Switzerland** (Rene Kammerer, coach) GK—Dominique Slongo, Florence Schelling—Christine Meier, Daniela Diaz, Laura Ruhnke, Kathrin Lehmann, Ruth Kunzle, Stefanie Marty, Julia Marty, Katrin Nabholz, Monika Leuenberger, Nicole Bullo, Melanie Hafliger, Yasmina Monteiro, Lucrece Nussbaum, Helga Schneiter, Silvia Bruggmann, Stephanie Gyseler, Rachel Rochat, Stefanie Wyss

**Sweden** (Peter Elander, coach) GK—Sara Grahn, Kim Martin—Pernilla Winberg, Maria Rooth, Erika Holst, Gunilla Andersson, Nanna Jansson, Joa Elfsberg, Katarina Timglas, Danijella Rundqvist, Elin Holmlov, Jenni Asserholt, Tina Enstrom, Emma Eliasson, Ann-Louise Edstrand, Frida Nevalainen, Angelica Lorsell, Emilia Andersson, Chanette Svensson, Helena Tageson

**United States** (Mark Johnson, coach) GK—Chanda Gunn, Jessie Vetter—Krissy Wendell, Natalie Darwitz, Sarah Parsons, Erika Lawler, Molly Engstrom, Jenny Potter, Caitlin Cahow, Kristin King, Angela Ruggiero, Gigi Marvin, Jinelle Zaugg, Julie Chu, Helen Resor, Meghan Duggan, Kerry Weiland, Hilary Knight, Tiffany Hagge, Kelli Halcisak

## 11th WOMEN'S WORLD CHAMPIONSHIP
## April 4-12, 2008
## Harbin, China

**Final Placing**

Gold ........United States
Silver ......Canada
Bronze ....Finland
4th ..........Switzerland
5th ..........Sweden
6th .........Russia
7th .........Japan^
8th .........China
9th .........Germany*

^promoted from Division I in 2007
*demoted to Division I for 2009

**Tournament Format**

Nine nations were divided into three groups of three and played a round-robin series within each. The top team from each group advanced to one group (D); the second-place teams advanced to a second group (E); and, the bottom three advanced to a last group (F). Once again, they played a round-robin series within each new group. The top two teams from group D advanced to the gold-medal game. The third team from this group played the top team from the second-place group (E) for the bronze medal. The last team from the final group (F) was relegated to Division I for the following year.

Teams received three points for a regulation time victory. All games tied after 60 minutes went to overtime and, if needed, a shootout. The winner in OT/SO received two points and the loser one point.

**Results & Standings**
**PRELIMINARY ROUND**
**GROUP A**

| | GP | W | OTW | OTL | L | GF | GA | P |
|---|---|---|---|---|---|---|---|---|
| Canada | 2 | 2 | 0 | 0 | 0 | 19 | 1 | 6 |
| Russia | 2 | 1 | 0 | 0 | 1 | 6 | 11 | 3 |
| China | 2 | 0 | 0 | 0 | 2 | 3 | 16 | 0 |

April 4 Canada 8 Russia 1
April 5 Russia 5 China 3
April 6 Canada 11 China 0

**GROUP B**

| | GP | W | OTW | OTL | L | GF | GA | P |
|---|---|---|---|---|---|---|---|---|
| United States | 2 | 2 | 0 | 0 | 0 | 15 | 2 | 6 |
| Switzerland | 2 | 1 | 0 | 0 | 1 | 4 | 7 | 3 |
| Germany | 2 | 0 | 0 | 0 | 2 | 1 | 11 | 0 |

April 4 United States 8 Germany 1
April 5 Switzerland 3 Germany 0
April 6 United States 7 Switzerland 1

**GROUP C**

| | GP | W | OTW | OTL | L | GF | GA | P |
|---|---|---|---|---|---|---|---|---|
| Finland | 2 | 1 | 1 | 0 | 0 | 9 | 3 | 5 |
| Sweden | 2 | 1 | 0 | 1 | 0 | 7 | 3 | 4 |
| Japan | 2 | 0 | 0 | 0 | 2 | 1 | 11 | 0 |

April 4 Sweden 5 Japan 0
April 5 Finland 6 Japan 1
April 6 Finland 3 Sweden 2 (Mari Pehkonen 3:00 OT)

**QUALIFICATION ROUND**
**GROUP D**

| | GP | W | OTW | OTL | L | GF | GA | P |
|---|---|---|---|---|---|---|---|---|
| United States | 2 | 1 | 0 | 1 | 0 | 4 | 3 | 4 |
| Canada | 2 | 1 | 0 | 0 | 1 | 6 | 6 | 3 |
| Finland | 2 | 0 | 1 | 0 | 1 | 3 | 4 | 2 |

April 8 Finland 1 United States 0 (Heidi Pelttari 3:42 OT)
April 9 Canada 4 Finland 2
April 10 United States 4 Canada 2

**GROUP E**

| | GP | W | OTW | OTL | L | GF | GA | P |
|---|---|---|---|---|---|---|---|---|
| Switzerland | 2 | 1 | 1 | 0 | 0 | 6 | 4 | 5 |
| Sweden | 2 | 1 | 0 | 1 | 0 | 6 | 5 | 4 |
| Russia | 2 | 0 | 0 | 0 | 2 | 2 | 5 | 0 |

April 8 Switzerland 4 Sweden 3 (5:00 OT/GWS—Kathrin Lehmann)
April 9 Sweden 3 Russia 1
April 10 Switzerland 2 Russia 1

**GROUP F**

| | GP | W | OTW | OTL | L | GF | GA | P |
|---|---|---|---|---|---|---|---|---|
| Japan | 2 | 1 | 0 | 0 | 1 | 4 | 3 | 3 |
| China | 2 | 1 | 0 | 0 | 1 | 5 | 5 | 3 |
| Germany | 2 | 1 | 0 | 0 | 1 | 4 | 5 | 3 |

April 8 Germany 2 Japan 1
April 9 Japan 3 China 1
April 10 China 4 Germany 2

**BRONZE MEDAL GAME**

April 12 Finland 4 Switzerland 1

**GOLD MEDAL GAME**

April 12 United States 4 Canada 3

**Rosters**

**Canada** (Peter Smith, coach) GK—Charline Labonte, Kim St. Pierre—Hayley Wickenheiser, Jennifer Botterill, Jayna Hefford, Cherie Piper, Sarah Vaillancourt, Caroline Ouellette, Becky Kellar, Carla MacLeod, Gina Kingsbury, Meghan Agosta, Katie Weatherston, Kelly Bechard, Colleen Sostorics, Gillian Apps, Delaney Collins, Gillian Ferrari, Meaghan Mikkelson, Rebecca Johnston

**China** (Steve Carlyle, coach) GK— Yao Shi, Dandan Jia—Rui Sun, Fengling Jin, Linuo Wang, Hong Sang, Xueting Qi, Shuang Zhang, Cui Huo, Ben Zhang, Rui Ma, Anqi Tan, Haijing Huang, Yue Fu, Baiwei Zu, Shanshan Cui, Fujin Gao, Na Jiang, Ziwei Su, Lu Zhang

**Finland** (Hannu Saintula, coach) GK— Noora Raty, Maija Hassinen—Mari Pehkonen, Mari Saarinen, Heidi Pelttari, Anne Helin, Emma Laaksonen, Karoliina Rantamaki, Jenni Hiirikoski, Marjo Voutilainen, Kati Kovalainen, Nora Tallus, Nina Tikkinen, Saija Sirvio, Mira Jalosuo, Eini Lehtinen, Piia Lallukka, Vilma Tarvainen, Venla Heikkila, Saara Tuominen

**Germany** (Peter Kathan, coach) GK—Viona Harrer, Jennifer Harss—Manuela Anwander, Andrea Lanzl, Jenny Tamas, Nina Ritter, Bettina Evers, Susann Gotz, Sabrina Kruck, Susanne Fellner, Sara Seiler, Stephanie Fruhwirt, Anja Scheytt, Nina Kamenik, Miriam Kresse, Lisa Schuster, Monika Bittner, Britta Schroder, Sarah Weyand, Franziska Busch

**Japan** (Yuji Ilzuka, coach) GK—Azusa Nakaoku, Nana Fujimoto—Yurie Adachi, Etsuko Wada, Aki Fujii, Yuka Hirano, Tomoko Sakagami, Yoko Kondo, Tomoe Yamane, Chiaki Yamanaka, Haruka Takashima, Yae Kawashima, Ami Nakamura, Shoko Nihonyanagi, Yuki Togawa, Nachi Fujimoto, Tomomi Iwahara, Haruna Kumano, Yoko Ohtani, Mai Takahashi

**Russia** (Vladimir Kucherenko, coach) GK—Maria Onolbayeva, Valentina Ostrovlyanchik—Yekaterina Smolentseva, Iya Gavrilova, Svetlana Terentieva, Alexandra Kapustina, Marina Sergina, Tatyana Burina, Alyona Khomich, Natalia Puzikova, Yelena Timofeyva, Inna Dyubanok, Yekaterina Lebedeva, Olga Permyakova, Olga Semenets, Anna Shukina, Galina Skiba, Yekaterina Smolina, Alexandra Vafina, Oxana Afonina

**Sweden** (Peter Elander, coach) GK—Kim Martin, Sara Grahn—Tina Enstrom, Isabelle Jordansson, Klara Myren, Emma Eliasson, Maria Rooth, Cecilia Ostberg, Katarina Timglas, Pernilla Winberg, Elin Holmlov, Danijela Rundqvist, Emma Nordin, Jenni Asserholt, Angelica Lorsell, Emilia Andersson, Frida Nevalainen, Ann-Louise Edstrand, Emelie Berggren, Erika Holst

**Switzerland** (Rene Kammerer, coach) GK—Florence Schelling, Dominique Slongo—Stefanie Marty, Kathrin Lehmann, Lucrece Nussbaum, Melanie Hafliger, Julia Marty, Christine Meier, Laura Ruhnke, Darcia Leimgruber, Silvia Bruggmann, Florence Schelling, Nadine Ehrbar, Angela Frautschi, Nicole Bullo, Rahel Michielin, Monika Leuenberger, Katrin Nabholz, Stefanie Wyss, Camille Balanche, Anja Stiefel

**United States** (Jackie Barto, coach) GK— Jessie Vetter, Molly Schaus—Natalie Darwitz, Jenny Potter, Julie Chu, Meghan Duggan, Caitlin Cahow, Angela Ruggiero, Sarah Parsons, Gigi Marvin, Rachael Drazan, Karen Thatcher, Molly Engstrom, Erika Lawler, Kacey Bellamy, Kelli Stack, Hilary Knight, Kerry Weiland, Sam Faber, Jessica Koizumi

## 12th WOMEN'S WORLD CHAMPIONSHIP
## April 4-12, 2009
## Hameenlinna, Finland

**Final Placing**

Gold ........United States
Silver ......Canada
Bronze ....Finland
4th ..........Sweden
5th ..........Russia
6th .........Kazakhstan^
7th .........Switzerland
8th .........Japan
9th .........China*

^promoted from Division I in 2008
*demoted to Division I for 2011

**Tournament Format**

Nine nations were divided into three groups of three and played a round-robin series within each. The top team from each group advanced to one group (D); the second-place teams advanced to a second group (E); and, the bottom three advanced to a last group (F). Once again, they played a round-robin series within each new group. The top two teams from group D advanced to the gold-medal game. The third team from this group played the top team from the second-place group (E) for the bronze medal. The last team from the final group (F) was relegated to Division I for the following year.

Teams received three points for a regulation time victory. All games tied after 60 minutes went to overtime and, if needed, a shootout. The winner in OT/SO received two points and the loser one point.

**Results & Final Standings**
**PRELIMINARY ROUND**
**GROUP A**

| | GP | W | OTW | OTL | L | GF | GA | P |
|---|---|---|---|---|---|---|---|---|
| United States | 2 | 2 | 0 | 0 | 0 | 16 | 0 | 6 |
| Russia | 2 | 1 | 0 | 0 | 1 | 3 | 9 | 3 |
| Japan | 2 | 0 | 0 | 0 | 2 | 1 | 11 | 0 |

| | | |
|---|---|---|
| April 4 | United States 8 | Japan 0 |
| April 5 | Russia 3 | Japan 1 |
| April 6 | United States 8 | Russia 0 |

**GROUP B**

| | GP | W | OTW | OTL | L | GF | GA | P |
|---|---|---|---|---|---|---|---|---|
| Canada | 2 | 2 | 0 | 0 | 0 | 20 | 1 | 6 |
| Sweden | 2 | 1 | 0 | 0 | 1 | 6 | 8 | 3 |
| China | 2 | 0 | 0 | 0 | 2 | 2 | 19 | 0 |

| | | |
|---|---|---|
| April 4 | Canada 13 | China 1 |
| April 5 | Sweden 6 | China 1 |
| April 6 | Canada 7 | Sweden 0 |

**GROUP C**

| | GP | W | OTW | OTL | L | GF | GA | P |
|---|---|---|---|---|---|---|---|---|
| Finland | 2 | 2 | 0 | 0 | 0 | 13 | 3 | 6 |
| Kazakhstan | 2 | 0 | 1 | 0 | 1 | 2 | 8 | 2 |
| Switzerland | 2 | 0 | 0 | 1 | 1 | 4 | 8 | 1 |

| | | |
|---|---|---|
| April 4 | Finland 7 | Kazakhstan 0 |
| April 5 | Kazakhstan 2 | Switzerland 1 (5:00 OT/GWS—Alena Fux) |
| April 6 | Finland 6 | Switzerland 3 |

**QUALIFYING ROUND**
**GROUP D**

| | GP | W | OTW | OTL | L | GF | GA | P |
|---|---|---|---|---|---|---|---|---|
| Canada | 2 | 2 | 0 | 0 | 0 | 10 | 1 | 6 |
| United States | 2 | 1 | 0 | 0 | 1 | 8 | 2 | 3 |
| Finland | 2 | 0 | 0 | 0 | 2 | 0 | 15 | 0 |

| | | |
|---|---|---|
| April 8 | Canada 8 | Finland 0 |
| April 9 | United States 7 | Finland 0 |
| April 10 | Canada 2 | United States 1 |

**GROUP E**

| | GP | W | OTW | OTL | L | GF | GA | P |
|---|---|---|---|---|---|---|---|---|
| Sweden | 2 | 2 | 0 | 0 | 0 | 17 | 0 | 6 |
| Russia | 2 | 1 | 0 | 0 | 1 | 9 | 10 | 3 |
| Kazakhstan | 2 | 0 | 0 | 0 | 2 | 2 | 18 | 0 |

| | | |
|---|---|---|
| April 8 | Sweden 9 | Kazakhstan 0 |
| April 9 | Russia 9 | Kazakhstan 2 |
| April 10 | Sweden 8 | Russia 0 |

**RELEGATION ROUND**
**GROUP E**

| | GP | W | OTW | OTL | L | GF | GA | P |
|---|---|---|---|---|---|---|---|---|
| Switzerland | 2 | 1 | 1 | 0 | 0 | 8 | 6 | 5 |
| Japan | 2 | 1 | 0 | 0 | 1 | 4 | 4 | 3 |
| China | 2 | 0 | 0 | 1 | 1 | 5 | 7 | 1 |

| | | |
|---|---|---|
| April 8 | Switzerland 5 | China 4 (5:00 OT/GWS—Nicole Bullo) |
| April 9 | Switzerland 3 | Japan 2 |
| April 10 | Japan 2 | China 1 |

**BRONZE MEDAL GAME**

April 12 Finland 4 Sweden 1

**GOLD MEDAL GAME**

April 12 United States 4 Canada 1

**Rosters**

**Canada** (Melody Davidson, coach) GK—Charline Labonte, Kim St. Pierre, Shannon Szabados—Meghan Agosta, Carla MacLeod, Becky Kellar, Colleen Sostorics, Rebecca Johnston, Gillian Ferrari, Gillian Apps, Meaghan Mikkelson, Caroline Ouellette, Jayna Hefford, Jennifer Botterill, Catherine Ward, Haley Irwin, Hayley Wickenheiser, Tessa Bonhomme, Sarah Vaillancourt, Gina Kingsbury, Marie-Philip Poulin

**China** (Don Strople, coach) GK—Yao Shi, Dandan Jia—Baiwei Yu, Ziwei Su, Yue Lou, Ben Zhang, Haijing Huang, Fengling Jin, Rui Sun, Rui Ma, Shanshan Cui, Linuo Wang, Na Jiang, Cui Huo, Liang Tang, Anqi Tan, Nan Wang, Fujin Gao, Xueting Qi, Shuang Zhang

**Finland** (Hannu Saintula, coach) GK—Maija Hassinen, Noora Raty, Mira Kuisma—Emma Laaksonen, Mariia Posa, Jenni Hiirikoski, Mira Jalosuo, Marjo Voutilainen, Venla Heikkila, Kati Kovalainen, Mari Saarinen, Satu Tuominen, Piia Lallukka, Saija Sirvio, Michelle Karvinen, Saara Tuominen, Nina Tikkinen, Mari Pehkonen, Heidi Pelttari, Anne Helin, Karoliina Rantamaki

**Japan** (Yuji Iizuka, coach) GK—Azusa Nakaoku, Eri Kiribuchi, Kumiko Okada—Haruna Kumano, Yoko Kondo, Emi Nonaka, Sena Suzuki, Etsuko Wada, Tomoe Yamane, Chiho Osawa, Haruna Yoneyama, Yurie Adachi, Aki Fujii, Saki Shimozawa, Yuka Hirano, Tomoko Sakagami, Mai Takahashi, Haruka Takashima, Chiaki Yamanaka, Nachi Fujimoto, Tomomi Iwahara

**Kazakhstan** (Alexander Maltsev, coach) GK—Daria Obydennova, Natalya Trunova, Anna Kossenko—Galina Shu, Lyubov Ibragimova, Olga Potapova, Yelena Shtelmaister, Viktoria Mussatayeva, Larisa Sviridova, Galia Nurgalieva, Olga Konysheva, Olga Kryukova, Natalya Yakovchuk, Viktoria Sazonova, Tatyana Korolyova, Albina Suprun, Alyona Fux, Yulia Chernukhina, Daria Moldabai, Arai Shegebayeva

**Russia** (Valentin Gureyev, coach) GK—Irina Gashennikova, Nadezhda Alexandrova, Maria Onolbayeva—Alyona Khomich, Olga Sosina, Iya Gavrilova, Alexandra Vafina, Marina Sergina, Yekaterina Ananina, Olga Permyakova, Yekaterina Smolentseva, Yekaterina Smolina, Kristina Petrovskaya, Anna Shukina, Svetlana Terentieva, Tatyana Burina, Yekaterina Lebedeva, Zoya Polunina, Inna Dyubanok, Tatyana Sotnikova, Alexandra Kapustina

**Sweden** (Peter Elander, coach) GK—Valentina Lizana, Sara Grahn, Kim Martin—Elin Holmlov, Frida Nevalainen, Jenni Asserholt, Maria Rooth, Erika Holst, Tina Enstrom, Emilia Andersson, Cecilia Ostberg, Isabelle Jordansson, Erica Uden-Johansson, Katarina Timglas, Pernilla Winberg, Emma Nordin, Klara Myren, Emma Eliasson, Gunilla Andersson, Frida Svedin-Thunstrom, Danijela Rundqvist

**Switzerland** (Rene Kammerer, coach) GK—Florence Schelling, Dominique Slongo, Patricia Elsmore-Sautter—Katrin Nabholz, Julia Marty, Darcia Leimgruber, Stefanie Marty, Nicole Bullo, Angela Frautschi, Sara Benz, Monika Waidacher, Christine Meier, Laura Benz, Lucrece Nussbaum, Rahel Michielin, Kathrin Lehmann, Monika Leuenberger, Sabrina Zollinger, Laura Ruhnke, Sandra Thalmann, Anja Stiefel

**United States** (Mark Johnson, coach) GK—Jessie Vetter, Molly Schaus, Megan Van Beusekom—Erika Lawler, Angela Ruggiero, Karen Thatcher, Helen Resor, Caitlin Cahow, Molly Engstrom, Meghan Duggan, Lisa Chesson, Jenny Potter, Julie Chu, Kelli Stack, Jocelyne Lamoureux, Gigi Marvin, Natalie Darwitz, Hilary Knight, Kacey Bellamy, Kerry Weiland, Monique Lamoureux

## 13th WOMEN'S WORLD CHAMPIONSHIP
## Zurich/Winterthur, Switzerland
## April 16-25, 2011

**Final Placing**

| | |
|---|---|
| Gold ........United States | 5th .........Sweden |
| Silver .......Canada | 6th .........Switzerland |
| Bronze ....Finland | 7th .........Slovakia^ |
| 4th..........Russia | 8th .........Kazakhstan+ |

^promoted from Division I in 2009
+demoted to Division I for 2012

**Tournament Format**

Eight teams were placed in two groups and played a round-robin series within each group. The top two teams from each advanced to a cross-over semi-finals. Those winners played for the gold, and the semi-finals losers played for the bronze medal.

**Results & Final Standings**
**GROUP A**

| | GP | W | OTW | OTL | L | GF | GA | P |
|---|---|---|---|---|---|---|---|---|
| United States | 3 | 3 | 0 | 0 | 0 | 27 | 2 | 9 |
| Sweden | 3 | 2 | 0 | 0 | 1 | 11 | 10 | 6 |
| Russia | 3 | 1 | 0 | 0 | 2 | 6 | 21 | 3 |
| Slovakia | 3 | 0 | 0 | 0 | 3 | 1 | 12 | 0 |

| | | | |
|---|---|---|---|
| April 17 | Zurich | United States 5 | Slovakia 0 |
| April 17 | Zurich | Sweden 7 | Russia 1 |
| April 18 | Zurich | Sweden 3 | Slovakia 0 |
| April 18 | Zurich | United States 13 | Russia 1 |
| April 20 | Winterthur | Russia 4 | Slovakia 1 |
| April 20 | Winterthur | United States 9 | Sweden 1 |

**GROUP B (WINTERTHUR)**

| | GP | W | OTW | OTL | L | GF | GA | P |
|---|---|---|---|---|---|---|---|---|
| Canada | 3 | 3 | 0 | 0 | 0 | 21 | 0 | 9 |
| Switzerland | 3 | 1 | 1 | 0 | 1 | 8 | 14 | 5 |
| Finland | 3 | 1 | 0 | 1 | 1 | 6 | 7 | 4 |
| Kazakhstan | 3 | 0 | 0 | 0 | 3 | 4 | 18 | 0 |

| | | |
|---|---|---|
| April 16 | Finland 5 | Kazakhstan 3 |
| April 16 | Canada 12 | Switzerland 0 |
| April 17 | Canada 7 | Kazakhstan 0 |
| April 17 | Switzerland 2 | Finland 1 (Stefanie Marty 1:50 OT) |
| April 19 | Canada 2 | Finland 0 |
| April 19 | Switzerland 6 | Kazakhstan 1 |

**RELEGATION ROUND (WINTERTHUR)**

| | GP | W | OTW | OTL | L | GF | GA | P |
|---|---|---|---|---|---|---|---|---|
| Slovakia | 2 | 1 | 1 | 0 | 0 | 3 | 1 | 5 |
| Kazakhstan | 2 | 0 | 0 | 1 | 1 | 1 | 3 | 1 |

April 22 Slovakia 1 Kazakhstan 0
April 24 Slovakia 2 Kazakhstan 1 (5:00 OT/GWS—Martina Velickova)

**FIFTH-PLACE GAME**
April 24 Zurich Sweden 3 Switzerland 2 (10:00 OT/GWS—Elin Holmlov)

**PLAYOFFS (ZURICH)**
**QUARTER-FINALS**
April 22 Finland 5 Sweden 1
April 22 Russia 5 Switzerland 4 (Tatiana Burina 2:58 OT)

**SEMI-FINALS**
April 23 Canada 4 Finland 1
April 23 United States 5 Russia 1

**BRONZE MEDAL GAME**
April 25 Finland 3 Russia 2 (Karoliina Rantamaki 2:49 OT)

**GOLD MEDAL GAME**
April 25 United States 3 Canada 2 (Hilary Knight 7:48 OT)

**Rosters**

**Canada** (Ryan Walter, coach) GK—Shannon Szabados, Charline Labonte, Kim St. Pierre—Rebecca Johnston, Hayley Wickenheiser, Jayna Hefford, Meghan Agosta, Marie-Philip Poulin-Nadeau, Cherie Piper, Haley Irwin, Tessa Bonhomme, Meaghan Mikkelson, Gillian Apps, Jennifer Wakefield, Caroline Ouellette, Natalie Spooner, Sarah Vaillancourt, Jocelyne Larocque, Tara Watchorn, Bobbi Jo Slusar, Catherine Ward

**Finland** (Pekka Hamalainen, coach) GK—Anna Vanhatalo, Maija Hassinen, Noora Raty—Mira Huhta, Rosa Lindstedt, Jenni Hiirikoski, Mira Jalosuo, Tea Villila, Essi Hallvar, Annina Rajahuhta, Susanna Tapani, Niina Makinen, Minnamari Tuominen, Terhi Mertanen, Michelle Karvinen, Tanja Niskanen, Pia Lund, Tiina Saarimaki, Anne Helin, Anne Tuomanen, Karoliina Rantamaki

**Kazakhstan** (Alexander Maltsev, coach) GK—Aizhan Raushanova, Daria Obydennova, Anna Kossenko—Alexandra Ashikhkina, Galina Shu, Lyubov Ibragimova, Olga Potapova, Yelena Shtelmaister, Zarina Tukhtieva, Viktoria Mussatayeva, Larisa Sviridova, Galia Nurgalieva, Olga Konysheva, Natalya Yakovchuk, Viktoria Sazonova, Tatyana Korolyova, Anastasia Orlova, Albina Suprun, Daria Moldabai, Natalya Karpeyeva, Alyona Fux

**Russia** (Valentin Gureyev, coach) GK—Anna Prugova, Valentina Ostrovlyanchik, Margarita Monakhova—Alyona Khomich, Olga Sosina, Iya Gavrilova, Alexandra Vafina, Marina Sergina, Olga Permyakova, Yekaterina Smolentseva, Anna Shukina, Olga Semenets, Tatyana Burina, Yekaterina Lebedeva, Zoya Polunina, Inna Dyubanok, Svetlana Terentieva, Yekaterina Solovyova, Svetlana Tkachyova, Alexandra Kapustina, Galina Skiba

**Slovakia** (Miroslav Karafiat, coach) GK—Zuzana Tomcikova, Romana Kiapesova, Jana Budajova—Petra Orszaghova, Jana Kapustova, Barbora Bremova, Romana Vargova, Maria Herichova, Petra Jurcova, Anna Dzurnakova, Martina Velickova, Janka Culikova, Iveta Karafiatova, Michaela Matejova, Nikola Gapova, Barbora Kezmarska, Petra Pravlikova, Maria Gajdosova, Nicol Cupkova, Alica Mihalikova, Lenka Srokova

**Sweden** (Niclas Hogberg, coach) GK—Sara Grahn, Kim Martin, Valentina Lizana—Elin Holmlov, Frida Nevalainen, Jenni Asserholt, Johanna Fallman, Johanna Malmstrom, Erika Holst, Tina Enstrom, Lina Wester, Pernilla Winberg, Linea Backman, Anna Borgqvist, Annie Svedin, Rebecca Stenberg, Emma Eliasson, Gunilla Andersson, Erika Grahm, Emma Nordin, Danijela Rundqvist

**Switzerland** (Rene Kammerer, coach) GK—Sophie Anthamatten, Dominique Slongo, Florence Schelling—Katrin Nabholz, Julia Marty, Darcia Leimgruber, Stefanie Marty, Nicole Bullo, Angela Frautschi, Sara Benz, Christine Meier, Lara Stalder, Evelina Raselli, Rahel Michielin, Kathrin Lehmann, Melanie Hafliger, Anja Stiefel, Stefanie Wyss, Sandra Thalmann, Sabrina Zollinger, Phoebe Stanz

**United States** (Katey Stone, coach) GK—Molly Schaus, Brianne McLaughlin, Jessie Vetter—Jen Schoullis, Angela Ruggiero, Monique Lamoureux-Kolls, Caitlin Cahow, Molly Engstrom, Meghan Duggan, Jenny Potter, Julie Chu, Brianna Decker, Anne Schleper, Kelli Stack, Jocelyne Lamoureux, Gigi Marvin, Hilary Knight, Kacey Bellamy, Josephine Pucci, Kendall Coyne, Kelley Steadman

## 14th WOMEN'S WORLD CHAMPIONSHIP
## Burlington, Vermont, United States
## April 7-14, 2012

**Final Placing**

Gold........Canada
Silver......United States
Bronze....Switzerland
4th..........Finland
5th .........Sweden
6th .........Russia
7th .........Germany^
8th .........Slovakia+

^promoted from Division I in 2011
+demoted to Division I for 2013

**Tournament Format**

Eight teams were placed in two groups and played a round-robin series within each group. For the first time, the groups were arranged vertically, not horizontally, so the top-ranked teams played in Group A and the lower-ranked in Group B. All teams from Group A advanced to the playoffs. The top two went directly to the semi-finals while the bottom two played a crossover quarter-finals with the top two from Group B. The bottom two in Group B played a best two-of-three series in the Relegation Round.

**Results & Final Standings**
**GROUP A**

| | GP | W | OTW | OTL | L | GF | GA | P |
|---|---|---|---|---|---|---|---|---|
| United States | 3 | 3 | 0 | 0 | 0 | 29 | 2 | 9 |
| Canada | 3 | 2 | 0 | 0 | 1 | 19 | 12 | 6 |
| Finland | 3 | 1 | 0 | 0 | 2 | 7 | 18 | 3 |
| Russia | 3 | 0 | 0 | 0 | 3 | 5 | 28 | 0 |

April 7 Finland 5 Russia 4
April 7 United States 9 Canada 2
April 8 Canada 3 Finland 2
April 8 United States 9 Russia 0
April 10 Canada 14 Russia 1
April 10 United States 11 Finland 0

**GROUP B**

| | GP | W | OTW | OTL | L | GF | GA | P |
|---|---|---|---|---|---|---|---|---|
| Switzerland | 3 | 2 | 0 | 0 | 1 | 7 | 6 | 6 |
| Sweden | 3 | 1 | 1 | 0 | 1 | 9 | 5 | 5 |
| Germany | 3 | 1 | 0 | 1 | 1 | 6 | 8 | 4 |
| Slovakia | 3 | 1 | 0 | 0 | 2 | 6 | 9 | 3 |

April 7 Sweden 5 Slovakia 1
April 7 Germany 3 Switzerland 2
April 8 Sweden 2 Germany 1 (Elin Holmlov 0:24 OT)
April 8 Switzerland 2 Slovakia 1
April 10 Switzerland 3 Sweden 2
April 10 Slovakia 4 Germany 2

**RELEGATION ROUND**

| | GP | W | OTW | OTL | L | GF | GA | P |
|---|---|---|---|---|---|---|---|---|
| Germany | 2 | 1 | 1 | 0 | 0 | 5 | 2 | 5 |
| Slovakia | 2 | 0 | 0 | 1 | 1 | 2 | 5 | 1 |

April 11 Germany 2 Slovakia 1 (5:00 OT/GWS—Manuela Anwander)
April 13 Germany 3 Slovakia 1

**FIFTH-PLACE GAME**
April 13 Sweden 2 Russia 1 (Elin Holmlov 0:34 OT)

**PLAYOFFS**
**QUARTER-FINALS**
April 11 Switzerland 5 Russia 2
April 11 Finland 2 Sweden 1

**SEMI-FINALS**
April 13 Canada 5 Finland 1
April 13 United States 10 Switzerland 0

**BRONZE MEDAL GAME**
April 14 Switzerland 6 Finland 2

**GOLD MEDAL GAME**
April 14 Canada 5 United States 4 (Caroline Ouellette 1:50 OT)

**Rosters**

**Canada** (Ben Church, coach) GK—Shannon Szabados, Charline Labonte, Genevieve Lacasse—Rebecca Johnston, Hayley Wickenheiser, Jayna Hefford, Meghan Agosta, Marie-Philip Poulin-Nadeau, Cherie Piper, Haley Irwin, Tessa Bonhomme, Meaghan Mikkelson, Gillian Apps, Jennifer Wakefield, Caroline Ouellette, Natalie Spooner, Sarah Vaillancourt, Jocelyne Larocque, Tara Watchorn, Bobbi Jo Slusar, Catherine Ward

**Finland** (Pekka Hamalainen, coach) GK—Anna Vanhatalo, Maija Hassinen, Noora Raty—Mira Huhta, Rosa Lindstedt, Jenni Hiirikoski, Mira Jalosuo, Tea Villila, Essi Hallvar, Annina Rajahuhta, Susanna Tapani, Niina Makinen, Minnamari Tuominen, Terhi Mertanen, Michelle Karvinen, Tanja Niskanen, Pia Lund, Tiina Saarimaki, Anne Helin, Anne Tuomanen, Karoliina Rantamaki

**Germany** (Peter Kathan, coach) GK—Viona Harrer, Jennifer Harss, Ivonne Schroder—Kerstin Spielberger, Jessica Hammerl, Manuela Anwander, Bettina Evers, Nina Kamenik, Julia Zorn, Anja Weisser, Britta Schroder, Susann Gotz, Andrea Lanzl, Rebecca Graeve, Sara Seiler, Susanne Fellner, Daria Gleissner, Ronja Richter, Tanja Eisenschmid, Lisa Schuster, Franziska Busch, Monika Bittner, Sarah Weyand

**Russia** (Valentin Gureyev, coach) GK—Anna Prugova, Valentina Ostrovlyanchik, Margarita Monakhova—Alyona Khomich, Olga Sosina, Iya Gavrilova, Alexandra Vafina, Marina Sergina, Olga Permyakova, Yekaterina Smolentseva, Anna Shukina, Olga Semenets, Tatyana Burina, Yekaterina Lebedeva, Zoya Polunina, Inna Dyubanok, Svetlana Terentieva, Yekaterina Solovyeva, Svetlana Tkachyova, Alexandra Kapustina, Galina Skiba

**Slovakia** (Miroslav Karafiat, coach) GK—Zuzana Tomcikova, Romana Kiapesova, Jana Budajova—Petra Orszaghova, Jana Kapustova, Barbora Bremova, Romana Vargova, Maria Herichova, Petra Jurcova, Anna Dzurnakova, Martina Velickova, Janka Culikova, Iveta Karafiatova, Michaela Matejova, Nikola Gapova, Barbora Kezmarska, Petra Pravlikova, Maria Gajdosova, Nicol Cupkova, Alica Mihalikova, Lenka Srokova

**Sweden** (Niclas Hogberg, coach) GK—Sara Grahn, Kim Martin, Valentina Lizana—Elin Holmlov, Frida Nevalainen, Jenny Asserholt, Johanna Fallman, Johanna Malmstrom, Erika Holst, Tina Enstrom, Lina Wester, Pernilla Winberg, Linea Backman, Anna Borgqvist, Annie Svedin, Rebecca Stenberg, Emma Eliasson, Gunilla Andersson, Erika Grahm, Emma Nordin, Danijela Rundqvist

**Switzerland** (Rene Kammerer, coach) GK—Sophie Anthamatten, Dominique Slongo, Florence Schelling—Katrin Nabholz, Julia Marty, Darcia Leimgruber, Stefanie Marty, Nicole Bullo, Angela Frautschi, Sara Benz, Christine Meier, Lara Stalder, Evelina Raselli, Rahel Michielin, Kathrin Lehmann, Melanie Hafliger, Anja Stiefel, Stefanie Wyss, Sandra Thalmann, Sabrina Zollinger, Phoebe Stanz

**United States** (Katey Stone, coach) GK—Molly Schaus, Brianne McLaughlin, Jesse Vetter—Jen Schoullis, Angela Ruggiero, Monique Lamoureux-Kolls, Caitlin Cahow, Molly Engstrom, Meghan Duggan, Jenny Potter, Julie Chu, Brianna Decker, Anne Schleper, Kelli Stack, Jocelyne Lamoureux, Gigi Marvin, Hilary Knight, Kacey Bellamy, Josehpine Pucci, Kendall Coyne, Kelley Steadman

*Canada and the United States staged one of the finest women's hockey games ever played, the former coming out on top, 5-4, to win the 2012 Women's World Championship for the first time since 2007. Photo: Dave Sandford / HHOF-IIHF Images.*

# U18 WOMEN'S WORLD CHAMPIONSHIP

## 1st U18 WOMEN'S WORLD CHAMPIONSHIP
**January 7-12, 2008**
**Calgary, Canada**

**Final Placing**

| | | | |
|---|---|---|---|
| Gold | United States | 5th | Germany |
| Silver | Canada | 6th | Finland |
| Bronze | Czech Republic | 7th | Switzerland |
| 4th | Sweden | 8th | Russia |

**Tournament Format**
The eight teams were divided into two groups of four and played a round robin within each group. The top two teams advanced to the playoffs where they played a cross-over semi-finals, while the bottom two teams played a series of placement games.

**Results & Standings**
**PRELIMINARY ROUND**
**GROUP A**

| | GP | W | OTW | OTL | L | GF | GA | P |
|---|---|---|---|---|---|---|---|---|
| Canada | 3 | 3 | 0 | 0 | 0 | 38 | 3 | 9 |
| Czech Republic | 3 | 2 | 0 | 0 | 1 | 10 | 16 | 6 |
| Germany | 3 | 1 | 0 | 0 | 2 | 7 | 15 | 3 |
| Finland | 3 | 0 | 0 | 0 | 3 | 5 | 26 | 0 |

| | | |
|---|---|---|
| January 7 | Germany 4 | Finland 2 |
| January 7 | Canada 11 | Czech Republic 2 |
| January 8 | Czech Republic 5 | Finland 3 |
| January 8 | Canada 10 | Germany 1 |
| January 9 | Czech Republic 3 | Germany 2 |
| January 9 | Canada 17 | Finland 0 |

**GROUP B**

| | GP | W | OTW | OTL | L | GF | GA | P |
|---|---|---|---|---|---|---|---|---|
| United States | 3 | 3 | 0 | 0 | 0 | 28 | 2 | 9 |
| Sweden | 3 | 2 | 0 | 0 | 1 | 20 | 7 | 6 |
| Switzerland | 3 | 1 | 0 | 0 | 2 | 7 | 17 | 3 |
| Russia | 3 | 0 | 0 | 0 | 3 | 2 | 31 | 0 |

| | | |
|---|---|---|
| January 7 | Sweden 4 | Switzerland 1 |
| January 7 | United States 11 | Russia 0 |
| January 8 | Sweden 14 | Russia 0 |
| January 8 | United States 11 | Switzerland 0 |
| January 9 | Switzerland 6 | Russia 2 |
| January 9 | United States 6 | Sweden 2 |

**PLACEMENT GAMES**
**QUALIFYING ROUND**

| | | |
|---|---|---|
| January 11 | Germany 2 | Russia 1 |
| January 11 | Finland 7 | Switzerland 2 |

**5TH-PLACE GAME**
January 12 Germany 4 Finland 1

**7TH-PLACE GAME**
January 12 Switzerland 4 Russia 1

**PLAYOFFS**
**SEMI-FINALS**

| | | |
|---|---|---|
| January 11 | United States 8 | Czech Republic 0 |
| January 11 | Canada 7 | Sweden 1 |

**BRONZE MEDAL GAME**
January 12 Czech Republic 4 Sweden 2

**GOLD MEDAL GAME**
January 12 United States 5 Canada 2

**Rosters**
**Canada** (Melody Davidson, coach) GK—Delayne Brian, Amanda Mazzotta—Samantha Watt, Tara Watchorn, Lauriane Rougeau, Brittany Haverstock, Jessica Jones, Leslie Oles, Rebecca Hewett, Marie-Philip Poulin, Brianne Jenner, Carolyne Prevost, Bailey Bram, Chelsea Karpenko, Laura McIntosh, Camille Dumais, Catherine White, Audrey Cournoyer, Natalie Spooner, Laura Fortino

**Czech Republic** (Tomas Vytisk, coach) GK—Katerina Becevova, Monika Pencikova (did not play)—Laura Peskova, Barbora Pekarkova, Alena Polenska, Andrea Vosykova, Lucie Novakova, Sabina Hajdova, Lucie Povova, Nikola Horakova, Nikola Dvorakova, Katerina Mrazova, Pavlina Horalkova, Petra Vojtechova, Tereza Stastna, Martina Krupkova, Dominika Navratilova, Denisa Ajchlerova, Lucie Manhartova, Nikola Tomigova

**Finland** (Seppo Karjalainen, coach) GK—Piia Raty, Jenna Juutilainen—Karoliina Maenpanen, Noora Jaakkola, Tiina Saarimaki, Tea Villila, Lotta Haarala, Linda Valimaki, Hanna-Riikka Turpeinen, Erika Aunio, Jutta Stoltenberg, Minnamari Tuominen, Tanja Niskanen, Niina Makinen, Susanna Ratinen, Maiju Yliniemi, Johanna Juutilainen, Pia Lund, Noora Sirvio, Elisa Rytkonen

**Germany** (Peter Kathan, coach) GK—Julia Zorn, Janine Steeger—Jenny Tamas, Carina Spuhler, Miriam Novotny, Michelle Grunewald, Alexandra Kuhn, Carina Hoffmann, Caroline Sauer, Yvonne Rothemund, Stephanie Trager, Tanja Golebiowski, Vanessa Anselm, Anja Weisser, Miriam Pokopec, Maike Hanke, Isabell Bruckl, Manuela Anwander, Angela Kohnle, Jessica Geml

**Russia** (Alexander Viryasov, coach) GK—Anna Vinogradova, Yulia Leskina—Alexandra Popova, Elizaveta Monakhova, Olga Bashurova, Katya Frolova, Zoya Polunina, Yekaterina Solovyova, Elina Mitrofanova, Alexandra Vafina, Anna Padyanova, Yekaterina Ananina, Yulia Vasyukova, Edit Spasich, Anna Kozlovskikh, Olga Sosina, Maria Kirilenko, Alexandra Vovrushko, Inna Dyubanok, Yelena Guslistaya

**Sweden** (Niklas Hogberg, coach) GK—Valentina Lizana, Hanna Emanuelsson—Johanna Fallman, Emma Holmbom, Emma Nordin, Annie Svedin, Miranda Tjarnstrom, Madeleine Ostling, Tina Enstrom, Linnea Backman, Cecilia Ostberg, Isabelle Jordansson, Fanny Rask, Deborah Eckefjord, Erika Grahm, Anna Borgqvist, Lisa Johansson, Elin Uusitalo, Klara Myren, Angelica Ostlund

**Switzerland** (Jorg Toggwiler, coach) GK—Sophie Anthamatten, Jessica Muller (did not play)—Sandra Thalmann, Nadja Hochuli, Fabiola Bachmann, Sandy Rigoli, Laura Benz, Seraina Hablutzel, Anja Stiefel, Lea Schmid, Sara Benz, Camille Balanche, Monika Waidacher, Nina Waidacher, Laura Muller, Evelina Raselli, Rahel Michielin, Bianca Landis, Aline Heiz, Andrea Fischer

**United States** (Katey Stone, coach) GK—Alyssa Grogan, Rebecca Ruegsegger—Blake Bolden, Kasey Boucher, Alev Kelter, Anne Schleper, Kelly Wild, Kate Bacon, Ashley Cottrell, Kendall Coyne, Brooke Ammerman, Brianna Decker, Sasha Sherry, Sarah Erickson, Kelley Steadman, Amanda Kessel, Meagan Mangene, Madison Packer, Corey Stearns, Elizabeth Turgeon

## 2nd U18 WOMEN'S WORLD CHAMPIONSHIP
**January 1-10, 2009**
**Fussen, Germany**

**Final Placing**

| | | | |
|---|---|---|---|
| Gold | United States | 5th | Finland |
| Silver | Canada | 6th | Germany |
| Bronze | Sweden | 7th | Russia |
| 4th | Czech Republic | 8th | Switzerland* |

*demoted to Division I for 2010

**Tournament Format**
The eight teams were divided into two groups of four and played a round robin within each group. The top two teams advanced to the playoffs where they played a cross-over semi-finals, while the bottom two teams played a series of placement games.

**Results & Standings**
**PRELIMINARY ROUND**
**GROUP A**

| | GP | W | OTW | OTL | L | GF | GA | P |
|---|---|---|---|---|---|---|---|---|
| United States | 3 | 3 | 0 | 0 | 0 | 37 | 2 | 9 |
| Sweden | 3 | 2 | 0 | 0 | 1 | 16 | 11 | 6 |
| Russia | 3 | 1 | 0 | 0 | 2 | 6 | 25 | 3 |
| Germany | 3 | 0 | 0 | 0 | 3 | 3 | 24 | 0 |

| | | |
|---|---|---|
| January 5 | United States 17 | Russia 0 |
| January 5 | Sweden 8 | Germany 1 |
| January 6 | Sweden 6 | Russia 1 |
| January 6 | United States 11 | Germany 0 |
| January 7 | United States 9 | Sweden 2 |
| January 7 | Russia 5 | Germany 2 |

**GROUP B**

| | GP | W | OTW | OTL | L | GF | GA | P |
|---|---|---|---|---|---|---|---|---|
| Canada | 3 | 3 | 0 | 0 | 0 | 35 | 1 | 9 |
| Czech Republic | 3 | 1 | 0 | 1 | 1 | 8 | 18 | 4 |
| Switzerland | 3 | 1 | 0 | 0 | 2 | 8 | 26 | 3 |
| Finland | 3 | 0 | 1 | 0 | 2 | 5 | 11 | 2 |

| | | |
|---|---|---|
| January 5 | Finland 2 | Czech Republic 1 (5:00 OT/GWS—Susanna Tapani) |
| January 5 | Canada 16 | Switzerland 1 |
| January 6 | Czech Republic 7 | Switzerland 3 |
| January 6 | Canada 6 | Finland 0 |
| January 7 | Switzerland 4 | Finland 3 |
| January 7 | Canada 13 | Czech Republic 0 |

**PLACEMENT GAMES**

| | | |
|---|---|---|
| January 9 | Germany 2 | Switzerland 1 (5:00 OT/GWS—Manuela Anwander) |
| January 9 | Finland 2 | Russia 1 (Susanna Tapani 3:40 OT) |

**5TH-PLACE GAME**

| | | |
|---|---|---|
| January 10 | Finland 2 | Germany 1 |

**7TH-PLACE GAME**

| | | |
|---|---|---|
| January 10 | Russia 3 | Switzerland 2 (5:00 OT/GWS—Olga Sosina) |

**PLAYOFFS**
**SEMI-FINALS**

| | | |
|---|---|---|
| January 9 | Canada 6 | Sweden 1 |
| January 9 | United States 18 | Czech Republic 0 |

**BRONZE MEDAL GAME**

| | | |
|---|---|---|
| January 10 | Sweden 9 | Czech Republic 1 |

**GOLD MEDAL GAME**

| | | |
|---|---|---|
| January 10 | United States 3 | Canada 2 (Kendall Coyne 6:47 OT) |

**Rosters**

**Canada** (Stephanie White, coach) GK—Roxanne Douville, Cassie Seguin—Brigette Lacquette, Stefanie McKeough, Rayna Cruickshank, Casandra Langan, Saige Pacholok, Christine Bestland, Breann Frykas, Marie-Philip Poulin, Brianne Jenner, Brittany Phillips, Kaleigh Fratkin, Jessica Campbell, Melodie Daoust, Jamie Lee Rattray, Laurie Kingsbury, Jillian Saulnier, Laura Fortino, Jessica Wong

**Czech Republic** (Tomas Vytisk, coach) GK—Monika Pencikova, Karolina Simunkova—Laura Peskova, Michaela Jackova, Pavlina Horalkova, Lucie Novakova, Denisa Ajchlerova, Lucie Povova, Katerina Solnickova, Katerina Pipkova, Marketa Sramkova, Nikola Tomigova, Dominika Navratilova, Petra Vojtechova, Martina Krupkova, Lucie Manhartova, Katerina Mrazova, Karolina Kovarova, Jana Fialova, Barbora Pekarkova

**Finland** (Pekka Hamalainen, coach) GK—Susanna Airaksinen, Vilma Vaattovaara (did not play)—Karoliina Maenpanen, Isa Rahunen, Noora Jaakkola, Tiina Saarimaki, Tea Villila, Lotta Haarala, Salla Rantanen, Susanna Tapani, Milla Heikkinen, Jutta Stoltenberg, Roosa Kujala, Heidi Hallikainen, Tanja Niskanen, Niina Makinen, Annukka Kinisjarvi, Reetta Aralinna, Tytti Lintula, Elisa Rytkonen

**Germany** (Werner Schneider, coach) GK—Jule Flotgen, Janna Ramajzl—Michaela Gritl, Miriam Novotny, Alexandra Kuhn, Maike Hanke, Jacqueline Janzen, Yvonne Rothemund, Tanja Eisenschmid, Anja Weisser, Miriam Pokopec, Tanja Golebiowski, Stefanie Wolfgruber, Ines Strohmaier, Katharina Gerstmeir, Manuela Anwander, Jessica Geml, Daria Gleissner, Vanessa Anselm, Rebecca Graeve

**Russia** (Yuri Rychkov, coach) GK—Anna Prugova, Yulia Leskina—Anastasia Yudina, Alexandra Vovrushko, Anastasia Mishlanova, Elizaveta Monakhova, Anastasia Shondra, Yekaterina Solovyova, Maria Vasilieva, Elina Mitrofanova, Anna Padyanova, Kristina Sherstyuk, Yekaterina Ananina, Tatyana Leushina, Arina Zvezdina, Olga Sosina, Yana Vershinina, Yekaterina Skorodumova, Edit Spasich, Maria Pechnikova

**Sweden** (Niclas Hogberg, coach) GK—Josephin Lennstrom, Madeleine Schelander—Emilia Bergius, Linnea Backman, Josefine Holmgren, Emma Nordin, Madeleine Siggelin-Alstermark, Annie Svdein, Tina Enstrom, Anna Borgfeldt, Cecilia Ostberg, Isabelle Jordansson, Fanny Rask, Erika Grahm, Anna Borgqvist, Lisa Johansson, Melinda Olsson, Klara Myren, Angelica Ostlund, Johanna Olofsson

**Switzerland** (Jorg Toggwiler, coach) GK—Sophie Anthamatten, Sarah Kung—Sandra Thalmann, Sarah Forster, Fabiola Bachmann, Jana Heuscher, Laura Benz, Nicole Riedi, Sarina Wuffli, Nathalie Roth, Sabrina Zollinger, Seraina Frautschi, Sara Benz, Nicole Schneider, Simona Teggi, Nina Waidacher, Laura Muller, Evelina Raselli, Elodie Genilloud, Alea Erb

**United States** (Mark Johnson, coach) GK—Alex Rigsby, Corinne Boyles—Kate Brock, Megan Bozek, Blake Bolden, Caroline Campbell, Alev Kelter, Jacqueline Young, Taylor Wasylk, Brittany Ammerman, Brianna Decker, Jillian Dempsey, Lyndsey Fry, Amanda Pelkey, Jamie Kenyon, Amanda Kessel, Kendall Coyne, Alex Nelson, Madison Packer, Meagan Mangene

## 3rd U18 WOMEN'S WORLD CHAMPIONSHIP
## March 27-April 3, 2010
## Chicago, United States

**Final Placing**

| | |
|---|---|
| Gold ........Canada | 5th .........Finland |
| Silver ......United States | 6th .........Japan^ |
| Bronze ....Sweden | 7th .........Czech Republic |
| 4th..........Germany | 8th .........Russia* |

^promoted from Division I in 2009
*demoted to Division I for 2011

**Tournament Format**

The eight teams were divided into two groups of four and played a round robin within each group. The top two teams advanced to the playoffs where they played a cross-over semi-finals, while the bottom team in each group played a best-of-three for relegation.

**Results & Standings**
**PRELIMINARY ROUND**
**GROUP A**

| | GP | W | OTW | OTL | L | GF | GA | P |
|---|---|---|---|---|---|---|---|---|
| United States | 3 | 3 | 0 | 0 | 0 | 31 | 1 | 9 |
| Finland | 3 | 1 | 0 | 0 | 2 | 6 | 9 | 3 |
| Japan | 3 | 1 | 0 | 0 | 2 | 7 | 17 | 3 |
| Czech Republic | 3 | 1 | 0 | 0 | 2 | 6 | 23 | 3 |

| | | |
|---|---|---|
| March 27 | Finland 5 | Czech Republic 1 |
| March 27 | United States 11 | Japan 1 |
| March 28 | Czech Republic 5 | Japan 3 |
| March 28 | United States 5 | Finland 0 |
| March 30 | Japan 3 | Finland 1 |
| March 30 | United States 15 | Czech Republic 0 |

**GROUP B**

| | GP | W | OTW | OTL | L | GF | GA | P |
|---|---|---|---|---|---|---|---|---|
| Canada | 3 | 3 | 0 | 0 | 0 | 29 | 3 | 9 |
| Sweden | 3 | 2 | 0 | 0 | 1 | 9 | 13 | 6 |
| Germany | 3 | 1 | 0 | 0 | 2 | 7 | 21 | 3 |
| Russia | 3 | 0 | 0 | 0 | 3 | 5 | 13 | 0 |

| | | |
|---|---|---|
| March 27 | Canada 6 | Russia 3 |
| March 27 | Sweden 5 | Germany 4 |
| March 28 | Sweden 4 | Russia 1 |
| March 28 | Canada 15 | Germany 0 |
| March 30 | Germany 3 | Russia 1 |
| March 30 | Canada 8 | Sweden 0 |

**RELEGATION ROUND (BEST-OF-THREE)**

| | | |
|---|---|---|
| March 31 | Czech Republic 5 | Russia 0 |
| April 2 | Czech Republic 3 | Russia 1 |

**5TH-PLACE GAME**

| | | |
|---|---|---|
| April 2 | Finland 4 | Japan 1 |

**PLAYOFFS**
**QUARTER-FINALS**

| | | |
|---|---|---|
| March 31 | Sweden 2 | Japan 1 |
| March 31 | Germany 2 | Finland 1 (Manuela Anwander 6:21 OT) |

**SEMI-FINALS**

| | | |
|---|---|---|
| April 2 | Canada 10 | Germany 0 |
| April 2 | United States 5 | Sweden 0 |

**BRONZE MEDAL GAME**

| | | |
|---|---|---|
| April 3 | Sweden 7 | Germany 3 |

**GOLD MEDAL GAME**

| | | |
|---|---|---|
| April 3 | Canada 5 | United States 4 (Jessica Campbell 3:10 OT) |

**Rosters**

**Canada** (Dan Church, coach) GK—Carmen MacDonald, Erica Howe—Shannon Doyle, Caitlin MacDonald, Cassandra Poudrier, Jessica Campbell, Carly Mercer, Christine Bestland, Emily Fulton, Erin Ambrose, Kelly Terry, Jenna McParland, Jamie Lee Rattray, Melodie Daoust, Laurie Kingsbury, Jillian Saulnier, Hannah Armstrong, Sarah Davis, Brigette Lacquette, Hayleigh Cudmore

**Czech Republic** (Tomas Vytisk, coach) GK—Veronika Hladikova, Lenka Craigova—Marketa Vytiskova, Stepanka Eibinova, Katerina Solnickova, Lucie Povova, Michaela Novakova, Denisa Krizova, Veronika Kuzelova, Nikola Horakova, Adela Maresova, Adela Kubatova, Klara Hudeckova, Katerina Kaplanova, Martina Vonkova, Katerina Mrazova, Karolina Kovarova, Jana Fialova, Barbora Pekarkova, Michaela Jackova

**Finland** (Harri Laurila, coach) GK—Susanna Airaksinen, Isabella Portnoj—Johanna Koivisto, Karoliina Maenpanen, Isa Rahunen, Katja Nurmesniemi, Jenni Oinonen, Salla Rantanen, Susanna Tapani, Milla Heikkinen, Emma Ritari, Anni Kettunen, Heidi Hallikainen, Tanja Niskanen, Niina Makinen, Katariina Laitila, Tytti Lintula, Julia Rouru, Maijaliisa Leppo, Janna Jokinen

**Germany** (Peter Kathan, coach) GK—Nadja Gruber, Stephanie Hruby—Miriam Novotny, Katharina Gerstmeir, Jacqueline Janzen, Rebecca Graeve, Yvonne Rothemund, Julia Seitz, Anna-Maria Fiegert, Tanja Eisenschmid, Miriam Pokopec, Kira Kanders, Ines Strohmaier, Marie Delarbre, Gesa Dinges, Manuela Anwander, Daria Gleissner, Nadine Marx, Valerie Offermann, Tatjana Voigt

**Japan** (Yuji Iizuka, coach) GK—Shizuka Takahashi, Ai Tokoro—Rina Takeda, Itsuki Baba, Miho Shishiuchi, Risa Ukita, Shiori Koike, Ayaka Toko, Chiho Osawa, Nene Sugisawa, Mai Morii, Runa Moritake, Mika Hori, Moeko Fujimoto, Nodoka Abe, Naho Terashima, Ami Suzuki, Yukina Ota, Sawako Takahashi, Fuka Ishiura

**Russia** (Yuri Rychkov, coach) GK—Anna Prugova, Margarita Monakhova—Elvira Markova, Alexandra Vovrushko, Alexandra Tsirkunova, Tatyana Shibanova, Yulia Lavelina, Elina Mitrofanova, Lyudmila Belyakova, Yevgenia Dyupina, Xenia Baybakova, Maria Bukshevannaya, Olga Sosina, Yana Vershinina, Yekaterina Skorodumova, Tatyana Akmanayeva, Angelina Goncharenko, Lilit Karoyan, Maria Pechnikova, Anna Shibanova

**Sweden** (Niclas Hogberg, coach) GK—Sofia Carlstrom, Annika Ferngren—Cajsa Lillback, Tami Jacobs, Josefine Holmgren, Lina Backlin, Madeleine Siggelin-Alstermark, Fanny Akesson, Anna Borgfeldt, Linnea Hedin, Rebecca Stenberg, Emelie Johansson, Astrid Lilja, Lisa Johansson, Melinda Olsson, Michelle Lowenhielm, Hanna Astrom, Emmy Alasalmi, Lina Wester, Lisa Hedengren

**United States** (Katie King, coach) GK—Alex Rigsby, Aubree Moore—Emily Pfalzer, Gabie Figueroa, Alexandra Carpenter, Melissa Bizzari, Marissa Gedman, Taylor Wasylk, Brittany Ammerman, Meghan Lorence, Michelle Picard, Lyndsey Fry, Amanda Pelkey, Haley Skarupa, Zoe Hickel, Kendall Coyne, Stephanie Anderson, Meagan Mangene, Rachael Bona, Jordan Slavin

## 4th U18 WOMEN'S WORLD CHAMPIONSHIP
## January 1-8, 2011
## Stockholm, Sweden

**Final Placing**

Gold ........United States
Silver ......Canada
Bronze ....Finland
4th ..........Czech Republic
5th .........Sweden
6th .........Germany
7th .........Switzerland^
8th .........Japan+

^promoted from Division I in 2010
+demoted to Division I for 2012

**Tournament Format**

The eight teams were divided into two groups of four and played a round robin within each group. The top two teams advanced to the playoffs where they played a cross-over semi-finals, while the bottom two teams played a series of placement games

**Results & Standings**

**PRELIMINARY ROUND**

**GROUP A**

| | GP | W | OTW | OTL | L | GF | GA | P |
|---|---|---|---|---|---|---|---|---|
| Canada | 3 | 3 | 0 | 0 | 0 | 23 | 2 | 9 |
| Germany | 3 | 2 | 0 | 0 | 1 | 6 | 10 | 6 |
| Finland | 3 | 1 | 0 | 0 | 2 | 4 | 8 | 3 |
| Switzerland | 3 | 0 | 0 | 0 | 3 | 4 | 17 | 0 |

| | | |
|---|---|---|
| January 1 | Canada 9 | Switzerland 1 |
| January 1 | Germany 1 | Finland 0 |
| January 2 | Germany 4 | Switzerland 2 |
| January 2 | Canada 6 | Finland 0 |
| January 4 | Finland 4 | Switzerland 1 |
| January 4 | Canada 8 | Germany 1 |

**GROUP B**

| | GP | W | OTW | OTL | L | GF | GA | P |
|---|---|---|---|---|---|---|---|---|
| United States | 3 | 3 | 0 | 0 | 0 | 28 | 1 | 9 |
| Sweden | 3 | 2 | 0 | 0 | 1 | 5 | 13 | 6 |
| Czech Republic | 3 | 1 | 0 | 0 | 2 | 6 | 15 | 3 |
| Japan | 3 | 0 | 0 | 0 | 3 | 3 | 13 | 0 |

| | | |
|---|---|---|
| January 1 | United States 11 | Czech Republic 0 |
| January 1 | Sweden 2 | Japan 1 |
| January 2 | United States 7 | Japan 1 |
| January 2 | Sweden 3 | Czech Republic 2 |
| January 4 | Czech Republic 4 | Japan 1 |
| January 4 | United States 10 | Sweden 0 |

**RELEGATION ROUND**

| | GP | W | OTW | OTL | L | GF | GA | P |
|---|---|---|---|---|---|---|---|---|
| Switzerland | 3 | 2 | 0 | 0 | 1 | 10 | 6 | 6 |
| Japan | 3 | 1 | 0 | 0 | 2 | 6 | 10 | 3 |

| | | |
|---|---|---|
| January 5 | Switzerland 4 | Japan 0 |
| January 7 | Japan 5 | Switzerland 1 |
| January 8 | Switzerland 5 | Japan 1 |

**FIFTH-PLACE GAME**

January 7 Sweden 2 Germany 0

**PLAYOFFS**

**QUARTER-FINALS**

| | | |
|---|---|---|
| January 5 | Czech Republic 3 | Germany 1 |
| January 5 | Finland 3 | Sweden 2 (Sanna Valkama 1:46 OT) |

**SEMI-FINALS**

| | | |
|---|---|---|
| January 7 | Canada 6 | Finland 1 |
| January 7 | United States 14 | Czech Republic 1 |

**BRONZE MEDAL GAME**

January 8 Finland 3 Czech Republic 0

**GOLD MEDAL GAME**

January 8 United States 5 Canada 2

**Rosters**

**Canada** (Sarah Hodges, coach) GK—Amanda Makela, Ann-Renee Desbiens—Jennifer Shields, Sarah Edney, Katarina Zgraja, Emily Fulton, Gabrielle Davidson, Shelby Bram, Erin Ambrose, Katy Josephs, Meghan Dufault, Sarah Robson, Nicole Kosta, Cayley Mercer, Cydney Roesler, Gina Repaci, Hailey Browne, Rebecca Kohler, Sarah MacDonnell, Laura Stacey

**Czech Republic** (Tomas Vytisk, coach) GK—Veronika Hladikova, Lenka Craigova—Aneta Tejralova, Marketa Vytiskova, Jana Fialova, Stepanka Eibinova, Katerina Vanouckova, Sara Sidilkova, Adela Kubatova, Katerina Solnickova, Denisa Krizova, Veronika Kuzelova, Veronika Jirsova, Klara Hudeckova, Katerina Kaplanova, Klara Chmelova, Adriena Pecinova, Martina Vonkova, Karolina Kovarova, Michaela Novakova

**Finland** (Juuso Toivola, coach) GK—Isabella Portnoj, Tiina Ranne—Johanna Koivisto, Anna Kilponen, Isa Rahunen, Katja Nurmesniemi, Ella Pietikainen, Jenni Oinonen, Susanna Tapani, Milla Heikkinen, Anni Kettunen, Venla Kotkaslahti, Suvi Ollikainen, Anni Rantanen, Christa Alanko, Marianne Tanninen, Noora Tulus, Salla-Maaria Raitala, Saana Valkama, Jenna Suokko

**Germany** (Werner Schneider, coach) GK—Franziska Albl, Nadja Gruber—Theresa Wagner, Lusia Brugger, Jacqueline Janzen, Rebecca Graeve, Karina Port, Julia Seitz, Anna-Maria Fiegert, Tanja Eisenschmid, Bianca Laggerbauer, Katja-Lisa Engel, Eva Byszio, Saskia Selzer, Marie Delarbre, Theresa Fritz, Daria Gleissner, Jennifer Rau, Valerie Offermann, Kerstin Spielberger

**Japan** (Yuji Iizuka, coach) GK—Shizuka Takahashi, Ai Tokoro—Shiori Koike, Rina Takeda, Riko Yamaya, Risa Sugawara, Ayaka Toko, Moe Kato, Mai Morii, Nodoka Abe, Risa Ukita, Nene Sugisawa, Naho Terashima, Fuka Ishiura, Yui Sawade, Seika Yuyama, Mizuho Nakagawa, Rina Saeki, Runa Moritake, Momoka Odaira

**Sweden** (Henrik Cedergren, coach) GK—Sofia Carlstrom, Elin Moberg—Cajsa Lillback, Josefine Holmgren, Anna Kjellbin, Lina Backlin, Emma Martinsson, Caroline Markstrom, Anna Borgfeldt, Anna Daniels, Linnea Hedin, Felicia Karlsson, Linn Peterson, Elin Johansson, Cornelia Gillberg, Maria Lind, Michelle Lowenhielm, Olivia Nystrom, Teddie Falkeborn, Anna Johansson

**Switzerland** (Dominik Schaer, coach) GK—Tamara Klossner, Sandra Heim—Selina Wuttke, Sarah Forster, Nadine Hofstetter, Karin Williner, Celine Abgottspon, Lara Stalder, Livia Altmann, Sabrina Zollinger, Jana Bigler, Nicole Schneider, Romy Eggimann, Stephanie Lehner, Mariko Dale, Carmen Hanggi, Phoebe Staenz, Isabel Waidacher, Tiziana Cipriani, Stephanie Kamber

**United States** (Jodi KcKenna, coach) GK—Shenae Lundberg, Megan Miller—Emily Pfalzer, Layla Marvin, Lee Stecklein, Alex Carpenter, Courtney Burke, Hannah Brandt, Shiann Darkangelo, Milica McMillen, Amanda Boulier, Michelle Picard, Amanda Pelkey, Haley Skarupa, Emily Field, Paige Savage, Karley Sylvester, Abby Ness, Dana Trivigno, Sydney Daniels

## 5th U18 WOMEN'S WORLD CHAMPIONSHIP
## December 31, 2011-January 7, 2012
## Zlin/Prerov, Czech Republic

**Final Placing**

Gold ........Canada
Silver ......United States
Bronze ....Sweden
4th ..........Germany
5th .........Finland
6th .........Czech Republic
7th .........Russia^
8th .........Switzerland+

^promoted from Division I in 2011
+demoted to Division I for 2013

**Tournament Format**

The eight teams were divided into two groups of four and played a round robin within each group. The top two teams advanced to the playoffs where they played a cross-over semi-finals, while the bottom two teams played a series of placement games

**Results & Standings**

**PRELIMINARY ROUND**

**GROUP A (ZLIN)**

| | GP | W | OTW | OTL | L | GF | GA | P |
|---|---|---|---|---|---|---|---|---|
| United States | 3 | 3 | 0 | 0 | 0 | 28 | 1 | 9 |
| Sweden | 3 | 2 | 0 | 0 | 1 | 10 | 10 | 6 |
| Czech Republic | 3 | 1 | 0 | 0 | 2 | 4 | 17 | 3 |
| Russia | 3 | 0 | 0 | 0 | 3 | 2 | 16 | 0 |

| | | |
|---|---|---|
| December 31 | Sweden 4 | Czech Republic 1 |
| December 31 | United States 8 | Russia 0 |
| January 1 | Czech Republic 2 | Russia 0 |
| January 1 | United States 7 | Sweden 0 |
| January 3 | Sweden 6 | Russia 2 |
| January 3 | United States 13 | Czech Republic 1 |

**GROUP B (PREROV)**

| | GP | W | OTW | OTL | L | GF | GA | P |
|---|---|---|---|---|---|---|---|---|
| Canada | 3 | 3 | 0 | 0 | 0 | 26 | 1 | 9 |
| Germany | 3 | 1 | 0 | 0 | 2 | 6 | 10 | 3 |
| Finland | 3 | 1 | 0 | 0 | 2 | 6 | 12 | 3 |
| Switzerland | 3 | 1 | 0 | 0 | 2 | 7 | 22 | 3 |

| | | |
|---|---|---|
| December 31 | Canada 13 | Switzerland 1 |
| December 31 | Finland 3 | Germany 0 |
| January 1 | Switzerland 5 | Finland 3 |
| January 1 | Canada 6 | Germany 0 |
| January 3 | Germany 6 | Switzerland 1 |
| January 3 | Canada 7 | Finland 0 |

**RELEGATION ROUND (PREROV)**

| | GP | W | OTW | OTL | L | GF | GA | P |
|---|---|---|---|---|---|---|---|---|
| Russia | 3 | 1 | 1 | 0 | 1 | 10 | 9 | 5 |
| Switzerland | 3 | 1 | 0 | 1 | 1 | 9 | 10 | 4 |

| | | |
|---|---|---|
| January 4 | Switzerland 4 | Russia 2 |
| January 6 | Russia 5 | Switzerland 3 |
| January 7 | Russia 3 | Switzerland 2 (Valeria Pavlova 1:44 OT) |

**FIFTH-PLACE GAME**

| | | | |
|---|---|---|---|
| January 6 | Prerov | Finland 5 | Czech Republic 3 |

**PLAYOFFS (ZLIN)**

**QUARTER-FINALS**

| | | |
|---|---|---|
| January 4 | Sweden 2 | Finland 1 (Matildah Andersson 7:27 OT) |
| January 4 | Germany 2 | Czech Republic 1 |

**SEMI-FINALS**

| | | |
|---|---|---|
| January 6 | United States 7 | Germany 1 |
| January 6 | Canada 7 | Sweden 0 |

**BRONZE MEDAL GAME**

| | | |
|---|---|---|
| January 7 | Sweden 4 | Germany 1 |

**GOLD MEDAL GAME**

| | | |
|---|---|---|
| January 7 | Canada 3 | United States 0 |

**Rosters**

**Canada** (Pierre Alain, coach) GK: Emerance Maschmeyer, Elaine Chuli—Morgan Richardson, Emily Clark, Ashleigh Brykaliuk, Laura Stacey, Alexis Crossley, Taylor Woods, Kristyn Capizzano, Erin Ambrose, Jordan Krause, Meghan Dufault, Sarah Lefort, Halli Krzyzaniak, Erika Sowchuk, Cayley Mercer, Cydney Roesler, Abbey Frazer, Nicole Connery, Rebecca Kohler, Shannon MacAulay, Catherine Dubois

**Czech Republic** (Tomas Vytisk, coach) GK: Veronika Hladikova, Lenka Craigova—Aneta Tejralova, Marketa Vytiskova, Samantha Kolowratova, Dominika Laskova, Katerina Vanouckova, Sara Sadilkova, Adela Kubatova, Denisa Nesutova, Aneta Ledlova, Denisa Krizova, Veronika Kuzelova, Tereza Vanisova, Klara Mazankova, Klara Hudeckova, Dominika Vopravilova, Dana Pelikanova, Klara Chmelova, Adriena Pecinova, Vendula Pribylova, Michaela Novakova

**Finland** (Juuso Toivola, coach) GK: Isabella Portnoj, Tiina Ranne—Johanna Koivisto, Anna Kilponen, Jenna Tuovinen, Reetta Lindholm, Kristiina Merilainen, Reetta Valkjarvi, Ella Viitasuo, Susanne Uppgard, Emma Ritari, Venla Kotkaslahti, Suvi Ollikainen, Anni Rantanen, Christa Alanko, Vilma Tanskanen, Noora Tulus, Emma Nuutinen, Laura Vainionpaa, Saana Valkama, Jenna Suokko, Jenni Maamaki

**Germany** (Maritta Becker, coach) GK: Franziska Albl, Janina Fuchs—Anne Bartsch, Michelle Lubbert, Theresa Wagner, Melanie Haringer, Leonie Bauer, Jessica Ujcik, Julia Seitz, Anna-Maria Fiegert, Ann-Kathrin Voog, Vanessa Gasde, Larissa Swikull, Katja-Lisa Engel, Bernadette Karpf, Marie Delarbre, Marie-Kristin Schmid, Thersa Fritz, Dana Reimann, Laura Kluge, Muriel Scheuerlein, Kerstin Spielberger

**Russia** (Alexander Ulyankin, coach) GK: Margarita Monakhova, Nadezhda Morozova—Kristina Timofeyeva, Maria Bukshevannaya, Viktoriya Yegorova, Yevgenia Dyupina, Maria Batalova, Yelena Dergacheva, Diana Bulatova, Tatyana Shibanova, Lyudmila Belyakova, Tatiana Kitayeva, Tatyana Akmanayeva, Xenia Baibakova, Renata Isanbayeva, Yekaterina Nikolayeva, Maria Shepelinskaya, Yekaterina Zakharova, Angelina Goncharenko, Valeria Pavlova, Anna Shibanova

**Sweden** (Henrik Cedergren, coach) GK: Jessica Hjorth, Sara Besseling—Cajsa Lillback, Wilma Ekstrom, Caroline Markstrom, Anna Kjellbin, Lina Backlin, Matildah Andersson, Linnea Hedin, Linn Peterson, Elin Johansson, Amanda Lindberg, Michelle Lowenhielm, Olivia Carlsson, Emmy Alasalmi, Johanna Eidensten, Isabell Palm, Julia Lennartsson, Emily Fridh, Sabina Kuller, Malin Wong, Michelle Yucel

**Switzerland** (Dominik Schar, coach) GK: Janine Alder, Sandra Heim, Anja Zanetti—Selina Wuttke, Nicole Gubler, Nadine Hofstetter, Karin Williner, Celine Abgottspon, Lara Stalder, Reica Steiger, Dominique Scheuer, Livia Altmann, Dominique Ruegg, Jana Bigler, Laura Desboeufs, Valeska Poschung, Romy Eggimann, Stephanie Lehner, Mariko Dale, Phoebe Stanz, Isabel Waidacher, Tiziana Cipriani

**United States** (Heather Linstad, coach) GK: Brianna Laing, Sidney Peters, Natasha Rachlin, Lee Stecklein, Alex Carpenter, Courtney Burke, Briana Mastel, Samantha Lashomb, Demi Crossman, Kate Flug, Kate Schipper, Miye D'Oench, Anne Pankowski, Haley Skarupa, Jordan Hampton, Dani Cameranesi, Paige Savage, Maryanne Kennedy-Menefee, Molly Illikainen, Dana Trivigno, Sydney Daniels, Kaliya Johnson

*Sweden beat Germany by a 4-1 score to take bronze at the 2012 Women's U18 World Championship in the Czech Republic. Photo: Phillip MacCallum / HHOF-IIHF Images.*

*Hockey Hall of Fame chairman Bill Hay announces the newest inductees for 2012—Russia's Pavel Bure (inducted by the IIHF earlier in 2012), Sweden's Mats Sundin, and Joe Sakic and Adam Oates of Canada. Photo: Steve Poirier / HHOF.*

# HEAD-TO-HEAD RESULTS

## AUSTRALIA (AUS)

Totals=GP-W-T-L-GF-GA

### OLYMPICS, MEN

Date Score
20-Feb-60 AUS 1-TCH 18
Totals: 1-0-0-1-1-18

22-Feb-60 AUS 1-FIN 14
25-Feb-60 AUS 2-FIN 19
Totals: 2-0-0-2-3-33

27-Feb-60 AUS 3-JPN 11
24-Feb-60 AUS 2-JPN 13
Totals: 2-0-0-2-5-24

21-Feb-60 AUS 1-USA 12
Totals: 1-0-0-1-1-12

## AUSTRIA (AUT)

Totals=GP-W-T-L-GF-GA

### OLYMPICS, MEN

Date Score
05-Feb-76 AUT 6-BUL 2
Totals: 1-1-0-0-6-2

08-Feb-36 AUT 2-CAN 5
07-Feb-48 AUT 0-CAN 12
27-Jan-56 AUT 0-CAN 23
09-Feb-84 AUT 1-CAN 8
Totals: 4-0-0-4-3-48

13-Feb-36 AUT 1-TCH 2
04-Feb-48 AUT 3-TCH 17
11-Feb-84 AUT 0-TCH 13
19-Feb-88 AUT 0-TCH 4
14-Feb-94 AUT 3-CZE 7
Totals: 5-0-0-5-7-43

07-Feb-84 AUT 3-FIN 4
18-Feb-94 AUT 2-FIN 6
Totals: 2-0-0-2-5-10

11-Feb-68 AUT 5-FRA 2
22-Feb-94 AUT 4-FRA 5 (10:00 OT/GWS)
Totals: 2-1-0-1-9-7

12-Feb-28 AUT 0-GER 0
29-Jan-56 AUT 0-GER 7
12-Feb-94 AUT 3-GER 4
10-Feb-02 AUT 2-GER 3
Totals: 4-0-1-3-5-14

31-Jan-48 AUT 4-GBR 5
Totals: 1-0-0-1-4-5

01-Feb-64 AUT 3-HUN 0
Totals: 1-1-0-0-3-0

05-Feb-48 AUT 16-ITA 5
26-Jan-56 AUT 2-ITA 2
01-Feb-56 AUT 2-ITA 8
06-Feb-64 AUT 5-ITA 3
10-Feb-98 AUT 2-ITA 5
Totals: 5-2-1-2-27-23

03-Feb-64 AUT 5-JPN 5
15-Feb-68 AUT 1-JPN 11
07-Feb-76 AUT 3-JPN 2
12-Feb-98 AUT 3-JPN 4
Totals: 4-1-1-2-12-22

08-Feb-98 AUT 5-KAZ 5
Totals: 1-0-1-0-5-5

09-Feb-36 AUT 7-LAT 1
09-Feb-02 AUT 2-LAT 4
Totals: 2-1-0-1-9-5

07-Feb-64 AUT 2-NOR 8
12-Feb-68 AUT 4-NOR 5
15-Feb-84 AUT 6-NOR 5
21-Feb-88 AUT 4-NOR 4
20-Feb-94 AUT 4-NOR 2
24-Feb-94 AUT 1-NOR 3
Totals: 6-2-1-3-21-27

07-Feb-36 AUT 2-POL 1
30-Jan-48 AUT 5-POL 7
02-Feb-56 AUT 3-POL 4
08-Feb-64 AUT 1-POL 5
23-Feb-88 AUT 3-POL 2
Totals: 5-2-0-3-14-19

05-Feb-64 AUT 2-RUM 5
07-Feb-68 AUT 2-RUM 3
09-Feb-76 AUT 3-ROM 4
Totals: 3-0-0-3-7-12

15-Feb-88 AUT 1-URS 8
16-Feb-94 AUT 1-RUS 9
Totals: 2-0-0-2-2-17

07-Feb-98 AUT 2-SVK 2
12-Feb-02 AUT 3-SVK 2
Totals: 2-1-1-0-5-4

11-Feb-36 AUT 0-SWE 1
02-Feb-48 AUT 2-SWE 7
Totals: 2-0-0-2-2-8

11-Feb-28 AUT 4-SUI 4
01-Feb-48 AUT 2-SUI 11
31-Jan-56 AUT 4-SUI 7
11-Feb-76 AUT 3-SUI 5
14-Feb-02 AUT 1-SUI 4
Totals: 5-0-1-4-14-31

12-Feb-36 AUT 0-USA 1
06-Feb-48 AUT 2-USA 13
13-Feb-84 AUT 3-USA 7
13-Feb-88 AUT 6-USA 10
Totals: 4-0-0-4-11-31

17-Feb-88 AUT 1-FRG 3
Totals: 1-0-0-1-1-3

30-Jan-64 AUT 6-YUG 2
09-Feb-68 AUT 0-YUG 6
13-Feb-76 AUT 3-YUG 1
Totals: 3-2-0-1-9-9

### WORLD CHAMPIONSHIPS, MEN

10-May-99 AUT 2-BLR 3
02-May-05 AUT 0-BLR 5
01-May-07 AUT 2-BLR 5
05-May-11 AUT 2-BLR 7
Totals: 4-0-0-4-6-20

20-Jan-35 AUT 6-BEL 1
17-Feb-47 AUT 14-BEL 5
Totals: 2-2-0-0-20-6

07-Feb-31 AUT 0-CAN 8
22-Feb-33 AUT 0-CAN 4
13-Feb-38 AUT 0-CAN 3
13-Feb-49 AUT 0-CAN 7
18-Feb-49 AUT 2-CAN 8
22-Apr-93 AUT 0-CAN 11
26-Apr-94 AUT 1-CAN 6
23-Apr-96 AUT 0-CAN 4
01-May-98 AUT 1-CAN 5
25-Apr-04 AUT 2-CAN 2
Totals: 10-0-1-9-6-58

05-Feb-31 AUT 1-TCH 2
19-Feb-33 AUT 1-TCH 2
26-Feb-33 AUT 0-TCH 2
07-Feb-34 AUT 0-TCH 4
19-Jan-35 AUT 1-TCH 2
12-Feb-38 AUT 0-TCH 1
18-Feb-47 AUT 5-TCH 13
16-Feb-49 AUT 1-TCH 7
24-Feb-57 AUT 0-TCH 9
26-Apr-95 AUT 2-CZE 5
01-May-99 AUT 0-CZE 7
28-Apr-03 AUT 1-CZE 8
30-Apr-04 AUT 0-CZE 2
29-Apr-07 AUT 1-CZE 6
Totals vs. TCH: 9-0-0-9-9-42
Totals vs. CZE: 5-0-0-5-4-28

14-Feb-49 AUT 25-DEN 1
08-May-05 AUT 3-DEN 4
04-May-09 AUT 2-DEN 5
Totals: 3-1-0-2-30-10

05-Mar-57 AUT 1-GDR 3
Totals: 1-0-0-1-1-3

02-Mar-57 AUT 2-FIN 9
05-May-94 AUT 0-FIN 10
29-Apr-95 AUT 2-FIN 7
02-May-00 AUT 3-FIN 3
28-Apr-01 AUT 1-FIN 5
02-May-02 AUT 1-FIN 3
26-Apr-03 AUT 1-FIN 5
Totals: 7-0-1-6-10-42

01-Feb-30 AUT 2-FRA 1
24-Jan-35 AUT 4-FRA 1
01-May-96 AUT 3-FRA 6
02-May-96 AUT 3-FRA 6
06-May-00 AUT 3-FRA 3
24-Apr-04 AUT 6-FRA 0
Totals: 6-3-1-2-21-17

23-Feb-33 AUT 2-GER 0
03-Feb-34 AUT 2-GER 1
25-Apr-94 AUT 2-GER 2
26-Apr-96 AUT 0-GER 3
03-May-03 AUT 1-GER 5
01-May-04 AUT 1-GER 3
06-May-05 AUT 2-GER 2
03-May-09 AUT 1-GER 0
Totals: 8-3-2-3-11-16

01-Feb-31 AUT 1-GBR 0 (OT)
09-Feb-34 AUT 2-GBR 1
23-Jan-35 AUT 1-GBR 4
03-May-94 AUT 10-GBR 0
Totals: 4-3-0-1-14-5

21-Feb-33 AUT 1-HUN 0
01-May-09 AUT 6-HUN 0
Totals: 2-2-0-0-7-0

18-Feb-33 AUT 3-ITA 0
05-Feb-34 AUT 0-ITA 1
11-Feb-34 AUT 2-ITA 2
26-Jan-35 AUT 2-ITA 1
26-Apr-93 AUT 1-ITA 1
01-May-94 AUT 1-ITA 3
03-May-99 AUT 1-ITA 5
04-May-00 AUT 0-ITA 3
Totals: 8-2-2-4-10-16

26-Feb-57 AUT 3-JPN 3
05-May-99 AUT 4-JPN 2
07-May-00 AUT 5-JPN 3
02-May-01 AUT 3-JPN 2
Totals: 4-3-1-0-15-10

08-May-99 AUT 5-LAT 2
03-May-04 AUT 2-LAT 5
06-May-07 AUT 1-LAT 5
29-Apr-09 AUT 0-LAT 2
08-May-11 AUT 1-LAT 4
Totals: 5-1-0-4-9-18

29-Apr-93 AUT 6-NOR 2
01-May-95 AUT 3-NOR 5
11-May-99 AUT 3-NOR 0
04-May-07 AUT 2-NOR 3 (OT)
04-May-11 AUT 0-NOR 5
Totals: 5-2-0-3-14-15

05-Feb-30 AUT 2-POL 0
06-Feb-31 AUT 2-POL 1
15-Feb-47 AUT 10-POL 2
03-Mar-57 AUT 1-POL 5
Totals: 4-3-0-1-15-8

03-Feb-31 AUT 7-ROM 0
20-Feb-33 AUT 7-ROM 1
10-Feb-34 AUT 3-ROM 1
21-Jan-35 AUT 2-ROM 1
21-Feb-47 AUT 12-ROM 1
Totals: 5-5-0-0-31-4

27-Feb-57 AUT 1-URS 22
19-Apr-93 AUT 2-RUS 4
29-Apr-94 AUT 1-RUS 4
28-Apr-96 AUT 0-RUS 6
28-Apr-02 AUT 3-RUS 6
30-Apr-05 AUT 2-RUS 4
Totals vs URS 1-0-0-1-1-22
Totals vs. RUS 5-0-0-5-8-24

25-Apr-96 AUT 2-SVK 1
05-May-98 AUT 1-SVK 5
30-Apr-00 AUT 0-SVK 2
30-Apr-01 AUT 0-SVK 5
03-May-02 AUT 3-SVK 6
04-May-03 AUT 1-SVK 7
04-May-05 AUT 1-SVK 8
Totals: 7-1-0-6-8-34

30-Apr-02 AUT 5-SLO 3
29-Apr-03 AUT 6-SLO 2
11-May-05 AUT 2-SLO 6
07-May-11 AUT 3-SLO 2
Totals: 4-3-0-1-16-13

02-Feb-31 AUT 1-SWE 3
08-Feb-31 AUT 1-SWE 0
27-Jan-35 AUT 1-SWE 3
15-Feb-38 AUT 1-SWE 1
23-Feb-47 AUT 2-SWE 1
15-Feb-49 AUT 0-SWE 18
01-Mar-57 AUT 0-SWE 10
18-Apr-93 AUT 0-SWE 1
27-Apr-95 AUT 0-SWE 5
04-May-01 AUT 0-SWE 11
26-Apr-02 AUT 3-SWE 5
25-Apr-09 AUT 1-SWE 7
02-May-11 AUT 0-SWE 3
Totals: 13-2-1-10-10-68

02-Feb-30 AUT 1-SUI 2
22-Jan-35 AUT 1-SUI 1 (30:00 OT)
22-Feb-47 AUT 0-SUI 5
19-Feb-49 AUT 1-SUI 10
23-Apr-93 AUT 1-SUI 5
02-May-95 AUT 4-SUI 0
03-May-95 AUT 4-SUI 4
27-Apr-04 AUT 4-SUI 4
Totals: 8-1-3-4-16-31

09-May-00 AUT 3-UKR 2
07-May-01 AUT 0-UKR 2
06-May-02 AUT 2-UKR 3
06-May-03 AUT 5-UKR 2
07-May-07 AUT 8-UKR 4
Totals: 5-3-0-2-18-13

04-Feb-31 AUT 1-USA 2
24-Feb-33 AUT 0-USA 4
08-Feb-34 AUT 0-USA 1
18-Feb-47 AUT 6-USA 5
20-Feb-49 AUT 1-USA 9
24-Apr-95 AUT 2-USA 5
22-Apr-96 AUT 1-USA 5
03-May-99 AUT 2-USA 5
06-May-01 AUT 3-USA 0
27-Apr-07 AUT 2-USA 6
27-Apr-09 AUT 1-USA 6
30-Apr-11 AUT 1-USA 5
Totals: 12-2-0-10-20-53

### WORLD U20 CHAMPIONSHIPS

30-Dec-80 AUT 1-CAN 11
Totals: 1-0-0-1-1-11

28-Dec-80 AUT 4-TCH 21
29-Dec-09 AUT 1-CZE 7
Totals vs. TCH: 1-0-0-1-4-21
Totals vs. CZE: 1-0-0-1-1-7

30-Dec-09 AUT 1-FIN 10
Totals: 1-0-0-1-1-10

04-Jan-10 AUT 4-LAT 6
Totals: 1-0-0-1-4-6

27-Dec-80 AUT 1-URS 19
29-Dec-03 AUT 1-RUS 3
26-Dec-09 AUT 2-RUS 6
Totals vs. URS: 1-0-0-1-1-19
Totals vs. RUS: 2-0-0-2-3-9

30-Dec-03 AUT 0-SVK 6
02-Jan-10 AUT 2-SVK 3
Totals: 2-0-0-2-2-9

27-Dec-03 AUT 0-SWE 7
27-Dec-09 AUT 3-SWE 7
Totals: 2-0-0-2-3-14

02-Jan-04 AUT 2-SUI 6
Totals: 1-0-0-1-2-6

03-Jan-04 AUT 2-UKR 2
Totals: 1-0-1-0-2-2

02-Jan-81 AUT 2-USA 7
26-Dec-03 AUT 0-USA 8
Totals: 2-0-0-2-2-15

31-Dec-80 AUT 1-FRG 9
Totals: 1-0-0-1-1-9

## BELARUS (BLR)

Totals=GP-W-T-L-GF-GA

### OLYMPICS, MEN

Date Score
13-Feb-98 BLR 0-CAN 5
22-Feb-02 BLR 1-CAN 7
Totals: 2-0-0-2-1-12

16-Feb-02 BLR 1-FIN 8
17-Feb-10 BLR 1-FIN 5
Totals: 2-0-0-2-2-13

07-Feb-98 BLR 4-FRA 0
11-Feb-02 BLR 3-FRA 1
Totals: 2-2-0-0-7-1

09-Feb-98 BLR 8-GER 2
20-Feb-10 BLR 5-GER 3
Totals: 2-2-0-0-13-5

10-Feb-98 BLR 2-JPN 2
Totals: 1-0-1-0-2-2

18-Feb-98 BLR 1-RUS 4
15-Feb-02 BLR 4-RUS 6
23-Feb-02 BLR 2-RUS 7
Totals: 3-0-0-3-7-17

16-Feb-98 BLR 2-SWE 5
20-Feb-02 BLR 4-SWE 3
19-Feb-10 BLR 2-SWE 4
Totals: 3-1-0-2-8-12

13-Feb-02 BLR 1-SUI 2
23-Feb-10 BLR 2-SUI 3 (10:00 OT/GWS)
Totals: 2-0-0-2-3-5

09-Feb-02 BLR 1-UKR 0
Totals: 1-1-0-0-1-0

14-Feb-98 BLR 2-USA 5
18-Feb-02 BLR 1-USA 8
Totals: 2-0-0-2-3-13

### WORLD CHAMPIONSHIPS, MEN

10-May-99 BLR 3-AUT 2
02-May-05 BLR 5-AUT 0
01-May-07 BLR 5-AUT 2
05-May-11 BLR 7-AUT 2
Totals: 4-4-0-2-20-6

07-May-98 BLR 2-CAN 6
26-Apr-03 BLR 0-CAN 3
04-May-07 BLR 3-CAN 6
24-Apr-09 BLR 1-CAN 6
29-Apr-11 BLR 1-CAN 4
15-May-12 BLR 1-CAN 5
Totals: 6-0-0-6-8-30

03-May-98 BLR 2-CZE 4
28-Apr-01 BLR 1-CZE 5
10-May-05 BLR 1-CZE 5
27-Apr-07 BLR 2-CZE 8
10-May-08 BLR 2-CZE 3 (5:00 OT/GWS)
03-May-09 BLR 0-CZE 3
Totals: 6-0-0-6-8-28

12-May-08 BLR 2-DEN 3 (OT)
17-May-10 BLR 2-DEN 1
Totals: 2-1-0-1-4-4

10-May-98 BLR 2-FIN 5
04-May-99 BLR 1-FIN 4
18-May-06 BLR 0-FIN 4
02-May-09 BLR 2-FIN 1 (5:00 OT/GWS)
14-May-10 BLR 0-FIN 2
04-May-12 BLR 0-FIN 1
Totals: 6-1-0-5-5-17

07-May-08 BLR 3-FRA 1
03-May-11 BLR 1-FRA 2 (OT)
14-May-12 BLR 1-FRA 2
Totals: 3-1-0-2-5-5

01-May-98 BLR 4-GER 2
02-May-01 BLR 2-GER 0
07-May-07 BLR 5-GER 6
16-May-10 BLR 2-GER 1 (OT)
Totals: 4-3-0-1-13-9

28-Apr-09 BLR 3-HUN 1
Totals: 1-1-0-0-3-1

05-May-98 BLR 6-JPN 4
07-May-01 BLR 4-JPN 1
02-May-03 BLR 3-JPN 1
Totals: 3-3-0-0-13-6

07-May-05 BLR 2-KAZ 0
10-May-06 BLR 7-KAZ 1
09-May-10 BLR 5-KAZ 2
08-May-12 BLR 3-KAZ 2
Totals: 4-4-0-0-17-5

11-May-99 BLR 2-LAT 1
02-May-00 BLR 3-LAT 6
04-May-01 BLR 2-LAT 2
29-Apr-03 BLR 0-LAT 4
07-May-11 BLR 3-LAT 6
Totals: 5-1-1-3-10-19

08-May-99 BLR 2-NOR 0
05-May-01 BLR 3-NOR 2
30-Apr-09 BLR 3-NOR 2 (OT)
Totals: 3-3-0-0-8-4

02-May-99 BLR 2-RUS 2
07-May-00 BLR 1-RUS 0
04-May-05 BLR 0-RUS 2
08-May-06 BLR 2-RUS 3
09-May-08 BLR 3-RUS 4 (5:00 OT/GWS)
06-May-09 BLR 3-RUS 4
13-May-10 BLR 1-RUS 3
Totals: 7-1-1-5-12-18

30-Apr-05 BLR 1-SVK 2
06-May-06 BLR 2-SVK 1
06-May-07 BLR 3-SVK 4
26-Apr-09 BLR 2-SVK 1 (5:00 OT/GWS)
11-May-10 BLR 2-SVK 4
12-May-12 BLR 1-SVK 5
Totals: 6-2-0-4-11-17

05-May-03 BLR 4-SLO 3
08-May-11 BLR 7-SLO 1
Totals: 2-2-0-0-11-4

09-May-98 BLR 1-SWE 2
04-May-00 BLR 0-SWE 7
27-Apr-03 BLR 1-SWE 2
12-May-06 BLR 1-SWE 4
03-May-08 BLR 5-SWE 6
Totals: 5-0-0-5-8-21

09-May-00 BLR 5-SUI 3
30-Apr-01 BLR 2-SUI 5
09-May-05 BLR 0-SUI 2
16-May-06 BLR 2-SUI 1
05-May-08 BLR 1-SUI 2
01-May-11 BLR 1-SUI 4
06-May-12 BLR 2-SUI 3
Totals: 7-2-0-5-13-20

06-May-99 BLR 6-UKR 1
30-Apr-00 BLR 7-UKR 3
13-May-06 BLR 9-UKR 1
Totals: 3-3-0-0-22-5

05-May-00 BLR 0-USA 1
05-May-03 BLR 2-USA 4
29-Apr-07 BLR 1-USA 5
10-May-12 BLR 3-USA 5
Totals: 4-0-0-4-6-15

**WORLD U20 CHAMPIONSHIPS**

26-Dec-00 BLR 0-CAN 9
Totals: 1-0-0-1-0-9

03-Jan-99 BLR 2-CZE 10
28-Dec-01 BLR 1-CZE 9
25-Dec-04 BLR 2-CZE 7
30-Dec-06 BLR 1-CZE 2
Totals: 4-0-0-4-6-28

30-Dec-00 BLR 0-FIN 5
26-Dec-06 BLR 4-FIN 3
Totals: 2-1-0-1-4-8

01-Jan-02 BLR 2-FRA 3
03-Jan-02 BLR 3-FRA 2
Totals: 2-1-0-1-5-5

04-Jan-03 BLR 0-GER 4
03-Jan-05 BLR 3-GER 4
03-Jan-07 BLR 3-GER 1
Totals: 3-1-0-2-6-9

27-Dec-98 BLR 2-KAZ 2
02-Jan-01 BLR 5-KAZ 2
03-Jan-01 BLR 5-KAZ 5
Totals: 3-1-2-0-12-9

29-Dec-98 BLR 0-RUS 10
27-Dec-00 BLR 1-RUS 12
29-Dec-02 BLR 1-RUS 5
28-Dec-04 BLR 2-RUS 7
29-Dec-06 BLR 1-RUS 6
Totals: 5-0-0-5-5-40

26-Dec-01 BLR 1-SVK 7
27-Dec-02 BLR 1-SVK 11
02-Jan-05 BLR 1-SVK 2
04-Jan-07 BLR 0-SVK 9
Totals: 4-0-0-4-3-29

30-Dec-98 BLR 4-SWE 5
25-Dec-01 BLR 0-SWE 5
03-Jan-03 BLR 4-SWE 5
Totals: 3-0-0-3-8-15

26-Dec-98 BLR 3-SUI 4
29-Dec-00 BLR 1-SUI 3
26-Dec-02 BLR 2-SUI 4
26-Dec-04 BLR 0-SUI 5
27-Dec-06 BLR 1-SUI 4
Totals: 5-0-0-5-7-20

04-Jan-99 BLR 2-USA 7
29-Dec-01 BLR 2-USA 5
30-Dec-02 BLR 2-USA 8
29-Dec-04 BLR 5-USA 3
Totals: 4-1-0-3-11-23

**WORLD U18 CHAMPIONSHIPS, MEN**

21-Apr-02 BLR 5-CAN 3
10-Apr-04 BLR 2-CAN 7
15-Apr-10 BLR 3-CAN 11
Totals: 3-1-0-2-10-21

18-Apr-02 BLR 1-CZE 5
14-Apr-06 BLR 2-CZE 5
Totals: 2-0-0-2-3-10

09-Apr-04 BLR 1-DEN 4
21-Apr-08 BLR 6-DEN 2
Totals: 2-1-0-1-7-6

19-Apr-00 BLR 1-FIN 11
12-Apr-02 BLR 3-FIN 4
14-Apr-03 BLR 6-FIN 8
15-Apr-04 BLR 2-FIN 5
17-Apr-08 BLR 3-FIN 4
Totals: 5-0-0-5-15-32

21-Apr-00 BLR 0-GER 10
16-Apr-06 BLR 1-GER 5
Totals: 2-0-0-2-1-15

20-Apr-03 BLR 8-KAZ 6
Totals: 1-1-0-0-8-6

22-Apr-10 BLR 4-LAT 5 (5:00 OT/GWS)
Totals: 1-0-0-1-4-5

16-Apr-04 BLR 4-NOR 3
20-Apr-06 BLR 6-NOR 6
Totals: 2-1-1-0-10-9

16-Apr-00 BLR 1-RUS 18
20-Apr-02 BLR 0-RUS 11
13-Apr-06 BLR 0-RUS 8
Totals: 3-0-0-3-1-37

15-Apr-00 BLR 1-SVK 7
17-Apr-03 BLR 2-SVK 8
19-Apr-06 BLR 2-SVK 0
20-Apr-08 BLR 1-SVK 6
20-Apr-10 BLR 1-SVK 5
Totals: 5-1-0-4-7-26

15-Apr-02 BLR 2-SWE 4
16-Apr-03 BLR 3-SWE 9
13-Apr-04 BLR 0-SWE 4
13-Apr-08 BLR 2-SWE 6
14-Apr-10 BLR 0-SWE 7
Totals: 5-0-0-5-7-30

14-Apr-02 BLR 6-SUI 3
19-Apr-03 BLR 5-SUI 3
16-Apr-08 BLR 2-SUI 4
17-Apr-10 BLR 2-SUI 3
Totals: 4-2-0-2-15-13

22-Apr-00 BLR 3-UKR 8
17-Apr-02 BLR 3-UKR 1
Totals: 2-1-0-1-6-9

18-Apr-00 BLR 1-USA 9
11-Apr-02 BLR 0-USA 9
12-Apr-03 BLR 3-USA 3
12-Apr-04 BLR 0-USA 9
17-Apr-06 BLR 1-USA 12
14-Apr-08 BLR 2-USA 5
18-Apr-10 BLR 1-USA 7
Totals: 7-0-1-6-8-54

## BELGIUM (BEL)

Totals=GP-W-T-L-GF-GA

**OLYMPICS, MEN**

**Date Score**

07-Feb-36 BEL 0-TCH 5
Totals: 1-0-0-1-0-5

31-Jan-24 BEL 5-FRA 7
16-Feb-28 BEL 3-FRA 1
08-Feb-36 BEL 2-FRA 4 (20:00 OT)
Totals: 3-1-0-2-10-12

30-Jan-24 BEL 3-GBR 19
11-Feb-28 BEL 3-GBR 7
Totals: 2-0-0-2-6-26

12-Feb-28 BEL 3-HUN 2
06-Feb-36 BEL 2-HUN 11
Totals: 2-1-0-1-5-13

23-Apr-20 BEL 0-SWE 8
Totals: 1-0-0-1-0-8

28-Jan-24 BEL 0-USA 19
Totals: 1-0-0-1-0-19

**WORLD CHAMPIONSHIPS, MEN**

20-Jan-35 BEL 1-AUT 6
17-Feb-47 BEL 5-AUT 14
Totals: 2-0-0-2-6-20

15-Mar-50 BEL 0-CAN 33
Totals: 1-0-0-1-0-33

21-Jan-35 BEL 0-TCH 22
21-Feb-47 BEL 0-TCH 24
Totals: 2-0-0-2-0-46

17-Feb-49 BEL 8-DEN 3
Totals: 1-1-0-0-8-3

18-Feb-49 BEL 2-FIN 17
Totals: 1-0-0-1-2-17

31-Jan-30 BEL 1-FRA 4
05-Feb-34 BEL 2-FRA 0
20-Mar-50 BEL 7-FRA 1
Totals: 3-2-0-1-10-5

18-Feb-33 BEL 0-GER 6
Totals: 1-0-0-1-0-6

06-Feb-34 BEL 0-GBR 3
04-Feb-39 BEL 1-GBR 3
Totals: 2-0-0-2-1-6

23-Jan-35 BEL 1-HUN 6
03-Feb-39 BEL 1-HUN 8
Totals: 2-0-0-2-2-14

06-Feb-39 BEL 1-LAT 5
Totals: 1-0-0-1-1-5

22-Mar-50 BEL 4-NED 2
Totals: 1-1-0-0-4-2

12-Feb-49 BEL 0-NOR 2
19-Feb-49 BEL 1-NOR 14
Totals: 2-0-0-2-1-16

20-Feb-33 BEL 0-POL 1
22-Jan-35 BEL 2-POL 12
20-Feb-47 BEL 1-POL 11
Totals: 3-0-0-3-3-24

24-Feb-33 BEL 2-ROM 3
04-Feb-34 BEL 2-ROM 3
19-Jan-35 BEL 1-ROM 2
22-Feb-47 BEL 4-ROM 6
Totals: 4-0-0-4-9-14

16-Feb-47 BEL 1-SWE 24
Totals: 1-0-0-1-1-24

03-Feb-34 BEL 1-SUI 20
19-Feb-47 BEL 2-SUI 12
13-Feb-49 BEL 2-SUI 18
13-Mar-50 BEL 3-SUI 24
Totals: 4-0-0-4-8-74

18-Feb-47 BEL 2-USA 13
14-Feb-49 BEL 0-USA 12
Totals: 2-0-0-2-2-25

07-Feb-39 BEL 3-YUG 3
Totals: 1-0-1-0-3-3

## BULGARIA (BUL)

Totals=GP-W-T-L-GF-GA

**OLYMPICS, MEN**

**Date Score**

05-Feb-76 BUL 2-AUT 6
Totals: 1-0-0-1-2-6

13-Feb-76 BUL 5-JPN 7
Totals: 1-0-0-1-5-7

11-Feb-76 BUL 4-ROM 9
Totals: 1-0-0-1-4-9

07-Feb-76 BUL 3-SUI 8
Totals: 1-0-0-1-3-8

09-Feb-76 BUL 5-YUG 8
Totals: 1-0-0-1-5-8

## CANADA (CAN)

Totals=GP-W-T-L-GF-GA

**OLYMPICS, MEN**

**Date Score**

08-Feb-36 CAN 5-AUT 2
07-Feb-48 CAN 12-AUT 0
27-Jan-56 CAN 23-AUT 0
09-Feb-84 CAN 8-AUT 1
Totals: 4-4-0-0-48-3

13-Feb-98 CAN 5-BLR 0
22-Feb-02 CAN 7-BLR 1
Totals: 2-2-0-0-12-1

24-Apr-20 CAN 15-TCH 0
28-Jan-24 CAN 30-TCH 0
15-Feb-36 CAN 7-TCH 0
06-Feb-48 CAN 0-TCH 0
19-Feb-52 CAN 4-TCH 1
30-Jan-56 CAN 6-TCH 3
24-Feb-60 CAN 4-TCH 0
07-Feb-64 CAN 1-TCH 3
13-Feb-68 CAN 3-TCH 2
22-Feb-80 CAN 1-TCH 6
15-Feb-84 CAN 0-TCH 4
27-Feb-88 CAN 6-TCH 3
14-Feb-92 CAN 5-TCH 1
21-Feb-92 CAN 4 -TCH 2
23-Feb-94 CAN 3-CZE 2 (OT)
20-Feb-98 CAN 1 -CZE 2 (10:00 OT/GWS)
18-Feb-02 CAN 3-CZE 3
21-Feb-06 CAN 3-CZE 2
Totals vs. TCH: 14-10-1-3-86-25
Totals vs. CZE: 4-2-1-1-10-9

09-Feb-68 CAN 11-GDR 0
Totals: 1-1-0-0-11-0

17-Feb-52 CAN 1-FIN 3
05-Feb-64 CAN 4-FIN 2
09-Feb-68 CAN 2-FIN 1
16-Feb-80 CAN 2-FIN 5
11-Feb-84 CAN 0-FIN 2
18-Feb-88 CAN 5-FIN 3
25-Feb-94 CAN 2-FIN 3
21-Feb-98 CAN 3-FIN 4
20-Feb-02 CAN 6-FIN 2
19-Feb-06 CAN 13-FIN 3
Totals: 10-5-0-5-38-28

08-Feb-68 CAN 3-FRA 1
08-Feb-92 CAN 9-FRA 5
15-Feb-94 CAN 3-FRA 2
Totals: 3-3-0-0-15-8

06-Feb-32 CAN 15-GER 1
08-Feb-32 CAN 4-GER 0
13-Feb-36 CAN 4-GER 2
15-Feb-52 CAN 5-GER 1
26-Jan-56 CAN 10-GER 0
02-Feb-56 CAN 12-GER 0
22-Feb-60 CAN 4-GER 1
02-Feb-64 CAN 3-GER 2
20-Feb-88 CAN 5-GER 0
17-Feb-02 CAN 8-GER 2
16-Feb-06 CAN 6-GER 2
23-Feb-10 CAN 4-GER 3 (10:00 OT/GWS)
Totals: 12-12-0-0-80-14

01-Feb-24 CAN 1-GBR 2
18-Feb-28 CAN 3-GBR 0
01-Feb-48 CAN 19-GBR 2
18-Feb-92 CAN 14-GBR 0
Totals: 4-3-0-1-37-4

11-Feb-36 CAN 15-HUN 0
Totals: 1-1-0-0-15-0

12-Feb-36 CAN 21-ITA 1
03-Feb-48 CAN 3-ITA 1
28-Jan-56 CAN 7-ITA 2
13-Feb-94 CAN 7-ITA 2
Totals: 4-4-0-0-38-6

18-Feb-80 CAN 19-JPN 1
15-Feb-06 CAN 6-JPN 0
Totals: 2-2-0-0-25-1

20-Feb-60 CAN 4-KAZ 1
Totals: 1-1-0-0-4-1

18-Feb-98 CAN 11-LAT 0
Totals: 1-1-0-0-11-0

12-Feb-80 CAN 10-NED 1
Totals: 1-1-0-0-10-1

23-Feb-52 CAN 11-NOR 2
13-Feb-84 CAN 8-NOR 1
12-Feb-92 CAN 10-NOR 0
16-Feb-10 CAN 8-NOR 0
Totals: 4-4-0-0-37-3

07-Feb-32 CAN 9-POL 0
09-Feb-32 CAN 10-POL 0
06-Feb-36 CAN 8-POL 1
02-Feb-48 CAN 15-POL 0
18-Feb-52 CAN 11-POL 0
14-Feb-80 CAN 5-POL 1
14-Feb-88 CAN 1-POL 0
Totals: 7-7-0-0-59-2

04-Feb-56 CAN 0-URS 2
28-Feb-60 CAN 8-URS 5
08-Feb-64 CAN 2-URS 3
17-Feb-68 CAN 0-URS 5
20-Feb-80 CAN 4-URS 6
17-Feb-84 CAN 0-URS 4
24-Feb-88 CAN 0-URS 5
16-Feb-92 CAN 4-RUS 5
23-Feb-92 CAN 1-RUS 3

22-Feb-06 CAN 0-RUS 2
24-Feb-10 CAN 7-RUS 3
Totals vs. URS
7-1-0-6-14-30
Totals vs. RUS
4-1-0-3-12-13

19-Feb-94 CAN 1-SVK 3
26-Feb-10 CAN 3-SVK 2
Totals: 2-1-0-1-4-5

26-Apr-20 CAN 12-SWE 1
29-Jan-24 CAN 22-SWE 0
17-Feb-28 CAN 11-SWE 0
30-Jan-48 CAN 3-SWE 1
22-Feb-52 CAN 3-SWE 2
03-Feb-56 CAN 6-SWE 2
19-Feb-60 CAN 5-SWE 2
27-Feb-60 CAN 6-SWE 5
30-Jan-64 CAN 3-SWE 1
15-Feb-68 CAN 3-SWE 0
19-Feb-84 CAN 0-SWE 2
22-Feb-88 CAN 2-SWE 2
21-Feb-94 CAN 3-SWE 2
27-Feb-94 CAN 2-SWE 3
(10:00 OT/GWS)
14-Feb-98 CAN 3-SWE 2
15-Feb-02 CAN 2-SWE 5
Totals: 16-12-1-3-86-30

30-Jan-24 CAN 33-SUI 0
19-Feb-28 CAN 13-SUI 0
08-Feb-48 CAN 3-SUI 0
21-Feb-52 CAN 11-SUI 2
29-Jan-64 CAN 8-SUI 0
16-Feb-88 CAN 4-SUI 2
10-Feb-92 CAN 6-SUI 1
18-Feb-06 CAN 0-SUI 2
18-Feb-10 CAN 3-SUI 2
(5:00 OT/GWS)
Totals: 9-8-0-1-81-9

25-Apr-20 CAN 2-USA 0
03-Feb-24 CAN 6-USA 1
04-Feb-32 CAN 2-USA 1
(10:00 OT)
13-Feb-32 CAN 2-USA 2
(30:00 OT)
16-Feb-36 CAN 1-USA 0
05-Feb-48 CAN 12-USA 3
24-Feb-52 CAN 3-USA 3
31-Jan-56 CAN 1-USA 4
25-Feb-60 CAN 1-USA 2
03-Feb-64 CAN 8-USA 6
11-Feb-68 CAN 3-USA 2
07-Feb-84 CAN 4-USA 2
17-Feb-94 CAN 3-USA 3
16-Feb-98 CAN 4-USA 1
24-Feb-02 CAN 5-USA 2
21-Feb-10 CAN 3-USA 5
28-Feb-10 CAN 3-USA 2
(OT)
Totals: 17-11-3-3-63-39

06-Feb-68 CAN 6-FRG 1
26-Feb-88 CAN 8-FRG 1
Totals: 2-2-0-0-14-2

**WORLD CHAMPIONSHIPS, MEN**

07-Feb-31 CAN 8-AUT 0
22-Feb-33 CAN 4-AUT 0
13-Feb-38 CAN 3-AUT 0
13-Feb-49 CAN 7-AUT 0
18-Feb-49 CAN 8-AUT 2
22-Apr-93 CAN 11-AUT 0
26-Apr-94 CAN 6-AUT 1
23-Apr-96 CAN 4-AUT 0
01-May-98 CAN 5-AUT 1
25-Apr-04 CAN 2-AUT 2
Totals: 10-9-1-0-58-6

07-May-98 CAN 6-BLR 2
26-Apr-03 CAN 3-BLR 0
04-May-07 CAN 6-BLR 3
24-Apr-09 CAN 6-BLR 1
29-Apr-11 CAN 4-BLR 1
15-May-12 CAN 5-BLR 1
Totals: 6-6-0-0-30-8

15-Mar-50 CAN 33-BEL 0
Totals: 1-1-0-0-33-0

04-Feb-31 CAN 2-TCH 0
24-Feb-33 CAN 4-TCH 0
24-Jan-35 CAN 2-TCH 1
20-Feb-37 CAN 3-TCH 0
15-Feb-38 CAN 3-TCH 0
08-Feb-39 CAN 2-TCH 1
11-Feb-39 CAN 4-TCH 0
15-Feb-49 CAN 2-TCH 3
05-Mar-54 CAN 5-TCH 2
26-Feb-55 CAN 5-TCH 3
07-Mar-58 CAN 6-TCH 0
07-Mar-59 CAN 7-TCH 2
15-Mar-59 CAN 3-TCH 5
09-Mar-61 CAN 1-TCH 1
12-Mar-63 CAN 4-TCH 4
11-Mar-65 CAN 0-TCH 8
10-Mar-66 CAN 1-TCH 2
25-Mar-67 CAN 1-TCH 1
15-Mar-69 CAN 1-TCH 6
23-Mar-69 CAN 2-TCH 3
26-Apr-77 CAN 3-TCH 3
08-May-77 CAN 8-TCH 2
04-May-78 CAN 0-TCH 5
12-May-78 CAN 2-TCH 3
15-Apr-79 CAN 1-TCH 4
23-Apr-79 CAN 6-TCH 10
18-Apr-81 CAN 4-TCH 7
24-Apr-81 CAN 2-TCH 4
16-Apr-82 CAN 2-TCH 6
27-Apr-82 CAN 4-TCH 2
21-Apr-83 CAN 3-TCH 1
28-Apr-83 CAN 4-TCH 5
23-Apr-85 CAN 4-TCH 4
03-May-85 CAN 3-TCH 5
22-Apr-86 CAN 1-TCH 3
18-Apr-87 CAN 1-TCH 1
01-May-87 CAN 2-TCH 4
24-Apr-89 CAN 4-TCH 2
01-May-89 CAN 4-TCH 3
22-Apr-90 CAN 5-TCH 3
28-Apr-90 CAN 2-TCH 3
28-Apr-91 CAN 3-TCH 4
03-May-92 CAN 2-TCH 5
01-May-93 CAN 1-CZE 5
05-May-94 CAN 3-CZE 2
06-May-95 CAN 4-CZE 1
05-May-96 CAN 2-CZE 4
07-May-97 CAN 3-CZE 5
12-May-99 CAN 2-CZE 1
13-May-99 CAN 4-CZE 6*
03-May-00 CAN 1-CZE 2
12-May-00 CAN 1-CZE 2
08-May-01 CAN 2-CZE 4
05-May-02 CAN 1-CZE 5
09-May-03 CAN 8-CZE 4
03-May-04 CAN 2-CZE 6
15-May-05 CAN 0-CZE 3
14-May-06 CAN 4-CZE 6
06-May-07 CAN 4-CZE 3
(OT)
30-Apr-09 CAN 5-CZE 1
18-May-10 CAN 2-CZE 3
Totals vs. TCH:
43-17-6-20-128-131
Totals vs. CZE:
18-6-0-12-49-63
*Game 2, best-of-two, semi-finals. Czech won the game 5-4 and clinched the series in GWS.

12-Feb-49 CAN 47-DEN 0
02-May-03 CAN 2-DEN 2
05-May-06 CAN 5-DEN 3
Totals: 3-2-1-0-54-5

07-Mar-61 CAN 5-GDR 2
09-Mar-63 CAN 11-GDR 5
10-Mar-65 CAN 8-GDR 1
08-Mar-66 CAN 6-GDR 0
18-Mar-67 CAN 6-GDR 3
01-May-78 CAN 6-GDR 2
24-Apr-83 CAN 5-GDR 2
17-Apr-85 CAN 9-GDR 1
Totals: 8-8-0-0-56-16

10-Mar-51 CAN 11-FIN 1
04-Mar-54 CAN 20-FIN 1
28-Feb-55 CAN 12-FIN 0
03-Mar-58 CAN 24-FIN 0
09-Mar-59 CAN 6-FIN 0
11-Mar-61 CAN 12-FIN 1
08-Mar-62 CAN 8-FIN 1
14-Mar-63 CAN 12-FIN 2
05-Mar-65 CAN 4-FIN 0
06-Mar-66 CAN 9-FIN 1
19-Mar-67 CAN 5-FIN 1
16-Mar-69 CAN 5-FIN 1
29-Mar-69 CAN 6-FIN 1
27-Apr-77 CAN 5-FIN 1
27-Apr-78 CAN 4-FIN 6
17-Apr-79 CAN 5-FIN 4
12-Apr-81 CAN 4-FIN 3
15-Apr-82 CAN 9-FIN 2
22-Apr-83 CAN 5-FIN 1
21-Apr-85 CAN 5-FIN 2
15-Apr-86 CAN 2-FIN 3
28-Apr-86 CAN 4-FIN 3
26-Apr-87 CAN 7-FIN 2
15-Apr-89 CAN 6-FIN 4
19-Apr-90 CAN 6-FIN 5
23-Apr-91 CAN 5-FIN 3
06-May-92 CAN 3-FIN 4
28-Apr-93 CAN 5-FIN 1
08-May-94 CAN 2-FIN 1
(10:00 OT/GWS)
30-Apr-96 CAN 3-FIN 1
06-May-97 CAN 1-FIN 0
09-May-98 CAN 3-FIN 3
10-May-99 CAN 2-FIN 4
05-May-00 CAN 5-FIN 1
14-May-00 CAN 1-FIN 2
06-May-04 CAN 5-FIN 4
(OT)
08-May-05 CAN 3-FIN 3
15-May-06 CAN 4-FIN 2
21-May-06 CAN 0-FIN 5
13-May-07 CAN 4-FIN 2
12-May-08 CAN 6-FIN 3
04-May-09 CAN 3-FIN 4
(5:00 OT/GWS)
11-May-12 CAN 5-FIN 3
Totals: 43-34-2-7-256-92

01-Feb-31 CAN 9-FRA 0
06-Feb-34 CAN 9-FRA 0
17-Feb-37 CAN 12-FRA 0
23-Feb-37 CAN 13-FRA 1
28-Apr-92 CAN 4-FRA 3
25-Apr-95 CAN 1-FRA 4
27-Apr-04 CAN 3-FRA 0
01-May-11 CAN 9-FRA 1
07-May-12 CAN 7-FRA 2
Totals: 9-8-0-1-67-11

10-Feb-30 CAN 6-GER 1
21-Feb-33 CAN 5-GER 0
07-Feb-34 CAN 6-GER 0
22-Feb-37 CAN 5-GER 0
25-Feb-37 CAN 5-GER 0
16-Feb-38 CAN 3-GER 2
(OT)
19-Feb-38 CAN 1-GER 0
09-Feb-39 CAN 9-GER 0
28-Apr-94 CAN 3-GER 2
27-Apr-95 CAN 5-GER 2
24-Apr-96 CAN 1-GER 5
05-May-01 CAN 3-GER 3
02-May-02 CAN 3-GER 1
07-May-03 CAN 3-GER 2
(OT)
02-May-04 CAN 6 -GER 1
28-Apr-07 CAN 3-GER 2
10-May-08 CAN 10-GER 1
Totals: 17-15-1-1-77-22

19-Jan-35 CAN 4-GBR 2
26-Jan-35 CAN 6-GBR 0
26-Feb-37 CAN 3-GBR 0
20-Feb-38 CAN 3-GBR 1
07-Feb-39 CAN 4-GBR 0
21-Mar-50 CAN 12-GBR 0
13-Mar-51 CAN 17-GBR 1
17-Mar-62 CAN 12-GBR 2
30-Apr-94 CAN 8-GBR 2
Totals: 9-9-0-0-69-8

23-Feb-33 CAN 3-HUN 1
18-Feb-38 CAN 1-HUN 1
26-Apr-09 CAN 9-HUN 0
Totals: 3-2-1-0-13-2

23-Jan-35 CAN 9-ITA 0
21-Apr-82 CAN 3-ITA 3
16-Apr-83 CAN 6-ITA 0
24-Apr-93 CAN 11-ITA 2
25-Apr-94 CAN 4-ITA 1
29-Apr-95 CAN 2-ITA 2
03-May-97 CAN 6-ITA 0
05-May-98 CAN 5-ITA 2
05-May-99 CAN 5-ITA 2
07-May-00 CAN 6-ITA 0
30-Apr-01 CAN 3-ITA 1
29-Apr-02 CAN 5-ITA 0
08-May-10 CAN 5-ITA 1
Totals: 13-11-2-0-70-14

29-Apr-00 CAN 6-JPN 0
Totals: 1-1-0-0-6-0

12-May-12 CAN 8-KAZ 0
Totals: 1-1-0-0-8-0

20-Jan-35 CAN 14-LAT 0
30-Apr-97 CAN 3-LAT 3
27-Apr-02 CAN 4-LAT 1
27-Apr-03 CAN 6-LAT 1
30-Apr-04 CAN 2-LAT 0
30-Apr-05 CAN 6-LAT 4
11-May-06 CAN 11-LAT 0
04-May-08 CAN 7-LAT 0
07-May-09 CAN 4-LAT 2
10-May-10 CAN 6-LAT 1
Totals: 10-9-1-0-63-12

03-Feb-39 CAN 8-NED 0
13-Apr-81 CAN 8-NED 1
Totals: 2-2-0-0-16-1

20-Mar-50 CAN 11-NOR 1
11-Mar-51 CAN 8-NOR 0
28-Feb-54 CAN 8-NOR 0
02-Mar-58 CAN 12-NOR 0
13-Mar-62 CAN 14-NOR 1
06-Mar-65 CAN 6-NOR 0
20-Apr-90 CAN 8-NOR 0
01-May-92 CAN 4-NOR 3
26-Apr-97 CAN 7-NOR 0
03-May-99 CAN 4-NOR 2
01-May-00 CAN 3-NOR 4
28-Apr-01 CAN 5-NOR 0
07-May-06 CAN 7-NOR 1
30-Apr-07 CAN 4-NOR 2
08-May-08 CAN 2-NOR 1
14-May-08 CAN 8-NOR 2
03-May-09 CAN 5-NOR 1
14-May-10 CAN 12-NOR 1
07-May-11 CAN 3-NOR 2
Totals: 19-18-0-1-131-21

05-Feb-31 CAN 3-POL 0
18-Feb-37 CAN 8-POL 2
05-Feb-39 CAN 4-POL 0
27-Feb-55 CAN 8-POL 0
01-Mar-58 CAN 14-POL 1
05-Mar-59 CAN 9-POL 0
05-Mar-66 CAN 6-POL 0
16-Apr-86 CAN 8-POL 3
16-Apr-89 CAN 11-POL 0
Totals: 9-9-0-0-71-6

01-May-77 CAN 7-ROM 2
Totals: 1-1-0-0-7-2

07-Mar-54 CAN 2-URS 7
06-Mar-55 CAN 5-URS 0
09-Mar-58 CAN 4-URS 2
11-Mar-59 CAN 3-URS 1
12-Mar-61 CAN 5-URS 1
16-Mar-63 CAN 2-URS 4
14-Mar-65 CAN 1-URS 4
11-Mar-66 CAN 0-URS 3
27-Mar-67 CAN 1-URS 2
18-Mar-69 CAN 1-URS 7
30-Mar-69 CAN 2-URS 4
24-Apr-77 CAN 1-URS 11
06-May-77 CAN 1-URS 8
08-May-78 CAN 2-URS 4
10-May-78 CAN 1-URS 5
19-Apr-79 CAN 2-URS 5
25-Apr-79 CAN 2-URS 9
15-Apr-81 CAN 2-URS 8
22-Apr-81 CAN 4-URS 4
24-Apr-82 CAN 3-URS 4
25-Apr-82 CAN 4-URS 6
19-Apr-83 CAN 2-URS 8
02-May-83 CAN 2-URS 8
25-Apr-85 CAN 1-URS 9
01-May-85 CAN 3-URS 1
18-Apr-86 CAN 0-URS 4
24-Apr-86 CAN 4-URS 7
24-Apr-87 CAN 2-URS 3
29-Apr-87 CAN 0-URS 0
22-Apr-89 CAN 3-URS 4
29-Apr-89 CAN 3-URS 5
26-Apr-90 CAN 3-URS 3
30-Apr-90 CAN 1-URS 7
25-Apr-91 CAN 3-URS 5
02-May-91 CAN 3-URS 3
04-May-92 CAN 4-RUS 6
25-Apr-93 CAN 3-RUS 1
30-Apr-93 CAN 4-RUS 7
02-May-94 CAN 3-RUS 1
30-Apr-95 CAN 4-RUS 5
26-Apr-96 CAN 4-RUS 6
03-May-96 CAN 3-RUS 2
(10:00 OT/GWS)
09-May-97 CAN 2-RUS 1
02-May-01 CAN 5-RUS 1
05-May-03 CAN 5-RUS 2
14-May-05 CAN 4-RUS 3
18-May-08 CAN 4-RUS 5
(OT)
10-May-09 CAN 1-RUS 2
20-May-10 CAN 2-RUS 5
12-May-11 CAN 1-RUS 2
Totals vs. URS
35-5-4-26-78-166
Totals vs. RUS
15-7-0-8-49-49

21-Apr-96 CAN 3-SVK 3
03-May-98 CAN 2-SVK 2
01-May-99 CAN 3-SVK 2
09-May-00 CAN 4-SVK 3
07-May-02 CAN 2-SVK 3
08-May-04 CAN 2-SVK 1
12-May-05 CAN 5-SVK 4
17-May-06 CAN 4-SVK 1
02-May-07 CAN 5-SVK 4
28-Apr-09 CAN 7-SVK 3
04-May-12 CAN 3-SVK 2
17-May-12 CAN 3-SVK 4
Totals: 12-8-2-2-43-32

03-May-05 CAN 8-SLO 0
02-May-08 CAN 5-SLO 1
Totals: 2-2-0-0-13-1

06-Feb-31 CAN 0-SWE 0
22-Jan-35 CAN 5-SWE 2
19-Feb-37 CAN 9-SWE 0
12-Feb-38 CAN 3-SWE 2
16-Feb-49 CAN 2-SWE 2
22-Mar-50 CAN 3-SWE 1
17-Mar-51 CAN 5-SWE 1
01-Mar-54 CAN 8-SWE 0
03-Mar-55 CAN 3-SWE 0
06-Mar-58 CAN 10-SWE 2
12-Mar-59 CAN 5-SWE 0
02-Mar-61 CAN 6-SWE 1
13-Mar-62 CAN 3-SWE 5
15-Mar-63 CAN 1-SWE 4
13-Mar-65 CAN 4-SWE 6
13-Mar-66 CAN 4-SWE 2
29-Mar-67 CAN 0-SWE 6
21-Mar-69 CAN 1-SWE 5
27-Mar-69 CAN 2-SWE 4
22-Apr-77 CAN 2-SWE 4
04-May-77 CAN 7-SWE 0
06-May-78 CAN 7-SWE 5
14-May-78 CAN 3-SWE 2
21-Apr-79 CAN 3-SWE 5
27-Apr-79 CAN 6-SWE 3
20-Apr-81 CAN 1-SWE 3
26-Apr-81 CAN 3-SWE 4
18-Apr-82 CAN 3-SWE 3
29-Apr-82 CAN 6-SWE 0
17-Apr-83 CAN 2-SWE 3
30-Apr-83 CAN 3-SWE 1
27-Apr-85 CAN 6-SWE 3
13-Apr-86 CAN 1-SWE 4
26-Apr-86 CAN 5-SWE 6
23-Apr-87 CAN 3-SWE 4
03-May-87 CAN 0-SWE 9
21-Apr-89 CAN 5-SWE 6
27-Apr-89 CAN 5-SWE 3
24-Apr-90 CAN 3-SWE 1
02-May-90 CAN 4-SWE 6
26-Apr-91 CAN 3-SWE 3
30-Apr-91 CAN 3-SWE 3
20-Apr-93 CAN 4-SWE 1
07-May-94 CAN 6-SWE 0
05-May-95 CAN 2-SWE 3
(OT)
27-Apr-97 CAN 2-SWE 7
11-May-97 CAN 2-SWE 3
13-May-97 CAN 3-SWE 1
14-May-97 CAN 2-SWE 1
10-May-98 CAN 1-SWE 7
15-May-99 CAN 2-SWE 3
29-Apr-03 CAN 3-SWE 1
11-May-03 CAN 3-SWE 2
(OT)
09-May-04 CAN 5-SWE 3
07-May-05 CAN 4-SWE 5
20-May-06 CAN 4-SWE 5
12-May-07 CAN 4-SWE 1
16-May-08 CAN 5-SWE 4
08-May-09 CAN 3-SWE 1
16-May-10 CAN 1-SWE 3
09-May-11 CAN 3-SWE 2
Totals: 61-31-5-25-217-177

10-Feb-34 CAN 2-SUI 1
(OT)
27-Jan-35 CAN 4-SUI 2
27-Feb-37 CAN 2-SUI 1
(OT)
10-Feb-39 CAN 7-SUI 0
20-Feb-49 CAN 1-SUI 1
14-Mar-50 CAN 13-SUI 2
17-Mar-50 CAN 11-SUI 1
16-Mar-51 CAN 5-SUI 1
27-Feb-54 CAN 8-SUI 1
02-Mar-55 CAN 11-SUI 1
06-Mar-59 CAN 23-SUI 0
11-Mar-62 CAN 7-SUI 2
20-Apr-87 CAN 6-SUI 1

20-Apr-91 CAN 3-SUI 0
30-Apr-92 CAN 1-SUI 1
19-Apr-93 CAN 2-SUI 0
24-Apr-95 CAN 5-SUI 3
07-May-99 CAN 8-SUI 2
11-May-00 CAN 5-SUI 3
04-May-01 CAN 6-SUI 2
03-May-02 CAN 3-SUI 2
04-May-03 CAN 2-SUI 0
28-Apr-04 CAN 3-SUI 1
10-May-07 CAN 5-SUI 1
12-May-10 CAN 1-SUI 4
03-May-11 CAN 4-SUI 3 (OT)
09-May-12 CAN 3-SUI 2
Totals: 27-24-2-1-151-38

10-May-05 CAN 2 -UKR 1
Totals: 1-1-0-0-2-1

08-Feb-31 CAN 2-USA 0
26-Feb-33 CAN 1-USA 2 (10:00 OT)
11-Feb-34 CAN 2-USA 1
12-Feb-39 CAN 4-USA 0
17-Feb-49 CAN 7-USA 2
18-Mar-50 CAN 5-USA 0
15-Mar-51 CAN 16-USA 2
25-Feb-55 CAN 12-USA 1
08-Mar-58 CAN 12-USA 1
14-Mar-59 CAN 4-USA 1
05-Mar-61 CAN 7-USA 4
18-Mar-62 CAN 6-USA 1
11-Mar-63 CAN 10-USA 4
08-Mar-65 CAN 5-USA 2
03-Mar-66 CAN 7-USA 2
23-Mar-67 CAN 2-USA 1
20-Mar-69 CAN 5-USA 0
25-Mar-69 CAN 1-USA 0
21-Apr-77 CAN 4-USA 1
30-Apr-78 CAN 7-USA 2
14-Apr-79 CAN 6-USA 3
22-Apr-82 CAN 5-USA 3
20-Apr-85 CAN 3-USA 4
29-Apr-85 CAN 3-USA 2
20-Apr-86 CAN 4-USA 2
17-Apr-87 CAN 3-USA 1
18-Apr-89 CAN 8-USA 0
17-Apr-90 CAN 6-USA 3
19-Apr-91 CAN 4-USA 3
04-May-91 CAN 9-USA 4
03-May-95 CAN 4-USA 1
28-Apr-96 CAN 5-USA 1
01-May-97 CAN 5-USA 1
09-May-99 CAN 4-USA 1
10-May-01 CAN 3-USA 4 (OT)
30-Apr-02 CAN 2-USA 1
05-May-05 CAN 3-USA 1
09-May-06 CAN 2-USA 1
07-May-07 CAN 6-USA 3
06-May-08 CAN 5-USA 4
06-May-11 CAN 4-USA 3 (5:00 OT/GWS)
05-May-12 CAN 4-USA 5 (OT)
Totals: 42-38-0-4-217-78

03-Mar-54 CAN 8-FRG 1
04-Mar-55 CAN 10-FRG 1
04-Mar-61 CAN 9-FRG 1
10-Mar-62 CAN 8-FRG 0
08-Mar-63 CAN 6-FRG 0
21-Mar-67 CAN 13-FRG 1
29-Apr-77 CAN 9-FRG 3
28-Apr-78 CAN 6-FRG 2
19-Apr-82 CAN 7-FRG 1
25-Apr-83 CAN 3-FRG 1
18-Apr-85 CAN 5-FRG 0
12-Apr-86 CAN 8-FRG 3
21-Apr-87 CAN 3-FRG 5
19-Apr-89 CAN 8-FRG 2
16-Apr-90 CAN 5-FRG 1
22-Apr-91 CAN 3-FRG 2
Totals: 16-15-0-1-111-24

**WORLD U20 CHAMPIONSHIPS**

30-Dec-80 CAN 11-AUT 1
Totals: 1-1-0-0-11-1

26-Dec-00 CAN 9-BLR 0
Totals: 1-1-0-0-9-0

25-Dec-76 CAN 4-TCH 4
25-Dec-77 CAN 9-TCH 3
31-Dec-77 CAN 6-TCH 3
27-Dec-80 CAN 3-TCH 3
02-Jan-82 CAN 3-TCH 3
01-Jan-83 CAN 7-TCH 7
03-Jan-84 CAN 4-TCH 6
01-Jan-85 CAN 2-TCH 2
04-Jan-86 CAN 3-TCH 5
29-Dec-86 CAN 1-TCH 5
28-Dec-87 CAN 4-TCH 2
01-Jan-89 CAN 2-TCH 2
04-Jan-90 CAN 2-TCH 1
02-Jan-91 CAN 5-TCH 6
02-Jan-92 CAN 1-TCH 6
04-Jan-93 CAN 4-CZE/SVK 7
02-Jan-94 CAN 6-CZE 4
30-Dec-94 CAN 7-CZE 5
31-Dec-96 CAN 3-CZE 3
28-Dec-97 CAN 5-CZE 0
30-Dec-98 CAN 2-CZE 0
28-Dec-99 CAN 1-CZE 1
28-Dec-02 CAN 4-CZE 0
31-Dec-03 CAN 5-CZE 2
03-Jan-04 CAN 7-CZE 1
02-Jan-05 CAN 3-CZE 1
26-Dec-07 CAN 3-CZE 0
26-Dec-08 CAN 8-CZE 1
28-Dec-10 CAN 7-CZE 2
28-Dec-11 CAN 5-CZE 0
Totals vs. TCH: 16-4-6-6-60-65
Totals vs. CZE: 14-12-2-0-66-20

31-Dec-07 CAN 4-DEN 1
29-Dec-11 CAN 10-DEN 2
Totals: 2-2-0-0-14-3

26-Dec-76 CAN 6-FIN 4
27-Dec-78 CAN 1-FIN 3
27-Dec-79 CAN 1-FIN 2
22-Dec-81 CAN 5-FIN 1
29-Dec-82 CAN 6-FIN 3
25-Dec-83 CAN 2-FIN 4
31-Dec-84 CAN 4-FIN 4
01-Jan-86 CAN 6-FIN 5
27-Dec-86 CAN 6-FIN 6
29-Dec-87 CAN 4-FIN 4
03-Jan-89 CAN 4-FIN 3
31-Dec-89 CAN 3-FIN 3
01-Jan-91 CAN 5-FIN 1
30-Dec-91 CAN 2-FIN 2
30-Dec-92 CAN 3-FIN 2
30-Dec-93 CAN 6-FIN 3
01-Jan-95 CAN 6-FIN 4
29-Dec-95 CAN 3-FIN 1
25-Dec-97 CAN 2-FIN 3
28-Dec-98 CAN 6-FIN 4
25-Dec-99 CAN 3-FIN 2
28-Dec-00 CAN 2-FIN 2
03-Jan-01 CAN 2-FIN 5
30-Dec-01 CAN 1-FIN 4
31-Dec-02 CAN 5-FIN 3
26-Dec-03 CAN 3-FIN 0
30-Dec-04 CAN 8-FIN 1
26-Dec-05 CAN 5-FIN 1
03-Jan-06 CAN 4-FIN 0
02-Jan-08 CAN 4-FIN 2
26-Dec-11 CAN 8-FIN 1
05-Jan-12 CAN 4-FIN 0
Totals: 32-20-6-6-130-83

25-Dec-01 CAN 15-FRA 0
Totals: 1-1-0-0-15-0

26-Dec-91 CAN 5-GER 4
01-Jan-93 CAN 5-GER 2
27-Dec-93 CAN 5-GER 2
27-Dec-94 CAN 9-GER 1
27-Dec-96 CAN 4-GER 1
30-Dec-97 CAN 2-GER 0
29-Dec-02 CAN 4-GER 1
28-Dec-04 CAN 9-GER 0
29-Dec-06 CAN 3-GER 1
29-Dec-08 CAN 5-GER 1
Totals: 10-10-0-0-51-13

02-Jan-93 CAN 8-JPN 1
Totals: 1-1-0-0-8-1

03-Jan-98 CAN 3-KAZ 6
02-Jan-99 CAN 12-KAZ 2
28-Dec-08 CAN 15-KAZ 0
Totals: 3-2-0-1-30-8

26-Dec-09 CAN 16-LAT 0
Totals: 1-1-0-0-16-0

31-Dec-78 CAN 10-NOR 1
04-Jan-83 CAN 13-NOR 0
26-Dec-88 CAN 7-NOR 1
29-Dec-89 CAN 6-NOR 3
29-Dec-90 CAN 10-NOR 1
29-Dec-05 CAN 4-NOR 0
29-Dec-10 CAN 10-NOR 1
Totals: 7-7-0-0-60-7

23-Dec-76 CAN 14-POL 0
25-Dec-84 CAN 12-POL 1
30-Dec-86 CAN 18-POL 3
04-Jan-88 CAN 9-POL 1
28-Dec-89 CAN 12-POL 0
Totals: 5-5-0-0-65-5

02-Jan-77 CAN 4-URS 6
28-Dec-77 CAN 2-URS 3
28-Dec-79 CAN 5-URS 8
28-Dec-80 CAN 3-URS 7
26-Dec-81 CAN 7-URS 0
30-Dec-82 CAN 3-URS 7
02-Jan-84 CAN 3-URS 3
29-Dec-84 CAN 5-URS 0
02-Jan-86 CAN 1-URS 4
04-Jan-87 CAN 4-URS 2*
01-Jan-88 CAN 3-URS 2
04-Jan-89 CAN 2-URS 7
01-Jan-90 CAN 6-URS 4
04-Jan-91 CAN 3-URS 2
04-Jan-92 CAN 2-RUS 7
29-Dec-92 CAN 9-RUS 1
29-Dec-93 CAN 3-RUS 3
02-Jan-95 CAN 8-RUS 5
03-Jan-96 CAN 4-RUS 3
03-Jan-97 CAN 3-RUS 2
31-Dec-97 CAN 1-RUS 2 (OT)
05-Jan-99 CAN 2-RUS 3 (OT)
03-Jan-00 CAN 2-RUS 3
29-Dec-00 CAN 1-RUS 3
29-Dec-01 CAN 5-RUS 2
04-Jan-02 CAN 4-RUS 5
05-Jan-03 CAN 2-RUS 3
04-Jan-05 CAN 6-RUS 1
05-Jan-06 CAN 5-RUS 0
05-Jan-07 CAN 4-RUS 2
03-Jan-09 CAN 6-RUS 5 (10:00 OT/GWS)
26-Dec-10 CAN 6-RUS 3
05-Jan-11 CAN 3-RUS 5
03-Jan-12 CAN 5-RUS 6
Totals vs. URS: 14-6-1-7-51-55
Totals vs. RUS: 20-10-1-9-81-64
*Game suspended because of brawl—score and stats not counted

01-Jan-97 CAN 7-SVK 2
27-Dec-98 CAN 0-SVK 0
29-Dec-99 CAN 4-SVK 1
25-Dec-04 CAN 7-SVK 3
31-Dec-06 CAN 3-SVK 0
27-Dec-07 CAN 2-SVK 0
29-Dec-09 CAN 8-SVK 2
Totals: 7-6-1-0-31-8

28-Dec-76 CAN 5-SWE 3
01-Jan-78 CAN 5-SWE 6
30-Dec-78 CAN 0-SWE 1
23-Dec-81 CAN 3-SWE 2
02-Jan-83 CAN 2-SWE 5
31-Dec-83 CAN 6-SWE 2
23-Dec-84 CAN 8-SWE 2
30-Dec-85 CAN 9-SWE 2
02-Jan-87 CAN 4-SWE 3
26-Dec-87 CAN 4-SWE 2
31-Dec-88 CAN 4-SWE 5
03-Jan-90 CAN 4-SWE 5
30-Dec-90 CAN 7-SWE 4
29-Dec-91 CAN 2-SWE 2
27-Dec-92 CAN 5-SWE 4
04-Jan-94 CAN 6-SWE 4
04-Jan-95 CAN 4-SWE 3
04-Jan-96 CAN 4-SWE 1
26-Dec-97 CAN 0-SWE 4
04-Jan-99 CAN 6-SWE 1
05-Jan-01 CAN 2-SWE 1 (OT)
01-Jan-02 CAN 5-SWE 2
26-Dec-02 CAN 8-SWE 2
27-Dec-04 CAN 8-SWE 1
26-Dec-06 CAN 2-SWE 0
29-Dec-07 CAN 3-SWE 4
05-Jan-08 CAN 3-SWE 2 (OT)
05-Jan-09 CAN 5-SWE 1
31-Dec-10 CAN 5-SWE 6 (5:00 OT/GWS)
Totals: 29-20-1-8-129-80

30-Dec-79 CAN 9-SUI 5
01-Jan-82 CAN 11-SUI 1
28-Dec-83 CAN 12-SUI 0
26-Dec-85 CAN 12-SUI 1
26-Dec-86 CAN 6-SUI 4
26-Dec-90 CAN 6-SUI 0
27-Dec-91 CAN 6-SUI 4
26-Dec-93 CAN 5-SUI 1
27-Dec-95 CAN 2-SUI 1
30-Dec-96 CAN 4-SUI 1
01-Jan-00 CAN 8-SUI 3
31-Dec-00 CAN 8-SUI 4
27-Dec-01 CAN 6-SUI 1
02-Jan-02 CAN 4-SUI 0
28-Dec-03 CAN 7-SUI 2
28-Dec-05 CAN 4-SUI 3
28-Dec-09 CAN 6-SUI 0
03-Jan-10 CAN 6-SUI 1
02-Jan-11 CAN 4-SUI 1
Totals: 19-19-0-0-126-33

26-Dec-94 CAN 7-UKR 1
31-Dec-95 CAN 8-UKR 1
29-Dec-03 CAN 10-UKR 0
Totals: 3-3-0-0-25-2

01-Jan-77 CAN 8-USA 2
22-Dec-77 CAN 6-USA 3
02-Jan-79 CAN 6-USA 3
01-Jan-80 CAN 4-USA 2
31-Dec-80 CAN 3-USA 7
27-Dec-81 CAN 5-USA 4
27-Dec-82 CAN 4-USA 2
26-Dec-83 CAN 5-USA 2
28-Dec-84 CAN 7-USA 5
29-Dec-85 CAN 5-USA 2
01-Jan-87 CAN 6-USA 2
31-Dec-87 CAN 5-USA 4
29-Dec-88 CAN 5-USA 1
26-Dec-89 CAN 3-USA 2
27-Dec-90 CAN 4-USA 4
01-Jan-92 CAN 3-USA 5
26-Dec-92 CAN 3-USA 0
01-Jan-94 CAN 8-USA 3
29-Dec-94 CAN 8-USA 3
26-Dec-95 CAN 6-USA 1
28-Dec-96 CAN 4-USA 4
04-Jan-97 CAN 2-USA 0
02-Jan-98 CAN 0-USA 3
31-Dec-98 CAN 2-USA 5
31-Dec-99 CAN 1-USA 1
04-Jan-00 CAN 4-USA 3 (10:00 OT/GWS)
02-Jan-01 CAN 2-USA 1
03-Jan-03 CAN 3-USA 2
05-Jan-04 CAN 3-USA 4
31-Dec-05 CAN 3-USA 2
27-Dec-06 CAN 6-USA 3
03-Jan-07 CAN 2-USA 1 (10:00 OT/GWS)
04-Jan-08 CAN 4-USA 1
31-Dec-08 CAN 7-USA 4
31-Dec-09 CAN 5-USA 4 (5:00 OT/GWS)
05-Jan-10 CAN 5-USA 6 (OT)
03-Jan-11 CAN 4-USA 1
31-Dec-11 CAN 3-USA 2
Totals: 38-29-3-6-164-104

29-Dec-76 CAN 9-FRG 1
23-Dec-77 CAN 8-FRG 0
28-Dec-78 CAN 6-FRG 2
02-Jan-80 CAN 6-FRG 1
02-Jan-81 CAN 6-FRG 7
29-Dec-81 CAN 11-FRG 3
26-Dec-82 CAN 4-FRG 0
29-Dec-83 CAN 7-FRG 0
26-Dec-84 CAN 6-FRG 0
27-Dec-85 CAN 18-FRG 2
03-Jan-88 CAN 8-FRG 1
28-Dec-88 CAN 7-FRG 4
Totals: 12-11-0-1-96-21

**WORLD U18 CHAMPIONSHIPS, MEN**

21-Apr-02 CAN 3-BLR 5
10-Apr-04 CAN 7-BLR 2
15-Apr-10 CAN 11-BLR 3
Totals: 3-2-0-1-21-10

15-Apr-02 CAN 1-CZE 4
14-Apr-03 CAN 3-CZE 3
18-Apr-04 CAN 2-CZE 3
22-Apr-05 CAN 3-CZE 2 (OT)
22-Apr-06 CAN 1-CZE 4
13-Apr-09 CAN 4-CZE 3 (OT)
15-Apr-11 CAN 5-CZE 0
16-Apr-12 CAN 6-CZE 2
Totals: 8-4-1-3-25-21

11-Apr-04 CAN 2-DEN 1
18-Apr-05 CAN 15-DEN 1
15-Apr-08 CAN 4-DEN 1
12-Apr-12 CAN 6-DEN 1
Totals: 4-4-0-0-27-4

20-Apr-02 CAN 1-FIN 3
17-Apr-06 CAN 0-FIN 0
20-Apr-06 CAN 2-FIN 3 (OT)
20-Apr-08 CAN 2-FIN 1
19-Apr-09 CAN 4-FIN 5 (10:00 OT/GWS)
16-Apr-11 CAN 5-FIN 4
14-Apr-12 CAN 2-FIN 4
22-Apr-12 CAN 5-FIN 4 (OT)
Totals: 8-3-1-4-21-24

12-Apr-02 CAN 9-GER 1
14-Apr-05 CAN 2-GER 1
12-Apr-07 CAN 7-GER 3
13-Apr-08 CAN 9-GER 2
09-Apr-09 CAN 11-GER 2
21-Apr-11 CAN 4-GER 3
Totals: 6-6-0-0-42-12

16-Apr-03 CAN 8-KAZ 1
Totals: 1-1-0-0-8-1

14-Apr-07 CAN 9-LAT 1
21-Apr-10 CAN 5-LAT 1
Totals: 2-2-0-0-14-2

17-Apr-02 CAN 4-NOR 3
13-Apr-06 CAN 9-NOR 2
18-Apr-11 CAN 5-NOR 0
Totals: 3-3-0-0-18-5

11-Apr-02 CAN 4-RUS 8
12-Apr-03 CAN 3-RUS 6
16-Apr-04 CAN 2-RUS 5
19-Apr-05 CAN 6-RUS 3
19-Apr-06 CAN 4-RUS 1
17-Apr-07 CAN 5-RUS 2
16-Apr-08 CAN 2-RUS 4
23-Apr-08 CAN 8-RUS 0
24-Apr-11 CAN 4-RUS 6
19-Apr-12 CAN 4-RUS 2
Totals: 10-5-0-5-42-37

14-Apr-02 CAN 3-SVK 1
22-Apr-03 CAN 3-SVK 0
15-Apr-04 CAN 3-SVK 1
12-Apr-06 CAN 3-SVK 1
18-Apr-08 CAN 6-SVK 0
22-Apr-10 CAN 4-SVK 2
Totals: 6-6-0-0-22-5

19-Apr-03 CAN 8-SWE 1
08-Apr-04 CAN 5-SWE 0
16-Apr-05 CAN 1-SWE 2
15-Apr-06 CAN 0-SWE 2
22-Apr-07 CAN 3-SWE 8
21-Apr-08 CAN 3-SWE 2
14-Apr-09 CAN 4-SWE 2
18-Apr-10 CAN 4-SWE 5
19-Apr-11 CAN 2-SWE 4
Totals: 9-4-0-5-30-26

17-Apr-03 CAN 5-SUI 0
11-Apr-09 CAN 8-SUI 1
13-Apr-10 CAN 1-SUI 3
Totals: 3-2-0-1-14-4

18-Apr-02 CAN 3-USA 10
20-Apr-03 CAN 2-USA 1 (OT)
13-Apr-04 CAN 1-USA 2
24-Apr-05 CAN 1-USA 5
15-Apr-07 CAN 3-USA 2 (5:00 OT/GWS)
20-Apr-07 CAN 3-USA 4 (10:00 OT/GWS)
17-Apr-09 CAN 1-USA 2
16-Apr-10 CAN 0-USA 5
23-Apr-11 CAN 4-USA 5 (OT)
17-Apr-12 CAN 3-USA 5
20-Apr-12 CAN 1-USA 2
Totals: 11-2-0-9-22-43

**OLYMPICS, WOMEN**

09-Feb-98 CAN 2-CHN 0
Totals: 1-1-0-0-2-0

12-Feb-98 CAN 4-FIN 2
19-Feb-02 CAN 7-FIN 3
17-Feb-06 CAN 6-FIN 0
22-Feb-10 CAN 5-FIN 0
Totals: 4-4-0-0-22-5

11-Feb-06 CAN 16-ITA 0
Totals: 1-1-0-0-16-0

08-Feb-98 CAN 13-JPN 0
Totals: 1-1-0-0-13-0

11-Feb-02 CAN 7-KAZ 0
Totals: 1-1-0-0-7-0

13-Feb-02 CAN 7-RUS 0
12-Feb-06 CAN 12-RUS 0
Totals: 2-2-0-0-19-0

13-Feb-10 CAN 18-SVK 0
Totals: 1-1-0-0-18-0

11-Feb-98 CAN 5-SWE 3
16-Feb-02 CAN 11-SWE 0
14-Feb-06 CAN 8-SWE 1
20-Feb-06 CAN 4-SWE 1
17-Feb-10 CAN 13-SWE 1
Totals: 5-5-0-0-41-6

15-Feb-10 CAN 10-SUI 1
Totals: 1-1-0-0-10-1

14-Feb-98 CAN 4-USA 7
17-Feb-98 CAN 1-USA 3
21-Feb-02 CAN 3-USA 2
25-Feb-10 CAN 2-USA 0
Totals: 4-2-0-2-10-12

**WOMEN'S WORLD CHAMPIONSHIPS**
20-Apr-92 CAN 8-CHN 0
11-Apr-94 CAN 7-CHN 1
03-Apr-97 CAN 7-CHN 1
04-Apr-00 CAN 8-CHN 1
30-Mar-04 CAN 11-CHN 0
06-Apr-08 CAN 11-CHN 0
04-Apr-09 CAN 13-CHN 1
Totals: 7-7-0-0-65-4

21-Apr-92 CAN 10-DEN 0
Totals: 1-1-0-0-10-0

24-Mar-90 CAN 6-FIN 5
25-Apr-92 CAN 6-FIN 2
15-Apr-94 CAN 4-FIN 1
05-Apr-97 CAN 2-FIN 1
11-Mar-99 CAN 1-FIN 0
08-Apr-00 CAN 3-FIN 2
07-Apr-01 CAN 8-FIN 0
08-Apr-05 CAN 3-FIN 0
09-Apr-07 CAN 5-FIN 0
09-Apr-08 CAN 4-FIN 2
08-Apr-09 CAN 8-FIN 0
19-Apr-11 CAN 2-FIN 0
23-Apr-11 CAN 4-FIN 1
08-Apr-12 CAN 3-FIN 2
13-Apr-12 CAN 5-FIN 1
Totals: 15-15-0-0-64-17

21-Mar-90 CAN 17-GER 0
09-Mar-99 CAN 13-GER 0
01-Apr-04 CAN 13-GER 0
05-Apr-07 CAN 8-GER 0
Totals: 4-4-0-0-51-0

22-Mar-90 CAN 18-JPN 0
03-Apr-00 CAN 9-JPN 0
Totals: 2-2-0-0-27-0

02-Apr-01 CAN 11-KAZ 0
03-Apr-05 CAN 13-KAZ 0
17-Apr-11 CAN 7-KAZ 0
Totals: 3-3-0-0-31-0

12-Apr-94 CAN 12-NOR 0
Totals: 1-1-0-0-12-0

01-Apr-97 CAN 9-RUS 1
03-Apr-01 CAN 5-RUS 1
04-Apr-05 CAN 12-RUS 0
04-Apr-08 CAN 8-RUS 1
10-Apr-12 CAN 14-RUS 1
Totals: 5-5-0-0-48-4

19-Mar-90 CAN 15-SWE 1
23-Apr-92 CAN 6-SWE 1
14-Apr-94 CAN 8-SWE 2
13-Mar-99 CAN 4-SWE 1
06-Apr-00 CAN 4-SWE 0
05-Apr-01 CAN 13-SWE 0
04-Apr-04 CAN 7-SWE 1
06-Apr-05 CAN 10-SWE 0
06-Apr-09 CAN 7-SWE 0
Totals: 9-9-0-0-74-6

31-Mar-97 CAN 6-SUI 0
08-Mar-99 CAN 10-SUI 0
03-Apr-07 CAN 9-SUI 0
16-Apr-11 CAN 12-SUI 0
Totals: 4-4-0-0-37-0

25-Mar-90 CAN 5-USA 2
26-Apr-92 CAN 8-USA 0
17-Apr-94 CAN 6-USA 3
06-Apr-97 CAN 4-USA 3 (OT)
14-Mar-99 CAN 3-USA 1
09-Apr-00 CAN 3-USA 2
08-Apr-01 CAN 3-USA 2
03-Apr-04 CAN 1-USA 3
06-Apr-04 CAN 2-USA 0
09-Apr-05 CAN 0-USA 1 (20:00 OT/GWS)
07-Apr-07 CAN 5-USA 4
10-Apr-07 CAN 5-USA 1
10-Apr-08 CAN 2-USA 4
12-Apr-08 CAN 3-USA 4
10-Apr-09 CAN 2-USA 1
12-Apr-09 CAN 1-USA 4
25-Apr-11 CAN 2-USA 3 (OT)
07-Apr-12 CAN 2-USA 9
14-Apr-12 CAN 5-USA 4 (OT)
Totals: 19-12-0-7-62-51

**WOMEN'S U18 WORLD CHAMPIONSHIPS**
07-Jan-08 CAN 11-CZE 2
07-Jan-09 CAN 13-CZE 0
Totals: 2-2-0-0-24-2

09-Jan-08 CAN 17-FIN 0
06-Jan-09 CAN 6-FIN 0
02-Jan-11 CAN 6-FIN 0
07-Jan-11 CAN 6-FIN 1
03-Jan-12 CAN 7-FIN 0
Totals: 5-5-0-0-42-1

08-Jan-08 CAN 10-GER 1
28-Mar-10 CAN 15-GER 0
02-Apr-10 CAN 10-GER 0
04-Jan-11 CAN 8-GER 1
01-Jan-12 CAN 6-GER 0
Totals: 5-5-0-0-49-2

27-Mar-10 CAN 6-RUS 3
Totals: 1-1-0-0-6-3

11-Jan-08 CAN 7-SWE 1
09-Jan-09 CAN 6-SWE 1
30-Mar-10 CAN 8-SWE 0
06-Jan-12 CAN 7-SWE 0
Totals: 4-4-0-0-28-2

05-Jan-09 CAN 16-SUI 1
01-Jan-11 CAN 9-SUI 1
31-Dec-11 CAN 13-SUI 1
Totals: 3-3-0-0-38-3

12-Jan-08 CAN 2-USA 5
10-Jan-09 CAN 2-USA 3 (OT)
03-Apr-10 CAN 5-USA 4 (OT)
08-Jan-11 CAN 2-USA 5
07-Jan-12 CAN 3-USA 0
Totals: 5-2-0-3-14-17

# CHINA (CHN)

Totals=GP-W-T-L-GF-GA

**OLYMPICS, WOMEN**
**Date Score**
09-Feb-98 CHN 0-CAN 2
Totals: 1-0-0-1-0-2

14-Feb-98 CHN 1-FIN 6
17-Feb-98 CHN 1-FIN 4
12-Feb-02 CHN 0-FIN 4
16-Feb-10 CHN 1-FIN 2
Totals: 4-0-0-4-3-16

16-Feb-02 CHN 5-GER 5
Totals: 1-0-1-0-5-5

11-Feb-98 CHN 6-JPN 1
Totals: 1-1-0-0-6-1

19-Feb-02 CHN 2-KAZ 1 (OT)
Totals: 1-1-0-0-2-1

17-Feb-02 CHN 1-RUS 4
18-Feb-10 CHN 1-RUS 2
Totals: 2-0-0-2-2-6

22-Feb-10 CHN 3-SVK 1
Totals: 1-1-0-0-3-1

12-Feb-98 CHN 3-SWE 1
Totals: 1-1-0-0-3-1

20-Feb-10 CHN 0-SUI 6
Totals: 1-0-0-1-0-6

08-Feb-98 CHN 0-USA 5
14-Feb-02 CHN 1-USA 12
14-Feb-10 CHN 1-USA 12
Totals: 3-0-0-3-2-29

**WOMEN'S WORLD CHAMPIONSHIPS**
20-Apr-92 CHN 0-CAN 8
11-Apr-94 CHN 1-CAN 7
03-Apr-97 CHN 1-CAN 7
04-Apr-00 CHN 1-CAN 8
30-Mar-04 CHN 0-CAN 11
06-Apr-08 CHN 0-CAN 11
04-Apr-09 CHN 1-CAN 13
Totals: 7-0-0-7-4-65

23-Apr-92 CHN 5-DEN 2
Totals: 1-1-0-0-5-2

17-Apr-94 CHN 1-FIN 8
06-Apr-97 CHN 0-FIN 3
02-Apr-01 CHN 6-FIN 7
05-Apr-05 CHN 1-FIN 5
Totals: 4-0-0-4-8-23

08-Apr-00 CHN 3-GER 0
05-Apr-01 CHN 0 -GER 0
08-Apr-01 CHN 0-GER 1
31-Mar-04 CHN 2-GER 4
06-Apr-05 CHN 3-GER 3
09-Apr-05 CHN 0-GER 3
10-Apr-08 CHN 4-GER 2
Totals: 7-2-2-3-12-13

06-Apr-00 CHN 3-JPN 0
04-Apr-04 CHN 5-JPN 2
09-Apr-08 CHN 1-JPN 3
10-Apr-09 CHN 1-JPN 2
Totals: 4-2-0-2-10-7

06-Apr-01 CHN 4-KAZ 1
08-Apr-05 CHN 3-KAZ 0
04-Apr-07 CHN 7-KAZ 0
Totals: 3-3-0-0-14-1

26-Apr-92 CHN 2-NOR 1
14-Apr-94 CHN 8-NOR 1
Totals: 2-2-0-0-10-2

31-Mar-97 CHN 6-RUS 2
09-Mar-99 CHN 3-RUS 2
14-Mar-99 CHN 4-RUS 1
09-Apr-00 CHN 0-RUS 4
05-Apr-08 CHN 3-RUS 5
Totals: 5-3-0-2-16-14

21-Apr-92 CHN 2-SWE 6
12-Apr-94 CHN 4-SWE 4
08-Mar-99 CHN 1-SWE 3
03-Apr-00 CHN 1-SWE 1
08-Apr-07 CHN 2-SWE 12
05-Apr-09 CHN 1-SWE 6
Totals: 6-0-2-4-11-32

24-Apr-92 CHN 2-SUI 1 (10:00 OT/GWS)
01-Apr-97 CHN 11-SUI 3
12-Mar-99 CHN 3-SUI 2
03-Apr-04 CHN 6-SUI 3
07-Apr-07 CHN 1-SUI 5
08-Apr-09 CHN 4-SUI 5 (5:00 OT/GWS)
Totals: 6-4-0-2-27-19

15-Apr-94 CHN 3-USA 14
05-Apr-97 CHN 0-USA 6
11-Mar-99 CHN 0-USA 6
03-Apr-01 CHN 0-USA 13
03-Apr-05 CHN 2-USA 8
05-Apr-07 CHN 1-USA 9
Totals: 6-0-0-6-6-56

# CZECH REPUBLIC (CZE—TCH)

Totals=GP-W-T-L-GF-GA

**OLYMPICS, MEN**
**Date Score**
20-Feb-60 TCH 18-AUS 1
Totals: 1-1-0-0-18-1

13-Feb-36 TCH 2-AUT 1
04-Feb-48 TCH 17-AUT 3
11-Feb-84 TCH 13-AUT 0
19-Feb-88 TCH 4-AUT 0
14-Feb-94 CZE 7-AUT 3
Totals: 5-5-0-0-43-7

07-Feb-36 TCH 5-BEL 0
Totals: 1-1-0-0-5-0

24-Apr-20 TCH 0-CAN 15
28-Jan-24 TCH 0-CAN 30
15-Feb-36 TCH 0-CAN 7
06-Feb-48 TCH 0-CAN 0
19-Feb-52 TCH 1-CAN 4
30-Jan-56 TCH 3-CAN 6
24-Feb-60 TCH 0-CAN 4
07-Feb-64 TCH 3-CAN 1
13-Feb-68 TCH 2-CAN 3
22-Feb-80 TCH 6-CAN 1
15-Feb-84 TCH 4-CAN 0
27-Feb-88 TCH 3-CAN 6
14-Feb-92 TCH 1-CAN 5
21-Feb-92 TCH 2-CAN 4
23-Feb-94 CZE 2-CAN 3 (OT)
20-Feb-98 CZE 2-CAN 1 (10:00 OT/GWS)
18-Feb-02 CZE 3-CAN 3
21-Feb-06 CZE 2-CAN 3
Totals: 18-4-2-12-34-96

12-Feb-68 TCH 10-GDR 3
Totals: 1-1-0-0-10-3

21-Feb-52 TCH 11-FIN 2
01-Feb-64 TCH 4-FIN 0
10-Feb-68 TCH 4-FIN 3
08-Feb-72 TCH 7-FIN 1
06-Feb-76 TCH 2-FIN 1
13-Feb-84 TCH 7-FIN 2
26-Feb-88 TCH 5-FIN 2
12-Feb-94 CZE 1-FIN 3
13-Feb-98 CZE 3-FIN 0
18-Feb-06 CZE 2-FIN 4
24-Feb-10 CZE 0-FIN 2
Totals: 11-8-0-3-46-20

09-Feb-36 TCH 2-FRA 0
10-Feb-92 TCH 6-FRA 4
Totals: 2-2-0-0-8-4

17-Feb-52 TCH 6-GER 1
03-Feb-56 TCH 9-GER 3
27-Feb-60 TCH 9-GER 1
29-Jan-64 TCH 11-GER 1
16-Feb-94 CZE 1-GER 0
15-Feb-02 CZE 8-GER 2
15-Feb-06 CZE 4-GER 1
Totals: 7-7-0-0-48-9

14-Feb-36 TCH 0-GBR 5
02-Feb-48 TCH 11-GBR 4
Totals: 2-1-0-1-11-9

08-Feb-36 TCH 3-HUN 0
Totals: 1-1-0-0-3-0

30-Jan-48 TCH 22-ITA 3
19-Feb-06 CZE 4-ITA 1
Totals: 2-2-0-0-26-4

15-Feb-98 CZE 8-KAZ 2
Totals: 1-1-0-0-8-2

19-Feb-10 CZE 5-LAT 2
23-Feb-10 CZE 3-LAT 2 (OT)
Totals: 2-2-0-0-8-4

16-Feb-52 TCH 6-NOR 0
12-Feb-80 TCH 11-NOR 0
07-Feb-84 TCH 10-NOR 4
17-Feb-88 TCH 10-NOR 1
08-Feb-92 TCH 10-NOR 1
18-Feb-94 CZE 4-NOR 1
Totals: 6-6-0-0-51-7

13-Feb-28 TCH 3-POL 2
01-Feb-48 TCH 13-POL 1
15-Feb-52 TCH 8-POL 2
29-Jan-56 TCH 8-POL 3
05-Feb-72 TCH 14-POL 1
10-Feb-76 TCH 0-POL 1*
Totals: 6-5-0-1-46-10
* TCH won 7-1, but a failed doping test reversed result to 1-0 for POL

16-Feb-80 TCH 7-ROM 2
Totals: 1-1-0-0-7-2

02-Feb-56 TCH 4-URS 7
22-Feb-60 TCH 5-URS 8
31-Jan-64 TCH 5-URS 7
15-Feb-68 TCH 5-URS 4
13-Feb-72 TCH 2-URS 5
14-Feb-76 TCH 3-URS 4
19-Feb-84 TCH 0-URS 2
21-Feb-88 TCH 1-URS 6
12-Feb-92 TCH 4-RUS 3
20-Feb-94 CZE 3-RUS 4
16-Feb-98 CZE 1-RUS 2
22-Feb-98 CZE 1-RUS 0
20-Feb-02 CZE 0-RUS 1
25-Feb-06 CZE 3-RUS 0
21-Feb-10 CZE 2-RUS 4
Totals TCH vs. URS: 8-1-0-7-25-43
Totals TCH vs. RUS: 1-1-0-0-4-3
Totals CZE vs. RUS: 6-2-0-4-10-11

26-Feb-94 CZE 7-SVK 1
22-Feb-06 CZE 3-SVK 1
17-Feb-10 CZE 3-SVK 1
Totals: 3-3-0-0-13-3

29-Apr-20 TCH 1 -SWE 0
31-Jan-24 TCH 3-SWE 9
11-Feb-28 TCH 0-SWE 3
12-Feb-36 TCH 4-SWE 1
31-Jan-48 TCH 6-SWE 3
24-Feb-52 TCH 4-SWE 0
25-Feb-52 TCH 3-SWE 5
31-Jan-56 TCH 0-SWE 5
25-Feb-60 TCH 3-SWE 1
08-Feb-64 TCH 3-SWE 8
17-Feb-68 TCH 2-SWE 2
10-Feb-72 TCH 2-SWE 1
20-Feb-80 TCH 2-SWE 4
17-Feb-84 TCH 2-SWE 0
24-Feb-88 TCH 2-SWE 6
19-Feb-92 TCH 3-SWE 1
17-Feb-02 CZE 1-SWE 2
24-Feb-06 CZE 3-SWE 7
Totals: 18-8-1-9-44-58

01-Feb-24 TCH 11-SUI 2
07-Feb-48 TCH 7-SUI 1
22-Feb-52 TCH 8-SUI 3
04-Feb-64 TCH 5-SUI 1
16-Feb-92 TCH 4-SUI 2
16-Feb-06 CZE 2-SUI 3
Totals: 6-5-0-1-37-12

28-Apr-20 TCH 0-USA 16
11-Feb-36 TCH 0-USA 2
08-Feb-48 TCH 4-USA 3
23-Feb-52 TCH 3-USA 6
27-Jan-56 TCH 4-USA 3
04-Feb-56 TCH 4-USA 9
19-Feb-60 TCH 5-USA 7
28-Feb-60 TCH 4-USA 9
05-Feb-64 TCH 7-USA 1
06-Feb-68 TCH 5-USA 1
07-Feb-72 TCH 1-USA 5
08-Feb-76 TCH 5-USA 0
14-Feb-80 TCH 3-USA 7
09-Feb-84 TCH 4-USA 1
15-Feb-88 TCH 7-USA 5
22-Feb-92 TCH 6-USA 1
24-Feb-94 CZE 5-USA 3
18-Feb-98 CZE 4-USA 1
Totals: 18-10-0-8-71-80

08-Feb-68 TCH 5-FRG 1
12-Feb-76 TCH 7-FRG 4
18-Feb-80 TCH 11-FRG 3
13-Feb-88 TCH 1-FRG 2
Totals: 4-3-0-1-24-10

**WORLD CHAMPIONSHIPS, MEN**
05-Feb-31 TCH 2-AUT 1
19-Feb-33 TCH 2-AUT 1
26-Feb-33 TCH 2-AUT 0
07-Feb-34 TCH 4-AUT 0
19-Jan-35 TCH 2-AUT 1
12-Feb-38 TCH 1-AUT 0
18-Feb-47 TCH 13-AUT 5

16-Feb-49 TCH 7-AUT 1
24-Feb-57 TCH 9-AUT 0
26-Apr-95 CZE 5-AUT 2
01-May-99 CZE 7-AUT 0
28-Apr-03 CZE 8-AUT 1
30-Apr-04 CZE 2-AUT 0
29-Apr-07 CZE 6-AUT 1
Totals: 14-14-0-0-70-13

03-May-98 CZE 4-BLR 2
28-Apr-01 CZE 5-BLR 1
10-May-05 CZE 5-BLR 1
27-Apr-07 CZE 8-BLR 2
10-May-08 CZE 3-BLR 2 (5:00 OT/GWS)
03-May-09 CZE 3-BLR 0
Totals: 6-6-0-0-28-8

21-Jan-35 TCH 22-BEL 0
21-Feb-47 TCH 24-BEL 0
Totals: 2-2-0-0-46-0

04-Feb-31 TCH 0-CAN 2
24-Feb-33 TCH 0-CAN 4
24-Jan-35 TCH 1-CAN 2
20-Feb-37 TCH 0-CAN 3
15-Feb-38 TCH 0-CAN 3
08-Feb-39 TCH 1-CAN 2
11-Feb-39 TCH 0-CAN 4
15-Feb-49 TCH 3-CAN 2
05-Mar-54 TCH 2-CAN 5
26-Feb-55 TCH 3-CAN 5
07-Mar-58 TCH 0-CAN 6
07-Mar-59 TCH 2-CAN 7
15-Mar-59 TCH 5-CAN 3
09-Mar-61 TCH 1-CAN 1
12-Mar-63 TCH 4-CAN 4
11-Mar-65 TCH 8-CAN 0
10-Mar-66 TCH 2-CAN 1
25-Mar-67 TCH 1-CAN 1
15-Mar-69 TCH 6-CAN 1
23-Mar-69 TCH 3-CAN 2
26-Apr-77 TCH 3 CAN 3
08-May-77 TCH 2-CAN 8
04-May-78 TCH 5-CAN 0
12-May-78 TCH 3-CAN 2
15-Apr-79 TCH 4-CAN 1
23-Apr-79 TCH 10-CAN 6
18-Apr-81 TCH 7-CAN 4
24-Apr-81 TCH 4-CAN 2
16-Apr-82 TCH 6-CAN 2
27-Apr-82 TCH 2-CAN 4
21-Apr-83 TCH 1-CAN 3
28-Apr-83 TCH 5-CAN 4
23-Apr-85 TCH 4-CAN 4
03-May-85 TCH 5-CAN 3
22-Apr-86 TCH 3-CAN 1
18-Apr-87 TCH 1-CAN 1
01-May-87 TCH 4-CAN 2
24-Apr-89 TCH 2-CAN 4
01-May-89 TCH 3-CAN 4
22-Apr-90 TCH 3-CAN 5
28-Apr-90 TCH 3-CAN 2
28-Apr-91 TCH 4-CAN 3
03-May-92 TCH 5-CAN 2
01-May-93 CZE 5-CAN 1
05-May-94 CZE 2-CAN 3
06-May-95 CZE 1-CAN 4
05-May-96 CZE 4-CAN 2
07-May-97 CZE 5-CAN 3
12-May-99 CZE 1-CAN 2
13-May-99 CZE 6-CAN 4*
03-May-00 CZE 2-CAN 1
12-May-00 CZE 2-CAN 1
08-May-01 CZE 4-CAN 2
05-May-02 CZE 5-CAN 1
09-May-03 CZE 4-CAN 8
03-May-04 CZE 6 -CAN 2
15-May-05 CZE 3-CAN 0
14-May-06 CZE 6-CAN 4
06-May-07 CZE 3-CAN 4 (OT)
30-Apr-09 CZE 1-CAN 5
18-May-10 CZE 3-CAN 2
Totals: 61-32-6-23-194-177
*Game 2, best-of-two, semi-finals. Czech won the game 5-4 and clinched the series in GWS

02-May-08 CZE 5-DEN 2
25-Apr-09 CZE 5-DEN 0
02-May-11 CZE 6-DEN 0
04-May-12 CZE 2-DEN 0
Totals: 4-4-0-0-18-2

25-Feb-57 TCH 15-GDR 1
11-Mar-61 TCH 5-GDR 1
10-Mar-63 TCH 8-GDR 3
04-Mar-65 TCH 5-GDR 1
03-Mar-66 TCH 6-GDR 0
20-Mar-67 TCH 6-GDR 0
17-Mar-70 TCH 4-GDR 1
25-Mar-70 TCH 7-GDR 3
08-Apr-74 TCH 8-GDR 0
16-Apr-74 TCH 9-GDR 2
08-Apr-76 TCH 10-GDR 0
29-Apr-78 TCH 8-GDR 2
17-Apr-83 TCH 6-GDR 1
18-Apr-85 TCH 6-GDR 1
Totals: 14-14-0-0-103-16

14-Feb-49 TCH 19-FIN 2
01-Mar-54 TCH 12-FIN 1
06-Mar-55 TCH 18-FIN 2
28-Feb-57 TCH 3-FIN 0
28-Feb-58 TCH 5-FIN 1
10-Mar-59 TCH 8-FIN 2
02-Mar-61 TCH 6-FIN 0
15-Mar-63 TCH 5-FIN 2
10-Mar-65 TCH 5-FIN 2
05-Mar-66 TCH 8-FIN 1
23-Mar-67 TCH 1-FIN 3
18-Mar-69 TCH 7-FIN 4
25-Mar-69 TCH 4-FIN 2
20-Mar-70 TCH 9-FIN 1
30-Mar-70 TCH 3-FIN 5
26-Mar-71 TCH 5-FIN 0
03-Apr-71 TCH 4-FIN 2
14-Apr-72 TCH 5-FIN 3
22-Apr-72 TCH 8-FIN 2
07-Apr-73 TCH 4-FIN 2
15-Apr-73 TCH 8-FIN 0
12-Apr-74 TCH 5-FIN 0*
20-Apr-74 TCH 4-FIN 5
10-Apr-75 TCH 6-FIN 2
19-Apr-75 TCH 5-FIN 1
13-Apr-76 TCH 7-FIN 1
21-Apr-77 TCH 11-FIN 3
28-Apr-78 TCH 6-FIN 4
14-Apr-79 TCH 5-FIN 0
21-Apr-82 TCH 3-FIN 0
16-Apr-83 TCH 4-FIN 2
17-Apr-85 TCH 5-FIN 0
16-Apr-86 TCH 1-FIN 1
17-Apr-87 TCH 5-FIN 2
16-Apr-89 TCH 3-FIN 1
17-Apr-90 TCH 4-FIN 2
19-Apr-91 TCH 0-FIN 2
03-May-91 TCH 2-FIN 3
09-May-92 TCH 2-FIN 3 (10:00 OT/GWS)
25-Apr-93 CZE 3-FIN 1
25-Apr-94 CZE 4-FIN 4
23-Apr-95 CZE 3-FIN 0
05-May-95 CZE 0-FIN 3
23-Apr-96 CZE 4-FIN 2
27-Apr-97 CZE 2-FIN 1
12-May-98 CZE 1-FIN 4
14-May-98 CZE 2-FIN 2
15-May-99 CZE 3-FIN 1
16-May-99 CZE 1-FIN 4**
07-May-00 CZE 4-FIN 6
13-May-01 CZE 3-FIN 2 (OT)
30-Apr-03 CZE 2-FIN 1
09-May-06 CZE 3-FIN 3
20-May-06 CZE 3-FIN 1
29-Apr-09 CZE 3-FIN 4
20-May-10 CZE 2-FIN 1 (10:00 OT/GWS)
04-May-11 CZE 2-FIN 1
20-May-12 CZE 3-FIN 2
Totals: 58-43-4-11-273-112
*TCH won game 5-2 but FIN failed doping test resulting in an official score of 5-0
**Game 2, best-of-two gold-medal game. FIN won the game 4-0 but Czechs clinched the series in OT

22-Feb-37 TCH 8-FRA 1
26-Feb-37 TCH 3-FRA 1
30-Apr-92 TCH 3-FRA 0
24-Apr-93 CZE 6-FRA 2
26-Apr-94 CZE 5-FRA 2
27-Apr-96 CZE 9-FRA 2
03-May-97 CZE 9-FRA 3
09-May-10 CZE 6-FRA 2
Totals: 8-8-0-0-49-13

09-Feb-34 TCH 0-GER 1 (OT)
23-Feb-37 TCH 1-GER 2 (30:00 OT)
20-Feb-38 TCH 3-GER 0
07-Feb-39 TCH 1-GER 1 (30:00 OT)
20-Apr-93 CZE 5-GER 0
01-May-96 CZE 6-GER 1
26-Apr-97 CZE 2-GER 1
05-May-98 CZE 8-GER 1
29-Apr-01 CZE 2-GER 2
29-Apr-02 CZE 7-GER 5
04-May-03 CZE 4-GER 0
28-Apr-04 CZE 5-GER 1
03-May-05 CZE 2-GER 0
03-May-07 CZE 0-GER 2
09-May-11 CZE 5-GER 2
15-May-12 CZE 8-GER 1
Totals: 16-11-2-3-59-20

04-Feb-34 TCH 1-GBR 2
27-Jan-35 TCH 1-GBR 2
19-Feb-38 TCH 0-GBR 1
09-Feb-39 TCH 2-GBR 0
Totals: 4-1-0-3-4-5

01-Feb-31 TCH 4-HUN 1
05-Feb-34 TCH 1-HUN 0
10-Feb-34 TCH 1-HUN 0
27-Feb-37 TCH 0-HUN 0
Totals: 4-3-1-0-6-1

20-Feb-33 TCH 3-ITA 1
22-Jan-35 TCH 5-ITA 1
24-Apr-82 TCH 10-ITA 0
26-Apr-83 TCH 11-ITA 0
28-Apr-93 CZE 8-ITA 1
28-Apr-96 CZE 9-ITA 5
05-May-00 CZE 9-ITA 2
06-May-01 CZE 11-ITA 0
06-May-08 CZE 7-ITA 2
11-May-12 CZE 6-ITA 0
Totals: 10-10-0-0-79-12

04-Mar-57 TCH 25-JPN 1
01-May-98 CZE 8-JPN 2
03-May-99 CZE 12-JPN 2
01-May-00 CZE 6-JPN 3
28-Apr-02 CZE 5-JPN 3
Totals: 5-5-0-0-56-11

26-Apr-04 CZE 7-KAZ 0
05-May-05 CZE 1-KAZ 0
Totals: 2-2-0-0-8-0

04-Feb-39 TCH 9-LAT 0
11-May-00 CZE 3-LAT 1
02-May-02 CZE 3-LAT 1
24-Apr-04 CZE 3-LAT 1
05-May-06 CZE 1-LAT 1
17-May-10 CZE 3-LAT 1
30-Apr-11 CZE 4-LAT 2
10-May-12 CZE 3-LAT 1
Totals: 8-7-1-0-29-8

17-Feb-37 TCH 7-NOR 0
03-Mar-54 TCH 7-NOR 1
08-Mar-58 TCH 2-NOR 0
08-Mar-65 TCH 9-NOR 2
19-Apr-90 TCH 9-NOR 1
28-Apr-92 TCH 6-NOR 1
21-Apr-93 CZE 2-NOR 0
30-Apr-94 CZE 2-NOR 2
29-Apr-95 CZE 3-NOR 1
24-Apr-96 CZE 2-NOR 2
29-Apr-00 CZE 4-NOR 0
12-May-06 CZE 3-NOR 1
27-Apr-09 CZE 5-NOR 2
11-May-10 CZE 2-NOR 3
07-May-12 CZE 4-NOR 3 (5:00 OT/GWS)
Totals: 15-12-2-1-67-19

02-Feb-31 TCH 4-POL 1
08-Feb-31 TCH 0-POL 0
21-Feb-33 TCH 1-POL 0
25-Feb-37 TCH 1-POL 0
19-Feb-47 TCH 12-POL 0
05-Mar-55 TCH 17-POL 2
05-Mar-57 TCH 12-POL 3
03-Mar-58 TCH 7-POL 1
06-Mar-59 TCH 13-POL 1
06-Mar-66 TCH 6-POL 1
14-Mar-70 TCH 6-POL 3
22-Mar-70 TCH 10-POL 2
31-Mar-73 TCH 14-POL 1
08-Apr-73 TCH 4-POL 1
05-Apr-74 TCH 8-POL 0
13-Apr-74 TCH 12-POL 3
03-Apr-75 TCH 5-POL 0
12-Apr-75 TCH 8-POL 2
09-Apr-76 TCH 12-POL 0
12-Apr-86 TCH 1-POL 2
23-Apr-86 TCH 8-POL 1
18-Apr-89 TCH 15-POL 0
Totals: 22-20-1-1-176-24

18-Feb-33 TCH 8-ROM 0
20-Jan-35 TCH 4-ROM 2
15-Feb-47 TCH 23-ROM 1
24-Apr-77 TCH 13-ROM 1
Totals: 4-4-0-0-48-4

02-Mar-54 TCH 2-URS 5
27-Feb-55 TCH 0-URS 4
02-Mar-57 TCH 2-URS 2
04-Mar-58 TCH 4-URS 4
12-Mar-59 TCH 3-URS 4
07-Mar-61 TCH 6-URS 4
14-Mar-63 TCH 1-URS 3
13-Mar-65 TCH 1-URS 3
13-Mar-66 TCH 1-URS 7
29-Mar-67 TCH 2-URS 4
21-Mar-69 TCH 2-URS 0
28-Mar-69 TCH 4-URS 3
18-Mar-70 TCH 1-URS 3
27-Mar-70 TCH 1-URS 5
24-Mar-71 TCH 3-URS 3
01-Apr-71 TCH 5-URS 2
12-Apr-72 TCH 3-URS 3
20-Apr-72 TCH 3-URS 2
05-Apr-73 TCH 2-URS 3
13-Apr-73 TCH 2-URS 4
10-Apr-74 TCH 7-URS 2
18-Apr-74 TCH 1-URS 3
08-Apr-75 TCH 2-URS 5
17-Apr-75 TCH 1-URS 4
17-Apr-76 TCH 3-URS 2
25-Apr-76 TCH 3-URS 3
28-Apr-77 TCH 1-URS 6
04-May-77 TCH 4-URS 3
06-May-78 TCH 6-URS 4
14-May-78 TCH 1-URS 3
21-Apr-79 TCH 1-URS 11
27-Apr-79 TCH 1-URS 6
20-Apr-81 TCH 3-URS 8
26-Apr-81 TCH 1-URS 1
18-Apr-82 TCH 3-URS 5
29-Apr-82 TCH 0-URS 0
23-Apr-83 TCH 1-URS 5
30-Apr-83 TCH 1-URS 1
27-Apr-85 TCH 1-URS 5
29-Apr-85 TCH 2-URS 1
20-Apr-86 TCH 2-URS 4
21-Apr-87 TCH 1-URS 6
03-May-87 TCH 1-URS 2
21-Apr-89 TCH 2-URS 4
27-Apr-89 TCH 0-URS 1
24-Apr-90 TCH 1-URS 4
02-May-90 TCH 0-URS 5
26-Apr-91 TCH 2-URS 6
01-May-92 TCH 2-RUS 4
03-May-95 CZE 2-RUS 0
01-May-97 CZE 2-RUS 3
10-May-97 CZE 4-RUS 3
10-May-98 CZE 2-RUS 2
07-May-99 CZE 1-RUS 6
05-May-01 CZE 4-RUS 3
07-May-02 CZE 1-RUS 3
07-May-03 CZE 3-RUS 0
08-May-05 CZE 1-RUS 2
18-May-06 CZE 4-RUS 3 (OT)
09-May-07 CZE 0-RUS 4
04-May-08 CZE 4-RUS 5 (OT)
23-May-10 CZE 2-RUS 1
08-May-11 CZE 3-RUS 2
15-May-11 CZE 7-RUS 4
13-May-12 CZE 0-RUS 2
Totals TCH vs. URS: 48-10-8-30-100-178
Totals TCH vs. RUS: 1-0-0-1-2-4
Totals CZE vs. RUS: 16-8-1-7-40-43

30-Apr-97 CZE 3-SVK 1
07-May-98 CZE 1-SVK 0
09-May-99 CZE 8-SVK 2
08-May-00 CZE 6-SVK 2
14-May-00 CZE 5-SVK 3
10-May-01 CZE 2-SVK 0
05-May-03 CZE 3-SVK 3
10-May-03 CZE 2-SVK 4
07-May-05 CZE 5-SVK 1
05-May-07 CZE 2-SVK 3
02-May-09 CZE 8-SVK 0
06-May-11 CZE 3-SVK 2
19-May-12 CZE 1-SVK 3
Totals: 13-9-1-3-49-24

26-Apr-03 CZE 5-SLO 2
07-May-06 CZE 5-SLO 4
Totals: 2-2-0-0-10-6

07-Feb-31 TCH 0-SWE 1
23-Jan-35 TCH 2-SWE 1 (OT)
13-Feb-38 TCH 0-SWE 0 (30:00 OT)
22-Feb-47 TCH 1-SWE 2
13-Feb-49 TCH 2-SWE 4
20-Feb-49 TCH 3-SWE 0
10-Mar-53 TCH 3-SWE 5
06-Mar-54 TCH 2-SWE 4
01-Mar-55 TCH 6-SWE 5
27-Feb-57 TCH 0-SWE 2
09-Mar-58 TCH 1-SWE 7
09-Mar-59 TCH 4-SWE 1
12-Mar-61 TCH 5-SWE 2
17-Mar-63 TCH 3-SWE 2
14-Mar-65 TCH 3-SWE 2
11-Mar-66 TCH 2-SWE 1
27-Mar-67 TCH 5-SWE 5
19-Mar-69 TCH 0-SWE 2
30-Mar-69 TCH 0-SWE 1
15-Mar-70 TCH 4-SWE 5
24-Mar-70 TCH 2-SWE 2
21-Mar-71 TCH 5-SWE 6
29-Mar-71 TCH 3-SWE 1
09-Apr-72 TCH 4-SWE 1
17-Apr-72 TCH 2-SWE 0
02-Apr-73 TCH 0-SWE 2
10-Apr-73 TCH 3-SWE 3
07-Apr-74 TCH 3-SWE 2
15-Apr-74 TCH 0-SWE 3
05-Apr-75 TCH 5-SWE 2
14-Apr-75 TCH 7-SWE 0
11-Apr-76 TCH 3-SWE 1
23-Apr-76 TCH 5-SWE 3
30-Apr-77 TCH 3-SWE 1
06-May-77 TCH 2-SWE 1
08-May-78 TCH 3-SWE 2
10-May-78 TCH 6-SWE 1
19-Apr-79 TCH 3-SWE 3
25-Apr-79 TCH 6-SWE 3
15-Apr-81 TCH 3-SWE 3
22-Apr-81 TCH 2-SWE 4
22-Apr-82 TCH 3-SWE 3
25-Apr-82 TCH 3-SWE 2
19-Apr-83 TCH 4-SWE 1
02-May-83 TCH 4-SWE 1
25-Apr-85 TCH 7-SWE 2
15-Apr-86 TCH 2-SWE 3
20-Apr-87 TCH 3-SWE 2
29-Apr-87 TCH 3-SWE 3
22-Apr-89 TCH 3-SWE 3
29-Apr-89 TCH 2-SWE 1
26-Apr-90 TCH 1-SWE 5
30-Apr-90 TCH 5-SWE 5
25-Apr-91 TCH 1-SWE 2
30-Apr-93 CZE 3-SWE 4 (OT)
02-May-94 CZE 1-SWE 4
30-Apr-95 CZE 1-SWE 2
21-Apr-96 CZE 3-SWE 1
08-May-97 CZE 0-SWE 1
10-May-99 CZE 2-SWE 0
12-May-01 CZE 3-SWE 2 (10:00 OT/GWS)
14-May-05 CZE 3-SWE 2 (OT)
21-May-06 CZE 0-SWE 4
11-May-08 CZE 3-SWE 5
14-May-08 CZE 2-SWE 3 (OT)
07-May-09 CZE 1-SWE 3
13-May-10 CZE 2-SWE 1
22-May-10 CZE 3-SWE 2 (10:00 OT/GWS)
13-May-11 CZE 2-SWE 5
05-May-12 CZE 1-SWE 4
17-May-12 CZE 4-SWE 3
Totals: 71-34-10-27-191-175

01-Feb-30 TCH 1-SUI 3
22-Feb-33 TCH 1-SUI 0
26-Jan-35 TCH 0-SUI 4
19-Feb-37 TCH 2-SUI 2
18-Feb-38 TCH 3-SUI 2 (20:00 OT)
05-Feb-39 TCH 0-SUI 1
12-Feb-39 TCH 0-SUI 0 (30:00 OT)
05-Mar-39 TCH 0-SUI 2
20-Feb-47 TCH 6-SUI 1
18-Feb-49 TCH 8-SUI 1
08-Mar-53 TCH 9-SUI 4
26-Feb-54 TCH 7-SUI 1
25-Feb-55 TCH 7-SUI 0
05-Mar-59 TCH 9-SUI 0
07-Apr-72 TCH 19-SUI 1
15-Apr-72 TCH 12-SUI 2
23-Apr-87 TCH 5-SUI 2
22-Apr-91 TCH 4-SUI 1
29-Apr-91 TCH 3-SUI 4
04-May-92 TCH 2-SUI 0
10-May-92 TCH 5-SUI 2
09-May-98 CZE 3-SUI 1
15-May-98 CZE 4-SUI 0

01-May-01 CZE 3-SUI 1
26-Apr-02 CZE 5-SUI 0
02-May-04 CZE 3-SUI 1
01-May-05 CZE 3-SUI 1
08-May-08 CZE 5-SUI 0
15-May-10 CZE 2-SUI 3
Totals: 29-21-2-6-131-40

02-May-03 CZE 5-UKR 2
Totals: 1-1-0-0-5-2

06-Feb-31 TCH 0-USA 1
23-Feb-33 TCH 0-USA 6
06-Feb-34 TCH 0-USA 1
16-Feb-38 TCH 2-USA 0
10-Feb-39 TCH 0-USA 1
(20:00 OT)
23-Feb-47 TCH 6-USA 1
19-Feb-49 TCH 0-USA 2
03-Mar-55 TCH 4-USA 4
06-Mar-58 TCH 2-USA 2
13-Mar-59 TCH 2-USA 4
05-Mar-61 TCH 4-USA 1
09-Mar-63 TCH 10-USA 1
06-Mar-65 TCH 12-USA 0
08-Mar-66 TCH 7-USA 4
21-Mar-67 TCH 8-USA 3
16-Mar-69 TCH 8-USA 3
26-Mar-69 TCH 6-USA 2
19-Mar-71 TCH 1-USA 5
27-Mar-71 TCH 5-USA 0
06-Apr-75 TCH 8-USA 3
15-Apr-75 TCH 8-USA 0
15-Apr-76 TCH 10-USA 2
21-Apr-76 TCH 5-USA 1
02-May-77 TCH 6-USA 3
02-May-78 TCH 8-USA 3
17-Apr-79 TCH 2-USA 2
12-Apr-81 TCH 11-USA 2
19-Apr-82 TCH 6-USA 0
21-Apr-85 TCH 1-USA 3
01-May-85 TCH 11-USA 2
18-Apr-86 TCH 5-USA 2
27-Apr-86 TCH 10-USA 2
27-Apr-87 TCH 4-USA 2
19-Apr-89 TCH 5-USA 0
16-Apr-90 TCH 7-USA 1
20-Apr-91 TCH 1-USA 4
07-May-92 TCH 8-USA 1
18-Apr-93 CZE 1-USA 1
28-Apr-94 CZE 3-USA 5
27-Apr-95 CZE 2-USA 4
03-May-96 CZE 5-USA 0
05-May-97 CZE 3-USA 4
05-May-99 CZE 4-USA 3
04-May-02 CZE 5-USA 4
05-May-04 CZE 2-USA 3
(10:00 OT/GWS)
12-May-05 CZE 3 -USA 2
(10:00 OT/GWS)
16-May-06 CZE 1-USA 3
01-May-07 CZE 4-USA 3
11-May-11 CZE 4-USA 0
Totals: 49-31-4-14-230-106

07-Mar-53 TCH 11-FRG 2
12-Mar-53 TCH 9-FRG 4
27-Feb-54 TCH 9-FRG 4
02-Mar-55 TCH 8-FRG 0
05-Mar-61 TCH 6-FRG 0
07-Mar-63 TCH 10-FRG 1
18-Mar-67 TCH 6-FRG 2
22-Mar-71 TCH 9-FRG 1
30-Mar-71 TCH 4-FRG 0
10-Apr-72 TCH 8-FRG 1
18-Apr-72 TCH 8-FRG 1
03-Apr-73 TCH 4-FRG 2
11-Apr-73 TCH 7-FRG 2
19-Apr-76 TCH 9-FRG 1
22-Apr-77 TCH 9-FRG 3
26-Apr-78 TCH 8-FRG 0
14-Apr-81 TCH 6-FRG 2
15-Apr-82 TCH 2-FRG 4
24-Apr-83 TCH 3-FRG 3
20-Apr-85 TCH 6-FRG 1
13-Apr-86 TCH 3-FRG 4
25-Apr-86 TCH 3-FRG 1
25-Apr-87 TCH 5-FRG 2
15-Apr-89 TCH 3-FRG 3
20-Apr-90 TCH 3-FRG 0
23-Apr-91 TCH 7-FRG 1
01-May-91 TCH 4-FRG 1
Totals: 27-23-2-2-170-46

03-Feb-39 TCH 24-YUG 0
Totals: 1-1-0-0-24-0

**WORLD U20 CHAMPIONSHIPS**

28-Dec-80 TCH 21-AUT 4
29-Dec-09 CZE 7-AUT 1
Totals: 2-2-0-0-28-5

03-Jan-99 CZE 10-BLR 2
28-Dec-01 CZE 9-BLR 1
25-Dec-04 CZE 7-BLR 2
30-Dec-06 CZE 2-BLR 1
Totals: 4-4-0-0-28-6

25-Dec-76 TCH 4-CAN 4
25-Dec-77 TCH 3-CAN 9
31-Dec-77 TCH 3-CAN 6
27-Dec-80 TCH 3-CAN 3
02-Jan-82 TCH 3-CAN 3
01-Jan-83 TCH 7-CAN 7
03-Jan-84 TCH 6-CAN 4
01-Jan-85 TCH 2-CAN 2
04-Jan-86 TCH 5-CAN 3
29-Dec-86 TCH 5-CAN 1
28-Dec-87 TCH 2-CAN 4
01-Jan-89 TCH 2-CAN 2
04-Jan-90 TCH 1-CAN 2
02-Jan-91 TCH 6-CAN 5
02-Jan-92 TCH 6-CAN 1
04-Jan-93 CZE/SVK 7-CAN 4
02-Jan-94 CZE 4-CAN 6
30-Dec-94 CZE 5-CAN 7
31-Dec-96 CZE 3-CAN 3
28-Dec-97 CZE 0-CAN 5
30-Dec-98 CZE 0-CAN 2
28-Dec-99 CZE 1-CAN 1
28-Dec-02 CZE 0-CAN 4
31-Dec-03 CZE 2-CAN 5
03-Jan-04 CZE 1-CAN 7
02-Jan-05 CZE 1-CAN 3
26-Dec-07 CZE 0-CAN 3
26-Dec-08 CZE 1-CAN 8
28-Dec-10 CZE 2-CAN 7
28-Dec-11 CZE 0-CAN 5
Totals: 30-6-8-16-85-126

27-Dec-07 CZE 5-DEN 2
27-Dec-11 CZE 7-DEN 0
Totals: 2-2-0-0-12-2

30-Dec-76 TCH 2-FIN 3
03-Jan-79 TCH 6-FIN 5
02-Jan-80 TCH 2-FIN 4
02-Jan-81 TCH 6-FIN 6
26-Dec-81 TCH 5-FIN 1
04-Jan-83 TCH 5-FIN 3
26-Dec-83 TCH 7-FIN 8
29-Dec-84 TCH 1-FIN 1
02-Jan-86 TCH 2-FIN 0
04-Jan-87 TCH 3-FIN 5
04-Jan-88 TCH 1-FIN 2
04-Jan-89 TCH 7-FIN 2
26-Dec-89 TCH 7-FIN 1
04-Jan-91 TCH 6-FIN 1
27-Dec-91 TCH 1-FIN 4
26-Dec-92 CZE/SVK 2-FIN 5
27-Dec-93 CZE 3-FIN 7
26-Dec-94 CZE 3-FIN 0
01-Jan-97 CZE 3-FIN 2
(10:00 OT/GWS)
30-Dec-97 CZE 5-FIN 5
31-Dec-98 CZE 3-FIN 4
31-Dec-99 CZE 4-FIN 2
05-Jan-01 CZE 2-FIN 1
01-Jan-02 CZE 1-FIN 3
30-Dec-02 CZE 2-FIN 2
28-Dec-03 CZE 2-FIN 3
05-Jan-04 CZE 1-FIN 2
01-Jan-05 CZE 3-FIN 0
28-Dec-06 CZE 2-FIN 6
04-Jan-07 CZE 6-FIN 2
03-Jan-08 CZE 5-FIN 1
27-Dec-09 CZE 3-FIN 4
31-Dec-11 CZE 0-FIN 4
Totals: 33-14-4-15-111-99

29-Dec-91 TCH 8-GER 2
02-Jan-93 CZE/SVK 6-GER 3
30-Dec-93 CZE 6-GER 2
02-Jan-95 CZE 14-GER 3
27-Dec-95 CZE 6-GER 3
26-Dec-96 CZE 8-GER 2
27-Dec-97 CZE 9-GER 1
27-Dec-02 CZE 3-GER 0
30-Dec-08 CZE 6-GER 0
02-Jan-11 CZE 3-GER 2
Totals: 10-10-0-0-69-18

01-Jan-93 CZE/SVK 14-JPN 2
Totals: 1-1-0-0-14-2

01-Jan-00 CZE 6-KAZ 3
27-Dec-00 CZE 9-KAZ 1
31-Dec-08 CZE 10-KAZ 2
Totals: 3-3-0-0-25-6

26-Dec-05 CZE 5-LAT 1
03-Jan-10 CZE 10-LAT 2
Totals: 2-2-0-0-15-3

28-Dec-78 TCH 6-NOR 4
29-Dec-82 TCH 9-NOR 2
27-Dec-88 TCH 7-NOR 1
30-Dec-89 TCH 13-NOR 2
26-Dec-90 TCH 11-NOR 3
27-Dec-10 CZE 2-NOR 0
Totals: 6-6-0-0-48-12

01-Jan-77 TCH 9-POL 0
26-Dec-84 TCH 6-POL 2
01-Jan-87 TCH 9-POL 2
29-Dec-87 TCH 6-POL 1
29-Dec-89 TCH 11-POL 1
Totals: 5-5-0-0-41-6

23-Dec-76 TCH 0-URS 4
01-Jan-78 TCH 1-URS 6
30-Dec-78 TCH 1-URS 9
02-Jan-79 TCH 2-URS 2
01-Jan-80 TCH 2-URS 6
30-Dec-80 TCH 1-URS 5
23-Dec-81 TCH 3-URS 2
27-Dec-82 TCH 3-URS 4
31-Dec-83 TCH 4-URS 6
31-Dec-84 TCH 3-URS 1
01-Jan-86 TCH 3-URS 4
30-Dec-86 TCH 5-URS 3
26-Dec-87 TCH 4-URS 6
02-Jan-89 TCH 5-URS 3
02-Jan-90 TCH 5-URS 8
01-Jan-91 TCH 3-URS 5
01-Jan-92 TCH 5-RUS 2
30-Dec-92 CZE/SVK 1-RUS 1
26-Dec-93 CZE 1-RUS 5
27-Dec-94 CZE 3-RUS 4
26-Dec-95 CZE 5-RUS 3
04-Jan-96 CZE 1-RUS 4
04-Jan-97 CZE 1-RUS 4
01-Jan-98 CZE 1-RUS 5
04-Jan-00 CZE 1-RUS 0
(10:00 OT/GWS)
27-Dec-04 CZE 1-RUS 4
31-Dec-05 CZE 2-RUS 7
26-Dec-06 CZE 2-RUS 3
02-Jan-08 CZE 1-RUS 4
02-Jan-09 CZE 1-RUS 5
31-Dec-09 CZE 2-RUS 5
31-Dec-10 CZE 3-RUS 8
02-Jan-12 CZE 1-RUS 2
Totals TCH vs. URS:
16-4-1-11-45-74
Totals TCH vs. RUS:
2-1-1-0-6-3
Totals CZE vs. RUS:
15-2-0-13-26-63

29-Dec-95 CZE 4-SVK 4
26-Dec-98 CZE 2-SVK 3
25-Dec-99 CZE 5-SVK 2
31-Dec-00 CZE 5-SVK 0
27-Dec-01 CZE 0-SVK 1
04-Jan-02 CZE 6-SVK 2
04-Jan-03 CZE 0-SVK 2
02-Jan-04 CZE 4-SVK 2
30-Dec-05 CZE 5-SVK 3
29-Dec-07 CZE 5-SVK 2
04-Jan-10 CZE 5-SVK 2
04-Jan-11 CZE 5-SVK 2
04-Jan-12 CZE 5-SVK 2
Totals: 13-9-1-3-51-27

02-Jan-77 TCH 4-SWE 2
28-Dec-77 TCH 1-SWE 2
31-Dec-78 TCH 1-SWE 1
30-Dec-79 TCH 4-SWE 10
31-Dec-80 TCH 3-SWE 3
27-Dec-81 TCH 4-SWE 6
30-Dec-82 TCH 4-SWE 2
02-Jan-84 TCH 5-SWE 2
25-Dec-84 TCH 4-SWE 3
29-Dec-85 TCH 2-SWE 3
26-Dec-86 TCH 4-SWE 3
01-Jan-88 TCH 5-SWE 5
26-Dec-88 TCH 3-SWE 5
01-Jan-90 TCH 7-SWE 2
27-Dec-90 TCH 3-SWE 4
26-Dec-91 TCH 4-SWE 8
29-Dec-92 CZE/SVK 2-SWE 7
01-Jan-94 CZE 4-SWE 6
29-Dec-94 CZE 3-SWE 4
31-Dec-95 CZE 0-SWE 0
03-Jan-96 CZE 2-SWE 8
25-Dec-97 CZE 2-SWE 1
26-Dec-00 CZE 2-SWE 1
03-Jan-01 CZE 1-SWE 0
30-Dec-01 CZE 1-SWE 2
31-Dec-02 CZE 3-SWE 1
28-Dec-05 CZE 2-SWE 3
04-Jan-06 CZE 1-SWE 3
02-Jan-07 CZE 1-SWE 5
31-Dec-07 CZE 2-SWE 4
26-Dec-09 CZE 1-SWE 10
30-Dec-10 CZE 3-SWE 6
Totals: 32-10-4-18-88-122

29-Dec-81 TCH 16-SUI 0
29-Dec-83 TCH 13-SUI 2
30-Dec-85 TCH 7-SUI 2
02-Jan-87 TCH 8-SUI 1
29-Dec-90 TCH 10-SUI 0
30-Dec-91 TCH 2-SUI 4
29-Dec-93 CZE 6-SUI 0
27-Dec-96 CZE 1-SUI 1
03-Jan-98 CZE 3-SUI 4
(10:00 OT/GWS)
04-Jan-99 CZE 5-SUI 4
02-Jan-01 CZE 4-SUI 3
30-Dec-03 CZE 2-SUI 1
29-Dec-04 CZE 5-SUI 2
31-Dec-06 CZE 4-SUI 2
Totals: 14-11-1-2-86-26

01-Jan-95 CZE 10-UKR 1
26-Dec-03 CZE 8-UKR 0
Totals: 2-2-0-0-18-1

28-Dec-76 TCH 5-USA 2
23-Dec-77 TCH 8-USA 5
27-Dec-78 TCH 3-USA 2
27-Dec-79 TCH 7-USA 3
22-Dec-81 TCH 6-USA 4
26-Dec-82 TCH 6-USA 4
28-Dec-83 TCH 10-USA 1
23-Dec-84 TCH 9-USA 1
27-Dec-85 TCH 2-USA 5
27-Dec-86 TCH 2-USA 8
03-Jan-88 TCH 11-USA 1
30-Dec-88 TCH 1-USA 5
27-Dec-89 TCH 7-USA 1
30-Dec-90 TCH 5-USA 1
04-Jan-92 TCH 2-USA 3
27-Dec-92 CZE/SVK 6-USA 5
04-Jan-94 CZE 7-USA 3
04-Jan-95 CZE 5-USA 7
29-Dec-96 CZE 1-USA 2
03-Jan-97 CZE 2-USA 5
31-Dec-97 CZE 4-USA 1
28-Dec-98 CZE 6-USA 3
26-Dec-99 CZE 2-USA 2
03-Jan-00 CZE 4-USA 1
29-Dec-00 CZE 4-USA 2
25-Dec-01 CZE 1-USA 3
02-Jan-02 CZE 3-USA 4
02-Jan-03 CZE 3-USA 4
30-Dec-04 CZE 3-USA 1
04-Jan-05 CZE 3-USA 2
(OT)
02-Jan-06 CZE 1-USA 2
28-Dec-08 CZE 3-USA 4
04-Jan-09 CZE 2-USA 3
(OT)
30-Dec-11 CZE 5-USA 2
Totals: 34-20-1-13-149-102

26-Dec-76 TCH 8-FRG 2
22-Dec-77 TCH 5-FRG 4
28-Dec-79 TCH 13-FRG 4
31-Dec-81 TCH 7-FRG 1
02-Jan-83 TCH 9-FRG 0
25-Dec-83 TCH 6-FRG 1
28-Dec-84 TCH 7-FRG 3
26-Dec-85 TCH 9-FRG 3
31-Dec-87 TCH 7-FRG 4
29-Dec-88 TCH 11-FRG 1
Totals: 10-10-0-0-82-23

**WORLD U18 CHAMPIONSHIPS, MEN**

18-Apr-02 CZE 5-BLR 1
14-Apr-06 CZE 5-BLR 2
Totals: 2-2-0-0-10-3

15-Apr-02 CZE 4-CAN 1
14-Apr-03 CZE 3-CAN 3
18-Apr-04 CZE 3-CAN 2
22-Apr-05 CZE 2-CAN 3
(OT)
22-Apr-06 CZE 4-CAN 1
13-Apr-09 CZE 3-CAN 4
(OT)
15-Apr-11 CZE 0-CAN 5
16-Apr-12 CZE 2-CAN 6
Totals: 8-3-1-4-21-25

13-Apr-12 CZE 8-DEN 4
Totals: 1-1-0-0-8-4

16-Apr-99 CZE 1-FIN 3
21-Apr-00 CZE 0-FIN 3
22-Apr-01 CZE 1-FIN 2
21-Apr-02 CZE 4-FIN 2
13-Apr-04 CZE 1-FIN 1
18-Apr-05 CZE 6-FIN 1
15-Apr-07 CZE 2-FIN 4
18-Apr-10 CZE 3-FIN 4
(5:00 OT/GWS)
19-Apr-11 CZE 3-FIN 5
17-Apr-12 CZE 2-FIN 6
Totals: 10-2-1-7-23-31

08-Apr-99 CZE 4-GER 2
14-Apr-00 CZE 5-GER 3
17-Apr-01 CZE 1-GER 3
14-Apr-02 CZE 6-GER 1
12-Apr-06 CZE 4-GER 2
20-Apr-07 CZE 3-GER 6
12-Apr-09 CZE 3-GER 4
Totals: 7-4-0-3-26-21

12-Apr-03 CZE 5-KAZ 3
Totals: 1-1-0-0-5-3

19-Apr-07 CZE 4 -LAT 1
16-Apr-10 CZE 5-LAT 4
20-Apr-12 CZE 7-LAT 4
Totals: 3-3-0-0-16-9

16-Apr-01 CZE 7-NOR 2
12-Apr-02 CZE 7-NOR 4
12-Apr-04 CZE 7-NOR 0
17-Apr-11 CZE 3-NOR 2
Totals: 4-4-0-0-24-8

16-Apr-99 CZE 5-RUS 2
12-Apr-01 CZE 3-RUS 8
20-Apr-01 CZE 3-RUS 8
17-Apr-02 CZE 3-RUS 5
17-Apr-03 CZE 2-RUS 4
10-Apr-04 CZE 1-RUS 1
21-Apr-05 CZE 5-RUS 1
17-Apr-06 CZE 0-RUS 2
13-Apr-10 CZE 1-RUS 4
Totals: 9-2-1-6-23-35

18-Apr-99 CZE 0-SVK 1
24-Apr-00 CZE 3-SVK 4
(10:00 OT/GWS)
11-Apr-02 CZE 5-SVK 1
19-Apr-03 CZE 1-SVK 2
08-Apr-04 CZE 1-SVK 1
16-Apr-05 CZE 3-SVK 0
14-Apr-07 CZE 3-SVK 2
(5:00 OT/GWS)
14-Apr-10 CZE 4-SVK 3
21-Apr-11 CZE 4-SVK 3
Totals: 9-5-1-3-24-17

11-Apr-99 CZE 4-SWE 4
17-Apr-00 CZE 2-SWE 6
14-Apr-01 CZE 2-SWE 1
21-Apr-03 CZE 2-SWE 3
(OT)
15-Apr-04 CZE 5-SWE 1
24-Apr-05 CZE 2-SWE 4
19-Apr-06 CZE 3-SWE 0
17-Apr-07 CZE 0-SWE 3
09-Apr-09 CZE 0-SWE 7
18-Apr-09 CZE 2-SWE 4
14-Apr-11 CZE 2-SWE 1
Totals: 11-4-1-6-24-34

13-Apr-99 CZE 2-SUI 3
19-Apr-00 CZE 2-SUI 3
16-Apr-03 CZE 4-SUI 1
14-Apr-05 CZE 4-SUI 1
12-Apr-07 CZE 4-SUI 2
10-Apr-09 CZE 6-SUI 2
22-Apr-10 CZE 5-SUI 6
23-Apr-11 CZE 2-SUI 4
19-Apr-12 CZE 2-SUI 4
Totals: 9-4-0-5-31-26

10-Apr-99 CZE 6-UKR 1
16-Apr-00 CZE 6-UKR 0
Totals: 2-2-0-0-12-1

19-Apr-01 CZE 5-USA 4
(10:00 OT/GWS)
20-Apr-02 CZE 1-USA 0
16-Apr-04 CZE 2-USA 3
19-Apr-05 CZE 3-USA 4
15-Apr-06 CZE 0-USA 5
20-Apr-06 CZE 3-USA 4
(OT)
16-Apr-09 CZE 2-USA 6
20-Apr-10 CZE 0-USA 6
14-Apr-12 CZE 0-USA 5
Totals: 9-2-0-7-16-37

**WOMEN'S U18 WORLD CHAMPIONSHIPS**

07-Jan-08 CZE 2-CAN 11
07-Jan-09 CZE 0-CAN 13
Totals: 2-0-0-2-2-24

08-Jan-08 CZE 5-FIN 3
05-Jan-09 CZE 1-FIN 2 (5:00 OT/GWS)
27-Mar-10 CZE 1-FIN 5
08-Jan-11 CZE 0-FIN 3
06-Jan-12 CZE 3-FIN 5
Totals: 5-1-0-4-10-18

09-Jan-08 CZE 3-GER 2
05-Jan-11 CZE 3-GER 1
04-Jan-12 CZE 1-GER 2
Totals: 3-2-0-1-7-5

28-Mar-10 CZE 5-JPN 3
04-Jan-11 CZE 4-JPN 1
Totals: 2-2-0-0-9-4

31-Mar-10 CZE 5-RUS 0
02-Apr-10 CZE 3-RUS 1
01-Jan-12 CZE 2-RUS 0
Totals: 3-3-0-0-10-1

12-Jan-08 CZE 4-SWE 2
10-Jan-09 CZE 1-SWE 9
02-Jan-11 CZE 2-SWE 3
31-Dec-11 CZE 1-SWE 4
Totals: 4-1-0-3-8-18

06-Jan-09 CZE 7-SUI 3
Totals: 1-1-0-0-7-3

11-Jan-08 CZE 0-USA 8
09-Jan-09 CZE 0-USA 18
30-Mar-10 CZE 0-USA 15
01-Jan-11 CZE 0-USA 11
07-Jan-11 CZE 1-USA 14
03-Jan 3 CZE 1-USA 13
Totals: 6-0-0-6-2-79

# DENMARK (DEN)

Totals=GP-W-T-L-GF-GA

**WORLD CHAMPIONSHIPS, MEN**

**Date Score**
14-Feb-49 DEN 1-AUT 25
08-May-05 DEN 4-AUT 3
04-May-09 DEN 5-AUT 2
Totals: 3-2-0-1-10-30

12-May-08 DEN 3-BLR 2 (OT)
17-May-10 DEN 1-BLR 2
Totals: 2-1-0-1-4-4

17-Feb-49 DEN 3-BEL 8
Totals: 1-0-0-1-3-8

12-Feb-49 DEN 0-CAN 47
02-May-03 DEN 2-CAN 2
05-May-06 DEN 3-CAN 5
Totals: 3-0-1-2-5-54

02-May-08 DEN 2-CZE 5
25-Apr-09 DEN 0-CZE 5
02-May-11 DEN 0-CZE 6
04-May-12 DEN 0-CZE 2
Totals: 4-0-0-4-2-18

01-May-04 DEN 0-FIN 6
30-Apr-05 DEN 1-FIN 2
29-Apr-07 DEN 2-FIN 6
27-Apr-09 DEN 1-FIN 5
08-May-10 DEN 4-FIN 1
30-Apr-11 DEN 1-FIN 5
Totals: 6-1-0-5-9-25

10-May-05 DEN 3-GER 2
01-May-09 DEN 3-GER 1
12-May-10 DEN 1-GER 3
07-May-11 DEN 4-GER 3 (5:00 OT/GWS)
12-May-12 DEN 1-GER 2
Totals: 5-3-0-2-12-11

03-May-09 DEN 5-HUN 1
Totals: 1-1-0-0-5-1

13-May-06 DEN 5-ITA 0
07-May-07 DEN 5-ITA 2
04-May-08 DEN 6-ITA 2
06-May-12 DEN 3-ITA 4 (OT)
Totals: 4-3-0-1-19-8

27-Apr-04 DEN 4-JPN 3
Totals: 1-1-0-0-4-3

15-May-06 DEN 3-KAZ 2
Totals: 1-1-0-0-3-2

06-May-03 DEN 2-LAT 4
04-May-11 DEN 3-LAT 2 (5:00OT/GWS)
14-May-12 DEN 2-LAT 0
Totals: 3-2-0-1-7-6

09-May-06 DEN 3-NOR 6
29-Apr-09 DEN 4-NOR 5 (OT)
15-May-12 DEN 2-NOR 6
Totals: 3-0-0-3-9-17

27-Apr-03 DEN 1-RUS 6
25-Apr-04 DEN 2-RUS 6
27-Apr-07 DEN 1-RUS 9
06-May-08 DEN 1-RUS 4
16-May-10 DEN 1-RUS 6
05-May-11 DEN 3-RUS 4
10-May-12 DEN 1-RUS 3
Totals: 7-0-0-7-10-38

02-May-04 DEN 0-SVK 8
14-May-10 DEN 6-SVK 0
09-May-11 DEN 1-SVK 4
Totals: 3-1-0-2-7-12

06-May-05 DEN 3-SLO 4
12-May-06 DEN 3-SLO 3
Totals: 2-0-1-1-6-7

03-May-03 DEN 1-SWE 7
24-Apr-04 DEN 1-SWE 5
02-May-05 DEN 0-SWE 7
03-May-07 DEN 2-SWE 5
08-May-08 DEN 1-SWE 8
20-May-10 DEN 2-SWE 4
07-May-12 DEN 4-SWE 6
Totals: 7-0-0-7-11-42

29-Apr-03 DEN 2-SUI 6
05-May-07 DEN 1-SUI 4
11-May-08 DEN 2-SUI 7
Totals: 3-0-0-3-5-17

04-May-05 DEN 1-UKR 2
01-May-07 DEN 4-UKR 3
Totals: 2-1-0-1-5-5

26-Apr-03 DEN 5-USA 2
04-May-04 DEN 3-USA 8
07-May-06 DEN 0-USA 3
10-May-10 DEN 2-USA 1 (OT)
Totals: 4-2-0-2-10-14

**WORLD U20 CHAMPIONSHIPS**

31-Dec-07 DEN 1-CAN 4
29-Dec-11 DEN 2-CAN 10
Totals: 2-0-0-2-3-14

27-Dec-07 DEN 2-CZE 5
27-Dec-11 DEN 0-CZE 7
Totals: 2-0-0-2-2-12

30-Dec-11 DEN 1-FIN 10
Totals: 1-0-0-1-1-10

02-Jan-08 DEN 3-KAZ 6
Totals: 1-0-0-1-3-6

04-Jan-12 DEN 1-LAT 2 (OT)
Totals: 1-0-0-1-1-2

30-Dec-07 DEN 3 -SVK 4
Totals: 1-0-0-1-3-4

28-Dec-07 DEN 1 -SWE 10
Totals: 1-0-0-1-1-10

03-Jan-08 DEN 2-SUI 5
02-Jan-12 DEN 3-SUI 4 (OT)
Totals: 2-0-0-2-5-9

26-Dec-11 DEN 3-USA 11
Totals: 1-0-0-1-3-11

**WORLD U18 CHAMPIONSHIPS, MEN**

09-Apr-04 DEN 4-BLR 1
21-Apr-08 DEN 2-BLR 6
Totals: 2-1-0-1-6-7

11-Apr-04 DEN 1-CAN 2
18-Apr-05 DEN 1-CAN 15
15-Apr-08 DEN 1 -CAN 4
12-Apr-12 DEN 1-CAN 6
Totals: 4-0-0-4-4-27

13-Apr-12 DEN 4-CZE 8
Totals: 1-0-0-1-4-8

16-Apr-04 DEN 1-FIN 4
21-Apr-05 DEN 2-FIN 3
16-Apr-12 DEN 1-FIN 5
Totals: 3-0-0-3-4-12

15-Apr-05 DEN 1-GER 3
17-Apr-08 DEN 0-GER 4
Totals: 2-0-0-2-1-7

19-Apr-12 DEN 4-LAT 3 (OT)
Totals: 1-1-0-0-4-3

15-Apr-04 DEN 7-NOR 4
Totals: 1-1-0-0-7-4

16-Apr-05 DEN 1-RUS 2
18-Apr-08 DEN 1-RUS 10
Totals: 2-0-0-2-2-12

14-Apr-08 DEN 2-SVK 5
Totals: 1-0-0-1-2-5

12-Apr-04 DEN 1-SWE 2
19-Apr-05 DEN 1-SWE 3
Totals: 2-0-0-2-2-5

22-Apr-05 DEN 2-SUI 4
20-Apr-08 DEN 1-SUI 6
20-Apr-12 DEN 1-SUI 2
Totals: 3-0-0-3-4-12

08-Apr-04 DEN 2-USA 5
15-Apr-12 DEN 0-USA 4
Totals: 2-0-0-2-2-9

**WOMEN'S WORLD CHAMPIONSHIPS**

21-Apr-92 DEN 0-CAN 10
Totals: 1-0-0-1-0-10

23-Apr-92 DEN 2-CHN 5
Totals: 1-0-0-1-2-5

24-Apr-92 DEN 0-NOR 2
Totals: 1-0-0-1-0-2

20-Apr-92 DEN 1-SWE 4
Totals: 1-0-0-1-1-4

26-Apr-92 DEN 4-SUI 3 (OT)
Totals: 1-1-0-0-4-3

# EAST GERMANY (GDR)

Totals=GP-W-T-L-GF-GA

**OLYMPICS, MEN**

**Date Score**
09-Feb-68 GDR 0-CAN 11
Totals: 1-0-0-1-0-11

12-Feb-68 GDR 3-TCH 10
Totals: 1-0-0-1-3-10

14-Feb-68 GDR 2-FIN 3
Totals: 1-0-0-1-2-3

07-Feb-68 GDR 0-URS 9
Totals: 1-0-0-1-0-9

10-Feb-68 GDR 2-SWE 5
Totals: 1-0-0-1-2-5

15-Feb-68 GDR 4-USA 6
Totals: 1-0-0-1-4-6

17-Feb-68 GDR 2-FRG 4
Totals: 1-0-0-1-2-4

**WORLD CHAMPIONSHIPS, MEN**

05-Mar-57 GDR 3-AUT 1
Totals: 1-1-0-0-3-1

07-Mar-61 GDR 2-CAN 5
09-Mar-63 GDR 5-CAN 11
10-Mar-65 GDR 1-CAN 8
08-Mar-66 GDR 0-CAN 6
18-Mar-67 GDR 3-CAN 6
01-May-78 GDR 2-CAN 6
24-Apr-83 GDR 2-CAN 5
17-Apr-85 GDR 1-CAN 9
Totals: 8-0-0-8-16-56

25-Feb-57 GDR 1-TCH 15
11-Mar-61 GDR 1-TCH 5
10-Mar-63 GDR 3-TCH 8
04-Mar-65 GDR 1-TCH 5
03-Mar-66 GDR 0-TCH 6
20-Mar-67 GDR 0-TCH 6
17-Mar-70 GDR 1-TCH 4
25-Mar-70 GDR 3-TCH 7
08-Apr-74 GDR 0-TCH 8
16-Apr-74 GDR 2-TCH 9
08-Apr-76 GDR 0-TCH 10
29-Apr-78 GDR 2-TCH 8
17-Apr-83 GDR 1-TCH 6
18-Apr-85 GDR 1-TCH 6
Totals: 14-0-0-14-16-103

27-Feb-57 GDR 3-FIN 5
04-Mar-61 GDR 4-FIN 6
13-Mar-63 GDR 1-FIN 0
13-Mar-65 GDR 3-FIN 2
12-Mar-66 GDR 4-FIN 3
28-Mar-67 GDR 1-FIN 5
19-Mar-70 GDR 0-FIN 1
28-Mar-70 GDR 4-FIN 3
06-Apr-74 GDR 3-FIN 7
14-Apr-74 GDR 1-FIN 7
18-Apr-76 GDR 2-FIN 1
24-Apr-76 GDR 3-FIN 9
09-May-78 GDR 4-FIN 4
25-Apr-83 GDR 6-FIN 4
27-Apr-83 GDR 6-FIN 2
23-Apr-85 GDR 4-FIN 4
28-Apr-85 GDR 2-FIN 6
Totals: 17-7-2-8-51-69

13-Mar-59 GDR 8-ITA 6
19-Apr-83 GDR 3-ITA 1
29-Apr-83 GDR 1-ITA 3
Totals: 3-2-0-1-12-10

01-Mar-57 GDR 9-JPN 2
Totals: 1-1-0-0-9-2

07-Mar-59 GDR 3-NOR 6
14-Mar-59 GDR 1-NOR 4
12-Mar-65 GDR 5-NOR 1
Totals: 3-1-0-2-9-11

02-Mar-57 GDR 6-POL 2
09-Mar-59 GDR 5-POL 1
09-Mar-66 GDR 4-POL 0
21-Mar-70 GDR 2-POL 2
30-Mar-70 GDR 5-POL 2
11-Apr-74 GDR 5-POL 3
19-Apr-74 GDR 3-POL 3
11-Apr-76 GDR 4-POL 6
20-Apr-76 GDR 4-POL 5
Totals: 9-5-2-2-38-24

04-Mar-57 GDR 0-URS 12
05-Mar-59 GDR 1-URS 6
09-Mar-61 GDR 1-URS 9
12-Mar-63 GDR 0-URS 12
07-Mar-65 GDR 0-URS 8
06-Mar-66 GDR 0-URS 10
21-Mar-67 GDR 0-URS 12
15-Mar-70 GDR 1-URS 12
24-Mar-70 GDR 1-URS 7
05-Apr-74 GDR 0-URS 5
13-Apr-74 GDR 3-URS 10
09-Apr-76 GDR 0-URS 4
27-Apr-78 GDR 4-URS 7
16-Apr-83 GDR 0-URS 3
20-Apr-85 GDR 0-URS 6
Totals: 15-0-0-15-11-123

24-Feb-57 GDR 1-SWE 11
05-Mar-61 GDR 2-SWE 3
07-Mar-63 GDR 1-SWE 5
05-Mar-65 GDR 1-SWE 5
05-Mar-66 GDR 4-SWE 1
23-Mar-67 GDR 2-SWE 8
14-Mar-70 GDR 1-SWE 6
22-Mar-70 GDR 2-SWE 6
09-Apr-74 GDR 1-SWE 10
17-Apr-74 GDR 3-SWE 9
17-Apr-76 GDR 2-SWE 8
26-Apr-78 GDR 2-SWE 6
20-Apr-83 GDR 4-SWE 5
21-Apr-85 GDR 0-SWE 11
30-Apr-85 GDR 2-SWE 7
Totals: 15-1-0-14-28-101

10-Mar-59 GDR 6-SUI 2
Totals: 1-1-0-0-6-2

06-Mar-59 GDR 2-USA 9
08-Mar-61 GDR 6-USA 5
17-Mar-63 GDR 3-USA 3
09-Mar-65 GDR 7-USA 4
11-Mar-66 GDR 0-USA 4
25-Mar-67 GDR 0-USA 0
12-Apr-76 GDR 2-USA 1
03-May-78 GDR 7-USA 4
13-May-78 GDR 8-USA 4
24-Apr-85 GDR 5-USA 5
Totals: 10-5-3-2-40-39

11-Mar-59 GDR 0-FRG 8
16-Mar-63 GDR 3-FRG 4
26-Mar-67 GDR 8-FRG 1
14-Apr-76 GDR 1-FRG 7
22-Apr-76 GDR 1-FRG 1
07-May-78 GDR 1-FRG 1
11-May-78 GDR 0-FRG 0
22-Apr-83 GDR 3-FRG 4
01-May-83 GDR 3-FRG 7
26-Apr-85 GDR 0-FRG 6
02-May-85 GDR 1-FRG 4
Totals: 11-1-3-7-21-43

# FINLAND (FIN)

Totals=GP-W-T-L-GF-GA

**OLYMPICS, MEN**

**Date Score**
22-Feb-60 FIN 14-AUS 1
25-Feb-60 FIN 19-AUS 2
Totals: 2-2-0-0-33-3

07-Feb-84 FIN 4-AUT 3
18-Feb-94 FIN 6-AUT 2
Totals: 2-2-0-0-10-5

16-Feb-02 FIN 8-BLR 1
17-Feb-10 FIN 5-BLR 1
Totals: 2-2-0-0-13-2

17-Feb-52 FIN 3-CAN 13
05-Feb-64 FIN 2-CAN 6
08-Feb-68 FIN 5-CAN 2
16-Feb-80 FIN 4-CAN 3
11-Feb-84 FIN 2-CAN 4
18-Feb-88 FIN 3-CAN 1
25-Feb-94 FIN 3-CAN 5
21-Feb-98 FIN 3-CAN 2
20-Feb-02 FIN 1-CAN 2
19-Feb-06 FIN 2-CAN 0
Totals: 10-5-0-5-28-38

21-Feb-52 FIN 2-TCH 11
01-Feb-64 FIN 0-TCH 4
10-Feb-68 FIN 3-TCH 4
08-Feb-72 FIN 1-TCH 7
06-Feb-76 FIN 1-TCH 2
13-Feb-84 FIN 2-TCH 7
26-Feb-88 FIN 2-TCH 5
12-Feb-94 FIN 3-CZE 1
13-Feb-98 FIN 0-CZE 3
18-Feb-06 FIN 4-CZE 2
24-Feb-10 FIN 2-CZE 0
Totals vs. TCH:
7-0-0-7-11-40
Totals vs. CZE:
4-3-0-1-9-6

14-Feb-68 FIN 3-GDR 2
Totals: 1-1-0-0-3-2

16-Feb-88 FIN 10-FRA 1
22-Feb-92 FIN 4-FRA 1
Totals: 2-2-0-0-14-2

22-Feb-52 FIN 5-GER 1
21-Feb-60 FIN 1-GER 4
08-Feb-64 FIN 1-GER 2
09-Feb-92 FIN 5 -GER 1
20-Feb-94 FIN 7-GER 1
21-Feb-06 FIN 2-GER 0
19-Feb-10 FIN 5-GER 0
Totals: 7-5-0-2-26-9

17-Feb-92 FIN 5-ITA 3
16-Feb-06 FIN 6-ITA 0
Totals: 2-2-0-0-11-3

23-Feb-60 FIN 6-JPN 6
26-Feb-60 FIN 11-JPN 2
14-Feb-80 FIN 6-JPN 3
Totals: 3-2-1-0-23-11

16-Feb-98 FIN 8-KAZ 2
Totals: 1-1-0-0-8-2

20-Feb-80 FIN 10-NED 3
Totals: 1-1-0-0-10-3

20-Feb-52 FIN 5-NOR 2
09-Feb-84 FIN 16-NOR 2
16-Feb-94 FIN 4-NOR 0
Totals: 3-3-0-0-25-4

23-Feb-52 FIN 2-POL 4
07-Feb-72 FIN 5-POL 1
14-Feb-76 FIN 7-POL 1
12-Feb-80 FIN 4-POL 5
22-Feb-88 FIN 5-POL 1
11-Feb-92 FIN 9-POL 1
Totals: 6-4-0-2-32-13

20-Feb-60 FIN 4-URS 8
04-Feb-64 FIN 0-URS 10
06-Feb-68 FIN 0-URS 8
05-Feb-72 FIN 3-URS 9
12-Feb-76 FIN 2-URS 7
18-Feb-80 FIN 2-URS 4
28-Feb-88 FIN 2-URS 1
19-Feb-92 FIN 1-RUS 6
14-Feb-94 FIN 5-RUS 0
26-Feb-94 FIN 4-RUS 0
15-Feb-98 FIN 3-RUS 4
20-Feb-98 FIN 4-RUS 7
18-Feb-02 FIN 3-RUS 1
24-Feb-06 FIN 4-RUS 0
Totals vs. URS:
7-1-0-6-13-47
Totals vs. RUS:
7-4-0-3-24-18

27-Feb-10 FIN 5-SVK 3
Totals: 1-1-0-0-5-3

15-Feb-52 FIN 2-SWE 9
02-Feb-64 FIN 0-SWE 7
12-Feb-68 FIN 1-SWE 5
13-Feb-72 FIN 4-SWE 3
22-Feb-80 FIN 3-SWE 3
20-Feb-88 FIN 3-SWE 3
15-Feb-92 FIN 2-SWE 2
20-Feb-92 FIN 2-SWE 3
18-Feb-98 FIN 2-SWE 1
26-Feb-06 FIN 2-SWE 3
21-Feb-10 FIN 0-SWE 3
Totals: 11-2-3-6-21-42

16-Feb-52 FIN 0-SUI 12
30-Jan-64 FIN 4-SUI 0
14-Feb-88 FIN 1-SUI 2
15-Feb-06 FIN 5-SUI 0
Totals: 4-2-0-2-10-14

18-Feb-52 FIN 2-USA 8
07-Feb-64 FIN 3-USA 2
17-Feb-68 FIN 1-USA 1
10-Feb-72 FIN 1-USA 4
10-Feb-76 FIN 4-USA 5
24-Feb-80 FIN 2-USA 4
15-Feb-84 FIN 3-USA 3
13-Feb-92 FIN 1-USA 4
23-Feb-94 FIN 6-USA 1
15-Feb-02 FIN 0-USA 6
22-Feb-06 FIN 4-USA 3
26-Feb-10 FIN 1-USA 6
Totals: 12-3-2-7-28-47

16-Feb-68 FIN 4-FRG 1
08-Feb-76 FIN 5-FRG 3
17-Feb-84 FIN 4-FRG 7
24-Feb-88 FIN 8-FRG 0
Totals: 4-3-0-1-21-11

**WORLD CHAMPIONSHIPS, MEN**

02-Mar-57 FIN 9-AUT 2
05-May-94 FIN 10-AUT 0
29-Apr-95 FIN 7-AUT 2
02-May-00 FIN 3-AUT 3
28-Apr-01 FIN 5-AUT 1
02-May-02 FIN 3-AUT 1
26-Apr-03 FIN 5-AUT 1
Totals: 7-6-1-0-42-10

10-May-98 FIN 5-BLR 2
04-May-99 FIN 4-BLR 1
18-May-06 FIN 4-BLR 0
02-May-09 FIN 1-BLR 2 (5:00 OT/GWS)
14-May-10 FIN 2-BLR 0
04-May-12 FIN 1-BLR 0
Totals: 6-5-0-1-17-5

18-Feb-49 FIN 17-BEL 2
Totals: 1-1-0-0-17-2

10-Mar-51 FIN 1-CAN 11
04-Mar-54 FIN 1-CAN 20
28-Feb-55 FIN 0-CAN 12
03-Mar-58 FIN 0-CAN 24
09-Mar-59 FIN 0-CAN 6
11-Mar-61 FIN 1-CAN 12
08-Mar-62 FIN 1-CAN 8
14-Mar-63 FIN 2-CAN 12
05-Mar-65 FIN 0-CAN 4
06-Mar-66 FIN 1-CAN 9
19-Mar-67 FIN 1-CAN 5
16-Mar-69 FIN 1-CAN 5
29-Mar-69 FIN 1-CAN 6
27-Apr-77 FIN 1-CAN 5
27-Apr-78 FIN 6-CAN 4
17-Apr-79 FIN 4-CAN 5
12-Apr-81 FIN 3-CAN 4
15-Apr-82 FIN 2-CAN 9
22-Apr-83 FIN 1-CAN 5
21-Apr-85 FIN 2-CAN 5
15-Apr-86 FIN 3-CAN 2
28-Apr-86 FIN 3-CAN 4
26-Apr-87 FIN 2-CAN 7
15-Apr-89 FIN 4-CAN 6
19-Apr-90 FIN 5-CAN 6
23-Apr-91 FIN 3-CAN 5
06-May-92 FIN 4-CAN 3
28-Apr-93 FIN 1-CAN 5
08-May-94 FIN 1-CAN 2 (10:00 OT/GWS)
30-Apr-96 FIN 1-CAN 3
06-May-97 FIN 0-CAN 1
09-May-98 FIN 3-CAN 3
10-May-99 FIN 4-CAN 2
05-May-00 FIN 1-CAN 5
14-May-00 FIN 2-CAN 1
06-May-04 FIN 4-CAN 5 (OT)
08-May-05 FIN 3-CAN 3
15-May-06 FIN 2-CAN 4
21-May-06 FIN 5-CAN 0
13-May-07 FIN 2-CAN 4
12-May-08 FIN 3-CAN 6
04-May-09 FIN 4-CAN 3 (5:00 OT/GWS)
11-May-12 FIN 3-CAN 5
Totals: 43-7-2-34-92-256

14-Feb-49 FIN 2-TCH 19
01-Mar-54 FIN 1-TCH 12
06-Mar-55 FIN 2-TCH 18
28-Feb-57 FIN 0-TCH 3
28-Feb-58 FIN 1-TCH 5
10-Mar-59 FIN 2-TCH 8
02-Mar-61 FIN 0-TCH 6
15-Mar-63 FIN 2-TCH 5
10-Mar-65 FIN 2-TCH 5
05-Mar-66 FIN 1-TCH 8
23-Mar-67 FIN 3-TCH 1
18-Mar-69 FIN 4-TCH 7
25-Mar-69 FIN 2-TCH 4
20-Mar-70 FIN 1-TCH 9
30-Mar-70 FIN 5-TCH 3
26-Mar-71 FIN 0-TCH 5
03-Apr-71 FIN 2-TCH 4
14-Apr-72 FIN 3-TCH 5
22-Apr-72 FIN 2-TCH 8
07-Apr-73 FIN 2-TCH 4
15-Apr-73 FIN 0-TCH 8
12-Apr-74 FIN 0-TCH 5*
20-Apr-74 FIN 5-TCH 4
10-Apr-75 FIN 2-TCH 6
19-Apr-75 FIN 1-TCH 5
13-Apr-76 FIN 1-TCH 7
21-Apr-77 FIN 3-TCH 11
28-Apr-78 FIN 4-TCH 6
14-Apr-79 FIN 0-TCH 5
21-Apr-82 FIN 0-TCH 3
16-Apr-83 FIN 2-TCH 4
17-Apr-85 FIN 0-TCH 5
16-Apr-86 FIN 1-TCH 1
17-Apr-87 FIN 2-TCH 5
16-Apr-89 FIN 1-TCH 3
17-Apr-90 FIN 2-TCH 4
19-Apr-91 FIN 2-TCH 0
03-May-91 FIN 3-TCH 2
09-May-92 FIN 3-TCH 2 (10:00 OT/GWS)
25-Apr-93 FIN 1-CZE 3
25-Apr-94 FIN 4-CZE 4
23-Apr-95 FIN 0-CZE 3
05-May-95 FIN 3-CZE 0
23-Apr-96 FIN 2-CZE 4
27-Apr-97 FIN 1-CZE 2
12-May-98 FIN 4-CZE 1
14-May-98 FIN 2-CZE 2
15-May-99 FIN 1-CZE 3
16-May-99 FIN 4-CZE 1**
07-May-00 FIN 6-CZE 4
13-May-01 FIN 2-CZE 3 (OT)
30-Apr-03 FIN 1-CZE 2
09-May-06 FIN 3-CZE 3
20-May-06 FIN 1-CZE 3
29-Apr-09 FIN 4-CZE 3
20-May-10 FIN 1-CZE 2 (10:00 OT/GWS)
04-May-11 FIN 1-CZE 2
20-May-12 FIN 2-CZE 3
Totals vs. TCH:
39-6-1-32-69-225
Totals vs. CZE:
19-5-3-11-43-48
*TCH won game 5-2 but FIN failed doping test resulting in an official score of 5-0
**Game 2, best-of-two gold-medal game. FIN won the game 4-0 but Czechs clinched the series in OT

01-May-04 FIN 6 -DEN 0
30-Apr-05 FIN 2-DEN 1
29-Apr-07 FIN 6-DEN 2
27-Apr-09 FIN 5-DEN 1
08-May-10 FIN 1-DEN 4
30-Apr-11 FIN 5-DEN 1
Totals: 6-5-0-1-25-9

27-Feb-57 FIN 5-GDR 3
04-Mar-61 FIN 6-GDR 4
13-Mar-63 FIN 0-GDR 1
13-Mar-65 FIN 2-GDR 3
12-Mar-66 FIN 3-GDR 4
28-Mar-67 FIN 5-GDR 1
19-Mar-70 FIN 1-GDR 0
28-Mar-70 FIN 3-GDR 4
06-Apr-74 FIN 7-GDR 3
14-Apr-74 FIN 7-GDR 1
18-Apr-76 FIN 1-GDR 2
24-Apr-76 FIN 9-GDR 3
09-May-78 FIN 4-GDR 4
25-Apr-83 FIN 4-GDR 6
27-Apr-83 FIN 2-GDR 6
23-Apr-85 FIN 4-GDR 4
28-Apr-85 FIN 6-GDR 2
Totals: 17-8-2-7-69-51

19-Apr-93 FIN 2-FRA 0
30-Apr-94 FIN 8-FRA 1
02-May-95 FIN 5-FRA 0
25-Apr-96 FIN 6-FRA 3
26-Apr-97 FIN 6-FRA 1
10-May-12 FIN 7-FRA 1
Totals: 6-6-0-0-34-6

03-Feb-39 FIN 1-GER 12
28-Apr-92 FIN 6-GER 3
23-Apr-93 FIN 1-GER 3
29-Apr-97 FIN 6-GER 0
10-May-01 FIN 4-GER 1
06-May-03 FIN 2-GER 2
03-May-08 FIN 5-GER 1
10-May-10 FIN 1-GER 0
06-May-11 FIN 5-GER 4 (5:00 OT/GWS)
Totals: 9-6-1-2-31-26

17-Mar-51 FIN 3-GBR 6
09-Mar-62 FIN 5-GBR 7
Totals: 2-0-0-2-8-13

04-Feb-39 FIN 2-ITA 5
08-Feb-39 FIN 1-ITA 2
07-Mar-59 FIN 4-ITA 5
22-Apr-82 FIN 7-ITA 3
21-Apr-83 FIN 6-ITA 2
01-May-83 FIN 4-ITA 4
04-May-92 FIN 6-ITA 1
26-Apr-96 FIN 9-ITA 2
30-Apr-00 FIN 6-ITA 0
05-May-07 FIN 3-ITA 0
Totals: 10-6-1-3-48-24

05-Mar-57 FIN 5-JPN 2
30-Apr-01 FIN 8-JPN 0
Totals: 2-2-0-0-13-2

04-May-98 FIN 4-KAZ 0
14-May-12 FIN 4-KAZ 1
Totals: 2-2-0-0-8-1

02-May-98 FIN 6-LAT 0
09-May-05 FIN 0-LAT 0
07-May-06 FIN 5-LAT 0
09-May-08 FIN 2-LAT 1
02-May-11 FIN 3-LAT 2 (5:00 OT/GWS)
Totals: 5-4-1-0-16-3

06-Feb-39 FIN 1-NED 2
15-Apr-81 FIN 12-NED 3
21-Apr-81 FIN 4-NED 2
Totals: 3-2-0-1-17-7

17-Feb-49 FIN 7-NOR 3
16-Mar-51 FIN 3-NOR 0
02-Mar-54 FIN 2-NOR 0
06-Mar-58 FIN 2-NOR 1
17-Mar-62 FIN 5-NOR 2
09-Mar-65 FIN 4-NOR 1
22-Apr-90 FIN 3-NOR 3
27-Apr-90 FIN 8-NOR 1
22-Apr-93 FIN 2-NOR 0
29-Apr-94 FIN 5-NOR 1
26-Apr-95 FIN 5-NOR 2
21-Apr-96 FIN 1-NOR 1
08-May-00 FIN 7-NOR 4
14-May-06 FIN 3-NOR 0
05-May-08 FIN 3-NOR 2 (OT)
25-Apr-09 FIN 5-NOR 0
12-May-11 FIN 4-NOR 1
Totals: 17-15-2-0-69-22

03-Mar-55 FIN 3-POL 6
24-Feb-57 FIN 5-POL 3
05-Mar-58 FIN 2-POL 2
11-Mar-66 FIN 6-POL 3
15-Mar-70 FIN 9-POL 1
24-Mar-70 FIN 4-POL 0
04-Apr-73 FIN 5-POL 0
12-Apr-73 FIN 1-POL 1
09-Apr-74 FIN 2-POL 2
17-Apr-74 FIN 6-POL 2
07-Apr-75 FIN 5-POL 2
16-Apr-75 FIN 4-POL 1
17-Apr-76 FIN 3-POL 3
22-Apr-76 FIN 5-POL 5
20-Apr-79 FIN 4-POL 3
26-Apr-79 FIN 4-POL 2
18-Apr-86 FIN 4-POL 2
21-Apr-89 FIN 7-POL 2
28-Apr-89 FIN 4-POL 0
29-Apr-92 FIN 11-POL 2
29-Apr-02 FIN 8-POL 0
Totals: 21-15-5-1-102-42

29-Apr-77 FIN 4-ROM 2
03-May-77 FIN 14-ROM 1
Totals: 2-2-0-0-18-3

26-Feb-54 FIN 1-URS 7
25-Feb-55 FIN 2-URS 10
25-Feb-57 FIN 1-URS 11
02-Mar-58 FIN 0-URS 10
14-Mar-59 FIN 1-URS 6
05-Mar-61 FIN 3-URS 7
07-Mar-63 FIN 1-URS 6
04-Mar-65 FIN 4-URS 8
08-Mar-66 FIN 2-URS 13
18-Mar-67 FIN 2-URS 8
19-Mar-69 FIN 1-URS 6
26-Mar-69 FIN 3-URS 7
14-Mar-70 FIN 1-URS 2
22-Mar-70 FIN 1-URS 16
21-Mar-71 FIN 1-URS 8
29-Mar-71 FIN 1-URS 10
09-Apr-72 FIN 2-URS 10
17-Apr-72 FIN 2-URS 7
02-Apr-73 FIN 2-URS 8
10-Apr-73 FIN 1-URS 9
07-Apr-74 FIN 1-URS 7
15-Apr-74 FIN 1-URS 6
05-Apr-75 FIN 4-URS 8
14-Apr-75 FIN 2-URS 5
11-Apr-76 FIN 1-URS 8
22-Apr-77 FIN 6-URS 11
30-Apr-78 FIN 3-URS 6
13-Apr-81 FIN 1-URS 7
19-Apr-82 FIN 1-URS 8
17-Apr-83 FIN 0-URS 3
18-Apr-85 FIN 1-URS 5
13-Apr-86 FIN 1-URS 4
26-Apr-86 FIN 0-URS 8
23-Apr-87 FIN 0-URS 4
18-Apr-89 FIN 1-URS 4
20-Apr-90 FIN 1-URS 6
22-Apr-91 FIN 0-URS 3
03-May-97 FIN 7-RUS 4
06-May-98 FIN 2-RUS 4
06-May-99 FIN 3-RUS 3
04-May-02 FIN 1-RUS 0
09-May-02 FIN 2-RUS 3 (10:00 OT/GWS)
03-May-04 FIN 4-RUS 0
12-May-05 FIN 3-RUS 4 (10:00 OT/GWS)
01-May-07 FIN 4-RUS 5
12-May-07 FIN 2-RUS 1 (OT)
16-May-08 FIN 0-RUS 4
18-May-10 FIN 0-RUS 5
09-May-11 FIN 3-RUS 2 (5:00 OT/GWS)
13-May-11 FIN 3-RUS 0
19-May-12 FIN 2-RUS 6
Totals vs. URS:
37-0-0-37-56-272
Totals vs. RUS:
14-6-1-7-36-41

02-May-97 FIN 5-SVK 2
04-May-00 FIN 2-SVK 2
12-May-00 FIN 1-SVK 3
02-May-01 FIN 5-SVK 2
30-Apr-02 FIN 3-SVK 1
02-May-03 FIN 1-SVK 5
28-Apr-04 FIN 2-SVK 5
07-May-08 FIN 3-SVK 2
01-May-09 FIN 2-SVK 1 (OT)
17-May-10 FIN 5-SVK 2
07-May-11 FIN 2-SVK 1
06-May-12 FIN 1-SVK 0
Totals: 12-8-1-3-32-26

28-Apr-03 FIN 12-SLO 0
05-May-06 FIN 5-SLO 3
Totals: 2-2-0-0-17-3

12-Feb-49 FIN 1-SWE 12
15-Mar-51 FIN 3-SWE 11
28-Feb-54 FIN 3-SWE 5
02-Mar-55 FIN 0-SWE 9
04-Mar-57 FIN 3-SWE 9
01-Mar-58 FIN 2-SWE 5
06-Mar-59 FIN 4-SWE 4
13-Mar-59 FIN 1-SWE 2
07-Mar-61 FIN 4-SWE 6
12-Mar-62 FIN 2-SWE 12
10-Mar-63 FIN 0-SWE 4
07-Mar-65 FIN 2-SWE 2
03-Mar-66 FIN 1-SWE 5
21-Mar-67 FIN 1-SWE 5
15-Mar-69 FIN 3-SWE 6
23-Mar-69 FIN 0-SWE 5
17-Mar-70 FIN 3-SWE 1
26-Mar-70 FIN 3-SWE 4
24-Mar-71 FIN 1-SWE 1
01-Apr-71 FIN 1-SWE 2
12-Apr-72 FIN 1-SWE 2
20-Apr-72 FIN 5-SWE 4
05-Apr-73 FIN 2-SWE 3
13-Apr-73 FIN 1-SWE 2
10-Apr-74 FIN 3-SWE 3
18-Apr-74 FIN 2-SWE 6
08-Apr-75 FIN 0-SWE 1
17-Apr-75 FIN 2-SWE 1
15-Apr-76 FIN 3-SWE 4
24-Apr-77 FIN 1-SWE 5
02-May-78 FIN 1-SWE 6
24-Apr-82 FIN 3-SWE 3
24-Apr-83 FIN 4-SWE 4
20-Apr-85 FIN 5-SWE 0
02-May-85 FIN 6-SWE 1
21-Apr-86 FIN 4-SWE 4
24-Apr-86 FIN 4-SWE 4
24-Apr-87 FIN 4-SWE 1
19-Apr-89 FIN 3-SWE 6
16-Apr-90 FIN 2-SWE 4
20-Apr-91 FIN 4-SWE 4
03-May-92 FIN 3-SWE 1
10-May-92 FIN 2-SWE 5
27-Apr-94 FIN 5-SWE 3
25-Apr-95 FIN 6-SWE 3
07-May-95 FIN 4-SWE 1
28-Apr-96 FIN 5-SWE 5
07-May-97 FIN 2-SWE 5
07-May-98 FIN 0-SWE 1
16-May-98 FIN 0-SWE 1
17-May-98 FIN 0-SWE 0
12-May-99 FIN 3-SWE 1
13-May-99 FIN 1-SWE 2*
11-May-00 FIN 2-SWE 1
08-May-01 FIN 5-SWE 4
05-May-02 FIN 2-SWE 4
10-May-02 FIN 3-SWE 5
07-May-03 FIN 5-SWE 6

30-Apr-04 FIN 1-SWE 1
04-May-05 FIN 1-SWE 5
06-May-07 FIN 0-SWE 1
17-May-08 FIN 4-SWE 0
15-May-11 FIN 6-SWE 1
Totals: 63-15-12-36-158-234
*Game 2, best-of-two semi-finals. SWE won the game 2-0 but FIN clinched the series in OT

13-Mar-51 FIN 1-SUI 4
06-Mar-54 FIN 3-SUI 3
05-Mar-55 FIN 7-SUI 2
14-Mar-62 FIN 7-SUI 4
11-Apr-72 FIN 2-SUI 3
19-Apr-72 FIN 9-SUI 1
18-Apr-87 FIN 3-SUI 2
30-Apr-87 FIN 7-SUI 4
26-Apr-91 FIN 6-SUI 1
01-May-91 FIN 6-SUI 2
09-May-99 FIN 5-SUI 1
03-May-07 FIN 2-SUI 0
08-May-12 FIN 5-SUI 2
Totals: 13-10-1-2-63-29

02-May-99 FIN 3-UKR 1
06-May-01 FIN 7-UKR 1
27-Apr-02 FIN 3-UKR 0
03-May-03 FIN 9-UKR 0
26-Apr-04 FIN 5-UKR 1
02-May-05 FIN 4-UKR 1
27-Apr-07 FIN 5-UKR 0
Totals: 7-7-0-0-36-4

05-Feb-39 FIN 0-USA 4
12-Mar-51 FIN 4-USA 5
26-Feb-55 FIN 1-USA 8
09-Mar-58 FIN 2-USA 4
11-Mar-59 FIN 3-USA 10
12-Mar-61 FIN 2-USA 5
11-Mar-62 FIN 3-USA 6
08-Mar-63 FIN 11-USA 3
12-Mar-65 FIN 0-USA 4
09-Mar-66 FIN 4-USA 1
26-Mar-67 FIN 0-USA 2
22-Mar-69 FIN 4-USA 3
30-Mar-69 FIN 7-USA 3
23-Mar-71 FIN 7-USA 4
31-Mar-71 FIN 7-USA 3
04-Apr-75 FIN 7-USA 4
13-Apr-75 FIN 9-USA 1
08-Apr-76 FIN 3-USA 3
26-Apr-77 FIN 3-USA 2
07-May-77 FIN 2-USA 3
07-May-78 FIN 3-USA 3
11-May-78 FIN 3-USA 4
16-Apr-79 FIN 1-USA 1
22-Apr-79 FIN 2-USA 6
19-Apr-81 FIN 4-USA 6
25-Apr-81 FIN 3-USA 3
18-Apr-82 FIN 4-USA 2
26-Apr-85 FIN 8-USA 3
12-Apr-86 FIN 5-USA 4
21-Apr-87 FIN 5-USA 2
28-Apr-87 FIN 6-USA 4
23-Apr-89 FIN 3-USA 3
30-Apr-89 FIN 6-USA 2
25-Apr-90 FIN 1-USA 2
01-May-90 FIN 2-USA 3
28-Apr-91 FIN 1-USA 2
01-May-92 FIN 6-USA 1
20-Apr-93 FIN 1-USA 1
02-May-94 FIN 7-USA 0
07-May-94 FIN 8-USA 0
30-Apr-95 FIN 4-USA 4
09-May-97 FIN 2-USA 0
07-May-99 FIN 4-USA 3
05-May-01 FIN 1-USA 4
12-May-01 FIN 3-USA 1
07-May-02 FIN 3-USA 1
24-Apr-04 FIN 4-USA 2
06-May-05 FIN 4-USA 4
12-May-06 FIN 4-USA 0
10-May-07 FIN 5-USA 4 (10:00 OT/GWS)
11-May-08 FIN 3-USA 2
14-May-08 FIN 3-USA 2 (OT)
06-May-09 FIN 2-USA 3
12-May-10 FIN 3-USA 2
13-May-12 FIN 0-USA 5
17-May-12 FIN 3-USA 2
Totals: 56-29-8-19-206-169

05-Mar-54 FIN 1-FRG 5
01-Mar-55 FIN 1-FRG 7
05-Mar-59 FIN 5-FRG 3
09-Mar-61 FIN 3-FRG 3
15-Mar-62 FIN 9-FRG 3
11-Mar-63 FIN 4-FRG 4
25-Mar-67 FIN 2-FRG 2
20-Mar-71 FIN 4-FRG 3
28-Mar-71 FIN 7-FRG 2
08-Apr-72 FIN 8-FRG 5
16-Apr-72 FIN 13-FRG 3
01-Apr-73 FIN 8-FRG 3
09-Apr-73 FIN 2-FRG 1
10-Apr-76 FIN 5-FRG 2
20-Apr-76 FIN 4-FRG 4
01-May-77 FIN 4-FRG 1
05-May-77 FIN 7-FRG 2
03-May-78 FIN 3-FRG 4
05-May-78 FIN 3-FRG 5
13-May-78 FIN 7-FRG 2
18-Apr-79 FIN 5-FRG 2
24-Apr-79 FIN 7-FRG 3
17-Apr-81 FIN 6-FRG 3
23-Apr-81 FIN 4-FRG 4
16-Apr-82 FIN 4-FRG 3
19-Apr-83 FIN 3-FRG 4
29-Apr-83 FIN 4-FRG 2
24-Apr-85 FIN 3-FRG 3
30-Apr-85 FIN 4-FRG 5
19-Apr-86 FIN 10-FRG 1
20-Apr-87 FIN 1-FRG 3
02-May-87 FIN 2-FRG 2
25-Apr-89 FIN 3-FRG 1
26-Apr-89 FIN 3-FRG 0
23-Apr-90 FIN 4-FRG 2
29-Apr-90 FIN 1-FRG 1
25-Apr-91 FIN 6-FRG 0
29-Apr-91 FIN 4-FRG 2
Totals: 38-23-8-7-174-105

### WORLD U20 CHAMPIONSHIPS

30-Dec-09 FIN 10-AUT 1
Totals: 1-1-0-0-10-1

30-Dec-00 FIN 5-BLR 0
26-Dec-06 FIN 3-BLR 4
Totals: 2-1-0-1-8-4

26-Dec-76 FIN 4-CAN 6
27-Dec-78 FIN 3-CAN 1
27-Dec-79 FIN 2-CAN 1
22-Dec-81 FIN 1-CAN 5
29-Dec-82 FIN 3-CAN 6
25-Dec-83 FIN 4-CAN 2
31-Dec-84 FIN 4-CAN 4
01-Jan-86 FIN 5-CAN 6
27-Dec-86 FIN 6-CAN 6
29-Dec-87 FIN 4-CAN 4
03-Jan-89 FIN 3-CAN 4
31-Dec-89 FIN 3-CAN 3
01-Jan-91 FIN 1-CAN 5
30-Dec-91 FIN 2-CAN 2
30-Dec-92 FIN 2-CAN 3
30-Dec-93 FIN 3-CAN 6
01-Jan-95 FIN 4-CAN 6
29-Dec-95 FIN 1-CAN 3
25-Dec-97 FIN 3-CAN 2
28-Dec-98 FIN 4-CAN 6
25-Dec-99 FIN 2-CAN 3
28-Dec-00 FIN 2-CAN 2
03-Jan-01 FIN 5-CAN 2
30-Dec-01 FIN 4-CAN 1
31-Dec-02 FIN 3-CAN 5
26-Dec-03 FIN 0-CAN 3
30-Dec-04 FIN 1-CAN 8
26-Dec-05 FIN 1-CAN 5
03-Jan-06 FIN 0-CAN 4
02-Jan-08 FIN 2-CAN 4
26-Dec-11 FIN 1-CAN 8
05-Jan-12 FIN 0-CAN 4
Totals: 32-6-6-20-83-130

30-Dec-76 FIN 3-TCH 2
03-Jan-79 FIN 5-TCH 6
02-Jan-80 FIN 4-TCH 2
02-Jan-81 FIN 6-TCH 6
26-Dec-81 FIN 1-TCH 5
04-Jan-83 FIN 3-TCH 5
26-Dec-83 FIN 8-TCH 7
29-Dec-84 FIN 1-TCH 1
02-Jan-86 FIN 0-TCH 2
04-Jan-87 FIN 5-TCH 3
04-Jan-88 FIN 2-TCH 1
04-Jan-89 FIN 2-TCH 7
26-Dec-89 FIN 1-TCH 7
04-Jan-91 FIN 1-TCH 6
27-Dec-91 FIN 4-TCH 1
26-Dec-92 FIN 5-CZE/SVK 2
27-Dec-93 FIN 7-CZE 3
26-Dec-94 FIN 0-CZE 3
01-Jan-97 FIN 2-CZE 3 (10:00 OT/GWS)
30-Dec-97 FIN 5-CZE 5
31-Dec-98 FIN 4-CZE 3
31-Dec-99 FIN 2-CZE 4
05-Jan-01 FIN 1-CZE 2
01-Jan-02 FIN 3-CZE 1
30-Dec-02 FIN 2-CZE 2
28-Dec-03 FIN 3-CZE 2
05-Jan-04 FIN 2-CZE 1
01-Jan-05 FIN 0-CZE 3
28-Dec-06 FIN 6-CZE 2
04-Jan-07 FIN 2-CZE 6
03-Jan-08 FIN 1-CZE 5
27-Dec-09 FIN 4-CZE 3
31-Dec-11 FIN 4-CZE 0
Totals vs. TCH: 16-7-2-7-51-63
Totals vs. CZE: 17-8-2-7-48-48

30-Dec-11 FIN 10-DEN 1
Totals: 1-1-0-0-10-1

28-Dec-01 FIN 8-FRA 0
Totals: 1-1-0-0-8-0

01-Jan-92 FIN 2-GER 0
29-Dec-92 FIN 11-GER 0
02-Jan-94 FIN 2-GER 0
29-Dec-94 FIN 7-GER 1
26-Dec-97 FIN 5-GER 0
26-Dec-02 FIN 4-GER 0
25-Dec-04 FIN 4-GER 1
04-Jan-09 FIN 3-GER 1
29-Dec-10 FIN 5-GER 1
Totals: 9-9-0-0-43-4

27-Dec-92 FIN 7-JPN 0
Totals: 1-1-0-0-7-0

31-Dec-97 FIN 14-KAZ 1
04-Jan-99 FIN 6-KAZ 1
04-Jan-00 FIN 9-KAZ 1
29-Dec-07 FIN 5-KAZ 0
03-Jan-09 FIN 7-KAZ 1
Totals: 5-5-0-0-41-4

30-Dec-08 FIN 5-LAT 1
Totals: 1-1-0-0-5-1

27-Dec-82 FIN 10-NOR 2
29-Dec-88 FIN 9-NOR 3
01-Jan-90 FIN 8-NOR 2
31-Dec-90 FIN 10-NOR 2
30-Dec-05 FIN 9-NOR 1
Totals: 5-5-0-0-46-10

28-Dec-76 FIN 8-POL 2
28-Dec-84 FIN 11-POL 2
02-Jan-87 FIN 13-POL 3
31-Dec-87 FIN 9-POL 1
03-Jan-90 FIN 7-POL 1
26-Dec-96 FIN 7-POL 0
Totals: 6-6-0-0-55-9

01-Jan-77 FIN 6-URS 10
26-Dec-77 FIN 4-URS 10
31-Dec-78 FIN 2-URS 4
30-Dec-79 FIN 1-URS 2
31-Dec-80 FIN 6-URS 3
31-Dec-81 FIN 6-URS 3
02-Jan-83 FIN 2-URS 7
28-Dec-83 FIN 1-URS 3
01-Jan-85 FIN 5-URS 6
04-Jan-86 FIN 3-URS 4
29-Dec-86 FIN 5-URS 4
28-Dec-87 FIN 2-URS 6
01-Jan-89 FIN 3-URS 9
29-Dec-89 FIN 2-URS 3
03-Jan-91 FIN 5-URS 5
29-Dec-91 FIN 1-RUS 4
01-Jan-93 FIN 1-RUS 1
04-Jan-94 FIN 4-RUS 5
04-Jan-95 FIN 2-RUS 6
01-Jan-96 FIN 2-RUS 6
29-Dec-96 FIN 2-RUS 4
03-Jan-98 FIN 2-RUS 1
02-Jan-99 FIN 2-RUS 3
01-Jan-00 FIN 0-RUS 4
31-Dec-00 FIN 3-RUS 1
27-Dec-01 FIN 2-RUS 1
02-Jan-02 FIN 1-RUS 2 (OT)
03-Jan-03 FIN 1-RUS 4
02-Jan-04 FIN 4-RUS 3
31-Dec-06 FIN 0-RUS 5
26-Dec-07 FIN 4-RUS 1
28-Dec-08 FIN 2-RUS 5
28-Dec-09 FIN 0-RUS 2
04-Jan-10 FIN 4-RUS 3
02-Jan-11 FIN 3-RUS 4 (OT)
Totals vs. URS: 15-3-1-11-53-79
Totals vs. RUS: 20-6-1-13-40-65

31-Dec-96 FIN 4-SVK 3
03-Jan-97 FIN 6-SVK 4
29-Dec-98 FIN 3-SVK 4
26-Dec-99 FIN 1-SVK 1
02-Jan-01 FIN 3-SVK 1
02-Jan-03 FIN 6-SVK 0
27-Dec-04 FIN 0-SVK 2
31-Dec-08 FIN 2-SVK 3 (5:00 OT/GWS)
31-Dec-10 FIN 6-SVK 0
02-Jan-12 FIN 8-SVK 5
Totals: 10-6-1-3-39-23

23-Dec-76 FIN 4-SWE 5
22-Dec-77 FIN 4-SWE 4
28-Dec-78 FIN 1-SWE 2
02-Jan-79 FIN 2-SWE 5
01-Jan-80 FIN 3-SWE 2
30-Dec-80 FIN 1-SWE 2
30-Dec-81 FIN 9-SWE 6
26-Dec-82 FIN 6-SWE 4
29-Dec-83 FIN 4-SWE 1
26-Dec-84 FIN 5-SWE 3
26-Dec-85 FIN 0-SWE 2
30-Dec-86 FIN 0-SWE 5
03-Jan-88 FIN 5-SWE 2
28-Dec-88 FIN 2-SWE 6
28-Dec-89 FIN 5-SWE 2
26-Dec-90 FIN 8-SWE 5
04-Jan-92 FIN 4-SWE 6
02-Jan-93 FIN 2-SWE 9
29-Dec-93 FIN 2-SWE 6
02-Jan-95 FIN 3-SWE 3
28-Dec-96 FIN 4-SWE 2
28-Dec-97 FIN 4-SWE 3
28-Dec-02 FIN 3-SWE 2
29-Dec-04 FIN 5-SWE 4
03-Jan-05 FIN 4-SWE 3
02-Jan-06 FIN 1-SWE 0
26-Dec-08 FIN 1-SWE 3
31-Dec-09 FIN 1-SWE 7
03-Jan-12 FIN 2 -SWE 3 (10:00 OT/GWS)
Totals: 29-14-2-13-95-107

23-Dec-77 FIN 18-SUI 1
30-Dec-77 FIN 9-SUI 1
28-Dec-79 FIN 19-SUI 1
23-Dec-81 FIN 14-SUI 2
02-Jan-84 FIN 12-SUI 4
27-Dec-85 FIN 9-SUI 2
01-Jan-87 FIN 12-SUI 1
28-Dec-90 FIN 7-SUI 1
02-Jan-92 FIN 7-SUI 3
01-Jan-94 FIN 4-SUI 2
26-Dec-95 FIN 5-SUI 1
01-Jan-98 FIN 2-SUI 1
03-Jan-00 FIN 2-SUI 5
27-Dec-00 FIN 3-SUI 2
25-Dec-01 FIN 0-SUI 3
04-Jan-02 FIN 5-SUI 1
31-Dec-03 FIN 2-SUI 0
31-Dec-05 FIN 4-SUI 1
30-Dec-06 FIN 4-SUI 0
27-Dec-07 FIN 4-SUI 3 (5:00 OT/GWS)
28-Dec-10 FIN 4-SUI 0
04-Jan-11 FIN 2-SUI 3 (5:00 OT/GWS)
Totals: 22-19-0-3-148-38

27-Dec-94 FIN 6-UKR 2
28-Dec-95 FIN 4-UKR 1
30-Dec-03 FIN 14-UKR 1
Totals: 3-3-0-0-24-4

22-Dec-76 FIN 6-USA 3
31-Dec-77 FIN 6-USA 8
27-Dec-80 FIN 8-USA 1
02-Jan-82 FIN 8-USA 4
30-Dec-82 FIN 2-USA 4
31-Dec-83 FIN 7-USA 2
25-Dec-84 FIN 7-USA 4
30-Dec-85 FIN 7-USA 5
26-Dec-86 FIN 4-USA 1
01-Jan-88 FIN 8-USA 6
26-Dec-88 FIN 5-USA 5
04-Jan-90 FIN 6-USA 3
29-Dec-90 FIN 3-USA 6
26-Dec-91 FIN 1-USA 5
04-Jan-93 FIN 3-USA 5
26-Dec-93 FIN 5-USA 2
30-Dec-94 FIN 7-USA 5
31-Dec-95 FIN 4-USA 5
04-Jan-96 FIN 7-USA 8 (OT)
26-Dec-98 FIN 6-USA 3
29-Dec-99 FIN 3-USA 1
05-Jan-03 FIN 3-USA 2
03-Jan-04 FIN 1-USA 2
28-Dec-05 FIN 5-USA 6
05-Jan-06 FIN 4-USA 2
02-Jan-07 FIN 3-USA 6
31-Dec-07 FIN 3-USA 5
02-Jan-10 FIN 2-USA 6
26-Dec-10 FIN 2-USA 3 (OT)
28-Dec-11 FIN 4-USA 1
Totals: 30-16-1-13-140-119

25-Dec-76 FIN 4-FRG 1
28-Dec-77 FIN 4-FRG 1
30-Dec-78 FIN 7-FRG 1
28-Dec-80 FIN 8-FRG 6
27-Dec-81 FIN 8-FRG 4
01-Jan-83 FIN 9-FRG 1
03-Jan-84 FIN 8-FRG 2
23-Dec-84 FIN 9-FRG 0
29-Dec-85 FIN 7-FRG 2
26-Dec-87 FIN 6-FRG 0
31-Dec-88 FIN 5-FRG 3
Totals: 11-11-0-0-75-21

### WORLD U18 CHAMPIONSHIPS, MEN

19-Apr-00 FIN 11 -BLR 1
12-Apr-02 FIN 4-BLR 3
14-Apr-03 FIN 8-BLR 6
15-Apr-04 FIN 5-BLR 2
17-Apr-08 FIN 4-BLR 3
Totals: 5-5-0-0-32-15

20-Apr-02 FIN 3-CAN 1
17-Apr-06 FIN 0-CAN 0
20-Apr-06 FIN 3-CAN 2 (OT)
20-Apr-08 FIN 1-CAN 2
19-Apr-09 FIN 5-CAN 4 (10:00 OT/GWS)
16-Apr-11 FIN 4-CAN 5
14-Apr-12 FIN 4-CAN 2
22-Apr-12 FIN 4 -CAN 5 (OT)
Totals: 8-4-1-3-24-21

16-Apr-99 FIN 3-CZE 1
21-Apr-00 FIN 3-CZE 0
22-Apr-01 FIN 2-CZE 1
21-Apr-02 FIN 2-CZE 4
13-Apr-04 FIN 1-CZE 1
18-Apr-05 FIN 1-CZE 6
15-Apr-07 FIN 4-CZE 2
18-Apr-10 FIN 4-CZE 3 (5:00 OT/GWS)
19-Apr-11 FIN 5-CZE 3
17-Apr-12 FIN 6-CZE 2
Totals: 10-7-1-2-31-23

16-Apr-04 FIN 4-DEN 1
21-Apr-05 FIN 3-DEN 2
16-Apr-12 FIN 5-DEN 1
Totals: 3-3-0-0-12-4

22-Apr-05 FIN 4-GER 2
19-Apr-07 FIN 4-GER 3
22-Apr-08 FIN 3-GER 4
23-Apr-11 FIN 6-GER 0
19-Apr-12 FIN 8-GER 0
Totals: 5-4-0-1-25-9

19-Apr-03 FIN 5-KAZ 4
Totals: 1-1-0-0-5-4

20-Apr-07 FIN 6-LAT 3
13-Apr-10 FIN 7-LAT 2
Totals: 2-2-0-0-13-5

13-Apr-99 FIN 10-NOR 2
09-Apr-04 FIN 9-NOR 0
16-Apr-06 FIN 2-NOR 1
13-Apr-09 FIN 10-NOR 1
14-Apr-11 FIN 5-NOR 2
Totals: 5-5-0-0-36-6

11-Apr-99 FIN 3-RUS 1
17-Apr-00 FIN 2-RUS 5
24-Apr-00 FIN 3-RUS 1
18-Apr-02 FIN 3-RUS 4
12-Apr-04 FIN 2-RUS 5
09-Apr-09 FIN 7-RUS 4
17-Apr-09 FIN 0-RUS 4
16-Apr-10 FIN 5-RUS 4
23-Apr-10 FIN 5-RUS 1
21-Apr-11 FIN 2-RUS 5
Totals: 10-5-0-5-32-34

08-Apr-99 FIN 3-SVK 2
14-Apr-00 FIN 3-SVK 1
12-Apr-01 FIN 3-SVK 0
16-Apr-03 FIN 3-SVK 4

10-Apr-04 FIN 2-SVK 2
19-Apr-05 FIN 2-SVK 3
13-Apr-06 FIN 6-SVK 3
17-Apr-07 FIN 0-SVK 1
14-Apr-09 FIN 7-SVK 0
15-Apr-10 FIN 5-SVK 2
Totals: 10-6-1-3-34-18

18-Apr-99 FIN 2-SWE 2
22-Apr-00 FIN 4-SWE 2
11-Apr-02 FIN 2-SWE 0
12-Apr-03 FIN 3-SWE 3
14-Apr-06 FIN 4-SWE 3
11-Apr-07 FIN 1-SWE 2 (5:00 OT/GWS)
15-Apr-08 FIN 3-SWE 5
17-Apr-11 FIN 2-SWE 5
20-Apr-12 FIN 3-SWE 7
Totals: 9-3-2-4-24-29

16-Apr-99 FIN 1-SUI 6
17-Apr-01 FIN 3-SUI 0
20-Apr-01 FIN 2-SUI 4
17-Apr-02 FIN 8-SUI 1
20-Apr-03 FIN 2-SUI 2
15-Apr-05 FIN 3-SUI 1
13-Apr-07 FIN 1-SUI 5
14-Apr-08 FIN 5-SUI 3
Totals: 8-4-1-3-25-22

15-Apr-01 FIN 7-UKR 0
15-Apr-02 FIN 6-UKR 0
Totals: 2-2-0-0-13-0

09-Apr-99 FIN 5-USA 0
15-Apr-00 FIN 3-USA 2
14-Apr-01 FIN 4-USA 3
14-Apr-02 FIN 2-USA 3
17-Apr-03 FIN 0-USA 2
16-Apr-05 FIN 0-USA 3
22-Apr-06 FIN 1-USA 3
18-Apr-08 FIN 3-USA 4
11-Apr-09 FIN 3-USA 4
21-Apr-10 FIN 0-USA 5
12-Apr-12 FIN 0-USA 4
Totals: 11-3-0-8-21-33

**OLYMPICS, WOMEN**
12-Feb-98 FIN 2-CAN 4
19-Feb-02 FIN 3-CAN 7
17-Feb-06 FIN 0-CAN 6
22-Feb-10 FIN 0-CAN 5
Totals: 4-0-0-4-5-22

14-Feb-98 FIN 6-CHN 1
17-Feb-98 FIN 4-CHN 1
12-Feb-02 FIN 4-CHN 0
16-Feb-10 FIN 2-CHN 1
Totals: 4-4-0-0-16-3

14-Feb-02 FIN 3-GER 1
11-Feb-06 FIN 3-GER 0
Totals: 2-2-0-0-6-1

09-Feb-98 FIN 11-JPN 1
Totals: 1-1-0-0-11-1

14-Feb-10 FIN 5-RUS 1
Totals: 1-1-0-0-5-1

08-Feb-98 FIN 6-SWE 0
21-Feb-02 FIN 1-SWE 2
25-Feb-10 FIN 3-SWE 2 (OT)
Totals: 3-2-0-1-10-4

13-Feb-06 FIN 4-SUI 0
Totals: 1-1-0-0-4-0

11-Feb-98 FIN 2-USA 4
16-Feb-02 FIN 0-USA 5
14-Feb-06 FIN 3-USA 7
20-Feb-06 FIN 0-USA 4
18-Feb-10 FIN 0-USA 6
Totals: 5-0-0-5-5-26

**WOMEN'S WORLD CHAMPIONSHIPS**
24-Mar-90 FIN 5-CAN 6
25-Apr-92 FIN 2-CAN 6
15-Apr-94 FIN 1-CAN 4
05-Apr-97 FIN 1-CAN 2
11-Mar-99 FIN 0-CAN 1
08-Apr-00 FIN 2-CAN 3
07-Apr-01 FIN 0-CAN 8
08-Apr-05 FIN 0-CAN 3
09-Apr-07 FIN 0-CAN 5
09-Apr-08 FIN 2-CAN 4
08-Apr-09 FIN 0-CAN 8
19-Apr-11 FIN 0-CAN 2
23-Apr-11 FIN 1-CAN 4
08-Apr-12 FIN 2-CAN 3
13-Apr-12 FIN 1-CAN 5
Totals: 15-0-0-15-17-64

17-Apr-94 FIN 8-CHN 1
06-Apr-97 FIN 3-CHN 0
02-Apr-01 FIN 7-CHN 6
05-Apr-05 FIN 5-CHN 1
Totals: 4-4-0-0-23-8

11-Apr-94 FIN 17-GER 1
08-Mar-99 FIN 9-GER 0
04-Apr-00 FIN 4 -GER 1
03-Apr-01 FIN 5-GER 2
04-Apr-04 FIN 4-GER 0
03-Apr-05 FIN 5-GER 1
Totals: 6-6-0-0-44-5

31-Mar-04 FIN 1-JPN 0
05-Apr-08 FIN 6-JPN 1
Totals: 2-2-0-0-7-1

04-Apr-09 FIN 7-KAZ 0
16-Apr-11 FIN 5-KAZ 3
Totals: 2-2-0-0-12-3

19-Mar-90 FIN 10-NOR 1
20-Apr-92 FIN 11-NOR 3
03-Apr-97 FIN 10-NOR 0
Totals: 3-3-0-0-31-4

03-Apr-00 FIN 7-RUS 1
08-Apr-01 FIN 1-RUS 2
05-Apr-04 FIN 2-RUS 1
04-Apr-07 FIN 4-RUS 0
25-Apr-11 FIN 3-RUS 2 (OT)
07-Apr-12 FIN 5-RUS 4
Totals: 6-5-0-1-22-10

25-Mar-90 FIN 6-SWE 3
26-Apr-92 FIN 5-SWE 4 (10:00 OT/GWS)
31-Mar-97 FIN 3-SWE 0
14-Mar-99 FIN 8-SWE 2
09-Apr-00 FIN 7-SWE 1
01-Apr-04 FIN 2-SWE 2
06-Apr-04 FIN 3-SWE 2
09-Apr-05 FIN 2-SWE 5
05-Apr-07 FIN 1-SWE 0 (5:00 OT/GWS)
10-Apr-07 FIN 0-SWE 1
06-Apr-08 FIN 3-SWE 2 (OT)
12-Apr-09 FIN 4-SWE 1
22-Apr-11 FIN 5-SWE 1
11-Apr-12 FIN 2-SWE 1
Totals: 14-11-1-2-51-25

21-Mar-90 FIN 10-SUI 0
21-Apr-92 FIN 13-SUI 1
12-Apr-94 FIN 13-SUI 0
09-Mar-99 FIN 7-SUI 0
12-Apr-08 FIN 4-SUI 1
06-Apr-09 FIN 6-SUI 3
17-Apr-11 FIN 1-SUI 2 (OT)
14-Apr-12 FIN 2-SUI 6
Totals: 8-6-0-2-56-13

22-Mar-90 FIN 4-USA 5
23-Apr-92 FIN 3-USA 5
14-Apr-94 FIN 1-USA 2
01-Apr-97 FIN 3-USA 3
13-Mar-99 FIN 1-USA 3
06-Apr-00 FIN 3-USA 4
05-Apr-01 FIN 0-USA 9
06-Apr-05 FIN 1-USA 8
08-Apr-07 FIN 0-USA 4
08-Apr-08 FIN 1-USA 0 (OT)
09-Apr-09 FIN 0-USA 7
10-Apr-12 FIN 0-USA 11
Totals: 12-1-1-10-17-61

**WOMEN'S U18 WORLD CHAMPIONSHIPS**
09-Jan-08 FIN 0-CAN 17
06-Jan-09 FIN 0-CAN 6
02-Jan-11 FIN 0-CAN 6
07-Jan-11 FIN 1-CAN 6
03-Jan-12 FIN 0-CAN 7
Totals: 5-0-0-5-1-42

08-Jan-08 FIN 3-CZE 5
05-Jan-09 FIN 2-CZE 1 (5:00 OT/GWS)
27-Mar-10 FIN 5-CZE 1
08-Jan-11 FIN 3-CZE 0
06-Jan-12 FIN 5-CZE 3
Totals: 5-4-0-1-18-10

07-Jan-08 FIN 2-GER 4
12-Jan-08 FIN 1-GER 4
10-Jan-09 FIN 2-GER 1
31-Mar-10 FIN 1-GER 2 (OT)
01-Jan-11 FIN 0-GER 1
31-Dec-11 FIN 3-GER 0
Totals: 6-2-0-4-9-12

30-Mar-10 FIN 1-JPN 3
02-Apr-10 FIN 4-JPN 1
Totals: 2-1-0-1-5-4

09-Jan-09 FIN 2-RUS 1 (OT)
Totals: 1-1-0-0-2-1

05-Jan-11 FIN 3-SWE 2 (OT)
04-Jan-12 FIN 1-SWE 2 (OT)
Totals: 2-1-0-1-4-4

11-Jan-08 FIN 7-SUI 2
07-Jan-09 FIN 3-SUI 4
04-Jan-11 FIN 4-SUI 1
01-Jan-12 FIN 3-SUI 5
Totals: 4-2-0-2-17-12

28-Mar-10 FIN 0-USA 5
Totals: 1-0-0-1-0-5

# FRANCE (FRA)

Totals=GP-W-T-L-GF-GA

**OLYMPICS, MEN**
**Date Score**
11-Feb-68 FRA 2-AUT 5
22-Feb-94 FRA 5-AUT 4 (10:00 OT/GWS)
Totals: 2-1-0-1-7-9

07-Feb-98 FRA 0-BLR 4
11-Feb-02 FRA 1-BLR 3
Totals: 2-0-0-2-1-7

31-Jan-24 FRA 7-BEL 5
16-Feb-28 FRA 1-BEL 3
08-Feb-36 FRA 4-BEL 2 (20:00 OT)
Totals: 3-2-0-1-12-10

20-Feb-88 FRA 5-CAN 9
08-Feb-92 FRA 2-CAN 3
15-Feb-94 FRA 1-CAN 3
Totals: 3-0-0-3-8-15

09-Feb-36 FRA 0-TCH 2
10-Feb-92 FRA 4-TCH 6
Totals: 2-0-0-2-4-8

16-Feb-88 FRA 1-FIN 10
22-Feb-92 FRA 1-FIN 4
Totals: 2-0-0-2-2-14

20-Feb-92 FRA 4-GER 5
10-Feb-98 FRA 0-GER 2
Totals: 2-0-0-2-4-7

29-Jan-24 FRA 2-GBR 15
12-Feb-28 FRA 3-GBR 2
Totals: 2-1-0-1-5-17

11-Feb-28 FRA 2-HUN 0
07-Feb-36 FRA 0-HUN 3
Totals: 2-1-0-1-2-3

19-Feb-94 FRA 3-ITA 7
24-Feb-94 FRA 2-ITA 3
12-Feb-98 FRA 5-ITA 1
Totals: 3-1-0-2-10-11

17-Feb-68 FRA 2-JPN 6
09-Feb-98 FRA 5-JPN 2
Totals: 2-1-0-1-7-8

08-Feb-68 FRA 1-NOR 4
23-Feb-88 FRA 7-NOR 6 (10:00 OT/GWS)
16-Feb-92 FRA 4-NOR 2
Totals: 3-2-0-1-12-12

18-Feb-88 FRA 2-POL 0*
Totals: 1-1-0-0-2-0
*POL won game 6-2 but POL failed doping test resulting in an official score of FRA 2-0

09-Feb-68 FRA 3-RUM 7
Totals: 1-0-0-1-3-7

14-Feb-92 FRA 0-RUS 8
Totals: 1-0-0-1-0-8

21-Feb-94 FRA 2-SVK 6
14-Feb-02 FRA 1-SVK 7
Totals: 2-0-0-2-3-13

25-Apr-20 FRA 0-SWE 4
14-Feb-88 FRA 2-SWE 13
17-Feb-94 FRA 1-SWE 7
Totals: 3-0-0-3-3-24

22-Feb-88 FRA 0-SUI 9
12-Feb-92 FRA 4-SUI 3
09-Feb-02 FRA 3-SUI 3
Totals: 3-1-1-1-7-15

13-Feb-02 FRA 2-UKR 4
Totals: 1-0-0-1-2-4

30-Jan-24 FRA 0-USA 22
18-Feb-92 FRA 1-USA 4
13-Feb-94 FRA 4-USA 4
Totals: 3-0-1-2-5-30

13-Feb-68 FRA 1-YUG 10
Totals: 1-0-0-1-1-10

**WORLD CHAMPIONSHIPS, MEN**
01-Feb-30 FRA 1-AUT 2
24-Jan-35 FRA 1-AUT 4
01-May-96 FRA 6-AUT 3
02-May-96 FRA 6-AUT 3
06-May-00 FRA 3-AUT 3
24-Apr-04 FRA 0-AUT 6
Totals: 6-2-1-3-17-21

07-May-08 FRA 1-BLR 3
03-May-11 FRA 2-BLR 1 (OT)
14-May-12 FRA 2-BLR 1
Totals: 3-2-0-1-5-5

31-Jan-30 FRA 4-BEL 1
05-Feb-34 FRA 0-BEL 2
20-Mar-50 FRA 1-BEL 7
Totals: 3-1-0-2-5-10

01-Feb-31 FRA 0-CAN 9
06-Feb-34 FRA 0-CAN 9
17-Feb-37 FRA 0-CAN 12
23-Feb-37 FRA 1-CAN 13
28-Apr-92 FRA 3-CAN 4
25-Apr-95 FRA 4-CAN 1
27-Apr-04 FRA 0-CAN 3
01-May-11 FRA 1-CAN 9
07-May-12 FRA 2-CAN 7
Totals: 9-1-0-8-11-67

22-Feb-37 FRA 1-TCH 8
26-Feb-37 FRA 1-TCH 3
30-Apr-92 FRA 0-TCH 3
24-Apr-93 FRA 2-CZE 6
26-Apr-94 FRA 2-CZE 5
27-Apr-96 FRA 2-CZE 9
03-May-97 FRA 3-CZE 9
09-May-10 FRA 2-CZE 6
Totals vs. TCH:
3-0-0-3-2-14
Totals vs. CZE:
5-0-0-5-11-35

19-Apr-93 FRA 0-FIN 2
30-Apr-94 FRA 1-FIN 8
02-May-95 FRA 0-FIN 5
25-Apr-96 FRA 3-FIN 6
26-Apr-97 FRA 1-FIN 6
10-May-12 FRA 1-FIN 7
Totals: 6-0-0-6-6-34

08-Feb-34 FRA 0-GER 4
21-Jan-35 FRA 2-GER 1
20-Feb-37 FRA 0-GER 5
21-Apr-93 FRA 3-GER 5
23-Apr-95 FRA 4-GER 0
02-May-97 FRA 2-GER 1
28-Apr-09 FRA 2-GER 1
Totals: 7-4-0-3-13-17

05-Feb-31 FRA 1-GBR 2
22-Jan-35 FRA 0-GBR 1
14-Mar-50 FRA 0-GBR 9
Totals: 3-0-0-3-1-12

07-Feb-31 FRA 0-HUN 1
25-Feb-37 FRA 1-HUN 5
Totals: 2-0-0-2-1-6

20-Jan-35 FRA 1-ITA 1
01-May-95 FRA 2-ITA 5
22-Apr-96 FRA 5-ITA 6
10-May-97 FRA 1-ITA 8
09-May-08 FRA 3-ITA 2
10-May-08 FRA 6-ITA 4
15-May-10 FRA 2-ITA 1
Totals: 7-3-1-3-20-27

09-May-00 FRA 7-JPN 2
04-May-04 FRA 2-JPN 2
Totals: 2-1-1-0-9-4

30-Apr-04 FRA 0-KAZ 5
18-May-10 FRA 5-KAZ 3
06-May-12 FRA 6-KAZ 3
Totals: 3-2-0-1-11-11

08-May-97 FRA 2-LAT 6
04-May-99 FRA 5-LAT 8
02-May-09 FRA 1-LAT 7
Totals: 3-0-0-3-8-21

21-Mar-50 FRA 2-NED 4
Totals: 1-0-0-1-2-4

14-Mar-50 FRA 0-NOR 11
04-May-92 FRA 0-NOR 1
26-Apr-93 FRA 4-NOR 5
02-May-94 FRA 4-NOR 1
29-Apr-96 FRA 1-NOR 3
07-May-97 FRA 4-NOR 3
13-May-10 FRA 1-NOR 5
09-May-11 FRA 2-NOR 5
Totals: 8-2-0-6-16-34

03-Feb-31 FRA 1-POL 2 (OT)
19-Jan-35 FRA 3-POL 2
19-Feb-37 FRA 1-POL 7
06-May-92 FRA 3-POL 1
Totals: 4-2-0-2-8-12

04-Feb-31 FRA 7-ROM 1
03-Feb-34 FRA 4-ROM 1
Totals: 2-2-0-0-11-2

03-May-92 FRA 0-RUS 8
26-Apr-95 FRA 1-RUS 3
30-Apr-97 FRA 4-RUS 5
29-Apr-00 FRA 1-RUS 8
26-Apr-09 FRA 2-RUS 7
Totals: 5-0-0-5-8-31

28-Apr-97 FRA 3-SVK 5
15-May-12 FRA 4-SVK 5
Totals: 2-0-0-2-7-10

26-Jan-35 FRA 1-SWE 2
18-Feb-37 FRA 2-SWE 1
28-Apr-94 FRA 0-SWE 6
24-Apr-96 FRA 1-SWE 2
02-May-98 FRA 1-SWE 6
02-May-99 FRA 1-SWE 4
05-May-08 FRA 0-SWE 9
04-May-09 FRA 3-SWE 6
11-May-10 FRA 2-SWE 3
06-May-11 FRA 0-SWE 4
Totals: 10-1-0-9-11-43

04-Feb-34 FRA 0-SUI 3
23-Jan-35 FRA 1-SUI 5
01-May-92 FRA 5-SUI 6
29-Apr-93 FRA 3-SUI 1
28-Apr-95 FRA 3-SUI 2
06-May-98 FRA 1-SUI 5
06-May-99 FRA 0-SUI 6
01-May-00 FRA 4-SUI 2
25-Apr-04 FRA 0-SUI 6
03-May-08 FRA 1-SUI 4
24-Apr-09 FRA 0-SUI 1
29-Apr-11 FRA 0-SUI 1 (OT)
12-May-12 FRA 4-SUI 2
Totals: 13-4-0-9-22-44

07-May-00 FRA 2-UKR 3
02-May-04 FRA 2-UKR 6
Totals: 2-0-0-2-4-9

22-Apr-93 FRA 1-USA 6
25-Apr-94 FRA 1-USA 5
04-May-98 FRA 3-USA 1
03-May-00 FRA 2-USA 3
01-May-09 FRA 2-USA 6
16-May-10 FRA 0-USA 4
07-May-11 FRA 2-USA 3

04-May-12 FRA 2-USA 7
Totals: 8-1-0-7-13-35

**WORLD U20 CHAMPIONSHIPS**
01-Jan-02 FRA 3-BLR 2
03-Jan-02 FRA 2-BLR 3
Totals: 2-1-0-1-5-5

25-Dec-01 FRA 0-CAN 15
Totals: 1-0-0-1-0-15

28-Dec-01 FRA 0-FIN 8
Totals: 1-0-0-1-0-8

26-Dec-01 FRA 1-RUS 5
Totals: 1-0-0-1-1-5

29-Dec-01 FRA 0-SUI 8
Totals: 1-0-0-1-0-8

# GERMANY (GER)

Totals=GP-W-T-L-GF-GA

**OLYMPICS, MEN**
**Date Score**
12-Feb-28 GER 0-AUT 0
29-Jan-56 GER 7-AUT 0
12-Feb-94 GER 4-AUT 3
10-Feb-02 GER 3-AUT 2
Totals: 4-3-1-0-14-5

09-Feb-98 GER 2-BLR 8
20-Feb-10 GER 3-BLR 5
Totals: 2-0-0-2-5-13

06-Feb-32 GER 1-CAN 4
08-Feb-32 GER 0-CAN 5
13-Feb-36 GER 2-CAN 6
15-Feb-52 GER 1-CAN 15
26-Jan-56 GER 0-CAN 4
02-Feb-56 GER 0-CAN 10
22-Feb-60 GER 0-CAN 12
02-Feb-64 GER 2-CAN 4
18-Feb-92 GER 3-CAN 4 (10:00 OT/GWS)
17-Feb-02 GER 2-CAN 3
16-Feb-06 GER 1-CAN 5
23-Feb-10 GER 2-CAN 8
Totals: 12-0-0-12-14-80

17-Feb-52 GER 1-TCH 6
03-Feb-56 GER 3-TCH 9
27-Feb-60 GER 1-TCH 9
29-Jan-64 GER 1-TCH 11
16-Feb-94 GER 0-CZE 1
15-Feb-02 GER 2-CZE 8
15-Feb-06 GER 1-CZE 4
Totals vs. TCH:
4-0-0-4-6-35
Totals vs. CZE:
3-0-0-3-3-13

22-Feb-52 GER 1-FIN 5
21-Feb-60 GER 4-FIN 1
08-Feb-64 GER 2-FIN 1
09-Feb-92 GER 1-FIN 5
20-Feb-94 GER 1-FIN 7
21-Feb-06 GER 0-FIN 2
19-Feb-10 GER 0-FIN 5
Totals: 7-2-0-5-9-26

20-Feb-92 GER 5-FRA 4
10-Feb-98 GER 2-FRA 0
Totals: 2-2-0-0-7-4

12-Feb-36 GER 1-GBR 1 (30:00 OT)
Totals: 1-0-1-0-1-1

11-Feb-36 GER 2-HUN 1
Totals: 1-1-0-0-2-1

07-Feb-36 GER 3-ITA 0
27-Jan-56 GER 2-ITA 2
15-Feb-92 GER 5-ITA 2
18-Feb-06 GER 3-ITA 3
Totals: 4-2-2-0-13-7

07-Feb-98 GER 3-JPN 1
Totals: 1-1-0-0-3-1

12-Feb-02 GER 4-LAT 1
Totals: 1-1-0-0-4-1

21-Feb-52 GER 6-NOR 2
14-Feb-94 GER 2-NOR 1
Totals: 2-2-0-0-8-3

04-Feb-32 GER 2-POL 1
13-Feb-32 GER 4-POL 1
20-Feb-52 GER 4-POL 4
17-Feb-92 GER 4-POL 0
Totals: 4-3-1-0-14-6

31-Jan-56 GER 0-URS 8
19-Feb-60 GER 0-URS 8
25-Feb-60 GER 1-URS 7
05-Feb-64 GER 0-URS 10
18-Feb-94 GER 4-RUS 2
Totals vs. URS:
4-0-0-4-1-33
Totals vs. RUS:
1-1-0-0-4-2

24-Feb-94 GER 5-SVK 6 (OT)
12-Feb-98 GER 4-SVK 2
09-Feb-02 GER 3-SVK 0
Totals: 3-2-0-1-12-8

18-Feb-52 GER 3-SWE 7
04-Feb-56 GER 1-SWE 1
28-Feb-60 GER 2-SWE 8
04-Feb-64 GER 2-SWE 10
13-Feb-92 GER 1-SWE 3
22-Feb-92 GER 3-SWE 4
23-Feb-94 GER 0-SWE 3
18-Feb-02 GER 1-SWE 7
17-Feb-10 GER 0-SWE 2
Totals: 9-0-1-8-13-45

16-Feb-28 GER 0-SUI 1
08-Feb-36 GER 2-SUI 0
24-Feb-52 GER 3-SUI 6
07-Feb-64 GER 6-SUI 5
19-Feb-06 GER 2-SUI 2
Totals: 5-2-1-2-13-14

07-Feb-32 GER 0-USA 7
10-Feb-32 GER 0-USA 8
06-Feb-36 GER 0-USA 1
16-Feb-52 GER 2-USA 8
30-Jan-56 GER 2-USA 7
24-Feb-60 GER 1-USA 9
31-Jan-64 GER 0-USA 8
11-Feb-92 GER 0-USA 2
26-Feb-94 GER 4-USA 3
20-Feb-02 GER 0-USA 5
Totals: 10-1-0-9-9-58

**WORLD CHAMPIONSHIPS, MEN**
23-Feb-33 GER 0-AUT 2
03-Feb-34 GER 1-AUT 2
25-Apr-94 GER 2-AUT 2
26-Apr-96 GER 3-AUT 0
03-May-03 GER 5-AUT 1
01-May-04 GER 3-AUT 1
06-May-05 GER 2-AUT 2
03-May-09 GER 0-AUT 1
Totals: 8-3-2-3-16-11

01-May-98 GER 2-BLR 4
02-May-01 GER 0-BLR 2
07-May-07 GER 6-BLR 5
16-May-10 GER 1-BLR 2 (OT)
Totals: 4-1-0-3-9-13

18-Feb-33 GER 6-BEL 0
Totals: 1-1-0-0-6-0

10-Feb-30 GER 1-CAN 6
21-Feb-33 GER 0-CAN 5
07-Feb-34 GER 0-CAN 6
22-Feb-37 GER 0-CAN 5
25-Feb-37 GER 0-CAN 5
16-Feb-38 GER 2-CAN 3 (OT)
19-Feb-38 GER 0-CAN 1
09-Feb-39 GER 0-CAN 9
28-Apr-94 GER 2-CAN 3
27-Apr-95 GER 2-CAN 5
24-Apr-96 GER 5-CAN 1
05-May-01 GER 3-CAN 3
02-May-02 GER 1-CAN 3
07-May-03 GER 2-CAN 3 (OT)
02-May-04 GER 1-CAN 6
28-Apr-07 GER 2-CAN 3
10-May-08 GER 1-CAN 10
Totals: 17-1-1-15-22-77

09-Feb-34 GER 1-TCH 0 (OT)
23-Feb-37 GER 2-TCH 1 (30:00 OT)
20-Feb-38 GER 0-TCH 3
07-Feb-39 GER 1-TCH 1 (30:00 OT)
20-Apr-93 GER 0-CZE 5
01-May-96 GER 1-CZE 6
26-Apr-97 GER 1-CZE 2
05-May-98 GER 1-CZE 8
29-Apr-01 GER 2-CZE 2
29-Apr-02 GER 5-CZE 7
04-May-03 GER 0-CZE 4
28-Apr-04 GER 1-CZE 5
03-May-05 GER 0-CZE 2
03-May-07 GER 2-CZE 0
09-May-11 GER 2-CZE 5
15-May-12 GER 1-CZE 8
Totals vs. TCH:
4-2-1-1-4-5
Totals vs. CZE:
12-1-1-10-16-54

10-May-05 GER 2-DEN 3
01-May-09 GER 1-DEN 3
12-May-10 GER 3-DEN 1
07-May-11 GER 3-DEN 4 (5:00 OT/GWS)
12-May-12 GER 2-DEN 1
Totals: 5-2-0-3-11-12

03-Feb-39 GER 12-FIN 1
28-Apr-92 GER 3-FIN 6
23-Apr-93 GER 3-FIN 1
29-Apr-97 GER 0-FIN 6
10-May-01 GER 1-FIN 4
06-May-03 GER 2-FIN 2
03-May-08 GER 1-FIN 5
10-May-10 GER 0-FIN 1
06-May-11 GER 4-FIN 5 (5:00 OT/GWS)
Totals: 9-2-1-6-26-31

08-Feb-34 GER 4-FRA 0
21-Jan-35 GER 1-FRA 2
20-Feb-37 GER 5-FRA 0
21-Apr-93 GER 5-FRA 3
23-Apr-95 GER 0-FRA 4
02-May-97 GER 1-FRA 2
28-Apr-09 GER 1-FRA 2
Totals: 7-3-0-4-17-13

31-Jan-30 GER 4-GBR 2
17-Feb-37 GER 0-GBR 6
27-Feb-37 GER 0-GBR 5
11-Feb-38 GER 0-GBR 1
08-Feb-39 GER 1-GBR 0
27-Apr-94 GER 4-GBR 0
Totals: 6-3-0-3-9-14

01-Feb-30 GER 4-HUN 1
22-Feb-33 GER 4-HUN 0
19-Feb-37 GER 2-HUN 2 (30:00 OT)
17-Feb-38 GER 1-HUN 0
11-Feb-39 GER 6-HUN 2
04-May-09 GER 2-HUN 1
Totals: 6-5-1-0-19-6

04-Feb-34 GER 3-ITA 2
19-Jan-35 GER 0-ITA 2
05-Feb-39 GER 4-ITA 4 (30:00 OT)
06-Feb-39 GER 0-ITA 0
03-May-92 GER 6-ITA 2
02-May-94 GER 1-ITA 3
24-Apr-95 GER 1-ITA 2
07-May-97 GER 2-ITA 5
11-May-98 GER 4-ITA 4
04-May-01 GER 1-ITA 3
04-May-12 GER 3-ITA 0
Totals: 11-3-3-5-25-27

03-May-98 GER 5-JPN 1
26-Apr-02 GER 9-JPN 2
27-Apr-03 GER 5-JPN 4
Totals: 3-3-0-0-19-7

24-Apr-04 GER 4 -KAZ 2
01-May-05 GER 1-KAZ 2
Totals: 2-1-0-1-5-4

24-Jan-35 GER 3-LAT 1
13-Feb-38 GER 1-LAT 0
06-May-97 GER 0-LAT 8
10-May-98 GER 0-LAT 5
03-May-02 GER 3-LAT 2
26-Apr-04 GER 1-LAT 1
12-May-08 GER 5-LAT 3
06-May-12 GER 2-LAT 3
Totals: 8-4-1-3-15-23

22-Jan-35 GER 5-NED 0
Totals: 1-1-0-0-5-0

15-Feb-38 GER 8-NOR 0
18-Apr-93 GER 6-NOR 0
09-May-97 GER 4-NOR 2
02-May-07 GER 5-NOR 3
07-May-08 GER 2-NOR 3
13-May-12 GER 4-NOR 12
Totals: 6-4-0-2-29-20

02-Feb-30 GER 4-POL 1
19-Feb-33 GER 2-POL 0
20-Jan-35 GER 1-POL 3
27-Jan-35 GER 5-POL 1
12-Feb-39 GER 4-POL 0
04-May-92 GER 11-POL 1
Totals: 6-5-0-1-27-6

25-Jan-35 GER 3-ROM 0
18-Feb-37 GER 4-ROM 2
Totals: 2-2-0-0-7-2

27-Apr-93 GER 1-RUS 5
30-Apr-94 GER 0-RUS 6
28-Apr-95 GER 3-RUS 6
21-Apr-96 GER 1-RUS 2
28-Apr-97 GER 1-RUS 5
08-May-01 GER 1-RUS 3
24-Apr-09 GER 0-RUS 5
15-May-10 GER 2-RUS 3
22-May-10 GER 1-RUS 2
29-Apr-11 GER 2-RUS 0
08-May-12 GER 0-RUS 2
Totals: 11-1-0-10-12-39

29-Apr-96 GER 1-SVK 4
03-May-97 GER 1-SVK 0
30-Apr-03 GER 1-SVK 3
30-Apr-07 GER 1-SVK 5
05-May-08 GER 4-SVK 2
18-May-10 GER 2-SVK 1
01-May-11 GER 4-SVK 3
Totals: 7-4-0-3-14-18

09-May-05 GER 9-SLO 1
03-May-11 GER 3-SLO 2 (5:00 OT/GWS)
Totals: 2-2-0-0-12-3

01-May-92 GER 5-SWE 2
07-May-02 GER 2-SWE 6
23-May-10 GER 1-SWE 3
11-May-11 GER 2-SWE 5
09-May-12 GER 2-SWE 5
Totals: 5-1-0-4-12-21

09-Feb-30 GER 2-SUI 1
24-Feb-33 GER 1-SUI 1
11-Feb-34 GER 2-SUI 1 (20:00 OT)
26-Feb-37 GER 0-SUI 6
07-May-92 GER 1-SUI 3
30-Apr-95 GER 5-SUI 3
28-Apr-01 GER 3-SUI 1
28-Apr-02 GER 3-SUI 0
04-May-04 GER 0-SUI 1
05-May-05 GER 1-SUI 5
26-Apr-09 GER 2-SUI 3 (OT)
20-May-10 GER 1-SUI 0
Totals: 12-6-1-5-21-25

29-Apr-03 GER 3-UKR 1
Totals: 1-1-0-0-3-1

10-Feb-34 GER 0-USA 3
14-Feb-38 GER 0-USA 1
04-Feb-39 GER 0-USA 4
29-Apr-92 GER 5-USA 3
25-Apr-93 GER 6-USA 3
23-Apr-96 GER 2-USA 4
08-May-98 GER 1-USA 1
05-May-02 GER 2-USA 2
05-May-07 GER 0-USA 3
08-May-08 GER 4-USA 6
07-May-10 GER 2-USA 1 (OT)
Totals: 11-3-2-6-22-31

**WORLD U20 CHAMPIONSHIPS**
04-Jan-03 GER 4-BLR 0
03-Jan-05 GER 4-BLR 3
03-Jan-07 GER 1-BLR 3
Totals: 3-2-0-1-9-6

26-Dec-91 GER 4-CAN 5
01-Jan-93 GER 2-CAN 5
27-Dec-93 GER 2-CAN 5
27-Dec-94 GER 1-CAN 9
27-Dec-96 GER 1-CAN 4
30-Dec-97 GER 0-CAN 2
29-Dec-02 GER 1-CAN 4
28-Dec-04 GER 0-CAN 9
29-Dec-06 GER 1-CAN 3
29-Dec-08 GER 1-CAN 5
Totals: 10-0-0-10-13-51

29-Dec-91 GER 2-TCH 8
02-Jan-93 GER 3-CZE/SVK 6
30-Dec-93 GER 2-CZE 6
02-Jan-95 GER 3-CZE 14
27-Dec-95 GER 3-CZE 6
26-Dec-96 GER 2-CZE 8
27-Dec-97 GER 1-CZE 9
27-Dec-02 GER 0-CZE 3
30-Dec-08 GER 0-CZE 6
02-Jan-11 GER 2-CZE 3
Totals vs. TCH:
1-0-0-1-2-8
Totals vs. CZE:
9-0-0-9-16-61

01-Jan-92 GER 0-FIN 2
29-Dec-92 GER 0-FIN 11
02-Jan-94 GER 0-FIN 2
29-Dec-94 GER 1-FIN 7
26-Dec-97 GER 0-FIN 5
26-Dec-02 GER 0-FIN 4
25-Dec-04 GER 1-FIN 4
04-Jan-09 GER 1-FIN 3
29-Dec-10 GER 1-FIN 5
Totals: 9-0-0-9-4-43

04-Jan-93 GER 6-JPN 3
Totals: 1-1-0-0-6-3

27-Dec-08 GER 9-KAZ 0
Totals: 1-1-0-0-9-0

02-Jan-09 GER 1-LAT 7
Totals: 1-0-0-1-1-7

04-Jan-11 GER 1-NOR 3
Totals: 1-0-0-1-1-3

03-Jan-97 GER 7-POL 0
Totals: 1-1-0-0-7-0

30-Dec-91 GER 0-RUS 7
27-Dec-92 GER 0-RUS 4
01-Jan-94 GER 0-RUS 1
30-Dec-94 GER 1-RUS 8
31-Dec-95 GER 2-RUS 8
Totals: 5-0-0-5-3-28

30-Dec-95 GER 4-SVK 4
01-Jan-98 GER 0-SVK 9
03-Jan-98 GER 3-SVK 8
29-Dec-04 GER 0-SVK 5
27-Dec-06 GER 4-SVK 2
27-Dec-10 GER 1-SVK 2 (OT)
Totals: 6-1-1-4-12-30

02-Jan-92 GER 1-SWE 10
26-Dec-92 GER 2-SWE 4
26-Dec-93 GER 1-SWE 4
26-Dec-94 GER 2-SWE 10
28-Dec-95 GER 2-SWE 6
02-Jan-97 GER 2-SWE 8
29-Dec-97 GER 0-SWE 8
30-Dec-02 GER 2-SWE 7
26-Dec-04 GER 0-SWE 6
30-Dec-06 GER 1-SWE 3
Totals: 10-0-0-10-13-66

04-Jan-92 GER 6-SUI 2
04-Jan-94 GER 3-SUI 1
02-Jan-96 GER 3-SUI 3
29-Dec-96 GER 2-SUI 6
02-Jan-03 GER 2-SUI 6
01-Jan-05 GER 0-SUI 5
04-Jan-07 GER 3-SUI 5
26-Dec-10 GER 3-SUI 4
Totals: 8-2-1-5-22-32

04-Jan-95 GER 6-UKR 2
03-Jan-96 GER 5-UKR 0
Totals: 2-2-0-0-11-2

27-Dec-91 GER 2-USA 6
30-Dec-92 GER 3-USA 4
29-Dec-93 GER 2-USA 7
01-Jan-95 GER 3-USA 5
31-Dec-96 GER 0-USA 8
26-Dec-06 GER 2-USA 1 (OT)
26-Dec-08 GER 2-USA 8
30-Dec-10 GER 0-USA 4
Totals: 8-1-0-7-14-43

**WORLD U18 CHAMPIONSHIPS, MEN**
21-Apr-00 GER 10-BLR 0
16-Apr-06 GER 5-BLR 1
Totals: 2-2-0-0-15-1

12-Apr-02 GER 1-CAN 9
14-Apr-05 GER 1-CAN 2
12-Apr-07 GER 3-CAN 7
13-Apr-08 GER 2-CAN 9
09-Apr-09 GER 2-CAN 11
21-Apr-11 GER 3-CAN 4
Totals: 6-0-0-6-12-42

08-Apr-99 GER 2-CZE 4
14-Apr-00 GER 3-CZE 5
17-Apr-01 GER 3-CZE 1
14-Apr-02 GER 1-CZE 6
12-Apr-06 GER 2-CZE 4
20-Apr-07 GER 6-CZE 3
12-Apr-09 GER 4-CZE 3
Totals: 7-3-0-4-21-26

15-Apr-05 GER 3-DEN 1
17-Apr-08 GER 4-DEN 0
Totals: 2-2-0-0-7-1

22-Apr-05 GER 2-FIN 4
19-Apr-07 GER 3-FIN 4
22-Apr-08 GER 4-FIN 3
23-Apr-11 GER 0-FIN 6
19-Apr-12 GER 0-FIN 8
Totals: 5-1-0-4-9-25

16-Apr-07 GER 3-LAT 2
16-Apr-12 GER 4-LAT 5
Totals: 2-1-0-1-7-7

16-Apr-99 GER 4 -NOR 2
13-Apr-01 GER 2-NOR 2
11-Apr-02 GER 2-NOR 2
19-Apr-06 GER 2-NOR 2
18-Apr-09 GER 2-NOR 5
Totals: 5-1-3-1-12-13

14-Apr-01 GER 3-RUS 8
15-Apr-02 GER 2-RUS 8
17-Apr-05 GER 4-RUS 12
15-Apr-06 GER 5-RUS 9
15-Apr-07 GER 1-RUS 3
14-Apr-08 GER 2-RUS 6
16-Apr-11 GER 4-RUS 5 (5:00 OT/GWS)
14-Apr-12 GER 4-RUS 2
21-Apr-12 GER 1-RUS 4
Totals: 9-1-0-8-26-57

17-Apr-02 GER 1-SVK 4
20-Apr-06 GER 1-SVK 2
16-Apr-08 GER 5-SVK 4 (5:00 OT/GWS)
17-Apr-09 GER 5-SVK 4 (5:00 OT/GWS)
18-Apr-11 GER 0-SVK 4
Totals: 5-2-0-3-12-18

09-Apr-99 GER 2-SWE 5
15-Apr-00 GER 0-SWE 3
16-Apr-01 GER 2-SWE 1
18-Apr-02 GER 0-SWE 4
18-Apr-05 GER 2-SWE 3
11-Apr-09 GER 4-SWE 5
12-Apr-12 GER 1-SWE 8
Totals: 7-1-0-6-11-29

11-Apr-99 GER 0-SUI 3
17-Apr-00 GER 1-SUI 3
19-Apr-01 GER 1-SUI 7
20-Apr-02 GER 2-SUI 5
21-Apr-05 GER 2-SUI 0
14-Apr-09 GER 3-SUI 8
15-Apr-11 GER 4-SUI 1
17-Apr-12 GER 6-SUI 2
Totals: 8-3-0-5-19-29

12-Apr-99 GER 0-UKR 4
18-Apr-00 GER 4-UKR 4
21-Apr-02 GER 4-UKR 1
Totals: 3-1-1-1-8-9

15-Apr-99 GER 0-USA 6
22-Apr-00 GER 3-USA 1
22-Apr-01 GER 2-USA 1
13-Apr-06 GER 0-USA 9
13-Apr-07 GER 1-USA 9
20-Apr-08 GER 1-USA 4
19-Apr-11 GER 3-USA 7
Totals: 7-2-0-5-10-37

**OLYMPICS, WOMEN**
16-Feb-02 GER 5-CHN 5
Totals: 1-0-1-0-5-5

14-Feb-02 GER 1-FIN 3
11-Feb-06 GER 0-FIN 3
Totals: 2-0-0-2-1-6

17-Feb-06 GER 5-ITA 2
Totals: 1-1-0-0-5-2

17-Feb-02 GER 4-KAZ 0
Totals: 1-1-0-0-4-0

19-Feb-02 GER 0-RUS 5
20-Feb-06 GER 1-RUS 0 (10:00 OT/GWS)
Totals: 2-1-0-1-1-5

14-Feb-06 GER 2-SUI 1
Totals: 1-1-0-0-2-1

12-Feb-02 GER 0-USA 10
12-Feb-06 GER 0-USA 5
Totals: 2-0-0-2-0-15

**WOMEN'S WORLD CHAMPIONSHIPS**
21-Mar-90 GER 0-CAN 17
09-Mar-99 GER 0-CAN 13
01-Apr-04 GER 0-CAN 13
05-Apr-07 GER 0-CAN 8
Totals: 4-0-0-4-0-51

08-Apr-00 GER 0-CHN 3
05-Apr-01 GER 0-CHN 0
08-Apr-01 GER 1-CHN 0
31-Mar-04 GER 4-CHN 2
06-Apr-05 GER 3-CHN 3
09-Apr-05 GER 3-CHN 0
10-Apr-08 GER 2-CHN 4
Totals: 7-3-2-2-13-12

11-Apr-94 GER 1-FIN 17
08-Mar-99 GER 0-FIN 9
04-Apr-00 GER 1-FIN 4
03-Apr-01 GER 2-FIN 5
04-Apr-04 GER 0-FIN 4
03-Apr-05 GER 1-FIN 5
Totals: 6-0-0-6-5-44

19-Mar-90 GER 4-JPN 1
25-Mar-90 GER 9-JPN 2
09-Apr-00 GER 3-JPN 2
08-Apr-08 GER 2-JPN 1
Totals: 4-4-0-0-18-6

07-Apr-07 GER 3-KAZ 0
Totals: 1-1-0-0-3-0

24-Mar-90 GER 3-NOR 6
Totals: 1-0-0-1-3-6

12-Mar-99 GER 2-RUS 6
06-Apr-00 GER 2-RUS 7
03-Apr-04 GER 2-RUS 4
08-Apr-05 GER 2-RUS 1
09-Apr-07 GER 1-RUS 4
Totals: 5-1-0-4-9-22

10-Apr-12 GER 2-SVK 4
11-Apr-12 GER 2-SVK 1 (5:00 OT/GWS)
13-Apr-12 GER 3-SVK 1
Totals: 3-2-0-1-7-6

22-Mar-90 GER 0-SWE 7
16-Apr-94 GER 1-SWE 7
06-Apr-01 GER 6-SWE 2
08-Apr-12 GER 1-SWE 2 (OT)
Totals: 4-1-0-3-8-18

14-Apr-94 GER 1-SUI 2
17-Apr-94 GER 3-SUI 4
11-Mar-99 GER 5-SUI 4
14-Mar-99 GER 3-SUI 0
04-Apr-07 GER 0-SUI 1
05-Apr-08 GER 0-SUI 3
07-Apr-12 GER 3-SUI 2
Totals: 7-3-0-4-15-16

12-Apr-94 GER 0-USA 16
03-Apr-00 GER 1-USA 16
02-Apr-01 GER 0-USA 13
05-Apr-05 GER 0-USA 7
04-Apr-08 GER 1-USA 8
Totals: 5-0-0-5-2-60

**WOMEN'S U18 WORLD CHAMPIONSHIPS**
08-Jan-08 GER 1-CAN 10
28-Mar-10 GER 0-CAN 15
02-Apr-10 GER 0-CAN 10
04-Jan-11 GER 1-CAN 8
01-Jan-12 GER 0-CAN 6
Totals: 5-0-0-5-2-49

09-Jan-08 GER 2-CZE 3
05-Jan-11 GER 1-CZE 3
04-Jan-12 GER 2-CZE 1
Totals: 3-1-0-2-5-7

07-Jan-08 GER 4-FIN 2
12-Jan-08 GER 4-FIN 1
10-Jan-09 GER 1-FIN 2
31-Mar-10 GER 2-FIN 1 (OT)
01-Jan-11 GER 1-FIN 0
31-Dec-11 GER 0-FIN 3
Totals: 6-4-0-2-12-9

11-Jan-08 GER 2-RUS 1
07-Jan-09 GER 2-RUS 5
30-Mar-10 GER 3-RUS 1
Totals: 3-2-0-1-7-7

05-Jan-09 GER 1-SWE 8
27-Mar-10 GER 4-SWE 5
03-Apr-10 GER 3-SWE 7
07-Jan-11 GER 0-SWE 2
07-Jan-12 GER 1-SWE 4
Totals: 5-0-0-5-9-26

09-Jan-09 GER 2-SUI 1 (5:00 OT/GWS)
02-Jan-11 GER 4-SUI 2
03-Jan-12 GER 6-SUI 1
Totals: 3-3-0-0-12-4

06-Jan-09 GER 0-USA 11
06-Jan-12 GER 1-USA 7
Totals: 2-0-0-2-1-18

# GREAT BRITAIN (GBR)

Totals=GP-W-T-L-GF-GA

**OLYMPICS, MEN**
**Date Score**
31-Jan-48 GBR 5-AUT 4
Totals: 1-1-0-0-5-4

30-Jan-24 GBR 19-BEL 3
11-Feb-28 GBR 7-BEL 3
Totals: 2-2-0-0-26-6

01-Feb-24 GBR 2-CAN 19
18-Feb-28 GBR 0-CAN 14
11-Feb-36 GBR 2-CAN 1
01-Feb-48 GBR 0-CAN 3
Totals: 4-1-0-3-4-37

14-Feb-36 GBR 5-TCH 0
02-Feb-48 GBR 4-TCH 11
Totals: 2-1-0-1-9-11

29-Jan-24 GBR 15-FRA 2
12-Feb-28 GBR 2-FRA 3
Totals: 2-1-0-1-17-5

12-Feb-36 GBR 1-GER 1 (30:00 OT)
Totals: 1-0-1-0-1-1

16-Feb-28 GBR 1-HUN 0
13-Feb-36 GBR 5-HUN 1
Totals: 2-2-0-0-6-1

08-Feb-48 GBR 14-ITA 7
Totals: 1-1-0-0-14-7

08-Feb-36 GBR 3-JPN 0
Totals: 1-1-0-0-3-0

05-Feb-48 GBR 8-POL 2
Totals: 1-1-0-0-8-2

03-Feb-24 GBR 4-SWE 3
19-Feb-28 GBR 1-SWE 3
07-Feb-36 GBR 1-SWE 0
06-Feb-48 GBR 2-SWE 4
Totals: 4-2-0-2-8-10

17-Feb-28 GBR 0-SUI 4
04-Feb-48 GBR 3-SUI 12
Totals: 2-0-0-2-3-16

31-Jan-24 GBR 0-USA 11
15-Feb-36 GBR 0-USA 0 (30:00 OT)
07-Feb-48 GBR 3-USA 4
Totals: 3-0-1-2-3-15

**WORLD CHAMPIONSHIPS, MEN**
01-Feb-31 GBR 0-AUT 1 (OT)
09-Feb-34 GBR 1-AUT 2
23-Jan-35 GBR 4-AUT 1
03-May-94 GBR 0-AUT 10
Totals: 4-1-0-3-5-14

06-Feb-34 GBR 3-BEL 0
04-Feb-39 GBR 3-BEL 1
Totals: 2-2-0-0-6-1

19-Jan-35 GBR 2-CAN 4
26-Jan-35 GBR 0-CAN 6
26-Feb-37 GBR 0-CAN 3
20-Feb-38 GBR 1-CAN 3
07-Feb-39 GBR 0-CAN 4
21-Mar-50 GBR 0-CAN 12
13-Mar-51 GBR 1-CAN 17
17-Mar-62 GBR 2-CAN 12
30-Apr-94 GBR 2-CAN 8
Totals: 9-0-0-9-8-69

04-Feb-34 GBR 2-TCH 1
27-Jan-35 GBR 2-TCH 1
19-Feb-38 GBR 1-TCH 0
09-Feb-39 GBR 0-TCH 2
Totals: 4-3-0-1-5-4

17-Mar-51 GBR 6-FIN 3
09-Mar-62 GBR 7-FIN 5
Totals: 2-2-0-0-13-8

05-Feb-31 GBR 2-FRA 1
22-Jan-35 GBR 1-FRA 0
14-Mar-50 GBR 9-FRA 0
Totals: 3-3-0-0-12-1

31-Jan-30 GBR 2-GER 4
17-Feb-37 GBR 6-GER 0
27-Feb-37 GBR 5-GER 0
11-Feb-38 GBR 1-GER 0
08-Feb-39 GBR 0-GER 1
27-Apr-94 GBR 0-GER 4
Totals: 6-3-0-3-14-9

03-Feb-31 GBR 1-HUN 3
03-Feb-34 GBR 0-HUN 2
18-Feb-37 GBR 7-HUN 0
23-Feb-37 GBR 5-HUN 0
05-Feb-39 GBR 1-HUN 0
Totals: 5-3-0-2-14-5

10-Feb-34 GBR 4-ITA 1
29-Apr-94 GBR 2-ITA 10
Totals: 2-1-0-1-6-11

21-Jan-35 GBR 5-LAT 1
14-Feb-38 GBR 5-LAT 1
Totals: 2-2-0-0-10-2

12-Feb-38 GBR 8-NOR 0
15-Mar-50 GBR 2-NOR 0
17-Mar-50 GBR 4-NOR 3
15-Mar-51 GBR 3-NOR 4
11-Mar-62 GBR 2-NOR 12
06-May-94 GBR 2-NOR 5
Totals: 6-3-0-3-21-24

21-Feb-37 GBR 11-POL 0
18-Feb-38 GBR 7-POL 1
Totals: 2-2-0-0-18-1

06-Feb-31 GBR 11-ROM 0
11-Feb-34 GBR 2-ROM 1
19-Feb-37 GBR 11-ROM 0
Totals: 3-3-0-0-24-1

26-Apr-94 GBR 3-RUS 12
Totals: 1-0-0-1-3-12

17-Feb-38 GBR 3-SWE 2
18-Mar-50 GBR 5-SWE 4
10-Mar-51 GBR 1-SWE 5
15-Mar-62 GBR 0-SWE 17
Totals: 4-2-0-2-9-28

24-Jan-35 GBR 0-SUI 1
20-Feb-37 GBR 3-SUI 0
25-Feb-37 GBR 2-SUI 0 (20:00 OT)
22-Mar-50 GBR 3-SUI 10
12-Mar-51 GBR 1-SUI 7
08-Mar-62 GBR 3-SUI 6
Totals: 6-2-0-4-12-24

15-Feb-38 GBR 1-USA 1
20-Mar-50 GBR 2-USA 3
16-Mar-51 GBR 6-USA 6
14-Mar-62 GBR 5-USA 12
Totals: 4-0-2-2-14-22

12-Mar-62 GBR 0-FRG 9
Totals: 1-0-0-1-0-9

# HUNGARY (HUN)

Totals=GP-W-T-L-GF-GA

**OLYMPICS, MEN**
**Date Score**
01-Feb-64 HUN 0-AUT 3
Totals: 1-0-0-1-0-3

12-Feb-28 HUN 2-BEL 3
06-Feb-36 HUN 11-BEL 2
Totals: 2-1-0-1-13-5

12-Feb-36 HUN 0-CAN 15
Totals: 1-0-0-1-0-15

08-Feb-36 HUN 0-TCH 3
Totals: 1-0-0-1-0-3

11-Feb-28 HUN 0-FRA 2
07-Feb-36 HUN 3-FRA 0
Totals: 2-1-0-1-3-2

11-Feb-36 HUN 1-GER 2
Totals: 1-0-0-1-1-2

16-Feb-28 HUN 0-GBR 1
13-Feb-36 HUN 1-GBR 5
Totals: 2-0-0-2-1-6

30-Jan-64 HUN 4-ITA 6
Totals: 1-0-0-1-4-6

07-Feb-64 HUN 2-JPN 6
Totals: 1-0-0-1-2-6

05-Feb-64 HUN 1-NOR 6
Totals: 1-0-0-1-1-6

03-Feb-64 HUN 2-POL 6
Totals: 1-0-0-1-2-6

08-Feb-64 HUN 3-RUM 8
Totals: 1-0-0-1-3-8

06-Feb-64 HUN 2-YUG 4
Totals: 1-0-0-1-2-4

**WORLD CHAMPIONSHIPS, MEN**
21-Feb-33 HUN 0-AUT 1
01-May-09 HUN 0-AUT 6
Totals: 2-0-0-2-0-7

28-Apr-09 HUN 1-BLR 3
Totals: 1-0-0-1-1-3

23-Jan-35 HUN 6-BEL 1
03-Feb-39 HUN 8-BEL 1
Totals: 2-2-0-0-14-2

23-Feb-33 HUN 1-CAN 3
18-Feb-38 HUN 1-CAN 1
26-Apr-09 HUN 0-CAN 9
Totals: 3-0-1-2-2-13

01-Feb-31 HUN 1-TCH 4
05-Feb-34 HUN 0-TCH 1
10-Feb-34 HUN 0-TCH 1
27-Feb-37 HUN 0-TCH 0
Totals: 4-0-1-3-1-6

03-May-09 HUN 1-DEN 5
Totals: 1-0-0-1-1-5

07-Feb-31 HUN 1-FRA 0
25-Feb-37 HUN 5-FRA 1
Totals: 2-2-0-0-6-1

01-Feb-30 HUN 1-GER 4
22-Feb-33 HUN 0-GER 4
19-Feb-37 HUN 2-GER 2 (30:00 OT)
17-Feb-38 HUN 0-GER 1
11-Feb-39 HUN 2-GER 6
04-May-09 HUN 1-GER 2
Totals: 6-0-1-5-6-19

03-Feb-31 HUN 3-GBR 1
03-Feb-34 HUN 2-GBR 0
18-Feb-37 HUN 0-GBR 7
23-Feb-37 HUN 0-GBR 5
05-Feb-39 HUN 0-GBR 1
Totals: 5-2-0-3-5-14

31-Jan-30 HUN 2-ITA 0
06-Feb-34 HUN 0-ITA 0 (30:00 OT)
Totals: 2-1-1-0-2-0

20-Feb-33 HUN 3-LAT 0
Totals: 1-1-0-0-3-0

13-Feb-38 HUN 10-LTU 1
Totals: 1-1-0-0-10-1

19-Jan-35 HUN 6-NED 0
Totals: 1-1-0-0-6-0

24-Feb-33 HUN 1-POL 1
25-Jan-35 HUN 1-POL 1
20-Feb-37 HUN 0-POL 4
14-Feb-38 HUN 0-POL 3
08-Feb-39 HUN 3-POL 5
10-Feb-39 HUN 0-POL 3
Totals: 6-0-2-4-5-17

05-Feb-31 HUN 9-ROM 1
17-Feb-37 HUN 4-ROM 1
15-Feb-38 HUN 3-ROM 1
Totals: 3-3-0-0-16-3

24-Apr-09 HUN 3-SVK 4
Totals: 1-0-0-1-3-4

21-Jan-35 HUN 0-SWE 3
Totals: 1-0-0-1-0-3

19-Feb-33 HUN 0-SUI 1
07-Feb-34 HUN 0-SUI 1
20-Jan-35 HUN 1-SUI 1
22-Feb-37 HUN 2-SUI 4
11-Feb-38 HUN 0-SUI 1
09-Feb-39 HUN 2-SUI 5
Totals: 6-0-1-5-5-13

07-Feb-39 HUN 0-USA 3
Totals: 1-0-0-1-0-3

# ITALY (ITA)

Totals=GP-W-T-L-GF-GA

**OLYMPICS, MEN**

**Date Score**
05-Feb-48 ITA 5-AUT 16
26-Jan-56 ITA 2-AUT 2
01-Feb-56 ITA 8-AUT 2
06-Feb-64 ITA 3-AUT 5
10-Feb-98 ITA 5-AUT 2
Totals: 5-2-1-2-23-27

03-Feb-48 ITA 1-CAN 21
28-Jan-56 ITA 1-CAN 3
13-Feb-94 ITA 2-CAN 7
15-Feb-06 ITA 2-CAN 7
Totals: 4-0-0-4-6-38

30-Jan-48 ITA 3-TCH 22
19-Feb-06 ITA 1-CZE 4
Totals: vs. TCH: 1-0-0-1-3-22
Totals: vs. CZE: 1-0-0-1-1-4

17-Feb-92 ITA 3-FIN 5
16-Feb-06 ITA 0-FIN 6
Totals: 2-0-0-2-3-11

19-Feb-94 ITA 7-FRA 3
24-Feb-94 ITA 3-FRA 2
12-Feb-98 ITA 1-FRA 5
Totals: 3-2-0-1-11-10

07-Feb-36 ITA 0-GER 3
27-Jan-56 ITA 2-GER 2
15-Feb-92 ITA 2-GER 5
18-Feb-06 ITA 3-GER 3
Totals: 4-0-2-2-7-13

08-Feb-48 ITA 7-GBR 14
Totals: 1-0-0-1-7-14

30-Jan-64 ITA 6-HUN 4
Totals: 1-1-0-0-6-4

08-Feb-64 ITA 8-JPN 6
Totals: 1-1-0-0-8-6

07-Feb-98 ITA 3-KAZ 5
Totals: 1-0-0-1-3-5

02-Feb-64 ITA 2-NOR 9
18-Feb-92 ITA 3-NOR 5
22-Feb-94 ITA 6-NOR 3
Totals: 3-1-0-2-11-17

04-Feb-48 ITA 7-POL 13
03-Feb-56 ITA 5-POL 2
05-Feb-64 ITA 0-POL 7
11-Feb-84 ITA 6-POL 1
13-Feb-92 ITA 7-POL 1
20-Feb-92 ITA 1-POL 4
Totals: 6-3-0-3-26-28

07-Feb-64 ITA 2-RUM 6
Totals: 1-0-0-1-2-6

17-Feb-94 ITA 4-SVK 10
08-Feb-98 ITA 3-SVK 4
Totals: 2-0-0-2-7-14

09-Feb-84 ITA 1-URS 5
Totals: 1-0-0-1-1-5

07-Feb-48 ITA 0-SWE 23
07-Feb-84 ITA 1-SWE 11
11-Feb-92 ITA 3-SWE 7
15-Feb-94 ITA 1-SWE 4
Totals: 4-0-0-4-5-45

09-Feb-36 ITA 0-SUI 1
31-Jan-48 ITA 0-SUI 16
02-Feb-56 ITA 8-SUI 3
21-Feb-06 ITA 3-SUI 3
Totals: 4-1-1-2-11-23

08-Feb-36 ITA 2-USA 1 (20:00 OT)
01-Feb-48 ITA 1-USA 31
09-Feb-92 ITA 3-USA 6
21-Feb-94 ITA 1-USA 7
Totals: 4-1-0-3-7-45

15-Feb-84 ITA 4-FRG 9
Totals: 1-0-0-1-4-9

01-Feb-64 ITA 3-YUG 5
13-Feb-84 ITA 1-YUG 5
Totals: 2-0-0-2-4-10

**WORLD CHAMPIONSHIPS, MEN**

18-Feb-33 ITA 0-AUT 3
05-Feb-34 ITA 1-AUT 0
11-Feb-34 ITA 2-AUT 2
26-Jan-35 ITA 1-AUT 2
26-Apr-93 ITA 1-AUT 1
01-May-94 ITA 3-AUT 1
03-May-98 ITA 5-AUT 1
04-May-00 ITA 3-AUT 0
Totals: 8-4-2-2-16-10

23-Jan-35 ITA 0-CAN 9
21-Apr-82 ITA 3-CAN 3
16-Apr-83 ITA 0-CAN 6
24-Apr-93 ITA 2-CAN 11
25-Apr-94 ITA 1-CAN 4
29-Apr-95 ITA 2-CAN 2
03-May-97 ITA 0-CAN 6
05-May-98 ITA 2-CAN 5
05-May-99 ITA 2-CAN 5
07-May-00 ITA 0-CAN 6
30-Apr-01 ITA 1-CAN 3
29-Apr-02 ITA 0-CAN 5
08-May-10 ITA 1-CAN 5
Totals: 13-0-2-11-14-70

20-Feb-33 ITA 1-TCH 3
22-Jan-35 ITA 1-TCH 5
24-Apr-82 ITA 0-TCH 10
26-Apr-83 ITA 0-TCH 11
28-Apr-93 ITA 1-CZE 8
28-Apr-96 ITA 5-CZE 9
05-May-00 ITA 2-CZE 9
06-May-01 ITA 0-CZE 11
06-May-08 ITA 2-CZE 7
11-May-12 ITA 0-CZE 6
Totals vs. TCH: 4-0-0-4-2-29
Totals vs. CZE: 6-0-0-6-10-50

13-May-06 ITA 0-DEN 5
07-May-07 ITA 2-DEN 5
04-May-08 ITA 2-DEN 6
06-May-12 ITA 4-DEN 3 (OT)
Totals: 4-1-0-3-8-19

13-Mar-59 ITA 6-GDR 8
19-Apr-83 ITA 1-GDR 3
29-Apr-83 ITA 3-GDR 1
Totals: 3-1-0-2-10-12

04-Feb-39 ITA 5-FIN 2
08-Feb-39 ITA 2-FIN 1
07-Mar-59 ITA 5-FIN 4
22-Apr-82 ITA 3-FIN 7
21-Apr-83 ITA 2-FIN 6
01-May-83 ITA 4-FIN 4
04-May-92 ITA 1-FIN 6
26-Apr-96 ITA 2-FIN 9
30-Apr-00 ITA 0-FIN 6
05-May-07 ITA 0-FIN 3
Totals: 10-3-1-6-24-48

20-Jan-35 ITA 1-FRA 1
01-May-95 ITA 5-FRA 2
22-Apr-96 ITA 6-FRA 5
10-May-97 ITA 8-FRA 1
09-May-08 ITA 2-FRA 3
10-May-08 ITA 4-FRA 6
15-May-10 ITA 1-FRA 2
Totals: 7-3-1-3-27-20

04-Feb-34 ITA 2-GER 3
19-Jan-35 ITA 2-GER 0
05-Feb-39 ITA 4-GER 4 (30:00 OT)
06-Feb-39 ITA 0-GER 0
03-May-92 ITA 2-GER 6
02-May-94 ITA 3-GER 1
24-Apr-95 ITA 2-GER 1
07-May-97 ITA 5-GER 2
11-May-98 ITA 4-GER 4
04-May-01 ITA 3-GER 1
04-May-12 ITA 0-GER 3
Totals: 11-5-3-3-27-25

10-Feb-34 ITA 1-GBR 4
29-Apr-94 ITA 10-GBR 2
Totals: 2-1-0-1-11-6

31-Jan-30 ITA 0-HUN 2
06-Feb-34 ITA 0-HUN 0 (30:00 OT)
Totals: 2-0-1-1-0-2

03-May-02 ITA 6-JPN 2
Totals: 1-1-0-0-6-2

12-May-06 ITA 3-KAZ 2
16-May-10 ITA 2-KAZ 1
Totals: 2-2-0-0-5-3

24-Feb-33 ITA 0-LAT 2
09-Feb-39 ITA 2-LAT 1
28-Apr-97 ITA 5-LAT 4
08-May-98 ITA 1-LAT 1
30-Apr-02 ITA 1-LAT 4
02-May-07 ITA 4-LAT 3 (OT)
12-May-10 ITA 2-LAT 5
08-May-12 ITA 0-LAT 5
Totals: 8-3-1-4-15-25

07-Feb-39 ITA 2-NED 1
Totals: 1-1-0-0-2-1

10-Mar-59 ITA 3-NOR 4
23-Apr-96 ITA 4-NOR 0
02-May-97 ITA 2-NOR 2
01-May-99 ITA 2-NOR 5
09-May-00 ITA 1-NOR 1
01-May-01 ITA 1-NOR 1
09-May-12 ITA 2-NOR 6
Totals: 7-1-3-3-15-19

21-Jan-35 ITA 1-POL 1
14-Mar-59 ITA 5-POL 2
01-May-92 ITA 7-POL 5
02-May-02 ITA 1-POL 5
Totals: 4-2-1-1-14-13

19-Feb-33 ITA 2-ROM 0
09-Feb-34 ITA 3-ROM 0
Totals: 2-2-0-0-5-0

15-Apr-82 ITA 2-URS 9
24-Apr-83 ITA 1-URS 11
18-Apr-93 ITA 2-RUS 2
27-Apr-94 ITA 0-RUS 7
23-Apr-95 ITA 2-RUS 4
01-May-96 ITA 2-RUS 5
28-Apr-01 ITA 0-RUS 7
04-May-07 ITA 0-RUS 3
02-May-08 ITA 1-RUS 7
14-May-12 ITA 0-RUS 4
Totals vs. URS: 2-0-0-2-3-20
Totals vs. RUS: 8-0-1-7-7-39

08-May-97 ITA 3-SVK 4
01-May-98 ITA 1-SVK 2
03-May-99 ITA 4-SVK 7
02-May-00 ITA 2-SVK 6
Totals: 4-0-0-4-10-19

05-May-02 ITA 0-SLO 4
15-May-06 ITA 3-SLO 3
Totals: 2-0-1-1-3-7

24-Jan-35 ITA 1-SWE 1
05-Mar-59 ITA 0-SWE 11
19-Apr-82 ITA 2-SWE 5
23-Apr-83 ITA 1-SWE 5
29-Apr-92 ITA 0-SWE 0
21-Apr-93 ITA 2-SWE 6
04-May-94 ITA 2-SWE 7
02-May-95 ITA 0-SWE 7
25-Apr-96 ITA 3-SWE 3
26-Apr-97 ITA 3-SWE 5
08-May-06 ITA 0-SWE 4
28-Apr-07 ITA 1-SWE 7
12-May-12 ITA 0-SWE 4
Totals: 13-0-3-10-15-65

08-Feb-34 ITA 0-SUI 3
11-Mar-59 ITA 4-SUI 1
20-Apr-93 ITA 1-SUI 0
27-Apr-95 ITA 3-SUI 2
07-May-01 ITA 1-SUI 8
06-May-06 ITA 1-SUI 3
30-Apr-07 ITA 1-SUI 2
10-May-10 ITA 0-SUI 3
Totals: 8-3-0-5-11-22

10-May-06 ITA 2-UKR 4
Totals: 1-0-0-1-2-4

03-Feb-39 ITA 0-USA 5
16-Apr-82 ITA 7-USA 5
28-Apr-92 ITA 0-USA 1
30-Apr-97 ITA 2-USA 4
10-May-98 ITA 4-USA 0
27-Apr-02 ITA 2-USA 5
18-May-10 ITA 2-USA 3 (5:00 OT/GWS)
Totals: 7-2-0-5-17-23

06-Mar-59 ITA 2-FRG 7
09-Mar-59 ITA 2-FRG 2
18-Apr-82 ITA 2-FRG 5
17-Apr-83 ITA 0-FRG 4
27-Apr-83 ITA 4-FRG 5
Totals: 5-0-1-4-10-23

**OLYMPICS, WOMEN**

11-Feb-06 ITA 0-CAN 16
Totals: 1-0-0-1-0-16

17-Feb-06 ITA 2-GER 5
Totals: 1-0-0-1-2-5

14-Feb-06 ITA 1-RUS 5
Totals: 1-0-0-1-1-5

13-Feb-06 ITA 0-SWE 11
Totals: 1-0-0-1-0-11

20-Feb-06 ITA 0-SUI 11
Totals: 1-0-0-1-0-11

# JAPAN (JPN)

Totals=GP-W-T-L-GF-GA

**OLYMPICS, MEN**

**Date Score**
24-Feb-60 JPN 13-AUS 2
27-Feb-60 JPN 11-AUS 3
Totals: 2-2-0-0-24-5

03-Feb-64 JPN 5-AUT 5
15-Feb-68 JPN 11-AUT 1
07-Feb-76 JPN 2-AUT 3
12-Feb-98 JPN 4-AUT 3
Totals: 4-2-1-1-22-12

10-Feb-98 JPN 2-BLR 2
Totals: 1-0-1-0-2-2

13-Feb-76 JPN 7-BUL 5
Totals: 1-1-0-0-7-5

20-Feb-60 JPN 1-CAN 19
18-Feb-80 JPN 0-CAN 6
Totals: 2-0-0-2-1-25

23-Feb-60 JPN 6-FIN 6
26-Feb-60 JPN 2-FIN 11
14-Feb-80 JPN 3-FIN 6
Totals: 3-0-1-2-11-23

17-Feb-68 JPN 6-FRA 2
09-Feb-98 JPN 2-FRA 5
Totals: 2-1-0-1-8-7

07-Feb-98 JPN 1-GER 3
Totals: 1-0-0-1-1-3

08-Feb-36 JPN 0-GBR 3
Totals: 1-0-0-1-0-3

07-Feb-64 JPN 6-HUN 2
Totals: 1-1-0-0-6-2

08-Feb-64 JPN 6-ITA 8
Totals: 1-0-0-1-6-8

16-Feb-80 JPN 3-NED 3
Totals: 1-0-1-0-3-3

30-Jan-64 JPN 6-NOR 3
10-Feb-68 JPN 4-NOR 0
10-Feb-72 JPN 4-NOR 5
Totals: 3-2-0-1-14-8

06-Feb-64 JPN 4-POL 3
20-Feb-80 JPN 1-POL 5
Totals: 2-1-0-1-5-8

31-Jan-64 JPN 6-RUM 4
12-Feb-68 JPN 5-RUM 4
05-Feb-76 JPN 1-ROM 3
Totals: 3-2-0-1-12-11

12-Feb-80 JPN 0-URS 16
Totals: 1-0-0-1-0-16

06-Feb-36 JPN 0-SWE 2
21-Feb-60 JPN 0-SWE 19
Totals: 2-0-0-2-0-21

07-Feb-72 JPN 3-SUI 3
09-Feb-76 JPN 6-SUI 4
Totals: 2-1-1-0-9-7

12-Feb-72 JPN 7-FRG 6
Totals: 1-1-0-0-7-6

04-Feb-64 JPN 4-YUG 6
07-Feb-68 JPN 1-YUG 5
09-Feb-72 JPN 3-YUG 2
11-Feb-76 JPN 4-YUG 3
Totals: 4-2-0-2-12-16

**WORLD CHAMPIONSHIPS, MEN**

26-Feb-57 JPN 3-AUT 3
05-May-99 JPN 2-AUT 4
07-May-00 JPN 3-AUT 5
02-May-01 JPN 2-AUT 3
Totals: 4-0-1-3-10-15

05-May-98 JPN 4-BLR 6
07-May-01 JPN 1-BLR 4
02-May-03 JPN 1-BLR 3
Totals: 3-0-0-3-6-13

29-Apr-00 JPN 0-CAN 6
Totals: 1-0-0-1-0-6

04-Mar-57 JPN 1-TCH 25
01-May-98 JPN 2-CZE 8
03-May-99 JPN 2-CZE 12
01-May-00 JPN 3-CZE 6
28-Apr-02 JPN 3-CZE 5
Totals vs. TCH: 1-0-0-1-1-25
Totals vs. CZE: 4-0-0-4-10-31

27-Apr-04 JPN 3-DEN 4
Totals: 1-0-0-1-3-4

01-Mar-57 JPN 2-GDR 9
Totals: 1-0-0-1-2-9

05-Mar-57 JPN 2-FIN 5
30-Apr-01 JPN 0-FIN 8
Totals: 2-0-0-2-2-13

09-May-00 JPN 2-FRA 7
04-May-04 JPN 2-FRA 2
Totals: 2-0-1-1-4-9

03-May-98 JPN 1-GER 5
26-Apr-02 JPN 2-GER 9
27-Apr-03 JPN 4-GER 5
Totals: 3-0-0-3-7-19

03-May-02 JPN 2-ITA 6
Totals: 1-0-0-1-2-6

01-May-04 JPN 3-KAZ 5
Totals: 1-0-0-1-3-5

05-May-01 JPN 2-LAT 8
Totals: 1-0-0-1-2-8

03-May-00 JPN 0-NOR 9
04-May-01 JPN 3-NOR 3
Totals: 2-0-1-1-3-12

01-Feb-30 JPN 0-POL 5
27-Feb-57 JPN 3-POL 8
05-May-02 JPN 2-POL 5
Totals: 3-0-0-3-5-18

24-Feb-57 JPN 0-URS 16
28-Apr-04 JPN 1-RUS 6
Totals vs. URS:
1-0-0-1-0-16
Totals vs. RUS:
1-0-0-1-1-6

29-Apr-01 JPN 4-SVK 8
28-Apr-03 JPN 1-SVK 10
Totals: 2-0-0-2-5-18

02-May-02 JPN 3-SLO 4
03-May-03 JPN 3-SLO 3
Totals: 2-0-1-1-6-7

02-Mar-57 JPN 0-SWE 18
25-Apr-04 JPN 1-SWE 5
Totals: 2-0-0-2-1-23

29-Apr-02 JPN 1-SUI 5
Totals: 1-0-0-1-1-5

06-May-00 JPN 0-UKR 4
30-Apr-03 JPN 1-UKR 5
30-Apr-04 JPN 2-UKR 2
Totals: 3-0-1-2-3-11

01-May-99 JPN 1-USA 7
05-May-03 JPN 1-USA 8
Totals: 2-0-0-2-2-15

**WORLD U20 CHAMPIONSHIPS**
02-Jan-93 JPN 1-CAN 8
Totals: 1-0-0-1-1-8

01-Jan-93 JPN 2-CZE/SVK 14
Totals: 1-0-0-1-2-14

27-Dec-92 JPN 0-FIN 7
Totals: 1-0-0-1-0-7

04-Jan-93 JPN 3-GER 6
Totals: 1-0-0-1-3-6

26-Dec-92 JPN 0-RUS 16
Totals: 1-0-0-1-0-16

30-Dec-92 JPN 1-SWE 20
Totals: 1-0-0-1-1-20

29-Dec-92 JPN 2-USA 12
Totals: 1-0-0-1-2-12

**OLYMPICS, WOMEN**
08-Feb-98 JPN 0-CAN 13
Totals: 1-0-0-1-0-13

11-Feb-98 JPN 1-CHN 6
Totals: 1-0-0-1-1-6

09-Feb-98 JPN 1-FIN 11
Totals: 1-0-0-1-1-11

14-Feb-98 JPN 0-SWE 5
Totals: 1-0-0-1-0-5

12-Feb-98 JPN 0-USA 10
Totals: 1-0-0-1-0-10

**WOMEN'S WORLD CHAMPIONSHIPS**
22-Mar-90 JPN 0-CAN 18
03-Apr-00 JPN 0-CAN 9
Totals: 2-0-0-2-0-27

06-Apr-00 JPN 0-CHN 3
04-Apr-04 JPN 2-CHN 5

09-Apr-08 JPN 3-CHN 1
10-Apr-09 JPN 2-CHN 1
Totals: 4-2-0-2-7-10

31-Mar-04 JPN 0-FIN 1
05-Apr-08 JPN 1-FIN 6
Totals: 2-0-0-2-1-7

19-Mar-90 JPN 1-GER 4
25-Mar-90 JPN 2-GER 9
09-Apr-00 JPN 2-GER 3
08-Apr-08 JPN 1-GER 2
Totals: 4-0-0-4-6-18

08-Apr-00 JPN 4-RUS 8
05-Apr-09 JPN 1-RUS 3
Totals: 2-0-0-2-5-11

21-Mar-90 JPN 4-SWE 11
04-Apr-00 JPN 0-SWE 10
30-Mar-04 JPN 2-SWE 8
04-Apr-08 JPN 0-SWE 5
Totals: 4-0-0-4-6-34

24-Mar-90 JPN 4-SUI 5
05-Apr-04 JPN 0-SUI 4
09-Apr-09 JPN 2-SUI 3
Totals: 3-0-0-3-6-12

04-Apr-09 JPN 0-USA 8
Totals: 1-0-0-1-0-8

**WOMEN'S U18 WORLD CHAMPIONSHIPS**
28-Mar-10 JPN 3-CZE 5
04-Jan-11 JPN 1-CZE 4
Totals: 2-0-0-2-4-9

30-Mar-10 JPN 3-FIN 1
02-Apr-10 JPN 1-FIN 4
Totals: 2-1-0-1-4-5

31-Mar-10 JPN 1-SWE 2
01-Jan-11 JPN 1-SWE 2
Totals: 2-0-0-2-2-4

05-Jan-11 JPN 0-SUI 4
07-Jan-11 JPN 5-SUI 1
08-Jan-11 JPN 1-SUI 5
Totals: 3-1-0-2-6-10

27-Mar-10 JPN 1-USA 11
02-Jan-11 JPN 1-USA 7
Totals: 2-0-0-2-2-18

# KAZAKHSTAN (KAZ)

Totals=GP-W-T-L-GF-GA

**OLYMPICS, MEN**
**Date Score**
08-Feb-98 KAZ 5-AUT 5
Totals: 1-0-1-0-5-5

18-Feb-98 KAZ 1-CAN 4
Totals: 1-0-0-1-1-4

15-Feb-98 KAZ 2-CZE 8
Totals: 1-0-0-1-2-8

16-Feb-98 KAZ 2-FIN 8
Totals: 1-0-0-1-2-8

07-Feb-98 KAZ 5-ITA 3
Totals: 1-1-0-0-5-3

21-Feb-06 KAZ 5-LAT 2
Totals: 1-1-0-0-5-2

13-Feb-98 KAZ 2-RUS 9
18-Feb-06 KAZ 0-RUS 1
Totals: 2-0-0-2-2-10

10-Feb-98 KAZ 4-SVK 3
19-Feb-06 KAZ 1-SVK 2
Totals: 2-1-0-1-5-5

15-Feb-06 KAZ 2-SWE 7
Totals: 1-0-0-1-2-7

16-Feb-06 KAZ 1-USA 4
Totals: 1-0-0-1-1-4

**WORLD CHAMPIONSHIPS, MEN**
07-May-05 KAZ 0-BLR 2
10-May-06 KAZ 1-BLR 7
09-May-10 KAZ 2-BLR 5
08-May-12 KAZ 2-BLR 3
Totals: 4-0-0-4-5-17

12-May-12 KAZ 0-CAN 8
Totals: 1-0-0-1-0-8

26-Apr-04 KAZ 0-CZE 7
05-May-05 KAZ 0-CZE 1
Totals: 2-0-0-2-0-8

15-May-06 KAZ 2-DEN 3
Totals: 1-0-0-1-2-3

04-May-98 KAZ 0-FIN 4
14-May-12 KAZ 1-FIN 4
Totals: 2-0-0-2-1-8

30-Apr-04 KAZ 5-FRA 0
18-May-10 KAZ 3-FRA 5
06-May-12 KAZ 3-FRA 6
Totals: 3-1-0-2-11-11

24-Apr-04 KAZ 2-GER 4
01-May-05 KAZ 2-GER 1
Totals: 2-1-0-1-4-5

12-May-06 KAZ 2-ITA 3
16-May-10 KAZ 1-ITA 2
Totals: 2-0-0-2-3-5

01-May-04 KAZ 5-JPN 3
Totals: 1-1-0-0-5-3

06-May-98 KAZ 2-LAT 7
27-Apr-04 KAZ 1-LAT 3
Totals: 2-0-0-2-3-10

02-May-98 KAZ 4-RUS 8
09-May-05 KAZ 1-RUS 3
06-May-06 KAZ 1-RUS 10
11-May-10 KAZ 1-RUS 4
Totals: 4-0-0-4-7-25

10-May-05 KAZ 1-SVK 3
08-May-06 KAZ 0-SVK 6
13-May-10 KAZ 1-SVK 5
09-May-12 KAZ 2-SVK 4
Totals: 4-0-0-4-4-18

13-May-06 KAZ 5-SLO 0
Totals: 1-1-0-0-5-0

03-May-05 KAZ 1-SUI 2
05-May-12 KAZ 1-SUI 5
Totals: 2-0-0-2-2-7

03-May-04 KAZ 2-UKR 2
Totals: 1-0-1-0-2-2

15-May-10 KAZ 0-USA 10
11-May-12 KAZ 2-USA 3 (OT)
Totals: 2-0-0-2-2-13

**WORLD U20 CHAMPIONSHIPS**
27-Dec-98 KAZ 2-BLR 2
02-Jan-01 KAZ 2-BLR 5
03-Jan-01 KAZ 5-BLR 5
Totals: 3-0-2-1-9-12

03-Jan-98 KAZ 6-CAN 3
02-Jan-99 KAZ 2-CAN 12
28-Dec-08 KAZ 0-CAN 15
Totals: 3-1-0-2-8-30

01-Jan-00 KAZ 3-CZE 6
27-Dec-00 KAZ 1-CZE 9
31-Dec-08 KAZ 2-CZE 10
Totals: 3-0-0-3-6-25

02-Jan-08 KAZ 6-DEN 3
Totals: 1-1-0-0-6-3

31-Dec-97 KAZ 1-FIN 14
04-Jan-99 KAZ 1-FIN 6
04-Jan-00 KAZ 1-FIN 9
29-Dec-07 KAZ 0 -FIN 5
03-Jan-09 KAZ 1-FIN 7
Totals: 5-0-0-5-4-41

27-Dec-08 KAZ 0-GER 9
Totals: 1-0-0-1-0-9

04-Jan-09 KAZ 1-LAT 7
Totals: 1-0-0-1-1-7

25-Dec-97 KAZ 1-RUS 12
28-Dec-98 KAZ 0-RUS 7
25-Dec-99 KAZ 1-RUS 14
27-Dec-07 KAZ 4-RUS 5
Totals: 4-0-0-4-6-38

28-Dec-97 KAZ 5-SVK 2
30-Dec-00 KAZ 0-SVK 7
03-Jan-08 KAZ 0-SVK 8
Totals: 3-1-0-2-5-17

02-Jan-98 KAZ 1-SWE 5
31-Dec-98 KAZ 4-SWE 11
31-Dec-99 KAZ 1-SWE 13
03-Jan-00 KAZ 2-SWE 12
29-Dec-00 KAZ 2-SWE 8
Totals: 5-0-0-5-10-49

29-Dec-97 KAZ 0-SUI 7
30-Dec-98 KAZ 3-SUI 0
28-Dec-99 KAZ 0-SUI 5
30-Dec-07 KAZ 1-SUI 1
30-Dec-07 KAZ 3-SUI 1
Totals: 5-2-1-2-7-14

29-Dec-99 KAZ 5-UKR 2
Totals: 1-1-0-0-5-2

26-Dec-97 KAZ 2-USA 8
26-Dec-00 KAZ 1-USA 9
26-Dec-07 KAZ 1-USA 5
30-Dec-08 KAZ 0-USA 12
Totals: 4-0-0-4-4-34

**WORLD U18 CHAMPIONSHIPS, MEN**
20-Apr-03 KAZ 6-BLR 8
Totals: 1-0-0-1-6-8

16-Apr-03 KAZ 1-CAN 8
Totals: 1-0-0-1-1-8

12-Apr-03 KAZ 3-CZE 5
Totals: 1-0-0-1-3-5

19-Apr-03 KAZ 4-FIN 5
Totals: 1-0-0-1-4-5

15-Apr-03 KAZ 0 -RUS 5
Totals: 1-0-0-1-0-5

13-Apr-03 KAZ 2-SUI 13
Totals: 1-0-0-1-2-13

**OLYMPICS, WOMEN**
11-Feb-02 KAZ 0-CAN 7
Totals: 1-0-0-1-0-7

19-Feb-02 KAZ 1-CHN 2 (OT)
Totals: 1-0-0-1-1-2

17-Feb-02 KAZ 0-GER 4
Totals: 1-0-0-1-0-4

15-Feb-02 KAZ 1-RUS 4
Totals: 1-0-0-1-1-4

13-Feb-02 KAZ 0-SWE 7
Totals: 1-0-0-1-0-7

**WOMEN'S WORLD CHAMPIONSHIPS**
02-Apr-01 KAZ 0-CAN 11
03-Apr-05 KAZ 0-CAN 13
17-Apr-11 KAZ 0-CAN 7
Totals: 3-0-0-3-0-31

06-Apr-01 KAZ 1-CHN 4
08-Apr-05 KAZ 0-CHN 3
04-Apr-07 KAZ 0-CHN 7
Totals: 3-0-0-3-1-14

04-Apr-09 KAZ 0-FIN 7
16-Apr-11 KAZ 3-FIN 5
Totals: 2-0-0-2-3-12

07-Apr-07 KAZ 0-GER 3
Totals: 1-0-0-1-0-3

05-Apr-01 KAZ 2-RUS 8
06-Apr-05 KAZ 2-RUS 2
09-Apr-05 KAZ 2-RUS 1 (10:00 OT/GWS)
08-Apr-07 KAZ 0-RUS 7
09-Apr-09 KAZ 2-RUS 9
Totals: 5-1-1-3-8-27

22-Apr-11 KAZ 0-SVK 1
24-Apr-11 KAZ 1-SVK 2 (5:00 OT/GWS)
Totals: 2-0-0-2-1-3

03-Apr-01 KAZ 1-SWE 3
08-Apr-01 KAZ 1-SWE 3
04-Apr-05 KAZ 1-SWE 5
08-Apr-09 KAZ 0-SWE 9
Totals: 4-0-0-4-3-20

05-Apr-09 KAZ 2-SUI 1 (5:00 OT/GWS)
19-Apr-11 KAZ 1-SUI 6
Totals: 2-1-0-1-3-7

03-Apr-07 KAZ 0-USA 9
Totals: 1-0-0-1-0-9

# LATVIA (LAT)

Totals=GP-W-T-L-GF-GA

**OLYMPICS, MEN**
**Date Score**
09-Feb-36 LAT 1-AUT 7
09-Feb-02 LAT 4-AUT 2
Totals: 2-1-0-1-5-9

07-Feb-36 LAT 0-CAN 11
Totals: 1-0-0-1-0-11

19-Feb-10 LAT 2-CZE 5
23-Feb-10 LAT 2-CZE 3 (OT)
Totals: 2-0-0-2-4-8

12-Feb-02 LAT 1-GER 4
Totals: 1-0-0-1-1-4

21-Feb-06 LAT 2-KAZ 5
Totals: 1-0-0-1-2-5

08-Feb-36 LAT 2-POL 9
Totals: 1-0-0-1-2-9

19-Feb-06 LAT 2-RUS 9
16-Feb-10 LAT 2-RUS 8
Totals: 2-0-0-2-4-17

10-Feb-02 LAT 6-SVK 6
16-Feb-06 LAT 3-SVK 6
20-Feb-10 LAT 0-SVK 6
Totals: 3-0-1-2-9-18

18-Feb-06 LAT 1-SWE 6
Totals: 1-0-0-1-1-6

14-Feb-02 LAT 9-UKR 2
Totals: 1-1-0-0-9-2

15-Feb-06 LAT 3-USA 3
Totals: 1-0-1-0-3-3

**WORLD CHAMPIONSHIPS, MEN**
08-May-99 LAT 2-AUT 5
03-May-04 LAT 5-AUT 2
06-May-07 LAT 5-AUT 1
29-Apr-09 LAT 2-AUT 0
08-May-11 LAT 4-AUT 1
Totals: 5-4-0-1-18-9

11-May-99 LAT 1-BLR 2
02-May-00 LAT 6-BLR 3
04-May-01 LAT 2-BLR 2
29-Apr-03 LAT 4-BLR 0
07-May-11 LAT 6-BLR 3
Totals: 5-3-1-1-19-10

06-Feb-39 LAT 5-BEL 1
Totals: 1-1-0-0-5-1

20-Jan-35 LAT 0-CAN 14
30-Apr-97 LAT 3-CAN 3
27-Apr-02 LAT 1-CAN 4
27-Apr-03 LAT 1-CAN 6
30-Apr-04 LAT 0-CAN 2
30-Apr-05 LAT 4-CAN 6

11-May-06 LAT 0-CAN 11
04-May-08 LAT 0-CAN 7
07-May-09 LAT 2-CAN 4
10-May-10 LAT 1-CAN 6
Totals: 10-0-1-9-12-63

04-Feb-39 LAT 0-TCH 9
11-May-00 LAT 1-CZE 3
02-May-02 LAT 1-CZE 3
24-Apr-04 LAT 1-CZE 3
05-May-06 LAT 1-CZE 1
17-May-10 LAT 1-CZE 3
30-Apr-11 LAT 2-CZE 4
10-May-12 LAT 1-CZE 3
Totals vs. TCH:
1-0-0-1-0-9
Totals vs. CZE:
7-0-1-6-8-20

06-May-03 LAT 4-DEN 2
04-May-11 LAT 2-DEN 3 (5:00 OT/GWS)
14-May-12 LAT 0-DEN 2
Totals: 3-1-0-2-6-7

02-May-98 LAT 0-FIN 6
09-May-05 LAT 0-FIN 0
07-May-06 LAT 0-FIN 5
09-May-08 LAT 1-FIN 2
02-May-11 LAT 2-FIN 3 (5:00 OT/GWS)
Totals: 5-1-0-4-3-16

08-May-97 LAT 6-FRA 2
04-May-99 LAT 8-FRA 5
02-May-09 LAT 7-FRA 1
Totals: 3-3-0-0-21-8

24-Jan-35 LAT 1-GER 3
13-Feb-38 LAT 0-GER 1
06-May-97 LAT 8-GER 0
10-May-98 LAT 5-GER 0
03-May-02 LAT 2-GER 3
26-Apr-04 LAT 1-GER 1
12-May-08 LAT 3-GER 5
06-May-12 LAT 3-GER 2
Totals: 8-3-1-4-23-15

21-Jan-35 LAT 1-GBR 5
14-Feb-38 LAT 1-GBR 5
Totals: 2-0-0-2-2-10

20-Feb-33 LAT 0-HUN 3
Totals: 1-0-0-1-0-3

24-Feb-33 LAT 2-ITA 0
09-Feb-39 LAT 1-ITA 2
28-Apr-97 LAT 4-ITA 5
08-May-98 LAT 1-ITA 1
30-Apr-02 LAT 4-ITA 1
02-May-07 LAT 3-ITA 4 (OT)
12-May-10 LAT 5-ITA 2
08-May-12 LAT 5-ITA 0
Totals: 8-4-1-3-25-15

05-May-01 LAT 8-JPN 2
Totals: 1-1-0-0-8-2

06-May-98 LAT 7-KAZ 2
27-Apr-04 LAT 3 -KAZ 1
Totals: 2-2-0-0-10-3

25-Jan-35 LAT 7-NED 0
Totals: 1-1-0-0-7-0

11-Feb-38 LAT 3-NOR 1
03-May-97 LAT 6-NOR 3
10-May-99 LAT 7-NOR 1
07-May-01 LAT 3-NOR 0
16-May-06 LAT 4-NOR 2
07-May-07 LAT 4-NOR 7
11-May-08 LAT 4-NOR 1
16-May-10 LAT 5-NOR 0
12-May-12 LAT 0-NOR 3
Totals: 9-7-0-2-36-18

25-Feb-33 LAT 0-ROM 1
23-Jan-35 LAT 2-ROM 3
Totals: 2-0-0-2-2-4

04-May-98 LAT 5-RUS 7
05-May-00 LAT 3-RUS 2
04-May-03 LAT 2-RUS 1
03-May-09 LAT 1-RUS 6
05-May-12 LAT 2-RUS 5
Totals: 5-2-0-3-13-21

10-May-97 LAT 5-SVK 4
Totals: 1-1-0-0-5-4

05-May-05 LAT 3 -SLO 1
09-May-06 LAT 5-SLO 1
06-May-08 LAT 3-SLO 0
05-May-11 LAT 2-SLO 5
Totals: 4-3-0-1-13-7

02-May-97 LAT 1-SWE 1
06-May-99 LAT 3-SWE 4
30-Apr-00 LAT 1-SWE 3
29-Apr-01 LAT 2-SWE 5
26-Apr-03 LAT 1-SWE 3
05-May-04 LAT 1-SWE 4
10-May-05 LAT 1-SWE 9
30-Apr-07 LAT 2-SWE 8
27-Apr-09 LAT 3-SWE 2 (5:00 OT/GWS)
14-May-10 LAT 2-SWE 4
15-May-12 LAT 0-SWE 4
Totals: 11-1-1-9-17-47

18-Feb-33 LAT 1-SUI 5
03-Feb-39 LAT 0-SUI 12
02-May-99 LAT 3-SUI 5
08-May-00 LAT 1-SUI 4
05-May-02 LAT 4-SUI 6
03-May-03 LAT 2-SUI 4
01-May-04 LAT 1-SUI 1
28-Apr-07 LAT 1-SUI 2
30-Apr-09 LAT 2-SUI 1 (5:00 OT/GWS)
08-May-10 LAT 1-SUI 3
Totals: 10-1-1-8-16-43

04-May-00 LAT 2-UKR 1
02-May-01 LAT 2-UKR 4
07-May-05 LAT 3-UKR 0
04-May-07 LAT 5-UKR 0
Totals: 4-3-0-1-12-5

12-Feb-38 LAT 0-USA 1
27-Apr-97 LAT 4-USA 5
11-May-98 LAT 3-USA 2
07-May-00 LAT 1-USA 1
30-Apr-01 LAT 2-USA 0
29-Apr-02 LAT 2-USA 3
03-May-05 LAT 1-USA 3
13-May-06 LAT 2-USA 4
02-May-08 LAT 0-USA 4
25-Apr-09 LAT 2-USA 4
Totals: 10-2-1-7-17-27

05-Feb-39 LAT 6-YUG 0
08-Feb-39 LAT 4-YUG 0
Totals: 2-2-0-0-10-0

**WORLD U20 CHAMPIONSHIPS**
04-Jan-10 LAT 6-AUT 4
Totals: 1-1-0-0-6-4

26-Dec-09 LAT 0-CAN 16
Totals: 1-0-0-1-0-16

26-Dec-05 LAT 1-CZE 5
03-Jan-10 LAT 2-CZE 10
Totals: 2-0-0-2-3-15

04-Jan-12 LAT 2-DEN 1
Totals: 1-1-0-0-2-1

30-Dec-08 LAT 1-FIN 5
Totals: 1-0-0-1-1-5

02-Jan-09 LAT 7-GER 1
Totals: 1-1-0-0-7-1

04-Jan-09 LAT 7-KAZ 1
Totals: 1-1-0-0-7-1

04-Jan-06 LAT 4-NOR 0
Totals: 1-1-0-0-4-0

29-Dec-05 LAT 1-RUS 3
26-Dec-08 LAT 1-RUS 4
29-Dec-11 LAT 0-RUS 14
Totals: 3-0-0-3-2-21

27-Dec-05 LAT 4-SVK 7
27-Dec-08 LAT 2-SVK 7
27-Dec-09 LAT 3-SVK 8
27-Dec-11 LAT 1-SVK 3
Totals: 4-0-0-4-10-25

30-Dec-05 LAT 2-SWE 10
29-Dec-08 LAT 1-SWE 10
26-Dec-11 LAT 4-SWE 9
Totals: 3-0-0-3-7-29

02-Jan-06 LAT 2-SUI 5
30-Dec-09 LAT 5-SUI 7
30-Dec-11 LAT 3-SUI 5
Totals: 3-0-0-3-10-17

29-Dec-09 LAT 1-USA 12
02-Jan-12 LAT 2-USA 12
Totals: 2-0-0-2-3-24

**WORLD U18 CHAMPIONSHIPS**
22-Apr-10 LAT 5-BLR 4 (5:00 OT/GWS)
Totals: 1-1-0-0-5-4

14-Apr-07 LAT 1-CAN 9
21-Apr-10 LAT 1-CAN 5
Totals: 2-0-0-2-2-14

19-Apr-07 LAT 1-CZE 4
16-Apr-10 LAT 4-CZE 5
20-Apr-12 LAT 4-CZE 7
Totals: 3-0-0-3-9-16

19-Apr-12 LAT 3-DEN 4 (OT)
Totals: 1-0-0-1-3-4

20-Apr-07 LAT 3-FIN 6
13-Apr-10 LAT 2-FIN 7
Totals: 2-0-0-2-5-13

16-Apr-07 LAT 2-GER 3
16-Apr-12 LAT 5-GER 4
Totals: 2-1-0-1-7-7

13-Apr-07 LAT 3-RUS 6
14-Apr-10 LAT 0-RUS 9
12-Apr-12 LAT 1-RUS 6
Totals: 3-0-0-3-4-21

17-Apr-10 LAT 3-SVK 4
Totals: 1-0-0-1-3-4

15-Apr-12 LAT 1-SWE 3
Totals: 1-0-0-1-1-3

13-Apr-12 LAT 4-SUI 2
Totals: 1-1-0-0-4-2

17-Apr-07 LAT 0-USA 8
Totals: 1-0-0-1-0-8

# LITHUANIA (LTU)

Totals=GP-W-T-L-GF-GA

**WORLD CHAMPIONSHIPS, MEN**

**Date Score**
13-Feb-38 LTU 1-HUN 10
Totals: 1-0-0-1-1-10

12-Feb-38 LTU 1-POL 8
Totals: 1-0-0-1-1-8

11-Feb-38 LTU 1-ROM 0
Totals: 1-1-0-0-1-0

14-Feb-38 LTU 0-SUI 15
Totals: 1-0-0-1-0-15

# NETHERLANDS (NED)

Totals=GP-W-T-L-GF-GA

**OLYMPICS, MEN**

**Date Score**
12-Feb-80 NED 1-CAN 10
Totals: 1-0-0-1-1-10

20-Feb-80 NED 3-FIN 10
Totals: 1-0-0-1-3-10

16-Feb-80 NED 3-JPN 3
Totals: 1-0-1-0-3-3

18-Feb-80 NED 5-POL 3
Totals: 1-1-0-0-5-3

14-Feb-80 NED 4-URS 17
Totals: 1-0-0-1-4-17

**WORLD CHAMPIONSHIPS, MEN**
22-Mar-50 NED 2-BEL 4
Totals: 1-0-0-1-2-4

03-Feb-39 NED 0-CAN 8
13-Apr-81 NED 1-CAN 8
Totals: 2-0-0-2-1-16

06-Feb-39 NED 2-FIN 1
15-Apr-81 NED 3-FIN 12
21-Apr-81 NED 2-FIN 4
Totals: 3-1-0-2-7-17

21-Mar-50 NED 4-FRA 2
Totals: 1-1-0-0-4-2

22-Jan-35 NED 0-GER 5
Totals: 1-0-0-1-0-5

19-Jan-35 NED 0-HUN 6
Totals: 1-0-0-1-0-6

07-Feb-39 NED 1-ITA 2
Totals: 1-0-0-1-1-2

25-Jan-35 NED 0-LAT 7
Totals: 1-0-0-1-0-7

04-Feb-39 NED 0-POL 9
Totals: 1-0-0-1-0-9

24-Jan-35 NED 0-ROM 6
Totals: 1-0-0-1-0-6

12-Apr-81 NED 1-URS 10
Totals: 1-0-0-1-1-10

20-Jan-35 NED 0-SWE 6
14-Mar-50 NED 0-SWE 10
Totals: 2-0-0-2-0-16

21-Jan-35 NED 0-SUI 4
Totals: 1-0-0-1-0-4

15-Mar-50 NED 1-USA 17
17-Apr-81 NED 6-USA 7
23-Apr-81 NED 3-USA 7
Totals: 3-0-0-3-10-31

19-Apr-81 NED 2-FRG 9
25-Apr-81 NED 6-FRG 12
Totals: 2-0-0-2-8-21

# NORWAY (NOR)

Totals=GP-W-T-L-GF-GA

**OLYMPICS, MEN**

**Date Score**
07-Feb-64 NOR 8-AUT 2
12-Feb-68 NOR 5-AUT 4
15-Feb-84 NOR 5-AUT 6
21-Feb-88 NOR 4-AUT 4
20-Feb-94 NOR 2-AUT 4
24-Feb-94 NOR 3-AUT 1
Totals: 6-3-1-2-27-21

23-Feb-52 NOR 2-CAN 11
13-Feb-84 NOR 1-CAN 8
12-Feb-92 NOR 0-CAN 10
16-Feb-10 NOR 0-CAN 8
Totals: 4-0-0-4-3-37

16-Feb-52 NOR 0-TCH 6
12-Feb-80 NOR 0-TCH 11
07-Feb-84 NOR 4-TCH 10
17-Feb-88 NOR 1-TCH 10
08-Feb-92 NOR 1-TCH 10
18-Feb-94 NOR 1-CZE 4
Totals vs. TCH:
5-0-0-5-6-47
Totals vs. CZE:
1-0-0-1-1-4

20-Feb-52 NOR 2-FIN 5
09-Feb-84 NOR 2-FIN 16
16-Feb-94 NOR 0-FIN 4
Totals: 3-0-0-3-4-25

08-Feb-68 NOR 4-FRA 1
23-Feb-88 NOR 6-FRA 7 (10:00 OT/GWS)
16-Feb-92 NOR 2-FRA 4
Totals: 3-1-0-2-12-12

21-Feb-52 NOR 2-GER 6
14-Feb-94 NOR 1-GER 2
Totals: 2-0-0-2-3-8

05-Feb-64 NOR 6-HUN 1
Totals: 1-1-0-0-6-1

02-Feb-64 NOR 9-ITA 2
18-Feb-92 NOR 5-ITA 3
22-Feb-94 NOR 3-ITA 6
Totals: 3-2-0-1-17-11

30-Jan-64 NOR 3-JPN 6
10-Feb-68 NOR 0-JPN 4
10-Feb-72 NOR 5-JPN 4
Totals: 3-1-0-2-8-14

25-Feb-52 NOR 3-POL 4
31-Jan-64 NOR 2-POL 6
Totals: 2-0-0-2-5-10

06-Feb-64 NOR 4-RUM 2
14-Feb-68 NOR 4-RUM 3
20-Feb-80 NOR 3-ROM 3
Totals: 3-2-1-0-11-8

13-Feb-88 NOR 0-URS 5
10-Feb-92 NOR 1-RUS 8
12-Feb-94 NOR 1-RUS 5
Totals vs. URS:
1-0-0-1-0-5
Totals vs. RUS:
2-0-0-2-2-13

23-Feb-10 NOR 3-SVK 4
Totals: 1-0-0-1-3-4

17-Feb-52 NOR 2-SWE 4
18-Feb-80 NOR 1-SWE 7
Totals: 2-0-0-2-3-11

18-Feb-52 NOR 2-SUI 7
12-Feb-72 NOR 5-SUI 3
14-Feb-92 NOR 3-SUI 6
21-Feb-92 NOR 5-SUI 2
20-Feb-10 NOR 4-SUI 5 (OT)
Totals: 5-2-0-3-19-23

15-Feb-52 NOR 2-USA 3
16-Feb-80 NOR 1-USA 5
11-Feb-84 NOR 3-USA 3
19-Feb-88 NOR 3-USA 6
18-Feb-10 NOR 1-USA 6
Totals: 5-0-1-4-10-23

09-Feb-72 NOR 1-FRG 5
14-Feb-80 NOR 4-FRG 10
15-Feb-88 NOR 3-FRG 7
Totals: 3-0-0-3-8-22

08-Feb-64 NOR 8-YUG 4
17-Feb-68 NOR 2-YUG 3
06-Feb-72 NOR 5-YUG 2
Totals: 3-2-0-1-15-9

**WORLD CHAMPIONSHIPS, MEN**
29-Apr-93 NOR 2-AUT 6
01-May-95 NOR 5-AUT 3
11-May-99 NOR 0-AUT 3
04-May-07 NOR 3-AUT 2 (OT)
04-May-11 NOR 5-AUT 0
Totals: 5-3-0-2-15-14

08-May-99 NOR 0-BLR 2
05-May-01 NOR 2-BLR 3
30-Apr-09 NOR 2-BLR 3 (OT)
Totals: 3-0-0-3-4-8

12-Feb-49 NOR 2-BEL 0
19-Feb-49 NOR 14-BEL 1
Totals: 2-2-0-0-16-1

20-Mar-50 NOR 1-CAN 11
11-Mar-51 NOR 0-CAN 8
28-Feb-54 NOR 0-CAN 8
02-Mar-58 NOR 0-CAN 12
13-Mar-62 NOR 1-CAN 14
06-Mar-65 NOR 0-CAN 6
20-Apr-90 NOR 0-CAN 8
01-May-92 NOR 3-CAN 4
26-Apr-97 NOR 0-CAN 7
03-May-99 NOR 2-CAN 4
01-May-00 NOR 4-CAN 3
28-Apr-01 NOR 0-CAN 5
07-May-06 NOR 1-CAN 7
30-Apr-07 NOR 2-CAN 4
08-May-08 NOR 1-CAN 2
14-May-08 NOR 2-CAN 8
03-May-09 NOR 1-CAN 5

14-May-10 NOR 1-CAN 12
07-May-11 NOR 2-CAN 3
Totals: 19-1-0-18-21-131

17-Feb-37 NOR 0-TCH 7
03-Mar-54 NOR 1-TCH 7
08-Mar-58 NOR 0-TCH 2
08-Mar-65 NOR 2-TCH 9
19-Apr-90 NOR 1-TCH 9
28-Apr-92 NOR 1-TCH 6
21-Apr-93 NOR 0-CZE 2
30-Apr-94 NOR 2-CZE 2
29-Apr-95 NOR 1-CZE 3
24-Apr-96 NOR 2-CZE 2
29-Apr-00 NOR 0-CZE 4
12-May-06 NOR 1-CZE 3
27-Apr-09 NOR 2-CZE 5
11-May-10 NOR 3-CZE 2
07-May-12 NOR 3-CZE 4 (5:00 OT/GWS)
Totals vs. TCH: 6-0-0-6-5-40
Totals vs. CZE: 9-1-2-6-14-27

09-May-06 NOR 6-DEN 3
29-Apr-09 NOR 5-DEN 4 (OT)
15-May-12 NOR 6-DEN 2
Totals: 3-3-0-0-17-9

07-Mar-59 NOR 6-GDR 3
14-Mar-59 NOR 4-GDR 1
12-Mar-65 NOR 1-GDR 5
Totals: 3-2-0-1-11-9

17-Feb-49 NOR 3-FIN 7
16-Mar-51 NOR 0-FIN 3
02-Mar-54 NOR 0-FIN 2
06-Mar-58 NOR 1-FIN 2
17-Mar-62 NOR 2-FIN 5
09-Mar-65 NOR 1-FIN 4
22-Apr-90 NOR 3-FIN 3
27-Apr-90 NOR 1-FIN 8
22-Apr-93 NOR 0-FIN 2
29-Apr-94 NOR 1-FIN 5
26-Apr-95 NOR 2-FIN 5
21-Apr-96 NOR 1-FIN 1
08-May-00 NOR 4-FIN 7
14-May-06 NOR 0-FIN 3
05-May-08 NOR 2-FIN 3 (OT)
25-Apr-09 NOR 0-FIN 5
12-May-11 NOR 1-FIN 4
Totals: 17-0-2-15-22-69

14-Mar-50 NOR 11-FRA 0
04-May-92 NOR 1-FRA 0
26-Apr-93 NOR 5-FRA 4
02-May-94 NOR 1-FRA 4
29-Apr-96 NOR 3-FRA 1
07-May-97 NOR 3-FRA 4
13-May-10 NOR 5-FRA 1
09-May-11 NOR 5-FRA 2
Totals: 8-6-0-2-34-16

15-Feb-38 NOR 0-GER 8
18-Apr-93 NOR 0-GER 6
09-May-97 NOR 2-GER 4
02-May-07 NOR 3-GER 5
07-May-08 NOR 3-GER 2
13-May-12 NOR 12-GER 4
Totals: 6-2-0-4-20-29

12-Feb-38 NOR 0-GBR 8
15-Mar-50 NOR 0-GBR 2
17-Mar-50 NOR 3-GBR 4
15-Mar-51 NOR 4-GBR 3
11-Mar-62 NOR 12-GBR 2
06-May-94 NOR 5-GBR 2
Totals: 6-3-0-3-24-21

10-Mar-59 NOR 4-ITA 3
23-Apr-96 NOR 0-ITA 4
02-May-97 NOR 2-ITA 2
01-May-99 NOR 5-ITA 2
09-May-00 NOR 1-ITA 1
01-May-01 NOR 1-ITA 1
09-May-12 NOR 6-ITA 2
Totals: 7-3-3-1-19-15

03-May-00 NOR 9-JPN 0
04-May-01 NOR 3-JPN 3
Totals: 2-1-1-0-12-3

11-Feb-38 NOR 1-LAT 3
03-May-97 NOR 3-LAT 6
10-May-99 NOR 1-LAT 7
07-May-01 NOR 0-LAT 3
16-May-06 NOR 2-LAT 4
07-May-07 NOR 7-LAT 4
11-May-08 NOR 1-LAT 4
16-May-10 NOR 0-LAT 5
12-May-12 NOR 3-LAT 0
Totals: 9-2-0-7-18-36

09-Mar-58 NOR 8-POL 3
11-Mar-59 NOR 4-POL 3
Totals: 2-2-0-0-12-6

27-Feb-54 NOR 0-URS 7
01-Mar-58 NOR 2-URS 10
06-Mar-59 NOR 1-URS 13
05-Mar-65 NOR 2-URS 14
16-Apr-90 NOR 1-URS 9
30-Apr-92 NOR 2-RUS 3
29-Apr-01 NOR 0-RUS 4
06-May-12 NOR 2-RUS 4
17-May-12 NOR 2-RUS 5
Totals vs. URS: 5-0-0-5-6-53
Totals vs. RUS: 4-0-0-4-6-16

05-May-97 NOR 1-SVK 2
05-May-99 NOR 2-SVK 8
06-May-00 NOR 1-SVK 9
28-Apr-07 NOR 0-SVK 3
03-May-08 NOR 1-SVK 5
04-May-09 NOR 2-SVK 3 (OT)
Totals: 6-0-0-6-7-30

21-Mar-50 NOR 1-SWE 6
13-Mar-51 NOR 2-SWE 5
26-Feb-54 NOR 1-SWE 10
28-Feb-58 NOR 0-SWE 9
16-Mar-62 NOR 2-SWE 10
11-Mar-65 NOR 0-SWE 10
17-Apr-90 NOR 3-SWE 4
25-Apr-94 NOR 3-SWE 3
23-Apr-95 NOR 0-SWE 5
27-Apr-96 NOR 0-SWE 3
29-Apr-97 NOR 1-SWE 4
09-May-10 NOR 2-SWE 5
30-Apr-11 NOR 5-SWE 4 (5:00 OT/GWS)
04-May-12 NOR 1-SWE 3
Totals: 14-1-1-12-21-81

18-Feb-37 NOR 2-SUI 13
14-Feb-49 NOR 1-SUI 7
18-Mar-50 NOR 4-SUI 12
10-Mar-51 NOR 1-SUI 8
04-Mar-54 NOR 3-SUI 2
09-Mar-59 NOR 4-SUI 4
12-Mar-62 NOR 7-SUI 5
03-May-92 NOR 1-SUI 3
01-May-93 NOR 5-SUI 2
17-May-10 NOR 3-SUI 2
05-May-11 NOR 3-SUI 2
Totals: 11-5-1-5-34-60

06-May-07 NOR 2-UKR 3
Totals: 1-0-0-1-2-3

13-Feb-38 NOR 1-USA 7
13-Feb-49 NOR 1-USA 12
22-Mar-50 NOR 6-USA 12
09-Mar-51 NOR 3-USA 0
03-Mar-58 NOR 1-USA 6
05-Mar-59 NOR 3-USA 10
08-Mar-62 NOR 2-USA 14
14-Mar-65 NOR 6-USA 8
23-Apr-90 NOR 4-USA 9
29-Apr-90 NOR 1-USA 4
24-Apr-93 NOR 1-USA 3
27-Apr-94 NOR 2-USA 7
25-Apr-95 NOR 1-USA 2
28-Apr-97 NOR 1-USA 3
05-May-06 NOR 1-USA 3
12-May-08 NOR 1-USA 9
02-May-11 NOR 2-USA 4
Totals: 17-1-0-16-37-113

07-Mar-54 NOR 1-FRG 7
13-Mar-59 NOR 4-FRG 9
09-Mar-62 NOR 6-FRG 4
25-Apr-90 NOR 7-FRG 3
01-May-90 NOR 0-FRG 4
Totals: 5-2-0-3-18-27

**WORLD U20 CHAMPIONSHIPS**

31-Dec-78 NOR 1-CAN 10
04-Jan-83 NOR 0-CAN 13
26-Dec-88 NOR 1-CAN 7
29-Dec-89 NOR 3-CAN 6
29-Dec-90 NOR 1-CAN 10
29-Dec-05 NOR 0-CAN 4
29-Dec-10 NOR 1-CAN 10
Totals: 7-0-0-7-7-60

28-Dec-78 NOR 4-TCH 6
29-Dec-82 NOR 2-TCH 9
27-Dec-88 NOR 1-TCH 7
30-Dec-89 NOR 2-TCH 13
26-Dec-90 NOR 3-TCH 11
27-Dec-10 NOR 0-CZE 2
Totals vs. TCH: 5-0-0-5-12-46
Totals vs. CZE: 1-0-0-1-0-2

27-Dec-82 NOR 2-FIN 10
29-Dec-88 NOR 3-FIN 9
01-Jan-90 NOR 2-FIN 8
31-Dec-90 NOR 2-FIN 10
30-Dec-05 NOR 1-FIN 9
Totals: 5-0-0-5-10-46

04-Jan-11 NOR 3-GER 1
Totals: 1-1-0-0-3-1

04-Jan-06 NOR 0-LAT 4
Totals: 1-0-0-1-0-4

04-Jan-90 NOR 7-POL 3
Totals: 1-1-0-0-7-3

27-Dec-78 NOR 0-URS 17
26-Dec-82 NOR 1-URS 10
30-Dec-88 NOR 0-URS 10
27-Dec-89 NOR 2-URS 12
28-Dec-90 NOR 0-URS 13
30-Dec-10 NOR 2-RUS 8
Totals vs. URS: 5-0-0-5-3-62
Totals vs. RUS: 1-0-0-1-2-8

03-Jan-06 NOR 3-SVK 4
02-Jan-11 NOR 0-SVK 5
Totals: 2-0-0-2-3-9

01-Jan-83 NOR 3-SWE 15
01-Jan-89 NOR 1-SWE 9
26-Dec-89 NOR 3-SWE 4
04-Jan-91 NOR 0-SWE 10
26-Dec-10 NOR 1-SWE 7
Totals: 5-0-0-5-8-45

03-Jan-91 NOR 1-SUI 2
27-Dec-05 NOR 0-SUI 2
Totals: 2-0-0-2-1-4

30-Dec-78 NOR 1-USA 7
02-Jan-83 NOR 3-USA 8
02-Jan-89 NOR 4-USA 12
02-Jan-90 NOR 6-USA 5
01-Jan-91 NOR 1-USA 19
26-Dec-05 NOR 2-USA 11
Totals: 6-1-0-5-17-62

02-Jan-79 NOR 0-FRG 6
30-Dec-82 NOR 2-FRG 4
04-Jan-89 NOR 4-FRG 2
Totals: 3-1-0-2-6-12

**WORLD U18 CHAMPIONSHIPS**

16-Apr-04 NOR 3-BLR 4
20-Apr-06 NOR 6-BLR 6
Totals: 2-0-1-1-9-10

17-Apr-02 NOR 3-CAN 4
13-Apr-06 NOR 2-CAN 9
18-Apr-11 NOR 0-CAN 5
Totals: 3-0-0-3-5-18

16-Apr-01 NOR 2-CZE 7
12-Apr-02 NOR 4-CZE 7
12-Apr-04 NOR 0-CZE 7
17-Apr-11 NOR 2-CZE 3
Totals: 4-0-0-4-8-24

15-Apr-04 NOR 4-DEN 7
Totals: 1-0-0-1-4-7

13-Apr-99 NOR 2-FIN 10
09-Apr-04 NOR 0-FIN 9
16-Apr-06 NOR 1-FIN 2
13-Apr-09 NOR 1-FIN 10
14-Apr-11 NOR 2-FIN 5
Totals: 5-1-0-4-9-33

16-Apr-99 NOR 2-GER 4
13-Apr-01 NOR 2-GER 2
11-Apr-02 NOR 2-GER 2
19-Apr-06 NOR 2-GER 2
18-Apr-09 NOR 5-GER 2
Totals: 5-1-3-1-13-12

10-Apr-99 NOR 2-RUS 8
15-Apr-01 NOR 1-RUS 10
14-Apr-02 NOR 0-RUS 7
08-Apr-04 NOR 4-RUS 8
12-Apr-09 NOR 1-RUS 8
Totals: 5-0-0-5-8-41

09-Apr-99 NOR 0-SVK 7
19-Apr-01 NOR 4-SVK 4
15-Apr-02 NOR 4-SVK 3
11-Apr-04 NOR 2-SVK 8
15-Apr-06 NOR 2-SVK 5
10-Apr-09 NOR 2-SVK 5
23-Apr-11 NOR 6-SVK 2
Totals: 7-2-1-4-20-34

12-Apr-01 NOR 3-SWE 4
21-Apr-02 NOR 2-SWE 3
12-Apr-06 NOR 2-SWE 5
15-Apr-11 NOR 2-SWE 10
Totals: 4-0-0-4-7-22

18-Apr-02 NOR 2-SUI 7
16-Apr-09 NOR 3-SUI 7
21-Apr-11 NOR 1-SUI 4
Totals: 3-0-0-3-6-18

15-Apr-99 NOR 0-UKR 3
20-Apr-01 NOR 5-UKR 2
20-Apr-02 NOR 2-UKR 5
Totals: 3-1-0-2-7-10

12-Apr-99 NOR 2-USA 10
09-Apr-09 NOR 0-USA 8
Totals: 2-0-0-2-2-18

**WOMEN'S WORLD CHAMPIONSHIPS**

12-Apr-94 NOR 0-CAN 12
Totals: 1-0-0-1-0-12

26-Apr-92 NOR 1-CHN 2
14-Apr-94 NOR 1-CHN 8
Totals: 2-0-0-2-2-10

24-Apr-92 NOR 2-DEN 0
Totals: 1-1-0-0-2-0

19-Mar-90 NOR 1-FIN 10
20-Apr-92 NOR 3-FIN 11
03-Apr-97 NOR 0-FIN 10
Totals: 3-0-0-3-4-31

24-Mar-90 NOR 6-GER 3
Totals: 1-1-0-0-6-3

04-Apr-97 NOR 1-RUS 2
Totals: 1-0-0-1-1-2

11-Apr-94 NOR 1-SWE 3
17-Apr-94 NOR 3-SWE 6
01-Apr-97 NOR 2-SWE 2
Totals: 3-0-1-2-6-11

22-Mar-90 NOR 3-SUI 8
25-Mar-90 NOR 6-SUI 7
23-Apr-92 NOR 4-SUI 1
16-Apr-94 NOR 7-SUI 4
06-Apr-97 NOR 0-SUI 1
Totals: 5-2-0-3-20-21

21-Mar-90 NOR 0-USA 17
21-Apr-92 NOR 1-USA 9
31-Mar-97 NOR 0-USA 7
Totals: 3-0-0-3-1-33

# POLAND (POL)

Totals=GP-W-T-L-GF-GA

**OLYMPICS, MEN**

**Date Score**

07-Feb-36 POL 1-AUT 2
30-Jan-48 POL 7-AUT 5
02-Feb-56 POL 4-AUT 3
08-Feb-64 POL 5-AUT 1
23-Feb-88 POL 2-AUT 3
Totals: 5-3-0-2-19-14

07-Feb-32 POL 0-CAN 9
09-Feb-32 POL 0-CAN 10
06-Feb-36 POL 1-CAN 8
02-Feb-48 POL 0-CAN 15
18-Feb-52 POL 0-CAN 11
14-Feb-80 POL 1-CAN 5
14-Feb-88 POL 0-CAN 1
Totals: 7-0-0-7-2-59

13-Feb-28 POL 2-TCH 3
01-Feb-48 POL 1-TCH 13
15-Feb-52 POL 2-TCH 8
29-Jan-56 POL 3-TCH 8
05-Feb-72 POL 1-TCH 14
10-Feb-76 POL 1-TCH 0*
Totals: 6-1-0-5-10-46
*TCH won 7-1, but a failed doping test reversed result

23-Feb-52 POL 4-FIN 2
07-Feb-72 POL 1-FIN 5
14-Feb-76 POL 1-FIN 7
12-Feb-80 POL 5-FIN 4
22-Feb-88 POL 1-FIN 5
11-Feb-92 POL 1-FIN 9
Totals: 6-2-0-4-13-32

18-Feb-88 POL 0-FRA 2*
Totals: 1-0-0-1-0-2
*POL won game 6-2 but a failed doping test reversed result to 2-0 for FRA

04-Feb-32 POL 1-GER 2
13-Feb-32 POL 1-GER 4
20-Feb-52 POL 4-GER 4
17-Feb-92 POL 0-GER 4
Totals: 4-0-1-3-6-14

05-Feb-48 POL 2-GBR 8
Totals: 1-0-0-1-2-8

03-Feb-64 POL 6-HUN 2
Totals: 1-1-0-0-6-2

04-Feb-48 POL 13-ITA 7
03-Feb-56 POL 2-ITA 5
05-Feb-64 POL 7-ITA 0
11-Feb-84 POL 1-ITA 6
13-Feb-92 POL 1-ITA 7
20-Feb-92 POL 4-ITA 1
Totals: 6-3-0-3-28-26

06-Feb-64 POL 3-JPN 4
20-Feb-80 POL 5-JPN 1
Totals: 2-1-0-1-8-5

08-Feb-36 POL 9-LAT 2
Totals: 1-1-0-0-9-2

18-Feb-80 POL 3-NED 5
Totals: 1-0-0-1-3-5

25-Feb-52 POL 4-NOR 3
31-Jan-64 POL 6-NOR 2
Totals: 2-2-0-0-10-5

30-Jan-64 POL 6-RUM 1
Totals: 1-1-0-0-6-1

10-Feb-72 POL 3-URS 9
08-Feb-76 POL 1-URS 16
16-Feb-80 POL 1-URS 8
07-Feb-84 POL 1-URS 12
Totals: 4-0-0-4-6-45

12-Feb-28 POL 2-SWE 2
08-Feb-48 POL 2-SWE 13
16-Feb-52 POL 1-SWE 17
09-Feb-72 POL 3-SWE 5
13-Feb-84 POL 1-SWE 10
16-Feb-88 POL 1-SWE 1
09-Feb-92 POL 2-SWE 7
Totals: 7-0-2-5-12-55

06-Feb-48 POL 0-SUI 14
17-Feb-52 POL 3-SUI 6
01-Feb-56 POL 6-SUI 2
20-Feb-88 POL 1-SUI 4
19-Feb-92 POL 2-SUI 7
Totals: 5-1-0-4-12-33

05-Feb-32 POL 1-USA 4
08-Feb-32 POL 0-USA 5
31-Jan-48 POL 4-USA 23
22-Feb-52 POL 3-USA 5
28-Jan-56 POL 0-USA 4
12-Feb-72 POL 1-USA 6
12-Feb-76 POL 2-USA 7
17-Feb-84 POL 4-USA 7
15-Feb-92 POL 0-USA 3
Totals: 9-0-0-9-15-64

06-Feb-76 POL 4-FRG 7
09-Feb-84 POL 5-FRG 8
Totals: 2-0-0-2-9-15

07-Feb-64 POL 9-YUG 3
15-Feb-84 POL 8-YUG 1
Totals: 2-2-0-0-17-4

**WORLD CHAMPIONSHIPS, MEN**
05-Feb-30 POL 0-AUT 2
06-Feb-31 POL 1-AUT 2
15-Feb-47 POL 2-AUT 10
03-Mar-57 POL 5-AUT 1
Totals: 4-1-0-3-8-15

20-Feb-33 POL 1-BEL 0
22-Jan-35 POL 12-BEL 2
20-Feb-47 POL 11-BEL 1
Totals: 3-3-0-0-24-3

05-Feb-31 POL 0-CAN 3
18-Feb-37 POL 2-CAN 8
05-Feb-39 POL 0-CAN 4
27-Feb-55 POL 0-CAN 8
01-Mar-58 POL 1-CAN 14
05-Mar-59 POL 0-CAN 9
05-Mar-66 POL 0-CAN 6
16-Apr-86 POL 3-CAN 8
16-Apr-89 POL 0-CAN 11
Totals: 9-0-0-9-6-71

02-Feb-31 POL 1-TCH 4
08-Feb-31 POL 0-TCH 0
21-Feb-33 POL 0-TCH 1
25-Feb-37 POL 0-TCH 1
19-Feb-47 POL 0-TCH 12
05-Mar-55 POL 2-TCH 17
05-Mar-57 POL 3-TCH 12
03-Mar-58 POL 1-TCH 7
06-Mar-59 POL 1-TCH 13
06-Mar-66 POL 1-TCH 6
14-Mar-70 POL 3-TCH 6
22-Mar-70 POL 2-TCH 10
31-Mar-73 POL 1-TCH 14
08-Apr-73 POL 1-TCH 4
05-Apr-74 POL 0-TCH 8
13-Apr-74 POL 3-TCH 12
03-Apr-75 POL 0-TCH 5
12-Apr-75 POL 2-TCH 8
09-Apr-76 POL 0-TCH 12
12-Apr-86 POL 2-TCH 1
23-Apr-86 POL 1-TCH 8
18-Apr-89 POL 0-TCH 15
Totals: 22-1-1-20-24-176

02-Mar-57 POL 2-GDR 6
09-Mar-59 POL 1-GDR 5
09-Mar-66 POL 0-GDR 4
21-Mar-70 POL 2-GDR 2
30-Mar-70 POL 2-GDR 5
11-Apr-74 POL 3-GDR 5
19-Apr-74 POL 3-GDR 3
11-Apr-76 POL 6-GDR 4
20-Apr-76 POL 5-GDR 4
Totals: 9-2-2-5-24-38

03-Mar-55 POL 6-FIN 3
24-Feb-57 POL 3-FIN 5
05-Mar-58 POL 2-FIN 2
11-Mar-66 POL 3-FIN 6
15-Mar-70 POL 1-FIN 9
24-Mar-70 POL 0-FIN 4
04-Apr-73 POL 0-FIN 5
12-Apr-73 POL 1-FIN 1
09-Apr-74 POL 2-FIN 2
17-Apr-74 POL 2-FIN 6
07-Apr-75 POL 2-FIN 5
16-Apr-75 POL 1-FIN 4
17-Apr-76 POL 3-FIN 3
22-Apr-76 POL 5-FIN 5
20-Apr-79 POL 3-FIN 4
26-Apr-79 POL 2-FIN 4
18-Apr-86 POL 2-FIN 4
21-Apr-89 POL 2-FIN 7
28-Apr-89 POL 0-FIN 4
29-Apr-92 POL 2-FIN 11
29-Apr-02 POL 0-FIN 8
Totals: 21-1-5-15-42-102

03-Feb-31 POL 2-FRA 1 (OT)
19-Jan-35 POL 2-FRA 3
19-Feb-37 POL 7-FRA 1
06-May-92 POL 1-FRA 3
Totals: 4-2-0-2-12-8

02-Feb-30 POL 1-GER 4
19-Feb-33 POL 0-GER 2
20-Jan-35 POL 3-GER 1
27-Jan-35 POL 1-GER 5
12-Feb-39 POL 0-GER 4
04-May-92 POL 1-GER 11
Totals: 6-1-0-5-6-27

21-Feb-37 POL 0-GBR 11
18-Feb-38 POL 1-GBR 7
Totals: 2-0-0-2-1-18

24-Feb-33 POL 1-HUN 1
25-Jan-35 POL 1-HUN 1
20-Feb-37 POL 4-HUN 0
14-Feb-38 POL 3-HUN 0
08-Feb-39 POL 5-HUN 3
10-Feb-39 POL 3-HUN 0
Totals: 6-4-2-0-17-5

21-Jan-35 POL 1-ITA 1
14-Mar-59 POL 2-ITA 5
01-May-92 POL 5-ITA 7
02-May-02 POL 5-ITA 1
Totals: 4-1-1-2-13-14

01-Feb-30 POL 5-JPN 0
27-Feb-57 POL 8-JPN 3
05-May-02 POL 5-JPN 2
Totals: 3-3-0-0-18-5

12-Feb-38 POL 8-LTU 1
Totals: 1-1-0-0-8-1

04-Feb-39 POL 9-NED 0
Totals: 1-1-0-0-9-0

09-Mar-58 POL 3-NOR 8
11-Mar-59 POL 3-NOR 4
Totals: 2-0-0-2-6-12

13-Feb-38 POL 3-ROM 0
16-Feb-47 POL 6-ROM 0
Totals: 2-2-0-0-9-0

27-Apr-02 POL 0-SVK 7
Totals: 1-0-0-1-0-7

03-May-02 POL 2-SLO 4
Totals: 1-0-0-1-2-4

28-Feb-55 POL 2-URS 8
28-Feb-57 POL 1-URS 10
06-Mar-58 POL 1-URS 10
03-Mar-66 POL 1-URS 8
17-Mar-70 POL 0-URS 7
25-Mar-70 POL 0-URS 11
03-Apr-73 POL 3-URS 9
11-Apr-73 POL 0-URS 20
08-Apr-74 POL 3-URS 8
16-Apr-74 POL 0-URS 17
06-Apr-75 POL 2-URS 13
15-Apr-75 POL 1-URS 15
08-Apr-76 POL 6-URS 4
14-Apr-79 POL 0-URS 7
15-Apr-86 POL 2-URS 7
19-Apr-89 POL 1-URS 12
Totals: 16-1-0-15-23-166

04-Feb-31 POL 2-SWE 0
17-Feb-37 POL 3-SWE 0
16-Feb-38 POL 0-SWE 1
18-Feb-47 POL 3-SWE 5
06-Mar-55 POL 0-SWE 9
25-Feb-57 POL 3-SWE 8
07-Mar-58 POL 2-SWE 12
08-Mar-66 POL 2-SWE 8
19-Mar-70 POL 0-SWE 11
28-Mar-70 POL 1-SWE 5
01-Apr-73 POL 2-SWE 11
09-Apr-73 POL 0-SWE 7
06-Apr-74 POL 5-SWE 0*
14-Apr-74 POL 1-SWE 3
04-Apr-75 POL 0-SWE 10
13-Apr-75 POL 0-SWE 13
19-Apr-76 POL 1-SWE 4
15-Apr-79 POL 5-SWE 6
19-Apr-86 POL 3-SWE 12
15-Apr-89 POL 1-SWE 5
28-Apr-92 POL 0-SWE 7
Totals: 21-3-0-18-34-137
*SWE won game 4-1 but SWE failed doping test resulting in an official score of POL 5-0

23-Feb-33 POL 1-SUI 3
23-Feb-37 POL 0-SUI 1
15-Feb-38 POL 1-SUI 7
07-Feb-39 POL 0-SUI 4
23-Feb-47 POL 3-SUI 9
01-Mar-55 POL 2-SUI 4
07-Mar-59 POL 3-SUI 8
13-Mar-59 POL 2-SUI 1
Totals: 8-1-0-7-12-37

30-Apr-02 POL 0-UKR 3
Totals: 1-0-0-1-0-3

07-Feb-31 POL 0-USA 1
22-Feb-33 POL 0-USA 4
09-Feb-39 POL 0-USA 4
21-Feb-47 POL 2-USA 3
04-Mar-55 POL 2-USA 6
28-Feb-58 POL 4-USA 12
12-Mar-66 POL 4-USA 6
09-Apr-75 POL 5-USA 3
18-Apr-75 POL 5-USA 2
14-Apr-76 POL 2-USA 4
18-Apr-79 POL 5-USA 5
24-Apr-79 POL 1-USA 5
13-Apr-86 POL 2-USA 7
25-Apr-86 POL 5-USA 7
25-Apr-89 POL 1-USA 6
26-Apr-89 POL 2-USA 11
03-May-92 POL 0-USA 5
Totals: 17-2-1-14-40-91

26-Feb-55 POL 5-FRG 4
10-Mar-59 POL 3-FRG 5
06-Apr-73 POL 2-FRG 4
14-Apr-73 POL 4-FRG 1
12-Apr-76 POL 3-FRG 5
24-Apr-76 POL 1-FRG 2
17-Apr-79 POL 3-FRG 3
22-Apr-79 POL 1-FRG 8
21-Apr-86 POL 1-FRG 4
27-Apr-86 POL 5-FRG 5
23-Apr-89 POL 5-FRG 3
30-Apr-89 POL 0-FRG 2
Totals: 12-3-2-7-33-46

**WORLD U20 CHAMPIONSHIPS**
23-Dec-76 POL 0-CAN 14
25-Dec-84 POL 1-CAN 12
30-Dec-86 POL 3-CAN 18
04-Jan-88 POL 1-CAN 9
28-Dec-89 POL 0-CAN 12
Totals: 5-0-0-5-5-65

01-Jan-77 POL 0-TCH 9
26-Dec-84 POL 2-TCH 6
01-Jan-87 POL 2-TCH 9
29-Dec-87 POL 1-TCH 6
29-Dec-89 POL 1-TCH 11
Totals: 5-0-0-5-6-41

28-Dec-76 POL 2-FIN 8
28-Dec-84 POL 2-FIN 11
02-Jan-87 POL 3-FIN 13
31-Dec-87 POL 1-FIN 9
03-Jan-90 POL 1-FIN 7
26-Dec-96 POL 0-FIN 7
Totals: 6-0-0-6-9-55

03-Jan-97 POL 0-GER 7
Totals: 1-0-0-1-0-7

04-Jan-90 POL 3-NOR 7
Totals: 1-0-0-1-3-7

25-Dec-76 POL 1-URS 10
23-Dec-84 POL 0-URS 10
26-Dec-86 POL 3-URS 7
03-Jan-88 POL 2-URS 7
26-Dec-89 POL 0-URS 11
27-Dec-96 POL 0-RUS 12
Totals vs. URS: 5-0-0-5-6-45
Totals vs. RUS: 1-0-0-1-0-12

29-Dec-96 POL 4-SVK 7
Totals: 1-0-0-1-4-7

29-Dec-76 POL 5-SWE 6
29-Dec-84 POL 0-SWE 11
27-Dec-86 POL 0-SWE 15
28-Dec-87 POL 0-SWE 13
31-Dec-89 POL 0-SWE 14
30-Dec-96 POL 2-SWE 7
Totals: 6-0-0-6-7-66

04-Jan-87 POL 8-SUI 3
02-Jan-97 POL 1-SUI 6
Totals: 2-1-0-1-9-9

26-Dec-76 POL 2-USA 2
31-Dec-84 POL 2-USA 6
29-Dec-86 POL 2-USA 15
26-Dec-87 POL 4-USA 3
01-Jan-90 POL 2 USA 3
Totals: 5-1-1-3-12-29

02-Jan-77 POL 2-FRG 9
01-Jan-85 POL 3-FRG 3
01-Jan-88 POL 3-FRG 6
Totals: 3-0-1-2-8-18

# ROMANIA (ROU-ROM/RUM)

Totals=GP-W-T-L-GF-GA

**OLYMPICS, MEN**

**Date Score**
05-Feb-64 RUM 5-AUT 2
07-Feb-68 RUM 3-AUT 2
09-Feb-76 ROM 4-AUT 3
Totals: 3-3-0-0-12-7

11-Feb-76 ROM 9-BUL 4
Totals: 1-1-0-0-9-4

16-Feb-80 ROM 2-TCH 7
Totals: 1-0-0-1-2-7

09-Feb-68 RUM 7-FRA 3
Totals: 1-1-0-0-7-3

08-Feb-64 RUM 8-HUN 3
Totals: 1-1-0-0-8-3

07-Feb-64 RUM 6-ITA 2
Totals: 1-1-0-0-6-2

31-Jan-64 RUM 4-JPN 6
12-Feb-68 RUM 4-JPN 5
05-Feb-76 ROM 3-JPN 1
Totals: 3-1-0-2-11-12

06-Feb-64 RUM 2-NOR 4
14-Feb-68 RUM 3-NOR 4
20-Feb-80 ROM 3-NOR 3
Totals: 3-0-1-2-8-11

30-Jan-64 RUM 1-POL 6
Totals: 1-0-0-1-1-6

14-Feb-80 ROM 0-SWE 8
Totals: 1-0-0-1-0-8

13-Feb-76 ROM 4-SUI 3
Totals: 1-1-0-0-4-3

18-Feb-80 ROM 2-USA 7
Totals: 1-0-0-1-2-7

12-Feb-80 ROM 6-FRG 4
Totals: 1-1-0-0-6-4

02-Feb-64 RUM 5-YUG 5
16-Feb-68 RUM 5-YUG 9
07-Feb-76 ROM 3-YUG 4
Totals: 3-0-1-2-13-18

**WORLD CHAMPIONSHIPS, MEN**
03-Feb-31 ROM 0-AUT 7
20-Feb-33 ROM 1-AUT 7
10-Feb-34 ROM 1-AUT 3
21-Jan-35 ROM 1-AUT 2
21-Feb-47 ROM 1-AUT 12
Totals: 5-0-0-5-4-31

24-Feb-33 ROM 3-BEL 2
04-Feb-34 ROM 3-BEL 2
19-Jan-35 ROM 2-BEL 1
22-Feb-47 ROM 6-BEL 4
Totals: 4-4-0-0-14-9

01-May-77 ROM 2-CAN 7
Totals: 1-0-0-1-2-7

18-Feb-33 ROM 0-TCH 8
20-Jan-35 ROM 2-TCH 4
15-Feb-47 ROM 1-TCH 23
24-Apr-77 ROM 1-TCH 13
Totals: 4-0-0-4-4-48

29-Apr-77 ROM 2-FIN 4
03-May-77 ROM 1-FIN 14
Totals: 2-0-0-2-3-18

04-Feb-31 ROM 1-FRA 7
03-Feb-34 ROM 1-FRA 4
Totals: 2-0-0-2-2-11

25-Jan-35 ROM 0-GER 3
18-Feb-37 ROM 2-GER 4
Totals: 2-0-0-2-2-7

06-Feb-31 ROM 0-GBR 11
11-Feb-34 ROM 1-GBR 2
19-Feb-37 ROM 0-GBR 11
Totals: 3-0-0-3-1-24

05-Feb-31 ROM 1-HUN 9
17-Feb-37 ROM 1-HUN 4
15-Feb-38 ROM 1-HUN 3
Totals: 3-0-0-3-3-16

19-Feb-33 ROM 0-ITA 2
09-Feb-34 ROM 0-ITA 3
Totals: 2-0-0-2-0-5

25-Feb-33 ROM 1-LAT 0
23-Jan-35 ROM 3-LAT 2
Totals: 2-2-0-0-4-2

11-Feb-38 ROM 0-LTU 1
Totals: 1-0-0-1-0-1

24-Jan-35 ROM 6-NED 0
Totals: 1-1-0-0-6-0

13-Feb-38 ROM 0-POL 3
16-Feb-47 ROM 0-POL 6
Totals: 2-0-0-2-0-9

25-Apr-77 ROM 1-URS 18
Totals: 1-0-0-1-1-18

19-Feb-47 ROM 3-SWE 15
21-Apr-77 ROM 1-SWE 8
Totals: 2-0-0-2-4-23

05-Feb-34 ROM 2-SUI 7
12-Feb-38 ROM 1-SUI 8
17-Feb-47 ROM 3-SUI 13
Totals: 3-0-0-3-6-28

01-Feb-31 ROM 0-USA 15
20-Feb-47 ROM 3-USA 15
22-Apr-77 ROM 2-USA 7
05-May-77 ROM 5-USA 4
Totals: 4-1-0-3-10-41

27-Apr-77 ROM 3-FRG 6
07-May-77 ROM 2-FRG 3
Totals: 2-0-0-2-5-9

# RUSSIA (RUS—URS)

Totals=GP-W-T-L-GF-GA

**OLYMPICS, MEN**

**Date Score**
15-Feb-88 URS 8-AUT 1
16-Feb-94 RUS 9-AUT 1
Totals: 2-2-0-0-17-2

18-Feb-98 RUS 4-BLR 1
15-Feb-02 RUS 6-BLR 4
23-Feb-02 RUS 7-BLR 2
Totals: 3-3-0-0-17-7

04-Feb-56 URS 2-CAN 0
28-Feb-60 URS 5-CAN 8
08-Feb-64 URS 3-CAN 2
17-Feb-68 URS 5-CAN 0
20-Feb-80 URS 6-CAN 4
17-Feb-84 URS 4-CAN 0
24-Feb-88 URS 5-CAN 0
16-Feb-92 RUS 5-CAN 4
23-Feb-92 RUS 3-CAN 1
22-Feb-06 RUS 2-CAN 0
24-Feb-10 RUS 3-CAN 7
Totals: 11-9-0-2-43-26

02-Feb-56 URS 7-TCH 4
22-Feb-60 URS 8-TCH 5
31-Jan-64 URS 7-TCH 5
15-Feb-68 URS 4-TCH 5
13-Feb-72 URS 5-TCH 2
14-Feb-76 URS 4-TCH 3
19-Feb-84 URS 2-TCH 0
21-Feb-88 URS 6-TCH 1
12-Feb-92 RUS 3-TCH 4
20-Feb-94 RUS 4-CZE 3
16-Feb-98 RUS 2-CZE 1
22-Feb-98 RUS 0-CZE 1
20-Feb-02 RUS 1-CZE 0
25-Feb-06 RUS 0-CZE 3
21-Feb-10 RUS 4-CZE 2
Totals URS vs. TCH: 8-7-0-1-43-25
Totals RUS vs. TCH: 1-0-0-1-3-4
Totals RUS vs. CZE: 6-4-0-2-11-10

07-Feb-68 URS 9-GDR 0
Totals: 1-1-0-0-9-0

20-Feb-60 URS 8-FIN 4
04-Feb-64 URS 10-FIN 0
06-Feb-68 URS 8-FIN 0
05-Feb-72 URS 9-FIN 3
12-Feb-76 URS 7 FIN 2
18-Feb-80 URS 4-FIN 2
28-Feb-88 URS 1-FIN 2
19-Feb-92 RUS 6-FIN 1
14-Feb-94 RUS 0-FIN 5
26-Feb-94 RUS 0-FIN 4
15-Feb-98 RUS 4-FIN 3
20-Feb-98 RUS 7-FIN 4
18-Feb-02 RUS 1-FIN 3
24-Feb-06 RUS 0-FIN 4
Totals: 14-9-0-5-65-37

14-Feb-92 RUS 8-FRA 0
Totals: 1-1-0-0-8-0

31-Jan-56 URS 8-GER 0
19-Feb-60 URS 8-GER 0
25-Feb-60 URS 7-GER 1
05-Feb-64 URS 10-GER 0
18-Feb-94 RUS 2-GER 4
Totals: 5-4-0-1-35-5

09-Feb-84 URS 5-ITA 1
Totals: 1-1-0-0-5-1

12-Feb-80 URS 16-JPN 0
Totals: 1-1-0-0-16-0

13-Feb-98 RUS 9-KAZ 2
18-Feb-06 RUS 1-KAZ 0
Totals: 2-2-0-0-10-2

19-Feb-06 RUS 9-LAT 2
16-Feb-10 RUS 8-LAT 2
Totals: 2-2-0-0-17-4

14-Feb-80 URS 17-NED 4
Totals: 1-1-0-0-17-4

13-Feb-88 URS 5-NOR 0
10-Feb-92 RUS 8-NOR 1
12-Feb-94 RUS 5-NOR 1
Totals: 3-3-0-0-18-2

10-Feb-72 URS 9-POL 3
08-Feb-76 URS 16-POL 1
16-Feb-80 URS 8-POL 1
07-Feb-84 URS 12-POL 1
Totals: 4-4-0-0-45-6

23-Feb-94 RUS 3-SVK 2 (OT)
15-Feb-06 RUS 3-SVK 5
18-Feb-10 RUS 1-SVK 2 (5:00 OT/GWS)
Totals: 3-1-0-2-7-9

27-Jan-56 URS 5-SWE 1
30-Jan-56 URS 4-SWE 1
24-Feb-60 URS 2-SWE 2
07-Feb-64 URS 4-SWE 2
13-Feb-68 URS 3-SWE 2
07-Feb-72 URS 3-SWE 3
24-Feb-80 URS 9-SWE 2
15-Feb-84 URS 10-SWE 1
26-Feb-88 URS 7-SWE 1
25-Feb-94 RUS 3-SWE 4
16-Feb-06 RUS 5-SWE 0
Totals: 11-8-2-1-55-19

29-Jan-56 URS 10-SUI 3
01-Feb-64 URS 15-SUI 0
08-Feb-92 RUS 8-SUI 1
Totals: 3-3-0-0-33-4

03-Feb-56 URS 4-USA 0
27-Feb-60 URS 2-USA 3
29-Jan-64 URS 5-USA 1
09-Feb-68 URS 10-USA 2
09-Feb-72 URS 7-USA 2
06-Feb-76 URS 6-USA 2
22-Feb-80 URS 3-USA 4
17-Feb-88 URS 7-USA 5
21-Feb-92 RUS 5-USA 2
16-Feb-02 RUS 2-USA 2
22-Feb-02 RUS 2-USA 3
21-Feb-06 RUS 5-USA 4
Totals: 12-8-1-3-58-30

11-Feb-68 URS 9-FRG 1
10-Feb-76 URS 7-FRG 3
13-Feb-84 URS 6-FRG 1
19-Feb-88 URS 6-FRG 3
Totals: 4-4-0-0-28-8

11-Feb-84 URS 9-YUG 1
Totals: 1-1-0-0-9-1

**WORLD CHAMPIONSHIPS, MEN**

27-Feb-57 URS 22-AUT 1
19-Apr-93 RUS 4-AUT 2
29-Apr-94 RUS 4-AUT 1
28-Apr-96 RUS 6-AUT 0
28-Apr-02 RUS 6-AUT 3
30-Apr-05 RUS 4 -AUT 2
Totals: 6-6-0-0-46-9

02-May-99 RUS 2-BLR 2
07-May-00 RUS 0-BLR 1
04-May-05 RUS 2-BLR 0
08-May-06 RUS 3-BLR 2
09-May-08 RUS 4-BLR 3 (5:00 OT/GWS)
06-May-09 RUS 4-BLR 3
13-May-10 RUS 3-BLR 1
Totals: 7-5-1-1-18-12

07-Mar-54 URS 7-CAN 2
06-Mar-55 URS 0-CAN 5
09-Mar-58 URS 2-CAN 4
11-Mar-59 URS 1-CAN 3
12-Mar-61 URS 1-CAN 5
16-Mar-63 URS 4-CAN 2
14-Mar-65 URS 4-CAN 1
11-Mar-66 URS 3-CAN 0
27-Mar-67 URS 2-CAN 1
18-Mar-69 URS 7-CAN 1
30-Mar-69 URS 4-CAN 2
24-Apr-77 URS 11-CAN 1
06-May-77 URS 8-CAN 1
08-May-78 URS 4-CAN 2
10-May-78 URS 5-CAN 1
19-Apr-79 URS 5-CAN 2
25-Apr-79 URS 9-CAN 2
15-Apr-81 URS 8-CAN 2
22-Apr-81 URS 4-CAN 4
24-Apr-82 URS 4-CAN 3
25-Apr-82 URS 6-CAN 4
19-Apr-83 URS 8-CAN 2
02-May-83 URS 8-CAN 2
25-Apr-85 URS 9-CAN 1
01-May-85 URS 1-CAN 3
18-Apr-86 URS 4-CAN 0
24-Apr-86 URS 7-CAN 4
24-Apr-87 URS 3-CAN 2
29-Apr-87 URS 0-CAN 0
22-Apr-89 URS 4-CAN 3
29-Apr-89 URS 5-CAN 3
26-Apr-90 URS 3-CAN 3
30-Apr-90 URS 7-CAN 1
25-Apr-91 URS 5-CAN 3
02-May-91 URS 3-CAN 3
04-May-92 RUS 6-CAN 4
25-Apr-93 RUS 1-CAN 3
30-Apr-93 RUS 7-CAN 4
02-May-94 RUS 1-CAN 3
30-Apr-95 RUS 5-CAN 4
26-Apr-96 RUS 6-CAN 4
03-May-96 RUS 2-CAN 3 (10:00 OT/GWS)
09-May-97 RUS 1-CAN 2
02-May-01 RUS 1-CAN 5
05-May-03 RUS 2-CAN 5
14-May-05 RUS 3-CAN 4
18-May-08 RUS 5-CAN 4 (OT)
10-May-09 RUS 2-CAN 1
20-May-10 RUS 5-CAN 2
12-May-11 RUS 2-CAN 1
Totals: 50-34-4-12-215-127

02-Mar-54 URS 5-TCH 2
27-Feb-55 URS 4-TCH 0
02-Mar-57 URS 2-TCH 2
04-Mar-58 URS 4-TCH 4
12-Mar-59 URS 4-TCH 3
07-Mar-61 URS 4-TCH 6
14-Mar-63 URS 3-TCH 1
13-Mar-65 URS 3-TCH 1
13-Mar-66 URS 7-TCH 1
29-Mar-67 URS 4-TCH 2
21-Mar-69 URS 0-TCH 2
28-Mar-69 URS 3-TCH 4
18-Mar-70 URS 3-TCH 1
27-Mar-70 URS 5-TCH 1
24-Mar-71 URS 3-TCH 3
01-Apr-71 URS 2-TCH 5
12-Apr-72 URS 3-TCH 3
20-Apr-72 URS 2-TCH 3
05-Apr-73 URS 3-TCH 2
13-Apr-73 URS 4-TCH 2
10-Apr-74 URS 2-TCH 7
18-Apr-74 URS 3-TCH 1
08-Apr-75 URS 5-TCH 2
17-Apr-75 URS 4-TCH 1
17-Apr-76 URS 2-TCH 3
25-Apr-76 URS 3-TCH 3
28-Apr-77 URS 6-TCH 1
04-May-77 URS 3-TCH 4
06-May-78 URS 4-TCH 6
14-May-78 URS 3-TCH 1
21-Apr-79 URS 11-TCH 1
27-Apr-79 URS 6-TCH 1
20-Apr-81 URS 8-TCH 3
26-Apr-81 URS 1-TCH 1
18-Apr-82 URS 5-TCH 3
29-Apr-82 URS 0-TCH 0
23-Apr-83 URS 5-TCH 1
30-Apr-83 URS 1-TCH 1
27-Apr-85 URS 5-TCH 1
29-Apr-85 URS 1-TCH 2
20-Apr-86 URS 4-TCH 2
21-Apr-87 URS 6-TCH 1
03-May-87 URS 2-TCH 1
21-Apr-89 URS 4-TCH 2
27-Apr-89 URS 1-TCH 0
24-Apr-90 URS 4-TCH 1
02-May-90 URS 5-TCH 0
26-Apr-91 URS 6-TCH 2
01-May-92 RUS 4-TCH 2
03-May-95 RUS 0-CZE 2
01-May-97 RUS 3-CZE 2
10-May-97 RUS 3-CZE 4
10-May-98 RUS 2-CZE 2
07-May-99 RUS 6-CZE 1
05-May-01 RUS 3-CZE 4
07-May-02 RUS 3-CZE 1
07-May-03 RUS 0-CZE 3
08-May-05 RUS 2-CZE 1
18-May-06 RUS 3-CZE 4 (OT)
09-May-07 RUS 4-CZE 0
04-May-08 RUS 5-CZE 4 (OT)
23-May-10 RUS 1-CZE 2
08-May-11 RUS 2-CZE 3
15-May-11 RUS 4-CZE 7
13-May-12 RUS 2-CZE 0
Totals URS vs. TCH:
48-30-8-10-178-100
Totals RUS vs. TCH:
1-1-0-0-4-2
Totals RUS vs. CZE:
16-7-1-8-43-40

27-Apr-03 RUS 6-DEN 1
25-Apr-04 RUS 6-DEN 2
27-Apr-07 RUS 9-DEN 1
06-May-08 RUS 4-DEN 1
16-May-10 RUS 6-DEN 1
05-May-11 RUS 4-DEN 3
10-May-12 RUS 3-DEN 1
Totals: 7-7-0-0-38-10

04-Mar-57 URS 12-GDR 0
05-Mar-59 URS 6-GDR 1
09-Mar-61 URS 9-GDR 1
12-Mar-63 URS 12-GDR 0
07-Mar-65 URS 8-GDR 0
06-Mar-66 URS 10-GDR 0
21-Mar-67 URS 12-GDR 0
15-Mar-70 URS 12-GDR 1
24-Mar-70 URS 7-GDR 1
05-Apr-74 URS 5-GDR 0
13-Apr-74 URS 10-GDR 3
09-Apr-76 URS 4-GDR 0
27-Apr-78 URS 7-GDR 4
16-Apr-83 URS 3-GDR 0
20-Apr-85 URS 6-GDR 0
Totals: 15-15-0-0-123-11

26-Feb-54 URS 7-FIN 1
25-Feb-55 URS 10-FIN 2
25-Feb-57 URS 11-FIN 1
02-Mar-58 URS 10-FIN 0
14-Mar-59 URS 6-FIN 1
05-Mar-61 URS 7-FIN 3
07-Mar-63 URS 6-FIN 1
04-Mar-65 URS 8-FIN 4
08-Mar-66 URS 13-FIN 2
18-Mar-67 URS 8-FIN 2
19-Mar-69 URS 6-FIN 1
26-Mar-69 URS 7-FIN 3
14-Mar-70 URS 2-FIN 1
22-Mar-70 URS 16-FIN 1
21-Mar-71 URS 8-FIN 1
29-Mar-71 URS 10-FIN 1
09-Apr-72 URS 10-FIN 2
17-Apr-72 URS 7-FIN 2
02-Apr-73 URS 8-FIN 2
10-Apr-73 URS 9-FIN 1
07-Apr-74 URS 7-FIN 1
15-Apr-74 URS 6-FIN 1
05-Apr-75 URS 8-FIN 4
14-Apr-75 URS 5-FIN 2
11-Apr-76 URS 8-FIN 1
22-Apr-77 URS 11-FIN 6
30-Apr-78 URS 6-FIN 3
13-Apr-81 URS 7-FIN 1
19-Apr-82 URS 8-FIN 1
17-Apr-83 URS 3-FIN 0
18-Apr-85 URS 5-FIN 1
13-Apr-86 URS 4-FIN 1
26-Apr-86 URS 8-FIN 0
23-Apr-87 URS 4-FIN 0
18-Apr-89 URS 4-FIN 1
20-Apr-90 URS 6-FIN 1
22-Apr-91 URS 3-FIN 0
03-May-97 RUS 4-FIN 7
06-May-98 RUS 4-FIN 2
06-May-99 RUS 3-FIN 3
04-May-02 RUS 0-FIN 1
09-May-02 RUS 3-FIN 2 (10:00 OT/GWS)
03-May-04 RUS 0-FIN 4
12-May-05 RUS 4-FIN 3 (10:00 OT/GWS)
01-May-07 RUS 5-FIN 4
12-May-07 RUS 1-FIN 2 (OT)
16-May-08 RUS 4-FIN 0
18-May-10 RUS 5-FIN 0
09-May-11 RUS 2-FIN 3 (5:00 OT/GWS)
13-May-11 RUS 0-FIN 3
19-May-12 RUS 6-FIN 2
Totals: 51-44-1-6-313-92

03-May-92 RUS 8-FRA 0
26-Apr-95 RUS 3-FRA 1
30-Apr-97 RUS 5-FRA 4
29-Apr-00 RUS 8-FRA 1
26-Apr-09 RUS 7-FRA 2
Totals: 5-5-0-0-31-8

27-Apr-93 RUS 5-GER 1
30-Apr-94 RUS 6-GER 0
28-Apr-95 RUS 6-GER 3
21-Apr-96 RUS 2-GER 1
28-Apr-97 RUS 5-GER 1
08-May-01 RUS 3-GER 1
24-Apr-09 RUS 5-GER 0
15-May-10 RUS 3-GER 2
22-May-10 RUS 2-GER 1
29-Apr-11 RUS 0-GER 2
08-May-12 RUS 2-GER 0
Totals: 11-10-0-1-39-12

26-Apr-94 RUS 12-GBR 3
Totals: 1-1-0-0-12-3

15-Apr-82 URS 9-ITA 2
24-Apr-83 URS 11-ITA 1
18-Apr-93 RUS 2-ITA 2
27-Apr-94 RUS 7-ITA 0
23-Apr-95 RUS 4-ITA 2
01-May-96 RUS 5-ITA 2
28-Apr-01 RUS 7-ITA 0
04-May-07 RUS 3-ITA 0
02-May-08 RUS 7-ITA 1
14-May-12 RUS 4-ITA 0
Totals: 10-9-1-0-59-10

24-Feb-57 URS 16-JPN 0
28-Apr-04 RUS 6-JPN 1
Totals: 2-2-0-0-22-1

02-May-98 RUS 8-KAZ 4
09-May-05 RUS 3-KAZ 1
06-May-06 RUS 10-KAZ 1
11-May-10 RUS 4-KAZ 1
Totals: 4-4-0-0-25-7

04-May-98 RUS 7-LAT 5
05-May-00 RUS 2-LAT 3
04-May-03 RUS 1-LAT 2
03-May-09 RUS 6-LAT 1
05-May-12 RUS 5-LAT 2
Totals: 5-3-0-2-21-13

12-Apr-81 URS 10-NED 1
Totals: 1-1-0-0-10-1

27-Feb-54 URS 7-NOR 0
01-Mar-58 URS 10-NOR 2
06-Mar-59 URS 13-NOR 1
05-Mar-65 URS 14-NOR 2
16-Apr-90 URS 9-NOR 1
30-Apr-92 RUS 3-NOR 2
29-Apr-01 RUS 4-NOR 0
06-May-12 RUS 4-NOR 2
17-May-12 RUS 5-NOR 2
Totals: 9-9-0-0-69-12

28-Feb-55 URS 8-POL 2
28-Feb-57 URS 10-POL 1
06-Mar-58 URS 10-POL 1
03-Mar-66 URS 8-POL 1
17-Mar-70 URS 7-POL 0
25-Mar-70 URS 11-POL 0
03-Apr-73 URS 9-POL 3
11-Apr-73 URS 20-POL 0
08-Apr-74 URS 8-POL 3
16-Apr-74 URS 17-POL 0
06-Apr-75 URS 13-POL 2
15-Apr-75 URS 15-POL 1
08-Apr-76 URS 4-POL 6
14-Apr-79 URS 7-POL 0
15-Apr-86 URS 7-POL 2
19-Apr-89 URS 12-POL 1
Totals: 16-15-0-1-166-23

25-Apr-77 URS 18-ROM 1
Totals: 1-1-0-0-18-1

22-Apr-96 RUS 6-SVK 2
27-Apr-97 RUS 2-SVK 2
09-May-98 RUS 6-SVK 1
10-May-99 RUS 2-SVK 2
06-May-02 RUS 4-SVK 6
11-May-02 RUS 3-SVK 4
30-Apr-04 RUS 0-SVK 2
02-May-05 RUS 3-SVK 3
10-May-06 RUS 4-SVK 3
09-May-10 RUS 3-SVK 1
03-May-11 RUS 4-SVK 3
20-May-12 RUS 5-SVK 2
Totals: 12-6-3-3-42-31

26-Apr-02 RUS 8-SLO 1
01-May-11 RUS 6-SLO 4
Totals: 2-2-0-0-14-5

05-Mar-54 URS 1-SWE 1
26-Feb-55 URS 2-SWE 1
05-Mar-57 URS 4-SWE 4
08-Mar-58 URS 4-SWE 3
15-Mar-59 URS 4-SWE 2
04-Mar-61 URS 6-SWE 2
08-Mar-63 URS 1-SWE 2
10-Mar-65 URS 5-SWE 3
10-Mar-66 URS 3-SWE 3
25-Mar-67 URS 9-SWE 1
16-Mar-69 URS 4-SWE 2
24-Mar-69 URS 3-SWE 2
20-Mar-70 URS 2-SWE 4
30-Mar-70 URS 3-SWE 1
26-Mar-71 URS 8-SWE 0
03-Apr-71 URS 6-SWE 3
14-Apr-72 URS 11-SWE 2
22-Apr-72 URS 3-SWE 3
07-Apr-73 URS 6-SWE 1
15-Apr-73 URS 6-SWE 4
12-Apr-74 URS 3-SWE 1
20-Apr-74 URS 3-SWE 1
10-Apr-75 URS 4-SWE 1
19-Apr-75 URS 13-SWE 4
13-Apr-76 URS 6-SWE 1
21-Apr-76 URS 3-SWE 4
02-May-77 URS 1-SWE 5
08-May-77 URS 1-SWE 3
04-May-78 URS 6-SWE 1
12-May-78 URS 7-SWE 1
17-Apr-79 URS 9-SWE 3
23-Apr-79 URS 11-SWE 3
18-Apr-81 URS 4-SWE 1
24-Apr-81 URS 13-SWE 1
16-Apr-82 URS 7-SWE 3
27-Apr-82 URS 4-SWE 0
26-Apr-83 URS 4-SWE 0
28-Apr-83 URS 4-SWE 0
23-Apr-85 URS 6-SWE 2
12-Apr-86 URS 4-SWE 2
28-Apr-86 URS 3-SWE 2
26-Apr-87 URS 4-SWE 2
01-May-87 URS 2-SWE 2
24-Apr-89 URS 3-SWE 2
01-May-89 URS 5-SWE 1
22-Apr-90 URS 1-SWE 3
28-Apr-90 URS 3-SWE 0
28-Apr-91 URS 5-SWE 5
04-May-91 URS 1-SWE 2
06-May-92 RUS 0-SWE 2
24-Apr-93 RUS 2-SWE 5
02-May-93 RUS 3-SWE 1
05-May-97 RUS 4-SWE 1
09-May-99 RUS 1-SWE 4
09-May-00 RUS 4-SWE 2
10-May-01 RUS 3-SWE 4 (OT)
30-Apr-02 RUS 0-SWE 2
02-May-03 RUS 2-SWE 4
27-Apr-04 RUS 2-SWE 3
15-May-05 RUS 6-SWE 3
15-May-06 RUS 3-SWE 3
07-May-07 RUS 4-SWE 2
13-May-07 RUS 3-SWE 1
10-May-08 RUS 3-SWE 2

30-Apr-09 RUS 6-SWE 5 (OT)
11-May-12 RUS 7-SWE 3
Totals: 66-45-7-14-284-147

03-Mar-54 URS 4-SUI 2
04-Mar-55 URS 7-SUI 2
10-Apr-72 URS 10-SUI 2
18-Apr-72 URS 14-SUI 0
17-Apr-87 URS 13-SUI 5
19-Apr-91 URS 3-SUI 1
28-Apr-92 RUS 2-SUI 2
22-Apr-93 RUS 6-SUI 0
25-Apr-95 RUS 8-SUI 0
07-May-98 RUS 2-SUI 4
03-May-00 RUS 2-SUI 3
06-May-01 RUS 2-SUI 1
26-Apr-03 RUS 5-SUI 2
06-May-05 RUS 3-SUI 3
14-May-06 RUS 6-SUI 3
06-May-07 RUS 6-SUI 3
12-May-08 RUS 5-SUI 3
14-May-08 RUS 6-SUI 0
28-Apr-09 RUS 4-SUI 2
Totals: 19-15-2-2-108-38

04-May-99 RUS 4-UKR 1
03-May-02 RUS 3-UKR 3
11-May-06 RUS 6-UKR 0
29-Apr-07 RUS 8-UKR 1
Totals: 4-3-1-0-21-5

02-Mar-55 URS 3-USA 0
07-Mar-58 URS 4-USA 1
07-Mar-59 URS 5-USA 3
09-Mar-59 URS 5-USA 1
02-Mar-61 URS 13-USA 2
15-Mar-63 URS 9-USA 0
11-Mar-65 URS 9-USA 2
05-Mar-66 URS 11-USA 0
19-Mar-67 URS 7-USA 2
15-Mar-69 URS 17-USA 2
23-Mar-69 URS 8-USA 4
22-Mar-71 URS 10-USA 2
30-Mar-71 URS 7-USA 5
03-Apr-75 URS 10-USA 5
12-Apr-75 URS 13-USA 1
19-Apr-76 URS 5-USA 2
23-Apr-76 URS 7-USA 1
30-Apr-77 URS 8-USA 2
26-Apr-78 URS 9-USA 5
21-Apr-82 URS 8-USA 4
17-Apr-85 URS 11-USA 1
03-May-85 URS 10-USA 3
22-Apr-86 URS 5-USA 1
20-Apr-87 URS 11-USA 2
15-Apr-89 URS 4-USA 2
19-Apr-90 URS 10-USA 1
23-Apr-91 URS 12-USA 2
30-Apr-91 URS 6-USA 4
04-May-94 RUS 1-USA 3
25-Apr-96 RUS 3-USA 1
04-May-96 RUS 3-USA 4 (OT)
06-May-97 RUS 1-USA 1
01-May-00 RUS 0-USA 3
29-Apr-03 RUS 3-USA 2
01-May-04 RUS 2-USA 3
02-May-09 RUS 4-USA 1
08-May-09 RUS 3-USA 2
Totals: 37-32-1-4-257-80

01-Mar-54 URS 6-FRG 2
03-Mar-55 URS 5-FRG 1
11-Mar-61 URS 11-FRG 1
10-Mar-63 URS 15-FRG 3
23-Mar-67 URS 16-FRG 1
19-Mar-71 URS 11-FRG 2
27-Mar-71 URS 12-FRG 1
07-Apr-72 URS 11-FRG 2
15-Apr-72 URS 7-FRG 0
31-Mar-73 URS 17-FRG 1
08-Apr-73 URS 18-FRG 2
15-Apr-76 URS 8-FRG 2
21-Apr-77 URS 10-FRG 0
01-May-78 URS 10-FRG 2
15-Apr-79 URS 3-FRG 2
22-Apr-82 URS 7-FRG 0
20-Apr-83 URS 6-FRG 0
21-Apr-85 URS 10-FRG 2
16-Apr-86 URS 4-FRG 1
18-Apr-87 URS 7-FRG 0
16-Apr-89 URS 5-FRG 1
17-Apr-90 URS 5-FRG 2
20-Apr-91 URS 7-FRG 3
Totals: 23-23-0-0-211-31

**WORLD U20 CHAMPIONSHIPS**

27-Dec-80 URS 19-AUT 1
29-Dec-03 RUS 3-AUT 1
26-Dec-09 RUS 6-AUT 2
Totals: 3-3-0-0-28-4

29-Dec-98 RUS 10-BLR 0
27-Dec-00 RUS 12-BLR 1
29-Dec-02 RUS 5-BLR 1
28-Dec-04 RUS 7-BLR 2
29-Dec-06 RUS 6-BLR 1
Totals: 5-5-0-0-40-5

02-Jan-77 URS 6-CAN 4
28-Dec-77 URS 3-CAN 2
28-Dec-79 URS 8-CAN 5
28-Dec-80 URS 7-CAN 3
26-Dec-81 URS 0-CAN 7
30-Dec-82 URS 7-CAN 3
02-Jan-84 URS 3-CAN 3
29-Dec-84 URS 0-CAN 5
02-Jan-86 URS 4-CAN 1
04-Jan-87 URS 2-CAN 4*
01-Jan-88 URS 2-CAN 3
04-Jan-89 URS 7-CAN 2
01-Jan-90 URS 4-CAN 6
04-Jan-91 URS 2-CAN 3
04-Jan-92 RUS 7-CAN 2
29-Dec-92 RUS 1-CAN 9
29-Dec-93 RUS 3-CAN 3
02-Jan-95 RUS 5-CAN 8
03-Jan-96 RUS 3-CAN 4
03-Jan-97 RUS 2-CAN 3
31-Dec-97 RUS 2-CAN 1 (OT)
05-Jan-99 RUS 3-CAN 2 (OT)
03-Jan-00 RUS 3-CAN 2
29-Dec-00 RUS 3-CAN 1
29-Dec-01 RUS 2-CAN 5
04-Jan-02 RUS 5-CAN 4
05-Jan-03 RUS 3-CAN 2
04-Jan-05 RUS 1-CAN 6
05-Jan-06 RUS 0-CAN 5
05-Jan-07 RUS 2-CAN 4
03-Jan-09 RUS 5-CAN 6 (10:00 OT/GWS)
26-Dec-10 RUS 3-CAN 6
05-Jan-11 RUS 5-CAN 3
03-Jan-12 RUS 6-CAN 5
Totals: 34-16-2-16-119-132
*Game suspended because of brawl—score and stats not counted

23-Dec-76 URS 4-TCH 0
01-Jan-78 URS 6-TCH 1
30-Dec-78 URS 9-TCH 1
02-Jan-79 URS 2-TCH 2
01-Jan-80 URS 6-TCH 2
30-Dec-80 URS 5-TCH 1
23-Dec-81 URS 2-TCH 3
27-Dec-82 URS 4-TCH 3
31-Dec-83 URS 6-TCH 4
31-Dec-84 URS 1-TCH 3
01-Jan-86 URS 4-TCH 3
30-Dec-86 URS 3-TCH 5
26-Dec-87 URS 6-TCH 4
02-Jan-89 URS 3-TCH 5
02-Jan-90 URS 8-TCH 5
01-Jan-91 URS 5-TCH 3
01-Jan-92 RUS 2-TCH 5
30-Dec-92 RUS 1-CZE/SVK 1
26-Dec-93 RUS 5-CZE 1
27-Dec-94 RUS 4-CZE 3
26-Dec-95 RUS 3-CZE 5
04-Jan-96 RUS 4-CZE 1
04-Jan-97 RUS 4-CZE 1
01-Jan-98 RUS 5-CZE 1
04-Jan-00 RUS 0-CZE 1 (10:00 OT/GWS)
27-Dec-04 RUS 4-CZE 1
31-Dec-05 RUS 7-CZE 2
26-Dec-06 RUS 3-CZE 2
02-Jan-08 RUS 4-CZE 1
02-Jan-09 RUS 5-CZE 1
31-Dec-09 RUS 5-CZE 2
31-Dec-10 RUS 8-CZE 3
02-Jan-12 RUS 2-CZE 1
Totals URS vs. TCH: 16-11-1-4-74-45
Totals RUS vs. TCH: 2-0-1-1-3-6
Totals RUS vs. CZE: 15-13-0-2-63-26

01-Jan-77 URS 10-FIN 6
26-Dec-77 URS 10-FIN 4
31-Dec-78 URS 4-FIN 2
30-Dec-79 URS 2-FIN 1
31-Dec-80 URS 3-FIN 6
31-Dec-81 URS 3-FIN 6
02-Jan-83 URS 7-FIN 2
28-Dec-83 URS 3-FIN 1
01-Jan-85 URS 6-FIN 5
04-Jan-86 URS 4-FIN 3
29-Dec-86 URS 4-FIN 5
28-Dec-87 URS 6-FIN 2
01-Jan-89 URS 9-FIN 3
29-Dec-89 URS 3-FIN 2
03-Jan-91 URS 5-FIN 5
29-Dec-91 RUS 4-FIN 1
01-Jan-93 RUS 1-FIN 1
04-Jan-94 RUS 5-FIN 4
04-Jan-95 RUS 6-FIN 2
01-Jan-96 RUS 6-FIN 2
29-Dec-96 RUS 4-FIN 2
03-Jan-98 RUS 1-FIN 2
02-Jan-99 RUS 3-FIN 2
01-Jan-00 RUS 4-FIN 0
31-Dec-00 RUS 1-FIN 3
27-Dec-01 RUS 1-FIN 2
02-Jan-02 RUS 2-FIN 1 (OT)
03-Jan-03 RUS 4-FIN 1
02-Jan-04 RUS 3-FIN 4
31-Dec-06 RUS 5-FIN 0
26-Dec-07 RUS 1-FIN 4
28-Dec-08 RUS 5-FIN 2
28-Dec-09 RUS 2-FIN 0
04-Jan-10 RUS 3-FIN 4
02-Jan-11 RUS 4-FIN 3 (OT)
Totals: 35-24-2-9-144-93

26-Dec-01 RUS 5-FRA 1
Totals: 1-1-0-0-5-1

30-Dec-91 RUS 7-GER 0
27-Dec-92 RUS 4-GER 0
01-Jan-94 RUS 1-GER 0
30-Dec-94 RUS 8-GER 1
31-Dec-95 RUS 8-GER 2
Totals: 5-5-0-0-28-3

26-Dec-92 RUS 16-JPN 0
Totals: 1-1-0-0-16-0

25-Dec-97 RUS 12-KAZ 1
28-Dec-98 RUS 7-KAZ 0
25-Dec-99 RUS 14-KAZ 1
27-Dec-07 RUS 5-KAZ 4
Totals: 4-4-0-0-38-6

29-Dec-05 RUS 3-LAT 1
26-Dec-08 RUS 4-LAT 1
29-Dec-11 RUS 14-LAT 0
Totals: 3-3-0-0-21-2

27-Dec-78 URS 17-NOR 0
26-Dec-82 URS 10-NOR 1
30-Dec-88 URS 10-NOR 0
27-Dec-89 URS 12-NOR 2
28-Dec-90 URS 13-NOR 0
30-Dec-10 RUS 8-NOR 2
Totals: 6-6-0-0-70-5

25-Dec-76 URS 10-POL 1
23-Dec-84 URS 10-POL 0
26-Dec-86 URS 7-POL 3
03-Jan-88 URS 7-POL 2
26-Dec-89 URS 11-POL 0
27-Dec-96 RUS 12-POL 0
Totals: 6-6-0-0-57-6

27-Dec-95 RUS 3-SVK 3
26-Dec-96 RUS 4-SVK 3
30-Dec-97 RUS 4-SVK 0
04-Jan-99 RUS 3-SVK 2
05-Jan-01 RUS 4-SVK 3 (10:00 OT/GWS)
28-Dec-02 RUS 4-SVK 0
26-Dec-03 RUS 2-SVK 2
04-Jan-04 RUS 3-SVK 2
28-Dec-05 RUS 6-SVK 2
30-Dec-08 RUS 8-SVK 1
05-Jan-09 RUS 5-SVK 2
28-Dec-11 RUS 3-SVK 1
Totals: 12-10-2-0-49-21

26-Dec-76 URS 4-SWE 2
23-Dec-77 URS 3-SWE 6
31-Dec-77 URS 5-SWE 0
03-Jan-78 URS 5-SWE 2
03-Jan-79 URS 7-SWE 5
02-Jan-80 URS 2-SWE 1
02-Jan-81 URS 2-SWE 3
02-Jan-82 URS 7-SWE 2
04-Jan-83 URS 5-SWE 1
03-Jan-84 URS 8-SWE 2
28-Dec-84 URS 5-SWE 1
27-Dec-85 URS 6-SWE 1
01-Jan-87 URS 3-SWE 3
31-Dec-87 URS 4-SWE 2
29-Dec-88 URS 3-SWE 2
04-Jan-90 URS 5-SWE 5
29-Dec-90 URS 5-SWE 1
27-Dec-91 RUS 4-SWE 3
04-Jan-93 RUS 1-SWE 5
27-Dec-93 RUS 0-SWE 3
01-Jan-95 RUS 6-SWE 4
29-Dec-95 RUS 5-SWE 2
31-Dec-96 RUS 0-SWE 0
26-Dec-98 RUS 2-SWE 4
29-Dec-99 RUS 5-SWE 1
02-Jan-01 RUS 2-SWE 3
28-Dec-03 RUS 5-SWE 3
26-Dec-05 RUS 5-SWE 1
03-Jan-07 RUS 4-SWE 2
04-Jan-08 RUS 1-SWE 2 (OT)
31-Dec-08 RUS 0-SWE 5
29-Dec-09 RUS 1-SWE 4
28-Dec-10 RUS 0-SWE 2
03-Jan-11 RUS 4-SWE 3 (10:00 OT/GWS)
31-Dec-11 RUS 3-SWE 4 (OT)
05-Jan-12 RUS 0-SWE 1 (OT)
Totals: 36-21-3-12-127-91

22-Dec-77 URS 18-SUI 1
27-Dec-79 URS 6-SUI 0
27-Dec-81 URS 11-SUI 4
25-Dec-83 URS 14-SUI 2
29-Dec-85 URS 7-SUI 3
27-Dec-86 URS 8-SUI 0
31-Dec-90 URS 10-SUI 1
26-Dec-91 RUS 10-SUI 2
02-Jan-94 RUS 5-SUI 3
27-Dec-97 RUS 3-SUI 3
31-Dec-98 RUS 6-SUI 0
31-Dec-99 RUS 7-SUI 1
26-Dec-00 RUS 3-SUI 3
03-Jan-01 RUS 2-SUI 3
30-Dec-01 RUS 4-SUI 0
31-Dec-02 RUS 7-SUI 5
30-Dec-04 RUS 6-SUI 1
28-Dec-06 RUS 6-SUI 0
31-Dec-07 RUS 4-SUI 3
02-Jan-10 RUS 2-SUI 3 (OT)
26-Dec-11 RUS 3-SUI 0
Totals: 21-17-2-2-142-38

29-Dec-94 RUS 4-UKR 2
26-Dec-99 RUS 4-UKR 1
Totals: 2-2-0-0-8-3

30-Dec-76 URS 15-USA 5
28-Dec-78 URS 7-USA 1
29-Dec-81 URS 7-USA 0
01-Jan-83 URS 5-USA 3
29-Dec-83 URS 7-USA 4
26-Dec-84 URS 4-USA 2
26-Dec-85 URS 7-USA 3
02-Jan-87 URS 2-USA 4
29-Dec-87 URS 7-USA 3
27-Dec-88 URS 4-USA 2
30-Dec-89 URS 7-USA 3
26-Dec-90 URS 4-USA 2
02-Jan-92 RUS 5-USA 0
02-Jan-93 RUS 2-USA 4
30-Dec-93 RUS 4-USA 3
26-Dec-94 RUS 3-USA 4
28-Dec-97 RUS 3-USA 2
01-Jan-02 RUS 6-USA 1
26-Dec-02 RUS 5-USA 1
31-Dec-03 RUS 1-USA 4
25-Dec-04 RUS 4-USA 5
02-Jan-05 RUS 7-USA 2
03-Jan-06 RUS 5-USA 1
29-Dec-07 RUS 2-USA 3
05-Jan-08 RUS 4-USA 2
Totals: 25-19-0-6-127-64

28-Dec-76 URS 2-FRG 1
22-Dec-81 URS 12-FRG 3
29-Dec-82 URS 12-FRG 2
26-Dec-83 URS 9-FRG 1
25-Dec-84 URS 12-FRG 1
30-Dec-85 URS 10-FRG 0
04-Jan-88 URS 12-FRG 2
26-Dec-88 URS 15-FRG 0
Totals: 8-8-0-0-84-10

**WORLD U18 CHAMPIONSHIPS**

16-Apr-00 RUS 18-BLR 1
20-Apr-02 RUS 11-BLR 0
13-Apr-06 RUS 8-BLR 0
Totals: 3-3-0-0-37-1

11-Apr-02 RUS 8-CAN 4
12-Apr-03 RUS 6-CAN 3
16-Apr-04 RUS 5-CAN 2
19-Apr-05 RUS 3-CAN 6
19-Apr-06 RUS 1-CAN 4
17-Apr-07 RUS 2-CAN 5
16-Apr-08 RUS 4-CAN 2
23-Apr-08 RUS 0-CAN 8
24-Apr-11 RUS 6-CAN 4
19-Apr-12 RUS 2-CAN 4
Totals: 10-5-0-5-37-42

16-Apr-99 RUS 2-CZE 5
12-Apr-01 RUS 8-CZE 3
20-Apr-01 RUS 8-CZE 3
17-Apr-02 RUS 5-CZE 3
17-Apr-03 RUS 4-CZE 2
10-Apr-04 RUS 1-CZE 1
21-Apr-05 RUS 1-CZE 5
17-Apr-06 RUS 2-CZE 0
13-Apr-10 RUS 4-CZE 1
Totals: 9-6-1-2-35-23

16-Apr-05 RUS 2-DEN 1
18-Apr-08 RUS 10-DEN 1
Totals: 2-2-0-0-12-2

11-Apr-99 RUS 1-FIN 3
17-Apr-00 RUS 5-FIN 2
24-Apr-00 RUS 1-FIN 3
18-Apr-02 RUS 4-FIN 3
12-Apr-04 RUS 5-FIN 2
09-Apr-09 RUS 4-FIN 7
17-Apr-09 RUS 4-FIN 0
16-Apr-10 RUS 4-FIN 5
23-Apr-10 RUS 1-FIN 5
21-Apr-11 RUS 5-FIN 2
Totals: 10-5-0-5-34-32

14-Apr-01 RUS 8-GER 3
15-Apr-02 RUS 8-GER 2
17-Apr-05 RUS 12-GER 4
15-Apr-06 RUS 9-GER 5
15-Apr-07 RUS 3-GER 1
14-Apr-08 RUS 6-GER 2
16-Apr-11 RUS 5-GER 4 (5:00 OT/GWS)
14-Apr-12 RUS 2-GER 4
21-Apr-12 RUS 4-GER 1
Totals: 9-8-0-1-57-26

15-Apr-03 RUS 5-KAZ 0
Totals: 1-1-0-0-5-0

13-Apr-07 RUS 6-LAT 3
14-Apr-10 RUS 9-LAT 0
12-Apr-12 RUS 6-LAT 1
Totals: 3-3-0-0-21-4

10-Apr-99 RUS 8-NOR 2
15-Apr-01 RUS 10-NOR 1
14-Apr-02 RUS 7-NOR 0
08-Apr-04 RUS 8-NOR 4
12-Apr-09 RUS 8-NOR 1
Totals: 5-5-0-0-41-8

13-Apr-99 RUS 2-SVK 3
19-Apr-00 RUS 5-SVK 0
12-Apr-02 RUS 6-SVK 1
20-Apr-03 RUS 1-SVK 2 (10:00 OT/GWS)
13-Apr-04 RUS 2-SVK 2
23-Apr-05 RUS 5-SVK 2
13-Apr-08 RUS 6-SVK 4
11-Apr-09 RUS 7-SVK 2
18-Apr-10 RUS 3-SVK 1
14-Apr-11 RUS 8-SVK 2
Totals: 10-7-1-2-45-19

15-Apr-99 RUS 3-SWE 2
17-Apr-01 RUS 3-SWE 4
14-Apr-05 RUS 2-SWE 1
21-Apr-06 RUS 5-SWE 2
20-Apr-07 RUS 5-SWE 4
16-Apr-09 RUS 4-SWE 1
21-Apr-10 RUS 1-SWE 3
23-Apr-11 RUS 1-SWE 3
17-Apr-12 RUS 0-SWE 2
Totals: 9-5-0-4-24-22

18-Apr-99 RUS 1-SUI 4
22-Apr-00 RUS 4-SUI 1
22-Apr-01 RUS 6-SUI 2
14-Apr-03 RUS 12-SUI 3
19-Apr-07 RUS 4-SUI 3 (OT)
20-Apr-10 RUS 4-SUI 3
19-Apr-11 RUS 8-SUI 3
16-Apr-12 RUS 6-SUI 0
Totals: 8-7-0-1-45-19

08-Apr-99 RUS 2-USA 1
14-Apr-00 RUS 5-USA 1
21-Apr-02 RUS 1-USA 3
22-Apr-03 RUS 6-USA 3
18-Apr-04 RUS 3-USA 2
12-Apr-06 RUS 2-USA 4
12-Apr-07 RUS 5-USA 3
22-Apr-07 RUS 6-USA 5
21-Apr-08 RUS 3-USA 1
14-Apr-09 RUS 6-USA 5
19-Apr-09 RUS 0-USA 5
17-Apr-11 RUS 3-USA 4
Totals: 12-8-0-4-42-37

**OLYMPICS, WOMEN**
13-Feb-02 RUS 0-CAN 7
12-Feb-06 RUS 0-CAN 12
Totals: 2-0-0-2-0-19

17-Feb-02 RUS 4-CHN 1
18-Feb-10 RUS 2-CHN 1
Totals: 2-2-0-0-6-2

14-Feb-10 RUS 1-FIN 5
Totals: 1-0-0-1-1-5

19-Feb-02 RUS 5-GER 0
20-Feb-06 RUS 0-GER 1 (10:00 OT/GWS)
Totals: 2-1-0-1-5-1

14-Feb-06 RUS 5-ITA 1
Totals: 1-1-0-0-5-1

15-Feb-02 RUS 4-KAZ 1
Totals: 1-1-0-0-4-1

20-Feb-10 RUS 4-SVK 2
Totals: 1-1-0-0-4-2

11-Feb-02 RUS 2-SWE 3
11-Feb-06 RUS 1-SWE 3
Totals: 2-0-0-2-3-6

17-Feb-06 RUS 6-SUI 2
22-Feb-10 RUS 1-SUI 2 (10:00 OT/GWS)
Totals: 2-1-0-1-7-4

16-Feb-10 RUS 0-USA 13
Totals: 1-0-0-1-0-13

**WOMEN'S WORLD CHAMPIONSHIPS**
01-Apr-97 RUS 1-CAN 9
03-Apr-01 RUS 1-CAN 5
04-Apr-05 RUS 0-CAN 12
04-Apr-08 RUS 1-CAN 8
10-Apr-12 RUS 1-CAN 14
Totals: 5-0-0-5-4-48

31-Mar-97 RUS 2-CHN 6
09-Mar-99 RUS 2-CHN 3
14-Mar-99 RUS 1-CHN 4
09-Apr-00 RUS 4-CHN 0
05-Apr-08 RUS 5-CHN 3
Totals: 5-2-0-3-14-16

03-Apr-00 RUS 1-FIN 7
08-Apr-01 RUS 2-FIN 1
05-Apr-04 RUS 1-FIN 2
04-Apr-07 RUS 0-FIN 4
25-Apr-11 RUS 2-FIN 3 (OT)
07-Apr-12 RUS 4-FIN 5
Totals: 6-1-0-5-10-22

12-Mar-99 RUS 6-GER 2
06-Apr-00 RUS 7-GER 2
03-Apr-04 RUS 4-GER 2
08-Apr-05 RUS 1-GER 2
09-Apr-07 RUS 4-GER 1
Totals: 5-4-0-1-22-9

08-Apr-00 RUS 8-JPN 4
05-Apr-09 RUS 3-JPN 1
Totals: 2-2-0-0-11-5

05-Apr-01 RUS 8-KAZ 2
06-Apr-05 RUS 2-KAZ 2
09-Apr-05 RUS 1-KAZ 2 (10:00 OT/GWS)
08-Apr-07 RUS 7-KAZ 0
09-Apr-09 RUS 9-KAZ 2
Totals: 5-3-1-1-27-8

04-Apr-97 RUS 2-NOR 1
Totals: 1-1-0-0-2-1

20-Apr-11 RUS 4-SVK 1
Totals: 1-1-0-0-4-1

06-Apr-97 RUS 1-SWE 3
11-Mar-99 RUS 0-SWE 7
02-Apr-01 RUS 3-SWE 0
02-Apr-05 RUS 1-SWE 3
03-Apr-07 RUS 2-SWE 3
09-Apr-08 RUS 1-SWE 3
10-Apr-09 RUS 0-SWE 8
17-Apr-11 RUS 1-SWE 7
13-Apr-12 RUS 1-SWE 2
Totals: 9-1-0-8-10-36

03-Apr-97 RUS 3-SUI 3
31-Mar-04 RUS 2-SUI 1
10-Apr-08 RUS 1-SUI 2
22-Apr-11 RUS 5-SUI 4 (OT)
11-Apr-12 RUS 2-SUI 5
Totals: 5-2-1-2-13-15

08-Mar-99 RUS 2-USA 10
04-Apr-00 RUS 0-USA 15
07-Apr-01 RUS 1-USA 6
01-Apr-04 RUS 0-USA 8
06-Apr-09 RUS 0-USA 8
18-Apr-11 RUS 1-USA 13
23-Apr-11 RUS 1-USA 5
08-Apr-12 RUS 0-USA 9
Totals: 8-0-0-8-5-74

**WOMEN'S U18 WORLD CHAMPIONSHIPS**
27-Mar-10 RUS 3-CAN 6
Totals: 1-0-0-1-3-6

31-Mar-10 RUS 0-CZE 5
02-Apr-10 RUS 1-CZE 3
01-Jan-12 RUS 0-CZE 2
Totals: 3-0-0-3-1-10

09-Jan-09 RUS 1-FIN 2 (OT)
Totals: 1-0-0-1-1-2

11-Jan-08 RUS 1-GER 2
07-Jan-09 RUS 5-GER 2
30-Mar-10 RUS 1-GER 3
Totals: 3-1-0-2-7-7

08-Jan-08 RUS 0-SWE 14
06-Jan-09 RUS 1-SWE 6
28-Mar-10 RUS 1-SWE 4
03-Jan-12 RUS 2-SWE 6
Totals: 4-0-0-4-4-30

09-Jan-08 RUS 2-SUI 6
12-Jan-08 RUS 1-SUI 4
10-Jan-09 RUS 3-SUI 2 (5:00 OT/GWS)
04-Jan-12 RUS 2-SUI 4
06-Jan-12 RUS 5-SUI 3
07-Jan-12 RUS 3-SUI 2 (OT)
Totals: 6-3-0-3-16-21

07-Jan-08 RUS 0-USA 11
05-Jan-09 RUS 0-USA 17

31-Dec-11 RUS 0-USA 8
Totals: 3-0-0-3-0-36

# SLOVAKIA (SVK)

Totals=GP-W-T-L-GF-GA

**OLYMPICS, MEN**
**Date Score**
07-Feb-98 SVK 2-AUT 2
12-Feb-02 SVK 2-AUT 3
Totals: 2-0-1-1-4-5

19-Feb-94 SVK 3-CAN 1
26-Feb-10 SVK 2-CAN 3
Totals: 2-1-0-1-5-4

26-Feb-94 SVK 1-CZE 7
22-Feb-06 SVK 1-CZE 3
17-Feb-10 SVK 1-CZE 3
Totals: 3-0-0-3-3-13

27-Feb-10 SVK 3-FIN 5
Totals: 1-0-0-1-3-5

21-Feb-94 SVK 6-FRA 2
14-Feb-02 SVK 7-FRA 1
Totals: 2-2-0-0-13-3

24-Feb-94 SVK 6-GER 5 (OT)
12-Feb-98 SVK 2-GER 4
09-Feb-02 SVK 0-GER 3
Totals: 3-1-0-2-8-12

17-Feb-94 SVK 10-ITA 4
08-Feb-98 SVK 4-ITA 3
Totals: 2-2-0-0-14-7

10-Feb-98 SVK 3-KAZ 4
19-Feb-06 SVK 2-KAZ 1
Totals: 2-1-0-1-5-5

10-Feb-02 SVK 6-LAT 6
16-Feb-06 SVK 6-LAT 3
20-Feb-10 SVK 6-LAT 0
Totals: 3-2-1-0-18-9

23-Feb-10 SVK 4-NOR 3
Totals: 1-1-0-0-4-3

23-Feb-94 SVK 2-RUS 3 (OT)
15-Feb-06 SVK 5-RUS 3
18-Feb-10 SVK 2-RUS 1 (5:00 OT/GWS)
Totals: 3-2-0-1-9-7

13-Feb-94 SVK 4-SWE 4
21-Feb-06 SVK 3-SWE 0
24-Feb-10 SVK 4-SWE 3
Totals: 3-2-1-0-11-7

15-Feb-94 SVK 3-USA 3
18-Feb-06 SVK 2-USA 1
Totals: 2-1-1-0-5-4

**WORLD CHAMPIONSHIPS, MEN**
25-Apr-96 SVK 1-AUT 2
05-May-98 SVK 5-AUT 1
30-Apr-00 SVK 2-AUT 0
30-Apr-01 SVK 5-AUT 0
03-May-02 SVK 6-AUT 3
04-May-03 SVK 7-AUT 1
04-May-05 SVK 8-AUT 1
Totals: 7-6-0-1-34-8

30-Apr-05 SVK 2-BLR 1
06-May-06 SVK 1-BLR 2
06-May-07 SVK 4-BLR 3
26-Apr-09 SVK 1-BLR 2 (5:00 OT/GWS)
11-May-10 SVK 4-BLR 2
12-May-12 SVK 5-BLR 1
Totals: 6-4-0-2-17-11

21-Apr-96 SVK 3-CAN 3
03-May-98 SVK 2-CAN 2
01-May-99 SVK 2-CAN 3
09-May-00 SVK 3-CAN 4
07-May-02 SVK 3-CAN 2
08-May-04 SVK 1-CAN 2
12-May-05 SVK 4-CAN 5
17-May-06 SVK 1-CAN 4
02-May-07 SVK 4-CAN 5
28-Apr-09 SVK 3-CAN 7
04-May-12 SVK 2-CAN 3
17-May-12 SVK 4-CAN 3
Totals: 12-2-2-8-32-43

30-Apr-97 SVK 1-CZE 3
07-May-98 SVK 0-CZE 1
09-May-99 SVK 2-CZE 8
08-May-00 SVK 2-CZE 6
14-May-00 SVK 3-CZE 5
10-May-01 SVK 0-CZE 2
05-May-03 SVK 3-CZE 3
10-May-03 SVK 4-CZE 2
07-May-05 SVK 1-CZE 5
05-May-07 SVK 3-CZE 2
02-May-09 SVK 0-CZE 8
06-May-11 SVK 2-CZE 3
19-May-12 SVK 3-CZE 1
Totals: 13-3-1-9-24-49

02-May-04 SVK 8-DEN 0
14-May-10 SVK 0-DEN 6
09-May-11 SVK 4-DEN 1
Totals: 3-2-0-1-12-7

02-May-97 SVK 2-FIN 5
04-May-00 SVK 2-FIN 2
12-May-00 SVK 3-FIN 1
02-May-01 SVK 2-FIN 5
30-Apr-02 SVK 1-FIN 3
02-May-03 SVK 5-FIN 1
28-Apr-04 SVK 5-FIN 2
07-May-08 SVK 2-FIN 3
01-May-09 SVK 1-FIN 2 (OT)
17-May-10 SVK 2-FIN 5
07-May-11 SVK 1-FIN 2
06-May-12 SVK 0-FIN 1
Totals: 12-3-1-8-26-32

28-Apr-97 SVK 5-FRA 3
15-May-12 SVK 5-FRA 4
Totals: 2-2-0-0-10-7

29-Apr-96 SVK 4-GER 1
03-May-97 SVK 0-GER 1
30-Apr-03 SVK 3-GER 1
30-Apr-07 SVK 5-GER 1
05-May-08 SVK 2-GER 4
18-May-10 SVK 1-GER 2
01-May-11 SVK 3-GER 4
Totals: 7-3-0-4-18-14

24-Apr-09 SVK 4-HUN 3
Totals: 1-1-0-0-4-3

08-May-97 SVK 4-ITA 3
01-May-98 SVK 2-ITA 1
03-May-99 SVK 7-ITA 4
02-May-00 SVK 6-ITA 2
Totals: 4-4-0-0-19-10

29-Apr-01 SVK 8-JPN 4
28-Apr-03 SVK 10-JPN 1
Totals: 2-2-0-0-18-5

10-May-05 SVK 3-KAZ 1
08-May-06 SVK 6-KAZ 0
13-May-10 SVK 5-KAZ 1
09-May-12 SVK 4-KAZ 2
Totals: 4-4-0-0-18-4

10-May-97 SVK 4-LAT 5
Totals: 1-0-0-1-4-5

05-May-97 SVK 2-NOR 1
05-May-99 SVK 8-NOR 2
06-May-00 SVK 9-NOR 1
28-Apr-07 SVK 3-NOR 0
03-May-08 SVK 5-NOR 1
04-May-09 SVK 3-NOR 2 (OT)
Totals: 6-6-0-0-30-7

27-Apr-02 SVK 7-POL 0
Totals: 1-1-0-0-7-0

22-Apr-96 SVK 2-RUS 6
27-Apr-97 SVK 2-RUS 2
09-May-98 SVK 1-RUS 6
10-May-99 SVK 2-RUS 2
06-May-02 SVK 6-RUS 4
11-May-02 SVK 4-RUS 3
30-Apr-04 SVK 2-RUS 0
02-May-05 SVK 3-RUS 3
10-May-06 SVK 3-RUS 4
09-May-10 SVK 1-RUS 3
03-May-11 SVK 3-RUS 4
20-May-12 SVK 2-RUS 5
Totals: 12-3-3-6-31-42

09-May-08 SVK 5-SLO 1
10-May-08 SVK 4-SLO 3 (5:00 OT/GWS)
29-Apr-11 SVK 3-SLO 1
Totals: 3-3-0-0-12-5

07-May-99 SVK 1-SWE 2
05-May-01 SVK 1-SWE 3
02-May-02 SVK 2-SWE 1
09-May-02 SVK 3-SWE 2 (10:00 OT/GWS)
09-May-03 SVK 1-SWE 4
03-May-04 SVK 0-SWE 0
14-May-06 SVK 5-SWE 2
09-May-07 SVK 4-SWE 7
Totals: 8-3-1-4-17-21

10-May-98 SVK 1-SUI 1
07-May-03 SVK 3-SUI 1
06-May-04 SVK 3-SUI 1
08-May-05 SVK 3-SUI 1
12-May-06 SVK 2-SUI 2
13-May-12 SVK 1-SUI 0
Totals: 6-4-2-0-13-6

04-May-01 SVK 3-UKR 1
29-Apr-02 SVK 5-UKR 4
27-Apr-03 SVK 9-UKR 3
24-Apr-04 SVK 2-UKR 0
16-May-06 SVK 8-UKR 0
Totals: 5-5-0-0-27-8

27-Apr-96 SVK 3-USA 4
11-May-00 SVK 4-USA 1
08-May-01 SVK 1-USA 3
26-Apr-04 SVK 3-USA 3
09-May-04 SVK 0-USA 1 (10:00 OT/GWS)
03-May-07 SVK 2-USA 4
07-May-12 SVK 4-USA 2
Totals: 7-2-1-4-17-18

**WORLD U20 CHAMPIONSHIPS**
30-Dec-03 SVK 6-AUT 0
02-Jan-10 SVK 3-AUT 2
Totals: 2-2-0-0-9-2

26-Dec-01 SVK 7-BLR 1
27-Dec-02 SVK 11-BLR 1
02-Jan-05 SVK 2-BLR 1
04-Jan-07 SVK 9-BLR 0
Totals: 4-4-0-0-29-3

01-Jan-97 SVK 2-CAN 7
27-Dec-98 SVK 0-CAN 0
29-Dec-99 SVK 1-CAN 4
25-Dec-04 SVK 3-CAN 7
31-Dec-06 SVK 0-CAN 3
27-Dec-07 SVK 0-CAN 2
29-Dec-09 SVK 2-CAN 8
Totals: 7-0-1-6-8-31

29-Dec-95 SVK 4-CZE 4
26-Dec-98 SVK 3-CZE 2
25-Dec-99 SVK 2-CZE 5
31-Dec-00 SVK 0-CZE 5
27-Dec-01 SVK 1-CZE 0
04-Jan-02 SVK 2-CZE 6
04-Jan-03 SVK 2-CZE 0
02-Jan-04 SVK 2-CZE 4
30-Dec-05 SVK 3-CZE 5
29-Dec-07 SVK 2-CZE 5
04-Jan-10 SVK 2-CZE 5
04-Jan-11 SVK 2-CZE 5
04-Jan-12 SVK 2-CZE 5
Totals: 13-3-1-9-27-51

30-Dec-07 SVK 4-DEN 3
Totals: 1-1-0-0-4-3

31-Dec-96 SVK 3-FIN 4
03-Jan-97 SVK 4-FIN 6
29-Dec-98 SVK 4-FIN 3
26-Dec-99 SVK 1-FIN 1
02-Jan-01 SVK 1-FIN 3
02-Jan-03 SVK 0-FIN 6
27-Dec-04 SVK 2-FIN 0
31-Dec-08 SVK 3-FIN 2 (5:00 OT/GWS)
31-Dec-10 SVK 0-FIN 6
02-Jan-12 SVK 5-FIN 8
Totals: 10-3-1-6-23-39

30-Dec-95 SVK 4-GER 4
01-Jan-98 SVK 9-GER 0
03-Jan-98 SVK 8-GER 3
29-Dec-04 SVK 5-GER 0
27-Dec-06 SVK 2-GER 4
27-Dec-10 SVK 2-GER 1 (OT)
Totals: 6-4-1-1-30-12

28-Dec-97 SVK 2-KAZ 5
30-Dec-00 SVK 7-KAZ 0
03-Jan-08 SVK 8-KAZ 0
Totals: 3-2-0-1-17-5

27-Dec-05 SVK 7-LAT 4
27-Dec-08 SVK 7-LAT 2
27-Dec-09 SVK 8-LAT 3
27-Dec-11 SVK 3-LAT 1
Totals: 4-4-0-0-25-10

03-Jan-06 SVK 4-NOR 3
02-Jan-11 SVK 5-NOR 0
Totals: 2-2-0-0-9-3

29-Dec-96 SVK 7-POL 4
Totals: 1-1-0-0-7-4

27-Dec-95 SVK 3-RUS 3
26-Dec-96 SVK 3-RUS 4
30-Dec-97 SVK 0-RUS 4
04-Jan-99 SVK 2-RUS 3
05-Jan-01 SVK 3-RUS 4 (10:00 OT/GWS)
28-Dec-02 SVK 0-RUS 4
26-Dec-03 SVK 2-RUS 2
04-Jan-04 SVK 2-RUS 3
28-Dec-05 SVK 2-RUS 6
30-Dec-08 SVK 1-RUS 8
05-Jan-09 SVK 2-RUS 5
28-Dec-11 SVK 1-RUS 3
Totals: 12-0-2-10-21-49

26-Dec-95 SVK 0-SWE 6
27-Dec-96 SVK 4-SWE 1
05-Jan-99 SVK 5-SWE 4
27-Dec-00 SVK 1-SWE 3
29-Dec-01 SVK 2-SWE 2
02-Jan-02 SVK 2-SWE 3
31-Dec-03 SVK 1-SWE 0
30-Dec-04 SVK 0-SWE 3
31-Dec-05 SVK 0-SWE 6
28-Dec-06 SVK 3-SWE 6
26-Dec-07 SVK 3-SWE 4
28-Dec-08 SVK 1-SWE 3
03-Jan-09 SVK 3-SWE 5
30-Dec-11 SVK 1-SWE 9
Totals: 14-3-1-10-26-55

03-Jan-96 SVK 7-SUI 3
26-Dec-97 SVK 1-SUI 3
01-Jan-02 SVK 2-SUI 3 (10:00 OT/GWS)
30-Dec-02 SVK 3-SUI 0
03-Jan-05 SVK 3-SUI 2
04-Jan-06 SVK 3-SUI 3
02-Jan-07 SVK 1-SUI 2
02-Jan-08 SVK 5-SUI 2
31-Dec-09 SVK 1-SUI 4
30-Dec-10 SVK 4-SUI 6
31-Dec-11 SVK 6-SUI 4
Totals: 11-5-1-5-36-32

02-Jan-96 SVK 6-UKR 3
02-Jan-00 SVK 1-UKR 3
04-Jan-00 SVK 5-UKR 1
Totals: 3-2-0-1-12-7

25-Dec-97 SVK 6-USA 3
30-Dec-98 SVK 3-USA 2
28-Dec-99 SVK 0-USA 1
28-Dec-00 SVK 2-USA 7
03-Jan-01 SVK 2-USA 3
30-Dec-01 SVK 4-USA 4
31-Dec-02 SVK 1-USA 3
28-Dec-03 SVK 0-USA 5
30-Dec-06 SVK 1-USA 6
02-Jan-09 SVK 5-USA 3
26-Dec-09 SVK 3-USA 7
28-Dec-10 SVK 1-USA 6
Totals: 12-3-1-8-28-50

**WORLD U18 CHAMPIONSHIPS, MEN**
15-Apr-00 SVK 7-BLR 1
17-Apr-03 SVK 8-BLR 2
19-Apr-06 SVK 0-BLR 2
20-Apr-08 SVK 6-BLR 1
20-Apr-10 SVK 5-BLR 1
Totals: 5-4-0-1-26-7

14-Apr-02 SVK 1-CAN 3
22-Apr-03 SVK 0-CAN 3
15-Apr-04 SVK 1-CAN 3
12-Apr-06 SVK 1-CAN 3
18-Apr-08 SVK 0-CAN 6
22-Apr-10 SVK 2-CAN 4
Totals: 6-0-0-6-5-22

18-Apr-99 SVK 1-CZE 0
24-Apr-00 SVK 4-CZE 3 (10:00 OT/GWS)
11-Apr-02 SVK 1-CZE 5
19-Apr-03 SVK 2-CZE 1
08-Apr-04 SVK 1-CZE 1
16-Apr-05 SVK 0-CZE 3
14-Apr-07 SVK 2-CZE 3 (5:00 OT/GWS)
14-Apr-10 SVK 3-CZE 4
21-Apr-11 SVK 3-CZE 4
Totals: 9-3-1-5-17-24

14-Apr-08 SVK 5-DEN 2
Totals: 1-1-0-0-5-2

08-Apr-99 SVK 2-FIN 3
14-Apr-00 SVK 1-FIN 3
12-Apr-01 SVK 0-FIN 3
16-Apr-03 SVK 4-FIN 3
10-Apr-04 SVK 2-FIN 2
19-Apr-05 SVK 3-FIN 2
13-Apr-06 SVK 3-FIN 6
17-Apr-07 SVK 1-FIN 0
14-Apr-09 SVK 0-FIN 7
15-Apr-10 SVK 2-FIN 5
Totals: 10-3-1-6-18-34

17-Apr-02 SVK 4-GER 1
20-Apr-06 SVK 2-GER 1
16-Apr-08 SVK 4-GER 5 (5:00 OT/GWS)
17-Apr-09 SVK 4-GER 5 (5:00 OT/GWS)
18-Apr-11 SVK 4-GER 0
Totals: 5-3-0-2-18-12

17-Apr-10 SVK 4-LAT 3
Totals: 1-1-0-0-4-3

09-Apr-99 SVK 7-NOR 0
19-Apr-01 SVK 4-NOR 4
15-Apr-02 SVK 3-NOR 4
11-Apr-04 SVK 8-NOR 2
15-Apr-06 SVK 5-NOR 2
10-Apr-09 SVK 5-NOR 2
23-Apr-11 SVK 2-NOR 6
Totals: 7-4-1-2-34-20

13-Apr-99 SVK 3-RUS 2
19-Apr-00 SVK 0-RUS 5
12-Apr-02 SVK 1-RUS 6
20-Apr-03 SVK 2-RUS 1 (10:00 OT/GWS)
13-Apr-04 SVK 2-RUS 2
23-Apr-05 SVK 2-RUS 5
13-Apr-08 SVK 4-RUS 6
11-Apr-09 SVK 2-RUS 7
18-Apr-10 SVK 1-RUS 3
14-Apr-11 SVK 2-RUS 8
Totals: 10-2-1-7-19-45

16-Apr-99 SVK 1-SWE 4
20-Apr-01 SVK 1-SWE 5
20-Apr-02 SVK 5-SWE 3
13-Apr-03 SVK 4-SWE 1
17-Apr-04 SVK 4-SWE 5
21-Apr-05 SVK 3-SWE 5
17-Apr-06 SVK 2-SWE 5
13-Apr-07 SVK 6-SWE 3
Totals: 8-3-0-5-26-31

15-Apr-99 SVK 6-SUI 3
21-Apr-00 SVK 0-SUI 3
14-Apr-01 SVK 2-SUI 5
21-Apr-02 SVK 0-SUI 3
18-Apr-05 SVK 2-SUI 1
16-Apr-07 SVK 0-SUI 4
21-Apr-07 SVK 4-SUI 1
21-Apr-08 SVK 3-SUI 2
18-Apr-09 SVK 4-SUI 2
17-Apr-11 SVK 2-SUI 3
Totals: 10-5-0-5-23-27

16-Apr-01 SVK 10-UKR 1
18-Apr-02 SVK 3-UKR 0
Totals: 2-2-0-0-13-1

11-Apr-99 SVK 6-USA 5
17-Apr-00 SVK 4-USA 1
17-Apr-01 SVK 2-USA 6
14-Apr-03 SVK 2-USA 3
14-Apr-05 SVK 1-USA 3
19-Apr-07 SVK 2-USA 7
13-Apr-09 SVK 0-USA 12
15-Apr-11 SVK 1-USA 8
Totals: 8-2-0-6-18-45

**OLYMPICS, WOMEN**
13-Feb-10 SVK 0-CAN 18
Totals: 1-0-0-1-0-18

22-Feb-10 SVK 1-CHN 3
Totals: 1-0-0-1-1-3

20-Feb-10 SVK 2-RUS 4
Totals: 1-0-0-1-2-4

15-Feb-10 SVK 2-SWE 6
Totals: 1-0-0-1-2-6

17-Feb-10 SVK 2-SUI 5
Totals: 1-0-0-1-2-5

**WOMEN'S WORLD CHAMPIONSHIPS**
10-Apr-12 SVK 4-GER 2
11-Apr-12 SVK 1-GER 2 (5:00 OT/GWS)
13-Apr-12 SVK 1-GER 3
Totals: 3-1-0-2-6-7

22-Apr-11 SVK 1-KAZ 0
24-Apr-11 SVK 2-KAZ 1 (5:00 OT/GWS)
Totals: 2-2-0-0-3-1

20-Apr-11 SVK 1-RUS 4
Totals: 1-0-0-1-1-4

18-Apr-11 SVK 0-SWE 3
07-Apr-12 SVK 1-SWE 5
Totals: 2-0-0-2-1-8

08-Apr-12 SVK 1-SUI 2
Totals: 1-0-0-1-1-2

17-Apr-11 SVK 0-USA 5
Totals: 1-0-0-1-0-5

# SLOVENIA (SLO)

Totals=GP-W-T-L-GF-GA

**WORLD CHAMPIONSHIPS, MEN**

**Date Score**
30-Apr-02 SLO 3-AUT 5
29-Apr-03 SLO 2-AUT 6
11-May-05 SLO 6-AUT 2
07-Apr-11 SLO 2-AUT 3
Totals: 4-1-0-3-3-16

05-May-03 SLO 3-BLR 4
08-May-11 SLO 1-BLR 7
Totals: 2-0-0-2-4-11

03-May-05 SLO 0-CAN 8
02-May-08 SLO 1-CAN 5
Totals: 2-0-0-2-1-13

26-Apr-03 SLO 2-CZE 5
07-May-06 SLO 4-CZE 5
Totals: 2-0-0-2-6-10

06-May-05 SLO 4-DEN 3
12-May-06 SLO 3-DEN 3
Totals: 2-1-1-0-7-6

28-Apr-03 SLO 0-FIN 12
05-May-06 SLO 3-FIN 5
Totals: 2-0-0-2-3-17

09-May-05 SLO 1-GER 9
03-May-11 SLO 2-GER 3 (5:00 OT/GWS)
Totals: 2-0-0-2-3-12

05-May-02 SLO 4-ITA 0
15-May-06 SLO 3-ITA 3
Totals: 2-1-1-0-7-3

02-May-02 SLO 4-JPN 3
03-May-03 SLO 3-JPN 3
Totals: 2-1-1-0-7-6

13-May-06 SLO 0-KAZ 5
Totals: 1-0-0-1-0-5

05-May-05 SLO 1-LAT 3
09-May-06 SLO 1-LAT 5
06-May-08 SLO 0-LAT 3
05-May-11 SLO 5-LAT 2
Totals: 4-1-0-3-7-13

03-May-02 SLO 4-POL 2
Totals: 1-1-0-0-4-2

26-Apr-02 SLO 1-RUS 8
01-May-11 SLO 4-RUS 6
Totals: 2-0-0-2-5-14

09-May-08 SLO 1-SVK 5
10-May-08 SLO 3-SVK 4 (5:00 OT/GWS)
29-Apr-11 SLO 1-SVK 3
Totals: 3-0-0-3-5-12

28-Apr-02 SLO 2-SWE 8
Totals: 1-0-0-1-2-8

02-May-03 SLO 2-USA 7
01-May-05 SLO 0-USA 7
04-May-08 SLO 1-USA 5
Totals: 3-0-0-3-3-19

# SWEDEN (SWE)

Totals=GP-W-T-L-GF-GA

**OLYMPICS, MEN**

**Date Score**
11-Feb-36 SWE 1-AUT 0
02-Feb-48 SWE 7-AUT 2
Totals: 2-2-0-0-8-2

16-Feb-98 SWE 5-BLR 2
20-Feb-02 SWE 3-BLR 4
19-Feb-10 SWE 4-BLR 2
Totals: 3-2-0-1-12-8

23-Apr-20 SWE 8-BEL 0
Totals: 1-1-0-0-8-0

26-Apr-20 SWE 1-CAN 12
29-Jan-24 SWE 0-CAN 22
17-Feb-28 SWE 0-CAN 11
30-Jan-48 SWE 1-CAN 3
22-Feb-52 SWE 2-CAN 3
03-Feb-56 SWE 2-CAN 6
19-Feb-60 SWE 2-CAN 5
27-Feb-60 SWE 5-CAN 6
30-Jan-64 SWE 1-CAN 3
15-Feb-68 SWE 0-CAN 3
19-Feb-84 SWE 2-CAN 0
22-Feb-88 SWE 2-CAN 2
21-Feb-94 SWE 2-CAN 3
27-Feb-94 SWE 3-CAN 2 (10:00 OT/GWS)
14-Feb-98 SWE 2-CAN 3
15-Feb-02 SWE 5-CAN 2
Totals: 16-3-1-12-30-86

29-Apr-20 SWE 0-TCH 1
31-Jan-24 SWE 9-TCH 3
11-Feb-28 SWE 3-TCH 0
12-Feb-36 SWE 1-TCH 4
31-Jan-48 SWE 3-TCH 6
24-Feb-52 SWE 0-TCH 4
25-Feb-52 SWE 5-TCH 3
31-Jan-56 SWE 5-TCH 0
25-Feb-60 SWE 1-TCH 3
08-Feb-64 SWE 8-TCH 3
17-Feb-68 SWE 2-TCH 2
10-Feb-72 SWE 1-TCH 2
20-Feb-80 SWE 4-TCH 2
17-Feb-84 SWE 0-TCH 2
24-Feb-88 SWE 6-TCH 2
19-Feb-92 SWE 1-TCH 3
17-Feb-02 SWE 2-CZE 1
24-Feb-06 SWE 7-CZE 3
Totals vs. TCH:
16-7-1-8-49-40
Totals vs. CZE:
2-2-0-0-9-4

10-Feb-68 SWE 5-GDR 2
Totals: 1-1-0-0-5-2

15-Feb-52 SWE 9-FIN 2
02-Feb-64 SWE 7-FIN 0
12-Feb-68 SWE 5-FIN 1
13-Feb-72 SWE 3-FIN 4
22-Feb-80 SWE 3-FIN 3
20-Feb-88 SWE 3-FIN 3
15-Feb-92 SWE 2-FIN 2
20-Feb-92 SWE 3-FIN 2
18-Feb-98 SWE 1-FIN 2
26-Feb-06 SWE 3-FIN 2
21-Feb-10 SWE 3-FIN 0
Totals: 11-6-3-2-42-21

25-Apr-20 SWE 4-FRA 0
14-Feb-88 SWE 13-FRA 2
17-Feb-94 SWE 7-FRA 1
Totals: 3-3-0-0-24-3

18-Feb-52 SWE 7-GER 3
04-Feb-56 SWE 1-GER 1
28-Feb-60 SWE 8-GER 2
04-Feb-64 SWE 10-GER 2
13-Feb-92 SWE 3-GER 1
22-Feb-92 SWE 4-GER 3
23-Feb-94 SWE 3-GER 0
18-Feb-02 SWE 7-GER 1
17-Feb-10 SWE 2-GER 0
Totals: 9-8-1-0-45-13

03-Feb-24 SWE 3-GBR 4
19-Feb-28 SWE 3-GBR 1
07-Feb-36 SWE 0-GBR 1
06-Feb-48 SWE 4-GBR 2
Totals: 4-2-0-2-10-8

07-Feb-48 SWE 23-ITA 0
07-Feb-84 SWE 11-ITA 1
11-Feb-92 SWE 7-ITA 3
15-Feb-94 SWE 4-ITA 1
Totals: 4-4-0-0-45-5

06-Feb-36 SWE 2-JPN 0
21-Feb-60 SWE 19-JPN 0
Totals: 2-2-0-0-21-0

15-Feb-06 SWE 7-KAZ 2
Totals: 1-1-0-0-7-2

18-Feb-06 SWE 6-LAT 1
Totals: 1-1-0-0-6-1

17-Feb-52 SWE 4-NOR 2
18-Feb-80 SWE 7-NOR 1
Totals: 2-2-0-0-11-3

12-Feb-28 SWE 2-POL 2
08-Feb-48 SWE 13-POL 2
16-Feb-52 SWE 17-POL 1
09-Feb-72 SWE 5-POL 3
13-Feb-84 SWE 10-POL 1
16-Feb-88 SWE 1-POL 1
09-Feb-92 SWE 7-POL 2
Totals: 7-5-2-0-55-12

14-Feb-80 SWE 8-ROM 0
Totals: 1-1-0-0-8-0

27-Jan-56 SWE 1-URS 5
30-Jan-56 SWE 1-URS 4
24-Feb-60 SWE 2-URS 2
07-Feb-64 SWE 2-URS 4
13-Feb-68 SWE 2-URS 3
07-Feb-72 SWE 3-URS 3
24-Feb-80 SWE 2-URS 9
15-Feb-84 SWE 1-URS 10
26-Feb-88 SWE 1-URS 7
25-Feb-94 SWE 4-RUS 3
16-Feb-06 SWE 0-RUS 5
Totals vs. URS:
9-0-2-7-15-47
Totals vs. RUS:
2-1-0-1-4-8

13-Feb-94 SWE 4-SVK 4
21-Feb-06 SWE 0-SVK 3
24-Feb-10 SWE 3-SVK 4
Totals: 3-0-1-2-7-11

28-Apr-20 SWE 4-SUI 0
28-Jan-24 SWE 9-SUI 0
18-Feb-28 SWE 4-SUI 0
05-Feb-48 SWE 2-SUI 8
23-Feb-52 SWE 5-SUI 2
28-Jan-56 SWE 6-SUI 5
05-Feb-64 SWE 12-SUI 0
18-Feb-88 SWE 4-SUI 2
22-Feb-06 SWE 6-SUI 2
Totals: 9-8-0-1-52-19

27-Apr-20 SWE 0-USA 7
01-Feb-24 SWE 0-USA 20
13-Feb-36 SWE 1-USA 2
03-Feb-48 SWE 2-USA 5
21-Feb-52 SWE 4-USA 2
02-Feb-56 SWE 1-USA 6
22-Feb-60 SWE 3-USA 6
01-Feb-64 SWE 7-USA 4
07-Feb-68 SWE 4-USA 3
05-Feb-72 SWE 5-USA 1
12-Feb-80 SWE 2-USA 2
17-Feb-92 SWE 3-USA 3
19-Feb-94 SWE 6-USA 4
13-Feb-98 SWE 4-USA 2
19-Feb-06 SWE 2-USA 1
Totals: 15-7-2-6-44-68

09-Feb-68 SWE 5-FRG 4
16-Feb-80 SWE 5-FRG 2
11-Feb-84 SWE 1-FRG 1
28-Feb-88 SWE 3-FRG 2
Totals: 4-3-1-0-14-9

09-Feb-84 SWE 11-YUG 0
Totals: 1-1-0-0-11-0

**WORLD CHAMPIONSHIPS, MEN**
02-Feb-31 SWE 3-AUT 1
08-Feb-31 SWE 0-AUT 1
27-Jan-35 SWE 3-AUT 1
15-Feb-38 SWE 1-AUT 1
23-Feb-47 SWE 1-AUT 2
15-Feb-49 SWE 18-AUT 0
01-Mar-57 SWE 10-AUT 0
18-Apr-93 SWE 1-AUT 0
27-Apr-95 SWE 5-AUT 0
04-May-01 SWE 11-AUT 0
26-Apr-02 SWE 5-AUT 3
25-Apr-09 SWE 7-AUT 1
02-May-11 SWE 3-AUT 0
Totals: 13-10-1-2-68-10

09-May-98 SWE 2-BLR 1
04-May-00 SWE 7-BLR 0
27-Apr-03 SWE 2-BLR 1
12-May-06 SWE 4-BLR 1
03-May-08 SWE 6-BLR 5
Totals: 5-5-0-0-21-8

16-Feb-47 SWE 24-BEL 1
Totals: 1-1-0-0-24-1

06-Feb-31 SWE 0-CAN 0
22-Jan-35 SWE 2-CAN 5
19-Feb-37 SWE 0-CAN 9
12-Feb-38 SWE 2-CAN 3
16-Feb-49 SWE 2-CAN 2
22-Mar-50 SWE 1-CAN 3
17-Mar-51 SWE 1-CAN 5
01-Mar-54 SWE 0-CAN 8
03-Mar-55 SWE 0-CAN 3
06-Mar-58 SWE 2-CAN 10
12-Mar-59 SWE 0-CAN 5
02-Mar-61 SWE 1-CAN 6
13-Mar-62 SWE 5-CAN 3
15-Mar-63 SWE 4-CAN 1
13-Mar-65 SWE 6-CAN 4
13-Mar-66 SWE 2-CAN 4
29-Mar-67 SWE 6-CAN 0
21-Mar-69 SWE 5-CAN 1
27-Mar-69 SWE 4-CAN 2
22-Apr-77 SWE 4-CAN 2
04-May-77 SWE 0-CAN 7
06-May-78 SWE 5-CAN 7
14-May-78 SWE 2-CAN 3
21-Apr-79 SWE 5-CAN 3
27-Apr-79 SWE 3-CAN 6
20-Apr-81 SWE 3-CAN 1
26-Apr-81 SWE 4-CAN 3
18-Apr-82 SWE 3-CAN 3
29-Apr-82 SWE 0-CAN 6
17-Apr-83 SWE 3-CAN 2
30-Apr-83 SWE 1-CAN 3
27-Apr-85 SWE 3-CAN 6
13-Apr-86 SWE 4-CAN 1
26-Apr-86 SWE 6-CAN 5
23-Apr-87 SWE 4-CAN 3
03-May-87 SWE 9-CAN 0
21-Apr-89 SWE 6-CAN 5
27-Apr-89 SWE 3-CAN 5
24-Apr-90 SWE 1-CAN 3
02-May-90 SWE 6-CAN 4
26-Apr-91 SWE 3-CAN 3
30-Apr-91 SWE 3-CAN 3
20-Apr-93 SWE 1-CAN 4
07-May-94 SWE 0-CAN 6
05-May-95 SWE 3-CAN 2 (OT)
27-Apr-97 SWE 7-CAN 2
11-May-97 SWE 3-CAN 2
13-May-97 SWE 1-CAN 3
14-May-97 SWE 1-CAN 2
10-May-98 SWE 7-CAN 1
15-May-99 SWE 3-CAN 2
29-Apr-03 SWE 1-CAN 3
11-May-03 SWE 2-CAN 3 (OT)
09-May-04 SWE 3-CAN 5
07-May-05 SWE 5-CAN 4
20-May-06 SWE 5-CAN 4
12-May-07 SWE 1-CAN 4
16-May-08 SWE 4-CAN 5
08-May-09 SWE 1-CAN 3
16-May-10 SWE 3-CAN 1
09-May-11 SWE 2-CAN 3
Totals: 61-25-5-31-177-217

07-Feb-31 SWE 1-TCH 0
23-Jan-35 SWE 1-TCH 2 (OT)
13-Feb-38 SWE 0-TCH 0 (30:00 OT)
22-Feb-47 SWE 2-TCH 1
13-Feb-49 SWE 4-TCH 2
20-Feb-49 SWE 0-TCH 3
10-Mar-53 SWE 5-TCH 3
06-Mar-54 SWE 4-TCH 2
01-Mar-55 SWE 5-TCH 6
27-Feb-57 SWE 2-TCH 0
09-Mar-58 SWE 7-TCH 1
09-Mar-59 SWE 1-TCH 4
12-Mar-61 SWE 2-TCH 5
17-Mar-63 SWE 2-TCH 3
14-Mar-65 SWE 2-TCH 3
11-Mar-66 SWE 1-TCH 2
27-Mar-67 SWE 5-TCH 5
19-Mar-69 SWE 2-TCH 0
30-Mar-69 SWE 1-TCH 0
15-Mar-70 SWE 5-TCH 4
24-Mar-70 SWE 2-TCH 2
21-Mar-71 SWE 6-TCH 5
29-Mar-71 SWE 1-TCH 3
09-Apr-72 SWE 1-TCH 4
17-Apr-72 SWE 0-TCH 2
02-Apr-73 SWE 2-TCH 0
10-Apr-73 SWE 3-TCH 3
07-Apr-74 SWE 2-TCH 3
15-Apr-74 SWE 3-TCH 0
05-Apr-75 SWE 2-TCH 5
14-Apr-75 SWE 0-TCH 7
11-Apr-76 SWE 1-TCH 3
23-Apr-76 SWE 3-TCH 5
30-Apr-77 SWE 1-TCH 3
06-May-77 SWE 1-TCH 2
08-May-78 SWE 2-TCH 3
10-May-78 SWE 1-TCH 6
19-Apr-79 SWE 3-TCH 3
25-Apr-79 SWE 3-TCH 6
15-Apr-81 SWE 3-TCH 3
22-Apr-81 SWE 4-TCH 2
22-Apr-82 SWE 3-TCH 3
25-Apr-82 SWE 2-TCH 3
19-Apr-83 SWE 1-TCH 4
02-May-83 SWE 1-TCH 4
25-Apr-85 SWE 2-TCH 7
15-Apr-86 SWE 3-TCH 2
20-Apr-87 SWE 2-TCH 3
29-Apr-87 SWE 3-TCH 3
22-Apr-89 SWE 3-TCH 3
29-Apr-89 SWE 1-TCH 2
26-Apr-90 SWE 5-TCH 1
30-Apr-90 SWE 5-TCH 5
25-Apr-91 SWE 2-TCH 1
30-Apr-93 SWE 4-CZE 3 (OT)
02-May-94 SWE 4-CZE 1
30-Apr-95 SWE 2-CZE 1
21-Apr-96 SWE 1-CZE 3
08-May-97 SWE 1-CZE 0
10-May-99 SWE 0-CZE 2
12-May-01 SWE 2-CZE 3 (10:00 OT/GWS)
14-May-05 SWE 2-CZE 3 (OT)
21-May-06 SWE 4-CZE 0
11-May-08 SWE 5-CZE 3
14-May-08 SWE 3-CZE 2 (OT)
07-May-09 SWE 3-CZE 1
13-May-10 SWE 1-CZE 2
22-May-10 SWE 2-CZE 3 (10:00 OT/GWS)
13-May-11 SWE 5-CZE 2
05-May-12 SWE 4-CZE 1
17-May-12 SWE 3-CZE 4
Totals vs. TCH:
54-17-10-27-129-157
Totals vs. CZE:
17-10-0-7-46-34

03-May-03 SWE 7-DEN 1
24-Apr-04 SWE 5-DEN 1
02-May-05 SWE 7-DEN 0
03-May-07 SWE 5-DEN 2
08-May-08 SWE 8-DEN 1
20-May-10 SWE 4-DEN 2
07-May-12 SWE 6-DEN 4
Totals: 7-7-0-0-42-11

24-Feb-57 SWE 11-GDR 1
05-Mar-61 SWE 3-GDR 2
07-Mar-63 SWE 5-GDR 1
05-Mar-65 SWE 5-GDR 1
05-Mar-66 SWE 1-GDR 4
23-Mar-67 SWE 8-GDR 2
14-Mar-70 SWE 6-GDR 1
22-Mar-70 SWE 6-GDR 2
09-Apr-74 SWE 10-GDR 1
17-Apr-74 SWE 9-GDR 3
17-Apr-76 SWE 8-GDR 2
26-Apr-78 SWE 6-GDR 2
20-Apr-83 SWE 5-GDR 4
21-Apr-85 SWE 11-GDR 0
30-Apr-85 SWE 7-GDR 2
Totals: 15-14-0-1-101-28

12-Feb-49 SWE 12-FIN 1
15-Mar-51 SWE 11-FIN 3
28-Feb-54 SWE 5-FIN 3
02-Mar-55 SWE 9-FIN 0
04-Mar-57 SWE 9-FIN 3
01-Mar-58 SWE 5-FIN 2
06-Mar-59 SWE 4-FIN 4
13-Mar-59 SWE 2-FIN 1
07-Mar-61 SWE 6-FIN 4
12-Mar-62 SWE 12-FIN 2
10-Mar-63 SWE 4-FIN 0
07-Mar-65 SWE 2-FIN 2
03-Mar-66 SWE 5-FIN 1
21-Mar-67 SWE 5-FIN 1
15-Mar-69 SWE 6-FIN 3
23-Mar-69 SWE 5-FIN 0
17-Mar-70 SWE 1-FIN 3
26-Mar-70 SWE 4-FIN 3
24-Mar-71 SWE 1-FIN 1
01-Apr-71 SWE 2-FIN 1
12-Apr-72 SWE 2-FIN 1
20-Apr-72 SWE 4-FIN 5
05-Apr-73 SWE 3-FIN 2
13-Apr-73 SWE 2-FIN 1
10-Apr-74 SWE 3-FIN 3
18-Apr-74 SWE 6-FIN 2
08-Apr-75 SWE 1-FIN 0
17-Apr-75 SWE 1-FIN 2
15-Apr-76 SWE 4-FIN 3
24-Apr-77 SWE 5-FIN 1
02-May-78 SWE 6-FIN 1
24-Apr-82 SWE 3-FIN 3
24-Apr-83 SWE 4-FIN 4
20-Apr-85 SWE 0-FIN 5
02-May-85 SWE 1-FIN 6
21-Apr-86 SWE 4-FIN 4
24-Apr-86 SWE 4-FIN 4
24-Apr-87 SWE 1-FIN 4
19-Apr-89 SWE 6-FIN 3
16-Apr-90 SWE 4-FIN 2
20-Apr-91 SWE 4-FIN 4
03-May-92 SWE 1-FIN 3
10-May-92 SWE 5-FIN 2
27-Apr-94 SWE 3-FIN 5
25-Apr-95 SWE 3-FIN 6
07-May-95 SWE 1-FIN 4
28-Apr-96 SWE 5-FIN 5
07-May-97 SWE 5-FIN 2
07-May-98 SWE 1-FIN 0
16-May-98 SWE 1-FIN 0
17-May-98 SWE 0-FIN 0
12-May-99 SWE 1-FIN 3
13-May-99 SWE 2-FIN 1*
11-May-00 SWE 1-FIN 2
08-May-01 SWE 4-FIN 5
05-May-02 SWE 4-FIN 2
10-May-02 SWE 5-FIN 3
07-May-03 SWE 6-FIN 5
30-Apr-04 SWE 1-FIN 1
04-May-05 SWE 5-FIN 1
06-May-07 SWE 1-FIN 0
17-May-08 SWE 0-FIN 4
15-May-11 SWE 1-FIN 6
Totals: 63-36-12-15-234-158
*Game 2, best-of-two semi-finals. SWE won the game 2-0 but FIN clinched the series in OT.

26-Jan-35 SWE 2-FRA 1
18-Feb-37 SWE 1-FRA 2
28-Apr-94 SWE 6-FRA 0
24-Apr-96 SWE 2-FRA 1
02-May-98 SWE 6-FRA 1
02-May-99 SWE 4-FRA 1
05-May-08 SWE 9-FRA 0
04-May-09 SWE 6-FRA 3
11-May-10 SWE 3-FRA 2
06-May-11 SWE 4-FRA 0
Totals: 10-9-0-1-43-11

01-May-92 SWE 2-GER 5
07-May-02 SWE 6-GER 2
23-May-10 SWE 3-GER 1
11-May-11 SWE 5-GER 2
09-May-12 SWE 5-GER 2
Totals: 5-4-0-1-21-12

17-Feb-38 SWE 2-GBR 3
18-Mar-50 SWE 4-GBR 5
10-Mar-51 SWE 5-GBR 1
15-Mar-62 SWE 17-GBR 0
Totals: 4-2-0-2-28-9

21-Jan-35 SWE 3-HUN 0
Totals: 1-1-0-0-3-0

24-Jan-35 SWE 1-ITA 1
05-Mar-59 SWE 11-ITA 0
19-Apr-82 SWE 5-ITA 2
23-Apr-83 SWE 5-ITA 1
29-Apr-92 SWE 0-ITA 0
21-Apr-93 SWE 6-ITA 2
04-May-94 SWE 7-ITA 2
02-May-95 SWE 7-ITA 0
25-Apr-96 SWE 3-ITA 3
26-Apr-97 SWE 5-ITA 3
08-May-06 SWE 4-ITA 0
28-Apr-07 SWE 7-ITA 1
12-May-12 SWE 4-ITA 0
Totals: 13-10-3-0-65-15

02-Mar-57 SWE 18-JPN 0
25-Apr-04 SWE 5-JPN 1
Totals: 2-2-0-0-23-1

02-May-97 SWE 1-LAT 1
06-May-99 SWE 4-LAT 3
30-Apr-00 SWE 3-LAT 1
29-Apr-01 SWE 5-LAT 2
26-Apr-03 SWE 3-LAT 1
05-May-04 SWE 4-LAT 1
10-May-05 SWE 9-LAT 1
30-Apr-07 SWE 8-LAT 2
27-Apr-09 SWE 2-LAT 3 (5:00 OT/GWS)
14-May-10 SWE 4-LAT 2
15-May-12 SWE 4-LAT 0
Totals: 11-9-1-1-47-17

20-Jan-35 SWE 6-NED 0
14-Mar-50 SWE 10-NED 0
Totals: 2-2-0-0-16-0

21-Mar-50 SWE 6-NOR 1
13-Mar-51 SWE 5-NOR 2
26-Feb-54 SWE 10-NOR 1
28-Feb-58 SWE 9-NOR 0
16-Mar-62 SWE 10-NOR 2
11-Mar-65 SWE 10-NOR 0
17-Apr-90 SWE 4-NOR 3
25-Apr-94 SWE 3-NOR 3
23-Apr-95 SWE 5-NOR 0
27-Apr-96 SWE 3-NOR 0
29-Apr-97 SWE 4-NOR 1
09-May-10 SWE 5-NOR 2
30-Apr-11 SWE 4-NOR 5 (5:00 OT/GWS)
04-May-12 SWE 3-NOR 1
Totals: 14-12-1-1-81-21

04-Feb-31 SWE 0-POL 2
17-Feb-37 SWE 0-POL 3
16-Feb-38 SWE 1-POL 0
18-Feb-47 SWE 5-POL 3
06-Mar-55 SWE 9-POL 0
25-Feb-57 SWE 8-POL 3
07-Mar-58 SWE 12-POL 2
08-Mar-66 SWE 8-POL 2
19-Mar-70 SWE 11-POL 0
28-Mar-70 SWE 5-POL 1
01-Apr-73 SWE 11-POL 2
09-Apr-73 SWE 7-POL 0
06-Apr-74 SWE 0-POL 5*
14-Apr-74 SWE 3-POL 1
04-Apr-75 SWE 10-POL 0
13-Apr-75 SWE 13-POL 0
19-Apr-76 SWE 4-POL 1
15-Apr-79 SWE 6-POL 5
19-Apr-86 SWE 12-POL 3
15-Apr-89 SWE 5-POL 1
28-Apr-92 SWE 7-POL 0
Totals: 21-18-0-3-137-34
*SWE won game 4-1 but SWE failed doping test resulting in an official score of POL 5-0

19-Feb-47 SWE 15-ROM 3
21-Apr-77 SWE 8-ROM 1
Totals: 2-2-0-0-23-4

05-Mar-54 SWE 1-URS 1
26-Feb-55 SWE 1-URS 2
05-Mar-57 SWE 4-URS 4
08-Mar-58 SWE 3-URS 4
15-Mar-59 SWE 2-URS 4
04-Mar-61 SWE 2-URS 6
08-Mar-63 SWE 2-URS 1
10-Mar-65 SWE 3-URS 5
10-Mar-66 SWE 3-URS 3
25-Mar-67 SWE 1-URS 9
16-Mar-69 SWE 2-URS 4
24-Mar-69 SWE 2-URS 3
20-Mar-70 SWE 4-URS 2
30-Mar-70 SWE 1-URS 3
26-Mar-71 SWE 0-URS 8
03-Apr-71 SWE 3-URS 6
14-Apr-72 SWE 2-URS 11
22-Apr-72 SWE 3-URS 3
07-Apr-73 SWE 1-URS 6
15-Apr-73 SWE 4-URS 6
12-Apr-74 SWE 1-URS 3
20-Apr-74 SWE 1-URS 3
10-Apr-75 SWE 1-URS 4
19-Apr-75 SWE 4-URS 13
13-Apr-76 SWE 1-URS 6
21-Apr-76 SWE 4-URS 3
02-May-77 SWE 5-URS 1
08-May-77 SWE 3-URS 1
04-May-78 SWE 1-URS 6
12-May-78 SWE 1-URS 7
17-Apr-79 SWE 3-URS 9
23-Apr-79 SWE 3-URS 11
18-Apr-81 SWE 1-URS 4
24-Apr-81 SWE 1-URS 13
16-Apr-82 SWE 3-URS 7
27-Apr-82 SWE 0-URS 4
26-Apr-83 SWE 0-URS 4
28-Apr-83 SWE 0-URS 4
23-Apr-85 SWE 2-URS 6
12-Apr-86 SWE 2-URS 4
28-Apr-86 SWE 2-URS 3
26-Apr-87 SWE 2-URS 4
01-May-87 SWE 2-URS 2
24-Apr-89 SWE 2-URS 3
01-May-89 SWE 1-URS 5
22-Apr-90 SWE 3-URS 1
28-Apr-90 SWE 0-URS 3
28-Apr-91 SWE 5-URS 5
04-May-91 SWE 2-URS 1
06-May-92 SWE 2-RUS 0
24-Apr-93 SWE 5-RUS 2
02-May-93 SWE 1-RUS 3
05-May-97 SWE 1-RUS 4
09-May-99 SWE 4-RUS 1
09-May-00 SWE 2-RUS 4
10-May-01 SWE 4-RUS 3 (OT)
30-Apr-02 SWE 2-RUS 0
02-May-03 SWE 4-RUS 2
27-Apr-04 SWE 3-RUS 2
15-May-05 SWE 3-RUS 6
15-May-06 SWE 3-RUS 3
07-May-07 SWE 2-RUS 4
13-May-07 SWE 1-RUS 3
10-May-08 SWE 2-RUS 3
30-Apr-09 SWE 5-RUS 6 (OT)
11-May-12 SWE 3-RUS 7
Totals vs. URS:
49-7-6-36-100-232
Totals vs. RUS:
17-7-1-9-47-52

07-May-99 SWE 2-SVK 1
05-May-01 SWE 3-SVK 1
02-May-02 SWE 1-SVK 2
09-May-02 SWE 2-SVK 3 (10:00 OT/GWS)
09-May-03 SWE 4-SVK 1
03-May-04 SWE 0-SVK 0
14-May-06 SWE 2-SVK 5
09-May-07 SWE 7-SVK 4
Totals: 8-4-1-3-21-17

28-Apr-02 SWE 8-SLO 2
Totals: 1-1-0-0-8-2

19-Jan-35 SWE 1-SUI 6
18-Feb-38 SWE 2-SUI 0
15-Feb-47 SWE 4-SUI 4
17-Feb-49 SWE 3-SUI 1
20-Mar-50 SWE 2-SUI 3
14-Mar-51 SWE 3-SUI 3
07-Mar-53 SWE 9-SUI 2
12-Mar-53 SWE 9-SUI 1
02-Mar-54 SWE 6-SUI 3
27-Feb-55 SWE 10-SUI 0
09-Mar-62 SWE 17-SUI 2
08-Apr-72 SWE 12-SUI 1
16-Apr-72 SWE 8-SUI 5
21-Apr-87 SWE 12-SUI 1
23-Apr-91 SWE 4-SUI 3
09-May-92 SWE 4-SUI 1
25-Apr-93 SWE 4-SUI 6
04-May-98 SWE 4-SUI 2
12-May-98 SWE 4-SUI 1
14-May-98 SWE 7-SUI 2
04-May-99 SWE 6-SUI 1
06-May-00 SWE 1-SUI 1
06-May-03 SWE 5-SUI 2
12-May-05 SWE 2-SUI 1
10-May-06 SWE 4-SUI 4
02-May-07 SWE 6-SUI 0
07-May-08 SWE 2-SUI 4
03-May-09 SWE 4-SUI 1
18-May-10 SWE 5-SUI 0
08-May-11 SWE 2-SUI 0
Totals: 30-22-4-4-162-61

02-May-00 SWE 7-UKR 2
01-May-01 SWE 5-UKR 0
04-May-02 SWE 7-UKR 0
01-May-05 SWE 3-UKR 2
06-May-06 SWE 4-UKR 2
Totals: 5-5-0-0-26-6

05-Feb-31 SWE 0-USA 3
17-Feb-47 SWE 4-USA 1
18-Feb-49 SWE 3-USA 6
13-Mar-50 SWE 8-USA 3
17-Mar-50 SWE 2-USA 4
11-Mar-51 SWE 8-USA 0
05-Mar-55 SWE 1-USA 1
04-Mar-58 SWE 8-USA 3
10-Mar-59 SWE 1-USA 7
11-Mar-61 SWE 7-USA 3
10-Mar-62 SWE 2-USA 1
12-Mar-63 SWE 17-USA 2
04-Mar-65 SWE 5-USA 2
06-Mar-66 SWE 6-USA 1
18-Mar-67 SWE 3-USA 4
18-Mar-69 SWE 8-USA 2
29-Mar-69 SWE 10-USA 4
20-Mar-71 SWE 4-USA 2
28-Mar-71 SWE 4-USA 3
07-Apr-75 SWE 7-USA 0
16-Apr-75 SWE 12-USA 3
10-Apr-76 SWE 0-USA 2
25-Apr-76 SWE 7-USA 3

28-Apr-77 SWE 9-USA 0
27-Apr-78 SWE 5-USA 1
14-Apr-81 SWE 4-USA 2
15-Apr-82 SWE 4-USA 2
18-Apr-85 SWE 3-USA 4
16-Apr-86 SWE 5-USA 2
18-Apr-87 SWE 6-USA 2
16-Apr-89 SWE 4-USA 2
20-Apr-90 SWE 6-USA 1
22-Apr-91 SWE 4-USA 4
02-May-91 SWE 8-USA 4
04-May-92 SWE 4-USA 4
27-Apr-93 SWE 5-USA 2
30-Apr-94 SWE 6-USA 2
08-May-94 SWE 7-USA 2
28-Apr-95 SWE 2-USA 2
30-Apr-96 SWE 2-USA 3
03-May-97 SWE 3-USA 1
06-May-98 SWE 6-USA 1
08-May-00 SWE 3-USA 5
02-May-01 SWE 2-USA 2
13-May-01 SWE 3-USA 2
02-May-04 SWE 3-USA 1
08-May-04 SWE 3-USA 2
08-May-05 SWE 1-USA 5
17-May-06 SWE 6-USA 0
29-Apr-09 SWE 6-USA 5 (OT)
10-May-09 SWE 4-USA 2
04-May-11 SWE 6-USA 2
Totals: 52-37-5-10-257-127

08-Mar-53 SWE 8-FRG 6
13-Mar-53 SWE 12-FRG 2
04-Mar-54 SWE 4-FRG 0
25-Feb-55 SWE 5-FRG 4
07-Mar-59 SWE 6-FRG 1
08-Mar-61 SWE 12-FRG 1
17-Mar-62 SWE 4-FRG 0
13-Mar-63 SWE 10-FRG 2
20-Mar-67 SWE 3-FRG 1
23-Mar-71 SWE 7-FRG 2
31-Mar-71 SWE 1-FRG 2
11-Apr-72 SWE 10-FRG 0
19-Apr-72 SWE 7-FRG 1
04-Apr-73 SWE 8-FRG 2
12-Apr-73 SWE 12-FRG 1
08-Apr-76 SWE 4-FRG 1
25-Apr-77 SWE 7-FRG 1
29-Apr-78 SWE 10-FRG 1
14-Apr-79 SWE 7-FRG 3
12-Apr-81 SWE 4-FRG 2
21-Apr-82 SWE 3-FRG 1
16-Apr-83 SWE 5-FRG 1
17-Apr-85 SWE 3-FRG 2
28-Apr-85 SWE 5-FRG 2
18-Apr-86 SWE 4-FRG 2
17-Apr-87 SWE 3-FRG 0
18-Apr-89 SWE 3-FRG 3
19-Apr-90 SWE 6-FRG 0
19-Apr-91 SWE 8-FRG 1
Totals: 29-27-1-1-181-45

**WORLD U20 CHAMPIONSHIPS**

27-Dec-03 SWE 7-AUT 0
27-Dec-09 SWE 7-AUT 3
Totals: 2-2-0-0-14-3

30-Dec-98 SWE 5-BLR 4
25-Dec-01 SWE 5-BLR 0
03-Jan-03 SWE 5-BLR 4
Totals: 3-3-0-0-15-8

28-Dec-76 SWE 3-CAN 5
01-Jan-78 SWE 6-CAN 5
30-Dec-78 SWE 1-CAN 0
23-Dec-81 SWE 2-CAN 3
02-Jan-83 SWE 5-CAN 2
31-Dec-83 SWE 2-CAN 6
23-Dec-84 SWE 2-CAN 8
30-Dec-85 SWE 2-CAN 9
02-Jan-87 SWE 3-CAN 4
26-Dec-87 SWE 2-CAN 4
31-Dec-88 SWE 5-CAN 4
03-Jan-90 SWE 5-CAN 4
30-Dec-90 SWE 4-CAN 7
29-Dec-91 SWE 2-CAN 2
27-Dec-92 SWE 4-CAN 5
04-Jan-94 SWE 4-CAN 6
04-Jan-95 SWE 3-CAN 4
04-Jan-96 SWE 1-CAN 4
26-Dec-97 SWE 4-CAN 0
04-Jan-99 SWE 1-CAN 6
05-Jan-01 SWE 1-CAN 2 (OT)
01-Jan-02 SWE 2-CAN 5
26-Dec-02 SWE 2-CAN 8
27-Dec-04 SWE 1-CAN 8
26-Dec-06 SWE 0-CAN 2
29-Dec-07 SWE 4-CAN 3
05-Jan-08 SWE 2-CAN 3 (OT)
05-Jan-09 SWE 1-CAN 5
31-Dec-10 SWE 6-CAN 5 (5:00 OT/GWS)
Totals: 29-8-1-20-80-129

02-Jan-77 SWE 2-TCH 4
28-Dec-77 SWE 2-TCH 1
31-Dec-78 SWE 1-TCH 1
30-Dec-79 SWE 10-TCH 4
31-Dec-80 SWE 3-TCH 3
27-Dec-81 SWE 6-TCH 4
30-Dec-82 SWE 2-TCH 4
02-Jan-84 SWE 2-TCH 5
25-Dec-84 SWE 3-TCH 4
29-Dec-85 SWE 3-TCH 2
26-Dec-86 SWE 3-TCH 4
01-Jan-88 SWE 5-TCH 5
26-Dec-88 SWE 5-TCH 3
01-Jan-90 SWE 2-TCH 7
27-Dec-90 SWE 4-TCH 3
26-Dec-91 SWE 8-TCH 4
29-Dec-92 SWE 7-CZE/SVK 2
01-Jan-94 SWE 6-CZE 4
29-Dec-94 SWE 4-CZE 3
31-Dec-95 SWE 0-CZE 0
03-Jan-96 SWE 8-CZE 2
25-Dec-97 SWE 1-CZE 2
26-Dec-00 SWE 1-CZE 2
03-Jan-01 SWE 0-CZE 1
30-Dec-01 SWE 2-CZE 1
31-Dec-02 SWE 1-CZE 3
28-Dec-05 SWE 3-CZE 2
04-Jan-06 SWE 3-CZE 1
02-Jan-07 SWE 5-CZE 1
31-Dec-07 SWE 4-CZE 2
26-Dec-09 SWE 10-CZE 1
30-Dec-10 SWE 6-CZE 3
Totals vs. TCH:
17-8-3-6-68-60
Totals vs. CZE:
15-10-1-4-54-28

28-Dec-07 SWE 10-DEN 1
Totals: 1-1-0-0-10-1

23-Dec-76 SWE 5-FIN 4
22-Dec-77 SWE 4-FIN 4
28-Dec-78 SWE 2-FIN 1
02-Jan-79 SWE 5-FIN 2
01-Jan-80 SWE 2-FIN 3
30-Dec-80 SWE 2-FIN 1
30-Dec-81 SWE 6-FIN 9
26-Dec-82 SWE 4-FIN 6
29-Dec-83 SWE 1-FIN 4
26-Dec-84 SWE 3-FIN 5
26-Dec-85 SWE 2-FIN 0
30-Dec-86 SWE 5-FIN 0
03-Jan-88 SWE 2-FIN 5
28-Dec-88 SWE 6-FIN 2
28-Dec-89 SWE 2-FIN 5
26-Dec-90 SWE 5-FIN 8
04-Jan-92 SWE 6-FIN 4
02-Jan-93 SWE 9-FIN 2
29-Dec-93 SWE 6-FIN 2
02-Jan-95 SWE 3-FIN 3
28-Dec-96 SWE 2-FIN 4
28-Dec-97 SWE 3-FIN 4
28-Dec-02 SWE 2-FIN 3
29-Dec-04 SWE 4-FIN 5
03-Jan-05 SWE 3-FIN 4
02-Jan-06 SWE 0-FIN 1
26-Dec-08 SWE 3-FIN 1
31-Dec-09 SWE 7-FIN 1
03-Jan-12 SWE 3-FIN 2 (10:00 OT/GWS)
Totals: 29-13-2-14-107-95

02-Jan-92 SWE 10-GER 1
26-Dec-92 SWE 4-GER 2
26-Dec-93 SWE 4-GER 1
26-Dec-94 SWE 10-GER 2
28-Dec-95 SWE 6-GER 2
02-Jan-97 SWE 8-GER 2
29-Dec-97 SWE 8-GER 0
30-Dec-02 SWE 7-GER 2
26-Dec-04 SWE 6-GER 0
30-Dec-06 SWE 3-GER 1
Totals: 10-10-0-0-66-13

30-Dec-92 SWE 20-JPN 1
Totals: 1-1-0-0-20-1

02-Jan-98 SWE 5-KAZ 1
31-Dec-98 SWE 11-KAZ 4
31-Dec-99 SWE 13-KAZ 1
03-Jan-00 SWE 12-KAZ 2
29-Dec-00 SWE 8-KAZ 2
Totals: 5-5-0-0-49-10

30-Dec-05 SWE 10-LAT 2
29-Dec-08 SWE 10-LAT 1
26-Dec-11 SWE 9-LAT 4
Totals: 3-3-0-0-29-7

01-Jan-83 SWE 15-NOR 3
01-Jan-89 SWE 9-NOR 1
26-Dec-89 SWE 4-NOR 3
04-Jan-91 SWE 10-NOR 0
26-Dec-10 SWE 7-NOR 1
Totals: 5-5-0-0-45-8

29-Dec-76 SWE 6-POL 5
29-Dec-84 SWE 11-POL 0
27-Dec-86 SWE 15-POL 0
28-Dec-87 SWE 13-POL 0
31-Dec-89 SWE 14-POL 0
30-Dec-96 SWE 7-POL 2
Totals: 6-6-0-0-66-7

26-Dec-76 SWE 2-URS 4
23-Dec-77 SWE 6-URS 3
31-Dec-77 SWE 0-URS 5
03-Jan-78 SWE 2-URS 5
03-Jan-79 SWE 5-URS 7
02-Jan-80 SWE 1-URS 2
02-Jan-81 SWE 3-URS 2
02-Jan-82 SWE 2-URS 7
04-Jan-83 SWE 1-URS 5
03-Jan-84 SWE 2-URS 8
28-Dec-84 SWE 1-URS 5
27-Dec-85 SWE 1-URS 6
01-Jan-87 SWE 3-URS 3
31-Dec-87 SWE 2-URS 4
29-Dec-88 SWE 2-URS 3
04-Jan-90 SWE 5-URS 5
29-Dec-90 SWE 1-URS 5
27-Dec-91 SWE 3-RUS 4
04-Jan-93 SWE 5-RUS 1
27-Dec-93 SWE 3-RUS 0
01-Jan-95 SWE 4-RUS 6
29-Dec-95 SWE 2-RUS 5
31-Dec-96 SWE 0-RUS 0
26-Dec-98 SWE 4-RUS 2
29-Dec-99 SWE 1-RUS 5
02-Jan-01 SWE 3-RUS 2
28-Dec-03 SWE 3-RUS 5
26-Dec-05 SWE 1-RUS 5
03-Jan-07 SWE 2-RUS 4
04-Jan-08 SWE 2-RUS 1 (OT)
31-Dec-08 SWE 5-RUS 0
29-Dec-09 SWE 4-RUS 1
28-Dec-10 SWE 2-RUS 0
03-Jan-11 SWE 3-RUS 4 (10:00 OT/GWS)
31-Dec-11 SWE 4-RUS 3 (OT)
05-Jan-12 SWE 1-RUS 0 (OT)
Totals vs. URS:
17-2-2-13-39-79
Totals vs. RUS:
19-10-1-8-52-48

26-Dec-95 SWE 6-SVK 0
27-Dec-96 SWE 1-SVK 4
05-Jan-99 SWE 4-SVK 5
27-Dec-00 SWE 3-SVK 1
29-Dec-01 SWE 2-SVK 2
02-Jan-02 SWE 3-SVK 2
31-Dec-03 SWE 0-SVK 1
30-Dec-04 SWE 3-SVK 0
31-Dec-05 SWE 6-SVK 0
28-Dec-06 SWE 6-SVK 3
26-Dec-07 SWE 4-SVK 3
28-Dec-08 SWE 3-SVK 1
03-Jan-09 SWE 5-SVK 3
30-Dec-11 SWE 9-SVK 1
Totals: 14-10-1-3-55-26

26-Dec-77 SWE 8-SUI 1
22-Dec-81 SWE 17-SUI 0
26-Dec-83 SWE 5-SUI 2
01-Jan-86 SWE 7-SUI 1
29-Dec-86 SWE 8-SUI 0
01-Jan-91 SWE 6-SUI 1
01-Jan-92 SWE 4-SUI 3
30-Dec-93 SWE 6-SUI 2
03-Jan-97 SWE 2-SUI 6
31-Dec-97 SWE 1-SUI 2 (10:00 OT/GWS)
28-Dec-98 SWE 5-SUI 1
26-Dec-99 SWE 7-SUI 1
04-Jan-00 SWE 5-SUI 2
04-Jan-03 SWE 3-SUI 5
03-Jan-04 SWE 4-SUI 3
05-Jan-10 SWE 11-SUI 4
28-Dec-11 SWE 4-SUI 3 (5:00 OT/GWS)
Totals: 17-14-0-3-103-37

30-Dec-94 SWE 7-UKR 1
28-Dec-99 SWE 6-UKR 1
02-Jan-04 SWE 4-UKR 0
Totals: 3-3-0-0-17-2

25-Dec-76 SWE 5-USA 8
28-Dec-79 SWE 5-USA 1
28-Dec-80 SWE 10-USA 2
31-Dec-81 SWE 4-USA 2
29-Dec-82 SWE 4-USA 1
25-Dec-83 SWE 4-USA 1
01-Jan-85 SWE 7-USA 3
04-Jan-86 SWE 1-USA 5
04-Jan-87 SWE 8-USA 0
04-Jan-88 SWE 7-USA 5
04-Jan-89 SWE 3-USA 1
29-Dec-89 SWE 6-USA 5
02-Jan-91 SWE 2-USA 5
30-Dec-91 SWE 8-USA 6
01-Jan-93 SWE 4-USA 2
02-Jan-94 SWE 6-USA 1
27-Dec-94 SWE 4-USA 2
01-Jan-96 SWE 3-USA 0
03-Jan-98 SWE 3-USA 4
01-Jan-00 SWE 1-USA 5
31-Dec-00 SWE 1-USA 3
27-Dec-01 SWE 2-USA 2
04-Jan-02 SWE 2-USA 3
30-Dec-03 SWE 3-USA 4
01-Jan-05 SWE 2-USA 8
31-Dec-06 SWE 2-USA 3 (OT)
05-Jan-07 SWE 1-USA 2
03-Jan-10 SWE 2-USA 5
05-Jan-11 SWE 2-USA 4
Totals: 29-15-1-13-112-93

01-Jan-77 SWE 5-FRG 0
27-Dec-78 SWE 5-FRG 2
27-Dec-79 SWE 5-FRG 1
27-Dec-80 SWE 7-FRG 3
26-Dec-81 SWE 5-FRG 1
27-Dec-82 SWE 4-FRG 2
28-Dec-83 SWE 11-FRG 2
31-Dec-84 SWE 5-FRG 1
02-Jan-86 SWE 10-FRG 0
29-Dec-87 SWE 5-FRG 1
03-Jan-89 SWE 9-FRG 0
Totals: 11-11-0-0-71-13

**WORLD U18 CHAMPIONSHIPS**

15-Apr-02 SWE 4-BLR 2
16-Apr-03 SWE 9-BLR 3
13-Apr-04 SWE 4-BLR 0
13-Apr-08 SWE 6-BLR 2
14-Apr-10 SWE 7-BLR 0
Totals: 5-5-0-0-30-7

19-Apr-03 SWE 1-CAN 8
08-Apr-04 SWE 0-CAN 5
16-Apr-05 SWE 2-CAN 1
15-Apr-06 SWE 2-CAN 0
22-Apr-07 SWE 8-CAN 3
21-Apr-08 SWE 2-CAN 3
14-Apr-09 SWE 2-CAN 4
18-Apr-10 SWE 5-CAN 4
19-Apr-11 SWE 4-CAN 2
Totals: 9-5-0-4-26-30

11-Apr-99 SWE 4-CZE 4
17-Apr-00 SWE 6-CZE 2
14-Apr-01 SWE 1-CZE 2
21-Apr-03 SWE 3-CZE 2 (OT)
15-Apr-04 SWE 1-CZE 5
24-Apr-05 SWE 4-CZE 2
19-Apr-06 SWE 0-CZE 3
17-Apr-07 SWE 3-CZE 0
09-Apr-09 SWE 7-CZE 0
18-Apr-09 SWE 4-CZE 2
14-Apr-11 SWE 1-CZE 2
Totals: 11-6-1-4-34-24

12-Apr-04 SWE 2-DEN 1
19-Apr-05 SWE 3-DEN 1
Totals: 2-2-0-0-5-2

18-Apr-99 SWE 2-FIN 2
22-Apr-00 SWE 2-FIN 4
11-Apr-02 SWE 0-FIN 2
12-Apr-03 SWE 3-FIN 3
14-Apr-06 SWE 3-FIN 4
11-Apr-07 SWE 2-FIN 1 (5:00 OT/GWS)
15-Apr-08 SWE 5-FIN 3
17-Apr-11 SWE 5-FIN 2
20-Apr-12 SWE 7-FIN 3
Totals: 9-4-2-3-29-24

09-Apr-99 SWE 5-GER 2
15-Apr-00 SWE 3-GER 0
16-Apr-01 SWE 1-GER 2
18-Apr-02 SWE 4-GER 0
18-Apr-05 SWE 3-GER 2
11-Apr-09 SWE 5-GER 4
12-Apr-12 SWE 8-GER 1
Totals: 7-6-0-1-29-11

15-Apr-12 SWE 3-LAT 1
Totals: 1-1-0-0-3-1

12-Apr-01 SWE 4-NOR 3
21-Apr-02 SWE 3-NOR 2
12-Apr-06 SWE 5-NOR 2
15-Apr-11 SWE 10-NOR 2
Totals: 4-4-0-0-22-9

15-Apr-99 SWE 2-RUS 3
17-Apr-01 SWE 4-RUS 3
14-Apr-05 SWE 1-RUS 2
21-Apr-06 SWE 2-RUS 5
20-Apr-07 SWE 4-RUS 5
16-Apr-09 SWE 1-RUS 4
21-Apr-10 SWE 3-RUS 1
23-Apr-11 SWE 3-RUS 1
17-Apr-12 SWE 2-RUS 0
Totals: 9-4-0-5-22-24

16-Apr-99 SWE 4-SVK 1
20-Apr-01 SWE 5-SVK 1
20-Apr-02 SWE 3-SVK 5
13-Apr-03 SWE 1-SVK 4
17-Apr-04 SWE 5-SVK 4
21-Apr-05 SWE 5-SVK 3
17-Apr-06 SWE 5-SVK 2
13-Apr-07 SWE 3-SVK 6
Totals: 8-5-0-3-31-26

08-Apr-99 SWE 3-SUI 0
14-Apr-00 SWE 8-SUI 2
24-Apr-00 SWE 7-SUI 1
12-Apr-02 SWE 2-SUI 3
15-Apr-07 SWE 3-SUI 0
18-Apr-08 SWE 7-SUI 0
13-Apr-09 SWE 11-SUI 0
16-Apr-10 SWE 10-SUI 2
14-Apr-12 SWE 7-SUI 2
Totals: 9-8-0-1-58-10

13-Apr-99 SWE 10-UKR 2
19-Apr-00 SWE 4-UKR 1
19-Apr-01 SWE 9-UKR 4
14-Apr-02 SWE 8-UKR 3
Totals: 4-4-0-0-31-10

17 Apr 02 SWE 2-USA 6
15-Apr-03 SWE 2-USA 3
10-Apr-04 SWE 2-USA 6
22-Apr-05 SWE 2-USA 6
16-Apr-08 SWE 5-USA 4
23-Apr-08 SWE 3-USA 6
13-Apr-10 SWE 4-USA 2
23-Apr-10 SWE 1-USA 3
24-Apr-11 SWE 3-USA 4 (OT)
22-Apr-12 SWE 0-USA 7
Totals: 10-2-0-8-24-47

**OLYMPICS, WOMEN**

11-Feb-98 SWE 3-CAN 5
16-Feb-02 SWE 0-CAN 11
14-Feb-06 SWE 1-CAN 8
20-Feb-06 SWE 1-CAN 4
17-Feb-10 SWE 1-CAN 13
Totals: 5-0-0-5-6-41

12-Feb-98 SWE 1-CHN 3
Totals: 1-0-0-1-1-3

08-Feb-98 SWE 0-FIN 6
21-Feb-02 SWE 2-FIN 1
25-Feb-10 SWE 2-FIN 3 (OT)
Totals: 3-1-0-2-4-10

13-Feb-06 SWE 11-ITA 0
Totals: 1-1-0-0-11-0

14-Feb-98 SWE 5-JPN 0
Totals: 1-1-0-0-5-0

13-Feb-02 SWE 7-KAZ 0
Totals: 1-1-0-0-7-0

11-Feb-02 SWE 3-RUS 2
11-Feb-06 SWE 3-RUS 1
Totals: 2-2-0-0-6-3

15-Feb-10 SWE 6-SVK 2
Totals: 1-1-0-0-6-2

13-Feb-10 SWE 3-SUI 0
Totals: 1-1-0-0-3-0

09-Feb-98 SWE 1-USA 7
19-Feb-02 SWE 0-USA 4
17-Feb-06 SWE 3-USA 2 (10:00 OT/GWS)
22-Feb-10 SWE 1-USA 9
Totals: 4-1-0-3-5-22

**WOMEN'S WORLD CHAMPIONSHIPS**

19-Mar-90 SWE 1-CAN 15
23-Apr-92 SWE 1-CAN 6
14-Apr-94 SWE 2-CAN 8
13-Mar-99 SWE 1-CAN 4
06-Apr-00 SWE 0-CAN 4
05-Apr-01 SWE 0-CAN 13
04-Apr-04 SWE 1-CAN 7
06-Apr-05 SWE 0-CAN 10
06-Apr-09 SWE 0-CAN 7
Totals: 9-0-0-9-6-74

21-Apr-92 SWE 6-CHN 2
12-Apr-94 SWE 4-CHN 4
08-Mar-99 SWE 3-CHN 1
03-Apr-00 SWE 1-CHN 1
08-Apr-07 SWE 12-CHN 2
05-Apr-09 SWE 6-CHN 1
Totals: 6-4-2-0-32-11

20-Apr-92 SWE 4-DEN 1
Totals: 1-1-0-0-4-1

25-Mar-90 SWE 3-FIN 6
26-Apr-92 SWE 4-FIN 5 (10:00 OT/GWS)
31-Mar-97 SWE 0-FIN 3
14-Mar-99 SWE 2-FIN 8
09-Apr-00 SWE 1-FIN 7
01-Apr-04 SWE 2-FIN 2
06-Apr-04 SWE 2-FIN 3
09-Apr-05 SWE 5-FIN 2
05-Apr-07 SWE 0-FIN 1 (5:00 OT/GWS)
10-Apr-07 SWE 1-FIN 0
06-Apr-08 SWE 2-FIN 3 (OT)
12-Apr-09 SWE 1-FIN 4
22-Apr-11 SWE 1-FIN 5
11-Apr-12 SWE 1-FIN 2
Totals: 14-2-1-11-25-51

22-Mar-90 SWE 7-GER 0
16-Apr-94 SWE 7-GER 1
06-Apr-01 SWE 2-GER 6
08-Apr-12 SWE 2-GER 1 (OT)
Totals: 4-3-0-1-18-8

21-Mar-90 SWE 11-JPN 4
04-Apr-00 SWE 10-JPN 0
30-Mar-04 SWE 8-JPN 2
04-Apr-08 SWE 5-JPN 0
Totals: 4-4-0-0-34-6

03-Apr-01 SWE 3-KAZ 1
08-Apr-01 SWE 3-KAZ 1
04-Apr-05 SWE 5-KAZ 1
08-Apr-09 SWE 9-KAZ 0
Totals: 4-4-0-0-20-3

11-Apr-94 SWE 3-NOR 1
17-Apr-94 SWE 6-NOR 3
01-Apr-97 SWE 2-NOR 2
Totals: 3-2-1-0-11-6

06-Apr-97 SWE 3-RUS 1
11-Mar-99 SWE 7-RUS 0
02-Apr-01 SWE 0-RUS 3
02-Apr-05 SWE 3-RUS 1
03-Apr-07 SWE 3-RUS 2
09-Apr-08 SWE 3-RUS 1
10-Apr-09 SWE 8-RUS 0
17-Apr-11 SWE 7-RUS 1
13-Apr-12 SWE 2-RUS 1
Totals: 9-8-0-1-36-10

18-Apr-11 SWE 3-SVK 0
07-Apr-12 SWE 5-SVK 1
Totals: 2-2-0-0-8-1

04-Apr-97 SWE 7-SUI 1
09-Apr-07 SWE 4-SUI 0
08-Apr-08 SWE 3-SUI 4 (5:00 OT/GWS)
24-Apr-11 SWE 3-SUI 2 (5:00 OT/GWS)
10-Apr-12 SWE 2-SUI 3
Totals: 5-3-0-2-19-10

24-Mar-90 SWE 3-USA 10
25-Apr-92 SWE 4-USA 6
03-Apr-97 SWE 0-USA 10
09-Mar-99 SWE 0-USA 11
08-Apr-00 SWE 1-USA 7
05-Apr-04 SWE 2-USA 9
08-Apr-05 SWE 1-USA 4
20-Apr-11 SWE 1-USA 9
Totals: 8-0-0-8-12-66

**WOMEN'S U18 WORLD CHAMPIONSHIPS**

11-Jan-08 SWE 1-CAN 7
09-Jan-09 SWE 1-CAN 6
30-Mar-10 SWE 0-CAN 8
06-Jan-12 SWE 0-CAN 7
Totals: 4-0-0-4-2-28

12-Jan-08 SWE 2-CZE 4
10-Jan-09 SWE 9-CZE 1
02-Jan-11 SWE 3-CZE 2
31-Dec-11 SWE 4-CZE 1
Totals: 4-3-0-1-18-8

05-Jan-11 SWE 2-FIN 3 (OT)
04-Jan-12 SWE 2-FIN 1 (OT)
Totals: 2-1-0-1-4-4

05-Jan-09 SWE 8-GER 1
27-Mar-10 SWE 5-GER 4
03-Apr-10 SWE 7-GER 3
07-Jan-11 SWE 2-GER 0
07-Jan-12 SWE 4-GER 1
Totals: 5-5-0-0-26-9

31-Mar-10 SWE 2-JPN 1
01-Jan-11 SWE 2-JPN 1
Totals: 2-2-0-0-4-2

08-Jan-08 SWE 14-RUS 0
06-Jan-09 SWE 6-RUS 1
28-Mar-10 SWE 4-RUS 1
03-Jan-12 SWE 6-RUS 2
Totals: 4-4-0-0-30-4

07-Jan-08 SWE 4-SUI 1
Totals: 1-1-0-0-4-1

09-Jan-08 SWE 2-USA 6
07-Jan-09 SWE 2-USA 9
02-Apr-10 SWE 0-USA 5
04-Jan-11 SWE 0-USA 10
01-Jan-12 SWE 0-USA 7
Totals: 5-0-0-5-4-37

# SWITZERLAND (SUI)

Totals=GP-W-T-L-GF-GA

**OLYMPICS, MEN**

**Date** **Score**

11-Feb-28 SUI 4-AUT 4
01-Feb-48 SUI 11-AUT 2
31-Jan-56 SUI 7-AUT 4
11-Feb-76 SUI 5-AUT 3
14-Feb-02 SUI 4-AUT 1
Totals: 5-4-1-0-31-14

13-Feb-02 SUI 2-BLR 1
23-Feb-10 SUI 3-BLR 2 (10:00 OT/GWS)
Totals: 2-2-0-0-5-3

07-Feb-76 SUI 8-BUL 3
Totals: 1-1-0-0-8-3

30-Jan-24 SUI 0-CAN 33
19-Feb-28 SUI 0-CAN 13
08-Feb-48 SUI 0-CAN 3
21-Feb-52 SUI 2-CAN 11
29-Jan-64 SUI 0-CAN 8
16-Feb-88 SUI 2-CAN 4
10-Feb-92 SUI 1-CAN 6
18-Feb-06 SUI 2-CAN 0
18-Feb-10 SUI 2-CAN 3 (5:00 OT/GWS)
Totals: 9-1-0-8-9-81

01-Feb-24 SUI 2-TCH 11
07-Feb-48 SUI 1-TCH 7
22-Feb-52 SUI 3-TCH 8
04-Feb-64 SUI 1-TCH 5
16-Feb-92 SUI 2-TCH 4
16-Feb-06 SUI 3-CZE 2
Totals vs. TCH:
5-0-0-5-9-35
Totals vs. CZE:
1-1-0-0-3-2

16-Feb-52 SUI 12-FIN 0
30-Jan-64 SUI 0-FIN 4
14-Feb-88 SUI 2-FIN 1
15-Feb-06 SUI 0-FIN 5
Totals: 4-2-0-2-14-10

22-Feb-88 SUI 9-FRA 0
12-Feb-92 SUI 3-FRA 4
09-Feb-02 SUI 3-FRA 3
Totals: 3-1-1-1-15-7

16-Feb-28 SUI 1-GER 0
08-Feb-36 SUI 0-GER 2
24-Feb-52 SUI 6-GER 3
07-Feb-64 SUI 5-GER 6
19-Feb-06 SUI 2-GER 2
Totals: 5-2-1-2-14-13

17-Feb-28 SUI 4-GBR 0
04-Feb-48 SUI 12-GBR 3
Totals: 2-2-0-0-16-3

09-Feb-36 SUI 1-ITA 0
31-Jan-48 SUI 16-ITA 0
02-Feb-56 SUI 3-ITA 8
21-Feb-06 SUI 3-ITA 3
Totals: 4-2-1-1-23-11

07-Feb-72 SUI 3-JPN 3
09-Feb-76 SUI 4-JPN 6
Totals: 2-0-1-1-7-9

18-Feb-52 SUI 7-NOR 2
12-Feb-72 SUI 3-NOR 5
14-Feb-92 SUI 6-NOR 3
21-Feb-92 SUI 2-NOR 5
20-Feb-10 SUI 5-NOR 4 (OT)
Totals: 5-3-0-2-23-19

06-Feb-48 SUI 14-POL 0
17-Feb-52 SUI 6-POL 3
01-Feb-56 SUI 2-POL 6
20-Feb-88 SUI 4-POL 1
19-Feb-92 SUI 7-POL 2
Totals: 5-4-0-1-33-12

13-Feb-76 SUI 3-ROM 4
Totals: 1-0-0-1-3-4

29-Jan-56 SUI 3-URS 10
01-Feb-64 SUI 0-URS 15
08-Feb-92 SUI 1-RUS 8
Totals vs. URS:
2-0-0-2-3-25
Totals vs. RUS:
1-0-0-1-1-8

28-Apr-20 SUI 0-SWE 4
28-Jan-24 SUI 0-SWE 9
18-Feb-28 SUI 0-SWE 4
05-Feb-48 SUI 8-SWE 2
23-Feb-52 SUI 2-SWE 5
28-Jan-56 SUI 5-SWE 6
05-Feb-64 SUI 0-SWE 12
18-Feb-88 SUI 2-SWE 4
22-Feb-06 SUI 2-SWE 6
Totals: 9-1-0-8-19-52

11-Feb-02 SUI 2-UKR 5
Totals: 1-0-0-1-2-5

24-Apr-20 SUI 0-USA 29
07-Feb-36 SUI 0-USA 3
30-Jan-48 SUI 5-USA 4
19-Feb-52 SUI 2-USA 8
08-Feb-64 SUI 3-USA 7
25-Feb-88 SUI 4-USA 8
16-Feb-10 SUI 1-USA 3
24-Feb-10 SUI 0-USA 2
Totals: 8-1-0-7-15-64

06-Feb-72 SUI 0-FRG 5
Totals: 1-0-0-1-0-5

10-Feb-72 SUI 3-YUG 3
05-Feb-76 SUI 4-YUG 6
Totals: 2-0-1-1-7-9

**WORLD CHAMPIONSHIPS, MEN**

02-Feb-30 SUI 2-AUT 1
22-Jan-35 SUI 1-AUT 1 (30:00 OT)
22-Feb-47 SUI 5-AUT 0
19-Feb-49 SUI 10-AUT 1
23-Apr-93 SUI 5-AUT 1
02-May-95 SUI 0-AUT 4
03-May-95 SUI 4-AUT 4
27-Apr-04 SUI 4-AUT 4
Totals: 8-4-3-1-31-16

09-May-00 SUI 3-BLR 5
30-Apr-01 SUI 5-BLR 2
09-May-05 SUI 2-BLR 0
16-May-06 SUI 1-BLR 2
05-May-08 SUI 2-BLR 1
01-May-11 SUI 4-BLR 1
06-May-12 SUI 3-BLR 2
Totals: 7-5-0-2-20-13

03-Feb-34 SUI 20-BEL 1
19-Feb-47 SUI 12-BEL 2
13-Feb-49 SUI 18-BEL 2
13-Mar-50 SUI 24-BEL 3
Totals: 4-4-0-0-74-8

10-Feb-34 SUI 1-CAN 2 (OT)
27-Jan-35 SUI 2-CAN 4
27-Feb-37 SUI 1-CAN 2 (OT)
10-Feb-39 SUI 0-CAN 7
20-Feb-49 SUI 1-CAN 1
14-Mar-50 SUI 2-CAN 13
17-Mar-50 SUI 1-CAN 11
16-Mar-51 SUI 1-CAN 5
27-Feb-54 SUI 1-CAN 8
02-Mar-55 SUI 1-CAN 11
06-Mar-59 SUI 0-CAN 23
11-Mar-62 SUI 2-CAN 7
20-Apr-87 SUI 1-CAN 6
20-Apr-91 SUI 0-CAN 3
30-Apr-92 SUI 1-CAN 1
19-Apr-93 SUI 0-CAN 2
24-Apr-95 SUI 3-CAN 5
07-May-99 SUI 2-CAN 8
11-May-00 SUI 3-CAN 5
04-May-01 SUI 2-CAN 6
03-May-02 SUI 2-CAN 3
04-May-03 SUI 0-CAN 2
28-Apr-04 SUI 1-CAN 3
10-May-07 SUI 1-CAN 5
12-May-10 SUI 4-CAN 1
03-May-11 SUI 3-CAN 4 (OT)
09-May-12 SUI 2-CAN 3
Totals: 27-1-2-24-38-151

01-Feb-30 SUI 3-TCH 1
22-Feb-33 SUI 0-TCH 1
26-Jan-35 SUI 4-TCH 0
19-Feb-37 SUI 2-TCH 2
18-Feb-38 SUI 2-TCH 3 (20:00 OT)
05-Feb-39 SUI 1-TCH 0
12-Feb-39 SUI 0-TCH 0 (30:00 OT)
05-Mar-39 SUI 2-TCH 0
20-Feb-47 SUI 1-TCH 6
18-Feb-49 SUI 1-TCH 8
08-Mar-53 SUI 4-TCH 9
26-Feb-54 SUI 1-TCH 7
25-Feb-55 SUI 0-TCH 7
05-Mar-59 SUI 0-TCH 9
07-Apr-72 SUI 1-TCH 19
15-Apr-72 SUI 2-TCH 12
23-Apr-87 SUI 2-TCH 5
22-Apr-91 SUI 1-TCH 4
29-Apr-91 SUI 4-TCH 3
04-May-92 SUI 0-TCH 2
10-May-92 SUI 2-TCH 5
09-May-98 SUI 1-CZE 3
15-May-98 SUI 0-CZE 4
01-May-01 SUI 1-CZE 3
26-Apr-02 SUI 0-CZE 5
02-May-04 SUI 1-CZE 3
01-May-05 SUI 1-CZE 3
08-May-08 SUI 0-CZE 5
15-May-10 SUI 3-CZE 2
Totals vs. TCH:
21-5-2-14-33-103
Totals vs. CZE:
8-1-0-7-7-28

29-Apr-03 SUI 6-DEN 2
05-May-07 SUI 4-DEN 1
11-May-08 SUI 7-DEN 2
Totals: 3-3-0-0-17-5

10-Mar-59 SUI 2-GDR 6
Totals: 1-0-0-1-2-6

13-Mar-51 SUI 4-FIN 1
06-Mar-54 SUI 3-FIN 3
05-Mar-55 SUI 2-FIN 7
14-Mar-62 SUI 4-FIN 7
11-Apr-72 SUI 3-FIN 2
19-Apr-72 SUI 1-FIN 9
18-Apr-87 SUI 2-FIN 3
30-Apr-87 SUI 4-FIN 7
26-Apr-91 SUI 1-FIN 6
01-May-91 SUI 2-FIN 6
09-May-99 SUI 1-FIN 5
03-May-07 SUI 0-FIN 2
08-May-12 SUI 2-FIN 5
Totals: 13-2-1-10-29-63

04-Feb-34 SUI 3-FRA 0
23-Jan-35 SUI 5-FRA 1
01-May-92 SUI 6-FRA 5
29-Apr-93 SUI 1-FRA 3
28-Apr-95 SUI 2-FRA 3
06-May-98 SUI 5-FRA 1
06-May-99 SUI 6-FRA 0
01-May-00 SUI 2-FRA 4
25-Apr-04 SUI 6-FRA 0
03-May-08 SUI 4-FRA 1
24-Apr-09 SUI 1-FRA 0
29-Apr-11 SUI 1-FRA 0 (OT)
12-May-12 SUI 2-FRA 4
Totals: 13-9-0-4-44-22

09-Feb-30 SUI 1-GER 2
24-Feb-33 SUI 1-GER 1
11-Feb-34 SUI 1-GER 2 (20:00 OT)
26-Feb-37 SUI 6-GER 0
07-May-92 SUI 3-GER 1
30-Apr-95 SUI 3-GER 5
28-Apr-01 SUI 1-GER 3
28-Apr-02 SUI 0-GER 3
04-May-04 SUI 1-GER 0
05-May-05 SUI 5-GER 1
26-Apr-09 SUI 3-GER 2 (OT)
20-May-10 SUI 0-GER 1
Totals: 12-5-1-6-25-21

24-Jan-35 SUI 1-GBR 0
20-Feb-37 SUI 0-GBR 3
25-Feb-37 SUI 0-GBR 2 (20:00 OT)
22-Mar-50 SUI 10-GBR 3
12-Mar-51 SUI 7-GBR 1
08-Mar-62 SUI 6-GBR 3
Totals: 6-4-0-2-24-12

19-Feb-33 SUI 1-HUN 0
07-Feb-34 SUI 1-HUN 0
20-Jan-35 SUI 1-HUN 1
22-Feb-37 SUI 4-HUN 2
11-Feb-38 SUI 1-HUN 0
09-Feb-39 SUI 5-HUN 2
Totals: 6-5-1-0-13-5

08-Feb-34 SUI 3-ITA 0
11-Mar-59 SUI 1-ITA 4
20-Apr-93 SUI 0-ITA 1
27-Apr-95 SUI 2-ITA 3
07-May-01 SUI 8-ITA 1
06-May-06 SUI 3-ITA 1
30-Apr-07 SUI 2-ITA 1
10-May-10 SUI 3-ITA 0
Totals: 8-5-0-3-22-11

29-Apr-02 SUI 5-JPN 1
Totals: 1-1-0-0-5-1

03-May-05 SUI 2-KAZ 1
05-May-12 SUI 5-KAZ 1
Totals: 2-2-0-0-7-2

18-Feb-33 SUI 5-LAT 1
03-Feb-39 SUI 12-LAT 0
02-May-99 SUI 5-LAT 3
08-May-00 SUI 4-LAT 1
05-May-02 SUI 6-LAT 4
03-May-03 SUI 4-LAT 2
01-May-04 SUI 1-LAT 1
28-Apr-07 SUI 2-LAT 1
30-Apr-09 SUI 1-LAT 2 (5:00 OT/GWS)
08-May-10 SUI 3-LAT 1
Totals: 10-8-1-1-43-16

14-Feb-38 SUI 15-LTU 0
Totals: 1-1-0-0-15-0

21-Jan-35 SUI 4-NED 0
Totals: 1-1-0-0-4-0

18-Feb-37 SUI 13-NOR 2
14-Feb-49 SUI 7-NOR 1
18-Mar-50 SUI 12-NOR 4
10-Mar-51 SUI 8-NOR 1
04-Mar-54 SUI 2-NOR 3
09-Mar-59 SUI 4-NOR 4
12-Mar-62 SUI 5-NOR 7
03-May-92 SUI 3-NOR 1
01-May-93 SUI 2-NOR 5
17-May-10 SUI 2-NOR 3
05-May-11 SUI 2-NOR 3
Totals: 11-5-1-5-60-34

23-Feb-33 SUI 3-POL 1
23-Feb-37 SUI 1-POL 0
15-Feb-38 SUI 7-POL 1
07-Feb-39 SUI 4-POL 0
23-Feb-47 SUI 9-POL 3
01-Mar-55 SUI 4-POL 2
07-Mar-59 SUI 8-POL 3
13-Mar-59 SUI 1-POL 2
Totals: 8-7-0-1-37-12

05-Feb-34 SUI 7-ROM 2
12-Feb-38 SUI 8-ROM 1
17-Feb-47 SUI 13-ROM 3
Totals: 3-3-0-0-28-6

03-Mar-54 SUI 2-URS 4
04-Mar-55 SUI 2-URS 7
10-Apr-72 SUI 2-URS 10
18-Apr-72 SUI 0-URS 14
17-Apr-87 SUI 5-URS 13
19-Apr-91 SUI 1-URS 3
28-Apr-92 SUI 2-RUS 2
22-Apr-93 SUI 0-RUS 6
25-Apr-95 SUI 0-RUS 8
07-May-98 SUI 4-RUS 2
03-May-00 SUI 3-RUS 2
06-May-01 SUI 1-RUS 2
26-Apr-03 SUI 2-RUS 5
06-May-05 SUI 3-RUS 3
14-May-06 SUI 3-RUS 6
06-May-07 SUI 3-RUS 6
12-May-08 SUI 3-RUS 5
14-May-08 SUI 0-RUS 6
28-Apr-09 SUI 2-RUS 4
Totals vs. URS:
6-0-0-6-12-51
Totals vs. RUS:
13-2-2-9-26-57

10-May-98 SUI 1-SVK 1
07-May-03 SUI 1-SVK 3
06-May-04 SUI 1-SVK 3
08-May-05 SUI 1-SVK 3
12-May-06 SUI 2-SVK 2
13-May-12 SUI 0-SVK 1
Totals: 6-0-2-4-6-13

19-Jan-35 SUI 6-SWE 1
18-Feb-38 SUI 0-SWE 2
15-Feb-47 SUI 4-SWE 4
17-Feb-49 SUI 1-SWE 3
20-Mar-50 SUI 3-SWE 2
14-Mar-51 SUI 3-SWE 3
07-Mar-53 SUI 2-SWE 9
12-Mar-53 SUI 1-SWE 9
02-Mar-54 SUI 3-SWE 6
27-Feb-55 SUI 0-SWE 10
09-Mar-62 SUI 2-SWE 17
08-Apr-72 SUI 1-SWE 12
16-Apr-72 SUI 5-SWE 8
21-Apr-87 SUI 1-SWE 12
23-Apr-91 SUI 3-SWE 4
09-May-92 SUI 1-SWE 4
25-Apr-93 SUI 6-SWE 4
04-May-98 SUI 2-SWE 4
12-May-98 SUI 1-SWE 4
14-May-98 SUI 2-SWE 7
04-May-99 SUI 1-SWE 6
06-May-00 SUI 1-SWE 1
06-May-03 SUI 2-SWE 5
12-May-05 SUI 1-SWE 2
10-May-06 SUI 4-SWE 4
02-May-07 SUI 0-SWE 6
07-May-08 SUI 4-SWE 2
03-May-09 SUI 1-SWE 4
18-May-10 SUI 0-SWE 5
08-May-11 SUI 0-SWE 2
Totals: 30-4-4-22-61-162

08-May-06 SUI 2-UKR 1
Totals: 1-1-0-0-2-1

21-Feb-33 SUI 0-USA 7
17-Feb-38 SUI 1-USA 0
08-Feb-39 SUI 3-USA 2
11-Feb-39 SUI 1-USA 2
16-Feb-47 SUI 3-USA 4
12-Feb-49 SUI 5-USA 12
15-Feb-49 SUI 5-USA 4
21-Mar-50 SUI 5-USA 10
17-Mar-51 SUI 5-USA 1
28-Feb-55 SUI 3-USA 7
16-Mar-62 SUI 1-USA 12
25-Apr-87 SUI 3-USA 6
02-May-87 SUI 4-USA 7
25-Apr-91 SUI 2-USA 4
02-May-98 SUI 1-USA 5
10-May-99 SUI 0-USA 3
29-Apr-00 SUI 3-USA 3
02-May-02 SUI 0-USA 3
27-Apr-03 SUI 1-USA 0
04-May-09 SUI 4-USA 3 (OT)
09-May-11 SUI 5-USA 3
15-May-12 SUI 1-USA 5
Totals: 22-7-1-14-56-103

10-Mar-53 SUI 3-FRG 2
15-Mar-53 SUI 3-FRG 7
28-Feb-54 SUI 3-FRG 3
06-Mar-55 SUI 3-FRG 8
14-Mar-59 SUI 0-FRG 6
14-Mar-62 SUI 1-FRG 7
13-Apr-72 SUI 3-FRG 6
21-Apr-72 SUI 1-FRG 4
27-Apr-87 SUI 3-FRG 4
28-Apr-87 SUI 1-FRG 8
28-Apr-91 SUI 5-FRG 2
03-May-91 SUI 3-FRG 3
Totals: 12-2-2-8-29-60

04-Feb-39 SUI 23-YUG 0
Totals: 1-1-0-0-23-0

**WORLD U20 CHAMPIONSHIPS**

02-Jan-04 SUI 6-AUT 2
Totals: 1-1-0-0-6-2

26-Dec-98 SUI 4-BLR 3
29-Dec-00 SUI 3-BLR 1
26-Dec-02 SUI 4-BLR 2
26-Dec-04 SUI 5-BLR 0
27-Dec-06 SUI 4 -BLR 1
Totals: 5-5-0-0-20-7

30-Dec-79 SUI 5-CAN 9
01-Jan-82 SUI 1-CAN 11
28-Dec-83 SUI 0-CAN 12
26-Dec-85 SUI 1-CAN 12
26-Dec-86 SUI 4-CAN 6
26-Dec-90 SUI 0-CAN 6
27-Dec-91 SUI 4-CAN 6
26-Dec-93 SUI 1-CAN 5
27-Dec-95 SUI 1-CAN 2
30-Dec-96 SUI 1-CAN 4
01-Jan-00 SUI 3-CAN 8
31-Dec-00 SUI 4-CAN 8
27-Dec-01 SUI 1-CAN 6
02-Jan-02 SUI 0-CAN 4
28-Dec-03 SUI 2-CAN 7
28-Dec-05 SUI 3-CAN 4
28-Dec-09 SUI 0-CAN 6
03-Jan-10 SUI 1-CAN 6
02-Jan-11 SUI 1-CAN 4
Totals: 19-0-0-19-33-126

29-Dec-81 SUI 0-TCH 16
29-Dec-83 SUI 2-TCH 13
30-Dec-85 SUI 2-TCH 7
02-Jan-87 SUI 1-TCH 8
29-Dec-90 SUI 0-TCH 10
30-Dec-91 SUI 4-TCH 2
29-Dec-93 SUI 0-CZE 6
27-Dec-96 SUI 1-CZE 1
03-Jan-98 SUI 4-CZE 3 (10:00 OT/GWS)
04-Jan-99 SUI 4-CZE 5
02-Jan-01 SUI 3-CZE 4
30-Dec-03 SUI 1-CZE 2
29-Dec-04 SUI 2-CZE 5
31-Dec-06 SUI 2-CZE 4
Totals vs. TCH:
6-1-0-5-9-56
Totals vs. CZE:
8-1-1-6-17-30

03-Jan-08 SUI 5-DEN 2
02-Jan-12 SUI 4-DEN 3 (OT)
Totals: 2-2-0-0-9-5

23-Dec-77 SUI 1-FIN 18
30-Dec-77 SUI 1-FIN 9
28-Dec-79 SUI 1-FIN 19
23-Dec-81 SUI 2-FIN 14
02-Jan-84 SUI 4-FIN 12
27-Dec-85 SUI 2-FIN 9
01-Jan-87 SUI 1-FIN 12
28-Dec-90 SUI 1-FIN 7
02-Jan-92 SUI 3-FIN 7
01-Jan-94 SUI 2-FIN 4
26-Dec-95 SUI 1-FIN 5
01-Jan-98 SUI 1-FIN 2
03-Jan-00 SUI 5-FIN 2
27-Dec-00 SUI 2-FIN 3
25-Dec-01 SUI 3-FIN 0
04-Jan-02 SUI 1-FIN 5
31-Dec-03 SUI 0-FIN 2
31-Dec-05 SUI 1-FIN 4
30-Dec-06 SUI 0-FIN 4
27-Dec-07 SUI 3-FIN 4 (5:00 OT/GWS)
28-Dec-10 SUI 0-FIN 4
04-Jan-11 SUI 3-FIN 2 (5:00 OT/GWS)
Totals: 22-3-0-19-38-148

29-Dec-01 SUI 8-FRA 0
Totals: 1-1-0-0-8-0

04-Jan-92 SUI 2-GER 6
04-Jan-94 SUI 1-GER 3
02-Jan-96 SUI 3-GER 3
29-Dec-96 SUI 6-GER 2
02-Jan-03 SUI 6-GER 2
01-Jan-05 SUI 5-GER 0
04-Jan-07 SUI 5-GER 3
26-Dec-10 SUI 4-GER 3
Totals: 8-5-1-2-32-22

29-Dec-97 SUI 7-KAZ 0
30-Dec-98 SUI 0-KAZ 3
28-Dec-99 SUI 5-KAZ 0
30-Dec-07 SUI 1-KAZ 1
30-Dec-07 SUI 1-KAZ 3
Totals: 5-2-1-2-14-7

02-Jan-06 SUI 5-LAT 2
30-Dec-09 SUI 7-LAT 5
30-Dec-11 SUI 5-LAT 3
Totals: 3-3-0-0-17-10

03-Jan-91 SUI 2-NOR 1
27-Dec-05 SUI 2-NOR 0
Totals: 2-2-0-0-4-1

04-Jan-87 SUI 3-POL 8
02-Jan-97 SUI 6-POL 1
Totals: 2-1-0-1-9-9

22-Dec-77 SUI 1-URS 18
27-Dec-79 SUI 0-URS 6
27-Dec-81 SUI 4-URS 11
25-Dec-83 SUI 2-URS 14
29-Dec-85 SUI 3-URS 7
27-Dec-86 SUI 0-URS 8
31-Dec-90 SUI 1-URS 10
26-Dec-91 SUI 2-RUS 10
02-Jan-94 SUI 3-RUS 5
27-Dec-97 SUI 3-RUS 3
31-Dec-98 SUI 0-RUS 6
31-Dec-99 SUI 1-RUS 7
26-Dec-00 SUI 3-RUS 3
03-Jan-01 SUI 3-RUS 2
30-Dec-01 SUI 0-RUS 4
31-Dec-02 SUI 5-RUS 7
30-Dec-04 SUI 1-RUS 6
28-Dec-06 SUI 0-RUS 6
31-Dec-07 SUI 3-RUS 4
02-Jan-10 SUI 3-RUS 2 (OT)
26-Dec-11 SUI 0-RUS 3
Totals vs. URS:
7-0-0-7-11-74
Totals vs. RUS:
14-2-2-10-27-68

03-Jan-96 SUI 3-SVK 7
26-Dec-97 SUI 3-SVK 1
01-Jan-02 SUI 3-SVK 2 (10:00 OT/GWS)
30-Dec-02 SUI 0-SVK 3
03-Jan-05 SUI 2-SVK 3
04-Jan-06 SUI 3-SVK 3
02-Jan-07 SUI 2-SVK 1
02-Jan-08 SUI 2-SVK 5
31-Dec-09 SUI 4-SVK 1
30-Dec-10 SUI 6-SVK 4
31-Dec-11 SUI 4-SVK 6
Totals: 11-5-1-5-32-36

26-Dec-77 SUI 1-SWE 8
22-Dec-81 SUI 0-SWE 17
26-Dec-83 SUI 2-SWE 5
01-Jan-86 SUI 1-SWE 7
29-Dec-86 SUI 0-SWE 8
01-Jan-91 SUI 1-SWE 6
01-Jan-92 SUI 3-SWE 4
30-Dec-93 SUI 2-SWE 6
03-Jan-97 SUI 6-SWE 2
31-Dec-97 SUI 2-SWE 1 (10:00 OT/GWS)
28-Dec-98 SUI 1-SWE 5
26-Dec-99 SUI 1-SWE 7
04-Jan-00 SUI 2-SWE 5
04-Jan-03 SUI 5-SWE 3
03-Jan-04 SUI 3-SWE 4
05-Jan-10 SUI 4-SWE 11
28-Dec-11 SUI 3-SWE 4 (5:00 OT/GWS)
Totals: 17-3-0-14-37-103

30-Dec-95 SUI 5-UKR 3
25-Dec-99 SUI 6-UKR 2
27-Dec-03 SUI 11-UKR 0
Totals: 3-3-0-0-22-5

28-Dec-77 SUI 1-USA 11
02-Jan-80 SUI 5-USA 9
26-Dec-81 SUI 3-USA 6
03-Jan-84 SUI 3-USA 12
02-Jan-86 SUI 3-USA 11
30-Dec-86 SUI 6-USA 12
04-Jan-91 SUI 0-USA 8
29-Dec-91 SUI 1-USA 5
27-Dec-93 SUI 1-USA 1
29-Dec-95 SUI 3-USA 4
26-Dec-96 SUI 0-USA 4
30-Dec-97 SUI 1-USA 4
03-Jan-99 SUI 4-USA 5
05-Jan-01 SUI 0-USA 4
28-Dec-02 SUI 1-USA 3
27-Dec-04 SUI 4-USA 6
30-Dec-05 SUI 2-USA 2
28-Dec-07 SUI 2-USA 4
27-Dec-09 SUI 0-USA 3
31-Dec-10 SUI 1-USA 2
04-Jan-12 SUI 1-USA 2
Totals: 21-0-2-19-42-118

31-Dec-77 SUI 2-FRG 6
01-Jan-80 SUI 2-FRG 4
02-Jan-82 SUI 5-FRG 6
31-Dec-83 SUI 3-FRG 4
04-Jan-86 SUI 7-FRG 1
Totals: 5-1-0-4-19-21

**WORLD U18 CHAMPIONSHIPS, MEN**

14-Apr-02 SUI 3-BLR 6
19-Apr-03 SUI 3-BLR 5
16-Apr-08 SUI 4-BLR 2
17-Apr-10 SUI 3-BLR 2
Totals: 4-2-0-2-13-15

17-Apr-03 SUI 0-CAN 5
11-Apr-09 SUI 1-CAN 8
13-Apr-10 SUI 3-CAN 1
Totals: 3-1-0-2-4-14

13-Apr-99 SUI 3-CZE 2
19-Apr-00 SUI 3-CZE 2
16-Apr-03 SUI 1-CZE 4
14-Apr-05 SUI 1-CZE 4
12-Apr-07 SUI 2-CZE 4
10-Apr-09 SUI 2-CZE 6
22-Apr-10 SUI 6-CZE 5
23-Apr-11 SUI 4-CZE 2
19-Apr-12 SUI 4-CZE 2
Totals: 9-5-0-4-26-31

22-Apr-05 SUI 4-DEN 2
20-Apr-08 SUI 6-DEN 1
20-Apr-12 SUI 2-DEN 1
Totals: 3-3-0-0-12-4

16-Apr-99 SUI 6-FIN 1
17-Apr-01 SUI 0-FIN 3
20-Apr-01 SUI 4-FIN 2
17-Apr-02 SUI 1-FIN 8
20-Apr-03 SUI 2-FIN 2
15-Apr-05 SUI 1-FIN 3
13-Apr-07 SUI 5-FIN 1
14-Apr-08 SUI 3-FIN 5
Totals: 8-3-1-4-22-25

11-Apr-99 SUI 3-GER 0
17-Apr-00 SUI 3-GER 1
19-Apr-01 SUI 7-GER 1
20-Apr-02 SUI 5-GER 2
21-Apr-05 SUI 0-GER 2
14-Apr-09 SUI 8-GER 3
15-Apr-11 SUI 1-GER 4
17-Apr-12 SUI 2-GER 6
Totals: 8-5-0-3-29-19

13-Apr-03 SUI 13-KAZ 2
Totals: 1-1-0-0-13-2

13-Apr-12 SUI 2-LAT 4
Totals: 1-0-0-1-2-4

18-Apr-02 SUI 7-NOR 2
16-Apr-09 SUI 7-NOR 3
21-Apr-11 SUI 4-NOR 1
Totals: 3-3-0-0-18-6

18-Apr-99 SUI 4-RUS 1
22-Apr-00 SUI 1-RUS 4
22-Apr-01 SUI 2-RUS 6
14-Apr-03 SUI 3-RUS 12
19-Apr-07 SUI 3-RUS 4 (OT)
20-Apr-10 SUI 3-RUS 4
19-Apr-11 SUI 3-RUS 8
16-Apr-12 SUI 0-RUS 6
Totals: 8-1-0-7-19-45

15-Apr-99 SUI 3-SVK 6
21-Apr-00 SUI 3-SVK 0
14-Apr-01 SUI 5-SVK 2
21-Apr-02 SUI 3-SVK 0
18-Apr-05 SUI 1-SVK 2
16-Apr-07 SUI 4-SVK 0
21-Apr-07 SUI 1-SVK 4
21-Apr-08 SUI 2-SVK 3
18-Apr-09 SUI 2-SVK 4
17-Apr-11 SUI 3-SVK 2
Totals: 10-5-0-5-27-23

08-Apr-99 SUI 0-SWE 3
14-Apr-00 SUI 2-SWE 8
24-Apr-00 SUI 1-SWE 7
12-Apr-02 SUI 3-SWE 2
15-Apr-07 SUI 0-SWE 3
18-Apr-08 SUI 0-SWE 7
13-Apr-09 SUI 0-SWE 11
16-Apr-10 SUI 2-SWE 10
14-Apr-12 SUI 2-SWE 7
Totals: 9-1-0-8-10-58

09-Apr-99 SUI 4-UKR 1
15-Apr-00 SUI 10-UKR 1
12-Apr-01 SUI 6-UKR 2
11-Apr-02 SUI 10-UKR 0
Totals: 4-4-0-0-30-4

16-Apr-01 SUI 1-USA 3
15-Apr-02 SUI 1-USA 5
17-Apr-05 SUI 1-USA 7
13-Apr-08 SUI 2-USA 7
14-Apr-10 SUI 1-USA 5
14-Apr-11 SUI 1-USA 2
Totals: 6-0-0-6-7-29

**OLYMPICS, WOMEN**

15-Feb-10 SUI 1-CAN 10
Totals: 1-0-0-1-1-10

20-Feb-10 SUI 6-CHN 0
Totals: 1-1-0-0-6-0

13-Feb-06 SUI 0-FIN 4
Totals: 1-0-0-1-0-4

14-Feb-06 SUI 1-GER 2
Totals: 1-0-0-1-1-2

20-Feb-06 SUI 11-ITA 0
Totals: 1-1-0-0-11-0

17-Feb-06 SUI 2-RUS 6
22-Feb-10 SUI 2-RUS 1 (10:00 OT/GWS)
Totals: 2-1-0-1-4-7

17-Feb-10 SUI 5-SVK 2
Totals: 1-1-0-0-5-2

13-Feb-10 SUI 0-SWE 3
Totals: 1-0-0-1-0-3

11-Feb-06 SUI 0-USA 6
Totals: 1-0-0-1-0-6

**WOMEN'S WORLD CHAMPIONSHIPS**

31-Mar-97 SUI 0-CAN 6
08-Mar-99 SUI 0-CAN 10
03-Apr-07 SUI 0-CAN 9
16-Apr-11 SUI 0-CAN 12
Totals: 4-0-0-4-0-37

24-Apr-92 SUI 1-CHN 2 (10:00 OT/GWS)
01-Apr-97 SUI 3-CHN 11
12-Mar-99 SUI 2-CHN 3
03-Apr-04 SUI 3-CHN 6

07-Apr-07 SUI 5-CHN 1
08-Apr-09 SUI 5-CHN 4 (5:00 OT/GWS)
Totals: 6-2-0-4-19-27

26-Apr-92 SUI 3-DEN 4 (OT)
Totals: 1-0-0-1-3-4

21-Mar-90 SUI 0-FIN 10
21-Apr-92 SUI 1-FIN 13
12-Apr-94 SUI 0-FIN 13
09-Mar-99 SUI 0-FIN 7
12-Apr-08 SUI 1-FIN 4
06-Apr-09 SUI 3-FIN 6
17-Apr-11 SUI 2-FIN 1 (OT)
14-Apr-12 SUI 6-FIN 2
Totals: 8-2-0-6-13-56

14-Apr-94 SUI 2-GER 1
17-Apr-94 SUI 4-GER 3
11-Mar-99 SUI 4-GER 5
14-Mar-99 SUI 0-GER 3
04-Apr-07 SUI 1-GER 0
05-Apr-08 SUI 3-GER 0
07-Apr-12 SUI 2-GER 3
Totals: 7-4-0-3-16-15

24-Mar-90 SUI 5-JPN 4
05-Apr-04 SUI 4-JPN 0
09-Apr-09 SUI 3-JPN 2
Totals: 3-3-0-0-12-6

05-Apr-09 SUI 1-KAZ 2 (5:00 OT/GWS)
19-Apr-11 SUI 6-KAZ 1
Totals: 2-1-0-1-7-3

22-Mar-90 SUI 8-NOR 3
25-Mar-90 SUI 7-NOR 6
23-Apr-92 SUI 1-NOR 4
16-Apr-94 SUI 4-NOR 7
06-Apr-97 SUI 1-NOR 0
Totals: 5-3-0-2-21-20

03-Apr-97 SUI 3-RUS 3
31-Mar-04 SUI 1-RUS 2
10-Apr-08 SUI 2-RUS 1
22-Apr-11 SUI 4-RUS 5 (OT)
11-Apr-12 SUI 5-RUS 2
Totals: 5-2-1-2-15-13

08-Apr-12 SUI 2-SVK 1
Totals: 1-1-0-0-2-1

04-Apr-97 SUI 1-SWE 7
09-Apr-07 SUI 0-SWE 4
08-Apr-08 SUI 4-SWE 3 (5:00 OT/GWS)
24-Apr-11 SUI 2-SWE 3 (5:00 OT/GWS)
10-Apr-12 SUI 3-SWE 2
Totals: 5-2-0-3-10-19

19-Mar-90 SUI 3-USA 16
20-Apr-92 SUI 0-USA 17
11-Apr-94 SUI 0-USA 6
30-Mar-04 SUI 1-USA 9
06-Apr-08 SUI 1-USA 7
13-Apr-12 SUI 0-USA 10
Totals: 6-0-0-6-5-65

**WOMEN'S U18 WORLD CHAMPIONSHIPS**

05-Jan-09 SUI 1-CAN 16
01-Jan-11 SUI 1-CAN 9
31-Dec-11 SUI 1-CAN 13
Totals: 3-0-0-3-3-38

06-Jan-09 SUI 3-CZE 7
Totals: 1-0-0-1-3-7

11-Jan-08 SUI 2-FIN 7
07-Jan-09 SUI 4-FIN 3
04-Jan-11 SUI 1-FIN 4
01-Jan-12 SUI 5-FIN 3
Totals: 4-2-0-2-12-17

09-Jan-09 SUI 1-GER 2 (5:00 OT/GWS)
02-Jan-11 SUI 2-GER 4
03-Jan-12 SUI 1-GER 6
Totals: 3-0-0-3-4-12

05-Jan-11 SUI 4-JPN 0
07-Jan-11 SUI 1-JPN 5
08-Jan-11 SUI 5-JPN 1
Totals: 3-2-0-1-10-6

09-Jan-08 SUI 6-RUS 2
12-Jan-08 SUI 4-RUS 1
10-Jan-09 SUI 2-RUS 3 (5:00 OT/GWS)
04-Jan-12 SUI 4-RUS 2
06-Jan-12 SUI 3-RUS 5
07-Jan-12 SUI 2-RUS 3 (OT)
Totals: 6-3-0-3-21-16

07-Jan-08 SUI 1-SWE 4
Totals: 1-0-0-1-1-4

08-Jan-08 SUI 0-USA 11
Totals: 1-0-0-1-0-11

# UKRAINE (UKR)

Totals=GP-W-T-L-GF-GA

**OLYMPICS, MEN**

**Date Score**
09-Feb-02 UKR 0-BLR 1
Totals: 1-0-0-1-0-1

13-Feb-02 UKR 4-FRA 2
Totals: 1-1-0-0-4-2

14-Feb-02 UKR 2-LAT 9
Totals: 1-0-0-1-2-9

11-Feb-02 UKR 5-SUI 2
Totals: 1-1-0-0-5-2

**WORLD CHAMPIONSHIPS, MEN**

09-May-00 UKR 2-AUT 3
07-May-01 UKR 2-AUT 0
06-May-02 UKR 3-AUT 2
06-May-03 UKR 2-AUT 5
07-May-07 UKR 4-AUT 8
Totals: 5-2-0-3-13-18

06-May-99 UKR 1-BLR 6
30-Apr-00 UKR 3-BLR 7
13-May-06 UKR 1-BLR 9
Totals: 3-0-0-3-5-22

10-May-05 UKR 1-CAN 2
Totals: 1-0-0-1-1-2

02-May-03 UKR 2-CZE 5
Totals: 1-0-0-1-2-5

04-May-05 UKR 2-DEN 1
01-May-07 UKR 3-DEN 4
Totals: 2-1-0-1-5-5

02-May-99 UKR 1-FIN 3
06-May-01 UKR 1-FIN 7
27-Apr-02 UKR 0-FIN 3
03-May-03 UKR 0-FIN 9
26-Apr-04 UKR 1-FIN 5
02-May-05 UKR 1-FIN 4
27-Apr-07 UKR 0-FIN 5
Totals: 7-0-0-7-4-36

07-May-00 UKR 3-FRA 2
02-May-04 UKR 6 -FRA 2
Totals: 2-2-0-0-9-4

29-Apr-03 UKR 1-GER 3
Totals: 1-0-0-1-1-3

10-May-06 UKR 4-ITA 2
Totals: 1-1-0-0-4-2

06-May-00 UKR 4-JPN 0
30-Apr-03 UKR 5-JPN 1
30-Apr-04 UKR 2-JPN 2
Totals: 3-2-1-0-11-3

03-May-04 UKR 2-KAZ 2
Totals: 1-0-1-0-2-2

04-May-00 UKR 1-LAT 2
02-May-01 UKR 4-LAT 2
07-May-05 UKR 0-LAT 3
04-May-07 UKR 0-LAT 5
Totals: 4-1-0-3-5-12

06-May-07 UKR 3-NOR 2
Totals: 1-1-0-0-3-2

30-Apr-02 UKR 3-POL 0
Totals: 1-1-0-0-3-0

04-May-99 UKR 1-RUS 4
03-May-02 UKR 3-RUS 3
11-May-06 UKR 0-RUS 6
29-Apr-07 UKR 1-RUS 8
Totals: 4-0-1-3-5-21

04-May-01 UKR 1-SVK 3
29-Apr-02 UKR 4-SVK 5
27-Apr-03 UKR 3-SVK 9
24-Apr-04 UKR 0-SVK 2
16-May-06 UKR 0-SVK 8
Totals: 5-0-0-5-8-27

02-May-00 UKR 2-SWE 7
01-May-01 UKR 0-SWE 5
04-May-02 UKR 0-SWE 7
01-May-05 UKR 2-SWE 3
06-May-06 UKR 2-SWE 4
Totals: 5-0-0-5-6-26

08-May-06 UKR 1-SUI 2
Totals: 1-0-0-1-1-2

28-Apr-01 UKR 3-USA 6
28-Apr-04 UKR 1-USA 7
09-May-05 UKR 1-USA 1
Totals: 3-0-1-2-5-14

**WORLD U20 CHAMPIONSHIPS**

03-Jan-04 UKR 2-AUT 2
Totals: 1-0-1-0-2-2

26-Dec-94 UKR 1-CAN 7
31-Dec-95 UKR 1-CAN 8
29-Dec-03 UKR 0-CAN 10
Totals: 3-0-0-3-2-25

01-Jan-95 UKR 1-CZE 10
26-Dec-03 UKR 0-CZE 8
Totals: 2-0-0-2-1-18

27-Dec-94 UKR 2-FIN 6
28-Dec-95 UKR 1-FIN 4
30-Dec-03 UKR 1-FIN 14
Totals: 3-0-0-3-4-24

04-Jan-95 UKR 2-GER 6
03-Jan-96 UKR 0-GER 5
Totals: 2-0-0-2-2-11

29-Dec-99 UKR 2-KAZ 5
Totals: 1-0-0-1-2-5

29-Dec-94 UKR 2-RUS 4
26-Dec-99 UKR 1-RUS 4
Totals: 2-0-0-2-3-8

02-Jan-96 UKR 3-SVK 6
02-Jan-00 UKR 3-SVK 1
04-Jan-00 UKR 1-SVK 5
Totals: 3-1-0-2-7-12

30-Dec-94 UKR 1-SWE 7
28-Dec-99 UKR 1-SWE 6
02-Jan-04 UKR 0-SWE 4
Totals: 3-0-0-3-2-17

30-Dec-95 UKR 3-SUI 5
25-Dec-99 UKR 2-SUI 6
27-Dec-03 UKR 0-SUI 11
Totals: 3-0-0-3-5-22

02-Jan-95 UKR 3-USA 2
27-Dec-95 UKR 4-USA 3
Totals: 2-2-0-0-7-5

**WORLD U18 CHAMPIONSHIPS, MEN**

22-Apr-00 UKR 8-BLR 3
17-Apr-02 UKR 1-BLR 3
Totals: 2-1-0-1-9-6

10-Apr-99 UKR 1-CZE 6
16-Apr-00 UKR 0-CZE 6
Totals: 2-0-0-2-1-12

15-Apr-01 UKR 0-FIN 7
15-Apr-02 UKR 0-FIN 6
Totals: 2-0-0-2-0-13

12-Apr-99 UKR 4-GER 0
18-Apr-00 UKR 4-GER 4
21-Apr-02 UKR 1-GER 4
Totals: 3-1-1-1-9-8

15-Apr-99 UKR 3-NOR 0
20-Apr-01 UKR 2-NOR 5
20-Apr-02 UKR 5-NOR 2
Totals: 3-2-0-1-10-7

16-Apr-01 UKR 1-SVK 10
18-Apr-02 UKR 0-SVK 3
Totals: 2-0-0-2-1-13

13-Apr-99 UKR 2-SWE 10
19-Apr-00 UKR 1-SWE 4
19-Apr-01 UKR 4-SWE 9
14-Apr-02 UKR 3-SWE 8
Totals: 4-0-0-4-10-31

09-Apr-99 UKR 1-SUI 4
15-Apr-00 UKR 1-SUI 10
12-Apr-01 UKR 2-SUI 6
11-Apr-02 UKR 0-SUI 10
Totals: 4-0-0-4-4-30

16-Apr-99 UKR 0-USA 6
21-Apr-00 UKR 0-USA 6
13-Apr-01 UKR 0-USA 11
12-Apr-02 UKR 0-USA 10
Totals: 4-0-0-4-0-33

# UNITED STATES (USA)

Totals=GP-W-T-L-GF-GA

**OLYMPICS, MEN**

**Date Score**
21-Feb-60 USA 12-AUS 1
Totals: 1-1-0-0-12-1

12-Feb-36 USA 1-AUT 0
06-Feb-48 USA 13-AUT 2
13-Feb-84 USA 7-AUT 3
13-Feb-88 USA 10-AUT 6
Totals: 4-4-0-0-31-11

14-Feb-98 USA 5-BLR 2
18-Feb-02 USA 8-BLR 1
Totals: 2-2-0-0-13-3

28-Jan-24 USA 19-BEL 0
Totals: 1-1-0-0-19-0

25-Apr-20 USA 0-CAN 2
03-Feb-24 USA 1-CAN 6
04-Feb-32 USA 1-CAN 2 (10:00 OT)
13-Feb-32 USA 2-CAN 2 (30:00 OT)
16-Feb-36 USA 0-CAN 1
05-Feb-48 USA 3-CAN 12
24-Feb-52 USA 3-CAN 3
31-Jan-56 USA 4-CAN 1
25-Feb-60 USA 2-CAN 1
03-Feb-64 USA 6-CAN 8
11-Feb-68 USA 2-CAN 3
07-Feb-84 USA 2-CAN 4
17-Feb-94 USA 3-CAN 3
16-Feb-98 USA 1-CAN 4
24-Feb-02 USA 2-CAN 5
21-Feb-10 USA 5-CAN 3
28-Feb-10 USA 2-CAN 3 (OT)
Totals: 17-3-3-11-39-63

28-Apr-20 USA 16-TCH 0
11-Feb-36 USA 2-TCH 0
08-Feb-48 USA 3-TCH 4
23-Feb-52 USA 6-TCH 3
27-Jan-56 USA 3-TCH 4
04-Feb-56 USA 9-TCH 4
19-Feb-60 USA 7-TCH 5
28-Feb-60 USA 9-TCH 4
05-Feb-64 USA 1-TCH 7
06-Feb-68 USA 1-TCH 5
07-Feb-72 USA 5-TCH 1
08-Feb-76 USA 0-TCH 5
14-Feb-80 USA 7-TCH 3
09-Feb-84 USA 1-TCH 4
15-Feb-88 USA 5-TCH 7
22-Feb-92 USA 1-TCH 6
24-Feb-94 USA 3-CZE 5
18-Feb-98 USA 1-CZE 4
Totals vs. TCH: 16-8-0-8-76-62
Totals vs. CZE : 2-0-0-2-4-9

15-Feb-68 USA 6-GDR 4
Totals: 1-1-0-0-6-4

18-Feb-52 USA 8-FIN 2
07-Feb-64 USA 2-FIN 3
17-Feb-68 USA 1-FIN 1
10-Feb-72 USA 4-FIN 1
10-Feb-76 USA 5-FIN 4
24-Feb-80 USA 4-FIN 2
15-Feb-84 USA 3-FIN 3
13-Feb-92 USA 4-FIN 1
23-Feb-94 USA 1-FIN 6
15-Feb-02 USA 6-FIN 0
22-Feb-06 USA 3-FIN 4
26-Feb-10 USA 6-FIN 1
Totals: 12-7-2-3-47-28

30-Jan-24 USA 22-FRA 0
18-Feb-92 USA 4-FRA 1
13-Feb-94 USA 4-FRA 4
Totals: 3-2-1-0-30-5

07-Feb-32 USA 7-GER 0
10-Feb-32 USA 8-GER 0
06-Feb-36 USA 1-GER 0
16-Feb-52 USA 8-GER 2
30-Jan-56 USA 7-GER 2
24-Feb-60 USA 9-GER 1
31-Jan-64 USA 8-GER 0
11-Feb-92 USA 2-GER 0
26-Feb-94 USA 3-GER 4
20-Feb-02 USA 5-GER 0
Totals: 10-9-0-1-58-9

31-Jan-24 USA 11-GBR 0
15-Feb-36 USA 0-GBR 0 (30:00 OT)
07-Feb-48 USA 4-GBR 3
Totals: 3-2-1-0-15-3

08-Feb-36 USA 1-ITA 2 (20:00 OT)
01-Feb-48 USA 31-ITA 1
09-Feb-92 USA 6-ITA 3
21-Feb-94 USA 7-ITA 1
Totals: 4-3-0-1-45-7

16-Feb-06 USA 4-KAZ 1
Totals: 1-1-0-0-4-1

15-Feb-06 USA 3-LAT 3
Totals: 1-0-1-0-3-3

15-Feb-52 USA 3-NOR 2
16-Feb-80 USA 5-NOR 1
11-Feb-84 USA 3-NOR 3
19-Feb-88 USA 6-NOR 3
18-Feb-10 USA 6-NOR 1
Totals: 5-4-1-0-23-10

05-Feb-32 USA 4-POL 1
08-Feb-32 USA 5-POL 0
31-Jan-48 USA 23-POL 4
22-Feb-52 USA 5-POL 3
28-Jan-56 USA 4-POL 0
12-Feb-72 USA 6-POL 1
12-Feb-76 USA 7-POL 2
17-Feb-84 USA 7-POL 4
15-Feb-92 USA 3-POL 0
Totals: 9-9-0-0-64-15

18-Feb-80 USA 7-ROM 2
Totals: 1-1-0-0-7-2

03-Feb-56 USA 0-URS 4
27-Feb-60 USA 3-URS 2
29-Jan-64 USA 1-URS 5
09-Feb-68 USA 2-URS 10
09-Feb-72 USA 2-URS 7
06-Feb-76 USA 2-URS 6
22-Feb-80 USA 4-URS 3
17-Feb-88 USA 5-URS 7
21-Feb-92 USA 2-RUS 5
16-Feb-02 USA 2-RUS 2
22-Feb-02 USA 3-RUS 2
21-Feb-06 USA 4-RUS 5
Totals vs. URS: 8-2-0-6-19-44
Totals vs. RUS: 4-1-1-2-11-14

15-Feb-94 USA 3-SVK 3
18-Feb-06 USA 1-SVK 2
Totals: 2-0-1-1-4-5

27-Apr-20 USA 7-SWE 0
01-Feb-24 USA 20-SWE 0
13-Feb-36 USA 2-SWE 1
03-Feb-48 USA 5-SWE 2

21-Feb-52 USA 2-SWE 4
02-Feb-56 USA 6-SWE 1
22-Feb-60 USA 6-SWE 3
01-Feb-64 USA 4-SWE 7
07-Feb-68 USA 3-SWE 4
05-Feb-72 USA 1-SWE 5
12-Feb-80 USA 2-SWE 2
17-Feb-92 USA 3-SWE 3
19-Feb-94 USA 4-SWE 6
13-Feb-98 USA 2-SWE 4
19-Feb-06 USA 1-SWE 2
Totals: 15-6-2-7-68-44

24-Apr-20 USA 29-SUI 0
07-Feb-36 USA 3-SUI 0
30-Jan-48 USA 4-SUI 5
19-Feb-52 USA 8-SUI 2
08-Feb-64 USA 7-SUI 3
25-Feb-88 USA 8-SUI 4
16-Feb-10 USA 3-SUI 1
24-Feb-10 USA 2-SUI 0
Totals: 8-7-0-1-64-15

12-Feb-68 USA 8-FRG 1
14-Feb-76 USA 1-FRG 4
20-Feb-80 USA 4-FRG 2
21-Feb-88 USA 1-FRG 4
Totals: 4-2-0-2-14-11

**WORLD CHAMPIONSHIPS, MEN**

04-Feb-31 USA 2-AUT 1
24-Feb-33 USA 4-AUT 0
08-Feb-34 USA 1-AUT 0
18-Feb-47 USA 5-AUT 6
20-Feb-49 USA 9-AUT 1
24-Apr-95 USA 5-AUT 2
22-Apr-96 USA 5-AUT 1
03-May-99 USA 5-AUT 2
06-May-01 USA 0-AUT 3
27-Apr-07 USA 6-AUT 2
27-Apr-09 USA 6-AUT 1
30-Apr-11 USA 5-AUT 1
Totals: 12-10-0-2-53-20

05-May-00 USA 1-BLR 0
03-May-03 USA 4-BLR 2
29-Apr-07 USA 5-BLR 1
10-May-12 USA 5-BLR 3
Totals: 4-4-0-0-15-6

18-Feb-47 USA 13-BEL 2
14-Feb-49 USA 12-BEL 0
Totals: 2-2-0-0-25-2

08-Feb-31 USA 0-CAN 2
26-Feb-33 USA 2-CAN 1 (10:00 OT)
11-Feb-34 USA 1-CAN 2
12-Feb-39 USA 0-CAN 4
17-Feb-49 USA 2-CAN 7
18-Mar-50 USA 0-CAN 5
15-Mar-51 USA 2-CAN 16
25-Feb-55 USA 1-CAN 12
08-Mar-58 USA 1-CAN 12
14-Mar-59 USA 1-CAN 4
05-Mar-61 USA 4-CAN 7
18-Mar-62 USA 1-CAN 6
11-Mar-63 USA 4-CAN 10
08-Mar-65 USA 2-CAN 5
03-Mar-66 USA 2-CAN 7
23-Mar-67 USA 1-CAN 2
20-Mar-69 USA 0-CAN 5
25-Mar-69 USA 0-CAN 1
21-Apr-77 USA 1-CAN 4
30-Apr-78 USA 2-CAN 7
14-Apr-79 USA 3-CAN 6
22-Apr-82 USA 3-CAN 5
20-Apr-85 USA 4-CAN 3
29-Apr-85 USA 2-CAN 3
20-Apr-86 USA 2-CAN 4
17-Apr-87 USA 1-CAN 3
18-Apr-89 USA 0-CAN 8
17-Apr-90 USA 3-CAN 6
19-Apr-91 USA 3-CAN 4
04-May-91 USA 4-CAN 9
03-May-95 USA 1-CAN 4
28-Apr-96 USA 1-CAN 5
01-May-97 USA 1-CAN 5
09-May-99 USA 1-CAN 4
10-May-01 USA 4-CAN 3 (OT)
30-Apr-02 USA 1-CAN 2 (OT)
05-May-05 USA 1-CAN 3
09-May-06 USA 1-CAN 2
07-May-07 USA 3-CAN 6
06-May-08 USA 4-CAN 5
06-May-11 USA 3-CAN 4 (5:00 OT/GWS)
05-May-12 USA 5-CAN 4
Totals: 42-4-0-38-78-217

06-Feb-31 USA 1-TCH 0
23-Feb-33 USA 6-TCH 0
06-Feb-34 USA 1-TCH 0
16-Feb-38 USA 0-TCH 2
10-Feb-39 USA 1-TCH 0 (20:00 OT)
23-Feb-47 USA 1-TCH 6
19-Feb-49 USA 2-TCH 0
03-Mar-55 USA 4-TCH 4
06-Mar-58 USA 2-TCH 2
13-Mar-59 USA 4-TCH 2
05-Mar-61 USA 1-TCH 4
09-Mar-63 USA 1-TCH 10
06-Mar-65 USA 0-TCH 12
08-Mar-66 USA 4-TCH 7
21-Mar-67 USA 3-TCH 8
16-Mar-69 USA 3-TCH 8
26-Mar-69 USA 2-TCH 6
19-Mar-71 USA 5-TCH 1
27-Mar-71 USA 0-TCH 5
06-Apr-75 USA 3-TCH 8
15-Apr-75 USA 0-TCH 8
15-Apr-76 USA 2-TCH 10
21-Apr-76 USA 1-TCH 5
02-May-77 USA 3-TCH 6
02-May-78 USA 3-TCH 8
17-Apr-79 USA 2-TCH 2
12-Apr-81 USA 2-TCH 11
19-Apr-82 USA 0-TCH 6
21-Apr-85 USA 3-TCH 1
01-May-85 USA 2-TCH 11
18-Apr-86 USA 2-TCH 5
27-Apr-86 USA 2-TCH 10
27-Apr-87 USA 2-TCH 4
19-Apr-89 USA 0-TCH 5
16-Apr-90 USA 1-TCH 7
20-Apr-91 USA 4-TCH 1
07-May-92 USA 1-TCH 8
18-Apr-93 USA 1-CZE 1
28-Apr-94 USA 5-CZE 3
27-Apr-95 USA 4-CZE 2
03-May-96 USA 0-CZE 5
05-May-97 USA 4-CZE 3
05-May-99 USA 3-CZE 4
04-May-02 USA 4-CZE 5
05-May-04 USA 3-CZE 2 (10:00 OT/GWS)
12-May-05 USA 2-CZE 3 (10:00 OT/GWS)
16-May-06 USA 3-CZE 1
01-May-07 USA 3-CZE 4
11-May-11 USA 0-CZE 4
Totals vs. TCH:
37-9-3-25-74-193
Totals vs. CZE:
12-5-1-6-32-37

26-Apr-03 USA 2-DEN 5
04-May-04 USA 8 -DEN 3
07-May-06 USA 3-DEN 0
10-May-10 USA 1-DEN 2 (OT)
Totals: 4-2-0-2-14-10

06-Mar-59 USA 9-GDR 2
08-Mar-61 USA 5-GDR 6
17-Mar-63 USA 3-GDR 3
09-Mar-65 USA 4-GDR 7
11-Mar-66 USA 4-GDR 0
25-Mar-67 USA 0-GDR 0
12-Apr-76 USA 1-GDR 2
03-May-78 USA 4-GDR 7
13-May-78 USA 4-GDR 8
24-Apr-85 USA 5-GDR 5
Totals: 10-2-3-5-39-40

05-Feb-39 USA 4-FIN 0
12-Mar-51 USA 5-FIN 4
26-Feb-55 USA 8-FIN 1
09-Mar-58 USA 4-FIN 2
11-Mar-59 USA 10-FIN 3
12-Mar-61 USA 5-FIN 2
11-Mar-62 USA 6-FIN 3
08-Mar-63 USA 3-FIN 11
12-Mar-65 USA 4-FIN 0
09-Mar-66 USA 1-FIN 4
26-Mar-67 USA 2-FIN 0
22-Mar-69 USA 3-FIN 4
30-Mar-69 USA 3-FIN 7
23-Mar-71 USA 4-FIN 7
31-Mar-71 USA 3-FIN 7
04-Apr-75 USA 4-FIN 7
13-Apr-75 USA 1-FIN 9
08-Apr-76 USA 3-FIN 3
26-Apr-77 USA 2-FIN 3
07-May-77 USA 3-FIN 2
07-May-78 USA 3-FIN 3
11-May-78 USA 4-FIN 3
16-Apr-79 USA 1-FIN 1
22-Apr-79 USA 6-FIN 2
19-Apr-81 USA 6-FIN 4
25-Apr-81 USA 3-FIN 3
18-Apr-82 USA 2-FIN 4
26-Apr-85 USA 3-FIN 8
12-Apr-86 USA 4-FIN 5
21-Apr-87 USA 2-FIN 5
28-Apr-87 USA 4-FIN 6
23-Apr-89 USA 3-FIN 3
30-Apr-89 USA 2-FIN 6
25-Apr-90 USA 2-FIN 1
01-May-90 USA 3-FIN 2
28-Apr-91 USA 2-FIN 1
01-May-92 USA 1-FIN 6
20-Apr-93 USA 1-FIN 1
02-May-94 USA 0-FIN 7
07-May-94 USA 0-FIN 8
30-Apr-95 USA 4-FIN 4
09-May-97 USA 0-FIN 2
07-May-99 USA 3-FIN 4
05-May-01 USA 4-FIN 1
12-May-01 USA 1-FIN 3
07-May-02 USA 1-FIN 3
24-Apr-04 USA 2-FIN 4
06-May-05 USA 4-FIN 4
12-May-06 USA 0-FIN 4
10-May-07 USA 4-FIN 5 (10:00 OT/GWS)
11-May-08 USA 2-FIN 3
14-May-08 USA 2-FIN 3 (OT)
06-May-09 USA 3-FIN 2
12-May-10 USA 2-FIN 3
13-May-12 USA 5-FIN 0
17-May-12 USA 2-FIN 3
Totals: 56-19-8-29-169-206

22-Apr-93 USA 6-FRA 1
25-Apr-94 USA 5-FRA 1
04-May-98 USA 1-FRA 3
03-May-00 USA 3-FRA 2
01-May-09 USA 6-FRA 2
16-May-10 USA 4-FRA 0
07-May-11 USA 3-FRA 2
04-May-12 USA 7-FRA 2
Totals: 8-7-0-1-35-13

10-Feb-34 USA 3-GER 0
14-Feb-38 USA 1-GER 0
04-Feb-39 USA 4-GER 0
29-Apr-92 USA 3-GER 5
25-Apr-93 USA 3-GER 6
23-Apr-96 USA 4-GER 2
08-May-98 USA 1-GER 1
05-May-02 USA 2-GER 2
05-May-07 USA 3-GER 0
08-May-08 USA 6-GER 4
07-May-10 USA 1-GER 2 (OT)
Totals: 11-6-2-3-31-22

15-Feb-38 USA 1-GBR 1
20-Mar-50 USA 3-GBR 2
16-Mar-51 USA 6-GBR 6
14-Mar-62 USA 12-GBR 5
Totals: 4-2-2-0-22-14

07-Feb-39 USA 3-HUN 0
Totals: 1-1-0-0-3-0

03-Feb-39 USA 5-ITA 0
16-Apr-82 USA 5-ITA 7
28-Apr-92 USA 1-ITA 0
30-Apr-97 USA 4-ITA 2
10-May-98 USA 0-ITA 4
27-Apr-02 USA 5-ITA 2
18-May-10 USA 3-ITA 2 (5:00 OT/GWS)
Totals: 7-5-0-2-23-17

01-May-99 USA 7-JPN 1
05-May-03 USA 8-JPN 1
Totals: 2-2-0-0-15-2

15-May-10 USA 10-KAZ 0
11-May-12 USA 3-KAZ 2 (OT)
Totals: 2-2-0-0-13-2

12-Feb-38 USA 1-LAT 0
27-Apr-97 USA 5-LAT 4
11-May-98 USA 2-LAT 3
07-May-00 USA 1-LAT 1
30-Apr-01 USA 0-LAT 2
29-Apr-02 USA 3-LAT 2
03-May-05 USA 3-LAT 1
13-May-06 USA 4-LAT 2
02-May-08 USA 4-LAT 0
25-Apr-09 USA 4-LAT 2
Totals: 10-7-1-2-27-17

15-Mar-50 USA 17-NED 1
17-Apr-81 USA 7-NED 6
23-Apr-81 USA 7-NED 3
Totals: 3-3-0-0-31-10

13-Feb-38 USA 7-NOR 1
13-Feb-49 USA 12-NOR 1
22-Mar-50 USA 12-NOR 6
09-Mar-51 USA 0-NOR 3
03-Mar-58 USA 6-NOR 1
05-Mar-59 USA 10-NOR 3
08-Mar-62 USA 14-NOR 2
14-Mar-65 USA 8-NOR 6
23-Apr-90 USA 9-NOR 4
29-Apr-90 USA 4-NOR 1
24-Apr-93 USA 3-NOR 1
27-Apr-94 USA 7-NOR 2
25-Apr-95 USA 2-NOR 1
28-Apr-97 USA 3-NOR 1
05-May-06 USA 3-NOR 1
12-May-08 USA 9-NOR 1
02-May-11 USA 4-NOR 2
Totals: 17-16-0-1-113-37

07-Feb-31 USA 1-POL 0
22-Feb-33 USA 4-POL 0
09-Feb-39 USA 4-POL 0
21-Feb-47 USA 3-POL 2
04-Mar-55 USA 6-POL 2
28-Feb-58 USA 12-POL 4
12-Mar-66 USA 6-POL 4
09-Apr-75 USA 3-POL 5
18-Apr-75 USA 2-POL 5
14-Apr-76 USA 4-POL 2
18-Apr-79 USA 5-POL 5
24-Apr-79 USA 5-POL 1
13-Apr-86 USA 7-POL 2
25-Apr-86 USA 7-POL 5
25-Apr-89 USA 6-POL 1
26-Apr-89 USA 11-POL 2
03-May-92 USA 5-POL 0
Totals: 17-14-1-2-91-40

01-Feb-31 USA 15-ROM 0
20-Feb-47 USA 15-ROM 3
22-Apr-77 USA 7-ROM 2
05-May-77 USA 4-ROM 5
Totals: 4-3-0-1-41-10

02-Mar-55 USA 0-URS 3
07-Mar-58 USA 1-URS 4
07-Mar-59 USA 3-URS 5
09-Mar-59 USA 1-URS 5
02-Mar-61 USA 2-URS 13
15-Mar-63 USA 0-URS 9
11-Mar-65 USA 2-URS 9
05-Mar-66 USA 0-URS 11
19-Mar-67 USA 2-URS 7
15-Mar-69 USA 2-URS 17
23-Mar-69 USA 4-URS 8
22-Mar-71 USA 2-URS 10
30-Mar-71 USA 5-URS 7
03-Apr-75 USA 5-URS 10
12-Apr-75 USA 1-URS 13
19-Apr-76 USA 2-URS 5
23-Apr-76 USA 1-URS 7
30-Apr-77 USA 2-URS 8
26-Apr-78 USA 5-URS 9
21-Apr-82 USA 4-URS 8
17-Apr-85 USA 1-URS 11
03-May-85 USA 3-URS 10
22-Apr-86 USA 1-URS 5
20-Apr-87 USA 2-URS 11
15-Apr-89 USA 2-URS 4
19-Apr-90 USA 1-URS 10
23-Apr-91 USA 2-URS 12
30-Apr-91 USA 4-URS 6
04-May-94 USA 3-RUS 1
25-Apr-96 USA 1-RUS 3
04-May-96 USA 4-RUS 3 (OT)
06-May-97 USA 1-RUS 1
01-May-00 USA 3-RUS 0
29-Apr-03 USA 2-RUS 3
01-May-04 USA 3-RUS 2
02-May-09 USA 1-RUS 4
08-May-09 USA 2-RUS 3
Totals vs. URS:
28-0-0-28-60-237
Totals vs. RUS:
9-4-1-4-20-20

27-Apr-96 USA 4-SVK 3
11-May-00 USA 1-SVK 4
08-May-01 USA 3-SVK 1
26-Apr-04 USA 3-SVK 3
09-May-04 USA 1-SVK 0 (10:00 OT/GWS)
03-May-07 USA 4-SVK 2
07-May-12 USA 2-SVK 4
Totals: 7-4-1-2-18-17

02-May-03 USA 7-SLO 2
01-May-05 USA 7-SLO 0
04-May-08 USA 5-SLO 1
Totals: 3-3-0-0-19-3

05-Feb-31 USA 3-SWE 0
17-Feb-47 USA 1-SWE 4
18-Feb-49 USA 6-SWE 3
13-Mar-50 USA 3-SWE 8
17-Mar-50 USA 4-SWE 2
11-Mar-51 USA 0-SWE 8
05-Mar-55 USA 1-SWE 1
04-Mar-58 USA 3-SWE 8
10-Mar-59 USA 7-SWE 1
11-Mar-61 USA 3-SWE 7
10-Mar-62 USA 1-SWE 2
12-Mar-63 USA 2-SWE 17
04-Mar-65 USA 2-SWE 5
06-Mar-66 USA 1-SWE 6
18-Mar-67 USA 4-SWE 3
18-Mar-69 USA 2-SWE 8
29-Mar-69 USA 4-SWE 10
20-Mar-71 USA 2-SWE 4
28-Mar-71 USA 3-SWE 4
07-Apr-75 USA 0-SWE 7
16-Apr-75 USA 3-SWE 12
10-Apr-76 USA 2-SWE 0
25-Apr-76 USA 3-SWE 7
28-Apr-77 USA 0-SWE 9
27-Apr-78 USA 1-SWE 5
14-Apr-81 USA 2-SWE 4
15-Apr-82 USA 2-SWE 4
18-Apr-85 USA 4-SWE 3
16-Apr-86 USA 2-SWE 5
18-Apr-87 USA 2-SWE 6
16-Apr-89 USA 2-SWE 4
20-Apr-90 USA 1-SWE 6
22-Apr-91 USA 4-SWE 4
02-May-91 USA 4-SWE 8
04-May-92 USA 4-SWE 4
27-Apr-93 USA 2-SWE 5
30-Apr-94 USA 2-SWE 6
08-May-94 USA 2-SWE 7
28-Apr-95 USA 2-SWE 2
30-Apr-96 USA 3-SWE 2
03-May-97 USA 1-SWE 3
06-May-98 USA 1-SWE 6
08-May-00 USA 5-SWE 3
02-May-01 USA 2-SWE 2
13-May-01 USA 2-SWE 3
02-May-04 USA 1-SWE 3
08-May-04 USA 2-SWE 3
08-May-05 USA 5-SWE 1
17-May-06 USA 0-SWE 6
29-Apr-09 USA 5-SWE 6 (OT)
10-May-09 USA 2-SWE 4
04 May-11 USA 2-SWE 6
Totals: 52-10-5-37-127-257

21-Feb-33 USA 7-SUI 0
17-Feb-38 USA 0-SUI 1
08-Feb-39 USA 2-SUI 3
11-Feb-39 USA 2-SUI 1
16-Feb-47 USA 4-SUI 3
12-Feb-49 USA 12-SUI 5
15-Feb-49 USA 4-SUI 5
21-Mar-50 USA 10-SUI 5
17-Mar-51 USA 1-SUI 5
28-Feb-55 USA 7-SUI 3
16-Mar-62 USA 12-SUI 1
25-Apr-87 USA 6-SUI 3
02-May-87 USA 7-SUI 4
25-Apr-91 USA 4-SUI 2
02-May-98 USA 5-SUI 1
10-May-99 USA 3-SUI 0
29-Apr-00 USA 3-SUI 3
02-May-02 USA 3-SUI 0
27-Apr-03 USA 0-SUI 1
04-May-09 USA 3-SUI 4 (OT)
09-May-11 USA 3-SUI 5
15-May-12 USA 5-SUI 1
Totals: 22-14-1-7-103-56

28-Apr-01 USA 6-UKR 3
28-Apr-04 USA 7-UKR 1
09-May-05 USA 1-UKR 1
Totals: 3-2-1-0-14-5

27-Feb-55 USA 6-FRG 3
07-Mar-61 USA 4-FRG 4
13-Mar-62 USA 8-FRG 4
14-Mar-63 USA 8-FRG 4
28-Mar-67 USA 8-FRG 3
25-Mar-71 USA 2-FRG 7
02-Apr-71 USA 5-FRG 1
18-Apr-76 USA 5-FRG 1
24-Apr-77 USA 3-FRG 3

03-May-77 USA 4-FRG 1
05-May-78 USA 7-FRG 3
09-May-78 USA 5-FRG 5
20-Apr-79 USA 3-FRG 6
26-Apr-79 USA 2-FRG 5
15-Apr-81 USA 10-FRG 6
21-Apr-81 USA 2-FRG 6
24-Apr-82 USA 5-FRG 5
23-Apr-85 USA 4-FRG 3
15-Apr-86 USA 9-FRG 2
23-Apr-86 USA 5-FRG 0
23-Apr-87 USA 6-FRG 4
30-Apr-87 USA 6-FRG 3
21-Apr-89 USA 7-FRG 4
28-Apr-89 USA 4-FRG 3
22-Apr-90 USA 6-FRG 3
27-Apr-90 USA 5-FRG 3
26-Apr-91 USA 4-FRG 4
Totals: 27-18-5-4-143-96

**WORLD U20 CHAMPIONSHIPS**
02-Jan-81 USA 7-AUT 2
26-Dec-03 USA 8-AUT 0
Totals: 2-2-0-0-15-2

04-Jan-99 USA 7-BLR 2
29-Dec-01 USA 5-BLR 2
30-Dec-02 USA 8-BLR 2
29-Dec-04 USA 3-BLR 5
Totals: 4-3-0-1-23-11

01-Jan-77 USA 2-CAN 8
22-Dec-77 USA 3-CAN 6
02-Jan-79 USA 3-CAN 6
01-Jan-80 USA 2-CAN 4
31-Dec-80 USA 7-CAN 3
27-Dec-81 USA 4-CAN 5
27-Dec-82 USA 2-CAN 4
26-Dec-83 USA 2-CAN 5
28-Dec-84 USA 5-CAN 7
29-Dec-85 USA 2-CAN 5
01-Jan-87 USA 2-CAN 6
31-Dec-87 USA 4-CAN 5
29-Dec-88 USA 1-CAN 5
26-Dec-89 USA 2-CAN 3
27-Dec-90 USA 4-CAN 4
01-Jan-92 USA 5-CAN 3
26-Dec-92 USA 0-CAN 3
01-Jan-94 USA 3-CAN 8
29-Dec-94 USA 3-CAN 8
26-Dec-95 USA 1-CAN 6
28-Dec-96 USA 4-CAN 4
04-Jan-97 USA 0-CAN 2
02-Jan-98 USA 3-CAN 0
31-Dec-98 USA 5-CAN 2
31-Dec-99 USA 1-CAN 1
04-Jan-00 USA 3-CAN 4 (10:00 OT/GWS)
02-Jan-01 USA 1-CAN 2
03-Jan-03 USA 2-CAN 3
05-Jan-04 USA 4-CAN 3
31-Dec-05 USA 2-CAN 3
27-Dec-06 USA 3-CAN 6
03-Jan-07 USA 1-CAN 2 (10:00 OT/GWS)
04-Jan-08 USA 1-CAN 4
31-Dec-08 USA 4-CAN 7
31-Dec-09 USA 4-CAN 5 (5:00 OT/GWS)
05-Jan-10 USA 6-CAN 5 (OT)
03-Jan-11 USA 1-CAN 4
31-Dec-11 USA 2-CAN 3
Totals: 38-6-3-29-104-164

28-Dec-76 USA 2-TCH 5
23-Dec-77 USA 5-TCH 8
27-Dec-78 USA 2-TCH 3
27-Dec-79 USA 3-TCH 7
22-Dec-81 USA 4-TCH 6
26-Dec-82 USA 4-TCH 6
28-Dec-83 USA 1-TCH 10
23-Dec-84 USA 1-TCH 9
27-Dec-85 USA 5-TCH 2
27-Dec-86 USA 8-TCH 2
03-Jan-88 USA 1-TCH 11
30-Dec-88 USA 5-TCH 1
27-Dec-89 USA 1-TCH 7
30-Dec-90 USA 1-TCH 5
04-Jan-92 USA 3-TCH 2
27-Dec-92 USA 5-CZE/SVK 6
04-Jan-94 USA 3-CZE 7
04-Jan-95 USA 7-CZE 5
29-Dec-96 USA 2-CZE 1
03-Jan-97 USA 5-CZE 2
31-Dec-97 USA 1-CZE 4
28-Dec-98 USA 3-CZE 6
26-Dec-99 USA 2-CZE 2
03-Jan-00 USA 1-CZE 4
29-Dec-00 USA 2-CZE 4
25-Dec-01 USA 3-CZE 1
02-Jan-02 USA 4-CZE 3
02-Jan-03 USA 4-CZE 3
30-Dec-04 USA 1-CZE 3
04-Jan-05 USA 2-CZE 3 (OT)
02-Jan-06 USA 2-CZE 1
28-Dec-08 USA 4-CZE 3
04-Jan-09 USA 3-CZE 2 (OT)
30-Dec-11 USA 2-CZE 5
Totals vs. TCH: 16-4-0-12-51-90
Totals vs. CZE: 18-9-1-8-51-59

26-Dec-11 USA 11-DEN 3
Totals: 1-1-0-0-11-3

22-Dec-76 USA 3-FIN 6
31-Dec-77 USA 8-FIN 6
27-Dec-80 USA 1-FIN 8
02-Jan-82 USA 4-FIN 8
30-Dec-82 USA 4-FIN 2
31-Dec-83 USA 2-FIN 7
25-Dec-84 USA 4-FIN 7
30-Dec-85 USA 5-FIN 7
26-Dec-86 USA 1-FIN 4
01-Jan-88 USA 6-FIN 8
26-Dec-88 USA 5-FIN 5
04-Jan-90 USA 3-FIN 6
29-Dec-90 USA 6-FIN 3
26-Dec-91 USA 5-FIN 1
04-Jan-93 USA 5-FIN 3
26-Dec-93 USA 2-FIN 5
30-Dec-94 USA 5-FIN 7
31-Dec-95 USA 5-FIN 4
04-Jan-96 USA 8-FIN 7 (OT)
26-Dec-98 USA 3-FIN 6
29-Dec-99 USA 1-FIN 3
05-Jan-03 USA 2-FIN 3
03-Jan-04 USA 2-FIN 1
28-Dec-05 USA 6-FIN 5
05-Jan-06 USA 2-FIN 4
02-Jan-07 USA 6-FIN 3
31-Dec-07 USA 5-FIN 3
02-Jan-10 USA 6-FIN 2
26-Dec-10 USA 3-FIN 2 (OT)
28-Dec-11 USA 1-FIN 4
Totals: 30-13-1-16-119-140

27-Dec-91 USA 6-GER 2
30-Dec-92 USA 4-GER 3
29-Dec-93 USA 7-GER 2
01-Jan-95 USA 5-GER 3
31-Dec-96 USA 8-GER 0
26-Dec-06 USA 1-GER 2 (OT)
26-Dec-08 USA 8-GER 2
30-Dec-10 USA 4-GER 0
Totals: 8-7-0-1-43-14

29-Dec-92 USA 12-JPN 2
Totals: 1-1-0-0-12-2

26-Dec-97 USA 8-KAZ 2
26-Dec-00 USA 9-KAZ 1
26-Dec-07 USA 5-KAZ 1
30-Dec-08 USA 12-KAZ 0
Totals: 4-4-0-0-34-4

29-Dec-09 USA 12-LAT 1
03-Jan-12 USA 12-LAT 2
Totals: 2-2-0-0-24-3

30-Dec-78 USA 7-NOR 1
02-Jan-83 USA 8-NOR 3
02-Jan-89 USA 12-NOR 4
02-Jan-90 USA 5-NOR 6
01-Jan-91 USA 19-NOR 1
26-Dec-05 USA 11-NOR 2
Totals: 6-5-0-1-62-17

26-Dec-76 USA 2-POL 2
31-Dec-84 USA 6-POL 2
29-Dec-86 USA 15-POL 2
26-Dec-87 USA 3-POL 4
01-Jan-90 USA 3-POL 2
Totals: 5-3-1-1-29-12

30-Dec-76 USA 5-URS 15
28-Dec-78 USA 1-URS 7
29-Dec-81 USA 0-URS 7
01-Jan-83 USA 3-URS 5
29-Dec-83 USA 4-URS 7
26-Dec-84 USA 2-URS 4
26-Dec-85 USA 3-URS 7
02-Jan-87 USA 4-URS 2
29-Dec-87 USA 3-URS 7
27-Dec-88 USA 2-URS 4
30-Dec-89 USA 3-URS 7
26-Dec-90 USA 2-URS 4
02-Jan-92 USA 0-RUS 5
02-Jan-93 USA 4-RUS 2
30-Dec-93 USA 3-RUS 4
26-Dec-94 USA 4-RUS 3
28-Dec-97 USA 2-RUS 3
01-Jan-02 USA 1-RUS 6
26-Dec-02 USA 1-RUS 5
31-Dec-03 USA 4-RUS 1
25-Dec-04 USA 5-RUS 4
02-Jan-05 USA 2-RUS 7
03-Jan-06 USA 1-RUS 5
29-Dec-07 USA 3-RUS 2
05-Jan-08 USA 2-RUS 4
Totals vs. URS: 12-1-0-11-32-76
Totals vs. RUS: 13-5-0-8-32-51

25-Dec-97 USA 3-SVK 6
30-Dec-98 USA 2-SVK 3
28-Dec-99 USA 1-SVK 0
28-Dec-00 USA 7-SVK 2
03-Jan-01 USA 3-SVK 2
30-Dec-01 USA 4-SVK 4
31-Dec-02 USA 3-SVK 1
28-Dec-03 USA 5-SVK 0
30-Dec-06 USA 6-SVK 1
02-Jan-09 USA 3-SVK 5
26-Dec-09 USA 7-SVK 3
28-Dec-10 USA 6-SVK 1
Totals: 12-8-1-3-50-28

25-Dec-76 USA 8-SWE 5
28-Dec-79 USA 1-SWE 5
28-Dec-80 USA 2-SWE 10
31-Dec-81 USA 2-SWE 4
29-Dec-82 USA 1-SWE 4
25-Dec-83 USA 1-SWE 4
01-Jan-85 USA 3-SWE 7
04-Jan-86 USA 5-SWE 1
04-Jan-87 USA 0-SWE 8
04-Jan-88 USA 5-SWE 7
04-Jan-89 USA 1-SWE 3
29-Dec-89 USA 5-SWE 6
02-Jan-91 USA 5-SWE 2
30-Dec-91 USA 6-SWE 8
01-Jan-93 USA 2-SWE 4
02-Jan-94 USA 1-SWE 6
27-Dec-94 USA 2-SWE 4
01-Jan-96 USA 0-SWE 3
03-Jan-98 USA 4-SWE 3
01-Jan-00 USA 5-SWE 1
31-Dec-00 USA 3-SWE 1
27-Dec-01 USA 2-SWE 2
04-Jan-02 USA 3-SWE 2
30-Dec-03 USA 4-SWE 3
01-Jan-05 USA 8-SWE 2
31-Dec-06 USA 3-SWE 2 (OT)
05-Jan-07 USA 2-SWE 1
03-Jan-10 USA 5-SWE 2
05-Jan-11 USA 4-SWE 2
Totals: 29-13-1-15-93-112

28-Dec-77 USA 11-SUI 1
02-Jan-80 USA 9-SUI 5
26-Dec-81 USA 6-SUI 3
03-Jan-84 USA 12-SUI 3
02-Jan-86 USA 11-SUI 3
30-Dec-86 USA 12-SUI 6
04-Jan-91 USA 8-SUI 0
29-Dec-91 USA 5-SUI 1
27-Dec-93 USA 1-SUI 1
29-Dec-95 USA 4-SUI 3
26-Dec-96 USA 4-SUI 0
30-Dec-97 USA 4-SUI 1
03-Jan-99 USA 5-SUI 4
05-Jan-01 USA 4-SUI 0
28-Dec-02 USA 3-SUI 1
27-Dec-04 USA 6-SUI 4
30-Dec-05 USA 2-SUI 2
28-Dec-07 USA 4-SUI 2
27-Dec-09 USA 3-SUI 0
31-Dec-10 USA 2-SUI 1
04-Jan-12 USA 2-SUI 1
Totals: 21-19-2-0-118-42

02-Jan-95 USA 2-UKR 3
27-Dec-95 USA 3-UKR 4
Totals: 2-0-0-2-5-7

23-Dec-76 USA 3-FRG 4
25-Dec-77 USA 8-FRG 4
30-Dec-77 USA 6-FRG 5
31-Dec-78 USA 8-FRG 6
30-Dec-79 USA 2-FRG 5
30-Dec-80 USA 2-FRG 4
23-Dec-81 USA 8-FRG 1
04-Jan-83 USA 6-FRG 5
02-Jan-84 USA 10-FRG 2
29-Dec-84 USA 2-FRG 1
01-Jan-86 USA 4-FRG 1
28-Dec-87 USA 6-FRG 4
01-Jan-89 USA 15-FRG 3
Totals: 13-10-0-3-80-45

**WORLD U18 CHAMPIONSHIPS, MEN**
18-Apr-00 USA 9-BLR 1
11-Apr-02 USA 9-BLR 0
12-Apr-03 USA 3-BLR 3
12-Apr-04 USA 9-BLR 0
17-Apr-06 USA 12-BLR 1
14-Apr-08 USA 5-BLR 2
18-Apr-10 USA 7-BLR 1
Totals: 7-6-1-0-54-8

18-Apr-02 USA 10-CAN 3
20-Apr-03 USA 1-CAN 2 (OT)
13-Apr-04 USA 2-CAN 1
24-Apr-05 USA 5-CAN 1
15-Apr-07 USA 2-CAN 3 (5:00 OT/GWS)
20-Apr-07 USA 4 -CAN 3 (10:00 OT/GWS)
17-Apr-09 USA 2-CAN 1
16-Apr-10 USA 5-CAN 0
23-Apr-11 USA 5-CAN 4 (OT)
17-Apr-12 USA 5-CAN 3
20-Apr-12 USA 2-CAN 1
Totals: 11-9-0-2-43-22

19-Apr-01 USA 4-CZE 5 (10:00 OT/GWS)
20-Apr-02 USA 0-CZE 1
16-Apr-04 USA 3-CZE 2
19-Apr-05 USA 4-CZE 3
15-Apr-06 USA 5-CZE 0
20-Apr-06 USA 4-CZE 3 (OT)
16-Apr-09 USA 6-CZE 2
20-Apr-10 USA 6-CZE 0
14-Apr-12 USA 5-CZE 0
Totals: 9-7-0-2-37-16

08-Apr-04 USA 5-DEN 2
15-Apr-12 USA 4-DEN 0
Totals: 2-2-0-0-9-2

09-Apr-99 USA 0-FIN 5
15-Apr-00 USA 2-FIN 3
14-Apr-01 USA 3-FIN 4
14-Apr-02 USA 3-FIN 2
17-Apr-03 USA 2-FIN 0
16-Apr-05 USA 3-FIN 0
22-Apr-06 USA 3-FIN 1
18-Apr-08 USA 4-FIN 3
11-Apr-09 USA 4-FIN 3
21-Apr-10 USA 5-FIN 0
12-Apr-12 USA 4-FIN 0
Totals: 11-8-0-3-33-21

15-Apr-99 USA 6-GER 0
22-Apr-00 USA 1-GER 3
22-Apr-01 USA 1-GER 2
13-Apr-06 USA 9-GER 0
13-Apr-07 USA 9-GER 1
20-Apr-08 USA 4-GER 1
19-Apr-11 USA 7-GER 3
Totals: 7-5-0-2-37-10

17-Apr-07 USA 8 -LAT 0
Totals: 1-1-0-0-8-0

12-Apr-99 USA 10-NOR 2
09-Apr-09 USA 8-NOR 0
Totals: 2-2-0-0-18-2

08-Apr-99 USA 1-RUS 2
14-Apr-00 USA 1-RUS 5
21-Apr-02 USA 3-RUS 1
22-Apr-03 USA 3-RUS 6
18-Apr-04 USA 2-RUS 3
12-Apr-06 USA 4-RUS 2
12-Apr-07 USA 3-RUS 5
22-Apr-07 USA 5-RUS 6
21-Apr-08 USA 1-RUS 3
14-Apr-09 USA 5-RUS 6
19-Apr-09 USA 5-RUS 0
17-Apr-11 USA 4-RUS 3
Totals: 12-4-0-8-37-42

11-Apr-99 USA 5-SVK 6
17-Apr-00 USA 1-SVK 4
17-Apr-01 USA 6-SVK 2
14-Apr-03 USA 3-SVK 2
14-Apr-05 USA 3-SVK 1
19-Apr-07 USA 7-SVK 2
13-Apr-09 USA 12-SVK 0
15-Apr-11 USA 8-SVK 1
Totals: 8-6-0-2-45-18

17-Apr-02 USA 6-SWE 2
15-Apr-03 USA 3-SWE 2
10-Apr-04 USA 6-SWE 2
22-Apr-05 USA 6-SWE 2
16-Apr-08 USA 4-SWE 5
23-Apr-08 USA 6-SWE 3
13-Apr-10 USA 2-SWE 4
23-Apr-10 USA 3-SWE 1
24-Apr-11 USA 4-SWE 3 (OT)
22-Apr-12 USA 7-SWE 0
Totals: 10-8-0-2-47-24

16-Apr-01 USA 3-SUI 1
15-Apr-02 USA 5-SUI 1
17-Apr-05 USA 7-SUI 1
13-Apr-08 USA 7-SUI 2
14-Apr-10 USA 5-SUI 1
14-Apr-11 USA 2-SUI 1
Totals: 6-6-0-0-29-7

16-Apr-99 USA 6-UKR 0
21-Apr-00 USA 6-UKR 0
13-Apr-01 USA 11-UKR 0
12-Apr-02 USA 10-UKR 0
Totals: 4-4-0-0-33-0

**OLYMPICS, WOMEN**
14-Feb-98 USA 7-CAN 4
17-Feb-98 USA 3-CAN 1
21-Feb-02 USA 2-CAN 3
25-Feb-10 USA 0-CAN 2
Totals: 4-2-0-2-12-10

08-Feb-98 USA 5-CHN 0
14-Feb-02 USA 12-CHN 1
14-Feb-10 USA 12-CHN 1
Totals: 3-3-0-0-29-2

11-Feb-98 USA 4-FIN 2
16-Feb-02 USA 5-FIN 0
14-Feb-06 USA 7-FIN 3
20-Feb-06 USA 4-FIN 0
18-Feb-10 USA 6-FIN 0
Totals: 5-5-0-0-26-5

12-Feb-02 USA 10-GER 0
12-Feb-06 USA 5-GER 0
Totals: 2-2-0-0-15-0

12-Feb-98 USA 10-JPN 0
Totals: 1-1-0-0-10-0

16-Feb-10 USA 13-RUS 0
Totals: 1-1-0-0-13-0

09-Feb-98 USA 7-SWE 1
19-Feb-02 USA 4-SWE 0
17-Feb-06 USA 2-SWE 3 (10:00 OT/GWS)
22-Feb-10 USA 9-SWE 1
Totals: 4-3-0-1-22-5

11-Feb-06 USA 6-SUI 0
Totals: 1-1-0-0-6-0

**WOMEN'S WORLD CHAMPIONSHIPS**
25-Mar-90 USA 2-CAN 5
26-Apr-92 USA 0-CAN 8
17-Apr-94 USA 3-CAN 6
06-Apr-97 USA 3-CAN 4 (OT)
14-Mar-99 USA 1-CAN 3
09-Apr-00 USA 2-CAN 3
08-Apr-01 USA 2-CAN 3
03-Apr-04 USA 3-CAN 1
06-Apr-04 USA 0-CAN 2
09-Apr-05 USA 1-CAN 0 (20:00 OT/GWS)
07-Apr-07 USA 4-CAN 5
10-Apr-07 USA 1-CAN 5
10-Apr-08 USA 4-CAN 2
12-Apr-08 USA 4-CAN 3
10-Apr-09 USA 1-CAN 2
12-Apr-09 USA 4-CAN 1
25-Apr-11 USA 3-CAN 3 (OT)
07-Apr-12 USA 9-CAN 2
14-Apr-12 USA 4-CAN 5 (OT)
Totals: 19-7-0-12-51-62

15-Apr-94 USA 14-CHN 3
05-Apr-97 USA 6-CHN 0
11-Mar-99 USA 6-CHN 0
03-Apr-01 USA 13-CHN 0
03-Apr-05 USA 8-CHN 2
05-Apr-07 USA 9-CHN 1
Totals: 6-6-0-0-56-6

22-Mar-90 USA 5-FIN 4
23-Apr-92 USA 5-FIN 3
14-Apr-94 USA 2-FIN 1
01-Apr-97 USA 3-FIN 3
13-Mar-99 USA 3-FIN 1
06-Apr-00 USA 4-FIN 3
05-Apr-01 USA 9-FIN 0
06-Apr-05 USA 8-FIN 1
08-Apr-07 USA 4-FIN 0
08-Apr-08 USA 0-FIN 1 (OT)
09-Apr-09 USA 7-FIN 0
10-Apr-12 USA 11-FIN 0
Totals: 12-10-1-1-61-17

12-Apr-94 USA 16-GER 0
03-Apr-00 USA 16-GER 1
02-Apr-01 USA 13-GER 0
05-Apr-05 USA 7-GER 0
04-Apr-08 USA 8-GER 1
Totals: 5-5-0-0-60-2

04-Apr-09 USA 8-JPN 0
Totals: 1-1-0-0-8-0

03-Apr-07 USA 9-KAZ 0
Totals: 1-1-0-0-9-0

21-Mar-90 USA 17-NOR 0
21-Apr-92 USA 9-NOR 1
31-Mar-97 USA 7-NOR 0
Totals: 3-3-0-0-33-1

08-Mar-99 USA 10-RUS 2
04-Apr-00 USA 15-RUS 0
07-Apr-01 USA 6-RUS 1
01-Apr-04 USA 8-RUS 0
06-Apr-09 USA 8-RUS 0
18-Apr-11 USA 13-RUS 1
23-Apr-11 USA 5-RUS 1
08-Apr-12 USA 9-RUS 0
Totals: 8-8-0-0-74-5

17-Apr-11 USA 5-SVK 0
Totals: 1-1-0-0-5-0

24-Mar-90 USA 10-SWE 3
25-Apr-92 USA 6-SWE 4
03-Apr-97 USA 10-SWE 0
09-Mar-99 USA 11-SWE 0
08-Apr-00 USA 7-SWE 1
05-Apr-04 USA 9-SWE 2
08-Apr-05 USA 4-SWE 1
20-Apr-11 USA 9-SWE 1
Totals: 8-8-0-0-66-12

19-Mar-90 USA 16-SUI 3
20-Apr-92 USA 17-SUI 0
11-Apr-94 USA 6-SUI 0
30-Mar-04 USA 9-SUI 1
06-Apr-08 USA 7-SUI 1
13-Apr-12 USA 10-SUI 0
Totals: 6-6-0-0-65-5

**WOMEN'S U18 WORLD CHAMPIONSHIPS**

12-Jan-08 USA 5-CAN 2
10-Jan-09 USA 3-CAN 2 (OT)
03-Apr-10 USA 4-CAN 5 (OT)
08-Jan-11 USA 5-CAN 2
07-Jan-12 USA 0-CAN 3
Totals: 5-3-0-2-17-14

11-Jan-08 USA 8-CZE 0
09-Jan-09 USA 18-CZE 0
30-Mar-10 USA 15-CZE 0
01-Jan-11 USA 11-CZE 0
07-Jan-11 USA 14-CZE 1
03-Jan 3 USA 13-CZE 1
Totals: 6-6-0-0-79-2

28-Mar-10 USA 5-FIN 0
Totals: 1-1-0-0-5-0

06-Jan-09 USA 11-GER 0
06-Jan-12 USA 7-GER 1
Totals: 2-2-0-0-18-1

27-Mar-10 USA 11-JPN 1
02-Jan-11 USA 7-JPN 1
Totals: 2-2-0-0-18-2

07-Jan-08 USA 11-RUS 0
05-Jan-09 USA 17-RUS 0
31-Dec-11 USA 8-RUS 0
Totals: 3-3-0-0-36-0

09-Jan-08 USA 6-SWE 2
07-Jan-09 USA 9-SWE 2
02-Apr-10 USA 5-SWE 0
04-Jan-11 USA 10-SWE 0
01-Jan-12 USA 7-SWE 0
Totals: 5-5-0-0-37-4

08-Jan-08 USA 11-SUI 0
Totals: 1-1-0-0-11-0

# WEST GERMANY (FRG)

Totals=GP-W-T-L-GF-GA

**OLYMPICS, MEN**

**Date Score**
17-Feb-88 FRG 3-AUT 1
Totals: 1-1-0-0-3-1

06-Feb-68 FRG 1-CAN 6
26-Feb-88 FRG 1-CAN 8
Totals: 2-0-0-2-2-14

08-Feb-68 FRG 1-TCH 5
12-Feb-76 FRG 4-TCH 7
18-Feb-80 FRG 3-TCH 11
13-Feb-88 FRG 2-TCH 1
Totals: 4-1-0-3-10-24

17-Feb-68 FRG 4-GDR 2
Totals: 1-1-0-0-4-2

16-Feb-68 FRG 1-FIN 4
08-Feb-76 FRG 3-FIN 5
17-Feb-84 FRG 7-FIN 4
24-Feb-88 FRG 0-FIN 8
Totals: 4-1-0-3-11-21

15-Feb-84 FRG 9-ITA 4
Totals: 1-1-0-0-9-4

12-Feb-72 FRG 6-JPN 7
Totals: 1-0-0-1-6-7

09-Feb-72 FRG 5-NOR 1
14-Feb-80 FRG 10-NOR 4
15-Feb-88 FRG 7-NOR 3
Totals: 3-3-0-0-22-8

06-Feb-76 FRG 7-POL 4
09-Feb-84 FRG 8-POL 5
Totals: 2-2-0-0-15-9

12-Feb-80 FRG 4-ROM 6
Totals: 1-0-0-1-4-6

11-Feb-68 FRG 1-URS 9
10-Feb-76 FRG 3-URS 7
13-Feb-84 FRG 1-URS 6
19-Feb-88 FRG 3-URS 6
Totals: 4-0-0-4-8-28

09-Feb-68 FRG 4-SWE 5
16-Feb-80 FRG 2-SWE 5
11-Feb-84 FRG 1-SWE 1
28-Feb-88 FRG 2-SWE 3
Totals: 4-0-1-3-9-14

06-Feb-72 FRG 5-SUI 0
Totals: 1-1-0-0-5-0

12-Feb-68 FRG 1-USA 8
14-Feb-76 FRG 4-USA 1
20-Feb-80 FRG 2-USA 4
21-Feb-88 FRG 4-USA 1
Totals: 4-2-0-2-11-14

07-Feb-72 FRG 6-YUG 2
07-Feb-84 FRG 8-YUG 1
Totals: 2-2-0-0-14-3

**WORLD CHAMPIONSHIPS, MEN**

03-Mar-54 FRG 1-CAN 8
04-Mar-55 FRG 1-CAN 10
04-Mar-61 FRG 1-CAN 9
10-Mar-62 FRG 0-CAN 8
08-Mar-63 FRG 0-CAN 6
21-Mar-67 FRG 1-CAN 13
29-Apr-77 FRG 3-CAN 9
28-Apr-78 FRG 2-CAN 6
19-Apr-82 FRG 1-CAN 7
25-Apr-83 FRG 1-CAN 3
18-Apr-85 FRG 0-CAN 5
12-Apr-86 FRG 3-CAN 8
21-Apr-87 FRG 5-CAN 3
19-Apr-89 FRG 2-CAN 8
16-Apr-90 FRG 1-CAN 5
22-Apr-91 FRG 2-CAN 3
Totals: 16-1-0-15-24-111

07-Mar-53 FRG 2-TCH 11
12-Mar-53 FRG 4-TCH 9
27-Feb-54 FRG 4-TCH 9
02-Mar-55 FRG 0-TCH 8
05-Mar-61 FRG 0-TCH 6
07-Mar-63 FRG 1-TCH 10
18-Mar-67 FRG 2-TCH 6
22-Mar-71 FRG 1-TCH 9
30-Mar-71 FRG 0-TCH 4
10-Apr-72 FRG 1-TCH 8
18-Apr-72 FRG 1-TCH 8
03-Apr-73 FRG 2-TCH 4
11-Apr-73 FRG 2-TCH 7
19-Apr-76 FRG 1-TCH 9
22-Apr-77 FRG 3-TCH 9
26-Apr-78 FRG 0-TCH 8
14-Apr-81 FRG 2-TCH 6
15-Apr-82 FRG 4-TCH 2
24-Apr-83 FRG 3-TCH 3
20-Apr-85 FRG 1-TCH 6
13-Apr-86 FRG 4-TCH 3
25-Apr-86 FRG 1-TCH 3
25-Apr-87 FRG 2-TCH 5
15-Apr-89 FRG 3-TCH 3
20-Apr-90 FRG 0-TCH 3
23-Apr-91 FRG 1-TCH 7
01-May-91 FRG 1-TCH 4
Totals: 27-2-2-23-46-170

11-Mar-59 FRG 8-GDR 0
16-Mar-63 FRG 4-GDR 3
26-Mar-67 FRG 1-GDR 8
14-Apr-76 FRG 7-GDR 1
22-Apr-76 FRG 1-GDR 1
07-May-78 FRG 1-GDR 1
11-May-78 FRG 0-GDR 0
22-Apr-83 FRG 4-GDR 3
01-May-83 FRG 7-GDR 3
26-Apr-85 FRG 6-GDR 0
02-May-85 FRG 4-GDR 1
Totals: 11-7-3-1-43-21

05-Mar-54 FRG 5-FIN 1
01-Mar-55 FRG 7-FIN 1
05-Mar-59 FRG 3-FIN 5
09-Mar-61 FRG 3-FIN 3
15-Mar-62 FRG 3-FIN 9
11-Mar-63 FRG 4-FIN 4
25-Mar-67 FRG 2-FIN 2
20-Mar-71 FRG 3-FIN 4
28-Mar-71 FRG 2-FIN 7
08-Apr-72 FRG 5-FIN 8
16-Apr-72 FRG 3-FIN 13
01-Apr-73 FRG 3-FIN 8
09-Apr-73 FRG 1-FIN 2
10-Apr-76 FRG 2-FIN 5
20-Apr-76 FRG 4-FIN 4
01-May-77 FRG 1-FIN 4
05-May-77 FRG 2-FIN 7
03-May-78 FRG 4-FIN 3
05-May-78 FRG 5-FIN 3
13-May-78 FRG 2-FIN 7
18-Apr-79 FRG 2-FIN 5
24-Apr-79 FRG 3-FIN 7
17-Apr-81 FRG 3-FIN 6
23-Apr-81 FRG 4-FIN 4
16-Apr-82 FRG 3-FIN 4
19-Apr-83 FRG 4-FIN 3
29-Apr-83 FRG 2-FIN 4
24-Apr-85 FRG 3-FIN 3
30-Apr-85 FRG 5-FIN 4
19-Apr-86 FRG 1-FIN 10
20-Apr-87 FRG 3-FIN 1
02-May-87 FRG 2-FIN 2
25-Apr-89 FRG 1-FIN 3
26-Apr-89 FRG 0-FIN 3
23-Apr-90 FRG 2-FIN 4
29-Apr-90 FRG 1-FIN 1
25-Apr-91 FRG 0-FIN 6
29-Apr-91 FRG 2-FIN 4
Totals: 38-7-8-23-105-174

12-Mar-62 FRG 9-GBR 0
Totals: 1-1-0-0-9-0

06-Mar-59 FRG 7-ITA 2
09-Mar-59 FRG 2-ITA 2
18-Apr-82 FRG 5-ITA 2
17-Apr-83 FRG 4-ITA 0
27-Apr-83 FRG 5-ITA 4
Totals: 5-4-1-0-23-10

19-Apr-81 FRG 9-NED 2
25-Apr-81 FRG 12-NED 6
Totals: 2-2-0-0-21-8

07-Mar-54 FRG 7-NOR 1
13-Mar-59 FRG 9-NOR 4
09-Mar-62 FRG 4-NOR 6
25-Apr-90 FRG 3-NOR 7
01-May-90 FRG 4-NOR 0
Totals: 5-3-0-2-27-18

26-Feb-55 FRG 4-POL 5
10-Mar-59 FRG 5-POL 3
06-Apr-73 FRG 4-POL 2
14-Apr-73 FRG 1-POL 4
12-Apr-76 FRG 5-POL 3
24-Apr-76 FRG 2-POL 1
17-Apr-79 FRG 3-POL 3
22-Apr-79 FRG 8-POL 1
21-Apr-86 FRG 4-POL 1
27-Apr-86 FRG 5-POL 5
23-Apr-89 FRG 3-POL 5
30-Apr-89 FRG 2-POL 0
Totals: 12-7-2-3-46-33

27-Apr-77 FRG 6-ROM 3
07-May-77 FRG 3-ROM 2
Totals: 2-2-0-0-9-5

01-Mar-54 FRG 2-URS 6
03-Mar-55 FRG 1-URS 5
11-Mar-61 FRG 1-URS 11
10-Mar-63 FRG 3-URS 15
23-Mar-67 FRG 1-URS 16
19-Mar-71 FRG 2-URS 11
27-Mar-71 FRG 1-URS 12
07-Apr-72 FRG 2-URS 11
15-Apr-72 FRG 0-URS 7
31-Mar-73 FRG 1-URS 17
08-Apr-73 FRG 2-URS 18
15-Apr-76 FRG 2-URS 8
21-Apr-77 FRG 0-URS 10
01-May-78 FRG 2-URS 10
15-Apr-79 FRG 2-URS 3
22-Apr-82 FRG 0-URS 7
20-Apr-83 FRG 0-URS 6
21-Apr-85 FRG 2-URS 10
16-Apr-86 FRG 1-URS 4
18-Apr-87 FRG 0-URS 7
16-Apr-89 FRG 1-URS 5
17-Apr-90 FRG 2-URS 5
20-Apr-91 FRG 3-URS 7
Totals: 23-0-0-23-31-211

08-Mar-53 FRG 6-SWE 8
13-Mar-53 FRG 2-SWE 12
04-Mar-54 FRG 0-SWE 4
25-Feb-55 FRG 4-SWE 5
07-Mar-59 FRG 1-SWE 6
08-Mar-61 FRG 1-SWE 12
17-Mar-62 FRG 0-SWE 4
13-Mar-63 FRG 2-SWE 10
20-Mar-67 FRG 1-SWE 3
23-Mar-71 FRG 2-SWE 7
31-Mar-71 FRG 2-SWE 1
11-Apr-72 FRG 0-SWE 10
19-Apr-72 FRG 1-SWE 7
04-Apr-73 FRG 2-SWE 8
12-Apr-73 FRG 1-SWE 12
08-Apr-76 FRG 1-SWE 4
25-Apr-77 FRG 1-SWE 7
29-Apr-78 FRG 1-SWE 10
14-Apr-79 FRG 3-SWE 7
12-Apr-81 FRG 2-SWE 4
21-Apr-82 FRG 1-SWE 3
16-Apr-83 FRG 1-SWE 5
17-Apr-85 FRG 2-SWE 3
28-Apr-85 FRG 2-SWE 5
18-Apr-86 FRG 2-SWE 4
17-Apr-87 FRG 0-SWE 3
18-Apr-89 FRG 3-SWE 3
19-Apr-90 FRG 0-SWE 6
19-Apr-91 FRG 1-SWE 8
Totals: 29-1-1-27-45-181

10-Mar-53 FRG 2-SUI 3
15-Mar-53 FRG 7-SUI 3
28-Feb-54 FRG 3-SUI 3
06-Mar-55 FRG 8-SUI 3
14-Mar-59 FRG 6-SUI 0
14-Mar-62 FRG 7-SUI 1
13-Apr-72 FRG 6-SUI 3
21-Apr-72 FRG 4-SUI 1
27-Apr-87 FRG 4-SUI 3
28-Apr-87 FRG 8-SUI 1
28-Apr-91 FRG 2-SUI 5
03-May-91 FRG 3-SUI 3
Totals: 12-8-2-2-60-29

27-Feb-55 FRG 3-USA 6
07-Mar-61 FRG 4-USA 4
13-Mar-62 FRG 4-USA 8
14-Mar-63 FRG 4-USA 8
28-Mar-67 FRG 3-USA 8
25-Mar-71 FRG 7-USA 2
02-Apr-71 FRG 1-USA 5
18-Apr-76 FRG 1-USA 5
24-Apr-77 FRG 3-USA 3
03-May-77 FRG 1-USA 4
05-May-78 FRG 3-USA 7
09-May-78 FRG 5-USA 5
20-Apr-79 FRG 6-USA 3
26-Apr-79 FRG 5-USA 2
15-Apr-81 FRG 6-USA 10
21-Apr-81 FRG 6-USA 2
24-Apr-82 FRG 5-USA 5
23-Apr-85 FRG 3-USA 4
15-Apr-86 FRG 2-USA 9
23-Apr-86 FRG 0-USA 5
23-Apr-87 FRG 4-USA 6
30-Apr-87 FRG 3-USA 6
21-Apr-89 FRG 4-USA 7
28-Apr-89 FRG 3-USA 4
22-Apr-90 FRG 3-USA 6
27-Apr-90 FRG 3-USA 5
26-Apr-91 FRG 4-USA 4
Totals: 27-4-5-18-96-143

**WORLD U20 CHAMPIONSHIPS**

31-Dec-80 FRG 9-AUT 1
Totals: 1-1-0-0-9-1

29-Dec-76 FRG 1-CAN 9
23-Dec-77 FRG 0-CAN 8
28-Dec-78 FRG 2-CAN 6
02-Jan-80 FRG 1-CAN 6
02-Jan-81 FRG 7-CAN 6
29-Dec-81 FRG 3-CAN 11
26-Dec-82 FRG 0-CAN 4
29-Dec-83 FRG 0-CAN 7
26-Dec-84 FRG 0-CAN 6
27-Dec-85 FRG 2-CAN 18
03-Jan-88 FRG 1-CAN 8
28-Dec-88 FRG 4-CAN 7
Totals: 12-1-0-11-21-96

26-Dec-76 FRG 2-TCH 8
22-Dec-77 FRG 4-TCH 5
28-Dec-79 FRG 4-TCH 13
31-Dec-81 FRG 1-TCH 7
02-Jan-83 FRG 0-TCH 9
25-Dec-83 FRG 1-TCH 6
28-Dec-84 FRG 3-TCH 7
26-Dec-85 FRG 3-TCH 9
31-Dec-87 FRG 4-TCH 7
29-Dec-88 FRG 1-TCH 11
Totals: 10-0-0-10-23-82

25-Dec-76 FRG 1-FIN 4
28-Dec-77 FRG 1-FIN 4
30-Dec-78 FRG 1-FIN 7
28-Dec-80 FRG 6-FIN 8
27-Dec-81 FRG 4-FIN 8
01-Jan-83 FRG 1-FIN 9
03-Jan-84 FRG 2-FIN 8
23-Dec-84 FRG 0-FIN 9
29-Dec-85 FRG 2-FIN 7
26-Dec-87 FRG 0-FIN 6
31-Dec-88 FRG 3-FIN 5
Totals: 11-0-0-11-21-75

02-Jan-79 FRG 6-NOR 0
30-Dec-82 FRG 4-NOR 2
04-Jan-89 FRG 2-NOR 4
Totals: 3-2-0-1-12-6

02-Jan-77 FRG 9-POL 2
01-Jan-85 FRG 3-POL 3
01-Jan-88 FRG 6-POL 3
Totals: 3-2-1-0-18-8

28-Dec-76 FRG 1-URS 2
22-Dec-81 FRG 3-URS 12
29-Dec-82 FRG 2-URS 12
26-Dec-83 FRG 1-URS 9
25-Dec-84 FRG 1-URS 12
30-Dec-85 FRG 0-URS 10
04-Jan-88 FRG 2-URS 12
26-Dec-88 FRG 0-URS 15
Totals: 8-0-0-8-10-84

01-Jan-77 FRG 0-SWE 5
27-Dec-78 FRG 2-SWE 5
27-Dec-79 FRG 1-SWE 5
27-Dec-80 FRG 3-SWE 7
26-Dec-81 FRG 1-SWE 5
27-Dec-82 FRG 2-SWE 4
28-Dec-83 FRG 2-SWE 11

31-Dec-84 FRG 1-SWE 5
02-Jan-86 FRG 0-SWE 10
29-Dec-87 FRG 1-SWE 5
03-Jan-89 FRG 0-SWE 9
Totals: 11-0-0-11-13-71

31-Dec-77 FRG 6-SUI 2
01-Jan-80 FRG 4-SUI 2
02-Jan-82 FRG 6-SUI 5
31-Dec-83 FRG 4-SUI 3
04-Jan-86 FRG 1-SUI 7
Totals: 5-4-0-1-21-19

23-Dec-76 FRG 4-USA 3
25-Dec-77 FRG 4-USA 8
30-Dec-77 FRG 5-USA 6
31-Dec-78 FRG 6-USA 8
30-Dec-79 FRG 5-USA 2
30-Dec-80 FRG 4-USA 2
23-Dec-81 FRG 1-USA 8
04-Jan-83 FRG 5-USA 6
02-Jan-84 FRG 2-USA 10
29-Dec-84 FRG 1-USA 2
01-Jan-86 FRG 1-USA 4
28-Dec-87 FRG 4-USA 6
01-Jan-89 FRG 3-USA 15
Totals: 13-3-0-10-45-80

# YUGOSLAVIA (YUG)

Totals=GP-W-T-L-GF-GA

**OLYMPICS, MEN**

| Date | Score |
|---|---|
| 30-Jan-64 | YUG 2-AUT 6 |
| 09-Feb-68 | YUG 6-AUT 0 |
| 13-Feb-76 | YUG 1-AUT 3 |

Totals: 3-1-0-2-9-9

09-Feb-76 YUG 8-BUL 5
Totals: 1-1-0-0-8-5

13-Feb-68 YUG 10-FRA 1
Totals: 1-1-0-0-10-1

06-Feb-64 YUG 4-HUN 2
Totals: 1-1-0-0-4-2

01-Feb-64 YUG 5-ITA 3
13-Feb-84 YUG 5-ITA 1
Totals: 2-2-0-0-10-4

04-Feb-64 YUG 6-JPN 4
07-Feb-68 YUG 5-JPN 1
09-Feb-72 YUG 2-JPN 3
11-Feb-76 YUG 3-JPN 4
Totals: 4-2-0-2-16-12

08-Feb-64 YUG 4-NOR 8
17-Feb-68 YUG 3-NOR 2
06-Feb-72 YUG 2-NOR 5
Totals: 3-1-0-2-9-15

07-Feb-64 YUG 3-POL 9
15-Feb-84 YUG 1-POL 8
Totals: 2-0-0-2-4-17

02-Feb-64 YUG 5-ROM 5
16-Feb-68 YUG 9-ROM 5
07-Feb-76 YUG 4-ROM 3
Totals: 3-2-1-0-18-13

11-Feb-84 YUG 1-URS 9
Totals: 1-0-0-1-1-9

09-Feb-84 YUG 0-SWE 11
Totals: 1-0-0-1-0-11

10-Feb-72 YUG 3-SUI 3
05-Feb-76 YUG 6-SUI 4
Totals: 2-1-1-0-9-7

07-Feb-72 YUG 2-FRG 6
07-Feb-84 YUG 1-FRG 8
Totals: 2-0-0-2-3-14

**WORLD CHAMPIONSHIPS, MEN**

07-Feb-39 YUG 3-BEL 3
Totals: 1-0-1-0-3-3

03-Feb-39 YUG 0-TCH 24
Totals: 1-0-0-1-0-24

05-Feb-39 YUG 0-LAT 6
08-Feb-39 YUG 0-LAT 4
Totals: 2-0-0-2-0-10

04-Feb-39 YUG 0-SUI 23
Totals: 1-0-0-1-0-23

*It's always a battle of epic proportions when the Czech Republic and Slovakia face off, as in this 2012 World Championship encounter in Helsinki. Photo: Andre Ringuette / HHOF-IIHF Images.*

*The almost annual Canada-United States U20 game on New Year's Eve has become one of the fiercest and most anticipated games on the hockey calendar. Photo: Andy Devlin / HHOF-IIHF Images.*

# THE RECORD BOOK

## Olympics, Men

### All-Time Team Records

**LONGEST WINNING STREAK**
20 games CAN, April 24, 1920-February 8, 1936

**LONGEST UNDEFEATED STREAK**
24 games CAN, February 12, 1936-January 30, 1956
16 games URS, February 17, 1968-February 20, 1980

**LONGEST LOSING STREAK**
11 games HUN, February 8, 1936-present
9 games SUI, February 1, 1956-February 8, 1964
9 games POL, February 13, 1928-February 7, 1936

**LONGEST WINLESS STREAK**
21 games NOR, February 12, 1980-February 16, 1992

### Goal-Scoring Team Records

**MOST GOALS, TEAM, GAME**

**(EARLY ERA, 1920-1952)**
33 CAN 33-SUI 0, January 30, 1924
31 USA 31-ITA 1, February 1, 1948
30 CAN 30-TCH 0, January 28, 1924
29 USA 29-SUI 0, April 24, 1920
23 SWE 23-ITA 0, February 7, 1948
23 USA 23-POL 4, January 31, 1948

**(MODERN ERA, 1956-2010)**
23 CAN 23-AUT 0, January 27, 1956
19 CAN 19-JPN 1, February 20, 1960
19 SWE 19-JPN 0, February 21, 1960
19 FIN 19-AUS 2, February 25, 1960
18 TCH 18-AUS 1, February 20, 1960

**MOST GOALS BOTH TEAMS, GAME (BOTH TEAMS SCORING)**

**(EARLY ERA, 1920-1952)**
32 USA 31-ITA 1, February 1, 1948
27 USA 23-POL 4, January 31, 1948
25 TCH 22-ITA 3, January 30, 1948
22 CAN 21-ITA 1, February 3, 1948

**(MODERN ERA, 1956-2010)**
21 URS 17-NED 4, February 14, 1980
21 FIN 19-AUS 2, February 25, 1960
20 CAN 19-JPN 1, February 20, 1960
19 TCH 18-AUS 1, February 20, 1960
18 FIN 16-NOR 2, February 9, 1984
17 URS 16-POL 1, February 8, 1976
16 USA 10-AUT 6, February 13, 1988

**MOST GOALS, TEAM, PERIOD**

**(EARLY ERA, 1920-1952)**
15 USA, 1st half, April 24, 1920 vs. SUI
14 USA, 3rd period, February 1, 1948
14 CAN, 3rd period, January 30, 1924 vs. SUI
14 CAN, 2nd period, January 28, 1924 vs. TCH
14 USA, 2nd half, April 24, 1920 vs. SUI

**(MODERN ERA, 1956-2010)**
11 CAN, 2nd period, January 27, 1956 vs. AUT
9 SWE, 2nd period, February 14, 1988 vs. FRA
8 URS, 1st period, February 14, 1980 vs. NED
8 URS, 1st period, February 13, 1980 vs. JPN
8 FIN, 3rd period, February 25, 1960 vs. AUS
8 SWE, 1st period, February 21, 1960 vs. JPN
8 CZE, 3rd period, February 20, 1960 vs. AUS

**MOST GOALS BOTH TEAMS, PERIOD (BOTH TEAMS SCORING)**

**(EARLY ERA, 1920-1952)**
12 USA (11) & ITA (1), 2nd period, February 1, 1948
12 USA (9) & POL (3), 3rd period, January 31, 1948
11 TCH (10) & ITA (1), 2nd period, January 30, 1948
10 SWE (9) & POL (1), 2nd period, February 16, 1952
10 TCH (8) & AUT (2), 3rd period, February 4, 1948
10 USA (9) & POL (1), 2nd period, January 31, 1948

**(MODERN ERA, 1956-2010)**
10 CAN 7-FRA 3, 1st period, February 20, 1988
10 SWE 9-FRA 1, 2nd period, February 14, 1988
9 AUT 5-USA 4, 3rd period, February 13, 1988
9 URS 8-NED 1, 1st period, February 14, 1980
9 FIN 8-AUS 1, 1st period, February 22, 1960
8 URS 7-NED 1, 2nd period, February 14, 1980
8 BUL 4-YUG 4, 3rd period, February 9, 1976
8 URS 7-POL 1, 1st period, February 8, 1976
8 YUG 5-ROM 3, 1st period, February 16, 1968
8 ITA 4-JPN 4, 3rd period, February 9, 1964
8 JPN 6-AUS 2, 3rd period, February 24, 1960
8 CAN 7-JPN 1, 2nd period, February 20, 1960
8 CZE 7-AUS 1, 1st period, February 20, 1960
8 CZE 6-POL 2, 2nd period, January 29, 1956

**SCORELESS GAMES**
February 6, 1948 CAN-TCH
February 15, 1936 GBR-USA
February 12, 1928 GER-AUT

### Power-Play and Short-Handed Goals Records

**MOST POWER-PLAY GOALS, TEAM, GAME**
6 SWE, February 21, 1960 vs. JPN
5 FIN, February 16, 2006 vs. ITA
5 FIN, February 16, 1998 vs. KAZ
5 FIN, February 20, 1980 vs. NED

**MOST POWER-PLAY GOALS TEAM, PERIOD**
5 FIN, 3rd period, February 20, 1980 vs. NED
4 FIN, 2nd period, February 16, 2006 vs. ITA
4 URS, 1st period, February 14, 1980 vs. NED
4 SWE, 3rd period, February 21, 1960 vs. JPN

**MOST POWER-PLAY GOALS, BOTH TEAMS, GAME**
7 FIN (5) & KAZ (2), February 16, 1998

**MOST POWER-PLAY GOALS, BOTH TEAMS, PERIOD**
4 TCH (3) & NOR (1), 3rd period, February 17, 1988

**MOST SHORT-HANDED GOALS, TEAM, GAME**
2 SVK, February 21, 1994 vs. FRA
2 RUS, February 12, 1994 vs. NOR
2 TCH, February 15, 1988 vs. USA
2 JPN, February 24, 1960 vs. AUS
2 USA, February 19, 1960 vs. TCH

**MOST SHORT-HANDED GOALS, TEAM, PERIOD**
2 TCH, 3rd period, February 15, 1988 vs. USA
2 USA, 3rd period, February 19, 1960 vs. TCH

**MOST SHORT-HANDED GOALS, BOTH TEAMS, GAME**
3 TCH (2) & POL (1), February 5, 1972

### All-Time Individual Records

**MOST OLYMPICS PLAYED**
6 Raimo Helminen (FIN)
5 Dieter Hegen (FRG/GER)
5 Udo Kiessling (FRG/GER)
5 Jere Lehtinen (FIN)
5 Denis Perez (FRA)
5 Teemu Selanne (FIN)
5 Petter Thoresen (NOR)

**MOST GOLD MEDALS**
3 Vitali Davydov (URS), Anatoli Firsov (URS), Andrei Khomutov (URS/RUS), Viktor Kuzkin (URS), Alexander Ragulin (URS), Vladislav Tretiak (URS)

**MOST MEDALS**
4 (3G, S) Vladislav Tretiak (URS)
4 (2G,S,B) Igor Kravchuk (RUS)
4 (2S, 2B) Jiri Holik (TCH)
4 (S, 3B) Jere Lehtinen (FIN)
4 (B, 3S) Saku Koivu (FIN)
3 (3G) Vitali Davydov (URS), Anatoli Firsov (URS), Andrei Khomutov (URS/RUS), Viktor Kuzkin (URS), Alexander Ragulin (URS)
3 (2G, S) Alexei Kasatonov (URS), Valeri Kharlamov (URS), Vladimir Krutov (URS), Sergei Makarov (URS), Alexander Maltsev (URS), Boris Mikhailov (URS), Vladimir Petrov (URS), Sergei Starikov (URS), Valeri Vasilyev (URS)
3 (2G, B) Veniamin Alexandrov (URS), Vyacheslav Fetisov (URS), Igor Larionov (URS/RUS)
3 (G, S, B) Darius Kasparaitis (RUS), Alexei Zhamnov (RUS)
3 (G, 2B) Robert Lang (TCH/CZE)
3 (2S, B) Oldrich Machac (TCH), Frantisek Pospisil (TCH)
3 (S, 2B) Josef Cerny (TCH), Vladimir Dzurilla (TCH), Raimo Helminen (FIN), Jarmo Myllys (FIN), Ville Peltonen (FIN), Teemu Selanne (FIN)

**MOST GAMES PLAYED**
39 Raimo Helminen (FIN)
33 Dieter Hegen (FRG/GER)
32 Udo Kiessling (FRG/GER)
32 Jere Lehtinen (FIN)
31 Teemu Selanne (FIN)
29 Vlastimil Bubnik (TCH)
29 Sven "Tumba" Johansson (SWE)
29 Andreas Niederberger (FRG/GER)
29 Petter Thoresen (NOR)

**MOST POINTS, CAREER**
37 Teemu Selanne (FIN) 20+17=37
36 Vlastimil Bubnik# (TCH) 22+14=36
36 Valeri Kharlamov (URS) 14+22=36
36 Harry Watson* (CAN, 1924) 36+0=36
33 Herb Drury* (USA) 33+0=33
33 Vyacheslav Fetisov (URS) 12+21=33
32 Sven "Tumba" Johansson# (SWE) 25+7=32
31 Vladimir Krutov (URS) 16+15=31
30 Anatoli Firsov (URS) 18+12=30
30 Erich Kuhnhackl (FRG) 15+15=30
30 Saku Koivu (FIN) 9+21=30
*early era
#played early & modern era

**MOST POINTS, ONE OLYMPICS**

**(EARLY ERA, 1920-1952)**
36 Harry Watson (CAN, 1924) 36+0=36
23 Herb Drury (USA, 1924) 23+0=23
23 Wally Halder (CAN, 1948) 15+8=23
23 Bruce Mather (USA, 1948) 15+8=23
23 Vladimir Zabrodsky (TCH, 1948) 23+0=23
20 Bert McCaffery (CAN, 1924) 20=0=20
19 Billy Gibson (CAN, 1952) 12+7=19
18 Reginald "Hooley" Smith (CAN, 1924) 18+0=18

**(MODERN ERA, 1956-2010)**
18 Bob Attersley (CAN, 1960) 6+12=18
16 Anatoli Firsov (URS, 1968) 12+4=16
16 Valeri Kharlamov (URS, 1972) 9+7=16
15 Joe Juneau (CAN, 1992) 6+9=15
15 Vladimir Krutov (URS, 1988) 6+9=15
15 Milan Novy (TCH, 1980) 7+8=15

**MOST GOALS, CAREER**

**(EARLY ERA, 1920-1952)**

36 Harry Watson (CAN, 1924)
33 Herb Drury (USA)
21 Uli Poltera (SUI)
20 Bert McCaffery (CAN)
18 Eric Carruthers (GBR)
18 Reginald "Hooley" Smith (CAN)
18 Hans-Martin Trepp (SUI)
17 Dunc Munro (CAN)
17 Jack Riley (USA)

**(MODERN ERA, 1956-2010)**

25 Sven "Tumba" Johansson (SWE)=
25 Vladimir Zabrodsky (TCH)=
22 Vlastimil Bubnik (TCH)
20 Teemu Selanne (FIN)
17 Albin Felc (YUG)*
16 Dieter Hegen (FRG/GER)
16 Vladimir Krutov (URS)

*played only against B pool teams
=played in early and modern era

**MOST GOALS, ONE OLYMPICS**

**(EARLY ERA, 1920-1952)**

36 Harry Watson (CAN, 1924)
23 Herb Drury (USA, 1924)
23 Vladimir Zabrodsky (TCH, 1948)
20 Bert McCaffery (CAN, 1924)
18 Reginald "Hooley" Smith (CAN, 1924)
17 Bruce Cunliffe (USA, 1948)
17 Dunc Munro (CAN, 1924)
17 Jack Riley (USA, 1948)

**(MODERN ERA, 1956-2010)**

12 Albin Felc (YUG, 1964)*
12 Masahiro Sato (JPN, 1964)*
10 Nikolai Drozdetski (URS, 1984)

*played only against B pool teams

**MOST ASSISTS, CAREER**

22 Valeri Kharlamov (URS)
21 Vyacheslav Fetisov (URS)
21 Saku Koivu (FIN)
19 Mats Naslund (SWE)
18 Raimo Helminen (FIN)
17 Peter Forsberg (SWE)
17 Robert Lang (TCH/CZE)
17 Sergei Makarov (URS)
17 Teemu Selanne (FIN)

**MOST ASSISTS, ONE OLYMPICS**

12 Bob Attersley (CAN, 1960)
12 Fred Etcher (CAN, 1960)
10 Vladimir Vikulov (URS, 1968)
9 Vyacheslav Fetisov (URS, 1988)
9 Joe Juneau (CAN, 1992)
9 Valeri Kharlamov (URS, 1980)
9 Vladimir Krutov (URS, 1988)
9 Igor Larionov (URS, 1988)
9 George Mara (CAN, 1948)+
9 Vasili Pervukhin (URS, 1980)
9 Ab Renaud (CAN, 1948)+

+early era

**MOST PENALTY MINUTES, CAREER**

70 Pat Flatley (CAN)
54 Erich Goldmann (GER)
49 Jarkko Ruutu (FIN)
48 Paul Ambros (FRG)

**MOST PENALTY MINUTES, ONE OLYMPICS**

70 Pat Flatley (CAN, 1984)
43 Daniel Kunce (GER, 2002)
39 Petr Svoboda (CZE, 1998)
31 Ilya Kovalchuk (RUS, 2006)
31 Jarkko Ruutu (FIN, 2006)

**MOST POINTS, ONE GAME**
**(MODERN ERA, 1956-2010)**

8 Vaclav Nedomansky (TCH), 6 goals, 2 assists, February 5, 1972 vs. POL
7 Paul Knox (CAN), 5 goals, 2 assists, January 27, 1956 vs. AUT
7 Ronald Pettersson (SWE), 3 goals, 4 assists, February 21, 1960 vs. JPN
6 Fred Etcher (CAN), 2 goals, 4 assists, February 20, 1960 vs. JPN
6 Valeri Kharlamov (URS), 3 goals, 3 assists, February 5, 1972 vs. FIN
6 Yuri Lebedev (URS), 3 goals, 3 assists, February 14, 1980 vs. NED
6 Alexander Maltsev (URS), 2 goals, 4 assists, February 14, 1980 vs. NED
6 Raimo Summanen (FIN), 2 goals, 4 assists, February 9, 1984 vs. NOR

**MOST POINTS, ONE PERIOD**
**(MODERN ERA, 1956-2010)**

4 Paul Knox (CAN), 3 goals, 1 assist, 1st period, January 27, 1956 vs. AUT
4 Ken Laufman (CAN), 1 goal, 3 assists, 2nd period, January 27, 1956 vs. AUT
4 John Mayasich (USA), 1 goal, 3 assists, 3rd period, February 4, 1956 vs. TCH
4 Carl-Goran Oberg (SWE), 2 goals, 2 assists, 1st period, February 21, 1960 vs. JPN
4 Yuri Lebedev (URS), 2 goals, 2 assists, 1st period, February 14, 1980 vs. NED
4 Alexander Maltsev (URS), 1 goals, 3 assists, 1st period, February 14, 1980 vs. NED

**MOST GOALS, ONE GAME**

**(EARLY ERA, 1920-1952)**

13 Harry Watson, CAN, January 30, 1924 vs. SUI
11 Harry Watson, CAN, January 28, 1924 vs. TCH
8 Tony Conroy, USA, April 24, 1920 vs. SUI
8 Bert McCaffery, CAN, January 30, 1924 vs. SUI
8 Lars Ljungman, SWE, February 7, 1948 vs. ITA
7 Joe McCormick, USA, April 24, 1920 vs. SUI
7 Slim Halderson, CAN, April 24, 1920 vs. TCH
7 Frank Fredrickson, CAN, April 26, 1920 vs. SWE
7 Larry McCormick, USA, April 28, 1920 vs. TCH

**(MODERN ERA, 1956-2010)**

6 Vaclav Nedomansky (TCH), February 5, 1972 vs. POL
5 Paul Knox (CAN), January 27, 1956 vs. AUT
5 Pavel Bure (RUS), February 20, 1998 vs. FIN
4 Vsevolod Bobrov (URS), January 29, 1956 vs. SUI
4 Bobby Rousseau (CAN), February 20, 1960 vs. JPN
4 Jozef Golonka (TCH), February 20, 1960 vs. AUS
4 Raimo Kilpio (FIN), February 22, 1960 vs. AUS
4 Bill Cleary (USA), February 24, 1960 vs. GER
4 Roger Christian (USA), February 28, 1960 vs. TCH
4 Morris Mott (CAN), February 9, 1968 vs. GDR
4 Jozef Horesovsky (TCH), February 12, 1968 vs. GDR
4 Peter Gradin (SWE), February 13, 1984 vs. POL
4 Franck Pajonkowski (FRA), February 23, 1988 vs. NOR
4 Ilya Kovalchuk (RUS), February 19, 2006 vs. LAT

**MOST GOALS, ONE PERIOD**

**(EARLY ERA, 1920-1952)**

6 Harry Watson (CAN) 2nd period, January 28, 1924 vs. TCH
5 Larry McCormick (USA) 2nd half, April 28, 1920 vs. TCH
5 Harry Watson (CAN) 2nd period, January 30, 1924 vs. SUI

**(MODERN ERA, 1956-2010—ALL HAT TRICKS)**

3 Paul Knox (CAN), 1st period, January 27, 1956 vs. AUT
3 Dick Dougherty (USA), 3rd period, February 4, 1956 vs. TCH
3 Miroslav Vlach (TCH), 3rd period, February 20, 1960 vs. AUS
3 Raimo Kilpio (FIN), 1st period, February 22, 1960 vs. AUS
3 Juji Iwaoka (JPN), 3rd period, February 24, 1960 vs. AUS
3 Kalevi Numminen (FIN), 2nd period, February 25, 1960 vs. AUS
3 Jouni Seistamo (FIN), 3rd period, February 25, 1960 vs. AUS
3 Roger Christian (USA), 3rd period, February 28, 1960 vs. TCH
3 Josef Horesovsky (TCH), 1st period, February 12, 1968 vs. GDR
3 Vaclav Nedomansky (TCH), 3rd period, February 5, 1972 vs. POL
3 Arto Sirvio (FIN), 3rd period, February 9, 1984 vs. NOR
3 Peter Gradin (SWE), 2nd period, February 13, 1984 vs. POL
3 Erich Kuhnhackl (FRG), 2nd period, February 17, 1984 vs. FIN
3 Franck Pajonkowski (FRA), 2nd period, February 23, 1988 vs. NOR
3 Petr Rosol (TCH), 2nd period, February 8, 1992 vs. NOR

**MOST ASSISTS, ONE GAME**

5 Valeri Kharlamov (URS), February 13, 1980 vs. JPN
4 Fred Etcher (CAN), February 20, 1960 vs. JPN
4 Ronald Pettersson (SWE), February 21, 1960 vs. JPN
4 Bob Attersley (CAN), February 28, 1960 vs. URS
4 Vincent Lukac (TCH), February 12, 1980 vs. NOR
4 Boris Mikhailov (URS), February 13, 1980 vs. JPN
4 Alexander Maltsev (URS), February 14, 1980 vs. NED
4 Vasili Pervukhin (URS), February 24, 1980 vs. SWE
4 Viktor Tyumenev (URS), February 7, 1984 vs. POL
4 Darius Rusnak (TCH), February 7, 1984 vs. NOR
4 Raimo Summanen (FIN), February 9, 1984 vs. NOR
4 Ed Olczyk (USA), February 13, 1984 vs. AUT
4 Anders Eldebrink (SWE), February 14, 1988 vs. FRA
4 Erkki Lehtonen (FIN), February 16, 1988 vs. FRA
4 Joe Juneau (CAN), February 12, 1992 vs. NOR
4 Andrei Nikolishin (RUS), February 16, 1994 vs. AUT

**MOST ASSISTS, ONE PERIOD**

3 Ken Laufman (CAN), 2nd period, January 27, 1956 vs. AUT
3 John Mayasich (USA), 3rd period, February 4, 1956 vs. TCH
3 Yrjo Hakala (FIN), 2nd period, February 25, 1960 vs. AUS
3 Bob Attersley (CAN), 1st period, February 28, 1960 vs. URS
3 Anatoli Firsov (URS), 3rd period, February 1, 1964 vs. SUI
3 Eduard Pana (ROM), 3rd period, February 9, 1976 vs. AUT
3 Erich Kuhnhackl (FRG), 3rd period, February 14, 1976 vs. USA
3 Alexander Maltsev (URS), 1st period, February 14, 1980 vs. NED
3 Viktor Zhluktov (URS), 1st period, February 16, 1980 vs. POL

**PENALTY SHOTS**

Traian Cazacu (ROM) stopped by Karel Lang (TCH), 8:16, 3rd period, February 16, 1980
Martin Hinterstocker (FRG) stopped by Pelle Lindbergh (SWE), 3:39, 3rd period, February 16, 1980
Jiri Hrdina (TCH) stopped by Peter Lindmark (SWE), 10:10, 2nd period, February 24, 1988
Germany stopped by Mariusz Kieca (POL), 16:42, 3rd period, February 17, 1992
Petr Nedved (CAN) beat Garth Snow (USA), 12:09, 2nd period, February 17, 1994
Canada stopped by Garth Snow (USA), 12:11, 3rd period, February 17, 1994
Andrei Kovalyov (BLR) stopped by Cristobal Huet (FRA), 8:28, 2nd period, February 11, 2002
Andrejs Maticins (LAT) beat Kostyantyn Simchuk (UKR), 19:11, 1st period, February 14, 2002
Hnat Domenichelli (SUI) stopped by Pal Grotnes (NOR), 0:58, 1st period, February 20, 2010

## Goaltender Records

**MOST GOLD MEDALS**

3 Vladislav Tretiak (URS)
2 Martin Brodeur (CAN)

**MOST MEDALS**

4 (3 gold, silver) Vladislav Tretiak (URS)
3 (silver, 2 bronze) Vladimir Dzurilla (TCH), Jarmo Myllys (FIN)

**MOST OLYMPICS PARTICIPATED IN, GOALIE**

4 Dominik Hasek (CZE)
4 Jim Marthinsen (NOR)
4 Vladislav Tretiak (URS)

**MOST GAMES PLAYED, GOALIE, CAREER**
19 Vladislav Tretiak (URS)
17 Jim Marthinsen (NOR)
16 Dominik Hasek (TCH/CZE)
15 Anton Gale (YUG)
15 Andrei Mezin (BLR)
15 Jarmo Myllys (FIN)
15 Vladimir Nadrchal (TCH)

**MOST MINUTES PLAYED, GOALIE, CAREER**
1,059:41 Vladislav Tretiak (URS)
897:33 Jarmo Myllys (FIN)
882:28 Jim Marthinsen (NOR)
862:18 Anton Gale (YUG)
835:17 Dominik Hasek (TCH/CZE)
820:19 Vladimir Nadrchal (TCH)

**MOST WINS, GOALIE, CAREER**
17 Vladislav Tretiak (URS)
11 Mikhail Shtalenkov (RUS)
10 Viktor Konovalenko (URS)
10 Jarmo Myllys (FIN)

**MOST WINS, GOALIE, ONE OLYMPICS**
7 Murray Dowey, 1948 (CAN)
7 Jack McCartan, 1960 (USA)
7 Sergei Mylnikov, 1988 (URS)
7 Nikolai Puchkov, 1956 (URS)
7 Mikhail Shtalenkov, 1992 (RUS)

**MOST LOSSES, GOALIE, CAREER**
10 Andrei Mezin (BLR)
9 Jim Marthinsen (NOR)
9 Jozef Stogowski (POL)
8 Ulrich Jansen (FRG)
8 Petri Ylonen (FRA)

**MOST LOSSES, GOALIE, ONE OLYMPICS**
7 Per Dahl, 1952 (NOR)
6 Jozef Stogowski, 1932* (POL)
5 Michael Hobelsberger, 1960 (FRG)
5 Jim Marthinsen, 1994 (NOR)
5 Alfred Puls, 1956 (AUT)
5 Robert Reid, 1960 (AUS)
5 Gerald Rigolet, 1964 (SUI)
5 Josef Schramm, 1968 (FRG)
5 Petri Ylonen, 1992 (FRA)
* games consisted of three periods of 15 minutes

**MOST SHUTOUTS, CAREER**
5 Murray Dowey (CAN)+
5 Tom Moone (USA)+
4 Jimmy Foster (GBR)+
3 Hans Banninger (SUI)
3 Frank Farrell (USA)+
3 Viktor Konovalenko (URS)
3 Alphonse "Frenchy" Lacroix (USA)+
3 Jarmo Myllys (FIN)
3 Yevgeni Nabokov (RUS)
3 Antero Niittymaki (FIN)
3 Nikolai Puchkov (URS)
3 Jaromir Sindel (TCH)
3 Kjell Svensson (SWE)
+early era

**MOST SHUTOUTS, ONE OLYMPICS**
5 Murray Dowey, 1948 (CAN)+
5 Tom Moone, 1936* (USA)+
4 Jimmy Foster, 1936* (GBR)+
3 Frank Farrell, 1932* (USA)+
3 Alphonse "Frenchy" Lacroix, 1924 (USA)+
3 Yevgeni Nabokov, 2006 (RUS)
3 Antero Niittymaki, 2006 (FIN)
3 Nikolai Puchkov, 1956 (URS)
* games consisted of three periods of 15 minutes
+early era

**LONGEST SHUTOUT SEQUENCE (IN MINUTES), TEAM**
245:00 USA, January 28-February 3, 1924+
200:15 URS, January 31-February 7, 1964
194:03 FIN, February 12-18, 1994
+early era

**LONGEST SHUTOUT SEQUENCE (IN MINUTES), GOALIE**
225:25 Murray Dowey (CAN), January 30-February 3, 1948+
205:00 Alphonse "Frenchy" Lacroix (USA), January 28-February 3, 1924+
195:30 Murray Dowey (CAN), February 5-8, 1948+
164:19 Don Head (CAN), February 22-25, 1960
+early era

**BEST GOALS AGAINST AVERAGE, CAREER**
(minimum 500 minutes—career minutes played in brackets)
1.64 Mikhail Shtalenkov (730:57), RUS
1.74 Jaromir Sindel (621:02), TCH
1.78 Viktor Konovalenko (640:00), URS
1.87 Jarmo Myllys (897:33), FIN
1.87 Vladislav Tretiak (1,059:41), URS
1.89 Martin Brodeur (538:40), CAN
2.21 Tommy Salo (787:26), SWE
2.25 Vladimir Dzurilla (612:46), TCH

**ALL GOALIE ASSISTS**
2 Tomas Vokoun (CZE)
1 Petr Briza (TCH)
1 Miikka Kiprusoff (FIN)
1 Ryan Miller (USA)
1 Patrick Roy (CAN)
1 Tommy Soderstrom (SWE)

**MOST PENALTY MINUTES, GOALIE, CAREER**
16 Sean Burke (CAN)
12 Bernard Deschamps (FRA)

## Shots On Goal Records

(shots on goal have been officially recorded since 1960)

**MOST SHOTS, TEAM, GAME**
105 URS, February 5, 1964 vs. GER
103 URS, February 1, 1964 vs. SUI
95 CAN, February 20, 1960 vs. JPN

**MOST SHOTS, BOTH TEAMS, GAME**
139 FIN (84) & GER (55), February 8, 1964
124 URS (105) & GER (19), February 5, 1964

**MOST SHOTS, TEAM, PERIOD**
42 URS, 2nd period, February 5, 1964 vs. GER
41 URS, 3rd period, February 1, 1964 vs. SUI
40 URS, 1st period, February 5, 1964 vs. SUI

**MOST SHOTS, BOTH TEAMS, PERIOD**
51 FIN (36) & GER (15), 2nd period, February 8, 1964
47 URS (40) & GER (7), 1st period, February 5, 1964
45 URS (41) & SUI (4), 3rd period, February 1, 1964

**FEWEST SHOTS, TEAM, GAME**
8 AUS, February 22, 1960 vs. FIN
10 FIN, February 10, 1968 vs. TCH
10 POL, February 5, 1972 vs. TCH
10 NOR, February 12, 1980 vs. TCH
10 FRA, February 15, 1994 vs. CAN
10 FRA, February 17, 1994 vs. SWE

**FEWEST SHOTS, BOTH TEAMS, GAME**
34 SWE (22) & SUI (12), February 18, 1988
36 FIN (19) & SWE (17), February 18, 1998
38 FIN (24) & CZE (14), February 12, 1994

**FEWEST SHOTS, TEAM, PERIOD**
0 NOR, 3rd period, February 12, 1992 vs. CAN
0 SWE, 3rd period, February 20, 1992 vs. FIN
0 KAZ, 2nd period, February 16, 1998 vs. FIN

**FEWEST SHOTS, BOTH TEAMS, PERIOD**
6 ITA (3) & KAZ (3), 2nd period, February 7, 1998
7 FIN (5) & RUS (2), 3rd period, February 14, 1994

## Penalty Records

**FEWEST PENALTY MINUTES & PENALTIES, BOTH TEAMS, GAME**
0 USA & FIN, February 7, 1964
0 CAN & POL, February 14, 1980

**FEWEST PENALTY MINUTES & PENALTIES, TEAM, GAME**
0 GER, January 26, 1956 vs. CAN
0 POL, February 2, 1956 vs. AUT
0 TCH, February 4, 1956 vs. USA
0 USA, February 21, 1960 vs. AUS
0 GDR, February 10, 1968 vs. SWE
0 TCH, February 13, 1972 vs. URS
0 CAN February 22, 1988 vs. SWE
0 CAN, February 18, 1992 vs. GER

**MOST PENALTY MINUTES, TEAM, GAME**
70 CAN, February 19, 1984 vs. SWE
58 ITA, February 19, 2006 vs. CZE
43 CZE, February 15, 1998 vs. KAZ
42 SUI, February 18, 2006 vs. CAN

**MOST PENALTY MINUTES, TEAM, PERIOD**
62 CAN, 2nd period, February 19, 1984 vs. SWE
40 ITA, 2nd period, February 19, 2006 vs. CZE
33 FRA, 1st period, February 9, 1998 vs. JPN

**MOST PENALTY MINUTES, BOTH TEAMS, GAME**
84 CZE (43) & KAZ (41), February 15, 1998
78 ITA (58) & CZE (20), February 19, 2006
76 CAN (70) & SWE (6), February 19, 1984
76 SUI (42) & CAN (34), February 18, 2006

**MOST PENALTY MINUTES, BOTH TEAMS, PERIOD**
64 CAN (62) & SWE (2), 2nd period, February 19, 1984
62 CZE (31) & KAZ (31), 3rd period, February 15, 1998
52 GER (27) & SVK (25), 3rd period, February 12, 1998
50 ITA (40) & CZE (10), 2nd period, February 19, 2006

**MOST PENALTIES, TEAM, GAME**
16 ITA, February 19, 2006 vs. CZE
15 NOR, February 17, 1988
14 AUT, February 9, 1968 vs. YUG

**MOST PENALTIES, TEAM, PERIOD**
9 NOR, 3rd period, February 17, 1988 vs. TCH
8 FRG, 3rd period, February 16, 1980 vs. SWE
8 ITA, 3rd period, February 19, 2006

**MOST PENALTIES, BOTH TEAMS, GAME**
30 SUI (17) & CAN (13), February 18, 2006
27 NOR (15) & TCH (12), February 17, 1988
26 ITA (16) & CZE (10), February 19, 2006
24 FIN (12) & TCH (12), February 13, 1984

**MOST PENALTIES, BOTH TEAMS, PERIOD**
14 FIN (7) & NOR (7), 2nd period, February 9, 1984
12 AUT (7) & YUG (5), 2nd period, February 9, 1968
12 SVK (7) & USA (5), 3rd period, February 15, 1994
12 SUI (7) & CAN (), 3rd period, February 18, 2006
12 ITA (8) & CZE (4), 3rd period, February 19, 2006

**MOST PENALTY MINUTES, INDIVIDUAL, GAME**
60 Pat Flatley (CAN), February 19, 1984 vs. SWE (abuse of official)
32 Tony Tuzzolino (ITA), February 19, 2006 vs. CZE (minor, misconduct, gross misconduct)
29 Petr Svoboda (CZE), February 15, 1998 vs. KAZ (2 minors, major, game misconduct)

**MOST PENALTY MINUTES, INDIVIDUAL, PERIOD**
60 Pat Flatley (CAN), 2nd period, February 19, 1984 vs. SWE (abuse of official)
30 Tony Tuzzolino (ITA), 2nd period, February 19, 2006 vs. CZE (misconduct, gross misconduct)
27 Petr Svoboda (CZE), February 15, 1998 vs. KAZ (minor, major, game misconduct)

**MOST PENALTIES, INDIVIDUAL, GAME**

5 Paulin Bordeleau (FRA), February 18, 1988 vs. POL (4 minors, misconduct)
5 Waldemar Klisiak (POL), February 11, 1992 vs. FIN (all minors)
4 Toni Biersack (GER), January 27, 1956 vs. ITA (all minors)
4 Vilgot Larsson (SWE), Janua 27, 1956 vs. URS (all minors)
4 John Nicholas (AUS), February 25, 1960 vs. FIN (all minors)
4 Michel Caux (FRA), February 13, 1968 vs. YUG (all minors)
4 Dick Lamby (USA), February 6, 1976 vs. URS (all minors)
4 Andreas Beutler (SUI), February 10, 1992 vs. CAN (all minors)
4 Dave Archibald (CAN), February 10, 1992 vs. SUI (all minors)
4 Derek Mayer (CAN), February 21, 1994 vs. SWE (all minors)
4 Gerhard Puschnik (AUT), February 12, 1998 vs. JPN (3 minors, misconduct)
4 Petr Svoboda (CZE), February 15, 1998 vs. KAZ (2 minors, major, misconduct)
4 Richard Zednik (SVK), February 15, 2006 vs. RUS (4 minors)

**MOST PENALTIES, INDIVIDUAL, PERIOD**

4 Michel Caux (FRA), 3rd period, February 13, 1968 vs. YUG (2 minors, misconduct)
3 Mieczyslaw Chmura (POL), 3rd period, January 28, 1956 vs. USA (all minors)
3 Howie Lee (CAN), 2nd period, January 28, 1956 vs. ITA (all minors)
3 Marian Feter (POL), 3rd period, February 5, 1972 vs. CZE (2 minors, major)
3 Dick Lamby (USA), 1st period, February 6, 1976 vs. URS (all minors)
3 Milan Kajkl (TCH), 1st period, February 12, 1976 vs. GER (all minors)
3 Chris Chelios (USA), 2nd period, February 9, 1984 vs. TCH (all minors)
3 Drago Mlinarec (YUG), 3rd period, February 13, 1984 vs. ITA (all minors)
3 Petteri Lehto (FIN), 3rd period, February 17, 1984 vs. FRG (all minors)
3 Petter Thoresen (NOR), 3rd period, February 17, 1988 vs. TCH (2 minors, major)
3 Paulin Bordeleau (FRA), 3rd period, February 18, 1988 vs. POL (2 minors, misconduct)
3 Reijo Mikolainen (FIN), 3rd period, February 26, 1988 vs. TCH (all minors)
3 Dave Archibald (CAN), 2nd period, February 10, 1992 vs. SUI (all minors)
3 Waldemar Klisiak (POL), 3rd period, February 11, 1992 vs. FIN (all minors)
3 Bob Manno (ITA), 3rd period, February 18, 1992 vs. NOR (2 minors, misconduct)
3 Oleg Antonenko (BLR), 3rd period, February 13, 2002 vs. SUI (all minors)
3 Niklas Kronwall (SWE), 2nd period, February 24, 2006 vs. CZE (all minors)

## Speed Records

**FASTEST GOAL FROM START OF GAME**

8 seconds Miroslav Vlach (TCH), February 28, 1960 vs. USA
8 seconds Albin Felc (YUG), February 7, 1968 vs. JPN
10 seconds Stefan Chowaniec (POL), February 6, 1976 vs. GER

**FASTEST TWO GOALS FROM START OF GAME**

42 seconds Stephen Foyn (NOR, 0:12) & Kurt Harand (AUT, 0:42), February 15, 1984
54 seconds Frank Reichart (USA, 0:40) & Pio Parolini (SUI, 0:54), February 8, 1964

**FASTEST THREE GOALS FROM START OF GAME**

1:45 Stefan Chowaniec (POL, 0:10), Erich Kuhnhackl (GER, 1:00), Martin Hinterstocker (GER, 1:45), February 6, 1976

**FASTEST GOAL FROM START OF PERIOD**

6 seconds Jorma Peltonen (FIN), 2nd period, January 30, 1964 vs. SUI
6 seconds Vladimir Petrov (URS), 2nd period, February 13, 1980 vs. JPN
9 seconds Ray Cadieux (CAN), 2nd period, February 6, 1968 vs. GER

**FASTEST TWO GOALS, INDIVIDUAL**

8 seconds Carl-Goran Oberg (SWE), 1st period, February 21, 1960 vs. JPN (7:15 & 7:23)
9 seconds Helmuts Balderis (URS), 1st period, February 16, 1980 vs. POL (10:27 & 10:36)
15 seconds Erich Kuhnhackl (FRG), 1st period, February 6, 1972 vs. SUI (4:25 & 4:40)

**FASTEST TWO GOALS, TEAM**

5 seconds Vsevolod Bobrov (URS, 15:40) & Valentin Kuzin (URS, 15:45), 3rd period, February 3, 1956 vs. USA
10 seconds Gerry Theberge (CAN, 14:00) & George Scholes (CAN, 14:10), 2nd period, January 27, 1956 vs. AUT
10 seconds Valeri Kharlamov (URS, 13:31) & Vladimir Vikulov (URS, 13:41), 1st period, February 10, 1972 vs. POL

**FASTEST TWO GOALS, BOTH TEAMS**

7 seconds Dave Cunningham (AUS, 9:28) & Isao Ono (JPN, 9:35), 3rd period, February 24, 1960
7 seconds Heinz Schupp (AUT, 18:13) & Gyula Szabo (ROM, 18:20), 1st period, February 7, 1968

**FASTEST THREE GOALS, INDIVIDUAL**

4:28 Vladimir Golikov, URS (14:59, 19:00, 19:27, 1st period), February 13, 1980 vs. JPN
6:45 Vaclav Nedomansky, TCH (6:18, 12:45, 13:03, 3rd period), February 5, 1972 vs. POL
7:42 Paul Knox, CAN (12:17, 18:29, 19:59, 1st period), January 27, 1956 vs. AUT

**FASTEST THREE GOALS, TEAM**

36 seconds SWE, February 21, 1960 vs. JPN, 1st period (Carl-Goran Oberg 7:15 & 7:23, Anders Andersson 7:51)
44 seconds YUG, February 16, 1968 vs. ROM, 1st period (Janez Mlakar 2:05, Rudi Hiti 2:32, Viktor Tisler 2:49)
44 seconds BUL, February 9, 1976 vs. YUG, 3rd period (Miltcho Nenov 13:08, Ilia Batcharov 13:31, Nenov 13:52)
44 seconds FRG, February 14, 1980 vs. NOR, 1st period (Udo Kiessling 8:49, Hans Zach 9:08, Horst Kretschmer 9:33)

**FASTEST THREE GOALS, BOTH TEAMS**

31 seconds February 10, 1976, 3rd period (Matti Murto FIN 14:16, Bob Dobek USA 14:35, Matti Hagman FIN 14:47)
35 seconds February 17, 1984, 2nd period (David A. Jensen USA 18:38, Krystian Sikorski POL 18:57, Phil Verchota USA 19:13)

**FASTEST FOUR GOALS, TEAM**

1:18 CAN, January 27, 1956 vs. AUT, 2nd period (Jack MacKenzie 12:52, Ken Laufman 13:13, Gerry Theberge 14:00, George Scholes 14:10)

**FASTEST FIVE GOALS, TEAM**

1:30 CAN, January 27, 1956 vs. AUT, 2nd period (Jack MacKenzie 12:52, Ken Laufman 13:13, Gerry Theberge 14:00, George Scholes 14:10, Bob White 15:22)

**FASTEST SIX GOALS, BOTH TEAMS**

3:04 1st period, February 20, 1988 (Antoine Richer (FRA 16:16, Ken Yaremchuk CAN 16:57, Merlin Malinowski CAN 17:24, Philippe Bozon FRA 17:57, Marc Habscheid CAN 18:58, Steve Tambellini CAN 19:20)

*Vaclav Nedomansky, flanked by brothers Jiri (left) and Jaroslav Holik (right) celebrates one of Czechoslovakia's two wins over the Soviet Union at the 1969 World Championship in Stockholm, Sweden. Photo: IIHF.*

# World Championship (Men)

## All-Time Team Records

**LONGEST WINNING STREAK (NOT INCLUDING OLYMPICS COUNTED AS WM)**

27 games RUS, May 13, 2007-May 22, 2010
24 games CAN, February 6, 1934-February 16, 1938

**LONGEST WINNING STREAK (INCLUDING OLYMPICS COUNTED AS WM)**

21 games URS, April 12, 1974-February 14, 1976
20 games CAN, March 14, 1950-February 23, 1952

**LONGEST UNDEFEATED STREAK (NOT INCLUDING OLYMPICS COUNTED AS WM)**

47 games URS, May 8, 1978-April 27, 1985
37 games CAN, February 6, 1934-February 15, 1949
35 games URS, May 3, 1985-April 20, 1990

**LONGEST UNDEFEATED STREAK (INCLUDING OLYMPICS COUNTED AS WM)**

38 games URS, March 10, 1963-February 13, 1968
28 games CAN, April 24, 1920-February 24, 1933

**LONGEST LOSING STREAK (NOT INCLUDING OLYMPICS COUNTED AS WM)**

20 games JPN, February 27, 1957-May 2, 2001

**LONGEST LOSING STREAK (INCLUDING OLYMPICS COUNTED AS WM)**

14 games NOR, March 16, 1951-March 3, 1954
12 games BEL, February 6, 1934-February 6, 1939

**LONGEST WINLESS STREAK (NOT INCLUDING OLYMPICS COUNTED AS WM)**

44 games JPN, February 1, 1930-present

**LONGEST WINLESS STREAK (INCLUDING OLYMPICS COUNTED AS WM)**

20 games SUI, March 9, 1962-April 10, 1972
18 games AUT, February 15, 1949-March 5, 1957

**MOST GOALS, TEAM, GAME**

**(EARLY ERA, 1930-1976)**
47 CAN, February 12, 1949 vs. DEN
33 CAN, March 15, 1950 vs. BEL
25 AUT, February 13, 1949 vs. DEN
25 TCH, March 4, 1957 vs. JPN
24 TCH, February 3, 1939 vs. YUG
24 SWE, February 16, 1947 vs. BEL
24 TCH, February 21, 1947 vs. BEL
24 SUI, March 13, 1950 vs. BEL
24 CAN, March 3, 1958 vs. FIN
**(OPEN ERA, 1977-2010)**
18 URS, April 25, 1977 vs. ROM
15 TCH, April 18, 1989 vs. POL
14 FIN, May 3, 1977 vs. ROM
13 TCH, April 24, 1977 vs. ROM
13 URS, April 24, 1981 vs. SWE
13 URS, April 17, 1987 vs. SUI

**MOST GOALS, BOTH TEAMS, GAME (BOTH TEAMS SCORING)**

**(EARLY ERA, 1930-1976)**
27 SUI 24-BEL 3, March 13, 1950
26 AUT 25-DEN 1, February 14, 1949
26 TCH 25-JPN 1, March 4, 1957
25 SWE 24-BEL 1, February 16, 1947
24 TCH 23-ROM 1, February 15, 1947
**(OPEN ERA, 1977-2010)**
19 URS 18-ROM 1, April 25, 1977
18 FRG 12-NED 6, April 25, 1981
18 URS 13-SUI 5, April 17, 1987
17 URS 11-FIN 6, April 22, 1977
15 FIN 14-ROM 1, May 3, 1977
15 RUS 12-GBR 3, April 26, 1994

**MOST GOALS, TEAM, PERIOD**

**(EARLY ERA, 1930-1976)**
18 CAN, 3rd period, February 12, 1949 vs. DEN
16 CAN, 2nd period, February 12, 1949 vs. DEN
14 CAN, 1st period, March 15, 1950 vs. BEL
13 CAN, 1st period, February 12, 1949 vs. DEN
12 TCH, 3rd period, February 15, 1947 vs. ROM
12 SUI, 3rd period, March 13, 1950 vs. BEL
**(OPEN ERA, 1977-2010)**
8 URS, 2nd period, April 25, 1977
8 URS, 3rd period, May 1, 1978 vs. GDR
8 FIN, 2nd period, April 15, 1981 vs. NED
8 TCH, 2nd period, April 18, 1989 vs. POL

**MOST GOALS, BOTH TEAMS, PERIOD (BOTH TEAMS SCORING)**

**(EARLY ERA, 1930-1976)**
13 SUI 12-BEL 1, 3rd period, March 13, 1950
12 AUT 11-DEN 1, 3rd period, February 14, 1949
11 AUT 6-BEL 5, 3rd period, February 17, 1947
11 SUI 10-BEL 1, 2nd period, February 13, 1949
11 URS 10-USA 1, 3rd period, April 12, 1975
**(OPEN ERA, 1977-2010)**
10 FRG 7-NED 3, 3rd period, April 25, 1981
9 TCH 7-FIN 2, 1st period, April 21, 1977
9 FIN 8-NED 1, 2nd period, April 15, 1981

**SCORELESS GAMES**

February 6, 1931 Canada-Sweden
February 8, 1931 Czechoslovakia-Poland
February 6, 1935 Hungary-Italy (30:00 OT)
February 27, 1937 Hungary-Czechoslovakia
February 15, 1938 Sweden-Czechoslovakia (30:00 OT)
February 6, 1939 Germany-Italy
February 12, 1939 Switzerland-Czechoslovakia (30:00 OT)
March 25, 1967 United States-East Germany
May 11, 1978 East Germany-West Germany
April 29, 1982 Soviet Union-Czechoslovakia
April 29, 1987 Canada-Soviet Union
April 29, 1992 Sweden-Italy
May 17, 1998 Sweden-Finland
May 3, 2004 Slovakia-Sweden
May 9, 2005 Finland-Latvia
April 29, 2011 Switzerland 1-France 0 (GWS)

## Power-Play and Short-Handed Goals Records

**MOST POWER-PLAY GOALS, TEAM, GAME**

9 CAN, May 11, 2006 vs. LAT

**MOST POWER-PLAY GOALS, TEAM, PERIOD**

4 CAN, 1st period, May 11, 2006 vs. LAT
4 CAN, 3rd period, May 11, 2006 vs. LAT

**MOST POWER-PLAY GOALS, BOTH TEAMS, GAME**

7 ITA 4-FRA 3, April 22, 1996
7 SVK 4-ITA 3, May 3, 1999
7 FIN 4-SLO 3, May 5, 2006
7 NOR 4-DEN 3, May 9, 2006
7 CZE 4-RUS 3, May 4, 2008
7 CAN 5-SVK 2, April 28, 2009

**MOST SHORT-HANDED GOALS, TEAM, GAME**

3 USA, April 26, 1989 vs. POL
3 FIN, April 23, 1990 vs. FRG

**MOST SHORT-HANDED GOALS, TEAM, PERIOD**

3 FIN, 3rd period, April 23, 1990 vs. FRG

**MOST SHORT-HANDED GOALS, BOTH TEAMS, GAME**

4 FIN 3-FRG 1, April 23, 1990

## All-Time Individual Records

**MOST WORLD CHAMPIONSHIPS (NOT INCLUDING OLYMPICS COUNTED AS WM)**

15 Petteri Nummelin (FIN)
14 Mathias Seger (SUI)
13 Dieter Hegen (FRG/GER), Tommy Jakobsen (NOR), Dieter Kalt (AUT), Udo Kiessling (FRG), Aleksandrs Nizivijs (LAT), Ville Peltonen (FIN), Roland Ramoser (ITA), Gerhard Unterluggauer (AUT)
12 Mario Chittaroni (ITA), Jiri Holik (TCH), Jorgen Jonsson (SWE), Alexander Maltsev (URS), Ivo Ruthemann (SUI), Mark Streit (SUI), Martin Ulrich (AUT), David Vyborny (CZE)
11 Vyacheslav Fetisov (URS), Raimo Helminen (FIN), Ivan Hlinka (TCH), Sandy Jeannin (SUI), Valeri Kharlamov (URS), Vladimir Lutchenko (URS), Oldrich Machac (TCH), Sergei Makarov (URS), Boris Mikhailov (URS), Lasse Oksanen (FIN), Vladimir Petrov (URS), Martin Pluss (SUI), Aleksandrs Semjonovs (LAT), Leonids Tambijevs (LAT), Valeri Vasilyev (URS)

**MOST WORLD CHAMPIONSHIPS (INCLUDING OLYMPICS COUNTED AS WM)**

15 Petteri Nummelin (FIN)
14 Jiri Holik (TCH), Sven "Tumba" Johansson (SWE), Mathias Seger (SUI)
13 Dieter Hegen (FRG/GER), Tommy Jakobsen (NOR), Dieter Kalt (AUT), Udo Kiessling (FRG), Aleksandrs Nizivijs (LAT), Lasse Oksanen (FIN), Ville Peltonen (FIN), Roland Ramoser (ITA), Ronald Pettersson (SWE), Vladislav Tretiak (URS), Gerhard Unterluggauer (AUT)
12 Josef Cerny (TCH), Mario Chittaroni (ITA), Jorgen Jonsson (SWE), Oldrich Machac (TCH), Alexander Maltsev (URS), Alexander Ragulin (URS), Roland Stoltz (SWE), Martin Ulrich (AUT), David Vyborny (CZE)

**MOST WORLD CHAMPIONSHIPS (ALL POOLS/LEVELS)**

20 Viktor Szelig (HUN)
18 Tommy Jakobsen (NOR)
18 Krisztian Palkovics (HUN)
17 Balasz Kangyal (HUN)
17 Martin Ulrich (AUT)
16 Dieter Kalt (AUT)

**MOST GOLD MEDALS**

10 Vladislav Tretiak (URS)
9 Alexander Maltsev (URS), Vladimir Petrov (URS)
8 Valeri Kharlamov (URS), Vladimir Lutchenko (URS), Boris Mikhailov (URS), Valeri Vasilyev (URS), Sergei Makarov (URS), Alexander Ragulin (URS)
7 Vyacheslav Fetisov (URS), Sergei Kapustin (URS), Andrei Khomutov (URS), Vyacheslav Starshinov (URS), Alexander Yakushev (URS)

**MOST MEDALS**

| | |
|---|---|
| 13 (10 gold, 2 silver, bronze) | Vladislav Tretiak (URS) |
| 12 (9 gold, 2 silver, 1 bronze) | Alexander Maltsev (URS) |
| 11 (9 gold, 1 silver, 1 bronze) | Vladimir Petrov (URS) |
| 11 (8 gold, 2 silver, 1 bronze) | Valeri Kharlamov (URS), Vladimir Lutchenko (URS), Boris Mikhailov (URS), Valeri Vasilyev (URS) |
| 11 (8 gold, 1 silver, 2 bronze) | Sergei Makarov (URS) |
| 11 (7 gold, 1 silver, 3 bronze) | Vyacheslav Fetisov (URS) |
| 11 (3 gold, 5 silver, 3 bronze) | Ivan Hlinka (TCH), Jiri Holik (TCH) |
| 10 (8 gold, 1 silver, 1 bronze) | Alexander Ragulin (URS) |
| 10 (7 gold, 2 silver, 1 bronze) | Alexander Yakushev (URS) |
| 10 (6 gold, 2 silver, 2 bronze) | Vasili Pervukhin (URS) |
| 10 (3 gold, 5 silver, 2 bronze) | Vladimir Martinec (TCH) |
| 10 (3 gold, 4 silver, 3 bronze) | Oldrich Machac (TCH) |
| 9 (7 gold, 1 silver, 1 bronze) | Sergei Kapustin (URS), Andrei Khomutov (URS) |
| 9 (6 gold, 2 silver, 1 bronze) | Gennadi Tsygankov (URS) |
| 9 (3 gold, 5 silver, 1 bronze) | Jiri Bubla (TCH), Jiri Holecek (TCH) |
| 9 (3 gold, 3 silver, 3 bronze) | Frantisek Pospisil (TCH) |
| 9 (2 gold, 6 silver, 1 bronze) | Miroslav Dvorak (TCH) |
| 9 (2 gold, 3 silver, 4 bronze) | Jorgen Jonsson (SWE) |
| 8 (7 gold, 1 bronze) | Vyacheslav Starshinov (URS) |
| 8 (6 gold, 2 bronze) | Vladimir Myshkin (URS) |
| 8 (5 gold, 2 silver, 1 bronze) | Vladimir Shadrin (URS) |

8 (5 gold, 1 silver, 2 bronze) Vyacheslav Bykov (URS), Alexei Kasatonov (URS), David Vyborny (CZE)
8 (3 gold, 2 silver, 3 bronze) Vladimir Dzurilla (TCH)
8 (2 gold, 3 silver, 3 bronze) Mikael Nylander (SWE)
8 (1 gold, 4 silver, 3 bronze) Vaclav Nedomansky (TCH), Ville Peltonen (FIN)
8 (4 silver, 4 bronze) Josef Cerny (TCH)

### MOST GAMES PLAYED
119 Udo Kiessling (FRG)
110 Alexander Maltsev (URS)
109 Jiri Holik (TCH)
107 Oldrich Machac (TCH), Ville Peltonen (FIN)
106 Vyacheslav Fetisov (URS), Dieter Hegen (FRG/GER)
105 Valeri Kharlamov (URS), Boris Mikhailov (URS)
104 Jorgen Jonsson (SWE), Petteri Nummelin (FIN), David Vyborny (CZE)
103 Vladimir Lutchenko (URS)
102 Vladimir Petrov (URS)
101 Sergei Makarov (URS), Lasse Oksanen (FIN), Valeri Vasiliev (URS)

### MOST POINTS, CAREER
164 Boris Mikhailov (URS)
156 Valeri Kharlamov (URS)
153 Alexander Maltsev (URS)
152 Vladimir Petrov (URS)
123 Sergei Makarov (URS)
100 Sven "Tumba" Johansson (SWE)
107 Vladimir Martinec (TCH)
95 Vyacheslav Fetisov (URS)
95 Jiri Holik (TCH)

### MOST POINTS, ONE WM
34 Vladimir Petrov (URS, 1973)
29 Boris Mikhailov (URS, 1973)
26 Vladimir Zabrodsky (TCH, 1947)
23 Valeri Kharlamov (URS, 1973), Bill Warwick (CAN, 1955)
22 Anatoli Firsov (URS, 1967), Alexander Maltsev (URS, 1972)
21 Alexander Maltsev (URS, 1970), Vladimir Petrov (URS, 1977), Uli Poltera (SUI, 1950)
20 Dany Heatley (CAN, 2008), Lars Ljungman (SWE, 1947), Vladimir Martinec (TCH, 1976)

### MOST GOALS, CAREER
98 Boris Mikhailov (URS)
77 Alexander Maltsev (URS)
74 Valeri Kharlamov (URS), Vladimir Petrov (URS)
65 Vaclav Nedomansky (TCH)
60 Sven "Tumba" Johansson (SWE), Alexander Yakushev (URS)
55 Sergei Kapustin (URS), Bibi Torriani (SUI)
55 Sergei Makarov (URS)
52 Jiri Holik (TCH)
51 Pic Cattini (SUI), Vyacheslav Starshinov (URS)
50 Vladimir Martinec (TCH)

### MOST GOALS, ONE WM
26 Vladimir Zabrodsky (TCH, 1947)
18 Vladimir Petrov (URS, 1973)
17 Uli Poltera (SUI, 1950)
16 Vlastimil Bubnik (TCH, 1955), Boris Mikhailov (URS, 1973), Bill Warwick (CAN, 1955)
15 Alexander Maltsev (URS, 1970)
14 Fritz Demmer (AUT, 1947), Jaroslav Drobny (TCH, 1947), "Bibi" Torriani (SUI, 1934)
13 Slavomir Barton (TCH, 1955), Oskar Nowak (AUT, 1947), Vladimir Zabrodsky (TCH, 1955)
12 Vsevelod Bobrov (URS, 1957), Pic Cattini (SUI, 1939), Dany Heatley (CAN, 2008), Oldrich Kucera (TCH, 1935), Albert Lemay (CAN 1935), Jack MacKenzie (CAN, 1958), Josef Malecek (TCH, 1939), Boris Mikhailov (URS, 1977), Nils Nilsson (SWE, 1962), Ralph Redding (CAN, 1937), "Bibi" Torriani (SUI, 1939)

### MOST ASSISTS, CAREER
82 Valeri Kharlamov (URS)
78 Vladimir Petrov (URS)
76 Alexander Maltsev (URS)
68 Sergei Makarov (URS)
66 Boris Mikhailov (URS)
59 Vyacheslav Fetisov (URS)
57 Vladimir Martinec (TCH)
49 Petteri Nummelin (FIN)
48 Raimo Helminen (FIN)
47 Ville Peltonen (FIN)
45 Mikael Nylander (SWE)

### MOST ASSISTS, ONE WM
16 Vladimir Petrov (URS, 1973)
14 Valeri Kharlamov (URS, 1973), Sergei Makarov (URS, 1986), Vladimir Petrov (URS, 1977)
13 Boris Mikhailov (URS, 1973)
12 Mats Ahlberg (SWE, 1975), Valeri Kharlamov (URS, 1971), Saku Koivu (FIN, 1999), Petteri Nummelin (FIN, 2001), Vladimir Petrov (URS, 1975), Henrik Zetterberg (SWE, 2012)

### MOST PENALTY MINUTES, CAREER
150 Udo Kiessling (FRG)
146 Mario Chittaroni (ITA)
141 Tommy Jakobsen (NOR)
138 Sergiy Klimentyev (UKR)
127 Jarkko Ruutu (FIN)
126 Erich Kuhnhackl (FRG)
124 Jan Benda (GER)
120 Horst Kretschmer (FRG)

### MOST PENALTY MINUTES, ONE WM
60 Mario Chittaroni (ITA, 2001)
52 Ilya Kovalchuk (RUS, 2008)
49 Cory Cross (CAN, 1997)
47 Todd Bertuzzi (CAN, 2000)
46 Sergiy Klimentyev (UKR, 2007)

### MOST POINTS, GAME
10 Boris Mikhailov, URS, April 11, 1973 vs. POL (7 goals, 3 assists)
10 Vladimir Petrov, URS, April 11, 1973 vs. POL (5 goals, 5 assists)
9 Alexander Martinyuk, URS, April 8, 1973 vs. FRG (8 goals, 1 assist)
7 John Mayasich, USA, February 28, 1958 vs. POL (6 goals, 1 assist)
7 Jackie McLeod, CAN, March 17, 1962 vs. GBR (4 goals, 3 assists)
7 Vaclav Nedomansky, TCH, April 7, 1972 vs. SUI (4 goals, 3 assists)

### MOST POINTS, PERIOD
5 John Mayasich, USA, 3rd period, February 28, 1958 vs. POL (4 goals, 1 assist)
5 Alexander Martinyuk, URS, 1st period, April 8, 1973 vs. FRG (4 goals, 1 assist)
5 Vladimir Petrov, URS, 3rd period, April 11, 1973 vs. POL (3 goals, 2 assists)

### MOST GOALS, GAME
**(EARLY ERA, 1930-1976)**
12 Lars Ljungman, SWE, February 16, 1947 vs. BEL
12 Vladimir Zabrodsky, TCH, February 21, 1947 vs. BEL
9 Rudolf Wurmbrand, AUT, February 19, 1948 vs. DEN
8 Vladimir Zabrodsky, TCH, February 15, 1947 vs. ROM
8 Jim Russell, CAN, February 12, 1949 vs. DEN
8 Uli Poltera, SUI, March 13, 1950 vs. BEL
8 Vlastimil Bubnik, TCH, March 6, 1955 vs. FIN
8 Alexander Martinyuk, URS, April 8, 1973 vs. FRG

**(OPEN ERA, 1977-2010)**
4 Alexander Yakushev (URS), April 24, 1977 vs. CAN
4 Bohuslav Ebermann (TCH), April 23, 1979 vs. CAN
4 Markus Kuhl (FRG), April 26, 1979 vs. USA
4 Jiri Lala (TCH), April 12, 1981 vs. USA
4 Sergei Makarov (URS), April 17, 1985 vs. USA
4 Thomas Steen (SWE), April 19, 1986 vs. POL
4 Andrew McBain (CAN), April 16, 1989 vs. POL
4 Oldrich Valek (TCH), April 18, 1989 vs. POL
4 Magnus Svensson (SWE), May 8, 1994 vs. USA

### MOST GOALS, PERIOD
**(EARLY ERA, 1930-1976)**
5 Pic Cattini, SUI, 3rd period, February 4, 1939* vs. YUG
5 Vladimir Zabrodsky, TCH, 3rd period, February 21, 1947 vs. BEL

*period 15 mins.

**(OPEN ERA, 1977-2010)**
3 Thomas Steen (SWE), 3rd period, April 19, 1986 vs. POL
3 Alexander Suglobov (RUS), 2nd period, April 27, 2003 vs. DEN
3 Karlis Skrastins (LAT), 2nd period, April 29, 2003 vs. BLR
3 Shane Doan (CAN), 2nd period, May 4, 2007 vs. BLR

### MOST ASSISTS, GAME
6 Jiri Holik, TCH, March 31, 1973 vs. POL
5 Jaroslav Holik, TCH, March 18, 1969 vs. FIN
5 Vladimir Petrov, URS, April 11, 1973
5 Mats Ahlberg, SWE, Apr. 13, 1975 vs. POL
5 John McLean, CAN, April 16, 1989 vs. POL
5 Mats Sundin, SWE, May 8, 1994 vs. USA
5 Linus Omark, SWE, April 25, 2009 vs. AUT

### MOST ASSISTS, PERIOD
4 Mats Sundin, SWE, 3rd period, May 8, 1994 vs. USA

### PENALTY SHOTS
Ken Nicholson (GBR) beat Unto Wiitala (FIN), March 17, 1951
Kazimierz Malysiak (POL) stopped by Jean Ayer (SUI), March 7, 1959
Raimo Kilpio (FIN) beat Harry Lindner (FRG), March 9, 1961
Ulf Nilsson (SWE) beat Walery Kosyl (POL), April 6, 1974
Karl-Heinz Egger (FRG) stopped by Jiri Crha (TCH), April 3, 1973
Dave Christian (USA) beat Ted Lenssen (NED), April 17, 1981
Miroslav Frycer (TCH) beat Vladimir Myshkin (URS), April 26, 1981
Sergei Makarov (URS) stopped by Jiri Kralik (TCH), April 18, 1982
Sergei Shepelev (URS) stopped by Karl Friesen (FRG), April 22, 1982
United States stopped by Dominik Hasek (TCH), April 16, 1990
Switzerland stopped by Klaus Merk (FRG), April 28, 1991
Canada stopped by Tommy Soderstrom (SWE), April 20, 1993
Czech Republic stopped by Robert Schistad (NOR), April 21, 1993
United States stopped by Robert Schistad (NOR), April 24, 1993
Czech Republic stopped by Jarmo Myllys (FIN), April 23, 1995
France stopped by Corey Hirsch (CAN), April 25, 1995
Finland stopped by Claus Dalpiaz (AUT), April 29, 1995
Russia stopped by Parris Duffus (USA), April 25, 1996
Germany stopped by Andrei Mezin (BLR), May 1, 1998
Tim Connolly (USA) beat Kostyantyn Simchuk (UKR), April 28, 2001
J-J Aeschlimann (SUI) beat Jiro Nihei (JPN), April 29, 2002
J-J Aeschlimann (SUI) beat Sergejs Naumovs (LAT), May 5, 2002
Mark Szucs (AUT) beat Kostyantyn Simchuk (UKR), May 6, 2002
Vesa Viitakoski (FIN) beat Ryan Miller (USA), May 7, 2002
J-J Aeschlimann (SUI) beat Sergejs Naumovs (LAT), May 5, 2002
Austria stopped by Kostyantyn Simchuk (UKR), May 6, 2002
Finland stopped by Ryan Miller (USA), 2nd period, May 7, 2002
Finland stopped by Ryan Miller (USA), 3rd period, May 7, 2002
Klaus Kathan (GER) beat Kostyantyn Simchuk (UKR), April 29, 2003
Yoshikazu Kabayama (JPN) beat Kostyantyn Simchuk (UKR), April 30, 2003
Martin Pluss (SUI) stopped by Jason Muzzatti (ITA), May 6, 2006
Yan Stastny (USA) stopped by Antero Niitymaki (FIN), May 12, 2006
Martin Cibak (SVK) stopped by Igor Karpenko (UKR), May 16, 2006
Jakub Klepis (CZE) stopped by Peter Hirsch (DEN), May 2, 2008
Lee Stempniak (USA) stopped by Edgars Masalskis (LAT), May 2, 2008
Martins Cipulis (LAT) stopped by Robert Kristan (SLO), May 6, 2008
Aleksandrs Nizivijs (LAT) beat Robert Kristan (SLO), May 6, 2008
Patrick Bartschi (SUI) stopped by Patrick Galbraith (DEN), May 11, 2008
Kim Staal (DEN) beat Martin Gerber (SUI), May 11, 2008
Kim Staal (DEN) stopped by Vitali Koval (BLR), May 12, 2008
Radim Vrbata (CZE) beat Henrik Lundqvist (SWE), May 14, 2008
Jakub Klepis (CZE) stopped by Fabrice Lhenry (FRA), May 9, 2010
Aleksandrs Nizivijs (LAT) stopped by Adam Russo (ITA), May 12, 2010
Tomas Tatar (SVK) beat Vitali Yeremeyev (KAZ), May 13, 2010
Pavel Datsyuk (RUS) beat Frederik Andersen (DEN), May 16, 2010

Chris Stewart (CAN) stopped by Andrei Mezin (BLR), April 29, 2011
Jeff Skinner (CAN) beat Fabrice Lhenry (FRA), May 1, 2011
Patrick Reimer (GER) stopped by Jaroslav Halak (SVK), May 1, 2011
Patrik Elias (CZE) stopped by Patrick Galbraith (DEN), May 2, 2011
Matthias Bieber (SUI) stopped by James Reimer (CAN), May 3, 2011
Andrei Stas (BLR) stopped by Cristobal Huet (FRA), May 3, 2011
Anders Fredriksen (NOR) stopped by Jurgen Penker (AUT), May 4, 2011
Tomas Plekanec (CZE) beat Konstantin Barulin (RUS), May 8, 2011
Martins Cipulis (LAT) stopped by Fabian Weinhandl (AUT), May 8, 2011
Ken Andre Olimb (NOR) stopped by Cristobal Huet (FRA), May 9, 2011
Ken Andre Olimb (NOR) beat Petri Vehanen (FIN), May 12, 2011
Loui Eriksson (SWE) stopped by Ondrej Pavelec (CZE), May 13, 2011
Mikhail Grabovski (BLR) stopped by Tobias Stephan (SUI), May 6, 2012
Nikolai Kulyomin (RUS) stopped by Simon Nielsen (DEN), May 10, 2012
Yevgeni Kovyrshin (BLR) stopped by Jan Laco (SVK), May 12, 2012
David Krejci (CZE) stopped by Dennis Endras (GER), May 15, 2012

## Goaltender Records

### MOST GOLD MEDALS
10 Vladislav Tretiak (URS)
6 Vladimir Myshkin (URS), Viktor Konovalenko (URS)

### MOST MEDALS (3 GOLD OR 6 TOTAL MEDALS)
13 (10 gold, 2 silver, bronze) Vladislav Tretiak (URS)
9 (3 gold, 5 silver, bronze) Jiri Holecek (TCH)
8 (6 gold, 2 bronze) Vladimir Myshkin (URS)
8 (3 gold, 2 silver, 3 bronze) Vladimir Dzurilla (TCH)
7 (6 gold, bronze) Viktor Konovalenko (URS)
7 (gold, 2 silver, 4 bronze) Tommy Salo (SWE)
6 (3 gold, silver, 2 bronze) Milan Hnilicka (CZE)
6 (3 silver, 3 bronze) Leif Holmqvist (SWE)
4 (4 gold) Viktor Zinger (URS)
4 (3 gold, bronze) Sergei Mylnikov (URS)

### MOST TOURNAMENTS, GOALIE
13 Vladislav Tretiak (URS, 1970-83)
11 Andrei Mezin (BLR, 1998-2011)
10 Jiri Holecek (TCH, 1966-1978)
10 Arturs Irbe (URS/LAT, 1989-2005)
9 Jan Lasak (SVK, 2000-2009)
9 Jorma Valtonen (FIN, 1970-79)

### MOST GAMES PLAYED, GOALIE, CAREER
96 Vladislav Tretiak (URS)
66 Jiri Holecek (TCH)
55 Andrei Mezin (BLR)
54 Tommy Salo (SWE)
53 Jorma Valtonen (FIN)
51 Arturs Irbe (URS/LAT)
48 Vladimir Dzurilla (TCH)

### MOST MINUTES PLAYED, GOALIE, CAREER
5,344:37 Vladislav Tretiak (URS)
3,686:38 Jiri Holecek (TCH)
3,166:51 Tommy Salo (SWE)
3,139:50 Andrei Mezin (BLR)
3,120:41 Jorma Valtonen (FIN)
2,931:04 Arturs Irbe (URS/LAT)
2,737:20 Milan Hnilicka (CZE)

### MOST WINS, GOALIE, CAREER
76 Vladislav Tretiak (URS)
44 Jiri Holecek (TCH)
35 Vladimir Dzurilla (TCH)
34 Viktor Konovalenko (URS)
34 Tommy Salo (SWE)

### MOST LOSSES, GOALIE, CAREER
27 Andrei Mezin (BLR)
25 Juhani Lahtinen (FIN)
25 Jorma Valtonen (FIN)
24 Toni Kehle (FRG)
20 Karl Friesen (FRG)
20 Martin Gerber (SUI)
20 Istvan Hircsak (HUN)
20 Urpo Ylonen (FIN)

### MOST SHUTOUTS, CAREER
12 Jimmy Foster (GBR)*
12 Jiri Holecek (TCH)
12 Bohumil Modry (TCH)**
9 Arnold Hirtz (SUI)*
9 Vladislav Tretiak (URS)
8 Wilhelm Egginger (GER)*
8 Jan Peka (TCH)*
8 Tommy Salo (SWE)
7 Milan Hnilicka (CZE)
7 Leif Holmqvist (SWE)
7 Arturs Irbe (URS/LAT)
7 Fredrik Norrena (FIN)
7 Jozef Stogowski (POL)*
*played exclusively during era when games were 3 x 15
**played part of his career when games were 3 x 15

### MOST SHUTOUTS, ONE WM
8 Jimmy Foster (GBR, 1937)*
6 Ken Campbell (CAN, 1937)*
6 Hugo Muller (SUI, 1939)*
6 Art Puttee (CAN, 1931)*
4 Gerry Cosby (USA, 1933)*
4 Jiri Kralik (TCH, 1982)
4 Ivan McLelland (CAN, 1955)
4 Bohumil Modry (TCH, 1938)*
4 Jan Peka (TCH, 1933)*
*played exclusively during era when games were 3 x 15

### BEST GOALS AGAINST AVERAGE, CAREER (MINIMUM 1,000 MINUTES)
1.13 Jimmy Foster (GBR)
1.27 Bohumil Modry (TCH)
1.33 Vladimir Myshkin (URS)
1.44 Jan Peka (TCH)
1.47 Tomas Vokoun (CZE)
1.53 Yevgeni Belosheikin (URS)
1.63 Arnold Hirtz (SUI)
1.68 Nikolai Puchkov (URS)

## Shots On Goal Records

### MOST SHOTS, TEAM, GAME
114 CAN, March 15, 1950 vs. BEL
78 URS, March 22, 1971 vs. USA
65 CAN, May 2, 2008 vs. SLO

### MOST SHOTS, BOTH TEAMS, GAME
105 URS 78-USA 27, March 22, 1971
97 SWE 65-FRG 32, April 8, 1976
94 CAN 61-SUI 33, May 3, 2011
94 FRG 50-USA 44, April 15, 1986
91 FIN 64-LAT 27, May 9, 2008

### MOST SHOTS, TEAM, PERIOD
36 FIN, 1st period, May 9, 2008
32 URS, 3rd period, April 8, 1973 vs. FRG
31 FIN, 2nd period, May 7, 1999 vs. USA

### MOST SHOTS, BOTH TEAMS, PERIOD
41 FIN 36-LAT 5, 1st period, May 9, 2008
39 CAN 30-POL 9, 2nd period, April 16, 1989
38 USA 21-FIN 17, 3rd period, March 12, 1965
38 RUS 24-USA 14, 2nd period, May 4, 1994
38 FIN 31-USA 7, 2nd period, May 7, 1999
38 AUT 28-HUN 10, 2nd period, May 1, 2009

### FEWEST SHOTS, TEAM, GAME
7 SUI, May 4, 1992 vs. TCH
7 SLO, April 28, 2003 vs. FIN
8 FRA, April 19, 1993 vs. FIN
8 UKR, May 4, 2002 vs. SWE
8 UKR, May 4, 2002 vs. SWE
8 SUI, May 2, 2007 vs. SWE

### FEWEST SHOTS, BOTH TEAMS, GAME
29 TCH 22-SUI 7, May 4, 1992
32 GBR 17-USA 15, March 20, 1950
34 SUI 23-SWE 11, March 20, 1950
34 SUI 19-SVK 15, May 12, 2006

### FEWEST SHOTS, TEAM, PERIOD
0 SUI, 2nd period, May 4, 1992 vs. TCH
0 FRA, 1st period, April 24, 1993 vs. TCH
0 ITA, 2nd period, May 4, 1994 vs. SWE
0 AUT, 1st period, April 22, 1996 vs. USA
0 GER, 1st period, May 6, 1997 vs. LAT
0 SLO, 3rd period, May 3, 2005 vs. CAN
0 FIN, 3rd period, May 7, 2008 vs. SVK

### FEWEST SHOTS, BOTH TEAMS, PERIOD
5 GDR 4-FRG 1, 3rd period, May 7, 1978
6 TCH 6-SUI 0, 2nd period, May 4, 1992
6 RUS 4-SVK 2, 1st period, May 10, 1999
6 SVK 3-FIN 3, 3rd period, May 12, 2000
7 USA 7-AUT 0, 1st period, April 22, 1996
7 CAN 5-USA 2, 1st period, May 1, 1997
7 NOR 6-ITA 1, 1st period, May 9, 2000
7 SVK 6-CAN 1, 1st period, May 9, 2000

## Penalty Records

### FEWEST PENALTIES & PENALTY MINUTES, BOTH TEAMS, GAME
0 GBR-GER, February 17, 1937
0 SUI-NOR, February 18, 1937
0 FRA-SWE, February 18, 1937
0 CAN-TCH, February 20, 1937
0 SWE-NOR, February 26, 1954
0 TCH-USA, March 3, 1955
0 TCH-FIN, March 6, 1955
0 TCH-FRG, March 7, 1963
0 URS-USA, March 15, 1963
0 POL-URS, March 25, 1970
0 URS-SWE, April 19, 1975
0 URS-ROM, April 25, 1977
0 USA-TCH, May 2, 1978

### MOST PENALTY MINUTES, TEAM, GAME
106 USA, May 11, 2008 vs. FIN
80 CAN, May 7, 1997 vs. CZE
80 CZE, May 7, 1997 vs. CAN
80 SUI, May 20, 2010 vs. GER
77 AUT, April 26, 1996 vs. GER
76 ITA, May 7, 2001 vs. SUI
72 FRA, April 21, 1993 vs. GER

### MOST PENALTY MINUTES, TEAM, PERIOD
94 USA, 3rd period, May 11, 2008 vs. FIN
70 CAN, 3rd period, May 7, 1997 vs. CZE
70 CZE, 3rd period, May 7, 1997 vs. CAN
64 FRA, 3rd period, April 21, 1993 vs. GER
62 ITA, 3rd period, May 7, 2001 vs. SUI
60 GER, 3rd period, April 21, 1993 vs. FRA

### MOST PENALTY MINUTES, BOTH TEAMS, GAME
202 USA 106-FIN 96, May 11, 2008
160 CAN 80-CZE 80, May 7, 1997
140 FRA 72-GER 68, April 21, 1993
121 SUI 80-GER 41, May 20, 2010
117 ITA 76-SUI 41, May 7, 2001
116 AUT 77-GER 39, April 26, 1996

### MOST PENALTY MINUTES, BOTH TEAMS, PERIOD
149 USA 94-FIN 55, 3rd period, May 11, 2008
140 CAN 70-CZE 70, 3rd period, May 7, 1997
124 FRA 64-GER 60, 3rd period, April 21, 1993
92 AUT 55-GER 37, 3rd period, April 26, 1996
92 SUI 53-GER 39, 3rd period, May 20, 2010

### MOST PENALTIES, TEAM, GAME

19 UKR, May 2, 2000 vs. SWE
17 CAN, May 7, 1997 vs. CZE
17 CZE, May 7, 1997 vs. CAN
17 ITA, May 7, 2001 vs. SUI

### MOST PENALTIES, TEAM, PERIOD

12 CZE, 3rd period, May 7, 1997
12 CAN, 3rd period, May 7, 1997 vs. CZE

### MOST PENALTIES, BOTH TEAMS, GAME

34 CAN 17-CZE 17, May 7, 1997
34 URKR 19-SWE 15, May 2, 2000
28 CZE 16-RUS 12, May 7, 1999
27 ITA 17-SUI 10, May 7, 2001

### MOST PENALTIES, BOTH TEAMS, PERIOD

24 CZE 12-CAN 12, 3rd period, May 7, 1997
19 UKR 11-SWE 8, 2nd period, May 2, 2000
16 AUT 8-GER 8, 3rd period, April 26, 1996

### MOST PENALTY MINUTES, INDIVIDUAL, GAME

36 Jack Kirrane (USA), March 8, 1963 vs. FIN
34 Sergiy Klimentyev (UKR), May 6, 2007 vs. NOR

### MOST PENALTY MINUTES, INDIVIDUAL, PERIOD

32 Jack Kirrane (USA), 3rd period, March 8, 1963 vs. FIN
32 Sergiy Klimentyev (UKR), 3rd period, May 6, 2007 vs. NOR

### MOST PENALTIES, INDIVIDUAL, GAME

6 Mike Foligno (CAN), May 1, 1987 vs. TCH (4 minors, misconduct, game misconduct)
6 Christian Pouget (FRA), April 29, 1996 vs. NOR (4 minors, major, game misconduct)
6 Roman Simicek (CZE), May 7, 1999 vs. RUS (5 minors, misconduct)
6 Todd Bertuzzi (CAN), May 12, 2000 vs. TCH (4 minors, major, game misconduct)
5 Jack Kirrane (USA), March 8, 1963 vs. FIN (3 minors, misconduct, game misconduct)
5 Erich Kuhnhackl (FRG), May 1, 1983 vs. GDR (4 minors, misconduct)
5 Jiri Slegr (TCH), May 1, 1991 vs. FRG (3 minors, 2 match misconducts)
5 Christophe Ville (FRA), April 22, 1996 vs. ITA (4 minors, misconduct)

### MOST PENALTIES, INDIVIDUAL, PERIOD

5 Mike Foligno (CAN), May 1, 1987 vs. TCH (3 minors, misconduct, game misconduct)
4 Lou Nanne (USA), 1st period, April 18, 1976 vs. FRG (4 minors)

## Speed Records

### FASTEST GOAL FROM START OF GAME

5 seconds Sergei Demagin (BLR), May 2, 2009 vs. FIN
8 seconds Jay McClement (CAN), May 7, 2007 vs. USA

### FASTEST GOAL FROM START OF PERIOD

7 seconds Stefan Karlsson (SWE), 2nd period, March 29, 1969 vs. USA
8 seconds Bengt-Ake Gustafsson (SWE), 2nd period, April 15, 1979 vs. POL

### FASTEST TWO GOALS FROM START OF PERIOD

19 seconds Jiri Lala (TCH, 0:09) & Vladimir Ruzicka (TCH, 0:19), 3rd period, May 1, 1985

### FASTEST TWO GOALS, INDIVIDUAL

6 seconds Bohuslav Stastny (TCH), March 22, 1971 vs. GDR (9:14 & 9:20, 2nd period)
9 seconds Anders Carlsson (SWE), April 24, 1986 vs. FIN (19:20 & 19:29, 3rd period)
9 seconds Sergei Berezin (RUS), April 24, 1996 vs. AUT (19:38 & 19:47, 2nd period)

### FASTEST TWO GOALS, TEAM

5 seconds URS, Alexander Ragulin 1:58 & Vyacheslav Starshinov 2:03, 1st period, March 3, 1966 vs. POL
5 seconds URS, Alexander Yakushev 5:10 & Valeri Kharlamov 5:15, 2nd period, April 9, 1972 vs. FIN
6 seconds TCH, Jiri Holik 16:22 & Jiri Kochta 16:28, 3rd period, April 7, 1972 vs. SUI
6 seconds SWE, Lars-Goran Nilsson 6:00 & Tord Lundstrom 6:06, 1st period, April 19, 1972 vs. FRG

### FASTEST TWO GOALS, BOTH TEAMS

5 seconds Hakan Pettersson (SWE, 15:24) & Valeri Vasiliev (URS, 15:29), 3rd period, April 19, 1975
6 seconds Jukka Alkula (FIN, 14:59) & Milan Novy (TCH, 15:05), 1st period, April 21, 1977

### FASTEST THREE GOALS, TEAM

31 seconds CAN, April 16, 1986 vs. POL (Craig Redmond 6:59, Mark Hardy 7:17, Tony Tanti 7:30, 2nd period
38 seconds URS, March 19, 1971 vs. GDR (Yevgeni Mishakov 11:51, Yevgeni Zimin 12:14, Vladimir Vikulov 12:29, 3rd period)
43 seconds SVK, May 4, 2005 vs. AUT (Michal Handzus 15:05, Martin Strbak 15:28, Zigmund Palffy 15:47, 3rd period)

### FASTEST THREE GOALS, BOTH TEAMS

15 seconds Alexander Maltsev (URS, 15:14), Hakan Pettersson (SWE, 15:24), Valeri Vasiliev (URS, 15:29), 3rd period, April 19, 1975
26 seconds Jan Suchy (TCH, 1:02), Julius Haas (TCH, 1:19), Feliks Goralczyk (POL, 1:28), 2nd period, March 14, 1970

### FASTEST FOUR GOALS, TEAM

1:29 URS, March 15, 1969 vs. USA (Yevgeni Mishakov 7:52, Vladimir Petrov 8:35, Boris Mikhailov 9:08, Mikhailov 9:21, 2nd period)

### FASTEST FOUR GOALS, BOTH TEAMS

1:14 Alexander Kozhevnikov (URS, 3:35), Tom Milani (ITA, 3:53), Sergei Makarov (URS, 4:33), Cary Farelli (ITA, 4:49), 3rd period, April 15, 1982

### FASTEST FIVE GOALS, TEAM

2:55 URS, March 15, 1969 vs. USA (Yevgeni Mishakov 7:52, Vladimir Petrov 8:35, Boris Mikhailov 9:08, Mikhailov 9:21, Vladimir Yursinov 10:47, 2nd period)

*Sweden's Bengt-Ake Gustafsson (right) scored two goals in 8 seconds vs. Poland in the 1979 IIHF World Championships. Photo: IIHF.*

# U20 World Championship

## All-Time Team Records

### LONGEST WINNING STREAK
20 games CAN December 25, 2004-December27, 2007
18 games CAN December 30, 1993-December 27, 1996
13 games URS January 2, 1982-December 31, 1983

### LONGEST UNDEFEATED STREAK
27 games CAN December 26, 1993-January 4, 1997
20 games CAN December 25, 2004-December 27, 2007
19 games URS January 2, 1982-December 28, 1984
19 games URS December 26, 1977-December 30, 1980

### LONGEST LOSING STREAK
31 games SUI December 22, 1977-January 2, 1986
18 games NOR December 27, 1978-January 2, 1989
14 games NOR December 26, 1991-January 2, 2011

### LONGEST WINLESS STREAK
20 games POL December 28, 1987-present
20 games POL December 23, 1976-January 2, 1987
19 games FRG January 2, 1984-December 31, 1987

## Goal-Scoring Team Records

### MOST GOALS, TEAM, GAME
21 December 28, 1980 (Czechoslovakia 21-Austria 4)
20 December 30, 1992 (Sweden 20-Japan 1)
19 January 1, 1991 (United States 19-Norway 1)
19 December 27, 1980 (Soviet Union 19-Austria 1)
19 December 28, 1979 (Finland 19-Switzerland 1)
18 December 30, 1986 (Canada 18-Poland 3)
18 December 27, 1985 (Canada 18-West Germany 2)
18 December 23, 1977 (Finland 18-Switzerland 1)
18 December 22, 1977 (Soviet Union 18-Switzerland 0)

### MOST GOALS, BOTH TEAMS SCORING, GAME
25 December 28, 1980 (Czechoslovakia 21-Austria 4)
21 December 30, 1992 (Sweden 20-Japan 1)
21 December 30, 1986 (Canada 18-Poland 3)
20 January 1, 1991 (United States 19-Norway 1)
20 December 27, 1985 (Canada 18-West Germany 2)
20 December 27, 1980 (Soviet Union 19-Austria 1)
20 December 28, 1979 (Finland 19-Switzerland 1)
20 December 30, 1976 (Soviet Union 15-United States 5)

### MOST GOALS, TEAM, PERIOD
10 URS (December 27, 1978 3rd period vs. NOR)
10 USA (January 1, 1991 1st period vs. NOR)
9 FIN (December 23, 1977 3rd period vs. SUI)
9 TCH (December 28, 1980 3rd period vs. AUT)
9 SWE (December 30, 1992 2nd period vs. JPN)
9 CZE (January 2, 1995 2nd period vs. GER)

### MOST GOALS, BOTH TEAMS SCORING, PERIOD
11 January 1, 1983 2nd period, (TCH 6-CAN 5)
10 January 2, 1995 2nd period, (CZE 9-GER 1)
9 December 28, 1980 2nd period, (TCH 6-AUT 3)
9 December 29, 1983 3rd period, (TCH 8-SUI 1)

### SCORELESS GAMES
December 27, 1998 Canada 0 Slovakia 0
December 31, 1996 Sweden 0 Russia 0
December 31, 1995 Sweden 0 Czech Republic 0
January 4, 2000 Czech Republic 1 Russia 0 (GWS)

## Power-Play and Short-Handed Goals Records

### MOST POWER-PLAY GOALS, TEAM, GAME
8 FIN (December 30, 2009 vs. AUT)
8 CAN (December 28, 2008 vs. KAZ)
7 SWE (January 2, 1993 vs. FIN)
6 CAN (December 26, 2009 vs. LAT)
6 CAN (December 26, 2002 vs. SWE)
6 FIN (December 28, 1979 vs. SUI)

### MOST POWER-PLAY GOALS TEAM, PERIOD
4 TCH (2nd period January 3, 1988 vs. USA)

### MOST POWER-PLAY GOALS, BOTH TEAMS, GAME
8 SWE 7-FIN 1, January 2, 1993
7 SWE 4-SUI 3, January 5, 2010
7 AUT 4-LAT 3, January 4, 2010
7 USA 5-NOR 2, December 26, 2005
7 SVK 4-POL 3, December 29, 1996
7 USA 5-FIN 2, January 4, 1996
7 USA 4-SWE 3, December 30, 1991
7 TCH 5-AUT 2, December 28, 1980

### MOST POWER-PLAY GOALS, BOTH TEAMS, PERIOD
5 SUI 3-SWE 2, January 5, 2010, 2nd period
5 USA 4-FIN 1, January 2, 2007, 3rd period

### MOST SHORT-HANDED GOALS, TEAM, GAME
3 SWE (December 28,1987 vs. POL)

### MOST SHORT-HANDED GOALS, TEAM, PERIOD
2 USA (2nd period, December 31, 2009 vs. CAN)
2 SWE (2nd period, December 28, 2007 vs. DEN)
2 URS (2nd period, January 2, 1990 vs. TCH)
2 USA (1st period, December 29, 1986 vs. POL)
2 SWE (1st period, January 1, 1986 vs. SUI)

## All-Time Individual Records

### MOST WM20 CHAMPIONSHIPS
4 Michael Frolik, CZE (2005-08)
4 Andrei Kostitsyn, BLR (2001-05)
4 Konstantin Zakharov, BLR (2001-05)
4 Bjorn Christen, SUI (1997-2000)
4 Michel Riesen, SUI (1996-99)
4 Jochen Hecht, GER (1994-97)
4 Robert Sterflinger, FRG (1981-84)
4 Reijo Ruotsalainen, FIN (1977-80)

### MOST GOLD MEDALS
3 Jason Botterill, CAN (3G)

### MOST MEDALS
3 Jason Botterill (CAN)

3 Yevgeni Belosheikin, URS (2G, B)
3 Alexander Semak, URS (2G, B)
3 Mikhail Tatarinov, URS (2G, B)

3 Ryan Ellis, CAN (G, 2S)
3 Denis Shvidki, RUS (G, 2S)
3 Dmitri Yushkevich, URS (G, 2S)

3 Mikhail Donika, RUS (G, S, B)
3 Roman Lyashenko, RUS (G, S, B)

3 Johan Davidsson, SWE (2S, B)
3 Jari Munck, FIN (2S, B)
3 Frantisek Musil, TCH (2S, B)
3 Mattias Ohlund, SWE (2S, B)
3 Magnus Pajaarvi-Svensson (2S, B)
3 Petr Rosol, TCH (2S, B)
3 Niklas Sundstrom, SWE (2S, B)

3 Jay Bouwmeester, CAN (S, 2B)
3 Tomas Jonsson, SWE (S, 2B)
3 Kari Lehtonen, FIN (S, 2B)
3 Tuomo Ruutu, FIN (S, 2B)
3 Tommy Samuelsson, SWE (S, 2B)
3 Jason Spezza, CAN (S, 2B)
3 Thomas Steen, SWE (S, 2B)
3 Vyacheslav Voinov, RUS (S, 2B)

3 Sean Bergenheim, FIN (3B)

### MOST GAMES PLAYED
26 Bjorn Christen, SUI (1997-2000)
26 Jochen Hecht, GER (1994-97)
25 Michael Frolik, CZE (2005-08)
25 Michel Riesen, SUI (1996-99)
25 Robert Sterflinger, FRG (1981-84)

### MOST POINTS, CAREER
42 Peter Forsberg, SWE (10+32=42)
40 Robert Reichel, TCH (18+22=40)
39 Pavel Bure, URS (27+12=39)
35 Alexander Mogilny, URS (19+16=35)
35 Esa Tikkanen, FIN (17+18=35)
34 Vladimir Ruzicka, TCH (25+9=34)
34 Markus Naslund, SWE (21+13=34)
33 Niklas Sundstrom, SWE (18+15=33)
32 Esa Keskinen, FIN (10+22=32)
31 Eric Lindros, CAN (12+19=31)
30 Petr Rosol, TCH (18+12=30)

### MOST POINTS, ONE WM20
31 Peter Forsberg, SWE (1993-7+24=31)
24 Markus Naslund, SWE (1993-13+11=24)
22 Raimo Helminen, FIN (1984-11+11=22)
21 Robert Reichel, TCH (1990-11+10=21)
20 Vladimir Ruzicka, TCH (1983-12+8=20)
20 Esa Keskinen, FIN (1985-6+14=20)

### MOST GOALS, WM20 CAREER
27 Pavel Bure, URS (1989-91)
25 Vladimir Ruzicka, TCH (1981-83)
21 Markus Naslund, SWE (1992-93)
19 Alexander Mogilny, URS (1987-89)
18 Alexander Ovechkin, RUS (2003-05)
18 Robert Reichel, TCH (1988-90)
18 Petr Rosol, TCH (1982-84)
18 Niklas Sundstrom, SWE (1993-95)
17 Esa Tikkanen, FIN (1983-85)

### MOST GOALS, ONE WM20
13 Markus Naslund, SWE (1993)
12 Pavel Bure, URS (1991)
12 Vladimir Ruzicka, TCH (1983)
11 Raimo Helminen, FIN (1984)
11 Mikko Makela, FIN (1985)
11 Robert Reichel, TCH (1990)
11 German Volgin, URS (1983)

### MOST ASSISTS, WM20 CAREER
32 Peter Forsberg, SWE (1992-93)
22 Robert Reichel, TCH (1988-90)
20 Ryan Ellis, CAN (2009-11)
20 Jordan Schroeder, USA (2008-10)
19 Eric Lindros, CAN (1990-92)
19 Henrik Sedin, SWE (1998-2000)
18 Jason Allison, CAN (1994-95)
18 Esa Tikkanen, FIN (1983-85)

### MOST ASSISTS, ONE WM20
24 Peter Forsberg, SWE (1993)
14 Esa Keskinen, FIN (1985)
14 Doug Weight, USA (1991)
13 Jaromir Jagr, TCH (1990)
12 Jason Allison, CAN (1995)
12 Esa Tikkanen, FIN (1985)

### MOST PENALTY MINUTES, WM20 CAREER
74 Teemu Laakso, FIN (2005-07)
63 Sven Felski, GER (1993-94)
62 Alexi Lazarenko, UKR (1995-96)
62 Thomas Nussli, SUI (2001-02)
59 Roman Azanov, KAZ (2000-01)
59 Jack Johnson, USA (2006-07)
58 David Stich, CZE (2009)
57 Vadim Sozinov, KAZ (2000-01)
57 Marco Sturm, GER (1995-96)

### MOST PENALTY MINUTES, ONE WM20
68 Petr Cajanek, CZE (1995)
58 David Stich, CZE (2009)
53 David Wolf, GER (2009)
52 Teemu Laakso, FIN (2007)
51 Marco Sturm, GER (1996)

### MOST POINTS, ONE GAME

10 Peter Forsberg, SWE, December 30, 1992 vs. JPN (3+7=10)
9 Yevgeni Kuznetsov, RUS December 29, 2011 vs. LAT (3+6=9)
8 Ola Rosander, SWE, December 28, 1987 vs. POL (6+2=8)
7 Gabriel Bourque, CAN, December 26, 2009 vs. LAT (3+4=7)
7 Markus Naslund, SWE, December 30, 1992 vs. JPN (5+2=7)
7 Igor Alexandrov, RUS, December 26, 1992 vs. JPN (3+4=7)
7 Doug Weight, USA, January 1, 1991 vs. NOR (1+6=7)
7 Ted Drury, USA, January 1, 1991 vs. NOR (2+5=7)
7 Alexander Mogilny, URS, January 4, 1988 vs. FRG (5+2=7)
7 Par Edlund, SWE, December 27, 1986 vs. POL (2+5=7)
7 Roger Ohman, SWE, December 27, 1986 vs. POL (3+4=7)
7 Dave Andreychuk, CAN, January 4, 1983 vs. NOR (3+4=7)
7 Pekka Jarvela, FIN, December 23, 1981 vs. SUI (2+5=7)
7 Jari Kurri, FIN, December 28, 1979 vs. SUI (2+5=7)
7 Gerd Truntschka, FRG, January 2, 1977 vs. POL (4+3=7)
7 Nikita Gusev, RUS December 29, 2011 vs. LAT (2+5=7)
7 Austin Watson, USA January 3, 2012 vs. LAT (3+4=7)

### MOST POINTS, ONE PERIOD

6 Ted Drury, USA, 1st period, January 1, 1991 vs. NOR (2+4=6)
5 Peter Forsberg, SWE, 2nd period, December 30, 1992 vs. JPN (2+3=5)
5 Yevgeni Kuznetsov, RUS, 2nd period, December 29, 2011 vs. LAT (2+3=5)

### MOST GOALS, ONE GAME

6 Ola Rosander, SWE, December 28, 1987 vs. POL
5 Chris Bourque, USA, December 26, 2005 vs. NOR
5 Markus Naslund, SWE, December 30, 1992 vs. JPN
5 Alexander Mogilny, URS, January 4, 1988 vs. FRG
5 Wally Chapman, USA, January 3, 1984 vs. SUI
5 Tommy Lehmann, SWE, December 28, 1983 vs. FRG
5 Magnus Roupe, SWE, December 22, 1981 vs. SUI
5 Jan Vodila, TCH, December 27, 1979 vs. USA
5 Rainer Risku, FIN, December 23, 1977 vs. SUI

### MOST GOALS, ONE PERIOD

4 Teemu Pulkkinen, FIN, 3rd period December 30, 2011 vs. DEN
4 Jan Vodila, TCH, 3rd period December 27, 1979 vs. USA
3 Austin Watson, USA, 1st period, January 3, 2012 vs. LAT
3 Jan Kana, CZE, 2nd period December 31, 2008 vs. KAZ
3 Yevgeni Rymarev, KAZ, 3rd period January 2, 2008 vs. DEN
3 Michael Frolik, CZE, 1st period December 27, 2007 vs. DEN
3 Chris Bourque, USA, 2nd period December 26, 2005 vs. NOR
3 Jeff Carter, CAN, 2nd period December 30, 2004 vs. FIN
3 Vadim Sozinov, KAZ, 3rd period December 29, 1999 vs. UKR
3 Mikhail Medvedev, KAZ, 3rd period December 31, 1998 vs. SWE
3 Oleg Kvasha, RUS, 2nd period December 25, 1997 vs. KAZ
3 Patric Englund, SWE, 1st period December 31, 1989 vs. POL
3 Alexander Mogilny, URS, 2nd period January 4, 1989 vs. CAN
3 Mike Modano, USA, 2nd period January 2, 1989 vs. NOR
3 Adam Graves, CAN, 2nd period January 3, 1988 vs. FRG
3 Alexander Mogilny, URS, 3rd period January 4, 1988 vs. FRG
3 Ola Rosander, SWE, 1st period December 28, 1987 vs. POL
3 Arto Kulmala, FIN, 2nd period December 26, 1987 vs. FRG
3 Juraj Jurik, TCH, 1st period January 1, 1987 vs. POL
3 Jim Sandlak, CAN, 1st period December 26, 1985 vs. SUI
3 Wally Chapman, USA, 3rd period January 3, 1984 vs. SUI
3 Tommy Lehmann, SWE, 1st period December 28, 1983 vs. FRG
3 Bobby Carpenter, USA, 3rd period December 31, 1980 vs. CAN
3 Peter Stastny, TCH, 2nd period December 23, 1977 vs. USA
3 Kevin Hartzell, USA, 2nd period December 28, 1977 vs. SUI
3 Erkki Laine, FIN, 1st period December 22, 1976 vs. USA

### MOST ASSISTS, ONE GAME

6 Brenden Morrow, CAN, January 2, 1999 vs. KAZ
6 Doug Weight, USA, January 1, 1991 vs. NOR
6 Ilka Sinisalo, FIN, December 23, 1977 vs. SUI
5 Phil Kessel, USA, December 26, 2005 vs. NOR
5 Alexander Serikow, GER, January 4, 1995 vs. UKR
5 Ted Drury, USA, January 1, 1991 vs. NOR
5 Calle Johansson, SWE, January 4, 1987 vs. USA
5 Par Edlund, SWE, December 27, 1986 vs. POL
5 Konstantin Kudashov, URS, December 27, 1980 vs. AUT
5 Jari Kurri, FIN, December 28, 1979 vs. SUI
5 Tomas Jurco, SVK, December 31, 2011 vs. SUI

### MOST ASSISTS, ONE PERIOD

4 Michael Nylander, SWE, 2nd period December 26, 1991 vs. TCH
4 Ted Drury, USA, 1st period, January 1, 1991 vs. NOR
4 Austin Watson, USA, 3rd period, January 3, 2012 vs. LAT

### PENALTY SHOTS

Josef Lukac (TCH) stopped by Al Jensen (CAN), December 25, 1976
Steve Tambellini (CAN) stopped by Jaromir Sindel (TCH), December 25, 1977
Pius Kuonen (SUI) beat Terry Wright (CAN), December 30, 1979
Arkadi Obukhov (URS) beat Matti Rautiainen (FIN), January 2, 1983
Ladislav Lubina (TCH) stopped by Shawn Simpson (CAN), December 29, 1986
Ulf Sandstrom (SWE) stopped by Jimmy Waite (CAN), January 2, 1987
Vyacheslav Kozlov (URS) stopped by Wojciech Baca (POL), December 26, 1989
Robert Reichel (TCH) beat Wojciech Baca (POL), December 29, 1989
David Vyborny (CZE) beat Philippe DeRouville (CAN), January 4, 1993
Unknown (SWE) stopped by Robert Slavic (CZE), January 1, 1994
Sergi Chubenko (UKR) stopped by Jussi Markkanen (FIN), December 27, 1994
Veli-Pekka Nutikka (FIN) beat Dan Cloutier (CAN), January 1, 1995
Unknown (CZE) stopped by Oliver Hausler (GER), January 2, 1995
Danil Didkovsky (UKR) beat Stanislav Petrik (SVK), January 2, 1996
Kristian Huselius (SWE) beat Stanislav Petrik (SVK), December 27, 1996
Marian Gaborik (SVK) beat Zdenek Smid (CZE), December 25, 1999
Jamie Lundmark (CAN) beat Rastislav Stana (SVK), December 29, 1999
Unknown (FIN) stopped by Martin Zerzuben (SUI), December 27, 2000
Alexander Kulakov (BLR) beat Jason Bacashihua (USA), December 29, 2001
Clarke MacArthur (CAN) beat Jaroslav Halak (SVK), December 25, 2004
Sergei Shirokov (RUS) beat Al Montoya (USA), December 25, 2004
Alexei Yemelin (RUS) beat Michael Tobler (SUI), December 30, 2004
Mathias Trygg (NOR) beat Vladimir Kovac (SVK), January 3, 2006
Jonathan Toews (CAN) beat Jeff Zatkoff (USA) December 27, 2006
Fredrik Pettersson (SWE) stopped by Sebastian Stefaniszin (GER), December 30, 2006
Perttu Lindgren (FIN) stopped by Jakub Kovar (CZE), January 4, 2007
Tomas Marcinko (SVK) stopped by Michal Neuvirth (CZE), December 29, 2007
Oscar Moller (SWE) stopped by Harri Sateri (FIN), December 26, 2008
Roman Szturc (CZE) beat Andrei Yankov (KAZ), December 31, 2008
Jordan Schroeder (USA) stopped by Jaroslav Janus (SVK), January 2, 2009
Chris Kreider (USA) stopped by Jake Allen (CAN), December 31, 2009
Tomas Kubalik (CZE) stopped by Raimonds Ermics (LAT), January 3, 2010
Patrik Cehlin (SWE) stopped by Lars Volden (NOR), December 26, 2010
Tom Kuhnhackl (GER) stopped by Dominik Riecicky (SVK), December 27, 2010
Juraj Majdan (SVK) stopped by Benjamin Conz (SUI), December 30, 2010
Mark Stone (CAN) stopped by Petr Mrazek (CZE), December 28, 2011
Josh Archibald (USA) stopped by Petr Mrazek (CZE), December 30, 2011
Patrick Bjorkstrand (DEN) beat Christopher Gibson (FIN), December 30, 2011
Gregory Hofmann (SUI) beat Sebastian Feuk (DEN), January 2, 2012
Teemu Pulkkinen (FIN) stopped by Mark Visentin (CAN), January 5, 2012

## Goaltender Records

### MOST WM20 CHAMPIONSHIPS, GOALIE

3 Vitali Arystov, BLR (1999-2002)
3 Yevgeni Belosheikin, URS (1984-86)
3 Kai Fischer, GER (1995-97)
3 Vaclav Fuerbacher, TCH (1981-83)
3 Josef Heiss, FRG (1981-83)
3 Jan Hrabak, TCH (1977-79)
3 Kari Lehtonen, FIN (2001-03)
3 Sam Lindstahl, SWE (1985-87)
3 Andrei Medvedev, RUS (2001-03)
3 Mika Noronen, FIN (1997-99)
3 Alan Perry, USA (1984-86)
3 Tuukka Rask, FIN (2005-07)
3 Marek Schwarz, CZE (2004-06)
3 Marc Seliger, GER (1992-94)

### MOST GAMES PLAYED, GOALIE, CAREER

18 Alan Perry, USA (1984-86)
17 Tuukka Rask, FIN (2005-07)
17 Andrei Medvedev, RUS (2001-03)
17 Marc Seliger, GER (1992-94)
16 Yevgeni Belosheikin, URS (1984-86)
16 Marek Schwarz, CZE (2004-06)
15 Josef Heiss, FRG (1981-83)
15 Alexander Kolyuzhny, KAZ (1999-2001)

### MOST MINUTES PLAYED, GOALIE, CAREER

1,054:00 Yevgeni Belosheikin, URS (1984-86)
1,017:30 Marc Seliger, GER (1992-94)
968:33 Alan Perry, USA (1984-86)
945:06 Tuukka Rask, FIN (2005-07)
891:05 Marek Schwarz, CZE (2004-06)
880:47 Andrei Medvedev, RUS (2001-03)
838:06 Henrik Lundqvist, SWE (2001-02)

### MOST WINS, GOALIE, CAREER

11 Andrei Medvedev, RUS (2001-03)
11 Alexander Tyzhnykh, URS (1977-78)
9 Yevgeni Belosheikin, URS (1984-86)
9 Dominik Hasek, TCH (1983-85)
9 Al Montoya, USA (2004-05)
9 Alexei Volkov, RUS (1999-2000)
9 Jimmy Waite, CAN (1987-88)

### MOST WINS, GOALIE, ONE WM20

7 Tomas Duba, CZE (2001)
6 Andrei Karpin, URS (1983)
6 Manny Legace, CAN (1993)

6 Al Montoya, USA (2004)
6 Peter Olsson, SWE (1994)
6 Justin Pogge, CAN (2006)
6 Carey Price, CAN (2007)
6 Alexei Sheblanov, URS (1988)
6 Alexander Tyzhnykh, URS (1977)
6 Alexei Volkov, RUS (1999)
6 Jimmy Waite, CAN (1988)

**MOST LOSSES, GOALIE, CAREER**
14 Marc Seliger, GER (1992-94)
11 Igor Karpenko, UKR (1995-96)
10 Josef Heiss, FRG (1981-83)
9 Pauli Jaks, SUI (1991-92)
8 Beat Aebischer, SUI (1986-87)
8 Marek Schwarz, CZE (2004-06)

**MOST LOSSES, GOALIE, ONE WM20 CHAMPIONSHIP**
6 Sebastian Feuk, DEN (2012)
6 Oliver Hausler, GER (1995)
6 Igor Karpenko, UKR (1995)
6 Wlodzimierz Krauzowicz, POL (1987)
6 Klaus Merk, FRG (1986)
6 Marc Seliger, GER (1994)
6 Stefan Wadas, POL (1977)
6 Lars Weibel, SUI (1994)

**MOST SHUTOUTS, CAREER**
4 Jaroslav Halak, SVK (2004-05)
3 Nikolai Khabibulin, RUS (1992-93)
3 Denis Khlopotnov, RUS (1997-98)
3 Kari Lehtonen, FIN (2001-03)
3 Henrik Lundqvist, SWE (2001-02)
3 Justin Pogge, CAN (2006)

**MOST SHUTOUTS, ONE WM20**
3 Justin Pogge, CAN (2006)
2 Jake Allen, CAN (2010)
2 Brian Boucher, USA (1997)
2 Tomas Duba, CZE (2001)
2 Mathieu Garon, CAN (1998)
2 Jaroslav Halak, SVK (2004 & 2005)
2 Johan Holmqvist, SWE (1998)
2 Nikolai Khabibulin, RUS (1992)
2 Denis Khlopotnov, RUS (1997)
2 Pascal Leclaire, CAN (2002)
2 Kari Lehtonen, FIN (2003)
2 Henrik Lundqvist, SWE (2001)
2 Roberto Luongo, CAN (1999)
2 Al Montoya, USA (2004)
2 Michael Tobler, SUI (2005)
2 Semyon Varlamov, RUS (2007)
2 Andrei Vasilevski, RUS (2012)

**LONGEST SHUTOUT SEQUENCE (IN MINUTES), TEAM**
215:09 RUS, December 26, 1998-January 2, 1999
203:31 SWE, December 26, 1986-January 1, 1987

**LONGEST SHUTOUT SEQUENCE (IN MINUTES), GOALIE**
215:09 Alexei Volkov, RUS, December 26, 1998-January 2, 1999
151:50 Justin Pogge, CAN, December 31, 2005-January 5, 2006
151:38 Per Ragnar Bergkvist, SWE, December 29,1995-January 3,1996
146:52 Jaroslav Halak, SVK, December 28, 2003-January 2, 2004

**BEST GOALS AGAINST AVERAGE, CAREER**
(minimum 480 minutes-career minutes played listed in brackets)
1.42 Alexei Volkov, RUS (592:38)
1.55 Rick DiPitero, USA (658:40)
1.66 Maxime Ouellet, CAN (759:01)
1.67 Marc Denis, CAN (540:00)
1.70 Kari Lehtonen, FIN (776:16)
1.70 Marc-Andre Fleury, CAN (566:19)

**MOST ASSISTS, GOALIE, CAREER**
2 Janis Kalnins, LAT
2 Henrik Lundqvist, SWE
2 Joni Ortio, FIN

**MOST PENALTY MINUTES, GOALIE, CAREER**
26 Bernd Engelbrecht, FRG
22 Raimonds Ermics, LAT
20 Jussi Markkanen, FIN

## Shots On Goal Records

**MOST SHOTS, TEAM, GAME**
95 CAN, January 4, 1988 vs. POL
83 TCH, December 31, 1982 vs. FRG
81 FIN, December 26, 1987 vs. FRG

**MOST SHOTS, BOTH TEAMS, GAME**
125 CAN 95-POL 30, January 4, 1988
115 FIN 66-CAN 49, December 30, 1991
114 CAN 80-FRG 34, December 29, 1976
112 TCH 83-FRG 29, December 31, 1982

**MOST SHOTS, TEAM, PERIOD**
41 CAN, 3rd period, January 4, 1988 vs. POL
34 SWE, 2nd period, December 30, 1992 vs. JPN
33 RUS, 2nd period, December 27, 1996 vs. POL
33 CAN, 2nd period, January 4, 1988 vs. POL

**MOST SHOTS, BOTH TEAMS, PERIOD**
46 URS 34-POL 12, 3rd period, January 3, 1988
45 CAN 31-SUI 14, 2nd period, December 27, 1991
45 CAN 33-POL 12, 2nd period, January 4, 1988
44 CAN 41-POL 3, 3rd period, January 4, 1988
44 USA 28-FRG 16, 2nd period, December 28, 1987

**FEWEST SHOTS, TEAM, GAME**
6 BLR, December 27, 2000 vs. RUS
7 FRG, December 27, 1979 vs. SWE
8 SUI, December 31, 2003 vs. FIN
8 POL, December 27, 1996 vs. RUS
8 JPN, December 30, 1992 vs. SWE

**FEWEST SHOTS, BOTH TEAMS, GAME**
30 TCH 17-SWE 13, December 28, 1977
33 CZE 18-FIN 15, January 1, 2002
35 CZE 19-SWE 16, December 25, 1997

**FEWEST SHOTS, TEAM, PERIOD**
0 AUT, 1st period, December 30, 2009 vs. FIN
0 LAT, 2nd period, December 27, 2008 vs. SVK
0 NOR, 2nd period, January 4, 1983 vs. CAN
0 SUI, 3rd period, December 26, 1985 vs. CAN

**FEWEST SHOTS, BOTH TEAMS, PERIOD**
5 SUI 4-RUS 1, 3rd period, December 27, 1997
6 CZE 4-SWE 2, 1st period, December 25, 1997

## Penalty Records

**FEWEST PENALTY MINUTES, TEAM, GAME**
0 KAZ, December 29, 1997 vs. SUI
0 FIN, January 3, 1990 vs. POL
0 TCH, December 27, 1988 vs. NOR
0 FRG, January 4, 1989 vs. NOR
0 SUI, January 3, 1984 vs. USA
0 TCH, January 2, 1981 vs. FIN
0 SUI, December 30, 1979 vs. CAN

**FEWEST PENALTY MINUTES, BOTH TEAMS, GAME**
2 FIN 2-TCH 0, January 2, 1981
4 RUS 2-CZE 2, January 4, 2000
4 POL 2-SWE 2, December 29, 1984
4 USA 4-SUI 0, January 3, 1984

**FEWEST PENALTIES, GAME, TEAM**
0 KAZ, December 29, 1997 vs. SUI
0 FIN, January 3, 1990 vs. POL
0 TCH, December 27, 1988 vs. NOR
0 FRG, January 4, 1989 vs. NOR
0 SUI, January 3, 1984 vs. USA
0 TCH, January 2, 1981 vs. FIN
0 SUI, December 30, 1979 vs. CAN

**FEWEST PENALTIES, BOTH TEAMS, GAME**
1 FIN 1-TCH 0, January 2, 1981
2 RUS 1-CZE 1, January 4, 2000
2 POL 1-SWE 1, December 29, 1984
2 USA 2-SUI 0, January 3, 1984

**MOST PENALTY MINUTES, TEAM, GAME**
126 GER, January 3, 1998 vs. SVK
122 SUI, December 30, 1995 vs. UKR
100 UKR, December 30, 1995 vs. SUI

**MOST PENALTY MINUTES, TEAM, PERIOD**
118 GER, January 3, 1998 vs. SVK, 3rd period
86 SUI, December 30, 1995 vs. UKR, 3rd period
86 UKR, December 30, 1995 vs. SUI, 3rd period
85 SVK, January 3, 1998 vs. GER, 3rd period

**MOST PENALTY MINUTES, BOTH TEAMS, GAME**
222 SUI 122-UKR 100, December 30, 1995
219 GER 126-SVK 93, January 3, 1998
186 SUI 97-RUS 89, January 3, 2001

**MOST PENALTY MINUTES, BOTH TEAMS, PERIOD**
203 GER 118-SVK 85, January 3, 1998, 3rd period
172 SUI 86-UKR 86, December 30, 1995, 3rd period
162 RUS 81-SUI 81, January 3, 2001, 3rd period

**MOST PENALTIES, TEAM, GAME**
27 NOR, December 29, 2005 vs. CAN
25 CAN, December 29, 2005 vs. NOR
20 USA, January 4, 1996 vs. FIN
20 FIN, January 4, 1996 vs. USA

**MOST PENALTIES, TEAM, PERIOD**
15 NOR, December 29, 2005 vs. CAN, 3rd period
15 CAN, December 29, 2005 vs. NOR, 3rd period
12 FIN, January 4, 1996 vs. USA, 2nd period
11 CAN, December 27, 1979 vs. FIN, 3rd period

**MOST PENALTIES, BOTH TEAMS, GAME**
52 NOR 27-CAN 25, December 29, 2005
40 FIN 20-USA 20, January 4, 1996
36 FIN 19-UKR 17, December 27, 1994
32 NOR 18-USA 14, December 26, 2005

**MOST PENALTIES, BOTH TEAMS, PERIOD**
30 NOR 15-CAN 15, December 29, 2005, 3rd period

**MOST PENALTY MINUTES, INDIVIDUAL, GAME**
52 David Stich, CZE, January 4, 2009 vs. USA (minor, major, match, game)
32 Tomas Slovak, SVK, December 31, 2002 vs. USA (abuse of official, misconduct, minor)
31 Alexei Yemelin, RUS, January 3, 2006 vs. USA (3 minors, major, game misconduct)
31 Vadim Sozinov, KAZ, January 4, 2000 vs. FIN (3 minors, major, game misconduct)
31 Timo Salonen, FIN, January 4, 1996 vs. USA (3 minors, major, match misconduct)

**MOST PENALTY MINUTES, INDIVIDUAL, PERIOD**
50 David Stich, CZE, 2nd period, January 4, 2009 vs. USA (major, match, game)
32 Tomas Slovak, SVK, 3rd period, December 31, 2002 vs. USA (abuse of official, misconduct, minor)
31 Timo Salonen, FIN, 2nd period, January 4, 1996 vs. USA (3 minors, major, match misconduct)
30 Konstantin Koltsov, BLR, 3rd period, January 4, 1999 vs. USA (abuse of official, misconduct)

**MOST PENALTIES, INDIVIDUAL, GAME**
6 Eirik Grafsronningen, NOR, December 29, 2005 vs. CAN (5 minors, misconduct)
6 Oldrich Valek, TCH, December 30, 1979 vs. SWE (6 minors)

**MOST PENALTIES, INDIVIDUAL, PERIOD**
5 Timo Salonen, FIN, 2nd period, January 4, 1996 vs. USA (3 minors, major, match misconduct)
4 Eirik Grafsronningen, NOR, 3rd period, December 29, 2005 vs. CAN (3 minors, misconduct)
4 Oleksiy Lubnin, UKR, 3rd period, January 2, 2004 vs. SWE (3 minors, game misconduct)
4 Wlodzimierz Krol, POL, 3rd period, December 27, 1986 vs. SWE (4 minors)
4 Peter Baldinger, SUI, 2nd period, December 28, 1979 vs. FIN (3 minors, misconduct)

## Speed Records

**FASTEST GOAL FROM START OF GAME**
7 seconds Daniel Rydmark, SWE, December 28, 1989 vs. FIN
8 seconds Pavel Bure, URS, December 26, 1989 vs. POL
11 seconds Jim Sandlak, CAN, December 26, 1985 vs. SUI
11 seconds German Volgin, URS, December 29, 1982 vs. FRG

**FASTEST TWO GOALS FROM START OF GAME, TEAM**
1:03 SWE, January 2, 1997 vs. GER (Henrik Rehnberg 0:18, Linus Fagemo 1:03)

**FASTEST THREE GOALS FROM START OF GAME, TEAM**
1:33 URS, December 29, 1982 vs. FRG (German Volgin 0:11, Sergei Priakhin 1:05, Yevgeni Shtepa 1:33)

**FASTEST FOUR GOALS FROM START OF GAME, TEAM**
1:41 URS, December 29, 1982 vs. FRG (German Volgin 0:11, Sergei Priakhin 1:05, Yevgeni Shtepa 1:33, Sergei Kharin 1:41)

**FASTEST GOAL FROM START OF PERIOD**
8 seconds Eric Daze, CAN, 3rd period, January 4, 1995 vs. SWE
8 seconds Vesa Viitakoski, FIN, 2nd period, December 31, 1990 vs. NOR
8 seconds Richard Panik, SVK, 2nd period, December 27, 2010 vs. GER

**FASTEST TWO GOALS, INDIVIDUAL**
9 seconds Dave Gagner, CAN, December 28, 1983 vs. SUI (18:29 & 18:38 of 2nd)
10 seconds Andrei Sidorov, URS, January 4, 1988 vs. FRG (11:48 & 11:58 of 1st)

**FASTEST TWO GOALS, TEAM**
6 seconds RUS, December 29, 2005 vs. LAT (Yevgeni Malkin 3:54,Nikolai Lemtyugov 4:00,1st)
6 seconds FIN, December 28, 1979 vs. SUI (Mika Helkearo 16:18, Pekka Arbelius 16:24, 3rd)

**FASTEST TWO SHORT-HANDED GOALS, TEAM**
36 seconds SWE, January 1, 1986 vs. SUI (Fredrik Olausson 5:41 & Roger Johansson 6:17 of 1st)
41 seconds URS, January 2, 1990 vs. TCH (Vyacheslav Kozlov 3:50 & Roman Oksiuta 4:31 of 2nd)
47 seconds SUI, January 3, 1996 vs. SVK (Sandy Jeannin 2:04 & Reto von Arx 2:51 of 2nd)

**FASTEST TWO GOALS, BOTH TEAMS**
6 seconds USA-SWE, January 4, 1988 (Johan Garpenlov (SWE) 14:34, Joe Day (USA) 14:40, 2nd)
7 seconds SWE-LAT, December 30, 2005 (Edzus Karklins (LAT) 11:52, Mattias Ritola (SWE) 11:59, 3rd)
7 seconds URS-FIN, January 3, 1991 (Jere Lehtinen (FIN) 14:55, Sergei Zholtok (URS) 15:02, 2nd)

**FASTEST THREE GOALS, INDIVIDUAL**
4:01 Oleg Kvasha, RUS, December 25, 1997 vs. KAZ (2:13, 3:01, 6:14 of 2nd)
4:41 Patric Englund, SWE, December 31, 1989 vs. POL (13:54, 14:37, 18:35 of 1st)
5:09 Erkki Laine, FIN, December 22, 1976 vs. USA (4:51, 8:00, 10:00 of 1st)

**FASTEST THREE GOALS, TEAM**
23 seconds CAN, December 28, 1983 vs. SUI (Russ Courtnall 18:15, Dave Gagner 18:29, Dave Gagner 18:38, 2nd)
36 seconds TCH, January 1, 1993 vs. JPN (Radim Bicanek 7:42, Stanislav Neckar 8:05, David Vyborny 8:18, 3rd)
36 seconds URS, December 29, 1982 vs. FRG (Sergei Priakhin 1:05, Yevgeni Shtepa 1:33, Sergei Kharin 1:41, 1st)

**FASTEST THREE POWER-PLAY GOALS, TEAM**
38 seconds CAN, January 2, 1995 vs. RUS (Todd Harvey 2:29, Jeff O'Neill 2:48, Marty Murray 3:07 of 3rd)
49 seconds USA, January 4, 1996 vs. FIN (Matt Cullen 9:52, Mike York 10:08, Matt Herr 10:41 of 2nd)

**FASTEST THREE GOALS, BOTH TEAMS**
26 seconds SWE-FRG, December 28, 1983 (Tomas Sandstrom (SWE) 16:16, Tommy Lehmann (SWE) 16:29, Peter Draisaitl (FRG) 16:42, 1st)
33 seconds SWE-SUI, January 3, 2004 (Fredrik Johansson (SWE) 1:28, Christoph Roder (SUI) 1:41, Peter Guggisberg (SUI) 2:01, 2nd)

**FASTEST FOUR GOALS, TEAM**
1:08 CAN, December 28, 1983 vs. SUI (Russ Courtnall 18:15, Dave Gagner 18:29, Dave Gagner 18:38, Dean Evason 19:23, 2nd)

**FASTEST FOUR GOALS, BOTH TEAMS**
42 seconds URS-USA, December 26, 1985 (Sergei Garpenko (URS) 16:19, Mike Kelfer (USA) 16:27, Ravil Kaidarov (URS) 19:36, Scott Young (USA) 17:01, 2nd)
1:03 TCH-SUI, December 29, 1983 (Philipp Neuenschwander (SUI) 7:08, Kamil Kastak (TCH) 7:25, Petr Rosol (TCH), 7:49, Igor Talpas (TCH) 8:11, 3rd)

**FASTEST FIVE GOALS, TEAM**
1:55 URS, December 25, 1983 vs. SUI (Sergei Nemchinov 10:15, Igor Vyazmikin 10:31, Alexander Smirnov 11:15, Andrei Lomakin 11:49, Yevgeni Chizamin 12:10, 1st)

**FASTEST FIVE GOALS, BOTH TEAMS**
2:12 TCH-SUI, December 29, 1983 (Vladimir Kames (TCH) 5:59, Philipp Neuenschwander (SUI) 7:08, Kamil Kastak (TCH) 7:25, Petr Rosol (TCH) 7:49, Igor Talpas (TCH) 8:11, 3rd)

**FASTEST SIX GOALS, TEAM**
3:59 USA, January 1, 1991 vs. NOR (Bill Lindsay 9:47, Pat Neaton 10:36, Ted Drury 11:50, Chris Gotziaman 12:57, Keith Tkachuk 13:00, Aaron Miller 13:46, 1st)
4:35 CAN, December 30, 1986 vs. POL (Everett Sanipass 13:30, Brendan Shanahan 13:43, Theo Fleury 15:22, Scott Metcalfe 16:17, Pierre Turgeon 16:53, Everett Sanipass 18:05, 1st)

**FASTEST SIX GOALS, BOTH TEAMS**
4:19 FIN-URS, January 1, 1977 (Risto Siltanen (FIN) 12:10, Alexander Frolikov (URS) 12:46, Juha Jyrkkio (FIN) 13:06, Juha Jyrkkio (FIN) 14:02, Alexander Khabanov (URS) 15:05, Alexander Frolikov (URS) 6:29, 3rd)

*Canada's Eric Daze once scored eight seconds from the start of a period to tie a U20 record. Photo: Matthew Manor / HHOF.*

# U18 World Championship (Men)

## All-Time Team Records

### LONGEST WINNING STREAK
18 games United States, April 14, 2010-present
12 games United States, April 14, 2005-April 22, 2006

### LONGEST UNDEFEATED STREAK
18 games United States, April 14, 2010-present
12 games United States, April 14, 2005-April 22, 2006
9 games Russia, April 22, 2003-April 16, 2005

### LONGEST LOSING STREAK
17 games Denmark, April 16, 2004-April 16, 2012
12 games Ukraine, April 12, 2001-April 18, 2002

### LONGEST WINLESS STREAK
19 games Norway, April 18, 2002-April 16, 2009
19 games Ukraine, April 16, 1999-April 18, 2002

## Goal-Scoring Team Records

### MOST GOALS, GAME
15 CAN 15-DEN 1, April 18, 2005
13 SUI 13-KAZ 2, April 13, 2003
12 USA 12-BLR 1, April 17, 2006
12 RUS 12-GER 4, April 17, 2005
12 RUS 12-SUI 3, April 14, 2003

### MOST GOALS, BOTH TEAMS SCORING, GAME
16 CAN 15-DEN 1, April 18, 2005
16 RUS 12-GER 4, April 17, 2005
15 RUS 12-SUI 3, April 14, 2003
15 SUI 13-KAZ 2, April 13, 2003

### MOST GOALS, PERIOD
7 Canada, 2nd period vs. Germany, April 9, 2009
7 Russia, 1st period vs. Germany, April 17, 2005
7 Russia, 2nd period vs. Belarus, April 20, 2002
7 Russia, 2nd period vs. Norway, April 15, 2001
7 Russia, 2nd period vs. Belarus, April 16, 2000

### MOST GOALS, BOTH TEAMS SCORING, PERIOD
9 USA 8-BLR 1, 2nd period, April 17, 2006
9 CAN 8-DEN 1, 3rd period, April 18, 2005

### SCORELESS GAMES
CAN-FIN, April 17, 2006

## Power-Play and Short-Handed Goals Records

### MOST POWER-PLAY GOALS, TEAM, GAME
7 USA, April 12, 2004 vs. BLR
7 USA, April 17, 2006 vs. BLR
6 USA, April 11, 2002 vs. BLR
6 USA, April 15, 2011 vs. SVK

### MOST POWER-PLAY GOALS, INDIVIDUAL, GAME
3 Phil Kessel, USA, April 12, 2004 vs. BLR
3 Justin Azevedo, April 13, 2006 vs. NOR
3 Erik Johnson, USA, April 17, 2006 vs. BLR
3 Matt Duchene, CAN, April 18, 2008 vs. SVK

### MOST POWER-PLAY GOALS, TEAM, PERIOD
5 USA, 3rd period, April 11, 2002 vs. BLR
4 RUS, 1st period, April 17, 2005 vs. GER
4 USA, 2nd period, April 17, 2006 vs. BLR

### MOST POWER-PLAY GOALS, BOTH TEAMS, PERIOD
5 USA 5, BLR 0, 3rd period, April 11, 2002
5 USA 4, BLR 1, 2nd period, April 17, 2006
4 RUS 4, GER 0, 1st period, April 17, 2005
4 CAN 3, NOR 1, 2nd period, April 13, 2006
4 USA 4, BLR 0, 2nd period, April 17, 2006
4 SUI 2, CZE 2, 2nd period, April 10, 2009
4 BLR 2, CAN 2, 2nd period, April 15, 2010

### MOST POWER-PLAY GOALS, BOTH TEAMS, GAME
7 RUS 5, SUI 2, April 14, 2003
7 CAN 5, NOR 2, April 13, 2006
6 USA 4, NOR 2, April 12, 1999
6 SVK 4, SWE 2, April 13, 2007
6 USA 4, RUS 2, April 14, 2009
6 SUI 3, NOR 3, April 16, 2009

### MOST SHORT-HANDED GOALS, TEAM, GAME
3 SWE, April 16, 2003 vs. BLR

### MOST SHORT-HANDED GOALS, INDIVIDUAL, GAME & PERIOD
2 Igor Makarov (RUS), 3rd period, April 17, 2005 vs. GER
2 Toni Rajala, FIN, 2nd period, April 13, 2009 vs. NOR

### MOST SHORT-HANDED GOALS, TEAM, PERIOD
2 RUS, 2nd period, April 16, 2000 vs. BLR
2 RUS, 2nd period, April 15, 2001 vs. NOR
2 SWE, 2nd period, April 16, 2003 vs. BLR
2 RUS, 3rd period, April 17, 2005 vs. GER
2 RUS, 1st period, April 15, 2006 vs. GER
2 USA, 3rd period, April 23, 2011 vs. CAN

### MOST SHORT-HANDED GOALS, BOTH TEAMS, GAME
3 RUS 2, GER 1, April 15, 2006

## All-Time Individual Records

### MOST U18 WORLD CHAMPIONSHIPS PLAYED
3 Michael Frolik (CZE)
3 Andrei Kostitsyn (BLR)
3 Alexei Shagov (BLR)
3 Olexander Skorokhod (UKR)
3 Konstantin Zakharov (BLR)

### MOST GOLD MEDALS
2 Tyler Biggs (USA), Jack Campbell (USA), Adam Clendening (USA), Rocco Grimaldi (USA), Erik Johnson (USA), John Merrill (USA), Matt Nieto (USA), Jason Zucker (USA)

### MOST MEDALS
2 (2 gold) Tyler Biggs (USA), Jack Campbell (USA), Adam Clendening (USA), Rocco Grimaldi (USA), Erik Johnson (USA), John Merrill (USA), Matt Nieto (USA), Jason Zucker (USA)
2 (gold, silver) Anton Babchuk (RUS), Maxim Chudinov (RUS), Cade Fairchild (USA), Nikita Filatov (RUS), Jeff Frazee (USA), Nathan Gerbe (USA), Ryan Hayes (USA), Jack Johnson (USA), Zachary Jones (USA), Phil Kessel (USA), Igor Knyazev (RUS), Ilya Kovalchuk (RUS), Dmitri Kugryshev (RUS), Dmitri Kulikov (RUS), Andrei Loktionov (RUS), Andrei Medvedev (RUS), Jim O'Brien (USA), Kirill Petrov (RUS), Jack Skille (USA), Yuri Trubachev (RUS), James van Riemsdyk (USA), Vyacheslav Voinov (RUS), Colin Wilson (USA)
2 (gold, bronze) Anton Belov (RUS), Ryan Bourque (USA), Mikko Koivu (FIN), Kari Lehtonen (FIN), Yevgeni Malkin (RUS), Jeremy Morin (USA)
2 (2 silver) Jonas Brodin (SWE), Joachim Nermark (SWE), Victor Rask (SWE), Dmitri Orlov (RUS)
2 (silver, bronze) Tim Eriksson (SWE), Magnus Hedlund (SWE), Jonas Nordqvist (SWE), Alexander Ovechkin (RUS), Martin Samuelsson (SWE), Vinny Saponari (USA), Jordan Schroeder (USA)
2 (2 bronze) Michael Frolik (CZE), Mikael Granlund (FIN), Teemu Pulkkinen (FIN)

### MOST GAMES PLAYED
20 Andrei Kostitsyn (BLR)
19 Alexei Shagov (BLR)
19 Konstantin Zakharov (BLR)
16 Michael Frolik (CZE)
16 Olexander Skorokhod (UKR)

### MOST POINTS, CAREER
31 Alexander Ovechkin (RUS—23+8)
26 Mikael Granlund (FIN—6+20)
26 Phil Kessel (USA—16+10))
26 Kevin Romy (SUI—13+13)
25 Andrei Kostitsyn (BLR—13+12)
25 Yevgeni Kuznetsov (RUS—11+14)
24 Tony Rajala (FIN—13+11)
22 Konstantin Zakharov (BLR—6+16)
21 Nikita Kucherov (RUS—11+10)

### MOST POINTS, ONE U18
21 Nikita Kucherov (RUS, 2011—11+10)
19 Tony Rajala (FIN, 2009—10+9)
18 Mikhail Grigorenko (RUS, 2011—4+14)
18 Alexander Ovechkin (RUS, 2002—14+4)
16 Phil Kessel (USA, 2005—9+7)
16 Konstantin Zakharov (BLR, 2003—5+11)

### MOST GOALS, CAREER
23 Alexander Ovechkin (RUS)
17 Teemu Pulkkinen (FIN)
16 Phil Kessel (USA)
13 Andrei Kostitsyn (BLR)
13 Ilya Kovalchuk (RUS)
13 Tony Rajala (FIN)
13 Kevin Romy (SUI)

### MOST GOALS, ONE U18
14 Alexander Ovechkin (RUS, 2002)
11 Nikita Kucherov (RUS, 2011)
11 Ilya Kovalchuk (RUS, 2001)
10 Tony Rajala (FIN, 2009)
9 Phil Kessel (USA, 2005)
9 Alexander Ovechkin (RUS, 2003)
9 Konstantin Pushkaryov (KAZ, 2003)
9 Kevin Romy (SUI, 2002)
9 Brett Sterling (USA, 2002)

### MOST ASSISTS, CAREER
20 Mikael Granlund (FIN)
16 Konstantin Zakharov (BLR)
14 Rocco Grimaldi (USA)
14 Yevgeni Kuznetsov (RUS)
13 Markus Granlund (FIN)
13 Kevin Romy (SUI)

### MOST ASSISTS, ONE U18
14 Mikhail Grigorenko (RUS, 2011)
11 Mikael Granlund (FIN, 2009)
11 Konstantin Zakharov (BLR, 2003)
11 Albert Yarullin (RUS, 2011)
10 Cody Hodgson (CAN, 2008)
10 Nikita Kucherov (RUS, 2011)

### MOST PENALTY MINUTES, CAREER
70 Alexei Shagov (BLR)
68 Philippe Seydoux (SUI)
62 David Ruzicka (CZE)
60 Boris Valabik (SVK)

### MOST PENALTY MINUTES, ONE U18
68 Philippe Seydoux (SUI, 2003)
52 David Ruzicka (CZE, 2006)
49 Tyler Biggs (USA, 2011)
47 Alan Tallarini (SUI, 2002)
46 Yevgeni Haranin (BLR, 2004)
46 Ilmari Pitkanen (FIN, 2008)

### MOST POINTS, GAME
7 Toni Rajala (FIN), April 13, 2009 vs. NOR (3 goals, 4 assists)
6 Kevin Romy (SUI), April 11, 2002 vs. UKR (4 goals, 2 assists)
6 Kevin Romy (SUI), April 13, 2003 vs. KAZ (3 goals, 3 assists)
6 Ben Maxwell (CAN), April 13, 2006 vs. NOR (1 goal, 5 assists)
6 Teemu Pulkkinen (FIN), April 13, 2009 vs. NOR (3 goals, 3 assists)
6 Mikael Granlund (FIN), April 13, 2009 vs. NOR (1 goal, 5 assists)

6 Mika Zibanejad (SWE), April 15, 2011 vs. NOR (3 goals, 3 assists)
6 Mikhail Grigorenko (RUS), April 19, 2011 vs. SUI (2 goals, 4 assists)

**MOST POINTS, PERIOD**
5 Ben Maxwell (CAN), 2nd period, April 13, 2006 vs. NOR (1 goal, 4 assists)
5 Toni Rajala (FIN), 2nd period, April 13, 2009 vs. NOR (3 goals, 2 assists)
4 Michal Kolarik (SVK), 1st period, April 15, 2000 vs. BLR (1 goal, 3 assists)
4 Konstantin Pushkarov (KAZ), 2nd period, April 20, 2003 vs. BLR (3 goals, 1 assist)
4 Mikael Granlund (FIN), 2nd period, April 13, 2009 vs. NOR (1 goal, 3 assists)
4 Mikael Granlund (SWE), 3rd period, April 23, 2010 vs. RUS (1 goal, 3 assists)
4 Nail Yakupov (RUS), 1st period, April 19, 2011 vs. SUI (1 goal, 3 assists)

**MOST GOALS, ONE GAME**
4 Marian Gaborik (SVK), April 15, 2000 vs. BLR
4 Tuomo Ruutu (FIN), April 19, 2000 vs. BLR
4 Kevin Romy (SUI), April 11, 2002 vs. UKR
4 Alexander Ovechkin (RUS), April 12, 2002 vs. SVK
4 Roman Tomanek (SVK), April 11, 2004 vs. NOR
4 Ruslan Bashkirov (RUS), April 15, 2006 vs. GER
4 Erik Johnson (USA), April 17, 2006 vs. BLR

**MOST GOALS, PERIOD**
3 Marian Gaborik (SVK), 1st period, April 15, 2000 vs. BLR
3 Konstantin Pushkarov (KAZ), 2nd period, April 20, 2003 vs. BLR
3 Toni Rajala (FIN), 2nd period, April 13, 2009 vs. NOR

**MOST ASSISTS, GAME**
5 Ben Maxwell (CAN), April 13, 2006 vs. NOR
5 Mikael Granlund (FIN), April 13, 2009 vs. NOR
4 John Sabo (USA), April 15, 1999 vs. GER
4 Adam Bezak (SVK), April 13, 2007 vs. SWE
4 Toni Rajala (FIN), April 13, 2009 vs. NOR
4 Mikhail Grigorenko (RUS), April 19, 2011 vs. SUI

**MOST ASSISTS, PERIOD**
4 Ben Maxwell (CAN), 2nd period, April 13, 2006 vs. NOR
3 Michal Kolarik (SVK), 1st period, April 15, 2000 vs. BLR
3 Pelle Andersson (SWE), 2nd period, April 24, 2000 vs. SUI
3 Michael Eskesen (DEN), 3rd period, April 15, 2004 vs. NOR
3 Tomas Kudelka (CZE), 2nd period, April 18, 2005 vs. FIN
3 Dennis Persson (SWE), 1st period, April 17, 2006 vs. SVK
3 Eetu Poysti (FIN), 1st period, April 15, 2007 vs. CZE
3 Marcus Johansson (SWE), 3rd period, April 22, 2007 vs. CAN
3 Anton Lander (SWE), 3rd period, April 13, 2009 vs. SUI
3 Teemu Pulkkinen (FIN), 2nd period, April 13, 2009 vs. NOR
3 Mikael Granlund (SWE), 2nd period, April 13, 2010 vs. LAT
3 Nail Yakupov (RUS), 1st period, April 19, 2011 vs. SUI

**PENALTY SHOTS**
April 14, 2000 United States stopped by Andrei Medvedev (RUS)
April 14, 2000 United States stopped by Andrei Medvedev (RUS)
April 15, 2000 Alexander Dubovik (BLR) scored on Peter Budaj (SVK)
April 15, 2000 Finland stopped by Nick Pannoni (USA)
April 16, 2000 Russia stopped by Yuri Melnikov (BLR)
April 22, 2000 Marcel Goc (GER) scored on Nick Pannoni (USA)
April 12, 2002 Milan Michalek (CZE) scored on Vegard Sagbakken (NOR)
April 14, 2002 Alexander Steen (SWE) scored on Yevgeniy Galyuk (UKR)
April 18, 2002 Denys Ryabtsev (UKR) stopped by Jaroslav Halak (SVK)
April 21, 2002 Konstantin Zakharov (BLR) stopped by Tyler Weiman (CAN)
April 12, 2003 Konstantin Pushkarev (KAZ) scored on Jakub Cech (CZE)
April 8, 2004 Mathis Olimb (NOR) stopped by Anton Khudobin (RUS)
April 9, 2004 Lauri Tuokonen (FIN) scored on Lars Haugen (NOR)
April 12, 2004 Kevin Porter (USA) scored on Ihar Brikun (BLR)
April 12, 2004 Denis Parshin (RUS) stopped by Tuukka Rask (FIN)
April 13, 2004 Roman Tomanek (SVK) stopped by Anton Khudobin (RUS)
April 12, 2006 Bill Sweatt (USA) scored on Semyon Varlamov (RUS)
April 14, 2006 Michael Frolik (CZE) stopped by Vitali Trus (BLR)
April 20, 2007 Mikael Backlund (SWE) scored on Alexander Pechurski (RUS)
April 14, 2008 Nikita Filatov (RUS) stopped by Felix Bruckmann (GER)
April 16, 2008 Danny Kristo (USA) stopped by Jacob Markstrom (SWE)
April 10, 2009 Andrej Nestrasil (CZE) stopped by Benjamin Conz (SUI)
April 13, 2009 A.J. Treais (USA) stopped by Tomas Pek (SVK)
April 16, 2009 Yevgeni Kuznetsov (RUS) scored on Robin Lehner (SWE)
April 17, 2009 Tomas Jurko (SVK) stopped by Lukas Steinhauer (GER)
April 18, 2009 Mats Rosseli-Olsen (NOR) stopped by Lukas Steinhauer (GER)
April 16, 2011 Maxim Shalunov (RUS) scored on Marvin Cupper (GER)
April 19, 2011 William Karlsson (SWE) stopped by Malcolm Subban (CAN)
April 21, 2011 Lukas Sedlak (CZE) scored on Patrik Rybar (SVK)
Gustav Possler (SWE) stopped by Niklas Schlegel (SUI), April 14, 2012
Matt Lane (USA) stopped by Matt Murray (CAN), April 17, 2012
Brendan Gaunce (CAN) stopped by Joonas Korpisalo (FIN), April 22, 2012

## Goaltender Records

**MOST GOLD MEDALS**
2 Jack Campbell (USA)

**MOST MEDALS**
2 (2 gold) Jack Campbell (USA)
2 (gold, silver) Jeff Frazee (USA), Andrei Medvedev (RUS)
2 (gold, bronze) Kari Lehtonen (FIN)

**MOST U18 PARTICIPATED IN, GOALIE**
(listed alphabetically)
2 Valentyn Chernenko (UKR), Benjamin Conz (SUI), Sebastian Dahm (DEN), Jhonas Enroth (SWE), Jeff Frazee (USA), Johann Gustafsson (SWE), Jaroslav Halak (SVK), Peter Hamerlik (SVK), Christopher Heino-Lindberg (SWE), Alexei Gritsenko (BLR), Kari Lehtonen (FIN), Andrei Medvedev (RUS), Dmitri Milchakov (BLR), Dimitri Patzold (GER), Alexander Pechurski (RUS), Timo Pielmeier (GER), Tuukka Rask (FIN), Vegard Sagbakken (NOR), Marek Schwarz (CZE), Tobias Stephan (SUI), Semyon Varlamov (RUS), Andrei Vasilevski (RUS), Travis Weber (USA)

**MOST GAMES PLAYED, GOALIE, CAREER**
14 Jaroslav Halak (SVK)
14 Tobias Stephan (SUI)
12 Valentyn Chernenko (UKR)
12 Dimitri Patzold (GER)
12 Timo Pielmeier (GER)
12 Marek Schwarz (CZE)

**MOST MINUTES PLAYED, GOALIE, CAREER**
846:02 Jaroslav Halak (SVK)
800:00 Tobias Stephan (SUI)
720:00 Dimitri Patzold (GER)
707:41 Marek Schwarz (CZE)
669:37 Timo Pielmeier (GER)

**MOST WINS, GOALIE, CAREER**
9 Jack Campbell (USA)
9 Tobias Stephan (SWE)
8 Jaroslav Halak (SVK)
8 Kari Lehtonen (FIN)
7 Andrei Medvedev (RUS)

**MOST WINS, GOALIE, ONE U18**
6 John Gibson (USA, 2011)
6 Jake Allen (CAN, 2008)
6 Jeff Frazee (USA, 2005)
6 Lukas Mensator (CZE, 2002)

**MOST LOSSES, GOALIE, CAREER**
9 Valentyn Chernenko (UKR)
8 Sebastian Dahm (DEN)
7 Timo Pielmeier (GER)

**MOST LOSSES, GOALIE, ONE U18**
6 Sebastian Dahm (DEN, 2005)
6 Andrei Podoinikov (KAZ, 2003)

**MOST SHUTOUTS, CAREER**
5 Jack Campbell (USA)
3 Kari Lehtonen (FIN)

**MOST SHUTOUTS, ONE U18**
3 Jack Campbell (USA, 2010)
3 Collin Olson (USA, 2012)
2 Jake Allen (CAN, 2008)
2 Konstantin Barulin (RUS, 2002)
2 Jack Campbell (USA, 2009)
2 Peter Hamerlik (SVK, 1999)
2 Kari Lehtonen (FIN, 2001)
2 Ryan Munce (CAN, 2003)
2 Mark Owuya (SWE, 2007)
2 Vadym Seliverstov (UKR, 1999)
2 Tobias Stephan (SUI, 2002)

**BEST GOALS AGAINST AVERAGE, CAREER**
(minimum 400 minutes)
0.80 Jack Campbell (USA)
1.43 Jake Allen (CAN)
1.57 Lukas Mensator (CZE)
1.61 Marek Schwarz (CZE)

**GOALIE GOALS**
Anton Khudobin (RUS) scored into the empty net on April 12, 2004 vs. FIN (RUS 5-FIN 2)

**MOST ASSISTS, GOALIE, CAREER**
2 Rick DiPietro (USA, 1999)
2 Jack Campbell (USA, 2010)

**MOST PENALTY MINUTES, GOALIE, CAREER**
6 Samu Perhonen (FIN)

**LONGEST SHUTOUT SEQUENCE, TEAM (IN MINUTES)**
227:19 USA, April 12-17, 2006
202:45 USA, April 12-17. 2012
191:22 USA, April 18-23, 2010

## Shots On Goal Records

**MOST SHOTS, TEAM, GAME**
88 RUS, April 16, 2000 vs. BLR
79 FIN, April 19, 2000 vs. BLR
77 SWE, April 15, 2011 vs. NOR
76 GER, April 21, 2000 vs. BLR

**MOST SHOTS, BOTH TEAMS, GAME**
111 SWE 69-FIN 42, April 22, 2000
107 RUS 88-BLR 19, April 16, 2000
101 GER 76-BLR 25, April 21, 2000
100 RUS 70-FIN 30, April 17, 2000
100 FIN 79-BLR 21, April 19, 2000

**MOST SHOTS, TEAM, PERIOD**
41 SWE, 3rd period, April 15, 1999 vs. RUS
36 RUS, 1st period, April 16, 2000 vs. BLR
32 USA, 2nd period, April 17, 2006 vs. BLR

**MOST SHOTS, BOTH TEAMS, PERIOD**
59 SWE 41-RUS 18, 3rd period, April 15, 1999
41 FIN 25-SVK 16, 2nd period, April 14, 2000
40 FIN 27-BLR 13, 2nd period, April 12, 2002

#### FEWEST SHOTS, TEAM, GAME
6 GER, April 15, 1999 vs. USA
8 UKR, April 13, 2001 vs. USA
8 BLR, Apr 14, 2010 vs. SWE

#### FEWEST SHOTS, BOTH TEAMS, GAME
41 SWE 24-GER 17, April 18, 2002
42 SUI 26-DEN 16, April 22, 2005

#### FEWEST SHOTS, TEAM, PERIOD
0 BLR, 2nd period, April 15, 2004 vs. FIN
0 SVK, 3rd period, April 17, 2007 vs. FIN

#### FEWEST SHOTS, BOTH TEAMS, PERIOD
5 FIN 4-CZE 1, 3rd period, April 18, 2005
7 NOR 4-GER 3, 2nd period, April 16, 1999
7 RUS 5-DEN 2, 2nd period, April 18, 2008

## Penalty Records

#### FEWEST PENALTIES, TEAM, GAME
1 NOR, April 12, 2001 vs. SWE
1 LAT, April 14, 2007 vs. CAN
1 SUI, April 19, 2007 vs. RUS
1 FIN, April 20, 2007 vs. LAT
1 CAN, April 13, 2008 vs. GER
1 FIN, April 19, 2012 vs. GER
1 SWE, April 22, 2012 vs. USA

#### FEWEST PENALTY MINUTES, TEAM, GAME
2 NOR, April 12, 2001 vs. SWE
2 LAT, April 14, 2007 vs. CAN
2 SUI, April 19, 2007 vs. RUS
2 FIN, April 20, 2007 vs. LAT
2 CAN, April 13, 2008 vs. GER
2 FIN, April 19, 2012 vs. GER
2 SWE, April 22, 2012 vs. USA

#### FEWEST PENALTIES, BOTH TEAMS, GAME
3 SWE 2-NOR 1, April 12, 2001

#### FEWEST PENALTY MINUTES, BOTH TEAMS, GAME
6 SWE 4-NOR 2, April 12, 2001

#### MOST PENALTY MINUTES, TEAM, GAME
141 DEN, April 20, 2012 vs. SUI
131 SUI, April 20, 2012 vs. DEN
126 CZE, April 20, 2002 vs. USA
111 RUS, April 18, 1999 vs. SUI
110 USA, April 20, 2002 vs. CZE

#### MOST PENALTY MINUTES, BOTH TEAMS, GAME
272 DEN 141-SUI 131, April 20, 2012
236 CZE 126-USA 110, April 20, 2002
192 RUS 99-FIN 93, April 23, 2010

#### MOST PENALTY MINUTES, TEAM, PERIOD
129 SUI, 3rd period, April 20, 2012 vs. DEN
127 DEN, 3rd period, April 20. 2012 vs. SUI
116 CZE, 3rd period, April 20, 2002 vs. USA
104 USA, 3rd period, April 20, 2002 vs. CZE
103 RUS, 3rd period, April 18, 1999 vs. SUI

#### MOST PENALTY MINUTES, BOTH TEAMS, PERIOD
256 SUI 129-DEN 127, 3rd period, April 20, 2012
220 CZE 116-USA 104, 3rd period, April 20, 2002
174 RUS 87-FIN 87, 3rd period, April 23, 2010
153 RUS 103-SUI 50, 3rd period, April 18, 1999

#### MOST PENALTIES, TEAM, GAME
25 RUS, April 19, 2000 vs. SVK
21 RUS, April 17, 2001 vs. SWE
19 SVK, April 19, 2000 vs. RUS
18 UKR, April 13, 1999 vs. SWE
18 BLR, April 14, 2003 vs. FIN

#### MOST PENALTIES, BOTH TEAMS, GAME
44 RUS 25-SVK 19, April 19, 2000
36 RUS 21-SWE 15, April 17, 2001
30 NOR 16-USA 14, April 12, 1999
30 CZE 17-USA 13, April 20, 2002

#### MOST PENALTIES, TEAM, PERIOD
12 RUS, 3rd period, April 18, 1999 vs. SUI
12 CZE, 3rd period, April 20, 2002 vs. USA
11 RUS, 3rd period, April 19, 2000 vs. SVK
11 RUS, 3rd period, April 23, 2010 vs. FIN
11 SUI, 3rd period, April 20, 2012 vs. DEN

#### MOST PENALTIES, BOTH TEAMS, PERIOD
22 CZE 12-USA 10, 3rd period, April 20, 2002
21 SUI 11-DEN 10, 3rd period, April 20. 2012
20 RUS 10-SVK 10, 3rd period, April 19, 2000
18 RUS 11-FIN 7, 3rd period, April 23, 2010
16 RUS 12-SUI 4, 3rd period, April 18, 1999
16 SWE 9-CAN 7, 2nd period, April 15, 2006

#### MOST PENALTY MINUTES, INDIVIDUAL, GAME
36 David Ruzicka (CZE), April 22, 2006 vs. CAN (game misconduct, misconduct, 3 minors)
33 Vyacheslav Kulyomin (RUS), April 23, 2008 vs. CAN (3 minors, major, game misconduct)
31 Vadim Karaga (BLR), April 16, 2003 vs. SWE (3 minors, major, game misconduct)
30 Ilmari Pitkanen (FIN), 3rd period, April 22, 2008 (misconduct, game misconduct)

#### MOST PENALTY MINUTES, INDIVIDUAL, PERIOD
33 Vyacheslav Kulyomin (RUS), 3rd period, April 23, 2008 vs. CAN (3 minors, major, game misconduct)
32 David Ruzicka (CZE), 3rd period, April 22, 2006 vs. CAN (game misconduct, misconduct, minor)
30 Ilmari Pitkanen (FIN), 3rd period, April 22, 2008 (misconduct, game misconduct)

#### MOST PENALTIES, INDIVIDUAL, GAME
5 Vyacheslav Kulyomin (RUS), April 23, 2008 vs. CAN (3 minors, major, game misconduct)
5 Andy Rogers, CAN, April 8, 2004 vs. SWE (4 minors, 1 misconduct)
5 Joonas Lehtivuori, FIN, April 17, 2006 (5 minors)
5 Jan Platil (CZE), April 16, 2001 vs. NOR (4 minors, misconduct)
5 Gustav Grassberg (SWE), April 17, 2001 vs. RUS (5 minors)
5 Vadim Karaga (BLR), April 16, 2003 vs. SWE (3 minors, major, game misconduct)

#### MOST PENALTIES, INDIVIDUAL, PERIOD
5 Vyacheslav Kulyomin (RUS), 3rd period, April 23, 2008 vs. CAN (3 minors, major, game misconduct)
4 Adam Berti, CAN, 1st period, April 11, 2004 vs. DEN (3 minors, misconduct)

## Speed Records

#### FASTEST GOAL FROM START OF GAME
9 seconds Peter Guggisberg (SUI), April 16, 2003 vs. CZE
9 seconds Maximilian Forster (GER), April 16, 2008 vs. SVK

#### FASTEST GOAL FROM START OF PERIOD
8 seconds Jarod Palmer (USA), 2nd period, April 10, 2004 vs. SWE
12 seconds Mikael Granlund (FIN), 3rd period, April 11, 2009 vs. USA

#### FASTEST TWO GOALS, INDIVIDUAL
23 seconds Simon Hjalmarsson (SWE), 1:10 & 1:33, 2nd period, April 20, 2007 vs. RUS
25 seconds Peter Rohn (NOR), 16:18 & 16:43, 3rd period, April 20, 2006 vs. BLR

#### FASTEST TWO GOALS, TEAM
5 seconds RUS—Ilya Krikunov (14:22) & Yevgeni Tunik (14:27), 3rd period, April 15, 2002 vs. GER
8 seconds RUS—Sergei Ogorodnikov (8:19) & Dmitri Shitikov (8:27), 2nd period, April 8, 2004 vs. NOR

#### FASTEST TWO GOALS, BOTH TEAMS
7 seconds Alexander Dubovik (BLR) 7:04 & Vladislav Luchkin (RUS), 7:11, 3rd period, April 16, 2000

#### FASTEST TWO POWER-PLAY GOALS, TEAM
11 seconds CAN—Ryan Spooner (18:58) & Christian Thomas (19:09), 1st period, April 22, 2010 vs. SVK

#### FASTEST TWO POWER-PLAY GOALS, INDIVIDUAL
40 seconds Dmitri Malkov (BLR), April 18, 2000 vs. GER

#### FASTEST TWO SHORT-HANDED GOALS, TEAM
33 seconds USA—Zach Larraza (6:43) & Reid Boucher (7:16), 3rd period, April 23, 2011 vs. CAN

#### FASTEST TWO SHORT-HANDED GOALS, INDIVIDUAL
24 seconds Igor Makarov (RUS), 17:45 & 18:09, 3rd period, April 17, 2005 vs. GER

#### FASTEST THREE GOALS, INDIVIDUAL
7:14 Konstantin Pushkarev (KAZ), April 20, 2003 vs. BLR (11:26, 13:16, 18:40, 2nd period)

#### FASTEST THREE GOALS, TEAM
45 seconds RUS—Alexander Svitov (2:25), Vladislav Lutchkin (2:39), Alexander Tatarinov (3:1), 1st period, April 16, 2000 vs. BLR

#### FASTEST THREE GOALS, BOTH TEAMS
1:02 Emil Bejmo (SWE) 11:22, Mikael Backlund (SWE) 12:14, Angelo Esposito (CAN) 12:24, 3rd period, April 22, 2007

#### FASTEST THREE POWER-PLAY GOALS, TEAM
2:15 USA—Zach Parise (11:13), Patrick O'Sullivan (12:49), Steve Werner (13:28), 3rd period, April 11, 2002 vs. BLR

#### FASTEST FOUR GOALS, TEAM
2:02 CAN—Ryan O'Marra (7:51), Dan Bertram (8:26), Colton Yellowhorn (9:34), Devin Setoguchi (9:53), 3rd period, April 18, 2005 vs. DEN

#### FASTEST FOUR GOALS, BOTH TEAMS
2:00 Sebastian Uvira (GER) 8:26, Rocco Grimaldi (USA) 9:16, Daniel Fischbuch (GER) 10:00, Reid Boucher (USA) 10:26, 2nd period, April 19, 2011

#### FASTEST FOUR POWER-PLAY GOALS, TEAM
4:00 USA—Brett Sterling (9:28), Zach Parise (11:13), Patrick O'Sullivan (12:49), Steve Werner (13:28), 3rd period, April 11, 2002 vs. BLR

#### FASTEST FIVE GOALS, TEAM
3:52 CAN—Ryan O'Marra (6:01), O'Marra (7:51), Dan Bertram (8:26), Colton Yellowhorn (9:34), Devin Setoguchi (9:53), 3rd period, April 18, 2005 vs. DEN
4:21 RUS—Dmitri Zyuzin (2:43), Alexander Bumagin (4:03), Ilya Zubov (4:43), Alexei Sopin (6:27), Denis Pakhomov (7:04), 1st period, April 17, 2005 vs. GER

#### FASTEST FIVE POWER-PLAY GOALS, TEAM
5:25 USA—Ryan Suter (8:03), Brett Sterling (9:28), Zach Parise (11:13), Patrick O'Sullivan (12:49), Steve Werner (13:28), 3rd period, April 11, 2002 vs. BLR

# Olympics, Women

## All-Time Team Records

**LONGEST WINNING & UNDEFEATED STREAK**
15 games CAN, February 11, 2002-present
10 games USA, February 8, 1998-February 19, 2002

**LONGEST LOSING STREAK**
5 games SVK, February 13-22, 2010
5 games ITA, February 11-20, 2006
5 games KAZ, February 11-19, 2002
5 games JPN, February 8-14, 1998

**MOST GOALS, TEAM, ONE OG-W**
48 CAN, 2010
46 CAN, 2006
40 USA, 2010
36 USA, 1998

**FEWEST GOALS, TEAM, ONE OG-W**
2 JPN, 1998
2 KAZ, 2002

**MOST GOALS, TEAM, GAME**
18 February 13, 2010 Canada 18-Slovakia 0
16 February 11, 2006 Canada 16-Italy 0
13 February 17, 2010 Canada 13-Sweden 1
13 February 16, 2010 United States 13-Russia 0
13 February 8, 1998 Canada 13-Japan 0

**MOST GOALS, BOTH TEAMS, GAME (BOTH TEAMS SCORING)**
14 February 17, 2010 Canada 13-Sweden 1
13 February 14, 2002 United States 12-China 1

**MOST GOALS, TEAM, PERIOD**
7 CAN, 2nd period, February 17, 2010 vs. SWE
7 CAN, 1st period, February 13, 2010 vs. SWE
7 CAN, 1st period, February 12, 2006 vs. RUS
7 CAN, 3rd period, February 11, 2006 vs. ITA

**MOST GOALS, BOTH TEAMS, PERIOD (BOTH TEAMS SCORING)**
9 USA (6 goals) & CAN (3 goals), 3rd period, February 14, 1998

## Power-Play and Short-Handed Goals Records

**MOST POWER-PLAY GOALS, TEAM, GAME**
7 USA, February 16, 2010 vs. RUS
5 CAN, February 17, 2006 vs. FIN
5 CAN, February 11, 2002 vs. KAZ

**MOST POWER-PLAY GOALS, BOTH TEAMS, GAME (BOTH TEAMS SCORING)**
7 CAN (4) & USA (3), February 14, 1998

**MOST POWER-PLAY GOALS, INDIVIDUAL, GAME**
3 Kirsi Haninen, FIN, February 9, 1998 vs. JPN
2 Danielle Goyette, CAN, February 14, 2006 vs. SWE
2 Svetlana Trefilova, RUS, February 14, 2006 vs. ITA
2 Therese Sjolander, SWE, February 13, 2006 vs. ITA
2 Hayley Wickenheiser, CAN, February 11, 2002 vs. KAZ
2 Therese Brisson, CAN, February 19, 2002 vs. FIN
2 Lori Dupuis, CAN, February 14, 1998 vs. USA
2 Cammi Granato, USA, February 14, 1998 vs. CAN

**MOST POWER-PLAY GOALS, TEAM, PERIOD**
4 USA, 2nd, period, February 16, 2010 vs. RUS
3 CAN, 2nd period, February 14, 2006 vs. SWE
3 CAN, 3rd period, February 14, 1998 vs. USA

**MOST POWER-PLAY GOALS, BOTH TEAMS, PERIOD (BOTH TEAMS SCORING)**
4 CAN (3) & SWE (1), 2nd period, February 14, 2006

**MOST SHORT-HANDED GOALS, TEAM, GAME**
2 USA, February 16, 2010 vs. RUS
2 CAN, February 12, 2006 vs. RUS
2 USA, February 9, 1998 vs. SWE

**MOST SHORT-HANDED GOALS, TEAM, PERIOD**
2 CAN, February 12, 2006, 1st period, vs. RUS

## All-Time Individual Records

**MOST OLYMPICS**
4 (by country)
CAN Jennifer Botterill, Jayna Hefford, Becky Kellar, Hayley Wickenheiser
FIN Emma Laaksonen, Karoliina Rantamaki
SWE Gunilla Andersson, Erika Holst, Maria Rooth
USA Jenny Potter (-Schmidgall), Angela Ruggiero

**MOST GOLD MEDALS**
3 Jennifer Botterill (CAN), Jayna Hefford (CAN), Becky Kellar (CAN), Hayley Wickenheiser (CAN)

**MOST MEDALS**
4 (3G, 1S) Jennifer Botterill (CAN)
4 (3G, 1S) Jayna Hefford (CAN)
4 (3G, 1S) Becky Kellar (CAN)
4 (3G, 1S) Hayley Wickenheiser (CAN)
4 (1G, 2S, 1B) Jenny Potter (-Schmidgall) (USA)
4 (1G, 2S, 1B) Angela Ruggiero, (USA)

**MOST GAMES PLAYED**
21 (by country)
CAN Jennifer Botterill, Jayna Hefford, Becky Kellar, Hayley Wickenheiser
FIN Karoliina Rantamaki
USA Jenny Potter (-Schmidgall), Angela Ruggiero

20
SWE Gunilla Andersson, Erika Holst, Maria Rooth

**MOST POINTS, CAREER**
46 Hayley Wickenheiser, CAN
32 Jenny Potter (-Schmidgall), USA
30 Cherie Piper, CAN
27 Jayna Hefford, CAN
26 Caroline Ouellette, CAN
25 Natalie Darwitz, USA
25 Danielle Goyette, CAN
23 Katie King, USA
21 Gillian Apps, CAN

**MOST POINTS, ONE OG-W**
17 Hayley Wickenheiser, CAN, 2006
15 Meghan Agosta, CAN, 2010
15 Cherie Piper, CAN, 2006
14 Gillian Apps, CAN, 2006
12 Jayna Hefford, CAN, 2010
12 Riikka Nieminen (-Valila), 1998

**MOST GOALS, CAREER**
16 Hayley Wickenheiser, CAN
15 Danielle Goyette, CAN
15 Cherie Piper, CAN
14 Katie King, USA
14 Natalie Darwitz, USA

**MOST GOALS, ONE OG-W**
9 Meghan Agosta, CAN, 2010
8 Danielle Goyette, CAN, 1998
7 Gillian Apps, CAN, 2006
7 Cherie Piper, CAN, 2006
7 Natalie Darwitz, USA, 2002
7 Hayley Wickenheiser, CAN, 2002
7 Riikka Nieminen (-Valila), FIN, 1998

**MOST ASSISTS, CAREER**
30 Hayley Wickenheiser, CAN
21 Jenny Potter (-Schmidgall), USA
17 Caroline Ouellette, CAN
15 Cherie Piper, CAN
15 Jayna Hefford, CAN

**MOST ASSISTS, ONE OG-W**
12 Hayley Wickenheiser, CAN, 2006
9 Caroline Ouellette, CAN, 2010
9 Hayley Wickenheiser, CAN, 2010
8 Cherie Piper, CAN, 2006

**MOST PENALTY MINUTES, CAREER**
49 Tricia Dunn (-Luoma), USA
38 Angela Ruggiero, USA
36 Gunilla Andersson, SWE

**MOST PENALTY MINUTES, ONE OG-W**
34 Linda de Rocco, ITA, 2006
29 Tricia Dunn (-Luoma), USA, 2002
29 Kathrin Lehmann, SUI, 2006
20 Gunilla Andersson, SWE, 1998

**MOST GOALS, GAME**
4 Stephanie Marty (SUI), February 20, 2010 vs. CHN
4 Pernilla Winberg (SWE), February 15, 2010 vs. SVK

**MOST GOALS, PERIOD**
3 Larisa Mishina, RUS, 2nd period, February 17, 2006 vs. SUI
3 Caroline Ouellette, CAN, 1st period, February 11, 2006 vs. ITA

**MOST POINTS, GAME**
6 Jayna Hefford (CAN), February 13, 2010 vs. SVK (3 goals, 3 assists)
6 Cherie Piper (CAN), February 11, 2006 vs. ITA (1 goal, 5 assists)

**MOST POINTS, PERIOD**
4 Larisa Mishina, RUS, 2nd period, February 17, 2006 vs. SUI (3 goals, 1 assist)

**MOST ASSISTS, GAME**
5 Cherie Piper (CAN), February 11, 2006 vs. ITA

**MOST ASSISTS, PERIOD**
3 Hilary Knight (USA), 1st period, February 16, 2010 vs. RUS

**PENALTY SHOTS**
~there has never been a penalty shot in women's Olympic hockey

## Goaltender Records

**MOST TOURNAMENTS, GOALIE**
3 Kim St. Pierre (CAN), Irina Gashennikova (RUS), Kim Martin (SWE)

**MOST GAMES PLAYED, GOALIE, CAREER**
14 Irina Gashennikova, RUS
11 Hong Guo, CHN
10 Tuula Puputti, FIN
9 Kim Martin, SWE

**MOST MINUTES PLAYED, GOALIE, CAREER**
816:25 Irina Gashennikova, RUS
651:08 Hong Guo, CHN
570:04 Tuula Puputti, FIN
518:47 Kim Martin, SWE

**MOST WINS, GOALIE, CAREER**
8 Kim St. Pierre, CAN
7 Irina Gashennikova, RUS
5 Sara Decosta, USA
5 Kim Martin, SWE
5 Tuula Puputti, FIN
5 Sarah Tueting, USA

**MOST LOSSES, GOALIE, CAREER**
7 Irina Gashennikova, RUS
6 Hong Guo, CHN
5 Zuzana Tomcikova, SVK
4 Annica Ahlen, SWE
4 Stephanie Wartosch-Kurten, GER

**MOST SHUTOUTS, CAREER**
4 Kim St. Pierre, CAN
3 Sara Decosta, USA

**MOST SHUTOUTS, ONE OG-W**
2 Shannon Szabados, CAN, 2010
2 Jesse Vetter, USA, 2010
2 Charline Labonte, CAN, 2006
2 Sara Decosta, USA, 2002
2 Kim St. Pierre, CAN, 2002

**BEST GOALS AGAINST AVERAGE, CAREER**
(minimum 200 minutes)
0.78 Kim St. Pierre
0.91 Sarah Tueting
1.15 Manon Rheaume
1.27 Sara Decosta

**ALL GOALIE ASSISTS, CAREER**
1 Sara Decosta (USA)
1 Florence Schelling (SUI)
1 Kim St. Pierre (CAN)
1 Stephanie Wartosch-Kurten (GER)

**MOST PENALTY MINUTES, GOALIE, CAREER**
4 Hong Guo, CHN

## Shots On Goal Records

**MOST SHOTS, TEAM, GAME**
91 USA, February 12, 1998 vs. JPN
71 USA, February 14, 2002 vs. CHN
70 CAN, February 16, 2002 vs. SWE

**MOST SHOTS, BOTH TEAMS, GAME**
97 USA (91) & JPN (6), February 12, 1998
92 CAN (70) & SWE (22), February 16, 2002
91 CAN (70) & SWE (21), February 11, 1998

**MOST SHOTS, TEAM, PERIOD**
34 USA, 2nd period, February 12, 1998 vs. JPN
33 CAN, 3rd period, February 16, 2002 vs. SWE

**MOST SHOTS, BOTH TEAMS, PERIOD**
39 CAN (33) & SWE (6), 3rd period, February 16, 2002
36 USA (34) & JPN (2), 2nd period, February 12, 1998
36 CAN (28) & SWE (8), 2nd period, February 11, 1998

**FEWEST SHOTS, TEAM, GAME**
3 SWE, February 9, 1998 vs. USA
3 JPN, February 8, 1998 vs. CAN

**FEWEST SHOTS, BOTH TEAMS, GAME**
32 February 17, 1998 (FIN 23, CHN 9)
34 February 20, 2006 (CAN 26, SWE 8)
34 February 20, 2006 (USA 20, FIN 14)

**FEWEST SHOTS, TEAM, PERIOD**
0 ITA, 3rd period, February 13, 2006 vs. SWE
0 ITA, 3rd period, February 11, 2006 vs. CAN
0 JPN, 2nd period, February 11, 1998 vs. CHN
0 CHN, 1st period, February 8, 1998 vs. USA
0 JPN, 1st period, February 8, 1998 vs. CAN

**FEWEST SHOTS, BOTH TEAMS, PERIOD**
5 RUS 3-USA 2, 3rd period, February 16, 2010
7 USA 4-FIN 3, 2nd period, February 20, 2006
7 CAN 4-SWE 3, 3rd period, February 20, 2006

## Penalty Records

**FEWEST PENALTIES & PENALTY MINUTES, TEAM, GAME**
0 FIN, February 17, 1998 vs. CHN

**FEWEST PENALTY MINUTES, BOTH TEAMS, GAME**
8 February 17, 1998 (CHN 8, FIN 0)

**FEWEST PENALTIES, BOTH TEAMS, GAME**
4 February 17, 1998 (CHN 4, FIN 0)

**MOST PENALTY MINUTES, TEAM, GAME**
42 JPN, February 9, 1998 vs. FIN
41 SUI, February 14, 2006 vs. GER
38 USA, February 14, 2006 vs. FIN

**MOST PENALTY MINUTES, BOTH TEAMS, GAME**
60 February 14, 2006 (USA 38, FIN 22)
59 February 14, 2006 (SUI 41, GER 18)
58 February 9, 1998 (JPN, 42, FIN 16)
56 February 11, 1998 (SWE 36, CAN 20)

**MOST PENALTY MINUTES, TEAM, PERIOD**
31 SUI, 3rd period, February 14, 2006 vs. GER
30 JPN, 2nd period, February 9, 1998 vs. FIN

**MOST PENALTY MINUTES, BOTH TEAMS, PERIOD**
35 3rd period, February 14, 2006 (SUI 31, GER 4)
32 2nd period, February 9, 1998 (JPN 30, FIN 2)

**MOST PENALTIES, TEAM, GAME**
15 USA, February 14, 2006 vs. FIN
13 CAN, February 21, 2002 vs. USA
13 JPN, February 9, 1998 vs. FIN

**MOST PENALTIES, BOTH TEAMS, GAME**
26 February 14, 2006 (USA 15, FIN 11)
24 February 11, 1998 (SWE 14, CAN 10)
23 February 13, 2002 (KAZ 12, SWE 11)

**MOST PENALTIES, TEAM, PERIOD**
7 KAZ, 2nd period, February 13, 2002 vs. SWE
7 JPN, 2nd period, February 9, 1998 vs. FIN

**MOST PENALTIES, BOTH TEAMS, PERIOD**
10 2nd period, February 14, 2006 (USA 6, FIN 4)
10 3rd period, February 16, 2002 (USA 5, FIN 5)
10 2nd period, February 13, 2002 (KAZ 7, SWE 3)

**MOST PENALTY MINUTES, INDIVIDUAL, GAME**
27 Kathrin Lehmann, SUI, February 14, 2006 vs. GER
27 Tricia Dunn, USA, February 14, 2002 vs. CHN

**MOST PENALTY MINUTES, INDIVIDUAL, PERIOD**
27 Kathrin Lehmann, SUI, 3rd period, February 14, 2006 vs. GER
27 Tricia Dunn, USA, 1st period, February 14, 2002 vs. CHN

**MOST PENALTIES, INDIVIDUAL, GAME**
4 Darcia Leimgruber (SUI), February 20, 2010 vs. CHN (4 minors)
4 Linda de Rocco (ITA), February 20, 2006 vs. SUI (3 minors, 1 misconduct)
4 Linda de Rocco (ITA), February 13, 2006 vs. SWE (4 minors)
4 Monika Leuenberger (SUI), February 13, 2006 vs. FIN (4 minors)
4 Oxana Taikevich (KAZ), February 11, 2002 vs. CAN (4 minors)

**MOST PENALTIES, INDIVIDUAL, PERIOD**
3 Oxana Taikevich, KAZ, 2nd period, February 11, 2002 vs. CAN (3 minors)

## Speed Records

**FASTEST GOAL FROM START OF GAME**
13 seconds Mari Pehkonen (FIN), February 14, 2006 vs. USA

**FASTEST GOAL FROM START OF PERIOD**
19 seconds Janka Culikova (SVK), 3rd period, February 17, 2010 vs. SUI

**FASTEST TWO GOALS, INDIVIDUAL**
16 seconds Caroline Ouellette (CAN), February 11, 2006 vs. ITA (1:36 & 1:52, 1st period)

**FASTEST TWO GOALS, TEAM**
6 seconds CAN, February 19, 2002 vs. FIN (Hayley Wickenheiser 3:19, Jayna Hefford 3:25, 3rd period)

**FASTEST TWO GOALS, BOTH TEAMS**
13 seconds FIN & CHN, February 14, 1998 (Sari Fisk (FIN) 4:37, Hongmei Liu (CHN) 4:50, 2nd period)

**FASTEST THREE GOALS, INDIVIDUAL**
5:17 Caroline Ouellette (CAN), February 11, 2006 vs. ITA (1:36, 1:52, 6:53, 1st period)

**FASTEST THREE GOALS, TEAM**
59 seconds February 17, 2010 vs. SWE (Jayna Hefford 5:14, Hayley Wickenheiser 5:36, Gillian Apps 6:13, 2nd)
1:04 February 12, 1998 vs. JPN (Sandra Whyte 13:32, Shelley Looney 14:14, A.J. Mleczko, 14:36)

**FASTEST THREE GOALS, BOTH TEAMS**
1:27 GER, February 17, 2006 vs. ITA (Sara Seiler (GER) 5:32, Maria Leitner (ITA) 6:18, Maria Leitner (ITA) 6:59)

**FASTEST FOUR GOALS, TEAM**
2:43 USA, February 14, 2002 vs. CHN (Katie King 7:48, Laurie Baker 9:22, Julie Chu 9:57, Katie King 10:31, 2nd period)
2:45 CAN, February 17, 2010 vs. SWE (Jayna Hefford 5:14, Hayley Wickenheiser 5:36, Gillian Apps 6:13, Meghan Agosta 7:59, 2nd period)

**FASTEST FOUR GOALS, BOTH TEAMS**
2:15 GER, February 17, 2006 vs. ITA (Sara Seiler (GER) 5:32, Maria Leitner (ITA) 6:18, Maria Leitner (ITA) 6:59, Nikola Holmes (GER) 7:47)

**FASTEST FIVE GOALS, TEAM**
4:03 CAN, February 17, 2010 vs. SWE (Jayna Hefford 5:14, Hayley Wickenheiser 5:36, Gillian Apps 6:13, Meghan Agosta 7:59, Cherie Piper 9:17, 2nd period)

**FASTEST SIX GOALS, BOTH TEAMS**
7:20 CAN & USA, February 14, 1998 (Jayna Hefford (CAN) 5:28, Therese Brisson (CAN) 5:53, Laurie Baker (USA) 7:05, Cammi Granato (USA) 10:57, Jenny Schmidgall (USA) 12:25, Tricia Dunn (USA) 12:48, 3rd period)

# Women's World Championship

## All-Time Team Records

### LONGEST WINNING & UNDEFEATED STREAK
37 games CAN, March 19, 1990-April 3, 2004

### LONGEST LOSING STREAK
17 games JPN, March 19, 1990-April 9, 2008

### MOST GOALS, TEAM, ONE WW
61 CAN (1990—5 games)
50 USA (1990—5 games)

### FEWEST GOALS, TEAM, ONE WW
0 KAZ (2007—4 games)

### MOST GOALS, TEAM, GAME
18 March 22, 1990 Canada 18-Japan 0
17 April 11, 1994 Finland 17-Germany 1
17 April 20, 1992 USA 17-Switzerland 0
17 March 21, 1990 USA 17-Norway 0
17 March 21, 1990 Canada 17-Germany 0

### MOST GOALS, BOTH TEAMS, GAME (BOTH TEAMS SCORING)
19 March 19, 1990 United States 16-Switzerland 3
18 April 11, 1994 Finland 17-Germany 1
17 April 15, 1994 United States 14-China 3

### MOST GOALS, TEAM/BOTH TEAMS, PERIOD
10 USA, 3rd period, March 19, 1990 vs. SUI
9 CAN, 1st period, March 22, 1990 vs. JPN
8 CAN, 1st period, April 1, 2004 vs. GER
8 FIN, 3rd period, April 11, 1994 vs. GER
8 FIN, 2nd period, April 21, 1992 vs. SUI

### SCORELESS GAMES
April 5, 2001 China 0-Germany 0
April 9, 2005 United States 1-Canada 0 (GWS)
April 5, 2007 Finland 1-Sweden 0 (GWS)

## Power-Play and Short-Handed Goals Records

### MOST POWER-PLAY GOALS, TEAM, GAME
7 USA, April 12, 1994 vs. GER
6 CAN, April 5, 2001 vs. SWE
6 SWE, March 11, 1999 vs. RUS
6 CHN, April 1, 1997 vs. SUI

### MOST POWER-PLAY GOALS, INDIVIDUAL, GAME
3 Hanna Teerijoki (FIN), April 11, 1994 vs. GER
3 Hilary Knight (USA), April 18, 2011 vs. RUS

### MOST POWER-PLAY GOALS, TEAM, PERIOD
4 FIN, 3rd period, April 5, 2008 vs. JPN
4 CHN, 1st period, April 1, 1997 vs. SUI

### MOST POWER-PLAY GOALS, BOTH TEAMS, PERIOD
5 JPN 3, RUS 2—April 7, 2000, 1st period

### MOST SHORT-HANDED GOALS, TEAM, GAME
4 USA, March 19, 1990 vs. SUI

### MOST SHORT-HANDED GOALS, INDIVIDUAL, GAME
2 Cammi Granato (USA), March 19, 1990 vs. SUI

### MOST SHORT-HANDED GOALS, TEAM, PERIOD
3 USA, 3rd period, March 19, 1990 vs. SUI

## All-Time Individual Records

### MOST WOMEN'S WORLD CHAMPIONSHIPS
11 Gunilla Andersson (SWE—1992-2011)
11 Jayna Hefford (CAN—1997-2012)
11 Hayley Wickenheiser (CAN—1997-2012)
10 Erika Holst (SWE—1997-2011)
10 Karoliina Rantamaki (FIN—1997-2011)
10 Angela Ruggiero (USA—1997-2011)

### MOST GOLD MEDALS
9 Danielle Goyette (CAN)
7 Jayna Hefford (CAN), Hayley Wickenheiser (CAN)
6 Caroline Ouellette (CAN)

### MOST MEDALS
11 (7 gold, 4 silver) Jayna Hefford (CAN)
11 (7 gold, 4 silver) Hayley Wickenheiser (CAN)
10 (9 gold, 1 silver) Danielle Goyette (CAN)
10 (6 gold, 4 silver) Caroline Ouellette (CAN)
10 (4 gold, 6 silver) Jenny Potter (-Schmidgall) (USA)
10 (4 gold, 6 silver) Angela Ruggiero (USA)
9 (1 gold, 8 silver) Cammi Granato (USA)

### MOST GAMES PLAYED
57 Karoliina Rantamaki (FIN—1997-2012)
55 Jayna Hefford (CAN—1997-2012)
54 Gunilla Andersson (SWE—1992-2011)
53 Hayley Wickenheiser (CAN—1994-2012)
50 Caroline Ouellette (CAN—1999-2012)
50 Jenny Potter (-Schmidgall) (USA—1999-2012)
50 Angela Ruggiero (USA—1997-2011)

### MOST POINTS, CAREER
85 Hayley Wickenheiser (CAN—37+48)
78 Cammi Granato (USA—44+34)
77 Jayna Hefford (CAN—38+39)
68 Danielle Goyette (CAN—37+31)
61 Jenny Potter (-Schmidgall) (USA—23+38)
59 Katie King (USA—33+26)
59 Jennifer Botterill (CAN—26+33)
59 Krissy Wendell (USA—21+38)

### MOST POINTS, ONE WW
23 Cindy Curley (USA, 1990—11+12=23)
15 Tina Cardinale (USA, 1990—5+10=15)
14 Hayley Wickenheiser (CAN, 2007—8+6=14)
14 Cammi Granato (USA, 1990—9+5=14)
14 Kim Urech (SUI, 1990—8+6=14)
14 Monique Lamoureux-Kolls (USA, 2012—7+7=14)

### MOST GOALS, CAREER
44 Cammi Granato (USA)
38 Jayna Hefford (CAN)
37 Hayley Wickenheiser (CAN)
37 Danielle Goyette (CAN)
33 Katie King (USA)
30 Riikka Nieminen (FIN)

### MOST GOALS, ONE WW
11 Krissy Wendell (USA, 2000)
11 Cindy Curley (USA, 1990)
11 Angela James (CAN, 1990)
9 Krissy Wendell (USA, 2001)
9 Danielle Goyette (CAN, 1994)
9 Cammi Granato (USA, 1990)
8 Hayley Wickenheiser (CAN, 2007)
8 Jennifer Botterill (CAN, 2001)
8 Karyn Bye (USA, 2000)
8 Hongmei Liu (CHN, 1994)
8 Cammi Granato (USA, 1992)
8 Riikka Nieminen (FIN, 1990)
8 Kim Urech (SUI, 1990)

### MOST ASSISTS, CAREER
48 Hayley Wickenheiser (CAN)
41 Caroline Ouellette (CAN)
39 Jayna Hefford (CAN)
38 Jenny Potter (-Schmidgall) (USA)
38 Krissy Wendell (USA)
35 Julie Chu (USA)
34 Cammi Granato (USA)
34 Geraldine Heaney (CAN)

### MOST ASSISTS, ONE WW
12 Cindy Curley (USA, 1990)
11 Krissy Wendell (USA, 2000)
10 Tina Cardinale (USA, 1990)
9 Kelly Bechard (CAN, 2001)
9 Krissy Wendell (USA, 2001)
9 Riikka Nieminen (FIN, 1994)
9 Liisa Karikoski (FIN, 1990)

### MOST PENALTY MINUTES, CAREER
61 Yekaterina Smolentseva (RUS)
56 Angela Ruggiero (USA)
55 Xueting Qi (CHN)
54 Monika Leuenberger (SUI)
54 Olga Kryukova (KAZ)
53 Joa Elfsberg (SWE)

### MOST PENALTY MINUTES, ONE WW
35 Xueting Qi (CHN, 2009)
33 Yekaterina Smolentseva (RUS, 2008)
29 Tricia Dunn (USA, 2002)
29 Regula Mueller (SUI, 1997)

### MOST GOALS, ONE GAME
5 Hanna Teerijoki (FIN), April 11, 1994 vs. GER
5 Cindy Curley (USA), March 21, 1990 vs. NOR
4 Alana Blahoski (USA), April 4, 2000 vs. RUS
4 Danielle Goyette (CAN), April 12, 1994 vs. NOR
4 Birgitte Lersbryggen (NOR), April 16, 1994 vs. SUI
4 Cammi Granato (USA), April 20, 1992 vs. SUI
4 Riikka Nieminen (FIN), April 20, 1992 vs. NOR
4 Inger-Lise Fagernes (NOR), March 24, 1990 vs. FRG
4 Angela James (CAN), March 21, 1990 vs. FRG
4 Laura Schuler (CAN), March 21, 1990 vs. FRG

### MOST POINTS, GAME
9 Cindy Curley (USA), March 21, 1990 vs. NOR
8 Tina Cardinale (USA), March 19, 1990 vs. SUI

### MOST ASSISTS, GAME
5 Alana Blahoski (USA), April 4, 2000 vs. RUS
5 Lisa Brown (USA), March 19, 1990 vs. SUI
5 Tina Cardinale (USA), March 19, 1990 vs. SUI

### MOST POINTS, PERIOD
6 Cindy Curley, USA, 1st period, March 21, 1990 vs. NOR (4 goals, 2 assists)
5 Tiia Reima, FIN, 3rd period, April 11, 1994 vs. GER (3 goals, 2 assists)
4 Hayley Wickenheiser, 3rd period, April 4, 2009 vs. CHN (1 goal, 3 assists)
4 Alana Blahoski, USA, 1st period, April 4, 2000 vs. RUS (3 goals, 1 assist)
4 Hongmei Liu, CHN, 3rd period, April 14, 1994 vs. NOR (2 goals, 2 assists)
4 Shelley Looney, USA, 1st period, April 15, 1994 vs. CHN (3 goals, 1 assist)
4 Tina Cardinale, USA, 3rd period, March 19, 1990 vs. SUI (1 goal, 4 assists)

### MOST GOALS, PERIOD
4 Hanna Teerijoki, FIN, 2nd period, April 11, 1994 vs. GER
4 Cindy Curley, USA, 1st period, March 21, 1990 vs. NOR
3 Alana Blahoski, USA, 1st period, April 4, 2000 vs. RUS
3 Shelley Looney, USA, 1st period, April 15, 1994 vs. CHN
3 Tiia Reima, FIN, 3rd period, April 11, 1994 vs. GER
3 Charlotte Almblad, SWE, 3rd period, April 21, 1992 vs. CHN
3 Cammi Granato, USA, 3rd period, March 19, 1990 vs. SUI
3 Angela James, CAN, 3rd period, March 21, 1990 vs. FRG

### MOST ASSISTS, PERIOD
4 Sari Krooks, FIN, 2nd period, April 11, 1994 vs. GER
3 Carla MacLeod, CAN, 3rd period, April 6, 2009 vs. SWE
3 Hayley Wickenheiser, CAN, 3rd period, April 4, 2009 vs. CHN
3 Cherie Piper, CAN, 3rd period, April 6, 2008 vs. CHN
3 Vicky Sunohara, CAN, 1st period, April 9, 2007 vs. FIN
3 Caroline Ouellette, CAN, 2nd period, April 4, 2005 vs. RUS
3 Hayley Wickenheiser, CAN, 2nd period, April 3, 2005 vs. KAZ
3 Kirsi Hanninen, FIN, 3rd period, March 8, 1999 vs. GER

3 Jayna Hefford, CAN, 2nd period, March 8, 1999 vs. SUI
3 Stephanie O'Sullivan, USA, 3rd period, March 11, 1999 vs. CHN
3 Caroline Ouellette, CAN, 2nd period, March 9, 1999 vs. GER
3 Xuan Li, CHN, 1st period, April 1, 1997 vs. SUI
3 Lisa Brown, USA, 3rd period, April 20, 1992 vs. SUI
3 Beth Beagan, USA, 1st period, March 21, 1990 vs. NOR
3 Tina Cardinale, USA, 3rd period, March 19, 1990 vs. SUI
3 Cindy Curley, USA, 3rd period, March 19, 1990 vs. SUI

### PENALTY SHOTS

| | |
|---|---|
| April 5, 2007 | Jayna Hefford (CAN) stopped by Viona Harrer (GER) at 13:38 of 2nd period in 8-0 win by CAN |
| April 6, 2005 | Rui Sun (CHN) stopped by Stephanie Wartosch-Kurten (GER) at 11:25 of 3rd period in 3-3 tie |
| April 3, 2000 | Sweden stopped by Hong Guo (CHN) at 12:12 of 1st period in 1-1 tie |
| March 14, 1999 | Germany stopped by Patricia Sautter (SUI) at 19:12 of 1st period in 3-0 win by GER |
| March 12, 1999 | Germany stopped by Irina Votintseva (RUS) at 1:42 of 2nd period in 6-2 win by RUS |
| April 6, 1997 | Maria Rooth (SWE) stopped by Irina Gashennikova (RUS) at 8:59 of 2nd period in 3-1 win by SWE |
| April 1, 1997 | Xiuqing Yang (CHN) scored on Patricia Sautter (SUI) at 19:17 of 3rd period in 11-3 win by CHN |
| April 10, 2012 | Meghan Agosta (CAN) beat Valentina Ostrovlyanchik (RUS) |

## Goaltender Records

### MOST GOLD MEDALS
5 Kim St. Pierre (CAN)
4 Sami Jo Small (CAN)

### MOST MEDALS

| | |
|---|---|
| 9 (5 gold, 4 silver) | Kim St. Pierre (CAN) |
| 6 (2 gold, 4 silver) | Charline Labonte (CAN) |
| 4 (4 gold) | Sami Jo Small (CAN) |
| 4 (2 gold, 2 silver) | Jessie Vetter (USA) |
| 4 (4 silver) | Erin Whitten (USA) |
| 4 (4 bronze) | Liisa-Maria Sneck (FIN) |
| 3 (1 gold, 2 silver) | Chanda Gunn (USA) |
| 3 (3 silver) | Kelly Dyer (USA) |
| 3 (3 silver) | Sarah Tueting (USA) |
| 3 (3 bronze) | Tuula Puputti (FIN) |

### MOST TOURNAMENTS, GOALIE
8 Kim St. Pierre (CAN, 1999-2009)
7 Irina Gashennikova (RUS, 1997-2009)
7 Hong Guo (CHN, 1992-2004)
7 Kim Martin (SWE, 2001-12)
6 Lina Huo (CHN, 1994-2005)
6 Stephanie Wartosch-Kurten (GER, 1994-2005)

### MOST GAMES PLAYED, GOALIE, CAREER
31 Hong Guo (CHN—1992-2004)
28 Irina Gashennikova (RUS—1997-2009)
25 Florence Schelling (SUI, 2004-12)
24 Kim Martin (SWE—2001-12)
24 Stephanie Wartosch-Kurten (GER—1994-2005)
23 Kim St. Pierre (CAN—1999-2011)
22 Noora Raty (FIN, 2005-12)

### MOST MINUTES PLAYED, GOALIE, CAREER
1,655:10 Hong Guo (CHN)
1,513:48 Irina Gashennikova (RUS)
1,432:42 Florence Schelling (SUI)
1,373:07 Tuula Puputti (FIN)
1,349:42 Kim St. Pierre (CAN)
1,324:40 Kim Martin (SWE)
1,284:22 Noora Raty (FIN)
1,266:39 Stephanie Wartosch-Kurten (GER)

### MOST WINS, GOALIE, CAREER
19 Kim St. Pierre (CAN)
14 Hong Guo (CHN)
12 Irina Gashennikova (RUS)
10 Sami Jo Small (CAN)
10 Erin Whitten (USA)
10 Charline Labonte (CAN)

### MOST LOSSES, GOALIE, CAREER
13 Irina Gashennikova (RUS)
13 Natalya Trunova (KAZ)
12 Stephanie Wartosch-Kurten (GER)
12 Annica Ahlen (SWE)
12 Patricia Elsmore-Sautter (SUI)

### MOST SHUTOUTS, CAREER
13 Kim St. Pierre (CAN)
5 Charline Labonte (CAN)
5 Sami Jo Small (CAN)
5 Erin Whitten (USA)
4 Sarah Tueting (USA)
4 Stephanie Wartosch-Kurten (GER)

### MOST SHUTOUTS, ONE WW
3 Kim St. Pierre (CAN, 2005)
3 Liisa-Maria Sneck (FIN, 1997)
3 Erin Whitten (USA, 1997)

### LONGEST SHUTOUT SEQUENCE (IN MINUTES)
580:26 CAN April 4, 2004-February 14, 2006
210:38 USA April 12, 2008-April 10, 2009
200:54 CAN April 8, 2001-February 19, 2002

### MOST CONSECUTIVE SHUTOUTS
3 Kim St. Pierre (CAN, 2005)

### BEST GOALS AGAINST AVERAGE, CAREER
(minimum 550 minutes)
0.53 Sami Jo Small (CAN)
0.80 Kim St. Pierre (CAN)
1.12 Charline Labonte (CAN)

### BEST GOALS AGAINST AVERAGE, ONE WW
(minimum 180 minutes)
0.00 Liisa-Maria Sneck (FIN, 1997)
0.30 Kim St. Pierre (CAN, 2005)
0.33 Kim St. Pierre (CAN, 2007)
0.33 Sami Jo Small (CAN, 1999)
0.52 Chanda Gunn (USA, 2005)

### MOST ASSISTS, GOALIE, CAREER
2 Tuula Puputti (FIN)
2 Stephanie Wartosch-Kurten (GER)
2 Florence Schelling (SUI)

### MOST PENALTY MINUTES, GOALIE, CAREER
12 Hong Guo (CHN)
8 Stephanie Wartosch-Kurten (GER)
6 Natalya Trunova (KAZ)

## Shots On Goal Records

### MOST SHOTS, TEAM, GAME
82 USA, April 3, 1997 vs. SWE
80 USA, April 13, 2012 vs. SUI
79 USA, April 3, 2005 vs. CHN
76 SWE, April 4, 2005 vs. KAZ
76 USA, April 11, 1994 vs. SUI

### MOST SHOTS, BOTH TEAMS, GAME
108 SWE (75) & SUI (33), April 24, 2011
103 CAN (53) & USA (50), April 25, 2011
94 RUS (72) & KAZ (22), April 9, 2009
93 USA (79) & CHN (14), April 3, 2005
92 CAN (73) & SUI (19), March 8, 1999

### MOST SHOTS, TEAM, PERIOD
38 USA, 2nd period, April 3, 2005 vs. CHN
33 USA, 1st period, April 3, 1997 vs. SWE
33 USA, 1st period, April 23, 2011 vs. RUS

### MOST SHOTS, BOTH TEAMS, PERIOD
42 RUS (31) & KAZ (11), 3rd period, April 9, 2009
42 USA (38) & CHN (4), 2nd period, April 3, 2005
40 SWE (30) & SUI (10), 1st period, April 24, 2011
38 USA (33) & RUS (5), 1st period, April 23, 2011
37 USA (27) & CHN (10), 3rd period, April 3, 2001

### FEWEST SHOTS, TEAM, GAME
2 SUI, April 6, 2008 vs. USA
2 KAZ, April 3, 2005 vs. CAN
3 DEN, April 21, 1992 vs. CAN
4 GER, April 4, 2008 vs. USA
4 RUS, April 1, 2004 vs. USA

### FEWEST SHOTS, BOTH TEAMS, GAME
30 April 8, 2008 (GER 16, JPN 14)
31 April 6, 2008 (FIN 19, SWE 12)
36 April 14, 1994 (CHN 22, NOR 14)

### FEWEST SHOTS, TEAM, PERIOD
0 CHN, 3rd period, April 6, 2008 vs. CAN
0 SUI, 1st period, April 6, 2008 vs. USA
0 JPN, 1st period, April 5, 2008 vs. FIN
0 GER, 2nd period, April 4, 2008 vs. USA
0 KAZ, 1st period, April 3, 2005 vs. CAN
0 RUS, 1st period, April 1, 2004 vs. USA
0 KAZ, 1st period, April 2, 2001 vs. CAN
0 CHN, 1st period, April 6, 1997 vs. FIN
0 NOR, 1st period, April 3, 1997 vs. FIN
0 RUS, 1st period, April 1, 1997 vs. CAN
0 SUI, 1st period, March 31, 1997 vs. CAN
0 DEN, 1st period, April 21, 1992 vs. CAN

### FEWEST SHOTS, BOTH TEAMS, PERIOD
7 SUI & NOR, 1st period, April 6, 1997 (SUI 4, NOR 3)
7 SUI & NOR, 2nd period, April 6, 1997 (NOR 4, SUI 3)
8 CAN & FIN, 1st period, April 8, 2005 (CAN 6, FIN 2)

## Penalty Records

### FEWEST PENALTIES & PENALTY MINUTES, TEAM, GAME
0 USA, April 12, 2009 vs. CAN
0 CHN, April 4, 2007 vs. KAZ
0 RUS, April 7, 2001 vs. USA
0 USA, March 9, 1999 vs. SWE
0 SWE, April 16, 1994 vs. GER
0 SVK, April 22, 2011 vs. KAZ

### FEWEST PENALTY MINUTES, BOTH TEAMS, GAME
4 April 12, 2009 (CAN 4, USA 0)
4 April 7, 2001 (USA 4, RUS 0)
4 April 16, 1994 (GER 2, SWE 2)
6 April 4, 2009 (FIN 4, KAZ 2)
6 April 6, 2008 (CHN 2, CAN 1)
6 April 8, 2000 (CAN 4, FIN 2)
6 March 9, 1999 (SWE 6, USA 0)
6 April 22, 2011 (KAZ 6, SVK 0)

### FEWEST PENALTIES, BOTH TEAMS, GAME
2 April 12, 2009 (CAN 2, USA 0)
2 April 7, 2001 (USA 2, RUS 0)
2 April 16, 1994 (GER 2, SWE 0)
3 April 6, 2008 (CHN 2, CAN 1)
3 April 8, 2000 (CAN 2, FIN 1)
3 March 9, 1999 (SWE 3, USA 0)
3 April 4, 2009 (FIN 2, KAZ 1)
3 April 22, 2011 (KAZ 3, SVK 0)

### MOST PENALTY MINUTES, TEAM, GAME
50 RUS, March 11, 1999 vs. SWE
41 SUI, February 14, 2006 vs. GER
38 USA, February 14, 2006 vs. FIN

### MOST PENALTY MINUTES, BOTH TEAMS, GAME
63 April 10, 2008 (RUS 37, SUI 26)
60 March 11, 1999 (RUS 50, SWE 10)
57 April 8, 2009 (CHN 33, SUI 24)

### MOST PENALTY MINUTES, TEAM, PERIOD
37 SWE, 1st period, April 3, 2000 vs. CHN
33 RUS, 1st period, April 10, 2008 vs. SUI
29 CAN, 2nd period, March 8, 1999 vs. SUI
25 CHN, 2nd period, April 8, 2009 vs. SUI
24 SUI, 3rd period, April 9, 2007 vs. SWE
22 RUS, 3rd period, March 11, 1999 vs. SWE
22 CHN, 1st period, April 12, 1994 vs. SWE

**MOST PENALTY MINUTES, BOTH TEAMS, PERIOD**
43 1st period, April 10, 2008 (RUS 33, SUI 10)
39 1st period, April 3, 2000 (SWE 37, CHN 2)
35 2nd period, March 8, 1999 (CAN 29, SUI 6)
31 2nd period, April 8, 2009 (CHN 25, SUI 6)
30 3rd period, March 11, 1999 (RUS 22, SWE 8)

**MOST PENALTIES, TEAM, GAME**
17 RUS, March 11, 1999 vs. SWE
14 SWE, April 24, 2011 vs. SUI
13 CAN, April 12, 2008 vs. USA
13 SUI, April 10, 2008 vs. RUS
13 SWE, April 4, 2004 vs. CAN

**MOST PENALTIES, BOTH TEAMS, GAME**
24 April 12, 2008 (CAN 13, USA 11)
23 April 24, 2011 (SWE 14, SUI 9)
22 March 11, 1999 (RUS 17, SWE 5)
22 March 31, 1997 (CHN 11, RUS 11)
22 March 19, 1990 (CAN 11, SWE 11)

**MOST PENALTIES, TEAM, PERIOD**
8 SUI, 3rd period, April 9, 2007 vs. SWE
7 KAZ, 2nd period, April 8, 2001 vs. SWE
7 RUS, 2nd period, March 11, 1999 vs. SWE
7 RUS, 1st period, March 11, 1999 vs. SWE
7 FIN, 1st period, April 19, 2011 vs. CAN

**MOST PENALTIES, BOTH TEAMS, PERIOD**
11 3rd period, March 11, 1999 (RUS 7, SWE 4)
11 3rd period, April 10, 2012 (CAN 7, RUS 4)
10 3rd period, April 12, 2008 (CAN 5, USA 5)
10 1st period, April 10, 2008 (RUS 5, SUI 5)
10 2nd period, April 8, 2001 (KAZ 7, SWE 3)
10 1st period, April 11, 2012 (RUS 6, SUI 4)

**MOST PENALTY MINUTES, INDIVIDUAL, GAME**
29 Ekaterina Smolentseva, RUS, April 10, 2008 vs. SUI
27 Xueting Qi, CHN, April 8, 2009 vs. SUI
25 Nathalie Rivard, CAN, March 8, 1999 vs. SUI
25 Regula Muller, SUI, April 1, 1997 vs. CHN

**MOST PENALTY MINUTES, INDIVIDUAL, PERIOD**
29 Ekaterina Smolentseva, RUS, 1st period, April 10, 2008 vs. SUI
25 Xueting Qi, CHN, April 8, 2009 vs. SUI
25 Nathalie Rivard, CAN, 2nd period, March 8, 1999 vs. SUI
25 Regula Muller, SUI, 1st period, April 1, 1997 vs. CHN

**MOST PENALTIES, INDIVIDUAL, GAME**
4 Olga Kryukova, KAZ, April 5, 2009 vs. SUI (3 minors, 1 misconduct)
4 Stephanie Marty, SUI, April 6, 2008 vs. USA (4 minors)
4 Etsuko Wada, JPN, April 5, 2008 vs. FIN (4 minors)
4 Alena Khomich, RUS, March 11, 1999 vs. SWE (3 minors, 1 misconduct)
4 Yan Lu, CHN, April 20, 1992 vs. CAN (4 minors)

**MOST PENALTIES, INDIVIDUAL, PERIOD**
4 Alena Khomich, RUS, 1st period, March 11, 1999 vs. SWE (3 minors, 1 misconduct)
3 Yan Lu, CHN, 3rd period, April 20, 1992 vs. CAN (3 minors)
3 Monika Leuenberger, SUI, 3rd period, April 9, 2007 vs. SWE (2 minors, 1 misconduct)

## Speed Records

**FASTEST GOAL FROM START OF GAME**
13 seconds Maren Valenti (GER), April 17, 1994 vs. SUI
20 seconds Olga Volkova (RUS), April 5, 2004 vs. FIN

**FASTEST GOAL FROM START OF PERIOD**
4 seconds Inger Lise Fagernes (NOR), March 24, 1990, 2nd period, vs. FRG
6 seconds Ekaterina Pashkevich (RUS), March 31, 1997, 2nd period, vs. CHN
7 seconds Angela Ruggiero (USA), April 5, 2004, 3rd period, vs. SWE

**FASTEST TWO GOALS, INDIVIDUAL**
13 seconds Vicky Sunohara (CAN), March 22, 1990 vs. JPN (2:39 & 2:52, 1st period)

**FASTEST TWO GOALS, TEAM**
6 seconds USA, April 5, 2005 vs. GER (Kathleen Kauth 3:26, Katie King 3:32, 1st period)
7 seconds FIN, March 19, 1990 vs. NOR (Sari Krooks 18:45, Marianne Ihalainen 18:52, 1st period)
7 seconds USA, March 21, 1990 vs. NOR (Kelly O'Leary 4:31, Heidi Chalupnik 4:38, 3rd period)
7 seconds USA, April 5, 2005 vs. GER (Julie Chu 3:19, Kathleen Kauth 3:26, 1st period)

**FASTEST TWO GOALS, BOTH TEAMS**
12 seconds USA & CAN, April 17, 1994 (Stacy Wilson (CAN) 11:51, Cammi Granato (USA) 12:03, 3rd period)
14 seconds SWE & RUS, April 2, 2005 (Svetlana Trefilova (RUS) 10:43, Danijela Rundqvist (SWE) 10:57, 2nd period)

**FASTEST THREE GOALS, INDIVIDUAL**
5:48 Alana Blahoski (USA), April 4, 2000 vs. RUS (6:59, 10:16, 12:47, 1st period)
5:49 Hanna Teerijoki (FIN), April 11, 1994 vs. GER (13:14, 16:19, 19:03, 1st period)

**FASTEST THREE GOALS, TEAM**
13 seconds USA, April 5, 2005 vs. GER (Julie Chu 3:19, Kathleen Kauth 3:26, Katie King 3:32, 1st period)
46 seconds CAN, April 4, 2009 vs. CHN (Carla MacLeod 3:43, Caroline Ouellette 3:53, Sarah Vaillancourt 4:29, 1st period)
49 seconds USA, April 13, 2012 vs. SUI (Megan Bozek 4:56, Josephine Pucci 5:24, Erika Lawler 5:45)

**FASTEST THREE GOALS, BOTH TEAMS**
57 seconds JPN & SWE, March 21, 1990 (Annika Persson (SWE) 7:31, Rie Sato (JPN) 7:43, Sato (JPN) 8:28, 1st period)

**FASTEST FOUR GOALS, TEAM**
2:02 SWE, April 8, 2009 vs. KAZ (Danijela Rundqvist 16:38, Erika Holst 17:17, Erica Uden Johansson 17:41, Elin Holmlov 18:40, 3rd period)
2:29 USA, March 19, 1990 vs. SUI (Cammi Granato 13:58, Kimberly Eisenreid 14:34, Granato 16:18, Beth Beagan 16:27, 3rd period)
2:31 USA, April 4, 2000 vs. RUS (Cammi Granato 13:26, Brandy Fisher 14:14, Karyn Bye 14:34, Alana Blahoski 15:57, 2nd period)

**FASTEST FOUR GOALS, BOTH TEAMS**
1:58 CHN & SUI, April 1, 1997 (Hongmei Liu (CHN) 7:44, Lan Zhang (CHN) 8:27, Lei Xu (CHN) 8:54, Nicole Walder (SUI) 9:42, 1st period)
2:04 FIN & CHN, April 2, 2001 (Hongmei Liu (CHN) 17:39, Katja Riipi (FIN) 17:53, Hongmei Liu (CHN) 19:01, Vilja Lipsonen (FIN) 19:43, 1st period)

**FASTEST FIVE GOALS, TEAM**
3:28 USA, March 19, 1990 vs. SUI (Cammi Granato 13:58, Kimberley Eisenreid 14:34, Granato 16:18, Beth Beagan 16:27, Jeanine Sobek 17:26, 3rd period)
3:36 USA, April 4, 2000 vs. RUS (Cammi Granato 13:26, Brandy Fisher 14:14, Karyn Bye 14:34, Alana Blahoski 15:57, Tricia Dunn 17:02, 2nd period)

**FASTEST SIX GOALS, TEAM**
7:47 USA, March 19, 1990 vs. SUI (Shawna Davidson 9:39, Cammi Granato 13:58, Kimberley Eisenreid 14:34, Granato 16:18, Beth Beagan 16:27, Jeanine Sobek 17:26, 3rd period)

*Canada's Vicky Sunohara once scored two goals in 13 seconds, a Women's World Championship record.*

# U18 Women's World Championship

## All-Time Team Records

**LONGEST WINNING & UNDEFEATED STREAK**
14 games USA, January 7, 2008-April 3, 2010

**LONGEST LOSING STREAK**
7 games RUS, January 7, 2008-January 7, 2009

**MOST GOALS, TEAM, ONE WW18**
58 USA, 2009

**FEWEST GOALS, TEAM, ONE WW18**
4 RUS, 2008

**MOST GOALS, TEAM/BOTH TEAMS, GAME**
18 USA, January 9, 2009 vs. CZE
17 USA, January 5, 2009 vs. RUS
16 CAN, January 5, 2009 vs. SUI

**MOST GOALS, TEAM/BOTH TEAMS, PERIOD**
9 USA, January 5, 2009 vs. RUS, 1st period
8 USA, January 9, 2009 vs. CZE, 1st period
8 CAN, January 9, 2008 vs. FIN, 2nd period

## Power-Play and Short-Handed Goals Records

**MOST POWER-PLAY GOALS, TEAM, GAME**
4 CAN, January 8, 2008 vs. GER
4 CAN, January 11, 2008 vs. SWE
4 USA, January 5, 2009 vs. RUS
4 USA, January 7, 2009 vs. SWE
4 USA, January 9, 2009 vs. CZE
4 CAN, March 28, 2010 vs. GER
4 USA, March 30, 2010 vs. CZE

**MOST POWER-PLAY GOALS, BOTH TEAMS, GAME**
5 USA 4-SWE 1, January 7, 2009
5 SWE 3-GER 2, April 3, 2010
5 CAN 4-GER 1, January 4, 2011

**MOST POWER-PLAY GOALS, INDIVIDUAL, GAME**
2 Natalie Spooner, CAN, January 7, 2008 vs. CZE
2 Brianne Jenner, CAN, January 8, 2008 vs. GER
2 Marie-Philip Poulin, CAN, January 9, 2008 vs. FIN
2 Alena Polenska, CZE, January 12, 2008 vs. SWE
2 Kendall Coyne, USA, January 9, 2009 vs. CZE
2 Emma Nordin, SWE, January 10, 2009 vs. CZE
2 Kendall Coyne, USA, March 28, 2010 vs. FIN
2 Rebecca Stenberg, SWE, April 3, 2010 vs. GER
2 Ines Strohmaier, GER, April 3, 2010 vs. SWE
2 Sarah MacDonnell, CAN, January 4, 2011 vs. GER
2 Lara Stalder, SUI, January 5, 2011 vs. JPN

**MOST POWER-PLAY GOALS, INDIVIDUAL, PERIOD**
2 Natalie Spooner, CAN, January 7, 2008 vs. CZE, 1st period
2 Marie-Philip Poulin, CAN, January 9, 2008 vs. FIN, 1st period
2 Emma Nordin, January 10, 2009 vs. CZE, 1st period
2 Rebecca Stenberg, SWE, April 3, 2010 vs. GER, 1st period
2 Ines Strohmaier, GER, April 3, 2010 vs. SWE, 3rd period
2 Sabrina Zollinger, SUI, January 8, 2011 vs. JPN, 2nd period

**MOST POWER-PLAY GOALS, TEAM, PERIOD**
~no team has scored more than 2 power-play goals in any period

**MOST SHORT-HANDED GOALS, TEAM, GAME**
2 SWE, January 5, 2009 vs. GER
2 USA, January 7, 2009 vs. SWE
2 FIN, January 4, 2011 vs. SUI
2 SWE, April 2, 1010 vs USA, 1st period
2 GER, April 3, 2010 vs SUI, 2nd period

**MOST SHORT-HANDED GOALS, INDIVIDUAL, GAME**
2 Anna Borgqvist, SWE, January 5, 2009 vs. GER

**MOST SHORT-HANDED GOALS, TEAM, PERIOD**
~no team has scored more than one short-handed goal in any period

## All-Time Individual Records

**MOST WORLD WOMEN'S U18 CHAMPIONSHIPS**
3 (listed by nation)
CZE Jana Fialova, Karolina Kovarova, Katerina Solnickova, Katerina Mrazova, Barbora Pekarkova, Lucie Povova
FIN Milla Heikkinen, Niina Makinen, Tanja Niskanen, Isa Rahunen, Susanna Tapani
GER Manuela Anwander, Daria Gleissner, Rebecca Graeve, Jacqueline Janzen, Miriam Novotny, Miriam Pokopec, Yvonne Rothemund
RUS Elina Mitrofanova, Olga Sosina, Alexandra Vovrushko
SWE Anna Borgfeldt, Josephine Holmgren, Lisa Johansson
USA Kendall Coyne, Meagan Mangene, Amanda Pelkey

**MOST GOLD MEDALS**
2 Kendall Coyne (USA), Meagan Mangene (USA), Amanda Pelkey (USA)

**MOST MEDALS**
3 (2 gold, 1 silver) Kendall Coyne (USA)
3 (2 gold, 1 silver) Meagan Mangene (USA)
3 (2 gold, 1 silver) Amanda Pelkey (USA)

**MOST GAMES PLAYED**
16 (listed by nation)
CZE Jana Fialova, Karolina Kovarova
FIN Milla Heikkinen, Isa Rahunen, Susanna Tapani
GER Miriam Novotny, Miriam Pokopec, Yvonne Rothemund, Manuela Anwander, Daria Gleissner, Rebecca Graeve, Tanja Eisenschmid
SWE Josephine Holmgren, Lisa Johansson
USA Amanda Pelkey

**MOST POINTS, CAREER**
33 Kendall Coyne, USA
30 Amanda Kessel, USA
26 Marie-Philip Poulin, CAN
24 Jessica Campbell, CAN
23 Amanda Pelkey, USA
21 Cecilia Ostberg, SWE
20 Melodie Daoust, CAN
20 Madison Packer, USA

**MOST POINTS, ONE WW18**
19 Amanda Kessel, USA, 2009 (6+13)
15 Jessica Campbell, CAN, 2010 (7+8)
15 Kendall Coyne, USA, 2009 (8+7)
14 Marie-Philip Poulin, CAN, 2008 (8+6)
14 Camille Dumais, CAN, 2008 (5+9)

**MOST GOALS, CAREER**
22 Kendall Coyne, USA
14 Alex Carpenter, USA
13 Marie-Philip Poulin, CAN
11 Brianna Decker, USA
11 Brianne Jenner, CAN
11 Cecilia Ostberg, SWE
11 Madison Packer, USA

**MOST GOALS, ONE WW18**
11 Haley Skarupa, USA, 2012
10 Kendall Coyne, USA, 2010
8 Alex Carpenter, USA, 2010
8 Kendall Coyne, USA, 2009
8 Brianna Decker, USA, 2009
8 Marie-Philip Poulin, CAN, 2008
8 Kerstin Spielberger, GER, 2012

**MOST ASSISTS, CAREER**
20 Amanda Kessel, USA
16 Amanda Pelkey, USA
15 Jessica Campbell, CAN
15 Brigette Lacquette, CAN
13 Marie-Philip Poulin, CAN

**MOST ASSISTS, ONE WW18**
13 Amanda Kessel, USA, 2009
11 Brigette Lacquette, CAN, 2010
9 Erin Amrose, CAN, 2010
9 Camille Dumais, CAN, 2008
8 Jessica Campbell, CAN, 2010
8 Jessica Wong, CAN, 2009
8 Natalie Spooner, CAN, 2008

**MOST PENALTY MINUTES, CAREER**
53 Tanja Eisenschmid, GER
49 Elina Mitrofanova, RUS
48 Sandra Thalmann, SUI
37 Maike Hanke, GER
37 Susanna Tapani, FIN

**MOST PENALTY MINUTES, ONE WW18**
36 Sandra Thalmann, SUI, 2009
33 Maike Hanke, GER, 2008
33 Susanna Tapani, FIN, 2011
31 Tanja Eisenschmid, GER, 2011

**MOST GOALS, GAME**
4 Alex Carpenter, USA, March 30, 2010 vs. CZE
4 Kendall Coyne, USA, March 30, 2010 vs. CZE
4 Cecilia Ostberg, SWE, January 10, 2009 vs. CZE
4 Kendall Coyne, USA, January 7, 2009 vs. SWE
4 Cassandra Langan, CAN, January 5, 2009 vs. SUI

**MOST GOALS, PERIOD**
3 Rebecca Stenberg, SWE, 1st period, April 3, 2010 vs. GER
3 Kendall Coyne, USA, 3rd period, March 27, 2010 vs. JPN
3 Kendall Coyne, USA, 3rd period, January 7, 2009 vs. SWE
3 Cassandra Langan, CAN, 1st period, January 5, 2009 vs. SUI
3 Kerstin Spielberger, GER, 3rd period, January 3, 2012 vs. SUI

**MOST POINTS, GAME**
6 Haley Skarupa, USA, March 30, 2010 vs. CZE (2 goals, 4 assists)
6 Jessica Campbell, CAN, March 28, 2010 vs. GER (2 goals, 4 assists)
6 Amanda Kessel, USA, January 5, 2009 vs. RUS (3 goals, 3 assists)
5 Haley Skarupa, USA, January 7, 2011 vs. CZE (3 goals, 2 assists)
5 Klara Myren, SWE, January 10, 2009 vs. CZE (5 assists)
5 Cecilia Ostberg, SWE, January 10, 2009 vs. CZE (4 goals, 1 assist)
5 Amanda Kessel, USA, January 9, 2009 vs. CZE (2 goals, 3 assists)
5 Marie-Philip Poulin, CAN, January 7, 2008 vs. CZE (3 goals, 2 assists)
5 Cecilia Ostberg, SWE, January 8, 2008 vs. RUS (3 goals, 2 assists)
5 Ashley Cottrell, USA, January 8, 2008 vs. SUI (2 goals, 3 assists)
5 Laura Fortino, CAN, January 9, 2008 vs. FIN (1 goal, 4 assists)
5 Natalie Spooner, CAN, January 9, 2008 vs. FIN (5 assists)
5 Aamanda Kessel, USA, January 7, 2009 vs. SWE (5 assists)
5 Kendall Coyne, USA, January 5, 2009 vs. RUS (5 assists)
5 Marie Delarbre, GER, January 3, 2012 vs. SUI (2 goals, 3 assists)

**MOST POINTS, PERIOD**
4 Natalie Spooner, CAN, January 9, 2008 vs. FIN, 2nd period (4 assists)

**MOST ASSISTS, GAME**
5 Klara Myren, SWE, January 10, 2009 vs. CZE
5 Amanda Kessel, USA, January 7, 2009 vs. SWE
5 Kendall Coyne, USA, January 5, 2009 vs. RUS
5 Natalie Spooner, CAN, January 9, 2008 vs. FIN

**MOST ASSISTS, PERIOD**
4 Natalie Spooner, CAN, 2nd period, January 9, 2008 vs. FIN
3 Erin Ambrose, CAN, 1st period, March 30, 2010 vs. SWE
3 Amanda Kessel, USA, 3rd period, January 7, 2009 vs. SWE
3 Kendall Coyne, USA, 1st period, January 5, 2009 vs. RUS
3 Saige Pacholok, CAN, 3rd period, January 7, 2009 vs. CZE

**PENALTY SHOTS**
Phoebe Stanz (SUI) scored on Isabella Portnoj (FIN), January 4, 2011
Seika Yuyama (JPN) stopped by Tamara Klosser (SUI), January 8, 2011
Phoebe Stanz (SUI) stopped by Franziska Albl (GER), January 3, 2012
Lyudmila Belyakova (RUS) stopped by Janine Alder (SUI), January 4, 2012

## Goaltender Records

**MOST MEDALS**
2 (gold, silver) Alex Rigsby, USA

**MOST TOURNAMENTS, GOALIE**
2 Susanna Airaksinen (FIN)
2 Sophie Anthamatten (SUI)
2 Anna Prugova (RUS)
2 Alex Rigsby (USA)

**MOST GAMES PLAYED, GOALIE, CAREER**
10 Sophie Anthamatten, SUI
10 Anna Prugova, RUS
10 Veronika Hladikova, CZE
10 Shizuka Takahashi, JPN

**MOST MINUTES PLAYED, GOALIE, CAREER**
589:30 Sophie Anthamatten, SUI
532:58 Anna Prugova, RUS
489:54 Veronika Hladikova, CZE

**MOST WINS, GOALIE, CAREER**
5 Susanna Airaksinen, FIN
5 Alyssa Grogan, USA
5 Alex Rigsby, USA
5 Sofia Carlstrom, SWE

**MOST WINS, GOALIE, ONE WW18**
5 Alyssa Grogan, USA, 2008

**MOST LOSSES, GOALIE, CAREER**
7 Anna Prugova, RUS
6 Sophie Anthamatten, SUI
6 Shizuka Takahashi, JPN

**MOST LOSSES, GOALIE, ONE WW18**
5 Anna Prugova, RUS, 2010
5 Anna Vinogradova, RUS, 2008

**MOST SHUTOUTS, CAREER**
3 Alex Rigsby, USA

**MOST SHUTOUTS, ONE WW18**
2 Carmen MacDonald, CAN, 2010
2 Alex Rigsby, USA, 2010
2 Corrine Boyles, USA, 2009
2 Megan Miller, USA, 2011

**LONGEST SHUTOUT SEQUENCE (IN MINUTES)**
294:48 CAN, December 31, 2011-present
192:57 USA, March 27-April 3, 2010
192:37 CAN, March 27-April 3, 2010

**LONGEST SHUTOUT SEQUENCE, GOALIE**
158:35 Corrine Boyles, USA, 2009
150:42 Carmen MacDonald, CAN, 2010

**ALL GOALIE ASSISTS, CAREER**
~none to date

**MOST GOALIE PENALTY MINUTES, CAREER**
2 Sophie Anthamatten, SUI
2 Katerina Becevova, CZE
2 Annika Ferngren, SWE
2 Alyssa Grogan, USA
2 Monika Pencikova, CZE

## Shots On Goal Records

**MOST SHOTS, TEAM, GAME**
95 CAN, January 3, 2012 vs. FIN
88 SWE, January 6, 2009 vs. RUS
86 USA, January 6, 2012 vs. GER
80 CAN, January 5, 2009 vs. SUI
80 CAN, January 1, 2012 vs. GER

**MOST SHOTS, BOTH TEAMS, GAME**
108 SUI 61-GER 47, January 3, 2012
105 SUI 59-RUS 46, January 7, 2012
105 CAN 95-FIN 10, January 3, 2012
105 RUS 54-SUI 51, January 4, 2012
98 CAN 72-SUI 26, December 31, 2011
98 CAN 80-GER 18, January 1, 2012

**MOST SHOTS, TEAM, PERIOD**
39 SWE, January 6, 2009 vs. RUS, 2nd period
35 USA, January 2, 2011 vs. JPN, 3rd period
35 CAN, January 3, 2012 vs. FIN, 2nd period

**MOST SHOTS, BOTH TEAMS, PERIOD**
44 SUI 26-RUS 18, January 7, 2012, 1st period
43 GER 23-SUI 20, January 3, 2012, 2nd period
41 SWE 39-RUS 2, January 6, 2009, 2nd period
39 FIN 26-SUI 13, January 11, 2008, 1st period
39 CAN 35-FIN 4, January 3, 2012, 2nd period

**FEWEST SHOTS, TEAM, GAME**
3 RUS, January 5, 2009 vs. USA
3 RUS, January 7, 2008 vs. USA
4 SWE, January 4, 2011 vs. USA
5 SUI, January 8, 2008 vs. USA

**FEWEST SHOTS, BOTH TEAMS, GAME**
35 CZE 19-GER 16, January 9, 2008

**FEWEST SHOTS, TEAM, PERIOD**
0 January 7, 2008 FIN vs GER, 3rd period
January 7, 2008 RUS vs. USA, 1st period
January 9, 2008 FIN vs. CAN, 2nd period
January 9, 2008 CZE vs GER, 1st period
January 12, 2008 GER vs FIN, 3rd period
January 5, 2009 RUS vs. USA, 1st period
January 6, 2009 FIN vs. CAN, 3rd period
January 9, 2009 CZE vs. USA, 3rd period
March 30, 2010 SWE vs. CAN, 3rd period
April 2, 2010 SWE vs. USA, 1st period
April 3, 2010 GER vs. SWE, 2nd period

**FEWEST SHOTS, BOTH TEAMS, PERIOD**
5 GER 5-CZE 0, January 9, 2008, 1st period

## Penalty Records

**FEWEST PENALTIES & PENALTY MINUTES, TEAM, GAME**
0 USA, January 7, 2008 vs. RUS
2 USA, January 5, 2009 vs. RUS
2 SWE, January 10, 2009 vs. CZE

**FEWEST PENALTY MINUTES, BOTH TEAMS, GAME**
8 RUS 8-USA 0, January 7, 2008
8 USA 4-GER 4, January 6, 2012
12 FIN 8-CAN 4, January 9, 2009
12 CZE 10-SWE 2, January 10, 2009
12 USA 6-JPN 6, March 27, 2010

**FEWEST PENALTIES, BOTH TEAMS, GAME**
4 RUS 4-USA 0, January 7, 2008
4 USA 2-GER 2, January 6, 2012
6 FIN 4-CAN 2, January 9, 2009
6 CZE 5-SWE 1, January 10, 2009
6 USA 3-JPN 3, March 27, 2010

**MOST PENALTY MINUTES, TEAM, GAME**
49 RUS, January 10, 2009 vs. SUI
49 USA, January 7, 2009 vs. SWE
42 SUI, January 9, 2009 vs. GER

**MOST PENALTY MINUTES, BOTH TEAMS, GAME**
87 USA 49-SWE 38, January 7, 2009
68 SUI 42-GER 26, January 9, 2009
67 RUS 49-SUI 18, January 10, 2009

**MOST PENALTY MINUTES, TEAM, PERIOD**
31 RUS, January 10, 2009 vs. SUI, 2nd period
31 USA, January 7, 2009 vs. SWE, 3rd period
29 GER, January 12, 2008 vs. FIN, 3rd period
29 GER, January 5, 2011 vs. CZE, 3rd period

**MOST PENALTY MINUTES, BOTH TEAMS, PERIOD**
53 CZE 29-SUI 24, January 6, 2009, 1st period
43 USA 31-SWE 12, January 7, 2009, 3rd period
37 RUS 31-SUI 6, January 10, 2009, 2nd period

**MOST PENALTIES, TEAM, PERIOD**
8 SUI January 6, 2009 vs. CZE, 1st period
8 SWE January 7, 2008 vs. SUI, 2nd period
7 RUS January 8, 2008 vs. SWE, 2nd period

**MOST PENALTIES, BOTH TEAMS, PERIOD**
13 SUI 7-GER 6, January 9, 2009, 2nd period
12 SUI 8-CZE 4, January 6, 2009, 1st period
11 SWE 6-USA 5, January 7, 2009, 3rd period
11 USA 6-SWE 5, January 7, 2009, 2nd period
11 SWE 6-SUI 5, January 7, 2008, 1st period

**MOST PENALTIES, TEAM, GAME**
18 SWE January 7, 2008 vs. SUI
17 SUI January 9, 2009 vs GER
15 SWE January 7, 2009 vs. USA
15 RUS January 8, 2008 vs. SWE

**MOST PENALTIES, BOTH TEAMS, GAME**
30 SUI 17-GER 13, January 9, 2009
29 SWE 15-USA 14, January 7, 2009
29 SWE 18-SUI 11, January 7, 2008

**MOST PENALTY MINUTES, INDIVIDUAL, GAME**
29 Tanja Eisenschmid, GER, January 5, 2011 vs. CZE (2 minors, major, game misconduct)
27 Elina Mitrofanova, RUS, January 10, 2009 vs. SUI (minor, major, game misconduct)
27 Klara Mazankova, CZE, January 1, 2012 vs. RUS (minor, major, game misconduct)

**MOST PENALTY MINUTES, INDIVIDUAL, PERIOD**
27 Tanja Eisenschmid, GER, January 5, 2011 vs. CZE, 3rd period (minor, major, game misconduct)

**MOST PENALTIES, INDIVIDUAL, GAME**
6 Sandra Thalmann, SUI, January 10, 2009 vs. RUS (6 minors)
5 Sandra Thalmann, SUI, January 9, 2009 vs. GER (4 minors, 1 misconduct)
4 Emma Nordin, SWE, January 7, 2009 vs. USA (4 minors)
4 Lucie Povova, CZE, January 12, 2008 vs. SWE (4 minors)

4 Laura Benz, SUI, January 12, 2008 vs. RUS (4 minors)
4 Inna Dyubanok, RUS, January 8, 2008 vs. SWE (3 minors, 1 misconduct)
4 Phoebe Stanz, SUI, January 4, 2011 vs. FIN (4 minors)

**MOST PENALTIES, INDIVIDUAL, PERIOD**
3 Sandra Thalmann, January 9, 2009 vs. GER (3 minors, 1 misconduct)
3 Laura Benz, SUI, January 12, 2008 vs. RUS, 3rd period (3 minors)
3 Tanja Eisenschmid, GER, January 5, 2011 vs. CZE, 3rd period (minor, major, game misconduct)

## Speed Records

**FASTEST GOAL FROM START OF GAME & PERIOD**
17 seconds CAN (Brigette Lacquette), January 7, 2009 vs. CZE

**FASTEST TWO GOALS, INDIVIDUAL**
21 seconds Olga Sosina (RUS) 5:41 & 6:02, 3rd period, January 7, 2009 vs. GER
34 seconds Kendall Coyne (USA) 16:05 & 16:39, 2nd period, March 30, 2010 vs. CZE
35 seconds Brianne Jenner (CAN) 1:18 & 1:53, 2nd period, January 9, 2008 vs. FIN

**FASTEST TWO GOALS, TEAM**
7 seconds USA (Alexandra Carpenter 15:58 & Kendall Koyne 16:05, 2nd period), March 30, 2010 vs. CZE
7 seconds USA (Abby Ness 18:59 & Sydney Daniels 19:06, 3rd period), January 7, 2011

**FASTEST TWO GOALS, BOTH TEAMS**
7 seconds Hayley Skarupa (USA) 6:52 & Denisa Krizova (CZE) 6:59, 1st period, January 7, 2011

**FASTEST THREE GOALS, INDIVIDUAL**
6:51 Kendall Coyne (USA), 9:18, 12:49, 16:09, 3rd period, March 27, 2010 vs. JPN

**FASTEST THREE GOALS, TEAM**
41 seconds USA (Alex Carpenter 15:58, Kendall Coyne 16:05, Kendall Coyne 16:39, 2nd period), March 30, 2010 vs. CZE
50 seconds USA (Lyndsey Fry 13:15, Alev Kelter 13:44, Taylor Wasylk 14:05, 1st period), January 5, 2009 vs. RUS

**FASTEST THREE GOALS, BOTH TEAMS**
29 seconds Katerina Solnickova (CZE) 7:35, Runa Moritake (JPN) 7:57, Chiho Osawa (JPN) 8:04, 1st period, March 28, 2010

**FASTEST FOUR GOALS, TEAM**
3:08 USA (Brittany Ammerman 10:57, Lyndsey Fry 13:15, Alev Kelter 13:44, Taylor Wasylk 14:05, 1st period), January 5, 2009 vs. RUS
3:17 CAN (Jessica Campbell 11:21, Jillian Saulnier 11:41, Melodie Daoust 13:04, Christine Bestland 14:38, 3rd period), April 2, 2010 vs. GER

**FASTEST FIVE GOALS, TEAM**
6:04 SWE (Klara Myren 10:23, Anna Borgqvist 12:00, Angelica Ostlund 12:44, Anna Borgqvist 15:06, Tina Enstrom 16:27, 3rd period), January 5, 2009 vs. GER

*Russia's Olga Sosina (left) holds the WW18 record for fastest two goals by a player, scoring twice in just 21 seconds against Germany on January 7, 2009. Photo: Phillip MacCallum / HHOF-IIHF Images.*

*One of the most talked about images from the 2012 World Championships is this featuring Slovakian captain Zdeno Chara and American forward Max Pacioretty, the two meeting for the first time since a Montreal-Boston NHL game in which Pacioretty was badly injured by a Chara hit along the boards. Photo: Jeff Vinnick / HHOF-IIHF Images.*

# IIHF-NHL INTERNATIONAL

## Europeans in the NHL Draft

*bold denotes yearly leader

| | | | | | | TOP EUROPEAN NATIONS | | | | | REST OF THE WORLD | | | | | | | | | | | | | | | | | | |
|---|---|---|---|---|---|---|---|---|---|---|---|---|---|---|---|---|---|---|---|---|---|---|---|---|---|---|---|---|---|
| Year | Teams | Total | Euros | % | Euros/ Team | CZE TCH | FIN | RUS URS | SVK | SWE | AUT | BLR | CRO | DEN | FRA | GER FRG | GBR | HUN | ITA | JPN | KAZ | KOR | LAT | LTU | NOR | POL | SLO | SUI | UKR |
| 1969 | 12 | 84 | 1 | 1.19% | 0.08 | 0 | **1** | 0 | 0 | 0 | 0 | 0 | 0 | 0 | 0 | 0 | 0 | 0 | 0 | 0 | 0 | 0 | 0 | 0 | 0 | 0 | 0 | 0 | 0 |
| 1970 | 14 | 115 | 0 | 0 | 0 | 0 | 0 | 0 | 0 | 0 | 0 | 0 | 0 | 0 | 0 | 0 | 0 | 0 | 0 | 0 | 0 | 0 | 0 | 0 | 0 | 0 | 0 | 0 | 0 |
| 1971 | 14 | 117 | 0 | 0 | 0 | 0 | 0 | 0 | 0 | 0 | 0 | 0 | 0 | 0 | 0 | 0 | 0 | 0 | 0 | 0 | 0 | 0 | 0 | 0 | 0 | 0 | 0 | 0 | 0 |
| 1972 | 14 | 152 | 0 | 0 | 0 | 0 | 0 | 0 | 0 | 0 | 0 | 0 | 0 | 0 | 0 | 0 | 0 | 0 | 0 | 0 | 0 | 0 | 0 | 0 | 0 | 0 | 0 | 0 | 0 |
| 1973 | 16 | 168 | 0 | 0 | 0 | 0 | 0 | 0 | 0 | 0 | 0 | 0 | 0 | 0 | 0 | 0 | 0 | 0 | 0 | 0 | 0 | 0 | 0 | 0 | 0 | 0 | 0 | 0 | 0 |
| 1974 | 18 | 247 | 6 | 2.43% | 0.33 | 0 | 1 | 0 | 0 | **5** | 0 | 0 | 0 | 0 | 0 | 0 | 0 | 0 | 0 | 0 | 0 | 0 | 0 | 0 | 0 | 0 | 0 | 0 | 0 |
| 1975 | 18 | 217 | 6 | 2.76% | 0.33 | 0 | **3** | 1 | 0 | 2 | 0 | 0 | 0 | 0 | 0 | 0 | 0 | 0 | 0 | 0 | 0 | 0 | 0 | 0 | 0 | 0 | 0 | 0 | 0 |
| 1976 | 18 | 135 | 8 | 5.93% | 0.44 | 0 | 2 | 0 | 0 | **5** | 0 | 0 | 0 | 0 | 0 | 0 | 0 | 0 | 0 | 0 | 0 | 0 | 0 | 0 | 0 | 0 | 0 | 1 | 0 |
| 1977 | 18 | 185 | 5 | 2.70% | 0.28 | 0 | **3** | 0 | 0 | 2 | 0 | 0 | 0 | 0 | 0 | 0 | 0 | 0 | 0 | 0 | 0 | 0 | 0 | 0 | 0 | 0 | 0 | 0 | 0 |
| 1978 | 17 | 234 | 16 | 6.84% | 0.94 | 2 | 2 | 2 | 0 | **8** | 0 | 0 | 0 | 0 | 0 | **2** | 0 | 0 | 0 | 0 | 0 | 0 | 0 | 0 | 0 | 0 | 0 | 0 | 0 |
| 1979 | 21 | 126 | 6 | 4.76% | 0.29 | 1 | 0 | 0 | 0 | **5** | 0 | 0 | 0 | 0 | 0 | 0 | 0 | 0 | 0 | 0 | 0 | 0 | 0 | 0 | 0 | 0 | 0 | 0 | 0 |
| 1980 | 21 | 210 | 13 | 6.19% | 0.62 | 0 | 4 | 0 | 0 | **9** | 0 | 0 | 0 | 0 | 0 | 0 | 0 | 0 | 0 | 0 | 0 | 0 | 0 | 0 | 0 | 0 | 0 | 0 | 0 |
| 1981 | 21 | 211 | 32 | 15.17% | 1.52 | 4 | 12 | 0 | 0 | **14** | 0 | 0 | 0 | 0 | 0 | **2** | 0 | 0 | 0 | 0 | 0 | 0 | 0 | 0 | 0 | 0 | 0 | 0 | 0 |
| 1982 | 21 | 252 | 35 | 13.89% | 1.67 | **13** | 6 | 3 | 0 | **13** | 0 | 0 | 0 | 0 | 0 | 0 | 0 | 0 | 0 | 0 | 0 | 0 | 0 | 0 | 0 | 0 | 0 | 0 | 0 |
| 1983 | 21 | 252 | 34 | 13.49% | 1.62 | 9 | 9 | 5 | 0 | **10** | 0 | 0 | 0 | 0 | 0 | **1** | 0 | 0 | 0 | 0 | 0 | 0 | 0 | 0 | 0 | 0 | 0 | 0 | 0 |
| 1984 | 21 | 250 | 40 | 16.00% | 1.9 | 13 | 10 | 1 | 0 | **14** | 0 | 0 | 0 | 0 | 0 | **2** | 0 | 0 | 0 | 0 | 0 | 0 | 0 | 0 | 0 | 0 | 0 | 0 | 0 |
| 1985 | 21 | 252 | 31 | 12.30% | 1.48 | 8 | 4 | 2 | 0 | **16** | 0 | 0 | 0 | 0 | 0 | **1** | 0 | 0 | 0 | 0 | 0 | 0 | 0 | 0 | 0 | 0 | 0 | 0 | 0 |
| 1986 | 21 | 252 | 28 | 11.11% | 1.33 | 6 | **11** | 1 | 0 | 8 | 0 | 0 | 0 | **1** | 0 | 0 | **1** | 0 | 0 | 0 | 0 | 0 | 0 | 0 | 0 | 0 | 0 | 0 | 0 |
| 1987 | 21 | 252 | 38 | 15.08% | 1.81 | 11 | 6 | 2 | 0 | **15** | 0 | 0 | 0 | 1 | 0 | 1 | 0 | 0 | 0 | 0 | 0 | 0 | 0 | 0 | **2** | 0 | 0 | 0 | 0 |
| 1988 | 21 | 252 | 39 | 15.48% | 1.86 | 5 | 7 | 10 | 0 | **14** | 0 | 0 | 0 | 0 | 0 | **2** | 0 | 0 | 0 | 0 | 0 | 0 | 0 | 0 | 0 | 0 | 0 | 0 | 1 |
| 1989 | 21 | 252 | 38 | 15.08% | 1.81 | 8 | 3 | **18** | 0 | 9 | 0 | 0 | 0 | 0 | 0 | 0 | 0 | 0 | 0 | 0 | 0 | 0 | 0 | 0 | 0 | 0 | 0 | 0 | 0 |
| 1990 | 21 | 252 | 56 | 22.22% | 2.67 | **22** | 9 | 14 | 0 | 8 | 0 | 0 | 0 | 0 | 0 | 0 | 0 | 0 | 0 | 0 | 0 | 0 | 0 | 0 | **3** | 0 | 0 | 0 | 0 |
| 1991 | 22 | 264 | 56 | 21.21% | 2.55 | 10 | 6 | **25** | 0 | 11 | 0 | 0 | 0 | 0 | 0 | **1** | 0 | 0 | 0 | 0 | 0 | 0 | 0 | 0 | **1** | **1** | 0 | **1** | 0 |
| 1992 | 24 | 264 | 91 | 34.47% | 3.79 | 17 | 10 | **44** | 3 | 11 | 0 | 0 | 0 | 0 | 0 | 1 | 0 | 0 | 0 | 1 | 0 | 1 | **2** | 0 | 0 | 0 | 0 | 0 | 1 |
| 1993 | 26 | 266 | 93 | 34.96% | 3.58 | 14 | 8 | **36** | 4 | 18 | 0 | 2 | 0 | 0 | 0 | 1 | 0 | 0 | 0 | 0 | 1 | 0 | 1 | 0 | 1 | 2 | 0 | 1 | **4** |
| 1994 | 26 | 286 | 85 | 29.72% | 3.27 | 17 | 8 | **32** | 3 | 17 | 0 | 0 | 0 | 0 | 0 | 2 | 0 | 0 | 0 | 0 | **3** | 0 | 0 | 0 | 0 | 0 | 0 | 1 | 2 |
| 1995 | 26 | 234 | 79 | 33.76% | 3.04 | 21 | 13 | **25** | 7 | 8 | 1 | 0 | 0 | 0 | 0 | 1 | 0 | 0 | 0 | 0 | 0 | 0 | 0 | 0 | 0 | 0 | 0 | 0 | **3** |
| 1996 | 26 | 241 | 69 | 28.63% | 2.65 | 11 | 7 | **20** | 7 | 14 | 0 | 1 | 0 | 1 | 0 | **3** | 0 | 0 | 0 | 0 | 0 | 0 | 0 | 1 | 0 | 0 | 0 | 1 | **3** |
| 1997 | 26 | 246 | 78 | 31.70% | 3 | 16 | 12 | **20** | 6 | 15 | 0 | 1 | 0 | 0 | 0 | 2 | 0 | 0 | 0 | 0 | 0 | 0 | 1 | 0 | 1 | 0 | 0 | **3** | 1 |
| 1998 | 27 | 258 | 88 | 34.11% | 3.26 | **20** | 12 | 19 | 6 | 18 | 1 | 0 | 0 | 0 | 0 | 0 | 0 | 0 | 0 | 0 | 3 | 0 | 1 | 0 | 0 | 0 | 1 | 2 | **5** |
| 1999 | 28 | 272 | 115 | 42.28% | 4.11 | 18 | 17 | **25** | 12 | 24 | 2 | 2 | 1 | 0 | 1 | 0 | 0 | 1 | 0 | 0 | **5** | 0 | 2 | 0 | 1 | 0 | 0 | 3 | 1 |
| 2000 | 30 | 293 | 139 | 47.44% | 4.63 | 24 | 19 | **41** | 16 | 23 | 1 | 0 | 0 | 0 | 0 | 0 | 1 | 1 | 0 | 0 | 3 | 0 | 2 | 0 | 0 | 0 | 1 | **6** | 1 |
| 2001 | 30 | 289 | 142 | 49.13% | 4.73 | 31 | 23 | **37** | 15 | 17 | 2 | 0 | 0 | 0 | 1 | **6** | 0 | 0 | 0 | 0 | 2 | 0 | 1 | 0 | 0 | 0 | 1 | 5 | 1 |
| 2002 | 30 | 291 | 121 | 41.58% | 4.03 | 26 | 25 | **32** | 3 | 20 | 1 | 1 | 0 | 1 | 0 | 0 | 0 | 1 | 0 | 0 | 0 | 0 | 3 | 0 | 2 | 0 | 0 | **5** | 2 |
| 2003 | 30 | 292 | 103 | 35.27% | 3.43 | 18 | 13 | **30** | 10 | 16 | 1 | 2 | 0 | 0 | 0 | **4** | 0 | 0 | 0 | 0 | 2 | 0 | 2 | 0 | 0 | 1 | 0 | **4** | 0 |
| 2004 | 30 | 291 | 97 | 33.33% | 3.23 | **21** | 13 | 18 | 6 | 18 | 0 | **4** | 0 | 2 | 0 | 2 | 0 | 0 | 0 | 1 | 3 | 0 | 1 | 0 | 0 | 0 | **4** | **4** | 0 |
| 2005 | 30 | 230 | 57 | 24.78% | 1.9 | **13** | 9 | 12 | 7 | 11 | 0 | **1** | 0 | **1** | 0 | **1** | 0 | 0 | 0 | 0 | 0 | 0 | **1** | 0 | 0 | 0 | **1** | 0 | 0 |
| 2006 | 30 | 213 | 71 | 33.33% | 2.37 | 8 | 14 | 15 | 4 | **18** | 2 | 0 | 0 | 0 | 0 | **4** | 0 | 0 | 0 | 0 | 0 | 0 | 2 | 0 | 0 | 0 | 1 | 3 | 0 |
| 2007 | 30 | 211 | 45 | 21.33% | 1.5 | 5 | 4 | 9 | 3 | **17** | 0 | 0 | 0 | 1 | 0 | **4** | 0 | 0 | 0 | 0 | 0 | 0 | 0 | 0 | 0 | 0 | 0 | 2 | 0 |
| 2008 | 30 | 211 | 45 | 21.33% | 1.5 | 3 | 7 | 8 | 0 | **17** | 0 | 1 | 0 | 2 | 0 | 1 | 0 | 0 | 0 | 0 | 0 | 0 | 1 | 0 | **3** | 0 | 0 | 2 | 0 |
| 2009 | 30 | 210 | 53 | 25.24% | 1.77 | 3 | 10 | 7 | 4 | **24** | 0 | **1** | 0 | **1** | 0 | **1** | 0 | 0 | **1** | 0 | 0 | 0 | 0 | 0 | 0 | 0 | **1** | 0 | 0 |
| 2010 | 30 | 210 | 52 | 24.76% | 1.73 | 5 | 7 | 8 | 2 | **20** | 0 | 0 | 0 | 1 | 0 | **5** | 0 | 0 | 0 | 0 | 0 | 0 | 1 | 0 | 1 | 0 | 0 | 2 | 0 |
| 2011 | 30 | 211 | 68 | 32.2% | 2.27 | 10 | 10 | 9 | 4 | **28** | 0 | 0 | 0 | 1 | 0 | **2** | 0 | 0 | 0 | 0 | 0 | 0 | 0 | 0 | **2** | 0 | 0 | **2** | 0 |
| 2012 | 30 | 211 | 56 | 26.54% | 1.87 | 6 | 9 | 11 | 0 | **22** | 0 | 1 | 0 | **2** | 1 | 0 | 0 | 0 | 0 | 0 | 0 | 0 | **2** | 0 | 0 | 0 | 0 | **2** | 0 |
| Year | Teams | Total | Euros | % | Euros/ Team | CZE TCH | FIN | RUS URS | SVK | SWE | AUT | BLR | CRO | DEN | FRA | GER FRG | GBR | HUN | ITA | JPN | KAZ | KOR | LAT | LTU | NOR | POL | SLO | SUI | UKR |

# European Rookies in the NHL

*bold denotes yearly leader

| | | | | | | TOP EUROPEAN NATIONS | | | | | REST OF THE WORLD | | | | | | | | | | | | |
|---|---|---|---|---|---|---|---|---|---|---|---|---|---|---|---|---|---|---|---|---|---|---|---|
| Year | Teams | Rookies | Euros | % | Euros/ Team | CZE TCH | FIN | RUS URS | SVK | SWE | AUT | BLR | DEN | FRA | GER FRG | JPN | KAZ | LAT | NOR | POL | SLO | SUI | UKR |
| 1964-65 | 6 | 23 | 1 | 4.35% | 0.17 | 0 | 0 | 0 | 0 | **1** | 0 | 0 | 0 | 0 | 0 | 0 | 0 | 0 | 0 | 0 | 0 | 0 | 0 |
| 1965-66 | 6 | 21 | 0 | 0 | 0 | 0 | 0 | 0 | 0 | 0 | 0 | 0 | 0 | 0 | 0 | 0 | 0 | 0 | 0 | 0 | 0 | 0 | 0 |
| 1966-67 | 6 | 17 | 0 | 0 | 0 | 0 | 0 | 0 | 0 | 0 | 0 | 0 | 0 | 0 | 0 | 0 | 0 | 0 | 0 | 0 | 0 | 0 | 0 |
| 1967-68 | 12 | 95 | 1 | 1.05% | 0.83 | 0 | 0 | 0 | 0 | 0 | 0 | 0 | 0 | 0 | **1** | 0 | 0 | 0 | 0 | 0 | 0 | 0 | 0 |
| 1968-69 | 12 | 64 | 0 | 0 | 0 | 0 | 0 | 0 | 0 | 0 | 0 | 0 | 0 | 0 | 0 | 0 | 0 | 0 | 0 | 0 | 0 | 0 | 0 |
| 1969-70 | 12 | 55 | 1 | 1.81% | 0.08 | **1** | 0 | 0 | 0 | 0 | 0 | 0 | 0 | 0 | 0 | 0 | 0 | 0 | 0 | 0 | 0 | 0 | 0 |
| 1970-71 | 14 | 75 | 0 | 0 | 0 | 0 | 0 | 0 | 0 | 0 | 0 | 0 | 0 | 0 | 0 | 0 | 0 | 0 | 0 | 0 | 0 | 0 | 0 |
| 1971-72 | 14 | 61 | 0 | 0 | 0 | 0 | 0 | 0 | 0 | 0 | 0 | 0 | 0 | 0 | 0 | 0 | 0 | 0 | 0 | 0 | 0 | 0 | 0 |
| 1972-73 | 14 | 100 | 1 | 1.00% | 0.07 | 0 | 0 | 0 | 0 | **1** | 0 | 0 | 0 | 0 | 0 | 0 | 0 | 0 | 0 | 0 | 0 | 0 | 0 |
| 1973-74 | 16 | 98 | 3 | 3.06% | 0.19 | 0 | 0 | 0 | 0 | **3** | 0 | 0 | 0 | 0 | 0 | 0 | 0 | 0 | 0 | 0 | 0 | 0 | 0 |
| 1974-75 | 18 | 114 | 0 | 0 | 0 | 0 | 0 | 0 | 0 | 0 | 0 | 0 | 0 | 0 | 0 | 0 | 0 | 0 | 0 | 0 | 0 | 0 | 0 |
| 1975-76 | 18 | 81 | 0 | 0 | 0 | 0 | 0 | 0 | 0 | 0 | 0 | 0 | 0 | 0 | 0 | 0 | 0 | 0 | 0 | 0 | 0 | 0 | 0 |
| 1976-77 | 18 | 84 | 3 | 3.57% | 0.17 | 0 | 1 | 0 | 0 | **2** | 0 | 0 | 0 | 0 | 0 | 0 | 0 | 0 | 0 | 0 | 0 | 0 | 0 |
| 1977-78 | 18 | 93 | 6 | 6.45% | 0.33 | 1 | 0 | 0 | 0 | **5** | 0 | 0 | 0 | 0 | 0 | 0 | 0 | 0 | 0 | 0 | 0 | 0 | 0 |
| 1978-79 | 17 | 87 | 9 | 10.34% | 0.53 | 0 | 0 | 0 | 0 | **8** | 0 | 0 | 0 | 0 | 0 | 0 | 0 | 0 | **1** | 0 | 0 | 0 | 0 |
| 1979-80 | 21 | 202 | 11 | 5.45% | 0.52 | 1 | **5** | 0 | 0 | **5** | 0 | 0 | 0 | 0 | 0 | 0 | 0 | 0 | 0 | 0 | 0 | 0 | 0 |
| 1980-81 | 21 | 132 | 11 | 8.33% | 0.52 | 3 | 2 | 0 | 0 | **6** | 0 | 0 | 0 | 0 | 0 | 0 | 0 | 0 | 0 | 0 | 0 | 0 | 0 |
| 1981-82 | 21 | 157 | 25 | 15.92% | 1.19 | 4 | **10** | 0 | 0 | **10** | 0 | 0 | 0 | 0 | **1** | 0 | 0 | 0 | 0 | 0 | 0 | 0 | 0 |
| 1982-83 | 21 | 103 | 12 | 11.65% | 0.57 | **5** | 1 | 1 | 0 | **5** | 0 | 0 | 0 | 0 | 0 | 0 | 0 | 0 | 0 | 0 | 0 | 0 | 0 |
| 1983-84 | 21 | 126 | 7 | 5.56% | 0.33 | 0 | 2 | 0 | 0 | **5** | 0 | 0 | 0 | 0 | 0 | 0 | 0 | 0 | 0 | 0 | 0 | 0 | 0 |
| 1984-85 | 21 | 108 | 17 | 15.74% | 0.81 | 3 | **7** | 0 | 0 | 6 | 0 | 0 | 0 | 0 | **1** | 0 | 0 | 0 | 0 | 0 | 0 | 0 | 0 |
| 1985-86 | 21 | 111 | 14 | 12.61% | 0.67 | 2 | **7** | 0 | 0 | 5 | 0 | 0 | 0 | 0 | 0 | 0 | 0 | 0 | 0 | 0 | 0 | 0 | 0 |
| 1986-87 | 21 | 93 | 8 | 8.60% | 0.38 | 2 | **3** | 0 | 0 | 2 | 0 | 0 | 0 | 0 | **1** | 0 | 0 | 0 | 0 | 0 | 0 | 0 | 0 |
| 1987-88 | 21 | 122 | 8 | 6.56% | 0.38 | 2 | 0 | 0 | 0 | **6** | 0 | 0 | 0 | 0 | 0 | 0 | 0 | 0 | 0 | 0 | 0 | 0 | 0 |
| 1988-89 | 21 | 116 | 12 | 10.34% | 0.57 | 4 | **7** | 1 | 0 | 0 | 0 | 0 | 0 | 0 | 0 | 0 | 0 | 0 | 0 | 0 | 0 | 0 | 0 |
| 1989-90 | 21 | 118 | 18 | 15.25% | 0.86 | 3 | 1 | **9** | 0 | 4 | 0 | 0 | 0 | 0 | 0 | 0 | 0 | 0 | 0 | 0 | 0 | 0 | 0 |
| 1990-91 | 21 | 123 | 23 | 18.70% | 1.1 | **13** | 0 | 7 | 0 | 3 | 0 | 0 | 0 | 0 | 0 | 0 | 0 | 0 | 0 | 0 | 0 | 0 | 0 |
| 1991-92 | 22 | 118 | 23 | 19.49% | 1.05 | 4 | 1 | **14** | 0 | 3 | 0 | 0 | 0 | **1** | 0 | 0 | 0 | 0 | 0 | 0 | 0 | 0 | 0 |
| 1992-93 | 24 | 117 | 44 | 37.61% | 1.83 | 9 | 1 | **22** | 1 | 7 | 0 | 1 | 0 | 0 | 0 | 0 | 0 | **3** | 0 | 0 | 0 | 0 | 0 |
| 1993-94 | 26 | 149 | 38 | 25.50% | 1.46 | 8 | 3 | **16** | 3 | 4 | 0 | 1 | 0 | 0 | 0 | 0 | 0 | **2** | 0 | 1 | 0 | 0 | 0 |
| 1994-95 | 26 | 110 | 24 | 21.82% | 0.92 | 5 | 2 | **10** | 1 | 5 | 0 | 0 | 0 | 0 | 0 | 0 | 0 | 0 | 0 | 0 | 0 | **1** | 0 |
| 1995-96 | 26 | 144 | 37 | 25.69% | 1.42 | 9 | 7 | 6 | 2 | **10** | 0 | **1** | 0 | 0 | **1** | 0 | 0 | 0 | **1** | 0 | 0 | 0 | 0 |
| 1996-97 | 26 | 107 | 29 | 27.10% | 1.12 | 5 | 6 | **8** | 0 | 7 | 0 | **1** | 0 | 0 | 0 | 0 | **1** | 0 | 0 | **1** | 0 | 0 | 0 |
| 1997-98 | 26 | 118 | 39 | 33.05% | 1.5 | 6 | 4 | **10** | 6 | 8 | 0 | 0 | 0 | 0 | **2** | 0 | 0 | 1 | 1 | 0 | 0 | 0 | 1 |
| 1998-99 | 27 | 122 | 31 | 25.41% | 1.15 | **11** | 3 | 5 | 2 | 6 | 0 | 0 | 0 | 0 | 1 | 0 | 0 | **3** | 0 | 0 | 0 | 0 | 0 |
| 1999-00 | 28 | 137 | 51 | 37.23% | 1.82 | 12 | 7 | **16** | 4 | 8 | 0 | 0 | 0 | 0 | **1** | 0 | **1** | **1** | 0 | 0 | 0 | 0 | **1** |
| 2000-01 | 30 | 151 | 65 | 43.05% | 2.17 | **18** | 8 | 8 | 13 | 9 | 0 | 0 | 0 | 0 | 1 | 0 | 1 | 0 | 0 | 0 | 0 | **4** | 3 |
| 2001-02 | 30 | 132 | 50 | 37.88% | 1.67 | **17** | 13 | 5 | 5 | 9 | **1** | 0 | 0 | 0 | 0 | 0 | 0 | 0 | 0 | 0 | 0 | 0 | 0 |
| 2002-03 | 30 | 128 | 41 | 32.03% | 1.37 | 8 | 5 | **9** | 7 | 8 | 0 | **1** | 0 | **1** | **1** | 0 | 0 | 0 | 0 | 0 | 0 | **1** | 0 |
| 2003-04 | 30 | 160 | 48 | 30.63% | 1.6 | 9 | **12** | 11 | 3 | 7 | **2** | 0 | 0 | 0 | **2** | 0 | 0 | 0 | 0 | 0 | 0 | **2** | 0 |
| 2004-05 | 30 | * | * | * | * | * | * | * | * | * | * | * | * | * | * | * | * | * | * | * | * | * | * |
| 2005-06 | 30 | 211 | 45 | 21.33% | 1.5 | **11** | 8 | 3 | 5 | 9 | 1 | 0 | 0 | 0 | 1 | 0 | **3** | 1 | 1 | 0 | 0 | 2 | 0 |
| 2006-07 | 30 | 139 | 41 | 29.50% | 1.37 | **11** | 7 | 4 | 2 | 8 | 0 | 1 | **2** | 0 | 0 | 1 | 0 | 1 | 1 | 0 | 1 | 1 | 1 |
| 2007-08 | 30 | 146 | 34 | 23.29% | 1.13 | 6 | 8 | 3 | 2 | **9** | 0 | 1 | 0 | 0 | 2 | 0 | 0 | 0 | 0 | 0 | 0 | **3** | 0 |
| 2008-09 | 30 | 170 | 41 | 24.12% | 1.37 | 7 | 8 | 6 | 2 | **10** | 1 | 0 | **2** | 0 | 1 | 0 | 0 | **2** | 0 | 0 | 0 | **2** | 0 |
| 2009-10 | 30 | 137 | 32 | 23.06% | 1.07 | 3 | 5 | 7 | 1 | **9** | 1 | 0 | 2 | 0 | 0 | 0 | 1 | **3** | 0 | 0 | 0 | 0 | 0 |
| 2010-11 | 30 | 139 | 36 | 25.90% | 1.20 | 2 | 2 | 6 | 1 | **16** | 0 | 0 | 0 | 1 | **3** | 0 | 0 | 0 | 2 | 0 | 1 | 2 | 0 |
| 2011-12 | 30 | 135 | 26 | 19.26% | 0.87 | 2 | 3 | 3 | 1 | **13** | 0 | 0 | 0 | 1 | 0 | 0 | 0 | 0 | 0 | 0 | 0 | **3** | 0 |
| Year | Teams | Rookies | Euros | % | Euros/ Team | CZE TCH | FIN | RUS URS | SVK | SWE | AUT | BLR | DEN | FRA | GER FRG | JPN | KAZ | LAT | NOR | POL | SLO | SUI | UKR |

# Europeans in the NHL

*bold denotes yearly leader

| | | | | | | TOP EUROPEAN NATIONS | | | | | REST OF THE WORLD | | | | | | | | | | | | | |
|---|---|---|---|---|---|---|---|---|---|---|---|---|---|---|---|---|---|---|---|---|---|---|---|---|
| Year | Teams | Total | Euros | % | Euros/ Team | CZE TCH | FIN | RUS URS | SVK | SWE | AUT | BLR | DEN | FRA | GER FRG | JPN | KAZ | LAT | LTU | NOR | POL | SLO | SUI | UKR |
| 1964-65 | 6 | 171 | 1 | 0.006% | 0.17 | 0 | 0 | 0 | 0 | **1** | 0 | 0 | 0 | 0 | 0 | 0 | 0 | 0 | 0 | 0 | 0 | 0 | 0 | 0 |
| 1965-66 | 6 | 184 | 0 | 0 | 0 | 0 | 0 | 0 | 0 | 0 | 0 | 0 | 0 | 0 | 0 | 0 | 0 | 0 | 0 | 0 | 0 | 0 | 0 | 0 |
| 1966-67 | 6 | 176 | 0 | 0 | 0 | 0 | 0 | 0 | 0 | 0 | 0 | 0 | 0 | 0 | 0 | 0 | 0 | 0 | 0 | 0 | 0 | 0 | 0 | 0 |
| 1967-68 | 12 | 317 | 0 | 0 | 0 | 0 | 0 | 0 | 0 | 0 | 0 | 0 | 0 | 0 | 0 | 0 | 0 | 0 | 0 | 0 | 0 | 0 | 0 | 0 |
| 1968-69 | 12 | 326 | 0 | 0 | 0 | 0 | 0 | 0 | 0 | 0 | 0 | 0 | 0 | 0 | 0 | 0 | 0 | 0 | 0 | 0 | 0 | 0 | 0 | 0 |
| 1969-70 | 12 | 327 | 1 | 0.003% | 0.08 | **1** | 0 | 0 | 0 | 0 | 0 | 0 | 0 | 0 | 0 | 0 | 0 | 0 | 0 | 0 | 0 | 0 | 0 | 0 |
| 1970-71 | 14 | 392 | 0 | 0 | 0 | 0 | 0 | 0 | 0 | 0 | 0 | 0 | 0 | 0 | 0 | 0 | 0 | 0 | 0 | 0 | 0 | 0 | 0 | 0 |
| 1971-72 | 14 | 381 | 0 | 0 | 0 | 0 | 0 | 0 | 0 | 0 | 0 | 0 | 0 | 0 | 0 | 0 | 0 | 0 | 0 | 0 | 0 | 0 | 0 | 0 |
| 1972-73 | 14 | 403 | 1 | 0.002% | 0.07 | 0 | 0 | 0 | 0 | **1** | 0 | 0 | 0 | 0 | 0 | 0 | 0 | 0 | 0 | 0 | 0 | 0 | 0 | 0 |
| 1973-74 | 16 | | 4 | | 0.25 | 0 | 0 | 0 | 0 | **4** | 0 | 0 | 0 | 0 | 0 | 0 | 0 | 0 | 0 | 0 | 0 | 0 | 0 | 0 |
| 1974-75 | 18 | | 3 | | 0.17 | 0 | 0 | 0 | 0 | **3** | 0 | 0 | 0 | 0 | 0 | 0 | 0 | 0 | 0 | 0 | 0 | 0 | 0 | 0 |
| 1975-76 | 18 | | 2 | | 0.11 | 0 | 0 | 0 | 0 | **2** | 0 | 0 | 0 | 0 | 0 | 0 | 0 | 0 | 0 | 0 | 0 | 0 | 0 | 0 |
| 1976-77 | 18 | | 5 | | 0.28 | 0 | 1 | 0 | 0 | **4** | 0 | 0 | 0 | 0 | 0 | 0 | 0 | 0 | 0 | 0 | 0 | 0 | 0 | 0 |
| 1977-78 | 18 | | 11 | | 0.61 | 1 | 1 | 0 | 0 | **9** | 0 | 0 | 0 | 0 | 0 | 0 | 0 | 0 | 0 | 0 | 0 | 0 | 0 | 0 |
| 1978-79 | 17 | | 16 | | 0.94 | 1 | 0 | 0 | 0 | **14** | 0 | 0 | 0 | 0 | 0 | 0 | 0 | 0 | 0 | **1** | 0 | 0 | 0 | 0 |
| 1979-80 | 21 | | 26 | | 1.24 | 2 | 5 | 0 | 0 | **19** | 0 | 0 | 0 | 0 | 0 | 0 | 0 | 0 | 0 | 0 | 0 | 0 | 0 | 0 |
| 1980-81 | 21 | | 32 | | 1.52 | 5 | 6 | 0 | 0 | **21** | 0 | 0 | 0 | 0 | 0 | 0 | 0 | 0 | 0 | 0 | 0 | 0 | 0 | 0 |
| 1981-82 | 21 | | 48 | | 2.29 | 7 | 14 | 0 | 0 | **26** | 0 | 0 | 0 | 0 | **1** | 0 | 0 | 0 | 0 | 0 | 0 | 0 | 0 | 0 |
| 1982-83 | 21 | | 51 | | 2.43 | 13 | 13 | 1 | 0 | **24** | 0 | 0 | 0 | 0 | 0 | 0 | 0 | 0 | 0 | 0 | 0 | 0 | 0 | 0 |
| 1983-84 | 21 | 689 | 47 | 6.82% | 2.24 | 9 | 12 | 0 | 0 | **26** | 0 | 0 | 0 | 0 | 0 | 0 | 0 | 0 | 0 | 0 | 0 | 0 | 0 | 0 |
| 1984-85 | 21 | 672 | 58 | 8.63% | 2.76 | 12 | 16 | 0 | 0 | **29** | 0 | 0 | 0 | 0 | **1** | 0 | 0 | 0 | 0 | 0 | 0 | 0 | 0 | 0 |
| 1985-86 | 21 | 687 | 55 | 8.01% | 2.62 | 10 | 15 | 0 | 0 | **29** | 0 | 0 | 0 | 0 | **1** | 0 | 0 | 0 | 0 | 0 | 0 | 0 | 0 | 0 |
| 1986-87 | 21 | 683 | 52 | 7.61% | 2.48 | 11 | 17 | 0 | 0 | **22** | 0 | 0 | 0 | 0 | **2** | 0 | 0 | 0 | 0 | 0 | 0 | 0 | 0 | 0 |
| 1987-88 | 21 | 736 | 48 | 6.52% | 2.29 | 11 | 12 | 0 | 0 | **24** | 0 | 0 | 0 | 0 | **1** | 0 | 0 | 0 | 0 | 0 | 0 | 0 | 0 | 0 |
| 1988-89 | 21 | 717 | 59 | 8.23% | 2.81 | 16 | 18 | 1 | 0 | **23** | 0 | 0 | 0 | 0 | **1** | 0 | 0 | 0 | 0 | 0 | 0 | 0 | 0 | 0 |
| 1989-90 | 21 | 725 | 63 | 8.69% | 3 | 13 | 16 | 11 | 0 | **22** | 0 | 0 | 0 | 0 | **1** | 0 | 0 | 0 | 0 | 0 | 0 | 0 | 0 | 0 |
| 1990-91 | 21 | 736 | 64 | 8.7% | 3.05 | **23** | 11 | 14 | 0 | 15 | 0 | 0 | 0 | 0 | **1** | 0 | 0 | 0 | 0 | 0 | 0 | 0 | 0 | 0 |
| 1991-92 | 22 | 783 | 78 | 9.96% | 3.55 | **25** | 10 | **25** | 0 | 16 | 0 | 0 | 0 | **1** | **1** | 0 | 0 | 0 | 0 | 0 | 0 | 0 | 0 | 0 |
| 1992-93 | 24 | 788 | 112 | 15.23% | 4.67 | 25 | 9 | **42** | 5 | 22 | 0 | 1 | 0 | 1 | 1 | 0 | 0 | **4** | 0 | 0 | 0 | 0 | 0 | 2 |
| 1993-94 | 26 | 871 | 140 | 16.07% | 5.38 | 31 | 11 | **56** | 8 | 22 | 0 | 1 | 0 | 1 | 1 | 0 | 0 | **6** | 0 | 0 | 1 | 0 | 0 | 2 |
| 1994-95 | 26 | 806 | 145 | 17.99% | 5.58 | 30 | 12 | **59** | 8 | 26 | 0 | 1 | 0 | 1 | 1 | 0 | 0 | **3** | 0 | 0 | 1 | 0 | 1 | 2 |
| 1995-96 | 26 | 855 | 163 | 19.06% | 6.27 | 37 | 15 | **57** | 9 | 34 | 0 | 2 | 0 | 0 | 2 | 0 | 0 | **3** | 0 | 1 | 1 | 0 | 0 | 2 |
| 1996-97 | 26 | 846 | 168 | 19.86% | 6.46 | 37 | 17 | **57** | 8 | 36 | 0 | 2 | 0 | 0 | 2 | 0 | 1 | **3** | 0 | 1 | 2 | 0 | 0 | 2 |
| 1997-98 | 26 | 836 | 174 | 20.81% | 6.69 | 38 | 17 | **53** | 13 | 39 | 0 | 2 | 0 | 0 | 3 | 0 | 0 | **4** | 0 | 1 | 2 | 0 | 0 | 2 |
| 1998-99 | 27 | 902 | 196 | 21.73% | 7.26 | 51 | 19 | **58** | 13 | 41 | 0 | 2 | 0 | 0 | 4 | 0 | 0 | **7** | 0 | 0 | 2 | 0 | 0 | 1 |
| 1999-00 | 28 | 921 | 237 | 25.73% | 8.46 | 55 | 26 | **71** | 19 | 46 | 0 | 2 | 0 | 0 | 5 | 0 | 1 | **7** | 0 | | 2 | 0 | 0 | 3 |
| 2000-01 | 30 | 996 | 277 | 27.81% | 9.23 | **70** | 34 | 69 | 29 | 47 | 0 | 1 | 0 | 0 | 6 | 0 | 1 | 3 | 2 | 2 | 2 | 0 | 4 | 7 |
| 2001-02 | 30 | 981 | 293 | 29.87% | 9.77 | **78** | 42 | 62 | 32 | 53 | 1 | 1 | 0 | 0 | **6** | 0 | 2 | **6** | 2 | 1 | 2 | 0 | 1 | 4 |
| 2002-03 | 30 | 1,001 | 293 | 29.27% | 9.77 | **80** | 38 | 65 | 30 | 58 | 1 | 1 | 0 | 0 | **6** | 0 | 2 | 5 | 1 | 1 | 2 | 0 | 2 | 1 |
| 2003-04 | 30 | 1,028 | 300 | 29.18% | 10 | **76** | 37 | 64 | 35 | 53 | 3 | 2 | 0 | 0 | **7** | 0 | 4 | 4 | 2 | 2 | 2 | 0 | 4 | 5 |
| 2004-05 | 30 | * | * | * | * | * | * | * | * | * | * | * | * | * | * | * | * | * | * | * | * | * | * | * |
| 2005-06 | 30 | 961 | 263 | 27.37% | 8.77 | **65** | 39 | 51 | 32 | 47 | 3 | 3 | 0 | 1 | **8** | 0 | 2 | 3 | 1 | 1 | 2 | 0 | 4 | 1 |
| 2006-07 | 30 | 942 | 259 | 27.49% | 8.63 | **65** | 42 | 44 | 26 | 50 | 2 | 3 | 2 | 1 | **7** | 1 | 1 | 4 | 1 | 2 | 0 | 1 | 5 | 2 |
| 2007-08 | 30 | 941 | 242 | 25.72% | 8.01 | **59** | 41 | 32 | 23 | 53 | 2 | 4 | 2 | 1 | **9** | 0 | 1 | 3 | 1 | 2 | 0 | 1 | 6 | 2 |
| 2008-09 | 30 | 974 | 242 | 24.85% | 8.01 | **57** | 42 | 36 | 18 | 54 | 3 | 4 | 4 | 1 | **8** | 0 | 1 | 4 | 1 | 1 | 0 | 1 | 6 | 2 |
| 2009-10 | 30 | 962 | 229 | 23.8% | 7.6 | 48 | 38 | 34 | 18 | **54** | 3 | 4 | 6 | 1 | **8** | 0 | 1 | 5 | 1 | 1 | 0 | 1 | 4 | 2 |
| 2010-11 | 30 | 978 | 223 | 22.8% | 7.47 | 42 | 30 | 33 | 14 | **63** | 3 | 4 | 6 | 1 | **9** | 0 | 1 | 4 | 1 | 2 | 0 | 2 | 6 | 2 |
| 2011-12 | 30 | 985 | 222 | 22.5% | 7.4 | 43 | 29 | 31 | 12 | **69** | 3 | 3 | 6 | 1 | 7 | 0 | 1 | 3 | 1 | 1 | 0 | 2 | **8** | 2 |
| Year | Teams | Total | Euros | % | Euros/ Team | CZE TCH | FIN | RUS URS | SVK | SWE | AUT | BLR | DEN | FRA | GER FRG | JPN | KAZ | LAT | LTU | NOR | POL | SLO | SUI | UKR |

# IIHF-NHL Rule Comparison

| Rule | IIHF | NHL |
|---|---|---|
| Abuse of Officials | A player is assessed a match penalty and the Disciplinary Panel decides the length of suspension. | A player is assessed a game misconduct. and officials decide on the category of punishment. |
| Bench Minor Penalty | Any player can serve the penalty. | Only a player on ice when the infraction is called can serve the penalty. |
| Cage & Visor | Players born on or after January 1, 1975 must wear a visor. Tinted visors are not permitted. Players who are 16 years old or younger and who wish to play in a senior event must have parental permission and must wear a full cage. | Visors are not compulsory. Tinted visors are permitted. |
| Change of Players | Each team is allowed 5 seconds to change its players following a stoppage throughout the entire game. | The visiting team is allowed 5 seconds to change players at a stoppage, and the home team is allowed 8 seconds. This ruling does not apply in overtime or in the last 2 minutes of regulation time. |
| Checking From Behind | Minor penalty plus 10-minute misconduct or a 5-minute major plus game misconduct or match penalty and minimum of one-game suspension. Play automatically reviewed by tournament directorate. | No minor penalty. Only possible discipline is either 5-minute major and game misconduct or match penalty. |
| Checking to the Head | There is no such thing as a 'clean hit to the head' and neck area. Minor plus 10-minute misconduct or 5-minute major and game misconduct or match penalty and minimum of one-game suspension. Play automatically reviewed by tournament directorate. | Major penalty and game misconduct for a player who delivers a "lateral, backside or blindside" hit "where the head is the principal point of contact." |
| Delayed Penalty | A team cannot score into its own empty net if it has pulled the goalie for an extra attacker on a delayed penalty | Any own goal a team scores on its own empty net counts if it has pulled the goalie for an extra attacker on a delayed penalty. |
| Exposed Equipment | If a player comes onto the ice with exposed equipment, he is given a warning by the referee. If he comes on a second time, he is given a 10-minute misconduct. | No rule for exposed equipment. |
| Drop of puck at centre ice | One of the referees drops the puck to start every period and after every goal. | One of the referees drops the puck to start every period, but the linesmen drop the puck after goals. |
| Faceoffs | 1—The attacking player must place his stick on the ice in the offensive zone.<br>2—A player cannot win a faceoff by kicking the puck. | 1—The player from the visiting team must place his stick on the ice for all faceoffs.<br>2—A player can win the faceoff with his stick or body in any way. |
| Fighting | 1—Five-minute major and game misconduct or match penalty. No "tiedown" rule.<br>2—Referee may order players to their benches. | 1—(a) Five-minute major if both players started the fight at the same time; (b) minor penalty, five-minute major, and 10-minute misconduct for the instigator. Game misconduct if sweater not "tied down".<br>2—Players must go to their benches when a fight begins. |
| Goal-crease infraction | A player can pass through the goalie's crease but is not allowed to establish position there. If he does, the referee blows the whistle and a faceoff is held outside the offensive end. | A player can remain in the crease as long as he wants so long as he doesn't interfere with the goalie. |
| Goalkeeper Freezing Puck | Goaltender may freeze puck anywhere in the defending zone provided he is being checked. | Goaltender incurs a minor penalty for falling on the puck beyond hash marks or behind the goal line. |
| Goalkeeper Stick | The top of the shaft must have a form of protection. | A minimum 0.5" knob of tape or protective covering must affixed to the top of the shaft. |
| Goalkeeper Handling the Puck | A goaltender can handle the puck anywhere inside his half of the ice. | A goaltender can handle the puck anywhere inside his half of the ice with the exception of the trapezoid area behind the goal. |
| Goalkeeper Penalty | Any player on the ice at the stoppage of play is eligible to serve the penalty. | Any player on the ice at the time the foul was committed is eligible to serve the penalty. |
| Helmet | 1—A player whose helmet comes off during play must go directly to the players bench. Failure to do so results in a minor penalty.<br>2—A player must wear a helmet during the pre-game warmup. | 1—A player whose helmet comes off during play is permitted to finish his shift bare-headed.<br>2—A player may skate during the pre-game warmup without a helmet. |
| High-Sticking (puck) | The ensuing faceoff will be held at the nearest spot to where the puck was hit illegally at any time during a game. | The ensuing faceoff will take place in the defensive end if the offending team had a man advantage at the time the puck was hit illegally. |
| Icing the Puck | 1—Automatic icing as soon as the puck crosses the end red line.<br>2—Any icing of the puck subject to whistle. | 1—A player from the defending team must touch the puck first after it has crossed the end red line.<br>2—An attempted pass—deemed receivable by a linesman—can be waived off to prevent icing. |
| Kicking the Puck | A goal is allowed only if the kicked puck subsequently deflects off the stick of an attacking player and goes into the net. | A goal is allowed if the kicked puck deflects off any stick except the goalkeeper's and goes into the net. |
| Major Penalty | The replacement player must go to the penalty box immediately. | The replacement player must only be in the penalty box at the time the penalty expires. |
| Offside | On a delayed offside, any shot on goal will bring about a stoppage. | On a delayed offside, any shot on goal will not bring about a stoppage. |
| Penalties | No such ruling. | In the last 5 minutes or in overtime differential then play 3 minutes or 1 minute shorthanded. |
| Penalty Shot | A player must be in control of the puck in order to be awarded a penalty shot. | A player must be in control of the puck or could have obtained control of the puck to be awarded a penalty shot. |
| Players Dressed | A maximum of 20 players and 2 goalkeepers can be dressed. | A maximum of 18 players and 2 goalkeepers can be dressed. |
| Protective Equipment | The first violation of any equipment by any player after a warning to a team by the Referee will result in a misconduct penalty being assessed to the player. | A second violation of the same player who was previously warned for his equipment by the Referee will result in a minor penalty being assessed to that player. |
| Slew Footing | Minor penalty or five-minute major and game misconduct or match penalty. | Match penalty. |
| Stick Measurement | Only one measurement by one team per stoppage is allowed. | Only one measurement per team per stoppage is allowed. |
| Time-Outs | Only one team is permitted a time-out during a stoppage. | Both teams are permitted a time-out during same stoppage. |

# The NHL and Europe: Games Across the World

**1938 NHL TOUR OF EUROPE**

| | | |
|---|---|---|
| April 21, 1938 | Montreal Canadiens 5 | Detroit Red Wings 4 (London) |
| April 23, 1938 | Montreal Canadiens 5 | Detroit Red Wings 5 (Brighton) |
| April 25, 1938 | Montreal Canadiens 10 | Detroit Red Wings 8 (Paris) |
| April 27, 1938 | Detroit Red Wings 4 | Montreal Canadiens 3 (Paris) |
| April 29, 1938 | Montreal Canadiens 7 | Detroit Red Wings 5 (Paris) |
| May 5, 1938 | Montreal Canadiens 6 | Detroit Red Wings 3 (London) |
| May 7, 1938 | Detroit Red Wings 10 | Montreal Canadiens 5 (Brighton) |
| May 10, 1938 | Montreal Canadiens 5 | Detroit Red Wings 4 (London) |
| May 14, 1938 | Detroit Red Wings 5 | Montreal Canadiens 2 (Brighton) |

**1959 NHL TOUR OF EUROPE**

| | | |
|---|---|---|
| April 29, 1959 | Boston Bruins 7 | NY Rangers 5 (London) |
| April 30, 1959 | NY Rangers 4 | Boston Bruins 2 (London) |
| May 2, 1959 | NY Rangers 4 | Boston Bruins 3 (Geneva) |
| May 3, 1959 | Boston Bruins 12 | NY Rangers 4 (Geneva) |
| May 4, 1959 | NY Rangers 6 | Boston Bruins 2 (Paris) |
| May 5, 1959 | Boston Bruins 6 | NY Rangers 4 (Paris) |
| May 6, 1959 | Boston Bruins 6 | NY Rangers 3 (Antwerp) |
| May 7, 1959 | NY Rangers 6 | Boston Bruins 3 (Antwerp) |
| May 8, 1959 | NY Rangers 8 | Boston Bruins 4 (Antwerp) |
| May 9, 1959 | NY Rangers 7 | Boston Bruins 6 (Zurich) |
| May 10, 1959 | Boston Bruins 4 | NY Rangers 2 (Zurich) |
| May 12, 1959 | NY Rangers 4 | Boston Bruins 2 (Dortmund) |
| May 13, 1959 | Boston Bruins 6 | NY Rangers 4 (Dortmund) |
| May 14, 1959 | Boston Bruins 6 | NY Rangers 4 (Essen) |
| May 15, 1959 | NY Rangers 4 | Boston Bruins 3 (Essen) |
| May 16, 1959 | NY Rangers 8 | Boston Bruins 0 (Krefeld) |
| May 17, 1959 | NY Rangers 7 | Boston Bruins 2 (Krefeld) |
| May 19, 1959 | NY Rangers 6 | Boston Bruins 6 (Berlin) |
| May 20, 1959 | NY Rangers 3 | Boston Bruins 2 (Berlin) |
| May 21, 1959 | Boston Bruins 8 | NY Rangers 2 (Berlin) |
| May 22, 1959 | Boston Bruins 2 | NY Rangers 2 (Vienna) |
| May 23, 1959 | Boston Bruins 5 | NY Rangers 3 (Vienna) |
| May 24, 1959 | Boston Bruins 4 | NY Rangers 4 (Vienna) |

**1975-76 SOVIET TOUR OF NHL**

| | | |
|---|---|---|
| December 28, 1975 | CSKA Moscow 7 | NY Rangers 3 |
| December 29, 1975 | Krylya Sovietov 7 | Pittsburgh Penguins 4 |
| December 31, 1975 | Montreal Canadiens 3 | CSKA Moscow 3 |
| January 4, 1976 | Buffalo Sabres 12 | Krylya Sovietov 6 |
| January 7, 1976 | Krylya Sovietov 4 | Chicago Black Hawks 2 |
| January 8, 1976 | CSKA Moscow 5 | Boston Bruins 2 |
| January 10, 1976 | Krylya Sovietov 2 | NY Islanders 1 |
| January 11, 1976 | Philadelphia Flyers 4 | CSKA Moscow 1 |

**1975-76 NHL POST-SEASON TOUR OF JAPAN**

| | | |
|---|---|---|
| April 14, 1976 | Washington Capitals 5 | Kansas City Scouts 2 (Sapporo) |
| April 15, 1976 | Washington Capitals 6 | Kansas City Scouts 2 (Sapporo) |
| April 17, 1976 | Washington Capitals 6 | Kansas City Scouts 2 (Tokyo) |
| April 18, 1976 | Kansas City Scouts 4 | Washington Capitals 2 (Tokyo) |

**1977-78 SOVIET/CZECHOSLOVAK TOUR OF NHL**

| | | |
|---|---|---|
| December 26, 1977 | NY Rangers 4 | Poldi Kladno 4 |
| December 26, 1977 | Philadelphia Flyers 6 | Tesla Pardubice 1 |
| December 28, 1977 | Vancouver Canucks 2 | Spartak Moscow 0 |
| December 31, 1977 | Poldi Kladno 6 | Chicago Blackhawks 4 |
| December 31, 1977 | Tesla Pardubice 4 | Minnesota North Stars 2 |
| January 2, 1977 | Poldi Kladno 8 | Toronto Maple Leafs 5 |
| January 2, 1977 | Detroit Red Wings 5 | Tesla Pardubice 4 |
| January 3, 1978 | Spartak Moscow 8 | Colorado Rockies 3 |
| January 4, 1978 | Cleveland Barons 4 | Poldi Kladno 3 |
| January 4, 1978 | NY Islanders 8 | Tesla Pardubice 3 |
| January 5, 1978 | Spartak Moscow 2 | St. Louis Blues 1 |
| January 6, 1978 | Montreal Canadiens 5 | Spartak Moscow 2 |
| January 8, 1978 | Spartak Moscow 2 | Atlanta Flames 1 |

**1978-79 SOVIET TOUR OF NHL**

| | | |
|---|---|---|
| December 31, 1978 | Krylya Sovietov 8 | Minnesota North Stars 5 |
| January 2, 1979 | Philadelphia Flyers 4 | Krylya Sovietov 4 |
| January 4, 1979 | Detroit Red Wings 6 | Krylya Sovietov 5 |
| January 9, 1979 | Krylya Sovietov 4 | Boston Bruins 1 |

**1979 CHALLENGE CUP (MADISON SQUARE GARDEN, NEW YORK)**

| | | |
|---|---|---|
| February 8, 1979 | NHL All-Stars 4 | Soviet Union 2 |
| February 10, 1979 | Soviet Union 5 | NHL All-Stars 4 |
| February 11, 1979 | Soviet Union 6 | NHL All-Stars 0 |

**1979-80 SOVIET TOUR OF NHL**

| | | |
|---|---|---|
| December 26, 1979 | Vancouver Canucks 6 | Dynamo Moscow 2 |
| December 27, 1979 | CSKA Moscow 5 | NY Rangers 2 |
| December 29, 1979 | CSKA Moscow 3 | NY Islanders 2 |
| December 31, 1979 | Montreal Canadiens 4 | CSKA Moscow 2 |
| January 2, 1980 | Dynamo Moscow 7 | Winnipeg Jets 0 |
| January 3, 1980 | Buffalo Sabres 6 | CSKA Moscow 1 |
| January 4, 1980 | Dynamo Moscow 4 | Edmonton Oilers 1 |
| January 6, 1980 | CSKA Moscow 6 | Quebec Nordiques 4 |
| January 8, 1980 | Washington Capitals 5 | Dynamo Moscow 5 |

**1980-81 PRE-SEASON—DAGENS NYHETER CUP CHALLENGE (STOCKHOLM)**

| | | |
|---|---|---|
| September 22, 1980 | Washington Capitals 4 | Minnesota North Stars 3 (OT) |
| September 23, 1980 | Minnesota North Stars 8 | Djurgarden Stockholm 0 |
| September 24, 1980 | Washington Capitals 2 | AIK Stockholm 1 |
| September 25, 1980 | Minnesota North Stars 4 | AIK Stockholm 3 |
| September 26, 1980 | Washington Capitals 3 | Djurgarden Stockholm 2 |

**1981-82 PRE-SEASON—DAGENS NYHETER CUP CHALLENGE**

| | | |
|---|---|---|
| September 17, 1981 | HIFK Helsinki 4 | New York Rangers 1 (Helsinki) |
| September 17, 1981 | Vastra Frolunda 7 | Washington Capitals 4 (Gothenburg) |
| September 18, 1981 | AIK Stockholm 6 | Washington Capitals 1 (Stockholm) |
| September 18, 1981 | New York Rangers 5 | Djurgarden Stockholm 1 (Stockholm) |
| September 20, 1981 | New York Rangers 4 | Washington Capitals 1 (Stockholm) |
| September 22, 1981 | Washington Capitals 5 | Djurgarden Stockholm 2 (Stockholm) |
| September 22, 1981 | New York Rangers 7 | Vastra Frolunda 1 (Gothenburg) |
| September 23, 1981 | New York Rangers 4 | AIK Stockholm 1 (Stockholm) |
| September 24, 1981 | Washington Capitals 5 | Karpat Oulu 3 (Oulu) |

**1982-83 SOVIET TOUR OF NHL**

| | | |
|---|---|---|
| December 28, 1982 | Edmonton Oilers 4 | Soviet Union 3 |
| December 30, 1982 | Soviet Union 3 | Quebec Nordiques 0 |
| December 31, 1982 | Soviet Union 5 | Montreal Canadiens 0 |
| January 2, 1983 | Calgary Flames 3 | Soviet Union 2 |
| January 4, 1983 | Soviet Union 6 | Minnesota North Stars 3 |
| January 6, 1983 | Soviet Union 5 | Philadelphia Flyers 1 |

**1985-86 SOVIET TOUR OF NHL**

| | | |
|---|---|---|
| December 26, 1985 | CSKA Moscow 5 | Los Angeles Kings 2 |
| December 27, 1985 | CSKA Moscow 6 | Edmonton Oilers 3 |
| December 29, 1985 | Quebec Nordiques 5 | CSKA Moscow 1 |
| December 29, 1985 | Calgary Flames 4 | Dynamo Moscow 3 |
| December 31, 1985 | CSKA Moscow 6 | Montreal Canadiens 1 |
| January 2, 1986 | CSKA Moscow 4 | St. Louis Blues 2 |
| January 4, 1986 | CSKA Moscow 4 | Minnesota North Stars 3 |
| January 4, 1986 | Pittsburgh Penguins 3 | Dynamo Moscow 3 |
| January 6, 1986 | Dynamo Moscow 6 | Boston Bruins 4 |
| January 8, 1986 | Dynamo Moscow 7 | Buffalo Sabres 4 |

**RENDEZ-VOUS '87 (QUEBEC CITY)**

| | | |
|---|---|---|
| February 11, 1987 | NHL All-Stars 4 | Soviet Union 3 |
| February 13, 1987 | Soviet Union 5 | NHL All-Stars 3 |

**1988-89 SOVIET TOUR OF NHL**

| | | |
|---|---|---|
| December 26, 1988 | Quebec Nordiques 5 | CSKA Moscow 5 |
| December 27, 1988 | Calgary Flames 2 | Dynamo Riga 2 |
| December 28, 1988 | Edmonton Oilers 2 | Dynamo Riga 1 |
| December 29, 1988 | CSKA Moscow 3 | NY Islanders 2 |
| December 30, 1988 | Vancouver Canucks 6 | Dynamo Riga 1 |
| December 31, 1988 | CSKA Moscow 5 | Boston Bruins 4 |
| December 31, 1988 | Dynamo Riga 5 | Los Angeles 2 |
| January 2, 1989 | CSKA Moscow 5 | New Jersey Devils 0 |
| January 4, 1989 | Pittsburgh Penguins 4 | CSKA Moscow 2 |
| January 4, 1989 | Chicago Blackhawks 4 | Dynamo Riga 1 |
| January 5, 1989 | St. Louis Blues 5 | Dynamo Riga 0 |
| January 7, 1989 | Dynamo Riga 2 | Minnesota North Stars 1 |
| January 7, 1989 | CSKA Moscow 6 | Hartford Whalers 3 |
| January 9, 1989 | Buffalo Sabres 6 | CSKA Moscow 5 |

**1989-90 NHL PRE-SEASON IN EUROPE**

| | | |
|---|---|---|
| September 12, 1989 | Washington Capitals 7 | Farjestad Karlstad 4 (Karlstad) |
| September 13, 1989 | Washington Capitals 3 | Brynas Gavle 1 (Gavle) |

**1989-90 NHL PRE-SEASON—FRIENDSHIP TOUR**

| | | |
|---|---|---|
| September 10, 1989 | Czechoslovakia 4 | Calgary Flames 2 (Czechoslovakia) |
| September 11, 1989 | Czechoslovakia 4 | Calgary Flames 1 (Czechoslovakia) |
| September 14, 1989 | Calgary Flames 4 | Khimik 2 (Leningrad) |
| September 15, 1989 | Washington Capitals 8 | Spartak Moscow 7 (Moscow) |
| September 16, 1989 | Calgary Flames 5 | Sokol Kiev 2 (Kiev) |
| September 17, 1989 | Dynamo Moscow 7 | Washington Capitals 2 (Moscow) |
| September 18, 1989 | Calgary Flames 3 | Krylya Sovietov 2 (Moscow) |
| September 19, 1989 | Washington Capitals 2 | Dynamo Riga 1 (Riga) |
| September 20, 1989 | CSKA Moscow 2 | Calgary Flames 1 (Moscow) |
| September 21, 1989 | Washington Capitals 5 | SKA Leningrad 4 (Leningrad) |

**1989-90 SOVIET TOUR OF NHL**

| | | |
|---|---|---|
| December 4, 1989 | Khimik Voskresensk 6 | Los Angeles Kings 3 |
| December 6, 1989 | Edmonton Oilers 6 | Khimik Voskresensk 2 |
| December 8, 1989 | Calgary Flames 6 | Khimik Voskresensk 3 |
| December 11, 1989 | Khimik Voskresensk 4 | Detroit Red Wings 2 |
| December 12, 1989 | Washington Capitals 5 | Khimik Voskresensk 2 |
| December 14, 1989 | St. Louis Blues 3 | Khimik Voskresensk 0 |
| December 26, 1989 | NY Islanders 5 | Krylya Sovietov 4 |
| December 27, 1989 | Hartford Whalers 4 | Krylya Sovietov 3 |
| December 27, 1989 | Winnipeg Jets 4 | CSKA Moscow 1 |
| December 29, 1989 | Dynamo Moscow 5 | Pittsburgh Penguins 2 |
| December 29, 1989 | CSKA Moscow 6 | Vancouver Canucks 0 |
| December 31, 1989 | Quebec Nordiques 4 | Krylya Sovietov 4 |
| December 31, 1989 | Dynamo Moscow 7 | Toronto Maple Leafs 4 |
| January 1, 1990 | Krylya Sovietov 3 | NY Rangers 1 |
| January 2, 1990 | CSKA Moscow 4 | Minnesota North Stars 2 |
| January 3, 1990 | Montreal Canadiens 2 | Krylya Sovietov 1 |
| January 3, 1990 | Buffalo Sabres 4 | Dynamo Moscow 2 |
| January 6, 1990 | New Jersey Devils 7 | Dynamo Moscow 1 |
| January 7, 1990 | CSKA Moscow 6 | Chicago Blackhawks 4 |
| January 9, 1990 | CSKA Moscow 5 | Philadelphia Flyers 4 |
| January 9, 1990 | Dynamo Moscow 3 | Boston Bruins 1 |

**1990-91 PRE-SEASON—EPSON CUP (DUSSELDORF, GERMANY)**

| | | |
|---|---|---|
| September 6, 1990 | St. Louis Blues 3 | Dusseldorf 1 |
| September 7, 1990 | Edmonton Oilers 2 | Dusseldorf 0 |
| September 8, 1990 | St. Louis Blues 10 | Edmonton Oilers 1 |

**1990-91 NHL PRE-SEASON IN EUROPE**

| | | |
|---|---|---|
| September 9, 1990 | Edmonton Oilers 12 | Graz 3 (Graz) |
| September 10, 1990 | Montreal Canadiens 7 | AIK Stockholm 1 (Stockholm) |
| September 12, 1990 | Montreal Canadiens 5 | Leningrad/Yaroslavl 3 (Leningrad) |
| September 13, 1990 | Spartak Moscow 8 | Minnesota North Stars 5 (Moscow) |
| September 14, 1990 | Montreal Canadiens 4 | Dynamo Riga 2 (Riga) |
| September 15, 1990 | Krylya Sovietov 3 | Minnesota North Stars 2 (OT) (Moscow) |
| September 16, 1990 | Moscow Dynamo 4 | Montreal Canadiens 1 (Moscow) |
| September 17, 1990 | Minnesota North Stars 3 | Khimik Voskresensk 2 (Voskresensk) |
| September 18, 1990 | CSKA Moscow 3 | Montreal Canadiens 2 (OT) (Moscow) |
| September 19, 1990 | Sokol Kiev 5 | Minnesota North Stars 0 (Kiev) |

**1990-91 SOVIET TOUR OF NHL**

| | | |
|---|---|---|
| December 3, 1990 | Los Angeles Kings 5 | Khimik Voskresensk 1 |
| December 5, 1990 | St. Louis Blues 4 | Khimik Voskresensk 2 |
| December 8, 1990 | NY Islanders 2 | Khimik Voskresensk 2 |
| December 10, 1990 | Khimik Voskresensk 6 | Montreal Canadiens 3 |
| December 12, 1990 | Khimik Voskresensk 5 | Buffalo Sabres 4 |
| December 16, 1990 | Khimik Voskresensk 5 | Boston Bruins 2 |
| December 18, 1990 | Minnesota North Stars 6 | Khimik Voskresensk 4 |
| December 26, 1990 | CSKA Moscow 5 | Detroit Red Wings 2 |
| December 31, 1990 | CSKA Moscow 6 | NY Rangers 1 |
| January 1, 1991 | Toronto Maple Leafs 7 | Dynamo Moscow 4 |
| January 1, 1991 | CSKA Moscow 4 | Chicago Blackhawks 2 |
| January 3, 1991 | Hartford Whalers 0 | Dynamo Moscow 0 |
| January 4, 1991 | CSKA Moscow 6 | Calgary Flames 4 |
| January 6, 1991 | New Jersey Devils 2 | Dynamo Moscow 2 |
| January 6, 1991 | Edmonton Oilers 4 | CSKA Moscow 2 |
| January 8, 1991 | Washington Capitals 3 | Dynamo Moscow 2 |
| January 9, 1991 | CSKA Moscow 6 | Winnipeg Jets 4 |
| January 10, 1991 | Dynamo Moscow 4 | Philadelphia Flyers 1 |
| January 12, 1991 | Dynamo Moscow 4 | Pittsburgh Penguins 3 |
| January 13, 1991 | CSKA Moscow 4 | Vancouver Canucks 3 |
| January 15, 1991 | Dynamo Moscow 4 | Quebec Nordiques 1 |

**1992-93 NHL PRE-SEASON (LONDON, ENGLAND)**

| | | |
|---|---|---|
| September 12, 1992 | Montreal Canadiens 3 | Chicago Blackhawks 2 |
| September 13, 1992 | Chicago Blackhawks 5 | Montreal Canadiens 4 (OT) |

**1993-94 NHL PRE-SEASON—FRENCH'S CUP (LONDON, ENGLAND)**

| | | |
|---|---|---|
| September 11, 1993 | NY Rangers 5 | Toronto Maple Leafs 3 |
| September 12, 1993 | NY Rangers 3 | Toronto Maple Leafs 1 |

**1994-95 NHL PRE-SEASON, NIKE INTERNATIONAL CHALLENGE (HELSINKI, FINLAND)**

| | | |
|---|---|---|
| September 9, 1994 | Winnipeg Jets 8 | Tappara Tampere 2 |
| September 11, 1994 | Winnipeg Jets 5 | HIFK Helsinki 3 |

**1997-98 NHL REGULAR SEASON (TOKYO, JAPAN)**

| | | |
|---|---|---|
| October 3, 1997 | Vancouver Canucks 3 | Mighty Ducks of Anaheim 2 |
| October 4, 1997 | Might Ducks of Anaheim 3 | Vancouver Canucks 2 |

**1998-99 NHL PRE-SEASON (AUSTRIA)**

| | | |
|---|---|---|
| September 15, 1998 | Tampa Bay Lightning 4 | VEU Feldkirch 1 (Klagenfurt) |
| September 16, 1998 | Buffalo Sabres 5 | KAC Klagenfurt 1 (Klagenfurt) |
| September 18, 1998 | Tampa Bay Lightning 3 | Buffalo Sabres 1 (Innsbruck) |

**1998-99 NHL REGULAR SEASON (TOKYO, JAPAN)**

| | | |
|---|---|---|
| October 9, 1998 | Calgary Flames 3 | San Jose Sharks 3 |
| October 10, 1998 | Calgary Flames 5 | San Jose Sharks 2 |

**2000-01 NHL PRE-SEASON, NHL CHALLENGE (STOCKHOLM, SWEDEN)**

| | |
|---|---|
| September 13, 2000 | Vancouver Canucks 5 at MoDo 2 |
| September 15, 2000 | Vancouver Canucks 2 at Djurgarden 1 (OT) |

**2000-01 NHL REGULAR SEASON (TOKYO, JAPAN)**

| | | |
|---|---|---|
| October 7, 2000 | Nashville Predators 3 | Pittsburgh Penguins 1 |
| October 8, 2000 | Pittsburgh Penguins 3 | Nashville Predators 1 |

**2001-02 NHL PRE-SEASON (STOCKHOLM, SWEDEN—GAMES FEATURING DJURGARDEN AND JOKERIT CANCELLED BECAUSE OF 9/11)**

| | |
|---|---|
| Colorado Avalanche 5 | Brynas Gavle 3 |

**2003-04 NHL PRE-SEASON**

| | | |
|---|---|---|
| September 16, 2003 | Toronto Maple Leafs 5 | Jokerit 3 (Helsinki) |
| September 18, 2003 | Toronto Maple Leafs 9 | Djurgarden 2 (Stockholm) |
| September 19, 2003 | Toronto Maple Leafs 3 | Farjestad 0 (Stockholm) |

**2007-08 RED BULL SALUTE (SALZBURG, AUSTRIA)**

| | | |
|---|---|---|
| September 25, 2007 | Los Angeles Kings 7 | Red Bulls Salzburg 6 |
| September 26, 2007 | Los Angeles Kings 4 | Farjestad Karlstad 3 |

**2007-08 NHL REGULAR SEASON (LONDON, ENGLAND)**

| | | |
|---|---|---|
| September 29, 2007 | Los Angeles Kings 4 | Anaheim Ducks 1 |
| September 30, 2007 | Anaheim Ducks 4 | Los Angeles Kings 1 |

**2008-09 NHL PRE-SEASON**

| | | |
|---|---|---|
| September 28, 2008 | Tampa Bay Lightning 4 | Eisbaren Berlin 1 (Berlin) |
| September 30, 2008 | Tampa Bay Lightning 3 | Slovan Bratislava 2 (GWS) (Bratislava) |

**1ST VICTORIA CUP (BERNE, SWITZERLAND)**

| | | |
|---|---|---|
| **Exhibition** | | |
| September 30, 2008 | New York Rangers 8 | SC Bern 1 |
| **Final** | | |
| October 1, 2008 | New York Rangers 4 | Metallurg Magnitigorsk 3 |

**2008-09 NHL PRE-SEASON**

| | | |
|---|---|---|
| October 2, 2008 | Pittsburgh Penguins 4 | IFK Helsinki 1 (Helsinki) |
| October 2, 2008 | Ottawa Senators 4 | Frolunda Gothenburg 1 (Gothenburg) |

**2008-09 NHL REGULAR SEASON**

| | | |
|---|---|---|
| October 4, 2008 | Pittsburgh Penguins 4 | Ottawa Senators 3 (OT) (Stockholm) |
| October 5, 2008 | New York Rangers 2 | Tampa Bay Lightning 1 (Prague) |
| October 5, 2008 | Ottawa Senators 3 | Pittsburgh Penguins 1 (Stockholm) |

**2ND VICTORIA CUP (ZURICH, SWITZERLAND)**

| | | |
|---|---|---|
| **Exhibition** | | |
| September 28, 2009 | Chicago Blackhawks 9 | HC Davos 2 |
| **Final** | | |
| September 29, 2009 | ZSC Lions Zurich 2 | Chicago Blackhawks 1 |

**2009-10 NHL PRE-SEASON**

| | | |
|---|---|---|
| September 28, 2009 | Tappara Tampere 3 | Florida Panthers 2 (GWS) (Tampere) |
| September 29, 2009 | St. Louis Blues 6 | Linkopings HC 0 (Linkoping) |
| September 30, 2009 | Florida Panthers 4 | Jokerit Helsinki 2 (Helsinki) |
| September 30, 2009 | Detroit Red Wings 6 | Farjestad Karlstad 2 (Karlstad) |

**2009-10 NHL REGULAR SEASON**

| | | |
|---|---|---|
| October 2, 2009 | Florida Panthers 4 | Chicago Blackhawks 3 (GWS) (Helsinki) |
| October 2, 2009 | St. Louis Blues 4 | Detroit Red Wings 3 (Stockholm) |
| October 3, 2009 | Chicago Blackhawks 4 | Florida Panthers 0 (Helsinki) |
| October 3, 2009 | St. Louis Blues 5 | Detroit Red Wings 3 (Stockholm) |

**2010-11 PRE-SEASON**

| | | |
|---|---|---|
| October 2, 2010 | San Jose Sharks 3 | Adler Mannheim 2 (OT) (Mannheim) |
| October 2, 2010 | Boston Bruins 5 | Belfast Giants Selects 1 (Belfast) |
| October 4, 2010 | SKA St. Petersburg 5 | Carolina Hurricanes 3 (St. Petersburg) |
| October 4, 2010 | Minnesota Wild 5 | Ilves Tampere 1 (Tampere) |
| October 5, 2010 | Columbus Blue Jackets 4 | Malmo Redhawks 1 (Malmo) |
| October 5, 2010 | Boston Bruins 7 | HC Liberec 1 (Liberec) |
| October 6, 2010 | Phoenix Coyotes 3 | Dynamo Riga 1 (Riga) |

**2010-11 NHL REGULAR SEASON**

| | | |
|---|---|---|
| October 7, 2010 | Carolina Hurricanes 4 | Minnesota Wild 3 (Helsinki) |
| October 8, 2010 | Minnesota Wild 3 | Carolina Hurricanes 2 (Helsinki) |
| October 8, 2010 | San Jose Sharks 3 | Columbus Blue Jackets 2 (Stockholm) |
| October 9, 2010 | Columbus Blue Jackets 3 | San Jose Sharks 2 (Stockholm) |
| October 9, 2010 | Phoenix Coyotes 5 | Boston Bruins 2 (Prague) |
| October 10, 2010 | Boston Bruins 3 | Phoenix Coyotes 0 (Prague) |

**2011-12 PRE-SEASON**

| | | |
|---|---|---|
| September 29, 2011 | NY Rangers 2 | HC Sparta 0 (Prague) |
| September 30, 2011 | NY Rangers 4 | Frolunda 2 (Gothenburg) |
| October 2, 2011 | NY Rangers 4 | HC Slovan Bratislava 1 (Bratislava) |
| October 3, 2011 | EV Zug 8 | NY Rangers 4 (Zug) |
| October 4, 2011 | Anaheim 4 | Jokerit 3 (OT) (Helsinki) |
| October 4, 2011 | Los Angeles 5 | Hamburg Freezers 4 (Hamburg) |
| October 4, 2011 | Buffalo 8 | Adler Mannheim 3 (Mannheim) |

**2011-12 NHL REGULAR SEASON**

| | | |
|---|---|---|
| October 7, 2011 | Los Angeles 3 | NY Rangers 2 (OT) (Stockholm) |
| October 7, 2011 | Buffalo 4 | Anaheim 1(Helsinki) |
| October 8, 2011 | Anaheim 2 | NY Rangers 1(SO) (Stockholm) |
| October 8, 2011 | Buffalo 4 | Los Angeles 2 (Berlin) |

# Stanley Cup Winning Players from Europe

**ALL EUROPEAN* PLAYERS WHO HAVE WON THE STANLEY CUP**
*players born in Europe who acquired their basic ice hockey skills in Europe

**1980 New York Islanders (2):** Anders Kallur (SWE), Stefan Persson (SWE)
**1981 New York Islanders (2):** Anders Kallur (SWE), Stefan Persson (SWE)
**1982 New York Islanders (3):** Tomas Jonsson (SWE), Anders Kallur (SWE), Stefan Persson (SWE)
**1983 New York Islanders (4):** Mats Hallin (SWE), Tomas Jonsson (SWE), Anders Kallur (SWE), Stefan Persson (SWE)
**1984 Edmonton Oilers (3):** Jari Kurri (FIN), Willy Lindstrom (SWE), Jaroslav Pouzar (TCH)
**1985 Edmonton Oilers (4):** Jari Kurri (FIN), Willy Lindstrom (SWE), Jaroslav Pouzar (TCH), Esa Tikkanen (FIN)
**1986 Montreal Canadiens (3):** Kjell Dahlin (SWE), Mats Naslund (SWE), Petr Svoboda (TCH)
**1987 Edmonton Oilers (5):** Jari Kurri (FIN), Kent Nilsson (SWE), Jaroslav Pouzar (TCH), Reijo Ruotsalainen (FIN), Esa Tikkanen (FIN)
**1988 Edmonton Oilers (2):** Jari Kurri (FIN), Esa Tikkanen (FIN)
**1989 Calgary Flames (2):** Jiri Hrdina (TCH), Hakan Loob (SWE)
**1990 Edmonton Oilers (4):** Petr Klima (TCH), Jari Kurri (FIN), Reijo Ruotsalainen (FIN), Esa Tikkanen (FIN)
**1991 Pittsburgh Penguins (3):** Jiri Hrdina (TCH), Jaromir Jagr (TCH), Ulf Samuelsson (SWE)
**1992 Pittsburgh Penguins (4):** Jiri Hrdina (TCH), Jaromir Jagr (TCH), Kjell Samuelsson (SWE), Ulf Samuelsson (SWE)
**1993 Montreal Canadiens (0):** none
**1994 New York Rangers (5):** Alexander Karpovtsev (RUS), Alexei Kovalyov (RUS), Sergei Nemchinov (RUS), Esa Tikkanen (FIN), Sergei Zubov (RUS)
**1995 New Jersey Devils (4):** Tommy Albelin (SWE), Sergei Brylin (RUS), Robert (Bobby) Holik (CZE), Valeri Zelepukin (RUS)
**1996 Colorado Avalanche (5):** Peter Forsberg (SWE), Alexei Gusarov (RUS), Valeri Kamensky (RUS), Uwe Krupp (GER), Sandis Ozolinsh (LAT)
**1997 Detroit Red Wings (8):** Sergei Fyodorov (RUS), Vyacheslav Fetisov (RUS), Tomas Holmstrom (SWE), Vladimir Konstantinov (RUS), Vyacheslav Kozlov (RUS), Igor Larionov (RUS), Nicklas Lidstrom (SWE), Tomas Sandstrom (SWE)
**1998: Detroit Red Wings (8):** Anders Eriksson (SWE), Sergei Fyodorov (RUS), Vyacheslav Fetisov (RUS), Tomas Holmstrom (SWE), Vyacheslav Kozlov (RUS), Igor Larionov (RUS), Nicklas Lidstrom (SWE), Dmitri Mironov (RUS)
**1999 Dallas Stars (3):** Jere Lehtinen (FIN), Roman Turek (CZE), Sergei Zubov (RUS)
**2000 New Jersey Devils (8):** Sergei Brylin (RUS), Patrik Elias (CZE), Robert (Bobby) Holik (CZE), Vladimir Malakhov (RUS), Alexander Mogilny (RUS), Sergei Nemchinov (RUS), Krzysztof Oliwa (POL), Petr Sykora (CZE)
**2001 Colorado Avalanche (5):** David Aebischer (SUI), Peter Forsberg (SWE), Milan Hejduk (CZE), Ville Nieminen (FIN), Martin Skoula (CZE)
**2002 Detroit Red Wings (9):** Pavel Datsyuk (RUS), Sergei Fyodorov (RUS), Jiri Fischer (CZE), Dominik Hasek (CZE), Tomas Holmstrom (SWE), Igor Larionov (RUS), Nicklas Lidstrom (SWE), Fredrik Olausson (SWE), Jiri Slegr (CZE)
**2003 New Jersey Devils (6):** Tommy Albelin (SWE), Jiri Bicek (SVK), Sergei Brylin (RUS), Patrik Elias (CZE), Richard Smehlik (CZE), Oleg Tverdovsky (RUS)
**2004 Tampa Bay Lightning (7):** Dimitry Afanasenkov (RUS), Martin Cibak (SVK), Ruslan Fedotenko (UKR), Nikolai Khabibulin (RUS), Pavel Kubina (CZE), Fredrik Modin (SWE), Stanislav Neckar (CZE)
**2006 Carolina Hurricanes (6):** Anton Babchuk (RUS), Martin Gerber (SUI), Frantisek Kaberle (CZE), Oleg Tverdovsky (RUS), Josef Vasicek (CZE), Niclas Wallin (SWE)
**2007 Anaheim Ducks (3):** Ilya Bryzgalov (RUS), Samuel Pahlsson (SWE), Teemu Selanne (FIN)
**2008 Detroit Red Wings (12):** Pavel Datsyuk (RUS), Valtteri Filppula (FIN), Johan Franzen (SWE), Dominik Hasek (CZE), Tomas Holmstrom (SWE), Jiri Hudler (CZE), Tomas Kopecky (CZE), Niklas Kronwall (SWE), Nicklas Lidstrom (SWE), Andreas Lilja (SWE), Mikael Samuelsson (SWE), Henrik Zetterberg (SWE)
**2009 Pittsburgh Penguins (5):** Ruslan Fedotenko (UKR), Sergei Gonchar (RUS), Yevgeni Malkin (RUS), Miroslav Satan (SVK), Petr Sykora (CZE)
**2010 Chicago Blackhawks (5):** Niklas Hjalmarsson (SWE), Marian Hossa (SVK), Cristobal Huet (FRA), Tomas Kopecky (SVK), Antti Niemi (FIN)
**2011 Boston Bruins (5):** David Krejci (CZE), Zdeno Chara (SVK), Dennis Seidenberg (GER), Tuuka Rask (FIN), Tomas Kaberle (CZE)
**2012 Los Angeles Kings (3):** Anze Kopitar (SLO), Slava Voynov (RUS), Andrei Loktionov (RUS)

**FIRST PLAYER FROM EACH EUROPEAN COUNTRY TO WIN THE STANLEY CUP**

| | |
|---|---|
| CZE (TCH) | Jaroslav Pouzar—1983-84 Edmonton Oilers |
| FIN | Jari Kurri—1983-84 Edmonton Oilers |
| FRA | Cristobal Huet—2009-10 Chicago Blackhawks |
| GER | Uwe Krupp—1995-96 Colorado Avalanche |
| LAT | Sandis Ozolinsh—1995-96 Colorado Avalanche |
| POL | Krzysztof Oliwa—1999-2000 New Jersey Devils |
| RUS (URS) | Alexander Karpovtsev, Alexei Kovalyov, Sergei Nemchinov, Sergei Zubov—1993-94 New York Rangers |
| SLO | Anze Kopitar—2011-12 Los Angeles Kings |
| SUI | David Aebischer—2000-01 Colorado Avalanche |
| SVK | Jiri Bicek—2002-03 New Jersey Devils |
| SWE | Anders Kallur, Stefan Persson—1979-80 New York Islanders |
| UKR | Ruslan Fedotenko—2003-04 Tampa Bay Lightning |

**STANLEY CUP WINNING GOALS BY EUROPEANS**

| | |
|---|---|
| 1987 | Jari Kurri (FIN), Edmonton Oilers |
| 1991 | Ulf Samuelsson (SWE), Pittsburgh Penguins |
| 1995 | Sergei Brylin (RUS), New Jersey Devils |
| 1996 | Uwe Krupp (GER), Colorado Avalanche |
| 2004 | Ruslan Fedotenko (UKR), Tampa Bay Lightning |
| 2006 | Frantisek Kaberle (CZE), Carolina Hurricanes |
| 2008 | Henrik Zetterberg (SWE), Detroit Red Wings |

**EUROPEAN STANLEY CUP CAPTAINS**
Nicklas Lidstrom (SWE), Detroit Red Wings, 2007-08
Zdeno Chara (SVK), Boston Bruins, 2010-11

**EUROPEANS IN THE HOCKEY HALL OF FAME**
Vyacheslav Fetisov (RUS), Player, 2001
Valeri Kharlamov (RUS), Player, 2005
Jari Kurri (FIN), Player, 2001
Igor Larionov (RUS), Player, 2008
Paul Loicq (BEL), Builder, 1961
Gunther Sabetzki (GER), Builder, 1995
Borje Salming (SWE), Player, 1996
Lord Stanley of Preston (GBR), Builder, 1945
Peter Stastny (SVK), Player, 1998
Anatoli Tarasov (RUS), Builder, 1974
Vladislav Tretiak (RUS), Player, 1989

**FIRST EUROPEAN IN NHL**
Ulf Sterner (SWE), NY Rangers, January 27, 1965

**FIRST EUROPEAN CAPTAIN IN NHL**
Lars-Erik Sjoberg (SWE), Winnipeg Jets, 1979-80

**FIRST (AND ONLY) EUROPEAN HEAD COACHES IN NHL**
Alpo Suhonen (FIN), Chicago, October 5, 2000 (Chicago 2 at Buffalo 4)
Ivan Hlinka (CZE), Pittsburgh, October 13, 2000 (Tampa Bay 2 at Pittsburgh 3)

**FIRST EUROPEAN ON-ICE OFFICIAL IN NHL**
Marcus Vinnerborg (SWE), November 16, 2010 (Anaheim at Dallas)

*Slovenia's Anze Kopitar became the first player from his homeland to win the Stanley Cup, leading the Los Angeles Kings to victory in 2012 and taking the Cup home to Hrusica, Slovenia in the summer. Photo: Mike Bolt / HHOF.*

# CHAMPIONS, MEN

## European Club Champions

**EUROPEAN CUP**

1966 ZKL Brno, TCH
1967 ZKL Brno, TCH
1968 ZKL Brno, TCH
1969 CSKA Moscow, URS
1970 CSKA Moscow, URS
1971 CSKA Moscow, URS
1972 CSKA Moscow, URS
1973 CSKA Moscow, URS
1974 CSKA Moscow, URS
1975 Krylia Sovetov, URS
1976 CSKA Moscow, URS
1977 Poldi Kladno, TCH
1978 CSKA Moscow, URS
1979 CSKA Moscow, URS
1980 CSKA Moscow, URS
1981 CSKA Moscow, URS
1982 CSKA Moscow, URS
1983 CSKA Moscow, URS
1984 CSKA Moscow, URS
1985 CSKA Moscow, URS
1986 CSKA Moscow, URS
1987 CSKA Moscow, URS
1988 CSKA Moscow, URS
1989 CSKA Moscow, URS
1990 CSKA Moscow, URS
1991 Djurgardens IF, SWE
1992 Djurdardens IF, SWE
1993 Malmo IF, SWE
1994 TPS Turku, FIN
1995 Jokerit Helsinki, FIN
1996 Jokerit Helsinki, FIN
1997 Lada Togliatti, RUS

**EUROPEAN HOCKEY LEAGUE**

1997 TPS Turku, FIN
1998 VEU Feldkirch, AUT
1999 M. Magnitogorsk, RUS
2000 M. Magnitogorsk, RUS

**EUROPEAN CHAMPIONS CUP**

2005 Avangard Omsk, RUS
2006 Dynamo Moscow, RUS
2007 Ak Bars Kazan, RUS
2008 M. Magnitogorsk, RUS

**CHAMPIONS HOCKEY LEAGUE**

2009 ZSC Lions Zurich, SUI

**CONTINENTAL CUP**

1998 HC Kosice, SVK
1999 Ambri-Piotta, SUI
2000 Ambri-Piotta, SUI
2001 ZSC Lions Zurich, SUI
2002 ZSC Lions Zurich, SUI
2003 Jokerit Helsinki, FIN
2004 Slovan Bratislava, SVK
2005 HKm Zvolen, SVK
2006 Lada Togliatti, RUS
2007 Yunost Minsk, BLR
2008 Ak Bars Kazan, RUS
2009 MHC Martin, SVK
2010 Salzburg, AUT
2011 Yunost Minsk, BLR

## Victoria Cup

(European club champion vs. NHL team)
2008 New York Rangers
2009 ZSC Lions Zurich

## National Champions of Member Federations, Men

**ARMENIA**

1999-2000 ASC Yerevan
2000-01 ASC Yerevan
2001-02 *no champion*
2002-03 Dinamo Yerevan
2003-04 Dinamo Yerevan
2004-05 Dinamo Yerevan
2005-06 Urartu Yerevan
2006-07 Urartu Yerevan
2007-08 Urartu Yerevan
2008-09 Urartu Yerevan
2009-10 Urartu Yerevan
2010-11 Urartu Yerevan
2011-12 *no champion*

**AUSTRALIA**

1909 Victoria
1910 Victoria
1911 New South Wales
1912 New South Wales
1913 Victoria
1914 *no champion*
1921 New South Wales
1922 Victoria
1923 New South Wales
1924 New South Wales
1925 New South Wales
1926 New South Wales
1927 New South Wales
1928 New South Wales
1929 New South Wales
1930 New South Wales
1931 New South Wales
1932 New South Wales
1933 New South Wales
1934 New South Wales
1935 New South Wales
1936 New South Wales
1937 New South Wales
1938 New South Wales
1939 New South Wales
1940 *no champion*
1947 Victoria
1948 New South Wales
1949 Victoria
1950 New South Wales
1951 Victoria
1952 Victoria
1953 Victoria
1954 Victoria
1955 *no champion*
1961 Victoria
1962 Victoria
1963 New South Wales
1964 New South Wales
1965 Victoria
1966 Victoria
1967 Victoria
1968 Victoria
1969 New South Wales
1970 New South Wales
1971 New South Wales
1972 Victoria
1973 Victoria
1974 Victoria
1975 Victoria
1976 Victoria
1977 Queensland
1978 Victoria
1979 Victoria
1980 New South Wales
1981 New South Wales
1982 Victoria
1983 New South Wales
1984 New South Wales
1985 New South Wales
1986 South Australia
1987 South Australia
1988 New South Wales
1989 New South Wales
1990 South Australia
1991 South Australia
1992 New South Wales
1993 *no champion*
1994 New South Wales
1995 South Australia
1996 New South Wales
1997 South Australia
1998 Australia Capital Territory
1999 New South Wales
2000 New South Wales
2001 New South Wales
2002 Sydney Bears
2003 Newcastle Northstars
2004 West Sydney IceDogs
2005 Newcastle Northstars
2006 Newcastle Northstars
2007 Penrith Bears
2008 Newcastle Northstars
2009 Adelaide Adrenaline
2010 Melbourne Ice
2011 Melbourne Ice
2012 Melbourne Ice

**AUSTRIA**

1922-23 Wiener EV
1923-24 Wiener EV
1924-25 Wiener EV
1925-26 Wiener EV
1926-27 Wiener EV
1927-28 Wiener EV
1928-29 Wiener EV
1929-30 Wiener EV
1930-31 Wiener EV
1931-32 Potzleinsdorfer SK
1932-33 Wiener EV
1933-34 Klagenfurter AC
1934-35 Klagenfurter AC
1935-36 *no champion*
1936-37 Wiener EV
1937-38 EK Engelmann, Wien
1938-1945 *no champion*
1945-46 EK Engelmann, Wien
1946-47 Wiener EV
1947-48 Wiener EV
1948-49 Wiener Eissport-Gemeinschaft
1949-50 Wiener Eissport-Gemeinschaft
1950-51 Wiener Eissport-Gemeinschaft
1951-52 Klagenfurter AC
1952-53 Innsbrucker EV
1953-54 Innsbrucker EV
1954-55 Klagenfurter AC
1955-56 EK Engelmann, Wien
1956-57 EK Engelmann, Wien
1957-58 Innsbrucker EV
1958-59 Innsbrucker EV
1959-60 Klagenfurter AC
1960-61 Innsbrucker EV
1961-62 Wiener EV
1962-63 Innsbrucker EV
1963-64 Klagenfurter AC
1964-65 Klagenfurter AC
1965-66 Klagenfurter AC
1966-67 Klagenfurter AC
1967-68 Klagenfurter AC
1968-69 Klagenfurter AC
1969-70 Klagenfurter AC
1970-71 Klagenfurter AC
1971-72 Klagenfurter AC
1972-73 Klagenfurter AC
1973-74 Klagenfurter AC
1974-75 ATSE Graz
1975-76 Klagenfurter AC
1976-77 Klagenfurter AC
1977-78 ATSE Graz
1978-79 Klagenfurter AC
1979-80 Klagenfurter AC
1980-81 Villacher SV
1981-82 VEU Feldkirch
1982-83 VEU Feldkirch
1983-84 VEU Feldkirch
1984-85 Klagenfurter AC
1985-86 Klagenfurter AC
1986-87 Klagenfurter AC
1987-88 Klagenfurter AC
1988-89 GEV Innsbruck
1989-90 VEU Feldkirch
1990-91 Klagenfurter AC
1991-92 Villacher SV
1992-93 Villacher SV
1993-94 VEU Feldkirch
1994-95 VEU Feldkirch
1995-96 VEU Feldkirch
1996-97 VEU Feldkirch
1997-98 VEU Feldkirch
1998-99 Villacher SV
1999-2000 Klagenfurter AC
2000-01 Klagenfurter AC
2001-02 Villacher SV
2002-03 Black Wings Linz
2003-04 Klagenfurter AC
2004-05 Vienna Capitals
2005-06 Villacher SV
2006-07 Red Bull Salzburg
2007-08 Red Bull Salzburg
2008-09 Klagenfurter AC
2009-10 Red Bull Salzburg
2010-11 Red Bull Salzburg
2011-12 Black Wings Linz

**BELARUS**

1992-93 Dynamo Minsk
1993-94 Tivali Minsk
1994-95 Tivali Minsk
1995-96 Polimir Novopolotsk
1996-97 Polimir Novopolotsk
1997-98 Neman Grodno
1998-99 Neman Grodno
1999-2000 Tivali Minsk
2000-01 Neman Grodno

2001-02 Keramin Minsk
2002-03 HC Gomel
2003-04 Yunost Minsk
2004-05 Yunost Minsk
2005-06 Yunost Minsk
2006-07 Dynamo Minsk
2007-08 Keramin Minsk
2008-09 Yunost Minsk
2009-10 Yunost Minsk
2010-11 Yunost Minsk
2011-12 Metallurg Zhlobin

**BELGIUM**

1911-12 Brussels IHSC
1912-13 Brussels IHSC
1913-14 CDP Bruxelles
1914-19 *no champion*
1919-20 CDP Bruxelles
1920-21 CDP Bruxelles
1921-22 Brussels IHSC
1922-23 Brussels IHSC
1923-24 Le Puck Anvers
1924-25 Le Puck Anvers
1925-26 Le Puck Anvers
1926-27 Le Puck Anvers
1927-28 Le Puck Anvers
1928-29 CDP Anvers
1929-33 *no champion*
1933-34 CDP Anvers
1934-35 CDP Anvers
1935-36 CDP Anvers
1936-37 CDP Anvers
1937-38 Brussels IHSC
1938-39 Brussels IHSC
1939-40 Brussels IHSC
1940-41 Brussels IHSC
1941-42 Brussels IHSC
1942-43 Brussels IHSC
1943-44 *no champion*
1944-45 Brussels IHSC
1945-46 Brussels IHSC
1946-47 Brussels IHSC
1947-48 Brussels IHSC
1948-49 Brussels IHSC
1949-50 Brabo Antwerpen
1950-53 *no champion*
1953-54 Brabo Antwerpen
1954-59 *no champion*
1959-60 CPL Liege
1960-61 CPL Liege
1961-62 Brussels IHSC
1962-63 Brussels IHSC
1963-64 Brussels IHSC
1964-66 *no champion*
1966-67 Brussels IHSC
1967-68 Brussels IHSC
1968-69 *no champion*
1969-70 Brussels IHSC
1970-71 Brussels IHSC
1971-72 Brussels IHSC
1972-74 *no champion*
1974-75 Brussels IHSC
1975-76 Brussels IHSC
1976-77 Brussels IHSC
1977-78 Brussels IHSC
1978-79 Olympia Heist op den Berg
1979-80 Olympia Heist op den Berg
1980-81 HYC Herentals
1981-82 Brussels IHSC
1982-83 Olympia Heist op den Berg
1983-84 HYC Herentals
1984-85 HYC Herentals
1985-86 Olympia Heist op den Berg
1986-87 Olympia Heist op den Berg
1987-88 Phantoma Deurne
1988-89 Olympia Heist op den Berg
1989-90 Olympia Heist op den Berg
1990-91 Olympia Heist op den Berg
1991-92 Olympia Heist op den Berg
1992-93 HYC Herentals
1993-94 HYC Herentals
1994-95 *no champion*
1995-96 HYC Herentals
1996-97 HYC Herentals
1997-98 HYC Herentals
1998-99 Olympia Heist op den Berg
1999-2000 Phantoms Deurne
2000-01 Phantoms Deurne
2001-02 Phantoms Deurne
2002-03 Phantoms Deurne
2003-04 Olympia Heist op den Berg
2004-05 IHC Leuven
2005-06 White Caps Turnhout
2006-07 White Caps Turnhout
2007-08 White Caps Turnhout
2008-09 HYC Herentals
2009-10 IHC Leuven
2010-11 White Caps Turnhout
2011-12 HYC Herentals

**BOSNIA & HERZEGOVINA**

2009-10 HK Stari Grad Sarajevo
2010-11 Bosna Centar Sarajevo
2011-12 *no champion*

**BRAZIL**

2007-08 Sociedade Hipica de Campinas Sao Paulo
2008-09 Sociedade Hipica de Campinas Sao Paulo
2009-10 Sociedade Hipica de Campinas Sao Paulo
2010-12 *no champion*

**BULGARIA**

1951-52 Cerveno zname Sofia
1952-53 Udarnik Sofia
1953-54 Udarnik Sofia
1954-55 Torpedo Sofia
1955-56 Cerveno zname Sofia
1956-57 Cerveno zname Sofia
1957-58 *no champion*
1958-59 Cerveno zname Sofia
1959-60 Cerveno zname Sofia
1960-61 Cerveno zname Sofia
1961-62 Cerveno zname Sofia
1962-63 Cerveno zname Sofia
1963-64 CDNA Sofia
1964-65 CSKA Cerveno zname Sofia
1965-66 CSKA Cerveno zname Sofia
1966-67 CSKA Cerveno zname Sofia
1967-68 Metallurg Pernik
1968-69 CSKA Septemvriisko zname S
1969-70 Krakra Pernik
1970-71 CSKA Septemvriisko zname S
1971-72 CSKA Septemvriisko zname S
1972-73 CSKA Septemvriisko zname S
1973-74 CSKA Septemvriisko zname S
1974-75 CSKA Septemvriisko zname S
1975-76 Levski-Spartak Sofia
1976-77 Levski-Spartak Sofia
1977-78 Levski-Spartak Sofia
1978-79 Levski-Spartak Sofia
1979-80 Levski-Spartak Sofia
1980-81 Levski-Spartak Sofia
1981-82 Levski-Spartak Sofia
1982-83 CSKA Septemvriisko zname S
1983-84 CSKA Septemvriisko zname S
1984-85 Slavia Sofia
1985-86 CSKA Septemvriisko zname S
1986-87 Slavia Sofia
1987-88 Slavia Sofia
1988-89 Levski-Spartak Sofia
1989-90 Levski-Spartak Sofia
1990-91 Slavia Sofia
1991-92 DFS Levski-Spartak Sofia
1992-93 DFS Levski-Spartak Sofia
1993-94 DFS Levski-Spartak Sofia
1994-95 HC Levski Sofia
1995-96 Slavia SF Sofia
1996-97 Slavia SF Sofia
1997-98 Slavia SF Sofia
1998-99 HC Levski Sofia
1999-2000 Slavia Sofia
2000-01 Slavia Sofia
2001-02 Slavia Sofia
2002-03 Levski Sofia
2003-04 Slavia Sofia
2004-05 Slavia Sofia
2005-06 Akademika Sofia
2006-07 Akademika Sofia
2007-08 Slavia Sofia
2008-09 Slavia Sofia
2009-10 Slavia Sofia
2010-11 Slavia Sofia
2011-12 Slavia Sofia

**CANADA & USA (STANLEY CUP/NHL)**

1892-93 Montreal AAA
1893-94 Montreal AAA
1894-95 Montreal Victorias
1895-96 Winnipeg Victorias/ Montreal Victorias
1896-97 Montreal Victorias
1897-98 Montreal Victorias
1898-99 Montreal Victorias/Montreal Shamrocks
1899-1900 Montreal Shamrocks
1900-01 Winnipeg Victorias
1901-02 Montreal AAA/ Winnipeg Victorias
1902-03 Montreal AAA/Ottawa Silver Seven
1903-04 Ottawa Silver Seven
1904-05 Ottawa Silver Seven
1905-06 Ottawa Silver Seven/Montreal Wanderers
1906-07 Kenora Thistles/ Montreal Wanderers
1907-08 Montreal Wanderers
1908-09 Ottawa Senators
1909-10 Ottawa Senators/ Montreal Wanderers
1910-11 Ottawa Senators
1911-12 Quebec Bulldogs
1912-13 Quebec Bulldogs
1913-14 Toronto Blueshirts
1914-15 Vancouver Millionaires
1915-16 Montreal Canadiens
1916-17 Seattle Metropolitans
1917-18 Toronto Arenas
1918-19 *no winner—flu epidemic*
1919-20 Ottawa Senators
1920-21 Ottawa Senators
1921-22 Toronto St. Pats
1922-23 Ottawa Senators
1923-24 Montreal Canadiens
1924-25 Victoria Cougars
1925-26 Montreal Maroons
1926-27 Ottawa Senators
1927-28 New York Rangers
1928-29 Boston Bruins
1929-30 Montreal Canadiens
1930-31 Montreal Canadiens
1931-32 Toronto Maple Leafs
1932-33 New York Rangers
1933-34 Chicago Black Hawks
1934-35 Montreal Maroons
1935-36 Detroit Red Wings
1936-37 Detroit Red Wings
1937-38 Chicago Black Hawks
1938-39 Boston Bruins
1939-40 New York Rangers
1940-41 Boston Bruins
1941-42 Toronto Maple Leafs
1942-43 Detroit Red Wings
1943-44 Montreal Canadiens
1944-45 Toronto Maple Leafs
1945-46 Montreal Canadiens
1946-47 Toronto Maple Leafs
1947-48 Toronto Maple Leafs
1948-49 Toronto Maple Leafs
1949-50 Detroit Red Wings
1950-51 Toronto Maple Leafs
1951-52 Detroit Red Wings
1952-53 Montreal Canadiens
1953-54 Detroit Red Wings
1954-55 Detroit Red Wings
1955-56 Montreal Canadiens
1956-57 Montreal Canadiens
1957-58 Montreal Canadiens
1958-59 Montreal Canadiens
1959-60 Montreal Canadiens
1960-61 Chicago Black Hawks
1961-62 Toronto Maple Leafs
1962-63 Toronto Maple Leafs
1963-64 Toronto Maple Leafs
1964-65 Montreal Canadiens
1965-66 Montreal Canadiens
1966-67 Toronto Maple Leafs
1967-68 Montreal Canadiens
1968-69 Montreal Canadiens
1969-70 Boston Bruins
1970-71 Montreal Canadiens
1971-72 Boston Bruins
1972-73 Montreal Canadiens
1973-74 Philadelphia Flyers
1974-75 Philadelphia Flyers
1975-76 Montreal Canadiens
1976-77 Montreal Canadiens
1977-78 Montreal Canadiens
1978-79 Montreal Canadiens
1979-80 New York Islanders
1980-81 New York Islanders
1981-82 New York Islanders
1982-83 New York Islanders
1983-84 Edmonton Oilers
1984-85 Edmonton Oilers
1985-86 Montreal Canadiens
1986-87 Edmonton Oilers
1987-88 Edmonton Oilers
1988-89 Calgary Flames
1989-90 Edmonton Oilers
1990-91 Pittsburgh Penguins
1991-92 Pittsburgh Penguins
1992-93 Montreal Canadiens
1993-94 New York Rangers
1994-95 New Jersey Devils
1995-96 Colorado Avalanche
1996-97 Detroit Red Wings
1997-98 Detroit Red Wings
1998-99 Dallas Stars
1999-2000 New Jersey Devils
2000-01 Detroit Red Wings
2001-02 Colorado Avalanche
2002-03 New Jersey Devils
2003-04 Tampa Bay Lightning
2004-05 *no champion*
2005-06 Carolina Hurricanes
2006-07 Anaheim Ducks
2007-08 Detroit Red Wings
2008-09 Pittsburgh Penguins
2009-10 Chicago Blackhawks
2010-11 Boston Bruins
2011-12 Los Angeles Kings

**CANADA**

**Allan Cup Champions (senior)**

1907-08 Ottawa Cliffsides
1908-09 Kingston Queen's University
1909-10 Toronto St. Michael's
1910-11 Winnipeg Victorias
1911-12 Winnipeg Victorias
1912-13 Winnipeg Hockey Club
1913-14 Regina Victorias
1914-15 Winnipeg Monarchs
1915-16 Winnipeg 61st Battalion
1916-17 Toronto Dentals
1917-18 Kitchener Hockey Club
1918-19 Hamilton Tigers
1919-20 Winnipeg Falcons
1920-21 University of Toronto
1921-22 Toronto Granites
1922-23 Toronto Granites
1923-24 Sault Ste. Marie Greyhounds
1924-25 Port Arthur Seniors
1925-26 Port Arthur Seniors
1926-27 Toronto Varsity Grads
1927-28 University of Manitoba
1928-29 Port Arthur Seniors
1929-30 Montreal AAA
1930-31 Winnipeg Hockey Club
1931-32 Toronto Nationals
1932-33 Moncton Hawks
1933-34 Moncton Hawks
1934-35 Halifax Wolverines

| | |
|---|---|
| 1935-36 | Kimberley Dynamiters |
| 1936-37 | Sudbury Tigers |
| 1937-38 | Trail Smoke Eaters |
| 1938-39 | Trail Smoke Eaters |
| 1939-40 | Kirkland Lake Blue Devils |
| 1940-41 | Regina Rangers |
| 1941-42 | Ottawa RCAF |
| 1942-43 | Ottawa Commandos |
| 1943-44 | Quebec Aces |
| 1944-45 | no tournament |
| 1945-46 | Calgary Stampeders |
| 1946-47 | Montreal Royals |
| 1947-48 | Edmonton Flyers |
| 1948-49 | Ottawa Senators |
| 1949-50 | Toronto Marlboros |
| 1950-51 | Owen Sound Mercurys |
| 1951-52 | Fort Frances Canadians |
| 1952-53 | Kitchener-Waterloo Dutchmen |
| 1953-54 | Penticton V's |
| 1954-55 | Kitchener-Waterloo Dutchmen |
| 1955-56 | Vernon Canadians |
| 1956-57 | Whitby Dunlops |
| 1957-58 | Belleville McFarlands |
| 1958-59 | Whitby Dunlops |
| 1959-60 | Chatham Maroons |
| 1960-61 | Galt Terriers |
| 1961-62 | Trail Smoke Eaters |
| 1962-63 | Windsor Bulldogs |
| 1963-64 | Winnipeg Maroons |
| 1964-65 | Sherbrooke Beavers |
| 1965-66 | Drumheller Miners |
| 1966-67 | Drummondville Eagles |
| 1967-68 | Victoriaville Tigers |
| 1968-69 | Galt Hornets |
| 1969-70 | Spokane Jets |
| 1970-71 | Galt Hornets |
| 1971-72 | Spokane Jets |
| 1972-73 | Orillia Terriers |
| 1973-74 | Barrie Flyers |
| 1974-75 | Thunder Bay Twins |
| 1975-76 | Spokane Flyers |
| 1976-77 | Brantford Alexanders |
| 1977-78 | Kimberley Dynamiters |
| 1978-79 | Petrolia Squires |
| 1979-80 | Spokane Flyers |
| 1980-81 | Petrolia Squires |
| 1981-82 | Cranbrook Royals |
| 1982-83 | Cambridge Hornets |
| 1983-84 | Thunder Bay Twins |
| 1984-85 | Thunder Bay Twins |
| 1985-86 | Cornerbrook Royals |
| 1986-87 | Brantford Motts Clamatos |
| 1987-88 | Thunder Bay Twins |
| 1988-89 | Thunder Bay Twins |
| 1989-90 | Chomedy Laval Warriors |
| 1990-91 | Charlottetown Islanders |
| 1991-92 | Saint John Vitos |
| 1992-93 | Whitehorse Huskies |
| 1993-94 | Warroad Lakers |
| 1994-95 | Warroad Lakers |
| 1995-96 | Warroad Lakers |
| 1996-97 | Powell River Regals |
| 1997-98 | Truro Bearcats |
| 1998-99 | Stony Plain Eagles |
| 1999-00 | Powell River Regals |
| 2000-01 | Lloydminster BorderKings |
| 2001-02 | St. Georges Garaga |
| 2002-03 | Ile-des-Chenes North Stars |
| 2003-04 | St. Georges Garaga |
| 2004-05 | Thunder Bay Bombers |
| 2005-06 | Powell River Regals |
| 2006-07 | Lloydminster BorderKings |
| 2007-08 | Brantford Blast |
| 2008-09 | Bentley Generals |
| 2009-10 | Fort St. John Flyers |
| 2010-11 | Clarenville Caribous |
| 2011-12 | South East Prairie Thunder |

**Memorial Cup Champions (junior)**

| | |
|---|---|
| 1918-19 | University of Toronto Schools |
| 1919-20 | Toronto Canoe Club |
| 1920-21 | Winnipeg Falcons |
| 1921-22 | Fort William War Veterans |
| 1922-23 | University of Manitoba |
| 1923-24 | Owen Sound Greys |
| 1924-25 | Regina Pats |
| 1925-26 | Calgary Canadians |
| 1926-27 | Owen Sound Greys |
| 1927-28 | Regina Monarchs |
| 1928-29 | Toronto Marlboros |
| 1929-30 | Regina Pats |
| 1930-31 | Winnipeg Millionaires |
| 1931-32 | Sudbury Wolves |
| 1932-33 | Newmarket Reds |
| 1933-34 | Toronto St. Michael's |
| 1934-35 | Winnipeg Monarchs |
| 1935-36 | West Toronto Nationals |
| 1936-37 | Winnipeg Monarchs |
| 1937-38 | St. Boniface Seals |
| 1938-39 | Oshawa Generals |
| 1939-40 | Oshawa Generals |
| 1940-41 | Winnipeg Rangers |
| 1941-42 | Portage La Prairie Terriers |
| 1942-43 | Winnipeg Rangers |
| 1943-44 | Oshawa Generals |
| 1944-45 | Toronto St. Michael's |
| 1945-46 | Winnipeg Monarchs |
| 1946-47 | Toronto St. Michael's |
| 1947-48 | Port Arthur West End Bruins |
| 1948-49 | Montreal Royals |
| 1949-50 | Montreal Canadiens |
| 1950-51 | Barrie Flyers |
| 1951-52 | Guelph Biltmores |
| 1952-53 | Barrie Flyers |
| 1953-54 | St. Catharines Tee Pees |
| 1954-55 | Toronto Marlboros |
| 1955-56 | Toronto Marlboros |
| 1956-57 | Flin Flon Bombers |
| 1957-58 | Ottawa-Hull Canadiens |
| 1958-59 | Winnipeg Braves |
| 1959-60 | St. Catharines Tee Pees |
| 1960-61 | Toronto St. Michael's |
| 1961-62 | Hamilton Red Wings |
| 1962-63 | Edmonton Oil Kings |
| 1963-64 | Toronto Marlboros |
| 1964-65 | Niagara Falls Flyers |
| 1965-66 | Edmonton Oil Kings |
| 1966-67 | Toronto Marlboros |
| 1967-68 | Niagara Falls Flyers |
| 1968-69 | Montreal Junior Canadiens |
| 1969-70 | Montreal Junior Canadiens |
| 1970-71 | Quebec Remparts |
| 1971-72 | Cornwall Royals |
| 1972-73 | Toronto Marlboros |
| 1973-74 | Regina Pats |
| 1974-75 | Toronto Marlboros |
| 1975-76 | Hamilton Fincups |
| 1976-77 | New Westminster Bruins |
| 1977-78 | New Westminster Bruins |
| 1978-79 | Peterborough Petes |
| 1979-80 | Cornwall Royals |
| 1980-81 | Cornwall Royals |
| 1981-82 | Kitchener Rangers |
| 1982-83 | Portland Winter Hawks |
| 1983-84 | Ottawa 67's |
| 1984-85 | Prince Albert Raiders |
| 1985-86 | Guelph Platers |
| 1986-87 | Medicine Hat Tigers |
| 1987-88 | Medicine Hat Tigers |
| 1988-89 | Swift Current Broncos |
| 1989-90 | Oshawa Generals |
| 1990-91 | Spokane Chiefs |
| 1991-92 | Kamloops Blazers |
| 1992-93 | Sault Ste. Marie Greyhounds |
| 1993-94 | Kamloops Blazers |
| 1994-95 | Kamloops Blazers |
| 1995-96 | Granby Predateurs |
| 1996-97 | Hull Olympiques |
| 1997-98 | Portland Winter Hawks |
| 1998-99 | Ottawa 67's |
| 1999-2000 | Rimouski Oceanic |
| 2000-01 | Red Deer Rebels |
| 2001-02 | Kootenay Ice |
| 2002-03 | Kitchener Rangers |
| 2003-04 | Kelowna Rockets |
| 2004-05 | London Knights |
| 2005-06 | Quebec Remparts |
| 2006-07 | Vancouver Giants |
| 2007-08 | Spokane Chiefs |
| 2008-09 | Windsor Spitfires |
| 2009-10 | Windsor Spitfires |
| 2010-11 | Saint John Sea Dogs |
| 2011-12 | Shawinigan Cataractes |

**CHINA**

| | |
|---|---|
| 1987-88 | Changchun |
| 1988-89 | Harbin |
| 1989-90 | *no champion* |
| 1990-91 | Nei Menggol |
| 1991-92 | *no champion* |
| 1992-93 | Qiqihar |
| 1993-94 | Qiqihar |
| 1994-95 | Qiqihar |
| 1995-96 | Qiqihar |
| 1996-97 | Qiqihar |
| 1997-98 | Qiqihar |
| 1998-99 | Harbin |
| 1999-2000 | Qiqihar |
| 2000-01 | Qiqihar |
| 2001-02 | Harbin |
| 2002-03 | Harbin |
| 2003-04 | Qiqihar |
| 2004-05 | Qiqihar |
| 2005-06 | Qiqihar |
| 2006-07 | Harbin |
| 2007-08 | Qiqihar |
| 2008-09 | Qiqihar |
| 2009-10 | Qiqihar |
| 2010-11 | Harbin |
| 2011-12 | Qiqihar |

**CHINESE TAIPEI**

| | |
|---|---|
| 2000-01 | *no champion* |
| 2001-02 | Husky Kaohsiung |
| 2002-04 | *no champion* |
| 2004-05 | Taipei Raptors |
| 2005-06 | Chaiyi Sharks |
| 2006-07 | Taipei Bears |
| 2007-08 | Chaiyi Sharks |
| 2008-09 | Hsinchu Raptors |
| 2009-10 | Sababa Bears Taipei |
| 2010-11 | Sababa Bears Taipei |
| 2011-12 | Taipei Wolves |

**CROATIA**

| | |
|---|---|
| 1991-92 | HK Zagreb |
| 1992-93 | HK Zagreb |
| 1993-94 | HK Zagreb |
| 1994-95 | Medvescak Zagreb |
| 1995-96 | HK Zagreb |
| 1996-97 | Medvescak Zagreb |
| 1997-98 | Medvescak Zagreb |
| 1998-99 | Medvescak Zagreb |
| 1999-2000 | Medvescak Zagreb |
| 2000-01 | Medvescak Zagreb |
| 2001-02 | Medvescak Zagreb |
| 2002-03 | Medvescak Zagreb |
| 2003-04 | Medvescak Zagreb |
| 2004-05 | Medvescak Zagreb |
| 2005-06 | Medvescak Zagreb |
| 2006-07 | Medvescak Zagreb |
| 2007-08 | Mladost Zagreb |
| 2008-09 | Medvescak Zagreb |
| 2009-10 | Medvescak Zagreb |
| 2010-11 | Medvescak Zagreb |
| 2011-12 | Medvescak Zagreb |

**CZECHOSLOVAKIA**

| | |
|---|---|
| 1936-37 | LTC Praha |
| 1937-38 | LTC Praha |
| 1938-1945 | *no champion* |
| 1945-46 | LTC Praha |
| 1946-47 | LTC Praha |
| 1947-48 | LTC Praha |
| 1948-49 | LTC Praha |
| 1949-50 | ATK Praha |
| 1950-51 | SKP C. Budejovice |
| 1951-52 | YZKG Ostrava |
| 1952-53 | Sparta Praha Sokolovo |
| 1953-54 | Sparta Praha Sokolovo |
| 1954-55 | RH Brno |
| 1955-56 | RH Brno |
| 1956-57 | RH Brno |
| 1957-58 | RH Brno |
| 1958-59 | SONP Kladno |
| 1959-60 | RH Brno |
| 1960-61 | RH Brno |
| 1961-62 | RH Brno |
| 1962-63 | RH Brno |
| 1963-64 | ZKL Brno |
| 1964-65 | ZKL Brno |
| 1965-66 | ZKL Brno |
| 1966-67 | Dukla Jihlava |
| 1967-68 | Dukla Jihlava |
| 1968-69 | Dukla Jihlava |
| 1969-70 | Dukla Jihlava |
| 1970-71 | Dukla Jihlava |
| 1971-72 | Dukla Jihlava |
| 1972-73 | Tesla Pardubice |
| 1973-74 | Dukla Jihlava |
| 1974-75 | Poldi Kladno |
| 1975-76 | Poldi Kladno |
| 1976-77 | Poldi Kladno |
| 1977-78 | Poldi Kladno |
| 1978-79 | Slovan Bratislava |
| 1979-80 | Poldi Kladno |
| 1980-81 | TJ Vitkovice |
| 1981-82 | Dukla Jihlava |
| 1982-83 | Dukla Jihlava |
| 1983-84 | Dukla Jihlava |
| 1984-85 | Dukla Jihlava |
| 1985-86 | VSZ Kosice |
| 1986-87 | Tesla Pardubice |
| 1987-88 | VSZ Kosice |
| 1988-89 | Tesla Pardubice |
| 1989-90 | Sparta Praha |
| 1990-91 | Dukla Jihlava |

**CZECH REPUBLIC**

| | |
|---|---|
| 1991-92 | Dukla Trencin |
| 1992-93 | Sparta Praha |
| 1993-94 | HC Olomouc |
| 1994-95 | HC Vsetin |
| 1995-96 | HC Vsetin |
| 1996-97 | HC Vsetin |
| 1997-98 | HC Vsetin |
| 1998-99 | HC Vsetin |
| 1999-2000 | Sparta Praha |
| 2000-01 | HC Vsetin |
| 2001-02 | Sparta Praha |
| 2002-03 | Slavia Praha |
| 2003-04 | HC Zlin |
| 2004-05 | HC Pardubice |
| 2005-06 | Sparta Praha |
| 2006-07 | Sparta Praha |
| 2007-08 | Slavia Praha |
| 2008-09 | HC Karlovy Vary |
| 2009-10 | HC Pardubice |
| 2010-11 | Ocelari Trinec |
| 2011-12 | HC Pardubice |

**DENMARK**

| | |
|---|---|
| 1954-55 | Rungsted IK |
| 1955-56 | Kobenhavns SF |
| 1956-1959 | *no champion* |
| 1959-60 | Kobenhavns SF |
| 1960-61 | Kobenhavns SF |
| 1961-62 | Kobenhavns SF |
| 1962-63 | Rungsted IK |
| 1963-64 | Kobenhavns SF |
| 1964-65 | Kobenhavns SF |
| 1965-66 | Kobenhavns SF |
| 1966-67 | Gladsaxe SF |
| 1967-68 | Gladsaxe SF |
| 1968-69 | Esbjerg IK |
| 1969-70 | Kobenhavns SF |
| 1970-71 | Gladsaxe SF |
| 1971-72 | Kobenhavns SF |
| 1972-73 | Herning IK |
| 1973-74 | Gladsaxe SF |
| 1974-75 | Gladsaxe SF |
| 1975-76 | Kobenhavns SF |
| 1976-77 | Herning IK |
| 1977-78 | Rodovre SolK |
| 1978-79 | Vojens IK |
| 1979-80 | Vojens IK |

1980-81 Aalborg BK af 1885
1981-82 Vojens IK
1982-83 Rodovre SolK
1983-84 Herlev IK
1984-85 Rodovre SolK
1985-86 Rodovre SolK
1986-87 Herning IK
1987-88 Esbjerg IK
1988-89 Frederikshavn IK
1989-90 Rodovre SolK
1990-91 Herning IK
1991-92 Herning IK
1992-93 Esbjerg IK
1993-94 Herning IK
1994-95 Herning IK
1995-96 Esbjerg IK
1996-97 Herning IK
1997-98 Herning IK
1998-99 Rodovre IK
1999-2000 Frederikshavn IK
2000-2001 Herning IK
2001-02 Rungsted IK
2002-03 Herning IK
2003-04 Esbjerg IK
2004-05 Herning IK
2005-06 Sonderjyske Vojens
2006-07 Herning IK
2007-08 Herning IK
2008-09 Sonderjyske Vojens
2009-10 Sonderjyske Vojens
2010-11 Blue Fox Herning
2011-12 Herning Blue Fox

**DPR (NORTH) KOREA**
2000-01 Pyongchol Pyongyang
2001-02 *no champion*
2002-03 Pyongchol Pyongyang
2003-04 Pyongchol Pyongyang
2004-05 Pyongyang
2005-06 Pyongchol Pyongyang
2006-07 Pyongchol Pyongyang
2007-08 Pyongyang
2008-09 Pyongyang
2009-10 Pyongchol Pyongyang
2010-11 Pyongchol Pyongyang
2011-12 *no champion*

**ESTONIA**
1933-34 Kalev Tallinn
1934-35 *no champion*
1935-36 ASC Tartu
1936-37 Kalev Tallinn
1937-38 *no champion*
1938-39 ASC Tartu
1939-40 Sport Tallinn

1992-93 Kreenholm Narva
1993-94 Kreenholm Narva
1994-95 Kreenholm Narva
1995-96 Kreenholm Narva
1996-97 Valk 494 Tartu
1997-98 Kreenholm Narva
1998-99 Valk 494 Tartu
1999-2000 Valk 494 Tartu
2000-01 Narva 2000
2001-02 Valk 494 Tartu
2002-03 Valk 494 Tartu
2003-04 Panter-Hansa Sport Tallinn
2004-05 Tallinn Stars
2005-06 Tallinn Stars
2006-07 Tallinn Stars
2007-08 Kalev-Valk Tartu
2008-09 Tallinn Stars
2009-10 Viru-Sputnik Kohtla-Jarve
2010-11 Kalev-Valk Tartu
2011-12 Kalev-Valk Tartu

**FINLAND**
1927-28 Reipas Viipuri
1928-29 HJK Helsinki
1929-30 *no champion*
1930-31 TaPa Tampere
1931-32 HJK Helsinki
1932-33 HSK Helsinki
1933-34 HSK Helsinki
1934-35 HJK Helsinki
1935-36 Ilves Tampere
1936-37 Ilves Tampere
1937-38 Ilves Tampere
1938-39 KIF Helsinki
1939-40 *no champion*
1940-41 KIF Helsinki
1941-42 *no champion*
1942-43 KIF Helsinki
1943-44 *no champion*
1944-45 Ilves Tampere
1945-46 Ilves Tampere
1946-47 Ilves Tampere
1947-48 Tarmo Hameenlinna
1948-49 Tarmo Hameenlinna
1949-50 Ilves Tampere
1950-51 Ilves Tampere
1951-52 Ilves Tampere
1952-53 TBK Tampere
1953-54 TBK Tampere
1954-55 TBK Tampere
1955-56 TPS Turku
1956-57 Ilves Tampere
1957-58 Ilves Tampere
1958-59 Tappara Tampere
1959-60 Ilves Tampere
1960-61 Tappara Tampere
1961-62 Ilves Tampere
1962-63 Lukko Rauma
1963-64 Tappara Tampere
1964-65 Karhut Pori
1965-66 Ilves Tampere
1966-67 RU-38 Pori
1967-68 KooVee Tampere
1968-69 HIFK Helsinki
1969-70 HIFK Helsinki
1970-71 Assat Pori
1971-72 Ilves Tampere
1972-73 Jokerit Helsinki
1973-74 HIFK Helsinki
1974-75 Tappara Tampere
1975-76 TPS Turku
1976-77 Tappara Tampere
1977-78 Assat Pori
1978-79 Tappara Tampere
1979-80 HIFK Helsinki
1980-81 Karpat Oulu
1981-82 Tappara Tampere
1982-83 HIFK Helsinki
1983-84 Tappara Tampere
1984-85 Ilves Tampere
1985-86 Tappara Tampere
1986-87 Tappara Tampere
1987-88 Tappara Tampere
1988-89 TPS Turku
1989-90 TPS Turku
1990-91 TPS Turku
1991-92 Jokerit Helsinki
1992-93 TPS Turku
1993-94 Jokerit Helsinki
1994-95 TPS Turku
1995-96 Jokerit Helsinki
1996-97 Jokerit Helsinki
1997-98 HIFK Helsinki
1998-99 TPS Turku
1999-2000 TPS Turku
2000-01 TPS Turku
2001-02 Jokerit Helsinki
2002-03 Tappara Tampere
2003-04 Karpat Oulu
2004-05 Karpat Oulu
2005-06 HPK Hameenlinna
2006-07 Karpat Oulu
2007-08 Karpat Oulu
2008-09 JYP Jyvaskyla
2009-10 TPS Turku
2010-11 HIFK Helsinki
2011-12 JYP Jyvaskyla

**FRANCE**
1904-05 Patineurs de Paris
1905-06 Patineurs de Paris
1906-07 Lyon
1907-08 Patineurs de Paris
1908-1911 *no champion*
1911-12 Patineurs de Paris
1912-13 Patineurs de Paris
1913-14 Patineurs de Paris
1914-1919 *no champion*
1919-20 Ice Skating Club Paris
1920-21 Club des Sports d'Hiver Paris
1921-22 Club des Sports d'Hiver Paris
1922-23 Chamonix HC
1923-24 Chamonix HC
1924-25 Chamonix HC
1925-26 Club des Sports d'Hiver Paris
1926-27 Chamonix HC
1927-28 *no champion*
1928-29 Chamonix HC
1929-30 Chamonix HC
1930-31 Sports Alpins Chamonix
1931-32 Stade Francais Paris
1932-33 Stade Francais Paris
1933-34 Rapid de Paris
1934-35 Stade Francais Paris
1935-36 Francais Volants Paris
1936-37 *no champion*
1937-38 Francais Volants Paris
1938-39 Chamonix HC
1939-1941 *no champion*
1941-42 Sports Alpins Chamonix
1942-43 *no champion*
1943-44 Sports Alpins Chamonix
1944-45 *no champion*
1945-46 Sports Alpins Chamonix
1946-1948 *no champion*
1948-49 Chamonix HC
1949-50 Racing Club Paris
1950-51 Racing Club Paris
1951-52 Chamonix HC
1952-53 Paris Universite Club
1953-54 Chamonix HC
1954-55 Chamonix HC
1955-56 Patineurs de Lyon
1956-57 AC Boulogne-Billancourt
1957-58 Chamonix HC
1958-59 Chamonix HC
1959-60 AC Boulogne-Billancourt
1960-61 Chamonix HC
1961-62 AC Boulogne-Billancourt
1962-63 Chamonix HC
1963-64 Chamonix HC
1964-65 Chamonix HC
1965-66 Chamonix HC
1966-67 Chamonix HC
1967-68 Chamonix HC
1968-69 HC Saint Gervais
1969-70 Chamonix HC
1970-71 Chamonix HC
1971-72 Chamonix HC
1972-73 Chamonix HC
1973-74 HC Saint Gervais
1974-75 HC Saint Gervais
1975-76 Chamonix HC
1976-77 HC Gap
1977-78 HC Gap
1978-79 Chamonix HC
1979-80 ASG Tours
1980-81 CSG Grenoble
1981-82 CSG Grenoble
1982-83 HC Saint Gervais
1983-84 Club de Sports Megeve
1984-85 HC Saint Gervais
1985-86 HC Saint Gervais
1986-87 HC Mont Blanc
1987-88 HC Mont Blanc
1988-89 Francais Volants de Paris
1989-90 Rouen HC
1990-91 CSG Grenoble
1991-92 Rouen HC
1992-93 Rouen HC
1993-94 Rouen HC
1994-95 Rouen HC
1995-96 HC Brest
1996-97 HC Brest
1997-98 HC Grenoble
1998-99 HC Amiens
1999-2000 HC Reims
2000-01 Rouen Hockey Elite 76
2001-02 HC Reims
2002-03 Rouen Hockey Elite 76
2003-04 HC Amiens
2004-05 HC Mulhouse
2005-06 Rouen Hockey Elite 76
2006-07 Grenoble Metropole Hockey 38
2007-08 Rouen Hockey Elite 76
2008-09 Grenoble Metropole Hockey 38
2009-10 Rouen Hockey Elite 76
2010-11 Rouen Hockey Elite 76
2011-12 Rouen Dragons

**GEORGIA**
2007-08 Ruchi Mglebi Tbilisi
2008-12 *no champion*

**GERMANY (GDR/EAST)**
1950-51 Ostglas Weisswasser
1951-52 Chemie Weisswasser
1952-53 Chemie Weisswasser
1953-54 Dynamo Weisswasser
1954-55 Dynamo Weisswasser
1955-56 Dynamo Weisswasser
1956-57 Dynamo Weisswasser
1957-58 Dynamo Weisswasser
1958-59 Dynamo Weisswasser
1959-60 Dynamo Weisswasser
1960-61 Dynamo Weisswasser
1961-62 Dynamo Weisswasser
1962-63 Dynamo Weisswasser
1963-64 Dynamo Weisswasser
1964-65 Dynamo Weisswasser
1965-66 Dynamo Berlin
1966-67 Dynamo Berlin
1967-68 Dynamo Berlin
1968-69 Dynamo Weisswasser
1969-70 Dynamo Weisswasser
1970-71 Dynamo Weisswasser
1971-72 Dynamo Weisswasser
1972-73 Dynamo Weisswasser
1973-74 Dynamo Weisswasser
1974-75 Dynamo Weisswasser
1975-76 Dynamo Berlin
1976-77 Dynamo Berlin
1977-78 Dynamo Berlin
1978-79 Dynamo Berlin
1979-80 Dynamo Berlin
1980-81 Dynamo Weisswasser
1981-82 Dynamo Berlin
1982-83 Dynamo Berlin
1983-84 Dynamo Berlin
1984-85 Dynamo Berlin
1985-86 Dynamo Berlin
1986-87 Dynamo Berlin
1987-88 Dynamo Berlin
1988-89 Dynamo Weisswasser
1989-90 Dynamo Weisswasser

**GERMANY (FRG/WEST)**
1911-12 Berliner SC
1912-13 Berliner SC
1913-14 Berliner SC
1914-1919 *no champion*
1919-20 Berliner SC
1920-21 Berliner SC
1921-22 MTV Muenchen
1922-23 Berliner SC
1923-24 Berliner SC
1924-25 Berliner SC
1925-26 Berliner SC
1926-27 SC Riessersee
1927-28 Berliner SC
1928-29 Berliner SC
1929-30 Berliner SC
1930-31 Berliner SC
1931-32 Berliner SC
1932-33 Berliner SC
1933-34 SC Brandenburg Berlin
1934-35 SC Riessersee
1935-36 Berliner SC
1936-37 Berliner SC
1937-38 SC Riessersee

1938-39 Engelmann Wien
1939-40 Wiener EG (Vienna)
1940-41 SC Riessersee
1941-1943 *no champion*
1943-44 KSG Brandenburg/ Berliner SC
1944-1946 *no champion*
1946-47 SC Riessersee
1947-48 SC Riessersee
1948-49 EV Fussen
1949-50 SC Riessersee
1950-51 Preussen Krefeld
1951-52 Krefelder EV
1952-53 EV Fussen
1953-54 EV Fussen
1954-55 EV Fussen
1955-56 EV Fussen
1956-57 EV Fussen
1957-58 EV Fussen
1958-59 EV Fussen
1959-60 SC Riessersee
1960-61 EV Fussen
1961-62 EC Bad Tolz
1962-63 EV Fussen
1963-64 EV Fussen
1964-65 EV Fussen
1965-66 EC Bad Tolz
1966-67 Dusseldorfer EG
1967-68 EV Fussen
1968-69 EV Fussen
1969-70 EV Landshut
1970-71 EV Fussen
1971-72 Dusseldorfer EG
1972-73 EV Fuessen
1973-74 Berliner SC
1974-75 Dusseldorfer EG
1975-76 Berliner SC
1976-77 Kolner EC
1977-78 SC Riessersee
1978-79 Kolner EC
1979-80 Mannheimer ERC
1980-81 SC Riessersee
1981-82 SB Rosenheim
1982-83 EV Landshut
1983-84 Kolner EC
1984-85 SB Rosenheim
1985-86 Kolner EC
1986-87 Kolner EC
1987-88 Kolner EC
1988-89 SB Rosenheim
1989-90 Dusseldorfer EG
1990-91 Dusseldorfer EG

**GERMANY**
1991-92 Dusseldorfer EG
1992-93 Dusseldorfer EG
1993-94 Munich Maddogs
1994-95 Kolner Haie
1995-96 Dusseldorfer EG
1996-97 Adler Mannheim
1997-98 Adler Mannheim
1998-99 Adler Mannheim
1999-2000 Munchen Barons
2000-01 Adler Mannheim
2001-02 Kolner Haie
2002-03 Krefeld Penguins
2003-04 Frankfurt Lions
2004-05 Eisbaren Berlin
2005-06 Eisbaren Berlin
2006-07 Adler Mannheim
2007-08 Eisbaren Berlin
2008-09 Eisbaren Berlin
2009-10 Hannover Scorpions
2010-11 Eisbaren Berlin
2011-12 Eisbaren Berlin

**GREAT BRITAIN**
1898-99 Princes' Skating Club, London
1899-1900 Princes' Skating Club, London
1900-01 Princes' Skating Club, London
1901-02 Cambridge University
1902-03 London Canadians
1903-04 London Canadians
1904-05 Princes' Skating Club, London
1905-06 Princes' Skating Club, London
1906-07 Oxford Canadians
1907-08 Princes' Skating Club, London
1908-09 Princes' Skating Club, London
1909-10 Oxford Canadians
1910-11 Oxford Canadians
1911-12 Princes' Skating Club, London
1912-13 Oxford Canadians
1913-14 Princes' Skating Club, London
1914-27 *no champion*
1927-28 United Services
1928-29 United Services
1929-30 London Lions
1930-31 London Lions
1931-32 Oxford University
1932-33 Oxford University
1933-34 Grosvenor House Canadians
1934-35 Streatham
1935-36 Wembley Lions
1936-37 Wembley Lions
1937-38 Harringay Racers
1938-39 Harringay Greyhounds
1939-40 Harringay Greyhounds
1940-46 *no champion*
1946-47 Brighton Tigers
1947-48 Brighton Tigers
1948-49 Harringay Racers
1949-50 Streatham
1950-51 Nottingham Panthers
1951-52 Wembley Lions
1952-53 Streatham
1953-54 Nottingham Panthers
1954-55 Harringay Racers
1955-56 Nottingham Panthers
1956-57 Wembley Lions
1957-58 Brighton Tigers
1958-59 Paisley Pirates
1959-60 Brighton Tigers
1960-75 *no champion*
1975-76 Ayr Bruins
1976-77 Fife Flyers
1977-78 Fife Flyers
1978-79 Murrayfield Racers
1979-80 Murrayfield Racers
1980-81 Murrayfield Racers
1981-82 Dundee Rockets
1982-83 Dundee Rockets
1983-84 Dundee Rockets
1984-85 Fife Flyers
1985-86 Murrayfield Racers
1986-87 Durham Wasps
1987-88 Durham Wasps
1988-89 Nottingham Panthers
1989-90 Cardiff Devils
1990-91 Durham Wasps
1991-92 Durham Wasps
1992-93 Cardiff Devils
1993-94 Cardiff Devils
1994-95 Sheffield Steelers
1995-96 Sheffield Steelers
1996-97 Sheffield Steelers
1997-98 Ayr Scottish Eagles
1998-99 Cardiff Devils
1999-2000 London Knights
2000-01 Sheffield Steelers
2001-02 Sheffield Steelers
2002-03 Belfast Giants
2003-04 Sheffield Steelers
2004-05 Coventry Blaze
2005-06 Newcastle Vipers
2006-07 Nottingham Panthers
2007-08 Sheffield Steelers
2008-09 Sheffield Steelers
2009-10 Belfast Giants
2010-11 Sheffield Steelers
2011-12 Belfast Giants

**GREECE**
1988-89 Aris Thessaloniki
1989-90 Aris Thessaloniki
1990-91 Aris Thessaloniki
1991-92 Aris Thessaloniki
1992-93 Athens Ice Flyers
1993-99 *no champion*
1999-2000 Iptameni Athens
2000-01 Iptameni Athens
2001-07 *no champion*
2007-08 Iptameni Athens
2008-09 Iptameni Athens
2009-10 Iptameni Athens
2010-11 Aris Thessaloniki
2011-12 *no champion*

**HONG KONG**
2004-05 Hongkong 3
2005-06 Hongkong Penguins
2006-07 *no champion*
2007-08 Dragon Centre Hongkong
2008-09 Returning Hope Hongkong
2009-10 Smirnoff Ice Hongkong
2010-11 Hongkong Penguins
2011-12 Coors Light Hongkong

**HUNGARY**
1936-37 BKE Budapest
1937-38 BKE Budapest
1938-39 BKE Budapest
1939-40 BKE Budapest
1940-41 BBTE Budapest
1941-42 BKE Budapest
1942-43 BBTE Budapest
1943-44 BKE Budapest
1944-45 *no champion*
1945-46 BKE Budapest
1946-47 MTK Budapest
1947-48 MTK Budapest
1948-49 MTK Budapest
1949-50 BVM Budapest
1950-51 Budapesti Kinizsi
1951-52 BVM Budapest
1952-53 Budapesti Postas
1953-54 Budapesti Postas
1954-55 Budapesti Kinizsi
1955-56 Budapesti Kinizsi
1956-57 BVM Budapest
1957-58 Ujpesti Dozsa Budapest
1958-59 BVM Budapest
1959-60 Ujpesti Dozsa Budapest
1960-61 Ferencvarosi TC Budapest
1961-62 Ferencvarosi TC Budapest
1962-63 BVM Budapest
1963-64 Ferencvarosi TC Budapest
1964-65 Ujpesti Dozsa Budapest
1965-66 Ujpesti Dozsa Budapest
1966-67 Ujpesti Dozsa Budapest
1967-68 Ujpesti Dozsa Budapest
1968-69 Ujpesti Dozsa Budapest
1969-70 Ujpesti Dozsa Budapest
1970-71 Ferencvarosi TC Budapest
1971-72 Ferencvarosi TC Budapest
1972-73 Ferencvarosi TC Budapest
1973-74 Ferencvarosi TC Budapest
1974-75 Ferencvarosi TC Budapest
1975-76 Ferencvarosi TC Budapest
1976-77 Ferencvarosi TC Budapest
1977-78 Ferencvarosi TC Budapest
1978-79 Ferencvarosi TC Budapest
1979-80 Ferencvarosi TC Budapest
1980-81 Volan Szekesfehervar
1981-82 Ujpesti Dozsa Budapest
1982-83 Ujpesti Dozsa Budapest
1983-84 Ferencvarosi TC Budapest
1984-85 Ujpesti Dozsa Budapest
1985-86 Ujpesti Dozsa Budapest
1986-87 Ujpesti Dozsa Budapest
1987-88 Ujpesti Dozsa Budapest
1988-89 Ferencvarosi TC Budapest
1989-90 Lehel Jaszberenyi
1990-91 Ferencvarosi TC Budapest
1991-92 Ferencvarosi TC Budapest
1992-93 Ferencvarosi TC Budapest
1993-94 Ferencvarosi TC Budapest
1994-95 Ferencvarosi TC Budapest
1995-96 Dunaferr SE Dunaujvaros
1996-97 Ferencvarosi TC Budapest
1997-98 Dunaferr SE Dunaujvaros
1998-99 Alba Volan Szekesfehervar
1999-2000 Dunaferr SE Dunaujvaros
2000-01 Alba Volan Szekesfehervar
2001-02 Dunaferr SE Dunaujvaros
2002-03 Alba Volan Szekesfehervar
2003-04 Alba Volan Szekesfehervar
2004-05 Alba Volan Szekesfehervar
2005-06 Alba Volan Szekesfehervar
2006-07 Alba Volan Szekesfehervar
2007-08 Alba Volan Szekesfehervar
2008-09 Alba Volan Szekesfehervar
2009-10 Fehervar AV19
2010-11 Fehervar AV19
2011-12 Fehervar AV19

**ICELAND**
1967-68 Skautafelag Akureyri
1968-69 Skautafelag Akureyri
1969-70 Skautafelag Reykjavík
1970-78 *no champion*
1978-79 Skautafelag Reykjavík
1979-80 Skautafelag Akureyri
1980-81 *no champion*
1981-82 Skautafelag Akureyri
1982-83 Skautafelag Akureyri
1983-84 Skautafelag Akureyri
1984-85 Skautafelag Reykjavík
1985-86 *no champion*
1986-87 Skautafelag Akureyri
1987-88 Skautafelag Akureyri
1988-91 *no champion*
1991-92 Skautafelag Akureyri
1992-93 Skautafelag Akureyri
1993-94 Skautafelag Akureyri
1994-95 Skautafelag Akureyri
1995-96 Skautafelag Akureyri
1996-97 Skautafelag Akureyri
1997-98 Skautafelag Akureyri
1998-99 Skautafelag Reykjavík
1999-2000 Skautafelag Reykjavík
2000-01 Skautafelag Akureyri
2001-02 Skautafelag Akureyri
2002-03 Skautafelag Akureyri
2003-04 Skautafelag Akureyri
2004-05 Skautafelag Akureyri
2005-06 Skautafelag Reykjavík
2006-07 Skautafelag Reykjavik
2007-08 Skautafelag Akureyri
2008-09 Skautafelag Reykjavik
2009-10 Skautafelag Akureyri
2010-11 Skautafelag Akureyri
2011-12 Bjorninn Reykjavik

**INDIA**
2007-08 Rimo club Leh
2008-09 Rimo club Leh
2009-10 Indo-Tibetian Border Police
2010-12 *no champion*

**IRELAND**
2007-08 Dundalk Bulls
2008-09 Dundalk Bulls
2009-10 Charlestown Chiefs
2010-12 *no champion*

**ISRAEL**
1989-90 HC Haifa
1990-91 HC Haifa
1991-93 *no champion*
1993-94 HC Haifa
1994-95 HC Bat Yam
1995-96 Jerusalem Lions
1996-97 Jerusalem Lions
1997-98 Maccabi Amos Lod
1998-99 SC Metulla
1999-2000 HC Maalot
2000-01 Macabi Amos Lod
2001-02 HC Maalot
2002-03 HC Maalot
2003-04 Maccabi Amos Lod
2004-05 Maccabi Amos Lod
2005-06 Haifa Hawks
2006-07 Haifa Hawks
2007-08 Haifa Hawks

2008-09 Ice Time Hertzliya
2009-10 Monfort Maalot
2010-11 HC Metulla
2011-12 Maccabi Metulla

**ITALY**
1924-25 HC Milano
1925-26 HC Milano
1926-27 HC Milano
1927-1929 *no champion*
1929-30 HC Milano
1930-31 HC Milano
1931-32 HC Cortina
1932-33 HC Milano
1933-34 HC Milano
1934-35 HC Diavoli Rosso-Neri
1935-36 HC Diavoli Rosso-Neri
1936-37 Associazione Milanese Disco Ghiaccio
1937-38 Associazione Milanese Disco Ghiaccio
1938-1940 *no champion*
1940-41 Associazione Milanese Disco Ghiaccio
1941-1946 *no champion*
1946-47 HC Milano
1947-48 HC Milano
1948-49 HC Diavoli Rosso-Neri
1949-50 HC Milano
1950-51 HC Milano Inter
1951-52 HC Milano Inter
1952-53 HC Diavoli Rosso-Neri
1953-54 HC Milano Inter
1954-55 HC Milano Inter
1955-56 *no champion*
1956-57 SG Cortina
1957-58 HC Milano Inter
1958-59 SG Cortina
1959-60 Diavoli HC Milano
1960-61 SG Cortina Rex
1961-62 SG Cortina Rex
1962-63 HC Bolzano
1963-64 SG Cortina Rex
1964-65 SG Cortina Rex
1965-66 SG Cortina Rex
1966-67 SG Cortina Rex
1967-68 SG Cortina Rex
1968-69 HC Val Gardena
1969-70 SG Cortina
1970-71 SG Cortina
1971-72 SG Cortina
1972-73 HC Bolzano
1973-74 SG Cortina
1974-75 SG Cortina
1975-76 HC Gardena
1976-77 HC Bolzano
1977-78 HC Bolzano
1978-79 HC Bolzano
1979-80 HC Gardena
1980-81 HC Gardena
1981-82 HC Bolzano
1982-83 HC Bolzano
1983-84 HC Bolzano
1984-85 HC Bolzano
1985-86 HC Bolzano
1986-87 A.S. Varese Hockey
1987-88 HC Bolzano
1988-89 A.S. Varese Hockey
1989-90 HC Bolzano
1990-91 HC Milano Saima
1991-92 HC Devils Milano
1992-93 Lion Hockey Milano
1993-94 Milan Hockey
1994-95 HC Bolzano
1995-96 HC Bolzano
1996-97 HC Bolzano
1997-98 HC Bolzano
1998-99 HC Meran Merano
1999-2000 HC Bolzano
2000-01 HC Asiago
2001-02 Milano Vipers
2002-03 Milano Vipers
2003-04 Milano Vipers
2004-05 Milano Vipers
2005-06 Milano Vipers
2006-07 SG Cortina
2007-08 Bolzano Foxes
2008-09 Bolzano Foxes
2009-10 HC Asiago
2010-11 HC Asiago
2011-12 Bolzano Foxes

**JAPAN**
1974-75 Kokudo Keikaku Tokyo
1975-76 Oji Seishi Tomakomai
1976-77 Oji Seishi Tomakomai
1977-78 Seibu Tetsudo Tokyo
1978-79 Seibu Tetsudo Tokyo
1979-80 Oji Seishi Tomakomai
1980-81 Oji Seishi Tomakomai
1981-82 Kokudo Keikaku Tokyo
1982-83 Oji Seishi Tomakomai
1983-84 Oji Seishi Tomakomai
1984-85 Oji Seishi Tomakomai
1985-86 Oji Seishi Tomakomai
1986-87 Oji Seishi Tomakomai
1987-88 Kokudo Keikaku Tokyo
1988-89 Oji Seishi Tomakomai
1989-90 Oji Seishi Tomakomai
1990-91 Oji Seishi Tomakomai
1991-92 Kokudo Keikaku Tokyo
1992-93 Kokudo Tokyo
1993-94 New Oji Tomakomai
1994-95 Kokudo Tokyo
1995-96 Seibu Tokyo
1996-97 Seibu Tokyo
1997-98 Kokudo Tokyo
1998-99 Kokudo Tokyo
1999-2000 Seibu Tokyo
2000-01 Seibu Tokyo
2001-02 Oji Tomakomai
2002-03 Seibu Tokyo
2003-04 Kokudo Tokyo
2004-05 Oji Tomakomai
2005-06 Nippon Paper Cranes Kushiro
2006-07 Nippon Paper Cranes Kushiro
2007-08 Seibu Tokyo
2008-09 Seibu Tokyo
2009-10 Nippon Paper Cranes Kushiro
2010-11 Nippon Paper Cranes Kushiro
2011-12 Nippon Paper Cranes Kushiro

**KAZAKHSTAN**
1992-93 Torpedo Ust-Kamenogorsk
1993-94 Torpedo Ust-Kamenogorsk
1994-95 Torpedo Ust-Kamenogorsk
1995-96 Torpedo Ust-Kamenogorsk
1996-97 Torpedo Ust-Kamenogorsk
1997-98 Torpedo Ust-Kamenogorsk
1998-99 Bulat Temirtau
1999-2000 Torpedo Ust-Kamenogorsk
2000-01 Torpedo Ust-Kamenogorsk
2001-02 Torpedo Ust-Kamenogorsk
2002-03 Torpedo Ust-Kamenogorsk
2003-04 Torpedo Ust-Kamenogorsk
2004-05 Torpedo Ust-Kamenogorsk
2005-06 Kazakhmys Karaganda
2006-07 Torpedo Ust-Kamenogorsk
2007-08 Barys Astana
2008-09 Barys Astana
2009-10 Sary-Arka Karaganda
2010-11 Beibarys Atyrau
2011-12 Beibarys Atyrau

**KOREA**
2000-01 Dongwon Dreams
2001-02 Dongwon Dreams
2002-03 Korea University
2003-04 Yonsei University
2004-05 Anyang Halla
2005-06 Anyang Halla
2006-07 High One Chuncheon
2007-08 High One Chuncheon
2008-09 High One Chuncheon
2009-10 Anyang Halla
2010-11 Anyang Halla
2011-12 HighOne Chuncheon

**KYRGYZSTAN**
2010-11 Gornyak Ak-Tuz
2011-12 Arstan Bishkek

**LATVIA**
1931-32 Union Riga
1932-33 Union Riga
1933-34 ASK Riga
1934-35 ASK Riga
1935-36 ASK Riga
1936-37 Universitates Sports Riga
1937-38 ASK Riga
1938-39 ASK Riga
1939-40 Universitates Sports Riga
1940-41 *no champion*
1941-42 Universitates Sports Riga
1942-43 *no champion*
1943-44 Universitates Sports Riga
1944-45 *no champion*

1991-92 HK Saga Kekeva Riga
1992-93 Pardaugava Riga
1993-94 Pardaugava Riga
1994-95 Nik's Brih Riga
1995-96 Riga Alianse
1996-97 Essamika
1997-98 Nik's Brih Riga
1998-99 Nik's Brih Riga
1999-2000 Liepajas Metalurgs
2000-01 HK Riga 2000
2001-02 Liepajas Metalurgs
2002-03 Liepajas Metalurgs
2003-04 HK Riga 2000
2004-05 HK Riga 2000
2005-06 HK Riga 2000
2006-07 HK Riga 2000
2007-08 Liepajas Metalurgs
2008-09 Liepajas Metalurgs
2009-10 Dinamo Riga Juniors
2010-11 Liepajas Metalurgs
2011-12 Liepajas Metalurgs

**LITHUANIA**
1925-26 LFLS Kaunas
1926-27 LFLS Kaunas
1927-28 LFLS Kaunas
1928-29 STSK Kaunas
1929-30 *no champion*
1930-31 LFLS Kaunas
1931-32 LGSF Kaunas
1932-33 LGSF Kaunas
1933-34 LFLS Kaunas
1934-36 *no champion*
1936-37 LGSF Kaunas
1937-38 Tauras Kaunas
1938-39 KJK Kaunas
1939-40 Tauras Kaunas
1940-41 Spartakus
1941-42 Tauras Kaunas
1942-43 *no champion*
1992-93 Energija Elektrenai
1993-94 Energija Elektrenai
1994-95 Energija Elektrenai
1995-96 Energija Elektrenai
1996-97 Energija Elektrenai
1997-98 Energija Elektrenai
1998-99 Energija Elektrenai
1999-2000 Viltis Kaunas
2000-01 Energija Elektrenai
2001-02 Garsu Pasaulis Vilnius
2002-03 Energija Elektrenai
2003-04 Energija Elektrenai
2004-05 Energija Elektrenai
2005-06 Energija Elektrenai
2006-07 Energija Elektrenai
2007-08 Energija Elektrenai
2008-09 Energija Elektrenai
2009-10 Sporto Centras Elektrenai
2010-11 Sporto Centras Elektrenai
2011-12 Energija Elektrenai

**LUXEMBOURG**
1993-94 Tornado Luxembourg
1994-95 *no champion*
1995-96 Tornado Luxembourg
1996-97 Tornado Luxembourg
1997-98 Tornado Luxembourg
1998-99 Tornado Luxembourg
1999-2000 Tornado Luxembourg
2000-01 Tornado Luxembourg
2001-02 Tornado Luxembourg
2002-03 Tornado Luxembourg
2003-11 *no champion*
2011-12 Tornado Luxembourg

**MACAU**
2006-07 Hongkong
2007-08 Guangzhou
2008-09 Shenzhen
2009-10 Shenzhen
2010-12 *no champion*

**MALAYSIA**
2001-02 Devils Kuala Lumpur
2002-03 Blackhawks Kuala Lumpur
2003-04 Metro Wildcats Kuala Lumpur
2004-05 Inferno Ice Kuala Lumpur
2005-06 Wildcats Kuala Lumpur
2006-07 Inferno Ice Kuala Lumpur
2007-08 Fangs Kuala Lumpur
2008-09 Cobras Kuala Lumpur
2009-10 Cobras Kuala Lumpur
2010-11 Asian Tigers Kuala Lumpu
2011-12 Asian Tigers Kuala Lumpur

**MEXICO**
1997 Estado de Mexico
1998 Estado de Mexico
1999 Estado de Mexico
2000 Universidad Nacional Autonoma de Mexico
2001 Distrito Federal
2002 Distrito Federal
2003 Distrito Federal
2004 Lomas Verdes
2005 San Jeronimo Jurasicos
2006 San Jeronimo Osos
2007 San Jeronimo Osos
2008 San Jeronimo Osos
2009 Lomas Vedes Halcones
2010 San Jeronimo Jurasicos
2011 Teotihuacan Priests
2012 Aztec Eagle Warriors

**MONGOLIA**
1999-2000 Baganuur
2000-01 Ulaanbaatar Economical University
2001-02 Ulaanbaatar Economical University
2002-03 Ulaanbaatar Economical University
2003-04 Baganuur
2004-05 Baganuur
2005-06 Baganuur
2006-07 Otgon od Ulaanbaatar
2007-08 Otgon od Ulaanbaatar
2008-09 Otgon od Ulaanbaatar
2009-10 Khangarid Erdenet
2010-11 Baganuur
2011-12 Zaluus San Ulaanbaatar

**NETHERLANDS**
1937-38 HIJC Den Haag
1938-39 HIJC Den Haag
1939-45 *no champion*
1945-46 HIJC Den Haag
1946-47 TIJSC Tilburg
1947-48 HIJC Den Haag
1948-49 *no champion*
1949-50 Ijsvogels Amsterdam
1950-64 *no champion*
1964-65 HIJC Den Haag
1965-66 HIJC Den Haag
1966-67 HIJC Den Haag

| | |
|---|---|
| 1967-68 | HIJC Den Haag |
| 1968-69 | HIJC Den Haag |
| 1969-70 | SIJ Den Bosch |
| 1970-71 | Tilburg Trappers |
| 1971-72 | Tilburg Trappers |
| 1972-73 | Tilburg Trappers |
| 1973-74 | Tilburg Trappers |
| 1974-75 | Tilburg Trappers |
| 1975-76 | Tilburg Trappers |
| 1976-77 | Feenstra Flyers Heerenveen |
| 1977-78 | Feenstra Flyers Heerenveen |
| 1978-79 | Feenstra Flyers Heerenveen |
| 1979-80 | Feenstra Flyers Heerenveen |
| 1980-81 | Feenstra Flyers Heerenveen |
| 1981-82 | Feenstra Flyers Heerenveen |
| 1982-83 | Feenstra Flyers Heerenveen |
| 1983-84 | Vissers Nijmegen |
| 1984-85 | Deko Builders Amsterdam |
| 1985-86 | Noorder Stores GIJS Gronin |
| 1986-87 | Rotterdam Pandas |
| 1987-88 | Nijmegen Spitman |
| 1988-89 | Rotterdam Pandas |
| 1989-90 | Rotterdam Pandas |
| 1990-91 | Peter Langhout Utrecht |
| 1991-92 | Pro Badge Utrecht |
| 1992-93 | Nijmegen Flames Guards |
| 1993-94 | Tilburg Trappers |
| 1994-95 | Tilburg Trappers |
| 1995-96 | Tilburg Trappers |
| 1996-97 | Nijmegen Tigers |
| 1997-98 | Nijmegen Tigers |
| 1998-99 | Nijmegen Tigers |
| 1999-2000 | Nijmegen Tigers |
| 2000-01 | Tilburg Trappers |
| 2001-02 | Amsterdam Tigers |
| 2002-03 | Amsterdam Tigers |
| 2003-04 | Bulldogs Amsterdam |
| 2004-05 | Bulldogs Amsterdam |
| 2005-06 | Nijmegen Emperors |
| 2006-07 | Tilburg Trappers |
| 2007-08 | Tilburg Trappers |
| 2008-09 | HYS The Hague |
| 2009-10 | Nijmegen Devils |
| 2010-11 | HYS The Hague |
| 2011-12 | Smoke Eaters Geleen |

**NEW ZEALAND**

| | |
|---|---|
| 1987 | Canterbury |
| 1988 | Auckland |
| 1989 | Christchurch |
| 1990 | Auckland |
| 1991 | Auckland |
| 1992 | Auckland |
| 1993 | Auckland |
| 1994 | Auckland |
| 1995 | North Island |
| 1996 | Southern District |
| 1997 | Auckland |
| 1998 | Southern District |
| 1999 | Auckland |
| 2000 | Auckland |
| 2001 | Auckland |
| 2002 | Auckland |
| 2003 | Auckland |
| 2004 | Auckland |
| 2005 | Southern Stampede |
| 2006 | Southern Stampede |
| 2007 | Botany Swarm |
| 2008 | Botany Swarm |
| 2009 | Canterbury Red Devils |
| 2010 | Botany Swarm |
| 2011 | Botany Swarm |
| 2012 | Canterbury Red Devils |

**NORWAY**

| | |
|---|---|
| 1934-35 | Trygg Oslo |
| 1935-36 | Grane Sandvika |
| 1936-37 | Grane Sandvika |
| 1937-38 | Trygg Oslo |
| 1938-39 | Grane Sandvika |
| 1939-40 | Grane Sandvika |
| 1940-1945 | *no champion* |
| 1945-46 | Forward Oslo |
| 1946-47 | Stabaek Oslo |
| 1947-48 | Strong Oslo |
| 1948-49 | Furuset Oslo |
| 1949-50 | Gamlebyen Oslo |
| 1950-51 | Furuset Oslo |
| 1951-52 | Furuset Oslo |
| 1952-53 | Gamlebyen Oslo |
| 1953-54 | Furuset Oslo |
| 1954-55 | Gamlebyen Oslo |
| 1955-56 | Gamlebyen Oslo |
| 1956-57 | Tigrene Oslo |
| 1957-58 | Gamlebyen Oslo |
| 1958-59 | Gamlebyen Oslo |
| 1959-60 | Valerenga Oslo |
| 1960-61 | Tigrene Oslo |
| 1961-62 | Valerenga Oslo |
| 1962-63 | Valerenga Oslo |
| 1963-64 | Gamlebyen Oslo |
| 1964-65 | Valerenga Oslo |
| 1965-66 | Valerenga Oslo |
| 1966-67 | Valerenga Oslo |
| 1967-68 | Valerenga Oslo |
| 1968-69 | Valerenga Oslo |
| 1969-70 | Valerenga Oslo |
| 1970-71 | Valerenga Oslo |
| 1971-72 | Hasle/Loren Oslo |
| 1972-73 | Valerenga Oslo |
| 1973-74 | Hasle/Loren Oslo |
| 1974-75 | Frisk Asker |
| 1975-76 | Hasle/Loren Oslo |
| 1976-77 | Manglerud/Star Oslo |
| 1977-78 | Manglerud/Star Oslo |
| 1978-79 | Frisk Asker |
| 1979-80 | Furuset Oslo |
| 1980-81 | Stjernen Fredrikstad |
| 1981-82 | Valerenga Oslo |
| 1982-83 | Furuset Oslo |
| 1983-84 | Sparta Sarpsborg |
| 1984-85 | Valerenga Oslo |
| 1985-86 | Stjernen Fredrikstad |
| 1986-87 | Valerenga Oslo |
| 1987-88 | Valerenga Oslo |
| 1988-89 | Sparta Sarpsborg |
| 1989-90 | Furuset Oslo |
| 1990-91 | Valerenga Oslo |
| 1991-92 | Valerenga Oslo |
| 1992-93 | Valerenga Oslo |
| 1993-94 | Lillehammer |
| 1994-95 | Storhamar Hamar |
| 1995-96 | Storhamar Hamar |
| 1996-97 | Storhamar Hamar |
| 1997-98 | Valerenga Oslo |
| 1998-99 | Valerenga Oslo |
| 1999-2000 | Storhamar Hamar |
| 2000-01 | Valerenga Oslo |
| 2001-02 | Frisk Tigers |
| 2002-03 | Valerenga Oslo |
| 2003-04 | Storhamar Dragons |
| 2004-05 | Valerenga Oslo |
| 2005-06 | Valerenga Oslo |
| 2006-07 | Valerenga Oslo |
| 2007-08 | Storhamar Dragons |
| 2008-09 | Valerenga Oslo |
| 2009-10 | Stavanger Oilers |
| 2010-11 | Sparta Sarpsborg |
| 2011-12 | Stavanger Oilers |

**POLAND**

| | |
|---|---|
| 1926-27 | AZS Warsaw |
| 1927-28 | AZS Warsaw |
| 1928-29 | AZS Warsaw |
| 1929-30 | AZS Warsaw |
| 1930-31 | AZS Warsaw |
| 1931-32 | *no champion* |
| 1932-33 | Legia Warsaw & Pogon Lwow |
| 1933-34 | AZS Poznan |
| 1934-35 | Czarni Lwow |
| 1935-36 | *no champion* |
| 1936-37 | Cracovia Krakow |
| 1937-38 | *no champion* |
| 1938-39 | Dab Katowice |
| 1939-45 | *no champion* |
| 1945-46 | Cracovia Krakow |
| 1946-47 | Cracovia Krakow |
| 1947-48 | *no champion* |
| 1948-49 | Cracovia Krakow |
| 1949-50 | KTH Krynica |
| 1950-51 | CWKS Warsaw |
| 1951-52 | CWKS Warsaw |
| 1952-53 | CWKS Warsaw |
| 1953-54 | CWKS Warsaw |
| 1954-55 | Legia Warsaw |
| 1955-56 | Legia Warsaw |
| 1956-57 | Legia Warsaw |
| 1957-58 | Gornik Katowice |
| 1958-59 | Legia Warsaw |
| 1959-60 | Gornik Katowice |
| 1960-61 | Legia Warsaw |
| 1961-62 | Gornik Katowice |
| 1962-63 | Legia Warsaw |
| 1963-64 | Legia Warsaw |
| 1964-65 | GKS Katowice |
| 1965-66 | Podhale Nowy Targ |
| 1966-67 | Legia Warsaw |
| 1967-68 | GKS Katowice |
| 1968-69 | Podhale Nowy Targ |
| 1969-70 | GKS Katowice |
| 1970-71 | Podhale Nowy Targ |
| 1971-72 | Podhale Nowy Targ |
| 1972-73 | Podhale Nowy Targ |
| 1973-74 | Podhale Nowy Targ |
| 1974-75 | Podhale Nowy Targ |
| 1975-76 | Podhale Nowy Targ |
| 1976-77 | Podhale Nowy Targ |
| 1977-78 | Podhale Nowy Targ |
| 1978-79 | Podhale Nowy Targ |
| 1979-80 | Zaglebie Sosnowiec |
| 1980-81 | Zaglebie Sosnowiec |
| 1981-82 | Zaglebie Sosnowiec |
| 1982-83 | Zaglebie Sosnowiec |
| 1983-84 | Polonia Bytom |
| 1984-85 | Zaglebie Sosnowiec |
| 1985-86 | Polonia Bytom |
| 1986-87 | Podhale Nowy Targ |
| 1987-88 | Polonia Bytom |
| 1988-89 | Polonia Bytom |
| 1989-90 | Polonia Bytom |
| 1990-91 | Polonia Bytom |
| 1991-92 | Unia Oswiecim |
| 1992-93 | Podhale Nowy Targ |
| 1993-94 | Podhale Nowy Targ |
| 1994-95 | Podhale Nowy Targ |
| 1995-96 | Podhale Nowy Targ |
| 1996-97 | Podhale Nowy Targ |
| 1997-98 | Podhale Nowy Targ |
| 1998-99 | Unia Oswiecim |
| 1999-2000 | Unia Oswiecim |
| 2000-01 | Unia Oswiecim |
| 2001-02 | Unia Oswiecim |
| 2002-03 | Unia Oswiecim |
| 2003-04 | Unia Oswiecim |
| 2004-05 | Tychy |
| 2005-06 | Cracovia Krakow |
| 2006-07 | Podhale Nowy Targ |
| 2007-08 | Cracovia Krakow |
| 2008-09 | Cracovia Krakow |
| 2009-10 | Podhale Nowy Targ |
| 2010-11 | Cracovia Krakow |
| 2011-12 | KH Sanok |

**PORTUGAL**

| | |
|---|---|
| 2000-01 | Viseu Lobos |
| 2001-02 | *no champion* |
| 2002-03 | Lisabon Pirates |
| 2003-12 | *no champion* |

**ROMANIA**

| | |
|---|---|
| 1924-25 | Brasovia Brasov |
| 1925-26 | *no champion* |
| 1926-27 | HC Roman Bucharest |
| 1927-28 | HC Roman Bucharest |
| 1928-29 | HC Roman Bucharest |
| 1929-30 | TC Roman Bucharest |
| 1930-31 | TC Roman Bucharest |
| 1931-32 | TC Roman Bucharest |
| 1932-33 | TC Roman Bucharest |
| 1933-34 | TC Roman Bucharest |
| 1934-35 | TC Bucuresti |
| 1935-36 | HC Bragadiru Bucharest |
| 1936-37 | TC Roman Bucharest |
| 1937-38 | Dragos Vota Cernauti |
| 1938-39 | *no champion* |
| 1939-40 | HC Rapid Bucharest |
| 1940-41 | HC Juventus Bucharest |
| 1941-42 | HC Rapid Bucharest |
| 1942-43 | *no champion* |
| 1943-44 | Venus Bucharest |
| 1944-45 | HC Juventus Bucharest |
| 1945-46 | HC Juventus Bucharest |
| 1946-47 | HC Ciocanul Bucharest |
| 1947-48 | *no champion* |
| 1948-49 | Avintil Miercurea Ciuc |
| 1949-50 | Locomotiva RTA Tirgu Mures |
| 1950-51 | Locomotiva RTA Tirgu Mures |
| 1951-52 | Avintil Miercurea Ciuc |
| 1952-53 | CCA Bucharest |
| 1953-54 | Stiinta Kluz |
| 1954-55 | CCA Bucharest |
| 1955-56 | CCA Bucharest |
| 1956-57 | Recolta Miercurea Ciuc |
| 1957-58 | CCA Bucharest |
| 1958-59 | CCA Bucharest |
| 1959-60 | Vointa Miercurea Ciuc |
| 1960-61 | CCA Bucharest |
| 1961-62 | CCA Bucharest |
| 1962-63 | Vointa Miercurea Ciuc |
| 1963-64 | Steaua Bucharest |
| 1964-65 | Steaua Bucharest |
| 1965-66 | Steaua Bucharest |
| 1966-67 | Steaua Bucharest |
| 1967-68 | Dinamo Bucharest |
| 1968-69 | Steaua Bucharest |
| 1969-70 | Dinamo Bucharest |
| 1970-71 | Steaua Bucharest |
| 1971-72 | Dinamo Bucharest |
| 1972-73 | Dinamo Bucharest |
| 1973-74 | Steaua Bucharest |
| 1974-75 | Steaua Bucharest |
| 1975-76 | Steaua Bucharest |
| 1976-77 | Steaua Bucharest |
| 1977-78 | Steaua Bucharest |
| 1978-79 | Dinamo Bucharest |
| 1979-80 | Steaua Bucharest |
| 1980-81 | Dinamo Bucharest |
| 1981-82 | Steaua Bucharest |
| 1982-83 | Steaua Bucharest |
| 1983-84 | Steaua Bucharest |
| 1984-85 | Steaua Bucharest |
| 1985-86 | Steaua Bucharest |
| 1986-87 | Steaua Bucharest |
| 1987-88 | Steaua Bucharest |
| 1988-89 | Steaua Bucharest |
| 1989-90 | Steaua Bucharest |
| 1990-91 | Steaua Bucharest |
| 1991-92 | Steaua Bucharest |
| 1992-93 | Steaua Bucharest |
| 1993-94 | Steaua Bucharest |
| 1994-95 | Steaua Bucharest |
| 1995-96 | Steaua Bucharest |
| 1996-97 | SC Miercurea Ciuc |
| 1997-98 | Steaua Bucharest |
| 1998-99 | Steaua Bucharest |
| 1999-2000 | SC Miercurea Ciuc |
| 2000-01 | Steaua Bucharest |
| 2001-02 | Steaua Bucharest |
| 2002-03 | Steaua Bucharest |
| 2003-04 | SC Miercurea Ciuc |
| 2004-05 | Steaua Bucharest |
| 2005-06 | Steaua Bucharest |
| 2006-07 | SC Miercurea Ciuc |
| 2007-08 | SC Miercurea Ciuc |
| 2008-09 | SC Miercurea Ciuc |
| 2009-10 | SC Miercurea Ciuc |
| 2010-11 | HSC Csikszereda |
| 2011-12 | HSC Csikszereda |

**RUSSIA (see also SOVIET UNION)**

| | |
|---|---|
| 1991-92 | Dynamo Moscow |
| 1992-93 | Dynamo Moscow |
| 1993-94 | Lada Togliatti |
| 1994-95 | Dynamo Moscow |
| 1995-96 | Lada Togliatti |
| 1996-97 | Torpedo Yaroslavl |
| 1997-98 | Metallurg Magnitogorsk |
| 1998-99 | Metallurg Magnitogorsk |
| 1999-2000 | Dynamo Moscow |
| 2000-01 | Metallurg Magnitogorsk |
| 2001-02 | Lokomotiv Yaroslavl |
| 2002-03 | Lokomotiv Yaroslavl |
| 2003-04 | Avangard Omsk |
| 2004-05 | Dynamo Moscow |
| 2005-06 | Ak Bars Kazan |
| 2006-07 | Metallurg Magnitogorsk |
| 2007-08 | Salavat Yulayev Ufa |
| 2008-09 | Ak Bars Kazan |
| 2009-10 | Ak Bars Kazan |
| 2010-11 | Salavat Yulayev Ufa |
| 2011-12 | Dynamo Moscow |

**SERBIA**

| | |
|---|---|
| 2000-01 | Vojvodina Novi Sad |
| 2001-02 | Vojvodina Novi Sad |
| 2002-03 | Vojvodina Novi Sad |
| 2003-04 | Vojvodina Novi Sad |
| 2004-05 | Crvena Zvezda Belgrade |
| 2005-06 | Partizan Belgrade |
| 2006-07 | Partizan Belgrade |
| 2007-08 | Partizan Belgrade |
| 2008-09 | Partizan Belgrade |
| 2009-10 | Partizan Belgrade |
| 2010-11 | Partizan Belgrade |
| 2011-12 | Partizan Belgrade |

**SINGAPORE**

| | |
|---|---|
| 1995-96 | Singapore Recreation Club |
| 1996-97 | Singapore Indian Association |
| 1997-98 | Singapore Recreation Club |
| 1998-99 | Singapore Recreation Club |
| 1999-2000 | Chenab |
| 2000-01 | Linear Technology Lions |
| 2001-02 | Continental Wings |
| 2002-03 | Continental Wings |
| 2003-04 | Brewerkz Bruins |
| 2004-05 | Linear Technology Lions |
| 2005-06 | M 1 |
| 2006-07 | San Miguel |
| 2007-08 | Harrys |
| 2008-09 | White team |
| 2009-11 | *no champion* |
| 2011-12 | Singapore Leafs |

**SLOVAKIA**

| | |
|---|---|
| 1939-40 | VS Bratislava |
| 1940-41 | VS Bratislava |
| 1941-42 | SK Bratislava |
| 1942-43 | SK Bratislava |
| 1943-44 | OAP Bratislava |
| 1944-45 | OAP Bratislava |
| | |
| 1993-94 | Dukla Trencin |
| 1994-95 | HC Kosice |
| 1995-96 | HC Kosice |
| 1996-97 | Dukla Trencin |
| 1997-98 | HC Slovan Bratislava |
| 1998-99 | HC Kosice |
| 1999-2000 | HC Slovan Bratislava |
| 2000-01 | HKM Zvolen |
| 2001-02 | HC Slovan Bratislava |
| 2002-03 | HC Slovan Bratislava |
| 2003-04 | Dukla Trencin |
| 2004-05 | HC Slovan Bratislava |
| 2005-06 | MsHK Zilina |
| 2006-07 | HC Slovan Bratislava |
| 2007-08 | HC Slovan Bratislava |
| 2008-09 | HC Kosice |
| 2009-10 | HC Kosice |
| 2010-11 | HC Kosice |
| 2011-12 | Slovan Bratislava |

**SLOVENIA (see also YUGOSLAVIA)**

| | |
|---|---|
| 1991-92 | HC Jesenice |
| 1992-93 | HC Jesenice |
| 1993-94 | HC Jesenice |
| 1994-95 | Olimpija Ljubljana |
| 1995-96 | Olimpija Ljubljana |
| 1996-97 | Olimpija Ljubljana |
| 1997-98 | Olimpija Ljubljana |
| 1998-99 | Olimpija Ljubljana |
| 1999-2000 | Olimpija Ljubljana |
| 2001-02 | Olimpija Ljubljana |
| 2002-03 | Olimpija Ljubljana |
| 2003-04 | Olimpija Ljubljana |
| 2004-05 | Acroni Jesenice |
| 2005-06 | Acroni Jesenice |
| 2006-07 | Olimpija Ljubljana |
| 2007-08 | Acroni Jesenice |
| 2008-09 | Acroni Jesenice |
| 2009-10 | Acroni Jesenice |
| 2010-11 | Acroni Jesenice |
| 2011-12 | Olimpija Ljubljana |

**SOUTH AFRICA**

| | |
|---|---|
| 1962 | Lions Johannesburg |
| 1963 | *no champion* |
| 1964 | Wembley Lions Johannesburg |
| 1965 | Swiss Bears Johannesburg |
| 1966 | Swiss Bears Johannesburg |
| 1967 | *no champion* |
| 1968 | Swiss Bears Johannesburg |
| 1969 | Canadian Hush Puppies Johannesburg |
| 1970 | Maple Leafs Johannesburg |
| 1971 | Edelweis Johannesburg |
| 1972 | Swiss Bears Johannesburg |
| 1973 | Swiss Bears Johannesburg |
| 1974 | Jungle Jets Johannesburg |
| 1975 | Jungle Jets Johannesburg |
| 1976 | Maple Leafs Johannesburg |
| 1977 | Maple Leafs Johannesburg |
| 1978 | North Stars Pretoria |
| 1979 | Flyers Roodenpoort |
| 1980 | Flyers Roodenpoort |
| 1981 | Flyers Roodenpoort |
| 1982 | Bullets Benoni |
| 1983 | North Stars Pretoria |
| 1984 | North Stars Pretoria |
| 1985 | Johannesburg Bullets |
| 1986 | Flyers Roodenpoort |
| 1987 | Flyers Johannesburg |
| 1988 | Flyers Johannesburg |
| 1989 | Johannesburg Bullets |
| 1990 | Johannesburg Bullets |
| 1991 | Flyers Roodenpoort |
| 1992 | Flyers Roodenpoort |
| 1993 | Flyers Roodenpoort |
| 1994 | Can-Ams Johannesburg |
| 1995 | Can-Ams Johannesburg |
| 1996 | Can-Ams Johannesburg |
| 1997 | Pretoria Capitals |
| 1998 | Pretoria Capitals |
| 1999 | Wildcats Krugersdorp |
| 2000 | Wildcats Krugersdorp |
| 2001 | Ama-Horney Pretoria |
| 2002 | Wildcats Krugersdorp |
| 2003 | Wildcats Krugersdorp |
| 2004 | *no champion* |
| 2005 | Ama-Horney Pretoria |
| 2006 | Warriors Pretoria |
| 2007 | Wildcats Krugersdorp |
| 2008 | Scorpions Kempton Park |
| 2009 | Scorpions Kempton Park |
| 2010 | Gauteng |
| 2011 | Gauteng |
| 2012 | Gauteng Miners |

**SOVIET UNION (see also RUSSIA)**

| | |
|---|---|
| 1946-47 | Dynamo Moscow |
| 1947-48 | CSKA Moscow |
| 1948-49 | CSKA Moscow |
| 1949-50 | CSKA Moscow |
| 1950-51 | VVS Moscow |
| 1951-52 | VVS Moscow |
| 1952-53 | VVS Moscow |
| 1953-54 | Dynamo Moscow |
| 1954-55 | CSKA Moscow |
| 1955-56 | CSKA Moscow |
| 1956-57 | Krylya Sovietov Moscow |
| 1957-58 | CSKA Moscow |
| 1958-59 | CSKA Moscow |
| 1959-60 | CSKA Moscow |
| 1960-61 | CSKA Moscow |
| 1961-62 | Spartak Moscow |
| 1962-63 | CSKA Moscow |
| 1963-64 | CSKA Moscow |
| 1964-65 | CSKA Moscow |
| 1965-66 | CSKA Moscow |
| 1966-67 | Spartak Moscow |
| 1967-68 | CSKA Moscow |
| 1968-69 | Spartak Moscow |
| 1969-70 | CSKA Moscow |
| 1970-71 | CSKA Moscow |
| 1971-72 | CSKA Moscow |
| 1972-73 | CSKA Moscow |
| 1973-74 | Krylya Sovietov Moscow |
| 1974-75 | CSKA Moscow |
| 1975-76 | Spartak Moscow |
| 1976-77 | CSKA Moscow |
| 1977-78 | CSKA Moscow |
| 1978-79 | CSKA Moscow |
| 1979-80 | CSKA Moscow |
| 1980-81 | CSKA Moscow |
| 1981-82 | CSKA Moscow |
| 1982-83 | CSKA Moscow |
| 1983-84 | CSKA Moscow |
| 1984-85 | CSKA Moscow |
| 1985-86 | CSKA Moscow |
| 1986-87 | CSKA Moscow |
| 1987-88 | CSKA Moscow |
| 1988-89 | CSKA Moscow |
| 1989-90 | Dynamo Moscow |
| 1990-91 | Dynamo Moscow |

**SPAIN**

| | |
|---|---|
| 1952-53 | Atletico Madrid |
| 1953-54 | Club Alpine Nurin |
| 1954-72 | *no champion* |
| 1972-73 | Real Sociedad San Sebastian |
| 1973-74 | Real Sociedad San Sebastian |
| 1974-75 | Txuri Urdin San Sebastian |
| 1975-76 | Txuri Urdin San Sebastian |
| 1976-77 | Casco Viejo Bilbao |
| 1977-78 | Casco Viejo Bilbao |
| 1978-79 | Casco Viejo Bilbao |
| 1979-80 | Txuri Urdin San Sebastian |
| 1980-81 | Casco Viejo Bilbao |
| 1981-82 | Vizcaya Bilbao |
| 1982-83 | CH Jaca |
| 1983-84 | CH Jaca |
| 1984-85 | Txuri Urdin San Sebastian |
| 1985-86 | CG Puigcerda |
| 1986-87 | *no champion* |
| 1987-88 | FC Barcelona |
| 1988-89 | CG Puigcerda |
| 1989-90 | Txuri Urdin San Sebastian |
| 1990-91 | CH Jaca |
| 1991-92 | Txuri Urdin San Sebastian |
| 1992-93 | Txuri Urdin San Sebastian |
| 1993-94 | CH Jaca |
| 1994-95 | Txuri Urdin San Sebastian |
| 1995-96 | CH Jaca |
| 1996-97 | FC Barcelona |
| 1997-98 | CH Majadahonda |
| 1998-99 | Txuri Urdin San Sebastian |
| 1999-2000 | Txuri Urdin San Sebastian |
| 2000-01 | CH Jaca |
| 2001-02 | FC Barcelona |
| 2002-03 | CH Jaca |
| 2003-04 | CH Jaca |
| 2004-05 | CH Jaca |
| 2005-06 | CG Puigcerda |
| 2006-07 | CG Puigcerda |
| 2007-08 | CG Puigcerda |
| 2008-09 | FC Barcelona |
| 2009-10 | CH Jaca |
| 2010-11 | CH Jaca |
| 2011-12 | CH Jaca |

**SWEDEN**

| | |
|---|---|
| 1921-22 | IK Gota |
| 1922-23 | IK Gota |
| 1923-24 | IK Gota |
| 1924-25 | Sodertalje SK |
| 1925-26 | Djurgarden Stockholm |
| 1926-27 | IK Gota |
| 1927-28 | IK Gota |
| 1928-29 | IK Gota |
| 1929-30 | IK Gota |
| 1930-31 | Sodertalje SK |
| 1931-32 | Hammarby Stockholm |
| 1932-33 | Hammarby Stockholm |
| 1933-34 | AIK Stockholm |
| 1934-35 | AIK Stockholm |
| 1935-36 | Hammarby Stockholm |
| 1936-37 | Hammarby Stockholm |
| 1937-38 | AIK Stockholm |
| 1938-39 | *no champion* |
| 1939-40 | IK Gota |
| 1940-41 | Sodertalje SK |
| 1941-42 | Hammarby Stockholm |
| 1942-43 | Hammarby Stockholm |
| 1943-44 | Sodertalje SK |
| 1944-45 | Hammarby Stockholm |
| 1945-46 | AIK Stockholm |
| 1946-47 | AIK Stockholm |
| 1947-48 | IK Gota |
| 1948-49 | *no champion* |
| 1949-50 | Djurgarden Stockholm |
| 1950-51 | Hammarby Stockholm |
| 1951-52 | *no champion* |
| 1952-53 | Sodertalje SK |
| 1953-54 | Djurgarden Stockholm |
| 1954-55 | Djurgarden Stockholm |
| 1955-56 | Sodertalje SK |
| 1956-57 | Gavle Godtemplares |
| 1957-58 | Djurgarden Stockholm |
| 1958-59 | Djurgarden Stockholm |
| 1959-60 | Djurgarden Stockholm |
| 1960-61 | Djurgarden Stockholm |
| 1961-62 | Djurgarden Stockholm |
| 1962-63 | Djurgarden Stockholm |
| 1963-64 | Brynas Gavle |
| 1964-65 | Vastra Frolunda Gothenburg |
| 1965-66 | Brynas Gavle |
| 1966-67 | Brynas Gavle |
| 1967-68 | Brynas Gavle |
| 1968-69 | Leksands IF |
| 1969-70 | Brynas Gavle |
| 1970-71 | Brynas Gavle |
| 1971-72 | Brynas Gavle |
| 1972-73 | Leksands IF |
| 1973-74 | Leksands IF |
| 1974-75 | Leksands IF |
| 1975-76 | Brynas Gavle |
| 1976-77 | Brynas Gavle |
| 1977-78 | Skelleftea AIK |
| 1978-79 | MoDo Ornskoldsvik |
| 1979-80 | Brynas Gavle |
| 1980-81 | Farjestads BK |
| 1981-82 | AIK Stockholm |
| 1982-83 | Djurgarden Stockholm |
| 1983-84 | AIK Stockholm |
| 1984-85 | Sodertalje SK |
| 1985-86 | Farjestad Karlstad |
| 1986-87 | Bjorkloven Umea |
| 1987-88 | Farjestad Karlstad |
| 1988-89 | Djurgarden Stockholm |
| 1989-90 | Djurgarden Stockholm |
| 1990-91 | Djurgarden Stockholm |
| 1991-92 | Malmo IF |
| 1992-93 | Brynas Gavle |
| 1993-94 | Malmo IF |
| 1994-95 | HV71 Jonkoving |
| 1995-96 | Lulea HF |
| 1996-97 | Farjestads Karlstad |
| 1997-98 | Farjestads Karlstad |
| 1998-99 | Brynas IF |
| 1999-2000 | Djurgarden Stockholm |
| 2000-01 | Djurgarden Stockholm |
| 2001-02 | Farjestad Karlstad |
| 2002-03 | Vastra Frolunda Gothenburg |
| 2003-04 | HV71 Jonkoping |

2004-05 Frolunda HC
2005-06 Farjestad Karlstad
2006-07 MoDo Ornskoldsvik
2007-08 HV71 Jonkoping
2008-09 Farjestad Karlstad
2009-10 HV71 Jonkoping
2010-11 Farjestad Karlstad
2011-12 Brynas Gavle

**SWITZERLAND**
1908-09 HC Davos
1909-10 HC Bellerive Vevey
1910-11 HC La Villa Lausanne
1911-12 Club de Patineurs Lausanne
1912-13 HC Les Avants
1913-14 HC Les Avants
1914-16 *no champion*
1916-17 Akademischer EHC Zurich
1917-18 HC Les Avants
1918-19 HC Bellerive Vevey
1919-20 HC Bellerive Vevey
1920-21 HC Rosey Gstaad
1921-22 EHC St Moritz
1922-23 EHC St Moritz
1923-24 HC Rosey Gstaad
1924-25 HC Rosey Gstaad
1925-26 HC Davos
1926-27 HC Davos
1927-28 EHC St Moritz
1928-29 HC Davos
1929-30 HC Davos
1930-31 HC Davos
1931-32 HC Davos
1932-33 HC Davos
1933-1937 *no champion*
1937-38 HC Davos
1938-39 HC Davos
1939-40 *no champion*
1940-41 HC Davos
1941-42 HC Davos
1942-43 HC Davos
1943-44 HC Davos
1944-45 HC Davos
1945-46 HC Davos
1946-47 HC Davos
1947-48 HC Davos
1948-49 Zurcher SC
1949-50 HC Davos
1950-51 EHC Arosa
1951-52 EHC Arosa
1952-53 EHC Arosa
1953-54 EHC Arosa
1954-55 EHC Arosa
1955-56 EHC Arosa
1956-57 EHC Arosa
1957-58 HC Davos
1958-59 SC Bern
1959-60 HC Davos
1960-61 Zurcher SC
1961-62 EHC Visp
1962-63 HC Villars
1963-64 HC Villars
1964-65 SC Bern
1965-66 Grasshopper Club Zurich
1966-67 EHC Kloten
1967-68 HC La Chaux-de-Fonds
1968-69 HC La Chaux-de-Fonds
1969-70 HC La Chaux-de-Fonds
1970-71 HC La Chaux-de-Fonds
1971-72 HC La Chaux-de-Fonds
1972-73 HC La Chaux-de-Fonds
1973-74 SC Bern
1974-75 SC Bern
1975-76 SC Langanau
1976-77 SC Bern
1977-78 EHC Biel
1978-79 SC Bern
1979-80 EHC Arosa
1980-81 EHC Biel
1981-82 EHC Arosa
1982-83 EHC Biel
1983-84 HC Davos
1984-85 HC Davos
1985-86 HC Lugano
1986-87 HC Lugano
1987-88 HC Lugano
1988-89 SC Bern
1989-90 HC Lugano
1990-91 SC Bern
1991-92 SC Bern
1992-93 EHC Kloten
1993-94 EHC Kloten
1994-95 EHC Kloten
1995-96 EHC Kloten
1996-97 SC Bern
1997-98 EV Zug
1998-99 HC Lugano
1999-2000 ZSC Lions Zurich
2000-01 ZSC Lions Zurich
2001-02 HC Davos
2002-03 HC Lugano
2003-04 SC Bern
2004-05 HC Davos
2005-06 HC Lugano
2006-07 HC Davos
2007-08 ZSC Lions Zurich
2008-09 HC Davos
2009-10 SC Bern
2010-11 HC Davos
2011-12 ZSC Lions Zurich

**THAILAND**
1999-2000 Blue Wave Bangkok
2000-01 Canstars Bangkok
2001-02 Canstars Bangkok
2002-03 Flying Farangs Bangkok
2003-04 Din-Daeng Jets Bangkok
2004-05 Canstars Bangkok
2005-06 Curve Coyotes Bangkok
2006-07 Jamcomb Sports Leafs Bangkok
2007-08 Curve Coyotes Bangkok
2008-09 Wall Street Warriors Bangkok
2009-10 Roadhouse Smokers Bangkok
2010-11 Pattaya Oilers Bangkok
2011-12 Hospital Blades Bangkok

**TURKEY**
1991-92 Belpa Ankara
1992-93 Ankara Buyuksehir Belediyesi
1993-94 Ankara Buyuksehir Belediyesi
1994-95 Ankara Buyuksehir Belediyesi
1995-96 Kavaklidere Ankara
1996-97 Ankara Buyuksehir Belediyesi
1997-98 Istanbul Paten Kulubu
1998-99 Gumus Patenler Spor Kulubu Ankara
1999-2000 Ankara Buyuksehir Belediyesi
2000-01 Polis Akademisi Ankara
2001-02 Ankara Buyuksehir Belediyesi
2002-03 Ankara Buyuksehir Belediyesi
2003-04 Polis Akademisi Ankara
2004-05 Polis Akademisi Ankara
2005-06 Polis Akademisi Ankara
2006-07 Kocaeli Buyuksehir Belediyesi Kagit Spor Izmit
2007-08 Polis Akademisi Ankara
2008-09 Polis Akademisi Ankara
2009-10 Ankara Universitesi SK
2010-11 Baskent Yildizlari Ankara
2011-12 Baskent Yildizlari Ankara

**UKRAINE**
1991-92 Sokil Kyiv
1992-93 Sokil Kyiv
1993-94 Masters Klub Kyiv
1994-95 Sokil Kyiv
1995-96 *no champion*
1996-97 Sokil Kyiv
1997-98 Sokil Kyiv
1998-99 Sokil Kyiv
1999-2000 Berkut Kyiv
2000-01 Berkut Kyiv
2001-02 Berkut Kyiv
2002-03 Sokil Kyiv
2003-04 Sokil Kyiv
2004-05 Sokil Kyiv
2005-06 Sokil Kyiv
2006-07 ATEK Kyiv
2007-08 Sokil Kyiv
2008-09 Sokil Kyiv
2009-10 Sokil Kyiv
2010-11 Donbas Donetsk
2011-12 Donbas Donetsk

**UNITED ARAB EMIRATES**
2009-10 Al Ain Vipers
2010-11 Abu Dhabi Storm
2011-12 Dubai Mighty Camels

**UNITED STATES (see also CANADA/NHL)**
**NCAA Champions**
1947-48 Michigan Wolverines
1948-49 Boston College Eagles
1949-50 Colorado College Tigers
1950-51 Michigan Wolverines
1951-52 Michigan Wolverines
1952-53 Michigan Wolverines
1953-54 RPI Engineers
1954-55 Michigan Wolverines
1955-56 Michigan Wolverines
1956-57 Colorado College Tigers
1957-58 Denver Pioneers
1958-59 North Dakota Fighting Sioux
1959-60 Denver Pioneers
1960-61 Denver Pioneers
1961-62 Michigan Tech Huskies
1962-63 North Dakota Fighting Sioux
1963-64 Michigan Wolverines
1964-65 Michigan Tech Huskies
1965-66 Michigan State Spartans
1966-67 Cornell Big Red
1967-68 Denver Pioneers
1968-69 Denver Pioneers
1969-70 Cornell Big Red
1970-71 Boston University Terriers
1971-72 Boston University Terriers
1972-73 Wisconsin Badgers
1973-74 Minnesota Golden Gophers
1974-75 Michigan Tech Huskies
1975-76 Minnesota Golden Gophers
1976-77 Wisconsin Badgers
1977-78 Boston University Terriers
1978-79 Minnesota Golden Gophers
1979-80 North Dakota Fighting Sioux
1980-81 Wisconsin Badgers
1981-82 North Dakota Fighting Sioux
1982-83 Wisconsin Badgers
1983-84 Bowling Green Falcons
1984-85 RPI Engineers
1985-86 Michigan State Spartans
1986-87 North Dakota Fighting Sioux
1987-88 Lake Superior State Lakers
1988-89 Harvard Crimson
1989-90 Wisconsin Badgers
1990-91 Northern Michigan Wildcats
1991-92 Lake Superior State Lakers
1992-93 Maine Black Bears
1993-94 Lake Superior State Lakers
1994-95 Boston University Terriers
1995-96 Michigan Wolverines
1996-97 North Dakota Fighting Sioux
1997-98 Michigan Wolverines
1998-99 Maine Black Bears
1999-2000 North Dakota Fighting Sioux
2000-01 Boston College Eagles
2001-02 Minnesota Golden Gophers
2002-03 Minnesota Golden Gophers
2003-04 Denver Pioneers
2004-05 Denver Pioneers
2005-06 Wisconsin Badgers
2006-07 Michigan State Spartans
2007-08 Boston College Eagles
2008-09 Boston University Terriers
2009-10 Boston College Eagles
2010-11 University of Minnesota Duluth
2011-12 Boston College Eagles

**YUGOSLAVIA (SEE ALSO SLOVENIA)**
1938-39 Ilirija Ljubljana
1939-40 Ilirija Ljubljana
1940-41 Ilirija Ljubljana
1941-1946 Not Played
1946-47 Mladost Zagreb
1947-48 Partizan Belgrade
1948-49 Mladost Zagreb
1949-50 Not Played
1950-51 Partizan Belgrade
1951-52 Partizan Belgrade
1952-53 Partizan Belgrade
1953-54 Partizan Belgrade
1954-55 Partizan Belgrade
1955-56 SD Zagreb
1956-57 HK Jesenice
1957-58 HK Jesenice
1958-59 HK Jesenice
1959-60 HK Jesenice
1960-61 HK Jesenice
1961-62 HK Jesenice
1962-63 HK Jesenice
1963-64 HK Jesenice
1964-65 HK Jesenice
1965-66 HK Jesenice
1966-67 HK Jesenice
1967-68 HK Jesenice
1968-69 HK Jesenice
1969-70 HK Jesenice
1970-71 HK Jesenice
1971-72 Olimpija Ljubljana
1972-73 HK Jesenice
1973-74 Olimpija Ljubljana
1974-75 Olimpija Ljubljana
1975-76 Olimpija Ljubljana
1976-77 HK Jesenice
1977-78 HK Jesenice
1978-79 Olimpija Ljubljana
1979-80 Olimpija Ljubljana
1980-81 HK Jesenice
1981-82 HK Jesenice
1982-83 Olimpija Ljubljana
1983-84 Olimpija Ljubljana
1984-85 HK Jesenice
1985-86 Partizan Belgrade
1986-87 HK Jesenice
1987-88 HK Jesenice
1988-89 Medvescak Zagreb
1989-90 Medvescak Zagreb
1990-91 Medvescak Zagreb

*The Los Angeles Kings claimed the Stanley Cup for the first time in the franchise's 45 years of existence, beating New Jersey in five games in 2012. Photo: Craig Campbell / HHOF.*

# CHAMPIONS, WOMEN

## European Women's Championships

| | |
|---|---|
| 1989 | Finland |
| 1991 | Finland |
| 1993 | Finland |
| 1995 | Finland |
| 1996 | Sweden |

## European Women's Champions Cup

| | |
|---|---|
| 2004-05 | AIK Solna (SWE) |
| 2005-06 | AIK Solna (SWE) |
| 2006-07 | AIK Solna (SWE) |
| 2007-08 | AIK Solna (SWE) |
| 2008-09 | SKIF Nizhni Novgorod (RUS) |
| 2009-10 | Tornado Moscow (RUS) |
| 2010-11 | Ilves Tampere (FIN) |
| 2011-12 | Tornado Moscow (RUS) |

## 3 Nations Cup

| Year | Host | Gold | Silver | Bronze |
|---|---|---|---|---|
| 1996 | Ottawa | Canada | United States | Finland |
| 1997 | Lake Placid | United States | Canada | Finland |
| 1998 | Kuortane | Canada | United States | Finland |
| 1999 | Montreal | Canada | United States | Finland |

## 4 Nations Cup

| Year | Host | Gold | Silver | Bronze |
|---|---|---|---|---|
| 2000 | Provo | Canada | United States | Finland |
| 2001* | Vierumaki | Canada | Finland | Sweden |
| 2002 | Kitchener | Canada | United States | Finland |
| 2003 | Skovde | United States | Canada | Finland |
| 2004 | Lake Placid | Canada | United States | Finland |
| 2005 | Hameenlinna | Canada | United States | Finland |
| 2006 | Kitchener | Canada | United States | Sweden |
| 2007 | Leksand | Canada | United States | Finland |
| 2008 | Lake Placid | United States | Canada | Sweden |
| 2009 | Vierumaki | Canada | United States | Sweden |
| 2010 | Clarenville** | Canada | United States | Finland |
| 2011 | Nykoping | United States | Canada | Sweden |

*United States didn't compete because of 9/11
**St. John's co-host

## National Champions of Member Federations, Women

**AUSTRIA**

| | |
|---|---|
| 2001-02 | EHV Sabres Vienna |
| 2002-03 | EHV Sabres Vienna |
| 2003-04 | EHV Sabres Vienna |
| 2004-05 | EHV Sabres Vienna |
| 2005-06 | The Ravens Salzburg |
| 2006-07 | EHV Sabres Vienna |
| 2007-08 | EHV Sabres Vienna |
| 2008-09 | The Ravens Salzburg |
| 2009-10 | EHV Sabres Vienna |
| 2010-11 | EHV Sabres Vienna |
| 2011-12 | EHV Sabres Vienna |

**CANADA**
**NWHL**

| | |
|---|---|
| 1999-2000 | Beatrice Aeros |
| 2000-01 | Beatrice Aeros |
| 2001-02 | Beatrice Aeros |
| 2002-03 | Calgary X-Treme |
| 2003-04 | Calgary X-Treme |
| 2004-05 | Toronto Aeros |
| 2005-06 | Montreal Axion |
| 2006-07 | Brampton Thunder |

**CWHL**

| | |
|---|---|
| 2007-08 | Mississauga Chiefs |

**CWHL (Clarkson Cup)**

| | |
|---|---|
| 2008-09 | Montreal Stars |
| 2009-10 | Minnesota Whitecaps |
| 2010-11 | Montreal Stars |
| 2011-12 | Montreal Stars |

**CIAU (CIS as of 2001)**

| | |
|---|---|
| 1997-98 | Concordia University Stingers |
| 1998-99 | Concordia University Stingers |
| 1999-2000 | University of Alberta Golden Bears |
| 2000-01 | University of Toronto Blues |
| 2001-02 | University of Alberta Golden Bears |
| 2002-03 | University of Alberta Golden Bears |
| 2003-04 | University of Alberta Golden Bears |
| 2004-05 | Laurier University Golden Hawks |
| 2005-06 | University of Alberta Golden Bears |
| 2006-07 | University of Alberta Golden Bears |
| 2007-08 | McGill University Martlets |
| 2008-09 | McGill University Martlets |
| 2009-10 | University of Alberta Golden Bears |
| 2010-11 | McGill University Martlets |
| 2011-12 | University of Calgary Dinos |

**DENMARK**

| | |
|---|---|
| 1989-90 | HIK (now Gentofte) |
| 1990-91 | HIK (now Gentofte) |
| 1991-92 | HIK (now Gentofte) |
| 1992-93 | HIK (now Gentofte) |
| 1993-94 | HIK (now Gentofte) |
| 1994-95 | HIK (now Gentofte) |
| 1995-96 | Herlev |
| 1996-97 | Herlev |
| 1997-98 | Herlev |
| 1998-99 | Rodovre |
| 1999-2000 | Rodovre |
| 2000-01 | Frederikshavn |
| 2001-02 | Herlev |
| 2002-03 | Rodovre |
| 2003-04 | Herlev |
| 2004-05 | Rodovre |
| 2005-06 | Herlev |
| 2006-07 | Herlev |
| 2007-08 | Herlev |
| 2008-09 | Herlev |
| 2009-10 | Herlev |
| 2010-11 | Hvidovre |
| 2011-12 | Hvidovre |

**EWHL (Elite Women's Hockey League)**

| | |
|---|---|
| 2004-05 | EHV Sabres Wien (AUT) |
| 2005-06 | HC Slovan Bratislava (SVK) |
| 2006-07 | HC Slovan Bratislava (SVK) |
| 2007-08 | HC Slavia Prag (CZE) |
| 2008-09 | HC Slavia Prag (CZE) |
| 2009-10 | ESC Planegg (GER) |
| 2010-11 | EHV Sabres Wien (AUT) |
| 2011-12 | EHV Sabres Wien (AUT) |

**FINLAND**

| | |
|---|---|
| 1982-83 | HJK Helsinki |
| 1983-84 | HJK Helsinki |
| 1984-85 | Ilves Tampere |
| 1985-86 | Ilves Tampere |
| 1986-87 | Ilves Tampere |
| 1987-88 | Ilves Tampere |
| 1988-89 | EVU Vantaa |
| 1989-90 | Ilves Tampere |
| 1990-91 | Ilves Tampere |
| 1991-92 | Ilves Tampere |
| 1992-93 | Ilves Tampere |
| 1993-94 | Shakers Kerava |
| 1994-95 | Shakers Kerava |
| 1995-96 | Shakers Kerava |
| 1996-97 | JyP Jyvaskyla |
| 1997-98 | JyP Jyvaskyla |
| 1999-2000 | Blues Espoo |
| 2000-01 | Blues Espoo |
| 2001-02 | Blues Espoo |
| 2002-03 | Blues Espoo |
| 2003-04 | Blues Espoo |
| 2004-05 | Blues Espoo |
| 2005-06 | Ilves Tampere |
| 2006-07 | Blues Espoo |
| 2007-08 | Blues Espoo |
| 2008-09 | Blues Espoo |
| 2009-10 | Ilves Tampere |
| 2010-11 | HPK Hamennlinna |
| 2011-12 | Karpat Oulu |

**GERMANY**

| | |
|---|---|
| 1983-84 | ESG Esslingen |
| 1984-85 | EHC Eisbaren Dusseldorf |
| 1985-86 | EHC Eisbaren Dusseldorf |
| 1986-87 | EHC Eisbaren Dusseldorf |
| 1987-88 | Mannheimer ERC WildCats |
| 1988-89 | EHC Eisbaren Dusseldorf |
| 1989-90 | Mannheimer ERC WildCats |
| 1990-91 | OSC Berlin |
| 1991-92 | Mannheimer ERC WildCats |
| 1992-93 | Neusser EC |
| 1993-94 | TuS Geretsried |
| 1994-95 | ESG Esslingen |
| 1995-96 | ESG Esslingen |
| 1996-97 | ESG Esslingen |
| 1997-98 | ESG Esslingen |
| 1998-99 | Mannheimer ERC WildCats |
| 1999-2000 | Mannheimer ERC WildCats |
| 2000-01 | TV Kornwestheim |
| 2001-02 | TV Kornwestheim |
| 2002-03 | TV Kornwestheim |
| 2003-04 | TV Kornwestheim |
| 2004-05 | EC Bergkamener Baren |
| 2005-06 | OSC Berlin |
| 2006-07 | OSC Berlin |
| 2007-08 | ESC Planegg |
| 2008-09 | OSC Berlin |
| 2009-10 | OSC Berlin |
| 2010-11 | ESC Planegg |
| 2011-12 | ESC Planegg |

**RUSSIA**

| | |
|---|---|
| 1995-96 | Luzhniki Moscow |
| 1996-97 | CSK VVS Moscow |
| 1997-98 | CSK VVS Moscow |
| 1998-99 | Viking Moscow |
| 1999-2000 | Spartak-Mercury Yekaterinburg |
| 2000-01 | SKIF Moscow |
| 2001-02 | SKIF Moscow |
| 2002-03 | SKIF Moscow |
| 2003-04 | SKIF Moscow |
| 2004-05 | SKIF Moscow |
| 2005-06 | Tornado Dmitrov |
| 2006-07 | Tornado Dmitrov |
| 2007-08 | SKIF Nizhny Novgorod |
| 2008-09 | Tornado Dmitrov |
| 2009-10 | SKIF Nizhny Novgorod |
| 2010-11 | Tornado Dmitrov |
| 2011-12 | Tornado Dmitrov |

**SLOVAKIA**

| | |
|---|---|
| 1991-92 | Zilina |
| 1992-93 | Dubnica |
| 1993-94 | Dubnica |
| 1994-95 | Zilina |
| 1995-96 | Dubnica |
| 1996-97 | Poprad |
| 1997-98 | Turcianske Teplice |
| 1998-99 | MHK Martin |
| 1999-2000 | MHK Martin |
| 2000-01 | MHK Martin |
| 2001-02 | Topolcany |
| 2002-03 | Topolcany |
| 2003-04 | MHK Martin |
| 2004-05 | MHK Martin |
| 2005-06 | MHK Martin |
| 2006-07 | MHK Martin |
| 2007-08 | MHK Martin |
| 2008-09 | MHK Martin |
| 2009-10 | HC Spisska Nova Ves |
| 2010-11 | HC Spisska Nova Ves |
| 2011-12 | HK Poprad |

**SWEDEN**

| | |
|---|---|
| 1987-88 | Nacka HK |
| 1988-89 | Nacka HK |
| 1989-90 | Nacka HK |
| 1990-91 | Nacka HK |
| 1991-92 | Nacka HK |
| 1992-93 | Nacka HK |
| 1993-94 | Nacka HK |
| 1994-95 | FoC Farsta |
| 1995-96 | Nacka HK |
| 1996-97 | FoC Farsta |
| 1997-98 | Nacka HK |
| 1998-99 | Malarhojden/Bredang Hockey |
| 1999-2000 | Malarhojden/Bredang Hockey |
| 2000-01 | Malarhojden/Bredang Hockey |
| 2001-02 | Malarhojden/Bredang Hockey |
| 2002-03 | Malarhojden/Bredang Hockey |
| 2003-04 | AIK Stockholm |
| 2004-05 | Malarhojden/Bredang Hockey |
| 2005-06 | Malarhojden/Bredang Hockey |
| 2006-07 | AIK Stockholm |
| 2007-08 | Segeltorps IF |
| 2008-09 | AIK Stockholm |
| 2009-10 | Segeltorps IF |
| 2010-11 | Segeltorps IF |
| 2011-12 | Modo |

**SWITZERLAND**

| | |
|---|---|
| 1986-87 | EHC Kloten |
| 1987-88 | EHC Kloten |
| 1988-89 | Grasshopper-Club Zurich |
| 1989-90 | Grasshopper-Club Zurich |
| 1990-91 | Grasshopper-Club Zurich |
| 1991-92 | EHC Bulach |
| 1992-93 | SC Lyss |
| 1993-94 | DHC Langenthal |
| 1994-95 | SC Lyss |
| 1995-96 | SC Lyss |
| 1996-97 | DHC Lyss |
| 1997-98 | EV Zug |
| 1998-99 | EV Zug |
| 1999-2000 | DSC St. Gallen |
| 2000-01 | SC Reinach |
| 2001-02 | SC Reinach |
| 2002-03 | SC Reinach |
| 2003-04 | EV Zug/Seewen |
| 2004-05 | EV Zug/Seewen |
| 2005-06 | HC Lugano |
| 2006-07 | HC Lugano |
| 2007-08 | DHC Langenthal |
| 2008-09 | HC Lugano |
| 2009-10 | HC Lugano |
| 2010-11 | ZSC Lions Zurich |
| 2011-12 | ZSC Lions Zurich |

**UNITED STATES (NCAA)**

| | |
|---|---|
| 2000-01 | University of Minnesota-Duluth Bulldogs |
| 2001-02 | University of Minnesota-Duluth Bulldogs |
| 2002-03 | University of Minnesota-Duluth Bulldogs |
| 2003-04 | University of Minnesota-Twin Cities Golden Gophers |
| 2004-05 | University of Minnesota-Twin Cities Golden Gophers |
| 2005-06 | University of Wisconsin Badgers |
| 2006-07 | University of Wisconsin Badgers |
| 2007-08 | University of Minnesota-Duluth Bulldogs |
| 2008-09 | University of Wisconsin Badgers |
| 2009-10 | University of Minnesota-Duluth Bulldogs |
| 2010-11 | University of Wisconsin Badgers |
| 2011-12 | University of Minnesota Golden Gophers |

*Tornado Moscow Region won the 2012 European Women's Champions Cup. Photo: Veli-Matti A. Pitkanen*

# PLAYERS' REGISTER, MEN

## Active Skaters, Men

(event-by-event summary for recently-active skaters internationally who play in the top level)

At 1992 WM20, the Soviet Union played as Commonwealth of Independent States beginning January 1, 1992; at 1992 OG-M, Russia played as the Unified Team but the name was later changed to Russia for historical consistency; at 1993 WM20, Czechoslovakia played as Czech/Slovak Republics. Where a player's summary statistics include participation from an earlier national incarnation and a current one (i.e., TCH and CZE), the more recent abbreviation is used.

Year Event #-Pos NAT GP G A P Pim Finish

**Aagaard, Mikkel**
**b. Frederikshavn, Denmark, October 18, 1995**

| Year Event | #-Pos | NAT | GP | G | A | P | Pim | Finish |
|---|---|---|---|---|---|---|---|---|
| 2012 WM18 | 14-F | DEN | 6 | 0 | 0 | 0 | 2 | 10th |

**Aaltonen, Juhamatti**
**b. Ii, Finland, June 4, 1985**

| Year Event | #-Pos | NAT | GP | G | A | P | Pim | Finish |
|---|---|---|---|---|---|---|---|---|
| 2003 WM18 | 12-F | FIN | 6 | 0 | 1 | 1 | 4 | 7th |
| 2010 WM | 50-F | FIN | 7 | 1 | 2 | 3 | 2 | 6th |
| 2011 WM | 50-F | FIN | 9 | 1 | 2 | 3 | 6 | G |
| **Totals WM** | | | **16** | **2** | **4** | **6** | **8** | **G** |

**Aaltonen, Mikael**
**b. Turku, Finland, January 12, 1991**

| Year Event | #-Pos | NAT | GP | G | A | P | Pim | Finish |
|---|---|---|---|---|---|---|---|---|
| 2009 WM18 | 2-D | FIN | 6 | 3 | 3 | 6 | 37 | B |

**Aaltonen, Miro**
**b. Joensuu, Finland, June 7, 1993**

| Year Event | #-Pos | NAT | GP | G | A | P | Pim | Finish |
|---|---|---|---|---|---|---|---|---|
| 2011 WM18 | 12-F | FIN | 6 | 4 | 0 | 4 | 2 | 5th |
| 2012 WM20 | 15-F | FIN | 7 | 1 | 3 | 4 | 0 | 4th |

**Aaltonen, Nico**
**b. Hyvinkaa, Finland, June 15, 1988**

| Year Event | #-Pos | NAT | GP | G | A | P | Pim | Finish |
|---|---|---|---|---|---|---|---|---|
| 2006 WM18 | 10-F | FIN | 5 | 0 | 1 | 1 | 4 | S |
| 2007 WM20 | 20-F | FIN | 5 | 0 | 0 | 0 | 0 | 6th |
| 2008 WM20 | 21-F | FIN | 6 | 3 | 1 | 4 | 0 | 6th |
| **Totals WM20** | | | **11** | **3** | **1** | **4** | **0** | **—** |

**Abakunchik, Alexander**
**b. Minsk, Soviet Union (Belarus), May 31, 1987**

| Year Event | #-Pos | NAT | GP | G | A | P | Pim | Finish |
|---|---|---|---|---|---|---|---|---|
| 2007 WM20 | 22-F | BLR | 6 | 0 | 1 | 1 | 4 | 10th |

**Abdelkader, Justin**
**b. Muskegon, Michigan, United States, February 25, 1987**

| Year Event | #-Pos | NAT | GP | G | A | P | Pim | Finish |
|---|---|---|---|---|---|---|---|---|
| 2007 WM20 | 18-F | USA | 7 | 0 | 2 | 2 | 10 | B |
| 2012 WM | 18-F | USA | 8 | 1 | 3 | 4 | 4 | 7th |

**Abeltshauser, Konrad**
**b. Bad Tolz, Germany, September 2, 1992**

| Year Event | #-Pos | NAT | GP | G | A | P | Pim | Finish |
|---|---|---|---|---|---|---|---|---|
| 2009 WM18 | 6-D | GER | 6 | 0 | 0 | 0 | 2 | 10th |
| 2011 WM20 | 6-D | GER | 6 | 0 | 0 | 0 | 2 | 10th |

**Abmiotka, Artur**
**b. Minsk, Belarus, June 15, 1992**

| Year Event | #-Pos | NAT | GP | G | A | P | Pim | Finish |
|---|---|---|---|---|---|---|---|---|
| 2010 WM18 | 13-F | BLR | 6 | 1 | 1 | 2 | 4 | 10th |

**Abolins, Andis**
**b. Riga, Soviet Union (Latvia), June 26, 1986**

| Year Event | #-Pos | NAT | GP | G | A | P | Pim | Finish |
|---|---|---|---|---|---|---|---|---|
| 2006 WM20 | 19-F | LAT | 6 | 1 | 1 | 2 | 2 | 9th |

**Ackermann, Alexander**
**b. Mannheim, Germany, January 18, 1993**

| Year Event | #-Pos | NAT | GP | G | A | P | Pim | Finish |
|---|---|---|---|---|---|---|---|---|
| 2011 WM18 | 16-F | GER | 6 | 2 | 2 | 4 | 14 | 6th |

**Ackermann, Nicolas**
**b. Mannheim, West Germany (Germany), December 31, 1989**

| Year Event | #-Pos | NAT | GP | G | A | P | Pim | Finish |
|---|---|---|---|---|---|---|---|---|
| 2007 WM18 | 27-D | GER | 6 | 0 | 2 | 2 | 0 | 8th |

**Adam, Luke**
**b. St. John's, Newfoundland, Canada, June 18, 1990**

| Year Event | #-Pos | NAT | GP | G | A | P | Pim | Finish |
|---|---|---|---|---|---|---|---|---|
| 2010 WM20 | 20-F | CAN | 6 | 4 | 4 | 8 | 8 | S |

**Adamovics, Edgars**
**b. Riga, Soviet Union (Latvia), April 1, 1986**

| Year Event | #-Pos | NAT | GP | G | A | P | Pim | Finish |
|---|---|---|---|---|---|---|---|---|
| 2006 WM20 | 13-D | LAT | 6 | 0 | 1 | 1 | 8 | 9th |

**Afinogenov, Maxim**
**b. Moscow, Soviet Union (Russia), September 4, 1979**

| Year Event | #-Pos | NAT | GP | G | A | P | Pim | Finish |
|---|---|---|---|---|---|---|---|---|
| 1998 WM20 | 29-F | RUS | 7 | 3 | 2 | 5 | 4 | S |
| 1999 WM20 | 29-F | RUS | 7 | 3 | 5 | 8 | 0 | G |
| 1999 WM | 61-F | RUS | 6 | 2 | 1 | 3 | 2 | 5th |
| 2000 WM | 61-F | RUS | 6 | 1 | 0 | 1 | 4 | 6th |
| 2002 OG-M | 61-F | RUS | 6 | 2 | 2 | 4 | 4 | B |
| 2002 WM | 61-F | RUS | 9 | 3 | 0 | 3 | 6 | S |
| 2004 WM | 61-F | RUS | 5 | 1 | 1 | 2 | 4 | 10th |
| 2004 WCH | 61-F | RUS | 4 | 0 | 1 | 1 | 2 | 6th |
| 2005 WM | 61-F | RUS | 9 | 3 | 2 | 5 | 6 | B |
| 2006 OG-M | 61-F | RUS | 8 | 1 | 0 | 1 | 10 | 4th |
| 2008 WM | 61-F | RUS | 8 | 5 | 1 | 6 | 2 | G |
| 2010 OG-M | 61-F | RUS | 4 | 1 | 1 | 2 | 0 | 6th |
| 2010 WM | 61-F | RUS | 9 | 3 | 4 | 7 | 18 | S |
| 2011 WM | 61-F | RUS | 9 | 1 | 2 | 3 | 6 | 4th |
| **Totals WM20** | | | **14** | **6** | **7** | **13** | **4** | **G,S** |
| **Totals WM** | | | **61** | **19** | **11** | **30** | **46** | **G,2S,B** |
| **Totals OG-M** | | | **18** | **4** | **3** | **7** | **14** | **B** |

~WM20 IIHF Directorate Best Forward (1999)

**Ageyenko, Yegor**
**b. Novopolotsk, Russia, October 3, 1992**

| Year Event | #-Pos | NAT | GP | G | A | P | Pim | Finish |
|---|---|---|---|---|---|---|---|---|
| 2010 WM18 | 11-F | BLR | 6 | 1 | 0 | 1 | 6 | 10th |

**Ahlen, Mikael**
**b. Salem, Sweden, April 14, 1988**

| Year Event | #-Pos | NAT | GP | G | A | P | Pim | Finish |
|---|---|---|---|---|---|---|---|---|
| 2006 WM18 | 10-F | SWE | 6 | 0 | 1 | 1 | 24 | 6th |

**Ahnelov, Jonas**
**b. Huddinge, Sweden, December 11, 1987**

| Year Event | #-Pos | NAT | GP | G | A | P | Pim | Finish |
|---|---|---|---|---|---|---|---|---|
| 2007 WM20 | 8-D | SWE | 7 | 0 | 1 | 1 | 6 | 4th |

**Ahsberg, Daniel**
**b. Gothenburg, Sweden, April 14, 1985**

| Year Event | #-Pos | NAT | GP | G | A | P | Pim | Finish |
|---|---|---|---|---|---|---|---|---|
| 2005 WM20 | 22-F | SWE | 6 | 1 | 1 | 2 | 0 | 6th |

**Akdag, Sinan**
**b. Rosenheim, West Germany (Germany), November 5, 1989**

| Year Event | #-Pos | NAT | GP | G | A | P | Pim | Finish |
|---|---|---|---|---|---|---|---|---|
| 2007 WM18 | 4-D | GER | 6 | 0 | 2 | 2 | 29 | 8th |
| 2009 WM20 | 7-D | GER | 6 | 0 | 1 | 1 | 0 | 9th |
| 2012 WM | 82-D | GER | 4 | 0 | 0 | 0 | 2 | 12th |

**Akerman, Johan**
**b. Stockholm, Sweden, November 20, 1972**

| Year Event | #-Pos | NAT | GP | G | A | P | Pim | Finish |
|---|---|---|---|---|---|---|---|---|
| 2007 WM | 44-D | SWE | 9 | 3 | 3 | 6 | 4 | 4th |
| 2009 WM | 4-D | SWE | 9 | 0 | 1 | 1 | 6 | B |
| **Totals WM** | | | **18** | **3** | **4** | **7** | **10** | **B** |

**Aksenenko, Alexander**
**b. Novosibirsk, Soviet Union (Russia), March 8, 1986**

| Year Event | #-Pos | NAT | GP | G | A | P | Pim | Finish |
|---|---|---|---|---|---|---|---|---|
| 2004 WM18 | 24-D | RUS | 6 | 0 | 0 | 0 | 4 | G |
| 2006 WM20 | 13-D | RUS | 6 | 0 | 2 | 2 | 8 | S |

**Alatalo, Jonas**
**b. Stockholm, Sweden, May 31, 1989**

| Year Event | #-Pos | NAT | GP | G | A | P | Pim | Finish |
|---|---|---|---|---|---|---|---|---|
| 2007 WM18 | 28-D | FIN | 6 | 0 | 2 | 2 | 0 | 7th |

**Albanese, Adrian**
**b. Bad Tolz, West Germany (Germany), April 1, 1988**

| Year Event | #-Pos | NAT | GP | G | A | P | Pim | Finish |
|---|---|---|---|---|---|---|---|---|
| 2006 WM18 | 14-F | GER | 6 | 0 | 0 | 0 | 0 | 8th |

**Albert, John**
**b. Concord, Ohio, United States, January 19, 1989**

| Year Event | #-Pos | NAT | GP | G | A | P | Pim | Finish |
|---|---|---|---|---|---|---|---|---|
| 2007 WM18 | 15-F | USA | 7 | 1 | 2 | 3 | 2 | S |

**Alberts, Andrew**
**b. Minneapolis, Minnesota, United States, June 30, 1981**

| Year Event | #-Pos | NAT | GP | G | A | P | Pim | Finish |
|---|---|---|---|---|---|---|---|---|
| 2006 WM | 41-D | USA | 7 | 1 | 0 | 1 | 14 | 7th |
| 2007 WM | 41-D | USA | 7 | 0 | 1 | 1 | 14 | 5th |
| **Totals WM** | | | **14** | **1** | **1** | **2** | **28** | **—** |

**Albrecht, Danny**
**b. Bad Muskau, East Germany (Germany), January 17, 1985**

| Year Event | #-Pos | NAT | GP | G | A | P | Pim | Finish |
|---|---|---|---|---|---|---|---|---|
| 2005 WM20 | 9-F | GER | 3 | 0 | 0 | 0 | 10 | 9th |

**Alcen, Johan**
**b. Sandviken, Sweden, March 11, 1988**

| Year Event | #-Pos | NAT | GP | G | A | P | Pim | Finish |
|---|---|---|---|---|---|---|---|---|
| 2008 WM20 | 29-F | SWE | 6 | 1 | 3 | 4 | 2 | S |

**Alexandrov, Yuri**
**b. Cherepovets, Soviet Union (Russia), June 24, 1988**

| Year Event | #-Pos | NAT | GP | G | A | P | Pim | Finish |
|---|---|---|---|---|---|---|---|---|
| 2006 WM18 | 2-D | RUS | 6 | 1 | 2 | 3 | 10 | 5th |
| 2007 WM20 | 23-D | RUS | 6 | 0 | 0 | 0 | 4 | S |
| 2008 WM20 | 23-D | RUS | 7 | 1 | 0 | 1 | 4 | B |
| **Totals WM20** | | | **13** | **1** | **0** | **1** | **8** | **S,B** |

**Alfredsson, Daniel**
**b. Gothenburg, Sweden, December 11, 1972**

| Year Event | #-Pos | NAT | GP | G | A | P | Pim | Finish |
|---|---|---|---|---|---|---|---|---|
| 1995 WM | 24-F | SWE | 8 | 3 | 1 | 4 | 4 | S |
| 1996 WM | 11-F | SWE | 6 | 1 | 2 | 3 | 4 | 6th |
| 1996 WCH | 11-F | SWE | 4 | 0 | 0 | 0 | 2 | 3rd |
| 1998 OG-M | 11-F | SWE | 4 | 2 | 3 | 5 | 2 | 5th |
| 1999 WM | 11-F | SWE | 10 | 4 | 5 | 9 | 8 | B |
| 2001 WM | 24-F | SWE | 9 | 3 | 5 | 8 | 6 | B |
| 2002 OG-M | 11-F | SWE | 4 | 1 | 4 | 5 | 2 | 5th |
| 2004 WM | 11-F | SWE | 8 | 4 | 2 | 6 | 8 | S |
| 2004 WCH | 11-F | SWE | 4 | 0 | 6 | 6 | 2 | 5th |
| 2005 WM | 11-F | SWE | 9 | 3 | 6 | 9 | 6 | 4th |
| 2006 OG-M | 11-F | SWE | 8 | 5 | 5 | 10 | 4 | G |
| 2010 OG-M | 11-F | SWE | 4 | 3 | 0 | 3 | 0 | 5th |
| 2012 WM | 11-F | SWE | 8 | 1 | 6 | 7 | 2 | 6th |
| **Totals WM** | | | **58** | **19** | **27** | **46** | **38** | **2S,2B** |
| **Totals OG-M** | | | **20** | **11** | **12** | **23** | **8** | **G** |
| **Totals IIHF-NHL** | | | **8** | **0** | **6** | **6** | **4** | **—** |

**Alikoski, Mikko**
**b. Oulu, Finland, July 28, 1986**

| Year Event | #-Pos | NAT | GP | G | A | P | Pim | Finish |
|---|---|---|---|---|---|---|---|---|
| 2004 WM18 | 10-F | FIN | 6 | 0 | 0 | 0 | 0 | 7th |
| 2006 WM20 | 10-F | FIN | 7 | 1 | 0 | 1 | 0 | B |

**Alm, Johan**
**b. Skelleftea, Sweden, January 28, 1992**

| Year Event | #-Pos | NAT | GP | G | A | P | Pim | Finish |
|---|---|---|---|---|---|---|---|---|
| 2010 WM18 | 2-D | SWE | 6 | 0 | 0 | 0 | 4 | S |

**Altmann, Mario**
**b. Vienna, Austria, November 4, 1986**

| Year Event | #-Pos | NAT | GP | G | A | P | Pim | Finish |
|---|---|---|---|---|---|---|---|---|
| 2009 WM | 41-D | AUT | 3 | 0 | 0 | 0 | 0 | 14th |
| 2011 WM | 41-D | AUT | 6 | 0 | 0 | 0 | 0 | 15th |
| **Totals WM** | | | **9** | **0** | **0** | **0** | **0** | **—** |

**Alzner, Karl**
**b. Burnaby, British Columbia, Canada, September 24, 1988**

| Year Event | #-Pos | NAT | GP | G | A | P | Pim | Finish |
|---|---|---|---|---|---|---|---|---|
| 2007 WM20 | 3-D | CAN | 6 | 0 | 1 | 1 | 2 | G |
| 2008 WM20 | 27-D | CAN | 7 | 1 | 1 | 2 | 0 | G |
| **Totals WM20** | | | **13** | **1** | **2** | **3** | **2** | **2G** |

**Amar, Baptiste**
**b. Gap, France, November 11, 1979**

| Year Event | #-Pos | NAT | GP | G | A | P | Pim | Finish |
|---|---|---|---|---|---|---|---|---|
| 2000 WM | 27-D | FRA | 6 | 0 | 0 | 0 | 0 | 15th |
| 2002 OG-M | 27-D | FRA | 4 | 0 | 0 | 0 | 0 | 14th |
| 2004 WM | 27-D | FRA | 6 | 0 | 0 | 0 | 2 | 16th |
| 2008 WM | 27-D | FRA | 5 | 2 | 3 | 5 | 6 | 14th |
| 2009 WM | 27-D | FRA | 6 | 0 | 1 | 1 | 2 | 12th |
| 2010 WM | 27-D | FRA | 6 | 2 | 1 | 3 | 4 | 14th |
| 2012 WM | 27-D | FRA | 7 | 0 | 1 | 1 | 2 | 9th |
| **Totals WM** | | | **36** | **4** | **6** | **10** | **16** | **—** |

**Ambuhl, Andres**
**b. Davos, Switzerland, September 14, 1983**

| 2001 WM18 | 10-F | SUI | 7 | 1 | 2 | 3 | 2 | S |
|---|---|---|---|---|---|---|---|---|
| 2002 WM20 | 22-F | SUI | 7 | 1 | 3 | 4 | 16 | 4th |
| 2003 WM20 | 10-F | SUI | 6 | 0 | 6 | 6 | 6 | 7th |
| 2004 WM | 16-F | SUI | 7 | 1 | 1 | 2 | 6 | 8th |
| 2005 WM | 10-F | SUI | 6 | 0 | 0 | 0 | 2 | 8th |
| 2006 OG-M | 10-F | SUI | 1 | 0 | 0 | 0 | 0 | 6th |
| 2006 WM | 10-F | SUI | 6 | 1 | 1 | 2 | 8 | 9th |
| 2007 WM | 10-F | SUI | 7 | 0 | 0 | 0 | 12 | 8th |
| 2008 WM | 10-F | SUI | 7 | 2 | 3 | 5 | 2 | 7th |
| 2009 WM | 10-F | SUI | 6 | 2 | 1 | 3 | 6 | 9th |
| 2010 OG-M | 10-F | SUI | 5 | 0 | 0 | 0 | 0 | 8th |
| 2010 WM | 10-F | SUI | 7 | 4 | 2 | 6 | 4 | 5th |
| 2011 WM | 10-F | SUI | 6 | 1 | 1 | 2 | 4 | 9th |
| 2012 WM | 10-F | SUI | 7 | 1 | 0 | 1 | 2 | 11th |
| **Totals WM20** | | | **13** | **1** | **9** | **10** | **22** | **—** |
| **Totals WM** | | | **59** | **12** | **9** | **21** | **46** | **—** |
| **Totals OG-M** | | | **6** | **0** | **0** | **0** | **0** | **—** |

**Amstutz, Reto**
**b. Sigriswil, Switzerland, February 24, 1993**

| 2011 WM18 | 17-F | SUI | 6 | 1 | 0 | 1 | 0 | 7th |
|---|---|---|---|---|---|---|---|---|
| 2012 WM20 | 19-F | SUI | 6 | 0 | 1 | 1 | 0 | 8th |

**Ancicka, Martin**
**b. Kladno, Czechoslovakia (Czech Republic), October 1, 1974**

| 2007 WM | 27-D | GER | 5 | 0 | 3 | 3 | 6 | 9th |
|---|---|---|---|---|---|---|---|---|

**Andersen, Jonas**
**b. Sarpsborg, Norway, March 8, 1981**

| 1999 WM18 | 21-F | NOR | 6 | 1 | 0 | 1 | 0 | 9th |
|---|---|---|---|---|---|---|---|---|
| 2006 WM | 24-F | NOR | 6 | 0 | 0 | 0 | 0 | 11th |
| 2007 WM | 24-F | NOR | 6 | 2 | 1 | 3 | 4 | 14th |
| 2010 OG-M | 42-F | NOR | 4 | 0 | 0 | 0 | 0 | 10th |
| **Totals WM** | | | **12** | **2** | **1** | **3** | **4** | **—** |

**Andersen, Niclas**
**b. Grums, Sweden, April 28, 1988**

| 2005 WM18 | 27-D | SWE | 7 | 0 | 0 | 0 | 12 | B |
|---|---|---|---|---|---|---|---|---|
| 2006 WM18 | 27-D | SWE | 6 | 1 | 1 | 2 | 14 | 6th |
| 2008 WM20 | 9-D | SWE | 6 | 0 | 2 | 2 | 6 | S |
| **Totals WM18** | | | **13** | **1** | **1** | **2** | **26** | **B** |

**Andersen, Robin**
**b. Fredrikstad, Norway, February 9, 1991**

| 2009 WM18 | 10-F | NOR | 6 | 0 | 1 | 1 | 4 | 9th |
|---|---|---|---|---|---|---|---|---|
| 2011 WM20 | 29-D | NOR | 6 | 0 | 1 | 1 | 2 | 9th |

**Andersons, Janis**
**b. Riga, Soviet Union (Latvia), October 7, 1986**

| 2006 WM20 | 22-D | LAT | 6 | 0 | 1 | 1 | 2 | 9th |
|---|---|---|---|---|---|---|---|---|
| 2010 WM | 14-D | LAT | 5 | 0 | 0 | 0 | 2 | 11th |
| 2011 WM | 5-D | LAT | 3 | 0 | 1 | 1 | 4 | 13th |
| 2012 WM | 3-D | LAT | 4 | 0 | 0 | 0 | 0 | 10th |
| **Totals WM** | | | **12** | **0** | **1** | **1** | **6** | **—** |

**Andersons, Toms**
**b. November 25, 1993**

| 2012 WM20 | 23-F | LAT | 6 | 2 | 0 | 2 | 4 | 9th |
|---|---|---|---|---|---|---|---|---|

**Andersson, Calle**
**b. Limhamn, Sweden, May 16, 1994**

| 2012 WM18 | 4-D | SWE | 6 | 0 | 3 | 3 | 0 | S |
|---|---|---|---|---|---|---|---|---|

**Andersson, Erik**
**b. Ljungby, Sweden, September 18, 1986**

| 2006 WM20 | 11-F | SWE | 6 | 0 | 4 | 4 | 2 | 5th |
|---|---|---|---|---|---|---|---|---|

**Andersson, Fredric**
**b. Gnesta, Sweden, October 13, 1988**

| 2006 WM18 | 28-F | SWE | 6 | 0 | 0 | 0 | 12 | 6th |
|---|---|---|---|---|---|---|---|---|

**Andersson, Jimmy**
**b. Stockholm, Sweden, August 29, 1989**

| 2007 WM18 | 9-F | SWE | 6 | 1 | 0 | 1 | 2 | B |
|---|---|---|---|---|---|---|---|---|

**Andersson, Joakim**
**b. Munkedal, Sweden, February 5, 1989**

| 2006 WM18 | 20-F | SWE | 6 | 0 | 0 | 0 | 4 | 6th |
|---|---|---|---|---|---|---|---|---|
| 2007 WM18 | 10-F | SWE | 6 | 0 | 1 | 1 | 4 | B |
| 2008 WM20 | 18-F | SWE | 6 | 0 | 6 | 6 | 2 | S |
| 2009 WM20 | 18-F | SWE | 6 | 2 | 4 | 6 | 6 | S |
| **Totals WM18** | | | **12** | **0** | **1** | **1** | **8** | **B** |
| **Totals WM20** | | | **12** | **2** | **10** | **12** | **8** | **2S** |

**Andersson, Johan**
**b. Mjolby, Sweden, May 18, 1984**

| 2004 WM20 | 26-F | SWE | 6 | 1 | 4 | 5 | 4 | 7th |
|---|---|---|---|---|---|---|---|---|
| 2008 WM | 16-F | SWE | 9 | 0 | 1 | 1 | 2 | 4th |
| 2009 WM | 16-F | SWE | 9 | 1 | 1 | 2 | 6 | B |
| **Totals WM** | | | **18** | **1** | **2** | **3** | **8** | **B** |

**Andersson, Johan**
**b. Nynashamn, Sweden, May 2, 1987**

| 2005 WM18 | 22-F | SWE | 7 | 0 | 2 | 2 | 0 | B |
|---|---|---|---|---|---|---|---|---|

**Andersson, Jonas**
**b. Stockholm, Sweden, February 24, 1981**

| 1999 WM18 | 11-F | SWE | 7 | 2 | 0 | 2 | 4 | S |
|---|---|---|---|---|---|---|---|---|
| 2001 WM20 | 23-F | SWE | 7 | 0 | 0 | 0 | 6 | 4th |
| 2010 WM | 71-F | SWE | 9 | 6 | 0 | 6 | 6 | B |

**Andersson, Niklas**
**b. Danderyd, Sweden, March 5, 1986**

| 2004 WM18 | 2-D | SWE | 6 | 1 | 0 | 1 | 6 | 5th |
|---|---|---|---|---|---|---|---|---|
| 2006 WM20 | 2-D | SWE | 6 | 0 | 1 | 1 | 4 | 5th |

**Andersson, Peter**
**b. Kvidinge, Sweden, April 13, 1991**

| 2009 WM18 | 19-D | SWE | 6 | 1 | 0 | 1 | 6 | 5th |
|---|---|---|---|---|---|---|---|---|
| 2010 WM20 | 6-D | SWE | 6 | 0 | 3 | 3 | 4 | B |

**Andreasen, Andreas**
**b. Esbjerg, Denmark, March 1, 1976**

| 2003 WM | 25-D | DEN | 6 | 0 | 0 | 0 | 2 | 11th |
|---|---|---|---|---|---|---|---|---|
| 2004 WM | 25-D | DEN | 6 | 0 | 1 | 1 | 2 | 12th |
| 2005 WM | 25-D | DEN | 6 | 1 | 1 | 2 | 8 | 14th |
| 2006 WM | 25-D | DEN | 6 | 0 | 0 | 0 | 4 | 13th |
| 2007 WM | 25-D | DEN | 6 | 0 | 1 | 1 | 8 | 10th |
| 2008 WM | 25-D | DEN | 6 | 0 | 1 | 1 | 0 | 12th |
| **Totals WM** | | | **36** | **1** | **4** | **5** | **24** | **—** |

**Andrews, Brent**
**b. Hunter River, Prince Edward Island, Canada, January 19, 1993**

| 2011 WM18 | 9-F | CAN | 7 | 0 | 1 | 1 | 14 | 4th |
|---|---|---|---|---|---|---|---|---|

**Andreychikov, Ruslan**
**b. Gomel, Belarus, July 28, 1992**

| 2010 WM18 | 22-D | BLR | 6 | 0 | 0 | 0 | 2 | 10th |
|---|---|---|---|---|---|---|---|---|

**Andrighetto, Sven**
**b. Zurich, Switzerland, March 21, 1993**

| 2010 WM18 | 5-F | SUI | 6 | 0 | 3 | 3 | 2 | 5th |
|---|---|---|---|---|---|---|---|---|
| 2011 WM18 | 22-F | SUI | 6 | 3 | 2 | 5 | 8 | 7th |
| 2012 WM20 | 22-F | SUI | 6 | 1 | 1 | 2 | 2 | 8th |
| **Totals WM18** | | | **12** | **3** | **5** | **8** | **10** | **—** |

**Andronov, Sergei**
**b. Penza, Soviet Union (Russia), July 19, 1989**

| 2007 WM18 | 11-F | RUS | 7 | 0 | 2 | 2 | 0 | G |
|---|---|---|---|---|---|---|---|---|
| 2009 WM20 | 16-F | RUS | 7 | 3 | 5 | 8 | 2 | B |

**Anisimov, Artyom**
**b. Yaroslavl, Soviet Union (Russia), May 24, 1988**

| 2006 WM18 | 12-F | RUS | 6 | 3 | 2 | 5 | 2 | 5th |
|---|---|---|---|---|---|---|---|---|
| 2007 WM20 | 12-F | RUS | 6 | 2 | 1 | 3 | 4 | S |
| 2008 WM20 | 12-F | RUS | 7 | 1 | 3 | 4 | 6 | B |
| 2010 WM | 42-F | RUS | 9 | 1 | 2 | 3 | 6 | S |
| **Totals WM20** | | | **13** | **3** | **4** | **7** | **10** | **S,B** |

**Ankerst, Jaka**
**b. Kranj, Yugoslavia (Slovenia), March 27, 1989**

| 2011 WM | 26-F | SLO | 3 | 0 | 0 | 0 | 2 | 16th |
|---|---|---|---|---|---|---|---|---|

**Ankipans, Girts**
**b. Riga, Soviet Union (Latvia), November 29, 1975**

| 2003 WM | 9-F | LAT | 6 | 0 | 1 | 1 | 0 | 9th |
|---|---|---|---|---|---|---|---|---|
| 2005 WM | 9-F | LAT | 6 | 2 | 4 | 6 | 0 | 9th |
| 2006 OG-M | 9-F | LAT | 5 | 0 | 0 | 0 | 0 | 12th |
| 2009 WM | 75-F | LAT | 7 | 1 | 2 | 3 | 6 | 7th |
| 2010 OG-M | 75-F | LAT | 4 | 2 | 0 | 2 | 4 | 12th |
| 2011 WM | 75-F | LAT | 6 | 0 | 0 | 0 | 2 | 13th |
| **Totals WM** | | | **25** | **3** | **7** | **10** | **8** | **—** |
| **Totals OG-M** | | | **9** | **2** | **0** | **2** | **4** | **—** |

**Ankudinov, Andrei**
**b. Ufa, Soviet Union (Russia), February 11, 1991**

| 2009 WM18 | 12-F | RUS | 7 | 1 | 0 | 1 | 26 | S |
|---|---|---|---|---|---|---|---|---|

**Ansoldi, Luca**
**b. Merano, Italy, January 5, 1982**

| 2012 WM | 71-F | ITA | 7 | 2 | 0 | 2 | 2 | 15th |
|---|---|---|---|---|---|---|---|---|

**Antipin, Viktor**
**b. Ust-Kamenogorsk, Kazakhstan, June 12, 1992**

| 2010 WM18 | 4-D | RUS | 7 | 1 | 1 | 2 | 6 | 4th |
|---|---|---|---|---|---|---|---|---|
| 2012 WM20 | 4-D | RUS | 7 | 0 | 2 | 2 | 2 | S |

**Antonen, Joose**
**b. Tampere, Finland, April 28, 1995**

| 2012 WM18 | 20-F | FIN | 7 | 1 | 0 | 1 | 0 | 4th |
|---|---|---|---|---|---|---|---|---|

**Antonietti, Benjamin**
**b. Orbe, Switzerland, July 7, 1991**

| 2009 WM18 | 13-F | SUI | 6 | 1 | 2 | 3 | 0 | 8th |
|---|---|---|---|---|---|---|---|---|
| 2010 WM20 | 16-F | SUI | 7 | 1 | 1 | 2 | 4 | 4th |
| 2011 WM20 | 23-F | SUI | 6 | 0 | 0 | 0 | 4 | 5th |
| **Totals WM20** | | | **13** | **1** | **1** | **2** | **8** | **—** |

**Antonov, Andrei**
**b. Voskresensk, Soviet Union (Russia), April 27, 1985**

| 2009 WM | 85-D | BLR | 7 | 0 | 0 | 0 | 2 | 8th |
|---|---|---|---|---|---|---|---|---|

**Apalkov, Danil**
**b. Chelyabinsk, Russia, January 1, 1992**

| 2010 WM18 | 14-F | RUS | 7 | 0 | 0 | 0 | 6 | 4th |
|---|---|---|---|---|---|---|---|---|
| 2012 WM20 | 14-F | RUS | 7 | 1 | 2 | 3 | 0 | S |

**Apelis, Edgars**
**b. Daugavpils, Soviet Union (Latvia), November 23, 1989**

| 2007 WM18 | 13-D | LAT | 6 | 0 | 1 | 1 | 2 | 10th |
|---|---|---|---|---|---|---|---|---|

**Archibald, Josh**
**b. Regina, Saskatchewan, Canada, October 6, 1992**

| 2012 WM20 | 21-F | USA | 6 | 0 | 2 | 2 | 6 | 7th |
|---|---|---|---|---|---|---|---|---|

**Arkhipov, Dmitri**
**b. Novocheboksarsk, Russia, February 2, 1993**

| 2010 WM18 | 28-F | RUS | 3 | 0 | 0 | 0 | 2 | 4th |
|---|---|---|---|---|---|---|---|---|

**Armia, Joel**
**b. Pori, Finland, May 31, 1993**

| 2011 WM18 | 23-F | FIN | 6 | 4 | 9 | 13 | 8 | 5th |
|---|---|---|---|---|---|---|---|---|
| 2011 WM20 | 20-F | FIN | 6 | 0 | 1 | 1 | 2 | 6th |
| 2012 WM20 | 10-F | FIN | 7 | 5 | 2 | 7 | 16 | 4th |
| **Totals WM20** | | | **13** | **5** | **3** | **8** | **18** | **—** |

**Armstrong, Colby**
**b. Lloydminster, Saskatchewan, Canada, November 23, 1982**

| 2007 WM | 20-F | CAN | 9 | 1 | 1 | 2 | 4 | G |
|---|---|---|---|---|---|---|---|---|
| 2009 WM | 20-F | CAN | 9 | 0 | 3 | 3 | 4 | S |
| **Totals WM** | | | **18** | **1** | **4** | **5** | **8** | **G,S** |

**Arnason, Tyler**
**b. Oklahoma City, Oklahoma, United States, March 16, 1979**

| 2007 WM | 39-F | USA | 7 | 1 | 3 | 4 | 0 | 5th |
|---|---|---|---|---|---|---|---|---|

**Arnesson, Linus**
**b. Stockholm, Sweden, September 21, 1994**

| 2012 WM18 | 5-D | SWE | 6 | 0 | 0 | 0 | 4 | S |
|---|---|---|---|---|---|---|---|---|

**Arniel, Jamie**
**b. Kingston, Ontario, Canada, November 16, 1989**

| 2007 WM18 | 11-F | CAN | 6 | 3 | 5 | 8 | 10 | 4th |
|---|---|---|---|---|---|---|---|---|

**Arnold, Bill**
**b. Needham, Massachusetts, United States, May 13, 1992**

| 2010 WM18 | 10-F | USA | 6 | 1 | 2 | 3 | 6 | G |
|---|---|---|---|---|---|---|---|---|
| 2012 WM20 | 14-F | USA | 6 | 3 | 3 | 6 | 4 | 7th |

**Arnold, Eric**
**b. Seedorf, Switzerland, November 30, 1992**

| | | | | | | | | |
|---|---|---|---|---|---|---|---|---|
| 2010 WM18 | 18-F | SUI | 5 | 0 | 0 | 0 | 0 | 5th |

**Arrosamena, Nicolas**
**b. Saint-Pierre-et-Miquelon, France, January 9, 1990**

| | | | | | | | | |
|---|---|---|---|---|---|---|---|---|
| 2011 WM | 23-F | FRA | 5 | 0 | 0 | 0 | 2 | 12th |

**Artyukhin, Yevgeni**
**b. Moscow, Soviet Union (Russia), April 4, 1983**

| | | | | | | | | |
|---|---|---|---|---|---|---|---|---|
| 2001 WM18 | 25-D | RUS | 6 | 1 | 1 | 2 | 4 | G |
| 2003 WM20 | 23-F | RUS | 6 | 1 | 0 | 1 | 10 | G |
| 2011 WM | 49-F | RUS | 9 | 2 | 1 | 3 | 24 | 4th |

**Arvidsson, Viktor**
**b. Kusmark, Sweden, April 8, 1993**

| | | | | | | | | |
|---|---|---|---|---|---|---|---|---|
| 2011 WM18 | 13-F | SWE | 5 | 0 | 1 | 1 | 8 | S |

**Arzamastsev, Zakhar**
**b. Novokuznetsk, Soviet Union (Russia), November 6, 1992**

| | | | | | | | | |
|---|---|---|---|---|---|---|---|---|
| 2010 WM18 | 24-D | RUS | 7 | 0 | 3 | 3 | 27 | 4th |
| 2012 WM20 | 24-D | RUS | 7 | 0 | 2 | 2 | 2 | S |

**Ashton, Carter**
**b. Winnipeg, Manitoba, Canada, April 1, 1991**

| | | | | | | | | |
|---|---|---|---|---|---|---|---|---|
| 2011 WM20 | 25-F | CAN | 7 | 1 | 2 | 3 | 6 | S |

**Ask, Morten**
**b. Oslo, Norway, May 14, 1980**

| | | | | | | | | |
|---|---|---|---|---|---|---|---|---|
| 2001 WM | 26-F | NOR | 6 | 1 | 2 | 3 | 10 | 15th |
| 2006 WM | 21-F | NOR | 6 | 1 | 3 | 4 | 4 | 11th |
| 2007 WM | 21-F | NOR | 6 | 3 | 4 | 7 | 10 | 14th |
| 2008 WM | 21-F | NOR | 7 | 3 | 2 | 5 | 8 | 8th |
| 2009 WM | 21-F | NOR | 6 | 0 | 2 | 2 | 10 | 11th |
| 2011 WM | 21-F | NOR | 7 | 1 | 3 | 4 | 10 | 6th |
| 2012 WM | 21-F | NOR | 8 | 2 | 8 | 10 | 6 | 8th |
| **Totals WM** | | | **46** | **11** | **24** | **35** | **58** | **—** |

**Aslaksen, Adrian**
**b. Sarpsborg, Norway, August 2, 1993**

| | | | | | | | | |
|---|---|---|---|---|---|---|---|---|
| 2011 WM18 | 19-F | NOR | 6 | 0 | 0 | 0 | 4 | 9th |

**Asperup, Matthias**
**b. Rodovre, Denmark, March 3, 1995**

| | | | | | | | | |
|---|---|---|---|---|---|---|---|---|
| 2012 WM18 | 19-F | DEN | 6 | 1 | 0 | 1 | 12 | 10th |

**Asten, Micke**
**b. Helsinki, Finland, June 10, 1992**

| | | | | | | | | |
|---|---|---|---|---|---|---|---|---|
| 2010 WM18 | 16-F | FIN | 6 | 1 | 1 | 2 | 12 | B |

**Atkinson, Cam**
**b. Greenwich, Connecticut, United States, June 5, 1989**

| | | | | | | | | |
|---|---|---|---|---|---|---|---|---|
| 2012 WM | 13-F | USA | 8 | 1 | 2 | 3 | 4 | 7th |

**Atyushov, Vitali**
**b. Penza, Soviet Union (Russia), July 4, 1979**

| | | | | | | | | |
|---|---|---|---|---|---|---|---|---|
| 2006 WM | 27-D | RUS | 7 | 0 | 2 | 2 | 10 | 5th |
| 2007 WM | 27-D | RUS | 9 | 0 | 3 | 3 | 4 | B |
| 2009 WM | 27-D | RUS | 9 | 2 | 5 | 7 | 0 | G |
| 2010 WM | 27-D | RUS | 9 | 0 | 4 | 4 | 4 | S |
| 2011 WM | 27-D | RUS | 9 | 1 | 2 | 3 | 4 | 4th |
| **Totals WM** | | | **43** | **3** | **16** | **19** | **22** | **G,S,B** |

**Augsburger, Gaetan**
**b. St-Imier, Switzerland, April 4, 1988**

| | | | | | | | | |
|---|---|---|---|---|---|---|---|---|
| 2007 WM20 | 26-F | SUI | 6 | 0 | 1 | 1 | 0 | 7th |
| 2008 WM20 | 29-F | SUI | 6 | 0 | 0 | 0 | 0 | 9th |
| **Totals WM20** | | | **12** | **0** | **1** | **1** | **0** | **—** |

**Augstkalns, Edmunds**
**b. August 25, 1994**

| | | | | | | | | |
|---|---|---|---|---|---|---|---|---|
| 2012 WM18 | 8-D | LAT | 6 | 1 | 2 | 3 | 22 | 9th |

**Aulie, Keith**
**b. Rouleau, Saskatchewan, Canada, July 11, 1989**

| | | | | | | | | |
|---|---|---|---|---|---|---|---|---|
| 2009 WM20 | 32-D | CAN | 6 | 0 | 1 | 1 | 2 | G |

**Auvinen, Henri**
**b. Jyvaskyla, Finland, February 21, 1993**

| | | | | | | | | |
|---|---|---|---|---|---|---|---|---|
| 2011 WM18 | 3-D | FIN | 6 | 0 | 0 | 0 | 10 | 5th |

**Auvitu, Yohann**
**b. Ivry-sur-Seine, France, July 27, 1989**

| | | | | | | | | |
|---|---|---|---|---|---|---|---|---|
| 2010 WM | 18-D | FRA | 6 | 0 | 2 | 2 | 4 | 14th |
| 2011 WM | 18-D | FRA | 6 | 0 | 1 | 1 | 2 | 12th |
| 2012 WM | 18-D | FRA | 6 | 2 | 2 | 4 | 0 | 9th |
| **Totals WM** | | | **18** | **2** | **5** | **7** | **6** | **—** |

**Avdosev, Yevgeni**
**b. Novopolotsk, Soviet Union (Belarus), August 11, 1988**

| | | | | | | | | |
|---|---|---|---|---|---|---|---|---|
| 2006 WM18 | 21-F | BLR | 6 | 0 | 1 | 1 | 6 | 9th |

**Averin, Yegor**
**b. Omsk, Soviet Union (Russia), August 25, 1989**

| | | | | | | | | |
|---|---|---|---|---|---|---|---|---|
| 2007 WM18 | 19-F | RUS | 7 | 3 | 2 | 5 | 6 | G |

**Avgustincic, Jaka**
**b. Ljubljana, Yugoslavia (Slovenia), October 27, 1976**

| | | | | | | | | |
|---|---|---|---|---|---|---|---|---|
| 2002 WM | 7-F | SLO | 6 | 0 | 0 | 0 | 0 | 13th |
| 2003 WM | 21-F | SLO | 5 | 0 | 0 | 0 | 4 | 15th |
| 2005 WM | 21-F | SLO | 6 | 0 | 0 | 0 | 0 | 13th |
| 2006 WM | 21-F | SLO | 6 | 0 | 0 | 0 | 2 | 16th |
| **Totals WM** | | | **23** | **0** | **0** | **0** | **6** | **—** |

**Axelsson, Anton**
**b. Ytterby, Sweden, January 16, 1986**

| | | | | | | | | |
|---|---|---|---|---|---|---|---|---|
| 2006 WM20 | 16-F | SWE | 6 | 1 | 0 | 1 | 6 | 5th |

**Baca, Martin**
**b. Liptovsky Mikulas, Czechoslovakia (Slovakia), February 2, 1989**

| | | | | | | | | |
|---|---|---|---|---|---|---|---|---|
| 2007 WM18 | 11-D | SVK | 6 | 0 | 1 | 1 | 24 | 5th |

**Bacek, Igor**
**b. Bratislava, Czechoslovakia (Slovakia), January 30, 1986**

| | | | | | | | | |
|---|---|---|---|---|---|---|---|---|
| 2004 WM18 | 10-F | SVK | 6 | 0 | 3 | 3 | 2 | 6th |
| 2006 WM20 | 11-F | SVK | 6 | 1 | 3 | 4 | 2 | 8th |

**Bacher, Jens Ulrich**
**b. Asker, Norway, October 2, 1992**

| | | | | | | | | |
|---|---|---|---|---|---|---|---|---|
| 2009 WM18 | 6-D | NOR | 6 | 0 | 0 | 0 | 6 | 9th |
| 2011 WM20 | 6-D | NOR | 6 | 0 | 0 | 0 | 2 | 9th |

**Bachet, Vincent**
**b. St. Maurice-le-Girard, France, April 29, 1978**

| | | | | | | | | |
|---|---|---|---|---|---|---|---|---|
| 2000 WM | 35-D | FRA | 6 | 1 | 0 | 1 | 4 | 15th |
| 2002 OG-M | 3-D | FRA | 4 | 0 | 1 | 1 | 4 | 14th |
| 2004 WM | 3-D | FRA | 6 | 0 | 0 | 0 | 0 | 16th |
| 2008 WM | 3-D | FRA | 5 | 0 | 1 | 1 | 6 | 14th |
| 2009 WM | 3-D | FRA | 6 | 0 | 1 | 1 | 6 | 12th |
| 2010 WM | 3-D | FRA | 6 | 0 | 0 | 0 | 6 | 14th |
| 2011 WM | 3-D | FRA | 6 | 0 | 0 | 0 | 10 | 12th |
| 2012 WM | 3-D | FRA | 7 | 0 | 1 | 1 | 0 | 9th |
| **Totals WM** | | | **36** | **1** | **3** | **4** | **26** | **—** |

**Backes, David**
**b. Blaine, Minnesota, United States, May 1, 1984**

| | | | | | | | | |
|---|---|---|---|---|---|---|---|---|
| 2007 WM | 18-F | USA | 7 | 1 | 2 | 3 | 6 | 5th |
| 2008 WM | 42-F | USA | 6 | 0 | 1 | 1 | 35 | 6th |
| 2009 WM | 42-F | USA | 9 | 1 | 4 | 5 | 33 | 4th |
| 2010 OG-M | 42-F | USA | 6 | 1 | 2 | 3 | 2 | S |
| **Totals WM** | | | **22** | **2** | **7** | **9** | **74** | **—** |

**Backlund, Mikael**
**b. Vasteras, Sweden, March 17, 1989**

| | | | | | | | | |
|---|---|---|---|---|---|---|---|---|
| 2006 WM18 | 21-F | SWE | 3 | 1 | 0 | 1 | 0 | 6th |
| 2007 WM18 | 11-F | SWE | 6 | 6 | 1 | 7 | 6 | B |
| 2008 WM20 | 22-F | SWE | 6 | 3 | 4 | 7 | 10 | S |
| 2009 WM20 | 22-F | SWE | 6 | 5 | 2 | 7 | 6 | S |
| 2010 WM | 60-F | SWE | 6 | 0 | 1 | 1 | 2 | B |
| 2011 WM | 60-F | SWE | 9 | 3 | 2 | 5 | 2 | S |
| **Totals WM18** | | | **9** | **7** | **1** | **8** | **6** | **B** |
| **Totals WM20** | | | **12** | **8** | **6** | **14** | **16** | **2S** |
| **Totals WM** | | | **15** | **3** | **3** | **6** | **4** | **S,B** |

**Backman, Christian**
**b. Alingsas, Sweden, April 28, 1980**

| | | | | | | | | |
|---|---|---|---|---|---|---|---|---|
| 1999 WM20 | 3-D | SWE | 6 | 0 | 3 | 3 | 0 | 4th |
| 2000 WM20 | 8-D | SWE | 7 | 1 | 1 | 2 | 6 | 5th |
| 2004 WM | 8-D | SWE | 9 | 1 | 1 | 2 | 6 | S |
| 2005 WM | 8-D | SWE | 9 | 1 | 1 | 2 | 6 | 4th |
| 2006 OG-M | 8-D | SWE | 8 | 1 | 2 | 3 | 6 | G |
| 2010 WM | 5-D | SWE | 9 | 0 | 3 | 3 | 10 | B |
| **Totals WM20** | | | **13** | **1** | **4** | **5** | **6** | **—** |
| **Totals WM** | | | **27** | **2** | **5** | **7** | **22** | **S,B** |

**Backman, Mattias**
**b. Linkoping, Sweden, October 3, 1992**

| | | | | | | | | |
|---|---|---|---|---|---|---|---|---|
| 2012 WM20 | 5-D | SWE | 6 | 0 | 3 | 3 | 4 | G |

**Backstrom, Nicklas**
**b. Gavle, Sweden, November 23, 1987**

| | | | | | | | | |
|---|---|---|---|---|---|---|---|---|
| 2005 WM18 | 25-F | SWE | 7 | 2 | 3 | 5 | 4 | B |
| 2006 WM20 | 19-F | SWE | 6 | 4 | 3 | 7 | 2 | 5th |
| 2006 WM | 19-F | SWE | 4 | 0 | 0 | 0 | 0 | G |
| 2007 WM20 | 19-F | SWE | 7 | 0 | 7 | 7 | 20 | 4th |
| 2007 WM | 19-F | SWE | 9 | 1 | 5 | 6 | 4 | 4th |
| 2008 WM | 19-F | SWE | 9 | 3 | 4 | 7 | 4 | 4th |
| 2010 OG-M | 19-F | SWE | 4 | 1 | 5 | 6 | 0 | 5th |
| 2012 WM | 19-F | SWE | 2 | 0 | 1 | 1 | 0 | 6th |
| **Totals WM20** | | | **13** | **4** | **10** | **14** | **22** | **—** |
| **Totals WM** | | | **24** | **4** | **10** | **14** | **8** | **G** |

**Bagin, Emil**
**b. Ilava, Slovakia, September 8, 1993**

| | | | | | | | | |
|---|---|---|---|---|---|---|---|---|
| 2011 WM18 | 6-D | SVK | 6 | 0 | 1 | 1 | 8 | 10th |

**Bahensky, Zdenek**
**b. Most, Czechoslovakia (Czech Republic), January 3, 1986**

| | | | | | | | | |
|---|---|---|---|---|---|---|---|---|
| 2004 WM18 | 20-F | CZE | 7 | 1 | 3 | 4 | 2 | B |
| 2006 WM20 | 20-F | CZE | 6 | 0 | 1 | 1 | 10 | 6th |

**Bajaruns, Lauris**
**b. Ventspils, Soviet Union (Latvia), March 31, 1989**

| | | | | | | | | |
|---|---|---|---|---|---|---|---|---|
| 2007 WM18 | 25-F | LAT | 6 | 1 | 0 | 1 | 0 | 10th |
| 2009 WM20 | 25-F | LAT | 6 | 0 | 0 | 0 | 6 | 8th |

**Bakos, Martin**
**b. Spisska Nova Ves, Czechoslovakia (Slovakia), April 18, 1990**

| | | | | | | | | |
|---|---|---|---|---|---|---|---|---|
| 2010 WM20 | 7-F | SVK | 6 | 2 | 2 | 4 | 2 | 8th |

**Bakos, Michael**
**b. Augsburg, West Germany (Germany), March 2, 1979**

| | | | | | | | | |
|---|---|---|---|---|---|---|---|---|
| 1997 WM20 | 6-D | GER | 6 | 0 | 0 | 0 | 12 | 9th |
| 1998 WM20 | 6-D | GER | 6 | 1 | 0 | 1 | 2 | 10th |
| 2005 WM | 25-D | GER | 5 | 0 | 0 | 0 | 0 | 15th |
| 2007 WM | 22-D | GER | 5 | 0 | 2 | 2 | 6 | 9th |
| 2008 WM | 22-D | GER | 6 | 1 | 1 | 2 | 8 | 10th |
| 2009 WM | 22-D | GER | 6 | 1 | 1 | 2 | 6 | 15th |
| 2010 OG-M | 22-D | GER | 4 | 0 | 0 | 0 | 0 | 11th |
| **Totals WM20** | | | **12** | **1** | **0** | **1** | **14** | **—** |
| **Totals WM** | | | **22** | **2** | **4** | **6** | **20** | **—** |

**Balis, Milan**
**b. Bratislava, Czechoslovakia (Slovakia), June 8, 1988**

| | | | | | | | | |
|---|---|---|---|---|---|---|---|---|
| 2006 WM18 | 23-D | SVK | 6 | 1 | 1 | 2 | 10 | 7th |
| 2008 WM20 | 23-D | SVK | 6 | 1 | 2 | 3 | 14 | 7th |

**Balisy, Chase**
**b. Fullerton, California, United States, February 2, 1992**

| | | | | | | | | |
|---|---|---|---|---|---|---|---|---|
| 2010 WM18 | 13-F | USA | 7 | 1 | 2 | 3 | 4 | G |

**Ballard, Keith**
**b. Baudette, Minnesota, United States, November 26, 1982**

| | | | | | | | | |
|---|---|---|---|---|---|---|---|---|
| 2000 WM18 | 2-D | USA | 6 | 1 | 1 | 2 | 4 | 8th |
| 2002 WM20 | 2-D | USA | 7 | 1 | 1 | 2 | 4 | 5th |
| 2004 WM | 31-D | USA | 8 | 1 | 0 | 1 | 2 | B |
| 2007 WM | 44-D | USA | 7 | 0 | 3 | 3 | 16 | 5th |
| 2008 WM | 2-D | USA | 5 | 0 | 2 | 2 | 16 | 6th |
| 2009 WM | 2-D | USA | 9 | 1 | 2 | 3 | 2 | 4th |
| **Totals WM** | | | **29** | **2** | **7** | **9** | **36** | **B** |

**Balmelli, Lukas**
**b. Mendrisio, Switzerland, January 3, 1994**

| | | | | | | | | |
|---|---|---|---|---|---|---|---|---|
| 2011 WM18 | 18-F | SUI | 6 | 0 | 1 | 1 | 2 | 7th |
| 2012 WM18 | 8-F | SUI | 6 | 1 | 1 | 2 | 33 | 7th |
| Totals WM18 | | | 12 | 1 | 2 | 3 | 35 | |

**Baltisberger, Phil**
**b. Zofingen, Switzerland, November 13, 1995**

| | | | | | | | | |
|---|---|---|---|---|---|---|---|---|
| 2012 WM18 | 14-D | SUI | 6 | 0 | 1 | 1 | 8 | 7th |
| 2012 WM20 | 4-D | SUI | 6 | 0 | 0 | 0 | 0 | 8th |

**Bar, Steven**
**b. Mannheim, Germany, May 25, 1993**

| | | | | | | | | |
|---|---|---|---|---|---|---|---|---|
| 2011 WM18 | 10-D | GER | 6 | 0 | 1 | 1 | 8 | 6th |

**Barabanov, Alexander**
**b. St. Petersburg, Russia, June 17, 1994**

| | | | | | | | | |
|---|---|---|---|---|---|---|---|---|
| 2012 WM18 | 21-F | RUS | 6 | 1 | 1 | 2 | 0 | 5th |

**Baranka, Ivan**
**b. Ilava, Czechoslovakia (Slovakia), May 19, 1985**

| | | | | | | | | |
|---|---|---|---|---|---|---|---|---|
| 2003 WM18 | 9-D | SVK | 7 | 1 | 1 | 2 | 8 | S |
| 2004 WM20 | 6-D | SVK | 6 | 1 | 1 | 2 | 8 | 6th |
| 2005 WM20 | 6-D | SVK | 6 | 0 | 2 | 2 | 4 | 7th |
| 2009 WM | 7-D | SVK | 6 | 0 | 1 | 1 | 4 | 10th |
| 2010 OG-M | 7-D | SVK | 7 | 1 | 0 | 1 | 0 | 4th |
| 2011 WM | 7-D | SVK | 6 | 0 | 0 | 0 | 4 | 10th |
| 2012 WM | 7-D | SVK | 10 | 0 | 3 | 3 | 2 | S |
| **Totals WM20** | | | **12** | **1** | **3** | **4** | **12** | **—** |
| **Totals WM** | | | **22** | **0** | **4** | **4** | **10** | **S** |

**Barbashev, Sergei**
**b. Moscow, Russia, July 26, 1992**

| | | | | | | | | |
|---|---|---|---|---|---|---|---|---|
| 2010 WM18 | 22-F | RUS | 7 | 2 | 6 | 8 | 6 | 4th |
| 2012 WM20 | 22-F | RUS | 7 | 0 | 3 | 3 | 0 | S |

**Barber, Riley**
**b. Livonia, Michigan, United States, February 7, 1994**

| | | | | | | | | |
|---|---|---|---|---|---|---|---|---|
| 2012 WM18 | 22-F | USA | 6 | 1 | 2 | 3 | 2 | G |

**Bardreau, Cole**
**b. Fairport, New York, United States, July 22, 1993**

| | | | | | | | | |
|---|---|---|---|---|---|---|---|---|
| 2011 WM18 | 18-F | USA | 6 | 0 | 0 | 0 | 4 | G |

**Barinka, Michal**
**b. Vyskov, Czechoslovakia (Czech Republic), June 12, 1984**

| | | | | | | | | |
|---|---|---|---|---|---|---|---|---|
| 2002 WM18 | 25-D | CZE | 8 | 4 | 2 | 6 | 6 | B |
| 2004 WM20 | 7-D | CZE | 5 | 1 | 1 | 2 | 6 | 4th |
| 2007 WM | 5-D | CZE | 7 | 1 | 2 | 3 | 8 | 7th |
| 2009 WM | 11-D | CZE | 5 | 0 | 0 | 0 | 2 | 6th |
| 2010 WM | 8-D | CZE | 4 | 0 | 0 | 0 | 4 | G |
| **Totals WM** | | | **16** | **1** | **2** | **3** | **14** | **G** |

**Barker, Cam**
**b. Winnipeg, Manitoba, Canada, April 4, 1986**

| | | | | | | | | |
|---|---|---|---|---|---|---|---|---|
| 2005 WM20 | 25-D | CAN | 3 | 1 | 0 | 1 | 4 | G |
| 2006 WM20 | 25-D | CAN | 6 | 2 | 4 | 6 | 18 | G |
| **Totals WM20** | | | **9** | **3** | **4** | **7** | **22** | **2G** |

**Barkov, Aleksander**
**b. Tampere, Finland, September 2, 1995**

| | | | | | | | | |
|---|---|---|---|---|---|---|---|---|
| 2012 WM18 | 9-F | FIN | 7 | 1 | 2 | 3 | 27 | 4th |
| 2012 WM20 | 16-F | FIN | 7 | 1 | 3 | 4 | 0 | 4th |

**Barrie, Tyson**
**b. Victoria, British Columbia, Canada, July 26, 1991**

| | | | | | | | | |
|---|---|---|---|---|---|---|---|---|
| 2011 WM20 | 22-D | CAN | 7 | 1 | 2 | 3 | 0 | S |

**Barta, Alexander**
**b. Berlin, West Germany (Germany), February 2, 1983**

| | | | | | | | | |
|---|---|---|---|---|---|---|---|---|
| 2003 WM20 | 15-F | GER | 6 | 0 | 1 | 1 | 4 | 9th |
| 2005 WM | 29-F | GER | 6 | 1 | 1 | 2 | 2 | 15th |
| 2006 OG-M | 29-F | GER | 5 | 0 | 0 | 0 | 4 | 10th |
| 2007 WM | 29-F | GER | 6 | 2 | 0 | 2 | 4 | 9th |
| 2009 WM | 29-F | GER | 6 | 0 | 0 | 0 | 0 | 15th |
| 2010 WM | 29-F | GER | 9 | 3 | 1 | 4 | 0 | 4th |
| 2011 WM | 29-F | GER | 7 | 2 | 1 | 3 | 0 | 7th |
| 2012 WM | 29-F | GER | 7 | 0 | 0 | 0 | 0 | 12th |
| **Totals WM** | | | **34** | **6** | **2** | **8** | **6** | **—** |

**Bartanus, Marek**
**b. Liptovsky Mikulas, Czechoslovakia (Slovakia), February 13, 1987**

| | | | | | | | | |
|---|---|---|---|---|---|---|---|---|
| 2005 WM18 | 23-F | SVK | 6 | 1 | 1 | 2 | 2 | 6th |
| 2006 WM20 | 23-F | SVK | 5 | 1 | 0 | 1 | 4 | 8th |
| 2007 WM20 | 23-F | SVK | 6 | 1 | 2 | 3 | 8 | 8th |
| **Totals WM20** | | | **11** | **2** | **2** | **4** | **12** | **—** |

**Bartecko, Lubos**
**b. Kezmarok, Czechoslovakia (Slovakia), July 14, 1976**

| | | | | | | | | |
|---|---|---|---|---|---|---|---|---|
| 2000 WM | 23-F | SVK | 7 | 2 | 3 | 5 | 14 | S |
| 2002 OG-M | 23-F | SVK | 4 | 0 | 1 | 1 | 0 | 13th |
| 2002 WM | 23-F | SVK | 9 | 2 | 2 | 4 | 2 | G |
| 2004 WM | 23-F | SVK | 9 | 2 | 2 | 4 | 6 | 4th |
| 2004 WCH | 23-F | SVK | 4 | 0 | 1 | 1 | 2 | 7th |
| 2005 WM | 23-F | SVK | 7 | 0 | 1 | 1 | 4 | 5th |
| 2006 OG-M | 23-F | SVK | 6 | 0 | 0 | 0 | 6 | 5th |
| 2009 WM | 23-F | SVK | 6 | 3 | 0 | 3 | 6 | 10th |
| 2010 OG-M | 23-F | SVK | 7 | 0 | 1 | 1 | 0 | 4th |
| 2011 WM | 23-F | SVK | 4 | 1 | 1 | 2 | 8 | 10th |
| **Totals WM** | | | **42** | **10** | **9** | **19** | **40** | **G,S** |
| **Totals OG-M** | | | **17** | **0** | **2** | **2** | **6** | **—** |

**Bartek, Daniel**
**b. Olomouc, Czechoslovakia (Czech Republic), October 2, 1988**

| | | | | | | | | |
|---|---|---|---|---|---|---|---|---|
| 2008 WM20 | 11-F | CZE | 6 | 2 | 1 | 3 | 0 | 5th |

**Barton, Jaroslav**
**b. Novy Jicin, Czechoslovakia (Czech Republic), March 26, 1987**

| | | | | | | | | |
|---|---|---|---|---|---|---|---|---|
| 2007 WM20 | 15-D | CZE | 6 | 1 | 1 | 2 | 14 | 5th |

**Bartosek, Michal**
**b. Vyskov, Czechoslovakia (Czech Republic), March 18, 1989**

| | | | | | | | | |
|---|---|---|---|---|---|---|---|---|
| 2007 WM18 | 9-F | CZE | 6 | 0 | 0 | 0 | 2 | 9th |

**Bartovic, Milan**
**b. Trencin, Czechoslovakia (Slovakia), April 9, 1981**

| | | | | | | | | |
|---|---|---|---|---|---|---|---|---|
| 1999 WM18 | 10-F | SVK | 7 | 5 | 2 | 7 | 6 | B |
| 2000 WM20 | 28-F | SVK | 7 | 0 | 2 | 2 | 0 | 9th |
| 2001 WM20 | 8-F | SVK | 7 | 1 | 2 | 3 | 6 | 8th |
| 2006 WM | 16-F | SVK | 7 | 2 | 4 | 6 | 8 | 8th |
| 2009 WM | 10-F | SVK | 6 | 0 | 0 | 0 | 2 | 10th |
| 2010 WM | 61-F | SVK | 6 | 2 | 2 | 4 | 2 | 12th |
| 2012 WM | 61-F | SVK | 10 | 3 | 0 | 3 | 6 | S |
| **Totals WM20** | | | **14** | **1** | **4** | **5** | **6** | **—** |
| **Totals WM** | | | **29** | **7** | **6** | **13** | **18** | **S** |

**Bartschi, Patrik**
**b. Bulach, Switzerland, August 20, 1984**

| | | | | | | | | |
|---|---|---|---|---|---|---|---|---|
| 2001 WM18 | 23-F | SUI | 7 | 5 | 2 | 7 | 4 | S |
| 2002 WM18 | 11-F | SUI | 8 | 5 | 4 | 9 | 4 | 7th |
| 2002 WM20 | 11-F | SUI | 7 | 2 | 2 | 4 | 2 | 4th |
| 2003 WM20 | 11-F | SUI | 6 | 6 | 4 | 10 | 0 | 7th |
| 2003 WM | 24-F | SUI | 6 | 1 | 0 | 1 | 0 | 8th |
| 2004 WM20 | 11-F | SUI | 6 | 3 | 5 | 8 | 0 | 8th |
| 2005 WM | 61-F | SUI | 2 | 0 | 0 | 0 | 0 | 8th |
| 2008 WM | 61-F | SUI | 7 | 1 | 2 | 3 | 0 | 7th |
| **Totals WM18** | | | **15** | **10** | **6** | **16** | **8** | **S** |
| **Totals WM20** | | | **19** | **11** | **11** | **22** | **2** | **—** |
| **Totals WM** | | | **15** | **2** | **2** | **4** | **0** | **—** |

**Bartschi, Sven**
**b. Langenthal, Switzerland, October 5, 1992**

| | | | | | | | | |
|---|---|---|---|---|---|---|---|---|
| 2009 WM18 | 27-F | SUI | 6 | 1 | 2 | 3 | 2 | 8th |
| 2010 WM18 | 27-F | SUI | 6 | 1 | 2 | 3 | 2 | 5th |
| 2011 WM20 | 15-F | SUI | 6 | 1 | 1 | 2 | 4 | 5th |
| 2012 WM20 | 15-F | SUI | 2 | 0 | 0 | 0 | 0 | 8th |
| **Totals WM18** | | | **12** | **2** | **4** | **6** | **4** | **—** |
| **Totals WM20** | | | **8** | **1** | **1** | **2** | **4** | **—** |

**Bartulis, Oskars**
**b. Ogre, Soviet Union (Latvia), January 21, 1987**

| | | | | | | | | |
|---|---|---|---|---|---|---|---|---|
| 2005 WM | 15-D | LAT | 1 | 0 | 0 | 0 | 2 | 9th |
| 2006 WM20 | 2-D | LAT | 3 | 0 | 0 | 0 | 0 | 9th |
| 2009 WM | 3-D | LAT | 4 | 0 | 0 | 0 | 0 | 7th |
| 2010 OG-M | 8-D | LAT | 4 | 0 | 0 | 0 | 2 | 12th |
| 2012 WM | 8-D | LAT | 6 | 1 | 2 | 3 | 2 | 10th |
| **Totals WM** | | | **11** | **1** | **2** | **3** | **4** | **—** |

**Bashko, Andrei**
**b. Minsk, Soviet Union (Belarus), May 23, 1982**

| | | | | | | | | |
|---|---|---|---|---|---|---|---|---|
| 2000 WM18 | 29-D | BLR | 6 | 0 | 2 | 2 | 2 | 10th |
| 2001 WM20 | 4-D | BLR | 6 | 0 | 0 | 0 | 2 | 9th |
| 2002 WM20 | 4-D | BLR | 5 | 0 | 0 | 0 | 0 | 9th |
| 2005 WM | 25-D | BLR | 6 | 0 | 1 | 1 | 2 | 10th |
| 2008 WM | 29-D | BLR | 3 | 0 | 0 | 0 | 0 | 9th |
| 2009 WM | 29-D | BLR | 7 | 0 | 1 | 1 | 2 | 8th |
| **Totals WM20** | | | **11** | **0** | **0** | **0** | **2** | **—** |
| **Totals WM** | | | **16** | **0** | **2** | **2** | **4** | **—** |

**Bastiansen, Anders**
**b. Oslo, Norway, October 31, 1980**

| | | | | | | | | |
|---|---|---|---|---|---|---|---|---|
| 2006 WM | 20-F | NOR | 6 | 0 | 2 | 2 | 4 | 11th |
| 2007 WM | 20-F | NOR | 6 | 4 | 1 | 5 | 4 | 14th |
| 2008 WM | 20-F | NOR | 7 | 1 | 5 | 6 | 4 | 8th |
| 2009 WM | 20-F | NOR | 6 | 2 | 1 | 3 | 0 | 11th |
| 2010 OG-M | 20-F | NOR | 4 | 1 | 0 | 1 | 4 | 10th |
| 2010 WM | 20-F | NOR | 6 | 3 | 1 | 4 | 4 | 9th |
| 2011 WM | 20-F | NOR | 7 | 3 | 4 | 7 | 4 | 6th |
| 2012 WM | 20-F | NOR | 8 | 1 | 4 | 5 | 8 | 8th |
| **Totals WM** | | | **46** | **14** | **18** | **32** | **32** | **—** |

**Bau-Hansen, Mathias**
**b. Glostrup, Denmark, July 3, 1993**

| | | | | | | | | |
|---|---|---|---|---|---|---|---|---|
| 2012 WM20 | 13-F | DEN | 5 | 2 | 2 | 4 | 0 | 10th |

**Baumgartner, Gregor**
**b. Kapfenberg, Austria, July 13, 1979**

| | | | | | | | | |
|---|---|---|---|---|---|---|---|---|
| 2000 WM | 28-F | AUT | 6 | 0 | 0 | 0 | 0 | 13th |
| 2007 WM | 67-F | AUT | 6 | 0 | 1 | 1 | 0 | 15th |
| 2009 WM | 79-F | AUT | 6 | 0 | 1 | 1 | 2 | 14th |
| **Totals WM** | | | **18** | **0** | **2** | **2** | **2** | **—** |

**Baur, Oliver**
**b. Wettswil am Albis, Switzerland, April 7, 1990**

| | | | | | | | | |
|---|---|---|---|---|---|---|---|---|
| 2008 WM18 | 19-F | SUI | 6 | 1 | 0 | 1 | 4 | 8th |

**Baxmann, Jens**
**b. Berlin, West Germany (Germnay), March 24, 1985**

| | | | | | | | | |
|---|---|---|---|---|---|---|---|---|
| 2005 WM20 | 29-D | GER | 6 | 0 | 0 | 0 | 8 | 9th |

**Beauchemin, Francois**
**b. Sorel, Quebec, Canada, June 4, 1980**

| | | | | | | | | |
|---|---|---|---|---|---|---|---|---|
| 2010 WM | 22-D | CAN | 7 | 0 | 1 | 1 | 0 | 7th |

**Beaulieu, Nathan**
**b. Strathroy, Ontario, Canada, December 5, 1992**

| | | | | | | | | |
|---|---|---|---|---|---|---|---|---|
| 2012 WM20 | 28-D | CAN | 6 | 0 | 1 | 1 | 16 | B |

**Bednar, Jaroslav**
**b. Prague, Czechoslovakia (Czech Republic), November 9, 1976**

| | | | | | | | | |
|---|---|---|---|---|---|---|---|---|
| 2006 WM | 25-F | CZE | 7 | 0 | 0 | 0 | 0 | S |
| 2007 WM | 25-F | CZE | 7 | 1 | 0 | 1 | 0 | 7th |
| **Totals WM** | | | **14** | **1** | **0** | **1** | **0** | **S** |

**Behal, Jiri**
**b. May 25, 1994**

| | | | | | | | | |
|---|---|---|---|---|---|---|---|---|
| 2012 WM18 | 3-D | CZE | 6 | 0 | 0 | 0 | 2 | 8th |

**Bejmo, Emil**
**b. Karlstad, Sweden, October 10, 1989**

| | | | | | | | | |
|---|---|---|---|---|---|---|---|---|
| 2007 WM18 | 12-F | SWE | 6 | 4 | 2 | 6 | 0 | B |

**Beleskey, Matt**
**b. Windsor, Ontario, Canada, June 7, 1988**

| | | | | | | | | |
|---|---|---|---|---|---|---|---|---|
| 2006 WM18 | 11-F | CAN | 7 | 0 | 1 | 1 | 37 | 4th |

**Belle, Shawn**
**b. Edmonton, Alberta, Canada, January 3, 1985**

| | | | | | | | | |
|---|---|---|---|---|---|---|---|---|
| 2003 WM18 | 5-D | CAN | 7 | 1 | 1 | 2 | 0 | G |
| 2004 WM20 | 37-D | CAN | 6 | 0 | 1 | 1 | 0 | S |
| 2005 WM20 | 4-D | CAN | 6 | 1 | 0 | 1 | 6 | G |
| **Totals WM20** | | | **12** | **1** | **1** | **2** | **6** | **G,S** |

**Bellemare, Pierre-Edouard**
**b. Blanc-Mesnil, France, March 6, 1985**

| | | | | | | | | |
|---|---|---|---|---|---|---|---|---|
| 2004 WM | 41-F | FRA | 3 | 0 | 0 | 0 | 2 | 16th |
| 2008 WM | 41-F | FRA | 5 | 0 | 0 | 0 | 18 | 14th |
| 2009 WM | 41-F | FRA | 6 | 2 | 1 | 3 | 2 | 12th |
| 2010 WM | 41-F | FRA | 6 | 1 | 2 | 3 | 4 | 14th |
| 2011 WM | 41-F | FRA | 6 | 1 | 1 | 2 | 2 | 12th |
| 2012 WM | 41-F | FRA | 5 | 2 | 4 | 6 | 4 | 9th |
| **Totals WM** | | | **31** | **6** | **8** | **14** | **32** | **—** |

**Belov, Anton**
**b. Ryazan, Soviet Union (Russia), July 29, 1986**

| | | | | | | | | |
|---|---|---|---|---|---|---|---|---|
| 2003 WM18 | 6-D | RUS | 5 | 0 | 0 | 0 | 2 | B |
| 2004 WM18 | 3-D | RUS | 6 | 1 | 1 | 2 | 6 | G |
| **Totals WM18** | | | **11** | **1** | **1** | **2** | **8** | |

**Belov, Nikolai**
**b. Moscow, Soviet Union (Russia), August 13, 1987**

| | | | | | | | | |
|---|---|---|---|---|---|---|---|---|
| 2011 WM | 44-D | RUS | 6 | 0 | 0 | 0 | 4 | 4th |

**Bena, Adam**
**b. Skalica, Czechoslovakia (Slovakia), March 14, 1988**

| | | | | | | | | |
|---|---|---|---|---|---|---|---|---|
| 2007 WM20 | 3-D | SVK | 6 | 0 | 0 | 0 | 12 | 8th |
| 2008 WM20 | 17-D | SVK | 6 | 0 | 1 | 1 | 8 | 7th |
| **Totals WM20** | | | **12** | **0** | **1** | **1** | **20** | **—** |

**Bender, Tim**
**b. Mannheim, Germany, March 19, 1995**

| | | | | | | | | |
|---|---|---|---|---|---|---|---|---|
| 2012 WM18 | 8-D | GER | 6 | 2 | 2 | 4 | 2 | 6th |

**Bene, Matej**
**b. Nitra, Slovakia, April 11, 1992**

| 2012 WM20 | 16-F | SVK | 6 | 0 | 1 | 1 | 6 | 6th |
|---|---|---|---|---|---|---|---|---|

**Bengstsson, Rasmus**
**b. Landskrona, Sweden, May 14, 1993**

| 2011 WM18 | 3-D | SWE | 6 | 0 | 4 | 4 | 2 | S |
|---|---|---|---|---|---|---|---|---|

**Benn, Jamie**
**b. Victoria, British Columbia, Canada, July 18, 1989**

| 2009 WM20 | 24-F | CAN | 6 | 4 | 2 | 6 | 4 | G |
|---|---|---|---|---|---|---|---|---|
| 2012 WM | 24-F | CAN | 8 | 3 | 2 | 5 | 4 | 5th |

**Beran, Matej**
**b. Plzen, Czech Republic, November 11, 1993**

| 2011 WM18 | 27-F | CZE | 6 | 0 | 0 | 0 | 2 | 8th |
|---|---|---|---|---|---|---|---|---|

**Beranek, Petr**
**b. Brno, Czech Republic, July 8, 1993**

| 2011 WM18 | 25-F | CZE | 6 | 0 | 0 | 0 | 0 | 8th |
|---|---|---|---|---|---|---|---|---|

**Berdnikov, Roman**
**b. Omsk, Soviet Union (Russia), May 18, 1992**

| 2010 WM18 | 9-F | RUS | 7 | 2 | 4 | 6 | 4 | 4th |
|---|---|---|---|---|---|---|---|---|

**Berdyukov, Georgi**
**b. Khabarovsk, Russia, August 19, 1991**

| 2011 WM20 | 6-D | RUS | 7 | 1 | 2 | 3 | 4 | G |
|---|---|---|---|---|---|---|---|---|

**Bereglazov, Alexei**
**b.Magnitogorsk, Russia, April 20, 1994**

| 2012 WM18 | 5-D | RUS | 6 | 0 | 6 | 6 | 2 | 5th |
|---|---|---|---|---|---|---|---|---|

**Berezin, Maxim**
**b. Izhevsk, Soviet Union (Russia), January 29, 1991**

| 2011 WM20 | 5-D | RUS | 7 | 0 | 3 | 3 | 8 | G |
|---|---|---|---|---|---|---|---|---|

**Bergenheim, Sean**
**b. Helsinki, Finland, February 8, 1984**

| 2001 WM18 | 27-F | FIN | 6 | 3 | 1 | 4 | 8 | B |
|---|---|---|---|---|---|---|---|---|
| 2002 WM18 | 10-F | FIN | 8 | 8 | 4 | 12 | 6 | 4th |
| 2002 WM20 | 10-F | FIN | 7 | 0 | 1 | 1 | 4 | B |
| 2003 WM20 | 10-F | FIN | 7 | 2 | 4 | 6 | 6 | B |
| 2004 WM20 | 10-F | FIN | 7 | 1 | 3 | 4 | 2 | B |
| 2006 WM | 10-F | FIN | 9 | 2 | 1 | 3 | 4 | B |
| 2007 WM | 10-F | FIN | 9 | 1 | 2 | 3 | 31 | S |
| 2008 WM | 20-F | FIN | 4 | 0 | 0 | 0 | 2 | B |
| **Totals WM18** | | | **14** | **11** | **5** | **16** | **14** | **B** |
| **Totals WM20** | | | **21** | **3** | **8** | **11** | **12** | **3B** |
| **Totals WM** | | | **22** | **3** | **3** | **6** | **37** | **S,2B** |

**Berger, Alain**
**b. Burgdorf, Switzerland, December 27, 1990**

| 2008 WM18 | 21-F | SUI | 6 | 2 | 0 | 2 | 6 | 8th |
|---|---|---|---|---|---|---|---|---|

**Berger, Nils**
**b. Niederurnen, Switzerland, January 2, 1991**

| 2009 WM18 | 21-F | SUI | 5 | 1 | 1 | 2 | 4 | 8th |
|---|---|---|---|---|---|---|---|---|

**Berger, Pascal**
**b. Burgdorf, Switzerland, March 24, 1989**

| 2007 WM18 | 10-F | SUI | 6 | 2 | 2 | 4 | 6 | 6th |
|---|---|---|---|---|---|---|---|---|
| 2008 WM20 | 25-F | SUI | 6 | 0 | 0 | 0 | 0 | 9th |

**Bergeron, Patrice**
**b. Ancienne-Lorette, Quebec, Canada, July 24, 1985**

| 2004 WM | 37-F | CAN | 9 | 1 | 0 | 1 | 4 | G |
|---|---|---|---|---|---|---|---|---|
| 2005 WM20 | 37-F | CAN | 6 | 5 | 8 | 13 | 6 | G |
| 2006 WM | 37-F | CAN | 9 | 6 | 8 | 14 | 2 | 4th |
| 2010 OG-M | 37-F | CAN | 7 | 0 | 1 | 1 | 2 | G |
| **Totals WM** | | | **18** | **7** | **8** | **15** | **6** | **G** |

~Triple Gold Club
~WM20 MVP (2005), WM20 All-Star Team/Forward (2005)

**Bergfors, Nicklas**
**b. Sodertalje, Sweden, March 7, 1987**

| 2004 WM18 | 23-F | SWE | 6 | 1 | 2 | 3 | 6 | 5th |
|---|---|---|---|---|---|---|---|---|
| 2005 WM18 | 10-F | SWE | 7 | 6 | 0 | 6 | 0 | B |
| 2005 WM20 | 16-F | SWE | 6 | 2 | 1 | 3 | 2 | 6th |
| 2006 WM20 | 18-F | SWE | 6 | 3 | 3 | 6 | 2 | 5th |
| 2007 WM20 | 18-F | SWE | 7 | 0 | 2 | 2 | 0 | 4th |
| **Totals WM18** | | | **13** | **7** | **2** | **9** | **6** | **B** |
| **Totals WM20** | | | **19** | **5** | **6** | **11** | **4** | **—** |

**Berglind, Victor**
**b. Karlstad, Sweden, October 2, 1992**

| 2010 WM18 | 3-D | SWE | 6 | 0 | 7 | 7 | 4 | S |
|---|---|---|---|---|---|---|---|---|

**Berglund, Kristofer**
**b. Umea, Sweden, August 12, 1988**

| 2006 WM18 | 4-D | SWE | 6 | 0 | 0 | 0 | 2 | 6th |
|---|---|---|---|---|---|---|---|---|
| 2008 WM20 | 4-D | SWE | 6 | 0 | 1 | 1 | 2 | S |

**Berglund, Patrik**
**b. Vasteras, Sweden, June 2, 1988**

| 2006 WM18 | 19-F | SWE | 6 | 4 | 1 | 5 | 2 | 6th |
|---|---|---|---|---|---|---|---|---|
| 2007 WM20 | 15-F | SWE | 7 | 1 | 2 | 3 | 0 | 4th |
| 2008 WM20 | 15-F | SWE | 6 | 3 | 4 | 7 | 14 | S |
| 2009 WM | 14-F | SWE | 7 | 0 | 1 | 1 | 0 | B |
| 2011 WM | 18-F | SWE | 9 | 8 | 2 | 10 | 8 | S |
| **Totals WM20** | | | **13** | **4** | **6** | **10** | **14** | **S** |
| **Totals WM** | | | **16** | **8** | **3** | **11** | **8** | **S,B** |

~WM All-Star Team/Forward (2011), WM20 All-Star Team/Forward (2008)

**Bernard, Anton**
**b. Bolzano, Italy, April 18, 1989**

| 2012 WM | 18-F | ITA | 7 | 0 | 0 | 0 | 2 | 15th |
|---|---|---|---|---|---|---|---|---|

**Bertaggia, Alessio**
**b. Lugano, Switzerland, July 30, 1993**

| 2011 WM18 | 10-F | SUI | 6 | 1 | 2 | 3 | 4 | 7th |
|---|---|---|---|---|---|---|---|---|
| 2012 WM20 | 10-F | SUI | 6 | 1 | 3 | 4 | 2 | 8th |

**Bertilsson, Simon**
**b. Karlskoga, Sweden, April 19, 1991**

| 2009 WM18 | 3-D | SWE | 6 | 0 | 1 | 1 | 6 | 5th |
|---|---|---|---|---|---|---|---|---|
| 2011 WM20 | 15-D | SWE | 6 | 0 | 1 | 1 | 4 | 4th |

**Bertram, Daniel**
**b. Calgary, Alberta, Canada, January 14, 1987**

| 2005 WM18 | 28-F | CAN | 6 | 4 | 0 | 4 | 8 | S |
|---|---|---|---|---|---|---|---|---|
| 2006 WM20 | 22-F | CAN | 6 | 0 | 0 | 0 | 22 | G |
| 2007 WM20 | 22-F | CAN | 6 | 0 | 0 | 0 | 4 | G |
| **Totals WM20** | | | **12** | **0** | **0** | **0** | **26** | **2G** |

**Bertrand, Charles**
**b. Paris, France, February 5, 1991**

| 2012 WM | 26-F | FRA | 7 | 0 | 1 | 1 | 2 | 9th |
|---|---|---|---|---|---|---|---|---|

**Bertschy, Christoph**
**b. Le Mouret, Switzerland, April 5, 1994**

| 2011 WM18 | 26-F | SUI | 6 | 1 | 0 | 1 | 12 | 7th |
|---|---|---|---|---|---|---|---|---|
| 2012 WM20 | 28-F | SUI | 6 | 2 | 2 | 4 | 4 | 8th |

**Berzins, Armands**
**b. Riga, Soviet Union (Latvia), December 27, 1983**

| 2006 OG-M | 21-F | LAT | 5 | 0 | 1 | 1 | 4 | 12th |
|---|---|---|---|---|---|---|---|---|
| 2007 WM | 21-F | LAT | 6 | 1 | 2 | 3 | 10 | 13th |
| 2008 WM | 21-F | LAT | 6 | 0 | 1 | 1 | 8 | 11th |
| 2009 WM | 21-F | LAT | 7 | 0 | 0 | 0 | 4 | 7th |
| 2010 OG-M | 21-F | LAT | 4 | 0 | 1 | 1 | 2 | 12th |
| 2011 WM | 21-F | LAT | 6 | 0 | 2 | 2 | 4 | 13th |
| 2012 WM | 21-F | LAT | 6 | 1 | 1 | 2 | 14 | 10th |
| **Totals WM** | | | **31** | **2** | **6** | **8** | **40** | **—** |
| **Totals OG-M** | | | **9** | **0** | **2** | **2** | **6** | **—** |

**Besch, Nicolas**
**b. Le Havre, France, October 25, 1984**

| 2008 WM | 74-D | FRA | 5 | 0 | 0 | 0 | 6 | 14th |
|---|---|---|---|---|---|---|---|---|
| 2010 WM | 74-D | FRA | 6 | 0 | 1 | 1 | 12 | 14th |
| 2011 WM | 74-D | FRA | 6 | 0 | 0 | 0 | 10 | 12th |
| 2012 WM | 74-D | FRA | 7 | 2 | 0 | 2 | 2 | 9th |
| **Totals WM** | | | **24** | **2** | **1** | **3** | **30** | **—** |

**Beukeboom, Brock**
**b. Uxbridge, Ontario, Canada, April 1, 1992**

| 2010 WM18 | 25-D | CAN | 4 | 0 | 1 | 1 | 2 | 7th |
|---|---|---|---|---|---|---|---|---|

**Bezak, Adam**
**b. Bratislava, Czechoslovakia (Slovakia), July 4, 1989**

| 2006 WM18 | 12-F | SVK | 6 | 0 | 0 | 0 | 2 | 7th |
|---|---|---|---|---|---|---|---|---|
| 2007 WM18 | 12-F | SVK | 6 | 4 | 5 | 9 | 6 | 5th |
| 2009 WM20 | 12-F | SVK | 7 | 4 | 1 | 5 | 6 | 4th |
| **Totals WM18** | | | **12** | **4** | **5** | **9** | **8** | **—** |

**Bezina, Goran**
**b. Split, Yugoslavia (Croatia), March 21, 1980**

| 1999 WM20 | 27-D | SUI | 6 | 1 | 1 | 2 | 2 | 9th |
|---|---|---|---|---|---|---|---|---|
| 2000 WM20 | 13-D | SUI | 7 | 0 | 0 | 0 | 8 | 6th |
| 2001 WM | 13-D | SUI | 6 | 0 | 1 | 1 | 43 | 9th |
| 2003 WM | 13-D | SUI | 6 | 1 | 1 | 2 | 0 | 8th |
| 2004 WM | 57-D | SUI | 7 | 0 | 1 | 1 | 4 | 8th |
| 2005 WM | 57-D | SUI | 7 | 1 | 0 | 1 | 8 | 8th |
| 2006 OG-M | 57-D | SUI | 6 | 0 | 2 | 2 | 0 | 6th |
| 2006 WM | 57-D | SUI | 6 | 2 | 1 | 3 | 4 | 9th |
| 2007 WM | 57-D | SUI | 7 | 1 | 1 | 2 | 6 | 8th |
| 2008 WM | 57-D | SUI | 7 | 0 | 2 | 2 | 6 | 7th |
| 2009 WM | 57-D | SUI | 6 | 0 | 0 | 0 | 6 | 9th |
| 2010 WM | 57-D | SUI | 7 | 0 | 2 | 2 | 16 | 5th |
| 2011 WM | 57-D | SUI | 3 | 1 | 0 | 1 | 4 | 9th |
| 2012 WM | 57-D | SUI | 5 | 1 | 1 | 2 | 29 | 11th |
| **Totals WM20** | | | **13** | **1** | **1** | **2** | **10** | **—** |
| **Totals WM** | | | **67** | **7** | **10** | **17** | **126** | **—** |

**Bezuch, Juraj**
**b. Skalica, Slovakia, December 20, 1993**

| 2011 WM18 | 18-F | SVK | 6 | 0 | 0 | 0 | 0 | 10th |
|---|---|---|---|---|---|---|---|---|

**Bezuska, Peter**
**b. Bojnice, Slovakia, March 30, 1993**

| 2011 WM18 | 5-D | SVK | 6 | 0 | 1 | 1 | 20 | 10th |
|---|---|---|---|---|---|---|---|---|
| 2012 WM20 | 5-D | SVK | 6 | 0 | 0 | 0 | 4 | 6th |

**Bicek, Jiri**
**b. Kosice, Czechoslovakia (Slovakia), December 3, 1978**

| 1996 WM20 | 12-F | SVK | 6 | 2 | 5 | 7 | 4 | 7th |
|---|---|---|---|---|---|---|---|---|
| 1997 WM20 | 12-F | SVK | 6 | 2 | 1 | 3 | 4 | 6th |
| 1997 WM | 26-F | SVK | 8 | 1 | 0 | 1 | 4 | 9th |
| 2009 WM | 4-F | SVK | 6 | 0 | 0 | 0 | 2 | 10th |
| **Totals WM20** | | | **12** | **4** | **6** | **10** | **8** | **—** |
| **Totals WM** | | | **14** | **1** | **0** | **1** | **6** | **—** |

**Bieber, Matthias**
**b. Zurich, Switzerland, March 14, 1986**

| 2005 WM20 | 14-F | SUI | 6 | 0 | 0 | 0 | 2 | 8th |
|---|---|---|---|---|---|---|---|---|
| 2006 WM20 | 14-F | SUI | 6 | 0 | 7 | 7 | 10 | 7th |
| 2011 WM | 44-F | SUI | 6 | 0 | 1 | 1 | 2 | 9th |
| 2012 WM | 48-F | SUI | 7 | 0 | 1 | 1 | 4 | 11th |
| **Totals WM20** | | | **12** | **0** | **7** | **7** | **12** | **—** |
| **Totals WM** | | | **13** | **0** | **2** | **2** | **6** | **—** |

**Bielke, Dominik**
**b. Berlin, West Germany (Germany), October 23, 1990**

| 2008 WM18 | 27-D | GER | 6 | 0 | 1 | 1 | 12 | 5th |
|---|---|---|---|---|---|---|---|---|
| 2009 WM20 | 29-D | GER | 6 | 0 | 0 | 0 | 4 | 9th |

**Biersack, Tobias**
**b. Garmisch-Partenkirchen, West Germany (Germany), March 20, 1990**

| 2008 WM18 | 26-F | GER | 6 | 1 | 0 | 1 | 4 | 5th |
|---|---|---|---|---|---|---|---|---|

**Biggs, Tyler**
**b. Cincinnati, Ohio, United States, April 30, 1993**

| 2010 WM18 | 4-F | USA | 7 | 0 | 0 | 0 | 4 | G |
|---|---|---|---|---|---|---|---|---|
| 2011 WM18 | 22-F | USA | 6 | 2 | 1 | 3 | 49 | G |
| **Totals WM18** | | | **13** | **2** | **1** | **3** | **53** | **2G** |

**Bigler, Emil**
**b. Gladsaxe, Denmark, July 3, 1988**

| 2008 WM20 | 6-D | DEN | 5 | 0 | 0 | 0 | 0 | 10th |
|---|---|---|---|---|---|---|---|---|

**Bires, Andrej**
**b. Banska Bystrica, Slovakia, November 19, 1993**

| 2011 WM18 | 7-F | SVK | 6 | 1 | 0 | 1 | 4 | 10th |
|---|---|---|---|---|---|---|---|---|

**Birner, Michal**
**b. Litomerice, Czechoslovakia (Czech Republic), March 2, 1986**

| 2004 WM18 | 16-F | CZE | 7 | 3 | 2 | 5 | 8 | B |
|---|---|---|---|---|---|---|---|---|
| 2006 WM20 | 16-F | CZE | 6 | 0 | 2 | 2 | 4 | 6th |

**Biro, Marek**
**b. Banska Bystrica, Czechoslovakia (Slovakia), February 8, 1988**

| 2005 WM18 | 2-D | SVK | 6 | 0 | 0 | 0 | 2 | 6th |
|---|---|---|---|---|---|---|---|---|
| 2006 WM18 | 13-D | SVK | 6 | 0 | 2 | 2 | 16 | 7th |
| 2008 WM20 | 8-D | SVK | 6 | 0 | 1 | 1 | 12 | 7th |
| **Totals WM18** | | | **12** | **0** | **2** | **2** | **18** | **—** |

**Biryukov, Igor**
**b. Moscow, Soviet Union (Russia), September 25, 1990**

| | | | | | | | | |
|---|---|---|---|---|---|---|---|---|
| 2008 WM18 | 25-F | RUS | 6 | 1 | 0 | 1 | 8 | S |

**Biryukov, Yevgeni**
**b. Kasli, Soviet Union (Russia), April 19, 1986**

| | | | | | | | | |
|---|---|---|---|---|---|---|---|---|
| 2004 WM18 | 15-D | RUS | 6 | 0 | 0 | 0 | 4 | G |
| 2006 WM20 | 15-D | RUS | 6 | 0 | 4 | 4 | 6 | S |
| 2012 WM | 48-D | RUS | 7 | 1 | 3 | 4 | 4 | G |

**Birzins, Ricards**
**b. Riga, Soviet Union (Latvia), April 24, 1989**

| | | | | | | | | |
|---|---|---|---|---|---|---|---|---|
| 2007 WM18 | 7-D | LAT | 6 | 0 | 0 | 0 | 6 | 10th |

**Bittner, Dominik**
**b. Weilheim, Germany, June 10, 1992**

| | | | | | | | | |
|---|---|---|---|---|---|---|---|---|
| 2011 WM20 | 7-D | GER | 6 | 0 | 1 | 1 | 6 | 10th |

**Bjerrum, Rasmus**
**b. Esbjerg, Denmark, April 20, 1992**

| | | | | | | | | |
|---|---|---|---|---|---|---|---|---|
| 2012 WM20 | 25-F | DEN | 6 | 0 | 0 | 0 | 0 | 10th |

**Bjorklund, Gustav**
**b. Huddinge, Sweden, February 23, 1993**

| | | | | | | | | |
|---|---|---|---|---|---|---|---|---|
| 2011 WM18 | 11-F | SWE | 6 | 5 | 3 | 8 | 0 | S |

**Bjorklund, Henrik**
**b. Karlstad, Sweden, September 22, 1990**

| | | | | | | | | |
|---|---|---|---|---|---|---|---|---|
| 2007 WM18 | 20-F | SWE | 6 | 0 | 0 | 0 | 0 | B |
| 2008 WM18 | 13-F | SWE | 6 | 2 | 2 | 4 | 4 | 4th |
| **Totals WM18** | | | **12** | **2** | **2** | **4** | **4** | **B** |

**Bjorkstrand, Oliver**
**b. Herning, Denmark, April 10, 1995**

| | | | | | | | | |
|---|---|---|---|---|---|---|---|---|
| 2012 WM18 | 13-F | DEN | 6 | 4 | 3 | 7 | 0 | 10th |
| 2012 WM20 | 12-F | DEN | 6 | 2 | 0 | 2 | 0 | 10th |

**Bjorkstrand, Patrick**
**b. Herning, Denmark, July 1, 1992**

| | | | | | | | | |
|---|---|---|---|---|---|---|---|---|
| 2012 WM20 | 11-F | DEN | 6 | 1 | 5 | 6 | 4 | 10th |

**Bjorsland, Martin**
**b. Fredrikstad, Norway, August 15, 1993**

| | | | | | | | | |
|---|---|---|---|---|---|---|---|---|
| 2011 WM18 | 5-D | NOR | 6 | 0 | 0 | 0 | 4 | 9th |

**Bjugstad, Nick**
**b. Coon Rapids, Minnesota, United States, July 17, 1992**

| | | | | | | | | |
|---|---|---|---|---|---|---|---|---|
| 2011 WM20 | 27-F | USA | 6 | 2 | 2 | 4 | 0 | B |
| 2012 WM20 | 27-F | USA | 6 | 4 | 2 | 6 | 0 | 7th |
| Totals WM20 | | | 12 | 6 | 4 | 10 | 0 | B |

**Blake, Jason**
**b. Moorhead, Minnesota, United States, September 2, 1973**

| | | | | | | | | |
|---|---|---|---|---|---|---|---|---|
| 2000 WM | 55-F | USA | 7 | 1 | 1 | 2 | 2 | 5th |
| 2004 WCH | 55-F | USA | 4 | 1 | 0 | 1 | 2 | 4th |
| 2006 OG-M | 55-F | USA | 6 | 0 | 0 | 0 | 2 | 8th |
| 2009 WM | 55-F | USA | 9 | 1 | 3 | 4 | 4 | 4th |
| **Totals WM** | | | **16** | **2** | **4** | **6** | **6** | **—** |

**Blank, Sachar**
**b. Karaganda, Soviet Union (Kazakhstan), July 10, 1985**

| | | | | | | | | |
|---|---|---|---|---|---|---|---|---|
| 2005 WM20 | 23-F | GER | 6 | 0 | 2 | 2 | 10 | 9th |

**Blaser, Yannick**
**b. Langnau, Switzerland, April 1, 1989**

| | | | | | | | | |
|---|---|---|---|---|---|---|---|---|
| 2007 WM18 | 2-D | SUI | 6 | 1 | 0 | 1 | 6 | 6th |

**Blatak, Miroslav**
**b. Gottwaldov (Zlin), Czechoslovakia (Czech Republic), May 25, 1982**

| | | | | | | | | |
|---|---|---|---|---|---|---|---|---|
| 2000 WM18 | 7-D | CZE | 6 | 0 | 1 | 1 | 4 | 6th |
| 2002 WM20 | 11-D | CZE | 7 | 3 | 4 | 7 | 2 | 7th |
| 2009 WM | 44-D | CZE | 7 | 3 | 1 | 4 | 8 | 6th |
| 2010 OG-M | 44-D | CZE | 5 | 0 | 2 | 2 | 2 | 7th |
| 2010 WM | 44-D | CZE | 9 | 2 | 1 | 3 | 4 | G |
| 2012 WM | 44-D | CZE | 10 | 1 | 1 | 2 | 0 | B |
| **Totals WM** | | | **26** | **6** | **3** | **9** | **12** | **G,B** |

**Blindenbacher, Severin**
**b. Zurich, Switzerland, March 15, 1983**

| | | | | | | | | |
|---|---|---|---|---|---|---|---|---|
| 2000 WM18 | 8-D | SUI | 7 | 0 | 0 | 0 | 8 | 4th |
| 2001 WM18 | 6-D | SUI | 7 | 2 | 3 | 5 | 10 | S |
| 2001 WM20 | 5-D | SUI | 7 | 0 | 0 | 0 | 10 | 6th |
| 2002 WM20 | 5-D | SUI | 7 | 0 | 0 | 0 | 4 | 4th |
| 2003 WM20 | 5-D | SUI | 6 | 2 | 3 | 5 | 4 | 7th |
| 2003 WM | 10-D | SUI | 7 | 0 | 1 | 1 | 0 | 8th |
| 2005 WM | 5-D | SUI | 6 | 1 | 1 | 2 | 12 | 8th |
| 2006 OG-M | 5-D | SUI | 6 | 0 | 1 | 1 | 6 | 6th |
| 2006 WM | 5-D | SUI | 5 | 0 | 2 | 2 | 12 | 9th |
| 2007 WM | 5-D | SUI | 7 | 0 | 1 | 1 | 2 | 8th |
| 2008 WM | 5-D | SUI | 6 | 0 | 3 | 3 | 2 | 7th |
| 2009 WM | 5-D | SUI | 6 | 0 | 2 | 2 | 6 | 9th |
| 2010 OG-M | 5-D | SUI | 5 | 1 | 1 | 2 | 4 | 8th |
| 2012 WM | 5-D | SUI | 7 | 0 | 3 | 3 | 2 | 11th |
| **Totals WM18** | | | **14** | **2** | **3** | **5** | **18** | **S** |
| **Totals WM20** | | | **20** | **2** | **3** | **5** | **18** | **—** |
| **Totals WM** | | | **44** | **1** | **13** | **14** | **36** | **—** |
| **Totals OG-M** | | | **11** | **1** | **2** | **3** | **10** | **—** |

**Blinovs, Viktors**
**b. Riga, Soviet Union (Latvia), June 26, 1981**

| | | | | | | | | |
|---|---|---|---|---|---|---|---|---|
| 2002 WM | 11-F | LAT | 6 | 0 | 0 | 0 | 0 | 11th |
| 2006 WM | 9-F | LAT | 6 | 1 | 0 | 1 | 2 | 10th |
| 2008 WM | 8-F | LAT | 3 | 0 | 0 | 0 | 2 | 11th |
| **Totals WM** | | | **15** | **1** | **0** | **1** | **4** | **—** |

**Bliznak, Mario**
**b. Trencin, Czechoslovakia (Slovakia), March 6, 1987**

| | | | | | | | | |
|---|---|---|---|---|---|---|---|---|
| 2005 WM18 | 20-F | SVK | 6 | 1 | 0 | 1 | 0 | 6th |
| 2007 WM20 | 13-F | SVK | 6 | 1 | 0 | 1 | 4 | 8th |
| 2012 WM | 55-F | SVK | 10 | 0 | 3 | 3 | 2 | S |

**Blokh, Roman**
**b. Grodno, Soviet Union (Belarus), November 22, 1986**

| | | | | | | | | |
|---|---|---|---|---|---|---|---|---|
| 2003 WM18 | 16-F | BLR | 6 | 0 | 1 | 1 | 0 | 8th |
| 2004 WM18 | 9-F | BLR | 6 | 2 | 0 | 2 | 10 | 9th |
| 2005 WM20 | 13-F | BLR | 6 | 0 | 0 | 0 | 2 | 10th |
| **Totals WM18** | | | **12** | **2** | **1** | **3** | **10** | |

**Blomkvist, Albin**
**b. Kristianstad, Sweden, January 8, 1993**

| | | | | | | | | |
|---|---|---|---|---|---|---|---|---|
| 2011 WM18 | 4-D | SWE | 6 | 1 | 1 | 2 | 10 | S |

**Blomstrand, Ludwig**
**b. Uppsala, Sweden, March 8, 1993**

| | | | | | | | | |
|---|---|---|---|---|---|---|---|---|
| 2011 WM18 | 15-F | SWE | 6 | 0 | 0 | 0 | 0 | S |

**Blugers, Teodors**
**b. Riga, Latvia, August 15, 1994**

| | | | | | | | | |
|---|---|---|---|---|---|---|---|---|
| 2012 WM18 | 21-F | LAT | 6 | 2 | 2 | 4 | 6 | 9th |
| 2012 WM20 | 21-F | LAT | 6 | 1 | 2 | 3 | 2 | 9th |

**Blum, Eric**
**b. Pfaffnau, Switzerland, June 13, 1986**

| | | | | | | | | |
|---|---|---|---|---|---|---|---|---|
| 2006 WM20 | 3-D | SUI | 6 | 2 | 3 | 5 | 4 | 7th |

**Blum, Jonathon**
**b. Rancho Santa Margarita, California, United States, January 30, 1989**

| | | | | | | | | |
|---|---|---|---|---|---|---|---|---|
| 2008 WM20 | 24-D | USA | 6 | 0 | 1 | 1 | 0 | 4th |
| 2009 WM20 | 24-D | USA | 6 | 2 | 2 | 4 | 0 | 5th |
| **Totals WM20** | | | **12** | **2** | **3** | **5** | **0** | **—** |

**Blunden, Michael**
**b. Toronto, Ontario, Canada, December 15, 1986**

| | | | | | | | | |
|---|---|---|---|---|---|---|---|---|
| 2006 WM20 | 21-F | CAN | 6 | 2 | 3 | 5 | 8 | G |

**Bobocky, Miroslav**
**b. Topolcany, Czechoslovakia (Slovakia), September 23, 1991**

| | | | | | | | | |
|---|---|---|---|---|---|---|---|---|
| 2009 WM18 | 4-F | SVK | 6 | 1 | 0 | 1 | 4 | 7th |

**Bocharov, Stanislav**
**b. Khabarovsk, Soviet Union (Russia), June 20, 1991**

| | | | | | | | | |
|---|---|---|---|---|---|---|---|---|
| 2011 WM20 | 18-F | RUS | 7 | 0 | 2 | 2 | 2 | G |

**Bochenski, Brandon**
**b. Blaine, Minnesota, United States, April 4, 1982**

| | | | | | | | | |
|---|---|---|---|---|---|---|---|---|
| 2007 WM | 10-F | USA | 7 | 2 | 3 | 5 | 6 | 5th |

**Bochkaryov, Konstantin**
**b. Kazan, Soviet Union (Russia), August 10, 1991**

| | | | | | | | | |
|---|---|---|---|---|---|---|---|---|
| 2009 WM18 | 21-D | RUS | 7 | 0 | 0 | 0 | 6 | S |

**Bodker, Mads**
**b. Copenhagen, Denmark, August 31, 1987**

| | | | | | | | | |
|---|---|---|---|---|---|---|---|---|
| 2004 WM18 | 5-D | DEN | 6 | 0 | 0 | 0 | 12 | 8th |
| 2005 WM18 | 4-D | DEN | 6 | 1 | 1 | 2 | 6 | 10th |
| 2006 WM | 4-D | DEN | 5 | 1 | 0 | 1 | 4 | 13th |
| 2007 WM | 4-D | DEN | 6 | 0 | 0 | 0 | 0 | 10th |
| 2008 WM | 4-D | DEN | 6 | 0 | 0 | 0 | 0 | 12th |
| 2009 WM | 4-D | DEN | 6 | 0 | 0 | 0 | 2 | 13th |
| 2010 WM | 4-D | DEN | 7 | 0 | 1 | 1 | 2 | 8th |
| 2011 WM | 4-D | DEN | 6 | 1 | 1 | 2 | 0 | 11th |
| 2012 WM | 4-D | DEN | 7 | 0 | 0 | 0 | 0 | 13th |
| **Totals WM18** | | | **12** | **1** | **1** | **2** | **18** | **—** |
| **Totals WM** | | | **43** | **2** | **2** | **4** | **8** | **—** |

**Bodker, Mikkel**
**b. Brondby, Denmark, December 16, 1989**

| | | | | | | | | |
|---|---|---|---|---|---|---|---|---|
| 2005 WM18 | 16-F | DEN | 6 | 1 | 1 | 2 | 6 | 10th |
| 2008 WM20 | 8-F | DEN | 6 | 2 | 4 | 6 | 2 | 10th |
| 2009 WM | 89-F | DEN | 6 | 3 | 1 | 4 | 4 | 13th |
| 2011 WM | 89-F | DEN | 6 | 3 | 1 | 4 | 2 | 11th |
| **Totals WM** | | | **12** | **6** | **2** | **8** | **6** | **—** |

**Bodrov, Denis**
**b. Moscow, Soviet Union (Russia), August 22, 1986**

| | | | | | | | | |
|---|---|---|---|---|---|---|---|---|
| 2006 WM20 | 23-D | RUS | 6 | 0 | 3 | 3 | 2 | S |

**Bodrov, Yevgeni**
**b. Togliatti, Soviet Union (Russia), January 8, 1988**

| | | | | | | | | |
|---|---|---|---|---|---|---|---|---|
| 2006 WM18 | 26-F | RUS | 6 | 2 | 2 | 4 | 14 | 5th |
| 2008 WM20 | 10-F | RUS | 7 | 1 | 3 | 4 | 6 | B |

**Bogner, Julian**
**b. Straubing, West Germany (Germany), March 4, 1991**

| | | | | | | | | |
|---|---|---|---|---|---|---|---|---|
| 2009 WM18 | 26-F | GER | 6 | 1 | 2 | 3 | 2 | 10th |

**Bogoleisha, Sergei**
**b. Grodno, Soviet Union (Belarus), February 20, 1990**

| | | | | | | | | |
|---|---|---|---|---|---|---|---|---|
| 2008 WM18 | 5-D | BLR | 6 | 0 | 0 | 0 | 18 | 9th |

**Bogosian, Zach**
**b. Massena, New York, United States, July 15, 1990**

| | | | | | | | | |
|---|---|---|---|---|---|---|---|---|
| 2009 WM | 4-D | USA | 9 | 0 | 1 | 1 | 2 | 4th |

**Bolf, Lukas**
**b. Vrchlabi, Czechoslovakia (Czech Republic), February 20, 1985**

| | | | | | | | | |
|---|---|---|---|---|---|---|---|---|
| 2003 WM18 | 6-D | CZE | 6 | 1 | 2 | 3 | 30 | 6th |
| 2005 WM20 | 10-D | CZE | 7 | 0 | 4 | 4 | 8 | B |

**Bolland, David**
**b. Toronto, Ontario, Canada, June 5, 1986**

| | | | | | | | | |
|---|---|---|---|---|---|---|---|---|
| 2006 WM20 | 19-F | CAN | 6 | 3 | 2 | 5 | 14 | G |

**Boltun, Peter**
**b. Michalovce, Slovakia, January 2, 1993**

| | | | | | | | | |
|---|---|---|---|---|---|---|---|---|
| 2011 WM18 | 17-F | SVK | 6 | 1 | 1 | 2 | 4 | 10th |

**Bolyakin, Yevgeni**
**b. Karaganda, Soviet Union (Kazakhstan), April 20, 1990**

| | | | | | | | | |
|---|---|---|---|---|---|---|---|---|
| 2008 WM20 | 14-D | KAZ | 6 | 0 | 1 | 1 | 8 | 8th |
| 2009 WM20 | 14-D | KAZ | 6 | 0 | 0 | 0 | 4 | 10th |
| **Totals WM20** | | | **12** | **0** | **1** | **1** | **12** | **—** |

**Bondra, David**
**b. Annapolis, Maryland, United States, August 26, 1992**

| | | | | | | | | |
|---|---|---|---|---|---|---|---|---|
| 2010 WM18 | 29-F | SVK | 6 | 0 | 3 | 3 | 16 | 8th |

**Bonnet, Jerome**
**b. Lois, Switzerland, September 9, 1987**

| | | | | | | | | |
|---|---|---|---|---|---|---|---|---|
| 2007 WM20 | 28-F | SUI | 6 | 0 | 0 | 0 | 4 | 7th |

**Bonsaksen, Alexander**
**b. Oslo, Norway, January 24, 1987**

| | | | | | | | | |
|---|---|---|---|---|---|---|---|---|
| 2006 WM20 | 25-D | NOR | 6 | 0 | 0 | 0 | 20 | 10th |
| 2009 WM | 47-D | NOR | 6 | 0 | 0 | 0 | 4 | 11th |
| 2010 OG-M | 47-D | NOR | 4 | 0 | 0 | 0 | 2 | 10th |
| 2010 WM | 47-D | NOR | 6 | 0 | 0 | 0 | 6 | 9th |
| 2011 WM | 47-D | NOR | 7 | 0 | 2 | 2 | 6 | 6th |
| 2012 WM | 47-D | NOR | 8 | 0 | 1 | 1 | 0 | 8th |
| **Totals WM** | | | **27** | **0** | **3** | **3** | **16** | **—** |

**Booth, David**
**b. Detroit, Michigan, United States, November 24, 1984**

| | | | | | | | | |
|---|---|---|---|---|---|---|---|---|
| 2002 WM18 | 7-F | USA | 8 | 2 | 2 | 4 | 10 | G |
| 2004 WM20 | 21-F | USA | 6 | 0 | 1 | 1 | 2 | G |
| 2008 WM | 7-F | USA | 7 | 1 | 0 | 1 | 2 | 6th |

**Bordeleau, Sebastien**
**b. Vancouver, British Columbia, February 15, 1975**

| 2004 WM | 71-F | FRA | 5 | 0 | 0 | 0 | 4 | 16th |
|---|---|---|---|---|---|---|---|---|
| 2008 WM | 71-F | FRA | 5 | 2 | 4 | 6 | 6 | 14th |
| **Totals WM** | | | **10** | **2** | **4** | **6** | **10** | **—** |

**Borer, Casey**
**b. Minneapolis, Minnesota, United States, July 28, 1985**

| 2003 WM18 | 23-D | USA | 6 | 0 | 0 | 0 | 2 | 4th |
|---|---|---|---|---|---|---|---|---|
| 2005 WM20 | 6-D | USA | 6 | 0 | 0 | 0 | 6 | 4th |

**Borgatello, Christian**
**b. Merano, Italy, February 10, 1982**

| 2002 WM | 30-F | ITA | 6 | 0 | 1 | 1 | 0 | 15th |
|---|---|---|---|---|---|---|---|---|
| 2006 OG-M | 50-D | ITA | 5 | 1 | 0 | 1 | 4 | 11th |
| 2006 WM | 50-D | ITA | 6 | 1 | 1 | 2 | 4 | 14th |
| 2007 WM | 50-D | ITA | 6 | 1 | 1 | 2 | 4 | 12th |
| 2008 WM | 50-D | ITA | 5 | 0 | 1 | 1 | 2 | 16th |
| 2010 WM | 50-D | ITA | 6 | 1 | 1 | 2 | 2 | 15th |
| 2012 WM | 50-D | ITA | 1 | 0 | 0 | 0 | 0 | 15th |
| **Totals WM** | | | **30** | **3** | **5** | **8** | **12** | **—** |

**Borge, Henrik**
**b. Sarpsborg, Norway, October 13, 1986**

| 2006 WM20 | 6-D | NOR | 6 | 0 | 0 | 0 | 6 | 10th |
|---|---|---|---|---|---|---|---|---|

**Borovansky, Michal**
**b. Prague, Czechoslovakia (Czech Republic), March 15, 1985**

| 2005 WM20 | 24-F | CZE | 6 | 0 | 0 | 0 | 2 | B |
|---|---|---|---|---|---|---|---|---|

**Borovkov, Alexander**
**b. Moscow, Soviet Union (Russia), January 28, 1982**

| 2007 WM | 45-F | BLR | 6 | 0 | 0 | 0 | 2 | 11th |
|---|---|---|---|---|---|---|---|---|

**Borresen, Eirik**
**b. Vang, Norway, August 7, 1991**

| 2009 WM18 | 24-F | NOR | 4 | 0 | 0 | 0 | 0 | 9th |
|---|---|---|---|---|---|---|---|---|
| 2011 WM20 | 14-F | NOR | 6 | 1 | 0 | 1 | 0 | 9th |

**Bortnak, Dalibor**
**b. Presov, Czechoslovakia (Slovakia), February 17, 1991**

| 2009 WM18 | 20-F | SVK | 5 | 1 | 1 | 2 | 4 | 7th |
|---|---|---|---|---|---|---|---|---|
| 2011 WM20 | 19-F | SVK | 6 | 0 | 2 | 2 | 8 | 8th |

**Boruta, Antonin**
**b. Zlin, Czechoslovakia (Czech Republic), October 26, 1988**

| 2008 WM20 | 15-D | CZE | 6 | 1 | 1 | 2 | 0 | 5th |
|---|---|---|---|---|---|---|---|---|

**Boucher, Reid**
**b. Grand Ledge, Michigan, United States, September 8, 1993**

| 2011 WM18 | 14-F | USA | 6 | 8 | 2 | 10 | 8 | G |
|---|---|---|---|---|---|---|---|---|

**Bourke, Troy**
**b. Onoway, Alberta, Canada, March 30, 1994**

| 2012 WM18 | 19-F | CAN | 7 | 0 | 7 | 7 | 2 | B |
|---|---|---|---|---|---|---|---|---|

**Bournival, Michael**
**b. Shawinigan, Quebec, Canada, May 31, 1992**

| 2010 WM18 | 15-F | CAN | 6 | 2 | 1 | 3 | 2 | 7th |
|---|---|---|---|---|---|---|---|---|
| 2012 WM20 | 10-F | CAN | 6 | 0 | 1 | 1 | 0 | B |

**Bourque, Chris**
**b. Boston, Massachusetts, United States, January 29, 1986**

| 2005 WM20 | 27-F | USA | 3 | 1 | 1 | 2 | 0 | 4th |
|---|---|---|---|---|---|---|---|---|
| 2006 WM20 | 27-F | USA | 7 | 7 | 1 | 8 | 12 | 4th |
| **Totals WM20** | | | **10** | **8** | **2** | **10** | **12** | **—** |

**Bourque, Gabriel**
**b. Rimouski, Quebec, Canada, September 23, 1990**

| 2010 WM20 | 7-F | CAN | 6 | 3 | 6 | 9 | 4 | S |
|---|---|---|---|---|---|---|---|---|

**Bourque, Rene**
**b. Lac La Biche, Alberta, Canada, December 10, 1981**

| 2010 WM | 17-F | CAN | 7 | 1 | 1 | 2 | 14 | 7th |
|---|---|---|---|---|---|---|---|---|

**Bourque, Ryan**
**b. Boxford, Massachusetts, United States, January 3, 1991**

| 2008 WM18 | 17-F | USA | 7 | 2 | 3 | 5 | 4 | B |
|---|---|---|---|---|---|---|---|---|
| 2009 WM18 | 17-F | USA | 7 | 1 | 6 | 7 | 12 | G |
| 2010 WM20 | 17-F | USA | 7 | 0 | 3 | 3 | 8 | G |
| 2011 WM20 | 17-F | USA | 6 | 0 | 3 | 3 | 4 | B |
| **Totals WM18** | | | **14** | **3** | **9** | **12** | **16** | **G,B** |
| **Totals WM20** | | | **13** | **0** | **6** | **6** | **12** | **G,B** |

**Bouwmeester, Jay**
**b. Edmonton, Alberta, Canada, September 27, 1983**

| 2000 WM20 | 3-D | CAN | 7 | 0 | 0 | 0 | 2 | B |
|---|---|---|---|---|---|---|---|---|
| 2001 WM20 | 4-D | CAN | 7 | 0 | 2 | 2 | 6 | B |
| 2002 WM20 | 4-D | CAN | 7 | 0 | 2 | 2 | 10 | S |
| 2003 WM | 4-D | CAN | 9 | 3 | 4 | 7 | 4 | G |
| 2004 WM | 4-D | CAN | 9 | 2 | 1 | 3 | 0 | G |
| 2004 WCH | 3-D | CAN | 4 | 0 | 0 | 0 | 0 | 1st |
| 2006 OG-M | 3-D | CAN | 6 | 0 | 0 | 0 | 0 | 7th |
| 2008 WM | 4-D | CAN | 9 | 0 | 0 | 0 | 4 | S |
| 2012 WM | 4-D | CAN | 8 | 0 | 2 | 2 | 0 | 5th |
| **Totals WM20** | | | **21** | **0** | **4** | **4** | **18** | **S,2B** |
| **Totals WM** | | | **35** | **5** | **7** | **12** | **8** | **2G,S** |

~WM IIHF Directorate Best Defenceman (2003), WM All-Star Team/Defence (2003), WM20 All-Star Team/Defence (2002)

**Bowman, Drayson**
**b. Littleton, Colorado, United States, March 8, 1989**

| 2009 WM20 | 27-F | USA | 6 | 3 | 1 | 4 | 6 | 5th |
|---|---|---|---|---|---|---|---|---|

**Boychuk, Zac**
**b. Airdrie, Alberta, Canada, October 4, 1989**

| 2007 WM18 | 14-F | CAN | 6 | 4 | 3 | 7 | 4 | 4th |
|---|---|---|---|---|---|---|---|---|
| 2008 WM20 | 11-F | CAN | 7 | 0 | 0 | 0 | 2 | G |
| 2009 WM20 | 11-F | CAN | 6 | 4 | 3 | 7 | 0 | G |
| **Totals WM20** | | | **13** | **4** | **3** | **7** | **2** | **2G** |

**Boyce Rotevall, Jeremy**
**b. Stockholm, Sweden, August 28, 1993**

| 2011 WM18 | 14-F | SWE | 6 | 4 | 2 | 6 | 12 | S |
|---|---|---|---|---|---|---|---|---|
| 2012 WM20 | 11-F | SWE | 6 | 0 | 0 | 0 | 2 | G |

**Boyd, Dustin**
**b. Winnipeg, Manitoba, Canada, July 16, 1986**

| 2006 WM20 | 16-F | CAN | 6 | 4 | 2 | 6 | 0 | G |
|---|---|---|---|---|---|---|---|---|

**Boyd, Travis**
**b. Hopkins, Minnesota, United States, September 14, 1993**

| 2011 WM18 | 26-F | USA | 6 | 2 | 4 | 6 | 2 | G |
|---|---|---|---|---|---|---|---|---|

**Boyes, Brad**
**b. Mississauga, Ontario, Canada, April 17, 1982**

| 2001 WM20 | 34-F | CAN | 7 | 1 | 3 | 4 | 2 | B |
|---|---|---|---|---|---|---|---|---|
| 2002 WM20 | 17-F | CAN | 7 | 5 | 4 | 9 | 16 | S |
| 2006 WM | 26-F | CAN | 9 | 4 | 4 | 8 | 4 | 7th |
| **Totals WM20** | | | **14** | **6** | **7** | **13** | **18** | **S,B** |

**Boyle, Dan**
**b. Ottawa, Ontario, Canada, July 12, 1976**

| 2005 WM | 27-D | CAN | 9 | 0 | 3 | 3 | 6 | S |
|---|---|---|---|---|---|---|---|---|
| 2010 OG-M | 22-D | CAN | 7 | 1 | 5 | 6 | 2 | G |

**Bozic, Dennis**
**b. Sodertalje, Sweden, August 2, 1990**

| 2008 WM18 | 8-D | SWE | 6 | 1 | 2 | 3 | 4 | 4th |
|---|---|---|---|---|---|---|---|---|

**Brandi, Nicola**
**b. March 2, 1994**

| 2012 WM18 | 12-F | SUI | 6 | 1 | 1 | 2 | 29 | 7th |
|---|---|---|---|---|---|---|---|---|

**Brandl, Thomas**
**b. Landshut, West Germany (Germany), February 8, 1991**

| 2009 WM18 | 11-F | GER | 6 | 1 | 4 | 5 | 6 | 10th |
|---|---|---|---|---|---|---|---|---|
| 2011 WM20 | 11-F | GER | 6 | 0 | 1 | 1 | 4 | 10th |

**Brassard, Austen**
**b. Windsor, Ontario, Canada, March 14, 1993**

| 2011 WM18 | 10-F | CAN | 7 | 0 | 1 | 1 | 2 | 4th |
|---|---|---|---|---|---|---|---|---|

**Braun, Constantin**
**b. Lampertheim, West Germany (Germany), March 11, 1988**

| 2005 WM18 | 9-F | GER | 6 | 1 | 2 | 3 | 12 | 8th |
|---|---|---|---|---|---|---|---|---|
| 2006 WM18 | 20-F | GER | 6 | 3 | 3 | 6 | 4 | 8th |
| 2007 WM20 | 20-F | GER | 6 | 1 | 0 | 1 | 18 | 9th |
| 2010 WM | 90-D | GER | 9 | 0 | 0 | 0 | 4 | 4th |
| 2011 WM | 90-D | GER | 7 | 0 | 2 | 2 | 4 | 7th |
| **Totals WM18** | | | **12** | **4** | **5** | **9** | **16** | **—** |

**Braun, Justin**
**b. Vadnais Heights, Minnesota, United States, February 10, 1987**

| 2012 WM | 20-D | USA | 8 | 0 | 0 | 0 | 2 | 7th |
|---|---|---|---|---|---|---|---|---|

**Braun, Laurin**
**b. Lampertheim, West Germany (Germany), March 11, 1988**

| 2009 WM18 | 18-F | GER | 6 | 2 | 2 | 4 | 6 | 10th |
|---|---|---|---|---|---|---|---|---|
| 2011 WM20 | 18-F | GER | 6 | 0 | 0 | 0 | 2 | 10th |

**Brehmer, Anton**
**b. Orebro, Sweden, February 6, 1994**

| 2012 WM18 | 17-F | SWE | 6 | 0 | 0 | 0 | 4 | S |
|---|---|---|---|---|---|---|---|---|

**Breitbach, Robin**
**b. Hamburg, West Germany (Germany), March 5, 1982**

| 1999 WM18 | 3-D | GER | 4 | 0 | 2 | 2 | 6 | 9th |
|---|---|---|---|---|---|---|---|---|
| 2000 WM18 | 10-D | GER | 6 | 0 | 3 | 3 | 10 | 7th |
| 2007 WM | 25-D | GER | 5 | 0 | 0 | 0 | 8 | 9th |
| **Totals WM18** | | | **10** | **0** | **5** | **5** | **16** | **—** |

**Brejcak, Jan**
**b. Poprad, Czechoslovakia (Slovakia), June 29, 1989**

| 2009 WM20 | 19-D | SVK | 7 | 0 | 0 | 0 | 6 | 4th |
|---|---|---|---|---|---|---|---|---|

**Brekke, Simen**
**b. Oslo, Norway, October 19, 1991**

| 2009 WM18 | 21-F | NOR | 4 | 0 | 1 | 1 | 2 | 9th |
|---|---|---|---|---|---|---|---|---|
| 2011 WM20 | 28-F | NOR | 6 | 0 | 1 | 1 | 2 | 9th |

***Bremberg, Fredrik**
**b. Malmo, Sweden, June 21, 1973**

| 1993 WM20 | 23-F | SWE | 7 | 5 | 3 | 8 | 2 | S |
|---|---|---|---|---|---|---|---|---|
| 2000 WM | 23-F | SWE | 6 | 1 | 1 | 2 | 0 | 7th |
| 2007 WM | 23-F | SWE | 8 | 2 | 4 | 6 | 8 | 4th |

*played 1993 WM20 and 2000 WM as Fredrik Lindquist

**Brent, Tim**
**b. Cambridge, Ontario, Canada, March 10, 1984**

| 2004 WM20 | 8-F | CAN | 6 | 1 | 2 | 3 | 4 | S |
|---|---|---|---|---|---|---|---|---|

**Brewer, Eric**
**b. Kamloops, British Columbia, Canada, April 17, 1979**

| 1998 WM20 | 3-D | CAN | 7 | 0 | 2 | 2 | 8 | 8th |
|---|---|---|---|---|---|---|---|---|
| 2001 WM | 2-D | CAN | 7 | 0 | 2 | 2 | 6 | 5th |
| 2002 OG-M | 3-D | CAN | 6 | 2 | 0 | 2 | 0 | G |
| 2002 WM | 2-D | CAN | 7 | 2 | 3 | 5 | 4 | 6th |
| 2003 WM | 2-D | CAN | 9 | 1 | 2 | 3 | 8 | G |
| 2004 WM | 2-D | CAN | 9 | 1 | 1 | 2 | 6 | G |
| 2004 WCH | 2-D | CAN | 6 | 1 | 3 | 4 | 4 | 1st |
| 2007 WM | 4-D | CAN | 9 | 1 | 3 | 4 | 6 | G |
| **Totals WM** | | | **41** | **5** | **11** | **16** | **30** | **3G** |

**Brickley, Connor**
**b. Everett, Massachusetts, United States, February 25, 1992**

| 2010 WM18 | 20-F | USA | 7 | 0 | 4 | 4 | 4 | G |
|---|---|---|---|---|---|---|---|---|
| 2012 WM20 | 23-F | USA | 3 | 0 | 0 | 0 | 0 | 7th |

**Brittain, Josh**
**b. Milton, Ontario, Canada, January 3, 1990**

| 2008 WM18 | 27-F | CAN | 7 | 0 | 1 | 1 | 4 | G |
|---|---|---|---|---|---|---|---|---|

**Brnak, Tomas**
**b. Povazska Bystrica, Czechoslovakia (Slovakia), April 20, 1987**

| 2005 WM18 | 4-D | SVK | 6 | 0 | 1 | 1 | 4 | 6th |
|---|---|---|---|---|---|---|---|---|
| 2007 WM20 | 9-D | SVK | 6 | 0 | 2 | 2 | 2 | 8th |

**Brodersen, Morten**
**b. Aarhus, Denmark, March 16, 1994**

| 2012 WM18 | 16-F | DEN | 6 | 0 | 1 | 1 | 27 | 10th |
|---|---|---|---|---|---|---|---|---|

**Brodin, Daniel**
**b. Stockholm, Sweden, February 9, 1990**

| 2010 WM20 | 26-F | SWE | 6 | 3 | 2 | 5 | 6 | B |
|---|---|---|---|---|---|---|---|---|

**Brodin, Jonas**
**b. Karlstad, Sweden, July 12, 1993**

| | | | | | | | | |
|---|---|---|---|---|---|---|---|---|
| 2010 WM18 | 4-D | SWE | 6 | 0 | 2 | 2 | 0 | S |
| 2011 WM18 | 2-D | SWE | 4 | 0 | 1 | 1 | 2 | S |
| 2012 WM20 | 25-D | SWE | 6 | 0 | 4 | 4 | 14 | G |
| 2012 WM | 28-D | SWE | 7 | 1 | 0 | 1 | 0 | 6th |
| **Totals WM18** | | | **10** | **0** | **3** | **3** | **2** | **2S** |

**Brown, Chris**
**b. Flower Mound, Texas, United States, February 3, 1991**

| | | | | | | | | |
|---|---|---|---|---|---|---|---|---|
| 2009 WM18 | 12-F | USA | 7 | 4 | 3 | 7 | 8 | G |
| 2011 WM20 | 10-F | USA | 6 | 2 | 1 | 3 | 4 | B |

**Brown, Dustin**
**b. Ithaca, New York, United States, November 4, 1984**

| | | | | | | | | |
|---|---|---|---|---|---|---|---|---|
| 2002 WM20 | 23-F | USA | 7 | 1 | 3 | 4 | 10 | 5th |
| 2003 WM20 | 23-F | USA | 7 | 2 | 2 | 4 | 10 | 4th |
| 2004 WM | 9-F | USA | 9 | 1 | 3 | 4 | 4 | B |
| 2006 WM | 23-F | USA | 7 | 5 | 2 | 7 | 10 | 7th |
| 2008 WM | 23-F | USA | 7 | 5 | 4 | 9 | 22 | 6th |
| 2009 WM | 23-F | USA | 9 | 3 | 5 | 8 | 8 | 4th |
| 2010 OG-M | 32-F | USA | 6 | 0 | 0 | 0 | 0 | S |
| **Totals WM20** | | | **14** | **3** | **5** | **8** | **20** | **—** |
| **Totals WM** | | | **32** | **14** | **14** | **28** | **44** | **B** |

**Brown, J.T. (Joshua Thomas)**
**b. Burnsville, Minnesota, United States, July 2, 1990**

| | | | | | | | | |
|---|---|---|---|---|---|---|---|---|
| 2012 WM | 23-F | USA | 6 | 1 | 1 | 2 | 0 | 7th |

**Brown, Mike**
**b. Northbrook, Illinois, United States, June 24, 1985**

| | | | | | | | | |
|---|---|---|---|---|---|---|---|---|
| 2005 WM20 | 13-F | USA | 7 | 1 | 1 | 2 | 2 | 4th |
| 2011 WM | 18-F | USA | 7 | 0 | 0 | 0 | 0 | 8th |

**Bruckner, Benedikt**
**b. Marktoberdorf, Germany, January 1, 1990**

| | | | | | | | | |
|---|---|---|---|---|---|---|---|---|
| 2007 WM18 | 7-D | GER | 6 | 0 | 0 | 0 | 4 | 8th |
| 2008 WM18 | 20-D | GER | 6 | 0 | 2 | 2 | 4 | 5th |
| 2009 WM20 | 20-D | GER | 6 | 0 | 0 | 0 | 2 | 9th |
| **Totals WM18** | | | **12** | **0** | **2** | **2** | **8** | **—** |

**Brunner, Damien**
**b. Zurich, Switzerland, March 9, 1986**

| | | | | | | | | |
|---|---|---|---|---|---|---|---|---|
| 2010 WM | 96-F | SUI | 7 | 1 | 4 | 5 | 2 | 5th |
| 2012 WM | 96-F | SUI | 7 | 3 | 4 | 7 | 6 | 11th |
| **Totals WM** | | | **14** | **4** | **8** | **12** | **8** | **—** |

**Bryhnisveen, Nicolai**
**b. Oslo, Norway, October 31, 1991**

| | | | | | | | | |
|---|---|---|---|---|---|---|---|---|
| 2009 WM18 | 5-D | NOR | 6 | 0 | 2 | 2 | 18 | 9th |
| 2011 WM20 | 3-D | NOR | 6 | 0 | 0 | 0 | 16 | 9th |

**Brykun, Kirill**
**b. Vitebsk, Soviet Union (Belarus), September 17, 1990**

| | | | | | | | | |
|---|---|---|---|---|---|---|---|---|
| 2008 WM18 | 11-F | BLR | 6 | 0 | 1 | 1 | 10 | 9th |

**Brylin, Sergei**
**b. Moscow, Soviet Union (Russia), January 13, 1974**

| | | | | | | | | |
|---|---|---|---|---|---|---|---|---|
| 1993 WM20 | 17-F | RUS | 7 | 3 | 3 | 6 | 6 | 6th |
| 1994 WM20 | 13-F | RUS | 7 | 1 | 5 | 6 | 0 | B |
| 1996 WM | 21-F | RUS | 8 | 3 | 2 | 5 | 12 | 4th |
| 2007 WM | 18-F | RUS | 2 | 0 | 0 | 0 | 0 | B |
| **Totals WM20** | | | **14** | **4** | **8** | **12** | **6** | **B** |
| **Totals WM** | | | **10** | **3** | **2** | **5** | **12** | **B** |

**Bubela, Milos**
**b. Banska Bystrica, Slovakia, August 25, 1992**

| | | | | | | | | |
|---|---|---|---|---|---|---|---|---|
| 2012 WM20 | 22-F | SVK | 6 | 2 | 3 | 5 | 4 | 6th |

**Buc, David**
**b. Piestany, Czechoslovakia (Slovakia), January 22, 1987**

| | | | | | | | | |
|---|---|---|---|---|---|---|---|---|
| 2005 WM18 | 22-F | SVK | 6 | 0 | 0 | 0 | 0 | 6th |
| 2007 WM20 | 18-F | SVK | 6 | 1 | 3 | 4 | 2 | 8th |

**Bukarts, Rihards**
**b. Jurmala, Latvia, December 31, 1995**

| | | | | | | | | |
|---|---|---|---|---|---|---|---|---|
| 2012 WM18 | 10-F | LAT | 6 | 0 | 5 | 5 | 2 | 9th |

**Bukarts, Roberts**
**b. Jurmala, Soviet Union (Latvia), June 27, 1990**

| | | | | | | | | |
|---|---|---|---|---|---|---|---|---|
| 2007 WM18 | 11-F | LAT | 6 | 1 | 3 | 4 | 0 | 10th |
| 2009 WM20 | 11-F | LAT | 6 | 4 | 2 | 6 | 10 | 8th |
| 2010 WM20 | 11-F | LAT | 6 | 6 | 1 | 7 | 4 | 9th |
| 2011 WM | 9-F | LAT | 6 | 3 | 0 | 3 | 2 | 13th |
| 2012 WM | 9-F | LAT | 3 | 0 | 0 | 0 | 0 | 10th |
| **Totals WM20** | | | **12** | **10** | **3** | **13** | **14** | **—** |
| **Totals WM** | | | **9** | **3** | **0** | **3** | **2** | **—** |

**Bulik, Tomas**
**b. Presov, Czechoslovakia (Slovakia), August 27, 1985**

| | | | | | | | | |
|---|---|---|---|---|---|---|---|---|
| 2003 WM18 | 17-F | SVK | 7 | 2 | 2 | 4 | 0 | S |
| 2004 WM20 | 11-F | SVK | 6 | 0 | 3 | 3 | 2 | 6th |
| 2005 WM20 | 11-F | SVK | 6 | 2 | 3 | 5 | 20 | 7th |
| 2010 WM | 88-F | SVK | 6 | 0 | 0 | 0 | 4 | 12th |
| **Totals WM20** | | | **12** | **2** | **6** | **8** | **22** | **—** |

**Bulis, Jan**
**b. Pardubice, Czechoslovakia (Czech Republic), March 18, 1978**

| | | | | | | | | |
|---|---|---|---|---|---|---|---|---|
| 2006 OG-M | 38-F | CZE | 8 | 0 | 0 | 0 | 10 | B |
| 2006 WM | 38-F | CZE | 9 | 0 | 0 | 0 | 0 | S |

**Bullitis, Eduards**
**b. Riga, Soviet Union (Latvia), January 14, 1986**

| | | | | | | | | |
|---|---|---|---|---|---|---|---|---|
| 2006 WM20 | 25-F | LAT | 6 | 1 | 1 | 2 | 8 | 9th |

**Bumagin, Alexander**
**b. Togliatti, Soviet Union (Russia), March 1, 1987**

| | | | | | | | | |
|---|---|---|---|---|---|---|---|---|
| 2005 WM18 | 18-F | RUS | 6 | 2 | 1 | 3 | 6 | 5th |
| 2007 WM20 | 29-F | RUS | 6 | 2 | 6 | 8 | 16 | S |

**Bumagin, Yevgeni**
**b. Belgorod, Soviet Union (Russia), April 7, 1982**

| | | | | | | | | |
|---|---|---|---|---|---|---|---|---|
| 2010 WM | 27-F | KAZ | 6 | 0 | 0 | 0 | 2 | 16th |
| 2012 WM | 27-F | KAZ | 7 | 0 | 0 | 0 | 6 | 16th |
| **Totals WM** | | | **13** | **0** | **0** | **0** | **8** | **—** |

**Burakowsky, Andre**
**b. Klagenfurt, Austria, February 9, 1995**

| | | | | | | | | |
|---|---|---|---|---|---|---|---|---|
| 2012 WM18 | 24-F | SWE | 6 | 0 | 3 | 3 | 0 | S |

**Buravchikov, Vyacheslav**
**b. Moscow, Soviet Union (Russia), May 22, 1987**

| | | | | | | | | |
|---|---|---|---|---|---|---|---|---|
| 2005 WM18 | 9-D | RUS | 6 | 3 | 4 | 7 | 4 | 5th |
| 2006 WM20 | 21-D | RUS | 6 | 0 | 2 | 2 | 4 | S |
| 2007 WM20 | 9-D | RUS | 6 | 2 | 2 | 4 | 2 | S |
| **Totals WM20** | | | **12** | **2** | **4** | **6** | **6** | **2S** |

**Burdasov, Anton**
**b. Chelyabinsk, Soviet Union (Russia), May 9, 1991**

| | | | | | | | | |
|---|---|---|---|---|---|---|---|---|
| 2011 WM20 | 7-F | RUS | 7 | 0 | 1 | 1 | 6 | G |

**Burgler, Dario**
**b. Illgau, Switzerland, December 18, 1987**

| | | | | | | | | |
|---|---|---|---|---|---|---|---|---|
| 2005 WM18 | 17-F | SUI | 6 | 1 | 0 | 1 | 4 | 9th |
| 2006 WM20 | 17-F | SUI | 6 | 2 | 1 | 3 | 6 | 7th |
| 2007 WM20 | 17-F | SUI | 6 | 1 | 2 | 3 | 8 | 7th |
| **Totals WM20** | | | **12** | **3** | **3** | **6** | **14** | **—** |

**Burish, Adam**
**b. Madison, Wisconsin, United States, January 6, 1983**

| | | | | | | | | |
|---|---|---|---|---|---|---|---|---|
| 2008 WM | 37-F | USA | 7 | 0 | 3 | 3 | 27 | 6th |

**Burmistrov, Alexander**
**b. Kazan, Soviet Union (Russia), October 21, 1991**

| | | | | | | | | |
|---|---|---|---|---|---|---|---|---|
| 2009 WM18 | 8-F | RUS | 7 | 4 | 7 | 11 | 6 | S |
| 2010 WM20 | 8-F | RUS | 6 | 3 | 1 | 4 | 6 | 6th |

**Burns, Brent**
**b. Ajax, Ontario, Canada, March 9, 1985**

| | | | | | | | | |
|---|---|---|---|---|---|---|---|---|
| 2004 WM20 | 22-F | CAN | 6 | 0 | 6 | 6 | 20 | S |
| 2008 WM | 8-D | CAN | 9 | 3 | 6 | 9 | 16 | S |
| 2010 WM | 8-D | CAN | 7 | 0 | 5 | 5 | 12 | 7th |
| 2011 WM | 8-D | CAN | 7 | 2 | 2 | 4 | 8 | 5th |
| **Totals WM** | | | **23** | **5** | **13** | **18** | **36** | **S** |

~WM IIHF Directorate Best Defenceman (2008)

**Burrows, Alexandre**
**b. Pincourt, Quebec, Canada, April 11, 1981**

| | | | | | | | | |
|---|---|---|---|---|---|---|---|---|
| 2012 WM | 41-F | CAN | 5 | 3 | 0 | 3 | 2 | 5th |

**Busch, Florian**
**b. Tegernsee, West Germany (Germany), January 2, 1985**

| | | | | | | | | |
|---|---|---|---|---|---|---|---|---|
| 2005 WM20 | 26-F | GER | 6 | 1 | 1 | 2 | 14 | 9th |
| 2006 OG-M | 46-F | GER | 5 | 0 | 0 | 0 | 6 | 10th |
| 2007 WM | 46-F | GER | 6 | 1 | 0 | 1 | 4 | 9th |
| 2008 WM | 46-F | GER | 6 | 2 | 3 | 5 | 0 | 10th |
| **Totals WM** | | | **12** | **3** | **3** | **6** | **4** | **—** |

**Busser, Xeno**
**b. Zurich, Switzerland, April 30, 1995**

| | | | | | | | | |
|---|---|---|---|---|---|---|---|---|
| 2012 WM18 | 27-D | SUI | 6 | 1 | 3 | 4 | 4 | 7th |

**Bustreo, Paolo**
**b. Feltre, Italy, March 29, 1983**

| | | | | | | | | |
|---|---|---|---|---|---|---|---|---|
| 2006 WM | 18-F | ITA | 6 | 0 | 0 | 0 | 2 | 14th |
| 2007 WM | 18-F | ITA | 2 | 0 | 0 | 0 | 4 | 12th |
| 2008 WM | 18-F | ITA | 5 | 0 | 1 | 1 | 4 | 16th |
| **Totals WM** | | | **13** | **0** | **1** | **1** | **10** | **—** |

**Butcher, Will**
**b. Sun Prairie, Wisconsin, United States, January 6, 1995**

| | | | | | | | | |
|---|---|---|---|---|---|---|---|---|
| 2012 WM18 | 6-D | USA | 6 | 0 | 0 | 0 | 2 | G |

**Butenschon, Sven**
**b. Itzehoe, West Germany (Germany), March 22, 1976**

| | | | | | | | | |
|---|---|---|---|---|---|---|---|---|
| 2009 WM | 6-D | GER | 6 | 0 | 2 | 2 | 2 | 15th |
| 2010 OG-M | 6-D | GER | 4 | 0 | 0 | 0 | 2 | 11th |
| 2010 WM | 6-D | GER | 7 | 0 | 0 | 0 | 2 | 4th |
| **Totals WM** | | | **13** | **0** | **2** | **2** | **4** | **—** |

**Butler, Chris**
**b. St. Louis, Missouri, United States, October 27, 1986**

| | | | | | | | | |
|---|---|---|---|---|---|---|---|---|
| 2006 WM20 | 4-D | USA | 4 | 0 | 0 | 0 | 2 | 4th |
| 2012 WM | 34-D | USA | 8 | 1 | 1 | 2 | 0 | 7th |

**Buzas, Patrick**
**b. Augsburg, West Germany (Germany), May 17, 1987**

| | | | | | | | | |
|---|---|---|---|---|---|---|---|---|
| 2007 WM20 | 11-F | GER | 6 | 0 | 0 | 0 | 4 | 9th |

**Buzats, Kristaps**
**b. Liepaja, Soviet Union (Latvia), January 4, 1989**

| | | | | | | | | |
|---|---|---|---|---|---|---|---|---|
| 2007 WM18 | 12-D | LAT | 6 | 0 | 1 | 1 | 4 | 10th |

**Bykov, Andrei**
**b. Moscow, Soviet Union (Russia), February 10, 1988**

| | | | | | | | | |
|---|---|---|---|---|---|---|---|---|
| 2007 WM20 | 19-F | SUI | 6 | 1 | 0 | 1 | 6 | 7th |
| 2008 WM20 | 19-F | SUI | 5 | 1 | 3 | 4 | 4 | 9th |
| **Totals WM20** | | | **11** | **2** | **3** | **5** | **10** | **—** |

**Bystrom, Ludwig**
**b. Ornskoldsvik, Sweden, July 20, 1994**

| | | | | | | | | |
|---|---|---|---|---|---|---|---|---|
| 2012 WM18 | 28-D | SWE | 6 | 0 | 1 | 1 | 2 | S |

**Cajanek, Petr**
**b. Gottwaldov (Zlin), Czechoslovakia (Czech Republic), August 18, 1975**

| | | | | | | | | |
|---|---|---|---|---|---|---|---|---|
| 1995 WM20 | 18-F | CZE | 7 | 3 | 5 | 8 | 68 | 5th |
| 2000 WM | 16-F | CZE | 9 | 1 | 3 | 4 | 2 | G |
| 2001 WM | 16-F | CZE | 9 | 2 | 6 | 8 | 4 | G |
| 2002 OG-M | 16-F | CZE | 4 | 0 | 0 | 0 | 0 | 7th |
| 2002 WM | 16-F | CZE | 7 | 3 | 2 | 5 | 2 | 5th |
| 2004 WCH | 16-F | CZE | 4 | 1 | 2 | 3 | 0 | 3rd |
| 2005 WM | 16-F | CZE | 9 | 2 | 2 | 4 | 8 | G |
| 2006 OG-M | 16-F | CZE | 7 | 1 | 0 | 1 | 4 | B |
| 2007 WM | 16-F | CZE | 6 | 0 | 2 | 2 | 12 | 7th |
| 2009 WM | 16-F | CZE | 7 | 5 | 5 | 10 | 10 | 6th |
| 2010 OG-M | 16-F | CZE | 5 | 0 | 0 | 0 | 6 | 7th |
| **Totals WM** | | | **47** | **13** | **20** | **33** | **38** | **3G** |
| **Totals OG-M** | | | **16** | **1** | **0** | **1** | **10** | **B** |

**Cajkovsky, Michal**
**b. Skalica, Czechoslovakia (Slovakia), May 6, 1992**

| | | | | | | | | |
|---|---|---|---|---|---|---|---|---|
| 2010 WM18 | 28-D | SVK | 6 | 0 | 0 | 0 | 6 | 8th |
| 2012 WM20 | 11-D | SVK | 6 | 0 | 0 | 0 | 12 | 6th |

**Caladi, Erik**
**b. Nitra, Czechoslovakia (Slovakia), April 1, 1988**

| | | | | | | | | |
|---|---|---|---|---|---|---|---|---|
| 2006 WM18 | 18-F | SVK | 6 | 1 | 1 | 2 | 8 | 7th |
| 2008 WM20 | 18-F | SVK | 6 | 4 | 2 | 6 | 0 | 7th |

**Callahan, Mitch**
**b. Whittier, California, August 17, 1991**

| | | | | | | | | |
|---|---|---|---|---|---|---|---|---|
| 2011 WM20 | 24-F | USA | 6 | 1 | 0 | 1 | 2 | B |

**Callahan, Ryan**
**b. Rochester, New York, United States, March 21, 1985**

| | | | | | | | | |
|---|---|---|---|---|---|---|---|---|
| 2005 WM20 | 24-F | USA | 7 | 1 | 2 | 3 | 29 | 4th |
| 2010 OG-M | 24-F | USA | 6 | 0 | 1 | 1 | 2 | S |

**Camichel, Duri**
**b. Samedan, Switzerland, May 6, 1982**

| | | | | | | | | |
|---|---|---|---|---|---|---|---|---|
| 2000 WM18 | 24-F | SUI | 7 | 2 | 2 | 4 | 6 | 4th |
| 2001 WM20 | 24-F | SUI | 7 | 0 | 1 | 1 | 12 | 6th |
| 2007 WM | 24-F | SUI | 7 | 0 | 1 | 1 | 0 | 8th |

**Cammalleri, Mike**
**b. Richmond Hill, Ontario, Canada, June 8, 1982**

| | | | | | | | | |
|---|---|---|---|---|---|---|---|---|
| 2001 WM20 | 29-F | CAN | 7 | 4 | 2 | 6 | 2 | B |
| 2002 WM20 | 13-F | CAN | 7 | 7 | 4 | 11 | 10 | S |
| 2006 WM | 13-F | CAN | 8 | 1 | 4 | 5 | 4 | 4th |
| 2007 WM | 13-F | CAN | 9 | 4 | 3 | 7 | 6 | G |
| **Totals WM20** | | | **14** | **11** | **6** | **17** | **12** | **S,B** |
| **Totals WM** | | | **17** | **5** | **7** | **12** | **10** | **G** |

~WM20 IIHF Directorate Best Forward (2002), WM20 All-Star Team/Forward (2002)

**Camperchioli, Luca**
**b. Basel, Switzerland, January 22, 1991**

| | | | | | | | | |
|---|---|---|---|---|---|---|---|---|
| 2009 WM18 | 11-D | SUI | 5 | 0 | 1 | 1 | 6 | 8th |
| 2010 WM20 | 2-D | SUI | 7 | 0 | 0 | 0 | 6 | 4th |
| 2011 WM20 | 7-D | SUI | 6 | 2 | 0 | 2 | 6 | 5th |
| **Totals WM20** | | | **13** | **2** | **0** | **2** | **12** | **—** |

**Carciola, Fabio**
**b. Kassel, West Germany (Germany), August 25, 1985**

| | | | | | | | | |
|---|---|---|---|---|---|---|---|---|
| 2005 WM20 | 16-F | GER | 6 | 1 | 1 | 2 | 4 | 9th |

**Carle, Matt**
**b. Anchorage, Alaska, United States, September 25, 1984**

| | | | | | | | | |
|---|---|---|---|---|---|---|---|---|
| 2002 WM18 | 5-D | USA | 8 | 0 | 3 | 3 | 2 | G |
| 2004 WM20 | 4-D | USA | 6 | 1 | 0 | 1 | 4 | G |

**Carlsen, Nicklas**
**b. Fredriksberg, Denmark, September 20, 1990**

| | | | | | | | | |
|---|---|---|---|---|---|---|---|---|
| 2008 WM18 | 23-F | DEN | 6 | 1 | 0 | 1 | 0 | 10th |

**Carlson, Dan**
**b. Corcoran, Minnesota, United States, May 14, 1993**

| | | | | | | | | |
|---|---|---|---|---|---|---|---|---|
| 2011 WM18 | 25-F | USA | 6 | 1 | 1 | 2 | 2 | G |

**Carlson, John**
**b. Natick, Massachusetts, United States, January 10, 1990**

| | | | | | | | | |
|---|---|---|---|---|---|---|---|---|
| 2010 WM20 | 11-D | USA | 7 | 4 | 3 | 7 | 2 | G |

~WM20 All-Star Team/Defence (2010)

**Carlsson, Jonathan**
**b. Uppsala, Sweden, August 5, 1988**

| | | | | | | | | |
|---|---|---|---|---|---|---|---|---|
| 2008 WM20 | 7-D | SWE | 6 | 1 | 1 | 2 | 2 | S |

**Carman, Mike**
**b. Apple Valley, Minnesota, United States, April 14, 1988**

| | | | | | | | | |
|---|---|---|---|---|---|---|---|---|
| 2006 WM18 | 20-F | USA | 6 | 4 | 4 | 8 | 10 | G |
| 2007 WM20 | 16-F | USA | 7 | 1 | 0 | 1 | 4 | B |
| 2008 WM20 | 19-F | USA | 6 | 2 | 1 | 3 | 10 | 4th |
| **Totals WM20** | | | **13** | **3** | **1** | **4** | **14** | **B** |

**Caron, Jordan**
**b. Sayabec, Quebec, Canada, November 2, 1990**

| | | | | | | | | |
|---|---|---|---|---|---|---|---|---|
| 2010 WM20 | 26-F | CAN | 6 | 0 | 4 | 4 | 6 | S |

**Carrick, Connor**
**b. Orland Park, Illinois, United States, April 13, 1994**

| | | | | | | | | |
|---|---|---|---|---|---|---|---|---|
| 2012 WM18 | 24-D | USA | 6 | 2 | 2 | 4 | 2 | G |

**Carrier, William**
**b. Pierrefonds, Quebec, Canada, December 20, 1994**

| | | | | | | | | |
|---|---|---|---|---|---|---|---|---|
| 2012 WM18 | 25-F | CAN | 7 | 0 | 0 | 0 | 0 | B |

**Carter, Jeff**
**b. London, Ontario, Canada, January 1, 1985**

| | | | | | | | | |
|---|---|---|---|---|---|---|---|---|
| 2003 WM18 | 17-F | CAN | 7 | 2 | 4 | 6 | 2 | G |
| 2004 WM20 | 9-F | CAN | 6 | 5 | 2 | 7 | 2 | S |
| 2005 WM20 | 7-F | CAN | 6 | 7 | 3 | 10 | 6 | G |
| 2006 WM | 7-F | CAN | 9 | 4 | 2 | 6 | 2 | 4th |
| **Totals WM20** | | | **12** | **12** | **5** | **17** | **8** | **G,S** |

~WM20 All-Star Team/Forward (2004, 2005)

**Carter, Ryan**
**b. White Bear Lake, Minnesota, United States, August 3, 1983**

| | | | | | | | | |
|---|---|---|---|---|---|---|---|---|
| 2010 WM | 22-F | USA | 6 | 1 | 1 | 2 | 4 | 13th |

**Caslava, Petr**
**b. Kolin, Czechoslovakia (Czech Republic), September 3, 1979**

| | | | | | | | | |
|---|---|---|---|---|---|---|---|---|
| 1999 WM20 | 7-D | CZE | 6 | 0 | 2 | 2 | 4 | 7th |
| 2007 WM | 36-D | CZE | 7 | 2 | 0 | 2 | 6 | 7th |
| 2008 WM | 36-D | CZE | 7 | 0 | 0 | 0 | 4 | 5th |
| 2009 WM | 36-D | CZE | 7 | 0 | 2 | 2 | 6 | 6th |
| 2010 WM | 36-D | CZE | 9 | 0 | 0 | 0 | 6 | G |
| 2011 WM | 36-D | CZE | 9 | 0 | 1 | 1 | 8 | B |
| 2012 WM | 36-D | CZE | 10 | 2 | 3 | 5 | 4 | B |
| **Totals WM** | | | **49** | **4** | **6** | **10** | **34** | **G,2B** |

**Catenacci, Dan**
**b. Richmond Hill, Ontario, Canada, March 9, 1993**

| | | | | | | | | |
|---|---|---|---|---|---|---|---|---|
| 2011 WM18 | 7-F | CAN | 7 | 0 | 2 | 2 | 22 | 4th |

**Ceci, Cody**
**b. Orleans, Ontario, Canada, December 21, 1993**

| | | | | | | | | |
|---|---|---|---|---|---|---|---|---|
| 2011 WM18 | 8-D | CAN | 7 | 0 | 1 | 1 | 2 | 4th |

**Cehlin, Patrick**
**b. Stockholm, Sweden, July 27, 1991**

| | | | | | | | | |
|---|---|---|---|---|---|---|---|---|
| 2009 WM18 | 9-F | SWE | 6 | 2 | 2 | 4 | 37 | 5th |
| 2011 WM20 | 29-F | SWE | 6 | 4 | 2 | 6 | 18 | 4th |

**Celio, Yannic**
**b. Quinto, Switzerland, August 14, 1993**

| | | | | | | | | |
|---|---|---|---|---|---|---|---|---|
| 2011 WM18 | 7-F | SUI | 6 | 0 | 1 | 1 | 14 | 7th |

**Ceresnak, Peter**
**b. Trencin, Slovakia, January 26, 1993**

| | | | | | | | | |
|---|---|---|---|---|---|---|---|---|
| 2010 WM18 | 23-D | SVK | 6 | 0 | 0 | 0 | 6 | 8th |
| 2011 WM18 | 20-D | SVK | 6 | 0 | 1 | 1 | 0 | 10th |
| 2011 WM20 | 26-D | SVK | 6 | 0 | 0 | 0 | 2 | 8th |
| 2012 WM20 | 14-D | SVK | 6 | 0 | 0 | 0 | 2 | 6th |
| **Totals WM18** | | | **12** | **0** | **1** | **1** | **6** | **—** |
| **Totals WM20** | | | **12** | **0** | **0** | **0** | **4** | **—** |

**Cerny, Jakub**
**b. Ceske Krumlov, Czechoslovakia (Czech Republic), March 5, 1987**

| | | | | | | | | |
|---|---|---|---|---|---|---|---|---|
| 2005 WM18 | 18-F | CZE | 2 | 0 | 0 | 0 | 0 | 4th |
| 2007 WM20 | 18-F | CZE | 6 | 0 | 0 | 0 | 4 | 5th |

**Cervenka, Roman**
**b. Prague, Czechoslovakia (Czech Republic), December 10, 1985**

| | | | | | | | | |
|---|---|---|---|---|---|---|---|---|
| 2005 WM20 | 29-F | CZE | 7 | 1 | 0 | 1 | 8 | B |
| 2009 WM | 10-F | CZE | 7 | 2 | 1 | 3 | 2 | 6th |
| 2010 OG-M | 10-F | CZE | 5 | 0 | 2 | 2 | 0 | 7th |
| 2010 WM | 10-F | CZE | 9 | 1 | 1 | 2 | 2 | G |
| 2011 WM | 10-F | CZE | 9 | 4 | 6 | 10 | 4 | B |
| **Totals WM** | | | **25** | **7** | **8** | **15** | **8** | **G,B** |

**Cerveny, Rudolf**
**b. Ceske Budejovice, Czechoslovakia (Czech Republic), August 6, 1989**

| | | | | | | | | |
|---|---|---|---|---|---|---|---|---|
| 2007 WM18 | 11-F | CZE | 6 | 0 | 1 | 1 | 2 | 9th |
| 2009 WM20 | 21-F | CZE | 6 | 0 | 1 | 1 | 0 | 6th |

**Cesik, Matej**
**b. Banska Bystrica, Czechoslovakia (Slovakia), June 26, 1988**

| | | | | | | | | |
|---|---|---|---|---|---|---|---|---|
| 2008 WM20 | 22-F | SVK | 6 | 1 | 1 | 2 | 8 | 7th |

**Chara, Zdeno**
**b. Trencin, Czechoslovakia (Slovakia), March 18, 1977**

| | | | | | | | | |
|---|---|---|---|---|---|---|---|---|
| 1999 WM | 4-D | SVK | 6 | 1 | 0 | 1 | 6 | 7th |
| 2000 WM | 5-D | SVK | 9 | 0 | 0 | 0 | 12 | S |
| 2001 WM | 3-D | SVK | 7 | 0 | 1 | 1 | 10 | 7th |
| 2004 WM | 3-D | SVK | 9 | 2 | 0 | 2 | 2 | 4th |
| 2004 WCH | 3-D | SVK | 4 | 0 | 2 | 2 | 8 | 7th |
| 2005 WM | 3-D | SVK | 7 | 0 | 2 | 2 | 2 | 5th |
| 2006 OG-M | 3-D | SVK | 6 | 1 | 1 | 2 | 2 | 5th |
| 2007 WM | 3-D | SVK | 7 | 3 | 1 | 4 | 4 | 6th |
| 2010 OG-M | 33-D | SVK | 7 | 0 | 3 | 3 | 6 | 4th |
| 2012 WM | 33-D | SVK | 10 | 2 | 2 | 4 | 4 | S |
| **Totals WM** | | | **55** | **8** | **6** | **14** | **40** | **2S** |
| **Totals OG-M** | | | **13** | **1** | **4** | **5** | **8** | **—** |

~WM IIHF Directorate Best Defenceman (2012), WM All-Star Team/Defence (2004, 2012)

**Chernaok, Pavel**
**b. Novopotolsk, Soviet Union (Belarus), September 28, 1986**

| | | | | | | | | |
|---|---|---|---|---|---|---|---|---|
| 2012 WM | 82-D | BLR | 7 | 0 | 0 | 0 | 0 | 14th |

**Chernov, Pavel**
**b. Novopolotsk, Soviet Union (Russia), January 30, 1990**

| | | | | | | | | |
|---|---|---|---|---|---|---|---|---|
| 2008 WM18 | 8-F | RUS | 6 | 2 | 3 | 5 | 4 | S |
| 2009 WM20 | 10-F | RUS | 7 | 3 | 2 | 5 | 12 | B |

**Chiarlitti, Nate**
**b. Maple, Ontario, Canada, February 4, 1992**

| | | | | | | | | |
|---|---|---|---|---|---|---|---|---|
| 2010 WM18 | 5-D | CAN | 6 | 0 | 0 | 0 | 0 | 7th |

**Chiesa, Alessandro**
**b. Lugano, Switzerland, February 1, 1987**

| | | | | | | | | |
|---|---|---|---|---|---|---|---|---|
| 2005 WM18 | 7-D | SUI | 6 | 0 | 1 | 1 | 6 | 9th |
| 2006 WM20 | 7-D | SUI | 6 | 1 | 0 | 1 | 10 | 7th |

**Chimera, Jason**
**b. Edmonton, Alberta, Canada, May 2, 1979**

| | | | | | | | | |
|---|---|---|---|---|---|---|---|---|
| 1999 WM20 | 23-F | CAN | 7 | 2 | 2 | 4 | 2 | S |
| 2007 WM | 25-F | CAN | 9 | 1 | 5 | 6 | 8 | G |
| 2008 WM | 25-F | CAN | 9 | 0 | 2 | 2 | 6 | S |
| **Totals WM** | | | **18** | **1** | **7** | **8** | **14** | **G,S** |

**Chipchura, Kyle**
**b. Westlock, Alberta, Canada, February 19, 1986**

| | | | | | | | | |
|---|---|---|---|---|---|---|---|---|
| 2004 WM18 | 17-F | CAN | 7 | 3 | 2 | 5 | 28 | 4th |
| 2006 WM20 | 17-F | CAN | 6 | 4 | 1 | 5 | 0 | G |

**Chlapik, Adam**
**b.Prague, Czech Republic, February 4, 1994**

| | | | | | | | | |
|---|---|---|---|---|---|---|---|---|
| 2012 WM18 | 16-F | CZE | 6 | 0 | 1 | 1 | 4 | 8th |

**Chorney, Taylor**
**b. Thunder Bay, Ontario, Canada, April 27, 1987**

| | | | | | | | | |
|---|---|---|---|---|---|---|---|---|
| 2005 WM18 | 4-D | USA | 6 | 1 | 0 | 1 | 8 | G |
| 2006 WM20 | 2-D | USA | 7 | 0 | 0 | 0 | 6 | 4th |
| 2007 WM20 | 4-D | USA | 7 | 1 | 5 | 6 | 4 | B |
| 2010 WM | 41-D | USA | 6 | 0 | 0 | 0 | 2 | 13th |
| **Totals WM20** | | | **14** | **1** | **5** | **6** | **10** | **B** |

**Chovan, Matus**
**b. Kosice, Slovakia, February 14, 1992**

| | | | | | | | | |
|---|---|---|---|---|---|---|---|---|
| 2012 WM20 | 26-F | SVK | 6 | 5 | 1 | 6 | 27 | 6th |

**Christen, Bjorn**
**b. Berne, Switzerland, April 5, 1980**

| | | | | | | | | |
|---|---|---|---|---|---|---|---|---|
| 1997 WM20 | 17-F | SUI | 6 | 1 | 0 | 1 | 8 | 7th |
| 1998 WM20 | 17-F | SUI | 7 | 3 | 1 | 4 | 4 | B |
| 1999 WM20 | 17-F | SUI | 6 | 0 | 0 | 0 | 2 | 9th |
| 2000 WM20 | 17-F | SUI | 7 | 4 | 3 | 7 | 29 | 6th |
| 2002 OG-M | 37-F | SUI | 4 | 0 | 0 | 0 | 6 | 11th |
| 2002 WM | 37-F | SUI | 6 | 0 | 1 | 1 | 2 | 10th |
| 2003 WM | 37-F | SUI | 6 | 1 | 0 | 1 | 2 | 8th |
| 2010 WM | 37-F | SUI | 2 | 0 | 0 | 0 | 0 | 5th |
| **Totals WM20** | | | **26** | **8** | **4** | **12** | **43** | **B** |
| **Totals WM** | | | **14** | **1** | **1** | **2** | **4** | **—** |

**Christensen, Jannik**
**b. Esbjerg, Denmark, June 9, 1992**

| | | | | | | | | |
|---|---|---|---|---|---|---|---|---|
| 2012 WM20 | 3-D | DEN | 6 | 0 | 1 | 1 | 6 | 10th |

**Christensen, Kennie**
**b. Frederikshavn, Denmark, March 30, 1990**

| | | | | | | | | |
|---|---|---|---|---|---|---|---|---|
| 2008 WM18 | 8-F | DEN | 6 | 2 | 1 | 3 | 4 | 10th |

**Christensen, Mads**
**b. Fredrikshavn, Denmark, November 3, 1984**

| | | | | | | | | |
|---|---|---|---|---|---|---|---|---|
| 2005 WM | 14-D | DEN | 1 | 0 | 0 | 0 | 0 | 14th |
| 2008 WM | 14-D | DEN | 5 | 0 | 0 | 0 | 0 | 12th |
| 2010 WM | 27-D | DEN | 7 | 0 | 0 | 0 | 2 | 8th |
| **Totals WM** | | | **13** | **0** | **0** | **0** | **2** | **—** |

**Christensen, Mads**
**b. Herning, Denmark, April 2, 1987**

| | | | | | | | | |
|---|---|---|---|---|---|---|---|---|
| 2004 WM18 | 12-F | DEN | 6 | 1 | 1 | 2 | 2 | 8th |
| 2005 WM18 | 12-F | DEN | 6 | 1 | 2 | 3 | 14 | 10th |
| 2007 WM | 18-F | DEN | 6 | 1 | 1 | 2 | 14 | 10th |
| 2008 WM | 18-F | DEN | 4 | 0 | 0 | 0 | 2 | 12th |
| 2010 WM | 60-F | DEN | 7 | 2 | 0 | 2 | 2 | 8th |
| 2011 WM | 60-F | DEN | 6 | 4 | 1 | 5 | 6 | 11th |
| **Totals WM18** | | | **12** | **2** | **3** | **5** | **16** | **—** |
| **Totals WM** | | | **23** | **7** | **2** | **9** | **24** | **—** |

**Christensen, Rasmus**
**b. Fredrikshavn, Denmark, July 31, 1990**

| | | | | | | | | |
|---|---|---|---|---|---|---|---|---|
| 2008 WM18 | 2-D | DEN | 6 | 0 | 0 | 0 | 4 | 10th |

**Christiansen, Soren**
**b. Esbjerg, Denmark, April 15, 1991**

| | | | | | | | | |
|---|---|---|---|---|---|---|---|---|
| 2008 WM18 | 17-F | DEN | 6 | 0 | 0 | 0 | 6 | 10th |

**Chudinov, Maxim**
**b. Cherepovets, Soviet Union (Russia), March 25, 1990**

| | | | | | | | | |
|---|---|---|---|---|---|---|---|---|
| 2007 WM18 | 27-D | RUS | 7 | 2 | 2 | 4 | 8 | G |
| 2008 WM18 | 27-D | RUS | 6 | 1 | 4 | 5 | 27 | S |
| 2008 WM20 | 28-D | RUS | 7 | 0 | 1 | 1 | 0 | B |
| 2009 WM20 | 27-D | RUS | 7 | 0 | 5 | 5 | 6 | B |
| 2010 WM20 | 27-D | RUS | 6 | 2 | 2 | 4 | 6 | 6th |
| **Totals WM18** | | | **13** | **3** | **6** | **9** | **35** | **G,S** |
| **Totals WM20** | | | **20** | **2** | **8** | **10** | **12** | **2B** |

**Chuprys, Yaroslav**
**b. Minsk, Soviet Union (Belarus), September 12, 1981**

| | | | | | | | | |
|---|---|---|---|---|---|---|---|---|
| 2001 WM20 | 9-F | BLR | 6 | 2 | 3 | 5 | 4 | 9th |
| 2003 WM | 19-F | BLR | 5 | 0 | 1 | 1 | 6 | 14th |
| 2006 WM | 68-F | BLR | 7 | 1 | 1 | 2 | 10 | 6th |
| 2008 WM | 68-F | BLR | 6 | 1 | 1 | 2 | 2 | 9th |
| 2009 WM | 68-F | BLR | 7 | 0 | 1 | 1 | 0 | 8th |
| 2010 WM | 68-F | BLR | 6 | 0 | 1 | 1 | 2 | 10th |
| **Totals WM** | | | **31** | **2** | **5** | **7** | **20** | **—** |

**Chvanov, Sergei**
**b. Cherepovets, Soviet Union (Russia), May 20, 1991**

| | | | | | | | | |
|---|---|---|---|---|---|---|---|---|
| 2009 WM18 | 9-F | RUS | 7 | 3 | 5 | 8 | 6 | S |

**Chvatal, Marek**
**b. Jihlava, Czechoslovakia (Czech Republic), January 27, 1984**

| | | | | | | | | |
|---|---|---|---|---|---|---|---|---|
| 2002 WM18 | 4-D | CZE | 8 | 0 | 1 | 1 | 6 | B |
| 2004 WM20 | 10-D | CZE | 6 | 0 | 1 | 1 | 10 | 4th |

**Cibak, Martin**
**b. Liptovsky Mikulas, Czechoslovakia (Slovakia), May 17, 1980**

| | | | | | | | | |
|---|---|---|---|---|---|---|---|---|
| 1999 WM20 | 17-F | SVK | 6 | 2 | 3 | 5 | 6 | B |
| 2000 WM20 | 20-F | SVK | 7 | 2 | 1 | 3 | 4 | 9th |
| 2004 WCH | 8-F | SVK | 4 | 1 | 0 | 1 | 0 | 7th |
| 2006 WM | 8-F | SVK | 7 | 2 | 1 | 3 | 8 | 8th |
| 2010 OG-M | 8-F | SVK | 7 | 0 | 0 | 0 | 6 | 4th |
| 2011 WM | 8-F | SVK | 3 | 0 | 1 | 1 | 2 | 10th |
| **Totals WM20** | | | **13** | **4** | **4** | **8** | **10** | **B** |
| **Totals WM** | | | **10** | **2** | **2** | **4** | **10** | **—** |

**Cibulskis, Oskars**
**b. Riga, Soviet Union (Latvia), April 9, 1988**

| | | | | | | | | |
|---|---|---|---|---|---|---|---|---|
| 2011 WM | 44-D | LAT | 6 | 0 | 1 | 1 | 0 | 13th |
| 2012 WM | 44-D | LAT | 7 | 0 | 0 | 0 | 4 | 10th |
| **Totals WM** | | | **13** | **0** | **1** | **1** | **4** | **—** |

**Ciernik, Ivan**
**b. Levice, Czechoslovakia (Slovakia), October 30, 1977**

| | | | | | | | | |
|---|---|---|---|---|---|---|---|---|
| 1996 WM20 | 6-F | SVK | 6 | 2 | 0 | 2 | 2 | 7th |
| 1997 WM20 | 13-F | SVK | 6 | 1 | 2 | 3 | 18 | 6th |
| 2006 WM | 28-F | SVK | 7 | 2 | 3 | 5 | 8 | 8th |
| 2007 WM | 28-F | SVK | 5 | 0 | 0 | 0 | 0 | 6th |
| 2008 WM | 27-F | SVK | 5 | 2 | 2 | 4 | 6 | 13th |
| 2010 WM | 27-F | SVK | 6 | 3 | 0 | 3 | 4 | 12th |
| **Totals WM20** | | | **12** | **3** | **2** | **5** | **20** | **—** |
| **Totals WM** | | | **23** | **7** | **5** | **12** | **18** | **—** |

**Cingel, Lukas**
**b. Zilina, Czechoslovakia (Slovakia), June 10, 1992**

| | | | | | | | | |
|---|---|---|---|---|---|---|---|---|
| 2010 WM18 | 26-F | SVK | 6 | 2 | 2 | 4 | 6 | 8th |

**Cinks, Ronalds**
**b. Riga, Soviet Union (Latvia), March 11, 1990**

| | | | | | | | | |
|---|---|---|---|---|---|---|---|---|
| 2007 WM18 | 10-F | LAT | 6 | 0 | 2 | 2 | 0 | 10th |
| 2009 WM20 | 21-F | LAT | 6 | 2 | 3 | 5 | 6 | 8th |
| 2010 WM20 | 21-F | LAT | 6 | 0 | 5 | 5 | 6 | 9th |
| **Totals WM20** | | | **12** | **2** | **8** | **10** | **12** | **—** |

**Cipulis, Martins**
**b. Cesis, Soviet Union (Latvia), November 29, 1980**

| | | | | | | | | |
|---|---|---|---|---|---|---|---|---|
| 2005 WM | 47-F | LAT | 6 | 1 | 2 | 3 | 0 | 9th |
| 2006 OG-M | 47-F | LAT | 5 | 1 | 1 | 2 | 0 | 12th |
| 2006 WM | 47-F | LAT | 6 | 1 | 1 | 2 | 2 | 10th |
| 2007 WM | 29-F | LAT | 6 | 1 | 4 | 5 | 2 | 13th |
| 2008 WM | 47-F | LAT | 6 | 1 | 2 | 3 | 2 | 11th |
| 2009 WM | 47-F | LAT | 7 | 4 | 2 | 6 | 4 | 7th |
| 2010 OG-M | 47-F | LAT | 4 | 1 | 1 | 2 | 0 | 12th |
| 2010 WM | 47-F | LAT | 6 | 1 | 1 | 2 | 0 | 11th |
| 2011 WM | 47-F | LAT | 6 | 4 | 2 | 6 | 2 | 13th |
| 2012 WM | 47-F | LAT | 7 | 0 | 1 | 1 | 0 | 10th |
| **Totals WM** | | | **50** | **13** | **15** | **28** | **12** | **—** |
| **Totals OG-M** | | | **9** | **2** | **2** | **4** | **0** | **—** |

**Cizikas, Casey**
**b. Mississauga, Ontario, Canada, February 27, 1991**

| | | | | | | | | |
|---|---|---|---|---|---|---|---|---|
| 2011 WM20 | 11-F | CAN | 7 | 2 | 1 | 3 | 6 | S |

**Claesson, Fredrik**
**b. Stockholm, Sweden, November 24, 1992**

| | | | | | | | | |
|---|---|---|---|---|---|---|---|---|
| 2010 WM18 | 28-D | SWE | 6 | 0 | 1 | 1 | 0 | S |
| 2012 WM20 | 7-D | SWE | 6 | 0 | 0 | 0 | 0 | G |

**Clark, Chris**
**b. Manchester, Connecticut, United States, March 8, 1976**

| | | | | | | | | |
|---|---|---|---|---|---|---|---|---|
| 2002 WM | 17-F | USA | 7 | 2 | 0 | 2 | 6 | 7th |
| 2007 WM | 17-F | USA | 6 | 2 | 1 | 3 | 4 | 5th |
| **Totals WM** | | | **13** | **4** | **1** | **5** | **10** | **—** |

**Clendening, Adam**
**b. Niagara Falls, New York, United States, October 26, 1992**

| | | | | | | | | |
|---|---|---|---|---|---|---|---|---|
| 2009 WM18 | 8-D | USA | 7 | 0 | 2 | 2 | 4 | G |
| 2010 WM18 | 5-D | USA | 7 | 3 | 7 | 10 | 4 | G |
| 2012 WM20 | 5-D | USA | 6 | 1 | 4 | 5 | 6 | 7th |
| **Totals WM18** | | | **14** | **3** | **9** | **12** | **8** | **2G** |

~WM18 All-Star Team/Defence (2010)

**Cliche, Marc-Andre**
**b. Rouyn-Noranda, Quebec, Canada, March 23, 1987**

| | | | | | | | | |
|---|---|---|---|---|---|---|---|---|
| 2007 WM20 | 11-F | CAN | 6 | 0 | 0 | 0 | 4 | G |

**Clifford, Kyle**
**b. Ayr, Ontario, Canada, January 13, 1991**

| | | | | | | | | |
|---|---|---|---|---|---|---|---|---|
| 2009 WM18 | 23-F | CAN | 6 | 0 | 0 | 0 | 16 | 4th |

**Clutterbuck, Cal**
**b. Welland, Ontario, Canada, November 18, 1987**

| | | | | | | | | |
|---|---|---|---|---|---|---|---|---|
| 2011 WM | 22-F | CAN | 7 | 0 | 1 | 1 | 4 | 5th |

**Coburn, Braydon**
**b. Calgary, Alberta, Canada, February 27, 1985**

| | | | | | | | | |
|---|---|---|---|---|---|---|---|---|
| 2003 WM18 | 3-D | CAN | 7 | 0 | 0 | 0 | 12 | G |
| 2004 WM20 | 29-D | CAN | 6 | 2 | 1 | 3 | 2 | S |
| 2005 WM20 | 29-D | CAN | 6 | 0 | 2 | 2 | 8 | G |
| 2009 WM | 55-D | CAN | 5 | 0 | 1 | 1 | 4 | S |
| **Totals WM20** | | | **12** | **2** | **3** | **5** | **10** | **G,S** |

**Cogliano, Andrew**
**b. Toronto, Ontario, Canada, June 14, 1987**

| | | | | | | | | |
|---|---|---|---|---|---|---|---|---|
| 2006 WM20 | 9-F | CAN | 6 | 1 | 4 | 5 | 4 | G |
| 2007 WM20 | 9-F | CAN | 6 | 1 | 2 | 3 | 0 | G |
| **Totals WM20** | | | **12** | **2** | **6** | **8** | **4** | **2G** |

**Colaiacovo, Carlo**
**b. Toronto, Ontario, Canada, January 27, 1983**

| | | | | | | | | |
|---|---|---|---|---|---|---|---|---|
| 2002 WM20 | 8-D | CAN | 7 | 0 | 3 | 3 | 2 | S |
| 2003 WM20 | 8-D | CAN | 6 | 1 | 9 | 10 | 2 | S |
| 2011 WM | 28-D | CAN | 5 | 0 | 0 | 0 | 0 | 5th |
| **Totals WM20** | | | **13** | **1** | **12** | **13** | **4** | **2S** |

~WM20 All-Star Team/Defence (2003)

**Cole, Erik**
**b. Oswego, New York, United States, November 6, 1978**

| | | | | | | | | |
|---|---|---|---|---|---|---|---|---|
| 2005 WM | 21-F | USA | 7 | 1 | 5 | 6 | 6 | 6th |
| 2006 OG-M | 26-F | USA | 6 | 1 | 2 | 3 | 0 | 8th |
| 2007 WM | 26-F | USA | 7 | 1 | 4 | 5 | 2 | 5th |
| **Totals WM** | | | **14** | **2** | **9** | **11** | **8** | **—** |

**Cole, Ian**
**b. Ann Arbor, Michigan, United States, February 21, 1989**

| | | | | | | | | |
|---|---|---|---|---|---|---|---|---|
| 2007 WM18 | 28-D | USA | 7 | 4 | 1 | 5 | 6 | S |
| 2008 WM20 | 28-D | USA | 6 | 0 | 0 | 0 | 6 | 4th |
| 2009 WM20 | 28-D | USA | 6 | 2 | 2 | 4 | 4 | 5th |
| **Totals WM20** | | | **12** | **2** | **2** | **4** | **10** | **—** |

**Collberg, Sebastian**
**b. Mariestad, Sweden, February 23, 1994**

| | | | | | | | | |
|---|---|---|---|---|---|---|---|---|
| 2012 WM18 | 15-F | SWE | 6 | 4 | 5 | 9 | 14 | S |
| 2012 WM20 | 15-F | SWE | 6 | 4 | 3 | 7 | 0 | G |

**Colliton, Jeremy**
**b. Blackie, Alberta, Canada, January 13, 1985**

| | | | | | | | | |
|---|---|---|---|---|---|---|---|---|
| 2003 WM18 | 21-F | CAN | 7 | 1 | 5 | 6 | 18 | G |
| 2004 WM20 | 21-F | CAN | 6 | 0 | 0 | 0 | 2 | S |
| 2005 WM20 | 21-F | CAN | 1 | 0 | 0 | 0 | 0 | G |
| **Totals WM20** | | | **7** | **0** | **0** | **0** | **2** | **G,S** |

**Comeau, Blake**
**b. Meadow Lake, Saskatchewan, Canada, February 18, 1986**

| | | | | | | | | |
|---|---|---|---|---|---|---|---|---|
| 2006 WM20 | 14-F | CAN | 6 | 3 | 4 | 7 | 8 | G |

**Compher, J.T. (Joseph Taylor)**
**b. Northbrook, Illinois, United States, April 8, 1995**

| | | | | | | | | |
|---|---|---|---|---|---|---|---|---|
| 2012 WM18 | 11-F | USA | 6 | 2 | 3 | 5 | 4 | G |

**Connolly, Brett**
**b. Prince George, British Columbia, Canada, May 2, 1992**

| | | | | | | | | |
|---|---|---|---|---|---|---|---|---|
| 2009 WM18 | 8-F | CAN | 6 | 3 | 3 | 6 | 4 | 4th |
| 2010 WM18 | 8-F | CAN | 4 | 1 | 0 | 1 | 10 | 7th |
| 2011 WM20 | 28-F | CAN | 7 | 0 | 3 | 3 | 0 | S |
| 2012 WM20 | 14-F | CAN | 6 | 5 | 1 | 6 | 4 | B |
| **Totals WM18** | | | **10** | **4** | **3** | **7** | **14** | **—** |
| **Totals WM20** | | | **13** | **5** | **4** | **9** | **4** | **S,B** |

**Copp, Andrew**
**b. Ann Arbor, Michigan, United States, July 8, 1994**

| | | | | | | | | |
|---|---|---|---|---|---|---|---|---|
| 2012 WM18 | 26-F | USA | 6 | 0 | 1 | 1 | 0 | G |

**Coqueux, Olivier**
**b. Saumur, France, November 29, 1973**

| | | | | | | | | |
|---|---|---|---|---|---|---|---|---|
| 2004 WM | 19-F | FRA | 6 | 0 | 1 | 1 | 8 | 16th |
| 2008 WM | 19-F | FRA | 5 | 1 | 0 | 1 | 4 | 14th |
| **Totals WM** | | | **11** | **1** | **1** | **2** | **12** | **—** |

**Cormier, Patrice**
**b. Moncton, New Brunswick, Canada, June 14, 1990**

| | | | | | | | | |
|---|---|---|---|---|---|---|---|---|
| 2009 WM20 | 28-F | CAN | 6 | 1 | 2 | 3 | 6 | G |
| 2010 WM20 | 28-F | CAN | 6 | 2 | 3 | 5 | 4 | S |
| **Totals WM20** | | | **12** | **3** | **5** | **8** | **10** | **G,S** |

**Cousins, Nick**
**b. Belleville, Ontario, Canada, July 20, 1993**

| | | | | | | | | |
|---|---|---|---|---|---|---|---|---|
| 2011 WM18 | 19-F | CAN | 7 | 4 | 4 | 8 | 10 | 4th |

**Couturier, Sean**
**b. Phoenix, Arizona, United States, December 7, 1992**

| | | | | | | | | |
|---|---|---|---|---|---|---|---|---|
| 2011 WM20 | 7-F | CAN | 7 | 2 | 1 | 3 | 0 | S |

**Cowen, Jared**
**b. Allan, Saskatchewan, Canada, January 25, 1991**

| | | | | | | | | |
|---|---|---|---|---|---|---|---|---|
| 2010 WM20 | 22-D | CAN | 6 | 0 | 1 | 1 | 2 | S |
| 2011 WM20 | 2-D | CAN | 7 | 1 | 0 | 1 | 0 | S |
| **Totals WM20** | | | **13** | **1** | **1** | **2** | **2** | **2S** |

**Coyle, Charlie**
**b. East Weymouth, Massachusetts, March 2, 1992**

| | | | | | | | | |
|---|---|---|---|---|---|---|---|---|
| 2011 WM20 | 3-F | USA | 6 | 2 | 4 | 6 | 4 | B |
| 2012 WM20 | 3-F | USA | 6 | 4 | 1 | 5 | 2 | 7th |
| **Totals WM20** | | | **12** | **6** | **5** | **11** | **6** | **B** |

**Crabb, Joey**
**b. Anchorage, Alaska, United States, April 3, 1983**

| | | | | | | | | |
|---|---|---|---|---|---|---|---|---|
| 2012 WM | 15-F | USA | 8 | 0 | 3 | 3 | 4 | 7th |

**Crosby, Sidney**
**b. Cole Harbour, Nova Scotia, Canada, August 7, 1987**

| | | | | | | | | |
|---|---|---|---|---|---|---|---|---|
| 2004 WM20 | 28-F | CAN | 6 | 2 | 3 | 5 | 4 | S |
| 2005 WM20 | 9-F | CAN | 6 | 6 | 3 | 9 | 4 | G |
| 2006 WM | 87-F | CAN | 9 | 8 | 8 | 16 | 10 | 4th |
| 2010 OG-M | 87-F | CAN | 7 | 4 | 3 | 7 | 4 | G |
| **Totals WM20** | | | **12** | **8** | **6** | **14** | **8** | **G,S** |

~WM IIHF Directorate Best Forward (2006), WM All-Star Team/Forward (2006)

**Csiszar, Brede**
**b. Oslo, Norway, March 26, 1987**

| | | | | | | | | |
|---|---|---|---|---|---|---|---|---|
| 2010 WM | 44-D | NOR | 2 | 0 | 0 | 0 | 0 | 9th |
| 2011 WM | 44-D | NOR | 7 | 0 | 0 | 0 | 0 | 6th |
| **Totals WM** | | | **9** | **0** | **0** | **0** | **0** | **—** |

**Cuma, Tyler**
**b. Toronto, Ontario, Canada, January 19, 1990**

| | | | | | | | | |
|---|---|---|---|---|---|---|---|---|
| 2008 WM18 | 6-D | CAN | 7 | 1 | 3 | 4 | 6 | G |

**Culek, Jakub**
**b. Klatovy, Czechoslovakia (Czech Republic), September 7, 1992**

| | | | | | | | | |
|---|---|---|---|---|---|---|---|---|
| 2009 WM18 | 18-F | CZE | 6 | 0 | 1 | 1 | 4 | 6th |
| 2011 WM20 | 14-F | CZE | 6 | 1 | 1 | 2 | 0 | 7th |
| 2012 WM20 | 14-F | CZE | 5 | 1 | 3 | 4 | 0 | 5th |
| **Totals WM20** | | | **11** | **2** | **4** | **6** | **0** | **—** |

**Cumiskey, Kyle**
**b. Abbotsford, British Columbia, Canada, December 2, 1986**

| | | | | | | | | |
|---|---|---|---|---|---|---|---|---|
| 2010 WM | 28-D | CAN | 7 | 0 | 3 | 3 | 0 | 7th |

**Cunik, Matej**
**b. Spisska Nova Ves, Czechoslovakia (Slovakia), January 25, 1987**

| | | | | | | | | |
|---|---|---|---|---|---|---|---|---|
| 2004 WM18 | 4-D | SVK | 6 | 0 | 1 | 1 | 2 | 6th |
| 2005 WM18 | 5-D | SVK | 6 | 0 | 0 | 0 | 6 | 6th |
| 2007 WM20 | 5-D | SVK | 6 | 0 | 1 | 1 | 8 | 8th |
| **Totals WM18** | | | **12** | **0** | **1** | **1** | **8** | **—** |

**Czarnik, Austin**
**b. Washington, Michigan, United States, December 12, 1992**

| | | | | | | | | |
|---|---|---|---|---|---|---|---|---|
| 2010 WM18 | 18-F | USA | 7 | 5 | 1 | 6 | 4 | G |
| 2012 WM20 | 2-F | USA | 6 | 2 | 2 | 4 | 0 | 7th |

**Czarnik, Robbie**
**b. Roseville, Michigan, United States, January 25, 1990**

| | | | | | | | | |
|---|---|---|---|---|---|---|---|---|
| 2008 WM18 | 7-F | USA | 7 | 3 | 5 | 8 | 10 | G |

**Da Costa, Stephane**
**b. Paris, France, July 11, 1989**

| | | | | | | | | |
|---|---|---|---|---|---|---|---|---|
| 2009 WM | 14-F | FRA | 6 | 0 | 2 | 2 | 0 | 12th |
| 2010 WM | 14-F | FRA | 5 | 1 | 2 | 3 | 14 | 14th |
| 2011 WM | 14-F | FRA | 5 | 0 | 1 | 1 | 6 | 12th |
| 2012 WM | 14-F | FRA | 7 | 1 | 5 | 6 | 4 | 9th |
| **Totals WM** | | | **23** | **2** | **10** | **12** | **24** | **—** |

**Da Costa, Teddy**
**b. Melun, France, February 17, 1986**

| | | | | | | | | |
|---|---|---|---|---|---|---|---|---|
| 2011 WM | 80-F | FRA | 6 | 0 | 0 | 0 | 10 | 12th |
| 2012 WM | 80-F | FRA | 7 | 2 | 1 | 3 | 6 | 9th |
| **Totals WM** | | | **13** | **2** | **1** | **3** | **16** | **—** |

**Dadonov, Yevgeni**
**b. Chelyabinsk, Soviet Union (Russia), March 12, 1989**

| | | | | | | | | |
|---|---|---|---|---|---|---|---|---|
| 2007 WM18 | 26-F | RUS | 7 | 2 | 2 | 4 | 2 | G |
| 2008 WM20 | 27-F | RUS | 7 | 0 | 0 | 0 | 4 | B |
| 2009 WM20 | 26-F | RUS | 7 | 2 | 5 | 7 | 2 | B |
| **Totals WM20** | | | **14** | **2** | **5** | **7** | **6** | **2B** |

**Dahlbeck, Klas**
**b. Katrineholm, Sweden, July 6, 1991**

| | | | | | | | | |
|---|---|---|---|---|---|---|---|---|
| 2011 WM20 | 6-D | SWE | 6 | 0 | 2 | 2 | 2 | 4th |

**Dahlmann, Morten**
**b. Horsholm, Denmark, September 22, 1976**

| | | | | | | | | |
|---|---|---|---|---|---|---|---|---|
| 2005 WM | 26-D | DEN | 6 | 0 | 0 | 0 | 4 | 14th |
| 2006 WM | 26-D | DEN | 6 | 1 | 0 | 1 | 10 | 13th |
| 2008 WM | 26-D | DEN | 5 | 0 | 1 | 1 | 4 | 12th |
| **Totals WM** | | | **17** | **1** | **1** | **2** | **18** | **—** |

**Dalidovich, Denis**
**b. Minsk, Belarus, May 28, 1993**

| | | | | | | | | |
|---|---|---|---|---|---|---|---|---|
| 2010 WM18 | 5-F | BLR | 6 | 0 | 1 | 1 | 4 | 10th |

**Daloga, Marek**
**b. Zvolen, Czechoslovakia (Slovakia), March 10, 1989**

| | | | | | | | | |
|---|---|---|---|---|---|---|---|---|
| 2007 WM18 | 7-D | SVK | 6 | 1 | 1 | 2 | 2 | 5th |
| 2008 WM20 | 7-D | SVK | 6 | 0 | 0 | 0 | 2 | 7th |
| 2009 WM20 | 7-D | SVK | 7 | 0 | 1 | 1 | 2 | 4th |
| **Totals WM20** | | | **13** | **0** | **1** | **1** | **4** | **—** |

**Daloga, Martin**
**b. Svolen, Slovakia, July 27, 1992**

| | | | | | | | | |
|---|---|---|---|---|---|---|---|---|
| 2012 WM20 | 20-F | SVK | 6 | 1 | 2 | 3 | 0 | 6th |

**Dalsgaard, Simon**
**b. Herning, Denmark, April 24, 1990**

| | | | | | | | | |
|---|---|---|---|---|---|---|---|---|
| 2008 WM18 | 13-F | DEN | 4 | 0 | 0 | 0 | 4 | 10th |

**D'Amigo, Jerry**
**b. Binghamton, New York, United States, February 19, 1991**

| | | | | | | | | |
|---|---|---|---|---|---|---|---|---|
| 2009 WM18 | 9-F | USA | 7 | 4 | 9 | 13 | 8 | G |
| 2010 WM20 | 19-F | USA | 7 | 6 | 6 | 12 | 0 | G |
| 2011 WM20 | 9-F | USA | 6 | 1 | 1 | 2 | 2 | B |
| **Totals WM20** | | | **13** | **7** | **7** | **14** | **2** | **G,B** |

~WM18 All-Star Team/Forward (2009)

**Danielsen, Adrian**
**b. Hamar, Norway, September 27, 1992**

| | | | | | | | | |
|---|---|---|---|---|---|---|---|---|
| 2011 WM20 | 8-D | NOR | 6 | 0 | 0 | 0 | 2 | 9th |

**Daniska, Tomas**
**b. Nitra, Czechoslovakia (Slovakia), May 29, 1991**

| | | | | | | | | |
|---|---|---|---|---|---|---|---|---|
| 2009 WM18 | 16-F | SVK | 6 | 1 | 2 | 3 | 4 | 7th |

**Dano, Marko**
**b. Eisenstadt, Austria, November 30, 1994**

| | | | | | | | | |
|---|---|---|---|---|---|---|---|---|
| 2011 WM18 | 19-F | SVK | 6 | 1 | 3 | 4 | 14 | 10th |
| 2012 WM20 | 29-F | SVK | 6 | 1 | 2 | 3 | 6 | 6th |

**Daras, Viliam**
**b. Bratislava, Czechoslovakia (Slovakia), September 28, 1992**

| | | | | | | | | |
|---|---|---|---|---|---|---|---|---|
| 2010 WM18 | 22-F | SVK | 6 | 0 | 1 | 1 | 0 | 8th |

**Darcy, Cam**
**b. South Boston, Massachusetts, United States, March 2, 1994**

| | | | | | | | | |
|---|---|---|---|---|---|---|---|---|
| 2012 WM18 | 19-F | USA | 6 | 0 | 0 | 0 | 0 | G |

**Darzins, Lauris**
**b. Riga, Soviet Union (Latvia), January 28, 1985**

| | | | | | | | | |
|---|---|---|---|---|---|---|---|---|
| 2006 WM | 10-F | LAT | 6 | 2 | 0 | 2 | 6 | 10th |
| 2007 WM | 10-F | LAT | 6 | 3 | 2 | 5 | 2 | 13th |
| 2008 WM | 10-F | LAT | 6 | 2 | 1 | 3 | 16 | 11th |
| 2009 WM | 10-F | LAT | 7 | 2 | 0 | 2 | 18 | 7th |
| 2010 OG-M | 10-F | LAT | 4 | 0 | 1 | 1 | 10 | 12th |
| 2010 WM | 10-F | LAT | 6 | 1 | 0 | 1 | 0 | 11th |
| 2011 WM | 10-F | LAT | 3 | 1 | 0 | 1 | 4 | 13th |
| **Totals WM** | | | **34** | **11** | **3** | **14** | **46** | **—** |

**Dasutins, Artjoms**
**b. Riga, Latvia, January 10, 1993**

| | | | | | | | | |
|---|---|---|---|---|---|---|---|---|
| 2010 WM18 | 17-F | LAT | 6 | 1 | 1 | 2 | 0 | 9th |

**Datsyuk, Pavel**
**b. Sverdlovsk (Yekaterinburg), Soviet Union (Russia), July 20, 1978**

| | | | | | | | | |
|---|---|---|---|---|---|---|---|---|
| 2001 WM | 14-F | RUS | 7 | 0 | 4 | 4 | 0 | 6th |
| 2002 OG-M | 26-F | RUS | 6 | 1 | 2 | 3 | 0 | B |
| 2003 WM | 13-F | RUS | 7 | 1 | 4 | 5 | 0 | 7th |
| 2004 WCH | 13-F | RUS | 4 | 1 | 0 | 1 | 0 | 6th |
| 2005 WM | 13-F | RUS | 9 | 3 | 4 | 7 | 0 | B |
| 2006 OG-M | 13-F | RUS | 8 | 1 | 7 | 8 | 10 | 4th |
| 2010 OG-M | 13-F | RUS | 4 | 1 | 2 | 3 | 2 | 6th |
| 2010 WM | 13-F | RUS | 6 | 6 | 1 | 7 | 0 | S |
| 2012 WM | 13-F | RUS | 10 | 3 | 4 | 7 | 2 | G |
| **Totals WM** | | | **39** | **13** | **17** | **30** | **2** | **G,S,B** |
| **Totals OG-M** | | | **18** | **3** | **11** | **14** | **12** | **B** |

~WM IIHF Directorate Best Forward (2010), WM All-Star Team/Forward (2010)

**Daugavins, Kaspars**
**b. Riga, Soviet Union (Latvia), May 18, 1988**

| | | | | | | | | |
|---|---|---|---|---|---|---|---|---|
| 2006 WM20 | 16-F | LAT | 6 | 0 | 2 | 2 | 4 | 9th |
| 2006 WM | 21-F | LAT | 3 | 0 | 1 | 1 | 2 | 10th |
| 2007 WM | 20-F | LAT | 6 | 3 | 3 | 6 | 0 | 13th |
| 2008 WM | 11-F | LAT | 6 | 0 | 0 | 0 | 0 | 11th |
| 2010 OG-M | 16-F | LAT | 4 | 0 | 0 | 0 | 2 | 12th |
| 2010 WM | 16-F | LAT | 6 | 2 | 1 | 3 | 0 | 11th |
| 2012 WM | 16-F | LAT | 7 | 1 | 1 | 2 | 8 | 10th |
| **Totals WM** | | | **28** | **6** | **6** | **12** | **10** | **—** |

**Davis, Nate**
**b. Cleveland, Ohio, United States, May 23, 1986**

| | | | | | | | | |
|---|---|---|---|---|---|---|---|---|
| 2004 WM18 | 15-F | USA | 6 | 1 | 1 | 2 | 2 | S |
| 2006 WM20 | 10-F | USA | 7 | 0 | 1 | 1 | 4 | 4th |
| 2007 WM | 16-F | USA | 7 | 0 | 0 | 0 | 2 | 5th |

**Dawes, Nigel**
**b. Winnipeg, Manitoba, Canada, February 9, 1985**

| | | | | | | | | |
|---|---|---|---|---|---|---|---|---|
| 2004 WM20 | 27-F | CAN | 6 | 6 | 5 | 11 | 0 | S |
| 2005 WM20 | 27-F | CAN | 6 | 2 | 4 | 6 | 6 | G |
| **Totals WM20** | | | **12** | **8** | **9** | **17** | **6** | **G,S** |

**Daxlberger, Dominik**
**b. Rosenheim, Germany, February 7, 1993**

| | | | | | | | | |
|---|---|---|---|---|---|---|---|---|
| 2011 WM18 | 18-F | GER | 6 | 1 | 0 | 1 | 4 | 6th |

**De Bettin, Giorgio**
**b. Pieve di Cadore, Italy, August 7, 1972**

| | | | | | | | | |
|---|---|---|---|---|---|---|---|---|
| 2002 WM | 19-F | ITA | 6 | 0 | 0 | 0 | 0 | 15th |
| 2006 OG-M | 9-F | ITA | 5 | 0 | 4 | 4 | 0 | 11th |
| 2006 WM | 9-F | ITA | 6 | 0 | 2 | 2 | 14 | 14th |
| 2007 WM | 9-F | ITA | 6 | 2 | 0 | 2 | 4 | 12th |
| 2008 WM | 9-F | ITA | 5 | 0 | 1 | 1 | 2 | 16th |
| 2010 WM | 9-F | ITA | 3 | 0 | 0 | 0 | 2 | 15th |
| **Totals WM** | | | **26** | **2** | **3** | **5** | **22** | **—** |

**Debrunner, Fabian**
**b. Zurich, Switzerland, March 19, 1985**

| | | | | | | | | |
|---|---|---|---|---|---|---|---|---|
| 2003 WM18 | 24-F | SUI | 6 | 0 | 1 | 1 | 2 | 9th |
| 2005 WM20 | 9-F | SUI | 6 | 0 | 0 | 0 | 0 | 8th |

**Dedunov, Pavel**
**b. Bolshoy Kamen, Soviet Union (Russia), April 8, 1990**

| | | | | | | | | |
|---|---|---|---|---|---|---|---|---|
| 2010 WM20 | 19-F | RUS | 6 | 0 | 0 | 0 | 2 | 6th |

**Degn, Kasper**
**b. Herning, Denmark, February 25, 1982**

| | | | | | | | | |
|---|---|---|---|---|---|---|---|---|
| 2004 WM | 24-F | DEN | 3 | 1 | 0 | 1 | 2 | 12th |
| 2005 WM | 9-F | DEN | 6 | 3 | 0 | 3 | 0 | 14th |
| 2006 WM | 9-F | DEN | 6 | 0 | 0 | 0 | 2 | 13th |
| 2008 WM | 9-F | DEN | 6 | 2 | 0 | 2 | 2 | 12th |
| 2009 WM | 9-F | DEN | 6 | 1 | 0 | 1 | 0 | 13th |
| 2010 WM | 9-F | DEN | 7 | 0 | 2 | 2 | 2 | 8th |
| 2011 WM | 9-F | DEN | 6 | 0 | 0 | 0 | 2 | 11th |
| **Totals WM** | | | **40** | **7** | **2** | **9** | **10** | **—** |

**De Haan, Calvin**
**b. Carp, Ontario, Canada, May 9, 1991**

| | | | | | | | | |
|---|---|---|---|---|---|---|---|---|
| 2009 WM18 | 24-D | CAN | 6 | 0 | 6 | 6 | 0 | 4th |
| 2010 WM20 | 24-D | CAN | 4 | 0 | 1 | 1 | 0 | S |
| 2011 WM20 | 24-D | CAN | 6 | 0 | 5 | 5 | 4 | S |
| **Totals WM20** | | | **10** | **0** | **6** | **6** | **4** | **2S** |

**De la Rose, Jacob**
**b. Arvika, Sweden, May 20, 1995**

| | | | | | | | | |
|---|---|---|---|---|---|---|---|---|
| 2012 WM18 | 19-F | SWE | 6 | 1 | 2 | 3 | 4 | S |

**Della Rovere, Stefan**
**b. Maple, Ontario, Canada, February 25, 1990**

| | | | | | | | | |
|---|---|---|---|---|---|---|---|---|
| 2009 WM20 | 15-F | CAN | 6 | 1 | 1 | 2 | 26 | G |
| 2010 WM20 | 19-F | CAN | 6 | 3 | 3 | 6 | 8 | S |
| **Totals WM20** | | | **12** | **4** | **4** | **8** | **34** | **G,S** |

**Delnov, Alexander**
**b.Moscow, Russia, January 14, 1994**

| | | | | | | | | |
|---|---|---|---|---|---|---|---|---|
| 2012 WM18 | 28-F | RUS | 6 | 1 | 2 | 3 | 12 | 5th |

**Del Zotto, Michael**
**b. Stouffville, Ontario, Canada, June 24, 1990**

| | | | | | | | | |
|---|---|---|---|---|---|---|---|---|
| 2010 WM | 4-D | CAN | 5 | 0 | 0 | 0 | 0 | 7th |

**Demagin, Sergei**
**b. Minsk, Soviet Union (Belarus), July 19, 1986**

| | | | | | | | | |
|---|---|---|---|---|---|---|---|---|
| 2007 WM | 21-F | BLR | 3 | 0 | 0 | 0 | 2 | 11th |
| 2009 WM | 59-F | BLR | 7 | 1 | 1 | 2 | 4 | 8th |
| 2010 OG-M | 59-F | BLR | 4 | 0 | 1 | 1 | 2 | 9th |
| 2010 WM | 59-F | BLR | 6 | 2 | 0 | 2 | 0 | 10th |
| 2011 WM | 59-F | BLR | 6 | 3 | 0 | 3 | 4 | 14th |
| **Totals WM** | | | **22** | **6** | **1** | **7** | **8** | **—** |

**De Marchi, Matt**
**b. Bemidji, Minnesota, United States, May 4, 1981**

| | | | | | | | | |
|---|---|---|---|---|---|---|---|---|
| 2010 WM | 19-D | ITA | 6 | 0 | 0 | 0 | 10 | 15th |
| 2012 WM | 19-D | ITA | 7 | 2 | 0 | 2 | 14 | 15th |
| **Totals WM** | | | **13** | **2** | **0** | **2** | **24** | **—** |

**Demiters, Renars**
**b. Riga, Soviet Union (Latvia), August 12, 1986**

| | | | | | | | | |
|---|---|---|---|---|---|---|---|---|
| 2006 WM20 | 8-D | LAT | 6 | 0 | 2 | 2 | 8 | 9th |

**Demkov, Artyom**
**b. Minsk, Soviet Union (Belarus), September 16, 1989**

| | | | | | | | | |
|---|---|---|---|---|---|---|---|---|
| 2011 WM | 17-F | BLR | 3 | 1 | 2 | 3 | 0 | 14th |

**Denisenko, Igor**
**b. Kazakhstanskaya, Soviet Union (Kazakhstan), July 16, 1989**

| | | | | | | | | |
|---|---|---|---|---|---|---|---|---|
| 2009 WM20 | 3-F | KAZ | 6 | 0 | 0 | 0 | 6 | 10th |

**Denisov, Denis**
**b. Kharkov, Soviet Union (Ukraine), December 31, 1981**

| | | | | | | | | |
|---|---|---|---|---|---|---|---|---|
| 2012 WM | 6-D | RUS | 10 | 2 | 1 | 3 | 2 | G |

**Denisov, Vladimir**
**b. Novopolotsk, Soviet Union (Belarus), June 29, 1984**

| | | | | | | | | |
|---|---|---|---|---|---|---|---|---|
| 2006 WM | 70-D | BLR | 6 | 0 | 1 | 1 | 35 | 6th |
| 2007 WM | 7-D | BLR | 6 | 0 | 1 | 1 | 14 | 11th |
| 2008 WM | 7-D | BLR | 6 | 0 | 3 | 3 | 6 | 9th |
| 2009 WM | 7-D | BLR | 5 | 0 | 0 | 0 | 6 | 8th |
| 2010 OG-M | 7-D | BLR | 4 | 0 | 0 | 0 | 0 | 9th |
| 2010 WM | 7-D | BLR | 6 | 0 | 1 | 1 | 2 | 10th |
| 2011 WM | 7-D | BLR | 4 | 0 | 1 | 1 | 4 | 14th |
| 2012 WM | 7-D | BLR | 7 | 0 | 1 | 1 | 10 | 14th |
| **Totals WM** | | | **40** | **0** | **8** | **8** | **77** | **—** |

**Deruns, Thomas**
**b. La Chaux-de-Fonds, Switzerland, March 1, 1982**

| | | | | | | | | |
|---|---|---|---|---|---|---|---|---|
| 2002 WM20 | 28-F | SUI | 7 | 0 | 1 | 1 | 2 | 4th |
| 2006 WM | 18-F | SUI | 6 | 0 | 1 | 1 | 29 | 9th |
| 2008 WM | 18-F | SUI | 7 | 0 | 3 | 3 | 10 | 7th |
| 2009 WM | 18-F | SUI | 5 | 0 | 0 | 0 | 0 | 9th |
| 2010 OG-M | 18-F | SUI | 5 | 0 | 0 | 0 | 0 | 8th |
| 2010 WM | 18-F | SUI | 7 | 1 | 2 | 3 | 16 | 5th |
| **Totals WM** | | | **25** | **1** | **6** | **7** | **55** | **—** |

**Dervaric, Damjan**
**b. Ljubljana, Yugoslavia (Slovenia), February 6, 1982**

| | | | | | | | | |
|---|---|---|---|---|---|---|---|---|
| 2003 WM | 23-D | SLO | 6 | 1 | 0 | 1 | 8 | 15th |
| 2005 WM | 23-D | SLO | 6 | 1 | 0 | 1 | 10 | 13th |
| 2008 WM | 23-D | SLO | 5 | 0 | 1 | 1 | 4 | 15th |
| 2011 WM | 23-D | SLO | 6 | 0 | 0 | 0 | 0 | 16th |
| **Totals WM** | | | **23** | **2** | **1** | **3** | **22** | **—** |

**Deschamps, Nicolas**
**b. LaSalle, Quebec, Canada, January 6, 1990**

| | | | | | | | | |
|---|---|---|---|---|---|---|---|---|
| 2008 WM18 | 17-F | CAN | 7 | 3 | 0 | 3 | 2 | G |

**Desjardins, Gabriel**
**b. Montreal, Quebec, Canada, November 9, 1992**

| | | | | | | | | |
|---|---|---|---|---|---|---|---|---|
| 2010 WM18 | 12-F | CAN | 6 | 0 | 3 | 3 | 2 | 7th |

**Despres, Simon**
**b. Laval, Quebec, Canada, June 27, 1991**

| | | | | | | | | |
|---|---|---|---|---|---|---|---|---|
| 2009 WM18 | 4-D | CAN | 6 | 0 | 2 | 2 | 8 | 4th |
| 2011 WM20 | 3-D | CAN | 7 | 0 | 3 | 3 | 0 | S |

**Desrosiers, Julien**
**b. St. Anaclet-de-Lessard, Quebec, Canada,**
October 14, 1980

| | | | | | | | | |
|---|---|---|---|---|---|---|---|---|
| 2008 WM | 24-F | FRA | 5 | 2 | 3 | 5 | 6 | 14th |
| 2011 WM | 24-F | FRA | 5 | 0 | 1 | 1 | 2 | 12th |
| 2012 WM | 24-F | FRA | 7 | 1 | 3 | 4 | 4 | 9th |
| **Totals WM** | | | **17** | **3** | **7** | **10** | **12** | **—** |

**De Toni, Manuel**
**b. Feltre, Italy, January 10, 1979**

| | | | | | | | | |
|---|---|---|---|---|---|---|---|---|
| 1999 WM | 18-F | ITA | 3 | 0 | 0 | 0 | 2 | 13th |
| 2000 WM | 18-F | ITA | 6 | 0 | 0 | 0 | 0 | 9th |
| 2001 WM | 18-F | ITA | 6 | 0 | 0 | 0 | 2 | 12th |
| 2002 WM | 18-F | ITA | 6 | 1 | 0 | 1 | 2 | 15th |
| 2006 OG-M | 28-F | ITA | 5 | 0 | 0 | 0 | 2 | 11th |
| 2006 WM | 28-F | ITA | 6 | 0 | 0 | 0 | 10 | 14th |
| 2007 WM | 28-F | ITA | 6 | 0 | 0 | 0 | 2 | 12th |
| 2008 WM | 28-F | ITA | 5 | 0 | 0 | 0 | 0 | 16th |
| 2010 WM | 28-F | ITA | 6 | 0 | 0 | 0 | 2 | 15th |
| 2012 WM | 28-F | ITA | 7 | 0 | 0 | 0 | 2 | 15th |
| **Totals WM** | | | **51** | **1** | **0** | **1** | **22** | **—** |

**Deyl, Radek**
**b. Kosice, Czechoslovakia (Slovakia), September 14, 1989**

| | | | | | | | | |
|---|---|---|---|---|---|---|---|---|
| 2009 WM20 | 25-D | SVK | 7 | 0 | 1 | 1 | 4 | 4th |

**Diaz, Rafael**
**b. Baar, Switzerland, January 9, 1986**

| | | | | | | | | |
|---|---|---|---|---|---|---|---|---|
| 2005 WM20 | 16-D | SUI | 6 | 1 | 1 | 2 | 8 | 8th |
| 2006 WM20 | 16-D | SUI | 6 | 0 | 1 | 1 | 6 | 7th |
| 2008 WM | 16-D | SUI | 7 | 0 | 0 | 0 | 0 | 7th |
| 2010 OG-M | 16-D | SUI | 5 | 0 | 0 | 0 | 4 | 8th |
| 2011 WM | 16-D | SUI | 6 | 3 | 1 | 4 | 4 | 9th |
| **Totals WM20** | | | **12** | **1** | **2** | **3** | **14** | **—** |

**Diem, Ramon**
**b. Zurich, Switzerland, November 11, 1994**

| | | | | | | | | |
|---|---|---|---|---|---|---|---|---|
| 2012 WM18 | 19-F | SUI | 6 | 0 | 1 | 1 | 0 | 7th |

**Di Domenico, Chris**
**b. North York (Toronto), Ontario, Canada, February 20, 1989**

| | | | | | | | | |
|---|---|---|---|---|---|---|---|---|
| 2009 WM20 | 25-F | CAN | 6 | 2 | 5 | 7 | 4 | G |

**Dilevka, Maris**
**b. Riga, Latvia, March 3, 1992**

| | | | | | | | | |
|---|---|---|---|---|---|---|---|---|
| 2010 WM18 | 21-F | LAT | 6 | 3 | 2 | 5 | 4 | 9th |
| 2012 WM20 | 16-F | LAT | 6 | 0 | 0 | 0 | 2 | 9th |

**DiPauli, Thomas**
**b. Woodbridge, Illinois, United States, April 29, 1994**

| | | | | | | | | |
|---|---|---|---|---|---|---|---|---|
| 2012 WM18 | 14-F | USA | 6 | 1 | 0 | 1 | 0 | G |

**Dixon, Stephen**
**b. Halifax, Nova Scotia, Canada, September 7, 1985**

| | | | | | | | | |
|---|---|---|---|---|---|---|---|---|
| 2003 WM18 | 14-F | CAN | 7 | 3 | 3 | 6 | 4 | G |
| 2004 WM20 | 24-F | CAN | 6 | 0 | 1 | 1 | 0 | S |
| 2005 WM20 | 14-F | CAN | 6 | 0 | 1 | 1 | 2 | G |
| **Totals WM20** | | | **12** | **0** | **2** | **2** | **2** | **G,S** |

**Djoos, Christian**
**b. Gothenburg, Sweden, August 6, 1994**

| | | | | | | | | |
|---|---|---|---|---|---|---|---|---|
| 2012 WM18 | 3-D | SWE | 6 | 1 | 2 | 3 | 2 | S |

**Doan, Shane**
**b. Halkirk, Alberta, Canada, October 10, 1976**

| | | | | | | | | |
|---|---|---|---|---|---|---|---|---|
| 1999 WM | 19-F | CAN | 4 | 0 | 0 | 0 | 0 | 4th |
| 2003 WM | 19-F | CAN | 9 | 4 | 2 | 6 | 12 | G |
| 2004 WCH | 19-F | CAN | 6 | 1 | 1 | 2 | 2 | 1st |
| 2005 WM | 19-F | CAN | 9 | 1 | 3 | 4 | 2 | S |
| 2006 OG-M | 19-F | CAN | 6 | 2 | 1 | 3 | 2 | 7th |
| 2007 WM | 19-F | CAN | 9 | 5 | 5 | 10 | 8 | G |
| 2008 WM | 19-F | CAN | 9 | 2 | 4 | 6 | 6 | S |
| 2009 WM | 19-F | CAN | 9 | 1 | 6 | 7 | 14 | S |
| **Totals WM** | | | **49** | **13** | **20** | **33** | **42** | **2G,3S** |

**Doczy, Milan**
**b. Zlin, Czechoslovakia (Czech Republic), January 27, 1990**

| | | | | | | | | |
|---|---|---|---|---|---|---|---|---|
| 2009 WM20 | 5-D | CZE | 6 | 0 | 2 | 2 | 8 | 6th |

**Doherty, Taylor**
**b. Cambridge, Ontario, Canada, March 2, 1991**

| | | | | | | | | |
|---|---|---|---|---|---|---|---|---|
| 2009 WM18 | 26-D | CAN | 6 | 0 | 0 | 0 | 8 | 4th |

**Dolezal, Ondrej**
**b. Prague, Czechoslovakia (Czech Republic), January 2, 1991**

| | | | | | | | | |
|---|---|---|---|---|---|---|---|---|
| 2009 WM18 | 26-D | CZE | 6 | 0 | 0 | 0 | 6 | 6th |

**Dolezal, Tomas**
**b. Prague, Czechoslovakia (Czech Republic), September 29, 1990**

| | | | | | | | | |
|---|---|---|---|---|---|---|---|---|
| 2010 WM20 | 12-F | CZE | 6 | 0 | 0 | 0 | 2 | 7th |

**Dolnik, Vladimir**
**b. Banska Bystrica, Slovakia, January 10, 1993**

| | | | | | | | | |
|---|---|---|---|---|---|---|---|---|
| 2011 WM18 | 27-F | SVK | 6 | 2 | 1 | 3 | 6 | 10th |
| 2012 WM20 | 19-F | SVK | 6 | 0 | 0 | 0 | 4 | 6th |

**Domenichelli, Hnat**
**b. Edmonton, Alberta, Canada, February 17, 1976**

| | | | | | | | | |
|---|---|---|---|---|---|---|---|---|
| 1996 WM20 | 17-F | CAN | 6 | 2 | 3 | 5 | 6 | G |
| 2010 OG-M | 17-F | SUI | 5 | 1 | 2 | 3 | 4 | 8th |

**Donati, Gianni**
**b. Obervas, Switzerland, March 6, 1989**

| | | | | | | | | |
|---|---|---|---|---|---|---|---|---|
| 2007 WM18 | 17-F | SUI | 6 | 1 | 0 | 1 | 2 | 6th |
| 2008 WM20 | 15-F | SUI | 6 | 0 | 0 | 0 | 2 | 9th |

**Donovan, Matt**
**b. Edmond, Oklahoma, United States, May 2, 1990**

| | | | | | | | | |
|---|---|---|---|---|---|---|---|---|
| 2010 WM20 | 4-D | USA | 7 | 3 | 2 | 5 | 2 | G |

**Donskoi, Joonas**
**b. Raahe, Finland, April 13, 1992**

| | | | | | | | | |
|---|---|---|---|---|---|---|---|---|
| 2010 WM18 | 12-F | FIN | 6 | 1 | 7 | 8 | 0 | B |
| 2011 WM20 | 27-F | FIN | 6 | 3 | 3 | 6 | 2 | 6th |
| 2012 WM20 | 27-F | FIN | 7 | 2 | 3 | 5 | 0 | 4th |
| Totals WM20 | | | 13 | 5 | 6 | 11 | 2 | — |

**Doronin, Pavel**
**b. Ufa, Soviet Union (Russia), August 21, 1988**

| | | | | | | | | |
|---|---|---|---|---|---|---|---|---|
| 2006 WM18 | 4-D | RUS | 6 | 0 | 1 | 1 | 12 | 5th |
| 2008 WM20 | 3-D | RUS | 7 | 0 | 2 | 2 | 2 | B |

**Doughty, Drew**
**b. London, Ontario, Canada, December 8, 1989**

| | | | | | | | | |
|---|---|---|---|---|---|---|---|---|
| 2007 WM18 | 20-D | CAN | 6 | 2 | 3 | 5 | 8 | 4th |
| 2008 WM20 | 8-D | CAN | 7 | 0 | 4 | 4 | 0 | G |
| 2009 WM | 3-D | CAN | 9 | 1 | 6 | 7 | 4 | S |
| 2010 OG-M | 8-D | CAN | 7 | 0 | 2 | 2 | 2 | G |

~WM20 IIHF Directorate Best Defenceman (2008), WM 20 All-Star Team/Defence (2008)

**Dowell, Jake**
**b. Eau Claire, Wisconsin, United States, March 4, 1985**

| | | | | | | | | |
|---|---|---|---|---|---|---|---|---|
| 2003 WM18 | 17-F | USA | 6 | 0 | 1 | 1 | 10 | 4th |
| 2004 WM20 | 16-F | USA | 6 | 0 | 2 | 2 | 2 | G |
| 2005 WM20 | 16-F | USA | 7 | 0 | 3 | 3 | 12 | 4th |
| **Totals WM20** | | | **13** | **0** | **5** | **5** | **14** | |

**Downie, Steve**
**b. Newmarket, Ontario, Canada, April 3, 1987**

| | | | | | | | | |
|---|---|---|---|---|---|---|---|---|
| 2006 WM20 | 7-F | CAN | 6 | 2 | 4 | 6 | 16 | G |
| 2007 WM20 | 7-F | CAN | 6 | 3 | 3 | 6 | 16 | G |
| 2010 WM | 9-F | CAN | 7 | 2 | 0 | 2 | 28 | 7th |
| **Totals WM20** | | | **12** | **5** | **7** | **12** | **32** | **2G** |

~WM20 All-Star Team/Forward (2006)

**Doyle, Eric**
**b. Calgary, Alberta, Canada, April 5, 1989**

| | | | | | | | | |
|---|---|---|---|---|---|---|---|---|
| 2007 WM18 | 2-D | CAN | 6 | 0 | 1 | 1 | 4 | 4th |

**Drabek, Jakub**
**b. Zilina, Czechoslovakia (Slovakia), March 3, 1987**

| | | | | | | | | |
|---|---|---|---|---|---|---|---|---|
| 2005 WM18 | 10-F | SVK | 6 | 0 | 0 | 0 | 10 | 6th |
| 2007 WM20 | 11-F | SVK | 6 | 0 | 1 | 1 | 6 | 8th |

**Draisaitl, Leon**
**b. Cologne, Germany, October 27, 1995**

| | | | | | | | | |
|---|---|---|---|---|---|---|---|---|
| 2012 WM18 | 15-F | GER | 6 | 2 | 5 | 7 | 2 | 6th |

**Dravecky, Vladimir**
**b. Kosice, Czechoslovakia (Slovakia), June 3, 1985**

| | | | | | | | | |
|---|---|---|---|---|---|---|---|---|
| 2003 WM18 | 19-F | SVK | 7 | 0 | 3 | 3 | 0 | S |
| 2010 WM | 22-F | SVK | 6 | 0 | 0 | 0 | 2 | 12th |

**Draxinger, Tobias**
**b. Munich, West Germany (Germany), January 3, 1985**

| | | | | | | | | |
|---|---|---|---|---|---|---|---|---|
| 2005 WM20 | 14-D | GER | 6 | 0 | 0 | 0 | 12 | 9th |
| 2007 WM | 9-D | GER | 6 | 0 | 0 | 0 | 6 | 9th |

**Dresler, Thor**
**b. Herlev, Denmark, March 10, 1979**

| | | | | | | | | |
|---|---|---|---|---|---|---|---|---|
| 2003 WM | 8-F | DEN | 5 | 0 | 0 | 0 | 0 | 11th |
| 2004 WM | 8-F | DEN | 2 | 0 | 0 | 0 | 0 | 12th |
| 2005 WM | 8-F | DEN | 3 | 0 | 0 | 0 | 2 | 14th |
| 2007 WM | 21-F | DEN | 5 | 0 | 1 | 1 | 4 | 10th |
| 2008 WM | 21-F | DEN | 3 | 0 | 1 | 1 | 0 | 12th |
| 2009 WM | 21-F | DEN | 6 | 0 | 0 | 0 | 2 | 13th |
| 2010 WM | 21-F | DEN | 7 | 0 | 1 | 1 | 0 | 8th |
| 2011 WM | 21-F | DEN | 6 | 0 | 0 | 0 | 4 | 11th |
| **Totals WM** | | | **37** | **0** | **3** | **3** | **12** | **—** |

**Drozd, Sergei**
**b. Minsk, Soviet Union (Belarus), April 14, 1990**

| | | | | | | | | |
|---|---|---|---|---|---|---|---|---|
| 2008 WM18 | 9-F | BLR | 6 | 2 | 4 | 6 | 4 | 9th |
| 2010 WM | 13-F | BLR | 3 | 0 | 0 | 0 | 0 | 10th |
| 2011 WM | 13-F | BLR | 4 | 0 | 0 | 0 | 2 | 14th |
| 2012 WM | 13-F | BLR | 6 | 0 | 0 | 0 | 2 | 14th |
| **Totals WM** | | | **13** | **0** | **0** | **0** | **4** | **—** |

**Drury, Chris**
**b. Trumbull, Connecticut, United States, August 20, 1976**

| | | | | | | | | |
|---|---|---|---|---|---|---|---|---|
| 1996 WM20 | 15-F | USA | 6 | 2 | 2 | 4 | 2 | 5th |
| 1997 WM | 17-F | USA | 8 | 0 | 1 | 1 | 2 | 6th |
| 1998 WM | 9-F | USA | 6 | 1 | 2 | 3 | 12 | 12th |
| 2002 OG-M | 18-F | USA | 6 | 0 | 0 | 0 | 0 | S |
| 2004 WM | 23-F | USA | 9 | 3 | 3 | 6 | 27 | B |
| 2004 WCH | 37-F | USA | 5 | 0 | 0 | 0 | 0 | 4th |
| 2006 OG-M | 18-F | USA | 6 | 0 | 3 | 3 | 2 | 8th |
| 2010 OG-M | 23-F | USA | 6 | 2 | 0 | 2 | 0 | S |
| **Totals WM** | | | **23** | **4** | **6** | **10** | **41** | **B** |
| **Totals OG-M** | | | **18** | **2** | **3** | **5** | **2** | **2S** |

**Dubinin, Anton**
**b. Moscow, Soviet Union (Russia), July 22, 1985**

| | | | | | | | | |
|---|---|---|---|---|---|---|---|---|
| 2003 WM18 | 10-F | RUS | 5 | 2 | 0 | 2 | 4 | B |

**Dubinsky, Brandon**
**b. Anchorage, Alaska, United States, April 29, 1986**

| | | | | | | | | |
|---|---|---|---|---|---|---|---|---|
| 2008 WM | 16-F | USA | 4 | 3 | 0 | 3 | 2 | 6th |
| 2010 WM | 17-F | USA | 6 | 3 | 7 | 10 | 2 | 13th |

**Du Bois, Felicien**
**b. La Chaux-de-Fonds, Switzerland, October 18, 1983**

| | | | | | | | | |
|---|---|---|---|---|---|---|---|---|
| 2009 WM | 13-D | SUI | 5 | 0 | 2 | 2 | 6 | 9th |
| 2010 WM | 13-D | SUI | 7 | 0 | 0 | 0 | 4 | 5th |
| 2011 WM | 13-D | SUI | 6 | 1 | 1 | 2 | 2 | 9th |
| 2012 WM | 13-D | SUI | 7 | 1 | 1 | 2 | 2 | 11th |
| **Totals WM** | | | **25** | **2** | **4** | **6** | **14** | **—** |

**Duca, Paolo**
**b. Locarno, Switzerland, June 3, 1981**

| | | | | | | | | |
|---|---|---|---|---|---|---|---|---|
| 1999 WM18 | 17-F | SUI | 7 | 0 | 5 | 5 | 2 | 4th |
| 2000 WM20 | 19-F | SUI | 7 | 4 | 1 | 5 | 14 | 6th |
| 2001 WM20 | 19-F | SUI | 7 | 0 | 2 | 2 | 4 | 6th |
| 2010 WM | 46-F | SUI | 7 | 0 | 0 | 0 | 0 | 5th |
| **Totals WM20** | | | **14** | **4** | **3** | **7** | **18** | **—** |

**Duchene, Matt**
**b. Haliburton, Ontario, Canada, January 16, 1991**

| | | | | | | | | |
|---|---|---|---|---|---|---|---|---|
| 2008 WM18 | 29-F | CAN | 7 | 5 | 3 | 8 | 6 | G |
| 2010 WM | 92-F | CAN | 7 | 4 | 3 | 7 | 0 | 7th |
| 2011 WM | 92-F | CAN | 7 | 0 | 0 | 0 | 2 | 5th |
| **Totals WM** | | | **14** | **4** | **3** | **7** | **2** | **—** |

**Dudarev, Dmitri**
**b. Ust-Kamenogorsk, Soviet Union (Kazakhstan), February 23, 1976**

| | | | | | | | | |
|---|---|---|---|---|---|---|---|---|
| 1998 OG-M | 18-F | KAZ | 7 | 1 | 1 | 2 | 0 | 8th |
| 1998 WM | 18-F | KAZ | 3 | 0 | 1 | 1 | 2 | 16th |
| 2004 WM | 12-F | KAZ | 6 | 0 | 0 | 0 | 4 | 13th |
| 2005 WM | 12-F | KAZ | 6 | 1 | 0 | 1 | 4 | 12th |
| 2006 OG-M | 21-F | KAZ | 5 | 0 | 0 | 0 | 2 | 9th |
| 2010 WM | 21-F | KAZ | 6 | 4 | 0 | 4 | 8 | 16th |
| 2012 WM | 21-F | KAZ | 5 | 0 | 3 | 3 | 0 | 16th |
| **Totals WM** | | | **26** | **5** | **4** | **9** | **18** | **—** |
| **Totals OG-M** | | | **12** | **1** | **1** | **2** | **2** | **—** |

**Dudik, Dmitri**
**b. Minsk, Soviet Union (Belarus), November 2, 1977**

| | | | | | | | | |
|---|---|---|---|---|---|---|---|---|
| 2000 WM | 18-F | BLR | 6 | 0 | 0 | 0 | 2 | 9th |
| 2002 OG-M | 24-F | BLR | 9 | 2 | 1 | 3 | 6 | 4th |
| 2005 WM | 77-F | BLR | 6 | 0 | 0 | 0 | 2 | 10th |
| 2006 WM | 77-F | BLR | 7 | 3 | 0 | 3 | 2 | 6th |
| 2007 WM | 77-F | BLR | 6 | 2 | 1 | 3 | 8 | 11th |
| 2008 WM | 77-F | BLR | 6 | 1 | 1 | 2 | 2 | 9th |
| **Totals WM** | | | **31** | **6** | **2** | **8** | **16** | **—** |

**Dudins, Vladislavs**
**b. Riga, Latvia, March 9, 1992**

| | | | | | | | | |
|---|---|---|---|---|---|---|---|---|
| 2010 WM18 | 29-D | LAT | 6 | 1 | 0 | 1 | 4 | 9th |

**Dumba, Matt**
**b. Calgary, Alberta, Canada, July 25, 1994**

| | | | | | | | | |
|---|---|---|---|---|---|---|---|---|
| 2012 WM18 | 24-D | CAN | 7 | 5 | 7 | 12 | 20 | B |

~WM18 IIHF Directorate Best Defenceman (2012)

**Dumoulin, Brian**
**b. Biddeford, Maine, United States, September 6, 1991**

| | | | | | | | | |
|---|---|---|---|---|---|---|---|---|
| 2011 WM20 | 4-D | USA | 6 | 0 | 2 | 2 | 2 | B |

**Dunner, Nico**
**b. Langrickenbach, Switzerland, April 19, 1994**

| | | | | | | | | |
|---|---|---|---|---|---|---|---|---|
| 2012 WM18 | 23-F | SUI | 6 | 0 | 0 | 0 | 6 | 7th |

**Duris, Oliver**
**b. Povazska Bystrica, Czechoslovakia (Slovakia), September 13, 1988**

| | | | | | | | | |
|---|---|---|---|---|---|---|---|---|
| 2008 WM20 | 28-F | SVK | 6 | 2 | 0 | 2 | 4 | 7th |

**Duus, Jesper**
**b. Glostrup, Denmark, November 24, 1967**

| | | | | | | | | |
|---|---|---|---|---|---|---|---|---|
| 2003 WM | 3-D | DEN | 6 | 0 | 1 | 1 | 2 | 11th |
| 2004 WM | 3-D | DEN | 6 | 0 | 1 | 1 | 4 | 12th |
| 2010 WM | 40-D | DEN | 2 | 0 | 0 | 0 | 0 | 8th |
| **Totals WM** | | | **14** | **0** | **2** | **2** | **6** | **—** |

**Dvoracek, David**
**b. Brno, Czech Republic, June 4, 1992**

| | | | | | | | | |
|---|---|---|---|---|---|---|---|---|
| 2010 WM18 | 23-F | CZE | 6 | 0 | 2 | 2 | 0 | 6th |

**Dvurechenski, Nikita**
**b. Lipetsk, Soviet Union (Russia), July 30, 1991**

| | | | | | | | | |
|---|---|---|---|---|---|---|---|---|
| 2009 WM18 | 25-F | RUS | 7 | 0 | 0 | 0 | 6 | S |
| 2011 WM20 | 17-F | RUS | 7 | 3 | 3 | 6 | 18 | G |

**Dwyer, Pat**
**b. Great Falls, Montana, United States, June 22, 1983**

| | | | | | | | | |
|---|---|---|---|---|---|---|---|---|
| 2012 WM | 39-F | USA | 8 | 1 | 2 | 3 | 0 | 7th |

**Dzerins, Andris**
**b. Jekabpils, Soviet Union (Latvia), February 14, 1988**

| | | | | | | | | |
|---|---|---|---|---|---|---|---|---|
| 2010 WM | 23-F | LAT | 6 | 0 | 1 | 1 | 4 | 11th |
| 2011 WM | 23-F | LAT | 6 | 0 | 5 | 5 | 2 | 13th |
| 2012 WM | 12-F | LAT | 4 | 0 | 0 | 0 | 4 | 10th |
| **Totals WM** | | | **16** | **0** | **6** | **6** | **10** | **—** |

**Dzerins, Guntis**
**b. Varaklana, Soviet Union (Latvia), February 17, 1985**

| | | | | | | | | |
|---|---|---|---|---|---|---|---|---|
| 2007 WM | 28-F | LAT | 1 | 0 | 0 | 0 | 0 | 13th |
| 2009 WM | 14-F | LAT | 7 | 1 | 0 | 1 | 0 | 7th |
| **Totals WM** | | | **8** | **1** | **0** | **1** | **0** | **—** |

**Eakin, Cody**
**b. Winnipeg, Manitoba, Canada, May 25, 1991**

| | | | | | | | | |
|---|---|---|---|---|---|---|---|---|
| 2009 WM18 | 21-F | CAN | 6 | 2 | 0 | 2 | 2 | 4th |
| 2011 WM20 | 21-F | CAN | 7 | 1 | 2 | 3 | 2 | S |

**Eaves, Patrick**
**b. Calgary, Alberta, Canada, May 1, 1984**

| | | | | | | | | |
|---|---|---|---|---|---|---|---|---|
| 2002 WM18 | 9-F | USA | 8 | 4 | 8 | 12 | 45 | G |
| 2004 WM20 | 9-F | USA | 6 | 1 | 5 | 6 | 8 | G |

**Eberle, Jan**
**b. Kladno, Czechoslovakia (Czech Republic), May 20, 1989**

| | | | | | | | | |
|---|---|---|---|---|---|---|---|---|
| 2009 WM20 | 24-F | CZE | 6 | 0 | 1 | 1 | 0 | 6th |

**Eberle, Jordan**
**b. Regina, Saskatchewan, Canada, May 15, 1990**

| | | | | | | | | |
|---|---|---|---|---|---|---|---|---|
| 2008 WM18 | 7-F | CAN | 7 | 4 | 6 | 10 | 0 | G |
| 2009 WM20 | 14-F | CAN | 6 | 6 | 7 | 13 | 2 | G |
| 2010 WM20 | 14-F | CAN | 6 | 8 | 5 | 13 | 4 | S |
| 2010 WM | 14-F | CAN | 4 | 1 | 3 | 4 | 0 | 7th |
| 2011 WM | 14-F | CAN | 7 | 4 | 0 | 4 | 2 | 5th |
| 2012 WM | 14-F | CAN | 8 | 4 | 4 | 8 | 0 | 5th |
| **Totals WM20** | | | **12** | **14** | **12** | **26** | **6** | **G,S** |
| **Totals WM** | | | **19** | **9** | **7** | **16** | **2** | **—** |

~WM20 MVP (2010), WM20 IIHF Directorate Best Forward (2010), WM20 All-Star Team/Forward (2010)

**Ebner, Bernhard**
**b. Schongau, Germany, September 12, 1990**

| | | | | | | | | |
|---|---|---|---|---|---|---|---|---|
| 2008 WM18 | 22-D | GER | 6 | 0 | 0 | 0 | 10 | 5th |

**Edler, Alexander**
**b. Ostersund, Sweden, April 21, 1986**

| | | | | | | | | |
|---|---|---|---|---|---|---|---|---|
| 2006 WM20 | 10-D | SWE | 6 | 0 | 1 | 1 | 6 | 5th |
| 2008 WM | 23-D | SWE | 8 | 1 | 2 | 3 | 12 | 4th |

**Edman, Niclas**
**b. Stockholm, Sweden, March 26, 1991**

| | | | | | | | | |
|---|---|---|---|---|---|---|---|---|
| 2009 WM18 | 5-D | SWE | 6 | 0 | 0 | 0 | 14 | 5th |

**Edwardson, Derek**
**b. Morton Grove, Illinois, United States, August 26, 1981**

| | | | | | | | | |
|---|---|---|---|---|---|---|---|---|
| 2012 WM | 9-F | ITA | 7 | 0 | 0 | 0 | 2 | 15th |

**Egger, Alexander**
**b. Bolzano, Italy, December 22, 1979**

| | | | | | | | | |
|---|---|---|---|---|---|---|---|---|
| 2006 WM | 7-D | ITA | 6 | 0 | 0 | 0 | 2 | 14th |
| 2010 WM | 17-F | ITA | 5 | 1 | 2 | 3 | 0 | 15th |
| 2012 WM | 17-F | ITA | 7 | 1 | 0 | 1 | 4 | 15th |
| **Totals WM** | | | **18** | **2** | **2** | **4** | **6** | **—** |

**Ehrensperger, Gianni**
**b. Zurich, Switzerland, May 5, 1985**

| | | | | | | | | |
|---|---|---|---|---|---|---|---|---|
| 2003 WM18 | 14-F | SUI | 6 | 2 | 0 | 2 | 2 | 9th |
| 2004 WM20 | 3-F | SUI | 6 | 5 | 2 | 7 | 2 | 8th |
| 2005 WM20 | 3-F | SUI | 6 | 0 | 2 | 2 | 0 | 8th |
| **Totals WM20** | | | **12** | **5** | **4** | **9** | **2** | **—** |

**Ehrhoff, Christian**
**b. Moers, West Germany (Germany), July 6, 1982**

| | | | | | | | | |
|---|---|---|---|---|---|---|---|---|
| 1999 WM18 | 29-F | GER | 6 | 1 | 2 | 3 | 6 | 9th |
| 2000 WM18 | 24-D | GER | 6 | 1 | 0 | 1 | 20 | 7th |
| 2002 OG-M | 10-D | GER | 7 | 0 | 0 | 0 | 8 | 8th |
| 2002 WM | 10-D | GER | 7 | 2 | 3 | 5 | 4 | 8th |
| 2003 WM | 10-D | GER | 7 | 0 | 0 | 0 | 8 | 6th |
| 2004 WCH | 10-D | GER | 4 | 0 | 0 | 0 | 2 | 8th |
| 2005 WM | 10-D | GER | 6 | 0 | 1 | 1 | 4 | 15th |
| 2006 OG-M | 10-D | GER | 5 | 1 | 1 | 2 | 4 | 10th |
| 2010 OG-M | 10-D | GER | 4 | 0 | 0 | 0 | 4 | 11th |
| 2010 WM | 10-D | GER | 6 | 1 | 1 | 2 | 0 | 4th |
| **Totals WM18** | | | **12** | **2** | **2** | **4** | **26** | **—** |
| **Totals WM** | | | **26** | **3** | **5** | **8** | **16** | **—** |
| **Totals OG-M** | | | **16** | **1** | **1** | **2** | **16** | **—** |

~WM All-Star Team/Defence (2010)

**Eikeland, Torbjorn**
**b. Lillehammer, Norway, July 6, 1991**

| | | | | | | | | |
|---|---|---|---|---|---|---|---|---|
| 2009 WM18 | 2-D | NOR | 6 | 0 | 0 | 0 | 6 | 9th |

**Eisenschmid, Markus**
**b. Marktoberdorf, Germany, January 22, 1995**

| | | | | | | | | |
|---|---|---|---|---|---|---|---|---|
| 2012 WM18 | 16-F | GER | 6 | 1 | 1 | 2 | 0 | 6th |

**Ekbom, Viktor**
**b. Falkoping, Sweden, June 1, 1989**

| | | | | | | | | |
|---|---|---|---|---|---|---|---|---|
| 2009 WM20 | 8-D | SWE | 6 | 0 | 2 | 2 | 2 | S |

**Ekholm Mattias**
**b. Borlange, Sweden, May 24, 1990**

| | | | | | | | | |
|---|---|---|---|---|---|---|---|---|
| 2008 WM18 | 2-D | SWE | 6 | 1 | 0 | 1 | 2 | 4th |
| 2010 WM20 | 14-D | SWE | 6 | 1 | 0 | 1 | 6 | B |

**Eklund, Oscar**
**b. Stockholm, Sweden, August 27, 1988**

| | | | | | | | | |
|---|---|---|---|---|---|---|---|---|
| 2008 WM20 | 8-D | SWE | 6 | 0 | 0 | 0 | 8 | S |

**Ekman-Larsson, Oliver**
**b. Karlskrona, Sweden, July 17, 1991**

| | | | | | | | | |
|---|---|---|---|---|---|---|---|---|
| 2009 WM18 | 7-D | SWE | 6 | 2 | 6 | 8 | 2 | 5th |
| 2010 WM20 | 3-D | SWE | 6 | 2 | 3 | 5 | 12 | B |
| 2010 WM | 3-D | SWE | 9 | 1 | 2 | 3 | 2 | B |
| 2011 WM | 3-D | SWE | 7 | 1 | 3 | 4 | 2 | S |
| **Totals WM** | | | **16** | **2** | **5** | **7** | **4** | **S,B** |

**Elias, Patrik**
**b. Trebic, Czechoslovakia (Czech Republic), April 13, 1976**

| | | | | | | | | |
|---|---|---|---|---|---|---|---|---|
| 1998 WM | 26-F | CZE | 3 | 1 | 0 | 1 | 0 | B |
| 2002 OG-M | 25-F | CZE | 4 | 1 | 1 | 2 | 0 | 7th |
| 2004 WCH | 25-F | CZE | 5 | 3 | 2 | 5 | 10 | 3rd |
| 2006 OG-M | 62-F | CZE | 1 | 0 | 0 | 0 | 2 | B |
| 2008 WM | 26-F | CZE | 7 | 6 | 3 | 9 | 6 | 5th |
| 2009 WM | 26-F | CZE | 3 | 2 | 0 | 2 | 2 | 6th |
| 2010 OG-M | 26-F | CZE | 5 | 2 | 2 | 4 | 2 | 7th |
| 2011 WM | 26-F | CZE | 9 | 4 | 5 | 9 | 6 | B |
| **Totals WM** | | | **22** | **13** | **8** | **21** | **14** | **2B** |
| **Totals OG-M** | | | **10** | **3** | **3** | **6** | **4** | **B** |

**Eller, Lars**
**b. Rodovre, Denmark, May 8, 1989**

| | | | | | | | | |
|---|---|---|---|---|---|---|---|---|
| 2008 WM20 | 16-F | DEN | 6 | 3 | 3 | 6 | 37 | 10th |
| 2008 WM | 20-F | DEN | 6 | 0 | 2 | 2 | 0 | 12th |
| 2010 WM | 61-F | DEN | 7 | 2 | 3 | 5 | 8 | 8th |
| 2012 WM | 81-F | DEN | 7 | 3 | 2 | 5 | 14 | 13th |
| **Totals WM** | | | **20** | **5** | **7** | **12** | **22** | **—** |

**Eller, Mads**
**b. Rodovre, Denmark, June 25, 1995**

| | | | | | | | | |
|---|---|---|---|---|---|---|---|---|
| 2012 WM18 | 11-F | DEN | 6 | 0 | 3 | 3 | 6 | 10th |
| 2012 WM20 | 19-F | DEN | 6 | 0 | 0 | 0 | 2 | 10th |

**Elliott, Stefan**
**b. North Vancouver, British Columbia, Canada, January 30, 1991**

| | | | | | | | | |
|---|---|---|---|---|---|---|---|---|
| 2009 WM18 | 6-D | CAN | 6 | 0 | 2 | 2 | 0 | 4th |

**Ellis, Ryan**
**b. Freelton, Ontario, Canada, January 3, 1991**

| | | | | | | | | |
|---|---|---|---|---|---|---|---|---|
| 2008 WM18 | 26-D | CAN | 7 | 3 | 4 | 7 | 0 | G |
| 2009 WM20 | 8-D | CAN | 6 | 1 | 6 | 7 | 0 | G |
| 2010 WM20 | 6-D | CAN | 6 | 1 | 7 | 8 | 2 | S |
| 2011 WM20 | 6-D | CAN | 7 | 3 | 7 | 10 | 2 | S |
| **Totals WM20** | | | **19** | **5** | **20** | **25** | **4** | **G,2S** |

~WM20 IIHF Directorate Best Defenceman (2011), WM20 All-Star Team/Defence (2011)

**Elo, Eero**
**b. Rauma, Finland, April 26, 1990**

| | | | | | | | | |
|---|---|---|---|---|---|---|---|---|
| 2010 WM20 | 16-F | FIN | 6 | 2 | 1 | 3 | 0 | 5th |

**El-Sayed, Marc**
**b. Wetzlar, Germany, January 18, 1991**

| | | | | | | | | |
|---|---|---|---|---|---|---|---|---|
| 2008 WM18 | 15-F | GER | 6 | 1 | 0 | 1 | 2 | 5th |
| 2009 WM18 | 21-F | GER | 6 | 3 | 3 | 6 | 0 | 10th |
| 2011 WM20 | 21-F | GER | 6 | 0 | 0 | 0 | 0 | 10th |
| **Totals WM18** | | | **12** | **4** | **3** | **7** | **2** | **—** |

**Emvall, Fredrik**
**b. Vaxjo, Sweden, June 28, 1976**

| | | | | | | | | |
|---|---|---|---|---|---|---|---|---|
| 2006 WM | 33-F | SWE | 9 | 3 | 2 | 5 | 4 | G |
| 2007 WM | 33-F | SWE | 9 | 1 | 2 | 3 | 2 | 4th |
| **Totals WM** | | | **18** | **4** | **4** | **8** | **6** | **G** |

**Engel, Florian**
**b. Munich, West Germany (Germany), January 2, 1990**

| | | | | | | | | |
|---|---|---|---|---|---|---|---|---|
| 2008 WM18 | 13-F | GER | 6 | 0 | 0 | 0 | 4 | 5th |

**Engler, Renato**
**b. Zivers, Switzerland, August 22, 1991**

| | | | | | | | | |
|---|---|---|---|---|---|---|---|---|
| 2008 WM18 | 26-F | SUI | 6 | 0 | 1 | 1 | 8 | 8th |
| 2009 WM18 | 14-F | SUI | 6 | 0 | 1 | 1 | 2 | 8th |
| 2011 WM20 | 21-F | SUI | 5 | 0 | 1 | 1 | 2 | 5th |
| **Totals WM18** | | | **12** | **0** | **2** | **2** | **10** | **—** |

**Engqvist, Andreas**
**b. Stockholm, Sweden, December 23, 1987**

| | | | | | | | | |
|---|---|---|---|---|---|---|---|---|
| 2010 WM | 20-F | SWE | 9 | 1 | 3 | 4 | 6 | B |

**Enlund, Jonas**
**b. Helsinki, Finland, November 3, 1987**

| | | | | | | | | |
|---|---|---|---|---|---|---|---|---|
| 2005 WM18 | 14-F | FIN | 6 | 1 | 3 | 4 | 0 | 7th |
| 2007 WM20 | 26-F | FIN | 6 | 1 | 0 | 1 | 6 | 6th |

**Ennis, Tyler**
**b. Edmonton, Alberta, Canada, October 6, 1989**

| | | | | | | | | |
|---|---|---|---|---|---|---|---|---|
| 2009 WM20 | 22-F | CAN | 6 | 3 | 4 | 7 | 0 | G |

**Enstrom, Tobias**
**b. Nordingra, Sweden, November 5, 1984**

| | | | | | | | | |
|---|---|---|---|---|---|---|---|---|
| 2002 WM18 | 15-D | SWE | 8 | 2 | 1 | 3 | 6 | 9th |
| 2003 WM20 | 6-D | SWE | 6 | 1 | 1 | 2 | 4 | 8th |
| 2004 WM20 | 6-D | SWE | 6 | 0 | 2 | 2 | 0 | 7th |
| 2007 WM | 2-D | SWE | 9 | 0 | 2 | 2 | 10 | 4th |
| 2009 WM | 39-D | SWE | 2 | 0 | 0 | 0 | 0 | B |
| 2010 OG-M | 39-D | SWE | 4 | 0 | 2 | 2 | 4 | 5th |
| **Totals WM20** | | | **12** | **1** | **3** | **4** | **4** | **—** |
| **Totals WM** | | | **11** | **0** | **2** | **2** | **10** | **B** |

**Erat, Martin**
**b. Trebic, Czechoslovakia (Czech Republic), August 29, 1981**

| | | | | | | | | |
|---|---|---|---|---|---|---|---|---|
| 1999 WM18 | 11-F | CZE | 6 | 0 | 2 | 2 | 12 | 5th |
| 2001 WM20 | 22-F | CZE | 7 | 2 | 1 | 3 | 16 | G |
| 2006 OG-M | 91-F | CZE | 8 | 1 | 1 | 2 | 4 | B |
| 2006 WM | 91-F | CZE | 9 | 3 | 5 | 8 | 6 | S |
| 2008 WM | 10-F | CZE | 7 | 2 | 4 | 6 | 14 | 5th |
| 2010 OG-M | 91-F | CZE | 5 | 0 | 1 | 1 | 2 | 7th |
| 2012 WM | 10-F | CZE | 5 | 3 | 1 | 4 | 2 | B |
| **Totals WM** | | | **21** | **8** | **10** | **18** | **22** | **S,B** |
| Totals OG | | | 13 | 1 | 2 | 3 | 6 | B |

**Ericsson, Jimmie**
**b. Skelleftea, Sweden, Febraury 22, 1980**

| | | | | | | | | |
|---|---|---|---|---|---|---|---|---|
| 2010 WM | 21-F | SWE | 3 | 0 | 0 | 0 | 4 | B |
| 2011 WM | 42-F | SWE | 8 | 2 | 1 | 3 | 2 | S |
| **Totals WM** | | | **11** | **2** | **1** | **3** | **6** | **S,B** |

**Ericsson, Jonathan**
**b. Karlskrona, Sweden, March 2, 1984**

| | | | | | | | | |
|---|---|---|---|---|---|---|---|---|
| 2010 WM | 52-D | SWE | 7 | 0 | 3 | 3 | 2 | B |
| 2012 WM | 52-D | SWE | 2 | 1 | 0 | 1 | 2 | 6th |
| **Totals WM** | | | **9** | **1** | **3** | **4** | **4** | **B** |

**Eriksson, Alexander**
**b. Anaset, Sweden, March 21, 1989**

| | | | | | | | | |
|---|---|---|---|---|---|---|---|---|
| 2007 WM18 | 2-D | SWE | 6 | 0 | 0 | 0 | 8 | B |

**Eriksson, Henrik**
**b. Vasterhaninge, Sweden, April 15, 1990**

| | | | | | | | | |
|---|---|---|---|---|---|---|---|---|
| 2008 WM18 | 14-F | SWE | 6 | 1 | 3 | 4 | 4 | 4th |

**Eriksson, Loui**
**b. Gothenburg, Sweden, July 17, 1985**

| | | | | | | | | |
|---|---|---|---|---|---|---|---|---|
| 2003 WM18 | 12-F | SWE | 6 | 5 | 2 | 7 | 12 | 5th |
| 2004 WM20 | 21-F | SWE | 6 | 1 | 1 | 2 | 2 | 7th |
| 2005 WM20 | 21-F | SWE | 6 | 2 | 3 | 5 | 0 | 6th |
| 2009 WM | 21-F | SWE | 9 | 3 | 4 | 7 | 0 | B |
| 2010 OG-M | 91-F | SWE | 4 | 3 | 1 | 4 | 0 | 5th |
| 2011 WM | 21-F | SWE | 9 | 3 | 1 | 4 | 2 | S |
| 2012 WM | 21-F | SWE | 8 | 5 | 8 | 13 | 2 | 6th |
| **Totals WM20** | | | **12** | **3** | **4** | **7** | **2** | **—** |
| **Totals WM** | | | **26** | **11** | **13** | **24** | **4** | **S,B** |

**Erixon, Sebastian**
**b. Sundsvall, Sweden, September 12, 1989**

| | | | | | | | | |
|---|---|---|---|---|---|---|---|---|
| 2007 WM18 | 3-D | SWE | 6 | 0 | 1 | 1 | 6 | B |
| 2009 WM20 | 3-D | SWE | 6 | 0 | 2 | 2 | 4 | S |

**Erixon, Tim**
**b. Port Chester, New York, United States, February 24, 1991**

| | | | | | | | | |
|---|---|---|---|---|---|---|---|---|
| 2009 WM18 | 24-D | SWE | 6 | 3 | 6 | 9 | 12 | 5th |
| 2009 WM20 | 16-D | SWE | 5 | 0 | 0 | 0 | 0 | S |
| 2010 WM20 | 4-D | SWE | 5 | 1 | 2 | 3 | 10 | B |
| 2011 WM20 | 4-D | SWE | 6 | 1 | 2 | 3 | 0 | 4th |
| 2011 WM | 44-D | SWE | 9 | 0 | 1 | 1 | 2 | S |
| **Totals WM20** | | | **16** | **2** | **4** | **6** | **10** | **S,B** |

~WM18 All-Star Team/Defence (2009)

**Erni, Samuel**
**b. Aadors, Switzerland, April 9, 1991**

| | | | | | | | | |
|---|---|---|---|---|---|---|---|---|
| 2009 WM18 | 6-D | SUI | 6 | 0 | 0 | 0 | 2 | 8th |

**Eronen, Teemu**
**b. Vantaa, Finland, November 22, 1990**

| | | | | | | | | |
|---|---|---|---|---|---|---|---|---|
| 2008 WM18 | 3-D | FIN | 6 | 0 | 0 | 0 | 4 | 6th |
| 2010 WM20 | 4-D | FIN | 6 | 1 | 2 | 3 | 4 | 5th |

**Eskesen, Michael**
**b. Odense, Denmark, June 5, 1986**

| | | | | | | | | |
|---|---|---|---|---|---|---|---|---|
| 2004 WM18 | 7-D | DEN | 6 | 1 | 3 | 4 | 2 | 8th |
| 2011 WM | 26-D | DEN | 6 | 0 | 0 | 0 | 0 | 11th |
| 2012 WM | 26-D | DEN | 3 | 0 | 0 | 0 | 0 | 13th |
| **Totals WM** | | | **9** | **0** | **0** | **0** | **0** | **—** |

**Esposito, Angelo**
**b. Montreal, Quebec, Canada, February 20, 1989**

| | | | | | | | | |
|---|---|---|---|---|---|---|---|---|
| 2007 WM18 | 9-F | CAN | 6 | 3 | 3 | 6 | 0 | 4th |
| 2009 WM20 | 7-F | CAN | 6 | 3 | 1 | 4 | 4 | G |

**Etem, Emerson**
**b. Long Beach, California, United States, June 16, 1992**

| | | | | | | | | |
|---|---|---|---|---|---|---|---|---|
| 2011 WM20 | 26-F | USA | 6 | 1 | 0 | 1 | 0 | B |
| 2012 WM20 | 10-F | USA | 6 | 0 | 4 | 4 | 2 | 7th |

**Ewanyk, Travis**
**b. St. Albert, Alberta, Canada, March 29, 1993**

| | | | | | | | | |
|---|---|---|---|---|---|---|---|---|
| 2011 WM18 | 22-F | CAN | 7 | 0 | 1 | 1 | 4 | 4th |

**Faber, Maximilian**
**b. Hagen, Germany, May 18, 1993**

| | | | | | | | | |
|---|---|---|---|---|---|---|---|---|
| 2011 WM18 | 5-D | GER | 6 | 0 | 0 | 0 | 0 | 6th |

**Fabricius, Karl**
**b. Kalix, Sweden, September 29, 1982**

| | | | | | | | | |
|---|---|---|---|---|---|---|---|---|
| 2008 WM | 12-F | SWE | 9 | 1 | 3 | 4 | 6 | 4th |

**Fabry, Branislav**
**b. Bratislava, Czechoslovakia (Slovakia), January 15, 1985**

| | | | | | | | | |
|---|---|---|---|---|---|---|---|---|
| 2003 WM18 | 24-F | SVK | 7 | 3 | 2 | 5 | 2 | S |
| 2004 WM20 | 15-F | SVK | 6 | 3 | 1 | 4 | 0 | 6th |
| 2005 WM20 | 15-F | SVK | 6 | 0 | 1 | 1 | 2 | 7th |
| **Totals WM20** | | | **12** | **3** | **2** | **5** | **2** | **—** |

**Fabus, Peter**
**b. Ilava, Czechoslovakia (Slovakia), July 15, 1979**

| | | | | | | | | |
|---|---|---|---|---|---|---|---|---|
| 2008 WM | 79-F | SVK | 5 | 0 | 2 | 2 | 4 | 13th |

**Fadeyev, Yevgeni**
**b. V-Kazakhstanskaya, Soviet Union (Kazakhstan), July 9, 1982**

| | | | | | | | | |
|---|---|---|---|---|---|---|---|---|
| 2001 WM20 | 3-D | KAZ | 6 | 0 | 0 | 0 | 14 | 10th |
| 2010 WM | 37-D | KAZ | 3 | 0 | 0 | 0 | 4 | 16th |
| 2012 WM | 37-D | KAZ | 7 | 0 | 0 | 0 | 4 | 16th |
| **Totals WM** | | | **10** | **0** | **0** | **0** | **8** | **—** |

**Fairchild, Cade**
**b. Duluth, Minnesota, United States, January 15, 1989**

| | | | | | | | | |
|---|---|---|---|---|---|---|---|---|
| 2006 WM18 | 2-D | USA | 6 | 0 | 0 | 0 | 0 | G |
| 2007 WM18 | 27-D | USA | 7 | 1 | 6 | 7 | 10 | S |
| 2008 WM20 | 27-D | USA | 6 | 0 | 1 | 1 | 4 | 4th |
| 2009 WM20 | 4-D | USA | 6 | 1 | 3 | 4 | 2 | 5th |
| **Totals WM18** | | | **13** | **1** | **6** | **7** | **10** | **G,S** |
| **Totals WM20** | | | **12** | **1** | **4** | **5** | **6** | **—** |

**Faksa, Radek**
**b. Opava, Czech Republic, January 9, 1994**

| | | | | | | | | |
|---|---|---|---|---|---|---|---|---|
| 2011 WM18 | 24-F | CZE | 6 | 0 | 0 | 0 | 2 | 8th |
| 2012 WM20 | 16-F | CZE | 6 | 2 | 0 | 2 | 4 | 5th |

**Fast, Konstantin**
**b. Chelyabinsk, Soviet Union (Russia), March 2, 1988**

| | | | | | | | | |
|---|---|---|---|---|---|---|---|---|
| 2008 WM20 | 16-D | KAZ | 5 | 0 | 1 | 1 | 4 | 8th |

**Fasth, Jesper**
**b. Nassjo, Sweden, December 2, 1991**

| | | | | | | | | |
|---|---|---|---|---|---|---|---|---|
| 2011 WM20 | 18-F | SWE | 6 | 4 | 2 | 6 | 0 | 4th |

**Faulk, Justin**
**b. South St. Paul, Minnesota, United States, March 20, 1992**

| | | | | | | | | |
|---|---|---|---|---|---|---|---|---|
| 2010 WM18 | 27-D | USA | 7 | 1 | 3 | 4 | 6 | G |
| 2011 WM20 | 25-D | USA | 6 | 1 | 3 | 4 | 0 | B |
| 2012 WM | 27-D | USA | 8 | 4 | 4 | 8 | 2 | 7th |

**Fauser, Gerrit**
**b. Nuremberg, West Germany (Germany), July 13, 1989**

| | | | | | | | | |
|---|---|---|---|---|---|---|---|---|
| 2007 WM18 | 23-F | GER | 6 | 1 | 2 | 3 | 4 | 8th |
| 2009 WM20 | 23-F | GER | 5 | 1 | 3 | 4 | 10 | 9th |

**Fayne, Mark**
**b. Sagamore Beach, Massachusetts, United States,** May 15, 1987

| | | | | | | | | |
|---|---|---|---|---|---|---|---|---|
| 2011 WM | 34-D | USA | 4 | 0 | 1 | 1 | 0 | 8th |

**Fedorov, Sergei** ~see Fyodorov, Sergei

**Fedosenko, Vyacheslav**
**b. Ust-Kamenogorsk, Soviet Union (Kazakhstan), February 6, 1990**

| | | | | | | | | |
|---|---|---|---|---|---|---|---|---|
| 2009 WM20 | 17-F | KAZ | 6 | 0 | 0 | 0 | 2 | 10th |

**Felicetti, Luca**
**b. Cavalese, Italy, August 18, 1981**

| | | | | | | | | |
|---|---|---|---|---|---|---|---|---|
| 2012 WM | 15-F | ITA | 7 | 0 | 0 | 0 | 2 | 15th |

**Felski, Sven**
**b. Berlin, East Germany (Germany), November 18, 1974**

| | | | | | | | | |
|---|---|---|---|---|---|---|---|---|
| 1993 WM20 | 11-F | GER | 7 | 2 | 0 | 2 | 28 | 7th |
| 1994 WM20 | 11-F | GER | 7 | 1 | 1 | 2 | 35 | 7th |
| 1998 WM | 11-F | GER | 6 | 0 | 2 | 2 | 18 | 11th |
| 2001 WM | 11-F | GER | 1 | 0 | 0 | 0 | 0 | 5th |
| 2003 WM | 11-F | GER | 6 | 2 | 0 | 2 | 14 | 6th |
| 2005 WM | 11-F | GER | 6 | 0 | 1 | 1 | 10 | 15th |
| 2006 OG-M | 11-F | GER | 5 | 2 | 0 | 2 | 4 | 10th |
| 2007 WM | 11-F | GER | 6 | 1 | 3 | 4 | 8 | 9th |
| 2008 WM | 11-F | GER | 6 | 0 | 1 | 1 | 6 | 10th |
| 2009 WM | 11-F | GER | 6 | 0 | 0 | 0 | 4 | 15th |

| | | | | | | | | |
|---|---|---|---|---|---|---|---|---|
| 2010 OG-M | 11-F | GER | 4 | 0 | 0 | 0 | 2 | 11th |
| 2010 WM | 11-F | GER | 9 | 0 | 3 | 3 | 8 | 4th |
| **Totals WM20** | | | **14** | **3** | **1** | **4** | **63** | **—** |
| **Totals WM** | | | **46** | **3** | **10** | **13** | **68** | **—** |
| **Totals OG-M** | | | **9** | **2** | **0** | **2** | **6** | **—** |

**Fernholm, Daniel**
**b. Stockholm, Sweden, December 20, 1983**

| | | | | | | | | |
|---|---|---|---|---|---|---|---|---|
| 2008 WM | 5-D | SWE | 8 | 0 | 3 | 3 | 4 | 4th |
| 2011 WM | 5-D | SWE | 9 | 0 | 1 | 1 | 4 | S |
| **Totals WM** | | | **17** | **0** | **4** | **4** | **8** | **S** |

**Ferraro, Landon**
**b. Burnaby, British Columbia, Canada, August 8, 1991**

| | | | | | | | | |
|---|---|---|---|---|---|---|---|---|
| 2009 WM18 | 16-F | CAN | 5 | 2 | 2 | 4 | 2 | 4th |

**Fical, Petr**
**b. Jindruchev Hradec, Czechoslovakia (Czech Republic), September 23, 1977**

| | | | | | | | | |
|---|---|---|---|---|---|---|---|---|
| 2004 WCH | 72-F | GER | 4 | 0 | 0 | 0 | 0 | 8th |
| 2005 WM | 72-F | GER | 6 | 0 | 1 | 1 | 0 | 15th |
| 2006 OG-M | 72-F | GER | 5 | 0 | 0 | 0 | 4 | 10th |
| 2007 WM | 72-F | GER | 6 | 0 | 0 | 0 | 10 | 9th |
| 2008 WM | 72-F | GER | 6 | 0 | 0 | 0 | 2 | 10th |
| **Totals WM** | | | **18** | **0** | **1** | **1** | **12** | **—** |

**Ficenec, Jakub**
**b. Hradec Kralove, Czechoslovakia (Czech Republic), February 11, 1977**

| | | | | | | | | |
|---|---|---|---|---|---|---|---|---|
| 2010 OG-M | 38-D | GER | 4 | 0 | 0 | 0 | 4 | 11th |

**Figren, Robin**
**b. Stockholm, Sweden, March 7, 1988**

| | | | | | | | | |
|---|---|---|---|---|---|---|---|---|
| 2006 WM18 | 13-F | SWE | 6 | 3 | 2 | 5 | 14 | 6th |
| 2008 WM20 | 23-F | SWE | 6 | 5 | 2 | 7 | 2 | S |

**Filatov, Nikita**
**b. Moscow, Soviet Union (Russia), May 25, 1990**

| | | | | | | | | |
|---|---|---|---|---|---|---|---|---|
| 2007 WM18 | 28-F | RUS | 7 | 4 | 5 | 9 | 6 | G |
| 2008 WM18 | 28-F | RUS | 6 | 3 | 6 | 9 | 29 | S |
| 2008 WM20 | 21-F | RUS | 7 | 4 | 5 | 9 | 10 | B |
| 2009 WM20 | 28-F | RUS | 7 | 8 | 3 | 11 | 6 | B |
| 2010 WM20 | 28-F | RUS | 6 | 1 | 5 | 6 | 6 | 6th |
| **Totals WM18** | | | **13** | **7** | **11** | **18** | **35** | |
| **Totals WM20** | | | **20** | **13** | **13** | **26** | **22** | **2B** |

~WM20 All-Star Team/Forward (2009), WM18 All-Star Team/Forward (2008)

**Filin, Igor**
**b. Minsk, Soviet Union (Belarus), November 29, 1987**

| | | | | | | | | |
|---|---|---|---|---|---|---|---|---|
| 2007 WM20 | 10-F | BLR | 6 | 1 | 1 | 2 | 4 | 10th |

**Filippi, Tomas**
**b. Rychnov nad Kneznou, Czech Republic, May 4, 1992**

| | | | | | | | | |
|---|---|---|---|---|---|---|---|---|
| 2010 WM18 | 14-F | CZE | 6 | 1 | 1 | 2 | 4 | 6th |
| 2012 WM20 | 22-F | CZE | 6 | 4 | 0 | 4 | 2 | 5th |

**Filippov, Alexei**
**b. Chelyabinsk, Russia, March 8, 1994**

| | | | | | | | | |
|---|---|---|---|---|---|---|---|---|
| 2012 WM18 | 11-F | RUS | 6 | 1 | 2 | 3 | 10 | 5th |

**Filppula, Valtteri**
**b. Vantaa, Finland, March 20, 1984**

| | | | | | | | | |
|---|---|---|---|---|---|---|---|---|
| 2002 WM18 | 12-F | FIN | 8 | 4 | 6 | 10 | 2 | 4th |
| 2003 WM20 | 12-F | FIN | 6 | 0 | 1 | 1 | 2 | B |
| 2004 WM20 | 12-F | FIN | 7 | 4 | 5 | 9 | 2 | B |
| 2010 OG-M | 51-F | FIN | 6 | 3 | 0 | 3 | 0 | B |
| 2012 WM | 51-F | FIN | 10 | 4 | 6 | 10 | 6 | 4th |
| **Totals WM20** | | | **13** | **4** | **6** | **10** | **4** | **2B** |

~WM20 All-Star Team/Forward (2004)

**Fischbuch, Daniel**
**b. Bad Friedrichshall, Germany, August 19, 1993**

| | | | | | | | | |
|---|---|---|---|---|---|---|---|---|
| 2011 WM18 | 15-F | GER | 6 | 2 | 1 | 3 | 6 | 6th |

**Fischer, Christpoher**
**b. Heidelberg, West Germany (Germany), January 24, 1988**

| | | | | | | | | |
|---|---|---|---|---|---|---|---|---|
| 2006 WM18 | 17-F | GER | 6 | 0 | 0 | 0 | 4 | 8th |
| 2007 WM20 | 3-D | GER | 6 | 1 | 1 | 2 | 6 | 9th |
| 2012 WM | 12-D | GER | 7 | 2 | 2 | 4 | 4 | 12th |

**Fischer, Jannick**
**b. Baar, Switzerland, June 29, 1990**

| | | | | | | | | |
|---|---|---|---|---|---|---|---|---|
| 2008 WM18 | 28-D | SUI | 6 | 0 | 1 | 1 | 4 | 8th |
| 2010 WM20 | 28-D | SUI | 7 | 0 | 0 | 0 | 2 | 4th |

**Fischer, Magnus**
**b. Oslo, Norway, May 10, 1994**

| | | | | | | | | |
|---|---|---|---|---|---|---|---|---|
| 2011 WM18 | 11-F | NOR | 5 | 0 | 0 | 0 | 2 | 9th |

**Fischhaber, Simon**
**b. Greiling, Germany, February 19, 1990**

| | | | | | | | | |
|---|---|---|---|---|---|---|---|---|
| 2007 WM18 | 14-F | GER | 6 | 1 | 1 | 2 | 4 | 8th |
| 2009 WM20 | 5-F | GER | 6 | 1 | 2 | 3 | 0 | 9th |

**Fisenko, Mikhail**
**b. Magnitogorsk, Soviet Union (Russia), June 1, 1990**

| | | | | | | | | |
|---|---|---|---|---|---|---|---|---|
| 2008 WM18 | 14-F | RUS | 6 | 0 | 2 | 2 | 2 | S |

**Fisher, Mike**
**b. Peterborough, Ontario, Canada, June 5, 1980**

| | | | | | | | | |
|---|---|---|---|---|---|---|---|---|
| 2005 WM | 17-F | CAN | 9 | 0 | 1 | 1 | 4 | S |
| 2009 WM | 12-F | CAN | 9 | 2 | 3 | 5 | 14 | S |
| **Totals WM** | | | **18** | **2** | **4** | **6** | **18** | **2S** |

**Flaake, Jerome**
**b. Guben, Germany, March 2, 1990**

| | | | | | | | | |
|---|---|---|---|---|---|---|---|---|
| 2007 WM18 | 16-F | GER | 6 | 4 | 2 | 6 | 12 | 8th |
| 2008 WM18 | 9-F | GER | 6 | 1 | 2 | 3 | 6 | 5th |
| 2009 WM20 | 9-F | GER | 6 | 3 | 2 | 5 | 12 | 9th |
| **Totals WM18** | | | **12** | **5** | **4** | **9** | **18** | **—** |

**Fleischmann, Tomas**
**b. Koprivnice, Czechoslovakia (Czech Republic), May 16, 1984**

| | | | | | | | | |
|---|---|---|---|---|---|---|---|---|
| 2002 WM18 | 14-F | CZE | 8 | 1 | 2 | 3 | 2 | B |
| 2003 WM20 | 23-F | CZE | 6 | 2 | 0 | 2 | 0 | 6th |
| 2004 WM20 | 16-F | CZE | 7 | 2 | 2 | 4 | 2 | 4th |
| 2008 WM | 43-F | CZE | 7 | 2 | 3 | 5 | 0 | 5th |
| 2010 OG-M | 34-F | CZE | 5 | 1 | 2 | 3 | 2 | 7th |
| **Totals WM20** | | | **13** | **4** | **2** | **6** | **2** | **—** |

**Fleury, Damien**
**b. Caen, France, February 1, 1986**

| | | | | | | | | |
|---|---|---|---|---|---|---|---|---|
| 2009 WM | 86-F | FRA | 6 | 0 | 0 | 0 | 0 | 12th |
| 2011 WM | 9-F | FRA | 6 | 1 | 0 | 1 | 2 | 12th |
| 2012 WM | 9-F | FRA | 7 | 1 | 0 | 1 | 8 | 9th |
| **Totals WM** | | | **19** | **2** | **0** | **2** | **10** | **—** |

**Florek, Justin**
**b. Marquette, Michigan, United States, May 18, 1990**

| | | | | | | | | |
|---|---|---|---|---|---|---|---|---|
| 2008 WM18 | 19-F | USA | 7 | 3 | 0 | 3 | 4 | G |

**Flynn, Ryan**
**b. St. Paul, Minnesota, United States, March 22, 1988**

| | | | | | | | | |
|---|---|---|---|---|---|---|---|---|
| 2006 WM18 | 12-F | USA | 6 | 2 | 1 | 3 | 4 | G |
| 2008 WM20 | 22-F | USA | 6 | 0 | 0 | 0 | 16 | 4th |

**Foligno, Marcus**
**b. Buffalo, New York, United States, August 10, 1991**

| | | | | | | | | |
|---|---|---|---|---|---|---|---|---|
| 2011 WM20 | 17-F | CAN | 7 | 2 | 2 | 4 | 2 | S |

**Foligno, Nick**
**b. Buffalo, New York, United States, October 31, 1987**

| | | | | | | | | |
|---|---|---|---|---|---|---|---|---|
| 2009 WM | 17-F | USA | 9 | 0 | 2 | 2 | 4 | 4th |
| 2010 WM | 71-F | USA | 6 | 3 | 0 | 3 | 0 | 13th |
| **Totals WM** | | | **15** | **3** | **2** | **5** | **4** | **—** |

**Follestad-Johansen, Erik**
**b. Oslo, Norway, June 22, 1989**

| | | | | | | | | |
|---|---|---|---|---|---|---|---|---|
| 2011 WM | 3-D | NOR | 4 | 0 | 0 | 0 | 0 | 6th |

**Fomin, Alexander**
**b. Minsk, Soviet Union (Belarus), November 12, 1990**

| | | | | | | | | |
|---|---|---|---|---|---|---|---|---|
| 2008 WM18 | 24-F | BLR | 6 | 6 | 2 | 8 | 0 | 9th |

**Fontanive, Nicola**
**b. Agordo, Italy, October 25, 1985**

| | | | | | | | | |
|---|---|---|---|---|---|---|---|---|
| 2012 WM | 11-F | ITA | 7 | 0 | 1 | 1 | 4 | 15th |

**Forbort, Derek**
**b. Duluth, Minnesota, United States, March 4, 1992**

| | | | | | | | | |
|---|---|---|---|---|---|---|---|---|
| 2010 WM18 | 3-D | USA | 7 | 0 | 2 | 2 | 6 | G |
| 2011 WM20 | 7-D | USA | 6 | 0 | 0 | 0 | 0 | B |
| 2012 WM20 | 4-D | USA | 3 | 0 | 2 | 2 | 0 | 7th |
| **Totals WM20** | | | **9** | **0** | **2** | **2** | **0** | **B** |

**Forsberg, Filip**
**b. Ostervala, Sweden, August 13, 1994**

| | | | | | | | | |
|---|---|---|---|---|---|---|---|---|
| 2011 WM18 | 29-F | SWE | 6 | 4 | 2 | 6 | 2 | S |
| 2012 WM18 | 16-F | SWE | 6 | 5 | 2 | 7 | 6 | S |
| 2012 WM20 | 16-F | SWE | 6 | 0 | 1 | 1 | 2 | G |
| **Totals WM18** | | | **12** | **9** | **4** | **13** | **8** | **2S** |

~WM18 IIHF Directorate Best Forward (2012)

**Forsberg, Kristian**
**b. Oslo, Norway, May 5, 1986**

| | | | | | | | | |
|---|---|---|---|---|---|---|---|---|
| 2004 WM18 | 7-F | NOR | 6 | 0 | 1 | 1 | 2 | 10th |
| 2006 WM20 | 7-F | NOR | 6 | 1 | 1 | 2 | 18 | 10th |
| 2007 WM | 29-F | NOR | 6 | 0 | 0 | 0 | 0 | 14th |
| 2008 WM | 26-F | NOR | 7 | 0 | 0 | 0 | 0 | 8th |
| 2009 WM | 26-F | NOR | 6 | 0 | 0 | 0 | 4 | 11th |
| 2010 OG-M | 26-F | NOR | 4 | 0 | 0 | 0 | 0 | 10th |
| 2010 WM | 26-F | NOR | 6 | 0 | 1 | 1 | 0 | 9th |
| 2011 WM | 26-F | NOR | 7 | 1 | 0 | 1 | 2 | 6th |
| 2012 WM | 26-F | NOR | 6 | 0 | 0 | 0 | 2 | 8th |
| **Totals WM** | | | **38** | **1** | **1** | **2** | **8** | **—** |

**Forsberg, Tobias**
**b. Pitea, Sweden, April 5, 1988**

| | | | | | | | | |
|---|---|---|---|---|---|---|---|---|
| 2008 WM20 | 16-F | SWE | 6 | 2 | 1 | 3 | 6 | S |

**Forster, Beat**
**b. Davos, Switzerland, February 2, 1983**

| | | | | | | | | |
|---|---|---|---|---|---|---|---|---|
| 2000 WM18 | 16-D | SUI | 7 | 0 | 0 | 0 | 24 | 4th |
| 2001 WM18 | 4-D | SUI | 7 | 2 | 2 | 4 | 34 | S |
| 2001 WM20 | 11-D | SUI | 7 | 0 | 1 | 1 | 4 | 6th |
| 2002 WM20 | 4-D | SUI | 7 | 0 | 2 | 2 | 10 | 4th |
| 2003 WM20 | 29-D | SUI | 6 | 1 | 3 | 4 | 2 | 7th |
| 2003 WM | 29-D | SUI | 7 | 1 | 2 | 3 | 8 | 8th |
| 2004 WM | 29-D | SUI | 7 | 1 | 2 | 3 | 6 | 8th |
| 2005 WM | 29-D | SUI | 7 | 1 | 1 | 2 | 12 | 8th |
| 2006 OG-M | 29-D | SUI | 6 | 0 | 0 | 0 | 6 | 6th |
| 2006 WM | 29-D | SUI | 6 | 1 | 0 | 1 | 12 | 9th |
| 2007 WM | 29-D | SUI | 7 | 0 | 0 | 0 | 4 | 8th |
| 2008 WM | 29-D | SUI | 7 | 2 | 2 | 4 | 2 | 7th |
| **Totals WM18** | | | **14** | **2** | **2** | **4** | **58** | **—** |
| **Totals WM20** | | | **20** | **1** | **6** | **7** | **16** | **—** |
| **Totals WM** | | | **41** | **6** | **7** | **13** | **44** | **—** |

*played WM18 as Beat Schiess-Forster

**Forster, Maximilian**
**b. Landshut, West Germany (Germany), September 19, 1990**

| | | | | | | | | |
|---|---|---|---|---|---|---|---|---|
| 2008 WM18 | 28-F | GER | 6 | 2 | 1 | 3 | 4 | 5th |
| 2009 WM20 | 26-F | GER | 3 | 0 | 1 | 1 | 2 | 9th |

**Fortier, Olivier**
**b. Ancienne-Lorette, Quebec, Canada, March 31, 1991**

| | | | | | | | | |
|---|---|---|---|---|---|---|---|---|
| 2007 WM18 | 29-F | CAN | 6 | 0 | 1 | 1 | 0 | 4th |

**Fowler, Cam**
**b. Windsor, Ontario, Canada, December 5, 1991**

| | | | | | | | | |
|---|---|---|---|---|---|---|---|---|
| 2009 WM18 | 4-D | USA | 7 | 1 | 7 | 8 | 4 | G |
| 2010 WM20 | 24-D | USA | 7 | 0 | 2 | 2 | 4 | G |
| 2011 WM | 7-D | USA | 7 | 1 | 2 | 3 | 2 | 8th |
| 2012 WM | 4-D | USA | 8 | 1 | 4 | 5 | 2 | 7th |
| **Totals WM** | | | **15** | **2** | **6** | **8** | **4** | **—** |

~WM18 IIHF Directorate Best Defenceman (2009), WM18 All-Star Team/Defence (2009)

**Franson, Cody**
**b. Sicamous, British Columbia, Canada, August 8, 1987**

| | | | | | | | | |
|---|---|---|---|---|---|---|---|---|
| 2007 WM20 | 26-D | CAN | 6 | 0 | 2 | 2 | 4 | G |

**Fransson, Johan**
**b. Kalix, Sweden, February 18, 1985**

| | | | | | | | | |
|---|---|---|---|---|---|---|---|---|
| 2004 WM20 | 5-D | SWE | 6 | 3 | 0 | 3 | 2 | 7th |
| 2005 WM20 | 5-D | SWE | 6 | 0 | 0 | 0 | 12 | 6th |
| **Totals WM20** | | | **12** | **3** | **0** | **3** | **14** | **—** |

**Franzen, Johan**
**b. Landsbro, Sweden, December 23, 1979**

| | | | | | | | | |
|---|---|---|---|---|---|---|---|---|
| 2005 WM | 16-F | SWE | 5 | 1 | 0 | 1 | 0 | 4th |
| 2006 WM | 39-F | SWE | 8 | 0 | 3 | 3 | 12 | G |
| 2010 OG-M | 93-F | SWE | 4 | 1 | 1 | 2 | 2 | 5th |
| 2012 WM | 93-F | SWE | 7 | 4 | 5 | 9 | 8 | 6th |
| **Totals WM** | | | **20** | **5** | **8** | **13** | **20** | **G** |

**Fraser, Colin**
**b. Sicamous, British Columbia, Canada, January 28, 1985**

| | | | | | | | | |
|---|---|---|---|---|---|---|---|---|
| 2005 WM20 | 11-F | CAN | 6 | 1 | 4 | 5 | 2 | G |

**Fraser, Jim**
**b. Port Huron, Michigan, United States, January 16, 1987**

| | | | | | | | | |
|---|---|---|---|---|---|---|---|---|
| 2005 WM18 | 11-F | USA | 6 | 1 | 1 | 2 | 10 | G |
| 2007 WM20 | 11-F | USA | 7 | 0 | 0 | 0 | 2 | B |

**Frederiksen, Christopher**
**b. Frederikshavn, Denmark, October 6, 1994**

| | | | | | | | | |
|---|---|---|---|---|---|---|---|---|
| 2012 WM18 | 23-F | DEN | 5 | 0 | 0 | 0 | 2 | 10th |

**Fredriksen, Anders**
**b. Fredrikstad, Norway, February 17, 1981**

| | | | | | | | | |
|---|---|---|---|---|---|---|---|---|
| 1999 WM18 | 27-F | NOR | 4 | 0 | 1 | 1 | 2 | 9th |
| 2000 WM | 33-F | NOR | 6 | 0 | 0 | 0 | 0 | 9th |
| 2001 WM | 25-F | NOR | 6 | 0 | 0 | 0 | 2 | 15th |
| 2010 WM | 52-F | NOR | 6 | 1 | 3 | 4 | 0 | 9th |
| 2011 WM | 52-F | NOR | 7 | 0 | 0 | 0 | 0 | 6th |
| **Totals WM** | | | **25** | **1** | **3** | **4** | **2** | **—** |

**Fredriksson, David**
**b. Barnarp, Sweden, October 4, 1985**

| | | | | | | | | |
|---|---|---|---|---|---|---|---|---|
| 2003 WM18 | 27-F | SWE | 6 | 0 | 0 | 0 | 29 | 5th |
| 2005 WM20 | 19-F | SWE | 5 | 1 | 0 | 1 | 20 | 6th |

**Freibergs, Kristers**
**b. Priekule, Latvia, July 3, 1992**

| | | | | | | | | |
|---|---|---|---|---|---|---|---|---|
| 2010 WM18 | 4-D | LAT | 5 | 1 | 1 | 2 | 2 | 9th |
| 2012 WM20 | 10-D | LAT | 6 | 0 | 0 | 0 | 0 | 9th |

**Freibergs, Ralfs**
**b. Riga, Soviet Union (Latvia), May 17, 1991**

| | | | | | | | | |
|---|---|---|---|---|---|---|---|---|
| 2009 WM20 | 29-D | LAT | 6 | 1 | 1 | 2 | 10 | 8th |
| 2010 WM20 | 29-D | LAT | 6 | 0 | 3 | 3 | 12 | 9th |
| **Totals WM20** | | | **12** | **1** | **4** | **5** | **22** | **—** |

**Freimanis, Martins**
**b. Liepaja, Latvia, January 19, 1994**

| | | | | | | | | |
|---|---|---|---|---|---|---|---|---|
| 2012 WM18 | 5-D | LAT | 6 | 0 | 1 | 1 | 8 | 9th |

**Friberg, Max**
**b. Skovde, Sweden, Noevmber 20, 1992**

| | | | | | | | | |
|---|---|---|---|---|---|---|---|---|
| 2010 WM18 | 10-F | SWE | 6 | 2 | 3 | 5 | 14 | S |
| 2011 WM20 | 14-F | SWE | 6 | 2 | 0 | 2 | 4 | 4th |
| 2012 WM20 | 14-F | SWE | 6 | 9 | 2 | 11 | 22 | G |
| **Totals WM20** | | | **12** | **11** | **2** | **13** | **26** | **G** |

~WM20 All-Star Team/Forward (2012)

**Friedli, Samuel**
**b. Rapperswil, Switzerland, April 8, 1987**

| | | | | | | | | |
|---|---|---|---|---|---|---|---|---|
| 2007 WM20 | 24-F | SUI | 6 | 1 | 1 | 2 | 4 | 7th |

**Fritsche, Dan**
**b. Parma, Ohio, United States, July 13, 1985**

| | | | | | | | | |
|---|---|---|---|---|---|---|---|---|
| 2004 WM20 | 22-F | USA | 6 | 2 | 2 | 4 | 4 | G |
| 2005 WM20 | 9-F | USA | 7 | 3 | 4 | 7 | 22 | 4th |
| **Totals WM20** | | | **13** | **5** | **6** | **11** | **26** | **G** |

**Fritsche, Tom**
**b. Parma, Ohio, United States, September 30, 1986**

| | | | | | | | | |
|---|---|---|---|---|---|---|---|---|
| 2004 WM18 | 18-F | USA | 6 | 2 | 3 | 5 | 6 | S |
| 2006 WM20 | 26-F | USA | 7 | 1 | 4 | 5 | 4 | 4th |

**Frk, Martin**
**b. Bochov, Czech Republic, October 5, 1993**

| | | | | | | | | |
|---|---|---|---|---|---|---|---|---|
| 2010 WM18 | 25-F | CZE | 6 | 2 | 5 | 7 | 6 | 6th |
| 2011 WM18 | 5-F | CZE | 6 | 1 | 4 | 5 | 2 | 8th |
| 2011 WM20 | 5-F | CZE | 6 | 3 | 3 | 6 | 31 | 7th |
| **Totals WM18** | | | **12** | **3** | **9** | **12** | **8** | **—** |

**Froberg, Linus**
**b. Karlstad, Sweden, June 16, 1993**

| | | | | | | | | |
|---|---|---|---|---|---|---|---|---|
| 2011 WM18 | 28-F | SWE | 6 | 1 | 0 | 1 | 2 | S |

**Froese, Byron**
**b. Winkler, Manitoba, Canada, March 12, 1991**

| | | | | | | | | |
|---|---|---|---|---|---|---|---|---|
| 2009 WM18 | 14-F | CAN | 6 | 4 | 3 | 7 | 4 | 4th |

**Frogren, Jonas**
**b. Falun, Sweden, August 28, 1980**

| | | | | | | | | |
|---|---|---|---|---|---|---|---|---|
| 2000 WM20 | 24-D | SWE | 7 | 0 | 2 | 2 | 6 | 5th |
| 2008 WM | 24-D | SWE | 9 | 0 | 3 | 3 | 8 | 4th |

**Froidevaux, Etienne**
**b. Biel, Switzerland, March 20, 1989**

| | | | | | | | | |
|---|---|---|---|---|---|---|---|---|
| 2007 WM18 | 23-F | SUI | 6 | 1 | 1 | 2 | 2 | 6th |
| 2007 WM20 | 10-F | SUI | 6 | 1 | 1 | 2 | 2 | 7th |
| 2008 WM20 | 10-F | SUI | 6 | 1 | 5 | 6 | 4 | 9th |
| **Totals WM20** | | | **12** | **2** | **6** | **8** | **6** | **—** |

**Frolik, Michael**
**b. Kladno, Czechoslovakia (Czech Republic), February 17, 1988**

| | | | | | | | | |
|---|---|---|---|---|---|---|---|---|
| 2004 WM18 | 28-F | CZE | 2 | 0 | 0 | 0 | 0 | B |
| 2005 WM18 | 14-F | CZE | 7 | 3 | 1 | 4 | 2 | 4th |
| 2006 WM18 | 27-F | CZE | 7 | 2 | 3 | 5 | 10 | B |
| 2007 WM20 | 27-F | CZE | 6 | 4 | 2 | 6 | 4 | 5th |
| 2008 WM20 | 14-F | CZE | 6 | 5 | 0 | 5 | 14 | 5th |
| 2011 WM | 18-F | CZE | 9 | 3 | 2 | 5 | 0 | B |
| 2012 WM | 67-F | CZE | 10 | 2 | 1 | 3 | 0 | B |
| **Totals WM18** | | | **16** | **5** | **4** | **9** | **12** | **2B** |
| **Totals WM20** | | | **12** | **9** | **2** | **11** | **18** | **—** |
| **Totals WM** | | | **19** | **5** | **3** | **8** | **0** | **2B** |

**Frolov, Alexander**
**b. Moscow, Soviet Union (Russia), June 19, 1982**

| | | | | | | | | |
|---|---|---|---|---|---|---|---|---|
| 2000 WM18 | 11-F | RUS | 6 | 5 | 1 | 6 | 10 | S |
| 2002 WM20 | 11-F | RUS | 7 | 6 | 2 | 8 | 4 | G |
| 2003 WM | 11-F | RUS | 7 | 3 | 2 | 5 | 6 | 7th |
| 2004 WCH | 24-F | RUS | 4 | 0 | 2 | 2 | 2 | 6th |
| 2006 OG-M | 24-F | RUS | 3 | 0 | 1 | 1 | 0 | 4th |
| 2007 WM | 24-F | RUS | 9 | 5 | 6 | 11 | 0 | B |
| 2009 WM | 24-F | RUS | 7 | 3 | 1 | 4 | 2 | G |
| 2010 WM | 24-F | RUS | 8 | 0 | 1 | 1 | 2 | S |
| **Totals WM** | | | **31** | **11** | **10** | **21** | **10** | **G,S,B** |

**Froshaug, Mats**
**b. Oslo, Norway, July 31, 1988**

| | | | | | | | | |
|---|---|---|---|---|---|---|---|---|
| 2006 WM18 | 21-F | NOR | 6 | 0 | 3 | 3 | 6 | 10th |
| 2008 WM | 27-F | NOR | 7 | 0 | 0 | 0 | 4 | 8th |

**Fruhauf, Peter**
**b. Presov, Czechoslovakia (Slovakia), August 15, 1982**

| | | | | | | | | |
|---|---|---|---|---|---|---|---|---|
| 2000 WM18 | 7-D | SVK | 6 | 2 | 2 | 4 | 12 | 5th |
| 2002 WM20 | 7-D | SVK | 7 | 1 | 0 | 1 | 6 | 8th |
| 2010 WM | 43-D | SVK | 4 | 0 | 1 | 1 | 2 | 12th |

**Fuglister, Jeffrey**
**b. Killwangen, Switzerland, January 15, 1990**

| | | | | | | | | |
|---|---|---|---|---|---|---|---|---|
| 2010 WM20 | 15-F | SUI | 7 | 2 | 2 | 4 | 33 | 4th |

**Fujerik, Dominik**
**b. Ilava, Slovakia, March 24, 1993**

| | | | | | | | | |
|---|---|---|---|---|---|---|---|---|
| 2011 WM18 | 16-F | SVK | 1 | 0 | 1 | 1 | 0 | 10th |

**Furchner, Sebastian**
**b. Kaufbeuren, West Germany (Germany), May 3, 1982**

| | | | | | | | | |
|---|---|---|---|---|---|---|---|---|
| 2012 WM | 67-F | GER | 7 | 0 | 0 | 0 | 2 | 12th |

**Furrer, Philippe**
**b. Staldenried, Switzerland, June 16, 1985**

| | | | | | | | | |
|---|---|---|---|---|---|---|---|---|
| 2002 WM18 | 29-D | SUI | 8 | 2 | 0 | 2 | 0 | 7th |
| 2003 WM18 | 3-D | SUI | 6 | 1 | 3 | 4 | 20 | 9th |
| 2003 WM20 | 7-D | SUI | 6 | 0 | 0 | 0 | 4 | 7th |
| 2005 WM20 | 7-D | SUI | 6 | 0 | 0 | 0 | 10 | 8th |
| 2008 WM | 54-D | SUI | 7 | 1 | 1 | 2 | 16 | 7th |
| 2009 WM | 54-D | SUI | 4 | 0 | 0 | 0 | 6 | 9th |
| 2010 OG-M | 54-D | SUI | 5 | 0 | 1 | 1 | 2 | 8th |
| 2011 WM | 54-D | SUI | 6 | 0 | 0 | 0 | 4 | 9th |
| 2012 WM | 54-D | SUI | 7 | 0 | 1 | 1 | 0 | 11th |
| **Totals WM18** | | | **14** | **3** | **3** | **6** | **20** | **—** |
| **Totals WM20** | | | **12** | **0** | **0** | **0** | **14** | **—** |
| **Totals WM** | | | **24** | **1** | **2** | **3** | **26** | **—** |

**Fusdahl, Tor Egil**
**b. Oslo, Norway, September 29, 1991**

| | | | | | | | | |
|---|---|---|---|---|---|---|---|---|
| 2009 WM18 | 12-F | NOR | 6 | 1 | 2 | 3 | 2 | 9th |

**Gaborik, Marian**
**b. Trencin, Czechoslovakia (Slovakia), February 14, 1982**

| | | | | | | | | |
|---|---|---|---|---|---|---|---|---|
| 1999 WM18 | 11-F | SVK | 7 | 3 | 7 | 10 | 2 | B |
| 1999 WM20 | 10-F | SVK | 6 | 3 | 0 | 3 | 2 | B |
| 2000 WM18 | 12-F | SVK | 6 | 6 | 2 | 8 | 12 | 5th |
| 2000 WM20 | 23-F | SVK | 7 | 3 | 1 | 4 | 0 | 9th |
| 2001 WM | 10-F | SVK | 7 | 2 | 1 | 3 | 0 | 7th |
| 2004 WM | 10-F | SVK | 9 | 4 | 2 | 6 | 4 | 4th |
| 2004 WCH | 10-F | SVK | 4 | 1 | 0 | 1 | 2 | 7th |
| 2005 WM | 10-F | SVK | 7 | 3 | 1 | 4 | 6 | 5th |
| 2006 OG-M | 10-F | SVK | 6 | 3 | 4 | 7 | 4 | 5th |
| 2007 WM | 10-F | SVK | 6 | 5 | 6 | 11 | 14 | 6th |
| 2010 OG-M | 10-F | SVK | 7 | 4 | 1 | 5 | 6 | 4th |
| 2011 WM | 10-F | SVK | 6 | 2 | 1 | 3 | 0 | 10th |
| **Totals WM18** | | | **13** | **9** | **9** | **18** | **14** | **B** |
| **Totals WM20** | | | **13** | **6** | **1** | **7** | **2** | **B** |
| **Totals WM** | | | **35** | **16** | **11** | **27** | **24** | **—** |
| **Totals OG-M** | | | **13** | **7** | **5** | **12** | **10** | **—** |

**Gade, Nikolai**
**b. Gentofte, Denmark, February 7, 1994**

| | | | | | | | | |
|---|---|---|---|---|---|---|---|---|
| 2012 WM18 | 17-F | DEN | 6 | 0 | 1 | 1 | 25 | 10th |

**Gagne, Simon**
**b. Ste. Foy, Quebec, Canada, February 29, 1980**

| | | | | | | | | |
|---|---|---|---|---|---|---|---|---|
| 1999 WM20 | 12-F | CAN | 7 | 7 | 1 | 8 | 2 | S |
| 2002 OG-M | 21-F | CAN | 6 | 1 | 3 | 4 | 0 | G |
| 2004 WCH | 21-F | CAN | 6 | 1 | 1 | 2 | 0 | 1st |
| 2005 WM | 21-F | CAN | 9 | 3 | 7 | 10 | 0 | S |
| 2006 OG-M | 21-F | CAN | 6 | 1 | 2 | 3 | 6 | 7th |
| **Totals OG-M** | | | **12** | **2** | **5** | **7** | **6** | **G** |

**Gagner, Sam**
**b. London, Ontario, Canada, August 10, 1989**

| | | | | | | | | |
|---|---|---|---|---|---|---|---|---|
| 2007 WM20 | 38-F | CAN | 6 | 0 | 0 | 0 | 8 | G |
| 2008 WM | 89-F | CAN | 1 | 0 | 0 | 0 | 0 | S |

**Galiardi, T.J. (Terry Joseph)**
**b. Calgary, Alberta, Canada, April 22, 1988**

| | | | | | | | | |
|---|---|---|---|---|---|---|---|---|
| 2010 WM | 18-F | USA | 6 | 0 | 3 | 3 | 8 | 13th |

**Galimov, Emil**
**b. Nizknekamsk, Russia, May 9, 1992**

| | | | | | | | | |
|---|---|---|---|---|---|---|---|---|
| 2010 WM18 | 27-F | RUS | 7 | 2 | 1 | 3 | 10 | 4th |

**Galin, Damir**
**b. January 17, 1994**

| | | | | | | | | |
|---|---|---|---|---|---|---|---|---|
| 2012 WM18 | 24-D | RUS | 6 | 0 | 0 | 0 | 0 | 5th |

**Gallagher, Brendan**
**b. Delta, British Columbia, May 6, 1992**

| | | | | | | | | |
|---|---|---|---|---|---|---|---|---|
| 2012 WM20 | 12-F | CAN | 6 | 3 | 3 | 6 | 12 | B |

**Galvins, Guntis**
**b. Talsi, Soviet Union (Latvia), January 25, 1986**

| | | | | | | | | |
|---|---|---|---|---|---|---|---|---|
| 2005 WM | 8-D | LAT | 6 | 0 | 1 | 1 | 0 | 9th |
| 2006 WM20 | 23-D | LAT | 5 | 1 | 1 | 2 | 29 | 9th |
| 2006 WM | 8-D | LAT | 6 | 0 | 0 | 0 | 8 | 10th |
| 2007 WM | 7-D | LAT | 6 | 1 | 2 | 3 | 8 | 13th |
| 2008 WM | 13-D | LAT | 6 | 0 | 0 | 0 | 2 | 11th |
| 2009 WM | 13-D | LAT | 7 | 1 | 2 | 3 | 2 | 7th |
| 2010 OG-M | 13-D | LAT | 2 | 0 | 0 | 0 | 0 | 12th |
| 2010 WM | 13-D | LAT | 6 | 1 | 1 | 2 | 8 | 11th |
| 2012 WM | 13-D | LAT | 7 | 0 | 3 | 3 | 2 | 10th |
| **Totals WM** | | | **44** | **3** | **9** | **12** | **30** | **—** |

**Ganz, Fabian**
**b. Embrach, Switzerland, January 31, 1990**

| | | | | | | | | |
|---|---|---|---|---|---|---|---|---|
| 2008 WM18 | 11-D | SUI | 6 | 0 | 0 | 0 | 6 | 8th |

**Gardiner, Jake**
**b. Deephaven, Minnesota, United States, July 4, 1990**

| | | | | | | | | |
|---|---|---|---|---|---|---|---|---|
| 2010 WM20 | 28-D | USA | 7 | 0 | 3 | 3 | 4 | G |

**Gardner, Ryan**
**b. Akron, Ontario, Canada, April 18, 1978**

| | | | | | | | | |
|---|---|---|---|---|---|---|---|---|
| 2009 WM | 51-F | SUI | 5 | 1 | 0 | 1 | 0 | 9th |
| 2011 WM | 51-F | SUI | 6 | 3 | 2 | 5 | 2 | 9th |
| **Totals WM** | | | **11** | **4** | **2** | **6** | **2** | **—** |

**Gareyev, Stanislav**
**b. Ivanovo, Russia, August 13, 1994**

| | | | | | | | | |
|---|---|---|---|---|---|---|---|---|
| 2012 WM18 | 3-D | RUS | 6 | 0 | 0 | 0 | 0 | 5th |

**Gasnikov, Yevgeni**
**b. Ust-Kamenogorsk, Soviet Union (Kazakhstan), January 18, 1988**

| | | | | | | | | |
|---|---|---|---|---|---|---|---|---|
| 2008 WM20 | 19-F | KAZ | 6 | 1 | 2 | 3 | 6 | 8th |

**Gasparovic, Jakub**
**b. Trencin, Czechoslovakia (Slovakia), February 26, 1990**

| | | | | | | | | |
|---|---|---|---|---|---|---|---|---|
| 2010 WM20 | 18-F | SVK | 6 | 2 | 1 | 3 | 4 | 8th |

**Gaul, Patrick**
**b. Pittsburgh, Pennsylvania, United States, February 27, 1990**

| | | | | | | | | |
|---|---|---|---|---|---|---|---|---|
| 2008 WM18 | 6-F | USA | 7 | 0 | 0 | 0 | 0 | G |

**Gaunce, Brendan**
**b. Markham, Ontario, March 25, 1994**

| | | | | | | | | |
|---|---|---|---|---|---|---|---|---|
| 2012 WM18 | 10-F | CAN | 7 | 3 | 1 | 4 | 8 | B |

**Gaustad, Paul**
**b. Fargo, North Dakota, United States, February 3, 1982**

| | | | | | | | | |
|---|---|---|---|---|---|---|---|---|
| 2011 WM | 28-F | USA | 6 | 0 | 1 | 1 | 4 | 8th |

**Gavrilenok, Alexei**
**b. Minsk, Soviet Union (Belarus), October 20, 1987**

| | | | | | | | | |
|---|---|---|---|---|---|---|---|---|
| 2007 WM20 | 3-D | BLR | 6 | 0 | 0 | 0 | 8 | 10th |

**Gavrilin, Andrei**
**b. Karaganda, Soviet Union (Kazakhstan), July 24, 1978**

| | | | | | | | | |
|---|---|---|---|---|---|---|---|---|
| 1998 WM20 | 29-F | KAZ | 6 | 2 | 1 | 3 | 6 | 7th |
| 2010 WM | 33-F | KAZ | 6 | 0 | 1 | 1 | 2 | 16th |

**Gavrus, Artur**
**b. Grodno, Belarus, January 3, 1994**

| | | | | | | | | |
|---|---|---|---|---|---|---|---|---|
| 2010 WM18 | 10-F | BLR | 6 | 1 | 0 | 1 | 0 | 10th |

**Gawlik, Christoph**
**b. Deggendorf, West Germany (Germany), August 10, 1987**

| | | | | | | | | |
|---|---|---|---|---|---|---|---|---|
| 2007 WM20 | 9-F | GER | 6 | 1 | 4 | 5 | 4 | 9th |

**Gay, Nicolas**
**b. Eysins, Switzerland, April 15, 1990**

| | | | | | | | | |
|---|---|---|---|---|---|---|---|---|
| 2008 WM18 | 3-F | SUI | 6 | 0 | 0 | 0 | 8 | 8th |
| 2010 WM20 | 3-F | SUI | 7 | 0 | 0 | 0 | 0 | 4th |

**Geering, Patrick**
**b. Zurich, Switzerland, February 12, 1990**

| | | | | | | | | |
|---|---|---|---|---|---|---|---|---|
| 2007 WM18 | 25-D | SUI | 6 | 0 | 0 | 0 | 4 | 6th |
| 2008 WM18 | 4-D | SUI | 6 | 3 | 2 | 5 | 8 | 8th |
| 2008 WM20 | 3-D | SUI | 6 | 0 | 0 | 0 | 0 | 9th |
| 2010 WM20 | 4-D | SUI | 7 | 0 | 5 | 5 | 2 | 4th |
| 2010 WM | 4-D | SUI | 1 | 0 | 0 | 0 | 0 | 5th |
| **Totals WM18** | | | **12** | **3** | **2** | **5** | **12** | **—** |
| **Totals WM20** | | | **13** | **0** | **5** | **5** | **2** | **—** |

**Gelazis, Matiss**
**b. Jelgava, Latvia, May 15, 1994**

| | | | | | | | | |
|---|---|---|---|---|---|---|---|---|
| 2012 WM18 | 6-D | LAT | 6 | 0 | 1 | 1 | 0 | 9th |

**Gemperli, Pascal**
**b. Mogelsberg, Switzerland, April 2, 1990**

| | | | | | | | | |
|---|---|---|---|---|---|---|---|---|
| 2008 WM18 | 14-F | SUI | 6 | 1 | 0 | 1 | 4 | 8th |

**Geoffrion, Blake**
**b. Brentwood, Tennessee, United States, February 3, 1988**

| | | | | | | | | |
|---|---|---|---|---|---|---|---|---|
| 2006 WM18 | 5-F | USA | 6 | 1 | 4 | 5 | 8 | G |
| 2007 WM20 | 5-F | USA | 7 | 0 | 1 | 1 | 6 | B |
| 2008 WM20 | 5-F | USA | 6 | 0 | 1 | 1 | 8 | 4th |
| **Totals WM20** | | | **13** | **0** | **2** | **2** | **14** | **B** |

**Gerasimov, Alexander**
**b. Ust-Kamenogorsk, Soviet Union (Kazakhstan), January 1, 1988**

| | | | | | | | | |
|---|---|---|---|---|---|---|---|---|
| 2008 WM20 | 13-D | KAZ | 6 | 0 | 0 | 0 | 8 | 8th |

**Gerbe, Nathan**
**b. Oxford, Michigan, United States, July 24, 1987**

| | | | | | | | | |
|---|---|---|---|---|---|---|---|---|
| 2004 WM18 | 21-F | USA | 6 | 0 | 2 | 2 | 20 | S |
| 2005 WM18 | 9-F | USA | 6 | 4 | 4 | 8 | 14 | G |
| 2006 WM20 | 20-F | USA | 7 | 0 | 0 | 0 | 6 | 4th |
| 2007 WM20 | 9-F | USA | 7 | 0 | 6 | 6 | 2 | B |
| **Totals WM18** | | | **12** | **4** | **6** | **10** | **34** | |
| **Totals WM20** | | | **14** | **0** | **6** | **6** | **8** | **B** |

**Gerber, Beat**
**b. Oberlangenegg, Switzerland, May 16, 1982**

| | | | | | | | | |
|---|---|---|---|---|---|---|---|---|
| 1999 WM18 | 11-D | SUI | 7 | 0 | 1 | 1 | 2 | 4th |
| 2000 WM18 | 2-D | SUI | 7 | 0 | 2 | 2 | 12 | 4th |
| 2001 WM20 | 2-D | SUI | 7 | 0 | 0 | 0 | 10 | 6th |
| 2002 WM20 | 2-D | SUI | 7 | 1 | 2 | 3 | 4 | 4th |
| 2002 WM | 21-D | SUI | 6 | 0 | 0 | 0 | 4 | 10th |
| 2006 WM | 2-D | SUI | 2 | 0 | 0 | 0 | 2 | 9th |
| 2007 WM | 2-D | SUI | 7 | 0 | 0 | 0 | 8 | 8th |
| 2008 WM | 2-D | SUI | 6 | 0 | 0 | 0 | 8 | 7th |
| 2011 WM | 2-D | SUI | 5 | 0 | 1 | 1 | 2 | 9th |
| **Totals WM18** | | | **14** | **0** | **3** | **3** | **14** | **—** |
| **Totals WM20** | | | **14** | **1** | **2** | **3** | **14** | **—** |
| **Totals WM** | | | **26** | **0** | **1** | **1** | **24** | **—** |

**Gerhat, Frantisek**
**b. Bratislava, Czechoslovakia (Slovakia), April 28, 1990**

| | | | | | | | | |
|---|---|---|---|---|---|---|---|---|
| 2010 WM20 | 12-F | SVK | 6 | 0 | 0 | 0 | 0 | 8th |

**Gernat, Martin**
**b. Presov, Slovakia, April 11, 1993**

| | | | | | | | | |
|---|---|---|---|---|---|---|---|---|
| 2011 WM18 | 28-D | SVK | 6 | 0 | 1 | 1 | 2 | 10th |
| 2012 WM20 | 25-D | SVK | 6 | 1 | 1 | 2 | 2 | 6th |

**Getzlaf, Ryan**
**b. Regina, Saskatchewan, Canada, May 10, 1985**

| | | | | | | | | |
|---|---|---|---|---|---|---|---|---|
| 2003 WM18 | 15-F | CAN | 7 | 2 | 2 | 4 | 10 | G |
| 2004 WM20 | 15-F | CAN | 6 | 3 | 3 | 6 | 4 | S |
| 2005 WM20 | 15-F | CAN | 6 | 3 | 9 | 12 | 8 | G |
| 2008 WM | 51-F | CAN | 9 | 3 | 11 | 14 | 10 | S |
| 2010 OG-M | 51-F | CAN | 7 | 3 | 4 | 7 | 2 | G |
| 2012 WM | 15-F | CAN | 8 | 2 | 7 | 9 | 27 | 5th |
| **Totals WM20** | | | **12** | **6** | **12** | **18** | **12** | **G,S** |
| **Totals WM** | | | **17** | **5** | **18** | **23** | **37** | **S** |

**Giebe, Christopher**
**b. Berlin, West Germany (Germany), May 13, 1987**

| | | | | | | | | |
|---|---|---|---|---|---|---|---|---|
| 2007 WM20 | 6-D | GER | 6 | 1 | 0 | 1 | 0 | 9th |

**Gilbert, Tom**
**b. Minneapolis, Minnesota, United States, January 10, 1983**

| | | | | | | | | |
|---|---|---|---|---|---|---|---|---|
| 2008 WM | 77-D | USA | 7 | 1 | 3 | 4 | 0 | 6th |

**Gill, Hal**
**b. Concord, Massachusetts, United States, April 6, 1975**

| | | | | | | | | |
|---|---|---|---|---|---|---|---|---|
| 2000 WM | 25-D | USA | 7 | 0 | 0 | 0 | 14 | 4th |
| 2001 WM | 25-D | USA | 9 | 0 | 0 | 0 | 4 | 7th |
| 2004 WM | 26-D | USA | 9 | 0 | 2 | 2 | 12 | B |
| 2005 WM | 25-D | USA | 7 | 0 | 0 | 0 | 6 | 6th |
| 2006 WM | 25-D | USA | 7 | 0 | 0 | 0 | 14 | 7th |
| **Totals WM** | | | **39** | **0** | **2** | **2** | **50** | **B** |

**Gillies, Colton**
**b. White Rock, British Columbia, Canada, February 12, 1989**

| | | | | | | | | |
|---|---|---|---|---|---|---|---|---|
| 2007 WM18 | 15-F | CAN | 6 | 2 | 1 | 3 | 10 | 4th |
| 2008 WM20 | 18-F | CAN | 7 | 1 | 0 | 1 | 6 | G |

**Gilroy, Matt**
**b. North Bellmore, New York, United States, July 30, 1984**

| | | | | | | | | |
|---|---|---|---|---|---|---|---|---|
| 2010 WM | 97-D | USA | 6 | 3 | 1 | 4 | 0 | 13th |

**Gimbatov, Magomed**
**b. Makhachkala, Soviet Union (Russia), November 11, 1990**

| | | | | | | | | |
|---|---|---|---|---|---|---|---|---|
| 2010 WM20 | 25-F | RUS | 6 | 0 | 0 | 0 | 2 | 6th |

**Giordano, Mark**
**b. Toronto, Ontario, Canada, October 3, 1983**

| | | | | | | | | |
|---|---|---|---|---|---|---|---|---|
| 2010 WM | 5-D | CAN | 7 | 3 | 1 | 4 | 10 | 7th |

**Gipters, Martins**
**b. Riga, Soviet Union (Latvia), April 5, 1989**

| | | | | | | | | |
|---|---|---|---|---|---|---|---|---|
| 2007 WM18 | 6-D | LAT | 6 | 0 | 0 | 0 | 4 | 10th |
| 2009 WM20 | 6-D | LAT | 3 | 0 | 0 | 0 | 4 | 8th |

**Girard, Felix**
**b. Levis, Quebec, Canada, May 9, 1994**

| | | | | | | | | |
|---|---|---|---|---|---|---|---|---|
| 2012 WM18 | 16-F | CAN | 5 | 1 | 0 | 1 | 6 | B\ |

**Girgensons, Zemgus**
**b. Riga, Latvia, January 5, 1994**

| | | | | | | | | |
|---|---|---|---|---|---|---|---|---|
| 2010 WM18 | 27-F | LAT | 6 | 1 | 1 | 2 | 2 | 9th |
| 2012 WM20 | 22-F | LAT | 6 | 2 | 0 | 2 | 6 | 9th |

**Giro, Sergei**
**b. Minsk, Soviet Union (Belarus), July 5, 1985**

| | | | | | | | | |
|---|---|---|---|---|---|---|---|---|
| 2003 WM18 | 5-D | BLR | 3 | 0 | 0 | 0 | 6 | 8th |
| 2005 WM20 | 24-D | BLR | 6 | 0 | 1 | 1 | 0 | 10th |

**Giroux, Claude**
**b. Hearst, Ontario, Canada, January 12, 1988**

| | | | | | | | | |
|---|---|---|---|---|---|---|---|---|
| 2008 WM20 | 28-F | CAN | 7 | 2 | 4 | 6 | 8 | G |

**Gleason, Tim**
**b. Clawson, Michigan, United States, January 29, 1983**

| | | | | | | | | |
|---|---|---|---|---|---|---|---|---|
| 2001 WM20 | 4-D | USA | 7 | 0 | 1 | 1 | 2 | 5th |
| 2003 WM20 | 4-D | USA | 1 | 0 | 0 | 0 | 0 | 4th |
| 2008 WM | 6-D | USA | 6 | 0 | 1 | 1 | 6 | 6th |
| 2010 OG-M | 4-D | USA | 6 | 0 | 0 | 0 | 0 | S |
| **Totals WM20** | | | **8** | **0** | **1** | **1** | **2** | **—** |

**Glovatski, Anton**
**b. Magnitogorsk, Soviet Union (Russia), August 6, 1988**

| | | | | | | | | |
|---|---|---|---|---|---|---|---|---|
| 2006 WM18 | 28-F | RUS | 6 | 4 | 1 | 5 | 2 | — |
| 2007 WM20 | 13-F | RUS | 6 | 0 | 1 | 1 | 2 | S |

**Gobbi, John**
**b. Faido, Switzerland, September 25, 1981**

| | | | | | | | | |
|---|---|---|---|---|---|---|---|---|
| 2011 WM | 19-D | SUI | 3 | 0 | 0 | 0 | 0 | 9th |

**Goc, Marcel**
**b. Calw, West Germany (Germany), August 24, 1983**

| | | | | | | | | |
|---|---|---|---|---|---|---|---|---|
| 2000 WM18 | 13-F | GER | 6 | 2 | 1 | 3 | 10 | 7th |
| 2001 WM18 | 7-F | GER | 6 | 2 | 4 | 6 | 0 | 5th |
| 2001 WM | 7-F | GER | 7 | 0 | 0 | 0 | 2 | 5th |
| 2003 WM | 57-F | GER | 7 | 1 | 2 | 3 | 0 | 6th |
| 2004 WCH | 57-F | GER | 3 | 0 | 1 | 1 | 2 | 8th |
| 2005 WM | 57-F | GER | 6 | 2 | 0 | 2 | 0 | 15th |
| 2006 OG-M | 57-F | GER | 5 | 1 | 0 | 1 | 0 | 10th |
| 2008 WM | 57-F | GER | 3 | 0 | 0 | 0 | 0 | 10th |
| 2010 OG-M | 57-F | GER | 4 | 2 | 1 | 3 | 0 | 11th |
| 2010 WM | 57-F | GER | 9 | 2 | 0 | 2 | 4 | 4th |
| 2012 WM | 57-F | GER | 7 | 0 | 0 | 0 | 2 | 12th |
| Totals WM18 | | | 12 | 4 | 5 | 9 | 10 | — |
| **Totals WM** | | | **39** | **5** | **2** | **7** | **8** | **—** |
| **Totals OG-M** | | | **9** | **3** | **1** | **4** | **0** | **—** |

**Goc, Nicolai**
**b. Calw, West Germany (Germany), June 17, 1986**

| | | | | | | | | |
|---|---|---|---|---|---|---|---|---|
| 2009 WM | 77-D | GER | 2 | 0 | 0 | 0 | 0 | 15th |
| 2010 WM | 77-D | GER | 9 | 1 | 0 | 1 | 4 | 4th |
| 2011 WM | 77-D | GER | 6 | 0 | 1 | 1 | 4 | 7th |
| 2012 WM | 77-D | GER | 7 | 0 | 0 | 0 | 14 | 12th |
| **Totals WM** | | | **24** | **1** | **1** | **2** | **22** | **—** |

**Godfrey, Josh**
**b. Collingwood, Ontario, Canada, January 15, 1988**

| | | | | | | | | |
|---|---|---|---|---|---|---|---|---|
| 2008 WM20 | 2-D | CAN | 7 | 0 | 5 | 5 | 8 | G |

**Gogulla, Philip**
**b. Dusseldorf, West Germany (Germany), July 31, 1987**

| | | | | | | | | |
|---|---|---|---|---|---|---|---|---|
| 2005 WM18 | 19-F | GER | 6 | 1 | 2 | 3 | 4 | 8th |
| 2007 WM20 | 19-F | GER | 6 | 0 | 6 | 6 | 8 | 9th |
| 2007 WM | 87-F | GER | 6 | 0 | 5 | 5 | 4 | 9th |
| 2008 WM | 87-F | GER | 6 | 1 | 3 | 4 | 6 | 10th |
| 2009 WM | 87-F | GER | 6 | 0 | 1 | 1 | 2 | 15th |
| 2010 WM | 87-F | GER | 7 | 1 | 0 | 1 | 0 | 4th |
| 2011 WM | 87-F | GER | 7 | 0 | 2 | 2 | 4 | 7th |
| 2012 WM | 87-F | GER | 7 | 2 | 7 | 9 | 4 | 12th |
| **Totals WM** | | | **39** | **4** | **18** | **22** | **20** | **—** |

**Golicic, Bostjan**
**b. Kranj, Yugoslavia (Slovenia), June 12, 1989**

| | | | | | | | | |
|---|---|---|---|---|---|---|---|---|
| 2011 WM | 71-F | SLO | 6 | 2 | 1 | 3 | 0 | 16th |

**Golicic, Jurij**
**b. Kranj, Yugoslavia (Slovenia), April 6, 1981**

| | | | | | | | | |
|---|---|---|---|---|---|---|---|---|
| 2003 WM | 17-F | SLO | 6 | 0 | 1 | 1 | 2 | 15th |
| 2005 WM | 17-F | SLO | 6 | 1 | 1 | 2 | 4 | 13th |
| 2006 WM | 17-F | SLO | 6 | 0 | 0 | 0 | 10 | 16th |
| 2008 WM | 17-F | SLO | 5 | 0 | 0 | 0 | 2 | 15th |
| **Totals WM** | | | **23** | **1** | **2** | **3** | **18** | **—** |

**Goligoski, Alex**
**b. Grand Rapids, Minnesota, United States, July 30, 1985**

| | | | | | | | | |
|---|---|---|---|---|---|---|---|---|
| 2005 WM20 | 10-D | USA | 7 | 0 | 1 | 1 | 2 | 4th |
| 2012 WM | 7-D | USA | 8 | 1 | 4 | 5 | 2 | 7th |

**Goloubef, Cody**
**b. Oakville, Ontario, Canada, November 30, 1989**

| | | | | | | | | |
|---|---|---|---|---|---|---|---|---|
| 2009 WM20 | 17-D | CAN | 6 | 0 | 1 | 1 | 8 | G |

**Golovkov, Igor**
**b. Moscow, Soviet Union (Russia), May 17, 1990**

| | | | | | | | | |
|---|---|---|---|---|---|---|---|---|
| 2008 WM18 | 2-D | RUS | 6 | 1 | 1 | 2 | 14 | S |
| 2009 WM20 | 2-D | RUS | 7 | 1 | 1 | 2 | 0 | B |

**Golovkovs, Georgs**
**b. Riga, Latvia, July 11, 1995**

| | | | | | | | | |
|---|---|---|---|---|---|---|---|---|
| 2012 WM18 | 18-F | LAT | 6 | 3 | 2 | 5 | 2 | 9th |

**Golubev, Denis**
**b. Magnitogorsk, Russia, July 11, 1991**

| | | | | | | | | |
|---|---|---|---|---|---|---|---|---|
| 2011 WM20 | 28-F | RUS | 7 | 3 | 3 | 6 | 6 | G |

**Golubtsov, Vadim**
**b. Lipetsk, Soviet Union (Russia), January 2, 1988**

| | | | | | | | | |
|---|---|---|---|---|---|---|---|---|
| 2006 WM18 | 21-F | RUS | 4 | 0 | 1 | 1 | 6 | 5th |
| 2008 WM20 | 16-F | RUS | 7 | 1 | 2 | 3 | 2 | B |

**Gonchar, Sergei**
**b. Chelyabinsk, Soviet Union (Russia), April 13, 1974**

| | | | | | | | | |
|---|---|---|---|---|---|---|---|---|
| 1993 WM20 | 3-D | RUS | 7 | 0 | 2 | 2 | 10 | 6th |
| 1996 WCH | 55-D | RUS | 4 | 2 | 2 | 4 | 2 | 4th |
| 1998 OG-M | 55-D | RUS | 6 | 0 | 2 | 2 | 0 | S |
| 2000 WM | 55-D | RUS | 6 | 1 | 0 | 1 | 2 | 9th |
| 2002 OG-M | 55-D | RUS | 6 | 0 | 0 | 0 | 2 | B |
| 2004 WCH | 55-D | RUS | 4 | 1 | 2 | 3 | 6 | 6th |
| 2006 OG-M | 55-D | RUS | 8 | 0 | 2 | 2 | 8 | 4th |
| 2007 WM | 55-D | RUS | 9 | 1 | 4 | 5 | 4 | B |
| 2010 OG-M | 55-D | RUS | 4 | 1 | 0 | 1 | 2 | 6th |
| 2010 WM | 55-D | RUS | 5 | 0 | 4 | 4 | 0 | S |
| **Totals WM** | | | **20** | **2** | **8** | **10** | **6** | **S,B** |
| **Totals OG-M** | | | **24** | **1** | **4** | **5** | **12** | **S,B** |
| **Totals IIHF-NHL** | | | **8** | **3** | **4** | **7** | **8** | **—** |

**Goncharov, Maxim**
**b. Moscow, Soviet Union (Russia), June 15, 1989**

| | | | | | | | | |
|---|---|---|---|---|---|---|---|---|
| 2007 WM18 | 5-D | RUS | 7 | 0 | 0 | 0 | 6 | G |
| 2009 WM20 | 5-D | RUS | 7 | 5 | 1 | 6 | 12 | B |

**Goranin, Yevgeni**
**b. Novopolotsk, Soviet Union (Belarus), March 20, 1986**

| | | | | | | | | |
|---|---|---|---|---|---|---|---|---|
| 2003 WM18 | 2-D | BLR | 6 | 0 | 1 | 1 | 8 | 8th |
| 2004 WM18 | 24-D | BLR | 6 | 1 | 0 | 1 | 46 | 9th |
| 2005 WM20 | 6-D | BLR | 6 | 0 | 1 | 1 | 4 | 10th |
| **Totals WM18** | | | **12** | **1** | **1** | **2** | **54** | **—** |

**Gordeyev, Artyom**
**b. Ufa, Soviet Union (Russia), September 15, 1988**

| | | | | | | | | |
|---|---|---|---|---|---|---|---|---|
| 2008 WM20 | 9-F | RUS | 7 | 2 | 2 | 4 | 2 | B |

**Gorges, Josh**
**b. Kelowna, British Columbia, Canada, August 14, 1984**

| | | | | | | | | |
|---|---|---|---|---|---|---|---|---|
| 2004 WM20 | 5-D | CAN | 6 | 0 | 3 | 3 | 4 | S |

**Gormley, Brandon**
**b. Murray River, Prince Edward Island, Canada, February 18, 1992**

| | | | | | | | | |
|---|---|---|---|---|---|---|---|---|
| 2012 WM20 | 3-D | CAN | 6 | 3 | 3 | 6 | 2 | B |

~WM20 IIHF Directorate Best Defenceman (2012), WM20 All-Star Team/Defence (2012)

**Goroshko, Oleg**
**b.Grodno, Soviet Union (Belarus), November 19, 1989**

| | | | | | | | | |
|---|---|---|---|---|---|---|---|---|
| 2011 WM | 22-D | BLR | 6 | 0 | 1 | 1 | 0 | 14th |
| 2012 WM | 22-D | BLR | 7 | 0 | 1 | 1 | 2 | 14th |
| **Totals WM** | | | **13** | **0** | **2** | **2** | **2** | **—** |

**Gorovikov, Konstantin**
**b. Novosibirsk, Soviet Union (Russia), August 31, 1977**

| | | | | | | | | |
|---|---|---|---|---|---|---|---|---|
| 2006 WM | 18-F | RUS | 7 | 1 | 3 | 4 | 8 | 5th |
| 2008 WM | 21-F | RUS | 9 | 2 | 2 | 4 | 8 | G |
| 2009 WM | 21-F | RUS | 9 | 1 | 4 | 5 | 4 | G |
| 2011 WM | 21-F | RUS | 9 | 0 | 2 | 2 | 2 | 4th |
| **Totals WM** | | | **34** | **4** | **11** | **15** | **22** | **2G** |

**Gotovets, Kirill**
**b. Minsk, Belarus, June 25, 1991**

| | | | | | | | | |
|---|---|---|---|---|---|---|---|---|
| 2008 WM18 | 3-D | BLR | 5 | 0 | 4 | 4 | 6 | 9th |
| 2010 WM | 91-D | BLR | 3 | 0 | 0 | 0 | 2 | 10th |
| 2011 WM | 91-D | BLR | 3 | 0 | 0 | 0 | 2 | 14th |
| **Totals WM** | | | **6** | **0** | **0** | **0** | **4** | **—** |

**Graborenko, Roman**
**b. Mogilyov, Belarus, August 24, 1992**

| | | | | | | | | |
|---|---|---|---|---|---|---|---|---|
| 2008 WM18 | 2-D | BLR | 6 | 0 | 0 | 0 | 2 | 9th |
| 2012 WM | 92-D | BLR | 7 | 0 | 1 | 1 | 0 | 14th |

**Grabovski, Mikhail**
**b. Potsdam, East Germany (Germany), January 31, 1984**

| | | | | | | | | |
|---|---|---|---|---|---|---|---|---|
| 2002 WM18 | 26-F | BLR | 8 | 2 | 1 | 3 | 2 | 5th |
| 2002 WM20 | 30-F | BLR | 6 | 0 | 1 | 1 | 2 | 9th |
| 2003 WM20 | 26-F | BLR | 6 | 2 | 0 | 2 | 2 | 10th |
| 2005 WM | 84-F | BLR | 6 | 4 | 1 | 5 | 2 | 10th |
| 2006 WM | 84-F | BLR | 7 | 5 | 4 | 9 | 2 | 6th |
| 2008 WM | 84-F | BLR | 5 | 0 | 3 | 3 | 0 | 9th |
| 2009 WM | 84-F | BLR | 7 | 3 | 6 | 9 | 2 | 8th |
| 2010 WM | 84-F | BLR | 6 | 0 | 3 | 3 | 6 | 10th |
| 2011 WM | 84-F | BLR | 6 | 2 | 2 | 4 | 2 | 14th |
| 2012 WM | 84-F | BLR | 7 | 1 | 3 | 4 | 4 | 14th |
| **Totals WM20** | | | **12** | **2** | **1** | **3** | **4** | **—** |
| **Totals WM** | | | **44** | **15** | **22** | **37** | **18** | **—** |

**Grachyov, Yevgeni**
**b. Khabarovsk, Soviet Union (Russia), February 21, 1990**

| | | | | | | | | |
|---|---|---|---|---|---|---|---|---|
| 2008 WM18 | 19-F | RUS | 6 | 2 | 3 | 5 | 2 | S |
| 2009 WM20 | 15-F | RUS | 7 | 2 | 3 | 5 | 4 | B |

**Gracik, Juraj**
**b. Topolcany, Czechoslovakia (Slovakia), August 14, 1986**

| | | | | | | | | |
|---|---|---|---|---|---|---|---|---|
| 2004 WM18 | 25-F | SVK | 6 | 2 | 0 | 2 | 4 | 6th |
| 2005 WM20 | 12-F | SVK | 6 | 0 | 0 | 0 | 2 | 7th |
| 2006 WM20 | 25-F | SVK | 6 | 2 | 2 | 4 | 4 | 8th |
| **Totals WM20** | | | **12** | **2** | **2** | **4** | **6** | **—** |

**Grafsronningen, Eirik**
**b. Lillehammer, Norway, May 5, 1986**

| | | | | | | | | |
|---|---|---|---|---|---|---|---|---|
| 2004 WM18 | 15-D | NOR | 6 | 0 | 0 | 0 | 0 | 10th |
| 2006 WM20 | 23-D | NOR | 6 | 0 | 1 | 1 | 26 | 10th |

**Gragnani, Marc-Andre**
**b. Montreal, Quebec, Canada, March 11, 1987**

| | | | | | | | | |
|---|---|---|---|---|---|---|---|---|
| 2011 WM | 17-D | CAN | 6 | 1 | 1 | 2 | 2 | 5th |

**Granak, Dominik**
**b. Havirov, Czechoslovakia (Czech Republic), June 11, 1983**

| | | | | | | | | |
|---|---|---|---|---|---|---|---|---|
| 2001 WM18 | 4-D | SVK | 6 | 0 | 1 | 1 | 2 | 8th |
| 2003 WM20 | 8-D | SVK | 6 | 0 | 1 | 1 | 6 | 5th |
| 2004 WM | 13-D | SVK | 9 | 0 | 1 | 1 | 4 | 4th |
| 2005 WM | 83-D | SVK | 7 | 0 | 0 | 0 | 4 | 5th |
| 2006 WM | 15-D | SVK | 7 | 0 | 0 | 0 | 6 | 8th |
| 2007 WM | 15-D | SVK | 1 | 0 | 0 | 0 | 0 | 6th |
| 2008 WM | 15-D | SVK | 5 | 0 | 1 | 1 | 4 | 13th |
| 2009 WM | 15-D | SVK | 6 | 1 | 1 | 2 | 2 | 10th |
| 2010 WM | 15-D | SVK | 6 | 0 | 1 | 1 | 2 | 12th |
| 2011 WM | 51-D | SVK | 6 | 0 | 1 | 1 | 0 | 10th |
| 2012 WM | 51-D | SVK | 6 | 2 | 1 | 3 | 6 | S |
| **Totals WM** | | | **53** | **3** | **6** | **9** | **28** | **S** |

**Granath, Elias**
**b. Borlange, Sweden, September 6, 1985**

| | | | | | | | | |
|---|---|---|---|---|---|---|---|---|
| 2003 WM18 | 2-D | SWE | 6 | 1 | 0 | 1 | 0 | 5th |
| 2005 WM20 | 4-D | SWE | 6 | 1 | 2 | 3 | 6 | 6th |

**Granberg, Petter**
**b. Gallivare, Sweden, August 27, 1992**

| | | | | | | | | |
|---|---|---|---|---|---|---|---|---|
| 2010 WM18 | 8-D | SWE | 6 | 0 | 1 | 1 | 2 | S |
| 2012 WM20 | 8-D | SWE | 5 | 0 | 1 | 1 | 4 | G |

**Granlund, Markus**
**b. Oulu, Finland, April 16, 1993**

| | | | | | | | | |
|---|---|---|---|---|---|---|---|---|
| 2010 WM18 | 23-F | FIN | 6 | 1 | 5 | 6 | 4 | B |
| 2011 WM18 | 22-F | FIN | 6 | 2 | 8 | 10 | 6 | 5th |
| 2012 WM20 | 11-F | FIN | 7 | 2 | 5 | 7 | 6 | 4th |
| **Totals WM18** | | | **12** | **3** | **13** | **16** | **10** | **B** |

**Granlund, Mattias**
**b. Glommertrask, Sweden, June 14, 1992**

| | | | | | | | | |
|---|---|---|---|---|---|---|---|---|
| 2010 WM18 | 20-F | SWE | 6 | 3 | 0 | 3 | 2 | S |

**Granlund, Mikael**
**b. Oulu, Finland, February 26, 1992**

| | | | | | | | | |
|---|---|---|---|---|---|---|---|---|
| 2009 WM18 | 11-F | FIN | 6 | 2 | 11 | 13 | 0 | B |
| 2009 WM20 | 12-F | FIN | 6 | 2 | 1 | 3 | 0 | 7th |
| 2010 WM18 | 27-F | FIN | 6 | 4 | 9 | 13 | 4 | B |
| 2010 WM20 | 22-F | FIN | 6 | 1 | 6 | 7 | 4 | 5th |
| 2011 WM | 64-F | FIN | 9 | 2 | 7 | 9 | 2 | G |
| 2012 WM20 | 20-F | FIN | 7 | 2 | 9 | 11 | 0 | 4th |
| 2012 WM | 64-F | FIN | 10 | 1 | 4 | 5 | 2 | 4th |
| **Totals WM18** | | | **12** | **6** | **20** | **26** | **4** | **2B** |
| **Totals WM20** | | | **19** | **5** | **16** | **21** | **4** | **—** |
| **Totals WM** | | | **19** | **3** | **11** | **14** | **4** | **G** |

~WM20 All-Star Team/Forward (2012)

**Granstrom, Jonathan**
**b. Mora, Sweden, March 9, 1986**

| | | | | | | | | |
|---|---|---|---|---|---|---|---|---|
| 2006 WM20 | 23-F | SWE | 6 | 0 | 4 | 4 | 8 | 5th |

**Grant, Alex**
**b. Antigonish, Nova Scotia, Canada, January 20, 1989**

| | | | | | | | | |
|---|---|---|---|---|---|---|---|---|
| 2007 WM18 | 22-D | CAN | 6 | 0 | 0 | 0 | 0 | 4th |

**Gras, Laurent**
**b. Chamonix, France, March 15, 1976**

| | | | | | | | | |
|---|---|---|---|---|---|---|---|---|
| 1997 WM | 40-F | FRA | 8 | 0 | 0 | 0 | 2 | 10th |
| 1998 OG-M | 40-F | FRA | 4 | 0 | 0 | 0 | 2 | 11th |
| 1998 WM | 40-F | FRA | 3 | 0 | 0 | 0 | 2 | 13th |
| 2002 OG-M | 28-F | FRA | 4 | 0 | 0 | 0 | 0 | 14th |
| 2004 WM | 28-F | FRA | 6 | 1 | 1 | 2 | 2 | 16th |
| 2008 WM | 28-F | FRA | 5 | 0 | 0 | 0 | 4 | 14th |
| 2009 WM | 28-F | FRA | 6 | 0 | 0 | 0 | 0 | 12th |
| 2010 WM | 28-F | FRA | 6 | 2 | 0 | 2 | 2 | 14th |
| 2011 WM | 28-F | FRA | 6 | 0 | 0 | 0 | 4 | 12th |
| **Totals WM** | | | **40** | **3** | **1** | **4** | **16** | **—** |
| **Totals OG-M** | | | **8** | **0** | **0** | **0** | **2** | **—** |

**Grassi, Daniele**
**b. Locarno, Switzerland, January 27, 1993**

| | | | | | | | | |
|---|---|---|---|---|---|---|---|---|
| 2011 WM18 | 12-F | SUI | 6 | 0 | 2 | 2 | 6 | 7th |

**Grauwiler, Lukas**
**b. Zurich, Switzerland, April 13, 1984**

| | | | | | | | | |
|---|---|---|---|---|---|---|---|---|
| 2002 WM18 | 14-F | SUI | 8 | 2 | 0 | 2 | 2 | 7th |
| 2004 WM20 | 13-F | SUI | 6 | 2 | 0 | 2 | 4 | 8th |

**Gravel, Kevin**
**b. Kingsford, Michigan, United States, March 6, 1992**

| | | | | | | | | |
|---|---|---|---|---|---|---|---|---|
| 2012 WM20 | 12-D | USA | 6 | 1 | 0 | 1 | 0 | 7th |

**Grebeshkov, Denis**
**b. Yaroslavl, Soviet Union (Russia), October 11, 1983**

| | | | | | | | | |
|---|---|---|---|---|---|---|---|---|
| 2001 WM18 | 5-D | RUS | 6 | 1 | 3 | 4 | 0 | G |
| 2001 WM20 | 6-D | RUS | 7 | 2 | 1 | 3 | 0 | 7th |
| 2002 WM20 | 5-D | RUS | 7 | 1 | 2 | 3 | 0 | G |
| 2003 WM20 | 5-D | RUS | 6 | 0 | 2 | 2 | 6 | G |
| 2007 WM | 7-D | RUS | 9 | 1 | 2 | 3 | 0 | B |
| 2008 WM | 37-D | RUS | 9 | 0 | 6 | 6 | 2 | G |
| 2009 WM | 37-D | RUS | 9 | 0 | 2 | 2 | 2 | G |
| 2010 OG-M | 37-D | RUS | 4 | 0 | 1 | 1 | 2 | 6th |
| 2010 WM | 37-D | RUS | 9 | 1 | 0 | 1 | 0 | S |
| 2011 WM | 37-D | RUS | 2 | 0 | 0 | 0 | 0 | 4th |
| **Totals WM20** | | | **20** | **3** | **5** | **8** | **6** | **2G** |
| **Totals WM** | | | **38** | **2** | **10** | **12** | **4** | **2G,S,B** |

**Green, Mike**
**b. Calgary, Alberta, Canada, October 12, 1985**

| | | | | | | | | |
|---|---|---|---|---|---|---|---|---|
| 2003 WM18 | 27-D | CAN | 7 | 0 | 0 | 0 | 2 | G |
| 2008 WM | 52-D | CAN | 9 | 4 | 8 | 12 | 2 | S |

~WM All-Star Team/Defence (2008)

**Green, Morten**
**b. Horsholm, Denmark, March 19, 1981**

| | | | | | | | | |
|---|---|---|---|---|---|---|---|---|
| 2003 WM | 29-F | DEN | 6 | 0 | 2 | 2 | 0 | 11th |
| 2004 WM | 29-F | DEN | 6 | 1 | 1 | 2 | 6 | 12th |
| 2005 WM | 13-F | DEN | 6 | 1 | 4 | 5 | 4 | 14th |
| 2006 WM | 13-F | DEN | 6 | 1 | 5 | 6 | 6 | 13th |
| 2007 WM | 13-F | DEN | 6 | 0 | 1 | 1 | 33 | 10th |
| 2008 WM | 13-F | DEN | 6 | 1 | 5 | 6 | 10 | 12th |
| 2009 WM | 13-F | DEN | 6 | 2 | 6 | 8 | 4 | 13th |
| 2010 WM | 13-F | DEN | 6 | 1 | 2 | 3 | 10 | 8th |
| 2011 WM | 13-F | DEN | 5 | 0 | 2 | 2 | 0 | 11th |
| 2012 WM | 13-F | DEN | 7 | 3 | 1 | 4 | 10 | 13th |
| **Totals WM** | | | **60** | **10** | **29** | **39** | **83** | **—** |

**Greene, Andy**
**b. Trenton, Michigan, United States, October 30, 1982**

| | | | | | | | | |
|---|---|---|---|---|---|---|---|---|
| 2010 WM | 6-D | USA | 6 | 0 | 2 | 2 | 0 | 13th |

**Greene, Matt**
**b. Grand Ledge, Michigan, United States, May 13, 1983**

| | | | | | | | | |
|---|---|---|---|---|---|---|---|---|
| 2001 | WM18 | 12-D | USA | 6 | 0 | 1 | 1 | 10 | 6th |
| 2003 | WM20 | 5-D | USA | 7 | 0 | 1 | 1 | 34 | 4th |
| 2007 | WM | 5-D | USA | 7 | 0 | 2 | 2 | 6 | 5th |
| 2008 | WM | 5-D | USA | 7 | 0 | 0 | 0 | 38 | 6th |
| 2010 | WM | 2-D | USA | 6 | 0 | 1 | 1 | 4 | 13th |
| **Totals WM** | | | | **20** | **0** | **3** | **3** | **48** | **—** |

**Gregorc, Blaz**
**b. Jesenice, Yugoslavia (Slovenia), January 18, 1990**

| | | | | | | | | | |
|---|---|---|---|---|---|---|---|---|---|
| 2011 | WM | 15-D | SLO | 6 | 0 | 2 | 2 | 4 | 16th |

**Gregorek, Petr**
**b. Ceske Tesin, Czechoslovakia (Czech Republic), May 25, 1978**

| | | | | | | | | | |
|---|---|---|---|---|---|---|---|---|---|
| 2010 | WM | 23-D | CZE | 9 | 1 | 0 | 1 | 4 | G |

**Greilinger, Thomas**
**b. Deggendorf, West Germany (Germany), August 6, 1981**

| | | | | | | | | | |
|---|---|---|---|---|---|---|---|---|---|
| 1999 | WM18 | 26-F | GER | 6 | 0 | 1 | 1 | 8 | 10th |
| 2001 | WM | 29-F | GER | 6 | 0 | 0 | 0 | 2 | 5th |
| 2004 | WM | 39-F | GER | 5 | 0 | 0 | 0 | 0 | 9th |
| 2010 | OG-M | 39-F | GER | 4 | 0 | 0 | 0 | 2 | 11th |
| 2011 | WM | 39-F | GER | 5 | 2 | 1 | 3 | 2 | 7th |
| 2012 | WM | 39-F | GER | 7 | 2 | 0 | 2 | 4 | 12th |
| **Totals WM** | | | | **23** | **4** | **1** | **5** | **8** | **—** |

**Gribko, Denis**
**b. Minsk, Soviet Union (Belarus), June 19, 1990**

| | | | | | | | | | |
|---|---|---|---|---|---|---|---|---|---|
| 2008 | WM18 | 7-D | BLR | 6 | 0 | 0 | 0 | 2 | 9th |

**Griffith, Seth**
**b. Wallaceburg, Ontario, Canada, January 4, 1993**

| | | | | | | | | | |
|---|---|---|---|---|---|---|---|---|---|
| 2011 | WM18 | 21-F | CAN | 7 | 0 | 0 | 0 | 6 | 4th |

**Grigorenko, Mikhail**
**b. Khabarovsk, Russia, May 16, 1994**

| | | | | | | | | | |
|---|---|---|---|---|---|---|---|---|---|
| 2011 | WM18 | 25-F | RUS | 7 | 4 | 14 | 18 | 18 | B |
| 2012 | WM20 | 17-F | RUS | 6 | 2 | 3 | 5 | 0 | S |

**Grigorenko, Yevgeni**
**b. Chelyabinsk, Russia, August 11, 1992**

| | | | | | | | | | |
|---|---|---|---|---|---|---|---|---|---|
| 2010 | WM18 | 18-F | RUS | 7 | 0 | 0 | 0 | 2 | 4th |

**Grimaldi, Rocco**
**b. Rossmoor, California, United States, February 8, 1993**

| | | | | | | | | | |
|---|---|---|---|---|---|---|---|---|---|
| 2010 | WM18 | 21-F | USA | 7 | 2 | 8 | 10 | 6 | G |
| 2011 | WM18 | 23-F | USA | 6 | 2 | 6 | 8 | 6 | G |
| **Totals WM18** | | | | **13** | **4** | **14** | **18** | **12** | **2G** |

**Grimshaw, Ryan**
**b. Rochester, New York, United States, January 28, 1990**

| | | | | | | | | | |
|---|---|---|---|---|---|---|---|---|---|
| 2008 | WM18 | 5-D | USA | 7 | 0 | 3 | 3 | 16 | G |

**Gritans, Rolands**
**b. Daugavpils, Soviet Union (Latvia), January 19, 1991**

| | | | | | | | | | |
|---|---|---|---|---|---|---|---|---|---|
| 2010 | WM20 | 24-D | LAT | 6 | 0 | 0 | 0 | 6 | 9th |

**Gron, Stanislav**
**b. Bratislava, Czechoslovakia (Slovakia), October 28, 1978**

| | | | | | | | | | |
|---|---|---|---|---|---|---|---|---|---|
| 1998 | WM20 | 23-F | SVK | 6 | 0 | 1 | 1 | 0 | 9th |
| 2010 | WM | 97-F | SVK | 3 | 0 | 0 | 0 | 2 | 12th |

**Grondahl, Ari**
**b. Helsinki, Finland, August 11, 1989**

| | | | | | | | | | |
|---|---|---|---|---|---|---|---|---|---|
| 2009 | WM20 | 2-D | FIN | 6 | 0 | 0 | 0 | 0 | 7th |

**Gronvaldt, Simon**
**b. Rodovre, Denmark, January 30, 1991**

| | | | | | | | | | |
|---|---|---|---|---|---|---|---|---|---|
| 2008 | WM18 | 9-D | DEN | 6 | 0 | 1 | 1 | 10 | 10th |
| 2008 | WM20 | 7-D | DEN | 6 | 0 | 1 | 1 | 6 | 10th |

**Grosaft, Maros**
**b. Nove Zamky, Czechoslovakia (Slovakia), February 15, 1990**

| | | | | | | | | | |
|---|---|---|---|---|---|---|---|---|---|
| 2010 | WM20 | 6-F | SVK | 6 | 0 | 0 | 0 | 2 | 8th |

**Grossman, Nicklas**
**b. Nacka, Sweden, January 22, 1985**

| | | | | | | | | | |
|---|---|---|---|---|---|---|---|---|---|
| 2005 | WM20 | 12-D | SWE | 6 | 0 | 0 | 0 | 37 | 6th |
| 2009 | WM | 2-D | SWE | 9 | 0 | 1 | 1 | 4 | B |
| 2011 | WM | 2-D | SWE | 2 | 0 | 0 | 0 | 4 | S |
| **Totals WM** | | | | **11** | **0** | **1** | **1** | **8** | **S,B** |

**Grossmann, Robin**
**b. Baden, Switzerland, August 17, 1987**

| | | | | | | | | | |
|---|---|---|---|---|---|---|---|---|---|
| 2005 | WM18 | 22-D | SUI | 6 | 0 | 1 | 1 | 4 | 9th |
| 2007 | WM20 | 5-D | SUI | 6 | 1 | 1 | 2 | 10 | 7th |

**Grozinger, Lars**
**b. Stuttgart, Germany, June 11, 1993**

| | | | | | | | | | |
|---|---|---|---|---|---|---|---|---|---|
| 2011 | WM18 | 13-F | GER | 6 | 1 | 2 | 3 | 6 | 6th |

**Groznik, Bostjan**
**b. Brezje, Yugoslavia (Slovenia), July 8, 1982**

| | | | | | | | | | |
|---|---|---|---|---|---|---|---|---|---|
| 2006 | WM | 6-D | SLO | 6 | 0 | 0 | 0 | 2 | 16th |

**Grundel, Anton**
**b. Karlstad, Sweden, March 5, 1990**

| | | | | | | | | | |
|---|---|---|---|---|---|---|---|---|---|
| 2008 | WM18 | 7-D | SWE | 6 | 0 | 1 | 1 | 8 | 4th |

**Grundling, Martin**
**b. Holic, Czechoslovakia (Slovakia), February 13, 1987**

| | | | | | | | | | |
|---|---|---|---|---|---|---|---|---|---|
| 2005 | WM18 | 7-D | SVK | 6 | 0 | 0 | 0 | 2 | 6th |
| 2006 | WM20 | 7-D | SVK | 6 | 0 | 0 | 0 | 6 | 8th |
| 2007 | WM20 | 7-D | SVK | 6 | 0 | 2 | 2 | 6 | 8th |
| **Totals WM20** | | | | **12** | **0** | **2** | **2** | **12** | **—** |

**Grundmanis, Kriss**
**b. Riga, Soviet Union (Latvia), February 13, 1989**

| | | | | | | | | | |
|---|---|---|---|---|---|---|---|---|---|
| 2007 | WM18 | 26-D | LAT | 6 | 0 | 1 | 1 | 4 | 10th |
| 2009 | WM20 | 26-D | LAT | 6 | 0 | 1 | 1 | 2 | 8th |

**Grzelcyk, Matt**
**b. Charlestown, Massachusetts, United States, January 5, 1994**

| | | | | | | | | | |
|---|---|---|---|---|---|---|---|---|---|
| 2012 | WM18 | 7-D | USA | 6 | 1 | 0 | 1 | 2 | G |

**Gubarev, Danil**
**b. Chelyabinsk, Soviet Union (Russia), October 15, 1991**

| | | | | | | | | | |
|---|---|---|---|---|---|---|---|---|---|
| 2009 | WM18 | 26-F | RUS | 7 | 0 | 0 | 0 | 0 | S |

**Gudas, Radko**
**b. Prague, Czechoslovakia (Czech Republic), June 5, 1990**

| | | | | | | | | | |
|---|---|---|---|---|---|---|---|---|---|
| 2009 | WM20 | 3-D | CZE | 6 | 2 | 1 | 3 | 8 | 6th |
| 2010 | WM20 | 3-D | CZE | 6 | 0 | 2 | 2 | 14 | 7th |
| **Totals WM20** | | | | **12** | **2** | **3** | **5** | **22** | **—** |

**Gudbranson, Erik**
**b. Orleans, Ontario, Canada, January 7, 1992**

| | | | | | | | | | |
|---|---|---|---|---|---|---|---|---|---|
| 2009 | WM18 | 5-D | CAN | 6 | 1 | 3 | 4 | 0 | 4th |
| 2010 | WM18 | 4-D | CAN | 6 | 0 | 1 | 1 | 4 | 7th |
| 2011 | WM20 | 5-D | CAN | 7 | 3 | 2 | 5 | 4 | S |
| **Totals WM18** | | | | **12** | **1** | **4** | **5** | **4** | **—** |

**Guerra, Samuel**
**b. Isone, Switzerland, May 11, 1993**

| | | | | | | | | | |
|---|---|---|---|---|---|---|---|---|---|
| 2010 | WM18 | 28-D | SUI | 6 | 2 | 0 | 2 | 2 | 5th |
| 2011 | WM18 | 27-D | SUI | 6 | 0 | 1 | 1 | 6 | 7th |
| 2011 | WM20 | 28-D | SUI | 6 | 0 | 0 | 0 | 2 | 5th |
| **Totals WM18** | | | | **12** | **2** | **1** | **3** | **8** | **—** |

**Guggisberg, Peter**
**b. Zimmerwald, Switzerland, January 20, 1985**

| | | | | | | | | | |
|---|---|---|---|---|---|---|---|---|---|
| 2003 | WM18 | 15-F | SUI | 6 | 6 | 4 | 10 | 4 | 9th |
| 2004 | WM20 | 15-F | SUI | 5 | 3 | 3 | 6 | 0 | 8th |
| 2008 | WM | 94-F | SUI | 2 | 0 | 0 | 0 | 0 | 7th |

**Gulasi, Michal**
**b. Ostrava, Czechoslovakia (Czech Republic), July 18, 1986**

| | | | | | | | | | |
|---|---|---|---|---|---|---|---|---|---|
| 2004 | WM18 | 27-D | CZE | 7 | 1 | 0 | 1 | 4 | B |
| 2005 | WM20 | 21-D | CZE | 6 | 0 | 2 | 2 | 14 | B |
| 2006 | WM20 | 24-D | CZE | 2 | 0 | 0 | 0 | 0 | 6th |
| **Totals WM20** | | | | **8** | **0** | **2** | **2** | **14** | **B** |

**Gunnarsson, Carl**
**b. Orebro, Sweden, November 9, 1986**

| | | | | | | | | | |
|---|---|---|---|---|---|---|---|---|---|
| 2004 | WM18 | 26-D | SWE | 6 | 0 | 0 | 0 | 24 | 5th |
| 2009 | WM | 11-D | SWE | 6 | 2 | 0 | 2 | 4 | B |
| 2010 | WM | 11-D | SWE | 9 | 1 | 1 | 2 | 2 | B |
| 2011 | WM | 11-D | SWE | 9 | 0 | 2 | 2 | 2 | S |
| **Totals WM** | | | | **24** | **3** | **3** | **6** | **8** | **S,2B** |

**Gunnarsson, Filip**
**b. Karlstad, Sweden, May 19, 1991**

| | | | | | | | | | |
|---|---|---|---|---|---|---|---|---|---|
| 2009 | WM18 | 18-F | SWE | 6 | 0 | 0 | 0 | 4 | 5th |

**Gurkin, Yefim**
**b. Ufa, Russia, November 13, 1992**

| | | | | | | | | | |
|---|---|---|---|---|---|---|---|---|---|
| 2010 | WM18 | 7-D | RUS | 7 | 2 | 2 | 4 | 6 | 4th |

**Gusev, Nikita**
**b. Moscow, Russia, July 8, 1992**

| | | | | | | | | | |
|---|---|---|---|---|---|---|---|---|---|
| 2012 | WM20 | 8-F | RUS | 7 | 3 | 6 | 9 | 0 | S |

**Gustafsson, Carl**
**b. San Juan, Puerto Rico, October 23, 1989**

| | | | | | | | | | |
|---|---|---|---|---|---|---|---|---|---|
| 2007 | WM18 | 15-F | SWE | 6 | 2 | 2 | 4 | 0 | B |
| 2009 | WM20 | 28-D | SWE | 6 | 0 | 2 | 2 | 0 | S |

**Guttig, Anthony**
**b. Dijon, France, October 30, 1988**

| | | | | | | | | | |
|---|---|---|---|---|---|---|---|---|---|
| 2012 | WM | 71-F | FRA | 5 | 1 | 1 | 2 | 8 | 9th |

**Haaland, Iver**
**b. Lillehammer, Norway, July 3, 1993**

| | | | | | | | | | |
|---|---|---|---|---|---|---|---|---|---|
| 2011 | WM18 | 25-D | NOR | 6 | 0 | 1 | 1 | 8 | 9th |

**Haapala, Henrik**
**b. Lempaala, Finland, February 28, 1994**

| | | | | | | | | | |
|---|---|---|---|---|---|---|---|---|---|
| 2012 | WM18 | 25-F | FIN | 7 | 4 | 6 | 10 | 2 | 4th |

**Haas, Gaetan**
**b. Bonfol, Switzerland, January 31, 1992**

| | | | | | | | | | |
|---|---|---|---|---|---|---|---|---|---|
| 2009 | WM18 | 24-F | SUI | 6 | 2 | 3 | 5 | 0 | 8th |
| 2010 | WM18 | 11-F | SUI | 6 | 0 | 2 | 2 | 2 | 5th |
| 2011 | WM20 | 11-F | SUI | 6 | 0 | 0 | 0 | 0 | 5th |
| 2012 | WM20 | 11-F | SUI | 6 | 3 | 0 | 3 | 2 | 8th |
| **Totals WM18** | | | | **12** | **2** | **5** | **7** | **2** | **—** |
| **Totals WM20** | | | | **12** | **3** | **0** | **3** | **2** | **—** |

**Haase, Henry**
**b. Berlin, Germany, June 25, 1993**

| | | | | | | | | | |
|---|---|---|---|---|---|---|---|---|---|
| 2011 | WM18 | 4-D | GER | 6 | 0 | 1 | 1 | 0 | 6th |

**Hachler, Cedric**
**b. Seengen, Switzerland, July 1, 1993**

| | | | | | | | | | |
|---|---|---|---|---|---|---|---|---|---|
| 2010 | WM18 | 2-D | SUI | 6 | 1 | 0 | 1 | 2 | 5th |
| 2011 | WM18 | 5-D | SUI | 6 | 0 | 1 | 1 | 12 | 7th |
| 2012 | WM20 | 2-D | SUI | 6 | 0 | 1 | 1 | 0 | 8th |
| **Totals WM18** | | | | **12** | **1** | **1** | **2** | **14** | **—** |

**Hackert, Michael**
**b. Heilbron, West Germany (Germany), June 21, 1981**

| | | | | | | | | | |
|---|---|---|---|---|---|---|---|---|---|
| 2007 | WM | 33-F | GER | 6 | 3 | 4 | 7 | 2 | 9th |
| 2008 | WM | 33-F | GER | 6 | 3 | 1 | 4 | 2 | 10th |
| 2009 | WM | 33-F | GER | 6 | 0 | 1 | 1 | 4 | 15th |
| **Totals WM** | | | | **18** | **6** | **6** | **12** | **8** | **—** |

**Hafner, Tomo**
**b. Jesenice, Yugoslavia (Slovenia), July 19, 1980**

| | | | | | | | | | |
|---|---|---|---|---|---|---|---|---|---|
| 2005 | WM | 15-F | SLO | 3 | 0 | 0 | 0 | 2 | 13th |
| 2006 | WM | 18-D | SLO | 6 | 0 | 1 | 1 | 4 | 16th |
| 2008 | WM | 91-F | SLO | 5 | 0 | 0 | 0 | 0 | 15th |
| **Totals WM** | | | | **14** | **0** | **1** | **1** | **6** | **—** |

**Haga, Michael**
**b. Asker, Norway, March 10, 1992**

| | | | | | | | | | |
|---|---|---|---|---|---|---|---|---|---|
| 2009 | WM18 | 16-F | NOR | 6 | 0 | 0 | 0 | 0 | 9th |
| 2011 | WM20 | 15-F | NOR | 6 | 0 | 0 | 0 | 0 | 9th |

**Hagelin, Carl**
**b. Sodertalje, Sweden, August 23, 1988**

| | | | | | | | | | |
|---|---|---|---|---|---|---|---|---|---|
| 2008 | WM20 | 12-F | SWE | 6 | 0 | 0 | 0 | 0 | S |

**Hagemo, Nate**
**b. Minneapolis, Minnesota, United States, October 8, 1985**

| | | | | | | | | | |
|---|---|---|---|---|---|---|---|---|---|
| 2003 | WM18 | 26-D | USA | 6 | 1 | 0 | 1 | 2 | 4th |
| 2004 | WM18 | 8-D | USA | 6 | 2 | 1 | 3 | 8 | S |
| 2005 | WM20 | 18-D | USA | 7 | 0 | 0 | 0 | 14 | 4th |
| **Totals WM18** | | | | **12** | **3** | **1** | **4** | **10** | **S** |

**Hagen, Martin**
**b. Oslo, Norway, March 14, 1986**

| | | | | | | | | | |
|---|---|---|---|---|---|---|---|---|---|
| 2004 | WM18 | 18-F | NOR | 6 | 2 | 0 | 2 | 2 | 10th |
| 2006 | WM20 | 10-F | NOR | 6 | 0 | 1 | 1 | 0 | 10th |

**Hager, Patrick**
**b. Stuttgart, West Germany (Germany), September 8, 1988**

| | | | | | | | | |
|---|---|---|---|---|---|---|---|---|
| 2006 WM18 | 23-F | GER | 6 | 1 | 2 | 3 | 6 | 8th |
| 2009 WM | 50-F | GER | 5 | 0 | 1 | 1 | 2 | 15th |
| 2010 WM | 50-F | GER | 7 | 0 | 0 | 0 | 8 | 4th |
| **Totals WM** | | | **12** | **0** | **1** | **1** | **10** | **—** |

**Haggerty, Ryan**
**b. Stamford, Connecticut, United States, March 4, 1993**

| | | | | | | | | |
|---|---|---|---|---|---|---|---|---|
| 2011 WM18 | 21-F | USA | 6 | 2 | 0 | 2 | 0 | G |

**Hagman, Niklas**
**b. Espoo, Finland, December 5, 1979**

| | | | | | | | | |
|---|---|---|---|---|---|---|---|---|
| 1998 WM20 | 9-F | FIN | 7 | 4 | 1 | 5 | 0 | G |
| 1999 WM20 | 9-F | FIN | 6 | 3 | 5 | 8 | 2 | 5th |
| 2002 OG-M | 16-F | FIN | 4 | 1 | 2 | 3 | 0 | 6th |
| 2002 WM | 10-F | FIN | 9 | 5 | 2 | 7 | 2 | 4th |
| 2003 WM | 14-F | FIN | 7 | 2 | 1 | 3 | 14 | 5th |
| 2004 WM | 9-F | FIN | 5 | 0 | 0 | 0 | 0 | 6th |
| 2004 WCH | 9-F | FIN | 5 | 1 | 0 | 1 | 2 | 2nd |
| 2005 WM | 14-F | FIN | 7 | 2 | 0 | 2 | 2 | 7th |
| 2006 OG-M | 14-F | FIN | 8 | 0 | 1 | 1 | 2 | S |
| 2009 WM | 14-F | FIN | 7 | 1 | 5 | 6 | 0 | 5th |
| 2010 OG-M | 10-F | FIN | 6 | 4 | 2 | 6 | 2 | B |
| **Totals WM20** | | | **13** | **7** | **6** | **13** | **2** | **G** |
| **Totals WM** | | | **35** | **10** | **8** | **18** | **18** | **—** |
| **Totals OG-M** | | | **18** | **5** | **5** | **10** | **4** | **S,B** |

~WM IIHF Directorate Best Forward (2002), WM All-Star Team/Forward (2002)

**Hahl, Riku**
**b. Hameenlinna, Finland, November 1, 1980**

| | | | | | | | | |
|---|---|---|---|---|---|---|---|---|
| 1999 WM20 | 17-F | FIN | 6 | 0 | 0 | 0 | 2 | 5th |
| 2000 WM20 | 24-F | FIN | 7 | 0 | 1 | 1 | 2 | 7th |
| 2004 WCH | 36-F | FIN | 2 | 1 | 0 | 1 | 0 | 2nd |
| 2005 WM | 23-F | FIN | 5 | 0 | 0 | 0 | 2 | 7th |
| 2006 WM | 23-F | FIN | 9 | 3 | 2 | 5 | 4 | B |
| 2008 WM | 23-F | FIN | 9 | 0 | 0 | 0 | 0 | B |
| 2010 WM | 23-F | FIN | 6 | 0 | 1 | 1 | 0 | 6th |
| **Totals WM20** | | | **13** | **0** | **1** | **1** | **4** | **—** |
| **Totals WM** | | | **29** | **3** | **3** | **6** | **6** | **2B** |

**Hainsey, Ron**
**b. Bolton, Connecticut, United States, March 24, 1981**

| | | | | | | | | |
|---|---|---|---|---|---|---|---|---|
| 1999 WM18 | 2-D | USA | 6 | 2 | 1 | 3 | 8 | 7th |
| 2000 WM20 | 2-D | USA | 7 | 1 | 1 | 2 | 4 | 4th |
| 2001 WM20 | 2-D | USA | 7 | 0 | 5 | 5 | 2 | 5th |
| 2009 WM | 6-D | USA | 9 | 2 | 4 | 6 | 2 | 4th |
| **Totals WM20** | | | **14** | **1** | **6** | **7** | **6** | **—** |

**Hakanpaa, Jani**
**b. Kirkkonummi, Finland, March 31, 1992**

| | | | | | | | | |
|---|---|---|---|---|---|---|---|---|
| 2010 WM18 | 26-D | FIN | 6 | 1 | 1 | 2 | 6 | B |
| 2012 WM20 | 7-D | FIN | 7 | 1 | 2 | 3 | 6 | 4th |

**Haldimann, Christian**
**b. Bowil, Switzerland, March 15, 1985**

| | | | | | | | | |
|---|---|---|---|---|---|---|---|---|
| 2005 WM20 | 18-D | SUI | 6 | 0 | 0 | 0 | 2 | 8th |

**Halinen, Petteri**
**b. Espoo, Finland, April 8, 1992**

| | | | | | | | | |
|---|---|---|---|---|---|---|---|---|
| 2010 WM18 | 13-F | FIN | 6 | 1 | 0 | 1 | 0 | B |

**Halischuk, Matt**
**b. Toronto, Ontario, Canada, June 1, 1988**

| | | | | | | | | |
|---|---|---|---|---|---|---|---|---|
| 2008 WM20 | 32-F | CAN | 7 | 2 | 3 | 5 | 2 | G |

**Hall, Taylor**
**b. Calgary, Alberta, Canada, November 14, 1991**

| | | | | | | | | |
|---|---|---|---|---|---|---|---|---|
| 2008 WM18 | 11-F | CAN | 7 | 4 | 5 | 9 | 4 | G |
| 2010 WM20 | 4-F | CAN | 6 | 6 | 6 | 12 | 0 | S |

**Hallberg, Per**
**b. Ornskoldsvik, Sweden, March 24, 1978**

| | | | | | | | | |
|---|---|---|---|---|---|---|---|---|
| 1997 WM20 | 7-F | SWE | 6 | 1 | 1 | 2 | 8 | 8th |
| 1998 WM20 | 7-F | SWE | 7 | 1 | 1 | 2 | 12 | 6th |
| 2004 WM | 4-D | SWE | 9 | 0 | 0 | 0 | 10 | S |
| 2006 WM | 18-D | SWE | 9 | 1 | 2 | 3 | 16 | G |
| 2007 WM | 18-D | SWE | 9 | 1 | 4 | 5 | 8 | 4th |
| **Totals WM20** | | | **13** | **2** | **2** | **4** | **20** | **—** |
| **Totals WM** | | | **27** | **2** | **6** | **8** | **34** | **G,S** |

**Halpern, Jeff**
**b. Potomac, Maryland, United States, May 3, 1976**

| | | | | | | | | |
|---|---|---|---|---|---|---|---|---|
| 2000 WM | 17-F | USA | 7 | 1 | 1 | 2 | 4 | 5th |
| 2001 WM | 15-F | USA | 9 | 1 | 1 | 2 | 8 | 4th |
| 2004 WM | 11-F | USA | 9 | 2 | 2 | 4 | 4 | B |
| 2004 WCH | 27-F | USA | 4 | 0 | 0 | 0 | 7 | 4th |
| 2005 WM | 11-F | USA | 7 | 1 | 0 | 1 | 6 | 6th |
| 2008 WM | 11-F | USA | 3 | 0 | 1 | 1 | 4 | 6th |
| **Totals WM** | | | **35** | **5** | **5** | **10** | **26** | **B** |

**Hamalainen, Roope**
**b. Lapeenranta, Finland, August 18, 1992**

| | | | | | | | | |
|---|---|---|---|---|---|---|---|---|
| 2010 WM18 | 14-F | FIN | 6 | 0 | 1 | 1 | 0 | B |
| 2012 WM20 | 14-F | FIN | 7 | 1 | 0 | 1 | 0 | 4th |

**Hamhuis, Dan**
**b. Smithers, British Columbia, Canada, December 13, 1982**

| | | | | | | | | |
|---|---|---|---|---|---|---|---|---|
| 2001 WM20 | 5-D | CAN | 7 | 0 | 1 | 1 | 8 | B |
| 2002 WM20 | 5-D | CAN | 6 | 0 | 3 | 3 | 8 | S |
| 2006 WM | 2-D | CAN | 9 | 1 | 4 | 5 | 10 | 4th |
| 2007 WM | 2-D | CAN | 9 | 1 | 2 | 3 | 2 | G |
| 2008 WM | 2-D | CAN | 9 | 1 | 1 | 2 | 8 | S |
| 2009 WM | 2-D | CAN | 9 | 2 | 2 | 4 | 16 | S |
| **Totals WM20** | | | **13** | **0** | **4** | **4** | **16** | **S,B** |
| **Totals WM** | | | **36** | **5** | **9** | **14** | **36** | **G,2S** |

**Hamilton, Curtis**
**b. Tacoma, Washington, United States, December 4, 1991**

| | | | | | | | | |
|---|---|---|---|---|---|---|---|---|
| 2009 WM18 | 22-F | CAN | 6 | 1 | 4 | 5 | 4 | 4th |
| 2011 WM20 | 16-F | CAN | 7 | 4 | 0 | 4 | 2 | S |

**Hamilton, Dougie**
**b. Toronto, Ontario, Canada, June 17, 1993**

| | | | | | | | | |
|---|---|---|---|---|---|---|---|---|
| 2012 WM20 | 4-D | CAN | 6 | 2 | 4 | 6 | 6 | B |

**Hamilton, Freddie**
**b. Toronto, Ontario, Canada, January 1, 1992**

| | | | | | | | | |
|---|---|---|---|---|---|---|---|---|
| 2010 WM18 | 23-F | CAN | 6 | 1 | 5 | 6 | 0 | 7th |
| 2012 WM20 | 13-F | CAN | 6 | 1 | 6 | 7 | 2 | B |

**Hamonic, Travis**
**b. St. Malo, Manitoba, Canada. August 16, 1990**

| | | | | | | | | |
|---|---|---|---|---|---|---|---|---|
| 2008 WM18 | 23-D | CAN | 7 | 0 | 2 | 2 | 14 | G |
| 2010 WM20 | 3-D | CAN | 6 | 1 | 2 | 3 | 0 | S |

**Hampl, Ondrej**
**b. Melnik, Czech Republic, January 26, 1993**

| | | | | | | | | |
|---|---|---|---|---|---|---|---|---|
| 2011 WM18 | 18-F | CZE | 6 | 0 | 2 | 2 | 4 | 8th |

**Hampl, Zbynek**
**b. Prerov, Czechoslovakia (Czech Republic), March 22, 1988**

| | | | | | | | | |
|---|---|---|---|---|---|---|---|---|
| 2008 WM20 | 21-D | CZE | 6 | 1 | 0 | 1 | 4 | 5th |

**Handzus, Michal**
**b. Banska Bystrica, Czechoslovakia (Slovakia), March 11, 1977**

| | | | | | | | | |
|---|---|---|---|---|---|---|---|---|
| 1996 WM20 | 20-F | SVK | 6 | 0 | 3 | 3 | 2 | 7th |
| 1997 WM20 | 20-F | SVK | 6 | 2 | 4 | 6 | 2 | 6th |
| 2000 WM | 36-F | SVK | 6 | 1 | 4 | 5 | 4 | S |
| 2002 OG-M | 26-F | SVK | 2 | 1 | 0 | 1 | 6 | 13th |
| 2002 WM | 26-F | SVK | 6 | 1 | 4 | 5 | 4 | G |
| 2005 WM | 26-F | SVK | 7 | 3 | 0 | 3 | 2 | 5th |
| 2009 WM | 26-F | SVK | 6 | 0 | 4 | 4 | 6 | 10th |
| 2010 OG-M | 26-F | SVK | 7 | 3 | 3 | 6 | 0 | 4th |
| 2011 WM | 26-F | SVK | 5 | 0 | 2 | 2 | 0 | 10th |
| 2012 WM | 26-F | SVK | 8 | 2 | 5 | 7 | 0 | S |
| **Totals WM20** | | | **12** | **2** | **7** | **9** | **4** | **—** |
| **Totals WM** | | | **38** | **7** | **19** | **26** | **16** | **G,2S** |
| **Totals OG-M** | | | **9** | **4** | **3** | **7** | **6** | **—** |

**Hannikainen, Markus**
**b. Helsinki, Finland, March 26, 1993**

| | | | | | | | | |
|---|---|---|---|---|---|---|---|---|
| 2011 WM18 | 13-F | FIN | 6 | 1 | 0 | 1 | 0 | 5th |
| 2012 WM20 | 13-F | FIN | 7 | 0 | 1 | 1 | 0 | 4th |

**Hansen, Jannik**
**b. Herlev, Denmark, March 15, 1986**

| | | | | | | | | |
|---|---|---|---|---|---|---|---|---|
| 2004 WM18 | 22-F | DEN | 6 | 3 | 4 | 7 | 32 | 8th |
| 2005 WM | 17-F | DEN | 4 | 0 | 0 | 0 | 2 | 14th |
| 2006 WM | 17-F | DEN | 6 | 2 | 0 | 2 | 6 | 13th |
| 2008 WM | 17-F | DEN | 6 | 2 | 2 | 4 | 0 | 12th |
| 2012 WM | 36-F | DEN | 6 | 0 | 2 | 2 | 29 | 13th |
| **Totals WM** | | | **22** | **4** | **4** | **8** | **37** | **—** |

**Hansen, Mads**
**b. Oslo, Norway, September 16, 1978**

| | | | | | | | | |
|---|---|---|---|---|---|---|---|---|
| 2000 WM | 8-F | NOR | 6 | 0 | 0 | 0 | 0 | 9th |
| 2001 WM | 8-F | NOR | 6 | 0 | 0 | 0 | 2 | 15th |
| 2006 WM | 8-F | NOR | 6 | 1 | 1 | 2 | 6 | 11th |
| 2007 WM | 8-F | NOR | 6 | 2 | 2 | 4 | 6 | 14th |
| 2008 WM | 8-F | NOR | 7 | 1 | 2 | 3 | 8 | 8th |
| 2009 WM | 8-F | NOR | 6 | 0 | 0 | 0 | 12 | 11th |
| 2010 OG-M | 8-F | NOR | 4 | 1 | 0 | 1 | 2 | 10th |
| 2011 WM | 8-F | NOR | 7 | 0 | 1 | 1 | 16 | 6th |
| 2012 WM | 8-F | NOR | 8 | 2 | 7 | 9 | 4 | 8th |
| **Totals WM** | | | **52** | **6** | **13** | **19** | **54** | **—** |

**Hansen, Tobias**
**b. Herlev, Denmark, January 4, 1992**

| | | | | | | | | |
|---|---|---|---|---|---|---|---|---|
| 2012 WM20 | 5-D | DEN | 6 | 0 | 0 | 0 | 2 | 10th |

**Hanson, Christian**
**b. Glens Falls, New York, United States, March 10, 1986**

| | | | | | | | | |
|---|---|---|---|---|---|---|---|---|
| 2010 WM | 20-F | USA | 6 | 0 | 1 | 1 | 2 | 13th |

**Hantak, Filip**
**b. Prague, Czech Republic, January 10, 1992**

| | | | | | | | | |
|---|---|---|---|---|---|---|---|---|
| 2010 WM18 | 11-F | CZE | 6 | 1 | 0 | 1 | 6 | 6th |

**Hanusch, Steve**
**b. Cottbus, Germany, December 2, 1990**

| | | | | | | | | |
|---|---|---|---|---|---|---|---|---|
| 2008 WM18 | 8-D | GER | 6 | 1 | 0 | 1 | 18 | 5th |

**Hanzal, Martin**
**b. Pisek, Czechoslovakia (Czech Republic), February 20, 1987**

| | | | | | | | | |
|---|---|---|---|---|---|---|---|---|
| 2005 WM18 | 26-F | CZE | 7 | 4 | 3 | 7 | 10 | 4th |
| 2006 WM20 | 22-F | CZE | 6 | 0 | 2 | 2 | 4 | 6th |
| 2007 WM20 | 12-F | CZE | 6 | 2 | 1 | 3 | 6 | 5th |
| 2008 WM | 11-F | CZE | 6 | 0 | 3 | 3 | 8 | 5th |
| **Totals WM20** | | | **12** | **2** | **3** | **5** | **10** | **—** |

**Harand, Christoph**
**b. Vienna, Austria, May 27, 1981**

| | | | | | | | | |
|---|---|---|---|---|---|---|---|---|
| 2004 WM | 61-F | AUT | 5 | 1 | 0 | 1 | 0 | 11th |
| 2005 WM | 61-F | AUT | 6 | 0 | 0 | 0 | 4 | 16th |
| 2009 WM | 61-F | AUT | 3 | 0 | 0 | 0 | 2 | 14th |
| **Totals WM** | | | **14** | **1** | **0** | **1** | **6** | **—** |

**Harand, Patrick**
**b. Vienna, Austria, March 15, 1984**

| | | | | | | | | |
|---|---|---|---|---|---|---|---|---|
| 2004 WM20 | 16-F | AUT | 6 | 1 | 4 | 5 | 27 | 9th |
| 2005 WM | 19-F | AUT | 6 | 0 | 0 | 0 | 6 | 16th |
| 2007 WM | 16-F | AUT | 6 | 0 | 0 | 0 | 2 | 15th |
| 2011 WM | 16-F | AUT | 6 | 0 | 0 | 0 | 10 | 15th |
| **Totals WM** | | | **18** | **0** | **0** | **0** | **18** | **—** |

**Harant, Tomas**
**b. Zilina, Czechoslovakia (Slovakia), April 28, 1980**

| | | | | | | | | |
|---|---|---|---|---|---|---|---|---|
| 2006 WM | 71-D | SVK | 7 | 0 | 0 | 0 | 4 | 8th |
| 2007 WM | 71-F | SVK | 7 | 0 | 0 | 0 | 0 | 6th |
| **Totals WM** | | | **14** | **0** | **0** | **0** | **4** | **—** |

**Hardt, Nichlas**
**b. Rodovre, Denmark, July 6, 1988**

| | | | | | | | | |
|---|---|---|---|---|---|---|---|---|
| 2008 WM20 | 22-F | DEN | 6 | 2 | 2 | 4 | 6 | 10th |
| 2008 WM | 32-F | DEN | 6 | 0 | 0 | 0 | 2 | 12th |
| 2009 WM | 44-F | DEN | 6 | 2 | 0 | 2 | 4 | 13th |
| 2010 WM | 44-F | DEN | 7 | 0 | 0 | 0 | 6 | 8th |
| 2011 WM | 44-F | DEN | 6 | 4 | 1 | 5 | 2 | 11th |
| 2012 WM | 44-F | DEN | 7 | 2 | 2 | 4 | 0 | 13th |
| **Totals WM** | | | **32** | **8** | **3** | **11** | **14** | **—** |

**Harju, Johan**
**b. Overtornea, Sweden, May 15, 1986**

| | | | | | | | | |
|---|---|---|---|---|---|---|---|---|
| 2009 WM | 24-F | SWE | 9 | 2 | 2 | 4 | 4 | B |
| 2010 WM | 24-F | SWE | 9 | 4 | 1 | 5 | 4 | B |
| **Totals WM** | | | **18** | **6** | **3** | **9** | **8** | **2B** |

**Harrington, Scott**
**b. Kingston, Ontario, Canada, January 1, 1993**

| | | | | | | | | |
|---|---|---|---|---|---|---|---|---|
| 2011 WM18 | 6-D | CAN | 7 | 0 | 0 | 0 | 8 | 4th |
| 2012 WM20 | 6-D | CAN | 5 | 1 | 3 | 4 | 0 | B |

**Harrold, Peter**
**b. Kirtland Hills, Ohio, United States, June 8, 1983**

| | | | | | | | | |
|---|---|---|---|---|---|---|---|---|
| 2009 WM | 7-D | USA | 3 | 0 | 0 | 0 | 0 | 4th |

**Hartikainen, Teemu**
**b. Kuopio, Finland, May 3, 1990**

| | | | | | | | | |
|---|---|---|---|---|---|---|---|---|
| 2008 WM18 | 10-F | FIN | 6 | 2 | 1 | 3 | 6 | 6th |
| 2009 WM20 | 35-F | FIN | 6 | 3 | 6 | 9 | 4 | 7th |
| 2010 WM20 | 35-F | FIN | 6 | 4 | 2 | 6 | 4 | 5th |
| **Totals WM20** | | | **12** | **7** | **8** | **15** | **8** | **—** |

**Hartl, Nikolaus**
**b. Zell am See, Austria, December 18, 1991**

| | | | | | | | | |
|---|---|---|---|---|---|---|---|---|
| 2010 WM20 | 13-D | AUT | 6 | 1 | 1 | 2 | 6 | 10th |

**Hartman, Ryan**
**b. West Dundee, Illinois, United States, September 20, 1994**

| | | | | | | | | |
|---|---|---|---|---|---|---|---|---|
| 2012 WM18 | 18-F | USA | 6 | 2 | 4 | 6 | 22 | G |

**Hartmanis, Toms**
**b. Liepaja, Soviet Union (Latvia), December 12, 1987**

| | | | | | | | | |
|---|---|---|---|---|---|---|---|---|
| 2006 WM20 | 7-F | LAT | 6 | 0 | 0 | 0 | 0 | 9th |

**Hascak, Marcel**
**b. Poprad, Czechoslovakia (Slovakia), February 3, 1987**

| | | | | | | | | |
|---|---|---|---|---|---|---|---|---|
| 2012 WM | 87-F | SVK | 10 | 0 | 1 | 1 | 2 | S |

**Hascak, Marek**
**b. Trencin, Czechoslovakia (Slovakia), December 8, 1985**

| | | | | | | | | |
|---|---|---|---|---|---|---|---|---|
| 2005 WM20 | 18-F | SVK | 6 | 1 | 0 | 1 | 2 | 7th |

**Haula, Erik**
**b. Pori, Finland, March 23, 1991**

| | | | | | | | | |
|---|---|---|---|---|---|---|---|---|
| 2008 WM18 | 11-F | FIN | 6 | 1 | 3 | 4 | 2 | 6th |
| 2009 WM18 | 12-F | FIN | 6 | 3 | 1 | 4 | 2 | B |
| 2011 WM20 | 10-F | FIN | 6 | 4 | 3 | 7 | 10 | 6th |
| **Totals WM18** | | | **12** | **4** | **4** | **8** | **4** | **B** |

**Hauner, Norman**
**b. Huckeswagen, Germany, December 4, 1991**

| | | | | | | | | |
|---|---|---|---|---|---|---|---|---|
| 2009 WM18 | 10-F | GER | 6 | 0 | 4 | 4 | 2 | 10th |
| 2011 WM20 | 10-F | GER | 4 | 2 | 1 | 3 | 0 | 10th |

**Haverinen, Joni**
**b. Uusikaupunki, Finland, May 17, 1987**

| | | | | | | | | |
|---|---|---|---|---|---|---|---|---|
| 2005 WM18 | 9-D | FIN | 6 | 0 | 0 | 0 | 2 | 7th |
| 2007 WM20 | 3-D | FIN | 6 | 0 | 0 | 0 | 4 | 6th |

**Havlat, Martin**
**b. Mlada Boleslav, Czechoslovakia (Czech Republic), April 19, 1981**

| | | | | | | | | |
|---|---|---|---|---|---|---|---|---|
| 1999 WM18 | 14-F | CZE | 7 | 2 | 4 | 6 | 2 | 5th |
| 2000 WM20 | 15-F | CZE | 7 | 3 | 2 | 5 | 4 | G |
| 2000 WM | 15-F | CZE | 9 | 2 | 1 | 3 | 2 | G |
| 2002 OG-M | 9-F | CZE | 4 | 3 | 1 | 4 | 27 | 7th |
| 2004 WM | 69-F | CZE | 3 | 0 | 0 | 0 | 4 | 5th |
| 2004 WCH | 69-F | CZE | 5 | 3 | 3 | 6 | 2 | 3rd |
| 2010 OG-M | 24-F | CZE | 5 | 0 | 2 | 2 | 0 | 7th |
| 2011 WM | 24-F | CZE | 6 | 2 | 4 | 6 | 4 | B |
| **Totals WM** | | | **18** | **4** | **5** | **9** | **10** | **G,B** |
| **Totals OG-M** | | | **9** | **3** | **3** | **6** | **31** | **—** |

**Hayes, Jimmy**
**b. Dorchester, Massachusetts, United States, November 21, 1989**

| | | | | | | | | |
|---|---|---|---|---|---|---|---|---|
| 2007 WM18 | 12-F | USA | 7 | 1 | 2 | 3 | 2 | S |
| 2009 WM20 | 12-F | USA | 6 | 2 | 0 | 2 | 2 | 5th |

**Heatley, Dany**
**b. Freiburg, West Germany (Germany), January 21, 1981**

| | | | | | | | | |
|---|---|---|---|---|---|---|---|---|
| 2000 WM20 | 11-F | CAN | 7 | 2 | 2 | 4 | 4 | B |
| 2001 WM20 | 15-F | CAN | 7 | 3 | 2 | 5 | 10 | B |
| 2002 WM | 15-F | CAN | 7 | 2 | 2 | 4 | 2 | 6th |
| 2003 WM | 15-F | CAN | 9 | 7 | 3 | 10 | 10 | G |
| 2004 WM | 15-F | CAN | 9 | 8 | 3 | 11 | 4 | G |
| 2004 WCH | 15-F | CAN | 6 | 0 | 2 | 2 | 2 | 1st |
| 2005 WM | 15-F | CAN | 9 | 3 | 4 | 7 | 16 | S |
| 2006 OG-M | 15-F | CAN | 6 | 2 | 1 | 3 | 8 | 7th |
| 2008 WM | 15-F | CAN | 9 | 12 | 8 | 20 | 4 | S |
| 2009 WM | 15-F | CAN | 9 | 6 | 4 | 10 | 8 | S |
| 2010 OG-M | 15-F | CAN | 7 | 4 | 3 | 7 | 4 | G |
| **Totals WM20** | | | **14** | **5** | **4** | **9** | **14** | **2B** |
| **Totals WM** | | | **52** | **38** | **24** | **62** | **44** | **2G,3S** |
| **Totals OG-M** | | | **13** | **6** | **4** | **10** | **12** | **G** |

~WM MVP (2004, 2008), WM IIHF Directorate Best Forward (2004, 2008), WM All-Star Team/Forward (2003, 2004, 2008)

**Hebar, Andrej**
**b. Ljubljana, Yugoslavia (Slovenia), September 7, 1984**

| | | | | | | | | |
|---|---|---|---|---|---|---|---|---|
| 2006 WM | 84-F | SLO | 6 | 0 | 0 | 0 | 2 | 16th |
| 2008 WM | 84-F | SLO | 5 | 0 | 0 | 0 | 6 | 15th |
| 2011 WM | 84-F | SLO | 6 | 1 | 0 | 1 | 4 | 16th |
| **Totals WM** | | | **17** | **1** | **0** | **1** | **12** | **—** |

**Hebeisen, Silvan**
**b. Eggiwil, Switzerland, July 15, 1993**

| | | | | | | | | |
|---|---|---|---|---|---|---|---|---|
| 2011 WM18 | 20-D | SUI | 6 | 0 | 1 | 1 | 4 | 7th |

**Hecht, Jochen**
**b. Mannheim, West Germany (Germany), June 21, 1977**

| | | | | | | | | |
|---|---|---|---|---|---|---|---|---|
| 1994 WM20 | 20-F | GER | 7 | 0 | 0 | 0 | 4 | 7th |
| 1995 WM20 | 19-F | GER | 7 | 5 | 3 | 8 | 18 | 8th |
| 1996 WM20 | 20-F | GER | 6 | 1 | 4 | 5 | 18 | 8th |
| 1996 WM | 29-F | GER | 6 | 1 | 2 | 3 | 8 | 8th |
| 1996 WCH | 29-F | GER | 4 | 1 | 0 | 1 | 2 | 6th |
| 1997 WM20 | 19-F | GER | 6 | 1 | 0 | 1 | 2 | 9th |
| 1997 WM | 29-F | GER | 8 | 2 | 0 | 2 | 6 | 11th |
| 1998 OG-M | 29-F | GER | 4 | 1 | 0 | 1 | 6 | 9th |
| 1998 WM | 29-F | GER | 5 | 1 | 1 | 2 | 2 | 11th |
| 2002 OG-M | 17-F | GER | 4 | 1 | 1 | 2 | 2 | 8th |
| 2004 WM | 17-F | GER | 6 | 3 | 0 | 3 | 4 | 9th |
| 2004 WCH | 17-F | GER | 4 | 1 | 0 | 1 | 2 | 8th |
| 2005 WM | 17-F | GER | 6 | 3 | 1 | 4 | 6 | 15th |
| 2009 WM | 17-F | GER | 6 | 1 | 0 | 1 | 4 | 15th |
| 2010 OG-M | 17-F | GER | 4 | 0 | 1 | 1 | 2 | 11th |
| **Totals WM20** | | | **26** | **7** | **7** | **14** | **42** | **—** |
| **Totals WM** | | | **37** | **11** | **4** | **15** | **30** | **—** |
| **Totals IIHF-NHL** | | | **8** | **2** | **0** | **2** | **4** | **—** |
| **Totals OG-M** | | | **12** | **2** | **2** | **4** | **10** | **—** |

**Hecquefeuille, Kevin**
**b. Amiens, France, November 20, 1984**

| | | | | | | | | |
|---|---|---|---|---|---|---|---|---|
| 2008 WM | 84-F | FRA | 5 | 0 | 0 | 0 | 4 | 14th |
| 2009 WM | 84-F | FRA | 6 | 1 | 1 | 2 | 8 | 12th |
| 2010 WM | 84-F | FRA | 6 | 0 | 1 | 1 | 6 | 14th |
| 2011 WM | 84-D | FRA | 6 | 1 | 3 | 4 | 4 | 12th |
| 2012 WM | 84-D | FRA | 7 | 3 | 1 | 4 | 4 | 9th |
| **Totals WM** | | | **30** | **5** | **6** | **11** | **26** | **—** |

**Hedman, Oscar**
**b. Sjalevad, Sweden, April 21, 1986**

| | | | | | | | | |
|---|---|---|---|---|---|---|---|---|
| 2004 WM18 | 25-D | SWE | 6 | 3 | 1 | 4 | 0 | 5th |
| 2005 WM20 | 8-D | SWE | 6 | 0 | 0 | 0 | 0 | 6th |
| 2006 WM20 | 8-D | SWE | 6 | 1 | 3 | 4 | 2 | 5th |
| **Totals WM20** | | | **12** | **1** | **3** | **4** | **2** | **—** |

**Hedman, Victor**
**b. Ornskoldsvik, Sweden, December 18, 1990**

| | | | | | | | | |
|---|---|---|---|---|---|---|---|---|
| 2007 WM18 | 5-D | SWE | 6 | 1 | 2 | 3 | 10 | B |
| 2008 WM18 | 4-D | SWE | 4 | 1 | 3 | 4 | 10 | 4th |
| 2008 WM20 | 6-D | SWE | 6 | 0 | 1 | 1 | 4 | S |
| 2009 WM20 | 4-D | SWE | 6 | 0 | 2 | 2 | 6 | S |
| 2010 WM | 77-D | SWE | 9 | 1 | 1 | 2 | 6 | B |
| 2012 WM | 77-D | SWE | 8 | 0 | 1 | 1 | 14 | 6th |
| **Totals WM18** | | | **10** | **2** | **5** | **7** | **20** | **B** |
| **Totals WM20** | | | **12** | **0** | **3** | **3** | **10** | **2S** |
| **Totals WM** | | | **17** | **1** | **2** | **3** | **20** | **B** |

~WM20 All-Star Team/Defence (2008), WM18 All-Star Team/Defence (2007, 2008)

**Hedstrom, Jonathan**
**b. Skelleftea, Sweden, December 27, 1977**

| | | | | | | | | |
|---|---|---|---|---|---|---|---|---|
| 2004 WM | 17-F | SWE | 8 | 1 | 1 | 2 | 6 | S |
| 2005 WM | 17-F | SWE | 9 | 3 | 4 | 7 | 10 | 4th |
| 2007 WM | 17-F | SWE | 8 | 3 | 2 | 5 | 18 | 4th |
| **Totals WM** | | | **25** | **7** | **7** | **14** | **34** | **S** |

**Hegarty, Ryan**
**b. Arlington, Massachusetts, United States, May 16, 1990**

| | | | | | | | | |
|---|---|---|---|---|---|---|---|---|
| 2008 WM18 | 24-D | USA | 7 | 0 | 3 | 3 | 8 | G |

**Heier, Andreas**
**b. Fredrikstad, Norway, December 5, 1993**

| | | | | | | | | |
|---|---|---|---|---|---|---|---|---|
| 2011 WM18 | 9-F | NOR | 6 | 2 | 0 | 2 | 8 | 9th |

**Heino, Henri**
**b. Lahti, Finland, June 14, 1986**

| | | | | | | | | |
|---|---|---|---|---|---|---|---|---|
| 2006 WM20 | 29-F | FIN | 7 | 1 | 0 | 1 | 0 | B |

**Heinrich, Dominique**
**b. Vienna, Austria, July 31, 1990**

| | | | | | | | | |
|---|---|---|---|---|---|---|---|---|
| 2010 WM20 | 19-F | AUT | 6 | 3 | 4 | 7 | 4 | 10th |

**Hejda, Jan**
**b. Prague, Czechoslovakia (Czech Republic), June 18, 1978**

| | | | | | | | | |
|---|---|---|---|---|---|---|---|---|
| 1998 WM20 | 7-D | CZE | 7 | 0 | 1 | 1 | 2 | 4th |
| 2003 WM | 25-D | CZE | 9 | 0 | 0 | 0 | 4 | 4th |
| 2004 WM | 35-D | CZE | 7 | 1 | 1 | 2 | 8 | 5th |
| 2005 WM | 35-D | CZE | 9 | 0 | 0 | 0 | 2 | G |
| 2006 WM | 35-D | CZE | 9 | 0 | 0 | 0 | 4 | S |
| 2008 WM | 35-D | CZE | 7 | 1 | 0 | 1 | 0 | 5th |
| 2010 OG-M | 35-D | CZE | 5 | 0 | 0 | 0 | 4 | 7th |
| **Totals WM** | | | **50** | **2** | **1** | **3** | **18** | **G,S** |

**Helbling, Timo**
**b. Basel, Switzerland, July 21, 1981**

| | | | | | | | | |
|---|---|---|---|---|---|---|---|---|
| 1999 WM18 | 2-D | SUI | 7 | 1 | 0 | 1 | 35 | 4th |
| 2000 WM20 | 3-D | SUI | 7 | 0 | 2 | 2 | 16 | 6th |
| 2001 WM20 | 3-D | SUI | 7 | 1 | 1 | 2 | 10 | 6th |
| 2006 WM | 6-D | SUI | 4 | 0 | 0 | 0 | 2 | 9th |
| 2010 WM | 6-D | SUI | 7 | 0 | 1 | 1 | 25 | 5th |
| **Totals WM20** | | | **14** | **1** | **3** | **4** | **26** | **—** |
| **Totals WM** | | | **11** | **0** | **1** | **1** | **27** | **—** |

**Helenius, Jani**
**b. Helsinki, Finland, January 18, 1990**

| | | | | | | | | |
|---|---|---|---|---|---|---|---|---|
| 2009 WM20 | 22-F | FIN | 6 | 0 | 0 | 0 | 2 | 7th |

**Helfer, Armin**
**b. Brunico, Italy, May 31, 1980**

| | | | | | | | | |
|---|---|---|---|---|---|---|---|---|
| 2012 WM | 26-D | ITA | 4 | 0 | 0 | 0 | 0 | 15th |

**Hellstrom, Alexander**
**b. Falun, Sweden, April 17, 1987**

| | | | | | | | | |
|---|---|---|---|---|---|---|---|---|
| 2005 WM18 | 3-D | SWE | 7 | 0 | 0 | 0 | 4 | B |
| 2007 WM20 | 3-D | SWE | 7 | 0 | 0 | 0 | 8 | 4th |

**Hellstrom, Mattias**
**b. Nordingra, Sweden, June 18, 1986**

| | | | | | | | | |
|---|---|---|---|---|---|---|---|---|
| 2004 WM18 | 4-F | SWE | 6 | 0 | 2 | 2 | 2 | 5th |
| 2005 WM20 | 15-F | SWE | 6 | 0 | 1 | 1 | 2 | 6th |
| 2006 WM20 | 4-F | SWE | 6 | 0 | 0 | 0 | 0 | 5th |
| **Totals WM20** | | | **12** | **0** | **1** | **1** | **2** | **—** |

**Helm, Darren**
**b. Winnipeg, Manitoba, Canada, January 21, 1987**

| | | | | | | | | |
|---|---|---|---|---|---|---|---|---|
| 2007 WM20 | 15-F | CAN | 6 | 2 | 0 | 2 | 10 | G |

**Hemsky, Ales**
**b. Pardubice, Czechoslovakia (Czech Republic), August 13, 1983**

| | | | | | | | | |
|---|---|---|---|---|---|---|---|---|
| 2002 WM20 | 12-F | CZE | 7 | 3 | 6 | 9 | 6 | 7th |
| 2005 WM | 83-F | CZE | 7 | 2 | 0 | 2 | 2 | G |
| 2006 OG-M | 83-F | CZE | 8 | 1 | 2 | 3 | 2 | B |
| 2009 WM | 83-F | CZE | 7 | 2 | 4 | 6 | 4 | 6th |
| 2012 WM | 83-F | CZE | 10 | 5 | 3 | 8 | 8 | B |
| **Totals WM** | | | **24** | **9** | **7** | **16** | **14** | **G,B** |

**Henderson, Brian**
**b. Amiens, France, April 14, 1958**

| | | | | | | | | |
|---|---|---|---|---|---|---|---|---|
| 2010 WM | 22-F | FRA | 6 | 0 | 0 | 0 | 0 | 14th |
| 2011 WM | 22-F | FRA | 6 | 0 | 0 | 0 | 2 | 12th |
| 2012 WM | 22-F | FRA | 7 | 1 | 0 | 1 | 0 | 9th |
| **Totals WM** | | | **19** | **1** | **0** | **1** | **2** | **—** |

**Henriksen, Jeppe**
**b. Ballerup, Denmark, June 9, 1989**

| | | | | | | | | |
|---|---|---|---|---|---|---|---|---|
| 2008 WM20 | 12-F | DEN | 6 | 0 | 0 | 0 | 0 | 10th |

**Henrion, John**
**b. Holden, Massachusetts, United States, January 19, 1991**

| | | | | | | | | |
|---|---|---|---|---|---|---|---|---|
| 2009 WM18 | 16-F | USA | 7 | 2 | 2 | 4 | 10 | G |

**Henrique, Adam**
**b. Brantford, Ontario, Canada, February 6, 1990**

| | | | | | | | | |
|---|---|---|---|---|---|---|---|---|
| 2010 WM20 | 12-F | CAN | 6 | 1 | 0 | 1 | 2 | S |

**Henritius, Teemu**
**b. Helsinki, Finland, April 20, 1993**

| | | | | | | | | |
|---|---|---|---|---|---|---|---|---|
| 2011 WM18 | 24-F | FIN | 6 | 0 | 0 | 0 | 4 | 5th |

**Hensick, Tim**
**b. Lansing, Michigan, United States, December 10, 1985**
2003 WM18 9-F USA 6 6 4 10 0 4th
2005 WM20 11-F USA 7 2 1 3 0 4th
~WM18 All-Star Team/Forward (2003)

**Herman, Jakub**
**b. Prerov, Czech Republic, February 21, 1992**
2010 WM18 15-F CZE 6 0 0 0 0 6th

**Herman, Radim**
**b. Brandys, Czechoslovakia (Czech Republic), April 13, 1991**
2009 WM18 25-F CZE 6 1 1 2 30 6th

**Herpich, Kai**
**b. Villingen-Schwenningen, Germany, December 10, 1994**
2012 WM18 13-F GER 6 0 0 0 0 6th

**Herren, Yannick**
**b. Saas Grund, Switzerland, February 7, 1991**
2011 WM20 27-F SUI 6 1 1 2 2 5th

**Hersby, Philip**
**b. Malmo, Sweden, July 25, 1984**
2009 WM 2-D DEN 5 0 0 0 6 13th
2011 WM 84-D DEN 6 0 1 1 2 11th
2012 WM 84-D DEN 7 0 1 1 2 13th
**Totals WM 18 0 2 2 10 —**

**Hertl, Tomas**
**b. Prague, Czech Republic, November 12, 1993**
2011 WM18 20-F CZE 6 1 0 1 12 8th
2012 WM20 19-F CZE 6 3 2 5 0 5th

**Hertzberg, Sonny**
**b. Herning, Denmark, April 21, 1995**
2012 WM18 8-D DEN 6 0 0 0 4 10th

**Herzog, Fabrice**
**b. December 9, 1994**
2012 WM18 26-F SUI 6 2 0 2 0 7th

**Hickey, Tom**
**b. Calgary, Alberta, Canada, February 8, 1989**
2008 WM20 4-D CAN 7 0 1 1 4 G
2009 WM20 4-D CAN 6 0 3 3 2 G
**Totals WM20 13 0 4 4 6 2G**

**Hietanen, Juuso**
**b. Hameenlinna, Finland, June 14, 1985**
2005 WM20 26-D FIN 6 1 1 2 2 5th
2010 WM 11-D FIN 2 0 0 0 0 6th
2012 WM 38-D FIN 10 1 4 5 0 4th
**Totals WM 12 1 4 5 0 —**

**Hietikko, Ville**
**b. Hyvinkaa, Finland, March 31, 1990**
2008 WM18 4-D FIN 6 0 0 0 4 6th

**Higgins, Chris**
**b. Smithtown, New York, United States, June 2, 1983**
2002 WM20 21-F USA 7 4 2 6 6 5th
2003 WM20 18-F USA 7 3 3 6 4 4th
2009 WM 18-F USA 6 1 0 1 2 4th
**Totals WM20 14 7 5 12 10 —**

**Hillen, Jack**
**b. Minnetonka, Minnesota, United States, January 24, 1986**
2010 WM 38-D USA 6 0 1 1 2 13th

**Hindos, Matej**
**b. Michalovce, Slovakia, September 12, 1993**
2011 WM18 24-F SVK 6 0 4 4 4 10th
2012 WM20 10-F SVK 6 0 1 1 0 6th

**Hirschi, Steve**
**b. Grosshochstetten, Switzerland, September 18, 1981**
1999 WM18 8-D SUI 7 0 0 0 4 4th
2001 WM20 8-D SUI 7 1 0 1 8 6th
2002 WM 33-D SUI 6 0 1 1 2 10th
2004 WM 33-D SUI 6 0 0 0 2 8th
2006 OG-M 33-D SUI 6 0 0 0 4 6th
2007 WM 33-D SUI 3 0 0 0 2 8th
2010 WM 33-D SUI 7 0 0 0 0 5th
**Totals WM 22 0 1 1 6 —**

**Hishon, Joey**
**b. Stratford, Ontario, Canada, October 20, 1991**
2009 WM18 18-F CAN 6 5 5 10 0 4th

**Hjalmarsson, Niklas**
**b. Eksjo, Sweden, June 6, 1987**
2005 WM18 5-D SWE 7 1 4 5 6 B
2007 WM20 28-D SWE 7 2 1 3 4 —
2012 WM 44-D SWE 8 0 3 3 2 6th

**Hjalmarsson, Simon**
**b. Varnamo, Sweden, February 1, 1989**
2007 WM18 16-F SWE 6 4 5 9 4 B
2009 WM20 29-F SWE 6 4 2 6 4 S

**Hjulmand, Sune**
**b. Esbjerg, Denmark, February 26, 1989**
2008 WM20 20-F DEN 6 1 1 2 8 10th

**Hlinka, Jaroslav**
**b. Prague, Czechoslovakia (Czech Republic), November 10, 1976**
2001 WM 17-F CZE 9 1 0 1 2 G
2002 WM 17-F CZE 7 1 5 6 2 5th
2003 WM 17-F CZE 9 2 1 3 6 4th
2004 WM 17-F CZE 2 0 1 1 2 5th
2006 WM 17-F CZE 9 2 4 6 2 S
2007 WM 17-F CZE 7 3 4 7 0 7th
2008 WM 17-F CZE 6 1 3 4 2 5th
2009 WM 17-F CZE 7 1 2 3 4 6th
**Totals WM 56 11 20 31 20 G,S**

**Hlinka, Michal**
**b. Novy Jicin, Czechoslovakia (Czech Republic), March 19, 1991**
2009 WM18 12-F CZE 6 0 2 2 6 6th
2010 WM20 26-F CZE 5 0 0 0 0 7th
2011 WM20 8-F CZE 6 3 1 4 2 7th
**Totals WM20 11 3 1 4 2 —**

**Hluchy, Milan**
**b. Rakovnik, Czechoslovakia (Czech Republic), January 13, 1985**
2003 WM18 11-F CZE 6 0 1 1 6 6th
2005 WM20 23-F CZE 7 1 2 3 6 B

**Hocevar, Matej**
**b. Ljubljana, Yugoslavia (Slovenia), April 30, 1982**
2011 WM 14-F SLO 6 0 2 2 6 16th

**Hodgson, Cody**
**b. Markham, Ontario, Canada, February 18, 1990**
2008 WM18 9-F CAN 7 2 10 12 8 G
2009 WM20 18-F CAN 6 5 11 16 2 G
~WM20 All-Star Team/Forward (2009)

**Hoeffel, Mike**
**b. North Oaks, Minnesota, United States, April 9, 1989**
2009 WM20 11-F USA 6 1 2 3 14 5th

**Hofbauer, Maximilian**
**b. Landshut, West Germany (Germany), January 2, 1990**
2008 WM18 23-F GER 6 1 1 2 0 5th

**Hofer, Armin**
**b. Brunico, Italy, March 19, 1987**
2008 WM 7-D ITA 5 0 0 0 0 16th
2010 WM 7-D ITA 5 0 0 0 2 15th
**Totals WM 10 0 0 0 2 —**

**Hofer, Fabio**
**b. Lustenau, Austria, January 23, 1991**
2010 WM20 14-F AUT 6 0 0 0 4 10th

**Hofer, Roland**
**b. Vipiteno, Italy, June 24, 1990**
2012 WM 5-D ITA 3 0 0 0 0 15th

**Hoff, Magnus**
**b. Oslo, Norway, October 7, 1993**
2011 WM18 10-F NOR 6 3 2 5 2 9th

**Hofflin, Mirko**
**b. Freiburg, Germany, June 18, 1992**
2009 WM18 13-F GER 6 0 1 1 4 10th
2011 WM20 19-F GER 6 0 1 1 4 10th

**Hoffmann, Luka**
**b. Zurich, Switzerland, January 17, 1993**
2011 WM18 25-F SUI 5 0 1 1 0 7th

**Hofmann, Gregory**
**b. Biel, Switzerland, November 13, 1992**
2010 WM18 13-F SUI 6 5 0 5 2 5th
2011 WM20 13-F SUI 6 1 3 4 2 5th
2012 WM20 13-F SUI 6 1 1 2 6 8th
Totals WM20 12 2 4 6 8 —

**Hokkanen, Iivo**
**b. Hameenlinna, Finland, May 3, 1985**
2005 WM20 8-F FIN 6 1 1 2 0 5th

**Holgaard, Lasse**
**b. Copenhagen, Denmark, January 30, 1989**
2008 WM20 10-F DEN 6 0 1 1 4 10th

**Holik, Petr**
**b. Zlin, Czechoslovakia (Czech Republic), March 3, 1992**
2010 WM18 21-F CZE 6 5 2 7 0 6th
2011 WM20 17-F CZE 6 1 2 3 2 7th
2012 WM20 17-F CZE 6 4 1 5 2 5th
Totals WM20 12 5 3 8 4 —

**Holland, Jason**
**b. Morinville, Alberta, April 30, 1976**
1996 WM20 3-D CAN 6 2 1 3 4 G
2008 WM 3-D GER 2 0 1 1 2 10th*
*suspended after two games due to IIHF eligibility violation because it was determined the Canadian-born player had not yet fulfilled four years' playing in Germany

**Holland, Peter**
**b. Caldeon, Ontario, Canada, January 14, 1991**
2009 WM18 11-F CAN 6 1 4 5 8 4th

**Hollenstein, Denis**
**b. Zurich, Switzerland, October 15, 1989**
2007 WM18 11-F SUI 6 2 2 4 8 6th
2008 WM20 11-F SUI 6 0 0 0 0 9th
2012 WM 70-F SUI 7 0 2 2 2 11th

**Hollstedt, Hans Kristian**
**b. Oslo, Norway, August 2, 1991**
2009 WM18 27-F NOR 4 0 0 0 2 9th
2011 WM20 22-F NOR 6 1 0 1 0 9th

**Holmqvist, Mikael**
**b. Stockholm, Sweden, June 8, 1979**
1998 WM20 14-F SWE 7 0 1 1 28 6th

**Holmstedt, Matthias**
**b. Karlskoga, Norway, November 25, 1980**
2008 WM 17-D NOR 1 0 0 0 2 8th

**Holos, Jonas**
**b. Sarpsborg, Norway, August 27, 1987**
2004 WM18 5-D NOR 6 0 1 1 2 10th
2006 WM20 11-D NOR 6 0 0 0 12 10th
2006 WM 6-D NOR 6 0 0 0 2 11th
2007 WM 6-D NOR 6 0 1 1 6 14th
2008 WM 6-D NOR 7 0 1 1 6 8th
2009 WM 6-D NOR 6 0 0 0 2 11th
2010 OG-M 6-D NOR 4 0 1 1 2 10th
2010 WM 6-D NOR 6 1 1 2 8 9th
2011 WM 6-D NOR 7 2 3 5 2 6th
2012 WM 6-D NOR 8 4 5 9 2 8th
**Totals WM 46 7 11 18 28 —**

**Holten Moller, Mikkel**
**b. Horsholm, Denmark, April 19, 1990**
2008 WM18 7-D DEN 6 0 0 0 2 10th

**Holtet, Marius**
**b. Hamar, Norway, August 31, 1984**
2001 WM18 19-F NOR 6 2 2 4 6 9th
2002 WM18 19-F NOR 8 5 3 8 12 11th

| | | | | | | | | |
|---|---|---|---|---|---|---|---|---|
| 2006 WM | 9-F | NOR | 6 | 1 | 1 | 2 | 4 | 11th |
| 2008 WM | 9-F | NOR | 7 | 1 | 1 | 2 | 4 | 8th |
| 2009 WM | 9-F | NOR | 2 | 0 | 0 | 0 | 0 | 11th |
| 2010 OG-M | 9-F | NOR | 4 | 1 | 0 | 1 | 0 | 10th |
| 2010 WM | 9-F | NOR | 4 | 0 | 0 | 0 | 4 | 9th |
| 2011 WM | 9-F | NOR | 7 | 6 | 2 | 8 | 4 | 6th |
| 2012 WM | 9-F | NOR | 7 | 2 | 3 | 5 | 4 | 8th |
| Totals WM18 | | 14 | 7 | 5 | 12 | 18 | — | |
| **Totals WM** | | | **33** | **10** | **7** | **17** | **20** | **—** |

**Holzapfel, Riley**
**b. Regina, Saskatchewan, Canada, August 18, 1988**

| | | | | | | | | |
|---|---|---|---|---|---|---|---|---|
| 2008 WM20 | 21-F | CAN | 7 | 0 | 0 | 0 | 8 | G |

**Holzer, Korbinian**
**b. Munich, West Germany (Germany), February 16, 1988**

| | | | | | | | | |
|---|---|---|---|---|---|---|---|---|
| 2005 WM18 | 12-D | GER | 6 | 2 | 1 | 3 | 4 | 8th |
| 2006 WM18 | 27-D | GER | 6 | 1 | 2 | 3 | 18 | 8th |
| 2007 WM20 | 27-D | GER | 6 | 0 | 0 | 0 | 8 | 9th |
| 2010 OG-M | 5-D | GER | 4 | 0 | 0 | 0 | 2 | 11th |
| 2010 WM | 5-D | GER | 8 | 0 | 0 | 0 | 22 | 4th |
| 2011 WM | 5-D | GER | 7 | 0 | 1 | 1 | 10 | 7th |
| **Totals WM18** | | | **12** | **3** | **3** | **6** | **22** | **—** |
| **Totals WM** | | | **15** | **0** | **1** | **1** | **32** | **—** |

**Honejsek, Antonin**
**b. Prostevjov, Czech Republic, February 19, 1991**

| | | | | | | | | |
|---|---|---|---|---|---|---|---|---|
| 2009 WM18 | 7-F | CZE | 6 | 4 | 2 | 6 | 2 | 6th |
| 2011 WM20 | 19-F | CZE | 6 | 2 | 2 | 4 | 0 | 7th |

**Honkaheimo, Otto**
**b. Rauma, Finland, August 3, 1985**

| | | | | | | | | |
|---|---|---|---|---|---|---|---|---|
| 2003 WM18 | 4-D | FIN | 6 | 0 | 3 | 3 | 4 | 7th |
| 2005 WM20 | 4-D | FIN | 6 | 1 | 0 | 1 | 0 | 5th |

**Horak, Oldrich**
**b. Zlin, Czechoslovakia (Czech Republic), January 9, 1991**

| | | | | | | | | |
|---|---|---|---|---|---|---|---|---|
| 2009 WM18 | 4-D | CZE | 6 | 0 | 0 | 0 | 6 | 6th |
| 2011 WM20 | 4-D | CZE | 6 | 0 | 0 | 0 | 8 | 7th |

**Horak, Roman**
**b. Ceske Budejovice, Czech Republic, May 21, 1991**

| | | | | | | | | |
|---|---|---|---|---|---|---|---|---|
| 2009 WM18 | 23-F | CZE | 6 | 2 | 1 | 3 | 4 | 6th |
| 2010 WM20 | 10-F | CZE | 6 | 1 | 1 | 2 | 0 | 7th |
| 2011 WM20 | 23-F | CZE | 5 | 0 | 1 | 1 | 4 | 7th |
| **Totals WM20** | | | **11** | **1** | **2** | **3** | **4** | **—** |

**Horcoff, Shawn**
**b. Trail, British Columbia, Canada, September 17, 1978**

| | | | | | | | | |
|---|---|---|---|---|---|---|---|---|
| 2003 WM | 10-F | CAN | 9 | 3 | 4 | 7 | 0 | G |
| 2004 WM | 10-F | CAN | 9 | 3 | 4 | 7 | 8 | G |
| 2009 WM | 10-F | CAN | 9 | 1 | 1 | 2 | 6 | S |
| **Totals WM** | | | **27** | **7** | **9** | **16** | **14** | **2G,S** |

**Hordler, Frank**
**b. Bad Muskau, East Germany (Germany), January 26, 1985**

| | | | | | | | | |
|---|---|---|---|---|---|---|---|---|
| 2002 WM18 | 24-D | GER | 8 | 0 | 0 | 0 | 8 | 10th |
| 2007 WM | 48-D | GER | 6 | 0 | 0 | 0 | 14 | 9th |
| 2008 WM | 48-D | GER | 6 | 1 | 0 | 1 | 6 | 10th |
| 2009 WM | 48-D | GER | 6 | 0 | 0 | 0 | 10 | 15th |
| 2010 WM | 48-D | GER | 1 | 0 | 0 | 0 | 0 | 4th |
| 2011 WM | 48-D | GER | 7 | 2 | 2 | 4 | 0 | 7th |
| **Totals WM** | | | **26** | **3** | **2** | **5** | **30** | **—** |

**Hornqvist, Patric**
**b. Sollentuna, Sweden, January 1, 1987**

| | | | | | | | | |
|---|---|---|---|---|---|---|---|---|
| 2005 WM18 | 18-F | SWE | 7 | 1 | 0 | 1 | 2 | B |
| 2007 WM20 | 10-F | SWE | 7 | 1 | 2 | 3 | 4 | 4th |
| 2007 WM | 8-F | SWE | 9 | 2 | 4 | 6 | 6 | 4th |
| 2008 WM | 10-F | SWE | 9 | 6 | 0 | 6 | 12 | 4th |
| 2010 OG-M | 27-F | SWE | 4 | 1 | 0 | 1 | 4 | 5th |
| 2012 WM | 27-F | SWE | 3 | 0 | 0 | 0 | 4 | 6th |
| **Totals WM** | | | **21** | **8** | **4** | **12** | **22** | **—** |

**Horsky, Marek**
**b. Bratislava, Czechoslovakia (Slovakia), December 30, 1986**

| | | | | | | | | |
|---|---|---|---|---|---|---|---|---|
| 2006 WM20 | 15-F | SVK | 6 | 1 | 1 | 2 | 4 | 8th |

**Hospelt, Kai**
**b. Cologne, West Germany (Germany), August 23, 1985**

| | | | | | | | | |
|---|---|---|---|---|---|---|---|---|
| 2002 WM18 | 22-F | GER | 8 | 0 | 0 | 0 | 2 | 10th |
| 2003 WM20 | 16-F | GER | 6 | 0 | 1 | 1 | 0 | 9th |
| 2005 WM20 | 18-F | GER | 6 | 0 | 0 | 0 | 6 | 9th |
| 2009 WM | 18-F | GER | 6 | 0 | 1 | 1 | 2 | 15th |
| 2010 OG-M | 18-F | GER | 4 | 0 | 1 | 1 | 2 | 11th |
| 2010 WM | 18-F | GER | 9 | 0 | 2 | 2 | 2 | 4th |
| 2011 WM | 18-F | GER | 7 | 1 | 2 | 3 | 4 | 7th |
| 2012 WM | 18-F | GER | 7 | 1 | 3 | 4 | 4 | 12th |
| Totals WM20 | | 12 | 0 | 1 | 1 | 6 | — | |
| **Totals WM** | | | **29** | **2** | **8** | **10** | **12** | **—** |

**Hossa, Marcel**
**b. Ilava, Czechoslovakia (Slovakia), October 12, 1981**

| | | | | | | | | |
|---|---|---|---|---|---|---|---|---|
| 1999 WM18 | 28-F | SVK | 7 | 2 | 0 | 2 | 14 | B |
| 2000 WM20 | 19-F | SVK | 7 | 0 | 1 | 1 | 8 | 9th |
| 2001 WM20 | 19-F | SVK | 7 | 1 | 3 | 4 | 8 | 8th |
| 2005 WM | 13-F | SVK | 2 | 0 | 0 | 0 | 0 | 5th |
| 2006 OG-M | 91-F | SVK | 6 | 0 | 0 | 0 | 0 | 5th |
| 2006 WM | 91-F | SVK | 7 | 1 | 3 | 4 | 6 | 8th |
| 2008 WM | 81-F | SVK | 5 | 2 | 5 | 7 | 2 | 13th |
| 2009 WM | 81-F | SVK | 6 | 3 | 2 | 5 | 4 | 10th |
| 2010 OG-M | 91-F | SVK | 7 | 0 | 1 | 1 | 0 | 4th |
| 2011 WM | 88-F | SVK | 6 | 1 | 0 | 1 | 2 | 10th |
| 2012 WM | 81-F | SVK | 6 | 0 | 0 | 0 | 0 | S |
| **Totals WM20** | | | **14** | **1** | **4** | **5** | **16** | **—** |
| **Totals WM** | | | **32** | **7** | **10** | **17** | **14** | **S** |
| **Totals OG-M** | | | **13** | **0** | **1** | **1** | **0** | **—** |

**Hossa, Marian**
**b. Stara Lubovna, Czechoslovakia (Slovakia), January 12, 1979**

| | | | | | | | | |
|---|---|---|---|---|---|---|---|---|
| 1997 WM20 | 24-F | SVK | 6 | 5 | 2 | 7 | 2 | 6th |
| 1997 WM | 14-F | SVK | 8 | 0 | 2 | 2 | 0 | 9th |
| 1998 WM20 | 24-F | SVK | 6 | 4 | 4 | 8 | 12 | 9th |
| 1999 WM | 22-F | SVK | 6 | 5 | 2 | 7 | 8 | 7th |
| 2001 WM | 18-F | SVK | 6 | 1 | 2 | 3 | 2 | 7th |
| 2002 OG-M | 81-F | SVK | 2 | 4 | 2 | 6 | 0 | 13th |
| 2004 WM | 81-F | SVK | 9 | 2 | 5 | 7 | 2 | 4th |
| 2004 WCH | 81-F | SVK | 4 | 1 | 0 | 1 | 2 | 7th |
| 2005 WM | 81-F | SVK | 7 | 4 | 3 | 7 | 6 | 5th |
| 2006 OG-M | 81-F | SVK | 6 | 5 | 5 | 10 | 4 | 5th |
| 2006 WM | 81-F | SVK | 5 | 1 | 6 | 7 | 0 | 8th |
| 2007 WM | 81-F | SVK | 6 | 2 | 4 | 6 | 6 | 6th |
| 2010 OG-M | 81-F | SVK | 7 | 3 | 6 | 9 | 6 | 4th |
| 2011 WM | 81-F | SVK | 5 | 1 | 1 | 2 | 2 | 10th |
| **Totals WM20** | | | **12** | **9** | **6** | **15** | **14** | **—** |
| **Totals WM** | | | **52** | **16** | **25** | **41** | **26** | **—** |
| **Totals OG-M** | | | **15** | **12** | **13** | **25** | **10** | **—** |

**Houfek, Jakub**
**b. Plzen, Czech Republic, January 20, 1994**

| | | | | | | | | |
|---|---|---|---|---|---|---|---|---|
| 2012 WM18 | 6-D | CZE | 6 | 1 | 0 | 1 | 4 | 8th |

**Hovinen, Miro**
**b. Espoo, Finland, April 29, 1992**

| | | | | | | | | |
|---|---|---|---|---|---|---|---|---|
| 2010 WM18 | 4-D | FIN | 6 | 1 | 0 | 1 | 33 | B |
| 2012 WM20 | 8-D | FIN | 7 | 0 | 0 | 0 | 2 | 4th |

**Hovorka, Marek**
**b. Ilava, Czechoslovakia (Slovakia), October 8, 1984**

| | | | | | | | | |
|---|---|---|---|---|---|---|---|---|
| 2012 WM | 25-F | SVK | 4 | 0 | 0 | 0 | 2 | S |

**Howden, Quinton**
**b. Oak Bank, Manitoba, Canada, January 21, 1992**

| | | | | | | | | |
|---|---|---|---|---|---|---|---|---|
| 2010 WM18 | 22-F | CAN | 6 | 4 | 2 | 6 | 4 | 7th |
| 2011 WM20 | 12-F | CAN | 7 | 2 | 3 | 5 | 4 | S |
| 2012 WM20 | 21-F | CAN | 6 | 3 | 3 | 6 | 2 | B |
| **Totals WM20** | | | **13** | **5** | **6** | **11** | **6** | **S,B** |

**Hoygard, Stian**
**b. Lorenskog, Norway, March 28, 1987**

| | | | | | | | | |
|---|---|---|---|---|---|---|---|---|
| 2006 WM20 | 15-F | NOR | 6 | 0 | 0 | 0 | 20 | 10th |

**Hrasko, Peter**
**b. Detva, Czehoslovakia (Slovakia), November 6, 1991**

| | | | | | | | | |
|---|---|---|---|---|---|---|---|---|
| 2010 WM20 | 16-D | SVK | 6 | 0 | 4 | 4 | 6 | 8th |
| 2011 WM20 | 16-D | SVK | 3 | 0 | 0 | 0 | 25 | 8th |
| **Totals WM20** | | | **9** | **0** | **4** | **4** | **31** | **—** |

**Hrbas, Marek**
**b. Plzen, Czech Republic, March 4, 1993**

| | | | | | | | | |
|---|---|---|---|---|---|---|---|---|
| 2011 WM18 | 28-D | CZE | 6 | 0 | 4 | 4 | 2 | 8th |
| 2012 WM20 | 13-D | CZE | 6 | 0 | 1 | 1 | 2 | 5th |

**Hrdel, Zbynek**
**b. Pisek, Czechoslovakia (Czech Republic), August 19, 1985**

| | | | | | | | | |
|---|---|---|---|---|---|---|---|---|
| 2003 WM18 | 10-F | CZE | 6 | 1 | 0 | 1 | 29 | 6th |
| 2005 WM20 | 15-F | CZE | 7 | 1 | 0 | 1 | 4 | B |

**Hricina, Tomas**
**b. Kosice, Czechoslovakia (Slovakia), May 31, 1990**

| | | | | | | | | |
|---|---|---|---|---|---|---|---|---|
| 2008 WM18 | 22-F | SVK | 6 | 5 | 1 | 6 | 0 | 7th |

**Hrivik, Marek**
**b. Cadca, Slovakia, August 28, 1991**

| | | | | | | | | |
|---|---|---|---|---|---|---|---|---|
| 2008 WM18 | 12-F | SVK | 6 | 1 | 0 | 1 | 2 | 7th |
| 2009 WM18 | 12-F | SVK | 6 | 2 | 3 | 5 | 0 | 7th |
| 2009 WM20 | 17-F | SVK | 7 | 1 | 0 | 1 | 2 | 4th |
| 2011 WM20 | 27-F | SVK | 6 | 2 | 0 | 2 | 2 | 8th |
| **Totals WM18** | | | **12** | **3** | **3** | **6** | **2** | **—** |
| **Totals WM20** | | | **13** | **3** | **0** | **3** | **4** | **—** |

**Hromas, Karel**
**b. Beroun, Czechoslovakia (Czech Republic), January 27, 1986**

| | | | | | | | | |
|---|---|---|---|---|---|---|---|---|
| 2003 WM18 | 14-F | CZE | 6 | 0 | 0 | 0 | 6 | 6th |
| 2004 WM18 | 17-F | CZE | 7 | 1 | 1 | 2 | 2 | B |
| 2004 WM20 | 15-F | CZE | 7 | 1 | 0 | 1 | 2 | 4th |
| 2006 WM20 | 17-F | CZE | 6 | 1 | 3 | 4 | 8 | 6th |
| **Totals WM18** | | | **13** | **1** | **1** | **2** | **8** | **B** |
| **Totals WM20** | | | **13** | **2** | **3** | **5** | **10** | **—** |

**Hruska, Milan**
**b. Topolcany, Czechoslovakia (Slovakia), April 26, 1985**

| | | | | | | | | |
|---|---|---|---|---|---|---|---|---|
| 2003 WM18 | 10-D | SVK | 7 | 0 | 1 | 1 | 4 | S |
| 2004 WM20 | 18-D | SVK | 6 | 0 | 1 | 1 | 6 | 6th |
| 2005 WM20 | 21-D | SVK | 6 | 0 | 0 | 0 | 6 | 7th |
| **Totals WM20** | | | **12** | **0** | **1** | **1** | **12** | **—** |

**Hubacek, Petr**
**b. Brno, Czechoslovakia (Czech Republic), September 2, 1979**

| | | | | | | | | |
|---|---|---|---|---|---|---|---|---|
| 2006 WM | 10-F | CZE | 9 | 1 | 0 | 1 | 6 | S |
| 2007 WM | 10-F | CZE | 7 | 0 | 0 | 0 | 2 | 7th |
| 2010 WM | 11-F | CZE | 9 | 2 | 0 | 2 | 0 | G |
| 2011 WM | 11-F | CZE | 9 | 0 | 2 | 2 | 2 | B |
| **Totals WM** | | | **34** | **3** | **2** | **5** | **10** | **G,S,B** |

**Huberdeau, Jonathan**
**b. St. Jerome, Quebec, Canada, June 4, 1993**

| | | | | | | | | |
|---|---|---|---|---|---|---|---|---|
| 2012 WM20 | 11-F | CAN | 6 | 1 | 8 | 9 | 16 | B |

**Hudacek, Libor**
**b. Levoca, Czechoslovakia (Slovakia), November 7, 1990**

| | | | | | | | | |
|---|---|---|---|---|---|---|---|---|
| 2008 WM18 | 29-F | SVK | 6 | 0 | 3 | 3 | 8 | 7th |
| 2010 WM20 | 13-F | SVK | 6 | 0 | 2 | 2 | 2 | 8th |
| 2012 WM | 21-F | SVK | 10 | 2 | 3 | 5 | 0 | S |

**Hudec, Denis**
**b. Trencin, Slovakia, June 20, 1993**

| | | | | | | | | |
|---|---|---|---|---|---|---|---|---|
| 2011 WM18 | 22-F | SVK | 3 | 1 | 0 | 1 | 0 | 10th |

**Hudecek, Jan**
**b. Ostrava, Czech Republic, October 7, 1994**

| | | | | | | | | |
|---|---|---|---|---|---|---|---|---|
| 2012 WM18 | 24-F | CZE | 6 | 2 | 0 | 2 | 6 | 8th |

**Hudon, Charles**
**b. Boisbriand, Quebec, Canada, June 23, 1994**

| | | | | | | | | |
|---|---|---|---|---|---|---|---|---|
| 2011 WM18 | 16-F | CAN | 7 | 0 | 1 | 1 | 2 | 4th |

**Huebscher, Andre**
**b. Moers, West Germany (Germany), January 8, 1989**

| | | | | | | | | |
|---|---|---|---|---|---|---|---|---|
| 2007 WM18 | 17-F | GER | 6 | 1 | 2 | 3 | 2 | 8th |
| 2009 WM20 | 6-F | GER | 6 | 1 | 1 | 2 | 4 | 9th |

**Hufner, Benjamin**
**b. Berlin, West Germany (Germany), January 7, 1991**

| | | | | | | | | |
|---|---|---|---|---|---|---|---|---|
| 2009 WM18 | 5-D | GER | 6 | 1 | 2 | 3 | 10 | 10th |
| 2011 WM20 | 5-D | GER | 6 | 0 | 1 | 1 | 2 | 10th |

**Huhtanen, Tuomas**
**b. Noormarkku, Finland, March 16, 1987**

| | | | | | | | | |
|---|---|---|---|---|---|---|---|---|
| 2007 WM20 | 11-F | FIN | 6 | 0 | 1 | 1 | 2 | 6th |

**Hundertpfund, Thomas**
**b. Klagenfurt, Austria, December 14, 1989**

| | | | | | | | | |
|---|---|---|---|---|---|---|---|---|
| 2011 WM | 77-F | AUT | 6 | 0 | 1 | 1 | 0 | 15th |

**Hunwick, Matt**
**b. Warren, Michigan, United States, May 21, 1985**

| | | | | | | | | |
|---|---|---|---|---|---|---|---|---|
| 2003 WM18 | 22-D | USA | 6 | 0 | 3 | 3 | 6 | 4th |
| 2004 WM20 | 5-D | USA | 6 | 0 | 0 | 0 | 0 | G |
| 2005 WM20 | 22-D | USA | 7 | 0 | 4 | 4 | 0 | 4th |
| **Totals WM20** | | | **13** | **0** | **4** | **4** | **0** | **G** |

**Huovinen, Joonas**
**b. Oulu, Finland, February 23, 1994**

| | | | | | | | | |
|---|---|---|---|---|---|---|---|---|
| 2012 WM18 | 8-F | FIN | 6 | 0 | 0 | 0 | 0 | 4th |

**Hurlimann, Stefan**
**b. Einsiedeln, Switzerland, March 13, 1985**

| | | | | | | | | |
|---|---|---|---|---|---|---|---|---|
| 2003 WM18 | 16-F | SUI | 6 | 0 | 0 | 0 | 8 | 9th |
| 2005 WM20 | 13-F | SUI | 6 | 3 | 0 | 3 | 0 | 8th |

**Hurri, Joonas**
**b. Lahti, Finland, March 31, 1991**

| | | | | | | | | |
|---|---|---|---|---|---|---|---|---|
| 2009 WM18 | 3-D | FIN | 6 | 0 | 0 | 0 | 4 | B |

**Huselius, Kristian**
**b. Osterhaninge, Sweden, November 10, 1978**

| | | | | | | | | |
|---|---|---|---|---|---|---|---|---|
| 1997 WM20 | 14-F | SWE | 6 | 1 | 4 | 5 | 4 | 8th |
| 1998 WM20 | 11-F | SWE | 2 | 0 | 0 | 0 | 0 | 6th |
| 2000 WM | 22-F | SWE | 7 | 4 | 1 | 5 | 4 | 7th |
| 2001 WM | 22-F | SWE | 9 | 2 | 3 | 5 | 0 | B |
| 2002 WM | 44-F | SWE | 9 | 5 | 6 | 11 | 0 | B |
| 2009 WM | 60-F | SWE | 8 | 4 | 3 | 7 | 6 | B |
| **Totals WM20** | | | **8** | **1** | **4** | **5** | **4** | **—** |
| **Totals WM** | | | **33** | **15** | **13** | **28** | **10** | **3B** |

**Huzevka, Peter**
**b. Povazska Bystrica, Czechoslovakia (Slovakia), September 9, 1976**

| | | | | | | | | |
|---|---|---|---|---|---|---|---|---|
| 2008 WM | 9-F | SVK | 5 | 0 | 1 | 1 | 0 | 13th |

**Hvorostinins, Vitailijs**
**b. Preili, Latvia, August 17, 1992**

| | | | | | | | | |
|---|---|---|---|---|---|---|---|---|
| 2012 WM20 | 14-F | LAT | 6 | 1 | 1 | 2 | 0 | 9th |

**Hyka, Tomas**
**b. Mlada Boleslav, Czech Republic, March 23, 1993**

| | | | | | | | | |
|---|---|---|---|---|---|---|---|---|
| 2011 WM18 | 15-F | CZE | 6 | 1 | 1 | 2 | 0 | 8th |
| 2012 WM20 | 27-F | CZE | 5 | 0 | 2 | 2 | 4 | 5th |

**Hytonen, Juha-Pekka**
**b. Jyvaskyla, Finland, May 22, 1981**

| | | | | | | | | |
|---|---|---|---|---|---|---|---|---|
| 1999 WM18 | 15-F | FIN | 7 | 2 | 2 | 4 | 2 | G |
| 2001 WM20 | 15-F | FIN | 7 | 0 | 1 | 1 | 4 | S |
| 2009 WM | 51-F | FIN | 7 | 0 | 0 | 0 | 2 | 5th |
| 2010 WM | 15-F | FIN | 7 | 1 | 0 | 1 | 2 | 6th |
| **Totals WM** | | | **14** | **1** | **0** | **1** | **4** | **—** |

**Hyvarinen, Ville**
**b. Kuopio, Finland, June 6, 1991**

| | | | | | | | | |
|---|---|---|---|---|---|---|---|---|
| 2009 WM18 | 7-D | FIN | 6 | 0 | 2 | 2 | 0 | B |

**Hyvonen, Hannes**
**b. Oulu, Finland, August 29, 1975**

| | | | | | | | | |
|---|---|---|---|---|---|---|---|---|
| 2008 WM | 18-F | FIN | 6 | 1 | 3 | 4 | 29 | B |
| 2009 WM | 8-F | FIN | 7 | 2 | 4 | 6 | 12 | 5th |
| **Totals WM** | | | **13** | **3** | **7** | **10** | **41** | **B** |

**Iannone, Pat**
**b. Fruitvale, British Columbia, February 9, 1982**

| | | | | | | | | |
|---|---|---|---|---|---|---|---|---|
| 2008 WM | 17-F | ITA | 5 | 1 | 2 | 3 | 16 | 16th |
| 2010 WM | 16-F | ITA | 6 | 0 | 1 | 1 | 4 | 15th |
| 2012 WM | 41-F | ITA | 7 | 0 | 0 | 0 | 4 | 15th |
| **Totals WM** | | | **18** | **1** | **3** | **4** | **24** | **—** |

**Igier, Kevin**
**b. Paris, France, March 4, 1987**

| | | | | | | | | |
|---|---|---|---|---|---|---|---|---|
| 2009 WM | 71-D | FRA | 6 | 0 | 0 | 0 | 0 | 12th |
| 2010 WM | 8-D | FRA | 3 | 0 | 0 | 0 | 0 | 14th |
| **Totals WM** | | | **9** | **0** | **0** | **0** | **0** | **—** |

**Iginla, Jarome**
**b. St. Albert, Alberta, Canada, July 1, 1977**

| | | | | | | | | |
|---|---|---|---|---|---|---|---|---|
| 1996 WM20 | 12-F | CAN | 6 | 5 | 7 | 12 | 4 | G |
| 1997 WM | 12-F | CAN | 11 | 2 | 3 | 5 | 2 | G |
| 2002 OG-M | 12-F | CAN | 6 | 3 | 1 | 4 | 0 | G |
| 2004 WCH | 12-F | CAN | 6 | 2 | 1 | 3 | 2 | 1st |
| 2006 OG-M | 12-F | CAN | 6 | 2 | 1 | 3 | 4 | 7th |
| 2010 OG-M | 12-F | CAN | 7 | 5 | 2 | 7 | 0 | G |
| **Totals OG-M** | | | **19** | **10** | **4** | **14** | **4** | **2G** |

~WM20 IIHF Directorate Best Forward (1996), WM20 All-Star Team/Forward (1996)

**Ignatovich, Maxim**
**b. Novosibirsk, Soviet Union (Russia), April 7, 1991**

| | | | | | | | | |
|---|---|---|---|---|---|---|---|---|
| 2011 WM20 | 23-D | RUS | 7 | 0 | 1 | 1 | 0 | G |

**Ikonen, Henri**
**b. Savonlinna, Finland, April 17, 1994**

| | | | | | | | | |
|---|---|---|---|---|---|---|---|---|
| 2012 WM18 | 24-F | FIN | 7 | 2 | 0 | 2 | 4 | 4th |

**Ikonen, Jasse**
**b. Kuopio, Finland, June 13, 1990**

| | | | | | | | | |
|---|---|---|---|---|---|---|---|---|
| 2008 WM18 | 12-F | FIN | 6 | 0 | 0 | 0 | 32 | 6th |
| 2010 WM20 | 21-F | FIN | 6 | 0 | 2 | 2 | 14 | 5th |

**Ikonen, Juuso**
**b. Espoo, Finland, January 3, 1995**

| | | | | | | | | |
|---|---|---|---|---|---|---|---|---|
| 2012 WM18 | 10-F | FIN | 5 | 0 | 1 | 1 | 0 | 4th |

**Ilin, Yuri**
**b. Chelyabinsk, Soviet Union (Russia), June 24, 1987**

| | | | | | | | | |
|---|---|---|---|---|---|---|---|---|
| 2007 WM20 | 14-F | BLR | 6 | 1 | 0 | 1 | 0 | 10th |

**Ilisko, Alberts**
**b. Riga, Soviet Union (Latvia), October 11, 1990**

| | | | | | | | | |
|---|---|---|---|---|---|---|---|---|
| 2007 WM18 | 3-D | LAT | 6 | 0 | 1 | 1 | 0 | 10th |
| 2009 WM20 | 3-D | LAT | 6 | 0 | 1 | 1 | 4 | 8th |
| 2010 WM20 | 3-D | LAT | 6 | 0 | 1 | 1 | 6 | 9th |
| **Totals WM20** | | | **12** | **0** | **2** | **2** | **10** | **—** |

**Illemann, Marco**
**b. Rodovre, Denmark, May 11, 1994**

| | | | | | | | | |
|---|---|---|---|---|---|---|---|---|
| 2012 WM18 | 10-D | DEN | 6 | 1 | 0 | 1 | 6 | 10th |

**Illo, Radoslav**
**b. Povazska Bystrica, Czechoslovakia (Slovakia), January 21, 1990**

| | | | | | | | | |
|---|---|---|---|---|---|---|---|---|
| 2010 WM20 | 17-F | SVK | 6 | 2 | 3 | 5 | 6 | 8th |

**Immonen, Jarkko**
**b. Rantasalmi, Finland, April 19, 1982**

| | | | | | | | | |
|---|---|---|---|---|---|---|---|---|
| 2000 WM18 | 12-F | FIN | 7 | 3 | 4 | 7 | 4 | G |
| 2002 WM20 | 12-F | FIN | 7 | 4 | 3 | 7 | 6 | B |
| 2009 WM | 26-F | FIN | 7 | 1 | 4 | 5 | 2 | 5th |
| 2010 OG-M | 62-F | FIN | 6 | 0 | 0 | 0 | 0 | B |
| 2010 WM | 26-F | FIN | 7 | 3 | 1 | 4 | 4 | 6th |
| 2011 WM | 26-F | FIN | 9 | 9 | 3 | 12 | 2 | G |
| 2012 WM | 26-F | FIN | 10 | 3 | 2 | 5 | 0 | 4th |
| **Totals WM** | | | **33** | **16** | **10** | **26** | **8** | **G** |

~WM All-Star Team/Forward (2011)

**Imrich, Michal**
**b. Piestany, Czechoslovakia (Slovakia), January 6, 1991**

| | | | | | | | | |
|---|---|---|---|---|---|---|---|---|
| 2009 WM18 | 3-D | SVK | 6 | 0 | 1 | 1 | 16 | 7th |

**Indrasis, Miks**
**b. Riga, Soviet Union (Latvia), September 30, 1990**

| | | | | | | | | |
|---|---|---|---|---|---|---|---|---|
| 2010 WM20 | 10-F | LAT | 6 | 1 | 2 | 3 | 8 | 9th |
| 2012 WM | 70-F | LAT | 7 | 3 | 2 | 5 | 2 | 10th |

**Insam, Marco**
**b. Selva Gardena, Italy, June 5, 1989**

| | | | | | | | | |
|---|---|---|---|---|---|---|---|---|
| 2008 WM | 8-F | ITA | 1 | 0 | 0 | 0 | 0 | 16th |
| 2012 WM | 8-F | ITA | 7 | 0 | 0 | 0 | 0 | 15th |
| **Totals WM** | | | **8** | **0** | **0** | **0** | **0** | **—** |

**Iori, Diego**
**b. Cavalese, Italy, May 20, 1986**

| | | | | | | | | |
|---|---|---|---|---|---|---|---|---|
| 2012 WM | 4-F | ITA | 7 | 0 | 0 | 0 | 4 | 15th |

**Irgl, Zbynek**
**b. Ostrava, Czechoslovakia (Czech Republic), November 29, 1980**

| | | | | | | | | |
|---|---|---|---|---|---|---|---|---|
| 2000 WM20 | 16-F | CZE | 7 | 2 | 1 | 3 | 6 | G |
| 2006 WM | 24-F | CZE | 6 | 2 | 2 | 4 | 0 | S |
| 2007 WM | 24-F | CZE | 7 | 2 | 2 | 4 | 4 | 7th |
| 2008 WM | 24-F | CZE | 7 | 1 | 2 | 3 | 2 | 5th |
| 2009 WM | 24-F | CZE | 5 | 0 | 0 | 0 | 2 | 6th |
| **Totals WM** | | | **25** | **5** | **6** | **11** | **8** | **S** |

**Isaksson, Magnus**
**b. Pitea, Sweden, January 16, 1987**

| | | | | | | | | |
|---|---|---|---|---|---|---|---|---|
| 2007 WM20 | 20-F | SWE | 7 | 2 | 0 | 2 | 2 | 4th |

**Isangulov, Ildar**
**b. Ufa, Russia, May 20, 1992**

| | | | | | | | | |
|---|---|---|---|---|---|---|---|---|
| 2012 WM20 | 26-D | RUS | 6 | 0 | 0 | 0 | 6 | S |

**Isopp, Maximilian Oliver**
**b. St. Veit an der Glan, Austria, February 5, 1990**

| | | | | | | | | |
|---|---|---|---|---|---|---|---|---|
| 2010 WM20 | 11-D | AUT | 6 | 0 | 0 | 0 | 6 | 10th |

**Ivanins, Raitis**
**b. Riga, Soviet Union (Latvia), January 3, 1979**

| | | | | | | | | |
|---|---|---|---|---|---|---|---|---|
| 2008 WM | 41-F | LAT | 6 | 0 | 0 | 0 | 31 | 11th |

**Ivanov, Nikita**
**b. Temirtau, Soviet Union (Kazakstan), March 31, 1989**

| | | | | | | | | |
|---|---|---|---|---|---|---|---|---|
| 2008 WM20 | 8-F | KAZ | 6 | 0 | 0 | 0 | 10 | 8th |
| 2009 WM20 | 10-F | KAZ | 6 | 0 | 0 | 0 | 10 | 10th |
| **Totals WM20** | | | **12** | **0** | **0** | **0** | **20** | **—** |

**Ivanyuzhenkov, Anton**
**b. Moscow Region, Russia, January 2, 1994**

| | | | | | | | | |
|---|---|---|---|---|---|---|---|---|
| 2011 WM18 | 12-F | RUS | 7 | 1 | 1 | 2 | 4 | B |

**Ivashin, Viktor**
**b. Ust-Kamenogorsk, Soviet Union (Kazakhstan), January 1, 1991**

| | | | | | | | | |
|---|---|---|---|---|---|---|---|---|
| 2009 WM20 | 12-D | KAZ | 6 | 0 | 0 | 0 | 4 | 10th |

**Jaakola, Topi**
**b. Oulu, Finland, November 15, 1983**

| | | | | | | | | |
|---|---|---|---|---|---|---|---|---|
| 2001 WM18 | 3-D | FIN | 6 | 1 | 1 | 2 | 4 | B |
| 2002 WM20 | 3-D | FIN | 6 | 0 | 0 | 0 | 2 | B |
| 2003 WM20 | 3-D | FIN | 7 | 1 | 1 | 2 | 4 | B |
| 2009 WM | 6-D | FIN | 7 | 0 | 0 | 0 | 4 | 5th |
| 2010 WM | 6-D | FIN | 7 | 0 | 1 | 1 | 4 | 6th |
| 2011 WM | 6-D | FIN | 9 | 0 | 1 | 1 | 6 | G |
| 2012 WM | 6-D | FIN | 10 | 0 | 0 | 0 | 2 | 4th |
| **Totals WM20** | | | **13** | **1** | **1** | **2** | **6** | **2B** |
| **Totals WM** | | | **33** | **0** | **2** | **2** | **16** | **—** |

**Jabornik, Henrich**
**b. Skalica, Czechoslovakia (Slovakia), February 18, 1991**

| | | | | | | | | |
|---|---|---|---|---|---|---|---|---|
| 2009 WM18 | 27-D | SVK | 6 | 0 | 0 | 0 | 8 | 7th |
| 2010 WM20 | 4-D | SVK | 6 | 0 | 0 | 0 | 10 | 8th |
| 2011 WM20 | 24-D | SVK | 6 | 0 | 1 | 1 | 4 | 8th |
| **Totals WM20** | | | **12** | **0** | **1** | **1** | **14** | **—** |

**Jackman, Barret**
**b. Trail, British Columbia, Canada, March 5, 1981**

| | | | | | | | | |
|---|---|---|---|---|---|---|---|---|
| 2000 WM20 | 20-D | CAN | 7 | 0 | 1 | 1 | 8 | B |
| 2001 WM20 | 2-D | CAN | 7 | 0 | 3 | 3 | 10 | B |
| 2007 WM | 5-D | CAN | 9 | 0 | 2 | 2 | 6 | G |
| **Totals WM20** | | | **14** | **0** | **4** | **4** | **18** | **2B** |

**Jacquemet, Arnaud**
**b. Sion, Switzerland, March 29, 1988**

| | | | | | | | | |
|---|---|---|---|---|---|---|---|---|
| 2005 WM18 | 28-F | SUI | 6 | 0 | 1 | 1 | 0 | 9th |
| 2007 WM20 | 27-F | SUI | 6 | 1 | 0 | 1 | 2 | 7th |
| 2008 WM20 | 17-F | SUI | 6 | 2 | 6 | 8 | 4 | 9th |
| **Totals WM20** | | | **12** | **3** | **6** | **9** | **6** | **—** |

**Jagr, Jaromir**
**b. Kladno, Czechoslovakia (Czech Republic), February 15, 1972**

| | | | | | | | | |
|---|---|---|---|---|---|---|---|---|
| 1990 WM20 | 6-F | TCH | 7 | 5 | 13 | 18 | 6 | B |
| 1990 WM | 22-F | TCH | 10 | 3 | 2 | 5 | 2 | B |
| 1991 CC | 15-F | TCH | 5 | 1 | 0 | 1 | 0 | 6th |
| 1994 WM | 21-F | CZE | 3 | 0 | 2 | 2 | 2 | 7th |
| 1996 WCH | 68-F | CZE | 3 | 1 | 0 | 1 | 2 | 8th |
| 1998 OG-M | 68-F | CZE | 6 | 1 | 4 | 5 | 2 | G |
| 2002 OG-M | 68-F | CZE | 4 | 2 | 3 | 5 | 4 | 7th |
| 2002 WM | 68-F | CZE | 7 | 4 | 4 | 8 | 2 | 5th |
| 2004 WM | 68-F | CZE | 7 | 5 | 4 | 9 | 6 | 5th |
| 2004 WCH | 68-F | CZE | 5 | 1 | 1 | 2 | 2 | 3rd |
| 2005 WM | 68-F | CZE | 8 | 2 | 7 | 9 | 2 | G |
| 2006 OG-M | 68-F | CZE | 8 | 2 | 5 | 7 | 6 | B |
| 2009 WM | 68-F | CZE | 7 | 3 | 6 | 9 | 6 | 6th |
| 2010 OG-M | 68-F | CZE | 5 | 2 | 1 | 3 | 6 | 7th |
| 2010 WM | 68-F | CZE | 9 | 3 | 4 | 7 | 12 | G |
| 2011 WM | 68-F | CZE | 9 | 5 | 4 | 9 | 4 | B |
| **Totals WM** | | | **60** | **25** | **33** | **58** | **36** | **2G,2B** |

| **Totals OG-M** | | | **23** | **7** | **13** | **20** | **18** | **G,B** |
|---|---|---|---|---|---|---|---|---|
| **Totals IIHF-NHL** | | | **13** | **3** | **1** | **4** | **4** | **—** |

~Triple Gold Club

~WM IIHF Directorate Best Forward (2011), WM All-Star Team/Forward (2004, 2005, 2011), WM20 All-Star Team/ Forward (1990)

**Jakobsen, Julian**
**b. Aalborg, Denmark, April 11, 1987**

| 2005 WM18 | 9-F | DEN | 6 | 1 | 2 | 3 | 4 | 10th |
|---|---|---|---|---|---|---|---|---|
| 2009 WM | 33-F | DEN | 6 | 2 | 1 | 3 | 2 | 13th |
| 2010 WM | 33-F | DEN | 7 | 1 | 1 | 2 | 4 | 8th |
| 2011 WM | 33-F | DEN | 6 | 0 | 5 | 5 | 4 | 11th |
| 2012 WM | 33-F | DEN | 7 | 0 | 0 | 0 | 12 | 13th |
| **Totals WM** | | | **26** | **3** | **7** | **10** | **22** | **—** |

**Jakobsen, Tommy**
**b. Oslo, Norway, December 10, 1970**

| 1989 WM20 | 8-D | NOR | 7 | 0 | 1 | 1 | 6 | 7th |
|---|---|---|---|---|---|---|---|---|
| 1990 WM20 | 8-D | NOR | 7 | 0 | 1 | 1 | 6 | 6th |
| 1992 OG-M | 7-D | NOR | 7 | 0 | 1 | 1 | 14 | 9th |
| 1992 WM | 7-D | NOR | 5 | 0 | 1 | 1 | 10 | 10th |
| 1993 WM | 7-D | NOR | 7 | 0 | 0 | 0 | 12 | 11th |
| 1994 OG-M | 7-D | NOR | 7 | 1 | 0 | 1 | 8 | 11th |
| 1994 WM | 7-D | NOR | 5 | 0 | 0 | 0 | 8 | 11th |
| 1995 WM | 7-D | NOR | 5 | 0 | 2 | 2 | 8 | 10th |
| 1996 WM | 7-D | NOR | 5 | 0 | 0 | 0 | 6 | 9th |
| 1997 WM | 7-D | NOR | 8 | 0 | 1 | 1 | 12 | 12th |
| 1999 WM | 7-D | NOR | 6 | 1 | 0 | 1 | 2 | 12th |
| 2000 WM | 7-D | NOR | 6 | 0 | 2 | 2 | 8 | 10th |
| 2006 WM | 7-D | NOR | 6 | 1 | 1 | 2 | 10 | 11th |
| 2007 WM | 7-D | NOR | 6 | 0 | 2 | 2 | 8 | 14th |
| 2008 WM | 7-D | NOR | 7 | 0 | 0 | 0 | 18 | 8th |
| 2009 WM | 7-D | NOR | 6 | 2 | 1 | 3 | 10 | 11th |
| 2010 OG-M | 7-D | NOR | 4 | 0 | 1 | 1 | 8 | 10th |
| 2010 WM | 7-D | NOR | 4 | 0 | 1 | 1 | 29 | 9th |
| **Totals WM20** | | | **14** | **0** | **2** | **2** | **12** | **—** |
| **Totals WM** | | | **76** | **4** | **11** | **15** | **141** | **—** |
| **Totals OG-M** | | | **18** | **1** | **2** | **3** | **30** | **—** |

**Jakovlevs, Martins**
**b. Jekabpils, Soviet Union (Latvia), May 4, 1991**

| 2010 WM20 | 25-D | LAT | 6 | 0 | 0 | 0 | 2 | 9th |
|---|---|---|---|---|---|---|---|---|

**Jalvanti, Joonas**
**b. Lahti, Finland, September 9, 1988**

| 2006 WM18 | 25-D | FIN | 6 | 2 | 0 | 2 | 0 | S |
|---|---|---|---|---|---|---|---|---|
| 2007 WM20 | 8-D | FIN | 6 | 0 | 0 | 0 | 0 | 6th |
| 2008 WM20 | 7-D | FIN | 6 | 1 | 3 | 4 | 4 | 6th |
| **Totals WM20** | | | **12** | **1** | **2** | **3** | **4** | **—** |

**Jamtin, Andreas**
**b. Danderyd, Sweden, May 4, 1983**

| 2001 WM18 | 19-F | SWE | 6 | 3 | 4 | 7 | 26 | 7th |
|---|---|---|---|---|---|---|---|---|
| 2002 WM20 | 28-F | SWE | 7 | 2 | 1 | 3 | 10 | 6th |
| 2003 WM20 | 28-F | SWE | 6 | 1 | 4 | 5 | 10 | 8th |
| 2011 WM | 8-F | SWE | 1 | 0 | 0 | 0 | 0 | S |
| **Totals WM20** | | | **13** | **3** | **5** | **8** | **20** | **—** |

**Janil, Jonathan**
**b. Caen, France, September 24, 1987**

| 2011 WM | 21-D | FRA | 6 | 0 | 0 | 0 | 0 | 12th |
|---|---|---|---|---|---|---|---|---|

**Jank, Bohumil**
**b. Pisek, Czech Republic, July 6, 1992**

| 2010 WM18 | 3-D | CZE | 6 | 1 | 4 | 5 | 8 | 6th |
|---|---|---|---|---|---|---|---|---|
| 2011 WM20 | 28-D | CZE | 2 | 0 | 0 | 0 | 0 | 7th |
| 2012 WM20 | 28-D | CZE | 6 | 0 | 0 | 0 | 2 | 5th |
| Totals WM20 | | | 8 | 0 | 0 | 0 | 2 | — |

**Jankovic, Dalimir**
**b. Martin, Czechoslovakia (Slovakia), January 28, 1989**

| 2008 WM20 | 25-F | SVK | 6 | 2 | 1 | 3 | 8 | 7th |
|---|---|---|---|---|---|---|---|---|

**Jankovic, Ivan**
**b. Myjava, Czechoslovakia (Slovakia), May 15, 1990**

| 2010 WM20 | 29-D | SVK | 6 | 0 | 1 | 1 | 4 | 8th |
|---|---|---|---|---|---|---|---|---|

**Janosik, Adam**
**b. Spissa nova ves, Czechoslovakia (Slovakia), September 7, 1992**

| 2009 WM18 | 7-D | SVK | 6 | 1 | 4 | 5 | 2 | 7th |
|---|---|---|---|---|---|---|---|---|
| 2011 WM20 | 3-D | SVK | 6 | 0 | 5 | 5 | 2 | 8th |
| 2012 WM20 | 3-D | SVK | 6 | 0 | 1 | 1 | 2 | 6th |
| Totals WM20 | | | 12 | 0 | 6 | 6 | 4 | — |

**Janosik, Filip**
**b. Krompachy, Czechoslovakia (Slovakia), April 6, 1991**

| 2009 WM18 | 8-F | SVK | 4 | 0 | 0 | 0 | 0 | 7th |
|---|---|---|---|---|---|---|---|---|

**Janzen, Alexander**
**b. Yarowoe, Soviet Union (Russia), July 20, 1985**

| 2005 WM20 | 19-F | GER | 6 | 1 | 0 | 1 | 4 | 9th |
|---|---|---|---|---|---|---|---|---|

**Jarnkrok, Calle**
**b. Gavle, Sweden, September 25, 1991**

| 2009 WM18 | 25-F | SWE | 6 | 2 | 7 | 9 | 4 | 5th |
|---|---|---|---|---|---|---|---|---|
| 2011 WM20 | 19-F | SWE | 6 | 2 | 3 | 5 | 2 | 4th |
| 2012 WM | 16-F | SWE | 8 | 0 | 1 | 1 | 0 | 6th |

**Jarrov, Sebastian**
**b. Herning, Denmark, September 21, 1990**

| 2008 WM18 | 11-F | DEN | 5 | 0 | 0 | 0 | 4 | 10th |
|---|---|---|---|---|---|---|---|---|

**Jarvelainen, Ville**
**b. Hameenlinna, Finland, February 24, 1993**

| 2011 WM18 | 15-F | FIN | 6 | 2 | 2 | 4 | 4 | 5th |
|---|---|---|---|---|---|---|---|---|

**Jarvinen, Joonas**
**b. Turku, Finland, January 5, 1989**

| 2007 WM18 | 3-D | FIN | 6 | 0 | 0 | 0 | 2 | 7th |
|---|---|---|---|---|---|---|---|---|
| 2008 WM20 | 3-D | FIN | 5 | 0 | 0 | 0 | 2 | 6th |
| 2009 WM20 | 7-D | FIN | 6 | 0 | 2 | 2 | 0 | 7th |
| 2012 WM | 56-D | FIN | 10 | 0 | 3 | 3 | 4 | 4th |
| **Totals WM20** | | | **11** | **0** | **2** | **2** | **2** | **—** |

**Jaskin, Dmitrij**
**b. Omsk, Russia, March 23, 1993**

| 2011 WM18 | 26-F | CZE | 6 | 4 | 1 | 5 | 10 | 8th |
|---|---|---|---|---|---|---|---|---|
| 2012 WM20 | 20-F | CZE | 6 | 1 | 1 | 2 | 4 | 5th |

**Jass, Koba**
**b. Riga, Soviet Union (Latvia), May 4, 1990**

| 2009 WM20 | 15-F | LAT | 6 | 0 | 0 | 0 | 0 | 8th |
|---|---|---|---|---|---|---|---|---|
| 2012 WM | 90-F | LAT | 7 | 0 | 0 | 0 | 27 | 10th |

**Jass, Maris**
**b. Riga, Soviet Union (Latvia), January 18, 1985**

| 2006 WM | 11-D | LAT | 6 | 0 | 0 | 0 | 6 | 10th |
|---|---|---|---|---|---|---|---|---|
| 2010 WM | 22-D | LAT | 6 | 0 | 0 | 0 | 6 | 11th |
| **Totals WM** | | | **12** | **0** | **0** | **0** | **12** | **—** |

**Jeannin, Sandy**
**b. Neuchatel, Switzerland, February 28, 1976**

| 1996 WM20 | 21-F | SUI | 6 | 3 | 2 | 5 | 6 | 9th |
|---|---|---|---|---|---|---|---|---|
| 1998 WM | 35-F | SUI | 9 | 0 | 0 | 0 | 4 | 4th |
| 1999 WM | 35-F | SUI | 6 | 0 | 0 | 0 | 6 | 8th |
| 2001 WM | 35-F | SUI | 6 | 0 | 1 | 1 | 6 | 9th |
| 2002 OG-M | 35-F | SUI | 4 | 1 | 1 | 2 | 0 | 11th |
| 2002 WM | 35-F | SUI | 6 | 3 | 0 | 3 | 2 | 10th |
| 2003 WM | 35-F | SUI | 7 | 0 | 1 | 1 | 2 | 8th |
| 2004 WM | 35-F | SUI | 7 | 0 | 0 | 0 | 14 | 8th |
| 2005 WM | 35-F | SUI | 7 | 1 | 1 | 2 | 2 | 8th |
| 2006 OG-M | 35-F | SUI | 6 | 0 | 0 | 0 | 2 | 6th |
| 2006 WM | 35-F | SUI | 6 | 1 | 4 | 5 | 2 | 9th |
| 2007 WM | 35-F | SUI | 7 | 1 | 1 | 2 | 4 | 8th |
| 2008 WM | 35-F | SUI | 7 | 1 | 1 | 2 | 2 | 7th |
| 2009 WM | 35-F | SUI | 6 | 0 | 2 | 2 | 4 | 9th |
| 2010 OG-M | 35-F | SUI | 5 | 0 | 1 | 1 | 2 | 8th |
| **Totals WM** | | | **74** | **7** | **11** | **18** | **48** | **—** |
| **Totals OG-M** | | | **15** | **1** | **2** | **3** | **4** | **—** |

**Jeglic, Ziga**
**b. Kranj, Yugoslavia (Slovenia), February 24, 1988**

| 2011 WM | 8-F | SLO | 6 | 1 | 2 | 3 | 10 | 16th |
|---|---|---|---|---|---|---|---|---|

**Jekimovs, Roberts**
**b. Riga, Soviet Union (Latvia), November 11, 1989**

| 2007 WM18 | 14-F | LAT | 6 | 0 | 2 | 2 | 4 | 10th |
|---|---|---|---|---|---|---|---|---|
| 2009 WM20 | 14-F | LAT | 6 | 4 | 3 | 7 | 0 | 8th |
| 2009 WM | 28-F | LAT | 4 | 0 | 0 | 0 | 4 | 7th |

**Jelisejevs, Nikolajs**
**b. Riga, Latvia, July 7, 1994**

| 2012 WM18 | 17-F | LAT | 6 | 1 | 0 | 1 | 2 | 9th |
|---|---|---|---|---|---|---|---|---|

**Jencik, Richard**
**b. Kosice, Czechoslovakia (Slovakia), January 1, 1985**

| 2005 WM20 | 25-F | SVK | 6 | 0 | 2 | 2 | 0 | 7th |
|---|---|---|---|---|---|---|---|---|

**Jenik, Stepan**
**b. Prague, Czech Republic, February 12, 1993**

| 2011 WM18 | 22-D | CZE | 6 | 0 | 0 | 0 | 8 | 8th |
|---|---|---|---|---|---|---|---|---|

**Jenks, A.J.**
**b. Wolverine Lake, Michigan, United States, June 27, 1990**

| 2010 WM20 | 22-F | USA | 7 | 3 | 2 | 5 | 6 | G |
|---|---|---|---|---|---|---|---|---|

**Jenner, Boone**
**b. Dorchester, Ontario, Canada, June 15, 1993**

| 2012 WM20 | 20-F | CAN | 5 | 0 | 2 | 2 | 29 | B |
|---|---|---|---|---|---|---|---|---|

**Jenni, Marcel**
**b. Niederhuningen, Switzerland, March 2, 1974**

| 1994 WM20 | 25-F | SUI | 7 | 0 | 1 | 1 | 2 | 8th |
|---|---|---|---|---|---|---|---|---|
| 1995 WM | 30-F | SUI | 7 | 1 | 0 | 1 | 8 | 12th |
| 1998 WM | 30-F | SUI | 9 | 3 | 5 | 8 | 14 | 4th |
| 1999 WM | 30-F | SUI | 6 | 2 | 0 | 2 | 0 | 8th |
| 2000 WM | 30-F | SUI | 7 | 2 | 3 | 5 | 4 | 5th |
| 2001 WM | 30-F | SUI | 6 | 1 | 2 | 3 | 12 | 9th |
| 2002 OG-M | 30-F | SUI | 2 | 0 | 0 | 0 | 0 | 11th |
| 2003 WM | 30-F | SUI | 4 | 0 | 0 | 0 | 2 | 8th |
| 2004 WM | 30-F | SUI | 7 | 2 | 2 | 4 | 12 | 8th |
| 2006 OG-M | 30-F | SUI | 6 | 0 | 0 | 0 | 4 | 6th |
| 2010 WM | 30-F | SUI | 7 | 0 | 0 | 0 | 0 | 5th |
| **Totals WM** | | | **53** | **11** | **12** | **23** | **52** | **—** |
| **Totals OG-M** | | | **8** | **0** | **0** | **0** | **4** | **—** |

**Jensen, Alexander**
**b. Hellerup, Denmark, July 16, 1990**

| 2008 WM18 | 15-F | DEN | 6 | 2 | 0 | 2 | 4 | 10th |
|---|---|---|---|---|---|---|---|---|
| 2008 WM20 | 15-F | DEN | 6 | 0 | 0 | 0 | 2 | 10th |

**Jensen, Jesper**
**b. Nybro, Sweden, February 5, 1987**

| 2005 WM18 | 19-F | DEN | 6 | 1 | 0 | 1 | 0 | 10th |
|---|---|---|---|---|---|---|---|---|
| 2009 WM | 61-F | DEN | 3 | 0 | 0 | 0 | 0 | 13th |
| 2010 WM | 22-F | DEN | 4 | 0 | 0 | 0 | 0 | 8th |
| 2011 WM | 40-F | DEN | 6 | 0 | 0 | 0 | 4 | 11th |
| 2012 WM | 40-F | DEN | 7 | 2 | 0 | 2 | 12 | 13th |
| **Totals WM** | | | **20** | **2** | **0** | **2** | **16** | **—** |

**Jensen, Jesper**
**b. Rodovre, Denmark, July 30, 1991**

| 2008 WM18 | 3-D | DEN | 6 | 0 | 0 | 0 | 6 | 10th |
|---|---|---|---|---|---|---|---|---|
| 2011 WM | 41-D | DEN | 6 | 0 | 0 | 0 | 4 | 11th |
| 2012 WM | 41-D | DEN | 7 | 0 | 1 | 1 | 0 | 13th |
| **Totals WM** | | | **13** | **0** | **1** | **1** | **4** | **—** |

**Jensen, Joakim**
**b. Baerum, Norway, August 8, 1987**

| 2004 WM18 | 21-F | NOR | 6 | 0 | 1 | 1 | 0 | 10th |
|---|---|---|---|---|---|---|---|---|
| 2006 WM20 | 21-F | NOR | 6 | 0 | 0 | 0 | 14 | 10th |

**Jensen, John**
**b. Hvidovre, Denmark, April 26, 1988**

| 2008 WM20 | 24-D | DEN | 6 | 0 | 0 | 0 | 2 | 10th |
|---|---|---|---|---|---|---|---|---|

**Jensen, Kasper**
**b. Hvidovre, Denmark, May 28, 1987**

| 2005 WM18 | 18-D | DEN | 6 | 0 | 0 | 0 | 2 | 10th |
|---|---|---|---|---|---|---|---|---|
| 2011 WM | 18-D | DEN | 6 | 0 | 1 | 1 | 2 | 11th |
| 2012 WM | 18-D | DEN | 7 | 0 | 0 | 0 | 0 | 13th |
| **Totals WM** | | | **13** | **0** | **1** | **1** | **2** | **—** |

**Jensen, Nicholas**
**b. Copenhagen, Denmark, April 8, 1989**

| 2008 WM20 | 13-F | DEN | 4 | 0 | 0 | 0 | 4 | 10th |
|---|---|---|---|---|---|---|---|---|

**Jensen, Nicklas**
**b. Herning, Denmark, March 16, 1993**

| 2012 WM20 | 17-F | DEN | 6 | 2 | 4 | 6 | 4 | 10th |
|---|---|---|---|---|---|---|---|---|

**Jerabek, Jakub**
**b. Plzen, Czechoslovakia (Czech Republic), May 12, 1991**

| | | | | | | | | |
|---|---|---|---|---|---|---|---|---|
| 2009 WM18 | 15-D | CZE | 6 | 1 | 1 | 2 | 22 | 6th |
| 2010 WM20 | 5-D | CZE | 6 | 1 | 1 | 2 | 0 | 7th |
| 2011 WM20 | 12-D | CZE | 6 | 1 | 7 | 8 | 4 | 7th |
| **Totals WM20** | | | **12** | **2** | **8** | **10** | **4** | **—** |

**Jerofejevs, Aleksandrs**
**b. Riga, Soviet Union (Latvia), April 12, 1984**

| | | | | | | | | |
|---|---|---|---|---|---|---|---|---|
| 2006 WM | 6-D | LAT | 6 | 1 | 0 | 1 | 6 | 10th |
| 2007 WM | 15-D | LAT | 5 | 0 | 3 | 3 | 6 | 13th |
| 2008 WM | 15-D | LAT | 6 | 0 | 0 | 0 | 8 | 11th |
| 2009 WM | 15-D | LAT | 7 | 1 | 0 | 1 | 6 | 7th |
| 2010 WM | 15-D | LAT | 6 | 0 | 1 | 1 | 4 | 11th |
| **Totals WM** | | | **30** | **2** | **4** | **6** | **30** | **—** |

**Jevpalovs, Nikita**
**b. Riga, Latvia, September 9, 1994**

| | | | | | | | | |
|---|---|---|---|---|---|---|---|---|
| 2012 WM18 | 14-F | LAT | 6 | 1 | 2 | 3 | 0 | 9th |
| 2012 WM20 | 28-F | LAT | 6 | 2 | 3 | 5 | 4 | 9th |

**Joensuu, Jesse**
**b. Pori, Finland, October 5, 1987**

| | | | | | | | | |
|---|---|---|---|---|---|---|---|---|
| 2004 WM18 | 19-F | FIN | 4 | 0 | 0 | 0 | 6 | 7th |
| 2005 WM18 | 19-F | FIN | 6 | 2 | 1 | 3 | 0 | 7th |
| 2005 WM20 | 15-F | FIN | 6 | 1 | 0 | 1 | 2 | 5th |
| 2006 WM20 | 19-F | FIN | 7 | 2 | 2 | 4 | 8 | B |
| 2007 WM20 | 18-F | FIN | 6 | 1 | 1 | 2 | 14 | 6th |
| 2012 WM | 18-F | FIN | 9 | 2 | 3 | 5 | 24 | 4th |
| **Totals WM18** | | | **10** | **2** | **1** | **3** | **6** | **—** |
| **Totals WM20** | | | **19** | **4** | **3** | **7** | **24** | **B** |

**Joggi, Mathias**
**b. Biel, Switzerland, January 22, 1986**

| | | | | | | | | |
|---|---|---|---|---|---|---|---|---|
| 2006 WM20 | 9-F | SUI | 6 | 4 | 3 | 7 | 14 | 7th |

**Johansen, Ryan**
**b. Port Moody, British Columbia, Canada, July 31, 1992**

| | | | | | | | | |
|---|---|---|---|---|---|---|---|---|
| 2011 WM20 | 19-F | CAN | 7 | 3 | 6 | 9 | 2 | S |

~WM20 All-Star Team/Forward (2011)

**Johansson, Jonathan**
**b. Gothenburg, Sweden, June 30, 1991**

| | | | | | | | | |
|---|---|---|---|---|---|---|---|---|
| 2009 WM18 | 21-F | SWE | 6 | 0 | 0 | 0 | 4 | 5th |

**Johansson, Karl**
**b. Ostersund, Sweden, January 21, 1993**

| | | | | | | | | |
|---|---|---|---|---|---|---|---|---|
| 2011 WM18 | 6-D | SWE | 6 | 0 | 2 | 2 | 4 | S |

**Johansson, Magnus**
**b. Linkoping, Sweden, September 4, 1973**

| | | | | | | | | |
|---|---|---|---|---|---|---|---|---|
| 2002 WM | 6-D | SWE | 9 | 1 | 0 | 1 | 6 | B |
| 2003 WM | 6-D | SWE | 9 | 0 | 0 | 0 | 6 | S |
| 2005 WM | 6-D | SWE | 9 | 1 | 4 | 5 | 2 | 4th |
| 2006 WM | 6-D | SWE | 9 | 2 | 3 | 5 | 2 | G |
| 2007 WM | 6-D | SWE | 8 | 3 | 0 | 3 | 2 | 4th |
| 2008 WM | 6-D | SWE | 9 | 1 | 2 | 3 | 8 | 4th |
| 2009 WM | 6-D | SWE | 9 | 3 | 5 | 8 | 6 | B |
| 2010 OG-M | 6-D | SWE | 4 | 0 | 2 | 2 | 2 | 5th |
| 2010 WM | 6-D | SWE | 9 | 0 | 4 | 4 | 6 | B |
| **Totals WM** | | | **71** | **11** | **18** | **29** | **38** | **G,S,3B** |

**Johansson, Marcus**
**b. Landskrona, Sweden, October 6, 1990**

| | | | | | | | | |
|---|---|---|---|---|---|---|---|---|
| 2007 WM18 | 22-F | SWE | 6 | 0 | 4 | 4 | 0 | B |
| 2008 WM18 | 11-F | SWE | 6 | 3 | 2 | 5 | 14 | 4th |
| 2009 WM20 | 11-F | SWE | 6 | 2 | 0 | 2 | 0 | S |
| 2010 WM20 | 11-F | SWE | 5 | 1 | 5 | 6 | 29 | B |
| **Totals WM18** | | | **12** | **3** | **6** | **9** | **14** | **B** |
| **Totals WM20** | | | **11** | **3** | **5** | **8** | **29** | **S,B** |

**Johansson, Martin**
**b. Landskrona, Sweden, October 24, 1987**

| | | | | | | | | |
|---|---|---|---|---|---|---|---|---|
| 2005 WM18 | 12-F | SWE | 4 | 0 | 0 | 0 | 0 | B |
| 2007 WM20 | 16-F | SWE | 7 | 3 | 2 | 5 | 0 | 4th |

**Johns, Stephen**
**b. Wampum, Pennsylvania, United States, April 18, 1992**

| | | | | | | | | |
|---|---|---|---|---|---|---|---|---|
| 2010 WM18 | 28-D | USA | 7 | 0 | 3 | 3 | 10 | G |
| 2012 WM20 | 28-D | USA | 6 | 1 | 1 | 2 | 2 | 7th |

**Johnson, Erik**
**b. Bloomington, Minnesota, United States, March 21, 1988**

| | | | | | | | | |
|---|---|---|---|---|---|---|---|---|
| 2005 WM18 | 5-D | USA | 6 | 0 | 0 | 0 | 0 | G |
| 2006 WM18 | 6-D | USA | 6 | 4 | 6 | 10 | 27 | G |
| 2007 WM20 | 6-D | USA | 7 | 4 | 6 | 10 | 16 | B |
| 2007 WM | 6-D | USA | 7 | 0 | 2 | 2 | 4 | 5th |
| 2010 OG-M | 6-D | USA | 6 | 1 | 0 | 1 | 4 | S |
| **Totals WM18** | | | **12** | **4** | **6** | **10** | **27** | **2G** |

~WM20 IIHF Directorate Best Defenceman (2007), WM20 All-Star Team/Defence (2007)

**Johnson, Jack**
**b. Indianapolis, Indiana, United States, January 13, 1987**

| | | | | | | | | |
|---|---|---|---|---|---|---|---|---|
| 2004 WM18 | 27-D | USA | 6 | 2 | 0 | 2 | 18 | S |
| 2005 WM18 | 27-D | USA | 6 | 0 | 2 | 2 | 35 | G |
| 2006 WM20 | 3-D | USA | 7 | 1 | 5 | 6 | 45 | 4th |
| 2007 WM20 | 3-D | USA | 7 | 3 | 0 | 3 | 14 | B |
| 2007 WM | 3-D | USA | 7 | 1 | 0 | 1 | 0 | 5th |
| 2009 WM | 3-D | USA | 9 | 5 | 2 | 7 | 10 | 4th |
| 2010 OG-M | 3-D | USA | 6 | 0 | 1 | 1 | 2 | S |
| 2010 WM | 3-D | USA | 6 | 0 | 3 | 3 | 4 | 13th |
| 2011 WM | 3-D | USA | 7 | 1 | 2 | 3 | 8 | 8th |
| 2012 WM | 3-D | USA | 8 | 3 | 1 | 4 | 16 | 7th |
| **Totals WM18** | | | **12** | **2** | **2** | **4** | **53** | **G,S** |
| **Totals WM20** | | | **14** | **4** | **5** | **9** | **59** | **B** |
| **Totals WM** | | | **37** | **10** | **8** | **18** | **38** | **—** |

~WM20 All-Star Team/Defence (2006)

**Johnson, Trevor**
**b. Trail, British Columbia, Canada, January 25, 1982**

| | | | | | | | | |
|---|---|---|---|---|---|---|---|---|
| 2010 WM | 5-D | ITA | 6 | 0 | 1 | 1 | 6 | 15th |
| 2012 WM | 24-D | ITA | 7 | 0 | 0 | 0 | 4 | 15th |
| **Totals WM** | | | **13** | **0** | **1** | **1** | **10** | **—** |

**Johnson, Tyler**
**b. Spokane, Washington, United States, July 29, 1990**

| | | | | | | | | |
|---|---|---|---|---|---|---|---|---|
| 2009 WM20 | 10-F | USA | 6 | 1 | 0 | 1 | 2 | 5th |
| 2010 WM20 | 10-F | USA | 7 | 3 | 2 | 5 | 25 | G |
| **Totals WM20** | | | **13** | **4** | **2** | **6** | **27** | **G** |

**Jokel, Oliver**
**b. Kosice, Slovakia, August 7, 1991**

| | | | | | | | | |
|---|---|---|---|---|---|---|---|---|
| 2011 WM20 | 11-F | SVK | 6 | 0 | 0 | 0 | 8 | 8th |

**Jokela, Mikko**
**b. Lappeenranta, Finland, March 4, 1980**

| | | | | | | | | |
|---|---|---|---|---|---|---|---|---|
| 1999 WM20 | 7-D | FIN | 6 | 0 | 2 | 2 | 6 | 5th |
| 2000 WM20 | 7-D | FIN | 7 | 0 | 1 | 1 | 2 | 7th |
| 2008 WM | 27-D | FIN | 9 | 0 | 0 | 0 | 6 | B |
| **Totals WM20** | | | **13** | **0** | **3** | **3** | **8** | **—** |

**Jokinen, Juho**
**b. Kalajoki, Finland, July 25, 1986**

| | | | | | | | | |
|---|---|---|---|---|---|---|---|---|
| 2006 WM20 | 8-D | FIN | 3 | 1 | 1 | 2 | 0 | B |

**Jokinen, Jussi**
**b. Kalajoki, Finland, April 1, 1983**

| | | | | | | | | |
|---|---|---|---|---|---|---|---|---|
| 2001 WM18 | 10-F | FIN | 6 | 2 | 0 | 2 | 2 | B |
| 2002 WM20 | 20-F | FIN | 7 | 2 | 6 | 8 | 2 | B |
| 2003 WM20 | 20-F | FIN | 7 | 6 | 2 | 8 | 2 | B |
| 2005 WM | 8-F | FIN | 7 | 0 | 1 | 1 | 2 | 7th |
| 2006 OG-M | 36-F | FIN | 8 | 1 | 3 | 4 | 2 | S |
| 2006 WM | 36-F | FIN | 9 | 2 | 6 | 8 | 2 | B |
| 2008 WM | 36-F | FIN | 9 | 1 | 3 | 4 | 8 | B |
| 2010 WM | 36-F | FIN | 7 | 2 | 1 | 3 | 20 | 6th |
| 2012 WM | 36-F | FIN | 10 | 5 | 4 | 9 | 8 | 4th |
| **Totals WM20** | | | **14** | **8** | **8** | **16** | **4** | **2B** |
| **Totals WM** | | | **42** | **10** | **15** | **25** | **36** | **2B** |

**Jokinen, Olli**
**b. Kuopio, Finland, December 5, 1978**

| | | | | | | | | |
|---|---|---|---|---|---|---|---|---|
| 1997 WM20 | 16-F | FIN | 6 | 5 | 0 | 5 | 12 | 5th |
| 1997 WM | 9-F | FIN | 8 | 4 | 2 | 6 | 6 | 5th |
| 1998 WM20 | 12-F | FIN | 7 | 4 | 6 | 10 | 6 | G |
| 1998 WM | 12-F | FIN | 10 | 0 | 1 | 1 | 6 | S |
| 1999 WM | 12-F | FIN | 12 | 3 | 1 | 4 | 14 | S |
| 2000 WM | 62-F | FIN | 9 | 1 | 3 | 4 | 6 | B |
| 2002 OG-M | 12-F | FIN | 4 | 2 | 1 | 3 | 0 | 6th |
| 2002 WM | 12-F | FIN | 9 | 1 | 1 | 2 | 4 | 4th |
| 2003 WM | 12-F | FIN | 7 | 1 | 2 | 3 | 8 | 5th |
| 2004 WM | 12-F | FIN | 7 | 5 | 3 | 8 | 6 | 6th |
| 2004 WCH | 12-F | FIN | 6 | 2 | 1 | 3 | 6 | 2nd |
| 2005 WM | 12-F | FIN | 7 | 1 | 4 | 5 | 2 | 7th |
| 2006 OG-M | 12-F | FIN | 8 | 6 | 2 | 8 | 2 | S |
| 2006 WM | 12-F | FIN | 5 | 2 | 1 | 3 | 27 | B |
| 2008 WM | 12-F | FIN | 8 | 1 | 4 | 5 | 29 | B |
| 2010 OG-M | 12-F | FIN | 6 | 3 | 1 | 4 | 2 | B |
| **Totals WM20** | | | **13** | **9** | **6** | **15** | **18** | **G** |
| **Totals WM** | | | **82** | **19** | **22** | **41** | **108** | **2S,3B** |
| **Totals OG-M** | | | **18** | **11** | **4** | **15** | **4** | **S,B** |

~WM20 IIHF Directorate Best Forward (1998), WM20 All-Star Team/Forward (1998)

**Jokipakka, Jyrki**
**b. Tampere, Finland, August 20, 1991**

| | | | | | | | | |
|---|---|---|---|---|---|---|---|---|
| 2011 WM20 | 3-D | FIN | 6 | 1 | 2 | 3 | 4 | 6th |

**Jones, Seth**
**b. Plano, Texas, United States, October 3, 1994**

| | | | | | | | | |
|---|---|---|---|---|---|---|---|---|
| 2011 WM18 | 28-D | USA | 6 | 0 | 3 | 3 | 0 | G |
| 2012 WM18 | 4-D | USA | 6 | 3 | 5 | 8 | 0 | G |
| **Totals WM18** | | | **12** | **3** | **8** | **11** | **0** | **2G** |

**Jordan, Michal**
**b. Zlin, Czechoslovakia (Czech Republic), July 17, 1990**

| | | | | | | | | |
|---|---|---|---|---|---|---|---|---|
| 2007 WM18 | 3-D | CZE | 6 | 0 | 1 | 1 | 4 | 9th |
| 2008 WM20 | 9-D | CZE | 6 | 0 | 1 | 1 | 4 | 5th |
| 2009 WM20 | 19-D | CZE | 6 | 0 | 1 | 1 | 0 | 6th |
| 2010 WM20 | 23-D | CZE | 6 | 0 | 1 | 1 | 4 | 7th |
| **Totals WM20** | | | **18** | **0** | **3** | **3** | **8** | **—** |

**Jorg, Mauro**
**b. Chur, Switzerland, April 29, 1990**

| | | | | | | | | |
|---|---|---|---|---|---|---|---|---|
| 2008 WM18 | 15-F | SUI | 5 | 0 | 2 | 2 | 2 | 8th |
| 2010 WM20 | 21-F | SUI | 7 | 3 | 1 | 4 | 4 | 4th |

**Jormakka, Pekka**
**b. Jyvaskyla, Finland, September 14, 1990**

| | | | | | | | | |
|---|---|---|---|---|---|---|---|---|
| 2008 WM18 | 13-F | FIN | 6 | 2 | 2 | 4 | 2 | 6th |
| 2010 WM20 | 14-F | FIN | 6 | 1 | 0 | 1 | 0 | 5th |

**Josefson, Jacob**
**b. Stockholm, Sweden, March 2, 1991**

| | | | | | | | | |
|---|---|---|---|---|---|---|---|---|
| 2008 WM18 | 23-F | SWE | 3 | 4 | 1 | 5 | 0 | 4th |
| 2009 WM18 | 26-F | SWE | 6 | 3 | 4 | 7 | 2 | 5th |
| 2009 WM20 | 26-F | SWE | 6 | 0 | 0 | 0 | 2 | S |
| 2010 WM20 | 10-F | SWE | 6 | 3 | 3 | 6 | 4 | B |
| **Totals WM18** | | | **9** | **7** | **5** | **12** | **2** | **—** |
| **Totals WM20** | | | **12** | **3** | **3** | **6** | **6** | **S,B** |

**Josi, Roman**
**b. Berne, Switzerland, June 1, 1990**

| | | | | | | | | |
|---|---|---|---|---|---|---|---|---|
| 2007 WM18 | 28-D | SUI | 6 | 1 | 1 | 2 | 2 | 6th |
| 2007 WM20 | 34-D | SUI | 6 | 0 | 0 | 0 | 0 | 7th |
| 2008 WM18 | 7-D | SUI | 6 | 1 | 4 | 5 | 4 | 8th |
| 2008 WM20 | 27-D | SUI | 6 | 0 | 1 | 1 | 4 | 9th |
| 2009 WM | 90-D | SUI | 6 | 0 | 0 | 0 | 2 | 9th |
| 2010 WM20 | 27-D | SUI | 4 | 1 | 2 | 3 | 0 | 4th |
| 2010 WM | 90-D | SUI | 7 | 1 | 2 | 3 | 0 | 5th |
| 2012 WM | 90-D | SUI | 3 | 0 | 1 | 1 | 0 | 11th |
| **Totals WM18** | | | **12** | **2** | **5** | **7** | **6** | **—** |
| **Totals WM20** | | | **16** | **1** | **3** | **4** | **4** | **—** |
| **Totals WM** | | | **16** | **1** | **3** | **4** | **2** | **—** |

**Juell, Rasmus**
**b. Oslo, Norway, February 25, 1991**

| | | | | | | | | |
|---|---|---|---|---|---|---|---|---|
| 2009 WM18 | 14-F | NOR | 6 | 3 | 2 | 5 | 10 | 9th |
| 2011 WM20 | 12-F | NOR | 6 | 1 | 0 | 1 | 0 | 9th |

**Junland, Jonas**
**b. Linkoping, Sweden, November 15, 1987**

| | | | | | | | | |
|---|---|---|---|---|---|---|---|---|
| 2007 WM20 | 6-D | SWE | 7 | 1 | 1 | 2 | 18 | 4th |

**Junttila, Julius**
**b. Oulu, Finland, August 15, 1991**

| | | | | | | | | |
|---|---|---|---|---|---|---|---|---|
| 2011 WM20 | 13-F | FIN | 6 | 2 | 3 | 5 | 6 | 6th |

**Jurcina, Milan**
**b. Liptovsky Mikulas, Czechoslovakia (Slovakia), June 7, 1983**

| | | | | | | | | |
|---|---|---|---|---|---|---|---|---|
| 2001 WM18 | 3-D | SVK | 6 | 0 | 0 | 0 | 6 | 8th |
| 2002 WM20 | 29-D | SVK | 7 | 1 | 1 | 2 | 14 | 8th |
| 2003 WM20 | 6-D | SVK | 1 | 0 | 0 | 0 | 0 | 5th |
| 2006 OG-M | 68-D | SVK | 6 | 0 | 1 | 1 | 8 | 5th |
| 2006 WM | 68-D | SVK | 7 | 2 | 1 | 3 | 8 | 8th |
| 2007 WM | 68-D | SVK | 7 | 1 | 1 | 2 | 8 | 6th |
| 2010 OG-M | 68-D | SVK | 7 | 0 | 0 | 0 | 2 | 4th |
| 2011 WM | 68-D | SVK | 6 | 0 | 2 | 2 | 4 | 10th |

| **Totals WM20** | | | **8** | **1** | **1** | **2** | **14** | **—** |
|---|---|---|---|---|---|---|---|---|
| **Totals WM** | | | **20** | **3** | **4** | **7** | **20** | **—** |
| **Totals OG-M** | | | **13** | **0** | **1** | **1** | **10** | **—** |

**Jurco, Tomas**
**b. Kosice, Czechoslovakia (Slovakia), December 28, 1992**

| 2009 WM18 | 24-F | SVK | 6 | 2 | 3 | 5 | 2 | 7th |
|---|---|---|---|---|---|---|---|---|
| 2011 WM20 | 13-F | SVK | 6 | 1 | 0 | 1 | 0 | 8th |
| 2012 WM20 | 13-F | SVK | 5 | 1 | 7 | 8 | 4 | 6th |
| Totals WM20 | | | 11 | 2 | 7 | 9 | 4 | — |

**Jurik, Milan**
**b. Zvolen, Czechoslovakia (Slovakia), February 28, 1988**

| 2006 WM18 | 15-F | SVK | 6 | 2 | 0 | 2 | 0 | 7th |
|---|---|---|---|---|---|---|---|---|
| 2008 WM20 | 15-F | SVK | 6 | 0 | 0 | 0 | 2 | 7th |

**Juutilainen, Jan-Mikael**
**b. Helsinki, Finland, January 5, 1988**

| 2006 WM18 | 14-F | FIN | 6 | 3 | 2 | 5 | 0 | S |
|---|---|---|---|---|---|---|---|---|
| 2008 WM20 | 27-F | FIN | 5 | 1 | 5 | 6 | 2 | 6th |

**Juutinen, Janne**
**b. Hyvinkaa, Finland, February 15, 1994**

| 2012 WM18 | 22-F | FIN | 7 | 0 | 0 | 0 | 2 | 4th |
|---|---|---|---|---|---|---|---|---|

**Jyrkkio, Jesse**
**b. Hameenlinna, Finland, June 29, 1989**

| 2007 WM18 | 7-D | FIN | 6 | 1 | 2 | 3 | 6 | 7th |
|---|---|---|---|---|---|---|---|---|
| 2009 WM20 | 13-D | FIN | 6 | 0 | 4 | 4 | 10 | 7th |

**Kabanov, Kirill**
**b. Moscow, Russia, July 16, 1992**

| 2009 WM18 | 17-F | RUS | 7 | 4 | 7 | 11 | 18 | S |
|---|---|---|---|---|---|---|---|---|

**Kaberle, Tomas**
**b. Rakovnik, Czechoslovakia (Czech Republic), March 2, 1978**

| 1998 WM20 | 12-D | CZE | 7 | 1 | 1 | 2 | 2 | 4th |
|---|---|---|---|---|---|---|---|---|
| 2002 OG-M | 15-D | CZE | 4 | 0 | 1 | 1 | 2 | 7th |
| 2003 WM | 15-D | CZE | 7 | 0 | 7 | 7 | 2 | 4th |
| 2004 WCH | 15-D | CZE | 4 | 0 | 1 | 1 | 0 | 3rd |
| 2005 WM | 15-D | CZE | 9 | 1 | 3 | 4 | 4 | G |
| 2006 OG-M | 15-D | CZE | 8 | 2 | 2 | 4 | 2 | B |
| 2006 WM | 15-D | CZE | 9 | 1 | 5 | 6 | 31 | S |
| 2008 WM | 15-D | CZE | 7 | 1 | 9 | 10 | 0 | 5th |
| 2010 OG-M | 15-D | CZE | 5 | 1 | 2 | 3 | 0 | 7th |
| **Totals WM** | | | **32** | **3** | **24** | **27** | **37** | **G,S** |
| **Totals OG-M** | | | **17** | **3** | **5** | **8** | **4** | **B** |

~WM All-Star Team/Defence (2008)

**Kachulin, Georgi**
**b. Minsk, Soviet Union (Belarus), February 15, 1990**

| 2008 WM18 | 12-F | BLR | 6 | 0 | 0 | 0 | 31 | 9th |
|---|---|---|---|---|---|---|---|---|

**Kachulin, Mikhail**
**b. Ust-Kamenogorsk, Soviet Union (Kazakhstan), January 25, 1988**

| 2008 WM20 | 11-F | KAZ | 6 | 1 | 1 | 2 | 4 | 8th |
|---|---|---|---|---|---|---|---|---|

**Kadri, Nazem**
**b. London, Ontario, Canada, October 6, 1990**

| 2010 WM20 | 9-F | CAN | 6 | 3 | 5 | 8 | 14 | S |
|---|---|---|---|---|---|---|---|---|

**Kahun, Dominik**
**b. Plana, Czech Republic, July 2, 1995**

| 2012 WM18 | 11-F | GER | 6 | 1 | 2 | 3 | 0 | 6th |
|---|---|---|---|---|---|---|---|---|

**Kaib, Barrett**
**b. Upper St. Clair, Pennsylvania, United States, February 7, 1993**

| 2011 WM18 | 7-D | USA | 6 | 0 | 2 | 2 | 0 | G |
|---|---|---|---|---|---|---|---|---|

**Kaefer, Raphael**
**b. Ebersberg, Germany, July 30, 1994**

| 2012 WM18 | 22-F | GER | 6 | 0 | 0 | 0 | 12 | 6th |
|---|---|---|---|---|---|---|---|---|

**Kaigorodov, Alexei**
**b. Magnitogorsk, Soviet Union (Russia), July 29, 1983**

| 2001 WM18 | 14-F | RUS | 6 | 1 | 5 | 6 | 8 | G |
|---|---|---|---|---|---|---|---|---|
| 2003 WM20 | 9-F | RUS | 6 | 1 | 2 | 3 | 4 | G |
| 2003 WM | 21-F | RUS | 2 | 0 | 0 | 0 | 2 | 7th |
| 2011 WM | 55-F | RUS | 8 | 1 | 3 | 4 | 2 | 4th |
| **Totals WM** | | | **10** | **1** | **3** | **4** | **4** | **—** |

**Kainz, Pascal**
**b. Hohenems, Austria, April 30, 1990**

| 2010 WM20 | 24-F | AUT | 6 | 0 | 1 | 1 | 4 | 10th |
|---|---|---|---|---|---|---|---|---|

**Kalashnikov, Stanislav**
**b. Omsk, Soviet Union (Russia), October 26, 1991**

| 2009 WM18 | 4-D | RUS | 7 | 0 | 1 | 1 | 8 | S |
|---|---|---|---|---|---|---|---|---|

**Kalimulin, Azat**
**b. Saby, Soviet Union (Russia), May 28, 1990**

| 2008 WM18 | 26-F | RUS | 6 | 0 | 1 | 1 | 0 | S |
|---|---|---|---|---|---|---|---|---|

**Kalin, Mattias**
**b. Danderyd, Sweden, April 3, 1994**

| 2012 WM18 | 14-F | SWE | 6 | 4 | 0 | 4 | 0 | S |
|---|---|---|---|---|---|---|---|---|

**Kalinac, Martin**
**b. Bratislava, Czechoslovakia (Slovakia), April 4, 1992**

| 2010 WM18 | 18-F | SVK | 6 | 1 | 0 | 1 | 4 | 8th |
|---|---|---|---|---|---|---|---|---|

**Kalinin, Dmitri**
**b. Chelyabinsk, Soviet Union (Russia), July 22, 1980**

| 2002 WM | 45-D | RUS | 9 | 0 | 1 | 1 | 4 | S |
|---|---|---|---|---|---|---|---|---|
| 2003 WM | 45-D | RUS | 7 | 1 | 0 | 1 | 4 | 7th |
| 2004 WM | 45-D | RUS | 6 | 0 | 1 | 1 | 2 | 10th |
| 2004 WCH | 45-D | RUS | 3 | 0 | 0 | 0 | 0 | 6th |
| 2005 WM | 45-D | RUS | 9 | 0 | 0 | 0 | 0 | B |
| 2008 WM | 7-D | RUS | 9 | 1 | 2 | 3 | 4 | G |
| 2009 WM | 7-D | RUS | 9 | 2 | 3 | 5 | 4 | G |
| 2010 OG-M | 7-D | RUS | 4 | 1 | 1 | 2 | 0 | 6th |
| 2010 WM | 7-D | RUS | 9 | 0 | 1 | 1 | 0 | S |
| 2011 WM | 7-D | RUS | 9 | 0 | 3 | 3 | 4 | 4th |
| 2012 WM | 7-D | RUS | 5 | 1 | 3 | 4 | 25 | G |
| **Totals WM** | | | **72** | **5** | **14** | **19** | **47** | **3G,2S,B** |

**Kalinin, Sergei**
**b. Omsk, Russia, March 17, 1991**

| 2011 WM20 | 21-F | RUS | 7 | 1 | 2 | 3 | 4 | G |
|---|---|---|---|---|---|---|---|---|

**Kallela, Toni**
**b. Oulainen, Finland, January 10, 1993**

| 2011 WM18 | 10-F | FIN | 6 | 2 | 3 | 5 | 0 | 5th |
|---|---|---|---|---|---|---|---|---|

**Kalnins, Krists**
**b. September 13, 1992**

| 2012 WM20 | 26-D | LAT | 6 | 0 | 1 | 1 | 14 | 9th |
|---|---|---|---|---|---|---|---|---|

**Kalus, Petr**
**b. Vitkovice, Czechoslovakia (Czech Republic), June 29, 1987**

| 2005 WM18 | 3-F | CZE | 7 | 0 | 3 | 3 | 12 | 4th |
|---|---|---|---|---|---|---|---|---|
| 2006 WM20 | 3-F | CZE | 5 | 0 | 1 | 1 | 4 | 6th |

**Kalvitis, Karlis**
**b. Riga, Soviet Union (Latvia), March 25, 1991**

| 2010 WM20 | 26-D | LAT | 6 | 0 | 0 | 0 | 0 | 9th |
|---|---|---|---|---|---|---|---|---|

**Kalvitis, Rudolfs**
**b. Riga, Latvia, March 23, 1994**

| 2012 WM18 | 7-D | LAT | 6 | 1 | 1 | 2 | 4 | 9th |
|---|---|---|---|---|---|---|---|---|

**Kalyuzhny, Alexei**
**b. Minsk, Soviet Union (Belarus), June 13, 1977**

| 1998 OG-M | 17-F | BLR | 7 | 1 | 0 | 1 | 6 | 7th |
|---|---|---|---|---|---|---|---|---|
| 1998 WM | 17-F | BLR | 6 | 1 | 4 | 5 | 2 | 8th |
| 1999 WM | 17-F | BLR | 6 | 1 | 1 | 2 | 6 | 9th |
| 2000 WM | 17-F | BLR | 6 | 1 | 2 | 3 | 12 | 9th |
| 2001 WM | 17-F | BLR | 6 | 2 | 1 | 3 | 4 | 14th |
| 2002 OG-M | 17-F | BLR | 9 | 1 | 1 | 2 | 0 | 4th |
| 2003 WM | 71-F | BLR | 6 | 1 | 3 | 4 | 4 | 14th |
| 2008 WM | 71-F | BLR | 6 | 1 | 3 | 4 | 4 | 9th |
| 2009 WM | 71-F | BLR | 5 | 1 | 5 | 6 | 0 | 8th |
| 2010 OG-M | 71-F | BLR | 4 | 3 | 1 | 4 | 2 | 9th |
| 2010 WM | 71-F | BLR | 6 | 4 | 2 | 6 | 4 | 10th |
| 2012 WM | 71-F | BLR | 7 | 3 | 2 | 5 | 2 | 14th |
| **Totals WM** | | | **54** | **15** | **23** | **38** | **38** | **—** |
| **Totals OG-M** | | | **20** | **5** | **2** | **7** | **8** | **—** |

**Kamayev, Denis**
**b. Izhevsk, Russia, March 6, 1994**

| 2012 WM18 | 23-F | RUS | 6 | 1 | 2 | 3 | 0 | 5th |
|---|---|---|---|---|---|---|---|---|

**Kampf, Marc**
**b. Sigriswil, Switzerland, November 8, 1990**

| 2008 WM18 | 10-F | SUI | 6 | 4 | 1 | 5 | 4 | 8th |
|---|---|---|---|---|---|---|---|---|

**Kana, Jan**
**b. Ostrava, Czechoslovakia (Czech Republic), March 22, 1990**

| 2009 WM20 | 9-F | CZE | 6 | 6 | 3 | 9 | 0 | 6th |
|---|---|---|---|---|---|---|---|---|
| 2010 WM20 | 9-F | CZE | 6 | 4 | 3 | 7 | 30 | 7th |
| **Totals WM20** | | | **12** | **10** | **6** | **16** | **30** | **—** |

**Kana, Tomas**
**b. Opava, Czechoslovakia (Czech Republic), November 29, 1987**

| 2005 WM18 | 24-F | CZE | 7 | 2 | 4 | 6 | 8 | 4th |
|---|---|---|---|---|---|---|---|---|
| 2006 WM20 | 28-F | CZE | 6 | 2 | 0 | 2 | 6 | 6th |
| 2007 WM20 | 28-F | CZE | 6 | 2 | 3 | 5 | 6 | 5th |
| **Totals WM20** | | | **12** | **4** | **3** | **7** | **12** | **—** |

**Kane, Evander**
**b. Vancouver, British Columbia, Canada, August 2, 1991**

| 2009 WM20 | 29-F | CAN | 6 | 2 | 4 | 6 | 2 | G |
|---|---|---|---|---|---|---|---|---|
| 2010 WM | 19-F | CAN | 7 | 2 | 2 | 4 | 6 | 7th |
| 2011 WM | 9-F | CAN | 7 | 0 | 2 | 2 | 4 | 5th |
| 2012 WM | 9-F | CAN | 8 | 4 | 3 | 7 | 2 | 5th |
| **Totals WM** | | | **22** | **6** | **7** | **13** | **12** | **—** |

**Kane, Patrick**
**b. Buffalo, New York, United States, November 19, 1988**

| 2006 WM18 | 27-F | USA | 6 | 7 | 5 | 12 | 2 | G |
|---|---|---|---|---|---|---|---|---|
| 2007 WM20 | 27-F | USA | 7 | 5 | 4 | 9 | 4 | B |
| 2008 WM | 83-F | USA | 7 | 3 | 7 | 10 | 0 | 6th |
| 2010 OG-M | 88-F | USA | 6 | 3 | 2 | 5 | 2 | S |

~WM20 All-Star Team/Forward (2007)

**Kapanen, Niko**
**b. Hattula, Finland, April 29, 1978**

| 1997 WM20 | 25-F | FIN | 6 | 4 | 4 | 8 | 0 | 5th |
|---|---|---|---|---|---|---|---|---|
| 1998 WM20 | 25-F | FIN | 7 | 2 | 5 | 7 | 2 | G |
| 2000 WM | 28-F | FIN | 9 | 4 | 3 | 7 | 4 | B |
| 2001 WM | 21-F | FIN | 9 | 3 | 1 | 4 | 8 | S |
| 2002 WM | 21-F | FIN | 9 | 0 | 4 | 4 | 10 | 4th |
| 2004 WM | 21-F | FIN | 7 | 3 | 2 | 5 | 14 | 6th |
| 2004 WCH | 39-F | FIN | 6 | 1 | 2 | 3 | 0 | 2nd |
| 2005 WM | 39-F | FIN | 7 | 1 | 4 | 5 | 8 | 7th |
| 2006 OG-M | 39-F | FIN | 8 | 2 | 1 | 3 | 2 | S |
| 2007 WM | 39-F | FIN | 9 | 0 | 7 | 7 | 6 | S |
| 2008 WM | 39-F | FIN | 9 | 2 | 5 | 7 | 0 | B |
| 2009 WM | 39-F | FIN | 7 | 7 | 3 | 10 | 2 | 5th |
| 2010 OG-M | 39-F | FIN | 6 | 0 | 2 | 2 | 0 | B |
| 2011 WM | 39-F | FIN | 9 | 2 | 1 | 3 | 2 | G |
| 2012 WM | 39-F | FIN | 10 | 1 | 1 | 2 | 2 | 4th |
| **Totals WM20** | | | **13** | **6** | **9** | **15** | **2** | **G** |
| **Totals WM** | | | **85** | **23** | **31** | **54** | **56** | **G,2S,2B** |
| **Totals OG-M** | | | **14** | **2** | **3** | **5** | **2** | **S,B** |

**Kapzan, Raphael**
**b. Landshut, West Germany (Germany), June 30, 1985**

| 2002 WM18 | 21-D | GER | 8 | 0 | 0 | 0 | 4 | 10th |
|---|---|---|---|---|---|---|---|---|
| 2005 WM20 | 5-D | GER | 6 | 0 | 0 | 0 | 4 | 9th |

**Karabanov, Igor**
**b. Minsk, Belarus, May 5, 1992**

| 2010 WM18 | 18-F | BLR | 6 | 0 | 0 | 0 | 8 | 10th |
|---|---|---|---|---|---|---|---|---|

**Kardashev, Nikita**
**b. Minsk, Belarus, September 25, 1992**

| 2010 WM18 | 19-D | BLR | 6 | 1 | 0 | 1 | 2 | 10th |
|---|---|---|---|---|---|---|---|---|

**Karev, Andrei**
**b. Elektrostal, Soviet Union (Russia), February 12, 1985**

| 2005 WM20 | 3-D | BLR | 6 | 0 | 1 | 1 | 34 | 10th |
|---|---|---|---|---|---|---|---|---|
| 2010 OG-M | 33-D | BLR | 4 | 0 | 0 | 0 | 2 | 9th |

**Karjalainen, Joni**
**b. Helsinki, Finland, April 13, 1991**

| 2009 WM18 | 13-F | FIN | 6 | 2 | 2 | 4 | 4 | B |
|---|---|---|---|---|---|---|---|---|

**Karklins, Edzus**
**b. Riga, Soviet Union (Latvia), February 4, 1986**

| 2006 WM20 | 20-F | LAT | 6 | 1 | 0 | 1 | 0 | 9th |
|---|---|---|---|---|---|---|---|---|

**Karlsson, Erik**
**b. Landsbro, Sweden, May 31, 1990**

| | | | | | | | | |
|---|---|---|---|---|---|---|---|---|
| 2008 WM18 | 5-D | SWE | 6 | 0 | 7 | 7 | 4 | 4th |
| 2009 WM20 | 5-D | SWE | 6 | 2 | 7 | 9 | 0 | S |
| 2010 WM | 65-D | SWE | 9 | 1 | 3 | 4 | 2 | B |
| 2012 WM | 65-D | SWE | 8 | 3 | 4 | 7 | 2 | 6th |
| **Totals WM** | | | **17** | **4** | **7** | **11** | **4** | **B** |

~WM20 IIHF Directorate Best Defenceman (2009), WM20 All-Star Team/Defence (2009), WM18 IIHF Directorate Best Defenceman (2008)

**Karlsson, Erik**
**b. Lerum, Sweden, July 28, 1994**

| | | | | | | | | |
|---|---|---|---|---|---|---|---|---|
| 2012 WM18 | 23-F | SWE | 6 | 1 | 2 | 3 | 2 | S |

**Karlsson, Martin**
**b. Falun, Sweden, January 5, 1991**

| | | | | | | | | |
|---|---|---|---|---|---|---|---|---|
| 2009 WM18 | 11-F | SWE | 6 | 0 | 0 | 0 | 0 | 5th |

**Karlsson, Sebastian**
**b. Gothenburg, Sweden, September 19, 1986**

| | | | | | | | | |
|---|---|---|---|---|---|---|---|---|
| 2004 WM18 | 22-F | SWE | 6 | 1 | 0 | 1 | 2 | 5th |
| 2005 WM20 | 28-F | SWE | 6 | 0 | 1 | 1 | 0 | 6th |
| 2006 WM20 | 3-F | SWE | 6 | 3 | 3 | 6 | 8 | 5th |
| **Totals WM20** | | | **12** | **3** | **4** | **7** | **8** | **—** |

**Karlsson, William**
**b. Marsta, Sweden, January 8, 1993**

| | | | | | | | | |
|---|---|---|---|---|---|---|---|---|
| 2011 WM18 | 17-F | SWE | 6 | 2 | 3 | 5 | 6 | S |
| 2012 WM20 | 17-F | SWE | 6 | 1 | 1 | 2 | 0 | G |

**Karmeniemi, Lauri**
**b. Hameenlinna, Finland, April 17, 1991**

| | | | | | | | | |
|---|---|---|---|---|---|---|---|---|
| 2009 WM18 | 5-D | FIN | 6 | 0 | 1 | 1 | 2 | B |

**Karpushkin, Alexander**
**b. Moscow, Soviet Union (Russia), September 18, 1991**

| | | | | | | | | |
|---|---|---|---|---|---|---|---|---|
| 2009 WM18 | 13-D | RUS | 7 | 0 | 0 | 0 | 2 | S |

**Karsums, Martins**
**b. Riga, Soviet Union (Latvia), February 26, 1986**

| | | | | | | | | |
|---|---|---|---|---|---|---|---|---|
| 2006 WM20 | 9-F | LAT | 6 | 3 | 3 | 6 | 6 | 9th |
| 2008 WM | 9-F | LAT | 2 | 1 | 2 | 3 | 2 | 11th |
| 2009 WM | 9-F | LAT | 6 | 1 | 3 | 4 | 27 | 7th |
| 2010 OG-M | 9-F | LAT | 4 | 0 | 2 | 2 | 2 | 12th |
| 2010 WM | 9-F | LAT | 6 | 3 | 1 | 4 | 2 | 11th |
| **Totals WM** | | | **14** | **5** | **6** | **11** | **31** | **—** |

**Kartayev, Vladislav**
**b. Chelyabinsk Region, Russia, February 10, 1992**

| | | | | | | | | |
|---|---|---|---|---|---|---|---|---|
| 2010 WM18 | 11-F | RUS | 6 | 1 | 2 | 3 | 4 | 4th |

**Karterud, Jorgen**
**b. Oslo, Norway, May 6, 1994**

| | | | | | | | | |
|---|---|---|---|---|---|---|---|---|
| 2011 WM18 | 14-F | NOR | 6 | 1 | 0 | 1 | 2 | 9th |

**Kaser, Marco**
**b. Huttwil, Switzerland, March 26, 1985**

| | | | | | | | | |
|---|---|---|---|---|---|---|---|---|
| 2005 WM20 | 19-F | SUI | 6 | 3 | 3 | 6 | 6 | 8th |

**Kaspar, Lukas**
**b. Most, Czechoslovakia (Czech Republic), September 23, 1985**

| | | | | | | | | |
|---|---|---|---|---|---|---|---|---|
| 2003 WM18 | 15-F | CZE | 6 | 2 | 2 | 4 | 6 | 6th |
| 2004 WM20 | 28-F | CZE | 6 | 0 | 3 | 3 | 2 | 4th |
| 2005 WM20 | 22-F | CZE | 7 | 1 | 1 | 2 | 16 | B |
| 2010 WM | 22-F | CZE | 9 | 2 | 1 | 3 | 4 | G |
| 2012 WM | 22-F | CZE | 7 | 0 | 1 | 1 | 4 | B |
| Totals WM20 | | | 13 | 1 | 4 | 5 | 18 | B |
| **Totals WM** | | | **16** | **2** | **2** | **4** | **8** | **G,B** |

**Kaspitz, Roland**
**b. Spittal an der Drau, Austria, November 1, 1981**

| | | | | | | | | |
|---|---|---|---|---|---|---|---|---|
| 2002 WM | 27-F | AUT | 6 | 0 | 2 | 2 | 2 | 12th |
| 2004 WM | 8-F | AUT | 6 | 0 | 0 | 0 | 0 | 11th |
| 2005 WM | 8-F | AUT | 6 | 1 | 1 | 2 | 12 | 16th |
| 2009 WM | 8-F | AUT | 6 | 2 | 0 | 2 | 2 | 14th |
| 2011 WM | 8-F | AUT | 6 | 0 | 0 | 0 | 8 | 15th |
| **Totals WM** | | | **30** | **3** | **3** | **6** | **24** | **—** |

**Kassian, Zack**
**b. LaSalle, Ontario, Canada, January 24, 1991**

| | | | | | | | | |
|---|---|---|---|---|---|---|---|---|
| 2009 WM18 | 10-F | CAN | 6 | 2 | 3 | 5 | 0 | 4th |
| 2011 WM20 | 9-F | CAN | 5 | 2 | 1 | 3 | 27 | S |

**Kaufmann, Evan**
**b. Tonka Bay, Minnesota, United States, October 31, 1984**

| | | | | | | | | |
|---|---|---|---|---|---|---|---|---|
| 2012 WM | 19-F | GER | 7 | 0 | 1 | 1 | 4 | 12th |

**Kaunismaki, Juha**
**b. Helsinki, Finland, May 6, 1979**

| | | | | | | | | |
|---|---|---|---|---|---|---|---|---|
| 2008 WM | 5-D | NOR | 6 | 0 | 0 | 0 | 4 | 8th |
| 2009 WM | 5-D | NOR | 6 | 0 | 0 | 0 | 4 | 11th |
| 2010 OG-M | 5-D | NOR | 4 | 0 | 0 | 0 | 0 | 10th |
| 2010 WM | 5-D | NOR | 6 | 0 | 0 | 0 | 4 | 9th |
| 2012 WM | 5-D | NOR | 8 | 1 | 1 | 2 | 2 | 8th |
| **Totals WM** | | | **26** | **1** | **1** | **2** | **14** | **—** |

**Kauss, Gvido**
**b. Jurmala, Soviet Union (Latvia), March 14, 1990**

| | | | | | | | | |
|---|---|---|---|---|---|---|---|---|
| 2007 WM18 | 5-D | LAT | 6 | 0 | 0 | 0 | 4 | 10th |
| 2009 WM20 | 4-D | LAT | 6 | 0 | 0 | 0 | 8 | 8th |
| 2010 WM20 | 4-D | LAT | 6 | 1 | 0 | 1 | 2 | 9th |
| **Totals WM20** | | | **12** | **1** | **0** | **1** | **10** | **—** |

**Kazantsev, Anton**
**b. Rudny, Soviet Union (Kazakhstan), August 26, 1986**

| | | | | | | | | |
|---|---|---|---|---|---|---|---|---|
| 2010 WM | 4-D | KAZ | 1 | 0 | 0 | 0 | 2 | 16th |

**Kaznacheyev, Alexander**
**b. V-Kazakhstanskaya, Soviet Union (Kazakhstan), March 27, 1990**

| | | | | | | | | |
|---|---|---|---|---|---|---|---|---|
| 2008 WM20 | 7-F | KAZ | 6 | 0 | 0 | 0 | 4 | 8th |
| 2009 WM20 | 13-F | KAZ | 5 | 0 | 2 | 2 | 27 | 10th |
| **Totals WM20** | | | **11** | **0** | **2** | **2** | **31** | **—** |

**Keil, Bernhard**
**b. Amberg, Germany, January 21, 1992**

| | | | | | | | | |
|---|---|---|---|---|---|---|---|---|
| 2011 WM20 | 26-F | GER | 6 | 0 | 1 | 1 | 4 | 10th |

**Keith, Duncan**
**b. Winnipeg, Manitoba, Canada, July 16, 1983**

| | | | | | | | | |
|---|---|---|---|---|---|---|---|---|
| 2008 WM | 22-D | CAN | 9 | 0 | 2 | 2 | 6 | S |
| 2010 OG-M | 2-D | CAN | 7 | 0 | 6 | 6 | 2 | G |
| 2012 WM | 2-D | CAN | 8 | 1 | 10 | 11 | 0 | 5th |
| **Totals WM** | | | **17** | **1** | **12** | **13** | **6** | **S** |

**Kellenberger, Steve**
**b. Bulach, Switzerland, February 6, 1987**

| | | | | | | | | |
|---|---|---|---|---|---|---|---|---|
| 2005 WM18 | 19-F | SUI | 6 | 0 | 1 | 1 | 2 | 9th |
| 2006 WM20 | 27-F | SUI | 6 | 0 | 0 | 0 | 2 | 7th |
| 2007 WM20 | 29-F | SUI | 6 | 0 | 4 | 4 | 2 | 7th |
| **Totals WM20** | | | **12** | **0** | **4** | **4** | **4** | **—** |

**Keller, Kilian**
**b. Fussen, Germany, March 15, 1993**

| | | | | | | | | |
|---|---|---|---|---|---|---|---|---|
| 2011 WM18 | 27-D | GER | 6 | 1 | 2 | 3 | 2 | 6th |

**Keller, Samuel**
**b. Winterthur, Switzerland, February 9, 1991**

| | | | | | | | | |
|---|---|---|---|---|---|---|---|---|
| 2009 WM18 | 26-F | SUI | 6 | 0 | 0 | 0 | 0 | 8th |

**Kempe, Mario**
**b. Kramfors, Sweden, September 19, 1988**

| | | | | | | | | |
|---|---|---|---|---|---|---|---|---|
| 2006 WM18 | 25-F | SWE | 5 | 0 | 1 | 1 | 27 | 6th |
| 2008 WM20 | 10-F | SWE | 6 | 0 | 0 | 0 | 2 | S |

**Kempny, Michal**
**b. Hodonin, Czechoslovakia (Czech Republic), September 8, 1990**

| | | | | | | | | |
|---|---|---|---|---|---|---|---|---|
| 2010 WM20 | 29-D | CZE | 6 | 0 | 2 | 2 | 0 | 7th |

**Kemppainen, Joonas**
**b. Kajaani, Finland, April 7, 1988**

| | | | | | | | | |
|---|---|---|---|---|---|---|---|---|
| 2005 WM18 | 23-F | FIN | 6 | 0 | 0 | 0 | 2 | 7th |
| 2006 WM18 | 13-F | FIN | 6 | 1 | 1 | 2 | 2 | S |
| 2008 WM20 | 24-F | FIN | 6 | 2 | 1 | 3 | 4 | 6th |
| **Totals WM18** | | | **12** | **1** | **1** | **2** | **4** | **S** |

**Kenins, Ronalds**
**b. Riga, Soviet Union (Latvia), February 28, 1991**

| | | | | | | | | |
|---|---|---|---|---|---|---|---|---|
| 2010 WM20 | 15-F | LAT | 6 | 2 | 2 | 4 | 6 | 9th |
| 2011 WM | 15-F | LAT | 6 | 0 | 0 | 0 | 0 | 13th |
| 2012 WM | 15-F | LAT | 5 | 1 | 2 | 3 | 6 | 10th |
| **Totals WM** | | | **11** | **1** | **2** | **3** | **6** | **—** |

**Kennedy, Tim**
**b. Buffalo, New York, United States, April 30, 1986**

| | | | | | | | | |
|---|---|---|---|---|---|---|---|---|
| 2010 WM | 13-F | USA | 6 | 1 | 0 | 1 | 0 | 13th |

**Kentos, Jozef**
**b. Zvolen, Czechoslovakia (Slovakia), March 8, 1991**

| | | | | | | | | |
|---|---|---|---|---|---|---|---|---|
| 2009 WM18 | 25-F | SVK | 6 | 1 | 0 | 1 | 2 | 7th |

**Kerdiles, Nick**
**b. Irvine, California, United States, January 11, 1994**

| | | | | | | | | |
|---|---|---|---|---|---|---|---|---|
| 2011 WM18 | 12-F | USA | 6 | 0 | 2 | 2 | 2 | G |
| 2012 WM18 | 17-F | USA | 6 | 4 | 5 | 9 | 2 | G |
| Totals WM18 | | | 12 | 4 | 7 | 11 | 4 | 2G |

**Kerman, Kalle**
**b. Kuopio, Finland, February 10, 1979**

| | | | | | | | | |
|---|---|---|---|---|---|---|---|---|
| 2009 WM | 29-F | FIN | 6 | 0 | 0 | 0 | 2 | 5th |

**Kesler, Ryan**
**b. Detroit, Michigan, United States, August 31, 1984**

| | | | | | | | | |
|---|---|---|---|---|---|---|---|---|
| 2002 WM18 | 17-F | USA | 8 | 2 | 5 | 7 | 4 | G |
| 2003 WM20 | 17-F | USA | 7 | 3 | 4 | 7 | 6 | 4th |
| 2004 WM20 | 17-F | USA | 6 | 3 | 0 | 3 | 6 | G |
| 2006 WM | 17-F | USA | 7 | 0 | 1 | 1 | 0 | 7th |
| 2010 OG-M | 17-F | USA | 6 | 2 | 0 | 2 | 2 | S |
| **Totals WM20** | | | **13** | **6** | **4** | **10** | **12** | **G** |

**Kessel, Blake**
**b. Madison, Wisconsin, United States, April 13, 1989**

| | | | | | | | | |
|---|---|---|---|---|---|---|---|---|
| 2009 WM20 | 20-D | USA | 6 | 0 | 1 | 1 | 2 | 5th |

**Kessel, Phil**
**b. Madison, Wisconsin, United States, October 2, 1987**

| | | | | | | | | |
|---|---|---|---|---|---|---|---|---|
| 2004 WM18 | 26-F | USA | 6 | 7 | 3 | 10 | 6 | S |
| 2005 WM18 | 8-F | USA | 6 | 9 | 7 | 16 | 2 | G |
| 2005 WM20 | 26-F | USA | 7 | 4 | 2 | 6 | 2 | 4th |
| 2006 WM20 | 8-F | USA | 7 | 1 | 10 | 11 | 2 | 4th |
| 2006 WM | 8-F | USA | 7 | 1 | 1 | 2 | 2 | 7th |
| 2007 WM | 8-F | USA | 7 | 2 | 5 | 7 | 6 | 5th |
| 2008 WM | 8-F | USA | 7 | 6 | 4 | 10 | 6 | 6th |
| 2010 OG-M | 81-F | USA | 6 | 1 | 1 | 2 | 0 | S |
| **Totals WM18** | | | **12** | **16** | **10** | **26** | **8** | **G,S** |
| **Totals WM20** | | | **14** | **5** | **12** | **17** | **4** | **—** |
| **Totals WM** | | | **21** | **9** | **10** | **19** | **14** | **—** |

**Ketov, Yevgeni**
**b. Gubakha, Soviet Union (Russia), January 17, 1986**

| | | | | | | | | |
|---|---|---|---|---|---|---|---|---|
| 2006 WM20 | 8-F | RUS | 6 | 0 | 1 | 1 | 2 | S |
| 2012 WM | 80-F | RUS | 7 | 0 | 0 | 0 | 0 | G |

**Khafizullin, Dinar**
**b. Kazan, Soviet Union (Russia), January 1, 1989**

| | | | | | | | | |
|---|---|---|---|---|---|---|---|---|
| 2009 WM20 | 14-D | RUS | 2 | 0 | 0 | 0 | 0 | B |

**Khatsei, Arseni**
**b. Chelyabinsk, Russia, January 28, 1994**

| | | | | | | | | |
|---|---|---|---|---|---|---|---|---|
| 2012 WM18 | 25-F | RUS | 6 | 3 | 0 | 3 | 6 | 5th |

**Khokhlachev, Alexander**
**b. Moscow, Russia, September 9, 1993**

| | | | | | | | | |
|---|---|---|---|---|---|---|---|---|
| 2012 WM20 | 19-F | RUS | 7 | 4 | 1 | 5 | 6 | S |

**Khokhriakov, Pyotr**
**b. Nizhnekamsk, Soviet Union (Russia), January 16, 1990**

| | | | | | | | | |
|---|---|---|---|---|---|---|---|---|
| 2010 WM20 | 16-F | RUS | 6 | 1 | 2 | 3 | 4 | 6th |

**Kiiskinen, Tuomas**
**b. Kuopio, Finland, October 7, 1986**

| | | | | | | | | |
|---|---|---|---|---|---|---|---|---|
| 2012 WM | 19-F | FIN | 5 | 0 | 2 | 2 | 0 | 4th |

**Kilstrom, Lukas**
**b. Sodertalje, Sweden, April 18, 1990**

| | | | | | | | | |
|---|---|---|---|---|---|---|---|---|
| 2010 WM20 | 2-D | SWE | 6 | 0 | 1 | 1 | 4 | B |

**Kimmel, Tom-Patric**
**b. Dusseldorf, West Germany (Germany), May 5, 1990**

| | | | | | | | | |
|---|---|---|---|---|---|---|---|---|
| 2008 WM18 | 16-F | GER | 6 | 2 | 2 | 4 | 0 | 5th |

**Kindl, Denis**
**b. Pardubice, Czechoslovakia (Czech Republic), August 4, 1992**

| | | | | | | | | |
|---|---|---|---|---|---|---|---|---|
| 2010 WM18 | 28-F | CZE | 6 | 0 | 0 | 0 | 14 | 6th |

**Kindl, Jakub**
**b. Sumperk, Czechoslovakia (Czech Republic), February 10, 1987**

| | | | | | | | | |
|---|---|---|---|---|---|---|---|---|
| 2006 WM20 | 9-D | CZE | 6 | 0 | 1 | 1 | 10 | 6th |
| 2007 WM20 | 9-D | CZE | 6 | 0 | 4 | 4 | 8 | 5th |
| **Totals WM20** | | | **12** | **0** | **5** | **5** | **18** | |

**Kink, Marcus**
**b. Dusseldorf, West Germany (Germany), January 13, 1985**

| | | | | | | | | |
|---|---|---|---|---|---|---|---|---|
| 2002 WM18 | 27-F | GER | 8 | 1 | 0 | 1 | 24 | 10th |
| 2003 WM20 | 28-F | GER | 6 | 0 | 0 | 0 | 18 | 9th |
| 2005 WM20 | 17-F | GER | 6 | 1 | 1 | 2 | 8 | 9th |
| 2011 WM | 75-F | GER | 3 | 0 | 2 | 2 | 4 | 7th |
| 2012 WM | 17-F | GER | 6 | 1 | 0 | 1 | 2 | 12th |
| **Totals WM20** | | | **12** | **1** | **1** | **2** | **26** | **—** |
| **Totals WM** | | | **9** | **1** | **2** | **3** | **6** | **—** |

**Kisum, Nicki**
**b. Herlev, Denmark, December 16, 1993**

| | | | | | | | | |
|---|---|---|---|---|---|---|---|---|
| 2012 WM20 | 26-F | DEN | 4 | 0 | 0 | 0 | 0 | 10th |

**Kitarov, Alexander**
**b. Minsk, Soviet Union (Belraus), June 18, 1987**

| | | | | | | | | |
|---|---|---|---|---|---|---|---|---|
| 2011 WM | 77-F | BLR | 6 | 0 | 3 | 3 | 4 | 14th |
| 2012 WM | 77-F | BLR | 6 | 0 | 0 | 0 | 14 | 14th |
| **Totals WM** | | | **12** | **0** | **3** | **3** | **18** | **—** |

**Kitsyn, Kirill**
**b. Novokuznetsk, Soviet Union (Russia), August 13, 1988**

| | | | | | | | | |
|---|---|---|---|---|---|---|---|---|
| 2008 WM20 | 25-F | KAZ | 6 | 0 | 1 | 1 | 2 | 8th |

**Kitsyn, Maxim**
**b. Novokuznetsk, Soviet Union (Russia), December 24, 1991**

| | | | | | | | | |
|---|---|---|---|---|---|---|---|---|
| 2009 WM18 | 23-F | RUS | 7 | 4 | 4 | 8 | 16 | S |
| 2010 WM20 | 13-F | RUS | 6 | 0 | 3 | 3 | 0 | 6th |
| 2011 WM20 | 13-F | RUS | 7 | 5 | 4 | 9 | 0 | G |
| **Totals WM20** | | | **13** | **5** | **7** | **12** | **0** | **G** |

**Kivisto, Tommi**
**b. Vantaa, Finland, June 7, 1991**

| | | | | | | | | |
|---|---|---|---|---|---|---|---|---|
| 2008 WM18 | 2-D | FIN | 6 | 1 | 2 | 3 | 8 | 6th |
| 2009 WM18 | 4-D | FIN | 6 | 0 | 3 | 3 | 22 | B |
| 2009 WM20 | 3-D | FIN | 6 | 1 | 0 | 1 | 6 | 7th |
| 2010 WM20 | 3-D | FIN | 6 | 0 | 1 | 1 | 0 | 5th |
| 2011 WM20 | 4-D | FIN | 6 | 0 | 1 | 1 | 6 | 6th |
| **Totals WM18** | | | **12** | **1** | **5** | **6** | **30** | **B** |
| **Totals WM20** | | | **18** | **1** | **2** | **3** | **12** | **—** |

**Kjargaard, Christoffer**
**b. Herning, Denmark, May 3, 1980**

| | | | | | | | | |
|---|---|---|---|---|---|---|---|---|
| 2005 WM | 16-F | DEN | 6 | 0 | 1 | 1 | 2 | 14th |
| 2006 WM | 16-F | DEN | 6 | 1 | 3 | 4 | 2 | 13th |
| 2007 WM | 16-F | DEN | 5 | 1 | 1 | 2 | 2 | 10th |
| 2008 WM | 16-F | DEN | 6 | 0 | 1 | 1 | 0 | 12th |
| **Totals WM** | | | **23** | **2** | **5** | **8** | **6** | **—** |

**Klavins, Edgars**
**b. Talsi, Latvia, March 10, 1993**

| | | | | | | | | |
|---|---|---|---|---|---|---|---|---|
| 2010 WM18 | 15-F | LAT | 6 | 0 | 1 | 1 | 14 | 9th |
| 2012 WM20 | 19-F | LAT | 6 | 0 | 0 | 0 | 2 | 9th |

**Klefbom, Oscar**
**b. Karlstad, Sweden, July 20, 1993**

| | | | | | | | | |
|---|---|---|---|---|---|---|---|---|
| 2011 WM18 | 19-D | SWE | 6 | 1 | 3 | 4 | 4 | S |
| 2012 WM20 | 6-D | SWE | 6 | 1 | 1 | 2 | 2 | G |

~WM20 All-Star Team/Defence (2012)

**Klementiev, Anton**
**b. Togliatti, Soviet Union (Russia), March 25, 1990**

| | | | | | | | | |
|---|---|---|---|---|---|---|---|---|
| 2010 WM20 | 29-D | RUS | 6 | 0 | 0 | 0 | 4 | 6th |

**Klepis, Jakub**
**b. Prague, Czechoslovakia (Czech Republic), June 5, 1984**

| | | | | | | | | |
|---|---|---|---|---|---|---|---|---|
| 2002 WM18 | 21-F | CZE | 8 | 1 | 8 | 9 | 8 | B |
| 2003 WM20 | 21-F | CZE | 6 | 0 | 4 | 4 | 4 | 6th |
| 2004 WM20 | 21-F | CZE | 7 | 2 | 2 | 4 | 4 | 4th |
| 2008 WM | 20-F | CZE | 4 | 0 | 1 | 1 | 0 | 5th |
| 2009 WM | 20-F | CZE | 7 | 1 | 4 | 5 | 6 | 6th |
| 2010 WM | 20-F | CZE | 9 | 3 | 4 | 7 | 8 | G |
| **Totals WM20** | | | **13** | **2** | **6** | **8** | **8** | **—** |
| **Totals WM** | | | **20** | **4** | **9** | **13** | **14** | **G** |

**Klimicek, Jiri**
**b. Ostrava, Czech Republic, September 6, 1992**

| | | | | | | | | |
|---|---|---|---|---|---|---|---|---|
| 2010 WM18 | 9-D | CZE | 6 | 0 | 2 | 2 | 4 | 6th |

**Klingberg, Carl**
**b. Gothenburg, Sweden, January 28, 1991**

| | | | | | | | | |
|---|---|---|---|---|---|---|---|---|
| 2009 WM18 | 17-F | SWE | 6 | 2 | 2 | 4 | 0 | 5th |
| 2010 WM20 | 17-F | SWE | 5 | 1 | 0 | 1 | 2 | B |
| 2011 WM20 | 17-F | SWE | 6 | 3 | 1 | 4 | 4 | 4th |
| **Totals WM20** | | | **11** | **4** | **1** | **5** | **6** | **B** |

**Klingberg, John**
**b. Lerum, Sweden, August 14, 1992**

| | | | | | | | | |
|---|---|---|---|---|---|---|---|---|
| 2011 WM20 | 9-D | SWE | 6 | 1 | 1 | 2 | 0 | 4th |
| 2012 WM20 | 9-D | SWE | 6 | 0 | 3 | 3 | 4 | G |

**Klinge, Manuel**
**b. Kassel, West Germany (Germany), September 5, 1984**

| | | | | | | | | |
|---|---|---|---|---|---|---|---|---|
| 2010 OG-M | 9-F | GER | 4 | 1 | 0 | 1 | 0 | 11th |

**Klopov, Dmitri**
**b. Gorky (Nizhni Novgorod), Soviet Union (Russia), October 7, 1989**

| | | | | | | | | |
|---|---|---|---|---|---|---|---|---|
| 2009 WM20 | 9-F | RUS | 7 | 5 | 2 | 7 | 4 | B |

**Klopper, Patrick**
**b. Duisburg, Germany, December 3, 1994**

| | | | | | | | | |
|---|---|---|---|---|---|---|---|---|
| 2012 WM18 | 24-F | GER | 6 | 0 | 0 | 0 | 2 | 6th |

**Klujevskis, Jurijs**
**b. Riga, Soviet Union (Latvia), September 24, 1986**

| | | | | | | | | |
|---|---|---|---|---|---|---|---|---|
| 2006 WM20 | 28-F | LAT | 6 | 2 | 2 | 4 | 0 | 9th |

**Knot, Ronald**
**b. Prague, Czech Republic, August 3, 1994**

| | | | | | | | | |
|---|---|---|---|---|---|---|---|---|
| 2012 WM18 | 7-D | CZE | 6 | 0 | 0 | 0 | 6 | 8th |

**Knotek, Tomas**
**b. Kladno, Czechoslovakia (Czech Republic), January 13, 1990**

| | | | | | | | | |
|---|---|---|---|---|---|---|---|---|
| 2007 WM18 | 10-F | CZE | 6 | 1 | 0 | 1 | 0 | 9th |
| 2009 WM20 | 15-D | CZE | 6 | 3 | 2 | 5 | 0 | 6th |
| 2010 WM20 | 14-F | CZE | 6 | 4 | 5 | 9 | 2 | 7th |
| **Totals WM20** | | | **12** | **7** | **7** | **14** | **2** | **—** |

**Knutsen, Jonas**
**b. Oslo, Norway, April 2, 1993**

| | | | | | | | | |
|---|---|---|---|---|---|---|---|---|
| 2011 WM18 | 20-F | NOR | 6 | 3 | 1 | 4 | 6 | 9th |

**Koberger, Sebastian**
**b. Munich, Germany, July 19, 1994**

| | | | | | | | | |
|---|---|---|---|---|---|---|---|---|
| 2012 WM18 | 2-D | GER | 6 | 0 | 0 | 0 | 2 | 6th |

**Koch, Thomas**
**b. Klagenfurt, Austria, August 17, 1983**

| | | | | | | | | |
|---|---|---|---|---|---|---|---|---|
| 2003 WM | 11-F | AUT | 6 | 0 | 0 | 0 | 0 | 10th |
| 2004 WM | 18-F | AUT | 6 | 1 | 1 | 2 | 4 | 11th |
| 2007 WM | 18-F | AUT | 6 | 2 | 2 | 4 | 0 | 15th |
| 2009 WM | 18-F | AUT | 6 | 4 | 3 | 7 | 10 | 14th |
| 2011 WM | 18-F | AUT | 6 | 0 | 2 | 2 | 2 | 15th |
| **Totals WM** | | | **30** | **7** | **8** | **15** | **16** | **—** |

**Koekkoek, Slater**
**b. Mountain, Ontario, Canada, February 18, 1994**

| | | | | | | | | |
|---|---|---|---|---|---|---|---|---|
| 2011 WM18 | 3-D | CAN | 7 | 1 | 1 | 2 | 2 | 4th |

**Kohl, Benedikt Anton**
**b. Berchtesgaden, West Germany (Germany), March 31, 1988**

| | | | | | | | | |
|---|---|---|---|---|---|---|---|---|
| 2006 WM18 | 4-D | GER | 6 | 0 | 0 | 0 | 2 | 8th |
| 2007 WM20 | 4-D | GER | 6 | 0 | 0 | 0 | 0 | 9th |

**Kohl, Marc**
**b. Mannheim, West Germany (Germany), September 10, 1991**

| | | | | | | | | |
|---|---|---|---|---|---|---|---|---|
| 2008 WM18 | 3-D | GER | 6 | 0 | 0 | 0 | 8 | 5th |

**Kohler, Bedrich**
**b. Vitkovice, Czechoslovakia (Czech Republic), February 14, 1985**

| | | | | | | | | |
|---|---|---|---|---|---|---|---|---|
| 2005 WM20 | 9-F | CZE | 7 | 0 | 0 | 0 | 0 | B |

**Kohn, Ladislav**
**b. Uherske Hradiste, Czechoslovakia (Czech Republic), March 4, 1975**

| | | | | | | | | |
|---|---|---|---|---|---|---|---|---|
| 1995 WM20 | 17-F | CZE | 7 | 0 | 4 | 4 | 8 | 5th |
| 2008 WM | 18-F | CZE | 5 | 0 | 1 | 1 | 14 | 5th |

**Koistinen, Matti**
**b. Outokumpu, Finland, January 18, 1986**

| | | | | | | | | |
|---|---|---|---|---|---|---|---|---|
| 2006 WM20 | 2-D | FIN | 7 | 0 | 1 | 1 | 10 | B |

**Koistinen, Ville**
**b. Oulu, Finland, June 17, 1982**

| | | | | | | | | |
|---|---|---|---|---|---|---|---|---|
| 2007 WM | 4-D | FIN | 2 | 0 | 0 | 0 | 2 | S |
| 2008 WM | 4-D | FIN | 9 | 1 | 1 | 2 | 4 | B |
| 2009 WM | 4-D | FIN | 4 | 1 | 2 | 3 | 4 | 5th |
| **Totals WM** | | | **15** | **2** | **3** | **5** | **10** | **S,B** |

**Koivu, Eerikki**
**b. Kokkola, Finland, December 29, 1979**

| | | | | | | | | |
|---|---|---|---|---|---|---|---|---|
| 2011 WM | 5-D | NOR | 7 | 1 | 0 | 1 | 2 | 6th |

**Koivu, Mikko**
**b. Turku, Finland, March 12, 1983**

| | | | | | | | | |
|---|---|---|---|---|---|---|---|---|
| 2000 WM18 | 13-F | FIN | 7 | 0 | 4 | 4 | 8 | G |
| 2001 WM18 | 9-F | FIN | 6 | 2 | 3 | 5 | 6 | B |
| 2001 WM20 | 9-F | FIN | 7 | 0 | 3 | 3 | 8 | S |
| 2002 WM20 | 9-F | FIN | 7 | 1 | 5 | 6 | 4 | B |
| 2004 WCH | 21-F | FIN | 4 | 0 | 1 | 1 | 2 | 2nd |
| 2006 OG-M | 21-F | FIN | 8 | 0 | 0 | 0 | 6 | S |
| 2006 WM | 21-F | FIN | 9 | 2 | 2 | 4 | 8 | B |
| 2007 WM | 9-F | FIN | 9 | 2 | 2 | 4 | 26 | S |
| 2008 WM | 9-F | FIN | 9 | 4 | 5 | 9 | 6 | B |
| 2010 OG-M | 9-F | FIN | 6 | 0 | 4 | 4 | 2 | B |
| 2011 WM | 9-F | FIN | 9 | 2 | 6 | 8 | 4 | G |
| 2012 WM | 9-F | FIN | 10 | 3 | 8 | 11 | 4 | 4th |
| **Totals WM18** | | | **13** | **2** | **7** | **9** | **14** | **G,B** |
| **Totals WM20** | | | **14** | **1** | **8** | **9** | **12** | **S,B** |
| **Totals WM** | | | **46** | **13** | **23** | **36** | **48** | **G,S,2B** |
| **Totals OG-M** | | | **14** | **0** | **4** | **4** | **8** | **S,B** |

**Koivu, Saku**
**b. Turku, Finland, November 23, 1974**

| | | | | | | | | |
|---|---|---|---|---|---|---|---|---|
| 1993 WM20 | 9-F | FIN | 7 | 1 | 8 | 9 | 6 | 5th |
| 1993 WM | 13-F | FIN | 6 | 0 | 1 | 1 | 2 | 7th |
| 1994 WM20 | 9-F | FIN | 7 | 3 | 6 | 9 | 12 | 4th |
| 1994 OG-M | 11-F | FIN | 8 | 4 | 3 | 7 | 12 | B |
| 1994 WM | 11-F | FIN | 8 | 5 | 6 | 11 | 4 | S |
| 1995 WM | 11-F | FIN | 8 | 5 | 5 | 10 | 18 | G |
| 1996 WCH | 11-F | FIN | 4 | 1 | 3 | 4 | 4 | 5th |
| 1997 WM | 11-F | FIN | 6 | 2 | 2 | 4 | 2 | 5th |
| 1998 OG-M | 11-F | FIN | 6 | 2 | 8 | 10 | 4 | B |
| 1999 WM | 11-F | FIN | 10 | 4 | 12 | 16 | 4 | S |
| 2003 WM | 11-F | FIN | 7 | 1 | 10 | 11 | 4 | 5th |
| 2004 WCH | 11-F | FIN | 6 | 3 | 1 | 4 | 2 | 2nd |
| 2006 OG-M | 11-F | FIN | 8 | 3 | 8 | 11 | 12 | S |
| 2008 WM | 11-F | FIN | 6 | 0 | 3 | 3 | 4 | B |
| 2010 OG-M | 11-F | FIN | 6 | 0 | 2 | 2 | 6 | B |
| **Totals WM20** | | | **14** | **4** | **14** | **18** | **18** | **—** |
| **Totals WM** | | | **51** | **17** | **39** | **56** | **38** | **G,2S,B** |
| **Totals OG-M** | | | **28** | **9** | **21** | **30** | **34** | **S,3B** |
| **Totals IIHF-NHL** | | | **10** | **4** | **4** | **8** | **6** | **—** |

~OG-M All-Star Team/Forward (2006), WM IIHF Directorate Best Forward (1995, 1999), WM All-Star Team/Forward (1994, 1995, 1999), WCH All-Star Team/Forward (2004)

**Kokarev, Denis**
**b. Tver, Soviet Union (Russia), June 17, 1985**

| | | | | | | | | |
|---|---|---|---|---|---|---|---|---|
| 2012 WM | 19-F | RUS | 10 | 1 | 0 | 1 | 4 | G |

**Kolarz, Michael**
**b. Havirov, Czechoslovakia (Czech Republic), January 12, 1987**

| | | | | | | | | |
|---|---|---|---|---|---|---|---|---|
| 2007 WM20 | 3-D | CZE | 6 | 0 | 0 | 0 | 8 | 5th |

**Kolehmainen, Janne**
**b. Lappeenranta, Finland, March 22, 1986**

| | | | | | | | | |
|---|---|---|---|---|---|---|---|---|
| 2004 WM18 | 22-F | FIN | 6 | 1 | 1 | 2 | 4 | 7th |
| 2005 WM20 | 24-F | FIN | 6 | 1 | 0 | 1 | 2 | 5th |
| 2006 WM20 | 11-F | FIN | 7 | 2 | 1 | 3 | 14 | B |
| **Totals WM20** | | | **13** | **3** | **1** | **4** | **16** | **B** |

**Kolesnikov, Vladislav**
**b. Ust-Kamenogorsk, Soviet Union (Kazakhstan), July 27, 1984**

| | | | | | | | | |
|---|---|---|---|---|---|---|---|---|
| 2012 WM | 70-D | KAZ | 7 | 0 | 0 | 0 | 4 | 16th |

**Kolesnikovs, Nikita**
**b. Jelgava, Latvia, October 30, 1992**

| | | | | | | | | |
|---|---|---|---|---|---|---|---|---|
| 2010 WM18 | 13-D | LAT | 6 | 1 | 1 | 2 | 6 | 9th |
| 2012 WM20 | 3-D | LAT | 6 | 0 | 2 | 2 | 2 | 9th |

**Kollar, Andrej**
**b. Topolcany, Czechoslovakia (Slovakia), January 12, 1977**

| | | | | | | | | |
|---|---|---|---|---|---|---|---|---|
| 2006 WM | 27-F | SVK | 7 | 2 | 2 | 4 | 10 | 8th |
| 2008 WM | 72-F | SVK | 5 | 1 | 0 | 1 | 2 | 13th |
| **Totals WM** | | | **12** | **3** | **2** | **5** | **12** | **—** |

**Kolnik, Juraj**
**b. Nitra, Czechoslovakia (Slovakia), November 13, 1980**

| | | | | | | | | |
|---|---|---|---|---|---|---|---|---|
| 2000 WM20 | 27-F | SVK | 7 | 2 | 1 | 3 | 2 | 9th |
| 2004 WM | 39-F | SVK | 7 | 0 | 0 | 0 | 0 | 4th |
| 2008 WM | 13-F | SVK | 5 | 3 | 4 | 7 | 2 | 13th |
| **Totals WM** | | | **12** | **3** | **4** | **7** | **2** | **—** |

**Kolosov, Andrei**
**b. Novopotolsk, Soviet Union (Belarus), June 8, 1989**

| | | | | | | | | |
|---|---|---|---|---|---|---|---|---|
| 2012 WM | 8-F | BLR | 6 | 0 | 0 | 0 | 2 | 14th |

**Kolosov, Sergei**
**b. Novopolotsk, Soviet Union (Belarus), May 22, 1986**

| | | | | | | | | |
|---|---|---|---|---|---|---|---|---|
| 2003 WM18 | 7-D | BLR | 6 | 0 | 1 | 1 | 14 | 8th |
| 2004 WM18 | 7-D | BLR | 6 | 1 | 0 | 1 | 24 | 9th |
| 2005 WM20 | 7-D | BLR | 6 | 0 | 0 | 0 | 6 | 10th |
| 2008 WM | 25-D | BLR | 6 | 0 | 0 | 0 | 2 | 9th |
| 2010 OG-M | 25-D | BLR | 4 | 0 | 0 | 0 | 0 | 9th |
| 2010 WM | 25-D | BLR | 6 | 0 | 0 | 0 | 2 | 10th |
| 2011 WM | 25-D | BLR | 6 | 0 | 0 | 0 | 4 | 14th |
| **Totals WM18** | | | **12** | **1** | **1** | **2** | **38** | **—** |
| **Totals WM** | | | **18** | **0** | **0** | **0** | **8** | **—** |

**Koltsov, Konstantin**
**b. Minsk, Soviet Union (Belarus), April 17, 1981**

| | | | | | | | | |
|---|---|---|---|---|---|---|---|---|
| 1999 WM20 | 28-F | BLR | 6 | 4 | 3 | 7 | 30 | 10th |
| 1999 WM | 28-F | BLR | 6 | 0 | 0 | 0 | 4 | 9th |
| 2001 WM20 | 28-F | BLR | 6 | 4 | 1 | 5 | 2 | 9th |
| 2001 WM | 28-F | BLR | 6 | 0 | 0 | 0 | 4 | 14th |
| 2002 OG-M | 28-F | BLR | 2 | 0 | 0 | 0 | 0 | 4th |
| 2005 WM | 28-F | BLR | 6 | 3 | 3 | 6 | 2 | 10th |
| 2007 WM | 28-F | BLR | 3 | 2 | 2 | 4 | 2 | 11th |
| 2008 WM | 28-F | BLR | 3 | 1 | 2 | 3 | 0 | 9th |
| 2009 WM | 28-F | BLR | 5 | 1 | 0 | 1 | 2 | 8th |
| 2010 OG-M | 28-F | BLR | 4 | 0 | 2 | 2 | 0 | 9th |
| 2012 WM | 28-F | BLR | 7 | 2 | 0 | 2 | 8 | 14th |
| **Totals WM20** | | | **12** | **8** | **4** | **12** | **32** | **—** |
| **Totals WM** | | | **36** | **9** | **7** | **16** | **22** | **—** |
| **Totals OG-M** | | | **6** | **0** | **2** | **2** | **0** | **—** |

**Komarek, Konstantin**
**b. Vienna, Austria, November 8, 1992**

| | | | | | | | | |
|---|---|---|---|---|---|---|---|---|
| 2010 WM20 | 15-F | AUT | 6 | 5 | 1 | 6 | 8 | 10th |

**Komaristy, Alexander**
**b. Severodonetsk, Soviet Union (Ukraine), October 2, 1989**

| | | | | | | | | |
|---|---|---|---|---|---|---|---|---|
| 2009 WM20 | 13-F | RUS | 7 | 0 | 2 | 2 | 2 | B |

**Komarov, Leo**
**b. Narva, Soviet Union (Estonia), January 23, 1987**

| | | | | | | | | |
|---|---|---|---|---|---|---|---|---|
| 2006 WM20 | 16-F | FIN | 7 | 0 | 3 | 3 | 32 | B |
| 2007 WM20 | 22-F | FIN | 6 | 2 | 1 | 3 | 16 | 6th |
| 2009 WM | 41-F | FIN | 5 | 0 | 1 | 1 | 4 | 5th |
| 2010 WM | 71-F | FIN | 7 | 1 | 0 | 1 | 0 | 6th |
| 2011 WM | 71-F | FIN | 8 | 0 | 2 | 2 | 2 | G |
| 2012 WM | 71-F | FIN | 10 | 1 | 0 | 1 | 4 | 4th |
| **Totals WM20** | | | **13** | **2** | **4** | **6** | **48** | **B** |
| **Totals WM** | | | **30** | **2** | **3** | **5** | **10** | **G** |

**Komarov, Nikita**
**b. Novopolotsk, Soviet Union (Belarus), June 28, 1988**

| | | | | | | | | |
|---|---|---|---|---|---|---|---|---|
| 2007 WM20 | 17-F | BLR | 6 | 1 | 0 | 1 | 4 | 10th |

**Komisarek, Mike**
**b. West Islip, New York, United States, January 19, 1982**

| | | | | | | | | |
|---|---|---|---|---|---|---|---|---|
| 2000 WM18 | 6-D | USA | 6 | 0 | 0 | 0 | 12 | 8th |
| 2001 WM20 | 6-D | USA | 7 | 0 | 0 | 0 | 0 | 5th |
| 2002 WM20 | 8-D | USA | 7 | 0 | 2 | 2 | 14 | 5th |
| 2006 WM | 55-D | USA | 7 | 0 | 1 | 1 | 4 | 7th |
| 2011 WM | 8-D | USA | 7 | 1 | 1 | 2 | 6 | 8th |
| **Totals WM20** | | | **14** | **0** | **2** | **2** | **14** | **—** |
| **Totals WM** | | | **14** | **1** | **2** | **3** | **10** | **—** |

**Kondrats, Ricards**
**b. December 21, 1994**

| | | | | | | | | |
|---|---|---|---|---|---|---|---|---|
| 2012 WM18 | 9-F | LAT | 6 | 1 | 2 | 3 | 2 | 9th |

**Konkov, Roman**
**b. Nizhni Novgorod, Russia, March 4, 1993**

| | | | | | | | | |
|---|---|---|---|---|---|---|---|---|
| 2011 WM18 | 11-F | RUS | 7 | 2 | 2 | 4 | 22 | B |

**Konnov, Pavel**
**b. Minsk, Belarus, March 1, 1992**

| | | | | | | | | |
|---|---|---|---|---|---|---|---|---|
| 2010 WM18 | 8-F | BLR | 4 | 0 | 0 | 0 | 25 | 10th |

**Kontiola, Petri**
**b. Seinajoki, Finland, October 4, 1984**

| | | | | | | | | |
|---|---|---|---|---|---|---|---|---|
| 2004 WM20 | 26-F | FIN | 7 | 1 | 1 | 2 | 2 | B |
| 2007 WM | 41-F | FIN | 9 | 2 | 5 | 7 | 2 | S |
| 2010 WM | 27-F | FIN | 7 | 3 | 0 | 3 | 2 | 6th |
| 2012 WM | 27-F | FIN | 10 | 0 | 2 | 2 | 4 | 4th |
| **Totals WM** | | | **26** | **5** | **7** | **12** | **8** | **S** |

**Kopecky, Peter**
**b. Ilava, Czechoslovakia (Slovakia), January 19, 1989**

| | | | | | | | | |
|---|---|---|---|---|---|---|---|---|
| 2009 WM20 | 9-F | SVK | 7 | 0 | 1 | 1 | 6 | 4th |

**Kopecky, Tomas**
**b. Ilava, Czechoslovakia (Slovakia), February 5, 1982**

| | | | | | | | | |
|---|---|---|---|---|---|---|---|---|
| 2000 WM18 | 19-F | SVK | 1 | 0 | 0 | 0 | 0 | 5th |
| 2000 WM20 | 22-F | SVK | 7 | 0 | 2 | 2 | 4 | 9th |
| 2001 WM20 | 22-F | SVK | 7 | 2 | 2 | 4 | 16 | 8th |
| 2002 WM20 | 22-F | SVK | 7 | 3 | 5 | 8 | 22 | 8th |
| 2010 OG-M | 82-F | SVK | 7 | 1 | 0 | 1 | 2 | 4th |
| 2012 WM | 82-F | SVK | 10 | 5 | 1 | 6 | 4 | S |
| **Totals WM20** | | | **21** | **5** | **9** | **14** | **42** | **—** |

**Kopitar, Anze**
**b. Jesenice, Yugoslavia (Slovenia), August 24, 1987**

| | | | | | | | | |
|---|---|---|---|---|---|---|---|---|
| 2005 WM | 25-F | SLO | 6 | 1 | 0 | 1 | 2 | 13th |
| 2006 WM | 13-F | SLO | 6 | 3 | 6 | 9 | 2 | 16th |
| 2008 WM | 11-F | SLO | 5 | 3 | 1 | 4 | 2 | 15th |
| **Totals WM** | | | **17** | **7** | **7** | **14** | **6** | **—** |

**Korabeinikov, Andrei**
**b. V-Kazakhstanskaya, Soviet Union (Kazakhstan), April 1, 1987**

| | | | | | | | | |
|---|---|---|---|---|---|---|---|---|
| 2012 WM | 5-D | KAZ | 4 | 0 | 0 | 0 | 2 | 16th |

**Korenko, Michal**
**b. Poprad, Czechoslovakia (Slovakia), July 22, 1987**

| | | | | | | | | |
|---|---|---|---|---|---|---|---|---|
| 2006 WM20 | 6-D | SVK | 6 | 0 | 0 | 0 | 0 | 8th |
| 2007 WM20 | 6-D | SVK | 6 | 2 | 1 | 3 | 4 | 8th |
| **Totals WM20** | | | **12** | **2** | **1** | **3** | **4** | **—** |

**Koreshkov, Rostislav**
**b. Samara, Soviet Union (Russia), December 24, 1989**

| | | | | | | | | |
|---|---|---|---|---|---|---|---|---|
| 2008 WM20 | 17-F | KAZ | 6 | 0 | 0 | 0 | 0 | 8th |

**Korhonen, Risto**
**b. Sotkamo, Finland, November 27, 1986**

| | | | | | | | | |
|---|---|---|---|---|---|---|---|---|
| 2003 WM18 | 5-D | FIN | 6 | 0 | 2 | 2 | 6 | 7th |
| 2004 WM18 | 4-D | FIN | 6 | 1 | 1 | 2 | 4 | 7th |
| 2005 WM20 | 5-D | FIN | 6 | 0 | 1 | 1 | 10 | 5th |
| 2006 WM20 | 4-D | FIN | 7 | 0 | 0 | 0 | 2 | B |
| **Totals WM18** | | | **12** | **1** | **3** | **4** | **10** | **—** |
| **Totals WM20** | | | **13** | **0** | **1** | **1** | **12** | **B** |

**Korhonen, Ville**
**b. Tampere, Finland, May 20, 1987**

| | | | | | | | | |
|---|---|---|---|---|---|---|---|---|
| 2005 WM18 | 15-F | FIN | 6 | 0 | 0 | 0 | 2 | 7th |
| 2007 WM20 | 29-F | FIN | 6 | 0 | 0 | 0 | 4 | 6th |

**Korim, Karol**
**b. Nitra, Slovakia, August 20, 1993**

| | | | | | | | | |
|---|---|---|---|---|---|---|---|---|
| 2011 WM18 | 4-D | SVK | 6 | 1 | 3 | 4 | 10 | 10th |

**Kormann, Nicolas**
**b. Gerzensee, Switzerland, May 29, 1990**

| | | | | | | | | |
|---|---|---|---|---|---|---|---|---|
| 2008 WM18 | 23-F | SUI | 6 | 0 | 0 | 0 | 14 | 8th |

**Korner, Alexander**
**b. Linz, Austria, October 23, 1990**

| | | | | | | | | |
|---|---|---|---|---|---|---|---|---|
| 2010 WM20 | 25-F | AUT | 5 | 0 | 0 | 0 | 2 | 10th |

**Korneyev, Konstantin**
**b. Moscow, Soviet Union (Russia), June 5, 1984**

| | | | | | | | | |
|---|---|---|---|---|---|---|---|---|
| 2002 WM18 | 3-D | RUS | 8 | 2 | 5 | 7 | 0 | S |
| 2003 WM20 | 3-D | RUS | 6 | 0 | 2 | 2 | 4 | G |
| 2004 WM20 | 3-D | RUS | 6 | 0 | 5 | 5 | 6 | 5th |
| 2007 WM | 2-D | RUS | 1 | 0 | 0 | 0 | 0 | B |
| 2008 WM | 22-D | RUS | 9 | 1 | 5 | 6 | 0 | G |
| 2009 WM | 22-D | RUS | 6 | 0 | 1 | 1 | 2 | G |
| 2010 OG-M | 22-D | RUS | 4 | 0 | 0 | 0 | 4 | 6th |
| 2010 WM | 22-D | RUS | 9 | 0 | 0 | 0 | 2 | S |
| 2011 WM | 22-D | RUS | 9 | 0 | 3 | 3 | 0 | 4th |
| **Totals WM20** | | | **12** | **0** | **7** | **7** | **10** | **G** |
| **Totals WM** | | | **34** | **1** | **9** | **10** | **4** | **2G,S,B** |

~WM18 All-Star Team/Defence (2002)

**Korobov, Dmitri**
**b. Novopolotsk, Soviet Union (Belarus), March 12, 1989**

| | | | | | | | | |
|---|---|---|---|---|---|---|---|---|
| 2006 WM18 | 3-D | BLR | 6 | 2 | 0 | 2 | 6 | 9th |
| 2007 WM20 | 24-D | BLR | 6 | 0 | 0 | 0 | 10 | 10th |
| 2009 WM | 89-D | BLR | 3 | 0 | 0 | 0 | 0 | 8th |
| 2011 WM | 89-D | BLR | 6 | 2 | 3 | 5 | 0 | 14th |
| 2012 WM | 89-D | BLR | 7 | 0 | 3 | 3 | 4 | 14th |
| **Totals WM** | | | **16** | **2** | **5** | **8** | **4** | **—** |

**Korolik, Sergei**
**b. Mogilyov, Soviet Union (Belarus), March 7, 1990**

| | | | | | | | | |
|---|---|---|---|---|---|---|---|---|
| 2008 WM18 | 18-F | BLR | 6 | 1 | 0 | 1 | 4 | 9th |

**Korolyov, Anton**
**b. Moscow, Soviet Union (Russia), January 26, 1988**

| | | | | | | | | |
|---|---|---|---|---|---|---|---|---|
| 2008 WM20 | 13-F | RUS | 7 | 3 | 1 | 4 | 4 | B |

**Korostin, Sergei**
**b. Prokopiesk, Soviet Union (Russia), July 5, 1989**

| | | | | | | | | |
|---|---|---|---|---|---|---|---|---|
| 2007 WM18 | 21-F | RUS | 7 | 5 | 1 | 6 | 4 | G |
| 2009 WM20 | 23-F | RUS | 7 | 1 | 1 | 2 | 6 | B |

**Korotki, Yegor**
**b. Murmansk, Soviet Union (Russia), February 2, 1988**

| | | | | | | | | |
|---|---|---|---|---|---|---|---|---|
| 2006 WM18 | 17-D | BLR | 6 | 0 | 0 | 0 | 2 | 9th |
| 2007 WM20 | 16-D | BLR | 6 | 0 | 0 | 0 | 2 | 10th |

**Korovkin, Andrei**
**b. V-Kazakhstanskaya, Soviet Union (Kazakhstan), March 19, 1989**

| | | | | | | | | |
|---|---|---|---|---|---|---|---|---|
| 2009 WM20 | 5-D | KAZ | 4 | 0 | 0 | 0 | 2 | 10th |

**Korpikoski, Lauri**
**b. Turku, Finland, July 28, 1986**

| | | | | | | | | |
|---|---|---|---|---|---|---|---|---|
| 2004 WM18 | 26-F | FIN | 6 | 5 | 6 | 11 | 2 | 7th |
| 2005 WM20 | 25-F | FIN | 5 | 2 | 0 | 2 | 6 | 5th |
| 2006 WM20 | 25-F | FIN | 7 | 1 | 5 | 6 | 4 | B |
| 2010 WM | 29-F | FIN | 7 | 0 | 0 | 0 | 0 | 6th |
| **Totals WM20** | | | **12** | **3** | **5** | **8** | **10** | **B** |

**Korsgaard, Lasse**
**b. Aalborg, Denmark, March 2, 1994**

| | | | | | | | | |
|---|---|---|---|---|---|---|---|---|
| 2012 WM18 | 18-F | DEN | 6 | 0 | 0 | 0 | 2 | 10th |

**Kosmachuk, Scott**
**b. Toronto, Ontario, Canada, January 24, 1994**

| | | | | | | | | |
|---|---|---|---|---|---|---|---|---|
| 2012 WM18 | 14-F | CAN | 7 | 0 | 0 | 0 | 4 | B |

**Kosov, Yaroslav**
**b. Magnitogorsk, Russia, July 5, 1993**

| | | | | | | | | |
|---|---|---|---|---|---|---|---|---|
| 2012 WM20 | 18-F | RUS | 7 | 2 | 2 | 4 | 0 | S |

**Kostalek, Jan**
**b. Prague, Czech Republic, February 17, 1995**

| | | | | | | | | |
|---|---|---|---|---|---|---|---|---|
| 2012 WM18 | 5-D | CZE | 6 | 0 | 1 | 1 | 6 | 8th |

**Kostitsyn, Andrei**
**b. Novopolotsk, Soviet Union (Belarus), February 3, 1985**

| | | | | | | | | |
|---|---|---|---|---|---|---|---|---|
| 2000 WM18 | 23-F | BLR | 6 | 0 | 0 | 0 | 4 | 10th |
| 2001 WM20 | 21-F | BLR | 6 | 0 | 0 | 0 | 2 | 9th |
| 2002 WM18 | 23-F | BLR | 8 | 7 | 3 | 10 | 18 | 5th |
| 2002 WM20 | 21-F | BLR | 6 | 3 | 0 | 3 | 0 | 9th |
| 2003 WM18 | 23-F | BLR | 6 | 6 | 9 | 15 | 28 | 8th |
| 2003 WM20 | 23-F | BLR | 6 | 2 | 1 | 3 | 0 | 10th |
| 2005 WM20 | 23-F | BLR | 5 | 1 | 4 | 5 | 6 | 10th |

| 2003 WM | 23-F | BLR | 2 | 1 | 0 | 1 | 2 | 14th |
|---|---|---|---|---|---|---|---|---|
| 2005 WM | 23-F | BLR | 6 | 0 | 0 | 0 | 4 | 10th |
| 2006 WM | 23-F | BLR | 6 | 1 | 4 | 5 | 6 | 6th |
| 2008 WM | 23-F | BLR | 5 | 2 | 1 | 3 | 18 | 9th |
| 2011 WM | 23-F | BLR | 5 | 3 | 4 | 7 | 4 | 14th |
| 2012 WM | 23-F | BLR | 3 | 0 | 2 | 2 | 27 | 14th |
| **Totals WM18** | | | **20** | **13** | **12** | **25** | **50** | **—** |
| **Totals WM20** | | | **23** | **6** | **5** | **11** | **8** | **—** |
| **Totals WM** | | | **27** | **7** | **11** | **18** | **61** | **—** |

**Kostitsyn, Sergei**
**b. Novopolotsk, Soviet Union (Belarus), March 20, 1987**

| 2003 WM18 | 24-F | BLR | 6 | 2 | 0 | 2 | 4 | 8th |
|---|---|---|---|---|---|---|---|---|
| 2004 WM18 | 13-F | BLR | 6 | 1 | 3 | 4 | 8 | 9th |
| 2005 WM20 | 22-F | BLR | 6 | 0 | 0 | 0 | 2 | 10th |
| 2007 WM20 | 23-F | BLR | 6 | 1 | 4 | 5 | 33 | 10th |
| 2008 WM | 74-F | BLR | 4 | 0 | 1 | 1 | 0 | 9th |
| 2010 OG-M | 74-F | BLR | 4 | 2 | 3 | 5 | 0 | 9th |
| 2012 WM | 74-F | BLR | 3 | 1 | 1 | 2 | 2 | 14th |
| **Totals WM18** | | | **12** | **3** | **3** | **6** | **12** | **—** |
| **Totals WM20** | | | **12** | **1** | **4** | **5** | **35** | **—** |
| **Totals WM** | | | **7** | **1** | **2** | **3** | **2** | **—** |

**Kostromitin, Dmitri**
**b. Chelyabinsk, Soviet Union (Russia), January 22, 1990**

| 2008 WM18 | 5-D | RUS | 6 | 0 | 0 | 0 | 4 | S |
|---|---|---|---|---|---|---|---|---|
| 2010 WM20 | 5-D | RUS | 6 | 0 | 0 | 0 | 2 | 6th |

**Kostyuchenok, Viktor**
**b. Minsk, Soviet Union (Belarus), June 7, 1979**

| 2006 WM | 43-D | BLR | 7 | 1 | 1 | 2 | 0 | 6th |
|---|---|---|---|---|---|---|---|---|
| 2007 WM | 43-D | BLR | 6 | 1 | 3 | 4 | 0 | 11th |
| 2008 WM | 43-D | BLR | 6 | 1 | 2 | 3 | 10 | 9th |
| 2009 WM | 43-D | BLR | 7 | 0 | 0 | 0 | 10 | 8th |
| 2010 OG-M | 43-D | BLR | 4 | 0 | 1 | 1 | 2 | 9th |
| 2010 WM | 43-D | BLR | 6 | 0 | 1 | 1 | 0 | 10th |
| 2011 WM | 43-D | BLR | 6 | 1 | 1 | 2 | 8 | 14th |
| 2012 WM | 43-D | BLR | 7 | 0 | 0 | 0 | 2 | 14th |
| **Totals WM** | | | **45** | **4** | **8** | **12** | **30** | **—** |

**Kotalik, Ales**
**b. Jindrichuv Hradec, Czechoslovakia (Czech Republic), December 23, 1978**

| 1998 WM20 | 23-F | CZE | 7 | 3 | 1 | 4 | 0 | 4th |
|---|---|---|---|---|---|---|---|---|
| 2006 OG-M | 22-F | CZE | 4 | 0 | 0 | 0 | 0 | B |
| 2008 WM | 12-F | CZE | 7 | 5 | 2 | 7 | 0 | 5th |
| 2009 WM | 12-F | CZE | 7 | 2 | 1 | 3 | 4 | 6th |
| **Totals WM** | | | **14** | **7** | **3** | **10** | **4** | **—** |

**Koudela, David**
**b. Prague, Czech Republic, April 20, 1992**

| 2010 WM18 | 24-F | CZE | 6 | 0 | 1 | 1 | 2 | 6th |
|---|---|---|---|---|---|---|---|---|

**Koukal, Petr**
**b. Nove mesto na Morave, Czechoslovakia (Czech Republic), August 16, 1982**

| 2010 WM | 42-F | CZE | 9 | 0 | 2 | 2 | 2 | G |
|---|---|---|---|---|---|---|---|---|
| 2012 WM | 42-F | CZE | 7 | 2 | 1 | 3 | 0 | B |
| **Totals WM** | | | **16** | **2** | **3** | **5** | **2** | **G,B** |

**Kousa, Mikko**
**b. Lahti, Finland, May 11, 1988**

| 2008 WM20 | 8-D | FIN | 6 | 1 | 2 | 3 | 4 | 6th |
|---|---|---|---|---|---|---|---|---|

**Kousal, Robert**
**b. Pardubice, Czechoslovakia (Czech Republic), October 7, 1990**

| 2010 WM20 | 13-F | CZE | 6 | 2 | 6 | 8 | 2 | 7th |
|---|---|---|---|---|---|---|---|---|

**Kovacevic, Sabahudin**
**b. Jesenice, Yugoslavia (Slovenia), February 26, 1986**

| 2011 WM | 86-D | SLO | 6 | 0 | 0 | 0 | 0 | 16th |
|---|---|---|---|---|---|---|---|---|

**Kovacik, Miroslav**
**b. Nitra, Czechoslovakia (Slovakia), November 9, 1978**

| 1998 WM20 | 26-F | SVK | 6 | 0 | 0 | 0 | 4 | 9th |
|---|---|---|---|---|---|---|---|---|
| 2006 WM | 21-F | SVK | 7 | 2 | 1 | 3 | 4 | 8th |
| 2007 WM | 47-F | SVK | 7 | 0 | 1 | 1 | 0 | 6th |
| 2008 WM | 47-F | SVK | 5 | 1 | 0 | 1 | 4 | 13th |
| **Totals WM** | | | **19** | **3** | **2** | **5** | **8** | **—** |

**Kovalchuk, Ilya**
**b. Tver, Soviet Union (Russia), April 15, 1983**

| 2000 WM18 | 28-F | RUS | 6 | 2 | 3 | 5 | 6 | S |
|---|---|---|---|---|---|---|---|---|
| 2001 WM18 | 17-F | RUS | 6 | 11 | 4 | 15 | 26 | G |
| 2001 WM20 | 17-F | RUS | 7 | 4 | 2 | 6 | 37 | 7th |
| 2002 OG-M | 71-F | RUS | 6 | 1 | 2 | 3 | 14 | B |
| 2003 WM | 71-F | RUS | 7 | 4 | 0 | 4 | 6 | 7th |
| 2004 WM | 71-F | RUS | 6 | 3 | 1 | 4 | 6 | 10th |
| 2004 WCH | 71-F | RUS | 4 | 1 | 0 | 1 | 4 | 6th |
| 2005 WM | 71-F | RUS | 9 | 3 | 3 | 6 | 4 | B |
| 2006 OG-M | 71-F | RUS | 8 | 4 | 1 | 5 | 31 | 4th |
| 2007 WM | 71-F | RUS | 9 | 2 | 5 | 7 | 10 | B |
| 2008 WM | 71-F | RUS | 8 | 2 | 6 | 8 | 52 | G |
| 2009 WM | 71-F | RUS | 9 | 5 | 9 | 14 | 4 | G |
| 2010 OG-M | 71-F | RUS | 4 | 1 | 2 | 3 | 0 | 6th |
| 2010 WM | 71-F | RUS | 9 | 2 | 10 | 12 | 2 | S |
| 2011 WM | 71-F | RUS | 9 | 3 | 5 | 8 | 6 | 4th |
| **Totals WM18** | | | **12** | **13** | **7** | **20** | **32** | **G,S** |
| **Totals WM** | | | **66** | **24** | **39** | **63** | **90** | **2G,S,2B** |
| **Totals OG-M** | | | **18** | **6** | **5** | **11** | **45** | **B** |

~WM MVP (2009), WM IIHF Directorate Best Forward (2009), WM All-Star Team/Forward (2009)

**Kovalev, Alexei** ~see Kovalyov, Alexei

**Kovalyov, Alexei**
**b. Togliatti, Soviet Union (Russia), February 24, 1973**

| 1992 WM20 | 27-F | RUS | 7 | 5 | 5 | 10 | 2 | G |
|---|---|---|---|---|---|---|---|---|
| 1992 OG-M | 14-F | RUS | 8 | 1 | 2 | 3 | 14 | G |
| 1992 WM | 14-F | RUS | 6 | 0 | 1 | 1 | 0 | 5th |
| 1996 WCH | 27-F | RUS | 5 | 2 | 1 | 3 | 8 | 4th |
| 1998 WM | 27-F | RUS | 6 | 5 | 3 | 8 | 14 | 5th |
| 2002 OG-M | 27-F | RUS | 6 | 3 | 1 | 4 | 4 | B |
| 2004 WCH | 27-F | RUS | 4 | 2 | 1 | 3 | 4 | 6th |
| 2005 WM | 27-F | RUS | 9 | 3 | 4 | 7 | 16 | B |
| 2006 OG-M | 27-F | RUS | 8 | 4 | 2 | 6 | 4 | 4th |
| **Totals WM** | | | **21** | **8** | **8** | **16** | **30** | **B** |
| **Totals OG-M** | | | **22** | **8** | **5** | **13** | **22** | **G,B** |
| **Totals IIHF-NHL** | | | **9** | **4** | **2** | **6** | **12** | **—** |

~WM IIHF Directorate Best Forward (2005), WM20 All-Star Team/Forward (1992)

**Kovar, Jan**
**b. Pisek, Czechoslovakia (Czech Republic), March 20, 1990**

| 2010 WM20 | 24-F | CZE | 6 | 3 | 3 | 6 | 2 | 7th |
|---|---|---|---|---|---|---|---|---|

**Kovyrshin, Yevgeni**
**b. Elektrostal, Soviet Union (Russia), January 25, 1986**

| 2009 WM | 15-F | BLR | 7 | 0 | 0 | 0 | 4 | 8th |
|---|---|---|---|---|---|---|---|---|
| 2010 WM | 88-F | BLR | 6 | 0 | 2 | 2 | 0 | 10th |
| 2011 WM | 88-F | BLR | 6 | 1 | 3 | 4 | 4 | 14th |
| 2012 WM | 88-F | BLR | 7 | 2 | 2 | 4 | 0 | 14th |
| **Totals WM** | | | **26** | **3** | **7** | **10** | **8** | **—** |

**Kozak, Lukas**
**b. Martin, Czechoslovakia (Slovakia), October 29, 1991**

| 2009 WM18 | 5-D | SVK | 6 | 0 | 0 | 0 | 6 | 7th |
|---|---|---|---|---|---|---|---|---|
| 2011 WM20 | 5-D | SVK | 6 | 0 | 0 | 0 | 2 | 8th |

**Kozak, Michal**
**b. Michalovce, Czechoslovakia (Slovakia), January 27, 1989**

| 2007 WM18 | 3-D | SVK | 6 | 0 | 0 | 0 | 8 | 5th |
|---|---|---|---|---|---|---|---|---|
| 2008 WM20 | 4-D | SVK | 6 | 0 | 0 | 0 | 6 | 7th |

**Kozlov, Viktor**
**b. Togliatti, Soviet Union (Russia), February 14, 1975**

| 1993 WM20 | 23-F | RUS | 7 | 2 | 1 | 3 | 2 | 6th |
|---|---|---|---|---|---|---|---|---|
| 1996 WM | 25-F | RUS | 8 | 0 | 3 | 3 | 0 | 4th |
| 1998 WM | 25-F | RUS | 6 | 4 | 5 | 9 | 0 | 5th |
| 2000 WM | 25-F | RUS | 6 | 1 | 3 | 4 | 2 | 9th |
| 2004 WCH | 22-F | RUS | 4 | 1 | 0 | 1 | 0 | 6th |
| 2005 WM | 25-F | RUS | 9 | 1 | 0 | 1 | 0 | B |
| 2006 OG-M | 25-F | RUS | 8 | 2 | 3 | 5 | 2 | 4th |
| 2010 OG-M | 52-F | RUS | 4 | 1 | 0 | 1 | 0 | 6th |
| 2010 WM | 52-F | RUS | 9 | 1 | 2 | 3 | 2 | S |
| **Totals WM** | | | **38** | **7** | **13** | **20** | **4** | **B** |
| **Totals OG-M** | | | **12** | **3** | **3** | **6** | **2** | **—** |

**Kozun, Brandon**
**b. Los Angeles, California, United States, March 8, 1990**

| 2010 WM20 | 17-F | CAN | 6 | 3 | 4 | 7 | 0 | S |
|---|---|---|---|---|---|---|---|---|

**Kparghai, Clarence**
**b. Monrovia, Liberia, May 13, 1985**

| 2005 WM20 | 23-D | SUI | 6 | 0 | 1 | 1 | 10 | 8th |
|---|---|---|---|---|---|---|---|---|

**Krajcik, Kristian**
**b. Trnava, Czechoslovakia (Slovakia), March 21, 1988**

| 2008 WM20 | 3-D | SVK | 6 | 0 | 0 | 0 | 2 | 7th |
|---|---|---|---|---|---|---|---|---|

**Krajicek, Lukas**
**b. Prostejov, Czechoslovakia (Czech Republic), March 11, 1983**

| 2002 WM20 | 7-D | CZE | 7 | 1 | 3 | 4 | 6 | 7th |
|---|---|---|---|---|---|---|---|---|
| 2003 WM20 | 29-D | CZE | 6 | 2 | 2 | 4 | 2 | 6th |
| 2006 WM | 2-D | CZE | 9 | 0 | 0 | 0 | 8 | S |
| 2011 WM | 25-D | CZE | 8 | 0 | 1 | 1 | 8 | B |
| 2012 WM | 25-D | CZE | 10 | 1 | 3 | 4 | 6 | B |
| Totals WM20 | | | 13 | 3 | 5 | 8 | 8 | — |
| **Totals WM** | | | **27** | **1** | **4** | **5** | **22** | **S,2B** |

**Kramer, Rene**
**b. Berlin, West Germany (Germany), October 24, 1987**

| 2005 WM18 | 24-D | GER | 6 | 1 | 0 | 1 | 6 | 8th |
|---|---|---|---|---|---|---|---|---|
| 2007 WM20 | 24-D | GER | 6 | 1 | 1 | 2 | 2 | 9th |

**Kranjc, Ales**
**b. Jesenice, Yugoslavia (Slovenia), July 29, 1981**

| 2003 WM | 6-D | SLO | 6 | 0 | 1 | 1 | 2 | 15th |
|---|---|---|---|---|---|---|---|---|
| 2006 WM | 28-D | SLO | 6 | 4 | 2 | 6 | 10 | 16th |
| 2008 WM | 28-D | SLO | 5 | 0 | 1 | 1 | 0 | 15th |
| 2011 WM | 28-D | SLO | 6 | 1 | 0 | 1 | 8 | 16th |
| **Totals WM** | | | **23** | **5** | **4** | **9** | **20** | **—** |

**Krasnoslabotsev, Vadim**
**b. Karagandinskaya, Soviet Union (Kazakhstan), August 16, 1983**

| 2006 WM | 81-F | KAZ | 6 | 1 | 1 | 2 | 4 | 15th |
|---|---|---|---|---|---|---|---|---|
| 2010 WM | 62-F | KAZ | 6 | 1 | 0 | 1 | 14 | 16th |
| 2012 WM | 62-F | KAZ | 7 | 3 | 0 | 3 | 0 | 16th |
| **Totals WM** | | | **19** | **5** | **1** | **6** | **18** | **—** |

**Kreider, Chris**
**b. Boxford, Massachusetts, United States, April 30, 1991**

| 2010 WM20 | 20-F | USA | 7 | 6 | 1 | 7 | 2 | G |
|---|---|---|---|---|---|---|---|---|
| 2010 WM | 19-F | USA | 6 | 1 | 1 | 2 | 0 | 13th |
| 2011 WM20 | 19-F | USA | 6 | 4 | 2 | 6 | 0 | B |
| 2011 WM | 19-F | USA | 7 | 2 | 1 | 3 | 6 | 8th |
| **Totals WM20** | | | **13** | **10** | **3** | **13** | **2** | **G,B** |
| **Totals WM** | | | **13** | **3** | **2** | **5** | **6** | **—** |

**Kreis, Sami**
**b. Egnach, Switzerland, April 4, 1994**

| 2011 WM18 | 28-D | SUI | 6 | 0 | 1 | 1 | 2 | 7th |
|---|---|---|---|---|---|---|---|---|
| 2012 WM18 | 9-D | SUI | 6 | 0 | 0 | 0 | 0 | 7th |
| **Totals WM18** | | | **12** | **0** | **1** | **1** | **2** | **—** |

**Krejci, Daniel**
**b. Prague, Czech Republic, April 27, 1992**

| 2009 WM18 | 8-D | CZE | 6 | 0 | 1 | 1 | 4 | 6th |
|---|---|---|---|---|---|---|---|---|
| 2012 WM20 | 12-D | CZE | 6 | 0 | 4 | 4 | 2 | 5th |

**Krejci, David**
**b. Sternberk, Czechoslovakia (Czech Republic), April 28, 1986**

| 2004 WM18 | 23-F | CZE | 7 | 3 | 4 | 7 | 0 | B |
|---|---|---|---|---|---|---|---|---|
| 2005 WM20 | 16-F | CZE | 7 | 0 | 1 | 1 | 2 | B |
| 2006 WM20 | 23-F | CZE | 6 | 3 | 3 | 6 | 4 | 6th |
| 2008 WM | 64-F | CZE | 5 | 0 | 0 | 0 | 2 | 5th |
| 2010 OG-M | 46-F | CZE | 5 | 2 | 1 | 3 | 6 | 7th |
| 2012 WM | 46-F | CZE | 10 | 3 | 4 | 7 | 4 | B |
| **Totals WM20** | | | **13** | **3** | **4** | **7** | **6** | **B** |
| **Totals WM** | | | **15** | **3** | **4** | **7** | **6** | **B** |

**Krejcik, Jakub**
**b. Prague, (Czechoslovakia), Czech Republic, June 25, 1991**

| 2012 WM | 30-D | CZE | 6 | 0 | 0 | 0 | 0 | B |
|---|---|---|---|---|---|---|---|---|

**Krempasky, Boris**
**b. Levoca, Slovakia, October 28, 1992**

| 2010 WM18 | 10-F | SVK | 6 | 0 | 3 | 3 | 2 | 8th |
|---|---|---|---|---|---|---|---|---|

**Kretschmann, Christian**
**b. Monchengladbach, Germany, March 13, 1993**

| 2011 WM18 | 19-F | GER | 6 | 0 | 0 | 0 | 2 | 6th |
|---|---|---|---|---|---|---|---|---|

**Kreutzer, Daniel**
**b. Dusseldorf, West Germany (Germany), October 23, 1979**

| | | | | | | | | |
|---|---|---|---|---|---|---|---|---|
| 1997 WM20 | 12-F | GER | 3 | 0 | 2 | 2 | 0 | 9th |
| 1998 WM20 | 22-F | GER | 6 | 0 | 2 | 2 | 6 | 10th |
| 2001 WM | 26-F | GER | 7 | 2 | 2 | 4 | 4 | 5th |
| 2002 OG-M | 26-F | GER | 7 | 0 | 0 | 0 | 0 | 8th |
| 2002 WM | 26-F | GER | 7 | 1 | 2 | 3 | 27 | 8th |
| 2003 WM | 26-F | GER | 7 | 2 | 1 | 3 | 4 | 6th |
| 2004 WM | 26-F | GER | 6 | 1 | 2 | 3 | 4 | 9th |
| 2004 WCH | 26-F | GER | 4 | 1 | 1 | 2 | 4 | 8th |
| 2005 WM | 26-F | GER | 6 | 1 | 1 | 2 | 6 | 15th |
| 2006 OG-M | 26-F | GER | 5 | 0 | 2 | 2 | 2 | 10th |
| 2007 WM | 26-F | GER | 6 | 0 | 2 | 2 | 6 | 9th |
| 2009 WM | 26-F | GER | 6 | 0 | 0 | 0 | 2 | 15th |
| 2010 WM | 26-F | GER | 7 | 1 | 3 | 4 | 6 | 4th |
| 2011 WM | 26-F | GER | 5 | 0 | 0 | 0 | 2 | 7th |
| **Totals WM20** | | | **9** | **0** | **4** | **4** | **6** | **—** |
| **Totals WM** | | | **57** | **8** | **13** | **21** | **61** | **—** |
| **Totals OG-M** | | | **12** | **0** | **2** | **2** | **2** | **—** |

**Kristensen, Emil**
**b. Esbjerg, Denmark, September 20, 1992**

| | | | | | | | | |
|---|---|---|---|---|---|---|---|---|
| 2012 WM18 | 21-F | DEN | 6 | 0 | 0 | 0 | 2 | 10th |
| 2012 WM20 | 9-D | DEN | 6 | 1 | 0 | 1 | 0 | 10th |

**Kristensen, Kasper**
**b. Herning, Denmark, July 11, 1990**

| | | | | | | | | |
|---|---|---|---|---|---|---|---|---|
| 2008 WM18 | 10-F | DEN | 6 | 0 | 0 | 0 | 0 | 10th |

**Kristiansen, Tommy**
**b. Sarpsborg, Norway, May 26, 1989**

| | | | | | | | | |
|---|---|---|---|---|---|---|---|---|
| 2006 WM18 | 15-F | NOR | 6 | 1 | 0 | 1 | 10 | 10th |
| 2011 WM | 15-F | NOR | 3 | 0 | 0 | 0 | 4 | 6th |
| 2012 WM | 15-F | NOR | 6 | 0 | 0 | 0 | 2 | 8th |
| **Totals WM** | | | **9** | **0** | **0** | **0** | **6** | **—** |

**Kristler, Andreas**
**b. Lienz, Austria, August 30, 1990**

| | | | | | | | | |
|---|---|---|---|---|---|---|---|---|
| 2009 WM | 37-F | AUT | 6 | 0 | 0 | 0 | 4 | 14th |
| 2010 WM20 | 18-F | AUT | 6 | 2 | 4 | 6 | 10 | 10th |

**Kristo, Danny**
**b. Eden Prairie, Minnesota, United States, June 18, 1990**

| | | | | | | | | |
|---|---|---|---|---|---|---|---|---|
| 2008 WM18 | 8-F | USA | 7 | 3 | 3 | 6 | 2 | G |
| 2009 WM20 | 18-F | USA | 6 | 1 | 0 | 1 | 0 | 5th |
| 2010 WM20 | 8-F | USA | 7 | 5 | 3 | 8 | 0 | G |
| **Totals WM20** | | | **13** | **6** | **3** | **9** | **0** | **G** |

**Kristoffersen, Jon-Rene**
**b. Fredrikstad, Norway, August 5, 1991**

| | | | | | | | | |
|---|---|---|---|---|---|---|---|---|
| 2009 WM18 | 28-D | NOR | 6 | 0 | 0 | 0 | 0 | 9th |

**Kronthaler, Stephan**
**b. Landshut, Germany, May 2, 1993**

| | | | | | | | | |
|---|---|---|---|---|---|---|---|---|
| 2011 WM18 | 8-D | GER | 5 | 0 | 1 | 1 | 0 | 6th |

**Kronwall, Niklas**
**b. Jarfalla, Sweden, January 12, 1981**

| | | | | | | | | |
|---|---|---|---|---|---|---|---|---|
| 1999 WM18 | 22-D | SWE | 7 | 0 | 4 | 4 | 10 | S |
| 2000 WM20 | 4-D | SWE | 7 | 5 | 1 | 6 | 10 | 5th |
| 2001 WM20 | 4-D | SWE | 6 | 0 | 1 | 1 | 2 | 4th |
| 2003 WM | 8-D | SWE | 5 | 0 | 0 | 0 | 4 | S |
| 2005 WM | 7-D | SWE | 9 | 3 | 3 | 6 | 10 | 4th |
| 2006 OG-M | 7-D | SWE | 2 | 1 | 1 | 2 | 8 | G |
| 2006 WM | 7-D | SWE | 8 | 2 | 8 | 10 | 10 | G |
| 2010 OG-M | 55-D | SWE | 4 | 0 | 0 | 0 | 2 | 5th |
| 2012 WM | 7-D | SWE | 8 | 1 | 0 | 1 | 4 | 6th |
| **Totals WM20** | | | **13** | **5** | **2** | **7** | **12** | **—** |
| **Totals WM** | | | **30** | **6** | **11** | **17** | **28** | **G,S** |
| **Totals OG-M** | | | **6** | **1** | **1** | **2** | **10** | **G** |

~Triple Gold Club
~WM MVP (2006), WM IIHF Directorate Best Defenceman (2006), WM All-Star Team/Defence (2005, 2006)

**Kronwall, Staffan**
**b. Jarfalla, Sweden, September 10, 1982**

| | | | | | | | | |
|---|---|---|---|---|---|---|---|---|
| 2002 WM20 | 6-D | SWE | 7 | 0 | 0 | 0 | 4 | 6th |
| 2011 WM | 24-D | SWE | 9 | 1 | 3 | 4 | 4 | S |
| 2012 WM | 4-D | SWE | 8 | 1 | 1 | 2 | 2 | 6th |
| **Totals WM** | | | **17** | **2** | **4** | **6** | **6** | **S** |

**Krueger, Justin**
**b. Dusseldorf, West Germany (Germany), October 6, 1986**

| | | | | | | | | |
|---|---|---|---|---|---|---|---|---|
| 2010 WM | 3-D | GER | 9 | 0 | 1 | 1 | 0 | 4th |
| 2011 WM | 3-D | GER | 7 | 0 | 1 | 1 | 8 | 7th |
| 2012 WM | 3-D | GER | 7 | 1 | 0 | 1 | 2 | 12th |
| **Totals WM** | | | **23** | **1** | **2** | **3** | **10** | **—** |

**Kruger, Marcus**
**b. Stockholm, Sweden, May 27, 1990**

| | | | | | | | | |
|---|---|---|---|---|---|---|---|---|
| 2010 WM20 | 24-F | SWE | 6 | 0 | 6 | 6 | 2 | B |
| 2011 WM | 32-F | SWE | 9 | 2 | 1 | 3 | 10 | S |
| 2012 WM | 32-F | SWE | 8 | 3 | 2 | 5 | 6 | 6th |
| **Totals WM** | | | **17** | **5** | **3** | **8** | **16** | **S** |

**Krysanov, Anton**
**b. Togliatti, Soviet Union (Russia), March 25, 1987**

| | | | | | | | | |
|---|---|---|---|---|---|---|---|---|
| 2005 WM18 | 16-F | RUS | 6 | 0 | 3 | 3 | 8 | 5th |
| 2007 WM20 | 21-F | RUS | 6 | 0 | 3 | 3 | 0 | S |

**Kuba, Filip**
**b. Ostrava, Czechoslovakia (Czech Republic), December 29, 1976**

| | | | | | | | | |
|---|---|---|---|---|---|---|---|---|
| 2001 WM | 8-D | CZE | 9 | 1 | 1 | 2 | 8 | G |
| 2002 WM | 8-D | CZE | 7 | 0 | 3 | 3 | 18 | 5th |
| 2006 OG-M | 17-D | CZE | 8 | 1 | 0 | 1 | 0 | B |
| 2008 WM | 71-D | CZE | 7 | 1 | 2 | 3 | 4 | 5th |
| 2010 OG-M | 17-D | CZE | 5 | 0 | 1 | 1 | 0 | 7th |
| **Totals WM** | | | **23** | **2** | **6** | **8** | **30** | **G** |
| **Totals OG-M** | | | **13** | **1** | **1** | **2** | **0** | **B** |

**Kubalik, Tomas**
**b. Plzen, Czechoslovakia (Czech Republic), May 1, 1990**

| | | | | | | | | |
|---|---|---|---|---|---|---|---|---|
| 2007 WM18 | 22-F | CZE | 6 | 1 | 1 | 2 | 4 | 9th |
| 2009 WM20 | 18-F | CZE | 6 | 0 | 2 | 2 | 4 | 6th |
| 2010 WM20 | 18-F | CZE | 6 | 4 | 5 | 9 | 8 | 7th |
| **Totals WM20** | | | **12** | **4** | **7** | **11** | **12** | **—** |

**Kubena, Pavel**
**b. Blansko, Czechoslovakia (Czech Republic), April 1, 1988**

| | | | | | | | | |
|---|---|---|---|---|---|---|---|---|
| 2006 WM18 | 14-F | CZE | 7 | 0 | 0 | 0 | 6 | B |
| 2008 WM20 | 13-F | CZE | 6 | 0 | 1 | 1 | 0 | 5th |

**Kubina, Pavel**
**b. Celadna, Czechoslovakia (Czech Republic), April 15, 1977**

| | | | | | | | | |
|---|---|---|---|---|---|---|---|---|
| 1996 WM20 | 13-D | CZE | 6 | 0 | 2 | 2 | 8 | 4th |
| 1999 WM | 23-D | CZE | 12 | 2 | 6 | 8 | 12 | G |
| 2001 WM | 13-D | CZE | 9 | 2 | 3 | 5 | 18 | G |
| 2002 OG-M | 13-D | CZE | 4 | 0 | 1 | 1 | 0 | 7th |
| 2002 WM | 13-D | CZE | 7 | 3 | 4 | 7 | 8 | 5th |
| 2005 WM | 13-D | CZE | 9 | 2 | 2 | 4 | 10 | G |
| 2006 OG-M | 13-D | CZE | 8 | 1 | 1 | 2 | 12 | B |
| 2010 OG-M | 77-D | CZE | 5 | 0 | 0 | 0 | 2 | 7th |
| **Totals WM** | | | **37** | **9** | **15** | **24** | **48** | **3G** |
| **Totals OG-M** | | | **17** | **1** | **2** | **3** | **14** | **B** |

~WM All-Star Team/Defence (1999)

**Kuchejda, David**
**b. Vitkov, Czechoslovakia (Czech Republic), June 12, 1987**

| | | | | | | | | |
|---|---|---|---|---|---|---|---|---|
| 2005 WM18 | 21-F | CZE | 7 | 3 | 2 | 5 | 6 | 4th |
| 2007 WM20 | 24-F | CZE | 5 | 0 | 0 | 0 | 4 | 5th |

**Kucherov, Nikita**
**b. Maikop, Russia, June 17, 1993**

| | | | | | | | | |
|---|---|---|---|---|---|---|---|---|
| 2011 WM18 | 16-F | RUS | 7 | 11 | 10 | 21 | 6 | B |
| 2012 WM20 | 9-F | RUS | 7 | 2 | 5 | 7 | 2 | S |

~WM18 IIHF Directorate Best Forward (2011)

**Kucheryavenko, Alexander**
**b. Moscow, Soviet Union (Russia), August 27, 1987**

| | | | | | | | | |
|---|---|---|---|---|---|---|---|---|
| 2005 WM18 | 26-F | RUS | 6 | 1 | 4 | 5 | 8 | 5th |
| 2007 WM20 | 15-F | RUS | 6 | 0 | 1 | 1 | 2 | S |

**Kudelka, Tomas**
**b. Gottwaldov (Zlin), Czechoslovakia (Czech Republic), March 10, 1987**

| | | | | | | | | |
|---|---|---|---|---|---|---|---|---|
| 2005 WM18 | 10-D | CZE | 7 | 0 | 4 | 4 | 6 | 4th |
| 2006 WM20 | 15-D | CZE | 6 | 1 | 0 | 1 | 10 | 6th |
| 2007 WM20 | 8-D | CZE | 6 | 1 | 2 | 3 | 6 | 5th |
| **Totals WM20** | | | **12** | **2** | **2** | **4** | **16** | **—** |

**Kudrna, Andrej**
**b. Nove Zamky, Slovakia, May 11, 1991**

| | | | | | | | | |
|---|---|---|---|---|---|---|---|---|
| 2011 WM20 | 23-F | SVK | 6 | 0 | 1 | 1 | 4 | 8th |

**Kudroc, Kristian**
**b. Michalovce, Czechoslovakia (Slovakia), May 21, 1981**

| | | | | | | | | |
|---|---|---|---|---|---|---|---|---|
| 1999 WM18 | 12-D | SVK | 7 | 0 | 1 | 1 | 11 | B |
| 2000 WM20 | 8-D | SVK | 7 | 0 | 0 | 0 | 8 | — |
| 2012 WM | 78-D | SVK | 1 | 0 | 0 | 0 | 0 | S |

**Kugryshev, Dmitri**
**b. Balakovo, Soviet Union (Russia), January 18, 1990**

| | | | | | | | | |
|---|---|---|---|---|---|---|---|---|
| 2007 WM18 | 18-F | RUS | 7 | 2 | 4 | 6 | 4 | G |
| 2008 WM18 | 18-F | RUS | 3 | 2 | 1 | 3 | 4 | S |
| 2008 WM20 | 18-F | RUS | 7 | 1 | 3 | 4 | 4 | B |
| 2009 WM20 | 18-F | RUS | 7 | 1 | 1 | 2 | 6 | B |
| **Totals WM18** | | | **10** | **4** | **5** | **9** | **8** | **G,S** |
| **Totals WM20** | | | **14** | **2** | **4** | **6** | **10** | **2B** |

**Kuhnhackl, Tom**
**b. Landshut, Germany, January 21, 1992**

| | | | | | | | | |
|---|---|---|---|---|---|---|---|---|
| 2009 WM18 | 14-F | GER | 6 | 1 | 1 | 2 | 4 | 10th |
| 2011 WM20 | 14-F | GER | 6 | 1 | 0 | 1 | 16 | 10th |

**Kukan, Dean**
**b. Volketswil, Switzerland, July 8, 1993**

| | | | | | | | | |
|---|---|---|---|---|---|---|---|---|
| 2010 WM18 | 14-D | SUI | 6 | 0 | 3 | 3 | 0 | 5th |
| 2011 WM18 | 14-D | SUI | 6 | 0 | 2 | 2 | 0 | 7th |
| 2012 WM20 | 14-D | SUI | 6 | 1 | 1 | 2 | 0 | 8th |
| **Totals WM18** | | | **12** | **0** | **5** | **5** | **0** | **—** |

**Kukkonen, Lasse**
**b. Oulu, Finland, September 18, 1981**

| | | | | | | | | |
|---|---|---|---|---|---|---|---|---|
| 1999 WM18 | 5-D | FIN | 7 | 1 | 0 | 1 | 0 | G |
| 2001 WM20 | 5-D | FIN | 7 | 0 | 0 | 0 | 2 | S |
| 2005 WM | 2-D | FIN | 7 | 0 | 0 | 0 | 2 | 7th |
| 2006 OG-M | 5-D | FIN | 2 | 0 | 0 | 0 | 0 | S |
| 2006 WM | 5-D | FIN | 9 | 2 | 0 | 2 | 8 | S |
| 2007 WM | 5-D | FIN | 9 | 0 | 1 | 1 | 4 | B |
| 2009 WM | 5-D | FIN | 6 | 0 | 0 | 0 | 4 | 5th |
| 2010 OG-M | 5-D | FIN | 6 | 0 | 1 | 1 | 4 | B |
| 2010 WM | 5-D | FIN | 6 | 0 | 0 | 0 | 2 | 6th |
| 2011 WM | 5-D | FIN | 9 | 0 | 0 | 0 | 0 | G |
| 2012 WM | 5-D | FIN | 10 | 0 | 1 | 1 | 0 | 4th |
| **Totals WM** | | | **56** | **2** | **2** | **4** | **20** | **G,S,B** |
| **Totals OG-M** | | | **8** | **0** | **1** | **1** | **0** | **S,B** |

**Kukumberg, Roman**
**b. Bratislava, Czechoslovakia (Slovakia), April 8, 1980**

| | | | | | | | | |
|---|---|---|---|---|---|---|---|---|
| 2000 WM20 | 26-F | SVK | 7 | 1 | 2 | 3 | 4 | 9th |
| 2004 WM | 30-F | SVK | 9 | 0 | 0 | 0 | 2 | 4th |
| 2007 WM | 16-F | SVK | 7 | 1 | 1 | 2 | 8 | 6th |
| 2010 WM | 16-F | SVK | 6 | 0 | 1 | 1 | 0 | 12th |
| **Totals WM** | | | **22** | **1** | **2** | **3** | **10** | **—** |

**Kukushkin, Sergei**
**b. Minsk, Soviet Union (Belarus), July 24, 1985**

| | | | | | | | | |
|---|---|---|---|---|---|---|---|---|
| 2003 WM18 | 17-F | BLR | 6 | 0 | 3 | 3 | 2 | 8th |
| 2005 WM20 | 26-F | BLR | 6 | 1 | 0 | 1 | 14 | 10th |
| 2006 WM | 26-F | BLR | 7 | 0 | 0 | 0 | 0 | 6th |
| 2007 WM | 26-F | BLR | 6 | 0 | 1 | 1 | 2 | 11th |
| **Totals WM** | | | **13** | **0** | **1** | **1** | **2** | **—** |

**Kulakov, Alexander**
**b. Minsk, Soviet Union (Belarus), May 15, 1983**

| | | | | | | | | |
|---|---|---|---|---|---|---|---|---|
| 2000 WM18 | 15-F | BLR | 6 | 1 | 1 | 2 | 4 | 10th |
| 2001 WM20 | 11-F | BLR | 6 | 1 | 1 | 2 | 0 | 9th |
| 2002 WM20 | 11-F | BLR | 6 | 0 | 2 | 2 | 4 | 9th |
| 2003 WM20 | 11-F | BLR | 6 | 2 | 0 | 2 | 2 | 10th |
| 2007 WM | 11-F | BLR | 6 | 2 | 2 | 4 | 6 | 11th |
| 2008 WM | 11-F | BLR | 5 | 0 | 1 | 1 | 0 | 9th |
| 2009 WM | 11-F | BLR | 7 | 0 | 0 | 0 | 2 | 8th |
| 2010 OG-M | 11-F | BLR | 4 | 0 | 1 | 1 | 0 | 9th |
| 2010 WM | 11-F | BLR | 6 | 0 | 0 | 0 | 0 | 10th |
| 2011 WM | 11-F | BLR | 6 | 1 | 5 | 6 | 2 | 14th |
| 2012 WM | 11-F | BLR | 5 | 0 | 0 | 0 | 2 | 14th |
| **Totals WM20** | | | **18** | **3** | **3** | **6** | **6** | **—** |
| **Totals WM** | | | **35** | **3** | **8** | **11** | **12** | **—** |

**Kulda, Arturs**
**b. Riga, Soviet Union (Latvia), July 25, 1988**

| | | | | | | | | |
|---|---|---|---|---|---|---|---|---|
| 2010 WM | 32-D | LAT | 3 | 0 | 0 | 0 | 2 | 11th |
| 2011 WM | 32-D | LAT | 3 | 0 | 0 | 0 | 6 | 13th |
| **Totals WM** | | | **6** | **0** | **0** | **0** | **8** | **—** |

**Kulda, Edgars**
**b. November 13, 1994**

| | | | | | | | | |
|---|---|---|---|---|---|---|---|---|
| 2012 WM18 | 23-F | LAT | 6 | 3 | 1 | 4 | 0 | 9th |

**Kulemin, Nikolai** ~see Kulyomin, Nikolai

**Kulemin, Vyacheslav** ~see Kulyomin, Vyacheslav

**Kulikov, Dmitri**
**b. Lipetsk, Russia, October 29, 1990**

| | | | | | | | | |
|---|---|---|---|---|---|---|---|---|
| 2007 WM18 | 3-D | RUS | 7 | 0 | 4 | 4 | 6 | G |
| 2008 WM18 | 11-D | RUS | 6 | 0 | 2 | 2 | 6 | S |
| 2009 WM20 | 3-D | RUS | 7 | 0 | 4 | 4 | 4 | B |
| 2010 WM | 43-D | RUS | 9 | 0 | 2 | 2 | 8 | S |
| 2011 WM | 43-D | RUS | 9 | 2 | 1 | 3 | 4 | 4th |
| **Totals WM18** | | | **13** | **0** | **6** | **6** | **12** | **G,S** |
| **Totals WM** | | | **18** | **2** | **3** | **5** | **12** | **S** |

**Kulikov, Pavel**
**b. Nizhnekamsk, Russia, January 14, 1992**

| | | | | | | | | |
|---|---|---|---|---|---|---|---|---|
| 2010 WM18 | 15-F | RUS | 7 | 0 | 1 | 1 | 0 | 4th |
| 2012 WM20 | 15-F | RUS | 7 | 1 | 1 | 2 | 2 | S |

**Kulmala, Rasmus**
**b. Alastaro, Finland, June 21, 1994**

| | | | | | | | | |
|---|---|---|---|---|---|---|---|---|
| 2012 WM18 | 26-F | FIN | 7 | 5 | 4 | 9 | 2 | 4th |

**Kulyomin, Nikolai**
**b. Magnitogorsk, Soviet Union (Russia), July 14, 1986**

| | | | | | | | | |
|---|---|---|---|---|---|---|---|---|
| 2004 WM18 | 9-F | RUS | 6 | 0 | 2 | 2 | 2 | G |
| 2006 WM20 | 14-F | RUS | 4 | 4 | 2 | 6 | 25 | S |
| 2006 WM | 15-F | RUS | 7 | 1 | 3 | 4 | 2 | 5th |
| 2007 WM | 15-F | RUS | 9 | 2 | 1 | 3 | 0 | B |
| 2010 WM | 41-F | RUS | 9 | 3 | 2 | 5 | 25 | S |
| 2011 WM | 41-F | RUS | 9 | 1 | 0 | 1 | 2 | 4th |
| 2012 WM | 41-F | RUS | 10 | 1 | 3 | 4 | 0 | G |
| **Totals WM** | | | **44** | **8** | **9** | **17** | **29** | **G,S,B** |

**Kulyomin, Vyacheslav**
**b. Moscow, Soviet Union (Russia), June 14, 1990**

| | | | | | | | | |
|---|---|---|---|---|---|---|---|---|
| 2008 WM18 | 10-F | RUS | 6 | 1 | 3 | 4 | 35 | S |
| 2010 WM20 | 7-F | RUS | 6 | 0 | 1 | 1 | 2 | 6th |

**Kummer, Dario**
**b. Krattingen, Switzerland, November 3, 1994**

| | | | | | | | | |
|---|---|---|---|---|---|---|---|---|
| 2012 WM18 | 18-F | SUI | 4 | 1 | 0 | 1 | 2 | 7th |

**Kumpulainen, Janne**
**b. Jyvaskyla, Finland, March 12, 1991**

| | | | | | | | | |
|---|---|---|---|---|---|---|---|---|
| 2009 WM18 | 15-F | FIN | 6 | 1 | 1 | 2 | 2 | B |

**Kundratek, Tomas**
**b. Trinec, Czechoslovakia (Czech Republic), December 26, 1989**

| | | | | | | | | |
|---|---|---|---|---|---|---|---|---|
| 2007 WM18 | 4-D | CZE | 6 | 0 | 0 | 0 | 6 | 9th |
| 2008 WM20 | 23-D | CZE | 6 | 1 | 0 | 1 | 2 | 5th |
| 2009 WM20 | 23-D | CZE | 6 | 0 | 6 | 6 | 10 | 6th |
| **Totals WM20** | | | **12** | **1** | **6** | **7** | **12** | **—** |

**Kunitz, Chris**
**b. Regina, Saskatchewan, Canada, September 26, 1979**

| | | | | | | | | |
|---|---|---|---|---|---|---|---|---|
| 2008 WM | 14-F | CAN | 9 | 2 | 5 | 7 | 4 | S |

**Kuonen, Raphael**
**b. Visp, Switzerland, March 13, 1992**

| | | | | | | | | |
|---|---|---|---|---|---|---|---|---|
| 2010 WM18 | 20-F | SUI | 6 | 0 | 1 | 1 | 6 | 5th |

**Kuplais, Kristaps**
**b. Riga, Soviet Union (Latvia), March 31, 1989**

| | | | | | | | | |
|---|---|---|---|---|---|---|---|---|
| 2009 WM20 | 20-D | LAT | 6 | 0 | 0 | 0 | 6 | 8th |

**Kuptsov, Sergei**
**b. Yekaterinburg, Russia, June 10, 1994**

| | | | | | | | | |
|---|---|---|---|---|---|---|---|---|
| 2012 WM18 | 15-F | RUS | 6 | 0 | 1 | 1 | 2 | 5th |

**Kurali, Mario**
**b. January 17, 1992**

| | | | | | | | | |
|---|---|---|---|---|---|---|---|---|
| 2012 WM20 | 7-D | SVK | 6 | 0 | 0 | 0 | 0 | 6th |

**Kurbatov, Yevgeni**
**b. Sverdlovsk (Yekaterinburg), Soviet Union (Russia), May 18, 1988**

| | | | | | | | | |
|---|---|---|---|---|---|---|---|---|
| 2008 WM20 | 8-D | RUS | 7 | 2 | 3 | 5 | 6 | B |

**Kurilin, Yevgeni**
**b. Minsk, Soviet Union (Belarus), January 3, 1979**

| | | | | | | | | |
|---|---|---|---|---|---|---|---|---|
| 2006 WM | 17-F | BLR | 6 | 0 | 1 | 1 | 2 | 6th |
| 2007 WM | 93-F | BLR | 6 | 0 | 1 | 1 | 4 | 11th |
| 2008 WM | 93-F | BLR | 3 | 0 | 0 | 0 | 0 | 9th |
| **Totals WM** | | | **15** | **0** | **2** | **2** | **6** | **—** |

**Kurki, Mikael**
**b. Helsinki, Finland, January 13, 1987**

| | | | | | | | | |
|---|---|---|---|---|---|---|---|---|
| 2005 WM18 | 7-D | FIN | 6 | 0 | 0 | 0 | 4 | 7th |
| 2007 WM20 | 6-D | FIN | 6 | 0 | 2 | 2 | 4 | 6th |

**Kurmis, Edgars**
**b. Riga, Latvia, February 6, 1993**

| | | | | | | | | |
|---|---|---|---|---|---|---|---|---|
| 2010 WM18 | 28-F | LAT | 6 | 1 | 0 | 1 | 2 | 9th |

**Kuronen, Mikael**
**b. Tampere, Finland, March 14, 1992**

| | | | | | | | | |
|---|---|---|---|---|---|---|---|---|
| 2012 WM20 | 28-F | FIN | 7 | 1 | 1 | 2 | 4 | 4th |

**Kurshuk, Alexander**
**b. Ust-Kamenogorsk, Soviet Union (Kazakhstan), September 27, 1988**

| | | | | | | | | |
|---|---|---|---|---|---|---|---|---|
| 2008 WM20 | 9-D | KAZ | 6 | 1 | 0 | 1 | 8 | 8th |

**Kurth, Marcel**
**b. Donaueschingen, Germany, January 15, 1994**

| | | | | | | | | |
|---|---|---|---|---|---|---|---|---|
| 2012 WM18 | 14-F | GER | 6 | 3 | 1 | 4 | 0 | 6th |

**Kuryanov, Anton**
**b. Ust-Kamenogorsk, Soviet Union (Kazakhstan), March 11, 1983**

| | | | | | | | | |
|---|---|---|---|---|---|---|---|---|
| 2009 WM | 19-F | RUS | 9 | 3 | 3 | 6 | 6 | G |

**Kutlak, Zdenek**
**b. Ceske Budejovice, Czechoslovakia (Czech Republic), February 13, 1980**

| | | | | | | | | |
|---|---|---|---|---|---|---|---|---|
| 2012 WM | 80-D | CZE | 1 | 0 | 0 | 0 | 4 | B |

**Kutny, Vladimir**
**b. Trencin, Czechoslovakia (Slovakia), May 22, 1985**

| | | | | | | | | |
|---|---|---|---|---|---|---|---|---|
| 2004 WM20 | 29-F | SVK | 6 | 0 | 0 | 0 | 0 | 6th |
| 2005 WM20 | 24-F | SVK | 5 | 0 | 0 | 0 | 2 | 7th |
| **Totals WM20** | | | **11** | **0** | **0** | **0** | **2** | **—** |

**Kuukka, Mikko**
**b. Hameenkyro, Finland, November 3, 1985**

| | | | | | | | | |
|---|---|---|---|---|---|---|---|---|
| 2003 WM18 | 6-D | FIN | 6 | 1 | 1 | 2 | 2 | 7th |
| 2005 WM20 | 12-D | FIN | 6 | 0 | 0 | 0 | 2 | 5th |

**Kuvayev, Alexander**
**b. Moscow, Russia, May 2, 1993**

| | | | | | | | | |
|---|---|---|---|---|---|---|---|---|
| 2011 WM18 | 27-F | RUS | 7 | 0 | 1 | 1 | 8 | B |

**Kuzmenkovs, Arturs**
**b. Daugavpils, Latvia, December 1, 1993**

| | | | | | | | | |
|---|---|---|---|---|---|---|---|---|
| 2010 WM18 | 10-F | LAT | 6 | 1 | 5 | 6 | 14 | 9th |
| 2012 WM20 | 12-F | LAT | 6 | 0 | 2 | 2 | 2 | 9th |

**Kuznetsov, Yevgeni**
**b. Chelyabinsk, Russia, May 19, 1992**

| | | | | | | | | |
|---|---|---|---|---|---|---|---|---|
| 2009 WM18 | 7-F | RUS | 7 | 6 | 7 | 13 | 10 | S |
| 2010 WM18 | 25-F | RUS | 7 | 5 | 7 | 12 | 6 | 4th |
| 2011 WM20 | 25-F | RUS | 7 | 4 | 7 | 11 | 4 | G |
| 2012 WM20 | 25-F | RUS | 7 | 6 | 7 | 13 | 4 | S |
| 2012 WM | 92-F | RUS | 10 | 2 | 4 | 6 | 4 | G |
| **Totals WM18** | | | **14** | **11** | **14** | **25** | **16** | **S** |
| **Totals WM20** | | | **14** | **10** | **14** | **24** | **8** | **G,S** |

~WM20 MVP (2012), WM20 IIHF Directorate Best Forward (2012), WM20 All-Star Team/Forward (2011, 2012), WM18 All-Star Team/Forward (2010)

**Kuznik, Gregory**
**b. Prince George, British Columbia, Canada, June 12, 1978**

| | | | | | | | | |
|---|---|---|---|---|---|---|---|---|
| 2011 WM | 18-D | SLO | 6 | 0 | 1 | 1 | 0 | 16th |

**Kvapil, Marek**
**b. Ilava, Czechoslovakia (Slovakia), January 5, 1985**

| | | | | | | | | |
|---|---|---|---|---|---|---|---|---|
| 2005 WM20 | 19-F | CZE | 7 | 2 | 3 | 5 | 0 | B |
| 2010 WM | 91-F | CZE | 8 | 0 | 0 | 0 | 0 | G |

**Kvapil, Tomas**
**b. Plzen, Czech Republic, April 28, 1993**

| | | | | | | | | |
|---|---|---|---|---|---|---|---|---|
| 2011 WM18 | 21-D | CZE | 5 | 1 | 0 | 1 | 6 | 8th |

**Kveton, David**
**b. Novy Jicin, Czechoslovakia (Czech Republic), January 3, 1988**

| | | | | | | | | |
|---|---|---|---|---|---|---|---|---|
| 2005 WM18 | 17-F | CZE | 7 | 4 | 2 | 6 | 4 | 4th |
| 2006 WM18 | 23-F | CZE | 7 | 2 | 5 | 7 | 2 | B |
| 2007 WM20 | 29-F | CZE | 6 | 0 | 0 | 0 | 0 | 5th |
| 2008 WM20 | 17-F | CZE | 1 | 0 | 0 | 0 | 2 | 5th |
| **Totals WM18** | | | **14** | **6** | **7** | **13** | **6** | **B** |
| **Totals WM20** | | | **7** | **0** | **0** | **0** | **2** | **—** |

**Kwiatkowski, Joel**
**b. Saskatoon, Saskatchewan, Canada, March 22, 1977**

| | | | | | | | | |
|---|---|---|---|---|---|---|---|---|
| 2009 WM | 29-D | CAN | 5 | 0 | 0 | 0 | 2 | S |

**Kyrychenko, Vitali**
**b. Kiev (Kyiv), Soviet Union (Ukraine), January 4, 1985**

| | | | | | | | | |
|---|---|---|---|---|---|---|---|---|
| 2002 WM18 | 28-F | UKR | 8 | 2 | 0 | 2 | 8 | 12th |
| 2004 WM20 | 18-F | UKR | 6 | 0 | 1 | 1 | 4 | 10th |

**Kytnar, Milan**
**b. Topolcany, Czechoslovakia (Slovakia), May 19, 1989**

| | | | | | | | | |
|---|---|---|---|---|---|---|---|---|
| 2007 WM18 | 19-F | SVK | 6 | 2 | 5 | 7 | 10 | 5th |
| 2009 WM20 | 22-F | SVK | 7 | 0 | 6 | 6 | 4 | 4th |

**Laakso, Aleksi**
**b. Seinajoki, Finland, March 16, 1990**

| | | | | | | | | |
|---|---|---|---|---|---|---|---|---|
| 2010 WM20 | 12-D | FIN | 5 | 1 | 2 | 3 | 0 | 5th |

**Laakso, Teemu**
**b. Tuusula, Finland, August 27, 1987**

| | | | | | | | | |
|---|---|---|---|---|---|---|---|---|
| 2004 WM18 | 6-D | FIN | 6 | 2 | 4 | 6 | 18 | 7th |
| 2005 WM18 | 28-D | FIN | 6 | 0 | 0 | 0 | 8 | 7th |
| 2005 WM20 | 28-D | FIN | 5 | 0 | 1 | 1 | 10 | 5th |
| 2006 WM20 | 28-D | FIN | 7 | 3 | 1 | 4 | 12 | B |
| 2007 WM20 | 2-D | FIN | 6 | 3 | 2 | 5 | 52 | 6th |
| **Totals WM18** | | | **12** | **2** | **4** | **6** | **26** | **—** |
| **Totals WM20** | | | **18** | **6** | **4** | **10** | **74** | **B** |

**Laaksonen, Jere**
**b. Eurajoki, Finland, February 28, 1991**

| | | | | | | | | |
|---|---|---|---|---|---|---|---|---|
| 2009 WM18 | 16-F | FIN | 6 | 1 | 1 | 2 | 6 | B |

**Lacroix, Simon**
**b. Montreal, Quebec, Canada, November 1, 1974**

| | | | | | | | | |
|---|---|---|---|---|---|---|---|---|
| 2008 WM | 72-D | FRA | 5 | 0 | 1 | 1 | 2 | 14th |

**Ladd, Andrew**
**b. Maple Ridge, British Columbia, Canada,**
December 12, 1985

| | | | | | | | | |
|---|---|---|---|---|---|---|---|---|
| 2005 WM20 | 19-F | CAN | 6 | 3 | 4 | 7 | 2 | G |
| 2011 WM | 16-F | CAN | 7 | 0 | 0 | 0 | 2 | 5th |
| 2012 WM | 16-F | CAN | 8 | 1 | 4 | 5 | 2 | 5th |
| **Totals WM** | | | **15** | **1** | **4** | **5** | **4** | **—** |

**Lagace, Jacob**
**b. Beloeil, Quebec, Canada, January 9, 1990**

| | | | | | | | | |
|---|---|---|---|---|---|---|---|---|
| 2008 WM18 | 14-F | CAN | 7 | 1 | 2 | 3 | 6 | G |

**Lagerstrom, Tony**
**b. Stockholm, Sweden, July 19, 1988**

| | | | | | | | | |
|---|---|---|---|---|---|---|---|---|
| 2006 WM18 | 11-F | SWE | 6 | 3 | 3 | 6 | 10 | 6th |
| 2008 WM20 | 25-F | SWE | 6 | 3 | 3 | 6 | 4 | S |

**Lahde, Nestori**
**b. Nokia, Finland, August 12, 1989**

| | | | | | | | | |
|---|---|---|---|---|---|---|---|---|
| 2007 WM18 | 25-F | FIN | 6 | 0 | 0 | 0 | 2 | 7th |
| 2008 WM20 | 28-F | FIN | 6 | 0 | 0 | 0 | 4 | 6th |
| 2009 WM20 | 14-F | FIN | 6 | 2 | 0 | 2 | 2 | 7th |
| **Totals WM20** | | | **12** | **2** | **0** | **2** | **6** | **—** |

**Lahteenmaki, Sami**
**b. Riihimaki, Finland, September 19, 1989**

| | | | | | | | | |
|---|---|---|---|---|---|---|---|---|
| 2009 WM20 | 21-F | FIN | 6 | 0 | 0 | 0 | 0 | 7th |

**Lahti, Janne**
**b. Riihimaki, Finland, July 20, 1982**

| | | | | | | | | |
|---|---|---|---|---|---|---|---|---|
| 2011 WM | 47-F | FIN | 5 | 0 | 0 | 0 | 0 | G |

**Lahti, Miika**
**b. Konnevesi, Finland, February 6, 1987**

| | | | | | | | | |
|---|---|---|---|---|---|---|---|---|
| 2004 WM18 | 12-F | FIN | 6 | 0 | 1 | 1 | 2 | 7th |
| 2005 WM18 | 20-F | FIN | 6 | 0 | 1 | 1 | 4 | 7th |
| 2007 WM20 | 28-F | FIN | 6 | 0 | 1 | 1 | 31 | 6th |
| **Totals WM18** | | | **12** | **0** | **2** | **2** | **6** | **—** |

**Laich, Brooks**
**b. Wawota, Saskatchewan, Canada, June 23, 1983**

| | | | | | | | | |
|---|---|---|---|---|---|---|---|---|
| 2003 WM20 | 29-F | CAN | 6 | 2 | 4 | 6 | 0 | S |
| 2010 WM | 21-F | CAN | 7 | 1 | 0 | 1 | 0 | 7th |

**Lajunen, Jani**
**b. Espoo, Finland, June 16, 1990**

| | | | | | | | | |
|---|---|---|---|---|---|---|---|---|
| 2008 WM18 | 15-F | FIN | 6 | 1 | 0 | 1 | 2 | 6th |
| 2008 WM20 | 9-D | FIN | 6 | 1 | 0 | 1 | 0 | 7th |
| 2010 WM20 | 24-F | FIN | 6 | 1 | 4 | 5 | 6 | 5th |
| 2011 WM | 24-F | FIN | 4 | 2 | 1 | 3 | 2 | G |
| **Totals WM20** | | | **12** | **2** | **4** | **6** | **6** | **—** |

**Lajunen, Ville**
**b. Helsinki, Finland, March 8, 1988**

| | | | | | | | | |
|---|---|---|---|---|---|---|---|---|
| 2008 WM20 | 9-D | FIN | 6 | 0 | 3 | 3 | 6 | 6th |

**Lakos, Andre**
**b. Vienna, Austria, July 29, 1979**

| | | | | | | | | |
|---|---|---|---|---|---|---|---|---|
| 1999 WM | 5-D | AUT | 6 | 0 | 0 | 0 | 6 | 10th |
| 2000 WM | 22-D | AUT | 6 | 0 | 0 | 0 | 6 | 13th |
| 2002 OG-M | 32-D | AUT | 4 | 0 | 0 | 0 | 6 | 12th |
| 2002 WM | 32-D | AUT | 6 | 2 | 1 | 3 | 16 | 12th |
| 2003 WM | 32-D | AUT | 6 | 0 | 3 | 3 | 4 | 10th |
| 2004 WM | 32-D | AUT | 6 | 1 | 2 | 3 | 6 | 11th |
| 2005 WM | 32-D | AUT | 6 | 1 | 1 | 2 | 6 | 16th |
| 2007 WM | 32-D | AUT | 6 | 3 | 1 | 4 | 4 | 15th |
| 2009 WM | 32-D | AUT | 6 | 0 | 0 | 0 | 14 | 14th |
| **Totals WM** | | | **48** | **7** | **8** | **15** | **62** | **—** |

**Lakos, Philippe**
**b. Vienna, Austria, August 19, 1980**

| | | | | | | | | |
|---|---|---|---|---|---|---|---|---|
| 2003 WM | 47-D | AUT | 6 | 0 | 0 | 0 | 6 | 10th |
| 2004 WM | 11-D | AUT | 6 | 0 | 0 | 0 | 4 | 11th |
| 2005 WM | 30-D | AUT | 6 | 1 | 1 | 2 | 16 | 16th |
| 2007 WM | 11-D | AUT | 6 | 0 | 0 | 0 | 12 | 15th |
| 2009 WM | 11-D | AUT | 6 | 0 | 0 | 0 | 6 | 14th |
| 2011 WM | 11-D | AUT | 6 | 0 | 0 | 0 | 33 | 15th |
| **Totals WM** | | | **36** | **1** | **1** | **2** | **77** | **—** |

**Lammer, Dominic**
**b. Altstatten, Switzerland, October 2, 1992**

| | | | | | | | | |
|---|---|---|---|---|---|---|---|---|
| 2010 WM18 | 12-F | SUI | 6 | 3 | 2 | 5 | 0 | 5th |

**Lamperier, Loic**
**b. Mont St. Aignan, France, August 7, 1989**

| | | | | | | | | |
|---|---|---|---|---|---|---|---|---|
| 2010 WM | 19-F | FRA | 3 | 0 | 0 | 0 | 0 | 14th |
| 2011 WM | 19-F | FRA | 3 | 0 | 0 | 0 | 0 | 12th |
| 2012 WM | 19-F | FRA | 4 | 0 | 0 | 0 | 0 | 9th |
| **Totals WM** | | | **10** | **0** | **0** | **0** | **0** | **—** |

**Lander, Anton**
**b. Sundsvall, Sweden, April 24, 1991**

| | | | | | | | | |
|---|---|---|---|---|---|---|---|---|
| 2008 WM18 | 16-F | SWE | 6 | 0 | 2 | 2 | 4 | 4th |
| 2009 WM18 | 16-F | SWE | 6 | 2 | 7 | 9 | 16 | 5th |
| 2010 WM20 | 16-F | SWE | 6 | 5 | 3 | 8 | 4 | B |
| 2011 WM20 | 16-F | SWE | 6 | 1 | 3 | 4 | 4 | 4th |
| **Totals WM18** | | | **12** | **2** | **9** | **11** | **20** | **—** |
| **Totals WM20** | | | **12** | **6** | **6** | **12** | **8** | **B** |

**Landeskog, Gabriel**
**b. Stockholm, Sweden, November 23, 1992**

| | | | | | | | | |
|---|---|---|---|---|---|---|---|---|
| 2009 WM18 | 14-F | SWE | 6 | 4 | 0 | 4 | 24 | 5th |
| 2011 WM20 | 22-F | SWE | 1 | 1 | 1 | 2 | 0 | 4th |
| 2012 WM | 92-F | SWE | 8 | 1 | 4 | 5 | 6 | 6th |

**Lane, Matt**
**b. Rochester, New York, United States, March 15, 1994**

| | | | | | | | | |
|---|---|---|---|---|---|---|---|---|
| 2012 WM18 | 21-F | USA | 6 | 3 | 4 | 7 | 2 | G |

**Langenbrunner, Jamie**
**b. Duluth, Minnesota, United States, July 24, 1975**

| | | | | | | | | |
|---|---|---|---|---|---|---|---|---|
| 1994 WM20 | 14-F | USA | 7 | 2 | 0 | 2 | 13 | 6th |
| 1995 WM20 | 14-F | USA | 7 | 1 | 1 | 2 | 6 | 6th |
| 1998 OG-M | 25-F | USA | 3 | 0 | 0 | 0 | 4 | 5th |
| 2004 WCH | 15-F | USA | 3 | 0 | 0 | 0 | 4 | 4th |
| 2010 OG-M | 15-F | USA | 6 | 1 | 3 | 4 | 0 | S |
| **Totals WM20** | | | **14** | **3** | **1** | **4** | **19** | **—** |
| **Totals OG-M** | | | **9** | **1** | **3** | **4** | **4** | **S** |

**Langwieder, Stefan**
**b. Munich, West Germany (Germany), January 8, 1987**

| | | | | | | | | |
|---|---|---|---|---|---|---|---|---|
| 2005 WM18 | 7-D | GER | 6 | 0 | 1 | 1 | 6 | 8th |
| 2007 WM20 | 7-D | GER | 6 | 0 | 0 | 0 | 8 | 9th |

**Lanzarotti, Alessandro**
**b. February 25, 1994**

| | | | | | | | | |
|---|---|---|---|---|---|---|---|---|
| 2012 WM18 | 5-D | SUI | 6 | 0 | 1 | 1 | 0 | 7th |

**Lapsansky, Adam**
**b. Spisska Nova Ves, Czechoslovakia (Slovakia), April 10, 1990**

| | | | | | | | | |
|---|---|---|---|---|---|---|---|---|
| 2007 WM18 | 9-F | SVK | 5 | 0 | 1 | 1 | 2 | 5th |
| 2008 WM18 | 18-F | SVK | 6 | 2 | 1 | 3 | 6 | 7th |
| 2010 WM20 | 26-F | SVK | 6 | 0 | 0 | 0 | 2 | 8th |
| **Totals WM18** | | | **11** | **2** | **2** | **4** | **8** | **—** |

**Larkin, Thomas**
**b. London, Great Britain, December 31, 1990**

| | | | | | | | | |
|---|---|---|---|---|---|---|---|---|
| 2012 WM | 27-D | ITA | 7 | 0 | 1 | 1 | 4 | 15th |

**LaRose, Chad**
**b. Fraser, Michigan, United States, March 27, 1982**

| | | | | | | | | |
|---|---|---|---|---|---|---|---|---|
| 2002 WM20 | 10-F | USA | 7 | 2 | 2 | 4 | 0 | 5th |
| 2007 WM | 59-F | USA | 7 | 2 | 1 | 3 | 2 | 5th |

**Larraza, Zach**
**b. Scottsdale, Arizona, February 25, 1993**

| | | | | | | | | |
|---|---|---|---|---|---|---|---|---|
| 2011 WM18 | 16-F | USA | 6 | 1 | 4 | 5 | 4 | G |

**Larsen, Mads**
**b. June 10, 1995**

| | | | | | | | | |
|---|---|---|---|---|---|---|---|---|
| 2012 WM18 | 3-D | DEN | 6 | 0 | 0 | 0 | 27 | 10th |

**Larsen, Mark**
**b. Fredrikshavn, Denmark, July 29, 1992**

| | | | | | | | | |
|---|---|---|---|---|---|---|---|---|
| 2012 WM20 | 21-D | DEN | 6 | 0 | 0 | 0 | 2 | 10th |

**Larsen, Philip**
**b. Esbjerg, Denmark, December 7, 1989**

| | | | | | | | | |
|---|---|---|---|---|---|---|---|---|
| 2008 WM20 | 3-D | DEN | 6 | 1 | 1 | 2 | 6 | 10th |
| 2009 WM | 3-D | DEN | 6 | 0 | 0 | 0 | 8 | 13th |
| 2010 WM | 3-D | DEN | 7 | 2 | 0 | 2 | 4 | 8th |
| 2012 WM | 3-D | DEN | 7 | 0 | 2 | 2 | 2 | 13th |
| **Totals WM** | | | **20** | **2** | **2** | **4** | **14** | **—** |

**Larsson, Adam**
**b. Skelleftea, Sweden, November 12, 1992**

| | | | | | | | | |
|---|---|---|---|---|---|---|---|---|
| 2009 WM18 | 10-D | SWE | 6 | 0 | 2 | 2 | 4 | 5th |
| 2010 WM18 | 5-D | SWE | 5 | 2 | 1 | 3 | 12 | S |
| 2010 WM20 | 5-D | SWE | 6 | 1 | 3 | 4 | 0 | B |
| 2011 WM20 | 5-D | SWE | 6 | 1 | 3 | 4 | 4 | 4th |
| **Totals WM18** | | | **11** | **2** | **3** | **5** | **16** | **S** |
| **Totals WM20** | | | **12** | **2** | **6** | **8** | **4** | **B** |

~WM18 IIHF Directorate Best Defenceman (2010), WM18 All-Star Team/Defence (2010)

**Larsson, Johan**
**b. Lau, Sweden, July 25, 1992**

| | | | | | | | | |
|---|---|---|---|---|---|---|---|---|
| 2010 WM18 | 12-F | SWE | 5 | 6 | 8 | 14 | 0 | S |
| 2011 WM20 | 10-F | SWE | 6 | 1 | 3 | 4 | 4 | 4th |
| 2012 WM20 | 10-F | SWE | 6 | 0 | 6 | 6 | 0 | G |
| 2012 WM | 10-F | SWE | 7 | 0 | 2 | 2 | 0 | 6th |
| Totals WM20 | | | 12 | 1 | 9 | 10 | 4 | G |

~WM18 All-Star Team/Forward (2010)

**Larsson, Tomas**
**b. Skelleftea, Sweden, January 16, 1988**

| | | | | | | | | |
|---|---|---|---|---|---|---|---|---|
| 2006 WM18 | 7-F | SWE | 6 | 2 | 2 | 4 | 24 | 6th |
| 2008 WM20 | 24-F | SWE | 6 | 2 | 2 | 4 | 8 | S |

**Lascek, Stanislav**
**b. Martin, Czechoslovakia (Slovakia), January 17, 1986**

| | | | | | | | | |
|---|---|---|---|---|---|---|---|---|
| 2005 WM20 | 20-F | SVK | 6 | 1 | 1 | 2 | 4 | 7th |
| 2006 WM20 | 17-F | SVK | 6 | 6 | 3 | 9 | 8 | 8th |
| **Totals WM20** | | | **12** | **7** | **4** | **11** | **12** | **—** |

**Lasch, Ryan**
**b. Lake Forest, California, United States, January 22, 1987**

| | | | | | | | | |
|---|---|---|---|---|---|---|---|---|
| 2012 WM | 11-F | USA | 7 | 0 | 2 | 2 | 0 | 7th |

**Lashoff, Brian**
**b. Albany, New York, United States, July 16, 1990**

| | | | | | | | | |
|---|---|---|---|---|---|---|---|---|
| 2010 WM20 | 18-D | USA | 7 | 0 | 2 | 2 | 4 | G |

**Lassen, Lasse**
**b. Herning, Denmark, May 13, 1989**

| | | | | | | | | |
|---|---|---|---|---|---|---|---|---|
| 2008 WM20 | 14-F | DEN | 6 | 0 | 0 | 0 | 0 | 10th |

**Lassen, Stefan**
**b. Herning, Denmark, November 1, 1985**

| | | | | | | | | |
|---|---|---|---|---|---|---|---|---|
| 2007 WM | 6-D | DEN | 6 | 0 | 0 | 0 | 4 | 10th |
| 2008 WM | 6-D | DEN | 6 | 1 | 1 | 2 | 12 | 12th |
| 2010 WM | 6-D | DEN | 7 | 2 | 0 | 2 | 2 | 8th |
| 2011 WM | 6-D | DEN | 6 | 0 | 0 | 0 | 8 | 11th |
| 2012 WM | 6-D | DEN | 7 | 0 | 0 | 0 | 2 | 13th |
| **Totals WM** | | | **32** | **3** | **1** | **4** | **28** | **—** |

**Lasu, Nicklas**
**b. Molndal, Sweden, September 16, 1989**

| | | | | | | | | |
|---|---|---|---|---|---|---|---|---|
| 2009 WM20 | 23-F | SWE | 6 | 2 | 0 | 2 | 2 | S |

**Latal, Martin**
**b. Olomouc, Czechoslovakia (Czech Republic), March 17, 1988**

| | | | | | | | | |
|---|---|---|---|---|---|---|---|---|
| 2006 WM18 | 12-F | CZE | 7 | 1 | 2 | 3 | 37 | B |
| 2008 WM20 | 12-F | CZE | 6 | 2 | 0 | 2 | 4 | 5th |

**Latendresse, Guillaume**
**b. Ste. Catherine, Quebec, Canada, May 24, 1987**

| | | | | | | | | |
|---|---|---|---|---|---|---|---|---|
| 2005 WM18 | 18-F | CAN | 6 | 2 | 3 | 5 | 4 | S |
| 2006 WM20 | 20-F | CAN | 6 | 0 | 0 | 0 | 0 | G |

**Latta, Nickolas**
**b. Schongau, Germany, October 5, 1993**

| | | | | | | | | |
|---|---|---|---|---|---|---|---|---|
| 2011 WM18 | 28-F | GER | 6 | 1 | 0 | 1 | 4 | 6th |
| 2011 WM20 | 27-F | GER | 4 | 0 | 0 | 0 | 0 | 10th |

**Latusa, Manuel**
**b. Vienna, Austria, January 23, 1984**

| | | | | | | | | |
|---|---|---|---|---|---|---|---|---|
| 2011 WM | 15-F | AUT | 4 | 0 | 0 | 0 | 4 | 15th |

**Laughton, Scott**
**b. Oakville, Ontario, Canada, May 30, 1994**

| | | | | | | | | |
|---|---|---|---|---|---|---|---|---|
| 2012 WM18 | 21-F | CAN | 7 | 2 | 5 | 7 | 4 | B |

**Laumann-Ylven, Martin**
**b. Oslo, Norway, December 22, 1988**

| | | | | | | | | |
|---|---|---|---|---|---|---|---|---|
| 2006 WM18 | 12-F* | NOR | 6 | 2 | 5 | 7 | 4 | — |
| 2009 WM | 35-F | NOR | 6 | 0 | 0 | 0 | 6 | 11th |
| 2010 OG-M | 35-F | NOR | 4 | 0 | 0 | 0 | 0 | 10th |
| 2010 WM | 35-F | NOR | 4 | 0 | 0 | 0 | 31 | 9th |
| 2011 WM | 35-F | NOR | 3 | 0 | 0 | 0 | 0 | 6th |
| **Totals WM** | | | **13** | **0** | **0** | **0** | **37** | **—** |

*played as Martin Ylven

**Lauridsen, Kristoffer**
**b. Herning, Denmark, February 14, 1994**

| | | | | | | | | |
|---|---|---|---|---|---|---|---|---|
| 2012 WM18 | 15-F | DEN | 5 | 4 | 4 | 8 | 4 | 10th |

**Lauridsen, Markus**
**b. Gentofte, Denmark, February 28, 1991**

| | | | | | | | | |
|---|---|---|---|---|---|---|---|---|
| 2008 WM18 | 6-D | DEN | 6 | 0 | 1 | 1 | 8 | 10th |

**Lauridsen, Oliver**
**b. Gentofte, Denmark, March 24, 1989**

| | | | | | | | | |
|---|---|---|---|---|---|---|---|---|
| 2008 WM20 | 4-D | DEN | 6 | 0 | 2 | 2 | 14 | 10th |

**Lavallee, Kevin**
**b. Montreal, Quebec, Canada, December 12, 1981**

| | | | | | | | | |
|---|---|---|---|---|---|---|---|---|
| 2011 WM | 27-D | GER | 7 | 1 | 3 | 4 | 4 | 7th |
| 2012 WM | 27-D | GER | 7 | 0 | 2 | 2 | 6 | 12th |
| **Totals WM** | | | **14** | **1** | **5** | **6** | **10** | **—** |

**Lavins, Rodrigo**
**b. Riga, Soviet Union (Latvia), August 3, 1974**

| | | | | | | | | |
|---|---|---|---|---|---|---|---|---|
| 2012 WM | 2-D | LAT | 7 | 0 | 0 | 0 | 0 | 10th |

**Lavrovs, Martins**
**b. Tukums, Latvia, March 31, 1994**

| | | | | | | | | |
|---|---|---|---|---|---|---|---|---|
| 2012 WM18 | 11-F | LAT | 6 | 1 | 2 | 3 | 2 | 9th |

**Lawson, Kyle**
**b. Southfield, Michigan, United States, January 11, 1987**

| | | | | | | | | |
|---|---|---|---|---|---|---|---|---|
| 2005 WM18 | 2-D | USA | 6 | 1 | 1 | 2 | 0 | G |
| 2007 WM20 | 2-D | USA | 7 | 0 | 0 | 0 | 2 | B |

**Lazarev, Anton**
**b. Chelyabinsk, Soviet Union (Russia), May 29, 1990**

| | | | | | | | | |
|---|---|---|---|---|---|---|---|---|
| 2008 WM18 | 9-F | RUS | 6 | 3 | 4 | 7 | 6 | S |

**Lazorenko, Mikhail**
**b. Ust-Kamenogorsk, Soviet Union (Kazakhstan), June 29, 1989**

| | | | | | | | | |
|---|---|---|---|---|---|---|---|---|
| 2009 WM20 | 11-F | KAZ | 6 | 0 | 0 | 0 | 8 | 10th |

**Lebedev, Alexander**
**b. Rybinsk, Russia, July 30, 1994**

| | | | | | | | | |
|---|---|---|---|---|---|---|---|---|
| 2012 WM18 | 26-F | RUS | 6 | 0 | 0 | 0 | 2 | 5th |

**Leblanc, Louis**
**b. Pointe Claire, Quebec, Canada, January 26, 1991**

| | | | | | | | | |
|---|---|---|---|---|---|---|---|---|
| 2011 WM20 | 20-F | CAN | 7 | 3 | 4 | 7 | 2 | S |

**Lecavalier, Vincent**
**b. Ile Bizard, Quebec, Canada, April 21, 1980**

| | | | | | | | | |
|---|---|---|---|---|---|---|---|---|
| 1998 WM20 | 14-F | CAN | 7 | 1 | 1 | 2 | 4 | — |
| 2001 WM | 4-F | CAN | 7 | 3 | 2 | 5 | 29 | — |
| 2004 WCH | 4-F | CAN | 6 | 2 | 5 | 7 | 8 | 1st |
| 2006 OG-M | 40-F | CAN | 6 | 0 | 3 | 3 | 16 | — |

**Leddy, Nick**
**b. Eden Prairie, Minnesota, United States, March 20, 1991**

| | | | | | | | | |
|---|---|---|---|---|---|---|---|---|
| 2011 WM20 | 6-D | USA | 6 | 0 | 3 | 3 | 0 | B |

**Leder, Kevin**
**b. Hvidovre, Denmark, July 26, 1988**

| | | | | | | | | |
|---|---|---|---|---|---|---|---|---|
| 2008 WM20 | 25-F | DEN | 5 | 1 | 0 | 1 | 0 | 10th |

**Lee, Brian**
**b. Fargo, North Dakota, United States, March 26, 1987**

| | | | | | | | | |
|---|---|---|---|---|---|---|---|---|
| 2005 WM20 | 2-D | USA | 7 | 0 | 0 | 0 | 4 | 4th |
| 2006 WM20 | 22-D | USA | 7 | 1 | 0 | 1 | 8 | 4th |
| 2007 WM20 | 22-D | USA | 7 | 0 | 0 | 0 | 14 | B |
| **Totals WM20** | | | **21** | **1** | **0** | **1** | **26** | **B** |

**Legein, Stefan**
**b. Oakville, Ontario, Canada, November 24, 1988**

| | | | | | | | | |
|---|---|---|---|---|---|---|---|---|
| 2008 WM20 | 7-F | CAN | 7 | 1 | 1 | 2 | 8 | G |

**Lehkonen, Artturi**
**b. Piikkio, Finland, July 4, 1995**

| | | | | | | | | |
|---|---|---|---|---|---|---|---|---|
| 2012 WM18 | 28-F | FIN | 7 | 7 | 3 | 10 | 6 | 4th |

**Lehtera, Jori**
**b. Espoo, Finland, December 23, 1987**

| | | | | | | | | |
|---|---|---|---|---|---|---|---|---|
| 2010 WM | 52-F | FIN | 5 | 0 | 0 | 0 | 0 | 6th |

**Lehtivuori, Joonas**
**b. Pirkkala, Finland, July 19, 1988**

| | | | | | | | | |
|---|---|---|---|---|---|---|---|---|
| 2006 WM18 | 9-D | FIN | 6 | 1 | 2 | 3 | 12 | S |
| 2007 WM20 | 12-D | FIN | 6 | 0 | 0 | 0 | 4 | 6th |
| 2008 WM20 | 6-D | FIN | 6 | 0 | 1 | 1 | 6 | 6th |
| **Totals WM20** | | | **12** | **0** | **1** | **1** | **10** | **—** |

**Lehtonen, Mikko**
**b. Espoo, Finland, April 1, 1987**

| | | | | | | | | |
|---|---|---|---|---|---|---|---|---|
| 2005 WM18 | 13-F | FIN | 6 | 2 | 3 | 5 | 2 | 7th |
| 2006 WM20 | 23-F | FIN | 7 | 0 | 1 | 1 | 2 | B |
| 2006 WM | 33-D | FIN | 9 | 1 | 4 | 5 | 14 | B |
| 2007 WM20 | 13-F | FIN | 6 | 4 | 6 | 10 | 0 | 6th |
| 2009 WM | 33-D | FIN | 7 | 1 | 0 | 1 | 6 | 5th |
| **Totals WM20** | | | **13** | **4** | **7** | **11** | **2** | **B** |
| **Totals WM** | | | **16** | **2** | **4** | **6** | **20** | **B** |

**Lehtonen, Mikko**
**b. Turku, Finland, January 16, 1994**

| | | | | | | | | |
|---|---|---|---|---|---|---|---|---|
| 2012 WM18 | 2-D | FIN | 7 | 0 | 1 | 1 | 0 | 4th |

**Leinonen, Tommi**
**b. Kajaani, Finland, May 14, 1987**

| | | | | | | | | |
|---|---|---|---|---|---|---|---|---|
| 2005 WM18 | 8-D | FIN | 6 | 0 | 0 | 0 | 4 | 7th |
| 2006 WM20 | 14-D | FIN | 6 | 0 | 2 | 2 | 8 | B |
| 2007 WM20 | 7-D | FIN | 6 | 0 | 0 | 0 | 6 | 6th |
| **Totals WM20** | | | **12** | **0** | **2** | **2** | **14** | **B** |

**Lemachko, Vladislav**
**b. Brest, Belarus, April 11, 1992**

| | | | | | | | | |
|---|---|---|---|---|---|---|---|---|
| 2010 WM18 | 17-D | BLR | 6 | 0 | 1 | 1 | 8 | 10th |

**Lemesani, Branislav**
**b. Kosice, Czechoslovakia (Slovakia), June 22, 1986**

| | | | | | | | | |
|---|---|---|---|---|---|---|---|---|
| 2006 WM20 | 18-F | SVK | 6 | 0 | 0 | 0 | 6 | 8th |

**Lemm, Aurelio**
**b. Davos, Switzerland, May 16, 1988**

| | | | | | | | | |
|---|---|---|---|---|---|---|---|---|
| 2005 WM18 | 14-F | SUI | 6 | 1 | 0 | 1 | 0 | 9th |
| 2008 WM20 | 23-F | SUI | 6 | 3 | 3 | 6 | 0 | 9th |

**Lemm, Fadri**
**b. Samedan, Switzerland, April 6, 1987**

| | | | | | | | | |
|---|---|---|---|---|---|---|---|---|
| 2005 WM18 | 16-F | SUI | 6 | 0 | 2 | 2 | 6 | 9th |
| 2006 WM20 | 24-F | SUI | 6 | 0 | 0 | 0 | 0 | 7th |
| 2007 WM20 | 16-F | SUI | 6 | 1 | 1 | 2 | 6 | 7th |
| **Totals WM20** | | | **12** | **1** | **1** | **2** | **6** | **—** |

**Lemm, Romano**
**b. Zurich, Switzerland, June 25, 1984**

| | | | | | | | | |
|---|---|---|---|---|---|---|---|---|
| 2001 WM18 | 26-F | SUI | 7 | 1 | 5 | 6 | 4 | S |
| 2002 WM18 | 15-F | SUI | 8 | 3 | 3 | 6 | 4 | 7th |
| 2003 WM20 | 26-F | SUI | 6 | 0 | 0 | 0 | 2 | 7th |
| 2005 WM | 67-F | SUI | 7 | 1 | 3 | 4 | 0 | 8th |
| 2006 OG-M | 67-F | SUI | 6 | 2 | 0 | 2 | 8 | 6th |
| 2006 WM | 67-F | SUI | 6 | 0 | 2 | 2 | 2 | 9th |
| 2007 WM | 67-F | SUI | 7 | 0 | 4 | 4 | 6 | 8th |
| 2008 WM | 67-F | SUI | 7 | 1 | 0 | 1 | 2 | 7th |
| 2009 WM | 67-F | SUI | 6 | 2 | 1 | 3 | 0 | 9th |
| 2010 OG-M | 67-F | SUI | 5 | 2 | 0 | 2 | 2 | 8th |
| 2010 WM | 67-F | SUI | 7 | 0 | 0 | 0 | 2 | 5th |
| 2011 WM | 67-F | SUI | 4 | 0 | 1 | 1 | 2 | 9th |
| **Totals WM18** | | | **15** | **4** | **8** | **12** | **8** | **S** |
| **Totals WM** | | | **44** | **4** | **11** | **15** | **14** | **—** |
| **Totals OG-M** | | | **11** | **4** | **0** | **4** | **10** | **—** |

**Lemtyugov, Nikolai**
**b. Miass, Soviet Union (Russia), January 15, 1986**

| | | | | | | | | |
|---|---|---|---|---|---|---|---|---|
| 2006 WM20 | 28-F | RUS | 6 | 4 | 1 | 5 | 0 | S |

**Lenoch, Patrik**
**b. Chrudim, Czech Republic, April 10, 1992**

| | | | | | | | | |
|---|---|---|---|---|---|---|---|---|
| 2010 WM18 | 8-D | CZE | 6 | 0 | 1 | 1 | 4 | 6th |

**Leonov, Yevgeni**
**b. Vitebsk, Belarus, May 12, 1992**

| | | | | | | | | |
|---|---|---|---|---|---|---|---|---|
| 2010 WM18 | 7-D | BLR | 6 | 1 | 3 | 4 | 16 | 10th |

**Leopold, Jordan**
**b. Golden Valley, Minnesota, United States, August 3, 1980**

| | | | | | | | | |
|---|---|---|---|---|---|---|---|---|
| 1999 WM20 | 4-D | USA | 6 | 0 | 1 | 1 | 0 | 8th |
| 2000 WM20 | 4-D | USA | 7 | 1 | 2 | 3 | 0 | 4th |
| 2002 WM | 3-D | USA | 7 | 0 | 1 | 1 | 4 | 7th |
| 2003 WM | 4-D | USA | 6 | 1 | 3 | 4 | 2 | 13th |
| 2005 WM | 4-D | USA | 7 | 0 | 1 | 1 | 0 | 6th |
| 2006 OG-M | 4-D | USA | 6 | 1 | 0 | 1 | 4 | 8th |
| 2008 WM | 4-D | USA | 4 | 0 | 1 | 1 | 6 | 6th |
| **Totals WM20** | | | **13** | **1** | **3** | **4** | **0** | **—** |
| **Totals WM** | | | **24** | **1** | **6** | **7** | **12** | **—** |

**Lepisto, Sami**
**b. Espoo, Finland, October 17, 1984**

| | | | | | | | | |
|---|---|---|---|---|---|---|---|---|
| 2004 WM20 | 3-D | FIN | 7 | 4 | 4 | 8 | 10 | B |
| 2008 WM | 40-D | FIN | 7 | 1 | 1 | 2 | 10 | B |
| 2010 OG-M | 18-D | FIN | 6 | 0 | 1 | 1 | 6 | B |
| 2011 WM | 18-D | FIN | 9 | 0 | 3 | 3 | 6 | G |
| **Totals WM** | | | **16** | **1** | **4** | **5** | **16** | **G,B** |

~WM20 IIHF Directorate Best Defenceman (2004), WM20 All-Star Team/Forward (2004)

**Leppanen, Erkka**
**b. Jyvaskyla, Finland, November 25, 1986**

| | | | | | | | | |
|---|---|---|---|---|---|---|---|---|
| 2003 WM18 | 8-D | FIN | 6 | 0 | 1 | 1 | 2 | 7th |
| 2006 WM20 | 7-D | FIN | 7 | 0 | 0 | 0 | 2 | B |

**Lesund, Erlend**
**b. Oslo, Norway, December 11, 1994**

| | | | | | | | | |
|---|---|---|---|---|---|---|---|---|
| 2011 WM18 | 27-D | NOR | 6 | 0 | 0 | 0 | 10 | 9th |

**Letang, Kris**
**b. Montreal, Quebec, Canada, April 24, 1987**

| | | | | | | | | |
|---|---|---|---|---|---|---|---|---|
| 2005 WM18 | 6-D | CAN | 6 | 2 | 2 | 4 | 20 | S |
| 2006 WM20 | 12-D | CAN | 6 | 1 | 2 | 3 | 2 | G |
| 2007 WM20 | 5-D | CAN | 6 | 0 | 6 | 6 | 12 | G |
| **Totals WM20** | | | **12** | **1** | **8** | **9** | **14** | **2G** |

~WM20 All-Star Team/Defence (2007)

**Leu, Marwin**
**b. Hemmenthal, Switzerland, June 21, 1993**

| | | | | | | | | |
|---|---|---|---|---|---|---|---|---|
| 2010 WM18 | 3-D | SUI | 6 | 0 | 1 | 1 | 4 | 5th |
| 2011 WM18 | 6-D | SUI | 6 | 0 | 0 | 0 | 0 | 7th |
| **Totals WM18** | | | **12** | **0** | **1** | **1** | **4** | **—** |

**Leuenberger, Kaj**
**b. Ursenbach, Switzerland, January 30, 1992**

| | | | | | | | | |
|---|---|---|---|---|---|---|---|---|
| 2010 WM18 | 19-F | SUI | 5 | 1 | 0 | 1 | 0 | 5th |

**Leveque, Gary**
**b. St. Pierre-et-Miquelon, France, August 25, 1981**

| | | | | | | | | |
|---|---|---|---|---|---|---|---|---|
| 2009 WM | 72-D | FRA | 3 | 0 | 0 | 0 | 4 | 12th |

**Levsha, Artyom**
**b. Novopolotsk, Belarus, September 24, 1992**

| | | | | | | | | |
|---|---|---|---|---|---|---|---|---|
| 2010 WM18 | 21-F | BLR | 6 | 2 | 1 | 3 | 4 | 10th |

**Lewis, Trevor**
**b. Salt Lake City, Utah, United States, January 8, 1987**

| | | | | | | | | |
|---|---|---|---|---|---|---|---|---|
| 2007 WM20 | 24-F | USA | 7 | 1 | 1 | 2 | 2 | B |

**Liedes, Heikki**
**b. Helsinki, Finland, January 12, 1993**

| | | | | | | | | |
|---|---|---|---|---|---|---|---|---|
| 2011 WM18 | 16-F | FIN | 6 | 1 | 0 | 1 | 8 | 5th |

**Liivik, Siim**
**b. Paide, Soviet Union (Estonia), February 14, 1988**

| | | | | | | | | |
|---|---|---|---|---|---|---|---|---|
| 2008 WM20 | 14-F | FIN | 6 | 0 | 1 | 1 | 2 | 6th |

**Likens, Jeff**
**b. Barrington, Illinois, United States, August 28, 1985**

| | | | | | | | | |
|---|---|---|---|---|---|---|---|---|
| 2003 WM18 | 11-D | USA | 6 | 0 | 2 | 2 | 2 | 4th |
| 2004 WM20 | 10-D | USA | 6 | 0 | 1 | 1 | 8 | G |
| 2005 WM20 | 5-D | USA | 7 | 0 | 4 | 4 | 0 | 4th |
| **Totals WM20** | | | **13** | **0** | **5** | **5** | **8** | **G** |

**Liles, John-Michael**
**b. Zionsville, Indiana, United States, November 25, 1980**

| | | | | | | | | |
|---|---|---|---|---|---|---|---|---|
| 2004 WCH | 26-D | USA | 2 | 0 | 0 | 0 | 0 | 4th |
| 2005 WM | 8-D | USA | 7 | 0 | 0 | 0 | 0 | 6th |
| 2006 OG-M | 27-D | USA | 6 | 0 | 2 | 2 | 2 | 8th |
| 2009 WM | 15-D | USA | 9 | 1 | 8 | 9 | 2 | 4th |
| **Totals WM** | | | **16** | **1** | **8** | **9** | **2** | **—** |

**Lilliestrom Karlsson, David**
**b. Stockholm, Sweden, April 12, 1993**

| | | | | | | | | |
|---|---|---|---|---|---|---|---|---|
| 2011 WM18 | 20-F | SWE | 6 | 0 | 0 | 0 | 0 | S |

**Lindahl, Magnus**
**b. Oslo, Norway, June 6, 1991**

| | | | | | | | | |
|---|---|---|---|---|---|---|---|---|
| 2009 WM18 | 19-F | NOR | 6 | 1 | 1 | 2 | 4 | 9th |
| 2011 WM20 | 10-F | NOR | 6 | 0 | 0 | 0 | 0 | 9th |

**Lindberg, Oscar**
**b. Skelleftea, Sweden, October 29, 1991**

| | | | | | | | | |
|---|---|---|---|---|---|---|---|---|
| 2009 WM18 | 28-F | SWE | 6 | 0 | 2 | 2 | 8 | 5th |
| 2011 WM20 | 24-F | SWE | 6 | 2 | 2 | 4 | 6 | 4th |

**Lindbohm, Petteri**
**b. Helsinki, Finland, September 23, 1993**

| | | | | | | | | |
|---|---|---|---|---|---|---|---|---|
| 2011 WM18 | 26-D | FIN | 6 | 0 | 0 | 0 | 0 | 5th |

**Lindell, Esa**
**b. Helsinki, Finland, May 23, 1994**

| | | | | | | | | |
|---|---|---|---|---|---|---|---|---|
| 2012 WM18 | 18-D | FIN | 7 | 0 | 6 | 6 | 2 | 4th |

**Lindgren, Perttu**
**b. Tampere, Finland, August 26, 1987**

| | | | | | | | | |
|---|---|---|---|---|---|---|---|---|
| 2005 WM18 | 12-F | FIN | 6 | 2 | 0 | 2 | 2 | 7th |
| 2006 WM20 | 15-F | FIN | 7 | 2 | 4 | 6 | 2 | B |
| 2007 WM20 | 15-F | FIN | 6 | 2 | 8 | 10 | 8 | 6th |
| **Totals WM20** | | | **13** | **4** | **12** | **16** | **10** | **B** |

**Lindhoj, Christopher**
**b. Herning, Denmark, February 14, 1994**

| | | | | | | | | |
|---|---|---|---|---|---|---|---|---|
| 2012 WM18 | 2-D | DEN | 6 | 0 | 0 | 0 | 2 | 10th |

**Lindholm, Elias**
**b. Boden, Sweden, December 2, 1994**

| | | | | | | | | |
|---|---|---|---|---|---|---|---|---|
| 2012 WM18 | 22-F | SWE | 4 | 2 | 1 | 3 | 2 | S |

**Lindholm, Hampus**
**b. Helsingborg, Sweden, January 20, 1994**

| | | | | | | | | |
|---|---|---|---|---|---|---|---|---|
| 2012 WM18 | 9-D | SWE | 6 | 0 | 4 | 4 | 4 | S |

**Lindlbauer, Peter**
**b. Bad Tolz, Germany, March 24, 1991**

| | | | | | | | | |
|---|---|---|---|---|---|---|---|---|
| 2009 WM18 | 3-D | GER | 6 | 0 | 2 | 2 | 0 | 10th |
| 2011 WM20 | 3-D | GER | 6 | 0 | 0 | 0 | 2 | 10th |

**Lindqvist, Robin**
**b. Boden, Sweden, August 16, 1987**

| | | | | | | | | |
|---|---|---|---|---|---|---|---|---|
| 2005 WM18 | 13-F | SWE | 6 | 0 | 0 | 0 | 0 | B |
| 2006 WM20 | 27-F | SWE | 5 | 1 | 1 | 2 | 4 | 5th |
| 2007 WM20 | 27-F | SWE | 7 | 2 | 0 | 2 | 2 | 4th |
| **Totals WM20** | | | **12** | **3** | **1** | **4** | **6** | **—** |

**Lindstrom, Mattias**
**b. Lulea, Sweden, March 21, 1991**

| | | | | | | | | |
|---|---|---|---|---|---|---|---|---|
| 2009 WM18 | 27-F | SWE | 6 | 0 | 0 | 0 | 4 | 5th |

**Lindstrom, Sanny**
**b. Huddinge, Sweden, December 24, 1979**

| | | | | | | | | |
|---|---|---|---|---|---|---|---|---|
| 1999 WM20 | 4-D | SWE | 5 | 0 | 0 | 0 | 2 | 4th |
| 2005 WM | 5-D | SWE | 3 | 0 | 0 | 0 | 0 | 4th |
| 2010 WM | 8-D | SWE | 5 | 0 | 0 | 0 | 0 | B |
| **Totals WM** | | | **8** | **0** | **0** | **0** | **0** | **B** |

**Linke, Mads**
**b. Gentofte, Denmark, April 5, 1990**

| | | | | | | | | |
|---|---|---|---|---|---|---|---|---|
| 2008 WM18 | 16-F | DEN | 6 | 0 | 0 | 0 | 4 | 10th |

**Linnet, Joachim**
**b. Herning, Denmark, April 11, 1993**

| | | | | | | | | |
|---|---|---|---|---|---|---|---|---|
| 2012 WM20 | 22-F | DEN | 6 | 0 | 0 | 0 | 2 | 10th |

**Lintner, Richard**
**b. Trencin, Czechoslovakia (Slovakia), November 15, 1977**

| | | | | | | | | |
|---|---|---|---|---|---|---|---|---|
| 1996 WM20 | 22-D | SVK | 6 | 0 | 1 | 1 | 12 | 7th |
| 1997 WM20 | 22-D | SVK | 6 | 2 | 1 | 3 | 22 | 6th |
| 2001 WM | 41-D | SVK | 7 | 0 | 2 | 2 | 2 | 7th |
| 2002 OG-M | 41-D | SVK | 4 | 1 | 1 | 2 | 0 | 13th |
| 2002 WM | 41-D | SVK | 9 | 4 | 4 | 8 | 22 | G |
| 2003 WM | 41-D | SVK | 9 | 1 | 3 | 4 | 2 | B |
| 2004 WM | 41-D | SVK | 8 | 2 | 3 | 5 | 6 | 4th |
| 2004 WCH | 41-D | SVK | 3 | 0 | 0 | 0 | 2 | 7th |
| 2005 WM | 41-D | SVK | 7 | 0 | 0 | 0 | 0 | 5th |
| 2010 WM | 41-D | SVK | 6 | 0 | 3 | 3 | 2 | 12th |
| **Totals WM20** | | | **12** | **2** | **2** | **4** | **34** | **—** |
| **Totals WM** | | | **46** | **7** | **15** | **22** | **34** | **G,B** |

~WM All-Star Team/Defence (2002)

**Lipsbergs, Edgars**
**b. Riga, Soviet Union (Latvia), June 10, 1989**

| | | | | | | | | |
|---|---|---|---|---|---|---|---|---|
| 2007 WM18 | 16-F | LAT | 6 | 1 | 1 | 2 | 6 | 10th |
| 2009 WM20 | 27-F | LAT | 6 | 0 | 0 | 0 | 2 | 8th |

**Lipsbergs, Kriss**
**b. Riga, Latvia, April 3, 1993**

| | | | | | | | | |
|---|---|---|---|---|---|---|---|---|
| 2010 WM18 | 3-D | LAT | 6 | 0 | 0 | 0 | 2 | 9th |
| 2012 WM20 | 18-D | LAT | 6 | 0 | 1 | 1 | 0 | 9th |

**Lipsbergs, Miks**
**b. Riga, Soviet Union (Latvia), June 9, 1991**

| | | | | | | | | |
|---|---|---|---|---|---|---|---|---|
| 2010 WM20 | 20-F | LAT | 6 | 1 | 0 | 1 | 6 | 9th |

**Lipsbergs, Roberts**
**b. July 29, 1994**

| | | | | | | | | |
|---|---|---|---|---|---|---|---|---|
| 2012 WM18 | 22-F | LAT | 6 | 4 | 0 | 4 | 2 | 9th |
| 2012 WM20 | 11-F | LAT | 6 | 2 | 1 | 3 | 2 | 9th |

**Lisin, Enver**
**b. Moscow, Soviet Union (Russia), April 22, 1986**

| | | | | | | | | |
|---|---|---|---|---|---|---|---|---|
| 2004 WM18 | 26-F | RUS | 6 | 1 | 0 | 1 | 12 | G |
| 2005 WM20 | 26-F | RUS | 6 | 2 | 3 | 5 | 0 | S |
| 2006 WM20 | 7-F | RUS | 6 | 2 | 0 | 2 | 2 | S |
| **Totals WM20** | | | **12** | **4** | **3** | **7** | **2** | **2S** |

**Liska, Juraj**
**b. Ilava, Czechoslovakia (Slovakia), October 3, 1985**

| | | | | | | | | |
|---|---|---|---|---|---|---|---|---|
| 2004 WM20 | 4-D | SVK | 6 | 0 | 0 | 0 | 0 | 6th |
| 2005 WM20 | 29-D | SVK | 6 | 0 | 0 | 0 | 0 | 7th |
| **Totals WM20** | | | **12** | **0** | **0** | **0** | **0** | **—** |

**Lison, Marek**
**b. Bratislava, Czechoslovakia (Slovakia), November 15, 1990**

| | | | | | | | | |
|---|---|---|---|---|---|---|---|---|
| 2008 WM18 | 9-F | SVK | 6 | 1 | 0 | 1 | 2 | 7th |

**Lisov, Nikita**
**b. Zaporozhye, Ukraine, May 23, 1994**

| | | | | | | | | |
|---|---|---|---|---|---|---|---|---|
| 2012 WM18 | 4-D | RUS | 6 | 0 | 0 | 0 | 2 | 5th |

**Little, Bryan**
**b. Edmonton, Alberta, Canada, November 12, 1987**

| | | | | | | | | |
|---|---|---|---|---|---|---|---|---|
| 2007 WM20 | 20-F | CAN | 6 | 1 | 1 | 2 | 14 | G |

**Litvinenko, Alexei**
**b. Kazakhstanskaya, Kazakhstan, March 7, 1980**

| | | | | | | | | |
|---|---|---|---|---|---|---|---|---|
| 1999 WM20 | 7-D | KAZ | 6 | 0 | 1 | 1 | 33 | 6th |
| 2000 WM20 | 5-D | KAZ | 7 | 1 | 0 | 1 | 20 | 8th |
| 2005 WM | 5-D | KAZ | 3 | 1 | 0 | 1 | 0 | 12th |
| 2006 WM | 7-F | KAZ | 6 | 1 | 1 | 2 | 10 | 15th |
| 2010 WM | 5-D | KAZ | 6 | 0 | 0 | 0 | 0 | 16th |
| 2012 WM | 7-D | KAZ | 6 | 0 | 0 | 0 | 8 | 16th |
| **Totals WM20** | | | **13** | **1** | **1** | **2** | **53** | **—** |
| **Totals WM** | | | **21** | **2** | **1** | **3** | **18** | **—** |

**Ljostad, Henrik**
**b. Asker, Norway, April 13, 1991**

| | | | | | | | | |
|---|---|---|---|---|---|---|---|---|
| 2009 WM18 | 8-D | NOR | 6 | 0 | 0 | 0 | 6 | 9th |

**Locke, Eric**
**b. Mississauga, Ontario, Canada, November 21, 1993**

| | | | | | | | | |
|---|---|---|---|---|---|---|---|---|
| 2011 WM18 | 15-F | CAN | 7 | 2 | 1 | 3 | 6 | 4th |

**Loeffel, Romain**
**b. Colombier, Switzerland, March 10, 1991**

| | | | | | | | | |
|---|---|---|---|---|---|---|---|---|
| 2008 WM18 | 6-D | SUI | 6 | 0 | 1 | 1 | 18 | 8th |
| 2009 WM18 | 5-D | SUI | 6 | 0 | 4 | 4 | 12 | 8th |
| 2011 WM20 | 5-D | SUI | 6 | 1 | 0 | 1 | 4 | 5th |
| **Totals WM18** | | | **12** | **0** | **5** | **5** | **30** | **—** |

**Lofquist, Sam**
**b. Somerset, Wisconsin, United States, March 15, 1990**

| | | | | | | | | |
|---|---|---|---|---|---|---|---|---|
| 2008 WM18 | 28-D | USA | 7 | 0 | 0 | 0 | 6 | G |

**Loginov, Alexander**
**b. Ufa, Soviet Union (Russia), February 18, 1987**

| | | | | | | | | |
|---|---|---|---|---|---|---|---|---|
| 2007 WM20 | 18-D | RUS | 6 | 1 | 2 | 3 | 4 | S |

**Loichat, Michael**
**b. La Chaux-de-Fonds, Switzerland, May 31, 1990**

| | | | | | | | | |
|---|---|---|---|---|---|---|---|---|
| 2010 WM20 | 23-D | SUI | 7 | 2 | 1 | 3 | 0 | 4th |

**Lojek, Martin**
**b. Brno, Czechoslovakia (Czech Republic), August 19, 1985**

| | | | | | | | | |
|---|---|---|---|---|---|---|---|---|
| 2005 WM20 | 3-D | CZE | 7 | 0 | 0 | 0 | 2 | B |

**Lokken-Ostli, Lars**
**b. Hamar, Norway, November 21, 1986**

| | | | | | | | | |
|---|---|---|---|---|---|---|---|---|
| 2010 WM | 37-D | NOR | 6 | 0 | 2 | 2 | 2 | 9th |
| 2012 WM | 37-D | NOR | 8 | 0 | 0 | 0 | 0 | 8th |
| **Totals WM** | | | **14** | **0** | **2** | **2** | **2** | **—** |

**Loktionov, Andrei**
**b. Voskresensk, Soviet Union (Russia), May 30, 1990**

| | | | | | | | | |
|---|---|---|---|---|---|---|---|---|
| 2007 WM18 | 17-F | RUS | 7 | 2 | 4 | 6 | 2 | G |
| 2008 WM18 | 17-F | RUS | 6 | 3 | 5 | 8 | 29 | S |
| **Totals WM18** | | | **13** | **5** | **9** | **14** | **31** | **—** |

**Lombardi, Matt**
**b. Montreal, Quebec, Canada, March 18, 1982**

| | | | | | | | | |
|---|---|---|---|---|---|---|---|---|
| 2007 WM | 18-F | CAN | 9 | 6 | 6 | 12 | 4 | G |
| 2009 WM | 18-F | CAN | 9 | 2 | 2 | 4 | 6 | S |
| **Totals WM** | | | **18** | **8** | **8** | **16** | **10** | **G,S** |

**Lopachuk, Stanislav**
**b. Minsk, Belarus, February 16, 1992**

| | | | | | | | | |
|---|---|---|---|---|---|---|---|---|
| 2010 WM18 | 9-F | BLR | 6 | 2 | 5 | 7 | 2 | 10th |

**Lorentzen, Peter**
**b. Halden, Norway, September 2, 1983**

| | | | | | | | | |
|---|---|---|---|---|---|---|---|---|
| 2001 WM18 | 8-F | NOR | 6 | 2 | 3 | 5 | 0 | 9th |
| 2009 WM | 14-F | NOR | 6 | 0 | 0 | 0 | 0 | 11th |
| 2010 WM | 14-F | NOR | 5 | 1 | 0 | 1 | 2 | 9th |
| 2011 WM | 14-F | NOR | 7 | 0 | 0 | 0 | 2 | 6th |
| **Totals WM** | | | **18** | **1** | **0** | **1** | **4** | **—** |

**Lorenz, Sean**
**b. Littleton, Colorado, United States, March 10, 1990**

| | | | | | | | | |
|---|---|---|---|---|---|---|---|---|
| 2008 WM18 | 3-D | USA | 7 | 0 | 0 | 0 | 0 | G |

**Lotscher, Kevin**
**b. Visp, Switzerland, February 17, 1988**

| | | | | | | | | |
|---|---|---|---|---|---|---|---|---|
| 2007 WM20 | 13-F | SUI | 6 | 0 | 0 | 0 | 0 | 7th |
| 2008 WM20 | 13-F | SUI | 6 | 1 | 0 | 1 | 8 | 9th |
| 2011 WM | 71-F | SUI | 6 | 2 | 0 | 2 | 2 | 9th |
| **Totals WM20** | | | **12** | **1** | **0** | **1** | **8** | **—** |

**Louis, Anthony**
**b. Winfield, Illinois, United States, February 10, 1995**

| | | | | | | | | |
|---|---|---|---|---|---|---|---|---|
| 2012 WM18 | 28-F | USA | 6 | 0 | 1 | 1 | 2 | G |

**Louring, Mads**
**b. Charlottenlund, Denmark, January 8, 1990**

| | | | | | | | | |
|---|---|---|---|---|---|---|---|---|
| 2008 WM18 | 21-F | DEN | 6 | 0 | 0 | 0 | 0 | 10th |

**Lucenius, Niclas**
**b. Turku, Finland, May 3, 1989**

| | | | | | | | | |
|---|---|---|---|---|---|---|---|---|
| 2006 WM18 | 21-F | FIN | 6 | 0 | 0 | 0 | 0 | S |
| 2007 WM18 | 10-F | FIN | 4 | 1 | 1 | 2 | 4 | 7th |
| 2008 WM20 | 26-F | FIN | 6 | 2 | 4 | 6 | 2 | 6th |
| 2009 WM20 | 10-F | FIN | 6 | 1 | 2 | 3 | 8 | 7th |
| **Totals WM18** | | | **10** | **1** | **1** | **2** | **4** | **S** |
| **Totals WM20** | | | **12** | **3** | **6** | **9** | **10** | **—** |

**Lukas, Philipp**
**b. Vienna, Austria, December 4, 1979**

| | | | | | | | | |
|---|---|---|---|---|---|---|---|---|
| 2000 WM | 19-F | AUT | 6 | 0 | 0 | 0 | 2 | 13th |
| 2001 WM | 19-F | AUT | 6 | 1 | 0 | 1 | 0 | 11th |
| 2002 WM | 19-F | AUT | 6 | 1 | 2 | 3 | 4 | 12th |
| 2003 WM | 19-F | AUT | 6 | 0 | 3 | 3 | 2 | 10th |
| 2004 WM | 19-F | AUT | 5 | 1 | 0 | 1 | 0 | 11th |
| 2007 WM | 19-F | AUT | 6 | 2 | 1 | 3 | 0 | 15th |
| 2011 WM | 19-F | AUT | 6 | 0 | 1 | 1 | 6 | 15th |
| **Totals WM** | | | **41** | **5** | **7** | **12** | **14** | **—** |

**Lukas, Robert**
**b. Vienna, Austria, August 29, 1978**

| | | | | | | | | |
|---|---|---|---|---|---|---|---|---|
| 2002 OG-M | 13-D | AUT | 4 | 0 | 0 | 0 | 0 | 12th |
| 2002 WM | 19-D | AUT | 6 | 1 | 1 | 2 | 0 | 12th |
| 2003 WM | 55-D | AUT | 6 | 0 | 2 | 2 | 4 | 10th |
| 2004 WM | 55-D | AUT | 6 | 1 | 2 | 3 | 0 | 11th |
| 2005 WM | 55-D | AUT | 6 | 1 | 0 | 1 | 2 | 16th |
| 2007 WM | 55-D | AUT | 6 | 1 | 1 | 2 | 12 | 15th |
| 2009 WM | 55-D | AUT | 1 | 0 | 0 | 0 | 0 | 14th |
| 2011 WM | 55-D | AUT | 6 | 0 | 1 | 1 | 2 | 15th |
| **Totals WM** | | | **37** | **4** | **7** | **11** | **20** | **—** |

**Lukyanenko, Dmitri**
**b. Gomel, Belarus, July 18, 1992**

| | | | | | | | | |
|---|---|---|---|---|---|---|---|---|
| 2010 WM18 | 2-D | BLR | 6 | 0 | 0 | 0 | 2 | 10th |

**Lund, Lars Erik**
**b. Oslo, Norway, July 25, 1974**

| | | | | | | | | |
|---|---|---|---|---|---|---|---|---|
| 2006 WM | 36-D | NOR | 6 | 0 | 0 | 0 | 2 | 11th |
| 2007 WM | 36-D | NOR | 6 | 1 | 4 | 5 | 4 | 14th |
| 2009 WM | 36-D | NOR | 6 | 1 | 1 | 2 | 0 | 11th |
| 2010 OG-M | 36-D | NOR | 4 | 0 | 0 | 0 | 0 | 10th |
| **Totals WM** | | | **18** | **2** | **5** | **7** | **6** | **—** |

**Lund, Mads**
**b. Vojens, Denmark, November 24, 1988**

| | | | | | | | | |
|---|---|---|---|---|---|---|---|---|
| 2008 WM20 | 11-F | DEN | 1 | 0 | 0 | 0 | 0 | 10th |

**Lund, Martin**
**b. Fredrikstad, Norway, June 28, 1993**

| | | | | | | | | |
|---|---|---|---|---|---|---|---|---|
| 2011 WM18 | 7-F | NOR | 6 | 1 | 0 | 1 | 0 | 9th |

**Lundberg, Emil**
**b. Katrineholm, Sweden, September 17, 1993**

| | | | | | | | | |
|---|---|---|---|---|---|---|---|---|
| 2011 WM18 | 22-F | SWE | 6 | 1 | 0 | 1 | 4 | S |

**Lundberg, Martin**
**b. Skelleftea, Sweden, June 7, 1990**

| | | | | | | | | |
|---|---|---|---|---|---|---|---|---|
| 2008 WM18 | 15-F | SWE | 6 | 1 | 1 | 2 | 8 | 4th |
| 2010 WM20 | 27-F | SWE | 5 | 0 | 2 | 2 | 4 | B |

**Lundh, Patrik**
**b. Stockholm, Sweden, June 12, 1988**

| | | | | | | | | |
|---|---|---|---|---|---|---|---|---|
| 2006 WM18 | 24-F | SWE | 6 | 0 | 1 | 1 | 4 | 6th |
| 2008 WM20 | 17-F | SWE | 6 | 1 | 0 | 1 | 6 | S |

**Lundin, Mike**
**b. Burnsville, Minnesota, United States, September 24, 1984**

| | | | | | | | | |
|---|---|---|---|---|---|---|---|---|
| 2010 WM | 39-D | USA | 6 | 0 | 1 | 1 | 0 | 13th |

**Lundqvist, Joel**
**b. Are, Sweden, March 2, 1982**

| | | | | | | | | |
|---|---|---|---|---|---|---|---|---|
| 2000 WM18 | 10-F | SWE | 6 | 3 | 1 | 4 | 2 | B |
| 2002 WM20 | 27-F | SWE | 7 | 1 | 1 | 2 | 6 | 6th |
| 2006 WM | 20-F | SWE | 8 | 1 | 0 | 1 | 4 | G |
| 2009 WM | 20-F | SWE | 1 | 0 | 0 | 0 | 0 | B |
| 2012 WM | 20-F | SWE | 3 | 1 | 1 | 2 | 2 | 6th |
| **Totals WM** | | | **12** | **2** | **1** | **3** | **6** | **G,B** |

**Luoma, Mikko**
**b. Jyvaskyla, Finland, June 22, 1976**

| | | | | | | | | |
|---|---|---|---|---|---|---|---|---|
| 2006 WM | 9-D | FIN | 9 | 0 | 2 | 2 | 6 | B |
| 2008 WM | 19-D | FIN | 8 | 0 | 0 | 0 | 6 | B |
| **Totals WM** | | | **17** | **0** | **2** | **2** | **12** | **2B** |

**Lupul, Joffrey**
**b. Edmonton, Alberta, Canada, September 23, 1983**

| | | | | | | | | |
|---|---|---|---|---|---|---|---|---|
| 2003 WM20 | 15-F | CAN | 6 | 2 | 1 | 3 | 27 | S |

**Lusnak, Patrik**
**b. Trencin, Czechoslovakia (Slovakia), November 6, 1988**

| | | | | | | | | |
|---|---|---|---|---|---|---|---|---|
| 2008 WM20 | 14-F | SVK | 6 | 2 | 3 | 5 | 2 | 7th |

**Lussier, Anthoine**
**b. Bonneville, France, February 8, 1983**

| | | | | | | | | |
|---|---|---|---|---|---|---|---|---|
| 2008 WM | 26-F | FRA | 5 | 0 | 0 | 0 | 4 | 14th |
| 2009 WM | 26-F | FRA | 6 | 2 | 0 | 2 | 6 | 12th |
| 2010 WM | 26-F | FRA | 6 | 0 | 1 | 1 | 2 | 14th |
| **Totals WM** | | | **17** | **2** | **1** | **3** | **12** | **—** |

**Luthi, Simon**
**b. Langnau, Switzerland, September 12, 1986**

| | | | | | | | | |
|---|---|---|---|---|---|---|---|---|
| 2003 WM18 | 5-D | SUI | 6 | 0 | 2 | 2 | 27 | 9th |
| 2006 WM20 | 8-D | SUI | 6 | 0 | 2 | 2 | 2 | 7th |

**Lutz, Andreas**
**b. Merano, Italy, March 30, 1986**

| | | | | | | | | |
|---|---|---|---|---|---|---|---|---|
| 2008 WM | 25-D | ITA | 4 | 0 | 0 | 0 | 2 | 16th |

**Luza, Patrik**
**b. Bratislava, Slovakia, July 27, 1994**

| | | | | | | | | |
|---|---|---|---|---|---|---|---|---|
| 2011 WM18 | 3-D | SVK | 6 | 0 | 0 | 0 | 2 | 10th |

**Lyamin, Kirill**
**b. Moscow, Soviet Union (Russia), January 13, 1986**

| | | | | | | | | |
|---|---|---|---|---|---|---|---|---|
| 2004 WM18 | 4-D | RUS | 6 | 1 | 0 | 1 | 20 | G |
| 2006 WM20 | 6-D | RUS | 6 | 0 | 0 | 0 | 6 | S |

**Lydman, Toni**
**b. Lahti, Finland, September 25, 1977**

| | | | | | | | | |
|---|---|---|---|---|---|---|---|---|
| 1996 WM20 | 6-D | FIN | 6 | 0 | 2 | 2 | 6 | 6th |
| 1997 WM20 | 6-D | FIN | 6 | 2 | 0 | 2 | 6 | 5th |
| 1998 WM | 9-D | FIN | 10 | 0 | 1 | 1 | 31 | S |
| 1999 WM | 9-D | FIN | 10 | 0 | 0 | 0 | 4 | S |
| 2000 WM | 9-D | FIN | 9 | 1 | 0 | 1 | 12 | B |
| 2002 WM | 9-D | FIN | 9 | 1 | 1 | 2 | 10 | 4th |
| 2003 WM | 9-D | FIN | 7 | 2 | 1 | 3 | 6 | 5th |
| 2004 WCH | 32-D | FIN | 6 | 0 | 3 | 3 | 6 | 2nd |
| 2006 OG-M | 32-D | FIN | 8 | 1 | 0 | 1 | 10 | S |
| 2010 OG-M | 32-D | FIN | 6 | 0 | 0 | 0 | 2 | B |
| **Totals WM20** | | | **12** | **2** | **2** | **4** | **12** | **—** |
| **Totals WM** | | | **45** | **4** | **3** | **7** | **63** | **2S,B** |
| **Totals OG-M** | | | **14** | **1** | **0** | **1** | **12** | **S,B** |

**Lykkeskov, Kim**
**b. Vojens, Denmark, July 20, 1983**

| | | | | | | | | |
|---|---|---|---|---|---|---|---|---|
| 2008 WM | 11-F | DEN | 6 | 0 | 0 | 0 | 4 | 12th |
| 2009 WM | 15-F | DEN | 6 | 0 | 2 | 2 | 2 | 13th |
| 2010 WM | 23-F | DEN | 7 | 0 | 0 | 0 | 0 | 8th |
| 2012 WM | 23-F | DEN | 4 | 0 | 0 | 0 | 0 | 13th |
| **Totals WM** | | | **23** | **0** | **2** | **2** | **6** | **—** |

**Lynch, Kevin**
**b. Grosse Pointe, Michigan, United States, April 23, 1991**

| | | | | | | | | |
|---|---|---|---|---|---|---|---|---|
| 2009 WM18 | 14-F | USA | 7 | 5 | 5 | 10 | 6 | G |

**Lyoe, Rasmus**
**b. Odense, Denmark, June 19, 1994**

| | | | | | | | | |
|---|---|---|---|---|---|---|---|---|
| 2012 WM18 | 5-D | DEN | 6 | 0 | 0 | 0 | 0 | 10th |

**Lyubimov, Roman**
**b. Tver, Russia, June 1, 1992**

| | | | | | | | | |
|---|---|---|---|---|---|---|---|---|
| 2010 WM18 | 13-F | RUS | 7 | 0 | 1 | 1 | 6 | 4th |

**Maatta, Olli**
**b. Jyvaskyla, Finland, August 22, 1994**

| | | | | | | | | |
|---|---|---|---|---|---|---|---|---|
| 2011 WM18 | 4-D | FIN | 6 | 1 | 3 | 4 | 0 | 5th |
| 2011 WM20 | 15-D | FIN | 6 | 0 | 0 | 0 | 0 | 6th |
| 2012 WM20 | 2-D | FIN | 1 | 0 | 0 | 0 | 0 | 4th |
| **Totals WM20** | | | **7** | **0** | **0** | **0** | **0** | **—** |

**MacArthur, Clarke**
**b. Lloydminster, Alberta, Canada, April 6, 1985**

| | | | | | | | | |
|---|---|---|---|---|---|---|---|---|
| 2005 WM20 | 17-F | CAN | 6 | 4 | 0 | 4 | 10 | G |

**Macejko, Miroslav**
**b. Gelnica, Slovakia, April 9, 1992**

| | | | | | | | | |
|---|---|---|---|---|---|---|---|---|
| 2010 WM18 | 3-D | SVK | 6 | 0 | 0 | 0 | 0 | 8th |

**Machac, Patrik**
**b. Hyskov, Czech Republic, April 23, 1994**

| | | | | | | | | |
|---|---|---|---|---|---|---|---|---|
| 2012 WM18 | 11-F | CZE | 4 | 0 | 2 | 2 | 6 | 8th |

**Macho, Michal**
**b. Martin, Czechoslovakia (Slovakia), January 17, 1982**

| | | | | | | | | |
|---|---|---|---|---|---|---|---|---|
| 2000 WM18 | 17-F | SVK | 4 | 1 | 0 | 1 | 2 | 5th |
| 2002 WM20 | 17-F | SVK | 7 | 0 | 2 | 2 | 6 | 8th |
| 2009 WM | 17-F | SVK | 1 | 0 | 0 | 0 | 0 | 10th |
| 2010 WM | 17-F | SVK | 6 | 0 | 0 | 0 | 0 | 12th |
| **Totals WM** | | | **7** | **0** | **0** | **0** | **0** | **—** |

**Macijevskis, Aleksandrs**
**b. Riga, Soviet Union (Latvia), June 26, 1975**

| | | | | | | | | |
|---|---|---|---|---|---|---|---|---|
| 1997 WM | 8-F | LAT | 8 | 1 | 0 | 1 | 0 | 7th |
| 2001 WM | 12-F | LAT | 6 | 0 | 0 | 0 | 0 | 13th |
| 2002 OG-M | 12-F | LAT | 4 | 2 | 3 | 5 | 0 | 9th |
| 2002 WM | 12-F | LAT | 6 | 0 | 1 | 1 | 0 | 11th |
| 2003 WM | 81-F | LAT | 6 | 0 | 0 | 0 | 0 | 9th |
| 2004 WM | 81-F | LAT | 7 | 1 | 1 | 2 | 2 | 7th |
| 2005 WM | 25-F | LAT | 5 | 0 | 1 | 1 | 0 | 9th |
| 2007 WM | 26-F | LAT | 6 | 0 | 1 | 1 | 10 | 13th |
| 2008 WM | 35-F | LAT | 3 | 0 | 0 | 0 | 0 | 11th |
| **Totals WM** | | | **47** | **2** | **4** | **6** | **12** | **—** |

**Madsen, Morten**
**b. Rodovre, Denmark, January 16, 1987**

| | | | | | | | | |
|---|---|---|---|---|---|---|---|---|
| 2004 WM18 | 21-F | DEN | 6 | 3 | 5 | 8 | 2 | 8th |
| 2005 WM18 | 21-F | DEN | 6 | 2 | 2 | 4 | 2 | 10th |
| 2006 WM | 29-F | DEN | 3 | 0 | 0 | 0 | 0 | 13th |
| 2007 WM | 29-F | DEN | 5 | 1 | 0 | 1 | 4 | 10th |
| 2008 WM | 29-F | DEN | 6 | 1 | 1 | 2 | 4 | 12th |
| 2009 WM | 29-F | DEN | 6 | 1 | 2 | 3 | 2 | 13th |
| 2010 WM | 29-F | DEN | 7 | 2 | 2 | 4 | 6 | 8th |
| 2011 WM | 29-F | DEN | 6 | 0 | 1 | 1 | 2 | 11th |
| 2012 WM | 29-F | DEN | 7 | 2 | 0 | 2 | 6 | 13th |
| **Totals WM18** | | | **12** | **5** | **7** | **12** | **4** | **—** |
| **Totals WM** | | | **40** | **7** | **6** | **13** | **24** | **—** |

**Madesen, Patrick**
**b. Herning, Denmark, January 9, 1993**

| | | | | | | | | |
|---|---|---|---|---|---|---|---|---|
| 2012 WM20 | 4-D | DEN | 6 | 0 | 0 | 0 | 4 | 10th |

**Madso, Kenneth**
**b. Trondheim, Norway, January 25, 1991**

| | | | | | | | | |
|---|---|---|---|---|---|---|---|---|
| 2009 WM18 | 7-D | NOR | 4 | 0 | 2 | 2 | 4 | 9th |
| 2011 WM20 | 7-D | NOR | 6 | 0 | 0 | 0 | 2 | 9th |

**Maenpaa, Mikko**
**b. Tampere, Finland, April 19, 1983**

| | | | | | | | | |
|---|---|---|---|---|---|---|---|---|
| 2001 WM18 | 7-D | FIN | 6 | 0 | 1 | 1 | 4 | B |
| 2010 WM | 7-D | FIN | 7 | 0 | 1 | 1 | 2 | 6th |
| 2012 WM | 7-D | FIN | 10 | 1 | 4 | 5 | 6 | 4th |
| **Totals WM** | | | **17** | **1** | **5** | **6** | **8** | **—** |

**Magdeyev, Roman**
**b. Togliatti, Soviet Union (Russia), April 17, 1987**

| | | | | | | | | |
|---|---|---|---|---|---|---|---|---|
| 2007 WM20 | 21-F | BLR | 6 | 0 | 1 | 1 | 8 | 10th |

**Magusin, Tomas**
**b. Partizanske, Czechoslovakia (Slovakia), April 8, 1987**

| | | | | | | | | |
|---|---|---|---|---|---|---|---|---|
| 2007 WM20 | 10-D | SVK | 6 | 0 | 0 | 0 | 0 | 8th |

**Maier, Patrick**
**b. Klaus, Austria, April 17, 1990**

| | | | | | | | | |
|---|---|---|---|---|---|---|---|---|
| 2010 WM20 | 16-F | AUT | 6 | 0 | 1 | 1 | 2 | 10th |

**Majdan, Juraj**
**b. Ilava, Czechoslovakia (Slovakia), August 20, 1991**

| | | | | | | | | |
|---|---|---|---|---|---|---|---|---|
| 2009 WM18 | 19-F | SVK | 6 | 1 | 0 | 1 | 10 | 7th |
| 2011 WM20 | 9-F | SVK | 6 | 1 | 2 | 3 | 6 | 8th |

**Majesky, Ivan**
**b. Banska Bystrica, Czechoslovakia (Slovakia), September 2, 1976**

| | | | | | | | | |
|---|---|---|---|---|---|---|---|---|
| 2002 OG-M | 22-D | SVK | 4 | 0 | 1 | 1 | 4 | 13th |
| 2003 WM | 23-D | SVK | 9 | 0 | 0 | 0 | 4 | B |
| 2004 WM | 28-D | SVK | 9 | 0 | 0 | 0 | 6 | 4th |
| 2005 WM | 29-D | SVK | 1 | 0 | 0 | 0 | 0 | 5th |
| 2006 OG-M | 29-D | SVK | 6 | 0 | 0 | 0 | 4 | 5th |
| 2008 WM | 23-D | SVK | 5 | 0 | 0 | 0 | 8 | 13th |
| 2010 WM | 8-D | SVK | 6 | 1 | 1 | 2 | 0 | 12th |
| 2011 WM | 16-D | SVK | 6 | 0 | 2 | 2 | 6 | 10th |
| **Totals WM** | | | **36** | **1** | **3** | **4** | **24** | **B** |
| **Totals OG-M** | | | **10** | **0** | **1** | **1** | **8** | **—** |

**Makarov, Igor**
**b. Moscow, Soviet Union (Russia), September 19, 1987**

| | | | | | | | | |
|---|---|---|---|---|---|---|---|---|
| 2005 WM18 | 25-F | RUS | 6 | 5 | 0 | 5 | 2 | 5th |
| 2007 WM20 | 25-F | RUS | 6 | 2 | 4 | 6 | 2 | S |

**Makarovs, Ilja**
**b. January 5, 1994**

| | | | | | | | | |
|---|---|---|---|---|---|---|---|---|
| 2012 WM18 | 24-D | LAT | 6 | 0 | 0 | 0 | 0 | 9th |

**Makinen, Atte**
**b. Tampere, Finland, May 17, 1995**

| | | | | | | | | |
|---|---|---|---|---|---|---|---|---|
| 2012 WM18 | 3-D | FIN | 7 | 1 | 0 | 1 | 2 | 4th |

**Makinen, Konsta**
**b. Tampere, Finland, January 19, 1992**

| | | | | | | | | |
|---|---|---|---|---|---|---|---|---|
| 2010 WM18 | 29-D | FIN | 6 | 1 | 1 | 2 | 16 | B |
| 2012 WM20 | 4-D | FIN | 7 | 0 | 0 | 0 | 6 | 4th |

**Makkonen, Jussi**
**b. Turku, Finland, April 24, 1985**

| | | | | | | | | |
|---|---|---|---|---|---|---|---|---|
| 2005 WM20 | 29-F | FIN | 5 | 2 | 2 | 4 | 8 | 5th |

**Malenkikh, Yegor**
**b. Chelyabinsk, Russia, January 22, 1994**

| | | | | | | | | |
|---|---|---|---|---|---|---|---|---|
| 2012 WM18 | 8-D | RUS | 6 | 0 | 1 | 1 | 0 | 5th |

**Malinen, Jarkko**
**b. Kuopio, Finland, March 17, 1988**

| | | | | | | | | |
|---|---|---|---|---|---|---|---|---|
| 2008 WM20 | 15-F | FIN | 6 | 1 | 0 | 1 | 0 | 6th |

**Malinovski, Vladimir**
**b. Magnitogorsk, Soviet Union (Russia), June 9, 1991**

| | | | | | | | | |
|---|---|---|---|---|---|---|---|---|
| 2009 WM18 | 14-F | RUS | 7 | 0 | 0 | 0 | 8 | S |

**Malkamaki, Miko**
**b. Kokkola, Finland, May 1, 1988**

| | | | | | | | | |
|---|---|---|---|---|---|---|---|---|
| 2006 WM18 | 4-D | FIN | 6 | 0 | 1 | 1 | 2 | S |
| 2008 WM20 | 4-D | FIN | 6 | 0 | 0 | 0 | 33 | 6th |

**Malkin, Yevgeni**
**b. Magnitogorsk, Soviet Union (Russia), July 31, 1986**

| | | | | | | | | |
|---|---|---|---|---|---|---|---|---|
| 2003 WM18 | 17-F | RUS | 6 | 5 | 4 | 9 | 2 | B |
| 2004 WM18 | 17-F | RUS | 6 | 4 | 4 | 8 | 31 | G |
| 2004 WM20 | 17-F | RUS | 6 | 1 | 4 | 5 | 0 | 5th |
| 2005 WM20 | 17-F | RUS | 6 | 3 | 7 | 10 | 16 | S |
| 2005 WM | 18-F | RUS | 9 | 0 | 4 | 4 | 8 | B |
| 2006 WM20 | 17-F | RUS | 6 | 4 | 6 | 10 | 12 | S |
| 2006 OG-M | 18-F | RUS | 7 | 2 | 4 | 6 | 31 | 4th |
| 2006 WM | 71-F | RUS | 7 | 3 | 6 | 9 | 6 | 5th |
| 2007 WM | 11-F | RUS | 9 | 5 | 5 | 10 | 6 | B |
| 2010 OG-M | 11-F | RUS | 4 | 3 | 3 | 6 | 0 | 6th |
| 2010 WM | 11-F | RUS | 5 | 5 | 2 | 7 | 10 | S |
| 2012 WM | 11-F | RUS | 10 | 11 | 8 | 19 | 4 | G |
| **Totals WM18** | | | **12** | **9** | **8** | **17** | **33** | **G,B** |
| **Totals WM20** | | | **18** | **8** | **17** | **25** | **28** | **2S** |
| **Totals WM** | | | **40** | **24** | **25** | **49** | **34** | **G,S,2B** |
| **Totals OG-M** | | | **11** | **5** | **7** | **12** | **31** | **—** |

~WM MVP (2012), WM IIHF Directorate Best Forward (2012), WM All-Star Team/Forward (2007, 2010, 2012), WM20 MVP (2006), WM20 IIHF Directorate Best Forward (2006), WM20 All-Star Team/Forward (2006)

**Malle, Jesper**
**b. Vojens, Denmark, May 10, 1990**

| | | | | | | | | |
|---|---|---|---|---|---|---|---|---|
| 2008 WM18 | 24-F | DEN | 5 | 0 | 0 | 0 | 2 | 10th |

**Malone, Ryan**
**b. Pittsburgh, Pennsylvania, United States, December 1, 1979**

| | | | | | | | | |
|---|---|---|---|---|---|---|---|---|
| 2004 WM | 12-F | USA | 9 | 3 | 0 | 3 | 2 | B |
| 2006 WM | 12-F | USA | 7 | 2 | 2 | 4 | 12 | 7th |
| 2010 OG-M | 12-F | USA | 6 | 3 | 2 | 5 | 6 | S |
| **Totals WM** | | | **16** | **5** | **2** | **7** | **14** | **B** |

**Mamin, Maxim**
**b. Georgia, Soviet Union (Russia), May 17, 1988**

| | | | | | | | | |
|---|---|---|---|---|---|---|---|---|
| 2006 WM18 | 15-F | RUS | 6 | 0 | 2 | 2 | 16 | 5th |
| 2008 WM20 | 15-F | RUS | 7 | 0 | 3 | 3 | 6 | B |

**Manavian, Antonin**
**b. Paris, France, April 26, 1987**

| | | | | | | | | |
|---|---|---|---|---|---|---|---|---|
| 2009 WM | 44-D | FRA | 6 | 0 | 0 | 0 | 4 | 12th |
| 2010 WM | 44-D | FRA | 3 | 0 | 0 | 0 | 2 | 14th |
| 2012 WM | 4-D | FRA | 7 | 0 | 0 | 0 | 0 | 9th |
| **Totals WM** | | | **16** | **0** | **0** | **0** | **6** | **—** |

**Manelius, Nico**
**b. Helsinki, Finland, March 12, 1991**

| | | | | | | | | |
|---|---|---|---|---|---|---|---|---|
| 2008 WM18 | 5-D | FIN | 6 | 0 | 2 | 2 | 0 | 6th |
| 2011 WM20 | 5-D | FIN | 6 | 0 | 0 | 0 | 0 | 6th |

**Manfreda, Marjan**
**b. Bled, Yugoslavia (Slovenia), November 23, 1983**

| | | | | | | | | |
|---|---|---|---|---|---|---|---|---|
| 2008 WM | 81-F | SLO | 1 | 1 | 0 | 1 | 2 | 15th |

**Mankinen, Jesse**
**b. Lapeenranta, Finland, May 20, 1991**

| | | | | | | | | |
|---|---|---|---|---|---|---|---|---|
| 2009 WM18 | 14-F | FIN | 6 | 1 | 1 | 2 | 0 | B |

**Mannberg, Daniel**
**b. Boden, Sweden, December 27, 1992**

| | | | | | | | | |
|---|---|---|---|---|---|---|---|---|
| 2010 WM18 | 13-F | SWE | 6 | 0 | 4 | 4 | 8 | S |

**Mantha, Anthony**
**b. Longueuil, Quebec, Canada, September 16, 1994**

| | | | | | | | | |
|---|---|---|---|---|---|---|---|---|
| 2012 WM18 | 9-F | CAN | 7 | 1 | 0 | 1 | 0 | B |

**Mapes, Corey**
**b. Heilbronn, Germany, June 22, 1992**

| | | | | | | | | |
|---|---|---|---|---|---|---|---|---|
| 2011 WM20 | 9-D | GER | 6 | 1 | 1 | 2 | 14 | 10th |

**Marchand, Brad**
**b. Halifax, Nova Scotia, Canada, May 11, 1988**

| | | | | | | | | |
|---|---|---|---|---|---|---|---|---|
| 2007 WM20 | 17-F | CAN | 6 | 2 | 0 | 2 | 2 | G |
| 2008 WM20 | 17-F | CAN | 7 | 4 | 2 | 6 | 4 | G |
| **Totals WM20** | | | **13** | **6** | **2** | **8** | **6** | **2G** |

**Marchetti, Stefano**
**b. Trento, Italy, November 10, 1986**

| | | | | | | | | |
|---|---|---|---|---|---|---|---|---|
| 2010 WM | 23-D | ITA | 3 | 0 | 0 | 0 | 0 | 15th |
| 2012 WM | 23-D | ITA | 7 | 0 | 0 | 0 | 0 | 15th |
| **Totals WM** | | | **10** | **0** | **0** | **0** | **0** | **—** |

**Marcinko, Tomas**
**b. Poprad, Czechoslovakia (Slovakia), April 11, 1988**

| | | | | | | | | |
|---|---|---|---|---|---|---|---|---|
| 2005 WM18 | 6-F | SVK | 6 | 1 | 0 | 1 | 4 | 6th |
| 2006 WM18 | 6-F | SVK | 6 | 1 | 2 | 3 | 6 | 7th |
| 2007 WM20 | 8-F | SVK | 6 | 1 | 3 | 4 | 16 | 8th |
| 2008 WM20 | 6-F | SVK | 6 | 2 | 4 | 6 | 12 | 7th |
| **Totals WM18** | | | **12** | **2** | **2** | **4** | **10** | **—** |
| **Totals WM20** | | | **12** | **3** | **7** | **10** | **28** | **—** |

**Margoni, Stefano**
**b. Bolzano, Italy, May 12, 1975**

| | | | | | | | | |
|---|---|---|---|---|---|---|---|---|
| 1998 OG-M | 22-F | ITA | 2 | 0 | 0 | 0 | 0 | 12th |
| 1998 WM | 22-F | ITA | 6 | 0 | 0 | 0 | 2 | 10th |
| 1999 WM | 22-F | ITA | 3 | 0 | 0 | 0 | 0 | 13th |
| 2000 WM | 22-F | ITA | 6 | 0 | 0 | 0 | 0 | 9th |
| 2001 WM | 22-F | ITA | 6 | 0 | 0 | 0 | 0 | 12th |
| 2002 WM | 22-F | ITA | 6 | 1 | 0 | 1 | 4 | 15th |
| 2006 OG-M | 22-F | ITA | 5 | 0 | 0 | 0 | 0 | 11th |
| 2006 WM | 22-F | ITA | 6 | 0 | 1 | 1 | 8 | 14th |
| 2007 WM | 22-F | ITA | 6 | 0 | 2 | 2 | 4 | 12th |
| 2008 WM | 22-F | ITA | 5 | 0 | 0 | 0 | 4 | 16th |
| 2010 WM | 22-F | ITA | 6 | 1 | 0 | 1 | 4 | 15th |
| **Totals WM** | | | **50** | **2** | **3** | **5** | **26** | **—** |
| **Totals OG-M** | | | **7** | **0** | **0** | **0** | **0** | **—** |

**Marincin, Martin**
**b. Kosice, Slovakia, February 18, 1992**

| | | | | | | | | |
|---|---|---|---|---|---|---|---|---|
| 2009 WM18 | 13-D | SVK | 6 | 0 | 1 | 1 | 4 | 7th |
| 2010 WM18 | 21-D | SVK | 6 | 2 | 1 | 3 | 14 | 8th |
| 2010 WM20 | 25-D | SVK | 6 | 0 | 2 | 2 | 6 | 8th |
| 2011 WM20 | 21-D | SVK | 2 | 0 | 0 | 0 | 27 | 8th |
| 2012 WM20 | 21-D | SVK | 6 | 1 | 2 | 3 | 2 | 6th |
| **Totals WM18** | | | **12** | **2** | **2** | **4** | **18** | **—** |
| **Totals WM20** | | | **14** | **1** | **4** | **5** | **35** | **—** |

**Marjamaki, Masi**
**b. Pori, Finland, January 16, 1985**

| | | | | | | | | |
|---|---|---|---|---|---|---|---|---|
| 2004 WM20 | 29-F | FIN | 7 | 2 | 1 | 3 | 2 | B |
| 2005 WM20 | 19-F | FIN | 6 | 0 | 0 | 0 | 12 | 5th |
| **Totals WM20** | | | **13** | **2** | **1** | **3** | **14** | **B** |

**Markelov, Sergei**
**b. Minsk, Soviet Union (Belarus), August 23, 1990**

| | | | | | | | | |
|---|---|---|---|---|---|---|---|---|
| 2008 WM18 | 23-D | BLR | 6 | 0 | 0 | 0 | 0 | 9th |

**Markkula, Samu**
**b. Jyvaskyla, Finland, February 27, 1994**

| | | | | | | | | |
|---|---|---|---|---|---|---|---|---|
| 2012 WM18 | 12-F | FIN | 7 | 2 | 0 | 2 | 0 | 4th |

**Markov, Andrei**
**b. Voskresensk, Soviet Union (Russia), December 20, 1978**

| | | | | | | | | |
|---|---|---|---|---|---|---|---|---|
| 1997 WM20 | 21-D | RUS | 6 | 0 | 1 | 1 | 2 | B |
| 1998 WM20 | 21-D | RUS | 7 | 3 | 2 | 5 | 6 | S |
| 1999 WM | 32-D | RUS | 6 | 1 | 4 | 5 | 2 | 5th |
| 2000 WM | 32-D | RUS | 6 | 0 | 2 | 2 | 0 | 9th |
| 2004 WCH | 32-D | RUS | 2 | 0 | 1 | 1 | 2 | 6th |
| 2005 WM | 52-D | RUS | 9 | 1 | 4 | 5 | 20 | B |
| 2006 OG-M | 52-D | RUS | 8 | 1 | 2 | 3 | 6 | 4th |
| 2007 WM | 52-D | RUS | 8 | 3 | 5 | 8 | 2 | B |
| 2008 WM | 52-D | RUS | 6 | 0 | 2 | 2 | 4 | G |
| 2010 OG-M | 79-D | RUS | 4 | 0 | 2 | 2 | 0 | 6th |
| **Totals WM20** | | | **13** | **3** | **3** | **6** | **8** | **S,B** |
| **Totals WM** | | | **35** | **5** | **17** | **22** | **28** | **G,2B** |
| **Totals OG-M** | | | **12** | **1** | **4** | **5** | **6** | **—** |

~WM IIHF Directorate Best Defenceman (2007), WM All-Star Team/Defence (2007), WM20 All-Star Team/Defence (1998)

**Markovic, Jaroslav**
**b. Martin, Czechoslovakia (Slovakia), May 22, 1985**

| | | | | | | | | |
|---|---|---|---|---|---|---|---|---|
| 2003 WM18 | 25-F | SVK | 7 | 3 | 1 | 4 | 6 | S |
| 2005 WM20 | 13-F | SVK | 6 | 0 | 1 | 1 | 0 | 7th |

**Marleau, Patrick**
**b. Aneroid, Saskatchewan, Canada, September 15, 1979**

| | | | | | | | | |
|---|---|---|---|---|---|---|---|---|
| 1999 WM | 41-F | CAN | 7 | 1 | 1 | 2 | 0 | 4th |
| 2001 WM | 10-F | CAN | 7 | 2 | 3 | 5 | 4 | 5th |
| 2003 WM | 12-F | CAN | 9 | 0 | 4 | 4 | 4 | G |
| 2005 WM | 22-F | CAN | 9 | 2 | 2 | 4 | 4 | S |
| 2010 OG-M | 11-F | CAN | 7 | 2 | 3 | 5 | 0 | G |
| **Totals WM** | | | **32** | **5** | **10** | **15** | **12** | **G,S** |

**Marolf, Pascal**
**b. Oberdiessbach, Switzerland, October 25, 1990**

| | | | | | | | | |
|---|---|---|---|---|---|---|---|---|
| 2008 WM18 | 18-F | SUI | 6 | 0 | 1 | 1 | 6 | 8th |
| 2010 WM20 | 26-F | SUI | 7 | 0 | 2 | 2 | 0 | 4th |

**Martens, Henry**
**b. Engelskirchen, West Germany (Germany), May 24, 1987**

| | | | | | | | | |
|---|---|---|---|---|---|---|---|---|
| 2005 WM18 | 18-F | GER | 6 | 0 | 1 | 1 | 2 | 8th |
| 2007 WM20 | 21-D | GER | 6 | 0 | 0 | 0 | 8 | 9th |

**Martensson, Tony**
**b. Upplands Vasby, Sweden, June 23, 1980**

| | | | | | | | | |
|---|---|---|---|---|---|---|---|---|
| 2000 WM20 | 23-F | SWE | 7 | 2 | 4 | 6 | 2 | 5th |
| 2006 WM | 9-F | SWE | 9 | 1 | 1 | 2 | 4 | G |
| 2007 WM | 9-F | SWE | 9 | 4 | 7 | 11 | 8 | 4th |
| 2008 WM | 9-F | SWE | 9 | 4 | 5 | 9 | 4 | 4th |
| 2009 WM | 9-F | SWE | 9 | 1 | 9 | 10 | 8 | B |
| 2010 WM | 9-F | SWE | 9 | 2 | 4 | 6 | 6 | B |
| **Totals WM** | | | **45** | **12** | **26** | **38** | **30** | **G,2B** |

**Marti, Christian**
**b. Lufingen, Switzerland, March 29, 1993**

| | | | | | | | | |
|---|---|---|---|---|---|---|---|---|
| 2011 WM18 | 8-D | SUI | 6 | 0 | 0 | 0 | 16 | 7th |
| 2012 WM20 | 8-D | SUI | 6 | 1 | 0 | 1 | 0 | 8th |

**Martin, Paul**
**b. Minneapolis, Minnesota, United States, March 5, 1981**

| | | | | | | | | |
|---|---|---|---|---|---|---|---|---|
| 2001 WM20 | 27-D | USA | 7 | 0 | 4 | 4 | 2 | 5th |
| 2004 WCH | 10-D | USA | 3 | 0 | 1 | 1 | 0 | 4th |
| 2005 WM | 10-D | USA | 7 | 0 | 0 | 0 | 2 | 6th |
| 2008 WM | 10-D | USA | 7 | 1 | 7 | 8 | 0 | 6th |
| **Totals WM** | | | **14** | **1** | **7** | **8** | **2** | **—** |

**Martinek, Radek**
**b. Halickuv brod, Czechoslovakia (Czech Republic), August 31, 1976**

| | | | | | | | | |
|---|---|---|---|---|---|---|---|---|
| 2000 WM | 7-D | CZE | 9 | 0 | 0 | 0 | 4 | G |
| 2001 WM | 7-D | CZE | 9 | 0 | 2 | 2 | 8 | G |
| 2011 WM | 7-D | CZE | 1 | 0 | 0 | 0 | 0 | B |
| **Totals WM** | | | **19** | **0** | **2** | **2** | **12** | **2G,B** |

**Martinsen, Andreas**
**b. Asker, Norway, June 13, 1990**

| | | | | | | | | |
|---|---|---|---|---|---|---|---|---|
| 2010 WM | 25-F | NOR | 3 | 0 | 0 | 0 | 0 | 9th |
| 2011 WM | 24-F | NOR | 7 | 0 | 0 | 0 | 6 | 6th |
| 2012 WM | 24-F | NOR | 8 | 1 | 2 | 3 | 0 | 8th |
| **Totals WM** | | | **18** | **1** | **2** | **3** | **6** | **—** |

**Martschini, Lino**
**b. Zug, Switzerland, January 21, 1993**

| | | | | | | | | |
|---|---|---|---|---|---|---|---|---|
| 2010 WM18 | 24-F | SUI | 6 | 1 | 2 | 3 | 2 | 5th |
| 2011 WM18 | 16-F | SUI | 6 | 2 | 4 | 6 | 0 | 7th |
| 2012 WM20 | 12-F | SUI | 6 | 0 | 1 | 1 | 0 | 8th |
| **Totals WM18** | | | **12** | **3** | **6** | **9** | **2** | **—** |

**Maslov, Kirill**
**b. Voronezh, Russia, March 23, 1994**

| | | | | | | | | |
|---|---|---|---|---|---|---|---|---|
| 2012 WM18 | 7-D | RUS | 6 | 0 | 1 | 1 | 8 | 5th |

**Matai, Jakub**
**b. Kadan, Czech Republic, May 9, 1993**

| | | | | | | | | |
|---|---|---|---|---|---|---|---|---|
| 2011 WM18 | 8-F | CZE | 5 | 1 | 0 | 1 | 0 | 8th |

**Matejcek, Martin**
**b. Odolena Voda, Czech Republic, March 18, 1994**

| | | | | | | | | |
|---|---|---|---|---|---|---|---|---|
| 2012 WM18 | 14-F | CZE | 6 | 0 | 1 | 1 | 0 | 8th |

**Mathisrud, Marius**
**b. Oslo, Norway, April 27, 1987**

| | | | | | | | | |
|---|---|---|---|---|---|---|---|---|
| 2006 WM20 | 18-F | NOR | 6 | 0 | 0 | 0 | 4 | 10th |

**Matousek, Tomas**
**b. Banska Bystrica, Slovakia, June 15, 1992**

| | | | | | | | | |
|---|---|---|---|---|---|---|---|---|
| 2010 WM18 | 27-F | SVK | 6 | 2 | 0 | 2 | 0 | 8th |
| 2011 WM20 | 22-F | SVK | 6 | 0 | 0 | 0 | 2 | 8th |
| 2012 WM20 | 27-F | SVK | 6 | 1 | 0 | 1 | 8 | 6th |
| Totals WM20 | | | 12 | 1 | 0 | 1 | 10 | — |

**Matthias, Shawn**
**b. Mississauga, Ontario, Canada, February 19, 1988**

| | | | | | | | | |
|---|---|---|---|---|---|---|---|---|
| 2006 WM18 | 22-F | CAN | 7 | 1 | 0 | 1 | 2 | 4th |
| 2008 WM20 | 22-F | CAN | 7 | 3 | 1 | 4 | 4 | G |

**Mattsson, Joakim**
**b. Kramfors, Sweden, January 24, 1990**

| | | | | | | | | |
|---|---|---|---|---|---|---|---|---|
| 2008 WM18 | 17-F | SWE | 6 | 2 | 0 | 2 | 12 | 4th |

**Mattson, Nick**
**b. Chanhassen, Minnesota, United States, October 25, 1991**

| | | | | | | | | |
|---|---|---|---|---|---|---|---|---|
| 2009 WM18 | 27-D | USA | 7 | 1 | 2 | 3 | 2 | G |

**Mauer, Frank**
**b. Heidelberg, Germany, April 12, 1988**

| | | | | | | | | |
|---|---|---|---|---|---|---|---|---|
| 2006 WM18 | 26-F | GER | 6 | 0 | 0 | 0 | 2 | 8th |
| 2011 WM | 28-F | GER | 5 | 0 | 3 | 3 | 0 | 7th |

**Maurer, Marco**
**b. Affoltern am Albis, Switzerland, February 21, 1988**

| | | | | | | | | |
|---|---|---|---|---|---|---|---|---|
| 2007 WM20 | 4-D | SUI | 3 | 0 | 0 | 0 | 0 | 7th |
| 2008 WM20 | 4-D | SUI | 6 | 1 | 0 | 1 | 12 | 9th |
| **Totals WM20** | | | **9** | **1** | **0** | **1** | **12** | **—** |

**Maurer, Uli**
**b. Garmisch-Partenkirchen, West Germany (Germany), January 19, 1985**

| | | | | | | | | |
|---|---|---|---|---|---|---|---|---|
| 2005 WM20 | 15-F | GER | 2 | 0 | 0 | 0 | 0 | 9th |

**Mayers, Jamal**
**b. Toronto, Ontario, Canada, October 24, 1974**

| | | | | | | | | |
|---|---|---|---|---|---|---|---|---|
| 2000 WM | 21-F | CAN | 7 | 1 | 0 | 1 | 2 | 4th |
| 2007 WM | 21-F | CAN | 9 | 4 | 1 | 5 | 8 | G |
| 2008 WM | 21-F | CAN | 9 | 2 | 3 | 5 | 2 | S |
| **Totals WM** | | | **25** | **7** | **4** | **11** | **12** | **G,S** |

**Mazins, Roberts**
**b. Riga, Soviet Union (Latvia), December 5, 1990**

| | | | | | | | | |
|---|---|---|---|---|---|---|---|---|
| 2010 WM20 | 19-F | LAT | 6 | 2 | 0 | 2 | 10 | 9th |

**Mazula, Eduard**
**b. Karaganda, Soviet Union (Kazakhstan), March 21, 1990**

| | | | | | | | | |
|---|---|---|---|---|---|---|---|---|
| 2008 WM20 | 24-F | KAZ | 6 | 0 | 0 | 0 | 6 | 8th |
| 2009 WM20 | 18-F | KAZ | 6 | 0 | 0 | 0 | 8 | 10th |
| **Totals WM20** | | | **12** | **0** | **0** | **0** | **14** | **—** |

**McArdle, Kenndal**
**b. Toronto, Ontario, Canada, January 4, 1987**

| | | | | | | | | |
|---|---|---|---|---|---|---|---|---|
| 2007 WM20 | 12-F | CAN | 6 | 0 | 0 | 0 | 0 | G |

**McBain, Jamie**
**b. Faribault, Minnesota, United States, February 25, 1988**

| | | | | | | | | |
|---|---|---|---|---|---|---|---|---|
| 2006 WM18 | 4-D | USA | 6 | 2 | 9 | 11 | 0 | G |
| 2007 WM20 | 17-D | USA | 7 | 0 | 0 | 0 | 2 | B |
| 2008 WM20 | 4-D | USA | 6 | 0 | 1 | 1 | 0 | 4th |
| **Totals WM20** | | | **13** | **0** | **1** | **1** | **2** | **B** |

**McCabe, Jake**
**b. Eau Claire, Wisconsin, United States, October 12, 1993**

| | | | | | | | | |
|---|---|---|---|---|---|---|---|---|
| 2011 WM18 | 19-D | USA | 6 | 0 | 1 | 1 | 0 | G |

**McCarey, Kevin**
**b. Baldwinsville, New York, United States, March 24, 1990**

| | | | | | | | | |
|---|---|---|---|---|---|---|---|---|
| 2008 WM18 | 26-F | USA | 7 | 0 | 0 | 0 | 2 | G |

**McDonagh, Ryan**
**b. Arden Hills, Minnesota, United States, June 13, 1989**

| | | | | | | | | |
|---|---|---|---|---|---|---|---|---|
| 2007 WM18 | 4-D | USA | 7 | 0 | 3 | 3 | 4 | S |
| 2009 WM20 | 17-D | USA | 6 | 0 | 3 | 3 | 2 | 5th |
| 2011 WM | 2-D | USA | 7 | 0 | 1 | 1 | 2 | 8th |

**McFarland, John**
**b. Richmond Hill, Ontario, Canada, April 2, 1992**

| | | | | | | | | |
|---|---|---|---|---|---|---|---|---|
| 2009 WM18 | 17-F | CAN | 6 | 3 | 5 | 8 | 6 | 4th |
| 2010 WM18 | 18-F | CAN | 6 | 4 | 1 | 5 | 8 | 7th |
| **Totals WM18** | | | **12** | **7** | **6** | **13** | **14** | **—** |

**McGregor, Ryan**
**b. Morden, Manitoba, Canada, March 13, 1991**

| | | | | | | | | |
|---|---|---|---|---|---|---|---|---|
| 2008 WM18 | 16-F | SUI | 6 | 0 | 2 | 2 | 4 | 8th |
| 2009 WM18 | 19-F | SUI | 5 | 1 | 0 | 1 | 2 | 8th |
| 2010 WM20 | 19-F | SUI | 7 | 1 | 1 | 2 | 6 | 4th |
| 2011 WM20 | 19-F | SUI | 6 | 0 | 0 | 0 | 2 | 5th |
| **Totals WM18** | | | **11** | **1** | **2** | **3** | **6** | **—** |
| **Totals WM20** | | | **13** | **1** | **1** | **2** | **8** | **—** |

**McKegg, Greg**
**b. St. Thomas, Ontario, Canada, June 17, 1992**

| | | | | | | | | |
|---|---|---|---|---|---|---|---|---|
| 2010 WM18 | 24-F | CAN | 6 | 1 | 6 | 7 | 4 | 7th |

**McMillan, Brandon**
**b. Delta, British Columbia, Canada, March 22, 1990**

| | | | | | | | | |
|---|---|---|---|---|---|---|---|---|
| 2008 WM18 | 15-F | CAN | 7 | 1 | 2 | 3 | 10 | G |
| 2010 WM20 | 15-F | CAN | 6 | 4 | 4 | 8 | 0 | S |

**McNabb, Brayden**
**b. Davidson, Saskatchewan, Canada, January 21, 1991**

| | | | | | | | | |
|---|---|---|---|---|---|---|---|---|
| 2009 WM18 | 3-D | CAN | 6 | 0 | 0 | 0 | 2 | 4th |

**McNeill, Mark**
**b. Edmonton, Alberta, Canada, February 22, 1993**

| | | | | | | | | |
|---|---|---|---|---|---|---|---|---|
| 2011 WM18 | 24-F | CAN | 7 | 0 | 6 | 6 | 2 | 4th |

**McRae, Philip**
**b. Minneapolis, Minnesota, United States, March 15, 1990**

| | | | | | | | | |
|---|---|---|---|---|---|---|---|---|
| 2008 WM18 | 18-F | USA | 7 | 3 | 3 | 6 | 4 | G |
| 2010 WM20 | 9-F | USA | 7 | 1 | 4 | 5 | 2 | G |

**Mebus, Oliver**
**b. Dormagen, Germany, March 30, 1993**

| | | | | | | | | |
|---|---|---|---|---|---|---|---|---|
| 2011 WM18 | 12-D | GER | 6 | 0 | 2 | 2 | 2 | 6th |

**Medby, Endre**
**b. Gjovik, Norway, January 11, 1994**

| | | | | | | | | |
|---|---|---|---|---|---|---|---|---|
| 2011 WM18 | 8-F | NOR | 6 | 1 | 3 | 4 | 4 | 9th |

**Medvedev, Yevgeni**
**b. Chelyabinsk, Soviet Union (Russia), August 27, 1982**

| | | | | | | | | |
|---|---|---|---|---|---|---|---|---|
| 2012 WM | 82-D | RUS | 10 | 1 | 3 | 4 | 4 | G |

**Megalinski, Dmitri**
**b. Perm, Soviet Union (Russia), April 15, 1985**

| | | | | | | | | |
|---|---|---|---|---|---|---|---|---|
| 2005 WM20 | 14-D | RUS | 6 | 0 | 1 | 1 | 4 | S |

**Meidl, Radek**
**b. Prostejov, Czechoslovakia (Czech Republic), November 25, 1988**

| | | | | | | | | |
|---|---|---|---|---|---|---|---|---|
| 2008 WM20 | 18-F | CZE | 6 | 1 | 1 | 2 | 4 | 5th |

**Meidl, Vaclav**
**b. Prostejov, Czechoslovakia (Czech Republic), May 27, 1986**

| | | | | | | | | |
|---|---|---|---|---|---|---|---|---|
| 2003 WM18 | 23-F | CZE | 6 | 0 | 0 | 0 | 2 | 6th |
| 2006 WM20 | 12-F | CZE | 6 | 1 | 1 | 2 | 4 | 6th |

**Meija, Gints**
**b. Riga, Soviet Union (Latvia), September 4, 1987**

| | | | | | | | | |
|---|---|---|---|---|---|---|---|---|
| 2006 WM20 | 27-F | LAT | 6 | 2 | 0 | 2 | 4 | 9th |
| 2010 OG-M | 87-F | LAT | 4 | 0 | 0 | 0 | 2 | 12th |
| 2010 WM | 87-F | LAT | 6 | 1 | 1 | 2 | 0 | 11th |
| 2011 WM | 87-F | LAT | 6 | 0 | 3 | 3 | 4 | 13th |
| 2012 WM | 87-F | LAT | 7 | 1 | 0 | 1 | 0 | 10th |
| **Totals WM** | | | **19** | **2** | **4** | **6** | **4** | **—** |

**Meirandres, Max**
**b. Rosenheim, Germany, February 4, 1993**

| | | | | | | | | |
|---|---|---|---|---|---|---|---|---|
| 2011 WM18 | 7-D | GER | 6 | 0 | 2 | 2 | 8 | 6th |

**Melart, Ilari**
**b. Helsinki, Finland, February 11, 1989**

| | | | | | | | | |
|---|---|---|---|---|---|---|---|---|
| 2009 WM20 | 5-D | FIN | 6 | 0 | 1 | 1 | 4 | 7th |

**Meleshko, Dmitri**
**b. Minsk, Soviet Union (Belarus), November 8, 1982**

| | | | | | | | | |
|---|---|---|---|---|---|---|---|---|
| 2005 WM | 19-F | BLR | 3 | 0 | 0 | 0 | 2 | 10th |
| 2006 WM | 19-F | BLR | 7 | 1 | 2 | 3 | 4 | 6th |
| 2007 WM | 19-F | BLR | 6 | 2 | 4 | 6 | 2 | 11th |
| 2008 WM | 19-F | BLR | 6 | 2 | 1 | 3 | 4 | 9th |
| 2009 WM | 19-F | BLR | 3 | 0 | 0 | 0 | 4 | 8th |
| 2010 OG-M | 19-F | BLR | 4 | 2 | 0 | 2 | 2 | 9th |
| 2010 WM | 19-F | BLR | 6 | 1 | 3 | 4 | 0 | 10th |
| 2011 WM | 19-F | BLR | 6 | 1 | 3 | 4 | 6 | 14th |
| 2012 WM | 19-F | BLR | 7 | 0 | 0 | 0 | 0 | 14th |
| **Totals WM** | | | **44** | **7** | **13** | **20** | **22** | **—** |

**Merrill, Jon**
**b. Brighton, Michigan, United States, February 3, 1992**

| | | | | | | | | |
|---|---|---|---|---|---|---|---|---|
| 2009 WM18 | 6-D | USA | 7 | 0 | 2 | 2 | 4 | G |
| 2010 WM18 | 15-D | USA | 7 | 0 | 1 | 1 | 2 | G |
| 2011 WM20 | 12-D | USA | 6 | 1 | 4 | 5 | 0 | B |
| 2012 WM20 | 15-D | USA | 6 | 0 | 4 | 4 | 6 | 7th |
| **Totals WM18** | | | **14** | **0** | **3** | **3** | **6** | **2G** |
| **Totals WM20** | | | **12** | **1** | **8** | **9** | **6** | **B** |

**Mertel, Marek**
**b. Trnava, Czechoslovakia (Slovakia), June 7, 1989**

| | | | | | | | | |
|---|---|---|---|---|---|---|---|---|
| 2009 WM20 | 29-F | SVK | 7 | 1 | 3 | 4 | 2 | 4th |

**Meszaros, Andrej**
**b. Povazska Bystrica, Czechoslovakia (Slovakia), October 13, 1985**

| | | | | | | | | |
|---|---|---|---|---|---|---|---|---|
| 2002 WM18 | 6-D | SVK | 8 | 0 | 1 | 1 | 8 | 8th |
| 2003 WM18 | 26-D | SVK | 7 | 2 | 2 | 4 | 6 | S |
| 2004 WM20 | 14-D | SVK | 6 | 1 | 1 | 2 | 12 | 6th |
| 2004 WM | 14-D | SVK | 7 | 0 | 1 | 1 | 2 | 4th |
| 2005 WM20 | 16-D | SVK | 6 | 3 | 1 | 4 | 4 | 7th |
| 2006 OG-M | 14-D | SVK | 6 | 0 | 2 | 2 | 4 | 5th |
| 2006 WM | 14-D | SVK | 1 | 0 | 0 | 0 | 0 | 8th |
| 2010 OG-M | 14-D | SVK | 7 | 0 | 0 | 0 | 4 | 4th |
| **Totals WM18** | | | **15** | **2** | **3** | **5** | **14** | **S** |
| **Totals WM20** | | | **12** | **4** | **2** | **6** | **16** | **—** |
| **Totals WM** | | | **8** | **0** | **1** | **1** | **2** | **—** |
| **Totals OG-M** | | | **13** | **0** | **2** | **2** | **8** | **—** |

**Metalnikov, Leonid**
**b. Kazakhstanskaya, Soviet Union (Kazakhstan), April 25, 1990**

| | | | | | | | | |
|---|---|---|---|---|---|---|---|---|
| 2009 WM20 | 22-D | KAZ | 6 | 0 | 0 | 0 | 0 | 10th |

**Methot, Marc**
**b. Ottawa, Ontario, Canada, June 21, 1985**

| | | | | | | | | |
|---|---|---|---|---|---|---|---|---|
| 2011 WM | 33-D | CAN | 7 | 0 | 0 | 0 | 2 | 5th |
| 2012 WM | 33-D | CAN | 6 | 0 | 2 | 2 | 25 | 5th |
| **Totals WM** | | | **13** | **0** | **2** | **2** | **27** | **—** |

**Mettler, Thomas**
**b. Ebnat Kappel, Switzerland, April 29, 1991**

| | | | | | | | | |
|---|---|---|---|---|---|---|---|---|
| 2009 WM18 | 10-D | SUI | 6 | 1 | 2 | 3 | 8 | 8th |

**Meunier, Laurent**
**b. St. Martin d'Heres, France, January 16, 1979**

| | | | | | | | | |
|---|---|---|---|---|---|---|---|---|
| 1999 WM | 10-F | FRA | 3 | 0 | 0 | 0 | 0 | 15th |
| 2000 WM | 10-F | FRA | 6 | 4 | 3 | 7 | 2 | 15th |
| 2002 OG-M | 10-F | FRA | 4 | 0 | 1 | 1 | 6 | 14th |
| 2008 WM | 10-F | FRA | 3 | 0 | 0 | 0 | 0 | 14th |
| 2009 WM | 10-F | FRA | 4 | 0 | 3 | 3 | 14 | 12th |
| 2010 WM | 10-F | FRA | 5 | 2 | 1 | 3 | 4 | 14th |
| 2011 WM | 10-F | FRA | 6 | 2 | 1 | 3 | 8 | 12th |
| 2012 WM | 10-F | FRA | 7 | 1 | 6 | 7 | 22 | 9th |
| **Totals WM** | | | **34** | **9** | **14** | **23** | **50** | **—** |

**Meyer, Nicolai**
**b. Fredrikshavn, Denmark, July 21, 1993**

| | | | | | | | | |
|---|---|---|---|---|---|---|---|---|
| 2012 WM20 | 15-F | DEN | 6 | 1 | 0 | 1 | 12 | 10th |

**Mezei, Branislav**
**b. Nitra, Czechoslovakia (Slovakia), October 8, 1980**

| | | | | | | | | |
|---|---|---|---|---|---|---|---|---|
| 1999 WM20 | 7-D | SVK | 6 | 0 | 0 | 0 | 8 | B |
| 2000 WM20 | 7-D | SVK | 7 | 1 | 0 | 1 | 6 | 9th |
| 2001 WM | 2-D | SVK | 6 | 0 | 0 | 0 | 2 | 7th |
| 2004 WM | 2-D | SVK | 9 | 0 | 0 | 0 | 6 | 4th |
| 2004 WCH | 2-D | SVK | 2 | 0 | 0 | 0 | 0 | 7th |
| 2008 WM | 24-D | SVK | 5 | 0 | 0 | 0 | 8 | 13th |
| **Totals WM20** | | | **13** | **1** | **0** | **1** | **14** | **B** |
| **Totals WM** | | | **20** | **0** | **0** | **0** | **16** | **—** |

**Michalek, Milan**
**b. Jindrichuv Hradec, Czechoslovakia (Czech Republic), December 7, 1984**

| | | | | | | | | |
|---|---|---|---|---|---|---|---|---|
| 2001 WM18 | 15-F | CZE | 7 | 1 | 1 | 2 | 6 | 4th |
| 2002 WM18 | 10-F | CZE | 8 | 7 | 1 | 8 | 30 | B |
| 2003 WM20 | 15-F | CZE | 6 | 2 | 2 | 4 | 2 | 6th |
| 2003 WM | 18-F | CZE | 1 | 0 | 0 | 0 | 0 | 4th |
| 2009 WM | 19-F | CZE | 3 | 1 | 0 | 1 | 4 | 6th |
| 2010 OG-M | 9-F | CZE | 5 | 2 | 0 | 2 | 0 | 7th |
| 2011 WM | 9-F | CZE | 8 | 4 | 2 | 6 | 6 | B |
| 2012 WM | 9-F | CZE | 9 | 2 | 2 | 4 | 4 | B |
| **Totals WM18** | | | **15** | **8** | **2** | **10** | **36** | **B** |
| **Totals WM** | | | **21** | **7** | **4** | **11** | **14** | **2B** |

**Michalek, Zbynek**
**b. Jindrichuv Hradec, Czechoslovakia (Czech Republic), December 23, 1982**

| | | | | | | | | |
|---|---|---|---|---|---|---|---|---|
| 2006 WM | 4-D | CZE | 9 | 3 | 0 | 3 | 6 | S |
| 2007 WM | 4-D | CZE | 7 | 0 | 1 | 1 | 4 | 7th |
| 2008 WM | 4-D | CZE | 7 | 0 | 0 | 0 | 6 | 5th |
| 2010 OG-M | 4-D | CZE | 5 | 0 | 0 | 0 | 2 | 7th |
| 2011 WM | 2-D | CZE | 8 | 0 | 1 | 1 | 0 | B |
| **Totals WM** | | | **31** | **3** | **2** | **5** | **16** | **S,B** |

**Mickevics, Arturs**
**b. Virbu, Soviet Union (Latvia), January 2, 1991**

| | | | | | | | | |
|---|---|---|---|---|---|---|---|---|
| 2010 WM20 | 16-F | LAT | 6 | 0 | 2 | 2 | 4 | 9th |

**Miele, Andy**
**b. Grosse Pointe Woods, Michigan, United States, April 15, 1988**

| | | | | | | | | |
|---|---|---|---|---|---|---|---|---|
| 2011 WM | 21-F | USA | 2 | 0 | 2 | 2 | 2 | 8th |

**Mieritz, Mark**
**b. Copenhagen, Denmark, January 3, 1991**

| | | | | | | | | |
|---|---|---|---|---|---|---|---|---|
| 2008 WM18 | 18-F | DEN | 6 | 0 | 1 | 1 | 4 | 10th |

**Miettinen, Antti**
**b. Hattula, Finland, July 3, 1980**

| | | | | | | | | |
|---|---|---|---|---|---|---|---|---|
| 2000 WM20 | 21-F | FIN | 7 | 4 | 1 | 5 | 2 | 7th |
| 2002 WM | 20-F | FIN | 9 | 2 | 4 | 6 | 4 | 4th |
| 2003 WM | 20-F | FIN | 6 | 0 | 1 | 1 | 0 | 5th |
| 2006 WM | 20-F | FIN | 9 | 2 | 2 | 4 | 10 | B |
| 2007 WM | 20-F | FIN | 8 | 1 | 1 | 2 | 6 | S |
| 2009 WM | 20-F | FIN | 7 | 3 | 5 | 8 | 6 | 5th |
| 2010 OG-M | 20-F | FIN | 6 | 1 | 0 | 1 | 0 | B |
| 2010 WM | 20-F | FIN | 6 | 0 | 2 | 2 | 4 | 6th |
| **Totals WM** | | | **45** | **8** | **15** | **23** | **30** | **S,B** |

**Mihalik, Denis**
**b. Topolcany, Czechoslovakia (Slovakia), May 20, 1992**

| | | | | | | | | |
|---|---|---|---|---|---|---|---|---|
| 2010 WM18 | 11-F | SVK | 6 | 0 | 0 | 0 | 0 | 8th |

**Mihalik, Vladimir**
**b. Presov, Czechoslovakia (Slovakia), January 29, 1987**

| | | | | | | | | |
|---|---|---|---|---|---|---|---|---|
| 2005 WM18 | 16-D | SVK | 6 | 0 | 0 | 0 | 10 | 6th |
| 2006 WM20 | 16-D | SVK | 6 | 0 | 3 | 3 | 8 | 8th |
| 2007 WM20 | 16-D | SVK | 6 | 1 | 0 | 1 | 4 | 8th |
| 2010 WM | 56-D | SVK | 6 | 1 | 0 | 1 | 4 | 12th |
| **Totals WM20** | | | **12** | **1** | **3** | **4** | **12** | **—** |

**Mikhailov, Dmitri**
**b. Magnitogorsk, Russia, May 2, 1993**

| | | | | | | | | |
|---|---|---|---|---|---|---|---|---|
| 2011 WM18 | 8-F | RUS | 6 | 0 | 3 | 3 | 29 | B |

**Mikhalyov, Andrei**
**b. Minsk, Soviet Union (Belarus), February 23, 1978**

| | | | | | | | | |
|---|---|---|---|---|---|---|---|---|
| 2005 WM | 8-F | BLR | 5 | 0 | 0 | 0 | 4 | 10th |
| 2006 WM | 8-F | BLR | 7 | 0 | 2 | 2 | 4 | 6th |
| 2007 WM | 8-F | BLR | 2 | 0 | 0 | 0 | 4 | 11th |
| 2008 WM | 8-F | BLR | 6 | 1 | 1 | 2 | 6 | 9th |
| 2009 WM | 8-F | BLR | 7 | 0 | 0 | 0 | 2 | 8th |
| 2010 OG-M | 8-F | BLR | 4 | 0 | 0 | 0 | 2 | 9th |
| 2010 WM | 8-F | BLR | 6 | 1 | 0 | 1 | 2 | 10th |
| 2011 WM | 10-F | BLR | 6 | 3 | 1 | 4 | 6 | 14th |
| 2012 WM | 10-F | BLR | 4 | 0 | 0 | 0 | 2 | 14th |
| **Totals WM** | | | **43** | **5** | **4** | **9** | **30** | **—** |

**Miklik, Michel**
**b. Piestany, Czechoslovakia (Slovakia), July 31, 1982**

| | | | | | | | | |
|---|---|---|---|---|---|---|---|---|
| 2012 WM | 91-F | SVK | 10 | 1 | 1 | 2 | 0 | S |

**Mikula, Ondrej**
**b. Banovce nad Bebravou, Czechoslovakia (Slovakia), July 3, 1988**

| | | | | | | | | |
|---|---|---|---|---|---|---|---|---|
| 2006 WM18 | 2-F | SVK | 6 | 0 | 3 | 3 | 2 | — |
| 2007 WM20 | 25-F | SVK | 6 | 2 | 1 | 3 | 8 | 8th |

**Mikus, Juraj**
**b. Skalica, Czechoslovakia (Slovakia), February 22, 1987**

| | | | | | | | | |
|---|---|---|---|---|---|---|---|---|
| 2005 WM18 | 12-F | SVK | 6 | 0 | 7 | 7 | 12 | 6th |
| 2006 WM20 | 12-F | SVK | 6 | 0 | 0 | 0 | 6 | 8th |
| 2007 WM20 | 12-F | SVK | 6 | 5 | 1 | 6 | 0 | 8th |
| 2008 WM | 71-F | SVK | 2 | 0 | 0 | 0 | 0 | 13th |
| 2009 WM | 71-F | SVK | 6 | 0 | 1 | 1 | 2 | 10th |
| 2012 WM | 71-F | SVK | 10 | 1 | 3 | 4 | 4 | S |
| **Totals WM** | | | **18** | **1** | **4** | **5** | **6** | **S** |
| **Totals WM20** | | | **12** | **5** | **1** | **6** | **6** | **—** |

**Mikus, Juraj**
**b. Trencin, Czechoslovakia (Slovakia), November 30, 1988**

| | | | | | | | | |
|---|---|---|---|---|---|---|---|---|
| 2006 WM18 | 7-D | SVK | 6 | 0 | 2 | 2 | 6 | 7th |
| 2008 WM20 | 26-D | SVK | 6 | 1 | 2 | 3 | 0 | 7th |

**Mikus, Peter**
**b. Trencin, Czechoslovakia (Slovakia), January 10, 1985**

| | | | | | | | | |
|---|---|---|---|---|---|---|---|---|
| 2005 WM20 | 22-D | SVK | 6 | 0 | 2 | 2 | 2 | 7th |

**Mikus, Tomas**
**b. Skalica, Slovakia, July 1, 1993**

| | | | | | | | | |
|---|---|---|---|---|---|---|---|---|
| 2011 WM18 | 21-F | SVK | 6 | 1 | 0 | 1 | 4 | 10th |

**Milekhin, Mikhail**
**b. Chelyabinsk, Soviet Union (Russia), November 2, 1988**

| | | | | | | | | |
|---|---|---|---|---|---|---|---|---|
| 2008 WM20 | 29-F | RUS | 7 | 0 | 1 | 1 | 2 | B |

**Mille, Mathieu**
**b. Amiens, France, January 10, 1981**

| | | | | | | | | |
|---|---|---|---|---|---|---|---|---|
| 2008 WM | 29-D | FRA | 2 | 0 | 0 | 0 | 0 | 14th |
| 2009 WM | 29-D | FRA | 6 | 0 | 0 | 0 | 4 | 12th |
| **Totals WM** | | | **8** | **0** | **0** | **0** | **4** | **—** |

**Miller, J.T. (Jonathan Tanner)**
**b. East Palestine, Ohio, United States, March 14, 1993**

| | | | | | | | | |
|---|---|---|---|---|---|---|---|---|
| 2011 WM18 | 11-F | USA | 6 | 4 | 9 | 13 | 6 | G |
| 2012 WM20 | 11-F | USA | 6 | 2 | 2 | 4 | 0 | 7th |

**Milovanovic, Jakob**
**b. Kranj, Yugoslavia (Slovenia), March 18, 1984**

| | | | | | | | | |
|---|---|---|---|---|---|---|---|---|
| 2006 WM | 27-D | SLO | 1 | 0 | 0 | 0 | 0 | 16th |
| 2008 WM | 51-D | SLO | 5 | 0 | 1 | 1 | 2 | 15th |
| **Totals WM** | | | **6** | **0** | **1** | **1** | **2** | **—** |

**Mironov, Andrei**
**b. July 29, 1994**

| | | | | | | | | |
|---|---|---|---|---|---|---|---|---|
| 2012 WM18 | 2-D | RUS | 6 | 1 | 0 | 1 | 0 | 5th |

**Mitchell, Garrett**
**b. Regina, Saskatchewan, Canada, February 9, 1991**

| | | | | | | | | |
|---|---|---|---|---|---|---|---|---|
| 2009 WM18 | 15-F | CAN | 6 | 0 | 1 | 1 | 6 | 4th |

**Mitchell, Willie**
**b. Port McNeill, British Columbia, Canada, April 23, 1977**

| | | | | | | | | |
|---|---|---|---|---|---|---|---|---|
| 2004 WM | 8-D | CAN | 9 | 0 | 0 | 0 | 0 | G |

**Mitera, Mark**
**b. Royal Oak, Michigan, United States, October 22, 1987**

| | | | | | | | | |
|---|---|---|---|---|---|---|---|---|
| 2005 WM18 | 17-D | USA | 6 | 0 | 0 | 0 | 8 | G |
| 2006 WM20 | 23-D | USA | 7 | 0 | 0 | 0 | 27 | 4th |

**Mlynarovic, Samuel**
**b. Poprad, Czechoslovakia (Slovakia), May 23, 1990**

| | | | | | | | | |
|---|---|---|---|---|---|---|---|---|
| 2010 WM20 | 14-F | SVK | 6 | 1 | 1 | 2 | 4 | 8th |

**Mochel, Marius**
**b. Nuremberg, Germany, May 28, 1991**

| | | | | | | | | |
|---|---|---|---|---|---|---|---|---|
| 2011 WM20 | 28-F | GER | 6 | 1 | 0 | 1 | 16 | 10th |

**Moe, Eric**
**b. Sundsvall, Sweden, March 6, 1988**

| | | | | | | | | |
|---|---|---|---|---|---|---|---|---|
| 2006 WM18 | 2-D | SWE | 6 | 1 | 2 | 3 | 0 | 6th |
| 2008 WM20 | 2-D | SWE | 6 | 1 | 3 | 4 | 0 | S |

**Moffatt, Luke**
**b. Paradise Valley, Arizona, United States, June 11, 1992**

| | | | | | | | | |
|---|---|---|---|---|---|---|---|---|
| 2010 WM18 | 7-F | USA | 7 | 2 | 1 | 3 | 2 | G |

**Moisand, Maxime**
**b. Grenoble, France, June 11, 1990**

| | | | | | | | | |
|---|---|---|---|---|---|---|---|---|
| 2011 WM | 20-D | FRA | 4 | 0 | 0 | 0 | 0 | 12th |
| 2012 WM | 20-D | FRA | 5 | 0 | 0 | 0 | 0 | 9th |
| **Totals WM** | | | **9** | **0** | **0** | **0** | **0** | **—** |

**Moisio, Patrik**
**b. Turku, Finland, February 4, 1992**

| | | | | | | | | |
|---|---|---|---|---|---|---|---|---|
| 2010 WM18 | 21-F | FIN | 5 | 0 | 0 | 0 | 25 | B |

**Mojzis, Tomas**
**b. Klojn, Czechoslovakia, (Czech Republic), May 2, 1982**

| | | | | | | | | |
|---|---|---|---|---|---|---|---|---|
| 2000 WM18 | 22-D | CZE | 6 | 1 | 3 | 4 | 8 | 6th |
| 2002 WM20 | 23-D | CZE | 7 | 0 | 0 | 0 | 4 | 7th |
| 2010 WM | 6-D | CZE | 6 | 1 | 0 | 1 | 4 | G |
| 2012 WM | 6-D | CZE | 9 | 0 | 0 | 0 | 8 | B |
| **Totals WM** | | | **15** | **1** | **0** | **1** | **12** | **G,B** |

**Molinder, Andreas**
**b. Ramsele, Sweden, February 23, 1987**

| | | | | | | | | |
|---|---|---|---|---|---|---|---|---|
| 2005 WM18 | 14-F | SWE | 7 | 0 | 1 | 1 | 4 | B |
| 2007 WM20 | 29-F | SWE | 7 | 0 | 0 | 0 | 2 | 4th |

**Moller, Bjarke**
**b. Aalborg, Denmark, September 23, 1985**

| | | | | | | | | |
|---|---|---|---|---|---|---|---|---|
| 2012 WM | 12-F | DEN | 7 | 0 | 0 | 0 | 0 | 13th |

**Moller, Oscar**
**b. Stockholm, Sweden, January 22, 1989**

| | | | | | | | | |
|---|---|---|---|---|---|---|---|---|
| 2007 WM18 | 17-F | SWE | 6 | 1 | 4 | 5 | 20 | B |
| 2008 WM20 | 26-F | SWE | 6 | 3 | 2 | 5 | 0 | S |
| 2009 WM20 | 9-F | SWE | 6 | 1 | 3 | 4 | 4 | S |
| **Totals WM20** | | | **12** | **4** | **5** | **9** | **4** | **2S** |

**Molnar, Jozef**
**b. Presov, Czechoslovakia (Slovakia), April 8, 1989**

| | | | | | | | | |
|---|---|---|---|---|---|---|---|---|
| 2007 WM18 | 29-F | SVK | 6 | 2 | 0 | 2 | 0 | 5th |
| 2009 WM20 | 18-F | SVK | 7 | 1 | 1 | 2 | 0 | 4th |

**Monnet, Thibaut**
**b. Martigny, Switzerland, February 2, 1982**

| | | | | | | | | |
|---|---|---|---|---|---|---|---|---|
| 1999 WM18 | 4-F | SUI | 7 | 3 | 1 | 4 | 0 | 4th |
| 2000 WM18 | 7-F | SUI | 7 | 4 | 3 | 7 | 6 | 4th |
| 2001 WM20 | 7-F | SUI | 7 | 2 | 5 | 7 | 6 | 6th |
| 2002 WM20 | 7-F | SUI | 7 | 3 | 2 | 5 | 14 | 4th |
| 2007 WM | 25-F | SUI | 7 | 1 | 1 | 2 | 0 | 8th |
| 2008 WM | 25-F | SUI | 7 | 1 | 2 | 3 | 10 | 7th |
| 2009 WM | 25-F | SUI | 3 | 0 | 0 | 0 | 2 | 9th |
| 2010 OG-M | 25-F | SUI | 5 | 0 | 1 | 1 | 0 | 8th |
| 2010 WM | 25-F | SUI | 7 | 2 | 2 | 4 | 6 | 5th |
| 2011 WM | 25-F | SUI | 6 | 1 | 0 | 1 | 2 | 9th |
| 2012 WM | 25-F | SUI | 5 | 0 | 0 | 0 | 0 | 11th |
| **Totals WM18** | | | **14** | **7** | **4** | **11** | **6** | **—** |
| **Totals WM20** | | | **14** | **5** | **7** | **12** | **20** | **—** |
| **Totals WM** | | | **35** | **5** | **5** | **10** | **20** | **—** |

**Montgomery, Kevin**
**b. Rochester, New York, United States, April 4, 1988**

| | | | | | | | | |
|---|---|---|---|---|---|---|---|---|
| 2006 WM18 | 17-D | USA | 6 | 0 | 0 | 0 | 0 | G |
| 2008 WM20 | 23-D | USA | 6 | 0 | 0 | 0 | 2 | 4th |

**Moore, Colin**
**b. Medfield, Massachusetts, United States, May 21, 1990**

| | | | | | | | | |
|---|---|---|---|---|---|---|---|---|
| 2008 WM18 | 21-F | USA | 7 | 3 | 0 | 3 | 2 | G |

**Morandi, Antoine**
**b. Fribourg, Switzerland, February 1, 1987**

| | | | | | | | | |
|---|---|---|---|---|---|---|---|---|
| 2007 WM20 | 31-D | SUI | 6 | 0 | 0 | 0 | 16 | 7th |

**Moravec, Tomas**
**b. Tabor, Czech Republic, April 6, 1993**

| | | | | | | | | |
|---|---|---|---|---|---|---|---|---|
| 2011 WM18 | 9-F | CZE | 6 | 0 | 0 | 0 | 0 | 8th |

**Morin, Jeremy**
**b. Auburn, New York, United States, April 16, 1991**

| | | | | | | | | |
|---|---|---|---|---|---|---|---|---|
| 2008 WM18 | 11-F | USA | 7 | 6 | 2 | 8 | 6 | B |
| 2009 WM18 | 11-F | USA | 7 | 6 | 4 | 10 | 8 | G |
| 2010 WM20 | 26-F | USA | 7 | 2 | 5 | 7 | 0 | G |
| 2011 WM20 | 11-F | USA | 4 | 0 | 1 | 1 | 2 | B |
| **Totals WM18** | | | **14** | **12** | **6** | **18** | **14** | **G,B** |
| **Totals WM20** | | | **11** | **2** | **6** | **8** | **2** | **G,B** |

**Morozov, Alexei**
**b. Moscow, Soviet Union (Russia), February 16, 1977**

| | | | | | | | | |
|---|---|---|---|---|---|---|---|---|
| 1996 WM20 | 24-F | RUS | 7 | 5 | 3 | 8 | 2 | B |
| 1997 WM20 | 24-F | RUS | 6 | 5 | 3 | 8 | 6 | B |
| 1997 WM | 25-F | RUS | 9 | 3 | 3 | 6 | 2 | 4th |
| 1998 OG-M | 24-F | RUS | 6 | 2 | 2 | 4 | 0 | S |
| 1998 WM | 95-F | RUS | 4 | 0 | 3 | 3 | 2 | 5th |
| 2004 WM | 95-F | RUS | 6 | 1 | 1 | 2 | 4 | 10th |
| 2007 WM | 95-F | RUS | 7 | 8 | 5 | 13 | 6 | B |
| 2008 WM | 95-F | RUS | 8 | 5 | 2 | 7 | 4 | G |
| 2009 WM | 95-F | RUS | 9 | 1 | 4 | 5 | 0 | G |
| 2010 OG-M | 95-F | RUS | 4 | 2 | 0 | 2 | 0 | 6th |

| 2011 WM | 95-F | RUS | 9 | 1 | 3 | 4 | 8 | 4th |
|---|---|---|---|---|---|---|---|---|
| **Totals WM20** | | | **13** | **10** | **6** | **16** | **8** | **2B** |
| **Totals WM** | | | **52** | **19** | **21** | **40** | **26** | **2G,B** |
| **Totals OG-M** | | | **10** | **4** | **2** | **6** | **0** | **S** |

~WM IIHF Directorate Best Forward (2007), WM All-Star Team/Forward (2007), WM20 IIHF Directorate Best Forward (1997), WM20 All-Star Team/Forward (1996)

**Morrison, Conor**
**b. London, Ontario, Canada, February 24, 1989**

| 2009 WM20 | 28-F | GER | 6 | 1 | 2 | 3 | 2 | 9th |
|---|---|---|---|---|---|---|---|---|

**Morrissey, Josh**
**b. Calgary, Alberta, Canada, March 28, 1995**

| 2012 WM18 | 6-D | CAN | 7 | 0 | 3 | 3 | 25 | B |
|---|---|---|---|---|---|---|---|---|

**Morrow, Brenden**
**b. Carlyle, Saskatchewan, Canada, January 16, 1979**

| 1999 WM20 | 33-F | CAN | 7 | 1 | 7 | 8 | 4 | S |
|---|---|---|---|---|---|---|---|---|
| 2001 WM | 29-F | CAN | 1 | 0 | 0 | 0 | 0 | 5th |
| 2002 WM | 10-F | CAN | 7 | 0 | 1 | 1 | 2 | 6th |
| 2004 WM | 19-F | CAN | 9 | 0 | 3 | 3 | 12 | G |
| 2004 WCH | 10-F | CAN | 1 | 0 | 0 | 0 | 4 | 1st |
| 2005 WM | 10-F | CAN | 9 | 0 | 1 | 1 | 6 | S |
| 2010 OG-M | 10-F | CAN | 7 | 2 | 1 | 3 | 2 | G |
| **Totals WM** | | | **26** | **0** | **5** | **5** | **20** | **G,S** |

**Mortensen, Soren**
**b. Christiansfeld, Denmark, March 19, 1995**

| 2012 WM18 | 22-F | DEN | 6 | 0 | 1 | 1 | 25 | 10th |
|---|---|---|---|---|---|---|---|---|

**Moser, Janik**
**b. Mannheim, Germany, September 26, 1995**

| 2012 WM18 | 18-D | GER | 6 | 1 | 1 | 2 | 2 | 6th |
|---|---|---|---|---|---|---|---|---|

**Moser, Simon**
**b. Berne, Switzerland, March 10, 1989**

| 2011 WM | 82-F | SUI | 6 | 0 | 2 | 2 | 0 | 9th |
|---|---|---|---|---|---|---|---|---|
| 2012 WM | 82-F | SUI | 2 | 2 | 0 | 2 | 0 | 11th |
| **Totals WM** | | | **8** | **2** | **2** | **4** | **0** | **—** |

**Moser, Stephan**
**b. Berne, Switzerland, March 13, 1986**

| 2006 WM20 | 13-F | SUI | 6 | 1 | 0 | 1 | 0 | 7th |
|---|---|---|---|---|---|---|---|---|

**Moss, David**
**b. Livonia, Michigan, United States, December 28, 1981**

| 2010 WM | 25-F | USA | 6 | 1 | 2 | 3 | 2 | 13th |
|---|---|---|---|---|---|---|---|---|

**Motin, Johan**
**b. Karlskoga, Sweden, October 10, 1989**

| 2007 WM18 | 6-D | SWE | 5 | 0 | 3 | 3 | 6 | B |
|---|---|---|---|---|---|---|---|---|
| 2008 WM20 | 3-D | SWE | 6 | 0 | 0 | 0 | 6 | S |

**Mozik, Vojtech**
**b. Prague, Czech Republic, December 26, 1992**

| 2012 WM20 | 8-D | CZE | 6 | 1 | 2 | 3 | 8 | 5th |
|---|---|---|---|---|---|---|---|---|

**Mozyakin, Sergei**
**b. Yaroslavl, Soviet Union (Russia), March 30, 1981**

| 2006 WM | 10-F | RUS | 4 | 2 | 1 | 3 | 0 | 5th |
|---|---|---|---|---|---|---|---|---|
| 2008 WM | 10-F | RUS | 7 | 0 | 1 | 1 | 2 | G |
| 2009 WM | 10-F | RUS | 6 | 2 | 2 | 4 | 2 | G |
| 2010 WM | 10-F | RUS | 4 | 1 | 1 | 2 | 0 | S |
| **Totals WM** | | | **21** | **5** | **5** | **10** | **4** | **2G,S** |

**Mraz, Bruno**
**b. Bratsilava, Slovakia, April 13, 1993**

| 2010 WM18 | 14-F | SVK | 6 | 1 | 1 | 2 | 2 | 8th |
|---|---|---|---|---|---|---|---|---|
| 2011 WM18 | 15-F | SVK | 6 | 3 | 1 | 4 | 8 | 10th |
| **Totals WM18** | | | **12** | **4** | **2** | **6** | **10** | **—** |

**Mraz, Richard**
**b. Nitra, Slovakia, February 19, 1993**

| 2011 WM18 | 11-F | SVK | 4 | 0 | 0 | 0 | 0 | 10th |
|---|---|---|---|---|---|---|---|---|
| 2012 WM20 | 12-F | SVK | 6 | 1 | 4 | 5 | 0 | 6th |

**Mrazek, Jaroslav**
**b. Pisek, Czechoslovakia (Czech Republic), January 14, 1986**

| 2004 WM18 | 6-D | CZE | 7 | 0 | 0 | 0 | 6 | B |
|---|---|---|---|---|---|---|---|---|
| 2006 WM20 | 14-D | CZE | 6 | 0 | 0 | 0 | 8 | 6th |

**Mucka, Matej**
**b. Bratislava, Czechoslovakia (Slovakia), April 18, 1990**

| 2008 WM18 | 4-D | SVK | 6 | 0 | 1 | 1 | 10 | 7th |
|---|---|---|---|---|---|---|---|---|

**Mueller, Peter**
**b. Bloomington, Minnesota, United States, April 14, 1988**

| 2005 WM18 | 18-F | USA | 6 | 4 | 3 | 7 | 20 | G |
|---|---|---|---|---|---|---|---|---|
| 2007 WM20 | 88-F | USA | 7 | 3 | 3 | 6 | 8 | B |
| 2008 WM | 88-F | USA | 7 | 0 | 4 | 4 | 0 | 6th |

**Muhlstein, Florian**
**b. Salzburg, Austria, December 11, 1990**

| 2010 WM20 | 22-D | AUT | 6 | 0 | 0 | 0 | 4 | 10th |
|---|---|---|---|---|---|---|---|---|

**Muller, Florian**
**b. Landshut, West Germany (Germany), September 11, 1989**

| 2009 WM20 | 27-D | GER | 3 | 0 | 0 | 0 | 0 | 9th |
|---|---|---|---|---|---|---|---|---|

**Muller, Marcel**
**b. Berlin, West Germany (Germany), July 10, 1988**

| 2006 WM18 | 19-F | GER | 6 | 0 | 4 | 4 | 4 | 8th |
|---|---|---|---|---|---|---|---|---|
| 2007 WM20 | 16-F | GER | 6 | 1 | 0 | 1 | 4 | 9th |
| 2010 OG-M | 25-F | GER | 4 | 0 | 2 | 2 | 12 | 11th |
| 2010 WM | 25-F | GER | 9 | 1 | 1 | 2 | 0 | 4th |
| 2011 WM | 25-F | GER | 7 | 1 | 4 | 5 | 6 | 7th |
| **Totals WM** | | | **16** | **2** | **5** | **7** | **6** | **—** |

**Muller, Marco**
**b. Heilbronn, Germany, November 22, 1990**

| 2008 WM18 | 12-D | GER | 6 | 0 | 1 | 1 | 8 | 5th |
|---|---|---|---|---|---|---|---|---|

**Muller, Marco**
**b. Zuchwil, Switzerland, January 21, 1994**

| 2012 WM18 | 21-F | SUI | 6 | 1 | 0 | 1 | 0 | 7th |
|---|---|---|---|---|---|---|---|---|

**Muller, Moritz**
**b. Frankfurt, West Germany (Germany), November 19, 1986**

| 2005 WM20 | 12-D | GER | 6 | 0 | 0 | 0 | 24 | 9th |
|---|---|---|---|---|---|---|---|---|
| 2009 WM | 91-D | GER | 6 | 1 | 0 | 1 | 2 | 15th |

**Mulock, T.J. "Travis"**
**b. Langley, British Columbia, Canada, June 25, 1985**

| 2009 WM | 15-F | GER | 6 | 0 | 0 | 0 | 0 | 15th |
|---|---|---|---|---|---|---|---|---|
| 2010 OG-M | 15-F | GER | 4 | 0 | 0 | 0 | 2 | 11th |

**Murcek, Michal**
**b. Martin, Slovakia, January 29, 1992**

| 2010 WM18 | 15-F | SVK | 6 | 1 | 1 | 2 | 2 | 8th |
|---|---|---|---|---|---|---|---|---|

**Muric, Egon**
**b. Bled, Yugoslavia (Slovenia), January 15, 1982**

| 2006 WM | 15-F | SLO | 6 | 1 | 0 | 1 | 4 | 16th |
|---|---|---|---|---|---|---|---|---|
| 2008 WM | 15-F | SLO | 4 | 0 | 0 | 0 | 2 | 15th |
| **Totals WM** | | | **10** | **1** | **0** | **1** | **6** | **—** |

**Murphy, Connor**
**b. Dublin, Ohio, United States, March 26, 1993**

| 2011 WM18 | 5-D | USA | 6 | 3 | 1 | 4 | 2 | G |
|---|---|---|---|---|---|---|---|---|

**Murphy, Ryan**
**b. Aurora, Ontario, Canada, March 31, 1993**

| 2011 WM18 | 14-D | CAN | 7 | 4 | 9 | 13 | 2 | 4th |
|---|---|---|---|---|---|---|---|---|

~WM18 IIHF Directorate Best Defenceman (2011)

**Murray, Douglas**
**b. Bromma, Sweden, March 12, 1980**

| 2008 WM | 2-D | SWE | 5 | 0 | 0 | 0 | 27 | 4th |
|---|---|---|---|---|---|---|---|---|
| 2010 OG-M | 3-D | SWE | 4 | 0 | 0 | 0 | 0 | 5th |

**Murray, Ryan**
**b. Regina, Saskatchewan, Canada, September 27, 1993**

| 2010 WM18 | 7-D | CAN | 6 | 0 | 0 | 0 | 2 | 7th |
|---|---|---|---|---|---|---|---|---|
| 2011 WM18 | 5-D | CAN | 7 | 3 | 7 | 10 | 6 | 4th |
| 2012 WM20 | 27-D | CAN | 6 | 0 | 3 | 3 | 0 | B |
| 2012 WM | 27-D | CAN | 6 | 0 | 0 | 0 | 0 | 5th |
| **Totals WM18** | | | **13** | **3** | **7** | **10** | **8** | **—** |

**Musatov, Igor**
**b. Moscow, Soviet Union (Russia), September 23, 1987**

| 2007 WM20 | 26-F | RUS | 6 | 1 | 0 | 1 | 6 | S |
|---|---|---|---|---|---|---|---|---|

**Music, Ales**
**b. Ljubljana, Yugoslavia (Slovenia), June 28, 1982**

| 2008 WM | 16-F | SLO | 5 | 0 | 0 | 0 | 0 | 15th |
|---|---|---|---|---|---|---|---|---|

**Musienko, Pavel**
**b. Chelyabinsk, Soviet Union (Russia), February 15, 1987**

| 2007 WM20 | 12-F | BLR | 6 | 0 | 1 | 1 | 2 | 10th |
|---|---|---|---|---|---|---|---|---|

**Musil, David**
**b. Edmonton, Alberta, Canada, April 9, 1993**

| 2009 WM18 | 6-D | CZE | 6 | 0 | 1 | 1 | 6 | 6th |
|---|---|---|---|---|---|---|---|---|
| 2011 WM18 | 6-D | CZE | 5 | 0 | 0 | 0 | 6 | 8th |
| 2012 WM20 | 6-D | CZE | 5 | 0 | 0 | 0 | 4 | 5th |
| **Totals WM18** | | | **11** | **0** | **1** | **1** | **12** | **—** |

**Mustonen, Aleksi**
**b. Helsinki, Finland, March 28, 1995**

| 2012 WM18 | 13-F | FIN | 7 | 2 | 3 | 5 | 0 | 4th |
|---|---|---|---|---|---|---|---|---|

**Myers, Tyler**
**b. Houston, Texas, United States, February 1, 1990**

| 2008 WM18 | 3-D | CAN | 7 | 1 | 1 | 2 | 10 | G |
|---|---|---|---|---|---|---|---|---|
| 2009 WM20 | 3-D | CAN | 6 | 1 | 0 | 1 | 2 | G |
| 2010 WM | 57-D | CAN | 7 | 0 | 2 | 2 | 4 | 7th |

**Myllari, Anton**
**b. Vasteras, Sweden, February 27, 1991**

| 2008 WM18 | 6-D | SWE | 6 | 0 | 0 | 0 | 33 | 4th |
|---|---|---|---|---|---|---|---|---|

**Myrvold, Anders**
**b. Lorenskog, Norway, August 12, 1975**

| 1994 WM | 8-D | NOR | 6 | 1 | 0 | 1 | 6 | 11th |
|---|---|---|---|---|---|---|---|---|
| 1999 WM | 26-D | NOR | 6 | 0 | 1 | 1 | 10 | 12th |
| 2006 WM | 54-D | NOR | 6 | 0 | 3 | 3 | 12 | 11th |
| 2008 WM | 54-D | NOR | 7 | 0 | 0 | 0 | 22 | 8th |
| 2009 WM | 54-D | NOR | 6 | 0 | 1 | 1 | 12 | 11th |
| **Totals WM** | | | **31** | **1** | **5** | **6** | **62** | **—** |

**Myttynen, Matias**
**b. Tampere, Finland, March 12, 1990**

| 2008 WM18 | 16-F | FIN | 6 | 0 | 0 | 0 | 0 | 6th |
|---|---|---|---|---|---|---|---|---|
| 2010 WM20 | 10-F | FIN | 6 | 0 | 1 | 1 | 0 | 5th |

**Nabb, Kim**
**b. Vasa, Finland, April 30, 1985**

| 2005 WM20 | 23-F | FIN | 6 | 0 | 0 | 0 | 2 | 5th |
|---|---|---|---|---|---|---|---|---|

**Nagy, Ladislav**
**b. Saca, Czechoslovakia (Slovakia), June 1, 1979**

| 1998 WM20 | 27-F | SVK | 6 | 6 | 2 | 8 | 12 | 9th |
|---|---|---|---|---|---|---|---|---|
| 1999 WM20 | 27-F | SVK | 6 | 4 | 3 | 7 | 0 | B |
| 2001 WM | 27-F | SVK | 7 | 2 | 1 | 3 | 6 | 7th |
| 2002 WM | 27-F | SVK | 6 | 1 | 3 | 4 | 6 | G |
| 2003 WM | 27-F | SVK | 9 | 4 | 4 | 8 | 10 | B |
| 2004 WCH | 27-F | SVK | 4 | 1 | 0 | 1 | 0 | 7th |
| 2009 WM | 27-F | SVK | 6 | 1 | 2 | 3 | 2 | 10th |
| 2011 WM | 27-F | SVK | 4 | 3 | 2 | 5 | 4 | 10th |
| **Totals WM20** | | | **12** | **10** | **5** | **15** | **12** | **B** |
| **Totals WM** | | | **32** | **11** | **12** | **23** | **28** | **G,B** |

**Nakladal, Jakub**
**b. Hradec Kralove, Czechoslovakia (Czech Republic), December 30, 1987**

| 2012 WM | 87-D | CZE | 10 | 0 | 4 | 4 | 6 | B |
|---|---|---|---|---|---|---|---|---|

**Nakyva, Kristian**
**b. Helsinki, Finland, November 18, 1990**

| 2010 WM20 | 6-D | FIN | 6 | 0 | 1 | 1 | 2 | 5th |
|---|---|---|---|---|---|---|---|---|

**Namestnikov, Vladislav**
**b. Zhukovsky, Russia, November 22, 1992**

| 2010 WM18 | 8-F | RUS | 7 | 5 | 2 | 7 | 4 | 4th |
|---|---|---|---|---|---|---|---|---|

**Nasgaard, John Nikolay**
**b. Oslo, Norway, June 22, 1993**

| 2011 WM18 | 24-D | NOR | 6 | 0 | 0 | 0 | 10 | 9th |
|---|---|---|---|---|---|---|---|---|

**Nash, Rick**
**b. Brampton, Ontario, Canada, June 16, 1984**

| | | | | | | | | |
|---|---|---|---|---|---|---|---|---|
| 2002 WM20 | 38-F | CAN | 7 | 1 | 2 | 3 | 2 | S |
| 2005 WM | 61-F | CAN | 9 | 9 | 6 | 15 | 8 | S |
| 2006 OG-M | 61-F | CAN | 6 | 0 | 1 | 1 | 10 | 7th |
| 2007 WM | 61-F | CAN | 9 | 6 | 5 | 11 | 4 | G |
| 2008 WM | 61-F | CAN | 9 | 6 | 7 | 13 | 6 | S |
| 2010 OG-M | 61-F | CAN | 7 | 2 | 3 | 5 | 0 | G |
| 2011 WM | 61-F | CAN | 7 | 2 | 3 | 5 | 2 | 5th |
| **Totals WM** | | | **34** | **23** | **21** | **44** | **20** | **G,2S** |
| **Totals OG-M** | | | **13** | **2** | **4** | **6** | **10** | **G** |

~WM MVP (2007), WM All-Star Team/Forward (2005, 2007, 2008)

**Nattinen, Joonas**
**b. Jamsa, Finland, January 3, 1991**

| | | | | | | | | |
|---|---|---|---|---|---|---|---|---|
| 2008 WM18 | 18-F | FIN | 6 | 2 | 2 | 4 | 8 | 6th |
| 2009 WM18 | 18-F | FIN | 6 | 1 | 3 | 4 | 6 | B |
| 2009 WM20 | 29-F | FIN | 6 | 1 | 2 | 3 | 0 | 7th |
| 2010 WM20 | 29-F | FIN | 6 | 0 | 4 | 4 | 4 | 5th |
| 2011 WM20 | 29-F | FIN | 6 | 3 | 0 | 3 | 2 | 6th |
| **Totals WM18** | | | **12** | **3** | **5** | **8** | **14** | **B** |
| **Totals WM20** | | | **18** | **4** | **6** | **10** | **6** | **—** |

**Naumenkov, Mikhail**
**b. Moscow, Russia, February 19, 1993**

| | | | | | | | | |
|---|---|---|---|---|---|---|---|---|
| 2012 WM20 | 6-D | RUS | 7 | 1 | 1 | 2 | 8 | S |

**Neal, James**
**b. Oshawa, Ontario, Canada, September 3, 1987**

| | | | | | | | | |
|---|---|---|---|---|---|---|---|---|
| 2005 WM18 | 19-F | CAN | 6 | 1 | 1 | 2 | 6 | S |
| 2007 WM20 | 19-F | CAN | 6 | 0 | 0 | 0 | 8 | G |
| 2009 WM | 28-F | CAN | 3 | 1 | 2 | 3 | 2 | S |
| 2011 WM | 18-F | CAN | 6 | 2 | 3 | 5 | 10 | 5th |
| **Totals WM** | | | **9** | **3** | **5** | **8** | **12** | **S** |

**Nechala, Tomas**
**b. Ilava, Slovakia, March 21, 1993**

| | | | | | | | | |
|---|---|---|---|---|---|---|---|---|
| 2011 WM18 | 10-D | SVK | 6 | 0 | 1 | 1 | 4 | 10th |

**Nedved, Petr**
**b. Liberec, Czechoslovakia (Czech Republic), December 9, 1971**

| | | | | | | | | |
|---|---|---|---|---|---|---|---|---|
| 1994 OG-M | 93-F | CAN | 8 | 5 | 1 | 6 | 6 | S |
| 1996 WCH | 93-F | CZE | 3 | 0 | 1 | 1 | 8 | — |
| 2012 WM | 93-F | CZE | 9 | 3 | 2 | 5 | 2 | B |

**Neher, Lars**
**b. Zurich, Switzerland, March 30, 1992**

| | | | | | | | | |
|---|---|---|---|---|---|---|---|---|
| 2010 WM18 | 8-F | SUI | 6 | 0 | 0 | 0 | 0 | 5th |

**Nelson, Brock**
**b. Minneapolis, Minnesota, United States, October 15, 1991**

| | | | | | | | | |
|---|---|---|---|---|---|---|---|---|
| 2011 WM20 | 8-F | USA | 5 | 0 | 1 | 1 | 0 | B |

**Nemec, Ondrej**
**b. Trebic, Czechoslovakia (Czech Republic), April 18, 1984**

| | | | | | | | | |
|---|---|---|---|---|---|---|---|---|
| 2002 WM18 | 23-D | CZE | 8 | 1 | 6 | 7 | 45 | B |
| 2004 WM20 | 4-D | CZE | 7 | 2 | 2 | 4 | 8 | 4th |
| 2009 WM | 6-D | CZE | 7 | 0 | 1 | 1 | 2 | 6th |
| 2010 WM | 63-D | CZE | 6 | 0 | 1 | 1 | 0 | G |
| 2011 WM | 63-D | CZE | 6 | 0 | 0 | 0 | 0 | B |
| 2012 WM | 23-D | CZE | 9 | 0 | 2 | 2 | 4 | B |
| **Totals WM** | | | **28** | **0** | **4** | **4** | **6** | **G,2B** |

**Nemeth, Patrik**
**b. Stockholm, Sweden, February 8, 1992**

| | | | | | | | | |
|---|---|---|---|---|---|---|---|---|
| 2010 WM18 | 7-D | SWE | 6 | 0 | 2 | 2 | 8 | S |
| 2011 WM20 | 12-D | SWE | 6 | 0 | 1 | 1 | 2 | 4th |
| 2012 WM20 | 12-D | SWE | 6 | 0 | 5 | 5 | 2 | G |
| **Totals WM20** | | | **12** | **0** | **6** | **6** | **4** | **G** |

**Nemisz, Greg**
**b. Courtice, Ontario, Canada, June 5, 1990**

| | | | | | | | | |
|---|---|---|---|---|---|---|---|---|
| 2008 WM18 | 28-F | CAN | 7 | 2 | 1 | 3 | 6 | G |
| 2010 WM20 | 16-F | CAN | 6 | 1 | 0 | 1 | 0 | S |

**Nermark, Joachim**
**b. Sunne, Sweden, May 12, 1993**

| | | | | | | | | |
|---|---|---|---|---|---|---|---|---|
| 2010 WM18 | 26-F | SWE | 6 | 0 | 3 | 3 | 2 | S |
| 2011 WM18 | 16-F | SWE | 5 | 1 | 0 | 1 | 4 | S |
| **Totals WM18** | | | **11** | **1** | **3** | **4** | **6** | **2S** |

**Ness, Aaron**
**b. Roseau, Minnesota, United States, May 18, 1990**

| | | | | | | | | |
|---|---|---|---|---|---|---|---|---|
| 2008 WM18 | 20-D | USA | 7 | 0 | 6 | 6 | 2 | G |

**Nesterov, Nikita**
**b. Chelyabinsk, Russia, March 28, 1993**

| | | | | | | | | |
|---|---|---|---|---|---|---|---|---|
| 2010 WM18 | 16-D | RUS | 7 | 2 | 0 | 2 | 29 | 4th |
| 2011 WM18 | 9-D | RUS | 7 | 2 | 2 | 4 | 29 | B |
| 2012 WM20 | 29-D | RUS | 7 | 2 | 3 | 5 | 6 | S |
| **Totals WM18** | | | **14** | **4** | **2** | **6** | **58** | **B** |

**Nestrasil, Andrej**
**b. Prague, Czechoslovakia (Czech Republic), February 22, 1991**

| | | | | | | | | |
|---|---|---|---|---|---|---|---|---|
| 2009 WM18 | 27-F | CZE | 6 | 2 | 2 | 4 | 6 | 6th |
| 2010 WM20 | 11-F | CZE | 6 | 1 | 6 | 7 | 4 | 7th |
| 2011 WM20 | 11-F | CZE | 6 | 1 | 2 | 3 | 2 | 7th |
| **Totals WM20** | | | **12** | **2** | **8** | **10** | **6** | **—** |

**Netesov, Igor**
**b. Ust-Kamenogorsk, Soviet Union (Kazakhstan), April 23, 1990**

| | | | | | | | | |
|---|---|---|---|---|---|---|---|---|
| 2009 WM20 | 6-D | KAZ | 6 | 0 | 0 | 0 | 8 | 10th |

**Neuenschwander, Jan**
**b. Langnau, Switzerland, January 10, 1993**

| | | | | | | | | |
|---|---|---|---|---|---|---|---|---|
| 2011 WM18 | 21-F | SUI | 6 | 1 | 0 | 1 | 10 | 7th |

**Nevalainen, Patrik**
**b. Umea, Sweden, January 27, 1987**

| | | | | | | | | |
|---|---|---|---|---|---|---|---|---|
| 2007 WM20 | 2-D | SWE | 7 | 0 | 0 | 0 | 2 | 4th |

**Nichushkin, Valeri**
**b. Chelyabinsk, Russia, March 4, 1995**

| | | | | | | | | |
|---|---|---|---|---|---|---|---|---|
| 2012 WM18 | 27-F | RUS | 6 | 2 | 0 | 2 | 0 | 5th |

**Niederreiter, Nino**
**b. Chur, Switzerland, September 8, 1992**

| | | | | | | | | |
|---|---|---|---|---|---|---|---|---|
| 2008 WM18 | 22-F | SUI | 6 | 1 | 1 | 2 | 2 | 8th |
| 2009 WM18 | 17-F | SUI | 6 | 3 | 3 | 6 | 16 | 8th |
| 2010 WM20 | 22-F | SUI | 7 | 6 | 4 | 10 | 10 | 4th |
| 2010 WM | 21-F | SUI | 4 | 0 | 0 | 0 | 4 | 5th |
| 2011 WM20 | 22-F | SUI | 6 | 2 | 2 | 4 | 12 | 5th |
| 2012 WM | 22-F | SUI | 6 | 0 | 0 | 0 | 2 | 11th |
| **Totals WM18** | | | **12** | **4** | **4** | **8** | **18** | **—** |
| **Totals WM20** | | | **13** | **8** | **6** | **14** | **22** | **—** |
| **Totals WM** | | | **10** | **0** | **0** | **0** | **6** | **—** |

~WM20 All-Star Team/Forward (2010)

**Nielsen, Daniel**
**b. Herning, Denmark, October 31, 1980**

| | | | | | | | | |
|---|---|---|---|---|---|---|---|---|
| 2003 WM | 5-D | DEN | 6 | 0 | 1 | 1 | 2 | 11th |
| 2004 WM | 5-D | DEN | 6 | 0 | 0 | 0 | 2 | 12th |
| 2006 WM | 5-D | DEN | 6 | 0 | 4 | 4 | 2 | 13th |
| 2007 WM | 5-D | DEN | 6 | 0 | 3 | 3 | 4 | 10th |
| 2008 WM | 5-D | DEN | 6 | 1 | 2 | 3 | 4 | 12th |
| 2009 WM | 5-D | DEN | 5 | 1 | 1 | 2 | 4 | 13th |
| 2010 WM | 5-D | DEN | 7 | 0 | 3 | 3 | 4 | 8th |
| 2011 WM | 5-D | DEN | 6 | 0 | 1 | 1 | 8 | 11th |
| 2012 WM | 5-D | DEN | 7 | 0 | 2 | 2 | 2 | 13th |
| **Totals WM** | | | **55** | **2** | **17** | **19** | **32** | **—** |

**Nielsen, Frans**
**b. Herning, Denmark, April 24, 1984**

| | | | | | | | | |
|---|---|---|---|---|---|---|---|---|
| 2003 WM | 15-F | DEN | 6 | 0 | 0 | 0 | 4 | 11th |
| 2004 WM | 15-F | DEN | 6 | 0 | 3 | 3 | 0 | 12th |
| 2005 WM | 15-F | DEN | 6 | 3 | 0 | 3 | 0 | 14th |
| 2006 WM | 15-F | DEN | 6 | 3 | 0 | 3 | 4 | 13th |
| 2007 WM | 15-F | DEN | 6 | 0 | 3 | 3 | 6 | 10th |
| 2010 WM | 51-F | DEN | 7 | 2 | 3 | 5 | 6 | 8th |
| 2012 WM | 51-F | DEN | 7 | 0 | 3 | 3 | 8 | 13th |
| **Totals WM** | | | **44** | **8** | **12** | **20** | **28** | **—** |

**Nielsen, Rasmus**
**b. Herning, Denmark, September 8, 1990**

| | | | | | | | | |
|---|---|---|---|---|---|---|---|---|
| 2008 WM18 | 12-D | DEN | 6 | 0 | 1 | 1 | 10 | 10th |

**Niemi, Antti-Jussi**
**b. Vantaa, Finland, September 22, 1977**

| | | | | | | | | |
|---|---|---|---|---|---|---|---|---|
| 1996 WM20 | 7-D | FIN | 6 | 3 | 1 | 4 | 43 | 6th |
| 1997 WM20 | 7-D | FIN | 6 | 0 | 2 | 2 | 8 | 5th |
| 1998 WM | 27-D | FIN | 9 | 0 | 0 | 0 | 6 | S |
| 1999 WM | 7-D | FIN | 12 | 1 | 1 | 2 | 8 | S |
| 2000 WM | 7-D | FIN | 9 | 0 | 0 | 0 | 0 | B |
| 2001 WM | 40-D | FIN | 9 | 0 | 1 | 1 | 10 | S |
| 2004 WM | 7-D | FIN | 7 | 1 | 2 | 3 | 4 | 6th |
| 2005 WM | 7-D | FIN | 7 | 2 | 0 | 2 | 4 | 7th |
| 2006 OG-M | 77-D | FIN | 8 | 0 | 0 | 0 | 2 | S |
| 2008 WM | 7-D | FIN | 9 | 0 | 1 | 1 | 28 | B |
| **Totals WM20** | | | **12** | **3** | **3** | **6** | **51** | **—** |
| **Totals WM** | | | **62** | **4** | **5** | **9** | **60** | **3S,2B** |

**Niemi, Jyri**
**b. Hameenkyro, Finland, June 15, 1990**

| | | | | | | | | |
|---|---|---|---|---|---|---|---|---|
| 2009 WM20 | 8-D | FIN | 6 | 2 | 1 | 3 | 6 | 7th |
| 2010 WM20 | 8-D | FIN | 6 | 3 | 2 | 5 | 6 | 5th |
| **Totals WM20** | | | **12** | **5** | **3** | **8** | **12** | **—** |

**Nieto, Matt**
**b. Long Beach, California, United States, November 5, 1992**

| | | | | | | | | |
|---|---|---|---|---|---|---|---|---|
| 2009 WM18 | 18-F | USA | 7 | 4 | 0 | 4 | 12 | G |
| 2010 WM18 | 19-F | USA | 7 | 1 | 3 | 4 | 4 | G |
| **Totals WM18** | | | **14** | **5** | **3** | **8** | **16** | **2G** |

**Niinimaa, Janne**
**b. Raahe, Finland, May 22, 1975**

| | | | | | | | | |
|---|---|---|---|---|---|---|---|---|
| 1992 WM20 | 29-D | FIN | 5 | 0 | 0 | 0 | 2 | 4th |
| 1994 WM20 | 29-D | FIN | 7 | 0 | 0 | 0 | 10 | 4th |
| 1995 WM20 | 6-D | FIN | 7 | 2 | 3 | 5 | 6 | 4th |
| 1995 WM | 6-D | FIN | 8 | 1 | 2 | 3 | 10 | G |
| 1996 WM | 6-D | FIN | 5 | 1 | 0 | 1 | 10 | 5th |
| 1996 WCH | 6-D | FIN | 2 | 0 | 0 | 0 | 2 | 5th |
| 1998 OG-M | 44-D | FIN | 6 | 0 | 3 | 3 | 8 | B |
| 2000 WM | 44-D | FIN | 9 | 2 | 1 | 3 | 8 | B |
| 2002 OG-M | 44-D | FIN | 4 | 0 | 3 | 3 | 2 | 6th |
| 2002 WM | 44-D | FIN | 9 | 0 | 4 | 4 | 8 | 4th |
| 2003 WM | 44-D | FIN | 7 | 1 | 2 | 3 | 12 | 5th |
| 2004 WM | 44-D | FIN | 7 | 0 | 5 | 5 | 2 | 6th |
| 2004 WCH | 44-D | FIN | 3 | 0 | 0 | 0 | 0 | 2nd |
| 2009 WM | 44-D | FIN | 6 | 0 | 1 | 1 | 16 | 5th |
| **Totals WM20** | | | **19** | **2** | **3** | **5** | **18** | **—** |
| **Totals WM** | | | **51** | **5** | **15** | **20** | **66** | **G,B** |
| **Totals IIHF-NHL** | | | **5** | **0** | **0** | **0** | **2** | **—** |
| **Totals OG-M** | | | **10** | **0** | **6** | **6** | **10** | **B** |

**Nikitin, Nikita**
**b. Omsk, Soviet Union (Russia), June 16, 1986**

| | | | | | | | | |
|---|---|---|---|---|---|---|---|---|
| 2006 WM20 | 4-D | RUS | 6 | 0 | 0 | 0 | 6 | S |
| 2012 WM | 12-D | RUS | 10 | 0 | 4 | 4 | 4 | G |

**Nikulin, Alexander**
**b. Moscow, Soviet Union (Russia), August 25, 1985**

| | | | | | | | | |
|---|---|---|---|---|---|---|---|---|
| 2005 WM20 | 21-F | RUS | 6 | 1 | 1 | 2 | 2 | S |

**Nikulin, Ilya**
**b. Moscow, Soviet Union (Russia), March 12, 1982**

| | | | | | | | | |
|---|---|---|---|---|---|---|---|---|
| 1999 WM18 | 4-D | RUS | 7 | 0 | 1 | 1 | 4 | 6th |
| 2000 WM18 | 5-D | RUS | 6 | 1 | 1 | 2 | 10 | S |
| 2006 WM | 6-D | RUS | 7 | 1 | 5 | 6 | 8 | 5th |
| 2007 WM | 5-D | RUS | 9 | 2 | 0 | 2 | 4 | B |
| 2008 WM | 5-D | RUS | 9 | 0 | 1 | 1 | 0 | G |
| 2009 WM | 5-D | RUS | 9 | 1 | 3 | 4 | 4 | G |
| 2010 OG-M | 5-D | RUS | 4 | 0 | 1 | 1 | 2 | 6th |
| 2010 WM | 5-D | RUS | 9 | 0 | 2 | 2 | 2 | S |
| 2011 WM | 5-D | RUS | 9 | 3 | 1 | 4 | 2 | 4th |
| 2012 WM | 5-D | RUS | 10 | 2 | 5 | 7 | 8 | G |
| **Totals WM18** | | | **13** | **1** | **2** | **3** | **14** | **S** |
| **Totals WM** | | | **62** | **9** | **17** | **26** | **28** | **3G,S,B** |

~WM All-Star Team/Defence (2012)

**Nilson, Marcus**
**b. Jarfalla, Sweden, March 1, 1978**

| | | | | | | | | |
|---|---|---|---|---|---|---|---|---|
| 1996 WM20 | 27-F | SWE | 7 | 3 | 5 | 8 | 12 | S |
| 1997 WM20 | 10-F | SWE | 6 | 0 | 4 | 4 | 29 | 8th |
| 1998 WM20 | 10-F | SWE | 7 | 3 | 5 | 8 | 4 | 6th |
| 2003 WM | 18-F | SWE | 1 | 0 | 0 | 0 | 0 | S |
| 2004 WCH | 18-F | SWE | 4 | 1 | 0 | 1 | 4 | 5th |
| 2008 WM | 26-F | SWE | 9 | 4 | 2 | 6 | 2 | 4th |
| 2009 WM | 26-F | SWE | 9 | 3 | 3 | 6 | 6 | B |
| 2010 WM | 26-F | SWE | 9 | 1 | 1 | 2 | 2 | B |
| **Totals WM20** | | | **20** | **6** | **14** | **20** | **45** | **S** |
| **Totals WM** | | | **28** | **8** | **6** | **14** | **10** | **S,2B** |

**Nilsson, Ludvig**
**b. Stockholm, Sweden, March 28, 1994**

| | | | | | | | | |
|---|---|---|---|---|---|---|---|---|
| 2012 WM18 | 12-F | SWE | 6 | 0 | 0 | 0 | 0 | S |

**Nilsson, Mattias**
**b. Visby, Sweden, January 23, 1994**

| | | | | | | | | |
|---|---|---|---|---|---|---|---|---|
| 2012 WM18 | 10-D | SWE | 6 | 0 | 1 | 1 | 0 | S |

**Nilsson, Robert**
**b. Calgary, Alberta, Canada, January 10, 1985**

| | | | | | | | | |
|---|---|---|---|---|---|---|---|---|
| 2001 WM18 | 26-F | SWE | 6 | 2 | 0 | 2 | 0 | 7th |
| 2002 WM18 | 29-F | SWE | 8 | 2 | 3 | 5 | 8 | 9th |
| 2003 WM20 | 29-F | SWE | 6 | 4 | 2 | 6 | 4 | 8th |
| 2004 WM20 | 9-F | SWE | 6 | 2 | 5 | 7 | 6 | 7th |
| 2005 WM20 | 9-F | SWE | 6 | 1 | 3 | 4 | 8 | 6th |
| 2008 WM | 27-F | SWE | 9 | 2 | 4 | 6 | 6 | 4th |
| 2011 WM | 27-F | SWE | 9 | 1 | 6 | 7 | 0 | S |
| **Totals WM18** | | | **14** | **4** | **3** | **7** | **8** | **—** |
| **Totals WM20** | | | **18** | **7** | **10** | **17** | **18** | **—** |
| **Totals WM** | | | **18** | **3** | **10** | **13** | **6** | **S** |

**Nilsson, Tom**
**b. Tyreso, Sweden, August 19, 1993**

| | | | | | | | | |
|---|---|---|---|---|---|---|---|---|
| 2011 WM18 | 7-D | SWE | 6 | 0 | 1 | 1 | 6 | S |

**Nimanis, Kristaps**
**b. Liepaja, Latvia, July 21, 1993**

| | | | | | | | | |
|---|---|---|---|---|---|---|---|---|
| 2010 WM18 | 24-D | LAT | 6 | 0 | 1 | 1 | 6 | 9th |
| 2012 WM20 | 2-D | LAT | 6 | 0 | 1 | 1 | 6 | 9th |

**Niskala, Janne**
**b. Vasteras, Sweden, September 22, 1981**

| | | | | | | | | |
|---|---|---|---|---|---|---|---|---|
| 2001 WM20 | 7-D | FIN | 7 | 0 | 0 | 0 | 10 | S |
| 2008 WM | 21-D | FIN | 9 | 2 | 2 | 4 | 2 | B |
| 2009 WM | 21-D | FIN | 4 | 1 | 2 | 3 | 2 | 5th |
| 2010 OG-M | 21-D | FIN | 6 | 0 | 2 | 2 | 2 | B |
| 2010 WM | 21-D | FIN | 7 | 0 | 2 | 2 | 4 | 6th |
| 2011 WM | 21-D | FIN | 9 | 1 | 3 | 4 | 4 | G |
| 2012 WM | 21-D | FIN | 10 | 3 | 1 | 4 | 10 | 4th |
| **Totals WM** | | | **39** | **7** | **10** | **17** | **22** | **G,2B** |

**Niskanen, Matt**
**b. Virginia, Minnesota, United States, December 6, 1986**

| | | | | | | | | |
|---|---|---|---|---|---|---|---|---|
| 2006 WM20 | 15-D | USA | 7 | 0 | 0 | 0 | 6 | 4th |
| 2009 WM | 5-D | USA | 9 | 1 | 2 | 3 | 2 | 4th |

**Nizivijs, Aleksandrs**
**b. Riga, Soviet Union (Latvia), September 16, 1976**

| | | | | | | | | |
|---|---|---|---|---|---|---|---|---|
| 1998 WM | 71-F | LAT | 6 | 2 | 0 | 2 | 0 | 9th |
| 1999 WM | 26-F | LAT | 6 | 1 | 3 | 4 | 4 | 11th |
| 2000 WM | 17-F | LAT | 7 | 1 | 3 | 4 | 0 | 8th |
| 2002 OG-M | 17-F | LAT | 4 | 2 | 3 | 5 | 2 | 9th |
| 2002 WM | 17-F | LAT | 4 | 1 | 0 | 1 | 0 | 11th |
| 2003 WM | 17-F | LAT | 6 | 0 | 0 | 0 | 4 | 9th |
| 2004 WM | 17-F | LAT | 7 | 1 | 2 | 3 | 6 | 7th |
| 2005 WM | 17-F | LAT | 6 | 0 | 2 | 2 | 2 | 9th |
| 2006 OG-M | 17-F | LAT | 5 | 2 | 3 | 5 | 0 | 12th |
| 2006 WM | 17-F | LAT | 6 | 0 | 3 | 3 | 4 | 10th |
| 2007 WM | 17-F | LAT | 6 | 1 | 0 | 1 | 0 | 13th |
| 2008 WM | 17-F | LAT | 6 | 1 | 1 | 2 | 2 | 11th |
| 2009 WM | 17-F | LAT | 7 | 3 | 5 | 8 | 2 | 7th |
| 2010 OG-M | 17-F | LAT | 4 | 0 | 2 | 2 | 2 | 12th |
| 2010 WM | 17-F | LAT | 6 | 1 | 1 | 2 | 0 | 11th |
| 2011 WM | 17-F | LAT | 6 | 1 | 4 | 5 | 4 | 13th |
| **Totals WM** | | | **79** | **13** | **24** | **37** | **28** | **—** |
| **Totals OG-M** | | | **13** | **4** | **8** | **12** | **4** | **—** |

**Nodl, Andreas**
**b. Vienna, Austria, February 28, 1987**

| | | | | | | | | |
|---|---|---|---|---|---|---|---|---|
| 2004 WM20 | 10-F | AUT | 6 | 0 | 0 | 0 | 0 | 9th |
| 2009 WM | 14-F | AUT | 4 | 0 | 1 | 1 | 4 | 14th |

**Noebels, Marcel**
**b. Tonisvorst, Germany, March 14, 1992**

| | | | | | | | | |
|---|---|---|---|---|---|---|---|---|
| 2009 WM18 | 15-F | GER | 6 | 0 | 0 | 0 | 0 | 10th |
| 2011 WM20 | 15-F | GER | 6 | 1 | 2 | 3 | 0 | 10th |

**Nokelainen, Petteri**
**b. Imatra, Finland, January 16, 1986**

| | | | | | | | | |
|---|---|---|---|---|---|---|---|---|
| 2003 WM18 | 26-F | FIN | 6 | 1 | 0 | 1 | 6 | 7th |
| 2004 WM18 | 27-F | FIN | 6 | 5 | 6 | 11 | 16 | 7th |
| 2004 WM20 | 27-F | FIN | 7 | 1 | 0 | 1 | 0 | B |
| 2005 WM20 | 9-F | FIN | 6 | 1 | 4 | 5 | 2 | 5th |
| 2011 WM | 29-F | FIN | 9 | 1 | 1 | 2 | 8 | G |
| **Totals WM18** | | | **12** | **6** | **6** | **12** | **22** | **—** |
| **Totals WM20** | | | **13** | **2** | **4** | **6** | **2** | **B** |

**Nordby Tranholm, Bo**
**b. Aalborg, Denmark, March 22, 1979**

| | | | | | | | | |
|---|---|---|---|---|---|---|---|---|
| 2003 WM | 10-F | DEN | 6 | 1 | 0 | 1 | 14 | 11th* |
| 2004 WM | 10-F | DEN | 6 | 1 | 1 | 2 | 6 | 12th* |
| 2005 WM | 10-F | DEN | 6 | 0 | 2 | 2 | 4 | 14th* |
| 2006 WM | 10-F | DEN | 6 | 0 | 0 | 0 | 4 | 13th* |
| 2007 WM | 10-F | DEN | 4 | 1 | 0 | 1 | 2 | 10th** |
| 2008 WM | 10-F | DEN | 6 | 0 | 0 | 0 | 6 | 12th*** |
| **Totals WM** | | | **34** | **3** | **3** | **6** | **36** | **—** |

*played as Bo Nordby Andersen
**played as Bo Nordby Tranholm
***played as Bo Nordby

**Nordstrom, Joakim**
**b. Tyreso, Sweden, February 25, 1992**

| | | | | | | | | |
|---|---|---|---|---|---|---|---|---|
| 2010 WM18 | 27-F | SWE | 6 | 0 | 2 | 2 | 6 | S |
| 2012 WM20 | 19-F | SWE | 6 | 4 | 1 | 5 | 0 | G |

**Nosek, Tomas**
**b. Pardubice, Czech Republic, September 1, 1992**

| | | | | | | | | |
|---|---|---|---|---|---|---|---|---|
| 2012 WM20 | 18-F | CZE | 6 | 0 | 1 | 1 | 2 | 5th |

**Noteng, Markus**
**b. Trondheim, Norway, January 20, 1994**

| | | | | | | | | |
|---|---|---|---|---|---|---|---|---|
| 2011 WM18 | 22-D | NOR | 6 | 0 | 1 | 1 | 10 | 9th |

**Novak, Filip**
**b. Ceske Budejovice, Czechoslovakia (Czech Republic), May 7, 1982**

| | | | | | | | | |
|---|---|---|---|---|---|---|---|---|
| 1999 WM18 | 22-D | CZE | 7 | 1 | 2 | 3 | 4 | 5th |
| 2002 WM20 | 5-D | CZE | 7 | 0 | 2 | 2 | 4 | 7th |
| 2010 WM | 5-D | CZE | 3 | 0 | 1 | 1 | 4 | G |

**Novopashin, Vitali**
**b. Ust-Kamenogorsk, Soviet Union (Kazakhstan), September 28, 1978**

| | | | | | | | | |
|---|---|---|---|---|---|---|---|---|
| 2012 WM | 4-D | KAZ | 7 | 0 | 4 | 4 | 2 | 16th |

**Novotny, Jiri**
**b. Pelhrimov, Czechoslovakia (Czech Republic), August 12, 1983**

| | | | | | | | | |
|---|---|---|---|---|---|---|---|---|
| 2000 WM18 | 25-F | CZE | 6 | 0 | 2 | 2 | 0 | 6th |
| 2001 WM18 | 25-F | CZE | 6 | 4 | 3 | 7 | 2 | 4th |
| 2002 WM20 | 25-F | CZE | 7 | 0 | 2 | 2 | 4 | 7th |
| 2003 WM20 | 25-F | CZE | 6 | 0 | 1 | 1 | 2 | 6th |
| 2007 WM | 13-F | CZE | 6 | 0 | 0 | 0 | 8 | 7th |
| 2008 WM | 13-F | CZE | 7 | 1 | 1 | 2 | 2 | 5th |
| 2010 WM | 12-F | CZE | 9 | 1 | 5 | 6 | 12 | G |
| 2011 WM | 12-F | CZE | 9 | 0 | 2 | 2 | 0 | B |
| 2012 WM | 12-F | CZE | 10 | 4 | 1 | 5 | 0 | B |
| **Totals WM18** | | | **12** | **4** | **5** | **9** | **2** | **—** |
| **Totals WM20** | | | **13** | **0** | **3** | **3** | **6** | **—** |
| **Totals WM** | | | **41** | **6** | **9** | **15** | **22** | **G,2B** |

**Novotny, Stepan**
**b. Prague, Czechoslovakia (Czech Republic), September 21, 1990**

| | | | | | | | | |
|---|---|---|---|---|---|---|---|---|
| 2007 WM18 | 13-F | CZE | 6 | 1 | 1 | 2 | 0 | 9th |
| 2009 WM20 | 16-F | CZE | 5 | 0 | 1 | 1 | 0 | 6th |
| 2010 WM20 | 16-F | CZE | 6 | 3 | 2 | 5 | 2 | 7th |
| **Totals WM20** | | | **11** | **3** | **3** | **6** | **2** | **—** |

**Nowak, Marco**
**b. Dresden, East Germany (Germany), July 23, 1990**

| | | | | | | | | |
|---|---|---|---|---|---|---|---|---|
| 2008 WM18 | 10-D | GER | 6 | 0 | 0 | 0 | 2 | 5th |
| 2009 WM20 | 13-D | GER | 6 | 1 | 0 | 1 | 2 | 9th |

**Nugent-Hopkins, Ryan**
**b. Burnaby, British Columbia, Canada, April 12, 1993**

| | | | | | | | | |
|---|---|---|---|---|---|---|---|---|
| 2012 WM | 93-F | CAN | 8 | 4 | 2 | 6 | 4 | 5th |

**Nummelin, Petteri**
**b. Turku, Finland, November 25, 1972**

| | | | | | | | | |
|---|---|---|---|---|---|---|---|---|
| 1992 WM20 | 9-D | FIN | 6 | 0 | 1 | 1 | 4 | 4th |
| 1995 WM | 3-D | FIN | 5 | 0 | 0 | 0 | 6 | G |
| 1996 WM | 3-D | FIN | 5 | 0 | 0 | 0 | 2 | 5th |
| 1996 WCH | 3-D | FIN | 1 | 0 | 0 | 0 | 0 | 5th |
| 1997 WM | 3-D | FIN | 8 | 0 | 2 | 2 | 10 | 5th |
| 1998 WM | 3-D | FIN | 1 | 0 | 0 | 0 | 0 | S |
| 1999 WM | 3-D | FIN | 12 | 0 | 0 | 0 | 4 | S |
| 2000 WM | 3-D | FIN | 9 | 2 | 4 | 6 | 0 | B |
| 2001 WM | 3-D | FIN | 9 | 1 | 12 | 13 | 0 | S |
| 2002 WM | 3-D | FIN | 7 | 1 | 0 | 1 | 2 | 4th |
| 2003 WM | 3-D | FIN | 7 | 2 | 2 | 4 | 4 | 5th |
| 2004 WM | 3-D | FIN | 7 | 2 | 2 | 4 | 2 | 6th |
| 2005 WM | 3-D | FIN | 7 | 0 | 2 | 2 | 0 | 7th |
| 2006 OG-M | 3-D | FIN | 8 | 0 | 2 | 2 | 2 | S |
| 2006 WM | 3-D | FIN | 9 | 3 | 11 | 14 | 2 | B |
| 2007 WM | 3-D | FIN | 7 | 3 | 5 | 8 | 4 | S |
| 2009 WM | 3-D | FIN | 5 | 0 | 3 | 3 | 0 | 5th |
| 2010 WM | 3-D | FIN | 6 | 1 | 6 | 7 | 0 | 6th |
| **Totals WM** | | | **104** | **15** | **49** | **64** | **36** | **G,4S,2B** |

~WM IIHF Directorate Best Defenceman (2000, 2010), WM All-Star Team/Defence (2000, 2001, 2007, 2010)

**Nurek, Alexander**
**b. Ust-Kamenogorsk, Soviet Union (Kazakhstan), February 15, 1990**

| | | | | | | | | |
|---|---|---|---|---|---|---|---|---|
| 2009 WM20 | 9-F | KAZ | 6 | 0 | 0 | 0 | 6 | 10th |

**Nurmi, Teemu**
**b. Tampere, Finland, February 24, 1985**

| | | | | | | | | |
|---|---|---|---|---|---|---|---|---|
| 2002 WM18 | 14-F | FIN | 8 | 1 | 4 | 5 | 6 | 4th |
| 2003 WM18 | 21-F | FIN | 6 | 2 | 3 | 5 | 4 | 7th |
| 2004 WM20 | 22-F | FIN | 7 | 2 | 2 | 4 | 0 | B |
| 2005 WM20 | 11-F | FIN | 6 | 1 | 1 | 2 | 2 | 5th |
| **Totals WM18** | | | **14** | **3** | **7** | **10** | **10** | **—** |
| **Totals WM20** | | | **13** | **3** | **3** | **6** | **2** | **B** |

**Nurse, Darnell**
**b. Hamilton, Ontario, Canada, February 4, 1995**

| | | | | | | | | |
|---|---|---|---|---|---|---|---|---|
| 2012 WM18 | 2-D | CAN | 7 | 0 | 0 | 0 | 14 | B |

**Nygard, Jonas**
**b. Oslo, Norway, November 28, 1987**

| | | | | | | | | |
|---|---|---|---|---|---|---|---|---|
| 2006 WM20 | 5-D | NOR | 5 | 0 | 0 | 0 | 16 | 10th |

**Nygard, Kjell**
**b. Oslo, Norway, January 4, 1978**

| | | | | | | | | |
|---|---|---|---|---|---|---|---|---|
| 2001 WM | 28-F | NOR | 6 | 0 | 1 | 1 | 0 | 15th |
| 2006 WM | 28-F | NOR | 6 | 1 | 0 | 1 | 0 | 11th |
| 2007 WM | 28-F | NOR | 6 | 0 | 0 | 0 | 0 | 14th |
| 2008 WM | 28-F | NOR | 7 | 0 | 0 | 0 | 0 | 8th |
| **Totals WM** | | | **25** | **1** | **1** | **2** | **0** | **—** |

**Nylander, Michael**
**b. Stockholm, Sweden, October 3, 1972**

| | | | | | | | | |
|---|---|---|---|---|---|---|---|---|
| 1991 WM20 | 26-F | SWE | 7 | 6 | 5 | 11 | 8 | 6th |
| 1992 WM20 | 26-F | SWE | 7 | 8 | 9 | 17 | 6 | S |
| 1992 WM | 16-F | SWE | 6 | 0 | 1 | 1 | 0 | G |
| 1993 WM | 26-F | SWE | 7 | 1 | 7 | 8 | 4 | S |
| 1996 WM | 92-F | SWE | 3 | 2 | 3 | 5 | 0 | 6th |
| 1996 WCH | 92-F | SWE | 4 | 2 | 1 | 3 | 0 | 3rd |
| 1997 WM | 92-F | SWE | 11 | 6 | 5 | 11 | 6 | S |
| 1998 OG-M | 92-F | SWE | 4 | 0 | 0 | 0 | 6 | 5th |
| 1999 WM | 92-F | SWE | 10 | 2 | 4 | 6 | 8 | B |
| 2000 WM | 92-F | SWE | 7 | 1 | 5 | 6 | 6 | 7th |
| 2002 OG-M | 92-F | SWE | 4 | 1 | 2 | 3 | 0 | 5th |
| 2002 WM | 92-F | SWE | 8 | 1 | 6 | 7 | 0 | B |
| 2004 WM | 92-F | SWE | 7 | 2 | 4 | 6 | 8 | S |
| 2006 WM | 92-F | SWE | 6 | 1 | 8 | 9 | 4 | G |
| 2010 WM | 92-F | SWE | 8 | 1 | 2 | 3 | 4 | B |
| **Totals WM20** | | | **14** | **14** | **14** | **28** | **14** | **S** |
| **Totals WM** | | | **73** | **17** | **45** | **62** | **40** | **2G,3S,3B** |
| **Totals OG-M** | | | **8** | **1** | **2** | **3** | **6** | **—** |

~WM IIHF Directorate Best Forward (1997), WM All-Star Team/Forward (1997), WM20 IIHF Directorate Best Forward (1992), WM20 All-Star Team/Forward (1992)

**Nyqvist, Julius**
**b. Vantaa, Finland, October 29, 1992**

| | | | | | | | | |
|---|---|---|---|---|---|---|---|---|
| 2010 WM18 | 8-D | FIN | 6 | 0 | 0 | 0 | 2 | B |

**Nystrom, Eric**
**b. Syosset, New York, United States, February 14, 1983**

| | | | | | | | | |
|---|---|---|---|---|---|---|---|---|
| 2001 WM18 | 21-F | USA | 6 | 3 | 3 | 6 | 6 | 6th |
| 2002 WM20 | 17-F | USA | 7 | 0 | 0 | 0 | 0 | 5th |
| 2003 WM20 | 21-F | USA | 7 | 1 | 2 | 3 | 2 | 4th |
| 2010 WM | 23-F | USA | 6 | 0 | 0 | 0 | 4 | 13th |
| **Totals WM20** | | | **14** | **1** | **2** | **3** | **2** | **—** |

**Oberrauch, Max**
**b. Bolzano, Italy, April 26, 1984**

| | | | | | | | | |
|---|---|---|---|---|---|---|---|---|
| 2010 WM | 3-F | ITA | 6 | 0 | 0 | 0 | 2 | — |

**Oblinger, Alexander**
**b. Augsburg, West Germany (Germany), January 17, 1989**

| | | | | | | | | |
|---|---|---|---|---|---|---|---|---|
| 2006 WM18 | 21-F | GER | 6 | 0 | 0 | 0 | 4 | 8th |
| 2007 WM18 | 18-F | GER | 6 | 1 | 1 | 2 | 8 | 8th |
| 2009 WM20 | 14-F | GER | 6 | 0 | 1 | 1 | 12 | 9th |
| **Totals WM18** | | | **12** | **1** | **1** | **2** | **12** | **—** |

**O'Brien, Jim**
**b. Maplewood, Minnesota, United States, January 29, 1989**

| | | | | | | | | |
|---|---|---|---|---|---|---|---|---|
| 2006 WM18 | 19-F | USA | 6 | 3 | 1 | 4 | 6 | G |
| 2007 WM18 | 19-F | USA | 7 | 3 | 4 | 7 | 12 | S |
| 2009 WM20 | 15-F | USA | 6 | 1 | 3 | 4 | 2 | 5th |
| **Totals WM18** | | | **13** | **6** | **5** | **11** | **18** | **G,S** |

**Obsut, Jaroslav**
**b. Presov, Czechoslovakia (Slovakia), September 3, 1976**

| | | | | | | | | |
|---|---|---|---|---|---|---|---|---|
| 2002 OG-M | 5-D | SVK | 4 | 0 | 0 | 0 | 2 | 13th |
| 2004 WCH | 43-D | SVK | 3 | 0 | 0 | 0 | 0 | 7th |
| 2005 WM | 43-D | SVK | 4 | 0 | 0 | 0 | 2 | 5th |
| 2009 WM | 43-D | SVK | 6 | 0 | 1 | 1 | 0 | 10th |
| **Totals WM** | | | **10** | **0** | **1** | **1** | **2** | **—** |

**Obukhovski, Alexander**
**b. Grodno, Soviet Union (Belarus), March 1, 1990**

| | | | | | | | | |
|---|---|---|---|---|---|---|---|---|
| 2008 WM18 | 16-F | BLR | 5 | 0 | 0 | 0 | 0 | 9th |

**O'Connor, Ryan**
**b. Hamilton, Ontario, Canada, January 12, 1992**

| | | | | | | | | |
|---|---|---|---|---|---|---|---|---|
| 2010 WM18 | 10-D | CAN | 6 | 3 | 2 | 5 | 8 | 7th |

**Odegaard, Henrik**
**b. Asker, Norway, February 12, 1988**

| | | | | | | | | |
|---|---|---|---|---|---|---|---|---|
| 2006 WM18 | 7-D | NOR | 6 | 0 | 0 | 0 | 8 | 10th |
| 2008 WM | 24-D | NOR | 7 | 0 | 0 | 0 | 2 | 8th |

**O'Dell, Eric**
**b. Ottawa, Ontario, Canada, June 21, 1990**

| | | | | | | | | |
|---|---|---|---|---|---|---|---|---|
| 2008 WM18 | 16-F | CAN | 7 | 1 | 3 | 4 | 8 | G |

**Oduya, Johnny**
**b. Stockholm, Sweden, October 1, 1981**

| | | | | | | | | |
|---|---|---|---|---|---|---|---|---|
| 2009 WM | 7-D | SWE | 5 | 3 | 1 | 4 | 2 | B |
| 2010 OG-M | 29-D | SWE | 4 | 0 | 0 | 0 | 12 | 5th |

**Ofner, Harald**
**b. Klagenfurt, Austria, January 21, 1983**

| | | | | | | | | |
|---|---|---|---|---|---|---|---|---|
| 2009 WM | 47-F | AUT | 3 | 0 | 0 | 0 | 2 | 14th |

**Ogorodnikov, Sergei**
**b. Irkutsk, Soviet Union (Russia), January 21, 1986**

| | | | | | | | | |
|---|---|---|---|---|---|---|---|---|
| 2004 WM18 | 11-F | RUS | 6 | 3 | 0 | 3 | 4 | G |
| 2006 WM20 | 10-F | RUS | 6 | 0 | 1 | 1 | 6 | S |

**Ogorodnikovs, Artjoms**
**b. Kiev (Kyiv), Soviet Union (Ukraine), December 27, 1989**

| | | | | | | | | |
|---|---|---|---|---|---|---|---|---|
| 2009 WM20 | 24-F | LAT | 6 | 2 | 1 | 3 | 2 | 8th |

**Ohlund, Mattias**
**b. Pitea, Sweden, September 9, 1976**

| | | | | | | | | |
|---|---|---|---|---|---|---|---|---|
| 1994 WM20 | 7-D | SWE | 7 | 0 | 2 | 2 | 2 | S |
| 1995 WM20 | 7-D | SWE | 7 | 1 | 0 | 1 | 4 | B |
| 1996 WM20 | 16-D | SWE | 7 | 0 | 5 | 5 | 32 | S |
| 1997 WM | 26-D | SWE | 11 | 2 | 1 | 3 | 12 | S |
| 1998 OG-M | 2-D | SWE | 4 | 0 | 1 | 1 | 4 | 5th |
| 1998 WM | 2-D | SWE | 10 | 2 | 1 | 3 | 8 | G |
| 2001 WM | 2-D | SWE | 9 | 2 | 3 | 5 | 12 | B |
| 2002 OG-M | 2-D | SWE | 4 | 0 | 2 | 2 | 2 | 5th |
| 2004 WCH | 2-D | SWE | 4 | 1 | 0 | 1 | 0 | 5th |
| 2006 OG-M | 2-D | SWE | 6 | 0 | 2 | 2 | 2 | G |
| 2010 OG-M | 2-D | SWE | 4 | 1 | 0 | 1 | 2 | 5th |
| **Totals WM20** | | | **21** | **1** | **7** | **8** | **38** | **2S,B** |
| **Totals WM** | | | **30** | **6** | **5** | **11** | **32** | **G,S,B** |
| **Totals OG-M** | | | **18** | **1** | **5** | **6** | **10** | **G** |

~WM20 IIHF Directorate Best Defenceman (1996), WM20 All-Star Team/Defence (1996)

**Ohmann, Marcel**
**b. Neuss, West Germany (Germany), April 4, 1991**

| | | | | | | | | |
|---|---|---|---|---|---|---|---|---|
| 2009 WM18 | 20-F | GER | 5 | 4 | 0 | 4 | 16 | 10th |
| 2011 WM20 | 20-F | GER | 6 | 0 | 1 | 1 | 6 | 10th |

**Okal, Zdenek**
**b. Zlin, Czechoslovakia (Czech Republic), July 8, 1990**

| | | | | | | | | |
|---|---|---|---|---|---|---|---|---|
| 2009 WM20 | 11-F | CZE | 6 | 3 | 2 | 5 | 18 | 6th |

**Okposo, Kyle**
**b. St. Paul, Minnesota, United States, April 16, 1988**

| | | | | | | | | |
|---|---|---|---|---|---|---|---|---|
| 2007 WM20 | 8-F | USA | 7 | 0 | 1 | 1 | 12 | B |
| 2008 WM20 | 9-F | USA | 6 | 1 | 5 | 6 | 2 | 4th |
| 2009 WM | 9-F | USA | 9 | 2 | 3 | 5 | 10 | 4th |
| 2010 WM | 21-F | USA | 6 | 1 | 2 | 3 | 0 | 13th |
| 2012 WM | 21-F | USA | 8 | 2 | 1 | 3 | 0 | 7th |
| **Totals WM20** | | | **13** | **1** | **6** | **7** | **14** | **B** |
| **Totals WM** | | | **23** | **5** | **6** | **11** | **10** | **—** |

**Olden, Sondre**
**b. Oslo, Norway, August 29, 1992**

| | | | | | | | | |
|---|---|---|---|---|---|---|---|---|
| 2009 WM18 | 18-F | NOR | 6 | 2 | 1 | 3 | 2 | 9th |
| 2011 WM20 | 13-F | NOR | 6 | 0 | 0 | 0 | 6 | 9th |

**Oleksiak, Jamie**
**b. Toronto, Ontario, Canada, December 21, 1992**

| | | | | | | | | |
|---|---|---|---|---|---|---|---|---|
| 2012 WM20 | 2-D | CAN | 6 | 0 | 0 | 0 | 2 | B |

**Olesz, Rostislav**
**b. Bilovec, Czechoslovakia (Czech Republic), October 10, 1985**

| | | | | | | | | |
|---|---|---|---|---|---|---|---|---|
| 2003 WM18 | 26-F | CZE | 6 | 2 | 3 | 5 | 4 | 6th |
| 2004 WM20 | 25-F | CZE | 6 | 3 | 2 | 5 | 6 | 4th |
| 2005 WM20 | 25-F | CZE | 7 | 7 | 3 | 10 | 12 | B |
| 2006 OG-M | 85-F | CZE | 8 | 0 | 0 | 0 | 2 | B |
| 2007 WM | 85-F | CZE | 7 | 2 | 3 | 5 | 4 | 7th |
| 2009 WM | 85-F | CZE | 7 | 0 | 1 | 1 | 2 | 6th |
| **Totals WM20** | | | **13** | **10** | **5** | **15** | **18** | **B** |
| **Totals WM** | | | **14** | **2** | **4** | **6** | **6** | **—** |

**Olimb, Ken Andre**
**b. Oslo, Norway, January 21, 1989**

| | | | | | | | | |
|---|---|---|---|---|---|---|---|---|
| 2006 WM18 | 16-F | NOR | 6 | 1 | 0 | 1 | 4 | 10th |
| 2010 WM | 40-F | NOR | 6 | 0 | 0 | 0 | 0 | 9th |
| 2011 WM | 40-F | NOR | 7 | 3 | 1 | 4 | 0 | 6th |
| 2012 WM | 40-F | NOR | 8 | 0 | 2 | 2 | 0 | 8th |
| **Totals WM** | | | **21** | **3** | **3** | **6** | **0** | **—** |

**Olimb, Mathis**
**b. Oslo, Norway, February 1, 1986**

| | | | | | | | | |
|---|---|---|---|---|---|---|---|---|
| 2002 WM18 | 22-F | NOR | 8 | 3 | 4 | 7 | 0 | 11th |
| 2004 WM18 | 22-F | NOR | 6 | 0 | 6 | 6 | 14 | 10th |
| 2006 WM20 | 20-F | NOR | 6 | 2 | 1 | 3 | 8 | 10th |
| 2007 WM | 46-F | NOR | 6 | 0 | 3 | 3 | 8 | 14th |
| 2008 WM | 46-F | NOR | 7 | 2 | 0 | 2 | 4 | 8th |
| 2010 OG-M | 46-F | NOR | 4 | 0 | 2 | 2 | 0 | 10th |
| 2010 WM | 46-F | NOR | 6 | 1 | 3 | 4 | 0 | 9th |
| 2011 WM | 46-F | NOR | 7 | 1 | 8 | 9 | 4 | 6th |
| 2012 WM | 46-F | NOR | 8 | 1 | 6 | 7 | 16 | 8th |
| **Totals WM18** | | | **14** | **3** | **10** | **13** | **14** | **—** |
| **Totals WM** | | | **34** | **5** | **20** | **25** | **32** | **—** |

**Olsen, Dylan**
**b. Calgary, Alberta, Canada, January 3, 1991**

| | | | | | | | | |
|---|---|---|---|---|---|---|---|---|
| 2009 WM18 | 12-D | CAN | 6 | 2 | 2 | 4 | 14 | 4th |
| 2011 WM20 | 4-D | CAN | 7 | 0 | 2 | 2 | 0 | S |

**Olsen, Rasmus**
**b. Herlev, Denmark, May 30, 1980**

| | | | | | | | | |
|---|---|---|---|---|---|---|---|---|
| 2007 WM | 20-F | DEN | 6 | 1 | 0 | 1 | 2 | 10th |
| 2008 WM | 24-F | DEN | 3 | 0 | 0 | 0 | 0 | 12th |
| 2009 WM | 12-F | DEN | 3 | 0 | 0 | 0 | 0 | 13th |
| **Totals WM** | | | **12** | **1** | **0** | **1** | **2** | **—** |

**Olsson, Kalle**
**b. Munkedal, Sweden, January 31, 1985**

| | | | | | | | | |
|---|---|---|---|---|---|---|---|---|
| 2003 WM18 | 21-F | SWE | 6 | 0 | 1 | 1 | 2 | 5th |
| 2005 WM20 | 11-F | SWE | 6 | 0 | 3 | 3 | 4 | 6th |

**Olvecky, Peter**
**b. Nove Zamky, Czechoslovakia (Czech Republic), October 11, 1985**

| | | | | | | | | |
|---|---|---|---|---|---|---|---|---|
| 2005 WM20 | 26-F | SVK | 6 | 3 | 1 | 4 | 16 | 7th |
| 2009 WM | 28-F | SVK | 5 | 0 | 1 | 1 | 2 | 10th |

**Omark, Linus**
**b. Overtornea, Sweden, February 5, 1987**

| | | | | | | | | |
|---|---|---|---|---|---|---|---|---|
| 2007 WM20 | 26-F | SWE | 7 | 2 | 3 | 5 | 4 | 4th |
| 2009 WM | 23-F | SWE | 9 | 2 | 8 | 10 | 14 | B |
| 2010 WM | 23-F | SWE | 9 | 1 | 3 | 4 | 8 | B |
| **Totals WM** | | | **18** | **3** | **11** | **14** | **22** | **2B** |

**O'Marra, Ryan**
**b. Tokyo, Japan, June 9, 1987**

| | | | | | | | | |
|---|---|---|---|---|---|---|---|---|
| 2005 WM18 | 22-F | CAN | 6 | 5 | 0 | 5 | 12 | S |
| 2006 WM20 | 23-F | CAN | 6 | 0 | 2 | 2 | 18 | G |
| 2007 WM20 | 23-F | CAN | 6 | 0 | 2 | 2 | 8 | G |
| **Totals WM20** | | | **12** | **0** | **4** | **4** | **26** | **2G** |

**Ondracek, Jiri**
**b. Gottwaldov (Zlin), Czechoslovakia (Czech Republic), June 3, 1988**

| | | | | | | | | |
|---|---|---|---|---|---|---|---|---|
| 2008 WM20 | 24-F | CZE | 6 | 0 | 5 | 5 | 8 | 5th |

**Ondruschka, Florian**
**b. Selb, West Germany (Germany), June 24, 1987**

| | | | | | | | | |
|---|---|---|---|---|---|---|---|---|
| 2005 WM18 | 17-D | GER | 6 | 1 | 0 | 1 | 6 | 8th |
| 2007 WM20 | 17-D | GER | 6 | 1 | 0 | 1 | 2 | 9th |
| 2012 WM | 7-D | GER | 7 | 0 | 0 | 0 | 2 | 12th |

**Onishenko, Oleg**
**b. Ust-Kamenogorsk, Soviet Union (Kazakhstan), August 23, 1989**

| | | | | | | | | |
|---|---|---|---|---|---|---|---|---|
| 2009 WM20 | 27-F | KAZ | 5 | 1 | 0 | 1 | 6 | 10th |

**Oppoyen, Jonas**
**b. Oslo, Norway, January 20, 1991**

| | | | | | | | | |
|---|---|---|---|---|---|---|---|---|
| 2009 WM18 | 22-F | NOR | 6 | 3 | 0 | 3 | 4 | 9th |
| 2011 WM20 | 19-F | NOR | 6 | 1 | 1 | 2 | 4 | 9th |

**Oraze, Martin**
**b. Klagenfurt, Austria, October 9, 1984**

| | | | | | | | | |
|---|---|---|---|---|---|---|---|---|
| 2004 WM20 | 18-D | AUT | 6 | 0 | 1 | 1 | 6 | 9th |
| 2009 WM | 39-D | AUT | 6 | 1 | 0 | 1 | 2 | 14th |

**O'Regan, Danny**
**b. Needham, Massachusetts, United States, January 30, 1994**

| | | | | | | | | |
|---|---|---|---|---|---|---|---|---|
| 2012 WM18 | 15-F | USA | 6 | 1 | 3 | 4 | 0 | G |

**O'Reilly, Ryan**
**b. Varna, Ontario, Canada, February 7, 1991**

| | | | | | | | | |
|---|---|---|---|---|---|---|---|---|
| 2009 WM18 | 9-F | CAN | 6 | 2 | 3 | 5 | 0 | 4th |
| 2012 WM | 37-F | CAN | 7 | 2 | 2 | 4 | 4 | 5th |

**Orellana, Kewin**
**b. Lausanne, Switzerland, January 8, 1992**

| | | | | | | | | |
|---|---|---|---|---|---|---|---|---|
| 2010 WM18 | 6-D | SUI | 6 | 0 | 0 | 0 | 6 | 5th |

**Orendorz, Dieter**
**b. Iserlohn, Germany, August 1, 1992**

| | | | | | | | | |
|---|---|---|---|---|---|---|---|---|
| 2011 WM20 | 23-D | GER | 6 | 0 | 1 | 1 | 2 | 10th |

**Orlov, Dmitri**
**b. Novokuznetsk, Soviet Union (Russia), July 23, 1991**

| | | | | | | | | |
|---|---|---|---|---|---|---|---|---|
| 2008 WM18 | 12-D | RUS | 6 | 0 | 1 | 1 | 0 | S |
| 2009 WM18 | 28-D | RUS | 7 | 2 | 2 | 4 | 6 | S |
| 2010 WM20 | 9-D | RUS | 6 | 0 | 4 | 4 | 4 | 6th |
| 2011 WM20 | 9-D | RUS | 7 | 1 | 8 | 9 | 6 | G |
| **Totals WM18** | | | **13** | **2** | **3** | **5** | **6** | **—** |
| **Totals WM20** | | | **13** | **1** | **12** | **13** | **10** | **G** |

~WM20 All-Star Team/Defence (2011)

**Orpik, Richard "Brooks"**
**b. San Francisco, California, United States, September 26, 1980**

| | | | | | | | | |
|---|---|---|---|---|---|---|---|---|
| 2000 WM20 | 3-D | USA | 7 | 1 | 1 | 2 | 6 | 4th |
| 2006 WM | 44-D | USA | 7 | 0 | 0 | 0 | 10 | 7th |
| 2010 OG-M | 44-D | USA | 6 | 0 | 0 | 0 | 0 | S |

**Orsava, Jakub**
**b. Sumperk, Czechoslovakia (Czech Republic), February 27, 1991**

| | | | | | | | | |
|---|---|---|---|---|---|---|---|---|
| 2009 WM18 | 24-F | CZE | 1 | 0 | 0 | 0 | 0 | 6th |
| 2011 WM20 | 27-F | CZE | 6 | 1 | 2 | 3 | 4 | 7th |

**Osala, Oskar**
**b. Vasa, Finland, December 26, 1987**

| | | | | | | | | |
|---|---|---|---|---|---|---|---|---|
| 2005 WM18 | 18-F | FIN | 6 | 0 | 0 | 0 | 27 | 7th |
| 2007 WM20 | 24-F | FIN | 6 | 5 | 3 | 8 | 4 | 6th |
| 2010 WM | 45-F | FIN | 4 | 0 | 0 | 0 | 2 | 6th |

**Oshie, T.J. (Timothy, Jr.)**
**b. Mt. Vernon, Washington, United States, December 23, 1986**

| | | | | | | | | |
|---|---|---|---|---|---|---|---|---|
| 2006 WM20 | 7-F | USA | 7 | 1 | 0 | 1 | 10 | 4th |
| 2009 WM | 74-F | USA | 9 | 1 | 2 | 3 | 2 | 4th |
| 2010 WM | 74-F | USA | 6 | 4 | 2 | 6 | 2 | 13th |
| **Totals WM** | | | **15** | **5** | **4** | **9** | **4** | **—** |

**Osmolovski, Pavel**
**b. Minsk, Soviet Union (Belarus), October 18, 1985**

| | | | | | | | | |
|---|---|---|---|---|---|---|---|---|
| 2005 WM20 | 12-F | BLR | 6 | 0 | 1 | 1 | 2 | 10th |

**Osnovin, Vyacheslav**
**b. Chelyabinsk, Russia, March 5, 1994**

| | | | | | | | | |
|---|---|---|---|---|---|---|---|---|
| 2012 WM18 | 18-F | RUS | 6 | 1 | 2 | 3 | 29 | 5th |

**Osterberg, Kyle**
**b. Lakeville, Minnesota, United States, September 5, 1994**

| | | | | | | | | |
|---|---|---|---|---|---|---|---|---|
| 2012 WM18 | 9-F | USA | 6 | 1 | 2 | 3 | 0 | G |

**Osterloh, Sebastian**
**b. Kaufbeuren, West Germany (Germany), February 20, 1983**

| | | | | | | | | |
|---|---|---|---|---|---|---|---|---|
| 2007 WM | 8-D | GER | 6 | 0 | 0 | 0 | 6 | 9th |
| 2008 WM | 8-D | GER | 6 | 0 | 0 | 0 | 20 | 10th |
| 2009 WM | 8-D | GER | 6 | 0 | 0 | 0 | 2 | 15th |
| **Totals WM** | | | **18** | **0** | **0** | **0** | **28** | **—** |

**Ostli, Lars**
**b. Hamar, Norway, November 21, 1986**

| | | | | | | | | |
|---|---|---|---|---|---|---|---|---|
| 2004 WM18 | 14-D | NOR | 6 | 0 | 0 | 0 | 8 | 10th |
| 2006 WM20 | 17-D | NOR | 6 | 0 | 1 | 1 | 12 | 10th |
| 2011 WM | 37-D | NOR | 1 | 0 | 0 | 0 | 0 | 6th |

**Ostrizek, David**
**b. Frydek-Mistek, Czechoslovakia (Czech Republic), October 1, 1990**

| | | | | | | | | |
|---|---|---|---|---|---|---|---|---|
| 2010 WM20 | 27-F | CZE | 5 | 2 | 1 | 3 | 0 | 7th |

**Ostwald, Elia**
**b. Bad Muskau, East Germany (Germany), March 17, 1988**

| | | | | | | | | |
|---|---|---|---|---|---|---|---|---|
| 2005 WM18 | 27-F | GER | 6 | 1 | 1 | 2 | 0 | 8th |
| 2006 WM18 | 15-F | GER | 6 | 2 | 2 | 4 | 0 | 8th |
| 2007 WM20 | 23-F | GER | 6 | 0 | 1 | 1 | 2 | 9th |
| **Totals WM18** | | | **12** | **3** | **3** | **6** | **0** | **—** |

**O'Sullivan, Patrick**
**b. Winston Salem, North Carolina, United States, February 1, 1985**

| | | | | | | | | |
|---|---|---|---|---|---|---|---|---|
| 2002 WM18 | 19-F | USA | 8 | 7 | 8 | 15 | 37 | G |
| 2003 WM20 | 12-F | USA | 7 | 1 | 2 | 3 | 10 | 4th |
| 2004 WM20 | 12-F | USA | 6 | 3 | 0 | 3 | 12 | G |
| 2005 WM20 | 12-F | USA | 7 | 2 | 6 | 8 | 12 | 4th |
| 2006 WM | 10-F | USA | 3 | 1 | 0 | 1 | 0 | 7th |
| 2008 WM | 9-F | USA | 7 | 3 | 3 | 6 | 2 | 6th |
| 2009 WM | 12-F | USA | 9 | 4 | 3 | 7 | 6 | 4th |
| **Totals WM20** | | | **20** | **6** | **8** | **14** | **34** | **G** |
| **Totals WM** | | | **19** | **8** | **6** | **14** | **8** | **—** |

**Ott, Steve**
**b. Summerside, Prince Edward Island, Canada, August 19, 1982**

| | | | | | | | | |
|---|---|---|---|---|---|---|---|---|
| 2001 WM20 | 21-F | CAN | 7 | 2 | 1 | 3 | 6 | B |
| 2002 WM20 | 14-F | CAN | 7 | 3 | 3 | 6 | 8 | S |
| 2010 WM | 29-F | CAN | 7 | 0 | 1 | 1 | 20 | 7th |
| **Totals WM20** | | | **14** | **5** | **4** | **9** | **14** | **S,B** |

**Ottosson, Sebastian**
**b. Karlskrona, Sweden, February 7, 1992**

| | | | | | | | | |
|---|---|---|---|---|---|---|---|---|
| 2010 WM18 | 14-F | SWE | 6 | 0 | 2 | 2 | 6 | S |

**Ovechkin, Alexander**
**b. Moscow, Soviet Union (Russia), September 17, 1985**

| | | | | | | | | |
|---|---|---|---|---|---|---|---|---|
| 2002 WM18 | 8-F | RUS | 8 | 14 | 4 | 18 | 0 | S |
| 2003 WM18 | 8-F | RUS | 6 | 9 | 4 | 13 | 6 | B |
| 2003 WM20 | 8-F | RUS | 6 | 6 | 1 | 7 | 4 | G |
| 2004 WM20 | 8-F | RUS | 6 | 5 | 2 | 7 | 25 | 5th |
| 2004 WM | 8-F | RUS | 6 | 1 | 1 | 2 | 0 | 10th |
| 2004 WCH | 8-F | RUS | 2 | 1 | 0 | 1 | 0 | 6th |
| 2005 WM20 | 8-F | RUS | 6 | 7 | 4 | 11 | 4 | S |
| 2005 WM | 8-F | RUS | 8 | 5 | 3 | 8 | 4 | B |
| 2006 OG-M | 8-F | RUS | 8 | 5 | 0 | 5 | 8 | 4th |
| 2006 WM | 8-F | RUS | 7 | 6 | 3 | 9 | 6 | 5th |
| 2007 WM | 8-F | RUS | 8 | 1 | 2 | 3 | 29 | B |
| 2008 WM | 8-F | RUS | 9 | 6 | 6 | 12 | 8 | G |
| 2010 OG-M | 8-F | RUS | 4 | 2 | 2 | 4 | 2 | 6th |
| 2010 WM | 8-F | RUS | 9 | 5 | 1 | 6 | 4 | S |
| 2011 WM | 8-F | RUS | 5 | 0 | 0 | 0 | 4 | 4th |
| 2012 WM | 8-F | RUS | 3 | 2 | 2 | 4 | 2 | G |
| **Totals WM18** | | | **14** | **23** | **8** | **31** | **6** | **S,B** |
| **Totals WM20** | | | **18** | **18** | **7** | **25** | **33** | **G,S** |
| **Totals WM** | | | **55** | **26** | **18** | **44** | **57** | **2G,S,2B** |
| **Totals OG-M** | | | **12** | **7** | **2** | **9** | **10** | **—** |

~ OG-M All-Star Team/Forward (2006), WM All-Star Team/Forward (2006, 2008), WM20 IIHF Directorate Best Forward (2005), WM20 All-Star Team/Forward (2005), WM18 IIHF Directorate Best Forward (2003), WM18 All-Star Team/Forward (2002, 2003)

**Overmark, Anders**
**b. Ringkoebing, Denmark, March 22, 1990**

| | | | | | | | | |
|---|---|---|---|---|---|---|---|---|
| 2008 WM18 | 4-D | DEN | 6 | 0 | 1 | 1 | 4 | 10th |

**Ozhiganov, Igor**
**b. Krasnogorsk, Russia, October 13, 1992**

| | | | | | | | | |
|---|---|---|---|---|---|---|---|---|
| 2012 WM20 | 7-D | RUS | 7 | 1 | 0 | 1 | 4 | S |

**Ozolins, Janis**
**b. Riga, Soviet Union (Latvia), February 4, 1989**

| | | | | | | | | |
|---|---|---|---|---|---|---|---|---|
| 2007 WM18 | 15-F | LAT | 6 | 2 | 0 | 2 | 2 | 10th |
| 2009 WM20 | 16-F | LAT | 6 | 2 | 3 | 5 | 2 | 8th |

**Ozolins, Karlis**
**b. March 16, 1994**

| | | | | | | | | |
|---|---|---|---|---|---|---|---|---|
| 2012 WM18 | 16-F | LAT | 6 | 0 | 1 | 1 | 2 | 9th |

**Paajanen, Otto**
**b. Loppi, Finland, September 13, 1992**

| | | | | | | | | |
|---|---|---|---|---|---|---|---|---|
| 2010 WM18 | 19-F | FIN | 6 | 1 | 0 | 1 | 2 | B |
| 2012 WM20 | 29-F | FIN | 7 | 0 | 1 | 1 | 2 | 4th |

**Paajarvi-Svensson, Magnus**
**b. Norrkoping, Sweden, April 12, 1991**

| | | | | | | | | |
|---|---|---|---|---|---|---|---|---|
| 2008 WM18 | 20-F | SWE* | 6 | 2 | 3 | 5 | 6 | 4th |
| 2009 WM18 | 20-F | SWE | 6 | 6 | 6 | 12 | 0 | 5th |
| 2008 WM20 | 21-F | SWE | 6 | 1 | 1 | 2 | 0 | S |
| 2009 WM20 | 21-F | SWE | 6 | 2 | 5 | 7 | 6 | S |
| 2010 WM20 | 21-F | SWE | 6 | 3 | 7 | 10 | 2 | B |
| 2010 WM | 91-F | SWE | 9 | 5 | 4 | 9 | 2 | B |
| 2011 WM | 91-F | SWE* | 9 | 2 | 5 | 7 | 2 | S |
| Totals WM18 | | | 12 | 8 | 9 | 17 | 6 | — |
| Totals WM20 | | | 18 | 6 | 13 | 19 | 8 | 2S,B |
| Totals WM | | | 18 | 7 | 9 | 16 | 4 | S,B |

*played as Magnus Paajarvi
~WM All-Star Team/Forward (2010)

**Pacioretty, Max**
**b. New Canaan, Connecticut, United States, November 20, 1988**

| | | | | | | | | |
|---|---|---|---|---|---|---|---|---|
| 2008 WM20 | 17-F | USA | 6 | 0 | 0 | 0 | 8 | 4th |
| 2012 WM | 67-F | USA | 8 | 2 | 10 | 12 | 4 | 7th |

**Pahlsson, Samuel**
**b. Ange, Sweden, December 17, 1977**

| | | | | | | | | |
|---|---|---|---|---|---|---|---|---|
| 1996 WM20 | 23-F | SWE | 7 | 0 | 0 | 0 | 0 | S |
| 1999 WM | 26-F | SWE | 10 | 1 | 3 | 4 | 4 | B |
| 2000 WM | 16-F | SWE | 7 | 0 | 0 | 0 | 4 | 7th |
| 2004 WM | 26-F | SWE | 9 | 1 | 3 | 4 | 8 | S |
| 2004 WCH | 26-F | SWE | 4 | 0 | 0 | 0 | 6 | 5th |
| 2005 WM | 26-F | SWE | 9 | 2 | 5 | 7 | 28 | 4th |
| 2006 OG-M | 26-F | SWE | 8 | 2 | 2 | 4 | 8 | G |
| 2010 OG-M | 26-F | SWE | 3 | 0 | 1 | 1 | 2 | 5th |
| **Totals WM** | | | **35** | **4** | **11** | **15** | **44** | **S,B** |
| **Totals OG-M** | | | **11** | **2** | **3** | **5** | **10** | **G** |

**Pain, Erwan**
**b. Pointe-a-Pitre, France, February 14, 1986**

| | | | | | | | | |
|---|---|---|---|---|---|---|---|---|
| 2010 WM | 81-F | FRA | 2 | 0 | 0 | 0 | 0 | 14th |

**Pajic, Rok**
**b. Jesenice, Yugoslavia (Slovenia), September 26, 1985**

| | | | | | | | | |
|---|---|---|---|---|---|---|---|---|
| 2006 WM | 74-F | SLO | 1 | 0 | 0 | 0 | 0 | 16th |
| 2008 WM | 13-F | SLO | 5 | 0 | 0 | 0 | 2 | 15th |
| 2011 WM | 76-F | SLO | 6 | 2 | 1 | 3 | 6 | 16th |
| **Totals WM** | | | **12** | **2** | **1** | **3** | **8** | **—** |

**Pakarinen, Iiro**
**b. Suonenjoki, Finland, August 25, 1991**

| | | | | | | | | |
|---|---|---|---|---|---|---|---|---|
| 2009 WM18 | 10-F | FIN | 6 | 1 | 1 | 2 | 2 | B |
| 2010 WM20 | 18-F | FIN | 6 | 1 | 1 | 2 | 2 | 5th |
| 2011 WM20 | 18-F | FIN | 6 | 1 | 2 | 3 | 2 | 6th |
| **Totals WM20** | | | **12** | **2** | **3** | **5** | **4** | **—** |

**Palat, Ondrej**
**b. Frydek-Mistek, Czechoslovakia (Czech Republic), March 28, 1991**

| | | | | | | | | |
|---|---|---|---|---|---|---|---|---|
| 2009 WM18 | 14-F | CZE | 6 | 1 | 0 | 1 | 2 | 6th |
| 2011 WM20 | 18-F | CZE | 6 | 2 | 1 | 3 | 0 | 7th |

**Palausch, Lennart**
**b. Bremerhaven, Germany, August 27, 1994**

| | | | | | | | | |
|---|---|---|---|---|---|---|---|---|
| 2012 WM18 | 19-F | GER | 6 | 0 | 3 | 3 | 2 | 6th |

**Paliotta, Mike**
**b. West Port, Connecticut, United States, April 16, 1993**

| | | | | | | | | |
|---|---|---|---|---|---|---|---|---|
| 2011 WM18 | 4-D | USA | 6 | 0 | 1 | 1 | 2 | G |

**Pallestrang, Alexander**
**b. Bregenz, Austria, April 4, 1990**

| | | | | | | | | |
|---|---|---|---|---|---|---|---|---|
| 2010 WM20 | 6-D | AUT | 6 | 1 | 1 | 2 | 16 | 10th |

**Palmieri, Kyle**
**b. Montvale, New Jersey, United States, February 1, 1991**

| | | | | | | | | |
|---|---|---|---|---|---|---|---|---|
| 2008 WM18 | 16-F | USA | 7 | 2 | 2 | 4 | 4 | G |
| 2010 WM20 | 23-F | USA | 7 | 1 | 8 | 9 | 4 | G |
| 2011 WM20 | 23-F | USA | 6 | 2 | 4 | 6 | 0 | B |
| 2012 WM | 61-F | USA | 7 | 2 | 2 | 4 | 8 | 7th |
| **Totals WM20** | | | **13** | **3** | **12** | **15** | **4** | **G,B** |

**Palmieri, Nick**
**b. Utica, New York, United States, July 12, 1989**

| | | | | | | | | |
|---|---|---|---|---|---|---|---|---|
| 2011 WM | 25-F | USA | 6 | 2 | 1 | 3 | 0 | 8th |

**Palushaj, Aaron**
**b. Northville, Michigan, United States, September 7, 1989**

| | | | | | | | | |
|---|---|---|---|---|---|---|---|---|
| 2009 WM20 | 7-F | USA | 6 | 2 | 3 | 5 | 10 | 5th |

**Panarin, Artemi**
**b. Korkino, Soviet Union (Russia), October 30, 1991**

| | | | | | | | | |
|---|---|---|---|---|---|---|---|---|
| 2011 WM20 | 27-F | RUS | 7 | 3 | 2 | 5 | 4 | G |

**Pance, Ziga**
**b. Ljubljana, Yugoslavia (Slovenia), January 1, 1989**

| | | | | | | | | |
|---|---|---|---|---|---|---|---|---|
| 2011 WM | 19-F | SLO | 6 | 0 | 0 | 0 | 2 | 16th |

**Panik, Richard**
**b. Martin, Czechoslovakia (Slovakia), February 7, 1991**

| | | | | | | | | |
|---|---|---|---|---|---|---|---|---|
| 2007 WM18 | 16-F | SVK | 6 | 0 | 2 | 2 | 2 | 5th |
| 2008 WM18 | 14-F | SVK | 6 | 4 | 6 | 10 | 0 | 7th |
| 2009 WM20 | 28-F | SVK | 7 | 2 | 3 | 5 | 4 | 4th |
| 2010 WM20 | 28-F | SVK | 6 | 6 | 2 | 8 | 2 | 8th |
| 2010 WM | 28-F | SVK | 6 | 0 | 2 | 2 | 6 | 12th |
| 2011 WM20 | 28-F | SVK | 6 | 7 | 2 | 9 | 12 | 8th |
| **Totals WM18** | | | **12** | **4** | **8** | **12** | **2** | **—** |
| **Totals WM20** | | | **19** | **15** | **7** | **22** | **18** | **—** |

**Panin, Grigori**
**b. Karaganda, Soviet Union (Kazakhstan), November 24, 1985**

| | | | | | | | | |
|---|---|---|---|---|---|---|---|---|
| 2005 WM20 | 5-D | RUS | 6 | 0 | 1 | 1 | 6 | S |

**Papa, Cyril**
**b. Grenoble, France, February 14, 1984**

| | | | | | | | | |
|---|---|---|---|---|---|---|---|---|
| 2009 WM | 21-F | FRA | 2 | 0 | 0 | 0 | 0 | 12th |

**Paramzin, Semyon**
**b. V-Kazakhstanskaya, Soviet Union (Kazakhstan), June 3, 1988**

| | | | | | | | | |
|---|---|---|---|---|---|---|---|---|
| 2008 WM20 | 29-F | KAZ | 6 | 0 | 2 | 2 | 0 | 8th |

**Parati, Patrick**
**b. Wetzikon, Switzerland, April 24, 1986**

| | | | | | | | | |
|---|---|---|---|---|---|---|---|---|
| 2006 WM20 | 5-D | SUI | 6 | 0 | 0 | 0 | 6 | 7th |

**Parent, Ryan**
**b. Prince Albert, Saskatchewan, Canada, March 17, 1987**

| | | | | | | | | |
|---|---|---|---|---|---|---|---|---|
| 2005 WM18 | 7-D | CAN | 6 | 0 | 0 | 0 | 6 | S |
| 2006 WM20 | 4-D | CAN | 6 | 0 | 0 | 0 | 12 | G |
| 2007 WM20 | 4-D | CAN | 6 | 0 | 0 | 0 | 6 | G |
| **Totals WM20** | | | **12** | **0** | **0** | **0** | **18** | **2G** |

**Parfeyevets, Maxim**
**b. Minsk, Belarus, April 15, 1992**

| | | | | | | | | |
|---|---|---|---|---|---|---|---|---|
| 2010 WM18 | 15-F | BLR | 6 | 0 | 1 | 1 | 8 | 10th |

**Parise, Zach**
**b. Minneapolis, Minnesota, United States, July 28, 1984**

| | | | | | | | | |
|---|---|---|---|---|---|---|---|---|
| 2002 WM18 | 15-F | USA | 8 | 7 | 3 | 10 | 6 | G |
| 2003 WM20 | 11-F | USA | 7 | 4 | 4 | 8 | 4 | 4th |
| 2004 WM20 | 11-F | USA | 6 | 5 | 6 | 11 | 4 | G |
| 2005 WM | 23-F | USA | 3 | 0 | 2 | 2 | 0 | 6th |
| 2007 WM | 9-F | USA | 1 | 0 | 0 | 0 | 0 | 5th |
| 2008 WM | 17-F | USA | 7 | 5 | 3 | 8 | 2 | 6th |
| 2010 OG-M | 9-F | USA | 6 | 4 | 4 | 8 | 0 | S |
| **Totals WM20** | | | **13** | **9** | **10** | **19** | **8** | **G** |
| **Totals WM** | | | **11** | **5** | **5** | **10** | **2** | **—** |

~OG-M All-Star Team/Forward (2010), WM20 MVP (2004), WM20 IIHF Directorate Best Forward (2004), WM20 All-Star Team/Forward (2004)

**Parshin, Denis**
**b. Rybinsk, Soviet Union (Russia), February 1, 1986**

| | | | | | | | | |
|---|---|---|---|---|---|---|---|---|
| 2004 WM18 | 27-F | RUS | 6 | 0 | 3 | 3 | 0 | G |
| 2005 WM20 | 27-F | RUS | 6 | 0 | 2 | 2 | 8 | S |

**Partanen, Mika**
**b. Helsinki, Finland, October 18, 1992**

| | | | | | | | | |
|---|---|---|---|---|---|---|---|---|
| 2010 WM18 | 28-F | FIN | 6 | 1 | 3 | 4 | 27 | B |

**Paryzek, Martin**
**b. Ceske Budejovice, Czechoslovakia (Czech Republic), March 23, 1989**

| | | | | | | | | |
|---|---|---|---|---|---|---|---|---|
| 2008 WM20 | 6-D | CZE | 6 | 0 | 0 | 0 | 6 | 5th |
| 2009 WM20 | 6-D | CZE | 6 | 1 | 1 | 2 | 4 | 6th |
| **Totals WM20** | | | **12** | **1** | **1** | **2** | **10** | **—** |

**Pashnin, Mikhail**
**b. Chelyabinsk, Soviet Union (Russia), May 11, 1989**

| | | | | | | | | |
|---|---|---|---|---|---|---|---|---|
| 2009 WM20 | 6-D | RUS | 7 | 0 | 2 | 2 | 2 | B |

**Paterlini, Thierry**
**b. Chur, Switzerland, April 27, 1975**

| | | | | | | | | |
|---|---|---|---|---|---|---|---|---|
| 1994 WM20 | 24-F | SUI | 7 | 0 | 3 | 3 | 2 | 8th |
| 2002 WM | 23-F | SUI | 6 | 0 | 1 | 1 | 2 | 10th |
| 2003 WM | 23-F | SUI | 7 | 1 | 1 | 2 | 4 | 8th |
| 2004 WM | 23-F | SUI | 7 | 0 | 0 | 0 | 4 | 8th |
| 2005 WM | 23-F | SUI | 7 | 0 | 0 | 0 | 8 | 8th |
| 2006 OG-M | 23-F | SUI | 6 | 1 | 0 | 1 | 6 | 6th |
| 2006 WM | 23-F | SUI | 6 | 1 | 0 | 1 | 6 | 9th |
| 2007 WM | 23-F | SUI | 4 | 0 | 0 | 0 | 0 | 8th |
| 2008 WM | 23-F | SUI | 7 | 2 | 1 | 3 | 4 | 7th |
| 2009 WM | 23-F | SUI | 6 | 0 | 1 | 1 | 6 | 9th |
| 2010 OG-M | 23-F | SUI | 5 | 0 | 1 | 1 | 6 | 8th |
| **Totals WM** | | | **50** | **4** | **4** | **8** | **34** | **—** |
| **Totals OG-M** | | | **11** | **1** | **1** | **2** | **12** | **—** |

**Paukovich, Geoff**
**b. Englewood, Colorado, United States, April 24, 1986**

| | | | | | | | | |
|---|---|---|---|---|---|---|---|---|
| 2004 WM18 | 23-F | USA | 6 | 0 | 0 | 0 | 8 | S |
| 2006 WM20 | 12-F | USA | 7 | 1 | 0 | 1 | 2 | 4th |

**Pavelka, Tomas**
**b. Ostrava, Czech Republic, May 29, 1993**

| | | | | | | | | |
|---|---|---|---|---|---|---|---|---|
| 2011 WM18 | 3-D | CZE | 6 | 0 | 0 | 0 | 4 | 8th |

**Pavelski, Joe**
**b. Stevens Point, Wisconsin, United States, July 11, 1984**

| | | | | | | | | |
|---|---|---|---|---|---|---|---|---|
| 2009 WM | 8-F | USA | 5 | 1 | 1 | 2 | 0 | 4th |
| 2010 OG-M | 16-F | USA | 6 | 0 | 3 | 3 | 4 | S |

**Pavlik, Filip**
**b. Trebic, Czech Republic, July 20, 1992**

| | | | | | | | | |
|---|---|---|---|---|---|---|---|---|
| 2010 WM18 | 7-D | CZE | 6 | 0 | 0 | 0 | 8 | 6th |

**Pavlikovsky, Rastislav**
**b. Ilava, Czechoslovakia (Slovakia), March 2, 1977**

| | | | | | | | | |
|---|---|---|---|---|---|---|---|---|
| 1997 WM20 | 18-F | SVK | 6 | 2 | 7 | 9 | 6 | 6th |
| 2002 OG-M | 19-F | SVK | 4 | 2 | 3 | 5 | 6 | 13th |
| 2002 WM | 19-F | SVK | 9 | 2 | 4 | 6 | 14 | G |
| 2004 WM | 19-F | SVK | 9 | 1 | 1 | 2 | 6 | 4th |
| 2004 WCH | 82-F | SVK | 2 | 0 | 0 | 0 | 2 | 7th |
| 2006 WM | 19-F | SVK | 7 | 1 | 6 | 7 | 4 | 8th |
| 2009 WM | 19-F | SVK | 4 | 0 | 0 | 0 | 0 | 10th |
| **Totals WM** | | | **29** | **4** | **11** | **15** | **24** | **G** |

**Pavlin, Ziga**
**b. Kranj, Yugoslavia (Slovenia), April 30, 1985**

| | | | | | | | | |
|---|---|---|---|---|---|---|---|---|
| 2011 WM | 17-D | SLO | 3 | 0 | 0 | 0 | 0 | 16th |

**Pavlovich, Alexander**
**b. Grodno, Belarus, December 7, 1988**

| | | | | | | | | |
|---|---|---|---|---|---|---|---|---|
| 2011 WM | 81-F | BLR | 5 | 0 | 0 | 0 | 0 | 14th |

**Pavlovs, Vitalijs**
**b. Riga, Soviet Union (Latvia), June 17, 1989**

| | | | | | | | | |
|---|---|---|---|---|---|---|---|---|
| 2007 WM18 | 28-F | LAT | 6 | 0 | 1 | 1 | 2 | 10th |
| 2009 WM20 | 22-F | LAT | 6 | 1 | 1 | 2 | 29 | 8th |

**Pearson, Tanner**
**b. Kitchener, Ontario, Canada, August 10, 1992**

| | | | | | | | | |
|---|---|---|---|---|---|---|---|---|
| 2012 WM20 | 15-F | CAN | 6 | 1 | 5 | 6 | 6 | B |

**Pecura, Sergejs**
**b. Riga, Soviet Union (Latvia), June 14, 1987**

| | | | | | | | | |
|---|---|---|---|---|---|---|---|---|
| 2006 WM20 | 15-F | LAT | 6 | 1 | 0 | 1 | 6 | 9th |
| 2010 WM | 27-F | LAT | 6 | 1 | 0 | 1 | 0 | 11th |
| 2011 WM | 27-F | LAT | 6 | 0 | 0 | 0 | 2 | 13th |
| **Totals WM** | | | **12** | **1** | **0** | **1** | **2** | **—** |

**Pedan, Andrei**
**b. Kaunas, Lithuania, July 7, 1993**

| | | | | | | | | |
|---|---|---|---|---|---|---|---|---|
| 2011 WM18 | 5-D | RUS | 6 | 0 | 2 | 2 | 25 | B |

**Pedersen, Kasper**
**b. Rodovre, Denmark, March 2, 1984**

| | | | | | | | | |
|---|---|---|---|---|---|---|---|---|
| 2009 WM | 25-D | DEN | 6 | 0 | 0 | 0 | 0 | 13th |

**Pedersen, Markus**
**b. Oslo, Norway, March 25, 1994**

| | | | | | | | | |
|---|---|---|---|---|---|---|---|---|
| 2011 WM18 | 6-F | NOR | 4 | 0 | 1 | 1 | 2 | 9th |

**Pedersen, Mathias**
**b. Herning, Denmark, November 2, 1988**

| | | | | | | | | |
|---|---|---|---|---|---|---|---|---|
| 2008 WM20 | 17-D | DEN | 6 | 0 | 0 | 0 | 0 | 10th |

**Peintner, Markus**
**b. Lustenau, Austria, December 17, 1980**

| | | | | | | | | |
|---|---|---|---|---|---|---|---|---|
| 2004 WM | 34-F | AUT | 6 | 0 | 2 | 2 | 25 | 11th |
| 2005 WM | 34-F | AUT | 6 | 0 | 1 | 1 | 2 | 16th |
| 2007 WM | 34-F | AUT | 6 | 2 | 0 | 2 | 6 | 15th |
| 2009 WM | 34-F | AUT | 6 | 1 | 0 | 1 | 2 | 14th |
| 2011 WM | 34-F | AUT | 3 | 0 | 1 | 1 | 2 | 15th |
| **Totals WM** | | | **27** | **3** | **4** | **7** | **37** | **—** |

**Pelech, Adam**
**b. Toronto, Ontario, Canada, August 18, 1994**

| | | | | | | | | |
|---|---|---|---|---|---|---|---|---|
| 2012 WM18 | 27-D | CAN | 7 | 0 | 0 | 0 | 8 | B |

**Pelss, Kristians**
**b. Preili, Latvia, September 9, 1992**

| | | | | | | | | |
|---|---|---|---|---|---|---|---|---|
| 2010 WM18 | 19-F | LAT | 6 | 2 | 1 | 3 | 0 | 9th |
| 2012 WM20 | 9-F | LAT | 5 | 1 | 2 | 3 | 8 | 9th |

**Peltonen, Ville**
**b. Vantaa, Finland, May 24, 1973**

| | | | | | | | | |
|---|---|---|---|---|---|---|---|---|
| 1993 WM20 | 16-F | FIN | 7 | 5 | 6 | 11 | 20 | 5th |
| 1994 OG-M | 26-F | FIN | 8 | 4 | 3 | 7 | 0 | B |
| 1994 WM | 16-F | FIN | 8 | 4 | 1 | 5 | 4 | S |
| 1995 WM | 16-F | FIN | 8 | 6 | 5 | 11 | 4 | G |
| 1996 WM | 16-F | FIN | 6 | 3 | 2 | 5 | 6 | 5th |
| 1996 WCH | 16-F | FIN | 4 | 1 | 3 | 4 | 0 | 5th |
| 1997 WM | 16-F | FIN | 7 | 2 | 2 | 4 | 0 | 5th |
| 1998 OG-M | 16-F | FIN | 6 | 2 | 1 | 3 | 6 | B |
| 1998 WM | 16-F | FIN | 10 | 4 | 6 | 10 | 8 | S |
| 1999 WM | 16-F | FIN | 12 | 2 | 3 | 5 | 2 | S |
| 2000 WM | 16-F | FIN | 9 | 0 | 4 | 4 | 2 | B |
| 2003 WM | 16-F | FIN | 7 | 3 | 4 | 7 | 2 | 5th |
| 2004 WM | 16-F | FIN | 7 | 4 | 6 | 10 | 2 | 6th |
| 2004 WCH | 16-F | FIN | 6 | 1 | 2 | 3 | 2 | 2nd |
| 2005 WM | 16-F | FIN | 6 | 1 | 2 | 3 | 4 | 7th |
| 2006 OG-M | 16-F | FIN | 8 | 4 | 5 | 9 | 6 | S |
| 2006 WM | 16-F | FIN | 9 | 2 | 2 | 4 | 8 | B |
| 2007 WM | 16-F | FIN | 9 | 2 | 7 | 9 | 4 | S |
| 2008 WM | 16-F | FIN | 9 | 1 | 3 | 4 | 2 | B |
| 2010 OG-M | 16-F | FIN | 6 | 0 | 1 | 1 | 2 | B |
| **Totals WM** | | | **107** | **34** | **47** | **81** | **48** | **G,4S,3B** |
| **Totals OG-M** | | | **28** | **10** | **10** | **20** | **14** | **S,3B** |
| **Totals IIHF-NHL** | | | **10** | **2** | **5** | **7** | **2** | **—** |

~WM All-Star Team/Forward (1995, 1998, 2004)

**Peranen, Joona**
**b. Jyvaskyla, Finland, September 23, 1990**

| | | | | | | | | |
|---|---|---|---|---|---|---|---|---|
| 2008 WM18 | 23-F | FIN | 6 | 0 | 0 | 0 | 0 | 6th |

**Perezhogin, Alexander**
**b. Ust-Kamenogorsk, Soviet Union (Kazakhstan), August 10, 1983**

| | | | | | | | | |
|---|---|---|---|---|---|---|---|---|
| 2001 WM18 | 26-F | RUS | 6 | 4 | 3 | 7 | 0 | G |
| 2002 WM20 | 26-F | RUS | 5 | 0 | 0 | 0 | 4 | G |
| 2003 WM20 | 26-F | RUS | 6 | 3 | 6 | 9 | 4 | G |
| 2009 WM | 16-F | RUS | 9 | 3 | 3 | 6 | 6 | G |
| 2012 WM | 37-F | RUS | 10 | 4 | 5 | 9 | 4 | G |
| **Totals WM20** | | | **11** | **3** | **6** | **9** | **8** | **2G** |
| **Totals WM** | | | **19** | **7** | **8** | **15** | **10** | **2G** |

**Perry, Corey**
**b. Peterborough, Ontario, Canada, May 16, 1985**

| | | | | | | | | |
|---|---|---|---|---|---|---|---|---|
| 2005 WM20 | 24-F | CAN | 6 | 2 | 5 | 7 | 6 | G |
| 2010 OG-M | 24-F | CAN | 7 | 4 | 1 | 5 | 2 | G |
| 2010 WM | 10-F | CAN | 7 | 2 | 4 | 6 | 8 | 7th |
| 2012 WM | 10-F | CAN | 8 | 3 | 4 | 7 | 8 | 5th |
| **Totals WM** | | | **15** | **5** | **8** | **13** | **16** | **—** |

**Persson, Anton**
**b. Gavle, Sweden, January 4, 1989**

| | | | | | | | | |
|---|---|---|---|---|---|---|---|---|
| 2007 WM18 | 18-F | SWE | 6 | 0 | 0 | 0 | 2 | B |
| 2009 WM20 | 17-F | SWE | 6 | 0 | 0 | 0 | 2 | S |

**Persson, Linus**
**b. Hagfors, Sweden, December 29, 1985**

| | | | | | | | | |
|---|---|---|---|---|---|---|---|---|
| 2003 WM18 | 20-F | SWE | 6 | 1 | 6 | 7 | 4 | 5th |
| 2005 WM20 | 17-F | SWE | 2 | 2 | 0 | 2 | 0 | 6th |

**Persson, Niklas**
**b. Osmo, Sweden, March 26, 1979**

| | | | | | | | | |
|---|---|---|---|---|---|---|---|---|
| 1998 WM20 | 13-F | SWE | 7 | 0 | 2 | 2 | 10 | 6th |
| 1999 WM20 | 21-F | SWE | 6 | 2 | 2 | 4 | 2 | 4th |
| 2009 WM | 22-F | SWE | 9 | 2 | 4 | 6 | 4 | B |
| 2010 WM | 22-F | SWE | 9 | 0 | 4 | 4 | 0 | B |
| 2011 WM | 23-F | SWE | 8 | 3 | 0 | 3 | 8 | S |
| 2012 WM | 23-F | SWE | 8 | 2 | 1 | 3 | 2 | 6th |
| **Totals WM20** | | | **13** | **2** | **4** | **6** | **12** | **—** |
| **Totals WM** | | | **34** | **7** | **9** | **16** | **14** | **S,2B** |

**Pesonen, Harri**
**b. Muurame, Finland, August 6, 1988**

| | | | | | | | | |
|---|---|---|---|---|---|---|---|---|
| 2008 WM20 | 19-F | FIN | 6 | 2 | 1 | 3 | 0 | 6th |

**Pesonen, Janne**
**b. Suomussalmi, Finland, May 11, 1982**

| | | | | | | | | |
|---|---|---|---|---|---|---|---|---|
| 2011 WM | 20-F | FIN | 9 | 2 | 5 | 7 | 4 | G |
| 2012 WM | 20-F | FIN | 9 | 1 | 2 | 3 | 2 | 4th |
| **Totals WM** | | | **18** | **3** | **7** | **10** | **6** | **G** |

**Pestoni, Inti**
**b. Ambri, Switzerland, August 8, 1991**

| | | | | | | | | |
|---|---|---|---|---|---|---|---|---|
| 2011 WM20 | 16-F | SUI | 6 | 5 | 2 | 7 | 0 | 5th |

**Pestunov, Dmitri**
**b. Ust-Kamenogorsk, Soviet Union (Kazakhstan), January 22, 1985**

| | | | | | | | | |
|---|---|---|---|---|---|---|---|---|
| 2003 WM18 | 12-F | RUS | 6 | 1 | 3 | 4 | 2 | B |
| 2003 WM20 | 6-F | RUS | 6 | 0 | 0 | 0 | 6 | G |
| 2004 WM20 | 6-F | RUS | 6 | 0 | 3 | 3 | 16 | 5th |
| 2005 WM20 | 12-F | RUS | 6 | 2 | 2 | 4 | 2 | S |
| **Totals WM20** | | | **18** | **2** | **5** | **7** | **24** | **G,S** |

**Peter, Emanuel**
**b. Niederuzwil, Switzerland, June 9, 1984**

| | | | | | | | | |
|---|---|---|---|---|---|---|---|---|
| 2001 WM18 | 25-F | SUI | 7 | 3 | 1 | 4 | 4 | S |
| 2002 WM20 | 17-F | SUI | 7 | 0 | 0 | 0 | 0 | 4th |
| 2003 WM20 | 17-F | SUI | 6 | 0 | 2 | 2 | 14 | 7th |
| 2004 WM20 | 17-F | SUI | 6 | 3 | 1 | 4 | 8 | 8th |
| **Totals WM20** | | | **19** | **3** | **3** | **6** | **22** | **—** |

**Petersson, Andre**
**b. Olofstrom, Sweden, September 11, 1990**

| | | | | | | | | |
|---|---|---|---|---|---|---|---|---|
| 2007 WM18 | 19-F | SWE | 5 | 0 | 2 | 2 | 0 | B |
| 2008 WM18 | 19-F | SWE | 6 | 4 | 4 | 8 | 2 | 4th |
| 2009 WM20 | 20-F | SWE | 6 | 3 | 3 | 6 | 2 | S |
| 2010 WM20 | 20-F | SWE | 6 | 8 | 3 | 11 | 4 | B |
| **Totals WM18** | | | **11** | **4** | **6** | **10** | **2** | **B** |
| **Totals WM20** | | | **12** | **11** | **6** | **17** | **6** | **S,B** |

**Petrasek, David**
**b. Jonkoping, Sweden, February 1, 1976**

| | | | | | | | | |
|---|---|---|---|---|---|---|---|---|
| 1996 WM20 | 2-D | SWE | 7 | 1 | 0 | 1 | 6 | S |
| 2011 WM | 22-D | SWE | 9 | 2 | 4 | 6 | 10 | S |

~WM All-Star Team/Defence (2011)

**Petro, Juraj**
**b. Banska Bystrica, Czechoslovakia (Slovakia), October 12, 1991**

| | | | | | | | | |
|---|---|---|---|---|---|---|---|---|
| 2009 WM18 | 14-F | SVK | 6 | 0 | 1 | 1 | 2 | 7th |

**Petrov, Georgi**
**b. Ust-Kamenogorsk, Soviet Union (Kazakhstan), August 19, 1988**

| | | | | | | | | |
|---|---|---|---|---|---|---|---|---|
| 2010 WM | 16-D | KAZ | 3 | 0 | 0 | 0 | 2 | 16th |

**Petrov, Kirill**
**b. Kazan, Soviet Union (Russia), April 13, 1990**

| | | | | | | | | |
|---|---|---|---|---|---|---|---|---|
| 2007 WM18 | 20-F | RUS | 7 | 0 | 3 | 3 | 2 | G |
| 2008 WM18 | 21-F | RUS | 6 | 5 | 2 | 7 | 6 | S |
| 2009 WM20 | 31-F | RUS | 7 | 0 | 0 | 0 | 4 | B |
| 2010 WM20 | 21-F | RUS | 6 | 4 | 6 | 10 | 6 | 6th |
| **Totals WM18** | | | **13** | **5** | **5** | **10** | **8** | **G,S** |
| **Totals WM20** | | | **13** | **4** | **6** | **10** | **10** | **B** |

~WM18 IIHF Directorate Best Forward (2008), WM18 All-Star Team/Forward (2008)

**Petruska, Tomas**
**b. Presov, Czechoslovakia (Slovakia), March 1, 1986**

| | | | | | | | | |
|---|---|---|---|---|---|---|---|---|
| 2004 WM18 | 18-F | SVK | 6 | 0 | 0 | 0 | 2 | 6th |
| 2006 WM20 | 21-F | SVK | 6 | 0 | 4 | 4 | 2 | 8th |

**Petruzalek, Jakub**
**b. Most, Czechoslovakia (Czech Republic), April 24, 1985**

| | | | | | | | | |
|---|---|---|---|---|---|---|---|---|
| 2003 WM18 | 19-F | CZE | 6 | 1 | 0 | 1 | 0 | 6th |
| 2005 WM20 | 28-F | CZE | 7 | 1 | 1 | 2 | 4 | B |
| 2012 WM | 88-F | CZE | 10 | 1 | 3 | 4 | 0 | B |

**Petry, Jeff**
**b. Ann Arbor, Michigan, United States, December 9, 1987**

| | | | | | | | | |
|---|---|---|---|---|---|---|---|---|
| 2012 WM | 2-D | USA | 8 | 2 | 3 | 5 | 4 | 7th |

**Pettersson, Adam**
**b. Olofstrom, Sweden, January 13, 1992**

| | | | | | | | | |
|---|---|---|---|---|---|---|---|---|
| 2010 WM18 | 15-F | SWE | 6 | 0 | 1 | 1 | 4 | S |

**Pettersson, Fredrik**
**b. Gothenburg, Sweden, June 10, 1987**

| | | | | | | | | |
|---|---|---|---|---|---|---|---|---|
| 2005 WM18 | 16-F | SWE | 7 | 1 | 2 | 3 | 6 | B |
| 2006 WM20 | 22-F | SWE | 6 | 3 | 2 | 5 | 8 | 5th |
| 2007 WM20 | 24-F | SWE | 6 | 1 | 1 | 2 | 8 | 4th |
| 2010 WM | 12-F | SWE | 7 | 1 | 1 | 2 | 4 | B |
| 2012 WM | 12-F | SWE | 1 | 0 | 0 | 0 | 0 | 6th |
| **Totals WM20** | | | **12** | **4** | **3** | **7** | **16** | **—** |
| **Totals WM** | | | **8** | **1** | **1** | **2** | **4** | **B** |

**Pettersson, Jesper**
**b. Stockholm, Sweden, July 16, 1994**

| | | | | | | | | |
|---|---|---|---|---|---|---|---|---|
| 2012 WM18 | 6-D | SWE | 6 | 1 | 1 | 2 | 4 | S |

**Peverley, Rich**
**b. Guelph, Ontario, Canada, July 8, 1982**

| | | | | | | | | |
|---|---|---|---|---|---|---|---|---|
| 2010 WM | 47-F | CAN | 7 | 1 | 3 | 4 | 4 | 7th |

**Pewal, Marco**
**b. Villach, Austria, September 17, 1978**

| | | | | | | | | |
|---|---|---|---|---|---|---|---|---|
| 2011 WM | 36-F | AUT | 1 | 1 | 0 | 1 | 0 | 15th |

**Pfoderl, Leonhard**
**b. Bad Tolz, Germany, September 1, 1993**

| | | | | | | | | |
|---|---|---|---|---|---|---|---|---|
| 2011 WM18 | 11-F | GER | 6 | 2 | 3 | 5 | 0 | 6th |

**Phaneuf, Dion**
**b. Edmonton, Alberta, Canada, April 10, 1985**

| | | | | | | | | |
|---|---|---|---|---|---|---|---|---|
| 2004 WM20 | 3-D | CAN | 6 | 2 | 2 | 4 | 29 | S |
| 2005 WM20 | 3-D | CAN | 6 | 1 | 5 | 6 | 14 | G |
| 2007 WM | 3-D | CAN | 7 | 0 | 8 | 8 | 2 | G |
| 2011 WM | 3-D | CAN | 7 | 0 | 3 | 3 | 8 | 5th |
| 2012 WM | 3-D | CAN | 8 | 2 | 0 | 2 | 4 | 5th |
| Totals WM20 | | | 12 | 3 | 7 | 10 | 43 | G,S |
| **Totals WM** | | | **22** | **2** | **11** | **13** | **14** | **G** |

~WM20 IIHF Directorate Best Defenceman (2005), WM20 All-Star Team/Defence (2004, 2005)

**Phillips, Chris**
**b. Fort McMurray, Alberta, Canada, March 9, 1978**

| | | | | | | | | |
|---|---|---|---|---|---|---|---|---|
| 1996 WM20 | 4-D | CAN | 6 | 0 | 0 | 0 | 0 | G |
| 1997 WM20 | 7-D | CAN | 7 | 0 | 1 | 1 | 4 | G |
| 2000 WM | 4-D | CAN | 9 | 0 | 0 | 0 | 2 | 4th |
| 2005 WM | 4-D | CAN | 9 | 0 | 1 | 1 | 8 | S |
| 2009 WM | 4-D | CAN | 9 | 0 | 3 | 3 | 12 | S |
| **Totals WM20** | | | **13** | **0** | **1** | **1** | **4** | **2G** |
| **Totals WM** | | | **27** | **0** | **4** | **4** | **22** | **2S** |

~WM20 All-Star Team/Defence (1997)

**Piatak, Erik**
**b. Kezmarok, Czechoslovakia (Slovakia), March 6, 1986**

| | | | | | | | | |
|---|---|---|---|---|---|---|---|---|
| 2004 WM18 | 22-F | SVK | 6 | 1 | 1 | 2 | 2 | 6th |
| 2006 WM20 | 26-F | SVK | 6 | 1 | 1 | 2 | 6 | 8th |

**Pichnarcik, Michal**
**b. Presov, Czechoslovakia (Slovakia), November 20, 1990**

| | | | | | | | | |
|---|---|---|---|---|---|---|---|---|
| 2008 WM18 | 11-D | SVK | 6 | 0 | 1 | 1 | 8 | 7th |

**Pichukha, Andrei**
**b. Minsk, Soviet Union (Belarus), April 8, 1990**

| | | | | | | | | |
|---|---|---|---|---|---|---|---|---|
| 2008 WM18 | 19-F | BLR | 6 | 0 | 1 | 1 | 0 | 9th |

**Pielmeier, Thomas**
**b. Deggendorf, West Germany (Germany), April 14, 1987**

| | | | | | | | | |
|---|---|---|---|---|---|---|---|---|
| 2005 WM18 | 15-F | GER | 6 | 0 | 1 | 1 | 4 | 8th |
| 2007 WM20 | 13-F | GER | 6 | 0 | 0 | 0 | 2 | 9th |

**Pietila, Blake**
**b. Brighton, Michigan, United States, February 20, 1993**

| | | | | | | | | |
|---|---|---|---|---|---|---|---|---|
| 2011 WM18 | 10-F | USA | 6 | 1 | 0 | 1 | 0 | G |

**Pietrangelo, Alex**
**b. King City, Ontario, Canada, January 18, 1990**

| | | | | | | | | |
|---|---|---|---|---|---|---|---|---|
| 2009 WM20 | 10-D | CAN | 6 | 1 | 2 | 3 | 0 | G |
| 2010 WM20 | 27-D | CAN | 6 | 3 | 9 | 12 | 14 | S |
| 2011 WM | 27-D | CAN | 7 | 2 | 3 | 5 | 2 | 5th |
| **Totals WM20** | | | **12** | **4** | **11** | **15** | **14** | **G,S** |

~WM IIHF Directorate Best Defenceman (2011), WM20 IIHF Directorate Best Defenceman (2010), WM20 All-Star Team/Defence (2010)

**Pietsch, Jan**
**b. Bad Homburg, West Germany (Germany), March 25, 1991**

| | | | | | | | | |
|---|---|---|---|---|---|---|---|---|
| 2009 WM18 | 8-D | GER | 6 | 0 | 0 | 0 | 4 | 10th |

**Pietta, Daniel**
**b. Krefeld, West Germany (Germany), December 9, 1986**

| | | | | | | | | |
|---|---|---|---|---|---|---|---|---|
| 2012 WM | 86-F | GER | 4 | 0 | 0 | 0 | 0 | 12th |

**Pihlman, Tuomas**
**b. Espoo, Finland, November 13, 1982**

| | | | | | | | | |
|---|---|---|---|---|---|---|---|---|
| 2000 WM18 | 20-F | FIN | 7 | 3 | 2 | 5 | 8 | G |
| 2001 WM20 | 17-F | FIN | 7 | 0 | 0 | 0 | 6 | S |
| 2002 WM20 | 29-F | FIN | 7 | 2 | 2 | 4 | 2 | B |
| 2009 WM | 49-F | FIN | 6 | 2 | 1 | 3 | 4 | 5th |
| **Totals WM20** | | | **14** | **2** | **2** | **4** | **8** | **S,B** |

**Pihlstrom, Antti**
**b. Vantaa, Finland, October 22, 1984**

| | | | | | | | | |
|---|---|---|---|---|---|---|---|---|
| 2008 WM | 38-F | FIN | 9 | 5 | 2 | 7 | 0 | B |
| 2010 WM | 40-F | FIN | 7 | 0 | 1 | 1 | 4 | 6th |
| 2011 WM | 40-F | FIN | 9 | 2 | 1 | 3 | 0 | G |
| 2012 WM | 40-F | FIN | 9 | 1 | 1 | 2 | 0 | 4th |
| **Totals WM** | | | **34** | **8** | **5** | **13** | **4** | **G,B** |

**Piispanen, Arsi**
**b. Jyvaskyla, Finland, July 23, 1985**

| | | | | | | | | |
|---|---|---|---|---|---|---|---|---|
| 2003 WM18 | 18-F | FIN | 6 | 4 | 1 | 5 | 4 | 7th |
| 2004 WM20 | 13-F | FIN | 7 | 1 | 0 | 1 | 0 | B |
| 2005 WM20 | 16-F | FIN | 6 | 0 | 0 | 0 | 0 | 5th |
| **Totals WM20** | | | **13** | **1** | **0** | **1** | **0** | **B** |

**Pineault, Adam**
**b. Holyoke, Massachusetts, United States, May 23, 1986**

| | | | | | | | | |
|---|---|---|---|---|---|---|---|---|
| 2003 WM18 | 15-F | USA | 5 | 0 | 2 | 2 | 4 | 4th |
| 2005 WM20 | 8-F | USA | 7 | 0 | 1 | 1 | 2 | 4th |

**Pirnes, Esa**
**b. Oulu, Finland, April 1, 1977**

| | | | | | | | | |
|---|---|---|---|---|---|---|---|---|
| 1997 WM20 | 10-F | FIN | 6 | 1 | 0 | 1 | 0 | 5th |
| 2003 WM | 10-F | FIN | 6 | 2 | 3 | 5 | 4 | 5th |
| 2004 WM | 61-F | FIN | 7 | 0 | 0 | 0 | 6 | 6th |
| 2006 WM | 55-F | FIN | 8 | 1 | 3 | 4 | 4 | B |
| 2008 WM | 10-F | FIN | 4 | 0 | 0 | 0 | 0 | B |
| **Totals WM** | | | **25** | **3** | **6** | **9** | **14** | **2B** |

**Piskacek, Jan**
**b. Slany, Czechoslovakia (Czech Republic), September 11, 1989**

| | | | | | | | | |
|---|---|---|---|---|---|---|---|---|
| 2008 WM20 | 5-D | CZE | 5 | 0 | 2 | 2 | 2 | 5th |
| 2009 WM20 | 4-D | CZE | 6 | 0 | 1 | 1 | 4 | 6th |
| **Totals WM20** | | | **11** | **0** | **3** | **3** | **6** | **—** |

**Pitkanen, Ilmari**
**b. Viljakkala, Finland, July 18, 1990**

| | | | | | | | | |
|---|---|---|---|---|---|---|---|---|
| 2008 WM18 | 27-F | FIN | 6 | 1 | 1 | 2 | 46 | 6th |

**Pitkanen, Joni**
**b. Oulu, Finland, September 19, 1983**

| | | | | | | | | |
|---|---|---|---|---|---|---|---|---|
| 2002 WM20 | 4-D | FIN | 7 | 1 | 3 | 4 | 0 | B |
| 2003 WM20 | 4-D | FIN | 7 | 1 | 5 | 6 | 0 | B |
| 2010 OG-M | 25-D | FIN | 5 | 1 | 2 | 3 | 29 | B |
| **Totals WM20** | | | **14** | **2** | **8** | **10** | **0** | **2B** |

~WM20 IIHF Directorate Best Defenceman (2003), WM20 All-Star Team/Defence (2003)

**Pittis, Jonathan**
**b. Calgary, Alberta, Canada, January 25, 1982**

| | | | | | | | | |
|---|---|---|---|---|---|---|---|---|
| 2007 WM | 39-F | ITA | 3 | 0 | 0 | 0 | 0 | 12th |
| 2008 WM | 39-F | ITA | 5 | 2 | 0 | 2 | 10 | 16th |
| 2010 WM | 39-F | ITA | 1 | 0 | 0 | 0 | 0 | 15th |
| **Totals WM** | | | **9** | **2** | **0** | **2** | **10** | **—** |

**Pivtsakin, Nikita**
**b. Omsk, Soviet Union (Russia), July 23, 1991**

| | | | | | | | | |
|---|---|---|---|---|---|---|---|---|
| 2010 WM20 | 3-D | RUS | 6 | 0 | 1 | 1 | 2 | 6th |
| 2011 WM20 | 3-D | RUS | 7 | 0 | 1 | 1 | 2 | G |
| **Totals WM20** | | | **13** | **0** | **2** | **2** | **4** | **G** |

**Pizans, Aldis**
**b. Riga, Soviet Union (Latvia), March 1, 1989**

| | | | | | | | | |
|---|---|---|---|---|---|---|---|---|
| 2007 WM18 | 9-D | LAT | 6 | 0 | 0 | 0 | 2 | 10th |
| 2009 WM20 | 5-D | LAT | 6 | 1 | 0 | 1 | 4 | 8th |

**Plachta, Matthias**
**b. Freiburg, Germany, May 16, 1991**

| | | | | | | | | |
|---|---|---|---|---|---|---|---|---|
| 2009 WM18 | 22-F | GER | 6 | 3 | 2 | 5 | 6 | 10th |
| 2011 WM20 | 22-F | GER | 6 | 1 | 1 | 2 | 16 | 10th |

**Planek, Martin**
**b. Znojmo, Czechoslovakia (Czech Republic), July 12, 1991**

| | | | | | | | | |
|---|---|---|---|---|---|---|---|---|
| 2011 WM20 | 15-D | CZE | 6 | 0 | 1 | 1 | 2 | 7th |

**Plastino, Nicholas**
**b. Sault Ste. Marie, Ontario, Canada, February 20, 1986**

| | | | | | | | | |
|---|---|---|---|---|---|---|---|---|
| 2010 WM | 44-D | ITA | 6 | 0 | 1 | 1 | 2 | 15th |
| 2012 WM | 44-D | ITA | 7 | 0 | 1 | 1 | 4 | 15th |
| **Totals WM** | | | **13** | **0** | **2** | **2** | **6** | **—** |

**Plekanec, Tomas**
**b. Kladno, Czechoslovakia (Czech Republic), October 31, 1982**

| | | | | | | | | |
|---|---|---|---|---|---|---|---|---|
| 2000 WM18 | 14-F | CZE | 6 | 1 | 1 | 2 | 2 | 6th |
| 2001 WM20 | 14-F | CZE | 7 | 1 | 1 | 2 | 6 | G |
| 2002 WM20 | 14-F | CZE | 7 | 3 | 4 | 7 | 0 | 7th |
| 2006 WM | 14-F | CZE | 9 | 3 | 0 | 3 | 20 | S |
| 2007 WM | 14-F | CZE | 7 | 4 | 4 | 8 | 2 | 7th |
| 2008 WM | 14-F | CZE | 4 | 0 | 3 | 3 | 2 | 5th |
| 2009 WM | 14-F | CZE | 7 | 0 | 1 | 1 | 4 | 6th |

| | | | | | | | | |
|---|---|---|---|---|---|---|---|---|
| 2010 OG-M | 14-F | CZE | 5 | 2 | 1 | 3 | 2 | 7th |
| 2011 WM | 14-F | CZE | 8 | 6 | 4 | 10 | 6 | B |
| 2012 WM | 14-F | CZE | 10 | 1 | 6 | 7 | 4 | B |
| **Totals WM20** | | | **14** | **4** | **5** | **9** | **6** | **G** |
| **Totals WM** | | | **45** | **14** | **18** | **32** | **38** | **S,2B** |

**Pluss, Benjamin**
**b. Murgenthal, Switzerland, March 3, 1979**

| | | | | | | | | |
|---|---|---|---|---|---|---|---|---|
| 2012 WM | 11-F | SUI | 7 | 0 | 1 | 1 | 2 | 11th |

**Pluss, Martin**
**b. Bulach, Switzerland, April 5, 1977**

| | | | | | | | | |
|---|---|---|---|---|---|---|---|---|
| 1996 WM20 | 26-F | SUI | 6 | 0 | 0 | 0 | 0 | 9th |
| 1997 WM20 | 28-F | SUI | 6 | 3 | 1 | 4 | 4 | 7th |
| 1998 WM | 18-F | SUI | 9 | 0 | 1 | 1 | 4 | 4th |
| 1999 WM | 18-F | SUI | 6 | 0 | 1 | 1 | 2 | 8th |
| 2001 WM | 28-F | SUI | 6 | 3 | 2 | 5 | 0 | 9th |
| 2002 OG-M | 28-F | SUI | 4 | 2 | 0 | 2 | 2 | 11th |
| 2002 WM | 28-F | SUI | 6 | 2 | 1 | 3 | 0 | 10th |
| 2003 WM | 28-F | SUI | 7 | 5 | 1 | 6 | 2 | 8th |
| 2004 WM | 28-F | SUI | 7 | 1 | 1 | 2 | 2 | 8th |
| 2005 WM | 28-F | SUI | 7 | 3 | 2 | 5 | 6 | 8th |
| 2006 OG-M | 28-F | SUI | 6 | 0 | 3 | 3 | 8 | 6th |
| 2006 WM | 28-F | SUI | 6 | 2 | 3 | 5 | 14 | 9th |
| 2009 WM | 28-F | SUI | 6 | 3 | 1 | 4 | 4 | 9th |
| 2010 OG-M | 28-F | SUI | 5 | 0 | 3 | 3 | 0 | 8th |
| 2010 WM | 28-F | SUI | 7 | 4 | 2 | 6 | 25 | 5th |
| 2011 WM | 28-F | SUI | 6 | 0 | 3 | 3 | 4 | 9th |
| **Totals WM20** | | | **12** | **3** | **1** | **4** | **4** | **—** |
| **Totals WM** | | | **73** | **23** | **18** | **41** | **63** | **—** |
| **Totals OG-M** | | | **15** | **2** | **6** | **8** | **10** | **—** |

**Pock, Markus**
**b. Klagenfurt, Austria, January 15, 1992**

| | | | | | | | | |
|---|---|---|---|---|---|---|---|---|
| 2010 WM20 | 17-F | AUT | 6 | 0 | 0 | 0 | 2 | 10th |

**Podhradsky, Peter**
**b. Bratislava, Czechoslovakia (Slovakia), December 10, 1979**

| | | | | | | | | |
|---|---|---|---|---|---|---|---|---|
| 1999 WM20 | 14-D | SVK | 6 | 0 | 2 | 2 | 4 | B |
| 2000 WM | 14-D | SVK | 9 | 0 | 1 | 1 | 14 | S |
| 2007 WM | 37-D | SVK | 7 | 2 | 5 | 7 | 6 | 6th |
| 2008 WM | 37-D | SVK | 3 | 1 | 0 | 1 | 0 | 13th |
| 2011 WM | 37-D | SVK | 6 | 0 | 1 | 1 | 0 | 10th |
| **Totals WM** | | | **25** | **3** | **7** | **10** | **20** | **S** |

**Podkonicky, Andrei**
**b. Zvolen, Czechoslovakia (Slovakia), May 9, 1978**

| | | | | | | | | |
|---|---|---|---|---|---|---|---|---|
| 1996 WM20 | 23-F | SVK | 6 | 0 | 0 | 0 | 0 | 7th |
| 1998 WM20 | 22-F | SVK | 6 | 3 | 5 | 8 | 27 | 9th |
| 2007 WM | 14-F | SVK | 4 | 0 | 0 | 0 | 2 | 6th |
| 2008 WM | 41-F | SVK | 5 | 1 | 1 | 2 | 2 | 13th |
| 2010 WM | 14-F | SVK | 6 | 1 | 1 | 2 | 4 | 12th |
| **Totals WM20** | | | **12** | **3** | **5** | **8** | **27** | **—** |
| **Totals WM** | | | **15** | **2** | **2** | **4** | **8** | **—** |

**Pohl, Patrick**
**b. Berlin, West Germany (Germany), January 8, 1990**

| | | | | | | | | |
|---|---|---|---|---|---|---|---|---|
| 2008 WM18 | 18-F | GER | 6 | 2 | 1 | 3 | 6 | 5th |
| 2009 WM20 | 19-F | GER | 6 | 1 | 2 | 3 | 0 | 9th |

**Pohl, Petr**
**b. Prostejov, Czechoslovakia (Czech Republic), August 28, 1986**

| | | | | | | | | |
|---|---|---|---|---|---|---|---|---|
| 2006 WM20 | 18-F | CZE | 6 | 4 | 1 | 5 | 0 | 6th |

**Pokka, Ville**
**b. Tornio, Finland, June 3, 1994**

| | | | | | | | | |
|---|---|---|---|---|---|---|---|---|
| 2011 WM18 | 5-D | FIN | 6 | 0 | 0 | 0 | 2 | 5th |
| 2012 WM18 | 21-D | FIN | 7 | 1 | 5 | 6 | 4 | 4th |
| 2012 WM20 | 12-D | FIN | 7 | 1 | 3 | 4 | 4 | 4th |
| **Totals WM18** | | | **13** | **1** | **5** | **6** | **6** | **—** |

**Pokovic, Lubor**
**b. Bremerhaven, Germany, March 16, 1992**

| | | | | | | | | |
|---|---|---|---|---|---|---|---|---|
| 2010 WM18 | 7-D | SVK | 6 | 0 | 0 | 0 | 2 | 8th |

**Pokulok, Sasha**
**b. Montreal, Quebec, Canada, May 25, 1986**

| | | | | | | | | |
|---|---|---|---|---|---|---|---|---|
| 2006 WM20 | 36-D | CAN | 6 | 0 | 0 | 0 | 0 | G |

**Polak, Michal**
**b. Plzen, Czechoslovakia (Czech Republic), January 11, 1985**

| | | | | | | | | |
|---|---|---|---|---|---|---|---|---|
| 2003 WM18 | 27-F | CZE | 6 | 0 | 0 | 0 | 6 | 6th |
| 2005 WM20 | 26-F | CZE | 7 | 1 | 0 | 1 | 4 | B |

**Polak, Roman**
**b. Ostrava, Czechoslovakia (Czech Republic), April 28, 1986**

| | | | | | | | | |
|---|---|---|---|---|---|---|---|---|
| 2004 WM18 | 24-D | CZE | 7 | 0 | 0 | 0 | 8 | B |
| 2005 WM20 | 6-D | CZE | 7 | 0 | 2 | 2 | 4 | B |
| 2006 WM20 | 6-D | CZE | 6 | 0 | 2 | 2 | 6 | 6th |
| 2009 WM | 5-D | CZE | 7 | 0 | 1 | 1 | 6 | 6th |
| 2010 OG-M | 5-D | CZE | 5 | 0 | 0 | 0 | 4 | 7th |
| **Totals WM20** | | | **13** | **0** | **4** | **4** | **10** | **B** |

**Poletin, Michal**
**b. Prague, Czechoslovakia (Czech Republic), June 6, 1991**

| | | | | | | | | |
|---|---|---|---|---|---|---|---|---|
| 2009 WM18 | 20-F | CZE | 6 | 1 | 2 | 3 | 2 | 6th |
| 2010 WM20 | 25-F | CZE | 4 | 1 | 0 | 1 | 0 | 7th |

**Polishuk, Fyodor**
**b. Cherkassk, Soviet Union (Russia), July 4, 1979**

| | | | | | | | | |
|---|---|---|---|---|---|---|---|---|
| 2012 WM | 18-F | KAZ | 7 | 1 | 0 | 1 | 4 | 16th |

**Poloncic, Gregor**
**b. Ljubljana, Yugoslavia (Slovenia), February 5, 1981**

| | | | | | | | | |
|---|---|---|---|---|---|---|---|---|
| 2002 WM | 18-F | SLO | 6 | 1 | 0 | 1 | 4 | 13th |
| 2003 WM | 18-F | SLO | 6 | 0 | 0 | 0 | 6 | 15th |
| 2008 WM | 18-F | SLO | 4 | 0 | 0 | 0 | 2 | 15th |
| **Totals WM** | | | **16** | **1** | **0** | **1** | **12** | **—** |

**Pominville, Jason**
**b. Repentigny, Quebec, Canada, November 30, 1982**

| | | | | | | | | |
|---|---|---|---|---|---|---|---|---|
| 2008 WM | 29-F | USA | 7 | 2 | 3 | 5 | 0 | 6th |

**Popov, Alexander**
**b. Angarsk, Soviet Union (Russia), August 31, 1980**

| | | | | | | | | |
|---|---|---|---|---|---|---|---|---|
| 2012 WM | 24-F | RUS | 10 | 4 | 8 | 12 | 2 | G |

**Porter, Chris**
**b. Toronto, Ontario, Canada, May 29, 1984**

| | | | | | | | | |
|---|---|---|---|---|---|---|---|---|
| 2011 WM | 24-F | USA | 7 | 0 | 1 | 1 | 2 | 8th |

**Porter, Kevin**
**b. Detroit, Michigan, United States, March 12, 1986**

| | | | | | | | | |
|---|---|---|---|---|---|---|---|---|
| 2003 WM18 | 29-F | USA | 6 | 0 | 2 | 2 | 2 | 4th |
| 2004 WM18 | 9-F | USA | 6 | 2 | 6 | 8 | 4 | S |
| 2005 WM20 | 21-F | USA | 7 | 3 | 2 | 5 | 6 | 4th |
| 2006 WM20 | 11-F | USA | 7 | 2 | 4 | 6 | 2 | 4th |
| **Totals WM18** | | | **12** | **2** | **8** | **10** | **6** | **S** |
| **Totals WM20** | | | **14** | **5** | **6** | **11** | **8** | **—** |

**Pospisil, Tomas**
**b. Sumperk, Czechoslovakia (Czech Republic), August 25, 1987**

| | | | | | | | | |
|---|---|---|---|---|---|---|---|---|
| 2005 WM18 | 11-F | CZE | 7 | 0 | 2 | 2 | 4 | 4th |
| 2007 WM20 | 10-F | CZE | 5 | 0 | 0 | 0 | 2 | 5th |

**Possler, Gustav**
**b. Sodertalje, Sweden, November 11, 1994**

| | | | | | | | | |
|---|---|---|---|---|---|---|---|---|
| 2012 WM18 | 20-F | SWE | 6 | 4 | 4 | 8 | 0 | S |

**Potapov, Alexei**
**b. Gorky (Nizhni Novgorod), Soviet Union (Russia), March 2, 1989**

| | | | | | | | | |
|---|---|---|---|---|---|---|---|---|
| 2009 WM20 | 29-F | RUS | 6 | 0 | 2 | 2 | 0 | B |

**Poticny, Valerian**
**b. Bratislava, Czechoslovakia (Slovakia), February 27, 1990**

| | | | | | | | | |
|---|---|---|---|---|---|---|---|---|
| 2008 WM18 | 13-F | SVK | 6 | 0 | 0 | 0 | 2 | 7th |

**Potthoff, Matthias**
**b. Wickede, West Germany (Germany), October 26, 1987**

| | | | | | | | | |
|---|---|---|---|---|---|---|---|---|
| 2007 WM20 | 14-F | GER | 6 | 0 | 0 | 0 | 8 | 9th |

**Potulny, Ryan**
**b. Grand Forks, North Dakota, United States, September 5, 1984**

| | | | | | | | | |
|---|---|---|---|---|---|---|---|---|
| 2010 WM | 16-F | USA | 6 | 2 | 2 | 4 | 0 | 13th |

**Pouliot, Benoit**
**b. Alfred, Ontario, Canada, September 29, 1986**

| | | | | | | | | |
|---|---|---|---|---|---|---|---|---|
| 2006 WM20 | 37-F | CAN | 6 | 0 | 5 | 5 | 14 | G |

**Poulsen, Morten**
**b. Herning, Denmark, September 9, 1988**

| | | | | | | | | |
|---|---|---|---|---|---|---|---|---|
| 2008 WM20 | 18-F | DEN | 6 | 2 | 1 | 3 | 0 | 10th |
| 2011 WM | 38-F | DEN | 6 | 0 | 0 | 0 | 0 | 11th |
| 2012 WM | 38-F | DEN | 7 | 1 | 0 | 1 | 0 | 13th |
| **Totals WM** | | | **13** | **1** | **0** | **1** | **0** | **—** |

**Povlsen, Magnus**
**b. October 14, 1994**

| | | | | | | | | |
|---|---|---|---|---|---|---|---|---|
| 2012 WM18 | 6-D | DEN | 6 | 0 | 0 | 0 | 18 | 10th |

**Poyhonen, Marko**
**b. Hollola, Finland, September 10, 1987**

| | | | | | | | | |
|---|---|---|---|---|---|---|---|---|
| 2007 WM20 | 23-F | FIN | 6 | 0 | 1 | 1 | 2 | 6th |

**Poysti, Eetu**
**b. Helsinki, Finland, January 16, 1989**

| | | | | | | | | |
|---|---|---|---|---|---|---|---|---|
| 2007 WM18 | 19-F | FIN | 6 | 3 | 3 | 6 | 0 | 7th |
| 2008 WM20 | 16-F | FIN | 6 | 0 | 1 | 1 | 2 | 6th |
| 2009 WM20 | 9-F | FIN | 6 | 0 | 0 | 0 | 0 | 7th |
| **Totals WM20** | | | **12** | **0** | **1** | **1** | **2** | **—** |

**Pozivil, Ondrej**
**b. Most, Czechoslovakia (Czech Republic), April 22, 1987**

| | | | | | | | | |
|---|---|---|---|---|---|---|---|---|
| 2005 WM18 | 6-D | CZE | 7 | 0 | 2 | 2 | 0 | 4th |
| 2007 WM20 | 4-D | CZE | 6 | 0 | 0 | 0 | 8 | 5th |

**Preisinger, Miroslav**
**b. Bratislava, Czechoslovakia (Slovakia), February 3, 1991**

| | | | | | | | | |
|---|---|---|---|---|---|---|---|---|
| 2008 WM18 | 28-F | SVK | 6 | 3 | 0 | 3 | 0 | 7th |
| 2009 WM18 | 22-F | SVK | 4 | 0 | 0 | 0 | 14 | 7th |
| 2011 WM20 | 29-F | SVK | 6 | 1 | 2 | 3 | 4 | 8th |
| **Totals WM18** | | | **10** | **3** | **0** | **3** | **14** | **—** |

**Pretnar, Boris**
**b. Bled, Yugoslavia (Slovenia), April 8, 1978**

| | | | | | | | | |
|---|---|---|---|---|---|---|---|---|
| 2003 WM | 16-F | SLO | 3 | 0 | 0 | 0 | 0 | 15th |
| 2005 WM | 16-F | SLO | 3 | 0 | 0 | 0 | 2 | 13th |
| 2008 WM | 14-F | SLO | 4 | 0 | 0 | 0 | 4 | 15th |
| **Totals WM** | | | **10** | **0** | **0** | **0** | **6** | **—** |

**Pretnar, Klemen**
**b. Bled, Yugoslavia (Slovenia), August 31, 1986**

| | | | | | | | | |
|---|---|---|---|---|---|---|---|---|
| 2011 WM | 21-D | SLO | 3 | 0 | 0 | 0 | 0 | 16th |

**Pribyl, Daniel**
**b. Pisek, Czech Republic, December 18, 1992**

| | | | | | | | | |
|---|---|---|---|---|---|---|---|---|
| 2012 WM20 | 15-F | CZE | 5 | 0 | 1 | 1 | 0 | 5th |

**Prochazka, Martin**
**b. Roudnice, Czech Republic, March 1, 1994**

| | | | | | | | | |
|---|---|---|---|---|---|---|---|---|
| 2012 WM18 | 21-F | CZE | 6 | 2 | 0 | 2 | 2 | 8th |

**Prokop, Patrik**
**b. Ostrava, Czechoslovakia (Czech Republic), January 16, 1988**

| | | | | | | | | |
|---|---|---|---|---|---|---|---|---|
| 2006 WM18 | 5-D | CZE | 7 | 0 | 0 | 0 | 10 | B |
| 2008 WM20 | 4-D | CZE | 6 | 0 | 1 | 1 | 25 | 5th |

**Pronger, Chris**
**b. Dryden, Ontario, Canada, October 10, 1974**

| | | | | | | | | |
|---|---|---|---|---|---|---|---|---|
| 1993 WM20 | 6-D | CAN | 7 | 1 | 3 | 4 | 6 | G |
| 1997 WM | 24-D | CAN | 9 | 0 | 2 | 2 | 12 | G |
| 1998 OG-M | 24-D | CAN | 6 | 0 | 0 | 0 | 4 | 4th |
| 2002 OG-M | 44-D | CAN | 6 | 0 | 1 | 1 | 2 | G |
| 2006 OG-M | 44-D | CAN | 6 | 1 | 2 | 3 | 16 | 7th |
| 2010 OG-M | 20-D | CAN | 7 | 0 | 5 | 5 | 2 | G |
| **Totals OG-M** | | | **25** | **1** | **8** | **9** | **24** | **2G** |

~Triple Gold Club

**Proshkin, Vitali**
**b. Elektrostal, Soviet Union (Russia), May 8, 1976**

| | | | | | | | | |
|---|---|---|---|---|---|---|---|---|
| 2003 WM | 4-D | RUS | 7 | 1 | 0 | 1 | 10 | 7th |
| 2004 WM | 4-D | RUS | 6 | 0 | 2 | 2 | 4 | 10th |
| 2005 WM | 4-D | RUS | 9 | 0 | 0 | 0 | 6 | B |
| 2007 WM | 45-D | RUS | 9 | 1 | 1 | 2 | 16 | B |
| 2008 WM | 45-D | RUS | 8 | 0 | 3 | 3 | 12 | G |
| 2009 WM | 45-D | RUS | 9 | 2 | 0 | 2 | 4 | G |
| **Totals WM** | | | **48** | **4** | **6** | **10** | **52** | **2G,2B** |

**Prucha, Petr**
**b. Chrudim, Czechoslovakia (Czech Republic), September 14, 1982**

| | | | | | | | | |
|---|---|---|---|---|---|---|---|---|
| 2002 WM20 | 8-F | CZE | 7 | 1 | 0 | 1 | 2 | 7th |
| 2004 WM | 73-F | CZE | 7 | 3 | 1 | 4 | 6 | 5th |
| 2005 WM | 73-F | CZE | 3 | 0 | 0 | 0 | 0 | G |
| 2011 WM | 73-F | CZE | 9 | 3 | 2 | 5 | 2 | B |
| 2012 WM | 73-F | CZE | 10 | 1 | 2 | 3 | 4 | B |
| **Totals WM** | | | **29** | **7** | **5** | **12** | **12** | **G,2B** |

**Pryor, Nick**
**b. Woodbury, Minnesota, United States, September 6, 1990**

| | | | | | | | | |
|---|---|---|---|---|---|---|---|---|
| 2008 WM18 | 22-D | USA | 7 | 0 | 0 | 0 | 0 | G |

**Puistola, Pasi**
**b. Tampere, Finland, September 16, 1978**

| | | | | | | | | |
|---|---|---|---|---|---|---|---|---|
| 1998 WM20 | 5-D | FIN | 7 | 1 | 3 | 4 | 8 | G |
| 2010 WM | 41-D | FIN | 6 | 0 | 3 | 3 | 0 | 6th |
| 2011 WM | 41-D | FIN | 9 | 0 | 3 | 3 | 4 | G |
| **Totals WM** | | | **15** | **0** | **6** | **6** | **4** | **G** |

**Pujacs, Georgijs**
**b. Riga, Soviet Union (Latvia), June 11, 1981**

| | | | | | | | | |
|---|---|---|---|---|---|---|---|---|
| 2006 OG-M | 18-D | LAT | 5 | 0 | 0 | 0 | 0 | 12th |
| 2006 WM | 18-D | LAT | 6 | 0 | 0 | 0 | 18 | 10th |
| 2007 WM | 18-D | LAT | 5 | 0 | 0 | 0 | 4 | 13th |
| 2008 WM | 18-D | LAT | 6 | 0 | 1 | 1 | 6 | 11th |
| 2009 WM | 18-D | LAT | 7 | 0 | 0 | 0 | 10 | 7th |
| 2010 OG-M | 71-D | LAT | 4 | 0 | 1 | 1 | 2 | 12th |
| 2010 WM | 71-D | LAT | 6 | 1 | 2 | 3 | 2 | 11th |
| 2011 WM | 81-D | LAT | 6 | 2 | 1 | 3 | 33 | 13th |
| 2012 WM | 81-D | LAT | 7 | 0 | 1 | 1 | 2 | 10th |
| **Totals WM** | | | **43** | **3** | **5** | **8** | **75** | **—** |
| **Totals OG-M** | | | **9** | **0** | **1** | **1** | **2** | **—** |

**Pulkkinen, Teemu**
**b. Vantaa, Finland, January 2, 1992**

| | | | | | | | | |
|---|---|---|---|---|---|---|---|---|
| 2009 WM18 | 20-F | FIN | 6 | 7 | 6 | 13 | 4 | B |
| 2010 WM18 | 10-F | FIN | 6 | 10 | 5 | 15 | 10 | B |
| 2011 WM20 | 6-F | FIN | 6 | 3 | 6 | 9 | 6 | 6th |
| 2012 WM20 | 6-F | FIN | 7 | 6 | 4 | 10 | 2 | 4th |
| **Totals WM18** | | | **12** | **17** | **11** | **28** | **14** | **2B** |
| **Totals WM20** | | | **13** | **9** | **10** | **19** | **8** | **—** |

~WM18 IIHF Directorate Best Forward (2010), WM18 All-Star Team/Forward (2010)

**Pulock, Ryan**
**b. Dauphin, Manitoba, Canada, October 6, 1994**

| | | | | | | | | |
|---|---|---|---|---|---|---|---|---|
| 2012 WM18 | 3-D | CAN | 6 | 1 | 1 | 2 | 0 | B |

**Puna, David**
**b. Bratislava, Czechoslovakia (Slovakia), February 19, 1990**

| | | | | | | | | |
|---|---|---|---|---|---|---|---|---|
| 2008 WM18 | 20-F | SVK | 6 | 0 | 2 | 2 | 6 | 7th |

**Purcell, Teddy**
**b. St. John's, Newfoundland, Canada, September 8, 1985**

| | | | | | | | | |
|---|---|---|---|---|---|---|---|---|
| 2012 WM | 26-F | CAN | 8 | 1 | 1 | 2 | 0 | 5th |

**Purolinna, Juha-Petteri**
**b. Helsinki, Finland, July 11, 1988**

| | | | | | | | | |
|---|---|---|---|---|---|---|---|---|
| 2008 WM20 | 2-D | FIN | 6 | 0 | 1 | 1 | 6 | 6th |

**Puschnik, Kevin**
**b. Feldkirch, Austria, September 2, 1991**

| | | | | | | | | |
|---|---|---|---|---|---|---|---|---|
| 2010 WM20 | 12-F | AUT | 1 | 0 | 0 | 0 | 0 | 10th |

**Pushkaryov, Konstantin**
**b. Ust-Kamenogorsk, Soviet Union (Kazakhstan), February 12, 1985**

| | | | | | | | | |
|---|---|---|---|---|---|---|---|---|
| 2012 WM | 81-F | KAZ | 7 | 3 | 1 | 4 | 2 | 16th |

**Puustinen, Juuso**
**b. Kuopio, Finland, April 5, 1988**

| | | | | | | | | |
|---|---|---|---|---|---|---|---|---|
| 2006 WM18 | 11-F | FIN | 6 | 1 | 2 | 3 | 10 | S |
| 2008 WM20 | 10-F | FIN | 6 | 4 | 1 | 5 | 12 | 6th |

**Pyatt, Tom**
**b. Thunder Bay, Ontario, Canada, February 14, 1987**

| | | | | | | | | |
|---|---|---|---|---|---|---|---|---|
| 2005 WM18 | 27-F | CAN | 6 | 2 | 3 | 5 | 2 | S |
| 2006 WM20 | 27-F | CAN | 6 | 1 | 0 | 1 | 16 | G |
| 2007 WM20 | 27-F | CAN | 6 | 1 | 3 | 4 | 2 | G |
| **Totals WM20** | | | **12** | **2** | **3** | **5** | **18** | **2G** |

**Pyett, Logan**
**b. Regina, Saskatchewan, Canada, May 26, 1988**

| | | | | | | | | |
|---|---|---|---|---|---|---|---|---|
| 2006 WM18 | 21-D | CAN | 7 | 1 | 3 | 4 | 12 | 4th |
| 2008 WM20 | 3-D | CAN | 7 | 0 | 1 | 1 | 4 | G |

**Pyorala, Mika**
**b. Oulu, Finland, July 13, 1981**

| | | | | | | | | |
|---|---|---|---|---|---|---|---|---|
| 2007 WM | 22-F | FIN | 8 | 0 | 1 | 1 | 2 | S |
| 2008 WM | 37-F | FIN | 9 | 0 | 0 | 0 | 0 | B |
| 2009 WM | 37-F | FIN | 6 | 1 | 1 | 2 | 0 | 5th |
| 2011 WM | 37-F | FIN | 9 | 1 | 2 | 3 | 4 | G |
| 2012 WM | 37-F | FIN | 9 | 1 | 1 | 2 | 2 | 4th |
| **Totals WM** | | | **41** | **3** | **5** | **8** | **8** | **G,S,B** |

**Pysyk, Mark**
**b. Sherwood Park, Alberta, Canada, January 11, 1992**

| | | | | | | | | |
|---|---|---|---|---|---|---|---|---|
| 2012 WM20 | 5-D | CAN | 6 | 0 | 0 | 0 | 2 | B |

**Quessandier, Benoit**
**b. Rouen, France, December 2, 1985**

| | | | | | | | | |
|---|---|---|---|---|---|---|---|---|
| 2008 WM | 16-D | FRA | 5 | 0 | 0 | 0 | 0 | 14th |
| 2009 WM | 16-D | FRA | 6 | 0 | 0 | 0 | 31 | 12th |
| 2010 WM | 16-D | FRA | 6 | 0 | 0 | 0 | 2 | 14th |
| **Totals WM** | | | **17** | **0** | **0** | **0** | **33** | **—** |

**Quincey, Kyle**
**b. Kitchener, Ontario, Canada, August 12, 1985**

| | | | | | | | | |
|---|---|---|---|---|---|---|---|---|
| 2012 WM | 22-D | CAN | 6 | 0 | 0 | 0 | 4 | 5th |

**Quine, Alan**
**b. Belleville, Ontario, Canada, February 25, 1993**

| | | | | | | | | |
|---|---|---|---|---|---|---|---|---|
| 2011 WM18 | 18-F | CAN | 7 | 1 | 6 | 7 | 6 | 4th |

**Quinlan, Nicolai**
**b. Munich, Germany, June 11, 1994**

| | | | | | | | | |
|---|---|---|---|---|---|---|---|---|
| 2012 WM18 | 4-D | GER | 6 | 0 | 0 | 0 | 2 | 6th |

**Rachunek, Tomas**
**b. Zlin, Czechoslovakia (Czech Republic), February 21, 1991**

| | | | | | | | | |
|---|---|---|---|---|---|---|---|---|
| 2009 WM18 | 10-F | CZE | 6 | 1 | 2 | 3 | 4 | 6th |
| 2011 WM20 | 10-F | CZE | 6 | 2 | 0 | 2 | 0 | 7th |

**Radivojevic, Branko**
**b. Piestany, Czechoslovakia (Slovakia), November 24, 1980**

| | | | | | | | | |
|---|---|---|---|---|---|---|---|---|
| 2000 WM20 | 14-F | SVK | 7 | 0 | 0 | 0 | 4 | 9th |
| 2003 WM | 92-F | SVK | 9 | 2 | 1 | 3 | 8 | B |
| 2004 WCH | 19-F | SVK | 4 | 0 | 1 | 1 | 2 | 7th |
| 2007 WM | 19-F | SVK | 7 | 2 | 1 | 3 | 6 | 6th |
| 2009 WM | 92-F | SVK | 6 | 0 | 1 | 1 | 4 | 10th |
| 2010 OG-M | 92-F | SVK | 7 | 0 | 0 | 0 | 6 | 4th |
| 2011 WM | 92-F | SVK | 6 | 0 | 1 | 1 | 6 | 10th |
| 2012 WM | 92-F | SVK | 10 | 4 | 4 | 8 | 2 | S |
| **Totals WM** | | | **38** | **8** | **8** | **16** | **26** | **S,B** |

**Radulov, Alexander**
**b. Nizhy Tagil, Soviet Union (Russia), July 5, 1986**

| | | | | | | | | |
|---|---|---|---|---|---|---|---|---|
| 2004 WM18 | 22-F | RUS | 6 | 2 | 5 | 7 | 2 | G |
| 2005 WM20 | 22-F | RUS | 6 | 2 | 1 | 3 | 4 | S |
| 2006 WM20 | 22-F | RUS | 6 | 1 | 3 | 4 | 4 | S |
| 2007 WM | 22-F | RUS | 9 | 2 | 0 | 2 | 6 | B |
| 2008 WM | 47-F | RUS | 6 | 0 | 3 | 3 | 2 | G |
| 2009 WM | 47-F | RUS | 9 | 4 | 6 | 10 | 10 | G |
| 2010 OG-M | 47-F | RUS | 4 | 1 | 1 | 2 | 4 | 6th |
| 2011 WM | 47-F | RUS | 9 | 2 | 5 | 7 | 6 | 4th |
| **Totals WM20** | | | **12** | **3** | **4** | **7** | **8** | **2S** |
| **Totals WM** | | | **33** | **8** | **14** | **22** | **24** | **2G,B** |

**Raffl, Michael**
**b. Villach, Austria, December 1, 1988**

| | | | | | | | | |
|---|---|---|---|---|---|---|---|---|
| 2009 WM | 12-F | AUT | 2 | 0 | 0 | 0 | 0 | 14th |
| 2011 WM | 12-F | AUT | 3 | 0 | 1 | 1 | 0 | 15th |
| **Totals WM** | | | **5** | **0** | **1** | **1** | **0** | **—** |

**Raffl, Thomas**
**b. Villach, Austria, June 19, 1986**

| | | | | | | | | |
|---|---|---|---|---|---|---|---|---|
| 2011 WM | 5-F | AUT | 6 | 2 | 2 | 4 | 2 | 15th |

**Rahbek, Martin**
**b. Ringkobing, Denmark, May 19, 1992**

| | | | | | | | | |
|---|---|---|---|---|---|---|---|---|
| 2012 WM20 | 6-D | DEN | 6 | 0 | 1 | 1 | 0 | 10th |

**Rahimi, Daniel**
**b. Umea, Sweden, April 28, 1987**

| | | | | | | | | |
|---|---|---|---|---|---|---|---|---|
| 2007 WM20 | 22-D | SWE | 7 | 0 | 0 | 0 | 18 | 4th |

**Rais, Matus**
**b. Nitra, Czechoslovakia (Slovakia), November 21, 1990**

| | | | | | | | | |
|---|---|---|---|---|---|---|---|---|
| 2010 WM20 | 8-D | SVK | 6 | 1 | 2 | 3 | 4 | 8th |

**Raisov, Aslan**
**b. Grozny, Soviet Union (Russia), December 29, 1990**

| | | | | | | | | |
|---|---|---|---|---|---|---|---|---|
| 2008 WM18 | 22-F | RUS | 6 | 2 | 4 | 6 | 2 | S |

**Rajala, Toni**
**b. Parkano, Finland, March 29, 1991**

| | | | | | | | | |
|---|---|---|---|---|---|---|---|---|
| 2008 WM18 | 20-F | FIN | 6 | 3 | 2 | 5 | 2 | 6th |
| 2009 WM18 | 21-F | FIN | 6 | 10 | 9 | 19 | 6 | B |
| 2009 WM20 | 11-F | FIN | 6 | 2 | 1 | 3 | 4 | 7th |
| 2010 WM20 | 11-F | FIN | 6 | 1 | 2 | 3 | 0 | 5th |
| 2011 WM20 | 25-F | FIN | 6 | 0 | 4 | 4 | 2 | 6th |
| **Totals WM18** | | | **12** | **13** | **11** | **24** | **8** | **B** |
| **Totals WM20** | | | **18** | **3** | **7** | **10** | **6** | **—** |

~WM18 IIHF Directorate Best Forward (2009), WM18 All-Star Team/Forward (2009)

**Rakell, Rickard**
**b. Stockholm, Sweden, May 5, 1993**

| | | | | | | | | |
|---|---|---|---|---|---|---|---|---|
| 2011 WM20 | 27-F | SWE | 5 | 0 | 3 | 3 | 2 | 4th |
| 2012 WM20 | 24-F | SWE | 6 | 2 | 3 | 5 | 4 | G |

**Rakhshani, Rhett**
**b. Huntington Beach, California, United States, March 6, 1988**

| | | | | | | | | |
|---|---|---|---|---|---|---|---|---|
| 2006 WM18 | 10-F | USA | 6 | 5 | 1 | 6 | 4 | G |
| 2008 WM20 | 10-F | USA | 6 | 2 | 2 | 4 | 2 | 4th |

**Rakos, Daniel**
**b. Pardubice, Czechoslovakia (Czech Republic), May 25, 1987**

| | | | | | | | | |
|---|---|---|---|---|---|---|---|---|
| 2005 WM18 | 2-F | CZE | 7 | 0 | 2 | 2 | 4 | 4th |
| 2007 WM20 | 16-F | CZE | 6 | 0 | 0 | 0 | 4 | 5th |

**Ramage, John**
**b. St. Louis, Missouri, United States, February 7, 1991**

| | | | | | | | | |
|---|---|---|---|---|---|---|---|---|
| 2009 WM18 | 5-D | USA | 7 | 0 | 1 | 1 | 2 | G |
| 2010 WM20 | 2-D | USA | 7 | 0 | 3 | 3 | 0 | G |
| 2011 WM20 | 5-D | USA | 6 | 0 | 0 | 0 | 4 | B |
| **Totals WM20** | | | **13** | **0** | **3** | **3** | **4** | **G,B** |

**Ramazanov, Damir**
**b. Ust-Kamenogorsk, Soviet Union (Kazakhstan), August 17, 1988**

| | | | | | | | | |
|---|---|---|---|---|---|---|---|---|
| 2008 WM20 | 23-D | KAZ | 6 | 0 | 0 | 0 | 0 | 8th |

**Ramholt, Tim**
**b. Zurich, Switzerland, November 2, 1984**

| | | | | | | | | |
|---|---|---|---|---|---|---|---|---|
| 2001 WM18 | 9-D | SUI | 7 | 0 | 1 | 1 | 4 | S |
| 2002 WM18 | 6-D | SUI | 8 | 1 | 4 | 5 | 12 | 7th |
| 2002 WM20 | 6-D | SUI | 7 | 0 | 1 | 1 | 6 | 4th |
| 2003 WM20 | 6-D | SUI | 6 | 2 | 2 | 4 | 2 | 7th |
| 2004 WM20 | 6-D | SUI | 6 | 1 | 1 | 2 | 4 | 8th |
| **Totals WM18** | | | **15** | **1** | **5** | **6** | **16** | **S** |
| **Totals WM20** | | | **19** | **3** | **4** | **7** | **12** | **—** |

**Rankel, Andre**
**b. Berlin, West Germany (Germany), August 27, 1985**

| | | | | | | | | |
|---|---|---|---|---|---|---|---|---|
| 2005 WM20 | 24-F | GER | 6 | 0 | 1 | 1 | 6 | 9th |
| 2007 WM | 24-F | GER | 6 | 0 | 0 | 0 | 4 | 9th |
| 2008 WM | 24-F | GER | 2 | 0 | 0 | 0 | 2 | 10th |
| 2009 WM | 24-F | GER | 3 | 0 | 0 | 0 | 2 | 15th |
| 2010 OG-M | 24-F | GER | 4 | 0 | 1 | 1 | 0 | 11th |
| 2010 WM | 24-F | GER | 9 | 0 | 0 | 0 | 0 | 4th |
| 2011 WM | 24-F | GER | 7 | 1 | 2 | 3 | 2 | 7th |
| 2012 WM | 24-F | GER | 3 | 0 | 0 | 0 | 0 | 12th |
| **Totals WM** | | | **30** | **1** | **2** | **3** | **10** | **—** |

**Rapac, Branislav**
**b. Spisska Nova Ves, Slovakia, June 4, 1993**

| | | | | | | | | |
|---|---|---|---|---|---|---|---|---|
| 2011 WM18 | 23-F | SVK | 6 | 1 | 1 | 2 | 31 | 10th |

**Rask, Joonas**
**b. Savonlinna, Finland, March 24, 1990**

| | | | | | | | | |
|---|---|---|---|---|---|---|---|---|
| 2008 WM18 | 22-F | FIN | 6 | 1 | 4 | 5 | 0 | 6th |
| 2009 WM20 | 26-F | FIN | 6 | 1 | 3 | 4 | 0 | 7th |
| 2010 WM20 | 19-F | FIN | 6 | 2 | 0 | 2 | 0 | 5th |
| **Totals WM20** | | | **12** | **3** | **3** | **6** | **0** | **—** |

**Rask, Victor**
**b. Leksand, Sweden, March 3, 1993**

| | | | | | | | | |
|---|---|---|---|---|---|---|---|---|
| 2010 WM18 | 18-F | SWE | 6 | 3 | 2 | 5 | 0 | S |
| 2011 WM18 | 18-F | SWE | 6 | 2 | 3 | 5 | 4 | S |
| 2012 WM20 | 18-F | SWE | 6 | 0 | 1 | 1 | 6 | G |
| **Totals WM18** | | | **12** | **5** | **5** | **10** | **4** | **2S** |

**Rasmussen, Christoffer**
**b. Charlottenlund, Denmark, January 17, 1989**

| | | | | | | | | |
|---|---|---|---|---|---|---|---|---|
| 2008 WM20 | 5-D | DEN | 6 | 0 | 1 | 1 | 14 | 10th |

**Rasmussen, Dennis**
**b. Vasteras, Sweden, July 3, 1990**

| | | | | | | | | |
|---|---|---|---|---|---|---|---|---|
| 2010 WM20 | 12-F | SWE | 6 | 2 | 1 | 3 | 2 | B |

**Rau, Kyle**
**b. Hoffman Estates, Illinois, United States, October 24, 1992**

| | | | | | | | | |
|---|---|---|---|---|---|---|---|---|
| 2012 WM20 | 20-F | USA | 6 | 3 | 2 | 5 | 4 | 7th |

**Rautensilds, Rinalds**
**b. Riga, Latvia, January 15, 1993**

| | | | | | | | | |
|---|---|---|---|---|---|---|---|---|
| 2010 WM18 | 22-F | LAT | 6 | 0 | 0 | 0 | 2 | 9th |

**Rautiainen, Teemu**
**b. Nurmijarvi, Finland, March 13, 1992**

| | | | | | | | | |
|---|---|---|---|---|---|---|---|---|
| 2010 WM18 | 25-F | FIN | 5 | 1 | 1 | 2 | 0 | B |

**Raux, Damien**
**b. Rouen, France, November 3, 1984**

| | | | | | | | | |
|---|---|---|---|---|---|---|---|---|
| 2008 WM | 20-F | FRA | 2 | 0 | 0 | 0 | 0 | 14th |
| 2009 WM | 20-F | FRA | 3 | 0 | 0 | 0 | 2 | 12th |
| 2010 WM | 82-F | FRA | 6 | 0 | 0 | 0 | 0 | 14th |
| 2011 WM | 82-F | FRA | 6 | 0 | 1 | 1 | 4 | 12th |
| 2012 WM | 28-F | FRA | 7 | 0 | 0 | 0 | 0 | 9th |
| **Totals WM** | | | **24** | **0** | **1** | **1** | **6** | **—** |

**Raymond, Mason**
**b. Cochrane, Alberta, Canada, September 17, 1985**

| | | | | | | | | |
|---|---|---|---|---|---|---|---|---|
| 2010 WM | 11-F | CAN | 3 | 0 | 1 | 1 | 0 | 7th |

**Razingar, Tomaz**
**b. Jesenice, Yugoslavia (Slovenia), April 25, 1979**

| | | | | | | | | |
|---|---|---|---|---|---|---|---|---|
| 2002 WM | 9-F | SLO | 6 | 3 | 3 | 6 | 6 | 13th |
| 2003 WM | 9-F | SLO | 6 | 3 | 1 | 4 | 2 | 15th |
| 2005 WM | 9-F | SLO | 5 | 1 | 2 | 3 | 6 | 13th |
| 2006 WM | 9-F | SLO | 6 | 2 | 4 | 6 | 2 | 16th |
| 2008 WM | 9-F | SLO | 5 | 0 | 3 | 3 | 0 | 15th |
| 2011 WM | 9-F | SLO | 6 | 3 | 1 | 4 | 4 | 16th |
| **Totals WM** | | | **34** | **12** | **14** | **26** | **20** | **—** |

**Rebek, Jeremy**
**b. Sault Ste. Marie, Ontario, Canada, February 8, 1976**

| | | | | | | | | |
|---|---|---|---|---|---|---|---|---|
| 2007 WM | 27-D | AUT | 6 | 0 | 1 | 1 | 2 | 15th |
| 2009 WM | 27-D | AUT | 6 | 0 | 0 | 0 | 4 | 14th |
| **Totals WM** | | | **12** | **0** | **1** | **1** | **6** | **—** |

**Rebolj, Miha**
**b. Jesenice, Yugoslavia (Slovenia), September 22, 1977**

| | | | | | | | | |
|---|---|---|---|---|---|---|---|---|
| 2002 WM | 27-D | SLO | 5 | 0 | 0 | 0 | 2 | 13th |
| 2003 WM | 27-D | SLO | 6 | 0 | 0 | 0 | 6 | 15th |
| 2005 WM | 27-D | SLO | 3 | 0 | 0 | 0 | 2 | 13th |
| 2008 WM | 27-D | SLO | 5 | 0 | 0 | 0 | 8 | 15th |
| **Totals WM** | | | **19** | **0** | **0** | **0** | **18** | **—** |

**Redlihs, Jekabs**
**b. Riga, Soviet Union (Latvia), March 29, 1982**

| | | | | | | | | |
|---|---|---|---|---|---|---|---|---|
| 2008 WM | 20-D | LAT | 4 | 0 | 0 | 0 | 2 | 11th |
| 2010 WM | 25-D | LAT | 6 | 0 | 1 | 1 | 4 | 11th |
| 2011 WM | 25-D | LAT | 6 | 1 | 1 | 2 | 4 | 13th |
| **Totals WM** | | | **16** | **1** | **2** | **3** | **10** | **—** |

**Redlihs, Krisjanis**
**b. Riga, Soviet Union (Latvia), January 15, 1981**

| | | | | | | | | |
|---|---|---|---|---|---|---|---|---|
| 2002 WM | 25-D | LAT | 6 | 0 | 1 | 1 | 0 | 11th |
| 2003 WM | 25-D | LAT | 6 | 0 | 0 | 0 | 2 | 9th |
| 2004 WM | 25-D | LAT | 7 | 0 | 0 | 0 | 2 | 7th |
| 2006 OG-M | 25-D | LAT | 5 | 0 | 0 | 0 | 2 | 12th |
| 2008 WM | 25-D | LAT | 6 | 0 | 0 | 0 | 10 | 11th |
| 2009 WM | 26-D | LAT | 7 | 1 | 0 | 1 | 2 | 7th |
| 2010 OG-M | 26-D | LAT | 4 | 0 | 1 | 1 | 2 | 12th |
| 2011 WM | 26-D | LAT | 4 | 1 | 0 | 1 | 2 | 13th |
| 2012 WM | 26-D | LAT | 7 | 1 | 0 | 1 | 0 | 10th |
| **Totals WM** | | | **43** | **3** | **1** | **4** | **18** | **—** |
| **Totals OG-M** | | | **9** | **0** | **1** | **1** | **4** | **—** |

**Redlihs, Mikelis**
**b. Riga, Soviet Union (Russia), July 1, 1984**

| | | | | | | | | |
|---|---|---|---|---|---|---|---|---|
| 2005 WM | 24-F | LAT | 6 | 0 | 1 | 1 | 0 | 9th |
| 2006 OG-M | 24-F | LAT | 5 | 1 | 0 | 1 | 4 | 12th |
| 2006 WM | 24-F | LAT | 6 | 0 | 2 | 2 | 6 | 10th |
| 2007 WM | 24-F | LAT | 6 | 1 | 3 | 4 | 0 | 13th |
| 2008 WM | 24-F | LAT | 6 | 2 | 1 | 3 | 12 | 11th |
| 2009 WM | 19-F | LAT | 7 | 0 | 2 | 2 | 6 | 7th |
| 2010 OG-M | 24-F | LAT | 4 | 1 | 0 | 1 | 4 | 12th |
| 2010 WM | 24-F | LAT | 3 | 0 | 0 | 0 | 2 | 11th |
| 2011 WM | 24-F | LAT | 6 | 1 | 6 | 7 | 4 | 13th |
| 2012 WM | 24-F | LAT | 7 | 1 | 0 | 1 | 4 | 10th |
| **Totals WM** | | | **47** | **5** | **15** | **20** | **34** | **—** |
| **Totals OG-M** | | | **9** | **2** | **0** | **2** | **8** | **—** |

**Regin, Peter**
**b. Herning, Denmark, April 16, 1986**

| | | | | | | | | |
|---|---|---|---|---|---|---|---|---|
| 2004 WM18 | 9-F | DEN | 6 | 5 | 4 | 9 | 0 | 8th |
| 2005 WM | 12-F | DEN | 6 | 0 | 3 | 3 | 0 | 14th |
| 2006 WM | 12-F | DEN | 6 | 0 | 0 | 0 | 8 | 13th |
| 2007 WM | 9-F | DEN | 5 | 3 | 3 | 6 | 6 | 10th |
| 2008 WM | 93-F | DEN | 6 | 2 | 1 | 3 | 4 | 12th |
| 2009 WM | 93-F | DEN | 6 | 1 | 0 | 1 | 4 | 13th |
| 2010 WM | 93-F | DEN | 7 | 2 | 5 | 7 | 6 | 8th |
| **Totals WM** | | | **36** | **8** | **12** | **20** | **28** | **—** |

**Reichel, Johannes**
**b. Klagenfurt, Austria, April 29, 1982**

| | | | | | | | | |
|---|---|---|---|---|---|---|---|---|
| 2011 WM | 17-D | AUT | 6 | 0 | 0 | 0 | 2 | 15th |

**Reichert, Marc**
**b. Berne, Switzerland, March 22, 1980**

| | | | | | | | | |
|---|---|---|---|---|---|---|---|---|
| 1998 WM20 | 18-F | SUI | 7 | 0 | 1 | 1 | 4 | B |
| 1999 WM20 | 18-F | SUI | 6 | 1 | 1 | 2 | 2 | 9th |
| 2000 WM20 | 18-F | SUI | 7 | 0 | 3 | 3 | 0 | 6th |
| 2001 WM | 36-F | SUI | 6 | 1 | 2 | 3 | 2 | 9th |
| 2002 WM | 36-F | SUI | 6 | 0 | 1 | 1 | 2 | 10th |
| 2004 WM | 36-F | SUI | 4 | 1 | 0 | 1 | 2 | 8th |
| 2006 WM | 36-F | SUI | 6 | 1 | 1 | 2 | 0 | 9th |
| 2007 WM | 36-F | SUI | 7 | 1 | 2 | 3 | 6 | 8th |
| 2008 WM | 36-F | SUI | 7 | 1 | 0 | 1 | 2 | 7th |
| **Totals WM20** | | | **20** | **1** | **5** | **6** | **6** | **B** |
| **Totals WM** | | | **36** | **5** | **6** | **11** | **14** | **—** |

**Reid, Adam**
**b. Chino Hills, California, United States, January 29, 1993**

| | | | | | | | | |
|---|---|---|---|---|---|---|---|---|
| 2011 WM18 | 9-F | USA | 6 | 2 | 0 | 2 | 4 | G |

**Reimer, Dennis**
**b. Herford, Germany, June 6, 1993**

| | | | | | | | | |
|---|---|---|---|---|---|---|---|---|
| 2011 WM18 | 20-F | GER | 6 | 0 | 1 | 1 | 2 | 6th |

**Reimer, Patrick**
**b. Mindelheim, Germany, December 10, 1982**

| | | | | | | | | |
|---|---|---|---|---|---|---|---|---|
| 2011 WM | 37-F | GER | 7 | 2 | 1 | 3 | 4 | 7th |
| 2012 WM | 37-F | GER | 7 | 3 | 2 | 5 | 2 | 12th |
| **Totals WM** | | | **14** | **5** | **3** | **8** | **6** | **—** |

**Reinhart, Max**
**b. Vancouver, British Columbia, Canada, February 4, 1992**

| | | | | | | | | |
|---|---|---|---|---|---|---|---|---|
| 2010 WM18 | 14-F | CAN | 6 | 0 | 1 | 1 | 39 | 7th |

**Reinhart, Sam**
**b. West Vancouver, British Columbia, Canada, November 6, 1995**

| | | | | | | | | |
|---|---|---|---|---|---|---|---|---|
| 2012 WM18 | 23-F | CAN | 7 | 2 | 4 | 6 | 0 | B |

**Reiss, Andre**
**b. Hannover, West Germany (Germany), May 17, 1986**

| | | | | | | | | |
|---|---|---|---|---|---|---|---|---|
| 2005 WM20 | 20-F | GER | 6 | 1 | 0 | 1 | 10 | 9th |
| 2008 WM | 63-D | GER | 3 | 0 | 0 | 0 | 2 | 10th |

**Rekis, Arvids**
**b. Jurmala, Soviet Union (Latvia), January 1, 1979**

| | | | | | | | | |
|---|---|---|---|---|---|---|---|---|
| 2003 WM | 3-D | LAT | 6 | 0 | 0 | 0 | 4 | 9th |
| 2004 WM | 3-D | LAT | 7 | 1 | 1 | 2 | 12 | 7th |
| 2006 OG-M | 3-D | LAT | 5 | 0 | 0 | 0 | 6 | 12th |
| 2006 WM | 3-D | LAT | 6 | 1 | 0 | 1 | 4 | 10th |
| 2007 WM | 3-D | LAT | 4 | 0 | 0 | 0 | 2 | 13th |
| 2008 WM | 3-D | LAT | 6 | 0 | 0 | 0 | 10 | 11th |
| 2010 OG-M | 3-D | LAT | 4 | 0 | 0 | 0 | 10 | 12th |
| 2010 WM | 3-D | LAT | 6 | 1 | 0 | 1 | 2 | 11th |
| 2011 WM | 3-D | LAT | 6 | 0 | 2 | 2 | 10 | 13th |
| **Totals WM** | | | **41** | **3** | **3** | **6** | **44** | **—** |
| **Totals OG-M** | | | **9** | **0** | **0** | **0** | **16** | **—** |

**Rekonen, Aleksi**
**b. Helsinki, Finland, July 23, 1993**

| | | | | | | | | |
|---|---|---|---|---|---|---|---|---|
| 2011 WM18 | 19-F | FIN | 6 | 0 | 0 | 0 | 0 | 5th |

**Rempel, Brendan**
**b. Willington, Connecticut, United States, April 24, 1991**

| | | | | | | | | |
|---|---|---|---|---|---|---|---|---|
| 2009 WM18 | 2-D | USA | 7 | 1 | 1 | 2 | 0 | G |

**Rensfeldt, Ludvig**
**b. Gavle, Sweden, January 29, 1992**

| | | | | | | | | |
|---|---|---|---|---|---|---|---|---|
| 2010 WM18 | 16-F | SWE | 6 | 6 | 6 | 12 | 4 | S |
| 2012 WM20 | 23-F | SWE | 6 | 1 | 5 | 6 | 6 | G |

**Renz, Andreas**
**b. Villingen-Schwenningen, Germany, June 12, 1977**

| | | | | | | | | |
|---|---|---|---|---|---|---|---|---|
| 1995 WM20 | 7-D | GER | 7 | 0 | 0 | 0 | 6 | 8th |
| 1996 WM20 | 7-D | GER | 6 | 0 | 1 | 1 | 4 | 8th |
| 1997 WM20 | 7-D | GER | 6 | 0 | 0 | 0 | 6 | 9th |
| 2001 WM | 31-D | GER | 7 | 0 | 0 | 0 | 8 | 5th |
| 2002 OG-M | 31-D | GER | 7 | 0 | 0 | 0 | 8 | 8th |
| 2002 WM | 31-D | GER | 7 | 0 | 0 | 0 | 6 | 8th |
| 2003 WM | 31-D | GER | 7 | 0 | 0 | 0 | 6 | 6th |
| 2004 WM | 31-D | GER | 6 | 0 | 1 | 1 | 4 | 9th |
| 2004 WCH | 31-D | GER | 3 | 0 | 0 | 0 | 2 | 8th |
| 2005 WM | 31-D | GER | 6 | 0 | 0 | 0 | 2 | 15th |
| 2006 OG-M | 31-D | GER | 5 | 0 | 0 | 0 | 2 | 10th |
| 2008 WM | 31-D | GER | 6 | 0 | 2 | 2 | 4 | 10th |
| 2009 WM | 31-D | GER | 6 | 0 | 0 | 0 | 8 | 15th |
| **Totals WM20** | | | **19** | **0** | **1** | **1** | **16** | **—** |
| **Totals WM** | | | **45** | **0** | **3** | **3** | **38** | **—** |
| **Totals OG-M** | | | **12** | **0** | **0** | **0** | **10** | **—** |

**Repik, Michal**
**b. Vlasim, Czechoslovakia (Czech Republic), December 31, 1988**

| | | | | | | | | |
|---|---|---|---|---|---|---|---|---|
| 2007 WM20 | 26-F | CZE | 6 | 0 | 0 | 0 | 0 | 5th |

**Reul, Denis**
**b. Marktredwitz, West Germany (Germany), June 29, 1989**

| | | | | | | | | |
|---|---|---|---|---|---|---|---|---|
| 2006 WM18 | 3-D | GER | 6 | 0 | 2 | 2 | 6 | 8th |
| 2007 WM18 | 10-D | GER | 6 | 1 | 3 | 4 | 4 | 8th |
| 2009 WM20 | 10-D | GER | 6 | 0 | 0 | 0 | 27 | 9th |
| 2011 WM | 2-D | GER | 3 | 0 | 0 | 0 | 2 | 7th |
| 2012 WM | 2-D | GER | 7 | 0 | 0 | 0 | 12 | 12th |
| Totals WM18 | | | 12 | 1 | 5 | 6 | 10 | — |
| **Totals WM** | | | **10** | **0** | **0** | **0** | **14** | **—** |

**Revenko, Igor**
**b. Minsk, Belarus, May 2, 1990**

| | | | | | | | | |
|---|---|---|---|---|---|---|---|---|
| 2008 WM18 | 8-F | BLR | 6 | 3 | 8 | 11 | 6 | 9th |

**Rexha, Alban**
**b. Signau, Switzerland, October 9, 1992**

| | | | | | | | | |
|---|---|---|---|---|---|---|---|---|
| 2010 WM18 | 9-F | SUI | 6 | 0 | 1 | 1 | 4 | 5th |

**Reznicek, Dalibor**
**b. Uhersky Brod, Czechoslovakia (Czech Republic), August 25, 1991**

| | | | | | | | | |
|---|---|---|---|---|---|---|---|---|
| 2011 WM20 | 7-D | CZE | 6 | 0 | 0 | 0 | 2 | 7th |

**Ribbenstrand, Alexander**
**b. Stockholm, Sweden, January 9, 1987**

| | | | | | | | | |
|---|---|---|---|---|---|---|---|---|
| 2005 WM18 | 6-D | SWE | 7 | 0 | 1 | 1 | 8 | B |
| 2007 WM20 | 7-D | SWE | 7 | 0 | 0 | 0 | 12 | 4th |

**Richard, Tanner**
**b. Markham, Ontario, Canada, April 6, 1993**

| | | | | | | | | |
|---|---|---|---|---|---|---|---|---|
| 2011 WM18 | 9-F | SUI | 6 | 4 | 1 | 5 | 2 | 7th |
| 2012 WM20 | 29-F | SUI | 6 | 2 | 2 | 4 | 6 | 8th |

**Richards, Brad**
**b. Montague, Prince Edward Island, May 2, 1980**

| | | | | | | | | |
|---|---|---|---|---|---|---|---|---|
| 2000 WM20 | 9-F | CAN | 7 | 1 | 1 | 2 | 0 | B |
| 2001 WM | 9-F | CAN | 7 | 3 | 3 | 6 | 0 | 5th |
| 2004 WCH | 39-F | CAN | 6 | 1 | 3 | 4 | 0 | 1st |
| 2006 OG-M | 39-F | CAN | 6 | 2 | 2 | 4 | 6 | 7th |

**Richards, Mike**
**b. Kenora, Ontario, Canada, February 11, 1985**

| | | | | | | | | |
|---|---|---|---|---|---|---|---|---|
| 2004 WM20 | 18-F | CAN | 6 | 2 | 3 | 5 | 2 | S |
| 2005 WM20 | 18-F | CAN | 6 | 1 | 4 | 5 | 2 | G |
| 2006 WM | 18-F | CAN | 9 | 3 | 2 | 5 | 10 | 4th |
| 2010 OG-M | 18-F | CAN | 7 | 2 | 3 | 5 | 0 | G |
| **Totals WM20** | | | **12** | **3** | **7** | **10** | **4** | **G,S** |

**Rieder, Tobias**
**b. Landshut, Germany, January 10, 1993**

| | | | | | | | | |
|---|---|---|---|---|---|---|---|---|
| 2009 WM18 | 23-F | GER | 6 | 1 | 3 | 4 | 8 | 10th |
| 2011 WM18 | 22-F | GER | 3 | 3 | 0 | 3 | 0 | 6th |
| 2011 WM20 | 16-F | GER | 6 | 1 | 1 | 2 | 0 | 10th |
| **Totals WM18** | | | **9** | **4** | **3** | **7** | **8** | **—** |

**Riefers, Philip**
**b. Krefeld, West Germany (Germany), March 15, 1990**

| | | | | | | | | |
|---|---|---|---|---|---|---|---|---|
| 2008 WM18 | 25-F | GER | 6 | 0 | 1 | 1 | 4 | 5th |

**Riekstins, Daniels**
**b. Riga, Latvia, October 1, 1994**

| | | | | | | | | |
|---|---|---|---|---|---|---|---|---|
| 2012 WM18 | 19-F | LAT | 6 | 0 | 0 | 0 | 29 | 9th |

**Rielly, Morgan**
**b. West Vancouver, British Columbia, Canada, March 9, 1994**

| | | | | | | | | |
|---|---|---|---|---|---|---|---|---|
| 2011 WM18 | 4-D | CAN | 7 | 2 | 1 | 3 | 0 | 4th |

**Riha, Jiri**
**b. Opocno, Czech Republic, September 18, 1992**

| | | | | | | | | |
|---|---|---|---|---|---|---|---|---|
| 2012 WM20 | 4-D | CZE | 6 | 1 | 1 | 2 | 10 | 5th |

**Riikola, Simo-Pekka**
**b. Joensuu, Finland, February 3, 1992**

| | | | | | | | | |
|---|---|---|---|---|---|---|---|---|
| 2010 WM18 | 2-D | FIN | 6 | 0 | 0 | 0 | 0 | B |
| 2012 WM20 | 3-D | FIN | 6 | 0 | 0 | 0 | 8 | 4th |

**Riska, Filip**
**b. Pedersore, Finland, May 13, 1985**

| | | | | | | | | |
|---|---|---|---|---|---|---|---|---|
| 2005 WM20 | 13-F | FIN | 6 | 0 | 0 | 0 | 0 | 5th |

**Rissanen, Rasmus**
**b. Kuopio, Finland, July 13, 1991**

| | | | | | | | | |
|---|---|---|---|---|---|---|---|---|
| 2008 WM18 | 24-D | FIN | 6 | 0 | 2 | 2 | 18 | 6th |
| 2009 WM18 | 8-D | FIN | 6 | 0 | 0 | 0 | 10 | B |
| 2011 WM20 | 8-D | FIN | 6 | 0 | 0 | 0 | 14 | 6th |
| **Totals WM18** | | | **12** | **0** | **2** | **2** | **28** | **—** |

**Ristolainen, Rasmus**
**b. Turku, Finland, October 27, 1994**

| | | | | | | | | |
|---|---|---|---|---|---|---|---|---|
| 2012 WM18 | 6-D | FIN | 7 | 2 | 1 | 3 | 10 | 4th |
| 2012 WM20 | 5-D | FIN | 7 | 0 | 3 | 3 | 0 | 4th |

**Ritchie, Brett**
**b. Orangeville, Ontario, Canada, July 1, 1993**

| | | | | | | | | |
|---|---|---|---|---|---|---|---|---|
| 2011 WM18 | 20-F | CAN | 7 | 4 | 3 | 7 | 6 | 4th |

**Ritola, Mattias**
**b. Borlange, Sweden, March 14, 1987**

| | | | | | | | | |
|---|---|---|---|---|---|---|---|---|
| 2005 WM18 | 17-F | SWE | 7 | 1 | 3 | 4 | 8 | B |
| 2006 WM20 | 21-F | SWE | 6 | 2 | 2 | 4 | 4 | 5th |

**Ritter, Toni**
**b. Bad Muskau, West Germany (Germany), February 6, 1990**

| | | | | | | | | |
|---|---|---|---|---|---|---|---|---|
| 2008 WM18 | 17-F | GER | 6 | 2 | 1 | 3 | 2 | 5th |
| 2009 WM20 | 22-F | GER | 6 | 1 | 1 | 2 | 4 | 9th |

**Rivera, Christopher**
**b. Geneva, Switzerland, October 2, 1986**

| | | | | | | | | |
|---|---|---|---|---|---|---|---|---|
| 2006 WM20 | 26-F | SUI | 6 | 0 | 0 | 0 | 0 | 7th |

**Robak, Colby**
**b. Dauphin, Manitoba, Canada, April 24, 1990**

| | | | | | | | | |
|---|---|---|---|---|---|---|---|---|
| 2008 WM18 | 24-D | CAN | 7 | 0 | 1 | 1 | 8 | G |

**Robar, Mitja**
**b. Maribor, Yugoslavia (Slovenia), January 4, 1983**

| | | | | | | | | |
|---|---|---|---|---|---|---|---|---|
| 2005 WM | 5-D | SLO | 6 | 0 | 0 | 0 | 6 | 13th |
| 2006 WM | 37-D | SLO | 6 | 0 | 0 | 0 | 25 | 16th |
| 2008 WM | 37-D | SLO | 5 | 1 | 1 | 2 | 4 | 15th |
| 2011 WM | 51-D | SLO | 6 | 0 | 2 | 2 | 4 | 16th |
| **Totals WM** | | | **23** | **1** | **3** | **4** | **39** | **—** |

**Rocco, Vincent**
**b. Woodbridge, Ontario, Canada, June 26, 1987**

| | | | | | | | | |
|---|---|---|---|---|---|---|---|---|
| 2012 WM | 88-F | ITA | 7 | 0 | 1 | 1 | 4 | 15th |

**Rodin, Anton**
**b. Stockholm, Sweden, November 21, 1990**

| | | | | | | | | |
|---|---|---|---|---|---|---|---|---|
| 2010 WM20 | 18-F | SWE | 6 | 3 | 7 | 10 | 2 | B |

**Rodman, David**
**b. Jesenice, Yugoslavia (Slovenia), September 10, 1983**

| | | | | | | | | |
|---|---|---|---|---|---|---|---|---|
| 2005 WM | 12-F | SLO | 6 | 0 | 0 | 0 | 2 | 13th |
| 2006 WM | 12-D | SLO | 6 | 0 | 0 | 0 | 16 | 16th |
| 2008 WM | 12-F | SLO | 5 | 1 | 1 | 2 | 6 | 15th |
| 2011 WM | 12-F | SLO | 6 | 1 | 3 | 4 | 2 | 16th |
| **Totals WM** | | | **23** | **2** | **4** | **6** | **26** | **—** |

**Rodman, Marcel**
**b. Jesenice, Yugoslavia (Slovenia), September 25, 1981**

| | | | | | | | | |
|---|---|---|---|---|---|---|---|---|
| 2002 WM | 22-F | SLO | 6 | 6 | 1 | 7 | 2 | 13th |
| 2003 WM | 22-F | SLO | 6 | 1 | 1 | 2 | 0 | 15th |
| 2005 WM | 22-F | SLO | 6 | 1 | 2 | 3 | 0 | 13th |
| 2006 WM | 22-D | SLO | 6 | 0 | 4 | 4 | 6 | 16th |
| 2008 WM | 22-F | SLO | 5 | 0 | 1 | 1 | 6 | 15th |
| 2011 WM | 22-F | SLO | 6 | 0 | 3 | 3 | 4 | 16th |
| **Totals WM** | | | **35** | **8** | **12** | **20** | **18** | **—** |

**Roest, Niklas**
**b. Oslo, Norway, August 3, 1986**

| | | | | | | | | |
|---|---|---|---|---|---|---|---|---|
| 2006 WM20 | 28-F | NOR | 6 | 0 | 0 | 0 | 6 | 10th |

**Rohac, Ivan**
**b. Liptovsky Mikulas, Czechoslovakia (Slovakia), March 25, 1988**

| | | | | | | | | |
|---|---|---|---|---|---|---|---|---|
| 2006 WM18 | 9-F | SVK | 6 | 3 | 2 | 5 | 0 | 7th |
| 2008 WM20 | 12-F | SVK | 6 | 3 | 2 | 5 | 6 | 7th |

**Rokseth, Daniel**
**b. Oslo, Norway, August 15, 1991**

| | | | | | | | | |
|---|---|---|---|---|---|---|---|---|
| 2011 WM20 | 27-D | NOR | 6 | 0 | 0 | 0 | 6 | 9th |

**Rolinek, Tomas**
**b. Nove mesto na Morave, Czechoslovakia (Czech Republic), February 17, 1980**

| | | | | | | | | |
|---|---|---|---|---|---|---|---|---|
| 2006 WM | 60-F | CZE | 8 | 0 | 0 | 0 | 2 | S |
| 2007 WM | 60-F | CZE | 3 | 0 | 0 | 0 | 0 | 7th |
| 2008 WM | 60-F | CZE | 7 | 2 | 1 | 3 | 2 | 5th |
| 2009 WM | 60-F | CZE | 7 | 1 | 2 | 3 | 10 | 6th |
| 2010 OG-M | 60-F | CZE | 5 | 1 | 0 | 1 | 0 | 7th |
| 2010 WM | 60-F | CZE | 9 | 4 | 1 | 5 | 12 | G |
| 2011 WM | 60-F | CZE | 9 | 1 | 2 | 3 | 6 | B |
| **Totals WM** | | | **43** | **8** | **6** | **14** | **32** | **G,S,B** |

**Roman, Ondrej**
**b. Ostrava, Czechoslovakia (Czech Republic), February 8, 1989**

| | | | | | | | | |
|---|---|---|---|---|---|---|---|---|
| 2006 WM18 | 16-F | CZE | 7 | 0 | 1 | 1 | 2 | B |
| 2007 WM18 | 16-F | CZE | 6 | 2 | 4 | 6 | 0 | 9th |
| 2009 WM20 | 10-F | CZE | 6 | 4 | 4 | 8 | 0 | 6th |
| **Totals WM18** | | | **13** | **2** | **5** | **7** | **2** | **B** |

**Romand, Jeremie**
**b. Sallanches, France, February 28, 1988**

| | | | | | | | | |
|---|---|---|---|---|---|---|---|---|
| 2011 WM | 17-F | FRA | 6 | 0 | 0 | 0 | 4 | 12th |

**Romanov, Konstantin**
**b. Moscow, Soviet Union (Russia), March 14, 1985**

| | | | | | | | | |
|---|---|---|---|---|---|---|---|---|
| 2012 WM | 85-F | KAZ | 7 | 0 | 0 | 0 | 4 | 16th |

**Romy, Kevin**
**b. La Chaux-de-Fonds, Switzerland, January 31, 1985**

| | | | | | | | | |
|---|---|---|---|---|---|---|---|---|
| 2002 WM18 | 21-F | SUI | 8 | 9 | 5 | 14 | 4 | 7th |
| 2003 WM18 | 21-F | SUI | 6 | 4 | 8 | 12 | 4 | 9th |
| 2003 WM20 | 21-F | SUI | 6 | 2 | 3 | 5 | 0 | 7th |
| 2004 WM20 | 21-F | SUI | 1 | 0 | 0 | 0 | 0 | 8th |
| 2005 WM20 | 21-F | SUI | 6 | 3 | 2 | 5 | 8 | 8th |
| 2005 WM | 88-F | SUI | 7 | 0 | 0 | 0 | 0 | 8th |
| 2006 WM | 88-F | SUI | 6 | 0 | 0 | 0 | 2 | 9th |
| 2009 WM | 88-F | SUI | 6 | 0 | 0 | 0 | 0 | 9th |
| 2010 WM | 88-F | SUI | 7 | 0 | 1 | 1 | 4 | 5th |
| 2012 WM | 88-F | SUI | 7 | 1 | 5 | 6 | 2 | 11th |
| **Totals WM18** | | | **14** | **13** | **13** | **26** | **8** | **—** |
| **Totals WM20** | | | **13** | **5** | **5** | **10** | **8** | **—** |
| **Totals WM** | | | **33** | **1** | **6** | **7** | **8** | **—** |

**Roppo, Antti**
**b. Tampere, Finland, February 9, 1989**

| | | | | | | | | |
|---|---|---|---|---|---|---|---|---|
| 2007 WM18 | 13-F | FIN | 6 | 0 | 1 | 1 | 25 | 7th |
| 2009 WM20 | 19-F | FIN | 6 | 2 | 1 | 3 | 0 | 7th |

**Rosinskis, Rinalds**
**b. August 18, 1994**

| | | | | | | | | |
|---|---|---|---|---|---|---|---|---|
| 2012 WM18 | 2-D | LAT | 6 | 0 | 0 | 0 | 18 | 9th |

**Rosseli Olsen, Mats**
**b. Oslo, Norway, April 29, 1991**

| | | | | | | | | |
|---|---|---|---|---|---|---|---|---|
| 2009 WM18 | 15-F | NOR | 6 | 1 | 5 | 6 | 10 | 9th |
| 2011 WM20 | 21-F | NOR | 6 | 0 | 1 | 1 | 18 | 9th |
| 2012 WM | 51-F | NOR | 5 | 0 | 0 | 0 | 0 | 8th |

**Rossi, Matthias**
**b. Menzingen, Switzerland, January 9, 1991**

| | | | | | | | | |
|---|---|---|---|---|---|---|---|---|
| 2009 WM18 | 28-F | SUI | 6 | 1 | 0 | 1 | 2 | 8th |

**Roste Fossen, Petter**
**b. Kongsberg, Norway, February 16, 1991**

| | | | | | | | | |
|---|---|---|---|---|---|---|---|---|
| 2009 WM18 | 26-F | NOR | 6 | 1 | 0 | 1 | 2 | 9th |
| 2011 WM20 | 11-F | NOR | 6 | 1 | 0 | 1 | 6 | 9th |

**Roth, Vladimir**
**b. Prague, Czechoslovakia (Czech Republic), June 25, 1990**

| | | | | | | | | |
|---|---|---|---|---|---|---|---|---|
| 2007 WM18 | 15-D | CZE | 6 | 1 | 1 | 2 | 6 | 9th |
| 2010 WM20 | 15-D | CZE | 6 | 2 | 4 | 6 | 0 | 7th |

**Rotter, Rafael**
**b. Vienna, Austria, June 14, 1987**

| | | | | | | | | |
|---|---|---|---|---|---|---|---|---|
| 2011 WM | 6-F | AUT | 6 | 1 | 1 | 2 | 2 | 15th |

**Rouiller, Anthony**
**b. February 14, 1994**

| | | | | | | | | |
|---|---|---|---|---|---|---|---|---|
| 2012 WM18 | 7-D | SUI | 6 | 0 | 2 | 2 | 2 | 7th |

**Rouleau, Alexandre**
**b. Mont Laurier, Quebec, Canada, July 29, 1983**

| | | | | | | | | |
|---|---|---|---|---|---|---|---|---|
| 2012 WM | 32-D | FRA | 7 | 1 | 1 | 2 | 6 | 9th |

**Rousek, Tomas**
**b. Ceske Budejovice, Czech Republic, September 9, 1993**

| | | | | | | | | |
|---|---|---|---|---|---|---|---|---|
| 2011 WM18 | 16-F | CZE | 6 | 2 | 0 | 2 | 6 | 8th |

**Roussel, Antoine**
**b. Roubaix, France, November 21, 1989**

| | | | | | | | | |
|---|---|---|---|---|---|---|---|---|
| 2012 WM | 54-F | FRA | 7 | 1 | 2 | 3 | 6 | 9th |

**Roussel, Thomas**
**b. Amiens, France, November 25, 1985**

| | | | | | | | | |
|---|---|---|---|---|---|---|---|---|
| 2009 WM | 38-D | FRA | 6 | 0 | 1 | 1 | 2 | 12th |
| 2010 WM | 38-D | FRA | 6 | 0 | 0 | 0 | 2 | 14th |
| 2011 WM | 38-D | FRA | 6 | 0 | 0 | 0 | 6 | 12th |
| **Totals WM** | | | **18** | **0** | **1** | **1** | **10** | **—** |

**Roy, Derek**
**b. Ottawa, Ontario, Canada, May 4, 1983**

| | | | | | | | | |
|---|---|---|---|---|---|---|---|---|
| 2003 WM20 | 21-F | CAN | 6 | 1 | 2 | 3 | 4 | S |
| 2008 WM | 9-F | CAN | 9 | 5 | 5 | 10 | 6 | S |
| 2009 WM | 9-F | CAN | 9 | 4 | 4 | 8 | 4 | S |
| **Totals WM** | | | **18** | **9** | **9** | **18** | **10** | **2S** |

**Roymark, Martin**
**b. Oslo, Norway, November 10, 1986**

| | | | | | | | | |
|---|---|---|---|---|---|---|---|---|
| 2004 WM18 | 12-F | NOR | 6 | 0 | 3 | 3 | 2 | 10th |
| 2006 WM20 | 13-F | NOR | 6 | 0 | 1 | 1 | 4 | 10th |
| 2008 WM | 22-F | NOR | 7 | 0 | 1 | 1 | 2 | 8th |
| 2009 WM | 22-F | NOR | 6 | 0 | 0 | 0 | 0 | 11th |
| 2010 OG-M | 22-F | NOR | 4 | 0 | 0 | 0 | 0 | 10th |
| 2010 WM | 22-F | NOR | 6 | 0 | 1 | 1 | 4 | 9th |
| 2011 WM | 22-F | NOR | 7 | 1 | 2 | 3 | 2 | 6th |
| 2012 WM | 22-F | NOR | 8 | 1 | 0 | 1 | 8 | 8th |
| **Totals WM** | | | **34** | **2** | **4** | **6** | **16** | **—** |

**Rozenthal, Francois**
**b. Dunkirk, France, June 20, 1975**

| | | | | | | | | |
|---|---|---|---|---|---|---|---|---|
| 1996 WM | 14-F | FRA | 7 | 4 | 1 | 5 | 2 | 11th |
| 1998 OG-M | 18-F | FRA | 2 | 0 | 0 | 0 | 0 | 11th |
| 1998 WM | 14-F | FRA | 3 | 0 | 0 | 0 | 0 | 13th |
| 1999 WM | 11-F | FRA | 3 | 0 | 0 | 0 | 0 | 15th |
| 2000 WM | 11-F | FRA | 6 | 1 | 1 | 2 | 0 | 15th |
| 2002 OG-M | 11-F | FRA | 4 | 0 | 0 | 0 | 0 | 14th |
| 2004 WM | 11-F | FRA | 6 | 0 | 0 | 0 | 4 | 16th |
| 2008 WM | 11-F | FRA | 5 | 0 | 1 | 1 | 2 | 14th |
| 2009 WM | 11-F | FRA | 6 | 0 | 1 | 1 | 6 | 12th |
| **Totals WM** | | | **36** | **5** | **4** | **9** | **14** | **—** |
| **Totals OG-M** | | | **6** | **0** | **0** | **0** | **0** | **—** |

**Roznik, Juraj**
**b. Trencin, Czechoslovakia (Slovakia), October 14, 1992**

| | | | | | | | | |
|---|---|---|---|---|---|---|---|---|
| 2010 WM18 | 24-F | SVK | 6 | 0 | 2 | 2 | 0 | 8th |

**Rozsival, Michal**
**b. Vlasim, Czechoslovakia (Czech Republic), September 3, 1978**

| | | | | | | | | |
|---|---|---|---|---|---|---|---|---|
| 2008 WM | 28-D | CZE | 4 | 0 | 0 | 0 | 0 | 5th |
| 2010 WM | 3-D | CZE | 9 | 0 | 2 | 2 | 4 | G |
| **Totals WM** | | | **13** | **0** | **2** | **2** | **4** | **G** |

**Rubin, Daniel**
**b. Berne, Switzerland, July 29, 1985**

| | | | | | | | | |
|---|---|---|---|---|---|---|---|---|
| 2011 WM | 40-F | SUI | 3 | 0 | 0 | 0 | 2 | 9th |
| 2012 WM | 40-F | SUI | 4 | 0 | 0 | 0 | 4 | 11th |
| **Totals WM** | | | **7** | **0** | **0** | **0** | **6** | **—** |

**Ruegsegger, Tyler**
**b. Lakewood, Colorado, United States, January 19, 1988**

| | | | | | | | | |
|---|---|---|---|---|---|---|---|---|
| 2008 WM20 | 15-F | USA | 6 | 2 | 2 | 4 | 4 | 4th |

**Rumpel, Jakub**
**b. Hrnciarovce, Czechoslovakia (Slovakia), January 28, 1987**

| | | | | | | | | |
|---|---|---|---|---|---|---|---|---|
| 2007 WM20 | 29-F | SVK | 6 | 0 | 1 | 1 | 6 | 8th |

**Rundblad, David**
**b. Lycksele, Sweden, October 8, 1990**

| | | | | | | | | |
|---|---|---|---|---|---|---|---|---|
| 2008 WM18 | 3-D | SWE | 6 | 0 | 1 | 1 | 2 | 4th |
| 2009 WM20 | 7-D | SWE | 6 | 1 | 1 | 2 | 0 | S |
| 2010 WM20 | 7-D | SWE | 6 | 1 | 4 | 5 | 2 | B |
| 2011 WM | 7-D | SWE | 4 | 0 | 1 | 1 | 2 | S |
| **Totals WM20** | | | **12** | **2** | **5** | **7** | **2** | **S,B** |

**Rupprich, Steven**
**b. Berlin, West Germany (Germany), April 15, 1989**

| | | | | | | | | |
|---|---|---|---|---|---|---|---|---|
| 2007 WM18 | 22-F | GER | 6 | 2 | 1 | 3 | 4 | 8th |
| 2009 WM20 | 25-F | GER | 6 | 1 | 1 | 2 | 16 | 9th |

**Rusnak, Ondrej**
**b. Bratislava, Czechoslovakia (Slovakia), February 25, 1989**

| | | | | | | | | |
|---|---|---|---|---|---|---|---|---|
| 2007 WM18 | 15-F | SVK | 6 | 1 | 0 | 1 | 6 | 5th |
| 2009 WM20 | 15-F | SVK | 7 | 2 | 0 | 2 | 2 | 4th |

**Russell, Kris**
**b. Caroline, Alberta, Canada, May 2, 1987**

| | | | | | | | | |
|---|---|---|---|---|---|---|---|---|
| 2006 WM20 | 10-D | CAN | 6 | 1 | 3 | 4 | 4 | G |
| 2007 WM20 | 10-D | CAN | 6 | 4 | 2 | 6 | 0 | G |
| 2010 WM | 2-D | CAN | 7 | 1 | 3 | 4 | 2 | 7th |
| 2012 WM | 7-D | CAN | 4 | 0 | 3 | 3 | 2 | 5th |
| **Totals WM20** | | | **12** | **5** | **5** | **10** | **4** | **2G** |
| **Totals WM** | | | **11** | **1** | **6** | **7** | **4** | **—** |

**Russo, Robbie**
**b. Westmont, Illinois, United States, February 15, 1993**

| | | | | | | | | |
|---|---|---|---|---|---|---|---|---|
| 2011 WM18 | 8-D | USA | 6 | 1 | 7 | 8 | 4 | G |

**Rust, Bryan**
**b. Bloomfield Hills, Michigan, United States, May 11, 1992**

| | | | | | | | | |
|---|---|---|---|---|---|---|---|---|
| 2010 WM18 | 12-F | USA | 7 | 4 | 2 | 6 | 4 | G |

**Rust, Matt**
**b. Bloomfield Hills, Michigan, United States, March 23, 1989**

| | | | | | | | | |
|---|---|---|---|---|---|---|---|---|
| 2007 WM18 | 9-F | USA | 7 | 2 | 2 | 4 | 6 | S |
| 2008 WM20 | 11-F | USA | 6 | 0 | 0 | 0 | 8 | 4th |
| 2009 WM20 | 9-F | USA | 6 | 3 | 1 | 4 | 10 | 5th |
| **Totals WM20** | | | **12** | **3** | **1** | **4** | **18** | **—** |

**Ruth, Teddy**
**b. St. Charles, Massachusetts, United States, February 14, 1989**

| | | | | | | | | |
|---|---|---|---|---|---|---|---|---|
| 2007 WM18 | 5-D | USA | 7 | 0 | 1 | 1 | 0 | S |
| 2009 WM20 | 5-D | USA | 6 | 0 | 0 | 0 | 25 | 5th |

**Ruthemann, Ivo**
**b. St. Gallen, Switzerland, December 12, 1976**

| | | | | | | | | |
|---|---|---|---|---|---|---|---|---|
| 1996 WM20 | 24-F | SUI | 6 | 1 | 1 | 2 | 18 | 9th |
| 1998 WM | 11-F | SUI | 9 | 0 | 1 | 1 | 0 | 4th |
| 1999 WM | 11-F | SUI | 6 | 0 | 2 | 2 | 2 | 8th |
| 2000 WM | 32-F | SUI | 7 | 3 | 0 | 3 | 0 | 5th |
| 2002 OG-M | 32-F | SUI | 4 | 1 | 1 | 2 | 0 | 11th |
| 2002 WM | 32-F | SUI | 6 | 1 | 0 | 1 | 0 | 10th |
| 2004 WM | 32-F | SUI | 7 | 3 | 2 | 5 | 4 | 8th |
| 2005 WM | 32-F | SUI | 7 | 2 | 2 | 4 | 4 | 8th |
| 2006 OG-M | 32-F | SUI | 6 | 1 | 2 | 3 | 2 | 6th |
| 2006 WM | 32-F | SUI | 6 | 2 | 2 | 4 | 0 | 9th |
| 2007 WM | 32-F | SUI | 7 | 1 | 0 | 1 | 2 | 8th |
| 2009 WM | 32-F | SUI | 6 | 0 | 3 | 3 | 2 | 9th |
| 2010 OG-M | 32-F | SUI | 5 | 1 | 0 | 1 | 0 | 8th |
| 2010 WM | 32-F | SUI | 7 | 1 | 3 | 4 | 0 | 5th |
| 2011 WM | 32-F | SUI | 6 | 2 | 5 | 7 | 6 | 9th |
| 2012 WM | 32-F | SUI | 7 | 3 | 1 | 4 | 2 | 11th |
| **Totals WM** | | | **81** | **18** | **21** | **39** | **22** | **—** |
| **Totals OG-M** | | | **15** | **3** | **3** | **6** | **2** | **—** |

**Ruuttu, Alexander**
**b. Chicago, Illinois, United States, December 9, 1992**

| | | | | | | | | |
|---|---|---|---|---|---|---|---|---|
| 2012 WM20 | 9-F | FIN | 7 | 3 | 0 | 3 | 0 | 4th |

**Ruutu, Jarkko**
**b. Vantaa, Finland, August 23, 1975**

| | | | | | | | | |
|---|---|---|---|---|---|---|---|---|
| 1998 WM | 32-F | FIN | 10 | 1 | 0 | 1 | 16 | S |
| 2001 WM | 37-F | FIN | 9 | 1 | 0 | 1 | 10 | S |
| 2002 OG-M | 37-F | FIN | 4 | 0 | 0 | 0 | 4 | 6th |
| 2004 WM | 37-F | FIN | 6 | 0 | 0 | 0 | 20 | 6th |
| 2004 WCH | 37-F | FIN | 4 | 0 | 0 | 0 | 6 | 2nd |
| 2005 WM | 37-F | FIN | 7 | 1 | 0 | 1 | 4 | 7th |
| 2006 OG-M | 37-F | FIN | 8 | 0 | 0 | 0 | 31 | S |
| 2006 WM | 37-F | FIN | 9 | 0 | 3 | 3 | 34 | B |
| 2007 WM | 37-F | FIN | 9 | 0 | 1 | 1 | 29 | S |
| 2009 WM | 73-F | FIN | 7 | 0 | 2 | 2 | 14 | 5th |
| 2010 OG-M | 37-F | FIN | 6 | 2 | 1 | 3 | 14 | B |
| **Totals WM** | | | **57** | **3** | **6** | **9** | **127** | **3S,B** |
| **Totals OG-M** | | | **18** | **2** | **1** | **3** | **49** | **S,B** |

**Ruutu, Tuomo**
**b. Vantaa, Finland, February 16, 1983**

| | | | | | | | | |
|---|---|---|---|---|---|---|---|---|
| 2000 WM18 | 15-F | FIN | 7 | 6 | 2 | 8 | 0 | G |
| 2001 WM20 | 26-F | FIN | 7 | 1 | 3 | 4 | 4 | S |
| 2002 WM20 | 15-F | FIN | 7 | 4 | 1 | 5 | 10 | B |
| 2003 WM20 | 15-F | FIN | 7 | 2 | 8 | 10 | 6 | B |
| 2004 WCH | 15-F | FIN | 6 | 1 | 2 | 3 | 4 | 2nd |
| 2006 WM | 15-F | FIN | 9 | 0 | 0 | 0 | 49 | B |
| 2007 WM | 15-F | FIN | 8 | 3 | 3 | 6 | 20 | S |
| 2008 WM | 15-F | FIN | 9 | 4 | 2 | 6 | 8 | B |
| 2010 OG-M | 15-F | FIN | 6 | 1 | 0 | 1 | 2 | B |
| 2011 WM | 15-F | FIN | 9 | 6 | 0 | 6 | 8 | G |
| **Totals WM20** | | | **21** | **7** | **12** | **19** | **20** | **S,2B** |
| **Totals WM** | | | **35** | **13** | **5** | **18** | **85** | **G,S,2B** |

**Ruzicka, Antonin**
**b. Prague, Czech Republic, January 29, 1993**

| | | | | | | | | |
|---|---|---|---|---|---|---|---|---|
| 2011 WM18 | 23-D | CZE | 6 | 0 | 0 | 0 | 2 | 8th |

**Ruzicka, Dan**
**b. Plzen, Czechoslovakia (Czech Republic), December 31, 1991**

| | | | | | | | | |
|---|---|---|---|---|---|---|---|---|
| 2009 WM18 | 9-D | CZE | 5 | 0 | 1 | 1 | 4 | 6th |

**Ruzicka, Martin**
**b. Beroun, Czechoslovakia (Czech Republic), December 15, 1985**

| | | | | | | | | |
|---|---|---|---|---|---|---|---|---|
| 2010 WM | 27-F | CZE | 8 | 0 | 0 | 0 | 0 | G |

**Ruzicka, Stefan**
**b. Nitra, Czechoslovakia (Slovakia), February 17, 1985**

| | | | | | | | | |
|---|---|---|---|---|---|---|---|---|
| 2002 WM18 | 22-F | SVK | 8 | 3 | 0 | 3 | 2 | 8th |
| 2003 WM18 | 22-F | SVK | 7 | 5 | 3 | 8 | 2 | S |
| 2004 WM20 | 23-F | SVK | 6 | 3 | 3 | 6 | 2 | 6th |
| 2005 WM20 | 23-F | SVK | 6 | 3 | 3 | 6 | 4 | 7th |
| 2009 WM | 14-F | SVK | 6 | 2 | 1 | 3 | 2 | 10th |
| 2011 WM | 14-F | SVK | 5 | 0 | 1 | 1 | 2 | 10th |
| **Totals WM18** | | | **15** | **8** | **3** | **11** | **4** | **—** |
| **Totals WM20** | | | **12** | **6** | **6** | **12** | **6** | **—** |
| **Totals WM** | | | **11** | **2** | **2** | **4** | **4** | **—** |

**Ruzicka, Vladimir**
**b. Most, Czechoslovakia (Czech Republic), February 17, 1989**

| | | | | | | | | |
|---|---|---|---|---|---|---|---|---|
| 2006 WM18 | 17-F | CZE | 7 | 0 | 1 | 1 | 2 | B |
| 2007 WM18 | 17-F | CZE | 6 | 2 | 4 | 6 | 4 | 9th |
| 2009 WM20 | 17-F | CZE | 5 | 2 | 3 | 5 | 4 | 6th |
| **Totals WM18** | | | **13** | **2** | **5** | **7** | **6** | **B** |

**Ryadinski, Alexander**
**b. Minsk, Soviet Union (Belarus), April 1, 1978**

| | | | | | | | | |
|---|---|---|---|---|---|---|---|---|
| 2003 WM | 5-D | BLR | 6 | 0 | 2 | 2 | 4 | 14th |
| 2005 WM | 5-D | BLR | 6 | 0 | 0 | 0 | 0 | 10th |
| 2006 WM | 5-D | BLR | 4 | 0 | 0 | 0 | 2 | 6th |
| 2007 WM | 5-D | BLR | 5 | 1 | 1 | 2 | 6 | 11th |
| 2009 WM | 5-D | BLR | 7 | 0 | 0 | 0 | 8 | 8th |
| 2010 OG-M | 52-D | BLR | 4 | 0 | 1 | 1 | 2 | 9th |
| 2010 WM | 52-D | BLR | 6 | 0 | 0 | 0 | 2 | 10th |
| 2011 WM | 52-D | BLR | 5 | 0 | 0 | 0 | 4 | 14th |
| **Totals WM** | | | **39** | **1** | **3** | **4** | **26** | **—** |

**Ryan, Bobby**
**b. Cherry Hill, New Jersey, United States, March 17, 1987**

| | | | | | | | | |
|---|---|---|---|---|---|---|---|---|
| 2006 WM20 | 9-F | USA | 7 | 3 | 4 | 7 | 0 | 4th |
| 2010 OG-M | 54-F | USA | 6 | 1 | 1 | 2 | 2 | S |
| 2012 WM | 9-F | USA | 8 | 5 | 2 | 7 | 0 | 7th |

**Ryan, Kenny**
**b. Franklin, Michigan, United States, July 10, 1991**

| | | | | | | | | |
|---|---|---|---|---|---|---|---|---|
| 2009 WM18 | 26-F | USA | 7 | 4 | 1 | 5 | 6 | G |

**Ryasenski, Yevgeni**
**b. Tver, Soviet Union (Russia), July 18, 1987**

| | | | | | | | | |
|---|---|---|---|---|---|---|---|---|
| 2007 WM20 | 10-D | RUS | 6 | 1 | 3 | 4 | 6 | S |
| 2012 WM | 77-D | RUS | 7 | 0 | 1 | 1 | 0 | G |

**Rychel, Kerby**
**b. Los Angeles, California, United States, October 7, 1994**

| | | | | | | | | |
|---|---|---|---|---|---|---|---|---|
| 2012 WM18 | 12-F | CAN | 7 | 5 | 3 | 8 | 12 | B |

**Rylov, Yakov**
**b. Kirovo-Chepetsk, Soviet Union (Russia), January 15, 1985**

| | | | | | | | | |
|---|---|---|---|---|---|---|---|---|
| 2005 WM20 | 7-D | RUS | 6 | 1 | 1 | 2 | 14 | S |

**Rymarev, Yevgeni**
**b. Ust-Kamenogorsk, Soviet Union (Kazakhstan), September 9, 1988**

| | | | | | | | | |
|---|---|---|---|---|---|---|---|---|
| 2008 WM20 | 18-F | KAZ | 6 | 6 | 1 | 7 | 0 | 8th |
| 2010 WM | 88-F | KAZ | 6 | 0 | 0 | 0 | 0 | 16th |
| 2012 WM | 88-F | KAZ | 7 | 1 | 0 | 1 | 2 | 16th |
| **Totals WM** | | | **13** | **1** | **0** | **1** | **2** | **—** |

**Ryno, Johan**
**b. Orebro, Sweden, June 5, 1986**

| | | | | | | | | |
|---|---|---|---|---|---|---|---|---|
| 2006 WM20 | 29-F | SWE | 6 | 2 | 3 | 5 | 4 | 5th |

**Ryser, Sven**
**b. Durrenroth, Switzerland, July 2, 1990**

| | | | | | | | | |
|---|---|---|---|---|---|---|---|---|
| 2008 WM18 | 27-F | SUI | 6 | 3 | 1 | 4 | 2 | 8th |
| 2010 WM20 | 8-F | SUI | 7 | 0 | 2 | 2 | 4 | 4th |

**Saad, Brandon**
**b. Gibsonia, Pennsylvania, United States, October 27, 1992**

| | | | | | | | | |
|---|---|---|---|---|---|---|---|---|
| 2010 WM18 | 22-F | USA | 7 | 3 | 3 | 6 | 4 | G |
| 2012 WM20 | 22-F | USA | 6 | 1 | 5 | 6 | 0 | 7th |

**Sabinin, Gennadi**
**b. Moscow Region, Russia, September 29, 1993**

| | | | | | | | | |
|---|---|---|---|---|---|---|---|---|
| 2011 WM18 | 2-D | RUS | 7 | 0 | 0 | 0 | 2 | B |

**Sabolic, Robert**
**b. Jesenice, Yugoslavia (Slovenia), September 18, 1988**

| | | | | | | | | |
|---|---|---|---|---|---|---|---|---|
| 2011 WM | 55-F | SLO | 6 | 1 | 3 | 4 | 0 | 16th |

**Sadovik, Alexei**
**b. Novopolotsk, Soviet Union (Belarus), June 23, 1990**

| | | | | | | | | |
|---|---|---|---|---|---|---|---|---|
| 2008 WM18 | 6-D | BLR | 6 | 0 | 0 | 0 | 6 | 9th |

**Safonov, Nikolai**
**b. Chelyabinsk, Soviet Union (Russia), June 3, 1989**

| 2009 WM20 | 7-D | KAZ | 6 | 0 | 0 | 0 | 6 | 10th |
|---|---|---|---|---|---|---|---|---|

**Sailio, Jari**
**b. Hyvinkaa, Finland, March 18, 1986**

| 2004 WM18 | 14-F | FIN | 6 | 1 | 0 | 1 | 14 | 7th |
|---|---|---|---|---|---|---|---|---|
| 2006 WM20 | 21-F | FIN | 7 | 1 | 0 | 1 | 12 | B |

**Salija, Arturs**
**b. Riga, Latvia, May 15, 1992**

| 2010 WM18 | 5-D | LAT | 6 | 0 | 0 | 0 | 10 | 9th |
|---|---|---|---|---|---|---|---|---|
| 2012 WM20 | 6-D | LAT | 6 | 0 | 2 | 2 | 4 | 9th |

**Sallinen, Jere**
**b. Espoo, Finland, October 26, 1990**

| 2008 WM18 | 28-F | FIN | 6 | 2 | 1 | 3 | 31 | 6th |
|---|---|---|---|---|---|---|---|---|

**Sallinen, Tomi**
**b. Espoo, Finland, Fenruary 11, 1989**

| 2007 WM18 | 26-F | FIN | 6 | 2 | 0 | 2 | 0 | 7th |
|---|---|---|---|---|---|---|---|---|
| 2008 WM20 | 20-F | FIN | 6 | 0 | 1 | 1 | 0 | 6th |
| 2009 WM20 | 20-F | FIN | 6 | 2 | 3 | 5 | 0 | 7th |
| **Totals WM20** | | | **12** | **2** | **4** | **6** | **0** | **—** |

**Salmela, Anssi**
**b. Nokia, Finland, August 13, 1984**

| 2004 WM20 | 7-D | FIN | 7 | 1 | 2 | 3 | 6 | B |
|---|---|---|---|---|---|---|---|---|
| 2008 WM | 33-D | FIN | 8 | 0 | 0 | 0 | 37 | B |
| 2009 WM | 28-D | FIN | 7 | 1 | 0 | 1 | 2 | 5th |
| 2011 WM | 28-D | FIN | 9 | 1 | 2 | 3 | 4 | G |
| 2012 WM | 28-D | FIN | 7 | 0 | 2 | 2 | 25 | 4th |
| **Totals WM** | | | **31** | **2** | **4** | **6** | **68** | **G,B** |

**Salminen, Sakari**
**b. Pori, Finland, May 31, 1988**

| 2008 WM20 | 23-F | FIN | 6 | 1 | 3 | 4 | 4 | 6th |
|---|---|---|---|---|---|---|---|---|

**Salminen, Saku**
**b. Helsinki, Finland, October 20, 1994**

| 2012 WM18 | 16-F | FIN | 7 | 0 | 5 | 5 | 0 | 4th |
|---|---|---|---|---|---|---|---|---|

**Salmivirta, Mikael**
**b. Helsinki, Finland, February 8, 1992**

| 2010 WM18 | 15-F | FIN | 6 | 1 | 1 | 2 | 2 | B |
|---|---|---|---|---|---|---|---|---|

**Salmonsson, Johannes**
**b. Uppsala, Sweden, February 7, 1986**

| 2004 WM20 | 16-F | SWE | 6 | 0 | 1 | 1 | 4 | 7th |
|---|---|---|---|---|---|---|---|---|
| 2005 WM20 | 13-F | SWE | 6 | 5 | 3 | 8 | 0 | 6th |
| 2006 WM20 | 25-F | SWE | 5 | 2 | 2 | 4 | 4 | 5th |
| **Totals WM20** | | | **17** | **7** | **6** | **13** | **8** | **—** |

**Salo, Espen**
**b. Oslo, Norway, April 22, 1993**

| 2011 WM18 | 17-D | NOR | 6 | 1 | 2 | 3 | 4 | 9th |
|---|---|---|---|---|---|---|---|---|

**Salo, Sami**
**b. Turku, Finland, September 2, 1974**

| 2001 WM | 5-D | FIN | 9 | 3 | 6 | 9 | 6 | S |
|---|---|---|---|---|---|---|---|---|
| 2002 OG-M | 5-D | FIN | 4 | 0 | 0 | 0 | 0 | 4th |
| 2004 WM | 5-D | FIN | 7 | 0 | 3 | 3 | 0 | 6th |
| 2004 WCH | 6-D | FIN | 6 | 0 | 1 | 1 | 2 | 2nd |
| 2006 OG-M | 6-D | FIN | 6 | 1 | 3 | 4 | 0 | S |
| 2010 OG-M | 6-D | FIN | 6 | 1 | 1 | 2 | 4 | B |
| **Totals WM** | | | **16** | **3** | **9** | **12** | **6** | **S** |
| **Totals OG-M** | | | **16** | **2** | **4** | **6** | **4** | **S,B** |

**Salomaki, Miikka**
**b. Raahe, Finland, March 9, 1993**

| 2010 WM18 | 7-F | FIN | 5 | 0 | 1 | 1 | 4 | B |
|---|---|---|---|---|---|---|---|---|
| 2011 WM18 | 25-F | FIN | 6 | 4 | 2 | 6 | 2 | 5th |
| 2011 WM20 | 11-F | FIN | 6 | 2 | 1 | 3 | 14 | 6th |
| 2012 WM20 | 22-F | FIN | 7 | 3 | 3 | 6 | 4 | 4th |
| **Totals WM18** | | | **11** | **4** | **3** | **7** | **6** | **B** |
| **Totals WM20** | | | **13** | **5** | **4** | **9** | **18** | **—** |

**Salonen, Aleksi**
**b. Muurame, Finland, February 3, 1993**

| 2011 WM18 | 28-D | FIN | 6 | 0 | 3 | 3 | 4 | 5th |
|---|---|---|---|---|---|---|---|---|

**Salsten, Eirik**
**b. Hamar, Norway, June 17, 1994**

| 2011 WM18 | 23-F | NOR | 6 | 0 | 0 | 0 | 6 | 9th |
|---|---|---|---|---|---|---|---|---|

**Samokhin, Yevgeni**
**b. Minsk, Belarus, August 17, 1993**

| 2010 WM18 | 14-F | BLR | 6 | 0 | 0 | 0 | 2 | 10th |
|---|---|---|---|---|---|---|---|---|

**Samuelsson, Henrik**
**b. Leksand, Sweden, February 7, 1994**

| 2011 WM18 | 15-F | USA | 6 | 0 | 1 | 1 | 4 | G |
|---|---|---|---|---|---|---|---|---|

**Samuelsson, Mikael**
**b. Mariefred, Sweden, December 23, 1976**

| 2005 WM | 37-F | SWE | 9 | 1 | 4 | 5 | 4 | 4th |
|---|---|---|---|---|---|---|---|---|
| 2006 OG-M | 37-F | SWE | 8 | 1 | 3 | 4 | 2 | G |
| 2006 WM | 37-F | SWE | 8 | 4 | 5 | 9 | 4 | G |
| **Totals WM** | | | **17** | **5** | **9** | **14** | **8** | **G** |

~Triple Gold Club

**Samuelsson, Philip**
**b. Leksand, Sweden, July 26, 1991**

| 2009 WM18 | 24-D | USA | 7 | 0 | 3 | 3 | 4 | G |
|---|---|---|---|---|---|---|---|---|

**Sandberg, Filip**
**b. Jarfalla, Sweden, July 23, 1994**

| 2012 WM18 | 21-F | SWE | 6 | 1 | 3 | 4 | 0 | S |
|---|---|---|---|---|---|---|---|---|

**Sandell, Sami**
**b. Nokia, Finland, March 1, 1987**

| 2007 WM20 | 10-F | FIN | 6 | 0 | 0 | 0 | 24 | 6th |
|---|---|---|---|---|---|---|---|---|

**Sandstrom, Lucas**
**b. Fagersta, Sweden, March 23, 1990**

| 2008 WM18 | 10-F | SWE | 6 | 1 | 1 | 2 | 6 | 4th |
|---|---|---|---|---|---|---|---|---|

**Sanguinetti, Bobby**
**b. Trenton, New Jersey, United States, February 29, 1988**

| 2008 WM20 | 20-D | USA | 6 | 1 | 2 | 3 | 0 | 4th |
|---|---|---|---|---|---|---|---|---|

**Sannitz, Raffaele**
**b. Mendrisio, Switzerland, May 18, 1983**

| 2001 WM18 | 19-F | SUI | 7 | 2 | 2 | 4 | 12 | S |
|---|---|---|---|---|---|---|---|---|
| 2002 WM20 | 19-F | SUI | 7 | 1 | 0 | 1 | 10 | 4th |
| 2006 WM | 39-F | SUI | 6 | 2 | 0 | 2 | 10 | 9th |
| 2007 WM | 39-F | SUI | 2 | 0 | 0 | 0 | 0 | 8th |
| 2008 WM | 39-F | SUI | 7 | 2 | 2 | 4 | 10 | 7th |
| 2009 WM | 39-F | SUI | 6 | 0 | 0 | 0 | 2 | 9th |
| 2010 OG-M | 39-F | SUI | 5 | 1 | 1 | 2 | 8 | 8th |
| **Totals WM** | | | **21** | **4** | **2** | **6** | **22** | **—** |

**Santala, Tommi**
**b. Helsinki, Finland, June 27, 1979**

| 1999 WM20 | 10-F | FIN | 6 | 1 | 1 | 2 | 6 | 5th |
|---|---|---|---|---|---|---|---|---|
| 2003 WM | 23-F | FIN | 7 | 0 | 1 | 1 | 6 | 5th |
| 2006 WM | 22-F | FIN | 1 | 0 | 0 | 0 | 2 | B |
| 2009 WM | 22-F | FIN | 7 | 0 | 0 | 0 | 4 | 5th |
| 2010 WM | 22-F | FIN | 6 | 0 | 0 | 0 | 4 | 6th |
| **Totals WM** | | | **21** | **0** | **1** | **1** | **16** | **B** |

**Saponari, Vinny**
**b. Powder Springs, Georgia, United States, February 15, 1990**

| 2007 WM18 | 16-F | USA | 7 | 2 | 2 | 4 | 0 | S |
|---|---|---|---|---|---|---|---|---|
| 2008 WM18 | 27-F | USA | 7 | 0 | 3 | 3 | 33 | B |
| **Totals WM18** | | | **14** | **2** | **5** | **7** | **33** | **S,B** |

**Saprykin, Oleg**
**b. Moscow, Soviet Union (Russia), February 12, 1981**

| 2003 WM | 19-F | RUS | 7 | 1 | 3 | 4 | 6 | 7th |
|---|---|---|---|---|---|---|---|---|
| 2009 WM | 91-F | RUS | 9 | 4 | 3 | 7 | 0 | G |
| **Totals WM** | | | **16** | **5** | **6** | **11** | **6** | **G** |

**Sartori, Riccardo**
**b. Bosco-Gurin, Switzerland, September 10, 1994**

| 2012 WM18 | 20-D | SUI | 6 | 0 | 0 | 0 | 27 | 7th |
|---|---|---|---|---|---|---|---|---|

**Sass-Jensen, Jonas**
**b. Rodovre, Denmark, April 27, 1993**

| 2012 WM20 | 14-F | DEN | 5 | 0 | 0 | 0 | 4 | 10th |
|---|---|---|---|---|---|---|---|---|

**Satan, Miroslav**
**b. Topolcany, Czechoslovakia (Slovakia), October 22, 1974**

| 1994 OG-M | 18-F | SVK | 8 | 9 | 0 | 9 | 0 | 6th |
|---|---|---|---|---|---|---|---|---|
| 1996 WM | 18-F | SVK | 5 | 0 | 3 | 3 | 6 | 10th |
| 1996 WCH | 18-F | SVK | 3 | 0 | 0 | 0 | 2 | 7th |
| 2000 WM | 18-F | SVK | 9 | 10 | 2 | 12 | 14 | S |
| 2002 OG-M | 18-F | SVK | 2 | 0 | 1 | 1 | 0 | 13th |
| 2002 WM | 18-F | SVK | 9 | 5 | 8 | 13 | 2 | G |
| 2003 WM | 18-F | SVK | 9 | 6 | 4 | 10 | 2 | B |
| 2004 WM | 18-F | SVK | 9 | 4 | 4 | 8 | 4 | 4th |
| 2004 WCH | 18-F | SVK | 4 | 0 | 0 | 0 | 4 | 7th |
| 2005 WM | 18-F | SVK | 7 | 2 | 2 | 4 | 8 | 5th |
| 2006 OG-M | 18-F | SVK | 6 | 0 | 2 | 2 | 2 | 5th |
| 2007 WM | 18-F | SVK | 7 | 1 | 7 | 8 | 4 | 6th |
| 2010 OG-M | 18-F | SVK | 6 | 1 | 1 | 2 | 0 | 4th |
| 2010 WM | 18-F | SVK | 2 | 0 | 0 | 0 | 0 | 12th |
| 2011 WM | 18-F | SVK | 6 | 3 | 2 | 5 | 4 | 10th |
| 2012 WM | 18-F | SVK | 10 | 4 | 2 | 6 | 4 | S |
| **Totals WM** | | | **73** | **35** | **34** | **69** | **48** | **G,2S,B** |
| **Totals OG-M** | | | **22** | **10** | **4** | **14** | **2** | **—** |
| **Totals IIHF-NHL** | | | **7** | **0** | **0** | **0** | **6** | **—** |

~WM MVP (2002), WM IIHF Directorate Best Forward (2000), WM All-Star Team/Forward (2000, 2002)

**Saulietis, Kaspars**
**b. Riga, Soviet Union (Latvia), June 12, 1987**

| 2006 WM20 | 21-F | LAT | 6 | 0 | 3 | 3 | 4 | 9th |
|---|---|---|---|---|---|---|---|---|
| 2010 WM | 18-F | LAT | 3 | 0 | 1 | 1 | 4 | 11th |
| 2011 WM | 18-F | LAT | 6 | 3 | 1 | 4 | 2 | 13th |
| 2012 WM | 18-F | LAT | 7 | 0 | 0 | 0 | 6 | 10th |
| **Totals WM** | | | **16** | **3** | **2** | **5** | **12** | **—** |

**Sauve, Maxime**
**b. Tours, France, January 30, 1990**

| 2008 WM18 | 18-F | CAN | 7 | 0 | 6 | 6 | 2 | G |
|---|---|---|---|---|---|---|---|---|

**Savary, Paul**
**b. Geneva, Switzerland, November 2, 1982**

| 2000 WM18 | 11-F | SUI | 2 | 0 | 0 | 0 | 0 | 4th |
|---|---|---|---|---|---|---|---|---|
| 2010 WM | 9-F | SUI | 7 | 0 | 1 | 1 | 2 | 5th |

**Savchenko, Roman**
**b. Ust-Kamenogorsk, Soviet Union (Kazakhstan), July 28, 1988**

| 2008 WM20 | 4-D | KAZ | 6 | 0 | 3 | 3 | 12 | 8th |
|---|---|---|---|---|---|---|---|---|
| 2010 WM | 2-D | KAZ | 6 | 0 | 0 | 0 | 2 | 16th |
| 2012 WM | 2-D | KAZ | 7 | 1 | 1 | 2 | 14 | 16th |
| **Totals WM** | | | **13** | **1** | **1** | **2** | **16** | **—** |

**Saveliev, Anton**
**b. Moscow, Russia, February 4, 1993**

| 2011 WM18 | 24-D | RUS | 7 | 1 | 0 | 1 | 2 | B |
|---|---|---|---|---|---|---|---|---|

**Savenkov, Konstantin**
**b. V-Kazakhstanskaya, Soviet Union (Kazakhstan), March 25, 1990**

| 2008 WM20 | 26-F | KAZ | 6 | 1 | 1 | 2 | 0 | 8th |
|---|---|---|---|---|---|---|---|---|
| 2009 WM20 | 26-F | KAZ | 6 | 3 | 0 | 3 | 8 | 10th |
| 2012 WM | 26-F | KAZ | 3 | 0 | 0 | 0 | 2 | 16th |
| **Totals WM20** | | | **12** | **4** | **1** | **5** | **8** | **—** |

**Saves, Sebastian**
**b. Oslo, Norway, December 11, 1993**

| 2011 WM18 | 15-D | NOR | 4 | 0 | 0 | 0 | 0 | 9th |
|---|---|---|---|---|---|---|---|---|

**Saviels, Agris**
**b. Jurmala, Soviet Union (Latvia), January 15, 1982**

| 2004 WM | 2-D | LAT | 7 | 0 | 0 | 0 | 0 | 7th |
|---|---|---|---|---|---|---|---|---|
| 2005 WM | 4-D | LAT | 6 | 0 | 0 | 0 | 2 | 9th |
| 2006 OG-M | 4-D | LAT | 5 | 0 | 0 | 0 | 8 | 12th |
| 2006 WM | 4-D | LAT | 6 | 0 | 0 | 0 | 10 | 10th |
| 2007 WM | 4-D | LAT | 6 | 1 | 0 | 1 | 2 | 13th |
| 2008 WM | 4-D | LAT | 6 | 0 | 0 | 0 | 4 | 11th |
| **Totals WM** | | | **31** | **1** | **0** | **1** | **18** | **—** |

**Savilahti-Nagander, Per**
**b. Lulea, Sweden, April 22, 1985**

| 2005 WM20 | 14-D | SWE | 6 | 0 | 0 | 0 | 10 | 6th |
|---|---|---|---|---|---|---|---|---|

**Sayustov, Dmitri**
**b. Chelyabinsk, Soviet Union (Russia), February 13, 1988**

| 2008 WM20 | 17-F | RUS | 7 | 1 | 3 | 4 | 6 | B |
|---|---|---|---|---|---|---|---|---|

**Sbisa, Luca**
**b. Ozieri, Italy, January 9, 1990**

| | | | | | | | | |
|---|---|---|---|---|---|---|---|---|
| 2008 WM20 | 22-D | SUI | 6 | 0 | 0 | 0 | 4 | 9th |
| 2010 WM20 | 5-D | SUI | 3 | 0 | 0 | 0 | 0 | 4th |
| 2010 OG-M | 47-D | SUI | 5 | 0 | 0 | 0 | 0 | 8th |
| 2011 WM | 47-D | SUI | 6 | 0 | 1 | 1 | 4 | 9th |
| 2012 WM | 47-D | SUI | 7 | 0 | 1 | 1 | 8 | 11th |
| **Totals WM20** | | | **9** | **0** | **0** | **0** | **4** | **—** |
| **Totals WM** | | | **13** | **0** | **2** | **2** | **12** | **—** |

**Scalzo, Mario**
**b. St. Hubert, Quebec, Canada, November 11, 1984**

| | | | | | | | | |
|---|---|---|---|---|---|---|---|---|
| 2011 WM | 7-D | CAN | 3 | 0 | 2 | 2 | 0 | 5th |

**Scandella, Giulio**
**b. Montreal, Quebec, Canada, September 18, 1983**

| | | | | | | | | |
|---|---|---|---|---|---|---|---|---|
| 2006 OG-M | 10-F | ITA | 2 | 0 | 1 | 1 | 0 | 11th |
| 2007 WM | 10-F | ITA | 6 | 0 | 1 | 1 | 2 | 12th |
| 2008 WM | 10-F | ITA | 5 | 0 | 2 | 2 | 2 | 16th |
| 2010 WM | 10-F | ITA | 6 | 2 | 1 | 3 | 2 | 15th |
| 2012 WM | 10-F | ITA | 7 | 1 | 2 | 3 | 10 | 15th |
| **Totals WM** | | | **24** | **3** | **6** | **9** | **16** | **—** |

**Scandella, Marco**
**b. Montreal, Quebec, Canada, February 23, 1990**

| | | | | | | | | |
|---|---|---|---|---|---|---|---|---|
| 2008 WM18 | 5-D | CAN | 7 | 1 | 1 | 2 | 6 | G |
| 2010 WM20 | 5-D | CAN | 6 | 1 | 2 | 3 | 2 | S |

**Scarlett, Reece**
**b. Sherwood Park, Alberta, Canada, March 31, 1993**

| | | | | | | | | |
|---|---|---|---|---|---|---|---|---|
| 2011 WM18 | 11-D | CAN | 7 | 0 | 0 | 0 | 0 | 4th |

**Schaarup, Mads**
**b. Herning, Denmark, January 30, 1987**

| | | | | | | | | |
|---|---|---|---|---|---|---|---|---|
| 2004 WM18 | 20-D | DEN | 6 | 0 | 0 | 0 | 0 | 8th |
| 2005 WM18 | 20-D | DEN | 6 | 0 | 1 | 1 | 4 | 10th |
| 2008 WM | 2-D | DEN | 2 | 0 | 0 | 0 | 0 | 12th |
| **Totals WM18** | | | **12** | **0** | **1** | **1** | **4** | **—** |

**Schappi, Reto**
**b. Horgen, Switzerland, January 27, 1991**

| | | | | | | | | |
|---|---|---|---|---|---|---|---|---|
| 2008 WM18 | 24-F | SUI | 6 | 0 | 1 | 1 | 4 | 8th |
| 2009 WM18 | 9-F | SUI | 6 | 3 | 3 | 6 | 2 | 8th |
| 2010 WM20 | 9-F | SUI | 7 | 0 | 2 | 2 | 4 | 4th |
| 2011 WM20 | 9-F | SUI | 5 | 0 | 0 | 0 | 8 | 5th |
| **Totals WM18** | | | **12** | **3** | **4** | **7** | **6** | **—** |
| **Totals WM20** | | | **12** | **0** | **2** | **2** | **12** | **—** |

**Scheifele, Mark**
**b. Kitchener, Ontario, Canada, March 15, 1993**

| | | | | | | | | |
|---|---|---|---|---|---|---|---|---|
| 2011 WM18 | 23-F | CAN | 7 | 6 | 2 | 8 | 2 | 4th |
| 2012 WM20 | 19-F | CAN | 6 | 3 | 3 | 6 | 0 | B |

**Schellander, Paul**
**b. Klagenfurt, Austria, November 5, 1986**

| | | | | | | | | |
|---|---|---|---|---|---|---|---|---|
| 2009 WM | 15-F | AUT | 6 | 0 | 0 | 0 | 2 | 14th |

**Schemitsch, Geoff**
**b. Toronto, Ontario, Canada, April 1, 1992**

| | | | | | | | | |
|---|---|---|---|---|---|---|---|---|
| 2010 WM18 | 2-D | CAN | 6 | 0 | 1 | 1 | 2 | 7th |

**Schenn, Brayden**
**b. Saskatoon, Saskatchewan, Canada, August 22, 1991**

| | | | | | | | | |
|---|---|---|---|---|---|---|---|---|
| 2008 WM18 | 22-F | CAN | 7 | 1 | 2 | 3 | 6 | G |
| 2010 WM20 | 10-F | CAN | 6 | 2 | 6 | 8 | 4 | S |
| 2011 WM20 | 10-F | CAN | 7 | 8 | 10 | 18 | 0 | S |
| **Totals WM20** | | | **13** | **10** | **16** | **26** | **4** | **2S** |

~WM20 MVP (2011), WM20 IIHF Directorate Best Forward (2011), WM20 All-Star Team/Forward (2011)

**Schenn, Luke**
**b. Saskatoon, Saskatchewan, Canada, November 2, 1989**

| | | | | | | | | |
|---|---|---|---|---|---|---|---|---|
| 2007 WM18 | 15-D | CAN | 6 | 3 | 0 | 3 | 4 | 4th |
| 2008 WM20 | 15-D | CAN | 7 | 0 | 0 | 0 | 6 | G |
| 2009 WM | 5-D | CAN | 9 | 0 | 1 | 1 | 0 | S |
| 2011 WM | 2-D | CAN | 7 | 0 | 1 | 1 | 0 | 5th |
| 2012 WM | 5-D | CAN | 8 | 0 | 1 | 1 | 25 | 5th |
| **Totals WM** | | | **24** | **0** | **3** | **3** | **25** | **S** |

**Scherwey, Tristan**
**b. Wunnewil Flamatt, Switzerland, May 7, 1991**

| | | | | | | | | |
|---|---|---|---|---|---|---|---|---|
| 2009 WM18 | 22-F | SUI | 6 | 3 | 2 | 5 | 14 | 8th |
| 2010 WM20 | 10-F | SUI | 7 | 1 | 2 | 3 | 8 | 4th |
| 2011 WM20 | 10-F | SUI | 5 | 0 | 0 | 0 | 28 | 5th |
| **Totals WM20** | | | **12** | **1** | **2** | **3** | **36** | **—** |

**Schiechl, Michael**
**b. Judenburg, Austria, January 29, 1989**

| | | | | | | | | |
|---|---|---|---|---|---|---|---|---|
| 2011 WM | 13-F | AUT | 3 | 1 | 0 | 1 | 0 | 15th |

**Schietzold, Andre**
**b. Werdau, West Germany (Germany), January 11, 1987**

| | | | | | | | | |
|---|---|---|---|---|---|---|---|---|
| 2005 WM18 | 13-F | GER | 6 | 2 | 0 | 2 | 2 | 8th |
| 2007 WM20 | 10-F | GER | 6 | 0 | 1 | 1 | 2 | 9th |

**Schilt, Sebastian**
**b. Hasle-Ruegsau, Switzerland, May 16, 1987**

| | | | | | | | | |
|---|---|---|---|---|---|---|---|---|
| 2007 WM20 | 6-D | SUI | 6 | 0 | 1 | 1 | 10 | 7th |

**Schlagenhauf, Roman**
**b. Kloten, Switzerland, March 17, 1989**

| | | | | | | | | |
|---|---|---|---|---|---|---|---|---|
| 2007 WM18 | 8-F | SUI | 6 | 1 | 2 | 3 | 4 | 6th |
| 2008 WM20 | 8-F | SUI | 6 | 1 | 0 | 1 | 2 | 9th |

**Schlumpf, Dominik**
**b. Monchaltorf, Switzerland, March 3, 1991**

| | | | | | | | | |
|---|---|---|---|---|---|---|---|---|
| 2008 WM18 | 2-D | SUI | 6 | 1 | 1 | 2 | 4 | 8th |
| 2010 WM20 | 18-D | SUI | 7 | 1 | 1 | 2 | 6 | 4th |
| 2011 WM20 | 8-D | SUI | 6 | 1 | 0 | 1 | 2 | 5th |
| **Totals WM20** | | | **13** | **2** | **1** | **3** | **8** | **—** |

**Schmid, Thomas**
**b. Weilheim, Germany, March 23, 1994**

| | | | | | | | | |
|---|---|---|---|---|---|---|---|---|
| 2012 WM18 | 7-D | GER | 6 | 0 | 0 | 0 | 6 | 6th |

**Schmidt, Chris**
**b. Beaver Lodge, Alberta, Canada, March 1, 1976**

| | | | | | | | | |
|---|---|---|---|---|---|---|---|---|
| 2008 WM | 7-D | GER | 6 | 2 | 4 | 6 | 2 | 10th |
| 2009 WM | 7-D | GER | 6 | 0 | 0 | 0 | 4 | 15th |
| 2010 OG-M | 7-D | GER | 4 | 0 | 1 | 1 | 2 | 11th |
| **Totals WM** | | | **12** | **2** | **4** | **6** | **6** | **—** |

**Schmidt, Markus**
**b. Hagenow, East Germany (Germany), January 30, 1985**

| | | | | | | | | |
|---|---|---|---|---|---|---|---|---|
| 2005 WM20 | 21-F | GER | 6 | 0 | 0 | 0 | 0 | 9th |

**Schmutz, Julian**
**b. Vechigen, Switzerland, February 28, 1994**

| | | | | | | | | |
|---|---|---|---|---|---|---|---|---|
| 2011 WM18 | 15-F | SUI | 6 | 0 | 0 | 0 | 2 | 7th |
| 2012 WM18 | 13-F | SUI | 6 | 1 | 0 | 1 | 41 | 7th |

**Schmutz, Flavio**
**b. Wald, Switzerland, October 8, 1994**

| | | | | | | | | |
|---|---|---|---|---|---|---|---|---|
| 2012 WM18 | 10-F | SUI | 6 | 2 | 0 | 2 | 2 | 7th |

**Schmutz, Reto**
**b. Wald, Switzerland, November 9, 1992**

| | | | | | | | | |
|---|---|---|---|---|---|---|---|---|
| 2009 WM18 | 20-F | SUI | 2 | 0 | 0 | 0 | 0 | 8th |
| 2010 WM18 | 10-F | SUI | 6 | 1 | 1 | 2 | 10 | 5th |
| **Totals WM18** | | | **8** | **1** | **1** | **2** | **10** | **—** |

**Schneider, Peter**
**b. Klosterneuberg, Austria, April 4, 1991**

| | | | | | | | | |
|---|---|---|---|---|---|---|---|---|
| 2010 WM20 | 23-F | AUT | 6 | 0 | 1 | 1 | 4 | 10th |

**Schneuwly, Cedric**
**b. Fribourg, Switzerland, May 19, 1992**

| | | | | | | | | |
|---|---|---|---|---|---|---|---|---|
| 2012 WM20 | 23-F | SUI | 6 | 1 | 0 | 1 | 0 | 8th |

**Schnyder, Daniel**
**b. Zurich, Switzerland, June 21, 1985**

| | | | | | | | | |
|---|---|---|---|---|---|---|---|---|
| 2003 WM18 | 7-D | SUI | 6 | 0 | 1 | 1 | 2 | 9th |
| 2005 WM20 | 5-D | SUI | 6 | 0 | 1 | 1 | 0 | 8th |

**Schnyder, Fabian**
**b. Schupfheim, Switzerland, December 30, 1985**

| | | | | | | | | |
|---|---|---|---|---|---|---|---|---|
| 2005 WM20 | 28-F | SUI | 6 | 0 | 3 | 3 | 0 | 8th |

**Scholz, Fabian**
**b. Zell am See, Austria, January 8, 1990**

| | | | | | | | | |
|---|---|---|---|---|---|---|---|---|
| 2010 WM20 | 9-D | AUT | 4 | 0 | 1 | 1 | 6 | 10th |

**Schopper, Benedikt**
**b. Weiden, West Germany (Germany), February 18, 1985**

| | | | | | | | | |
|---|---|---|---|---|---|---|---|---|
| 2005 WM20 | 11-D | GER | 5 | 0 | 0 | 0 | 8 | 9th |

**Schremp, Robbie**
**b. Syracuse, New York, United States, July 1, 1986**

| | | | | | | | | |
|---|---|---|---|---|---|---|---|---|
| 2005 WM20 | 17-F | USA | 7 | 4 | 1 | 5 | 2 | 4th |
| 2006 WM20 | 17-F | USA | 7 | 1 | 5 | 6 | 4 | 4th |
| **Totals WM20** | | | **14** | **5** | **6** | **11** | **6** | **—** |

**Schroeder, Jordan**
**b. Prior Lake, Minnesota, United States, September 29, 1990**

| | | | | | | | | |
|---|---|---|---|---|---|---|---|---|
| 2007 WM18 | 14-F | USA | 7 | 4 | 7 | 11 | 0 | S |
| 2008 WM18 | 9-F | USA | 7 | 3 | 2 | 5 | 2 | B |
| 2008 WM20 | 29-F | USA | 6 | 1 | 7 | 8 | 2 | 4th |
| 2009 WM20 | 19-F | USA | 6 | 3 | 8 | 11 | 2 | 5th |
| 2010 WM20 | 19-F | USA | 7 | 3 | 5 | 8 | 2 | G |
| **Totals WM18** | | | **14** | **7** | **9** | **16** | **2** | **S,B** |
| **Totals WM20** | | | **19** | **7** | **20** | **27** | **6** | **G** |

**Schubert, Christoph**
**b. Munich, West Germany (Germany), February 5, 1982**

| | | | | | | | | |
|---|---|---|---|---|---|---|---|---|
| 2000 WM18 | 6-D | GER | 6 | 2 | 2 | 4 | 12 | 7th |
| 2001 WM | 13-D | GER | 1 | 0 | 0 | 0 | 0 | 5th |
| 2002 OG-M | 13-D | GER | 7 | 0 | 1 | 1 | 6 | 8th |
| 2002 WM | 13-D | GER | 7 | 1 | 0 | 1 | 8 | 8th |
| 2004 WCH | 13-D | GER | 2 | 0 | 0 | 0 | 6 | 8th |
| 2005 WM | 13-D | GER | 3 | 0 | 4 | 4 | 6 | 15th |
| 2006 OG-M | 13-D | GER | 5 | 0 | 1 | 1 | 2 | 10th |
| 2008 WM | 13-D | GER | 6 | 1 | 2 | 3 | 12 | 10th |
| 2009 WM | 13-D | GER | 4 | 2 | 0 | 2 | 6 | 15th |
| 2012 WM | 13-D | GER | 7 | 1 | 2 | 3 | 2 | 12th |
| **Totals WM** | | | **28** | **5** | **8** | **13** | **34** | **—** |
| **Totals OG-M** | | | **12** | **0** | **2** | **2** | **8** | **—** |

**Schule, Tim**
**b. Bietigheim, West Germany (Germany), September 9, 1990**

| | | | | | | | | |
|---|---|---|---|---|---|---|---|---|
| 2009 WM20 | 4-D | GER | 6 | 0 | 0 | 0 | 4 | 9th |

**Schuler, Beat**
**b. Schwyz, Switzerland, March 1, 1985**

| | | | | | | | | |
|---|---|---|---|---|---|---|---|---|
| 2005 WM20 | 25-F | SUI | 6 | 1 | 1 | 2 | 0 | 8th |

**Schuller, David**
**b. Kapfenberg, Austria, September 6, 1980**

| | | | | | | | | |
|---|---|---|---|---|---|---|---|---|
| 2005 WM | 45-F | AUT | 6 | 0 | 0 | 0 | 6 | 16th |
| 2007 WM | 45-F | AUT | 6 | 0 | 1 | 1 | 14 | 15th |
| 2009 WM | 45-F | AUT | 6 | 0 | 0 | 0 | 8 | 14th |
| **Totals WM** | | | **18** | **0** | **1** | **1** | **28** | **—** |

**Schultz, Anders**
**b. Hvidovre, Denmark, June 1, 1992**

| | | | | | | | | |
|---|---|---|---|---|---|---|---|---|
| 2012 WM20 | 28-F | DEN | 5 | 0 | 0 | 0 | 4 | 10th |

**Schultz, Nick**
**b. Regina, Saskatchewan, August 25, 1982**

| | | | | | | | | |
|---|---|---|---|---|---|---|---|---|
| 2001 WM20 | 3-D | CAN | 7 | 0 | 0 | 0 | 2 | B |
| 2002 WM20 | 7-D | CAN | 7 | 0 | 2 | 2 | 4 | S |
| 2004 WM | 55-D | CAN | 9 | 0 | 1 | 1 | 0 | G |
| 2006 WM | 55-D | CAN | 9 | 0 | 2 | 2 | 6 | 4th |
| 2007 WM | 55-D | CAN | 9 | 0 | 0 | 0 | 2 | G |
| **Totals WM20** | | | **14** | **0** | **2** | **2** | **6** | **S,B** |
| **Totals WM** | | | **27** | **0** | **3** | **3** | **8** | **2G** |

**Schumacher, Dustin**
**b. Cologne, West Germany (Germany), June 9, 1991**

| | | | | | | | | |
|---|---|---|---|---|---|---|---|---|
| 2009 WM18 | 12-D | GER | 1 | 0 | 0 | 0 | 0 | 10th |

**Schumnig, Martin**
**b. Klagenfurt, Austria, July 28, 1989**

| | | | | | | | | |
|---|---|---|---|---|---|---|---|---|
| 2011 WM | 28-D | AUT | 6 | 0 | 0 | 0 | 0 | 15th |

**Schutz, Felix**
**b. Erding, West Germany (Germany), November 3, 1987**

| | | | | | | | | |
|---|---|---|---|---|---|---|---|---|
| 2005 WM18 | 5-F | GER | 6 | 2 | 1 | 3 | 2 | 8th |
| 2005 WM20 | 10-F | GER | 6 | 0 | 0 | 0 | 0 | 9th |
| 2007 WM20 | 5-F | GER | 6 | 5 | 3 | 8 | 8 | 9th |
| 2010 WM | 55-F | GER | 9 | 2 | 2 | 4 | 4 | 4th |
| 2011 WM | 55-F | GER | 7 | 3 | 1 | 4 | 4 | 7th |
| 2012 WM | 55-F | GER | 4 | 0 | 1 | 1 | 0 | 12th |
| Totals WM20 | | | 12 | 5 | 3 | 8 | 8 | — |
| **Totals WM** | | | **20** | **5** | **4** | **9** | **8** | **—** |

**Schutz, Marco**
**b. Villingen-Schwenningen, West Germany (Germany), February 19, 1985**

| | | | | | | | | |
|---|---|---|---|---|---|---|---|---|
| 2005 WM20 | 8-D | GER | 6 | 0 | 0 | 0 | 6 | 9th |

**Schwartz, Jaden**
**b. Wilcox, Saskatchewan, Canada, June 25, 1992**

| | | | | | | | | |
|---|---|---|---|---|---|---|---|---|
| 2011 WM20 | 8-F | CAN | 2 | 1 | 2 | 3 | 0 | S |
| 2012 WM20 | 8-F | CAN | 6 | 2 | 3 | 5 | 4 | B |
| Totals WM20 | | | 8 | 3 | 5 | 8 | 4 | S,B |

**Schwarz, Andreas**
**b. Landshut, Germany, May 6, 1995**

| | | | | | | | | |
|---|---|---|---|---|---|---|---|---|
| 2012 WM18 | 6-D | GER | 6 | 0 | 0 | 0 | 4 | 6th |

**Sciaroni, Gregory**
**b. Bellinzona, Switzerland, April 7, 1989**

| | | | | | | | | |
|---|---|---|---|---|---|---|---|---|
| 2007 WM18 | 18-F | SUI | 6 | 2 | 2 | 4 | 6 | 6th |
| 2007 WM20 | 12-F | SUI | 6 | 0 | 1 | 1 | 2 | 7th |
| 2008 WM20 | 18-F | SUI | 6 | 1 | 0 | 1 | 2 | 9th |
| **Totals WM20** | | | **12** | **1** | **1** | **2** | **4** | **—** |

**Scurko, Ladislav**
**b. Spisska Nova Ves, Czechoslovakia (Slovakia), April 4, 1986**

| | | | | | | | | |
|---|---|---|---|---|---|---|---|---|
| 2003 WM18 | 23-F | SVK | 7 | 0 | 2 | 2 | 2 | S |
| 2004 WM18 | 20-F | SVK | 6 | 0 | 3 | 3 | 6 | 6th |
| 2005 WM20 | 19-F | SVK | 6 | 0 | 0 | 0 | 6 | 7th |
| 2006 WM20 | 20-F | SVK | 6 | 2 | 0 | 2 | 16 | 8th |
| **Totals WM18** | | | **13** | **0** | **5** | **5** | **8** | **S** |
| **Totals WM20** | | | **12** | **2** | **0** | **2** | **22** | **—** |

**Seabrook, Brent**
**b. Richmond, British Columbia, Canada, April 20, 1985**

| | | | | | | | | |
|---|---|---|---|---|---|---|---|---|
| 2003 WM18 | 7-D | CAN | 7 | 3 | 3 | 6 | 4 | G |
| 2004 WM20 | 32-D | CAN | 6 | 1 | 2 | 3 | 2 | S |
| 2005 WM20 | 2-D | CAN | 5 | 0 | 3 | 3 | 0 | G |
| 2006 WM | 5-D | CAN | 8 | 0 | 0 | 0 | 2 | 4th |
| 2010 OG-M | 7-D | CAN | 7 | 0 | 1 | 1 | 2 | G |
| **Totals WM20** | | | **11** | **1** | **5** | **6** | **2** | **G,S** |

~WM18 IIHF Directorate Best Defenceman (2003), WM18 All-Star Team/Defence (2003)

**Sedin, Daniel**
**b. Ornskoldsvik, Sweden, September 26, 1980**

| | | | | | | | | |
|---|---|---|---|---|---|---|---|---|
| 1998 WM20 | 12-F | SWE | 7 | 4 | 1 | 5 | 2 | 6th |
| 1999 WM20 | 12-F | SWE | 6 | 5 | 5 | 10 | 2 | 4th |
| 1999 WM | 12-F | SWE | 9 | 0 | 1 | 1 | 2 | B |
| 2000 WM20 | 12-F | SWE | 7 | 6 | 4 | 10 | 0 | 5th |
| 2000 WM | 12-F | SWE | 7 | 3 | 2 | 5 | 8 | 7th |
| 2001 WM | 12-F | SWE | 3 | 0 | 2 | 2 | 0 | B |
| 2005 WM | 12-F | SWE | 9 | 5 | 4 | 9 | 2 | 4th |
| 2006 OG-M | 12-F | SWE | 8 | 1 | 3 | 4 | 2 | G |
| 2010 OG-M | 22-F | SWE | 4 | 1 | 2 | 3 | 0 | 5th |
| **Totals WM20** | | | **20** | **15** | **10** | **25** | **4** | **—** |
| **Totals WM** | | | **28** | **8** | **9** | **17** | **12** | **2B** |
| **Totals OG-M** | | | **12** | **2** | **5** | **7** | **2** | **G** |

**Sedin, Henrik**
**b. Ornskoldsvik, Sweden, September 26, 1980**

| | | | | | | | | |
|---|---|---|---|---|---|---|---|---|
| 1998 WM20 | 20-F | SWE | 7 | 0 | 4 | 4 | 4 | 6th |
| 1999 WM20 | 20-F | SWE | 6 | 3 | 6 | 9 | 10 | 4th |
| 1999 WM | 20-F | SWE | 8 | 0 | 0 | 0 | 4 | B |
| 2000 WM20 | 20-F | SWE | 7 | 4 | 9 | 13 | 6 | 5th |
| 2000 WM | 20-F | SWE | 7 | 2 | 3 | 5 | 6 | 7th |
| 2001 WM | 15-F | SWE | 9 | 1 | 0 | 1 | 0 | B |
| 2005 WM | 20-F | SWE | 9 | 2 | 4 | 6 | 2 | 4th |
| 2006 OG-M | 20-F | SWE | 8 | 3 | 1 | 4 | 2 | G |
| 2010 OG-M | 20-F | SWE | 4 | 0 | 2 | 2 | 2 | 5th |
| **Totals WM20** | | | **20** | **7** | **19** | **26** | **20** | **—** |
| **Totals WM** | | | **33** | **5** | **7** | **12** | **8** | **2B** |
| **Totals OG-M** | | | **12** | **3** | **3** | **6** | **4** | **G** |

**Sedlacek, Pavel**
**b. Zlin, Czech Republic, March 19, 1994**

| | | | | | | | | |
|---|---|---|---|---|---|---|---|---|
| 2012 WM18 | 12-F | CZE | 6 | 0 | 1 | 1 | 2 | 8th |

**Sedlak, Adam**
**b. Ostrava, Czechoslovakia (Czech Republic), September 21, 1991**

| | | | | | | | | |
|---|---|---|---|---|---|---|---|---|
| 2011 WM20 | 24-D | CZE | 6 | 0 | 0 | 0 | 12 | 7th |

**Sedlak, Lukas**
**b. Ceske Budejovice, Czech Republic, February 25, 1993**

| | | | | | | | | |
|---|---|---|---|---|---|---|---|---|
| 2011 WM18 | 11-F | CZE | 5 | 3 | 1 | 4 | 2 | 8th |
| 2012 WM20 | 29-F | CZE | 6 | 0 | 0 | 0 | 0 | 5th |

**Seger, Mathias**
**b. Flawil, Switzerland, December 17, 1977**

| | | | | | | | | |
|---|---|---|---|---|---|---|---|---|
| 1996 WM20 | 15-D | SUI | 5 | 1 | 0 | 1 | 40 | 9th |
| 1997 WM20 | 15-D | SUI | 6 | 0 | 2 | 2 | 10 | 7th |
| 1998 WM | 31-D | SUI | 9 | 1 | 0 | 1 | 6 | 4th |
| 1999 WM | 31-D | SUI | 6 | 1 | 1 | 2 | 8 | 8th |
| 2000 WM | 31-D | SUI | 7 | 0 | 0 | 0 | 8 | 5th |
| 2001 WM | 31-D | SUI | 6 | 0 | 3 | 3 | 6 | 9th |
| 2002 OG-M | 31-D | SUI | 4 | 0 | 1 | 1 | 4 | 11th |
| 2002 WM | 31-D | SUI | 6 | 0 | 0 | 0 | 6 | 10th |
| 2003 WM | 31-D | SUI | 7 | 1 | 3 | 4 | 8 | 8th |
| 2004 WM | 31-D | SUI | 7 | 0 | 2 | 2 | 2 | 8th |
| 2005 WM | 31-D | SUI | 7 | 0 | 0 | 0 | 8 | 8th |
| 2006 OG-M | 31-D | SUI | 6 | 0 | 1 | 1 | 14 | 6th |
| 2006 WM | 31-D | SUI | 5 | 0 | 0 | 0 | 0 | 9th |
| 2008 WM | 31-D | SUI | 4 | 0 | 0 | 0 | 0 | 7th |
| 2009 WM | 31-D | SUI | 6 | 1 | 1 | 2 | 4 | 9th |
| 2010 OG-M | 31-D | SUI | 5 | 0 | 2 | 2 | 4 | 8th |
| 2010 WM | 31-D | SUI | 7 | 0 | 2 | 2 | 6 | 5th |
| 2011 WM | 31-D | SUI | 5 | 0 | 1 | 1 | 4 | 9th |
| 2012 WM | 31-D | SUI | 7 | 0 | 0 | 0 | 0 | 11th |
| **Totals WM20** | | | **11** | **1** | **2** | **3** | **50** | **—** |
| **Totals WM** | | | **89** | **4** | **13** | **17** | **66** | **—** |
| **Totals OG-M** | | | **15** | **0** | **4** | **4** | **22** | **—** |

**Segla, Martin**
**b. Presov, Czechoslovakia (Slovakia), October 12, 1985**

| | | | | | | | | |
|---|---|---|---|---|---|---|---|---|
| 2005 WM20 | 27-F | SVK | 6 | 0 | 0 | 0 | 0 | 7th |

**Seidenberg, Dennis**
**b. Schwenningen, West Germany (Germany), July 18, 1981**

| | | | | | | | | |
|---|---|---|---|---|---|---|---|---|
| 1999 WM18 | 12-D | GER | 4 | 0 | 0 | 0 | 2 | 10th |
| 2001 WM | 84-D | GER | 7 | 0 | 1 | 1 | 2 | 5th |
| 2002 OG-M | 84-D | GER | 7 | 1 | 1 | 2 | 4 | 8th |
| 2002 WM | 84-D | GER | 7 | 1 | 2 | 3 | 8 | 8th |
| 2004 WCH | 84-D | GER | 4 | 0 | 0 | 0 | 0 | 8th |
| 2006 OG-M | 84-D | GER | 5 | 0 | 0 | 0 | 6 | 10th |
| 2008 WM | 5-D | GER | 6 | 0 | 0 | 0 | 14 | 10th |
| 2010 OG-M | 84-D | GER | 4 | 1 | 0 | 1 | 2 | 11th |
| **Totals WM** | | | **20** | **1** | **3** | **4** | **24** | **—** |
| **Totals OG-M** | | | **16** | **2** | **1** | **3** | **12** | **—** |

**Seidenberg, Yannic**
**b. Villingen-Schwenningen, West Germany (Germany), January 11, 1984**

| | | | | | | | | |
|---|---|---|---|---|---|---|---|---|
| 2001 WM18 | 12-F | GER | 6 | 1 | 0 | 1 | 2 | 5th |
| 2002 WM18 | 12-F | GER | 8 | 2 | 6 | 8 | 4 | 10th |
| 2003 WM20 | 12-F | GER | 6 | 1 | 1 | 2 | 12 | 9th |
| 2007 WM | 85-F | GER | 1 | 0 | 0 | 0 | 0 | 9th |
| 2008 WM | 36-F | GER | 6 | 1 | 2 | 3 | 4 | 10th |
| 2009 WM | 36-F | GER | 4 | 0 | 1 | 1 | 2 | 15th |
| **Totals WM18** | | | **14** | **3** | **6** | **9** | **6** | **—** |
| **Totals WM** | | | **11** | **1** | **3** | **4** | **6** | **—** |

**Seitsonen, Aki**
**b. Riihimaki, Finland, February 5, 1986**

| | | | | | | | | |
|---|---|---|---|---|---|---|---|---|
| 2005 WM20 | 18-F | FIN | 6 | 1 | 0 | 1 | 0 | 5th |
| 2006 WM20 | 18-F | FIN | 7 | 4 | 2 | 6 | 4 | B |
| **Totals WM20** | | | **13** | **5** | **2** | **7** | **4** | **B** |

**Sekac, Jiri**
**b. As, Czech Republic, June 10, 1992**

| | | | | | | | | |
|---|---|---|---|---|---|---|---|---|
| 2010 WM18 | 13-F | CZE | 6 | 4 | 0 | 4 | 2 | 6th |
| 2012 WM20 | 26-F | CZE | 6 | 0 | 3 | 3 | 2 | 5th |

**Sekera, Andrej**
**b. Bojnice, Czechoslovakia (Slovakia), June 8, 1986**

| | | | | | | | | |
|---|---|---|---|---|---|---|---|---|
| 2004 WM18 | 3-D | SVK | 6 | 1 | 1 | 2 | 18 | 6th |
| 2005 WM20 | 3-D | SVK | 6 | 1 | 0 | 1 | 2 | 7th |
| 2006 WM20 | 3-D | SVK | 6 | 2 | 3 | 5 | 2 | 8th |
| 2008 WM | 44-D | SVK | 5 | 0 | 1 | 1 | 2 | 13th |
| 2009 WM | 44-D | SVK | 6 | 0 | 2 | 2 | 2 | 10th |
| 2010 OG-M | 44-D | SVK | 7 | 1 | 0 | 1 | 0 | 4th |
| 2010 WM | 44-D | SVK | 6 | 0 | 2 | 2 | 2 | 12th |
| 2012 WM | 44-D | SVK | 10 | 2 | 7 | 9 | 6 | S |
| **Totals WM20** | | | **12** | **3** | **3** | **6** | **4** | **—** |
| **Totals WM** | | | **27** | **2** | **12** | **14** | **12** | **S** |

**Sekesi, Huba**
**b. Munich, Germany, September 5, 1993**

| | | | | | | | | |
|---|---|---|---|---|---|---|---|---|
| 2011 WM18 | 9-F | GER | 6 | 0 | 2 | 2 | 2 | 6th |

**Selanne, Teemu**
**b. Helsinki, Finland, July 3, 1970**

| | | | | | | | | |
|---|---|---|---|---|---|---|---|---|
| 1989 WM20 | 8-F | FIN | 7 | 5 | 5 | 10 | 10 | 6th |
| 1991 WM | 8-F | FIN | 10 | 6 | 5 | 11 | 2 | 5th |
| 1991 CC | 8-F | FIN | 6 | 1 | 1 | 2 | 2 | 3rd |
| 1992 OG-M | 8-F | FIN | 8 | 7 | 4 | 11 | 6 | 7th |
| 1996 WM | 88-F | FIN | 6 | 5 | 3 | 8 | 0 | 5th |
| 1996 WCH | 8-F | FIN | 4 | 3 | 2 | 5 | 0 | 5th |
| 1998 OG-M | 8-F | FIN | 5 | 4 | 6 | 10 | 8 | B |
| 1999 WM | 8-F | FIN | 11 | 3 | 8 | 11 | 2 | S |
| 2002 OG-M | 8-F | FIN | 4 | 3 | 0 | 3 | 2 | 6th |
| 2003 WM | 8-F | FIN | 7 | 8 | 3 | 11 | 2 | 5th |
| 2004 WCH | 8-F | FIN | 6 | 1 | 3 | 4 | 4 | 2nd |
| 2006 OG-M | 8-F | FIN | 8 | 6 | 5 | 11 | 4 | S |
| 2008 WM | 8-F | FIN | 9 | 3 | 4 | 7 | 12 | B |
| 2010 OG-M | 8-F | FIN | 6 | 0 | 2 | 2 | 0 | B |
| **Totals WM** | | | **43** | **25** | **23** | **48** | **18** | **S,B** |
| **Totals OG-M** | | | **31** | **20** | **17** | **37** | **20Q** | **S,2B** |
| **Totals IIHF-NHL** | | | **16** | **5** | **6** | **11** | **6** | **—** |

~OG-M IIHF Directorate Best Forward (2006), OG-M All-Star Team/Forward (2006), WM MVP (1999), WM All-Star Team/Forward (1999)

**Seleznev, Yakov**
**b. Yelabuga, Soviet Union (Russia), August 4, 1989**

| | | | | | | | | |
|---|---|---|---|---|---|---|---|---|
| 2007 WM18 | 2-D | RUS | 7 | 0 | 2 | 2 | 4 | G |
| 2008 WM20 | 20-D | RUS | 7 | 1 | 0 | 1 | 8 | B |

**Semin, Alexander** ~see Syomin, Alexander

**Semochkin, Alexander** ~see Syomochkin, Alexander

**Semorad, Jan**
**b. Ceske Lipa, Czechoslovakia (Czech Republic), March 19, 1988**

| | | | | | | | | |
|---|---|---|---|---|---|---|---|---|
| 2006 WM18 | 13-F | CZE | 3 | 0 | 0 | 0 | 2 | B |
| 2008 WM20 | 25-F | CZE | 6 | 0 | 1 | 1 | 0 | 5th |

**Semyonov, Maxim**
**b. Ust-Kamenogorsk, Soviet Union (Kazakhstan), February 9, 1984**

| | | | | | | | | |
|---|---|---|---|---|---|---|---|---|
| 2010 WM | 7-D | KAZ | 6 | 0 | 1 | 1 | 4 | 16th |

**Senkerik, Petr**
**b. Zlin, Czech Republic, March 13, 1991**

| | | | | | | | | |
|---|---|---|---|---|---|---|---|---|
| 2011 WM20 | 9-D | CZE | 5 | 0 | 0 | 0 | 8 | 7th |

**Senkevich, Artyom**
**b. Minsk, Soviet Union (Belarus), May 4, 1982**

| | | | | | | | | |
|---|---|---|---|---|---|---|---|---|
| 2010 WM | 82-F | BLR | 4 | 0 | 0 | 0 | 2 | 10th |

**Seppanen, Timo**
**b. Helsinki, Finland, July 22, 1987**

| | | | | | | | | |
|---|---|---|---|---|---|---|---|---|
| 2005 WM18 | 5-D | FIN | 6 | 2 | 1 | 3 | 0 | 7th |
| 2006 WM20 | 5-D | FIN | 7 | 2 | 2 | 4 | 4 | B |
| 2007 WM20 | 5-D | FIN | 6 | 0 | 3 | 3 | 10 | 6th |
| **Totals WM20** | | | **13** | **2** | **5** | **7** | **14** | **B** |

**Sergeyev, Andrei**
**b. Simferopol, Soviet Union (Ukraine), March 26, 1991**

| | | | | | | | | |
|---|---|---|---|---|---|---|---|---|
| 2009 WM18 | 11-D | RUS | 7 | 0 | 2 | 2 | 6 | S |
| 2011 WM20 | 26-D | RUS | 7 | 1 | 0 | 1 | 6 | G |

**Sergeyev, Artyom**
**b. Moscow, Russia, February 20, 1993**

| | | | | | | | | |
|---|---|---|---|---|---|---|---|---|
| 2012 WM20 | 3-D | RUS | 7 | 1 | 1 | 2 | 12 | S |

**Sersen, Michal**
**b. Gelnica, Czechoslovakia (Slovakia), December 28, 1985**

| | | | | | | | | |
|---|---|---|---|---|---|---|---|---|
| 2011 WM | 4-D | SVK | 1 | 0 | 0 | 0 | 0 | 10th |
| 2012 WM | 4-D | SVK | 10 | 0 | 0 | 0 | 4 | S |
| **Totals WM** | | | **11** | **0** | **0** | **0** | **4** | **S** |

**Seryakov, Yuri**
**b. Minsk, Belarus, May 4, 1992**

| | | | | | | | | |
|---|---|---|---|---|---|---|---|---|
| 2010 WM18 | 23-F | BLR | 6 | 0 | 0 | 0 | 2 | 10th |

**Setzinger, Oliver**
**b. Horn-Niederhorst, Austria, July 11, 1983**

| | | | | | | | | |
|---|---|---|---|---|---|---|---|---|
| 2001 WM | 15-F | AUT | 6 | 0 | 0 | 0 | 0 | 11th |
| 2002 OG-M | 15-F | AUT | 4 | 1 | 0 | 1 | 2 | 12th |
| 2002 WM | 15-F | AUT | 6 | 2 | 1 | 3 | 2 | 12th |
| 2003 WM | 15-F | AUT | 6 | 0 | 1 | 1 | 2 | 10th |
| 2004 WM | 91-F | AUT | 6 | 1 | 2 | 3 | 10 | 11th |
| 2005 WM | 91-F | AUT | 6 | 1 | 1 | 2 | 2 | 16th |
| 2007 WM | 91-F | AUT | 6 | 1 | 3 | 4 | 0 | 15th |
| 2009 WM | 91-F | AUT | 6 | 2 | 1 | 3 | 6 | 14th |
| 2011 WM | 91-F | AUT | 6 | 1 | 0 | 1 | 2 | 15th |
| **Totals WM** | | | **48** | **8** | **9** | **17** | **24** | **—** |

**Sevcenko, Arturs**
**b. Daugavpils, Latvia, April 24, 1994**

| | | | | | | | | |
|---|---|---|---|---|---|---|---|---|
| 2012 WM18 | 13-F | LAT | 6 | 0 | 3 | 3 | 0 | 9th |

**Sevcenko, Eriks**
**b. Daugavpils, Soviet Union (Latvia), April 28, 1991**

| | | | | | | | | |
|---|---|---|---|---|---|---|---|---|
| 2010 WM20 | 5-D | LAT | 1 | 0 | 0 | 0 | 0 | 9th |

**Severson, Damon**
**b. Melville, Saskatchewan, Canada, August 7, 1994**

| | | | | | | | | |
|---|---|---|---|---|---|---|---|---|
| 2012 WM18 | 5-D | CAN | 7 | 0 | 2 | 2 | 8 | B |

**Sgarbossa, Mike**
**b. Campbelville, Ontario, Canada, July 25, 1992**

| | | | | | | | | |
|---|---|---|---|---|---|---|---|---|
| 2010 WM18 | 11-F | CAN | 6 | 1 | 1 | 2 | 4 | 7th |

**Shafigulin, Grigori**
**b. Chelyabinsk, Soviet Union (Russia), January 13, 1985**

| | | | | | | | | |
|---|---|---|---|---|---|---|---|---|
| 2003 WM18 | 24-F | RUS | 4 | 0 | 0 | 0 | 0 | B |
| 2004 WM20 | 24-F | RUS | 6 | 0 | 0 | 0 | 0 | 5th |
| 2005 WM20 | 19-F | RUS | 6 | 0 | 2 | 2 | 8 | S |
| **Totals WM20** | | | **12** | **0** | **2** | **2** | **8** | **S** |

**Shagov, Alexei**
**b. Minsk, Soviet Union (Belarus), January 2, 1986**

| | | | | | | | | |
|---|---|---|---|---|---|---|---|---|
| 2002 WM18 | 25-D | BLR | 8 | 0 | 0 | 0 | 4 | 5th |
| 2003 WM18 | 25-D | BLR | 6 | 2 | 1 | 3 | 34 | 8th |
| 2004 WM18 | 25-D | BLR | 5 | 0 | 1 | 1 | 32 | 9th |
| 2005 WM20 | 19-D | BLR | 6 | 0 | 0 | 0 | 12 | 10th |
| **Totals WM18** | | | **19** | **2** | **2** | **4** | **70** | **—** |

**Shalunov, Maxim**
**b. Chelyabinsk, Russia, January 31, 1993**

| | | | | | | | | |
|---|---|---|---|---|---|---|---|---|
| 2010 WM18 | 17-F | RUS | 7 | 3 | 1 | 4 | 31 | 4th |
| 2011 WM18 | 17-F | RUS | 6 | 2 | 1 | 3 | 0 | B |
| **Totals WM18** | | | **13** | **5** | **2** | **7** | **31** | **B** |

**Shamansky, Igor**
**b. Kiev (Kyiv), Soviet Union (Ukraine), July 27, 1984**

| | | | | | | | | |
|---|---|---|---|---|---|---|---|---|
| 2001 WM18 | 25-F | UKR | 6 | 0 | 0 | 0 | 2 | 10th |
| 2002 WM18 | 15-F | UKR | 8 | 1 | 0 | 1 | 6 | 12th |
| 2004 WM20 | 23-F | UKR | 6 | 1 | 1 | 2 | 4 | 10th |
| **Totals WM18** | | | **14** | **1** | **0** | **1** | **8** | **—** |

**Shannon, Ryan**
**b. Darien, Connecticut, United States, March 2, 1983**

| | | | | | | | | |
|---|---|---|---|---|---|---|---|---|
| 2003 WM20 | 22-D | USA | 7 | 0 | 2 | 2 | 4 | 4th |
| 2009 WM | 26-F | USA | 9 | 3 | 0 | 3 | 2 | 4th |
| 2011 WM | 26-F | USA | 7 | 1 | 3 | 4 | 0 | 8th |
| **Totals WM** | | | **16** | **4** | **3** | **7** | **2** | **—** |

**Sharp, Patrick**
**b. Thunder Bay, Ontario, Canada, December 27, 1981**

| | | | | | | | | |
|---|---|---|---|---|---|---|---|---|
| 2008 WM | 10-F | CAN | 9 | 3 | 0 | 3 | 4 | S |
| 2012 WM | 81-F | CAN | 8 | 1 | 7 | 8 | 2 | 5th |
| **Totals WM** | | | **17** | **4** | **7** | **11** | **6** | **S** |

**Shattenkirk, Kevin**
**b. New Rochelle, New York, United States, January 29, 1989**

| | | | | | | | | |
|---|---|---|---|---|---|---|---|---|
| 2007 WM18 | 8-D | USA | 7 | 1 | 4 | 5 | 2 | S |
| 2009 WM20 | 8-D | USA | 6 | 1 | 8 | 9 | 4 | 5th |
| 2011 WM | 12-D | USA | 7 | 1 | 2 | 3 | 6 | 8th |

~WM18 IIHF Directorate Best Defenceman (2007), WM18 All-Star Team/Defence (2007)

**Sheleg, Sergei**
**b. Minsk, Soviet Union (Belarus), May 24, 1990**

| | | | | | | | | |
|---|---|---|---|---|---|---|---|---|
| 2008 WM18 | 22-D | BLR | 6 | 2 | 3 | 5 | 6 | 9th |

**Shemelin, Denis**
**b. Ust-Kamenogorsk, Soviet Union (Kazakhstan), July 24, 1978**

| | | | | | | | | |
|---|---|---|---|---|---|---|---|---|
| 2012 WM | 12-D | KAZ | 5 | 0 | 1 | 1 | 8 | 16th |

**Shevyrin, Denis**
**b. St. Petersburg, Russia, March 29, 1995**

| | | | | | | | | |
|---|---|---|---|---|---|---|---|---|
| 2012 WM18 | 17-F | GER | 6 | 1 | 0 | 1 | 6 | 6th |

**Shin, Alexander**
**b. Ust-Kamenogorsk, Soviet Union (Kazakhstan), November 21, 1985**

| | | | | | | | | |
|---|---|---|---|---|---|---|---|---|
| 2003 WM18 | 4-F | KAZ | 6 | 0 | 0 | 0 | 0 | 10th |
| 2010 WM | 49-F | KAZ | 6 | 0 | 0 | 0 | 2 | 16th |

**Shinkaruk, Hunter**
**b. Calgary, Alberta, Canada, October 13, 1994**

| | | | | | | | | |
|---|---|---|---|---|---|---|---|---|
| 2012 WM18 | 8-F | CAN | 6 | 4 | 4 | 8 | 6 | B |

**Shipley, Steve**
**b. Ilderton, Ontario, Canada, April 22, 1992**

| | | | | | | | | |
|---|---|---|---|---|---|---|---|---|
| 2010 WM18 | 9-F | CAN | 6 | 1 | 2 | 3 | 4 | 7th |

**Shirokov, Sergei**
**b. Moscow, Soviet Union (Russia), March 10, 1986**

| | | | | | | | | |
|---|---|---|---|---|---|---|---|---|
| 2004 WM18 | 29-F | RUS | 6 | 2 | 0 | 2 | 6 | G |
| 2005 WM20 | 29-F | RUS | 6 | 4 | 4 | 8 | 0 | S |
| 2006 WM20 | 29-F | RUS | 6 | 3 | 2 | 5 | 8 | S |
| 2012 WM | 52-F | RUS | 10 | 1 | 5 | 6 | 2 | G |
| **Totals WM20** | | | **12** | **7** | **6** | **13** | **8** | **2S** |

**Shore, Drew**
**b. Denver, Colorado, United States, January 29, 1991**

| | | | | | | | | |
|---|---|---|---|---|---|---|---|---|
| 2009 WM18 | 15-F | USA | 7 | 2 | 7 | 9 | 6 | G |
| 2011 WM20 | 15-F | USA | 6 | 2 | 0 | 2 | 2 | B |

**Shore, Nick**
**b. Denver, Colorado, United States, September 26, 1992**

| | | | | | | | | |
|---|---|---|---|---|---|---|---|---|
| 2010 WM18 | 23-F | USA | 7 | 3 | 7 | 10 | 0 | G |

**Shore, Quentin**
**b. Denver, Colorado, United States, May 25, 1994**

| | | | | | | | | |
|---|---|---|---|---|---|---|---|---|
| 2012 WM18 | 27-F | USA | 6 | 3 | 2 | 5 | 2 | G |

**Shumski, Dmitri**
**b. Minsk, Soviet Union (Belarus), January 14, 1988**

| | | | | | | | | |
|---|---|---|---|---|---|---|---|---|
| 2006 WM18 | 6-D | BLR | 6 | 1 | 1 | 2 | 4 | 9th |
| 2007 WM20 | 6-D | BLR | 6 | 0 | 1 | 1 | 4 | 10th |

**Shurko, Alexander**
**b. Minsk, Soviet Union (Belarus), March 14, 1987**

| | | | | | | | | |
|---|---|---|---|---|---|---|---|---|
| 2007 WM20 | 4-F | BLR | 6 | 1 | 1 | 2 | 0 | 10th |

**Shvedov, Igor**
**b. Novopolotsk, Soviet Union (Belarus), March 6, 1987**

| | | | | | | | | |
|---|---|---|---|---|---|---|---|---|
| 2007 WM20 | 2-D | BLR | 6 | 0 | 0 | 0 | 10 | 10th |

**Shypila, Vyacheslav**
**b. Novopolotsk, Soviet Union (Belarus), August 30, 1985**

| | | | | | | | | |
|---|---|---|---|---|---|---|---|---|
| 2005 WM20 | 17-D | BLR | 6 | 0 | 0 | 0 | 4 | 10th |

**Sidlik, Petr**
**b. Jihlava, Czech Republic, January 18, 1994**

| | | | | | | | | |
|---|---|---|---|---|---|---|---|---|
| 2011 WM18 | 4-D | CZE | 6 | 0 | 0 | 0 | 20 | 8th |
| 2012 WM18 | 4-D | CZE | 6 | 0 | 4 | 4 | 6 | 8th |
| Totals WM18 | | | 12 | 0 | 4 | 4 | 26 | — |

**Sieber, Lukas**
**b. Widnau, Switzerland, February 20, 1994**

| | | | | | | | | |
|---|---|---|---|---|---|---|---|---|
| 2012 WM18 | 17-F | SUI | 6 | 0 | 0 | 0 | 6 | 7th |

**Sieloff, Pat**
**b. Ann Arbor, Michigan, United States, May 15, 1994**

| | | | | | | | | |
|---|---|---|---|---|---|---|---|---|
| 2012 WM18 | 10-D | USA | 6 | 0 | 0 | 0 | 0 | G |

**Siksna, Edgars**
**b. Liepaja, Latvia, January 15, 1993**

| | | | | | | | | |
|---|---|---|---|---|---|---|---|---|
| 2010 WM18 | 8-D | LAT | 6 | 1 | 1 | 2 | 12 | 9th |
| 2012 WM20 | 4-D | LAT | 6 | 0 | 1 | 1 | 0 | 9th |

**Silas, Steve**
**b. Georgetown, Ontario, Canada, June 26, 1992**

| | | | | | | | | |
|---|---|---|---|---|---|---|---|---|
| 2010 WM18 | 6-D | CAN | 6 | 0 | 2 | 2 | 0 | 7th |

**Silfverberg, Jakob**
**b. Gavle, Sweden, October 13, 1990**

| | | | | | | | | |
|---|---|---|---|---|---|---|---|---|
| 2008 WM18 | 18-F | SWE | 5 | 1 | 2 | 3 | 2 | 4th |
| 2010 WM20 | 13-F | SWE | 6 | 3 | 2 | 5 | 0 | B |
| 2011 WM | 33-F | SWE | 9 | 0 | 1 | 1 | 2 | S |
| 2012 WM | 33-F | SWE | 8 | 2 | 0 | 2 | 2 | 6th |
| **Totals WM** | | | **17** | **2** | **1** | **3** | **4** | **S** |

**Simcak, Dominik**
**b. Kosice, Slovakia, May 5, 1992**

| | | | | | | | | |
|---|---|---|---|---|---|---|---|---|
| 2010 WM18 | 19-F | SVK | 6 | 3 | 3 | 6 | 0 | 8th |
| 2011 WM20 | 18-F | SVK | 6 | 0 | 0 | 0 | 0 | 8th |

**Simek, Juraj**
**b. Presov, Czechoslovakia (Slovakia), September 29, 1987**

| | | | | | | | | |
|---|---|---|---|---|---|---|---|---|
| 2005 WM18 | 21-F | SUI | 6 | 2 | 0 | 2 | 2 | 9th |
| 2006 WM20 | 21-F | SUI | 6 | 1 | 3 | 4 | 6 | 7th |
| 2007 WM20 | 9-F | SUI | 6 | 4 | 1 | 5 | 2 | 7th |
| **Totals WM20** | | | **12** | **5** | **4** | **9** | **8** | **—** |

**Simion, Dario**
**b. Locarno, Switzerland, May 22, 1994**

| | | | | | | | | |
|---|---|---|---|---|---|---|---|---|
| 2011 WM18 | 24-F | SUI | 6 | 3 | 0 | 3 | 0 | 7th |
| 2012 WM18 | 24-F | SUI | 5 | 1 | 1 | 2 | 0 | 7th |
| 2012 WM20 | 25-F | SUI | 6 | 0 | 0 | 0 | 2 | 8th |

**Simka, Filip**
**b. Martin, Czechoslovakia (Slovakia), February 18, 1986**

| | | | | | | | | |
|---|---|---|---|---|---|---|---|---|
| 2004 WM18 | 23-D | SVK | 6 | 0 | 0 | 0 | 18 | 6th |
| 2006 WM20 | 14-D | SVK | 6 | 0 | 0 | 0 | 10 | 8th |

**Simmonds, Wayne**
**b. Toronto, Ontario, Canada, August 26, 1988**

| | | | | | | | | |
|---|---|---|---|---|---|---|---|---|
| 2008 WM20 | 34-F | CAN | 7 | 0 | 0 | 0 | 4 | G |

**Simon, Dominik**
**b. Prague, Czech Republic, August 8, 1994**

| | | | | | | | | |
|---|---|---|---|---|---|---|---|---|
| 2012 WM18 | 22-F | CZE | 6 | 4 | 4 | 8 | 4 | 8th |

**Simonelli, Frankie**
**b. Bensenville, Illinois, United States, October 29, 1992**

| | | | | | | | | |
|---|---|---|---|---|---|---|---|---|
| 2010 WM18 | 17-D | USA | 7 | 0 | 0 | 0 | 2 | G |

**Sindel, Jakub**
**b. Jihlava, Czechoslovakia (Czech Republic), January 24, 1986**

| | | | | | | | | |
|---|---|---|---|---|---|---|---|---|
| 2003 WM18 | 29-F | CZE | 6 | 4 | 1 | 5 | 4 | 6th |
| 2004 WM18 | 19-F | CZE | 7 | 3 | 3 | 6 | 6 | B |
| 2004 WM20 | 23-F | CZE | 5 | 0 | 1 | 1 | 0 | 4th |
| 2006 WM20 | 19-F | CZE | 6 | 0 | 1 | 1 | 0 | 6th |
| **Totals WM18** | | | **13** | **7** | **4** | **11** | **10** | **B** |
| **Totals WM20** | | | **11** | **0** | **2** | **2** | **0** | **—** |

**Sinisalo, Tomas**
**b. Philadelphia, Pennsylvania, United States, January 15, 1986**

| | | | | | | | | |
|---|---|---|---|---|---|---|---|---|
| 2006 WM20 | 24-F | FIN | 7 | 1 | 0 | 1 | 2 | B |

**Sinkovic, Julius**
**b. Bratislava, Czechoslovakia (Slovakia), March 24, 1988**

| | | | | | | | | |
|---|---|---|---|---|---|---|---|---|
| 2006 WM18 | 17-F | SVK | 6 | 1 | 1 | 2 | 0 | 7th |
| 2007 WM20 | 19-F | SVK | 6 | 1 | 2 | 3 | 2 | 8th |
| 2008 WM20 | 29-F | SVK | 6 | 0 | 2 | 2 | 2 | 7th |
| **Totals WM20** | | | **12** | **1** | **4** | **5** | **4** | **—** |

**Sirianni, Rob**
**b. Edmonton, Alberta, Canada, October 31, 1983**

| | | | | | | | | |
|---|---|---|---|---|---|---|---|---|
| 2012 WM | 93-F | ITA | 7 | 0 | 0 | 0 | 8 | 15th |

**Sirokovs, Aleksejs**
**b. Riga, Soviet Union (Latvia), February 20, 1981**

| | | | | | | | | |
|---|---|---|---|---|---|---|---|---|
| 2003 WM | 16-F | LAT | 6 | 1 | 0 | 1 | 2 | 9th |
| 2004 WM | 16-F | LAT | 7 | 0 | 0 | 0 | 2 | 7th |
| 2005 WM | 16-F | LAT | 6 | 0 | 1 | 1 | 4 | 9th |
| 2006 WM | 16-F | LAT | 6 | 1 | 2 | 3 | 2 | 10th |
| 2007 WM | 16-F | LAT | 5 | 1 | 0 | 1 | 2 | 13th |
| 2008 WM | 16-F | LAT | 6 | 2 | 0 | 2 | 4 | 11th |
| 2009 WM | 16-F | LAT | 3 | 0 | 2 | 2 | 0 | 7th |
| 2010 OG-M | 88-F | LAT | 4 | 0 | 0 | 0 | 2 | 12th |
| 2012 WM | 17-F | LAT | 7 | 1 | 0 | 1 | 2 | 10th |
| **Totals WM** | | | **46** | **6** | **5** | **11** | **18** | **—** |

**Siska, Michal**
**b. Zvolen, Czechoslovakia (Slovakia), March 30, 1990**

| | | | | | | | | |
|---|---|---|---|---|---|---|---|---|
| 2008 WM18 | 21-D | SVK | 6 | 1 | 2 | 3 | 4 | 7th |
| 2009 WM20 | 6-D | SVK | 7 | 0 | 0 | 0 | 0 | 4th |
| 2010 WM20 | 21-D | SVK | 6 | 0 | 2 | 2 | 4 | 8th |
| **Totals WM20** | | | **13** | **0** | **2** | **2** | **4** | **—** |

**Sisovsky, Peter**
**b. Ilava, Czechoslovakia (Slovakia), August 15, 1991**

| | | | | | | | | |
|---|---|---|---|---|---|---|---|---|
| 2009 WM18 | 17-F | SVK | 6 | 1 | 0 | 1 | 6 | 7th |
| 2011 WM20 | 8-F | SVK | 6 | 1 | 0 | 1 | 4 | 8th |

**Sivic, Mitja**
**b. Brezje, Yugoslavia (Slovenia), October 1, 1979**

| | | | | | | | | |
|---|---|---|---|---|---|---|---|---|
| 2011 WM | 10-F | SLO | 4 | 0 | 1 | 1 | 2 | 16th |

**Sjogren, Mattias**
**b. Landskrona, Sweden, November 27, 1987**

| | | | | | | | | |
|---|---|---|---|---|---|---|---|---|
| 2011 WM | 15-F | SWE | 9 | 1 | 3 | 4 | 2 | S |

**Skaarberg, Tobias**
**b. Sarpsborg, Norway, January 19, 1991**

| | | | | | | | | |
|---|---|---|---|---|---|---|---|---|
| 2009 WM18 | 4-D | NOR | 6 | 0 | 1 | 1 | 4 | 9th |
| 2011 WM20 | 5-D | NOR | 5 | 0 | 1 | 1 | 0 | 9th |

**Skabelka, Alexei**
**b. Minsk, Russia, December 7, 1992**

| | | | | | | | | |
|---|---|---|---|---|---|---|---|---|
| 2010 WM18 | 16-F | BLR | 6 | 0 | 1 | 1 | 4 | 10th |

**Skadsdammen, Eirik**
**b. Lunnerseter, Norway, May 23, 1981**

| | | | | | | | | |
|---|---|---|---|---|---|---|---|---|
| 2008 WM | 18-F | NOR | 6 | 0 | 0 | 0 | 2 | 8th |

**Skille, Jack**
**b. Madison, Wisconsin, United States, May 19, 1987**

| | | | | | | | | |
|---|---|---|---|---|---|---|---|---|
| 2004 WM18 | 20-F | USA | 6 | 1 | 1 | 2 | 4 | S |
| 2005 WM18 | 20-F | USA | 6 | 1 | 3 | 4 | 8 | G |
| 2006 WM20 | 21-F | USA | 7 | 2 | 0 | 2 | 4 | 4th |
| 2007 WM20 | 20-F | USA | 7 | 1 | 5 | 6 | 14 | B |
| 2011 WM | 20-F | USA | 7 | 1 | 0 | 1 | 2 | 8th |
| **Totals WM18** | | | **12** | **2** | **4** | **6** | **12** | **G,S** |
| **Totals WM20** | | | **14** | **3** | **5** | **8** | **18** | **B** |

**Skinner, Jeff**
**b. Markham, Ontario, Canada, May 16, 1992**

| | | | | | | | | |
|---|---|---|---|---|---|---|---|---|
| 2011 WM | 53-F | CAN | 7 | 3 | 3 | 6 | 8 | 5th |
| 2012 WM | 53-F | CAN | 8 | 3 | 2 | 5 | 4 | 5th |
| **Totals WM** | | | **15** | **6** | **5** | **11** | **12** | **—** |

**Skjei, Brady**
**b. Lakeville, Minnesota, United States, March 26, 1994**

| | | | | | | | | |
|---|---|---|---|---|---|---|---|---|
| 2012 WM18 | 16-D | USA | 6 | 0 | 1 | 1 | 4 | G |

**Skladany, Frantisek**
**b. Martin, Czechoslovakia (Slovakia), April 22, 1982**

| | | | | | | | | |
|---|---|---|---|---|---|---|---|---|
| 2000 WM18 | 20-F | SVK | 6 | 1 | 1 | 2 | 2 | 5th |
| 2002 WM20 | 20-F | SVK | 7 | 0 | 0 | 0 | 4 | 8th |
| 2008 WM | 20-F | SVK | 5 | 0 | 1 | 1 | 4 | 13th |

**Sklenar, Jakub**
**b. Znojmo, Czechoslovakia (Czech Republic), March 20, 1988**

| | | | | | | | | |
|---|---|---|---|---|---|---|---|---|
| 2006 WM18 | 18-F | CZE | 7 | 0 | 0 | 0 | 0 | B |
| 2008 WM20 | 16-F | CZE | 6 | 4 | 0 | 4 | 4 | 5th |

**Skokan, David**
**b. Poprad, Czechoslovakia (Slovakia), December 6, 1988**

| | | | | | | | | |
|---|---|---|---|---|---|---|---|---|
| 2007 WM20 | 22-F | SVK | 6 | 0 | 2 | 2 | 22 | 8th |
| 2008 WM20 | 19-F | SVK | 6 | 2 | 6 | 8 | 6 | 7th |
| **Totals WM20** | | | **12** | **2** | **8** | **10** | **28** | **—** |

**Skoula, Martin**
**b. Litomerice, Czechoslovakia (Czech Republic), October 28, 1979**

| | | | | | | | | |
|---|---|---|---|---|---|---|---|---|
| 2002 OG-M | 41-D | CZE | 4 | 0 | 0 | 0 | 0 | 5th |
| 2004 WM | 41-D | CZE | 7 | 1 | 0 | 1 | 4 | 5th |
| 2004 WCH | 41-D | CZE | 2 | 0 | 0 | 0 | 2 | 3rd |
| 2006 WM | 41-D | CZE | 9 | 0 | 2 | 2 | 6 | B |
| 2011 WM | 41-D | CZE | 9 | 0 | 2 | 2 | 0 | B |
| **Totals WM** | | | **25** | **1** | **4** | **5** | **10** | **2B** |

**Skroder, Per-Age**
**b. Sarpsborg, Norway, August 4, 1978**

| | | | | | | | | |
|---|---|---|---|---|---|---|---|---|
| 1997 WM | 24-F | NOR | 8 | 0 | 2 | 2 | 4 | 12th |
| 1999 WM | 19-F | NOR | 6 | 2 | 1 | 3 | 4 | 12th |
| 2000 WM | 19-F | NOR | 6 | 4 | 1 | 5 | 0 | 9th |
| 2006 WM | 19-F | NOR | 6 | 2 | 0 | 2 | 6 | 11th |
| 2008 WM | 19-F | NOR | 7 | 0 | 1 | 1 | 2 | 8th |
| 2009 WM | 19-F | NOR | 6 | 0 | 2 | 2 | 4 | 11th |
| 2010 OG-M | 19-F | NOR | 1 | 0 | 0 | 0 | 0 | 10th |
| 2011 WM | 19-F | NOR | 7 | 3 | 4 | 7 | 10 | 6th |
| 2012 WM | 19-F | NOR | 8 | 5 | 7 | 12 | 2 | 8th |
| **Totals WM** | | | **54** | **16** | **18** | **34** | **32** | **—** |

**Skuratovs, Patriks**
**b. Riga, Latvia, March 26, 1994**

| | | | | | | | | |
|---|---|---|---|---|---|---|---|---|
| 2012 WM18 | 4-D | LAT | 6 | 0 | 1 | 1 | 0 | 9th |

**Skvorcovs, Gunars**
**b. Saldus, Soviet Union (Latvia), January 13, 1990**

| | | | | | | | | |
|---|---|---|---|---|---|---|---|---|
| 2009 WM20 | 13-F | LAT | 6 | 0 | 1 | 1 | 2 | 8th |
| 2010 WM20 | 13-F | LAT | 6 | 1 | 0 | 1 | 2 | 9th |
| **Totals WM20** | | | **12** | **1** | **1** | **2** | **4** | **—** |

**Slater, Jim**
**b. Petoskey, Michigan, United States, December 9, 1982**

| | | | | | | | | |
|---|---|---|---|---|---|---|---|---|
| 2012 WM | 19-F | USA | 8 | 2 | 1 | 3 | 6 | 7th |

**Slepyshev, Anton**
**b. Penza, Russia, May 13, 1994**

| | | | | | | | | |
|---|---|---|---|---|---|---|---|---|
| 2011 WM18 | 21-F | RUS | 7 | 3 | 1 | 4 | 0 | B |
| 2012 WM18 | 9-F | RUS | 6 | 3 | 4 | 7 | 6 | 5th |
| Totals WM18 | | | 13 | 6 | 5 | 11 | 6 | B |

**Slimak, Peter**
**b. Kosice, Czechoslovakia (Slovakia), August 20, 1990**

| | | | | | | | | |
|---|---|---|---|---|---|---|---|---|
| 2008 WM18 | 8-D | SVK | 6 | 1 | 1 | 2 | 6 | 7th |

**Sloboda, Martin**
**b. Bratislava, Czechoslovakia (Slovakia), October 2, 1990**

| | | | | | | | | |
|---|---|---|---|---|---|---|---|---|
| 2008 WM18 | 26-F | SVK | 4 | 0 | 1 | 1 | 0 | 7th |

**Slovacek, Ondrej**
**b. Vsetin, Czech Republic, September 14, 1994**

| | | | | | | | | |
|---|---|---|---|---|---|---|---|---|
| 2012 WM18 | 15-F | CZE | 6 | 2 | 0 | 2 | 31 | 8th |

**Slovak, Marek**
**b. Nitra, Czechoslovakia (Slovakia), September 23, 1988**

| | | | | | | | | |
|---|---|---|---|---|---|---|---|---|
| 2006 WM18 | 4-F | SVK | 6 | 0 | 1 | 1 | 4 | 7th |
| 2008 WM20 | 9-F | SVK | 6 | 2 | 7 | 9 | 12 | 7th |

**Smach, Ondrej**
**b. Hodonin, Czechoslovakia (Czech Republic), July 21, 1986**

| | | | | | | | | |
|---|---|---|---|---|---|---|---|---|
| 2004 WM18 | 5-D | CZE | 7 | 0 | 1 | 1 | 6 | B |
| 2005 WM20 | 12-D | CZE | 7 | 0 | 0 | 0 | 2 | B |
| 2006 WM20 | 5-D | CZE | 6 | 0 | 2 | 2 | 6 | 6th |
| **Totals WM20** | | | **13** | **0** | **2** | **2** | **8** | **B** |

**Smid, Ladislav**
**b. Frydlant, Czechoslovakia (Czech Republic), February 1, 1986**

| | | | | | | | | |
|---|---|---|---|---|---|---|---|---|
| 2003 WM18 | 2-D | CZE | 6 | 0 | 0 | 0 | 2 | 6th |
| 2004 WM18 | 8-D | CZE | 5 | 0 | 2 | 2 | 0 | B |
| 2004 WM20 | 12-D | CZE | 6 | 1 | 2 | 3 | 4 | 4th |
| 2005 WM20 | 8-D | CZE | 7 | 0 | 2 | 2 | 4 | B |
| 2006 WM20 | 8-D | CZE | 6 | 1 | 1 | 2 | 0 | 6th |
| 2007 WM | 6-D | CZE | 6 | 0 | 0 | 0 | 31 | 7th |
| **Totals WM18** | | | **11** | **0** | **2** | **2** | **2** | **B** |
| **Totals WM20** | | | **19** | **2** | **5** | **7** | **8** | **B** |

**Smirnovs, Andrejs**
**b. Riga, Latvia, June 27, 1992**

| | | | | | | | | |
|---|---|---|---|---|---|---|---|---|
| 2010 WM18 | 20-D | LAT | 6 | 0 | 0 | 0 | 4 | 9th |

**Smith, Colin**
**b. Edmonton, Alberta, Canada, June 20, 1993**

| | | | | | | | | |
|---|---|---|---|---|---|---|---|---|
| 2011 WM18 | 17-F | CAN | 7 | 2 | 1 | 3 | 14 | 4th |

**Smith, Craig**
**b. Madison, Wisconsin, United States, September 5, 1989**

| | | | | | | | | |
|---|---|---|---|---|---|---|---|---|
| 2011 WM | 15-F | USA | 7 | 3 | 3 | 6 | 4 | 8th |
| 2012 WM | 25-F | USA | 4 | 0 | 2 | 2 | 2 | 7th |
| **Totals WM** | | | **11** | **3** | **5** | **8** | **6** | **—** |

**Smith, Gemel**
**b. Toronto, Ontario, Canada, April 16, 1994**

| | | | | | | | | |
|---|---|---|---|---|---|---|---|---|
| 2012 WM18 | 18-F | CAN | 7 | 2 | 3 | 5 | 2 | B |

**Smith-Pelly, Devante**
**b. Scarborough (Toronto), Ontario, Canada, June 14, 1992**

| | | | | | | | | |
|---|---|---|---|---|---|---|---|---|
| 2012 WM20 | 22-F | CAN | 1 | 0 | 0 | 0 | 0 | B |

**Smits, Janis**
**b. Riga, Soviet Union (Latvia), June 8, 1990**

| | | | | | | | | |
|---|---|---|---|---|---|---|---|---|
| 2009 WM20 | 8-D | LAT | 6 | 0 | 0 | 0 | 6 | 8th |
| 2010 WM20 | 8-D | LAT | 6 | 0 | 0 | 0 | 6 | 9th |
| **Totals WM20** | | | **12** | **0** | **0** | **0** | **12** | **—** |

**Smrek, Peter**
**b. Martin, Czechoslovakia (Slovakia), February 16, 1979**

| | | | | | | | | |
|---|---|---|---|---|---|---|---|---|
| 1999 WM20 | 4-D | SVK | 6 | 0 | 1 | 1 | 4 | B |
| 2002 OG-M | 4-D | SVK | 4 | 0 | 0 | 0 | 0 | 13th |
| 2002 WM | 8-D | SVK | 9 | 0 | 0 | 0 | 8 | G |
| 2009 WM | 6-D | SVK | 6 | 1 | 0 | 1 | 6 | 10th |
| **Totals WM** | | | **15** | **1** | **0** | **1** | **14** | **G** |

**Smurov, Sergei**
**b. Khabarovsk, Russia, July 26, 1993**

| | | | | | | | | |
|---|---|---|---|---|---|---|---|---|
| 2011 WM18 | 26-F | RUS | 7 | 1 | 0 | 1 | 4 | B |

**Smyth, Ryan**
**b. Banff, Alberta, Canada, February 21, 1976**

| | | | | | | | | |
|---|---|---|---|---|---|---|---|---|
| 1995 WM20 | 20-F | CAN | 7 | 2 | 5 | 7 | 4 | G |
| 1999 WM | 94-F | CAN | 10 | 0 | 2 | 2 | 12 | 4th |
| 2000 WM | 94-F | CAN | 9 | 3 | 6 | 9 | 0 | 4th |
| 2001 WM | 94-F | CAN | 7 | 2 | 3 | 5 | 4 | 5th |
| 2002 OG-M | 94-F | CAN | 6 | 0 | 1 | 1 | 0 | G |
| 2002 WM | 94-F | CAN | 7 | 4 | 0 | 4 | 2 | 6th |
| 2003 WM | 94-F | CAN | 9 | 2 | 2 | 4 | 2 | G |
| 2004 WM | 94-F | CAN | 9 | 2 | 2 | 4 | 2 | G |
| 2004 WCH | 94-F | CAN | 6 | 3 | 1 | 4 | 2 | 1st |
| 2005 WM | 94-F | CAN | 9 | 2 | 1 | 3 | 6 | S |
| 2006 OG-M | 94-F | CAN | 6 | 0 | 1 | 1 | 4 | 7th |
| 2010 WM | 94-F | CAN | 1 | 0 | 0 | 0 | 0 | 7th |
| **Totals WM** | | | **61** | **15** | **16** | **31** | **28** | **2G,S** |
| **Totals OG-M** | | | **12** | **0** | **2** | **2** | **4** | **G** |

**Snall, Henri**
**b. Haparanda, Sweden, April 6, 1992**

| | | | | | | | | |
|---|---|---|---|---|---|---|---|---|
| 2010 WM18 | 17-F | SWE | 6 | 2 | 1 | 3 | 4 | S |

**Soberg, Markus**
**b. Oslo, Norway, April 22, 1995**

| | | | | | | | | |
|---|---|---|---|---|---|---|---|---|
| 2011 WM18 | 16-F | NOR | 6 | 1 | 2 | 3 | 4 | 9th |

**Sobotka, Vladimir**
**b. Trebic, Czechoslovakia (Czech Republic), July 2, 1987**

| | | | | | | | | |
|---|---|---|---|---|---|---|---|---|
| 2004 WM18 | 18-F | CZE | 7 | 1 | 0 | 1 | 10 | B |
| 2005 WM18 | 16-F | CZE | 7 | 1 | 0 | 1 | 10 | 4th |
| 2006 WM20 | 11-F | CZE | 6 | 2 | 2 | 4 | 33 | 6th |
| 2007 WM20 | 11-F | CZE | 6 | 4 | 4 | 8 | 12 | 5th |
| **Totals WM18** | | | **14** | **2** | **0** | **2** | **20** | **B** |
| **Totals WM20** | | | **12** | **6** | **6** | **12** | **45** | **—** |

**Soderberg, Carl**
**b. Malmo, Sweden, October 12, 1985**

| | | | | | | | | |
|---|---|---|---|---|---|---|---|---|
| 2003 WM18 | 14-F | SWE | 6 | 2 | 0 | 2 | 4 | 5th |
| 2005 WM20 | 27-F | SWE | 6 | 4 | 2 | 6 | 4 | 6th |

**Sointu, Matias**
**b. Tampere, Finland, February 10, 1990**

| | | | | | | | | |
|---|---|---|---|---|---|---|---|---|
| 2008 WM18 | 21-F | FIN | 6 | 3 | 0 | 3 | 8 | 6th |
| 2010 WM20 | 13-F | FIN | 4 | 1 | 2 | 3 | 6 | 5th |

**Solarev, Ilya**
**b. Perm, Soviet Union (Russia), August 2, 1982**

| | | | | | | | | |
|---|---|---|---|---|---|---|---|---|
| 2010 WM | 25-F | KAZ | 6 | 0 | 0 | 0 | 2 | 16th |

**Solberg, Henrik**
**b. Trondheim, Norway, Aptil 15, 1987**

| | | | | | | | | |
|---|---|---|---|---|---|---|---|---|
| 2010 WM | 39-D | NOR | 6 | 1 | 0 | 1 | 2 | 9th |
| 2012 WM | 39-D | NOR | 8 | 0 | 1 | 1 | 4 | 8th |
| **Totals WM** | | | **14** | **1** | **1** | **2** | **6** | **—** |

**Solder, Niklas**
**b. Neuss, Germany, December 8, 1993**

| | | | | | | | | |
|---|---|---|---|---|---|---|---|---|
| 2011 WM18 | 25-F | GER | 6 | 0 | 0 | 0 | 0 | 6th |

**Solomonov, Yevgeni**
**b. Gomel, Soviet Union (Belarus), May 9, 1990**

| | | | | | | | | |
|---|---|---|---|---|---|---|---|---|
| 2008 WM18 | 10-F | BLR | 6 | 1 | 0 | 1 | 4 | 9th |

**Solovyov, Stanislav**
**b. Sverdlovsk (Yekaterinburg), Soviet Union (Russia), January 1, 1991**

| | | | | | | | | |
|---|---|---|---|---|---|---|---|---|
| 2009 WM18 | 27-F | RUS | 7 | 0 | 0 | 0 | 4 | S |

**Sondergaard, Thomas**
**b. Gaerum, Denmark, June 30, 1993**

| | | | | | | | | |
|---|---|---|---|---|---|---|---|---|
| 2012 WM20 | 18-F | DEN | 6 | 0 | 0 | 0 | 2 | 10th |

**Sonne, Brett**
**b. Maple Ridge, British Columbia, Canada, March 16, 1989**

| | | | | | | | | |
|---|---|---|---|---|---|---|---|---|
| 2009 WM20 | 12-F | CAN | 6 | 1 | 2 | 3 | 0 | G |

**Sopanen, Vili**
**b. Valkeala, Finland, October 21, 1987**

| | | | | | | | | |
|---|---|---|---|---|---|---|---|---|
| 2007 WM20 | 16-F | FIN | 6 | 0 | 0 | 0 | 4 | 6th |

**Sorokins, Olegs**
**b. Riga, Soviet Union (Latvia), January 4, 1974**

| | | | | | | | | |
|---|---|---|---|---|---|---|---|---|
| 2001 WM | 22-D | LAT | 6 | 0 | 0 | 0 | 0 | 13th |
| 2002 OG-M | 22-D | LAT | 4 | 0 | 2 | 2 | 4 | 9th |
| 2002 WM | 22-D | LAT | 6 | 0 | 2 | 2 | 4 | 11th |
| 2003 WM | 22-D | LAT | 6 | 1 | 3 | 4 | 2 | 9th |
| 2004 WM | 22-D | LAT | 7 | 0 | 2 | 2 | 2 | 7th |
| 2005 WM | 22-D | LAT | 6 | 0 | 0 | 0 | 4 | 9th |
| 2007 WM | 22-D | LAT | 6 | 2 | 4 | 6 | 6 | 13th |
| 2009 WM | 22-D | LAT | 5 | 0 | 0 | 0 | 2 | 7th |
| **Totals WM** | | | **42** | **3** | **11** | **14** | **20** | **—** |

**Sotnieks, Kristaps**
**b. Riga, Soviet Union (Latvia), January 29, 1987**

| | | | | | | | | |
|---|---|---|---|---|---|---|---|---|
| 2006 WM20 | 4-D | LAT | 6 | 0 | 2 | 2 | 6 | 9th |
| 2009 WM | 11-D | LAT | 7 | 0 | 1 | 1 | 8 | 7th |
| 2010 OG-M | 11-D | LAT | 4 | 1 | 0 | 1 | 4 | 12th |
| 2010 WM | 11-D | LAT | 6 | 0 | 1 | 1 | 0 | 11th |
| 2011 WM | 11-D | LAT | 6 | 0 | 4 | 4 | 6 | 13th |
| 2012 WM | 11-D | LAT | 7 | 0 | 0 | 0 | 0 | 10th |
| **Totals WM** | | | **26** | **0** | **6** | **6** | **14** | **—** |

**Soudek, Robin**
**b. Ceske Budejovice, Czechoslovakia (Czech Republic), July 31, 1991**

| | | | | | | | | |
|---|---|---|---|---|---|---|---|---|
| 2009 WM18 | 17-F | CZE | 6 | 1 | 1 | 2 | 6 | 6th |
| 2011 WM20 | 25-F | CZE | 6 | 0 | 0 | 0 | 6 | 7th |

**Soumelidis, Eustathios**
**b. Brno, Czech Republic, January 17, 1994**

| | | | | | | | | |
|---|---|---|---|---|---|---|---|---|
| 2012 WM18 | 20-F | CZE | 6 | 1 | 3 | 4 | 4 | 8th |

**Souza, Michael**
**b. Wakefield, Massachusetts, United States, January 28, 1978**

| | | | | | | | | |
|---|---|---|---|---|---|---|---|---|
| 2010 WM | 27-F | ITA | 6 | 1 | 4 | 5 | 2 | 15th |

**Spelling, Thomas**
**b. Herning, Denmark, February 9, 1993**

| | | | | | | | | |
|---|---|---|---|---|---|---|---|---|
| 2012 WM20 | 8-F | DEN | 6 | 1 | 3 | 4 | 0 | 10th |

**Spets, Knut**
**b. Trondheim, Norway, November 7, 1982**

| | | | | | | | | |
|---|---|---|---|---|---|---|---|---|
| 1999 WM18 | 16-F | NOR | 6 | 0 | 0 | 0 | 6 | 9th |
| 2007 WM | 12-F | NOR | 6 | 0 | 0 | 0 | 2 | 14th |
| 2010 WM | 16-F | NOR | 6 | 0 | 0 | 0 | 0 | 9th |
| **Totals WM** | | | **12** | **0** | **0** | **0** | **2** | **—** |

**Spets, Lars Erik**
**b. Trondheim, Norway, April 2, 1985**

| | | | | | | | | |
|---|---|---|---|---|---|---|---|---|
| 2002 WM18 | 16-F | NOR | 8 | 3 | 3 | 6 | 4 | 11th |
| 2006 WM | 10-F | NOR | 6 | 0 | 0 | 0 | 0 | 11th |
| 2007 WM | 10-F | NOR | 6 | 2 | 1 | 3 | 4 | 14th |
| 2008 WM | 10-F | NOR | 7 | 1 | 1 | 2 | 0 | 8th |
| 2009 WM | 10-F | NOR | 6 | 0 | 1 | 1 | 2 | 11th |
| 2010 OG-M | 10-F | NOR | 4 | 0 | 0 | 0 | 2 | 10th |
| 2010 WM | 10-F | NOR | 6 | 1 | 2 | 3 | 0 | 9th |
| 2011 WM | 10-F | NOR | 7 | 1 | 2 | 3 | 2 | 6th |
| 2012 WM | 10-F | NOR | 8 | 3 | 1 | 4 | 4 | 8th |
| **Totals WM** | | | **46** | **8** | **8** | **16** | **12** | **—** |

**Spezza, Jason**
**b. Mississauga, Ontario, Canada, June 13, 1983**

| | | | | | | | | |
|---|---|---|---|---|---|---|---|---|
| 2000 WM20 | 19-F | CAN | 7 | 0 | 2 | 2 | 2 | B |
| 2001 WM20 | 9-F | CAN | 7 | 3 | 3 | 6 | 2 | B |
| 2002 WM20 | 9-F | CAN | 7 | 0 | 4 | 4 | 8 | S |
| 2008 WM | 91-F | CAN | 9 | 1 | 2 | 3 | 0 | S |
| 2009 WM | 91-F | CAN | 9 | 7 | 4 | 11 | 2 | S |
| 2011 WM | 19-F | CAN | 7 | 4 | 3 | 7 | 4 | 5th |
| **Totals WM20** | | | **21** | **3** | **9** | **12** | **4** | **S,2B** |
| **Totals WM** | | | **25** | **12** | **9** | **21** | **6** | **2S** |

~WM20 All-Star Team/Forward (2001)

**Spiridonov, Andrei**
**b. Ust-Kamenogorsk, Soviet Union (Kazakhstan), May 21, 1982**

| | | | | | | | | |
|---|---|---|---|---|---|---|---|---|
| 2001 WM20 | 29-F | KAZ | 6 | 0 | 0 | 0 | 2 | 10th |
| 2006 WM | 36-F | KAZ | 6 | 1 | 2 | 3 | 4 | 15th |
| 2010 WM | 23-F | KAZ | 6 | 0 | 0 | 0 | 2 | 16th |
| 2012 WM | 23-F | KAZ | 7 | 0 | 0 | 0 | 2 | 16th |
| **Totals WM** | | | **19** | **1** | **2** | **3** | **8** | **—** |

**Spiridonov, Andrei**
**b. Moscow, Soviet Union (Russia), April 16, 1984**

| | | | | | | | | |
|---|---|---|---|---|---|---|---|---|
| 2004 WM20 | 4-D | RUS | 6 | 0 | 3 | 3 | 6 | 5th |

**Spolidoro, Nico**
**b. Langnau, Switzerland, March 19, 1986**

| | | | | | | | | |
|---|---|---|---|---|---|---|---|---|
| 2006 WM20 | 19-F | SUI | 6 | 0 | 1 | 1 | 2 | 7th |

**Spooner, Ryan**
**b. Kanata, Ontario, Canada, January 30, 1992**

| | | | | | | | | |
|---|---|---|---|---|---|---|---|---|
| 2010 WM18 | 21-F | CAN | 6 | 2 | 0 | 2 | 2 | 7th |

**Sprukts, Janis**
**b. Riga, Soviet Union (Latvia), January 31, 1982**

| | | | | | | | | |
|---|---|---|---|---|---|---|---|---|
| 2000 WM | 16-D | LAT | 7 | 0 | 0 | 0 | 0 | 8th |
| 2003 WM | 5-D | LAT | 6 | 0 | 2 | 2 | 2 | 9th |
| 2005 WM | 5-F | LAT | 6 | 2 | 1 | 3 | 0 | 9th |
| 2006 WM | 5-F | LAT | 6 | 0 | 1 | 1 | 2 | 10th |
| 2007 WM | 5-F | LAT | 3 | 0 | 2 | 2 | 0 | 13th |
| 2008 WM | 5-F | LAT | 6 | 0 | 2 | 2 | 2 | 11th |
| 2009 WM | 5-F | LAT | 7 | 0 | 1 | 1 | 0 | 7th |
| 2010 OG-M | 5-F | LAT | 4 | 0 | 1 | 1 | 0 | 12th |
| 2010 WM | 5-F | LAT | 6 | 2 | 3 | 5 | 2 | 11th |
| 2012 WM | 5-F | LAT | 7 | 0 | 4 | 4 | 2 | 10th |
| **Totals WM** | | | **54** | **4** | **16** | **20** | **10** | **—** |

**Sprunger, Julien**
**b. Fribourg, Switzerland, January 4, 1986**

| | | | | | | | | |
|---|---|---|---|---|---|---|---|---|
| 2005 WM20 | 26-F | SUI | 6 | 0 | 0 | 0 | 2 | 8th |
| 2006 WM20 | 12-F | SUI | 6 | 2 | 3 | 5 | 12 | 7th |
| 2007 WM | 86-F | SUI | 7 | 2 | 0 | 2 | 4 | 8th |
| 2008 WM | 86-F | SUI | 7 | 3 | 2 | 5 | 6 | 7th |
| 2009 WM | 86-F | SUI | 5 | 0 | 0 | 0 | 0 | 9th |
| 2010 OG-M | 86-F | SUI | 5 | 2 | 0 | 2 | 2 | 8th |
| 2011 WM | 86-F | SUI | 6 | 0 | 1 | 1 | 2 | 9th |
| **Totals WM20** | | | **12** | **2** | **3** | **5** | **14** | **—** |
| **Totals WM** | | | **25** | **5** | **3** | **8** | **12** | **—** |

**Staal, Eric**
**b. Thunder Bay, Ontario, Canada, October 29, 1984**

| | | | | | | | | |
|---|---|---|---|---|---|---|---|---|
| 2002 WM18 | 20-F | CAN | 8 | 2 | 5 | 7 | 4 | 6th |
| 2007 WM | 12-F | CAN | 9 | 5 | 5 | 10 | 6 | G |
| 2008 WM | 12-F | CAN | 8 | 4 | 3 | 7 | 6 | S |
| 2010 OG-M | 21-F | CAN | 7 | 1 | 5 | 6 | 6 | G |
| **Totals WM** | | | **17** | **9** | **8** | **17** | **12** | **G,S** |

~Triple Gold Club

**Staal, Jordan**
**b. Thunder Bay, Ontario, Canada, September 10, 1988**

| | | | | | | | | |
|---|---|---|---|---|---|---|---|---|
| 2007 WM | 10-F | CAN | 9 | 0 | 2 | 2 | 0 | G |

**Staal, Kim**
**b. Herlev, Denmark, March 10, 1978**

| | | | | | | | | |
|---|---|---|---|---|---|---|---|---|
| 2003 WM | 19-F | DEN | 5 | 2 | 3 | 5 | 6 | 11th |
| 2004 WM | 19-F | DEN | 6 | 3 | 1 | 4 | 4 | 12th |
| 2005 WM | 19-F | DEN | 1 | 0 | 0 | 0 | 0 | 14th |
| 2006 WM | 19-F | DEN | 6 | 5 | 1 | 6 | 2 | 13th |
| 2007 WM | 19-F | DEN | 5 | 2 | 3 | 5 | 2 | 10th |
| 2008 WM | 19-F | DEN | 6 | 4 | 2 | 6 | 2 | 12th |
| 2009 WM | 19-F | DEN | 6 | 1 | 0 | 1 | 2 | 13th |
| 2010 WM | 19-F | DEN | 7 | 0 | 1 | 1 | 2 | 8th |
| 2011 WM | 19-F | DEN | 6 | 0 | 0 | 0 | 0 | 11th |
| **Totals WM** | | | **48** | **17** | **11** | **28** | **20** | **—** |

**Staal, Marc**
**b. Thunder Bay, Ontario, Canada, January 13, 1987**

| | | | | | | | | |
|---|---|---|---|---|---|---|---|---|
| 2006 WM20 | 3-D | CAN | 6 | 0 | 1 | 1 | 4 | G |
| 2007 WM20 | 14-D | CAN | 6 | 0 | 0 | 0 | 4 | G |
| 2010 WM | 18-D | CAN | 7 | 0 | 1 | 1 | 2 | 7th |
| **Totals WM20** | | | **12** | **0** | **1** | **1** | **8** | **2G** |

~WM20 IIHF Directorate Best Defenceman (2006)

**Stach, David**
**b. Kladno, Czech Republic, February 22, 1992**

| | | | | | | | | |
|---|---|---|---|---|---|---|---|---|
| 2010 WM18 | 16-F | CZE | 6 | 0 | 0 | 0 | 4 | 6th |

**Stafford, Drew**
**b. Milwaukee, Wisconsin, United States, October 30, 1985**

| | | | | | | | | |
|---|---|---|---|---|---|---|---|---|
| 2003 WM18 | 25-F | USA | 6 | 3 | 2 | 5 | 8 | 4th |
| 2004 WM20 | 19-F | USA | 6 | 0 | 2 | 2 | 2 | G |
| 2005 WM20 | 19-F | USA | 7 | 5 | 4 | 9 | 14 | 4th |
| 2006 WM | 19-F | USA | 7 | 0 | 1 | 1 | 0 | 7th |
| 2008 WM | 19-F | USA | 7 | 1 | 3 | 4 | 6 | 6th |
| 2009 WM | 21-F | USA | 9 | 2 | 1 | 3 | 6 | 4th |
| **Totals WM20** | | | **13** | **5** | **6** | **11** | **16** | **G** |
| **Totals WM** | | | **23** | **3** | **5** | **8** | **12** | **—** |

**Stajnoch, Martin**
**b. Bojnice, Czechoslovakia (Slovakia), September 15, 1990**

| | | | | | | | | |
|---|---|---|---|---|---|---|---|---|
| 2008 WM18 | 3-D | SVK | 6 | 1 | 3 | 4 | 10 | 7th |
| 2009 WM20 | 3-D | SVK | 7 | 1 | 3 | 4 | 6 | 4th |
| 2010 WM20 | 3-D | SVK | 4 | 0 | 0 | 0 | 4 | 8th |
| **Totals WM20** | | | **11** | **1** | **3** | **4** | **10** | **—** |

**Stalberg, Viktor**
**b. Gothenburg, Sweden, January 17, 1986**

| | | | | | | | | |
|---|---|---|---|---|---|---|---|---|
| 2012 WM | 25-F | SWE | 8 | 3 | 1 | 4 | 2 | 6th |

**Stals, Juris**
**b. Riga, Soviet Union (Latvia), April 8, 1982**

| | | | | | | | | |
|---|---|---|---|---|---|---|---|---|
| 2006 WM | 20-F | LAT | 6 | 0 | 0 | 0 | 4 | 10th |
| 2008 WM | 6-F | LAT | 6 | 0 | 0 | 0 | 2 | 11th |
| 2010 WM | 6-F | LAT | 4 | 0 | 2 | 2 | 0 | 11th |
| 2011 WM | 6-F | LAT | 3 | 0 | 0 | 0 | 0 | 13th |
| 2012 WM | 60-F | LAT | 7 | 0 | 0 | 0 | 0 | 10th |
| **Totals WM** | | | **26** | **0** | **2** | **2** | **6** | **—** |

**Stamkos, Steve**
**b. Markham, Ontario, Canada, February 7, 1990**

| | | | | | | | | |
|---|---|---|---|---|---|---|---|---|
| 2007 WM18 | 19-F | CAN | 6 | 2 | 8 | 10 | 8 | 4th |
| 2008 WM20 | 10-F | CAN | 7 | 1 | 5 | 6 | 4 | G |
| 2009 WM | 17-F | CAN | 9 | 7 | 4 | 11 | 6 | S |
| 2010 WM | 91-F | CAN | 5 | 2 | 1 | 3 | 10 | 7th |
| **Totals WM** | | | **14** | **9** | **5** | **14** | **16** | **S** |

~WM All-Star Team/Forward (2009), WM18 All-Star Team/Forward (2007)

**Stancescu, Victor**
**b. Bucharest, Romania, March 10, 1985**

| | | | | | | | | |
|---|---|---|---|---|---|---|---|---|
| 2002 WM18 | 22-F | SUI | 8 | 0 | 3 | 3 | 2 | 7th |
| 2003 WM18 | 22-F | SUI | 6 | 0 | 0 | 0 | 12 | 9th |
| 2003 WM20 | 23-F | SUI | 6 | 0 | 1 | 1 | 2 | 7th |
| 2004 WM20 | 22-F | SUI | 6 | 2 | 1 | 3 | 2 | 8th |
| 2005 WM20 | 22-F | SUI | 6 | 5 | 2 | 7 | 10 | 8th |
| 2011 WM | 22-F | SUI | 5 | 0 | 1 | 1 | 2 | 9th |
| **Totals WM18** | | | **14** | **0** | **3** | **3** | **14** | **—** |
| **Totals WM20** | | | **18** | **7** | **4** | **11** | **14** | **—** |

**Stano, Tomas**
**b. Ilava, Czechoslovakia (Slovakia), January 4, 1991**

| | | | | | | | | |
|---|---|---|---|---|---|---|---|---|
| 2008 WM18 | 23-D | SVK | 6 | 0 | 1 | 1 | 8 | 7th |
| 2009 WM18 | 23-D | SVK | 5 | 1 | 3 | 4 | 10 | 7th |
| **Totals WM18** | | | **11** | **1** | **4** | **5** | **18** | **—** |

**Stapleton, Tim**
**b. La Grange, Illinois, United States, July 9, 1982**

| | | | | | | | | |
|---|---|---|---|---|---|---|---|---|
| 2011 WM | 23-F | USA | 7 | 0 | 1 | 1 | 0 | 8th |

**Starchenko, Roman**
**b. Ust-Kamenogorsk, Soviet Union (Kazakhstan),** May 12, 1986

| | | | | | | | | |
|---|---|---|---|---|---|---|---|---|
| 2006 WM | 48-F | KAZ | 3 | 2 | 0 | 2 | 0 | 15th |
| 2010 WM | 48-F | KAZ | 6 | 2 | 0 | 2 | 2 | 16th |
| 2012 WM | 48-F | KAZ | 2 | 0 | 2 | 2 | 0 | 16th |
| **Totals WM** | | | **11** | **4** | **2** | **6** | **2** | **—** |

**Starkov, Kirill**
**b. Sverdlovsk (Yekaterinburg), Soviet Union (Russia), March 31, 1987**

| 2007 WM | 14-F | DEN | 6 | 1 | 1 | 2 | 0 | 10th |
|---|---|---|---|---|---|---|---|---|
| 2011 WM | 14-F | DEN | 6 | 0 | 2 | 2 | 2 | 11th |
| 2012 WM | 14-F | DEN | 7 | 0 | 1 | 1 | 0 | 13th |
| **Totals WM** | | | **19** | **1** | **4** | **5** | **2** | **—** |

**Starosta, Tomas**
**b. Trencin, Czechoslovakia (Slovakia), May 20, 1981**

| 1999 WM18 | 19-D | SVK | 7 | 2 | 1 | 3 | 2 | B |
|---|---|---|---|---|---|---|---|---|
| 2000 WM20 | 10-D | SVK | 6 | 0 | 0 | 0 | 0 | 9th |
| 2001 WM20 | 11-D | SVK | 7 | 0 | 1 | 1 | 8 | 8th |
| 2007 WM | 55-D | SVK | 6 | 0 | 0 | 0 | 2 | 6th |
| 2008 WM | 19-D | SVK | 5 | 0 | 0 | 0 | 2 | 13th |
| 2010 WM | 19-D | SVK | 6 | 0 | 3 | 3 | 4 | 12th |
| 2012 WM | 19-D | SVK | 10 | 0 | 0 | 0 | 2 | S |
| **Totals WM20** | | | **13** | **0** | **1** | **1** | **8** | **—** |
| **Totals WM** | | | **27** | **0** | **3** | **3** | **10** | **S** |

**Stas, Andrei**
**b. Minsk, Soviet Union (Belarus), October 18, 1988**

| 2006 WM18 | 23-F | BLR | 6 | 0 | 1 | 1 | 6 | 9th |
|---|---|---|---|---|---|---|---|---|
| 2007 WM20 | 26-F | BLR | 6 | 1 | 0 | 1 | 2 | 10th |
| 2009 WM | 23-F | BLR | 7 | 1 | 0 | 1 | 6 | 8th |
| 2010 OG-M | 26-F | BLR | 4 | 0 | 0 | 0 | 2 | 9th |
| 2010 WM | 26-F | BLR | 6 | 1 | 2 | 3 | 4 | 10th |
| 2011 WM | 26-F | BLR | 6 | 0 | 0 | 0 | 0 | 14th |
| 2012 WM | 26-F | BLR | 7 | 0 | 0 | 0 | 12 | 14th |
| **Totals WM** | | | **26** | **2** | **2** | **4** | **22** | **—** |

**Stasenko, Nikolai**
**b. Roshino, Soviet Union (Russia), February 15, 1987**

| 2007 WM20 | 5-D | BLR | 6 | 0 | 0 | 0 | 25 | 10th |
|---|---|---|---|---|---|---|---|---|
| 2010 OG-M | 5-D | BLR | 4 | 0 | 3 | 3 | 2 | 9th |
| 2010 WM | 5-D | BLR | 6 | 0 | 1 | 1 | 4 | 10th |
| 2011 WM | 5-D | BLR | 6 | 0 | 1 | 1 | 0 | 14th |
| 2012 WM | 5-D | BLR | 7 | 0 | 0 | 0 | 10 | 14th |
| **Totals WM** | | | **19** | **0** | **2** | **2** | **14** | **—** |

**Stastny, Andrej**
**b. Povazska Bystrica, Czechoslovakia (Slovakia), January 24, 1991**

| 2009 WM18 | 26-F | SVK | 6 | 1 | 3 | 4 | 12 | 7th |
|---|---|---|---|---|---|---|---|---|
| 2010 WM20 | 27-F | SVK | 6 | 1 | 2 | 3 | 10 | 8th |
| 2011 WM20 | 17-F | SVK | 6 | 1 | 1 | 2 | 0 | 8th |
| **Totals WM20** | | | **12** | **2** | **3** | **5** | **10** | **—** |

**Stastny, Paul**
**b. Quebec City, Quebec, Canada, December 27, 1985**

| 2007 WM | 11-F | USA | 7 | 4 | 4 | 8 | 2 | 5th |
|---|---|---|---|---|---|---|---|---|
| 2010 OG-M | 26-F | USA | 6 | 1 | 2 | 3 | 0 | S |
| 2012 WM | 26-F | USA | 8 | 3 | 6 | 9 | 0 | 7th |
| **Totals WM** | | | **15** | **7** | **10** | **17** | **2** | **—** |

**Stastny, Yan**
**b. Quebec City, Quebec, Canada, September 30, 1982**

| 2005 WM | 22-F | USA | 7 | 2 | 0 | 2 | 6 | 6th |
|---|---|---|---|---|---|---|---|---|
| 2006 WM | 21-F | USA | 7 | 1 | 0 | 1 | 2 | 7th |
| 2011 WM | 22-F | USA | 7 | 1 | 1 | 2 | 4 | 8th |
| **Totals WM** | | | **21** | **4** | **1** | **5** | **12** | **—** |

**Steele, Warren**
**b. Williamsburg, Ontario, Canada, May 16, 1994**

| 2012 WM18 | 7-D | CAN | 7 | 0 | 0 | 0 | 4 | B |
|---|---|---|---|---|---|---|---|---|

**Steen, Alexander**
**b. Winnipeg, Manitoba, Canada, March 1, 1984**

| 2002 WM18 | 9-F | SWE | 8 | 2 | 6 | 8 | 8 | 9th |
|---|---|---|---|---|---|---|---|---|
| 2003 WM20 | 24-F | SWE | 6 | 4 | 2 | 6 | 6 | 8th |
| 2004 WM20 | 17-F | SWE | 6 | 2 | 1 | 3 | 4 | 7th |
| 2007 WM | 10-F | SWE | 9 | 2 | 2 | 4 | 6 | 4th |
| **Totals WM20** | | | **12** | **6** | **3** | **9** | **10** | **—** |

**Stefanka, Juraj**
**b. Nitra, Czechoslovakia (Slovakia), August 21, 1976**

| 1996 WM20 | 14-F | SVK | 6 | 1 | 4 | 5 | 6 | 7th |
|---|---|---|---|---|---|---|---|---|
| 2004 WM | 48-F | SVK | 3 | 0 | 0 | 0 | 0 | 4th |
| 2005 WM | 48-F | SVK | 7 | 0 | 0 | 0 | 0 | 5th |
| 2009 WM | 20-F | SVK | 4 | 0 | 0 | 0 | 6 | 10th |
| **Totals WM** | | | **14** | **0** | **0** | **0** | **6** | **—** |

**Stefanovich, Mikhail**
**b. Minsk, Soviet Union (Belarus), November 27, 1989**

| 2006 WM18 | 22-F | BLR | 6 | 2 | 4 | 6 | 24 | 9th |
|---|---|---|---|---|---|---|---|---|
| 2007 WM20 | 18-F | BLR | 6 | 4 | 1 | 5 | 8 | 10th |
| 2009 WM | 16-F | BLR | 4 | 0 | 0 | 0 | 0 | 8th |
| 2010 WM | 16-F | BLR | 6 | 2 | 0 | 2 | 2 | 10th |
| **Totals WM** | | | **10** | **2** | **0** | **2** | **2** | **—** |

**Steiner, Nicholas**
**b. Eggiwil, Switzerland, June 28, 1991**

| 2009 WM18 | 8-D | SUI | 5 | 0 | 0 | 0 | 2 | 8th |
|---|---|---|---|---|---|---|---|---|
| 2011 WM20 | 6-D | SUI | 6 | 0 | 1 | 1 | 4 | 5th |

**Steinhauer, Dennis**
**b. Villingen-Schwenningen, Germany, May 7, 1991**

| 2008 WM18 | 7-D | GER | 6 | 0 | 1 | 1 | 0 | 5th |
|---|---|---|---|---|---|---|---|---|
| 2009 WM18 | 7-D | GER | 6 | 2 | 2 | 4 | 4 | 10th |
| **Totals WM18** | | | **12** | **2** | **3** | **5** | **4** | **—** |

**Steinmann, Janick**
**b. Baar, Switzerland, February 10, 1987**

| 2005 WM18 | 23-F | SUI | 6 | 0 | 1 | 1 | 8 | 9th |
|---|---|---|---|---|---|---|---|---|
| 2006 WM20 | 11-F | SUI | 6 | 0 | 1 | 1 | 14 | 7th |
| 2007 WM20 | 11-F | SUI | 6 | 1 | 0 | 1 | 8 | 7th |
| **Totals WM20** | | | **12** | **1** | **1** | **2** | **22** | **—** |

**Stempniak, Lee**
**b. Buffalo, New York, United States, February 4, 1983**

| 2007 WM | 12-F | USA | 7 | 6 | 4 | 10 | 27 | 5th |
|---|---|---|---|---|---|---|---|---|
| 2008 WM | 12-F | USA | 7 | 0 | 3 | 3 | 6 | 6th |
| 2009 WM | 22-F | USA | 9 | 2 | 0 | 2 | 6 | 4th |
| **Totals WM** | | | **23** | **8** | **7** | **15** | **39** | **—** |

**Stencel, Jan**
**b. Opava, Czech Republic, February 26, 1995**

| 2012 WM18 | 10-D | CZE | 6 | 1 | 0 | 1 | 2 | 8th |
|---|---|---|---|---|---|---|---|---|

**Stene, Andreas**
**b. Oslo, Norway, March 1, 1991**

| 2009 WM18 | 9-F | NOR | 6 | 0 | 0 | 0 | 2 | 9th |
|---|---|---|---|---|---|---|---|---|
| 2011 WM20 | 9-F | NOR | 6 | 0 | 0 | 0 | 2 | 9th |

**Stensund, Per Ferdinand**
**b. Asker, Norway, March 4, 1987**

| 2004 WM18 | 25-F | NOR | 5 | 0 | 1 | 1 | 4 | 10th |
|---|---|---|---|---|---|---|---|---|
| 2006 WM20 | 9-F | NOR | 6 | 0 | 0 | 0 | 6 | 10th |

**Stepan, Derek**
**b. Hastings, Minnesota, United States, June 18, 1990**

| 2010 WM20 | 21-F | USA | 7 | 4 | 10 | 14 | 4 | G |
|---|---|---|---|---|---|---|---|---|
| 2011 WM | 9-F | USA | 7 | 2 | 5 | 7 | 2 | 8th |

~WM20 All-Star Team/Forward (2010)

**Stepanov, Andrei**
**b. Moscow, Soviet Union (Russia), April 14, 1986**

| 2011 WM | 61-F | BLR | 6 | 2 | 3 | 5 | 0 | 14th |
|---|---|---|---|---|---|---|---|---|
| 2012 WM | 16-F | BLR | 5 | 0 | 1 | 1 | 0 | 14th |
| **Totals WM** | | | **11** | **2** | **4** | **6** | **0** | **—** |

**Stepanov, Igor**
**b. Vitebsk, Soviet Union (Belarus), April 13, 1990**

| 2008 WM18 | 15-F | BLR | 6 | 1 | 1 | 2 | 12 | 9th |
|---|---|---|---|---|---|---|---|---|

**Stepanov, Stefan**
**b. Moscow, Russia, September 23, 1992**

| 2010 WM18 | 2-D | RUS | 7 | 0 | 3 | 3 | 8 | 4th |
|---|---|---|---|---|---|---|---|---|

**Stephan, Eric**
**b. Berlin, Germany, February 2, 1994**

| 2012 WM18 | 10-D | GER | 6 | 0 | 3 | 3 | 6 | 6th |
|---|---|---|---|---|---|---|---|---|

**Stewart, Anthony**
**b. Lasalle, Quebec, Canada, January 5, 1985**

| 2003 WM18 | 12-F | CAN | 7 | 6 | 0 | 6 | 6 | G |
|---|---|---|---|---|---|---|---|---|
| 2004 WM20 | 12-F | CAN | 6 | 5 | 6 | 11 | 2 | S |
| 2005 WM20 | 12-F | CAN | 6 | 3 | 1 | 4 | 0 | G |
| **Totals WM20** | | | **12** | **8** | **7** | **15** | **2** | **G,S** |

~WM18 All-Star Team/Forward (2003)

**Stewart, Chris**
**b. Toronto, Ontario, Canada, October 30, 1987**

| 2011 WM | 25-F | CAN | 7 | 2 | 2 | 4 | 0 | 5th |
|---|---|---|---|---|---|---|---|---|

**Stich, David**
**b. Plzen, Czechoslovakia (Czech Republic), April 15, 1989**

| 2006 WM18 | 8-D | CZE | 7 | 0 | 0 | 0 | 10 | B |
|---|---|---|---|---|---|---|---|---|
| 2007 WM18 | 28-D | CZE | 4 | 1 | 0 | 1 | 2 | 9th |
| 2009 WM20 | 7-D | CZE | 6 | 1 | 0 | 1 | 58 | 6th |
| **Totals WM18** | | | **11** | **1** | **0** | **1** | **12** | **—** |

**St. Louis, Martin**
**b. Laval, Quebec, Canada, June 18, 1975**

| 2004 WCH | 26-F | CAN | 6 | 2 | 2 | 4 | 0 | 1st |
|---|---|---|---|---|---|---|---|---|
| 2006 OG-M | 26-F | CAN | 6 | 2 | 1 | 3 | 0 | 7th |
| 2008 WM | 26-F | CAN | 9 | 2 | 8 | 10 | 0 | S |
| 2009 WM | 26-F | CAN | 9 | 4 | 11 | 15 | 2 | S |
| **Totals WM** | | | **18** | **6** | **19** | **25** | **2** | **2S** |

~WM All-Star Team/Forward (2009)

**Stoa, Ryan**
**b. Bloomington, Minnesota, United States, April 13, 1987**

| 2005 WM18 | 19-F | USA | 6 | 0 | 3 | 3 | 2 | G |
|---|---|---|---|---|---|---|---|---|
| 2007 WM20 | 19-F | USA | 7 | 1 | 1 | 2 | 8 | B |

**Stoll, Jarret**
**b. Melville, Saskatchewan, Canada, June 24, 1982**

| 2001 WM20 | 19-F | CAN | 7 | 0 | 2 | 2 | 6 | B |
|---|---|---|---|---|---|---|---|---|
| 2002 WM20 | 16-F | CAN | 7 | 2 | 4 | 6 | 4 | S |
| **Totals WM20** | | | **14** | **2** | **6** | **8** | **10** | **S,B** |

**Stone, Mark**
**b. Winnipeg, Manitoba, Canada, May 13, 1992**

| 2012 WM20 | 16-F | CAN | 6 | 7 | 3 | 10 | 2 | B |
|---|---|---|---|---|---|---|---|---|

**Stoop, Lukas**
**b. Zurich, Switzerland, March 1, 1990**

| 2007 WM18 | 7-D | SUI | 6 | 0 | 2 | 2 | 0 | 6th |
|---|---|---|---|---|---|---|---|---|
| 2008 WM18 | 20-D | SUI | 4 | 0 | 0 | 0 | 6 | 8th |
| 2008 WM20 | 5-D | SUI | 6 | 0 | 0 | 0 | 2 | 9th |
| 2010 WM20 | 7-D | SUI | 7 | 0 | 2 | 2 | 8 | 4th |
| **Totals WM18** | | | **10** | **0** | **2** | **2** | **6** | **—** |
| **Totals WM20** | | | **13** | **0** | **2** | **2** | **10** | **—** |

**Storm, Frederik**
**b. Gentofte, Denmark, February 20, 1989**

| 2011 WM | 8-F | DEN | 6 | 0 | 0 | 0 | 0 | 11th |
|---|---|---|---|---|---|---|---|---|
| 2012 WM | 8-F | DEN | 7 | 0 | 0 | 0 | 0 | 13th |
| **Totals WM** | | | **13** | **0** | **0** | **0** | **0** | **—** |

**Strait, Brian**
**b. Waltham, Massachusetts, United States, January 4, 1988**

| 2006 WM18 | 7-D | USA | 6 | 0 | 0 | 0 | 4 | G |
|---|---|---|---|---|---|---|---|---|
| 2008 WM20 | 7-D | USA | 6 | 0 | 0 | 0 | 6 | 4th |

**Straka, Petr**
**b. Plzen, Czech Republic, June 15, 1992**

| 2009 WM18 | 11-F | CZE | 6 | 0 | 0 | 0 | 2 | 6th |
|---|---|---|---|---|---|---|---|---|
| 2011 WM20 | 21-F | CZE | 6 | 1 | 2 | 3 | 4 | 7th |
| 2012 WM20 | 21-F | CZE | 6 | 0 | 1 | 1 | 27 | 5th |
| **Totals WM20** | | | **12** | **1** | **3** | **4** | **31** | **—** |

**Stralman, Anton**
**b. Tibro, Sweden, August 1, 1986**

| 2005 WM20 | 6-D | SWE | 5 | 0 | 0 | 0 | 2 | 6th |
|---|---|---|---|---|---|---|---|---|
| 2006 WM20 | 6-D | SWE | 6 | 0 | 1 | 1 | 6 | 5th |
| 2007 WM | 4-D | SWE | 9 | 1 | 1 | 2 | 0 | 4th |
| 2008 WM | 36-D | SWE | 8 | 4 | 3 | 7 | 31 | 4th |
| 2009 WM | 36-D | SWE | 7 | 1 | 4 | 5 | 6 | B |
| **Totals WM20** | | | **11** | **0** | **1** | **1** | **8** | **—** |
| **Totals WM** | | | **24** | **6** | **8** | **14** | **37** | **B** |

**Strapac, Petr**
**b. Ostrava, Czechoslovakia (Czech Republic), October 11, 1989**

| 2008 WM20 | 27-F | CZE | 6 | 1 | 0 | 1 | 0 | 5th |
|---|---|---|---|---|---|---|---|---|
| 2009 WM20 | 27-F | CZE | 6 | 0 | 0 | 0 | 0 | 6th |
| **Totals WM20** | | | **12** | **1** | **0** | **1** | **0** | **—** |

**Straupe, Davis**
**b. Riga, Latvia, August 5, 1992**

| 2010 WM18 | 9-F | LAT | 6 | 2 | 2 | 4 | 4 | 9th |
|---|---|---|---|---|---|---|---|---|
| 2012 WM20 | 17-F | LAT | 6 | 0 | 1 | 1 | 2 | 9th |

**Straupe, Janis**
**b. Riga, Soviet Union (Latvia), June 3, 1989**

| | | | | | | | | |
|---|---|---|---|---|---|---|---|---|
| 2007 WM18 | 19-F | LAT | 6 | 3 | 1 | 4 | 4 | 10th |
| 2009 WM20 | 19-F | LAT | 6 | 2 | 3 | 5 | 4 | 8th |

**Strazzabosco, Michele**
**b. Asiago, Italy, February 6, 1976**

| | | | | | | | | |
|---|---|---|---|---|---|---|---|---|
| 1998 WM | 6-D | ITA | 6 | 0 | 1 | 1 | 2 | 10th |
| 1999 WM | 6-D | ITA | 3 | 0 | 0 | 0 | 2 | 13th |
| 2000 WM | 6-D | ITA | 5 | 0 | 0 | 0 | 10 | 9th |
| 2001 WM | 6-D | ITA | 6 | 0 | 0 | 0 | 6 | 12th |
| 2002 WM | 6-D | ITA | 6 | 0 | 0 | 0 | 2 | 15th |
| 2006 OG-M | 6-D | ITA | 5 | 0 | 0 | 0 | 10 | 11th |
| 2006 WM | 6-D | ITA | 6 | 1 | 0 | 1 | 18 | 14th |
| 2007 WM | 6-D | ITA | 6 | 0 | 1 | 1 | 6 | 12th |
| 2008 WM | 6-D | ITA | 4 | 0 | 1 | 1 | 10 | 16th |
| 2010 WM | 6-D | ITA | 6 | 2 | 0 | 2 | 10 | 15th |
| **Totals WM** | | | **48** | **3** | **3** | **6** | **66** | **—** |

**Strbak, Martin**
**b. Presov, Czechoslovakia (Slovakia), January 15, 1975**

| | | | | | | | | |
|---|---|---|---|---|---|---|---|---|
| 2000 WM | 7-D | SVK | 3 | 1 | 0 | 1 | 8 | S |
| 2001 WM | 4-D | SVK | 6 | 0 | 1 | 1 | 6 | 7th |
| 2002 WM | 7-D | SVK | 9 | 0 | 2 | 2 | 10 | G |
| 2003 WM | 7-D | SVK | 9 | 0 | 7 | 7 | 12 | B |
| 2004 WM | 7-D | SVK | 9 | 1 | 1 | 2 | 2 | 4th |
| 2004 WCH | 7-D | SVK | 4 | 0 | 0 | 0 | 4 | 7th |
| 2005 WM | 7-D | SVK | 7 | 2 | 5 | 7 | 10 | 5th |
| 2006 OG-M | 7-D | SVK | 6 | 0 | 0 | 0 | 2 | 5th |
| 2006 WM | 7-D | SVK | 7 | 1 | 1 | 2 | 8 | 8th |
| 2007 WM | 7-D | SVK | 7 | 0 | 1 | 1 | 2 | 6th |
| 2008 WM | 7-D | SVK | 5 | 0 | 0 | 0 | 0 | 13th |
| 2010 OG-M | 77-D | SVK | 7 | 0 | 1 | 1 | 2 | 4th |
| 2011 WM | 77-D | SVK | 6 | 0 | 0 | 0 | 2 | 10th |
| **Totals WM** | | | **68** | **5** | **18** | **23** | **60** | **G,S,B** |
| **Totals OG-M** | | | **13** | **0** | **1** | **1** | **4** | **—** |

**Streit, Mark**
**b. Englisberg, Switzerland, December 11, 1977**

| | | | | | | | | |
|---|---|---|---|---|---|---|---|---|
| 1996 WM20 | 7-D | SUI | 5 | 1 | 0 | 1 | 4 | 9th |
| 1997 WM20 | 7-D | SUI | 6 | 2 | 0 | 2 | 31 | 7th |
| 1998 WM | 16-D | SUI | 9 | 0 | 0 | 0 | 2 | 4th |
| 1999 WM | 7-D | SUI | 6 | 4 | 0 | 4 | 2 | 8th |
| 2000 WM | 7-D | SUI | 7 | 0 | 1 | 1 | 4 | 5th |
| 2001 WM | 7-D | SUI | 6 | 0 | 3 | 3 | 2 | 9th |
| 2002 OG-M | 7-D | SUI | 4 | 1 | 1 | 2 | 0 | 11th |
| 2002 WM | 7-D | SUI | 6 | 0 | 3 | 3 | 4 | 10th |
| 2003 WM | 7-D | SUI | 7 | 0 | 4 | 4 | 10 | 8th |
| 2004 WM | 7-D | SUI | 7 | 1 | 1 | 2 | 2 | 8th |
| 2005 WM | 7-D | SUI | 7 | 1 | 6 | 7 | 4 | 8th |
| 2006 OG-M | 7-D | SUI | 6 | 2 | 1 | 3 | 6 | 6th |
| 2006 WM | 7-D | SUI | 6 | 0 | 3 | 3 | 6 | 9th |
| 2007 WM | 7-D | SUI | 7 | 1 | 3 | 4 | 6 | 8th |
| 2009 WM | 7-D | SUI | 6 | 1 | 4 | 5 | 8 | 9th |
| 2010 OG-M | 7-D | SUI | 5 | 0 | 3 | 3 | 0 | 8th |
| 2012 WM | 7-D | SUI | 7 | 2 | 2 | 4 | 6 | 11th |
| **Totals WM20** | | | **11** | **3** | **0** | **3** | **35** | **—** |
| **Totals WM** | | | **81** | **10** | **30** | **40** | **56** | **—** |
| **Totals OG-M** | | | **15** | **3** | **5** | **8** | **6** | **—** |

~WM20 All-Star Team/Defence (1997)

**Strobl, Florian**
**b. Starnberg, West Germany (Germany), February 21, 1990**

| | | | | | | | | |
|---|---|---|---|---|---|---|---|---|
| 2008 WM18 | 19-F | GER | 6 | 1 | 1 | 2 | 2 | 5th |

**Strome, Ryan**
**b. Mississauga, Ontario, Canada, July 11, 1993**

| | | | | | | | | |
|---|---|---|---|---|---|---|---|---|
| 2012 WM20 | 18-F | CAN | 6 | 3 | 6 | 9 | 8 | B |

**Stuart, Colin**
**b. Rochester, Minnesota, United States, July 8, 1982**

| | | | | | | | | |
|---|---|---|---|---|---|---|---|---|
| 2009 WM | 49-F | USA | 4 | 0 | 0 | 0 | 4 | 4th |

**Stuart, Mark**
**b. Rochester, Minnesota, United States, April 27, 1984**

| | | | | | | | | |
|---|---|---|---|---|---|---|---|---|
| 2002 WM18 | 2-D | USA | 8 | 1 | 2 | 3 | 29 | G |
| 2003 WM20 | 2-D | USA | 7 | 0 | 1 | 1 | 2 | 4th |
| 2004 WM20 | 2-D | USA | 6 | 0 | 2 | 2 | 4 | G |
| 2008 WM | 22-D | USA | 7 | 0 | 0 | 0 | 4 | 6th |
| 2011 WM | 5-D | USA | 7 | 1 | 0 | 1 | 8 | 8th |
| **Totals WM20** | | | **13** | **0** | **3** | **3** | **6** | **G** |
| **Totals WM** | | | **14** | **1** | **0** | **1** | **12** | **—** |

**Studer, Thomas**
**b. Roggwil, Switzerland, November 2, 1994**

| | | | | | | | | |
|---|---|---|---|---|---|---|---|---|
| 2012 WM18 | 11-F | SUI | 6 | 0 | 3 | 3 | 4 | 7th |

**Stumpel, Josef**
**b. Nitra, Czechoslovakia (Slovakia), July 20, 1972**

| | | | | | | | | |
|---|---|---|---|---|---|---|---|---|
| 1991 WM20 | 15-F | TCH | 7 | 4 | 4 | 8 | 2 | B |
| 1996 WCH | 16-F | SVK | 3 | 0 | 0 | 0 | 0 | 7th |
| 1997 WM | 11-F | SVK | 8 | 2 | 1 | 3 | 4 | 9th |
| 1998 WM | 16-F | SVK | 4 | 1 | 2 | 3 | 6 | 7th |
| 2002 OG-M | 15-F | SVK | 2 | 2 | 1 | 3 | 0 | 13th |
| 2002 WM | 15-F | SVK | 3 | 0 | 1 | 1 | 4 | G |
| 2003 WM | 15-F | SVK | 9 | 4 | 11 | 15 | 0 | B |
| 2004 WM | 15-F | SVK | 9 | 1 | 2 | 3 | 2 | 4th |
| 2004 WCH | 15-F | SVK | 4 | 0 | 0 | 0 | 2 | 7th |
| 2005 WM | 15-F | SVK | 7 | 0 | 7 | 7 | 6 | 5th |
| 2006 OG-M | 15-F | SVK | 3 | 0 | 0 | 0 | 0 | 5th |
| 2010 OG-M | 15-F | SVK | 7 | 1 | 4 | 5 | 0 | 4th |
| 2011 WM | 15-F | SVK | 6 | 2 | 1 | 3 | 2 | 10th |
| **Totals WM** | | | **46** | **10** | **25** | **35** | **24** | **G,B** |
| **Totals IIHF-NHL** | | | **7** | **0** | **0** | **0** | **2** | **—** |
| **Totals OG-M** | | | **12** | **3** | **5** | **8** | **0** | **—** |

**Sturm, Marco**
**b. Dingolfing, West Germany (Germany), September 8, 1978**

| | | | | | | | | |
|---|---|---|---|---|---|---|---|---|
| 1995 WM20 | 17-F | GER | 7 | 0 | 0 | 0 | 6 | 8th |
| 1996 WM20 | 17-F | GER | 6 | 4 | 6 | 10 | 51 | 8th |
| 1997 WM | 39-F | GER | 8 | 1 | 1 | 2 | 4 | 11th |
| 1998 OG-M | 39-F | GER | 2 | 0 | 0 | 0 | 0 | 9th |
| 2001 WM | 19-F | GER | 7 | 4 | 1 | 5 | 26 | 5th |
| 2002 OG-M | 19-F | GER | 5 | 0 | 1 | 1 | 0 | 8th |
| 2004 WCH | 19-F | GER | 4 | 2 | 0 | 2 | 0 | 8th |
| 2008 WM | 19-F | GER | 6 | 2 | 1 | 3 | 6 | 10th |
| 2010 OG-M | 19-F | GER | 4 | 0 | 1 | 1 | 0 | 11th |
| **Totals WM20** | | | **13** | **4** | **6** | **10** | **57** | **—** |
| **Totals WM** | | | **21** | **7** | **3** | **10** | **36** | **—** |
| **Totals OG-M** | | | **11** | **0** | **2** | **2** | **0** | **—** |

**Styk, Michal**
**b. Banska Bystrica, Slovakia, January 17, 1992**

| | | | | | | | | |
|---|---|---|---|---|---|---|---|---|
| 2010 WM18 | 16-D | SVK | 6 | 0 | 0 | 0 | 10 | 8th |

**Styrman, Fredrik**
**b. Kalix, Sweden, April 3, 1991**

| | | | | | | | | |
|---|---|---|---|---|---|---|---|---|
| 2009 WM18 | 8-D | SWE | 6 | 1 | 0 | 1 | 2 | 5th |
| 2011 WM20 | 2-D | SWE | 6 | 0 | 3 | 3 | 2 | 4th |

**Subban, Pernell Karl "P.K."**
**b. Toronto, Ontario, Canada, May 13, 1989**

| | | | | | | | | |
|---|---|---|---|---|---|---|---|---|
| 2008 WM20 | 23-D | CAN | 7 | 0 | 0 | 0 | 2 | G |
| 2009 WM20 | 5-D | CAN | 6 | 3 | 6 | 9 | 6 | G |
| **Totals WM20** | | | **13** | **3** | **6** | **9** | **8** | **2G** |

~WM20 All-Star Team/Defence (2009)

**Suchy, Jiri**
**b. Bruntal, Czechoslovakia (Czech Republic), January 3, 1988**

| | | | | | | | | |
|---|---|---|---|---|---|---|---|---|
| 2007 WM20 | 25-D | CZE | 6 | 0 | 0 | 0 | 4 | 5th |
| 2008 WM20 | 3-D | CZE | 2 | 0 | 0 | 0 | 2 | 5th |
| **Totals WM20** | | | **8** | **0** | **0** | **0** | **6** | **—** |

**Suja, Jakub**
**b. Kosice, Czechoslovakia (Slovakia), November 1, 1988**

| | | | | | | | | |
|---|---|---|---|---|---|---|---|---|
| 2008 WM20 | 11-F | SVK | 6 | 0 | 1 | 1 | 0 | 7th |

**Sulak, Libor**
**b. Pelhrimov, Czech Republic, March 4, 1994**

| | | | | | | | | |
|---|---|---|---|---|---|---|---|---|
| 2012 WM18 | 28-D | CZE | 6 | 0 | 3 | 3 | 4 | 8th |

**Sulzer, Alexander**
**b. Kaufbeuren, West Germany (Germany), May 30, 1984**

| | | | | | | | | |
|---|---|---|---|---|---|---|---|---|
| 2003 WM20 | 6-D | GER | 6 | 0 | 2 | 2 | 14 | 9th |
| 2005 WM | 52-D | GER | 3 | 0 | 0 | 0 | 4 | 15th |
| 2006 OG-M | 52-D | GER | 5 | 0 | 1 | 1 | 2 | 10th |
| 2007 WM | 52-D | GER | 6 | 0 | 0 | 0 | 4 | 9th |
| 2010 OG-M | 52-D | GER | 4 | 0 | 0 | 0 | 4 | 11th |
| 2010 WM | 52-D | GER | 9 | 0 | 2 | 2 | 4 | 4th |
| **Totals WM** | | | **18** | **0** | **2** | **2** | **12** | **—** |
| **Totals OG-M** | | | **9** | **0** | **1** | **1** | **6** | **—** |

**Summers, Chris**
**b. Ann Arbor, Michigan, United States, February 5, 1988**

| | | | | | | | | |
|---|---|---|---|---|---|---|---|---|
| 2006 WM18 | 16-F | USA | 6 | 1 | 0 | 1 | 35 | G |
| 2008 WM20 | 16-D | USA | 6 | 0 | 1 | 1 | 2 | 4th |

**Sundberg, Alexander**
**b. Gentofte, Denmark, January 19, 1981**

| | | | | | | | | |
|---|---|---|---|---|---|---|---|---|
| 2004 WM | 18-F | DEN | 6 | 0 | 0 | 0 | 2 | 12th |
| 2007 WM | 24-F | DEN | 3 | 0 | 0 | 0 | 2 | 10th |
| 2009 WM | 24-F | DEN | 6 | 1 | 0 | 1 | 4 | 13th |
| 2010 WM | 12-F | DEN | 7 | 0 | 0 | 0 | 2 | 8th |
| **Totals WM** | | | **22** | **1** | **0** | **1** | **10** | **—** |

**Sundelius, Joacim**
**b. Oslo, Norway, July 23, 1991**

| | | | | | | | | |
|---|---|---|---|---|---|---|---|---|
| 2011 WM20 | 24-F | NOR | 6 | 0 | 0 | 0 | 2 | 9th |

**Sundh, Oscar**
**b. Uppsala, Sweden, October 22, 1986**

| | | | | | | | | |
|---|---|---|---|---|---|---|---|---|
| 2004 WM18 | 18-F | SWE | 6 | 0 | 2 | 2 | 0 | 5th |
| 2006 WM20 | 17-F | SWE | 4 | 0 | 0 | 0 | 2 | 5th |

**Sundstrom, Alexander**
**b. Vancouver, British Columbia, Canada, March 14, 1987**

| | | | | | | | | |
|---|---|---|---|---|---|---|---|---|
| 2007 WM20 | 17-F | SWE | 7 | 2 | 0 | 2 | 2 | 4th |

**Sundstrom, Johan**
**b. Gothenburg, Sweden, September 21, 1992**

| | | | | | | | | |
|---|---|---|---|---|---|---|---|---|
| 2011 WM20 | 13-F | SWE | 6 | 0 | 1 | 1 | 0 | 4th |
| 2012 WM20 | 13-F | SWE | 6 | 1 | 4 | 5 | 2 | G |
| **Totals WM20** | | | **12** | **1** | **5** | **6** | **2** | **G** |

**Suri, Reto**
**b. Utzenstorf, Switzerland, March 25, 1989**

| | | | | | | | | |
|---|---|---|---|---|---|---|---|---|
| 2007 WM18 | 27-F | SUI | 6 | 1 | 0 | 1 | 4 | 6th |
| 2008 WM20 | 24-F | SUI | 6 | 2 | 2 | 4 | 0 | 9th |

**Surovy, Tomas**
**b. Banska Bystrica, Czechoslovakia (Slovakia), September 24, 1981**

| | | | | | | | | |
|---|---|---|---|---|---|---|---|---|
| 1999 WM18 | 15-F | SVK | 7 | 1 | 2 | 3 | 6 | B |
| 2000 WM20 | 29-F | SVK | 7 | 0 | 0 | 0 | 2 | 9th |
| 2001 WM20 | 13-F | SVK | 7 | 1 | 3 | 4 | 6 | 8th |
| 2006 OG-M | 43-F | SVK | 6 | 0 | 1 | 1 | 2 | 5th |
| 2006 WM | 43-F | SVK | 7 | 2 | 2 | 4 | 4 | 8th |
| 2007 WM | 43-F | SVK | 7 | 0 | 1 | 1 | 4 | 6th |
| 2009 WM | 34-F | SVK | 5 | 1 | 0 | 1 | 0 | 10th |
| 2011 WM | 43-F | SVK | 6 | 1 | 1 | 2 | 2 | 10th |
| 2012 WM | 43-F | SVK | 10 | 0 | 4 | 4 | 12 | S |
| **Totals WM20** | | | **14** | **1** | **3** | **4** | **8** | **—** |
| **Totals WM** | | | **35** | **4** | **8** | **12** | **22** | **S** |

**Sushinski, Maxim**
**b. Leningrad (St. Petersburg), Soviet Union (Russia), July 1, 1974**

| | | | | | | | | |
|---|---|---|---|---|---|---|---|---|
| 1994 WM20 | 22-F | RUS | 7 | 4 | 2 | 6 | 10 | B |
| 1999 WM | 15-F | RUS | 6 | 1 | 2 | 3 | 4 | 5th |
| 2000 WM | 8-F | RUS | 6 | 3 | 1 | 4 | 0 | 9th |
| 2002 WM | 33-F | RUS | 9 | 3 | 4 | 7 | 4 | S |
| 2004 WM | 33-F | RUS | 6 | 2 | 1 | 3 | 12 | 10th |
| 2006 OG-M | 33-F | RUS | 8 | 2 | 3 | 5 | 8 | 4th |
| 2006 WM | 33-F | RUS | 7 | 2 | 4 | 6 | 0 | 5th |
| 2008 WM | 33-F | RUS | 9 | 4 | 1 | 5 | 6 | G |
| 2010 WM | 33-F | RUS | 5 | 0 | 1 | 1 | 8 | S |
| **Totals WM** | | | **48** | **15** | **14** | **29** | **34** | **G,2S** |

**Sushko, Vadim**
**b. Novopolotsk, Soviet Union (Belarus), April 27, 1986**

| | | | | | | | | |
|---|---|---|---|---|---|---|---|---|
| 2003 WM18 | 2-D | BLR | 6 | 0 | 2 | 2 | 8 | 8th |
| 2004 WM18 | 5-D | BLR | 6 | 1 | 0 | 1 | 12 | 9th |
| 2005 WM20 | 5-D | BLR | 6 | 0 | 0 | 0 | 0 | 10th |
| **Totals WM18** | | | **12** | **1** | **2** | **3** | **20** | **—** |

**Suslo, Nikolai**
**b. Gomel, Soviet Union (Belarus), March 4, 1991**

| | | | | | | | | |
|---|---|---|---|---|---|---|---|---|
| 2008 WM18 | 21-F | BLR | 6 | 0 | 0 | 0 | 8 | 9th |

**Sustr, Andrej**
**b. Plzen, Czechoslovakia (Czech Republic), November 29, 1990**

| | | | | | | | | |
|---|---|---|---|---|---|---|---|---|
| 2010 WM20 | 7-D | CZE | 5 | 0 | 0 | 0 | 6 | 7th |

**Suter, Ryan**
**b. Madison, Wisconsin, United States, January 21, 1985**

| | | | | | | | | |
|---|---|---|---|---|---|---|---|---|
| 2002 WM18 | 4-D | USA | 8 | 1 | 6 | 7 | 12 | G |
| 2003 WM18 | 20-D | USA | 6 | 1 | 3 | 4 | 22 | 4th |
| 2003 WM20 | 7-D | USA | 7 | 2 | 1 | 3 | 2 | 4th |
| 2004 WM20 | 7-D | USA | 6 | 0 | 2 | 2 | 8 | G |
| 2005 WM20 | 7-D | USA | 7 | 1 | 7 | 8 | 20 | 4th |

| | | | | | | | | |
|---|---|---|---|---|---|---|---|---|
| 2005 WM | 20-D | USA | 1 | 0 | 0 | 0 | 0 | 6th |
| 2006 WM | 7-D | USA | 7 | 1 | 1 | 2 | 10 | 7th |
| 2007 WM | 7-D | USA | 7 | 1 | 2 | 3 | 12 | 5th |
| 2009 WM | 20-D | USA | 9 | 1 | 2 | 3 | 8 | 4th |
| 2010 OG-M | 20-D | USA | 6 | 0 | 4 | 4 | 2 | S |
| **Totals WM18** | | | **14** | **2** | **9** | **11** | **24** | **G** |
| **Totals WM20** | | | **20** | **3** | **10** | **13** | **30** | **G** |
| **Totals WM** | | | **24** | **3** | **5** | **8** | **30** | **—** |

~WM20 All-Star Team/Defence (2005), WM18 IIHF Directorate Best Defenceman (2002)

**Sutter, Brandon**
**b. Huntington, New York, United States, February 14, 1989**

| | | | | | | | | |
|---|---|---|---|---|---|---|---|---|
| 2006 WM18 | 12-F | CAN | 7 | 2 | 0 | 2 | 2 | 4th |
| 2007 WM18 | 12-F | CAN | 6 | 1 | 1 | 2 | 2 | 4th |
| 2008 WM20 | 12-F | CAN | 7 | 0 | 1 | 1 | 2 | G |
| **Totals WM18** | | | **13** | **3** | **1** | **4** | **4** | **—** |

**Sutter, Dave**
**b. Monthey, Switzerland, February 21, 1992**

| | | | | | | | | |
|---|---|---|---|---|---|---|---|---|
| 2010 WM18 | 25-D | SUI | 6 | 0 | 2 | 2 | 2 | 5th |
| 2012 WM20 | 7-D | SUI | 6 | 0 | 0 | 0 | 4 | 8th |

**Svanberg, Ola**
**b. Tranemo, Sweden, June 10, 1985**

| | | | | | | | | |
|---|---|---|---|---|---|---|---|---|
| 2003 WM18 | 7-D | SWE | 6 | 0 | 1 | 1 | 8 | 5th |
| 2005 WM20 | 20-D | SWE | 6 | 0 | 2 | 2 | 12 | 6th |

**Svarny, Ivan**
**b. Nitra, Czechoslovakia (Slovakia), October 31, 1984**

| | | | | | | | | |
|---|---|---|---|---|---|---|---|---|
| 2009 WM | 12-D | SVK | 3 | 0 | 0 | 0 | 0 | 10th |

**Svatos, Marek**
**b. Kosice, Czechoslovakia (Slovakia), June 17, 1982**

| | | | | | | | | |
|---|---|---|---|---|---|---|---|---|
| 2000 WM18 | 24-F | SVK | 6 | 2 | 0 | 2 | 0 | 5th |
| 2002 WM20 | 15-F | SVK | 7 | 7 | 1 | 8 | 6 | 8th |
| 2006 OG-M | 40-F | SVK | 6 | 0 | 0 | 0 | 0 | 5th |
| 2010 WM | 40-F | SVK | 6 | 1 | 1 | 2 | 6 | 12th |

~WM20 All-Star Team/Forward (2002)

**Svendsen, Sebastian**
**b. Hvidovre, Denmark, July 30, 1991**

| | | | | | | | | |
|---|---|---|---|---|---|---|---|---|
| 2008 WM18 | 19-F | DEN | 6 | 2 | 1 | 3 | 2 | 10th |
| 2008 WM20 | 28-F | DEN | 5 | 0 | 0 | 0 | 4 | 10th |

**Svensson, Bjorn**
**b. Malmo, Sweden, June 16, 1986**

| | | | | | | | | |
|---|---|---|---|---|---|---|---|---|
| 2005 WM20 | 29-F | SWE | 6 | 0 | 0 | 0 | 0 | 6th |

**Sveum, Dennis**
**b. Lillehammer, Norway, November 27, 1986**

| | | | | | | | | |
|---|---|---|---|---|---|---|---|---|
| 2004 WM18 | 17-D | NOR | 6 | 0 | 1 | 1 | 6 | 10th |
| 2006 WM20 | 27-D | NOR | 5 | 2 | 0 | 2 | 6 | 10th |

**Svihalek, Michal**
**b. Jindrichuv Hradec, Czech Republic, April 29, 1993**

| | | | | | | | | |
|---|---|---|---|---|---|---|---|---|
| 2011 WM18 | 12-F | CZE | 6 | 0 | 2 | 2 | 4 | 8th |

**Svistunov, Vitali**
**b. Ust-Kamenogorsk, Soviet Union (Kazakhstan), January 24, 1990**

| | | | | | | | | |
|---|---|---|---|---|---|---|---|---|
| 2009 WM20 | 8-D | KAZ | 6 | 0 | 0 | 0 | 8 | 10th |

**Svitov, Alexander**
**b. Omsk, Soviet Union (Russia), November 3, 1982**

| | | | | | | | | |
|---|---|---|---|---|---|---|---|---|
| 2012 WM | 15-F | RUS | 10 | 0 | 0 | 0 | 4 | G |

**Svoboda, Tomas**
**b. Litomerice, Czechoslovakia (Czech Republic),** February 24, 1987

| | | | | | | | | |
|---|---|---|---|---|---|---|---|---|
| 2005 WM18 | 23-F | CZE | 5 | 0 | 0 | 0 | 0 | 4th |
| 2007 WM20 | 23-F | CZE | 6 | 2 | 3 | 5 | 14 | 5th |

**Sweatt, Bill**
**b. Elburn, Illinois, United States, September 21, 1988**

| | | | | | | | | |
|---|---|---|---|---|---|---|---|---|
| 2006 WM18 | 21-F | USA | 6 | 5 | 2 | 7 | 4 | G |
| 2007 WM20 | 21-F | USA | 7 | 1 | 1 | 2 | 0 | B |
| 2008 WM20 | 21-F | USA | 6 | 0 | 1 | 1 | 0 | 4th |
| **Totals WM20** | | | **13** | **1** | **2** | **3** | **0** | **B** |

**Sykora, Tomas**
**b. Bratislava, Czechoslovakia (Slovakia), July 4, 1990**

| | | | | | | | | |
|---|---|---|---|---|---|---|---|---|
| 2008 WM18 | 17-F | SVK | 6 | 0 | 1 | 1 | 2 | 7th |

**Syomin, Alexander**
**b. Krasnoyarsk, Soviet Union (Russia), March 3, 1984**

| | | | | | | | | |
|---|---|---|---|---|---|---|---|---|
| 2002 WM18 | 10-F | RUS | 8 | 8 | 7 | 15 | 16 | S |
| 2003 WM | 32-F | RUS | 6 | 0 | 0 | 0 | 0 | 7th |
| 2004 WM20 | 10-F | RUS | 6 | 2 | 2 | 4 | 10 | 5th |
| 2005 WM | 32-F | RUS | 6 | 3 | 0 | 3 | 8 | B |
| 2006 WM | 32-F | RUS | 7 | 3 | 3 | 6 | 8 | 5th |
| 2008 WM | 28-F | RUS | 9 | 6 | 7 | 13 | 8 | G |
| 2010 OG-M | 28-F | RUS | 4 | 0 | 2 | 2 | 4 | 6th |
| 2010 WM | 28-F | RUS | 8 | 1 | 4 | 5 | 12 | S |
| 2012 WM | 28-F | RUS | 3 | 2 | 3 | 5 | 0 | G |
| **Totals WM** | | | **39** | **15** | **17** | **32** | **36** | **2G,S,B** |

**Syomochkin, Alexander**
**b. Vitebsk, Soviet Union (Belarus), March 21, 1990**

| | | | | | | | | |
|---|---|---|---|---|---|---|---|---|
| 2008 WM18 | 14-F | BLR | 6 | 0 | 0 | 0 | 0 | 9th |

**Syrei, Alexander**
**b. Grodno, Soviet Union (Belarus), August 26, 1988**

| | | | | | | | | |
|---|---|---|---|---|---|---|---|---|
| 2004 WM18 | 8-D | BLR | 6 | 0 | 0 | 0 | 0 | 9th |
| 2006 WM18 | 4-D | BLR | 6 | 1 | 0 | 1 | 16 | 9th |
| 2007 WM20 | 29-D | BLR | 6 | 0 | 2 | 2 | 4 | 10th |
| **Totals WM18** | | | **12** | **1** | **0** | **1** | **16** | **—** |

**Syvret, Danny**
**b. Burlington, Ontario, Canada, June 13, 1985**

| | | | | | | | | |
|---|---|---|---|---|---|---|---|---|
| 2005 WM20 | 20-D | CAN | 6 | 1 | 2 | 3 | 2 | G |

**Szturc, Roman**
**b. Karvina, Czechoslovakia (Czech Republic), September 25, 1989**

| | | | | | | | | |
|---|---|---|---|---|---|---|---|---|
| 2007 WM18 | 7-F | CZE | 6 | 2 | 0 | 2 | 6 | 9th |
| 2008 WM20 | 28-F | CZE | 6 | 0 | 1 | 1 | 14 | 5th |
| 2009 WM20 | 20-F | CZE | 6 | 1 | 3 | 4 | 4 | 6th |
| **Totals WM20** | | | **12** | **1** | **4** | **5** | **18** | **—** |

**Talbot, Maxime**
**b. Lemoyne, Quebec, Canada, February 11, 1984**

| | | | | | | | | |
|---|---|---|---|---|---|---|---|---|
| 2004 WM20 | 25-F | CAN | 6 | 0 | 3 | 3 | 2 | S |

**Tallberg, Teemu**
**b. Helsinki, Finland, May 13, 1991**

| | | | | | | | | |
|---|---|---|---|---|---|---|---|---|
| 2009 WM18 | 29-F | FIN | 6 | 0 | 1 | 1 | 2 | B |
| 2011 WM20 | 24-F | FIN | 6 | 0 | 2 | 2 | 0 | 6th |

**Tallinder, Henrik**
**b. Stockholm, Sweden, January 10, 1979**

| | | | | | | | | |
|---|---|---|---|---|---|---|---|---|
| 1998 WM20 | 4-D | SWE | 7 | 1 | 0 | 1 | 6 | 6th |
| 1999 WM20 | 25-D | SWE | 3 | 0 | 0 | 0 | 2 | 4th |
| 2010 OG-M | 10-D | SWE | 4 | 0 | 0 | 0 | 4 | 5th |
| **Totals WM20** | | | **10** | **1** | **0** | **1** | **8** | **—** |

**Tambellini, Jeff**
**b. Calgary, Alberta, Canada, April 13, 1984**

| | | | | | | | | |
|---|---|---|---|---|---|---|---|---|
| 2004 WM20 | 19-F | CAN | 6 | 2 | 3 | 5 | 0 | S |

**Tambijevs, Kirils**
**b. Riga, Latvia, February 4, 1992**

| | | | | | | | | |
|---|---|---|---|---|---|---|---|---|
| 2010 WM18 | 14-F | LAT | 1 | 0 | 0 | 0 | 0 | 9th |

**Tangradi, Eric**
**b. Philadelphia, Pennsylvania, United States, February 10, 1989**

| | | | | | | | | |
|---|---|---|---|---|---|---|---|---|
| 2009 WM20 | 25-F | USA | 6 | 1 | 2 | 3 | 6 | 5th |

**Tarasenko, Vladimir**
**b. Yaroslavl, Soviet Union (Russia), December 13, 1991**

| | | | | | | | | |
|---|---|---|---|---|---|---|---|---|
| 2009 WM18 | 10-F | RUS | 7 | 8 | 7 | 15 | 6 | S |
| 2010 WM20 | 10-F | RUS | 6 | 4 | 1 | 5 | 2 | 6th |
| 2011 WM20 | 10-F | RUS | 7 | 4 | 7 | 11 | 0 | G |
| 2011 WM | 91-F | RUS | 6 | 1 | 0 | 1 | 0 | 4th |
| **Totals WM20** | | | **13** | **8** | **8** | **16** | **2** | **G** |

~WM18 All-Star Team/Forward (2009)

**Tarasov, Alexander**
**b. Magnitogorsk, Soviet Union (Russia), December 24, 1990**

| | | | | | | | | |
|---|---|---|---|---|---|---|---|---|
| 2010 WM20 | 26-D | RUS | 6 | 0 | 0 | 0 | 2 | 6th |

**Tardif, Luc**
**b. Rouen, France, November 30, 1984**

| | | | | | | | | |
|---|---|---|---|---|---|---|---|---|
| 2008 WM | 18-F | FRA | 5 | 0 | 0 | 0 | 4 | 14th |
| 2009 WM | 18-F | FRA | 6 | 3 | 0 | 3 | 6 | 12th |
| 2010 WM | 13-F | FRA | 6 | 1 | 2 | 3 | 14 | 14th |
| 2011 WM | 13-F | FRA | 6 | 0 | 0 | 0 | 8 | 12th |
| **Totals WM** | | | **23** | **4** | **2** | **6** | **32** | **—** |

**Tarnstrom, Dick**
**b. Sundbyberg, Sweden, January 20, 1975**

| | | | | | | | | |
|---|---|---|---|---|---|---|---|---|
| 1994 WM20 | 5-D | SWE | 7 | 5 | 0 | 5 | 4 | S |
| 1995 WM20 | 6-D | SWE | 7 | 2 | 2 | 4 | 4 | B |
| 2003 WM | 28-D | SWE | 9 | 1 | 3 | 4 | 0 | S |
| 2004 WM | 28-D | SWE | 9 | 4 | 2 | 6 | 6 | S |
| 2004 WCH | 28-D | SWE | 2 | 0 | 0 | 0 | 0 | 5th |
| 2007 WM | 28-D | SWE | 9 | 1 | 8 | 9 | 14 | 4th |
| 2009 WM | 28-D | SWE | 8 | 2 | 1 | 3 | 16 | B |
| **Totals WM20** | | | **14** | **7** | **2** | **9** | **8** | **S,B** |
| **Totals WM** | | | **35** | **8** | **14** | **22** | **36** | **2S,B** |

~WM IIHF Directorate Best Defenceman (2004), WM All-Star Team/Defence (2004)

**Tatar, Tomas**
**b. Ilava, Czechoslovakia (Slovakia), December 1, 1990**

| | | | | | | | | |
|---|---|---|---|---|---|---|---|---|
| 2009 WM20 | 14-F | SVK | 7 | 7 | 4 | 11 | 4 | 4th |
| 2010 WM20 | 10-F | SVK | 6 | 3 | 2 | 5 | 6 | 8th |
| 2010 WM | 90-F | SVK | 6 | 2 | 0 | 2 | 4 | 12th |
| 2012 WM | 90-F | SVK | 10 | 2 | 3 | 5 | 0 | S |
| **Totals WM20** | | | **13** | **10** | **6** | **16** | **10** | **—** |
| **Totals WM** | | | **16** | **4** | **3** | **7** | **4** | **S** |

**Tavares, John**
**b. Mississauga, Ontario, Canada, September 20, 1990**

| | | | | | | | | |
|---|---|---|---|---|---|---|---|---|
| 2006 WM18 | 20-F | CAN | 7 | 2 | 3 | 5 | 4 | 4th |
| 2008 WM20 | 20-F | CAN | 7 | 4 | 1 | 5 | 2 | G |
| 2009 WM20 | 19-F | CAN | 6 | 8 | 7 | 15 | 0 | G |
| 2010 WM | 20-F | CAN | 7 | 7 | 0 | 7 | 6 | 7th |
| 2011 WM | 20-F | CAN | 7 | 5 | 4 | 9 | 12 | 5th |
| 2012 WM | 20-F | CAN | 8 | 4 | 5 | 9 | 12 | 5th |
| **Totals WM20** | | | **13** | **12** | **8** | **20** | **2** | **2G** |
| **Totals WM** | | | **22** | **16** | **9** | **25** | **30** | **—** |

~WM20 MVP (2009), WM20 IIHF Directorate Best Forward (2009), WM20 All-Star Team/Forward (2009)

**Tavzelj, Andrej**
**b. Jesenice, Yugoslavia (Slovenia), March 14, 1984**

| | | | | | | | | |
|---|---|---|---|---|---|---|---|---|
| 2011 WM | 4-D | SLO | 6 | 0 | 1 | 1 | 2 | 16th |

**Tedenby, Mattias**
**b. Vetlanda, Sweden, February 21, 1990**

| | | | | | | | | |
|---|---|---|---|---|---|---|---|---|
| 2007 WM18 | 21-F | SWE | 6 | 2 | 1 | 3 | 4 | B |
| 2008 WM18 | 21-F | SWE | 6 | 4 | 4 | 8 | 35 | 4th |
| 2009 WM20 | 10-F | SWE | 6 | 1 | 4 | 5 | 4 | S |
| 2010 WM20 | 9-F | SWE | 5 | 3 | 3 | 6 | 4 | B |
| 2011 WM | 9-F | SWE | 9 | 1 | 2 | 3 | 8 | S |
| **Totals WM18** | | | **12** | **6** | **5** | **11** | **39** | **B** |
| **Totals WM20** | | | **11** | **4** | **7** | **11** | **8** | **S,B** |

~WM18 All-Star Team/Forward (2008)

**Telegin, Ivan**
**b. Novokuznetsk, Russia, February 28, 1992**

| | | | | | | | | |
|---|---|---|---|---|---|---|---|---|
| 2010 WM20 | 14-F | RUS | 6 | 0 | 0 | 0 | 2 | 6th |
| 2012 WM20 | 23-F | RUS | 6 | 1 | 1 | 2 | 12 | S |
| **Totals WM20** | | | **12** | **1** | **1** | **2** | **14** | **S** |

**Tenkrat, Petr**
**b. Kladno, Czechoslovakia (Czech Republic), May 31, 1977**

| | | | | | | | | |
|---|---|---|---|---|---|---|---|---|
| 2012 WM | 62-F | CZE | 10 | 1 | 3 | 4 | 2 | B |

**Teppo, Miihkali**
**b. Helsinki, Finland, December 28, 1992**

| | | | | | | | | |
|---|---|---|---|---|---|---|---|---|
| 2010 WM18 | 22-D | FIN | 6 | 1 | 1 | 2 | 4 | B |

**Teravainen, Teuvo**
**b. Helsinki, Finland, September 11, 1994**

| | | | | | | | | |
|---|---|---|---|---|---|---|---|---|
| 2011 WM18 | 18-F | FIN | 6 | 0 | 0 | 0 | 4 | 5th |
| 2012 WM18 | 19-F | FIN | 6 | 2 | 6 | 8 | 2 | 4th |
| **Totals WM18** | | | **12** | **2** | **6** | **8** | **6** | **—** |

**Tereshenko, Alexei**
**b. Mozhaysk, Soviet Union (Russia), December 16, 1980**

| | | | | | | | | |
|---|---|---|---|---|---|---|---|---|
| 2000 WM20 | 27-F | RUS | 7 | 3 | 5 | 8 | 2 | S |
| 2008 WM | 27-F | RUS | 9 | 2 | 4 | 6 | 2 | G |
| 2009 WM | 23-F | RUS | 9 | 3 | 2 | 5 | 6 | G |
| 2010 WM | 23-F | RUS | 9 | 0 | 1 | 1 | 4 | S |
| 2011 WM | 23-F | RUS | 8 | 1 | 0 | 1 | 2 | 4th |
| 2012 WM | 27-F | RUS | 10 | 2 | 1 | 3 | 2 | G |
| **Totals WM** | | | **45** | **8** | **8** | **16** | **16** | **3G,S** |

~WM20 All-Star Team/Forward (2000)

**Terlikar, Anze**
**b. Kranj, Yugoslavia (Slovenia), November 30, 1980**

| | | | | | | | | |
|---|---|---|---|---|---|---|---|---|
| 2003 WM | 29-F | SLO | 3 | 0 | 0 | 0 | 4 | 15th |
| 2006 WM | 24-F | SLO | 5 | 0 | 0 | 0 | 2 | 16th |
| 2008 WM | 24-F | SLO | 2 | 0 | 0 | 0 | 0 | 15th |
| **Totals WM** | | | **10** | **0** | **0** | **0** | **6** | **—** |

**Teubert, Colten**
**b. White Rock, British Columbia, Canada, March 8, 1990**

| | | | | | | | | |
|---|---|---|---|---|---|---|---|---|
| 2008 WM18 | 2-D | CAN | 7 | 0 | 1 | 1 | 30 | G |
| 2009 WM20 | 2-D | CAN | 6 | 0 | 0 | 0 | 4 | G |
| 2010 WM20 | 2-D | CAN | 6 | 0 | 1 | 1 | 0 | S |
| **Totals WM20** | | | **12** | **0** | **1** | **1** | **4** | **G,S** |

**Thegel, Henrik**
**b. Stockholm, Sweden, January 4, 1990**

| | | | | | | | | |
|---|---|---|---|---|---|---|---|---|
| 2008 WM18 | 12-F | SWE | 6 | 0 | 3 | 3 | 0 | 4th |

**Themar, Andrej**
**b. Martin, Czechoslovakia (Slovakia), June 28, 1988**

| | | | | | | | | |
|---|---|---|---|---|---|---|---|---|
| 2007 WM20 | 21-F | SVK | 6 | 0 | 1 | 1 | 2 | 8th |

**Thinn, Fredrik**
**b. Oslo, Norway, May 17, 1986**

| | | | | | | | | |
|---|---|---|---|---|---|---|---|---|
| 2004 WM18 | 23-F | NOR | 6 | 2 | 1 | 3 | 6 | 10th |
| 2006 WM20 | 24-F | NOR | 4 | 0 | 0 | 0 | 2 | 10th |

**Thinnesen, Mathias**
**b. Esbjerg, Denmark, September 24, 1990**

| | | | | | | | | |
|---|---|---|---|---|---|---|---|---|
| 2008 WM18 | 14-F | DEN | 6 | 0 | 0 | 0 | 2 | 10th |

**Thode, Anders**
**b. Fredrikshavn, Denmark, February 11, 1993**

| | | | | | | | | |
|---|---|---|---|---|---|---|---|---|
| 2012 WM20 | 27-D | DEN | 5 | 0 | 0 | 0 | 0 | 10th |

**Thomas, Christian**
**b. Toronto, Ontario, Canada, May 26, 1992**

| | | | | | | | | |
|---|---|---|---|---|---|---|---|---|
| 2010 WM18 | 17-F | CAN | 6 | 2 | 1 | 3 | 6 | 7th |

**Thompson, Nate**
**b. Anchorage, Alaska, United States, October 5, 1984**

| | | | | | | | | |
|---|---|---|---|---|---|---|---|---|
| 2012 WM | 44-F | USA | 8 | 2 | 0 | 2 | 0 | 7th |

**Thorell, Erik**
**b. Karlstad, Sweden, March 3, 1992**

| | | | | | | | | |
|---|---|---|---|---|---|---|---|---|
| 2010 WM18 | 19-F | SWE | 6 | 3 | 0 | 3 | 4 | S |
| 2012 WM20 | 28-F | SWE | 6 | 3 | 3 | 6 | 0 | G |

**Thoresen, Patrick**
**b. Hamar, Norway, November 7, 1983**

| | | | | | | | | |
|---|---|---|---|---|---|---|---|---|
| 2001 WM18 | 18-F | NOR | 6 | 4 | 2 | 6 | 2 | 9th |
| 2006 WM | 41-F | NOR | 5 | 2 | 0 | 2 | 6 | 11th |
| 2007 WM | 41-F | NOR | 6 | 1 | 4 | 5 | 2 | 14th |
| 2009 WM | 41-F | NOR | 6 | 2 | 0 | 2 | 6 | 11th |
| 2010 OG-M | 41-F | NOR | 4 | 0 | 5 | 5 | 0 | 10th |
| 2010 WM | 41-F | NOR | 6 | 2 | 4 | 6 | 2 | 9th |
| 2012 WM | 41-F | NOR | 8 | 7 | 11 | 18 | 4 | 8th |
| **Totals WM** | | | **31** | **14** | **19** | **33** | **20** | **—** |

~WM All-Star Team/Forward (2012)

**Thornberg, Jesper**
**b. Jonkoping, Sweden, March 15, 1991**

| | | | | | | | | |
|---|---|---|---|---|---|---|---|---|
| 2011 WM20 | 28-F | SWE | 6 | 1 | 2 | 3 | 0 | 4th |

**Thornberg, Martin**
**b. Jonkoping, Sweden, August 6, 1983**

| | | | | | | | | |
|---|---|---|---|---|---|---|---|---|
| 2007 WM | 20-F | SWE | 7 | 2 | 1 | 3 | 6 | 4th |
| 2009 WM | 10-F | SWE | 9 | 0 | 3 | 3 | 2 | B |
| 2011 WM | 10-F | SWE | 9 | 2 | 4 | 6 | 4 | S |
| **Totals WM** | | | **25** | **4** | **8** | **12** | **12** | **S,B** |

**Thornton, Joe**
**b. London, Ontario, Canada, July 2, 1979**

| | | | | | | | | |
|---|---|---|---|---|---|---|---|---|
| 1997 WM20 | 25-F | CAN | 7 | 2 | 2 | 4 | 0 | G |
| 2001 WM | 19-F | CAN | 6 | 1 | 1 | 2 | 6 | 5th |
| 2004 WCH | 97-F | CAN | 6 | 1 | 5 | 6 | 0 | 1st |
| 2005 WM | 97-F | CAN | 9 | 6 | 10 | 16 | 4 | S |
| 2006 OG-M | 97-F | CAN | 6 | 1 | 2 | 3 | 0 | 7th |
| 2010 OG-M | 19-F | CAN | 7 | 1 | 1 | 2 | 0 | G |
| **Totals WM** | | | **15** | **7** | **11** | **18** | **10** | **S** |
| **Totals OG-M** | | | **13** | **2** | **3** | **5** | **0** | **G** |

~WM MVP (2005), WM All-Star Team/Forward (2005)

**Ticar, Rok**
**b. Jesenice, Yugoslavia (Slovenia), May 3, 1989**

| | | | | | | | | |
|---|---|---|---|---|---|---|---|---|
| 2011 WM | 24-F | SLO | 5 | 3 | 0 | 3 | 2 | 16th |

**Tieranta, Anssi**
**b. Lempaala, Finland, August 7, 1985**

| | | | | | | | | |
|---|---|---|---|---|---|---|---|---|
| 2005 WM20 | 3-D | FIN | 6 | 0 | 0 | 0 | 2 | 5th |

**Tiffels, Dominik**
**b. Cologne, Germany, February 20, 1994**

| | | | | | | | | |
|---|---|---|---|---|---|---|---|---|
| 2012 WM18 | 3-D | GER | 6 | 0 | 1 | 1 | 0 | 6th |

**Tiffels, Frederik**
**b. Cologne, Germany, May 20, 1995**

| | | | | | | | | |
|---|---|---|---|---|---|---|---|---|
| 2011 WM18 | 23-F | GER | 6 | 0 | 0 | 0 | 2 | 6th |
| 2012 WM18 | 23-F | GER | 6 | 2 | 0 | 2 | 25 | 6th |
| Totals WM18 | | | 12 | 2 | 0 | 2 | 27 | — |

**Tikhonov, Dmitri**
**b. Magnitogorsk, Soviet Union (Russia), March 22, 1989**

| | | | | | | | | |
|---|---|---|---|---|---|---|---|---|
| 2008 WM20 | 15-D | KAZ | 6 | 0 | 0 | 0 | 6 | 8th |
| 2009 WM20 | 4-D | KAZ | 6 | 0 | 0 | 0 | 10 | 10th |
| **Totals WM20** | | | **12** | **0** | **0** | **0** | **16** | **—** |

**Tikhonov, Viktor**
**b. Riga, Soviet Union (Latvia), May 12, 1988**

| | | | | | | | | |
|---|---|---|---|---|---|---|---|---|
| 2008 WM20 | 11-F | RUS | 7 | 5 | 2 | 7 | 6 | B |

~WM20 IIHF Directorate Best Forward (2008), WM20 All-Star Team/Forward (2008)

**Tikkinen, Niklas**
**b. Espoo, Finland, June 1, 1994**

| | | | | | | | | |
|---|---|---|---|---|---|---|---|---|
| 2012 WM18 | 27-D | FIN | 7 | 0 | 2 | 2 | 4 | 4th |

**Timkin, Yevgeni**
**b. Murmansk, Soviet Union (Russia), September 3, 1990**

| | | | | | | | | |
|---|---|---|---|---|---|---|---|---|
| 2010 WM20 | 22-F | RUS | 6 | 0 | 1 | 1 | 18 | 6th |

**Timonen, Kimmo**
**b. Kuopio, Finland, March 18, 1975**

| | | | | | | | | |
|---|---|---|---|---|---|---|---|---|
| 1993 WM20 | 5-D | FIN | 7 | 2 | 0 | 2 | 6 | 5th |
| 1994 WM20 | 7-D | FIN | 7 | 3 | 3 | 6 | 4 | 4th |
| 1995 WM20 | 7-D | FIN | 7 | 2 | 6 | 8 | 4 | 4th |
| 1996 WM | 32-D | FIN | 6 | 0 | 1 | 1 | 0 | 5th |
| 1998 OG-M | 4-D | FIN | 6 | 0 | 1 | 1 | 2 | B |
| 1998 WM | 4-D | FIN | 10 | 2 | 6 | 8 | 4 | S |
| 1999 WM | 4-D | FIN | 12 | 1 | 4 | 5 | 6 | S |
| 2001 WM | 4-D | FIN | 9 | 2 | 2 | 4 | 10 | S |
| 2002 OG-M | 4-D | FIN | 4 | 0 | 1 | 1 | 2 | 6th |
| 2002 WM | 4-D | FIN | 9 | 1 | 2 | 3 | 8 | 4th |
| 2003 WM | 4-D | FIN | 7 | 2 | 5 | 7 | 2 | 5th |
| 2004 WCH | 4-D | FIN | 6 | 1 | 5 | 6 | 2 | 2nd |
| 2005 WM | 4-D | FIN | 6 | 2 | 1 | 3 | 6 | 7th |
| 2006 OG-M | 4-D | FIN | 8 | 1 | 4 | 5 | 2 | S |
| 2010 OG-M | 44-D | FIN | 6 | 2 | 2 | 4 | 2 | B |
| **Totals WM20** | | | **21** | **7** | **9** | **16** | **14** | **—** |
| **Totals WM** | | | **59** | **10** | **21** | **31** | **36** | **3S** |
| **Totals OG-M** | | | **24** | **3** | **8** | **11** | **8** | **S,2B** |

~OG-M All-Star Team/Defence (2006), WM20 All-Star Team/Defence (1994)

**Tinordi, Jarred**
**b. Millersville, Maryland, United States, February 20, 1992**

| | | | | | | | | |
|---|---|---|---|---|---|---|---|---|
| 2010 WM18 | 24-D | USA | 7 | 1 | 1 | 2 | 10 | G |
| 2012 WM20 | 24-D | USA | 6 | 1 | 1 | 2 | 6 | 7th |

**Tkachev, Vladimir**
**b. Dnepropetrovsk, Ukraine, May 10, 1993**

| | | | | | | | | |
|---|---|---|---|---|---|---|---|---|
| 2011 WM18 | 28-F | RUS | 7 | 2 | 1 | 3 | 2 | B |

**Toews, Jonathan**
**b. Winnipeg, Manitoba, Canada, April 29, 1988**

| | | | | | | | | |
|---|---|---|---|---|---|---|---|---|
| 2006 WM20 | 29-F | CAN | 6 | 0 | 2 | 2 | 2 | G |
| 2007 WM20 | 29-F | CAN | 6 | 4 | 3 | 7 | 12 | G |
| 2007 WM | 16-F | CAN | 9 | 2 | 5 | 7 | 6 | G |
| 2008 WM | 16-F | CAN | 9 | 2 | 3 | 5 | 8 | S |
| 2010 OG-M | 16-F | CAN | 7 | 1 | 7 | 8 | 2 | G |
| **Totals WM20** | | | **12** | **4** | **5** | **9** | **14** | **2G** |
| **Totals WM** | | | **18** | **4** | **8** | **12** | **14** | **G,S** |

~Triple Gold Club
~OG-M IIHF Directorate Best Forward (2010), OG-M All-Star Team/Forward (2010), WM20 All-Star Team/Forward (2007)

**Tokranov, Vasili**
**b. Almetievsk, Soviet Union (Russia), August 2, 1989**

| | | | | | | | | |
|---|---|---|---|---|---|---|---|---|
| 2007 WM18 | 8-D | RUS | 7 | 0 | 0 | 0 | 4 | G |
| 2009 WM20 | 8-D | RUS | 7 | 0 | 1 | 1 | 6 | B |

**Tollefsen, Ole Kristian**
**b. Oslo, Norway, March 29, 1984**

| | | | | | | | | |
|---|---|---|---|---|---|---|---|---|
| 2001 WM18 | 26-D | NOR | 6 | 0 | 0 | 0 | 4 | 9th |
| 2002 WM18 | 9-D | NOR | 8 | 1 | 1 | 2 | 18 | 11th |
| 2010 OG-M | 55-D | NOR | 3 | 0 | 0 | 0 | 25 | 10th |
| 2010 WM | 55-D | NOR | 3 | 0 | 1 | 1 | 2 | 9th |
| 2011 WM | 55-D | NOR | 7 | 0 | 1 | 1 | 10 | 6th |
| 2012 WM | 55-D | NOR | 8 | 0 | 0 | 0 | 20 | 8th |
| Totals WM18 | | | 14 | 1 | 1 | 2 | 22 | — |
| **Totals WM** | | | **18** | **0** | **2** | **2** | **32** | **—** |

**Tolzer, Steffen**
**b. Zittau, East Germany (Germany), June 12, 1985**

| | | | | | | | | |
|---|---|---|---|---|---|---|---|---|
| 2005 WM20 | 13-D | GER | 6 | 0 | 0 | 0 | 4 | 9th |

**Toman, Michal**
**b. Bojnice, Slovakia, May 24, 1992**

| | | | | | | | | |
|---|---|---|---|---|---|---|---|---|
| 2010 WM18 | 9-F | SVK | 6 | 1 | 4 | 5 | 6 | 8th |
| 2012 WM20 | 8-F | SVK | 6 | 1 | 2 | 3 | 4 | 6th |

**Tomecek, Vojtech**
**b. Karlovy Vary, Czech Republic, August 12, 1994**

| | | | | | | | | |
|---|---|---|---|---|---|---|---|---|
| 2012 WM18 | 23-F | CZE | 6 | 1 | 3 | 4 | 0 | 8th |

**Tommila, Juho**
**b. Lappi, Finland, February 9, 1993**

| | | | | | | | | |
|---|---|---|---|---|---|---|---|---|
| 2011 WM18 | 7-D | FIN | 6 | 0 | 1 | 1 | 10 | 5th |

**Torniainen, Kalle**
**b. Huddinge, Sweden, March 28, 1994**

| | | | | | | | | |
|---|---|---|---|---|---|---|---|---|
| 2011 WM18 | 20-F | FIN | 6 | 1 | 0 | 1 | 0 | 5th |

**Tornkvist, Tobias**
**b. Helsingborg, Sweden, April 14, 1994**

| | | | | | | | | |
|---|---|---|---|---|---|---|---|---|
| 2012 WM18 | 13-F | SWE | 6 | 0 | 2 | 2 | 14 | S |

**Torp, Nichlas**
**b. Jonkoping, Sweden, April 10, 1989**

| | | | | | | | | |
|---|---|---|---|---|---|---|---|---|
| 2007 WM18 | 7-D | SWE | 6 | 0 | 1 | 1 | 6 | B |
| 2009 WM20 | 6-D | SWE | 6 | 0 | 1 | 1 | 2 | S |

**Torres, Raffi**
**b. Toronto, Ontario, Canada, October 8, 1981**

| | | | | | | | | |
|---|---|---|---|---|---|---|---|---|
| 2001 WM20 | 28-F | CAN | 7 | 3 | 2 | 5 | 10 | B |

**Trabichet, Teddy**
**b. Echirolles, France, March 10, 1987**

| | | | | | | | | |
|---|---|---|---|---|---|---|---|---|
| 2008 WM | 87-D | FRA | 2 | 0 | 0 | 0 | 2 | 14th |
| 2011 WM | 87-D | FRA | 2 | 0 | 0 | 0 | 0 | 12th |
| **Totals WM** | | | **4** | **0** | **0** | **0** | **2** | **—** |

**Trachsler, Morris**
**b. Zurich, Switzerland, July 15, 1984**

| | | | | | | | | |
|---|---|---|---|---|---|---|---|---|
| 2004 WM20 | 18-F | SUI | 6 | 0 | 4 | 4 | 8 | 8th |
| 2010 WM | 43-F | SUI | 5 | 0 | 0 | 0 | 0 | 5th |
| 2011 WM | 43-F | SUI | 6 | 0 | 2 | 2 | 2 | 9th |
| 2012 WM | 43-F | SUI | 7 | 1 | 0 | 1 | 2 | 11th |
| **Totals WM** | | | **18** | **1** | **2** | **3** | **4** | **—** |

**Trattnig, Matthias**
**b. Graz, Austria, April 22, 1979**

| | | | | | | | | |
|---|---|---|---|---|---|---|---|---|
| 1999 WM | 27-F | AUT | 6 | 2 | 0 | 2 | 4 | 10th |
| 2000 WM | 12-F | AUT | 6 | 1 | 1 | 2 | 6 | 13th |
| 2001 WM | 12-F | AUT | 6 | 0 | 1 | 1 | 10 | 11th |
| 2002 OG-M | 12-F | AUT | 4 | 1 | 1 | 2 | 2 | 12th |
| 2002 WM | 12-F | AUT | 6 | 1 | 1 | 2 | 12 | 12th |
| 2003 WM | 21-F | AUT | 6 | 0 | 1 | 1 | 6 | 10th |
| 2004 WM | 21-F | AUT | 6 | 2 | 2 | 4 | 2 | 11th |
| 2005 WM | 21-F | AUT | 6 | 0 | 2 | 2 | 4 | 16th |
| 2007 WM | 21-F | AUT | 6 | 0 | 1 | 1 | 12 | 15th |
| 2009 WM | 21-F | AUT | 6 | 0 | 1 | 1 | 2 | 14th |
| 2011 WM | 51-D | AUT | 6 | 0 | 1 | 1 | 10 | 15th |
| **Totals WM** | | | **60** | **6** | **11** | **17** | **68** | **—** |

**Treais, A.J.**
**b. Bloomfield Heights, Michigan, United States, February 4, 1991**

| | | | | | | | | |
|---|---|---|---|---|---|---|---|---|
| 2009 WM18 | 23-F | USA | 7 | 2 | 0 | 2 | 2 | G |

**Treille, Sacha**
**b. Cannes, France, November 6, 1987**

| | | | | | | | | |
|---|---|---|---|---|---|---|---|---|
| 2008 WM | 77-F | FRA | 5 | 0 | 1 | 1 | 4 | 14th |
| 2009 WM | 77-F | FRA | 6 | 1 | 0 | 1 | 2 | 12th |
| 2010 WM | 77-F | FRA | 6 | 1 | 1 | 2 | 4 | 14th |
| 2011 WM | 77-F | FRA | 6 | 2 | 2 | 4 | 16 | 12th |
| 2012 WM | 77-F | FRA | 2 | 1 | 1 | 2 | 27 | 9th |
| **Totals WM** | | | **25** | **5** | **5** | **10** | **53** | **—** |

**Treille, Yorick**
**b. Grenoble, France, July 15, 1980**

| | | | | | | | | |
|---|---|---|---|---|---|---|---|---|
| 2000 WM | 14-F | FRA | 6 | 0 | 1 | 1 | 0 | 15th |
| 2002 OG-M | 14-F | FRA | 4 | 0 | 0 | 0 | 4 | 14th |
| 2008 WM | 7-F | FRA | 5 | 3 | 1 | 4 | 12 | 14th |
| 2009 WM | 7-F | FRA | 6 | 1 | 1 | 2 | 8 | 12th |
| 2010 WM | 7-F | FRA | 6 | 2 | 0 | 2 | 2 | 14th |
| 2012 WM | 7-F | FRA | 7 | 1 | 1 | 2 | 6 | 9th |
| **Totals WM** | | | **30** | **7** | **4** | **11** | **28** | **—** |

**Trettenes, Mathias**
**b. Stavanger, Norway, November 8, 1993**

| | | | | | | | | |
|---|---|---|---|---|---|---|---|---|
| 2011 WM18 | 21-F | NOR | 6 | 0 | 2 | 2 | 16 | 9th |

**Tripp, John**
**b. Kingston, Ontario, Canada, May 4, 1977**

| | | | | | | | | |
|---|---|---|---|---|---|---|---|---|
| 2007 WM | 21-F | GER | 6 | 1 | 2 | 3 | 2 | 9th |
| 2008 WM | 21-F | GER | 6 | 0 | 1 | 1 | 0 | 10th |
| 2010 OG-M | 21-F | GER | 4 | 1 | 0 | 1 | 2 | 11th |
| 2010 WM | 21-F | GER | 9 | 0 | 0 | 0 | 6 | 4th |
| 2011 WM | 21-F | GER | 7 | 3 | 1 | 4 | 4 | 7th |
| 2012 WM | 21-F | GER | 7 | 1 | 0 | 1 | 2 | 12th |
| **Totals WM** | | | **35** | **5** | **4** | **9** | **14** | **—** |

**Trivino, Corey**
**b. Toronto, Ontario, Canada, January 12, 1990**

| | | | | | | | | |
|---|---|---|---|---|---|---|---|---|
| 2008 WM18 | 10-F | CAN | 7 | 4 | 3 | 7 | 2 | G |

**Troock, Branden**
**b. Edmonton, Alberta, Canada, March 3, 1994**

| | | | | | | | | |
|---|---|---|---|---|---|---|---|---|
| 2012 WM18 | 11-F | CAN | 7 | 0 | 1 | 1 | 10 | B |

**Troshinski, Alexei**
**b. V-Kazakhstanskaya, Soviet Union (Kazakhstan), October 9, 1973**

| | | | | | | | | |
|---|---|---|---|---|---|---|---|---|
| 2012 WM | 55-D | KAZ | 7 | 0 | 1 | 1 | 0 | 16th |

**Trouba, Jacob**
**b. Rochester, Minnesota, United States, February 26, 1994**

| | | | | | | | | |
|---|---|---|---|---|---|---|---|---|
| 2011 WM18 | 24-D | USA | 6 | 1 | 0 | 1 | 0 | G |
| 2012 WM18 | 8-D | USA | 6 | 1 | 2 | 3 | 8 | G |
| 2012 WM20 | 8-D | USA | 6 | 0 | 2 | 2 | 0 | 7th |

**Trska, Peter**
**b. Dubnica nad Vahom, Slovakia, June 1, 1992**

| | | | | | | | | |
|---|---|---|---|---|---|---|---|---|
| 2010 WM18 | 25-D | SVK | 6 | 1 | 2 | 3 | 8 | 8th |
| 2011 WM20 | 7-D | SVK | 6 | 0 | 0 | 0 | 4 | 8th |
| 2012 WM20 | 6-D | SVK | 6 | 0 | 0 | 0 | 6 | 6th |
| Totals WM20 | | | 12 | 0 | 0 | 0 | 10 | — |

**Trunyov, Maxim**
**b. Kirovo-Chepetsk, Soviet Union (Russia), September 7, 1990**

| | | | | | | | | |
|---|---|---|---|---|---|---|---|---|
| 2010 WM20 | 11-F | RUS | 6 | 2 | 2 | 4 | 4 | 6th |

**Trutmann, Dario**
**b. Zug, Switzerland, September 17, 1992**

| | | | | | | | | |
|---|---|---|---|---|---|---|---|---|
| 2009 WM18 | 25-D | SUI | 6 | 1 | 1 | 2 | 2 | 8th |
| 2010 WM18 | 17-D | SUI | 6 | 0 | 5 | 5 | 12 | 5th |
| 2011 WM20 | 17-D | SUI | 6 | 0 | 4 | 4 | 2 | 5th |
| 2012 WM20 | 17-D | SUI | 6 | 0 | 2 | 2 | 6 | 8th |
| **Totals WM18** | | | **12** | **1** | **6** | **7** | **14** | **—** |
| **Totals WM20** | | | **12** | **0** | **6** | **6** | **8** | **—** |

**Trygg, Mathias**
**b. Oslo, Norway, March 15, 1986**

| | | | | | | | | |
|---|---|---|---|---|---|---|---|---|
| 2004 WM18 | 19-F | NOR | 6 | 5 | 2 | 7 | 4 | 10th |
| 2006 WM20 | 19-F | NOR | 6 | 1 | 2 | 3 | 0 | 10th |

**Trygg, Mats**
**b. Oslo, Norway, June 1, 1976**

| | | | | | | | | |
|---|---|---|---|---|---|---|---|---|
| 1997 WM | 23-D | NOR | 8 | 1 | 0 | 1 | 2 | 12th |
| 1999 WM | 23-D | NOR | 5 | 1 | 1 | 2 | 2 | 12th |
| 2000 WM | 23-D | NOR | 6 | 1 | 4 | 5 | 6 | 9th |
| 2001 WM | 23-D | NOR | 5 | 0 | 2 | 2 | 0 | 15th |
| 2006 WM | 23-D | NOR | 5 | 1 | 2 | 3 | 12 | 11th |
| 2007 WM | 23-D | NOR | 6 | 2 | 5 | 7 | 8 | 14th |
| 2008 WM | 23-D | NOR | 7 | 1 | 4 | 5 | 8 | 8th |
| 2009 WM | 23-D | NOR | 6 | 1 | 0 | 1 | 6 | 11th |
| 2010 OG-M | 23-D | NOR | 4 | 0 | 0 | 0 | 2 | 10th |
| 2012 WM | 23-D | NOR | 8 | 5 | 1 | 6 | 14 | 8th |
| **Totals WM** | | | **56** | **13** | **19** | **32** | **58** | **—** |

**Tudin, Daniel**
**b. Orleans, Ontario, Canada, August 3, 1978**

| | | | | | | | | |
|---|---|---|---|---|---|---|---|---|
| 2012 WM | 16-F | ITA | 6 | 0 | 1 | 1 | 2 | 15th |

**Tukonen, Lauri**
**b. Hyvinkaa, Finland, September 1, 1986**

| | | | | | | | | |
|---|---|---|---|---|---|---|---|---|
| 2004 WM18 | 9-F | FIN | 6 | 5 | 6 | 11 | 10 | 7th |
| 2004 WM20 | 25-F | FIN | 7 | 2 | 1 | 3 | 2 | B |
| 2005 WM20 | 27-F | FIN | 6 | 1 | 1 | 2 | 2 | 5th |
| 2006 WM20 | 9-F | FIN | 7 | 3 | 7 | 10 | 0 | B |
| **Totals WM20** | | | **20** | **6** | **9** | **15** | **4** | **2B** |

~WM20 All-Star Team/Forward (2006)

**Tuma, David**
**b. Decin, Czechoslovakia (Czech Republic), May 4, 1991**

| | | | | | | | | |
|---|---|---|---|---|---|---|---|---|
| 2009 WM18 | 19-F | CZE | 6 | 0 | 0 | 0 | 4 | 6th |
| 2011 WM20 | 26-F | CZE | 6 | 0 | 1 | 1 | 2 | 7th |

**Tuma, Martin**
**b. Most, Czechoslovakia (Czech Republic), September 14, 1985**

| | | | | | | | | |
|---|---|---|---|---|---|---|---|---|
| 2003 WM18 | 8-D | CZE | 6 | 0 | 0 | 0 | 29 | 6th |
| 2005 WM20 | 7-D | CZE | 7 | 0 | 0 | 0 | 28 | B |

**Tumashov, Yevgeni**
**b. V-Kazakhstanskaya, Soviet Union (Kazakhstan), November 2, 1988**

| | | | | | | | | |
|---|---|---|---|---|---|---|---|---|
| 2008 WM20 | 28-D | KAZ | 6 | 0 | 0 | 0 | 6 | 8th |

**Tuominen, Henri**
**b. Turku, Finland, September 10, 1991**

| | | | | | | | | |
|---|---|---|---|---|---|---|---|---|
| 2011 WM20 | 16-F | FIN | 5 | 0 | 1 | 1 | 4 | 6th |

**Tuppurainen, Jani**
**b. Oulu, Finland, March 30, 1980**

| | | | | | | | | |
|---|---|---|---|---|---|---|---|---|
| 2012 WM | 12-F | FIN | 2 | 0 | 1 | 1 | 2 | 4th |

**Turesson, Andreas**
**b. Kristianstad, Sweden, November 18, 1987**

| | | | | | | | | |
|---|---|---|---|---|---|---|---|---|
| 2007 WM20 | 12-F | SWE | 7 | 1 | 2 | 3 | 4 | 4th |

**Turovets, Nikita**
**b. Minsk, Belarus, October 31, 1992**

| | | | | | | | | |
|---|---|---|---|---|---|---|---|---|
| 2010 WM18 | 4-D | BLR | 6 | 0 | 0 | 0 | 0 | 10th |

**Turris, Kyle**
**b. New Westminster, British Columbia, Canada, August 14, 1989**

| | | | | | | | | |
|---|---|---|---|---|---|---|---|---|
| 2007 WM18 | 10-F | CAN | 6 | 3 | 2 | 5 | 2 | 4th |
| 2008 WM20 | 19-F | CAN | 7 | 4 | 4 | 8 | 2 | G |

**Turtiainen, Jaakko**
**b. Helsinki, Finland, March 5, 1991**

| | | | | | | | | |
|---|---|---|---|---|---|---|---|---|
| 2009 WM18 | 28-F | FIN | 4 | 0 | 0 | 0 | 0 | B |
| 2011 WM20 | 28-F | FIN | 6 | 1 | 1 | 2 | 0 | 6th |

**Tverdovski, Oleg**
**b. Donetsk, Soviet Union (Ukraine), May 18, 1976**

| | | | | | | | | |
|---|---|---|---|---|---|---|---|---|
| 1994 WM20 | 10-D | RUS | 7 | 1 | 5 | 6 | 6 | B |
| 1996 WM | 26-D | RUS | 3 | 0 | 1 | 1 | 0 | 4th |
| 1996 WCH | 7-D | RUS | 4 | 1 | 0 | 1 | 0 | 4th |
| 2001 WM | 10-D | RUS | 7 | 2 | 2 | 4 | 2 | 6th |
| 2002 OG-M | 7-D | RUS | 6 | 1 | 1 | 2 | 0 | B |
| 2004 WM | 10-D | RUS | 6 | 0 | 1 | 1 | 6 | 10th |
| 2004 WCH | 10-D | RUS | 3 | 0 | 0 | 0 | 0 | 6th |
| 2009 WM | 10-D | RUS | 9 | 2 | 2 | 4 | 6 | G |
| **Totals WM** | | | **25** | **4** | **6** | **10** | **14** | **G** |
| **Totals IIHF-NHL** | | | **7** | **1** | **0** | **1** | **0** | **—** |

**Tvrdon, Marek**
**b. Nitra, Slovakia, January 31, 1993**

| | | | | | | | | |
|---|---|---|---|---|---|---|---|---|
| 2010 WM18 | 17-F | SVK | 6 | 3 | 1 | 4 | 4 | 8th |
| 2012 WM20 | 17-F | SVK | 6 | 3 | 1 | 4 | 14 | 6th |

**Tybor, Radoslav**
**b. Ilava, Czechoslovakia (Slovakia), November 23, 1989**

| | | | | | | | | |
|---|---|---|---|---|---|---|---|---|
| 2009 WM20 | 21-F | SVK | 7 | 2 | 1 | 3 | 0 | 4th |

**Tynan, T.J.**
**b. Orland Park, Illinois, United States, February 25, 1992**

| | | | | | | | | |
|---|---|---|---|---|---|---|---|---|
| 2012 WM20 | 19-F | USA | 6 | 1 | 3 | 4 | 2 | 7th |

**Tyutin, Fyodor**
**b. Izhevsk, Soviet Union (Russia), July 19, 1983**

| | | | | | | | | |
|---|---|---|---|---|---|---|---|---|
| 2001 WM18 | 7-D | RUS | 6 | 1 | 4 | 5 | 18 | G |
| 2002 WM20 | 7-D | RUS | 7 | 1 | 0 | 1 | 2 | G |
| 2003 WM20 | 7-D | RUS | 6 | 0 | 3 | 3 | 12 | G |
| 2006 OG-M | 51-D | RUS | 8 | 0 | 1 | 1 | 4 | 4th |
| 2008 WM | 51-D | RUS | 6 | 0 | 1 | 1 | 0 | G |
| 2010 OG-M | 51-D | RUS | 4 | 0 | 2 | 2 | 2 | 6th |
| 2011 WM | 51-D | RUS | 9 | 0 | 3 | 3 | 0 | 4th |
| **Totals WM20** | | | **13** | **1** | **3** | **4** | **14** | **2G** |
| **Totals WM** | | | **21** | **0** | **6** | **6** | **6** | **G** |

**Ugarov, Alexei**
**b. Nizhnekamsk, Soviet Union (Russia), January 2, 1985**

| | | | | | | | | |
|---|---|---|---|---|---|---|---|---|
| 2005 WM20 | 18-F | BLR | 6 | 3 | 0 | 3 | 6 | 10th |
| 2005 WM | 18-F | BLR | 6 | 0 | 0 | 0 | 2 | 10th |
| 2006 WM | 18-F | BLR | 7 | 0 | 2 | 2 | 4 | 6th |
| 2007 WM | 18-F | BLR | 6 | 3 | 2 | 5 | 6 | 11th |
| 2008 WM | 18-F | BLR | 6 | 4 | 1 | 5 | 0 | 9th |
| 2009 WM | 18-F | BLR | 7 | 2 | 0 | 2 | 2 | 8th |
| 2010 OG-M | 18-F | BLR | 4 | 1 | 1 | 2 | 4 | 9th |
| 2010 WM | 18-F | BLR | 6 | 0 | 2 | 2 | 0 | 10th |
| 2011 WM | 18-F | BLR | 6 | 0 | 1 | 1 | 2 | 14th |
| 2012 WM | 18-F | BLR | 7 | 2 | 1 | 3 | 0 | 14th |
| **Totals WM** | | | **51** | **11** | **9** | **20** | **16** | **—** |

**Uher, Dominik**
**b. Frydek Mistek, Czech Republic, December 31, 1992**

| | | | | | | | | |
|---|---|---|---|---|---|---|---|---|
| 2010 WM18 | 17-F | CZE | 6 | 1 | 1 | 2 | 0 | 6th |
| 2012 WM20 | 23-F | CZE | 6 | 1 | 2 | 3 | 4 | 5th |

**Uhnak, Martin**
**b. Nitra, Czechoslovakia (Slovakia), January 23, 1990**

| | | | | | | | | |
|---|---|---|---|---|---|---|---|---|
| 2008 WM18 | 27-F | SVK | 6 | 2 | 2 | 4 | 0 | 7th |
| 2009 WM20 | 10-F | SVK | 7 | 1 | 0 | 1 | 0 | 4th |

**Uldall, Bjorn**
**b. Herning, Denmark, April 10, 1994**

| | | | | | | | | |
|---|---|---|---|---|---|---|---|---|
| 2012 WM18 | 7-D | DEN | 6 | 1 | 0 | 1 | 2 | 10th |

**Ulehla, Marcel**
**b. Bratislava, Czechoslovakia (Slovakia), July 30, 1986**

| | | | | | | | | |
|---|---|---|---|---|---|---|---|---|
| 2004 WM18 | 29-F | SVK | 6 | 0 | 0 | 0 | 4 | 6th |
| 2006 WM20 | 29-F | SVK | 6 | 0 | 0 | 0 | 4 | 8th |

**Ulescenko, Edgars**
**b. Riga, Soviet Union (Latvia), March 10, 1990**

| | | | | | | | | |
|---|---|---|---|---|---|---|---|---|
| 2009 WM20 | 28-F | LAT | 6 | 0 | 1 | 1 | 6 | 8th |
| 2010 WM20 | 28-F | LAT | 6 | 0 | 1 | 1 | 4 | 9th |
| **Totals WM20** | | | **12** | **0** | **2** | **2** | **10** | **—** |

**Ullmann, Christoph**
**b. Altotting, West Germany (Germany), May 19, 1983**

| | | | | | | | | |
|---|---|---|---|---|---|---|---|---|
| 2004 WM | 47-F | GER | 3 | 0 | 0 | 0 | 0 | 9th |
| 2007 WM | 47-F | GER | 6 | 1 | 0 | 1 | 4 | 9th |
| 2008 WM | 47-F | GER | 6 | 1 | 3 | 4 | 0 | 10th |
| 2009 WM | 47-F | GER | 6 | 1 | 1 | 2 | 10 | 15th |
| 2010 WM | 47-F | GER | 9 | 0 | 1 | 1 | 4 | 4th |
| 2011 WM | 47-F | GER | 7 | 0 | 3 | 3 | 4 | 7th |
| 2012 WM | 47-F | GER | 7 | 0 | 5 | 5 | 0 | 12th |
| **Totals WM** | | | **44** | **3** | **13** | **16** | **22** | **—** |

**Ullman, Petter**
**b. Falun, Sweden, November 24, 1986**

| | | | | | | | | |
|---|---|---|---|---|---|---|---|---|
| 2006 WM20 | 15-D | SWE | 6 | 0 | 1 | 1 | 4 | 5th |

**Ullstrom, David**
**b. Jonkoping, Sweden, April 22, 1989**

| | | | | | | | | |
|---|---|---|---|---|---|---|---|---|
| 2009 WM20 | 24-F | SWE | 6 | 2 | 2 | 4 | 2 | S |

**Ulmer, Stefan**
**b. Dornbirn, Austria, December 1, 1990**

| | | | | | | | | |
|---|---|---|---|---|---|---|---|---|
| 2010 WM20 | 8-D | AUT | 6 | 0 | 6 | 6 | 10 | 10th |

**Umberger, Richard Allen "R.J."**
**b. Pittsburgh, Pennsylvania, United States, May 3, 1982**

| | | | | | | | | |
|---|---|---|---|---|---|---|---|---|
| 2000 WM18 | 18-F | USA | 6 | 1 | 0 | 1 | 2 | 8th |
| 2001 WM20 | 20-F | USA | 7 | 2 | 2 | 4 | 2 | 5th |
| 2002 WM20 | 22-F | USA | 7 | 1 | 4 | 5 | 0 | 5th |
| 2006 WM | 20-F | USA | 1 | 0 | 0 | 0 | 0 | 7th |
| **Totals WM20** | | | **14** | **3** | **6** | **9** | **2** | **—** |

**Untergaschnigg, Andreas**
**b. Salzburg, Austria, January 17, 1990**

| | | | | | | | | |
|---|---|---|---|---|---|---|---|---|
| 2010 WM20 | 3-D | AUT | 6 | 0 | 0 | 0 | 2 | 10th |

**Unterluggauer, Gerhard**
**b. Villach, Austria, August 15, 1976**

| | | | | | | | | |
|---|---|---|---|---|---|---|---|---|
| 1994 WM | 8-D | AUT | 4 | 0 | 0 | 0 | 0 | 8th |
| 1995 WM | 8-D | AUT | 6 | 0 | 0 | 0 | 2 | 11th |
| 1998 OG-M | 5-D | AUT | 4 | 0 | 0 | 0 | 4 | 14th |
| 1998 WM | 5-D | AUT | 3 | 0 | 1 | 1 | 2 | 15th |
| 1999 WM | 4-D | AUT | 6 | 1 | 0 | 1 | 4 | 10th |
| 2000 WM | 4-D | AUT | 6 | 2 | 0 | 2 | 4 | 13th |
| 2001 WM | 4-D | AUT | 6 | 0 | 0 | 0 | 8 | 11th |
| 2002 OG-M | 4-D | AUT | 4 | 2 | 0 | 2 | 4 | 12th |
| 2002 WM | 4-D | AUT | 6 | 1 | 2 | 3 | 8 | 12th |
| 2003 WM | 4-D | AUT | 6 | 0 | 1 | 1 | 2 | 10th |
| 2004 WM | 4-D | AUT | 6 | 2 | 0 | 2 | 4 | 11th |
| 2005 WM | 4-D | AUT | 6 | 3 | 1 | 4 | 14 | 16th |
| 2007 WM | 4-D | AUT | 6 | 0 | 1 | 1 | 4 | 15th |
| 2009 WM | 4-D | AUT | 6 | 0 | 1 | 1 | 4 | 14th |
| 2011 WM | 4-D | AUT | 6 | 1 | 0 | 1 | 2 | 15th |
| **Totals WM** | | | **73** | **10** | **7** | **17** | **58** | **—** |
| **Totals OG-M** | | | **8** | **2** | **0** | **2** | **8** | **—** |

**Untersander, Ramon**
**b. Alt St. Johann, Switzerland, January 21, 1991**

| | | | | | | | | |
|---|---|---|---|---|---|---|---|---|
| 2010 WM20 | 32-D | SUI | 7 | 0 | 0 | 0 | 2 | 4th |
| 2011 WM20 | 32-D | SUI | 6 | 0 | 0 | 0 | 0 | 5th |
| **Totals WM20** | | | **13** | **0** | **0** | **0** | **2** | **—** |

**Unterweger, Markus**
**b. Leoben, Austria, August 24, 1990**

| | | | | | | | | |
|---|---|---|---|---|---|---|---|---|
| 2010 WM20 | 7-F | AUT | 5 | 1 | 0 | 1 | 2 | 10th |

**Upenieks, Raimonds**
**b. Riga, Latvia, February 20, 1992**

| | | | | | | | | |
|---|---|---|---|---|---|---|---|---|
| 2010 WM18 | 11-F | LAT | 6 | 0 | 2 | 2 | 12 | 9th |

**Upitis, Juris**
**b. Riga, Soviet Union (Latvia), June 16, 1991**

| | | | | | | | | |
|---|---|---|---|---|---|---|---|---|
| 2010 WM20 | 9-F | LAT | 6 | 0 | 3 | 3 | 6 | 9th |

**Upper, Dmitri**
**b. Dmitrievka, Soviet Union (Russia), July 27, 1978**

| | | | | | | | | |
|---|---|---|---|---|---|---|---|---|
| 2012 WM | 36-F | KAZ | 7 | 0 | 3 | 3 | 0 | 16th |

**Upshall, Scottie**
**b. Fort McMurray, Alberta, Canada, October 7, 1983**

| | | | | | | | | |
|---|---|---|---|---|---|---|---|---|
| 2002 WM20 | 19-F | CAN | 7 | 3 | 3 | 6 | 10 | S |
| 2003 WM20 | 19-F | CAN | 6 | 4 | 1 | 5 | 18 | S |
| 2009 WM | 8-F | CAN | 8 | 0 | 1 | 1 | 27 | S |
| **Totals WM20** | | | **13** | **7** | **4** | **11** | **28** | **2S** |

~WM20 All-Star Team/Forward (2003)

**Usenko, Ivan**
**b. Gorky (Nizhni Novgorod), Soviet Union (Russia), February 12, 1983**

| | | | | | | | | |
|---|---|---|---|---|---|---|---|---|
| 2009 WM | 3-D | BLR | 7 | 0 | 0 | 0 | 0 | 8th |

**Uvira, Sebastian**
**b. Freiburg, Germany, January 26, 1993**

| | | | | | | | | |
|---|---|---|---|---|---|---|---|---|
| 2011 WM18 | 24-F | GER | 6 | 1 | 1 | 2 | 16 | 6th |

**Vaananen, Ossi**
**b. Vantaa, Finland, August 18, 1980**

| | | | | | | | | |
|---|---|---|---|---|---|---|---|---|
| 1999 WM20 | 5-D | FIN | 6 | 0 | 2 | 2 | 8 | 5th |
| 2000 WM20 | 9-D | FIN | 7 | 0 | 0 | 0 | 16 | 7th |
| 2001 WM | 6-D | FIN | 9 | 0 | 2 | 2 | 16 | S |
| 2002 OG-M | 6-D | FIN | 2 | 0 | 1 | 1 | 0 | 6th |
| 2003 WM | 6-D | FIN | 7 | 0 | 4 | 4 | 8 | 5th |
| 2004 WCH | 5-D | FIN | 4 | 1 | 2 | 3 | 0 | 2nd |
| 2005 WM | 6-D | FIN | 7 | 0 | 1 | 1 | 8 | 7th |
| 2008 WM | 6-D | FIN | 9 | 0 | 1 | 1 | 8 | B |
| 2011 WM | 4-D | FIN | 9 | 0 | 0 | 0 | 4 | G |
| 2012 WM | 4-D | FIN | 10 | 0 | 1 | 1 | 4 | 4th |
| **Totals WM20** | | | **13** | **0** | **2** | **2** | **24** | **—** |
| **Totals WM** | | | **51** | **0** | **9** | **9** | **48** | **G,S,B** |

**Vachovec, Michal**
**b. Parlavy Vary, Czech Republic, July 15, 1992**

| | | | | | | | | |
|---|---|---|---|---|---|---|---|---|
| 2010 WM18 | 18-F | CZE | 6 | 2 | 3 | 5 | 8 | 6th |

**Vahalahti, Ville**
**b. Parainen, Finland, November 7, 1977**

| | | | | | | | | |
|---|---|---|---|---|---|---|---|---|
| 2009 WM | 82-F | FIN | 4 | 0 | 0 | 0 | 2 | 5th |

**Vainonen, Mikko**
**b. Helsinki, Finland, April 11, 1994**

| | | | | | | | | |
|---|---|---|---|---|---|---|---|---|
| 2012 WM18 | 4-D | FIN | 7 | 0 | 4 | 4 | 8 | 4th |

**Vakiparta, Riku**
**b. Rauma, Finland, February 2, 1992**

| | | | | | | | | |
|---|---|---|---|---|---|---|---|---|
| 2010 WM18 | 5-D | FIN | 6 | 0 | 2 | 2 | 4 | B |

**Valabik, Boris**
**b. Nitra, Czechoslovakia (Slovakia), February 14, 1986**

| | | | | | | | | |
|---|---|---|---|---|---|---|---|---|
| 2003 WM18 | 27-D | SVK | 7 | 1 | 0 | 1 | 34 | S |
| 2004 WM18 | 27-D | SVK | 6 | 0 | 3 | 3 | 26 | 6th |
| 2005 WM20 | 9-D | SVK | 6 | 0 | 1 | 1 | 20 | 7th |
| 2006 WM20 | 28-D | SVK | 6 | 1 | 5 | 6 | 32 | 8th |
| 2009 WM | 48-D | SVK | 6 | 0 | 0 | 0 | 16 | 10th |
| **Totals WM18** | | | **13** | **1** | **3** | **4** | **60** | **S** |
| **Totals WM20** | | | **12** | **1** | **6** | **7** | **52** | **—** |

**Valach, Juraj**
**b. Zvolen, Czechoslovakia (Slovakia), February 1, 1989**

| | | | | | | | | |
|---|---|---|---|---|---|---|---|---|
| 2006 WM18 | 16-D | SVK | 6 | 0 | 0 | 0 | 8 | 7th |
| 2007 WM20 | 4-D | SVK | 6 | 0 | 0 | 0 | 8 | 8th |
| 2009 WM20 | 8-D | SVK | 7 | 0 | 3 | 3 | 16 | 4th |
| **Totals WM20** | | | **13** | **0** | **3** | **3** | **24** | **—** |

**Valchar, Radim**
**b. Karvina, Czechoslovakia (Czech Republic), April 20, 1989**

| | | | | | | | | |
|---|---|---|---|---|---|---|---|---|
| 2007 WM18 | 21-F | CZE | 6 | 3 | 0 | 3 | 2 | 9th |
| 2009 WM20 | 22-F | CZE | 6 | 0 | 1 | 1 | 2 | 6th |

**Valek, David**
**b. Orem, Utah, United States, March 19, 1991**

| | | | | | | | | |
|---|---|---|---|---|---|---|---|---|
| 2009 WM18 | 21-F | USA | 7 | 1 | 0 | 1 | 4 | G |

**Valenta, Tomas**
**b. Uherske Hradiste, Czech Republic, April 13, 1992**

| | | | | | | | | |
|---|---|---|---|---|---|---|---|---|
| 2010 WM18 | 4-D | CZE | 6 | 0 | 0 | 0 | 0 | 6th |

**Valentenko, Pavel**
**b. Moscow, Soviet Union (Russia), October 20, 1987**

| | | | | | | | | |
|---|---|---|---|---|---|---|---|---|
| 2007 WM20 | 4-D | RUS | 6 | 2 | 1 | 3 | 6 | S |

**Valivaara, Jyrki**
**b. Jyvaskyla, Finland, May 30, 1976**

| | | | | | | | | |
|---|---|---|---|---|---|---|---|---|
| 2011 WM | 19-D | FIN | 9 | 0 | 3 | 3 | 8 | G |

**Valkonen, Joonas**
**b. Vantaa, Finland, June 3, 1993**

| | | | | | | | | |
|---|---|---|---|---|---|---|---|---|
| 2011 WM18 | 8-D | FIN | 6 | 1 | 1 | 2 | 6 | 5th |

**Valuiski, Semyon**
**b. Samara Region, Soviet Union (Russia), February 10, 1991**

| | | | | | | | | |
|---|---|---|---|---|---|---|---|---|
| 2011 WM20 | 8-F | RUS | 7 | 0 | 2 | 2 | 4 | G |

**Vampola, Petr**
**b. Zdar nad Sazavou, Czechoslovakia (Czech Republic), January 21, 1982**

| | | | | | | | | |
|---|---|---|---|---|---|---|---|---|
| 2000 WM18 | 21-F | CZE | 6 | 0 | 0 | 0 | 4 | 6th |
| 2010 WM | 14-F | CZE | 9 | 0 | 2 | 2 | 4 | G |
| 2011 WM | 14-F | CZE | 3 | 0 | 0 | 0 | 0 | B |
| **Totals WM** | | | **12** | **0** | **2** | **2** | **4** | **G,B** |

**Vandas, Michael**
**b. Poprad, Czechoslovakia (Slovakia), February 2, 1991**

| | | | | | | | | |
|---|---|---|---|---|---|---|---|---|
| 2009 WM18 | 6-F | SVK | 6 | 2 | 0 | 2 | 2 | 7th |
| 2010 WM20 | 20-F | SVK | 6 | 0 | 0 | 0 | 0 | 8th |
| 2011 WM20 | 20-F | SVK | 5 | 0 | 3 | 3 | 0 | 8th |
| **Totals WM20** | | | **11** | **0** | **3** | **3** | **0** | **—** |

**Vanek, Thomas**
**b. Baden, Austria, January 19, 1984**

| | | | | | | | | |
|---|---|---|---|---|---|---|---|---|
| 2004 WM20 | 26-F | AUT | 6 | 3 | 1 | 4 | 37 | 9th |
| 2004 WM | 15-F | AUT | 6 | 2 | 5 | 7 | 0 | 11th |
| 2009 WM | 26-F | AUT | 6 | 1 | 3 | 4 | 2 | 14th |
| **Totals WM** | | | **12** | **3** | **8** | **11** | **2** | **—** |

**van Riemsdyk, James**
**b. Middletown, New Jersey, United States, May 4, 1989**

| | | | | | | | | |
|---|---|---|---|---|---|---|---|---|
| 2006 WM18 | 23-F | USA | 6 | 0 | 1 | 1 | 2 | G |
| 2007 WM18 | 21-F | USA | 7 | 5 | 7 | 12 | 4 | S |
| 2007 WM20 | 12-F | USA | 7 | 1 | 0 | 1 | 2 | B |
| 2008 WM20 | 12-F | USA | 6 | 5 | 6 | 11 | 2 | 4th |
| 2009 WM20 | 21-F | USA | 6 | 6 | 4 | 10 | 4 | 5th |
| 2011 WM | 16-F | USA | 2 | 1 | 0 | 1 | 2 | 8th |
| **Totals WM18** | | | **13** | **5** | **8** | **13** | **6** | **G,S** |
| **Totals WM20** | | | **19** | **12** | **10** | **22** | **8** | **B** |

~WM20 All-Star Team/Forward (2008), WM18 IIHF Directorate Best Forward (2007), WM18 All-Star Team/Forward (2007)

**Vantuch, Lukas**
**b. Jihlava, Czechoslovakia (Czech Republic), July 20, 1987**

| | | | | | | | | |
|---|---|---|---|---|---|---|---|---|
| 2007 WM20 | 20-F | CZE | 4 | 0 | 0 | 0 | 0 | 5th |

**Vasilchenko, Alexei**
**b. Ust-Kamenogorsk, Soviet Union (Kazakhstan), March 29, 1981**

| | | | | | | | | |
|---|---|---|---|---|---|---|---|---|
| 2000 WM20 | 8-D | KAZ | 7 | 0 | 1 | 1 | 6 | 8th |
| 2001 WM20 | 2-D | KAZ | 6 | 0 | 1 | 1 | 20 | 10th |
| 2005 WM | 6-D | KAZ | 1 | 0 | 0 | 0 | 0 | 12th |
| 2006 OG-M | 2-D | KAZ | 5 | 0 | 1 | 1 | 8 | 9th |
| 2010 WM | 29-D | KAZ | 6 | 0 | 1 | 1 | 10 | 16th |
| **Totals WM20** | | | **13** | **0** | **2** | **2** | **26** | **—** |
| **Totals WM** | | | **7** | **0** | **1** | **1** | **10** | **—** |

**Vasiliev, Valeri**
**b. Togliatti, Soviet Union (Russia), March 17, 1990**

| | | | | | | | | |
|---|---|---|---|---|---|---|---|---|
| 2008 WM18 | 4-D | RUS | 6 | 0 | 0 | 0 | 0 | S |

**Vasilevski, Alexei**
**b. Ufa, Russia, January 21, 1993**

| | | | | | | | | |
|---|---|---|---|---|---|---|---|---|
| 2011 WM18 | 3-D | RUS | 7 | 0 | 0 | 0 | 4 | B |

**Vasiljevs, Herberts**
**b. Riga, Soviet Union (Latvia), May 23, 1976**

| | | | | | | | | |
|---|---|---|---|---|---|---|---|---|
| 1998 WM | 26-F | LAT | 6 | 0 | 2 | 2 | 4 | 9th |
| 2000 WM | 22-F | LAT | 1 | 0 | 0 | 0 | 4 | 8th |
| 2004 WM | 12-F | LAT | 7 | 0 | 1 | 1 | 0 | 7th |
| 2005 WM | 12-F | LAT | 6 | 0 | 0 | 0 | 0 | 9th |
| 2006 OG-M | 12-F | LAT | 4 | 1 | 0 | 1 | 4 | 12th |
| 2006 WM | 12-F | LAT | 6 | 1 | 0 | 1 | 10 | 10th |
| 2007 WM | 12-F | LAT | 6 | 2 | 3 | 5 | 8 | 13th |
| 2008 WM | 12-F | LAT | 6 | 2 | 1 | 3 | 10 | 11th |
| 2009 WM | 12-F | LAT | 7 | 3 | 6 | 9 | 6 | 7th |
| 2010 OG-M | 12-F | LAT | 4 | 1 | 1 | 2 | 6 | 12th |
| 2010 WM | 12-F | LAT | 6 | 0 | 3 | 3 | 8 | 11th |
| 2011 WM | 12-F | LAT | 6 | 1 | 1 | 2 | 6 | 13th |
| **Totals WM** | | | **51** | **8** | **16** | **24** | **50** | **—** |
| **Totals OG-M** | | | **8** | **2** | **1** | **3** | **10** | **—** |

**Vasko, Filip**
**b. Humenne, Slovakia, December 10, 1993**

| | | | | | | | | |
|---|---|---|---|---|---|---|---|---|
| 2011 WM18 | 14-F | SVK | 6 | 2 | 3 | 5 | 6 | 10th |

**Vatanen, Sami**
**b. Jyvaskyla, Finland, June 3, 1991**

| | | | | | | | | |
|---|---|---|---|---|---|---|---|---|
| 2008 WM18 | 7-D | FIN | 6 | 0 | 3 | 3 | 4 | 6th |
| 2009 WM18 | 9-D | FIN | 6 | 0 | 5 | 5 | 6 | B |
| 2010 WM20 | 9-D | FIN | 6 | 2 | 3 | 5 | 0 | 5th |
| 2010 WM | 44-D | FIN | 7 | 0 | 0 | 0 | 6 | 6th |
| 2011 WM20 | 9-D | FIN | 6 | 0 | 4 | 4 | 4 | 6th |
| **Totals WM18** | | | **12** | **0** | **8** | **8** | **10** | **B** |
| **Totals WM20** | | | **12** | **2** | **7** | **9** | **4** | **—** |

**Vatrano, Frank**
**b. East Longmeadow, Massachusetts, United States, March 14, 1994**

| | | | | | | | | |
|---|---|---|---|---|---|---|---|---|
| 2012 WM18 | 13-F | USA | 6 | 2 | 2 | 4 | 2 | G |

**Vauclair, Julien**
**b. Delemont, Switzerland, October 2, 1979**

| | | | | | | | | |
|---|---|---|---|---|---|---|---|---|
| 1998 WM20 | 22-F | SUI | 7 | 1 | 2 | 3 | 12 | B |
| 1999 WM20 | 22-D | SUI | 6 | 1 | 1 | 2 | 6 | 9th |
| 2000 WM | 3-D | SUI | 7 | 0 | 0 | 0 | 0 | 5th |
| 2001 WM | 3-D | SUI | 6 | 1 | 0 | 1 | 27 | 9th |
| 2002 OG-M | 3-D | SUI | 4 | 1 | 0 | 1 | 2 | 11th |
| 2002 WM | 3-D | SUI | 6 | 0 | 2 | 2 | 2 | 10th |

| | | | | | | | | |
|---|---|---|---|---|---|---|---|---|
| 2004 WM | 3-D | SUI | 5 | 0 | 0 | 0 | 16 | 8th |
| 2005 WM | 3-D | SUI | 7 | 0 | 0 | 0 | 10 | 8th |
| 2006 OG-M | 3-D | SUI | 6 | 0 | 0 | 0 | 6 | 6th |
| 2006 WM | 3-D | SUI | 6 | 0 | 0 | 0 | 4 | 9th |
| 2007 WM | 3-D | SUI | 7 | 0 | 0 | 0 | 4 | 8th |
| 2008 WM | 3-D | SUI | 7 | 1 | 1 | 2 | 4 | 7th |
| 2010 WM | 3-D | SUI | 7 | 1 | 1 | 2 | 0 | 5th |
| 2011 WM | 3-D | SUI | 6 | 1 | 1 | 2 | 2 | 9th |
| **Totals WM20** | | | **13** | **2** | **3** | **5** | **18** | **B** |
| **Totals WM** | | | **64** | **4** | **5** | **9** | **69** | **—** |
| **Totals OG-M** | | | **10** | **1** | **0** | **1** | **8** | **—** |

**Vedel, Yannick**
**b. Gentofte, Denmark, April 18, 1994**

| | | | | | | | | |
|---|---|---|---|---|---|---|---|---|
| 2012 WM18 | 12-F | DEN | 6 | 0 | 2 | 2 | 6 | 10th |

**Vermeille, Mike**
**b. Porrentruy, Switzerland, April 5, 1992**

| | | | | | | | | |
|---|---|---|---|---|---|---|---|---|
| 2012 WM20 | 5-D | SUI | 6 | 0 | 1 | 1 | 12 | 8th |

**Vermette, Antoine**
**b. St. Agapit, Quebec, July 20, 1982**

| | | | | | | | | |
|---|---|---|---|---|---|---|---|---|
| 2011 WM | 50-F | CAN | 4 | 0 | 0 | 0 | 0 | 5th |

**Vermin, Joel**
**b. Frauenkappelen, Switzerland, February 5, 1992**

| | | | | | | | | |
|---|---|---|---|---|---|---|---|---|
| 2010 WM18 | 26-F | SUI | 6 | 3 | 2 | 5 | 0 | 5th |
| 2011 WM20 | 26-F | SUI | 6 | 0 | 1 | 1 | 2 | 5th |
| 2012 WM20 | 26-F | SUI | 6 | 4 | 1 | 5 | 2 | 8th |
| Totals WM20 | | | 12 | 4 | 2 | 6 | 4 | — |

**Versteeg, Kris**
**b. Lethbridge, Alberta, Canada, May 13, 1986**

| | | | | | | | | |
|---|---|---|---|---|---|---|---|---|
| 2004 WM18 | 9-F | CAN | 7 | 0 | 2 | 2 | 4 | 4th |

**Videll, Linus**
**b. Skarpnack, Sweden, May 5, 1985**

| | | | | | | | | |
|---|---|---|---|---|---|---|---|---|
| 2003 WM18 | 18-F | SWE | 6 | 2 | 0 | 2 | 12 | 5th |
| 2005 WM20 | 18-F | SWE | 6 | 0 | 4 | 4 | 0 | 6th |

**Vidmar, Uros**
**b. Jesenice, Yugoslavia (Slovenia), October 9, 1980**

| | | | | | | | | |
|---|---|---|---|---|---|---|---|---|
| 2006 WM | 19-D | SLO | 6 | 0 | 1 | 1 | 12 | 16th |
| 2008 WM | 77-D | SLO | 5 | 0 | 0 | 0 | 2 | 15th |
| **Totals WM** | | | **11** | **0** | **1** | **1** | **14** | **—** |

**Viedensky, Marek**
**b. Handlova, Czechoslovakia (Slovakia), August 18, 1990**

| | | | | | | | | |
|---|---|---|---|---|---|---|---|---|
| 2008 WM18 | 25-F | SVK | 6 | 1 | 5 | 6 | 6 | 7th |
| 2009 WM20 | 24-F | SVK | 7 | 0 | 4 | 4 | 4 | 4th |
| 2010 WM20 | 24-F | SVK | 6 | 1 | 5 | 6 | 0 | 8th |
| **Totals WM20** | | | **13** | **1** | **9** | **10** | **4** | **—** |

**Vigners, Rolands**
**b. Riga, Soviet Union (Latvia), March 7, 1991**

| | | | | | | | | |
|---|---|---|---|---|---|---|---|---|
| 2010 WM20 | 22-F | LAT | 6 | 1 | 2 | 3 | 0 | 9th |

**Vikingstad, Tore**
**b. Trondheim, Norway, October 8, 1975**

| | | | | | | | | |
|---|---|---|---|---|---|---|---|---|
| 1997 WM | 29-F | NOR | 8 | 0 | 1 | 1 | 6 | 12th |
| 1999 WM | 29-F | NOR | 6 | 1 | 2 | 3 | 2 | 12th |
| 2000 WM | 29-F | NOR | 6 | 3 | 2 | 5 | 10 | 9th |
| 2001 WM | 29-F | NOR | 6 | 1 | 1 | 2 | 10 | 15th |
| 2006 WM | 29-F | NOR | 6 | 1 | 5 | 6 | 10 | 11th |
| 2009 WM | 29-F | NOR | 6 | 1 | 3 | 4 | 10 | 11th |
| 2010 OG-M | 29-F | NOR | 4 | 4 | 0 | 4 | 4 | 10th |
| **Totals WM** | | | **38** | **7** | **14** | **21** | **48** | **—** |

**Viklund, Tobias**
**b. Kramfors, Sweden, May 8, 1986**

| | | | | | | | | |
|---|---|---|---|---|---|---|---|---|
| 2004 WM18 | 16-D | SWE | 6 | 0 | 0 | 0 | 4 | 5th |
| 2006 WM20 | 7-D | SWE | 6 | 1 | 0 | 1 | 6 | 5th |

**Vikstrand, Mikael**
**b. Karlstad, Sweden, November 5, 1993**

| | | | | | | | | |
|---|---|---|---|---|---|---|---|---|
| 2011 WM18 | 9-D | SWE | 6 | 0 | 1 | 1 | 8 | S |

**Vilkoits, Raimonds**
**b. Riga, Soviet Union (Latvia), April 10, 1990**

| | | | | | | | | |
|---|---|---|---|---|---|---|---|---|
| 2010 WM20 | 7-F | LAT | 6 | 2 | 2 | 4 | 6 | 9th |

**Vincour, Tomas**
**b. Brno, Czechoslovakia (Czech Republic), November 19, 1990**

| | | | | | | | | |
|---|---|---|---|---|---|---|---|---|
| 2009 WM20 | 28-F | CZE | 6 | 0 | 3 | 3 | 2 | 6th |
| 2010 WM20 | 22-F | CZE | 5 | 0 | 4 | 4 | 2 | 7th |
| **Totals WM20** | | | **11** | **0** | **7** | **7** | **4** | **—** |

**Violenti, Dmitri**
**b. Samara Region, Soviet Union (Russia), September 23, 1987**

| | | | | | | | | |
|---|---|---|---|---|---|---|---|---|
| 2007 WM20 | 19-F | BLR | 6 | 0 | 0 | 0 | 0 | 10th |

**Virkkunen, Valtteri**
**b. Espoo, Finland, February 18, 1991**

| | | | | | | | | |
|---|---|---|---|---|---|---|---|---|
| 2009 WM18 | 22-F | FIN | 6 | 0 | 1 | 1 | 4 | B |
| 2011 WM20 | 21-F | FIN | 6 | 1 | 0 | 1 | 2 | 6th |

**Virtanen, Jesse**
**b. Rauma, Finland, August 7, 1991**

| | | | | | | | | |
|---|---|---|---|---|---|---|---|---|
| 2011 WM20 | 23-D | FIN | 6 | 1 | 1 | 2 | 0 | 6th |

**Vishnevski, Vitali**
**b. Kharkov, Soviet Union (Ukraine), March 18, 1980**

| | | | | | | | | |
|---|---|---|---|---|---|---|---|---|
| 1998 WM20 | 14-D | RUS | 7 | 1 | 2 | 3 | 6 | S |
| 1999 WM20 | 5-D | RUS | 7 | 0 | 2 | 2 | 6 | G |
| 1999 WM | 2-D | RUS | 6 | 0 | 1 | 1 | 8 | 5th |
| 2001 WM | 2-D | RUS | 7 | 0 | 3 | 3 | 6 | 6th |
| 2004 WCH | 5-D | RUS | 3 | 0 | 0 | 0 | 0 | 6th |
| 2006 OG-M | 5-D | RUS | 8 | 0 | 1 | 1 | 4 | 4th |
| 2009 WM | 3-D | RUS | 9 | 0 | 0 | 0 | 29 | G |
| **Totals WM20** | | | **14** | **1** | **4** | **5** | **12** | **G,S** |
| **Totals WM** | | | **22** | **0** | **4** | **4** | **43** | **G** |

~WM20 IIHF Directorate Best Defenceman (1999), WM20 All-Star Team/Defence (1999)

**Visnovsky, Lubomir**
**b. Topolcany, Czechoslovakia (Czech Republic), August 11, 1976**

| | | | | | | | | |
|---|---|---|---|---|---|---|---|---|
| 1996 WM20 | 7-D | SVK | 6 | 1 | 5 | 6 | 4 | 7th |
| 1996 WM | 6-D | SVK | 5 | 0 | 1 | 1 | 4 | 10th |
| 1996 WCH | 6-D | SVK | 1 | 0 | 0 | 0 | 0 | 7th |
| 1997 WM | 17-D | SVK | 8 | 0 | 1 | 1 | 4 | 9th |
| 1998 OG-M | 6-D | SVK | 3 | 0 | 0 | 0 | 2 | 10th |
| 1998 WM | 6-D | SVK | 4 | 0 | 0 | 0 | 2 | 7th |
| 1999 WM | 17-D | SVK | 6 | 0 | 2 | 2 | 6 | 7th |
| 2000 WM | 17-D | SVK | 9 | 0 | 6 | 6 | 2 | S |
| 2002 OG-M | 17-D | SVK | 3 | 1 | 2 | 3 | 0 | 13th |
| 2002 WM | 17-D | SVK | 5 | 2 | 1 | 3 | 2 | G |
| 2003 WM | 17-D | SVK | 9 | 4 | 8 | 12 | 2 | B |
| 2004 WCH | 17-D | SVK | 4 | 0 | 0 | 0 | 6 | 7th |
| 2005 WM | 17-D | SVK | 7 | 2 | 6 | 8 | 0 | 5th |
| 2006 OG-M | 17-D | SVK | 6 | 1 | 1 | 2 | 0 | 5th |
| 2008 WM | 17-D | SVK | 5 | 2 | 7 | 9 | 0 | 13th |
| 2010 OG-M | 17-D | SVK | 7 | 2 | 1 | 3 | 0 | 4th |
| 2011 WM | 17-D | SVK | 3 | 0 | 2 | 2 | 0 | 10th |
| **Totals WM** | | | **61** | **10** | **34** | **44** | **22** | **G,S,B** |
| **Totals OG-M** | | | **19** | **4** | **4** | **8** | **2** | **—** |
| **Totals IIHF-NHL** | | | **5** | **0** | **0** | **0** | **6** | **—** |

~WM All-Star Team/Defence (2003)

**Vitoshkin, Stanislav**
**b. Togliatti, Soviet Union (Russia), January 16, 1988**

| | | | | | | | | |
|---|---|---|---|---|---|---|---|---|
| 2008 WM20 | 21-F | KAZ | 6 | 0 | 3 | 3 | 12 | 8th |

**Vittasmaki, Veli-Matti**
**b. Turku, Finland, July 3, 1990**

| | | | | | | | | |
|---|---|---|---|---|---|---|---|---|
| 2008 WM18 | 8-D | FIN | 6 | 0 | 0 | 0 | 6 | 6th |
| 2009 WM20 | 25-D | FIN | 6 | 0 | 1 | 1 | 0 | 7th |
| 2010 WM20 | 25-D | FIN | 6 | 0 | 1 | 1 | 2 | 5th |
| **Totals WM20** | | | **12** | **0** | **2** | **2** | **2** | **—** |

**Vizvary, Matus**
**b. Bratislava, Czechoslovakia (Slovakia), March 15, 1989**

| | | | | | | | | |
|---|---|---|---|---|---|---|---|---|
| 2009 WM20 | 16-D | SVK | 7 | 0 | 0 | 0 | 4 | 4th |

**Vlach, Jaroslav**
**b. Pabenice, Czech Republic, April 6, 1992**

| | | | | | | | | |
|---|---|---|---|---|---|---|---|---|
| 2010 WM18 | 26-F | CZE | 6 | 0 | 0 | 0 | 2 | 6th |

**Vlasic, Marc-Edouard**
**b. Montreal, Quebec, Canada, March 30, 1987**

| | | | | | | | | |
|---|---|---|---|---|---|---|---|---|
| 2009 WM | 44-D | CAN | 5 | 0 | 0 | 0 | 4 | S |
| 2012 WM | 44-D | CAN | 2 | 0 | 0 | 0 | 0 | 5th |
| **Totals WM** | | | **7** | **0** | **0** | **0** | **4** | **S** |

**Voinov, Vyacheslav**
**b. Chelyabinsk, Soviet Union (Russia), January 15, 1990**

| | | | | | | | | |
|---|---|---|---|---|---|---|---|---|
| 2007 WM18 | 24-D | RUS | 7 | 1 | 4 | 5 | 2 | G |
| 2007 WM20 | 30-D | RUS | 6 | 1 | 0 | 1 | 0 | S |
| 2008 WM18 | 24-D | RUS | 6 | 1 | 4 | 5 | 2 | S |
| 2008 WM20 | 24-D | RUS | 7 | 0 | 1 | 1 | 0 | B |
| 2009 WM20 | 24-D | RUS | 7 | 1 | 3 | 4 | 0 | B |
| **Totals WM18** | | | **13** | **2** | **8** | **10** | **4** | **G,S** |
| **Totals WM20** | | | **20** | **2** | **4** | **6** | **0** | **S,2B** |

~WM18 All-Star Team/Defence (2008)

**Vojta, Jakub**
**b. Usti Nad Labem, Czechoslovakia (Czech Republic), February 8, 1987**

| | | | | | | | | |
|---|---|---|---|---|---|---|---|---|
| 2005 WM18 | 22-D | CZE | 7 | 1 | 0 | 1 | 8 | 4th |
| 2007 WM20 | 22-D | CZE | 6 | 0 | 3 | 3 | 8 | 5th |

**Volchenkov, Anton**
**b. Moscow, Soviet Union (Russia), February 25, 1982**

| | | | | | | | | |
|---|---|---|---|---|---|---|---|---|
| 2000 WM18 | 4-D | RUS | 6 | 1 | 0 | 1 | 6 | S |
| 2001 WM20 | 4-D | RUS | 7 | 0 | 4 | 4 | 6 | 7th |
| 2002 WM20 | 13-D | RUS | 7 | 1 | 3 | 4 | 6 | G |
| 2002 WM | 6-D | RUS | 9 | 0 | 0 | 0 | 0 | S |
| 2004 WCH | 6-D | RUS | 1 | 0 | 0 | 0 | 0 | 6th |
| 2006 OG-M | 6-D | RUS | 8 | 0 | 0 | 0 | 2 | 4th |
| 2009 WM | 6-D | RUS | 1 | 0 | 1 | 1 | 0 | G |
| 2010 OG-M | 6-D | RUS | 4 | 0 | 1 | 1 | 2 | 6th |
| **Totals WM20** | | | **14** | **1** | **7** | **8** | **12** | **G** |
| **Totals WM** | | | **10** | **0** | **1** | **1** | **0** | **S,G** |
| **Totals OG-M** | | | **12** | **0** | **1** | **1** | **4** | **—** |

**Volek, Dominik**
**b. Prague, Czech Republic, January 12, 1994**

| | | | | | | | | |
|---|---|---|---|---|---|---|---|---|
| 2012 WM18 | 19-F | CZE | 6 | 2 | 2 | 4 | 4 | 8th |

**Volkov, Artyom**
**b. Novopolotsk, Soviet Union (Belarus), January 28, 1985**

| | | | | | | | | |
|---|---|---|---|---|---|---|---|---|
| 2002 WM18 | 14-F | BLR | 8 | 1 | 0 | 1 | 12 | 5th |
| 2003 WM18 | 28-F | BLR | 6 | 2 | 3 | 5 | 26 | 8th |
| 2003 WM20 | 14-F | BLR | 6 | 0 | 1 | 1 | 8 | 10th |
| 2005 WM20 | 28-F | BLR | 6 | 0 | 3 | 3 | 8 | 10th |
| 2007 WM | 30-F | BLR | 6 | 0 | 0 | 0 | 12 | 11th |
| **Totals WM18** | | | **14** | **3** | **3** | **6** | **38** | **—** |
| **Totals WM20** | | | **12** | **0** | **4** | **4** | **16** | **—** |

**Voloshenko, Roman**
**b. Brest, Soviet Union (Belarus), May 12, 1986**

| | | | | | | | | |
|---|---|---|---|---|---|---|---|---|
| 2004 WM18 | 12-F | RUS | 6 | 5 | 6 | 11 | 18 | G |
| 2005 WM20 | 25-F | RUS | 6 | 2 | 0 | 2 | 2 | S |
| 2006 WM20 | 16-F | RUS | 6 | 3 | 0 | 3 | 2 | S |
| **Totals WM20** | | | **12** | **5** | **0** | **5** | **4** | **2S** |

**Vondrka, Michal**
**b. Ceske Budejovice, Czechoslovakia (Czech Republic), May 17, 1982**

| | | | | | | | | |
|---|---|---|---|---|---|---|---|---|
| 2012 WM | 82-F | CZE | 9 | 0 | 1 | 1 | 0 | B |

**Von Gunten, Patrick**
**b. Sigriswil, Switzerland, February 10, 1985**

| | | | | | | | | |
|---|---|---|---|---|---|---|---|---|
| 2003 WM18 | 9-D | SUI | 6 | 0 | 1 | 1 | 6 | 9th |
| 2005 WM20 | 10-D | SUI | 6 | 0 | 1 | 1 | 2 | 8th |
| 2010 OG-M | 72-D | SUI | 5 | 1 | 0 | 1 | 0 | 8th |
| 2012 WM | 72-D | SUI | 7 | 0 | 0 | 0 | 0 | 11th |

**Voracek, Jakub**
**b. Kladno, Czechoslovakia (Czech Republic), August 15, 1989**

| | | | | | | | | |
|---|---|---|---|---|---|---|---|---|
| 2006 WM18 | 22-F | CZE | 7 | 3 | 3 | 6 | 6 | B |
| 2007 WM18 | 20-F | CZE | 4 | 1 | 2 | 3 | 2 | 9th |
| 2007 WM20 | 21-F | CZE | 6 | 1 | 2 | 3 | 4 | 5th |
| 2008 WM20 | 20-F | CZE | 6 | 0 | 6 | 6 | 4 | 5th |
| 2010 WM | 93-F | CZE | 9 | 0 | 2 | 2 | 6 | G |
| 2011 WM | 93-F | CZE | 9 | 1 | 2 | 3 | 2 | B |
| **Totals WM18** | | | **11** | **4** | **5** | **9** | **8** | **B** |
| **Totals WM20** | | | **12** | **1** | **8** | **9** | **8** | **—** |
| **Totals WM** | | | **18** | **1** | **4** | **5** | **8** | **G,B** |

**Voracek, Tomas**
**b. Ostrava, Czechoslovakia (Czech Republic), February 27, 1990**

| | | | | | | | | |
|---|---|---|---|---|---|---|---|---|
| 2010 WM20 | 4-D | CZE | 6 | 0 | 1 | 1 | 4 | 7th |

**Vorobyov, Dmitri**
**b. Togliatti, Soviet Union (Russia), October 18, 1985**

| | | | | | | | | |
|---|---|---|---|---|---|---|---|---|
| 2005 WM20 | 6-D | RUS | 6 | 1 | 5 | 6 | 27 | S |
| 2008 WM | 6-D | RUS | 5 | 0 | 1 | 1 | 4 | G |

**Vorobyov, Yakov**
**b. Ust-Kamenogorsk, Soviet Union (Kazakhstan), July 7, 1989**

| | | | | | | | | |
|---|---|---|---|---|---|---|---|---|
| 2008 WM20 | 12-F | KAZ | 6 | 4 | 0 | 4 | 8 | 8th |
| 2009 WM20 | 21-F | KAZ | 5 | 0 | 1 | 1 | 14 | 10th |
| **Totals WM20** | | | **11** | **4** | **1** | **5** | **22** | **—** |

**Voronin, Artyom**
**b. Vidnoe, Russia, July 22, 1991**

| | | | | | | | | |
|---|---|---|---|---|---|---|---|---|
| 2011 WM20 | 15-F | RUS | 7 | 1 | 2 | 3 | 10 | G |

**Vorontsov, Alexei**
**b. Ust-Kamenogorsk, Soviet Union (Kazakhstan), January 18, 1985**

| | | | | | | | | |
|---|---|---|---|---|---|---|---|---|
| 2010 WM | 54-F | KAZ | 3 | 0 | 0 | 0 | 16 | 16th |
| 2012 WM | 54-F | KAZ | 6 | 0 | 0 | 0 | 0 | 16th |
| **Totals WM** | | | **9** | **0** | **0** | **0** | **16** | **—** |

**Voroshilov, Igor**
**b. Polotsk, Soviet Union (Belarus), August 13, 1989**

| | | | | | | | | |
|---|---|---|---|---|---|---|---|---|
| 2006 WM18 | 16-F | BLR | 6 | 1 | 3 | 4 | 4 | 9th |
| 2007 WM20 | 11-F | BLR | 6 | 0 | 0 | 0 | 0 | 10th |

**Vorshev, Konstantin**
**b. Moscow Region, Russia, May 26, 1993**

| | | | | | | | | |
|---|---|---|---|---|---|---|---|---|
| 2011 WM18 | 7-D | RUS | 6 | 0 | 0 | 0 | 6 | B |

**Vrana, Jakub**
**b. Prague, Czech Republic, February 18, 1996**

| | | | | | | | | |
|---|---|---|---|---|---|---|---|---|
| 2012 WM18 | 13-F | CZE | 6 | 4 | 4 | 8 | 4 | 8th |

**Vrana, Petr**
**b. Sternberk, Czechoslovakia (Czech Republic), March 29, 1985**

| | | | | | | | | |
|---|---|---|---|---|---|---|---|---|
| 2005 WM20 | 20-F | CZE | 7 | 5 | 3 | 8 | 16 | B |

**Vrbata, Radim**
**b. Mlada Boleslav, Czechoslovakia (Czech Republic), June 13, 1981**

| | | | | | | | | |
|---|---|---|---|---|---|---|---|---|
| 2001 WM20 | 26-F | CZE | 7 | 1 | 2 | 3 | 4 | G |
| 2003 WM | 19-F | CZE | 9 | 3 | 3 | 6 | 2 | 4th |
| 2005 WM | 19-F | CZE | 3 | 0 | 1 | 1 | 0 | G |
| 2008 WM | 19-F | CZE | 7 | 5 | 2 | 7 | 4 | 5th |
| **Totals WM** | | | **19** | **8** | **6** | **14** | **6** | **G** |

**Vydareny, Rene**
**b. Bratislava, Czechoslovakia (Slovakia), May 6, 1981**

| | | | | | | | | |
|---|---|---|---|---|---|---|---|---|
| 1999 WM18 | 8-D | SVK | 7 | 0 | 0 | 0 | 2 | B |
| 2000 WM20 | 12-D | SVK | 7 | 0 | 0 | 0 | 2 | 9th |
| 2001 WM20 | 29-D | SVK | 7 | 0 | 3 | 3 | 0 | 8th |
| 2005 WM | 8-D | SVK | 7 | 0 | 0 | 0 | 12 | 5th |
| 2006 WM | 23-D | SVK | 7 | 1 | 0 | 1 | 6 | 8th |
| 2008 WM | 8-D | SVK | 2 | 0 | 0 | 0 | 0 | 13th |
| 2009 WM | 29-D | SVK | 6 | 0 | 1 | 1 | 0 | 10th |
| 2012 WM | 23-D | SVK | 10 | 0 | 0 | 0 | 2 | S |
| **Totals WM20** | | | **14** | **0** | **3** | **3** | **2** | **—** |
| **Totals WM** | | | **32** | **1** | **1** | **2** | **20** | **S** |

**Vyletelka, Tomas**
**b. Banovce nad Bebravou, Czechoslovakia (Slovakia), July 4, 1989**

| | | | | | | | | |
|---|---|---|---|---|---|---|---|---|
| 2009 WM20 | 27-F | SVK | 7 | 0 | 1 | 1 | 6 | 4th |

**Wagenhoffer, Jozef**
**b. Bratislava, Czechoslovakia (Slovakia), May 11, 1986**

| | | | | | | | | |
|---|---|---|---|---|---|---|---|---|
| 2004 WM18 | 19-D | SVK | 6 | 0 | 1 | 1 | 2 | 6th |
| 2006 WM20 | 19-D | SVK | 4 | 0 | 1 | 1 | 27 | 8th |

**Wahl, Mitch**
**b. Seal Beach, California, United States, January 22, 1990**

| | | | | | | | | |
|---|---|---|---|---|---|---|---|---|
| 2009 WM20 | 14-F | USA | 6 | 1 | 3 | 4 | 2 | 5th |

**Waitl, Maximilian**
**b. Landshut, West Germany (Germany), December 24, 1991**

| | | | | | | | | |
|---|---|---|---|---|---|---|---|---|
| 2009 WM18 | 24-D | GER | 6 | 1 | 0 | 1 | 6 | 10th |

**Walker, Luke**
**b. New Haven, Connecticut, United States, February 19, 1990**

| | | | | | | | | |
|---|---|---|---|---|---|---|---|---|
| 2010 WM20 | 14-F | USA | 7 | 0 | 0 | 0 | 6 | G |

**Wallen, William**
**b. Stockholm, Sweden, August 16, 1991**

| | | | | | | | | |
|---|---|---|---|---|---|---|---|---|
| 2009 WM18 | 22-F | SWE | 4 | 2 | 6 | 8 | 0 | 5th |

**Wallin, Rickard**
**b. Stockholm, Sweden, September 9, 1980**

| | | | | | | | | |
|---|---|---|---|---|---|---|---|---|
| 2000 WM20 | 29-F | SWE | 7 | 2 | 2 | 4 | 0 | 5th |
| 2007 WM | 15-F | SWE | 9 | 2 | 0 | 2 | 6 | 4th |
| 2008 WM | 15-F | SWE | 9 | 2 | 3 | 5 | 4 | 4th |
| 2009 WM | 15-F | SWE | 9 | 1 | 0 | 1 | 8 | B |
| 2010 WM | 51-F | SWE | 9 | 1 | 5 | 6 | 0 | B |
| 2011 WM | 51-F | SWE | 9 | 0 | 0 | 0 | 4 | S |
| **Totals WM** | | | **45** | **6** | **8** | **14** | **22** | **S,2B** |

**Walser, Samuel**
**b. Olten, Switzerland, June 5, 1992**

| | | | | | | | | |
|---|---|---|---|---|---|---|---|---|
| 2009 WM18 | 23-F | SUI | 6 | 1 | 1 | 2 | 8 | 8th |
| 2011 WM20 | 24-F | SUI | 6 | 1 | 0 | 1 | 4 | 5th |
| 2012 WM20 | 24-F | SUI | 6 | 0 | 1 | 1 | 6 | 8th |
| Totals WM20 | | | 12 | 1 | 1 | 2 | 10 | — |

**Wannstrom, Sebastian**
**b. Gavle, Sweden, March 3, 1991**

| | | | | | | | | |
|---|---|---|---|---|---|---|---|---|
| 2011 WM20 | 20-F | SWE | 6 | 2 | 3 | 5 | 2 | 4th |

**Warg, Fredrik**
**b. Skelleftea, Sweden, May 3, 1979**

| | | | | | | | | |
|---|---|---|---|---|---|---|---|---|
| 2007 WM | 79-F | SWE | 7 | 2 | 3 | 5 | 4 | 4th |
| 2008 WM | 79-F | SWE | 9 | 2 | 5 | 7 | 0 | 4th |
| **Totals WM** | | | **16** | **4** | **8** | **12** | **4** | **—** |

**Wargh, Tommy**
**b. Ornskoldsvik, Sweden, December 19, 1986**

| | | | | | | | | |
|---|---|---|---|---|---|---|---|---|
| 2006 WM20 | 12-D | SWE | 5 | 0 | 1 | 1 | 4 | 5th |

**Warn, Max**
**b. Helsinki, Finland, June 10, 1988**

| | | | | | | | | |
|---|---|---|---|---|---|---|---|---|
| 2005 WM18 | 24-F | FIN | 6 | 1 | 1 | 2 | 16 | 7th |
| 2006 WM18 | 26-F | FIN | 5 | 2 | 1 | 3 | 6 | S |
| 2008 WM20 | 18-F | FIN | 6 | 1 | 1 | 2 | 6 | 6th |
| **Totals WM18** | | | **11** | **3** | **2** | **5** | **22** | **S** |

**Warsofsky, David**
**b. South Weymouth, Massachusetts, United States, May 30, 1990**

| | | | | | | | | |
|---|---|---|---|---|---|---|---|---|
| 2008 WM18 | 2-D | USA | 7 | 0 | 7 | 7 | 8 | G |
| 2010 WM20 | 5-D | USA | 7 | 0 | 2 | 2 | 6 | G |

**Watson, Austin**
**b. Ann Arbour, Michigan, United States, January 13, 1992**

| | | | | | | | | |
|---|---|---|---|---|---|---|---|---|
| 2010 WM18 | 14-F | USA | 7 | 2 | 1 | 3 | 33 | G |
| 2012 WM20 | 26-F | USA | 6 | 3 | 6 | 9 | 0 | 7th |

**Weal, Jordan**
**b. North Vancouver, British Columbia, Canada, April 15, 1992**

| | | | | | | | | |
|---|---|---|---|---|---|---|---|---|
| 2010 WM18 | 19-F | CAN | 6 | 3 | 6 | 9 | 30 | 7th |

**Weber, Shea**
**b. Sicamous, British Columbia, Canada, August 14, 1985**

| | | | | | | | | |
|---|---|---|---|---|---|---|---|---|
| 2005 WM20 | 6-D | CAN | 6 | 0 | 0 | 0 | 10 | G |
| 2007 WM | 6-D | CAN | 6 | 1 | 1 | 2 | 31 | G |
| 2009 WM | 6-D | CAN | 9 | 4 | 8 | 12 | 6 | S |
| 2010 OG-M | 6-D | CAN | 7 | 2 | 4 | 6 | 2 | G |
| **Totals WM** | | | **15** | **5** | **9** | **14** | **37** | **G,S** |

~ OG-M All-Star Team/Defence (2010), WM IIHF Directorate Best Defenceman (2009), WM All-Star Team/Defence (2009)

**Weber, Tim**
**b. Murten, Switzerland, February 6, 1990**

| | | | | | | | | |
|---|---|---|---|---|---|---|---|---|
| 2010 WM20 | 17-F | SUI | 7 | 1 | 0 | 1 | 2 | 4th |

**Weber, Yannick**
**b. Morges, Switzerland, September 23, 1988**

| | | | | | | | | |
|---|---|---|---|---|---|---|---|---|
| 2005 WM18 | 8-D | SUI | 6 | 1 | 0 | 1 | 6 | 9th |
| 2007 WM20 | 7-D | SUI | 6 | 1 | 3 | 4 | 10 | 7th |
| 2008 WM20 | 7-D | SUI | 6 | 2 | 4 | 6 | 14 | 9th |
| 2009 WM | 77-D | SUI | 3 | 0 | 0 | 0 | 8 | 9th |
| 2010 OG-M | 77-D | SUI | 5 | 0 | 0 | 0 | 6 | 8th |
| **Totals WM20** | | | **12** | **3** | **7** | **10** | **24** | **—** |

**Weberg, Nicholas**
**b. Oslo, Norway, February 20, 1992**

| | | | | | | | | |
|---|---|---|---|---|---|---|---|---|
| 2011 WM20 | 18-F | NOR | 6 | 2 | 0 | 2 | 0 | 9th |

**Weberg, Sebastian**
**b. Oslo, Norway, December 8, 1993**

| | | | | | | | | |
|---|---|---|---|---|---|---|---|---|
| 2011 WM18 | 18-F | NOR | 6 | 0 | 2 | 2 | 12 | 9th |

**Wedin, Anton**
**b. Sundsvall, Sweden, March 1, 1993**

| | | | | | | | | |
|---|---|---|---|---|---|---|---|---|
| 2011 WM18 | 23-F | SWE | 6 | 0 | 0 | 0 | 0 | S |

**Weinhandl, Mattias**
**b. Ljungby, Sweden, June 1, 1980**

| | | | | | | | | |
|---|---|---|---|---|---|---|---|---|
| 1999 WM20 | 18-F | SWE | 6 | 0 | 3 | 3 | 2 | 4th |
| 2002 WM | 26-F | SWE | 9 | 3 | 4 | 7 | 4 | B |
| 2005 WM | 13-F | SWE | 8 | 0 | 1 | 1 | 0 | 4th |
| 2008 WM | 80-F | SWE | 9 | 5 | 8 | 13 | 2 | 4th |
| 2009 WM | 80-F | SWE | 9 | 5 | 7 | 12 | 8 | B |
| 2010 OG-M | 80-F | SWE | 4 | 0 | 2 | 2 | 2 | 5th |
| 2010 WM | 80-F | SWE | 2 | 3 | 0 | 3 | 0 | B |
| **Totals WM** | | | **37** | **16** | **20** | **36** | **4** | **3B** |

**Weiss, Alexander**
**b. Neustadt, West Germany (Germany), January 29, 1987**

| | | | | | | | | |
|---|---|---|---|---|---|---|---|---|
| 2007 WM20 | 26-F | GER | 6 | 0 | 1 | 1 | 2 | 9th |

**Weiss, Daniel**
**b. Titisee-Neustadt, West Germany (Germany), February 22, 1990**

| | | | | | | | | |
|---|---|---|---|---|---|---|---|---|
| 2007 WM18 | 28-F | GER | 6 | 1 | 1 | 2 | 2 | 8th |
| 2008 WM18 | 24-F | GER | 6 | 4 | 0 | 4 | 8 | 5th |
| 2009 WM20 | 24-F | GER | 6 | 2 | 2 | 4 | 2 | 9th |
| **Totals WM18** | | | **12** | **5** | **1** | **6** | **10** | |

**Weller, Shawn**
**b. Glens Falls, New York, United States, July 8, 1986**

| | | | | | | | | |
|---|---|---|---|---|---|---|---|---|
| 2005 WM20 | 15-F | USA | 7 | 0 | 0 | 0 | 2 | 4th |

**Welser, Daniel**
**b. Klagenfurt, Austria, February 16, 1983**

| | | | | | | | | |
|---|---|---|---|---|---|---|---|---|
| 2003 WM | 20-F | AUT | 6 | 2 | 1 | 3 | 4 | 10th |
| 2004 WM | 20-F | AUT | 6 | 1 | 1 | 2 | 8 | 11th |
| 2005 WM | 20-F | AUT | 6 | 1 | 1 | 2 | 10 | 16th |
| 2007 WM | 20-F | AUT | 6 | 1 | 1 | 2 | 0 | 15th |
| 2011 WM | 20-F | AUT | 6 | 0 | 0 | 0 | 2 | 15th |
| **Totals WM** | | | **30** | **5** | **4** | **9** | **24** | **—** |

**Welti, Marc**
**b. Zurich, Switzerland, January 27, 1988**

| | | | | | | | | |
|---|---|---|---|---|---|---|---|---|
| 2007 WM20 | 2-D | SUI | 6 | 0 | 2 | 2 | 0 | 7th |
| 2008 WM20 | 2-D | SUI | 6 | 0 | 0 | 0 | 2 | 9th |
| **Totals WM20** | | | **12** | **0** | **2** | **2** | **2** | **—** |

**Wennberg, Alexander**
**b. Nacka, Sweden, September 22, 1994**

| | | | | | | | | |
|---|---|---|---|---|---|---|---|---|
| 2012 WM18 | 25-F | SWE | 6 | 3 | 6 | 9 | 0 | S |

**Werek, Ethan**
**b. Stoufville, Ontario, Canada, June 7, 1991**

| | | | | | | | | |
|---|---|---|---|---|---|---|---|---|
| 2009 WM18 | 25-F | CAN | 6 | 4 | 2 | 6 | 6 | 4th |

**Werenka, Darcy**
**b. Edmonton, Alberta, Canada, May 13, 1973**

| | | | | | | | | |
|---|---|---|---|---|---|---|---|---|
| 1993 WM20 | 4-D | CAN | 7 | 1 | 0 | 1 | 18 | G |
| 2009 WM | 24-D | AUT | 6 | 0 | 0 | 0 | 10 | 14th |
| 2011 WM | 24-D | AUT | 6 | 0 | 1 | 1 | 6 | 15th |
| **Totals WM** | | | **12** | **0** | **1** | **1** | **16** | **—** |

**Westin, John**
**b. Kramfors, Sweden, May 19, 1992**

| | | | | | | | | |
|---|---|---|---|---|---|---|---|---|
| 2010 WM18 | 24-F | SWE | 6 | 3 | 1 | 4 | 6 | S |

**Wey, Patrick**
**b. Pittsburgh, Pennsylvania, March 21, 1991**

| | | | | | | | | |
|---|---|---|---|---|---|---|---|---|
| 2011 WM20 | 18-D | USA | 6 | 0 | 0 | 0 | 2 | B |

**Wheeler, Blake**
**b. Robbinsdale, Minnesota, United States, August 31, 1986**

| | | | | | | | | |
|---|---|---|---|---|---|---|---|---|
| 2006 WM20 | 16-F | USA | 7 | 2 | 0 | 2 | 6 | 4th |
| 2011 WM | 17-F | USA | 7 | 2 | 3 | 5 | 6 | 8th |

**White, Ian**
**b. Steinbach, Manitoba, Canada, May 4, 1984**

| | | | | | | | | |
|---|---|---|---|---|---|---|---|---|
| 2003 WM20 | 17-D | CAN | 6 | 2 | 4 | 6 | 0 | S |
| 2009 WM | 7-D | CAN | 5 | 1 | 2 | 3 | 0 | S |

**Whitney, Ray**
**b. Fort Saskatchewan, Alberta, Canada, May 8, 1972**

| | | | | | | | | |
|---|---|---|---|---|---|---|---|---|
| 1998 WM | 14-F | CAN | 6 | 4 | 2 | 6 | 4 | 4th |
| 1999 WM | 14-F | CAN | 10 | 1 | 5 | 6 | 20 | 4th |
| 2002 WM | 14-F | CAN | 7 | 1 | 3 | 4 | 2 | 6th |

| 2010 WM | 13-F | CAN | 7 | 2 | 6 | 8 | 0 | 7th |
|---|---|---|---|---|---|---|---|---|
| **Totals WM** | | | **30** | **8** | **16** | **24** | **26** | **—** |

**Whitney, Ryan**
**b. Boston, Massachusetts, United States, February 19, 1983**

| 2001 WM18 | 4-D | USA | 6 | 0 | 1 | 1 | 8 | 6th |
|---|---|---|---|---|---|---|---|---|
| 2002 WM20 | 3-D | USA | 7 | 1 | 2 | 3 | 20 | 5th |
| 2003 WM20 | 19-D | USA | 7 | 1 | 4 | 5 | 14 | 4th |
| 2010 OG-M | 19-D | USA | 6 | 0 | 0 | 0 | 0 | S |
| **Totals WM20** | | | **14** | **2** | **6** | **8** | **34** | **—** |

**Wichert, Christian**
**b. Munich, West Germany (Germany), May 10, 1987**

| 2005 WM18 | 20-F | GER | 6 | 0 | 1 | 1 | 6 | 8th |
|---|---|---|---|---|---|---|---|---|
| 2007 WM20 | 29-F | GER | 6 | 0 | 0 | 0 | 6 | 9th |

**Wick, Roman**
**b. Zuzwil, Switzerland, December 30, 1985**

| 2003 WM18 | 27-F | SUI | 6 | 4 | 0 | 4 | 2 | 9th |
|---|---|---|---|---|---|---|---|---|
| 2005 WM20 | 27-F | SUI | 6 | 1 | 3 | 4 | 0 | 8th |
| 2008 WM | 14-F | SUI | 3 | 1 | 1 | 2 | 2 | 7th |
| 2009 WM | 14-F | SUI | 6 | 2 | 2 | 4 | 2 | 9th |
| 2010 OG-M | 14-F | SUI | 5 | 2 | 3 | 5 | 2 | 8th |
| 2012 WM | 14-F | SUI | 7 | 1 | 1 | 2 | 0 | 11th |
| **Totals WM** | | | **16** | **4** | **4** | **8** | **4** | **—** |

**Wieser, Dino**
**b. Davos, Switzerland, June 13, 1989**

| 2008 WM20 | 6-F | SUI | 6 | 1 | 2 | 3 | 4 | 9th |
|---|---|---|---|---|---|---|---|---|

**Wilenius, Tomi**
**b. Nokia, Finland, January 15, 1993**

| 2011 WM18 | 21-F | FIN | 6 | 1 | 0 | 1 | 4 | 5th |
|---|---|---|---|---|---|---|---|---|

**Williams, Justin**
**b. Cobourg, Ontario, Canada, October 4, 1981**

| 2002 WM | 41-F | CAN | 5 | 0 | 3 | 3 | 6 | 6th |
|---|---|---|---|---|---|---|---|---|
| 2004 WM | 11-F | CAN | 9 | 0 | 0 | 0 | 4 | G |
| 2007 WM | 11-F | CAN | 9 | 1 | 2 | 3 | 16 | G |
| **Totals WM** | | | **23** | **1** | **5** | **6** | **26** | **2G** |

**Wilson, Clay**
**b. Fridley, Minnesota, United States, April 5, 1983**

| 2011 WM | 4-D | USA | 7 | 0 | 2 | 2 | 0 | 8th |
|---|---|---|---|---|---|---|---|---|

**Wilson, Colin**
**b. Greenwich, Connecticut, United States, October 20, 1989**

| 2006 WM18 | 24-F | USA | 6 | 0 | 1 | 1 | 8 | G |
|---|---|---|---|---|---|---|---|---|
| 2007 WM18 | 22-F | USA | 7 | 5 | 7 | 12 | 4 | S |
| 2008 WM20 | 33-F | USA | 6 | 6 | 1 | 7 | 4 | 4th |
| 2009 WM20 | 33-F | USA | 6 | 3 | 6 | 9 | 4 | 5th |
| **Totals WM18** | | | **13** | **5** | **8** | **13** | **12** | **—** |
| **Totals WM20** | | | **12** | **9** | **7** | **16** | **8** | **—** |

**Winther, Mike**
**b. Trochu, Alberta, Canada, July 9, 1994**

| 2012 WM18 | 15-F | CAN | 7 | 1 | 1 | 2 | 4 | B |
|---|---|---|---|---|---|---|---|---|

**Wirtanen, Petteri**
**b. Hyvinkaa, Finland, May 28, 1986**

| 2004 WM18 | 13-F | FIN | 6 | 0 | 2 | 2 | 6 | 7th |
|---|---|---|---|---|---|---|---|---|
| 2006 WM20 | 13-F | FIN | 7 | 0 | 1 | 1 | 2 | B |

**Wisniewski, James**
**b. Canton, Michigan, United States, February 21, 1984**

| 2002 WM18 | 20-D | USA | 3 | 1 | 2 | 3 | 6 | G |
|---|---|---|---|---|---|---|---|---|
| 2003 WM20 | 20-D | USA | 7 | 0 | 4 | 4 | 6 | 4th |
| 2004 WM20 | 20-D | USA | 6 | 2 | 3 | 5 | 4 | G |
| 2008 WM | 43-D | USA | 6 | 1 | 2 | 3 | 6 | 6th |
| **Totals WM20** | | | **13** | **2** | **7** | **9** | **10** | **G** |

**Wohlberg, David**
**b. South Lyon, Michigan, United States, July 18, 1990**

| 2008 WM18 | 14-F | USA | 7 | 3 | 0 | 3 | 16 | G |
|---|---|---|---|---|---|---|---|---|

**Woidtke, Jannik**
**b. Dusseldorf, Germany, May 14, 1991**

| 2011 WM20 | 12-D | GER | 6 | 0 | 0 | 0 | 10 | 10th |
|---|---|---|---|---|---|---|---|---|

**Wolf, David**
**b. Dusseldorf, West Germany (Germany), September 15, 1989**

| 2007 WM18 | 25-F | GER | 1 | 0 | 0 | 0 | 0 | 8th |
|---|---|---|---|---|---|---|---|---|
| 2009 WM20 | 11-F | GER | 6 | 1 | 0 | 1 | 53 | 9th |

**Wolf, Marcel**
**b. Hohenems, Austria, August 25, 1990**

| 2010 WM20 | 27-F | AUT | 6 | 0 | 1 | 1 | 4 | 10th |
|---|---|---|---|---|---|---|---|---|

**Wolf, Michael**
**b. Echenbichl, Austria, April 27, 1981**

| 2007 WM | 16-F | GER | 6 | 5 | 3 | 8 | 6 | 9th |
|---|---|---|---|---|---|---|---|---|
| 2008 WM | 16-F | GER | 6 | 1 | 2 | 3 | 4 | 10th |
| 2009 WM | 16-F | GER | 6 | 0 | 1 | 1 | 2 | 15th |
| 2010 OG-M | 16-F | GER | 4 | 0 | 0 | 0 | 2 | 11th |
| 2010 WM | 16-F | GER | 9 | 1 | 1 | 2 | 2 | 4th |
| 2011 WM | 16-F | GER | 7 | 2 | 1 | 3 | 0 | 7th |
| **Totals WM** | | | **34** | **9** | **8** | **17** | **14** | **—** |

**Wrenn, William**
**b. Anchorage, Alaska, United States, March 16, 1991**

| 2009 WM18 | 19-D | USA | 7 | 3 | 0 | 3 | 0 | G |
|---|---|---|---|---|---|---|---|---|

**Wurm, Armin**
**b. Fussen, West Germany (Germany), June 11, 1989**

| 2009 WM20 | 12-D | GER | 6 | 0 | 0 | 0 | 4 | 9th |
|---|---|---|---|---|---|---|---|---|

**Yakimov, Bogdan**
**b. Nizhnekamsk, Russia, October 4, 1994**

| 2011 WM18 | 22-F | RUS | 7 | 1 | 1 | 2 | 2 | B |
|---|---|---|---|---|---|---|---|---|
| 2012 WM18 | 10-F | RUS | 6 | 3 | 4 | 7 | 0 | 5th |
| Totals WM18 | | | 13 | 4 | 5 | 9 | 2 | B |

**Yakovenko, Sergei**
**b. Karaganda, Soviet Union (Kazakhstan), March 24, 1976**

| 2012 WM | 75-D | KAZ | 7 | 0 | 0 | 0 | 6 | 16th |
|---|---|---|---|---|---|---|---|---|

**Yakupov, Nail**
**b. Nizhnekamsk, Russia, October 6, 1993**

| 2011 WM18 | 10-F | RUS | 7 | 6 | 7 | 13 | 6 | B |
|---|---|---|---|---|---|---|---|---|
| 2012 WM20 | 10-F | RUS | 7 | 0 | 9 | 9 | 6 | S |

**Yandle, Keith**
**b. Boston, Massachusetts, United States, September 9, 1986**

| 2010 WM | 93-D | USA | 6 | 1 | 3 | 4 | 0 | 13th |
|---|---|---|---|---|---|---|---|---|

**Yarullin, Albert**
**b. Kazan, Russia, May 3, 1993**

| 2010 WM18 | 3-D | RUS | 7 | 0 | 0 | 0 | 2 | 4th |
|---|---|---|---|---|---|---|---|---|
| 2011 WM18 | 23-D | RUS | 7 | 0 | 11 | 11 | 4 | B |
| **Totals WM18** | | | **14** | **0** | **11** | **11** | **6** | **B** |

**Yaskevich, Georgi**
**b. Novopolotsk, Soviet Union (Belarus), November 29, 1988**

| 2007 WM20 | 7-D | BLR | 4 | 0 | 0 | 0 | 6 | 10th |
|---|---|---|---|---|---|---|---|---|

**Yedeshko, Dmitri**
**b. Minsk, Soviet Union (Belarus), April 25, 1985**

| 2005 WM20 | 4-D | BLR | 6 | 0 | 0 | 0 | 0 | 10th |
|---|---|---|---|---|---|---|---|---|

**Yefimenko, Alexei**
**b. Minsk, Soviet Union (Belarus), August 20, 1985**

| 2005 WM20 | 27-F | BLR | 6 | 2 | 1 | 3 | 0 | 10th |
|---|---|---|---|---|---|---|---|---|

**Yemelin, Alexei**
**b. Togliatti, Soviet Union (Russia), April 25, 1986**

| 2004 WM18 | 2-D | RUS | 6 | 0 | 0 | 0 | 10 | G |
|---|---|---|---|---|---|---|---|---|
| 2005 WM20 | 20-D | RUS | 6 | 1 | 0 | 1 | 8 | S |
| 2006 WM20 | 2-D | RUS | 6 | 2 | 5 | 7 | 39 | S |
| 2007 WM | 3-D | RUS | 9 | 1 | 2 | 3 | 6 | B |
| 2010 WM | 74-D | RUS | 9 | 1 | 1 | 2 | 33 | S |
| 2011 WM | 74-D | RUS | 9 | 0 | 0 | 0 | 29 | 4th |
| 2012 WM | 74-D | RUS | 9 | 2 | 2 | 4 | 4 | G |
| **Totals WM20** | | | **12** | **3** | **5** | **8** | **47** | **2S** |
| **Totals WM** | | | **36** | **4** | **5** | **9** | **72** | **G,S,B** |

**Yezhov, Denis**
**b. Samara Region, Soviet Union (Russia), February 28, 1985**

| 2002 WM18 | 19-D | RUS | 8 | 0 | 3 | 3 | 4 | S |
|---|---|---|---|---|---|---|---|---|
| 2003 WM18 | 4-D | RUS | 6 | 0 | 4 | 4 | 2 | B |
| 2003 WM20 | 4-D | RUS | 6 | 0 | 0 | 0 | 6 | G |
| 2004 WM20 | 2-D | RUS | 6 | 0 | 0 | 0 | 2 | 5th |
| 2005 WM20 | 24-D | RUS | 6 | 0 | 2 | 2 | 2 | S |
| **Totals WM18** | | | **14** | **0** | **7** | **7** | **6** | **S,B** |
| **Totals WM20** | | | **18** | **0** | **2** | **2** | **10** | **G,S** |

**Yunkov, Mikhail**
**b. Voskresensk, Soviet Union (Russia), February 16, 1986**

| 2004 WM18 | 19-F | RUS | 6 | 0 | 4 | 4 | 8 | G |
|---|---|---|---|---|---|---|---|---|
| 2005 WM20 | 23-F | RUS | 6 | 1 | 1 | 2 | 0 | S |
| 2006 WM20 | 19-F | RUS | 6 | 0 | 0 | 0 | 4 | S |
| **Totals WM20** | | | **12** | **1** | **1** | **2** | **4** | **2S** |

**Yuryev, Kirill**
**b. Perm Region, Soviet Union (Russia), February 22, 1991**

| 2009 WM18 | 5-D | RUS | 7 | 0 | 0 | 0 | 8 | S |
|---|---|---|---|---|---|---|---|---|

**Zaborsky, Tomas**
**b. Banska Bystrica, Czechoslovakia (Slovakia), November 14, 1987**

| 2007 WM20 | 14-F | SVK | 6 | 1 | 2 | 3 | 4 | 8th |
|---|---|---|---|---|---|---|---|---|

**Zackrisson, Patrik**
**b. Ekero, Sweden, March 27, 1987**

| 2005 WM18 | 21-F | SWE | 7 | 2 | 3 | 5 | 0 | B |
|---|---|---|---|---|---|---|---|---|
| 2007 WM20 | 25-F | SWE | 7 | 1 | 1 | 2 | 12 | — |

**Zadelenov, Sergei**
**b. Glazov, Soviet Union (Russia), February 27, 1976**

| 2003 WM | 22-F | BLR | 6 | 1 | 1 | 2 | 2 | — |
|---|---|---|---|---|---|---|---|---|
| 2005 WM | 22-F | BLR | 6 | 1 | 1 | 2 | 4 | 10th |
| 2006 WM | 22-F | BLR | 7 | 4 | 4 | 8 | 6 | 6th |
| 2007 WM | 22-F | BLR | 6 | 0 | 6 | 6 | 0 | 11th |
| 2008 WM | 22-F | BLR | 6 | 1 | 2 | 3 | 6 | 9th |
| 2010 OG-M | 22-F | BLR | 4 | 0 | 0 | 0 | 0 | 9th |
| **Totals WM** | | | **31** | **7** | **14** | **21** | **18** | **—** |

**Zadorov, Nikita**
**b. Moscow, Russia, April 16, 1995**

| 2012 WM18 | 16-D | RUS | 6 | 2 | 0 | 2 | 4 | 5th |
|---|---|---|---|---|---|---|---|---|

**Zadrazil, Matej**
**b. Lomnice, Czech Republic, February 12, 1994**

| 2012 WM18 | 18-F | CZE | 6 | 1 | 1 | 2 | 0 | 8th |
|---|---|---|---|---|---|---|---|---|

**Zagrapan, Marek**
**b. Presov, Czechoslovakia (Slovakia), December 6, 1986**

| 2003 WM18 | 8-F | SVK | 7 | 0 | 0 | 0 | 0 | S |
|---|---|---|---|---|---|---|---|---|
| 2004 WM18 | 21-F | SVK | 6 | 4 | 4 | 8 | 8 | 6th |
| 2005 WM20 | 8-F | SVK | 4 | 1 | 2 | 3 | 6 | 7th |
| 2006 WM20 | 8-F | SVK | 6 | 2 | 5 | 7 | 18 | 8th |
| 2010 WM | 21-F | SVK | 6 | 2 | 0 | 2 | 2 | 12th |
| **Totals WM18** | | | **13** | **4** | **4** | **8** | **8** | **S** |
| **Totals WM20** | | | **10** | **3** | **7** | **10** | **24** | **—** |

**Zaitsev, Nikita**
**b. Moscow, Soviet Union (Russia), October 29, 1991**

| 2009 WM18 | 22-D | RUS | 7 | 1 | 4 | 5 | 14 | S |
|---|---|---|---|---|---|---|---|---|
| 2010 WM20 | 2-D | RUS | 6 | 0 | 0 | 0 | 4 | 6th |
| 2011 WM20 | 2-D | RUS | 6 | 0 | 0 | 0 | 0 | G |
| **Totals WM20** | | | **12** | **0** | **0** | **0** | **4** | **G** |

**Zajac, Travis**
**b. Winnipeg, Mantioba, Canada, May 13, 1985**

| 2011 WM | 15-F | CAN | 7 | 1 | 2 | 3 | 2 | 5th |
|---|---|---|---|---|---|---|---|---|

**Zakharov, Konstantin**
**b. Minsk, Soviet Union (Belarus), May 2, 1985**

| 2000 WM18 | 13-F | BLR | 5 | 0 | 0 | 0 | 2 | 10th |
|---|---|---|---|---|---|---|---|---|
| 2001 WM20 | 20-F | BLR | 6 | 0 | 0 | 0 | 0 | 9th |
| 2002 WM18 | 21-F | BLR | 8 | 1 | 5 | 6 | 20 | 5th |
| 2002 WM20 | 20-F | BLR | 6 | 1 | 1 | 2 | 6 | 9th |
| 2003 WM18 | 21-F | BLR | 6 | 5 | 11 | 16 | 10 | 8th |
| 2003 WM20 | 21-F | BLR | 4 | 1 | 1 | 2 | 4 | 10th |
| 2005 WM20 | 21-F | BLR | 6 | 3 | 2 | 5 | 6 | 10th |
| 2010 OG-M | 21-F | BLR | 4 | 1 | 0 | 1 | 4 | 9th |
| **Totals WM18** | | | **19** | **6** | **16** | **22** | **32** | **—** |
| **Totals WM20** | | | **22** | **5** | **4** | **9** | **16** | **—** |

**Zalesak, Miroslav**
**b. Skalica, Czechoslovakia (Slovakia), January 2, 1980**

| 1999 WM20 | 4-F | SVK | 5 | 2 | 1 | 3 | 4 | B |
|---|---|---|---|---|---|---|---|---|
| 2000 WM20 | 18-F | SVK | 7 | 1 | 2 | 3 | 2 | 9th |
| 2006 WM | 6-F | SVK | 7 | 0 | 1 | 1 | 2 | 8th |
| 2010 WM | 20-F | SVK | 3 | 0 | 0 | 0 | 0 | 12th |
| **Totals WM20** | | | **12** | **3** | **3** | **6** | **6** | **B** |
| **Totals WM** | | | **10** | **0** | **1** | **1** | **2** | **—** |

**Zamorsky, Petr**
**b. Zlin, Czech Republic, August 3, 1992**

| | | | | | | | | |
|---|---|---|---|---|---|---|---|---|
| 2010 WM18 | 10-D | CZE | 6 | 1 | 1 | 2 | 2 | 6th |
| 2012 WM20 | 7-D | CZE | 5 | 0 | 2 | 2 | 6 | 5th |

**Zangger, Sandro**
**b. Jona, Switzerland, August 27, 1994**

| | | | | | | | | |
|---|---|---|---|---|---|---|---|---|
| 2012 WM18 | 16-F | SUI | 6 | 1 | 1 | 2 | 2 | 7th |

**Zaripov, Danis**
**b. Chelyabinsk, Soviet Union (Russia), March 26, 1981**

| | | | | | | | | |
|---|---|---|---|---|---|---|---|---|
| 2006 WM | 12-F | RUS | 6 | 2 | 3 | 5 | 4 | 5th |
| 2007 WM | 12-F | RUS | 9 | 3 | 9 | 12 | 6 | B |
| 2008 WM | 25-F | RUS | 8 | 3 | 4 | 7 | 0 | G |
| 2009 WM | 25-F | RUS | 2 | 2 | 1 | 3 | 0 | G |
| 2010 OG-M | 25-F | RUS | 4 | 2 | 0 | 2 | 2 | 6th |
| 2011 WM | 25-F | RUS | 9 | 1 | 5 | 6 | 0 | 4th |
| **Totals WM** | | | **34** | **11** | **22** | **33** | **10** | **2G,B** |

**Zelubovskis, Elviss**
**b. Riga, Soviet Union (Latvia), April 13, 1986**

| | | | | | | | | |
|---|---|---|---|---|---|---|---|---|
| 2006 WM20 | 17-F | LAT | 6 | 2 | 0 | 2 | 4 | 9th |

**Zemchenko, Ignat**
**b. Angarsk, Russia, April 24, 1992**

| | | | | | | | | |
|---|---|---|---|---|---|---|---|---|
| 2012 WM20 | 16-F | RUS | 7 | 2 | 3 | 5 | 2 | S |

**Zemitis, Girts**
**b. Jelgava, Latvia, June 13, 1995**

| | | | | | | | | |
|---|---|---|---|---|---|---|---|---|
| 2012 WM18 | 15-D | LAT | 6 | 0 | 0 | 0 | 0 | 9th |

**Zetterberg, Henrik**
**b. Njurunda, Sweden, October 9, 1980**

| | | | | | | | | |
|---|---|---|---|---|---|---|---|---|
| 2000 WM20 | 11-F | SWE | 7 | 3 | 2 | 5 | 8 | 5th |
| 2001 WM | 20-F | SWE | 9 | 1 | 3 | 4 | 2 | B |
| 2002 OG-M | 40-F | SWE | 4 | 0 | 1 | 1 | 0 | 5th |
| 2002 WM | 20-F | SWE | 9 | 0 | 7 | 7 | 4 | B |
| 2003 WM | 20-F | SWE | 9 | 3 | 4 | 7 | 2 | S |
| 2004 WCH | 40-F | SWE | 4 | 1 | 1 | 2 | 4 | 5th |
| 2005 WM | 40-F | SWE | 9 | 2 | 4 | 6 | 4 | 4th |
| 2006 OG-M | 40-F | SWE | 8 | 3 | 3 | 6 | 0 | G |
| 2006 WM | 40-F | SWE | 8 | 2 | 3 | 5 | 6 | G |
| 2010 OG-M | 40-F | SWE | 4 | 1 | 0 | 1 | 2 | 5th |
| 2012 WM | 40-F | SWE | 8 | 3 | 12 | 15 | 4 | 6th |
| **Totals WM** | | | **52** | **11** | **33** | **44** | **22** | **G,S,2B** |
| **Totals OG-M** | | | **16** | **4** | **4** | **8** | **2** | **G** |

~Triple Gold Club
~WM All-Star Team/Forward (2012)

**Zhailauov, Talgat**
**b. Kazakhstanskaya, Soviet Union (Kazakhstan), July 7, 1985**

| | | | | | | | | |
|---|---|---|---|---|---|---|---|---|
| 2003 WM18 | 23-F | KAZ | 6 | 1 | 5 | 6 | 2 | 10th |
| 2006 WM | 11-F | KAZ | 6 | 1 | 1 | 2 | 16 | 15th |
| 2010 WM | 8-F | KAZ | 6 | 0 | 0 | 0 | 0 | 16th |
| 2012 WM | 8-F | KAZ | 7 | 2 | 2 | 4 | 2 | 16th |
| **Totals WM** | | | **19** | **3** | **3** | **6** | **18** | **—** |

**Zharkov, Danil**
**b. St. Petersburg, Russia, February 6, 1994**

| | | | | | | | | |
|---|---|---|---|---|---|---|---|---|
| 2012 WM18 | 17-F | RUS | 6 | 1 | 4 | 5 | 8 | 5th |

**Zheldakov, Grigori**
**b. Moscow, Russia, February 11, 1992**

| | | | | | | | | |
|---|---|---|---|---|---|---|---|---|
| 2010 WM18 | 12-D | RUS | 7 | 1 | 1 | 2 | 12 | 4th |
| 2012 WM20 | 12-D | RUS | 7 | 2 | 1 | 3 | 4 | S |

**Zherdev, Nikolai**
**b. Kiev (Kyiv), Soviet Union (Ukraine), November 5, 1984**

| | | | | | | | | |
|---|---|---|---|---|---|---|---|---|
| 2002 WM18 | 13-F | RUS | 8 | 6 | 5 | 11 | 22 | S |
| 2003 WM20 | 13-F | RUS | 6 | 0 | 1 | 1 | 2 | G |
| 2009 WM | 13-F | RUS | 3 | 0 | 1 | 1 | 0 | G |
| 2012 WM | 93-F | RUS | 10 | 2 | 4 | 6 | 2 | G |
| **Totals WM** | | | **13** | **2** | **5** | **7** | **2** | **2G** |

~WM18 IIHF Directorate Best Forward (2002)

**Zhevlochenko, Dmitri**
**b. Minsk, Belarus, April 16, 1992**

| | | | | | | | | |
|---|---|---|---|---|---|---|---|---|
| 2010 WM18 | 3-D | BLR | 6 | 2 | 2 | 4 | 8 | 10th |

**Zholudev, Konstantin**
**b. Novopolotsk, Soviet Union (Belarus), May 9, 1990**

| | | | | | | | | |
|---|---|---|---|---|---|---|---|---|
| 2008 WM18 | 4-D | BLR | 6 | 0 | 0 | 0 | 2 | 9th |

**Zhurik, Alexander**
**b. Minsk, Soviet Union (Belarus), May 29, 1975**

| | | | | | | | | |
|---|---|---|---|---|---|---|---|---|
| 1998 OG-M | 25-D | BLR | 4 | 0 | 0 | 0 | 10 | 7th |
| 1999 WM | 25-D | BLR | 6 | 0 | 0 | 0 | 4 | 9th |
| 2001 WM | 27-D | BLR | 6 | 0 | 1 | 1 | 4 | 14th |
| 2002 OG-M | 27-D | BLR | 9 | 0 | 1 | 1 | 6 | 4th |
| 2003 WM | 27-D | BLR | 6 | 0 | 0 | 0 | 20 | 14th |
| 2005 WM | 27-D | BLR | 6 | 0 | 0 | 0 | 12 | 10th |
| 2006 WM | 27-D | BLR | 4 | 0 | 1 | 1 | 0 | 6th |
| 2007 WM | 27-D | BLR | 6 | 0 | 0 | 0 | 6 | 11th |
| 2008 WM | 27-D | BLR | 6 | 1 | 0 | 1 | 2 | 9th |
| **Totals WM** | | | **40** | **1** | **2** | **3** | **48** | **—** |
| **Totals OG-M** | | | **13** | **0** | **1** | **1** | **16** | **—** |

**Zhurnya, Ruslan**
**b. Novopolotsk, Belarus, March 1, 1992**

| | | | | | | | | |
|---|---|---|---|---|---|---|---|---|
| 2010 WM18 | 12-F | BLR | 6 | 0 | 0 | 0 | 4 | 10th |

**Zibanejad, Mika**
**b. Huddinge, Sweden, April 18, 1993**

| | | | | | | | | |
|---|---|---|---|---|---|---|---|---|
| 2011 WM18 | 21-F | SWE | 6 | 4 | 4 | 8 | 2 | S |
| 2012 WM20 | 20-F | SWE | 6 | 4 | 1 | 5 | 2 | G |

**Zidlicky, Marek**
**b. Most, Czechoslovakia (Czech Republic), February 3, 1977**

| | | | | | | | | |
|---|---|---|---|---|---|---|---|---|
| 1995 WM20 | 9-D | CZE | 7 | 0 | 2 | 2 | 36 | 5th |
| 1997 WM20 | 19-D | CZE | 7 | 0 | 5 | 5 | 12 | 4th |
| 2004 WCH | 3-D | CZE | 5 | 3 | 1 | 4 | 2 | 3rd |
| 2005 WM | 3-D | CZE | 9 | 1 | 3 | 4 | 18 | G |
| 2006 OG-M | 3-D | CZE | 7 | 4 | 1 | 5 | 16 | B |
| 2007 WM | 3-D | CZE | 7 | 1 | 5 | 6 | 6 | 7th |
| 2008 WM | 3-D | CZE | 7 | 1 | 4 | 5 | 6 | 5th |
| 2009 WM | 3-D | CZE | 7 | 0 | 1 | 1 | 6 | 6th |
| 2010 OG-M | 3-D | CZE | 5 | 0 | 5 | 5 | 2 | 7th |
| 2011 WM | 3-D | CZE | 9 | 1 | 4 | 5 | 6 | B |
| **Totals WM20** | | | **14** | **0** | **7** | **7** | **48** | **—** |
| **Totals WM** | | | **39** | **4** | **17** | **21** | **42** | **G,B** |
| **Totals OG-M** | | | **12** | **4** | **6** | **10** | **18** | **B** |

~WM All-Star Team/Defence (2005, 2011)

**Ziegler, Sven**
**b. Nuremberg, Germany, July 1, 1994**

| | | | | | | | | |
|---|---|---|---|---|---|---|---|---|
| 2012 WM18 | 21-F | GER | 6 | 2 | 0 | 2 | 4 | 6th |

**Ziegler, Thomas**
**b. Zurich, Switzerland, June 9, 1978**

| | | | | | | | | |
|---|---|---|---|---|---|---|---|---|
| 1998 WM20 | 21-F | SUI | 7 | 3 | 1 | 4 | 2 | B |
| 2000 WM | 38-F | SUI | 7 | 2 | 2 | 4 | 0 | 5th |
| 2001 WM | 39-F | SUI | 6 | 0 | 1 | 1 | 4 | 9th |
| 2002 WM | 38-F | SUI | 6 | 0 | 0 | 0 | 2 | 10th |
| 2004 WM | 38-F | SUI | 7 | 1 | 3 | 4 | 20 | 8th |
| 2005 WM | 38-F | SUI | 6 | 1 | 0 | 1 | 10 | 8th |
| 2006 OG-M | 38-F | SUI | 5 | 1 | 0 | 1 | 8 | 6th |
| 2008 WM | 38-F | SUI | 7 | 0 | 0 | 0 | 4 | 7th |
| 2009 WM | 38-F | SUI | 6 | 0 | 0 | 0 | 4 | 9th |
| **Totals WM** | | | **45** | **4** | **6** | **10** | **44** | **—** |

**Ziemins, Juris**
**b. Riga, Latvia, September 15, 1993**

| | | | | | | | | |
|---|---|---|---|---|---|---|---|---|
| 2010 WM18 | 26-F | LAT | 6 | 0 | 1 | 1 | 2 | 9th |
| 2012 WM20 | 15-D | LAT | 6 | 1 | 1 | 2 | 0 | 9th |

**Zientek, Benjamin**
**b. Augsburg, Germany, April 20, 1994**

| | | | | | | | | |
|---|---|---|---|---|---|---|---|---|
| 2012 WM18 | 12-F | GER | 6 | 1 | 0 | 1 | 4 | 6th |

**Zimmerman, Sean**
**b. Denver, Colorado, United States, May 24, 1987**

| | | | | | | | | |
|---|---|---|---|---|---|---|---|---|
| 2007 WM20 | 23-D | USA | 7 | 0 | 0 | 0 | 6 | B |

**Zinoviev, Sergei**
**b. Novokuznetsk, Soviet Union (Russia), March 4, 1980**

| | | | | | | | | |
|---|---|---|---|---|---|---|---|---|
| 2000 WM20 | 13-F | RUS | 7 | 2 | 3 | 5 | 6 | S |
| 2003 WM | 16-F | RUS | 7 | 0 | 2 | 2 | 22 | 7th |
| 2005 WM | 42-F | RUS | 6 | 1 | 2 | 3 | 20 | B |
| 2007 WM | 42-F | RUS | 9 | 3 | 10 | 13 | 12 | B |
| 2008 WM | 42-F | RUS | 9 | 1 | 5 | 6 | 12 | G |
| 2009 WM | 42-F | RUS | 9 | 1 | 4 | 5 | 6 | G |
| 2010 OG-M | 42-F | RUS | 4 | 0 | 2 | 2 | 0 | 6th |
| 2011 WM | 42-F | RUS | 9 | 4 | 3 | 7 | 4 | 4th |
| **Totals WM** | | | **49** | **10** | **26** | **36** | **76** | **2G,2B** |

**Zisser, Stefan**
**b. Bolzano, Italy, March 26, 1980**

| | | | | | | | | |
|---|---|---|---|---|---|---|---|---|
| 2000 WM | 23-F | ITA | 5 | 0 | 0 | 0 | 0 | 9th |
| 2002 WM | 2-F | ITA | 6 | 0 | 0 | 0 | 8 | 15th |
| 2006 OG-M | 2-F | ITA | 5 | 0 | 0 | 0 | 2 | 11th |
| 2010 WM | 2-F | ITA | 6 | 0 | 0 | 0 | 0 | 15th |
| **Totals WM** | | | **17** | **0** | **0** | **0** | **8** | **—** |

**Zorec, Marco**
**b. Villach, Austria, September 12, 1990**

| | | | | | | | | |
|---|---|---|---|---|---|---|---|---|
| 2010 WM20 | 4-D | AUT | 6 | 0 | 0 | 0 | 43 | 10th |

**Zorko, Nikolaj**
**b. June 2, 1994**

| | | | | | | | | |
|---|---|---|---|---|---|---|---|---|
| 2012 WM18 | 24-F | DEN | 6 | 0 | 0 | 0 | 0 | 10th |

**Zotov, Pavel**
**b. Moscow, Soviet Union (Russia), August 14, 1991**

| | | | | | | | | |
|---|---|---|---|---|---|---|---|---|
| 2009 WM18 | 16-F | RUS | 7 | 0 | 0 | 0 | 6 | S |

**Zovinec, Dusan**
**b. Prague, Czech Republic, October 5, 1992**

| | | | | | | | | |
|---|---|---|---|---|---|---|---|---|
| 2010 WM18 | 6-D | CZE | 5 | 0 | 1 | 1 | 4 | 6th |

**Zubarev, Andrei**
**b. Ufa, Soviet Union (Russia), March 3, 1987**

| | | | | | | | | |
|---|---|---|---|---|---|---|---|---|
| 2005 WM18 | 3-D | RUS | 6 | 1 | 1 | 2 | 4 | 5th |
| 2006 WM20 | 11-D | RUS | 6 | 0 | 2 | 2 | 4 | S |
| 2007 WM20 | 3-D | RUS | 6 | 0 | 2 | 2 | 2 | S |
| **Totals WM20** | | | **12** | **0** | **4** | **4** | **6** | **2S** |

**Zuber, Timon**
**b. Opfikon, Switzerland, May 24, 1994**

| | | | | | | | | |
|---|---|---|---|---|---|---|---|---|
| 2012 WM18 | 4-D | SUI | 6 | 0 | 0 | 0 | 0 | 7th |

**Zubov, Ilya**
**b. Chelyabinsk, Soviet Union (Russia), February 14, 1987**

| | | | | | | | | |
|---|---|---|---|---|---|---|---|---|
| 2005 WM18 | 12-F | RUS | 6 | 3 | 5 | 8 | 6 | 5th |
| 2007 WM20 | 11-F | RUS | 6 | 3 | 1 | 4 | 6 | S |

**Zuccarello-Aasen, Mats**
**b. Oslo, Norway, September 1, 1987**

| | | | | | | | | |
|---|---|---|---|---|---|---|---|---|
| 2004 WM18 | 16-F | NOR | 6 | 0 | 2 | 2 | 8 | 10th |
| 2006 WM20 | 16-F | NOR | 6 | 0 | 2 | 2 | 4 | 10th |
| 2008 WM | 48-F | NOR | 7 | 1 | 0 | 1 | 2 | 8th |
| 2009 WM | 48-F | NOR | 6 | 3 | 0 | 3 | 8 | 11th |
| 2010 OG-M | 48-F | NOR | 4 | 1 | 2 | 3 | 2 | 10th |
| 2010 WM | 48-F | NOR | 6 | 3 | 1 | 4 | 6 | 9th |
| **Totals WM** | | | **19** | **7** | **1** | **8** | **16** | **—** |

**Zucker, Jason**
**b. Newport Beach, California, United States, January 16, 1992**

| | | | | | | | | |
|---|---|---|---|---|---|---|---|---|
| 2009 WM18 | 7-F | USA | 7 | 1 | 5 | 6 | 0 | G |
| 2010 WM18 | 16-F | USA | 7 | 4 | 3 | 7 | 2 | G |
| 2010 WM20 | 16-F | USA | 7 | 2 | 0 | 2 | 2 | G |
| 2011 WM20 | 16-F | USA | 4 | 1 | 0 | 1 | 0 | B |
| 2012 WM20 | 16-F | USA | 6 | 3 | 4 | 7 | 2 | 7th |
| **Totals WM18** | | | **14** | **5** | **8** | **13** | **2** | **2G** |
| **Totals WM20** | | | **17** | **6** | **4** | **10** | **4** | **G,B** |

**Zukal, Marek**
**b. Bratislava, Czechoslovakia (Slovakia), August 23, 1988**

| | | | | | | | | |
|---|---|---|---|---|---|---|---|---|
| 2008 WM20 | 5-D | SVK | 6 | 0 | 0 | 0 | 2 | 7th |

**Zvirbulis, Pauls**
**b. Riga, Latvia, February 24, 1993**

| | | | | | | | | |
|---|---|---|---|---|---|---|---|---|
| 2012 WM20 | 7-D | LAT | 6 | 0 | 1 | 1 | 0 | 9th |

**Zwikel, Jonathan**
**b. Brussels, Belgium, July 16, 1975**

| | | | | | | | | |
|---|---|---|---|---|---|---|---|---|
| 1997 WM | 42-F | FRA | 8 | 0 | 1 | 1 | 4 | 10th |
| 1998 OG-M | 42-F | FRA | 4 | 0 | 0 | 0 | 0 | 11th |
| 1998 WM | 42-F | FRA | 3 | 1 | 0 | 1 | 6 | 13th |
| 2000 WM | 42-F | FRA | 6 | 1 | 2 | 3 | 2 | 15th |
| 2002 OG-M | 22-F | FRA | 4 | 0 | 0 | 0 | 4 | 14th |
| 2004 WM | 13-F | FRA | 6 | 0 | 1 | 1 | 4 | 16th |
| 2008 WM | 13-F | FRA | 5 | 1 | 1 | 2 | 2 | 14th |
| 2009 WM | 13-F | FRA | 6 | 0 | 1 | 1 | 14 | 12th |
| **Totals WM** | | | **34** | **3** | **6** | **9** | **32** | **—** |
| **Totals OG-M** | | | **8** | **0** | **0** | **0** | **4** | **—** |

**Zyryanov, Gleb**
**b. Kirovo-Chepetsk, Russia, April 16, 1992**

| | | | | | | | | |
|---|---|---|---|---|---|---|---|---|
| 2010 WM18 | 26-F | RUS | 7 | 0 | 0 | 0 | 2 | 4th |

# Active Goalies, Men

(event-by-event summary for recently-active goalies internationally who play in the top level)

| Year Event | #-Pos | NAT | GP | W-T-L | Mins | GA | SO | GAA | A | Pim | Medals |
|---|---|---|---|---|---|---|---|---|---|---|---|

| **Aebischer, David** | | | | | | | | | | | **b. Fribourg, Switzerland, February 7, 1978** |
|---|---|---|---|---|---|---|---|---|---|---|---|
| 1997 WM20 | 30-G | SUI | 5 | 3-1-1 | 300:00 | 10 | 0 | 2.00 | 0 | 0 | 7th |
| 1998 WM20 | 30-G | SUI | 6 | 4-1-1 | 378:47 | 10 | 1 | 1.58 | 0 | 0 | B |
| 1998 WM | 40-G | SUI | 7 | 2-1-4 | 375:59 | 18 | 0 | 2.87 | 0 | 0 | 4th |
| 1999 WM | 40-G | SUI | 4 | 1-0-2 | 173:33 | 13 | 1 | 4.49 | 0 | 2 | 8th |
| 2002 OG-M | 40-G | SUI | 2 | 0-1-1 | 81:19 | 6 | 0 | 4.43 | 0 | 0 | 11th |
| 2005 WM | 40-G | SUI | 1 | 0-1-0 | 60:00 | 3 | 0 | 3.00 | 0 | 0 | 8th |
| 2006 OG-M | 40-G | SUI | 4 | 1-2-0 | 200:00 | 7 | 0 | 2.10 | 0 | 0 | 6th |
| 2006 WM | 40-G | SUI | 6 | 2-2-2 | 359:00 | 16 | 0 | 2.67 | 0 | 0 | 9th |
| 2007 WM | 40-G | SUI | 1 | 0-0-1 | 60:00 | 6 | 0 | 6.00 | 0 | 10 | 8th |
| **Totals WM20** | | | **11** | **7-2-2** | **678:47** | **20** | **1** | **1.77** | **0** | **0** | **B** |
| **Totals WM** | | | **19** | **5-4-9** | **1,028:32** | **56** | **1** | **3.27** | **0** | **12** | **—** |
| **Totals OG-M** | | | **6** | **1-3-1** | **281:19** | **13** | **0** | **2.77** | **0** | **0** | **—** |

~WM20 IIHF Directorate Best Goalie (1998), WM20 All-Star Team/Goal (1998)

| **Ahres, Anton** | | | | | | | | | | | **b. Brest, Belarus, February 12, 1992** |
|---|---|---|---|---|---|---|---|---|---|---|---|
| 2010 WM18 | 1-G | BLR | 3 | 0-0-2 | 164:20 | 15 | 0 | 5.48 | 0 | 0 | 10th |

| **Aittokallio, Sami** | | | | | | | | | | | **b. Tampere, Finland, August 6, 1992** |
|---|---|---|---|---|---|---|---|---|---|---|---|
| 2011 WM20 | 30-G | FIN | 1 | 0-0-0 | 20:00 | 0 | 0 | 0.00 | 0 | 0 | 6th |
| 2012 WM20 | 30-G | FIN | 5 | 3-0-2 | 310:00 | 13 | 1 | 2.52 | 0 | 0 | 4th |
| **Totals WM20** | | | **6** | **3-0-2** | **330:00** | **13** | **1** | **2.36** | **0** | **0** | **—** |

| **Akerlund, Magnus** | | | | | | | | | | | **b. Osby, Sweden, April 25, 1986** |
|---|---|---|---|---|---|---|---|---|---|---|---|
| 2004 WM18 | 30-G | SWE | 5 | 2-0-3 | 300:00 | 17 | 1 | 3.40 | 0 | 0 | 5th |
| 2004 WM20 | 1-G | SWE | 1 | 0-0-1 | 58:36 | 4 | 0 | 4.10 | 0 | 0 | 7th |
| 2006 WM20 | 30-G | SWE | 2 | 1-0-1 | 120:00 | 7 | 0 | 3.50 | 0 | 0 | 5th |
| **Totals WM20** | | | **3** | **1-0-2** | **178:36** | **11** | **0** | **3.70** | **0** | **0** | **—** |

| **Alistratov, Danila** | | | | | | | | | | | **b. Chelyabinsk, Soviet Union (Russia), October 30, 1990** |
|---|---|---|---|---|---|---|---|---|---|---|---|
| 2008 WM18 | 1-G | RUS | 3 | 1-0-0 | 144:05 | 7 | 0 | 2.91 | 0 | 0 | S |
| 2009 WM20 | 20-G | RUS | 3 | 2-0-1 | 137:31 | 7 | 0 | 3.05 | 0 | 0 | B |

| **Allen, Jake** | | | | | | | | | | | **b. Fredericton, New Brunswick, Canada, August 7, 1990** |
|---|---|---|---|---|---|---|---|---|---|---|---|
| 2008 WM18 | 31-G | CAN | 7 | 6-0-1 | 420:00 | 10 | 2 | 1.43 | 0 | 2 | G |
| 2010 WM20 | 1-G | CAN | 5 | 4-0-0 | 291:23 | 10 | 2 | 2.06 | 0 | 0 | S |

~WM18 IIHF Directorate Best Goalie (2008), WM18 All-Star Team/Goal (2008)

| **Andersen, Frederik** | | | | | | | | | | | **b. Herning, Denmark, October 2, 1989** |
|---|---|---|---|---|---|---|---|---|---|---|---|
| 2008 WM20 | 1-G | DEN | 4 | 0-0-4 | 213:32 | 20 | 0 | 5.62 | 0 | 0 | 10th |
| 2010 WM | 30-G | DEN | 2 | 1-0-1 | 120:00 | 7 | 0 | 3.50 | 0 | 2 | 8th |
| 2011 WM | 30-G | DEN | 4 | 2-0-2 | 245:59 | 14 | 0 | 3.41 | 0 | 0 | 11th |
| 2012 WM | 30-G | DEN | 6 | 1-0-5 | 359:16 | 20 | 1 | 3.34 | 0 | 0 | 13th |
| **Totals WM** | | | **12** | **4-0-8** | **725:15** | **41** | **1** | **3.39** | **0** | **2** | **—** |

| **Andersen, Matthias** | | | | | | | | | | | **b. Herning, Denmark, September 29, 1994** |
|---|---|---|---|---|---|---|---|---|---|---|---|
| 2012 WM18 | | DEN | 3RD GK—DID NOT PLAY | | | | | | | | |

| **Anderson, Craig** | | | | | | | | | | | **b. Park Ridge, Illinois, United States, May 21, 1981** |
|---|---|---|---|---|---|---|---|---|---|---|---|
| 2006 WM | 31-G | USA | 5 | 3-0-2 | 280:00 | 11 | 1 | 2.36 | 0 | 0 | 7th |
| 2008 WM | 31-G | USA | 2 | 0-0-1 | 64:10 | 6 | 0 | 5.61 | 0 | 0 | 6th |
| **Totals WM** | | | **7** | **3-0-3** | **344:10** | **17** | **1** | **2.96** | **0** | **0** | **—** |

| **Auld, Alexander** | | | | | | | | | | | **b. Cold Lake, Alberta, Canada, January 7, 1981** |
|---|---|---|---|---|---|---|---|---|---|---|---|
| 2001 WM20 | 30-G | CAN | 1 | 0-0-0 | 20:00 | 4 | 0 | 12.00 | 0 | 0 | B |
| 2006 WM | 35-G | CAN | 5 | 2-0-2 | 273:42 | 13 | 0 | 2.85 | 0 | 2 | 4th |

| **Auren, Jean** | | | | | | | | | | | **b. Kruunupyy, Finland, March 20, 1994** |
|---|---|---|---|---|---|---|---|---|---|---|---|
| 2012 WM18 | 30-G | FIN | 2 | 1-0-0 | 64:49 | 3 | 0 | 2.78 | 0 | 0 | 4th |

| **Avotins, Ugis** | | | | | | | | | | | **b. Riga, Soviet Union (Latvia), April 18, 1986** |
|---|---|---|---|---|---|---|---|---|---|---|---|
| 2006 WM20 | 30-G | LAT | 6 | 1-0-5 | 333:57 | 28 | 1 | 5.03 | 0 | 0 | 9th |

| **Bacashihua, Jason** | | | | | | | | | | | **b. Garden City, Michigan, United States, September 20, 1982** |
|---|---|---|---|---|---|---|---|---|---|---|---|
| 2002 WM20 | 29-G | USA | 7 | 4-2-1 | 420:00 | 20 | 0 | 2.86 | 0 | 0 | 5th |
| 2006 WM | 33-G | USA | 3 | 1-0-1 | 140:00 | 5 | 0 | 2.14 | 0 | 0 | 7th |
| 2007 WM | 33-G | USA | 1 | 0-0-0 | 20:00 | 1 | 0 | 3.00 | 0 | 0 | 5th |
| **Totals WM** | | | **4** | **1-0-1** | **160:00** | **6** | **0** | **2.25** | **0** | **0** | **—** |

| **Bachman, Richard** | | | | | | | | | | | **b. Salt Lake City, Utah, United States, July 25, 1987** |
|---|---|---|---|---|---|---|---|---|---|---|---|
| 2012 WM | 31-G | USA | 1 | 1-0-0 | 64:38 | 2 | 0 | 1.86 | 0 | 0 | 7th |

| **Backlund, Johan** | | | | | | | | | | | **b. Skelleftea, Sweden, July 24, 1981** |
|---|---|---|---|---|---|---|---|---|---|---|---|
| 2007 WM | 31-G | SWE | 6 | 4-0-2 | 359:02 | 12 | 2 | 2.01 | 0 | 2 | 4th |

| **Backstrom, Niklas** | | | | | | | | | | | **b. Helsinki, Finland, February 13, 1978** |
|---|---|---|---|---|---|---|---|---|---|---|---|
| 1998 WM20 | 29-G | FIN | 2 | 1-1-0 | 120:00 | 5 | 1 | 2.50 | 0 | 0 | G |
| 2005 WM | 32-G | FIN | 5 | 1-3-1 | 310:00 | 12 | 1 | 2.32 | 1 | 0 | 7th |
| 2006 OG-M | | FIN | 3RD GK—DID NOT PLAY | | | | | | | | |
| 2006 WM | | FIN | 3RD GK—DID NOT PLAY | | | | | | | | |
| 2008 WM | 32-G | FIN | 8 | 6-0-2 | 483:22 | 17 | 1 | 2.11 | 1 | 2 | B |
| 2010 OG-M | 33-G | FIN | 2 | 1-0-0 | 109:52 | 2 | 1 | 1.09 | 0 | 2 | B |
| **Totals WM** | | | **13** | **7-3-3** | **793:22** | **29** | **2** | **2.19** | **2** | **2** | **B** |

| **Barulin, Konstantin** | | | | | | | | | | | **b. Karaganda, Soviet Union (Kazakhstan), September 4, 1984** |
|---|---|---|---|---|---|---|---|---|---|---|---|
| 2002 WM18 | 30-G | RUS | 3 | 2-0-0 | 125:12 | 0 | 2 | 0.00 | 0 | 0 | S |
| 2003 WM20 | 20-G | RUS | 1 | 1-0-0 | 60:00 | 1 | 0 | 1.00 | 0 | 0 | G |
| 2004 WM20 | 30-G | RUS | 4 | 1-1-2 | 200:00 | 12 | 0 | 3.60 | 0 | 0 | 5th |
| 2011 WM | 84-G | RUS | 7 | 2-0-4 | 342:19 | 16 | 0 | 2.80 | 0 | 0 | 4th |
| 2012 WM | 30-G | RUS | 2 | 2-0-0 | 120:00 | 1 | 1 | .050 | 0 | 0 | G |
| **Totals WM20** | | | **5** | **2-1-2** | **260:00** | **13** | **0** | **3.00** | **0** | **0** | **G** |
| **Totals WM** | | | **9** | **4-0-4** | **462:19** | **17** | **1** | **2.21** | **0** | **0** | **G** |

| **Baur, Rene** | | | | | | | | | | | **b. San Candido, Italy, January 19, 1985** |
|---|---|---|---|---|---|---|---|---|---|---|---|
| 2006 OG-M | | ITA | 3RD GK—DID NOT PLAY | | | | | | | | |
| 2006 WM | | ITA | 3RD GK—DID NOT PLAY | | | | | | | | |

| **Beauchemin, Rejean** | | | | | | | | | | | **b. Winnipeg, Manitoba, Canada, May 3, 1985** |
|---|---|---|---|---|---|---|---|---|---|---|---|
| 2003 WM18 | 30-G | CAN | 1 | 1-0-0 | 60:00 | 1 | 0 | 1.00 | 0 | 0 | G |
| 2005 WM20 | 35-G | CAN | 1 | 1-0-0 | 60:00 | 0 | 1 | 0.00 | 0 | 0 | G |

| **Bellissimo, Daniel** | | | | | | | | | | | **b. Toronto, Ontario, Canada, August 15, 1984** |
|---|---|---|---|---|---|---|---|---|---|---|---|
| 2010 WM | 30-G | ITA | 5 | 1-0-3 | 263:51 | 9 | 0 | 2.05 | 0 | 0 | 15th |
| 2012 WM | 30-G | ITA | 5 | 1-0-4 | 274:29 | 20 | 0 | 4.37 | 0 | 0 | 15th |
| **Totals WM** | | | **10** | **2-0-7** | **538:20** | **29** | **0** | **3.23** | **0** | **0** | **—** |

| **Benda, Marek** | | | | | | | | | | | **b. Plana, Czechoslovakia (Czech Republic), May 21, 1989** |
|---|---|---|---|---|---|---|---|---|---|---|---|
| 2007 WM18 | 1-G | CZE | 6 | 3-0-3 | 316:22 | 16 | 0 | 3.03 | 0 | 0 | 9th |

| **Bengtsberg, Christoffer** | | | | | | | | | | | **b. Stockholm, Sweden, November 1, 1899** |
|---|---|---|---|---|---|---|---|---|---|---|---|
| 2007 WM18 | 30-G | SWE | 1 | 0-0-0 | 19:45 | 1 | 0 | 3.04 | 0 | 0 | B |

| **Bennett, Brett** | | | | | | | | | | | **b. Williamsville, New York, United States, March 8, 1988** |
|---|---|---|---|---|---|---|---|---|---|---|---|
| 2006 WM18 | 31-G | USA | 2 | 2-0-0 | 120:00 | 1 | 1 | 0.50 | 0 | 2 | G |

| **Bernard, Andreas** | | | | | | | | | | | **b. Bolzano, Italy, June 9, 1990** |
|---|---|---|---|---|---|---|---|---|---|---|---|
| 2012 WM | | ITA | 3RD GK—DID NOT PLAY | | | | | | | | |

| **Bernier, Jonathan** | | | | | | | | | | | **b. Laval, Quebec, Canada, September 7, 1988** |
|---|---|---|---|---|---|---|---|---|---|---|---|
| 2006 WM18 | 1-G | CAN | 7 | 3-1-3 | 420:32 | 12 | 1 | 1.71 | 0 | 0 | 4th |
| 2008 WM20 | 1-G | CAN | 2 | 1-0-1 | 119:53 | 4 | 1 | 2.00 | 0 | 0 | G |
| 2011 WM | 45-G | CAN | 3 | 2-0-1 | 179:00 | 6 | 0 | 2.01 | 0 | 0 | 5th |

| **Berra, Reto** | | | | | | | | | | | **b. Bulach, Switzerland, January 3, 1987** |
|---|---|---|---|---|---|---|---|---|---|---|---|
| 2005 WM18 | 30-G | SUI | 2 | 1-0-1 | 120:00 | 9 | 0 | 4.50 | 0 | 0 | 9th |
| 2006 WM20 | 20-G | SUI | 6 | 2-2-2 | 358:40 | 14 | 0 | 2.34 | 0 | 2 | 7th |
| 2007 WM20 | 20-G | SUI | 6 | 3-0-3 | 359:33 | 19 | 0 | 3.17 | 0 | 2 | 7th |
| 2012 WM | 20-G | SUI | 4 | 1-0-3 | 239:29 | 12 | 0 | 3.01 | 0 | 0 | 11th |
| **Totals WM20** | | | **12** | **5-2-5** | **718:13** | **33** | **0** | **2.76** | **0** | **4** | **—** |

| **Biryukov, Mikhail** | | | | | | | | | | | **b. Yaroslavl, Soviet Union (Russia), October 13, 1985** |
|---|---|---|---|---|---|---|---|---|---|---|---|
| 2008 WM | 35-G | RUS | 3 | 3-0-0 | 162:26 | 6 | 0 | 2.22 | 0 | 0 | G |
| 2012 WM | 40-G | RUS | 1 | 0-0-0 | 40:00 | 0 | 0 | 0.00 | 0 | 0 | G |
| **Totals WM** | | | **4** | **3-0-0** | **202:26** | **6** | **0** | **1.78** | **0** | **0** | **2G** |

| **Bishop, Ben** | | | | | | | | | | | **b. Denver, Colorado, United States, November 21, 1986** |
|---|---|---|---|---|---|---|---|---|---|---|---|
| 2010 WM | 1-G | USA | 1 | 0-0-0 | 20:00 | 0 | 0 | 0.00 | 0 | 0 | 13th |

| **Bobkov, Igor** | | | | | | | | | | | **b. Surgut, Soviet Union (Russia), January 2, 1991** |
|---|---|---|---|---|---|---|---|---|---|---|---|
| 2009 WM18 | 29-G | RUS | 6 | 4-0-2 | 360:00 | 20 | 1 | 3.33 | 0 | 0 | S |
| 2010 WM20 | 20-G | RUS | 6 | 3-0-3 | 343:05 | 14 | 1 | 2.45 | 0 | 0 | 6th |
| 2011 WM20 | 30-G | RUS | 2 | 1-0-1 | 93:33 | 6 | 0 | 3.85 | 0 | 0 | G |
| **Totals WM20** | | | **8** | **4-0-4** | **436:38** | **20** | **1** | **2.75** | **0** | **0** | **G** |

~WM18 IIHF Directorate Best Goalie (2009)

| **Bobrovski, Sergei** | | | | | | | | | | | **b. Novokuznetsk, Soviet Union (Russia), September 20, 1988** |
|---|---|---|---|---|---|---|---|---|---|---|---|
| 2008 WM20 | 1-G | RUS | 6 | 4-0-2 | 366:07 | 15 | 0 | 2.46 | 0 | 2 | B |

| **Boltshauser, Luca** | | | | | | | | | | | **b. Zurich, Switzerland, July 17, 1993** |
|---|---|---|---|---|---|---|---|---|---|---|---|
| 2011 WM18 | 29-G | SUI | 6 | 3-0-3 | 332:44 | 16 | 0 | 2.89 | 0 | 0 | 7th |
| 2012 WM20 | | SUI | 3RD GK—DID NOT PLAY | | | | | | | | |

| **Borodulia, Alexander** | | | | | | | | | | | **b. Minsk, Soviet Union (Belarus), October 6, 1991** |
|---|---|---|---|---|---|---|---|---|---|---|---|
| 2008 WM18 | 25-G | BLR | 4 | 0-0-3 | 135:50 | 11 | 0 | 4.86 | 0 | 0 | 9th |

| **Brodeur, Martin** | | | | | | | | | | | **b. Montreal, Quebec, Canada, May 6, 1972** |
|---|---|---|---|---|---|---|---|---|---|---|---|
| 1996 WM | 30-G | CAN | 3 | 0-1-1 | 140:00 | 8 | 0 | 3.43 | 0 | 0 | S |
| 1996 WCH | 1-G | CAN | 2 | 0-0-1 | 60:02 | 4 | 0 | 4.00 | 0 | 0 | 2nd |
| 1998 OG-M | CAN | DID NOT PLAY | | | | | | | | | |
| 2002 OG-M | 30-G | CAN | 5 | 4-1-0 | 300:00 | 9 | 0 | 1.80 | 0 | 0 | G |
| 2004 WCH | 30-G | CAN | 5 | 5-0-0 | 300:00 | 5 | 1 | 1.00 | 0 | 2 | 1st |
| 2005 WM | 30-G | CAN | 7 | 5-0-2 | 418:36 | 20 | 0 | 2.87 | 0 | 0 | S |

| | | | | | | | | | | | |
|---|---|---|---|---|---|---|---|---|---|---|---|
| 2006 OG-M | 30-G | CAN | 4 | 2-0-2 | 238:40 | 8 | 0 | 2.01 | 0 | 0 | 7th |
| 2010 OG-M | 30-G | CAN | 2 | 1-0-1 | 124:18 | 6 | 0 | 2.90 | 0 | 0 | G |
| **Totals WM** | | | **10** | **5-1-3** | **558:36** | **28** | **0** | **3.01** | **0** | **0** | **2S** |
| **Totals IIHF-NHL** | | | **7** | **5-0-1** | **360:02** | **9** | **1** | **1.50** | **0** | **2** | **—** |
| **Totals OG-M** | | | **11** | **7-1-3** | **662:58** | **23** | **0** | **2.08** | **0** | **0** | **2G,S** |

~WCH All-Star Team/Goal (2004)

| **Bruckmann, Felix** | | | | | | | | | | | **b. Breisach am Rhein, West Germany (Germany), December 16, 1990** |
|---|---|---|---|---|---|---|---|---|---|---|---|
| 2008 WM18 | 1-G | GER | 2 | 1-0-1 | 120:00 | 9 | 0 | 4.50 | 0 | 0 | 5th |

| **Bruckler, Bernd** | | | | | | | | | | | **b. Graz, Austria, September 26, 1981** |
|---|---|---|---|---|---|---|---|---|---|---|---|
| 2004 WM | | AUT | 3RD GK—DID NOT PLAY | | | | | | | | |
| 2005 WM | 23-G | AUT | 5 | 0-1-4 | 288:32 | 19 | 0 | 3.95 | 0 | 0 | 16th |
| 2007 WM | 31-G | AUT | 2 | 0-0-2 | 120:00 | 11 | 0 | 5.50 | 0 | 0 | 15th |
| 2009 WM | 30-G | AUT | 5 | 2-0-3 | 299:24 | 13 | 2 | 2.61 | 0 | 0 | 14th |
| **Totals WM** | | | **12** | **2-1-9** | **447:56** | **43** | **2** | **5.76** | **0** | **0** | **—** |

| **Brul, Yevgeni** | | | | | | | | | | | **b. Kiev (Kyiv), Soviet Union (Ukraine), February 22, 1967** |
|---|---|---|---|---|---|---|---|---|---|---|---|
| 2000 WM | | UKR | 3RD GK—DID NOT PLAY | | | | | | | | |
| 2004 WM | | UKR | 3RD GK—DID NOT PLAY | | | | | | | | |

| **Bryzgalov, Ilya** | | | | | | | | | | | **b. Togliatti, Soviet Union (Russia), June 22, 1980** |
|---|---|---|---|---|---|---|---|---|---|---|---|
| 2000 WM20 | 20-G | RUS | 4 | 3-0-1 | 244:04 | 3 | 1 | 0.74 | 0 | 0 | S |
| 2000 WM | 20-G | RUS | 4 | 1-0-3 | 218:24 | 10 | 0 | 2.75 | 0 | 0 | 9th |
| 2002 OG-M | | RUS | 3RD GK—DID NOT PLAY | | | | | | | | |
| 2004 WCH | 30-G | RUS | 3 | 2-0-1 | 179:50 | 7 | 0 | 2.34 | 0 | 2 | 6th |
| 2006 OG-M | 30-G | RUS | 1 | 0-0-1 | 60:00 | 5 | 0 | 5.00 | 0 | 0 | 4th |
| 2009 WM | 30-G | RUS | 7 | 6-0-0 | 404:04 | 14 | 1 | 2.08 | 0 | 2 | G |
| 2010 OG-M | 30-G | RUS | 2 | 0-0-1 | 100:53 | 3 | 0 | 1.78 | 0 | 0 | 6th |
| **Totals WM** | | | **11** | **7-0-3** | **622:28** | **24** | **1** | **2.31** | **0** | **2** | **G** |
| **Totals OG-M** | | | **3** | **0-0-2** | **160:53** | **8** | **0** | **2.98** | **0** | **0** | **—** |

| **Budaj, Peter** | | | | | | | | | | | **b. Banska Bystrica, Czechoslovakia (Slovakia), September 18, 1982** |
|---|---|---|---|---|---|---|---|---|---|---|---|
| 2000 WM18 | 1-G | SVK | 5 | 3-0-2 | 289:24 | 13 | 0 | 2.70 | 0 | 4 | 5th |
| 2001 WM20 | 25-G | SVK | 4 | 0-0-4 | 249:12 | 17 | 0 | 4.09 | 0 | 0 | 8th |
| 2002 WM20 | 1-G | SVK | 4 | 1-1-2 | 212:29 | 11 | 1 | 3.11 | 0 | 0 | 8th |
| 2004 WCH | | SVK | 3RD GK—DID NOT PLAY | | | | | | | | |
| 2006 OG-M | 37-G | SVK | 3 | 2-0-1 | 179:24 | 6 | 0 | 2.01 | 0 | 0 | 5th |
| 2008 WM | 31-G | SVK | 1 | 0-0-1 | 59:29 | 3 | 0 | 3.03 | 0 | 0 | 13th |
| 2010 OG-M | | SVK | 3RD GK—DID NOT PLAY | | | | | | | | |
| 2010 WM | 31-G | SVK | 6 | 2-0-4 | 282:40 | 13 | 0 | 2.76 | 0 | 0 | 12th |
| **Totals WM20** | | | **8** | **1-1-6** | **461:41** | **28** | **1** | **3.64** | **0** | **0** | **—** |
| **Totals WM** | | | **7** | **2-0-5** | **342:09** | **16** | **0** | **2.81** | **0** | **0** | **—** |

| **Buhrer, Marco** | | | | | | | | | | | **b. Dielsdorf, Switzerland, October 9, 1979** |
|---|---|---|---|---|---|---|---|---|---|---|---|
| 1998 WM20 | 28-G | SUI | 1 | 0-0-1 | 60:00 | 4 | 0 | 4.00 | 0 | 0 | B |
| 1999 WM20 | 30-G | SUI | 6 | 1-0-5 | 358:27 | 26 | 0 | 4.35 | 0 | 0 | 9th |
| 2003 WM | 44-G | SUI | 5 | 3-0-2 | 297:25 | 9 | 1 | 1.82 | 0 | 0 | 8th |
| 2004 WM | 44-G | SUI | 1 | 0-0-1 | 60:00 | 3 | 0 | 3.00 | 0 | 0 | 8th |
| 2005 WM | | SUI | 3RD GK—DID NOT PLAY | | | | | | | | |
| 2006 OG-M | | SUI | 3RD GK—DID NOT PLAY | | | | | | | | |
| 2006 WM | | SUI | 3RD GK—DID NOT PLAY | | | | | | | | |
| **Totals WM20** | | | **7** | **1-0-6** | **418:27** | **30** | **0** | **4.30** | **0** | **0** | **B** |
| **Totals WM** | | | **6** | **3-0-3** | **357:25** | **12** | **1** | **2.01** | **0** | **0** | **—** |

| **Campbell, Jack** | | | | | | | | | | | **b. Port Huron, Michigan, United States, January 9, 1992** |
|---|---|---|---|---|---|---|---|---|---|---|---|
| 2009 WM18 | 1-G | USA | 5 | 4-0-0 | 240:58 | 3 | 2 | 0.75 | 0 | 0 | G |
| 2010 WM18 | 1-G | USA | 6 | 5-0-1 | 359:39 | 5 | 3 | 0.83 | 2 | 0 | G |
| 2010 WM20 | 1-G | USA | 3 | 2-0-1 | 165:35 | 7 | 1 | 2.54 | 0 | 0 | G |
| 2011 WM20 | 1-G | USA | 6 | 5-0-1 | 353:35 | 10 | 0 | 1.70 | 0 | 0 | B |
| 2011 WM | | USA | 3RD GK—DID NOT PLAY | | | | | | | | |
| 2012 WM20 | 1-G | USA | 5 | 3-0-2 | 297:36 | 13 | 0 | 2.62 | 0 | 0 | 7th |
| **Totals WM18** | | | **11** | **9-0-1** | **600:37** | **8** | **5** | **0.80** | **2** | **0** | **2G** |
| **Totals WM20** | | | **14** | **10-0-4** | **816:46** | **30** | **1** | **2.20** | **0** | **0** | **G,B** |

~WM20 IIHF Directorate Award Best Goalie (2011), WM20 All-Star Team/Goal (2011), WM18 IIHF Directorate Best Goalie (2010), WM18 All-Star Team/Goal (2009, 2010)

| **Cann, Trevor** | | | | | | | | | | | **b. Oakville, Ontario, Canada, March 30, 1989** |
|---|---|---|---|---|---|---|---|---|---|---|---|
| 2007 WM18 | 30-G | CAN | 6 | 4-0-2 | 366:10 | 18 | 0 | 2.95 | 0 | 0 | 4th |

| **Cannata, Joe** | | | | | | | | | | | **b. Wakefield, Massachusetts, United States, January 2, 1990** |
|---|---|---|---|---|---|---|---|---|---|---|---|
| 2008 WM18 | 31-G | USA | 2 | 1-0-1 | 120:00 | 7 | 0 | 3.50 | 1 | 0 | B |

| **Ciaccio, Damiano** | | | | | | | | | | | **b. Fontaines sur Grandson, Switzerland, February 10, 1989** |
|---|---|---|---|---|---|---|---|---|---|---|---|
| 2007 WM18 | 30-G | SUI | 1 | 0-0-1 | 59:52 | 3 | 0 | 3.01 | 0 | 0 | 6th |

| **Ciliak, Marek** | | | | | | | | | | | **b. Zvolen, Czechoslovakia (Slovakia), April 2, 1990** |
|---|---|---|---|---|---|---|---|---|---|---|---|
| 2008 WM18 | 1-G | SVK | 3 | 2-0-1 | 180:00 | 9 | 0 | 3.00 | 0 | 0 | 7th |
| 2010 WM20 | 1-G | SVK | 4 | 1-0-2 | 152:31 | 14 | 0 | 5.51 | 0 | 0 | 8th |

| **Cimermanis, Rihards** | | | | | | | | | | | **b. Riga, Latvia, March 22, 1993** |
|---|---|---|---|---|---|---|---|---|---|---|---|
| 2012 WM20 | 1-G | LAT | 1 | 0-0-0 | 19:04 | 5 | 0 | 15.73 | 0 | 0 | 9th |

| **Clemmensen, Scott** | | | | | | | | | | | **b. Des Moines, Iowa, United States, July 23, 1977** |
|---|---|---|---|---|---|---|---|---|---|---|---|
| 2010 WM | 30-G | USA | 6 | 3-0-3 | 346:46 | 9 | 1 | 1.56 | 0 | 0 | 13th |

| **Conklin, Ty** | | | | | | | | | | | **b. Anchorage, Alaska, United States, March 30, 1976** |
|---|---|---|---|---|---|---|---|---|---|---|---|
| 2004 WM | 29-G | USA | 5 | 3-0-1 | 280:00 | 10 | 1 | 2.14 | 0 | 0 | B |
| 2004 WCH | | USA | 3RD GK—DID NOT PLAY | | | | | | | | |
| 2005 WM | 30-G | USA | 3 | 1-0-2 | 179:39 | 6 | 0 | 2.00 | 0 | 2 | 6th |
| 2011 WM | 29-G | USA | 4 | 1-0-3 | 216:00 | 14 | 0 | 3.89 | 1 | 0 | 8th |
| **Totals WM** | | | **12** | **5-0-6** | **675:39** | **30** | **1** | **2.66** | **0** | **2** | **B** |

~WM IIHF Directorate Best Goalie (2004)

| **Conz, Benjamin** | | | | | | | | | | | **b. St-Ursanne, Switzerland, September 13, 1991** |
|---|---|---|---|---|---|---|---|---|---|---|---|
| 2008 WM18 | 1-G | SUI | 4 | 2-0-2 | 240:00 | 13 | 0 | 3.25 | 0 | 0 | 8th |
| 2009 WM18 | 1-G | SUI | 6 | 2-0-3 | 327:28 | 27 | 0 | 4.95 | 0 | 2 | 8th |
| 2010 WM20 | 1-G | SUI | 7 | 3-0-4 | 428:10 | 34 | 0 | 4.76 | 0 | 2 | 4th |
| 2011 WM20 | 1-G | SUI | 6 | 3-0-3 | 363:55 | 18 | 0 | 2.97 | 0 | 0 | 5th |
| **Totals WM18** | | | **10** | **4-0-5** | **567:28** | **40** | **0** | **4.23** | **0** | **2** | **—** |
| **Totals WM20** | | | **13** | **6-0-7** | **792:05** | **52** | **0** | **3.94** | **0** | **0** | **—** |

~WM20 IIHF Directorate Best Goalie (2010), WM20 All-Star Team/Goal (2010)

| **Cupper, Marvin** | | | | | | | | | | | **b. Cologne, Germany, February 16, 1994** |
|---|---|---|---|---|---|---|---|---|---|---|---|
| 2011 WM18 | 30-G | GER | 4 | 1-0-3 | 245:00 | 14 | 0 | 3.43 | 0 | 0 | 6th |
| 2012 WM18 | 1-G | GER | 4 | 1-0-2 | 199:05 | 13 | 0 | 3.92 | 0 | 0 | 6th |
| **Totals WM18** | | | **8** | **2-0-5** | **444:05** | **27** | **0** | **3.65** | **0** | **0** | **—** |

| **Curry, John** | | | | | | | | | | | **b. Shorewood, Minnesota, United States, February 27, 1984** |
|---|---|---|---|---|---|---|---|---|---|---|---|
| 2012 WM | | USA | 3RD GK—DID NOT PLAY | | | | | | | | |

| **D'Agostini, Andrew** | | | | | | | | | | | **b. Scarborough (Toronto), Ontario, Canada, August 16, 1993** |
|---|---|---|---|---|---|---|---|---|---|---|---|
| 2011 WM18 | 1-G | CAN | 2 | 1-0-1 | 117:30 | 5 | 1 | 2.55 | 0 | 0 | 4th |

| **Dahm, Sebastian** | | | | | | | | | | | **b. Copenhagen, Denmark, February 28, 1987** |
|---|---|---|---|---|---|---|---|---|---|---|---|
| 2004 WM18 | 2-G | DEN | 4 | 2-0-2 | 240:00 | 12 | 0 | 3.00 | 0 | 2 | 8th |
| 2005 WM18 | 1-G | DEN | 6 | 0-0-6 | 332:19 | 22 | 0 | 3.97 | 0 | 0 | 10th |
| 2009 WM | 31-G | DEN | 1 | 0-0-1 | 60:00 | 5 | 0 | 5.00 | 0 | 0 | 13th |
| **Totals WM18** | | | **10** | **2-0-8** | **572:19** | **34** | **0** | **3.56** | **0** | **2** | **—** |

| **Dansk, Oscar** | | | | | | | | | | | **b. Stockholm, Sweden, February 28, 1994** |
|---|---|---|---|---|---|---|---|---|---|---|---|
| 2012 WM18 | 1-G | SWE | 5 | 4-0-1 | 272:47 | 9 | 1 | 1.98 | 1 | 0 | S |

| **DiPietro, Rick** | | | | | | | | | | | **b. Winthrop, Massachusetts, United States, September 19, 1981** |
|---|---|---|---|---|---|---|---|---|---|---|---|
| 1999 WM18 | 29-G | USA | 4 | 1-0-3 | 240:00 | 13 | 1 | 3.25 | 2 | 2 | 7th |
| 2000 WM20 | 29-G | USA | 5 | 2-1-2 | 298:57 | 9 | 1 | 1.81 | 1 | 2 | 4th |
| 2001 WM20 | 29-G | USA | 6 | 5-0-1 | 359:43 | 8 | 1 | 1.33 | 0 | 0 | 5th |
| 2001 WM | 1-G | USA | 3 | 0-1-2 | 179:00 | 8 | 0 | 2.68 | 0 | 2 | 4th |
| 2004 WCH | 29-G | USA | 1 | 1-0-0 | 60:00 | 1 | 0 | 1.00 | 0 | 0 | 4th |
| 2005 WM | 29-G | USA | 4 | 2-0-2 | 250:00 | 7 | 1 | 1.68 | 0 | 2 | 6th |
| 2006 OG-M | 29-G | USA | 4 | 1-0-3 | 237:06 | 9 | 0 | 2.28 | 0 | 2 | 8th |
| **Totals WM20** | | | **11** | **7-1-3** | **658:40** | **17** | **2** | **1.55** | **1** | **2** | **—** |
| **Totals WM** | | | **7** | **2-1-4** | **429:00** | **15** | **1** | **2.10** | **0** | **4** | **—** |

~WM20 IIHF Directorate Best Goalie (2000), WM20 All-Star Team/Goal (2000)

| **Divis, Reinhard** | | | | | | | | | | | **b. Vienna, Austria, July 4, 1975** |
|---|---|---|---|---|---|---|---|---|---|---|---|
| 1996 WM | 25-G | AUT | 2 | 0-1-0 | 80:00 | 6 | 0 | 4.50 | 0 | 0 | 12th |
| 1998 OG-M | 25-G | AUT | 2 | 0-0-1 | 102:11 | 6 | 0 | 3.52 | 0 | 0 | 14th |
| 1998 WM | 38-G | AUT | 3 | 0-0-2 | 160:00 | 12 | 0 | 4.50 | 0 | 0 | 15th |
| 1999 WM | 38-G | AUT | 6 | 3-0-3 | 360:00 | 19 | 1 | 3.17 | 0 | 2 | 10th |
| 2000 WM | 38-G | AUT | 6 | 2-2-2 | 358:56 | 15 | 0 | 2.51 | 0 | 0 | 13th |
| 2001 WM | 38-G | AUT | 6 | 2-0-4 | 327:16 | 19 | 1 | 3.48 | 0 | 0 | 11th |
| 2002 OG-M | 38-G | AUT | 4 | 1-0-3 | 238:21 | 12 | 0 | 3.02 | 0 | 0 | 12th |
| 2004 WM | 38-G | AUT | 6 | 1-2-3 | 358:23 | 14 | 1 | 2.34 | 0 | 0 | 11th |
| 2007 WM | 38-G | AUT | 4 | 1-0-3 | 242:22 | 18 | 0 | 4.46 | 0 | 0 | 15th |
| **Totals WM** | | | **33** | **9-5-17** | **1,886:57** | **103** | **3** | **3.28** | **0** | **2** | **—** |
| **Totals OG-M** | | | **6** | **1-0-4** | **340:32** | **18** | **0** | **3.17** | **0** | **0** | **—** |

| **Dubnyk, Devan** | | | | | | | | | | | **b. Calgary, Alberta, Canada, May 4, 1986** |
|---|---|---|---|---|---|---|---|---|---|---|---|
| 2004 WM18 | 30-G | CAN | 6 | 3-0-3 | 356:50 | 12 | 1 | 2.02 | 0 | 2 | 4th |
| 2010 WM | | CAN | 3RD GK—DID NOT PLAY | | | | | | | | |
| 2011 WM | 40-G | CAN | 1 | 0-0-0 | 13:50 | 0 | 0 | 0.00 | 0 | 0 | 5th |
| 2012 WM | 40-G | CAN | 2 | 2-0-0 | 120:00 | 2 | 1 | 1.00 | 0 | 0 | 5th |
| **Totals WM** | | | **3** | **2-0-0** | **133:50** | **2** | **1** | **0.90** | **0** | **0** | **—** |

| **Ducret, Raphael** | | | | | | | | | | | **b. Lausanne, Switzerland, January 15, 1985** |
|---|---|---|---|---|---|---|---|---|---|---|---|
| 2003 WM18 | 1-G | SUI | 5 | 1-1-3 | 300:00 | 18 | 0 | 3.60 | 0 | 0 | 9th |

| **Endras, Dennis** | | | | | | | | | | | **b. Immenstadt, West Germany (Germany), July 17, 1985** |
|---|---|---|---|---|---|---|---|---|---|---|---|
| 2010 OG-M | | GER | 3RD GK—DID NOT PLAY | | | | | | | | |
| 2010 WM | 44-G | GER | 6 | 4-0-2 | 364:06 | 7 | 1 | 1.15 | 0 | 0 | 4th |
| 2011 WM | 44-G | GER | 6 | 2-0-4 | 375:00 | 21 | 1 | 3.36 | 0 | 0 | 7th |
| 2012 WM | 44-G | GER | 6 | 2-0-3 | 317:26 | 23 | 1 | 4.35 | 0 | 0 | 12th |
| **Totals WM** | | | **18** | **8-0-9** | **1,056:32** | **51** | **3** | **2.90** | **0** | **0** | **—** |

~WM MVP (2010), WM IIHF Directorate Best Goalie (2010), WM All-Star Team/Goal (2010)

| Engren, Atte | | | | | | | | | | | b. Rauma, Finland, February 19, 1988 |
|---|---|---|---|---|---|---|---|---|---|---|---|
| 2006 WM18 | 29-G | FIN | 1 | 0-0-0 | 0:29 | 0 | 0 | 0.00 | 0 | 0 | S |

| Enkuzens, Nauris | | | | | | | | | | | b. Riga, Soviet Union (Latvia), April 18, 1989 |
|---|---|---|---|---|---|---|---|---|---|---|---|
| 2007 WM18 | 1-G | LAT | 6 | 0-0-5 | 297:26 | 27 | 0 | 5.45 | 0 | 2 | 10th |
| 2009 WM20 | 1-G | LAT | 6 | 2-0-3 | 346:18 | 25 | 0 | 4.33 | 0 | 2 | 8th |

| Enroth, Jhonas | | | | | | | | | | | b. Stockholm, Sweden, June 25, 1988 |
|---|---|---|---|---|---|---|---|---|---|---|---|
| 2005 WM18 | 30-G | SWE | 3 | 2-0-0 | 141:08 | 4 | 0 | 1.70 | 0 | 0 | B |
| 2006 WM18 | 30-G | SWE | 5 | 3-0-2 | 298:26 | 9 | 0 | 1.81 | 0 | 0 | 6th |
| 2007 WM20 | 30-G | SWE | 3 | 2-0-1 | 144:16 | 7 | 0 | 2.91 | 0 | 0 | 4th |
| 2008 WM20 | 1-G | SWE | 5 | 4-0-1 | 308:56 | 12 | 0 | 2.33 | 0 | 0 | S |
| 2012 WM | 1-G | SWE | 2 | 2-0-0 | 120:00 | 5 | 0 | 2.50 | 0 | 0 | 6th |
| **Totals WM18** | | | **8** | **5-0-2** | **439:34** | **13** | **0** | **1.77** | **0** | **0** | **—** |
| **Totals WM20** | | | **8** | **6-0-2** | **453:12** | **19** | **0** | **2.52** | **0** | **0** | **S** |

| Ermics, Raimonds | | | | | | | | | | | b. Jurmala, Soviet Union (Latvia), January 21, 1990 |
|---|---|---|---|---|---|---|---|---|---|---|---|
| 2009 WM20 | 30-G | LAT | 1 | 0-0-1 | 13:42 | 3 | 0 | 13.14 | 0 | 22 | 8th |
| 2010 WM20 | 30-G | LAT | 4 | 0-0-3 | 87:39 | 15 | 0 | 10.27 | 0 | 0 | 9th |
| **Totals WM20** | | | **5** | **0-0-4** | **101:21** | **18** | **0** | **10.66** | **0** | **22** | **—** |

| Ersberg, Erik | | | | | | | | | | | b. Sala, Sweden, March 8, 1982 |
|---|---|---|---|---|---|---|---|---|---|---|---|
| 2007 WM | 30-G | SWE | 1 | 0-0-1 | 59:08 | 4 | 0 | 4.06 | 0 | 0 | 4th |
| 2011 WM | 40-G | SWE | 2 | 0-0-2 | 125:00 | 8 | 0 | 3.84 | 0 | 0 | S |
| **Totals WM** | | | **3** | **0-0-3** | **184:08** | **12** | **0** | **3.91** | **0** | **0** | **S** |

| Esche, Robert | | | | | | | | | | | b. Utica, New York, United States, January 22, 1978 |
|---|---|---|---|---|---|---|---|---|---|---|---|
| 1998 WM20 | 31-G | USA | 4 | 2-0-2 | 237:50 | 13 | 0 | 3.28 | 0 | 20 | 5th |
| 2000 WM | 31-G | USA | 2 | 1-1-0 | 120:00 | 1 | 1 | 0.50 | 0 | 0 | 5th |
| 2001 WM | 42-G | USA | 6 | 4-0-2 | 359:11 | 13 | 0 | 2.17 | 0 | 0 | 4th |
| 2004 WCH | 42-G | USA | 4 | 1-0-3 | 237:02 | 10 | 0 | 2.53 | 0 | 0 | 4th |
| 2006 OG-M | 42-G | USA | 1 | 0-0-1 | 58:52 | 5 | 0 | 5.10 | 0 | 0 | 8th |
| 2008 WM | 35-G | USA | 4 | 2-0-2 | 198:03 | 7 | 0 | 2.12 | 0 | 0 | 6th |
| 2009 WM | 31-G | USA | 8 | 3-0-5 | 480:04 | 25 | 0 | 3.12 | 0 | 2 | 4th |
| **Totals WM** | | | **20** | **10-1-9** | **1,157:18** | **46** | **1** | **2.38** | **0** | **2** | **—** |

| Fasth, Viktor | | | | | | | | | | | b. Kalix, Sweden, August 8, 1982 |
|---|---|---|---|---|---|---|---|---|---|---|---|
| 2011 WM | 30-G | SWE | 7 | 6-0-1 | 420:00 | 12 | 3 | 1.71 | 1 | 0 | S |
| 2012 WM | 30-G | SWE | 6 | 4-0-2 | 359:36 | 14 | 2 | 2.34 | 0 | 0 | 6th |
| **Totals WM** | | | **13** | **10-0-3** | **779:36** | **26** | **5** | **2.00** | **1** | **0** | **S** |

~WM MVP (2011), WM IIHF Directorate Best Goalie (2011), WM All-Star Team/Goal (2011)

| Fedorov, Olexander | | | | | | | | | | | b. Kiev (Kyiv), Soviet Union (Ukraine), April 12, 1978 |
|---|---|---|---|---|---|---|---|---|---|---|---|
| 2002 OG-M | | UKR | 3RD GK—DID NOT PLAY | | | | | | | | |
| 2005 WM | | UKR | 3RD GK—DID NOT PLAY | | | | | | | | |
| 2006 WM | | UKR | 3RD GK—DID NOT PLAY | | | | | | | | |

| Ferhi, Eddy | | | | | | | | | | | b. Charenton-le-Pont, France, November 26, 1979 |
|---|---|---|---|---|---|---|---|---|---|---|---|
| 2008 WM | | FRA | 3RD GK—DID NOT PLAY | | | | | | | | |
| 2009 WM | 1-G | FRA | 1 | 0-0-1 | 60:00 | 7 | 0 | 7.00 | 0 | 0 | 12th |
| 2010 WM | 1-G | FRA | 2 | 0-0-2 | 108:03 | 7 | 0 | 3.89 | 0 | 0 | 14th |
| **Totals WM** | | | **3** | **0-0-3** | **168:03** | **14** | **0** | **5.00** | **0** | **0** | **—** |

| Feuk, Sebastian | | | | | | | | | | | b. Horsholm, Denmark, June 17, 1993 |
|---|---|---|---|---|---|---|---|---|---|---|---|
| 2012 WM20 | 30-G | DEN | 6 | 0-0-6 | 335:31 | 40 | 0 | 7.15 | 0 | 0 | 10th |

| Fiala, Radek | | | | | | | | | | | b. Brno, Czechoslovakia (Czech Republic), February 9, 1986 |
|---|---|---|---|---|---|---|---|---|---|---|---|
| 2006 WM20 | 1-G | CZE | 4 | 1-0-2 | 217:33 | 12 | 1 | 3.31 | 0 | 0 | 6th |

| Fleury, Marc-Andre | | | | | | | | | | | b. Sorel, Quebec, Canada, November 28, 1984 |
|---|---|---|---|---|---|---|---|---|---|---|---|
| 2003 WM20 | 1-G | CAN | 5 | 4-0-1 | 267:28 | 7 | 1 | 1.57 | 1 | 0 | S |
| 2004 WM20 | 1-G | CAN | 5 | 4-0-1 | 298:51 | 9 | 1 | 1.81 | 0 | 2 | S |
| 2010 OG-M | | CAN | 3RD GK—DID NOT PLAY | | | | | | | | |
| **Totals WM20** | | | **10** | **8-0-2** | **566:19** | **16** | **2** | **1.70** | **1** | **2** | **2S** |

~WM20 IIHF Directorate Best Goalie (2003), WM20 All-Star Team/Goal (2003)

| Flueler, Lukas | | | | | | | | | | | b. Kloten, Switzerland, October 22, 1988 |
|---|---|---|---|---|---|---|---|---|---|---|---|
| 2008 WM20 | 30-G | SUI | 1 | 0-0-1 | 59:16 | 4 | 0 | 4.05 | 0 | 0 | 9th |
| 2012 WM | | SUI | 3RD GK—DID NOT PLAY | | | | | | | | |

| Forsberg, Anton | | | | | | | | | | | b. Harnosand, Sweden, November 27, 1992 |
|---|---|---|---|---|---|---|---|---|---|---|---|
| 2012 WM20 | 1-G | SWE | 2 | 1-0-0 | 60:24 | 1 | 0 | 0.99 | 0 | 0 | G |

| Francouz, Pavel | | | | | | | | | | | b. Plzen, Czechoslovakia (Czech Republic), June 3, 1990 |
|---|---|---|---|---|---|---|---|---|---|---|---|
| 2010 WM20 | 1-G | CZE | 2 | 1-0-0 | 100:55 | 8 | 0 | 4.76 | 0 | 0 | 7th |

| Frazee, Jeff | | | | | | | | | | | b. Edina, Minnesota, United States, May 13, 1987 |
|---|---|---|---|---|---|---|---|---|---|---|---|
| 2004 WM18 | 30-G | USA | 1 | 0-0-0 | 9:29 | 0 | 0 | 0.00 | 0 | 0 | S |
| 2005 WM18 | 30-G | USA | 6 | 6-0-0 | 360:00 | 8 | 1 | 1.33 | 0 | 0 | G |
| 2006 WM20 | 30-G | USA | 1 | 1-0-0 | 60:00 | 5 | 0 | 5.00 | 0 | 0 | 4th |
| 2007 WM20 | 30-G | USA | 5 | 4-0-1 | 313:16 | 9 | 0 | 1.72 | 0 | 0 | B |
| **Totals WM18** | | | **7** | **6-0-0** | **369:29** | **8** | **1** | **1.30** | **0** | **0** | **—** |
| **Totals WM20** | | | **6** | **5-0-1** | **373:16** | **14** | **0** | **2.25** | **0** | **0** | **B** |

| Furch, Dominik | | | | | | | | | | | b. Prague, Czechoslovakia (Czech Republic), April 19, 1990 |
|---|---|---|---|---|---|---|---|---|---|---|---|
| 2007 WM18 | 29-G | CZE | 2 | 0-0-0 | 47:36 | 1 | 0 | 1.26 | 0 | 0 | 9th |
| 2009 WM20 | 1-G | CZE | 5 | 2-0-2 | 265:41 | 14 | 1 | 3.16 | 0 | 0 | 6th |

| Fyodorov, Olexander | | | | | | | | | | | b. Kiev (Kyiv), Soviet Union (Ukraine), April 12, 1978 |
|---|---|---|---|---|---|---|---|---|---|---|---|
| 2007 WM | 1-G | UKR | 3 | 0-0-1 | 84:59 | 13 | 0 | 9.18 | 0 | 0 | 16th |

| Galbraith, Patrick | | | | | | | | | | | b. Haderslev, Denmark, March 11, 1986 |
|---|---|---|---|---|---|---|---|---|---|---|---|
| 2006 WM | | DEN | 3RD GK—DID NOT PLAY | | | | | | | | |
| 2008 WM | 30-G | DEN | 4 | 1-0-2 | 197:44 | 14 | 0 | 4.25 | 0 | 0 | 12th |
| 2009 WM | 1-G | DEN | 5 | 3-0-2 | 301:06 | 14 | 0 | 2.79 | 0 | 0 | 13th |
| 2010 WM | 1-G | DEN | 5 | 2-0-3 | 298:18 | 10 | 1 | 2.01 | 0 | 0 | 8th |
| 2011 WM | 1-G | DEN | 2 | 0-0-2 | 120:00 | 10 | 0 | 5.00 | 0 | 0 | 11th |
| 2012 WM | | DEN | 3RD GK—DID NOT PLAY | | | | | | | | |
| **Totals WM** | | | **16** | **6-0-9** | **917:08** | **48** | **1** | **3.14** | **0** | **0** | **—** |

| Galimov, Stanislav | | | | | | | | | | | b. Magnitogorsk, Soviet Union (Russia), February 12, 1988 |
|---|---|---|---|---|---|---|---|---|---|---|---|
| 2006 WM18 | 30-G | RUS | 1 | 1-0-0 | 60:00 | 0 | 1 | 0.00 | 0 | 0 | 5th |
| 2008 WM20 | 30-G | RUS | 1 | 1-0-0 | 60:00 | 4 | 0 | 4.00 | 0 | 0 | B |

| Garipov, Emil | | | | | | | | | | | b. Kazan, Russia, August 15, 1991 |
|---|---|---|---|---|---|---|---|---|---|---|---|
| 2009 WM18 | 30-G | RUS | 1 | 1-0-0 | 60:00 | 1 | 0 | 1.00 | 0 | 0 | S |

| Genoni, Leonardo | | | | | | | | | | | b. Semione, Switzerland, August 28, 1987 |
|---|---|---|---|---|---|---|---|---|---|---|---|
| 2005 WM18 | 1-G | SUI | 4 | 0-0-4 | 240:00 | 11 | 0 | 2.75 | 0 | 2 | 9th |
| 2006 WM20 | 30-G | SUI | 1 | 0-0-0 | 00:26 | 0 | 0 | 0.00 | 0 | 0 | 7th |
| 2011 WM | 63-G | SUI | 2 | 0-0-2 | 123:41 | 5 | 0 | 2.43 | 0 | 0 | 9th |

| Gerber, Martin | | | | | | | | | | | b. Burgdorf, Switzerland, September 3, 1974 |
|---|---|---|---|---|---|---|---|---|---|---|---|
| 2000 WM | 1-G | SUI | 2 | 0-1-1 | 120:00 | 7 | 0 | 3.50 | 0 | 0 | 5th |
| 2001 WM | 26-G | SUI | 6 | 2-0-4 | 357:50 | 16 | 0 | 2.68 | 0 | 0 | 9th |
| 2002 OG-M | 26-G | SUI | 3 | 2-0-0 | 157:44 | 4 | 0 | 1.52 | 0 | 0 | 11th |
| 2002 WM | 26-G | SUI | 4 | 1-0-3 | 240:00 | 12 | 0 | 3.00 | 0 | 2 | 10th |
| 2004 WM | 26-G | SUI | 6 | 2-2-2 | 358:20 | 11 | 2 | 1.84 | 0 | 0 | 8th |
| 2005 WM | 26-G | SUI | 6 | 3-0-3 | 359:17 | 10 | 1 | 1.67 | 0 | 2 | 8th |
| 2006 OG-M | 26-G | SUI | 3 | 1-0-2 | 160:00 | 11 | 1 | 4.13 | 0 | 0 | 6th |
| 2008 WM | 26-G | SUI | 5 | 3-0-2 | 266:50 | 14 | 0 | 3.15 | 1 | 0 | 7th |
| 2009 WM | 26-G | SUI | 6 | 3-0-3 | 363:54 | 14 | 1 | 2.31 | 0 | 0 | 9th |
| 2010 WM | 26-G | SUI | 5 | 3-0-2 | 297:56 | 7 | 1 | 1.41 | 0 | 0 | 5th |
| **Totals WM** | | | **40** | **17-3-20** | **2,364:07** | **91** | **5** | **2.31** | **1** | **4** | **—** |
| **Totals OG-M** | | | **6** | **3-0-2** | **317:44** | **15** | **1** | **2.83** | **0** | **0** | **—** |

| Gibson, Christopher | | | | | | | | | | | b. Karkkila, Finland, December 12, 1992 |
|---|---|---|---|---|---|---|---|---|---|---|---|
| 2012 WM20 | 31-G | FIN | 2 | 1-0-1 | 120:00 | 9 | 0 | 4.50 | 0 | 0 | 4th |

| Gibson, John | | | | | | | | | | | b. Pittsburgh, Pennsylvania, United States, July 14, 1993 |
|---|---|---|---|---|---|---|---|---|---|---|---|
| 2011 WM18 | 1-G | USA | 6 | 6-0-0 | 358:52 | 14 | 0 | 2.34 | 0 | 4 | G |
| 2012 WM20 | 35-G | USA | 1 | 0-0-1 | 60:00 | 4 | 0 | 4.00 | 0 | 2 | 7th |

~WM18 IIHF Directorate Best Goalie (2011)

| Giguere, Jean-Sebastien | | | | | | | | | | | b. Montreal, Quebec, Canada, May 16, 1977 |
|---|---|---|---|---|---|---|---|---|---|---|---|
| 2001 WM | | CAN | 3RD GK—DID NOT PLAY | | | | | | | | |
| 2002 WM | 35-G | CAN | 5 | 3-0-1 | 253:43 | 8 | 0 | 1.89 | 0 | 0 | 6th |
| 2004 WM | 35-G | CAN | 2 | 2-0-0 | 120:00 | 1 | 1 | 0.50 | 0 | 0 | G |
| **Totals WM** | | | **7** | **5-0-1** | **373:43** | **9** | **1** | **1.44** | **0** | **0** | **G** |

| Gistedt, Joel | | | | | | | | | | | b. Uddevalla, Sweden, December 7, 1987 |
|---|---|---|---|---|---|---|---|---|---|---|---|
| 2007 WM20 | 1-G | SWE | 5 | 1-0-3 | 275:34 | 9 | 0 | 1.96 | 0 | 0 | 4th |

| Glass, Jeff | | | | | | | | | | | b. Calgary, Alberta, Canada, November 19, 1985 |
|---|---|---|---|---|---|---|---|---|---|---|---|
| 2005 WM20 | 33-G | CAN | 5 | 5-0-0 | 300:00 | 7 | 0 | 1.40 | 0 | 0 | G |

| Glavic, Gaber | | | | | | | | | | | b. Jesenice, Yugoslavia (Slovenia), March 11, 1978 |
|---|---|---|---|---|---|---|---|---|---|---|---|
| 2002 WM | 30-G | SLO | 4 | 3-0-1 | 240:00 | 13 | 1 | 3.25 | 0 | 2 | 13th |
| 2003 WM | 30-G | SLO | 5 | 0-1-3 | 266:40 | 23 | 0 | 5.18 | 0 | 0 | 15th |
| 2005 WM | 30-G | SLO | 5 | 2-0-3 | 272:37 | 23 | 0 | 5.06 | 1 | 0 | 13th |
| 2006 WM | 30-G | SLO | 1 | 0-0-0 | 13:23 | 4 | 0 | 17.93 | 0 | 0 | 16th |
| 2008 WM | | SLO | 3RD GK—DID NOT PLAY | | | | | | | | |
| **Totals WM** | | | **15** | **5-1-7** | **792:40** | **63** | **1** | **4.77** | **1** | **2** | **—** |

| Goryachevskikh, Stepan | | | | | | | | | | | b. Nizhnekamsk, Soviet Union (Russia), June 26, 1985 |
|---|---|---|---|---|---|---|---|---|---|---|---|
| 2005 WM20 | 25-G | BLR | 6 | 1-0-5 | 350:11 | 28 | 0 | 4.80 | 0 | 0 | 10th |
| 2005 WM | | BLR | 3RD GK—DID NOT PLAY | | | | | | | | |
| 2006 WM | | BLR | 3RD GK—DID NOT PLAY | | | | | | | | |
| 2007 WM | 33-G | BLR | 1 | 0-0-1 | 60:00 | 6 | 0 | 6.00 | 0 | 0 | 11th |
| 2008 WM | | BLR | 3RD GK—DID NOT PLAY | | | | | | | | |

| Greiss, Thomas | | | | | | | | | | | b. Cologne, West Germany (Germany), January 29, 1986 |
|---|---|---|---|---|---|---|---|---|---|---|---|
| 2005 WM20 | 1-G | GER | 3 | 0-0-2 | 103:58 | 13 | 0 | 7.50 | 0 | 0 | 9th |
| 2006 OG-M | 40-G | GER | 1 | 0-0-1 | 60:00 | 5 | 0 | 5.00 | 0 | 0 | 10th |
| 2010 OG-M | 1-G | GER | 3 | 0-0-3 | 178:51 | 15 | 0 | 5.03 | 0 | 0 | 11th |
| **Totals OG-M** | | | **4** | **0-0-4** | **238:51** | **20** | **0** | **5.02** | **0** | **0** | **—** |

| **Grinfogels, Nils** | | | | | | | | | | | **b. Dobele, Latvia, May 28, 1994** |
|---|---|---|---|---|---|---|---|---|---|---|---|
| 2012 WM18 | | LAT | 3RD GK—DID NOT PLAY | | | | | | | | |

| **Grishukevich, Leonid** | | | | | | | | | | | **b. Minsk, Soviet Union (Belarus), March 30, 1978** |
|---|---|---|---|---|---|---|---|---|---|---|---|
| 1998 OG-M | | BLR | 3RD GK—DID NOT PLAY | | | | | | | | |
| 2003 WM | | BLR | 3RD GK—DID NOT PLAY | | | | | | | | |

| **Grotnes, Pal** | | | | | | | | | | | **b. Lorenskog, Norway, March 7, 1977** |
|---|---|---|---|---|---|---|---|---|---|---|---|
| 2006 WM | 30-G | NOR | 2 | 0-0-2 | 92:55 | 9 | 0 | 5.81 | 0 | 0 | 11th |
| 2007 WM | 33-G | NOR | 6 | 2-0-4 | 358:48 | 21 | 0 | 3.51 | 0 | 0 | 14th |
| 2008 WM | 33-G | NOR | 6 | 1-0-5 | 346:02 | 26 | 0 | 4.51 | 0 | 0 | 8th |
| 2009 WM | 33-G | NOR | 5 | 1-0-3 | 241:57 | 16 | 0 | 3.97 | 0 | 0 | 11th |
| 2010 OG-M | 33-G | NOR | 4 | 0-0-4 | 226:11 | 19 | 0 | 5.04 | 0 | 0 | 10th |
| 2010 WM | 33-G | NOR | 5 | 3-0-2 | 298:39 | 14 | 0 | 2.81 | 0 | 25 | 9th |
| 2011 WM | | NOR | 3RD GK—DID NOT PLAY | | | | | | | | |
| 2012 WM | | NOR | 3RD GK—DID NOT PLAY | | | | | | | | |
| **Totals WM** | | | **24** | **7-0-16** | **1,338:21** | **86** | **0** | **3.86** | **0** | **25** | **—** |

| **Grubauer, Philipp** | | | | | | | | | | | **b. Rosenheim, Germany, November 25, 1991** |
|---|---|---|---|---|---|---|---|---|---|---|---|
| 2008 WM18 | 30-G | GER | 4 | 2-0-2 | 245:00 | 17 | 1 | 4.16 | 0 | 0 | 5th |
| 2009 WM20 | 30-G | GER | 3 | 0-0-2 | 108:57 | 12 | 0 | 6.61 | 0 | 0 | 9th |
| 2011 WM20 | 30-G | GER | 4 | 0-0-4 | 175:49 | 13 | 0 | 4.44 | 0 | 0 | 10th |
| **Totals WM20** | | | **7** | **0-0-6** | **284:46** | **25** | **0** | **5.27** | **0** | **0** | **10th** |

| **Gryaznov, Maxim** | | | | | | | | | | | **b. Temirtau, Kazakhstan, August 11, 1992** |
|---|---|---|---|---|---|---|---|---|---|---|---|
| 2009 WM20 | 1-G | KAZ | 3 | 0-0-0 | 73:29 | 10 | 0 | 8.17 | 0 | 0 | 10th |

| **Gudlevskis, Kristers** | | | | | | | | | | | **b. Riga, Latvia, July 31, 1992** |
|---|---|---|---|---|---|---|---|---|---|---|---|
| 2010 WM18 | 30-G | LAT | 6 | 1-0-4 | 339:03 | 29 | 0 | 5.13 | 0 | 0 | 9th |
| 2012 WM20 | 25-G | LAT | 5 | 1-0-4 | 279:41 | 24 | 0 | 5.15 | 0 | 0 | 9th |

| **Gundersen, Matthias** | | | | | | | | | | | **b. Seoul, South Korea, September 16, 1985** |
|---|---|---|---|---|---|---|---|---|---|---|---|
| 2006 WM | 39-G | NOR | 5 | 1-0-3 | 267:05 | 14 | 0 | 3.15 | 0 | 0 | 11th |
| 2007 WM | | NOR | 3RD GK—DID NOT PLAY | | | | | | | | |

| **Gunnarsson, Jonas** | | | | | | | | | | | **b. Eksjo, Sweden, March 31, 1992** |
|---|---|---|---|---|---|---|---|---|---|---|---|
| 2010 WM18 | 30-G | SWE | 2 | 2-0-0 | 120:00 | 4 | 1 | 2.00 | 0 | 2 | S |

| **Gustafsson, Johan** | | | | | | | | | | | **b. Koping, Sweden, February 28, 1992** |
|---|---|---|---|---|---|---|---|---|---|---|---|
| 2009 WM18 | 1-G | SWE | 2 | 2-0-0 | 120:00 | 2 | 1 | 1.00 | 0 | 0 | 5th |
| 2010 WM18 | 1-G | SWE | 4 | 3-0-1 | 238:10 | 8 | 0 | 2.02 | 0 | 0 | S |
| 2012 WM20 | 30-G | SWE | 5 | 5-0-0 | 326:51 | 12 | 1 | 2.20 | 0 | 0 | G |
| **Totals WM18** | | | **6** | **5-0-1** | **358:10** | **10** | **1** | **1.68** | **0** | **0** | **S** |

| **Gustavsson, Jonas** | | | | | | | | | | | **b. Danderyd, Sweden, October 24, 1984** |
|---|---|---|---|---|---|---|---|---|---|---|---|
| 2009 WM | 50-G | SWE | 5 | 3-0-2 | 276:04 | 13 | 0 | 2.83 | 0 | 0 | B |
| 2010 OG-M | 50-G | SWE | 1 | 1-0-0 | 60:00 | 2 | 0 | 2.00 | 0 | 0 | 5th |
| 2010 WM | 50-G | SWE | 6 | 4-0-2 | 369:35 | 11 | 0 | 1.79 | 0 | 0 | B |
| **Totals WM** | | | **11** | **7-0-2** | **645:39** | **24** | **0** | **2.23** | **0** | **0** | **2B** |

| **Hackett, Matt** | | | | | | | | | | | **b. London, Ontario, Canada, March 7, 1990** |
|---|---|---|---|---|---|---|---|---|---|---|---|
| 2012 WM | | CAN | 3RD GK—DID NOT PLAY | | | | | | | | |

| **Hadelov, Andreas** | | | | | | | | | | | **b. Kiruna, Sweden, July 23, 1975** |
|---|---|---|---|---|---|---|---|---|---|---|---|
| 2000 WM | | SWE | 3RD GK—DID NOT PLAY | | | | | | | | |
| 2001 WM | | SWE | 3RD GK—DID NOT PLAY | | | | | | | | |

| **Halak, Jaroslav** | | | | | | | | | | | **b. Bratislava, Czechoslovakia (Slovakia), May 13, 1985** |
|---|---|---|---|---|---|---|---|---|---|---|---|
| 2002 WM18 | 30-G | SVK | 7 | 3-0-3 | 416:14 | 18 | 1 | 2.59 | 0 | 0 | 8th |
| 2003 WM18 | 30-G | SVK | 7 | 5-0-2 | 429:48 | 14 | 0 | 1.95 | 0 | 0 | S |
| 2004 WM20 | 1-G | SVK | 6 | 2-1-3 | 360:00 | 14 | 2 | 2.33 | 0 | 0 | 6th |
| 2005 WM20 | 30-G | SVK | 6 | 4-0-2 | 360:00 | 13 | 2 | 2.17 | 0 | 0 | 7th |
| 2007 WM | 41-G | SVK | 2 | 1-0-1 | 118:53 | 5 | 1 | 2.52 | 0 | 0 | 6th |
| 2009 WM | 41-G | SVK | 4 | 1-0-2 | 189:15 | 10 | 0 | 3.17 | 0 | 0 | 10th |
| 2010 OG-M | 41-G | SVK | 7 | 4-0-3 | 422:38 | 17 | 1 | 2.41 | 0 | 0 | 4th |
| 2011 WM | 30-G | SVK | 6 | 2-0-4 | 354:29 | 15 | 0 | 2.54 | 1 | 0 | 10th |
| **Totals WM18** | | | **14** | **8-0-5** | **846:02** | **32** | **1** | **2.27** | **0** | **0** | **S** |
| **Totals WM20** | | | **12** | **6-1-5** | **720:00** | **27** | **4** | **2.25** | **0** | **0** | **—** |
| **Totals WM** | | | **12** | **4-0-7** | **654:37** | **30** | **1** | **2.75** | **1** | **0** | **—** |

~WM18 IIHF Directorate Best Goalie (2003), WM18 All-Star Team/Goal (2003)

| **Halasz, Tomas** | | | | | | | | | | | **b. Kosice, Czechoslovakia (Slovakia), May 25, 1990** |
|---|---|---|---|---|---|---|---|---|---|---|---|
| 2010 WM20 | 2-G | SVK | 4 | 1-0-2 | 206:21 | 14 | 0 | 4.07 | 0 | 0 | 8th |

| **Hallikainen, Joonas** | | | | | | | | | | | **b. Helsinki, Finland, October 5, 1985** |
|---|---|---|---|---|---|---|---|---|---|---|---|
| 2005 WM20 | 1-G | FIN | 3 | 2-0-1 | 116:59 | 8 | 1 | 4.10 | 0 | 0 | 5th |

| **Haloschan, Dustin** | | | | | | | | | | | **b. Oberhausen, Germany, July 2, 1991** |
|---|---|---|---|---|---|---|---|---|---|---|---|
| 2009 WM18 | 30-G | GER | 1 | 0-0-1 | 40:00 | 8 | 0 | 12.00 | 0 | 0 | 10th |

| **Hamerlik, Peter** | | | | | | | | | | | **b. Myjava, Czechoslovakia (Slovakia), January 2, 1982** |
|---|---|---|---|---|---|---|---|---|---|---|---|
| 2011 WM | | SVK | 3RD GK—DID NOT PLAY | | | | | | | | |
| 2012 WM | 2-G | SVK | 2 | 0-0-1 | 74:17 | 4 | 0 | 3.23 | 0 | 0 | S |

| **Hansen, Matthias** | | | | | | | | | | | **b. Fredrikshavn, Denmark, July 29, 1994** |
|---|---|---|---|---|---|---|---|---|---|---|---|
| 2012 WM18 | 1-G | DEN | 2 | 0-0-1 | 86:02 | 10 | 0 | 6.97 | 0 | 0 | 10th |

| **Hardy, Florian** | | | | | | | | | | | **b. Nantes, France, February 8, 1985** |
|---|---|---|---|---|---|---|---|---|---|---|---|
| 2010 WM | | FRA | 3RD GK—DID NOT PLAY | | | | | | | | |
| 2012 WM | | FRA | 3RD GK—DID NOT PLAY | | | | | | | | |

| **Harma, Antti** | | | | | | | | | | | **b. Helsinki, Finland, January 5, 1987** |
|---|---|---|---|---|---|---|---|---|---|---|---|
| 2007 WM20 | 1-G | FIN | 1 | 0-0-1 | 26:25 | 4 | 0 | 9.09 | 0 | 0 | 6th |

| **Harstad-Evjen, Halvor** | | | | | | | | | | | **b. Asker, Norway, December 10, 1981** |
|---|---|---|---|---|---|---|---|---|---|---|---|
| 2007 WM | | NOR | 3RD GK—DID NOT PLAY | | | | | | | | |

| **Haugen, Lars** | | | | | | | | | | | **b. Oslo, Norway, March 19, 1987** |
|---|---|---|---|---|---|---|---|---|---|---|---|
| 2004 WM18 | 1-G | NOR | 4 | 0-0-2 | 168:55 | 17 | 0 | 6.04 | 0 | 0 | 10th |
| 2006 WM20 | 1-G | NOR | 4 | 0-0-2 | 199:14 | 19 | 0 | 5.72 | 0 | 0 | 10th |
| 2011 WM | 30-G | NOR | 7 | 4-0-3 | 422:18 | 19 | 1 | 2.70 | 0 | 0 | 6th |
| 2012 WM | 30-G | NOR | 7 | 4-0-3 | 424:53 | 20 | 1 | 2.82 | 1 | 0 | 8th |
| **Totals WM** | | | **14** | **8-0-6** | **847:11** | **39** | **2** | **2.76** | **1** | **0** | **—** |

| **Helenius, Riku** | | | | | | | | | | | **b. Palkane, Finland, March 1, 1988** |
|---|---|---|---|---|---|---|---|---|---|---|---|
| 2006 WM18 | 30-G | FIN | 6 | 4-1-1 | 360:40 | 11 | 1 | 1.83 | 0 | 0 | S |
| 2008 WM20 | 1-G | FIN | 4 | 2-0-2 | 214:09 | 12 | 1 | 3.36 | 0 | 2 | 6th |

| **Hell, Gunther** | | | | | | | | | | | **b. Bolzano, Italy, August 30, 1978** |
|---|---|---|---|---|---|---|---|---|---|---|---|
| 2006 OG-M | 73-G | ITA | 2 | 0-0-2 | 87:32 | 8 | 0 | 5.48 | 0 | 0 | 11th |
| 2007 WM | 73-G | ITA | 4 | 1-0-2 | 236:59 | 10 | 0 | 2.53 | 1 | 0 | 12th |
| 2008 WM | 73-G | ITA | 5 | 0-0-3 | 205:33 | 17 | 0 | 4.96 | 1 | 0 | 16th |
| **Totals WM** | | | **9** | **1-0-5** | **442:32** | **27** | **0** | **3.66** | **1** | **0** | **—** |

| **Hestmann, Robert** | | | | | | | | | | | **b. Lorenskog, Norway, July 23, 1988** |
|---|---|---|---|---|---|---|---|---|---|---|---|
| 2006 WM18 | 25-G | NOR | 2 | 0-0-2 | 99:22 | 10 | 0 | 6.04 | 0 | 0 | 10th |
| 2011 WM | | NOR | 3RD GK—DID NOT PLAY | | | | | | | | |

| **Hiadlovsky, Tomas** | | | | | | | | | | | **b. Trencin, Czechoslovakia (Slovakia), December 15, 1988** |
|---|---|---|---|---|---|---|---|---|---|---|---|
| 2006 WM18 | 30-G | SVK | 4 | 1-0-1 | 187:22 | 5 | 0 | 1.60 | 0 | 0 | 7th |

| **Hiller, Jonas** | | | | | | | | | | | **b. Felben Wellhausen, Switzerland, February 12, 1982** |
|---|---|---|---|---|---|---|---|---|---|---|---|
| 2006 WM | | SUI | 3RD GK—DID NOT PLAY | | | | | | | | |
| 2007 WM | 1-G | SUI | 6 | 3-0-3 | 358:50 | 15 | 0 | 2.51 | 0 | 0 | 8th |
| 2008 WM | 1-G | SUI | 3 | 1-0-1 | 150:47 | 7 | 0 | 2.79 | 0 | 2 | 7th |
| 2010 OG-M | 1-G | SUI | 5 | 2-0-3 | 315:57 | 13 | 0 | 2.47 | 0 | 0 | 8th |
| **Totals WM** | | | **9** | **4-0-4** | **509:37** | **22** | **0** | **2.59** | **0** | **2** | **—** |

| **Hirn, Lorenz** | | | | | | | | | | | **b. Feldkirch, Austria, April 20, 1990** |
|---|---|---|---|---|---|---|---|---|---|---|---|
| 2010 WM20 | 1-G | AUT | 5 | 0-0-4 | 288:13 | 27 | 0 | 5.62 | 0 | 0 | 10th |

| **Hirsch, Peter** | | | | | | | | | | | **b. Copenhagen, Denmark, March 6, 1979** |
|---|---|---|---|---|---|---|---|---|---|---|---|
| 2003 WM | 31-G | DEN | 6 | 1-1-4 | 331:02 | 27 | 0 | 4.89 | 1 | 0 | 11th |
| 2004 WM | 31-G | DEN | 5 | 1-0-3 | 217:52 | 20 | 0 | 5.51 | 0 | 0 | 12th |
| 2005 WM | 31-G | DEN | 6 | 1-0-4 | 316:24 | 20 | 0 | 3.79 | 0 | 0 | 14th |
| 2006 WM | 31-G | DEN | 6 | 2-1-3 | 359:03 | 18 | 1 | 3.01 | 0 | 0 | 13th |
| 2007 WM | 31-G | DEN | 3 | 2-0-1 | 152:13 | 13 | 0 | 5.12 | 0 | 0 | 10th |
| 2008 WM | 31-G | DEN | 3 | 1-0-2 | 163:55 | 14 | 0 | 5.12 | 1 | 0 | 12th |
| 2010 WM | | DEN | 3RD GK—DID NOT PLAY | | | | | | | | |
| **Totals WM** | | | **29** | **8-2-17** | **1,540:29** | **112** | **1** | **4.36** | **2** | **0** | **—** |

| **Hocevar, Andrei** | | | | | | | | | | | **b. Ljubljana, Yugoslavia (Slovenia), November 21, 1984** |
|---|---|---|---|---|---|---|---|---|---|---|---|
| 2005 WM | 20-G | SLO | 1 | 0-0-0 | 26:29 | 1 | 0 | 2.27 | 0 | 0 | 13th |
| 2006 WM | | SLO | 3RD GK—DID NOT PLAY | | | | | | | | |
| 2008 WM | 1-G | SLO | 2 | 0-0-1 | 85:00 | 4 | 0 | 2.82 | 0 | 0 | 15th |
| 2011 WM | 1-G | SLO | 2 | 0-0-1 | 80:00 | 8 | 0 | 6.00 | 0 | 0 | 16th |
| **Totals WM** | | | **5** | **0-0-2** | **191:29** | **13** | **0** | **4.07** | **0** | **0** | **—** |

| **Hogberg, Marcus** | | | | | | | | | | | **b. Orebro, Sweden, November 25, 1994** |
|---|---|---|---|---|---|---|---|---|---|---|---|
| 2012 WM18 | 30-G | SWE | 2 | 1-0-0 | 87:13 | 5 | 0 | 3.44 | 0 | 0 | S |

| **Holly, Juraj** | | | | | | | | | | | **b. Svaty Jur, Czechoslovakia (Slovakia), January 21, 1991** |
|---|---|---|---|---|---|---|---|---|---|---|---|
| 2009 WM18 | 1-G | SVK | 5 | 2-0-2 | 239:54 | 23 | 0 | 5.75 | 0 | 0 | 7th |
| 2011 WM20 | 1-G | SVK | 5 | 1-0-3 | 172:27 | 11 | 1 | 3.83 | 0 | 0 | 8th |

| **Holmqvist, Johan** | | | | | | | | | | | **b. Tierp, Sweden, May 24, 1978** |
|---|---|---|---|---|---|---|---|---|---|---|---|
| 1998 WM20 | 1-G | SWE | 6 | 2-0-4 | 306:00 | 12 | 2 | 2.35 | 0 | 2 | 6th |
| 2005 WM | 30-G | SWE | 1 | 0-0-1 | 40:00 | 3 | 0 | 4.50 | 0 | 0 | 4th |
| 2006 WM | 30-G | SWE | 7 | 5-2-0 | 420:00 | 14 | 2 | 2.00 | 0 | 0 | G |
| 2009 WM | 30-G | SWE | 2 | 1-0-0 | 87:56 | 4 | 0 | 2.73 | 0 | 0 | B |
| **Totals WM** | | | **10** | **6-2-1** | **547:56** | **21** | **2** | **2.30** | **0** | **0** | **G,B** |

~WM IIHF Directorate Best Goalie (2006)

| **Holtby, Braden** | | | | | | | | | | | **b. Marshall, Saskatchewan, Canada, September 16, 1989** |
|---|---|---|---|---|---|---|---|---|---|---|---|
| 2007 WM18 | 1-G | CAN | 1 | 0-0-0 | 8:50 | 2 | 0 | 13.58 | 0 | 0 | 4th |

| **Hovinen, Niko** | | | | | | | | | | | **b. Helsinki, Finland, March 16, 1988** |
|---|---|---|---|---|---|---|---|---|---|---|---|
| 2011 WM | | FIN | 3RD GK—DID NOT PLAY | | | | | | | | |

**Howard, Jimmy** — b. Syracuse, New York, United States, March 26, 1984

| 2002 WM18 | 33-G | USA | 6 | 5-0-1 | 360:00 | 8 | 1 | 1.33 | 0 | 0 | G |
|---|---|---|---|---|---|---|---|---|---|---|---|
| 2003 WM20 | 30-G | USA | 3 | 0-0-1 | 79:17 | 8 | 0 | 6.05 | 0 | 0 | 4th |
| 2012 WM | 35-G | USA | 7 | 5-0-2 | 421:08 | 17 | 1 | 2.42 | 0 | 2 | 7th |

**Hrachovina, Dominik** — b. Brno, Czech Republic, August 29, 1994

| 2012 WM18 | | CZE | 3RD GK—DID NOT PLAY | | | | | | | | |
|---|---|---|---|---|---|---|---|---|---|---|---|

**Hudacek, Julius** — b. Levoca, Czechoslovakia (Slovakia), August 9, 1988

| 2008 WM20 | 1-G | SVK | 6 | 3-0-3 | 359:08 | 16 | 1 | 2.67 | 0 | 0 | 7th |
|---|---|---|---|---|---|---|---|---|---|---|---|
| 2012 WM | | SVK | 3RD GK—DID NOT PLAY | | | | | | | | |

**Huet, Cristobal** — b. St. Martin d'Heres, France, September 3, 1975

| 1997 WM | 1-G | FRA | 3 | 0-0-0 | 101:01 | 12 | 0 | 7.13 | 0 | 0 | 10th |
|---|---|---|---|---|---|---|---|---|---|---|---|
| 1998 OG-M | 1-G | FRA | 2 | 1-0-1 | 120:00 | 5 | 0 | 2.50 | 0 | 0 | 11th |
| 1998 WM | 1-G | FRA | 1 | 0-0-1 | 5:24 | 3 | 0 | 33.33 | 0 | 0 | 13th |
| 1999 WM | 39-G | FRA | 1 | 0-0-1 | 60:00 | 6 | 0 | 6.00 | 0 | 0 | 15th |
| 2000 WM | 39-G | FRA | 4 | 1-1-2 | 239:13 | 11 | 0 | 2.76 | 0 | 0 | 15th |
| 2002 OG-M | 1-G | FRA | 3 | 0-1-2 | 178:41 | 10 | 0 | 3.36 | 0 | 0 | 14th |
| 2004 WM | 39-G | FRA | 4 | 0-1-3 | 196:22 | 17 | 0 | 5.19 | 0 | 0 | 16th |
| 2008 WM | 39-G | FRA | 5 | 2-0-2 | 250:00 | 15 | 0 | 3.60 | 0 | 0 | 14th |
| 2011 WM | 39-G | FRA | 6 | 1-0-5 | 281:47 | 16 | 0 | 3.41 | 0 | 0 | 12th |
| 2012 WM | 39-G | FRA | 5 | 3-0-2 | 299:10 | 18 | 0 | 3.61 | 0 | 0 | 9th |
| **Totals WM** | | | **29** | **7-2-16** | **1,432:57** | **98** | **0** | **4.10** | **0** | **0** | **—** |
| **Totals OG-M** | | | **5** | **1-1-3** | **298:41** | **15** | **0** | **3.01** | **0** | **0** | **—** |

**Iilahti, Jonathan** — b. Vaasa, Finland, April 27, 1992

| 2010 WM18 | 1-G | FIN | 6 | 5-0-1 | 365:00 | 17 | 0 | 2.79 | 0 | 0 | B |
|---|---|---|---|---|---|---|---|---|---|---|---|

**Iles, Andy** — b. Ithaca, New York, United States, January 30, 1992

| 2010 WM18 | 29-G | USA | 1 | 1-0-0 | 60:00 | 1 | 0 | 1.00 | 0 | 0 | G |
|---|---|---|---|---|---|---|---|---|---|---|---|
| 2011 WM20 | 29-G | USA | 1 | 0-0-0 | 9:33 | 0 | 0 | 0.00 | 0 | 0 | B |

**Ivanov, Alexei** — b. Omsk, Soviet Union (Russia), May 4, 1988

| 2012 WM | 1-G | KAZ | 2 | 0-0-0 | 34:53 | 3 | 0 | 5.16 | 0 | 0 | 16th |
|---|---|---|---|---|---|---|---|---|---|---|---|

**Janka, Markus** — b. Wolfratshausen, West Germany (Germany), March 21, 1980

| 2002 WM | | GER | 3RD GK—DID NOT PLAY | | | | | | | | |
|---|---|---|---|---|---|---|---|---|---|---|---|

**Janus, Jaroslav** — b. Presov, Czechoslovakia (Slovakia), September 21, 1989

| 2007 WM18 | 2-G | SVK | 5 | 2-0-2 | 267:37 | 14 | 0 | 3.14 | 0 | 0 | 5th |
|---|---|---|---|---|---|---|---|---|---|---|---|
| 2009 WM20 | 2-G | SVK | 7 | 3-0-3 | 393:32 | 21 | 0 | 3.20 | 0 | 2 | 4th |

~WM20 All-Star Team/Goal (2009)

**Jensen, Dennis** — b. Esbjerg, Denmark, January 26, 1992

| 2012 WM20 | 1-G | DEN | 1 | 0-0-0 | 29:39 | 4 | 0 | 8.09 | 0 | 0 | 10th |
|---|---|---|---|---|---|---|---|---|---|---|---|

**Johnson, Chad** — b. Calgary, Alberta, Canada, June 10, 1986

| 2010 WM | 30-G | CAN | 3 | 0-0-0 | 73:21 | 1 | 0 | 0.82 | 0 | 0 | 7th |
|---|---|---|---|---|---|---|---|---|---|---|---|

**Jonas, Oliver** — b. Munich, West Germany (Germany), May 14, 1979

| 2003 WM | 1-G | GER | 3 | 2-1-0 | 180:00 | 4 | 0 | 1.33 | 0 | 0 | 6th |
|---|---|---|---|---|---|---|---|---|---|---|---|
| 2004 WCH | 1-G | GER | 1 | 0-0-0 | 29:43 | 4 | 0 | 8.08 | 0 | 0 | 8th |
| 2005 WM | 1-G | GER | 2 | 0-0-2 | 118:25 | 6 | 0 | 3.04 | 0 | 0 | 15th |
| 2007 WM | 1-G | GER | 1 | 0-0-1 | 60:00 | 5 | 0 | 5.00 | 0 | 0 | 9th |
| **Totals WM** | | | **6** | **2-1-3** | **358:25** | **15** | **0** | **2.51** | **0** | **0** | **—** |

**Jones, Martin** — b. North Vancouver, British Columbia, Canada, January 10, 1990

| 2010 WM20 | 31-G | CAN | 2 | 1-0-1 | 78:08 | 3 | 0 | 2.30 | 0 | 0 | S |
|---|---|---|---|---|---|---|---|---|---|---|---|

**Johansen, Espen** — b. Nes, Norway, February 10, 1993

| 2011 WM18 | 29-G | NOR | 2 | 0-0-0 | 21:06 | 6 | 0 | 17.06 | 0 | 0 | 9th |
|---|---|---|---|---|---|---|---|---|---|---|---|

**Jucers, Maris** — b. Priekule, Soviet Union (Latvia), June 18, 1987

| 2011 WM | | LAT | 3RD GK—DID NOT PLAY | | | | | | | | |
|---|---|---|---|---|---|---|---|---|---|---|---|
| 2012 WM | 1-G | LAT | 2 | 0-0-1 | 78:13 | 4 | 0 | 3.07 | 0 | 0 | 10th |

**Kalnins, Janis** — b. Limbazi, Latvia, December 13, 1991

| 2010 WM20 | 2-G | LAT | 6 | 1-0-2 | 272:21 | 42 | 0 | 9.25 | 2 | 0 | 9th |
|---|---|---|---|---|---|---|---|---|---|---|---|

**Kasik, Libor** — b. Zlin, Czechoslovakia (Czech Republic), March 31, 1992

| 2010 WM18 | 29-G | CZE | 5 | 1-0-4 | 241:50 | 17 | 0 | 4.22 | 0 | 0 | 6th |
|---|---|---|---|---|---|---|---|---|---|---|---|
| 2012 WM20 | | CZE | 3RD GK—DID NOT PLAY | | | | | | | | |

**Khudobin, Anton** — b. Ust-Kamenogorsk, Soviet Union (Kazakhstan), May 7, 1986

| 2004 WM18* | 20-G | RUS | 6 | 4-2-0 | 360:00 | 13 | 0 | 2.17 | 0 | 2 | G |
|---|---|---|---|---|---|---|---|---|---|---|---|
| 2005 WM20 | 30-G | RUS | 5 | 3-0-2 | 263:33 | 12 | 0 | 2.73 | 0 | 0 | S |
| 2006 WM20 | 30-G | RUS | 5 | 4-0-1 | 300:00 | 11 | 0 | 2.20 | 0 | 4 | S |
| **Totals WM20** | | | **10** | **7-0-3** | **563:33** | **23** | **0** | **2.45** | **0** | **4** | **2S** |

*scored a goal April 12, 2004 (RUS 5-FIN 2)

**Khudyakov, Denis** — b. Chelyabinsk, Soviet Union (Russia), March 8, 1984

| 2002 WM18 | 20-G | RUS | 6 | 5-0-1 | 354:48 | 16 | 0 | 2.71 | 0 | 0 | S |
|---|---|---|---|---|---|---|---|---|---|---|---|
| 2004 WM20 | 20-G | RUS | 3 | 2-0-0 | 160:00 | 4 | 0 | 1.50 | 0 | 0 | 5th |

**Kiprusoff, Miikka** — b. Turku, Finland, October 26, 1976

| 1995 WM20 | 29-G | FIN | 2 | 1-0-1 | 116:25 | 5 | 0 | 2.58 | 0 | 2 | 4th |
|---|---|---|---|---|---|---|---|---|---|---|---|
| 1996 WM20 | 1-G | FIN | 3 | 1-0-2 | 159:21 | 9 | 0 | 3.39 | 0 | 0 | 6th |
| 1999 WM | 1-G | FIN | 3 | 2-1-0 | 155:49 | 2 | 1 | 0.77 | 0 | 0 | S |
| 2001 WM | 31-G | FIN | 3 | 2-0-1 | 140:00 | 5 | 1 | 2.14 | 1 | 0 | S |
| 2004 WCH | 34-G | FIN | 6 | 4-1-1 | 363:52 | 9 | 2 | 1.48 | 0 | 2 | 2nd |
| 2010 OG-M | 34-G | FIN | 5 | 3-0-2 | 250:08 | 11 | 1 | 2.64 | 1 | 0 | B |
| **Totals WM20** | | | **5** | **2-0-3** | **275:46** | **14** | **0** | **3.05** | **0** | **2** | **—** |
| **Totals WM** | | | **6** | **4-1-1** | **295:49** | **7** | **2** | **1.42** | **1** | **0** | **2S** |

**Klein, Patrick** — b. Duisburg, Germany, January 1, 1994

| 2012 WM18 | 20-G | GER | 3 | 1-0-2 | 160:00 | 16 | 0 | 6.00 | 0 | 0 | 6th |
|---|---|---|---|---|---|---|---|---|---|---|---|

**Klempa, Martin** — b. Poprad, Czechoslovakia (Slovakia), July 20, 1973

| 1996 WM | | SVK | 3RD GK—DID NOT PLAY | | | | | | | | |
|---|---|---|---|---|---|---|---|---|---|---|---|

**Kolesnik, Vitali** — b. Ust-Kamenogorsk, Soviet Union (Kazakhstan), August 20, 1979

| 2012 WM | 20-G | KAZ | 4 | 0-0-4 | 208:25 | 18 | 0 | 5.18 | 0 | 2 | 16th |
|---|---|---|---|---|---|---|---|---|---|---|---|

**Konrad, Branislav** — b. Nitra, Czechoslovakia (Slovakia), October 10, 1987

| 2005 WM18 | 30-G | SVK | 2 | 0-0-0 | 27:06 | 0 | 0 | 0.00 | 0 | 0 | 6th |
|---|---|---|---|---|---|---|---|---|---|---|---|
| 2007 WM20 | 1-G | SVK | 5 | 1-0-3 | 269:59 | 11 | 1 | 2.44 | 0 | 0 | 8th |

**Korpisalo, Joonas** — b. Pori, Finland, April 28, 1994

| 2012 WM18 | 1-G | FIN | 6 | 3-0-3 | 357:02 | 18 | 1 | 3.02 | 0 | 0 | 4th |
|---|---|---|---|---|---|---|---|---|---|---|---|

**Koshechkin, Vasili** — b. Togliatti, Soviet Union (Russia), March 27, 1983

| 2007 WM | 83-G | RUS | 3 | 3-0-0 | 180:00 | 8 | 0 | 2.67 | 1 | 0 | B |
|---|---|---|---|---|---|---|---|---|---|---|---|
| 2010 WM | 83-G | RUS | 3 | 3-0-0 | 180:00 | 3 | 0 | 1.00 | 0 | 0 | S |
| 2011 WM | | RUS | 3RD GK—DID NOT PLAY | | | | | | | | |
| **Totals WM** | | | **6** | **6-0-0** | **360:00** | **11** | **0** | **1.83** | **1** | **0** | **S,B** |

**Kostenko, Sergei** — b. Kenerovo Region, Russia, September 17, 1992

| 2010 WM18 | 1-G | RUS | 3 | 2-0-0 | 146:16 | 5 | 0 | 2.05 | 0 | 2 | 4th |
|---|---|---|---|---|---|---|---|---|---|---|---|
| 2012 WM20 | | RUS | 3RD GK—DID NOT PLAY | | | | | | | | |

**Kotschnew, Dimitrij** — b. Karaganda, Soviet Union (Kazakhstan), June 15, 1981

| 1999 WM18 | 28-G | GER | 3 | 0-0-2 | 154:51 | 12 | 0 | 4.65 | 0 | 0 | 9th |
|---|---|---|---|---|---|---|---|---|---|---|---|
| 2007 WM | 30-G | GER | 2 | 1-0-1 | 119:49 | 3 | 1 | 1.50 | 0 | 0 | 9th |
| 2008 WM | 1-G | GER | 1 | 0-0-1 | 20:00 | 4 | 0 | 12.00 | 0 | 0 | 10th |
| 2010 WM | 1-G | GER | 1 | 0-0-1 | 59:15 | 3 | 0 | 3.04 | 0 | 0 | 4th |
| 2012 WM | 1-G | GER | 2 | 0-0-2 | 101:39 | 8 | 0 | 4.72 | 0 | 0 | 12th |
| **Totals WM** | | | **6** | **1-0-5** | **300:43** | **18** | **1** | **3.59** | **0** | **0** | **—** |

**Kotvan, Zdenko** — b. Skalica, Czechoslovakia (Slovakia), August 12, 1989

| 2007 WM18 | 30-G | SVK | 4 | 1-0-1 | 97:23 | 4 | 1 | 2.46 | 0 | 0 | 5th |
|---|---|---|---|---|---|---|---|---|---|---|---|
| 2009 WM20 | 30-G | SVK | 1 | 0-0-1 | 28:32 | 5 | 0 | 10.51 | 0 | 0 | 4th |

**Koutsky, Vladislav** — b. Nachod, Czechoslovakia (Czech Republic), April 19, 1985

| 2005 WM20 | 2-G | CZE | 1 | 1-0-0 | 60:00 | 1 | 0 | 1.00 | 0 | 0 | B |
|---|---|---|---|---|---|---|---|---|---|---|---|

**Kovac, Vladimir** — b. Topolcany, Czechoslovakia (Slovakia), April 26, 1987

| 2005 WM18 | 29-G | SVK | 6 | 2-0-4 | 332:06 | 17 | 0 | 3.07 | 0 | 0 | 6th |
|---|---|---|---|---|---|---|---|---|---|---|---|
| 2006 WM20 | 30-G | SVK | 4 | 0-0-2 | 209:38 | 12 | 0 | 3.43 | 0 | 0 | 8th |

**Koval, Vitali** — b. Perm, Soviet Union (Russia), March 31, 1980

| 2008 WM | 1-G | BLR | 6 | 1-0-5 | 370:49 | 19 | 0 | 3.07 | 0 | 0 | 9th |
|---|---|---|---|---|---|---|---|---|---|---|---|
| 2009 WM | 1-G | BLR | 2 | 0-0-2 | 120:00 | 9 | 0 | 4.50 | 0 | 2 | 8th |
| 2010 OG-M | 1-G | BLR | 2 | 1-0-1 | 120:00 | 8 | 0 | 4.00 | 0 | 0 | 9th |
| 2010 WM | 1-G | BLR | 3 | 2-0-1 | 180:00 | 7 | 0 | 2.33 | 0 | 2 | 10th |
| 2012 WM | 1-G | BLR | 5 | 0-0-4 | 266:26 | 13 | 0 | 2.93 | 0 | 2 | 14th |
| **Totals WM** | | | **16** | **3-0-12** | **937:15** | **48** | **0** | **3.07** | **0** | **6** | **—** |

**Kovar, Jakub** — b. Pisek, Czechoslovakia (Czech Republic), July 19, 1988

| 2006 WM18 | 29-G | CZE | 2 | 0-0-2 | 105:08 | 2 | 0 | 1.14 | 0 | 0 | B |
|---|---|---|---|---|---|---|---|---|---|---|---|
| 2007 WM20 | 30-G | CZE | 2 | 1-0-0 | 84:02 | 4 | 0 | 2.86 | 0 | 0 | 5th |
| 2008 WM20 | 30-G | CZE | 2 | 1-0-1 | 120:00 | 6 | 0 | 3.00 | 0 | 0 | 5th |
| 2011 WM | | CZE | 3RD GK—DID NOT PLAY | | | | | | | | |
| 2012 WM | 1-G | CZE | 6 | 4-0-2 | 351:14 | 12 | 1 | 2.05 | 0 | 0 | B |
| **Totals WM20** | | | **4** | **2-0-1** | **204:02** | **10** | **0** | **2.94** | **0** | **0** | **—** |

**Kral, Tomas** — b. Plzen, Czech Republic, December 29, 1992

| 2012 WM20 | | CZE | 3RD GK—DID NOT PLAY | | | | | | | | |
|---|---|---|---|---|---|---|---|---|---|---|---|

**Kristan, Robert** — b. Jesenice, Yugoslavia (Slovenia), April 4, 1983

| 2002 WM | | SLO | 3RD GK—DID NOT PLAY | | | | | | | | |
|---|---|---|---|---|---|---|---|---|---|---|---|
| 2003 WM | 20-G | SLO | 1 | 0-0-1 | 60:00 | 7 | 0 | 7.00 | 0 | 0 | 15th |
| 2005 WM | 31-G | SLO | 1 | 0-0-1 | 60:00 | 7 | 0 | 7.00 | 0 | 2 | 13th |
| 2006 WM | 33-G | SLO | 6 | 0-2-4 | 346:14 | 22 | 0 | 3.81 | 0 | 0 | 16th |
| 2008 WM | 33-G | SLO | 4 | 0-0-4 | 218:54 | 17 | 0 | 4.66 | 0 | 0 | 15th |
| 2011 WM | 33-G | SLO | 5 | 1-0-4 | 283:37 | 15 | 0 | 3.17 | 1 | 2 | 16th |
| **Totals WM** | | | **17** | **1-2-14** | **968:45** | **68** | **0** | **4.21** | **1** | **4** | **—** |

| **Kristin, Matej** | **b. Ilava, Czechoslovakia (Slovakia), January 24, 1990** | | | | | | | | | | |
|---|---|---|---|---|---|---|---|---|---|---|---|
| 2008 WM18 | 2-G | SVK | 3 | 1-0-2 | 185:00 | 13 | 0 | 4.22 | 0 | 0 | 7th |

| **Krizan, Karol** | **b. Zilina, Czechoslovakia (Slovakia), June 5, 1980** | | | | | | | | | | |
|---|---|---|---|---|---|---|---|---|---|---|---|
| 2000 WM20 | 1-G | SVK | 4 | 2-0-1 | 165:22 | 7 | 0 | 2.54 | 0 | 0 | 9th |
| 2004 WM | 60-G | SVK | 1 | 1-0-0 | 20:00 | 0 | 0 | 0.00 | 0 | 0 | 4th |
| 2005 WM | | SVK | 3RD GK—DID NOT PLAY | | | | | | | | |
| 2006 OG-M | 60-G | SVK | 2 | 2-0-0 | 120:00 | 1 | 1 | 0.50 | 0 | 0 | 5th |
| 2006 WM | 60-G | SVK | 7 | 3-1-2 | 379:41 | 12 | 3 | 1.90 | 0 | 2 | 8th |
| 2007 WM | 60-G | SVK | 5 | 3-0-2 | 298:21 | 16 | 0 | 3.22 | 0 | 0 | 6th |
| 2008 WM | | SVK | 3RD GK—DID NOT PLAY | | | | | | | | |
| **Totals WM** | | | **13** | **7-1-4** | **698:02** | **28** | **3** | **2.41** | **0** | **2** | **—** |

| **Kuonen, Robin** | **b. Visp, Switzerland, March 2, 1994** | | | | | | | | | | |
|---|---|---|---|---|---|---|---|---|---|---|---|
| 2011 WM18 | 30-G | SUI | 1 | 0-0-0 | 26:23 | 2 | 0 | 4.55 | 0 | 0 | 7th |

| **Kuusela, Joonas** | **b. Espoo, Finland, May 30, 1990** | | | | | | | | | | |
|---|---|---|---|---|---|---|---|---|---|---|---|
| 2008 WM18 | 31-G | FIN | 2 | 1-0-1 | 118:35 | 7 | 0 | 3.54 | 0 | 0 | 6th |

| **Kuznetsov, Alexei** | **b. Ust-Kamenogorsk, Soviet Union (Kazakhstan), February 1, 1983** | | | | | | | | | | |
|---|---|---|---|---|---|---|---|---|---|---|---|
| 2010 WM | 20-G | KAZ | 1 | 0-0-1 | 20:00 | 4 | 0 | 12.00 | 0 | 2 | 16th |

| **Laco, Jan** | **b. Liptovsky Mikulas, Czechoslovakia (Slovakia), December 1, 1981** | | | | | | | | | | |
|---|---|---|---|---|---|---|---|---|---|---|---|
| 2012 WM | 50-G | SVK | 9 | 7-0-2 | 524:10 | 19 | 1 | 2.17 | 0 | 0 | S |

~WM IIHF Directorate Best Goalie (2012), WM All-Star Team/Goal (2012)

| **Laikovski, Maxim** | **b. Grodno, Soviet Union (Belarus), December 19, 1988** | | | | | | | | | | |
|---|---|---|---|---|---|---|---|---|---|---|---|
| 2006 WM18 | 25-G | BLR | 2 | 0-0-2 | 76:06 | 18 | 0 | 14.19 | 0 | 2 | 9th |

| **Langhammer, Marek** | **b. Moravska Trebova, Czechoslovakia, July 22, 1994** | | | | | | | | | | |
|---|---|---|---|---|---|---|---|---|---|---|---|
| 2012 WM18 | 30-G | CZE | 2 | 1-0-1 | 113:09 | 9 | 0 | 4.77 | 0 | 0 | 8th |

| **Larsen, Christian** | **b. Gentofte, Denmark, May 29, 1993** | | | | | | | | | | |
|---|---|---|---|---|---|---|---|---|---|---|---|
| 2012 WM20 | | DEN | 3RD GK—DID NOT PLAY | | | | | | | | |

| **Larsson, Daniel** | **b. Boden, Sweden, February 7, 1986** | | | | | | | | | | |
|---|---|---|---|---|---|---|---|---|---|---|---|
| 2004 WM18 | 1-G | SWE | 1 | 1-0-0 | 60:00 | 4 | 0 | 4.00 | 0 | 0 | 5th |
| 2006 WM20 | 1-G | SWE | 4 | 3-0-1 | 249:26 | 4 | 1 | 0.96 | 0 | 0 | 5th |

| **Lasak, Jan** | **b. Zvolen, Czechoslovakia (Slovakia), April 10, 1979** | | | | | | | | | | |
|---|---|---|---|---|---|---|---|---|---|---|---|
| 1999 WM20 | 25-G | SVK | 6 | 4-1-1 | 359:48 | 14 | 1 | 2.33 | 1 | 2 | B |
| 2000 WM | 1-G | SVK | 4 | 2-0-1 | 199:26 | 8 | 0 | 2.41 | 0 | 4 | S |
| 2001 WM | 31-G | SVK | 3 | 0-0-3 | 179:40 | 10 | 0 | 3.34 | 0 | 2 | 7th |
| 2002 OG-M | 25-G | SVK | 2 | 0-1-1 | 93:52 | 6 | 0 | 3.84 | 0 | 0 | 13th |
| 2002 WM | 25-G | SVK | 6 | 5-0-1 | 368:53 | 14 | 0 | 2.28 | 0 | 0 | G |
| 2003 WM | 25-G | SVK | 6 | 4-1-1 | 359:20 | 11 | 0 | 1.84 | 0 | 0 | B |
| 2004 WM | 25-G | SVK | 9 | 5-2-2 | 528:37 | 9 | 3 | 1.02 | 0 | 0 | 4th |
| 2004 WCH | 25-G | SVK | 3 | 0-0-3 | 151:44 | 12 | 0 | 4.75 | 0 | 0 | 7th |
| 2005 WM | 25-G | SVK | 6 | 3-1-1 | 327:02 | 11 | 0 | 2.02 | 1 | 0 | 5th |
| 2006 OG-M | 25-G | SVK | 1 | 1-0-0 | 60:00 | 3 | 0 | 3.00 | 0 | 0 | 5th |
| 2006 WM | 25-G | SVK | 1 | 0-0-1 | 40:00 | 2 | 0 | 3.00 | 0 | 0 | 8th |
| 2008 WM | 25-G | SVK | 4 | 3-0-1 | 245:00 | 9 | 0 | 2.20 | 0 | 0 | 13th |
| 2009 WM | 25-G | SVK | 2 | 0-0-1 | 56:31 | 10 | 0 | 10.62 | 0 | 0 | 10th |
| 2011 WM | | SVK | 3RD GK—DID NOT PLAY | | | | | | | | |
| **Totals WM** | | | **41** | **22-4-12** | **2,304:29** | **84** | **3** | **2.19** | **1** | **6** | **G,S,B** |
| **Totals OG-M** | | | **3** | **1-1-1** | **153:52** | **9** | **0** | **3.51** | **0** | **0** | **—** |

| **Lassila, Teemu** | **b. Helsinki, Finland, March 26, 1983** | | | | | | | | | | |
|---|---|---|---|---|---|---|---|---|---|---|---|
| 2011 WM | 35-G | FIN | 3 | 2-0-0 | 164:26 | 6 | 0 | 2.19 | 0 | 0 | G |

| **Leclaire, Pascal** | **b. Repentigny, Quebec, Canada, November 7, 1982** | | | | | | | | | | |
|---|---|---|---|---|---|---|---|---|---|---|---|
| 2002 WM20 | 31-G | CAN | 5 | 4-0-1 | 299:25 | 9 | 2 | 1.80 | 0 | 0 | S |
| 2008 WM | 31-G | CAN | 4 | 4-0-0 | 240:00 | 8 | 1 | 2.00 | 1 | 0 | S |

~WM20 All-Star Team/Goal (2002)

| **Lee, Mike** | **b. Roseau, Minnesota, United States, October 5, 1990** | | | | | | | | | | |
|---|---|---|---|---|---|---|---|---|---|---|---|
| 2010 WM20 | 30-G | USA | 5 | 4-0-0 | 263:56 | 11 | 0 | 2.50 | 0 | 0 | G |

| **Leggio, David** | **b. Williamsville, New York, United States, July 31, 1984** | | | | | | | | | | |
|---|---|---|---|---|---|---|---|---|---|---|---|
| 2010 WM | | USA | 3RD GK—DID NOT PLAY | | | | | | | | |

| **Lehner, Robin** | **b. Gothenburg, Sweden, July 24, 1991** | | | | | | | | | | |
|---|---|---|---|---|---|---|---|---|---|---|---|
| 2009 WM18 | 30-G | SWE | 4 | 2-0-2 | 235:42 | 11 | 1 | 2.80 | 0 | 0 | 5th |
| 2011 WM20 | 30-G | SWE | 3 | 2-0-1 | 195:00 | 9 | 1 | 2.77 | 0 | 2 | 4th |

| **Lehr, Philip** | **b. Berlin, Germany, June 3, 1993** | | | | | | | | | | |
|---|---|---|---|---|---|---|---|---|---|---|---|
| 2011 WM18 | 1-G | GER | 2 | 0-0-2 | 120:00 | 13 | 0 | 6.50 | 0 | 0 | 6th |

| **Lehtonen, Kari** | **b. Helsinki, Finland, November 16, 1983** | | | | | | | | | | |
|---|---|---|---|---|---|---|---|---|---|---|---|
| 2000 WM18 | 1-G | FIN | 6 | 5-0-1 | 307:11 | 9 | 1 | 1.76 | 0 | 2 | G |
| 2001 WM18 | 1-G | FIN | 4 | 3-0-1 | 239:10 | 7 | 2 | 1.76 | 0 | 0 | B |
| 2001 WM20 | 1-G | FIN | 1 | 0-1-0 | 60:00 | 2 | 0 | 2.00 | 0 | 0 | S |
| 2002 WM20 | 1-G | FIN | 6 | 4-0-2 | 359:36 | 7 | 1 | 1.17 | 0 | 0 | B |
| 2003 WM20 | 1-G | FIN | 6 | 3-1-2 | 356:40 | 13 | 2 | 2.19 | 0 | 0 | B |
| 2004 WCH | | FIN | 3RD GK—DID NOT PLAY | | | | | | | | |
| 2007 WM | 32-G | FIN | 6 | 4-0-2 | 373:59 | 12 | 1 | 1.93 | 0 | 0 | S |
| 2012 WM | 32-F | FIN | 4 | 2-0-2 | 231:57 | 11 | 1 | 2.85 | 0 | 0 | 4th |
| **Totals WM18** | | | **10** | **8-0-2** | **546:21** | **16** | **3** | **1.76** | **0** | **2** | **—** |
| **Totals WM20** | | | **13** | **7-2-4** | **776:16** | **22** | **3** | **1.70** | **0** | **0** | **S,2B** |
| **Totals WM** | | | **10** | **6-0-4** | **605:56** | **23** | **2** | **2.28** | **0** | **0** | **S** |

~WM IIHF Directorate Best Goalie (2007), WM All-Star Team/Goal (2007), WM20 IIHF Directorate Best Goalie (2002)

| **Lhenry, Fabrice** | **b. Lyon, France, June 29, 1972** | | | | | | | | | | |
|---|---|---|---|---|---|---|---|---|---|---|---|
| 1992 OG-M | | FRA | 3RD GK—DID NOT PLAY | | | | | | | | |
| 1994 OG-M | | FRA | 3RD GK—DID NOT PLAY | | | | | | | | |
| 1997 WM | | FRA | 3RD GK—DID NOT PLAY | | | | | | | | |
| 1998 OG-M | | FRA | 3RD GK—DID NOT PLAY | | | | | | | | |
| 1998 WM | 33-G | FRA | 2 | 0-0-0 | 79:57 | 4 | 0 | 3.00 | 0 | 0 | 13th |
| 1999 WM | | FRA | 3RD GK—DID NOT PLAY | | | | | | | | |
| 2000 WM | 33-G | FRA | 2 | 1-0-0 | 94:49 | 5 | 0 | 3.16 | 0 | 0 | 15th |
| 2002 OG-M | | FRA | 3RD GK—DID NOT PLAY | | | | | | | | |
| 2004 WM | 42-G | FRA | 4 | 0-0-2 | 163:38 | 11 | 0 | 4.03 | 0 | 0 | 16th |
| 2008 WM | 42-G | FRA | 1 | 0-0-1 | 49:22 | 7 | 0 | 8.51 | 0 | 0 | 14th |
| 2009 WM | 42-G | FRA | 5 | 1-0-4 | 299:35 | 21 | 0 | 4.21 | 1 | 2 | 12th |
| 2010 WM | 42-G | FRA | 5 | 2-0-2 | 250:34 | 15 | 0 | 3.59 | 0 | 0 | 14th |
| 2011 WM | 42-G | FRA | 2 | 0-0-0 | 80:00 | 7 | 0 | 5.25 | 0 | 0 | 12th |
| 2012 WM | 42-G | FRA | 2 | 0-0-2 | 120:00 | 14 | 0 | 7.00 | 0 | 0 | 9th |
| **Totals WM** | | | **23** | **4-0-11** | **1,137:55** | **84** | **0** | **4.43** | **1** | **2** | **—** |

| **Lindback, Anders** | **b. Gavle, Sweden, May 3, 1988** | | | | | | | | | | |
|---|---|---|---|---|---|---|---|---|---|---|---|
| 2010 WM | 35-G | SWE | 1 | 0-0-0 | 00:01 | 0 | 0 | 0.00 | 0 | 0 | B |

| **Lundqvist, Henrik** | **b. Are, Sweden, March 2, 1982** | | | | | | | | | | |
|---|---|---|---|---|---|---|---|---|---|---|---|
| 2000 WM18 | 30-G | SWE | 4 | 3-0-1 | 240:00 | 9 | 0 | 2.25 | 0 | 0 | B |
| 2001 WM20 | 30-G | SWE | 7 | 3-0-4 | 418:51 | 12 | 2 | 1.72 | 1 | 0 | 4th |
| 2002 WM20 | 30-G | SWE | 7 | 3-2-2 | 419:15 | 15 | 1 | 2.15 | 1 | 0 | 6th |
| 2003 WM | | SWE | 3RD GK—DID NOT PLAY | | | | | | | | |
| 2004 WM | 35-G | SWE | 8 | 5-2-1 | 476:14 | 13 | 1 | 1.64 | 0 | 2 | S |
| 2004 WCH | | SWE | 3RD GK—DID NOT PLAY | | | | | | | | |
| 2005 WM | 35-G | SWE | 9 | 6-0-2 | 510:00 | 20 | 1 | 2.35 | 0 | 0 | 4th |
| 2006 OG-M | 35-G | SWE | 6 | 5-0-1 | 360:00 | 14 | 0 | 2.33 | 0 | 0 | G |
| 2008 WM | 30-G | SWE | 5 | 3-0-2 | 283:15 | 14 | 0 | 2.97 | 0 | 10 | 4th |
| 2010 OG-M | 30-G | SWE | 3 | 2-0-1 | 179:05 | 4 | 2 | 1.34 | 0 | 0 | 5th |
| **Totals WM20** | | | **14** | **6-2-6** | **838:06** | **27** | **3** | **1.93** | **2** | **0** | **—** |
| **Totals WM** | | | **22** | **14-2-5** | **1,269:29** | **47** | **2** | **2.22** | **0** | **12** | **S** |
| **Totals OG-M** | | | **9** | **7-0-2** | **539:05** | **18** | **2** | **2.00** | **0** | **0** | **G** |

~WM All-Star Team/Goal (2004)

| **Lundstrom, Joakim** | **b. Gavle, Sweden, February 25, 1984** | | | | | | | | | | |
|---|---|---|---|---|---|---|---|---|---|---|---|
| 2002 WM18 | 1-G | SWE | 3 | 1-0-2 | 180:00 | 8 | 0 | 2.67 | 0 | 0 | 9th |
| 2004 WM20 | 30-G | SWE | 6 | 3-0-2 | 299:08 | 7 | 1 | 1.40 | 0 | 0 | 7th |

| **Lundstrom, Niklas** | **b. Varmdo, Sweden, January 10, 1993** | | | | | | | | | | |
|---|---|---|---|---|---|---|---|---|---|---|---|
| 2011 WM18 | 30-G | SWE | 6 | 4-0-2 | 364:43 | 13 | 0 | 2.14 | 0 | 2 | S |

| **Luongo, Roberto** | **b. Montreal, Quebec, Canada, April 4, 1979** | | | | | | | | | | |
|---|---|---|---|---|---|---|---|---|---|---|---|
| 1998 WM20 | 1-G | CAN | 3 | 0-0-2 | 145:02 | 8 | 0 | 3.31 | 0 | 2 | 8th |
| 1999 WM20 | 1-G | CAN | 7 | 4-1-2 | 405:13 | 13 | 2 | 1.92 | 1 | 0 | S |
| 2001 WM | 1-G | CAN | 2 | 2-0-0 | 83:36 | 2 | 0 | 1.44 | 0 | 0 | 5th |
| 2003 WM | 31-G | CAN | 4 | 4-0-0 | 211:50 | 7 | 1 | 1.98 | 0 | 0 | G |
| 2004 WM | 1-G | CAN | 7 | 5-1-1 | 440:00 | 17 | 1 | 2.32 | 0 | 0 | G |
| 2004 WCH | 1-G | CAN | 1 | 1-0-0 | 63:45 | 3 | 0 | 2.82 | 0 | 0 | 1st |
| 2005 WM | 1-G | CAN | 2 | 1-1-0 | 120:00 | 3 | 1 | 1.50 | 0 | 0 | S |
| 2006 OG-M | 1-G | CAN | 2 | 1-0-1 | 118:58 | 3 | 0 | 1.51 | 0 | 0 | 7th |
| 2010 OG-M | 1-G | CAN | 5 | 5-0-0 | 307:40 | 9 | 1 | 1.76 | 0 | 0 | G |
| **Totals WM20** | | | **10** | **4-1-4** | **550:15** | **21** | **2** | **2.29** | **1** | **2** | **S** |
| **Totals WM** | | | **15** | **12-2-1** | **855:26** | **29** | **3** | **2.03** | **0** | **0** | **2G,S** |
| **Totals OG-M** | | | **7** | **6-0-1** | **426:38** | **12** | **1** | **1.69** | **0** | **0** | **G** |

~WM20 IIHF Directorate Best Goalie (1999), WM20 All-Star Team/Goal (1999)

| **Lusins, Edgars** | **b. Riga, Soviet Union (Latvia), December 25, 1984** | | | | | | | | | | |
|---|---|---|---|---|---|---|---|---|---|---|---|
| 2010 WM | | LAT | 3RD GK—DID NOT PLAY | | | | | | | | |

| **Lysenstoen, Andre** | **b. Oslo, Norway, October 27, 1988** | | | | | | | | | | |
|---|---|---|---|---|---|---|---|---|---|---|---|
| 2006 WM18 | 1-G | NOR | 5 | 0-2-2 | 259:04 | 19 | 0 | 4.40 | 0 | 0 | 10th |
| 2008 WM | 34-G | NOR | 1 | 0-0-1 | 60:00 | 5 | 0 | 5.00 | 0 | 0 | 8th |
| 2009 WM | 34-G | NOR | 3 | 0-0-2 | 125:51 | 9 | 0 | 4.29 | 0 | 0 | 11th |
| 2010 OG-M | 34-G | NOR | 1 | 0-0-0 | 15:31 | 4 | 0 | 15.47 | 0 | 0 | 10th |
| 2010 WM | 34-G | NOR | 1 | 0-0-0 | 14:03 | 2 | 0 | 8.54 | 0 | 0 | 9th |
| **Totals WM** | | | **5** | **0-0-3** | **199:54** | **16** | **0** | **4.80** | **0** | **0** | **—** |

| **Macek, Jakub** | **b. Bratislava, Czechoslovakia (Slovakia), June 25, 1987** | | | | | | | | | | |
|---|---|---|---|---|---|---|---|---|---|---|---|
| 2007 WM20 | 2-G | SVK | 2 | 0-0-2 | 89:00 | 10 | 0 | 6.74 | 0 | 0 | 8th |

| **Machovsky, Matej** | **b. Opava, Czech Republic, July 25, 1993** | | | | | | | | | | |
|---|---|---|---|---|---|---|---|---|---|---|---|
| 2011 WM18 | 29-G | CZE | 5 | 3-0-2 | 300:00 | 16 | 0 | 3.20 | 0 | 0 | 8th |

| **Madsen, Michael** | | | | | | | | | | | **b. Vojens, Denmark, November 21, 1980** |
|---|---|---|---|---|---|---|---|---|---|---|---|
| 2003 WM | | DEN | 3RD GK—DID NOT PLAY | | | | | | | | |
| 2004 WM | 30-G | DEN | 2 | 0-0-0 | 67:25 | 5 | 0 | 4.45 | 0 | 0 | 12th |
| 2005 WM | 30-G | DEN | 1 | 1-0-0 | 41:21 | 0 | 0 | 0.00 | 0 | 0 | 14th |
| 2006 WM | | DEN | 3RD GK—DID NOT PLAY | | | | | | | | |
| 2007 WM | 30-G | DEN | 4 | 0-0-3 | 207:09 | 15 | 0 | 4.34 | 0 | 0 | 10th |
| **Totals WM** | | | **7** | **1-0-3** | **315:55** | **20** | **0** | **3.80** | **0** | **0** | **—** |

| **Makarov, Andrei** | | | | | | | | | | | **b. Kazan, Russia, April 20, 1993** |
|---|---|---|---|---|---|---|---|---|---|---|---|
| 2012 WM20 | 20-G | RUS | 3 | 1-0-1 | 135:52 | 2 | 0 | 0.88 | 0 | 0 | S |

| **Maliutin, Maxim** | | | | | | | | | | | **b. Yaroslavl, Soviet Union (Belarus), September 16, 1988** |
|---|---|---|---|---|---|---|---|---|---|---|---|
| 2010 OG-M | | BLR | 3RD GK—DID NOT PLAY | | | | | | | | |

| **Manzato, Daniel** | | | | | | | | | | | **b. Fribourg, Switzerland, January 17, 1984** |
|---|---|---|---|---|---|---|---|---|---|---|---|
| 2001 WM18 | 20-G | SUI | 1 | 0-0-1 | 60:00 | 3 | 0 | 3.00 | 0 | 0 | S |
| 2003 WM20 | 1-G | SUI | 2 | 1-0-1 | 120:00 | 5 | 0 | 2.50 | 0 | 0 | 7th |
| 2004 WM20 | 20-G | SUI | 5 | 1-0-3 | 249:10 | 13 | 1 | 3.13 | 0 | 0 | 8th |
| 2007 WM | | SUI | 3RD GK—DID NOT PLAY | | | | | | | | |
| 2010 WM | | SUI | 3RD GK—DID NOT PLAY | | | | | | | | |
| 2011 WM | | SUI | 3RD GK—DID NOT PLAY | | | | | | | | |
| **Totals WM20** | | | **7** | **2-0-4** | **369:10** | **18** | **1** | **2.93** | **0** | **0** | **—** |

| **Markstrom, Jakob** | | | | | | | | | | | **b. Gavle, Sweden, January 31, 1990** |
|---|---|---|---|---|---|---|---|---|---|---|---|
| 2008 WM18 | 1-G | SWE | 6 | 4-0-2 | 355:09 | 18 | 1 | 3.04 | 0 | 2 | 4th |
| 2009 WM20 | 25-G | SWE | 5 | 4-0-1 | 298:07 | 8 | 1 | 1.61 | 0 | 2 | S |
| 2010 WM20 | 25-G | SWE | 5 | 4-0-1 | 298:50 | 11 | 0 | 2.21 | 0 | 0 | B |
| 2010 WM | 25-G | SWE | 3 | 3-0-0 | 180:00 | 4 | 1 | 1.33 | 0 | 0 | B |
| **Totals WM20** | | | **10** | **8-0-2** | **596:57** | **19** | **1** | **1.91** | **0** | **2** | **S,B** |

~WM20 IIHF Directorate Best Goalie (2009)

| **Martin, Spencer** | | | | | | | | | | | **b. Okaville, Ontario, Canada, June 8, 1995** |
|---|---|---|---|---|---|---|---|---|---|---|---|
| 2012 WM18 | | CAN | DID NOT PLAY | | | | | | | | |

| **Masalskis, Edgars** | | | | | | | | | | | **b. Riga, Soviet Union (Latvia), March 31, 1980** |
|---|---|---|---|---|---|---|---|---|---|---|---|
| 2002 OG-M | | LAT | 3RD GK—DID NOT PLAY | | | | | | | | |
| 2002 WM | | LAT | 3RD GK—DID NOT PLAY | | | | | | | | |
| 2003 WM | | LAT | 3RD GK—DID NOT PLAY | | | | | | | | |
| 2004 WM | 32-G | LAT | 1 | 0-0-1 | 60:00 | 3 | 0 | 3.00 | 0 | 0 | 7th |
| 2005 WM | 31-G | LAT | 2 | 0-0-1 | 76:50 | 11 | 0 | 8.59 | 0 | 0 | 9th |
| 2006 OG-M | 31-G | LAT | 1 | 0-0-0 | 32:02 | 4 | 0 | 7.49 | 0 | 0 | 12th |
| 2006 WM | | LAT | 3RD GK—DID NOT PLAY | | | | | | | | |
| 2007 WM | 31-G | LAT | 4 | 2-0-2 | 220:00 | 12 | 1 | 3.27 | 1 | 0 | 13th |
| 2008 WM | 31-G | LAT | 6 | 2-0-4 | 320:42 | 18 | 1 | 3.37 | 1 | 0 | 11th |
| 2009 WM | 31-G | LAT | 7 | 4-0-3 | 426:26 | 18 | 1 | 2.53 | 0 | 0 | 7th |
| 2010 OG-M | 31-G | LAT | 4 | 0-0-4 | 244:35 | 21 | 0 | 5.15 | 0 | 0 | 12th |
| 2010 WM | 31-G | LAT | 6 | 2-0-4 | 326:40 | 15 | 1 | 2.76 | 0 | 0 | 11th |
| 2011 WM | 31-G | LAT | 6 | 2-0-4 | 351:27 | 19 | 0 | 3.24 | 0 | 2 | — |
| 2012 WM | 31-G | LAT | 6 | 2-0-4 | 340:00 | 15 | 1 | 2.65 | 0 | 0 | 10th |
| **Totals WM** | | | **38** | **14-0-23** | **2,122:05** | **111** | **5** | **3.14** | **2** | **2** | **—** |
| **Totals OG-M** | | | **5** | **0-0-4** | **276:37** | **25** | **0** | **5.42** | **0** | **0** | **—** |

| **Mason, Chris** | | | | | | | | | | | **b. Red Deer, Alberta, Canada, April 20, 1976** |
|---|---|---|---|---|---|---|---|---|---|---|---|
| 2006 WM | | CAN | 3RD GK—DID NOT PLAY | | | | | | | | |
| 2007 WM | | CAN | 3RD GK—DID NOT PLAY | | | | | | | | |
| 2009 WM | 50-G | CAN | 4 | 4-0-0 | 240:00 | 4 | 1 | 1.00 | 1 | 0 | S |
| 2010 WM | 50-G | CAN | 7 | 3-0-4 | 342:58 | 16 | 0 | 2.80 | 1 | 0 | 7th |
| **Totals WM** | | | **11** | **7-0-4** | **582:58** | **20** | **1** | **2.06** | **2** | **0** | **S** |

| **Mason, Steve** | | | | | | | | | | | **b. Oakville, Ontario, Canada, May 29, 1988** |
|---|---|---|---|---|---|---|---|---|---|---|---|
| 2008 WM20 | 30-G | CAN | 5 | 5-0-0 | 303:36 | 6 | 1 | 1.19 | 0 | 0 | G |

~WM20 IIHF Directorate Best Goalie (2008), WM20 All-Star Team/Goal (2008)

| **Mattsson, Johan** | | | | | | | | | | | **b. Huddinge, Sweden, April 25, 1992** |
|---|---|---|---|---|---|---|---|---|---|---|---|
| 2012 WM20 | | SWE | 3RD GK—DID NOT PLAY | | | | | | | | |

| **Maxwell, Brandon** | | | | | | | | | | | **b. Winter Park, Florida, United States, March 22, 1991** |
|---|---|---|---|---|---|---|---|---|---|---|---|
| 2008 WM18 | 29-G | USA | 5 | 4-0-1 | 298:23 | 11 | 0 | 2.21 | 0 | 0 | B |

| **Mayer, Robert** | | | | | | | | | | | **b. Havirov, Czechoslovakia (Czech Republic), October 9, 1989** |
|---|---|---|---|---|---|---|---|---|---|---|---|
| 2007 WM18 | 29-G | SUI | 5 | 2-0-3 | 304:15 | 11 | 1 | 2.17 | 0 | 2 | 6th |
| 2008 WM20 | 20-G | SUI | 5 | 1-0-4 | 303:04 | 16 | 0 | 3.17 | 0 | 0 | 9th |

| **Mazanec, Marek** | | | | | | | | | | | **b. Ceske Budejovice, Czechoslovakia (Czech Republic), July 18, 1991** |
|---|---|---|---|---|---|---|---|---|---|---|---|
| 2009 WM18 | 30-G | CZE | 3 | 1-0-0 | 116:08 | 7 | 0 | 3.62 | 0 | 0 | 6th |
| 2011 WM20 | 2-G | CZE | 3 | 1-0-2 | 111:48 | 10 | 1 | 5.37 | 0 | 0 | 7th |

| **McCollum, Tom** | | | | | | | | | | | **b. Amherst, New York, United States, December 7, 1989** |
|---|---|---|---|---|---|---|---|---|---|---|---|
| 2007 WM18 | 29-G | USA | 1 | 0-0-1 | 59:15 | 4 | 0 | 4.05 | 0 | 0 | S |
| 2009 WM20 | 30-G | USA | 5 | 3-0-2 | 297:05 | 14 | 1 | 2.83 | 0 | 0 | 5th |

| **McKee, David** | | | | | | | | | | | **b. Odessa, Texas, United States, December 5, 1983** |
|---|---|---|---|---|---|---|---|---|---|---|---|
| 2006 WM | | USA | 3RD GK—DID NOT PLAY | | | | | | | | |

| **McNeely, Matt** | | | | | | | | | | | **b. Burnsville, Minnesota, United States, February 16, 1993** |
|---|---|---|---|---|---|---|---|---|---|---|---|
| 2011 WM18 | 30-G | USA | 1 | 0-0-0 | 11:36 | 1 | 0 | 5.17 | 0 | 0 | G |

| **Meili, Lukas** | | | | | | | | | | | **b. Russikon, Switzerland, January 19, 1992** |
|---|---|---|---|---|---|---|---|---|---|---|---|
| 2010 WM18 | 29-G | SUI | 5 | 3-0-2 | 268:39 | 17 | 0 | 3.80 | 0 | 0 | 5th |
| 2012 WM20 | 20-G | SUI | 2 | 0-0-2 | 113:31 | 9 | 0 | 4.76 | 0 | 0 | 8th |

| **Merzlikins, Elvis** | | | | | | | | | | | **b. April 13, 1994** |
|---|---|---|---|---|---|---|---|---|---|---|---|
| 2012 WM18 | 20-G | LAT | 4 | 1-0-1 | 184:22 | 15 | 0 | 4.88 | 0 | 0 | 9th |
| 2012 WM20 | 30-G | LAT | 1 | 0-0-1 | 60:00 | 14 | 0 | 14.00 | 0 | 0 | 9th |

| **Metsola, Juha** | | | | | | | | | | | **b. Tampere, Finland, February 24, 1989** |
|---|---|---|---|---|---|---|---|---|---|---|---|
| 2007 WM18 | 1-G | FIN | 4 | 2-0-1 | 198:38 | 7 | 0 | 2.11 | 0 | 0 | 7th |
| 2009 WM20 | 1-G | FIN | 4 | 3-0-1 | 245:00 | 6 | 0 | 1.47 | 0 | 0 | 7th |

| **Mezin, Andrei** | | | | | | | | | | | **b. Chelyabinsk, Soviet Union (Russia), July 8, 1974** |
|---|---|---|---|---|---|---|---|---|---|---|---|
| 1998 OG-M | 30-G | BLR | 6 | 2-0-4 | 355:46 | 21 | 1 | 3.54 | 0 | 2 | 7th |
| 1998 WM | 30-G | BLR | 6 | 2-0-4 | 308:23 | 20 | 0 | 3.89 | 0 | 2 | 8th |
| 1999 WM | 31-G | BLR | 6 | 4-1-1 | 360:00 | 10 | 1 | 1.67 | 0 | 4 | 9th |
| 2000 WM | 31-G | BLR | 6 | 3-0-2 | 325:12 | 17 | 0 | 3.14 | 0 | 0 | 9th |
| 2001 WM | 31-G | BLR | 3 | 0-0-2 | 140:00 | 11 | 0 | 4.71 | 0 | 0 | 14th |
| 2002 OG-M | 31-G | BLR | 7 | 1-0-4 | 309:55 | 28 | 0 | 5.42 | 0 | 0 | 4th |
| 2003 WM | 31-G | BLR | 3 | 1-0-2 | 155:40 | 8 | 0 | 3.08 | 0 | 0 | 14th |
| 2005 WM | 31-G | BLR | 5 | 2-0-3 | 297:24 | 5 | 2 | 1.01 | 0 | 2 | 10th |
| 2006 WM | 31-G | BLR | 7 | 4-0-3 | 417:01 | 14 | 0 | 2.01 | 1 | 0 | 6th |
| 2007 WM | 31-G | BLR | 5 | 1-0-3 | 277:22 | 22 | 0 | 4.76 | 0 | 0 | 11th |
| 2009 WM | 31-G | BLR | 5 | 4-0-1 | 314:05 | 9 | 0 | 1.72 | 0 | 0 | 8th |
| 2010 OG-M | 31-G | BLR | 2 | 0-0-2 | 130:00 | 7 | 0 | 3.23 | 0 | 0 | 9th |
| 2010 WM | 31-G | BLR | 3 | 1-0-2 | 183:57 | 6 | 0 | 1.96 | 0 | 0 | 10th |
| 2011 WM | 31-G | BLR | 6 | 2-0-4 | 360:46 | 19 | 0 | 3.16 | 0 | 2 | 14th |
| 2012 WM | 31-G | BLR | 2 | 1-0-0 | 69:50 | 2 | 0 | 3.44 | 0 | 0 | 14th |
| **Totals WM** | | | **57** | **25-1-27** | **3,209:40** | **143** | **3** | **2.67** | **1** | **10** | **—** |
| **Totals OG-M** | | | **15** | **3-0-10** | **795:41** | **56** | **1** | **4.22** | **0** | **2** | **—** |

~WM IIHF Directorate Best Goalie (2009), WM All-Star Team/Goal (2006, 2009)

| **Milchakov, Dmitri** | | | | | | | | | | | **b. Minsk, Soviet Union (Belarus), March 2, 1986** |
|---|---|---|---|---|---|---|---|---|---|---|---|
| 2003 WM18 | 30-G | BLR | 2 | 0-0-1 | 77:35 | 10 | 0 | 7.73 | 0 | 2 | 8th |
| 2004 WM18 | 1-G | BLR | 6 | 1-0-5 | 340:00 | 29 | 0 | 5.12 | 0 | 0 | 9th |
| 2005 WM20 | 30-G | BLR | 1 | 0-0-0 | 8:48 | 0 | 0 | 0.00 | 0 | 0 | 10th |
| 2008 WM | | BLR | 3RD GK—DID NOT PLAY | | | | | | | | |
| 2011 WM | | BLR | 3RD GK—DID NOT PLAY | | | | | | | | |
| 2012 WM | 40-G | BLR | 2 | 0-0-2 | 81:17 | 6 | 0 | 4.43 | 0 | 0 | 14th |
| **Totals WM18** | | | **8** | **1-0-6** | **417:35** | **39** | **0** | **5.60** | **0** | **2** | **—** |

| **Miller, Ryan** | | | | | | | | | | | **b. East Lansing, Michigan, United States, July 17, 1980** |
|---|---|---|---|---|---|---|---|---|---|---|---|
| 2001 WM | | USA | 3RD GK—DID NOT PLAY | | | | | | | | |
| 2002 WM | 39-G | USA | 4 | 2-1-1 | 238:13 | 7 | 1 | 1.76 | 0 | 0 | 7th |
| 2003 WM | 30-G | USA | 4 | 2-0-2 | 192:56 | 8 | 0 | 2.49 | 0 | 0 | 13th |
| 2010 OG-M | 39-G | USA | 6 | 5-0-1 | 355:07 | 8 | 1 | 1.35 | 1 | 0 | S |
| **Totals WM** | | | **8** | **4-1-3** | **431:09** | **15** | **1** | **2.09** | **0** | **0** | **—** |

~OG-M MVP (2010), OG-M IIHF Directorate Best Goalie (2010), OG-M All-Star Team/Goal (2010)

| **Mischler, Matthias** | | | | | | | | | | | **b. Jegenstorf, Switzerland, March 21, 1990** |
|---|---|---|---|---|---|---|---|---|---|---|---|
| 2010 WM20 | 20-G | SUI | 1 | 0-0-0 | 1:25 | 0 | 0 | 0.00 | 0 | 0 | 4th |

| **Miscuks, Vadims** | | | | | | | | | | | **b. Ventspils, Latvia, October 1, 1993** |
|---|---|---|---|---|---|---|---|---|---|---|---|
| 2010 WM18 | 2-G | LAT | 1 | 0-0-1 | 25:51 | 5 | 0 | 11.61 | 0 | 0 | 9th |

| **Modig, Mattias** | | | | | | | | | | | **b. Lulea, Sweden, April 1, 1987** |
|---|---|---|---|---|---|---|---|---|---|---|---|
| 2005 WM18 | 1-G | SWE | 5 | 3-0-2 | 276:48 | 13 | 0 | 2.82 | 0 | 0 | B |

| **Moller, Christian** | | | | | | | | | | | **b. Copenhagen, Denmark, December 2, 1988** |
|---|---|---|---|---|---|---|---|---|---|---|---|
| 2008 WM20 | 2-G | DEN | 3 | 0-0-2 | 145:16 | 12 | 0 | 4.96 | 0 | 0 | 10th |

| **Montoya, Al** | | | | | | | | | | | **b. Chicago, Illinois, United States, February 13, 1985** |
|---|---|---|---|---|---|---|---|---|---|---|---|
| 2004 WM20 | 29-G | USA | 6 | 6-0-0 | 360:00 | 8 | 2 | 1.33 | 0 | 0 | G |
| 2005 WM20 | 29-G | USA | 7 | 3-0-4 | 393:15 | 22 | 0 | 3.36 | 0 | 0 | 4th |
| 2009 WM | 35-G | USA | 1 | 1-0-0 | 60:00 | 2 | 0 | 2.00 | 0 | 0 | 4th |
| 2011 WM | 35-G | USA | 4 | 2-0-1 | 207:59 | 9 | 0 | 2.60 | 0 | 0 | 8th |
| **Totals WM** | | | **5** | **3-0-1** | **267:59** | **11** | **0** | **2.46** | **0** | **0** | **—** |
| **Totals WM20** | | | **13** | **9-0-4** | **753:15** | **30** | **2** | **2.39** | **0** | **0** | **G** |

~WM20 IIHF Directorate Best Goalie (2004), WM20 All-Star Team/Goal (2004)

| **Mrazek, Petr** | | | | | | | | | | | **b. Ostrava, Czech Republic, February 14, 1992** |
|---|---|---|---|---|---|---|---|---|---|---|---|
| 2012 WM20 | 2-G | CZE | 6 | 3-0-3 | 361:30 | 15 | 1 | 2.49 | 0 | 0 | 5th |
| 2012 WM | 29-G | CZE | 1 | 0-0-0 | 9:12 | 0 | 0 | 0.00 | 0 | 0 | B |

~WM20 IIHF Directorate Best Goalie (2012), WM20 All-Star Team/Goal (2012)

| **Murray, Adam** | | | | | | | | | | | **b. Anchorage, Alaska, United States, March 28, 1991** |
|---|---|---|---|---|---|---|---|---|---|---|---|
| 2009 WM18 | 30-G | USA | 3 | 2-0-1 | 178:24 | 9 | 0 | 3.03 | 0 | 0 | G |

| **Murray, Matt** | | | | | | | | | | | **b. Fond du Lac, Wisconsin, United States, January 26, 1978** |
|---|---|---|---|---|---|---|---|---|---|---|---|
| 2012 WM18 | 30-G | CAN | 7 | 4-0-3 | 419:51 | 19 | 0 | 2.72 | 0 | 0 | |

| **Mustukovs, Ervins** | | | | | | | | | | | **b. Riga, Soviet Union (Latvia), April 7, 1984** |
|---|---|---|---|---|---|---|---|---|---|---|---|
| 2010 OG-M | | LAT | 3RD GK—DID NOT PLAY | | | | | | | | |
| 2012 WM | | LAT | 3RD GK—DID NOT PLAY | | | | | | | | |

| **Nabokov, Yevgeni** | | | | | | | | | | | **b. Ust-Kamenogorsk, Soviet Union (Kazakhstan), July 25, 1975** |
|---|---|---|---|---|---|---|---|---|---|---|---|
| 2006 OG-M | 20-G | RUS | 7 | 4-0-2 | 359:27 | 8 | 3 | 1.34 | 0 | 0 | 4th |
| 2008 WM | 20-G | RUS | 5 | 5-0-0 | 302:42 | 9 | 2 | 1.78 | 1 | 0 | G |
| 2010 OG-M | 20-G | RUS | 3 | 2-0-1 | 144:07 | 10 | 0 | 4.16 | 0 | 0 | 6th |
| 2011 WM | 20-G | RUS | 4 | 2-0-1 | 199:45 | 12 | 0 | 3.60 | 0 | 0 | 4th |
| **Totals WM** | | | **9** | **7-0-1** | **502:27** | **21** | **2** | **2.51** | **1** | **0** | **G** |
| **Totals OG-M** | | | **10** | **6-0-3** | **503:34** | **18** | **3** | **2.14** | **0** | **0** | **—** |

~WM IIHF Directorate Best Goalie (2008), WM All-Star Team/Goal (2008)

| **Nalimov, Ivan** | | | | | | | | | | | **b. Novokuznetsk, Russia, August 12, 1994** |
|---|---|---|---|---|---|---|---|---|---|---|---|
| 2012 WM18 | 29-G | RUS | 1 | 1-0-0 | 60:00 | 1 | 0 | 1.00 | 0 | 0 | 5th |

| **Neuvirth, Michal** | | | | | | | | | | | **b. Usti nad Laben, Czechoslovakia (Czech Republic), March 23, 1988** |
|---|---|---|---|---|---|---|---|---|---|---|---|
| 2006 WM18 | 30-G | CZE | 5 | 3-1-2 | 320:00 | 13 | 0 | 2.44 | 1 | 0 | B |
| 2008 WM20 | 29-G | CZE | 4 | 2-0-2 | 240:00 | 10 | 0 | 2.50 | 0 | 2 | 5th |

| **Nielsen, Simon** | | | | | | | | | | | **b. Herning, Denmark, October 27, 1986** |
|---|---|---|---|---|---|---|---|---|---|---|---|
| 2011 WM | | DEN | 3RD GK—DID NOT PLAY | | | | | | | | |
| 2012 WM | 31-G | DEN | 1 | 0-0-1 | 59:15 | 3 | 0 | 3.04 | 0 | 0 | 13th |

| **Niittymaki, Antero** | | | | | | | | | | | **b. Turku, Finland, June 18, 1980** |
|---|---|---|---|---|---|---|---|---|---|---|---|
| 2000 WM20 | 1-G | FIN | 5 | 1-1-2 | 244:48 | 10 | 0 | 2.45 | 0 | 0 | 7th |
| 2006 OG-M | 31-G | FIN | 6 | 5-0-1 | 358:51 | 8 | 3 | 1.34 | 0 | 0 | S |
| 2006 WM | 31-G | FIN | 4 | 2-1-1 | 211:51 | 6 | 2 | 1.70 | 0 | 2 | B |
| 2010 OG-M | | FIN | 3RD GK—DID NOT PLAY | | | | | | | | |

~OG-M MVP (2006), OG-M IIHF Directorate Best Goalie (2006), OG-M All-Star Team/Goal (2006)

| **Nilsson, Anders** | | | | | | | | | | | **b. Lulea, Sweden, March 19, 1990** |
|---|---|---|---|---|---|---|---|---|---|---|---|
| 2010 WM20 | 1-G | SWE | 1 | 1-0-0 | 60:00 | 3 | 0 | 3.00 | 0 | 0 | B |
| 2011 WM | | SWE | 3RD GK—DID NOT PLAY | | | | | | | | |

| **Nilstorp, Christopher** | | | | | | | | | | | **b. Malmo, Sweden, February 16, 1984** |
|---|---|---|---|---|---|---|---|---|---|---|---|
| 2012 WM | | SWE | 3RD GK—DID NOT PLAY | | | | | | | | |

| **Norbak, Nikolaj** | | | | | | | | | | | **b. Frederikshavn, Denmark, April 7, 1990** |
|---|---|---|---|---|---|---|---|---|---|---|---|
| 2008 WM18 | 1-G | DEN | 5 | 0-0-5 | 274:13 | 23 | 0 | 5.03 | 0 | 2 | 10th |

| **Novotny, Filip** | | | | | | | | | | | **b. Pelhrimov, Czechoslovakia (Czech Republic), May 6, 1991** |
|---|---|---|---|---|---|---|---|---|---|---|---|
| 2009 WM18 | 1-G | CZE | 5 | 0-0-5 | 245:07 | 19 | 0 | 4.65 | 0 | 4 | 6th |
| 2011 WM20 | 1-G | CZE | 5 | 2-0-1 | 248:12 | 15 | 0 | 3.63 | 0 | 2 | 7th |

| **Nyffeler, Melvin** | | | | | | | | | | | **b. Dubendorf, Switzerland, December 16, 1994** |
|---|---|---|---|---|---|---|---|---|---|---|---|
| 2012 WM18 | 30-G | SUI | 5 | 2-0-3 | 258:13 | 17 | 0 | 3.95 | 0 | 27 | 7th |

| **Nygård, Chris-Henrik** | | | | | | | | | | | **b. Fredrikstad, Norway, April 10, 1991** |
|---|---|---|---|---|---|---|---|---|---|---|---|
| 2009 WM18 | 29-G | NOR | 3 | 0-0-3 | 138:07 | 17 | 0 | 7.39 | 0 | 0 | 9th |

| **Olson, Collin** | | | | | | | | | | | **b. Apple Valley, Minnesota, United States, April 4, 1994** |
|---|---|---|---|---|---|---|---|---|---|---|---|
| 2012 WM18 | 29-G | USA | 5 | 5-0-0 | 300:00 | 4 | 3 | 0.80 | 0 | 0 | G |

~WM18 IIHF Directorate Best Goaltender (2012)

| **Ortio, Joni** | | | | | | | | | | | **b. Turku, Finland, April 16, 1991** |
|---|---|---|---|---|---|---|---|---|---|---|---|
| 2009 WM18 | 31-G | FIN | 5 | 3-0-2 | 308:55 | 15 | 1 | 2.91 | 0 | 0 | B |
| 2010 WM20 | 1-G | FIN | 6 | 3-0-3 | 317:44 | 16 | 0 | 3.02 | 2 | 0 | 5th |
| 2011 WM20 | 31-G | FIN | 6 | 3-0-3 | 354:52 | 11 | 1 | 1.86 | 0 | 0 | 6th |
| **Totals WM20** | | | **12** | **6-0-6** | **672:36** | **27** | **1** | **2.41** | **2** | **0** | **—** |

| **Owuya, Mark** | | | | | | | | | | | **b. Stockholm, Sweden, July 18, 1989** |
|---|---|---|---|---|---|---|---|---|---|---|---|
| 2007 WM18 | 1-G | SWE | 6 | 4-0-2 | 345:00 | 13 | 2 | 2.26 | 0 | 0 | B |
| 2009 WM20 | 30-G | SWE | 1 | 1-0-0 | 60:00 | 1 | 0 | 1.00 | 0 | 0 | S |

| **Palmer, Joe** | | | | | | | | | | | **b. Utica, New York, United States, February 19, 1988** |
|---|---|---|---|---|---|---|---|---|---|---|---|
| 2006 WM18 | 30-G | USA | 4 | 4-0-0 | 246:50 | 6 | 1 | 1.46 | 1 | 0 | G |
| 2008 WM20 | 34-G | USA | 2 | 0-0-0 | 60:00 | 4 | 0 | 4.00 | 0 | 0 | 4th |

| **Patzold, Dimitri** | | | | | | | | | | | **b. Ust-Kamenogorsk, Soviet Union (Kazakhstan), February 3, 1983** |
|---|---|---|---|---|---|---|---|---|---|---|---|
| 2000 WM18 | 30-G | GER | 6 | 2-1-3 | 360:00 | 16 | 1 | 2.67 | 0 | 0 | 7th |
| 2001 WM18 | 30-G | GER | 6 | 3-1-2 | 360:00 | 20 | 0 | 3.33 | 0 | 0 | 5th |
| 2003 WM20 | 30-G | GER | 5 | 0-0-5 | 245:37 | 21 | 0 | 5.13 | 0 | 2 | 9th |
| 2007 WM | 40-G | GER | 3 | 2-0-1 | 180:00 | 11 | 0 | 3.67 | 0 | 0 | 9th |
| 2008 WM | 32-G | GER | 3 | 1-0-2 | 178:28 | 13 | 0 | 4.37 | 0 | 0 | 10th |
| 2009 WM | 32-G | GER | 6 | 1-0-5 | 357:46 | 15 | 0 | 2.52 | 0 | 0 | 15th |
| 2010 OG-M | 32-G | GER | 1 | 0-0-1 | 60:00 | 5 | 0 | 5.00 | 0 | 0 | 11th |
| 2011 WM | 32-G | GER | 1 | 1-0-0 | 60:00 | 3 | 0 | 3.00 | 0 | 0 | 7th |
| 2012 WM | | GER | 3RD GK—DID NOT PLAY | | | | | | | | |
| **Totals WM18** | | | **12** | **5-2-5** | **720:00** | **36** | **1** | **3.00** | **0** | **0** | **—** |
| **Totals WM** | | | **13** | **5-0-8** | **776:14** | **42** | **0** | **3.25** | **0** | **0** | **—** |

| **Pavelec, Ondrej** | | | | | | | | | | | **b. Kladno, Czechoslovakia (Czech Republic), August 31, 1987** |
|---|---|---|---|---|---|---|---|---|---|---|---|
| 2005 WM18 | 1-G | CZE | 7 | 4-0-3 | 380:51 | 13 | 1 | 2.05 | 0 | 0 | 4th |
| 2007 WM20 | 1-G | CZE | 5 | 2-0-3 | 274:35 | 15 | 0 | 3.28 | 0 | 0 | 5th |
| 2010 WM | 31-G | CZE | 1 | 0-0-1 | 59:05 | 3 | 0 | 3.05 | 0 | 0 | G |
| 2010 OG-M | | CZE | 3RD GK—DID NOT PLAY | | | | | | | | |
| 2011 WM | 31-G | CZE | 8 | 7-0-1 | 479:16 | 15 | 2 | 1.88 | 0 | 0 | B |
| **Totals WM** | | | **9** | **7-0-2** | **538:21** | **18** | **2** | **2.01** | **0** | **0** | **G,B** |

| **Pavelka, Jaroslav** | | | | | | | | | | | **b. Hradec Kralove, Czech Republic, September 12, 1993** |
|---|---|---|---|---|---|---|---|---|---|---|---|
| 2011 WM18 | 1-G | CZE | 1 | 0-0-1 | 58:46 | 4 | 0 | 4.08 | 0 | 0 | 8th |

| **Pechurski, Alexander** | | | | | | | | | | | **b. Magnitogorsk, Soviet Union (Russia), June 4, 1990** |
|---|---|---|---|---|---|---|---|---|---|---|---|
| 2007 WM18 | 29-G | RUS | 3 | 1-0-0 | 76:31 | 5 | 0 | 3.92 | 0 | 0 | G |
| 2008 WM18 | 29-G | RUS | 5 | 4-0-1 | 215:55 | 11 | 0 | 3.06 | 0 | 0 | S |
| **Totals WM18** | | | **8** | **5-0-1** | **292:26** | **16** | **0** | **3.28** | **0** | **0** | **—** |

| **Pek, Tomas** | | | | | | | | | | | **b. Bratislava, Czechoslovakia (Slovakia), May 30, 1991** |
|---|---|---|---|---|---|---|---|---|---|---|---|
| 2009 WM18 | 30-G | SVK | 4 | 0-0-2 | 125:06 | 12 | 0 | 5.76 | 0 | 0 | 7th |

| **Penker, Jurgen** | | | | | | | | | | | **b. Bregenz, Austria, October 17, 1982** |
|---|---|---|---|---|---|---|---|---|---|---|---|
| 2005 WM | 31-G | AUT | 1 | 0-0-0 | 10:35 | 1 | 0 | 5.67 | 0 | 0 | 16th |
| 2009 WM | 29-G | AUT | 1 | 0-0-1 | 60:00 | 6 | 0 | 6.00 | 0 | 0 | 14th |
| 2011 WM | 29-G | AUT | 3 | 0-0-3 | 140:00 | 13 | 0 | 5.57 | 0 | 0 | 15th |
| **Totals WM** | | | **5** | **0-0-4** | **210:35** | **20** | **0** | **5.70** | **0** | **0** | **—** |

| **Perhonen, Samu** | | | | | | | | | | | **b. Jamsankoski, Finland, March 7, 1993** |
|---|---|---|---|---|---|---|---|---|---|---|---|
| 2011 WM18 | 1-G | FIN | 4 | 2-0-2 | 238:41 | 14 | 0 | 3.52 | 0 | 6 | 5th |

| **Petrik, Imrich** | | | | | | | | | | | **b. Michalovce, Czechoslovakia (Slovakia), July 2, 1983** |
|---|---|---|---|---|---|---|---|---|---|---|---|
| 2001 WM18 | 1-G | SVK | 6 | 1-1-4 | 323:09 | 23 | 0 | 4.27 | 0 | 0 | 8th |

| **Petersson-Wentzel, Fredrik** | | | | | | | | | | | **b. Uppsala, Sweden, July 23, 1991** |
|---|---|---|---|---|---|---|---|---|---|---|---|
| 2011 WM20 | 1-G | SWE | 3 | 2-0-1 | 178:30 | 8 | 0 | 2.69 | 0 | 0 | 4th |

| **Pickard, Cal** | | | | | | | | | | | **b. Winnipeg, Manitoba, Canada, April 15, 1992** |
|---|---|---|---|---|---|---|---|---|---|---|---|
| 2010 WM18 | 1-G | CAN | 6 | 3-0-3 | 313:50 | 15 | 0 | 2.87 | 0 | 0 | 7th |

| **Pickard, Chet** | | | | | | | | | | | **b. Winnipeg, Manitoba, Canada, November 29, 1989** |
|---|---|---|---|---|---|---|---|---|---|---|---|
| 2009 WM20 | 31-G | CAN | 2 | 2-0-0 | 120:00 | 1 | 1 | 0.50 | 0 | 0 | G |

| **Pielmeier, Timo** | | | | | | | | | | | **b. Deggendorf, West Germany (Germany), July 7, 1989** |
|---|---|---|---|---|---|---|---|---|---|---|---|
| 2006 WM18 | 1-G | GER | 6 | 1-1-4 | 339:45 | 25 | 0 | 4.42 | 0 | 0 | 8th |
| 2007 WM18 | 1-G | GER | 6 | 2-0-3 | 329:52 | 21 | 0 | 3.82 | 0 | 0 | 8th |
| 2007 WM20 | 2-G | GER | 1 | 0-0-1 | 60:00 | 3 | 0 | 3.00 | 0 | 0 | 9th |
| 2009 WM20 | 1-G | GER | 5 | 1-0-3 | 251:03 | 17 | 1 | 4.06 | 0 | 0 | 9th |
| Totals WM18 | 12 | 3-1-7669:37 | 46 | 0 | 4.12 | 0 | 0 | — | | | |
| **Totals WM20** | | | **6** | **1-0-4** | **311:03** | **20** | **1** | **3.86** | **0** | **0** | **—** |

| **Pinc, Marek** | | | | | | | | | | | **b. Most, Czechoslovakia (Czech Republic), March 20, 1979** |
|---|---|---|---|---|---|---|---|---|---|---|---|
| 2007 WM | 79-G | CZE | 1 | 0-0-1 | 0:23 | 1 | 0 | 156.52 | 0 | 0 | 7th |
| 2008 WM | 97-G | CZE | 1 | 1-0-0 | 60:00 | 2 | 0 | 2.00 | 0 | 0 | 5th |
| **Totals WM** | | | **2** | **1-0-1** | **60:23** | **3** | **0** | **2.98** | **0** | **0** | **—** |

| **Pintaric, Matija** | | | | | | | | | | | **b. Maribor, (Yugoslavia), Slovenia, August 11, 1989** |
|---|---|---|---|---|---|---|---|---|---|---|---|
| 2011 WM | | SLO | 3RD GK—DID NOT PLAY | | | | | | | | |

| **Pogge, Justin** | | | | | | | | | | | **b. Fort McMurray, Alberta, Canada, April 22, 1986** |
|---|---|---|---|---|---|---|---|---|---|---|---|
| 2004 WM18 | 1-G | CAN | 1 | 1-0-0 | 60:00 | 2 | 0 | 2.00 | 0 | 0 | 4th |
| 2006 WM20 | 33-G | CAN | 6 | 6-0-0 | 360:00 | 6 | 3 | 1.00 | 1 | 0 | G |

| **Polivka, Patrik** | | | | | | | | | | | **b. Plzen, Czech Republic, March 4, 1994** |
|---|---|---|---|---|---|---|---|---|---|---|---|
| 2012 WM18 | 1-G | CZE | 5 | 1-0-3 | 246:51 | 20 | 0 | 4.86 | 0 | 0 | 8th |

| **Price, Carey** | | | | | | | | | | | **b. Anahim Lake, British Columbia, Canada, August 16, 1987** |
|---|---|---|---|---|---|---|---|---|---|---|---|
| 2005 WM18 | 1-G | CAN | 4 | 2-0-2 | 248:36 | 11 | 0 | 2.65 | 0 | 0 | S |
| 2007 WM20 | 1-G | CAN | 6 | 6-0-0 | 370:00 | 7 | 2 | 1.14 | 0 | 0 | G |

~WM20 IIHF Directorate Best Goalie (2007), WM20 All-Star Team/Goal (2007)

| **Pronin, Valeri** | | | | | | | | | | | **b. Togliatti, Soviet Union (Russia), April 26, 1988** |
|---|---|---|---|---|---|---|---|---|---|---|---|
| 2007 WM20 | 30-G | BLR | 6 | 2-0-3 | 319:25 | 19 | 0 | 3.57 | 0 | 2 | 10th |

| **Proskuryakov, Ilya** | | | | | | | | | | | **b. Surgut, Soviet Union (Russia), February 21, 1987** |
|---|---|---|---|---|---|---|---|---|---|---|---|
| 2005 WM18 | 30-G | RUS | 4 | 2-0-1 | 180:06 | 9 | 0 | 3.00 | 0 | 4 | 5th |

| **Prusek, Martin** | | | | | | | | | | | **b. Ostrava, Czechoslovakia (Czech Republic), December 11, 1975** |
|---|---|---|---|---|---|---|---|---|---|---|---|
| 1997 WM | | CZE | 3RD GK—DID NOT PLAY | | | | | | | | |
| 1998 WM | | CZE | 3RD GK—DID NOT PLAY | | | | | | | | |
| 1999 WM | | CZE | 3RD GK—DID NOT PLAY | | | | | | | | |
| 2009 WM | CZE | 25-G | 3 | 2-0-0 | 136:01 | 4 | 0 | 1.76 | 0 | 0 | 6th |

| **Punnenovs, Ivars** | | | | | | | | | | | **b. Riga, Latvia, May 30, 1994** |
|---|---|---|---|---|---|---|---|---|---|---|---|
| 2012 WM18 | 1-G | LAT | 4 | 1-0-3 | 178:07 | 10 | 0 | 3.37 | 0 | 0 | 9th |

| Quemener, Ronan | | | | | | | | | | | b. Paris, France, February 13, 1988 |
|---|---|---|---|---|---|---|---|---|---|---|---|
| 2011 WM | | FRA | 3RD GK—DID NOT PLAY | | | | | | | | |

| Quick, Jonathan | | | | | | | | | | | b. Milford, Connecticut, United States, January 21, 1986 |
|---|---|---|---|---|---|---|---|---|---|---|---|
| 2010 OG-M | | USA | 3RD GK—DID NOT PLAY | | | | | | | | |

| Raitums, Martins | | | | | | | | | | | b. Talsi, Soviet Union (Latvia), April 14, 1985 |
|---|---|---|---|---|---|---|---|---|---|---|---|
| 2005 WM | | LAT | 3RD GK—DID NOT PLAY | | | | | | | | |
| 2006 WM | 1-G | LAT | 1 | 0-0-0 | 44:40 | 8 | 0 | 10.75 | 0 | 0 | 10th |
| 2007 WM | | LAT | 3RD GK—DID NOT PLAY | | | | | | | | |
| 2010 WM | 1-G | LAT | 1 | 0-0-0 | 32:25 | 2 | 0 | 3.70 | 0 | 0 | 11th |
| 2011 WM | 30-G | LAT | 1 | 0-0-0 | 18:33 | 0 | 0 | 0.00 | 0 | 0 | 13th |
| **Totals WM** | | | **3** | **0-0-0** | **95:38** | **10** | **0** | **6.27** | **0** | **0** | **—** |

| Ramo, Karri | | | | | | | | | | | b. Asikkala, Finland, July 1, 1986 |
|---|---|---|---|---|---|---|---|---|---|---|---|
| 2004 WM18 | 1-G | FIN | 1 | 1-0-0 | 60:00 | 1 | 0 | 1.00 | 0 | 0 | 7th |
| 2006 WM20 | 1-G | FIN | 1 | 0-0-1 | 57:59 | 6 | 0 | 6.21 | 0 | 0 | B |
| 2008 WM | | FIN | 3RD GK—DID NOT PLAY | | | | | | | | |
| 2009 WM | 31-G | FIN | 1 | 1-0-0 | 60:00 | 1 | 0 | 1.00 | 0 | 0 | 5th |
| 2012 WM | | FIN | 3RD GK—DID NOT PLAY | | | | | | | | |

| Rask, Tuukka | | | | | | | | | | | b. Savonlinna, Finland, March 10, 1987 |
|---|---|---|---|---|---|---|---|---|---|---|---|
| 2004 WM18 | 31-G | FIN | 5 | 2-2-1 | 298:42 | 8 | 0 | 1.61 | 0 | 0 | 7th |
| 2005 WM18 | 30-G | FIN | 5 | 2-0-3 | 278:07 | 14 | 0 | 3.02 | 0 | 0 | 7th |
| 2005 WM20 | 30-G | FIN | 5 | 1-0-2 | 243:26 | 12 | 0 | 2.96 | 0 | 0 | 5th |
| 2006 WM20 | 30-G | FIN | 6 | 4-0-2 | 369:26 | 13 | 1 | 2.11 | 0 | 2 | B |
| 2007 WM20 | 30-G | FIN | 6 | 2-0-3 | 332:14 | 19 | 1 | 3.43 | 0 | 0 | 6th |
| **Totals WM18** | | | **10** | **4-2-4** | **576:49** | **22** | **0** | **2.29** | **0** | **0** | **—** |
| **Totals WM20** | | | **17** | **7-0-7** | **945:06** | **44** | **2** | **2.79** | **0** | **2** | **B** |

~WM20 IIHF Directorate Best Goalie (2006), WM20 All-Star Team/Goal (2006)

| Rautio, David | | | | | | | | | | | b. Lulea, Sweden, July 8, 1985 |
|---|---|---|---|---|---|---|---|---|---|---|---|
| 2005 WM20 | 1-G | SWE | 4 | 1-0-2 | 197:36 | 13 | 1 | 3.95 | 0 | 0 | 6th |

| Reimer, James | | | | | | | | | | | b. Morweena, Manitoba, Canada, March 15, 1988 |
|---|---|---|---|---|---|---|---|---|---|---|---|
| 2011 WM | 34-G | CAN | 4 | 4-0-0 | 235:24 | 8 | 0 | 2.04 | 0 | 0 | 5th |

| Reimer, Jochen | | | | | | | | | | | b. Mindelheim, Germany, September 6, 1985 |
|---|---|---|---|---|---|---|---|---|---|---|---|
| 2011 WM | | GER | 3RD GK—DID NOT PLAY | | | | | | | | |

| Riksman, Juuso | | | | | | | | | | | b. Helsinki, Finland, April 1, 1977 |
|---|---|---|---|---|---|---|---|---|---|---|---|
| 2009 WM | | FIN | 3RD GK—DID NOT PLAY | | | | | | | | |

| Ridderwall, Stefan | | | | | | | | | | | b. Huddinge, Sweden, March 5, 1988 |
|---|---|---|---|---|---|---|---|---|---|---|---|
| 2006 WM18 | 1-G | SWE | 1 | 0-0-1 | 59:22 | 2 | 0 | 2.02 | 0 | 0 | 6th |
| 2008 WM20 | 30-G | SWE | 1 | 1-0-0 | 60:00 | 1 | 0 | 1.00 | 0 | 0 | S |

| Riecicky, Dominik | | | | | | | | | | | b. Kosice, Czechoslovakia (Slovakia), June 9, 1992 |
|---|---|---|---|---|---|---|---|---|---|---|---|
| 2010 WM18 | 30-G | SVK | 6 | 2-0-4 | 359:38 | 20 | 0 | 3.34 | 0 | 0 | 8th |
| 2011 WM20 | 30-G | SVK | 5 | 1-0-1 | 191:02 | 12 | 0 | 3.77 | 1 | 0 | 8th |
| 2012 WM20 | 30-G | SVK | 2 | 0-0-2 | 90:07 | 12 | 0 | 7.99 | 0 | 0 | 6th |
| **Totals WM20** | | | **7** | **1-0-3** | **281:09** | **24** | **0** | **5.12** | **1** | **0** | **—** |

| Rinne, Pekka | | | | | | | | | | | b. Kempele, Finland, November 3, 1982 |
|---|---|---|---|---|---|---|---|---|---|---|---|
| 2009 WM | 35-G | FIN | 6 | 4-0-2 | 372:38 | 12 | 1 | 1.93 | 0 | 2 | 5th |
| 2010 WM | 35-G | FIN | 4 | 2-0-2 | 249:27 | 7 | 1 | 1.68 | 1 | 0 | 6th |
| **Totals WM** | | | **10** | **6-0-4** | **622:05** | **19** | **2** | **1.83** | **1** | **2** | **—** |

| Rinne, Rasmus | | | | | | | | | | | b. Hyvinkaa, Finland, July 8, 1990 |
|---|---|---|---|---|---|---|---|---|---|---|---|
| 2008 WM18 | 1-G | FIN | 4 | 1-0-3 | 237:52 | 13 | 0 | 3.28 | 0 | 0 | 6th |

| Roy, Olivier | | | | | | | | | | | b. Amqui, Quebec, Canada, July 12, 1991 |
|---|---|---|---|---|---|---|---|---|---|---|---|
| 2011 WM20 | 31-G | CAN | 3 | 2-0-1 | 185:00 | 11 | 0 | 3.57 | 0 | 0 | S |

| Rudolf, Sergei | | | | | | | | | | | b. Ust-Kamenogorsk, Soviet Union (Kazakhstan), September 20, 1988 |
|---|---|---|---|---|---|---|---|---|---|---|---|
| 2008 WM20 | 30-G | KAZ | 3 | 1-0-0 | 78:34 | 2 | 0 | 1.53 | 0 | 0 | 8th |

| Russo, Adam | | | | | | | | | | | b. Montreal, Quebec, Canada, April 12, 1983 |
|---|---|---|---|---|---|---|---|---|---|---|---|
| 2008 WM | | ITA | 3RD GK—DID NOT PLAY | | | | | | | | |
| 2010 WM | 1-G | ITA | 2 | 0-0-2 | 99:22 | 8 | 0 | 4.83 | 0 | 0 | 15th |

| Rutledge, Jared | | | | | | | | | | | b. Chicago, Illinois, United States, August 4, 1994 |
|---|---|---|---|---|---|---|---|---|---|---|---|
| 2012 WM18 | 1-G | USA | 1 | 1-0-0 | 60:00 | 0 | 1 | 0.00 | 0 | 0 | G |

| Rybar, Patrik | | | | | | | | | | | b. Skalica, Slovakia, November 9, 1993 |
|---|---|---|---|---|---|---|---|---|---|---|---|
| 2011 WM18 | 29-G | SVK | 6 | 1-0-4 | 292:22 | 20 | 1 | 4.10 | 0 | 0 | 10th |

| Sabol, Richard | | | | | | | | | | | b. Presnov, Slovakia, January 31, 1994 |
|---|---|---|---|---|---|---|---|---|---|---|---|
| 2011 WM18 | 1-G | SVK | 2 | 0-0-1 | 66:02 | 8 | 0 | 7.27 | 0 | 0 | 10th |
| 2012 WM20 | 2-G | SVK | 1 | 0-0-0 | 23:37 | 1 | 0 | 2.54 | 0 | 0 | 6th |

| Sadikov, Ramis | | | | | | | | | | | b. Moscow, Soviet Union (Russia), February 26, 1991 |
|---|---|---|---|---|---|---|---|---|---|---|---|
| 2010 WM20 | 1-G | RUS | 1 | 0-0-0 | 26:32 | 1 | 0 | 2.26 | 0 | 0 | 6th |

| Saikkonen, Dennis | | | | | | | | | | | b. Berne, Switzerland, November 27, 1992 |
|---|---|---|---|---|---|---|---|---|---|---|---|
| 2010 WM18 | 30-G | SUI | 2 | 0-0-1 | 89:49 | 10 | 0 | 6.68 | 0 | 0 | 5th |

| Salak, Alexander | | | | | | | | | | | b. Strakonice, Czechoslovakia (Czech Republic), January 5, 1987 |
|---|---|---|---|---|---|---|---|---|---|---|---|
| 2005 WM18 | 30-G | CZE | 1 | 0-0-0 | 48:28 | 1 | 0 | 1.24 | 0 | 0 | 4th |

| Sarkis, Leon | | | | | | | | | | | b. Zurich, Switzerland, January 19, 1991 |
|---|---|---|---|---|---|---|---|---|---|---|---|
| 2009 WM18 | 30-G | SUI | 1 | 0-0-1 | 31:06 | 7 | 0 | 13.50 | 0 | 0 | 8th |

| Saros, Juuse | | | | | | | | | | | b. Hameenlinna, Finland |
|---|---|---|---|---|---|---|---|---|---|---|---|
| 2012 WM18 | | FIN | 3RD GK—DID NOT PLAY | | | | | | | | |

| Sateri, Harri | | | | | | | | | | | b. Toijola, Finland, December 29, 1989 |
|---|---|---|---|---|---|---|---|---|---|---|---|
| 2007 WM18 | 30-G | FIN | 4 | 1-0-2 | 165:10 | 9 | 0 | 3.27 | 0 | 0 | 7th |
| 2008 WM20 | 30-G | FIN | 3 | 0-0-2 | 150:38 | 10 | 0 | 3.98 | 0 | 0 | 6th |
| 2009 WM20 | 30-G | FIN | 2 | 0-0-2 | 118:39 | 7 | 0 | 3.54 | 0 | 0 | 7th |
| **Totals WM20** | | | **5** | **0-0-4** | **269:17** | **17** | **0** | **3.79** | **0** | **0** | **—** |

| Schlegel, Niklas | | | | | | | | | | | b. August 3, 1994 |
|---|---|---|---|---|---|---|---|---|---|---|---|
| 2012 WM18 | 1-G | SUI | 2 | 0-0-1 | 101:18 | 9 | 0 | 5.33 | 0 | 0 | 7th |

| Schneider, Cory | | | | | | | | | | | b. Salem, Massachusetts, United States, March 18, 1986 |
|---|---|---|---|---|---|---|---|---|---|---|---|
| 2004 WM18 | 1-G | USA | 6 | 5-0-1 | 350:31 | 10 | 0 | 1.71 | 0 | 0 | S |
| 2005 WM20 | 1-G | USA | 1 | 0-0-0 | 22:41 | 3 | 0 | 7.94 | 0 | 0 | 4th |
| 2006 WM20 | 1-G | USA | 6 | 2-1-3 | 359:06 | 16 | 0 | 2.67 | 0 | 0 | 4th |
| **Totals WM20** | | | **7** | **2-1-3** | **381:47** | **19** | **0** | **2.99** | **0** | **0** | **—** |

| Schwarz, Marek | | | | | | | | | | | b. Mlada Boleslav, Czechoslovakia (Czech Republic), April 1, 1986 |
|---|---|---|---|---|---|---|---|---|---|---|---|
| 2003 WM18 | 31-G | CZE | 5 | 1-1-3 | 288:20 | 10 | 0 | 2.08 | 0 | 0 | 6th |
| 2004 WM18 | 30-G | CZE | 7 | 3-3-1 | 419:21 | 9 | 1 | 1.29 | 0 | 2 | B |
| 2004 WM20 | 1-G | CZE | 7 | 3-0-4 | 388:46 | 18 | 1 | 2.78 | 0 | 0 | 4th |
| 2005 WM20 | 30-G | CZE | 6 | 4-0-2 | 361:57 | 13 | 1 | 2.15 | 0 | 0 | B |
| 2006 WM20 | 30-G | CZE | 3 | 1-0-2 | 140:22 | 6 | 0 | 2.56 | 0 | 0 | 6th |
| **Totals WM18** | | | **12** | **4-4-4** | **707:41** | **19** | **1** | **1.61** | **0** | **2** | **—** |
| **Totals WM20** | | | **16** | **8-0-8** | **891:05** | **37** | **2** | **2.49** | **0** | **0** | **B** |

~WM20 IIHF Directorate Best Goalie (2005), WM20 All-Star Team/Goal (2005), WM18 IIHF Directorate Best Goalie (2004)

| Sedlacek, Jakub | | | | | | | | | | | b. Zlin, Czechoslovakia (Czech Republic), April 5, 1990 |
|---|---|---|---|---|---|---|---|---|---|---|---|
| 2010 WM20 | 30-G | CZE | 5 | 2-0-3 | 259:05 | 16 | 0 | 3.71 | 0 | 0 | 7th |

| Shabanov, Sergei | | | | | | | | | | | b. Minsk, Soviet Union (Belarus), February 24, 1974 |
|---|---|---|---|---|---|---|---|---|---|---|---|
| 1999 WM | | BLR | 3RD GK—DID NOT PLAY | | | | | | | | |
| 2001 WM | 2-G | BLR | 1 | 1-0-0 | 60:00 | 1 | 0 | 1.00 | 0 | 0 | 14th |
| 2002 OG-M | 2-G | BLR | 6 | 2-0-2 | 230:05 | 14 | 1 | 3.65 | 0 | 0 | 4th |
| 2003 WM | 2-G | BLR | 4 | 1-0-2 | 204:20 | 9 | 0 | 2.64 | 0 | 0 | 14th |
| 2005 WM | 2-G | BLR | 1 | 0-0-1 | 60:00 | 5 | 0 | 5.00 | 0 | 0 | 10th |
| 2006 WM | | BLR | 3RD GK—DID NOT PLAY | | | | | | | | |
| 2007 WM | 2-G | BLR | 1 | 0-0-1 | 21:17 | 2 | 0 | 5.64 | 0 | 0 | 11th |
| 2010 WM | | BLR | 3RD GK—DID NOT PLAY | | | | | | | | |
| 2011 WM | | BLR | 3RD GK—DID NOT PLAY | | | | | | | | |
| **Totals WM** | | | **7** | **2-0-4** | **345:37** | **17** | **0** | **2.95** | **0** | **0** | **—** |

| Shegalo, Pavel | | | | | | | | | | | b. Moscow, Russia, February 7, 1993 |
|---|---|---|---|---|---|---|---|---|---|---|---|
| 2011 WM18 | 30-G | RUS | 4 | 1-0-0 | 81:00 | 6 | 0 | 4.44 | 0 | 0 | B |

| Shelepnev, Yan | | | | | | | | | | | b. Minsk, Belarus, February 16, 1993 |
|---|---|---|---|---|---|---|---|---|---|---|---|
| 2010 WM18 | 20-G | BLR | 4 | 0-0-3 | 171:53 | 19 | 0 | 6.63 | 0 | 0 | 10th |

| Shikin, Dmitri | | | | | | | | | | | b. Elektrostal, Soviet Union (Russia), August 28, 1991 |
|---|---|---|---|---|---|---|---|---|---|---|---|
| 2011 WM20 | 20-G | RUS | 6 | 4-0-1 | 342:11 | 16 | 0 | 2.81 | 0 | 0 | G |

| Simboch, Juraj | | | | | | | | | | | b. Bratislava, Slovakia, January 30, 1992 |
|---|---|---|---|---|---|---|---|---|---|---|---|
| 2012 WM20 | 1-G | SVK | 5 | 2-0-2 | 246:16 | 17 | 0 | 4.14 | 0 | 0 | 6th |

| Simila, Petteri | | | | | | | | | | | b. Oulu, Finland, April 9, 1990 |
|---|---|---|---|---|---|---|---|---|---|---|---|
| 2010 WM20 | 28-G | FIN | 2 | 0-0-0 | 40:00 | 5 | 0 | 7.50 | 0 | 0 | 5th |

| Simko, Marek | | | | | | | | | | | b. Zvolen, Czechoslovakia (Slovakia), January 11, 1988 |
|---|---|---|---|---|---|---|---|---|---|---|---|
| 2006 WM18 | 1-G | SVK | 4 | 1-0-3 | 171:25 | 13 | 0 | 4.55 | 0 | 0 | 7th |

| Simpson, Kent | | | | | | | | | | | b. Edmonton, Alberta, Canada, March 26, 1992 |
|---|---|---|---|---|---|---|---|---|---|---|---|
| 2010 WM18 | 30-G | CAN | 2 | 0-0-0 | 43:47 | 3 | 0 | 4.11 | 0 | 0 | 7th |

| Sionas, Ebbe | | | | | | | | | | | b. Faringso, Sweden, March 7, 1995 |
|---|---|---|---|---|---|---|---|---|---|---|---|
| 2012 WM18 | | SWE | 3RD GK—DID NOT PLAY | | | | | | | | |

| Smith, Jeremy | | | | | | | | | | | b. Dearborn, Minnesota, United States, April 13, 1989 |
|---|---|---|---|---|---|---|---|---|---|---|---|
| 2008 WM20 | 30-G | USA | 6 | 4-0-2 | 299:54 | 12 | 0 | 2.40 | 0 | 0 | 4th |

| **Smith, Ruben** | | | | | | | | | | | **b. Stavanger, Norway, April 15, 1987** |
|---|---|---|---|---|---|---|---|---|---|---|---|
| 2006 WM20 | 30-G | NOR | 4 | 0-0-4 | 159:34 | 15 | 0 | 5.64 | 0 | 0 | 10th |
| 2008 WM | 30-G | NOR | 1 | 0-0-0 | 13:19 | 1 | 0 | 4.51 | 0 | 0 | 8th |
| 2010 OG-M | | NOR | 3RD GK—DID NOT PLAY | | | | | | | | |
| 2010 WM | 30-G | NOR | 2 | 0-0-1 | 46:38 | 10 | 0 | 12.87 | 0 | 0 | 9th |
| **Totals WM** | | | **3** | **0-0-1** | **59:57** | **11** | **0** | **11.01** | **0** | **0** | **—** |

| **Smolnikov, Mikhail** | | | | | | | | | | | **b. Ust-Kamenogorsk, Soviet Union (Kazakhstan), March 15, 1988** |
|---|---|---|---|---|---|---|---|---|---|---|---|
| 2008 WM20 | 1-G | KAZ | 5 | 1-0-4 | 281:26 | 25 | 0 | 5.33 | 0 | 0 | 8th |

| **Soberg, Steffen** | | | | | | | | | | | **b. Oslo, Norway, August 6, 1993** |
|---|---|---|---|---|---|---|---|---|---|---|---|
| 2011 WM18 | 1-G | NOR | 6 | 1-0-5 | 338:46 | 22 | 0 | 3.90 | 0 | 0 | 9th |
| 2011 WM20 | 1-G | NOR | 3 | 1-0-2 | 134:34 | 8 | 0 | 3.57 | 0 | 0 | 9th |

| **Sorensen, George** | | | | | | | | | | | **b. Herning, Denmark, May 15, 1995** |
|---|---|---|---|---|---|---|---|---|---|---|---|
| 2012 WM18 | 25-G | DEN | 5 | 1-0-4 | 276:12 | 18 | 0 | 3.91 | 0 | 27 | 10th |

| **Sorensen, Martin** | | | | | | | | | | | **b. Hvidovre, Denmark, December 6, 1990** |
|---|---|---|---|---|---|---|---|---|---|---|---|
| 2008 WM18 | 25-G | DEN | 2 | 0-0-1 | 85:47 | 12 | 0 | 8.39 | 0 | 0 | 10th |

| **Stana, Rastislav** | | | | | | | | | | | **b. Kosice, Czechoslovakia (Slovakia), January 10, 1980** |
|---|---|---|---|---|---|---|---|---|---|---|---|
| 2000 WM20 | 30-G | SVK | 4 | 0-1-3 | 203:56 | 8 | 0 | 2.35 | 0 | 0 | 9th |
| 2001 WM | | SVK | 3RD GK—DID NOT PLAY | | | | | | | | |
| 2002 OG-M | 31-G | SVK | 1 | 1-0-0 | 60:00 | 1 | 0 | 1.00 | 0 | 0 | 13th |
| 2002 WM | 31-G | SVK | 3 | 3-0-0 | 180:00 | 8 | 1 | 2.67 | 0 | 0 | G |
| 2003 WM | 31-G | SVK | 2 | 2-0-0 | 120:00 | 4 | 0 | 2.00 | 0 | 0 | B |
| 2004 WM | | SVK | 3RD GK—DID NOT PLAY | | | | | | | | |
| 2004 WCH | 31-G | SVK | 2 | 0-0-1 | 88:12 | 6 | 0 | 4.08 | 0 | 0 | 7th |
| 2005 WM | 31-G | SVK | 2 | 1-0-1 | 92:23 | 6 | 0 | 3.90 | 1 | 0 | 5th |
| 2006 WM | | SVK | 3RD GK—DID NOT PLAY | | | | | | | | |
| 2009 WM | 31-G | SVK | 2 | 1-0-1 | 125:00 | 4 | 0 | 1.92 | 0 | 0 | 10th |
| 2010 OG-M | | SVK | 3RD GK—DID NOT PLAY | | | | | | | | |
| 2010 WM | 35-G | SVK | 2 | 0-0-0 | 74:50 | 4 | 0 | 3.21 | 0 | 0 | 12th |
| **Totals WM** | | | **11** | **7-0-2** | **592:13** | **26** | **1** | **2.63** | **1** | **0** | **G,B** |

| **Starkbaum, Bernhard** | | | | | | | | | | | **b. Vienna, Austria, February 19, 1986** |
|---|---|---|---|---|---|---|---|---|---|---|---|
| 2009 WM | | AUT | 3RD GK—DID NOT PLAY | | | | | | | | |

| **Staudt, Sebastian** | | | | | | | | | | | **b. Krefeld, West Germany (Germany), April 29, 1988** |
|---|---|---|---|---|---|---|---|---|---|---|---|
| 2006 WM18 | 2-G | GER | 1 | 0-0-0 | 20:00 | 2 | 0 | 6.00 | 0 | 0 | 8th |

| **Stefaniszin, Sebastian** | | | | | | | | | | | **b. Berlin, West Germany (Germany), July 22, 1987** |
|---|---|---|---|---|---|---|---|---|---|---|---|
| 2005 WM18 | 30-G | GER | 1 | 0-0-0 | 49:42 | 7 | 0 | 8.45 | 0 | 0 | 8th |
| 2007 WM20 | 1-G | GER | 5 | 2-0-3 | 299:00 | 14 | 0 | 2.81 | 0 | 2 | 9th |

| **Steinhauer, Lukas** | | | | | | | | | | | **b. Rosenheim, Germany, August 27, 1992** |
|---|---|---|---|---|---|---|---|---|---|---|---|
| 2009 WM18 | 1-G | GER | 6 | 2-0-3 | 324:22 | 28 | 0 | 5.18 | 0 | 0 | 10th |

| **Stepanek, Jakub** | | | | | | | | | | | **b. Vsetin, Czechoslovakia (Czech Republic), July 20, 1986** |
|---|---|---|---|---|---|---|---|---|---|---|---|
| 2009 WM | 33-G | CZE | 6 | 2-0-3 | 283:19 | 10 | 2 | 2.12 | 0 | 2 | 6th |
| 2010 WM | | CZE | 3RD GK—DID NOT PLAY | | | | | | | | |
| 2011 WM | 33-G | CZE | 1 | 1-0-0 | 60:00 | 2 | 0 | 2.00 | 0 | 0 | B |
| 2012 WM | 33-G | CZE | 5 | 3-0-1 | 242:07 | 6 | 1 | 1.49 | 0 | 0 | B |
| **Totals WM** | | | **12** | **6-0-4** | **585:26** | **18** | **3** | **1.84** | **0** | **0** | **2B** |

| **Stepanov, Sergei** | | | | | | | | | | | **b. Minsk, Belarus, January 23, 1993** |
|---|---|---|---|---|---|---|---|---|---|---|---|
| 2010 WM18 | 25-G | BLR | 1 | 0-0-1 | 27:41 | 4 | 0 | 8.67 | 0 | 0 | 10th |

| **Stephan, Tobias** | | | | | | | | | | | **b. Zurich, Switzerland, January 21, 1984** |
|---|---|---|---|---|---|---|---|---|---|---|---|
| 2001 WM18 | 30-G | SUI | 6 | 4-0-2 | 360:00 | 16 | 0 | 2.67 | 0 | 0 | S |
| 2002 WM18 | 30-G | SUI | 8 | 5-0-3 | 440:00 | 20 | 2 | 2.73 | 0 | 0 | 7th |
| 2002 WM20 | 20-G | SUI | 6 | 2-0-4 | 357:58 | 20 | 1 | 3.35 | 0 | 2 | 4th |
| 2003 WM20 | 30-G | SUI | 4 | 2-0-2 | 240:00 | 14 | 0 | 3.50 | 0 | 0 | 7th |
| 2003 WM | | SUI | 3RD GK—DID NOT PLAY | | | | | | | | |
| 2010 OG-M | | SUI | 3RD GK—DID NOT PLAY | | | | | | | | |
| 2010 WM | 52-G | SUI | 2 | 1-0-1 | 120:00 | 6 | 0 | 3.00 | 0 | 2 | 5th |
| 2011 WM | 52-G | SUI | 4 | 3-0-1 | 240:48 | 7 | 1 | 1.74 | 0 | 0 | 9th |
| 2012 WM | 52-G | SUI | 3 | 1-0-2 | 176:43 | 9 | 0 | 3.06 | 0 | 0 | 11th |
| **Totals WM18** | | | **14** | **9-0-5** | **800:00** | **36** | **2** | **2.70** | **0** | **0** | **—** |
| **Totals WM20** | | | **10** | **4-0-6** | **597:58** | **34** | **1** | **3.41** | **0** | **2** | **—** |
| **Totals WM** | | | **9** | **5-0-4** | **537:31** | **22** | **1** | **2.46** | **0** | **2** | **—** |

| **Stigis, Kristaps** | | | | | | | | | | | **b. Riga, Soviet Union (Latvia), May 1, 1987** |
|---|---|---|---|---|---|---|---|---|---|---|---|
| 2006 WM20 | 1-G | LAT | 1 | 0-0-0 | 26:03 | 2 | 0 | 4.61 | 0 | 0 | 9th |

| **Subban, Malcolm** | | | | | | | | | | | **b. Rexdale, Ontario, Canada, December 21, 1993** |
|---|---|---|---|---|---|---|---|---|---|---|---|
| 2011 WM18 | 30-G | CAN | 5 | 3-0-2 | 302:31 | 15 | 1 | 2.98 | 0 | 0 | 4th |

| **Suomalainen, Erno** | | | | | | | | | | | **b. Espoo, Finland, March 2, 1991** |
|---|---|---|---|---|---|---|---|---|---|---|---|
| 2009 WM18 | 30-G | FIN | 1 | 1-0-0 | 60:00 | 1 | 0 | 1.00 | 0 | 0 | B |

| **Swette, Rene** | | | | | | | | | | | **b. Lustenau, Austria, August 21, 1988** |
|---|---|---|---|---|---|---|---|---|---|---|---|
| 2011 WM | | AUT | 3RD GK—DID NOT PLAY | | | | | | | | |

| **Tanzer, Andreas** | | | | | | | | | | | **b. Garmisch-Partenkirchen, West Germany (Germany), April 3, 1989** |
|---|---|---|---|---|---|---|---|---|---|---|---|
| 2007 WM18 | 30-G | GER | 1 | 0-0-1 | 29:06 | 7 | 0 | 14:43 | 0 | 0 | 8th |

| **Tarkki, Iiro** | | | | | | | | | | | **b. Rauma, Finland, July 1, 1985** |
|---|---|---|---|---|---|---|---|---|---|---|---|
| 2010 WM | | FIN | 3RD GK—DID NOT PLAY | | | | | | | | |

| **Tellqvist, Mikael** | | | | | | | | | | | **b. Sundbyberg, Sweden, September 19, 1979** |
|---|---|---|---|---|---|---|---|---|---|---|---|
| 2000 WM | 32-G | SWE | 1 | 0-0-1 | 60:00 | 4 | 0 | 4.00 | 0 | 0 | 7th |
| 2001 WM | 32-G | SWE | 1 | 1-0-0 | 60:00 | 2 | 0 | 2.00 | 0 | 0 | B |
| 2002 OG-M | | SWE | 3RD GK—DID NOT PLAY | | | | | | | | |
| 2003 WM | 32-G | SWE | 7 | 6-0-1 | 393:16 | 9 | 0 | 1.37 | 0 | 0 | S |
| 2004 WCH | 32-G | SWE | 3 | 1-1-1 | 178:52 | 12 | 0 | 4.03 | 0 | 0 | 5th |
| 2006 OG-M | 32-G | SWE | 1 | 0-0-1 | 60:00 | 3 | 0 | 3.00 | 0 | 2 | G |
| 2008 WM | 32-G | SWE | 2 | 1-0-0 | 79:24 | 5 | 0 | 3.78 | 0 | 0 | 4th |
| **Totals WM** | | | **11** | **8-0-2** | **592:40** | **20** | **0** | **2.02** | **0** | **0** | **S,B** |

| **Theodore, Jose** | | | | | | | | | | | **b. Laval, Quebec, Canada, September 13, 1976** |
|---|---|---|---|---|---|---|---|---|---|---|---|
| 1996 WM20 | 1-G | CAN | 4 | 4-0-0 | 240:00 | 6 | 0 | 1.50 | 0 | 0 | G |
| 2000 WM | 60-G | CAN | 8 | 5-0-3 | 478:11 | 13 | 2 | 1.63 | 0 | 0 | 4th |
| 2004 WCH | | CAN | 3RD GK—DID NOT PLAY | | | | | | | | |

~WM20 IIHF Directorate Best Goalie (1996), WM20 All-Star Team/Goal (1996)

| **Thomas, Tim** | | | | | | | | | | | **b. Flint, Michigan, United States, April 15, 1974** |
|---|---|---|---|---|---|---|---|---|---|---|---|
| 1995 WM | | USA | 3RD GK—DID NOT PLAY | | | | | | | | |
| 1996 WM | 32-G | USA | 1 | 0-0-0 | 29:38 | 1 | 0 | 2.02 | 0 | 0 | B |
| 1998 WM | 32-G | USA | 1 | 0-0-0 | 58:17 | 2 | 0 | 2.06 | 0 | 0 | 12th |
| 1999 WM | 30-G | USA | 2 | 0-0-2 | 98:50 | 8 | 0 | 4.85 | 0 | 0 | 6th |
| 2005 WM | | USA | 3RD GK—DID NOT PLAY | | | | | | | | |
| 2008 WM | 30-G | USA | 3 | 2-0-0 | 160:00 | 4 | 1 | 1.50 | 0 | 0 | 6th |
| 2010 OG-M | 30-G | USA | 1 | 0-0-0 | 11:31 | 1 | 0 | 5.21 | 0 | 0 | S |
| **Totals WM** | | | **7** | **2-0-2** | **346:45** | **15** | **1** | **2.60** | **0** | **0** | **B** |

| **Tobler, Michael** | | | | | | | | | | | **b. Zurich, Switzerland, August 5, 1985** |
|---|---|---|---|---|---|---|---|---|---|---|---|
| 2003 WM18 | 20-G | SUI | 1 | 0-0-1 | 60:00 | 12 | 0 | 12.00 | 0 | 0 | 9th |
| 2004 WM20 | 1-G | SUI | 2 | 1-0-1 | 110:28 | 4 | 0 | 2.17 | 0 | 0 | 8th |
| 2005 WM20 | 20-G | SUI | 6 | 2-0-4 | 358:54 | 20 | 2 | 3.34 | 0 | 2 | 8th |
| **Totals WM20** | | | **8** | **3-0-5** | **469:22** | **24** | **2** | **3.07** | **0** | **2** | **—** |

| **Toivonen, Hannu** | | | | | | | | | | | **b. Kalvola, Finland, May 18, 1984** |
|---|---|---|---|---|---|---|---|---|---|---|---|
| 2002 WM18 | 30-G | FIN | 5 | 2-0-2 | 242:23 | 9 | 1 | 2.23 | 0 | 0 | 4th |
| 2004 WM20 | 30-G | FIN | 6 | 4-0-2 | 357:25 | 11 | 1 | 1.85 | 0 | 0 | B |

| **Toivonen, Juha** | | | | | | | | | | | **b. Hattula, Finland, June 10, 1987** |
|---|---|---|---|---|---|---|---|---|---|---|---|
| 2005 WM18 | 1-G | FIN | 2 | 1-0-0 | 79:59 | 3 | 0 | 2.25 | 0 | 2 | 7th |

| **Tokarski, Dustin** | | | | | | | | | | | **b. Watson, Saskatchewan, Canada, September 16, 1989** |
|---|---|---|---|---|---|---|---|---|---|---|---|
| 2009 WM20 | 30-G | CAN | 4 | 4-0-0 | 248:41 | 11 | 0 | 2.65 | 0 | 0 | G |

| **Tragust, Thomas** | | | | | | | | | | | **b. Silandro, Italy, May 28, 1986** |
|---|---|---|---|---|---|---|---|---|---|---|---|
| 2006 WM | 35-G | ITA | 2 | 0-1-0 | 54:35 | 1 | 0 | 1.10 | 0 | 0 | 14th |
| 2008 WM | 35-G | ITA | 4 | 0-0-2 | 91:17 | 12 | 0 | 7.89 | 0 | 0 | 16th |
| 2010 WM | | ITA | 3RD GK—DID NOT PLAY | | | | | | | | |
| 2012 WM | 34-G | ITA | 4 | 0-0-2 | 146:23 | 11 | 0 | 4.51 | 0 | 0 | 15th |
| **Totals WM** | | | **10** | **0-1-4** | **292:15** | **24** | **0** | **4.93** | **0** | **0** | **—** |

| **Treutle, Niklas** | | | | | | | | | | | **b. Nuremberg, Germany, April 29, 1991** |
|---|---|---|---|---|---|---|---|---|---|---|---|
| 2011 WM20 | 1-G | GER | 4 | 0-0-2 | 186:04 | 7 | 0 | 2.26 | 0 | 0 | 10th |

| **Trus, Vitali** | | | | | | | | | | | **b. Novopolotsk, Soviet Union (Belarus), June 24, 1988** |
|---|---|---|---|---|---|---|---|---|---|---|---|
| 2006 WM18 | 1-G | BLR | 6 | 1-1-2 | 283:54 | 18 | 1 | 3.80 | 0 | 0 | 9th |

| **Ullberg, Richard** | | | | | | | | | | | **b. Sipoo, Finland, July 16, 1993** |
|---|---|---|---|---|---|---|---|---|---|---|---|
| 2011 WM18 | 30-G | FIN | 2 | 1-0-1 | 120:00 | 5 | 1 | 2.50 | 0 | 0 | 5th |
| 2012 WM20 | | FIN | 3RD GK—DID NOT PLAY | | | | | | | | |

| **Unice, Josh** | | | | | | | | | | | **b. Holland, Ohio, United States, June 24, 1989** |
|---|---|---|---|---|---|---|---|---|---|---|---|
| 2007 WM18 | 30-G | USA | 6 | 4-0-2 | 373:49 | 15 | 1 | 2.41 | 0 | 0 | S |
| 2009 WM20 | 1-G | USA | 1 | 1-0-0 | 62:49 | 2 | 0 | 1.91 | 0 | 0 | 5th |

~WM20 All-Star Team/Goal (2007), WM18 IIHF Directorate Best Goalie (2007)

| **Ustinski, Igor** | | | | | | | | | | | **b. Tyumen, Russia, June 14, 1994** |
|---|---|---|---|---|---|---|---|---|---|---|---|
| 2012 WM18 | | RUS | 3RD GK—DID NOT PLAY | | | | | | | | |

| **Valent, Michal** | | | | | | | | | | | **b. Martin, Czechoslovakia (Slovakia), March 5, 1986** |
|---|---|---|---|---|---|---|---|---|---|---|---|
| 2004 WM18 | 1-G | SVK | 6 | 1-3-2 | 358:07 | 15 | 1 | 2.51 | 0 | 0 | 6th |
| 2006 WM20 | 1-G | SVK | 5 | 1-1-1 | 158:30 | 15 | 1 | 5.68 | 0 | 0 | 8th |

| Varlamov, Semyon | | | | | | | | | | | b. Samara, Soviet Union (Russia), April 27, 1988 |
|---|---|---|---|---|---|---|---|---|---|---|---|
| 2005 WM18 | 1-G | RUS | 4 | 2-0-1 | 179:52 | 10 | 0 | 3.34 | 0 | 0 | 5th |
| 2006 WM18 | 1-G | RUS | 5 | 3-0-2 | 298:20 | 14 | 1 | 2.82 | 0 | 0 | 5th |
| 2007 WM20 | 1-G | RUS | 6 | 5-0-1 | 358:12 | 9 | 2 | 1.51 | 0 | 0 | S |
| 2010 OG-M | | RUS | 3RD GK—DID NOT PLAY | | | | | | | | |
| 2010 WM | 40-G | RUS | 5 | 4-0-1 | 297:53 | 7 | 1 | 1.41 | 0 | 0 | S |
| 2012 WM | 1-G | RUS | 8 | 8-0-0 | 440:00 | 13 | 1 | 1.77 | 0 | 0 | G |
| **Totals WM18** | | | **9** | **5-0-3** | **478:12** | **24** | **1** | **3.01** | **0** | **0** | **—** |
| **Totals WM** | | | **13** | **12-0-1** | **737:53** | **20** | **2** | **1.63** | **0** | **0** | **G,S** |

| Vasilevski, Andrei | | | | | | | | | | | b. Tyumen, Russia, July 25, 1994 |
|---|---|---|---|---|---|---|---|---|---|---|---|
| 2010 WM18 | 30-G | RUS | 5 | 2-0-3 | 272:03 | 12 | 1 | 2.65 | 0 | 0 | 4th |
| 2011 WM18 | 1-G | RUS | 6 | 4-0-2 | 343:30 | 15 | 0 | 2.62 | 0 | 0 | B |
| 2012 WM18 | 30-G | RUS | 5 | 2-0-3 | 299:20 | 11 | 1 | 2.20 | 0 | 0 | 5th |
| 2012 WM20 | 30-G | RUS | 5 | 4-0-1 | 298:31 | 10 | 2 | 2.01 | 0 | 2 | S |
| **Totals WM18** | | | **16** | **8-0-8** | **914:53** | **38** | **2** | **2.49** | **0** | **0** | **B** |

| Vasiljevs, Dainis | | | | | | | | | | | b. Riga, Soviet Union (Latvia), January 27, 1990 |
|---|---|---|---|---|---|---|---|---|---|---|---|
| 2007 WM18 | 29-G | LAT | 2 | 0-0-1 | 62:34 | 9 | 0 | 8.63 | 0 | 0 | 10th |

| Vehanen, Petri | | | | | | | | | | | b. Rauma, Finland, October 9, 1977 |
|---|---|---|---|---|---|---|---|---|---|---|---|
| 2008 WM | 35-G | FIN | 1 | 1-0-0 | 61:27 | 2 | 0 | 1.95 | 0 | 0 | B |
| 2010 WM | 31-G | FIN | 3 | 2-0-1 | 180:00 | 7 | 1 | 2.33 | 0 | 0 | 6th |
| 2011 WM | 31-G | FIN | 8 | 6-0-1 | 388:13 | 8 | 1 | 1.24 | 0 | 0 | G |
| 2012 WM | 31-G | FIN | 7 | 4-0-2 | 366:43 | 13 | 1 | 2.13 | 0 | 0 | 4th |
| **Totals WM** | | | **19** | **13-0-4** | **996:23** | **30** | **3** | **1.81** | **0** | **0** | **G,B** |

| Visentin, Mark | | | | | | | | | | | b. Waterdown, Ontario, Canada, August 7, 1992 |
|---|---|---|---|---|---|---|---|---|---|---|---|
| 2011 WM20 | 30-G | CAN | 4 | 3-0-1 | 239:05 | 8 | 0 | 2.01 | 1 | 0 | S |
| 2012 WM20 | 29-G | CAN | 4 | 3-0-1 | 210:08 | 5 | 1 | 1.43 | 0 | 0 | B |
| **Totals WM20** | | | **8** | **6-0-2** | **449:13** | **13** | **1** | **1.74** | **1** | **0** | **S,B** |

| Vokoun, Tomas | | | | | | | | | | | b. Karlovy Vary, Czechoslovakia (Czech Republic), February 7, 1976 |
|---|---|---|---|---|---|---|---|---|---|---|---|
| 1996 WM20 | 30-G | CZE | 6 | 2-2-2 | 356:01 | 21 | 1 | 3.54 | 0 | 0 | 4th |
| 2003 WM | 29-G | CZE | 7 | 4-1-1 | 388:31 | 14 | 1 | 2.16 | 1 | 0 | 4th |
| 2004 WM | 29-G | CZE | 6 | 5-0-1 | 370:00 | 7 | 2 | 1.14 | 0 | 2 | 5th |
| 2004 WCH | 29-G | CZE | 5 | 2-0-3 | 302:00 | 15 | 0 | 2.98 | 0 | 0 | — |
| 2005 WM | 29-G | CZE | 8 | 7-0-1 | 499:17 | 9 | 2 | 1.08 | 0 | 6 | G |
| 2006 OG-M | 29-G | CZE | 7 | 3-0-3 | 341:38 | 14 | 1 | 2.46 | 2 | 0 | B |
| 2010 OG-M | 29-G | CZE | 5 | 3-0-2 | 303:35 | 9 | 0 | 1.78 | 0 | 0 | 7th |
| 2010 WM | 29-G | CZE | 8 | 7-0-1 | 496:27 | 13 | 0 | 1.57 | 2 | 2 | G |
| **Totals WM** | | | **29** | **23-1-4** | **1,754:15** | **43** | **5** | **1.47** | **3** | **10** | **2G** |
| **Totals OG-M** | | | **12** | **6-0-5** | **645:13** | **23** | **1** | **2.14** | **2** | **0** | **B** |

~WM IIHF Directorate Best Goalie (2005), WM All-Star Team/Goal (2005)

| Volden, Lars | | | | | | | | | | | b. Oslo, Norway, July 26, 1992 |
|---|---|---|---|---|---|---|---|---|---|---|---|
| 2009 WM18 | 30-G | NOR | 5 | 1-0-2 | 220:00 | 22 | 0 | 6.00 | 0 | 2 | 9th |
| 2011 WM20 | 25-G | NOR | 4 | 0-0-3 | 223:34 | 23 | 0 | 6.17 | 0 | 0 | 9th |
| 2012 WM | 34-G | NOR | 1 | 0-0-1 | 60:00 | 4 | 0 | 4.00 | 0 | 0 | 8th |

| Volkov, Dmitri | | | | | | | | | | | b. Mogilyov, Soviet Union (Belarus), July 7, 1990 |
|---|---|---|---|---|---|---|---|---|---|---|---|
| 2008 WM18 | 20-G | BLR | 4 | 1-0-2 | 222:22 | 14 | 0 | 3.78 | 0 | 0 | 9th |

| Vosvrda, Tomas | | | | | | | | | | | b. Ostrava, Czechoslovakia (Czech Republic), September 12, 1989 |
|---|---|---|---|---|---|---|---|---|---|---|---|
| 2009 WM20 | 2-G | CZE | 2 | 0-0-2 | 96:22 | 8 | 0 | 4.98 | 0 | 0 | 6th |

| Ward, Cam | | | | | | | | | | | b. Saskatoon, Saskatchewan, February 29, 1984 |
|---|---|---|---|---|---|---|---|---|---|---|---|
| 2007 WM | 30-G | CAN | 5 | 5-0-0 | 300:00 | 11 | 0 | 2.20 | 0 | 2 | G |
| 2008 WM | 30-G | CAN | 5 | 4-0-1 | 302:42 | 13 | 0 | 2.58 | 0 | 0 | S |
| 2012 WM | 30-G | CAN | 6 | 4-0-2 | 360:32 | 17 | 0 | 2.83 | 1 | 0 | 5th |
| **Totals WM** | | | **16** | **13-0-3** | **963:14** | **41** | **0** | **2.55** | **1** | **2** | **G,S** |

| Wedgewood, Scott | | | | | | | | | | | b. Brampton, Ontario, Canada, August 14, 1992 |
|---|---|---|---|---|---|---|---|---|---|---|---|
| 2012 WM20 | 30-G | CAN | 3 | 2-0-0 | 148:48 | 6 | 1 | 2.42 | 1 | 0 | B |

| Weinhandl, Fabian | | | | | | | | | | | b. Graz, Austria, January 3, 1987 |
|---|---|---|---|---|---|---|---|---|---|---|---|
| 2011 WM | 31-G | AUT | 4 | 1-0-2 | 220:00 | 13 | 0 | 3.55 | 0 | 0 | 15th |

| Whitney, Brandon | | | | | | | | | | | b. Kentville, Nova Scotia, Canada, May 11, 1994 |
|---|---|---|---|---|---|---|---|---|---|---|---|
| 2012 WM18 | CAN | DID NOT PLAY | | | | | | | | | |

| Wieser, Marco | | | | | | | | | | | b. Villach, Austria, December 15, 1990 |
|---|---|---|---|---|---|---|---|---|---|---|---|
| 2010 WM20 | 30-G | AUT | 2 | 0-0-2 | 71:07 | 12 | 0 | 10.12 | 0 | 0 | 10th |

| Will, Roman | | | | | | | | | | | b. Plzen, Czechoslovakia (Czech Republic), May 22, 1992 |
|---|---|---|---|---|---|---|---|---|---|---|---|
| 2010 WM18 | 30-G | CZE | 3 | 1-0-0 | 122:47 | 10 | 0 | 4.89 | 0 | 0 | 6th |

| Wolf, Tim | | | | | | | | | | | b. Zurich, Switzerland, January 25, 1992 |
|---|---|---|---|---|---|---|---|---|---|---|---|
| 2012 WM20 | 1-G | SUI | 5 | 2-0-2 | 253:14 | 12 | 0 | 2.84 | 0 | 2 | 8th |

| Yankov, Andrei | | | | | | | | | | | b. Kazakhstanskaya, Soviet Union (Kazakhstan), June 2, 1989 |
|---|---|---|---|---|---|---|---|---|---|---|---|
| 2009 WM20 | 20-G | KAZ | 6 | 0-0-6 | 286:31 | 50 | 0 | 10.47 | 0 | 0 | 10th |

| Yeremeyev, Vitali | | | | | | | | | | | b. Ust-Kamenogorsk, Soviet Union (Kazakhstan), September 23, 1975 |
|---|---|---|---|---|---|---|---|---|---|---|---|
| 1998 OG-M | 30-G | KAZ | 7 | 2-0-4 | 291:42 | 28 | 0 | 5.76 | 0 | 0 | 8th |
| 1998 WM | 30-G | KAZ | 3 | 0-0-2 | 143:27 | 11 | 0 | 4.60 | 0 | 0 | 16th |
| 2004 WM | 31-G | KAZ | 5 | 1-1-3 | 220:46 | 12 | 0 | 3.26 | 0 | 0 | 13th |
| 2006 OG-M | 31-G | KAZ | 3 | 1-0-2 | 180:00 | 10 | 0 | 3.33 | 0 | 0 | 9th |
| 2010 WM | 31-G | KAZ | 5 | 0-0-5 | 300:00 | 21 | 0 | 4.20 | 0 | 0 | 16th |
| 2012 WM | 31-G | KAZ | 4 | 0-0-3 | 180:08 | 12 | 0 | 4.00 | 1 | 2 | 16th |
| **Totals WM** | | | **17** | **1-1-13** | **844:21** | **56** | **0** | **3.98** | **1** | **2** | **—** |
| **Totals OG-M** | | | **10** | **3-0-6** | **471:42** | **38** | **0** | **4.83** | **0** | **0** | **—** |

| Yeryomenko, Alexander | | | | | | | | | | | b. Moscow, Soviet Union (Russia), April 10, 1980 |
|---|---|---|---|---|---|---|---|---|---|---|---|
| 2005 WM | | RUS | 3RD GK—DID NOT PLAY | | | | | | | | |
| 2007 WM | 30-G | RUS | 6 | 5-0-1 | 365:40 | 6 | 2 | 0.98 | 0 | 0 | B |
| 2008 WM | 30-G | RUS | 2 | 1-0-0 | 85:44 | 3 | 0 | 2.10 | 0 | 0 | G |
| 2009 WM | 1-G | RUS | 3 | 3-0-0 | 140:00 | 3 | 0 | 1.29 | 0 | 0 | G |
| 2010 WM | 30-G | RUS | 1 | 1-0-0 | 60:00 | 1 | 0 | 1.00 | 0 | 0 | S |
| **Totals WM** | | | **12** | **10-0-1** | **651:24** | **13** | **2** | **1.20** | **0** | **0** | **2G,S,B** |

| Zabotinskis, Dmitrijs | | | | | | | | | | | b. Ogre, Soviet Union (Latvia), January 19, 1980 |
|---|---|---|---|---|---|---|---|---|---|---|---|
| 2008 WM | | LAT | 3RD GK—DID NOT PLAY | | | | | | | | |
| 2009 WM | | LAT | 3RD GK—DID NOT PLAY | | | | | | | | |

| Zador, Michael | | | | | | | | | | | b. Toronto, Ontario, Canada, May 8, 1991 |
|---|---|---|---|---|---|---|---|---|---|---|---|
| 2009 WM18 | 30-G | CAN | 6 | 4-0-2 | 371:10 | 15 | 0 | 2.42 | 0 | 0 | 4th |

| Zatkoff, Jeff | | | | | | | | | | | b. Detroit, Michigan, United States, June 9, 1987 |
|---|---|---|---|---|---|---|---|---|---|---|---|
| 2007 WM20 | 37-G | USA | 2 | 0-0-2 | 121:29 | 7 | 0 | 3.46 | 0 | 0 | B |

| Zepp, Robert | | | | | | | | | | | b. Newmarket, Ontario, Canada, September 7, 1981 |
|---|---|---|---|---|---|---|---|---|---|---|---|
| 2010 WM | 72-G | GER | 2 | 0-0-2 | 116:52 | 3 | 0 | 1.54 | 0 | 0 | 4th |

| Zhelobnyuk, Vadim | | | | | | | | | | | b. Moscow, Soviet Union (Russia), April 22, 1989 |
|---|---|---|---|---|---|---|---|---|---|---|---|
| 2007 WM18 | 1-G | RUS | 7 | 5-0-1 | 350:06 | 19 | 0 | 3.26 | 0 | 0 | G |
| 2009 WM20 | 1-G | RUS | 5 | 3-0-1 | 292:29 | 11 | 0 | 2.26 | 0 | 0 | B |

| Zhitkov, Pavel | | | | | | | | | | | b. Karaganda, Soviet Union (Kazakhstan), June 4, 1984 |
|---|---|---|---|---|---|---|---|---|---|---|---|
| 2010 WM | 1-G | KAZ | 1 | 0-0-0 | 40:00 | 6 | 0 | 9.00 | 0 | 0 | 16th |

| Zhuravski, Dmitri | | | | | | | | | | | b. Krichev, Soviet Union (Belarus), July 11, 1987 |
|---|---|---|---|---|---|---|---|---|---|---|---|
| 2007 WM20 | 25-G | BLR | 1 | 0-0-1 | 40:00 | 6 | 0 | 9.00 | 0 | 0 | 10th |

| Ziffzer, Youri | | | | | | | | | | | b. Singapore, Singapore, August 21, 1986 |
|---|---|---|---|---|---|---|---|---|---|---|---|
| 2005 WM20 | 30-G | GER | 5 | 1-0-3 | 256:02 | 19 | 0 | 4.45 | 0 | 0 | 9th |

| Zurkirchen, Sandro | | | | | | | | | | | b. Schwyz, Switzerland, February 25, 1990 |
|---|---|---|---|---|---|---|---|---|---|---|---|
| 2008 WM18 | 30-G | SUI | 2 | 0-0-2 | 120:00 | 12 | 0 | 6.00 | 0 | 0 | 8th |

*Martin Brodeur is the only goalie not named Tretiak to have won more than one Olympic gold, having helped Canada to victory in both 2002 and 2010. Photo: Dave Sandford / HHOF.*

*U.S. goalie Ryan Miller was at the height of his powers at the 2010 Olympics when he was named tournament MVP and helped the Americans to a silver medal. Photo: Matthew Manor / HHOF-IIHF Images.*

# Retired Skaters, Men

(career summary for players who have retired from hockey or who have not played recently for their country)

First-Last

| Years | Event | NAT | GP | G | A | P | Pim | Medals |
|---|---|---|---|---|---|---|---|---|
| **Aaby, Henrik / b. Aug. 22, 1975** | | | | | | | | |
| 1995-99 | WM | NOR | 12 | 1 | 0 | 1 | 18 | — |
| **Aalto, Antti / b. Mar. 4, 1975** | | | | | | | | |
| 1994 | WM20 | FIN | 14 | 2 | 5 | 7 | 26 | — |
| 1997 | WM | FIN | 22 | 3 | 0 | 3 | 22 | B |
| 2002 | OG-M | FIN | 4 | 0 | 0 | 0 | 4 | — |
| **Aaltonen, Petri / b. May 31, 1970** | | | | | | | | |
| 1989-90 | WM20 | FIN | 14 | 7 | 5 | 12 | 10 | — |
| **Aaltonen, Risto / b. Dec. 29, 1930** | | | | | | | | |
| 1957 | WM | FIN | 3 | 1 | 0 | 1 | — | — |
| **Aarnio, Antti / b. May 14, 1981** | | | | | | | | |
| 1999 | WM18 | FIN | 7 | 0 | 2 | 2 | 30 | G |
| **Abbot, Reg / b. Feb. 4, 1930** | | | | | | | | |
| 1965 | WM | CAN | 7 | 2 | 2 | 4 | 0 | — |
| **Abdulayev, Eldar / b. Jan. 20, 1985** | | | | | | | | |
| 2003 | WM18 | KAZ | 6 | 0 | 2 | 2 | 4 | — |
| **Abel, Clarence "Taffy" / b. May 28, 1900 / d. Aug. 1, 1964** | | | | | | | | |
| 1924 | OG-M | USA | 5 | 15 | — | 15 | 8 | S |
| **Abel, George / b. Feb. 23, 1916 / d. Apr. 16, 1996** | | | | | | | | |
| 1952 | OG-M | CAN | 8 | 6 | 6 | 12 | 2 | G |
| **Abelstedt, Borje / b. June 14, 1913 / d. unknown** | | | | | | | | |
| 1935 | WM | SWE | 8 | 1 | — | 1 | — | — |
| **Abercrombie, Bobby / b. Jan. 5, 1983** | | | | | | | | |
| 2001 | WM18 | NOR | 5 | 0 | 0 | 0 | 12 | — |
| **Abols, Artis / b. Jan. 3, 1973** | | | | | | | | |
| 1999-2002 | WM | LAT | 23 | 1 | 3 | 4 | 10 | — |
| **Abrahamsen, Trond / b. July 16, 1960** | | | | | | | | |
| 1979 | WM20 | NOR | 5 | 1 | 0 | 1 | 4 | — |
| 1980-84 | OG-M | NOR | 10 | 1 | 0 | 1 | 10 | — |
| **Abrahamsson, Carl / b. May 1, 1896 / d Dec. 25, 1948** | | | | | | | | |
| 1928 | OG-M | SWE | 4 | 0 | 0 | 0 | 6 | S |
| 1931 | WM | SWE | 6 | 0 | 0 | 0 | — | — |
| **Abrahamsson, Thommy / b. Apr. 8, 1947** | | | | | | | | |
| 1970-74 | WM | SWE | 41 | 6 | 8 | 14 | 36 | 2S,3B |
| 1972 | OG-M | SWE | 5 | 1 | 0 | 1 | 0 | — |
| **Abstreiter, Tobias / b. July 6, 1970** | | | | | | | | |
| 1988-89 | WM20 | FRG | 14 | 1 | 3 | 4 | 13 | — |
| 1994-2004 | WM | GER | 27 | 1 | 7 | 8 | 18 | — |
| 2004 | WCH | GER | 4 | 0 | 0 | 0 | 2 | — |
| 2002 | OG-M | GER | 7 | 0 | 2 | 2 | 0 | — |
| **Acker, Gert / b. May 7, 1982** | | | | | | | | |
| 2000 | WM18 | GER | 6 | 2 | 1 | 3 | 6 | — |
| **Ackermann, Rene / b. Apr. 1, 1972** | | | | | | | | |
| 1991 | WM20 | SUI | 6 | 0 | 0 | 0 | 0 | — |
| **Acton, Ben / b. Dec. 12, 1927** | | | | | | | | |
| 1960 | OG-M | AUS | 5 | 0 | 0 | 0 | 11 | — |
| **Acton, Keith / b. Apr. 15, 1958** | | | | | | | | |
| 1987-92 | WM | CAN | 26 | 6 | 0 | 6 | 4 | S |
| **Adamek, Marek / b. Mar. 27, 1967** | | | | | | | | |
| 1987 | WM20 | POL | 7 | 0 | 1 | 1 | 25 | — |
| **Adamiec, Janusz / b. Apr. 29, 1962** | | | | | | | | |
| 1989-92 | WM | POL | 16 | 0 | 3 | 3 | 4 | — |
| 1984-92 | OG-M | POL | 19 | 2 | 1 | 3 | 0 | — |
| **Adamik, Petr / b. Mar. 29, 1952** | | | | | | | | |
| 1973 | WM | TCH | 3 | 0 | 0 | 0 | 2 | B |
| **Adamowski, Tadeusz / b. Nov. 19, 1901 / d. Aug. 1994** | | | | | | | | |
| 1930-33 | WM | POL | 16 | 3 | 0 | 3 | 0 | — |
| 1928 | OG-M | POL | 2 | 1 | — | 1 | — | — |
| **Adams, Greg / b. Aug. 1, 1963** | | | | | | | | |
| 1986-90 | WM | CAN | 11 | 9 | 1 | 10 | 10 | B |
| **Adams, Jurgen / b. Feb. 13, 1961** | | | | | | | | |
| 1979-81 | WM20 | FRG | 15 | 5 | 4 | 9 | 14 | — |
| **Adams, Kevyn / b. Oct. 8, 1974** | | | | | | | | |
| 1994 | WM20 | USA | 7 | 4 | 3 | 7 | 2 | — |
| 2005 | WM | USA | 1 | 0 | 0 | 0 | 0 | — |
| **Adams, Wally / b. unknown / d. unknown** | | | | | | | | |
| 1930 | WM | CAN | 1 | 0 | — | 0 | — | G |
| **Adamus, Damian / b. Feb. 20, 1967** | | | | | | | | |
| 1987 | WM20 | POL | 3 | 1 | 1 | 2 | 0 | — |
| **Adolfsen, Svein / b. unknown** | | | | | | | | |
| 1954 | WM | NOR | 6 | 0 | — | 0 | 0 | — |
| **Adolfson, Jan Erik / b. June 1, 1930 / d. Mar. 27, 2001** | | | | | | | | |
| 1950-54 | WM | NOR | 15 | 1 | 1 | 2 | 2 | — |
| 1952 | OG-M | NOR | 7 | 0 | 0 | 0 | — | — |
| **Adrian, Hans / b. Jan. 2, 1925** | | | | | | | | |
| 1950 | WM | SWE | 1 | 0 | 0 | 0 | 0 | — |
| **Aeberli, Patrick / b. July 14, 1981** | | | | | | | | |
| 2001 | WM20 | SUI | 7 | 0 | 0 | 0 | 0 | — |
| **Aeger, Florian / b. unknown** | | | | | | | | |
| 1983 | WM20 | FRG | 7 | 0 | 0 | 0 | 2 | — |
| **Aegertner, Daniel / b. Sept. 3, 1976** | | | | | | | | |
| 1996 | WM20 | SUI | 5 | 0 | 1 | 1 | 20 | — |
| **Aeschlimann, Jean-Jacques / b. May 30, 1967** | | | | | | | | |
| 1986-87 | WM20 | SUI | 14 | 3 | 0 | 3 | 2 | — |
| 1995-03 | WM | SUI | 31 | 8 | 0 | 8 | 14 | — |
| 2002 | OG-M | SUI | 4 | 3 | 3 | 6 | 2 | — |
| **Aeschlimann, Peter / b. July 12, 1946** | | | | | | | | |
| 1972 | OG-M | SUI | 4 | 0 | 0 | 0 | 2 | — |
| 1972 | WM | SUI | 10 | 1 | 1 | 2 | 12 | — |
| **Afanasenkov, Dmitri / b. May 12, 1980** | | | | | | | | |
| 2000 | WM20 | RUS | 7 | 5 | 1 | 6 | 6 | S |
| 2004 | WCH | RUS | 2 | 1 | 1 | 2 | 0 | — |
| **Afinogenov, Denis / b. Mar. 15, 1974** | | | | | | | | |
| 1997 | WM | RUS | 9 | 1 | 1 | 2 | 0 | — |
| **Agazzi, Giancarlo / b. Aug. 22, 1932** | | | | | | | | |
| 1959 | WM | ITA | 4 | 1 | 1 | 2 | 8 | — |
| 1956-64 | OG-M | ITA | 13 | 5 | 1 | 6 | 12 | — |
| **Ageikin, Sergei / b. June 13, 1963** | | | | | | | | |
| 1983 | WM20 | URS | 7 | 1 | 1 | 2 | 6 | G |
| 1986 | WM | URS | 6 | 1 | 1 | 2 | 2 | G |
| **Agnel, Benjamin / b. Nov. 29, 1973** | | | | | | | | |
| 1994 | OG-M | FRA | 6 | 1 | 0 | 1 | 2 | — |
| **Agu, Johan / b. Apr. 27, 1983** | | | | | | | | |
| 2003 | WM20 | SWE | 6 | 0 | 0 | 0 | 0 | — |
| **Ahearn, Kevin / b. June 20, 1948** | | | | | | | | |
| 1971 | WM | USA | 10 | 1 | 1 | 2 | 2 | — |
| 1972 | OG-M | USA | 5 | 4 | 3 | 7 | 0 | S |
| **Ahern, Fred / b. Feb. 12, 1952** | | | | | | | | |
| 1976 | CC | USA | 5 | 2 | 0 | 2 | 0 | — |
| **Ahlberg, Mats / b. May 16, 1947** | | | | | | | | |
| 1973-78 | WM | SWE | 60 | 30 | 31 | 61 | 56 | 2S,3B |
| 1976 | CC | SWE | 4 | 1 | 1 | 2 | 0 | — |
| 1972-80 | OG-M | SWE | 8 | 6 | 5 | 11 | 13 | B |
| **Ahlen, Thomas / b. Mar. 8, 1959** | | | | | | | | |
| 1984 | CC | SWE | 4 | 0 | 0 | 0 | 0 | 2nd |
| 1984 | OG-M | SWE | 7 | 3 | 1 | 4 | 4 | B |
| **Ahlen, Valter / b. Aug. 6, 1929** | | | | | | | | |
| 1957 | WM | SWE | 4 | 1 | 3 | 4 | — | G |
| **Ahlqvist, Timo / b. Apr. 2, 1940** | | | | | | | | |
| 1961 | WM | FIN | 6 | 2 | 0 | 2 | 8 | — |
| **Ahlroos, Kim / b. July 2, 1971** | | | | | | | | |
| 1991 | WM20 | FIN | 7 | 2 | 1 | 3 | 4 | — |
| **Ahlstrom, Bjorn / b. Apr. 7, 1971** | | | | | | | | |
| 1991 | WM20 | SWE | 2 | 0 | 1 | 1 | 14 | — |
| **Ahlund, Hakan / b. Aug. 16, 1967** | | | | | | | | |
| 1987 | WM20 | SWE | 6 | 2 | 1 | 3 | 4 | B |
| 1993 | WM | SWE | 5 | 0 | 0 | 0 | 2 | S |
| **Ahmaoja, Timo / b. Aug. 8, 1978** | | | | | | | | |
| 1998 | WM20 | FIN | 7 | 0 | 0 | 0 | 4 | G |
| **Ahne, Manfred / b. June 2, 1961** | | | | | | | | |
| 1980-81 | WM20 | FRG | 9 | 4 | 2 | 6 | 0 | — |
| 1985-89 | WM | FRG | 39 | 2 | 2 | 4 | 8 | — |
| 1984 | OG-M | FRG | 6 | 0 | 0 | 0 | 0 | — |
| **Aho, Harri / b. Mar. 11, 1968** | | | | | | | | |
| 1988 | WM20 | FIN | 5 | 1 | 0 | 1 | 4 | B |
| **Aho, Matti / b. Jan. 28, 1983** | | | | | | | | |
| 2003 | WM20 | FIN | 7 | 2 | 1 | 3 | 2 | B |
| **Ahokainen, Seppo / b. Jan. 19, 1952** | | | | | | | | |
| 1972-82 | WM | FIN | 67 | 15 | 9 | 24 | 34 | — |
| 1976 | OG-M | FIN | 5 | 1 | 3 | 4 | 6 | — |
| **Ahonen, Olli / b. Apr. 5, 1979** | | | | | | | | |
| 1998-99 | WM20 | FIN | 13 | 6 | 3 | 9 | 2 | G |
| **Ahosilta, Marko / b. Jan. 24, 1980** | | | | | | | | |
| 2000 | WM20 | FIN | 7 | 1 | 3 | 4 | 0 | — |
| **Aimonetto, Richard / b. Jan. 24, 1973** | | | | | | | | |
| 1998-00 | WM | FRA | 12 | 1 | 2 | 3 | 10 | — |
| 1998-02 | OG-M | FRA | 8 | 0 | 0 | 0 | 0 | — |
| **Air, Sandy / b. Mar. 25, 1928** | | | | | | | | |
| 1958 | WM | CAN | 2 | 1 | 2 | 3 | 0 | G |
| **Akazawa, Shikashi / b. Nov. 15, 1934** | | | | | | | | |
| 1960 | OG-M | JPN | 2 | 0 | 0 | 0 | 2 | — |
| **Akerblom, Bjorn / b. June 24, 1960** | | | | | | | | |
| 1979-80 | WM20 | SWE | 11 | 1 | 1 | 2 | 6 | 2B |
| **Akerblom, Markus / b. Nov. 22, 1969** | | | | | | | | |
| 1988-89 | WM20 | SWE | 14 | 5 | 6 | 11 | 12 | S |
| **Akerstrom, Roger / b. Apr. 5, 1967** | | | | | | | | |
| 1987 | WM20 | SWE | 6 | 0 | 0 | 0 | 8 | B |
| 1993 | WM | SWE | 8 | 1 | 1 | 2 | 6 | S |
| **Akervall, Hank / b. Aug. 24, 1937 / d. Feb. 18, 2000** | | | | | | | | |
| 1964 | OG-M | CAN | 7 | 2 | 0 | 2 | 9 | — |
| **Akesson, Frederik / b. Aug. 27, 1966** | | | | | | | | |
| 2003-05 | WM | DEN | 12 | 1 | 3 | 4 | 12 | — |
| **Akiba, Takeshi / b. May 4, 1944** | | | | | | | | |
| 1968-76 | OG-M | JPN | 14 | 0 | 1 | 1 | 8 | — |
| **Akkanen, Juuso / b. Dec. 22, 1983** | | | | | | | | |
| 2001 | WM18 | FIN | 6 | 0 | 0 | 0 | 6 | B |
| **Aksyutenko, Sergei / b. May 2, 1979** | | | | | | | | |
| 1998 | WM20 | KAZ | 7 | 0 | 0 | 0 | 2 | — |
| **Akymov, Pavlo / b. Mar. 5, 1986** | | | | | | | | |
| 2004 | WM20 | UKR | 6 | 0 | 0 | 0 | 2 | — |
| **Alanen, Johannes / b. Feb. 5, 1978** | | | | | | | | |
| 1998 | WM20 | FIN | 7 | 0 | 3 | 3 | 2 | G |
| **Alastalo, Juha / b. May 29, 1981** | | | | | | | | |
| 1999 | WM18 | FIN | 7 | 0 | 2 | 2 | 4 | G |
| **Alatalo, Mika / b. June 11, 1971** | | | | | | | | |
| 1989-91 | WM20 | FIN | 20 | 7 | 7 | 14 | 20 | — |
| 1993-98 | WM | FIN | 22 | 3 | 1 | 4 | 14 | 2S |
| 1994 | OG-M | FIN | 7 | 2 | 1 | 3 | 2 | B |
| **Albelin, Tommy / b. May 21, 1964** | | | | | | | | |
| 1983-84 | WM20 | SWE | 14 | 1 | 6 | 7 | 16 | — |
| 1985-97 | WM | SWE | 48 | 6 | 10 | 16 | 44 | G,2S |
| 1987-96 | CC | SWE | 16 | 3 | 2 | 5 | 10 | — |
| 1998 | OG-M | SWE | 3 | 0 | 0 | 0 | 4 | — |
| **Alber, Gerhard / b. July 21, 1960** | | | | | | | | |
| 1980 | WM20 | FRG | 4 | 1 | 0 | 1 | 6 | — |
| **Albert, Pierre-Yves / b. May 6, 1983** | | | | | | | | |
| 2002 | WM20 | FRA | 6 | 2 | 0 | 2 | 6 | — |
| **Alberton, Rino / b. Mar. 30, 1936** | | | | | | | | |
| 1956 | OG-M | ITA | 5 | 1 | 0 | 1 | 2 | — |
| **Albinsson, Andreas / b. Mar. 19, 1981** | | | | | | | | |
| 1999 | WM18 | SWE | 7 | 2 | 3 | 5 | 0 | S |
| **Albrecht, Zdenek / b. Aug. 14, 1961** | | | | | | | | |
| 1980 | WM20 | TCH | 4 | 0 | 2 | 2 | 4 | — |
| **Aldcorn, Gary / b. Mar. 7, 1935** | | | | | | | | |
| 1965 | WM | CAN | 7 | 5 | 1 | 6 | 8 | — |
| **Aldridge, Keith / b. July 20, 1973** | | | | | | | | |
| 1995-96 | WM | USA | 12 | 0 | 1 | 1 | 4 | B |
| **Aleksushin, Vladimir / b. July 3, 1969** | | | | | | | | |
| 1988 | WM20 | URS | 7 | 0 | 2 | 2 | 10 | S |
| **Alexandrov, Boris / b. Nov. 13, 1955** | | | | | | | | |
| 1976 | CC | URS | 5 | 2 | 4 | 6 | 2 | — |
| 1976 | OG-M | URS | 5 | 2 | 2 | 4 | 0 | G |
| **Alexandrov, Igor / b. Feb. 5, 1973** | | | | | | | | |
| 1993 | WM20 | RUS | 7 | 3 | 4 | 7 | 0 | — |
| **Alexandrov, Sergei / b. Apr. 29, 1978** | | | | | | | | |
| 1998 | WM20 | KAZ | 7 | 4 | 2 | 6 | 2 | — |
| 2004-05 | WM | KAZ | 12 | 2 | 0 | 2 | 4 | — |
| 2006 | OG-M | KAZ | 5 | 1 | 0 | 1 | 2 | — |
| **Alexandrov, Veniamin / b. Apr. 18, 1937** | | | | | | | | |
| 1958-67 | WM | URS | 50 | 43 | 32 | 75 | 26 | 4G,2S,B |
| 1960-68 | OG-M | URS | 18 | 14 | 12 | 26 | 23 | 2G,B |
| ~IIHF Hall of Fame | | | | | | | | |
| ~WM All-Star Team/Forward (1966, 1967) | | | | | | | | |
| **Alexandrov, Viktor / b. Dec. 28, 1985** | | | | | | | | |
| 2001 | WM20 | KAZ | 6 | 2 | 1 | 3 | 4 | — |
| **Alexeyev, Alexander / b. Jan. 8, 1968** | | | | | | | | |
| 2003 | WM | BLR | 6 | 0 | 1 | 1 | 0 | — |
| 1998 | OG-M | BLR | 7 | 1 | 1 | 2 | 0 | — |
| **Alinc, Jan / b. May 27, 1972** | | | | | | | | |
| 1992 | WM20 | TCH | 7 | 0 | 0 | 0 | 0 | — |
| 1994 | OG-M | CZE | 6 | 2 | 0 | 2 | 4 | — |
| **Alkula, Jukka / b. Sept. 19, 1947** | | | | | | | | |
| 1977 | WM | FIN | 10 | 7 | 2 | 9 | 4 | — |
| **Allan, Chad / b. July 12, 1976** | | | | | | | | |
| 1995-96 | WM20 | CAN | 13 | 1 | 0 | 1 | 10 | 2G |
| **Allard, Pierre / b. Aug. 9, 1972** | | | | | | | | |
| 1997-2000 | WM | FRA | 17 | 3 | 0 | 3 | 6 | — |
| 1998 | OG-M | FRA | 4 | 0 | 0 | 0 | 6 | — |
| **Allen, Bryan / b. Aug. 21, 1980** | | | | | | | | |
| 1999 | WM20 | CAN | 7 | 1 | 2 | 3 | 2 | S |
| **Allen, Harry / b. Jan. 23, 1923** | | | | | | | | |
| 1950 | WM | CAN | 7 | 8 | 2 | 10 | 0 | G |
| **Allen, Marko / b. Apr. 5, 1967** | | | | | | | | |
| 1987 | WM20 | FIN | 7 | 2 | 3 | 5 | 4 | G |
| **Allen, Percy / b. unknown / d. unknown** | | | | | | | | |
| 1938 | WM | CAN | 7 | 4 | — | 4 | — | G |
| **Allen, Peter / b. Mar. 6, 1970** | | | | | | | | |
| 1995-2000 | WM | CAN | 8 | 0 | 0 | 0 | 4 | B |
| **Allesoe, Morten / b. July 23, 1987** | | | | | | | | |
| 2005 | WM18 | DEN | 6 | 0 | 0 | 0 | 2 | — |

**Alley, Steve / b. Dec. 20, 1953**
1975-78 WM USA 12 1 1 2 2 —
1976 OG-M USA 5 0 0 0 4 —

**Allinger, Ruben / b. Dec. 23, 1891 / d. Jan. 9, 1979**
1924 OG-M SWE 5 0 — 0 — —

**Allison, Jason / b. May 29, 1975**
1994-95 WM20 CAN 14 6 18 24 8 2G
~WM20 All-Star Team/Forward (1995)

**Allison, Ray / b. Mar. 4, 1959**
1979 WM20 CAN 5 0 5 5 4 —

**Alm, Larry / b. 1937**
1965 WM USA 7 1 0 1 2 —

**Almack, Tom / b. 1914 / d. Jan. 25, 1979**
1937 WM CAN 2 0 0 0 0 G

**Almasy, Peter / b. Feb. 11, 1961**
1992-93 WM FRA 12 4 0 4 0 —
1988-92 OG-M FRA 14 6 4 10 8 —

**Almetov, Alexander / b. Jan. 18, 1940 / d. Jan. 18, 1992**
1961-67 WM URS 35 30 28 58 10 4G,B
1960-64 OG-M URS 14 5 6 11 2 G,B
~WM All-Star Team/Forward (1965, 1967)

**Almqvist, Gote / b. June 25, 1921 / d. Dec. 21, 1994**
1953-54 WM SWE 10 1 0 1 2 G,B
1952 OG-M SWE 8 1 0 1 — B

**Almtorp, Jonas / b. Nov. 17, 1983**
2001 WM18 SWE 6 1 2 3 2 —
2003 WM20 SWE 6 0 0 0 4 —

**Althoff, Christian / b. Mar. 3, 1972**
1992 WM20 GER 7 0 0 0 0 —

**Altmann, Karl / b. Feb. 7, 1959**
1978-79 WM20 FRG 11 0 2 2 14 —

**Alvera, Isidoro / b. Mar. 3, 1945**
1964 OG-M ITA 6 1 1 2 0 —

**Amann, Richard / b. Dec. 30, 1960**
1992-93 WM GER 11 1 4 5 32 —
1992-94 OG-M GER 16 0 2 2 8 —

**Ambros, Paul / b. June 22, 1934**
1959-63 WM FRG 27 4 3 7 44 —
1956-64 OG-M FRG 22 0 1 1 48 —

**Ambruz, Martin / b. Dec. 5, 1979**
1999 WM20 CZE 6 0 2 2 8 —

**Ames, Paul / b. Mar. 12, 1965**
1984 WM20 USA 7 0 0 0 6 —

**Amess, Ron / b. Aug. 9, 1937**
1960 OG-M AUS 5 0 0 0 2 —

**Amirovici, Caetan / b. unknown / d. unknown**
1947 WM ROM 2 0 — 0 — —

**Amodeo, Mike / b. June 22, 1952**
1982-83 WM ITA 17 1 1 2 20 —

**Amonte, Tony / b. Aug. 2, 1970**
1989-90 WM20 USA 14 6 5 11 6 —
1991-93 WM USA 16 3 7 10 12 —
1996-2004 WCH USA 12 2 4 6 6 1st
1998-2002 OG-M USA 10 2 3 5 4 S

**Anastasiu, Paul / b. 1913 / d. unknown**
1931-47 WM ROM 34 5 0 5 7 —

**Anciaux, Hubert / b. Nov. 25, 1925**
1947-50 WM BEL 17 5 1 6 0 —

**Andersen, Carl-Oscar Boe / b. Mar. 30, 1972**
1994-99 WM NOR 25 0 1 1 16 —

**Andersen, Cato / b. June 10, 1959**
1979 WM20 NOR 5 0 0 0 0 —
1984 OG-M NOR 5 2 1 3 2 —

**Andersen, Cato Tom / b. June 17, 1967**
1990-96 WM NOR 27 1 4 5 16 —
1988-94 OG-M NOR 12 0 2 2 10 —

**Andersen, Karl / b. Mar. 30, 1972**
1991 WM20 NOR 6 0 0 0 6 —

**Andersen, Kenneth / b. Feb. 8, 1983**
2001 WM18 NOR 5 0 0 0 4 —

**Andersen, Knut / b. 1959**
1979 WM20 NOR 5 1 0 1 4 —

**Andersen, Lars-Hakon / b. Jan. 13, 1974**
1996-99 WM NOR 10 3 1 4 0 —
1994 OG-M NOR 5 0 0 0 2 —

**Andersen, Morgan / b. Apr. 7, 1966**
1990 WM NOR 7 0 2 2 12 —
1988-94 OG-M NOR 14 1 1 2 14 —

**Anderson, Glenn / b. Oct. 2, 1960**
1989-92 WM CAN 12 4 3 7 20 2S
1984-87 CC CAN 15 3 5 8 20 2/1st
1980 OG-M CAN 6 2 2 4 4 —

**Anderson, Jimmy / b. Dec. 16, 1916 / d. unknown**
1937 WM GBR 7 3 2 5 4 S

**Anderson, John / b. Mar. 28, 1957**
1977 WM20 CAN 7 10 5 15 4 S
1983-85 WM CAN 15 7 4 11 24 S,B

**Anderson, John / b. Aug. 17, 1960**
1980 WM20 USA 5 1 0 1 2 —

**Anderson, Osborn "Ty" / b. Oct. 15, 1908 / d. Jan. 31, 1989**
1931 WM USA 6 3 — 3 — S
1932 OG-M USA 6 1 1 2 5 S
*birth name Asbjorn Andersen but changed when he moved to U.S.

**Anderson, Russ / b. Feb. 12, 1955**
1977 WM USA 10 0 0 0 12 —

**Anderson, Warren / b. Apr. 13, 1952**
1980-84 OG-M CAN 13 1 0 1 4 —

**Anderson, Wendell / b. Feb. 1, 1933**
1955 WM USA 8 2 0 2 5 —
1956 OG-M USA 7 0 1 1 2 S

**Andersson, Adam / b. May 21, 1983**
2001 WM18 SWE 6 0 1 1 0 —
2002-03 WM20 SWE 13 1 1 2 6 —

**Andersson, Ake / b. June 8, 1918 / d. May 11, 1982**
1938-54 WM SWE 39 7 1 8 4 G,2S,B
1948-52 OG-M SWE 17 6 0 6 0 B

**Andersson, Anders / b. Jan. 2, 1937 / d. Dec. 15, 1989**
1957-65 WM SWE 26 13 11 24 16 2G,B
1960-64 OG-M SWE 13 10 6 16 10 S

**Andersson, Erik / b. Aug. 19, 1971**
1991 WM20 SWE 7 2 1 3 4 —

**Andersson, Gunnar / b. Nov. 18, 1944**
1971-74 WM SWE 13 0 0 0 0 2B

**Andersson, Henrik / b. Jan. 19, 1970**
1990 WM20 SWE 5 0 1 1 2 —

**Andersson, Henrik / b. Apr. 12, 1977**
1997 WM20 SWE 6 1 0 1 0 —

**Andersson, Jesper / b. Apr. 30, 1986**
2004 WM18 SWE 6 2 0 2 0 —

**Andersson, Kenneth / b. Mar. 19, 1958**
1986 WM SWE 7 1 1 2 0 S

**Andersson, Kent Erik / b. May 24, 1951**
1977-78 WM SWE 20 9 2 11 12 S
1981 CC SWE 5 0 1 1 0 —

**Andersson, Leif / b. Mar. 3, 1940**
1962 WM SWE 4 3 1 4 0 G

**Andersson, Mikael / b. July 6, 1959**
1978-79 WM20 SWE 13 1 2 3 2 S,B
1987 WM SWE 10 4 2 6 10 G
1987 CC SWE 5 1 5 6 0 —
1988 OG-M SWE 8 3 3 6 4 B

**Andersson, Mikael / b. May 10, 1966**
1984-86 WM20 SWE 20 7 8 15 18 —
1992-94 WM SWE 21 5 3 8 2 G,S,B
1991-96 WCH SWE 10 0 2 2 4 —
1998 OG-M SWE 4 1 1 2 0 —

**Andersson, Niklas / b. May 20, 1971**
1989-91 WM20 SWE 21 10 6 16 14 S
1996-2004 WM SWE 43 6 11 17 24 3S,B
1991-96 CC SWE 7 0 1 1 0 —

**Andersson, Olle / b. July 1, 1914 / d. Apr. 28, 1990**
1935-38 WM SWE 14 3 0 3 0 —

**Andersson, Pelle / b. Mar. 1, 1982**
2000 WM18 SWE 6 0 6 6 4 B

**Andersson, Peter / b. Mar. 2, 1962**
1981-82 WM20 SWE 12 4 7 11 14 G
1982-91 WM SWE 58 4 10 14 32 2G,S
1984-91 CC SWE 19 2 2 4 8 2nd
1988-92 OG-M SWE 16 3 4 7 8 B

**Andersson, Peter / b. Aug. 29, 1965**
1983-85 WM20 SWE 21 7 11 18 40 —
1993-2001 WM SWE 29 2 10 12 28 S,2B
1992 OG-M SWE 8 0 1 1 4 —

**Andersson, Sivert / b. Mar. 4, 1959**
1979 WM20 SWE 6 2 1 3 12 B

**Andersson, Stig / b. Oct. 16, 1914 / d. Mar. 23, 2000**
1938-53 WM SWE 10 6 3 9 2 G
1936-48 OG-M SWE 4 0 0 0 0 —

**Andersson, Sture / b. Nov. 18, 1949**
1979 WM SWE 8 1 1 2 0 B
1980 OG-M SWE 7 2 0 2 0 B

**Andersson, Torbjorn / b. Feb. 1, 1957**
1977 WM20 SWE 7 4 1 5 17 —

**Andersson-Dettner, Thore / b. Oct. 18, 1908 / d. Oct. 7, 1984**
1931 WM SWE 6 0 — 0 — —

**Andersson-Junkka, Jonas / b. May 4, 1975**
1995 WM20 SWE 7 2 4 6 8 B

**Andersson-Tvilling, Hans / b. Sweden, July 15, 1928**
1951-55 WM SWE 22 11 1 12 2 G,S,B
1952-56 OG-M SWE 16 5 4 9 2 B

**Andersson-Tvilling, Stig / b. July 15, 1928 / d. Sept. 20, 1989**
1951-55 WM SWE 25 11 5 16 4 G,S,B
1952-56 OG-M SWE 16 6 2 8 0 B

**Andjelic, Alexander / b. Oct. 16, 1940**
1964 OG-M YUG 5 0 0 0 0 —

**Andrei, Nicolae / b. Dec. 8, 1939**
1964 OG-M ROM 7 3 2 5 2 —

**Andrejs, Rene / b. Sept. 25, 1958**
1977-78 WM20 TCH 13 0 4 4 8 B

**Andreossi, Munrezzan "Mezzi" / b. June 30, 1897 / d. Oct. 1958**
1928 OG-M SUI 2 0 — 0 4 B

**Andresen, Bjorn / b. Sept. 8, 1946**
1972 OG-M NOR 4 1 2 3 0 —

**Andresen, Knut / b. June 2, 1959**
1980 OG-M NOR 5 1 0 1 12 —

**Andreychuk, Dave / b. Sept. 29, 1963**
1983 WM20 CAN 7 6 5 11 14 B
1986 WM CAN 10 3 2 5 18 B

**Andreyev, Alexei / b. Apr. 8, 1979**
1999 WM20 BLR 6 1 0 1 22 —

**Andreyev, Andrei / b. Mar. 4, 1959**
1979 WM20 URS 6 6 1 7 4 G

**Andrievsky, Alexander / b. Aug. 10, 1968**
1998-2001 WM BLR 21 5 6 11 22 —
1998-2002 OG-M BLR 15 1 2 3 12 —

**Andrusak, Greg / b. Nov. 14, 1969**
1995 WM CAN 7 0 0 0 12 B

**Andrushenko, Igor / b. Feb. 12, 1983**
2000-01 WM18 UKR 12 0 2 2 4 —

**Andrushenko, Viktor / b. May 10, 1986**
2002 WM18 UKR 8 1 3 4 37 —
2004 WM20 UKR 6 0 0 0 6 —

**Andrys, Roman / b. Jan. 22, 1967**
1987 WM20 TCH 7 1 4 5 0 S

**Andrzejewski, Alfred / b. unknown / d. unknown**
1938-39 WM POL 5 0 0 0 0 —

**Anger, Niklas / b. July 14, 1977**
1996-97 WM20 SWE 13 8 0 8 4 S

**Anikeyenko, Vitali / b. Jan. 2, 1987 / d. Sept. 7, 2011**
2003-05 WM18 RUS 12 1 1 2 12 B
2007 WM20 RUS 6 0 1 1 10 S
~perished in Yaroslavl plane crash

**Anisimov, Artyom / b. May 24, 1988**
1995 WM20 RUS 7 0 0 0 0 S

**Anisin, Vyacheslav / b. July 11, 1951**
1972-75 WM URS 33 14 16 30 12 3G,S
1972 SS URS 7 1 3 4 2 2nd

**Ankert, Thorsten / b. June 22, 1988**
2005-06 WM18 GER 12 0 1 1 14 —

**Anshakov, Sergei / b. Jan. 13, 1984**
2002 WM18 RUS 8 2 2 4 2 S
2003-04 WM20 RUS 12 6 3 9 0 G

**Ansoldi, Luca / b. Jan. 5, 1982**
2006-10 WM ITA 23 5 1 6 18 —
2006 OG-M ITA 5 0 0 0 10 —

**Antal, Elod Gherghely / b. Mar. 11, 1955**
1977 WM ROM 10 0 1 1 6 —
1976-80 OG-M ROM 10 3 3 6 2 —

**Antal, Istvan / b. Sept. 18, 1958**
1980 OG-M ROM 5 0 0 0 2 —

**Anthamatten, Silvan / b. June 16, 1984**
2004 WM20 SUI 6 0 1 1 2 —

**Antipin, Vladimir / b. Apr. 18, 1970**
1998-2010 WM KAZ 21 1 2 3 16 —
1998-2006 OG-M KAZ 12 2 1 3 8 —

**Antipov, Anatoli / b. Jan. 29, 1959**
1979 WM20 URS 6 0 5 5 2 G

**Antipov, Vladimir / b. Jan. 17, 1978**
1997-98 WM20 RUS 13 1 4 5 0 S,B
2002-05 WM RUS 29 2 7 9 6 S,B

**Antisin, Misko / b. July 4, 1964**
1992-98 WM SUI 20 1 1 2 47 —

**Antonen, Juuso / b. Feb. 8, 1988**
2006 WM18 FIN 6 0 1 1 8 S

**Antonenko, Oleg / b. July 11, 1971**
1998-2009 WM BLR 40 15 9 24 18 —
2002-10 OG BLR 13 1 1 2 8 —

**Antonovich, Mike / b. Oct. 18, 1951**
1976-82 WM USA 21 1 3 4 18 —
**Antons, Heiko / b. Nov. 8, 1951**
1972 OG-M FRG 1 0 0 0 0 —
**Antons, Nils / b. Sept. 17, 1979**
1997-98 WM20 GER 12 1 0 1 10 —
**Antosik, Igor / b. Mar. 24, 1987**
2005 WM18 RUS 6 0 2 2 4 —
**Antropov, Nikolai / b. Feb. 18, 1980**
1998-99 WM20 KAZ 13 3 11 14 22 —
1998 WM KAZ 3 0 1 1 4 —
2006 OG-M KAZ 5 1 0 1 4 —
**Antuszewicz, Michal / b. Oct. 1, 1909 / d. Mar. 10, 1993**
1952 OG-M POL 2 0 0 0 — —
**Apollonio, Claudio / b. Aug. 21, 1921**
1948 OG-M ITA 3 1 — 1 — —
**Appel, Frank / b. May 12, 1976**
1996 WM20 GER 4 0 0 0 6 —
**Araki, Nobuhiro / b. Jan. 10, 1944**
1968 OG-M JPN 5 3 4 7 2 —
**Arbelius, Pekka / b. , June 19, 1960**
1980 WM20 FIN 5 3 3 6 6 S
1981-90 WM FIN 36 14 7 21 20 —
1981 CC FIN 5 0 0 0 2 —
**Arcangeloni, Stephane / b. June 6, 1972**
1994 OG-M FRA 7 1 0 1 2 —
**Archer, Alex "Sandy" / b. May 1, 1910 / d. July 29, 1997**
1937-38 WM GBR 17 12 6 18 2 2S
1936 OG-M GBR 7 2 1 3 0 G
**Archibald, Dave / b. Apr. 14, 1969**
1991 WM CAN 10 0 1 1 8 S
1992 OG-M CAN 8 7 1 8 18 S
**Argokov, Artyom / b. Jan. 16, 1976**
2004-06 WM KAZ 18 2 2 4 4 —
2006 OG-M KAZ 5 0 0 0 8 —
**Arima, Tony / b. Sept. 9, 1961**
1980-81 WM20 FIN 10 4 1 5 10 2S
1983 WM FIN 10 3 3 6 16 —
**Arkhipov, Denis / b. May 19, 1979**
1998-99 WM20 RUS 14 6 4 10 6 G,S
2003-06 WM RUS 14 4 5 9 18 —
**Arkiomaa, Tero / b. Feb. 20, 1968**
1988 WM20 FIN 7 1 3 4 4 B
**Arling, Adrian / b. Mar. 21, 1985**
2003 WM18 SWE 6 0 0 0 0 —
**Armstrong, Chris / b. June 26, 1975**
1994 WM20 CAN 6 0 1 1 0 G
**Armstrong, Howard / b. Apr. 1906 / d. Feb. 4, 1964**
1930 WM CAN 1 1 — 1 — G
**Arnesen, Christian / b. unknown**
1983 WM20 NOR 6 3 1 4 6 —
**Arniel, Scott / b. Sept. 17, 1962**
1981-82 WM20 CAN 12 8 7 15 8 G
**Arnott, Jason / b. Oct. 11, 1974**
1994 WM CAN 8 0 6 6 10 G
**Aro, Kari / b. Dec. 28, 1935**
1958-62 WM FIN 5 0 0 0 2 —
**Arthur, Fred / b. Mar. 6, 1961**
1981 WM20 CAN 5 0 2 2 10 —
**Artursson, Greger / b. Feb. 6, 1972**
1992 WM20 SWE 7 1 1 2 4 S
**Arvedson, Magnus / b. Nov. 25, 1971**
1997 WM SWE 10 2 1 3 6 S
2002 OG-M SWE 4 0 0 0 0 —
**Arvidsen, Patrick / b. May 1, 1987**
2005 WM18 DEN 6 0 0 0 14 —
**Arwe, Wilhelm / b. Jan. 28, 1898 / d. Apr. 8, 1980**
1920-24 OG-M SWE 8 3 — 3 2 —
**Asai, Isao / b. Dec. 25, 1942**
1968 OG-M JPN 5 0 0 0 4 —
**Ashton, Brent / b. May 18, 1960**
1989 WM CAN 10 3 3 6 2 S
**Aslan, Riri / b. unknown / d. unknown**
1931-33 WM ROM 1 1 — 1 — —
**Asland, Glenn / b. Apr. 25, 1970**
1989 WM20 NOR 7 1 0 1 2 —
**Aslund, Calle / b. Mar. 29, 1983**
2001 WM18 SWE 6 0 0 0 6 —
**Astasenko, Kaspars / b. Feb. 7, 1975**
2001-06 WM LAT 10 1 2 3 14 —
2002 OG-M LAT 3 0 1 1 0 —
**Astley, Mark / b. Mar. 30, 1969**
1994 OG-M CAN 8 0 1 1 4 S

**Astrakhantsev, Konstantin / b. Jan. 21, 1967**
1993 WM RUS 8 1 0 1 2 G
**Atanasov, Ivan / b. Apr. 30, 1957**
1976 OG-M BUL 5 1 1 2 4 —
**Atanasov, Malin / b. June 14, 1946**
1976 OG-M BUL 5 1 0 1 2 —
**Attersley, Bob / b. Aug. 13, 1933**
1958 WM CAN 7 10 7 17 0 G
1960 OG-M CAN 7 6 12 18 4 S
**Auckenthaler, Fred / b. 1899 / d/ unknown**
1924 OG-M SUI 2 0 — 0 — —
**Aucoin, Adrian / b. July 3, 1973**
1993 WM20 CAN 7 0 1 1 8 G
2000 WM CAN 9 3 3 6 14 —
1994 OG-M CAN 4 0 0 0 2 S
**Auffrey, Matt / b. Jan. 3, 1986**
2004 WM18 USA 6 2 3 5 8 S
**Aufiero, Pat / b. Apr. 1, 1980**
2000 WM20 USA 7 0 0 0 4 —
**Auge, Les / b. May 16, 1953 / d. Sept. 13, 2002**
1979 WM USA 8 1 0 1 4 —
**Augsten, Christoph / b. July 4, 1961**
1980-81 WM20 FRG 10 2 1 3 16 —
**Augusta, Josef / b. Nov. 24, 1946**
1969-78 WM TCH 33 3 6 9 20 3S,B
1976 CC TCH 7 3 2 5 6 2nd
1976 OG-M TCH 5 0 1 1 0 S
**Augusta, Patrik / b. Nov. 13, 1969**
1992 WM TCH 5 2 2 4 4 B
1992 OG-M TCH 8 3 2 5 0 B
**Auhuber, Klaus / b. Oct. 28, 1951**
1977-79 WM FRG 28 1 4 5 48 —
1976-80 OG-M FRG 10 1 1 2 19 B
**Aulin, Jared / b. Mar. 15, 1982**
2002 WM20 CAN 7 4 5 9 4 S
**Auzins, Aleksejs / b. Aug. 7, 1910 / d. Apr. 25, 1997**
1935-38 WM LAT 6 2 — 2 — —
1936 OG-M LAT 2 0 — 0 — —
**Avdeyev, Ivan / b. Jan. 10, 1958**
1977 WM20 URS 7 3 5 8 4 G
**Awrey, Don / b. July 18, 1943**
1972 SS CAN 2 0 0 0 0 1st
**Axelsson, Emil / b. Mar. 19, 1986**
2004 WM18 SWE 5 0 0 0 8 —
**Axelsson, Per-Johan / b. Feb. 26, 1975**
1995 WM20 SWE 7 2 3 5 2 B
2000-05 WM SWE 43 14 18 32 44 2S,2B
2004 WCH SWE 4 0 0 0 2 —
2002-06 OG-M SWE 12 3 3 6 2 G
**Axinte, Dumitru / b. May 9, 1952**
1977 WM ROM 10 3 0 3 0 —
1976-80 OG-M ROM 10 2 3 5 0 —
**Azanov, Roman / b. May 8, 1981**
2000-01 WM20 KAZ 13 0 3 3 59 —
**Azevedo, Justin / b. Apr. 1, 1988**
2006 WM18 CAN 7 4 4 8 20 —
**Azuma, Takeshi / b. Jan. 9, 1953**
1976-80 OG-M JPN 10 3 2 5 4 —
**Baarnhielm, Patrik / b. July 24, 1983**
2003 WM20 SWE 6 0 2 2 2 —
**Baban, Jozsef / b. May 25, 1935**
1964 OG-M HUN 7 0 1 1 6 —
**Babariko, Yevgeni / b. Feb. 3, 1974**
1994 WM20 RUS 7 1 2 3 0 B
**Babchuk, Anton / b. May 6, 1984**
2001-02 WM18 RUS 14 3 3 6 10 —
**Babe, Warren / b. Sept. 7, 1968**
1988 WM20 CAN 7 0 2 2 10 G
**Babich, Dmitri / b. Sept. 15, 1982**
2001 WM20 KAZ 6 0 0 0 0 —
**Babich, Yevgeni / b. Jan. 7, 1921 / d. unknown**
1954-57 WM URS 19 5 5 10 4 G,2S
1956 OG-M URS 7 2 3 5 4 G
**Babin, Michael / b. Mar. 20, 1970**
1992-94 WM FRA 17 0 1 1 2 —
1992 OG-M FRA 8 0 0 0 4 —
**Babin, Noah / b. Mar. 11, 1984**
2002 WM18 USA 8 0 0 0 4 G
**Babinov, Sergei / b. July 11, 1955**
1976-83 WM URS 47 9 9 18 32 4G,S,B
1976-81 CC URS 12 0 3 3 6 1st
1976 OG-M URS 5 2 2 4 15 G
**Babka, Daniel / b. Mar. 30, 1972**
1997-99 WM SVK 12 1 0 1 6 —

**Babych, Dave / b. May 23, 1961**
1981-89 WM CAN 17 2 2 4 12 S
**Babych, Wayne / b. June 6, 1958**
1978 WM20 CAN 6 5 5 10 4 B
1979 WM CAN 7 1 2 3 0 —
**Baca, Jergus / b. Jan. 4, 1965**
1989-2002 WM SVK 41 1 4 5 48 G,2B
1991 CC TCH 8 1 3 4 10 —
1994 OG-M SVK 8 1 2 3 10 —
**Bach, Alexander / b. June 18, 1987**
2005 WM18 DEN 6 0 1 1 0 —
**Bachelet, Benoit / b. Nov. 6, 1974**
1999-2004 WM FRA 15 3 2 5 6 —
2002 OG-M FRA 4 0 0 0 4 —
**Bacher, Enrico / b. Dec. 27, 1940**
1959 WM ITA 4 1 1 2 2 —
1964 OG-M ITA 7 3 0 3 6 —
**Bacho, Pavel / b. Sept. 19, 1978**
1998 WM20 CZE 7 1 3 4 0 —
**Bachtold, Jurg / b. unknown / d. unknown**
1933 WM SUI 6 0 — 0 2 —
**Bachura, Adolf / b. Apr. 10, 1933**
1957 WM AUT 7 0 — 0 — —
1964 OG-M AUT 7 2 1 3 2 —
**Bachvarov, Iliya / b. Oct. 10, 1943**
1976 OG-M BUL 5 3 0 3 12 —
**Bachvarov, Marin / b. June 30, 1947**
1976 OG-M BUL 5 1 1 2 2 —
**Bacilek, Stanislav / b. Nov. 13, 1929**
1954-59 WM TCH 30 6 0 6 8 3B
1956 OG-M TCH 6 0 0 0 6 —
**Bacinskas, A. / b. unknown / d. unknown**
1938 WM LTU 4 1 — 1 — —
**Back, Daniel / b. June 4, 1975**
1995 WM20 SWE 7 0 2 2 0 B
**Back, Rene / b. Sept. 8, 1982**
2000 WM18 SUI 7 1 1 2 8 —
2002 WM20 SUI 7 0 1 1 8 —
**Backer, Par / b. Jan. 4, 1982**
2001-02 WM20 SWE 14 4 1 5 8 —
**Backstrom, Anders / b. Dec. 9, 1960**
1980 WM20 SWE 5 0 0 0 0 B
**Backstrom, Kristoffer / b. Jan. 24, 1985**
2003 WM18 SWE 6 0 1 1 8 —
**Badal, Ales / b. Mar. 21, 1967**
1987 WM20 TCH 6 0 0 0 0 S
**Bader, Heinz / b. Oct. 10, 1940**
1962-67 WM FRG 21 1 2 3 18 —
1968 OG-M FRG 7 0 1 1 6 —
**Badertscher, Rolf / b. Feb. 2, 1977**
1997 WM20 SUI 6 0 0 0 2 —
**Badoucek, Vaclav / b. Feb. 9, 1962**
1981-82 WM20 TCH 12 1 3 4 10 S
**Badrov, Yuri / b. Sept. 4, 1982**
2000 WM18 BLR 6 0 0 0 0 —
**Badrutt, Christian / b. 1914 / d. unknown**
1935-39 WM SUI 25 5 0 5 1 S,2B
**Badyl, Pavel / b. Apr. 24, 1986**
2003-04 WM18 BLR 12 0 0 0 0 —
**Bagnoud, Bernhard / b. Feb. 10, 1932**
1959 WM SUI 3 1 1 2 0 —
1956 OG-M SUI 5 6 2 8 6 —
**Bailey, Jason / b. June 4, 1987**
2005 WM18 USA 6 0 1 1 4 G
**Baillie, George / b. Mar. 11, 1921 / d. unknown**
1948 OG-M GBR 6 0 — 0 — —
**Baker, Bill / b. Nov. 29, 1956**
1979-81 WM USA 14 2 2 4 10 —
1980 OG-M USA 7 1 0 1 4 G
1981 CC USA 1 0 0 0 0 —
**Baker, Bob / b. Dec. 21, 1926 / d. Nov. 25, 1994**
1948 OG-M USA 8 7 2 9 2 —
**Baker, Lennie / b. Sept. 13, 1918 / d. July 8, 2008**
1948 OG-M GBR 8 5 — 5 — —
**Bakkelund, Benjamin / b. Apr. 11, 1988**
2006 WM18 NOR 6 0 1 1 2 —
**Bakke-Pedersen, Roar / b. Nov. 24, 1927 / d. Nov. 9, 1989**
1949-62 WM NOR 46 8 7 15 21 —
1952 OG-M NOR 7 0 0 0 — —
**Bakos, Juraj / b. Sept. 3, 1960**
1979-80 WM20 TCH 11 1 0 1 4 S
**Bakrlik, Frantisek / b. June 2, 1983**
2001 WM18 CZE 7 2 1 3 8 —

**Bakula, Martin / b. June 23, 1970**
1989 WM20 TCH 7 1 1 2 8 B

**Bakunenko, Andri / b. Apr. 28, 1977**
1996 WM20 UKR 6 1 1 2 0 —

**Balakowicz, Wladyslaw / b. June 15, 1965**
1985 WM20 POL 7 1 1 2 0 —

**Balan, Stanislav / b. Jan. 30, 1986**
2004 WM18 CZE 7 0 2 2 2 B

**Balandin, Mikhail / b. June 27, 1980 / d. Sept. 7, 2011**
2000 WM20 RUS 7 0 1 1 4 S
~perished in Yaroslavl plane crash

**Balastik, Jaroslav / b. Nov. 28, 1979**
1999 WM20 CZE 6 2 3 5 0 —
2003-07 WM CZE 23 5 2 7 8 S

**Balaz, Vladislav / b. Jan. 28, 1984**
2004 WM20 SVK 6 0 1 1 8 —

**Balderis, Helmuts / b. July 31, 1952**
1976-83 WM URS 47 28 26 54 49 3G,S,B
1976 CC URS 5 2 3 5 6 —
1980 OG-M URS 7 5 4 9 5 S
~IIHF Hall of Fame
~WM IIHF Directorate Best Forward (1977), WM All-Star Team/Forward (1977)

**Baldi, Mattia / b. July 12, 1977**
1996-97 WM20 SUI 11 2 3 5 36 —
1998-2002 WM SUI 15 1 1 2 10 —

**Baldinger, Peter / b. Mar. 30, 1961**
1980 WM20 SUI 5 0 0 0 16 —

**Balej, Jozef / b. Feb. 22, 1982**
2000 WM18 SVK 6 0 5 5 4 —
2001 WM20 SVK 7 3 3 6 4 —

**Ball, Rudi / b. June 22, 1911 / d. Sept. 1975**
1930-38 WM GER 22 11 1 12 3 S
1932-36 OG-M GER 10 5 1 6 6 B
~IIHF Hall of Fame

**Ballet, Francis / b. Decemebr 3, 1983**
2002 WM20 FRA 6 0 1 1 0 —

**Balmer, Samuel / b. May 1, 1968**
1991-95 WM SUI 32 1 4 5 20 —
1992 OG-M SUI 7 3 0 3 0 —

**Balmochnykh, Maxim / b. Mar. 7, 1979**
1998-99 WM20 RUS 14 5 11 16 8 G,S
~WM20 All-Star Team/Forward (1998, 1999)

**Bankuti, Arpad / b. May 13, 1941**
1964 OG-M HUN 7 3 0 3 2 —

**Bannister, Drew / b. Sept. 4, 1974**
1994 WM20 CAN 7 0 4 4 10 G

**Baran, Maciej / b. Sept. 27, 1977**
1997 WM20 POL 6 0 0 0 0 —

**Barbanson, Jean / b. Dec. 19, 1915 / d. May 10, 1940**
1934-35 WM BEL 5 0 — 0 — —

**Barber, Bill / b. July 11, 1952**
1976 CC CAN 7 2 0 2 4 1st
1982 WM CAN 10 8 1 9 10 B
~WM All-Star Team/Forward (1982)

**Barbulescu, Andrei / b. Oct. 6, 1909 / d. July 30, 1987**
1947 WM ROM 1 0 — 0 — —

**Barcza, Miklos / b. Jan. 7, 1908 / d. 1948**
1930-39 WM HUN 28 0 0 0 8 —
1928-36 OG-M HUN 7 0 — 0 — —

**Bardet, Michael / b. Mar. 29, 1982**
2002 WM20 FRA 6 0 0 0 0 —

**Barensoi, Helmut / b. 1957**
1977 WM20 FRG 7 0 0 0 4 —

**Bares, Petr / b. Jan. 4, 1970**
1990 WM20 TCH 2 1 2 3 2 B

**Barin, Stephane / b. Aug. 8, 1971**
1992-2000 WM FRA 50 7 7 14 32 —
1992-2002 OG-M FRA 23 6 2 8 12 —

**Barinka, Peter / b. Apr. 6, 1977**
1997 WM20 SVK 4 0 0 0 2 —

**Barkov, Alexander / b. Apr., 17, 1965**
1992-99 WM RUS 21 3 9 12 29 —

**Barkunov, Alexander / b. May 13, 1981**
2001 WM20 RUS 7 0 2 2 10 —

**Barlie, Vegar / b. Aug. 7, 1972**
1990-91 WM20 NOR 14 1 3 4 6 —
1994 WM NOR 6 1 1 2 0 —
1994 OG-M NOR 6 0 1 1 2 —

**Barna, Frigyes / b. 1895 / d. unknown**
1930-31 WM HUN 6 0 — 0 — —
1928 OG-M HUN 1 0 — 0 — —

**Barnes, Norm / b. Aug. 24, 1953**
1981 WM CAN 6 0 1 1 6 —

**Barnes, Stu / b. Dec. 25, 1970**
1990 WM20 CAN 7 2 4 6 6 G

**Baroni, Gianmario / b. Jan. 21, 1910 / d. unknown**
1930-35 WM ITA 14 1 0 1 0 —
1936 OG-M ITA 1 0 0 0 — —

**Barsky, Olexander / b. Jan. 30, 1982**
1999 WM18 UKR 6 0 0 0 6 —

**Bart Hansen, Petter / b. Mar. 8, 1981**
1999 WM18 NOR 6 0 0 0 10 —

**Barta, Bjorn / b. May 22, 1980**
1998 WM20 GER 6 0 0 0 0 —

**Bartanus, Karol / b. June 6, 1978**
1998 WM20 SVK 6 0 4 4 34 —

**Bartek, Martin / b. July 17, 1980**
1999 WM20 SVK 6 1 0 1 4 B

**Bartek, Peter / b. Apr. 25, 1978**
1997-98 WM20 SVK 12 0 1 1 10 —

**Bartel, Robin / b. May 16, 1961**
1984 OG-M CAN 6 0 1 1 4 —

**Bartell, Adam / b. Apr. 27, 1973**
1993 WM20 USA 7 0 2 2 2 —

**Bartell, Fred / b. Dec. 13, 1960**
1983 WM GDR 9 2 2 4 2 —

**Barthelsson, Tony / b. July 1, 1966**
1986 WM20 SWE 7 0 2 2 4 —

**Bartlett, Anders / b. Dec. 2, 1984**
2001 WM18 NOR 6 0 0 0 0 —

**Bartlett, Mike / b. Jan. 6, 1985**
2003 WM18 USA 6 0 2 2 30 —

**Bartley, Victor / b. Feb. 17, 1988**
2006 WM18 CAN 7 1 1 2 10 —

**Bartlick, Robert / b. June 27, 1983**
2001 WM18 GER 6 0 0 0 4 —
2003 WM20 GER 6 0 0 0 4 —

**Bartolone, Christopher / b. Jan. 24, 1970**
1994-2002 WM ITA 53 9 9 18 98 —
1998 OG-M ITA 4 0 1 1 2 —

**Barton, Slavomir / b. Jan. 12, 1926 / d. Jan. 16, 2004**
1955-58 WM TCH 18 22 6 28 0 2B
1952-56 OG-M TCH 16 13 3 16 4 —

**Bartos, Martin / b. June 2, 1988**
2006 WM18 CZE 7 3 1 4 2 B

**Bartos, Peter / b. Sept. 5, 1973**
1998-2001 WM SVK 26 3 5 8 10 S
1996 WCH SVK 1 0 0 0 0 —

**Bartschi, Deny / b. Apr. 3, 1982**
2000 WM18 SUI 7 3 0 3 0 —
2002 WM20 SUI 7 0 1 1 0 —

**Bartschi, Peter / b. Jan. 19, 1967**
1987 WM20 SUI 4 1 0 1 2 —

**Barz, Benjamin / b. Aug. 8, 1983**
2001 WM18 GER 6 1 3 4 0 —
2003 WM20 GER 6 0 0 0 2 —

**Basa, Ion / b. June 4, 1944**
1968 OG-M ROM 5 0 2 2 0 —

**Bashkatov, Yegor / b. Apr. 23, 1971**
1991 WM20 URS 7 0 3 3 0 S

**Bashkirov, Andrei / b. June 22, 1970**
2004 WM RUS 6 2 0 2 2 —

**Bashkirov, Ruslan / b. Mar. 7, 1989**
2006 WM18 RUS 6 6 2 8 4 —

**Bass, Cody / b. Jan. 7, 1987**
2005 WM18 CAN 4 0 0 0 4 S

**Bassen, Bob / b. May 6, 1965**
1985 WM20 CAN 7 2 0 2 8 G
1992 WM CAN 3 1 1 2 0 S

**Bassett, Cole / b. July 23, 1982**
2000 WM18 USA 6 0 2 2 0 —

**Bassi, Giancarlo / b. Feb. 23, 1926**
1948 OG-M ITA 5 0 — 0 — —

**Bastenie, Walter / b. May 29, 1910 / d. unknown**
1936 OG-M BEL 3 0 — 0 — —

**Bastian, Frederic / b. Jan. 12, 1983**
2002 WM20 FRA 4 0 0 0 0 —

**Bastiansen, Harald / b. Mar. 7, 1962**
1979 WM20 NOR 5 1 0 1 2 —

**Bastien, Yves / b. Aug. 2, 1989**
2007 WM18 CAN 6 3 1 4 0 S

**Bates, Shawn / b. Apr. 3, 1975**
1995 WM20 USA 7 5 1 6 2 —

**Bathgate, Bernie / b. Mar. 15, 1923**
1955 WM CAN 6 1 0 1 0 G

**Batkiewicz, Jozef / b. Feb. 22, 1950**
1973-75 WM POL 20 0 1 1 12 —
1972 OG-M POL 5 0 1 1 2 —

**Batovsky, Zoltan / b. Mar. 27, 1979**
1999 WM20 SVK 6 2 3 5 4 B

**Battaglia, Jon "Bates" / b. Dec. 13, 1975**
1995 WM20 USA 7 3 2 5 2 —
1998-2004 WM USA 15 3 3 6 20 B

**Batyrshin, Ruslan / b. Feb. 19, 1975**
1995 WM20 RUS 7 1 4 5 10 S

**Bauer, Arnie / b. Aug. 10, 1924**
1955 WM USA 8 4 0 4 2 —

**Bauer, Reinhold / b. July 28, 1950**
1972-73 WM FRG 11 1 0 1 4 —
1972 OG-M FRG 2 0 0 0 2 —

**Bauer, Ray / b. unknown**
1949 WM CAN 6 5 — 5 — S

**Bauer, Robin / b. Mar. 24, 1974**
1994 WM20 SUI 7 0 2 2 0 —

**Baulin, Yuri / b. Oct. 5, 1933 / d. Dec. 5, 2006**
1959 WM URS 5 3 5 8 6 S
1960 OG-M URS 6 1 2 3 10 B

**Baumann, Andre / b. Oct. 27, 1977**
1996-97 WM20 SUI 12 3 1 4 28 —

**Baumgartner, Lukas / b. Mar. 15, 1984**
2001-02 WM18 SUI 15 3 2 5 38 —
2002-04 WM20 SUI 19 0 3 3 4 —

**Baumgartner, Nolan / b. Mar. 23, 1976**
1995-96 WM20 CAN 13 1 2 3 26 2G
~WM20 All-Star Team/Defence (1996)

**Baumgartner, Raoul / b. Mar. 15, 1971**
1991 WM20 SUI 7 1 0 1 4 —

**Bautier, Andre / b. 1907 / d. unknown**
1928 OG-M BEL 3 0 — 0 — —

**Bautin, Sergei / b. Mar. 11, 1967**
1992-99 WM RUS 19 1 5 6 30 —
1992 OG-M RUS 8 0 0 0 6 G

**Bayer, Marco / b. Sept. 20, 1972**
1991-92 WM20 SUI 14 1 2 3 28 —
1995 WM SUI 7 0 1 1 14 —

**Bayes, Richie / b. Mar. 21, 1948**
1969 WM CAN 8 2 2 4 0 —

**Bayon, Timo / b. Apr. 13, 1982**
2002 WM20 FRA 6 1 1 2 6 —

**Bazzi, Gian / b. Apr. 3, 1931**
1951-62 WM SUI 16 6 2 8 2 2B
1952 OG-M SUI 8 3 0 3 0 —

**Beattie, Scott / b. May 16, 1968**
1996-2001 WM ITA 11 0 1 1 2 —

**Beaudoin, Yves / b. Jan. 7, 1965**
1985 WM20 CAN 7 0 3 3 4 G

**Beaufait, Mark / b. May 13, 1970**
1994 OG-M USA 8 1 4 5 2 —

**Bebris, Janis / b. July 28, 1917 / d. May 2, 1969**
1936 OG-M LAT 3 1 — 1 — —

**Beccarelli, Fabio / b. May 18, 1979**
1999 WM20 SUI 6 0 0 0 2 —

**Beccarelli, Mauro / b. Dec. 2, 1981**
1999 WM18 SUI 7 3 1 4 6 —

**Beck, Barry / b. June 3, 1957**
1981 CC CAN 7 0 0 0 2 2nd

**Beck, Martin / b. Oct. 25, 1933**
1953-55 WM FRG 17 1 0 1 18 S
1956 OG-M FRG 8 0 0 0 8 —

**Beck, Mattias / b. Jan. 21, 1983**
2001 WM18 SWE 6 3 0 3 0 —
2003 WM20 SWE 6 0 3 3 0 —

**Beck, Roger / b. unknown**
1949 WM BEL 5 1 — 1 — —

**Becker, Bruce / b. Jan. 22, 1988**
2006 WM18 GER 6 0 0 0 8 —

**Beckon, Dave / b. Mar. 19, 1961**
1980 WM20 CAN 5 2 2 4 2 —

**Becuwe, Mathieu / b. May 6, 1982**
2002 WM20 FRA 6 0 0 0 2 —

**Bednar, Vladimir / b. Oct. 1, 1948**
1969-72 WM TCH 22 0 2 2 14 G,2B
1972 OG-M TCH 6 0 0 0 2 B

**Bednarski, Kazimierz / b. Jan. 27, 1958**
1977 WM20 POL 7 0 0 0 4 —

**Bedogni, Mario / b. Nov. 22, 1923**
1948-56 OG-M ITA 8 3 1 4 2 —

**Bedsvaag, Kenneth / b. Apr. 22, 1982**
1999 WM18 NOR 6 1 0 1 8 —

**Beers, Bob / b. May 20, 1967**
1993-97 WM USA 22 4 2 6 14 —

**Bega, Taras / b. Feb. 5, 1983**
2000-01 WM18 UKR 12 1 0 1 0 —

**Begg, Gary / b. Dec. 29, 1940**
1965-69 WM CAN 31 3 6 9 28 2B
1964 OG-M CAN 7 1 0 1 2 —
~WM All-Star Team/Defence (1966)

**Begin, Steve / b. June 14, 1978**
1998 WM20 CAN 7 0 0 0 10 —

**Bekbulatov, Vadim / b. Mar. 8, 1970**
1998-2003 WM BLR 18 2 5 7 26 —
1998-2002 OG-M BLR 14 3 4 7 12 —

**Bekesi-Bliesener, Pal / b. 1914 / d. unknown**
1933-38 WM HUN 11 0 0 0 4 —

**Bekkerud, Bjorn / b. Jan. 16, 1966**
1992-93 WM NOR 8 0 0 0 0 —

**Beland, Amedee / b. unknown**
1951 WM USA 4 1 — 1 0 —

**Belavskis, Aleksandrs / b. Jan. 17, 1964**
1997-2002 WM LAT 34 12 12 24 44 —
2002 OG-M LAT 4 1 1 2 4 —

**Belayev, Maxim / b. Aug. 24, 1979**
1998-99 WM20 KAZ 13 0 2 2 12 —
2006 WM KAZ 3 0 2 2 2 —

**Bell, Brendan / b. Mar. 31, 1983**
2003 WM20 CAN 6 1 1 2 6 S

**Bell, Mark / b. Aug. 5, 1980**
2000 WM20 CAN 7 2 0 2 8 B

**Bellefeuille, Blake / b. Dec. 27, 1977**
1997 WM20 USA 6 0 1 1 2 S

**Bellio, John / b. Dec. 19, 1954**
1982-83 WM ITA 17 2 2 4 32 —
1984 OG-M ITA 5 1 1 2 4 —

**Bellows, Brian / b. Sept. 1, 1964**
1987-90 WM CAN 28 12 15 27 18 S
1984 CC CAN 5 0 1 1 0 1st
~WM IIHF Directorate Best Forward (1989)

**Belohlav, Radek / b. Apr. 11, 1970**
1995-98 WM CZE 25 9 7 16 4 G,B

**Belov, Oleg / b. Apr. 20, 1973**
1993 WM20 RUS 7 1 2 3 2 —
1995-98 WM RUS 20 5 5 10 20 —

**Belousov, Valeri / b. Dec. 17, 1948**
1976 CC URS 5 0 1 1 2 —

**Belov, Yevgeni / b. Apr. 30, 1962**
1982 WM20 URS 7 3 1 4 4 —

**Bely, Pavel / b. Aug. 1, 1980**
1999 WM20 BLR 6 2 4 6 0 —

**Benak, Jaroslav / b. Apr. 3, 1962**
1983-87 WM TCH 36 1 11 12 36 G,S,B
1984-87 CC TCH 10 2 2 4 10 —
1984-88 OG-M TCH 15 2 5 7 16 S

**Ben-Amor, Semir / b. May 5, 1982**
2000 WM18 FIN 7 0 1 1 4 G

**Benda, Jan / b. Apr. 28, 1972**
1994-2005 WM GER 51 6 16 22 124 —
1996 WCH GER 4 1 1 2 0 —
1994-2002 OG-M GER 19 4 1 5 16 —

**Bender, Walt / b. Nov. 1, 1910 / d. Sept. 13, 1989**
1934 WM USA 4 0 — 0 — S

**Benedetti, Enrico / b. Aug. 16, 1940**
1964 OG-M ITA 7 1 1 2 2 —

**Bengtsson, Folke / b. Apr. 24, 1944**
1966-67 WM SWE 10 8 4 12 4 S
1968 OG-M SWE 6 3 1 4 0 —

**Benjamins, Dick / b. unknown / d. unknown**
1939 WM NED 2 0 — 0 — —

**Benk, Andras / b. Sept. 3, 1987**
2009 WM HUN 2 0 1 1 0 —

**Benko, Marek / b. Feb. 9, 1983**
2001 WM18 SVK 6 0 0 0 0 —

**Bennett, Curt / b. Mar. 27, 1948**
1978-79 WM USA 18 3 1 4 2 —
1976 CC USA 5 0 3 3 0 —

**Bennett, Harvey / b. Aug. 9, 1952**
1978 WM USA 8 3 0 3 19 —
1976 CC USA 4 0 2 2 2 —

**Benning, Brian / b. June 10, 1966**
1993 WM CAN 8 1 2 3 0 —

**Benoit, Andre / b. Jan. 6, 1984**
2002 WM18 CAN 8 1 3 4 4 —

**Benoit, Joe / b. Feb. 27, 1916 / d. Oct. 19, 1981**
1939 WM CAN 8 8 — 8 — G

**Benoit, Moe / b. July 26, 1933**
1959 WM CAN 8 3 0 3 12 G
1960 OG-M CAN 7 1 3 4 18 S

**Benoit, Yvan / b. Apr. 9, 1985**
2002 WM18 SUI 8 1 3 4 0 —
2004-05 WM20 SUI 12 3 2 5 43 —

**Benson, Bobby / b. May 18, 1894 / d. Sept. 7, 1965**
1920 OG-M CAN 3 1 — 1 — G

**Bent, John / b. Aug. 5, 1908 / d. June 5, 2004**
1932 OG-M USA 6 3 3 6 0 S

**Benysek, Ladislav / b. Mar. 24, 1975**
1997-2000 WM CZE 30 1 1 2 8 2G,B

**Beraldo, Paul / b. Oct. 5, 1967**
1994 WM ITA 6 2 1 3 6 —

**Beran, Marc / b. Jan. 8, 1970**
1990 WM20 USA 7 1 1 2 0 —

**Beranek, Josef / b. Oct. 25, 1969**
1989 WM20 TCH 7 4 9 13 6 B
1991-2004 WM CZE 38 8 12 20 44 2B
1991-96 CC CZE 8 1 1 2 8 —
1998 OG-M CZE 6 1 0 1 4 G

**Berard, Bryan / b. Mar. 5, 1977**
1995-96 WM20 USA 13 1 5 6 56 —
1997 WM USA 1 1 0 1 0 —
1998 OG-M USA 2 0 0 0 0 —

**Beravs, Bozidar / b. Dec. 24, 1948**
1972-76 OG-M YUG 8 0 1 1 4 —

**Beravs, Slavko / b. June 19, 1946**
1968-72 OG-M YUG 8 2 2 4 0 —

**Berchtold, Claudio / b. Jan. 16, 1986**
2006 WM20 SUI 6 0 0 0 6 —

**Berdila, Ion / b. Feb. 1, 1958**
1980 OG-M ROM 5 0 0 0 6 —

**Berenson, Gordon "Red" / b. Dec. 8, 1939**
1959 WM CAN 8 9 2 11 4 G
1972 SS CAN 2 0 1 1 0 1st

**Berezin, Sergei / b. Nov. 5, 1971**
1991 WM20 URS 7 3 1 4 6 S
1994-98 WM RUS 26 19 9 28 10 —
1996 WCH RUS 2 1 0 1 0 —
1994 OG-M RUS 8 3 2 5 2 —

**Berg, Aki-Petteri / b. July 28, 1977**
1997 WM20 FIN 6 0 2 2 8 —
1999-2007 WM FIN 47 5 3 8 69 3S,2B
2004 WCH FIN 5 0 1 1 2 2nd
1998-2006 OG-M FIN 18 1 0 1 12 S,B

**Berg, Arne / b. Sept. 15, 1931**
1951-54 WM NOR 13 1 — 1 2 —
1952 OG-M NOR 8 1 0 1 0 —

**Berg, Mikael / b. July 1, 1981**
1999 WM18 SWE 7 4 6 10 2 S

**Berg, Oivind / b. July 13, 1946**
1972 OG-M NOR 4 0 0 0 0 —

**Berg, Reg / b. Sept. 18, 1976**
1995-96 WM20 USA 13 2 2 4 33 —

**Bergeid, Trygve / b. Mar. 30, 1942**
1962 WM NOR 7 2 0 2 2 —
1968 OG-M NOR 5 1 1 2 2 —

**Bergen, Brad / b. Mar. 16, 1966**
1996-97 WM GER 14 2 1 3 10 —
1996 WCH GER 1 0 0 0 0 —
1998 OG-M GER 3 1 1 2 0 —

**Berger, Jurg / b. Feb. 5, 1954**
1976 OG-M SUI 5 1 3 4 6 —

**Bergevin, Marc / b. Aug. 11, 1965**
1994 WM CAN 8 0 0 0 2 G

**Bergland, Tim / b. Jan. 11, 1965**
1995 WM USA 5 2 1 3 2 —

**Bergloff, Bob / b. July 26, 1958**
1977 WM20 USA 7 2 2 4 6 —

**Berglund, Bo / b. Apr. 6, 1955**
1989 WM SWE 9 4 0 4 4 —
1980-88 OG-M SWE 14 5 7 12 8 2B

**Berglund, Charles / b. Jan. 18, 1965**
1991-95 WM SWE 32 4 9 13 8 G,2S,B
1991 CC SWE 6 1 0 1 0 —
1992-94 OG-M SWE 13 1 4 5 4 G

**Berglund, Christian / b. Mar. 12, 1980**
1999-2000 WM20 SWE 13 8 6 14 37 —

**Berglund, Rolf / b. Dec. 4, 1957**
1977 WM20 SWE 6 0 0 0 2 —

**Bergman, Emil / b. July 28, 1908 / d. Apr. 13, 1975**
1931 WM SWE 6 0 — 0 — —
1928 OG-M SWE 5 0 0 0 — S

**Bergman, Gary / b. Oct. 7, 1938 / d. Dec. 8, 2000**
1972 SS CAN 8 0 3 3 13 1st

**Bergman, Jan / b. Aug. 7, 1969**
1989 WM20 SWE 7 1 0 1 2 S

**Bergman, Thommie / b. Dec. 10, 1947**
1971-72 WM SWE 18 3 4 7 12 2B
1976 CC SWE 3 0 2 2 6 —
1972 OG-M SWE 4 1 1 2 6 —

**Bergqvist, Jonas / b. Sept. 26, 1962**
1982 WM20 SWE 7 4 5 9 9 —
1986-98 WM SWE 75 25 16 41 50 3G,3S,B
1987-96 WCH SWE 16 3 1 4 6 —
1988-94 OG-M SWE 16 4 3 7 8 G,B

**Bergqvist, Kenneth / b. May 19, 1980**
2000 WM20 SWE 7 3 4 7 2 —

**Bergqvist, Sven / b. Aug. 20, 1914 / d. Dec. 16, 1996**
1935-38 WM SWE 14 2 — 2 — —
1936 OG-M SWE 5 0 — 0 — —
~IIHF Hall of Fame

**Bergseng, Arne / b. Mar. 22, 1961**
1984 OG-M NOR 5 1 0 1 0 —

**Bergseng, Lars / b. May 14, 1963**
1983 WM20 NOR 7 0 2 2 11 —
1990 WM NOR 9 0 0 0 12 —
1988 OG-M NOR 3 2 1 3 2 —

**Beribak, Igor / b. May 18, 1964**
2002 WM SLO 6 0 1 1 6 —
1984 OG-M YUG 5 0 0 0 0 —

**Bernasconi, Roland / b. July 18, 1935**
1962 WM SUI 7 1 3 4 0 —

**Bernat, Adam / b. Aug. 4, 1958**
1977 WM20 POL 7 0 0 0 10 —

**Bernatsky, Oleksiy / b. Apr. 29, 1975**
1995 WM20 UKR 7 0 1 1 14 —

**Berndaner, Ignaz / b. July 4, 1954**
1973-83 WM FRG 64 7 7 14 38 —
1984 CC FRG 5 0 0 0 0 —
1976-84 OG-M FRG 11 3 2 5 0 —

**Bernhardt, Oliver / b. July 29, 1976**
1996 WM20 GER 6 0 0 0 10 —

**Bernier, Steve / b. Mar. 31, 1985**
2003 WM18 CAN 7 4 4 8 12 G

**Berntdsson, Peter / b. Jan. 17, 1965**
1985 WM20 SWE 7 1 2 3 2 —

**Berra, Rene / b. Feb. 13, 1942**
1972 WM SUI 6 1 0 1 0 —
1972 OG-M SUI 4 0 0 0 0 —

**Berry, Brad / b. Apr. 1, 1965**
1985 WM20 CAN 7 0 1 1 2 G

**Berry, Coco / b. Nov. 5, 1926**
1949 WM BEL 6 0 — 0 — —

**Berry, Don / b. unknown**
1955 WM CAN 5 1 0 1 2 G

**Berry, Franz / b. Nov. 21, 1938**
1959 WM SUI 8 0 0 0 4 —
1956-64 OG-M SUI 12 0 1 1 8 —

**Berry, Ken / b. June 21, 1960**
1980-88 OG-M CAN 14 6 5 11 12 —

**Bertaggia, Sandro / b. May 7, 1964**
1987-95 WM SUI 41 2 8 10 57 —
1992 OG-M SUI 7 0 2 2 2 —

**Berteling, Ron / b. Sept. 6, 1957**
1981 WM NED 8 2 0 2 0 —
1980 OG-M NED 5 0 0 0 0 —

**Berti, Adam / b. July 1, 1986**
2004 WM18 CAN 7 1 2 3 26 —

**Bertuzzi, Todd / b. Feb. 2, 1975**
1998-2000 WM CAN 15 6 6 12 63 —
2006 OG CAN 6 0 3 3 6 —

**Berube, Larry / b. June 30, 1930 / d. June 25, 1993**
1951 WM USA 6 1 — 1 0 —

**Berwanger, Markus / b. June 7, 1963**
1983 WM20 FRG 6 0 1 1 4 —
1985-91 WM FRG 29 3 1 4 32 —

**Bes, Jeff / b. July 31, 1973**
1993 WM20 CAN 7 3 2 5 4 G

**Besic, Mustafa / b. Mar. 12, 1961**
1984 OG-M YUG 5 3 0 3 2 —

**Beslagic, Elvis / b. July 4, 1973**
2002-03 WM SLO 12 0 2 2 16 —

**Bessard du Parc, Geoffroy / b. June 30, 1982**
2002 WM20 FRA 6 0 0 0 2 —

**Besse, Guillaume / b. Jan. 26, 1976**
1997 WM FRA 8 0 0 0 10 —
2002 OG-M FRA 4 0 0 0 0 —

**Bessone, Pete / b. Jan. 13, 1913 / d. Dec. 5, 1989**
1934 WM USA — 2 1 3 — S

**Bestagini, Luigi / b. Aug. 28, 1919 / d. May 2, 1993**
1948 OG-M ITA 7 0 — 0 — —

**Beszteri, Janos / b. Aug. 9, 1938**
1964 OG-M HUN 7 2 1 3 0 —

**Bethlen, Istvan / b. Mar. 8, 1904 / d. Feb. 6, 1982**
1931-35 WM HUN 11 1 — 1 1 —

**Bets, Maxim / b. Jan. 31, 1974**
1994 WM20 RUS 7 0 0 0 8 B

**Betts, Blair / b. Feb. 16, 1980**
1999 WM20 CAN 5 0 0 0 2 S

**Betz, Michael / b. Feb. 19, 1962**
1981-82 WM20 FRG 12 4 5 9 8 —
1983-85 WM FRG 19 3 3 6 20 —
1984 CC FRG 5 1 1 2 0 —
1984 OG-M FRG 6 1 0 1 2 —

**Beukeboom, Jeff / b. Mar. 28, 1965**
1985 WM20 CAN 3 1 0 1 4 G

**Beutler, Andreas / b. Jan. 26, 1963**
1982 WM20 SUI 7 1 0 1 8 —
1991 WM SUI 10 0 0 0 8 —
1992 OG-M SUI 7 0 1 1 14 —

**Bevis, Brett Topher / b. Apr. 2, 1986**
2004 WM18 USA 6 1 0 1 4 S

**Bevz, Alexei / b. Jan. 1, 1960**
1980 WM20 URS 5 0 1 1 4 G

**Bezak, Marian / b. July 4, 1958**
1978 WM20 TCH 6 2 1 3 4 —

**Bezshasny, Ruslan / b. June 26, 1979**
2000-03 WM UKR 12 0 3 3 2 —

**Bezukladnikov, Vyacheslav / b. Sept. 7, 1968**
1994 WM RUS 6 1 1 2 2 —
1994 OG-M RUS 8 0 0 0 4 —

**Biafore, Chad / b. Mar. 28, 1968**
1997-99 WM ITA 17 0 0 0 16 —
1998 OG-M ITA 4 0 1 1 6 —

**Bialotski, Denis / b. Mar. 30,1984**
2002 WM18 BLR 8 0 0 0 2 —

**Bialynicki-Birula, Krzysztof / b. Aug. 15, 1944**
1966-73 WM POL 20 6 2 8 0 —
1972 OG-M POL 4 0 1 1 0 —

**Bicanek, Radim / b. Jan. 18, 1975**
1993 WM20 TCH 7 1 0 1 0 B

**Bielak, Ryszard / b. Mar. 28, 1967**
1987 WM20 POL 6 0 0 0 2 —

**Bielas, Rolf / b. Sept. 2, 1950**
1970-78 WM GDR 39 10 3 13 8 —

**Bieler, Fredy / b. Apr. 18, 1923**
1949-51 WM SUI 21 24 2 26 4 2B
1948 OG-M SUI 5 5 — 5 — B

**Bianchi, Elias / b. Apr. 22, 1989**
2007 WM18 SUI 6 0 0 0 0 —

**Bielmann, Andre / b. Feb. 7, 1980**
2000 WM20 SUI 7 0 1 1 4 —

**Biermann, Karol / b. Nov. 15, 1984**
2004 WM20 SVK 5 0 1 1 2 —

**Bierenbroodspot, Piet / b. unknown**
1950 WM NED 3 0 0 0 0 —

**Biersack, Toni / b. July 14, 1927 / d. Mar. 30, 2007**
1953-54 WM FRG 11 4 3 7 20 S
1956 OG-M FRG 4 0 0 0 10 —

**Bierschel, Karl / b. Mar. 1, 1932**
1953-55 WM FRG 8 0 1 1 6 S
1952-56 OG-M FRG 13 0 0 0 0 —

**Bikar, Dejan / b. Mar. 13, 1907 / d. unknown**
1930-31 WM HUN 5 0 — 0 — —

**Bikar, Peter / b. Nov. 5, 1945**
1964 OG-M HUN 7 1 2 3 2 —

**Bilek, Roman / b. Feb. 23, 1984**
2002 WM18 CZE 8 1 0 1 2 B

**Billkvam, Arne / b. Apr. 7, 1960**
1979 WM20 NOR 5 0 1 1 2 —
1990-93 WM NOR 22 1 1 2 18 —
1988-94 OG-M NOR 18 2 4 6 12 —

**Bilodeau, Brent / b. Mar. 27, 1973**
1992-93 WM20 USA 14 0 2 2 18 B

**Bilyaletdinov, Zinetula / b. Mar. 13, 1955**
1978-87 WM URS 63 6 14 20 79 6G,S,B
1976-84 CC URS 18 0 2 2 24 1st
1980-84 OG-M URS 14 2 4 6 2 G,S

**Biotti, Chris / b. Apr. 22, 1967**
1985-87 WM20 USA 21 4 4 8 18 B

**Birbaum, Alain / b. Oct. 11, 1985**
2003 WM18 SUI 6 0 0 0 6 —
2005 WM20 SUI 6 0 1 1 14 —

**Birch, Martin / b. July 14, 1970**
1995 WM SUI 7 0 1 1 6 —

**Bird, Les / b. Apr. 1910 / d. unknown**
1934 WM CAN 1 0 0 0 — G

**Birk, Harald / b. Sept. 1, 1963**
1983 WM20 FRG 7 0 1 1 8 —
1989-90 WM FRG 14 2 0 2 12 —

**Birk, Klaus / b. Jan. 3, 1966**
1985-86 WM20 FRG 14 2 1 3 9 —

**Biro, Anton / b. Sept. 30, 1939**
1964 OG-M ROM 7 2 2 4 2 —

**Biro, Laszlo / b. July 22, 1913 / d. unknown**
1937-38 WM ROM 7 1 0 1 9 —

**Biron, Mathieu / b. Apr. 29, 1980**
2000 WM20 CAN 7 0 0 0 8 B
~WM20 All-Star Team/Defence (2000)

**Bissett, Tom / b. Mar. 13, 1966**
1992-99 WM USA 12 4 0 4 0 —

**Bissonnette, Paul / b. Mar. 11, 1985**
2003 WM18 CAN 7 0 1 1 0 G

**Bjerken, Bret / b. July 24, 1959**
1978 WM20 USA 5 2 4 6 2 —

**Bjerklund, Egil / b. Sept. 5, 1933**
1954-65 WM NOR 27 1 0 1 16 —
1952-64 OG-M NOR 15 4 3 7 2 —

**Bjolbakk, Steinar / b. Sept. 6, 1946**
1965 WM NOR 6 0 0 0 0 —
1968-72 OG-M NOR 9 5 3 8 20 —

**Bjonnes, Bjarte / b. Mar. 23, 1981**
1999 WM18 NOR 6 1 1 2 4 —

**Bjork, Johan / b. Aug. 28, 1984**
2002 WM18 SWE 8 0 0 0 2 —
2004 WM20 SWE 6 0 2 2 2 —

**Bjorklund, Anders / b. Mar. 14, 1961**
1981 WM20 SWE 5 0 0 0 0 G

**Bjorkman, Henrik / b. June 3, 1971**
1990-91 WM20 SWE 11 0 4 4 12 —

**Bjorkman, Ruben / b. Feb. 27, 1929**
1955 WM USA 8 2 0 2 0 —
1952 OG-M USA 8 3 3 6 — S

**Bjorn, Lars / b. Dec. 16, 1931**
1953-61 WM SWE 46 9 3 12 46 2G,2B
1952-60 OG-M SWE 15 3 2 5 12 B
~IIHF Hall of Fame
~WM IIHF Directorate Best Defenceman (1954)

**Bjornland, Lars / b. Jan. 20, 1984**
2002 WM18 NOR 8 0 0 0 6 —

**Bjornstad, Sven / b. Jan. 4, 1971**
1994 OG-M NOR 4 0 0 0 4 —

**Bjugstad, Scott / b. June 2, 1961**
1984 OG-M USA 6 3 1 4 6 —

**Bjuhr, Tomas / b. Feb. 28, 1966**
1986 WM20 SWE 7 0 0 0 2 —

**Blaeser, Jeff / b. May 11, 1970**
1990 WM20 USA 7 2 2 4 0 —

**Blagoi, Oleg / b. Dec. 4, 1979**
2007 WM UKR 3 1 0 1 0 —

**Blaha, Michael / b. Jan. 26, 1972**
1992 WM20 SUI 7 1 2 3 4 —

**Blaha, Miroslav / b. Dec. 4, 1963**
1983 WM20 TCH 7 0 1 1 2 S

**Blaho, Stefan / b. June 22, 1985 / d. Aug. 29, 2006**
2003 WM18 SVK 7 1 2 3 8 S
2004 WM20 SVK 6 0 0 0 10 —

**Blake, Rob / b. Dec. 10, 1969**
1991-99 WM CAN 36 5 11 16 46 2G,S
1996 WCH CAN 4 0 1 1 0 2nd
1998-2006 OG-M CAN 18 2 4 6 6 G
~Triple Gold Club
~OG-M IIHF Directorate Best Defenceman (1998), WM IIHF Directorate Best Defenceman (1997), WM All-Star Team/ Defence (1997)

**Blanchard, Claude / b. May 25, 1945**
1968 OG-M FRA 5 0 0 0 0 —

**Blanchard, Rene / b. July 12, 1947**
1968 OG-M FRA 5 0 0 0 2 —

**Blanchard, Sean / b. Mar. 29, 1978**
1998 WM20 CAN 7 0 2 2 8 —

**Blank, Boris / b. July 10, 1978**
1998 WM20 GER 6 0 0 0 25 —
2002-04 WM GER 15 4 0 4 0 —

**Blank, Francis / b. Dec. 30, 1930**
1952 OG-M SUI 5 0 0 0 — —
1953-55 WM SUI 16 2 1 3 4 B

**Blatny, Zdenek / b. Jan. 14, 1981**
2001 WM20 CZE 7 5 2 7 6 G

**Blatter, Florian / b. May 12, 1984**
2002 WM18 SUI 8 0 2 2 0 —
2004 WM20 SUI 6 0 0 0 2 —

**Blazejovski, Laszlo / b. Budapest, Hungary, 1910 / d. unknown**
1931-37 WM HUN 23 4 0 4 2 —

**Blazek, Michal / b. Apr. 2, 1982**
2000 WM18 CZE 6 0 2 2 2 —

**Blazek, Miloslav / b. June 22, 1922 / d. Feb. 19, 1985**
1952 OG-M TCH 8 3 2 5 — —

**Blazek, Tomas / b. Mar. 3, 1975**
1994-95 WM20 CZE 14 3 7 10 4 —

**Bleuer, Markus / b. Nov. 5, 1964**
1984 WM20 SUI 7 0 0 0 2 —

**Blinov, Yuri / b. Jan. 13, 1949**
1972 WM URS 9 4 6 10 4 S
1972 SS URS 5 2 1 3 2 2nd
1972 OG-M URS 5 3 3 6 0 G

**Blinovs, Viktors / b. June 26, 1981**
2002-08 WM LAT 15 1 0 1 4 —

**Blokhin, Yevgeni / b. May 29, 1979**
1999 WM20 KAZ 6 0 0 0 12 —
2005-06 WM KAZ 12 0 2 2 30 —
2006 OG-M KAZ 2 0 0 0 0 —

**Blomberg, Knut / b. unknown**
1954 WM NOR 7 0 — 0 2 —

**Blomdahl, Patric / b. Jan. 30, 1984**
2004 WM20 SWE 4 2 0 2 20 —

**Blome, Gert / b. Aug. 28, 1934**
1958-67 WM SWE 38 3 10 13 21 G,2S,2B
1960-64 OG-M SWE 13 5 6 11 0 S

**Blomqvist, Gote / b. Jan. 11, 1928 / d. Feb. 28, 2003**
1950-54 WM SWE 11 8 1 9 4 G,B
1952 OG-M SWE 9 9 1 10 — B

**Blomqvist, Henrik / b. Mar. 24, 1984**
2002 WM18 SWE 8 0 1 1 20 —
2004 WM20 SWE 6 0 1 1 6 —

**Blomqvist, Timo / b. Jan. 23, 1961**
1979-81 WM20 FIN 16 3 4 7 50 2S
1985-89 WM FIN 16 0 4 4 14 —
1987 CC FIN 4 0 0 0 0 —
1988-92 OG-M FIN 16 1 2 3 18 S

**Blomsten, Arto / b. Mar. 16, 1965**
1985 WM20 SWE 6 0 0 0 6 —
1992-93 WM SWE 16 4 0 4 22 G,S

**Blue, Steve / b. May 4, 1959**
1978 WM20 USA 6 2 0 2 0 —

**Blukis, Roberts / b. Apr. 4, 1913 / d. Apr. 14, 1998**
1933-39 WM LAT 17 5 — 5 0 —
1936 OG-M LAT 3 0 — 0 — —

**Blum, Rainer / b. Jan. 18, 1960**
1979-80 WM20 FRG 10 0 0 0 4 —
1985-86 WM FRG 19 0 2 2 18 —
1984 CC FRG 5 0 1 1 2 —

**Blumel, Wolfgang / b. Mar. 2, 1927**
1957-59 WM GDR 8 6 3 9 0 —

**Boback, Mike / b. Aug. 13, 1970**
1990 WM20 USA 7 0 4 4 6 —
1992 WM USA 4 0 0 0 2 —

**Bobkin, Olexander / b. Sept. 2, 1982**
2006-07 WM UKR 5 1 1 2 25 —

**Bobrov, Vsevolod / b. Dec. 1, 1922 / d. July 1, 1979**
1954-57 WM URS 18 25 6 31 11 G,2S
1956 OG-M URS 7 9 2 11 4 G
~IIHF Hall of Fame
~WM IIHF Directorate Best Forward (1954)

**Bobrovnikov, Vasyl / b. Nov. 8, 1971**
1999-2007 WM UKR 50 5 9 14 8 —
2002 OG-M UKR 4 0 1 1 2 —

**Bodemann, Yanick / b. Apr. 29, 1985**
2004 WM20 AUT 6 0 0 0 0 —

**Bodger, Doug / b. June 18, 1966**
1987-99 WM CAN 28 1 6 7 8 S

**Bodnar, Slavomir / b. Aug. 13, 1985**
2003 WM18 SVK 7 1 0 1 0 S

**Bodunov, Alexander / b. June 3, 1951**
1973-74 WM URS 19 7 9 16 6 2G
1972 SS URS 3 1 0 1 0 2nd

**Boe, Havard / b. Apr. 18, 1985**
2002 WM18 NOR 8 0 0 0 2 —

**Boe, Rene / b. May 2, 1983**
2001 WM18 NOR 6 3 2 5 2 —

**Boehm, Rick / b. Sept. 12, 1959**
1994 WM GER 5 0 2 2 2 —

**Boeser, Bob / b. June 30, 1927 / d. Oct. 29, 1995**
1948 OG-M USA 5 6 3 9 0 —

**Bogas, Chris / b. Nov. 12, 1976**
1996 WM20 USA 6 0 0 0 25 —

**Bogdanov, Anatoliy / b. May 17, 1985**
2002 WM18 UKR 8 1 1 2 4 —
2004 WM20 UKR 6 0 0 0 8 —

**Bogdanovs, Mihails / b. Sept. 18, 1976**
1999 WM LAT 6 0 0 0 2 —

**Bogelsack, Friedhelm / b. Sept. 25, 1955**
1978-85 WM GDR 30 5 7 12 6 —

**Bogh, Knut / b. unknown / d. unknown**
1937-38 WM NOR 6 1 0 1 0 —

**Bogue, Art / b. Apr. 30, 1914 / d. unknown**
1938-39 WM USA 15 9 — 9 — S

**Boguniecki, Eric / b. May 6, 1975**
2000 WM USA 7 0 1 1 2 —

**Bohac, Jan / b. Feb. 3, 1982**
2000 WM18 CZE 6 1 2 3 2 —
2000-02 WM20 CZE 14 0 1 1 2 G

**Bohm, Albert / b. July 9, 1926**
1949 WM AUT 7 4 — 4 — —
1948 OG-M AUT 1 0 — 0 — —

**Bohunicky, Lukas / b. Oct. 30, 1987**
2005 WM18 SVK 6 0 0 0 14 —

**Boichenko, Pavel / b. Apr. 30, 1975**
1995 WM20 RUS 7 0 2 2 2 S

**Boikov, Alexander / b. Feb. 3, 1975**
1995 WM20 RUS 7 0 0 0 0 S

**Boimistruck, Fred / b. Nov. 4, 1962**
1981 WM20 CAN 5 3 0 3 8 —

**Boisvert, Serge / b. June 1, 1959**
1988 OG-M CAN 8 7 2 9 2 —

**Bokros, Lukas / b. Sept. 9, 1982**
2000 WM18 SVK 6 0 1 1 2 —

**Boldavesko, Sergejs / b. Oct. 9, 1970**
1997 WM LAT 8 1 1 2 8 —

**Boldescu, Vasile / b. July 23, 1941**
1968 OG-M ROM 2 0 0 0 0 —

**Boldin, Igor / b. Feb. 2, 1964**
1983-84 WM20 URS 14 2 8 10 0 2G
1992 WM RUS 6 3 1 4 0 —
1992 OG-M RUS 8 2 6 8 0 G

**Bolduc, Alexandre / b. June 26, 1985**
2003 WM18 CAN 7 1 0 1 8 G

**Bolduc, Dan / b. Apr. 6, 1953**
1979 WM USA 8 3 0 3 2 —
1976 CC USA 2 0 0 0 0 —
1976 OG-M USA 5 1 0 1 4 —

**Bolke, Harald / b. Oct. 5, 1959**
1985 WM GDR 10 1 0 1 2 —

**Boller, Heini / b. Sept. 6, 1921 / d. July 3, 2007**
1947-50 WM SUI 22 2 0 2 4 B
1948 OG-M SUI 5 3 — 3 — B

**Bolshakov, Pavlo / b. Nov. 27, 1985**
2004 WM20 UKR 6 0 0 0 0 —

**Bombardir, Brad / b. May 5, 1972**
1992 WM20 CAN 7 0 3 3 4 —

**Bond, Roland / b. June 27, 1944**
1973-76 WM SWE 18 1 4 5 4 S,B

**Bondarev, Artyom / b. Jan. 12, 1983**
2000-01 WM18 UKR 12 3 3 6 10 —
2000 WM20 UKR 7 0 0 0 0 —

**Bondarevs, Igors / b. Feb. 9, 1974**
1997-2002 WM LAT 27 1 4 5 14 —
2002 OG-M LAT 4 2 2 4 0 —

**Bondra, Peter / b. Feb. 7, 1968**
2002-03 WM SVK 17 10 4 14 26 G,B
1996 WCH SVK 3 3 0 3 2 —
1998-2006 OG-M SVK 8 5 0 5 27 —
~WM All-Star Team/Forward (2002)

**Bongers, Lutz / b. Jan. 1, 1968**
1988 WM20 FRG 7 1 1 2 2 —

**Bonin, Brian / b. Nov. 28, 1973**
1996 WM USA 8 1 0 1 2 B

**Bonk, Radek / b. Jan. 9, 1976**
1996 WM CZE 8 2 2 4 14 G
1996 WCH CZE 3 1 0 1 0 —

**Bonnard, Jean-Francois / b. Sept. 14, 1971**
2008 WM FRA 5 0 0 0 0 —
2002 OG-M FRA 4 0 0 0 2 —

**Bonsignore, Jason / b. Apr. 15, 1976**
1994-95 WM20 USA 14 2 2 4 32 —

**Boos, Tino / b. Apr. 10, 1975**
1995 WM20 GER 19 3 4 7 18 —
2003-05 WM GER 19 3 4 7 18 —
2004 WCH GER 4 1 1 2 2 —
2006 OG-M GER 5 2 1 3 8 —

**Boos, Wolfgang / b. Jan. 13, 1946**
1976 WM FRG 10 0 0 0 2 —
1976 OG-M FRG 5 0 0 0 0 B

**Booten, Lowell / b. unknown**
1947 WM USA 5 5 — 5 — —

**Borberg, Gordon / b. Feb. 23, 1978**
1998 WM20 GER 6 0 1 1 6 —

**Bordeleau, Paulin / b. Jan. 28, 1953**
1988 OG-M FRA 6 2 2 4 24 —

**Borecki, Ryszard / b. Feb. 4, 1967**
1987 WM20 POL 6 0 0 0 8 —

**Borland, Jim / b. Mar. 25, 1911 / d. 1938**
1934 WM GBR 5 2 — 2 — —
1936 OG-M GBR 3 1 0 1 0 G

**Boroczi, Gabor / b. Apr. 2, 1939 / d. May 2, 1991**
1964 OG-M HUN 7 0 1 1 4 —

**Borodulin, Mikhail / b. July 8, 1967**
1998 WM KAZ 3 1 0 1 6 —
1998 OG-M KAZ 7 3 0 3 10 —

**Borsato, Luciano / b. Jan. 7, 1966**
1995 WM CAN 7 3 1 4 18 B

**Borshevski, Nikolai / b. Jan. 12, 1965**
1984 WM20 URS 7 6 7 13 4 G
1992 WM RUS 6 1 3 4 2 —
1992 OG-M RUS 8 7 2 9 0 G
~WM20 All-Star Team/Forward (1984)

**Bortolussi, Maurizio / b. Apr. 25, 1968**
1993 WM ITA 5 0 0 0 0 —

**Borysenko, Pavlo / b. June 4, 1987**
2002 WM18 UKR 8 0 0 0 0 —

**Borysenko, Ruslan / b. Apr. 22, 1983**
2000-01 WM18 UKR 12 0 1 1 4 —

**Borzecki, Adam / b. May 6, 1978**
1997 WM20 POL 6 0 0 0 8 —

**Bosch, Fredy / b. Nov. 21, 1963**
1982 WM20 SUI 6 0 1 1 2 —

**Boss, Daniel / b. Nov. 1, 1983**
2001 WM18 SUI 7 0 0 0 0 S

**Bossoney, Andre / b. unknown / d. unknown**
1934 WM FRA 4 0 — 0 — —

**Bossy, Mike / b. Jan. 22, 1957**
1981-84 CC CAN 15 13 7 20 4 1st,2nd

**Bostrom, Sigurd / b. Nov. 26, 1918 / d. unknown**
1947 WM SWE 5 0 — 0 — S

**Botez, Alexandru / b. 1909 / d. unknown**
1931-38 WM ROM 27 10 1 11 0 —

**Bottenheim, Jacques / b. unknown / d. unknown**
1934 WM FRA — 0 — 0 — —

**Botter, Cedric / b. Jan. 23, 1985**
2003 WM18 SUI 6 2 1 3 8 —

**Botteri, Stephane / b. Jan. 27, 1962**
1992-93 WM FRA 12 0 1 1 4 —
1988-94 OG-M FRA 21 0 2 2 20 —

**Botterill, Fred / b. Aug. 15, 1910 / d. Mar. 2, 1967**
1937 WM CAN 9 8 1 9 0 G

**Botterill, Jason / b. May 19, 1976**
1994-96 WM20 CAN 19 2 7 9 16 3G

**Botturi, Guido / b. unknown / d. unknown**
1930 WM ITA 1 0 0 0 — —

**Boucha, Henry / b. June 1, 1951**
1971 WM USA 10 7 1 8 2 —
1972 OG-M USA 5 2 3 5 6 S

**Bouchard, Francois / b. Apr. 26, 1988**
2006 WM18 CAN 7 3 5 8 6 —

**Bouchard, Joel / b. Jan. 23, 1974**
1993-94 WM20 CAN 14 0 1 1 10 2G
1997 WM CAN 11 0 1 1 2 G

**Bouchard, Kris / b. Oct. 7, 1982**
2000 WM18 USA 5 1 0 1 4 —

**Bouchard, Pierre-Marc / b. Apr. 27, 1984**
2002 WM18 CAN 8 4 8 12 16 —
2003 WM20 CAN 6 2 3 5 2 S

**Boucher, Denis / b. Sept. 20, 1933**
1959 WM CAN 8 8 1 9 4 G

**Boucher, Gaetan / b. May 5, 1956**
1987 WM SUI 7 3 2 5 12 —
1988 OG-M SUI 6 0 1 1 8 —

**Bouck, Tyler / b. Jan. 13, 1980**
1999-2000 WM20 CAN 14 2 2 4 22 S,B

**Bouillon, Francis / b. Oct. 17, 1975**
2003 WM USA 6 0 1 1 0 —

**Boulerice, Jesse / b. Aug. 10, 1978**
1997-98 WM20 USA 13 2 1 3 14 S

**Boumedienne, Josef / b. Jan. 12, 1978**
1997-98 WM20 SWE 7 1 0 1 4 —

**Bourbeau, Al / b. May 17, 1965**
1984-85 WM20 USA 14 8 5 13 26 —
1988 OG-M USA 5 3 1 4 2 —

**Bourbonnais, Roger / b. Oct. 26, 1942**
1965-69 WM CAN 31 6 10 16 24 2B
1964-68 OG-M CAN 14 4 7 11 0 B
~IIHF Hall of Fame
~OG-M All-Star Team/Forward (1964)

**Bourdon, Luc / b. Feb. 16, 1987**
2005 WM18 CAN 6 0 1 1 4 S
2006-07 WM20 CAN 12 3 7 10 10 2G
~WM20 All-Star Team/Defence (2006)

**Bourne, Bob / b. June 21, 1954**
1984 CC CAN 8 0 3 3 0 1st

**Bourque, Phil / b. June 8, 1962**
1994 WM USA 8 0 1 1 6 —

**Bourque, Ray / b. Dec. 28, 1960**
1981-87 CC CAN 24 3 14 17 24 —
1998 OG-M CAN 6 1 2 3 4 —

**Boutette, Pat / b. Mar. 1, 1952**
1981 WM CAN 8 1 1 2 16 —

**Boutillier, Paul / b. May 3, 1963**
1982-83 WM20 CAN 14 4 8 12 6 G,B

**Bouzek, Vladimir / b. Dec. 3, 1920 / d. d. July 31, 2006**
1947-49 WM TCH 4 4 — 4 — 2G
1948 OG-M TCH 1 3 — 3 — S
~IIHF Hall of Fame

**Bovair, Terry / b. Jan. 15, 1960**
1980 WM20 CAN 5 2 2 4 10 —

**Bovim, Patrick Andre / b. Apr. 24, 1988**
2006 WM18 NOR 6 3 2 5 0 —

**Bowen, Curtis / b. Mar. 24, 1974**
1994 WM20 CAN 7 2 0 2 10 G

**Bownass, Jack / b. July 27, 1930**
1967-69 WM CAN 11 0 2 2 16 B

**Boxer, Herb / b. June 4, 1947**
1975 WM USA 10 1 2 3 10 —

**Boyard, Philippe / b. Oct. 31, 1916 / d. unknown**
1935-37 WM FRA 11 2 0 2 10 —
1936 OG-M FRA 3 0 — 0 — —

**Boychuk, Johnny / b. Jan. 19, 1984**
2002 WM18 CAN 5 1 0 1 8 —

**Bozek, Roman / b. Mar. 24, 1974**
1983 WM20 TCH 7 1 0 1 2 S

**Bozek, Steve / b. Nov. 26, 1960**
1991 WM CAN 8 1 1 2 4 S

**Bozik, Mojmir / b. Feb. 26, 1962**
1981-82 WM20 TCH 11 0 4 4 18 S
1986-90 WM TCH 25 1 3 4 16 2B
1987 CC TCH 6 0 1 1 4 —
1988 OG-M TCH 8 1 3 4 2 —

**Bozon, Philippe / b. Nov. 30, 1966**
1992-2000 WM FRA 39 13 13 26 49 —
1988-2002 OG-M FRA 21 14 9 23 10 —
~IIHF Hall of Fame

**Brabec, Jaroslav / b. Feb. 1, 1971**
1991 WM20 TCH 6 2 1 3 2 B

**Brackl, Hans / b. unknown / d. unknown**
1933 WM ROM 5 0 — 0 0 —

**Bradley, Bart / b. July 29, 1930**
1959 WM CAN 8 5 4 9 8 G

**Bradley, Brian / b. Jan. 21, 1965**
1985 WM20 CAN 7 7 5 12 2 G
1988 OG-M CAN 7 0 4 4 0 —

**Bradley, Matt / b. June 13, 1978**
1998 WM20 CAN 7 1 1 2 0 —

**Bragnalo, Rick / b. Dec. 1, 1951**
1982-83 WM ITA 17 4 4 8 14 —

**Branch, James / b. 1946**
1969 WM USA 10 0 0 0 16 —

**Brandenburg, Otto / b. Oct. 1924 / d. Jan. 24, 2010**
1953 WM FRG 3 2 0 2 4 S

**Brandl, Maximilian / b. Feb. 13, 1988**
2005-06 WM18 GER 11 2 2 4 2 —

**Brandl, Thomas / b. Feb. 9, 1969**
1988-89 WM20 FRG 14 2 5 7 20 —
1990-95 WM GER 36 8 7 15 42 —
1996 WCH GER 4 1 1 2 8 —
1992-98 OG-M GER 19 1 6 7 22 —

**Brandner, Christoph / b. July 5, 1975**
1998-2003 WM AUT 33 7 11 18 18 —
1998-2002 OG-M AUT 8 0 1 1 4 —

**Brandrup, Paul / b. Mar. 28, 1960**
1980 WM20 USA 5 1 1 2 6 —

**Brandstetter, Ewald / b. 1963**
1981 WM20 AUT 5 1 0 1 2 —

**Brandting, Oscar / b. Feb. 29, 1984**
2002 WM18 SWE 8 0 0 0 0 —

**Branduardi, Gianpiero / b. Aug. 28, 1936**
1959 WM ITA 8 3 1 4 8 —
1956-64 OG-M ITA 13 2 0 2 4 —

**Brannstrom, Fabian / b. Aug. 1, 1974**
1993-94 WM20 GER 14 2 3 5 0 —

**Brannstrom, Niklas / b. Nov. 23, 1970**
1990 WM20 SWE 7 5 1 6 6 —

**Brasar, Per-Olov / b. Sept. 30, 1950**
1974-78 WM SWE 50 8 18 26 26 S,3B
1976 CC SWE 5 0 1 1 2 —

**Brasey, Patrice / b. Jan. 28, 1964**
1982 WM20 SUI 7 0 0 0 4 —
1987 WM SUI 6 0 0 0 9 —
1988-92 OG-M SUI 11 1 0 1 37 —

**Brashear, Donald / b. Jan. 7, 1972**
1997-98 WM USA 14 2 3 5 18 —

**Brassard, Derick / b. Sept. 22, 1987**
2005 WM18 CAN 6 0 4 4 6 S

**Bratianu, Dan / b. 1908 / d. 1991**
1931 WM ROM 5 0 — 0 — —

**Brattas, Per / b. 1935**
1958 WM NOR 4 0 0 0 2 —

**Bratz, Bjorn / b. Sept. 18, 1960**
1979 WM20 NOR 5 0 0 0 0 —

**Braun, Frank / b. Nov. 9, 1948**
1966-83 WM GDR 61 6 6 12 14 —

**Braun, Michael / b. May 2, 1961**
1978 WM20 SUI 4 1 0 1 6 —

**Brazda, Radomir / b. Oct. 11, 1967**
1987 WM20 TCH 7 2 1 3 6 S

**Brebant, Richard / b. Feb. 21, 1964**
1994 WM GBR 6 1 0 1 8 —

**Breistroff, Michel / b. Feb. 5, 1971**
1996 WM FRA 7 0 1 1 4 —

**Breiter, Robert / b. Mar. 28, 1909 / d. unknown**
1928 OG-M SUI 4 2 — 2 — B

**Breitschuh, Jurgen / b. July 19, 1950**
1976 WM GDR 9 1 0 1 2 —

**Brekke, Brent / b. Aug. 16, 1971**
1991 WM20 USA 7 0 0 0 8 —

**Brenchley, Edgar "Chirp" / b. Feb. 10, 1912 / d. Mar. 13, 1975**
1937 WM GBR 8 8 0 8 14 S
1936 OG-M GBR 7 4 0 4 0 G

**Brendl, Pavel / b. Mar. 23, 1981**
2001 WM20 CZE 7 4 6 10 8 G
~WM20 IIHF Directorate Best Forward (2001), WM20 All-Star Team/Forward (2001)

**Brennan, Billy / b. Jan. 13, 1934**
1962 WM GBR 7 2 5 7 44 —

**Brennan, Mickey / b. 1908 / d. unknown**
1939 WM CAN 8 2 — 2 — G

**Brennan, Mike / b. Jan. 24, 1986**
2004 WM18 USA 6 0 1 1 16 S

**Brennan, Rich / b. Nov. 26, 1972**
1992 WM20 USA 7 0 2 2 4 B

**Bresagk, Michael / b. Feb. 24, 1970**
1994-98 WM GER 14 0 0 0 12 —

**Brewer, Carl / b. Oct. 21, 1938 / d. Aug. 25, 2001**
1967 WM CAN 7 1 6 7 10 B
~WM All-Star Team/Defence (1967)

**Brezhnev, Vladimir / b. Mar. 5, 1945**
1961-66 WM URS 15 4 3 7 15 2G,B

**Briand, Arnaud / b. Apr. 29, 1970**
1993-2004 WM FRA 42 12 10 22 52 —
1992-2002 OG-M FRA 22 3 2 5 18 —

**Brickley, Andy / b. Aug. 9, 1961**
1981 WM20 USA 5 1 1 2 4 —
1992 WM USA 6 1 1 2 0 —

**Brickley, Mike / b. Jan. 13, 1981**
1999 WM18 USA 6 1 0 1 6 —

**Briere, Daniel / b. Oct. 6, 1977**
1997 WM20 CAN 7 2 4 6 4 G
2003-04 WM CAN 18 6 11 17 12 2G

**Brierley, Dan / b. Jan. 23, 1974**
1993 WM20 USA 7 0 0 0 4 —

**Bright, Chris / b. Oct. 14, 1970**
1995 WM CAN 8 0 3 3 8 B
2004 WM JPN 6 2 3 5 8 —
Totals WM 14 2 6 8 16 B

**Brind'Amour, Rod / b. Aug. 9, 1970**
1989 WM20 CAN 7 2 3 5 4 —
1992-94 WM CAN 22 8 4 12 12 G
1996 WCH CAN 5 1 2 3 0 2nd
1998 OG-M CAN 6 1 2 3 0 —

**Brink, Andy / b. Jan. 9, 1974**
1994 WM20 USA 7 0 1 1 12 —

**Brisebois, Patrice / b. Jan. 27, 1971**
1990-91 WM20 CAN 14 3 8 11 8 2G

**Brittig, Christian / b. Mar. 27, 1966**
1990 WM FRG 6 0 0 0 8 —
1988 OG-M FRG 8 1 0 1 0 —

**Broberg, Tage / b. May 4, 1909 / d. unknown**
1931 WM SWE 6 0 — 0 — —

**Brockmann, Andreas / b. June 11, 1967**
1985-86 WM20 FRG 14 0 2 2 6 —
1992 WM GER 6 1 2 3 6 —
1992 OG-M GER 8 3 2 5 2 —

**Brodahl, Ole / b. unknown / d. unknown**
1937 WM NOR 2 1 0 1 0 —

**Broden, Connie / b. Apr. 6, 1932**
1958 WM CAN 7 11 7 18 6 G

**Brodin, Michael / b. Sept. 16, 1982**
2002 WM20 FRA 6 1 2 3 10 —

**Brodmann, Mario / b. Apr. 2, 1966**
1992 WM SUI 8 1 0 1 10 —
1992 OG-M SUI 7 2 2 4 8 —

**Brodnik, Andrej / b. May 4, 1970**
2002-03 WM SLO 12 1 2 3 22 —

**Bromowicz, Henryk / b. Feb. 22, 1924 / d. Dec. 30, 1982**
1947-55 WM POL 11 0 0 0 2 —
1948-56 OG-M POL 20 1 0 1 0 —
~played under the name Henryk Brommer, 1947-50

**Broms, Sigurd / b. Jan. 10, 1932 / d. Jan. 13, 2007**
1953-61 WM SWE 36 20 6 26 17 2G,B
1956-60 OG-M SWE 13 2 1 3 2 —

**Brooke, Bob / b. Dec. 18, 1960**
1980 WM20 USA 5 3 2 5 8 —
1985-87 WM USA 20 2 2 4 22 —
1984-87 CC USA 10 1 1 2 8 —
1984 OG-M USA 6 1 1 2 10 —

**Brooker, Charlie / b. Mar. 25, 1932**
1956 OG-M CAN 5 4 1 5 2 B

**Brooks, David / b. Dec. 27, 1939**
1964 OG-M USA 6 1 0 1 33 —

**Brooks, Herb / b. Aug. 5, 1937 / d. Aug. 11, 2003**
1961-67 WM USA 26 8 4 12 12 B
1964-68 OG-M USA 14 1 3 4 6 —

**Bros, Michal / b. Jan. 25, 1976**
1996 WM20 CZE 6 3 3 6 4 —
2000-02 WM CZE 16 1 2 3 4 G

**Brost, Todd / b. Sept. 23, 1967**
1992 OG-M CAN 8 0 4 4 4 S

**Broten, Aaron / b. Nov. 14, 1960**
1979 WM20 USA 5 4 3 7 0 —
1981-87 WM USA 45 11 16 27 34 —
1984-87 CC USA 10 0 6 6 4 —

**Broten, Neal / b. Nov. 29, 1959**
1979 WM20 USA 5 2 4 6 10 —
1990 WM USA 8 1 5 6 4 —
1981-84 CC USA 12 6 3 9 4 —
1980 OG-M USA 7 2 1 3 2 G

**Brown, Bobby / b. Apr. 2, 1933**
1962 WM CAN 6 5 5 10 0 S

**Brown, Charlie / b. July 28, 1939**
1972 OG-M USA 5 0 0 0 6 S

**Brown, Curtis / b. Feb. 12, 1976**
1996 WM20 CAN 5 0 1 1 2 G
2000 WM CAN 9 1 3 4 8 —

**Brown, Doug / b. June 12, 1964**
1986-2001 WM USA 38 4 7 11 4 —
1991 CC USA 8 1 2 3 0 2nd

**Brown, Greg / b. Mar. 7, 1968**
1986-87 WM20 USA 14 1 3 4 10 B
1989-98 WM USA 33 3 5 8 33 —
1988-92 OG-M USA 13 0 4 4 4 —

**Brown, Joe / b. Mar. 19, 1926**
1962 WM GBR 6 0 0 0 8 —

**Brown, Keith / b. May 6, 1960**
1979 WM20 CAN 5 0 2 2 0 —

**Brown, Peter / b. May 21, 1954**
1975 WM USA 8 0 3 3 2 —

**Brown, Rob / b. Apr. 10, 1968**
1988 WM20 CAN 7 6 2 8 2 G

**Brown, Wayne / b. Nov. 16, 1930**
1959 WM CAN 5 2 1 3 7 G

**Brown, Wilbert / b. Sept. 24, 1899 / d. Apr. 6, 1964**
1928 OG-M GBR 2 0 — 0 — —

**Brownschidle, Jack / b. Oct. 2, 1955**
1975-79 WM USA 18 2 2 4 9 —

**Brownschidle, Jeff / b. Mar. 1, 1959**
1977-79 WM20 USA 12 1 3 4 2 —

**Bruce, Gordie / b. May 9, 1919 / d. July 15, 1997**
1938 WM CAN 7 4 — 4 — G

**Bruciamonte, Egidio / b. unknown / d. unknown**
1939 WM ITA 4 0 — 0 — —

**Bruck, Herbert / b. 1900 / d. unknown**
1931-33 WM AUT 12 4 — 4 0 B
1928 OG-M AUT 2 0 — 0 — —

**Bruck, Walter / b. unknown / d. unknown**
1930 WM AUT 3 1 — 1 — —
1928 OG-M AUT 2 0 — 0 4 —

**Bruderer, Martin / b. July 14, 1966**
1986 WM20 SUI 7 0 0 0 4 —

**Bruderer, Sandro / b. June 1, 1984**
2002 WM18 SUI 8 0 0 0 2 —

**Bruggemann, Lars / b. Mar. 2, 1976**
1995-96 WM20 GER 13 2 1 3 28 —
1998 WM GER 6 0 0 0 8 —
1998 OG-M GER 4 0 1 1 0 —

**Brugnoli, Patrick / b. Apr. 12, 1970**
1994-96 WM ITA 11 0 0 0 2 —
1994-98 OG-M ITA 11 1 0 1 2 —

**Bruininks, Brian / b. Mar. 30, 1970**
1990 WM20 USA 7 0 0 0 4 —

**Brunclik, Bedrich / b. July 6, 1946**
1971 WM TCH 4 1 0 1 4 S

**Brunner, Fritz / b. Nov. 3, 1965**
1984 WM20 FRG 7 0 2 2 8 —

**Brunner, Markus / b. May 18, 1973**
1997-98 WM ITA 14 1 0 1 4 —
1998 OG-M ITA 4 0 0 0 4 —

**Brunold, Alain / b. Feb. 12, 1985**
2003 WM18 SUI 6 0 1 1 2 —

**Bruun, Henrik / b. unknown**
1959 WM NOR 1 0 0 0 0 —

**Bryjak, Zbigniew / b. May 28, 1965**
1985 WM20 POL 7 2 0 2 8 —
1989-92 WM POL 15 0 0 0 4 —

**Bryniarski, Franciszek / b. May 16, 1957**
1977 WM20 POL 7 0 0 0 6 —

**Bryniarski, Kazimierz / b. Oct. 11, 1934**
1955-58 WM POL 14 1 0 1 0 —
1956 OG-M POL 5 3 0 3 0 —

**Bubenshikov, Ilya / b. Oct. 2, 1980**
1999 WM20 BLR 6 0 0 0 0 —

**Bubenshikov, Igor / b. Jan. 12, 1960**
1980 WM20 URS 4 0 1 1 2 G

**Bubla, Jiri / b. Jan. 27, 1950**
1971-79 WM TCH 87 10 20 30 48 3G,5S,B
1976 CC TCH 7 3 2 5 4 2nd
1976-80 OG-M TCH 10 0 5 5 8 S
~WM All-Star Team/Defence (1978, 1979)

**Bubnik, Gustav / b. Nov. 21, 1928**
1949 WM TCH 5 3 — 3 — G
1948 OG-M TCH 4 5 — 5 — S

**Bubnik, Vaclav / b. Jan. 1, 1926 / d. Mar. 27, 1990**
1954-55 WM TCH 11 1 2 3 2 B
1952-56 OG-M TCH 15 2 1 3 12 —

**Bubnik, Vlastimil / b. Mar. 18, 1931**
1954-63 WM TCH 29 33 13 46 14 S,2B
1952-64 OG-M TCH 29 22 14 36 8 B
~IIHF Hall of Fame
~WM IIHF Directorate Best Forward (1961)

**Buchberger, Kelly / b. Dec. 2, 1966**
1993-96 WM CAN 20 0 2 2 20 G,S

**Bucher, Laurent / b. June 23, 1972**
1992 WM20 SUI 7 2 1 3 4 —

**Bucher, Tobias / b. Feb. 3, 1989**
2007 WM18 SUI 5 0 1 1 2 —

**Buchetti, Giancarlo / b. unknown / d. unknown**
1948 OG-M ITA 3 0 — 0 — —

**Buchwieser, Hubert / b. Jan. 25, 1976**
1995 WM20 GER 7 0 0 0 4 —

**Buchwieser, Martin / b. May 28, 1989**
2007 WM18 GER 6 1 3 4 0 —

**Buckna, Matej / b. unknown**
1996 WCH SVK 1 0 0 0 0 —

**Buder, Manfred / b. Mar. 24, 1936**
1957-67 WM GDR 46 11 6 17 34 —
1968 OG-M GDR 7 0 0 0 2 —

**Buenzli, Daniel / b. June 3, 1967**
1987 WM20 SUI 7 0 0 0 4 —

**Buhler, Cyrill / b. Nov. 4, 1983**
2001 WM18 SUI 7 3 2 5 12 S
2003 WM20 SUI 6 2 1 3 4 —

**Buia, Gheorghe / b. 1915 / d. unknown**
1933-37 WM ROM 12 0 0 0 2 —

**Bujar, Krzysztof / b. Nov. 14, 1961**
1989-92 WM POL 16 3 1 4 12 —
1992 OG-M POL 7 0 1 1 2 —

**Bukac, Ludek / b. Aug. 4, 1935**
1961-63 WM TCH 12 4 3 7 4 S,B
~IIHF Hall of Fame

**Bukovinsky, Jozef / b. Aug. 6, 1949**
1979 WM TCH 5 0 0 0 0 S

**Bulgheroni, Carlo / b. June 6, 1928**
1948 OG-M ITA 7 1 — 1 — —

**Bulhakov, Yuri / b. June 20, 1985**
2003 WM18 BLR 6 1 1 2 2 —

**Bull, Petter / b. Apr. 4, 1983**
2001 WM18 NOR 6 0 0 0 4 —

**Bullard, Mike / b. Mar. 10, 1961**
1986 WM CAN 10 2 1 3 2 B

**Bulyin, Vladislav / b. May 18, 1972**
1992 WM20 RUS 7 0 0 0 10 G

**Bundi, Ralph / b. Feb. 15, 1978**
1998 WM20 SUI 7 0 1 1 12 B

**Bunter, Jaromir / b. Apr. 3, 1930**
1956 OG-M TCH 5 1 0 1 4 —

**Burakovsky, Mikael / b. June 23, 1977**
1997 WM20 SWE 6 0 1 1 12 —

**Burakovsky, Robert / b. Nov. 24, 1966**
1986 WM20 SWE 7 1 1 2 0 —

**Buran, Otto / b. unknown / d. unknown**
1938 WM NOR 4 0 — 0 — —

**Burda, Mieczyslaw / b. Apr. 19, 1916 / d. Apr. 29, 1990**
1937-39 WM POL 18 8 1 9 1 —
1948 OG-M POL 8 0 — 0 — —

**Burda, Vaclav / b. Jan. 14, 1973**
1993 WM20 TCH 5 0 1 1 0 B
1998 WM CZE 2 0 0 0 0 B

**Bure, Pavel / b. Mar. 31, 1971**
1989-91 WM20 URS 21 27 12 39 45 G,2S
1990-2000 WM RUS 26 9 13 22 22 G,B
1998-2002 OG-M RUS 12 11 1 12 10 S,B
~OG-M IIHF Directorate Best Forward (1998), WM20 IIHF Directorate Best Forward (1989), WM20 All-Star Team/Forward (1989)
~IIHF Hall of Fame

**Bure, Valeri / b. June 13, 1974**
1994 WM20 RUS 7 5 3 8 4 B
1994 WM RUS 6 3 0 3 2 —
1996 WCH RUS 1 0 0 0 2 —
1998-2002 OG-M RUS 12 2 0 2 2 S,B
~WM20 All-Star Team/Forward (1994)

**Bureau, Roger / b. Feb. 1, 1909 / d. Apr. 1945**
1939 WM BEL 4 0 — 0 — —
1928-36 OG-M BEL 6 0 — 0 — —

**Burek, Karol / b. Sept. 23, 1935**
1958 WM POL 5 2 0 2 0 —

**Burg, Dick / b. Mar. 24, 1936**
1959-61 WM USA 15 0 5 5 8 —

**Burger, Jiri / b. May 8, 1977**
1997 WM20 CZE 7 3 0 3 4 —

**Burghard, Alfred / b. Mar. 31, 1968**
1988 WM20 FRG 7 0 1 1 0 —

**Buril, Vladimir / b. May 17, 1969**
1989 WM20 TCH 7 0 2 2 8 B
1994 OG-M SVK 4 0 0 0 0 —

**Burillo, Thomas / b. Oct. 12, 1971**
1991 WM20 SUI 7 0 0 0 2 —

**Burkart, Urs / b. Jan. 9, 1963**
1982 WM20 SUI 7 0 0 0 4 —
1988 OG-M SUI 5 0 2 2 0 —

**Burkhalter, Loic / b. Feb. 11, 1980**
2000 WM20 SUI 7 1 3 4 4 —

**Burkhart, Gunther / b. Nov. 18, 1942**
1968 OG-M AUT 5 0 1 1 16 —

**Burman, Erik / b. Dec. 6, 1897 / d. Mar. 31, 1985**
1920-24 OG-M SWE 10 9 — 9 — —

**Burmistronak, Alexander / b. Mar. 27, 1986**
2004 WM18 BLR 6 0 0 0 4 —

**Burnett, William / b. 1914 / d. unknown**
1937 WM CAN 9 7 3 10 9 G

**Burnik, Dejan / b. Mar. 25, 1963**
1984 OG-M YUG 5 0 0 0 0 —

**Burns, Charlie / b. Feb. 14, 1936**
1958 WM CAN 7 3 3 6 0 G
~WM IIHF Directorate Best Forward (1958)

**Burns, Tony / b. Sept. 18, 1971**
1991 WM20 USA 7 0 0 0 2 —

**Burr, Shawn / b. July 1, 1966**
1990 WM CAN 10 4 1 5 14 —

**Burstrom, Anders / b. Jan. 28, 1976**
1995-96 WM20 SWE 14 2 0 2 6 S,B

**Burt, Adam / b. Jan. 15, 1969**
1987-89 WM20 USA 14 1 7 8 10 —
1993-98 WM USA 12 2 1 3 10 —

**Burtnett, Wellingon / b. Aug. 26, 1930**
1956 OG-M USA 1 0 0 0 0 S

**Burton, James / b. Nov. 13, 1961**
1993-95 WM AUT 19 3 7 10 10 —
1994 OG-M AUT 7 2 2 4 6 —

**Busch, Markus / b. May 30, 1981**
1999 WM18 GER 6 0 0 0 4 —

**Bushell, H.W. / b. unknown / d. unknown**
1931 WM GBR 2 0 — 0 — —

**Busillo, Giuseppe ("Joe") / b. May 13, 1970**
1995-2006 WM ITA 46 8 8 16 60 —
1998-2006 OG-M ITA 9 1 2 3 10 —

**Buskoven, Henrik / b. May 4, 1970**
1990 WM20 NOR 7 2 3 5 2 —

**But, Anton / b. July 3, 1980**
2000 WM20 RUS 7 2 3 5 2 S
2001 WM RUS 7 3 0 3 2 —

**Butcher, Garth / b. Jan. 8, 1963**
1982 WM20 CAN 7 1 3 4 0 G
1992 WM CAN 3 1 0 1 4 —

**Butochnov, Andri / b. July 8, 1980**
2000 WM20 UKR 7 0 2 2 2 —

**Butsayev, Vyacheslav / b. June 13, 1970**
1990 WM20 URS 7 3 4 7 14 S
1991-2004 WM RUS 47 8 9 17 46 G,S,B
1991 CC URS 5 2 0 2 0 —
1992 OG-M RUS 8 1 1 2 4 G

**Butsayev, Yuri / b. Oct. 11, 1978**
1997 WM20 RUS 6 1 0 1 0 B

**Butsenko, Konstyantyn / b. Mar. 10, 1969**
1999 WM UKR 3 0 0 0 2 —

**Buturlin, Alexander / b. Sept. 3, 1981**
1999 WM18 RUS 7 3 2 5 41 —
2001 WM20 RUS 7 4 1 5 8 —

**Buvik, Alf / b. May 12, 1984**
2001 WM18 NOR 6 1 0 1 4 —

**Buzek, Petr / b. Apr. 26, 1977**
1995 WM20 CZE 7 2 2 4 10 —
2000 WM CZE 9 1 3 4 24 G

**Byakin, Ilya / b. Feb. 2, 1963**
1982-83 WM20 URS 14 1 9 10 16 G
1989-94 WM URS 49 10 14 24 26 3G,B
1988 OG-M URS 8 1 4 5 4 G
~WM IIHF Directorate Best Defenceman (1993), WM All-Star Team/Defence (1993), WM20 IIHF Directorate Best Defenceman (1983), WM20 All-Star Team/Defence (1982, 1983)

**Byce, John / b. Aug. 9, 1967**
1992 WM USA 6 0 2 2 2 —

**Bychkov, Mikhail / b. May 22, 1926 / d. May 17, 1997**
1954-55 WM URS 12 3 1 4 2 G,S
1960 OG-M URS 7 1 3 4 4 B

**Bye, Bjarne / b. July 24, 1907 / d. unknown**
1937 WM NOR 2 0 0 0 0 —

**Byers, Dane / b. Feb. 21, 1986**
2004 WM18 CAN 7 0 1 1 8 —

**Byers, Lyndon / b. Feb. 29, 1964**
1984 WM20 CAN 6 1 1 2 4 —

**Bykov, Dmitri / b. May 5, 1977**
1999-2006 WM RUS 24 5 2 7 22 —

**Bykov, Mikhail / b. Sept. 3, 1981**
1999 WM18 RUS 7 0 1 1 6 —

**Bykov, Vyacheslav / b. July 24, 1960**
1983-95 WM URS 84 36 32 68 22 5G,S,2B
1987 CC URS 9 2 7 9 4 2nd
1988-92 OG-M RUS 15 6 10 16 2 2G
~OG-M All-Star Team/Forward (1992), WM All-Star Team/Forward (1989)

**Bykovsky, Boris / b. Mar. 19, 1969**
1989 WM20 URS 7 0 1 1 0 G

**Bylund, Lars / b. Feb. 15, 1938**
1966 WM SWE 7 0 1 1 0 —

**Bystrom, Lars / b. Oct. 7, 1965**
1984-85 WM20 SWE 14 3 4 7 10 —

**Bystrov, Valentin / b. Apr. 6, 1929**
1958 WM URS 1 0 0 0 0 S

**Bystryantsev, Viktor / b. Mar. 16, 1971**
1998 WM KAZ 3 0 0 0 2 —

**Cabana, Frederik / b. May 16, 1986**
2004 WM18 CAN 7 1 4 5 18 —

**Cabanis, Bernard / b. June 23, 1950**
1968 OG-M FRA 5 0 0 0 0 —

**Cadieux, Jan / b. Mar. 17, 1980**
1999 WM20 SUI 6 1 0 1 2 —

**Cadieux, Ray / b. Dec. 27, 1941**
1966-67 WM CAN 9 4 0 4 8 2B
1964-68 OG-M CAN 14 8 2 10 8 B

**Caduff, Andreas / b. Oct. 17, 1964**
1984 WM20 SUI 7 1 0 1 2 —

**Caffery, Terry / b. Apr. 1, 1949**
1969 WM CAN 10 4 4 8 8 —

**Cahenzli, Andrea / b. Mar. 29, 1964**
1984 WM20 SUI 7 0 0 0 4 —

**Cahoon, Ed / b. July 2, 1926**
1947 WM USA 3 3 — 3 — —

**Cajka, Ludek / b. Nov. 3, 1963**
1987 WM TCH 9 1 2 3 10 B
1987 CC TCH 3 0 3 3 0 —

**Cakajik, Martin / b. Dec. 12, 1979**
1999 WM20 SVK 6 0 3 3 18 B

**Calamar, Alexandru / b. June 20, 1941**
1964-68 OG-M ROM 12 4 4 8 6 —

**Calder, Eric / b. July 26, 1963**
1981 WM20 CAN 5 1 0 1 4 —

**Calder, Kyle / b. Jan. 5, 1979**
1999 WM20 CAN 7 2 6 8 2 S
2002-06 WM CAN 21 4 3 7 10 G

**Caldr, Vladimir / b. Nov. 26, 1958**
1977-78 WM20 TCH 13 4 4 8 0 B
1983-86 WM TCH 16 2 5 7 4 S
1984 CC TCH 5 0 0 0 0 —
1984 OG-M TCH 7 4 0 4 2 S

**Caloun, Jan / b. Dec. 20, 1972**
1992 WM20 TCH 7 8 1 9 20 —
1993-99 WM CZE 14 4 4 8 12 G,B
1998 OG-M CZE 3 0 0 0 6 G

**Camazzola, Jimmy / b. Jan. 5, 1964**
1992 WM ITA 5 1 1 2 10 —
1992-94 OG-M ITA 14 2 4 6 22 —

**Camenzind, Andreas / b. Feb. 1, 1982**
2000 WM18 SUI 7 1 0 1 2 —
2001-02 WM20 SUI 14 4 2 6 43 —

**Camenzind, Arthur / b. May 7, 1971**
1991 WM20 SUI 6 0 0 0 2 —

**Campbell, Bill / b. Mar. 24, 1964**
1981 WM20 CAN 5 0 1 1 2 —

**Campbell, Brian / b. May 23, 1979**
1999 WM20 CAN 7 1 1 2 4 S
~WM20 All-Star Team/Defence (1999)

**Campbell, Gene / b. Aug. 17, 1932**
1955 WM USA 8 3 1 4 2 —
1956 OG-M USA 7 1 0 1 6 S

**Campbell, Gregory / b. Dec. 17, 1983**
2003 WM20 CAN 6 1 1 2 4 S

**Campbell, Jim / b. Feb. 3, 1973**
1992-93 WM20 USA 14 7 6 13 6 B
1997-2001 WM USA 13 2 2 4 14 —
1994 OG-M USA 8 0 0 0 6 —

**Campbell, Tom / b. Mar. 10, 1922 / d. unknown**
1954 WM CAN 6 1 — 1 0 S

**Cannerheim, Kim / b. July 11, 1978**
1998 WM20 SWE 5 2 0 2 2 —

**Cantacuzino, Constantin / b. Nov. 11, 1905 / d. May 26, 1954**
1931-37 WM ROM 22 8 — 8 0 —

**Capla, Boris / b. Nov. 9, 1962**
1982 WM20 FRG 4 0 0 0 0 —

**Capla, Josef / b. Sept. 1938**
1965 WM TCH 6 3 2 5 6 S

**Capuano, Dave / b. July 27, 1968**
1987 WM20 USA 7 1 1 2 2 —

**Carcillo, Dan / b. Jan. 28, 1985**
2003 WM18 CAN 7 2 2 4 33 G

**Card, Ryan / b. Feb. 18, 1984**
2002 WM18 CAN 8 0 2 2 2 —

**Carez, Fernand / b. Oct. 28, 1905 / d. unknown**
1949 WM BEL 6 0 — 0 — —
1936 OG-M BEL 1 0 — 0 — —

**Carkner, Terry / b. Mar. 7, 1966**
1986 WM20 CAN 7 0 4 4 0 S
1993 WM CAN 8 0 0 0 0 —

**Carlassare, Franco / b. Sept. 24, 1913 / d. unknown**
1935-39 WM ITA 4 0 — 0 — —

**Carlson, Dan / b. Apr. 6, 1979**
1999 WM20 USA 6 1 0 1 0 —

**Carlsson, Anders / b. Nov. 25, 1960**
1986-97 WM SWE 55 15 14 29 40 2G,3S
1987 CC SWE 6 1 0 1 0 —

**Carlsson, Arne / b. Jan. 5, 1943**
1967-74 WM SWE 55 5 9 14 34 4S,2B
1968 OG-M SWE 7 0 0 0 4 —

**Carlsson, Calle / b. May 5, 1972**
1992 WM20 SWE 4 0 1 1 4 S

**Carlsson, Daniel / b. Feb. 24, 1977**
1997 WM20 SWE 6 1 2 3 6 —

**Carlsson, Leif / b. Mar. 15, 1957**
1977 WM20 SWE 6 0 0 0 4 —

**Carlsson, Leif / b. Feb. 18, 1965**
1985 WM20 SWE 7 3 3 6 6 —

**Carlsson, Ruben / b. Jan. 29, 1913 / d. Feb. 14, 2004**
1937 WM SWE 3 0 0 0 2 —
1936 OG-M SWE 2 1 — 1 — —

**Carlsson, Stig / b. Jan. 17, 1924 / d. Dec. 14, 1978**
1949-55 WM SWE 38 18 2 20 8 G,S,B
1948-56 OG-M SWE 11 8 0 8 4 —

**Carlsson, Thomas / b. Mar. 11, 1971**
1991 WM20 SWE 7 1 1 2 0 —

**Carlston, Scott / b. Apr. 4, 1960**
1980 WM20 USA 5 4 2 6 4 —

**Carlyle, Johnny / b. July 31, 1929**
1950-51 WM GBR 12 6 0 6 8 —

**Carlyle, Randy / b. Apr. 19, 1956**
1989 WM CAN 9 1 4 5 4 S

**Carnback, Patrik / b. Feb. 1, 1968**
1988 WM20 SWE 6 4 3 7 10 —
1992-94 WM SWE 16 3 2 5 24 G,B
1992 OG-M SWE 7 1 1 2 2 —

**Carnes, Neil / b. Aug. 19, 1970**
1989 WM20 USA 7 2 2 4 4 —

**Carney, Keith / b. Feb. 3, 1970**
1990 WM20 USA 7 0 3 3 2 —
1998 OG-M USA 4 0 0 0 2 —

**Carpenter, Bobby / b. July 13, 1963**
1981 WM20 USA 5 5 4 9 6 —
1987 WM USA 10 2 2 4 8 —
1984-87 CC USA 11 2 6 8 8 —

**Carpentier, Hugo / b. Mar. 17, 1988**
2006 WM18 CAN 7 0 0 0 4 —

**Carr-Harris, Brian / b. Jan. 26, 1903 / d. July 5, 1942**
1931 WM GBR 4 5 — 5 — —

**Carrier, Marcel / b. unknown**
1950 WM FRA 4 0 0 0 0 —

**Carriou, Allan / b. Feb. 2, 1976**
2004 WM FRA 6 0 0 0 6 —
2002 OG-M FRA 4 0 0 0 6 —

**Carruthers, Colin / b. July 17, 1890 / d. Nov. 10, 1957**
1924-28 OG-M GBR 11 12 — 12 — B

**Carruthers, Eric / b. Oct. 11, 1895 / d. Nov. 19, 1931**
1930 WM GBR 1 0 1 1 — —
1924-28 OG-M GBR 11 18 — 18 — B

**Carson, Jim / b. July 20, 1968**
1986 WM20 USA 7 4 1 5 0 B
1987 WM USA 10 2 3 5 4 —

**Cartelli, Mario / b. Nov. 16, 1979**
1999 WM20 CZE 6 0 2 2 2 —

**Carter, Anson / b. June 6, 1974**
1994 WM20 CAN 7 3 2 5 0 G
1997-2003 WM CAN 20 6 3 9 12 2G

**Carter, John / b. May 3, 1963**
1986 WM USA 9 1 2 3 14 —

**Casey, Terry / b. 1944**
1967 WM USA 7 2 0 2 2 —

**Cashman, Wayne / b. June 24, 1945**
1972 SS CAN 2 0 2 2 14 1st

**Cassels, Andrew / b. July 23, 1969**
1989 WM20 CAN 7 2 5 7 2 —
1996 WM CAN 6 1 0 1 0 S

**Cassidy, Bruce / b. May 20, 1965**
1984 WM20 CAN 7 0 0 0 6 —

**Cattaruzza, Beat / b. 1966**
1986 WM20 SUI 7 0 1 1 8 —

**Cattin, Raymond / b. 1931**
1955 WM SUI 6 0 0 0 0 —

**Cattini, Ferdinand "Pic" / b. Sept. 27, 1916 / d. Aug. 17, 1969**
1933-49 WM SUI 49 51 4 55 6 S,2B
1936-48 OG-M SUI 9 1 0 1 0 B
~IIHF Hall of Fame

**Cattini, Hans / b. Jan. 24, 1914 / d. Apr. 3, 1987**
1933-49 WM SUI 44 26 2 28 7 S,2B
1936-48 OG-M SUI 9 1 0 1 0 B
~IIHF Hall of Fame

**Caux, Michel / b. Aug. 30, 1946**
1968 OG-M FRA 5 1 0 1 22 —

**Cavanaugh, Dan / b. Mar. 3, 1980**
2000 WM20 USA 7 2 0 2 6 —

**Cavosie, Marc / b. Aug. 6, 1981**
2001 WM20 USA 7 2 4 6 4 —

**Cazan, Traian / b. Oct. 22, 1958**
1980 OG-M ROM 5 2 0 2 12 —

**Cedergren, Henrik / b. Aug. 17, 1964**
1984 WM20 SWE 7 1 2 3 8 —

**Ceglarski, Len / b. June 27, 1926**
1952 OG-M USA 8 2 1 3 — S

**Celio, Bixio / b. June 6, 1928**
1954 WM SUI 2 0 — 0 0 —
1952 OG-M SUI 4 1 0 1 — —

**Celio, Filippo / b. Sept. 30, 1966**
1986 WM20 SUI 7 1 1 2 10 —

**Celio, Manuele / b. June 9, 1966**
1986 WM20 SUI 7 2 5 7 2 —
1987-93 WM SUI 32 3 4 7 10 —
1988-92 OG-M SUI 13 2 1 3 0 —

**Celio, Nicola / b. June 19, 1972**
1991-92 WM20 SUI 14 5 3 8 4 —

**Cellar, Andreas / b. July 18, 1981**
1999 WM18 SUI 7 1 0 1 8 —

**Cereda, Luca / b. Sept. 7, 1981**
1999 WM18 SUI 7 1 7 8 8 —
1999-2000 WM20 SUI 13 3 4 7 24 —
2003-04 WM SUI 12 0 2 2 4 —

**Cernik, Frantisek / b. June 3, 1953**
1976-83 WM TCH 47 14 11 25 18 G,3S,B
1976-81 CC TCH 13 0 1 1 4 —
1984 OG-M TCH 7 3 0 3 4 S

**Cerny, Ales / b. June 24, 1982**
2000 WM18 CZE 6 0 2 2 6 —

**Cerny, Frantisek / b. July 28, 1959**
1977-79 WM20 TCH 19 4 4 8 4 S,B
1983-87 WM TCH 16 0 1 1 12 S,B

**Cerny, Ivan / b. Aug. 19, 1959**
1978-79 WM20 TCH 12 3 6 9 8 S
~WM20 All-Star Team/Defence (1979)

**Cerny, Josef / b. Sept. 18, 1939**
1959-71 WM TCH 59 20 17 37 34 4S,4B
1960-72 OG-M TCH 26 11 16 27 8 S,2B
~IIHF Hall of Fame
~OG-M All-Star Team/Forward (1964)

**Cerny, Michal / b. June 11, 1973**
1993 WM20 TCH 7 5 1 6 2 B

**Cerny, Milan / b. Mar. 27, 1963**
1983 WM20 TCH 7 0 2 2 17 S

**Cetkovsky, Alois / b. Sept. 5, 1908 / d. unknown**
1933-39 WM TCH 38 5 2 7 0 2B
1936 OG-M TCH 5 0 — 0 — —

**Chagodayev, Alexander / b. Jan. 15, 1981**
2001 WM20 RUS 7 0 2 2 2 —

**Chaland, Jean / b. 1892 / d. unknown**
1920 OG-M FRA 1 0 0 0 — —

**Chalupa, Milan / b. July 4, 1953**
1976-83 WM TCH 60 6 9 15 22 2G,4S,B
1976-81 CC TCH 13 1 3 4 14 2nd
1976-84 OG-M TCH 18 1 3 4 18 2S

**Chambers, Shawn / b. Oct. 11, 1966**
1994 WM USA 8 0 3 3 4 —
1996 WCH USA 1 0 0 0 0 1st

**Chandler, Bill / b. unknown**
1951 WM CAN 6 5 — 5 2 G

**Chapman, Benny / b. unknown**
1954 WM CAN 3 0 — 0 8 S

**Chapman, Brennan / b. Jan. 11, 1985**
2003 WM18 CAN 7 0 1 1 6 G

**Chapman, Wally / b. July 6, 1964**
1984 WM20 USA 7 6 3 9 0 —

**Chappell, Jimmy / b. Mar. 25, 1915 / d. Apr. 3, 1973**
1937-38 WM GBR 15 7 6 13 0 2S
1936-48 OG-M GBR 14 5 0 5 2 G

**Chappot, Roger / b. Oct. 17, 1940**
1959-72 WM SUI 22 4 5 9 12 —
1964 OG-M SUI 7 0 0 0 8 —

**Chaput, Stefan / b. Mar. 11, 1988**
2006 WM18 CAN 7 0 1 1 2 —

**Charest, Larry / b. 1914 / d. unknown**
1938-51 WM USA 7 3 — 3 0 —

**Charlet, Andre / b. Apr. 23, 1898 / d. Nov. 24, 1954**
1930-31 WM FRA 7 1 — 1 — —
1924-28 OG-M FRA 3 0 — 0 — —

**Charlet, Francois / b. unknown**
1950 WM FRA 4 0 0 0 0 —

**Charouzd, Miloslav / b. Augist 15, 1928**
1954 WM TCH 7 2 2 4 0 —
1952 OG-M TCH 9 6 2 8 — —

**Charpentier, Pierre / b. 1887 / d. unknown**
1920-24 OG-M FRA 4 0 0 0 — —

**Charron, Craig / b. Nov. 15, 1967**
1995 WM USA 6 1 1 2 18 —

**Charron, Guy / b. Jan. 24, 1949**
1977-79 WM CAN 17 1 4 5 2 B

**Chartrain, Andre / b. Mar. 24, 1962**
1981 WM20 CAN 5 2 1 3 2 —

**Chartraw, Rick / b. July 13, 1954**
1976 CC USA 5 0 0 0 8 —

**Chase, John / b. June 12, 1906 / d. Apr. 1, 1994**
1932 OG-M USA 6 4 2 6 1 S

**Chatelain, Alex / b. Feb. 22, 1978**
1998 WM20 SUI 6 2 1 3 0 B

**Chaudron, Jacques / b. June 5, 1889 / d. June 16, 1969**
1924 OG-M FRA 3 0 — 0 — —

**Chauvel, Brice / b. July 20, 1979**
2004 WM FRA 3 0 0 0 0 —

**Chebaturkin, Vladimir / b. Apr. 23, 1975**
1995 WM20 RUS 7 0 2 2 2 S

**Chebotarevski, Sergei / b. May 13, 1980**
1999-2000 WM20 KAZ 13 0 0 0 2 —

**Chelios, Chris / b. Jan. 25, 1962**
1982 WM20 USA 7 1 2 3 10 —
1994 WM USA 1 0 0 0 0 —
1984-2004 WCH USA 31 1 13 14 35 1st
1984-2006 OG-M USA 22 3 4 7 16 S
~OG-M IIHF Directorate Best Defenceman (2002), OG-M All-Star Team/Defence (2002)

**Chelodi, Armando / b. Jan. 12, 1973**
1995-2002 WM ITA 40 0 5 5 18 —

**Chelodi, Enrico / b. Sept. 19, 1982**
2006 WM ITA 5 0 0 0 0 —

**Chepurko, Andrei / b. Jan. 21, 1981**
1999 WM18 UKR 6 0 1 1 2 —

**Cherbayev, Alexander / b. May 13 13, 1973**
1992-93 WM20 RUS 10 7 2 9 10 G

**Cherepanov, Alexander / b. Aug. 15, 1932**
1957-58 WM URS 14 9 8 17 18 2S

**Cherepanov, Alexander / b. Feb. 16, 1985**
2003 WM18 KAZ 5 0 1 1 4 —

**Cherepanov, Alexei / b. Jan. 15, 1989 / d. Oct. 13, 2008**
2007 WM18 RUS 7 5 3 8 6 G
2007-08 WM20 RUS 12 8 6 14 4 S,B
~WM20 IIHF Directorate Best Forward (2007), WM20 All-Star Team/Forward (2007), WM18 All-Star Team/Forward (2007)

**Chernenko, Sergiy / b. Feb. 16, 1984**
2001-02 WM18 UKR 14 0 0 0 6 —
2004 WM20 UKR 6 0 1 1 2 —

**Chernenko, Volodym / b. July 11, 1982**
1999 WM18 UKR 6 0 0 0 0 —

**Chernomaz, Rich / b. Sept. 1, 1963**
1995 WM CAN 8 0 3 3 10 B

**Chernook, Pavel / b. Sept. 28, 1986**
2003-04 WM18 BLR 12 0 0 0 30 —

**Chernov, Artyom / b. Apr. 28, 1982**
2000 WM18 RUS 6 2 2 4 2 S
2001 WM20 RUS 7 1 0 1 0 —

**Chernov, Mikhail / b. Nov. 11, 1978**
1998 WM20 RUS 7 2 0 2 12 S

**Chernykh, Alexander / b. Sept. 12, 1965**
1983-85 WM20 URS 21 14 9 23 22 2G,B
1989 WM URS 7 0 1 1 8 G
1988 OG-M URS 8 2 2 4 4 G

**Chernykh, Dmitri / b. Feb. 27, 1985**
2003 WM18 RUS 6 4 1 5 4 B

**Chiasson, Steve / b. Apr. 14, 1967**
1987 WM20 CAN 5 2 1 3 16 —
1997 WM CAN 11 0 3 3 8 G

**Chibirev, Igor / b. Apr. 19, 1968**
1988 WM20 URS 7 4 3 7 0 S
2002 OG-M UKR 4 2 1 3 2 —

**Chikalin, Alexei / b. Oct. 24, 1974**
1994 WM20 RUS 7 0 0 0 4 B

**Chinn, Nicky / b. June 14, 1972**
1994 WM GBR 6 0 0 0 2 —

**Chipman, Reg / b. 1917 / d. unknown**
1938 WM CAN 7 2 — 2 — G

**Chisholm, Cliff / b. Mar. 1911 / d. unknown**
1933 WM CAN 4 1 — 1 0 S

**Chisholm, Jim / b. Jan. 8, 1962**
1981 WM20 USA 5 2 1 3 0 —

**Chistov, Stanislav / b. Apr. 17, 1983**
2001 WM18 RUS 4 4 2 6 0 G
2001-02 WM20 RUS 14 9 5 14 0 G
~WM20 All-Star Team/Forward (2002)

**Chitarroni, Mario / b. June 11, 1967**
1992-2008 WM ITA 67 14 19 33 146 —
1998-2006 OG-M ITA 9 2 1 3 18 —

**Chizhmin, Yevgeni / b. Jan. 14, 1964**
1984 WM20 URS 7 3 1 4 0 G

**Chlubna, Tomas / b. Nov. 6, 1972**
1992 WM20 TCH 5 0 0 0 6 —

**Chmelir, Lukas / b. Apr. 15, 1983**
2001 WM18 CZE 7 0 4 4 2 —
2003 WM20 CZE 6 0 2 2 0 —

**Chmelo, Lubomir / b. Jan. 13, 1986**
2004 WM18 SVK 6 0 0 0 2 —

**Chmura, Mieczyslaw / b. Jan. 1, 1934 / d. Apr. 9, 1980**
1957 WM POL 6 0 — 0 6 —
1956 OG-M POL 5 1 0 1 14 —

**Chodakowski, Kazimierz / b. June 20, 1929**
1955-59 WM POL 30 4 0 4 23 —
1952-56 OG-M POL 13 3 0 3 6 —

**Cholewa, Marek / b. July 1, 1963**
1986 WM POL 8 1 0 1 6 —
1984-92 OG-M POL 19 0 3 3 8 —

**Chorske, Tom / b. Sept. 18, 1966**
1986 WM20 USA 7 1 0 1 2 B
1989-99 WM USA 29 5 5 10 26 B

**Choteborsky, Jan / b. Jan. 28, 1981**
1999 WM18 CZE 7 1 3 4 6 —
2001 WM20 CZE 7 0 2 2 0 G

**Chouinard, Eric / b. July 8, 1980**
2000 WM20 CAN 7 3 0 3 0 B

**Chowaniec, Andrzej / b. Jan. 1, 1958**
1979 WM POL 4 0 0 0 0 —
1984 OG-M POL 6 1 0 1 2 —

**Chowaniec, Stefan / b. Apr. 21, 1953**
1973-79 WM POL 47 8 10 18 16 —
1972-80 OG-M POL 11 1 3 4 6 —

**Christ, Jerzy / b. Sept. 15, 1958**
1986-89 WM POL 20 6 3 9 12 —
1984-88 OG-M POL 12 7 3 10 2 —

**Christen, Gregory / b. Jan. 19, 1983**
2003 WM20 SUI 6 1 4 5 10 —

**Christensen, Bent / b. Nov. 16, 1975**
2004 WM DEN 5 0 0 0 4 —

**Christian, Bill / b. Jan. 28, 1938**
1958-65 WM USA 20 11 10 21 20 B
1960-64 OG-M USA 14 4 12 16 4 G
~IIHF Hall of Fame

**Christian, Dave / b. May 12, 1959**
1979 WM20 USA 5 2 1 3 0 —
1981-89 WM USA 14 12 6 18 8 —
1981-91 CC USA 19 4 2 6 6 2nd
1980 OG-M USA 7 0 8 8 6 G

**Christian, Gord / b. Nov. 21, 1927**
1955-58 WM USA 15 6 5 11 16 —
1956 OG-M USA 6 5 1 6 4 S

**Christian, Roger / b. Dec. 1, 1935**
1958-65 WM USA 20 15 5 20 14 B
1960-64 OG-M USA 13 11 4 15 28 G

**Christiansen, Carsten / b. unknown / d. unknown**
1937 WM NOR 1 0 0 0 0 —

**Christiansen, Keith / b. July 14, 1944**
1969-71 WM USA 20 6 4 10 22 —
1972 OG-M USA 5 1 1 2 6 S

**Christie, Mike / b. Dec. 20, 1949**
1976 CC USA 4 0 0 0 2 —

**Christoff, Steve / b. Jan. 23, 1958**
1979 WM USA 8 3 2 5 4 —
1981 CC USA 6 1 5 6 4 —
1980 OG-M USA 7 2 1 3 6 G

**Christoffersen, Magnus / b. Feb. 2, 1969**
1989 WM20 NOR 7 0 1 1 6 —

**Chromco, Michal / b. May 3, 1972**
1992 WM20 TCH 2 0 0 0 2 —

**Chubarov, Artyom / b. Dec. 13, 1979**
1998-99 WM20 RUS 14 7 5 12 4 G,S
2004 WCH RUS 4 0 1 1 0 —

**Chubenko, Sergiy / b. Mar. 4, 1976**
1995-96 WM20 UKR 13 2 1 3 8 —

**Chupin, Alexei / b. Nov. 11, 1972**
1997-98 WM RUS 15 2 3 5 12 —

**Churilov, Gennadi / b. May 5, 1987 / d. Sept. 7, 2011**
2006-07 WM20 RUS 12 3 4 7 18 2S
~perished in Yaroslavl plane crash

**Churin, Yuri / b. unknown**
1975 WM URS 8 3 3 6 6 G

**Churko, Alexander / b. Mar. 14, 1987**
2004 WM18 BLR 6 1 0 1 2 —

**Churlyayev, Mikhail / b. Oct. 22, 1989**
2006-07 WM18 RUS 11 0 0 0 6 —

**Chursin, Boris / b. May 14, 1975**
1995 WM20 UKR 7 0 3 3 2 —

**Chvojka, Petr / b. May 27, 1982**
2000 WM18 CZE 5 0 0 0 2 —
2002 WM20 CZE 7 1 0 1 6 —

**Chyzowski, Dave / b. July 11, 1971**
1990 WM20 CAN 7 9 4 13 2 G
~WM20 All-Star Team/Forward (1990)

**Ciarcia, Gerry / b. Oct. 23, 1956**
1982-83 WM ITA 17 0 0 0 8 —
1984 OG-M ITA 5 1 0 1 10 —

**Ciavaglia, Pete / b. July 15, 1969**
1989 WM20 USA 7 1 4 5 0 —
1994 WM USA 7 1 0 1 2 —
1994 OG-M USA 8 2 4 6 0 —

**Cibien, Pierangelo / b. Apr. 7, 1968**
1993 WM ITA 6 0 0 0 2 —

**Ciccarelli, Dino / b. Feb. 8, 1960**
1980 WM20 CAN 5 5 1 6 2 —
1982-87 WM CAN 19 6 3 9 4 B

**Ciccarello, Joe / b. Mar. 8, 1972**
1999 WM ITA 3 0 0 0 0 —

**Cichocki, Chris / b. Sept. 17, 1963**
1983 WM20 USA 7 0 1 1 0 —

**Cierny, Ladislav / b. Nov. 3, 1974**
2002-04 WM SVK 27 1 3 4 22 G,B
2004 WCH SVK 1 0 0 0 0 —

**Cieslik, Wlodzimierz / b. Oct. 10, 1965**
1985 WM20 POL 7 0 1 1 8 —

**Ciger, Zdeno / b. Oct. 19, 1969**
1988-89 WM20 TCH 14 8 7 15 10 B
1989-2003 WM TCH 53 15 15 30 34 3B
1991-96 WCH SVK 8 1 0 1 4 —
1998 OG-M SVK 4 1 1 2 4 —

**Ciglenecki, Robert / b. July 17, 1974**
2002-06 WM SLO 23 0 2 2 48 —

**Cihlar, Jiri / b. Aug. 19, 1969**
1989 WM20 TCH 7 2 3 5 6 B

**Cijan, Thomas / b. Dec. 29, 1960**
1996 WM AUT 7 0 0 0 0 —
1984-88 OG-M AUT 11 2 6 8 14 —

**Cimetta, Rob / b. Feb. 15, 1970**
1989 WM20 CAN 7 7 4 11 4 —

**Cimrman, Otto / b. May 1, 1925**
1956 OG-M TCH 3 0 2 2 2 —

**Cipruss, Aigars / b. Jan. 12, 1972**
1997-2009 WM LAT 61 8 14 22 12 —
2002-06 OG-M LAT 9 3 3 6 6 —

**Circelli, Toni / b. Nov. 18, 1961**
1992-95 WM ITA 23 2 3 5 16 —
1992-94 OG-M ITA 14 0 3 3 16 —

**Cirella, Carmine / b. Jan. 16, 1960**
1980 WM20 CAN 5 2 3 5 14 —

**Cirella, Joe / b. May 9, 1963**
1983 WM20 CAN 7 0 0 0 6 B

**Cirone, Jason / b. Feb. 21, 1971**
2006-08 WM ITA 17 5 5 10 22 —
2006 OG-M ITA 5 1 1 2 6 —

**Cisar, Jaroslav / b. 1913 / d. 1971**
1935-39 WM TCH 24 4 0 4 6 B

**Cisar, Marian / b. Feb. 25, 1978**
1998 WM20 SVK 6 4 1 5 29 —

**Cizek, Martin / b. May 17, 1984**
2002 WM18 CZE 8 0 0 0 4 B

**Claesson, Jan / b. Jan. 18, 1958**
1984 CC SWE 6 1 2 3 6 2nd

**Claesson, Stefan / b. Mar. 24, 1969**
1989 WM20 SWE 7 2 5 7 2 S

**Clancy, Terry / b. Apr. 2, 1943**
1964 OG-M CAN 7 1 1 2 2 —

**Claret, Marcel / b. unknown / d. unknown**
1934-50 WM FRA 8 0 0 0 4 —

**Claret, Pierre / b. July 1, 1911 / d. unknown**
1935-37 WM FRA 15 2 0 2 7 —
1936 OG-M FRA 3 0 — 0 — —

**Clark, Wendel / b. Oct. 25, 1966**
1985 WM20 CAN 7 4 2 6 10 G

**Clarke, Bobby / b. Aug. 13, 1949**
1982 WM CAN 9 0 1 1 6 B
1972 SS CAN 8 2 4 6 18 1st
1976 CC CAN 6 1 2 3 0 1st

**Clarkson, George "Guy" / b. Jan. 1, 1891 / d. Oct. 1974**
1924 OG-M GBR 3 0 — 0 — B

**Clayton, Bert / b. unknown / d. unknown**
1930 WM CAN 1 0 — 0 — G

**Cleary, Bill / b. Aug. 19, 1934**
1959 WM USA 8 7 1 8 2 —
1956-60 OG-M USA 14 11 10 21 2 G,S
~IIHF Hall of Fame
~WM IIHF Directorate Best Forward (1959)

**Cleary, Bob / b. Apr. 21, 1936**
1959 WM USA 8 3 5 8 2 —
1960 OG-M USA 7 6 4 10 6 G

**Cleary, Daniel / b. Dec. 18, 1978**
2002 WM CAN 7 2 1 3 2 —

**Clements, Earl / b. unknown**
1954 WM CAN 7 2 1 3 0 S

**Clune, Richard / b. Apr. 25, 1987**
2005 WM18 CAN 6 2 2 4 12 S

**Clutterbuck, Cal / b. Nov. 18, 1987**
2005 WM18 CAN 6 1 1 2 8 S

**Clymer, Ben / b. Apr. 11, 1978**
1996-97 WM20 USA 12 0 6 6 16 S
2000 WM USA 7 0 0 0 4 —

**Cocozza, Cato / b. Mar. 18, 1984**
2002 WM18 NOR 8 0 0 0 4 —

**Coffey, Paul / b. June 1, 1961**
1990 WM CAN 10 1 6 7 10 —
1984-96 WCH CAN 33 6 25 31 24 3/1st,2nd

**Cohen, Matt / b. Nov. 8, 1985**
2003 WM18 USA 6 0 0 0 2 —

**Cohen-Tervaert, Thijs / b. Feb. 11, 1915 / d. Jan. 1, 1945**
1939 WM NED 4 0 — 0 — —

**Cole, Danton / b. Jan. 10, 1967**
1990-94 WM USA 26 9 6 15 22 —

**Coleman, Jon / b. Mar. 9, 1975**
1994 WM20 USA 7 0 0 0 2 —

| Player / Year | Event | Team | GP | G | A | P | PIM | Medal |
|---|---|---|---|---|---|---|---|---|
| **Coletti, Alfredo / b. Sept. 12, 1937** | | | | | | | | |
| 1959 | WM | ITA | 1 | 0 | 0 | 0 | 0 | — |
| **Collard, Tony / b. July 28, 1961** | | | | | | | | |
| 1981 | WM | NED | 8 | 3 | 1 | 4 | 4 | — |
| **Collenberg, Franco / b. Aug. 25, 1985** | | | | | | | | |
| 2003 | WM18 | SUI | 6 | 0 | 0 | 0 | 0 | — |
| **Colley, Kevin / b. Jan. 4, 1979** | | | | | | | | |
| 1998 | WM20 | USA | 7 | 0 | 3 | 3 | 6 | — |
| **Collins, Dan / b. Feb. 26, 1987** | | | | | | | | |
| 2005 | WM18 | USA | 6 | 2 | 1 | 3 | 4 | G |
| **Collins, Dustin / b. Feb. 28, 1985** | | | | | | | | |
| 2003 | WM18 | USA | 6 | 0 | 0 | 0 | 2 | — |
| **Collins, Frank / b. Oct. 1903 / d. unknown** | | | | | | | | |
| 1933 | WM | CAN | 5 | 2 | — | 2 | 0 | S |
| **Collins, Joe / b. Sept. 12, 1915 / d. unknown** | | | | | | | | |
| 1939 | WM | GBR | 3 | 0 | — | 0 | — | — |
| **Collon, Albert / b. unknown / d. unknown** | | | | | | | | |
| 1930 | WM | BEL | 1 | 0 | — | 0 | — | — |
| 1928 | OG-M | BEL | 3 | 0 | — | 0 | — | — |
| **Collyard, Bob / b. Oct. 16, 1949** | | | | | | | | |
| 1978-79 | WM | USA | 18 | 3 | 5 | 8 | 10 | — |
| **Colvin, Bill / b. Dec. 3, 1934 / d. Nov. 3, 2010** | | | | | | | | |
| 1956 | OG-M | CAN | 4 | 0 | 4 | 4 | 0 | B |
| **Commodore, Mike / b. Nov. 7, 1979** | | | | | | | | |
| 2007 | WM | CAN | 9 | 0 | 2 | 2 | 14 | G |
| **Comploi, Georg / b. Nov. 9, 1968** | | | | | | | | |
| 1992-2000 | WM | ITA | 44 | 4 | 1 | 5 | 64 | — |
| 1992 | OG-M | ITA | 7 | 0 | 0 | 0 | 2 | — |
| **Comrie, Mike / b. Sept. 11, 1980** | | | | | | | | |
| 2002-06 | WM | CAN | 25 | 7 | 5 | 12 | 26 | G |
| **Conacher, Brian / b. Aug. 31, 1941** | | | | | | | | |
| 1965 | WM | CAN | 7 | 1 | 3 | 4 | 6 | — |
| 1964 | OG-M | CAN | 7 | 7 | 1 | 8 | 6 | — |
| **Conacher, Pete / b. July 29, 1932** | | | | | | | | |
| 1959 | WM | CAN | 8 | 7 | 4 | 11 | 2 | G |
| **Conlin, Paul / b. Jan. 26, 1943** | | | | | | | | |
| 1965-67 | WM | CAN | 19 | 2 | 2 | 4 | 14 | 2B |
| 1964-68 | OG-M | CAN | 14 | 0 | 0 | 0 | 4 | B |
| **Conne, Flavien / b. Apr. 1, 1980** | | | | | | | | |
| 1998-2000 | WM20 | SUI | 18 | 5 | 6 | 11 | 12 | B |
| 2000-05 | WM | SUI | 33 | 4 | 0 | 4 | 20 | — |
| 2002-06 | OG-M | SUI | 7 | 1 | 0 | 1 | 6 | — |
| **Connelly, Jim / b. Oct. 7, 1932** | | | | | | | | |
| 1960 | OG-M | CAN | 7 | 5 | 3 | 8 | 14 | S |
| **Connolly, Tim / b. May 7, 1981** | | | | | | | | |
| 1999 | WM20 | USA | 6 | 1 | 0 | 1 | 8 | — |
| 2001 | WM | USA | 9 | 3 | 4 | 7 | 4 | — |
| **Conroy, Al / b. Jan. 17, 1966** | | | | | | | | |
| 1986 | WM20 | CAN | 7 | 4 | 4 | 8 | 6 | S |
| **Conroy, Craig / b. Sept. 4, 1971** | | | | | | | | |
| 2004 | WCH | USA | 2 | 0 | 0 | 0 | 0 | — |
| 2006 | OG-M | USA | 6 | 1 | 4 | 5 | 2 | — |
| **Conroy, Tony / b. Oct. 19, 1895 / d. Jan. 11, 1978** | | | | | | | | |
| 1920 | OG-M | USA | 4 | 14 | — | 14 | 2 | S |
| **Contini, Joe / b. Jan. 29, 1957** | | | | | | | | |
| 1977 | WM20 | CAN | 7 | 4 | 6 | 10 | 38 | S |
| **Convery, Brandon / b. Feb. 4, 1974** | | | | | | | | |
| 1994 | WM20 | CAN | 7 | 1 | 0 | 1 | 2 | G |
| 1995 | WM | CAN | 8 | 0 | 1 | 1 | 0 | B |
| **Conway, Kevin / b. Mar. 27, 1927** | | | | | | | | |
| 1955 | WM | CAN | 7 | 0 | 0 | 0 | 17 | G |
| **Conway, Kevin / b. July 13, 1963** | | | | | | | | |
| 1994 | WM | GBR | 6 | 2 | 1 | 3 | 6 | — |
| **Conz, Florian / b. Oct. 20, 1984** | | | | | | | | |
| 2001-02 | WM18 | SUI | 14 | 4 | 10 | 14 | 6 | — |
| 2003 | WM20 | SUI | 6 | 0 | 1 | 1 | 4 | — |
| **Cook, John / b. Jan. 22, 1936** | | | | | | | | |
| 1962 | WM | GBR | 7 | 0 | 0 | 0 | 2 | — |
| **Cooke, Matt / b. Sept. 7, 1978** | | | | | | | | |
| 1998 | WM20 | CAN | 7 | 1 | 1 | 2 | 6 | — |
| 2004 | WM | CAN | 9 | 2 | 2 | 4 | 8 | G |
| **Cookman, John / b. Sept. 2, 1909 / d. Aug. 19, 1982** | | | | | | | | |
| 1932 | OG-M | USA | 5 | 2 | 1 | 3 | 0 | S |
| **Cooper, Ian / b. Nov. 29, 1968** | | | | | | | | |
| 1994 | WM | GBR | 6 | 1 | 0 | 1 | 4 | — |
| **Cooper, Stephen / b. Nov. 11, 1966** | | | | | | | | |
| 1994 | WM | GBR | 6 | 0 | 1 | 1 | 4 | — |
| **Copeland, Todd / b. May 18, 1968** | | | | | | | | |
| 1987 | WM20 | USA | 7 | 1 | 2 | 3 | 6 | — |
| 1992 | WM | USA | 6 | 1 | 0 | 1 | 2 | — |
| **Copija, Miroslaw / b. Aug. 1, 1965** | | | | | | | | |
| 1985 | WM20 | POL | 7 | 0 | 0 | 0 | 2 | — |
| 1989 | WM | POL | 10 | 0 | 0 | 0 | 6 | — |
| 1988 | OG-M | POL | 5 | 0 | 1 | 1 | 4 | — |
| **Coppo, Paul / b. Nov. 2, 1938** | | | | | | | | |
| 1962-69 | WM | USA | 24 | 13 | 16 | 29 | 0 | B |
| 1964 | OG-M | USA | 7 | 3 | 4 | 7 | 0 | — |
| **Corkum, Bob / b. Dec. 18, 1967** | | | | | | | | |
| 1987 | WM20 | USA | 7 | 4 | 0 | 4 | 6 | — |
| **Corrente, Matt / b. Mar. 17, 1988** | | | | | | | | |
| 2006 | WM18 | CAN | 7 | 0 | 0 | 0 | 28 | — |
| **Corriveau, Yvon / b. Feb. 8, 1967** | | | | | | | | |
| 1987 | WM20 | CAN | 6 | 2 | 1 | 3 | 4 | — |
| **Corso, Daniel / b. Apr. 3, 1978** | | | | | | | | |
| 1998 | WM20 | CAN | 7 | 0 | 3 | 3 | 4 | — |
| **Corson, Shayne / b. Aug. 13, 1966** | | | | | | | | |
| 1985-86 | WM20 | CAN | 14 | 10 | 10 | 20 | 8 | G,S |
| 1993-94 | WM | CAN | 15 | 6 | 7 | 13 | 10 | G |
| 1991 | CC | CAN | 8 | 0 | 5 | 5 | 12 | 1st |
| 1998 | OG-M | CAN | 6 | 1 | 1 | 2 | 2 | — |
| ~WM20 All-Star Team/Forward (1986) | | | | | | | | |
| **Corvo, Joe / b. June 20, 1977** | | | | | | | | |
| 1997 | WM20 | USA | 6 | 1 | 1 | 2 | 0 | S |
| 2003-06 | WM | USA | 13 | 0 | 1 | 1 | 2 | — |
| ~WM20 IIHF Directorate Best Defenceman (1997) | | | | | | | | |
| **Costea, Marian / b. June 13, 1952** | | | | | | | | |
| 1977 | WM | ROM | 10 | 0 | 3 | 3 | 26 | — |
| 1976-80 | OG-M | ROM | 10 | 6 | 5 | 11 | 24 | — |
| **Cote, Alain / b. Apr. 14, 1967** | | | | | | | | |
| 1986 | WM20 | CAN | 7 | 1 | 4 | 5 | 6 | S |
| **Cote, Matthew / b. Jan. 19, 1966** | | | | | | | | |
| 1994 | WM | GBR | 6 | 0 | 0 | 0 | 8 | — |
| **Cote, Sylvain / b. Jan. 19, 1966** | | | | | | | | |
| 1984-86 | WM20 | CAN | 14 | 1 | 6 | 7 | 17 | S |
| 1992 | WM | CAN | 1 | 0 | 0 | 0 | 0 | — |
| 1996 | WCH | CAN | 2 | 0 | 1 | 1 | 0 | 2nd |
| ~WM20 All-Star Team/Defence (1986) | | | | | | | | |
| **Coughlin, Kevin / b. Apr. 23, 1985** | | | | | | | | |
| 2003 | WM18 | USA | 6 | 0 | 0 | 0 | 25 | — |
| **Coulombe, Partick / b. Apr. 23, 1985** | | | | | | | | |
| 2003 | WM18 | CAN | 7 | 0 | 2 | 2 | 2 | G |
| **Courcelles, Sebastien / b. Nov. 19, 1984** | | | | | | | | |
| 2002 | WM18 | CAN | 8 | 2 | 0 | 2 | 20 | — |
| **Cournoyer, Yvan / b. Nov. 22, 1943** | | | | | | | | |
| 1972 | SS | CAN | 8 | 3 | 2 | 5 | 2 | 1st |
| **Courteau, Yves / b. Apr. 25, 1964** | | | | | | | | |
| 1984 | WM20 | CAN | 7 | 0 | 1 | 1 | 0 | — |
| **Courtnall, Geoff / b. Aug. 18, 1962** | | | | | | | | |
| 1991 | WM | CAN | 10 | 5 | 1 | 6 | 16 | S |
| **Courtnall, Russ / b. June 2, 1965** | | | | | | | | |
| 1984 | WM20 | CAN | 7 | 7 | 6 | 13 | 0 | — |
| 1991 | WM | CAN | 2 | 1 | 3 | 4 | 0 | S |
| 1991 | CC | CAN | 8 | 0 | 2 | 2 | 0 | 1st |
| 1984 | OG-M | CAN | 7 | 1 | 3 | 4 | 2 | — |
| **Courville, Larry / b. Apr. 2, 1975** | | | | | | | | |
| 1995 | WM20 | CAN | 7 | 2 | 3 | 5 | 6 | G |
| **Couttet, Henri / b. June 8, 1901 / d. Oct. 11, 1953** | | | | | | | | |
| 1920 | OG-M | FRA | 1 | 0 | 0 | 0 | — | — |
| **Couttet, Marcel / b. Apr. 27, 1912 / d. unknown** | | | | | | | | |
| 1937 | WM | FRA | 5 | 1 | 0 | 1 | 0 | — |
| 1936 | OG-M | FRA | 3 | 1 | — | 1 | — | — |
| **Couture, Logan / b. Mar. 28, 1989** | | | | | | | | |
| 2007 | WM18 | CAN | 6 | 2 | 2 | 4 | 2 | — |
| **Couvert, Marcial / b. unknown / d. unknown** | | | | | | | | |
| 1930-34 | WM | FRA | 12 | 2 | — | 2 | — | — |
| **Couvert, Raoul / b. 1903 / d. unknown** | | | | | | | | |
| 1930-31 | WM | FRA | 6 | 3 | — | 3 | — | — |
| 1924-28 | OG-M | FRA | 2 | 0 | — | 0 | — | — |
| **Coward, Johnny / b. Oct. 28, 1910 / d. 1989** | | | | | | | | |
| 1937 | WM | GBR | 5 | 0 | 0 | 0 | 2 | S |
| 1936 | OG-M | GBR | 6 | 1 | 0 | 1 | 0 | G |
| **Cox, Ralph / b. Feb. 27, 1957** | | | | | | | | |
| 1979 | WM | USA | 7 | 0 | 1 | 1 | 8 | — |
| **Crabb, Joey / b. Apr. 3, 1983** | | | | | | | | |
| 2001 | WM18 | USA | 6 | 5 | 2 | 7 | 2 | — |
| **Craig, Mike / b. June 6, 1971** | | | | | | | | |
| 1990-91 | WM20 | CAN | 14 | 9 | 5 | 14 | 16 | 2G |
| ~WM20 All-Star Team/Forward (1991) | | | | | | | | |
| **Craigwell, Dale / b. Apr. 24, 1971** | | | | | | | | |
| 1991 | WM20 | CAN | 6 | 1 | 2 | 3 | 0 | G |
| **Crameri, Gian-Marco / b. Dec. 13, 1972** | | | | | | | | |
| 1998-2002 | WM | SUI | 33 | 5 | 18 | 23 | 26 | — |
| 2002 | OG-M | SUI | 4 | 0 | 1 | 1 | 4 | — |
| **Cranston, Tim / b. Dec. 13, 1962** | | | | | | | | |
| 1994 | WM | GBR | 6 | 0 | 0 | 0 | 4 | — |
| **Craven, Murray / b. July 20, 1964** | | | | | | | | |
| 1990-91 | WM | CAN | 18 | 2 | 6 | 8 | 16 | S |
| **Crawford, Bill / b. 1932** | | | | | | | | |
| 1951 | WM | GBR | 5 | 2 | — | 2 | 0 | — |
| **Crawford, Bobby / b. May 27, 1960** | | | | | | | | |
| 1977-79 | WM20 | USA | 18 | 5 | 11 | 16 | 6 | — |
| **Crawford, Floyd / b. Nov. 28, 1928** | | | | | | | | |
| 1959 | WM | CAN | 8 | 1 | 0 | 1 | 6 | G |
| **Crawford, Marc / b. Feb. 13, 1961** | | | | | | | | |
| 1981 | WM20 | CAN | 5 | 1 | 3 | 4 | 4 | — |
| **Creighton, Adam / b. June 2, 1965** | | | | | | | | |
| 1985 | WM20 | CAN | 7 | 8 | 4 | 12 | 4 | G |
| **Creighton, Archie / b. July 23, 1912 / d. unknown** | | | | | | | | |
| 1935 | WM | CAN | 7 | 4 | — | 4 | — | G |
| **Crettanand, Yves / b. Apr. 29, 1963** | | | | | | | | |
| 1992 | OG-M | FRA | 8 | 0 | 0 | 0 | 2 | — |
| **Cristofoli, Ed / b. Jan. 2, 1939** | | | | | | | | |
| 1961 | WM | CAN | 1 | 0 | 1 | 1 | 0 | G |
| **Crombeen, B.J. / b. July 10, 1985** | | | | | | | | |
| 2003 | WM18 | CAN | 7 | 1 | 4 | 5 | 4 | G |
| **Cronie, Ab / b. Jan. 29, 1915 / d. Oct. 25, 1997** | | | | | | | | |
| 1939 | WM | CAN | 8 | 3 | — | 3 | — | G |
| **Cross, Cory / b. Jan. 3, 1971** | | | | | | | | |
| 1997-2003 | WM | CAN | 25 | 2 | 4 | 6 | 55 | 2G |
| **Cross, Tom / b. May 29, 1990** | | | | | | | | |
| 2007 | WM18 | USA | 7 | 0 | 1 | 1 | 4 | S |
| **Crossman, Doug / b. May 30, 1960** | | | | | | | | |
| 1980 | WM20 | CAN | 5 | 0 | 2 | 2 | 2 | — |
| 1987 | CC | CAN | 8 | 0 | 1 | 1 | 4 | 1st |
| **Crotti, Ernesto / b. July 18, 1936** | | | | | | | | |
| 1959 | WM | ITA | 8 | 4 | 4 | 8 | 2 | — |
| 1956 | OG-M | ITA | 6 | 4 | 7 | 11 | 0 | — |
| **Crouse, Art / b. Sep. 17, 1923 / d. Sept. 24, 1996** | | | | | | | | |
| 1949 | WM | USA | 8 | 2 | — | 2 | 2 | B |
| **Crowley, Cliff / b. June 13, 1906 / d. Apr. 27, 1948** | | | | | | | | |
| 1932 | OG-M | CAN | 1 | 0 | 0 | 0 | 0 | G |
| **Crowley, Dan / b. unknown** | | | | | | | | |
| 1949 | WM | USA | 3 | 0 | — | 0 | — | B |
| **Crowley, Mike / b. July 4, 1975** | | | | | | | | |
| 1995 | WM20 | USA | 7 | 0 | 3 | 3 | 8 | — |
| 1996-98 | WM | USA | 14 | 1 | 1 | 2 | 6 | B |
| **Crowley, Ted / b. May 3, 1970** | | | | | | | | |
| 1988-90 | WM20 | USA | 21 | 2 | 6 | 8 | 6 | — |
| 1994 | OG-M | USA | 8 | 0 | 2 | 2 | 8 | — |
| **Csabi, Tomas / b. Nov. 16, 1984** | | | | | | | | |
| 2002 | WM18 | CZE | 8 | 3 | 1 | 4 | 37 | B |
| **Csongei, Franz / b. Sept. 13, 1913 / d. unknown** | | | | | | | | |
| 1933-47 | WM | AUT | 30 | 1 | — | 1 | 1 | B |
| 1936-48 | OG-M | AUT | 13 | 6 | — | 6 | — | — |
| **Csorich, Stefan / b. Sept. 25, 1921 / d. July 15, 2008** | | | | | | | | |
| 1947-57 | WM | POL | 22 | 7 | 0 | 7 | 18 | — |
| 1948-52 | OG-M | POL | 15 | 6 | 4 | 10 | — | — |
| **Cubars, Sergejs / b. Apr. 23, 1976** | | | | | | | | |
| 2003 | WM | LAT | 6 | 1 | 1 | 2 | 2 | — |
| **Cudinovs, Sergejs / b. Sept. 10, 1962** | | | | | | | | |
| 1997-99 | WM | LAT | 20 | 7 | 5 | 12 | 32 | — |
| **Cuendet, Rodolphe / b. 1887 / d. Feb. 9, 1954** | | | | | | | | |
| 1920 | OG-M | SUI | 2 | 0 | 0 | 0 | — | — |
| **Cullen, Joe / b. Feb. 14, 1981** | | | | | | | | |
| 1999 | WM18 | USA | 6 | 2 | 0 | 2 | 4 | — |
| **Cullen, John / b. Aug. 2, 1964** | | | | | | | | |
| 1990 | WM | CAN | 10 | 1 | 3 | 4 | 0 | — |
| **Cullen, Mark / b. Oct. 28, 1978** | | | | | | | | |
| 2006 | WM | USA | 7 | 1 | 2 | 3 | 0 | — |
| **Cullen, Matt / b. Nov. 2, 1976** | | | | | | | | |
| 1996 | WM20 | USA | 6 | 3 | 1 | 4 | 0 | — |
| 1998-2004 | WM | USA | 27 | 6 | 12 | 18 | 14 | B |
| **Cullimore, Jassen / b. Dec. 4, 1972** | | | | | | | | |
| 1992 | WM20 | CAN | 7 | 1 | 0 | 1 | 2 | — |
| **Cunliffe, Bruce / b. Aug. 19, 1925 / d. Apr. 6, 1989** | | | | | | | | |
| 1948 | OG-M | USA | 8 | 17 | 6 | 23 | 12 | — |
| **Cunniff, John / b. July 9, 1944** | | | | | | | | |
| 1967-75 | WM | USA | 15 | 1 | 3 | 4 | 15 | — |
| 1968 | OG-M | USA | 7 | 1 | 4 | 5 | 4 | — |
| **Cunningham, Dave / b. Oct. 6, 1927** | | | | | | | | |
| 1960 | OG-M | AUS | 5 | 4 | 2 | 6 | 4 | — |
| **Cunningham, Richard / b. Mar. 3, 1951** | | | | | | | | |
| 1984 | OG-M | AUT | 5 | 1 | 1 | 2 | 8 | — |
| **Cunti, Luca / b. July 4, 1989** | | | | | | | | |
| 2005 | WM18 | SUI | 6 | 1 | 1 | 2 | 0 | — |
| **Cunti, Pietro / b. Mar. 9, 1962** | | | | | | | | |
| 1987 | WM | SUI | 10 | 2 | 2 | 4 | 6 | — |
| 1988 | OG-M | SUI | 2 | 1 | 1 | 2 | 2 | — |
| **Cupolo, Mark / b. Nov. 17, 1965** | | | | | | | | |
| 1993 | WM | ITA | 6 | 0 | 0 | 0 | 4 | — |

**Currie, Bob / b. Sept. 16, 1936**
1966-67 WM USA 14 0 2 2 24 —

**Currie, Dan / b. Mar. 15, 1968**
1988 WM20 CAN 7 4 3 7 2 G

**Curth, Christian / b. Mar. 17, 1970**
1989 WM20 FRG 7 0 0 0 0 —

**Curtis, Bob / b. Mar. 30, 1964**
1984 WM20 USA 7 1 2 3 2 —

**Cusson, Jean / b. Oct. 5, 1942**
1967 WM CAN 7 3 0 3 0 B

**Cuthbert, Cuthbert Ross / b. Feb. 6, 1892 / d. 1970**
1924-28 OG-M GBR 10 10 — 10 2 B

**Cutta, Jakub / b. Dec. 29, 1981**
2001 WM20 CZE 7 0 1 1 24 G

**Cychowski, Rafal / b. May 14, 1978**
1997 WM20 POL 6 0 0 0 8 —

**Cyr, Denis / b. Feb. 4, 1961**
1981 WM20 CAN 5 2 1 3 0 —

**Cyr, Paul / b. Oct. 31, 1963**
1982-83 WM20 CAN 14 5 9 14 31 G,B

**Czachowski, Ludwik / b. May 5, 1944 / d. July 10, 1999**
1970-74 WM POL 27 1 1 2 14 —
1972 OG-M POL 5 0 0 0 2 —

**Czaka, Zoltan / b. Dec. 2, 1932**
1964-68 OG-M ROM 12 2 0 2 2 —

**Czapka, Ludwik / b. May 27, 1966**
1989 WM POL 9 1 0 1 0 —
1985 WM20 POL 7 1 0 1 2 —

**Czarnota, Joe / b. Mar. 25, 1925 / d. Oct. 9, 1968**
1952 OG-M USA 8 2 2 4 — S

**Czech, Rudolf / b. Sept. 15, 1930 / d. 1975**
1957-58 WM POL 14 5 3 8 0 —
1952-56 OG-M POL 12 0 0 0 0 —

**Czerkawski, Mariusz / b. Apr. 13, 1972**
1990 WM20 POL 7 1 0 1 4 —
1992-2002 WM POL 9 2 2 4 8 —
1992 OG-M POL 5 0 1 1 4 —

**Czerwiec, Dariusz / b. Apr. 23, 1966**
1992 WM POL 5 0 1 1 4 —

**Czyzewski, Zygmunt / b. Oct. 4, 1910 / d. unknown**
1947 WM POL 5 0 — 0 — —

**Dackell, Andreas / b. Dec. 29, 1972**
1994-96 WM SWE 21 5 7 12 29 S,B
1994 OG-M SWE 4 0 0 0 0 G

**DaCorte, Luigi / b. June 10, 1973**
1994 WM ITA 2 0 0 0 0 —
1994 OG-M ITA 6 0 0 0 0 —

**Daffner, Thomas / b. Sept. 1, 1971**
2001 WM GER 7 1 3 4 4 —

**Dagnino, Edmond / b. May 19, 1903 / d. unknown**
1931 WM USA 6 2 — 2 — S

**Dahl, Bjorn / b. Aug. 21, 1971**
1995-96 WM NOR 10 0 0 0 4 —

**Dahl, Jan Morten / b. Dec. 11, 1973**
2001 WM NOR 6 0 0 0 4 —

**Dahl, Kevin / b. Dec. 30, 1968**
1992 OG-M CAN 8 2 0 2 6 S

**Dahl, Per / b. Mar. 21, 1916 / d. Feb. 17, 1989**
1937 WM NOR 2 0 0 0 0 —

**Dahlberg, Johan / b. Feb. 3, 1987**
2005 WM18 SWE 7 1 0 1 8 B

**Dahlberg, Lennart / b. Dec. 11, 1962**
1982 WM20 SWE 7 0 0 0 10 —

**Dahlen, Ulf / b. Jan. 21, 1967**
1986-87 WM20 SWE 14 10 12 22 6 B
1989-2002 WM SWE 35 15 9 24 4 G,S,B
1991-96 WCH SWE 10 3 2 5 5 —
1998-2002 OG-M SWE 8 2 2 4 2 —
~WM All-Star Team/Forward (1993), WM20 All-Star Team/Forward (1987)

**Dahlin, Kjell / b. Mar. 2, 1963**
1982-83 WM20 SWE 14 8 5 13 6 —

**Dahlquist, Chris / b. Dec. 14, 1962**
1990 WM USA 10 1 0 1 18 —

**Dahlstrom, Robin / b. Jan. 13, 1986**
2006 WM18 NOR 6 2 1 3 8 —

**Dahm, Win / b. Oct. 8, 1960**
1980 WM20 USA 5 1 2 3 6 —

**Dahlman, Toni / b. Sept. 3, 1979**
1998 WM20 FIN 6 2 0 2 0 G

**Dahlstrom, Ole Eskild / b. Mar. 4, 1970**
1989-90 WM20 NOR 14 2 11 13 18 —
1990-2000 WM NOR 44 8 7 15 31 —
1992-94 OG-M NOR 14 7 2 9 6 —

**Daigle, Alexandre / b. Feb. 7, 1975**
1993-95 WM20 CAN 14 2 14 16 31 2G

**Daigneault, Jean-Jacques "J-J" / b. Oct. 12, 1965**
1984 WM20 CAN 7 0 2 2 2 —
1984 OG-M CAN 7 1 1 2 0 —

**Daikawa, Daniel / b. July 30, 1971**
1998-2003 WM JPN 18 0 3 3 26 —

**Dailley, Gordon / b. July 24, 1911 / d. May 3, 1989**
1935-39 WM GBR 29 15 4 19 5 2S,B
1936 OG-M GBR 7 0 1 1 0 G

**Dale, John / b. Dec. 19, 1945**
1968 OG-M USA 7 0 1 1 0 —

**Dalene, Geir / b. May 16, 1970**
1990 WM20 NOR 7 0 0 0 4 —

**Daley, Bill / b. unknown**
1962-63 WM USA 11 4 3 7 10 B

**Daley, Pat / b. Mar. 27, 1959**
1978 WM20 CAN 6 3 2 5 2 B

**Daley, Trevor / b. Oct. 9, 1983**
2006 WM CAN 7 0 1 1 10 —

**Dallenbach, Jurg / b. Aug. 3, 1983**
2000-01 WM18 SUI 14 0 5 5 18 —
2002-03 WM20 SUI 13 1 0 1 22 —

**Dallman, Marty / b. Feb. 15, 1963**
1993 WM AUT 6 0 1 1 10 —
1994 OG-M AUT 7 4 4 8 8 —

**Dalsoren, Olav / b. Sept. 8, 1938**
1958-62 WM NOR 20 9 7 16 2 —
1964-68 OG-M NOR 12 6 7 13 0 —

**D'Alvise, Dan / b. Dec. 13, 1955**
1980 OG-M CAN 6 3 3 6 8 —

**Dame, Aurelia "Bunny" / b. Dec. 6, 1913 / d. unknown**
1939 WM CAN 8 9 — 9 — G

**Damgaard, Jesper / b. May 6, 1975**
2003-10 WM DEN 47 10 14 24 68 —

**Damphousse, Vincent / b. Dec. 17, 1967**
1996 WCH CAN 8 2 0 2 8 2nd

**Danda, Bronislav / b. Jan. 10, 1930**
1954-55 WM TCH 15 10 5 15 4 B
1952-60 OG-M TCH 18 4 10 14 0 —

**Dandenault, Mathieu / b. Feb. 3, 1976**
2003 WM CAN 9 2 3 5 12 G

**Danecek, Jan / b. Feb. 15, 1986**
2004 WM18 CZE 7 2 0 2 2 B

**Daneyko, Ken / b. Apr. 17, 1964**
1986-89 WM CAN 15 0 0 0 4 S,B

**Danicek, Ondrej / b. Apr. 6, 1983**
2001 WM18 CZE 7 0 0 0 0 —

**Daniel, Adrian / b. Jan. 15, 1979**
1998 WM20 SVK 6 0 0 0 0 —

**Daniels, Kimbi / b. Jan. 19, 1972**
1992 WM20 CAN 7 3 4 7 16 —

**Danielsson, Jan-Ake / b. Jan. 2, 1960**
1979-80 WM20 SWE 11 0 1 1 10 2B

**Danielsson, Nicklas / b. Dec. 7, 1984**
2004 WM20 SWE 6 2 1 3 8 —

**Danilovs, Sergejs / b. Feb. 16, 1989**
2007 WM18 LAT 5 2 1 3 2 —

**Danner, David / b. Feb. 19, 1983**
2001 WM18 GER 6 0 0 0 14 —
2003 WM20 GER 6 1 0 1 2 —

**Dano, Jozef / b. Dec. 28, 1968**
1996-99 WM SVK 18 9 6 15 12 —
1994-98 OG-M SVK 12 4 5 9 10 —

**D'Appolonia, Otello / b. unknown**
1939 WM ITA 3 1 — 1 — —

**Danry, Dan / b. unknown**
1949 WM DEN 3 0 — 0 — —

**Daramy, Xavier / b. Mar. 12, 1981**
2004 WM FRA 6 0 0 0 6 —

**Darby, Craig / b. Sept. 26, 1972**
2001 WM USA 9 0 2 2 2 —

**Da Rin, Alberto / b. Dec. 11, 1938**
1959 WM ITA 6 0 0 0 4 —
1964 OG-M ITA 7 5 2 7 8 —

**Da Rin, Gianfranco / b. June 15, 1935**
1959 WM ITA 8 0 0 0 2 —
1956-64 OG-M ITA 12 2 1 3 2 —

**Darling, Marsh / b. Jan. 30, 1919 / d. Oct. 27 2009**
1950 WM CAN 6 6 1 7 12 G

**Dary, Georges / b. Dec. 6, 1889 / d. unknown**
1920 OG-M FRA 1 0 0 0 — —

**Davey, Gerry / b. Sept. 5, 1914 / d. Feb. 12, 1977**
1934-38 WM GBR 29 24 3 27 0 2S,B
1936-48 OG-M GBR 13 12 0 12 0 G

**David, Jiri / b. Mar. 27, 1980**
2000 WM20 CZE 7 0 0 0 6 G

**David, Robert / b. 1918 / d. unknown**
1950 WM CAN 1 1 0 1 0 G

**Davidson, Lee / b. June 30, 1968**
1987-88 WM20 USA 14 4 6 10 14 —

**Davidson, Ron / b. July 16, 1957**
1980 OG-M CAN 6 1 4 5 0 —

**Davidsson, Johan / b. Jan. 6, 1976**
1994-96 WM20 SWE 20 8 12 20 12 2S,B
2002-07 WM SWE 32 8 9 17 8 2S,B
~WM20 All-Star Team/Forward (1996)

**Davies, Jack / b. July 14, 1928**
1950 WM CAN 7 2 3 5 2 G
1952 OG-M CAN 8 4 2 6 6 G

**Davis, Lorne / b. July 20, 1930**
1966 WM CAN 7 1 0 1 2 B

**Davydov, Marat / b. July 20, 1972**
1997-98 WM RUS 14 0 0 0 6 —

**Davydov, Oleg / b. Mar. 16, 1971**
1994 OG-M RUS 8 1 0 1 0 —

**Davydov, Vitali / b. Apr. 3, 1939**
1963-71 WM URS 54 1 6 7 14 7G
1964-72 OG-M URS 17 0 6 6 12 3G
~IIHF Hall of Fame
~WM IIHF Directorate Best Defenceman (1967)

**Davydov, Yevgeni / b. May 27, 1967**
1986-87 WM20 URS 13 6 1 7 6 G
1990 WM URS 9 5 4 9 6 G
1992 OG-M RUS 8 3 3 6 2 G

**Dawe, Billy / b. June 8, 1924**
1950 WM CAN 7 12 2 14 2 G
1952 OG-M CAN 8 6 5 11 2 G

**Dawe, Jason / b. May 29, 1973**
1993 WM20 CAN 7 3 3 6 8 G
1996 WM CAN 8 3 0 3 2 S

**Day, Joe / b. May 11, 1968**
1988 WM20 USA 7 2 1 3 14 —

**Daze, Eric / b. July 2, 1975**
1995 WM20 CAN 7 8 2 10 0 G
1998-99 WM CAN 8 1 5 6 0 —
~WM20 All-Star Team/Forward (1995)

**Dazzi, Marco / b. May 8, 1967**
1987 WM20 SUI 7 1 0 1 8 —

**Deacon, Maxwell "Bill" / b. Mar. 22, 1910 / d. Apr. 29, 1970**
1936 OG-M CAN 4 0 0 0 0 S

**Deadmarsh, Adam / b. May 10, 1975**
1993-95 WM20 USA 21 6 4 10 28 —
1996 WCH USA 7 2 2 4 8 1st
1998-2002 OG-M USA 10 2 1 3 4 S

**Dean, Kevin / b. Apr. 1, 1969**
1988 WM20 USA 7 0 0 0 0 —
1998 WM USA 3 0 0 0 0 —

**De Angelis, Michael / b. Jan. 27, 1966**
1992-2001 WM ITA 49 3 9 12 44 —
1992-98 OG-M ITA 18 0 3 3 26 —

**de Bastiani, Joe / b. unknown**
1949 WM CAN 7 9 — 9 — S

**de Beukelaer, Jan / b. Dec. 26, 1910 / d. Feb. 5, 2000**
1933-35 WM BEL 8 0 — 0 0 —

**Deblois, Lucien / b. June 21, 1957**
1981 WM CAN 8 3 0 3 4 —

**Debol, Dave / b. Mar. 27, 1956**
1977-81 WM USA 26 12 11 23 16 —

**De Bruyn, Brian / b. Sept. 9, 1954**
1981 WM NED 7 2 0 2 2 —
1980 OG-M NED 5 0 0 0 0 —

**Dechevyi, Sergiy / b. June 25, 1977**
1996 WM20 UKR 5 0 2 2 22 —

**De Cloe, Dick / b. May 20, 1953**
1980 OG-M NED 5 3 3 6 6 —

**de Craene, Jean / b. unknown / d. unknown**
1930 WM BEL 1 0 — 0 — —

**Defauw, Brad / b. Nov. 10, 1977**
2003 WM USA 6 1 1 2 4 —

**De Gaetano, Philip / b. Aug. 9, 1963**
1994 WM ITA 6 0 1 1 4 —

**Degn, Lasse / b. Oct. 7, 1977**
2003-05 WM DEN 12 2 0 2 8 —

**De Graauw, Corky / b. Feb. 23, 1951**
1981 WM NED 3 0 0 0 6 —
1980 OG-M NED 5 3 5 8 12 —

**DeGray, Dale / b. Sept. 1, 1963**
1995 WM CAN 6 1 1 2 6 B

**De Grio, Gary / b. Feb. 16, 1960**
1979 WM20 USA 5 1 1 2 2 —
1982 WM USA 7 3 1 4 4 —

**De Heer, Jack / b. May 17, 1953**
1981 WM NED 8 5 1 6 8 —
1980 OG-M NED 5 3 3 6 11 —

**de Jong, Felix / b. Feb. 26, 1913 / d. unknown**
1935-39 WM NED 10 0 0 0 — —

**Dekonski, Igor / b. Aug. 22, 1938**
1959 WM URS 7 5 3 8 4 S

**Dekumbis, Reto / b. Sept. 13, 1956**
1987 WM SUI 8 3 2 5 8 —

**de Laat, Alfons / b. Nov. 7, 1927**
1950 WM NED 4 1 0 1 0 —

**Delahey, Charlie / b. Mar. 19, 1905 / d. Mar. 17, 1973**
1928 OG-M CAN 1 0 — 0 — G

**Delarge, Constant / b. Mar. 26, 1922 / d. Dec. 18, 1991**
1949 WM BEL 6 0 — 0 — —

**Delesalle, Michel / b. Dec. 22, 1907 / d. unknown**
1935 WM FRA 5 2 — 2 — —
1936 OG-M FRA 3 1 — 1 — —

**Della Rossa, Patric / b. July 28, 1975**
1994 WM20 SUI 7 1 2 3 4 —
1999-2007 WM SUI 53 3 4 7 40 —
2002-06 OG-M SUI 10 0 3 3 6 —

**Dell'Jannone, Patrick / b. Oct. 7, 1954**
1982-83 WM ITA 17 2 4 6 6 —

**Delnon, Hugo / b. unknown / d. unknown**
1947-49 WM SUI 8 5 — 5 — —

**Delnon, Othmar / b. 1917 / d. unknown**
1947-50 WM SUI 18 10 7 17 2 B

**Delnon, Reto / b. May 1, 1920 / d. Nov. 6, 1983**
1939-55 WM SUI 44 23 7 30 0 3B
1952 OG-M SUI 7 0 2 2 — —

**Delorme, Gilbert / b. Nov. 25, 1962**
1981 WM20 CAN 5 1 0 1 0 —

**Delrez, Tony / b. Nov. 1, 1926**
1949 WM BEL 6 0 — 0 — —

**DeMarco, Ab / b. Feb. 27, 1949**
1969 WM CAN 9 1 0 1 6 —

**de Marwicz, Frank / b. Nov. 11, 1907 / d. 1990**
1930-34 WM GBR 5 0 0 0 — —

**de Mazzeri, Tino / b. Jan. 22, 1910 / d. unknown**
1930-39 WM ITA 24 2 0 2 0 —

**Demen Willaume, Richard / b. Jan. 28, 1986**
2004 WM18 SWE 6 1 1 2 10 —

**Dementiev, Roman / b. July 19, 1985**
2003 WM18 KAZ 6 0 0 0 6 —

**de Mezieres, Miguel / b. unknown / d. unknown**
1937 WM FRA 7 0 0 0 4 —

**de Mezieres, Jacques / b. unknown**
1950 WM FRA 3 0 0 0 2 —

**Demitra, Pavol / b. Nov. 29, 1974 / d. Sept. 7, 2011**
1993 WM20 TCH 7 4 4 8 8 B
1996-2011 WM SVK 38 12 17 29 24 B
1996-2004 WCH SVK 7 0 2 2 6 —
2002-10 OG-M SVK 15 6 14 20 6 —
~OG-M All-Star Team/Forward (2010)
~perished in Yaroslavl plane crash

**Demkov, Artyom / b. Sept. 26, 1989**
2006 WM18 BLR 6 1 2 3 4 —

**Demkowicz, Tomasz / b. Apr. 27, 1970**
2002 WM POL 6 1 0 1 4 —

**Demmer, Fritz / b. Apr. 17, 1911 / d. unknown**
1930-49 WM AUT 54 31 0 31 0 2B
1936-48 OG-M AUT 12 6 — 6 — —

**Demota, Glen / b. July 17, 1961**
1980 WM20 USA 5 0 1 1 0 —

**Demuth, Alain / b. June 3, 1979**
1999 WM20 SUI 6 2 0 2 6 —
2000-06 WM SUI 14 2 0 2 4 —

**Denisov, Denis / b. Dec. 31, 1981**
1999 WM18 RUS 7 0 2 2 0 —
2000-01 WM20 RUS 14 2 3 5 2 S
2005 WM RUS 9 0 1 1 4 B

**Denisov, Dmitri / b. July 5, 1970**
1994 OG-M RUS 8 3 1 4 4 —

**Denisov, Vladimir / b. June 29, 1984**
2002 WM18 BLR 8 0 1 1 27 —
2003 WM20 BLR 6 0 1 1 4 —

**De Nobili, Franco / b. Oct. 25, 1961**
1980-81 WM20 FRG 9 0 0 0 10 —

**De Piero, Bob / b. Dec. 25, 1954**
1982-83 WM ITA 17 3 4 7 6 —
1984 OG-M ITA 5 0 1 1 4 —

**de Pon, Huib / b. unknown / d. unknown**
1935 WM NED 4 0 0 0 — —

**Deprez, Maurice / b. 1886 / d. unknown**
1920 OG-M BEL 1 0 0 0 — —

**de Rauch, Alfred / b. June 13, 1887 / d. unknown**
1920-28 OG-M FRA 7 5 0 5 — —

**de Revay, Jozef / b. Oct. 20, 1902 / d. Apr. 19, 1945**
1930 WM HUN 2 0 — 0 — —
1928 OG-M HUN 2 0 — 0 — —

**de Ridder, Louis / b. June 9, 1902 / d. May 5, 1981**
1930-34 WM BEL 8 0 — 0 0 —
1924-36 OG-M BEL 4 1 — 1 — —

**Derkatch, Dale / b. Oct. 17, 1964**
1983-84 WM20 CAN 14 8 4 12 6 B

**Derrick, Noel / b. July 5, 1926**
1960 OG-M AUS 6 2 1 3 2 —

**Derungs, Harry / b. Mar. 30, 1971**
1991 WM20 SUI 7 1 0 1 0 —

**Desantis, Jason / b. Mar. 9, 1986**
2004 WM18 USA 6 1 0 1 4 S

**Desiatkov, Pavel / b. Feb. 28, 1975**
1994 WM20 RUS 7 0 0 0 0 B

**de Siebenthaler, Wilhelm / b. June 6, 1899 / d. unknown**
1924 OG-M SUI 3 0 — 0 — —

**Desjardins, Eric / b. June 14, 1969**
1988-89 WM20 CAN 14 1 4 5 12 G
1991-96 WCH CAN 16 2 4 6 10 1st,2nd
1998 OG-M CAN 6 0 0 0 2 —

**De Toni, Lino / b. Oct. 18, 1972**
1994-2002 WM ITA 39 2 3 5 16 —
1994 OG-M ITA 7 1 0 1 0 —

**Devaney, John / b. Apr. 10, 1958**
1980 OG-M CAN 6 4 3 7 6 —

**Devecka, Dusan / b. June 19, 1980**
2000 WM20 SVK 7 0 0 0 0 —

**Devereaux, Boyd / b. Apr. 16, 1978**
1997 WM20 CAN 7 4 0 4 0 G

**Devereaux, Gerald "Red" / b. 1937**
1962 WM GBR 4 0 0 0 0 —

**De Vos, Tjakko / b. July 12, 1956**
1981 WM NED 8 2 3 5 2 —

**Devyatkin, Petr / b. Mar. 8, 1977**
1998 OG-M KAZ 7 0 0 0 27 —

**Dewar, Tommy / b. June 10, 1913 / d. July 23, 1982**
1934 WM CAN — 0 — 0 — G

**Dewey, Jim / b. 1912 / d. Mar. 29, 1965**
1934 WM CAN 4 1 0 1 — G

**Dewitz, Dieter / b. Oct. 2, 1945**
1970 WM GDR 4 0 0 0 2 —

**De Wolf, Joshua / b. July 25, 1977**
2002 WM USA 7 0 0 0 2 —

**Dewolf, Karl / b. Feb. 21, 1972**
1997-2004 WM FRA 26 1 1 2 26 —
1998-2002 OG-M FRA 7 0 0 0 6 —

**Dewsbury, Al / b. Apr. 12, 1926**
1959 WM CAN 8 3 0 3 28 G

**De Zanna, Francesco / b. Jan. 18, 1905 / d. unknown**
1933 WM ITA 4 0 — 0 0 —

**Dick, Sven / b. Oct. 22, 1974**
1994 WM20 SUI 6 0 0 0 6 —

**Dickson, Bruce / b. Apr. 22, 1931**
1952 OG-M CAN 8 8 3 11 0 G

**Didkovsky, Danil / b. Sept. 3, 1976**
1995-96 WM20 UKR 13 4 2 6 10 —
1999 WM UKR 3 0 0 0 6 —

**Diduck, Gerald / b. Apr. 6, 1965**
1984 WM20 CAN 7 0 0 0 4 —

**Diener, Michael / b. May 11, 1973**
1992 WM20 SUI 7 0 0 0 0 —

**Diepold, Johann / b. June 23, 1958**
1978 WM20 FRG 5 1 3 4 7 —

**Diethelm, Gerhard / b. Dec. 6, 1934**
1962 WM SUI 6 1 0 1 0 —

**Diethelm, Rolf / b. May 15, 1940**
1964 OG-M SUI 6 1 0 1 0 —

**Dietiker, Heinz / b. unknown**
1955 WM SUI 6 0 — 0 2 —

**Dietrich, Edi / b. unknown / d. unknown**
1935 WM ROM 4 0 — 0 — —

**Dietrich, Robert / b. July 25, 1986 / d. Sept. 7, 2011**
2005 WM20 GER 6 0 0 0 6 —
2007-11 WM GER 22 2 2 4 4 —
~perished in Yaroslavl plane crash

**Dietrichstein, Jacques / b. unknown / d. unknown**
1930-34 WM AUT 12 1 — 1 3 B
1928 OG-M AUT 1 0 — 0 — —

**Dietz, Theo / b. Aug. 12, 1926**
1950 WM NED 2 0 0 0 0 —

**Di Fazio, Albert / b. May 9, 1955**
1982-83 WM ITA 17 2 4 6 14 —

**Di Fiore, Raphael / b. Apr. 20, 1966**
1993 WM ITA 6 0 0 0 4 —

**di Gaetano, Philip / b. Aug 9, 1963**
1994 OG-M ITA 7 1 0 1 8 —

**Dilworth, Dan / b. Feb. 23, 1942**
1961 WM USA 2 1 0 1 2 —
1964 OG-M USA 7 2 4 6 0 —

**Dimaio, Rob / b. Feb. 19, 1968**
1988 WM20 CAN 7 1 0 1 10 G

**Dimitrakos, Niko / b. May 21, 1979**
2003 WM USA 6 0 1 1 6 —

**Dimock, Bill / b. unknown**
1949 WM CAN 7 7 — 7 — S

**Dineen, Gary / b. Dec. 24, 1943 / d. Apr. 1, 2006**
1965-67 WM CAN 21 8 13 21 16 2B
1964-68 OG-M CAN 14 4 8 12 16 B

**Dineen, Kevin / b. Oct. 28, 1963**
1985-93 WM CAN 37 11 13 24 50 2S
1987 CC CAN 3 1 2 3 0 1st
1984 OG-M CAN 7 0 0 0 6 —

**Dinger, Jan / b. unknown**
1950 WM NED 2 0 0 0 0 —

**Dion, Tom / b. Apr. 22, 1969**
1989 WM20 USA 7 0 1 1 0 —

**Dionisi, Ignazio / b. Feb. 27, 1913 / d. unknown**
1933-39 WM ITA 24 7 1 8 2 —
1936-48 OG-M ITA 7 2 0 2 — —

**Dionne, Marcel / b. Aug. 3, 1951**
1978-86 WM CAN 38 21 11 32 16 3B
1976-81 CC CAN 13 5 6 11 8 1st,2nd
~WM IIHF Directorate Best Forward (1978)

**Di Pietro, Paul / b. Ontario, 8, 1970**
2005-08 WM SUI 21 5 8 13 10 —
2006 OG-M SUI 6 3 0 3 0 —

**Direr, Andrej / b. Feb. 16, 1987**
2004 WM18 SVK 6 0 0 0 0 —

**Disalvatore, Jon / b. Mar. 30, 1981**
2001 WM20 USA 7 6 3 9 2 —

**Dischler, Marius / b. July 5, 1986**
2004 WM18 NOR 6 1 1 2 2 —

**Divis, Raimund / b. Jan. 5, 1978**
2003-07 WM AUT 24 7 3 10 4 —

**Divisek, Tomas / b. July 19, 1979**
1999 WM20 CZE 6 2 7 9 6 —

**Djelloul, Serge / b. Mar. 28, 1966**
1995-97 WM FRA 21 1 2 3 8 —
1998 OG-M FRA 4 0 0 0 2 —

**Djoos, Per / b. May 11, 1968**
1988 WM20 SWE 7 0 2 2 4 —
1990-99 WM SWE 17 3 3 6 10 S,B

**Djordjevic, Miroljub / b. Nov. 27, 1938**
1964 OG-M YUG 7 3 3 6 2 —

**Dlugos, Hans / b. unknown**
1947 WM ROM 7 1 — 1 — —

**Dobek, Bob / b. Oct. 4, 1952**
1976 OG-M USA 5 3 4 7 4 —

**Dobner, Martin / b. May 8, 1984**
2004 WM20 AUT 6 0 0 0 2 —

**Dobry, Lukas / b. Apr. 15, 1983**
2001 WM18 CZE 7 0 0 0 0 —

**Dobryshkin, Yuri / b. July 19, 1979**
1999 WM20 RUS 7 5 2 7 0 G

**Dobrzynski, Ralf / b. Apr. 13, 1973**
1993 WM20 GER 7 0 2 2 2 —

**Doers, Mike / b. June 17, 1971**
1991 WM20 USA 8 2 2 4 2 —

**Doherty, Dick / b. unknown**
1955 WM USA 8 5 0 5 6 —

**Doig, Jason / b. Jan. 29, 1977**
1997 WM20 CAN 7 0 2 2 37 G

**Dolak, Thomas / b. Mar. 25, 1979**
1997-98 WM20 GER 12 0 2 2 10 —

**Dolana, Jiri / b. Mar. 16, 1937**
1961-63 WM TCH 14 12 3 15 21 S,B
1964 OG-M TCH 7 7 3 10 0 B

**Dolana, Libor / b. May 6, 1964**
1983-84 WM20 TCH 14 10 6 16 2 S,B
1987-91 WM TCH 24 8 4 12 0 2B

**Dolewski, Tadeusz / b. June 7, 1917 / d. Jan. 1, 1994**
1947 WM POL 2 0 — 0 — —
1948 OG-M POL 2 0 — 0 — —

**Dolezal, Jiri / b. Sept. 22, 1962**
1987-94 WM TCH 53 19 9 28 40 4B
1987 CC TCH 6 0 1 1 4 —
1988-94 OG-M CZE 14 3 3 6 8 —

**Dolinski, Adam / b. Jan. 18, 1966**
1985 WM20 POL 7 0 0 0 6 —

**Dollas, Bobby / b. Jan. 31, 1965**
1985 WM20 CAN 7 0 2 2 12 G
1994 WM CAN 8 0 1 1 4 G
~WM20 All-Star Team/Defence (1985)

**Doman, Matt / b. Feb. 10, 1980**
1999 WM20 USA 6 1 1 2 6 —

**Domeniconi, Claude / b. July 26, 1958**
1978 WM20 SUI 6 0 2 2 4 —

**Domian, Martin / b. Jan. 15, 1987**
2005 WM18 SVK 6 1 0 1 2 —

**Domin, Petr / b. Jan. 2, 1983**
2001 WM18 CZE 7 0 5 5 4 —
2003 WM20 CZE 6 0 1 1 0 —

**Donatelli, Clark / b. Nov. 22, 1965**
1984-85 WM20 USA 14 3 5 8 18 —
1985-87 WM USA 29 7 6 13 28 —
1988-92 OG-M USA 14 4 2 6 12 —

**Donato, Ted / b. Apr. 28, 1969**
1988 WM20 USA 7 3 2 5 18 —
1997-2002 WM USA 21 7 11 18 16 —
1992 OG-M USA 8 4 3 7 8 —

**Dondi, Ralph / b. May 11, 1915 / d. unknown**
1938-39 WM USA 15 3 — 3 — S

**Doner, Lexi / b. Nov. 1, 1960**
1980 WM20 USA 5 1 1 2 4 —

**Donika, Mikhail / b. May 15, 1979**
1997-99 WM20 RUS 20 0 3 3 4 G,S,B

**Donika, Vitaliy / b. May 12, 1982**
1999-2000 WM18 UKR 12 1 3 4 4 —
2006-07 WM UKR 6 0 0 0 2 —

**Donnelly, Dave / b. Feb. 2, 1963**
1984 OG-M CAN 7 1 1 2 12 —

**Donovan, Shean / b. Jan. 22, 1975**
1995 WM20 CAN 7 0 0 0 6 G
1997 WM CAN 10 0 1 1 31 G

**Dopita, Jiri / b. Dec. 2, 1968**
1994-2004 WM CZE 59 17 14 31 38 3G,2B
1996-2004 WCH CZE 7 1 1 2 2 —
1998-2002 OG-M CZE 10 3 4 7 2 G
~WM All-Star Team/Forward (2000)

**Dorasil, Wolfgang / b. Nov. 7, 1903 / d. unknown**
1930-34 WM TCH 20 4 0 4 0 B
1928 OG-M TCH 2 0 — 0 — —

**Dorfler, Andreas / b. Apr. 21, 1984**
2002 WM18 GER 8 0 1 1 4 —

**Dorian, Dan / b. Mar. 2, 1963**
1985 WM USA 5 2 3 5 2 —

**Dorn, Konrad / b. Oct. 29, 1962**
1981 WM20 AUT 5 0 1 1 12 —
1996 WM AUT 7 0 0 0 2 —
1984-88 OG-M AUT 10 0 2 2 2 —

**Dornas, V. / b. unknown / d. unknown**
1938 WM LTU 1 0 — 0 — —

**Dornbach, Greg / b. Jan. 11, 1966**
1985-86 WM20 USA 14 5 6 11 18 B

**Dornic, Ivan / b. May 26, 1962**
1982 WM20 TCH 7 3 2 5 0 S

**Dornic, Ivan / b. Apr. 12, 1985**
2003 WM18 SVK 7 1 1 2 6 S

**Dorofeyev, Igor / b. Aug. 10, 1968**
1988 WM20 URS 7 3 1 4 4 S

**Dorokhin, Igor / b. Aug. 15, 1962**
1998 OG-M KAZ 7 0 0 0 4 —

**Dostal, David / b. Aug. 27, 1973**
2004 WM FRA 6 0 0 0 2 —

**Dotzler, Alexander / b. Sept. 12, 1984**
2002 WM18 GER 8 0 0 0 6 —

**Douben, Dmitri / b. June 7, 1981**
2001 WM20 BLR 6 0 1 1 4 —

**Doucet, Benoit / b. Apr. 23, 1963**
1993-96 WM GER 17 5 3 8 30 —
1996 WCH GER 4 1 0 1 2 —
1994-98 OG-M GER 12 3 0 3 21 —

**Dougherty, Dick / b. Aug. 5, 1932**
1956 OG-M USA 7 4 1 5 0 S

**Douglas, Jack / b. Apr. 24, 1930**
1962 WM CAN 6 0 3 3 10 S
1960 OG-M CAN 7 3 2 5 6 S
~WM All-Star Team/Defence (1962)

**Douris, Peter / b. Feb. 19, 1966**
1986 WM20 CAN 7 4 2 6 6 S

**Doyle, Rob / b. Feb. 10, 1964**
1993-2003 WM AUT 31 5 6 11 59 —
1994 OG-M AUT 7 1 1 2 14 —

**Draisaitl, Peter / b. Dec. 7, 1965**
1984 WM20 FRG 7 3 2 5 2 —
1989-98 WM GER 48 9 10 19 14 —
1996 WCH GER 4 1 4 5 2 —
1988-98 OG-M GER 20 4 3 7 8 —

**Draper, Kris / b. May 24, 1971**
1990-91 WM20 CAN 14 1 5 6 4 2G
2000-05 WM CAN 28 2 7 9 16 G,S
2004 WCH CAN 5 2 2 4 2 1st
2006 OG-M CAN 6 0 0 0 0 —

**Drasyk, Marion / b. July 26, 1957**
1989 WM POL 10 1 0 1 6 —

**Draxler, Markus / b. Apr. 5, 1977**
1996 WM20 GER 6 0 1 1 2 —

**Drbohlav, Antonin / b. June 1, 1988**
2006 WM18 CZE 7 0 0 0 2 B

**Dreseler, James / b. May 22, 1974**
1993 WM20 GER 7 0 0 0 6 —

**Drgon, Adam / b. Feb. 16, 1985**
2003 WM18 SVK 7 1 0 1 12 S

**Drifan, Igor / b. Feb. 22, 1975**
1995 WM20 UKR 7 0 0 0 2 —

**Driver, Bruce / b. Apr. 29, 1962**
1987 WM CAN 8 0 0 0 4 —
1984 OG-M CAN 7 3 1 4 10 —

**Drobny, Jaroslav / b. Oct. 10, 1921 / d. Sept. 13, 2001**
1939-47 WM TCH 13 20 — 20 — G
1948 OG-M TCH 7 11 — 11 — S
~IIHF Hall of Fame

**Droppa, Ivan / b. Feb. 1, 1972**
1991-92 WM20 TCH 11 0 4 4 10
1997-2001 WM SVK 34 2 5 7 34 S
1996 WCH SVK 3 0 1 1 2 —
1998 OG-M SVK 4 0 0 0 0 —

**Droppa, Miroslav / b. Feb. 17, 1977**
1996-97 WM20 SVK 11 0 1 1 6 —

**Drotar, Martin / b. Nov. 5, 1981**
2001 WM20 SVK 7 0 0 0 2 —

**Drozdetski, Nikolai / b. June 14, 1957 / d. Nov. 24, 1995**
1981-85 WM URS 26 11 13 24 10 2G,B
1981 CC URS 7 2 2 4 2 1st
1984 OG-M URS 7 10 2 12 2 G

**Druken, Harold / b. Jan. 26, 1979**
1999 WM20 CAN 7 1 1 2 2 S

**Drury, Herb / b. Mar. 2, 1896 / d. July 1, 1965**
1920-24 OG-M USA 9 33 — 33 5 2S

**Drury, Ted / b. Sept. 13, 1971**
1990-91 WM20 USA 15 7 8 15 4 —
1993-2003 WM USA 18 2 3 5 6 —
1992-94 OG-M USA 14 2 3 5 2 —

**Drzik, Josef / b. Dec. 24, 1976**
1996 WM20 SVK 6 1 2 3 4 —

**Dube, Christian / b. Apr. 25, 1977**
1996-97 WM20 CAN 12 8 4 12 0 2G
~WM20 All-Star Team/Forward (1997)

**Dube, Roger / b. Oct. 2, 1965**
1994-98 WM FRA 26 13 5 18 10 —
1998 OG-M FRA 3 0 0 0 29 —

**Dube, Yanick / b. June 14, 1974**
1994 WM20 CAN 7 5 5 10 10 G

**Dubec, Marek / b. Feb. 26, 1982**
2000 WM18 SVK 6 0 0 0 2 —

**Dubec, Milan / b. Sept. 6, 1981**
2001 WM20 SVK 7 0 0 0 0 —

**Dubi, Gerard / b. Nov. 27, 1943**
1972 WM SUI 8 2 2 4 2 —
1972 OG-M SUI 4 0 1 1 0 —

**Dubinin, Anton / b. July 22, 1985**
2003 WM18 RUS 5 2 0 2 4 B

**Dubois, Daniel / b. 1959**
1978 WM20 SUI 6 0 0 0 0 —

**Dubois, Daniel / b. Oct. 30, 1964**
1984 WM20 SUI 7 4 0 4 2 —

**Dubois, Gilles / b. June 7, 1966**
1986 WM20 SUI 7 1 1 2 2 —

**Dubois, Gregory / b. Mar. 27, 1975**
1999-2000 WM FRA 9 0 0 0 4 —
1998 OG-M FRA 4 0 1 1 2 —

**Dubois, Guy / b. Jan. 14, 1950**
1972 WM SUI 9 0 0 0 2 —
1972-76 OG-M SUI 9 2 2 4 4 —

**Dubovik, Alexander / b. Mar. 11, 1983**
2000 WM18 BLR 6 1 0 1 2 —

**Duchesne, Steve / b. June 30, 1965**
1994-96 WM CAN 14 1 4 5 4 G,S

**Duda, Radek / b. Jan. 28, 1979**
1998 WM20 CZE 7 1 0 1 14 —
2003 WM CZE 8 1 4 5 43 —

**Duda, Ron / b. May 6, 1963**
1983 WM20 USA 6 0 0 0 2 —

**Dudacek, Jiri / b. Apr. 4, 1962**
1980-82 WM20 TCH 16 7 6 13 4 S
1981-84 CC TCH 10 4 2 6 4 —

**Due-Boije, Christian / b. Oct. 12, 1966**
1985-86 WM20 SWE 14 1 1 2 22 —
1994 OG-M SWE 6 1 0 1 12 G

**Dufour, Louis / b. July 26, 1901 / d. May 1960**
1920-28 OG-M SUI 6 3 0 3 — B

**Dugan, Tom / b. unknown**
1947 WM USA 6 6 — 6 — —

**Duguay, Ron / b. July 6, 1957**
1977 WM20 CAN 5 1 3 4 11 S
1981 CC CAN 7 0 2 2 6 2nd

**Dulak, Martin / b. Sept. 21, 1988**
2006 WM18 SVK 8 1 0 1 1 —

**Duleba, Mariusz / b. Aug. 2, 1975**
2002 WM POL 6 0 0 0 8 —

**Duma, Pavel / b. June 20, 1981**
2000-01 WM20 RUS 14 2 3 5 6 S

**Dumitru, Constantin / b. 1955**
1977 WM ROM 10 0 0 0 4 —

**Dumon, Roland / b. Jan. 14, 1922 / d. unknown**
1949-50 WM BEL 5 0 0 0 0 —

**Dumont, Jean-Pierre / b. Apr. 1, 1978**
1998 WM20 CAN 7 0 0 0 0 —
2004 WM CAN 9 0 1 1 0 G

**Duncanson, Bert / b. Oct. 2, 1911 / d. Mar. 24, 2000**
1932 OG-M CAN 1 1 0 1 0 G

**Dunkelman, Fred / b. Feb. 5, 1920 / d. July 23, 2010**
1948 OG-M GBR 5 1 — 1 — —

**Dunlop, Connor / b. Jan. 5, 1981**
1999 WM18 USA 6 2 3 5 6 —
2000-01 WM20 USA 14 1 4 5 12 —

**Dunn, Patrick / b. Mar. 15, 1963**
1992-96 WM FRA 28 3 1 4 20 —
1992 OG-M FRA 8 3 2 5 8 —

**Dunn, Richie / b. May 12, 1957**
1977 WM20 USA 7 2 1 3 2 —
1986 WM USA 10 1 1 2 2 —
1981 CC USA 6 1 3 4 4 —

**Dunsmore, Fred / b. Mar. 30, 1929**
1965 WM CAN 4 0 2 2 0 —

**Dunster, Frank / b. Mar. 24, 1921 / d. Apr. 8, 1995**
1948 OG-M CAN 8 1 — 1 8 G

**du Pon, Huib / b. unknown / d. unknown**
1939 WM NED 4 1 — 1 — —

**DuPont, Micki / b. Apr. 15, 1980**
2006 WM CAN 9 0 1 1 4 —

**Du Pre, Albert / b. May 7, 1927**
1950 WM BEL 1 0 0 0 — —

**Du Pre, Jules / b. Sept. 19, 1923 / d. unknown**
1947-49 WM BEL 12 3 — 3 — —

**Dupuis, Bob / b. unknown**
1951-59 WM USA 7 1 0 1 6 —

**Dupuis, Guy / b. Sept. 4, 1957**
1988 OG-M FRA 6 0 5 5 0 —

**Durak, Miroslav / b. June 9, 1981**
2001 WM20 SVK 7 1 1 2 4 —

**Durco, Juraj / b. July 16, 1977**
1996-97 WM20 SVK 12 1 3 4 20 —

**Duris, Vitezslav / b. Jan. 5, 1954**
1979 WM TCH 8 1 1 2 8 S
1980 OG-M TCH 6 0 1 1 0 —

**Durnov, Konstantin / b. Apr. 21, 1984**
2002 WM18 BLR 8 0 1 1 6 —
2002-03 WM20 BLR 11 0 0 0 10 —

**Durst, Hans / b. June 28, 1921 / d. unknown**
1948 OG-M SUI 7 5 — 5 — B

**Durst, Reto / b. unknown**
1978 WM20 SUI 6 3 0 3 6 —

**Durst, Walter / b. Feb. 28, 1927**
1950-53 WM SUI 17 7 4 11 2 3B
1948-52 OG-M SUI 12 8 0 8 — B

**Durst, Walter / b. June 4, 1950**
1972 WM SUI 8 1 2 3 6 —
1976 OG-M SUI 4 3 2 5 0 —

**Dusbabek, Joe / b. May 1, 1978**
1998 WM20 USA 7 2 0 2 14 —

**Duvivier, Emile / b. unknown / d. unknown**
1934-35 WM BEL 8 0 — 0 — —

**Dvorak, Miroslav / b. Oct. 11, 1951 / d. June 11, 2008**
1974-83 WM TCH 85 3 20 23 42 2G,6S,B
1976-81 CC TCH 13 0 4 4 6 2nd
1976-80 OG-M TCH 11 1 3 4 2 S

**Dvorak, Petr / b. Oct. 11, 1983**
2003 WM20 CZE 6 0 0 0 2 —

**Dvorak, Radek / b. Mar. 9, 1977**
1999-2005 WM CZE 37 9 16 25 34 3G
2004 WCH CZE 4 1 0 1 0 —
2002 OG-M CZE 4 0 0 0 0 —

**Dvoretsky, Pavlo / b. Sept. 25, 1982**
2000 WM18 UKR 6 0 0 0 2 —

**Dyachenko, Yuriy / b. June 2, 1982**
2006 WM UKR 6 1 2 3 6 —

**Dyatlov, Vyacheslav / b. July 16, 1982**
2000 WM18 UKR 6 0 1 1 10 —

**Dykhuis, Karl / b. July 8, 1972**
1991-92 WM20 CAN 14 0 3 3 10 G

**Dylla, Eric / b. Sept. 24, 1976**
1995 WM20 GER 7 0 0 0 2 —

**Dziubinski, Bogdan / b. Jan. 1, 1958**
1977 WM20 POL 7 3 1 4 13 —
1980 OG-M POL 5 1 1 2 0 —

**Dzhugelia, Adgur / b. May 6, 1986**
2004 WM18 RUS 6 0 2 2 2 G

**Eager, Ben / b. Jan. 22, 1984**
2002 WM18 CAN 8 1 3 4 45 —

**Eagles, Mike / b. Mar. 7, 1963**
1983 WM20 CAN 7 2 4 6 2 B

**Eakin, Bruce / b. Sept. 28, 1962**
1982 WM20 CAN 7 4 7 11 4 G

**Earl, Robbie / b. June 2, 1985**
2003 WM18 USA 6 2 2 4 8 —

**Eaton, Mark / b. May 6, 1977**
2001-02 WM USA 16 1 4 5 2 —

**Eatough, Jeff / b. June 2, 1963**
1981 WM20 CAN 5 1 2 3 4 —

**Eaves, Ben / b. Mar. 27, 1982**
2000 WM18 USA 6 1 3 4 0 —
2002 WM20 USA 6 1 4 5 2 —

**Eaves, Mike / b. June 10, 1956**
1976-78 WM USA 20 6 4 10 2 —
1981 CC USA 6 3 3 6 4 —

**Ebata, Yutaka / b. Oct. 19, 1974**
1993 WM20 JPN 7 0 0 0 8 —

**Eberl, Georg / b. May 11, 1936**
1959-62 WM FRG 21 7 4 11 14 —
1960 OG-M FRG 7 1 2 3 2 —

**Eberle, Jorg / b. Feb. 9, 1962**
1982 WM20 SUI 6 4 1 5 4 —
1987-93 WM SUI 32 7 5 12 12 —
1988-92 OG-M SUI 13 7 5 12 12 —

**Eberle, Milan / b. Sept. 30, 1962**
1981-82 WM20 TCH 12 7 5 12 8 S

**Ebermann, Bohuslav / b. Sept. 19, 1948**
1974-81 WM TCH 56 24 19 43 20 G,4S,B
1976 CC TCH 4 1 0 1 4 2nd
1976-80 OG-M TCH 11 3 2 5 4 S

**Ebert, Valentin / b. Mar. 4, 1981**
2001 WM20 BLR 4 0 0 0 8 —

**Ebina, Yutaka / b. Apr. 26, 1943**
1968 OG-M JPN 5 3 0 3 6 —

**Eckerblom, Niklas / b. Jan. 4, 1984**
2002 WM18 SWE 8 1 0 1 12 —
2004 WM20 SWE 4 0 2 2 2 —

**Eckstein, Ulrich / b. Apr. 6, 1927**
1955 WM FRG 8 0 1 1 0 —

**Edberg, Rolf / b. Sept. 29, 1950**
1977-79 WM SWE 26 16 9 25 8 S,B

**Eder, Hans-Georg / b. Oct. 28, 1963**
1982-83 WM20 FRG 14 2 1 3 0 —

**Edlund, Par / b. Apr. 9, 1967**
1986-87 WM20 SWE 14 7 6 13 16 B

**Edstrom, Lars / b. July 16, 1966**
1991 CC SWE 6 0 1 1 0 —
1992 OG-M SWE 8 4 0 4 6 —

**Edvardsen, Gustav / b. unknown / d. 1991**
1937 WM NOR 2 0 0 0 0 —

**Edvardsen, Ragnar / b. unknown**
1950 WM NOR 4 0 0 0 0 —

**Egen, Markus / b. Sept. 14, 1927**
1953-59 WM FRG 26 28 8 36 47 S
1952-60 OG-M FRG 21 14 3 17 21 —

**Egen, Uli / b. Aug. 24, 1956**
1979-82 WM FRG 23 7 3 10 6 —
1980 OG-M FRG 5 2 2 4 6 —

**Egener, Mike / b. Sept. 26, 1984**
2002 WM18 CAN 8 0 0 0 24 —

**Egger, Felix / b. unknown**
1947 WM AUT 6 1 — 1 — B

**Egger, Karl-Heinz / b. Oct. 2, 1949**
1971-73 WM FRG 29 3 4 7 10 —
1972 OG-M FRG 4 1 0 1 4 —

**Egger, Reinhold / b. unknown / d. unknown**
1934 WM AUT 5 0 — 0 — —

**Eggerbauer, Ernst / b. Apr. 16, 1932**
1954-59 WM FRG 23 2 1 3 8 —
1960 OG-M FRG 7 0 0 0 4 —

**Eggerbauer, Michael / b. Feb. 18, 1960**
1978-80 WM20 FRG 16 1 2 3 10 —

**Eggiman, Beat / b. Sept. 1, 1961**
1980 WM20 SUI 5 0 0 0 4 —

**Ego, Klaus / b. Dec. 4, 1947**
1971 WM FRG 2 0 0 0 0 —

**Eibl, Michael / b. Nov. 9, 1946**
1972 WM FRG 3 0 0 0 2 —

**Eichelkraut, Florian / b. May 25, 1984**
2002 WM18 GER 8 1 1 2 4 —

**Eickmann, Sebastian / b. Sept. 3, 1989**
2007 WM18 GER 6 0 1 1 2 —

**Eikeland, Tor / b. June 28, 1960**
1979 WM20 NOR 5 0 2 2 2 —
1990 WM NOR 10 1 2 3 6 —
1988 OG-M NOR 6 0 2 2 2 —

**Eimannsberger, Johann / b. Sept. 13, 1946**
1971-73 WM FRG 25 4 2 6 16 —
1972 OG-M FRG 4 2 1 3 7 —

**Eimannsberger, Peter / b. Sept. 2, 1958**
1977-78 WM20 FRG 12 0 0 0 8 —

**Eisenhardt, Rudolf / b. Dec. 1, 1915 / d. unknown**
1938 WM NOR 1 0 — 0 — —

**Ejdepalm, Johan / b. Jan. 4, 1982**
2002 WM20 SWE 7 1 0 1 0 —

**Ekberg, Victor / b. June 16, 1932**
1960 OG-M AUS 6 0 2 2 0 —

**Ekelund, Peter / b. Feb. 28, 1971**
1991 WM20 SWE 6 0 1 1 0 —

**Ekholm, Patrik / b. June 5, 1972**
1992 WM20 SWE 3 0 0 0 0 S

**Eklund, Per-Erik / b. Mar. 22, 1963**
1982-83 WM20 SWE 13 6 4 10 6 —
1985-97 WM SWE 59 9 23 32 16 G,4S
1984 CC SWE 8 1 1 2 0 2nd
1984 OG-M SWE 7 2 6 8 0 B

**Eklund, Thom / b. Oct. 28, 1958**
1983-87 WM SWE 30 7 6 13 26 G,S
1987 CC SWE 6 1 2 3 6 —
1984-88 OG-M SWE 14 1 1 2 8 2B

**Ekman, Kenneth / b. May 5, 1945**
1972 OG-M SWE 3 0 0 0 2 —

**Ekman, Nils / b. Mar. 11, 1976**
1996 WM20 SWE 7 2 1 3 4 S
2008 WM SWE 9 0 6 6 4 —

**Ekmo, Trond / b. unknown**
1962 WM NOR 4 0 0 0 0 —

**Elander, Peter / b. Mar. 1, 1960**
1980 WM20 SWE 5 2 1 3 2 B

**Eldebrink, Anders / b. Dec. 11, 1960**
1981-90 WM SWE 51 13 11 24 42 G,3S
1984-87 CC SWE 14 1 6 7 10 2nd
1988 OG-M SWE 8 4 6 10 4 B
~WM All-Star Team/Defence (1989)

**Eliasson, Roger / b. Apr. 3, 1963**
1983 WM20 SWE 7 0 1 1 0 —

**Elick, Mickey John / b. Mar. 17, 1974**
1998 WM CAN 6 0 0 0 4 —

**Eliesen, Glenn Stian / b. Mar. 6, 1986**
2004 WM18 NOR 6 0 0 0 2 —

**Elizarov, Vladimir / b. July 22, 1925**
1958 WM URS 7 6 5 11 0 S

**Eljar, Joakim / b. Aug. 29, 1984**
2002 WM18 NOR 7 2 1 3 2 —

**Ellerby, Keaton / b. Nov. 5, 1988**
2006 WM18 CAN 5 0 1 1 10 —

**Ellett, Dave / b. Mar. 30, 1964**
1989 WM CAN 10 4 2 6 14 S

**Ellingsen, Age / b. Nov. 5, 1962**
1990-92 WM NOR 13 0 1 1 16 —
1984-88 OG-M NOR 11 1 2 3 8 —

**Elliott, Robert / b. unknown / d. unknown**
1931 WM USA 6 3 — 3 — S

**Ellis, Ron / b. Jan. 8, 1945**
1977 WM CAN 10 5 4 9 2 —
1972 SS CAN 8 0 3 3 8 1st

**Elofsson, Jonas / b. Jan. 31, 1979**
1997-98 WM20 SWE 9 1 1 2 10 —

**Elomo, Miika / b. Apr. 21, 1977**
1995-96 WM20 FIN 13 4 6 10 16 —

**Elomo, Teemu / b. Jan. 13, 1979**
1998-99 WM20 FIN 13 6 3 9 10 G

**Eloranta, Kari / b. Feb. 29, 1956**
1979-89 WM FIN 34 5 6 11 24 —
1991 CC FIN 6 0 1 1 4 —
1980-92 OG-M FIN 23 0 12 12 6 S

**Eloranta, Mikko / b. Aug. 24, 1972**
1998-2005 WM FIN 36 3 4 7 34 2S
2004 WCH FIN 6 2 0 2 2 2nd
2002 OG-M FIN 4 2 0 2 2 —

**Elsen, Andre / b. July 27, 1921 / d. unknown**
1950 WM BEL 4 2 0 2 0 —

**Eltner, Marco / b. Apr. 26, 1975**
1994-95 WM20 GER 11 1 0 1 20 —

**Elvenes, Bjorn / b. June 12, 1944 / d. 1988**
1962-65 WM NOR 13 10 4 14 2 —
1964 OG-M NOR 7 7 2 9 0 —

**Elvenes, Stefan / b. Mar. 30, 1970**
1989 WM20 SWE 7 1 2 3 4 S

**Elynuik, Pat / b. Oct. 30, 1967**
1987 WM20 CAN 6 6 5 11 2 —

**Emerson, Nelson / b. Aug. 17, 1967**
1992-98 WM CAN 17 4 4 8 8 G

**Emhardt, Anton / b. unknown / d. unknown**
1931 WM AUT 2 0 — 0 — B

**Eminger, Steve / b. Oct. 31, 1983**
2003 WM20 CAN 6 0 2 2 16 S

**Emma, David / b. Jan. 14, 1969**
1988-89 WM20 USA 14 6 2 8 8 —
1991-99 WM USA 16 2 3 5 8 —
1992 OG-M USA 6 0 1 1 6 —

**Emmerton, Cory / b. June 1, 1988**
2006 WM18 CAN 7 1 1 2 2 —

**Emmons, John / b. Aug. 17, 1974**
1993-94 WM20 USA 14 3 3 6 10 —

**Emori, Toshihito / b. 1932**
1957 WM JPN 7 2 0 2 — —

**Endrass, Michael / b. Sept. 18, 1988**
2006 WM18 GER 6 3 0 3 4 —

**Endrass, Stefan / b. Mar. 25, 1982**
2000 WM18 GER 6 2 0 2 2 —

**Endres, Arthur / b. Feb. 6, 1932**
1956 OG-M FRG 8 1 0 1 4 —

**Eneqvist, Johan / b. Jan. 21, 1982**
2000 WM18 SWE 6 2 3 5 6 B

**Engberg, Holger / b. Jan. 4, 1909 / d. Feb. 28, 1993**
1937-38 WM SWE 9 2 0 2 0 —
1936 OG-M SWE 5 1 — 1 — —

**Engblom, Brian / b. Jan. 27, 1955**
1983 WM CAN 10 1 2 3 0 B
1981 CC CAN 5 1 0 1 4 2nd

**Engblom, David / b. June 2, 1977**
1997 WM20 SWE 6 0 0 0 8 —

**Engel, Egon / b. Feb. 1, 1918 / d. unknown**
1947 WM AUT 7 0 — 0 — B
1948 OG-M AUT 8 0 — 0 — —

**Engelmann, Bernd / b. May 20, 1950**
1974 WM GDR 9 1 0 1 4 —

**Engelmann, Werner / b. Dec. 13, 1939**
1963 WM GDR 1 0 0 0 — —

**Englund, Patric / b. June 3, 1970**
1990 WM20 SWE 7 9 2 11 2 —

**Engman, Gustav / b. Jan. 17, 1985**
2003 WM18 SWE 6 0 0 0 16 —

**Engqvist, Ake / b. Dec. 9, 1921 / d. Sept. 15,1981**
1949 WM SWE 1 1 — 1 — —

**Ennaffati, Omar / b. Apr. 26, 1980**
2009 WM HUN 6 0 0 0 4 —

**Enstrom, Tommy / b. July 30, 1986**
2004 WM18 SWE 6 3 1 4 8 —

**Enzler, Karl / b. Mar. 29, 1925**
1953-54 WM FRG 8 1 0 1 2 S
1952 OG-M FRG 8 0 1 1 — —

**Erdall, Rich / b. Jan. 31, 1963**
1982-83 WM20 USA 14 7 5 12 24 —

**Erdmann, Alexander / b. Apr. 14, 1977**
1997 WM20 GER 6 0 1 1 6 —

**Erdodi, Bela / b. unknown / d. unknown**
1938 WM HUN 2 0 — 0 — —

**Erhardt, Carl / b. Feb. 15, 1897 / d. May 3, 1988**
1931-35 WM GBR 15 4 — 4 — B
1936 OG-M GBR 6 0 0 0 0 G
~IIHF Hall of Fame

**Erhart, Hermann / b. July 12, 1943**
1968 OG-M AUT 4 0 0 0 2 —

**Erhart, Sven / b. Feb. 2, 1964**
1984 WM20 FRG 7 1 0 1 10 —

**Erickson, Bryan / b. Mar. 7, 1960**
1979-80 WM20 USA 9 4 3 7 8 —
1982-87 WM USA 27 13 6 19 24 —
1984 CC USA 6 2 2 4 4 —

**Erickson, Patrik / b. Mar. 13, 1969**
1989 WM20 SWE 7 4 6 10 6 S
1990-91 WM SWE 18 3 1 4 6 G,S
1992 OG-M SWE 8 2 2 4 2 —

**Ericson, Ake / b. May 16, 1913 / d. Nov. 16, 1986**
1937-38 WM SWE 8 0 0 0 2 —
1936-48 OG-M SWE 11 4 — 4 — —

**Ericson, Bo / b. Jan. 23, 1958**
1977-78 WM20 SWE 14 0 6 6 16 S
1983-85 WM SWE 18 3 3 6 18 —
1984 CC SWE 8 1 2 3 10 2nd
1984 OG-M SWE 6 1 1 2 8 B

**Ericsson, Hans / b. Nov. 24, 1932**
1957 WM SWE 4 0 — 0 — G

**Ericsson, Lars-Erik / b. July 5, 1950**
1976-79 WM SWE 26 7 4 11 18 S,2B
1976 CC SWE 3 1 2 3 0 —

**Ericsson, Tomaz / b. Mar. 23, 1967**
1987 WM20 SWE 5 2 4 6 6 B

**Eriksen, Rune / b. Feb. 19, 1964**
1983 WM20 NOR 7 0 0 0 4 —

**Eriksen, Tommie / b. Oct. 7, 1970**
1990 WM20 NOR 7 2 1 3 26 —

**Eriksson, Anders / b. Jan. 9, 1975**
1994-95 WM20 SWE 14 4 10 14 20 S,B
1999 WM SWE 10 0 3 3 14 B
~WM20 All-Star Team/Defence (1995)

**Eriksson, Clas / b. Feb. 20, 1973**
1993 WM20 SWE 6 0 1 1 0 S

**Eriksson, Eddy / b. Feb. 16, 1965**
1985 WM20 SWE 7 4 4 8 18 —

**Eriksson, Fredrik / b. July 18, 1983**
2001 WM18 SWE 6 4 2 6 2 —
2003 WM20 SWE 6 0 4 4 10 —

**Eriksson, Hakan / b. Jan. 24, 1956**
1979 WM SWE 5 0 0 0 2 B
1980-84 OG-M SWE 14 3 3 6 12 2B

**Eriksson, Jan / b. Jan. 14, 1958**
1978 WM20 SWE 7 1 2 3 2 S
1982 WM SWE 4 0 0 0 0 —
1980 OG-M SWE 7 1 0 1 7 B

**Eriksson, Johan / b. Feb. 26, 1978**
1998 WM20 SWE 7 1 1 2 2 —

**Eriksson, Jorgen / b. Mar. 26, 1971**
1991 WM20 SWE 6 0 1 1 2 —

**Eriksson, Kent / b. Apr. 8, 1957**
1977 WM20 SWE 7 1 0 1 5 —

**Eriksson, Niklas / b. Feb. 17, 1969**
1989 WM20 SWE 7 6 3 9 6 S
1994 OG-M SWE 8 0 1 1 0 G
~WM20 All-Star Team/Forward (1989)

**Eriksson, Patrik / b. Mar. 13, 1969**
1988 WM20 SWE 6 3 2 5 8 —

**Eriksson, Peter / b. July 12, 1965**
1989 WM SWE 7 0 1 1 8 —
1987 CC SWE 3 0 0 0 0 —
1988 OG-M SWE 3 0 1 1 0 B

**Eriksson, Robin / b. July 28, 1957**
1977 WM20 SWE 7 1 0 1 2 —

**Eriksson, Roland / b. Mar. 1, 1954**
1976-83 WM SWE 48 20 18 38 6 2S,B
1976 CC SWE 5 2 2 4 2 —

**Eriksson, Rolf / b. Nov. 18, 1918 / d. unknown**
1947-51 WM SWE 17 16 0 16 0 2S
1948 OG-M SWE 8 6 — 6 — —

**Eriksson, Thomas / b. Oct. 16, 1959**
1979-90 WM20 SWE 44 6 4 10 54 S,B
1981-84 CC SWE 10 0 3 3 2
1980-88 OG-M SWE 14 2 3 5 16 2B

**Eriksson, Tim / b. Feb. 5, 1982**
1999-2000 WM18 SWE 13 5 8 13 18
2001-02 WM20 SWE 14 0 5 5 8 —

**Eriksson, Tommy / b. Mar. 5, 1966**
1985 WM20 SWE 7 1 3 4 8 —

**Erixon, Jan / b. July 8, 1962**
1981 WM20 SWE 5 1 6 7 2 G
1982-83 WM SWE 17 5 4 9 12 —
1981 CC SWE 2 0 0 0 0 —
~WM20 All-Star Team/Forward (1981)

**Erkgards, Johan / b. Nov. 12, 1989**
2007 WM18 SWE 6 0 0 0 6 B

**Erkgards, Stefan / b. Mar. 23, 1985**
2003 WM18 SWE 6 1 1 2 4 —

**Erni, Bruno / b. Nov. 15, 1968**
1993-95 WM SUI 13 0 1 1 6 —

**Errey, Bob / b. Sept. 21, 1964**
1997 WM CAN 11 2 1 3 6 G

**Ertl, Hans / b. Jan. 30, 1909 / d. unknown**
1933 WM AUT 8 2 — 2 4 —
1928 OG-M AUT 1 0 — 0 — —

**Eruzione, Mike / b. Oct. 25, 1954**
1975-76 WM USA 18 1 2 3 4 —
1980 OG-M USA 7 3 2 5 2 G

**Erzen, Mirko / b. unknown / d. unknown**
1939 WM YUG 2 0 0 0 — —

**Esashika, Kiyoshi / b. Sept. 23, 1948**
1976 OG-M JPN 5 0 1 1 0 —

**Esau, Len / b. June 3, 1968**
1995 WM CAN 7 0 1 1 2 B

**Esbjors, Joacim / b. July 4, 1970**
1990 WM20 SWE 6 0 3 3 0 —
1992 WM SWE 8 0 0 0 0 G

**Esbjors, Lars-Erik / b. Oct. 11, 1949**
1976 WM SWE 10 1 1 2 5 B
1976 CC SWE 1 0 0 0 2 —

**Esipov, Andrei / b. May 9, 1980**
2000 WM20 RUS 7 0 1 1 4 S

**Eskesen, Michael / b. June 5, 1986**
2004 WM18 DEN 6 1 3 4 2 —

**Espe, David / b. Nov. 3, 1966**
1985 WM20 USA 7 0 0 0 8 —

**Espeland, Stefan / b. Mar. 24, 1989**
2006 WM18 NOR 6 0 0 0 8 —

**Esposito, Phil / b. Feb. 20, 1942**
1977 WM CAN 10 7 3 10 14 —
1972 SS CAN 8 7 6 13 15 1st
1976 CC CAN 7 4 3 7 0 1st

**Ete, Roger / b. unknown / d. unknown**
1937 WM FRA 4 0 0 0 0 —

**Etcher, Fred / b. Aug. 23, 1932 / d. Nov. 25, 2011**
1960 OG-M CAN 7 9 12 21 0 S

**Ethier, Pat / b. Mar. 17, 1961**
1980-81 WM20 USA 10 2 1 3 22 —

**Evason, Dean / b. Aug. 22, 1964**
1984 WM20 CAN 7 6 3 9 0 —
1997 WM CAN 11 2 3 5 20 G

**Everett, Doug / b. Apr. 3, 1905 / d. Sept. 14, 1996**
1932 OG-M USA 5 4 0 4 0 S

**Everwijn, Rein / b. June 30, 1916 / d. unknown**
1939 WM NED 4 0 — 0 — —

**Evtushevski, Greg / b. May 4, 1965**
1994 WM GER 5 1 1 2 8 —

**Fabian, Stefan / b. Feb. 10, 1981**
1999 WM18 SVK 7 0 2 2 6 B

**Fabris, Arnaldo / b. Aug. 16, 1916 / d. unknown**
1948 OG-M ITA 8 0 — 0 — —

**Fagarasi, Zoltan / b. Jan. 11, 1942**
1968 OG-M ROM 5 1 3 4 2 —

**Fagemo, Linus / b. Mar. 5, 1977**
1997 WM20 SWE 6 1 1 2 4 —

**Fagerhoi, Kim / b. Aug. 13, 1971**
1991 WM20 NOR 6 1 2 3 0 —

**Fagerli, Jan-Roar / b. Sept. 22, 1966**
1990-97 WM NOR 28 0 0 0 6 —
1992-94 OG-M NOR 14 0 1 1 6 —

**Fagerstedt, Juha / b. Apr. 15, 1983**
2001 WM18 FIN 6 0 0 0 0 B
2003 WM20 FIN 7 0 0 0 8 B

**Faggioni, Flavio / b. Aug. 18, 1981**
2007 WM ITA 6 0 0 0 4 —

**Fah, Michel / b. Oct. 18, 1977**
1997 WM20 SUI 6 0 1 1 4 —

**Fahey, Brian / b. Mar. 2, 1981**
1999 WM18 USA 6 1 0 1 4 —

**Fahey, Jim / b. May 11, 1979**
2003 WM USA 6 1 0 1 2 —

**Fair, Keith / b. Jan. 8, 1968**
1992 WM SUI 8 0 3 3 0 —
1992 OG-M SUI 7 2 5 7 6 —

**Fair, Peter / b. May 1906 / d. unknown**
1934 WM GBR 2 0 — 0 — —

**Fairburn, Jim / b. Sept. 12, 1927**
1955 WM CAN 8 6 3 9 0 G

**Fairchild, Kelly / b. Apr. 9, 1973**
2003 WM USA 6 5 0 5 2 —

**Faistl, Klaus / b. Oct. 1, 1962**
1982 WM20 FRG 7 1 2 3 12 —

**Fakhrutdinov, Dmitri / b. Apr. 13, 1983**
2003 WM20 RUS 6 0 1 1 2 G

**Fako, Karol / b. Nov. 24, 1931**
1959 WM TCH 8 3 5 8 0 B

**Falardeau, Lee / b. July 22, 1983**
2001 WM18 USA 6 0 3 3 2 —

**Falfudinov, Denis / b. Sept. 23, 1981**
2001 WM20 KAZ 6 0 0 0 2 —

**Falk, Andreas / b. Feb. 27, 1983**
2003 WM20 SWE 6 3 0 3 6 —

**Falk, Nichlas / b. Feb. 3, 1971**
1997-2002 WM SWE 37 4 5 9 16 G,S,2B
1991 WM20 SWE 7 0 3 3 10 —

**Falk, Stefan / b. May 5, 1966**
1986 WM20 SWE 7 1 1 2 0 —

**Falkman, Craig / b. Aug. 1, 1943**
1967-71 WM USA 16 5 1 6 18 —
1968 OG-M USA 2 1 1 2 4 —

**Falk-Nilsen, Tore / b. Apr. 27, 1948**
1980 OG-M NOR 5 1 2 3 12 —

**Falloon, Pat / b. Sept. 22, 1972**
1991 WM20 CAN 7 3 3 6 2 G
1992 WM CAN 6 2 1 3 2 —

**Famiglietti, Ron / b. 1940**
1963 WM USA 7 0 0 0 0 —

**Fanduls, Viaceslavs / b. Mar. 17, 1969**
1999-2004 WM LAT 35 8 10 18 30 —
2002 OG-M LAT 4 4 0 4 2 —

**Farda, Richard / b. Nov. 8, 1945**
1969-74 WM TCH 56 15 21 36 10 G,2S,3B
1972 OG-M TCH 5 1 5 6 0 B

**Fardella, Vincenzo / b. June 8, 1926**
1948 OG-M ITA 7 2 — 2 — —

**Farelli, Cary / b. June 19, 1957**
1982 WM ITA 7 3 2 5 6 —
1984 OG-M ITA 5 2 2 4 0 —

**Farkas, Jeff / b. Jan. 24, 1978**
1996-98 WM20 USA 19 8 6 14 16 S

**Farkas, Matyas / b. Aug. 13, 1893 / d. June 1, 1981**
1930-35 WM HUN 10 1 — 1 — —
1936 OG-M HUN 1 0 — 0 — —

**Farmer-Horn, Ken / b. July 26, 1912 / d. Jan. 12, 2005**
1936 OG-M CAN 8 8 2 10 0 S

**Farquharson, Hugh / b. Nov. 14, 1911 / d. Mar. 27, 1985**
1936 OG-M CAN 8 10 5 15 2 S

**Fata, Rico / b. Feb. 12, 1980**
1999 WM20 CAN 7 1 3 4 8 S

**Fatyka, Stanislav / b. Sept. 5, 1978**
1998 WM20 SVK 6 1 1 2 27 —

**Faucomprez, Gerard / b. Oct. 9, 1944**
1968 OG-M FRA 5 2 3 5 2 —

**Faulkner, George / b. Dec. 27, 1933**
1966 WM CAN 7 6 2 8 2 B

**Favarin, Nicolas / b. Apr. 29, 1980**
2004 WM FRA 6 0 0 0 2 —

**Favre, Andre / b. unknown**
1951 WM SUI 3 0 — 0 0 B

**Favrod, Philippe / b. 1959**
1978 WM20 SUI 6 0 1 1 0 —

**Fawcett, Bernard / b. Apr. 28, 1909 / d. Dec. 28, 1961**
1928 OG-M GBR — 0 — 0 — —

**Feamster, Dave / b. Sept. 10, 1958**
1978 WM20 USA 6 0 5 5 8 —

**Federici, Aldo / b. Sept. 6, 1920 / d. unknown**
1948-56 OG-M ITA 9 9 0 9 2 —

**Fedorov, Sergei ~see Fyodorov, Sergei**

**Fedotenko, Igor / b. Feb. 1, 1988**
2006 WM18 BLR 6 0 0 0 4 —

**Fedotenko, Ruslan / b. Jan. 18, 1979**
1996 WM20 UKR 6 0 1 1 2 —
2002 OG-M UKR 1 1 0 1 4 —

**Fedotov, Anatoli / b. May 11, 1966**
1985-86 WM20 URS 13 1 7 8 2 G,B
1997 WM RUS 9 2 2 4 10 —
1987 CC URS 8 0 1 1 4 2nd

**Fedotov, Sergei / b. Jan. 24, 1977**
1997 WM20 RUS 6 0 1 1 2 B

**Fedulov, Igor / b. July 4, 1966**
1994-95 WM RUS 12 6 7 13 8 —

**Feenstra, Jacques / b. unknown**
1950 WM NED 4 1 0 1 2 —

**Fehr, Nino / b. Sept. 3, 1988**
2005 WM18 SUI 6 0 0 0 0 —

**Feistl, Klaus / b. Oct. 1, 1962**
1981 WM20 FRG 5 0 1 1 18 —

**Feistritzer, Walter / b. Apr. 21, 1920 / d. unknown**
1938-49 WM AUT 24 18 — 18 — B
1948 OG-M AUT 8 5 — 5 — —

**Fekete, Daniel / b. Feb. 22, 1982**
2009 WM HUN 6 0 1 1 0 —

**Felber, Harald / b. June 1, 1949**
1976 WM GDR 10 0 0 0 2 —

**Felc, Albin / b. May 14, 1941**
1964-72 OG-M YUG 16 17 8 25 8 —

**Feldmanis, Vents / b. Mar. 7, 1977**
2003 WM LAT 6 0 0 0 0 —

**Felfernig, Gerhard / b. May 18, 1944**
1968 OG-M AUT 5 0 1 1 2 —

**Felicetti, Dino / b. Dec. 22, 1970**
1997-2001 WM ITA 23 4 4 8 37 —
1998 OG-M ITA 4 2 0 2 2 —

**Felicetti, Luca / b. Aug. 18, 1981**
2006 WM ITA 6 0 0 0 2 —

**Felix, Chris / b. May 27, 1964**
1988 OG-M CAN 6 1 2 3 2 —

**Fendt, Thorsten / b. Jan. 20, 1977**
1995-97 WM20 GER 19 2 1 3 10 —

**Fengler, Reinhardt / b. Feruary 5, 1957**
1976-85 WM GDR 40 5 1 6 18 —

**Fenke, Ferenc / b. unknown**
1947 WM ROM 3 0 — 0 — —

**Fenton, Paul / b. Dec. 22, 1959**
1985-89 WM USA 19 3 4 7 22 —

**Fenyves, Dave / b. Apr. 29, 1960**
1980 WM20 CAN 5 0 0 0 8 —

**Feoktistov, Ilya / b. Mar. 30, 1985**
2003 WM18 KAZ 6 0 0 0 2 —

**Fera, Rick / b. Aug. 13, 1964**
1994 WM GBR 6 1 2 3 4 —

**Ference, Andrew / b. Mar. 17, 1979**
1999 WM20 CAN 7 1 2 3 6 S

**Ference, Brad / b. Apr. 2, 1979**
1998-99 WM20 CAN 14 0 3 3 31 S
2002 WM CAN 6 0 0 0 4 —

**Ferencz, Ion / b. June 10, 1932**
1964 OG-M ROM 7 5 2 7 0 —

**Fergus, Tom / b. June 16, 1962**
1985 WM USA 8 4 2 6 14 —

**Ferguson, George / b. Apr. 1, 1935**
1961-63 WM CAN 13 3 5 8 24 G

**Ferm, Jonas / b. Aug. 15, 1981**
1999 WM18 SWE 7 3 3 6 0 S

**Ferrari, Marco / b. Nov. 25, 1971**
1991 WM20 SUI 7 0 0 0 4 —

**Ferraro, Chris / b. Jan. 24, 1973**
1992-93 WM20 USA 14 8 10 18 10 B
2003 WM USA 6 0 2 2 18 —

**Ferraro, Peter / b. Jan. 24, 1973**
1992-93 WM20 USA 14 10 9 19 20 B
2003 WM USA 6 1 4 5 10 —
1994 OG-M USA 8 6 0 6 6 —
~WM20 All-Star Team/Forward (1992)

**Ferraro, Ray / b. Aug. 23, 1964**
1989-96 WM CAN 23 3 10 13 16 2S

**Ferriero, Benn / b. Apr. 29, 1987**
2005 WM18 USA 6 1 3 4 4 G

**Feser, Till / b. Sept. 26, 1972**
1992 WM20 GER 7 3 0 3 16 —

**Feter, Marian / b. Mar. 13, 1946**
1970-75 WM POL 18 0 0 0 22 —
1972 OG-M POL 2 0 0 0 16 —

**Fetisov, Vyacheslav / b. Apr. 20, 1958**
1977-78 WM20 URS 14 6 9 15 8 2G
1977-91 WM URS 106 36 59 95 89 7G,S,3B
1981-96 WCH RUS 20 3 14 17 31 1st,2nd
1980-88 OG-M URS 22 12 21 33 24 2G,S
~IIHF Hall of Fame/Triple Gold Club
~WM IIHF Directorate Best Defenceman (1978, 1982, 1985, 1986, 1989), WM All-Star Team/Defence (1978, 1982, 1983, 1985, 1986, 1987, 1989, 1990, 1991), WM20 IIHF Directorate Best Defenceman (1977, 1978), WM 20 All-Styar Team/Defence (1978)

**Fiala, Ondrej / b. Nov. 4, 1987**
2005 WM18 CZE 7 2 1 3 8 —

**Fiala, Petr / b. Jan. 7, 1960**
1980 WM20 TCH 5 0 1 1 8 —

**Fichuk, Pete / b. Apr. 8, 1947**
1971 WM USA 1 0 0 0 0 —

**Fidler, Mike / b. Aug. 19, 1956**
1978 WM USA 10 8 2 10 18 —

**Fife, Jim / b. unknown**
1951 WM USA 6 1 — 1 4 —

**Figala, Milan / b. Nov. 23, 1955**
1979 WM TCH 7 2 1 3 6 S

**Figliuzzi, Stefan / b. July 23, 1968**
1992-96 WM ITA 23 9 5 14 14 —
1994-98 OG-M ITA 11 6 4 10 6 —

**Filatov, Anatoli / b. Mar. 29, 1975**
2004 WM KAZ 6 2 0 2 6 —

**Filewich, Jonathan / b. Oct. 2, 1984**
2002 WM18 CAN 8 4 3 7 22 —

**Filimonov, Dmitri / b. Oct. 14, 1971**
1991 CC URS 5 0 0 0 0 —

**Filin, Timofei / b. June 18, 1984**
2002 WM18 BLR 7 3 2 5 2 —
2005 WM BLR 1 0 0 0 0 —
*suspended for doping violation at 2005 WM and stats not counted officially

**Filipenko, Pavel / b. Feb. 1, 1982**
2001 WM20 KAZ 6 0 0 0 0 —

**Filippin, Jean-Christophe / b. May 18, 1969**
1997-2000 WM FRA 20 1 1 2 24 —
1998 OG-M FRA 4 0 0 0 4 —

**Filippov, Alexander / b. Feb. 20, 1951**
1975-76 WM URS 16 2 1 3 4 G,S

**Filo, Marian / b. May 18, 1984**
2002 WM18 SVK 8 0 0 0 0 —

**Filo, Martin / b. Feb. 6, 1989**
2007 WM18 SVK 6 0 1 1 4 —

**Finell, Joni / b. July 18, 1986**
2004 WM18 FIN 5 0 0 0 0 —

**Finley, Jeff / b. Apr. 14, 1967**
2000 WM CAN 7 1 1 2 0 —

**Finnstrom, Johan / b. Mar. 27, 1976**
1995-96 WM20 SWE 12 1 6 7 10 S,B

**Finstad, Morten / b. May 24, 1967**
1990-94 WM NOR 23 3 1 4 0 —
1994 OG-M NOR 7 0 0 0 4 —

**Firsov, Anatoli / b. Feb. 1, 1941 / d. July 24, 2000**
1965-71 WM URS 47 45 40 85 26 6G
1964-72 OG-M URS 19 18 12 30 6 3G
~IIHF Hall of Fame
~OG-M IIHF Directorate Best Forward (1968), WM IIHF Directorate Best Forward (1967, 1971), WM All-Star Team/Forward (1967, 1968, 1970), OG-M All-Star Team/Forward (1968)

**Fischer, Andreas / b. Nov. 25, 1966**
1986 WM20 SUI 7 0 1 1 8 —

**Fischer, Jiri / b. July 31, 1980**
2004 WCH CZE 4 0 0 0 2 —
2005 WM CZE 9 0 1 1 4 G
~suffered career-ending heart attack in an NHL game on Nov. 21, 2005

**Fischer, Marco / b. Apr. 19, 1972**
1991 WM20 SUI 7 0 2 2 2 —

**Fischer, Patrick / b. Sept. 6, 1975**
1994 WM20 SUI 7 1 0 1 8 —
1998-2005 WM SUI 42 13 8 21 36 —
2002-06 OG-M SUI 10 2 1 3 8 —

**Fischer, Patrick / b. June 18, 1978**
1997-98 WM20 SUI 13 0 1 1 16 B
2002-03 WM SUI 7 0 0 0 2 —

**Fischer, Ron / b. Apr. 12, 1959**
1989-92 WM GER 16 3 3 6 10 —
1988-92 OG-M GER 16 2 4 6 10 —

**Fischer, Thomas / b. Jan. 8, 1984**
2002 WM18 GER 8 0 0 0 14 —

**Fishback, Dan / b. May 7, 1961**
1981 WM20 USA 4 1 0 1 0 —

**Fisher, Frank / b. May 16, 1907 / d. Apr. 23, 1983**
1928 OG-M CAN 1 1 — 1 — G

**Fiskari, Harold / b. unknown**
1954 WM CAN 3 0 — 0 0 S

**Fistric, Boris / b. Sept. 15, 1960**
1979 WM20 CAN 5 0 0 0 22 —

**Fitzgerald, Ed / b. Aug. 3, 1890 / d. Apr. 18, 1966**
1920 OG-M USA 3 1 — 1 0 S

**Fitzgerald, Joe / b. Oct. 10, 1904 / d. Mar. 20, 1987**
1932 OG-M USA 1 0 0 0 1 S

**Fitzgerald, Tom / b. Aug. 28, 1968**
1987 WM20 USA 7 3 0 3 2 —
1989-91 WM USA 20 1 2 3 18 —

**Fitzpatrick, Rory / b. Jan. 11, 1975**
1995 WM20 USA 7 0 2 2 8 —

**Fjeld, Jon / b. unknown**
1983 WM20 NOR 6 0 0 0 0 —

**Fjeld, Morten / b. Mar. 4, 1976**
1997-2001 WM NOR 25 1 1 2 26 —

**Fjeldsgaard, Knut / b. May 19, 1952**
1980 OG-M NOR 5 0 0 0 0 —

**Fjeldstad, Erik / b. Feb. 20, 1944**
1964 OG-M NOR 5 0 3 3 0 —

**Fjeldstad, Rune / b. Dec. 23, 1971**
1991 WM20 NOR 7 0 1 1 4 —
1995-97 WM NOR 13 2 4 6 2 —

**Flamaropol, Mihai / b. Nov. 21, 1919 / d. unknown**
1947 WM ROM 2 0 — 0 — —

**Flanagan, Denny / b. unknown**
1951 WM CAN 6 8 — 8 2 G

**Flasar, Ales / b. Mar. 1, 1965**
1985 WM20 TCH 7 1 2 3 16 S
1993 WM CZE 7 0 0 0 0 B

**Flatley, Pat / b. Oct. 3, 1963**
1983 WM20 CAN 7 4 0 4 6 B
1983 WM CAN 6 0 0 0 2 B
1984 OG-M CAN 7 3 3 6 70 —

**Fleischmann, Jaroslav / b. July 6, 1885 / d. Sept. 23, 1939**
1924 OG-M TCH 1 0 — 0 — —

**Fleischmann, Miroslav / b. Sept. 4, 1886 / d. Aug. 12, 1955**
1924 OG-M TCH 3 0 — 0 — —

**Fleming, Jakob / b. Aug. 28, 1982**
2000 WM18 USA 5 1 0 1 29 —

**Flemming, Michael / b. Feb. 1, 1965**
1985 WM20 FRG 7 0 0 0 2 —

**Fletcher, Don / b. Mar. 28, 1931**
1961-63 WM CAN 14 5 6 11 23 G

**Fletcher, Jim / b. July 31, 1918 / d. unknown**
1947 WM USA 7 0 — 0 — —

**Fleury, Theo / b. June 29, 1968**
1987-88 WM20 CAN 13 8 5 13 6 G
1990-91 WM CAN 17 9 12 21 18 S
1991-96 WCH CAN 15 5 6 11 20 1st,2nd
1998-2002 OG-M CAN 12 1 5 6 8 G
~WM20 All-Star Team/Forward (1988)

**Flick, Bill / b. Ontario, 1925**
1951 WM CAN 6 2 — 2 4 G

**Flinck, Tapio / b. Aug. 14, 1950**
1976 WM FIN 10 1 1 2 6 —
1976 CC FIN 5 0 0 0 2 —

**Flodin, Niklas / b. Jan. 17, 1984**
2002 WM18 SWE 8 1 3 4 16 —

**Florescu, Iulian / b. Oct. 23, 1943**
1964-68 OG-M ROM 9 4 3 7 2 —

**Florio, Perry / b. July 15, 1967**
1985 WM20 USA 7 0 1 1 4 —

**Flotiront, Pierre / b. Mar. 29, 1958**
1978 WM20 SUI 4 0 2 2 2 —

**Flynn, Rob / b. Jan. 8, 1983**
2001 WM18 USA 6 1 1 2 2 —

**Foderl, Herbert / b. unknown**
1957 WM AUT 3 0 — 0 — —

**Foglietta, Giuseppe / b. Mar. 8, 1966**
1992 OG-M ITA 7 6 1 7 2 —

**Fogolin, Lee / b. Feb. 7, 1955**
1976 CC USA 2 0 0 0 6 —

**Fokin, Anatoli / b. July 25, 1982**
2001 WM20 KAZ 6 0 0 0 12 —

**Fokin, Sergei / b. May 2, 1963**
1995-98 WM RUS 29 0 3 3 16 —

**Folcke, Ghislain / b. Jan. 10, 1983**
2002 WM20 FRA 6 0 1 1 2 —

**Foley, Pat / b. Jan. 24, 1981**
1999 WM18 USA 6 1 3 4 8 —
2000 WM20 USA 7 1 0 1 31 —

**Folghera, Philipp / b. May 7, 1979**
1999 WM20 SUI 6 2 0 2 0 —

**Foligno, Mike / b. Jan. 29, 1959**
1981-87 WM CAN 27 2 9 11 58 B

**Fonfara, Andrzej / b. Sept. 21, 1939**
1959-66 WM POL 12 3 1 4 0 —
1964 OG-M POL 7 5 7 12 4 —

**Fonfara, Karol / b. Oct. 16, 1940**
1966 WM POL 7 2 1 3 0 —

**Fontana, Ruben / b. June 15, 1967**
1987 WM20 SUI 7 0 0 0 8 —

**Fontanive, Nicola / b. Oct. 25, 1985**
2006-10 WM ITA 17 2 1 3 10 —
2006 OG-M ITA 3 0 0 0 2 —

**Foote, Adam / b. July 10, 1971**
1996-2004 WCH CAN 14 1 3 4 14 1st,2nd
1998-2006 OG-M CAN 18 1 2 3 12 G

**Forbes, Ian / b. Mar. 30, 1927 / d. Oct. 13, 1989**
1950-62 WM GBR 20 10 2 12 26 —

**Forbes, Mike / b. Sept. 20, 1957**
1977 WM20 CAN 7 0 1 1 22 S

**Forbes, Sherman / b. June 11, 1909 / d. May 9, 1985**
1933 WM USA 5 3 — 3 2 G

**Forfang, Klas / b. May 10, 1969**
1989 WM20 NOR 7 1 2 3 0 —

**Forhan, Bob / b. Mar. 27, 1936**
1963-65 WM CAN 14 10 6 16 6 —
1960-64 OG-M CAN 13 8 5 13 0 S

**Forrest, Justin / b. Apr. 15, 1981**
1999 WM18 USA 6 1 2 3 10 —
2001 WM20 USA 7 1 1 2 8 —

**Forsander, Johan / b. Apr. 28, 1978**
1997-98 WM20 SWE 13 5 4 9 2 —

**Forsberg, Per / b. Mar. 27, 1964**
1984 WM20 SWE 7 1 0 1 6 —

**Forsberg, Peter / b. July 20, 1973**
1992-93 WM20 SWE 14 10 32 42 38 2S
1992-2004 WM SWE 33 15 14 29 26 2G,3S
1996-2004 WCH SWE 8 2 6 8 6 —
1994-2010 OG SWE 22 3 17 20 14 2G
~Triple Gold Club
~WM IIHF Directorate Best Forward (1998), WM All-Star Team/Forward (1998, 2003), WM20 IIHF Directorate Best Forward (1993), WM20 All-Star Team/Forward (1993)

**Forsey, Jack / b. Nov. 17, 1914 / d. Jan. 1, 1998**
1937 WM CAN 6 8 2 10 4 G

**Forslund, Tomas / b. Nov. 24, 1968**
1988 WM20 SWE 7 0 0 0 10 —
1994-96 WM SWE 19 4 3 7 16 S,B
1991 CC SWE 6 1 0 1 2 —

**Forss, Matti / b. May 17, 1957**
1977 WM20 FIN 7 3 5 8 4 —
1982 WM FIN 7 0 3 3 0 —

**Forsstrom, Karl / b. Sept. 6, 1915 / d. Aug. 22, 1987**
1938 WM SWE 5 0 — 0 — —

**Foschi, Mauro / b. Oct. 15, 1960**
1980 WM20 SUI 5 0 0 0 2 —

**Foster, Corey / b. Oct. 27, 1969**
1989 WM20 CAN 7 1 3 4 4 —

**Foster, Dwight / b. Apr. 2, 1957**
1977 WM20 CAN 6 2 3 5 4 S

**Foster, Kevin / b. Oct. 5, 1962**
1982 WM20 USA 7 2 6 8 14 —

**Fournier, Guy / b. Jan. 30, 1962**
1981 WM20 CAN 5 1 2 3 0 —

**Fox, Jim / b. May 18, 1960**
1980 WM20 CAN 5 3 2 5 0 —
1986 WM CAN 10 2 1 3 2 B

**Foyn, Stephen / b. June 23, 1959**
1979 WM20 NOR 5 1 0 1 26 —
1990 WM NOR 10 4 1 5 6 —
1980-88 OG-M NOR 16 6 2 8 21 —

**Francheterre, Patrick / b. Feb. 10, 1948**
1968 OG-M FRA 5 0 0 0 0 —

**Francis, Ron / b. Mar. 1, 1963**
1985 WM CAN 10 2 5 7 2 S

**Franck, Francois / b. 1904 / d. unknown**
1933-35 WM BEL 9 0 0 0 3 —
1924-28 OG-M BEL 5 0 — 0 — —

**Franck, Louis / b. 1904 / d. unknown**
1934 WM BEL 1 0 — 0 — —

**Francz, Robert / b. Mar. 30, 1978**
1998 WM20 GER 6 0 0 0 26 —

**Frank, David / b. unknown**
1961 WM USA 4 1 0 1 4 —

**Frank, Josef / b. Aug. 2, 1984**
2002 WM18 GER 8 0 0 0 4 —

**Franke, Joachim / b. Mar. 30, 1940**
1959-67 WM GDR 40 8 2 10 18 —

**Franke, Jurgen / b. Aug. 7, 1952**
1976-78 WM GDR 18 1 2 3 8 —

**Franz, Georg / b. Jan. 9, 1965**
1983-85 WM20 FRG 14 1 1 2 10 —
1985-95 WM GER 51 8 6 14 8 —
1988-94 OG-M GER 16 2 3 5 12 —

**Franzen, Rikard / b. Mar. 21, 1968**
1987-88 WM20 SWE 12 3 2 5 18 B
2000 WM SWE 5 0 1 1 6 —

**Fras, Adam / b. July 13, 1970**
1990 WM20 POL 6 1 0 1 2 —

**Fraser, Curt / b. Jan. 12, 1958**
1978 WM20 CAN 5 0 2 2 0 B
1987 CC USA 5 0 1 1 4 —

**Fraser, Iain / b. Aug. 10, 1969**
1995 WM CAN 8 2 7 9 8 B

**Frederick, Joe / b. June 8, 1969**
1995 WM USA 6 1 1 2 2 —

**Fredrickson, Frank / b. July 11, 1895 / d. May 28, 1979**
1920 OG-M CAN 3 12 — 12 7 G

**Fredriksen, Lasse / b. Jan. 24, 1981**
1999 WM18 NOR 6 2 0 2 6 —

**Freer, Mark / b. July 14, 1968**
1995 WM CAN 6 1 0 1 2 B

**Frei, Ratus / b. Sept. 8, 1932**
1955 WM SUI 7 1 0 1 2 —
1956 OG-M SUI 5 0 0 0 0 —

**Frenzel, Dieter / b. June 29, 1955**
1974-85 WM GDR 50 7 6 13 18 —

**Frenzel, Hans / b. Dec. 17, 1928**
1957-59 WM GDR 13 6 1 7 12 —

**Frenzel, Matthias / b. Apr. 5, 1982**
2000 WM18 GER 6 1 1 2 2 —

**Fresher, Rupert / b. Aug. 23, 1932**
1962 WM GBR 6 2 0 2 8 —

**Frick, James "Bud" / b. Jan. 1, 1928 / d. Sept. 14, 1996**
1950 WM USA 7 2 0 2 6 S

**Fridfinnsson, Chris / b. June 14, 1898 / d. Nov. 10, 1938**
1920 OG-M CAN 1 1 — 1 — G

**Friedrich, Elwin / b. July 25, 1933 / d. Feb. 2, 2012**
1962 WM SUI 7 0 3 3 10 —
1964 OG-M SUI 7 0 0 0 0 —

**Friesen, Jeff / b. Aug. 5, 1976**
1994-95 WM20 CAN 12 5 4 9 4 2G
1996-2004 WM CAN 42 8 10 18 32 2G,S

**Friis, Jarl / b. Nov. 2, 1964**
1983 WM20 NOR 7 1 2 3 4 —
1992 WM NOR 5 2 0 2 2 —
1988-92 OG-M NOR 11 2 3 5 8 —

**Friis, Martin / b. Nov. 18, 1965**
1992 OG-M NOR 4 0 0 0 0 —

**Friman, Kari-Pekka / b. Oct. 5, 1966**
1985-86 WM20 FIN 14 0 4 4 6 —

**Frischlander, Henry / b. unknown / d. unknown**
1931 WM ROM 3 0 — 0 — —

**Frisk, Andreas / b. Jan. 5, 1984**
2002 WM18 SWE 8 0 2 2 2 —

**Frison, Bruno / b. May 14, 1936**
1959 WM ITA 8 4 1 5 6 —
1964 OG-M ITA 6 3 0 3 8 —

**Fritsche, John / b. Mar. 5, 1966**
1990 WM USA 10 2 0 2 4 —

**Fritz, Georg / b. unknown**
1986 WM FRG 10 2 0 2 14 —

**Fritz, Johann / b. Feb. 6, 1958**
1984 OG-M AUT 5 1 0 1 2 —

**Frohlich, Vaclav / b. Feb. 22, 1930**
1958 WM TCH 7 1 0 1 0 —

**Frohlicher, Joel / b. Apr. 5, 1982**
2000 WM18 SUI 7 2 0 2 6 —

**Frolik, Martin / b. Feb. 10, 1982**
2000 WM18 CZE 3 3 1 4 2 —

**Frolikov, Alexei / b. Feb. 15, 1957**
1977 WM20 URS 7 6 5 11 12 G

**Frolo, Tomas / b. Jan. 26, 1982**
2000 WM18 SVK 6 0 0 0 14 —

**Frolov, Dmitri / b. Aug. 22, 1966**
1993-95 WM RUS 20 0 5 5 14 G

**Frolov, Oleg / b. Apr. 21, 1985**
2005 WM20 BLR 6 0 0 0 2 —

**From Bjork, Christopher / b. Mar. 28, 1987**
2005 WM18 SWE 7 3 0 3 6 B

**Frosch, Manfred / b. unknown**
1981 WM20 AUT 5 0 0 0 0 —

**Fruhauf, Peter / b. Aug. 15, 1982**
2000 WM18 SVK 6 2 2 4 12 —

**Fryberger, Walter / b. May 5, 1940**
1964 OG-M USA 7 3 1 4 0 —

**Frycer, Miroslav / b. Sept. 27, 1959**
1978-79 WM20 TCH 12 3 1 4 10 S
1979-81 WM TCH 9 1 2 3 2 S,B
1980 OG-M TCH 6 1 1 2 7 —

**Frylen, Edvin / b. Dec. 23, 1975**
1993-94 WM20 SWE 14 0 1 1 6 2S

**Fryzlewicz, Stanislaw / b. Aug. 4, 1946**
1970-74 WM POL 28 0 1 1 18 —
1972 OG-M POL 5 0 0 0 0 —

**Ftorek, Robbie / b. Jan. 2, 1952**
1976-81 CC USA 9 3 2 5 16 —
1972 OG-M USA 5 0 2 2 0 S

**Fuchs, Fritz / b. unknown / d. unknown**
1930 WM SUI 1 0 — 0 — B

**Fuchs, Lothar / b. June 18, 1941**
1966-70 WM GDR 22 1 1 2 2 —
1968 OG-M GDR 7 4 0 4 2 —

**Fujii, Tadamitsu / b. Jan. 24, 1954**
1980 OG-M JPN 5 1 0 1 6 —

**Fujimori, Jun / b. 1929**
1957 WM JPN 3 1 — 1 — —

**Fujita, Kiyoshi (Ryan) / b. June 25, 1972**
1998-2004 WM JPN 27 6 11 17 77 —
1998 OG-M JPN 4 1 1 2 2 —

**Fullerton, Billy / b. Nov. 23, 1913 / d. Jan. 17, 1941**
1939 WM GBR 5 1 — 1 — —

**Funiok, Maciej / b. Jan. 4, 1970**
1990 WM20 POL 7 0 0 0 4 —

**Funk, Lorenz / b. Mar. 17, 1947**
1967-79 WM FRG 72 9 9 18 38 —
1968-76 OG-M FRG 15 6 6 12 6 B

**Funk, Lorenz / b. Jan. 2, 1969**
1988-89 WM20 FRG 13 2 2 4 2 —

**Funk, Michael / b. Sept. 15, 1986**
2004 WM18 CAN 7 0 1 1 2 —

**Furca, Slawomir / b. Nov. 13, 1971**
1990 WM20 POL 7 1 1 2 10 —

**Furchner, Sebastian / b. May 3, 1982**
2000 WM18 GER 6 0 1 1 10 —
2005 WM GER 6 2 1 3 0 —
2006 OG-M GER 1 0 0 0 0 —

**Furlani, Giovanni / b. Sept. 4, 1936**
1959 WM ITA 8 3 2 5 6 —
1956 OG-M ITA 6 1 2 3 6 —

**Furrer, Gaston / b. May 10, 1945**
1972 WM SUI 10 0 0 0 28 —
1964-72 OG-M SUI 11 0 1 1 12 —

**Furuya, Kenichi / b. Nov. 8, 1912 / d. unknown**
1936 OG-M JPN 2 0 0 0 — —

**Fusco, Mark / b. Mar. 12, 1961**
1981 WM20 USA 3 0 0 0 2 —
1985 WM USA 10 0 1 1 4 —
1984 CC USA 1 0 0 0 2 —
1984 OG-M USA 6 0 0 0 6 —

**Fusco, Scott / b. Jan. 21, 1963**
1982 WM20 USA 6 5 4 9 0 —
1984-88 OG-M USA 12 5 6 11 8 —

**Fux, Andrei / b. Jan. 1, 1985**
2003 WM18 KAZ 6 0 0 0 0 —

**Fylling, Quinn / b. Jan. 16, 1982**
2000 WM18 USA 6 1 1 2 4 —

**Fyodorov, Fedor / b. June 11, 1981**
1999 WM18 RUS 7 0 0 0 6 —
2005 WM RUS 6 0 1 1 2 B

**Fyodorov, Sergei / b. Dec. 13, 1969**
1987-89 WM20 URS 20 9 15 24 12 G,S
1989-2010 WM URS 38 17 16 33 40 3G,S
1991-96 WCH URS 10 5 5 10 8 —
1998-2010 OG-M RUS 16 3 11 14 18 S,B

**Fyodorov, Yevgeni / b. Nov. 11, 1980**
2000 WM20 RUS 7 1 4 5 4 S

**Fyodorov, Yuri / b. July 8, 1949**
1975-78 WM URS 20 1 4 5 7 2G

**Gaare, Frode / b. unknown**
1979 WM20 NOR 5 0 0 0 0 —

**Gabdulin, Rustem / b. Nov. 20, 1977**
1997 WM20 RUS 6 1 1 2 0 B

**Gabrielsen, Jonas / b. June 10, 1982**
1999 WM18 NOR 6 0 0 0 2 —

**Gabris, Ladislav / b. Mar. 18, 1981**
2001 WM20 SVK 7 0 1 1 2 —

**Gachet, Stephane / b. Jan. 18, 1974**
1998 WM FRA 3 0 0 0 0 —

**Gagne, Emil / b. unknown / d. unknown**
1949 WM CAN 5 4 — 4 — S

**Gagner, Dave / b. Dec. 11, 1964**
1984 WM20 CAN 7 4 2 6 4 —
1993 WM CAN 8 3 1 4 6 —
1984 OG-M CAN 7 5 2 7 6 —

**Gagnon, Aaron / b. Apr. 24, 1986**
2004 WM18 CAN 7 0 3 3 10 —

**Gagnon, Charles "Bus" / b. Nov. 28, 1926**
1958 WM CAN 6 7 3 10 6 G

**Gahn, Kristian / b. Feb. 17, 1972**
1991-92 WM20 SWE 14 8 9 17 12 S
2000 WM SWE 7 1 2 3 10 —

**Gailer, Peter / b. Feb. 6, 1956**
1981-82 WM FRG 15 2 3 5 20 —

**Gailland, Jeremy / b. Apr. 6, 1988**
2005 WM18 SUI 6 0 0 0 2 —

**Gainey, Bob / b. Dec. 13, 1953**
1982-83 WM CAN 20 2 7 9 2 2B
1976-81 CC CAN 12 3 3 6 4 1st,2nd

**Gajdos, Peter / b. Feb. 13, 1982**
2000 WM18 SVK 6 0 0 0 8 —
2002 WM20 SVK 6 0 2 2 6 —

**Galambos, Peter / b. June 14, 1989**
2007 WM18 SVK 6 0 0 0 2 —

**Galanov, Maxim / b. Mar. 13, 1974**
1993 WM20 RUS 7 1 0 1 4 —
2000 WM RUS 6 0 0 0 0 —

**Galarneau, Michel / b. Mar. 1, 1961**
1995 WM FRA 6 1 1 2 2 —

**Galchenyuk, Alexander / b. July 28, 1967**
1986-87 WM20 URS 13 2 3 5 12 G
1998-2001 WM BLR 24 1 3 4 26 —
1991 CC URS 5 0 1 1 0 —
1998 OG-M BLR 7 1 2 3 0 —

**Galiani, Ed / b. June 6, 1960**
1990 WM USA 3 0 1 1 0 —

**Galimov, Alexander / b. May 2, 1985 / d. Sept. 12, 2011**
2005 WM20 RUS 6 1 2 3 0 S
~perished as a result of injuries sustained in Yaroslavl plane crash on Sept. 7, 2011

**Galipeau, Oscar "Gus" / b. 1922 / d. unknown**
1947 WM USA 7 4 — 4 — —

**Gall, Sandor / b. Nov. 23, 1955**
1977 WM ROM 10 1 2 3 13 —
1976-80 OG-M ROM 10 1 4 5 10 —

**Gallagher, John / b. unknown**
1950 WM USA 7 0 0 0 4 S

**Galland, Moe / b. 1929**
1954 WM CAN 7 16 4 20 0 S

**Gallant, Gerard / b. Sept. 2, 1963**
1989 WM CAN 8 2 3 5 10 S

**Galley, Garry / b. Apr. 16, 1963**
1993-96 WM CAN 16 1 4 5 6 S

**Gallo, Peter / b. Jan. 12, 1978**
1998 WM20 SVK 6 1 1 2 4 —

**Gallstedt, Niklas / b. Feb. 7, 1967**
1987 WM20 SWE 5 0 2 2 0 B

**Galvas, Lukas / b. Mar. 28, 1979**
1998-99 WM20 CZE 13 1 2 3 24 —

**Galyuk, Olexi / b. Aug. 4, 1983**
2001 WM18 UKR 6 0 0 0 0 —

**Gambucci, Andre / b. Nov. 12, 1928**
1952 OG-M USA 8 4 2 6 — S

**Gambucci, Gary / b. Sept. 27, 1946**
1969-76 WM USA 30 9 8 17 27 —

**Gandini, Dave / b. Mar. 6, 1958**
1977 WM20 USA 7 3 4 7 0 —

**Gandorfer, Thomas / b. June 9, 1959**
1978 WM20 FRG 6 0 4 4 14 —
1983 WM FRG 1 0 0 0 0 —

**Gansiniec, Alfred / b. Oct. 29, 1919 / d. Mar. 20, 1999**
1947-55 WM POL 15 2 1 3 4 —
1948-52 OG-M POL 13 7 0 7 — —

**Ganster, Fritz / b. Sept. 4, 1960**
1984 OG-M AUT 5 0 0 0 0 —

**Ganz, Bryan / b. Feb. 2, 1972**
1991 WM20 USA 6 0 0 0 4 —

**Gapeyenko, Sergei / b. Apr. 5, 1966**
1986 WM20 URS 7 5 0 5 2 G

**Garbocz, Dariusz / b. Jan. 11, 1971**
1990 WM20 POL 7 1 0 1 2 —
1992 WM POL 6 0 0 0 2 —
1992 OG-M POL 7 0 1 1 6 —

**Garbocz, Michal / b. Febraury 13, 1973**
2002 WM POL 6 0 0 0 2 —

**Garbutt, George / b. June 18, 1903 / d. Sept. 21, 1967**
1931 WM CAN 1 0 — 0 — G
1932 OG-M CAN 1 1 0 1 0 G

**Gardner, Bill / b. May 19, 1960**
1980 WM20 CAN 5 0 4 4 14 —

**Gardner, Bruce / b. unknown**
1950 WM USA 7 7 2 9 2 S

**Gardner, Jim / b. Dec. 16, 1960**
1980 WM20 USA 5 0 2 2 0 —

**Gardon, Radek / b. Apr. 19, 1969**
1988-89 WM20 TCH 14 3 4 7 8 B

**Gardstrom, Tuomas / b. July 12, 1986**
2004 WM18 FIN 6 0 1 1 16 —

**Gare, Danny / b. May 14, 1954**
1976-81 CC CAN 8 1 5 6 2 1st,2nd

**Garlock, Ryan / b. Apr. 24, 1986**
2004 WM18 CAN 7 1 4 5 6 —

**Garpenlov, Johan / b. Mar. 21, 1968**
1987-88 WM20 SWE 14 7 4 11 18 B
1990-92 WM SWE 28 9 5 14 20 2G,S
1991-96 WCH SWE 10 1 2 3 12 —

**Garrison, Jack / b. Feb. 13, 1909 / d. May 13, 1988**
1933 WM USA 5 2 — 2 2 G
1932-36 OG-M USA 13 7 3 10 14 S,B

**Garrity, Jack / b. Apr. 1, 1926**
1948 OG-M USA 3 1 1 2 4 —

**Garten, Marius / b. Feb. 8, 1988**
2006 WM18 GER 6 1 2 3 6 —

**Gartner, Mike / b. Oct. 29, 1959**
1978 WM20 CAN 6 3 3 6 4 B
1981-93 WM CAN 35 14 8 22 38 2B
1984-87 CC CAN 17 5 4 9 16 2/1st

**Garvey, Liam / b. Jan. 2, 1973**
1993 WM20 USA 7 0 0 0 8 —

**Gashkov, Dmytro / b. May 23, 1984**
2001 WM18 UKR 6 0 0 0 2 —

**Gasparini, Leo / b. Jan. 21, 1920 / d. Sep. 9, 1991**
1939 WM ITA 5 0 — 0 — —

**Gasser, Norbert / b. May 18, 1957**
1984 OG-M ITA 5 0 0 0 6 —

**Gatyatulin, Anvar / b. Mar. 21, 1976**
1995 WM20 RUS 7 1 0 1 4 S

**Gaudreau, Rob / b. Mar. 8, 1944**
1968 OG-M USA 6 0 0 0 2 —

**Gaudreau, Rob / b. Jan. 20, 1970**
1990 WM20 USA 7 3 1 4 6 —
1993 WM USA 5 3 3 6 2 —

**Gauf, Don / b. Jan. 1, 1927**
1950 WM CAN 2 2 0 2 4 G
1952 OG-M CAN 7 4 0 4 4 G

**Gaulin, Jean-Marc / b. Mar. 3, 1962**
1981 WM20 CAN 5 2 0 2 4 —

**Gauthier, Denis / b. Oct. 1, 1976**
1996 WM20 CAN 6 1 1 2 6 G

**Gautschi, Marc / b. Dec. 8, 1982**
2000 WM18 SUI 7 1 0 1 2 —

**Gauvin, Joel / b. July 24, 1939**
1968 OG-M FRA 5 0 0 0 11 —

**Gavalier, Michal / b. Jan. 7, 1984**
2002 WM18 SVK 8 0 1 1 8 —
2004 WM20 SVK 6 0 0 0 4 —

**Gavey, Aaron / b. Feb. 22, 1974**
1994 WM20 CAN 7 4 2 6 26 G

**Gavrylyuk, Vitali / b. Oct. 13, 1983**
2000-01 WM18 UKR 11 4 0 4 0 —

**Gazzaroli, Ivan / b. Jan. 1, 1973**
1992 WM20 SUI 7 0 0 0 2 —

**Gburek, Wiktor / b. Nov. 17, 1920 / d. unknown**
1955 WM POL 1 0 0 0 0 —

**Geary, Don / b. July 10, 1926**
1948 OG-M USA 2 0 0 0 0 —

**Gebauer, Andreas / b. Aug. 31, 1965**
1985 WM GDR 7 0 0 0 0 —

**Geffert, Pavel / b. May 7, 1968**
1995 WM CZE 8 1 1 2 2 —
1994 OG-M CZE 5 3 2 5 2 —

**Gegenfurtner, Christian / b. July 1, 1974**
1994 WM20 GER 7 0 0 0 4 —

**Gehri, Rene / b. Jan. 30, 1964**
1984 WM20 SUI 7 1 1 2 0 —

**Geiger, Patrick / b. Nov. 16, 1989**
2007 WM18 GER 6 3 1 4 2 —

**Geiger, Roger / b. unknown**
1978 WM20 SUI 6 0 1 1 0 —

**Geisert, Uwe / b. Dec. 26, 1960**
1985 WM GDR 9 0 0 0 4 —

**Gelinas, Martin / b. June 5, 1970**
1989 WM20 CAN 7 0 2 2 8 —
1998 WM CAN 6 1 0 1 6 —

**Gelzinus, Christian / b. Apr. 17, 1967**
1986 WM20 FRG 7 0 0 0 0 —

**Gendron, Martin / b. Feb. 15, 1974**
1993-94 WM20 CAN 14 11 6 17 8 2G

**Gens, Matt / b. Mar. 31, 1983**
2001 WM18 USA 6 1 0 1 2 —

**Gensel, Hardy / b. Sept. 27, 1982**
2000 WM18 GER 6 2 0 2 4 —

**Gentges, Frank / b. Feb. 25, 1965**
1984-85 WM20 FRG 13 0 0 0 6 —

**Gentile, Brandon / b. Apr. 23, 1987**
2005 WM18 USA 6 0 1 1 2 G

**George, Werner / b. Sept. 12, 1913 / d. unknown**
1934 WM GER 6 2 — 2 — B
1936 OG-M GER 2 0 — 0 — —

**Geran, George "Gerry" / b. Aug. 3, 1896 / d. Sept. 1981**
1920 OG-M USA 2 3 — 3 — S

**Gerarden, Dan / b. July 16, 1962**
1982 WM20 USA 5 0 1 1 8 —

**Gerasimov, Alexander / b. Jan. 3, 1946**
1978-79 WM20 URS 12 4 12 16 6 2G
1984 OG-M URS 7 2 3 5 6 G

**Gerasimov, Kirill / b. unknown**
1976 OG-M BUL 5 2 2 4 0 —

**Gerber, Bruno / b. Feb. 2, 1936**
1959-62 WM SUI 6 1 2 3 6 —

**Gerber, Lukas / b. Sept. 7, 1982**
2002 WM20 SUI 7 0 0 0 6 —
2003 WM SUI 7 0 0 0 8 —

**Gerber, Roland / b. May 21, 1984**
2002 WM18 SUI 8 1 1 2 6 —
2003-04 WM20 SUI 12 1 0 1 6 —

**Gergely, Andras / b. Jan. 20, 1916 / d. unknown**
1933-39 WM HUN 23 3 0 3 0 —
1936 OG-M HUN 2 0 — 0 — —

**Gergely, Laszlo / b. Jan. 20, 1916 / d. 1946**
1935 WM HUN 4 0 — 0 — —
1936 OG-M HUN 4 0 — 0 — —

**Gerhardsson, Peter / b. May 15, 1974**
1994 WM20 SWE 7 0 2 2 0 S

**Gerike, Sven / b. Jan. 5, 1977**
1997 WM20 GER 6 2 2 4 2 —

**Gerli, Umberto / b. Dec. 4, 1925**
1948 OG-M ITA 7 2 — 2 — —

**Gerlovski, Alexei / b. Mar. 27, 1984**
2002 WM18 BLR 8 0 0 0 2 —

**Germann, Reto / b. Oct. 27, 1974**
1994 WM20 SUI 7 1 0 1 2 —

**Geromini, Albert / b. Apr. 10, 1896 / d. Dec. 1961**
1930-39 WM SUI 22 5 1 6 3 3B
1928 OG-M SUI 4 1 — 1 3 B

**Geromini, Franz / b. unknown / d. unknown**
1937-39 WM SUI 23 3 0 3 9 2B

**Gerritsen, Hans / b. 1907 / d. unknown**
1935-39 WM NED 8 0 0 0 — —

**Geyer, Cyrill / b. Mar. 26, 1981**
2005 WM SUI 3 0 0 0 0 —

**Ghedina, Bruno / b. Feb. 21, 1943**
1964 OG-M ITA 6 0 0 0 0 —

**Ghiorghiu, Ion / b. Mar. 5, 1947**
1977 WM ROM 10 0 1 1 0 —
1968-76 OG-M ROM 8 0 2 2 0 —

**Ghezze, Ivo / b. Mar. 3, 1941**
1964 OG-M ITA 7 0 1 1 4 —

**Giachino, Philippe / b. Dec. 29, 1963**
1982 WM20 SUI 7 1 0 1 4 —

**Gianini, Tiziano / b. June 18, 1973**
1992 WM20 SUI 7 0 2 2 12 —

**Gibson, Billy / b. Apr. 22, 1927 / d. Aug. 29, 2006**
1951 WM CAN 6 8 — 8 6 G
1952 OG-M CAN 8 12 7 19 6 G

**Giger, Daniel / b. May 25, 1974**
1994 WM20 SUI 7 0 1 1 14 —

**Gil, Lukasz / b. Sept. 22, 1977**
1997 WM20 POL 6 2 0 2 2 —

**Gil, Piotr / b. Februry 4, 1972**
2002 WM POL 5 0 0 0 0 —

**Gilbert, John / b. unknown**
1955 WM USA 8 0 0 0 4 —

**Gilbert, Rod / b. July 1, 1941**
1977 WM CAN 10 2 2 4 12 —
1972 SS CAN 6 1 3 4 9 1st

**Giles, Curt / b. Nov. 30, 1958**
1982 WM CAN 10 0 1 1 12 B
1992 OG-M CAN 8 1 0 1 6 S

**Gill, Todd / b. Nov. 9, 1965**
1992 WM CAN 6 0 3 3 6 —

**Gillies, Clark / b. Apr. 7, 1954**
1981 CC CAN 7 2 5 7 8 2nd

**Gilligan, Bill / b. Aug. 5, 1954**
1978 WM USA 10 4 1 5 23 —

**Gilmour, Doug / b. June 25, 1963**
1981 WM20 CAN 5 0 0 0 0 —
1990 WM CAN 9 2 4 6 18 —
1987 CC CAN 8 2 0 2 4 1st

**Gimayev, Irek / b. Sept. 2, 1957**
1977 WM20 URS 7 2 3 5 6 G
1979-85 WM URS 26 5 4 9 38 3G,B
1981-84 CC URS 10 1 1 2 8 1st

**Gimayev, Sergei / b. Feb. 16, 1984**
2004 WM20 RUS 6 0 2 2 6 —

**Ginnetti, Robert / b. July 31, 1965**
1992 WM ITA 5 0 0 0 4 —
1992 OG-M ITA 7 2 0 2 6 —

**Gionta, Brian / b. Jan. 18, 1979**
1998-99 WM20 USA 13 11 8 19 10 —
2000-05 WM USA 23 6 2 8 14 —
2006 OG-M USA 6 4 0 4 2 —
~WM20 All-Star Team/Forward (1999)

**Gionta, Stephen / b. Oct. 9, 1983**
2001 WM18 USA 6 2 0 2 4 —

**Girard, Rick / b. May 1, 1974**
1994 WM20 CAN 7 6 3 9 2 G

**Girard, Sylvain / b. May 19, 1972**
1994 OG-M FRA 6 0 1 1 0 —

**Girardin, Pierre / b. Jan. 26, 1962**
1982 WM20 SUI 7 2 2 4 0 —

**Giving, Petter / b. Sept. 1, 1981**
1999 WM18 NOR 6 0 0 0 2 —

**Gjose, Anders / b. Dec. 12, 1984**
2002 WM18 NOR 7 0 3 3 6 —

**Glad, Jarkko / b. July 17, 1973**
1993 WM20 FIN 7 0 1 1 2 —

**Glazachev, Konstantin / b. Feb. 18, 1985**
2003 WM18 RUS 6 2 3 5 20 B

**Glebov, Andrei / b. Mar. 8, 1980**
2007 WM BLR 6 1 0 1 4 —

**Glennie, Brian / b. Aug. 29, 1946**
1968 OG-M CAN 7 0 1 1 10 B

**Globke, Rob / b. Oct. 24, 1982**
2000 WM18 USA 6 4 2 6 6 —
2001-02 WM20 USA 14 4 1 5 12 —

**Gloor, Kevin / b. Apr. 26, 1983**
2003 WM20 SUI 6 1 0 1 2 —

**Glovatski, Vadim / b. Jan. 1, 1970**
1998 WM KAZ 3 1 1 2 2 —
1998 OG-M KAZ 7 0 2 2 6 —

**Glowacki, Franciczek / b. Dec. 15, 1910 / d. May 3, 1989**
1935 WM POL 3 0 — 0 — —

**Glukhov, Mikhail / b. May 13, 1988**
2006 WM18 RUS 6 1 0 1 4 —

**Glushenkov, Viktor / b. Sept. 4, 1960**
1979-80 WM20 URS 11 0 3 3 6 2G

**Gmeiner, Manfred / b. Oct. 2, 1941**
1962-63 WM FRG 11 2 2 4 10 —
1968 OG-M FRG 7 0 0 0 2 —

**Gnidenko, Artyom / b. Feb. 3, 1980**
2004-07 WM UKR 15 0 0 0 12 —

**Gnyazdovsky, Vadym / b. Feb. 22, 1985**
2004 WM20 UKR 6 0 0 0 0 —

**Gobel, Josef / b. June 11, 1905 / d. unknown**
1930-35 WM AUT 22 6 — 6 0 B
1928-36 OG-M AUT 5 2 0 2 2 —

**Goble, George / b. Apr. 26, 1913 / d. unknown**
1937 WM CAN 9 5 3 8 7 G

**Goc, Marcel / b. Aug. 24, 1983**
2003 WM20 GER 6 1 2 3 2 —

**Goc, Sascha / b. Apr. 14, 1979**
1997-98 WM20 GER 12 0 2 2 31 —
1998-2003 WM GER 12 1 4 5 14 —
2004 WCH GER 3 0 0 0 2 —
2006 OG-M GER 5 0 0 0 10 —

**Godeau, Joel / b. Aug. 6, 1945**
1968 OG-M FRA 3 0 0 0 0 —

**Godfrey, Johnny / b. 1918 / d. unknown**
1938 WM CAN 7 2 — 2 — G

**Godlewski, Czeslaw / b. Jan. 4, 1904 / d. Feb. 4, 2001**
1933 WM POL 4 0 — 0 0 —

**Godlewski, Jozef / b. Mar. 26, 1907 / d. Mar. 4, 2004**
1931 WM POL 2 0 — 0 — —

**Godynyuk, Alexander / b. Jan. 27, 1970**
1989-90 WM20 URS 14 3 3 6 6 G,S
1999 WM UKR 3 0 0 0 0 —
~WM20 IIHF Directorate Best Defenceman (1990), WM20 All-Star Team/Defence (1990)

**Goegan, Grant / b. Jan. 15, 1955**
1982-83 WM ITA 17 2 2 4 8 —
1984 OG-M ITA 5 3 1 4 4 —

**Goeminne, Paul / b. 1888 / d. unknown**
1920 OG-M BEL 1 0 0 0 — —

**Gogala, Joze / b. Apr. 23, 1916 / d. unknown**
1939 WM YUG 5 1 — 1 — —

**Goheen, Frank "Moose" / b. Feb. 9, 1894 / d. Nov. 13, 1979**
1920 OG-M USA 4 7 — 7 7 S

**Goicoechea, Yannick / b. Apr. 2, 1965**
1992 WM FRA 6 0 0 0 2 —

**Gojanovic, Miroslav / b. Apr. 20, 1949**
1968-76 OG-M YUG 8 1 1 2 0 —

**Golaz, Milo / b. Sept. 21, 1927**
1950-55 WM SUI 12 1 0 1 12 2B
1952-56 OG-M SUI 13 3 1 4 2 —

**Golden, Mike / b. June 17, 1965**
1984 WM20 USA 7 1 3 4 0 —

**Goldmann, Erich / b. Apr. 7, 1976**
1994-96 WM20 GER 20 4 4 8 32 —
1996-2004 WM GER 35 1 1 2 28 —
1996 WCH GER 3 0 1 1 2 —
1998-2002 OG-M GER 11 0 1 1 54 —

**Goldsworthy, Bill / b. Aug. 24, 1944 / d. Mar. 29, 1996**
1972 SS CAN 3 1 1 2 4 1st

**Golinski, Adam / b. Feb. 10, 1966**
1985 WM20 POL 7 1 0 1 6 —

**Golikov, Alexander / b. Nov. 26, 1952**
1976-79 WM URS 38 11 14 25 6 2G,S,B
1976 CC URS 2 0 1 1 2 —
1980 OG-M URS 7 7 6 13 6 S

**Golikov, Vladimir / b. June 10, 1954**
1976-82 WM URS 46 19 19 38 18 4G,S
1981 CC URS 7 3 0 3 4 1st
1980 OG-M URS 7 2 5 7 2 S

**Golonka, Jozef / b. Jan. 6, 1938**
1959-69 WM TCH 39 21 24 45 24 2S,2B
1960-68 OG-M TCH 21 13 12 25 22 S,B
~IIHF Hall of Fame

**Golovin, Alexander / b. Mar. 26, 1983**
2001 WM18 RUS 6 2 3 5 0 G

**Golovkov, Vladimir / b. July 28, 1960**
1979-80 WM20 URS 11 3 2 5 0 2G

**Golts, Alexander / b. Mar. 12, 1972**
2001 WM RUS 7 2 2 4 2 —

**Golts, Alexander / b. Mar. 19, 1980**
2000 WM20 KAZ 7 0 0 0 6 —

**Golubev, Alexei / b. Jan. 26, 1988**
2006 WM18 BLR 6 0 0 0 8 —

**Gomez, Scott / b. Dec. 23, 1979**
1998-99 WM20 USA 13 4 7 11 6 —
2004 WCH USA 5 1 3 4 0 —
2006 OG-M USA 6 1 4 5 10 —

**Gomolyako, Sergei / b. Jan. 19, 1970**
1989 WM20 URS 7 4 2 6 4 G

**Goncharenko, Viktor / b. May 10, 1969**
1999 WM UKR 3 0 0 0 0 —

**Gonera, Sebastian / b. Dec. 18, 1971**
1992-2002 WM POL 12 1 2 3 0 —

**Goodman, Magnus "Mike" / b. Mar. 18, 1898 / d. July 18, 1991**
1920 OG-M CAN 3 3 — 3 — G

**Goosens, Jean Maurice / b. 1892 / d. unknown**
1920 OG-M BEL 1 0 0 0 — —

**Goralczyk, Feliks / b. June 16, 1950 / d. Jan. 14, 1980**
1970 WM POL 8 3 1 4 4 —
1972 OG-M POL 5 2 0 2 0 —

**Goralczyk, Robert / b. Mar. 21, 1943 / d. May 18, 1984**
1966-76 WM POL 43 4 4 8 33 —
1972-76 OG-M POL 7 0 0 0 0 —

**Gorbachyov, Eduard / b. Mar. 18, 1969**
1994 WM RUS 3 1 0 1 4 —

**Gorban, Yevgeni / b. Feb. 28, 1986**
2003 WM18 KAZ 6 0 3 3 8 —

**Gorbatuk, Olexander / b. Feb. 20, 1981**
1999 WM18 UKR 6 0 0 0 6 —

**Gorbenko, Vasyl / b. Jan. 14, 1982**
2000 WM18 UKR 6 0 1 1 18 —
2000 WM20 UKR 7 0 1 1 0 —

**Gorbunov, Sergei / b. May 20, 1963**
1983 WM20 URS 7 1 2 3 6 G

**Gordiyuk, Viktor / b. Apr. 11, 1970**
1989-90 WM20 URS 14 6 10 16 2 G,S
1991 CC URS 5 0 2 2 0 —

**Gordon, Boyd / b. Oct. 19, 1983**
2003 WM20 CAN 6 0 0 0 0 S

**Gordon, Grant / b. Oct. 1900 / d. unknown**
1928 OG-M CAN 1 0 — 0 — G

**Gordon, Robb / b. Jan. 13, 1976**
1996 WM20 CAN 6 0 4 4 0 G

**Gorenc, Marjan / b. Feb. 27, 1964**
1984 OG-M YUG 5 0 0 0 0 —

**Gorence, Tom / b. Mar. 11, 1957**
1982 WM USA 7 1 1 2 2 —
1981 CC USA 6 1 1 2 2 —

**Gorgenlander, Rudolf / b. Jan. 5, 1974**
1994 WM20 GER 7 1 0 1 8 —

**Goring, Butch / b. Oct. 22, 1949**
1981 CC CAN 7 3 2 5 4 2nd

**Gorokhov, Ilya / b. Aug. 23, 1977**
1996-97 WM20 RUS 13 0 2 2 8 2B

**Gorulko, Yuriy / b. Mar. 9, 1977**
1996 WM20 UKR 6 1 1 2 2 —

**Gosselin, George / b. Mar. 5, 1931**
1958-59 WM CAN 13 11 5 16 8 2G

**Gosselin, Guy / b. Jan. 6, 1964**
1986-91 WM USA 28 3 1 4 20 —
1988-92 OG-M USA 14 0 3 3 8 —

**Gossweiler, Manuel / b. Mar. 16, 1983**
2001 WM18 SUI 7 0 0 0 8 S

**Gosztonyi, Bela / b. Nov. 27, 1917 / d. unknown**
1939 WM HUN 4 0 — 0 — —

**Gosztyla, Bronislaw / b. Oct. 11, 1935 / d. Oct. 18, 1991**
1955-66 WM POL 31 5 6 11 21 —
1956-64 OG-M POL 12 7 6 13 4 —

**Gotalski, Jerzy / b. Oct. 12, 1957**
1977 WM20 POL 7 0 0 0 2 —

**Gotsch, Klaus / b. June 20, 1961**
1980-81 WM20 FRG 10 5 3 8 12 —

**Gottwald, Stephan / b. Sept. 20, 1983**
2001 WM18 GER 6 4 0 4 0 —

**Gotziaman, Chris / b. Nov. 29, 1971**
1991 WM20 USA 8 5 2 7 4 —

**Goulet, Michel / b. Apr. 21, 1960**
1983 WM CAN 10 1 8 9 6 B
1984-87 CC CAN 16 7 9 16 0 2/1st

**Govedaris, Chris / b. Feb. 2, 1970**
1995 WM CAN 8 1 0 1 6 B

**Govorun, Olexander / b. Mar. 4, 1975**
1995 WM20 UKR 7 0 0 0 0 —

**Gozzi, Anders / b. July 12, 1967**
1987 WM20 SWE 7 2 3 5 4 B

**Grabovsky, Ladislav / b. unknown**
1957 WM TCH 5 5 0 5 — B

**Grace, Norman / b. Dec. 11, 1907 / d. unknown**
1930-31 WM GBR 5 0 0 0 — —

**Grace, Tommy / b. Feb. 15, 1914 / d. unknown**
1939 WM GBR 2 0 — 0 — —

**Grade, Jeff / b. Apr. 1, 1963**
1981 WM20 USA 5 1 0 1 12 —

**Gradin, Peter / b. Dec. 9, 1958**
1985 WM SWE 9 3 1 4 6 —
1984 OG-M SWE 7 9 4 13 6 B

**Gradin, Thomas / b. Feb. 18, 1956**
1978 WM SWE 10 2 1 3 0 —
1981-84 CC SWE 13 3 4 7 10 —

**Graeffe, Jimmy / b. July 7, 1921 / d. unknown**
1939-50 WM BEL 11 1 0 1 2 —

**Graf, Markus / b. July 27, 1959**
1978 WM20 SUI 6 0 0 0 0 —

**Grafstrom, Myron / b. Aug. 3, 1933**
1965 WM USA 5 0 0 0 0 —

**Grafstrom, Sam / b. Dec. 16, 1935**
1961-65 WM USA 12 1 6 7 0 —

**Gragnani, Marc-Andre / b. Mar. 11, 1987**
2005 WM18 CAN 6 0 3 3 0 S

**Graham, Dirk / b. July 29, 1959**
1987 WM CAN 9 0 3 3 8 —
1991 CC CAN 8 3 1 4 0 1st

**Graiziger, Bob / b. Sept. 26, 1921 / d. unknown**
1950 WM USA 6 1 0 1 8 S

**Granath, Einar / b. Oct. 28, 1936 / d. Jan. 5, 1993**
1960 OG-M SWE 5 1 2 3 2 —

**Granato, Tony / b. July 25, 1964**
1983-84 WM20 USA 14 5 3 8 10 —
1985-87 WM USA 26 8 12 20 30 —
1991 CC USA 7 1 2 3 12 2nd
1988 OG-M USA 6 1 7 8 4 —

**Grando, Daniel / b. June 20, 1948**
1968 OG-M FRA 4 0 0 0 0 —

**Grandtner, Ivan / b. Jan. 10, 1943**
1967 WM TCH 5 1 0 1 0 —

**Granholm, Svante / b. Mar. 15, 1947**
1968 OG-M SWE 6 1 0 1 4 —

**Granlund, Svante / b. Feb. 1, 1921 / d. Nov. 28, 2010**
1948 OG-M SWE 6 3 — 3 — —

**Granstedt, Michael / b. Aug. 9, 1961**
1981 WM20 SWE 5 2 0 2 2 G

**Granstrom, Holger / b. Dec. 25, 1917 / d. July 22, 1941**
1939 WM FIN 5 4 — 4 — —

**Grant, Gordon / b. Mar. 31, 1905 / d. unknown**
1930 WM CAN 1 2 — 2 — G

**Grant, Joe / b. Jan. 23, 1957**
1980 OG-M CAN 6 0 1 1 2 —

**Grant, Perley / b. unknown**
1947 WM USA 7 7 — 7 — —

**Grant, Petre / b. July 25, 1904 / d. unknown**
1931-33 WM ROM 8 2 0 2 0 —

**Grant, Serban / b. unknown / d. unknown**
1931-33 WM ROM 9 0 — 0 0 —

**Grasberg, Gustav / b. Apr. 6, 1983**
2001 WM18 SWE 6 1 2 3 10 —
2002 WM20 SWE 7 0 0 0 29 —

**Gratton, Chris / b. July 5, 1975**
1993 WM20 CAN 7 2 2 4 6 G
1997-98 WM CAN 15 1 5 6 18 G

**Gratton, Dan / b. Dec. 17, 1966**
1985 WM20 CAN 7 2 3 5 16 G

**Graul, Thomas / b. Mar. 15, 1962**
1983-85 WM GDR 20 4 6 10 6 —

**Grauwiler, Stefan / b. Apr. 12, 1977**
1997 WM20 SUI 6 0 0 0 10 —

**Gravelle, Orval / b. Dec. 7, 1927 / d. Jan. 18, 1997**
1948 OG-M CAN 8 3 — 3 4 G

**Graves, Adam / b. Apr. 12, 1968**
1988 WM20 CAN 7 5 0 5 4 G
1993-99 WM CAN 18 7 5 12 16 —
1996 WCH CAN 7 0 1 1 2 2nd

**Gravnaas, Jorgen / b. Sept. 8, 1981**
1999 WM18 NOR 6 0 0 0 2 —

**Gray, Dick / b. Mar. 14, 1920 / d. unknown**
1951 WM CAN 6 3 — 3 4 G

**Gray, Norm / b. 1930 / d. Oct. 22, 2008**
1954 WM CAN 7 5 4 9 6 S

**Grazia, Gene / b. July 29, 1934**
1959 WM USA 7 2 0 2 0 —
1960 OG-M USA 2 0 0 0 0 G

**Grebennikov, Vladimir / b. Aug. 2, 1932 / d. Dec. 19, 1992**
1957 WM URS 4 4 0 4 — S
1960 OG-M URS 7 4 4 8 4 B

**Greely, Walt / b. unknown**
1955 WM USA 8 1 0 1 0 —

**Green, Art / b. May 12, 1921 / d. unknown**
1939 WM GBR 1 0 0 0 — —
1948 OG-M GBR 6 1 — 1 — —

**Green, Frank / b. Nov. 16, 1918 / d. unknown**
1948 OG-M GBR 8 15 — 15 — —

**Green, Mark / b. Feb. 11, 1958**
1978 WM20 USA 6 7 5 12 18 —

**Greene, Matt / b. May 13, 1983**
2003 WM20 USA 7 0 1 1 34 —

**Green, Rick / b. Feb. 20, 1956**
1979-90 WM CAN 34 2 7 9 8 B

**Green, Travis / b. Dec. 20, 1970**
1996-98 WM CAN 25 8 12 20 22 G,S

**Greenbank, Kelly / b. Nov. 17, 1955**
1984-88 OG-M AUT 11 0 3 3 12 —

**Greenlaw, Jeff / b. Feb. 28, 1968**
1986 WM20 CAN 7 3 1 4 4 S

**Greenwood, Harold / b. Nov. 15, 1894 / d. 1978**
1928 OG-M GBR — — — — — —

**Gregg, Randy / b. Feb. 19, 1956**
1984 CC CAN 3 0 1 1 4 1st
1980-88 OG-M CAN 14 2 3 5 10 —

**Gregor, Frantisek / b. Dec. 8, 1938**
1961-63 WM TCH 11 2 3 5 0 S,B
1964 OG-M TCH 7 1 1 2 0 B

**Gregoric, Otokar / b. unknown / d. unknown**
1939 WM YUG 5 0 — 0 — —

**Grein, Andre / b. Jan. 22, 1973**
1993 WM20 GER 7 4 1 5 10 —

**Greiner, Dieter / b. Dec. 27, 1937**
1959 WM GDR 5 0 0 0 6 —

**Gretzky, Wayne / b. Jan. 26, 1961**
1978 WM20 CAN 6 8 9 17 2 B
1982 WM CAN 10 6 8 14 0 B
1981-96 WCH CAN 39 20 43 63 10 3/1st,2/2nd
1998 OG-M CAN 6 0 4 4 2 —
~IIHF Hall of Fame
~WM20 IIHF Directorate Best Forward (1978), WM20 All-Star Team/Forward (1978), WM All-Star Team/Forward (1982)

**Grey, Mike / b. Apr. 28, 1975**
2003-05 WM DEN 18 3 0 3 6 —

**Gribko, Yevgeni / b. Apr. 3, 1973**
1995 WM RUS 6 0 0 0 2 —

**Grier, Mike / b. Jan. 5, 1975**
1995 WM20 USA 7 0 2 2 12 —
2004 WM USA 9 1 2 3 8 B

**Griffin, Joe / b. unknown / d. unknown**
1930 WM CAN 1 1 — 1 — G

**Griffin, Ron / b. May 16, 1958**
1978 WM20 USA 6 0 0 0 0 —

**Griffith, Steve / b. Mar. 12, 1961**
1981 WM20 USA 5 0 3 3 6 —
1984 OG-M USA 5 0 0 0 0 —

**Griga, Yvan / b. June 12, 1963**
1982 WM20 SUI 7 0 3 3 18 —

**Grigalauskas, Juozas / b. unknown / d. unknown**
1938 WM LTU 4 0 — 0 — —

**Grigorenko, Igor / b. Apr. 9, 1983**
2001 WM18 RUS 6 6 4 10 8 G
2002-03 WM20 RUS 13 7 6 13 8 2G
2003-06 WM RUS 14 3 3 6 24 —
~WM20 IIHF Directorate Best Forward (2003), WM20 All-Star Team/Forward (2003)

**Grigortsevich, Denis / b. Mar. 2, 1980**
1999 WM20 BLR 6 0 0 0 8 —

**Grimaldi, Joe / b. Aug. 23, 1986**
2004 WM18 USA 6 0 0 0 2 S

**Grimm, Siegried / b. Feb. 27, 1940**
1961 WM GDR 6 2 0 2 0 —

**Grishenko, Alexei / b. Mar. 10, 1965**
1985 WM20 URS 7 2 3 5 4 B

**Grocott, John / b. unknown**
1955 WM USA 8 1 0 1 10 —

**Grodinski, Dmitri / b. Feb. 20, 1984**
2002 WM18 BLR 8 0 0 0 4 —

**Groenteman, Dick / b. unknown**
1950 WM NED 4 0 0 0 0 —

**Grof, Jakub / b. May 16, 1981**
2001 WM20 CZE 7 0 0 0 2 G

**Groger, Andy / b. Nov. 3, 1958**
1977 WM20 FRG 7 0 0 0 4 —

**Groger, Thomas / b. Feb. 24, 1966**
1985-86 WM20 FRG 14 4 1 5 6 —

**Gron, Tomas / b. Jan. 6, 1981**
1999 WM18 SVK 7 1 0 1 4 B

**Gronlund, Tommi / b. Oct. 11, 1973**
1991 WM20 FIN 4 0 0 0 2 —

**Gronman, Tuomas / b. Mar. 22, 1974**
1992-94 WM20 FIN 21 2 6 8 34 —
1998 OG-M FIN 4 0 0 0 2 B

**Gronstrand, Jari / b. Nov. 14, 1962**
1986 WM FIN 9 0 2 2 8 —
1987 CC FIN 4 0 0 0 0 —

**Gronvall, Janne / b. July 17, 1973**
1991-93 WM20 FIN 20 3 3 6 22 —
2001 WM FIN 7 0 0 0 8 S
~WM20 IIHF Directorate Best Defenceman (1993), WM20 All-Star Team/Defence (1992)

**Grosev, Yevgeni / b. Apr. 3, 1937**
1959 WM URS 8 6 4 10 8 S
1960 OG-M URS 7 4 3 7 6 B

**Gross, Alexander / b. Aug. 19, 1959**
1978-79 WM20 FRG 10 0 3 3 0 —

**Gross, Aug. "Gustav" / b. Jan. 19, 1926**
1948 OG-M AUT 6 7 — 7 — —

**Gross, Jakob / b. Feb. 17, 1960**
1980 WM20 SUI 5 0 1 1 0 —

**Gross, Pavel / b. May 11, 1968**
1988 WM20 TCH 7 3 1 4 14 —

**Gross, Remo / b. Feb. 17, 1960**
1980 WM20 SUI 5 1 0 1 8 —

**Grot, Denis / b. Jan. 6, 1984**
2002 WM18 RUS 8 0 2 2 10 S
2004 WM20 RUS 6 0 0 0 6 —

**Groulx, Wayne / b. Feb. 2, 1965**
1993 WM AUT 6 0 0 0 10 —

**Gruber, Alexander / b. unknown**
1981 WM20 AUT 5 0 0 0 0 —

**Gruber, Ingemar / b. Mar. 25, 1977**
2000-02 WM ITA 12 0 1 1 2 —

**Gruber, Marco / b. May 29, 1983**
2001 WM18 SUI 7 1 1 2 4 S

**Gruden, John / b. June 4, 1970**
2003 WM USA 6 0 1 1 4 —

**Gruth, Henryk / b. Sept. 2, 1957**
1977 WM20 POL 6 0 0 0 2 —
1975-92 WM POL 53 4 4 8 24 —
1980-92 OG-M POL 24 0 5 5 6 —
~IIHF Hall of Fame

**Grygiel, Adrian / b. Aug. 13, 1983**
2001 WM18 GER 6 1 1 2 2 —
2003 WM20 GER 6 0 1 1 4 —

**Grzesiczek, Engelbert / b. Feb. 17, 1963**
1983 WM20 FRG 7 1 1 2 4 —

**Gschliesser, Alexander / b. May 11, 1973**
1998 WM ITA 6 0 0 0 4 —
1994 OG-M ITA 5 0 0 0 0 —

**Gschmeidler, Mario / b. Sept. 3, 1981**
1999 WM18 GER 6 1 0 1 6 —

**Gschwill, Timo / b. Mar. 5, 1972**
1992 WM20 GER 6 1 0 1 6 —

**Guay, Paul / b. Sept. 2, 1963**
1984 OG-M USA 6 1 0 1 8 —

**Gudas, Leo / b. May 20, 1965**
1985 WM20 TCH 7 1 3 4 14 S
1989-93 WM TCH 34 4 9 13 50 4B
1991 CC TCH 5 1 0 1 10 —
1992 OG-M TCH 8 0 2 2 6 B

**Gueguen, Thomas / b. July 24, 1982**
2002 WM20 FRA 6 0 0 0 4 —

**Guennelon, Gerald / b. June 22, 1967**
1992-99 WM FRA 11 0 0 0 12 —
1992-94 OG-M FRA 14 0 1 1 6 —

**Guerin, Bill / b. Nov. 9, 1970**
1989-90 WM20 USA 14 0 3 3 34 —
1996-2004 WCH USA 12 2 4 6 25 1st
1998-2006 OG-M USA 16 5 3 8 6 S

**Guggemos, George / b. Jan. 9, 1927**
1953 WM FRG 4 2 2 4 4 S
1952 OG-M FRG 8 1 1 2 — —

**Guggemos, Markus / b. Mar. 9, 1982**
1999-2000 WM18 GER 12 2 1 3 8 —

**Guggenbuhl, Walter / b. unknown**
1951 WM SUI 6 0 — 0 0 B

**Guignard, Fabian / b. Feb. 15, 1976**
1996 WM20 SUI 6 0 0 0 8 —

**Guilhem, Gael / b. Sept. 7, 1982**
2002 WM20 FRA 6 0 0 0 0 —

**Guillemard, Franck / b. Apr. 28, 1975**
1999 WM FRA 3 0 0 0 0 —

**Gulbrandsen, Bjorn / b. Sept. 17, 1925**
1949-54 WM NOR 20 19 1 20 4 —
1952 OG-M NOR 8 3 1 4 — —

**Gulbrandsen, Bjorn / b. Jan. 9, 1927 / d. May 20, 1988**
1954 WM NOR 4 0 — 0 0 —
1952 OG-M NOR 6 0 1 1 — —

**Gulda, Peter / b. July 4, 1966**
1994 WM GER 5 0 2 2 2 —

**Guliavtsev, Alexander / b. May 3, 1973**
1993 WM20 RUS 6 1 3 4 2 —

**Gulliksen, Rune / b. Jan. 23, 1963**
1983 WM20 NOR 7 4 0 4 4 —
1990 WM NOR 9 0 0 0 4 —
1988-92 OG-M NOR 11 1 1 2 6 —

**Gundersen, Carl / b. Sept. 1, 1967**
1990-93 WM NOR 22 1 2 3 26 —
1992 OG-M NOR 7 1 0 1 4 —

**Gundersen, Finn / b. Apr. 16, 1933**
1951-54 WM NOR 12 0 0 0 2 —
1952 OG-M NOR 8 0 0 0 — —

**Gundersen, Ingmar / b. unknown**
1983 WM20 NOR 5 0 0 0 0 —

**Gundersen, Jarle / b. Feb. 13, 1972**
1991 WM20 NOR 6 0 0 0 0 —

**Gundersen, Tor / b. Sept. 5, 1933**
1958-62 WM NOR 21 1 2 3 20 —
1964-68 OG-M NOR 11 2 0 2 4 —

**Gundmundsson, Martin / b. Aug. 21, 1986**
2004 WM18 SWE 6 0 1 1 0 —

**Gunko, Yuriy / b. Feb. 28, 1972**
1999-2007 WM UKR 38 2 4 6 40 —
2002 OG-M UKR 4 0 1 1 4 —

**Gunther, Petri / b. Aug. 20, 1973**
1992 WM20 FIN 4 1 1 2 2 —

**Guntner, Michael / b. Jan. 3, 1968**
1993-99 WM AUT 24 1 1 2 26 —
1994 OG-M AUT 4 0 0 0 2 —

**Gurcik, Pavol / b. Jan. 21, 1985**
2003 WM18 SVK 7 0 1 1 2 S

**Guren, Miroslav / b. Sept. 24, 1976**
1995-96 WM20 CZE 13 0 2 2 6 —

**Guryev, Alexander / b. Jan. 8, 1958**
1978 WM20 URS 7 1 6 7 2 G

**Guryshev, Alexei / b. Mar. 14, 1925 / d. Nov. 16, 1983**
1954-59 WM URS 33 28 9 37 6 G,4S
1956 OG-M URS 7 7 2 9 0 G

**Gusarov, Alexei / b. July 8, 1964**
1984 WM20 URS 7 4 5 9 8 G
1985-91 WM URS 58 8 13 21 32 3G,S,2B
1984-91 CC URS 13 1 3 4 10 2nd
1988-98 OG-M RUS 14 1 4 5 14 G,S
~Triple Gold Club
~WM20 IIHF Directorate Best Defenceman (1984), WM20 All-Star Team/Defence (1984)

**Guscetti, Gabriele / b. Sept. 1, 1960**
1980 WM20 SUI 5 0 0 0 4 —

**Gusev, Alexander / b. Jan. 21, 1947**
1972-77 WM URS 37 11 15 26 18 2G,S,B
1972 SS URS 6 1 0 1 2 2nd
1976 CC URS 5 0 5 5 0 —
1976 OG-M URS 5 1 2 3 2 G
~WM All-Star Team/Defence (1973)

**Gusev, Konstantin / b. Sept. 27, 1979**
1999 WM20 RUS 7 0 1 1 0 G

**Gusev, Sergei / b. July 31, 1975**
1995 WM20 RUS 7 1 2 3 4 S
2002-05 WM RUS 18 1 2 3 2 S,B

**Gusev, Vladimir / b. Nov. 24, 1982**
2000 WM18 RUS 6 1 1 2 4 S

**Guskov, Alexander / b. Nov. 26, 1976**
2002-04 WM RUS 21 1 4 5 16 S

**Gusmanov, Ravil / b. July 25, 1972**
1992 WM20 RUS 7 1 1 2 0 G
1999-2002 WM RUS 20 7 9 16 12 S
1994 OG-M RUS 8 3 1 4 0 —

**Gusov, Vyacheslav / b. Jan. 1, 1985**
2003 WM18 BLR 4 0 1 1 4 —

**Gustafsson, Bengt-Ake / b. Mar. 23, 1958**
1977-78 WM20 SWE 14 4 8 12 16 S
1979-91 WM SWE 44 12 24 36 24 2G,S,B
1984-87 CC SWE 11 4 3 7 6 2nd
1992 OG-M SWE 6 0 1 1 0 —
~IIHF Hall of Fame

**Gustafsson, Juha / b. Apr. 26, 1979**
1999 WM20 FIN 6 1 1 2 0 —

**Gustafsson, Per / b. June 6, 1970**
1996-2003 WM SWE 9 2 2 4 2 S

**Gustafsson, Per / b. Jan. 25, 1977**
1997 WM20 SWE 6 0 0 0 0 —

**Gut, Karel / b. Sept. 16, 1927**
1954-59 WM TCH 35 11 5 16 4 3B
1952-60 OG-M TCH 22 4 11 15 6 —
~IIHF Hall of Fame
~WM IIHF Directorate Best Defenceman (1955)

**Guttowski, Bruno / b. Nov. 8, 1924**
1953-59 WM FRG 27 6 2 8 10 S
1956 OG-M FRG 6 1 1 2 8 —

**Guy, Chris / b. July 30, 1962**
1982 WM20 USA 7 0 0 0 2 —

**Guyaz, Gilles / b. Mar. 9, 1972**
1992 WM20 SUI 7 0 1 1 2 —

**Guyaz, Noel / b. May 10, 1972**
1991-92 WM20 SUI 14 1 1 2 12 —

**Guyer, Gino / b. Oct. 14, 1983**
2003 WM20 USA 7 1 2 3 4 —

**Guzzo, Patrick / b. Oct. 14, 1917 / d. 1993**
1948 OG-M CAN 8 5 — 5 8 G

**Haagensen, Svein / b. Nov. 23, 1939**
1965 WM NOR 7 1 0 1 0 —
1968-72 OG-M NOR 8 5 0 5 6 —

**Haanpaa, Ari / b. Nov. 29, 1965**
1984-85 WM20 FIN 14 11 4 15 12 S

**Haapakoski, Mikko / b. Jan. 19, 1967**
1986-87 WM20 FIN 14 2 3 5 10 G
1993 WM FIN 6 0 1 1 4 —

**Haapalainen, Hannu / b. Feb. 28, 1951**
1977-82 WM FIN 23 1 2 3 6 —
1976-80 OG-M FIN 12 1 1 2 8 —

**Haapaniemi, Harri / b. June 2, 1960**
1980 WM20 FIN 5 0 0 0 0 S

**Haapaniemi, Matti / b. May 27, 1939**
1959-61 WM FIN 14 0 0 0 6 —

**Haas, Derek / b. May 1, 1955**
1988 OG-M FRA 6 2 0 2 2 —

**Haas, Julius / b. Sept. 28, 1948**
1970-72 WM TCH 15 11 3 14 8 G,B

**Haberl, Dieter / b. unknown**
1981 WM20 AUT 5 0 1 1 2 —

**Habisreutinger, Bruno / b. Mar. 5, 1975**
1994 WM20 SUI 7 0 0 0 4 —

**Habscheid, Marc / b. Mar. 1, 1963**
1982 WM20 CAN 7 6 6 12 2 G
1992 WM CAN 6 1 0 1 4 —
1988 OG-M CAN 8 5 3 8 6 —

**Hachula, Andrzej / b. Aug. 6, 1960**
1984 OG-M POL 6 0 2 2 0 —

**Hackert, Axel / b. Dec. 14, 1984**
2002 WM18 GER 8 3 1 4 0 —

**Hadfield, Vic / b. Oct. 4, 1940**
1972 SS CAN 2 0 0 0 0 1st

**Haffner, Rolf / b. Feb. 9, 1913 / d. unknown**
1937 WM GER 9 0 0 0 2 —

**Hafner, Adolf / b. Jan. 5, 1926**
1947 WM AUT 3 0 — 0 — B
1956 OG-M AUT 6 0 1 1 2 —

**Hafner, Eduard / b. Jan. 19, 1955**
1976-84 OG-M YUG 10 4 3 7 0 —

**Hagberg, Marius / b. Feb. 5, 1989**
2006 WM18 NOR 6 0 0 0 2 —

**Hagelberg, Jaakko / b. Nov. 3, 1982**
2000 WM18 FIN 7 1 3 4 6 G

**Hagelin, Bobbie / b. Feb. 1, 1984**
2002 WM18 SWE 2 0 0 0 2 —

**Hagfors, Per / b. unknown**
1951 WM NOR 6 0 — 0 0 —

**Haggarty, Jim / b. Apr. 14, 1914 / d. Mar. 8, 1998**
1936 OG-M CAN 2 2 3 5 0 S

**Haggerty, Sean / b. Feb. 11, 1976**
1995 WM20 USA 7 1 6 7 8 —
2000 WM USA 7 1 1 2 8 —

**Hagglund, Roger / b. July 2, 1961 / d. June 6, 1992**
1981 WM20 SWE 5 3 4 7 6 G
1982-83 WM SWE 14 0 3 3 4 —

**Hagman, Johan / b. May 9, 1974**
1994 WM20 SWE 6 0 1 1 2 S

**Hagman, Matti / b. Sept. 21, 1955**
1975-83 WM FIN 36 9 17 26 30 —
1976-87 CC FIN 15 4 6 10 10 —
1976 OG-M FIN 5 1 2 3 2 —

**Hagnauer, Jean-Pierre / b. Feb. 24, 1913 / d. unknown**
1930-35 WM FRA 11 2 — 2 — —
1936 OG-M FRA 3 1 — 1 — —

**Hagos, Yared / b. Mar. 27, 1983**
2001 WM18 SWE 6 1 4 5 0 —
2002-03 WM20 SWE 13 3 4 7 6 —

**Hagstrom, Anders / b. Aug. 14, 1946**
1970 WM SWE 1 0 0 0 2 S

**Hagstrom, Klaus / b. May 1, 1918 / d. Aug. 8, 2006**
1939 WM FIN 4 0 — 0 — —

**Haider, Klaus / b. Mar. 8, 1959**
1979 WM20 FRG 5 2 0 2 7 —

**Haight, Gary / b. Oct. 4, 1961**
1985 WM USA 2 0 2 2 0 —

**Haight, Jim / b. 1914 / d. unknown**
1939 WM CAN 1 0 — 0 — G

**Hajas, Stanislav / b. Mar. 30, 1956**
2002 WM18 SVK 6 0 0 0 2 —

**Hajduk, Pavol / b. Apr. 11, 1984**
2002 WM18 SVK 8 0 0 0 2 —
2004 WM20 SVK 5 0 0 0 2 —

**Hajdusek, Stanislav / b. Mar. 30, 1956**
1981 WM TCH 6 0 1 1 4 B
1981 CC TCH 6 0 1 1 4 —

**Hajek, David / b. June 13, 1980**
2000 WM20 CZE 7 1 2 3 6 G

**Hajnos, Janusz / b. Aug. 27, 1968**
1992 OG-M POL 6 2 1 3 0 —

**Hajny, Premysl / b. Dec. 18, 1925 / d. Mar. 3, 1978**
1949 WM TCH 7 1 — 1 — G
1948 OG-M TCH 5 2 — 2 — S

**Hajsman, Vlastimil / b. Feb. 26, 1928 / d. Oct. 24, 1993**
1954-55 WM TCH 14 3 3 6 0 B
1952 OG-M TCH 9 4 0 4 — —

**Hajt, Chris / b. July 5, 1978**
1997-98 WM20 USA 13 1 0 1 14 S

**Hakala, Yrjo / b. Apr. 20, 1932**
1951-59 WM FIN 41 13 7 20 31 —
1952-60 OG-M FIN 13 3 3 6 2 —

**Hakanen, Reijo / b. Aug. 20, 1943**
1965-67 WM FIN 21 7 2 9 2 —

**Hakansson, Anders / b. Apr. 27, 1956**
1981 WM SWE 7 4 0 4 8 S
1981-84 CC SWE 13 2 2 4 6 2nd

**Hakansson, Mikael / b. May 31, 1974**
1993-94 WM20 SWE 14 2 1 3 10 2S
2000 WM SWE 7 1 0 1 0 —

**Hakulinen, Markku / b. Feb. 27, 1956 / d. Oct. 9, 1990**
1980 OG-M FIN 7 2 4 6 2 —

**Halauca, Alexandru / b. Aug. 12, 1957**
1976-80 OG-M ROM 10 2 1 3 10 —
**Halberg, Erik / b. unknown**
1949 WM DEN 3 0 — 0 — —
**Halder, Wally / b. Sept. 15, 1925 / d. Oct. 27, 1994**
1948 OG-M CAN 8 15 — 15 18 G
**Halderson, Haldor "Slim" / b. Jan. 6, 1900 / d. Aug. 1, 1965**
1920 OG-M CAN 3 9 — 9 — G
**Hale, David / b. June 18, 1981**
2001 WM20 USA 7 0 2 2 8 —
**Halfnight, Ashlin / b. Mar. 14, 1975**
1994-95 WM20 USA 14 0 2 2 8 —
**Halford, Pete / b. 1912 / d. unknown**
1935-39 WM GBR 12 0 — 0 — S,B
**Hall, Adam / b. Aug. 14, 1980**
1999-2000 WM20 USA 13 2 1 3 6 —
2003-2007 WM USA 36 4 4 8 4 B
**Hall, Don / b. Apr. 2, 1930**
1962 WM USA 6 4 5 9 0 B
**Hall, Todd / b. Jan. 22, 1973**
1992-93 WM20 USA 14 0 2 2 10 B
**Haller, Kevin / b. Dec. 5, 1970**
1990 WM20 CAN 7 2 2 4 8 G
**Halliday, Craig / b. May 2, 1962**
1981 WM20 CAN 5 0 0 0 2 —
**Hallin, Mats / b. Mar. 9, 1958**
1978 WM20 SWE 7 5 3 8 17 S
**Hallin, Per / b. Oct. 17, 1980**
1999-2000 WM20 SWE 13 2 10 12 4 —
**Hallock, Gerard / b. June 14, 1906 / d. unknown**
1932 OG-M USA 1 0 0 0 0 S
**Halttunen, Niko / b. Apr. 13, 1975**
1995 WM20 FIN 7 1 3 4 8 —
**Halvardsson, David / b. Oct. 5, 1976**
1996 WM20 SWE 7 0 0 0 0 S
**Halvardsson, Johan / b. Dec. 26, 1979**
1999 WM20 SWE 6 0 0 0 4 —
**Halward, Doug / b. Nov. 1, 1955**
1983-85 WM CAN 20 2 4 6 10 S,B
**Hamalainen, Erik / b. Apr. 20, 1965**
1984-85 WM20 FIN 14 0 2 2 2 S
1992-95 WM FIN 30 2 2 4 25 G,2S
1994 OG-M FIN 8 1 0 1 6 B
**Hamalainen, Tommi / b. Mar. 27, 1975**
1994-95 WM20 FIN 12 1 1 2 6 —
**Hamalainen, Ville / b. July 6, 1981**
1999 WM18 FIN 7 4 2 6 2 G
2000-01 WM20 FIN 14 7 5 12 2 S
**Hamann, Borge / b. unknown**
1949 WM DEN 3 0 — 0 — —
**Hamilton, Clark / b. Jan. 12, 1955**
1975 WM USA 8 0 1 1 4 —
**Hamilton, Hugh / b. Feb. 11, 1977**
1997 WM20 CAN 7 0 0 0 6 G
**Hamilton, Jeff / b. Sept. 4, 1977**
2004 WM USA 6 1 0 1 2 B
**Hammarstrom, Inge / b. Jan. 20, 1948**
1971-81 WM SWE 41 18 6 24 12 2S,3B
1976 CC SWE 5 1 2 3 2 —
1972 OG-M SWE 5 4 1 5 0 —
**Hammarstrom, Peter / b. Mar. 23, 1969**
1989 WM20 SWE 7 2 0 2 10 S
**Hammer, Arild / b. unknown**
1965 WM NOR 6 0 1 1 6 —
**Hammer, Rolf / b. Feb. 25, 1969**
1989 WM20 FRG 7 2 1 3 0 —
**Hammerle, Robert / b. Feb. 17, 1962**
1982 WM20 FRG 7 1 0 1 0 —
**Hammerseng, Lars / b. Oct. 30, 1983**
2001 WM18 NOR 6 0 0 0 0 —
**Hammerstad, Tom / b. Apr. 28, 1983**
2001 WM18 NOR 6 0 2 2 2 —
**Hammond, Ray / b. 1928**
1950 WM GBR 7 0 0 0 0 —
**Hampton, Rick / b. June 14, 1956**
1977-78 WM CAN 20 1 2 3 13 B
**Hamr, Radek / b. June 15, 1974**
2007 WM CZE 7 0 0 0 0 —
**Hamrlik, Martin / b. May 6, 1973**
1991 WM20 TCH 7 2 0 2 2 B
**Hamrlik, Roman / b. Apr. 12, 1974**
1992 WM20 TCH 7 3 0 3 8 —
1994-2004 WM CZE 8 1 0 0 0 —
1996-2004 WCH CZE 7 0 2 2 4 —
1998-2002 OG-M CZE 10 1 1 2 4 G
**Hand, Tony / b. Aug. 15, 1967**
1994 WM GBR 6 0 0 0 0 —
**Handlovsky, Lukas / b.Aug. 3, 1986**
2004 WM18 SVK 6 2 3 5 0 —
**Handrick, Jorg / b. July 20, 1968**
1994 WM GER 5 0 0 0 2 —
1994 OG-M GER 8 1 2 3 0 —
**Handschin, Emil / b. Mar. 19, 1928 / d. May 27, 1990**
1947-59 WM SUI 52 7 4 11 14 3B
1948-56 OG-M SUI 18 4 1 5 2 B
**Handy, Henryk / b. July 9, 1940 / d. Mar. 13, 2007**
1964 OG-M POL 6 1 0 1 2 —
**Haneveer, Johny / b. Mar. 2, 1921 / d. unknown**
1947 WM BEL 3 1 — 1 — —
**Hanft, Jorg / b. Feb. 24, 1964**
1984 WM20 FRG 7 0 0 0 4 —
**Hangsleben, Alan / b. Feb. 22, 1953**
1981 WM USA 8 1 3 4 22 —
1976 CC USA 5 1 1 2 12 —
**Hanig, Gustav / b. Nov. 5, 1944**
1967-72 WM FRG 27 7 5 12 0 —
1968 OG-M FRG 6 2 1 3 0 —
**Hankinson, Casey / b. May 8, 1976**
1996 WM20 USA 6 0 0 0 25 —
**Hannan, Dave / b. Nov. 26, 1961**
1992 OG-M CAN 8 3 5 8 8 S
**Hannan, Scott / b. Jan. 23, 1979**
2005 WM CAN 9 0 0 0 8 S
2004 WCH CAN 5 0 1 1 4 1st
**Hannon, Brian / b. Sept. 26, 1965**
1985 WM20 USA 7 3 2 5 6 —
**Hannula, Mika / b. Apr. 2, 1979**
2003-06 WM SWE 17 6 1 7 37 G,S
2006 OG-M SWE 8 0 0 0 2 G
**Hansen, Basil / b. July 10, 1926**
1960 OG-M AUS 4 1 0 1 4 —
**Hansen, Geir / b. 1960**
1979 WM20 NOR 5 0 0 0 2 —
**Hansen, Jan-Erik / b. Sept. 24, 1940**
1962-65 WM NOR 10 1 1 2 10 —
1964 OG-M NOR 5 1 2 3 2 —
**Hansen, Kaare / b. unknown / d. unknown**
1938 WM NOR 4 1 — 1 — —
**Hansen, Odd / b. unknown**
1949-51 WM NOR 11 1 0 1 4 —
**Hansen, Rene / b. Oct. 17, 1972**
1990 WM20 NOR 7 1 0 1 10 —
1995-96 WM NOR 10 0 0 0 4 —
**Hansen, Svein Norman / b. Apr. 18, 1933**
1962 WM NOR 5 0 0 0 10 —
1964-72 OG-M NOR 16 2 0 2 12 —
**Hanson, Keith / b. May 26, 1957**
1977 WM20 USA 7 0 1 1 0 —
**Hansson, Hans / b. Nov. 26, 1949**
1972 OG-M SWE 1 0 0 0 0 —
**Hansson, Mats / b. Mar. 3, 1983**
2003 WM20 SWE 6 0 0 0 2 —
**Hansson, Roger / b. July 13, 1967**
1987 WM20 SWE 6 3 3 6 4 B
1992-95 WM SWE 20 6 6 12 4 G,S,B
1994 OG-M SWE 8 5 2 7 4 G
**Hantschke, Ralf / b. May 27, 1965**
1985 WM GDR 10 2 0 2 10 —
**Hanzawa, Tsutomu / b. Aug. 28, 1948**
1972-80 OG-M JPN 13 3 3 6 0 —
**Hanzlik, Jan / b. Mar. 21, 1982**
2000 WM18 CZE 6 1 3 4 4 —
2002 WM20 CZE 7 1 1 2 29 —
**Harabin, Ladislav / b. Sept. 12, 1980**
1998-2000 WM20 SVK 19 0 2 2 20 B
**Harand, Kurt / b. Sept. 11, 1957**
1984-88 OG-M AUT 11 3 0 3 4 —
**Haray, Bela / b. Mar. 25, 1915 / d. Mar. 9, 1988**
1934-39 WM HUN 22 7 1 8 9 —
1936 OG-M HUN 5 4 — 4 — —
**Harbakon, Raman / b. Aug. 18, 1984**
2002 WM18 BLR 8 1 2 3 4 —
**Harbavy, Vasili / b. June 4, 1983**
2002-03 WM20 BLR 12 2 1 3 2 —
**Hardin, Per-Olof / b. Sept. 17, 1937**
1961-63 WM SWE 16 9 10 19 6 G,S
**Hardy, Mark / b. Feb. 1, 1959**
1986 WM CAN 10 3 2 5 12 B
**Hargreaves, Ted / b. Nov. 4, 1943**
1967-69 WM CAN 17 3 3 6 12 B
1968 OG-M CAN 5 1 2 3 0 B
**Harikkala, Jaakko / b. Mar. 30, 1981**
1999 WM18 FIN 7 3 0 3 12 G
**Harila, Kari / b. Apr. 15, 1968**
1988 WM20 FIN 7 0 0 0 2 B
1993 WM FIN 6 1 0 1 2 —
**Harju, Matti / b. July 14, 1943**
1967-69 WM FIN 11 1 0 1 2 —
1968 OG-M FIN 7 2 1 3 2 —
**Harkins, Todd / b. Oct. 8, 1968**
1992-95 WM USA 12 1 7 8 38 —
**Harlock, David / b. Mar. 16, 1971**
1991 WM20 CAN 7 0 2 2 2 G
1994 OG-M CAN 8 0 0 0 8 S
**Harlow, Scott / b. Oct. 11, 1963**
1983 WM20 USA 7 2 2 4 0 —
**Harnett, Roy / b. 1929**
1950 WM GBR 7 0 0 0 0 —
**Harrington, John / b. May 24, 1957**
1982 WM USA 6 0 0 0 4 —
1980-84 OG-M USA 12 0 5 5 8 G
**Harris, Bob / b. Dec. 4, 1953**
1976 OG-M USA 5 1 0 1 2 —
**Harris, Paul / b. Mar. 23, 1981**
1999 WM18 USA 6 1 0 1 4 —
**Harrison, Cliff / b. Oct. 30, 1927 / d. Dec. 15, 1988**
1952 OG-M USA 8 5 2 7 — S
**Harrison, Jay / b. Nov. 3, 1982**
2001-02 WM20 CAN 14 0 1 1 8 S,B
**Harter, Ernst / b. unknown**
1949-50 WM SUI 2 0 0 0 0 B
**Hartman, Mike / b. Feb. 7, 1967**
1987 WM20 USA 6 2 1 3 14 —
**Hartmann, Karel / b. Aug. 24, 1888 / d. unknown**
1920 OG-M TCH 3 0 0 0 — B
**Hartmeyer, Georges / b. Dec. 12, 1923 / Oct. 31, 2009**
1947-50 WM BEL 12 3 0 3 0 —
**Hartnell, Scott / b. Apr. 18, 1982**
2006 WM CAN 9 1 0 1 4 —
**Hartog, Johny / b. unknown / d. unknown**
1939-47 WM BEL 11 2 — 2 — —
**Hartsburg, Craig / b. June 29, 1959**
1977-78 WM20 CAN 8 2 5 7 13 S,B
1982-87 WM CAN 25 4 6 10 28 2B
1981-87 CC CAN 16 0 3 3 12 1st,2nd
~WM IIHF Directorate Best Defenceman (1987)
**Hartung, Peter / b. Sept. 5, 1973**
1992 WM20 GER 7 0 0 0 0 —
**Hartzell, Kevin / b. Feb. 20, 1958**
1978 WM20 USA 6 5 2 7 4 —
**Harvey, Todd / b. Feb. 17, 1975**
1994-95 WM20 CAN 14 10 3 13 10 2G
**Hasani, Adam / b. June 3, 1989**
2007 WM18 SUI 6 0 0 0 4 —
**Hascak, Oto / b. Jan. 31, 1964**
1989-96 WM SVK 24 5 5 10 12 2B
1996 WCH SVK 3 0 1 1 0 —
1988-98 OG-M SVK 16 2 9 11 8 —
**Hashey, Bud / b. unknown**
1949 WM CAN 7 4 — 4 — S
**Hasler, Steivan / b. May 21, 1984**
2004 WM20 SUI 6 0 1 1 0 —
**Hassinen, Jani / b. May 11, 1975**
1994-95 WM20 FIN 14 1 1 2 4 —
**Hassler, Albert / b. Nov. 2, 1903 / d. Sept. 22, 1994**
1930-37 WM FRA 21 5 0 5 2 —
1924-36 OG-M FRA 9 2 — 2 — —
**Hatcher, Derian / b. June 4, 1972**
1993-2002 WM USA 13 1 3 4 8 —
1996 WCH USA 6 3 2 5 10 1st
1998-2006 OG-M USA 10 0 0 0 12 —
**Hatcher, Kevin / b. Sept. 9, 1966**
1984 WM20 USA 7 1 0 1 0 —
1987-96 WCH USA 20 0 7 7 20 1st,2nd
1998 OG-M USA 3 0 2 2 0 —
**Hatterscheid, Daniel / b. Sept. 18, 1984**
2002 WM18 GER 8 1 0 1 0 —
**Hauer, Brett / b. July 11, 1971**
1993-2005 WM USA 34 5 7 12 24 B
1994 OG-M USA 8 0 0 0 10 —
**Hauer, Jaroslav / b. May 5, 1962 / d. Dec. 27, 1998**
1981-82 WM20 TCH 12 4 3 7 6 S

**Hauger, Kjell / b. unknown**
1949 WM NOR 4 0 — 0 — —

**Haugom, Erik / b. Feb. 7, 1982**
1999 WM18 NOR 6 0 0 0 28 —

**Haukali, Terje / b. July 2, 1972**
1991 WM20 NOR 5 0 0 0 2 —

**Hausner, Gerhard / b. Sept. 25, 1947**
1968-76 OG-M AUT 9 0 0 0 0 —

**Havel, Jan / b. Nov. 10, 1942**
1967-71 WM TCH 18 8 7 15 8 S,B
1968 OG-M TCH 7 5 1 6 2 S

**Havel, Lukas / b. Nov. 10, 1981**
2001 WM20 CZE 7 1 1 2 6 G

**Havel, Marlan / b. Jan. 26, 1984**
2001 WM18 CZE 7 2 1 3 2 —

**Havelid, Niclas / b. Apr. 12, 1973**
1993 WM20 SWE 7 0 0 0 10 S
1998-2004 WM SWE 19 0 4 4 8 G,S
2006 OG-M SWE 7 0 0 0 4 G

**Havlicek, Libor / b. Oct. 13, 1953**
1979 WM TCH 8 0 4 4 2 S

**Havulinna, Kalle / b. Sept. 27, 1924**
1949-51 WM FIN 10 2 — 2 0 —

**Hawerchuk, Dale / b. Apr. 4, 1963**
1981 WM20 CAN 5 5 4 9 2 —
1982-89 WM CAN 28 9 13 22 10 S,2B
1987-91 CC CAN 17 6 5 11 0 2/1st

**Hawgood, Greg / b. Aug. 10, 1968**
1987-88 WM20 CAN 13 3 10 13 12 G
~WM20 All-Star Team/Defence (1988)

**Hay, Dwayne / b. Feb. 11, 1977**
1997 WM20 CAN 7 0 0 0 2 G

**Hayama, Masahiro / b. Jan. 23, 1910 / d. unknown**
1936 OG-M JPN 2 0 0 0 — —

**Hayashi, Seichi / b. unknown / d. unknown**
1930 WM JPN 1 0 0 0 — —

**Hayes, Benny / b. 1914 / d. unknown**
1939 WM CAN 1 0 — 0 — G

**Hayes, Ryan / b. June 4, 1989**
2006-07 WM18 USA 13 2 3 5 6 —

**Hazlett, Steve / b. Dec. 12, 1957**
1977 WM20 CAN 7 6 1 7 4 S

**Heaslip, Mark / b. Dec. 26, 1951**
1977 WM USA 10 0 1 1 8 —

**Heath, Randy / b. Nov. 11, 1964**
1984 WM20 CAN 7 3 6 9 12 —

**Heavern, Robert / b. unknown**
1947 WM USA 5 1 — 1 — —

**Heberlein, Marc / b. Sept. 16, 1981**
1999 WM18 SUI 7 2 2 4 6 —
2000-01 WM20 SUI 14 2 1 3 27 —

**Heckelsmuller, Horst / b. Jan. 3, 1958**
1977-78 WM20 FRG 13 1 0 1 2 —
1985 WM FRG 7 1 2 3 4 —

**Hecl, Radoslav / b. Oct. 11, 1974**
1999-2002 WM SVK 9 0 0 0 2 G

**Hedberg, Anders / b. Feb. 25, 1951**
1970-74 WM SWE 39 17 16 33 6 2S,2B
1976-81 CC SWE 10 7 4 11 4 —
~IIHF Hall of Fame

**Hedenstrom, Per / b. Mar. 4, 1963**
1983 WM20 SWE 3 1 0 1 4 —

**Hedican, Bret / b. Aug. 10, 1970**
1997-2001 WM USA 23 2 8 10 18 —
1992-2006 OG-M USA 14 0 1 1 10 —

**Hedin, Pierre / b. Feb. 19, 1978**
1998 WM20 SWE 7 3 2 5 4 —
2002 WM SWE 9 2 1 3 4 B
~WM20 All-Star Team/Defence (1998)

**Hedlund, Henric / b. Apr. 7, 1945**
1968 OG-M SWE 7 3 2 5 4 —

**Hedlund, Karl-Soren / b. Jan. 28, 1938**
1958 WM SWE 1 0 0 0 0 B

**Hedlund, Magnus / b. Apr. 24, 1982**
1999-2000 WM18 SWE 13 2 6 8 8 —
2000-02 WM20 SWE 21 4 7 11 14 —

**Hedman, Erik / b. unknown / d. unknown**
1939 WM FIN 4 0 — 0 — —

**Heed, Jonas / b. Jan. 3, 1967**
1987 WM20 SWE 5 0 3 3 2 B

**Heen, Henrik / b. Apr. 27, 1988**
2006 WM18 NOR 6 0 0 0 0 —

**Hegegy, Alexander / b. Oct. 21, 1987**
2005 WM18 CZE 7 2 0 2 0 —

**Hegen, Dieter / b. Apr. 29, 1962**
1981-82 WM20 FRG 12 15 3 18 24 —
1982-97 WM FRG 106 39 21 60 82 —
1984-96 WCH GER 7 1 1 2 6
1984-98 OG-M GER 33 16 7 23 16 —
~IIHF Hall of Fame

**Hegg, Jo Magnus / b. July 1, 1988**
2006 WM18 NOR 6 0 2 2 0 —

**Heidt, Mike / b. Nov. 4, 1963**
1992-96 WM GER 12 4 0 4 8 —
1996 WCH GER 4 0 1 1 2 —
1992 OG-M GER 8 0 1 1 6 —

**Heierling, Hans / b. unknown**
1950-51 WM SUI 13 2 0 2 14 2B

**Heikkila, Antti / b. Oct. 30, 1943**
1966 WM FIN 3 0 0 0 0 —

**Heikkila, Antti / b. Feb. 1, 1958**
1978 WM20 FIN 6 1 4 5 4 —

**Heikkila, Ilkka / b. July 1, 1988**
2006 WM18 FIN 6 1 0 1 6 S

**Heikkinen, Eetu / b. July 8, 1988**
2006 WM18 FIN 6 0 1 1 10 S

**Heim, Axel / b. Aug. 5, 1971**
1991 WM20 SUI 7 0 1 1 24 —

**Heindl, Bill / b. May 13, 1946 / d. Mar. 1, 1992**
1969 WM CAN 9 4 1 5 2 —

**Heinicke, Gunter / b. Jan. 8, 1934**
1959-61 WM GDR 7 1 0 1 8 —

**Heinicke, Werner / b. Mar. 13, 1932**
1957-59 WM GDR 11 2 1 3 10 —

**Heinrich, Alfred / b. Feb. 21, 1906 / d. unknown**
1930 WM GER 2 0 — 0 — S
1932 OG-M GER 6 0 0 0 18 B

**Heinrich, Herbert / b. Apr. 15, 1958**
1977 WM20 FRG 7 0 0 0 4 —

**Heinz, Wilhelm / b. unknown / d. unknown**
1931 WM TCH 1 0 — 0 — —

**Heinze, Horst / b. Nov. 28, 1937**
1959-63 WM GDR 14 3 2 5 0 —

**Heinze, Steve / b. Jan. 30, 1970**
1989 WM20 USA 7 2 1 3 2 —
2000 WM USA 7 0 3 3 8 —
1992 OG-M USA 8 1 3 4 8 —

**Heinzle, Karl / b. July 31, 1960**
1993-96 WM AUT 18 1 1 2 8 —
1994 OG-M AUT 7 0 0 0 4 —

**Heiskanen, Santeri / b. Apr. 13, 1977**
1997 WM20 FIN 6 0 2 2 6 —

**Heisten, Barrett / b. Mar. 19, 1980**
1999-2000 WM20 USA 13 4 5 9 28 —

**Heitzmann, Marc / b. Mar. 19, 1964**
1984 WM20 SUI 7 0 1 1 0 —

**Hejduk, Milan / b. Feb. 14, 1976**
1995-96 WM20 CZE 13 1 3 4 14 —
1998-2003 WM CZE 8 5 1 6 2 B
2004 WCH CZE 4 3 2 5 2 —
1998-2006 OG-M CZE 16 3 1 4 4 G,B

**Hejma, Peter / b. Apr. 24, 1944**
1968 OG-M TCH 7 3 0 3 4 S

**Hejma, Peter / b. Sept. 11, 1970**
1989 WM20 FRG 7 0 0 0 2 —

**Helander, Hannu / b. Sept. 23, 1956**
1982-83 WM FIN 16 1 5 6 6 —

**Helander, Peter / b. Dec. 4, 1951**
1981-82 WM SWE 18 2 4 6 22 S
1981 CC SWE 5 0 2 2 8 —

**Held, Daniel / b. Nov. 13, 1961**
1981 WM20 FRG 4 1 1 2 20 —
1987 WM FRG 10 1 3 4 4 —

**Heldner, Thomas / b. Aug. 4, 1970**
1995 WM SUI 6 0 0 0 2 —

**Helenius, Sami / b. Jan. 22, 1974**
1993 WM20 FIN 7 0 1 1 6 —
2003 WM FIN 2 0 0 0 0 —

**Helfenstein, Sven / b. July 30, 1982**
1999-2000 WM18 SUI 14 6 11 17 2 —
2000-02 WM20 SUI 21 5 7 12 8 —

**Helfer, Armin / b. May 31, 1980**
2000-10 WM ITA 39 3 2 5 54 —
2006 OG-M ITA 5 0 0 0 4 —

**Helisten, Mikko / b. June 17, 1975**
1995 WM20 FIN 7 1 0 1 0 —

**Helkearo, Mika / b. Oct. 4, 1960**
1980 WM20 FIN 5 3 2 5 0 S

**Hellen, Teuvo / b. Mar. 15, 1923**
1949 WM FIN 4 0 — 0 — —

**Heller, Otto / b. Nov. 30, 1914 / d. unknown**
1938 WM SUI 1 0 — 0 — —
1936 OG-M SUI 3 0 0 0 — —

**Hellerud, Terje / b. unknown**
1958-62 WM NOR 22 9 8 17 20 —

**Hellgren, Jens / b. Mar. 6, 1989**
2007 WM18 SWE 6 0 0 0 6 B

**Hellmann, Lennart / b. Dec. 2, 1914 / d. unknown**
1935-38 WM SWE 7 1 — 1 — —
1936 OG-M SWE 1 0 — 0 — —

**Helmeczi, Frigyes / b. Dec. 19, 1913 / d. unknown**
1938-39 WM HUN 10 1 — 1 — —
1936 OG-M HUN 1 0 — 0 — —

**Helmersson, Karl / b. Oct. 28, 1979**
1999 WM20 SWE 4 0 1 1 4 —

**Helmersson, Per / b. Oct. 2, 1982**
2000 WM18 SWE 5 1 3 4 12 B
2002 WM20 SWE 7 0 0 0 6 —

**Helminen, Dwight / b. June 22, 1983**
2001 WM18 USA 6 3 5 8 0 —
2002-03 WM20 USA 14 2 3 5 4 —

**Helminen, Raimo / b. Mar. 11, 1964**
1983-84 WM20 FIN 14 11 16 27 4 S
1985-2002 WM FIN 93 12 48 60 8 G,4S,B
1987-96 WCH FIN 8 0 5 5 0 —
1984-2002 OG-M FIN 39 6 18 24 16 S,2B
~WM20 IIHF Directorate Best Forward (1984), WM20 All-Star Team/Forward (1984)

**Hemmerling, Jan / b. Oct. 27, 1907 / d. unknown**
1931 WM POL 4 0 — 0 — —

**Hemming, Jonas / b. Feb. 3, 1970**
1990 WM20 FIN 5 3 2 5 0 —

**Hemstrom, Jens / b. Apr. 17, 1972**
1992 WM20 SWE 3 0 0 0 6 S

**Henderson, Paul / b. Jan. 28, 1943**
1972 SS CAN 8 7 3 10 4 1st

**Hendrickson, Darby / b. Aug. 28, 1972**
1996-2001 WM USA 44 6 8 14 28 B
1994 OG-M USA 8 0 0 0 6 —

**Hendry, Gian-Carlo / b. Oct. 3, 1981**
1999 WM18 SUI 5 0 0 0 2 —

**Henning, Brett / b. May 7, 1980**
2000 WM20 USA 7 0 0 0 0 —

**Henrich, Adam / b. Jan. 19, 1984**
2002 WM18 CAN 8 0 3 3 43 —

**Henriksson, Hannu / b. Apr. 18, 1963**
1982-83 WM20 FIN 11 3 0 3 22 B
1990-91 WM FIN 14 1 2 3 16 —

**Henriksson, Leif / b. May 26, 1943**
1967-69 WM SWE 14 3 3 6 8 2S
1968 OG-M SWE 6 2 3 5 4 —

**Hentunen, Jukka / b. May 3, 1974**
2000-07 WM FIN 50 15 14 29 46 2S,2B
2004 WCH FIN 6 1 1 2 2 2nd
2006 OG-M FIN 8 0 0 0 2 S

**Hentze, Frederik / b. Apr. 6, 1987**
2004-05 WM18 DEN 9 0 1 1 4 —

**Henzen, Charles / b. Oct. 4, 1945**
1972 WM SUI 10 0 1 1 4 —
1972-76 OG-M SUI 8 0 0 0 6 —

**Herda, Marian / b. Oct. 1, 1933**
1956 OG-M POL 2 0 0 0 2 —

**Herker, Erich / b. Sept. 25, 1905 / d. unknown**
1930 WM GER 5 0 — 0 — S
1932 OG-M GER 2 1 0 1 0 B

**Herlet, Casper / b. Aug. 9, 1987**
2005 WM18 DEN 6 0 0 0 4 —

**Hermansson, Dan / b. Jan. 30, 1958**
1977-78 WM20 SWE 14 7 3 10 44 S

**Hermansson, Daniel / b. Apr. 3, 1982**
2000 WM18 SWE 6 2 2 4 0 B
2002 WM20 SWE 2 1 0 1 2 —

**Hermansson, Lennart / b. Oct. 12, 1965**
1985 WM20 SWE 6 2 0 2 20 —

**Hern, John / b. 1911 / d. unknown**
1933 WM CAN 4 4 — 4 0 S

**Herr, Matt / b. May 26, 1976**
1996 WM20 USA 6 1 0 1 0 —

**Herter, Jason / b. Oct. 2, 1970**
1990 WM20 CAN 7 0 1 1 2 G

**Hertl, Jaroslav / b. Oct. 28, 1989**
2007 WM18 CZE 6 0 1 1 2 —

**Herzig, Bernd / b. May 21, 1941**
1961 WM FRG 4 0 0 0 4 —
1964 OG-M FRG 6 0 0 0 0 —

**Herzig, Tom / b. June 14, 1962**
1982 WM20 USA 7 2 2 4 0 —

**Herzog, Michael / b. Feb. 27, 1952 / d. Jan. 30, 2011**
1976 OG-M AUT 5 0 3 3 0 —

**Hessel, Mats / b. Mar. 13, 1961**
1984 OG-M SWE 7 1 1 2 2 B

**Heward, Jamie / b. Mar. 30, 1971**
1995-2003 WM CAN 17 0 5 5 8 G,B

**Heximer, Roy / b. Nov. 8, 1919 / d. unknown**
1938 WM CAN 7 0 — 0 — G

**Heyer, Jens / b. Feb. 11, 1989**
2007 WM18 GER 6 0 1 1 4 —

**Heylliard, Jacques / b. unknown**
1950 WM FRA 4 0 0 0 0 —

**Heynen, Fernando / b. May 27, 1987**
2005 WM18 SUI 6 0 0 0 8 —

**Hibberd, Ted / b. Apr. 22, 1926**
1948 OG-M CAN 8 3 — 3 4 G

**Hickey, Pat / b. May 15, 1953**
1978 WM CAN 10 5 1 6 4 B

**Hidber, Bruno / b. Jan. 19, 1963**
1982 WM20 SUI 7 0 0 0 0 —

**Hidi, Andre / b. June 5, 1960**
1980 WM20 CAN 5 2 0 2 2 —

**Hiekkaranta, Aarno / b. Dec. 23, 1932**
1954-55 WM FIN 14 3 0 3 2 —

**Hiemer, Jorg / b. July 20, 1958**
1977-78 WM20 FRG 13 1 0 1 14 —
1981 WM FRG 8 2 0 2 10 —

**Hiemer, Uli / b. Sept. 21, 1962**
1980-82 WM20 FRG 17 5 10 15 49 —
1981-95 WM GER 63 8 11 19 96 —
1984 CC FRG 3 0 0 0 4 —
1984-94 OG-M GER 20 2 1 3 16 —

**Hikigi, Takao / b. Oct. 30, 1944**
1968-72 OG-M JPN 9 7 4 11 8 —

**Hilbert, Andy / b. Feb. 6, 1981**
1999 WM18 USA 6 6 1 7 4 —
1999-2001 WM20 USA 20 7 9 16 6 —
2002-06 WM USA 20 2 4 6 18 B

**Hildebrand, Ike / b. May 27, 1927 / d. Aug. 27, 2006**
1959 WM CAN 8 6 4 10 6 G

**Hildebrand, Rolf / b. June 22, 1982**
2000 WM18 SUI 7 1 0 1 0 —

**Hilger, Raimond / b. Dec. 3, 1965**
1985 WM20 FRG 7 0 2 2 22 —
1990-95 WM FRG 41 11 6 17 30 —
1992-94 OG-M GER 13 2 1 3 12 —

**Hill, George / b. 1904 / d. unknown**
1931 WM CAN 6 2 — 2 — G

**Hill, Sean / b. Feb. 14, 1970**
1990 WM20 USA 7 0 3 3 10 —
1994 WM USA 8 0 2 2 6 —
1992 OG-M USA 8 2 0 2 6 —

**Hille, Henk / b. May 16, 1959**
1981 WM NED 8 0 0 0 22 —
1980 OG-M NED 5 1 0 1 6 —

**Hiller, Bernd / b. Feb. 26, 1942**
1961-70 WM GDR 29 5 8 13 6 —
1968 OG-M GDR 7 1 0 1 0 —

**Hiller, Guido / b. Oct. 1, 1964**
1983 WM GDR 6 0 1 1 4 —

**Hilliard, Channing / b. Oct. 17, 1908 / d. unknown**
1933 WM USA 5 3 — 3 0 G

**Hilpert, Daniel / b. July 27, 1981**
1999 WM18 GER 6 1 0 1 0 —

**Hilson, Barney / b. 1927**
1949 WM CAN 7 4 — 4 — S

**Hiltebrand, Christof / b. May 7, 1981**
1999 WM18 SUI 7 3 4 7 0 —

**Hilton, Kevin / b. Jan. 5, 1975**
1994-95 WM20 USA 14 4 2 6 2 —

**Himanka, Markus / b. Feb. 27, 1988**
2006 WM18 FIN 6 0 0 0 0 S

**Hindmar., Dave / b. Oct. 15, 1958**
1980 OG-M CAN 6 2 4 6 4 —

**Hinkel, Roy / b. 1907 / d. unknown**
1935 WM CAN 4 0 — 0 — G
1932 OG-M CAN 6 2 1 3 6 G

**Hinterkircher, Heinz / b. unknown**
1947-49 WM SUI 10 2 — 2 — —

**Hinterstocker, Benjamin / b. Nov. 26, 1979**
1997-98 WM20 GER 12 2 1 3 6 —

**Hinterstocker, Hermann / b. June 21, 1956**
1976-79 WM FRG 38 5 3 8 8 —
1980 OG-M FRG 5 0 1 1 0 —

**Hinterstocker, Martin / b. July 28, 1954**
1973-79 WM FRG 18 3 0 3 10 —
1976-80 OG-M FRG 10 5 4 9 9 B

**Hinterstocker, Martin / b. Feb. 1, 1983**
2000-01 WM18 GER 12 0 1 1 6 —
2003 WM20 GER 2 0 0 0 0 —

**Hinterstocker, Martin / b. Sept. 3, 1989**
2007 WM18 GER 6 0 1 1 0 —

**Hirano, Susumu / b. Apr. 23, 1910 / d. unknown**
1930 WM JPN 1 0 0 0 — —
1936 OG-M JPN 2 0 0 0 — —

**Hirsch, Tom / b. Jan. 27, 1963**
1982 WM USA 6 1 1 2 0 —
1984 CC USA 5 0 0 0 0 —
1984 OG-M USA 6 1 0 1 10 —

**Hirsch, Tyler / b. Jan. 4, 1984**
2002 WM18 USA 8 2 5 7 18 G

**Hirschovits, Kim / b. May 9, 1982**
2002 WM20 FIN 7 0 1 1 6 B

**Hirsimaki, Jukka / b. Jan. 25, 1957**
1977 WM20 FIN 7 0 1 1 6 —

**Hirtreiter, Frank / b. Jan. 19, 1968**
1988 WM20 FRG 6 0 0 0 2 —

**Hirvonen, Raimo / b. July 20, 1957**
1977 WM20 FIN 7 1 0 1 4 —
1982 WM FIN 5 0 2 2 0 —
1981 CC FIN 3 0 0 0 2 —

**Hirvonen, Timo / b. Dec. 5, 1973**
1993 WM20 FIN 7 0 2 2 10 —

**Hirvonen, Tomi / b. Jan. 11, 1977**
1996-97 WM20 FIN 12 2 3 5 31 —

**Hitch, Clive / b. May 17, 1931**
1960 OG-M AUS 6 0 0 0 0 —

**Hiti, Gorazd / b. Aug. 12, 1948**
1972-84 OG-M YUG 14 3 8 11 4 —

**Hiti, Rudi / b. Nov. 4, 1946**
1968-72 OG-M YUG 7 3 2 5 12 —
~IIHF Hall of Fame

**Hjalm, Mikael / b. Mar. 23, 1963**
1982-83 WM20 SWE 14 10 2 12 10 —
1985-86 WM SWE 20 3 6 9 10 S
1984-88 OG-M SWE 15 2 2 4 8 2B

**Hjelm, Hans / b. Dec. 16, 1926**
1947 WM SWE 3 0 — 0 — S

**Hlavac, Jan / b. Sept. 20, 1976**
1995-96 WM20 CZE 13 2 3 5 6 —
1998-2006 WM CZE 51 14 16 30 18 2G,S,B

**Hlinka, Ivan / b. Jan. 26, 1950 / d. Aug. 16, 2004**
1970-81 WM TCH 90 43 42 85 27 3G,5S,3B
1976 CC TCH 7 2 2 4 12 2nd
1972-76 OG-M TCH 10 4 5 9 11 S,B
~IIHF Hall of Fame
~WM All-Star Team/Forward (1978)

**Hlinka, Miroslav / b. Aug. 30, 1972**
2000-03 WM SVK 34 6 7 13 36 G,S,B
2004 WCH SVK 2 0 0 0 2 —

**Hlinkin, Artyom / b. Sept. 7, 1983**
2002-03 WM20 BLR 12 1 0 1 14 —

**Hlushko, Todd / b. Feb. 2, 1970**
1995 WM CAN 8 4 0 4 4 B
1994 OG-M CAN 8 5 0 5 6 S

**Hnidenko, Artyom / b. Feb. 3, 1980**
2000 WM20 UKR 7 4 1 5 0 —
2003 WM UKR 6 0 1 1 2 —

**Hobbins, Bill / b. Apr. 13, 1960**
1979 WM20 CAN 5 0 1 1 4 —

**Hobson, Adam / b. Jan. 9, 1987**
2005 WM18 CAN 6 1 2 3 4 S

**Hochuli, Simon / b. Feb. 6, 1972**
1991 WM20 SUI 4 0 0 0 4 —

**Hock, Robert / b. Jan. 12, 1973**
1992-93 WM20 GER 11 2 3 5 2 —

**Hockley, Cal / b. Mar. 21, 1931**
1961 WM CAN 7 1 1 2 4 G

**Hodek, Petr / b. Feb. 10, 1966**
1986 WM20 TCH 3 0 0 0 0 —

**Hodgson, Dan / b. Aug. 29, 1965**
1984-85 WM20 CAN 14 6 6 12 4 G

**Hoel, Jesper / b. Mar. 6, 1987**
2004 WM18 NOR 4 1 0 1 0 —

**Hofacker, Martin / b. 1966**
1986 WM20 SUI 7 0 0 0 4 —

**Hofer, Paul / b. Nov. 19, 1928**
1954-55 WM SUI 14 0 0 0 8 —
1952-56 OG-M SUI 10 0 0 0 2 —

**Hofer, Rudolf / b. unknown**
1981 WM20 AUT 5 1 0 1 0 —

**Hofer, Willi / b. May 1, 1960**
1979-80 WM20 FRG 9 1 1 2 2 —

**Hoff, Geir / b. Feb. 14, 1965**
1983 WM20 NOR 7 0 1 1 15 —
1990-96 WM NOR 35 6 7 13 32 —
1988-94 OG-M NOR 19 5 2 7 8 —

**Hoffmann, Olivier / b. Jan. 17, 1967**
1987 WM20 SUI 7 2 1 3 2 —

**Hoffmann, Ueli / b. Sept. 1, 1953**
1976 OG-M SUI 5 0 1 1 4 —

**Hofherr, Anton / b. Dec. 20, 1947**
1971-72 WM FRG 20 3 3 6 16 —
1972 OG-M FRG 3 2 3 5 8 —

**Hofherr, Franz / b. Mar. 15, 1949**
1971 WM FRG 6 0 0 0 0 —

**Hofmanas, A. / b. unknown / d. unknown**
1938 WM LTU 2 0 — 0 — —

**Hofner, Ernst / b. Sept. 21, 1957**
1977 WM20 FRG 7 5 3 8 2 —
1981-87 WM FRG 55 15 16 31 43 —
1984 CC FRG 5 1 5 6 4 —
1980-84 OG-M FRG 11 4 3 7 6 —

**Hofstetter, Christian / b. May 20, 1967**
1987 WM20 SUI 7 0 0 0 4 —

**Hofstetter, Christian / b. Apr. 16, 1972**
1992 WM20 SUI 2 0 0 0 0 —

**Hogan, Joe / b. Nov. 13, 1935**
1962 WM CAN 6 3 7 10 2 S

**Hogardh, Peter / b. May 15, 1976**
1996 WM20 SWE 7 2 2 4 2 S

**Hoglund, Johan / b. June 9, 1982**
2000 WM18 SWE 6 0 1 1 2 B

**Hoglund, Jonas / b. Aug. 29, 1972**
1992 WM20 SWE 7 3 2 5 0 S
1997-2005 WM SWE 38 13 10 23 10 3S

**Hohenadl, Frank / b. June 29, 1972**
1992 WM20 GER 7 0 0 0 14 —

**Hohenberger, Herbert / b. Feb. 8, 1969**
1993-2003 WM AUT 54 4 14 18 86 —
1994-98 OG-M AUT 11 0 0 0 20 —

**Hohenberger, Martin / b. Jan. 29, 1977**
2002-03 WM AUT 12 3 1 4 18 —
1998-2002 OG-M AUT 8 0 0 0 2 —

**Hohener, Martin / b. June 23, 1980**
2000 WM20 SUI 7 0 1 1 4 —
2002 WM SUI 5 0 0 0 2 —
2002 OG-M SUI 4 0 0 0 0 —

**Hoibye, Christoffer / b. Jan. 19, 1984**
2002 WM18 NOR 7 0 0 0 0 —

**Hoibyhagen, Andre / b. Mar. 16, 1981**
1999 WM18 NOR 6 0 0 0 16 —

**Hoja, Ralph / b. Feb. 11, 1961**
1980 WM20 FRG 5 0 0 0 0 —

**Hojmose, Dennis / b. Jan. 6, 1986**
2004 WM18 DEN 6 0 1 1 4 —

**Holan, Milos / b. Apr. 22, 1971**
1990-91 WM20 TCH 10 2 2 4 2 2B
1993-94 WM CZE 14 1 6 7 18 B

**Holbus, Mirko / b. Jan. 26, 1940**
1964 OG-M YUG 6 0 — 0 — —

**Holden, Josh / b. Jan. 18, 1978**
1998 WM20 CAN 6 4 0 4 16 —

**Holderied, Engelbert / b. June 26, 1924**
1952 OG-M FRG 2 0 0 0 — —

**Holecko, Peter / b. Jan. 13, 1982**
2002 WM20 SVK 7 0 2 2 0 —

**Holeczy, Roger / b. Oct. 19, 1976**
2009 WM HUN 6 1 0 1 2 —

**Holik, Jaroslav / b. Aug. 3, 1942**
1965-73 WM TCH 55 21 32 53 74 G,2S,3B
1972 OG-M TCH 3 2 1 3 0 B

**Holik, Jiri / b. July 9, 1944**
1965-77 WM TCH 109 52 43 95 87 3G,5S,3B
1976 CC TCH 7 0 3 3 0 2nd
1964-76 OG-M TCH 24 6 5 11 10 2S,2B
~IIHF Hall of Fame

**Holik, Robert "Bobby" / b. Jan. 1, 1971**
1989-90 WM20 TCH 14 11 8 19 14 2B
1990-91 WM TCH 20 4 8 12 18 B
1996 WCH CZE 3 0 0 0 0 —

**Holland, Frank / b. Nov. 23, 1904 / d. unknown**
1933 WM USA 5 2 — 2 0 G

**Hollenstein, Felix / b. Apr. 7, 1965**
1984 WM20 SUI 7 0 1 1 0 —
1992-95 WM SUI 22 3 1 4 12 —
1988 OG-M SUI 6 1 1 2 2 —

**Hollstrom, Filip / b. Feb. 23, 1985**
2003 WM18 SWE 6 0 0 0 2 —

**Hollweg, Ryan / b. Apr. 23, 1983**
2002 WM20 USA 7 2 3 5 33 —

**Holm, Kristoffer / b. Jan. 11, 1984**
2002 WM18 NOR 8 0 0 0 4 —

**Holmberg, Erik / b. Jan. 24, 1963**
1983 WM20 SWE 7 0 1 1 2 —

**Holmes, George / b. June 23, 1895 / d. unknown**
1924 OG-M GBR 4 1 — 1 — B

**Holmgren, Leif / b. May 25, 1953**
1978-83 WM SWE 28 4 6 10 16 B
1980 OG-M SWE 7 2 5 7 11 B

**Holmqvist, Andreas / b. July 23, 1981**
2001 WM20 SWE 6 0 2 2 4 —
2006 WM SWE 9 0 1 1 0 G

**Holmqvist, Birger / b. Dec. 28, 1900 / d. Apr. 9, 1989**
1924-28 OG-M SWE 9 8 — 8 2 S

**Holmqvist, David / b. Apr. 23, 1984**
2002 WM18 SWE 8 0 0 0 0 —

**Holmstrom, Tomas / b. Jan. 23, 1973**
1996 WM SWE 6 1 0 1 12 —
2004 WCH SWE 4 3 2 5 8 —
2002-06 OG-M SWE 12 2 3 5 12 —

**Holsboer, Max / b. 1882 / d. unknown**
1920 OG-M SUI 1 0 0 0 — —

**Holscher, Henrik / b. Sept. 20, 1972**
1992 WM20 GER 7 1 3 4 4 —

**Holt, Charles / b. July 17, 1922 / d. unknown**
1949 WM USA 2 3 — 3 — B

**Holten Moller, Joachim / b. July 30, 1987**
2005 WM18 DEN 6 0 1 1 2 —

**Holub, Jan / b. May 3, 1983**
2001 WM18 CZE 7 0 0 0 6 —
2003 WM20 CZE 6 0 0 0 14 —

**Holubar, Petr / b. Nov. 19, 1964**
1984 WM20 TCH 7 0 1 1 0 B

**Holy, Karel / b. Feb. 3, 1956**
1980 OG-M TCH 6 0 0 0 0 —

**Holy, Martin / b. Feb. 1, 1980**
2000 WM20 CZE 7 0 0 0 0 G

**Holzer, Mathias / b. Mar. 4, 1973**
1992 WM20 SUI 7 0 1 1 4 —

**Holzer, Renzo / b. Mar. 9, 1952**
1976 OG-M SUI 5 2 3 5 4 —

**Holzinger, Brian / b. Oct. 10, 1972**
1992 WM20 USA 7 1 1 2 2 B

**Holzmann, Georg / b. Mar. 5, 1961**
1979-81 WM20 FRG 15 8 9 17 55 —
1986-95 WM FRG 44 2 8 10 87 —
1988-92 OG-M FRG 12 3 5 8 12 —

**Homan, Viktor / b. May 9, 1984**
2002 WM18 BLR 8 1 3 4 2 —

**Homburg, Fred / b. Feb. 4, 1962**
1981 WM NED 4 0 1 1 6 —

**Home, William / b. unknown / d. unknown**
1930 WM GBR 1 1 0 1 — —

**Hommel, Christian / b. Jan. 23, 1981**
2003 WM GER 4 0 0 0 2 —

**Homola, Craig / b. Nov. 29, 1958**
1981 WM USA 7 0 2 2 4 —

**Honda, Yoshiaki / b. Apr. 5, 1951**
1976-80 OG-M* JPN 10 0 0 0 4 —
*played under birth name of Yoshiaki Kyoya at 1976 OG-M before adopting his wife's name (Honda) in 1978

**Honegger, Doug / b. Feb. 24, 1968**
1991-92 WM SUI 17 0 0 0 16 —
1992 OG-M SUI 2 0 0 0 0 —

**Honig, Herbert / b. Sept. 19, 1932**
1957 WM GDR 3 0 — 0 — —

**Honkanen, Jaakko / b. July 16, 1942**
1965 WM FIN 6 0 0 0 2 —

**Honkavaara, Aarne / b. July 7, 1924**
1949-51 WM FIN 10 8 — 8 0 —
1952 OG-M FIN 8 2 2 4 0 —

**Honma, Sadaki / b. June 4, 1953**
1976-80 OG-M JPN 10 1 2 3 6 —

**Honma, Shinichi / b. Nov. 3, 1934**
1957 WM JPN 7 2 0 2 — —
1960-64 OG-M JPN 12 3 2 5 16 —

**Honma, Teruyasu / b. Mar. 7, 1949**
1972 OG-M JPN 2 0 1 1 0 —

**Hope, Joe / b. Jan. 1, 1982**
2000 WM18 USA 6 2 3 5 4 —
2002 WM20 USA 7 0 1 1 4 —

**Hope, Shannon / b. Nov. 25, 1962**
1994 WM GBR 6 0 1 1 14 —

**Hopfer, Rupert / b. unknown**
1981 WM20 AUT 5 0 0 0 0 —

**Horacek, Jan / b. May 22, 1979**
1999 WM20 CZE 6 1 1 2 12 —

**Horak, Jakub / b. May 17, 1974**
1994 WM20 SUI 7 1 0 1 4 —

**Horak, Michal / b. Feb. 25, 1977**
1997 WM20 CZE 7 0 2 2 0 —

**Horak, Roman / b. Sept. 24, 1969**
1988 WM20 TCH 7 4 2 6 4 —
1993-95 WM CZE 22 1 2 3 4 B
1994 OG-M CZE 7 3 1 4 2 —

**Horansky, Stanislav / b. Mar. 2, 1965**
1985 WM20 TCH 7 0 1 1 4 S

**Horava, Miloslav / b. Aug. 14, 1961**
1980-81 WM20 TCH 10 2 4 6 8 —
1981-93 WM CZE 45 4 16 20 18 G,S,3B
1981-87 CC TCH 16 3 3 6 11 —
1984-94 OG-M CZE 28 2 5 7 24 S,B
~WM20 IIHF Directorate Best Defenceman (1981), WM20 All-Star Team/Defence (1981)

**Horava, Miloslav / b. Aug. 14, 1961**
2000 WM18 CZE 6 2 1 3 2 —
2002 WM20 CZE 7 2 3 5 2 —

**Horava, Petr / b. July 22, 1985**
2003 WM18 CZE 6 0 0 0 6 —

**Horesovsky, Josef / b. July 18, 1946**
1969-73 WM TCH 47 8 5 13 40 G,S,3B
1968-72 OG-M TCH 12 5 2 7 2 S,B
~OG-M IIHF Directorate Best Defenceman (1968)

**Hori, Hiroshi / b. Sept. 19, 1949**
1972-80 OG-M JPN 14 0 3 3 8 —

**Horna, Tomas / b. Nov. 20, 1980**
2000 WM20 CZE 7 0 1 1 0 G

**Hornak, Ernest / b. Apr. 16, 1964**
1983-84 WM20 TCH 14 12 3 15 9 S,B

**Hornak, Marek / b. July 2, 1983**
2001 WM18 SVK 6 3 0 3 0 —

**Hornby, Howie / b. Oct. 7, 1934**
1963 WM CAN 7 0 2 2 2 —

**Horne, Alfred / b. Oct. 4, 1931**
1956 OG-M CAN 3 1 0 1 0 B

**Horsky, Jaroslav / b. Jan. 20, 1960**
1979 WM20 TCH 6 1 1 2 0 S

**Horsky, Phillippe / b. Jan. 29, 1983**
2004-05 WM AUT 10 0 1 1 0 —

**Horvat, Drago / b. July 9, 1958**
1984 OG-M YUG 4 0 0 0 2 —

**Horvath, Andras / b. Apr. 8, 1976**
2009 WM HUN 6 1 0 1 10 —

**Horvath, Branislav / b. July 18, 1989**
2007 WM18 SVK 6 2 1 3 0 —

**Horvath, Marian / b. Nov. 28, 1965**
1985 WM20 TCH 7 1 0 1 2 S

**Hoshino, Yoshio / b. Nov. 2, 1950**
1972-80 OG-M JPN 14 4 2 6 6 —

**Hosoi, Mikio / b. Sept. 19, 1949**
1980 OG-M JPN 5 0 0 0 0 —

**Hospodar, Ed / b. Feb. 9, 1959**
1978 WM20 USA 6 3 4 7 10 —

**Hostak, Martin / b. Nov. 11, 1967**
1987 WM20 TCH 7 7 3 10 4 S
1990-95 WM CZE 16 4 4 8 6 2B
1994 OG-M CZE 7 1 0 1 0 —

**Houck, Terry / b. Jan. 11, 1957**
1977 WM20 USA 7 0 0 0 2 —

**Houle, Denis / b. Aug. 19, 1958**
1977 WM20 CAN 7 0 1 1 0 S

**Houriet, Pierre / b. unknown**
1978 WM20 SUI 6 1 0 1 0 —

**Housley, Phil / b. Mar. 9, 1964**
1982 WM20 USA 7 1 0 1 6 —
1982-2003 WM USA 46 9 15 24 18 —
1984-96 WCH USA 12 0 5 5 4 1st
2002 OG-M USA 6 1 4 5 0 S
~IIHF Hall of Fame

**Howald, Patrick / b. Dec. 26, 1969**
1991-95 WM SUI 28 11 1 12 12 —
1992 OG-M SUI 7 4 3 7 4 —

**Howe, Mark / b. May 28, 1955**
1981 CC USA 6 0 4 4 2 —
1972 OG-M USA 5 0 0 0 0 S

**Howe, Marty / b. Jan. 15, 1937**
1967 WM USA 7 3 2 5 36 —

**Howes, Bruce / b. July 4, 1960**
1979 WM20 CAN 5 0 1 1 2 —

**Hrbaty, Jan / b. Jan. 20, 1942**
1967-70 WM TCH 23 4 4 8 2 2B
1968 OG-M TCH 7 2 7 9 2 S

**Hrbek, Petr / b. Apr. 3, 1969**
1988-89 WM20 TCH 14 7 6 13 8 B
1992-93 WM TCH 16 10 1 11 4 2B
1991 CC TCH 1 0 0 0 0 —
1992-94 OG-M CZE 16 3 7 10 6 B
~WM All-Star Team/Forward (1992), WM20 All-Star Team/Forward (1988)

**Hrdina, Jan / b. Feb. 6, 1976**
1995 WM20 CZE 7 2 1 3 4 —
2002 WM CZE 7 2 1 3 12 —
2002 OG-M CZE 4 0 0 0 0 —

**Hrdina, Jiri / b. Jan. 5, 1958**
1977-78 WM20 TCH 13 3 5 8 2 B
1982-90 WM TCH 57 15 15 30 38 G,2S,2B
1984-87 CC TCH 11 1 3 4 4 —
1984-88 OG-M TCH 15 6 10 16 8 B

**Hrebejk, Stepan / b. May 28, 1982**
2000 WM18 CZE 6 0 1 1 8 —

**Hreus, Michal / b. Mar. 9, 1973**
2000 WM SVK 7 2 1 3 2 S

**Hromadka, Karel / b. May 23, 1905 / d. unknown**
1930-35 WM TCH 28 10 1 11 0 B
1928-36 OG-M TCH 7 1 — 1 — —

**Hrtus, Michal / b.July 9, 1987**
2005 WM18 SVK 6 0 1 1 2 —

**Hrubes, Milos / b. Mar. 21, 1964**
1983-84 WM20 TCH 14 1 3 4 10 S,B

**Hruska, Antonin / b. Jan. 25, 1989**
2007 WM18 SVK 6 0 0 0 8 —

**Hruska, David / b. Jan. 8, 1977**
1997 WM20 CZE 7 0 1 1 2 —

**Hruska, Radim / b. Oct. 12, 1985**
2004 WM20 CZE 7 1 1 2 0 —

**Huba, Peter / b. Feb. 17, 1986**
2004 WM18 SVK 6 0 0 0 2 —

**Hubay-Hruby, Istvan / b. unknown / d. unknown**
1938 WM HUN 2 0 — 0 — —

**Huber, Hans / b. Dec. 10, 1929**
1954-59 WM FRG 22 7 0 7 2 —
1956-60 OG-M FRG 14 7 0 7 2 —

**Huber, Willie / b. Jan. 15, 1958**
1977-78 WM20 CAN 13 1 4 5 13 S,B
1981 WM CAN 7 0 2 2 10 —

**Hubinsky, Peter / b. Apr. 4, 1987**
2005 WM18 SVK 5 0 0 0 0 —

**Hubl, Jaroslav / b. Oct. 4, 1957**
1977 WM20 TCH 7 0 7 7 2 B

**Huck, Fran / b. Dec. 4, 1945**
1966-69 WM CAN 24 12 12 24 26 2B
1968 OG-M CAN 7 4 5 9 10 B
~IIHF Hall of Fame
~OG-M All-Star Team/Forward (1968), WM All-Star Team/Forward (1966)

**Huddy, Charlie / b. June 2, 1959**
1984 CC CAN 7 0 2 2 2 1st

**Hudec, Michal / b. Oct. 23, 1979**
1999 WM20 SVK 6 1 1 2 0 B
2006 WM SVK 3 1 0 1 0 —

| | | | | | | | | |
|---|---|---|---|---|---|---|---|---|
| **Hudec, Stanislav / b. June 3, 1982** | | | | | | | | |
| 2000 | WM18 | SVK | 6 | 0 | 0 | 0 | 6 | — |
| 2002 | WM20 | SVK | 7 | 1 | 1 | 2 | 14 | — |
| **Hudler, Jiri / b. Jan. 4, 1984** | | | | | | | | |
| 2000-02 | WM18 | CZE | 14 | 7 | 9 | 16 | 16 | — |
| 2002-04 | WM20 | CZE | 20 | 6 | 9 | 15 | 8 | — |
| 2003 | WM | CZE | 9 | 2 | 4 | 6 | 2 | — |
| ~WM18 All-Star Team/Forward (2002) | | | | | | | | |
| **Hudson, Lou / b. May 16, 1898 / d. June 24, 1975** | | | | | | | | |
| 1928 | OG-M | CAN | 3 | 4 | — | 4 | — | G |
| **Huffman, Kerry / b. Jan. 3, 1968** | | | | | | | | |
| 1987 | WM20 | CAN | 6 | 0 | 1 | 1 | 4 | — |
| 1992 | WM | CAN | 6 | 1 | 0 | 1 | 2 | — |
| **Hug, Ernst / b. Oct. 23, 1910 / d. unknown** | | | | | | | | |
| 1934-35 | WM | SUI | 14 | 0 | — | 0 | — | S |
| 1936 | OG-M | SUI | 3 | 0 | 0 | 0 | — | — |
| **Hugaru, Alexandru / b. unknown / d. unknown** | | | | | | | | |
| 1938 | WM | ROM | 4 | 1 | — | 1 | — | — |
| **Huggins, Al / b. Dec. 21, 1910 / d. unknown** | | | | | | | | |
| 1933 | WM | CAN | 5 | 1 | — | 1 | 0 | S |
| **Hughes, Ryan / b. Jan. 17, 1972** | | | | | | | | |
| 1992 | WM20 | CAN | 7 | 0 | 1 | 1 | 0 | — |
| **Huglen, Mark / b. May 20, 1962** | | | | | | | | |
| 1981 | WM20 | USA | 5 | 0 | 0 | 0 | 6 | — |
| **Huguenin, Rene / b. Aug. 9, 1944** | | | | | | | | |
| 1972 | WM | SUI | 10 | 0 | 0 | 0 | 2 | — |
| 1972 | OG-M | SUI | 3 | 0 | 1 | 1 | 0 | — |
| **Huhtala, Jarmo / b. Apr. 16, 1957** | | | | | | | | |
| 1977 | WM20 | FIN | 7 | 3 | 1 | 4 | 2 | — |
| **Huhtala, Tommi / b. Dec. 7, 1987** | | | | | | | | |
| 2005 | WM18 | FIN | 6 | 1 | 0 | 1 | 6 | — |
| **Huikari, Juha / b. Jan. 8, 1960** | | | | | | | | |
| 1979-80 | WM20 | FIN | 11 | 3 | 3 | 6 | 28 | S |
| 1985 | WM | FIN | 10 | 1 | 2 | 3 | 12 | — |
| 1981 | CC | FIN | 3 | 0 | 0 | 0 | 4 | — |
| **Huizinga, Chuck / b. Oct. 29, 1953** | | | | | | | | |
| 1980 | OG-M | NED | 5 | 0 | 0 | 0 | 0 | — |
| **Hujsa, Martin / b. Sept. 9, 1979** | | | | | | | | |
| 1999 | WM20 | SVK | 6 | 0 | 1 | 1 | 2 | B |
| **Hull, Bobby / b. Jan. 3, 1939** | | | | | | | | |
| 1976 | CC | CAN | 7 | 5 | 3 | 8 | 2 | 1st |
| **Hull, Brett / b. Aug. 9, 1964** | | | | | | | | |
| 1986 | WM | USA | 10 | 7 | 4 | 11 | 16 | — |
| 1991-2004 | WCH | USA | 17 | 9 | 11 | 20 | 6 | 1st,2nd |
| 1998-2002 | OG-M | USA | 10 | 5 | 6 | 11 | 6 | S |
| **Hull, Dennis / b. Nov. 19, 1944** | | | | | | | | |
| 1972 | SS | CAN | 4 | 2 | 2 | 4 | 4 | 1st |
| **Hull, Jody / b. Feb. 2, 1969** | | | | | | | | |
| 1988 | WM20 | CAN | 7 | 2 | 1 | 3 | 2 | G |
| **Hult, Alexander / b. Nov. 19, 1984** | | | | | | | | |
| 2004 | WM20 | SWE | 6 | 0 | 2 | 2 | 2 | — |
| **Hultgren, Herman / b. June 25, 1980** | | | | | | | | |
| 2000 | WM20 | SWE | 6 | 1 | 3 | 4 | 0 | — |
| **Huml, Ivan / b. Sept. 6, 1981** | | | | | | | | |
| 1999 | WM18 | CZE | 7 | 0 | 0 | 0 | 4 | — |
| **Hunkes, Jiri / b. July 31, 1984** | | | | | | | | |
| 2002 | WM18 | CZE | 8 | 0 | 2 | 2 | 16 | B |
| **Hunter, Dave / b. Jan. 1, 1958** | | | | | | | | |
| 1977 | WM20 | CAN | 7 | 6 | 0 | 6 | 4 | S |
| **Hunter, Eric / b. Sept. 11, 1986** | | | | | | | | |
| 2004 | WM18 | CAN | 7 | 2 | 1 | 3 | 6 | — |
| **Huokko, Jan / b. June 11, 1974** | | | | | | | | |
| 1999 | WM | SWE | 10 | 0 | 2 | 2 | 2 | B |
| **Hurbanek, Kay / b. Mar. 24, 1982** | | | | | | | | |
| 2000 | WM18 | GER | 6 | 3 | 1 | 4 | 8 | — |
| **Hurley, Paul / b. July 12, 1945** | | | | | | | | |
| 1968 | OG-M | USA | 7 | 3 | 3 | 6 | 0 | — |
| **Hurley, Tom / b. Aug. 29, 1944** | | | | | | | | |
| 1967 | WM | USA | 7 | 1 | 2 | 3 | 2 | — |
| 1968 | OG-M | USA | 7 | 0 | 2 | 2 | 2 | — |
| **Hurst, Art / b. May 2, 1933 / d. Nov. 1993** | | | | | | | | |
| 1956 | OG-M | CAN | 8 | 3 | 3 | 6 | 22 | B |
| **Hurtaj, Lubomir / b. Nov. 28, 1975** | | | | | | | | |
| 2000 | WM | SVK | 8 | 1 | 2 | 3 | 2 | S |
| **Hurych, Oldrich / b. Dec. 4, 1917 / d. unknown** | | | | | | | | |
| 1939 | WM | TCH | 6 | 3 | — | 3 | — | — |
| **Huschto, Dieter / b. July 17, 1947** | | | | | | | | |
| 1974 | WM | GDR | 10 | 3 | 0 | 3 | 4 | — |
| **Huse, Tom / b. unknown** | | | | | | | | |
| 1979 | WM20 | NOR | 5 | 0 | 0 | 0 | 0 | — |
| **Huss, Anders / b. Apr. 6, 1964** | | | | | | | | |
| 1984 | WM20 | SWE | 6 | 4 | 1 | 5 | 4 | — |
| 1990-92 | WM | SWE | 18 | 1 | 5 | 6 | 12 | G,S |
| **Husse, Andrzej / b. May 27, 1967** | | | | | | | | |
| 1987 | WM20 | POL | 7 | 0 | 2 | 2 | 2 | — |
| **Hutanu, Vasile / b. June 1, 1954** | | | | | | | | |
| 1976 | OG-M | ROM | 5 | 1 | 0 | 1 | 2 | — |
| **Hutchinson, Andrew / b. Mar. 24, 1980** | | | | | | | | |
| 2007 | WM | USA | 7 | 3 | 1 | 4 | 2 | — |
| **Hutchinson, Don / b. unknown / d. unknown** | | | | | | | | |
| 1930 | WM | CAN | 1 | 0 | — | 0 | — | G |
| **Hutchinson, John / b. unknown / d. unknown** | | | | | | | | |
| 1938 | WM | USA | 2 | 0 | — | 0 | — | — |
| **Huttenmoser-Schefer, Marc / b. unknown** | | | | | | | | |
| 1999 | WM18 | SUI | 7 | 0 | 0 | 0 | 0 | — |
| **Hutz, Bernie / b. Apr. 30, 1961** | | | | | | | | |
| 1981 | WM20 | AUT | 5 | 0 | 0 | 0 | 6 | — |
| 1984-88 | OG-M | AUT | 8 | 0 | 2 | 2 | 2 | — |
| **Huura, Pasi / b. Mar. 23, 1966** | | | | | | | | |
| 1991 | CC | FIN | 6 | 0 | 0 | 0 | 4 | — |
| **Huusko, Anders / b. Aug. 24, 1971** | | | | | | | | |
| 1991 | WM20 | SWE | 7 | 3 | 1 | 4 | 10 | — |
| 1996-98 | WM | SWE | 16 | 1 | 2 | 3 | 18 | G |
| **Huusko, Erik / b. Aug. 24, 1971** | | | | | | | | |
| 1991 | WM20 | SWE | 7 | 2 | 1 | 3 | 2 | — |
| 1995 | WM | SWE | 8 | 2 | 2 | 4 | 6 | S |
| **Hviid, Erik / b. unknown** | | | | | | | | |
| 1949 | WM | DEN | 3 | 0 | — | 0 | — | — |
| **Hviid, Jorgen / b. Sept. 1, 1916 / d. unknown** | | | | | | | | |
| 1949 | WM | DEN | 3 | 4 | 0 | 4 | 0 | — |
| ~IIHF Hall of Fame (Builder) | | | | | | | | |
| **Hvila, Lukas / b. Nov. 30, 1981** | | | | | | | | |
| 1999 | WM18 | SVK | 7 | 3 | 1 | 4 | 8 | B |
| 2001 | WM20 | SVK | 7 | 0 | 0 | 0 | 0 | — |
| **Hymanson, Jeff / b. Mar. 11, 1954** | | | | | | | | |
| 1976 | WM | USA | 10 | 1 | 0 | 1 | 14 | — |
| 1976 | OG-M | USA | 5 | 0 | 0 | 0 | 4 | — |
| **Hynes, Dave / b. Apr. 17, 1951** | | | | | | | | |
| 1977 | WM | USA | 10 | 3 | 4 | 7 | 10 | — |
| **Hynes, Gord / b. July 22, 1966** | | | | | | | | |
| 1992 | OG-M | CAN | 8 | 3 | 3 | 6 | 6 | S |
| **Hynes, Wayne / b. May 29, 1969** | | | | | | | | |
| 2001-02 | WM | GER | 14 | 5 | 1 | 6 | 8 | — |
| 2002 | OG-M | GER | 7 | 0 | 0 | 0 | 6 | — |
| **Hynning, Fredrik / b. May 15, 1983** | | | | | | | | |
| 2001 | WM18 | SWE | 6 | 0 | 4 | 4 | 0 | — |
| **Hysing, Mats / b. Aug. 13, 1944** | | | | | | | | |
| 1969 | WM | SWE | 7 | 0 | 2 | 2 | 0 | S |
| **Hytiainen, Pentti / b. Sept. 20, 1941** | | | | | | | | |
| 1961-63 | WM | FIN | 19 | 1 | 4 | 5 | 4 | — |
| **Hytonen, Erkki / b. May 27, 1933** | | | | | | | | |
| 1954-58 | WM | FIN | 21 | 1 | 0 | 1 | 13 | — |
| 1952 | OG-M | FIN | 4 | 0 | 0 | 0 | 0 | — |
| **Hytti, Jari / b. Mar. 28, 1959** | | | | | | | | |
| 1979 | WM20 | FIN | 6 | 0 | 0 | 0 | 4 | — |
| **Hytia, Mikko / b. unknown** | | | | | | | | |
| 1999 | WM18 | FIN | 7 | 4 | 3 | 7 | 4 | G |
| **Iafrate, Al / b. Mar. 21, 1966** | | | | | | | | |
| 1998 | WM | USA | 4 | 0 | 2 | 2 | 6 | — |
| 1984 | OG-M | USA | 6 | 0 | 0 | 0 | 2 | — |
| **Ianovici, Andrei / b. unknown** | | | | | | | | |
| 1964 | OG-M | ROM | 1 | 0 | — | 0 | — | — |
| **Ibelherr, Franz / b. July 3, 1964** | | | | | | | | |
| 1983-84 | WM20 | FRG | 13 | 0 | 0 | 0 | 8 | — |
| **Iberer, Matthias / b. Apr. 29, 1985** | | | | | | | | |
| 2004 | WM20 | AUT | 6 | 0 | 0 | 0 | 2 | — |
| **Ibermajer, Frantisek / b. 1961** | | | | | | | | |
| 1981 | WM20 | TCH | 5 | 0 | 0 | 0 | 0 | — |
| **Ibounig, Christoph / b. Jan. 23, 1985** | | | | | | | | |
| 2004 | WM20 | AUT | 6 | 0 | 0 | 0 | 2 | — |
| **Ibragimov, Rinat / b. Mar. 7, 1986** | | | | | | | | |
| 2004 | WM18 | RUS | 6 | 0 | 0 | 0 | 0 | G |
| **Ichikawa, Tatsuo / b. Feb. 11, 1916 / d. unknown** | | | | | | | | |
| 1936 | OG-M | JPN | 2 | 0 | 0 | 0 | — | — |
| **Iga, Yuji / b. July 18, 1965** | | | | | | | | |
| 1998 | OG-M | JPN | 4 | 0 | 0 | 0 | 2 | — |
| **Iglehart, Stewart / b. Feb. 22, 1910 / d. unknown** | | | | | | | | |
| 1933 | WM | USA | 5 | 0 | — | 0 | 0 | G |
| **Ignatius, Panu / b. May 11, 1929** | | | | | | | | |
| 1954-55 | WM | FIN | 14 | 1 | 1 | 2 | 6 | — |
| **Ignatjevs, Viktors / b. Apr. 26, 1970** | | | | | | | | |
| 2000-05 | WM | LAT | 31 | 1 | 3 | 4 | 38 | — |
| 2002 | OG-M | LAT | 4 | 0 | 0 | 0 | 4 | — |
| **Ignatovics, Andrejs / b. Mar. 24, 1971** | | | | | | | | |
| 1997-99 | WM | LAT | 16 | 2 | 5 | 7 | 4 | — |
| **Ignatushkin, Igor / b. Apr. 7, 1984** | | | | | | | | |
| 2002 | WM18 | RUS | 8 | 2 | 9 | 11 | 2 | S |
| **Ihala, Hannu / b. Dec. 5, 1957** | | | | | | | | |
| 1977 | WM20 | FIN | 7 | 0 | 1 | 1 | 0 | — |
| **Ihalainen, Kalevi / b. Dec. 23, 1913 / d. unknown** | | | | | | | | |
| 1939 | WM | FIN | 2 | 0 | — | 0 | — | — |
| **Ihara, Akira / b. Jan. 16, 1974** | | | | | | | | |
| 1993 | WM20 | JPN | 7 | 2 | 2 | 4 | 6 | — |
| **Ihnacak, Peter / b. May 3, 1957** | | | | | | | | |
| 1977 | WM20 | TCH | 7 | 2 | 5 | 7 | 0 | B |
| 1982 | WM | TCH | 4 | 0 | 0 | 0 | 0 | S |
| **Iizuka, Yuji / b. May 17, 1974** | | | | | | | | |
| 1993 | WM20 | JPN | 7 | 0 | 0 | 0 | 0 | — |
| **Ikonen, Juha / b. June 7, 1970** | | | | | | | | |
| 1998 | WM | FIN | 10 | 2 | 2 | 4 | 12 | S |
| **Ilavsky, Slavomir / b. May 11, 1969** | | | | | | | | |
| 1996 | WCH | SVK | 1 | 1 | 1 | 2 | 0 | — |
| **Ilgunas, Vytautas / b. unknown / d. unknown** | | | | | | | | |
| 1938 | WM | LTU | 2 | 1 | — | 1 | — | — |
| **Iliev, Gheorghi / b. Jan. 18, 1946** | | | | | | | | |
| 1976 | OG-M | BUL | 5 | 1 | 0 | 1 | 6 | — |
| **Iljina, Timo / b. June 6, 1966** | | | | | | | | |
| 1986 | WM20 | FIN | 7 | 1 | 4 | 5 | 2 | — |
| **Imes, Chris / b. Aug. 27, 1972** | | | | | | | | |
| 1991-92 | WM20 | USA | 14 | 1 | 2 | 3 | 0 | B |
| 1995 | WM | USA | 6 | 1 | 0 | 1 | 0 | — |
| 1994 | OG-M | USA | 8 | 0 | 0 | 0 | 2 | — |
| **Immonen, Jarkko / b. Apr. 19, 1982** | | | | | | | | |
| 2002 | WM18 | FIN | 8 | 2 | 4 | 6 | 6 | — |
| 2004 | WM20 | FIN | 7 | 2 | 3 | 5 | 2 | B |
| **Immonen, Tuomas / b. May 16, 1983** | | | | | | | | |
| 2003 | WM20 | FIN | 7 | 1 | 2 | 3 | 4 | B |
| **Immonen, Waltteri / b. Apr. 3, 1967** | | | | | | | | |
| 1992-94 | WM | FIN | 13 | 3 | 2 | 5 | 0 | 2S |
| **Imrie, Tom / b. July 15, 1937** | | | | | | | | |
| 1962 | WM | GBR | 7 | 2 | 3 | 5 | 2 | — |
| **Inaba, Kiku / b. unknown / d. unknown** | | | | | | | | |
| 1930 | WM | JPN | 1 | 0 | 0 | 0 | — | — |
| **Inatsu, Hidenori / b. June 5, 1938** | | | | | | | | |
| 1960 | OG-M | JPN | 5 | 2 | 0 | 2 | 8 | — |
| **Incze, Gabor / b. unknown / d. unknown** | | | | | | | | |
| 1947 | WM | ROM | 7 | 4 | — | 4 | — | — |
| **Incze, Lajos / b. Oct. 17, 1918 / d. unknown** | | | | | | | | |
| 1947 | WM | ROM | 7 | 8 | — | 8 | — | — |
| **Ingman, Jan / b. Nov. 25, 1961** | | | | | | | | |
| 1981 | WM20 | SWE | 5 | 4 | 2 | 6 | 2 | G |
| **Inman, David / b. June 13, 1980** | | | | | | | | |
| 2000 | WM20 | USA | 7 | 0 | 0 | 0 | 4 | — |
| **Innocenti, Dino / b. Nov. 6, 1913 / d. unknown** | | | | | | | | |
| 1939 | WM | ITA | 7 | 2 | — | 2 | — | — |
| 1948 | OG-M | ITA | 6 | 4 | — | 4 | — | — |
| **Insam, Adolf / b. Aug. 4, 1951** | | | | | | | | |
| 1982-83 | WM | ITA | 8 | 1 | 0 | 1 | 2 | — |
| 1984 | OG-M | ITA | 5 | 0 | 0 | 0 | 0 | — |
| **Insam, Leo / b. Feb. 6, 1975** | | | | | | | | |
| 1995-2001 | WM | ITA | 36 | 2 | 3 | 5 | 32 | — |
| 1994-98 | OG-M | ITA | 5 | 0 | 1 | 1 | 0 | — |
| **Intranuovo, Ralph / b. Dec. 11, 1973** | | | | | | | | |
| 1993 | WM20 | CAN | 7 | 3 | 2 | 5 | 4 | G |
| 1995 | WM | CAN | 8 | 5 | 1 | 6 | 6 | B |
| **Iob, Tony / b. Jan. 2, 1971** | | | | | | | | |
| 1997-2006 | WM | ITA | 23 | 4 | 3 | 7 | 75 | — |
| 2006 | OG-M | ITA | 5 | 2 | 2 | 4 | 2 | — |
| **Ionescu, Ion / b. Feb. 17, 1935** | | | | | | | | |
| 1964-68 | OG-M | ROM | 12 | 2 | 6 | 8 | 10 | — |
| **Ionita, Ion / b. Jan. 9, 1951** | | | | | | | | |
| 1977 | WM | ROM | 10 | 0 | 1 | 1 | 6 | — |
| 1976 | OG-M | ROM | 5 | 0 | 1 | 1 | 2 | — |
| **Ionov, Anatoli / b. Aug. 6, 1939** | | | | | | | | |
| 1965-66 | WM | URS | 8 | 4 | 4 | 8 | 8 | 2G |
| 1968 | OG-M | URS | 6 | 1 | 2 | 3 | 2 | G |
| **Iovio, Emilio / b. Mar. 9, 1962** | | | | | | | | |
| 1982-94 | WM | ITA | 24 | 2 | 1 | 3 | 8 | — |
| 1992-94 | OG-M | ITA | 10 | 4 | 1 | 5 | 0 | — |
| **Irani, Michael / b. Oct. 6, 1982** | | | | | | | | |
| 2000 | WM18 | SWE | 6 | 1 | 1 | 2 | 4 | B |
| **Irie, Atsuo / b. Oct. 31, 1937** | | | | | | | | |
| 1960-64 | OG-M | JPN | 12 | 4 | 6 | 10 | 6 | — |
| **Irving, Randy / b. Aug. 12, 1959** | | | | | | | | |
| 1979 | WM20 | CAN | 5 | 4 | 2 | 6 | 8 | — |
| **Irving, Stu / b. Feb. 2, 1949** | | | | | | | | |
| 1972 | OG-M | USA | 5 | 1 | 1 | 2 | 6 | S |
| **Isakov, Yevgeni / b. Oct. 13, 1984** | | | | | | | | |
| 2002 | WM18 | RUS | 8 | 4 | 0 | 4 | 2 | S |
| **Isaksson, Esa / b. Apr. 21, 1947** | | | | | | | | |
| 1966-71 | WM | FIN | 23 | 5 | 6 | 11 | 2 | — |

**Isaksson, Ulf / b. Mar. 19, 1954**
1981-82 WM SWE 15 1 3 4 8 S
1981 CC SWE 1 0 0 0 0 —
**Isayenko, Denis / b. Mar. 17, 1980**
2000 WM20 UKR 7 0 1 1 10 —
2004-07 WM UKR 16 0 1 1 22 —
**Isbister, Brad / b. May 7, 1977**
1997 WM20 CAN 7 4 3 7 8 G
2000-01 WM CAN 16 9 3 12 34 —
**Iscacci, Ernesto / b. unknown / d. unknown**
1930 WM ITA 1 0 0 0 — —
**Ishiguro, Shiro / b. Feb. 12, 1975**
1993 WM20 JPN 7 0 0 0 0 —
**Ishioka, Gen / b. Jan. 13, 1976**
1993 WM20 JPN 5 0 0 0 0 —
**Iskrzycki, Andrzej / b. Nov. 20, 1951**
1975-79 WM POL 18 1 0 1 13 —
1976 OG-M POL 4 0 0 0 2 —
**Isojima, Akihito / b. July 24, 1973**
1993 WM20 JPN 7 0 0 0 2 —
1999-2001 WM JPN 13 0 2 2 2 —
**Isotalo, Pentti / b. Feb. 27, 1927**
1951 WM FIN 6 0 — 0 4 —
1952 OG-M FIN 8 0 0 0 2 —
**Isotalus, Petri / b. June 1, 1977**
1997 WM20 FIN 6 0 0 0 2 —
**Istomin, Denis / b. Jan. 12, 1987**
2005 WM18 RUS 4 0 2 2 2 —
**Itabashi, Shinichi / b. Jan. 15, 1974**
1993 WM20 JPN 7 0 1 1 6 —
**Itabashi, Toru / b. June 6, 1946**
1968 OG-M JPN 5 0 0 0 6 —
**Ito, Kengo / b. Dec. 4, 1978**
2000-04 WM JPN 30 3 6 9 22 —
**Ito, Masatushi / b. July 14, 1978**
2002-04 WM JPN 18 4 2 6 2 —
**Ito, Minoru / b. Mar. 26, 1948**
1968-76 OG-M JPN 14 9 2 11 6 —
**Ito, Norio / b. July 18, 1948**
1980 OG-M JPN 5 0 0 0 0 —
**Itzicsohn, Gilbert / b. Aug. 17, 1944**
1968 OG-M FRA 5 2 2 4 6 —
**Ivankovic, Vjeran / b. Feb. 24, 1975**
1994 WM20 SUI 7 0 1 1 0 —
1995 WM SUI 7 2 1 3 4 —
**Ivanov, Alexei / b. Jan. 5, 1985**
2003 WM18 RUS 6 1 2 3 6 B
**Ivanov, Eduard / b. Apr. 25, 1938**
1963-67 WM URS 21 6 5 11 20 3G
1964 OG-M URS 7 5 1 6 4 G
~OG-M IIHF Directorate Best Forward (1964)
**Ivanov, Igor / b. Oct. 26, 1970**
1989-90 WM20 URS 13 5 4 9 8 G,S
1994 OG-M RUS 8 0 0 0 2 —
**Ivanov, Igor / b. July 5, 1973**
1993 WM20 RUS 7 2 0 2 6 —
**Ivanov, Yevgeni / b. May 24, 1980**
1999-2000 WM20 KAZ 12 2 0 2 20 —
**Ivarsson, Lars / b. Oct. 21, 1963**
1988 OG-M SWE 2 1 2 3 0 B
**Iwamoto, Koji / b. Jan. 22, 1942**
1964-72 OG-M JPN 16 11 8 19 8 —
**Iwaoka, Juji / b. Sept. 28, 1933**
1960 OG-M JPN 5 3 0 3 0 —
**Iwata, Yasunori / b. Nov. 24, 1972**
1998-2004 WM JPN 30 3 3 6 10 —
**Jaakola, Seppo / b. Jan. 28, 1920 / d. unknown**
1939 WM FIN 1 0 — 0 — —
**Jaaskalainen, Teemu / b. June 7, 1983**
2001 WM18 FIN 6 2 0 2 2 B
2003 WM20 FIN 7 1 0 1 4 B
**Jaatinen, Antti / b. July 24, 1986**
2004 WM18 FIN 6 0 1 1 14 —
**Jablonski, Kurt / b. Jan. 10, 1931**
1957 WM GDR 6 1 — 1 4 —
**Jaccard, Marius / b. Mar. 27, 1898 / d. Jan. 19, 1978**
1920-24 OG-M SUI 4 0 0 0 — —
**Jachna, Leszek / b. May 9, 1958**
1977 WM20 POL 7 0 0 0 0 —
1986 WM POL 9 1 1 2 4 —
1980-88 OG-M POL 17 0 0 0 10 —
**Jackman, Richard / b. June 28, 1978**
1997 WM20 CAN 7 2 0 2 0 G
**Jackson, Don / b. Sept. 2, 1956**
1978-79 WM USA 18 1 2 3 20 —
**Jackson, Jeff / b. Apr. 24, 1965**
1985 WM20 CAN 7 1 7 8 10 G
**Jackson, Ted / b. 1899 / d. unknown**
1934-35 WM GBR 13 2 — 2 — B
**Jackson, Todd / b. Apr. 10, 1981**
1999 WM18 USA 6 2 1 3 2 —
**Jacobsen, Tom / b. Mar. 29, 1984**
2002 WM18 NOR 8 1 4 5 0 —
**Jacobsson, Peter / b. Dec. 18, 1972**
1991 WM20 SWE 3 0 2 2 4 —
**Jacquet, Emile / b. Sept. 25, 1886 / d. unknown**
1924 OG-M SUI 1 0 — 0 — —
**Jaenecke, Gustav / b. May 22, 1908 / d. May 30, 1985**
1930-39 WM GER 40 25 1 26 0 S,B
1928-36 OG-M GER 14 4 0 4 4 B
~IIHF Hall of Fame
**Jagersten, Markus / b. Mar. 11, 1984**
2002 WM18 NOR 8 0 1 1 6 —
**Jahns, Christoph / b. June 30, 1979**
1998 WM20 GER 6 0 0 0 0 —
**Jajszczok, Kordian / b. Sept. 4, 1950**
1976 WM POL 3 0 1 1 2 —
1976 OG-M POL 4 0 1 1 2 —
**Jakabhazi, Laszlo / b. Nov. 14, 1938**
1964 OG-M HUN 7 0 0 0 0 —
**Jakes, Jiri / b. Oct. 4, 1982**
2002 WM20 CZE 7 0 0 0 2 —
**Jakob, Thomas / b. Mar. 13, 1985**
2003 WM18 SUI 6 0 0 0 2 —
**Jakopic, Bogdan / b. Jan. 18, 1948**
1976 OG-M YUG 5 1 0 1 4 —
**Jaks, Peter / b. May 4, 1966**
1986 WM20 SUI 7 6 2 8 2 —
1987-98 WM SUI 29 5 6 11 16 —
1988-92 OG-M SUI 13 3 3 6 6 —
**Jalasvaara, Janne / b. Apr. 15, 1984**
2002 WM18 FIN 8 0 0 0 20 —
2003-04 WM20 FIN 14 1 2 3 10 2B
**Jalo, Risto / b. July 18, 1962**
1981-82 WM20 FIN 12 7 13 20 8 S,B
1983-90 WM FIN 39 4 10 14 16 —
1984 OG-M FIN 6 2 4 6 4 —
**Jalonen, Kari / b. Jan. 6, 1960**
1979-80 WM20 FIN 11 7 7 14 2 S
1981-89 WM FIN 50 21 27 48 11 —
1981 CC FIN 5 0 1 1 4 —
**Jamalainen, Jarmo / b. June 2, 1959**
1979 WM20 FIN 6 0 0 0 4 —
**Jamieson, Tom / b. Feb. 22, 1926**
1954 WM CAN 7 0 — 0 10 S
**Jaminki, Tommi / b. Feb. 11, 1983**
2001 WM18 FIN 6 2 2 4 4 B
**Jamtin, Andreas / b. May 4, 1983**
2001 WM18 SWE 6 3 4 7 26 —
2002-03 WM20 SWE 13 3 5 8 20 —
**Jan, Bogo / b. Feb. 20, 1944**
1964-72 OG-M YUG 15 5 3 8 6 —
**Jan, Ivo / b. Apr. 10, 1942**
1964-72 OG-M YUG 15 8 2 10 2 —
**Jan, Ivo / b. Apr. 3, 1975**
2002-05 WM SLO 17 7 6 13 6 —
**Jancek, Richard / b. Sept. 14, 1989**
2007 WM18 SVK 5 0 0 0 0 —
**Jancovic, Dalimir / b. Jan. 28, 1989**
2007 WM18 SVK 5 0 1 1 4 —
**Janczi, Andrzej / b. July 14, 1954**
1979 WM POL 4 0 0 0 0 —
1980 OG-M POL 5 0 0 0 2 —
**Janecky, Otakar / b. Dec. 26, 1960**
1980 WM20 TCH 2 0 2 2 0 —
1989-94 WM CZE 32 6 12 18 10 3B
1992-94 OG-M CZE 16 6 8 14 8 B
**Janiczko, Szymon / b. Jan. 9, 1930**
1955-59 WM POL 15 5 1 6 6 —
1956 OG-M POL 5 1 0 1 2 —
**Janik, Doug / b. Mar. 26, 1980**
1999-2000 WM20 USA 13 1 0 1 29 —
**Janikowski, Janusz / b. Mar. 10, 1968**
1987-88 WM20 POL 14 4 3 7 6 —
**Janiszewski, Henryk / b. Feb. 20, 1949**
1974 WM POL 5 0 0 0 2 —
1980 OG-M POL 5 1 2 3 2 —
**Jankowski, Jacek / b. May 9, 1968**
1987 WM20 POL 6 0 0 0 0 —
**Janku, Pavel / b. Apr. 28, 1969**
1995 WM CZE 8 1 0 1 2 —
**Janney, Craig / b. Sept. 26, 1967**
1985-86 WM20 USA 10 5 3 8 2 B
1987-94 WM USA 17 3 5 8 0 —
1991 CC USA 8 4 2 6 0 2nd
1988 OG-M USA 5 3 1 4 2 —
**Janos, Branislav / b. Jan. 8, 1971**
1991 WM20 TCH 7 4 4 8 6 B
1996-98 WM SVK 19 2 6 8 18 —
1994-98 OG-M SVK 12 2 4 6 6 —
**Janosi, Csaba / b. Mar. 10, 1981**
2009 WM HUN 6 0 0 0 0 —
**Jansen, Arve / b. Jan. 18, 1971**
1991 WM20 NOR 4 1 0 1 2 —
**Jansen, Birger / b. Jan. 7, 1948**
1972 OG-M NOR 4 0 0 0 2 —
**Jansen, Roy / b. May 6, 1950**
1972 OG-M NOR 4 2 0 2 6 —
**Janssen, Jan / b. Oct. 17, 1952**
1981 WM NED 8 1 2 3 0 —
1980 OG-M NED 5 0 3 3 4 —
**Jansson, Folke / b. Dec. 29, 1917 / d. Dec. 25, 1983**
1938 WM SWE 1 0 — 0 — —
**Jansson, Magnus / b. Nov. 16, 1969**
1989 WM20 SWE 7 1 2 3 4 S
**Jansson, Stefan / b. Mar. 23, 1966**
1986 WM20 SWE 7 0 1 1 2 —
**Jantunen, Marko / b. Feb. 14, 1971**
1991 WM20 FIN 7 3 10 13 12 —
1997 WM FIN 8 1 0 1 6 —
**Januszewski, Henryk / b. Feb. 20, 1949**
1979 WM POL 7 3 1 4 18 —
**Janzen, Sergej / b. Feb. 18, 1987**
2005 WM18 GER 6 1 1 2 2 —
**Janzon, Joachim / b. Oct. 25, 1959**
1979 WM20 FRG 5 0 0 0 0 —
**Jardine, Frank / b. Mar. 20, 1924**
1948 OG-M GBR 2 0 — 0 — —
**Jarecki, Henryk vel Fabian / b. 1919 / d. unknown**
1939 WM POL 5 1 — 1 — —
**Jarkko, Martti / b. Nov. 26, 1953**
1977-78 WM FIN 20 3 6 9 6 —
**Jarlsbo, Oystein / b. Apr. 3, 1961**
1979 WM20 NOR 5 0 1 1 8 —
1980-84 OG-M NOR 10 0 0 0 8 —
**Jarn, Heikki / b. Sept. 23, 1941**
1971 WM FIN 9 1 1 2 6 —
1972 OG-M FIN 5 2 0 2 2 —
**Jarvela, Pekka / b. Feb. 9, 1962**
1981-82 WM20 FIN 12 8 9 17 8 S,B
1985-87 WM FIN 19 5 10 15 14 —
**Jarvenpaa, Hannu / b. May 19, 1963**
1982-83 WM20 FIN 13 4 5 9 10 B
1985-92 WM FIN 43 19 12 31 62 S
1991 CC FIN 6 0 1 1 4 —
1992 OG-M FIN 8 5 6 11 14 —
**Jarvenpaa, Juha / b. Dec. 18, 1965**
1990 WM FIN 9 1 0 1 2 —
**Jarventie, Martti / b. Apr. 4, 1976**
1995-96 WM20 FIN 13 1 2 3 28 —
**Jarvi, Iiro / b. Mar. 23, 1965**
1983-85 WM20 FIN 21 8 5 13 12 S
1987-89 WM FIN 17 2 2 4 20 —
1987-91 CC FIN 10 0 0 0 8 —
1988 OG-M FIN 8 2 5 7 10 S
**Jarvinen, Jan-Mikael / b. Feb. 26, 1988**
2006 WM18 FIN 6 1 4 5 2 S
**Jarvinen, Jari / b. Oct. 3, 1960**
1979-80 WM20 FIN 11 0 5 5 0 S
**Jarvinen, Kari / b. Jan. 13, 1957**
1977 WM20 FIN 7 4 1 5 18 —
**Jarvinen, Pauli / b. May 4, 1965**
1989-91 WM FIN 25 5 1 6 16 —
**Jasecko, Stanislav / b. Dec. 5, 1972**
1996-2000 WM SVK 26 0 2 2 18 S
1996 WCH SVK 1 0 0 0 2 —
1998 OG-M SVK 4 0 0 0 4 —
**Jasinski, Tomasz / b. Dec. 29, 1916 / d. Mar. 23, 1998**
1947 WM POL 7 1 — 1 — —
1948 OG-M POL 6 0 — 0 — —

**Jaskierski, Mieczyslaw / b. Oct. 17, 1950**
1970-79 WM POL 50 18 8 26 20 —
1976 OG-M POL 3 0 0 0 4 —

**Jasko, Jan / b. June 20, 1959**
1978-79 WM20 TCH 12 3 5 8 4 —
1987 CC TCH 2 0 0 0 4 —

**Jasko, Tomas / b. Dec. 9, 1983**
2001 WM18 SVK 6 4 4 8 0 —
2002 WM20 SVK 7 1 0 1 4 —

**Jaspers, Jason / b. Apr. 8, 1981**
2001 WM20 CAN 7 1 0 1 6 B

**Jass, Mareks / b. July 22, 1976**
1999 WM LAT 6 0 1 1 2 —

**Jasu, Juhani / b. Jan. 19, 1988**
2006 WM18 FIN 6 0 0 0 4 S

**Javanainen, Arto / b. Apr. 8, 1959**
1977-79 WM20 FIN 19 7 12 19 10 —
1982-83 WM FIN 15 3 3 6 12 —
1981 CC FIN 5 1 0 1 2 —
1984 OG-M FIN 6 2 2 4 6 —

**Javorek, Justin / b. July 22, 1988**
2006 WM18 SVK 6 0 0 0 4 —

**Jax, Fredrik / b. Feb. 6, 1972**
1992 WM20 SWE 7 2 4 6 2 S

**Jax, Hans / b. Mar. 6, 1948**
1975-77 WM SWE 30 8 13 21 4 S,2B

**Jeandupeux, Eric / b. Apr. 30, 1963**
1982 WM20 SUI 7 0 4 4 2 —

**Jebavy, Jiri / b. Mar. 17, 1989**
2006-07 WM18 CZE 13 0 2 2 10 —

**Jedamzik, Rafael / b. Mar. 6, 1974**
1993-94 WM20 GER 14 1 1 2 12 —

**Jelinek, Tomas / b. Apr. 29, 1962**
1981-82 WM20 TCH 12 5 3 8 14 S
1989-92 WM TCH 23 6 10 16 26 3B
1991 CC TCH 5 2 3 5 10 —
1992 OG-M TCH 8 3 2 5 12 B

**Jeney, Zoltan / b. May 13, 1910 / d. unknown**
1930-39 WM HUN 40 11 1 12 7 —
1936 OG-M HUN 5 1 — 1 — —

**Jenni, Heinz / b. July 25, 1951**
1972 WM SUI 6 0 0 0 12 —
1972 OG-M SUI 4 1 0 1 0 —

**Jenny, Oscar / b. June 17, 1939**
1962 WM SUI 7 1 1 2 8 —
1964 OG-M SUI 3 0 0 0 2 —

**Jensen, Dan / b. Jan. 16, 1969**
2003-04 WM DEN 12 2 1 3 16 —

**Jensen, David A. / b. May 3, 1961**
1980-81 WM20 USA 10 0 3 3 8 —
1984 CC USA 4 1 1 2 2 —
1984 OG-M USA 6 5 1 6 0 —

**Jensen, David H. / b. May 3, 1961**
1986-92 WM USA 16 4 3 7 12 —
1984 OG-M USA 6 0 0 0 6 —

**Jensen, Hans / b. unknown / d. unknown**
1937-38 WM NOR 6 0 0 0 2 —

**Jensen, Jimmy / b. Jan. 24, 1988**
2006 WM18 SWE 6 0 2 2 0 —

**Jensen, Paul / b. May 1, 1955**
1976 OG-M USA 5 0 0 0 4 —

**Jensen, Steve / b. Apr. 14, 1955**
1975-78 WM USA 26 9 5 14 12 —
1976 CC USA 5 1 0 1 2 —
1976 OG-M USA 5 5 0 5 6 —

**Jerabek, Vladimir / b. Feb. 25, 1959**
1979 WM20 TCH 6 0 1 1 2 S

**Jerecinsky, Josef / b. unknown / d. unknown**
1931 WM ROM 1 0 — 0 1 —

**Jeremiah, Bob / b. Feb. 19, 1913 / d. unknown**
1934 WM USA 4 0 — 0 — S

**Jessens, Andrejs / b. Dec. 9, 1919 / d. unknown**
1935 WM LAT 5 3 — 3 — —

**Jestin, Mathieu / b. Apr. 14, 1983**
2002 WM20 FRA 6 0 1 1 27 —

**Jezak, Marian / b. Nov. 26, 1928**
1955-59 WM POL 14 3 0 3 0 —
1952 OG-M POL 8 3 1 4 — —

**Jillson, Jeff / b. July 14, 1980**
1999-2000 WM20 USA 13 0 0 0 10 —
2004 WM USA 9 1 1 2 6 B

**Jindra, Josef / b. June 12, 1980**
2000 WM20 CZE 7 1 1 2 0 G

**Jindrich, Robert / b. Oct. 14, 1976**
1996 WM20 CZE 6 0 2 2 2 —

**Jirik, Jaroslav / b. Feb. 10, 1939**
1958-69 WM TCH 47 30 17 47 32 2S,3B
1960-68 OG-M TCH 15 7 7 14 8 S,B
~WM All-Star Team/Forward (1965)

**Jirkovsky, Jaroslav / b. 1891 / d. unknown**
1924 OG-M TCH 3 1 — 1 — —

**Jirotka, Drahos / b. Sept. 20, 1915 / d. unknown**
1935-38 WM TCH 5 1 0 1 0 B
1936 OG-M TCH 8 4 — 4 — —

**Jirotka, Zdenek / b. Feb. 15, 1914 / d. unknown**
1934-38 WM TCH 11 0 0 0 0 B
1936 OG-M TCH 4 2 — 2 — —

**Jiroutek, Jiri / b. Feb. 13, 1964**
1983-84 WM20 TCH 14 4 7 11 8 S,B

**Jiskra, Pavel / b. June 19, 1960**
1980 WM20 TCH 5 1 1 2 2 —

**Jobczyk, Wieslaw / b. Feb. 23, 1954**
1976-79 WM POL 18 7 4 11 10 —
1976-84 OG-M POL 15 8 6 14 10 —

**Jobin, David / b. Sept. 27, 1981**
1999 WM18 SUI 7 1 3 4 31 —
1999-2001 WM20 SUI 20 0 3 3 31 —

**Jobs, Kristoffer / b. Jan. 30, 1983**
2001 WM18 SWE 6 0 0 0 2 —

**Jocham, Sascha / b. July 20, 1987**
2005 WM18 GER 6 0 0 0 4 —

**Jochems, Gunther / b. Nov. 5, 1928**
1954-55 WM FRG 15 1 0 1 4 —
1956 OG-M FRG 7 0 0 0 0 —

**Jocher, Markus / b. Oct. 6, 1978**
1998 WM20 GER 6 0 0 0 8 —

**Jochl, Wolfgang / b. May 10, 1930**
1957 WM AUT 7 0 — 0 2 —
1956 OG-M AUT 6 0 1 1 0 —

**Jocius, — / b. unknown / d. unknown**
1938 WM LTU 4 1 — 1 — —

**Johannessen, Ola / b. May 1, 1981**
1999 WM18 NOR 6 0 1 1 6 —

**Johannesson, Konrad "Konnie" / b. Aug. 10, 1896 / d. Oct. 28, 1968**
1920 OG-M CAN 3 2 — 2 — G

**Johannson, Jim / b. Mar. 10, 1964**
1983-84 WM20 USA 14 7 5 12 16 —
1992 WM USA 6 2 1 3 2 —
1988-92 OG-M USA 13 1 1 2 6 —

**Johannson, John / b. Oct. 18, 1961**
1981 WM20 USA 4 2 0 2 0 —

**Johannson, Ken / b. Oct. 6, 1930**
1962-66 WM USA 12 5 3 8 4 B

**Johansen, Bjorn / b. Feb. 3, 1944**
1965 WM NOR 7 1 0 1 2 —
1968-72 OG-M NOR 9 1 0 1 4 —

**Johansen, Erik / b. July 8, 1983**
2001 WM18 NOR 6 2 1 3 4 —

**Johansen, Knut / b. 1959**
1979 WM20 NOR 5 0 0 0 0 —

**Johansen, Morten / b. Dec. 25, 1952**
1980 OG-M NOR 5 0 2 2 0 —

**Johansen, Roy / b. Apr. 27, 1960**
1979 WM20 NOR 5 0 0 0 0 —
1992-93 WM NOR 12 2 0 2 8 —
1984-94 OG-M NOR 12 2 1 3 2 —

**Johansen, Stig / b. Mar. 8, 1970**
1989-90 WM20 NOR 14 4 3 7 6 —

**Johansen, Tom / b. July 19, 1967**
1994-95 WM NOR 6 0 0 0 2 —
1992-94 OG-M NOR 12 2 0 2 4 —

**Johansen, Trevor / b. Mar. 30, 1957**
1977 WM20 CAN 6 0 1 1 11 S
1979 WM CAN 8 2 1 3 4 —

**Johansen, Vidar / b. Dec. 17, 1951**
1980 OG-M NOR 2 1 0 1 0 —

**Johansson, Andreas / b. May 19, 1973**
1992-93 WM20 SWE 14 2 7 9 18 2S
1995-2004 WM SWE 33 7 14 21 46 2S,2B
1996-2004 WCH SWE 6 0 0 0 6 —
1998 OG-M SWE 3 0 0 0 2 —

**Johansson, Bjorn / b. Feb. 23, 1950**
1972-76 WM SWE 47 6 10 16 26 S,4B
1976 CC SWE 5 1 2 3 2 —

**Johansson, Calle / b. Feb. 14, 1967**
1986-87 WM20 SWE 13 1 9 10 12 B
1991-92 WM SWE 9 1 1 2 10 2G
1991-96 WCH SWE 10 2 7 9 8 —
1998 OG-M SWE 4 0 0 0 2 —
~WM20 IIHF Directorate Best Defenceman (1987)

**Johansson, Daniel / b. Sept. 10, 1974**
1993-94 WM20 SWE 13 5 7 12 10 2S

**Johansson, Daniel / b. July 5, 1981**
1999 WM18 SWE 7 4 2 6 2 S

**Johansson, David / b. June 15, 1981**
1999 WM18 SWE 7 1 2 3 31 S
2001 WM20 SWE 7 2 0 2 8 —

**Johansson, Erik / b. Sept. 29, 1927 / d. Dec. 16, 1992**
1947-55 WM SWE 35 11 4 15 2 G,2S,B
1952 OG-M SWE 8 4 3 7 — B

**Johansson, Fredrik / b. Mar. 12, 1975**
1995 WM20 SWE 7 3 1 4 2 B

**Johansson, Fredrik / b. Feb. 27, 1984**
2002 WM18 SWE 8 1 0 1 2 —
2004 WM20 SWE 6 2 2 4 6 —

**Johansson (-Brandius), Georg / b. May 10, 1898 / d. Apr. 20, 1964**
1920 OG-M SWE 6 3 — 3 2 —

**Johansson, Gosta / b. Mar. 2, 1929 / d. Apr. 10, 1997**
1949-55 WM SWE 34 28 5 33 4 G,S,B
1952 OG-M SWE 8 6 1 7 — B

**Johansson, Gustaf "Lulle" / b. Sept. 14, 1900 / d. July 1, 1971**
1931-35 WM SWE 14 5 — 5 — —
1924-28 OG-M SWE 10 9 — 9 0 —

**Johansson, Helge / b. Sept. 8, 1904 / d. June 6, 1987**
1924-28 OG-M SWE 5 0 0 0 4 S

**Johansson, Jakob / b. Jan. 3, 1979**
1999 WM20 SWE 6 2 2 4 2 —

**Johansson, Jens / b. Mar. 26, 1964**
1982-84 WM20 SWE 21 3 4 7 6 —

**Johansson, Jonas / b. Mar. 18, 1984**
2002 WM18 SWE 8 5 1 6 18 —

**Johansson, Kari / b. Feb. 14, 1947**
1967-69 WM FIN 13 1 0 1 0 —
1968 OG-M FIN 7 0 0 0 4 —

**Johansson, Kent / b. Apr. 13, 1956**
1983-85 WM SWE 20 5 2 7 6 —

**Johansson, Kim / b. Jan. 21, 1988**
2006 WM18 SWE 6 0 1 1 2 —

**Johansson, Lennart / b. June 7, 1941 / d. Oct. 23, 2010**
1964 OG-M SWE 7 0 1 1 2 S

**Johansson, Mathias / b. Feb. 22, 1974**
1994 WM20 SWE 7 2 2 4 0 S
2001-06 WM SWE 30 1 4 5 22 G,S,2B
2002 OG-M SWE 4 1 0 1 0 —

**Johansson, Mikael / b. June 12, 1966**
1986 WM20 SWE 7 2 3 5 6 —
1990-98 WM SWE 45 11 25 36 10 2G,2S,B
1988-92 OG-M SWE 16 4 7 11 2 B

**Johansson, Nicklas / b. June 12, 1984**
2002 WM18 SWE 8 0 1 1 4 —

**Johansson, Nils / b. July 24, 1938**
1962-70 WM SWE 51 3 20 23 10 G,4S,B
1964-68 OG-M SWE 14 1 2 3 4 S

**Johansson, Ragnar / b. Dec. 30, 1911 / d. unknown**
1938 WM SWE 2 0 — 0 — —

**Johansson, Roger / b. Apr. 17, 1967**
1986-87 WM20 SWE 14 3 5 8 10 B
1994-97 WM SWE 24 1 5 6 26 S,B
1996 WCH SWE 3 0 0 0 0 —
1994 OG-M SWE 8 2 0 2 8 G

**Johansson, Rune / b. Aug. 23, 1920 / d. Dec. 30, 1998**
1947-53 WM SWE 25 5 1 6 12 G,2S
1948-52 OG-M SWE 16 5 0 5 — B

**Johansson, Stig-Goran "Stisse" / b. July 18, 1943 / d. Apr. 20, 2002**
1967-74 WM SWE 54 19 12 31 20 3S,3B
1972 OG-M SWE 4 0 0 0 2 —

**Johansson, Sven "Tumba" / b. Aug. 27, 1931 / d. Oct 1, 2011**
1953-66 WM SWE 66 60 40 100 12 3G,S,3B
1952-64 OG-M SWE 29 25 7 32 9 S,B
~IIHF Hall of Fame
~WM IIHF Directorate Best Forward (1957, 1962)

**Johansson, Thomas / b. Aug. 18, 1970**
1999-2002 WM SWE 14 3 1 4 10 2B

**Johansson, Thomas / b. Mar. 24, 1972**
1991 WM20 NOR 5 0 0 0 0 —

**Johncke, Torsten / b. Mar. 14, 1912 / d. Nov. 8, 1984**
1935 WM SWE 8 2 — 2 — —
1936 OG-M SWE 4 0 — 0 — —

**Johnsen, Pal / b. Mar. 17, 1976**
1997-2001 WM NOR 26 1 3 4 2 —

**Johnsen, Thomas / b. Apr. 11, 1979**
2003-06 WM DEN 24 0 1 1 8 —

**Johnson, Al / b. Mar. 30, 1935**
1965 WM CAN 7 4 2 6 6 —

**Johnson, Bill / b. Apr. 16, 1928**
1965 WM CAN 6 0 2 2 0 —

**Johnson, Brian / b. Mar. 7, 1965**
1984-85 WM20 USA 11 1 4 5 4 —

**Johnson, Craig / b. Mar. 18, 1972**
1991 WM20 USA 2 0 2 2 0 —
1993-2003 WM USA 26 4 7 11 14 —
1994 OG-M USA 8 0 4 4 4 —

**Johnson, Gordon / b. unknown / d. unknown**
1935 WM GBR 7 2 — 2 — B

**Johnson, Greg / b. Mar. 16, 1971**
1991 WM20 CAN 7 4 2 6 0 G
1993 WM CAN 8 1 2 3 2 —
1994 OG-M CAN 8 0 3 3 0 S

**Johnson, Gregg / b. June 18, 1982**
2002 WM20 USA 7 1 0 1 2 —

**Johnson, Jim / b. Aug. 9, 1962**
1985-90 WM USA 37 0 6 6 76 —
1991 CC USA 8 0 0 0 20 2nd

**Johnson, Jonas / b. Mar. 23, 1970**
1995-2002 WM SWE 17 2 5 7 2 S,B

**Johnson, Larry / b. unknown**
1965 WM USA 7 1 0 1 14 —

**Johnson, Mark / b. Sept. 22, 1957**
1978-90 WM USA 63 15 18 33 34 —
1981-87 CC USA 17 3 7 10 2 —
1980 OG-M USA 7 5 6 11 6 G
~IIHF Hall of Fame

**Johnson, Mike / b. Oct. 3, 1974**
2000 WM CAN 9 1 1 2 10 —

**Johnson, Milton "Prince" / b. unknown**
1949-50 WM USA 15 8 7 15 10 S,B

**Johnson, Paul / b. May 18, 1937**
1958-61 WM USA 20 12 10 22 20 —
1960-64 OG-M USA 14 11 3 14 8 G

**Johnson, Peter / b. May 31, 1959**
1979 WM20 USA 4 0 0 0 6 —
1982 WM USA 6 0 0 0 4 —

**Johnson, Russell "Buzz" / b. unknown**
1949-50 WM USA 15 19 3 22 0 S,B

**Johnsson, Kim / b. Mar. 16, 1976**
1996 WM20 SWE 7 1 2 3 6 S
1998-2002 WM SWE 35 5 5 10 16 G,3B
2004 WCH SWE 4 1 3 4 0 —
2002 OG-M SWE 4 1 1 2 0 —
~WM IIHF Directorate Best Defenceman (2001), WM All-Star Team/Defence (2001)

**Johnsson, Pierre / b. Mar. 22, 1969**
1989 WM20 SWE 5 0 0 0 4 S

**Johnsson, Pierre / b. Feb. 7, 1984**
2004 WM20 SWE 6 1 0 1 4 —

**Johnston, Greg / b. Jan. 14, 1965**
1985 WM20 CAN 7 2 0 2 2 G

**Johnston, Marshall / b. June 6, 1941**
1966-67 WM CAN 14 5 5 10 4 2B
1964-68 OG-M CAN 14 2 9 11 10 B
~IIHF Hall of Fame

**Johnston, Tom / b. 1908 / d. unknown**
1939 WM CAN 7 1 — 1 — G

**Jokiharju, Juha / b. Aug. 17, 1968**
1988 WM20 FIN 7 2 2 4 2 B

**Jokila, Janne / b. Apr. 22, 1982**
2000 WM18 FIN 7 3 5 8 8 G
2002 WM20 FIN 7 1 0 1 2 B

**Jokila, Jarmo / b. Feb. 13, 1986**
2004 WM18 FIN 6 1 0 1 4 —

**Jokinen, Juho / b. Feb. 23, 1976**
1996 WM20 FIN 6 3 5 8 27 —

**Jokinen, Markku / b. Aug. 9, 1968**
1988 WM20 FIN 7 3 1 4 2 B

**Joly, Yvan / b. Feb. 6, 1960**
1979-80 WM20 CAN 10 5 0 5 10 —

**Jomphe, Jean-Francois / b. Dec. 28, 1972**
1995-96 WM CAN 16 4 1 5 10 S,B

**Jonak, Jiri / b. Aug. 20, 1963**
1983 WM20 TCH 7 1 3 4 8 S

**Jonczyk, Stanislaw / b. Apr. 14, 1935**
1957-58 WM POL 11 0 0 0 0 —

**Jones, Brad / b. June 26, 1965**
1995 WM USA 5 0 2 2 2 —

**Jones, Dave / b. unknown**
1959 WM CAN 1 1 0 1 0 G

**Jones, Harold "Hal" / b. 1933**
1961-63 WM CAN 14 10 13 23 4 G

**Jones, Matt / b. Aug. 8, 1983**
2003 WM20 USA 7 0 3 3 6 —

**Jones, Russell / b. Sept. 1, 1926**
1960 OG-M AUS 6 2 3 5 4 —

**Jones, Sebastian / b. Aug. 22, 1982**
2000 WM18 GER 6 0 0 0 6 —

**Jones, Terry / b. Jan. 9, 1959**
1978 WM20 USA 6 2 2 4 0 —

**Jones, Ty / b. Feb. 22, 1979**
1998 WM20 USA 7 0 2 2 6 —

**Jones, Zachary / b. Jan. 14, 1987**
2004-05 WM18 USA 12 0 0 0 18 —

**Jonsson, Anders / b. July 18, 1962**
1981-82 WM20 SWE 12 6 0 6 2 G

**Jonsson, Hans / b. Aug. 2, 1973**
1993 WM20 SWE 7 2 1 3 24 S
1996-99 WM SWE 26 1 1 2 22 G,B

**Jonsson, Johan / b. July 21, 1985**
2003 WM18 SWE 6 0 1 1 6 —

**Jonsson, Jorgen / b. Sept. 29, 1972**
1994-2007 WM SWE 104 26 31 57 58 2G,3S,4B
2004 WCH SWE 4 0 0 0 0 —
1994-2006 OG-M SWE 20 1 1 2 8 2G

**Jonsson, Kenny / b. Oct. 6, 1974**
1993-94 WM20 SWE 14 5 8 13 12 2S
1994-2009 WM SWE 49 11 15 26 28 G,2B
1996 WCH SWE 1 0 0 0 4 —
1994-2006 OG-M SWE 14 2 4 6 6 2G
~OG-M IIHF Directorate Best Defenceman (2006), WM All-Star Team/Defence (2009), WM20 IIHF Directorate Best Defenceman (1994), WM20 All-Star Team/Defence (1993, 1994)

**Jonsson, Lars / b. Jan. 2, 1982**
2000 WM18 SWE 6 0 0 0 2 B
2002 WM20 SWE 7 1 1 2 8 —

**Jonsson, Robin / b. Dec. 10, 1983**
2001 WM18 SWE 6 0 0 0 4 —

**Jonsson, Stefan / b. June 13, 1965**
1985 WM20 SWE 2 0 0 0 0 —

**Jonsson, Stig / b. Mar. 14, 1926**
1949-50 WM SWE 7 6 0 6 0 —

**Jonsson, Tomas / b. Apr. 12, 1960**
1978-80 WM20 SWE 18 4 4 8 24 S,2B
1979-95 WM SWE 44 1 15 16 48 G,4S,B
1981-87 CC SWE 8 1 2 3 6 —
1980-94 OG-M SWE 15 3 5 8 16 G,B
~IIHF Hall of Fame/Triple Gold Club
~WM20 All-Star Team/Defence (1980)

**Jorde, Marv / b. 1937**
1961 WM USA 7 4 2 6 6 —

**Jormakka, Kaarlo / b. July 2, 1988**
2006 WM18 FIN 6 0 0 0 4 S

**Josefsson, Daniel / b. Oct. 15, 1981**
1999 WM18 SWE 7 0 0 0 2 S
2001 WM20 SWE 7 1 2 3 0 —

**Joseph, Chris / b. Sept. 10, 1969**
1987-88 WM20 CAN 13 2 3 5 22 G

**Joseph, Fabian / b. Dec. 5, 1965**
1992-94 OG-M CAN 16 2 3 5 4 2S

**Jost, Richard / b. July 20, 1962**
1982 WM20 SUI 7 0 1 1 15 —

**Joubert, Jacques / b. Mar. 23, 1971**
1995 WM USA 6 1 1 2 2 —

**Jouhkimainen, Miikka / b. Apr. 10, 1985**
2003 WM18 FIN 6 2 0 2 2 —

**Jovanovski, Ed / b. June 26, 1976**
1995 WM20 CAN 7 2 0 2 4 G
1998-2008 WM CAN 33 4 5 9 26 2S
2004 WCH CAN 1 0 0 0 0 1st
2002 OG-M CAN 6 0 3 3 4 G

**Joyce, Bob / b. July 11, 1966**
1988 OG-M CAN 4 1 0 1 0 —

**Jug, Vlado / b. Apr. 6, 1947**
1968 OG-M YUG 5 1 2 3 0 —

**Juhlin, Patrik / b. Apr. 24, 1970**
1990 WM20 SWE 6 1 0 1 0 —
1993-94 WM SWE 9 2 1 3 4 S,B
1996 WCH SWE 4 0 0 0 2 —
1994 OG-M SWE 8 7 1 8 16 G

**Juhn, Julius / b. Dec. 19, 1921 / d. unknown**
1948 OG-M AUT 5 1 — 1 — —

**Jukes, Hamilton / b. May 28, 1895 / d. Jan. 8, 1951**
1924 OG-M GBR 3 3 — 3 — B

**Juneau, Joe / b. Jan. 5, 1968**
1992 OG-M CAN 8 6 9 15 4 S

**Jungbeck, Andreas / b. Oct. 7, 1982**
2000 WM18 SWE 6 3 0 3 2 B

**Junker, Steve / b. June 25, 1972**
1992 WM20 CAN 7 2 2 4 4 —

**Junnila, Jyri / b. Apr. 7, 1984**
2004 WM20 FIN 7 1 0 1 0 B

**Juntunen, Henrik / b. Apr. 24, 1983**
2001 WM18 FIN 6 1 2 3 18 B
2003 WM20 FIN 7 1 2 3 0 B

**Jurcak, Robert / b. Oct. 12, 1976**
1996 WM20 SVK 6 0 0 0 6 —

**Jurek, Kazimierz / b. Mar. 2, 1964**
1992 WM POL 6 1 0 1 4 —
1992 OG-M POL 7 1 1 2 2 —

**Jurgens, Arvids / b. May 27, 1905 / d. Dec. 17, 1955**
1933-35 WM LAT 9 2 — 2 0 —
1936 OG-M LAT 3 0 — 0 — —

**Jurik, Juraj / b. July 21, 1968**
1987-88 WM20 TCH 14 10 2 12 8 S
~WM20 All-Star Team/Forward (1987)

**Justinian, George / b. Jan. 25, 1954**
1977 WM ROM 10 0 0 0 2 —
1976-80 OG-M ROM 10 1 2 3 4 —

**Justka, Mariusz / b. July 19, 1974**
2002 WM POL 6 0 1 1 0 —

**Jutila, Timo / b. Dec. 24, 1963**
1981-83 WM20 FIN 19 3 7 10 30 S,B
1987-97 WM FIN 63 13 21 34 62 G,2S
1987-91 CC FIN 11 1 0 1 8 —
1984-94 OG-M FIN 22 3 4 7 16 B
~IIHF Hall of Fame
~WM All-Star Team/Defence (1992, 1994, 1995)

**Juttner, Franz / b. July 22, 1962**
1981-82 WM20 FRG 10 0 0 0 4 —

**Jylha, Juhani / b. Sept. 28, 1946**
1966-69 WM FIN 12 2 2 4 8 —

**Jyrkkio, Juha / b. Jan. 17, 1959**
1977-79 WM20 FIN 19 8 11 19 27 —

**Kaario, Matti / b. Nov. 29, 1953**
1983 WM FIN 9 0 2 2 2 —

**Kabanov, Alexander / b. Mar. 8, 1957**
1977 WM20 URS 7 4 4 8 12 G

**Kabayama, Matthew / b. Nov. 18, 1965**
1998 OG-M JPN 4 1 0 1 0 —

**Kabayama, Yoshikazu / b. Nov. 18, 1965**
1998-2003 WM JPN 24 1 6 7 16 —

**Kaberle, Frantisek, Sr. / b. Aug. 6, 1951**
1975-79 WM TCH 44 4 3 7 16 2G,3S
1976 CC TCH 2 0 0 0 0 2nd
1980 OG-M TCH 6 0 4 4 0 —

**Kaberle, Frantisek, Jr. / b. Aug. 11, 1973**
1992-93 WM20 TCH 14 1 1 2 10 B
1995-2005 WM CZE 84 10 20 30 28 5G,2B
1996 WCH CZE 2 0 0 0 0 —
2006 OG-M CZE 8 0 1 1 6 B

**Kablukov, Ilya / b. Jan. 18, 1988**
2006 WM18 RUS 6 0 0 0 2 —

**Kabrt, Pavel / b. Nov. 6, 1978**
1998 WM20 CZE 7 1 2 3 4 —

**Kachlik, Jakub / b. Apr. 2, 1989**
2007 WM18 CZE 6 0 0 0 6 —

**Kacic, Jule / b. unknown / d. unknown**
1939 WM YUG 4 0 — 0 — —

**Kacik, Tadeusz / b. Oct. 6, 1946 / d. May 17, 1988**
1970-74 WM POL 29 5 0 5 2 —
1972 OG-M POL 5 1 1 2 2 —

**Kacir, Marian / b. Sept. 29, 1974**
1998 WM CZE 7 2 2 4 4 B

**Kadera, Roman / b. Feb. 9, 1973**
1993 WM20 TCH 7 2 0 2 10 B

**Kadlec, Arnold / b. Jan. 8, 1959**
1978-79 WM20 TCH 12 0 4 4 8 S
1981-86 WM TCH 41 7 7 14 30 G,2S,B
1981-84 CC TCH 10 1 3 4 6 —
1980-84 OG-M TCH 13 3 3 6 12 S

**Kadlec, Drahomir / b. Nov. 29, 1965**
1985 WM20 TCH 7 1 2 3 2 S
1987-96 WM CZE 53 8 10 18 42 G,5B
1987-96 WCH CZE 5 0 1 1 14 —
1992-94 OG-M CZE 16 1 3 4 8 B

**Kadlec, Petr / b. Jan. 5, 1977**
1997 WM20 CZE 7 0 0 0 6 —
2003 WM CZE 9 1 6 7 12 —

**Kadow, Harald / b. Dec. 25, 1939**
1972 WM FRG 9 1 1 2 2 —

**Kadow, Werner / b. Mar. 24, 1933**
1957 WM POL 6 4 1 5 — —

**Kadziolka, Andrzej / b. Oct. 12, 1960**
1986-92 WM POL 26 3 6 9 18 —
1988-92 OG-M POL 13 1 2 3 8 —

**Kafer, Norbert / b. Feb. 24, 1958**
1978 WM20 FRG 6 1 0 1 8 —

**Kagarlitski, Dmitri / b. Aug. 1, 1989**
2007 WM18 RUS 7 1 1 2 0 G

**Kahnberg, Magnus / b. Feb. 25, 1980**
2004-07 WM SWE 16 3 1 4 8 S

**Kajkl, Milan / b. May 14, 1950**
1975-78 WM TCH 39 1 3 4 14 2G,2S
1976 CC TCH 7 0 1 1 2 2nd
1976 OG-M TCH 5 0 1 1 6 S

**Kajzerek, Marian / b. Aug. 27, 1946**
1970 WM POL 9 0 0 0 2 —
1976 OG-M POL 4 0 0 0 0 —

**Kakihara, Isao / b. May 1, 1944**
1972 OG-M JPN 4 0 0 0 0 —

**Kakihara, Takashi / b. Sept. 15, 1937**
1960 OG-M JPN 5 3 1 4 12 —

**Kakko, Erik / b. May 21, 1971**
1991 WM20 FIN 5 0 0 0 2 —

**Kakl, Horst / b. Jan. 16, 1942**
1964 OG-M AUT 7 1 0 1 4 —

**Kalev, Ivailo / b. May 9, 1946**
1976 OG-M BUL 5 1 2 3 4 —

**Kalgoum, Monir / b. Jan. 23, 1984**
2004 WM20 SWE 6 2 0 2 0 —

**Kalimulin, Marat / b. Aug. 20, 1988 / d. Sept. 7, 2011**
2008 WM20 RUS 7 1 3 4 8 B
~perished in Yaroslavl plane crash

**Kalitka, Andri / b. Jan. 22, 1982**
2000 WM18 UKR 6 0 0 0 8 —

**Kallarsson, Tomi / b. Mar. 15, 1979**
1998 WM20 FIN 7 0 0 0 4 G

**Kallio, Tomi / b. Jan. 27, 1977**
1996-97 WM20 FIN 12 7 6 13 4 —
1999-2007 WM FIN 78 21 24 45 53 3S,2B
2002 OG-M FIN 4 1 2 3 2 —

**Kalliokoski, Jouni / b. Nov. 24, 1963**
1983 WM20 FIN 7 3 0 3 2 —

**Kallur, Anders / b. July 6, 1952**
1981 CC SWE 5 3 1 4 0 —

**Kalmikov, Konstantin / b. June 14, 1978**
2000 WM UKR 6 2 0 2 0 —

**Kalt, Dieter, Sr. / b. July 29, 1941**
1964-68 OG-M AUT 12 3 2 5 20 —

**Kalt, Dieter, Jr. / b. June 26, 1974**
1993-2007 WM AUT 75 22 12 34 40 —
1994-2002 OG-M AUT 15 1 1 2 14 —

**Kalteva, Mikko / b. May 25, 1984**
2002 WM18 FIN 7 0 0 0 6 —
2003-04 WM20 FIN 14 0 2 2 4 2B

**Kalteva, Petri / b. July 20, 1971**
1991 WM20 FIN 7 1 1 2 2 —

**Kalto, Kari / b. July 7, 1978**
1998 WM20 FIN 7 1 3 4 4 G

**Kaluzik, Kamil / b. Nov. 20, 1961**
1980 WM20 TCH 2 0 0 0 0 —

**Kamarainen, Jouko / b. Aug. 14, 1957**
1977 WM20 FIN 7 0 2 2 2 —

**Kamei, Shinkichi / b. June 20, 1910 / d. unknown**
1936 OG-M JPN 2 0 0 0 — —

**Kamenev, Vasili / b. Jan. 8, 1964**
1984 WM20 URS 7 1 3 4 0 G

**Kamenski, Valeri / b. Apr. 18, 1966**
1985-86 WM20 URS 14 9 8 17 14 G,B
1986-2000 WM RUS 61 29 19 48 74 3G,S,B
1987 CC URS 9 6 1 7 6 2nd
1988-98 OG-M RUS 14 6 5 11 6 G,S
~Triple Gold Club
~WM IIHF Directorate Best Forward (1991), WM All-Star Team/Forward (1991)

**Kamentsev, Pavel / b. Aug. 15, 1969**
1998 WM KAZ 3 1 0 1 6 —
1998 OG-M KAZ 7 2 0 2 4 —

**Kames, Vladimir / b. Sept. 23, 1964**
1983-84 WM20 TCH 14 9 8 17 2 S,B
1985 WM TCH 9 1 2 3 6 G
1984 CC TCH 3 1 0 1 2 —

**Kaminski, Yan / b. July 28, 1971**
1990-91 WM20 URS 13 3 1 4 6 2S
1993 WM RUS 8 2 2 4 4 G

**Kammer, Fred / b. June 3, 1912 / d. Feb. 21, 1996**
1936 OG-M USA 1 0 0 0 0 B

**Kammerer, Axel / b. July 21, 1964**
1983-84 WM20 FRG 14 2 3 5 4 —
1985-91 WM FRG 58 5 3 8 10 —
1992 OG-M GER 8 0 0 0 6 —

**Kane, Kenny / b. May 1905 / d. unknown**
1933 WM CAN 5 3 — 3 0 S

**Kane, Shaun / b. Feb. 24, 1970**
1989-90 WM20 USA 14 1 1 2 10 —

**Kaneda, Yuso / b. unknown**
1957 WM JPN 7 0 — 0 — —

**Kaneiri, Takaki / b. Jan. 2, 1943**
1968 OG-M JPN 5 0 1 1 8 —

**Kanervo, Kari / b. Jan. 1, 1963**
1983 WM20 FIN 6 2 3 5 2 —

**Kangasalusta, Pekka / b. Sept. 22, 1977**
1997 WM20 FIN 6 0 1 1 0 —

**Kangasniemi, Miska / b. Jan. 6, 1975**
1995 WM20 FIN 7 0 0 0 2 —

**Kangyal, Balazs / b. July 24, 1969**
2009 WM HUN 6 0 1 1 8 —

**Kankaanpera, Ari / b. Apr. 27, 1955**
1976 WM FIN 10 0 0 0 10 —

**Kankaanpera, Markus / b. Apr. 7, 1980**
1999-2000 WM20 FIN 13 0 2 2 14 —

**Kankaanpera, Mikko / b. Mar. 30, 1982**
2000 WM18 FIN 7 3 4 7 2 G
2002 WM20 FIN 7 0 2 2 4 B

**Kankaanpera, Risto / b. Mar. 8, 1958**
1978 WM20 FIN 6 2 1 3 0 —

**Kanko, Petr / b. Feb. 7, 1984**
2001 WM18 CZE 7 6 1 7 4 —
2004 WM20 CZE 7 1 1 2 4 —

**Kanov, Jan / b. June 23, 1987**
2005 WM18 CZE 7 0 1 1 16 —

**Kantee, Kevin / b. Jan. 29, 1984**
2002 WM18 FIN 8 1 3 4 4 —
2004 WM20 FIN 7 0 1 1 4 B

**Kantola, Jouni / b. Apr. 18, 1966**
1986 WM20 FIN 7 2 4 6 2 —

**Kantor, Robert / b. Feb. 25, 1977**
1998 WM CZE 8 0 1 1 0 B

**Kaonpaa, Esko / b. July 4, 1942 / d. Jan. 9, 2002**
1964 OG-M FIN 1 0 0 0 0 —

**Kapanen, Hannu / b. Mar. 13, 1951**
1976 WM FIN 10 3 3 6 10 —
1976 CC FIN 2 0 1 1 0 —
1976 OG-M FIN 5 1 3 4 2 —

**Kapanen, Sami / b. June 14, 1973**
1992-93 WM20 FIN 14 2 7 9 10 —
1994-2010 WM FIN 54 22 18 40 20 G,3S
1996 WCH FIN 3 0 0 0 4 —
1994-2002 OG FIN 18 2 3 5 6 2B
~WM IIHF Directorate Best Forward (2001), WM All-Star Team/Forward (2001)

**Kapus, Richard / b. Feb. 9, 1973**
1993 WM20 TCH 7 2 2 4 10 B
1998-2007 WM SVK 53 11 16 27 26 S,B
2002-06 OG-M SVK 10 0 3 3 4 —

**Kapusta, Tomas / b. Feb. 23, 1967**
1985-87 WM20 TCH 21 7 7 14 8 2S
1993 WM CZE 8 2 2 4 6 B
1994 OG-M CZE 8 0 0 0 2 —

**Kapustin, Igor / b. Feb. 2, 1957**
1977 WM20 URS 7 0 2 2 0 G

**Kapustin, Sergei / b. Feb. 13, 1953**
1974-83 WM URS 81 55 34 89 53 7G,S,B
1976-81 CC URS 11 5 5 10 6 1st
1976 OG-M URS 5 3 1 4 8 G
~WM All-Star Team/Forward (1978, 1981)

**Kapynen, Tero / b. Feb. 11, 1958**
1978 WM20 FIN 6 4 1 5 0 —

**Karabin, Ladislav / b. Feb. 16, 1970**
1990 WM20 TCH 6 2 1 3 6 B

**Karachun, Viktor / b. Aug. 12, 1968**
1998-2001 WM BLR 18 3 3 6 10 —
1998 OG-M BLR 7 2 1 3 8 —

**Karaga, Vadim / b. Jan. 3, 1985**
2003 WM18 BLR 6 8 4 12 37 —
2003-05 WM20 BLR 12 3 3 6 24 —
2003 WM BLR 2 0 0 0 0 —

**Karagavrelidis, Jordan / b. Mar. 24, 1958**
1977 WM20 TCH 7 1 1 2 0 B

**Karalahti, Jere / b. Mar. 25, 1975**
1994-95 WM20 FIN 14 5 6 11 12 —
1998-2005 WM FIN 54 13 13 26 36 2S,B
~WM All-Star Team/Defence (1998, 1999)

**Karalius, Vladas / b. unknown / d. unknown**
1938 WM LTU 4 0 — 0 — —

**Karamnov, Vitali / b. July 6, 1968**
1996 WM RUS 8 0 2 2 0 —

**Karamnov, Vitali / b. Aug. 8, 1989**
2007 WM18 RUS 7 0 3 3 6 G

**Karatkevich, Alexander / b. Mar. 3, 1988**
2006 WM18 BLR 6 2 1 3 4 —

**Karaulshuk, Olexander / b. July 27, 1983**
2000-01 WM18 UKR 12 3 1 4 16 —

**Karchenko, Sergei / b. Apr. 17, 1976**
2004 WM UKR 6 1 2 3 4 —

**Karel, Helmut / b. May 21, 1970**
1995 WM AUT 7 0 0 0 0 —

**Karelius, Janne / b. Apr. 10, 1965**
1984 WM20 FIN 7 0 0 0 0 S

**Karetin, Sergei / b. Jan. 14, 1986**
2004 WM18 RUS 6 0 0 0 6 G

**Karger, Reinhard / b. Oct. 2, 1945**
1970-74 WM GDR 14 2 0 2 2 —

**Kariya, Paul / b. Oct. 16, 1974**
1992-93 WM20 CAN 13 3 7 10 4 G
1993-96 WM CAN 24 11 17 28 4 G,S
1994-2002 OG-M CAN 14 6 5 11 2 G,S
~WM IIHF Directorate Best Forward (1994), WM All-Star Team/Forward (1994, 1996), WM20 All-Star Team/Forward (1993)

**Karlberg, Ernst / b. Oct. 12, 1901 / d. Mar. 20, 1987**
1924-28 OG-M SWE 10 0 — 0 0 S

**Karlin, Mattias / b. July 4, 1979**
1998-99 WM20 SWE 13 4 3 7 8 —

**Karlsson, Andreas / b. Aug. 19, 1975**
1995 WM20 SWE 7 2 2 4 0 B
1996-2006 WM SWE 13 5 4 9 10 G

**Karlsson, Bertil / b. Jan. 1, 1938**
1959-63 WM SWE 14 1 8 9 18 G,S

**Karlsson, Gabriel / b. Jan. 22, 1980**
1999-2000 WM20 SWE 12 6 5 11 8 —

**Karlsson, Jakob / b. Feb. 20, 1972**
1992 WM20 SWE 7 0 3 3 4 S

**Karlsson, Jan / b. May 30, 1964**
1983-84 WM20 SWE 12 1 1 2 8 —

**Karlsson, Jens / b. Nov. 7, 1982**
2000 WM18 SWE 6 5 4 9 20 B
2002 WM20 SWE 7 0 0 0 8 —

**Karlsson, Lars / b. June 28, 1960**
1979-80 WM20 SWE 11 0 1 1 6 2B
1987-92 WM SWE 16 4 2 6 16 2G
1987 CC SWE 4 1 1 2 0 —
1988 OG-M SWE 7 1 3 4 4 B

**Karlsson, Martin / b. Apr. 26, 1952**
1976-77 WM SWE 20 1 2 3 6 S,B

**Karlsson, Mattias / b. Apr. 15, 1985**
2003 WM18 SWE 6 1 3 4 16 —

**Karlsson, Ragnar / b. Feb. 13, 1977**
1997 WM20 SWE 6 1 1 2 0 —

**Karlsson, Reine / b. Feb. 25, 1965**
1985 WM20 SWE 7 3 5 8 10 —

**Karlsson, Stefan / b. Sept. 11, 1946**
1969-74 WM SWE 55 23 18 41 14 3S,3B

**Karlsson, Yngve / b. Feb. 10, 1929**
1951 WM SWE 6 6 — 6 0 S

**Karlstad, Jon / b. Nov. 10, 1958**
1992-93 WM NOR 12 0 1 1 4 —
1984-92 OG-M NOR 12 0 2 2 8 —

**Karmanos, Jason / b. May 22, 1974**
1994 WM20 USA 7 1 2 3 6 —

**Karnaukh, Sergiy / b. Aug. 25, 1975**
1995 WM20 UKR 7 0 1 1 6 —

**Karotki, Alexander / b. Apr. 8, 1985**
2003 WM18 BLR 6 1 0 1 2 —

**Karpan, Vaughn / b. June 20, 1961**
1984-88 OG-M CAN 15 0 0 0 2 —

**Karpov, Nikolai / b. Nov. 8, 1929**
1960 OG-M URS 3 1 2 3 2 B

**Karpov, Sergei / b. Dec. 19, 1959**
1979 WM20 URS 6 0 1 1 6 G

**Karpov, Sergei / b. Mar. 11, 1984**
2004 WM20 RUS 6 0 0 0 0 —

**Karpov, Tomas / b. Mar. 9, 1989**
2007 WM18 CZE 6 0 3 3 6 —

**Karpov, Valeri / b. Aug. 5, 1971**
1991 WM20 URS 7 0 4 4 2 S
1993-2002 WM RUS 38 14 7 21 34 G,S
1994 OG-M RUS 8 3 1 4 2 —

**Karpovtsev, Alexander / b. Apr. 7, 1970 / d. Sept. 7, 2011**
1990 WM20 URS 7 0 1 1 8 S
1993-2005 WM RUS 16 0 2 2 12 G,B
1996 WCH RUS 1 0 0 0 0 —
~perished in Yaroslavl plane crash

**Karrbrandt, Thomas / b. Mar. 18, 1959**
1978-79 WM20 SWE 13 1 0 1 6 S,B

**Karrenbauer, Bernd / b. Mar. 5, 1944**
1965-74 WM GDR 39 7 4 11 16 —
1968 OG-M GDR 7 4 2 6 2 —

**Karshunov, Andrei / b. May 10, 1983**
2000 WM18 BLR 6 0 0 0 8 —
2002-03 WM20 BLR 12 1 0 1 18 —

**Kartchenko, Sergiy / b. unknown**
1995 WM20 UKR 7 0 1 1 8 —

**Karumaa, Matti / b. Nov. 25, 1924 / d. May 31, 1993**
1949-51 WM FIN 10 5 — 5 2 —
1952 OG-M FIN 7 3 0 3 — —

**Karvinen, Jannik / b. May 17, 1986**
2004 WM18 DEN 6 1 0 1 6 —

**Kasai, Hisashi / b. Apr. 11, 1943**
1968 OG-M JPN 3 0 0 0 0 —

**Kasan, Robert / b. unknown**
1981 WM20 AUT 5 0 0 0 4 —

**Kasatonov, Alexei / b. Oct. 14, 1959**
1978-79 WM20 URS 13 4 6 10 10 2G
1981-91 WM URS 77 18 33 51 64 5G,S,2B
1981-91 CC URS 27 3 19 22 20 1st,2nd
1980-88 OG-M URS 21 7 13 20 8 2G,S
~IIHF Hall of Fame
~WM IIHF Directorate Best Defenceman (1983), WM All-Star Team/Defence (1982, 1983, 1985, 1986, 1991), WM 20 IIHF Directorate Best Defenceman (1979), WM 20 All-Star Team/Defence (1979)

**Kaser, Roland / b. Oct. 15, 1979**
1999 WM20 SUI 6 1 0 1 6 —

**Kashtanov, Yevgeni / b. Aug. 8, 1984**
2002 WM18 BLR 8 1 0 1 0 —
2003 WM20 BLR 6 0 0 0 4 —

**Kasik, Peter / b. June 24, 1962**
1982 WM20 TCH 7 2 2 4 2 S

**Kasparaitis, Darius / b. Oct. 16, 1972**
1991-92 WM20 URS 13 2 8 10 24 G,S
1992-96 WM RUS 14 2 3 5 6 —
1996-2004 WCH RUS 9 0 3 3 22 —
1992-2006 OG-M RUS 28 1 6 7 20 G,S,B
~WM20 IIHF Directorate Best Defenceman (1992)

**Kasper, Jan / b. Sept. 21, 1932**
1955-63 WM TCH 32 8 1 9 12 S,4B
1956-60 OG-M TCH 14 3 4 7 12 —

**Kasper, Peter / b. Dec. 20, 1974**
1996-2003 WM AUT 31 1 0 1 18 —
2002 OG-M AUT 4 0 0 0 0 —

**Kasperczyk, Jedrzej / b. May 20, 1968**
1987-88 WM20 POL 14 4 2 6 4 —

**Kasprzak, Zbigniew / b. Sept. 30, 1908 / d. Mar. 6, 1965**
1937-38 WM POL 13 1 0 1 5 —

**Kasprzycki, Mieczyslaw / b. Dec. 13, 1910 / d. Oct. 21, 2001**
1937-47 WM POL 17 2 0 2 0 —
1936-48 OG-M POL 7 0 — 0 — —

**Kasslatter, Fabrizio / b. Sept. 6, 1954**
1984 OG-M ITA 5 1 0 1 0 —

**Kastak, Kamil / b. May 8, 1966**
1984-86 WM20 TCH 18 4 8 12 4 S,B
1992-94 WM CZE 22 3 8 11 6 2B
1991 CC TCH 5 1 2 3 0 —
1992-94 OG-M CZE 15 3 8 11 2 B

**Kastsyuchonak, Viktor / b. June 7, 1979**
1999 WM20 BLR 6 0 0 0 8 —

**Kasyanchuk, Kostyantyn / b. Oct. 24, 1979**
1999-2006 WM UKR 31 4 3 7 12 —

**Katayama, Tatsuki / b. Jan. 26, 1973**
1998-2001 WM JPN 18 1 0 1 10 —
1998 OG-M JPN 4 0 0 0 4 —

**Kathan, Klaus / b. Jan. 7, 1977**
1996-97 WM20 GER 12 2 1 3 16 —
2001-05 WM GER 30 5 7 12 10 —
2004 WCH GER 3 0 0 0 2 —
2002-06 OG-M GER 12 3 2 5 2 —

**Katic, Mark / b. May 9, 1989**
2007 WM18 CAN 6 0 1 1 0 —

**Katlaps, Ulvis / b. Mar. 20, 1968**
1988 WM20 URS 7 0 4 4 4 S

**Katrych, Kyrylo / b. Apr. 3, 1984**
2004 WM20 UKR 6 1 1 2 4 —

**Kaukokari, Mikko / b. June 11, 1980**
2000 WM20 FIN 7 1 1 2 4 —

**Kauppi, Ossi / b. Apr. 19, 1929 / d. Apr. 16, 2000**
1949-54 WM FIN 16 3 — 3 6 —
1952 OG-M FIN 8 0 0 0 — —

**Kauppila, Jari / b. Feb. 23, 1974**
1994 WM20 FIN 7 1 0 1 6 —

**Kauppinen, Marko / b. Mar. 23, 1979**
1998-99 WM20 FIN 13 4 4 8 12 G

**Kautonen, Veli-Pekka / b. May 9, 1970**
1989-90 WM20 FIN 14 2 12 14 26 —

**Kavec, Ignac / b. Feb. 20, 1953**
1976 OG-M YUG 5 1 2 3 4 —

**Kavulic, Ondrej / b. Feb. 1, 1981**
1999 WM18 CZE 7 0 1 1 0 —

**Kawabuchi, Isao / b. Dec. 13, 1936**
1964 OG-M JPN 7 3 2 5 0 —

**Kawaguchi, Yutaka / b. Apr. 5, 1973**
1993 WM20 JPN 6 0 1 1 4 —
1998-2003 WM JPN 28 1 2 3 14 —
1998 OG-M JPN 4 0 0 0 0 —

**Kawahira, Makoto / b. Aug. 25, 1971**
2001 WM JPN 6 1 3 4 31 —
1998 OG-M JPN 4 0 0 0 2 —

**Kawamura, Katsuyoshi / b. Jan. 18, 1954**
1980 OG-M JPN 5 0 0 0 0 —

**Kawanichi, Tsukasa / b. unknown**
1957 WM JPN — 0 — 0 — —

**Kawashima, Hironori / b. June 8, 1974**
1993 WM20 JPN 7 0 0 0 4 —

**Kawashima, Makoto / b. May 2, 1979**
2000-04 WM JPN 30 2 2 4 24 —

**Kazachok, Andrei / b. June 18, 1984**
2002 WM18 BLR 8 0 0 0 14 —
2003 WM20 BLR 6 0 0 0 2 —

**Kazahari, Kimio / b. Feb. 18, 1936**
1964 OG-M JPN 7 0 2 2 0 —

**Kazatel, Michal / b. Apr. 9, 1988**
2006 WM18 CZE 7 1 1 2 2 B

**Kazda, Mario / b. July 4, 1976**
1996 WM20 SVK 6 0 0 0 2 —

**Kazionov, Dmitri / b. May 13, 1984**
2002 WM18 RUS 1 0 0 0 0 S
2004 WM20 RUS 6 1 1 2 2 —

**Kazlovich, Maxim / b. Mar. 8, 1984**
2002 WM18 BLR 8 1 1 2 10 —

**Keane, Mike / b. May 29, 1967**
1987 WM20 CAN 6 0 1 1 4 —

**Kealty, Jeff / b. Apr. 9, 1976**
1996 WM20 USA 6 0 1 1 6 —

**Kearns, Dennis / b. Sept. 27, 1945**
1977-78 WM CAN 20 0 2 2 16 B

**Keating, Ed / b. unknown / d. unknown**
1934 WM USA 4 0 0 0 — S

**Keating, Mike / b. Jan. 21, 1957**
1977 WM20 CAN 7 0 2 2 0 S

**Kebede, Desta / b. June 25, 1989**
2007 WM18 SUI 6 0 1 1 2 —

**Keckeis, Herbert / b. unknown**
1981 WM20 AUT 5 2 1 3 4 —

**Keczmer, Dan / b. May 25, 1968**
1990-99 WM USA 16 2 0 2 8 —

**Kehle, Markus / b. May 13, 1972**
1992 WM20 GER 7 0 0 0 2 —

**Keinonen, Matti / b. Nov. 6, 1941**
1962-73 WM FIN 69 20 12 32 91 —
1968-72 OG-M FIN 11 4 0 4 14 —
~IIHF Hall of Fame

**Kekalainen, Janne / b. Oct. 14, 1970**
1990 WM20 FIN 5 0 2 2 0 —

**Kekalainen, Jarmo / b. July 7, 1966**
1986 WM20 FIN 7 4 3 7 4 —
1991 CC FIN 6 0 1 1 0 —

**Kelch, Gunther / b. unknown / d. unknown**
1937 WM GER 4 0 0 0 0 —

**Kelfer, Mike / b. Jan. 2, 1967**
1986-87 WM20 USA 14 5 4 9 8 B

**Kelland, Christopher / b. Dec. 22, 1957**
1994 WM GBR 6 0 0 0 8 —

**Kelleher, Chris / b. Mar. 23, 1975**
1995 WM20 USA 7 1 0 1 0 —

**Keller, Florian / b. Jan. 30, 1976**
1995-96 WM20 GER 13 4 9 13 8 —
1998 WM GER 6 0 1 1 4 —

**Keller, Hans / b. Mar. 24, 1944**
1972 WM SUI 8 2 2 4 4 —
1972 OG-M SUI 4 0 0 0 0 —

**Keller, Helmut / b. Nov. 16, 1952**
1973 WM FRG 6 0 0 0 4 —

**Keller, Matthias / b. Jan. 11, 1975**
1994 WM20 SUI 7 0 0 0 0 —

**Keller, Olivier / b. Mar. 20, 1971**
1991 WM20 SUI 7 0 0 0 4 —
1998-2005 WM SUI 43 2 5 7 44 —
2002-06 OG-M SUI 10 0 1 1 12 —

**Keller, Ruedi / b. Oct. 6, 1925**
1953-55 WM SUI 12 1 0 1 8 B
1956 OG-M SUI 1 0 0 0 0 —

**Keller, Ryan / b. Jan. 6, 1984**
2002 WM18 CAN 8 2 0 2 14 —

**Keller, Walter / b. Oct. 26, 1933**
1954 WM SUI 5 0 — 0 2 —
1956 OG-M SUI 5 2 1 3 2 —

**Kellett, Kevin / b. July 23, 1978**
1998 WM20 USA 7 0 0 0 8 —

**Kelley, John / b. July 10, 1927**
1949 WM USA 5 2 — 2 — B

**Kellin, Tony / b. Mar. 19, 1963**
1982-83 WM20 USA 14 2 4 6 14 —

**Kelly, Jimmy / b. 1912 / d. unknown**
1937-39 WM GBR 22 6 1 7 7 2S

**Kelly, John Paul / b. Nov. 15, 1959**
1979 WM20 CAN 5 0 0 0 10 —

**Kemp, Jim / b. Oct. 26, 1910 / d. unknown**
1937 WM CAN 9 10 2 12 2 G

**Kempf, Markus / b. Mar. 27, 1973**
1993 WM20 GER 7 1 0 1 2 —

**Kenig, Kaspar / b. Apr. 3, 1981**
1999 WM18 FIN 7 2 3 5 6 G

**Kenig, Maxim / b. Sept. 16, 1983**
2001 WM18 FIN 6 1 3 4 2 B

**Kennedy, Bob / b. unknown**
1954 WM CAN 7 6 1 7 10 S

**Kennedy, Sheldon / b. June 15, 1969**
1988-89 WM20 CAN 14 7 6 13 20 G

**Kennholt, Kenneth / b. Jan. 13, 1965**
1991-93 WM SWE 26 3 9 12 30 2G,S
1992 OG-M SWE 8 0 1 1 2 —

**Kentala, Ville / b. Feb. 21, 1966**
1986 WM20 FIN 7 1 4 5 4 —

**Kepak, Zdenek / b. Dec. 24, 1937**
1961-65 WM TCH 7 0 3 3 0 2S

**Keranen, Juho / b. Apr. 7, 1985**
2003 WM18 FIN 6 0 2 2 8 —

**Keranen, Matias / b. Feb. 14, 1985**
2003 WM18 FIN 6 1 0 1 12 —

**Kercs, Aleksandrs* / b. Mar. 16, 1967**
1987 WM20 URS 6 6 2 8 20 —
1997-2004 WM LAT 52 15 10 25 38 —
2002 OG-M LAT 4 0 3 3 2 —
*played in 1987 using the name Alexander Kerch

**Kerr, Gord / b. unknown / d. unknown**
1933 WM CAN 5 2 — 2 0 S

**Kertesz, Jozsef / b. Jan. 28, 1940**
1964 OG-M HUN 7 0 1 1 0 —

**Kerth, Werner / b. Dec. 7, 1966**
1993-96 WM AUT 25 6 2 8 18 —
1988-94 OG-M AUT 13 6 5 11 4 —

**Kesa, Teemu / b. June 7, 1981**
1999 WM18 FIN 6 0 0 0 16 G

**Keskinen, Esa / b. Feb. 3, 1965**
1984-85 WM20 FIN 14 10 22 32 4 S
1989-96 WM FIN 51 7 28 35 24 G,S
1988-94 OG-M FIN 16 3 5 8 8 S,B

**Keslers, Herberts / b. unknown / d. unknown**
1933 WM LAT 1 0 — 0 — —

**Kessler, Charles / b. Jan. 11, 1911 / d. unknown**
1933-39 WM SUI 42 6 4 10 0 S,2B
1936 OG-M SUI 3 1 0 1 — —

**Kessler, Dino / b. Dec. 23, 1966**
1986 WM20 SUI 7 0 1 1 0 —
1992-98 WM SUI 17 1 2 3 24 —
1992 OG-M SUI 7 0 0 0 10 —

**Kessler, Herbert / b. Dec. 28, 1912 / d. unknown**
1935-39 WM SUI 26 10 0 10 1 S,2B
1936 OG-M SUI 3 0 0 0 — —

**Kessler, Roman / b. unknown / d. unknown**
1934-38 WM GER 17 3 0 3 1 B

**Ketola, Juha-Pekka / b. Jan. 21, 1983**
2001 WM18 FIN 6 1 2 3 2 B

**Ketola, Stefan / b. Feb. 9, 1972**
1991-92 WM20 SWE 10 1 5 6 6 S

**Ketola, Veli-Pekka / b. Mar. 28, 1948**
1969-74 WM FIN 53 22 14 36 58 —
1976-81 CC FIN 10 0 0 0 8 —
1968-72 OG-M FIN 12 3 4 7 17 —

**Kevorkian, Aram / b. Apr. 20, 1982**
2002 WM20 FRA 6 2 0 2 6 —

**Kewley, Herb / b. 1927**
1949 WM CAN 6 2 — 2 — S

**Kezik, Viktor / b. Oct. 18, 1982**
2000 WM18 BLR 6 0 0 0 16 —

**Khaidarov, Ravil / b. Dec. 25, 1966**
1985-86 WM20 URS 14 11 6 17 18 G,B
1991 CC URS 5 2 0 2 6 —

**Khalizov, Svyatoslav / b. Feb. 8, 1963**
1982-83 WM20 URS 14 1 2 3 10 G
1989 WM URS 4 0 0 0 2 G

**Kharchenko, Sergiy / b. Apr. 17, 1978**
2002-07 WM UKR 16 2 0 2 6 —

**Kharin, Sergei / b. Feb. 20, 1963**
1983 WM20 URS 7 8 2 10 2 G

**Kharitonov, Alexander / b. Mar. 30, 1976**
2000-07 WM RUS 34 7 5 12 24 2B
2006 OG-M RUS 8 1 1 2 6 —

**Kharko, Dmitri / b. Feb. 8, 1985**
2003 WM18 KAZ 6 0 0 0 0 —

**Kharlamov, Alexander / b. Sept. 23, 1975**
1994-95 WM20 RUS 14 6 3 9 6 S,B

**Kharlamov, Valeri / b. Jan. 14, 1948 / d. Aug. 27, 1981**
1969-79 WM URS 105 74 82 156 79 8G,2S,B
1972 SS URS 7 3 4 7 16 2nd
1972-80 OG-M URS 17 14 22 36 10 2G,S
~IIHF Hall of Fame
~WM All-Star Team/Forward (1971, 1972, 1973, 1976)
~killed in a car accident

**Khatsko, Alexei / b. Mar. 29, 1982**
2000 WM18 BLR 6 0 1 1 10 —

**Khavanov, Alexander / b. Jan. 30, 1972**
1999-2003 WM RUS 14 0 3 3 6 —
2004 WCH RUS 4 0 1 1 4 —

**Khlebnikov, Valeri / b. Oct. 13, 1981**
2000 WM20 RUS 7 2 1 3 2 S

**Khlystov, Nikolai / b. Nov. 10, 1932 / d. Feb. 14, 1999**
1954-58 WM URS 27 6 8 14 2 G,3S
1956 OG-M URS 7 1 2 3 0 G

**Khmyl, Oleg / b. Jan. 30, 1970**
1998-2003 WM BLR 30 3 5 8 30 —
1998-2002 OG-M BLR 16 1 5 6 4 —

**Khmyl, Olexander / b. Dec. 6, 1980**
2000 WM20 UKR 7 1 1 2 0 —

**Khmylyov, Yuri / b. Oct. 29, 1964**
1984 WM20 URS 7 2 7 9 0 G
1986-92 WM URS 29 4 6 10 12 2G,S
1987 CC URS 9 0 1 1 2 2nd
1992 OG-M RUS 8 4 6 10 4 G

**Khomitski, Vadim / b. July 21, 1983**
2006 WM RUS 7 0 3 3 2 —

**Khomka, Sergei / b. June 6, 1983**
2003 WM20 BLR 6 0 0 0 0 —

**Khomutov, Andrei / b. Apr. 21, 1961**
1981 WM20 URS 5 3 1 4 4 B
1981-95 WM URS 84 30 37 67 40 7G,S,B
1981-87 CC URS 16 4 3 7 2 1st,2nd
1984-92 OG-M URS 23 11 12 23 10 3G
~WM All-Star Team/Forward (1990)

**Khristich, Dmitri / b. July 23, 1969**
1988-89 WM20 URS 14 7 3 10 2 G,S
1990-2003 WM URS 25 3 9 12 40 G
2002 OG-M UKR 2 2 0 2 0 —

**Kiberlein, Artur / b. Aug. 7, 1985**
2003 WM18 KAZ 6 0 0 0 2 —

**Kienass, Torsten / b. Feb. 23, 1971**
1993-97 WM GER 30 2 3 5 16 —
1996 WCH GER 1 0 0 0 2 —
1994 OG-M GER 7 0 0 0 2 —

**Kiessling, Udo / b. May 21, 1955**
1973-91 WM FRG 119 17 26 43 150 —
1984 CC FRG 4 0 1 1 4 —
1976-92 OG-M GER 32 5 9 14 42 B
~IIHF Hall of Fame
~WM All-Star Team/Defence (1987)

**Kiever, Doug / b. July 19, 1908 / d. unknown**
1937 WM CAN 4 1 3 4 0 G

**Kihlstrom, Mats / b. Jan. 3, 1964**
1983-84 WM20 SWE 12 3 2 5 18 —
1985-89 WM SWE 33 8 5 13 34 G,S
1988 OG-M SWE 8 1 2 3 4 B

**Kiimalainen, Markku / b. Oct. 8, 1955**
1981 WM FIN 8 4 4 8 2 —
1980 OG-M FIN 7 1 6 7 4 —

**Kikuchi, Takeshi / b. unknown**
1957 WM JPN 7 2 0 2 — —

**Kilanowicz, Tadeusz / b. June 8, 1940 / d. July 4, 1979**
1966 WM POL 7 2 2 4 0 —
1964 OG-M POL 7 4 2 6 2 —

**Kilburn, Doug / b. unknown**
1955 WM CAN 8 6 7 13 0 G

**Kilburn, Jim / b. unknown**
1950 WM CAN 6 3 1 4 14 G

**Kilmartin, Gerry / b. July 7, 1926 / d. June 17, 1970**
1947-49 WM USA 8 7 — 7 12 B
1952 OG-M USA 7 2 4 6 — S

**Kilpatrick, Jack / b. July 7, 1917 / d. Dec. 18, 1989**
1936 OG-M GBR 1 0 0 0 0 G

**Kilpio, Raimo / b. Feb. 2, 1936**
1957-67 WM FIN 56 16 9 25 22 —
1960-64 OG-M FIN 13 10 4 14 4 —

**Kimalainen, Markku / b. unknown**
1981 CC FIN 5 1 0 1 0 —

**Kinch, Matt / b. Feb. 17, 1980**
2000 WM20 CAN 7 0 0 0 0 B

**Kinder, Jan / b. May 26, 1944**
1972 OG-M NOR 4 0 1 1 6 —

**King, Derek / b. Feb. 11, 1967**
1992 WM CAN 6 1 1 2 6 —

**King, Steve / b. Sept. 28, 1948**
1969 WM CAN 10 3 1 4 2 —

**Kink, Georg / b. Aug. 26, 1949**
1972 OG-M FRG 4 0 1 1 6 —

**Kink, Philipp / b. Mar. 2, 1985**
2004 WM20 AUT 6 0 0 0 2 —

**Kinnunen, Veli-Pekka / b. Feb. 12, 1961**
1981 WM20 FIN 5 2 1 3 2 S

**Kinoshita, Kozue / b. Apr. 15, 1912 / d. unknown**
1930 WM JPN 1 0 0 0 — —
1936 OG-M JPN 2 0 0 0 — —

**Kinzel, Dieter / b. June 14, 1959**
1983 WM GDR 6 0 3 3 4 —

**Kiprusoff, Marko / b. June 6, 1972**
1992 WM20 FIN 7 2 2 4 2 —
1994-2003 WM FIN 59 6 13 19 16 G,4S
1996 WCH FIN 4 0 1 1 0 —
1994 OG-M FIN 8 3 3 6 4 B

**Kirchbaumer, Klaus / b. Oct. 7, 1944**
1968 OG-M AUT 4 1 0 1 4 —

**Kirchberger, Christian / b. Jan. 20, 1944**
1964 OG-M AUT 6 3 1 4 0 —

**Kirchberger, Karl / b. unknown / d. unknown**
1930-38 WM AUT 36 9 1 10 3 B

**Kirchmaier, Walter / b. Jan. 27, 1963**
1983 WM20 FRG 7 2 1 3 2 —

**Kirilenko, Dmitri / b. Aug. 4, 1979**
1999 WM20 RUS 7 3 5 8 6 G

**Kirisits, Johannes / b. Nov. 8, 1985**
2004 WM20 AUT 6 0 1 1 4 —

**Kirk, John / b. Sept. 15, 1961**
1981 WM20 CAN 5 4 3 7 24 —

**Kirkham, Terry / b. Feb. 4, 1959**
1979 WM20 CAN 5 2 1 3 2 —

**Kirrane, Jack / b. Aug. 20, 1930**
1958-63 WM USA 7 1 0 1 46 —
1948-60 OG-M USA 14 5 4 9 11 G

**Kirschbauer, Florian / b. July 28, 1988**
2006 WM18 GER 6 0 0 0 4 —

**Kiryukhin, Andrei / b. Aug. 4, 1987 / d. Sept. 7, 2011**
2007 WM20 RUS 6 0 3 3 2 S
~perished in Yaroslavl plane crash

**Kisela, Robert / b. June 3, 1968**
1988 WM20 TCH 7 3 4 7 2 —

**Kisslinger, Georg / b. unknown**
1983 WM20 FRG 7 0 0 0 2 —

**Kisum, Tobias / b. Mar. 12, 1986**
2004 WM18 DEN 6 0 1 1 2 —

**Kitagawa, Kiyoshi / b. unknown / d. unknown**
1930 WM JPN 1 0 0 0 — —

**Kitazawa, Masatatsu / b. Apr. 29, 1916 / d. unknown**
1936 OG-M JPN 2 0 0 0 — —

**Kitchen, Bill / b. Oct. 2, 1960**
1980 WM20 CAN 5 0 1 1 10 —

**Kitchen, Walter "Pud" / b. Dec. 18, 1912 / d. July 18, 1988**
1936 OG-M CAN 6 2 2 4 0 S

**Kittel, Wolfgang / b. Jan. 16, 1898 / d. unknown**
1928 OG-M GER 1 0 0 0 — —

**Kiuru, Jussi / b. July 9, 1973**
1992-93 WM20 FIN 13 1 1 2 8 —

**Kiuru, Marko / b. June 5, 1969**
1987-89 WM20 FIN 21 7 10 17 4 G,B

**Kivela, Teppo / b. Oct. 8, 1967**
1986-87 WM20 FIN 14 8 10 18 4 G
1991 WM FIN 10 0 0 0 4 —

**Kivi, Karri / b. Jan. 31, 1970**
1989-90 WM20 FIN 14 1 2 3 14 —

**Kiviaho, Tommy / b. June 27, 1971**
1991 WM20 FIN 6 1 2 3 2 —

**Kjellberg, Patric / b. June 17, 1969**
1989 WM20 SWE 7 3 4 7 4 S
1992-98 WM SWE 18 4 6 10 2 2G
1992-98 OG-M SWE 20 2 4 6 2 G

**Kjelsberg, Christian / b. July 5, 1971**
1991 WM20 NOR 5 0 0 0 2 —

**Kjelstadli, Magnus / b. Mar. 26, 1986**
2004 WM18 NOR 5 0 0 0 0 —

**Kjems, Mads / b. Apr. 24, 1986**
2004 WM18 DEN 6 1 0 1 14 —

**Klacl, Jaroslav / b. July 27, 1958**
1977 WM20 TCH 4 1 1 2 0 B

**Klang, Herbert / b. unknown / d. unknown**
1928 OG-M AUT 1 0 — 0 — —

**Klapac, Jan / b. Feb. 27, 1941**
1965-73 WM TCH 39 18 10 28 16 G,2S,2B
1964-68 OG-M TCH 12 1 1 2 6 S,B

**Klassen, Ralph / b. Sept. 15, 1955**
1977 WM CAN 10 1 5 6 0 —

**Klatt, Bill / b. Oct. 16, 1947**
1976 WM USA 10 3 1 4 2 —

**Klatt, Trent / b. Jan. 30, 1971**
1991 WM20 USA 8 6 6 12 6 —
1999 WM USA 6 3 0 3 0 —

**Klatt, Werner / b. Jan. 16, 1955**
1976-77 WM FRG 20 0 1 1 0 —

**Klaus, Josef / b. Feb. 24, 1958**
1977 WM20 FRG 6 0 0 0 16 —

**Klaus, Sepp / b. unknown**
1978 WM20 FRG 6 1 0 1 4 —

**Klavs, Edgars / b. July 20, 1913 / d. Aug. 28, 1983**
1938-39 WM LAT 10 2 — 2 — —

**Kleber, Fritz / b. Dec. 21, 1932**
1954 WM FRG 2 0 — 0 0 —

**Klee, Ken / b. Apr. 24, 1971**
1991 WM20 USA 8 1 1 2 2 —
1992-97 WM USA 10 1 0 1 12 —
2004 WCH USA 4 0 0 0 0 —

**Klein, Arie / b. Feb. 17, 1932**
1950 WM NED 4 0 0 0 0 —

**Klein, Kevin / b. Dec. 13, 1984**
2004 WM20 CAN 6 0 0 0 0 S

**Kleinendorst, Kurt / b. Dec. 31, 1960**
1982 WM USA 5 2 0 2 10 —

**Kleinendorst, Scot / b. Jan. 16, 1960**
1982 WM USA 4 0 0 0 2 —

**Kleinheinz, Andreas / b. Apr. 28, 1983**
2001 WM18 GER 6 1 2 3 4 —

**Klejna, Michal / b. Oct. 8, 1987**
2005 WM18 SVK 6 1 0 1 4 —

**Klemenc, Igor Peter / b. June 16, 1956**
1984 OG-M YUG 5 0 1 1 0 —

**Klempa, Tomas / b. Mar. 2, 1984**
2002 WM18 SVK 8 1 4 5 2 —

**Klenner, Sebastian / b. Nov. 26, 1976**
1996 WM20 GER 6 0 0 0 6 —

**Klesla, Rostislav / b. Mar. 21, 1982**
2001 WM20 CZE 7 3 4 7 4 G
2002-07 WM CZE 11 2 2 4 10 —
~WM20 IIHF Directorate Best Defenceman (2001), WM20 All-Star Team/Defence (2001)

**Klevakhin, Dmitri / b. Feb. 20, 1976**
1995-96 WM20 RUS 14 4 4 8 4 S,B

**Klima, Petr / b. Dec. 23, 1964**
1983-84 WM20 TCH 14 10 8 18 28 S,B
1984 CC TCH 5 2 1 3 4 —

**Klimas, Juozas / b. unknown / d. unknown**
1938 WM LTU 4 0 — 0 — —

**Klimbacher, Sven / b. Sept. 12, 1981**
2004-05 WM AUT 7 0 0 0 0 —

**Klimentyev, Sergiy / b. Apr. 5, 1975**
1999-2007 WM UKR 44 5 10 15 138 —
2002 OG-M UKR 4 0 1 1 8 —

**Klimiankov, Vitali / b. July 17, 1983**
2000 WM18 BLR 6 0 2 2 4 —
2001-02 WM20 BLR 12 1 0 1 14 —

**Klimin, Mikhail / b. Apr. 1, 1982**
2000 WM18 BLR 6 3 0 3 4 —
2001-02 WM20 BLR 12 0 3 3 8 —

**Klimovich, Sergei / b. May 8, 1974**
1993 WM20 RUS 7 2 2 4 10 —

**Klimt, Tomas / b. Dec. 26, 1973**
1993 WM20 TCH 7 0 0 0 4 B

**Klinar, Blaz / b. Feb. 27, 1981**
2005 WM SLO 3 0 0 0 0 —

**Klinar, Ciril / b. May 9, 1937**
1968 OG-M YUG 5 1 3 4 2 —

**Klinck, Byrle / b. June 20, 1934**
1956 OG-M CAN 4 0 1 1 4 B

**Klisiak, Waldemar / b. May 6, 1967**
2002 WM POL 6 2 0 2 4 —
1992 OG-M POL 6 1 0 1 12 —

**Klocek, Stanislaw / b. Oct. 17, 1955**
1980-84 OG-M POL 11 2 2 4 6 —

**Klockare, Stefan / b. May 30, 1972**
1992 WM20 SWE 7 1 2 3 0 S

**Klooster, William / b. Dec. 25, 1957**
1981 WM NED 8 0 0 0 6 —
1980 OG-M NED 5 3 2 5 8 —

**Kloti, Marco / b. Mar. 18, 1975**
1994 WM20 SUI 7 1 0 1 0 —

**Klotz, Helmut / b. unknown**
1967 WM FRG 2 0 0 0 5 —

**Klotz, Ko / b. unknown / d. unknown**
1939 WM NED 4 0 — 0 — —

**Klubertanz, Kyle / b. Sept. 23, 1985**
2003 WM18 USA 6 0 0 0 4 —

**Kluc, Miroslav / b.Dec. 1, 1922 / d. unknown**
1956 OG-M TCH 3 2 1 3 2 —

**Klucar, Martin / b. Aug. 4, 1987**
2005 WM18 SVK 6 0 0 0 4 —

**Klugel, Gerhard / b. Jan. 8, 1936**
1959-63 WM GDR 18 4 2 6 8 —

**Kluuskeri, Niko / b. Nov. 3, 1989**
2007 WM18 FIN 5 1 2 3 4 —

**Kluzak, Gord / b. Mar. 4, 1964**
1982 WM20 CAN 7 0 1 1 4 G
~WM20 IIHF Directorate Best Defenceman (1982), WM20 All-Star Team/Defence (1982)

**Klys, Jaroslaw / b. July 23, 1977**
1997 WM20 POL 6 0 0 0 8 —

**Klyukin, Nikita / b. Nov. 10, 1989 / d. Sept. 7, 2011**
2007 WM18 RUS 7 3 0 3 2 G
2009 WM20 RUS 7 0 8 8 2 B
~perished in Yaroslavl plane crash

**Knelsen, Dion / b. Jan. 4, 1989**
2007 WM18 CAN 6 2 2 4 2 —

**Knibbs, Bert / b. unknown**
1951 WM CAN 3 1 — 1 0 G

**Knight, Keith / b. Aug. 19, 1963**
1981 WM20 USA 5 2 1 3 6 —

**Knihs, Paul / b. May 7, 1983**
2001 WM18 GER 6 0 0 0 0 —

**Knobloch, Thomas / b. Apr. 10, 1974**
1993-94 WM20 GER 14 0 2 2 2 —

**Knoflach, Heinz / b. July 30, 1945**
1968 OG-M AUT 3 0 0 0 2 —

**Knold, Lars / b. July 24, 1984**
2002 WM18 NOR 8 0 1 1 2 —

**Knold, Martin / b. Jan. 14, 1976**
1999-2001 WM NOR 15 3 4 7 10 —

**Knold, Per Christian / b. May 4, 1968**
1990-97 WM NOR 36 4 1 5 6 —

**Knoll, Hermann / b. Dec. 10, 1931**
1957 WM AUT 7 0 — 0 8 —
1956-64 OG-M AUT 12 0 2 2 6 —

**Knox, Paul / b. Nov. 23, 1933**
1956 OG-M CAN 8 7 5 12 2 B

**Knuble, Mike / b. July 4, 1972**
1995-2005 WM USA 28 7 4 11 22 —
2006 OG-M USA 6 1 1 2 4 —

**Knutsen, Espen / b. Jan. 12, 1972**
1989-91 WM20 NOR 20 3 11 14 16 —
1994-97 WM NOR 24 8 8 16 4 —
1994 OG-M NOR 7 1 3 4 2 —

**Knuutinen, Olli / b. Feb. 11, 1932**
1954-57 WM FIN 9 2 1 3 2 —

**Knyazev, Igor / b. Jan. 27, 1983**
2000-01 WM18 RUS 12 1 5 6 28 G,S
2002 WM20 RUS 7 2 1 3 35 G
~WM20 IIHF Directorate Best Defenceman (2002), WM20 All-Star Team/Defence (2002)

**Kobach, Reto / b. Apr. 13, 1980**
2000 WM20 SUI 7 0 0 0 8 —
2004 WM SUI 2 0 0 0 0 —

**Kobasew, Chuck / b. Apr. 17, 1982**
2002 WM20 CAN 7 5 1 6 2 S

**Kobayashi, Tomohito / b. Apr. 28, 1974**
2000-04 WM JPN 24 2 3 5 4 —

**Koberle, Walter / b. Jan. 13, 1949**
1976-78 WM FRG 29 8 3 11 12 —
1976 OG-M FRG 5 1 0 1 6 B

**Kobori, Takayuki / b. Apr. 20, 1969**
1998-2004 WM JPN 24 2 4 6 12 —
1998 OG-M JPN 4 0 0 0 6 —

**Kobranov, Vladimir / b. Oct. 4, 1927**
1949 WM TCH 7 5 — 5 — G
1948 OG-M TCH 2 0 — 0 — S

**Koch, Les / b. Nov. 10, 1958**
1978 WM20 FRG 6 1 1 2 2 —

**Kocher, Wolfgang / b. Sept. 16, 1962**
1981 WM20 AUT 5 0 1 1 0 —

**Kochta, Jiri / b. Oct. 11, 1946**
1967-75 WM TCH 61 18 21 39 6 G,3S,2B
1968-72 OG-M TCH 9 4 3 7 0 S,B

**Kogel, Karl / b. Oct. 26, 1917 / d. unknown**
1935-39 WM GER 20 5 1 6 4 —
1936 OG-M GER 6 0 — 0 — —

**Koger, Daniel / b. Aug. 10, 1989**
2009 WM HUN 3 0 0 0 2 —

**Kohler, Arne / b. Apr. 4, 1984**
2002 WM18 FIN 8 0 0 0 2 —

**Kohler, Willy / b. June 30, 1962**
1982 WM20 SUI 7 1 2 3 0 —

**Kohvakka, Teemu / b. Jan. 27, 1974**
1994 WM20 FIN 7 1 2 3 12 —

**Koiso, Erkki / b. Apr. 13, 1934**
1957-61 WM FIN 22 0 0 0 21 —
1960 OG-M FIN 5 0 2 2 13 —

**Koivisto, Tom / b. June 4, 1974**
1993-94 WM20 FIN 14 1 1 2 6 —
2002 WM FIN 9 2 1 3 4 —

**Koivisto, Toni / b. Nov. 5, 1982**
2000 WM18 FIN 7 0 3 3 0 G
2001-02 WM20 FIN 14 3 5 8 2 S,B

**Koivulahti, Pertti / b. June 7, 1951**
1977-82 WM FIN 39 5 22 27 4 —
1976 CC FIN 5 0 4 4 2 —
1976 OG-M FIN 5 1 2 3 0 —

**Koivunen, Petro / b. May 30, 1970**
1989-90 WM20 FIN 14 5 6 11 20 —

**Koivunen, Toni / b. Nov. 21, 1971**
1991 WM20 FIN 6 1 1 2 2 —

**Kokavec, Michal / b. Mar. 1, 1983**
2003 WM20 SVK 6 2 1 3 4 —

**Kokkala, Lassi / b. Mar. 20, 1989**
2007 WM18 FIN 6 1 1 2 4 —

**Kokko, Petri / b. Feb. 1, 1975**
1995 WM20 FIN 7 1 0 1 22 —

**Kokkonen, Anton / b. Aug. 13, 1989**
2007 WM18 FIN 6 2 0 2 4 —

**Kokorev, Dmitri / b. Jan. 9, 1979**
1999 WM20 RUS 7 0 3 3 2 G

**Kokoszka, Leszek / b. Apr. 11, 1951**
1976-79 WM POL 16 7 2 9 8 —
1976-80 OG-M POL 9 5 2 7 4 —

**Kokrment, Jindrich / b. Dec. 20, 1957**
1977 WM20 TCH 7 3 3 6 2 B
1981-82 WM TCH 17 6 6 12 0 S,B
1981 CC TCH 6 2 3 5 2 —

**Koks, Milan / b. May 25, 1940**
1966 WM TCH 7 3 3 6 0 S

**Kolacek, Kamil / b. Sept. 21, 1973**
1993 WM20 TCH 7 1 4 5 4 B

**Kolafa, Tomas / b. Feb. 7, 1984**
2002 WM18 CZE 7 0 0 0 31 B

**Kolanos, Krys / b. July 27, 1981**
2003 WM CAN 9 0 1 1 6 G

**Kolar, Richard / b. Mar. 12, 1966**
1986 WM20 TCH 7 0 1 1 0 —

**Kolarik, Chad / b. Jan. 26, 1986**
2004 WM18 USA 6 1 3 4 2 S

**Kolarik, Michal / b. Oct. 8, 1982**
2000 WM18 SVK 6 2 3 5 20 —
2002 WM20 SVK 7 0 0 0 0 —

**Kolarik, Pavel / b. Oct. 24, 1972**
2003 WM CZE 5 0 1 1 2 —

**Kolasa, Boleslaw / b. Oct. 25, 1920 / d. unknown**
1947 WM POL 5 4 — 4 — —
1948 OG-M POL 4 2 — 2 — —

**Kolba, Marek / b. Jan. 14, 1980**
2000 WM20 SVK 7 0 0 0 8 —

**Kolda, Ladislav / b. Oct. 16, 1983**
2003 WM20 CZE 6 0 0 0 0 —

**Koledayev, Alexei / b. Mar. 27, 1976**
2005-10 WM KAZ 18 0 2 2 10 —
2006 OG-M KAZ 5 0 0 0 10 —

**Kolesnikov, Yuri / b. Aug. 15, 1984**
2001 WM18 UKR 6 0 0 0 6 —

**Kolijn, Patrick / b. Jan. 9, 1957**
1980 OG-M NED 5 0 0 0 9 —

**Kolkka, Vaino / b. Jan. 22, 1948**
1970 WM FIN 4 0 0 0 0 —

**Kolkunov, Alexei / b. Feb. 3, 1977**
1996-97 WM20 RUS 12 4 4 8 8 2B

**Kolliker, Jakob / b. July 21, 1953**
1987 WM SUI 10 1 1 2 8 —
1976-88 OG-M SUI 11 2 6 8 8 —
~IIHF Hall of Fame

**Kolnik, Lubomir / b. Jan. 23, 1968**
1991-99 WM SVK 29 7 7 14 16 2G,B
1991-96 CC SVK 8 2 0 2 2 —
1994-98 OG-M SVK 12 4 1 5 4 G

**Kolosov, Andrei / b. June 8, 1989**
2006 WM18 BLR 6 0 0 0 6 —

**Kolosov, Vitali / b. May 11, 1981**
1999 WM18 UKR 6 1 1 2 8 —

**Kolozvary, Ivan / b. Feb. 16, 1983**
2002-03 WM20 SVK 13 3 3 6 0 —

**Kolsrud, Bjorn / b. unknown**
1979 WM20 NOR 5 0 0 0 4 —

**Koltsov, Kirill / b. Feb. 1, 1983**
2001 WM18 RUS 6 1 6 7 16 G
2003 WM20 RUS 6 2 3 5 6 G
2006 WM RUS 6 0 0 0 27 —

**Komadoski, Neil / b. Feb. 10, 1982**
2000 WM18 USA 6 0 2 2 12 —

**Komarniski, Zenith / b. Aug. 13, 1978**
1998 WM20 CAN 7 0 0 0 26 —

**Komarov, Alexander / b. July 25, 1923 / d. unknown**
1954-55 WM URS 7 2 0 2 2 G,S

**Komissarov, Anton / b. Apr. 18, 1978**
1998 WM20 KAZ 7 1 0 1 2 —
2004-05 WM KAZ 12 0 0 0 4 —

**Komma, Michael / b. Dec. 20, 1964**
1984 WM20 FRG 7 0 0 0 0 —

**Komorski, Wlodzimierz / b. July 6, 1944**
1966-70 WM POL 15 0 1 1 24 —

**Kompajn, Gert / b. Sept. 13, 1960**
1988 OG-M AUT 5 0 0 0 4 —

**Komulainen, Olli-Pekka / b.July 24, 1985**
2003 WM18 FIN 4 0 1 1 0 —

**Kon, Yosuke / b. Sept. 21, 1978**
2000-04 WM JPN 21 0 2 2 37 —

**Kondrashkin, Sergei / b. Apr. 2, 1975**
1994 WM20 RUS 7 3 1 4 4 B

**Kondratiev, Maxim / b. Jan. 20, 1983**
2002-03 WM20 RUS 13 0 2 2 16 2G
2004-07 WM RUS 11 0 0 0 4 B

**Koneckis, Eriks / b. Feb. 9, 1920 / d. Feb. 2, 2006**
1939 WM LAT 1 0 — 0 — —

**Konecny, Rastislav / b.May 20, 1988**
2006 WM18 SVK 6 3 0 3 4 —

**Konig, Christoph / b. Mar. 26, 1979**
1999-2002 WM AUT 12 1 1 2 4 —

**Konig, Rudolf / b. Apr. 25, 1957**
1976-88 OG-M AUT 12 4 3 7 10 —

**Konig, Walter / b. June 9, 1944**
1968 OG-M AUT 3 0 0 0 2 —

**Konik, George / b. May 4, 1937**
1971 WM USA 9 1 1 2 8 —

**Konopasek, Stanislav / b. Apr. 18, 1923 / d. Mar. 6, 2008**
1947-49 WM TCH 13 25 — 25 — 2G
1948 OG-M TCH 6 11 — 11 — S

**Konowalchuk, Steve / b. Nov. 11, 1972**
1992 WM20 USA 7 4 0 4 8 B
2000-02 WM USA 14 4 2 6 6 —
1996-2004 WCH USA 6 0 0 0 4 1st

**Konradsson, Ulf / b. Jan. 15, 1965**
1985 WM20 SWE 7 0 1 1 0 —

**Konroyd, Steve / b. Feb. 10, 1961**
1985-91 WM CAN 20 1 6 7 0 2S

**Konstantinov, Vladimir / b. Mar. 19, 1967**
1986-87 WM20 URS 13 3 8 11 12 G
1986-91 WM URS 38 5 6 11 59 3G,B
~suffered career-ending injuries from a car accident, June 13, 1997

**Kontos, Chris / b. Dec. 10, 1963**
1994 OG-M CAN 8 3 1 4 2 S

**Kontrec, Dejan / b. Jan. 23, 1970**
2002-06 WM SLO 22 5 11 16 4 —

**Kontsek, Roman / b. June 11, 1970**
1989 WM20 TCH 6 5 3 8 4 B
1997 WM SVK 8 4 2 6 4 —
1994-98 OG-M SVK 12 4 1 5 10 —

**Konttinen, Tero / b. June 14, 1985**
2003 WM18 FIN 6 1 0 1 4 —

**Koopmans, Leo / b. Nov. 28, 1953**
1981 WM NED 8 4 1 5 4 —
1980 OG-M NED 5 0 0 0 0 —

**Kopat, Vladimir / b. Apr. 23, 1971**
1999-2006 WM BLR 35 1 2 3 26 —
2002 OG-M BLR 8 1 1 2 4 —

**Kopczynski, Adam / b. Aug. 2, 1948**
1973-75 WM POL 30 2 4 6 22 —
1972 OG-M POL 5 0 1 1 0 —

**Kopecky, Bill / b. Jan. 11, 1966**
1985 WM20 USA 7 2 0 2 4 —

**Kopecky, Jan / b. Mar. 21, 1979**
1999 WM20 CZE 6 1 2 3 6 —

**Kopecky, Ludvik / b. May 22, 1963**
1982-83 WM20 TCH 14 4 5 9 8 2S

**Kopf, Ernst / b. Feb. 10, 1940**
1962-76 WM FRG 24 3 7 10 8 —
1964-76 OG-M FRG 19 6 9 15 16 B

**Kopf, Ernst / b. June 24, 1968**
1988 WM20 FRG 6 5 1 6 4 —
1991-94 WM GER 27 10 4 14 10 —
1992 OG-M GER 8 3 1 4 0 —

**Kopitz, Lasse / b. May 21, 1980**
2003-05 WM GER 10 1 0 1 6 —
2004 WCH GER 3 0 0 0 4 —
2006 OG-M GER 4 0 0 0 0 —

**Kopot, Artyom / b. July 25, 1972**
1992 WM20 RUS 7 0 1 1 6 G

**Koppchen, Patrick / b. June 21, 1980**
2002 WM GER 7 0 0 0 0 —

**Kopylov, Yuri / b. Mar. 30, 1930**
1958 WM URS 7 6 4 10 2 S

**Korabov, Stanislav / b. May 29, 1982**
2000 WM18 BLR 6 1 3 4 2 —
2002 WM20 BLR 6 0 0 0 2 —

**Korbela, Jaroslav / b. May 20, 1957**
1977 WM20 TCH 7 6 2 8 10 B
1981-82 WM TCH 16 5 3 8 10 S,B
1981-84 CC TCH 10 0 1 1 12 —
1984 OG-M TCH 7 0 1 1 10 S

**Korber, Daniel / b. Nov. 8, 1974**
1994 WM20 GER 7 0 0 0 0 —

**Koreis, Jakub / b. June 26, 1984**
2002 WM18 CZE 8 1 2 3 6 B
2003-04 WM20 CZE 12 0 3 3 0 —

**Koren, Gunther / b. July 30, 1962**
1981 WM20 AUT 5 0 0 0 4 —
1988 OG-M AUT 6 2 1 3 0 —

**Koren, Helmut / b. Mar. 30, 1958**
1984 OG-M AUT 5 0 0 0 0 —

**Koreshkov, Alexander / b. Oct. 28, 1968**
1998-2010 WM KAZ 27 1 8 9 10 —
1998-2006 OG-M KAZ 12 4 8 12 2 —

**Koreshkov, Yevgeni / b. Mar. 11, 1970**
1998-2006 WM KAZ 21 5 3 8 28 —
1998-2006 OG-M KAZ 12 7 3 10 14 —

**Korff, Werner / b. Dec. 18, 1911 / d. unknown**
1933-35 WM GER 10 0 — 0 0 B
1932 OG-M GER 6 0 1 1 2 B

**Korn, Jim / b. July 28, 1957**
1979-81 WM USA 13 0 2 2 20 —

**Korneyev, Vladislav / b. Mar. 30, 1981**
1999 WM18 RUS 7 0 0 0 2 —
2001 WM20 RUS 7 0 0 0 2 —

**Kornusov, Vladimir / b. Mar. 16, 1983**
2001 WM18 RUS 6 0 3 3 10 G

**Korobeinikov, Sergei / b. Apr. 12, 1982**
2001 WM20 KAZ 6 0 0 0 2 —

**Korolyov, Igor / b. Sept. 6, 1970 / d. Sept. 7, 2011**
1992 WM RUS 6 2 1 3 2 —
1991 CC URS 5 0 0 0 0 —
~perished in Yaroslavl plane crash

**Korolyuk, Alexander / b. Jan. 15, 1976**
1995-96 WM20 RUS 14 13 4 17 51 S,B
1997-2001 WM RUS 13 3 4 7 12 —
2006 OG-M RUS 6 1 1 2 6 —

**Korotkov, Konstantin / b. Jan. 25, 1972**
1991-92 WM20 URS 14 8 3 11 14 G,S

**Korotkov, Sergei / b. Feb. 11, 1951**
1976 WM URS 10 1 2 3 2 S

**Korpikari, Oskari / b. Apr. 5, 1984**
2004 WM20 FIN 3 0 0 0 2 B

**Korpisalo, Jari / b. Feb. 17, 1966**
1986 WM20 FIN 6 3 6 9 4 —
1993 WM FIN 6 0 1 1 4 —

**Korsunov, Vladimir / b. Mar. 16, 1983**
2002 WM20 RUS 7 0 2 2 6 G

**Kosek, Jan / b. Jan. 11, 1914 / d. unknown**
1937 WM TCH 8 0 1 1 14 —
1936 OG-M TCH 3 0 — 0 — —

**Kosik, Michal / b. May 23, 1979**
1999 WM20 SVK 6 0 0 0 2 B

**Koskela, Ilpo / b. Jan. 29, 1945**
1969-73 WM FIN 40 6 4 10 4 —
1968-72 OG-M FIN 12 1 2 3 2 —
~WM All-Star Team/Defence (1971)

**Koskela, Timo / b. Jan. 23, 1979**
1999 WM20 FIN 6 1 1 2 0 —

**Koskilahti, Jukka / b. May 23, 1954**
1979 WM FIN 6 0 0 0 2 —
1980 OG-M FIN 7 1 0 1 0 —

**Koskimaki, Petteri / b. May 5, 1971**
1991 WM20 FIN 6 2 5 7 2 —

**Koskinen, Hannu / b. Nov. 23, 1953**
1981 WM FIN 8 0 0 0 4 —
1980 OG-M FIN 7 1 1 2 2 —

**Koskinen, Tapio / b. Jan. 22, 1953**
1976-79 WM FIN 18 7 6 13 14 —
1976 CC FIN 5 0 3 3 6 —
1976 OG-M FIN 5 0 0 0 0 —

**Koslow, Daniel / b. Jan. 6, 1982**
1999-2000 WM18 GER 12 0 2 2 4 —

**Kosmachev, Dmitri / b. June 7, 1985**
2002-03 WM18 RUS 14 0 2 2 8 S,B
2004 WM20 RUS 6 0 0 0 2 —

**Kossmann, Rainer / b. May 1, 1927**
1955 WM FRG 2 0 0 0 0 —
1956 OG-M FRG 4 0 0 0 0 —

**Kostarev, Vitali / b. May 1, 1929**
1957 WM URS 3 1 2 3 — S

**Kostichkin, Pavel / b. Nov. 9, 1968**
1987-88 WM20 URS 13 6 5 11 18 S

**Kostka, Vladimir / b. Mar. 14, 1953**
1975 WM TCH 6 0 0 0 2 S

**Kostner, Erwin / b. Apr. 7, 1958**
1983 WM ITA 3 0 1 1 0 —
1984 OG-M ITA 5 0 0 0 0 —

**Kostyuk, Dmitri / b. Oct. 6, 1984**
2002 WM18 RUS 8 0 0 0 0 S

**Koszowski, Marek / b. Mar. 9, 1969**
1988 WM20 POL 6 1 0 1 10 —
1992 WM POL 6 1 1 2 4 —

**Kotala, Lumir / b. Apr. 10, 1964**
1983-84 WM20 TCH 14 5 4 9 4 S,B

**Kotrla, Jindrich / b. Mar. 7, 1975**
2003 WM CZE 9 0 1 1 2 —

**Kottstorfer, Reiner / b. Aug. 2, 1981**
1999 WM18 GER 6 0 0 0 6 —

**Koudelka, Martin / b. Feb. 11, 1976**
1996 WM20 CZE 5 1 2 3 2 —

**Koutny, Lajos / b. Oct. 17, 1939**
1964 OG-M HUN 7 0 0 0 0 —

**Koutuaniemi, Jouni / b. Jan. 3, 1961**
1980-81 WM20 FIN 10 2 5 7 12 2S

**Kouwenhoven, Mike / b. Feb. 7, 1959**
1981 WM NED 2 0 1 1 2 —

**Kovac, Joze / b. Sept. 23, 1961**
1984 OG-M YUG 5 0 1 1 4 —

**Kovac, Kristian / b. Jan. 1, 1981**
1999 WM18 SVK 7 1 2 3 2 B

**Kovacs, Csaba / b. Mar. 18, 1984**
2009 WM HUN 6 0 1 1 2 —

**Koval, Oleksiy / b. Oct. 26, 1985**
2002 WM18 UKR 6 0 0 0 0 —
2004 WM20 UKR 6 0 0 0 4 —

**Kovalenko, Andrei / b. June 7, 1970**
1990-2002 WM20 RUS 26 6 10 16 8 S
1991-2004 WCH RUS 12 3 2 5 20 —
1992-98 OG-M RUS 14 5 2 7 16 G,S

**Kovalenko, Oleg / b. Feb. 11, 1975**
2004-06 WM KAZ 18 0 3 3 10 —
2006 OG-M KAZ 5 0 0 0 4 —

**Kovalyov, Andrei / b. Apr. 2, 1966**
1986 WM20 URS 7 0 1 1 0 G
1998-2003 WM BLR 29 4 7 11 12 —
1998-2002 OG-M BLR 16 2 5 7 14 —

**Kovich, John / b. Jan. 1, 1928**
1949 WM CAN 6 0 — 0 — S

**Kovin, Vladimir / b. June 20, 1954**
1985 WM URS 2 0 0 0 0 B
1976-84 CC URS 11 2 3 5 8
1984 OG-M URS 7 5 3 8 2 G

**Kowalczyk, Pavel / b. June 8, 1974**
1993-94 WM20 CZE 14 3 5 8 20 B

**Kowalski, Adam / b. Dec. 19, 1912 / d. Dec. 9, 1971**
1935-39 WM POL 21 8 0 8 4 —
1932-48 OG-M POL 16 6 0 6 0 —

**Kowalski, Alexander / b. Oct. 7, 1902 / d. Apr. 3, 1940**
1930-31 WM POL 8 2 — 2 — —
1928-32 OG-M POL 8 2 0 2 6 —

**Kowcinak, Dick / b. May 25, 1917 / d. unknown**
1939 WM CAN 8 6 — 6 — G

**Kozak, Paul / b. June 29, 1910 / d. unknown**
1937 WM CAN 8 2 1 3 2 G

**Kozhan, Stanislav / b. May 5, 1983**
2001 WM18 UKR 6 1 3 4 0 —
**Kozhevnikov, Alexander / b. Sept. 21, 1958**
1978 WM20 URS 7 5 4 9 4 G
1982 WM URS 10 6 1 7 2 G
1984 CC URS 5 0 1 1 0 —
1984-88 OG-M URS 9 5 5 10 6 2G
**Kozhevnikov, Alexander / b. Sept. 21, 1958**
2004 WM20 RUS 6 0 0 0 4 —
**Koziel, Zbigniew / b. May 12, 1964**
1992 WM POL 4 0 0 0 0 —
**Kozlov, Roman / b. Sept. 30, 1981**
2001 WM20 KAZ 6 0 0 0 2 —
2004-05 WM KAZ 12 1 1 2 6 —
**Kozlov, Vyacheslav / b. May 3, 1972**
1990-91 WM20 URS 14 7 16 23 12 2S
1991-94 WM RUS 11 3 4 7 14 B
1991-96 WCH RUS 10 2 4 6 16
**Kozlovich, Sergei / b. June 13, 1988**
2006 WM18 BLR 6 0 0 0 6 —
**Koznev, Alexei / b. Oct. 3, 1975**
2002 WM RUS 9 3 2 5 6 S
**Kraatz, Fritz / b. Feb. 4, 1906 / d. unknown**
1930 WM SUI 2 0 — 0 — B
1928 OG-M SUI 3 0 — 0 — B
**Kraft, Milan / b. Jan. 17, 1980**
2000 WM20 CZE 7 5 7 12 0 G
2004 WM CZE 7 1 1 2 2 —
~WM20 IIHF Directorate Best Forward (2000), WM20 All-Star Team/Forward (2000)
**Kraft, Rune / b. May 29, 1969**
1989 WM20 NOR 6 0 0 0 0 —
**Kraft, Ryan / b. Jan. 17, 1980**
2001 WM USA 9 0 2 2 0 —
**Krainz, Martin / b. May 20, 1967**
1993-96 WM AUT 13 0 0 0 31 —
1994 OG-M AUT 3 0 0 0 2 —
**Krajcovic, Eugen / b. Nov. 12, 1958**
1978 WM20 TCH 6 0 0 0 4 —
**Krajnc, Gregor / b. Jan. 27, 1976**
2002 WM SLO 6 0 0 0 4 —
**Kral, Josef / b. unknown / d. unknown**
1930-31 WM TCH 2 0 — 0 — —
**Kral, Norbert / b. July 21, 1956**
1981 WM TCH 1 0 1 1 0 B
1981 CC TCH 5 2 0 2 0 —
**Kralik, Dusan / b. May 10, 1966**
1986 WM20 TCH 7 0 0 0 8 —
**Kramer, Brady / b. June 13, 1973**
1993 WM20 USA 7 0 1 1 6 —
**Krapf, Andy / b. Apr. 13, 1971**
1991 WM20 SUI 7 0 0 0 0 —
**Krasl, Jan / b. Aug. 10, 1899 / d. Mar. 17, 1980**
1928 OG-M TCH 1 0 — 0 — —
**Krasotkin, Dmitri / b. Aug. 28, 1971**
1995-2001 WM RUS 21 1 3 4 6 —
**Krastinov, Dimo / b. Jan. 20, 1945**
1976 OG-M BUL 5 0 2 2 0 —
**Kratena, Ivo / b. May 7, 1985**
2003 WM18 CZE 6 2 3 5 0 —
**Kratena, Ondrej / b. Apr. 21, 1977**
1996-97 WM20 CZE 13 6 7 13 0 —
1997-2002 WM CZE 14 0 0 0 0 B
**Kratzsch, Dieter / b. June 2, 1939**
1961-67 WM GDR 31 8 0 8 2 —
1968 OG-M GDR 6 0 0 0 2 —
**Kraus, Jakub / b. Oct. 9, 1979**
1999 WM20 CZE 6 0 0 0 0 —
**Kravchuk, Igor / b. Sept. 13, 1966**
1985-86 WM20 URS 14 0 5 5 10 G,B
1990-2000 WM RUS 26 2 7 9 16 G,B
1987-91 CC URS 10 0 4 4 4 2nd
1988-2002 OG-M URS 26 4 6 10 8 2G,S,B
~OG-M All-Star Team/Defence (1992)
**Krawinkel, Markus / b. May 27, 1974**
1994 WM20 GER 7 1 0 1 2 —
**Krayer, Ed / b. June 6, 1967**
1987 WM20 USA 7 2 2 4 2 —
**Krayzel, Milos / b. Nov. 11, 1961**
1981 WM20 TCH 5 2 0 2 6 —
**Kreis, Harold / b. Jan. 19, 1959**
1979 WM20 FRG 5 0 1 1 4 —
1979-90 WM FRG 69 4 20 24 20 —
1984-88 OG-M FRG 14 1 3 4 2 —
**Kreisel, Franz / b. Jan. 6, 1890 / d. unknown**
1930 WM GER 5 0 — 0 — S
1928 OG-M GER 2 0 0 0 — —
**Kreitz, Willy / b. Sept. 21, 1903 / d. July 3, 1982**
1930-35 WM BEL 12 5 — 5 0 —
1924-36 OG-M BEL 4 0 — 0 — —
**Kremers, Nico / b. Apr. 22, 1927**
1950 WM NED 2 0 0 0 0 —
**Kremershoff, Walter / b. Dec. 3, 1922 / d. unknown**
1953-55 WM FRG 10 0 0 0 2 S
1952 OG-M FRG 8 5 1 6 — —
**Krempels, Peter / b. 1897 / d. unknown**
1930 WM HUN 2 0 — 0 — —
1928 OG-M HUN 2 0 — 0 — —
**Kreps, Kamil / b. Nov. 18, 1984**
2002 WM18 CZE 8 3 2 5 6 B
2004 WM20 CZE 7 0 0 0 0 —
**Krepuska, Istvan / b. 1899 / d. 1978**
1930 WM HUN 2 0 — 0 — —
1928 OG-M HUN — 0 — 0 — —
**Kress, Michael / b. Apr. 13, 1976**
1996 WM20 SUI 5 0 0 0 22 —
**Kretschmer, Horst / b. Oct. 19, 1955**
1976-87 WM FRG 63 6 4 10 120 —
1980-88 OG-M FRG 13 3 2 5 26 —
**Kreuzmann, Stephan / b. May 24, 1984**
2002 WM18 GER 8 0 1 1 14 —
**Krevsun, Alexander / b. June 2, 1980**
2000 WM20 KAZ 7 1 2 3 6 —
**Kriechbaum, Josef / b. Apr. 26, 1949**
1976 OG-M AUT 3 0 0 0 0 —
**Krieger, Bob / b. Oct. 5, 1952**
1977 WM USA 10 6 1 7 6 —
**Krikke, Henk / b. July 21, 1954**
1981 WM NED 7 0 0 0 2 —
**Krikunenko, Oleg / b. Sept. 4, 1977**
1996 WM20 UKR 5 0 1 1 24 —
**Krikunov, Ilya / b. Feb. 27, 1984**
2002 WM18 RUS 8 3 8 11 6 S
2004 WM20 RUS 6 0 2 2 2 —
**Krikunov, Vladimir / b. Mar. 24, 1950**
1976 CC URS 5 0 0 0 2 —
**Krinner, Toni / b. June 14, 1967**
1985-86 WM20 FRG 14 1 0 1 8 —
**Krisak, Patrik / b. Aug. 22, 1974**
1993 WM20 TCH 7 3 1 4 4 B
**Kristan, Marjan / b. July 16, 1937**
1964 OG-M YUG 6 0 — 0 — —
**Kristek, Jaroslav / b. Mar. 16, 1980**
2000 WM20 CZE 7 5 1 6 2 G
**Kristensen, Kjell / b. unknown**
1954 WM NOR 7 0 — 0 0 —
**Kristensen, Thom / b. unknown**
1972 OG-M NOR 1 0 0 0 0 —
**Kristiansen, Bjorn / b. unknown**
1949 WM NOR 3 0 — 0 — —
**Kristiansen, Erik / b. Mar. 12, 1961**
1990-94 WM NOR 28 8 2 10 22 —
1984-94 OG-M NOR 23 3 2 5 20 —
**Kristiansen, Kent Inge / b. Mar. 29, 1969**
1989 WM20 NOR 7 0 1 1 8 —
**Kristiansen, Pal / b. Jan. 21, 1970**
1989-90 WM20 NOR 14 3 1 4 4 —
1993 WM NOR 7 0 1 1 2 —
**Kristiansen, Per Arne / b. Sept. 9, 1959**
1984 OG-M NOR 5 0 0 0 4 —
**Kristiansen, Truls / b. Apr. 5, 1964**
1983 WM20 NOR 7 0 0 0 8 —
1988 OG-M NOR 6 0 3 3 2 —
**Kristin, Miroslav / b. Jan. 22, 1982**
2001-02 WM20 SVK 14 1 2 3 8 —
**Kristoffersson, Marcus / b. Jan. 22, 1979**
1999 WM20 SWE 6 3 4 7 33 —
**Krivokhizha, Yuri / b. May 30, 1968**
1988 WM20 URS 7 0 3 3 10 S
1999-2000 WM BLR 12 0 2 2 10 —
**Krivokrasov, Sergei / b. Apr. 15, 1974**
1992 WM20 RUS 7 3 3 6 22 G
1998 OG-M RUS 6 0 0 0 4 S
**Kriz, Pavel / b. Jan. 2, 1977**
1997 WM20 CZE 7 1 0 1 14 —
**Krmelj, Miran / b. Feb. 23, 1941 / d. Mar. 2, 2009**
1964 OG-M YUG 3 0 — 0 — —
**Kroge, Gunnar / b. Oct. 18, 1930 / d. Jan. 24, 2000**
1949-51 WM NOR 17 0 0 0 2 —
1952 OG-M NOR 6 0 0 0 — —
**Krol, Wladyslaw / b. Oct. 30, 1907 / d. Jan. 28, 1991**
1938 WM POL 6 4 — 4 — —
1936 OG-M POL 3 0 — 0 — —
**Krol, Wlodzimierz / b. July 5, 1968**
1987-88 WM20 POL 14 1 4 5 32 —
**Kromm, Bobby / b. June 28, 1928 / d. June 9, 2010**
1961 WM CAN 3 0 3 3 2 G
**Kromp, Wolfgang / b. Sept. 17, 1970**
1993-2001 WM AUT 27 0 2 2 6 —
1994-2002 OG-M AUT 15 1 2 3 10 —
**Kron, Robert / b. Feb. 27, 1967**
1985-87 WM20 TCH 19 7 8 15 14 2S
1989-90 WM TCH 20 2 3 5 2 2B
1991 CC TCH 5 0 0 0 0 —
~WM20 IIHF Directorate Best Forward (1987)
**Kropac, Radoslav / b. Apr. 5, 1975**
1998 WM SVK 6 0 0 0 0 —
**Kropf, Martin / b. June 15, 1976**
1996 WM20 GER 6 0 1 1 2 —
**Kroupa, Vlastimil / b. Apr. 27, 1975**
1995 WM20 CZE 7 4 2 6 10 —
1997 WM CZE 9 0 4 4 10 B
**Krovopuskov, Alexei / b. Oct. 11, 1978**
1998 WM20 RUS 7 4 3 7 8 S
**Krsnak, Peter / b. Aug. 25, 1988**
2006 WM18 SVK 6 0 0 0 2 —
**Krstev, Angel / b. Dec. 15, 1980**
2000 WM20 CZE 7 0 0 0 6 G
**Kruchinin, Andrei / b. May 18, 1978**
1998 WM20 RUS 7 0 2 2 2 S
2006 WM RUS 5 0 2 2 4 —
**Kruck, Andreas / b. Dec. 24, 1984**
2002 WM18 GER 8 1 0 1 10 —
**Krueger, Ralph / b. Aug. 31, 1959**
1981-86 WM FRG 16 0 2 2 4 —
**Kruger, Raphael / b. May 12, 1971**
1989 WM20 FRG 6 0 0 0 2 —
**Krull, Harald / b. Feb. 8, 1957**
1977 WM20 FRG 7 0 1 1 2 —
1979 WM FRG 8 0 1 1 10 —
1980 OG-M FRG 5 0 3 3 0 —
**Krumpschmid, Normand / b. Dec. 13, 1969**
1998-99 WM AUT 9 2 0 2 16 —
1998 OG-M AUT 4 0 0 0 2 —
**Krupp, Uwe / b. June 24, 1965**
1983-85 WM20 FRG 14 0 1 1 8 —
1986-90 WM FRG 5 2 1 3 4 —
1998 OG-M GER 2 0 2 2 4 —
**Krutikov, Alexei / b. Feb. 1, 1984**
2005 WM BLR 6 0 0 0 4 —
**Krutov, Vladimir / b. June 3, 1960**
1979-80 WM20 URS 11 15 10 25 7 2G
1981-89 WM URS 68 44 34 78 68 5G,S,B
1981-87 CC URS 22 14 16 30 18 1st,2nd
1980-88 OG-M URS 22 16 15 31 6 2G,S
~IIHF Hall of Fame
~WM IIHF Directorate Best Forward (1986, 1987), WM All-Star Team/Forward (1983, 1985, 1986, 1987), WM20 IIHF Directorate Best Forward (1979, 1980), WM20 All-Star Team/Forward (1979, 1980)
**Kryazhev, Oleg / b. Oct. 9, 1970**
1998 WM KAZ 3 0 1 1 0 —
1998 OG-M KAZ 7 0 0 0 0 —
**Krygier, Todd / b. Oct. 12, 1965**
1991-97 WM USA 19 5 5 10 20 —
**Krygier, Wlodzimierz / b. Jan. 29, 1900 / d. Sept. 17, 1975**
1930-31 WM POL 10 3 — 3 — —
1928-32 OG-M POL 7 0 0 0 2 —
**Krylov, Valeri / b. Feb. 8, 1959**
1979 WM20 URS 6 0 0 0 0 G
**Krylov, Yuri / b. Mar. 11, 1930 / d. Nov. 4, 1979**
1954-59 WM URS 29 11 1 12 10 G,3S
1956 OG-M URS 7 4 3 7 4 G
**Kryvamaz, Yevgeni / b. July 23, 1979**
1999 WM20 BLR 6 1 0 1 8 —
**Kryvorutski, Dmitri / b. May 16, 1982**
1999-2000 WM18 UKR 11 1 2 3 8
**Kubes, Ondrej / b. Nov. 11, 1981**
1999 WM18 CZE 7 0 0 0 0 —
**Kubista, Jan / b. Apr. 12, 1984**
2002 WM18 CZE 7 1 2 3 4 B

**Kubowicz, Jacek / b. June 19, 1967**
1987 WM20 POL 7 3 1 4 4 —

**Kubrak, Alexander / b. May 2, 1982**
2000 WM18 UKR 6 0 0 0 0 —

**Kuc, Jacek / b. May 5, 1971**
1990 WM20 POL 7 0 0 0 2 —

**Kuc, Jaroslaw / b. Feb. 23, 1978**
1997 WM20 POL 6 0 0 0 6 —

**Kucera, Frantisek / b. Feb. 3, 1968**
1987-88 WM20 TCH 14 2 4 6 4 S
1989-2000 WM CZE 39 6 9 15 24 2G,2B
1991 CC TCH 5 0 0 0 4 —
1998 OG-M CZE 6 0 0 0 0 G
~WM IIHF Directorate Best Defenceman (1998, 1999), WM All-Star Team/Defence (1998)

**Kucera, Jiri / b. Mar. 28, 1966**
1985-86 WM20 TCH 14 7 8 15 8 S
1987-96 WM TCH 68 16 13 29 35 G,4B
1987-96 WCH CZE 8 0 0 0 4 —
1994 OG-M CZE 8 6 2 8 4 —

**Kucera, Oldrich / b. July 1, 1914 / d. unknown**
1933-39 WM TCH 37 25 2 27 0 2B
1936 OG-M TCH 8 6 — 6 — —

**Kucera, Vojtech / b. Oct. 15, 1965**
1985 WM20 TCH 7 1 1 2 2 S

**Kucharcik, Tomas / b. May 10, 1970**
1999 WM CZE 6 0 0 0 0 G

**Kuchevski, Alfred / b. May 17, 1931 / d. May 15, 2000**
1954-58 WM URS 17 3 0 3 4 G,2S
1956-60 OG-M URS 11 0 4 4 16 G,B

**Kuchin, Sergei / b. Mar. 4, 1962**
1982 WM20 URS 7 5 2 7 4 —

**Kuchyna, Petr / b. Jan. 14, 1970**
1990 WM20 TCH 7 2 2 4 0 B
1995 WM CZE 8 0 1 1 4 —

**Kuczera, Heinz / b. June 16, 1935**
1957-63 WM GDR 26 3 3 6 12 —

**Kudashov, Alexei / b. July 21, 1971**
1990-91 WM20 URS 14 4 9 13 6 2S
1998-2000 WM RUS 15 1 5 6 12 —
1994 OG-M RUS 8 1 2 3 4 —

**Kudashov, Sergei / b. Jan. 16, 1962**
1981-82 WM20 URS 12 2 8 10 6 B

**Kudo, Atsuo / b. Jan. 9, 1965**
1998 OG-M JPN 4 0 1 1 0 —

**Kudo, Kimihisa / b. Sept. 6, 1939**
1964-68 OG-M JPN 9 3 5 9 2 —

**Kudriavtsev, Oleg / b. June 2, 1963**
1981 WM20 URS 5 1 0 1 4 B

**Kudrna, Jaroslav / b. Dec. 5, 1975**
1995 WM20 CZE 7 4 4 8 6 —

**Kuenzi, Andre / b. Jan. 10, 1967**
1987 WM20 SUI 7 1 1 2 6 —
1988-92 OG-M SUI 9 0 0 0 4 —

**Kuenzi, Andres / b. Nov. 4, 1941**
1962 WM SUI 3 0 0 0 0 —

**Kugut, Igor / b. Apr. 22, 1984**
2004 WM20 UKR 6 0 0 0 0 —

**Kuhl, Marcus / b. Mar. 15, 1956**
1978-87 WM FRG 46 21 14 35 6 —
1984 CC FRG 5 2 1 3 2 —
1980-84 OG-M FRG 11 3 4 7 4 —

**Kuhn, Alois / b. Nov. 23, 1910 / d. unknown**
1934-35 WM GER 11 1 — 1 — B
1936 OG-M GER 3 0 — 0 — —

**Kuhn, Bernd / b. Aug. 17, 1944**
1967-73 WM FRG 35 6 2 8 36 —
1968-72 OG-M FRG 11 1 1 2 8 —

**Kuhn, Ludwig / b. May 26, 1918 / d. unknown**
1938-39 WM GER 6 1 — 1 — 0
1952 OG-M FRG 7 0 0 0 — —

**Kuhnhackl, Erich / b. Oct. 17, 1950**
1973-85 WM FRG 75 40 35 75 126 —
1972-84 OG-M FRG 15 15 15 30 22 B
~IIHF Hall of Fame

**Kuhnhauser, Bernd / b. Aug. 27, 1971**
1996 WM GER 6 1 0 1 8 —

**Kuhnke, Harald / b. Nov. 17, 1958**
1983-85 WM GDR 13 2 5 7 4 —

**Kuk, Dustin / b. Jan. 29, 1979**
1998 WM20 USA 7 0 1 1 2 —

**Kuki, Arto / b. Feb. 22, 1976**
1996 WM20 FIN 6 1 1 2 2 —

**Kukkonen, Mikko / b. Jan. 19, 1988**
2006 WM18 FIN 6 0 0 0 2 S

**Kulczynski, Harry / b. Feb. 2, 1982**
2000 WM18 GER 6 0 0 0 4 —

**Kulej, Lucjan / b. Nov. 29, 1896 / d. July 13, 1971**
1930-31 WM POL 6 1 — 1 — —
1928 OG-M POL 2 0 — 0 — —

**Kuleshov, Mikhail / b. July 7, 1981**
1999 WM18 RUS 7 0 4 4 2 —

**Kulikov, Alexander / b. Apr. 20, 1951**
1976 CC URS 3 0 1 1 2 —

**Kulmala, Arto / b. Apr. 5, 1968**
1988 WM20 FIN 7 5 0 5 4 B

**Kulmala, Vesa / b. Mar. 4, 1986**
2004 WM18 FIN 6 0 0 0 18 —

**Kulonen, Jouni / b. Oct. 2, 1981**
1999 WM18 FIN 7 1 6 7 0 G
2001 WM20 FIN 7 0 1 1 0 S

**Kulonen, Timo / b. Nov. 1, 1967**
1986-87 WM20 FIN 12 2 3 5 12 G

**Kulyash, Denis / b. May 31, 1983**
2006 WM RUS 7 3 1 4 6 —

**Kumar, Bojan / b. Aug. 3, 1950**
1972-76 OG-M YUG 7 0 0 0 23 —

**Kummer, Franz / b. Jan. 5, 1962**
1982 WM20 FRG 7 0 3 3 18 —

**Kummer, Wolfgang / b. Mar. 29, 1970**
1989 WM20 FRG 7 2 1 3 4 —
1992-94 WM GER 16 1 1 2 6 —
1994 OG-M GER 8 2 0 2 10 —

**Kummetz, Gunther / b. unknown / d. unknown**
1930 WM GER 3 0 — 0 — S

**Kumpel, Mark / b. Mar. 7, 1961**
1984 OG-M USA 6 1 0 1 2 —

**Kunce, Daniel / b. July 17, 1971**
1997-2004 WM GER 18 1 0 1 16 —
1996 WCH GER 3 0 0 0 4 —
1998-2002 OG-M GER 10 1 1 2 45 —

**Kung, Andreas / b. May 17, 1983**
2001 WM18 SUI 7 0 0 0 4 S

**Kunstler, Werner / b. Apr. 30, 1934**
1957-59 WM GDR 14 2 0 2 0 —

**Kuntos, Jiri / b. Dec. 11, 1971**
1991 WM20 TCH 7 1 4 5 14 B

**Kunz, Torsten / b. Mar. 31, 1978**
1998 WM20 GER 6 1 0 1 2 —

**Kunzi, Andre / b. Jan. 10, 1967**
1986 WM20 SUI 7 0 3 3 0 —

**Kuonen, Pius / b. Sept. 23, 1961**
1980 WM20 SUI 5 2 0 2 0 —

**Kupaks, Arturs / b. July 14, 1973**
1997-2001 WM LAT 14 0 1 1 20 —

**Kupec, Martin / b. Feb. 15, 1988**
2006 WM18 CZE 7 0 0 0 0 B

**Kurashev, Konstantin / b. Jan. 13, 1962**
1982 WM20 URS 7 2 1 3 4 —

**Kurceba, Paul / b. Feb. 19, 1987**
2005 WM18 CAN 6 1 0 1 4 S

**Kurdin, Gennadi / b. Feb. 9, 1959**
1979 WM20 URS 6 4 2 6 2 G

**Kurek, Jozef / b. Jan. 2, 1933**
1955-66 WM POL 26 21 2 23 20 —
1956-64 OG-M POL 9 4 1 5 2 —

**Kurilko, Andri / b. Apr. 1975**
1995 WM20 UKR 7 0 0 0 4 —

**Kurka, Tomas / b. Dec. 14, 1981**
1999 WM18 CZE 7 5 1 6 2 —

**Kurkinen, Risto / b. Jan. 21, 1963**
1983 WM20 FIN 5 1 1 2 2 —
1987-91 WM FIN 15 5 3 8 0 —

**Kurokawa, Hideaki / b. May 8, 1944**
1972 OG-M JPN 4 0 0 0 4 —

**Kuronen, Juho / b. Feb. 18, 1982**
2000 WM18 FIN 6 0 0 0 4 G

**Kurowski, Jacek / b. Dec. 2, 1965**
1985 WM20 POL 7 1 0 1 0 —

**Kurri, Jari / b. May 18, 1960**
1979-80 WM20 FIN 11 6 10 16 2 S
1982-94 WM FIN 32 19 19 38 10 —
1981-96 WCH FIN 20 4 2 6 11 —
1980-98 OG-M FIN 13 3 5 8 8 B
~IIHF Hall of Fame
~WM All-Star Team/Forward (1991, 1994)

**Kurtenbach, Terry / b. Mar. 14, 1963**
1994 WM GBR 6 1 1 2 2 —

**Kurvers, Tom / b. Sept. 14, 1962**
1982 WM20 USA 7 3 3 6 16 —
1987-89 WM USA 20 5 3 8 19 —

**Kurylin, Yevgeni / b. Jan. 1, 1979**
1999 WM20 BLR 6 2 5 7 2 —

**Kurz, Kurt / b. Sept. 30, 1927**
1957 WM AUT 7 0 — 0 — —
1956 OG-M AUT 3 1 0 1 0 —

**Kus, Josef / b. June 1, 1921 / d. July 23, 2005**
1947 WM TCH 6 5 — 5 — G

**Kutlak, Zdenek / b. Feb. 13, 1980**
2000 WM20 CZE 7 0 0 0 2 G
2006 WM CZE 9 0 0 0 0 S

**Kutnyi, Mikhail / b. Nov. 7, 1981**
1999 WM18 UKR 5 0 0 0 4 —

**Kutsevich, Pavel / b. June 21, 1983**
2003 WM20 BLR 6 0 1 1 2 —

**Kuusela, Keijo / b. Jan. 6, 1921 / d. Apr. 27, 1984**
1949-51 WM FIN 10 9 — 9 0 —
1952 OG-M FIN 8 4 0 4 2 —

**Kuusisto, Jarmo / b. Apr. 5, 1961**
1981 WM20 FIN 5 0 0 0 4 S
1987-90 WM FIN 24 1 4 5 32 —

**Kuusisto, Matti / b. Apr. 6, 1982**
2000 WM18 FIN 7 0 1 1 14 G

**Kuusisto, Pekka / b. Jan. 17, 1945**
1967-73 WM FIN 16 4 0 4 10 —
1968 OG-M FIN 5 0 0 0 12 —

**Kuvaldin, Alexander / b. Mar. 16, 1974**
2001 WM RUS 7 1 1 2 2 —

**Kuwabara, Ryan / b. Mar. 23, 1972**
1998-2003 WM JPN 27 7 5 12 38 —
1998 OG-M JPN 4 2 0 2 4 —

**Kuzela, Milan / b. Apr. 27, 1946**
1972-79 WM TCH 35 0 8 8 22 G,2S,B

**Kuzin, Valentin / b. Sept. 23, 1926 / d. Aug. 13, 1994**
1954-55 WM URS 14 6 2 8 0 G,S
1956 OG-M URS 7 4 2 6 2 G

**Kuzkin, Viktor / b. July 6, 1940 / d. June 24, 2008**
1963-72 WM URS 50 8 7 15 32 6G,S
1972 SS URS 7 0 1 1 8 2nd
1964-72 OG-M URS 19 4 1 5 4 3G
~IIHF Hall of Fame

**Kuzmichev, Konstantin / b. Jan. 8, 1975**
1994 WM20 RUS 7 0 0 0 2 B

**Kuzmickas, Antanas / b. unknown / d. unknown**
1938 WM LTU 4 0 — 0 — —

**Kuzmickas, Bronius / b. unknown / d. unknown**
1938 WM LTU 3 0 — 0 — —

**Kuzmin, Yevgeni / b. July 8, 1974**
2004 WM KAZ 6 0 0 0 2 —

**Kuzminski, Alexander / b. Apr. 12, 1972**
1992 WM20 RUS 6 2 0 2 2 G

**Kuzminsky, Andri / b. Dec. 1975**
1995 WM20 UKR 7 1 3 4 2 —

**Kuznetsov, Viktor / b. May 14, 1950**
1974 WM URS 9 1 1 2 2 G

**Kuznetsov, Yuri / b. Aug. 10, 1971**
2001 WM RUS 7 1 2 3 2 —

**Kuzniecow, Krzysztof / b. June 16, 1968**
1988 WM20 POL 7 1 0 1 2 —
1992 WM POL 6 1 0 1 2 —
1992 OG-M POL 7 0 0 0 4 —

**Kvartalnov, Dmitri / b. Mar. 25, 1966**
1989-96 WM RUS 25 7 8 15 10 G,B

**Kvasha, Oleg / b. July 26, 1978**
1997-98 WM20 RUS 13 6 2 8 8 S,B
2004 WCH RUS 2 0 1 1 0 —
2002 OG-M RUS 5 0 0 0 0 B

**Kverka, Jaromir / b. Nov. 11, 1971**
1991 WM20 TCH 4 2 5 7 6 B

**Kwasigroch, Piotr / b. June 1, 1962**
1986-89 WM POL 18 2 1 3 6 —
1988 OG-M POL 6 0 0 0 2 —

**Kygyt, Igor / b. Apr. 22, 1984**
2002 WM18 UKR 8 0 0 0 20 —

**Kyhos, Vladimir / b. June 23, 1956**
1984 OG-M TCH 7 1 0 1 4 S

**Kyllonen, Markku / b. unknown**
1987 CC FIN 5 0 2 2 0 —

**Kyoya, Yoshiaki ~see Yoshiaki Honda**

**Kyro, Roger / b. Dec. 19, 1972**
1992 WM20 SWE 5 1 0 1 0 S

**Kysela, Robert / b. June 5, 1968**
1996 WM CZE 5 2 1 3 2 G

**Laaksonen, Antti / b. Oct. 3, 1973**
1993 WM20 FIN 7 2 0 2 2 —
2001-04 WM FIN 16 3 6 9 10 S
2004 WCH FIN 1 0 0 0 0 2nd
2006 OG-M FIN 8 0 0 0 6 S

**Laaksonen, Mikko / b. July 8, 1967**
1986-87 WM20 FIN 13 10 4 14 6 G

**Laamanen, Jukka-Pekka / b. Oct. 4, 1976**
1996 WM20 FIN 6 0 2 2 2 —
2007 WM FIN 4 0 1 1 4 S

**Laatikainen, Arto / b. May 24, 1980**
1999-2000 WM20 FIN 13 0 4 4 8 —

**LaBatte, Phil / b. July 5, 1911 / d. Sept. 6, 2002**
1936 OG-M USA 5 0 2 2 6 B

**La Bianca, Mike / b. Dec. 16, 1959**
1979 WM20 USA 5 0 1 1 0 —

**Labionak, Vitali / b. Sept. 15, 1986**
2004 WM18 BLR 6 0 0 1 4 —

**Labraaten, Dan / b. June 9, 1951**
1974-86 WM SWE 56 19 10 29 38 S,4B
1976 CC SWE 5 0 1 1 2 —

**Labuz, Sebastian / b. Feb. 12, 1978**
1997 WM20 POL 6 0 0 0 0 —
2002 WM POL 6 0 1 1 0 —

**Lacarriere, Jacques / b. Sept. 12, 1906 / d. July 28, 2005**
1930-37 WM FRA 21 2 0 2 4 —
1936 OG-M FRA 3 0 — 0 — —
~IIHF Hall of Fame

**Lacarriere, Philippe / b. Apr. 20, 1938**
1968 OG-M FRA 5 1 1 2 2 —

**Lacey, Gary / b. May 24, 1964**
1984 WM20 CAN 5 0 0 0 4 —

**Lachance, Rob / b. Feb. 1, 1974**
1994 WM20 USA 7 0 5 5 4 —

**Lachance, Scott / b. Oct. 22, 1972**
1991-92 WM20 USA 15 3 5 8 2 B
1996-99 WM USA 22 0 2 2 10 B
1992 OG-M USA 8 0 1 1 6 —
~WM20 All-Star Team/Defence (1991)

**Lack, Alfred / b. unknown / d. unknown**
1947 WM SUI 7 0 — 0 — —

**Lackey, Carl / b. 1943**
1969 WM USA 10 3 1 4 12 —

**Lackey, Jerry / b. 1945**
1969 WM USA 8 1 2 3 8 —

**Lacorne, Jean / b. unknown**
1950 WM FRA 4 0 0 0 0 —

**Lacouture, Dan / b. Apr. 18, 1977**
1997 WM20 USA 6 1 0 1 4 S
2002 WM USA 7 2 2 4 0 —

**Ladanyi, Balazs / b. Jan. 6, 1976**
2009 WM HUN 6 0 3 3 0 —

**Ladygin, Mykola / b. Dec. 7, 1983**
2001 WM18 UKR 6 0 1 1 6 —

**Lafayette, Nathan / b. Feb. 17, 1973**
1993 WM20 CAN 7 3 1 4 0 G

**Lafleur, Brian / b. Mar. 11, 1975**
1995 WM20 USA 7 0 0 0 4 —

**Lafleur, Guy / b. Sept. 20, 1951**
1981 WM CAN 7 1 0 1 2 —
1976-81 CC CAN 14 3 14 17 12 1st,2nd

**Lafontaine, Pat / b. Feb. 22, 1965**
1989 WM USA 10 5 3 8 8 —
1987-96 CC USA 16 8 3 11 4 1st
1984-98 OG-M USA 10 6 4 10 0 —

**Lahteenmaki, Ari / b. July 19, 1961**
1980-81 WM20 FIN 10 9 6 15 22 2S
~WM20 All-Star Team/Forward (1981)

**Laine, Erkki / b. Sept. 13, 1957**
1977 WM20 FIN 7 6 4 10 8 —
1984-88 OG-M FIN 13 4 6 10 6 S

**Laine, Rauni / b. Mar. 8, 1928**
1949 WM FIN 1 1 — 1 — —

**Laine, Teemu / b. Aug. 9, 1982**
2000 WM18 FIN 7 1 4 5 8 G
2000 WM20 FIN 7 1 0 1 6 —

**Lainesalo, Lenni / b. May 10, 1929**
1955 WM FIN 7 0 0 0 4 —

**Laitinen, Kari / b. Apr. 9, 1964**
1988 OG-M FIN 7 3 2 5 0 S

**Laitinen, Miro / b. Jan. 1, 1981**
1999 WM18 FIN 7 2 3 5 0 G
2001 WM20 FIN 7 1 0 1 4 S

**Lajovec, Vojko / b. Mar. 18, 1962**
1984 OG-M YUG 5 0 0 0 0 —

**Lake, Cliff / b. Aug. 1906 / d. unknown**
1934 WM CAN 4 5 — 5 — G

**Lakhmatov, Vitali / b. June 27, 1981**
2001 WM20 SUI 7 1 2 3 0 —

**Laksola, Pekka / b. May 25, 1964**
1983-84 WM20 FIN 14 1 3 4 22 S
1986-90 WM FIN 23 1 6 7 10 —

**Laksola, Reijo / b. Aug. 10, 1952**
1975 WM FIN 10 0 1 1 4 —
1976 OG-M FIN 5 1 0 1 4 —

**Lala, Jiri / b. Aug. 21, 1959**
1977-79 WM20 TCH 13 2 5 7 8 S,B
1981-86 WM TCH 48 31 17 48 12 G,2S,B
1981-84 CC TCH 11 4 2 6 0 —
1984-88 OG-M TCH 14 3 5 8 2 S
~WM IIHF Directorate Best Forward (1983)

**Lalor, Mike / b. Mar. 8, 1963**
1996 WM USA 8 0 0 0 4 B

**Lambert, Dan / b. Jan. 12, 1970**
1989 WM20 CAN 7 1 2 3 4 —

**Lambert, Michael / b. Mar. 10, 1984**
2002 WM18 CAN 8 2 2 4 2 —

**Lamby, Dick / b. May 3, 1955**
1978 WM USA 8 0 2 2 20 —
1976 OG-M USA 5 0 2 2 10 —

**Lamich, Martin / b. Jan. 9, 1979**
1999 WM20 CZE 6 2 2 4 31 —

**Lamirande, Jean-Paul / b. Aug. 21, 1924**
1958-59 WM CAN 15 1 8 9 2 2G
~WM IIHF Directorate Best Defenceman (1959)

**Lammers, John / b. Feb. 28, 1986**
2004 WM18 CAN 7 3 0 3 0 —

**Lammers, Martin / b. unknown / d. unknown**
1939 WM NED 4 2 — 2 — —

**Lammin, Dave / b. 1935**
1962 WM GBR 7 0 1 1 6 —

**Lampainen, Matti / b. Jan. 16, 1932**
1954-63 WM FIN 44 1 3 4 14 —
1960 OG-M FIN 6 2 0 2 4 —

**Lampert, Michael / b. July 17, 1972**
1998 WM AUT 3 0 0 0 4 —
1998 OG-M AUT 4 0 0 0 8 —

**Lampinen, Juha / b. Apr. 10, 1970**
1989 WM20 FIN 7 0 1 1 0 —

**Lampman, Bryce / b. Aug. 31, 1982**
2002 WM20 USA 7 0 0 0 8 —

**Landelius, Gunnar / b. Mar. 20, 1918 / d. unknown**
1947 WM SWE 7 3 — 3 — S
1948 OG-M SWE 7 1 — 1 — —

**Landolt, Patrick / b. Jan. 22, 1982**
2000 WM18 SUI 7 0 3 3 0 —

**Lane, Jesse / b. Mar. 2, 1983**
2001 WM18 USA 6 0 2 2 10 —

**Lang, Dieter / b. unknown**
1962 WM FRG 4 0 4 4 4 —

**Lang, Hans / b. unknown / d. unknown**
1933-38 WM GER 28 8 1 9 6 B

**Lang, Lukas / b. Oct. 14, 1988**
2006 WM18 CZE 7 1 0 1 2 B

**Lang, Martin / b. Dec. 1, 1968**
1987 WM20 SUI 4 0 1 1 0 —

**Lang, Robert / b. Dec. 19, 1970**
1992-97 WM CZE 24 8 7 15 29 G,2B
1996 WCH CZE 3 0 0 0 2 —
1992-2006 OG-M CZE 26 6 17 23 14 G,2B

**Langevin, Dave / b. May 15, 1954**
1976 WM USA 10 1 0 1 11 —
1981 CC USA 6 0 1 1 8 —

**Langhammer, Jakub / b. Aug. 17, 1984**
2002 WM18 CZE 8 1 0 1 0 B

**Langkow, Daymond / b. Sept. 27, 1976**
1996 WM20 CAN 5 3 3 6 2 G

**Langmaid, Ben / b. unknown / d. unknown**
1933 WM USA 5 4 — 4 2 G

**Langner, Gerhard / b. Feb. 15, 1943**
1964 OG-M POL 7 0 0 0 2 —

**Langner, Paul / b. Oct. 15, 1949**
1971-73 WM FRG 26 0 0 0 10 —
1972 OG-M FRG 3 0 1 1 2 —

**Langway, Rod / b. May 3, 1957**
1982 WM USA 6 0 2 2 4 —
1981-87 CC USA 17 1 3 4 22 —

**Laniel, Marc / b. Jan. 16, 1968**
1988 WM20 CAN 7 1 2 3 6 G

**Lanier, Jonas / b. Feb. 24, 1982**
2000 WM18 GER 6 3 0 3 6 —

**Lanz, Rick / b. Sept. 16, 1961**
1980 WM20 CAN 5 0 1 1 6 —
1983 WM CAN 6 0 2 2 2 B

**Lanzinger, Gunther / b. Jan. 4, 1972**
1993-2001 WM AUT 40 3 0 3 12 —
1994-2002 OG-M AUT 11 0 1 1 14 —

**Lap, Miroslav / b. Sept. 8, 1950**
1976 OG-M YUG 5 1 0 1 2 —

**Laperriere, Andre / b. June 12, 1925**
1948 OG-M CAN 8 1 — 1 14 G

**Lapin, Yevgeni / b. May 8, 1980**
2000 WM20 RUS 7 1 3 4 6 S

**Lapinkoski, Marko / b. Oct. 2, 1969**
1988-89 WM20 FIN 10 4 1 5 0 B

**Lapointe, Claude / b. Oct. 11, 1968**
1999 WM CAN 10 1 3 4 10 —

**Lapointe, Guy / b. May 18, 1948**
1972 SS CAN 7 0 1 1 6 1st
1976 CC CAN 7 0 4 4 2 1st

**Lapointe, Martin / b. Sept. 12, 1973**
1991-93 WM20 CAN 21 9 8 17 18 2G
2000 WM CAN 3 0 0 0 4 —

**Laporte, Benoit / b. June 14, 1960**
1992-94 WM FRA 16 4 0 4 32 —
1992-94 OG-M FRA 15 4 6 10 8 —

**Lappalainen, Joni / b. Mar. 21, 1984**
2002 WM18 FIN 8 3 2 5 2 —

**Lappalainen, Pentti / b. unknown / d. unknown**
1939 WM FIN 3 0 — 0 — —

**Lappin, Mike / b. Jan. 19, 1969**
1989 WM20 USA 7 2 4 6 2 —

**Larese-Fece, Igino / b. Oct. 6, 1931**
1959 WM ITA 4 0 0 0 0 —

**Larionov, Igor / b. Dec. 3, 1960**
1979-80 WM20 URS 10 5 7 12 12 2G
1982-89 WM URS 57 25 26 51 31 4G,S,B
1981-96 WCH RUS 26 6 9 15 22 1st,2nd
1984-2002 OG-M RUS 21 5 16 21 14 2G,B
~IIHF Hall of Fame/Triple Gold Club
~WM All-Star Team/Forward (1983, 1986), WM20 All-Star Team/Forward (1980)

**Larkin, Jim / b. Apr. 15, 1970**
1990 WM20 USA 7 1 1 2 2 —

**Larmer, Steve / b. June 16, 1961**
1991 WM CAN 10 5 3 8 4 S
1991 CC CAN 8 6 5 11 4 1st

**Larntvedt, Johnny / b. Oct. 27, 1916 / d. Sept. 27, 1996**
1949-51 WM NOR 18 2 0 2 4 —
1952 OG-M NOR 8 0 1 1 — —

**Larouche, Pierre / b. Nov. 16, 1955**
1977 WM CAN 10 7 8 15 16 —

**Larsen, Anders / b. Sept. 9, 1971**
1991 WM20 NOR 7 0 0 0 4 —

**Larsen, Bjorn Berg / b. Feb. 10, 1969**
1989 WM20 NOR 7 0 0 0 8 —

**Larsen, Brad / b. Jan. 28, 1977**
1996-97 WM20 CAN 13 1 2 3 10 2G

**Larsen, Einar Bruno / b. Nov. 17, 1931**
1958-62 WM NOR 20 8 11 19 20 —
1964 OG-M NOR 6 2 3 5 8 —

**Larsen, Johnny / b. unknown / d. unknown**
1938 WM NOR 4 0 — 0 — —

**Larsen, Martin / b. Apr. 30, 1986**
2004 WM18 DEN 6 0 1 1 2 —

**Larsen, Ronny / b. Dec. 31, 1971**
2003-04 WM DEN 12 4 2 6 31 —

**Larson, Bart / b. Nov. 2, 1958**
1978 WM20 USA 6 0 2 2 0 —

**Larson, Reed / b. July 30, 1956**
1981 WM USA 8 5 1 6 6 —
1981 CC USA 5 1 1 2 4 —

**Larsson, Bengt / b. Jan. 27, 1927**
1949-51 WM SWE 10 8 — 8 2 S

**Larsson, Erik / b. Jan. 18, 1905 / d. Mar. 8, 1970**
1928 OG-M SWE 5 0 0 0 — S

**Larsson, Jan / b. Sept. 4, 1965**
1992-99 WM SWE 40 5 6 11 36 G,S,2B

**Larsson, Peter / b. Apr. 9, 1968**
1988 WM20 SWE 5 1 5 6 6 —

**Larsson, Stefan / b. June 14, 1965**
1985 WM20 SWE 7 1 1 2 2 —
1993 WM SWE 8 0 1 1 0 S

**Larsson, Stig / b. Nov. 22, 1947**
1972 WM SWE 8 2 3 5 0 B

**Larsson, Vilgot / b. May 3, 1932**
1955-59 WM SWE 30 3 2 5 14 G,B
1956 OG-M SWE 7 0 1 1 10 —

**Lartama, Mika / b. Mar. 17, 1963**
1983 WM20 FIN 6 1 1 2 6 —

**Lassas, Ake / b. Aug. 21, 1924 / d. Apr. 16, 2009**
1949-55 WM SWE 27 1 0 1 12 S,B
1952-56 OG-M SWE 12 1 1 2 2 B

**Laszkiewicz, Leszek / b. Aug. 11, 1978**
1997 WM20 POL 6 1 0 1 0 —
2002 WM POL 6 1 1 2 4 —

**Latal, Jaromir / b. Nov. 12, 1963**
1983 WM20 TCH 7 0 1 1 12 S

**Latal, Jiri / b. Feb. 2, 1967**
1985-87 WM20 TCH 21 4 8 12 4 2S
1989 WM TCH 1 0 0 0 0 B
~WM20 All-Star Team/Defence (1987)

**Latal, Ondrej / b. Mar. 15, 1981**
1999 WM18 CZE 7 1 0 1 0 —

**Lator, Geza / b. 1889 / d. unknown**
1930-31 WM HUN 6 0 — 0 — —
1928 OG-M HUN 1 0 — 0 — —

**Latta, David / b. Jan. 3, 1967**
1987 WM20 CAN 6 4 6 10 12 —

**Lattuca, Frank / b. May 6, 1965**
1992 WM ITA 3 0 0 0 0 —

**Latusa, Manuel / b. Jan. 23, 1984**
2004 WM20 AUT 6 1 1 2 6 —

**Lauber, Bernhard / b. Feb. 24, 1964**
1984 WM20 SUI 7 0 1 1 0 —

**Lauen, Mike / b. Feb. 9, 1961**
1980 WM20 USA 5 2 0 2 2 —

**Lauer, Armin / b. June 2, 1958**
1977-78 WM20 FRG 9 0 1 1 10 —

**Laufman, Ken / b. Jan. 30, 1932**
1956-60 OG-M CAN 12 1 9 10 4 S,B

**Laukkanen, Janne / b. Mar. 19, 1970**
1990 WM20 FIN 7 0 1 1 4 —
1992-98 WM FIN 23 3 5 8 28 3S
1991-96 WCH FIN 10 1 2 3 2 —
1992-98 OG-M FIN 22 0 3 3 22 2B

**Laukkanen, Jari / b. June 21, 1967**
1987 WM20 FIN 5 0 1 1 2 G

**Laukkanen, Jukka / b. Feb. 18, 1958**
1977 WM20 FIN 7 0 1 1 0 —

**Laukkanen, Pekka / b. Apr. 9, 1959**
1978-79 WM20 FIN 12 1 3 4 0 —

**Lauper, Adrien / b.Aug. 14, 1987**
2005 WM18 SUI 6 1 0 1 2 —

**Laurencin, Charel / b. unknown**
1947 WM BEL 5 0 — 0 — —

**Laurila, Harri / b. Apr. 30, 1965**
1984-85 WM20 FIN 14 4 5 9 10 S
1992 WM FIN 8 0 1 1 2 S
1992 OG-M FIN 8 0 0 0 2 —

**Lautenschlager, Beat / b. Jan. 21, 1959**
1978 WM20 SUI 6 1 0 1 2 —

**Lauze, Gaston / b. Dec. 11, 1919 / d. unknown**
1951 WM USA 6 0 — 0 0 —

**LaVarre, Mark / b. Feb. 21, 1965**
1984 WM20 USA 7 1 1 2 14 —

**Lavins, Rodrigo / b. Aug. 3, 1974**
1997-2009 WM LAT 63 3 18 21 77 —
2002-10 OG LAT 13 0 1 1 6 —

**Laviolette, Peter / b. Dec. 7, 1964**
1988-94 OG-M USA 13 1 2 3 10 —

**Lavoie, Dominic / b. Nov. 21, 1967**
1999-2000 WM AUT 12 2 1 3 20 —
1998 OG-M AUT 4 5 1 6 8 —

**Lavoie, Joseph / b. Nov. 21, 1967**
2001-02 WM AUT 12 1 4 5 26 —
2002 OG-M AUT 4 0 1 1 2 —

**Lawman, Larry / b. unknown**
1958 WM USA 5 0 0 0 0 —

**Lawrence, Chris / b. Feb. 5, 1987**
2005 WM18 CAN 6 1 0 1 4 S

**Lawrence, Jason / b. Feb. 2, 1987**
2005 WM18 USA 6 3 2 5 4 G

**Lawton, Brian / b. June 29, 1965**
1983 WM20 USA 7 3 1 4 6 —
1987 WM USA 8 3 3 6 6 —
1984 CC USA 6 5 0 5 4 —

**Lax, John / b. July 23, 1911 / d. July 14, 2001**
1936 OG-M USA 3 0 0 0 2 B

**Lax, Peter / b. Nov. 7, 1941**
1963-67 WM FRG 12 4 1 5 2 —
1968 OG-M FRG 7 2 1 3 8 —

**Laxdal, Derek / b. Feb. 21, 1966**
1986 WM20 CAN 7 1 4 5 6 S

**Laylin, Cory / b. Jan. 24, 1970**
1990 WM20 USA 7 0 1 1 2 —

**Lays, Valentin / b. Jan. 7, 1987**
2002 WM18 UKR 6 0 0 0 4 —

**Lazarenko, Oleksiy / b. Mar. 1, 1976**
1995-96 WM20 UKR 11 4 1 5 62 —
2000-01 WM UKR 9 0 0 0 8 —

**Lazaro, Jeff / b. Mar. 21, 1968**
1993-94 WM USA 12 2 0 2 12 —
1994 OG-M USA 8 2 2 4 4 —

**Lazarov, Dimitre / b. June 18, 1946**
1976 OG-M BUL 5 0 0 0 0 —

**Leach, Jamie / b. Aug. 25, 1969**
1989 WM20 CAN 7 1 4 5 2 —

**Leach, Jay / b. Sept. 2, 1979**
1998 WM20 USA 7 0 1 1 8 —

**Leach, Reggie / b. Apr. 23, 1950**
1976 CC CAN 6 1 1 2 4 1st

**Leach, Steve / b. Jan. 16, 1966**
1984-86 WM20 USA 21 10 5 15 20 B
1988 OG-M USA 6 1 2 3 0 —

**Leacock, Ernie / b. Mar. 1906 / d. 1977**
1935 WM GBR 1 0 — 0 — B

**Leaky, Thomas / b. unknown / d. unknown**
1939 WM USA 3 0 — 0 — S

**Leask, Rob / b. June 9, 1971**
2004 WM GER 6 0 0 0 8 —
2004 WCH GER 4 0 1 1 6 —
2006 OG-M GER 5 0 0 0 6 —

**Le Bas, Michel / b. unknown**
1950 WM FRA 2 1 0 1 0 —

**Lebda, Brett / b. Jan. 15, 1982**
2002 WM20 USA 7 2 0 2 6 —

**Lebeau, Patrick / b. Mar. 17, 1970**
1992 OG-M CAN 8 1 3 4 4 S

**Lebech, Knud / b. unknown**
1949 WM DEN 3 0 — 0 — —

**Lebedev, Yuri / b. Mar. 1, 1951**
1973-81 WM URS 39 7 12 19 20 6G
1972 SS URS 3 1 0 1 2 2nd
1976 CC URS 4 0 0 0 0 —
1980 OG-M URS 7 3 5 8 4 S

**Leblanc, Michel / b. Dec. 17, 1959**
1992-94 WM FRA 17 1 0 1 6 —
1988-92 OG-M FRA 12 0 2 2 4 —

**Lebler, Eddy / b. May 20, 1958**
1984-88 OG-M AUT 11 4 4 8 12 —

**Lechl, Jurgen / b. Dec. 23, 1960**
1979-80 WM20 FRG 10 3 5 8 6 —

**LeClair, John / b. July 5, 1969**
1988-89 WM20 USA 14 10 6 16 24 —
1996 WCH USA 7 6 4 10 6 1st
1998-2002 OG-M USA 10 6 2 8 4 S
~OG-M All-Star Team/Forward (2002)

**Lecompte, Louis / b. July 28, 1914 / d. Feb. 1970**
1948 OG-M CAN 8 1 — 1 4 G

**Lecomte, Jules / b. unknown / d. unknown**
1930 WM BEL 1 0 — 0 — —

**Lecomte, Laurent / b. Aug. 2, 1965**
1997 WM FRA 8 0 1 1 2 —

**Lecy, Scott / b. Apr. 8, 1959**
1978 WM20 USA 6 3 4 7 4 —

**Lecy, Todd / b. Nov. 1, 1960**
1980 WM20 USA 5 2 2 4 2 —

**Lederer, Ulrich / b. Aug. 18, 1897 / d. unknown**
1930-31 WM AUT 10 1 — 1 — B
1928 OG-M AUT 2 2 0 2 2 —

**Ledin, Per / b. Sept. 14, 1978**
2008 WM SWE 7 0 5 5 4 —

**Ledock, Rene / b. Oct. 4, 1966**
1985-86 WM20 FRG 14 0 0 0 20 —

**Ledovskikh, Alexander / b. Feb. 17, 1961**
1981 WM20 URS 5 0 1 1 0 B

**Ledyard, Grant / b. Nov. 19, 1961**
1985-86 WM CAN 14 0 3 3 10 S,B

**Lee, Ed / b. Dec. 17, 1961**
1981 WM20 USA 5 2 2 4 8 —

**Lee, Howie / b. Oct. 13, 1929**
1956 OG-M CAN 8 2 0 2 12 B

**Leeb, Brad / b. Aug. 27, 1979**
1999 WM20 CAN 7 3 5 8 2 S

**Leeman, Gary / b. Feb. 19, 1964**
1983-84 WM20 CAN 14 4 8 12 14 B

**Leempoels, Andre / b. Nov. 22, 1921 / d. unknown**
1939 WM BEL 4 0 — 0 — —

**Leetch, Brian / b. Mar. 3, 1968**
1985-87 WM20 USA 21 2 6 8 12 B
1987-89 WM USA 20 7 9 16 8 —
1991-2004 WCH USA 19 1 11 12 12 1st
1988-2002 OG-M USA 16 2 11 13 4 S
~OG-M All-Star Team/Defence (2002), WM20 All-Star Team/Defence (1987)

**Leetma, Jonas / b. Mar. 26, 1983**
2001 WM18 SWE 6 1 1 2 2 —
2003 WM20 SWE 6 0 1 1 6 —

**Lefley, Chuck / b. Jan. 20, 1950**
1969 WM CAN 7 0 1 1 10 —

**Lefebvre, Patrice / b. June 28, 1967**
2007 WM ITA 5 0 0 0 2 —

**Legace, Mike / b. unknown**
1961 WM CAN 7 4 3 7 6 G
~WM All-Star Team/Forward (1961)

**Legachev, Pavlo / b. Aug. 15, 1984**
2001 WM18 UKR 5 1 0 1 0 —
2004 WM20 UKR 6 0 0 0 4 —

**Legwand, David / b. Aug. 17, 1980**
1998-99 WM20 USA 13 1 3 4 33 —
1999-2005 WM USA 28 3 8 11 16 —

**Lehmann, Peter / b. Jan. 28, 1946**
1972 OG-M SUI 3 1 0 1 0 —

**Lehmann, Tommy / b. Feb. 3, 1964**
1983-84 WM20 SWE 14 9 3 12 4 —

**Lehner, Josef / b. Feb. 15, 1972**
1992 WM20 GER 7 1 0 1 4 —

**Lehtera, Tero / b. Apr. 21, 1972**
1991-92 WM20 FIN 12 2 3 5 2 —
1995 WM FIN 8 1 0 1 0 G
1994 OG-M FIN 4 0 1 1 0 B

**Lehtinen, Jere / b. June 24, 1973**
1991-93 WM20 FIN 18 8 10 18 12 —
1992-2007 WM FIN 30 8 13 21 8 G,3S
1996-2004 WCH FIN 10 3 5 8 2 —
1994-2010 OG FIN 32 11 9 20 4 S,3B
~WM All-Star Team/Forward (1995)

**Lehtio, Rauno / b. Mar. 3, 1942**
1962-63 WM FIN 14 2 2 4 6 —
1964 OG-M FIN 7 1 0 1 0 —

**Lehtisalo, Juho / b. Jan. 4, 1983**
2003 WM20 FIN 7 0 1 1 2 B

**Lehto, Markus / b. Oct. 20, 1962**
1982 WM20 FIN 7 1 8 9 14 B
1985 WM FIN 10 1 1 2 10 —
1984 OG-M FIN 6 1 2 3 2 —

**Lehto, Petteri / b. Mar. 13, 1961**
1984 OG-M FIN 6 2 2 4 10 —

**Lehtonen, Antero / b. Dec. 4, 1954**
1977-81 WM FIN 26 4 8 12 6 —

**Lehtonen, Erkki / b. Jan. 9, 1957**
1986 WM FIN 10 3 4 7 2 —
1988 OG-M FIN 8 4 6 10 2 S

**Lehtonen, Pertti / b. Oct. 18, 1956**
1981-89 WM FIN 32 2 9 11 14 —
1984 OG-M FIN 6 0 1 1 6 —

**Lehtosaari, Pentti / b. Feb. 27, 1967**
1986-87 WM20 FIN 13 8 5 13 0 G

**Leibnitz, Jo Espen / b. Jan. 7, 1972**
1991 WM20 NOR 5 1 0 1 4 —

**Leime, Heikki / b. May 7, 1962**
1981-82 WM20 FIN 12 3 2 5 2 S,B
1990 WM FIN 7 0 0 0 8 —

**Leimu, Pekka / b. Apr. 11, 1947**
1969-70 WM FIN 18 8 4 12 12 —
1968 OG-M FIN 6 2 1 3 4 —

**Leinonen, Mikko / b. July 15, 1955**
1978-81 WM FIN 26 6 5 11 10 —
1981 CC FIN 5 0 1 1 0 —
1980 OG-M FIN 7 6 4 10 0 —

**Leisenring, Brady / b. Sept. 7, 1982**
2000 WM18 USA 6 1 2 3 8 —

**Leitner, Willi / b. unknown**
1967 WM FRG 7 1 1 2 0 —

**Lekens, Jef / b. Apr. 22, 1911 / d. Sept. 13, 1973**
1930-50 WM BEL 19 3 0 3 2 —
1936 OG-M BEL 3 0 — 0 — —

**Lelkes, Richard / b. Feb. 19, 1987**
2004-05 WM18 SVK 12 2 2 4 10 —

**Lemarque, Eric / b. July 1, 1969**
1994-95 WM FRA 11 1 2 3 4 —
1994 OG-M FRA 5 1 0 1 6 —

**Lemay, Albert / b. July 1910 / d. unknown**
1935 WM CAN 7 12 — 12 — G

**Lemay, Moe / b. Feb. 18, 1962**
1982 WM20 CAN 7 2 0 2 4 G

**Lemay, Tony / b. 1913 / d. unknown**
1935 WM CAN 7 8 — 8 — G

**Lemieux, Claude / b. July 16, 1965**
1985 WM20 CAN 6 3 2 5 6 G
1987-96 WCH CAN 14 2 2 4 23 1st,2nd

**Lemieux, Mario / b. Oct. 5, 1965**
1983 WM20 CAN 7 5 5 10 10 B
1985 WM CAN 10 4 6 10 2 S
1987-2004 WCH CAN 15 12 11 23 10 2/1st
2002 OG-M CAN 5 2 4 6 0 G
~IIHF Hall of Fame

**Lemieux, Ray / b. unknown / d. unknown**
1938 WM USA 6 0 — 0 — —

**Lemiszko, Wladyslaw / b. June 9, 1911 / d. Apr. 17, 1988**
1935 WM POL 3 0 — 0 — —

**Lemoine, Jean-Philippe / b. Sept. 11, 1964**
1992-99 WM FRA 41 1 1 2 90 —
1988-98 OG-M FRA 18 0 2 2 30 —

**Lempio, Joachim / b. Sept. 23, 1956**
1978-85 WM GDR 30 0 6 6 15 —

**Lenardon, Norm / b. Oct. 20, 1933**
1961-63 WM CAN 10 6 2 8 2 G

**Lennartsson, Jonas / b. Apr. 10, 1981**
1999 WM18 SWE 7 1 1 2 4 S
2001 WM20 SWE 7 0 0 0 0 —

**Leonov, Yuri / b. Apr. 2, 1963**
1990 WM URS 8 0 2 2 4 G

**Leontiev, Oleg / b. Nov. 15, 1970**
1999-2008 WM BLR 18 1 5 6 4 —

**Lepisto, Jussi / b. Feb. 28, 1960**
1979 WM20 FIN 6 0 0 0 6 —

**Leppa, Henry / b. Mar. 12, 1947**
1973-76 WM FIN 39 12 14 26 8 —
1976 OG-M FIN 5 2 3 5 0 —

**Leppanen, Janne / b. Sept. 21, 1969**
1989 WM20 FIN 7 0 1 1 6 —

**Leppanen, Reijo / b. Nov. 8, 1951**
1982 WM FIN 7 2 4 6 2 —
1980 OG-M FIN 6 5 4 9 0 —

**Lepre, Gilbert / b. Feb. 6, 1945**
1968 OG-M FRA 4 0 1 1 2 —

**Lepsa, Tomaz / b. June 11, 1955**
1976 OG-M YUG 5 1 0 1 2 —

**Lerg, Bryan / b. Jan. 20, 1986**
2004 WM18 USA 6 2 6 8 2 S

**Lerondeau, Jean / b. June 27, 1963**
1988 OG-M FRA 6 0 0 0 2 —

**Leschyshyn, Curtis / b. Sept. 21, 1969**
1990 WM CAN 9 0 0 0 4 —

**Lessard, Stephane / b. Feb. 2, 1962**
1988 OG-M FRA 6 0 1 1 2 —

**Letowski, Trevor / b. Apr. 5, 1977**
1997 WM20 CAN 7 2 1 3 4 G
2000 WM CAN 9 0 2 2 6 —

**Leuenberger, Markus / b. July 24, 1962**
1988 OG-M SUI 6 0 0 0 0 —

**Leuenberger, Rolf / b. unknown**
1978 WM20 SUI 6 0 0 0 0 —

**Leuenberger, Sven / b. Aug. 25, 1969**
1991-93 WM SUI 25 0 5 5 36 —
1992 OG-M SUI 7 1 0 1 8 —

**Leuzinger, Bruno / b. Jan. 6, 1886 / d. Dec. 23, 1952**
1920-24 OG-M SUI 1 0 0 0 — —

**Lever, Don / b. Nov. 14, 1952**
1978 WM CAN 10 4 3 7 4 B

**Levesque, Willie / b. Jan. 22, 1980**
2000 WM20 USA 7 1 0 1 10 —

**Levinski, Dmitri / b. June 23, 1981**
1999 WM18 RUS 7 2 1 3 4 —

**Levo, Tapio / b. Sept. 24, 1955**
1976-83 WM FIN 45 13 6 19 28 —
1976-81 CC FIN 9 1 3 4 4 —
1980 OG-M FIN 6 1 4 5 2 —

**Lewacki, Eugeniusz / b. Jan. 24, 1926**
1955 WM POL 7 2 0 2 0 —
1948-52 OG-M POL 14 8 2 10 — —

**Lewandowski, Eduard / b. May 3, 1980**
2002-05 WM GER 26 1 7 8 10 —
2004 WCH GER 4 0 1 1 4 —
2006 OG-M GER 5 0 2 2 0 —

**Lewerstrom, Erik / b. May 28, 1980**
2000 WM20 SWE 7 3 5 8 14 —

**Liapunov, Yevgeni / b. Sept. 9, 1978**
1998 WM20 KAZ 7 1 1 2 2 —

**Liba, Igor / b. Nov. 4, 1960**
1979-80 WM20 TCH 11 4 1 5 4 S
1982-92 WM TCH 58 13 23 36 62 G,2S,2B
1984-87 CC TCH 11 2 7 9 12 —
1984-92 OG-M TCH 19 9 10 19 18 S,B

**Libbett, Nick / b. Dec. 9, 1945**
1979 WM CAN 8 1 0 1 4 —

**Liberman, Charles / b. Aug. 8, 1945**
1968 OG-M FRA 5 1 1 2 0 —

**Lichnowski, Jan / b. unknown . d. unknown**
1928 OG-M TCH 1 0 — 0 — —

**Lidral, Jan / b. Mar. 19, 1929 / d. Jan. 24, 1982**
1955 WM TCH 7 0 0 0 12 B
1952 OG-M TCH 2 0 2 2 — —

**Lidster, Doug / b. Oct. 18, 1960**
1985-91 WM CAN 30 5 5 10 18 2S
1984 OG-M CAN 7 0 2 2 2 —

**Lidstrom, Nicklas / b. Apr. 28, 1970**
1990 WM20 SWE 7 3 3 6 2 —
1991-2004 WM SWE 16 4 4 8 6 G,S,B
1991-2004 WCH SWE 14 4 2 6 6 —
1998-2010 OG-M SWE 20 4 10 14 6 G
~Triple Gold Club
~OG-M All-Star Team/Defence (2006)

**Lie, Espen / b. Jan. 23, 1984**
2002 WM18 NOR 8 0 1 1 8 —

**Lien, Sven / b. Aug. 4, 1958**
1984 OG-M NOR 5 1 0 1 0 —

**Liimatainen, Petri / b. July 20, 1969**
1988-89 WM20 SWE 14 0 2 2 6 S
1992 WM SWE 1 0 0 0 0 G
1992 OG-M SWE 8 0 0 0 6 —

**Liitsola, Seppo / b. Feb. 7, 1933**
1955 WM FIN 2 0 1 1 0 —

**Lilja, Karl-Erik / b. Apr. 24, 1957**
1977 WM20 SWE 7 0 0 0 0 —

**Liljeberg, Yngve / b. July 23, 1909 / d. Oct. 5, 1978**
1935-37 WM SWE 11 6 0 6 0 —
1936 OG-M SWE 4 2 — 2 — —

**Liljeblad, Joni / b. Sept. 17, 1989**
2007 WM18 FIN 6 2 0 2 4 —

**Lill, Edgar / b. Sept. 28, 1962**
1982 WM20 FRG 7 0 0 0 2 —

**Lilley, John / b. Mar. 8, 1972**
1992 WM20 USA 7 3 4 7 10 B
1994 WM USA 8 1 0 1 29 —
1994 OG-M USA 8 3 1 4 16 —

**Lilyholm, Len / b. Apr. 1, 1941**
1966-71 WM USA 20 5 7 12 10 —
1968 OG-M USA 7 2 2 4 9 —

**Lind, John / b. Jan. 13, 1983**
2001 WM18 SWE 6 0 0 0 0 —

**Lind, Juha / b. Jan. 2, 1974**
1994 WM20 FIN 7 5 2 7 2 —
1997-2002 WM FIN 47 8 10 18 22 2S,B
1998-2002 OG-M FIN 10 0 1 1 6 B

**Lindahl, Henry / b. unknown / d. unknown**
1939 WM FIN 4 0 — 0 — —

**Lindberg, Bob / b. Dec. 31, 1945**
1971 WM USA 7 0 1 1 2 —

**Lindberg, Chris / b. Apr. 16, 1967**
1992 WM CAN 5 1 0 1 8 —
1992 OG-M CAN 8 1 4 5 4 S

**Lindberg, Hans "Virus" / b. Jan. 16, 1945**
1966-71 WM SWE 31 13 9 22 6 2S,B
1972 OG-M SWE 5 0 2 2 4 —

**Lindberg, Torbjorn / b. June 8, 1970**
1989-90 WM20 SWE 14 1 9 10 2 S

**Lindblom, Goran / b. Mar. 4, 1956**
1978-82 WM SWE 28 1 4 5 0 S
1984 OG-M SWE 7 0 1 1 0 B

**Lindbom, Johan / b. July 8, 1971**
1997 WM SWE 8 0 1 1 6 S

**Linde, Bertil / b. Feb. 28, 1907 / d. Mar. 25, 1990**
1931 WM SWE 6 3 — 3 — —
1928 OG-M SWE 4 0 0 0 — S

**Lindegren, Pentti / b. Dec. 18, 1940**
1965 WM FIN 4 0 0 0 0 —

**Lindemann, Sven / b. Apr. 23, 1978**
1998 WM20 SUI 7 0 1 1 6 B

**Linden, Trevor / b. Apr. 11, 1970**
1988 WM20 CAN 7 1 0 1 0 G
1991-98 WM CAN 16 2 8 10 8 S
1996 WCH CAN 6 1 1 2 0 2nd
1998 OG-M CAN 6 1 0 1 10 —

**Linder, Engelbert / b. July 18, 1962**
1993-98 WM AUT 28 1 1 2 16 —
1994-98 OG-M AUT 8 0 0 0 12 —

**Lindgren, Erik / b. Dec. 20, 1902 / d. unknown**
1931 WM SWE 6 0 — 0 — —

**Lindgren, Jari / b. Jan. 6, 1959**
1979 WM20 FIN 6 0 0 0 0 —

**Lindgren, Lars / b. Oct. 12, 1952**
1977-78 WM SWE 20 3 4 7 16 S
1981 CC SWE 5 0 1 1 6 —

**Lindgren, Mats / b. Oct. 1, 1974**
1993-94 WM20 SWE 14 6 6 12 10 2S
1998 OG-M SWE 4 0 0 0 2 —

**Lindgren, Victor / b. Jan. 8, 1985**
2004-05 WM20 AUT 11 0 2 2 6 —

**Lindgren, Viktor / b. Mar. 16, 1986**
2004 WM18 SWE 6 0 2 2 2 —

**Lindh, Mats / b. Sept. 12, 1947**
1972-75 WM SWE 12 2 7 9 0 2B
1972 OG-M SWE 4 1 0 1 0 —

**Lindholm, Christopher / b. May 11, 1985**
2003 WM18 SWE 6 3 2 5 6 —

**Lindholm, Jan / b. Apr. 16, 1955**
1984 CC SWE 4 0 0 0 4 2nd

**Lindholm, Miika / b. June 21, 1980**
2000 WM20 FIN 7 0 0 0 0 —

**Lindlof, Joni / b. May 17, 1984**
2002 WM18 FIN 8 1 2 3 10 —

**Lindmark, Orjan / b. Apr. 22, 1967**
1987 WM20 SWE 6 0 1 1 0 B

**Lindner, Heimo / b. July 22, 1978**
2001 WM AUT 6 0 0 0 4 —

**Lindquist, Vic / b. Mar. 22, 1908 / d. Dec. 1, 1983**
1935 WM CAN 7 4 — 4 — G
1932 OG-M CAN 5 3 6 9 2 G
~IIHF Hall of Fame

**Lindqvist, Einar / b. May 31, 1895 / d. Apr. 26, 1972**
1920 OG-M SWE 6 3 — 3 6 —

**Lindroos, Jari / b. Jan. 31, 1961**
1992 OG-M FIN 8 0 4 4 6 —

**Lindros, Eric / b. Feb. 28, 1973**
1990-92 WM20 CAN 21 12 19 31 32 2G
1993 WM CAN 8 11 6 17 10 —
1991-96 WCH CAN 16 6 5 11 18 1st,2nd
1992-2002 OG-M CAN 20 8 9 17 16 G,S
~WM IIHF Directorate Best Forward (1993), WM All-Star Team/Forward (1993), WM20 IIHF Directorate Best Forward (1991), WM20 All-Star Team/Forward (1991), OG-M All-Star Team/Forward (1992)

**Lindsay, Bill / b. May 17, 1971**
1991 WM20 USA 7 3 5 8 8 —
1994 WM USA 5 3 1 4 2 —

**Lindstrom, Anders / b. Feb. 5, 1966**
1986 WM20 SWE 7 0 0 0 2 —

**Lindstrom, Claes / b. Oct. 27, 1920 / d. June 2, 2009**
1948 OG-M SWE 6 5 — 5 — —

**Lindstrom, Erling / b. Aug. 9, 1937**
1957-59 WM SWE 21 15 6 21 2 G,B

| | | | | | | | | |
|---|---|---|---|---|---|---|---|---|
| **Lindstrom, Lars-Eje / b. June 16, 1957** | | | | | | | | |
| 1977 | WM20 | SWE | 7 | 0 | 2 | 2 | 8 | — |
| **Lindstrom, Joakim / b. Dec. 5, 1983** | | | | | | | | |
| 2001 | WM18 | SWE | 6 | 2 | 5 | 7 | 2 | — |
| 2003 | WM20 | SWE | 6 | 2 | 3 | 5 | 6 | — |
| **Lindstrom, Liam / b. Jan. 12, 1985** | | | | | | | | |
| 2003 | WM18 | SWE | 6 | 1 | 3 | 4 | 45 | — |
| **Lindstrom, Rainer / b. Sept. 29, 1930** | | | | | | | | |
| 1954-55 | WM | FIN | 12 | 2 | 0 | 2 | 4 | — |
| **Lindstrom, Roger / b. Nov. 28, 1955** | | | | | | | | |
| 1979 | WM | SWE | 3 | 0 | 0 | 0 | 0 | B |
| **Lindstrom, Seppo / b. May 16, 1941** | | | | | | | | |
| 1969-77 | WM | FIN | 69 | 5 | 6 | 11 | 28 | — |
| 1968-76 | OG-M | FIN | 17 | 0 | 2 | 2 | 10 | — |
| **Lindstrom, Willy / b. May 5, 1951** | | | | | | | | |
| 1974-75 | WM | SWE | 17 | 9 | 5 | 14 | 10 | 2B |
| 1976 | CC | SWE | 1 | 0 | 0 | 0 | 5 | — |
| **Lingemann, Boris / b. Aug. 25, 1977** | | | | | | | | |
| 1996-97 | WM20 | GER | 12 | 5 | 3 | 8 | 2 | — |
| **Linhart, Tomas / b. Feb. 16, 1984** | | | | | | | | |
| 2004 | WM20 | CZE | 7 | 0 | 0 | 0 | 4 | — |
| **Linke, Marcel / b. Apr. 23, 1981** | | | | | | | | |
| 1999 | WM18 | GER | 6 | 2 | 0 | 2 | 2 | — |
| **Linna, Kaj / b. Jan. 24, 1971** | | | | | | | | |
| 1998 | WM | FIN | 10 | 0 | 0 | 0 | 10 | S |
| **Linnes, Per / b. unknown / d. unknown** | | | | | | | | |
| 1938 | WM | NOR | 3 | 0 | — | 0 | — | — |
| **Linnonmaa, Harri / b. July 30, 1946** | | | | | | | | |
| 1970-75 | WM | FIN | 41 | 10 | 5 | 15 | 30 | — |
| 1976 | CC | FIN | 4 | 1 | 1 | 2 | 0 | — |
| 1972 | OG-M | FIN | 4 | 0 | 0 | 0 | 0 | — |
| **Linse, Martin / b. Oct. 13, 1962** | | | | | | | | |
| 1982 | WM20 | SWE | 7 | 2 | 4 | 6 | 4 | — |
| **Linseman, Ken / b. Aug. 11, 1959** | | | | | | | | |
| 1981 | CC | CAN | 4 | 0 | 1 | 1 | 4 | 2nd |
| **Lipiansky, Jan / b. July 23, 1974** | | | | | | | | |
| 1999 | WM | SVK | 6 | 0 | 0 | 0 | 4 | — |
| **Lipin, Alexander / b. Dec. 19, 1985** | | | | | | | | |
| 2003 | WM18 | KAZ | 6 | 0 | 0 | 0 | 8 | — |
| **Lipka, Rastislav / b. May 9, 1983** | | | | | | | | |
| 2001 | WM18 | SVK | 6 | 2 | 4 | 6 | 6 | — |
| 2003 | WM20 | SVK | 6 | 1 | 3 | 4 | 2 | — |
| **Lipkowski, Krzysztof / b. Mar. 27, 1979** | | | | | | | | |
| 1997 | WM20 | POL | 6 | 0 | 1 | 1 | 2 | — |
| **Lipovsky, Roman / b. Mar. 7, 1967** | | | | | | | | |
| 1986-87 | WM20 | TCH | 12 | 3 | 2 | 5 | 6 | S |
| **Lippit, Percy / b. Nov. 1, 1913 / d. unknown** | | | | | | | | |
| 1935-50 | WM | BEL | 18 | 0 | 0 | 0 | 0 | — |
| **Liprando, John / b. July 7, 1959** | | | | | | | | |
| 1978-79 | WM20 | USA | 11 | 5 | 4 | 9 | 16 | — |
| **Litma, Lasse / b. Apr. 5, 1954** | | | | | | | | |
| 1978-83 | WM | FIN | 29 | 3 | 4 | 7 | 20 | — |
| 1976 | CC | FIN | 2 | 0 | 0 | 0 | 4 | — |
| 1980 | OG-M | FIN | 7 | 0 | 4 | 4 | 10 | — |
| **Litvinov, Sergei / b. July 7, 1982** | | | | | | | | |
| 2001 | WM20 | KAZ | 6 | 0 | 0 | 0 | 2 | — |
| **Litvinov, Vitali / b. Nov. 16, 1978** | | | | | | | | |
| 1998 | WM20 | KAZ | 7 | 0 | 2 | 2 | 10 | — |
| **Litwin, Marek / b. Jan. 1, 1966** | | | | | | | | |
| 1985 | WM20 | POL | 7 | 0 | 0 | 0 | 6 | — |
| **Lius, Joni / b. Mar. 4, 1971** | | | | | | | | |
| 1998 | WM | FIN | 10 | 0 | 1 | 1 | 4 | S |
| **Livf, Mathias / b. Feb. 24, 1974** | | | | | | | | |
| 2007 | WM | NOR | 6 | 0 | 1 | 1 | 6 | — |
| **Living, Jonas / b. Jan. 29, 1983** | | | | | | | | |
| 2001 | WM18 | SWE | 6 | 1 | 1 | 2 | 8 | — |
| **Livingston, Bob / b. Nov. 3, 1908 / d. Apr. 2, 1974** | | | | | | | | |
| 1932 | OG-M | USA | 1 | 0 | 0 | 0 | 0 | S |
| **Ljungberg, Thomas / b. Feb. 19, 1963** | | | | | | | | |
| 1983 | WM20 | SWE | 3 | 0 | 1 | 1 | 0 | — |
| **Ljungkvist, Daniel / b. Sept. 18, 1981** | | | | | | | | |
| 1999 | WM18 | SWE | 7 | 0 | 0 | 0 | 10 | S |
| 2001 | WM20 | SWE | 7 | 0 | 1 | 1 | 8 | — |
| **Ljungman, Lars / b. Apr. 1, 1918 / d. Apr. 19, 1962** | | | | | | | | |
| 1947 | WM | SWE | 6 | 20 | — | 20 | — | S |
| 1948 | OG-M | SWE | 6 | 10 | — | 10 | — | — |
| **Ljustereng, Per / b. Mar. 13, 1968** | | | | | | | | |
| 1988 | WM20 | SWE | 7 | 0 | 2 | 2 | 2 | — |
| **Lluis, Pierre / b. unknown** | | | | | | | | |
| 1950 | WM | FRA | 4 | 0 | 0 | 0 | 0 | — |
| **Lob, Paul / b. unknown / d. unknown** | | | | | | | | |
| 1920 | OG-M | SUI | 2 | 0 | 0 | 0 | — | — |
| **Lobanovsky, Denis / b. Jan. 9, 1976** | | | | | | | | |
| 1995 | WM20 | UKR | 7 | 0 | 0 | 0 | 0 | — |

| | | | | | | | | |
|---|---|---|---|---|---|---|---|---|
| **Loek, Rijk / b. unknown** | | | | | | | | |
| 1950 | WM | NED | 4 | 0 | 0 | 0 | 0 | — |
| **Loewen, Darcy / b. Feb. 26, 1969** | | | | | | | | |
| 1989 | WM20 | CAN | 7 | 1 | 1 | 2 | 12 | — |
| **Lofgren, Borje / b. Oct. 13, 1926** | | | | | | | | |
| 1950-51 | WM | SWE | 12 | 0 | 0 | 0 | 0 | S |
| **Logan, Jim / b. Sept. 17, 1933** | | | | | | | | |
| 1956 | OG-M | CAN | 8 | 7 | 5 | 12 | 0 | B |
| **Logunov, Denis / b. May 5, 1985** | | | | | | | | |
| 2003 | WM18 | RUS | 6 | 1 | 0 | 1 | 4 | B |
| **Logvin, Vladimir / b. Jan. 27, 1980** | | | | | | | | |
| 1998-2000 | WM20 | KAZ | 20 | 0 | 0 | 0 | 10 | — |
| **Loher, Henry / b. Jan. 23, 1960** | | | | | | | | |
| 1980 | WM20 | SUI | 5 | 1 | 2 | 3 | 0 | — |
| **Lohrer, Heini / b. June 29, 1918 / d. Dec. 12, 2011** | | | | | | | | |
| 1937-49 | WM | SUI | 24 | 12 | 0 | 12 | 1 | 2B |
| 1948 | OG-M | SUI | 7 | 11 | — | 11 | — | B |
| **Lohrer, Werner / b. Mar. 4, 1917 / d. unknown** | | | | | | | | |
| 1948 | OG-M | SUI | 3 | 2 | — | 2 | — | B |
| **Loibl, Albert / b. Nov. 20, 1937** | | | | | | | | |
| 1964 | OG-M | FRG | 6 | 0 | 0 | 0 | 0 | — |
| **Loicq, Paul / b. Aug. 11, 1888 / d. Mar. 26, 1953** | | | | | | | | |
| 1920 | OG-M | BEL | 1 | 0 | 0 | 0 | 2 | — |
| ~IIHF Hall of Fame | | | | | | | | |
| **Loktev, Konstantin / b. Apr. 16, 1933 / d. Nov. 4, 1996** | | | | | | | | |
| 1957-66 | WM | URS | 41 | 38 | 24 | 62 | 28 | 2G,3S,B |
| 1960-64 | OG-M | URS | 13 | 10 | 8 | 18 | 16 | G,B |
| ~IIHF Hall of Fame | | | | | | | | |
| ~WM IIHF Directorate Best Forward (1966), WM All-Star Team/Forward (1965, 1966) | | | | | | | | |
| **Lomakin, Andrei / b. Aug. 9, 1964 / d. Dec. 9, 2006** | | | | | | | | |
| 1984 | WM20 | URS | 7 | 5 | 5 | 10 | 2 | G |
| 1991 | WM | URS | 10 | 3 | 3 | 6 | 4 | B |
| 1987-91 | CC | URS | 14 | 2 | 6 | 8 | 10 | 2nd |
| 1988 | OG-M | URS | 8 | 1 | 3 | 4 | 2 | G |
| **Lombar, Milan / b. unknown / d. unknown** | | | | | | | | |
| 1939 | WM | YUG | 5 | 0 | — | 0 | — | — |
| **Lombard, Raymond / b. Oct. 4, 1918 / d. unknown** | | | | | | | | |
| 1947-49 | WM | BEL | 12 | 4 | — | 4 | — | — |
| **Lomovsek, Blaz / b. Dec. 24, 1956** | | | | | | | | |
| 1984 | OG-M | YUG | 5 | 0 | 0 | 0 | 4 | — |
| **Long, Barry / b. Jan. 3, 1949** | | | | | | | | |
| 1981 | WM | CAN | 7 | 1 | 0 | 1 | 8 | — |
| **Longstaff, David / b. Aug. 26, 1974** | | | | | | | | |
| 1994 | WM | GBR | 6 | 0 | 0 | 0 | 6 | — |
| **Longuet, Andre / b. unknown** | | | | | | | | |
| 1950 | WM | FRA | 1 | 0 | 0 | 0 | 0 | — |
| **Lonsmin, Viktor / b. June 11, 1920 / d. unknown** | | | | | | | | |
| 1939 | WM | TCH | 10 | 1 | — | 1 | — | — |
| **Lonyai, Robert / b. unknown / d. unknown** | | | | | | | | |
| 1937 | WM | HUN | 2 | 0 | 0 | 0 | 0 | — |
| **Loob, Hakan / b. July 3, 1960** | | | | | | | | |
| 1979-80 | WM20 | SWE | 11 | 7 | 4 | 11 | 2 | 2B |
| 1982-91 | WM | SWE | 36 | 14 | 19 | 33 | 26 | 2G,S |
| 1984 | CC | SWE | 8 | 6 | 4 | 10 | 2 | 2nd |
| 1992-94 | OG-M | SWE | 16 | 8 | 9 | 17 | 2 | G |
| ~IIHF Hall of Fame/Triple Gold Club | | | | | | | | |
| ~OG-M All-Star Team/Forward (1992) | | | | | | | | |
| **Loob, Peter / b. July 23, 1957** | | | | | | | | |
| 1983 | WM | SWE | 3 | 1 | 2 | 3 | 8 | — |
| **Loos, Vilem / b. 1895 / d. 1942** | | | | | | | | |
| 1920-24 | OG-M | TCH | 6 | 4 | 0 | 4 | — | B |
| **Looser, Patrick / b. Jan. 23, 1974** | | | | | | | | |
| 1994 | WM20 | SUI | 7 | 1 | 1 | 2 | 14 | — |
| **Lorentsen, Simon / b. June 30, 1986** | | | | | | | | |
| 2004 | WM18 | DEN | 6 | 1 | 0 | 1 | 0 | — |
| **Lorenzi, Carlo / b. Sept. 2, 1974** | | | | | | | | |
| 1999-2008 | WM | ITA | 36 | 0 | 3 | 3 | 22 | — |
| 2006 | OG-M | ITA | 1 | 0 | 0 | 0 | 0 | — |
| **Lorin, Pierre / b. Oct. 25, 1912 / d. unknown** | | | | | | | | |
| 1935-37 | WM | FRA | 9 | 0 | 0 | 0 | 0 | — |
| 1936 | OG-M | FRA | 1 | 0 | — | 0 | — | — |
| **Lorincz, Ferenc / b. Jan. 23, 1933** | | | | | | | | |
| 1964 | OG-M | HUN | 7 | 0 | 0 | 0 | 0 | — |
| **Losamoen, Oivind / b. Oct. 13, 1957** | | | | | | | | |
| 1980-84 | OG-M | NOR | 9 | 2 | 1 | 3 | 6 | — |
| **Losch, Mike / b. Aug. 24, 1974** | | | | | | | | |
| 1993-94 | WM20 | GER | 14 | 2 | 1 | 3 | 16 | — |
| **Loth, Andreas / b. Feb. 26, 1972** | | | | | | | | |
| 1992 | WM20 | GER | 7 | 0 | 1 | 1 | 2 | — |
| 2001-02 | WM | GER | 14 | 2 | 2 | 4 | 12 | — |
| 2002 | OG-M | GER | 7 | 2 | 0 | 2 | 0 | — |
| **Lotvonen, Kimmo / b. Jan. 11, 1976** | | | | | | | | |
| 1996 | WM20 | FIN | 6 | 0 | 3 | 3 | 0 | — |

| | | | | | | | | |
|---|---|---|---|---|---|---|---|---|
| **Louette, Henri / b. 1900 / d. unknown** | | | | | | | | |
| 1924 | OG-M | BEL | 3 | 2 | — | 2 | — | — |
| **Louhi, Jyrki / b. Mar. 28, 1978** | | | | | | | | |
| 1998 | WM20 | FIN | 7 | 3 | 4 | 7 | 0 | G |
| **Lovdal, Orjan / b. Sept. 24, 1962** | | | | | | | | |
| 1979 | WM20 | NOR | 5 | 2 | 2 | 4 | 2 | — |
| 1990-96 | WM | NOR | 20 | 1 | 6 | 7 | 16 | — |
| 1984-92 | OG-M | NOR | 13 | 1 | 8 | 9 | 14 | — |
| **Loven, Fredrik / b. Mar. 14, 1977** | | | | | | | | |
| 1996-97 | WM20 | SWE | 13 | 1 | 3 | 4 | 2 | S |
| **Lovryk, Roman / b. Feb. 5, 1985** | | | | | | | | |
| 2002 | WM18 | UKR | 8 | 0 | 0 | 0 | 14 | — |
| **Lovsin, Ken / b. Dec. 4, 1966** | | | | | | | | |
| 1994 | OG-M | CAN | 8 | 0 | 0 | 0 | 8 | S |
| **Low, Evert / b. Dec. 16, 1913 / d. unknown** | | | | | | | | |
| 1935 | WM | SWE | 2 | 0 | — | 0 | — | — |
| **Lowdahl, Christer / b. Feb. 28, 1958** | | | | | | | | |
| 1978 | WM20 | SWE | 7 | 2 | 0 | 2 | 2 | S |
| **Lowe, Darren / b. Oct. 13, 1960** | | | | | | | | |
| 1984 | OG-M | CAN | 7 | 2 | 2 | 4 | 0 | — |
| **Lowe, Kevin / b. Apr. 15, 1959** | | | | | | | | |
| 1982 | WM | CAN | 9 | 1 | 1 | 2 | 2 | B |
| 1984 | CC | CAN | 7 | 0 | 4 | 4 | 8 | 1st |
| **Lozhkin, Alexei / b. Feb. 21, 1974** | | | | | | | | |
| 1998 | WM | BLR | 6 | 1 | 0 | 1 | 2 | — |
| 1998 | OG-M | BLR | 7 | 0 | 2 | 2 | 0 | — |
| **Lubina, Ladislav / b. Feb. 11, 1967** | | | | | | | | |
| 1985-87 | WM20 | TCH | 21 | 9 | 13 | 22 | 10 | 2S |
| 1990-98 | WM | TCH | 37 | 8 | 4 | 12 | 26 | 3B |
| 1987 | CC | TCH | 6 | 0 | 1 | 1 | 6 | — |
| 1992 | OG-M | TCH | 8 | 2 | 4 | 6 | 2 | B |
| **Lubnin, Oleksiy / b. Oct. 16, 1984** | | | | | | | | |
| 2001-02 | WM18 | UKR | 14 | 0 | 5 | 5 | 49 | — |
| 2004 | WM20 | UKR | 6 | 1 | 0 | 1 | 48 | — |
| **Lucchini, Leo / b. Aug. 12, 1928** | | | | | | | | |
| 1950 | WM | CAN | 7 | 11 | 9 | 20 | 0 | G |
| **Luchinkin, Sergei / b. Oct. 16, 1976** | | | | | | | | |
| 1996 | WM20 | RUS | 7 | 1 | 1 | 2 | 0 | B |
| **Luchkin, Vladislav / b. Feb. 3, 1982** | | | | | | | | |
| 2000 | WM18 | RUS | 6 | 2 | 0 | 2 | 4 | S |
| **Luciak, Matus / b. Oct. 24, 1983** | | | | | | | | |
| 2001 | WM18 | SVK | 6 | 2 | 3 | 5 | 6 | — |
| **Luckner, Harald / b. Mar. 27, 1957** | | | | | | | | |
| 1977 | WM20 | SWE | 7 | 4 | 2 | 6 | 4 | — |
| 1981 | WM | SWE | 6 | 0 | 0 | 0 | 0 | S |
| 1980 | OG-M | SWE | 6 | 0 | 2 | 2 | 0 | B |
| **Ludemann, Mirko / b. Dec. 15, 1973** | | | | | | | | |
| 1992-93 | WM20 | GER | 14 | 0 | 1 | 1 | 8 | — |
| 1994-2004 | WM | GER | 43 | 3 | 10 | 13 | 22 | — |
| 1996-2004 | WCH | GER | 8 | 1 | 0 | 1 | 4 | — |
| 1994-2002 | OG-M | GER | 12 | 1 | 2 | 3 | 0 | — |
| **Ludwiczak, Witalis / b. Apr. 20, 1910 / d. June 19, 1988** | | | | | | | | |
| 1933-38 | WM | POL | 25 | 1 | 0 | 1 | 1 | — |
| 1932-36 | OG-M | POL | 9 | 0 | 0 | 0 | 2 | — |
| **Ludwig, Andreas / b. Jan. 5, 1963** | | | | | | | | |
| 1983-85 | WM | GDR | 20 | 5 | 2 | 6 | 12 | — |
| **Ludwig, Craig / b. Mar. 15, 1961** | | | | | | | | |
| 1981 | WM20 | USA | 5 | 0 | 0 | 0 | 12 | — |
| **Ludwig, Horst / b. unknown** | | | | | | | | |
| 1967 | WM | FRG | 7 | 2 | 1 | 3 | 4 | — |
| **Lukac, Jozef / b. Mar. 13, 1957** | | | | | | | | |
| 1977 | WM20 | TCH | 7 | 4 | 1 | 5 | 2 | B |
| **Lukac, Michal / b. Aug. 26, 1984** | | | | | | | | |
| 2001-02 | WM18 | SVK | 13 | 3 | 4 | 7 | 22 | — |
| 2003-04 | WM20 | SVK | 11 | 1 | 2 | 3 | 2 | — |
| **Lukac, Vincent / b. Feb. 14, 1954** | | | | | | | | |
| 1977-85 | WM | TCH | 38 | 13 | 9 | 22 | 4 | 2G,2S |
| 1984 | CC | TCH | 5 | 2 | 1 | 3 | 0 | — |
| 1980-84 | OG-M | TCH | 13 | 6 | 10 | 16 | 2 | S |
| **Lukacovic, Adam / b. Apr. 16, 1986** | | | | | | | | |
| 2004 | WM18 | CZE | 7 | 0 | 2 | 2 | 6 | B |
| **Lukes, Christian / b. July 28, 1969** | | | | | | | | |
| 1988-89 | WM20 | FRG | 14 | 0 | 0 | 0 | 14 | — |
| **Lukes, Frantisek / b. Sept. 25, 1982** | | | | | | | | |
| 2000 | WM18 | CZE | 6 | 1 | 0 | 1 | 8 | — |
| 2002 | WM20 | CZE | 7 | 0 | 1 | 1 | 0 | — |
| **Lukin, Jarrett / b. Jan. 24, 1984** | | | | | | | | |
| 2002 | WM18 | CAN | 8 | 1 | 0 | 1 | 6 | — |
| **Lukowich, Morris / b. June 1, 1956** | | | | | | | | |
| 1981 | WM | CAN | 8 | 2 | 1 | 3 | 4 | — |
| **Lukyanchikov, Nikolai / b. May 23, 1989** | | | | | | | | |
| 2007 | WM18 | RUS | 7 | 1 | 0 | 1 | 4 | G |

**Lumme, Jyrki / b. July 16, 1966**
1986 WM20 FIN 7 1 4 5 2 —
1990-2000 WM FIN 38 5 17 22 26 B
1991-96 WCH FIN 10 2 3 5 12 —
1988-2002 OG-M FIN 16 1 2 3 18 S,B

**Lund, Bob / b. unknown**
1965 WM USA 7 0 3 3 6 —

**Lundberg, Joakim / b. Feb. 12, 1974**
1994 WM20 SWE 7 1 0 1 4 S

**Lundberg, Lars Gunnar / b. Jan. 12, 1952**
1976-78 WM SWE 29 11 4 15 26 S,B

**Lundby, Thor / b. Mar. 5, 1937**
1964 OG-M NOR 6 5 1 6 0 —

**Lundeen, Bob / b. Nov. 4, 1952**
1975-76 WM USA 20 0 1 1 2 —
1976 OG-M USA 5 0 0 0 2 —

**Lundeen, Charlie / b. Oct. 29, 1962**
1982 WM20 USA 7 1 4 5 10 —

**Lundell, Bertil / b. Sept. 6, 1908 / d. July 11, 1996**
1935-37 WM SWE 11 1 0 1 1 —
1936 OG-M SWE 5 0 — 0 — —

**Lundell, Einar / b. Jan. 9, 1894 / d. Mar. 29, 1976**
1920 OG-M SWE 5 0 — 0 4 —

**Lundell, Per / b. June 29, 1968**
1988 WM20 SWE 6 1 2 3 2 —

**Lundenes, Hakan / b. unknown**
1980 OG-M NOR 5 0 1 1 2 —

**Lundgren, Jeff / b. Jan. 10, 1959**
1978-79 WM20 USA 11 0 3 3 15 —

**Lundh, Staffan / b. Jan. 14, 1963**
1986 WM SWE 6 0 0 0 2 S

**Lundholm, Bengt / b. Aug. 4, 1955**
1976-79 WM SWE 36 12 13 25 18 S,2B
1981 CC SWE 5 1 0 1 2 —
1980 OG-M SWE 6 1 0 1 2 B

**Lundmark, Jamie / b. Jan. 16, 1981**
2000-01 WM20 CAN 14 6 6 12 6 2B

**Lundqvist, Per / b. Jan. 24, 1951**
1979 WM SWE 8 3 0 3 2 B
1980 OG-M SWE 7 4 3 7 6 B

**Lundstrom, Finn / b. June 4, 1947**
1975 WM SWE 9 0 0 0 6 B

**Lundstrom, Jon / b. Mar. 19, 1964**
1983-84 WM20 SWE 13 3 4 7 6 —

**Lundstrom, Mats / b. Apr. 23, 1966**
1985-86 WM20 SWE 14 9 8 17 8 —

**Lundstrom, Per Anton / b. Sept. 29, 1977**
1996-97 WM20 SWE 13 1 4 5 16 S

**Lundstrom, Tord / b. Mar. 4, 1945**
1965-75 WM SWE 73 40 26 66 34 3S,4B
1976 CC SWE 5 1 3 4 6 —
1968-72 OG-M SWE 12 5 4 9 12 S
~IIHF Hall of Fame

**Lundvall, Lars-Eric / b. Apr. 3, 1934**
1955-63 WM SWE 40 25 12 37 21 2G,S,B
1956-64 OG-M SWE 21 12 8 20 6 S

**Luojola, Hannu / b. Nov. 29, 1946**
1971 WM FIN 10 1 0 1 9 —

**Luongo, Chris / b. Mar. 17, 1967**
1996-2000 WM USA 19 2 0 2 8 B

**Luostarinen, Esko / b. May 8, 1935**
1957-63 WM FIN 35 2 4 6 22 —
1960-64 OG-M FIN 13 5 2 7 6 —

**Luovi, Mikko / b. Nov. 5, 1973**
1992-93 WM20 FIN 14 6 0 6 2 —

**Lupul, Gary / b. Apr. 4, 1959**
1979 WM20 CAN 5 2 1 3 2 —

**Lupzig, Andreas / b. Aug. 5, 1968**
1986-88 WM20 FRG 17 4 2 6 8 —
1990-98 WM GER 28 3 7 10 38 —
1996 WCH GER 4 1 1 2 0 —
1998 OG-M GER 4 0 0 0 4 —

**Lupzig, Verner / b. 1959**
1977 WM20 FRG 7 0 1 1 13 —

**Lussy, Silvan / b. Sept. 19, 1980**
2000 WM20 SUI 7 0 0 0 2 —

**Lusth, Mats / b. May 20, 1962**
1982 WM20 SWE 6 0 4 4 12 —

**Lutchenko, Vladimir / b. Jan. 2, 1949**
1969-79 WM URS 103 12 19 31 58 8G,2S,B
1972 SS URS 8 1 3 4 0 2nd
1976 CC URS 3 0 1 1 2 —
1972-76 OG-M URS 10 0 3 3 6 2G

**Luthi, Alfred "Fredy" / b. July 31, 1961**
1987-93 WM SUI 35 7 8 15 18 —
1988-92 OG-M SUI 13 2 6 8 18 —

**Luthi, Claude / b. Aug. 3, 1972**
1992 WM20 SUI 7 0 2 2 4 —

**Luthi, Ernst / b. Feb. 20, 1954**
1976 OG-M SUI 4 1 0 1 2 —

**Luthi, Ueli / b. Oct. 31, 1943**
1972 WM SUI 10 5 1 6 10 —

**Lutz, Rainer / b. Apr. 23, 1961**
1980-81 WM20 FRG 10 1 1 2 10 —
1983 WM FRG 8 0 1 1 0 —

**Luza, Patrik / b. Apr. 13, 1972**
1992 WM20 TCH 7 1 1 2 4 —

**Lyapkin, Yuri / b. Jan. 21, 1945**
1971-76 WM URS 40 7 9 16 28 4G,S
1972 SS URS 6 1 5 6 0 2nd
1976 OG-M URS 5 1 3 4 2 G

**Lyashenko, Roman / b. May 2, 1979 / d. July 6, 2003**
1997-99 WM20 RUS 20 4 7 11 10 G,S,B
2002 WM RUS 9 0 2 2 14 S

**Lyaskovsky, Yuriy / b. Oct. 29, 1975**
1995 WM20 UKR 7 0 0 0 0 —

**Lynov, Yuri / b. Nov. 12, 1967**
1985 WM20 URS 7 0 2 2 2 B

**Lyons, John / b. Mar. 31, 1900 / d. Jan. 15, 1971**
1924 OG-M USA 1 0 — 0 0 S

**Lysen, Goran / b. Aug. 30, 1939**
1959 WM SWE 4 1 0 1 0 —

**Lysenko, Alexander / b. May 25, 1964**
1984 WM20 URS 7 2 0 2 4 G

**Lysiak, Tom / b. Apr. 22, 1953**
1978 WM CAN 7 1 1 2 4 B

**Lytvynenko, Vitaliy / b. June 14, 1970**
1999-2006 WM UKR 39 6 9 15 12 —
2002 OG-M UKR 4 0 1 1 4 —

**Lyubimov, Alexander / b. Feb. 15, 1980**
2000 WM20 RUS 7 3 2 5 4 S

**Lyubomirov, Lubomir / b. Nov. 22, 1958**
1976 OG-M BUL 5 1 0 1 18 —

**Lyubushin, Mikhail / b. July 24, 1983**
2003 WM20 RUS 6 0 2 2 0 G

**Lyutkevych, Vitaliy / b. Apr. 4, 1980**
2001-07 WM UKR 18 1 2 3 8 —

**Maas, Hans / b. July 10, 1912 / d. Unknown**
1935 WM NED 6 0 0 0 — —

**Maass, Michael / b. June 21, 1973**
1993 WM20 GER 7 0 0 0 4 —

**Maatta, Eilert / b. Sept. 22, 1935**
1957-67 WM SWE 35 12 22 34 14 2G,2S,B
1964 OG-M SWE 7 2 3 5 6 S

**Maatta, Tero / b. Jan. 2, 1982**
2000 WM18 FIN 7 2 2 4 8 G
2001-02 WM20 FIN 14 1 2 3 6 S,B

**Maattanen, Pasi / b. June 11, 1972**
1992 WM20 FIN 4 0 0 0 0 —

**Maattanen, Raimo / b. Feb. 8, 1943**
1967 WM FIN 7 0 0 0 4 —

**MacAdam, Al / b. Mar. 16, 1952**
1977-79 WM CAN 18 8 8 16 0 —

**Macauley, Doug / b. July 22, 1929**
1950 WM CAN 7 6 4 10 4 G

**Macchietto, Francesco / b. July 31, 1932**
1956-64 OG-M ITA 13 1 2 3 4 —

**MacDonald, Lane / b. Mar. 3, 1966**
1986 WM20 USA 7 1 5 6 0 B
1987 WM USA 2 0 0 0 0 —
1988 OG-M USA 6 6 1 7 4 —

**Macdonell, Fred / b. unknown / d. unknown**
1934 WM USA 4 0 0 0 — S

**MacDougal, Mike / b. Apr. 30, 1958**
1977 WM20 USA 7 4 3 7 6 —

**Macejka, Filip / b. Apr. 17, 1984**
2002 WM18 SVK 8 1 3 4 26 —

**Macek, Peter / b. May 13, 1983**
2001 WM18 SVK 6 0 0 0 10 —
2003 WM20 SVK 1 0 0 0 0 —

**Macelis, Jiri / b. Jan. 7, 1923 / d. unknown**
1949 WM TCH 7 1 — 1 — G

**Mach, Miroslav / b. Jan. 30, 1970**
1990 WM20 TCH 6 1 1 2 2 B

**Machac, Oldrich / b. Apr. 18, 1946**
1967-78 WM TCH 107 17 26 43 74 3G,4S,3B
1976 CC TCH 7 0 4 4 4 2nd
1968-76 OG-M TCH 17 0 3 3 14 2S,B
~IIHF Hall of Fame
~WM All-Star Team/Defence (1972)

**Machacek, Petr / b. Oct. 19, 1985**
2003 WM18 CZE 6 0 0 0 2 —

**MacInnis, Al / b. July 11, 1963**
1990 WM CAN 9 1 3 4 10 —
1991 CC CAN 8 2 4 6 23 1st
1998-2002 OG-M CAN 12 2 0 2 10 G

**MacIver, Norm / b. Sept. 8, 1964**
1993 WM CAN 8 0 5 5 4 —

**Mack, Craig / b. Mar. 27, 1965**
1984 WM20 USA 7 1 1 2 6 —

**MacKay, Brian / b. Sept. 29, 1932**
1962 WM USA 7 3 5 8 0 B

**MacKay, Mark / b. May 28, 1964**
1996-2001 WM GER 21 3 3 6 16 —
1996 WCH GER 4 1 3 4 2 —
1998-2002 OG-M GER 11 1 6 7 8 —

**MacKenzie, Barry / b. Aug. 16, 1941**
1965-67 WM CAN 21 2 5 7 26 2B
1964-68 OG-M CAN 14 0 4 4 12 B
~IIHF Hall of Fame

**Mackenzie, Derek / b. June 11, 1981**
2001 WM20 CAN 7 1 2 3 4 B

**MacKenzie, Gord / b. Manitoba, 1930**
1931 WM CAN 5 2 — 2 — G

**MacKenzie, Jack / b. July 22, 1930**
1958 WM CAN 7 12 5 17 6 G
1956 OG-M CAN 8 7 4 11 6 B
~OG-M IIHF Directorate Best Forward (1956)

**MacKenzie, Jim / b. unknown**
1965 WM CAN 5 0 1 1 4 —

**MacLean, John / b. Nov. 20, 1964**
1984 WM20 CAN 7 7 1 8 4 —
1989 WM CAN 10 3 6 9 4 S

**MacLean, Paul / b. Mar. 9, 1958**
1980 OG-M CAN 6 2 3 5 8 —

**MacLellan, Brian / b. Oct. 27, 1958**
1985 WM CAN 4 0 0 0 0 S

**MacLeod, Scott / b. May 17, 1959**
1979 WM20 CAN 5 1 2 3 4 —

**MacMillan, Bill / b. Mar. 7, 1943**
1966-67 WM CAN 14 5 4 9 6 2B
1968 OG-M CAN 6 1 2 3 0 B

**MacMillan, Bob / b. Dec. 3, 1952**
1978 WM CAN 10 0 3 3 6 B

**Macoszek, Roman / b. June 11, 1980**
1999 WM20 SVK 6 1 1 2 27 B

**Macoun, Jamie / b. Aug. 17, 1961**
1985-91 WM CAN 25 5 2 7 26 2S
~WM IIHF Directorate Best Defenceman (1991)

**MacSwain, Steve / b. Aug. 8, 1965**
1990 WM USA 3 1 0 1 0 —

**Mader, Bob / b. Oct. 29, 1932**
1962 WM CAN 7 2 5 7 8 S

**Madach, Peter / b. Feb. 26, 1963**
1981-82 WM20 SWE 12 2 4 6 18 G

**Madera, Sergiy / b. June 26, 1984**
2004 WM20 UKR 6 0 0 0 0 —

**Madl, Michal / b. Nov. 2, 1966**
1986 WM20 TCH 7 0 2 2 0 —

**Madovy, Martin / b. Jan. 16, 1971**
1991 WM20 TCH 7 5 3 8 4 B

**Maef, Markus / b. Feb. 14, 1964**
1984 WM20 SUI 7 0 0 0 4 —

**Magerov, Sergei / b. Aug. 11, 1988**
2006 WM18 BLR 6 0 0 0 8 —

**Maglione, Matt / b. Apr. 20, 1982**
2000 WM18 USA 6 1 1 2 0 —

**Magnussen, Trond / b. Feb. 1, 1973**
1990 WM20 NOR 7 3 1 4 6 —
1992-2001 WM NOR 46 10 12 22 52 —
1994 OG-M NOR 7 0 1 1 2 —

**Magnusson, Mikael / b. Mar. 15, 1973**
1993 WM20 SWE 7 0 4 4 8 S
2000 WM SWE 7 0 0 0 14 —

**Magwood, John / b. Mar. 23, 1896 / d. unknown**
1931 WM GBR 4 4 — 4 — —

**Magyar, Sandor / b. Oct. 25, 1907 / d. May 17, 1983**
1936 OG-M HUN 6 2 — 2 — —

**Mahle, Oscar / b. Aug. 22, 1939 / d. May 21, 2006**
1958-62 WM USA 10 9 0 9 8 B

**Mahovlich, Frank / b. Jan. 10, 1938**
1972 SS CAN 6 1 1 2 0 1st

**Mahovlich, Pete / b. Oct. 10, 1946**
1972 SS CAN 7 1 1 2 4 1st
1976 CC CAN 7 1 4 5 0 1st

**Mai, Carletto / b. unknown / d. unknown**
1930 WM SUI 3 0 — 0 — B

**Maia, Pierrick / b. Feb. 16, 1967**
1993-94 WM FRA 11 1 0 1 6 —
1994 OG-M FRA 7 3 0 3 10 —

**Maidl, Anton / b. July 24, 1960**
1980 WM20 FRG 5 0 0 0 2 —

**Maier, Andreas / b. Sept. 10, 1987**
2005 WM18 GER 6 0 0 0 4 —

**Maier, Simon / b. Jan. 1, 1987**
2005 WM18 GER 6 0 1 1 2 —

**Maillot, Yannick / b. Apr. 20, 1982**
2002 WM20 FRA 6 0 0 0 8 —

**Maiocchi, Mario / b. Apr. 27, 1913 / d. unknown**
1935 WM ITA 6 0 — 0 — —
1936 OG-M ITA 3 0 0 0 — —

**Mair, Adam / b. Feb. 15, 1979**
1999 WM20 CAN 7 1 1 2 29 S

**Mair, Michael / b. Aug. 31, 1956**
1982-83 WM ITA 16 1 1 2 2 —
1984 OG-M ITA 5 1 2 3 2 —

**Maiser, Justin / b. June 29, 1983**
2001 WM18 USA 6 2 2 4 8 —

**Maisonneuve, Roger / b. Feb. 26, 1933**
1966 WM USA 3 0 0 0 0 —

**Maj, Boguslaw / b. Jan. 18, 1960**
1992 WM POL 6 0 1 1 2 —

**Majernik, Miroslav / b. Jan. 12, 1961**
1980-81 WM20 TCH 10 1 1 2 2 —

**Majesky, Boris / b. Sept. 3, 1978**
1998 WM20 SVK 6 1 0 1 2 —

**Majoross, Gergely / b. May 9, 1979**
2009 WM HUN 6 0 0 0 0 —

**Makarov, Konstantin / b. Sept. 17, 1985**
2003 WM18 RUS 6 2 0 2 2 B

**Makarov, Nikolai / b. Dec. 19, 1948**
1981 WM URS 1 0 0 0 0 G

**Makarov, Sergei / b. June 19, 1958**
1977-78 WM20 URS 14 12 14 26 8 2G
1978-91 WM URS 101 55 68 123 85 8G,S,2B
1981-87 CC URS 22 16 15 31 12 1st,2nd
1980-88 OG-M URS 22 11 17 28 18 2G,S
~IIHF Hall of Fame
~WM IIHF Directorate Best Forward (1985), WM All-Star Team/Forward (1979, 1981, 1982, 1983, 1985, 1986, 1987, 1989)

**Makarov, Yevgeni / b. July 16, 1981**
2001 WM20 BLR 6 0 0 0 2 —

**Makartsev, Konstantin / b. Mar. 29, 1958**
1977-78 WM20 URS 13 1 3 4 0 2G

**Makela, Mikko / b. Feb. 28, 1965**
1984-85 WM20 FIN 12 12 2 14 6 S
1985-94 WM FIN 24 9 14 23 8 2S
1987 CC FIN 5 1 1 2 12 —
1992-94 OG-M FIN 13 5 6 11 4 B
~WM20 All-Star Team/Forward (1985)

**Makela, Tuukka / b. May 24, 1982**
2000 WM18 FIN 7 1 1 2 22 G

**Maki, Ted / b. unknown**
1962-63 WM CAN 13 2 3 5 18 S

**Maki, Tomi / b. Aug. 19, 1983**
2001 WM18 FIN 6 1 0 1 8 B
2002-03 WM20 FIN 14 3 2 5 27 2B

**Makiaho, Toni / b. Jan. 11, 1975**
1995 WM20 FIN 7 0 1 1 2 —
1998 WM FIN 9 0 0 0 6 S

**Makinen, Ari / b. Apr. 5, 1957**
1977 WM20 FIN 6 0 0 0 2 —

**Makinen, Kauko / b. July 20, 1927 / d. Aug. 5, 1968**
1951 WM FIN 3 0 — 0 2 —
1952 OG-M FIN 5 0 0 0 — —

**Makinen, Marko / b. Mar. 31, 1977**
1996 WM20 FIN 5 0 0 0 4 —

**Makitalo, Jarmo / b. Oct. 8, 1960**
1979-80 WM20 FIN 11 6 4 10 4 S
1980-84 OG-M FIN 13 3 2 5 2 —

**Makkonen, Kari / b. Jan. 20, 1955**
1976-86 WM FIN 66 16 12 28 34 —
1976-81 CC FIN 8 3 1 4 2 —

**Makritski, Alexander / b. Aug. 11, 1971**
2000-10 WM BLR 37 2 3 5 32 —
2002-10 OG BLR 13 0 0 0 14 —

**Malacko, Jim "Shorty" / b. 1930**
1951 WM CAN 5 0 — 0 2 G

**Malakhov, Vladimir / b. Aug. 30, 1968**
1987-92 WM20 URS 26 2 2 4 18 G,B
1991-96 WCH RUS 9 1 0 1 12 —
1992-2002 OG-M RUS 14 4 3 7 8 G,B
~Triple Gold Club

**Malec, Tomas / b. May 13, 1982**
2000 WM18 SVK 6 0 2 2 8 —
2001-02 WM20 SVK 14 1 0 1 6 —

**Malecek, Josef / b. June 18, 1903 / d. Sept. 26, 1982**
1930-39 WM TCH 48 49 3 52 1 2B
1924-36 OG-M TCH 13 11 — 11 — —
~IIHF Hall of Fame

**Maley, David / b. Apr. 24, 1963**
1991 WM USA 8 0 1 1 2 —

**Maley, Dick / b. unknown / d. unknown**
1934-39 WM USA 13 4 0 4 — 2S

**Malgunas, Stewart / b. Apr. 21, 1970**
1990 WM20 CAN 7 0 1 1 0 G

**Malhotra, Manny / b. Apr. 18, 1980**
1998-2000 WM20 CAN 14 0 2 2 8 B
2002 WM CAN 7 0 0 0 4 —

**Malicki, Tadeusz / b. Feb. 17, 1948**
1970 WM POL 3 0 0 0 0 —

**Malik, Marek / b. June 24, 1975**
1994-95 WM20 CZE 14 4 9 13 32 —
2004 WCH CZE 4 0 0 0 4 —
2006 OG-M CZE 8 0 0 0 8 B

**Malinowski, Merlin / b. Sept. 27, 1958**
1988 OG-M CAN 8 3 2 5 0 —

**Malinsky, Jiri / b. Sept. 5, 1971**
1990-91 WM20 TCH 14 3 2 5 4 2B

**Malkov, Dmitri / b. Dec. 3, 1982**
2000 WM18 UKR 6 2 0 2 6 —

**Malloy, Charlie / b. Nov. 17, 1957**
1977 WM20 USA 7 0 0 0 0 —

**Malloy, Norm / b. Sept. 27, 1913 / d. Dec. 1964**
1932 OG-M CAN 5 3 3 6 4 G

**Malmberg, Ove / b. May 17, 1933**
1956 OG-M SWE 6 0 0 0 8 —

**Malmivaara, Olli / b. Mar. 13, 1982**
2000 WM18 FIN 7 1 1 2 6 G
2001-02 WM20 FIN 13 1 1 2 4 S,B

**Malo, Andre / b. May 10, 1965**
1994 WM GBR 5 0 0 0 8 —

**Malo, Joe / b. May 22, 1934**
1962 WM CAN 7 8 6 14 4 S

**Maloney, Don / b. Sept. 5, 1958**
1985 WM CAN 9 1 1 2 2 S

**Maltby, Kirk / b. Dec. 22, 1972**
2003-05 WM CAN 18 3 3 6 16 G,S

**Maltsev, Alexander / b. Apr. 20, 1949**
1969-83 WM URS 110 77 76 153 30 9G,2S,B
1972 SS URS 8 0 5 5 0 2nd
1976-81 CC URS 9 4 5 9 2 1st
1972-80 OG-M URS 17 15 12 27 0 2G,S
~IIHF Hall of Fame
~WM IIHF Directorate Best Forward (1970, 1972, 1981), WM All-Star Team/Forward (1970, 1971, 1972, 1978, 1981)

**Malver, Svend / b. unknown**
1949 WM DEN 3 0 — 0 — —

**Malykhin, Igor / b. June 6, 1969**
1988-89 WM20 URS 14 0 8 8 18 G,S

**Malysiak, Andrzej / b. June 30, 1957**
1977 WM20 POL 7 4 0 4 2 —
1979 WM POL 8 1 0 1 4 —
1980 OG-M POL 5 2 6 8 0 —

**Malysiak, Kazimierz / b. Apr. 11, 1936**
1958-59 WM POL 11 1 0 1 0 —

**Mamonovs, Vladimirs / b. Apr. 22, 1980**
2006 OG-M LAT 5 0 0 0 4 —

**Manderville, Kent / b. Apr. 12, 1971**
1990-91 WM20 CAN 14 2 8 10 0 2G
1992 OG-M CAN 8 1 2 3 0 S

**Mandes, Steve / b. Aug. 15, 1985**
2003 WM18 USA 6 2 0 2 2 —

**Maneluk, Mike / b. Oct. 1, 1973**
1995 WM CAN 8 0 2 2 0 B

**Mangold, Klaus / b. Jan. 15, 1950**
1976 WM FRG 9 0 0 0 0 —

**Maniacco, Aldo / b. Nov. 4, 1934**
1956 OG-M ITA 6 5 7 12 6 —

**Mann, Cameron / b. Apr. 20, 1977**
1997 WM20 CAN 7 3 4 7 10 G

**Mann, Stefan / b. June 2, 1975**
1993-95 WM20 GER 21 2 1 3 22 —

**Mannikko, Miikka / b. Mar. 27, 1979**
1999 WM20 FIN 6 2 3 5 4 —

**Manno, Bob / b. Oct. 31, 1956**
1982-83 WM ITA 17 1 5 6 28 —
1992 OG-M ITA 7 1 2 3 22 —

**Manowski, Jozef / b. Jan. 7, 1935**
1964 OG-M POL 7 7 1 8 2 —

**Mansi, Maurizio / b. Sept. 3, 1965**
1992-2002 WM ITA 53 11 18 29 56 —
1994-98 OG-M ITA 11 2 2 4 12 —

**Mansikka, Reijo / b. Jan. 23, 1959**
1978 WM20 FIN 6 1 2 3 0 —

**Manskow Hansen, Andre / b. June 17, 1975**
1999 WM NOR 6 1 0 1 2 —

**Manson, Dave / b. Jan. 27, 1967**
1993 WM CAN 8 3 7 10 22 —
~WM All-Star Team/Defence (1993)

**Mansson, Mathias / b. Sept. 20, 1981**
2001 WM20 SWE 7 0 0 0 14 —
2007 WM SWE 4 0 0 0 2 —

**Mantha, Moe / b. Jan. 21, 1961**
1982-91 WM USA 26 3 2 5 18 —
1992 OG-M USA 8 1 1 2 4 —

**Mantyla, Tuukka / b. May 25, 1981**
1999 WM18 FIN 6 1 0 1 8 G
2000-01 WM20 FIN 14 1 7 8 20 S
2004-07 WM FIN 21 0 4 4 10 S,B
~WM20 All-Star Team/Defence (2001)

**Mantymaa, Ville / b. Mar. 8, 1985**
2002-03 WM18 FIN 13 1 5 6 8 —
2005 WM20 FIN 4 1 1 2 2 —

**Mara, George / b. Dec. 12, 1921 / d. Aug. 30, 2006**
1948 OG-M CAN 8 12 — 12 4 G

**Mara, Paul / b. Sept. 7, 1979**
1997-99 WM20 USA 19 2 5 7 28 S
2004 WM USA 9 1 2 3 8 B

**Maras, Daniel / b. Feb. 21, 1981**
1999 WM18 SVK 7 1 0 1 4 B

**Marazza, Aldo / b. unknown / d. unknown**
1934 WM ITA 1 0 0 0 — —

**Marchant, Todd / b. Aug. 12, 1973**
1993 WM20 USA 7 2 3 5 2 —
1994 OG-M USA 8 1 1 2 6 —

**Marchetti, Giovanni / b. Feb. 12, 1968**
1992-99 WM ITA 38 0 1 1 39 —
1992 OG-M ITA 7 0 0 0 6 —

**Marchewczyk, Czeslaw / b. Oct. 1, 1912 / d. Nov. 10, 2003**
1930-39 WM POL 27 10 0 10 5 —
1932-48 OG-M POL 14 3 0 3 2 —

**Markov, Sergei / b. Mar. 12, 1973**
1993 WM20 RUS 7 1 1 2 4 —

**Marcinczak, Marek / b. Jan. 19, 1954**
1975-79 WM POL 26 1 3 4 14 —
1976-80 OG-M POL 9 0 3 3 2 —

**Marcinko, Miroslav / b. Jan. 16, 1964**
1994 OG-M SVK 8 0 1 1 6 —

**Marcos, Elie / b. July 8, 1983**
2002 WM20 FRA 6 0 0 0 4 —

**Marcotte, Ray / b. unknown**
1951 WM USA 6 0 — 0 2 —

**Marczell, Artur / b. Dec. 27, 1974**
1996-2000 WM AUT 13 2 0 2 2 —

**Marek, Jan / b. Dec. 31, 1979 / d. Sept. 7, 2011**
2007-11 WM CZE 29 8 6 14 26 G,B
~perished in Yaroslavl plane crash

**Marek, Miloslav / b. unknown**
1949 WM TCH 2 1 — 1 — G

**Mares, Tomas / b. Dec. 14, 1965**
1985 WM20 TCH 7 5 1 6 6 S

**Margerit, Pascal / b. Dec. 12, 1971**
1992 OG-M FRA 8 0 0 0 0 —

**Margo, Gyorgy / b. May 15, 1912 / d. unknown**
1933-38 WM HUN 18 3 0 3 2 —

**Marha, Josef / b. June 2, 1976**
1994-95 WM20 CZE 12 9 5 14 2 —

**Mariams, Artyom / b. July 19, 1980**
1999-2000 WM20 RUS 14 1 1 2 4 G,S

**Marien, Glen / b. unknown**
1963 WM USA 3 0 0 0 4 —

**Marinov, Erik / b. May 29, 1977**
1997 WM20 SVK 6 0 4 4 0 —

**Marinucci, Chris / b. Dec. 29, 1971**
1997 WM USA 8 1 0 1 2 —

**Marjamaki, Pekka / b. Dec. 18, 1947**
1967-79 WM FIN 90 15 12 27 55 —
1972-76 OG-M FIN 10 2 1 3 4 —
~IIHF Hall of Fame
~WM IIHF Directorate Best Defenceman (1975), WM All-Star Team/Defence (1975)

**Mark, Detlef / b. July 25, 1954**
1976-85 WM GDR 17 0 0 0 6 —

**Markevich, Fyodor / b. Jan. 3, 1988**
2006 WM18 BLR 6 0 0 0 2 —

**Markle, Peter / b. Sept. 24, 1946**
1969 WM USA 10 1 0 1 2 —

**Marklund, Jorgen / b. June 15, 1964**
1984 WM20 SWE 5 0 0 0 0 —

**Markov, Danil / b. July 30, 1976**
1998-2008 WM RUS 12 0 1 1 2 G
2002-06 OG-M RUS 13 0 3 3 4 B

**Markovski, Ivan / b. Aug. 18, 1935**
1976 OG-M BUL 5 0 0 0 4 —

**Markovsky, Dmytro / b. July 5, 1975**
1999-2002 WM UKR 9 0 0 0 2 —

**Marois, Daniel / b. Oct. 3, 1968**
2001 WM CAN 1 0 1 1 0 —

**Marois, Mario / b. Dec. 15, 1957**
1989 WM CAN 10 0 4 4 6 S

**Maron, Oliver / b. Sept. 30, 1983**
2001 WM18 SVK 6 1 1 2 10 —
2003 WM20 SVK 6 0 2 2 2 —

**Maroste, Mark / b. Jan. 30, 1963**
1982-83 WM20 USA 14 0 6 6 6 —

**Maroz, Andrei / b. Jan. 30, 1963**
1999-2001 WM20 BLR 12 1 1 2 6 —

**Marquis, Philippe / b. Jan. 19, 1976**
1996 WM20 SUI 6 0 3 3 14 —
1999 WM SUI 6 0 0 0 0 —

**Marsh, Brad / b. Mar. 31, 1958**
1977-78 WM20 CAN 13 1 7 8 18 S,B
1979 WM CAN 6 1 0 1 4 —

**Marsh, John / b. unknown**
1965 WM USA 7 0 0 0 4 —

**Marshall, Jack / b. unknown / d. unknown**
1938 WM CAN 5 0 — 0 — G

**Marshall, Jason / b. Feb. 22, 1971**
1991 WM20 CAN 7 0 4 4 6 G

**Martak, Igor / b. Feb. 3, 1981**
1999 WM18 SVK 7 0 1 1 0 B

**Martemianov, Andrei / b. Mar. 30, 1963**
1983 WM20 URS 7 0 0 0 2 G

**Marthinsen, Tommy / b. Dec. 24, 1976**
2001-06 WM NOR 12 2 0 2 6 —

**Martignoni, Adolf / b. July 28, 1909 / d. unknown**
1936 OG-M SUI 1 0 0 0 — —

**Martikainen, Kari / b. Sept. 15, 1968**
1999 WM FIN 12 0 4 4 2 S

**Martikainen, Sami / b. June 29, 1989**
2007 WM18 FIN 6 0 1 1 4 —

**Martin, Floyd / b. June 6, 1926**
1956-60 OG-M CAN 15 8 12 20 26 S,B
1962 WM CAN 7 9 5 14 15 S

**Martin, Louis-Phillipe / b. Oct. 2, 1984**
2002 WM18 CAN 8 2 2 4 2 —

**Martin, Matt / b. Apr. 30, 1971**
1997 WM USA 8 0 0 0 0 —
1994 OG-M USA 8 0 2 2 8 —

**Martin, Rick / b. July 26, 1951 / d. Mar. 13, 2011**
1976 CC CAN 4 3 2 5 0 1st

**Martin, Ronny / b. Mar. 17, 1972**
1992 WM20 GER 7 1 2 3 8 —

**Martin, Tom / b. July 5, 1938**
1962 WM USA 7 1 6 7 12 B
1964 OG-M USA 7 0 0 0 6 —

**Martineau, Hank / b. unknown**
1951 WM USA 6 3 — 3 4 —

**Martinec, Tomas / b. Mar. 5, 1976**
2002-05 WM GER 20 3 0 3 24 —
2004 WCH GER 3 0 0 0 2 —
2006 OG-M GER 5 1 0 1 2 —

**Martinec, Vladimir / b. Dec. 22, 1949**
1970-81 WM TCH 102 53 57 110 44 3G,5S,3B
1976 CC TCH 7 3 4 7 2 2nd
1972-80 OG-M TCH 11 10 6 16 2 S,B
~IIHF Hall of Fame
~WM IIHF Directorate Best Forward (1976), WM All-Star Team/Forward (1974, 1975, 1976, 1977)

**Martinek, Libor / b. Apr. 3, 1962**
1981 WM20 TCH 5 2 0 2 2 —

**Martinsen, Per / b. Jan. 1, 1970**
1990 WM20 NOR 7 0 0 0 0 —

**Martinsen, Thor / b. July 12, 1945**
1965 WM NOR 7 2 0 2 10 —
1964-80 OG-M NOR 21 1 0 1 8 —

**Martinyuk, Alexander / b. Sept. 11, 1945**
1971-73 WM URS 19 16 7 23 4 2G
1972 SS URS 1 0 0 0 0 2nd

**Martinyuk, Sergei / b. Jan. 30, 1971**
1990-91 WM20 URS 9 2 4 6 6 2S

**Marton, Jurg / b. May 22, 1963**
1982 WM20 SUI 7 0 0 0 20 —

**Marttila, Jukka / b. Apr. 15, 1968**
1987-88 WM20 FIN 11 0 1 1 4 G,B

**Marttila, Niko / b. Jan. 12, 1971**
1991 WM20 FIN 6 1 4 5 2 —

**Marttinen, Jyri / b. Sept. 1, 1982**
2002 WM20 FIN 7 1 2 3 8 B

**Martynov, Igor / b. Feb. 2, 1964**
1984 WM20 URS 7 3 2 5 12 G

**Maruk, Dennis / b. Nov. 17, 1955**
1979-83 WM CAN 25 10 7 17 12 B

**Masek, Ondrej / b. June 9, 1987**
2005 WM18 CZE 7 0 1 1 2 —

**Maskarinec, Martin / b. Feb. 3, 1969**
1989 WM20 TCH 7 1 5 6 10 B

**Maslan, Frantisek / b. Feb. 19, 1933**
1960 OG-M TCH 2 0 0 0 0 —

**Maslenikov, Maxim / b. Feb. 8, 1979**
1999 WM20 RUS 7 0 2 2 4 G

**Maslenikov, Yaroslav / b. Apr. 23, 1982**
2002 WM20 BLR 6 0 1 1 8 —

**Maslov, Nikolai / b. May 16, 1960**
1979 WM20 URS 6 2 2 4 8 G

**Mason, Brian / b. Apr. 1, 1965**
1994 WM GBR 5 0 0 0 0 —

**Masopust, Karel / b. Oct. 4, 1942**
1968 OG-M TCH 7 0 1 1 6 S

**Massara, John / b. May 20, 1966**
1995-96 WM ITA 9 1 1 2 0 —

**Masson, Romain / b. Apr. 26, 1983**
2002 WM20 FRA 6 0 0 0 2 —

**Massy, Didier / b. Jan. 5, 1963**
1991 WM SUI 3 0 0 0 0 —

**Mastel, Giovanni / b. May 6, 1943**
1964 OG-M ITA 1 0 0 0 0 —

**Mastrullo, Mike / b. May 5, 1957**
1982-83 WM ITA 16 0 0 0 4 —
1984 OG-M ITA 5 1 0 1 0 —

**Masuko, Shuji / b. July 8, 1978**
2003 WM JPN 6 0 1 1 0 —

**Matchefts, John / b. June 18, 1931**
1955 WM USA 6 1 0 1 12 —
1956 OG-M USA 7 2 2 4 2 S

**Matczak, Wojciech / b. Jan. 28, 1964**
1992 WM POL 6 0 1 1 2 —

**Matejka, Juraj / b. Jan. 4, 1983**
2001 WM18 SVK 6 0 0 0 0 —

**Matejovsky, Radek / b. Nov. 17, 1977**
1997 WM20 CZE 7 3 1 4 6 —

**Materski, Kazimierz / b. Sept. 23, 1906 / d. Feb. 3, 1971**
1931-33 WM POL 11 1 — 1 2 —
1932 OG-M POL 6 0 0 0 2 —

**Materukhin, Olexander / b. Oct. 17, 1981**
1999 WM18 UKR 6 0 3 3 10 —
2000 WM20 UKR 7 0 1 1 2 —
2006-07 WM UKR 12 1 1 2 18 —

**Mather, Bruce / b. July 25, 1926 / d. Oct. 1975**
1949 WM USA 7 19 — 19 — B
1948 OG-M USA 8 15 8 23 0 —

**Mathieu, Nando / b. Dec. 22, 1949**
1976 OG-M SUI 5 3 2 5 2 —

**Maticins, Andrejs / b. Jan. 30, 1963**
1997-2000 WM LAT 27 3 9 12 20 —
2002 OG-M LAT 4 1 2 3 2 —

**Matikainen, Petri / b. Jan. 7, 1967**
1986-87 WM20 FIN 14 2 4 6 19 G

**Matlakiewicz, Piotr / b. June 6, 1971**
1990 WM20 POL 5 0 0 0 2 —

**Matras, Jerzy / b. Jan. 7, 1966**
1985 WM20 POL 7 0 0 0 8 —

**Matsos, David / b. Nov. 12, 1973**
1996 WM CAN 8 0 0 0 4 S

**Matsuda, Kazuo / b. May 7, 1941**
1968 OG-M JPN 5 0 2 2 2 —

**Matsuda, Mikio / b. Aug. 18, 1949**
1980 OG-M JPN 5 0 1 1 0 —

**Matsura, Hiroshi / b. May 14, 1968**
1998-99 WM JPN 6 0 1 1 2 —
1998 OG-M JPN 1 0 0 0 0 —

**Matsura, Hiroyuki / b. Aug. 18, 1937**
1964 OG-M JPN 7 0 1 1 4 —

**Mattern, Jan / b. unknown / d. unknown**
1933 WM TCH 4 0 — 0 0 B

**Matthews, Terry / b. 1939**
1962 WM GBR 7 0 0 0 2 —

**Mattie, Jamie / b. June 28, 1980**
2007 WM AUT 6 0 0 0 0 —

**Mattioni, Romeo / b. Apr. 3, 1967**
1987 WM20 SUI 7 1 0 1 0 —

**Mattli, Georg / b. Oct. 18, 1954**
1976 OG-M SUI 5 0 0 0 0 —

**Mattsson, Hans-Jacob / b. June 2, 1890 / d. Dec. 1, 1980**
1920 OG-M SWE 1 0 — 0 — —

**Mattsson, Jesper / b. May 13, 1975**
1995 WM20 SWE 7 0 6 6 22 B
1999-2006 WM SWE 19 2 4 6 8 G,B

**Mattsson, Torbjorn / b. Oct. 22, 1960**
1980 WM20 SWE 5 0 0 0 2 B

**Matulevicius, Vladas / b. unknown / d. unknown**
1938 WM LTU 1 0 — 0 — —

**Matulik, Ivan / b. June 17, 1968**
1987 WM20 TCH 7 3 2 5 6 S

**Matushkin, Igor / b. Jan. 27, 1965**
1998-2000 WM BLR 18 1 5 6 8 —
1998-2002 OG-M BLR 16 1 3 4 4 —

**Matvichuk, Richard / b. Feb. 5, 1973**
1992 WM20 CAN 4 0 0 0 2 —
2002 WM CAN 7 1 0 1 6 —

**Matvichuk, Olexander / b. May 13, 1975**
2000-07 WM UKR 36 4 9 13 34 —

**Matytsin, Andrei / b. Jan. 30, 1963**
1983 WM20 URS 7 0 1 1 2 G

**Mauer, Albert / b. unknown / d. unknown**
1932 OG-M POL 1 0 0 0 0 —

**Maunula, Henrik / b. Mar. 8, 1987**
2005 WM18 FIN 6 0 2 2 8 —

**Mautin, Francois / b. May 9, 1907 / d. unknown**
1928 OG-M FRA — — — — — —

**Maximenko, Andrei / b. Oct. 13, 1981**
1999 WM18 RUS 7 0 1 1 29 —

**Maxwell, Ben / b. Mar. 30, 1988**
2006 WM18 CAN 7 2 5 7 10 —

**Maxwell, Brad / b. July 8, 1957**
1978-82 WM CAN 22 3 1 4 30 2B

**Maxwell, Kevin / b. Mar. 30, 1960**
1980 OG-M CAN 6 0 5 5 4 —

**May, Brad / b. Nov. 29, 1971**
1991 WM20 CAN 3 1 0 1 2 G
1996 WM CAN 8 0 0 0 6 S

**Mayasich, John / b. May 22, 1933**
1958-69 WM USA 42 16 13 29 10 B
1956-60 OG-M USA 14 14 8 22 4 G,S
~IIHF Hall of Fame
~WM IIHF Directorate Best Defenceman (1962)

**Mayer, Alois / b. unknown**
1959 WM FRG 5 1 0 1 0 —

**Mayer, Derek / b. May 21, 1967**
1993-96 WM CAN 16 1 1 2 4 S
1994 OG-M CAN 8 1 2 3 18 S

**Mayer, Hans-Jorg / b. Nov. 17, 1972**
1992 WM20 GER 7 2 3 5 4 —

**Mayer, Oliver / b. May 24, 1972**
1992 WM20 GER 7 0 0 0 10 —

**Mayer, Stefan / b. Aug. 11, 1975**
1998 WM GER 6 0 2 2 4 —

**Mayes, Harry / b. unknown / d. unknown**
1934 WM GBR 6 0 0 0 — —

**Maynart, Bruno / b. Feb. 25, 1971**
1993 WM FRA 6 0 0 0 0 —

**Mayor, Didier / b. unknown**
1978 WM20 SUI 6 1 1 2 0 —

**Mayorov, Boris / b. Feb. 11, 1938**
1961-67 WM URS 35 19 24 43 23 4G,B
1964-68 OG-M URS 14 8 7 15 2 2G
~IIHF Hall of Fame
~WM All-Star Team/Forward (1961)

**Mayorov, Yevgeni / b. Feb. 11, 1938 / d. Dec. 10, 1997**
1961-63 WM URS 14 7 6 13 8 G,B
1964 OG-M URS 5 2 2 4 0 G

**Mayr, Jorg / b. Jan. 3, 1970**
1988-89 WM20 FRG 14 1 3 4 24 —
1991-2001 WM GER 30 1 3 4 18 —
1992-2002 OG-M GER 17 1 2 3 2 —

**Maznyak, Alexander / b. Mar. 17, 1985**
2003 WM18 KAZ 6 0 2 2 8 —

**Mazunin, Yevgeni / b. Sept. 18, 1981**
2000-01 WM20 KAZ 13 1 1 2 8 —
2004-06 WM KAZ 15 0 0 0 20 —

**Mazza, Alain / b. Oct. 14, 1948**
1968 OG-M FRA 5 2 1 3 16 —

**Mazzoleni, Fausto / b. Nov. 15, 1960**
1980 WM20 SUI 4 2 1 3 0 —
1987 WM SUI 10 0 0 0 8 —
1988 OG-M SUI 6 3 0 3 2 —

**McAlpine, Scotty / b. unknown / d. unknown**
1933 WM CAN 4 0 — 0 0 S

**McAmmond, Dean / b. June 15, 1973**
1993 WM20 CAN 7 0 1 1 12 G
1996-2000 WM CAN 16 0 2 2 2 S

**McAvoy, George / b. June 21, 1931**
1955 WM CAN 8 3 0 3 14 G

**McBain, Andrew / b. Jan. 18, 1965**
1989 WM CAN 10 6 2 8 8 S

**McBain, Jason / b. Apr. 12, 1974**
1994 WM20 USA 7 1 1 2 10 —
1995 WM USA 6 0 1 1 4 —

**McBain, Mike / b. Jan. 12, 1977**
1996-97 WM20 USA 11 0 2 2 8 S

**McBean, Wayne / b. Feb. 21, 1969**
1988 WM20 CAN 7 1 0 1 2 G

**McCabe, Bryan / b. June 8, 1975**
1994-95 WM20 CAN 14 3 9 12 10 2G
1997-99 WM CAN 27 2 7 9 24 G
2006 OG-M CAN 6 0 0 0 18 —
~WM20 IIHF Directorate Best Defenceman (1995), WM20 All-Star Team/Defence (1995)

**McCaffery, Bert / b. Apr. 12, 1893 / d. 1955**
1924 OG-M CAN 5 20 — 20 0 G

**McCallum, Sammy / b. June 1899 / d. unknown**
1931 WM CAN 6 1 — 1 — G

**McCann, Rick / b. May 27, 1944**
1966 WM CAN 2 0 0 0 2 B

**McCardy, Russ / b. unknown**
1963 WM USA 7 0 1 1 6 —

**McCarthy, Charlie / b. unknown**
1963 WM USA 7 0 1 1 2 —

**McCarthy, Jeremiah / b. Mar. 1, 1976**
1996 WM20 USA 6 2 1 3 2 —

**McCarthy, Justin / b. Jan. 25, 1899 / d. Apr. 8, 1976**
1924 OG-M USA 5 8 — 8 0 S

**McCarthy, Steve / b. Feb. 3, 1981**
2000-01 WM20 CAN 14 1 3 4 6 2B

**McCauley, Alyn / b. May 29, 1977**
1996-97 WM20 CAN 13 2 8 10 4 2G

**McClanahan, Rob / b. Jan. 9, 1958**
1979 WM USA 8 1 2 3 6 —
1981 CC USA 6 0 0 0 2 —
1980 OG-M USA 7 5 3 8 2 G

**McClement, Jay / b. Mar. 2, 1983**
2002-03 WM20 CAN 13 2 3 5 6 2S
2007 WM CAN 9 2 2 4 4 G

**McCloskey, Kevin / b. May 13, 1957**
1977 WM20 USA 7 0 1 1 18 —

**McConnell, Brian / b. Feb. 1, 1983**
2001 WM18 USA 6 3 3 6 8 —
2003 WM20 USA 7 1 1 2 0 —

**McCormick, Joe / b. Aug. 12, 1894 / d. June 14, 1958**
1920 OG-M USA 3 8 — 8 5 S

**McCormick, Larry / b. July 12, 1890 / d. unknown**
1920 OG-M USA 1 7 — 7 0 S

**McCourt, Dale / b. Jan. 26, 1957**
1977 WM20 CAN 7 10 8 18 14 S
1979-81 WM CAN 12 1 3 4 8 —
~WM20 IIHF Directorate Best Forward (1977), WM20 All-Star Team/Forward (1977)

**McCoy, Jim / b. Jan. 2, 1942**
1964 OG-M USA 4 0 0 0 0 —

**McCrady, Scott / b. Oct. 30, 1968**
1988 WM20 CAN 7 0 1 1 8 G

**McCrae, Dave / b. Feb. 29, 1932**
1950-51 WM GBR 9 3 0 3 2 —

**McCreedy, John / b. Feb. 23, 1911 / d. unknown**
1939 WM CAN 8 3 — 3 — G

**McCrimmon, Brad / b. Mar. 29, 1959**
1978-79 WM20 CAN 11 1 4 5 6 B
~perished in Yaroslavl plane crash

**McDonald, Andy / b. Aug. 25, 1977**
2002 WM CAN 7 4 1 5 0 —

**McDonald, Jack / b. Aug. 26, 1932**
1955 WM CAN 8 6 1 7 6 G

**McDonald, Lanny / b. Aug. 26, 1932**
1981 WM CAN 8 3 0 3 4 —
1976 CC CAN 5 0 2 2 0 1st

**McDonald, Sam / b. 1934**
1962 WM GBR 7 1 2 3 0 —

**McDonnell, Kent / b. Mar. 1, 1979**
1999 WM20 CAN 7 1 1 2 4 S

**McDonough, Ryan / b. Jan. 2, 1988**
2006 WM18 CAN 7 0 0 0 14 —

**McDougal, Mike / b. Apr. 30, 1958**
1978 WM20 USA 6 3 5 8 10 —

**McEachern, Shawn / b. Feb. 28, 1969**
1991 WM USA 10 3 2 5 6 —
1996 WCH USA 1 0 1 1 0 1st
1992 OG-M USA 8 1 0 1 10 —

**McElmury, Jim / b. Oct. 3, 1949**
1971-77 WM USA 20 4 3 7 12 —
1972 OG-M USA 5 0 1 1 6 S

**McEwen, Doug / b. Oct. 2, 1963**
1994 WM GBR 6 1 2 3 0 —

**McFall, Dan / b. Apr. 8, 1963**
1982-83 WM20 USA 14 2 0 2 10 —

**McGillis, Dan / b. July 1, 1972**
2002 WM CAN 5 0 1 1 2 —

**McGinn, Jamie / b. Sept. 5, 1988**
2006 WM18 CAN 7 2 1 3 10 —

**McGlynn, Dick / b. June 19, 1948**
1971 WM USA 1 0 0 0 0 —
1972 OG-M USA 5 0 0 0 2 S

**McGowan, Cal / b. June 19, 1970**
1995 WM USA 6 1 3 4 6 —

**McGrath, Evan / b. Jan. 14, 1986**
2004 WM18 CAN 7 1 1 2 4 —

**McInnis, Marty / b. June 2, 1970**
1996-97 WM USA 15 2 4 6 6 B
1992 OG-M USA 8 5 2 7 4 —

**McInroy, Tommy / b. June 3, 1917 / d. unknown**
1939 WM GBR 5 2 — 2 — —

**McIntyre, Clare / b. Feb. 1909 / d. unknown**
1933 WM CAN 5 4 — 4 0 G

**McIntyre, Hugh "Pinoke" / b. 1934**
1961-63 WM CAN 11 8 5 13 6 G

**McIntyre, Jack / b. Oct. 15, 1926**
1955 WM CAN 8 8 8 16 4 G

**McIntyre, John / b. unknown**
1950 WM USA 7 7 1 8 0 S

**McIntyre, John / b. Apr. 29, 1969**
1989 WM20 CAN 7 1 0 1 4 —

**McIntyre, Ross / b. unknown**
1947 WM USA 6 5 — 5 — —

**McKechnie, Walt / b. June 19, 1947**
1977 WM CAN 10 1 6 7 28 —

**McKegney, Tony / b. Feb. 15, 1958**
1978 WM20 CAN 6 2 6 8 0 B

**McKim, Andrew / b. July 6, 1970**
1995 WM CAN 8 6 7 13 4 B

**McKinch, Jack / b. May 7, 1958**
1978 WM20 USA 6 0 1 1 0 —

**McKinnon, Dan / b. Apr. 21, 1922 / d. unknown**
1955-58 WM USA 12 4 0 4 6 —
1956 OG-M USA 6 1 1 2 4 S

**McKnight, Bob / b. Mar. 19, 1938**
1962-63 WM CAN 14 4 4 8 0 S
1960 OG-M CAN 2 2 2 4 2 S

**McLaren, Kyle / b. June 18, 1977**
2001 WM CAN 7 0 2 2 2 —

**McLean, Brett / b. Aug. 14, 1978**
1998 WM20 CAN 7 1 1 2 4 —

**McLean, Don / b. Oct. 6, 1926 / d. Aug. 23, 2009**
1951 WM CAN 5 5 — 5 6 G

**McLellan, John / b. Aug. 6, 1928 / d. Oct. 27, 1979**
1959 WM CAN 8 4 6 10 10 G

**McLeod, Jack / b. Apr. 30, 1930**
1961-66 WM CAN 28 30 17 47 22 G,S,B
~IIHF Hall of Fame
~WM All-Star Team/Forward (1962)

**McLlwain, Dave / b. Jan. 9, 1967**
1987 WM20 CAN 6 4 4 8 2 —

**McMunn, Harold / b. Oct. 6, 1902 / d. Feb. 5, 1964**
1924 OG-M CAN 5 5 — 5 0 G

**McNab, Peter / b. May 8, 1952**
1986 WM USA 10 0 1 1 2 —

**McNamara, Jim / b. Mar. 19, 1982**
2000 WM18 USA 6 0 0 0 0 —

**McNeill, Mike / b. July 22, 1966**
1991 WM USA 10 1 0 1 4 —

**McPhail, Paul / b. Jan. 8, 1915 / d. unknown**
1937 WM GBR 3 1 1 2 2 S

**McQuade, Norm / b. 1911 / d. unknown**
1937 WM GBR 6 3 2 5 0 S

**McReavy, Pat / b. Jan. 16, 1918 / d. Nov. 13, 2001**
1938 WM CAN 7 2 — 2 — G

**McSween, Don / b. June 9, 1964**
1994 WM USA 8 1 1 2 0 —

**McVey, Bob / b. Mar. 14, 1936**
1960 OG-M USA 6 2 4 6 12 G

**McVey, Ward / b. July 25, 1900 / d. Feb. 14, 1967**
1931 WM CAN 6 1 — 1 — G

**Meciar, Stanislav / b. Oct. 14, 1963**
1994 WM CZE 6 0 0 0 4 —

**Medicus, Dieter / b. Apr. 7, 1957**
1977 WM20 FRG 7 1 0 1 28 —
1983-87 WM FRG 17 1 1 2 12 —
1984 CC FRG 2 0 0 0 2 —
1988 OG-M FRG 7 0 0 0 0 —

**Medri, Giampiero / b. Mar. 17, 1909 / d. unknown**
1933-34 WM ITA 5 0 0 0 0 —

**Medrik, Stanislav / b. Apr. 4, 1966**
1985-86 WM20 TCH 14 0 2 2 14 S
1991-97 WM SVK 22 2 1 3 4 —
1996 WCH SVK 1 0 0 0 0 —
1994 OG-M SVK 8 0 0 0 4 —

**Medvedev, Dmitri / b. Jan. 12, 1967**
1987 WM20 URS 6 1 0 1 2 —

**Medvedev, Mikhail / b. Jan. 1, 1979**
1998-99 WM20 KAZ 13 4 0 4 4 —

**Meech, Derek / b. Apr. 21, 1984**
2004 WM20 CAN 6 0 1 1 2 S

**Meerkamper, Emil / b. unknown / d. unknown**
1933 WM SUI 6 0 — 0 4 —

**Meier, Daniel / b. Jan. 13, 1972**
1991-92 WM20 SUI 13 2 1 3 2 —

**Meier, Dominic / b. Dec. 26, 1976**
1996 WM20 SUI 6 0 0 0 18 —

**Meier, Marcel / b. Apr. 3, 1961**
1980 WM20 SUI 5 0 0 0 0 —

**Meier, Peter / b. Oct. 2, 1967**
1987 WM20 SUI 3 0 0 0 0 —

**Meijer, Sebastian / b. Sept. 1, 1984**
2002 WM18 SWE 8 3 5 8 2 —
2004 WM20 SWE 6 2 0 2 0 —

**Meindl, Horst / b. Feb. 6, 1946**
1967 WM FRG 7 0 0 0 2 —
1968 OG-M FRG 7 0 4 4 2 —

**Meitinger, Holger / b. Mar. 28, 1957**
1977 WM20 FRG 7 5 4 9 4 —
1979-83 WM FRG 33 13 14 27 18 —
1984 CC FRG 5 2 2 4 0 —
1980 OG-M FRG 5 0 2 2 20 —

**Meixner, Jaromir / b. Mar. 11, 1940**
1965-66 WM TCH 11 0 3 3 0 2S

**Melametsa, Anssi / b. June 21, 1961**
1980-81 WM20 FIN 10 1 7 8 6 2S
1983-85 WM FIN 20 8 5 13 30 —
1984 OG-M FIN 6 4 3 7 10 —

**Melenovsky, Marek / b. Mar. 3, 1977**
1996-97 WM20 CZE 13 5 3 8 4 —

**Melgaard, Svein / b. Mar. 16, 1982**
1999 WM18 NOR 2 0 0 0 0 —

**Meliakov, Igor / b. Dec. 23, 1976**
1995-96 WM20 RUS 14 7 7 14 8 S,B

**Melicharek, Tibor / b. Jan. 21, 1976**
2007-08 WM SVK 11 1 0 1 2 —

**Melin, Bjorn / b. July 4, 1981**
1999 WM18 SWE 3 1 2 3 2 S
2000-01 WM20 SWE 14 2 3 5 14 —
2006 WM SWE 6 0 2 2 0 G

**Melinder, Henrik / b. Jan. 6, 1979**
1999 WM20 SWE 6 0 0 0 4 —

**Melischko, Christoph / b. July 25, 1983**
2001 WM18 GER 6 0 1 1 2 —

**Mellanby, Scott / b. June 11, 1966**
1986 WM20 CAN 7 5 4 9 6 S

**Melland, Neville / b. Apr. 3, 1904 / d. Dec. 1990**
1930-34 WM GBR 10 3 0 3 — —
1928 OG-M GBR — 0 — 0 — —

**Mellor, Tom / b. Jan. 27, 1950**
1971 WM USA 10 1 3 4 2 —
1972 OG-M USA 5 0 0 0 2 S

**Melnyk, Larry / b. Feb. 21, 1960**
1979 WM20 CAN 5 1 1 2 2 —

**Meluzin, Roman / b. June 17, 1972**
1991-92 WM20 TCH 13 1 4 5 6 B
1995-99 WM CZE 28 3 3 6 2 2G

**Melynchuk, Gerry / b. unknown**
1967 WM USA 7 3 0 3 2 —

**Menardi, Dino / b. Aug. 23, 1923**
1948 OG-M ITA 4 0 — 0 — —

**Menauer, Josef / b. May 10, 1983**
2003 WM20 GER 6 0 2 2 2 —

**Mende, Karsten / b. Jan. 14, 1968**
1993 WM GER 6 0 2 2 2 —

**Mendel, Rob / b. Sept. 19, 1968**
1988 WM20 USA 7 1 1 2 4 —

**Meng, Heini / b. Nov. 20, 1902 / d. unknown**
1930 WM SUI 3 1 — 1 — B
1928 OG-M SUI 3 1 — 1 4 B

**Menge, Daniel / b. Jan. 14, 1983**
2001 WM18 GER 6 1 0 1 0 —
2003 WM20 GER 6 0 0 0 0 —

**Mengshoel, Lars Petter / b. Apr. 6, 1988**
2006 WM18 NOR 6 1 2 3 — —

**Mercier, Justin / b. June 25, 1987**
2005 WM18 USA 6 0 1 1 29 G

**Meredith, Dick / b. Dec. 22, 1932**
1958-59 WM USA 15 8 5 13 6 —
1956-60 OG-M USA 9 4 4 8 2 G,S

**Meredith, Wayne / b. Oct. 4, 1939**
1964 OG-M USA 4 0 0 0 8 —

**Merrick, Wayne / b. Apr. 23, 1952**
1977 WM CAN 10 4 3 7 10 —

**Merta, Jerzy / b. May 23, 1967**
1987 WM20 POL 7 3 1 4 2 —

**Mertl, Tomas / b. Mar. 11, 1986**
2004 WM18 CZE 1 0 0 0 0 B

**Mertzig, Jan / b. July 18, 1970**
1998 WM SWE 4 0 0 0 0 G

**Meserve, Reg / b. July 14, 1934**
1962 WM USA 7 5 6 11 8 B

**Mesikammen, Ilkka / b. Mar. 15, 1943**
1963-67 WM FIN 26 1 0 1 28 —
1964 OG-M FIN 7 0 0 0 0 —

**Messa, Peter / b. Sept. 19, 1980**
2000 WM20 SWE 7 2 2 4 14 —

**Messier, Mark / b. Jan. 18, 1961**
1989 WM CAN 6 3 3 6 8 S
1984-96 WCH CAN 32 6 20 26 36 3/1st,2nd

**Metcalfe, Scott / b. Jan. 6, 1967**
1987 WM20 CAN 6 2 5 7 12 —

**Metlicka, Josef / b. June 29, 1962**
1980 WM20 TCH 5 3 0 3 0 —

**Metlyuk, Denis / b. Jan. 30, 1972**
1992 WM20 RUS 7 5 2 7 4 G

**Metrailler, Cedric / b. Apr. 26, 1982**
2000 WM18 SUI 7 1 1 2 4 —

**Metropolit, Glen / b. June 25, 1974**
2006 WM CAN 9 0 2 2 6 —

**Metsaranta, Matias / b. June 18, 1981**
1999 WM18 FIN 7 0 1 1 2 G

**Metz, Stefan / b. Oct. 15, 1951**
1976 OG-M FRG 5 0 0 0 0 B

**Metzen, Dave / b. unknown**
1967 WM USA 7 0 0 0 2 —

**Meyer, Andreas / b. Oct. 20, 1954**
1976 OG-M SUI 5 0 1 1 4 —

**Meyer, David / b. unknown / d. unknown**
1930 WM BEL 1 0 — 0 — —
1928 OG-M BEL 3 1 — 1 — —

**Meyer, Dennis / b. Sept. 23, 1977**
1997 WM20 GER 6 0 1 1 2 —

**Meyer, Freddy / b. Jan. 4, 1981**
1999 WM18 USA 6 2 2 4 8 —
2001 WM20 USA 7 0 2 2 10 —
2006 WM USA 7 0 0 0 6 —

**Meyer, Jayson / b. Feb. 21, 1965**
1993-96 WM GER 22 2 1 3 16 —
1996 WCH GER 4 0 1 1 2 —
1994 OG-M GER 8 0 1 1 8 —

**Meyer, Thomas / b. Oct. 20, 1962**
1982 WM20 SUI 7 0 0 0 0 —

**Meyers, Bob / b. Aug. 11, 1924**
1952 OG-M CAN 2 2 0 2 0 G

**Miadzel, Ivan / b. Apr. 5, 1986**
2004 WM18 BLR 6 0 0 3 24 —

**Mialeshka, Dmitri / b. Nov. 8, 1982**
2000 WM18 BLR 6 0 0 0 4 —
2001-02 WM20 BLR 12 4 1 5 4 —

**Michalek, Jan / b. July 21, 1905 / d. unknown**
1933-39 WM TCH 25 0 0 0 6 2B

**Michalik, Wladyslaw / b. Mar. 28, 1911 / d. June 26, 2001**
1938-39 WM POL 7 0 — 0 — —

**Michaud, Dick / b. unknown**
1963 WM USA 7 1 0 1 12 —

**Micheletti, Joe / b. Oct. 24, 1954**
1977-82 WM USA 15 0 5 5 10 —

**Micheli, Claudio / b. Dec. 17, 1970**
1998-2000 WM SUI 16 0 3 3 0 —

**Micheller, Klaus / b. Apr. 20, 1967**
1986 WM20 FRG 7 0 3 3 20 —
1998 WM GER 6 0 1 1 4 —

**Micka, Tomas / b. June 7, 1983**
2001 WM18 CZE 7 1 2 3 0 —
2003 WM20 CZE 6 0 0 0 0 —

**Middendorf, Max / b. Aug. 18, 1967**
1986 WM20 USA 7 2 2 4 4 B

**Middleton, Jim / b. unknown**
1955 WM CAN 4 0 0 0 4 G

**Middleton, Rick / b. Dec. 4, 1953**
1981-84 CC CAN 14 5 6 11 0 1st,2nd

**Midsather, Oddvar / b. unknown**
1959 WM NOR 8 0 0 0 12 —

**Midttun, Teddy / b. May 16, 1984**
2002 WM18 NOR 8 2 0 2 16 —

**Mielonen, Juho / b. Mar. 1, 1987**
2005 WM18 FIN 6 1 1 2 4 —

**Mieszkowski, Tomasz / b. Apr. 9, 1972**
2002 WM POL 6 0 0 0 6 —

**Miettinen, Antti-Jussi / b. Mar. 30, 1983**
2001 WM18 FIN 5 0 1 1 2 B

**Miettinen, Tommi / b. Dec. 3, 1975**
1994-95 WM20 FIN 14 4 9 13 6 —

**Migacz, Bogdan / b. May 28, 1948 / d. June 18, 1998**
1970 WM POL 8 2 2 4 0 —

**Migliore, Lodovico / b. Dec. 27, 1956**
1983 WM ITA 10 0 0 0 4 —
1984 OG-M ITA 5 0 2 2 2 —

**Mihailescu, Dan / b. July 2, 1945**
1964 OG-M ROM 4 0 — 0 — —

**Mihalik, Tomas / b. Jan. 15, 1981**
1999 WM18 SVK 7 0 1 1 2 B

**Miikkulainen, Jarno / b. Nov. 2, 1972**
1992 WM20 FIN 3 0 0 0 0 —

**Mika, Petr / b. Feb. 12, 1979**
1999 WM20 CZE 6 6 1 7 2 —

**Mikalunas (Sarnasto), Romeo / b. July 5, 1916 / d. unknown**
1939 WM FIN 3 0 — 0 — —

**Mikesch, Pat / b. Feb. 15, 1973**
1993 WM20 USA 7 1 1 2 2 —

**Mikhailov, Boris / b. Oct. 6, 1944**
1969-79 WM URS 105 98 66 164 56 8G,2S,B
1972 SS URS 8 3 2 5 9 2nd
1972-80 OG-M URS 15 10 6 16 4 2G,S
~IIHF Hall of Fame
~WM IIHF Directorate Best Forward (1973), WM All-Star Team/Forward (1973, 1979)

**Mikhailov, Nikolai / b. Feb. 19, 1948**
1976 OG-M BUL 3 1 1 2 4 —

**Mikhailov, Valeri / b. Mar. 20, 1960**
1980 WM20 URS 5 0 3 3 4 G

**Mikhailov, Vladimir / b. Jan. 4, 1989**
2006 WM18 BLR 6 1 5 6 18 —

**Mikhailov, Yegor / b. July 23, 1978**
1998 WM20 RUS 7 0 1 1 2 S

**Mikhnov, Alexei / b. Aug. 31, 1982**
2006 WM RUS 7 4 2 6 2 —

**Mikhnov, Andri / b. Nov. 26, 1983**
2006 WM UKR 6 2 0 2 2 —

**Mikita, Stan / b. May 20, 1940**
1972 SS CAN 2 0 1 1 0 1st

**Mikkelsen, Arne / b. July 23, 1934**
1965 WM NOR 7 0 2 2 2 —
1968-72 OG-M NOR 9 4 3 7 10 —

**Mikkelson, Brendan / b. June 22, 1987**
2005 WM18 CAN 6 0 2 2 0 S

**Mikko, Roger / b. Sept. 7, 1957**
1977 WM20 SWE 7 3 3 6 2 —

**Mikkola, Ilkka / b. Jan. 18, 1979**
1997-99 WM20 FIN 19 1 6 7 35 G

**Mikkola, Niko / b. Jan. 9, 1974**
1994 WM20 FIN 6 2 1 3 6 —

**Mikkolainen, Reijo / b. May 14, 1964**
1987-90 WM FIN 20 3 1 4 10 S
1988 OG-M FIN 8 4 1 5 10 S

**Mikkonen, Tuomas / b. Mar. 25, 1983**
2003 WM20 FIN 7 0 2 2 0 B

**Miklos, Sandor / b. Mar. 5, 1915 / d. 1981**
1931-39 WM HUN 37 26 0 26 2 —
1936 OG-M HUN 6 8 — 8 — —

**Miklos, Tiberiu / b. Apr. 2, 1954**
1977 WM ROM 10 0 0 0 0 —
1976 OG-M ROM 5 0 1 1 0 —

**Mikolasek, Tomas / b. Dec. 24, 1971**
1991 WM20 TCH 1 0 2 2 2 B

**Mikulchik, Oleg / b. June 27, 1964**
1984 WM20 URS 7 0 3 3 2 G
1998-2005 WM BLR 24 0 2 2 22 —
2002 OG-M BLR 9 1 0 1 14 —

**Milani, Tom / b. Apr. 13, 1952**
1982-83 WM ITA 17 5 1 6 14 —
1984 OG-M ITA 5 1 2 3 2 —

**Milbury, Mike / b. June 17, 1952**
1976 CC USA 5 1 3 4 16 —

**Mild, Hans / b. July 31, 1934/ d. Dec. 23, 2007**
1959-63 WM SWE 22 9 6 15 10 S
1964 OG-M SWE 3 0 0 0 2 S
~WM All-Star Team/Forward (1963)

**Millen, Corey / b. Mar. 30, 1964**
1982 WM20 USA 7 2 4 6 4 —
1985 WM USA 10 3 1 4 10 —
1987 CC USA 1 1 0 1 0 —
1984-88 OG-M USA 12 6 5 11 6 —

**Miller, Aaron / b. Aug. 11, 1971**
1991 WM20 USA 8 1 1 2 0 —
2004-05 WM USA 16 0 3 3 10 B
2004 WCH USA 5 0 0 0 4 —
2002 OG-M USA 6 0 0 0 4 S

**Miller, Art / b. unknown**
1967 WM USA 6 1 2 3 2 —

**Miller, Bob / b. Sept. 28, 1956**
1977-85 WM USA 35 14 14 28 16 —
1981 CC USA 6 0 1 1 6 —
1976 OG-M USA 5 0 1 1 0 —

**Miller, Bryan / b. Feb. 17, 1983**
2001 WM18 USA 6 1 2 3 4 —

**Miller, David / b. Dec. 15, 1925 / d. Oct. 8, 1996**
1952 OG-M CAN 8 11 0 11 2 G

**Miller, Ed / b. unknown**
1958 WM USA 7 0 1 1 4 —

**Miller, Kelly / b. Mar. 3, 1963**
1981-83 WM20 USA 17 2 5 7 0 —
1985-99 WM USA 25 4 8 12 6 —
1987 CC USA 5 0 0 0 0 —

**Miller, Kevin / b. Sept. 2, 1965**
1991-2003 WM USA 20 3 8 11 43 —
1991 CC USA 8 2 3 5 16 2nd
1988 OG-M USA 5 1 3 4 4 —

**Miller, Kip / b. June 11, 1969**
1988 WM20 USA 7 2 2 4 2 —
1990 WM USA 9 1 1 2 10 —

**Miller, Kris / b. Mar. 30, 1969**
1988 WM20 USA 7 0 1 1 4 —

**Miller, Paul / b. Aug. 21, 1959**
1977 WM20 USA 7 6 0 6 12 —
1982 WM USA 4 0 0 0 0 —

**Miller, Warren / b. Jan. 1, 1954**
1977-81 WM USA 17 5 4 9 6 —
1981 CC USA 6 2 0 2 2 —

**Mills, Barry / b. Mar. 21, 1961**
1980 WM20 USA 1 0 0 0 0 —

**Mills, Craig / b. Aug. 27, 1976**
1996 WM20 CAN 6 0 0 0 4 G

**Milne, John / b. unknown**
1962 WM GBR 1 0 0 0 0 —

**Milo, Dusan / b. Mar. 5, 1973**
2002-06 WM SVK 25 6 6 12 12 G,B
2002 OG-M SVK 2 0 2 2 2 —

**Milroy, Andrew "Nap" / b. unknown**
1951 WM CAN 2 1 — 1 0 G

**Milton, Kjell-Rune / b. May 26, 1948**
1969-75 WM SWE 43 5 5 10 16 2S,3B
1972 OG-M SWE 3 0 0 0 2 —

**Milton, Ray / b. Aug. 27, 1912 / d. Sept. 17, 2003**
1936 OG-M CAN 2 0 0 0 0 S

**Mimochodek, Karel / b. Jan. 4, 1968**
1988 WM20 TCH 6 0 2 2 6 —

**Minder, Sandor / b. Oct. 25, 1907 / d. May 17, 1983**
1930-33 WM HUN 11 5 — 5 — —
1928-36 OG-M HUN 9 3 — 3 — —

**Miner, John / b. Aug. 28, 1965**
1985 WM20 CAN 7 0 2 2 12 G

**Minge, Leszek / b. Jan. 19, 1958**
1977 WM20 POL 7 1 1 2 2 —

**Mintchev, Bojidar / b. Aug. 1, 1946**
1976 OG-M BUL 5 2 1 3 0 —

**Mion, Giuseppe / b. Apr. 9, 1959**
1984 OG-M AUT 5 0 0 0 2 —

**Mironov, Boris / b. Mar. 21, 1972**
1991-92 WM20 URS 13 2 5 7 29 G,S
1996 WM RUS 8 1 4 5 12 —
1998-2002 OG-M RUS 12 1 2 3 12 S,B

**Mironov, Dmitri / b. Dec. 25, 1965**
1991-2000 WM RUS 22 5 3 8 12 B
1991 CC URS 5 0 1 1 4 —
1992-98 OG-M RUS 14 3 4 7 6 G,S
~OG-M All-Star Team/Defence (1992)

**Miroshnichenko, Sergei / b. June 21, 1979**
1999 WM20 KAZ 6 1 0 1 6 —

**Misawa, Satoru / b. June 25, 1943**
1980 OG-M JPN 5 1 2 3 0 —

**Misek, Petr / b. Mar. 23, 1959**
1981 WM TCH 8 1 0 1 6 B

**Mishakov, Yevgeni / b. Feb. 22, 1941 / d. May 30, 2007**
1967-72 WM URS 28 23 6 29 14 4G,S
1972 SS URS 6 0 0 0 11 2nd
1968-72 OG-M URS 11 6 2 8 4 2G

**Misharin, Georgi / b. May 11, 1985**
2003 WM18 RUS 6 0 2 2 2 B
2005 WM20 RUS 6 1 1 2 6 S
2006 WM RUS 3 0 1 1 4 —

**Mishler, Todd / b. Apr. 11, 1959**
1979 WM20 USA 5 1 0 1 4 —

**Miskovich, Aaron / b. Apr. 28, 1978**
1998 WM20 USA 7 1 0 1 0 —

**Misterka, Janusz / b. Jan. 9, 1970**
1990 WM20 POL 7 1 0 1 8 —

**Misura, Matej / b. Feb. 16, 1989**
2007 WM18 SVK 6 1 1 2 4 —

**Mitchell, Bill / b. Feb. 22, 1930**
1962 WM CAN 7 0 1 1 22 S

**Mitchell, Jeff / b. May 16, 1975**
1995 WM20 USA 7 0 0 0 4 —

**Mitchell, Jimmy / b. Feb. 13, 1925**
1951 WM GBR 6 0 — 0 4 —

**Miura, Hiroyuki / b. Dec. 31, 1973**
1993 WM20 JPN 7 1 0 1 10 —
1998-2004 WM JPN 19 0 2 2 22 —
1998 OG-M JPN 4 0 0 0 4 —

**Miura, Takayuki / b. Mar. 25, 1967**
1998 WM JPN 3 0 0 0 2 —
1998 OG-M JPN 4 0 0 0 2 —

**Miwa, Robert / b. May 12, 1970**
2002-04 WM JPN 12 1 0 1 2 —

**Miyauchi, Fumitaka / b. Nov. 6, 1972**
1998-2004 WM JPN 24 1 1 2 8 —

**Miyazaki, Naruhiro / b. unknown**
1957 WM JPN 7 0 — 0 2 —

**Miyazaki, Yoshihiro / b. May 10, 1930**
1960 OG-M JPN 6 2 1 3 10 —

**Mizera, Frantisek / b. Aug. 23, 1919 / d. unknown**
1949 WM TCH 4 1 — 1 — G

**Mlakar, Janez / b. May 31, 1944**
1968 OG-M YUG 5 1 2 3 6 —

**Mlinarec, Drago / b. Aug. 24, 1960**
1984 OG-M YUG 5 0 1 1 12 —

**Mloian, Artur / b. Mar. 17, 1981**
1999 WM18 UKR 6 1 2 3 0 —

**Moberg, Jonathan / b. Jan. 3, 1987**
2005 WM18 DEN 6 0 0 0 2 —

**Moc, Miroslav / b. 1959**
1978 WM20 TCH 6 1 0 1 2 —

**Modano, Mike / b. June 7, 1970**
1988-89 WM20 USA 14 10 10 20 20 —
1990-2005 WM USA 21 6 4 10 8 —
1991-2004 WCH USA 20 4 17 21 6 1st,2nd
1998-2006 OG-M USA 16 4 6 10 10 S

**Modes, Werner / b. Sept. 12, 1949**
1971 WM FRG 9 1 1 2 8 —
1972 OG-M FRG 4 1 0 1 0 —

**Modin, Fredrik / b. Oct. 8, 1974**
1994 WM20 SWE 7 2 2 4 2 S
1996-2001 WM SWE 27 10 7 10 20 G,B
2004 WCH SWE 4 4 4 8 2 —
2006-10 OG SWE 11 2 2 4 6 G
~Triple Gold Club

**Modry, Jaroslav / b. Feb. 27, 1971**
1991 WM20 TCH 6 0 1 1 2 B
2003 WM CZE 9 0 3 3 4 —

**Moe, Per / b. unknown**
1949-62 WM NOR 22 0 2 2 2 —

**Mogilny, Alexander / b. Feb. 18, 1969**
1987-89 WM20 URS 20 19 16 35 10 G,S
1989 WM URS 10 0 3 3 2 G
1996 WCH RUS 5 2 4 6 0 —
1988 OG-M URS 6 3 2 5 2 G
~Triple Gold Club
~WM20 IIHF Directorate Best Forward (1988), WM20 All-Star Team/Forward (1988)

**Mois, Aurel / b. Aug. 29, 1948**
1968 OG-M ROM 5 2 0 2 2 —

**Moiseyev, Yuri / b. July 15, 1940 / d. Sept. 23, 2005**
1968 OG-M URS 7 2 4 6 6 G

**Mokhov, Stepan / b. Jan. 22, 1981**
1999 WM18 RUS 7 1 1 2 6 —

**Molander, Nils / b. June 22, 1889 / d. Jan. 30, 1974**
1920-24 OG-M SWE 9 9 — 9 2 —

**Molberg, Patrik / b. June 16, 1988**
2006 WM18 NOR 6 1 1 2 6 —

**Molberg, Rune / b. Nov. 21, 1952**
1980 OG-M NOR 5 1 2 3 8 —

**Molgaard, Lars / b. Dec. 31, 1971**
2003 WM DEN 6 1 1 2 4 —

**Molin, Johan / b. Oct. 25, 1976**
1996 WM20 SWE 7 3 0 3 0 S

**Molin, Lars / b. May 7, 1956**
1981-87 WM SWE 22 4 5 9 14 G,S
1981 CC SWE 5 2 2 4 0 —
1980-88 OG-M SWE 14 2 7 9 4 2B

**Molin, Ove / b. May 27, 1971**
1991 WM20 SWE 5 0 4 4 0 —
1999 WM SWE 10 0 0 0 6 B

**Mollard, Aug.e / b. unknown / d. unknown**
1931 WM FRA 5 0 — 0 — —

**Moller, Fredrik / b. Dec. 16, 1976**
1996 WM20 SWE 7 0 0 0 2 S

**Moller, Mads / b. Feb. 14, 1982**
2005-07 WM DEN 12 0 0 0 2 —

**Moller, Mike / b. June 16, 1962**
1982 WM20 CAN 7 5 9 14 4 G
~WM20 All-Star Team/Forward (1982)

**Moller, Randy / b. Aug. 23, 1963**
1982 WM20 CAN 7 0 3 3 4 G

**Molling, Jochen / b. Aug. 9, 1973**
1993 WM20 GER 7 0 0 0 8 —
1997-2004 WM GER 30 0 1 1 18 —
1998 OG-M GER 4 0 0 0 4 —

**Molmy, Wilfried / b. Nov. 11, 1982**
2002 WM20 FRA 6 0 0 0 2 —

**Molteni, Andrea / b. Dec. 5, 1980**
2006 WM ITA 6 0 1 1 0 —

**Monard, Joseph / b. Feb. 11, 1901 / d. Feb. 3, 1973**
1924 OG-M FRA 1 0 — 0 0 —

**Monayenkov, Igor / b. Jan. 14, 1967**
1986-87 WM20 URS 13 2 0 2 10 G

**Monberg, Nicolas / b. Sept. 22, 1980**
2003-05 WM DEN 18 0 0 0 10 —

**Mondt, Niki / b. Aug. 9, 1978**
1996-98 WM20 GER 17 3 3 6 16 —

**Monitzer, Rudolf / b. unknown**
1957 WM AUT 7 4 0 4 — —

**Monji, Akira / b. unknown**
1957 WM JPN 4 0 — 0 — —

**Mononen, Erkki / b. May 29, 1943**
1966-71 WM FIN 13 1 3 4 4 —

**Mononen, Lauri / b. Mar. 22, 1950**
1969-75 WM FIN 51 21 18 39 35 —
1972 OG-M FIN 4 3 0 3 6 —

**Monson, Walter / b. Nov. 29, 1908 / d. Jan. 9, 1988**
1932 OG-M CAN 6 7 3 10 3 G

**Montandon, Gil / b. Apr. 28, 1965**
1987-93 WM SUI 33 5 5 10 16 —
1988-92 OG-M SUI 11 1 2 3 6 —

**Monteith, Steve / b. Sept. 21, 1943**
1968 OG-M CAN 7 1 0 1 0 B

**Montemurro, Carlo / b.Apr. 18, 1934**
1956 OG-M ITA 6 2 0 2 18 —

**Moore, Grant / b. Apr. 30, 1943**
1965 WM CAN 6 1 0 1 0 —

**Moore, Gregg / b. Mar. 26, 1984**
2002 WM18 USA 8 4 4 8 4 G
2003-04 WM20 USA 13 0 3 3 2 G

**Moore, Greg / b. Apr. 12, 1961**
1981 WM20 USA 4 0 0 0 0 —

**Moore, Ken / b. Feb. 17, 1910 / d. Dec. 1982**
1932 OG-M CAN 1 1 0 1 0 G

**Moran, Ian / b. Aug. 24, 1972**
1991 WM20 USA 6 0 2 2 2 —
1993 WM USA 6 0 0 0 0 —

**Moravec, David / b. Mar. 24, 1973**
1997-2002 WM CZE 46 5 9 14 34 2G,2B
1998 OG-M CZE 6 0 1 1 2 G
~WM MVP (2001)

**Morawiecki, Jaroslaw / b. Mar. 11, 1964**
1986 WM POL 10 1 2 3 0 —
1988 OG-M POL 3 2 1 3 0 —

**Morczinietz, Andreas / b. Mar. 11, 1978**
1996-98 WM20 GER 12 3 4 7 2 —
2002-05 WM GER 23 6 4 10 14 —
2002 OG-M GER 3 0 2 2 0 —

**Moreau, Albert / b. unknown**
1951 WM USA 6 2 — 2 0 —

**Morger, Hans / b. unknown**
1955 WM SUI 5 1 0 1 0 —

**Morin, George / b. unknown**
1951 WM USA 4 0 — 0 2 —

**Morin, Linus / b. Jan. 30, 1987**
2005 WM18 SWE 7 0 1 1 2 B

**Moris, Jacques / b. July 7, 1924 / d. unknown**
1950 WM BEL 3 3 1 4 0 —

**Morisset, Dave / b. Apr. 6, 1981**
2001 WM20 CAN 7 0 1 1 18 B

**Morocco, Rick / b. Feb. 14, 1963**
1992 OG-M ITA 7 2 1 3 6 —

**Morosan, Doru / b. May 15, 1953**
1977 WM ROM 10 0 0 0 2 —
1976-80 OG-M ROM 10 0 2 2 0 —

**Morosani, Anton / b. June 20, 1907 / d. Mar. 1993**
1928 OG-M SUI 4 1 — 1 — B

**Morozov, Andrei / b. Feb. 16, 1977**
1980 WM20 URS 5 0 0 0 0 G

**Morozov, Igor / b. Feb. 14, 1961**
1980 WM20 URS 5 0 0 0 0 G

**Morozov, Valentin / b. June 1, 1975**
1995 WM20 RUS 7 3 4 7 4 S

**Morris, Derek / b. Aug. 24, 1978**
1999-2004 WM CAN 26 1 10 11 47 G

**Morris, Frank / b. 1904 / d. unknown**
1931 WM CAN 6 6 — 6 — G

**Morris, Frank / b. Mar. 22, 1963**
1994 WM GBR 6 0 0 0 8 —

**Morris, Jim / b. 1912 / d. unknown**
1939 WM CAN 7 7 — 7 — G

**Morris, Jon / b. May 6, 1966**
1995 WM USA 6 3 5 8 4 —

**Morrison, Brendan / b. Aug. 15, 1975**
2000-05 WM CAN 25 6 9 15 18 G,S

**Morrison, Dave / b. June 12, 1962**
1982 WM20 CAN 7 1 2 3 0 G

**Morrison, John / b. Apr. 6, 1945**
1968 OG-M USA 7 2 6 8 10 —

**Morrison, Justin / b. Aug. 10, 1979**
1999 WM20 USA 6 3 2 5 2 —

**Morrison, Mark / b. Mar. 11, 1963**
1982-83 WM20 CAN 14 6 9 15 0 G,B

**Morrison, Scott / b. Aug. 12, 1964**
1994 WM GBR 4 0 1 1 4 —

**Morrow, Brad / b. July 15, 1954**
1976 WM USA 10 1 2 3 7 —

**Morrow, Ken / b. Oct. 17, 1956**
1978 WM USA 6 0 0 0 0 —
1981 CC USA 6 0 0 0 6 —
1980 OG-M USA 7 1 2 3 6 G

**Mortas, Anthony / b. Feb. 13, 1974**
1997-2004 WM FRA 26 1 0 1 6 —
1998-2002 OG-M FRA 8 0 2 2 2 —

**Morth, Tommy / b. July 16, 1959**
1979 WM20 SWE 6 2 2 4 4 B
1982-83 WM SWE 20 2 3 5 10 —
1984 OG-M SWE 6 1 2 3 2 B

**Mortl, Herbert / b. Nov. 4, 1948**
1976 OG-M AUT 5 3 1 4 0 —

**Morz, Jochen / b. May 6, 1957**
1981-82 WM FRG 15 0 0 0 2 —

**Mosebach, Matthias / b. Jan. 1, 1974**
1993 WM20 GER 7 0 1 1 2 —

**Moser, Marcel / b. Jan. 4, 1983**
2001 WM18 SUI 3 0 1 1 4 S

**Moser, Max / b. Sept. 24, 1949**
1976 OG-M AUT 5 2 2 4 8 —

**Moser, Peter / b. June 15, 1962**
1982 WM20 SUI 7 5 1 6 12 —

**Moser, Simon / b. Mar. 10, 1989**
2007 WM18 SUI 6 0 1 1 4 —

**Moskal, Patrik / b. Jan. 11, 1981**
1999 WM18 CZE 7 2 0 2 0 —
2001 WM20 CZE 7 1 1 2 0 G

**Mosnar, Miroslav / b. Aug. 10, 1968**
1998 OG-M SVK 3 0 0 0 6 —

**Mossmer, Eduard / b. Feb. 21, 1934**
1964 OG-M AUT 3 0 1 1 0 —

**Mossmer, Hans / b. Mar. 22, 1932**
1956 OG-M AUT 6 0 0 0 2 —

**Mossmer, Josef / b. Mar. 15, 1943**
1968 OG-M AUT 5 0 0 0 6 —

**Motkov, Dmitri / b. Feb. 23, 1971**
1991 WM20 URS 7 0 2 2 16 S

**Mott, Morris / b. May 25, 1946**
1966-69 WM CAN 24 9 3 12 8 2B
1968 OG-M CAN 7 5 1 6 2 B

**Mottau, Mike / b. Mar. 19, 1978**
1998 WM20 USA 7 2 2 4 4 —
1999-2003 WM USA 16 2 3 5 0 —

**Mottier, Ernest / b. Apr. 16, 1891 / d. unknown**
1924 OG-M SUI 3 0 — 0 — —

**Mouther, Michel / b. Jan. 10, 1978**
1997-98 WM20 SUI 13 1 4 5 18 B

**Mowers, Mark / b. Feb. 16, 1974**
2002 WM USA 7 1 2 3 4 —

**Moylan, Dave / b. Aug. 13, 1967**
1986 WM20 CAN 7 1 2 3 0 S

**Moyon, Christophe / b. May 12, 1963**
1994 WM FRA 5 0 1 1 2 —
1994 OG-M FRA 7 0 0 0 0 —

**Mozheiko, Dmitri / b. Apr. 2, 1976**
1995-96 WM20 UKR 13 0 0 0 4 —

**Mracka, Daniel / b. Jan. 12, 1984**
2002 WM18 SVK 8 2 1 3 8 —

**Mrazek, Frantisek / b. May 16, 1979**
1999 WM20 CZE 6 0 2 2 6 —

**Mrena, Jozef / b. May 2, 1980**
2000 WM20 SVK 7 0 0 0 0 —

**Mroz, Ryszard / b. Mar. 17, 1965**
1985 WM20 POL 7 1 0 1 2 —

**Mrozek, Michel / b. unknown**
1950 WM FRA 3 0 0 0 2 —

**Mucha, Jan / b. Jan. 11, 1984**
2002 WM18 SVK 8 0 0 0 4 —

**Mucha, Lukas / b. Mar. 26, 1985**
2003 WM18 SVK 7 0 0 0 2 S

**Mucke, Andre / b. Jan. 27, 1983**
2001 WM18 GER 6 0 1 1 2 —

**Mudroch, Petr / b. Oct. 12, 1978**
1997-98 WM20 CZE 14 0 2 2 12 —

**Mudry, Oscar / b. unknown**
1953 WM SUI 1 0 0 0 0 B

**Mudryi, Sergiy / b. Feb. 25, 1980**
2000 WM20 UKR 7 0 0 0 4 —

**Mueller, Brian / b. June 2, 1972**
1992 WM20 USA 7 0 0 0 0 B

**Mueller, Patrick / b. Feb. 20, 1965**
1984 WM20 SUI 6 0 1 1 0 —

**Mueller, Thomas / b. Mar. 26, 1964**
1984 WM20 SUI 7 4 1 5 4 —
1987 WM SUI 4 0 1 1 2 —

**Muhle, Ole Andre / b. June 25, 1986**
2004 WM18 NOR 6 1 1 2 6 —

**Muhlhausen, Hans / b. 1958**
1977 WM20 FRG 7 0 0 0 0 —

**Muhr, Manfred / b. May 31, 1967**
1993-96 WM AUT 26 6 2 8 20 —
1988-94 OG-M AUT 13 0 0 0 12 —

**Mukhanov, Olexander / b. May 17, 1976**
1995-96 WM20 UKR 8 1 0 1 8 —

**Mukhin, Yevgeni / b. Jan. 14, 1968**
1988 WM20 URS 7 1 0 1 8 S

**Mulhern, Jack / b. July 18, 1927 / d. Sept. 19, 2007**
1952 OG-M USA 8 5 1 6 — S

**Mulholland, R.D. / b. unknown / d. unknown**
1930 WM GBR 1 1 0 1 — —

**Mullen, Brian / b. Mar. 16, 1962**
1980-81 WM20 USA 10 2 5 7 6 —
1989-91 WM USA 20 6 7 13 10 —
1984 CC USA 4 0 0 0 0 —

**Mullen, Joe / b. Feb. 26, 1957**
1979 WM USA 8 7 1 8 2 —
1984-91 CC USA 19 6 6 12 2 2nd

**Muller, Gerhard / b. Aug. 15, 1954**
1974-83 WM GDR 37 5 4 9 39 —

**Muller, Hubert / b. Mar. 12, 1956**
1979 WM FRG 4 0 0 0 0 —

**Muller, Kirk / b. Feb. 8, 1966**
1984 WM20 CAN 7 2 1 3 16 —
1985-89 WM CAN 37 14 9 23 40 2S,B
1984 OG-M CAN 6 2 1 3 0 —

**Muller, Laurent / b. May 28, 1978**
1996-98 WM20 SUI 18 4 6 10 8 B
1999 WM SUI 4 0 0 0 2 —

**Muller, Marco / b. July 26, 1960**
1980 WM20 SUI 5 2 1 3 4 —
1987 WM SUI 6 1 0 1 4 —

**Muller, Martin / b. Apr. 27, 1958**
1978 WM20 FRG 6 4 2 6 4 —

**Muller, Paul / b. Feb. 20, 1896 / d. unknown**
1924 OG-M SUI 3 0 — 0 — —

**Muller, Pascal / b. Apr. 10, 1979**
1999 WM20 SUI 6 0 0 0 14 —

**Muller, Peter / b. unknown / d. unknown**
1933-35 WM SUI 20 5 — 5 0 S

**Muller, Yves / b. Feb. 8, 1989**
2007 WM18 SUI 6 0 4 4 4 —

**Mullernders, Jacques / b. Oct. 1, 1917 / d. unknown**
1947 WM BEL 7 0 — 0 — —

**Munck, Jari / b. Feb. 1, 1962**
1980-82 WM20 FIN 17 0 5 5 14 2S,B

**Munro, Dunc / b. Jan. 19, 1901 / d. Jan. 3, 1958**
1924 OG-M CAN 5 17 — 17 1 G

**Munroe, Don / b. unknown**
1949 WM CAN 6 10 — 10 — S

**Muntz, Charles / b. unknown / d. unknown**
1930-31 WM FRA 7 2 — 2 — —

**Murakami, Hiroyuki / b. Jan. 14, 1971**
1999-2001 WM JPN 9 0 0 0 20 —

**Murano, Masao / b. July 31, 1935**
1960 OG-M JPN 4 1 1 2 4 —

**Muratov, Yevgeni / b. Jan. 28, 1981**
2000-01 WM20 RUS 14 8 5 13 6 —
~WM20 All-Star Team/Forward (2000)

**Murdoch, Bob / b. Nov. 20, 1946**
1969 WM CAN 6 0 0 0 2 —

**Murphy, Cory / b. Feb. 13, 1978**
2007 WM CAN 9 1 6 7 8 G

**Murphy, Gord / b. Mar. 23, 1967**
1998 WM CAN 6 1 0 1 2 —

**Murphy, Joe / b. Oct. 16, 1967**
1986 WM20 CAN 7 4 10 14 2 S

**Murphy, Larry / b. Mar. 8, 1961**
1980 WM20 CAN 5 1 0 1 4 —
1985-2000 WM CAN 17 2 9 11 8 S
1987-91 CC CAN 16 1 7 8 4 2/1st

**Murphy, Mark / b. Aug. 6, 1976**
2002 WM USA 7 2 0 2 6 —

**Murphy, Mike / b. Sept. 12, 1950**
1978 WM CAN 10 1 4 5 16 B

**Murphy, Rob / b. Apr. 7, 1969**
1989 WM20 CAN 7 1 0 1 8 —

**Murphy, Ryan / b. Mar. 21, 1979**
1999 WM20 USA 5 1 2 3 2 —

**Murphy, Ryan / b. Jan. 23, 1983**
2001 WM18 USA 6 1 3 4 2 —

**Murphy, Steve / b. Mar. 1, 1961**
1979 WM20 USA 5 2 1 3 0 —

**Murray, Brady / b. Aug. 17, 1984**
2004 WM20 USA 6 2 0 2 0 G

**Murray, Garth / b. Sept. 17, 1982**
2002 WM20 CAN 7 3 3 6 12 S

**Murray, Glen / b. Nov. 1, 1972**
1998-2004 WM CAN 14 3 4 7 8 G

**Murray, Herman / b. Dec. 5, 1909 / d. unknown**
1936 OG-M CAN 8 5 0 5 2 S

**Murray, John / b. Jan. 27, 1924 / d. unknown**
1950-62 WM GBR 10 1 1 2 0 —
1948 OG-M GBR 6 1 — 1 — —

**Murray, Marty / b. Feb. 16, 1975**
1994-95 WM20 CAN 14 7 12 19 4 2G
~WM20 IIHF Directorate Best Forward (1995), WM20 All-Star Team/Forward (1995)

**Murray, Raymond "Rem" / b. Oct. 9, 1972**
2001 WM CAN 7 1 3 4 2 —

**Murray, Robert / b. Oct. 17, 1951**
1978-81 WM FRG 23 2 1 3 26 —

**Murray, Troy / b. July 31, 1962**
1982 WM20 CAN 7 4 4 8 6 G
1987 WM CAN 10 2 2 4 14 —

**Murto, Matti / b. Feb. 9, 1949**
1970-76 WM FIN 58 15 9 24 18 —
1972-76 OG-M FIN 10 4 2 6 4 —

**Musatov, Vadim / b. Apr. 17, 1967**
1987 WM20 URS 6 0 0 0 12 —

**Musial, Wojciech / b. Mar. 2, 1966**
1985 WM20 POL 7 0 1 1 0 —

**Musil, Frantisek / b. Dec. 17, 1964**
1982-84 WM20 TCH 20 1 5 6 26 2S,B
1983-94 WM TCH 43 6 5 11 106 G,S,B
1984-91 CC TCH 10 0 1 1 10 —
~WM All-Star Team/Defence (1992), WM20 All-Star Team/Defence (1984)

**Muske, Karlis / b. May 16, 1921 / d. unknown**
1939 WM LAT 3 0 — 0 — —

**Mussi, Camillo / b. Nov. 18, 1911 / d. unknown**
1933-35 WM ITA 18 3 1 4 0 —
1936 OG-M ITA 3 0 0 0 — —

**Mustala, Mikko / b. Apr. 12, 1965**
1985 WM20 FIN 7 0 1 1 0 —

**Mustonen, Tom / b. unknown**
1963 WM USA 7 5 3 8 0 —

**Mustonen, Tomi / b. May 31, 1983**
2001 WM18 FIN 6 3 1 4 2 B

**Mustonen, Toni / b. Apr. 29, 1982**
2000 WM18 FIN 7 1 0 1 0 G
2001 WM20 FIN 7 1 0 1 2 S

**Myhre, Geir / b. Apr. 7, 1954**
1980-84 OG-M NOR 10 12 6 8 26 —

**Myles, Gord / b. Nov. 27, 1931**
1958 WM CAN 2 3 1 4 0 G

**Myrra, Jouko / b. Mar. 20, 1969**
1989 WM20 FIN 7 0 1 1 0 —

**Naatanen, Matti / b. July 17, 1983**
2003 WM20 FIN 6 0 1 1 0 B

**Nabokov, Dmitri / b. Jan. 4, 1977**
1996 WM20 RUS 7 3 5 8 4 B

**Nadasdi, Tomas / b. May 14, 1980**
1999 WM20 SVK 6 0 0 0 2 B

**Nadzon, Ivan / b. Jan. 5, 1984**
2004 WM20 UKR 6 0 0 0 4 —

**Naef, Fritz / b. June 5, 1934**
1955-62 WM SUI 12 8 3 11 0 —
1956 OG-M SUI 5 6 2 8 4 —

**Nagel, Lars Peder / b. Feb. 25, 1981**
1999 WM18 NOR 6 0 0 0 0 —
2006 WM NOR 6 0 0 0 4 —

**Nagruzov, Sergiy / b. Aug. 22, 1984**
2001-02 WM18 UKR 14 0 0 0 12 —

**Nagy, Adalbert / b. Feb. 3, 1933**
1964 OG-M ROM 5 0 1 1 0 —

**Nagy, Bela / b. Dec. 18, 1957**
1980 OG-M ROM 5 0 0 0 6 —

**Nagy, Gergo / b. Oct. 10, 1989**
2009 WM HUN 3 0 0 0 0 —

**Nagy, Istvan / b. June 1, 1979**
1999 WM20 SVK 6 4 3 7 6 B

**Nagy, Zoltan / b. Aug. 19, 1955**
1980 OG-M ROM 5 0 0 0 0 —

**Nakajimaya, Yujiro / b. Feb. 16, 1971**
1999 WM JPN 3 1 0 1 2 —

**Nakamura, Hitoshi / b. Apr. 29, 1949**
1976-80 OG-M JPN 10 1 0 1 18 —

**Nakano, Minoru / b. Oct. 18, 1936**
1964 OG-M JPN 7 0 0 0 7 —

**Nakayama, Iwao / b. July 2, 1949**
1972-80 OG-M JPN 14 0 1 1 4 —

**Namestnikov, Yevgeni / b. Oct. 9, 1971**
1990-91 WM20 URS 14 1 1 2 16 2S

**Nanne, Lou / b. June 2, 1941**
1976-77 WM USA 20 3 5 8 45 —
1976 CC USA 5 0 2 2 6 —
1968 OG-M USA 7 2 2 4 12 —
~IIHF Hall of Fame

**Nanne, Marty / b. July 21, 1967**
1987 WM20 USA 7 1 1 2 6 —

**Nanzen, Tord / b. Aug. 23, 1954**
1979 WM SWE 7 0 0 0 2 B

**Napier, Mark / b. Jan. 28, 1957**
1982 WM CAN 9 3 1 4 0 B

**Nappila, Jarkko / b. July 6, 1988**
2006 WM18 FIN 6 0 0 0 6 S

**Nardella, Bob / b. Feb. 2, 1968**
1995-97 WM ITA 17 5 6 11 16 —
1998-2006 OG-M ITA 9 0 3 3 12 —

**Narimanov, Nikolai / b. Apr. 10, 1958**
1977-78 WM20 URS 14 6 6 12 22 2G

**Narvanmaa, Jouko / b. Sept. 10, 1962**
1985-89 WM FIN 15 1 3 4 14 —
1987 CC FIN 1 0 0 0 0 —

**Narvestad, Johan / b. unknown / d. unknown**
1937-38 WM NOR 4 0 0 0 2 —

**Nasheim, Rick / b. Jan. 15, 1963**
1993-99 WM AUT 32 6 4 10 16 —
1994-98 OG-M AUT 9 1 1 2 4 —

**Nasibullen, Lotfi / b. May 13, 1926**
1949-51 WM FIN 10 3 — 3 4 —

**Naslund, Fredrik / b. Sept. 15, 1986**
2004 WM18 SWE 6 0 1 1 4 —

**Naslund, Markus / b. July 30, 1973**
1992-93 WM20 SWE 14 21 13 34 45 2S
1993-2002 WM SWE 22 8 7 15 30 S,2B
1996-2004 WCH SWE 5 0 3 3 2 —
2002 OG-M SWE 4 2 1 3 0 —
~WM20 All-Star Team/Forward (1993)

**Naslund, Mats / b. Oct. 31, 1959**
1977-79 WM20 SWE 20 7 10 17 26 S,B
1979-91 WM SWE 46 13 18 31 22 G,S,B
1984-91 CC SWE 20 4 8 12 8 2nd
1980-94 OG-M SWE 23 4 19 23 33 G,B
~IIHF Hall of Fame/Triple Gold Club

**Naslund, Ron / b. Feb. 28, 1943**
1966-69 WM USA 24 4 2 6 16 —
1972 OG-M USA 5 1 1 2 2 S

**Naster, Mario / b. Dec. 11, 1965**
1985-91 WM GDR 12 0 1 1 4 —

**Nathe, Bryan / b. Feb. 8, 1983**
2000-01 WM18 USA 10 0 0 0 0 —

**Nattress, Ric / b. May 25, 1962**
1991 WM CAN 7 0 1 1 4 S

**Naumann, Andreas / b. Sept. 22, 1972**
1992 WM20 GER 7 1 0 1 2 —

**Naumenko, Dmytro / b. Apr. 23, 1986**
2002 WM18 UKR 8 0 0 0 0 —

**Naurov, Alexander / b. Mar. 4, 1985**
2003 WM18 RUS 6 3 2 5 2 B

**Navarenko, Yuriy / b. Sept. 10, 1979**
2006-07 WM UKR 12 1 2 3 76 —

**Navrat, Zdenek / b. May 25, 1931**
1956 OG-M TCH 7 3 2 5 0 —

**Navratil, Milan / b. Feb. 11, 1974**
1994 WM20 CZE 7 1 2 3 2 —

**Nazarov, Andrei / b. May 22, 1974**
1998 WM RUS 6 1 2 3 10 —

**Neaton, Pat / b. May 21, 1971**
1991 WM20 USA 8 4 2 6 6 —
1994-95 WM USA 12 3 0 3 20 —

**Neckar, Stanislav / b. Dec. 22, 1975**
1993 WM20 TCH 7 2 0 2 6 B
1996 WM CZE 8 1 3 4 2 G
1996 WCH CZE 3 0 0 0 0 —

**Nedoma, Milan / b. Mar. 29, 1972**
1992 WM20 TCH 7 0 4 4 6 —

**Nedomansky, Vaclav / b. Mar. 14, 1944**
1965-74 WM TCH 80 65 27 92 51 G,4S,3B
1968-72 OG-M TCH 12 11 5 16 4 S,B
~IIHF Hall of Fame
~WM IIHF Directorate Best Forward (1974), WM All-Star Team/Forward (1969, 1970, 1974)

**Nedorost, Andrei / b. Apr. 30, 1980**
2001 WM SVK 4 0 0 0 4 —

**Nedorost, David / b. Mar. 22, 1981**
1999 WM18 CZE 7 2 1 3 6 —

**Nedorost, Vaclav / b. Mar. 16, 1982**
2000 WM18 CZE 6 4 1 5 0 —
2000-01 WM20 CZE 14 4 6 10 6 2G

**Nedved, Zdenek / b. Mar. 3, 1975**
1994-95 WM20 CZE 14 8 7 15 20 —

**Needham, Mike / b. Mar. 25, 1970**
1990 WM20 CAN 7 3 4 7 2 G

**Neff, Claudio / b. July 10, 1981**
1999 WM18 SUI 7 0 1 1 0 —
2001 WM20 SUI 7 0 2 2 4 —

**Negrello, Hec / b. 1922 / d. unknown**
1951 WM CAN 6 5 — 5 0 G

**Negrin, John / b. Mar. 25, 1989**
2007 WM18 CAN 6 0 1 1 2 —

**Neil, Lawson / b. Mar. 24, 1930**
1950-51 WM GBR 13 3 2 5 4 —

**Neininger, Bernhard / b. Oct. 19, 1955**
1976 OG-M SUI 5 2 0 2 6 —

**Neininger, Toni / b. Aug. 8, 1950**
1972 WM SUI 10 2 1 3 4 —
1972-76 OG-M SUI 9 6 2 8 6 —

**Neliba, Jan / b. Sept. 5, 1953**
1981 WM TCH 6 0 0 0 6 B
1981 CC TCH 2 0 0 0 2 —
1980 OG-M TCH 6 0 1 1 2 —

**Nelson, Francis / b. Jan. 24, 1910 / d. Mar. 9, 1973**
1931 WM USA 1 0 — 0 — S
1932 OG-M USA 5 1 1 2 2 S

**Nelson, Jeff / b. Dec. 18, 1972**
1992 WM20 CAN 7 1 1 2 2 —

**Nelson, Levi / b. Apr. 28, 1988**
2006 WM18 CAN 7 0 0 0 10 —

**Nemcek, Martin / b. Feb. 10, 1978**
1998 WM20 SVK 6 0 1 1 4 —

**Nemchinov, Sergei / b. Jan. 14, 1964**
1983-84 WM20 URS 14 9 9 18 4 2G
1989-98 WM RUS 33 9 6 15 16 2G,B
1987-96 WCH RUS 10 1 2 3 8 2nd
1998 OG-M RUS 6 1 0 1 0 S

**Nemcicky, Roman / b. Sept. 14, 1968**
1987-88 WM20 TCH 12 0 4 4 2 S

**Nemcicky, Tomas / b. Mar. 27, 1973**
1993 WM20 TCH 7 3 0 3 8 B

**Nemcok, Martin / b. Aug. 5, 1984**
2002 WM18 SVK 8 0 0 0 2 —

**Nemec, Oldrich / b. July 16, 1922 / d. unknown**
1949 WM TCH 7 0 — 0 — G

**Nemec, Vladimir / b. Nov. 3, 1978**
1998 WM20 SVK 6 1 4 5 0 —

**Nemecek, Jan / b. Jan. 14, 1976**
1996 WM20 CZE 6 1 2 3 2 —

**Nemeth, Steve / b. Feb. 11, 1967**
1987 WM20 CAN 6 4 4 8 4 —

**Nemirka, Konstantin / b. Apr. 11, 1983**
2000 WM18 BLR 3 1 0 1 0 —
2001-02 WM20 BLR 12 0 1 1 0 —

**Nenov, Miltcho / b. Dec. 19, 1957**
1976 OG-M BUL 5 3 1 4 2 —

**Nentwich, Miro / b. Mar. 24, 1959**
1978-79 WM20 FRG 11 2 1 3 2 —

**Nepryayev, Ivan / b. Feb. 4, 1982**
2001-02 WM20 RUS 14 1 7 8 26 G
2005-07 WM RUS 15 1 3 4 12 2B
2006 OG-M RUS 2 0 0 0 2 —

**Nerell, Erik / b. Jan. 29, 1964**
1983 WM20 NOR 7 0 0 0 0 —
1984 OG-M NOR 5 0 0 0 0 —

**Nervik, Alexander / b. July 3, 1979**
2007 WM NOR 6 0 0 0 4 —

**Nesbitt, Ivor / b. July 1, 1910 / d. unknown**
1934 WM GBR 2 0 — 0 — —

**Netik, Tomas / b. Apr. 28, 1982**
2000 WM18 CZE 6 1 1 2 0 —

**Neubauer, Jiri / b. May 18, 1947**
1974 WM TCH 9 0 1 1 4 S

**Neuenschwander, Caryl / b. Jan. 16, 1984**
2002 WM18 SUI 8 3 6 9 0 —
2003 WM20 SUI 6 3 0 3 2 —

**Neuenschwander, Philipp / b. Dec. 29, 1964**
1984 WM20 SUI 7 2 3 5 2 —
1988 OG-M SUI 6 0 3 3 2 —

**Neumaier, Lambert / b. Feb. 13, 1910 / d. unknown**
1933 WM AUT 2 0 — 0 0 —
1936 OG-M AUT 2 0 — 0 — —

**Neumann, Jon / b. unknown**
1983 WM20 NOR 6 0 0 0 0 —

**Neuwirth, Theo / b. Dec. 15, 1940**
1964 OG-M AUT 5 0 — 0 — —

**Nevalainen, Unto / b. June 13, 1935**
1959 WM FIN 5 0 0 0 2 —

**Neville, Dave / b. May 2, 1908 / d. Oct. 14. 1991**
1936 OG-M CAN 8 9 3 12 6 S

**Nevstruyev, Sergei / b. Aug. 29, 1972**
2004 WM KAZ 3 0 0 0 4 —

**Newkirk, John / b. unknown**
1959 WM USA 8 1 0 1 16 —

**Newsome, Ab / b. unknown**
1950 WM CAN 7 10 7 17 2 G

**Nicholas, John / b. May 2, 1936**
1960 OG-M AUS 6 0 0 0 16 —

**Nicholls, Bernie / b. June 24, 1961**
1985 WM CAN 10 0 2 2 12 S

**Nicholson, Ed / b. unknown / d. unknown**
1939 WM USA 9 2 — 2 — S

**Nicholson, Ken / b. Sept. 20, 1922 / d. unknown**
1950-51 WM GBR 13 8 7 15 0 —

**Nickel, Hartmut / b. Nov. 16, 1944**
1970-74 WM GDR 20 2 4 6 6 —
1968 OG-M GDR 7 0 0 0 2 —

**Nickel, Wolfgang / b. Mar. 19, 1929**
1957 WM GDR 7 2 0 2 — —

**Nicklasson, Dan / b. Sept. 10, 1961**
1981 WM20 SWE 3 0 0 0 0 G

**Niederberger, Andreas / b. Apr. 20, 1963**
1981-83 WM20 FRG 17 1 4 5 4 —
1985-95 WM GER 78 5 19 24 48 —
1984 CC FRG 5 1 0 1 2 —
1984-94 OG-M GER 29 0 4 4 12 —

**Niederer, Marcel / b. Sept. 9, 1960**
1980 WM20 SUI 5 2 0 2 8 —

**Niederhausen, Patrice / b. Feb. 28, 1964**
1984 WM20 SUI 7 0 1 1 0 —

**Niedermayer, Rob / b. Dec. 28, 1974**
1993 WM20 CAN 7 0 2 2 2 G
1999-2004 WM CAN 19 4 5 9 30 G

**Niedermayer, Scott / b. Aug. 31, 1973**
1991-92 WM20 CAN 14 0 0 0 10 G
2004 WM CAN 9 3 2 5 12 G
1996-2004 WCH CAN 14 2 4 6 15 1st,2nd
2002-10 OG-M CAN 13 2 3 5 8 2G
~Triple Gold Club
~WM20 All-Star Team/Defence (1992)

**Niedospial, Zbigniew / b. Jan. 23, 1968**
1987-88 WM20 POL 14 3 0 3 10 —

**Niedziolka, Krzysztof / b. Feb. 9, 1969**
1988 WM20 POL 5 0 0 0 6 —

**Niedzwiedz, Czeslaw / b. Mar. 22, 1969**
1988 WM20 POL 7 0 0 0 0 —

**Nielsen, Bernard / b. unknown**
1965 WM USA 7 0 2 2 6 —

**Nielsen, Chris / b. Feb. 16, 1980**
2000 WM20 CAN 7 3 0 3 8 B

**Nielsen, Esben / b. June 4, 1986**
2004 WM18 DEN 6 0 0 0 4 —

**Nielsen, Jeff / b. Sept. 20, 1971**
2000 WM USA 7 1 1 2 2 —

**Nielsen, Jens / b. Oct. 23, 1969**
2003-07 WM DEN 23 2 7 9 16 —

**Nielsen, Jesper / b. May 14, 1987**
2005 WM18 DEN 6 0 0 0 4 —

**Nielsen, Ole / b. unknown**
1949 WM DEN 3 0 — 0 — —

**Nielsen, Poul / b. unknown**
1949 WM DEN 3 0 — 0 — —

**Nielsen, Ragnar / b. unknown**
1958 WM NOR 6 0 0 0 2 —

**Niemi, Marcus / b. Apr. 11, 1986**
2004 WM18 SWE 6 2 0 2 2 —

**Nieminen, Lasse / b. Aug. 29, 1966**
1986 WM20 FIN 7 2 4 6 0 —

**Nieminen, Mika / b. Jan. 1, 1966**
1991-97 WM FIN 54 22 22 44 22 G,2S
1996 WCH FIN 4 2 0 2 2 —
1992-98 OG-M FIN 21 8 13 21 8 2B

**Nieminen, Pertti / b. Dec. 9, 1936**
1957-62 WM FIN 35 6 1 7 41 —
1960 OG-M FIN 6 8 2 10 8 —

**Nieminen, Ville / b. Apr. 6, 1977**
1997 WM20 FIN 6 2 5 7 2 —
2004 WCH FIN 2 0 0 0 0 2nd
2002-06 OG-M FIN 12 0 2 2 6 S

**Nienhuis, Kraig / b. May 9, 1961**
1996 WM AUT 6 0 0 0 12 —

**Niess, Dieter / b. Mar. 19, 1926**
1953 WM FRG 3 1 1 2 0 S
1952 OG-M FRG 8 0 1 1 — —

**Nieuwendyk, Joe / b. Sept. 10, 1966**
1986 WM20 CAN 7 5 7 12 6 S
1990 WM CAN 1 0 0 0 0 —
1998-2002 OG-M CAN 12 3 4 7 2 G

**Niggli, Stefan / b. May 8, 1981**
1999 WM18 SUI 7 2 1 3 4 —
2000-01 WM20 SUI 14 1 1 2 6 —

**Nigro, Frank / b. Feb. 11, 1960**
1992 OG-M ITA 7 0 3 3 6 —

**Nihei, Taro / b. Mar. 9, 1971**
2000-02 WM JPN 18 2 3 5 4 —

**Niinimaki, Jesse / b. Aug. 19, 1983**
2003 WM20 FIN 7 1 3 4 0 B

**Nikander, Harry / b. June 18, 1957**
1977 WM20 FIN 7 0 1 1 8 —
1986 WM FIN 7 0 0 0 8 —

**Nikiforov, Viktor / b. Dec. 4, 1931**
1956 OG-M URS 1 0 0 0 0 G

**Nikitenko, Andrei / b. Jan. 13, 1979**
1999 WM20 RUS 7 0 5 5 2 G

**Nikitin, Igor / b. Mar. 23, 1973**
1985-86 WM20 URS 14 0 5 5 10 G,B
1998 WM KAZ 3 0 0 0 0 —
1998 OG-M KAZ 7 1 0 1 6 —

**Nikitin, Igor / b. Mar. 9, 1987**
2005 WM18 RUS 6 0 0 0 6 —

**Nikitin, Valeri / b. June 20, 1939**
1957 WM URS 7 0 4 4 4 S

**Nikitin, Valeri / b. June 20, 1939**
1967-70 WM URS 16 1 9 10 4 2G

**Nikkila, Seppo / b. Dec. 23, 1936**
1962-65 WM FIN 20 8 7 15 6 —
1964 OG-M FIN 6 2 1 3 0 —

**Nikko, Janne / b. June 7, 1974**
1992-94 WM20 FIN 21 0 1 1 10 —

**Nikkolainen, Reijo / b. May 14, 1964**
1984 WM20 FIN 7 2 2 4 0 S

**Nikolayev, Andri / b. Sept. 18, 1972**
2003 WM UKR 6 0 0 0 2 —

**Nikolishin, Andrei / b. Mar. 25, 1973**
1992 WM20 RUS 7 1 2 3 2 G
1993-2000 WM RUS 31 3 7 10 28 G
1996 WCH RUS 4 1 3 4 4 —
1994-2002 OG-M RUS 14 2 6 8 12 B

**Nikolov, Angel / b. Nov. 18, 1975**
1995 WM20 CZE 7 1 0 1 6 —

**Nikonov, Yuri / b. Mar. 28, 1966**
1986 WM20 URS 7 1 3 4 0 G

**Nilan, Chris / b. Feb. 9, 1958**
1987 CC USA 5 2 0 2 14 —

**Nill, Jim / b. Apr. 11, 1958**
1980 OG-M CAN 6 1 2 3 4 —

**Nilon, Bob / b. June 24, 1914 / d. unknown**
1934 WM USA 4 2 1 3 — S

**Nilsen, Johnny / b. Jan. 27, 1975**
1995-2006 WM NOR 20 0 1 1 12 —

**Nilsen, Morten / b. Aug. 15, 1984**
2002 WM18 NOR 8 0 0 0 6 —

**Nilsen, Nils / b. Dec. 29, 1952**
1980 OG-M NOR 5 0 1 1 2 —

**Nilsen, Sjur / b. Dec. 3, 1967**
1994-2000 WM NOR 36 2 3 5 40 —

**Nilson, Patrik / b. May 18, 1981**
1999 WM18 SWE 7 1 1 2 4 S

**Nilsson, Axel / b. Nov. 12, 1904 / d. unknown**
1937-38 WM SWE 8 0 0 0 0 —

**Nilsson, Birger / b. Mar. 30, 1921 / d. unknown**
1947 WM SWE 2 5 — 5 — S

**Nilsson, Eric / b. Feb. 4, 1983**
2001 WM18 SWE 6 0 1 1 0 —

**Nilsson, Fredrik / b. Apr. 16, 1971**
1990-91 WM20 SWE 12 3 1 4 16 —
1996 WCH SWE 4 0 1 1 2 —

**Nilsson, Henrik / b. Jan. 10, 1970**
1990 WM20 SWE 7 1 3 4 4 —

**Nilsson, Johan / b. Mar. 17, 1987**
2005 WM18 SWE 6 1 1 2 2 B

**Nilsson, Kent / b. Aug. 31, 1956**
1985-90 WM SWE 28 19 18 37 12 S
1981-87 CC SWE 19 3 14 17 8 —
~IIHF Hall of Fame

**Nilsson, Lars-Goran / b. Mar. 9, 1944**
1966-74 WM SWE 60 26 23 49 70 3S,3B
1976 CC SWE 4 0 0 0 2 —
1968-72 OG-M SWE 12 4 3 7 6 —

**Nilsson, Magnus / b. Sept. 21, 1976**
1998 WM20 SWE 7 2 1 3 10 —

**Nilsson, Mattias / b. Feb. 6, 1982**
2000 WM18 SWE 5 0 0 0 14 B

**Nilsson, Nils "Nisse" / b. Mar. 8, 1936**
1957-67 WM SWE 48 45 23 68 4 2G,2S,2B
1956-64 OG-M SWE 14 12 6 18 6 S
~IIHF Hall of Fame
~OG-M IIHF Directorate Best Forward (1960), WM All-Star Team/Forward (1962)

**Nilsson, Per / b. June 9, 1960**
1980 WM20 SWE 5 0 2 2 0 B

**Nilsson, Peter / b. June 10, 1962**
1981-82 WM20 SWE 11 1 3 4 0 G

**Nilsson, Stefan / b. Jan. 1965**
1985 WM20 SWE 5 1 1 2 16 —

**Nilsson, Stefan / b. Feb. 1968**
1988 WM20 SWE 7 1 0 1 12 —

**Nilsson, Stefan "Skuggan" / b. Apr. 5, 1968**
1988 WM20 SWE 4 0 3 3 2 —
1993-97 WM SWE 25 3 3 6 8 3S

**Nilsson, Stefan / b. Sept. 1968**
1988 WM20 SWE 7 3 0 3 4 —

**Nilsson, Ulf / b. May 11, 1950**
1973 WM SWE 10 5 3 8 4 S
1976-81 CC SWE 9 2 3 5 8 —

**Nishiuchi, Towohiko / b. unknown / d. unknown**
1930 WM JPN 1 0 0 0 — —

**Nistor, Constantin / b. May 22, 1954**
1977 WM ROM 10 0 1 1 2 —
1980 OG-M ROM 5 0 1 1 4 —

**Nitta, Mitsuaki / b. July 3, 1973**
1993 WM20 JPN 7 2 1 3 8 —

**Nitz, Rolf / b. May 24, 1960**
1985 WM GDR 9 0 0 0 2 —

**Nivet, Hubert / b. unknown**
1950 WM FRA 4 0 0 0 4 —

**Noack, Rudiger / b. Nov. 30, 1944**
1965-76 WM GDR 47 8 3 11 6 —
1968 OG-M GDR 7 1 2 3 0 —

**Noack, Ulrich / b. Nov. 2, 1942**
1965 WM GDR 5 1 2 3 2 —
1968 OG-M GDR 2 0 0 0 2 —

**Noah, John / b. Nov. 21, 1927**
1952 OG-M USA 8 0 1 1 — S

**Nobs, Kurt / b. Sept. 4, 1935**
1959-62 WM SUI 7 1 0 1 8 —

**Nolan, Owen / b. Feb. 12, 1972**
1997 WM CAN 10 4 3 7 31 G
2002 OG-M CAN 6 0 3 3 2 G

**Norberg, Bertil / b. July 14, 1910 / d. Mar. 24, 1995**
1937 WM SWE 3 0 0 0 0 —
1936 OG-M SWE 4 1 — 1 — —

**Norberg, Lennart / b. Jan. 21, 1949**
1978-81 WM SWE 23 7 0 7 0 S,B
1980 OG-M SWE 7 1 1 2 2 B

**Nord, Bjorn / b. Apr. 5, 1972**
1992 WM20 SWE 7 1 6 7 6 S
2000-01 WM SWE 16 3 5 8 10 B

**Nordin, Anders / b. Feb. 26, 1944**
1970 WM SWE 4 0 1 1 2 S

**Nordin, Hakan / b. Jan. 15, 1961**
1980-81 WM20 SWE 10 4 7 11 0 G,B
1984 OG-M SWE 7 0 5 5 2 B
~WM20 All-Star Team/Defence (1981)

**Nordlander, Bert-Ola / b. Aug. 12, 1938**
1961-71 WM SWE 47 5 12 17 20 G,3S,2B
1960-72 OG-M SWE 26 3 6 9 9 S

**Nordmark, Robert / b. Aug. 20, 1962**
1981-82 WM20 SWE 12 2 1 3 2 G
1986-95 WM SWE 23 5 5 10 30 G,2S

**Nordnes, Magne / b. June 23, 1969**
1989 WM20 NOR 7 0 0 0 0 —

**Nordqvist, Jonas / b. Apr. 26, 1982**
1999-2000 WM18 SWE 13 3 6 9 0 S,B
2001-02 WM20 SWE 14 1 6 7 2 —
2006 WM SWE 9 2 2 4 6 G

**Nordstrom, Peter / b. July 26, 1974**
1998-2005 WM SWE 44 5 14 19 16 G,S,B

**Noreen, Dale / b. unknown**
1961 WM USA 7 0 0 0 6 —

**Norgren, Johan / b. Feb. 3, 1972**
1992 WM20 SWE 7 0 1 1 2 S

**Noris, Joe / b. Oct. 26, 1951**
1976 CC USA 4 0 1 1 6 —

**Normio, Teemu / b. May 9, 1980**
2000 WM20 FIN 7 1 0 1 25 —

**Norppa, Timo / b. July 9, 1965**
1985 WM20 FIN 7 1 2 3 0 —

**Norqual, Don / b. unknown**
1963 WM USA 5 1 0 1 0 —

**Norris, Dwayne / b. Jan. 8, 1970**
1990 WM20 CAN 7 2 4 6 2 G
1994 OG-M CAN 8 2 2 4 4 S

**Norstebo, Svein Enok / b. Feb. 26, 1972**
1990-91 WM20 NOR 13 0 1 1 6 —
1992-2001 WM NOR 54 2 5 7 26 —
1994 OG-M NOR 7 0 1 1 0 —

**Norstrom, Mattias / b. Jan. 2, 1972**
1992 WM20 SWE 7 0 1 1 10 S
1996-2005 WM SWE 42 1 12 13 38 G,2S
1996-2004 WCH SWE 8 0 1 1 0 —
1998-2002 OG-M SWE 8 0 1 1 2 —

**Norton, Jeff / b. Nov. 25, 1965**
1989-90 WM USA 16 5 1 6 18 —
1988 OG-M USA 6 0 4 4 4 —

**Norwich, Craig / b. Dec. 15, 1955**
1978-81 WM USA 18 2 2 4 2 —

**Nosek, David / b. Feb. 19, 1981**
1999 WM18 CZE 7 0 0 0 4 —
2001 WM20 CZE 7 0 0 0 6 G

**Nosov, Artyom / b. Apr. 4, 1985**
2003 WM18 RUS 6 0 2 2 14 B

**Noterman, Gentil / b. Nov. 11, 1931**
1950 WM BEL 4 2 0 2 0 —

**Novajovsky, Peter / b. Sept. 27, 1989**
2007 WM18 SVK 6 0 0 0 2 —

**Novak, Eduard / b. Nov. 27, 1946**
1971-77 WM TCH 33 16 2 18 12 G,3S
1972-76 OG-M TCH 7 4 1 5 4 S,B

**Novak, Jan / b. Feb. 9, 1979**
2004 WM CZE 7 0 2 2 4 —

**Novak, Jiri / b. June 6, 1950**
1973-79 WM TCH 54 23 22 45 17 2G,3S,B
1976 CC TCH 5 0 2 2 0 2nd
1976-80 OG-M TCH 10 3 3 6 4 S

**Novak, Vladimir / b. June 26, 1980**
2000 WM20 CZE 7 0 0 0 0 G

**Novak, Zbynek / b. July 23, 1983**
2001 WM18 CZE 7 0 2 2 6 —
2003 WM20 CZE 6 0 0 0 4 —

**Novitski, Vadim / b. Jan. 23, 1979**
1999 WM20 BLR 5 0 2 2 4 —

**Novopashin, Vitali / b. Sept. 28, 1978**
1998 WM20 KAZ 7 0 3 3 2 —
2005 WM KAZ 3 0 0 0 0 —

**Novoselov, Sergei / b. Mar. 31, 1965**
1985 WM20 URS 7 3 9 12 18 B

**Novoseltsev, Ivan / b. Jan. 23, 1979**
2003 WM RUS 6 0 0 0 0 —

**Novotny, Ivo / b. Apr. 8, 1978**
1998 WM20 CZE 7 1 0 1 2 —

**Novotny, Jiri / b. Aug. 12, 1983**
1997 WM20 CZE 7 0 0 0 0 —

**Novy, Erich / b. Feb. 5, 1937**
1957-67 WM GDR 47 6 7 13 34 —

**Novy, Helmut / b. July 31, 1944**
1963-70 WM GDR 38 7 7 14 34 —
1968 OG-M GDR 7 1 0 1 6 —

**Novy, Milan / b. Sept. 23, 1951**
1975-82 WM TCH 66 33 25 58 26 2G,4S,B
1976-81 CC TCH 13 6 5 11 9 2nd
1976-80 OG-M TCH 11 14 10 24 0 S
~IIHF Hall of Fame
~WM All-Star Team/Forward (1976)

**Novy, Miroslav / b. Oct. 1, 1930**
1954 WM TCH 6 1 — 1 8 —
1952 OG-M TCH 8 0 0 0 — —

**Nowak, Andrzej / b. Feb. 7, 1956**
1984 OG-M POL 6 1 1 2 2 —

**Nowak, Brett / b. May 20, 1981**
1999 WM18 USA 6 0 2 2 4 —
2000 WM20 USA 7 0 1 1 2 —

**Nowak, Dan / b. Apr. 6, 1966**
1986 WM20 FRG 7 0 0 0 14 —
1995-98 WM GER 25 0 4 4 26 —
1996 WCH GER 4 1 0 1 2 —

**Nowak, James / b. May 20, 1981**
2001 WM20 USA 7 2 3 5 4 —

**Nowak, Oskar / b. Mar. 25, 1913 / d. unknown**
1934-47 WM AUT 29 21 — 21 — B
1936-48 OG-M AUT 12 3 — 3 — —

**Nowak, Zdzislaw / b. Feb. 25, 1928 / d. Nov. 25, 2000**
1955-57 WM POL 13 7 1 8 2 —
1956 OG-M POL 4 0 0 0 0 —

**Nowinski, Ryszard / b. June 19, 1951**
1976 WM POL 10 1 0 1 6 —

**Nugent, Marty / b. July 1909 / d. unknown**
1933 WM CAN 3 0 — 0 0 S

**Nummelin, Timo / b. Sept. 7, 1948**
1972-82 WM FIN 72 11 8 19 63 —
1976-81 CC FIN 7 0 1 1 0 —
1976 OG-M FIN 5 1 0 1 4 —
~WM All-Star Team/Defence (2006)

**Numminen, Kalevi / b. Jan. 31, 1940**
1959-67 WM FIN 47 7 7 14 52 —
1960-64 OG-M FIN 13 5 1 6 14 —

**Numminen, Teppo / b. July 3, 1968**
1988 WM20 FIN 7 5 2 7 4 B
1987-97 WM FIN 32 8 6 14 20 S
1987-2004 WCH FIN 18 2 3 5 4 —
1988-2006 OG-M FIN 24 3 8 11 4 2S,B
~~WM All-Star Team/Defence (1997), WM20 IIHF Directorate Best Defenceman (1988), WM20 All-Star Team/Defence (1988)

**Nurmela, Holger / b. Oct. 28, 1920 / d. Mar. 1, 2005**
1947-54 WM SWE 28 26 6 32 4 S,B
1948-56 OG-M SWE 14 4 0 4 0 B

**Nurmi, Juha / b. Feb. 25, 1959**
1979 WM20 FIN 6 0 0 0 0 —
1982-83 WM FIN 11 1 0 1 4 —

**Nurmi, Mauno / b. Dec. 23, 1936**
1957-62 WM FIN 24 7 3 10 28 —

**Nurminen, Aaro / b. May 8, 1937**
1959 WM FIN 7 0 0 0 0 —

**Nurminen, Kai / b. Mar. 29, 1969**
1996-97 WM FIN 12 7 2 9 6 —
1996 WCH FIN 2 0 1 1 0 —

**Nurro, Kimmo / b. Sept. 24, 1966**
1986 WM20 FIN 7 2 2 4 2 —

**Nuspliger, Beat / b. May 29, 1966**
1986 WM20 SUI 7 2 3 5 8 —

**Nussli, Thomas / b. Mar. 12, 1982**
2000 WM18 SUI 7 0 0 0 12 —
2001-02 WM20 SUI 14 5 4 9 62 —

**Nutikka, Veli-Pekka / b. Jan. 16, 1975**
1994-95 WM20 FIN 14 7 2 9 12 —

**Nuutinen, Sami / b. June 11, 1971**
1989-91 WM20 FIN 17 1 5 6 4 —

**Nyberg, Lars / b. Mar. 31, 1958**
1977 WM20 SWE 6 0 0 0 0 —

**Nyberg, Marcus / b. Jan. 16, 1986**
2004 WM18 SWE 6 0 0 0 4 —

**Nyffenegger, Toni / b. May 23, 1967**
1987 WM20 SUI 7 1 0 1 4 —

**Nygren, Hakan / b. July 7, 1944**
1969-71 WM SWE 13 3 2 5 10 S,B

**Nyholm, Olof / b. Jan. 14, 1918 / d. unknown**
1939 WM FIN 5 0 — 0 — —

**Nyholm, Robert / b. Mar. 7, 1988**
2005-06 WM18 FIN 9 2 1 3 2 S

**Nylander, Peter / b. Jan. 20, 1976**
1995-96 WM20 SWE 14 4 3 7 2 S,B

**Nylund, Gary / b. Oct. 28, 1963**
1982 WM20 CAN 7 1 3 4 0 G

**Nyman, Roland / b. Mar. 31, 1961**
1980 WM20 SWE 5 0 0 0 0 B

**Nyman, Stefan / b. June 1, 1972**
1991 WM20 SWE 6 1 1 2 8 —

**Nyrop, Bill / b. July 23, 1952 / d. Dec. 31, 1995**
1976 CC USA 5 1 1 2 0 —

**Nystrom, David / b. Feb. 21, 1980**
2000 WM20 SWE 7 2 6 8 2 —

**Nystrom, Harri / b. June 16, 1962**
1982 WM20 FIN 7 0 0 0 0 B

**Obara, Daisuke / b. June 4, 1981**
2003-04 WM JPN 7 1 0 1 0 —

**Oberg, Carl-Goran / b. Dec. 24, 1938**
1958-67 WM SWE 35 18 14 32 20 2S,2B
1960-68 OG-M SWE 19 7 8 15 12 S

**Oberg, Hans / b. Nov. 21, 1926**
1949-58 WM SWE 43 28 9 37 2 2G,2B
1952-56 OG-M SWE 16 5 1 6 0 B

**Oberg, Lars / b. Feb. 3, 1950**
1976 WM SWE 10 0 0 0 0 B

**Oberg, Mikael / b. Jan. 28, 1985**
2003 WM18 SWE 6 0 0 0 2 —

**Oberg, Peter / b. Aug. 3, 1982**
2000 WM18 SWE 6 1 0 1 4 B
2002 WM20 SWE 7 1 1 2 0 —

**Oberg, Sigfrid / b. Feb. 22, 1907 / d. Apr. 2, 1949**
1931-35 WM SWE 10 2 — 2 — —
1928 OG-M SWE 5 1 0 1 8 S

**Oberhammer, Giulio / b. Dec. 14, 1935**
1959 WM ITA 8 3 1 4 0 —
1956-64 OG-M ITA 13 2 0 2 0 —

**Oberhuber, Gunther / b. Apr. 22, 1954**
1976 OG-M AUT 5 0 1 1 4 —

**Oberrauch, Robert / b. Nov. 6, 1965**
1992-98 WM ITA 35 1 4 5 34 —
1992-98 OG-M ITA 17 0 2 2 20 —

**Obloj, Tadeusz / b. Aug. 29, 1950**
1970-79 WM POL 48 7 4 11 10 —
1972-80 OG-M POL 14 4 2 6 0 —

**Obodiac, Stan / b. unknown / d. unknown**
1951 WM CAN 6 10 — 10 0 G

**Obresa, Peter / b. Aug. 6, 1960**
1979-80 WM20 FRG 10 3 1 4 2 —
1989 WM FRG 5 0 0 0 4 —
1984 CC FRG 5 1 0 1 2 —
1988 OG-M FRG 8 2 1 3 4 —

**Obukhov, Arkadi / b. Jan. 15, 1963**
1983 WM20 URS 7 1 3 4 2 G

**O'Callahan, Jack / b. July 24, 1957**
1979-89 WM USA 18 0 3 3 26 —
1980 OG-M USA 5 0 1 1 2 G

**Ocelka, Rastislav / b. Apr. 11, 1983**
2001 WM18 SVK 6 0 2 2 2 —

**Ochsner, Sasha / b. Jan. 14, 1973**
1992 WM20 SUI 7 1 1 2 2 —

**O'Connell, Mike / b. Nov. 25, 1955**
1985 WM USA 8 1 0 1 2 —
1981 CC USA 4 1 3 4 2 —

**O'Connor, Mike / b. Jan. 25, 1963**
1982 WM20 USA 7 1 3 4 2 —
1994 WM GBR 6 0 0 0 14 —

**O'Connor, Ted / b. Nov. 15, 1930**
1958 WM CAN 7 6 3 9 16 G

**O'Connor, Tom / b. unknown**
1958 WM CAN 7 7 4 11 6 G

**Octeau, Jay / b. Mar. 24, 1965**
1985 WM20 USA 7 1 2 3 2 —

**Odelein, Lyle / b. July 21, 1968**
1996 WCH CAN 2 0 0 0 0 2nd

**Odelein, Selmar / b. Apr. 11, 1966**
1985-86 WM20 CAN 14 1 6 7 14 G,S

**Odintsov, Sergei / b. Oct. 6, 1962**
1981-82 WM20 URS 12 7 5 12 4 B

**O'Donnell, Sean / b. Oct. 13, 1971**
1999 WM CAN 9 1 2 3 2 —

**O'Flaherty, Gerry / b. Aug. 31, 1950**
1976 CC USA 4 0 1 1 0 —

**Ogawa, Jiro / b. Jan. 20, 1939**
1964 OG-M JPN 7 1 1 2 0 —

**Ogorczyk, Jerzy / b. Feb. 8, 1937**
1958-59 WM POL 14 0 0 0 8 —
1964 OG-M POL 7 1 0 1 2 —

**Ogorodnikov, Andrei / b. Aug. 29, 1982**
2001 WM20 KAZ 6 1 0 1 4 —
2005-06 WM KAZ 9 1 0 1 2 —
2006 OG-M KAZ 5 0 0 0 4 —

**Ogrodnick, John / b. June 20, 1959**
1979 WM20 CAN 5 3 1 4 4 —
1981 WM CAN 8 3 3 6 0 —

**Ohga, Kiyoshi / b. unknown / d. unknown**
1930 WM JPN 1 0 0 0 — —

**Ohling, Jens / b. Apr. 3, 1962**
1981-82 WM20 SWE 12 1 12 13 12 G
1985-89 WM SWE 19 1 3 4 8 —
1984-88 OG-M SWE 15 5 8 13 2 2B

**Ohman, Niklas / b. Jan. 8, 1987**
2005 WM18 SWE 7 0 1 1 2 B

**Ohman, Roger / b. June 5, 1967**
1986-87 WM20 SWE 14 6 8 14 16 B

**Ohno, Naoto / b. Dec. 11, 1975**
1993 WM20 JPN 7 0 0 0 0 —

**Ohrlund, Uno / b. May 22, 1937**
1962-65 WM SWE 21 19 5 24 2 G,S,B
1964 OG-M SWE 6 7 1 8 2 S

**Oijennus, Oiva / b. Jan. 31, 1953**
1975 WM FIN 8 1 0 1 0 —

**Ojanen, Janne / b. Apr. 9, 1968**
1987-88 WM20 FIN 14 8 15 23 22 G,B
1987-2002 WM FIN 46 11 15 26 39 G,S
1987-96 WCH FIN 15 3 4 7 2 —
1988-94 OG-M FIN 16 6 3 9 12 S,B

**Okajima, Toru / b. Jan. 21, 1943**
1968-72 OG-M JPN 8 7 2 9 6 —

**Okerlund, Todd / b. Sept. 6, 1964**
1984 WM20 USA 7 2 3 5 4 —
1988 OG-M USA 3 1 0 1 4 —

**Okhotnikov, Mikhail / b. Jan. 8, 1976**
1995-96 WM20 RUS 14 0 1 1 4 S,B

**Okland, Jorgen / b. Apr. 19, 1983**
2001 WM18 NOR 6 0 0 0 0 —

**Oksa, Tommi / b. Oct. 14, 1984**
2004 WM20 FIN 7 1 1 2 2 B

**Oksanen, Hannu / b. Nov. 15, 1957**
1986 WM FIN 5 0 1 1 2 —
1984 OG-M FIN 6 0 0 0 0 —

**Oksanen, Lasse / b. Dec. 7, 1942**
1965-77 WM FIN 101 25 24 49 23 —
1976 CC FIN 5 3 0 3 0 —
1964-72 OG-M FIN 19 5 2 7 6 —
~IIHF Hall of Fame

**Oksiuta, Roman / b. Aug. 21, 1970**
1989-90 WM20 URS 14 13 5 18 8 G,S
1996 WM RUS 8 3 0 3 2 —
**Oktyabryov, Artur / b. Nov. 26, 1973**
1993 WM20 RUS 7 0 1 1 12 —
1999 WM RUS 6 0 0 0 10 —
**Okvist, Tore / b. Sept. 30, 1957**
1977 WM20 SWE 7 5 2 7 11 —
**Olafsen, Franz / b. Apr. 20, 1944**
1964 OG-M NOR 7 4 1 5 0 —
**Olander, Jere / b. Oct. 2, 1989**
2007 WM18 FIN 6 0 0 0 4 —
**Olausson, Fredrik / b. Oct. 5, 1966**
1985-86 WM20 SWE 14 5 3 8 15 —
1986-89 WM SWE 19 4 1 5 10 S
2002 OG-M SWE 4 0 0 0 2 —
**Olausson, Niklas / b. May 12, 1986**
2004 WM18 SWE 6 0 1 1 0 —
**Olczyk, Ed / b. Aug. 16, 1966**
1986-93 WM USA 33 13 13 26 50 —
1984-91 CC USA 19 2 10 12 12 2nd
1984 OG-M USA 6 2 6 8 0 —
**Olczyk, Stanislaw / b. Oct. 15, 1932 / d. Jan. 23, 1996**
1955-59 WM POL 24 3 1 4 22 —
1956-64 OG-M POL 12 1 1 2 2 —
**Olds, Wally / b. Aug. 17, 1949**
1977-81 WM USA 26 3 5 8 8 —
1972 OG-M USA 5 0 0 0 0 S
**Olejowski, Dariusz / b. Feb. 1, 1968**
1988 WM20 POL 7 3 2 5 2 —
**Olenici, Adrian / b. Apr. 19, 1956**
1977 WM ROM 10 0 0 0 0 —
1980 OG-M ROM 5 1 0 1 2 —
**Oletskiy, Valentyn / b. June 2, 1971**
1999-2007 WM UKR 29 0 4 4 14 —
2002 OG-M UKR 4 2 1 3 4 —
**Oliwa, Krzysztof / b. Apr. 12, 1973**
2002 WM POL 6 1 2 3 22 —
**Ollila, Jukka / b. Mar. 1, 1973**
1992-93 WM20 FIN 14 0 0 0 8 —
**Olsen, Atle / b. Jan. 29, 1972**
1996-97 WM NOR 13 3 2 5 24 —
**Olsen, Christian / b. Oct. 8, 1987**
2004-05 WM18 DEN 12 1 1 2 26 —
**Olsen, Eivind / b. Apr. 16, 1971**
1991 WM20 NOR 7 0 0 0 6 —
**Olsen, Oystein / b. Jan. 11, 1969**
1989 WM20 NOR 4 0 0 0 4 —
1992-97 WM NOR 28 2 4 6 34 —
1992 OG-M NOR 7 0 0 0 0 —
**Olsen, Tom Erik / b. Mar. 20, 1970**
1989-90 WM20 NOR 14 6 2 8 4 —
1993-96 WM NOR 12 0 0 0 2 —
**Olson, Doug / b. Mar. 18, 1957**
1977 WM20 USA 7 1 0 1 16 —
**Olson, Gregg / b. Mar. 16, 1961**
1981 WM20 USA 5 1 1 2 0 —
**Olson, Weldon / b. Nov. 12, 1932**
1958-59 WM USA 14 5 3 8 6 —
1956-60 OG-M USA 14 7 0 7 16 G,S
**Olsson, Ake / b. Mar. 9, 1917 / d. unknown**
1947-49 WM SWE 8 0 — 0 — S
**Olsson, Bjorn / b. July 2, 1957**
1977 WM20 SWE 7 1 1 2 2 —
**Olsson, Christer / b. July 24, 1970**
1995-2001 WM SWE 37 5 5 10 34 G,S,2B
~WM IIHF Directorate Best Defenceman (1995)
**Olsson, Mattias / b. Apr. 1, 1971**
1990-91 WM20 SWE 14 5 9 14 10 —
**Olsson, Nils-Olof / b. May 28, 1951**
1977-78 WM SWE 20 1 7 8 8 S
**Olsson, Ove / b. Aug. 15, 1960**
1979-80 WM20 SWE 11 2 1 3 4 2B
1982 WM SWE 10 3 1 4 4 —
**Olsson, Robin / b. May 30, 1989**
2007 WM18 SWE 6 1 1 2 2 B
**Olsson, Roger / b. Jan. 30, 1944**
1969-70 WM SWE 10 5 1 6 6 2S
1968 OG-M SWE 7 1 1 2 6 —
**Olsvik, Christian / b. Nov. 13, 1970**
1989 WM20 NOR 7 0 1 1 0 —

**Olvestad, Jimmie / b. Feb. 16, 1980**
1999-2000 WM20 SWE 13 4 4 8 14 —
2001 WM SWE 3 0 0 0 0 B
**O'Malley, Brett / b. Mar. 14, 1984**
2002 WM18 CAN 8 1 2 3 0 —
**O'Malley, Terry / b. Oct. 21, 1940**
1965-69 WM CAN 31 1 5 6 26 2B
1964-80 OG-M CAN 19 1 6 7 6 B
~IIHF Hall of Fame
**Ondrejcik, Rastislav / b. Jan. 27, 1973**
2009 WM HUN 4 0 0 0 6 —
**O'Neill, Jeff / b. Feb. 23, 1976**
1995 WM20 CAN 7 2 4 6 2 G
**O'Neill, Wes / b. Mar. 3, 1986**
2004 WM18 CAN 7 1 1 2 2 —
**Ono, Isao / b. Aug. 5, 1933**
1957 WM JPN 7 1 — 1 — —
1960-64 OG-M JPN 13 8 7 15 12 —
**Ono, Yutaka / b. Mar. 26, 1974**
2000 WM JPN 6 0 0 0 0 —
**Onishenko, Yevgeniy / b. Aug. 5, 1985**
2004 WM20 UKR 6 0 0 0 8 —
**Opsahl, Al / b. Sept. 27, 1924 / d. July 25, 1990**
1948 OG-M USA 8 1 1 2 4 —
**Opulskis, Juris / b. Apr. 21, 1969**
1998-2001 WM LAT 19 2 5 7 0 —
**Oravec, Christopher / b. May 26, 1981**
1999 WM18 GER 6 0 0 0 0 —
**Oravec, Tomas / b. Mar. 11, 1982**
2000 WM18 SVK 6 2 2 4 2 —
2002 WM20 SVK 7 1 2 3 6 —
**Orbaek, Cato / b. Feb. 23, 1983**
2007 WM NOR 4 0 0 0 0 —
**Orbanowski, Horst / b. July 7, 1908 / d. unknown**
1933-37 WM GER 26 6 1 7 7 B
**O'Regan, Tom / b. Dec. 29, 1961**
1989-96 WM USA 32 3 4 7 24 B
**Orekhovski, Oleg / b. Nov. 3, 1977**
1997 WM20 RUS 6 0 1 1 2 B
2001 WM RUS 7 0 0 0 8 —
**Orlando, Gaetano "Gates" / b. Nov. 13, 1962**
1992-99 WM ITA 46 15 21 36 50 —
1994-98 OG-M ITA 11 4 8 12 8 —
**Orleski, Dave / b. Dec. 26, 1959**
1979 WM20 CAN 5 2 0 2 0 —
**Orlov, Maxim / b. Jan. 31, 1981**
1999 WM18 RUS 7 3 2 5 6 —
**Ornskog, Stefan / b. Apr. 4, 1969**
1989 WM20 SWE 7 1 1 2 0 S
1994-95 WM SWE 16 2 5 7 4 S,B
1994 OG-M SWE 8 2 0 2 2 G
**Orosz, Karoly / b. Jan. 28, 1945**
1964 OG-M HUN 7 0 2 2 2 —
**Orr, Bobby / b. Mar. 20, 1948**
1976 CC CAN 7 2 7 9 8 1st
**Orsolini, Lionel / b. Feb. 22, 1971**
1992-95 WM FRA 16 1 0 1 0 —
**Ortiz, Ray / b. June 10, 1984**
2002 WM18 USA 8 0 0 0 4 G
**Orszagh, Vladimir / b. May 24, 1977**
1996 WM20 SVK 6 5 1 6 18 —
2001-05 WM SVK 39 7 10 17 40 G,B
2004 WCH SVK 4 0 0 0 6 —
**Osadchi, Alexander / b. July 19, 1975**
1994 WM20 RUS 6 0 2 2 6 B
**O'Shea, Danny / b. June 15, 1945**
1968 OG-M CAN 7 3 2 5 10 B
**O'Shea, Kevin / b. May 28, 1947**
1969 WM CAN 7 0 0 0 23 —
**Oshiro, Joel / b. July 28, 1971**
2002-04 WM JPN 18 1 3 4 22 —
**Osiecki, Mark / b. July 23, 1968**
1992 WM USA 6 0 1 1 4 —
**Osipov, Denis / b. May 9, 1987**
2005 WM18 RUS 6 0 0 0 4 —
**Osipov, Sergei / b. Dec. 15, 1967**
1986-87 WM20 URS 13 3 7 10 2 G
**Oslizlo, Lubomir / b. Oct. 10, 1957**
1977 WM20 TCH 7 1 2 3 8 B
~WM20 All-Star Team/Defence (1977)
**Osmera, Miloslav / b. Jan. 21, 1924**
1954 WM TCH 4 0 — 0 6 —
1952 OG-M TCH 8 1 0 1 — —

**Oss, Arnold / b. Apr. 18, 1928**
1952 OG-M USA 8 7 4 11 — S
**Ostling, Stig / b. Dec. 31, 1948**
1972-81 WM SWE 41 2 6 8 24 S,3B
1976 CC SWE 1 0 0 0 0 —
1972 OG-M SWE 5 0 0 0 0 —
**Ostrcil, Radim / b. Jan. 15, 1989**
2007 WM18 CZE 6 1 1 2 4 —
**Ostrowski, Brian / b. unknown**
1977 WM20 CAN 2 0 2 2 2 S
**Ostrushko, Artyom / b. Mar. 18, 1974**
1999-2006 WM UKR 39 0 1 1 36 —
**O'Sullivan, Chris / b. May 15, 1974**
1994 WM20 USA 7 0 3 3 4 —
1995-2002 WM USA 20 0 1 1 10 —
**Oswald, Gunther / b. July 1, 1969**
1988-89 WM20 FRG 14 3 3 6 18 —
1991-95 WM GER 15 1 3 4 28 —
**Otcenas, Ondrej / b. Mar. 6, 1987**
2005 WM18 SVK 6 4 1 5 10 —
**Otomo, Tsutsumi / b. Sept. 15, 1975**
1993 WM20 JPN 7 1 0 1 8 —
1998 WM JPN 3 0 0 0 4 —
1998 OG-M JPN 4 1 1 2 12 —
**Otoupalik, Jiri / b. Nov. 15, 1958**
1977 WM20 TCH 7 3 0 3 0 B
**Ott, Andreas / b. June 9, 1969**
1989 WM20 FRG 7 1 0 1 0 —
**Ott, Christian / b. Dec. 26, 1966**
1986 WM20 FRG 7 0 0 0 8 —
**Ott, Hans / b. Feb. 28, 1930**
1954-55 WM SUI 14 6 0 6 0 —
1956 OG-M SUI 5 1 0 1 4 —
**Ott, Ladislav / b. unknown**
1954 WM SUI 7 0 — 0 2 —
**Otto, Andy / b. May 8, 1963**
1983 WM20 USA 7 3 1 4 20 —
**Otto, Joel / b. Oct. 29, 1961**
1985-90 WM USA 19 4 5 9 10 —
1987-96 CC USA 20 5 4 9 22 1st,2nd
1998 OG-M USA 4 0 0 0 0 —
**Ottosson, Kristoffer / b. Jan. 9, 1976**
1995-96 WM20 SWE 14 0 3 3 2 S,B
2001 WM SWE 9 4 4 8 0 B
**Ottosson, Peter / b. Sept. 4, 1965**
1992 WM SWE 8 0 2 2 2 G
1992 OG-M SWE 6 0 2 2 2 —
**Ouellet, Bob / b. Mar. 18, 1968**
1996-2000 WM FRA 19 1 4 5 10 —
1998 OG-M FRA 4 0 1 1 2 —
**Ouellet, Joseph / b. Mar. 18, 1968**
1997 WM FRA 8 0 4 4 0 —
**Ovcacik, Ctirad / b. Oct. 18, 1984**
2002 WM18 CZE 8 0 1 1 0 B
2004 WM20 CZE 7 2 0 2 4 —
**Ovchinnikov, Andri / b. May 1, 1961**
1981 WM20 URS 5 2 0 2 6 B
**Overakker, Dolf / b. unknown**
1950 WM NED 4 2 0 2 0 —
**Ovsyanikov, Andrei / b. Jan. 11, 1979**
1999 WM20 BLR 6 0 2 2 4 —
**Owen, Edwyn "Bob" / b. June 8, 1936 / d. Oct. 5, 2007**
1959 WM USA 8 1 3 4 2 —
1960 OG-M USA 7 1 2 3 4 G
**Oxley, John / b. Dec. 29, 1922 / d. June 1, 1976**
1948 OG-M GBR 7 7 — 7 — —
**Oystila, Jouko / b. Feb. 25, 1952**
1971-75 WM FIN 34 2 4 6 10 —
**Ozolins, Sandis* / b. Aug. 3, 1972**
1991-92 WM20 URS 14 2 7 9 10 G,S
1998-2002 WM LAT 16 3 8 11 18 —
2002-06 OG-M LAT 6 1 7 8 0 —
*also known as Sandis Ozolinsh
**Ozols, Juris / b. Apr. 6, 1977**
2004 WM LAT 6 0 0 0 2 —
**Ozols, Karlis / b. Mar. 2, 1989**
2007 WM18 LAT 6 0 0 0 2 —
**Paavola, Rodney / b. Aug. 21, 1939 / d. Dec. 3, 1995**
1959 WM USA 8 1 0 1 2 —
1960 OG-M USA 7 0 1 1 4 G
**Pabiska, Lukas / b. Feb. 24, 1984**
2002 WM18 CZE 8 2 1 3 6 B
**Pacalt, Frantisek / b. July 20, 1912 / d. unknown**
1937-47 WM TCH 26 0 0 0 0 G,B

**Pachucki, Maciej / b. June 9, 1970**
1990 WM20 POL 7 0 0 0 2 —
**Packard, Dennis / b. Feb. 9, 1982**
2000 WM18 USA 6 0 1 1 2 —
**Pacula, Ireneusz / b. Nov. 16, 1966**
1985 WM20 POL 7 1 1 2 2 —
1992 WM POL 6 1 1 2 4 —
1988 OG-M POL 5 1 0 1 2 —
**Paderhuber, Andreas / b. Apr. 26, 1978**
1998 WM20 GER 6 0 0 0 4 —
**Paegle, Karlis / b. Oct. 4, 1911 / d. Dec. 23, 1997**
1935-39 WM LAT 15 2 — 2 — —
1936 OG-M LAT 3 1 — 1 — —
**Paetsch, Nathan / b. Mar. 30, 1983**
2002-03 WM20 CAN 13 1 1 2 4 2S
**Paiement, Wilf / b. Oct. 16, 1955**
1977-79 WM CAN 28 14 10 24 46 B
~WM IIHF Directorate Best Forward (1979)
**Paille, Daniel / b. Apr. 15, 1984**
2003-04 WM20 CAN 12 4 0 4 4 2S
**Pajerski, Sebastian / b. Mar. 24, 1977**
1997 WM20 POL 6 1 2 3 0 —
**Pajic, Murajica / b. Aug. 24, 1961**
1984 OG-M YUG 5 0 0 0 6 —
**Pajonkowski, Franck / b. Jan. 21, 1964**
1993-96 WM FRA 20 4 2 6 50 —
1988-94 OG-M FRA 13 7 2 9 24 —
**Pakaslahti, Petri / b. Jan. 22, 1976**
2005 WM FIN 7 1 0 1 0 —
**Pakhomov, Denis / b. Apr. 8, 1987**
2005 WM18 RUS 6 1 0 1 10 —
**Paklin, Sergei / b. June 1, 1981**
1999-2001 WM20 BLR 12 2 1 3 6 —
**Paladiev, Yevgeni / b. May 12, 1948**
1969-73 WM URS 28 4 10 14 16 3G
1972 SS URS 3 0 0 0 0 2nd
**Palazzari, Doug / b. Nov. 3, 1952**
1976 CC USA 2 0 0 0 2 —
**Palazzi, Steve / b. Feb. 9, 1961**
1979 WM20 USA 5 2 0 2 2 —
**Palecek, Josef / b. May 5, 1949**
1972-74 WM TCH 25 5 12 17 6 G,S,B
**Palfalvy, Bela / b. 1917 / d. 1944**
1938-39 WM HUN 8 0 — 0 — —
**Palffy, Zigmund / b. May 5, 1972**
1991-92 WM20 TCH 13 10 7 17 8 B
1996-2005 WM SVK 30 20 23 43 46 G,B
1991-96 WCH SVK 8 2 2 4 4 —
1994-2010 OG-M SVK 16 3 10 13 16 —
**Palkovics, Krisztian / b. May 10, 1975**
2009 WM HUN 6 1 0 1 6 —
**Pallassalo, Tomi / b. Aug. 17, 1989**
2007 WM18 FIN 6 1 2 3 6 —
**Palm, Gustaf / b. Feb. 12, 1984**
2002 WM18 SWE 8 4 1 5 8 —
**Palm, Trent / b. June 10, 1988**
2006 WM18 USA 6 0 1 1 2 G
**Palmer, Jarod / b. Feb. 10, 1986**
2004 WM18 USA 6 1 1 2 0 S
**Palmer, Winthrop / b. Dec. 5, 1906 / d. Feb. 4, 1970**
1933 WM USA 5 9 — 9 0 G
1932 OG-M USA 6 8 3 11 2 S
**Palmqvist, Bjorn / b. Mar. 15, 1944**
1966-72 WM SWE 50 19 6 25 9 3S,2B
1968-72 OG-M SWE 11 4 2 6 0 —
**Palo, Marko / b. Aug. 29, 1967**
1993-95 WM FIN 22 2 3 5 10 G,S
1994 OG-M FIN 8 2 3 5 4 B
**Palous, Jan / b. Oct. 25, 1888 / d. Sept. 25, 1971**
1920-24 OG-M TCH 3 0 0 0 — B
**Palsola, Sakari / b. June 9, 1972**
1992 WM20 FIN 7 0 0 0 2 —
**Paluch, Scott / b. Mar. 9, 1966**
1986 WM20 USA 7 0 5 5 2 B
**Palus, Mieczyslaw / b. Aug. 31, 1921 / d. May 15, 1986**
1947 WM POL 7 4 — 4 — —
1948 OG-M POL 6 5 — 5 — —
**Pana, Eduard / b. unknown / d. unknown**
1947 WM ROM 7 2 — 2 — —
**Pana, Eduard / b. May 28, 1944**
1977 WM ROM 10 1 2 3 2 —
1964-76 OG-M ROM 12 7 9 16 2 —
~IIHF Hall of Fame
**Panchartek, Frantisek / b. Mar. 27, 1946**
1971 WM TCH 6 1 1 2 12 S
**Panchenko, Olexander / b. Apr. 13, 1980**
2000 WM20 UKR 7 2 1 3 0 —
**Pander, Rasmus / b. Mar. 19, 1976**
2006-07 WM DEN 11 1 3 4 10 —
**Pandolfo, Jay / b. Dec. 27, 1974**
1999 WM USA 2 0 0 0 0 —
1994 WM20 USA 7 0 0 0 2 —
**Pandolfo, Mike / b. Sept. 15, 1979**
1999 WM20 USA 6 0 1 1 4 —
**Panenka, Antonin / b. unknown / d. unknown**
1935-47 WM ROM 13 3 0 3 0 —
**Panfilenkov, Stanislav / b. Sept. 28, 1969**
1989 WM20 URS 7 2 3 5 0 G
**Panin, Igor / b. Sept. 27, 1960**
1980 WM20 URS 5 0 1 1 4 G
**Panin, Mikhail / b. Jan. 15, 1961**
1980-81 WM20 URS 10 4 6 10 6 G,B
**Pankov, Dmitri / b. Oct. 29, 1974**
1998-2003 WM BLR 30 7 8 15 8 —
2002 OG-M BLR 9 3 1 4 2 —
**Pankov, Vasili / b. Aug. 15, 1968**
1998-2001 WM BLR 24 5 9 14 80 —
1998-2002 OG-M BLR 16 2 1 3 10 —
**Pantelejevs, Grigorijs / b. Nov. 13, 1972**
2000-07 WM LAT 48 7 12 19 12 —
2002-06 OG-M LAT 9 2 3 5 2 —
**Pantsyrev, Dmitri / b. Aug. 6, 1986**
2003-04 WM18 BLR 11 1 2 3 18 —
**Pantucek, Vaclav / b. Nov. 24, 1934**
1954-61 WM TCH 35 17 9 26 12 S,2B
1956-60 OG-M TCH 13 11 5 16 4 —
**Pantyukhov, Yuri / b. Mar. 15, 1931 / d. Oct. 22, 1981**
1957-59 WM URS 21 11 8 19 4 3S
1956 OG-M URS 7 2 1 3 2 G
**Pappa, Hans / b. July 26, 1936**
1959 WM SUI 8 0 0 0 6 —
1956 OG-M SUI 4 0 0 0 0 —
**Paquet, Jean-Philippe / b. Jan. 7, 1987**
2005 WM18 CAN 6 0 0 0 2 S
**Paradise, Bob / b. Apr. 22, 1944**
1969-77 WM USA 18 0 0 0 36 —
1968 OG-M USA 6 0 0 0 0 —
**Parakhonka, Dmitri / b. Jan. 25, 1984**
2002 WM18 BLR 8 0 0 0 14 —
2003 WM20 BLR 6 0 1 1 6 —
**Paramanov, Sergei / b. June 2, 1958**
1978 WM20 URS 7 1 2 3 4 G
**Parco, John / b. Aug. 25, 1971**
2006 OG-M ITA 5 3 1 4 10 —
2006-10 WM ITA 18 0 2 2 8 —
**Pardavy, Jan / b. Sept. 8, 1971**
1997-2001 WM SVK 36 9 8 17 32 S
1998-2002 OG-M SVK 8 3 1 4 14 —
**Parent, Norm / b. unknown**
1951 WM USA 6 0 — 0 8 —
**Parenteau, Pierre-Alexandre / b. Mar. 24, 1983**
2003 WM20 CAN 6 4 3 7 2 S
**Parise, Jean-Paul "J-P" / b. Dec. 11, 1941**
1972 SS CAN 6 2 2 4 28 1st
**Park, Alex / b. unknown / d. unknown**
1930 WM CAN 1 2 — 2 — G
**Park, Brad / b. June 6, 1948**
1972 SS CAN 8 1 4 5 2 1st
**Park, Richard / b. May 27, 1976**
1994-95 WM20 USA 14 4 9 13 33 —
2002-06 WM USA 28 10 7 17 0 B
**Parker, H.G. / b. unknown / d. unknown**
1931 WM GBR — 0 — 0 — —
**Parks, Greg / b. Mar. 25, 1967**
1994 OG-M CAN 8 1 2 3 10 S
**Parolini, Pio / b. Feb. 19, 1940**
1962 WM SUI 6 2 3 5 4 —
1964 OG-M SUI 7 3 0 3 0 —
**Parrish, Mark / b. Feb. 2, 1977**
1996-97 WM20 USA 12 6 5 11 10 S
1998-2005 WM USA 16 6 0 6 12 —
2006 OG-M USA 6 0 0 0 4 —
**Parrott, Peter / b. May 27, 1936**
1960 OG-M AUS 4 0 0 0 0 —
**Parssinen, Timo / b. Jan. 17, 1977**
2001-07 WM FIN 41 9 18 27 14 2S
**Partinen, Lalli / b. Aug. 20, 1941**
1965-73 WM FIN 38 2 4 6 28 —
1968 OG-M FIN 7 0 0 0 2 —
**Parviainen, Jari / b. Aug. 20, 1967**
1987 WM20 FIN 4 0 0 0 4 G
**Parzyszek, Adrian / b. Oct. 18, 1975**
2002 WM POL 6 1 1 2 4 —
**Pasek, Dusan / b. Sept. 7, 1960 / d. Mar. 15, 1998**
1979-80 WM20 TCH 13 8 1 9 6 S
1982-87 WM TCH 50 17 12 29 34 G,2S,B
1981-87 CC TCH 17 4 3 7 18 —
1984-88 OG-M TCH 15 7 8 15 10 S
**Paska, Jiri / b. Aug. 3, 1964**
1984 WM20 TCH 7 0 3 3 2 B
**Pasqualloto, Gino / b. Nov. 10, 1955**
1982 WM ITA 1 0 0 0 0 —
1984 OG-M ITA 5 0 0 0 0 —
**Pata, Zdenek / b. Feb. 3, 1960**
1980 WM20 TCH 5 0 4 4 6 —
**Patera, Pavel / b. Sept. 6, 1971**
1995-2002 WM CZE 70 18 28 47 36 4G,2B
1996 WCH CZE 2 0 1 1 0 —
1998-2002 OG-M CZE 10 2 3 5 2 G
**Paterson, Mark / b. Feb. 22, 1964**
1984 WM20 CAN 7 0 2 2 10 —
**Paterson, Rick / b. Feb. 10, 1958**
1978 WM20 CAN 6 1 2 3 0 B
**Paton, Tom / b. Jan. 14, 1932**
1951 WM GBR 6 0 — 0 0 —
**Patrick, Craig / b. May 20, 1946**
1971-79 WM USA 18 3 5 8 4 —
1976 CC USA 5 2 2 4 0 —
**Patrick, Glenn / b. Apr. 26, 1950**
1978 WM USA 9 1 3 4 4 —
**Patrick, James / b. June 14, 1963**
1982-83 WM20 CAN 14 0 4 4 10 G,B
1983-2002 WM CAN 40 3 7 10 20 S,B
1987 CC CAN 6 0 1 1 2 1st
1984 OG-M CAN 7 0 3 3 4 —
**Patschinski, Rainer / b. Aug. 28, 1950**
1970-78 WM GDR 37 8 7 15 16 —
**Patt, Christian / b. unknown**
1978 WM20 SUI 6 0 0 0 0 —
**Patzner, Helmut / b. Apr. 2, 1962**
1982 WM20 FRG 7 1 0 1 2 —
**Paukkunen, Markku / b. Apr. 15, 1981**
1999 WM18 FIN 7 2 1 3 0 G
2001 WM20 FIN 7 1 1 2 4 S
**Paulsen, Andre / b. Feb. 14, 1983**
2001 WM18 NOR 6 0 0 0 0 —
**Paulsen, Christopher / b. Apr. 14, 1989**
2006 WM18 NOR 6 0 0 0 8 —
**Paulsen, Eirik / b. May 21, 1970**
1995 WM NOR 5 0 0 0 2 —
1992 OG-M NOR 7 2 1 3 6 —
**Paulsson, Marcus / b. Jan. 10, 1984**
2003 WM20 SWE 6 0 3 3 6 —
**Paulus, Albton / b. Dec. 20, 1957**
1977 WM20 FRG 5 1 0 1 9 —
**Pauna, Matti / b. Feb. 16, 1960**
1980 WM20 SWE 5 1 0 1 8 B
1985-87 WM SWE 27 5 3 8 2 G,S
**Paunio, Joel / b. Aug. 17, 1964**
1984 WM20 FIN 6 0 3 3 11 S
**Pavelec, Stanislav / b. Apr. 28, 1964**
1984 WM20 TCH 7 2 3 5 0 B
**Pavelich, Mark / b. Feb. 28, 1958**
1981 WM USA 8 2 3 5 4 —
1980 OG-M USA 7 1 6 7 2 G
**Pavlacka, Matus / b. Nov. 17, 1984**
2002 WM18 SVK 8 0 0 0 8 —
**Pavlas, Ales / b. Jan. 30, 1982**
2000 WM18 CZE 6 0 0 0 0 —
**Pavlas, Petr / b. Feb. 4, 1968**
1987-88 WM20 TCH 14 5 10 15 6 S
**Pavletic, Karel / b. unknown / d. unknown**
1939 WM YUG 5 1 — 1 — —
**Pavlikovsky, Richard / b. Mar. 3, 1975**
2001 WM SVK 7 1 0 1 8 —
2002 OG-M SVK 4 0 0 0 4 —
**Pavlis, Libor / b. Nov. 1, 1977**
1997 WM20 CZE 7 1 1 2 4 —

**Pavlov, Yevgeni / b. Jan. 10, 1981**
1999 WM18 RUS 7 2 3 5 2 —

**Pavlovs, Igors / b. Jan. 1, 1965**
1997-98 WM LAT 14 3 3 6 4 —

**Pavlu, Martin / b. July 8, 1962**
1982-97 WM ITA 49 5 8 13 4 —
1984-98 OG-M ITA 16 5 2 7 0 —

**Pawelczyk, Marian / b. Jan. 10, 1936**
1957-58 WM POL 13 1 1 2 0 —

**Pawlik, Bogdan / b. Sept. 10, 1956**
1986 WM POL 8 0 1 1 2 —

**Pawsey, Ken / b. Dec. 13, 1940**
1960 OG-M AUS 3 0 0 0 0 —

**Payette, Jean-Paul / b. Sept. 19, 1929**
1959 WM CAN 4 3 4 7 0 G

**Payne, Steve / b. Aug. 16, 1958**
1979 WM CAN 7 2 0 2 2 —

**Payot, Calixte / b. 1901 / d. unknown**
1924-28 OG-M FRA 3 0 — 0 — —

**Payot, Martin / b. unknown / d. unknown**
1937 WM FRA 8 0 0 0 5 —

**Payot, Philippe / b. Dec. 21, 1893 / d. Apr. 29, 1958**
1928 OG-M FRA 1 0 — 0 — —

**Payusov, Vasili / b. Jan. 22, 1957**
1977 WM20 URS 7 0 2 2 6 G

**Pazler, Lubos / b. Mar. 6, 1967**
1986-87 WM20 TCH 14 0 6 6 0 S

**Pchelyakov, Andrei / b. Feb. 19, 1972**
1998-2006 WM KAZ 15 3 3 6 26 —
1998-2006 OG-M KAZ 12 1 2 3 8 —

**Peacosh, Walt / b. Sept. 16, 1935**
1961-63 WM CAN 14 8 9 17 19 G

**Peake, Pat / b. May 28, 1973**
1992-93 WM20 USA 14 9 10 19 22 B

**Pearson, Fred / b. Mar. 23, 1923 / d. Sept. 10, 2009**
1948 OG-M USA 6 2 4 6 6 —

**Pearson, Harry / b. Mar. 18, 1934**
1962 WM GBR 7 4 1 5 8 —

**Peca, Giustino / b. Aug. 17, 1970**
2002 WM ITA 6 0 0 0 2 —

**Peca, Michael / b. Mar. 26, 1974**
1994 WM20 CAN 7 2 2 4 8 G
2001 WM CAN 3 1 3 4 0 —
2002 OG-M CAN 6 0 2 2 2 G

**Pecherin, Yuri / b. Jan. 30, 1982**
1999-2000 WM18 UKR 12 1 1 2 10 —

**Pedersen, Erik / b. Sept. 20, 1955**
1980 OG-M NOR 5 0 0 0 8 —

**Pedersen, Roar ~see Bakke-Pedersen, Roar**

**Pederson, Barry / b. Mar. 13, 1961**
1987 WM CAN 10 2 3 5 2 —

**Pederson, Denis / b. Sept. 10, 1975**
1995 WM20 CAN 7 2 2 4 0 G

**Pederson, Mark / b. Jan. 14, 1968**
1988 WM20 CAN 7 1 2 3 4 G

**Pederson, Tom / b. Jan. 14, 1970**
1989 WM20 USA 7 2 8 10 4 —
1991-96 WM USA 17 1 4 5 12 B

**Peitsoma, Jukka / b. July 12, 1958**
1977-78 WM20 FIN 11 1 2 3 8 —

**Pekarik, Pavol / b. Dec. 24, 1977**
1997 WM20 SVK 6 0 0 0 8 —

**Pekkala, Jose / b. Oct. 31, 1962**
1982 WM20 FIN 7 1 0 1 4 B

**Pelkonen, Tommi / b. Aug. 23, 1984**
2002 WM18 FIN 8 2 1 3 0 —

**Pellegrini, Giorgio / b. unknown / d. unknown**
1939 WM ITA 2 0 — 0 — —

**Pellerin, Scott / b. Jan. 9, 1970**
1990 WM20 CAN 7 2 0 2 2 G

**Peloffy, Andre / b. Feb. 25, 1951**
1988 OG-M FRA 6 0 2 2 0 —

**Pellegrino, Santino / b. Feb. 9, 1965**
1992 WM ITA 5 1 1 2 4 —
1992 OG-M ITA 5 2 1 3 0 —

**Peltomaa, Jussi / b. June 24, 1987**
2005 WM18 FIN 6 0 0 0 4 —

**Peltomaa, Timo / b. July 26, 1968**
1988 WM20 FIN 6 0 3 3 2 B
1991-93 WM FIN 20 4 3 7 18 S
1991 CC FIN 6 0 1 1 4 —
1992 OG-M FIN 8 0 0 0 2 —

**Peltonen, Esa / b. Feb. 25, 1947**
1967-78 WM FIN 81 29 17 46 26 —
1976 CC FIN 5 0 1 1 0 —
1968-80 OG-M FIN 24 5 5 10 6 —
~IIHF Hall of Fame

**Peltonen, Jorma / b. Jan. 11, 1944**
1966-75 WM FIN 52 10 11 26 12 —
1964-72 OG-M FIN 15 3 4 7 6 —

**Peltonen, Jouni / b. Jan. 21, 1955**
1976 WM FIN 10 0 0 0 0 —
1976 CC FIN 1 0 0 0 0 —

**Peltzer, Marc-Paul / b. unknown / d. unknown**
1930-35 WM BEL 10 4 — 4 — —
1928 OG-M BEL 3 4 — 4 — —

**Peluso, Mike / b. Sept. 2, 1974**
2000 WM USA 7 2 2 4 0 —

**Penczek, Roman / b. Dec. 10, 1929 / d. June 3, 1987**
1955 WM POL 8 0 0 0 0 —
1952 OG-M POL 7 0 0 0 — —

**Penelov, Ivan / b. May 18, 1948**
1976 OG-M BUL 5 1 1 2 0 —

**Penicka, Lubomir / b. May 8, 1954**
1981 CC TCH 6 0 2 2 2 —

**Penitz, Friedrich / b. unknown**
1949 WM AUT 2 0 0 0 — —

**Penner, Gerry / b. unknown**
1963 WM CAN 6 3 0 3 6 —

**Penney, Chad / b. Sept. 18, 1973**
1992 WM20 CAN 7 0 0 0 2 —

**Penningrowth, Jim / b. July 28, 1957**
1977 WM20 USA 7 2 0 2 8 —

**Pennington, Cliff / b. Apr. 18, 1940**
1960 OG-M CAN 4 0 2 2 6 S

**Pepin, Jean / b. unknown**
1950 WM FRA 4 1 0 1 0 —

**Peplinski, Jim / b. Oct. 24, 1960**
1988 OG-M CAN 7 0 1 1 6 —

**Pepper, Steve / b. July 29, 1959**
1978 WM20 USA 6 0 2 2 2 —

**Perez, Bryan / b. Feb. 5, 1982**
2000 WM18 USA 6 1 3 4 2 —

**Perez, Denis / b. Apr. 25, 1965**
1992-2000 WM FRA 50 1 5 6 42 —
1988-2002 OG-M FRA 29 0 4 4 18 —

**Pergl, Frantisek / b. Sept. 7, 1915 / d. unknown**
1935-39 WM TCH 24 5 0 5 0 B

**Perreault, Gilbert / b. Nov. 13, 1950**
1972 SS CAN 2 1 1 2 0 1st
1976-81 CC CAN 11 7 10 17 4 1st,2nd

**Perreault, Yanic / b. Apr. 4, 1971**
1996 WM CAN 8 6 3 9 0 S
~WM IIHF Directorate Best Forward (1996)

**Perrin, Pip / b. 1920 / d. unknown**
1939 WM GBR 3 0 — 0 — —

**Persson, Andre / b. Jan. 12, 1983**
2003 WM20 SWE 5 0 0 0 0 —

**Persson, Dennis / b. June 2, 1988**
2006 WM18 SWE 6 1 5 6 8 —

**Persson, Erik / b. Nov. 19, 1909 / d. unknown**
1937 WM SWE 1 0 0 0 0 —

**Persson, Gunnar / b. Aug. 24, 1958**
1978 WM20 SWE 7 0 0 0 0 S

**Persson, Joakim / b. May 15, 1966**
1986 WM20 SWE 7 2 4 6 18 —

**Persson, Ricard / b. Aug. 24, 1969**
1988-89 WM20 SWE 14 5 11 16 22 S
2000 WM SWE 7 0 0 0 6 —
~WM20 IIHF Directorate Best Defenceman (1989), WM20 All-Star Team/Defence (1989)

**Persson, Stefan / b. Dec. 22, 1954**
1977 WM SWE 10 2 0 2 20 S
1981 CC SWE 5 0 0 0 2 —

**Perthaler, Christian / b. July 21, 1968**
1993-2003 WM AUT 36 1 4 5 10 —
1998-2002 OG-M AUT 7 1 3 4 4 —

**Pervukhin, Vasili / b. Jan. 1, 1956**
1977-87 WM URS 78 4 14 18 8 6G,2S,2B
1981-87 CC URS 20 0 4 4 10 1st,2nd
1980-84 OG-M URS 14 0 11 11 2 G,S

**Pervyshin, Andrei / b. Feb. 2, 1985**
2003 WM18 RUS 6 0 3 3 12 B

**Pescher, Hans-Georg / b. Apr. 25, 1931**
1955 WM FRG 8 2 — 2 4 —
1952 OG-M FRG 8 0 0 0 — —

**Pesek-Kada, Karel / b. Sept. 20, 1895 / d. Sept. 30, 1970**
1920 OG-M TCH 3 0 0 0 — B

**Petac, Janez / b. Mar. 6, 1949 / d. May 23, 2011**
1976 OG-M YUG 5 0 0 0 0 —

**Petajaaho, Sakari / b. Jan. 29, 1962**
1981-82 WM20 FIN 12 5 5 10 12 S,B

**Peter, Kurt / b. May 29, 1934**
1962 WM SUI 7 0 2 2 0 —
1956 OG-M SUI 5 0 0 0 2 —

**Peterdi, Imre / b. May 31, 1980**
2009 WM HUN 6 2 0 2 0 —

**Petermann, Felix / b. Apr. 11, 1984**
2001-02 WM18 GER 14 0 2 2 28 —
2003 WM20 GER 6 0 0 0 2 —
2007 WM GER 3 0 0 0 4 —

**Peternousek, Jiri "George" / b. Mar. 11, 1947**
1981 WM NED 8 0 2 2 12 —
1980 OG-M NED 5 1 2 3 4 —

**Peters, Dan / b. Nov. 24, 1977**
1997 WM20 USA 5 0 0 0 2 S

**Peters, Dietmar / b. Aug. 8, 1949**
1970-85 WM GDR 55 4 12 16 39 —
1968 OG-M GDR 7 2 5 7 6 —

**Peters, Roland / b. Sept. 17, 1951**
1976-85 WM GDR 40 7 4 11 24 —

**Petersen, Annar / b. Nov. 23, 1931**
1950-58 WM NOR 13 3 0 3 2 —
1952 OG-M NOR 8 0 0 0 — —

**Petersen, Christian / b. Dec. 1, 1937 / d. Sept. 17, 2009**
1958-65 WM NOR 25 9 6 15 8 —
1964-68 OG-M NOR 12 7 6 13 4 —

**Petersen, Henrik / b. 1933**
1958-62 WM NOR 19 6 2 8 0 —

**Petersen, Toby / b. Oct. 27, 1978**
1997-98 WM20 USA 13 0 4 4 0 S
2007 WM USA 7 2 1 3 4 —

**Petersen, Wilhelm / b. Oct. 2, 1906 / d. Dec. 11, 1988**
1937 WM SWE 3 0 0 0 2 —
1928-36 OG-M SWE 9 2 0 2 2 S

**Petersons, Arvids / b. Oct. 24, 1913 / d. July 6, 1985**
1933-39 WM LAT 18 8 — 8 — —
1936 OG-M LAT 3 1 — 1 — —

**Petersons, Eriks / b. Oct. 7, 1909 / d. unknown**
1933 WM LAT 4 0 — 0 0 —

**Petey, Philippe / b. May 9, 1960**
1980 WM20 SUI 5 0 1 1 0 —

**Petho, Jozef / b. Apr. 17, 1964**
1984 WM20 TCH 7 2 3 5 0 B

**Petit, Michel / b. Feb. 12, 1964**
1990 WM CAN 8 0 1 1 8 —

**Petit, Simon / b. Nov. 2, 1983**
2002 WM20 FRA 6 0 1 1 2 —

**Petrakov, Andrei / b. Apr. 26, 1976**
1996 WM20 RUS 7 1 3 4 0 B

**Petre, Henrik / b. Apr. 9, 1979**
1998 WM20 SWE 7 1 3 4 6 —

**Petrell, Lennart / b. Apr. 13, 1984**
2004 WM20 FIN 5 0 0 0 27 B

**Petrenko, Sergei / b. Sept. 10, 1968**
1988 WM20 URS 7 0 0 0 2 S
1992-99 WM RUS 26 7 11 18 12 G
1992 OG-M RUS 8 3 2 5 0 G

**Petrik, Helmut / b. May 16, 1961**
1981 WM20 AUT 5 1 1 2 10 —
1984 OG-M AUT 5 0 0 0 0 —

**Petrik, Nikolas / b. Mar. 19, 1984**
2004 WM20 AUT 6 0 0 0 6 —

**Petrilainen, Pasi / b. May 5, 1978**
1996-98 WM20 FIN 13 1 5 6 6 —

**Petro, John / b. unknown**
1954 WM CAN 7 8 2 10 8 S

**Petroshinin, Yevgeni / b. Oct. 16, 1976**
1996 WM20 RUS 7 2 1 3 2 B
2001 WM RUS 7 0 0 0 14 —

**Petroske, Jack / b. Aug. 6, 1934**
1958 WM USA 7 0 0 0 6 —
1956 OG-M USA 7 0 0 0 4 S

**Petrov, Anton / b. May 13, 1978**
1998 WM20 KAZ 7 0 0 0 4 —

**Petrov, Dmitri / b. Oct. 2, 1985**
2003 WM18 RUS 6 0 1 1 0 B

**Petrov, Nikolai / b. May 2, 1952**
1976 OG-M BUL 5 1 0 1 4 —

**Petrov, Oleg / b. Apr. 18, 1971**
1991 WM20 URS 7 4 4 8 4 S
1998-2000 WM RUS 18 4 6 10 12 —

**Petrov, Vladimir / b. June 30, 1947**
1969-81 WM URS 102 74 78 152 84 9G,S,B
1972 SS URS 8 3 4 7 10 2nd
1972-80 OG-M URS 16 8 7 15 14 2G,S
~IIHF Hall of Fame
~WM All-Star Team/Forward (1973, 1975, 1977, 1979)

**Petrovici, Ion / b. unknown / d. unknown**
1937 WM ROM 2 0 0 0 0 —

**Petrovicky, Robert / b. Oct. 26, 1973**
1992 WM20 TCH 7 3 6 9 10 —
1996-2008 WM SVK 23 9 6 15 6 G
1994-2002 OG-M SVK 16 4 8 12 20 —

**Petrovicky, Ronald / b. Feb. 15, 1977**
2000-04 WM SVK 11 1 0 1 10 S
2006 OG-M SVK 6 1 0 1 2 —

**Petrovskis, Adolfs / b. unknown / d. unknown**
1933-38 WM LAT 13 3 — 3 0 —
1936 OG-M LAT 3 0 — 0 — —

**Petrs, Zbynek / b. unknown / d. unknown**
1931-33 WM TCH 4 0 — 0 0 B

**Petrukhin, Yevgeni / b. Aug. 31, 1980**
1999-2000 WM20 KAZ 13 0 0 0 12 —

**Petrunin, Andrei / b. Feb. 2, 1978**
1996-97 WM20 RUS 13 4 4 8 4 2B

**Pettersson, Bror / b. Jan. 31, 1924 / d. Oct. 15, 1978**
1947 WM SWE 6 2 — 2 — S
1948 OG-M SWE 5 4 — 4 — —

**Pettersson, Hakan / b. May 11, 1949 / d. May 10, 2008**
1971-75 WM SWE 18 5 5 10 2 4B
1972 OG-M SWE 5 0 0 0 2 —

**Pettersson, Jorgen / b. July 11, 1956**
1983 WM SWE 10 2 0 2 4 —
1981 CC SWE 5 0 0 0 0 —

**Pettersson, Lars / b. Mar. 19, 1925 / d. May 8, 1971**
1949-51 WM SWE 10 4 — 4 4 S
1952 OG-M SWE 9 6 2 8 — B

**Pettersson, Lars-Gunnar / b. Apr. 8, 1960**
1980 WM20 SWE 5 4 1 5 0 B
1985-87 WM SWE 26 9 7 16 24 G,S
1987 CC SWE 5 2 0 2 0 —
1988 OG-M SWE 8 3 4 7 2 B

**Pettersson, Martin / b. Jan. 19, 1961**
1981 WM20 SWE 5 0 2 2 2 G

**Pettersson, Ove / b. Feb. 2, 1962**
1981-82 WM20 SWE 12 0 1 1 8 G

**Pettersson, Robert / b. Oct. 23, 1904 / d. unknown**
1931 WM SWE 6 0 — 0 — —

**Pettersson, Rolf / b. Sept. 27, 1926**
1947-55 WM SWE 25 6 5 11 6 G,S,B
1948 OG-M SWE 6 2 — 2 — —

**Pettersson, Ronald "Sura-Pelle" / b. Apr. 16, 1935**
1955-67 WM SWE 65 42 21 63 15 2G,2S,2B
1956-64 OG-M SWE 21 8 12 20 4 S
~IIHF Hall of Fame

**Pettersson, Timmy / b. Mar. 15, 1977**
1997 WM20 SWE 6 0 3 3 2 —

**Petterstrom, Pontus / b. Apr. 21, 1982**
2000 WM18 SWE 6 2 1 3 6 B

**Pettinger, Matt / b. Oct. 22, 1980**
2000 WM20 CAN 7 4 0 4 4 B
2006 WM CAN 8 1 0 1 4 —

**Pettygrove, Marc / b. Jan. 18, 1960**
1979 WM20 USA 5 0 0 0 6 —

**Petukhov, Stanislav / b. Aug. 19, 1937**
1963 WM URS 7 4 4 8 4 G
1960-64 OG-M URS 11 8 5 13 6 G,B

**Pewal, Marco / b. Sept. 17, 1978**
2007 WM AUT 6 0 0 0 0 —

**Pfammatter, Kurt / b. Mar. 30, 1941**
1964 OG-M SUI 7 1 1 2 2 —

**Pfeffer, Thomas / b. Sept. 3, 1980**
2007 WM AUT 3 0 1 1 0 —

**Pfefferle, Max / b. unknown**
1959 WM FRG 5 3 1 4 4 —

**Pfister, Willi / b. Mar. 1, 1928**
1950-51 WM SUI 11 5 5 10 4 2B
1952 OG-M SUI 8 1 2 3 — —

**Pflugel, Harry / b. Mar. 26, 1959**
1978-79 WM20 FRG 11 4 1 5 37 —

**Pfosi, Guido / b. Jan. 16, 1965**
1984 WM20 SUI 7 1 0 1 2 —

**Philipp, Rainer / b. Mar. 8, 1950**
1971-81 WM FRG 73 29 16 45 22 —
1972-80 OG-M FRG 13 2 7 9 6 B

**Phillips, Nicholas / b. Apr. 15, 1987**
2005 WM18 DEN 6 0 0 0 2 —

**Phippen, Pat / b. unknown**
1976 WM USA 2 0 0 0 2 —

**Picard, Robert / b. May 25, 1957**
1978-79 WM CAN 17 1 2 3 6 B

**Picha, Zdenek / b. May 17, 1921 / d. Apr. 15, 1984**
1949 WM TCH 6 3 — 3 — G

**Pidcock, Jack / b. unknown / d. unknown**
1931 WM CAN 6 3 — 3 — G

**Piechota, Jan / b. July 10, 1910 / d. Oct. 12, 1991**
1933 WM POL 1 0 — 0 0 —

**Piecko, Jan / b. Feb. 3, 1955**
1974-79 WM POL 25 0 3 3 4 —
1984 OG-M POL 5 1 3 4 0 —

**Piekarski, Rafal / b. Feb. 2, 1977**
1997 WM20 POL 6 1 0 1 4 —

**Pienitz, Hans / b. Jan. 27, 1988**
2006 WM18 GER 6 0 2 2 22 —

**Pihlstrom, Mathias / b. May 26, 1975**
1995 WM20 SWE 7 1 1 2 0 B

**Piitulainen, Ossi / b. Apr. 13, 1965**
1985 WM20 FIN 7 0 1 1 0 —

**Pilar, Karel / b. Dec. 23, 1977**
2001 WM CZE 9 0 0 0 6 G

**Pillmaier, Klaus / b. Mar. 22, 1965**
1984 WM20 FRG 7 3 0 3 2 —

**Pilloni, Patrick / b. Feb. 21, 1970**
1994-2001 WM AUT 22 0 2 2 12 —
1998 OG-M AUT 4 0 0 0 2 —

**Pilyugin, Danil / b. Oct. 21, 1985**
2003 WM18 KAZ 6 1 0 1 6 —

**Pinc, Michal / b. Dec. 2, 1981**
1999 WM18 CZE 7 3 1 4 6 —

**Pinder, Gerry / b. Sept. 15, 1948**
1969 WM CAN 10 3 1 4 14 —
1968 OG-M CAN 7 1 0 1 2 B

**Pinder, Herb / b. Dec. 24, 1946**
1968 OG-M CAN 2 1 0 1 2 B

**Pinomaki, Matti / b. Feb. 8, 1986**
2004 WM18 FIN 6 0 0 0 2 —

**Pinter, Philipp / b. Jan. 18, 1985**
2004 WM20 AUT 6 0 0 0 0 —

**Piper, Elmer / b. 1911 / d. unknown**
1934 WM CAN — 0 — 0 — G

**Pirie, Brad / b. Oct. 21, 1955**
1980 OG-M CAN 6 1 2 3 2 —

**Pirjeta, Lasse / b. Apr. 4, 1974**
2002-04 WM FIN 21 4 0 4 2 —

**Piros, Kamil / b. Nov. 20, 1978**
1997-98 WM20 CZE 14 2 7 9 6 —

**Pisa, Ales / b. Jan. 2, 1977**
1996-97 WM20 CZE 13 0 2 2 35 —

**Pisaru, Marian / b. Jan. 4, 1954**
1977 WM ROM 10 1 0 1 6 —
1976-80 OG-M ROM 10 4 2 6 4 —

**Piskura, Ondrej / b. May 2, 1986**
2004 WM18 SVK 6 0 0 0 2 —

**Pistek, Lubomir / b. Aug. 7, 1980**
1999-2000 WM20 SVK 12 1 1 2 6 B

**Pitblado, Edward / b. Feb. 23, 1896 / d. Dec. 2, 1978**
1924 OG-M GBR 5 4 — 4 — B

**Pittl, Stefan / b. June 2, 1984**
2004 WM20 AUT 6 0 1 1 6 —

**Pittrich, Rudolf / b. June 19, 1935**
1955-62 WM FRG 13 2 3 5 18 —
1956 OG-M FRG 6 1 0 1 0 —

**Pivko, Libor / b. Mar. 29, 1980**
2000 WM20 CZE 7 1 2 3 4 G

**Pivonka, Michal / b. Jan. 28, 1966**
1984-86 WM20 TCH 21 15 11 26 24 S,B
1985-86 WM TCH 20 2 2 4 6 G
1991 CC TCH 5 0 3 3 2 —
~WM20 IIHF Directorate Best Forward (1985), WM20 All-Star Team/Forward (1985, 1986)

**Plachta, Jacek / b. May 18, 1969**
1988 WM20 POL 7 2 0 2 8 —
2002 WM POL 6 1 4 5 10 —

**Planovsky, Antonin / b. Nov. 10, 1959**
1979 WM20 TCH 6 0 0 0 2 S
1982 WM TCH 3 0 1 1 2 S

**Plante, Dan / b. Oct. 5, 1971**
1996-97 WM USA 15 2 2 4 6 B

**Plante, Derek / b. Jan. 17, 1971**
1991 WM20 USA 7 1 2 3 4 —
1992-2002 WM USA 43 5 6 11 14 B

**Plantery, Mark / b. Aug. 14, 1959**
1977 WM20 CAN 7 0 1 1 2 S

**Platek, Dariusz / b. July 26, 1966**
1992 OG-M POL 6 0 0 0 0 —

**Platil, Jan / b. Feb. 9, 1983**
2001 WM18 CZE 7 0 0 0 20 —
2007 WM CZE 4 0 0 0 8 —

**Platt, Geoff / b. July 10, 1985**
2003 WM18 CAN 7 3 0 3 0 G

**Platzer, Martin / b. Sept. 24, 1963**
1984-88 OG-M AUT 11 0 1 1 2 —

**Platzer, Michael / b. unknown**
1981 WM20 AUT 5 2 0 2 2 —

**Plavsic, Adrien / b. Jan. 13, 1970**
1990 WM20 CAN 7 0 1 1 8 G
1992 OG-M CAN 8 0 2 2 0 S

**Plavucha, Vlastimil / b. Nov. 6, 1968**
1996-2000 WM SVK 22 6 2 8 8 —
1996 WCH SVK 3 0 2 2 0 —
1994-98 OG-M SVK 9 4 0 4 2 —

**Plaxton, Bert / b. Apr. 22, 1901 / d. Nov. 7, 1970**
1928 OG-M CAN 1 2 — 2 — G

**Plaxton, Hugh / b. May 16, 1904 / d. Dec. 1, 1982**
1928 OG-M CAN 3 12 — 12 — G

**Plaxton, Rogers / b. June 2, 1904 / d. Dec. 20, 1963**
1928 OG-M CAN 1 0 — 0 — G

**Pleau, Larry / b. June 29, 1947**
1969 WM USA 10 5 0 5 8 —
1968 OG-M USA 7 2 4 6 2 —

**Pleban, Jim / b. unknown**
1950 WM USA 5 0 0 0 4 S

**Pleisch, Thomas / b. Dec. 17, 1913 / d. unknown**
1934-35 WM SUI 8 1 — 1 — S
1936 OG-M SUI 1 0 0 0 — —

**Pleschberger, Achim / b. Feb. 6, 1968**
1987 WM20 SUI 7 1 1 2 4 —

**Pletka, Vaclav / b. June 8, 1979**
1999 WM20 CZE 6 5 1 6 26 —

**Plihal, Tomas / b. Mar. 23, 1983**
2001 WM18 CZE 7 1 1 2 2 —

**Plotka, Wolfgang / b. May 16, 1941**
1963-70 WM GDR 32 4 5 9 25 —
1968 OG-M GDR 7 1 1 2 4 —

**Pluymers, Al / b. June 8, 1957**
1981 WM NED 8 0 1 1 4 —
1980 OG-M NED 5 0 1 1 2 —

**Plyushev, Alexander / b. Feb. 8, 1986**
2004 WM18 RUS 6 1 1 2 4 G

**Pobyedonostsev, Olexander / b. Nov. 19, 1981**
1999 WM18 UKR 6 0 1 1 12 —
2000 WM20 UKR 7 0 0 0 2 —
2005-07 WM UKR 7 0 0 0 12 —

**Pock, Herbert / b. Mar. 8, 1957**
1976-88 OG-M AUT 14 6 1 7 4 —

**Pock, Thomas / b. Dec. 2, 1981**
2002-05 WM AUT 21 2 2 4 20 —
2002 OG-M AUT 4 0 0 0 2 —

**Podein, Shjon / b. Mar. 5, 1968**
1993-98 WM USA 18 4 4 8 26 —

**Podlegayev, Dmitri / b. Sept. 12, 1974**
1994 WM20 RUS 7 0 0 0 0 B

**Podlesak, Martin / b. Sept. 26, 1982**
2002 WM20 CZE 7 2 0 2 2 —

**Podloski, Ray / b. Jan. 5, 1966**
1999 WM AUT 6 1 0 1 2 —

**Podlesak, Martin / b. Sept. 26, 1982**
2000 WM18 CZE 6 3 0 3 20 —

**Podollan, Jason / b. Feb. 18, 1976**
1996 WM20 CAN 6 2 3 5 2 G

**Podsiadlo, Krzysztof / b. Feb. 16, 1962**
1986-89 WM POL 20 0 4 4 12 —
1988 OG-M POL 6 0 1 1 2 —

**Pogacnik, Tone / b. Mar. 24, 1910 / d. unknown**
1939 WM YUG 5 0 — 0 — —

**Pohanka, Igor / b. July 5, 1983**
2001 WM18 SVK 6 2 3 5 4 —
2002-03 WM20 SVK 13 3 6 9 6 —

| | | | | | | | | |
|---|---|---|---|---|---|---|---|---|
| **Pohja, Tommy / b. July 18, 1964** | | | | | | | | |
| 1984 | WM20 | FIN | 6 | 1 | 0 | 1 | 8 | S |
| 1986 | WM | FIN | 8 | 0 | 3 | 3 | 0 | — |
| **Pohjavirta, Tuomo / b. Nov. 17, 1917 / d. unknown** | | | | | | | | |
| 1949 | WM | FIN | 4 | 0 | — | 0 | — | — |
| **Pohl, Anton / b. Aug. 22, 1944** | | | | | | | | |
| 1972 | WM | FRG | 5 | 0 | 1 | 1 | 0 | — |
| **Pohl, John / b. June 29, 1979** | | | | | | | | |
| 2003 | WM | USA | 6 | 3 | 4 | 7 | 0 | — |
| **Pohl, Michael / b. Jan. 25, 1968** | | | | | | | | |
| 1988 | WM20 | FRG | 5 | 1 | 0 | 1 | 2 | — |
| **Pohland, Heinz / b. Sept. 1, 1950** | | | | | | | | |
| 1976 | WM | GDR | 10 | 0 | 0 | 0 | 0 | — |
| **Pohorelec, Dusan / b. Nov. 20, 1972** | | | | | | | | |
| 1994 | OG-M | SVK | 5 | 0 | 0 | 0 | 0 | — |
| **Poindl, Bernd / b. Augist 30, 1941** | | | | | | | | |
| 1961-67 | WM | GDR | 33 | 3 | 3 | 6 | 16 | — |
| 1968 | OG-M | GDR | 6 | 0 | 0 | 0 | 0 | — |
| **Poirier, Chuck / b. unknown** | | | | | | | | |
| 1951 | WM | USA | 6 | 3 | — | 3 | 8 | — |
| **Poitsch, Fritz / b. Oct. 15, 1926** | | | | | | | | |
| 1953-54 | WM | FRG | 11 | 6 | 2 | 8 | 4 | S |
| 1952 | OG-M | FRG | 8 | 4 | 1 | 5 | — | — |
| **Pojkar, David / b. June 4, 1981** | | | | | | | | |
| 1999 | WM18 | CZE | 7 | 0 | 1 | 1 | 6 | — |
| 2001 | WM20 | CZE | 7 | 0 | 0 | 0 | 2 | G |
| **Pokladov, Alexander / b. Dec. 18, 1978** | | | | | | | | |
| 1998 | WM20 | KAZ | 6 | 0 | 0 | 0 | 2 | — |
| **Pokorny, Andreas / b. June 18, 1968** | | | | | | | | |
| 1988 | WM20 | FRG | 7 | 1 | 2 | 3 | 0 | — |
| 1989-91 | WM | FRG | 23 | 2 | 2 | 4 | 10 | — |
| **Pokorny, Miloslav / b. Oct. 5, 1926 / d. Nov. 8, 1948** | | | | | | | | |
| 1947-57 | WM | TCH | 13 | 9 | 2 | 11 | — | G,B |
| 1948 | OG-M | TCH | 7 | 2 | — | 2 | — | S |
| **Pokrivcak, Tomas / b. Oct. 10, 1984** | | | | | | | | |
| 2004 | WM20 | SVK | 6 | 1 | 2 | 3 | 0 | — |
| **Pokrovski, Valeri / b. May 17, 1978** | | | | | | | | |
| 1998 | WM20 | RUS | 7 | 0 | 0 | 0 | 2 | S |
| **Polaczek, Alexander / b. Aug. 9, 1980** | | | | | | | | |
| 2007 | WM | GER | 3 | 0 | 0 | 0 | 2 | — |
| **Polak, Jiri / b. Aug. 10, 1977** | | | | | | | | |
| 1996 | WM20 | CZE | 6 | 0 | 1 | 1 | 2 | — |
| **Polak, Vojtech / b. June 27, 1985** | | | | | | | | |
| 2003 | WM18 | CZE | 6 | 3 | 2 | 5 | 18 | — |
| 2004 | WM20 | CZE | 6 | 1 | 0 | 1 | 4 | — |
| **Polansky, Jiri / b. Dec. 18, 1981** | | | | | | | | |
| 1999 | WM18 | CZE | 7 | 0 | 0 | 0 | 2 | — |
| **Polcik, Peter / b. July 23, 1983** | | | | | | | | |
| 2001 | WM18 | SVK | 4 | 1 | 1 | 2 | 2 | — |
| **Poleshuk, Anton / b. Feb. 21, 1987** | | | | | | | | |
| 2005 | WM18 | RUS | 6 | 0 | 0 | 0 | 10 | — |
| **Polich, Mike / b. Dec. 19, 1952** | | | | | | | | |
| 1975 | WM | USA | 10 | 2 | 5 | 7 | 34 | — |
| 1976 | CC | USA | 5 | 1 | 1 | 2 | 4 | — |
| **Polischuk, Fyodor / b. July 4, 1979** | | | | | | | | |
| 1999 | WM20 | KAZ | 6 | 0 | 1 | 1 | 0 | — |
| 2004-05 | WM | KAZ | 12 | 0 | 1 | 1 | 10 | — |
| 2006 | OG-M | KAZ | 5 | 0 | 1 | 1 | 6 | — |
| **Poling, Sam / b. unknown** | | | | | | | | |
| 1950 | WM | USA | 4 | 1 | 0 | 1 | 0 | S |
| **Poliukh, Alexander / b. June 19, 1979** | | | | | | | | |
| 1999 | WM20 | BLR | 6 | 0 | 1 | 1 | 4 | — |
| **Polizu, Nicu / b. July 2, 1904 / d. unknown** | | | | | | | | |
| 1931-34 | WM | ROM | 16 | 1 | — | 1 | 1 | — |
| **Poljansek, Silvo / b. Dec. 25, 1951** | | | | | | | | |
| 1972-76 | OG-M | YUG | 9 | 1 | 2 | 3 | 2 | — |
| **Polkovnikov, Oleg / b. Dec. 13, 1973** | | | | | | | | |
| 2000-01 | WM | UKR | 11 | 0 | 0 | 0 | 10 | — |
| **Pollari, Eino / b. Apr. 11, 1935** | | | | | | | | |
| 1958 | WM | FIN | 7 | 1 | 0 | 1 | 0 | — |
| **Pollesol, Ed / b. unknown** | | | | | | | | |
| 1963 | WM | CAN | 1 | 1 | 0 | 1 | 0 | — |
| **Pollock, Tom / b. Aug. 1, 1925 / d. Aug. 17, 1994** | | | | | | | | |
| 1952 | OG-M | CAN | 8 | 2 | 1 | 3 | 6 | G |
| **Polonitsky, Vasyl / b. Feb. 28, 1977** | | | | | | | | |
| 1996 | WM20 | UKR | 5 | 0 | 1 | 1 | 40 | — |
| 2006 | WM | UKR | 6 | 0 | 0 | 0 | 4 | — |
| **Poltera, Gebi / b. Dec. 14, 1923 / d. Nov. 11, 2008** | | | | | | | | |
| 1947-54 | WM | SUI | 36 | 20 | 6 | 26 | 18 | 3B |
| 1948-52 | OG-M | SUI | 14 | 6 | 5 | 11 | — | B |
| **Poltera, Uli / b. July 17, 1922 / d. Mar. 1994** | | | | | | | | |
| 1947-54 | WM | SUI | 39 | 45 | 4 | 49 | 14 | 3B |
| 1948-52 | OG-M | SUI | 14 | 21 | 3 | 24 | — | B |
| **Polupanov, Viktor / b. Jan. 1, 1946** | | | | | | | | |
| 1966-70 | WM | URS | 21 | 14 | 14 | 28 | 18 | 3G |
| 1968 | OG-M | URS | 7 | 6 | 6 | 12 | 10 | G |
| **Polushin, Alexander / b. May 8, 1983** | | | | | | | | |
| 2001 | WM18 | RUS | 6 | 3 | 0 | 3 | 6 | G |
| 2002-03 | WM20 | RUS | 13 | 4 | 9 | 13 | 10 | 2G |
| **Pomaranski, Joe / b. Feb. 4, 1983** | | | | | | | | |
| 2001 | WM18 | USA | 6 | 1 | 1 | 2 | 6 | — |
| **Pomichter, Mike / b. Sept. 10, 1973** | | | | | | | | |
| 1993 | WM20 | USA | 7 | 0 | 2 | 2 | 4 | — |
| 1995 | WM | USA | 6 | 1 | 2 | 3 | 2 | — |
| **Ponikarovski, Olexi / b. Apr. 9, 1980** | | | | | | | | |
| 2002 | OG-M | UKR | 4 | 1 | 1 | 2 | 6 | — |
| **Poole, Jack / b. unknown** | | | | | | | | |
| 1961-63 | WM | USA | 20 | 13 | 8 | 21 | 16 | B |
| **Pootmans, Georges / b. May 19, 1917 / d. unknown** | | | | | | | | |
| 1934-39 | WM | BEL | 12 | 4 | — | 4 | — | — |
| 1936 | OG-M | BEL | 3 | 2 | — | 2 | — | — |
| **Popescu, Florin / b. unknown** | | | | | | | | |
| 1947 | WM | ROM | 7 | 0 | — | 0 | — | — |
| **Popescu, Mihai / b. Nov. 11, 1960** | | | | | | | | |
| 1980 | OG-M | ROM | 5 | 0 | 0 | 0 | 0 | — |
| **Popikhin, Yevgeni / b. Feb. 19, 1960** | | | | | | | | |
| 1980 | WM20 | URS | 5 | 0 | 1 | 1 | 4 | G |
| **Popko, Luke / b. Mar. 29, 1988** | | | | | | | | |
| 2006 | WM18 | USA | 6 | 2 | 1 | 3 | 8 | G |
| **Poplimont, Andre / b. Apr. 18, 1893 / d. unknown** | | | | | | | | |
| 1924 | OG-M | BEL | 3 | 1 | — | 1 | — | — |
| **Popov, Andrei / b. July 15, 1988** | | | | | | | | |
| 2006 | WM18 | RUS | 6 | 3 | 2 | 5 | 8 | — |
| **Popov, Valeri / b. Feb. 24, 1967** | | | | | | | | |
| 1987 | WM20 | URS | 6 | 1 | 2 | 3 | 4 | — |
| **Popovic, Mark / b. Oct. 11, 1982** | | | | | | | | |
| 2001-02 | WM20 | CAN | 14 | 0 | 3 | 3 | 8 | S,B |
| **Popovic, Miljan / b. unknown / d. unknown** | | | | | | | | |
| 1939 | WM | YUG | 4 | 0 | — | 0 | — | — |
| **Popovic, Peter / b. Feb. 10, 1968** | | | | | | | | |
| 1993 | WM | SWE | 8 | 0 | 1 | 1 | 2 | S |
| 1996 | WCH | SWE | 3 | 0 | 0 | 0 | 2 | — |
| **Popugayev, Andrei / b. Apr. 2, 1965** | | | | | | | | |
| 1985 | WM20 | URS | 7 | 0 | 0 | 0 | 12 | B |
| **Por, Grega / b. Oct. 3, 1977** | | | | | | | | |
| 2003 | WM | SLO | 6 | 1 | 0 | 1 | 0 | — |
| **Porkka, Toni / b. Jan. 4, 1970** | | | | | | | | |
| 1990 | WM20 | FIN | 7 | 1 | 0 | 1 | 6 | — |
| **Porter, John "Red" / b. Jan. 21, 1904 / d. unknown** | | | | | | | | |
| 1928 | OG-M | CAN | 3 | 3 | — | 3 | — | G |
| **Porter, Lyle / b. Feb. 12, 1941** | | | | | | | | |
| 1966 | WM | USA | 7 | 2 | 2 | 4 | 2 | — |
| **Portland, Buster / b. 1916 / d. unknown** | | | | | | | | |
| 1938 | WM | CAN | 7 | 1 | — | 1 | — | G |
| **Portner, Philipp / b. Nov. 11, 1977** | | | | | | | | |
| 1997 | WM20 | SUI | 6 | 0 | 0 | 0 | 2 | — |
| **Porvari, Jukka / b. Jan. 19, 1954** | | | | | | | | |
| 1977-81 | WM | FIN | 36 | 13 | 7 | 20 | 26 | — |
| 1981 | CC | FIN | 5 | 1 | 0 | 1 | 0 | — |
| 1980 | OG-M | FIN | 7 | 7 | 4 | 11 | 4 | — |
| **Posma, Mike / b. Dec. 16, 1967** | | | | | | | | |
| 1987 | WM20 | USA | 7 | 2 | 2 | 4 | 10 | — |
| **Posmetyev, Oleg / b. June 19, 1966** | | | | | | | | |
| 1985 | WM20 | URS | 7 | 2 | 1 | 3 | 2 | B |
| **Posmyk, Marek / b. Sept. 15, 1978** | | | | | | | | |
| 1996-98 | WM20 | CZE | 13 | 2 | 2 | 4 | 10 | — |
| **Pospisil, Frantisek / b. Apr. 2, 1944** | | | | | | | | |
| 1967-77 | WM | TCH | 97 | 9 | 36 | 45 | 38 | 3G,3S,3B |
| 1976 | CC | TCH | 7 | 1 | 1 | 2 | 0 | 2nd |
| 1968-76 | OG-M | TCH | 17 | 2 | 7 | 9 | 22 | 2S,B |
| ~IIHF Hall of Fame | | | | | | | | |
| ~WM IIHF Directorate Best Defenceman (1972, 1976), WM All-Star Team/Defence (1972, 1976, 1977) | | | | | | | | |
| **Pospisil, Miroslav / b. unknown** | | | | | | | | |
| 1954 | WM | TCH | 7 | 4 | 0 | 4 | 2 | — |
| **Potac, Jozef / b. June 6, 1978** | | | | | | | | |
| 1997 | WM20 | SVK | 6 | 0 | 0 | 0 | 4 | — |
| **Potaichuk, Andrei / b. Aug. 18, 1970** | | | | | | | | |
| 1990 | WM20 | URS | 7 | 3 | 2 | 5 | 2 | S |
| 1996 | WM | RUS | 7 | 1 | 5 | 6 | 0 | — |
| **Pothier, Brian / b. Apr. 15, 1977** | | | | | | | | |
| 2007 | WM | USA | 7 | 0 | 1 | 1 | 4 | — |
| **Poti, Tom / b. Mar. 22, 1977** | | | | | | | | |
| 1996-97 | WM20 | USA | 12 | 1 | 5 | 6 | 4 | S |
| 2002 | OG-M | USA | 6 | 0 | 1 | 1 | 4 | S |
| **Potsch, Rudolf / b. June 15, 1937** | | | | | | | | |
| 1959-66 | WM | TCH | 27 | 7 | 8 | 15 | 18 | 3S,2B |
| 1960-64 | OG-M | TCH | 14 | 4 | 4 | 8 | 8 | B |
| **Potter, Corey / b. Jan. 5, 1984** | | | | | | | | |
| 2002 | WM18 | USA | 8 | 0 | 2 | 2 | 29 | G |
| 2004 | WM20 | USA | 6 | 0 | 0 | 0 | 6 | G |
| **Pottinger, Markus / b. Jan. 5, 1978** | | | | | | | | |
| 1996-98 | WM20 | GER | 18 | 0 | 1 | 1 | 37 | — |
| **Potucek, Franz / b. May 28, 1927** | | | | | | | | |
| 1949-57 | WM | AUT | 14 | 0 | — | 0 | — | — |
| 1956 | OG-M | AUT | 6 | 1 | 0 | 1 | 4 | — |
| **Potvin, Denis / b. Oct. 29, 1953** | | | | | | | | |
| 1986 | WM | CAN | 7 | 1 | 4 | 5 | 6 | B |
| 1976-81 | CC | CAN | 14 | 3 | 13 | 16 | 28 | 1st,2nd |
| **Potz, Jerzy / b. Feb. 1, 1953 / d. Jan. 27, 2000** | | | | | | | | |
| 1973-89 | WM | POL | 57 | 1 | 3 | 4 | 37 | — |
| 1972-88 | OG-M | POL | 20 | 0 | 2 | 2 | 13 | — |
| **Poudrier, Serge / b. Apr. 22, 1966** | | | | | | | | |
| 1992-99 | WM | FRA | 33 | 6 | 5 | 11 | 45 | — |
| 1992-98 | OG-M | FRA | 19 | 3 | 7 | 10 | 12 | — |
| **Pouget, Christian / b. Jan. 11, 1966** | | | | | | | | |
| 1992-2004 | WM | FRA | 41 | 10 | 14 | 24 | 86 | — |
| 1988-98 | OG-M | FRA | 14 | 1 | 2 | 3 | 18 | — |
| **Poulin, Patrick / b. Apr. 23, 1973** | | | | | | | | |
| 1992 | WM20 | CAN | 7 | 2 | 2 | 4 | 2 | — |
| **Pouliot, Marc-Antoine / b. May 22, 1985** | | | | | | | | |
| 2003 | WM18 | CAN | 7 | 2 | 7 | 9 | 6 | G |
| **Pourtanel, Benoit / b. Apr. 12, 1974** | | | | | | | | |
| 2002 | OG-M | FRA | 4 | 0 | 0 | 0 | 0 | — |
| **Pourtanel, Patrice / b. Feb. 8, 1946** | | | | | | | | |
| 1968 | OG-M | FRA | 5 | 0 | 0 | 0 | 0 | — |
| **Pousaz, Jacques / b. Aug. 5, 1947** | | | | | | | | |
| 1972 | OG-M | SUI | 4 | 0 | 2 | 2 | 0 | — |
| **Pousse, Pierre / b. Feb. 27, 1966** | | | | | | | | |
| 1992-96 | WM | FRA | 30 | 3 | 3 | 6 | 8 | — |
| 1992-94 | OG-M | FRA | 15 | 1 | 1 | 2 | 4 | — |
| **Pousset, Nicolas / b. May 21, 1979** | | | | | | | | |
| 2004 | WM | FRA | 6 | 0 | 0 | 0 | 6 | — |
| **Pouzar, Jaroslav / b. Jan. 23, 1952** | | | | | | | | |
| 1976-82 | WM | TCH | 55 | 21 | 13 | 34 | 32 | 2G,3S,B |
| 1976-81 | CC | TCH | 11 | 3 | 1 | 4 | 8 | 2nd |
| 1976-80 | OG-M | TCH | 11 | 10 | 6 | 16 | 14 | S |
| **Pozivil, Lukas / b. Sept. 12, 1982** | | | | | | | | |
| 2002 | WM20 | CZE | 7 | 1 | 0 | 1 | 4 | — |
| **Prachar, Kamil / b. Aug. 24, 1963** | | | | | | | | |
| 1983 | WM20 | TCH | 7 | 0 | 2 | 2 | 15 | S |
| 1991 | CC | TCH | 5 | 0 | 0 | 0 | 0 | — |
| **Prajzler, Petr / b. Sept. 21, 1965** | | | | | | | | |
| 1985 | WM20 | TCH | 6 | 1 | 2 | 3 | 4 | S |
| **Prakopchyk, Andrei / b. Apr. 16, 1986** | | | | | | | | |
| 2004 | WM18 | BLR | 6 | 0 | 1 | 1 | 6 | — |
| **Precechtel, Kamil / b. May 12, 1962** | | | | | | | | |
| 1982 | WM20 | TCH | 7 | 2 | 4 | 6 | 0 | S |
| **Prechac, Olivier / b. Jan. 5, 1949** | | | | | | | | |
| 1968 | OG-M | FRA | 5 | 0 | 0 | 0 | 0 | — |
| **Prendergast, Mike / b. Oct. 22, 1972** | | | | | | | | |
| 1992 | WM20 | USA | 6 | 0 | 0 | 0 | 2 | B |
| **Presley, Wayne / b. Mar. 23, 1965** | | | | | | | | |
| 1987 | CC | USA | 5 | 1 | 0 | 1 | 12 | — |
| **Prete, Antonio / b. Oct. 30, 1918 / d. unknown** | | | | | | | | |
| 1939 | WM | ITA | 1 | 0 | — | 0 | — | — |
| **Preuss, Gunther / b. Mar. 3, 1964** | | | | | | | | |
| 1984 | WM20 | FRG | 7 | 0 | 1 | 1 | 0 | — |
| **Priddy, Stan / b. Feb. 26, 1921 / d. May 12, 1996** | | | | | | | | |
| 1948 | OG-M | USA | 8 | 1 | 0 | 1 | 2 | — |
| **Priechodsky, Marek / b. Oct. 24, 1979** | | | | | | | | |
| 1999 | WM20 | SVK | 6 | 0 | 0 | 0 | 6 | B |
| **Primeau, Keith / b. Nov. 24, 1971** | | | | | | | | |
| 1997-98 | WM | CAN | 17 | 6 | 4 | 10 | 18 | G |
| 1996 | WCH | CAN | 5 | 0 | 0 | 0 | 21 | 2nd |
| 1998 | OG-M | CAN | 6 | 2 | 1 | 3 | 4 | — |
| **Primeau, Kevin / b. Mar. 1, 1956** | | | | | | | | |
| 1980 | OG-M | CAN | 6 | 4 | 1 | 5 | 6 | — |
| **Princi, Didier / b. June 2, 1971** | | | | | | | | |
| 1991 | WM20 | SUI | 6 | 0 | 0 | 0 | 2 | — |
| **Prinz, Cornel / b. Apr. 19, 1979** | | | | | | | | |
| 1999 | WM20 | SUI | 6 | 0 | 0 | 0 | 18 | — |
| **Priondolo, Constantine / b. Sept. 10, 1959** | | | | | | | | |
| 1982-83 | WM | ITA | 17 | 6 | 2 | 8 | 4 | — |
| 1984 | OG-M | ITA | 4 | 0 | 4 | 4 | 2 | — |
| **Probst, Jakob / b. unknown** | | | | | | | | |
| 1954-59 | WM | FRG | 10 | 2 | 0 | 2 | 8 | — |

**Probst, Paul / b. May 3, 1950**
1972 WM SUI 7 0 3 3 4 —
1972 OG-M SUI 4 0 0 0 0 —

**Prochazka, Frantisek / b. Jan. 25, 1962 / d. Apr. 27, 2012**
1986-92 WM TCH 38 10 3 13 68 3B
1992 OG-M TCH 8 1 1 2 4 B

**Prochazka, Libor / b. Apr. 25, 1974**
1994 WM20 CZE 5 0 0 0 2 —
1997-99 WM CZE 29 4 7 11 52 G,2B
1998 OG-M CZE 1 0 0 0 0 G

**Prochazka, Martin / b. Mar. 3, 1972**
1990-92 WM20 TCH 21 9 5 14 2 2B
1995-2002 WM CZE 70 27 28 55 30 4G,2B
1996 WCH CZE 2 0 0 0 0 —
1998 OG-M CZE 6 1 1 2 0 G
~WM MVP (2000), WM All-Star Team/Forward (1997)

**Prochazka, Radek / b. Jan. 6, 1978**
1997-98 WM20 CZE 14 1 4 5 6 —

**Prokhorov, Vitali / b. Dec. 25, 1966**
1992-98 WM RUS 12 0 4 4 4 —
1991 CC URS 5 1 2 3 4 —
1992 OG-M RUS 8 2 4 6 6 G

**Prokop, Juraj / b. Sept. 18, 1985**
2003 WM18 SVK 7 0 3 3 2 S

**Prokopiev, Alexander / b. June 10, 1971**
1995-2004 WM RUS 57 15 14 29 38 S

**Prokupek, Ladislav / b. Apr. 21, 1975**
1994 WM20 CZE 6 1 2 3 4 —

**Prommersberger, Anton / b. July 15, 1981**
1999 WM18 GER 6 0 0 0 4 —

**Prommersberger, Max / b. Sept. 12, 1987**
2005 WM18 GER 6 0 0 0 6 —

**Pronin, Nikolai / b. Apr. 13, 1979**
2004 WM RUS 3 0 0 0 0 —

**Pronovost, Jean / b. Dec. 18, 1945**
1977-78 WM CAN 17 4 5 9 0 B

**Proposins, Aleksejs / b. Mar. 20, 1989**
2007 WM18 LAT 6 0 0 0 2 —

**Propp, Brian / b. Feb. 15, 1959**
1979 WM20 CAN 5 2 1 3 2 —
1982-83 WM CAN 20 7 5 13 10 2B
1987 CC CAN 9 2 2 4 2 1st

**Prorok, Ivo / b. Dec. 28, 1969**
2006 WM CZE 6 0 0 0 4 S

**Prorok, Pavel / b. Mar. 17, 1963**
1982 WM20 TCH 7 0 2 2 16 S

**Prosek, Bohumil / b. Mar. 26, 1931**
1957-61 WM TCH 17 6 1 7 10 S,2B
1956 OG-M TCH 7 2 2 4 4 —

**Proske, Frank / b. June 12, 1958**
1978-85 WM GDR 30 6 3 9 8 —

**Prospal, Vaclav / b. Feb. 17, 1975**
1994-95 WM20 CZE 14 4 8 12 18 —
2000-05 WM CZE 25 8 14 22 14 2G
2004 WCH CZE 4 1 3 4 0 —
2006 OG-M CZE 8 4 2 6 2 B

**Protsenko, Borys / b. Aug. 21, 1978**
2000-06 WM UKR 29 6 7 13 43 —

**Prunet, Lilian / b. Feb. 15, 1978**
2004 WM FRA 6 0 0 0 8 —

**Prunster, Norbert / b. Jan. 6, 1954**
1984 OG-M ITA 3 0 0 0 0 —

**Prusa, Peter / b. Feb. 19, 1944**
1967-74 WM GDR 26 5 3 8 17 —
1968 OG-M GDR 7 0 0 0 2 —

**Pryakhin, Sergei / b. Dec. 7, 1963**
1982-83 WM20 URS 14 4 5 9 17 G
1987-90 WM URS 11 0 3 3 10 G,S
1987 CC URS 9 0 2 2 6 2nd

**Pryazhnikov, Viktor / b. Dec. 23, 1933 / d. Apr. 17, 2008**
1959 WM URS 7 5 2 7 0 S
1960 OG-M URS 3 2 0 2 0 B

**Pryl, Stanislav / b. Nov. 23, 1942**
1963-70 WM TCH 30 14 9 23 36 2S,2B
1964 OG-M TCH 4 0 1 1 4 B

**Prymovych, Konstantin / b. Apr. 10, 1984**
2002 WM18 UKR 8 2 0 2 12 —

**Przedpelski, Rajmund / b. Mar. 18, 1916 / d. unknown**
1937-39 WM POL 9 3 0 3 2 —

**Psenka, Tomas / b. Dec. 16, 1982**
2000 WM18 SVK 6 0 1 1 2 —

**Psurny, Michal / b. Feb. 23, 1986**
2004 WM18 CZE 7 2 1 3 0 B

**Psurny, Roman / b. Feb. 23, 1986**
2004 WM18 CZE 7 2 3 5 16 B

**Ptacek, Frantisek / b. Apr. 4, 1975**
1995 WM20 CZE 7 1 0 1 8 —

**Pucher, Peter / b. Aug. 12, 1974**
1997-2005 WM SVK 48 5 9 14 16 G,S
1998 OG-M SVK 2 0 0 0 0 —

**Pucher, Rene / b. Dec. 2, 1970**
1996-99 WM SVK 17 1 0 1 8 —
1994 OG-M SVK 6 1 0 1 2 —

**Puhakka, Mika / b. Mar. 1, 1976**
1996 WM20 FIN 6 0 3 3 0 —

**Pukalovic, Robert / b. Oct. 28, 1960**
1997-98 WM SVK 14 0 1 1 10 —

**Pulawski, Tadeusz / b. Feb. 20, 1969**
1988 WM20 POL 4 0 1 1 0 —

**Pulka, Witold / b. May 16, 1957**
1977 WM20 POL 6 2 1 3 6 —

**Pulkkinen, Petri / b. June 5, 1968**
1988 WM20 FIN 7 2 1 3 4 B

**Pulli, Heino / b. Mar. 22, 1938**
1958-65 WM FIN 35 12 7 19 12 —
1960-64 OG-M FIN 13 8 6 14 6 —

**Pulliainen, Tuukka / b. Aug. 25, 1984**
2002 WM18 FIN 8 2 6 8 8 —

**Pullola, Tommi / b. May 18, 1971**
1990-91 WM20 FIN 12 4 7 11 12 —

**Pulpan, Lukas / b. June 23, 1985**
2003 WM18 CZE 6 1 4 5 10 —
~WM18 All-Star Team/Defence (2003)

**Pulver, Anton / b. July 29, 1981**
1999 WM20 BLR 6 0 0 0 2 —

**Puncochar, Petr / b. June 8, 1983**
2000-01 WM18 CZE 13 2 3 5 4 —
2003 WM20 CZE 6 1 0 1 2 —

**Puolanne, Lauri / b. Mar. 5, 1976**
1996 WM20 FIN 6 0 0 0 2 —

**Pupkov, Yevgeni / b. Jan. 18, 1976**
2006 WM KAZ 6 1 1 2 8 —
2006 OG-M KAZ 5 0 0 0 6 —

**Purola, Joni / b. June 23, 1983**
2001 WM18 FIN 6 0 1 1 0 B

**Purpur, Ken / b. Mar. 1, 1932 / d. June 5, 2011**
1956 OG-M USA 7 2 2 4 2 S

**Purvis, Al / b. Jan. 9, 1929 / d. Aug. 13, 2009**
1950 WM CAN 7 3 2 5 6 G
1952 OG-M CAN 8 2 1 3 2 G

**Pusbauer, Jaroslav / b. July 31, 1901 / d. June 6, 1974**
1931-38 WM TCH 32 2 — 2 1 2B
1924-36 OG-M TCH 11 0 — 0 — —

**Puschnig, Andreas / b. Sept. 7, 1972**
1993-2001 WM AUT 32 8 10 18 18 —
1994-98 OG-M AUT 11 4 2 6 8 —

**Puschnig, Josef / b. Sept. 12, 1946**
1964-76 OG-M AUT 17 9 3 12 35 —
~IIHF Hall of Fame

**Puschnik, Gerhard / b. Oct. 16, 1966**
1993-98 WM AUT 29 0 6 6 24 —
1988-98 OG-M AUT 15 4 4 8 22 —

**Pushkaryov, Konstantin / b. Feb. 12, 1985**
2003 WM18 KAZ 6 9 1 10 6 —

**Pushkov, Sergei / b. Feb. 25, 1964**
1993 WM RUS 8 0 1 1 2 G

**Puterle, Janez / b. Feb. 21, 1952**
1972-76 OG-M YUG 8 4 2 6 10 —

**Putnins, Ludvigs / b. 1920 / d. unknown**
1938-39 WM LAT 10 5 — 5 — —

**Puzio, Mariusz / b. Mar. 12, 1966**
1985 WM20 POL 7 1 1 2 2 —
1992 OG-M POL 7 2 0 2 4 —

**Pycha, Zdenek / b. May 29, 1926**
1952 OG-M TCH 5 0 0 0 — —

**Pyka, Daniel / b. May 17, 1984**
2002 WM18 GER 8 2 1 3 8 —

**Pyka, Nico / b. July 22, 1977**
1997 WM20 GER 6 0 0 0 0 —
2005 WM GER 6 0 0 0 2 —

**Pyka, Reemt / b. Jan. 14, 1969**
1989 WM20 FRG 7 0 2 2 2 —
1995-98 WM GER 19 1 1 2 14 —
1996 WCH GER 4 1 0 1 4 —
1998 OG-M GER 4 0 0 0 0 —

**Pyndt, Martin / b. July 13, 1977**
2006 WM DEN 6 0 0 0 0 —

**Pysarenko, Yevgeni / b. Apr. 12, 1980**
2000 WM20 UKR 7 1 0 1 12 —

**Pysz, Patryk / b. Jan. 15, 1975**
2002 WM POL 6 0 1 1 4 —

**Pytel, Henryk / b. Sept. 15, 1955**
1976-86 WM POL 27 2 6 8 6 —
1976-84 OG-M POL 15 2 4 6 16 —

**Quaglia, Leon / b. 1896 / d. unknown**
1930-35 WM FRA 19 6 — 6 — —
1920-28 OG-M FRA 7 7 0 7 — —

**Quales, Johnny / b. Aug. 10, 1928**
1950-51 WM GBR 8 2 2 4 8 —

**Quantschnig, Christoph / b. Mar. 8, 1985**
2004 WM20 AUT 6 0 0 0 2 —

**Quinlan, Dominik / b. Sept. 6, 1988**
2006 WM18 GER 6 0 1 1 0 —

**Quinn, Dan / b. June 1, 1965**
1987 WM CAN 10 2 2 4 12 —

**Quinn, David / b. July 30, 1966**
1986 WM20 USA 7 1 3 4 8 B

**Quint, Deron / b. Mar. 12, 1976**
1994-95 WM20 USA 14 3 4 7 8 —
2001 WM USA 9 0 0 0 4 —

**Quinn, Robert / b. unknown**
1963 WM USA 6 2 1 3 5 —

**Quintal, Stephane / b. Oct. 22, 1968**
1999 WM CAN 10 3 2 5 4 —

**Quirk, George / b. unknown / d. unknown**
1938-39 WM USA 15 9 — 9 — S

**Rabanser, Edmondo / b. Nov. 3, 1936**
1964 OG-M ITA 7 1 3 4 2 —

**Rabinovici, Iuliu ~see Radian, Jules**

**Rachunek, Ivan / b. July 6, 1981**
1999 WM18 CZE 7 2 3 5 12 —
2001 WM20 CZE 6 1 0 1 6 G

**Rachunek, Karel / b. Aug. 27, 1979 / d. Sept. 7, 2011**
1998-99 WM20 CZE 13 1 3 4 10 —
2009-11 WM CZE 25 3 8 11 18 G,B
~perished in Yaroslavl plane crash

**Racine, Yves / b. Feb. 7, 1969**
1989 WM20 CAN 7 0 0 0 6 —
1991-94 WM CAN 12 1 2 3 8 G,S

**Racovica, Ion / b. unknown / d. unknown**
1947 WM ROM 3 0 — 0 — —

**Radant, Detlef / b. Dec. 8, 1958**
1983-85 WM GDR 15 4 2 6 8 —

**Radevic, Radim / b. Dec. 16, 1966**
1988 OG-M TCH 3 0 1 1 0 —

**Radian, Jules / b. 1915 / d. unknown**
1933-37 WM ROM 17 1 0 1 0 —
*played under the name Iuliu Rabinovici before adopting his Jewish name

**Radin, Igor / b. May 1, 1938**
1964 OG-M YUG 5 0 — 0 — —

**Radke, Fred / b. Jan. 1906 / d. unknown**
1930 WM CAN 1 0 — 0 — G

**Raduns, Nate / b. May 17, 1984**
2002 WM18 USA 8 0 1 1 2 G

**Radwanski, Maciej / b. July 1, 1978**
1997 WM20 POL 6 0 1 1 0 —

**Rafalski, Brian / b. Sept. 28, 1973**
1992-93 WM20 USA 14 0 3 3 4 B
1995 WM USA 5 0 0 0 2 6th
2004 WCH USA 4 0 3 3 6 4th
2002-10 OG USA 17 5 8 13 4 2S
~OG-M IIHF Directorate Best Defenceman (2010), OG-M All-Star Team/Defence (2010)

**Raffa, Gyorgy / b. May 16, 1938**
1964 OG-M HUN 7 0 0 0 0 —

**Raffainer, Reto / b. Jan. 1, 1982**
2002 WM20 SUI 7 2 0 2 0 —

**Raffl, Peter / b. Feb. 2, 1960**
1984-88 OG-M AUT 11 1 2 3 6 —

**Ragnarsson, Marcus / b. Aug. 13, 1971**
1995-97 WM SWE 15 2 1 3 14 2S
2004 WCH SWE 3 0 0 0 0 —
1998-2002 OG-M SWE 7 0 3 3 2 —

**Ragulin, Alexander / b. May 5, 1941 / d. Nov. 17, 2004**
1961-73 WM URS 80 11 14 25 50 8G,S,B
1972 SS URS 6 0 1 1 4 2nd
1964-72 OG-M URS 19 3 8 11 2 3G
~IIHF Hall of Fame
~WM IIHF Directorate Best Defenceman (1966), WM All-Star Team/Defence (1963, 1965, 1966, 1967), OG-M All-Star Team/Defence (1964)

**Raiski, Andrei / b. Mar. 30, 1970**
1998 WM KAZ 3 0 1 1 2 —

**Raitanen, Rauli / b. Jan. 14, 1970**
1989-90 WM20 FIN 14 3 1 4 6 —
1992 WM FIN 7 2 5 7 2 S

**Rajamaki, Tommi / b. Feb. 29, 1976**
1995-96 WM20 FIN 13 2 2 4 47 —

**Rajnoha, Pavel / b. Feb. 23, 1974**
1993-94 WM20 TCH 14 1 4 5 0 B

**Rakhmatulin, Ildar / b. Jan. 9, 1961**
1980 WM20 URS 5 1 0 1 2 G

**Ramage, Rob / b. Jan. 11, 1959**
1977-78 WM20 CAN 13 1 5 6 8 S,B
1981 WM CAN 8 0 1 1 0 —

**Ramholt, Arne / b. May 20, 1976**
1996 WM20 SUI 6 1 0 1 0 —

**Rammelmayr, Fritz / b. July 27, 1893 / d. unknown**
1928 OG-M GER 2 0 0 0 — —

**Rammer, Karl / b. unknown / d. unknown**
1933-34 WM AUT 7 0 — 0 1 —

**Ramoser, Florian / b. Oct. 7, 1979**
2006-07 WM ITA 12 0 0 0 16 —
2006 OG-M ITA 5 0 0 0 10 —

**Ramoser, Roland / b. Sept. 3, 1972**
1994-2010 WM ITA 70 8 8 16 75 —
1994-98 OG ITA 11 2 3 5 10 —

**Rampf, Hans / b. Feb. 2, 1931 / d. May 6, 2001**
1953-63 WM FRG 30 7 5 12 14 S
1956-60 OG-M FRG 14 2 0 2 13 —
~IIHF Hall of Fame

**Ramsay, Beattie / b. Dec. 12, 1895 / d. Sept. 30, 1952**
1924 OG-M CAN 5 10 — 10 0 G

**Ramsey, Charles / b. unknown / d. unknown**
1931 WM USA 6 3 — 3 — S

**Ramsey, Mike / b. Dec. 3, 1960**
1979 WM20 USA 5 1 1 2 10 —
1982 WM USA 7 1 0 1 8 —
1984-87 CC USA 11 1 2 3 8 —
1980 OG-M USA 7 0 2 2 8 G

**Ramstedt, Teemu / b. Dec. 9, 1987**
2005 WM18 FIN 6 1 3 4 0 —

**Ramus, Ernie / b. Dec. 31, 1912 / d. unknown**
1935 WM GBR 7 2 — 2 — B

**Ranfilenkov, Stanislav / b. Sept. 28, 1969**
1988 WM20 URS 7 5 2 7 6 S

**Ranheim, Paul / b. Jan. 25, 1966**
1986 WM20 USA 7 6 3 9 8 B
1990-97 WM USA 23 8 1 9 10 —

**Ranta, Tommi / b. Mar. 16, 1989**
2007 WM18 FIN 6 0 2 2 0 —

**Rantasila, Juha / b. June 5, 1945**
1966-74 WM FIN 46 11 7 18 78 —
1968-72 OG-M FIN 9 2 1 3 8 —

**Rapac, Richard / b. July 28, 1987**
2005 WM18 SVK 6 0 1 1 2 —

**Rapp, Christian / b. May 22, 1928 / d. July 4, 2004**
1951-55 WM FIN 18 4 0 4 6 —
1952 OG-M FIN 7 4 3 7 — —

**Rasko, Igor / b. Oct. 7, 1966**
1985 WM20 URS 7 0 1 1 0 B

**Rasmussen, Carl / b. unknown**
1950 WM NOR 7 1 0 1 0 —

**Rasmussen, Erik / b. Mar. 28, 1977**
1996-97 WM20 USA 12 4 6 10 20 S
2002 WM USA 7 0 1 1 2 —

**Rasolko, Andrei / b. Sept. 13, 1968**
1988 WM20 URS 7 0 1 1 4 S
2003 WM BLR 5 1 0 1 4 —
2002 OG-M BLR 9 1 1 2 0 —

**Rassa, Kalevi / b. Feb. 3, 1936 / d. Oct. 24, 1963**
1960 OG-M FIN 4 0 1 1 0 —

**Rastio, Teppo / b. Feb. 15, 1934**
1954-62 WM FIN 47 21 11 32 12 —
1960 OG-M FIN 5 4 2 6 4 —

**Raszewski, Zbigniew / b. Mar. 9, 1968**
1987 WM20 POL 7 1 2 3 4 —

**Rataj, Igor / b. Nov. 3, 1973**
1998 WM SVK 6 0 0 0 6 —

**Rataj, Ivo / b. Sept. 11, 1941**
1964-72 OG-M YUG 13 0 0 0 4 —

**Ratchuk, Mike / b. Feb. 20, 1988**
2006 WM18 USA 6 0 3 3 4 G

**Ratelle, Jean / b. Oxct. 3, 1940**
1972 SS CAN 6 1 3 4 0 1st

**Rath, Marius / b. May 27, 1970**
1989-90 WM20 NOR 14 7 5 12 2 —
1993-95 WM NOR 18 4 1 5 6 —
1992-94 OG-M NOR 14 6 1 7 2 —

**Rathje, Mike / b. May 11, 1974**
1993 WM20 CAN 7 2 2 4 12 G

**Ratushny, Dan / b. Sept. 29, 1970**
1990 WM20 CAN 7 2 2 4 4 G
1992 OG-M CAN 8 0 0 0 4 S

**Raty, Topias / b. Apr. 11, 1989**
2007 WM18 FIN 6 0 0 0 0 —

**Rau, Chad / b. Jan. 18, 1987**
2005 WM18 USA 6 1 0 1 0 G

**Raubal, Michael / b. July 11, 1970**
1989 WM20 FRG 4 0 0 0 2 —

**Rauch, Eduard / b. May 2, 1961**
1987 WM SUI 7 0 0 0 4 —

**Rauch, Martin / b. Mar. 19, 1964**
1984 WM20 SUI 7 0 0 0 0 —
1991-98 WM SUI 26 0 5 5 14 —

**Rauchenwald, Gerald / b. Nov. 25, 1963**
1994-95 WM AUT 13 1 0 1 20 —

**Rauhala, Reine / b. Apr. 9, 1973**
1993 WM20 SWE 7 6 1 7 0 S

**Rausse, Errol / b. May 18, 1959**
1979 WM20 CAN 5 1 1 2 2 —

**Rautakallio, Pekka / b. July 25, 1953**
1972-83 WM FIN 58 10 18 28 10 —
1976-81 CC FIN 10 2 3 5 4 —

**Rautalin, Pentti / b. May 6, 1940**
1963-65 WM FIN 6 1 0 1 0 —

**Rautanen, Reino / b. Oct. 31, 1928**
1954 WM FIN 4 0 — 0 2 —

**Rauth, Otto / b. Jan. 22, 1914 / d. unknown**
1939 WM ITA 7 8 — 8 — —
1948 OG-M ITA 7 4 — 4 — —

**Rautiainen, Matti / b. Oct. 7, 1955**
1978-79 WM FIN 18 5 3 8 6 —
1976 CC FIN 4 1 1 2 0 —
1976 OG-M FIN 5 1 1 2 0 —

**Rautio, Kai / b. July 22, 1964**
1990-92 WM FIN 11 0 1 1 2 S

**Ravenscroft, Pete / b. Apr. 13, 1922 / d. unknown**
1950 WM GBR 5 0 0 0 0 —

**Ravnik, Viktor / b. Oct. 19, 1941**
1964-72 OG-M YUG 16 0 4 4 12 —

**Razin, Andrei / b. Oct. 23, 1973**
2001 WM RUS 7 3 4 7 4 —

**Razin, Gennadi / b. Feb. 3, 1978**
2000-04 WM UKR 8 0 2 2 4 —

**Razinger, Rado / b. Dec. 3, 1944**
1968 OG-M YUG 5 0 0 0 0 —

**Razpet, Bojan / b. Jan. 22, 1960**
1984 OG-M YUG 5 0 0 0 0 —

**Razvodovski, Pavel / b. Aug. 7, 1989**
2006 WM18 BLR 6 0 1 1 8 —

**Razym, Milan / b. Oct. 12, 1961**
1981 WM20 TCH 5 0 0 0 0 —

**Reardon, Kent / b. May 14, 1959**
1979 WM20 CAN 5 2 1 3 6 —

**Reasoner, Marty / b. Feb. 26, 1977**
1996-97 WM20 USA 12 4 5 9 14 S
2002-06 WM USA 20 1 4 5 16 —

**Reber, Jorg / b. May 6, 1974**
1994 WM20 SUI 7 0 0 0 6 —

**Recchi, Mark / b. Feb. 1, 1968**
1988 WM20 CAN 7 0 5 5 4 G
1990-97 WM CAN 22 5 10 15 4 G
1998 OG-M CAN 5 0 2 2 0 —

**Redden, Wade / b. June 12, 1977**
1995-96 WM20 CAN 13 3 4 7 2 2G
1999-2005 WM CAN 26 3 8 11 33 S
2004 WCH CAN 2 0 1 1 0 1st
2006 OG-M CAN 6 1 0 1 0 —
~WM IIHF Directorate Best Defenceman (2005)

**Redding, Ralph / b. Nov. 6, 1911 / d. unknown**
1937 WM CAN 9 12 1 13 2 G

**Reddox, Liam / b. Jan. 27, 1986**
2004 WM18 CAN 7 6 1 7 6 —

**Redmond, Craig / b. Sept. 22, 1965**
1986 WM CAN 10 3 2 5 14 B
1984 OG-M CAN 7 2 0 2 4 —

**Redmond, Mickey / b. Dec. 27, 1947**
1972 SS CAN 1 0 0 0 0 1st

**Reeds, Mark / b. Jan. 24, 1960**
1980 WM20 CAN 5 1 0 1 2 —

**Regehr, Robyn / b. Apr. 13, 1980**
1999 WM20 CAN 7 0 0 0 2 S
2000-05 WM CAN 15 0 0 0 6 S
2004 WCH CAN 6 0 0 0 6 1st
2006 OG-M CAN 6 0 1 1 2 —

**Rego, Mickey / b. Mar. 4, 1958**
1977 WM20 USA 7 0 4 4 4 —

**Regula, Henryk / b. Mar. 13, 1938**
1958-66 WM POL 14 2 2 4 16 —

**Rehnberg, Henrik / b. July 20, 1977**
1997 WM20 SWE 6 2 0 2 6 —

**Rehor, Jan / b. Apr. 30, 1983**
2001 WM18 CZE 7 0 1 1 6 —

**Rehus, Branislav / b. Dec. 24, 1988**
2006 WM18 SVK 6 0 0 0 10 —

**Reichart, Bill / b. July 3, 1935**
1969 WM USA 5 0 1 1 2 —
1964 OG-M USA 7 3 3 6 4 —

**Reichel, Johannes / b. Apr. 29, 1982**
2004 WM AUT 3 0 0 0 0 —

**Reichel, Martin / b. Nov. 7, 1973**
1994-2004 WM GER 43 1 7 8 10 —
2004 WCH GER 2 0 0 0 0 —
2002 OG-M GER 7 1 0 1 0 —

**Reichel, Robert / b. June 25, 1971**
1988-90 WM20 TCH 21 18 22 40 10 2B
1990-2003 WM CZE 77 24 39 63 30 3G,4B
1991-2004 WCH CZE 12 2 2 4 8 —
1998-2002 OG-M CZE 10 4 0 4 2 G
~WM All-Star Team/Forward (1990, 1996, 2001), WM20 IIHF Directorate Best Forward (1990), WM20 All-Star Team/Forward (1990)

**Reid, Brandon / b. Mar. 9, 1981**
2000-01 WM20 CAN 14 5 8 13 4 2B

**Reif, Josef / b. Sept. 5, 1937**
1961-67 WM FRG 26 9 4 13 26 —
1960-68 OG-M FRG 21 2 1 3 12 —

**Reil, Joakim / b. May 17, 1955**
1981-87 WM FRG 18 0 3 3 12 —
1984 CC FRG 3 0 0 0 4 —
1980-88 OG-M FRG 12 1 1 2 6 —

**Reime, Leif Jostein / b. unknown**
1999 WM18 NOR 6 0 0 0 4 —

**Reimers, Jason / b. Jan. 1, 1981**
1999 WM18 USA 6 1 1 2 26 —

**Reinbahs, Indrikis / b. Aug. 9, 1904 / d. unknown**
1933 WM LAT 4 0 — 0 0 —

**Reindl, Franz / b. Nov. 24, 1954**
1976-86 WM FRG 75 13 13 26 79 —
1984 CC FRG 5 0 2 2 0 —
1976-84 OG-M FRG 16 2 5 7 4 B

**Reineck, Johan / b. Apr. 7, 1981**
1999 WM18 SWE 7 0 1 1 0 S
2001 WM20 SWE 7 1 0 1 0 —

**Reinert, Thomas / b. Jan. 17, 1980**
2006 WM DEN 3 0 0 0 2 —

**Reinhard, Francis / b. May 20, 1944**
1972 WM SUI 8 1 0 1 0 —
1972 OG-M SUI 4 1 2 3 0 —

**Reinhart, Paul / b. Jan. 6, 1960**
1982-83 WM CAN 13 3 8 11 6 2B
1981 CC CAN 2 0 0 0 2 2nd

**Reinprecht, Steve / b. May 7, 1976**
2003 WM CAN 8 0 6 6 2 G

**Reist, Alain / b. Dec. 7, 1979**
1998-99 WM20 SUI 13 0 1 1 2 B

**Reitz, Erik / b. July 29, 1982**
2002 WM20 USA 7 0 1 1 12 —

**Rejman, Miroslav / b. Oct. 17, 1925 / d. Jan. 31, 2008**
1954-55 WM TCH 15 3 0 3 0 B
1952 OG-M TCH 9 2 3 5 — —

**Rekomaa, Esko / b. Dec. 24, 1932 / d. Feb. 14, 1985**
1954-55 WM FIN 15 7 2 9 4 —
1952 OG-M FIN 5 0 0 0 — —

**Remlein, Boleslaw / b. Mar. 19, 1958**
1977 WM20 POL 7 0 1 1 4 —

**Remmelg, Jan / b. Jan. 3, 1960**
1979 WM20 SWE 6 0 0 0 0 B

**Renaud, Ab / b. Oct. 2, 1920**
1948 OG-M CAN 8 4 — 4 4 G

**Renaud, Boris / b. Jan. 2, 1946**
1964-72 OG-M YUG 13 5 3 8 10 —

**Renault, Serge / b. Nov. 14, 1920 / d. unknown**
1937-50 WM FRA 12 0 0 0 0 —

**Renberg, Mikael / b. May 5, 1972**
1992 WM20 SWE 7 6 4 10 8 S
1993-2003 WM SWE 36 15 13 28 26 G,2S,B
1998-2002 OG-M SWE 8 2 2 4 8 —
~WM All-Star Team/Forward (1993)

**Rentzsch, Marco / b. Jan. 23, 1966**
1986 WM20 FRG 7 1 0 1 2 —
1991 WM FRG 10 0 0 0 6 —

**Repnyev, Vladimir / b. Jan. 9, 1949**
1974 WM URS 8 1 5 6 6 G

**Repo, Seppo / b. Sept. 21, 1947**
1971-82 WM FIN 66 18 10 28 49 —
1976 CC FIN 5 1 2 3 0 —
1972 OG-M FIN 4 0 0 0 4 —

**Reshetnikov, Kirill / b. Mar. 28, 1981**
1999 WM18 UKR 5 0 0 0 6 —

**Ressmann, Gerald / b. July 24, 1970**
1995-2005 WM AUT 41 3 6 9 40 —
1994-2002 OG-M AUT 15 3 0 3 10 —

**Retzer, Christian / b. Jan. 7, 1982**
2000 WM18 GER 6 0 2 2 0 —

**Retzer, Stephan / b. Oct. 11, 1976**
1994-96 WM20 GER 20 1 1 2 16 —
2003-05 WM GER 19 0 3 3 4 —
2004 WCH GER 2 0 0 0 0 —

**Reuille, Sebastien / b. June 22, 1981**
1999 WM18 SUI 7 2 2 4 6 —
2001 WM20 SUI 7 2 0 2 12 —

**Reunamaki, Matti / b. July 25, 1940**
1963-67 WM FIN 28 3 5 8 14 —
1964-68 OG-M FIN 14 1 2 3 2 —

**Reuter, Christian / b. Feb. 22, 1966**
1984-86 WM20 FRG 21 2 2 4 4 —

**Revenko, Sergi / b. Mar. 6, 1977**
1996 WM20 UKR 6 0 1 1 6 —

**Revoyaz, Paul / b. unknown / d. unknown**
1937 WM FRA 7 2 0 2 4 —

**Reyers, Zeger / b. unknown / d. unknown**
1935 WM NED 6 0 0 0 — —

**Reynolds, Bobby / b. July 14, 1967**
1987 WM20 USA 7 3 3 6 8 —
1990-96 WM USA 17 0 2 2 20 B

**Rezek, Spencer / b. July 16, 1984**
2002 WM18 SUI 8 1 0 1 6 —

**Reznicek, Josef / b. Nov. 30, 1966**
1986 WM20 TCH 7 1 2 3 4 —
1991 WM TCH 10 0 2 2 10 —

**Rhodin, Thomas / b. Apr. 8, 1971**
1991 WM20 SWE 7 1 0 1 0 —
2002-05 WM SWE 26 6 4 10 24 S,B
~WM All-Star Team/Defence (2002)

**Ribble, Pat / b. Apr. 26, 1954**
1978 WM CAN 10 0 0 0 15 B

**Ribeiro, Mike / b. Feb. 10, 1980**
2000 WM20 CAN 7 0 2 2 0 B

**Ricci, Mike / b. Oct. 27, 1971**
1989-90 WM20 CAN 12 5 6 11 6 G
1994 WM CAN 8 2 1 3 8 G

**Rice, Steve / b. May 26, 1971**
1990-91 WM20 CAN 14 6 1 7 24 2G

**Rice, Williard / b. Apr. 21, 1895 / d. July 21, 1967**
1924 OG-M USA 5 13 — 13 0 S

**Richards, Travis / b. Mar. 22, 1970**
1993 WM USA 5 0 1 1 0 —
1994 OG-M USA 8 0 0 0 2 —

**Richardson, Luke / b. Mar. 26, 1969**
1987 WM20 CAN 3 0 0 0 0 —
1994-96 WM CAN 16 0 1 1 18 G,S

**Richer, Antoine / b. Aug. 9, 1961**
1992-96 WM FRA 25 3 3 6 16 —
1988-94 OG-M FRA 20 2 2 4 18 —

**Richer, Stephane / b. June 7, 1966**
1985 WM20 CAN 7 4 3 7 2 G

**Richmond, Dan / b. Aug. 1, 1984**
2004 WM20 USA 6 0 4 4 4 G

**Richnak, Richard / b. Sept. 2, 1977**
1997 WM20 SVK 3 1 0 1 2 —

**Richter, Barry / b. Sept. 11, 1970**
1989-90 WM20 USA 14 3 1 4 2 —
1992-99 WM USA 24 3 0 3 18 —
1994 OG-M USA 8 0 3 3 4 —

**Richter, Martin / b. Dec. 6, 1977**
1997 WM20 CZE 7 0 0 0 8 —
2001-06 WM CZE 33 0 3 3 32 G,S

**Richter, Pavel / b. Dec. 5, 1954**
1978-85 WM TCH 48 12 16 28 40 G,3S,B
1981 CC TCH 3 1 2 3 2 —
1984 OG-M TCH 7 2 5 7 4 S

**Richter, Thomas / b. Jan. 26, 1983**
2001 WM18 GER 6 0 0 0 2 —

**Riddle, Troy / b. Aug. 24, 1981**
2001 WM20 USA 7 0 1 1 6 —

**Ridley, Art / b. 1918 / d. unknown**
1938-39 WM GBR 7 0 — 0 — S

**Rieciciar, Pavol / b. Jan. 19, 1978**
1997-98 WM20 SVK 12 2 4 6 6 —

**Riedel, Thomas / b. May 26, 1965**
1985 WM20 FRG 7 0 0 0 2 —

**Riedl, Walter / b. unknown**
1961-67 WM FRG 18 0 0 0 20 —

**Riedmeier, Erwin / b. May 27, 1941**
1971 WM FRG 9 0 0 0 2 —

**Riesch, Georg / b. Feb. 26, 1933**
1959 WM SUI 5 0 0 0 4 —
1956 OG-M SUI 4 0 0 0 10 —

**Riesen, Michel / b. Apr. 11, 1979**
1996-99 WM20 SUI 25 9 6 15 12 B
1998-2001 WM SUI 9 4 2 6 2 —

**Rifel, Vadim / b. Feb. 19, 1979**
1998-99 WM20 KAZ 13 2 1 3 8 —
2004-06 WM KAZ 9 0 1 1 6 —

**Rigoni, Luca / b. Jan. 1, 1975**
2006-07 WM ITA 8 0 0 0 4 —

**Riihijarvi, Juha / b. Dec. 15, 1969**
1992-96 WM FIN 20 7 3 10 8 S
1996 WCH FIN 4 0 4 4 0 —

**Riihijarvi, Teemu / b. Mar. 1, 1977**
1996-97 WM20 FIN 12 2 1 3 10 —

**Riihiranta, Heikki / b. Oct. 4, 1948**
1970-74 WM FIN 36 3 3 6 34 —
1976 CC FIN 5 0 3 3 12 —
1972 OG-M FIN 5 0 0 0 0 —

**Riise, Rodney / b. Dec. 21, 1942 / d. Dec. 31, 2009**
1968 OG-M NOR 1 0 0 0 2 —

**Rikala, Jorma / b. Aug. 24, 1937**
1961 WM FIN 3 0 0 0 4 —

**Riley, Jack / b. June 15, 1920**
1949 WM USA 7 5 — 5 — B
1948 OG-M USA 8 17 0 17 11 —

**Riley, Tom / b. unknown**
1961 WM USA 7 0 1 1 6 —

**Rimmel, Patrik / b. Dec. 28, 1972**
1992 WM20 TCH 4 0 4 4 4 —

**Rimstad, Walter / b. 1916 / d. unknown**
1951 WM CAN 5 4 — 4 0 G

**Rindal, Alexander / b. Sept. 4, 1989**
2006 WM18 NOR 6 0 1 1 0 —

**Rinne, Jouni / b. Feb. 12, 1956**
1976-79 WM FIN 18 6 5 11 4 —
1976 CC FIN 2 0 0 0 0 —

**Rintakoski, Matti / b. Sept. 18, 1924 / d. June 28, 1995**
1949-55 WM FIN 21 6 0 6 8 —
1952 OG-M FIN 8 0 0 0 2 —

**Rintala, Erkki / b. Apr. 10, 1918 / d. unknown**
1939 WM FIN 2 1 — 1 — —

**Rintanen, Kimmo / b. Aug. 7, 1973**
1993 WM20 FIN 7 3 3 6 6 —
1998-2004 WM FIN 62 13 15 28 6 3S,B
1998 OG-M FIN 6 1 0 1 0 B

**Rioux, Pierre / b. Feb. 1, 1962**
1982 WM20 CAN 7 3 3 6 4 G

**Risku, Rainer / b. Mar. 12, 1958**
1978 WM20 FIN 6 7 3 10 2 —

**Risler, Claude / b. unknown**
1950 WM FRA 4 1 0 1 0 —

**Rita, Jani / b. July 25, 1981**
1999-2001 WM20 FIN 20 9 5 14 2 S
2005-06 WM FIN 13 1 2 3 6 B
~WM20 All-Star Team/Forward (2001)

**Ritsch, Andreas / b. June 23, 1961**
1980 WM20 SUI 5 0 0 0 6 —
1987 WM SUI 10 2 0 2 4 —
1988 OG-M SUI 6 1 1 2 4 —

**Riutta, Bruce / b. Oct. 14, 1944**
1969-71 WM USA 20 2 1 3 14 —
1968 OG-M USA 7 1 1 2 10 —

**Riutta, Topi / b. May 8, 1980**
2000 WM20 FIN 7 0 3 3 0 —

**Riva, Luigi / b. May 13, 1968**
1987 WM20 SUI 7 0 0 0 2 —
1992 WM SUI 6 0 0 0 6 —

**Rivers, Jamie / b. Mar. 16, 1975**
1995 WM20 CAN 7 3 3 6 2 G

**Rivers, Joe / b. unknown / d. unknown**
1935 WM CAN 3 1 — 1 — G

**Rivers, Romeo / b. Mar. 28, 1907 / d. May 4, 1986**
1935 WM CAN 7 5 — 5 — G
1932 OG-M CAN 6 5 3 8 0 G

**Rivet, Craig / b. Sept. 13, 1974**
2003 WM CAN 9 0 1 1 6 G

**Rizitis, Janis / b. unknown / d. unknown**
1936 OG-M LAT 1 0 — 0 — —

**Rizk, Jean Michel / b. Mar. 24, 1986**
2004 WM18 CAN 7 2 1 3 8 —

**Rizzello, Antonio / b. Jan. 5, 1985**
2003 WM18 SUI 6 3 3 6 6 —
2004 WM20 SUI 6 0 0 0 0 —

**Rizzi, Sandro / b. Oct. 22, 1978**
1996-98 WM20 SUI 18 3 4 7 6 B
1999 WM SUI 6 0 0 0 0 —

**Roach, Andy / b. Aug. 22, 1973**
2004-05 WM USA 16 2 6 8 4 B

**Rob, Lubos / b. Aug. 5, 1970**
1989-90 WM20 TCH 14 5 7 12 8 2B

**Roberge, Richard / b. Apr. 7, 1934**
1962-66 WM USA 14 9 8 17 2 B

**Roberts, Dave / b. May 28, 1970**
1994 OG-M USA 8 1 5 6 4 —

**Roberts, Gary / b. May 23, 1966**
1986 WM20 CAN 7 6 3 9 6 S

**Roberts, Gord / b. Oct. 2, 1957**
1982-87 WM USA 17 3 5 8 45 —
1984 CC USA 6 1 0 1 6 —

**Robertson, Bob / b. Dec. 22, 1927**
1962 WM CAN 3 1 0 1 6 S

**Robertson, David / b. Oct. 11, 1985**
2003 WM18 USA 6 0 0 0 2 —

**Robertson, Gord / b. June 25, 1926**
1952 OG-M CAN 8 3 7 10 9 G

**Robertson, Harry / b. unknown / d. unknown**
1937 WM CAN 8 0 1 1 2 G

**Robertson, Russ / b. unknown**
1954 WM CAN 6 2 1 3 6 S

**Robidas, Stephane / b. Mar. 3, 1977**
2001-06 WM CAN 16 1 2 3 6 —

**Robinson, Larry / b. June 2, 1951**
1981 WM CAN 6 1 2 3 2 —
1976-84 CC CAN 22 1 3 4 4 2/1st,2nd
~WM IIHF Directorate Best Defenceman (1981), WM All-Star Team/Defence (1981)

**Robitaille, Luc / b. Feb. 17, 1966**
1986 WM20 CAN 7 3 5 8 2 S
1994 WM CAN 8 3 4 7 2 G
1991 CC CAN 8 1 2 3 10 1st

**Robson, Ed / b. unknown**
1955 WM USA 8 1 0 1 0 —

**Rochefort, Normand / b. Jan. 28, 1961**
1987 CC CAN 9 1 2 3 8 1st

**Rod, Jean-Luc / b. Aug. 4, 1965**
1984 WM20 SUI 7 2 0 2 2 —

**Rodenhiser, Dick / b. Oct. 17, 1932**
1955 WM USA 1 0 0 0 0 —
1956-60 OG-M USA 6 1 1 2 0 G,S

**Roder, Christoph / b. June 16, 1984**
2002 WM18 SUI 8 0 0 0 4 —
2004 WM20 SUI 6 1 0 1 0 —

**Rodionov, Alexei / b. May 13, 1980**
1999-2000 WM20 KAZ 13 0 0 0 4 —

**Roe, Tom / b. unknown**
1965 WM USA 5 3 0 3 10 —

**Roedger, Roy / b. Oct. 11, 1958**
1982-89 WM FRG 50 10 5 15 28 —
1984 CC FRG 5 0 0 0 4 —
1984-88 OG-M FRG 14 4 3 7 18 —

**Roenick, Jeremy / b. Jan. 17, 1970**
1988-89 WM20 USA 14 13 12 25 4 —
1991 WM USA 9 5 6 11 8 —
1991 CC USA 8 4 2 6 4 2nd
1998-2002 OG-M USA 10 1 5 6 8 S
~WM20 All-Star Team/Forward (1989)

**Roes, Horst / b. Sept. 6, 1944**
1967 WM FRG 6 0 0 0 4 —

**Rogenmoser, Harry / b. Mar. 13, 1968**
1995 WM SUI 7 0 2 2 2 —

**Rogers, Ab / b. 1911 / d. unknown**
1934 WM CAN — 4 — 4 — G

**Rogers, Andy / b. Sept. 25, 1986**
2004 WM18 CAN 7 1 2 3 26 —

**Rogers, Mike / b. Oct. 24, 1954**
1981 WM CAN 6 0 1 1 4 —

**Rogger, Bruno / b. Jan. 19, 1959**
1987 WM SUI 10 2 2 4 8 —
1988 OG-M SUI 6 3 1 4 10 —

**Rohatsch, Marian / b. June 15, 1983**
2001 WM18 GER 6 0 2 2 2 —

**Rohde, Peter / b. unknown**
1963 WM FRG 6 4 0 4 4 —

**Rohl, Dieter / b. Mar. 10, 1942**
1970 WM GDR 7 0 0 0 6 —

**Rohlicek, Jeff / b. Jan. 27, 1966**
1985 WM20 USA 7 0 2 2 2 —

**Rohlin, Leif / b. Feb. 26, 1968**
1988 WM20 SWE 7 1 1 2 10 —
1995-2001 WM SWE 17 1 4 5 6 S,B
1996 WCH SWE 1 0 0 0 2 —
1994 OG-M SWE 8 0 1 1 10 G

**Rohloff, Jon / b. Oct. 3, 1969**
1997 WM USA 8 0 2 2 10 —

**Rohloff, Todd / b. Jan. 16, 1974**
2002 WM USA 7 0 1 1 2 —

**Rohn, Peter / b. Jan. 4, 1988**
2006 WM18 NOR 6 3 0 3 20 —

**Rohrbach, Winfried / b. Mar. 20, 1943**
1970 WM GDR 6 0 0 0 0 —

**Rojkovic, Peter / b. Jan. 9, 1989**
2007 WM18 SVK 6 0 0 0 2 —

**Rolland, John / b. unknown**
1950-51 WM GBR 12 6 3 9 8 —

**Rolstad, Morten / b. Aug. 29, 1986**
2006 WM20 NOR 6 0 0 0 4 —

**Rolston, Brian / b. Feb. 21, 1973**
1991-93 WM20 USA 22 10 10 20 4 B
1996 WM USA 8 3 4 7 4 B
1996-2004 WCH USA 3 0 0 0 0 1st
1994-2006 OG-M USA 20 10 4 14 12 S

**Romanov, Oleg / b. Mar. 31, 1970**
1998-2001 WM BLR 24 4 4 8 16 —
1998-2002 OG-M BLR 16 2 4 6 4 —

**Romanov, Stanislav / b. Aug. 8, 1971**
1995 WM RUS 6 4 1 5 4 —

**Romanovski, Alexander / b. June 8, 1987**
2005 WM18 RUS 5 0 0 0 6 —

**Romanovskis, Vadims / b. July 30, 1978**
2003-04 WM LAT 13 2 0 2 8 —

**Romashin, Igor / b. Feb. 9, 1957**
1977 WM20 URS 7 6 6 12 4 G

**Romauch, Erich / b. June 2, 1894 / d. Mar. 26, 1987**
1964 OG-M AUT 7 0 2 2 0 —

**Romberg, Peter / b. Feb. 11, 1966**
1985 WM20 FRG 7 0 0 0 20 —

**Romer, Erich / b. June 2, 1894 / d. Mar. 26, 1987**
1930-35 WM GER 20 5 0 5 0 S,B
1928-32 OG-M GER 8 0 0 0 2 B

**Romishevski, Igor / b. Mar. 25, 1940**
1969-72 WM URS 32 2 8 10 14 3G,S
1968-72 OG-M URS 11 0 0 0 6 2G

**Rompre, Bob / b. Apr. 11, 1929**
1950 WM USA 7 3 1 4 8 S
1952 OG-M USA 8 5 3 8 — S

**Rona, Laszlo / b. May 20, 1913 / d. unknown**
1937-39 WM HUN 19 11 2 13 4 —
1936 OG-M HUN 6 1 — 1 — —

**Roncarelli, Francesco / b. Oct. 1, 1904 / d. unknown**
1930-34 WM ITA 6 0 1 1 1 —

**Ronning, Cliff / b. Oct. 1, 1965**
1991 WM CAN 10 1 4 5 8 S

**Ronningen, Jan Tore / b. Mar. 17, 1971**
1990-91 WM20 NOR 14 1 0 1 26 —

**Ronnqvist, Jonas / b. Aug. 22, 1973**
2000 WM SWE 7 0 3 3 0 —

**Rope, Don / b. Feb. 2, 1929**
1962 WM CAN 5 1 1 2 2 S
1956-60 OG-M CAN 15 8 4 12 4 S,B

**Rosa, Pavel / b. June 7, 1976**
1996 WM20 CZE 6 0 0 0 2 —

**Rosander, Ola / b. Apr. 2, 1969**
1988-89 WM20 SWE 13 13 10 23 6 S

**Rosen, Roger / b. Apr. 18, 1974**
1993-94 WM20 SWE 14 2 2 4 10 2S

**Roshin, Yevgeni / b. May 28, 1962**
1982 WM20 URS 7 2 5 7 4 —
1998 OG-M BLR 6 0 2 2 0 —

**Rosol, Petr / b. June 20, 1964**
1982-84 WM20 TCH 21 18 12 30 45 2S,B
1985-93 WM CZE 46 18 18 36 36 G,3B
1984-87 CC TCH 11 1 1 2 6 —
1988-92 OG-M CZE 15 7 5 12 16 B
~WM20 All-Star Team/Forward (1984)

**Ross, Don / b. Oct. 11, 1942**
1966-71 WM USA 24 3 4 7 36 —
1964-68 OG-M USA 14 2 2 4 2 —

**Ross, Doug / b. Oct. 9, 1951**
1976 OG-M USA 5 0 2 2 0 —

**Ross, Eldridge / b. Aug. 2, 1909 / d. Nov. 13, 1980**
1936 OG-M USA 8 1 0 1 2 B

**Ross, Gary / b. Dec. 8, 1953**
1976 WM USA 10 1 0 1 22 —
1976 OG-M USA 5 1 3 4 6 —

**Ross, Patrik / b. Feb. 27, 1970**
1990 WM20 SWE 7 1 4 5 6 —

**Ross, Tom / b. Jan. 17, 1954**
1975 WM USA 10 1 1 2 2 —

**Rossi De Mio, Ruggero / b. Mar. 7, 1976**
2002 WM ITA 6 0 0 0 4 —

**Rossi, Franco / b. Jan. 2, 1916 / d. Feb. 3, 2006**
1934-39 WM ITA 15 0 0 0 — —
1936-48 OG-M ITA 7 0 0 0 — —

**Rossi, Silvio / b. Feb. 14, 1920 / d. unknown**
1950-53 WM SUI 5 0 2 2 0 2B

**Rossiter, Kyle / b. June 9, 1980**
2000 WM20 CAN 7 0 0 0 20 B

**Roth, Mickey / b. unknown**
1951 WM CAN 6 7 — 7 0 G

**Rotheli, Andre / b. Oct. 12, 1970**
1991 WM SUI 10 1 0 1 2 —
1992-2002 OG-M SUI 11 1 3 4 6 —

**Rothen, Frederic / b. Jan. 26, 1976**
1996 WM20 SUI 6 1 5 6 29 —

**Rothkirch, Hans / b. Apr. 18, 1951**
1972 WM FRG 8 0 1 1 2 —
1972 OG-M FRG 4 2 0 2 4 —

**Rotsch, Jeff / b. unknown**
1975 WM USA 10 0 0 0 6 —

**Rottaris, Mario / b. Feb. 8, 1968**
1992 WM SUI 3 0 0 0 4 —
1992 OG-M SUI 7 2 1 3 4 —

**Rotter, Rafael / b. June 14, 1987**
2004 WM20 AUT 6 0 0 0 0 —

**Rouleau, Alexandre / b. July 29, 1983**
2003 WM20 CAN 6 0 1 1 0 S

**Roupe, Magnus / b. Mar. 23, 1963**
1982-83 WM20 SWE 13 8 5 13 16 —
1987 CC SWE 5 1 1 2 4 —
1990 WM SWE 10 0 3 3 8 S

**Rouse, Bob / b. June 18, 1964**
1987 WM CAN 4 0 0 0 4 —

**Rousseau, Bobby / b. July 26, 1940**
1960 OG-M CAN 7 5 4 9 2 S

**Rousseau, Hec / b. unknown**
1947 WM USA 7 5 — 5 — —

**Rousselin, Sebastien / b. July 1, 1982**
2002 WM20 FRA 6 0 0 0 6 —

**Roussin, Dany / b. Jan. 9, 1985**
2003 WM18 CAN 7 0 1 1 16 G

**Rovick, David / b. unknown**
1961-63 WM USA 11 0 3 3 8 —

**Rowe, Paul / b. May 5, 1914 / d. Aug. 28, 1993**
1936 OG-M USA 8 2 1 3 2 B

**Rowe, Tom / b. May 23, 1956**
1977 WM USA 3 0 0 0 2 —

**Roy, Jean-Yves / b. Feb. 17, 1969**
1994 OG-M CAN 8 1 0 1 0 S

**Roy, Serge / b. June 25, 1962**
1988 OG-M CAN 5 0 7 7 4 —

**Roy, Stephane / b. June 29, 1967**
1987 WM20 CAN 6 0 1 1 6 —

**Roymark, Tom / b. Apr. 23, 1950**
1972-80 OG-M NOR 9 1 1 2 2 —

**Rozakov, Rail / b. Mar. 29, 1981**
1999 WM18 RUS 7 0 1 1 4 —
2001 WM20 RUS 7 0 1 1 6 —

**Rozanski, Stanislaw / b. Apr. 2, 1933 / d. June 2, 1996**
1957 WM POL 4 0 — 0 2 —

**Rozanski, Jaroslaw / b. Aug. 29, 1976**
2002 WM POL 6 1 1 2 2 —

**Rozenthal, Maurice / b. June 20, 1975**
1996-2004 WM FRA 33 4 9 13 18 —
1998-2002 OG-M FRA 8 4 1 5 8 —

**Rozgonyi, Gyorgy / b. May 31, 1943**
1964 OG-M HUN 7 3 3 6 4 —

**Rozic, Peter / b. Feb. 17, 1974**
2002-05 WM SLO 17 2 0 2 2 —

**Rozinak, Vaclav / b. Dec. 7, 1922 / d. Mar. 1, 1997**
1947-49 WM TCH 8 7 — 7 — 2G
1948 OG-M TCH 6 8 — 8 — S

**Rozkalns, Karlis / b. Sept. 15, 1989**
2007 WM18 LAT 6 0 0 0 2 —

**Rucchin, Larry / b. May 12, 1967**
1996-2001 WM ITA 28 0 0 0 24 —
1998 OG-M ITA 4 0 0 0 4 —

**Rucchin, Steve / b. July 4, 1971**
1998 WM CAN 6 1 2 3 2 —

**Ruchala, Czeslaw / b. Feb. 26, 1951 / d. Nov. 11, 1996**
1970 WM POL 4 0 0 0 0 —

**Ruchala, Krzysztof / b. Sept. 3, 1967**
1987 WM20 POL 7 2 3 5 0 —

**Rucinsky, Martin / b. Mar. 11, 1971**
1991 WM20 TCH 7 9 5 14 2 B
1994-2005 WM CZE 43 15 20 35 82 3G
1991-2004 WCH CZE 11 1 3 4 16 —
1998-2006 OG-M CZE 18 4 7 11 6 G,B
~WM All-Star Team/Forward (1999, 2001), WM20 All-Star Team/Forward (1991)

**Rud, Christoph / b. Sept. 8, 1984**
2004 WM20 AUT 6 0 0 0 14 —

**Rudert, Joachim / b. Aug. 1, 1932**
1957-59 WM GDR 12 3 0 3 0 —

**Rudolf, Albert / b. unknown / d. unknown**
1930 WM SUI 3 0 — 0 — B

**Rudolph, Ferdinand / b. 1899 / d. unknown**
1924 OG-M BEL 3 1 — 1 — —

**Ruedi, Beat / b. Feb. 19, 1920 / d. Oct. 29, 2009**
1937-39 WM SUI 8 6 2 8 1 2B
1948 OG-M SUI 5 2 — 2 — B

**Ruedi, Luzius / b. June 12, 1900 / d. unknown**
1930 WM SUI 2 0 — 0 — B
1928 OG-M SUI 3 0 — 0 2 B

**Ruefenacht, Christof / b. Jan. 31, 1964**
1984 WM20 SUI 7 1 2 3 4 —

**Ruegg, Max / b. Mar. 12, 1942**
1964 OG-M SUI 7 0 0 0 0 —

**Ruelle, Emery / b. unknown**
1966 WM USA 7 3 1 4 4 —

**Rufanov, Yegor / b. Nov. 9, 1985**
2004 WM20 UKR 6 0 0 0 2 —

**Rufener, Andy / b. May 28, 1971**
1991 WM20 SUI 7 0 1 1 2 —

**Ruggeri, Rosario / b. June 8, 1984**
2002 WM18 CAN 8 1 0 1 14 —

**Ruisma, Veli-Matti / b. Sept. 28, 1954**
1977-79 WM FIN 16 1 1 2 4 —

**Rullier, Joe / b. Jan. 28, 1980**
2000 WM20 CAN 7 0 0 0 6 B

**Rumrich, Jurgen / b. Mar. 20, 1968**
1988 WM20 FRG 7 0 0 0 2 —
1992-2002 WM GER 40 4 4 8 4 —
1996 WCH GER 4 1 0 1 2 —
1992-2002 OG-M GER 19 2 1 3 2 —

**Rumrich, Michael / b. July 1, 1965**
1984 WM20 FRG 7 1 0 1 6 —
1991-94 WM GER 26 7 1 8 36 —
1992-94 OG-M GER 16 5 1 6 10 —

**Rundqvist, Emil / b. Nov. 14, 1905 / d. unknown**
1931 WM SWE 2 0 — 0 — —

**Rundqvist, Thomas / b. May 4, 1960**
1980 WM20 SWE 5 1 2 3 6 B
1982-93 WM SWE 76 16 28 44 42 2G,3S
1987-91 CC SWE 12 2 4 6 12 —
1984-92 OG-M SWE 23 6 8 14 14 2B
~IIHF Hall of Fame
~WM All-Star Team/Forward (1991)

**Ruohola, Jussi / b. Feb. 11, 1986**
2004 WM18 FIN 6 0 2 2 6 —

**Ruotanen, Arto / b. Apr. 11, 1961**
1981 WM20 FIN 5 0 1 1 0 S
1985-92 WM FIN 57 2 13 15 42 S
1991 CC FIN 6 0 0 0 2 —
1984-92 OG-M FIN 21 0 7 7 12 S

**Ruotsalainen, Reijo / b. Apr. 1, 1960**
1977-80 WM20 FIN 24 9 12 21 8 S
1978-89 WM FIN 44 8 12 20 20 —
1981-87 CC FIN 9 0 1 1 4 —
1988 OG-M FIN 8 4 2 6 0 S
~WM20 IIHF Directorate Best Defenceman (1980), WM20 All-Star Team/Defence (1980)

**Ruotsalainen, Vesa / b. Apr. 13, 1966**
1985-86 WM20 FIN 14 0 2 2 14 —

**Rusnak, Darius / b. Dec. 2, 1959**
1978-79 WM20 TCH 10 4 0 4 4 S
1981-86 WM TCH 44 15 11 26 20 G,2S,B
1981 CC TCH 6 4 0 4 10 —
1984 OG-M TCH 7 4 5 9 6 S

**Rusnell, Dave / b. July 31, 1933**
1961 WM CAN 7 5 5 10 15 G

**Russ, Othmar / b. Nov. 5, 1952**
1976 OG-M AUT 5 0 1 1 10 —

**Russell, Jimmy / b. Mar. 31, 1918 / d. unknown**
1938-49 WM CAN 13 12 — 12 — G,S

**Russell, Phil / b. July 21, 1952**
1977-86 WM CAN 18 0 4 4 26 B

**Russell, Roy / b. Apr. 7, 1963**
1981 WM20 CAN 5 0 0 0 0 —

**Russell, Tom / b. 1929**
1949 WM CAN 7 8 — 8 — S

**Russwurn, Erik / b. Nov. 10, 1984**
2002 WM18 NOR 8 0 2 2 0 —

**Rusznak, Karol / b. Nov. 26, 1967**
1987 WM20 TCH 7 0 5 5 2 S

**Rusznyak, Karol / b. Nov. 26, 1967**
1998 OG-M SVK 4 0 0 0 0 —

**Ruuttu, Christian / b. Feb. 20, 1964**
1983-84 WM20 FIN 14 2 3 5 22 S
1985-96 WM FIN 60 17 17 34 72 2S
1987-96 WCH FIN 15 4 6 10 16 —

**Ruzicka, David / b. Mar. 8, 1988**
2005-06 WM18 CZE 14 1 0 1 62 —

**Ruzicka, Vladimir / b. June 6, 1963**
1981-83 WM20 TCH 19 25 9 34 14 2S
1983-89 WM TCH 50 25 25 50 22 G,S,2B
1984-87 CC TCH 11 2 0 2 2 —
1984-98 OG-M TCH 21 11 9 20 12 G,S
~WM All-Star Team/Forward (1985), WM20 All-Star Team/Forward (1982, 1983)

**Ryabev, Alexander / b. Aug. 24, 1988**
2006 WM18 RUS 6 1 1 2 0 —

**Ryabtsev, Denis / b. Oct. 17, 1984**
2002 WM18 UKR 8 2 3 5 12 —

**Ryabikin, Dmitri / b. Mar. 24, 1976**
1996 WM20 RUS 7 1 1 2 0 B
2002 WM RUS 9 0 3 3 2 S

**Ryan, Barry / b. Feb. 11, 1958**
1977 WM20 USA 7 0 0 0 0 —

**Ryanov, Vyacheslav / b. Jan. 24, 1959**
1978-79 WM20 URS 13 12 5 17 4 2G

**Ryazantsev, Alexander / b. Mar. 15, 1980**
1999-2000 WM20 RUS 14 2 6 8 6 G,S
2005 WM RUS 9 0 3 3 0 B
~WM20 IIHF Directorate Best Defenceman (2000), WM20 All-Star Team/Defence (2000)

**Rybin, Maxim / b. June 15, 1981**
1999 WM18 RUS 7 1 2 3 8 —

**Rybovic, Lubomir / b. Feb. 18, 1972**
1996 WM SVK 5 0 0 0 0 —
1996 WCH SVK 3 1 0 1 0 —

**Rybski, Andrzej / b. July 19, 1953**
1975 WM POL 7 1 0 1 2 —

**Rydberg, Ake / b. Sept. 3, 1938**
1961 WM SWE 5 0 2 2 0 —

**Ryder, Brad / b. Oct. 16, 1961**
1980 WM20 CAN 4 1 1 2 14 —

**Ryder, Michael / b. Mar. 31, 1980**
2000 WM20 CAN 7 1 3 4 6 B

**Rydmark, Daniel / b. Feb. 23, 1970**
1989-90 WM20 SWE 14 6 10 16 20 S
1992 WM SWE 7 0 1 1 4 G
1992-94 OG-M SWE 14 1 1 2 10 B

**Rygel, Ragnar / b. May 25, 1930 / d. Sept. 13, 1999**
1949-54 WM NOR 23 10 1 11 2 —
1952 OG-M NOR 8 4 1 5 — —

**Rylko, Tadeusz / b. Sept. 22, 1958**
1977 WM20 POL 7 1 0 1 2 —

**Rylkov, Sergei / b. Mar. 1, 1986**
2003-04 WM18 BLR 10 0 1 1 2 —

**Rylski, Roman / b. Apr. 23, 1980**
1999-2000 WM20 KAZ 13 0 2 2 20 —

**Ryman, Erik / b. June 10, 1972**
2006-08 WM NOR 18 0 0 0 18 —

**Rys, Miroslav / b. Aug. 17, 1932**
1959 WM TCH 3 0 0 0 0 B

**Rytvinski, Vasili / b. July 12, 1980**
1999 WM20 BLR 6 0 0 0 2 —

**Rytz, Phillipp / b. Dec. 7, 1984**
2002 WM18 SUI 8 0 1 1 12 —

**Ryznar, Jason / b. Feb. 19, 1983**
2001 WM18 USA 6 1 2 3 0 —

**Saarela, Pasi / b. Aug. 24, 1973**
1993 WM20 FIN 7 2 0 2 8 —

**Saarenheimo, Pekka / b. May 6, 1982**
2000 WM18 FIN 7 1 1 2 0 G
2002 WM20 FIN 7 1 0 1 0 B

**Saarenoja, Juha / b. Apr. 2, 1961**
1981 WM20 FIN 5 0 0 0 0 S

**Saari, Eero / b. Sept. 18, 1928**
1951 WM FIN 5 1 — 1 2 —
1952 OG-M FIN 8 0 1 1 — —

**Saari, Len / b. July 9, 1909 / d. unknown**
1939 WM USA 9 0 — 0 — S

**Saari, Timo / b. Jan. 14, 1949**
1974-76 WM FIN 29 2 4 6 12 —
1976 CC FIN 3 0 0 0 2 —
1976 OG-M FIN 5 0 0 0 6 —

**Saarikoski, Timo / b. July 17, 1969**
1989 WM20 FIN 7 2 6 8 0 —
1992-93 WM FIN 14 3 5 8 6 S
1992 OG-M FIN 8 0 0 0 0 —

**Saarinen, Jesse / b. July 29, 1985**
2003 WM18 FIN 6 3 2 5 4 —

**Saarinen, Olli / b. July 29, 1953**
1980 OG-M FIN 7 0 1 1 4 —

**Saarinen, Simo / b. Feb. 14, 1963**
1982-83 WM20 FIN 14 6 6 12 10 B
1989-90 WM FIN 12 0 3 3 10 —
1984-92 OG-M FIN 18 1 3 4 24 S
~WM20 All-Star Team/Defence (1983)

**Sabinski, Roman / b. Dec. 28, 1908 / d. June 28, 1978**
1930-33 WM POL 16 0 0 0 0 —
1932 OG-M POL 6 0 0 0 6 —

**Sabo, John / b. Sept. 4, 1981**
1999 WM18 USA 6 2 6 8 8 —
2000-01 WM20 USA 14 1 1 2 16 —

**Sabybyn, Vadym / b. Apr. 21, 1982**
2000 WM18 UKR 6 0 2 2 0 —

**Sacco, David / b. July 31, 1970**
1993 WM USA 6 0 0 0 0 —
1994 OG-M USA 8 3 5 8 12 —

**Sacco, Joe / b. Feb. 4, 1969**
1989 WM20 USA 7 3 1 4 2 —
1990-2002 WM USA 49 7 7 14 30 B
1992 OG-M USA 8 0 2 2 0 —

**Sachko, Vladimir / b. May 26, 1988**
2006 WM18 BLR 6 1 0 1 10 —

**Sachs, Walter / b. Feb. 15, 1891 / d. unknown**
1928 OG-M GER 1 0 0 0 — —

**Sacratini, Vezio / b. Sept. 12, 1966**
1994-2002 WM ITA 23 4 6 10 38 —
1994 OG-M ITA 7 0 1 1 10 —

**Sadjina, Alexander / b. Nov. 14, 1954**
1976 OG-M AUT 4 1 0 1 0 —

**Sadler, Robin / b. Mar. 31, 1955**
1988 OG-M AUT 6 2 1 3 4 —

**Sadlocha, Piotr / b. Apr. 28, 1970**
1990 WM20 POL 7 0 0 0 4 —

**Sadowsky, Robert / b. Aug. 16, 1914 / d. unknown**
1937-47 WM ROM 10 0 0 0 0 —

**Sady, Sergi / b. July 13, 1978**
1996 WM20 UKR 6 0 0 0 2 —

**Saether, Joakim / b. July 24, 1977**
2000 WM NOR 6 1 0 1 2 —

**Safronov, Kirill / b. Feb. 26, 1981**
1999 WM18 RUS 7 0 1 1 28 —
1999-2000 WM20 RUS 14 0 5 5 14 G,S

**Safwenberg, David / b. Oct. 1, 1896 / d. July 31, 1957**
1920 OG-M SWE 1 1 — 1 — —

**Sagat, Martin / b. Nov. 11, 1984**
2002 WM18 SVK 8 2 2 4 0 —
2004 WM20 SVK 6 1 0 1 2 —

**Sagesser, Hanspeter / b. unknown**
1978 WM20 SUI 6 0 0 0 0 —

**Sagymbayev, Yerlan / b. Apr. 5, 1970**
1998 WM KAZ 3 0 0 0 4 —
1998 OG-M KAZ 7 1 0 1 4 —

**Sahlstedt, Kalle / b. Aug. 25, 1973**
1993 WM20 FIN 7 1 2 3 0 —

**Sahraj, Valerij / b. May 20, 1965**
2002 WM SLO 5 1 1 2 2 —

**Saifullin, Ramil / b. Apr. 8, 1976**
1995 WM20 RUS 7 0 1 1 0 S

**Sailynoja, Keijo / b. Feb. 17, 1970**
1989-90 WM20 FIN 14 6 3 9 4 —
1992-93 WM FIN 13 2 1 3 2 S
1992 OG-M FIN 8 1 0 1 4 —

**Sainomaa, Teemu / b. May 15, 1981**
2001 WM20 FIN 7 0 2 2 4 S

**Saito, Takeshi / b. Apr. 8, 1981**
2003-04 WM JPN 12 1 2 3 8 —

**Saito, Tetsuya / b. Dec. 14, 1983**
2003 WM JPN 6 1 0 1 2 —

**Sakai, Toshiyuki / b. Sept. 3, 1964**
1998-2002 WM JPN 12 4 0 4 4 —
1998 OG-M JPN 4 0 2 2 6 —

**Sakata, Junji / b. May 10, 1974**
1993 WM20 JPN 7 0 0 0 2 —
1998-2001 WM JPN 12 0 1 1 2 —

**Sakic, Joe / b. July 7, 1969**
1988 WM20 CAN 7 3 1 4 2 G
1991-94 WM CAN 18 10 8 18 0 G,S
1996-2004 WCH CAN 12 6 4 10 8 1st,2nd
1998-2006 OG-M CAN 16 6 7 13 4 G
~Triple Gold Club
~OG-M MVP (2002), OG-M IIHF Directorate Best Forward (2002), OG-M All-Star Team/Forward (2002)

**Sakurai, Hideo / b. Aug. 14, 1948**
1976-80 OG-M JPN 10 5 3 8 4 —

**Sakurai, Kunihiko / b. Apr. 11, 1972**
2003-04 WM JPN 12 0 3 3 10 —
1998 OG-M JPN 4 0 0 0 4 —

**Sakurai, Teruo / b. unknown**
1957 WM JPN 7 0 — 0 — —

**Sakurai, Toshi / b. unknown**
1957 WM JPN 2 0 — 0 — —

**Salaschenko, Alex / b. Mar. 8, 1981**
1999 WM18 UKR 6 3 0 3 33 —

**Salat, Michael / b. unknown**
1981 WM20 AUT 5 0 0 0 4 —

**Salei, Ruslan / b. Nov. 2, 1974 / d. Sept. 7, 2011**
1998-2010 WM BLR 31 4 8 12 57 —
1998-2010 OG-M BLR 17 4 1 5 8 —
~perished in Yaroslavl plane crash

**Salfi, Kent / b. June 10, 1971**
2002-03 WM AUT 12 0 1 1 14 —
2002 OG-M AUT 4 0 1 1 2 —

**Saliji, Samir / b. Mar. 3, 1984**
2002 WM18 SVK 8 1 2 3 2 —
2003 WM20 SVK 6 0 1 1 4 —

**Salis, Edgar / b. May 20, 1970**
1998-2001 WM SUI 22 3 2 5 8 —
2002 OG-M SUI 2 0 0 0 0 —

**Salisma, Eero / b. Dec. 16, 1916 / d. July 19, 1998**
1949 WM FIN 3 1 — 1 — —
1952 OG-M FIN 7 1 2 3 0 —

**Salmelainen, Tommi / b. Jan. 29, 1949**
1971 WM FIN 9 0 1 1 10 —

**Salmelainen, Tony / b. Aug. 8, 1981**
1999 WM18 FIN 6 1 2 3 8 G
2001 WM20 FIN 7 3 2 5 6 S

**Saimi, Jorma / b. May 6, 1933**
1957-59 WM FIN 21 9 6 15 4 —
1960 OG-M FIN 4 1 2 3 0 —

**Salming, Borje / b. Apr. 17, 1951**
1972-73 WM SWE 14 4 6 10 14 S,B
1976-91 CC SWE 16 4 5 9 22 —
1992 OG-M SWE 8 4 3 7 4 —
~IIHF Hall of Fame
~WM All-Star Team/Defence (1973)

**Salming, Stig / b. Oct. 15, 1947**
1975-78 WM SWE 40 5 5 10 51 S,2B
1976 CC SWE 5 0 1 1 2 —

**Salnikov, Roman / b. Feb. 18, 1976**
1995-96 WM20 UKR 13 1 2 3 55 —
1999-2007 WM UKR 45 7 4 11 26 —
2002 OG-M UKR 4 0 3 3 8 —

**Salnikov, Sergei / b. June 26, 1986**
2004 WM18 RUS 6 0 2 2 6 G

**Salo, Vesa / b. Apr. 17, 1965**
1984-85 WM20 FIN 14 0 3 3 6 S
~WM20 IIHF Directorate Best Defenceman (1985)

**Salomaa, Sami-Ville / b. July 25, 1977**
1997 WM20 FIN 6 1 1 2 2 —

**Salomatin, Alexei / b. Feb. 7, 1965**
1995 WM RUS 6 2 1 3 2 —

**Salomonsson, Andreas / b. Dec. 19, 1973**
1993 WM20 SWE 5 0 3 3 2 S
2001-04 WM SWE 18 7 1 8 16 S,B

**Salonen, Aki / b. June 26, 1929**
1957 WM FIN 5 0 0 0 — —

**Salonen, Anssi / b. Sept. 4, 1936**
1961 WM FIN 6 2 2 4 2 —

**Salonen, Pasi / b. Dec. 18, 1985**
2002-03 WM18 FIN 14 2 2 4 6 —

**Salonen, Sami / b. Apr. 17, 1977**
1997 WM20 FIN 6 0 1 1 2 —

**Salonen, Timo / b. Aug. 25, 1976**
1995-96 WM20 FIN 13 6 1 7 51 —

**Salpa, Janne / b. Oct. 28, 1976**
1996 WM20 FIN 6 1 2 3 2 —

**Salsten, Jorgen / b. May 4, 1963**
1990-94 WM NOR 15 0 1 1 20 —
1988 OG-M NOR 4 0 0 0 2 —

**Salsten, Petter / b. Mar. 11, 1965**
1990-96 WM NOR 36 3 6 9 44 —
1988-94 OG-M NOR 20 4 6 10 20 —

**Salzmann, Walter / b. May 13, 1936 / d. Sept. 12, 2012**
1964 OG-M SUI 7 0 0 0 2 —

**Sammalkangas, Tapio / b. Mar. 16, 1980**
2000 WM20 FIN 7 0 0 0 35 —

**Samokhvalov, Andrei / b. May 10, 1975**
2004-06 WM KAZ 11 4 0 4 4 0
2006 OG-M KAZ 5 0 0 0 0 —

**Samolenko, George / b. Dec. 20, 1930**
1958 WM CAN 5 2 3 5 0 G
1960 OG-M CAN 7 8 4 12 0 S

**Samonig, Paul / b. Sept. 2, 1947**
1968 OG-M AUT 5 1 1 2 0 —

**Samoylov, Igor / b. Jan. 23, 1982**
2000 WM18 RUS 6 0 2 2 0 S

**Sampson, Gary / b. Aug. 24, 1959**
1984 OG-M USA 6 1 2 3 2 —

**Sampson, Ed / b. Dec. 23, 1921 / d. Aug. 26, 1974**
1956 OG-M USA 7 0 0 0 8 S

**Samsoe-Jensen, Nick / b. Aug. 5, 1987**
2005 WM18 DEN 6 0 1 1 4 —

**Samsonov, Sergei / b. Oct. 27, 1978**
1996-97 WM20 RUS 13 10 3 13 0 2B
2004 WCH RUS 4 1 2 3 0 —
2002 OG-M RUS 6 1 2 3 4 B
~WM20 All-Star Team/Forward (1997)

**Samuelsen, Peter / b. Apr. 29, 1972**
1990-91 WM20 NOR 14 1 1 2 2 —

**Samuelsson, Kjell / b. Oct. 18, 1958**
1991 WM SWE 10 2 2 4 12 G
1991 CC SWE 6 1 0 1 16 —

**Samuelsson, Martin / b. Jan. 25, 1982**
1999-2000 WM18 SWE 13 5 8 13 14 —
2001-02 WM20 SWE 14 4 1 5 6 —

**Samuelsson, Tommy / b. Jan. 12, 1960**
1978-80 WM20 SWE 18 1 4 5 8 S,2B
1981-90 WM SWE 53 1 4 5 12 3S
1987 CC SWE 3 0 1 1 4 —
1980-88 OG-M SWE 15 0 4 4 4 2B

**Samuelsson, Ulf / b. Mar. 26, 1964**
1982-84 WM20 SWE 15 2 7 9 38 —
1985-90 WM SWE 16 3 2 5 40 S
1991 CC SWE 3 0 0 0 4 —
1998 OG-M SWE 3 0 1 1 4 —
*disqualified from 1998 OG-M after three games because he did not possess a valid Swedish passport.

**Sandberg, Gosta/ b. June 6, 1932 / d. Apr. 27, 2006**
1961 WM SWE 4 0 1 1 0 —

**Sandelin, Scott / b. Aug. 8, 1964**
1984 WM20 USA 7 0 1 1 10 —
1986 WM USA 10 2 0 2 2 —

**Sanders, Frank / b. Mar. 8, 1949 / d. Feb. 17, 2012**
1972 OG-M USA 5 3 0 3 0 S

**Sanderson, Geoff / b. Feb. 1, 1972**
1993-97 WM CAN 27 10 7 17 12 2G

**Sandlak, Jim / b. Dec. 12, 1966**
1985-86 WM20 CAN 12 6 7 13 22 G,S
~WM20 IIHF Directorate Best Forward (1986)

**Sandner, Christoph / b. Feb. 19, 1971**
1998 WM GER 6 0 0 0 0 —

**Sandstrom, Jan / b. Jan. 24, 1978**
1998 WM20 SWE 7 1 0 1 6 —
2007 WM SWE 3 0 0 0 2 —

**Sandstrom, Tomas / b. Sept. 4, 1964**
1983-84 WM20 SWE 14 13 6 19 22 —
1985-89 WM SWE 28 11 15 26 38 G
1984-91 CC SWE 14 2 3 5 10 2nd
1984-98 OG-M SWE 11 2 2 4 6 B
~WM20 IIHF Directorate Best Forward (1983), WM20 All-Star Team/Forward (1983)

**Sandstrom, Ulf / b. Apr. 24, 1967**
1987 WM20 SWE 5 3 1 4 0 B
1988 OG-M SWE 7 3 2 5 2 B

**Sanford, James / b. June 18, 1984**
2002 WM18 CAN 8 1 1 2 8 —

**Sanford, Larry / b. unknown / d. unknown**
1931-33 WM USA 11 3 — 3 0 G,S

**Sanger, Matthias / b. Nov. 4, 1975**
1995 WM20 GER 7 0 0 0 0 —

**Sanipass, Everett / b. Feb. 13, 1968**
1987 WM20 CAN 6 3 2 5 8 —

**Sano, Hideyuki / b. June 1, 1974**
1993 WM20 JPN 7 0 0 0 4 —

**Santavuori, Tuomas / b. Jan. 24, 1985**
2003 WM18 FIN 6 2 0 2 6 —

**Sapozhnikov, Andrei / b. June 15, 1971**
1993 WM RUS 8 0 0 0 29 G

**Sapozhnikov, Vladimir / b. Aug. 2, 1982**
2002 WM20 RUS 7 0 0 0 6 G

**Saravo, Pekka / b. Nov. 13, 1979**
2005-07 WM FIN 23 2 2 4 12 S,B

**Sargent, Gary / b. Feb. 18, 1954**
1976 CC USA 5 0 0 0 2 —

**Sarich, Cory / b. Aug. 16, 1978**
1997-98 WM20 CAN 14 0 1 1 12 G

**Saris, Mari / b. Jan. 9, 1958**
1981 WM NED 7 2 1 3 0 —

**Sarkijarvi, Hans / b. Mar. 3, 1957**
1977 WM20 SWE 7 2 4 6 12 —
1985 WM SWE 8 1 0 1 6 —

**Sarmatin, Mikhail / b. Oct. 26, 1972**
1997-99 WM RUS 21 4 2 5 16 —

**Sarner, Craig / b. June 20, 1949**
1976-79 WM USA 18 3 2 5 17 —
1972 OG-M USA 5 4 5 9 0 S

**Sarnik, Piotr / b. Feb. 15, 1977**
1997 WM20 POL 6 0 0 0 4 —

**Sasaki, Keiji / b. Dec. 18, 1977**
2003 WM JPN 5 0 0 0 4 —

**Sasaki, Yuichi / b. Apr. 5, 1974**
1993 WM20 JPN 6 0 1 1 12 —
2002 WM JPN 6 0 0 0 2 —

**Sasek, Miloslav / b. Mar. 25, 1933**
1957-58 WM TCH 12 4 5 9 0 B

**Sasoya, Daisuke / b. Oct. 23, 1974**
1993 WM20 JPN 7 2 3 5 6 —

**Sato, Hiroshi / b. Feb. 18, 1983**
2004 WM JPN 3 0 0 0 6 —

**Sato, Masami / b. 1927**
1957 WM JPN 7 0 — 0 — —

**Sato, Masahiro / b. Oct. 27, 1936**
1964 OG-M JPN 7 12 2 14 2 —

**Sato, Masakazu / b. Sept. 23, 1976**
1999-2000 WM JPN 9 0 0 0 4 —

**Sato, Michihiro / b. Nov. 18, 1943**
1968 OG-M JPN 5 0 3 3 2 —

**Saunier, Bruno / b. July 19, 1963**
1992-93 WM FRA 9 1 0 1 2 —
1992-94 OG-M FRA 13 0 1 1 4 —

**Saunier, Franck / b. Feb. 14, 1966**
1994 OG-M FRA 7 2 0 2 2 —

**Sauve, Yann / b. Feb. 18, 1990**
2007 WM18 CAN 6 0 1 1 4 —

**Savage, Brian / b. Feb. 24, 1971**
1993-99 WM CAN 16 3 3 6 4 —
1994 OG-M CAN 8 2 2 4 6 S

**Savage, Reginald / b. May 1, 1970**
1989 WM20 CAN 7 4 5 9 4 —

**Savard, Robert / b. Mar. 16, 1961**
1981 WM20 CAN 5 0 2 2 2 —

**Savard, Serge / b. Jan. 22, 1946**
1972 SS CAN 5 0 2 2 0 1st
1976 CC CAN 7 0 3 3 0 1st

**Savchenko, Kostya / b. Oct. 19, 1982**
2000 WM18 UKR 6 0 0 0 6 —

**Savchenkov, Alexander / b. Sept. 30, 1973**
2002 WM RUS 2 0 0 0 2 S

**Savenko, Bogdan / b. Nov. 20, 1974**
2000-05 WM UKR 30 2 4 6 10 —
2002 OG-M UKR 4 0 1 1 2 —

**Savenkov, Andrei / b. Mar. 7, 1975**
2004-06 WM KAZ 12 0 0 0 14 —
1998-2006 OG-M KAZ 9 0 2 2 4 —

**Savic, Dragomir / b. May 4, 1949**
1972-76 OG-M YUG 8 0 1 1 2 —

**Savilov, Gennadi / b. Aug. 15, 1976**
2003 WM BLR 6 0 0 0 2 —

**Savin, Alexei / b. May 15, 1986 / d. June 18, 2007**
2005 WM20 BLR 6 1 1 2 12 —
2006 WM BLR 3 0 0 0 0 —

**Savitsky, Olexander / b. May 3, 1971**
1999-2004 WM UKR 20 1 2 3 26 —

**Savoie, Pierre / b. unknown / d. unknown**
1934-35 WM FRA 6 0 — 0 — —

**Savolainen, Jani / b. Oct. 5, 1988**
2006 WM18 FIN 6 2 0 2 2 S

**Savolainen, Vesa / b. Jan. 14, 1968**
1988 WM20 FIN 3 1 0 1 2 B

**Sawatske, Tom / b. Jan. 12, 1984**
2002 WM18 USA 8 1 0 1 4 G

**Sawkins, Peter / b. Aug. 29, 1963**
1983 WM20 USA 6 0 0 0 0 —

**Saxrud, Simen / b. Jan. 4, 1984**
2002 WM18 NOR 8 2 1 3 2 —

**Sayliss, George / b. unknown**
1954 WM CAN 4 1 — 1 4 S

**Scap, Ivan / b. Dec. 3, 1955**
1976-84 OG-M YUG 10 1 1 2 10 —

**Scapinello, Marco / b. Feb. 18, 1964**
1992 OG-M ITA 6 0 0 0 0 —

**Scarsini, Hans / b. Oct. 3, 1924**
1956 OG-M AUT 2 0 0 0 4 —

**Scerban, Bedrich / b. May 31, 1964**
1987-95 WM TCH 70 4 11 15 48 5B
1987 CC TCH 6 0 0 0 2 —
1988-94 OG-M TCH 24 0 5 5 12 B

**Scero, Brandon / b. May 5, 1986**
2004 WM18 USA 6 2 6 8 2 S

**Schaden, Mario / b. Apr. 30, 1972**
1996-2005 WM AUT 40 2 0 2 18 —
1998-2002 OG-M AUT 8 0 1 1 2 —

**Schaefer, Peter / b. July 12, 1977**
1997 WM20 CAN 7 3 1 4 4 G
2000-02 WM CAN 15 1 1 2 6 —

**Schafhauser, Bill / b. Mar. 12, 1962**
1982 WM20 USA 7 1 0 1 6 —

| | | | | | | | | |
|---|---|---|---|---|---|---|---|---|
| **Schager, Gerd / b. June 18, 1944** | | | | | | | | |
| 1968 | OG-M | AUT | 5 | 0 | 2 | 2 | 8 | — |
| **Scharf, Peter / b. July 15, 1953** | | | | | | | | |
| 1977-86 | WM | FRG | 64 | 4 | 5 | 9 | 38 | — |
| 1984 | CC | FRG | 5 | 0 | 1 | 1 | 0 | — |
| 1980-84 | OG-M | FRG | 11 | 0 | 4 | 4 | 10 | — |
| **Scharfe, Bert / b. Nov. 17, 1914 / d. unknown** | | | | | | | | |
| 1934 | WM | CAN | — | 5 | — | 5 | — | G |
| **Schastlivy, Piotr / b. Apr. 18, 1979** | | | | | | | | |
| 1999 | WM20 | RUS | 7 | 3 | 4 | 7 | 4 | G |
| 2007 | WM | RUS | 8 | 3 | 1 | 4 | 2 | B |
| **Schauer, Stefan / b. Jan. 12, 1983** | | | | | | | | |
| 2000-01 | WM18 | GER | 12 | 2 | 3 | 5 | 24 | — |
| 2003 | WM20 | GER | 6 | 1 | 1 | 2 | 6 | — |
| 2005 | WM | GER | 6 | 0 | 1 | 1 | 2 | — |
| 2006 | OG-M | GER | 5 | 0 | 0 | 0 | 4 | — |
| **Schefler, Dwight / b. unknown / d. unknown** | | | | | | | | |
| 1931 | WM | USA | — | 0 | — | 0 | 1 | S |
| **Scheifele, Steve / b. Apr. 18, 1968** | | | | | | | | |
| 1988 | WM20 | USA | 7 | 0 | 2 | 2 | 6 | — |
| **Schellenberg, Marco / b. Mar. 27, 1974** | | | | | | | | |
| 1994 | WM20 | SUI | 7 | 0 | 0 | 0 | 2 | — |
| **Schenk, Philipp / b. Dec. 3, 1914 / d. unknown** | | | | | | | | |
| 1935-39 | WM | GER | 32 | 5 | 0 | 5 | 2 | — |
| 1936 | OG-M | GER | 4 | 0 | — | 0 | — | — |
| **Schenkel, Thomas / b. May 20, 1985** | | | | | | | | |
| 2002 | WM18 | GER | 8 | 0 | 1 | 1 | 14 | — |
| **Schenker, Filippo / b. May 23, 1983** | | | | | | | | |
| 2001 | WM18 | SUI | 7 | 0 | 0 | 0 | 6 | S |
| **Schertz, Jan / b. Nov. 27, 1969** | | | | | | | | |
| 1991-96 | WM | GER | 12 | 0 | 0 | 0 | 0 | — |
| **Scheurer, Gerald / b. unknown** | | | | | | | | |
| 1978 | WM20 | SUI | 6 | 0 | 1 | 1 | 0 | — |
| **Schiau, Razvan / b. Oct. 17, 1944** | | | | | | | | |
| 1968 | OG-M | ROM | 5 | 0 | 0 | 0 | 0 | — |
| **Schibukat, Herbert / b. Oct. 27, 1914 / d. unknown** | | | | | | | | |
| 1935-39 | WM | GER | 19 | 3 | 0 | 3 | 2 | — |
| 1936-52 | OG-M | GER | 14 | 3 | 0 | 3 | — | — |
| **Schichtl, Hans / b. Apr. 8, 1943** | | | | | | | | |
| 1971-72 | WM | FRG | 17 | 0 | 0 | 0 | 27 | — |
| 1968 | OG-M | FRG | 7 | 0 | 0 | 0 | 16 | — |
| **Schiffl, Heinz / b. Aug. 19, 1968** | | | | | | | | |
| 1988 | WM20 | FRG | 6 | 0 | 1 | 1 | 6 | — |
| **Schildan, Heinz / b. May 18, 1941** | | | | | | | | |
| 1961-66 | WM | GDR | 22 | 0 | 1 | 1 | 2 | — |
| **Schiller, Peter / b. June 29, 1957** | | | | | | | | |
| 1977 | WM20 | FRG | 7 | 1 | 1 | 2 | 22 | — |
| 1981-86 | WM | FRG | 32 | 2 | 2 | 4 | 36 | — |
| 1984 | CC | FRG | 5 | 0 | 0 | 0 | 0 | — |
| 1988 | OG-M | FRG | 8 | 2 | 1 | 3 | 6 | — |
| **Schilling, Paul / b. unknown** | | | | | | | | |
| 1971 | WM | USA | 10 | 0 | 1 | 1 | 4 | — |
| **Schinko, Thomas / b. May 8, 1969** | | | | | | | | |
| 1988 | WM20 | FRG | 7 | 0 | 4 | 4 | 4 | — |
| 1994 | WM | GER | 3 | 0 | 0 | 0 | 2 | — |
| **Schioldan, Christian / b. Dec. 6, 1978** | | | | | | | | |
| 2004-06 | WM | DEN | 18 | 0 | 2 | 2 | 12 | — |
| **Schira, Craig / b. Apr. 21, 1988** | | | | | | | | |
| 2006 | WM18 | CAN | 7 | 0 | 2 | 2 | 8 | — |
| **Schischefski, Gunther / b. Aug. 11, 1925 / d. July 15, 2007** | | | | | | | | |
| 1957 | WM | GDR | 5 | 1 | — | 1 | — | — |
| **Schlagenhauf, Peter / b. Mar. 19, 1960** | | | | | | | | |
| 1980 | WM20 | SUI | 5 | 3 | 1 | 4 | 2 | — |
| 1987 | WM | SUI | 7 | 3 | 1 | 4 | 2 | — |
| 1988 | OG-M | SUI | 6 | 2 | 0 | 2 | 0 | — |
| **Schlapfer, Otto / b. Mar. 11, 1931** | | | | | | | | |
| 1951-59 | WM | SUI | 33 | 14 | 1 | 15 | 22 | 2B |
| 1952-56 | OG-M | SUI | 13 | 2 | 0 | 2 | 8 | — |
| **Schlegel, Brad / b. July 22, 1968** | | | | | | | | |
| 1991-2002 | WM | CAN | 28 | 1 | 4 | 5 | 24 | S,B |
| 1992-94 | OG-M | CAN | 16 | 1 | 2 | 3 | 10 | 2S |
| **Schlenker, Chris / b. July 9, 1984** | | | | | | | | |
| 2002 | WM18 | CAN | 8 | 0 | 0 | 0 | 6 | — |
| **Schloder, Alois / b. Aug. 11, 1947** | | | | | | | | |
| 1967-78 | WM | FRG | 67 | 14 | 26 | 40 | 70 | — |
| 1968-76 | OG-M | FRG | 14 | 6 | 3 | 9 | 16 | B |
| ~IIHF Hall of Fame | | | | | | | | |
| **Schloder, Kurt / b. unknown** | | | | | | | | |
| 1967 | WM | FRG | 7 | 3 | 2 | 5 | 2 | — |
| **Schmalzbauer, Gary / b. Jan. 27, 1940** | | | | | | | | |
| 1964 | OG-M | USA | 7 | 3 | 0 | 3 | 0 | — |
| **Schmid, Hans / b. Dec. 28, 1898 / d. unknown** | | | | | | | | |
| 1928 | OG-M | GER | 1 | 0 | 0 | 0 | — | — |
| **Schmid, Wilhelm / b. Mar. 30, 1921 / d. unknown** | | | | | | | | |
| 1949 | WM | AUT | 4 | 2 | — | 2 | — | — |
| 1956 | OG-M | AUT | 5 | 1 | 0 | 1 | 6 | — |
| **Schmid, Udo / b. Jan. 4, 1965** | | | | | | | | |
| 1984-85 | WM20 | FRG | 14 | 4 | 2 | 6 | 6 | — |
| **Schmidt, Harvey / b. unknown** | | | | | | | | |
| 1966 | WM | CAN | 5 | 0 | 1 | 1 | 2 | B |
| **Schmidt, Michael / b. May 23, 1961** | | | | | | | | |
| 1980 | WM20 | FRG | 5 | 0 | 0 | 0 | 20 | — |
| 1989-92 | WM | GER | 36 | 3 | 7 | 10 | 18 | — |
| 1992 | OG-M | GER | 3 | 0 | 0 | 0 | 0 | — |
| **Schmidt, Moritz / b. June 9, 1973** | | | | | | | | |
| 1993 | WM20 | GER | 7 | 0 | 2 | 2 | 4 | — |
| **Schmidt, Oscar / b. May 27, 1908 / d. unknown** | | | | | | | | |
| 1934-35 | WM | SUI | 5 | 0 | — | 0 | — | S |
| 1936 | OG-M | SUI | 2 | 0 | 0 | 0 | — | — |
| **Schmiedinger, Walter / b. unknown / d. unknown** | | | | | | | | |
| 1937-39 | WM | GER | 17 | 4 | 0 | 4 | 0 | — |
| **Schmitt, Pierre / b. Dec. 19, 1965** | | | | | | | | |
| 1988 | OG-M | FRA | 6 | 0 | 0 | 0 | 2 | — |
| **Schmitz, Michael / b. Mar. 15, 1973** | | | | | | | | |
| 1993 | WM20 | GER | 7 | 0 | 0 | 0 | 2 | — |
| **Schmultzler, Jurgen / b. June 6, 1942** | | | | | | | | |
| 1963-67 | WM | GDR | 6 | 0 | 0 | 0 | 6 | — |
| **Schnabel, Robert / b. Nov. 10, 1978** | | | | | | | | |
| 1998 | WM20 | CZE | 7 | 0 | 0 | 0 | 2 | — |
| **Schneeberger, Andreas / b. unknown** | | | | | | | | |
| 1986 | WM20 | SUI | 7 | 0 | 3 | 3 | 10 | — |
| **Schneider, Andreas / b. 1966** | | | | | | | | |
| 1994 | WM20 | GER | 7 | 0 | 1 | 1 | 6 | — |
| **Schneider, Andy / b. Mar. 29, 1972** | | | | | | | | |
| 1992 | WM20 | CAN | 7 | 0 | 0 | 0 | 6 | — |
| **Schneider, Bill "Buzz" / b. Sept. 14, 1954** | | | | | | | | |
| 1975-82 | WM | USA | 37 | 12 | 3 | 15 | 20 | — |
| 1976-80 | OG-M | USA | 12 | 7 | 4 | 11 | 10 | G |
| **Schneider, Bjorn / b. Jan. 24, 1973** | | | | | | | | |
| 1991-92 | WM20 | SUI | 14 | 2 | 1 | 3 | 8 | — |
| **Schneider, Florian / b. Mar. 10, 1975** | | | | | | | | |
| 1995 | WM20 | GER | 7 | 0 | 0 | 0 | 4 | — |
| **Schneider, Johann Hans / b. Sept. 14, 1913 / d. unknown** | | | | | | | | |
| 1935-49 | WM | AUT | 15 | 5 | — | 5 | — | B |
| 1948 | OG-M | AUT | 1 | 1 | — | 1 | — | — |
| **Schneider, Mathieu / b. June 12, 1969** | | | | | | | | |
| 1988 | WM20 | USA | 7 | 0 | 2 | 2 | 16 | — |
| 1996 | WCH | USA | 7 | 2 | 0 | 2 | 8 | 1st |
| 1998-2006 | OG-M | USA | 10 | 1 | 2 | 3 | 22 | — |
| **Schneider, Rochus / b. Dec. 29, 1967** | | | | | | | | |
| 1996 | WM | GER | 6 | 0 | 1 | 1 | 4 | — |
| **Schneider, Sascha / b. Dec. 21, 1977** | | | | | | | | |
| 1997 | WM20 | SUI | 6 | 1 | 2 | 3 | 8 | — |
| **Schneider, Scott / b. May 18, 1965** | | | | | | | | |
| 1985 | WM20 | USA | 7 | 1 | 1 | 2 | 4 | — |
| **Schneider, Walter / b. Aug. 22, 1953** | | | | | | | | |
| 1976 | OG-M | AUT | 4 | 0 | 0 | 0 | 0 | — |
| **Schneitberger, Otto / b. Sept. 29, 1939** | | | | | | | | |
| 1961-72 | WM | FRG | 31 | 5 | 2 | 7 | 52 | — |
| 1960-72 | OG-M | FRG | 22 | 1 | 2 | 3 | 18 | — |
| **Schnitzer, Florian / b. Jan. 28, 1981** | | | | | | | | |
| 1999 | WM18 | GER | 6 | 1 | 0 | 1 | 8 | — |
| **Schnoll, Alexander / b. Dec. 27, 1962** | | | | | | | | |
| 1982 | WM20 | FRG | 7 | 0 | 0 | 0 | 0 | — |
| **Schnyder, Simon / b. Feb. 7, 1987** | | | | | | | | |
| 2005 | WM18 | SUI | 6 | 1 | 0 | 1 | 4 | — |
| **Schnyder, Stefan / b. May 13, 1983** | | | | | | | | |
| 2001 | WM18 | SUI | 7 | 2 | 2 | 4 | 0 | S |
| 2003 | WM20 | SUI | 6 | 0 | 2 | 2 | 0 | — |
| **Schocher, Mario / b. Apr. 26, 1978** | | | | | | | | |
| 1997-98 | WM20 | SUI | 13 | 2 | 2 | 4 | 12 | B |
| **Schodl, Christoph / b. Apr. 7, 1962** | | | | | | | | |
| 1981 | WM20 | FRG | 5 | 0 | 2 | 2 | 0 | — |
| **Scholes, George / b. Nov. 23, 1928 / d. Nov. 18, 2004** | | | | | | | | |
| 1956 | OG-M | CAN | 8 | 5 | 3 | 8 | 2 | B |
| **Scholz, Eckhard / b. Nov. 6, 1953** | | | | | | | | |
| 1978-85 | WM | GDR | 28 | 2 | 3 | 5 | 8 | — |
| **Scholz, Georg / b. June 24, 1937** | | | | | | | | |
| 1961-63 | WM | FRG | 12 | 7 | 1 | 8 | 2 | — |
| 1964 | OG-M | FRG | 7 | 0 | 1 | 1 | 2 | — |
| **Schommer, Patrick / b. Apr. 26, 1989** | | | | | | | | |
| 2007 | WM18 | SUI | 6 | 0 | 1 | 1 | 0 | — |
| **Schonberger, Sandro / b. Jan. 14, 1987** | | | | | | | | |
| 2005 | WM18 | GER | 6 | 1 | 0 | 1 | 0 | — |
| **Schonmoser, Christian / b. May 14, 1979** | | | | | | | | |
| 1997 | WM20 | GER | 6 | 0 | 0 | 0 | 2 | — |
| **Schoop, Steven / b. Apr. 11, 1987** | | | | | | | | |
| 2005 | WM18 | SUI | 6 | 0 | 0 | 0 | 8 | — |
| **Schopf, Robert / b. June 24, 1989** | | | | | | | | |
| 2007 | WM18 | GER | 6 | 1 | 1 | 2 | 0 | — |
| **Schreiber, Wally / b. Apr. 15, 1962** | | | | | | | | |
| 1988-94 | OG-M | CAN | 24 | 4 | 4 | 8 | 6 | 2S |
| **Schriner, Marty / b. May 20, 1972** | | | | | | | | |
| 1992 | WM20 | USA | 5 | 0 | 0 | 0 | 8 | B |
| **Schroder, Klaus / b. July 27, 1955** | | | | | | | | |
| 1978-83 | WM | GDR | 20 | 0 | 1 | 1 | 6 | — |
| **Schroder, Markus / b. Nov. 16, 1981** | | | | | | | | |
| 1999 | WM18 | GER | 6 | 1 | 0 | 1 | 8 | — |
| **Schroder, Stefan / b. Nov. 16, 1981** | | | | | | | | |
| 1999 | WM18 | GER | 6 | 0 | 1 | 1 | 8 | — |
| **Schroeter, Reg / b. Sept. 11, 1921 / d. July 30, 2002** | | | | | | | | |
| 1948 | OG-M | CAN | 8 | 12 | — | 12 | 2 | G |
| **Schrottle, Martin / b. Sept. 1, 1901 / d. unknown** | | | | | | | | |
| 1930-35 | WM | GER | 17 | 5 | 0 | 5 | 0 | S |
| 1928-32 | OG-M | GER | 7 | 1 | 1 | 2 | 0 | B |
| **Schubert, Siegfried / b. Oct. 4, 1939** | | | | | | | | |
| 1959-63 | WM | FRG | 26 | 2 | 5 | 7 | 16 | — |
| 1960-64 | OG-M | FRG | 12 | 3 | 2 | 5 | 8 | — |
| **Schubert, Thomas / b. Feb. 13, 1972** | | | | | | | | |
| 1992 | WM20 | GER | 7 | 0 | 2 | 2 | 4 | — |
| **Schubiger, Otto / b. Jan. 6, 1925** | | | | | | | | |
| 1947-55 | WM | SUI | 18 | 4 | 3 | 7 | 2 | B |
| 1948-52 | OG-M | SUI | 9 | 8 | 1 | 9 | — | B |
| **Schuldes, Horst / b. Mar. 18, 1939** | | | | | | | | |
| 1959-61 | WM | FRG | 12 | 0 | 1 | 1 | 0 | — |
| 1960-64 | OG-M | FRG | 13 | 1 | 1 | 2 | 10 | — |
| **Schuller, Johann / b. Aug. 5, 1953** | | | | | | | | |
| 1976 | OG-M | AUT | 3 | 0 | 0 | 0 | 0 | — |
| **Schultz, Jeff / b. Sept. 26, 1982** | | | | | | | | |
| 2004 | WM18 | CAN | 7 | 0 | 0 | 0 | 2 | — |
| **Schulz, David / b. Jan. 3, 1986** | | | | | | | | |
| 2004 | WM18 | CAN | 6 | 0 | 0 | 0 | 4 | — |
| **Schulz, Jurgen / b. Jan. 7, 1970** | | | | | | | | |
| 1989 | WM20 | FRG | 7 | 1 | 0 | 1 | 0 | — |
| **Schumperli, Bernhard / b. Jan. 18, 1972** | | | | | | | | |
| 1991-92 | WM20 | SUI | 14 | 2 | 2 | 4 | 4 | — |
| **Schupp, Heinz / b. Feb. 26, 1942** | | | | | | | | |
| 1968 | OG-M | AUT | 5 | 4 | 0 | 4 | 6 | — |
| **Schur, Hartwig / b. July 29, 1947** | | | | | | | | |
| 1974 | WM | GDR | 9 | 0 | 0 | 0 | 6 | — |
| **Schury, Daniel / b. June 21, 1976** | | | | | | | | |
| 1996 | WM20 | GER | 6 | 0 | 0 | 0 | 4 | — |
| **Schussler, Franz / b. Jan. 20, 1911 / d. unknown** | | | | | | | | |
| 1934-35 | WM | AUT | 15 | 0 | — | 0 | — | — |
| 1936 | OG-M | AUT | 1 | 0 | — | 0 | — | — |
| **Schuster, Manfred / b. Feb. 14, 1958** | | | | | | | | |
| 1977-78 | WM20 | FRG | 12 | 0 | 0 | 0 | 14 | — |
| 1985-87 | WM | FRG | 19 | 0 | 1 | 1 | 6 | — |
| 1988 | OG-M | FRG | 8 | 0 | 0 | 0 | 12 | — |
| **Schutte, Hans / b. unknown / d. unknown** | | | | | | | | |
| 1933 | WM | GER | 1 | 0 | — | 0 | 0 | — |
| **Schutz, Armin / b. unknown** | | | | | | | | |
| 1953 | WM | SUI | 3 | 0 | 0 | 0 | 0 | B |
| **Schwabe, Jens / b. Jan. 12, 1972** | | | | | | | | |
| 1992 | WM20 | GER | 7 | 3 | 4 | 7 | 0 | — |
| **Schwach, Frantisek / b. unknown** | | | | | | | | |
| 1958 | WM | TCH | 7 | 0 | 1 | 1 | 2 | — |
| **Schwalm, Bela / b. Oct. 25, 1941** | | | | | | | | |
| 1964 | OG-M | HUN | 6 | 3 | 0 | 3 | 0 | — |
| **Schwartz, Yvan / b. Feb. 10, 1962** | | | | | | | | |
| 1982 | WM20 | SUI | 6 | 0 | 0 | 0 | 2 | — |
| **Schwarzenbach, Diego / b. May 9, 1987** | | | | | | | | |
| 2005 | WM18 | SUI | 6 | 0 | 0 | 0 | 0 | — |
| **Schwencke, Cor / b. Apr. 22, 1924** | | | | | | | | |
| 1950 | WM | NED | 4 | 1 | 0 | 1 | 0 | — |
| **Schwimmbeck, Peter / b. Sept. 14, 1941** | | | | | | | | |
| 1964 | OG-M | FRG | 6 | 0 | 0 | 0 | 4 | — |
| **Schwitzer, Josef / b. Oct. 31, 1946** | | | | | | | | |
| 1968-76 | OG-M | AUT | 10 | 0 | 2 | 2 | 14 | — |
| **Sciba, Joshua / b. Feb. 6, 1985** | | | | | | | | |
| 2003 | WM18 | USA | 6 | 0 | 0 | 0 | 6 | — |
| **Scott, John / b. 1928** | | | | | | | | |
| 1954 | WM | CAN | 6 | 1 | — | 1 | 0 | S |
| **Scott, Patrick / b. Nov. 12, 1966** | | | | | | | | |
| 1994 | WM | GBR | 6 | 2 | 0 | 2 | 2 | — |
| **Scotti, Gianni / b. Sept. 1, 1911 / d. unknown** | | | | | | | | |
| 1934-35 | WM | ITA | 13 | 3 | 0 | 3 | — | — |
| 1936 | OG-M | ITA | 3 | 1 | 0 | 1 | — | — |

**Searle, Tom / b. Apr. 26, 1963**
1998-2001 WM AUT 21 2 5 7 16 —
1998-2002 OG-M AUT 8 1 2 3 4 —

**Sebek, Venci / b. May 25, 1963**
1980-83 WM20 USA 12 2 0 2 14 —

**Secco, Lou / b. Jan. 18, 1927 / d. Oct. 27, 2008**
1952 OG-M CAN 8 3 2 5 2 G

**Secemski, Andrzej / b. May 16, 1970**
1990 WM20 POL 7 1 0 1 0 —

**Sechny, Richard / b. Oct. 19, 1971**
1999 WM SVK 6 0 0 0 0 —
2002 OG-M SVK 4 0 0 0 6 —

**Secord, Al / b. Mar. 3, 1958**
1977 WM20 CAN 7 2 2 4 10 S
1987 WM CAN 10 0 2 2 16 —

**Sedin, Jim / b. June 25, 1930**
1952 OG-M USA 8 2 2 4 — S

**Sedlak, Oldrich / b. Sept. 3, 1922 / d. Sept. 4, 1985**
1955 WM TCH 8 4 0 4 0 B
1952 OG-M TCH 7 1 1 2 — —

**Sedlak, Zdenek / b. Jan. 18, 1974**
1994 WM20 CZE 7 1 1 2 2 —
2002 WM CZE 7 1 0 1 2 —

**Segawa, Akiyoshi / b. May 31, 1934**
1957 WM JPN — 1 — 1 — —
1960 OG-M JPN 6 2 8 10 2 —

**Segerblad, Henning / b. Aug. 25, 1983**
2001 WM18 NOR 6 0 2 2 6 —

**Seidler, Emil / b. Mar. 13, 1914 / d. unknown**
1936 OG-M AUT 2 2 — 2 — —

**Seikkula, Timo / b. May 27, 1978**
1998 WM20 FIN 7 3 2 5 4 G

**Seikola, Markus / b. June 5, 1982**
2000 WM18 FIN 7 1 4 5 4 G
2002 WM20 FIN 7 1 2 3 16 B

**Seiling, Ric / b. Dec. 15, 1957**
1977 WM20 CAN 7 3 3 6 8 S

**Seiling, Rod / b. Nov. 14, 1944**
1972 SS CAN 3 0 0 0 0 1st
1964 OG-M CAN 7 4 2 6 6 —
~OG-M All-Star Team/Defence (1964)

**Seistamo, Jouni / b. Nov. 9, 1939**
1959-63 WM FIN 26 7 3 10 16 —
1960-64 OG-M FIN 12 8 4 12 8 —

**Sejba, Jiri / b. July 22, 1962**
1985-89 WM TCH 38 7 9 16 28 G,2B
1987 CC TCH 5 1 2 3 2 —
1988 OG-M TCH 8 3 1 4 16 —

**Sejejs, Normunds / b. Feb. 12, 1968**
1997-2004 WM LAT 36 2 6 8 34 —

**Sejna, Peter / b. Oct. 5, 1979**
1999 WM20 SVK 6 1 2 3 0 B
2003 WM SVK 4 0 0 0 4 B

**Sekelj, Matjaz / b. Dec. 9, 1960**
1984 OG-M YUG 5 2 1 3 2 —

**Sekeras, Lubomir / b. Nov. 18, 1968**
1996-2001 WM SVK 38 4 13 17 50 S
1996 WCH SVK 1 0 0 0 0 —
1994-98 OG-M SVK 12 0 4 4 12 —

**Sekulic, Krunoslav / b. Oct. 19, 1961**
1984 OG-M AUT 5 0 0 0 0 —

**Sekyra, Jiri / b. Apr. 21, 1929 / d. Oct. 18, 1977**
1954-55 WM TCH 7 2 0 2 2 B
1952 OG-M TCH 8 9 1 10 — —

**Selega, Rafal / b. May 22, 1977**
1997 WM20 POL 6 1 0 1 2 —

**Selianin, Sergei / b. Sept. 20, 1966**
1986 WM20 URS 7 0 2 2 10 G

**Seliger, Pavel / b. June 15, 1978**
1998 WM20 CZE 7 2 1 3 0 —

**Sell, Walter / b. unknown / d. unknown**
1930-31 WM AUT 3 0 0 0 — B
1928 OG-M AUT 2 0 — 0 — —

**Sellgren, Martin / b. June 10, 1979**
2000-01 WM NOR 12 0 0 0 4 —

**Seluyanov, Alexander / b. Mar. 24, 1982**
2000 WM18 RUS 6 0 1 1 4 S
2001 WM20 RUS 7 0 2 2 4 —

**Semak, Alexander / b. Jan. 16, 1966**
1984-86 WM20 URS 21 10 14 24 18 2G,B
1987-91 WM URS 30 8 7 15 18 G,S,B
1987-96 WCH RUS 13 5 1 6 17 —

**Seman, Daniel / b. Jan. 1, 1979**
1999 WM20 CZE 6 0 0 0 6 —

**Seme, Stefan / b. Aug. 20, 1947**
1972 OG-M YUG 2 0 1 1 0 —

**Semenchenko, Vitali / b. July 6, 1974**
2004-07 WM UKR 21 0 2 2 14 —

**Semjonovs, Aleksandrs / b. June 8, 1972**
1997-2007 WM LAT 70 17 9 26 60 —
2002-06 OG-M LAT 9 1 1 2 6 —

**Semyonov, Alexander / b. Feb. 8, 1982**
2001 WM20 KAZ 6 0 1 1 2 —

**Semyonov, Anatoli / b. Mar. 5, 1962**
1981-82 WM20 URS 12 8 10 18 28 B
1987 WM URS 10 2 1 3 16 S
1984-87 CC URS 15 5 6 11 4 —
1988 OG-M URS 8 2 4 6 6 G

**Semyonov, Dmitri / b. Feb. 23, 1986**
2003 WM18 BLR 4 0 0 0 2 —

**Senftleben, Helmut / b. May 5, 1934**
1957 WM GDR 7 1 — 1 — —

**Senger, Patrick / b. July 9, 1978**
1997-98 WM20 GER 12 0 0 0 4 —

**Senko, Juraj / b. Oct. 10, 1984**
2004 WM20 SVK 6 0 0 0 0 —

**Senins, Sergejs / b. Apr. 16, 1972**
1997-2000 WM LAT 15 0 2 2 4 —
2002 OG-M LAT 4 0 1 1 4 —

**Sepp, Kurt / b. Sept. 4, 1935**
1953-63 WM FRG 36 12 9 21 16 S
1956-64 OG-M FRG 17 7 2 9 8 —

**Seppa, Jyrki / b. Nov. 14, 1961**
1981 WM20 FIN 5 2 0 2 4 S

**Seppo, Jukka / b. Jan. 22, 1968**
1987-88 WM20 FIN 14 4 14 18 32 G,B
1987-89 WM FIN 18 2 1 3 8 —
1987 CC FIN 4 1 0 1 0 —

**Serdyukov, Pavel / b. Mar. 10, 1981**
2000-01 WM20 KAZ 13 0 0 0 12 —

**Serikow, Alexander / b. June 23, 1975**
1993-95 WM20 GER 21 5 13 18 14 —
1995-97 WM GER 13 0 0 0 10 —
1994 OG-M GER 6 0 1 1 0 —

**Serov, Vladislav / b. June 14, 1978**
2004 WM UKR 5 0 0 0 0 —
2002 OG-M UKR 4 0 1 1 0 —

**Sersen, Michal / b. Dec. 28, 1985**
2003 WM18 SVK 7 0 1 1 8 S

**Sertich, Steve / b. Oct. 20, 1952**
1975 WM USA 9 1 0 1 2 —
1976 OG-M USA 5 1 2 3 0 —

**Sessa, Jason / b. July 17, 1977**
1997 WM20 USA 6 1 1 2 2 S

**Sethereng, Morten / b. Jan. 15, 1953**
1972-80 OG-M NOR 8 3 0 3 2 —

**Sethreng, Rene / b. May 5, 1981**
1999 WM18 NOR 6 1 5 6 20 —

**Setikovsky, Pavel / b. Feb. 3, 1960**
1979-80 WM20 TCH 11 1 3 4 8 S

**Setoguchi, Devin / b. Jan. 1, 1987**
2005 WM18 CAN 6 4 2 6 6 S

**Sevcik, Frantisek / b. Jan. 11, 1942**
1965-70 WM TCH 32 11 6 17 2 2S,2B
1968 OG-M TCH 7 3 2 5 4 S
~OG-M All-Star Team/Forward (1968)

**Sevcik, Jaroslav / b. May 15, 1965**
1985 WM20 TCH 7 1 0 1 2 S

**Severyn, C.J. / b. June 2, 1989**
2007 WM18 USA 7 2 1 3 4 S

**Sevigny, Pierre / b. Sept. 8, 1971**
1991 WM20 CAN 7 4 2 6 8 G

**Sevon, Jorma / b. Feb. 7, 1958**
1978 WM20 FIN 6 7 5 12 0 —
1981 WM FIN 8 3 1 4 2 —
1981 CC FIN 5 0 1 1 4 —

**Sexton, Blaine / b. May 3, 1891 / d. Apr. 29, 1966**
1930 WM GBR 1 0 0 0 — —
1924-28 OG-M GBR 5 3 0 3 0 B

**Seychel, Chris / b. July 27, 1964**
1983 WM20 USA 7 2 0 2 4 —

**Seydoux, Philippe / b. Feb. 23, 1985**
2003 WM18 SUI 5 0 1 1 68 —
2004 WM20 SUI 6 1 1 2 4 —

**Seyller, Bernhard / b. Apr. 8, 1960**
1979-80 WM20 FRG 10 2 1 3 29 —

**Seyller, Max / b. Jan. 15, 1984**
2002 WM18 GER 8 1 1 2 18 —
2003 WM20 GER 6 1 0 1 2 —

**Sgualdo, Marcel / b. Dec. 18, 1944**
1972 WM SUI 5 0 0 0 0 —
1972 OG-M SUI 3 0 1 1 5 —

**Shadilov, Igor / b. June 7, 1980**
2000 WM20 RUS 7 1 0 1 0 S

**Shadrin, Vladimir / b. June 6, 1948**
1970-77 WM URS 64 33 40 73 42 5G,2S,B
1972 SS URS 8 3 5 8 0 2nd
1972-76 OG-M URS 8 7 4 11 2 2G

**Shafarenko, Oleg / b. Oct. 31, 1981**
1999 WM18 UKR 6 1 2 3 0 —
2000 WM20 UKR 7 0 1 1 8 —
2006-07 WM UKR 11 0 3 3 10 —

**Shafikov, Ruslan / b. May 11, 1976**
1996 WM20 RUS 7 1 8 9 0 B

**Shafranov, Konstantin / b. Sept. 11, 1968**
1998-2010 WM KAZ 21 0 5 5 8 —
1998-2006 OG-M KAZ 12 4 3 7 6 —

**Shakhov, Dmitri / b. Mar. 21, 1985**
2003 WM18 KAZ 6 3 4 7 4 —

**Shakhraychuk, Vadim / b. June 12, 1974**
1999-2006 WM UKR 42 13 9 22 80 —
2002 OG-M UKR 4 2 0 2 4 —

**Shalamai, Sergei / b. June 12, 1976**
1996 WM20 RUS 7 0 1 1 0 B

**Shalimov, Viktor / b. Apr. 20, 1951**
1975-82 WM URS 48 29 22 51 10 3G,S,B
1976-81 CC URS 8 2 3 5 2 —
1976 OG-M URS 5 5 5 10 2 G
~WM IIHF Directorate Best Forward (1982)

**Shalnov, Stanislav / b. Mar. 28, 1973**
1993 WM20 RUS 7 2 0 2 2 —

**Shanahan, Brendan / b. Jan. 23, 1969**
1987 WM20 CAN 6 4 3 7 4 —
1994-2006 WM CAN 14 7 4 11 16 G
1991-96 WCH CAN 15 5 4 9 14 1st,2nd
1998-2002 OG-M CAN 12 2 1 3 0 G
~Triple Gold Club

**Shand, Dave / b. Aug. 11, 1956**
1978-79 WM CAN 17 0 3 3 14 B

**Shannon, Darrin / b. Dec. 8, 1969**
1989 WM20 CAN 7 1 3 4 10 —

**Shantz, Jeff / b. Oct. 10, 1973**
1993 WM20 CAN 7 2 4 6 2 G

**Sharapa, Ruslan / b. Apr. 6, 1982**
2001-02 WM20 BLR 12 0 0 0 22 —

**Shargorodski, Oleg / b. Nov. 16, 1969**
1994 OG-M RUS 8 0 0 0 4 —

**Sharifianov, Vadim / b. Dec. 23, 1975**
1993-95 WM20 RUS 21 8 10 18 20 S,B

**Sharkevich, Alexander / b. Jan. 20, 1982**
2000 WM18 BLR 6 0 0 0 18 —

**Sharpley, Glen / b. Sept. 6, 1956**
1978 WM CAN 10 1 3 4 16 B

**Shashov, Vladimir / b. July 29, 1960**
1980 WM20 URS 5 2 1 3 2 G

**Shastin, Yevgeni / b. July 14, 1960**
1980 WM20 URS 5 3 2 5 6 G

**Shastin, Yegor / b. Sept. 10, 1982**
2000 WM18 RUS 6 7 4 11 4 S
2001 WM20 RUS 7 2 2 4 35 —

**Shatalov, Yuri / b. June 13, 1945**
1974 WM URS 9 1 4 5 4 G
1972 SS URS 2 0 0 0 0 2nd

**Shaughnessy, Frank / b. June 21, 1911 / d. June 12, 1982**
1936 OG-M USA 8 0 0 0 4 B

**Shaw, Brad / b. Apr. 28, 1964**
1983-84 WM20 CAN 14 1 3 4 2 B

**Shaw, Evan / b. Mar. 24, 1984**
2002 WM18 USA 8 0 0 0 2 G

**Shaw, Geoff / b. Nov. 26, 1958**
1977 WM20 CAN 7 3 1 4 19 S

**Shea, Dan / b. Mar. 10, 1966**
1986 WM20 USA 7 3 4 7 4 B

**Shea, Michael / b. June 4, 1961**
1993-96 WM AUT 24 0 1 1 6 —
1988-94 OG-M AUT 13 0 1 1 8 —

**Shebaga, Mike / b. Aug. 19, 1922 / d. unknown**
1955 WM CAN 8 5 0 5 0 G

**Sheehan, Bobby / b. Jan. 11, 1949**
1981 WM USA 8 1 1 2 0 —

**Sheehy, Neil / b. Feb. 9, 1960**
1985-92 WM USA 14 0 0 0 16 —

**Sheehy, Tim / b. Sept. 3, 1948**
1969-71 WM USA 20 2 6 8 14 —
1972 OG-M USA 5 2 1 3 0 S

**Shefer, Andrei / b. July 26, 1981**
1999 WM18 RUS 7 3 2 5 20 —
2001 WM20 RUS 7 2 1 3 2 —

**Shemelin, Denis / b. July 24, 1978**
1998 WM20 KAZ 7 0 1 1 4 —
2004 WM KAZ 2 0 0 0 2 —
2006 OG-M KAZ 5 0 0 0 4 —

**Shemetov, Sergei / b. Sept. 3, 1984**
2002 WM18 RUS 8 2 3 5 2 S

**Shendelev, Sergei / b. Jan. 19, 1964**
1984 WM20 URS 7 1 0 1 2 G
1993-95 WM RUS 20 3 7 10 17 G
1994 OG-M RUS 8 0 0 0 6 —

**Shepelev, Sergei / b. Oct. 13, 1955**
1981-83 WM URS 28 14 8 22 16 3G
1981-84 CC URS 11 6 5 11 4 1st
1984 OG-M URS 7 2 4 6 0 G

**Shepherd, Roy / b. Aug. 4, 1931 / d. Apr. 11, 2008**
1951-62 WM GBR 13 1 2 3 6 —

**Shepler, Dwight / b. Aug. 11, 1905 / d. unknown**
1931 WM USA 6 1 — 1 — S

**Sherbatyuk, Roman / b. Jan. 23, 1981**
1999 WM18 UKR 6 1 0 1 22 —
2000 WM20 UKR 4 0 0 0 2 —

**Sherven, Gord / b. Aug. 21, 1963**
1983 WM20 CAN 7 1 3 4 0 B
1983 WM CAN 9 2 1 3 2 B
1988 OG-M CAN 8 4 4 8 4 —

**Shesterikov, Sergei / b. Feb. 6, 1967**
1987 WM20 URS 6 2 2 4 0 —

**Shevchenko, Olexander / b. Oct. 11, 1984**
2001-02 WM18 UKR 14 1 2 3 8 —
2004 WM20 UKR 6 0 0 0 4 —

**Shevchenko, Vladislav / b. Aug. 11, 1976**
1995-96 WM20 UKR 13 0 1 1 30 —

**Shevelev, Andrei / b. Oct. 23, 1979**
1999 WM20 BLR 6 2 0 2 20 —

**Shevyev, Maxim / b. July 5, 1984**
2002 WM18 RUS 8 1 5 6 2 S

**Shewan, Cam / b. Dec. 26, 1912 / d. unknown**
1935 WM CAN 7 0 — 0 — G

**Shikhanov, Sergei / b. Apr. 8, 1978**
1998 WM20 RUS 7 2 3 5 8 S

**Shill, Bill / b. Mar. 6, 1923**
1954 WM CAN 7 6 3 9 4 S

**Shimada, Shigeru / b. Oct. 16, 1935**
1960-64 OG-M JPN 13 0 5 5 0 —

**Shinin, Alexander / b. Jan. 7, 1984**
2002 WM18 RUS 8 0 1 1 0 S

**Shipitsin, Yuri / b. Sept. 6, 1962**
1981-82 WM20 URS 12 0 10 10 18 B

**Shirono, Masaki / b. Dec. 27, 1970**
1998-2001 WM JPN 12 2 0 2 8 —

**Shiryayev, Valeri / b. Aug. 28, 1963**
1983 WM20 URS 7 1 4 5 2 G
1999-2004 WM UKR 34 6 8 14 22 G
2002 OG-M UKR 4 0 2 2 0 —

**Shishkanov, Timofei / b. June 10, 1983**
2001 WM18 RUS 6 2 2 4 0 G
2003 WM20 RUS 6 1 0 1 2 G

**Shitikov, Dmitri / b. Jan. 21, 1986**
2003-04 WM18 RUS 12 7 5 12 8 G,B

**Shitkovski, Sergei / b. Aug. 31, 1970**
1998 WM BLR 5 1 0 1 0 —

**Shkotov, Alexei / b. June 22, 1984**
2002 WM18 RUS 8 2 4 6 12 S
2004 WM20 RUS 6 2 2 4 4 —

**Shoji, Toshihiko / b. Apr. 23, 1909 / d. unknown**
1930 WM JPN 1 0 0 0 — —
1936 OG-M JPN 2 0 0 0 — —

**Shostak, Mikhail / b. Apr. 26, 1957**
1977 WM20 URS 7 5 5 10 11 G

**Shtefan, Pavlo / b. Mar. 26, 1980**
2000 WM20 UKR 7 0 2 2 4 —

**Shtepa, Yevgeni / b. Feb. 28, 1963**
1982-83 WM20 URS 14 8 3 11 4 G

**Shutron, Ben / b. June 14, 1988**
2006 WM18 CAN 7 0 2 2 4 —

**Shutt, Steve / b. July 1, 1952**
1976 CC CAN 6 1 2 3 8 1st

**Shuvalov, Maxim / b. Apr. 23, 1993 / d. Sept. 7, 2011**
2011 WM18 RUS 7 0 0 0 4 B
~perished in Yaroslavl plane crash

**Shuvalov, Viktor / b. Dec. 15, 1923**
1954-55 WM URS 15 11 2 13 6 G,S
1956 OG-M URS 7 5 2 7 0 G

**Shvetzov, Vladimir / b. Nov. 23, 1957**
1977 WM20 URS 7 5 1 6 0 G

**Shvidki, Denis / b. Nov. 21, 1980**
1998-2000 WM20 RUS 21 3 7 10 6 G,2S

**Shymanski, Maxim / b. Jan. 30, 1982**
2000 WM18 BLR 5 0 0 0 8 —
2001-02 WM20 BLR 12 0 2 2 20 —

**Siankevich, Artyom / b. May 4, 1982**
2000 WM18 BLR 6 0 0 0 4 —
2001-02 WM20 BLR 12 0 3 3 6 —

**Sidiakin, Andrei / b. Jan. 20, 1979**
1998 WM20 RUS 7 1 1 2 2 S

**Sidorenko, Andrei / b. July 22, 1959**
1979 WM20 URS 6 1 2 3 4 G

**Sidorenko, Andrei / b. Nov. 1, 1978**
1998 WM20 KAZ 7 0 0 0 4 —

**Sidorenkov, Genrikh / b. Aug. 11, 1931**
1954-61 WM URS 31 6 7 13 6 G,3S,B
1956-60 OG-M URS 13 1 2 3 14 G,B

**Sidorov, Andrei / b. May 15, 1969**
1988-89 WM20 URS 14 11 7 18 16 G,S

**Sidulov, Konstantin / b. Jan. 1, 1977**
1997 WM20 RUS 6 0 2 2 2 B

**Sigalet, Jonathan / b. Feb. 12, 1986**
2004 WM18 CAN 7 0 2 2 4 —

**Sigg, Daniel / b. Apr. 13, 1972**
1991 WM20 SUI 7 0 0 0 6 —

**Signoretti, Andre / b. Jan. 16, 1979**
2007-08 WM ITA 8 1 3 4 6 —
2006 OG-M ITA 4 0 0 0 2 —

**Sihvonen, Toni / b. Feb. 19, 1971**
1999-2001 WM FIN 30 3 4 7 10 2S,B

**Sikora, Dariusz / b. Dec. 30, 1958**
1977 WM20 POL 7 0 0 0 2 —
1980 OG-M POL 5 0 0 0 0 —

**Sikora, Miroslaw / b. Oct. 5, 1957**
1977 WM20 POL 7 0 3 3 6 —
1987 WM FRG 4 2 1 3 2 —

**Sikorski, Krystian / b. Apr. 14, 1961**
1986 WM POL 10 1 1 2 6 —
1984-88 OG-M POL 12 3 1 4 2 —

**Silfver, Claes-Henrik / b. Nov. 3, 1958**
1978 WM20 SWE 7 2 1 3 0 S

**Silfverberg, Conny / b. Mar. 7, 1959**
1977-79 WM20 SWE 20 3 7 10 10 S,B

**Silfverberg, Jan-Erik / b. Jan. 21, 1953**
1977 WM SWE 10 0 0 0 0 S

**Silius, Jyrki / b. Mar. 27, 1967**
1987 WM20 FIN 7 2 5 7 4 G

**Silk, Dave / b. Jan. 1, 1958**
1980 OG-M USA 7 2 3 5 0 G

**Silka, Frank / b. unknown**
1963 WM USA 7 0 1 1 0 —

**Sillanpaa, Olli / b. Mar. 3, 1981**
1999 WM18 FIN 7 3 2 5 0 G

**Sillanpaa, Teemu / b. Apr. 7, 1971**
1989-91 WM20 FIN 20 2 1 3 20 —

**Sille, Tamas / b. Nov. 23, 1969**
2009 WM HUN 6 1 0 1 14 —

**Sillig, Max / b. Nov. 19, 1873 / d. Nov. 15, 1959**
1920 OG-M SUI 2 0 0 0 — —

**Sillinger, Mike / b. June 29, 1971**
1991 WM20 CAN 7 4 2 6 2 G
2000 WM CAN 9 3 0 3 4 —

**Siltanen, Risto / b. Oct. 31, 1958**
1977-78 WM20 FIN 11 5 4 9 12 —
1977-83 WM FIN 26 1 4 5 20 —
1981 CC FIN 5 1 1 2 6 —
~WM20 All-Star Team/Defence (1977, 1978)

**Silvan, Lauri / b. Mar. 13, 1932**
1954 WM FIN 7 1 — 1 4 —
1952 OG-M FIN 7 4 1 5 — —

**Silver, Ron / b. Sept. 22, 1907 / d. unknown**
1934 WM CAN — 0 — 0 — G

**Simensen, Alexander / b. Sept. 27, 1983**
2001 WM18 NOR 6 2 2 4 10 —

**Simicek, Roman / b. Nov. 4, 1971**
1997-99 WM CZE 21 2 6 8 32 G,B

**Simioni, Mario / b. Apr. 1, 1963**
1992 WM ITA 5 1 0 1 2 —

**Simko, Jan / b. Dec. 13, 1978**
1997-98 WM20 SVK 12 3 1 4 0 —

**Simmer, Charlie / b. Mar. 20, 1954**
1983 WM CAN 10 2 3 5 8 B

**Simon, Ben / b. June 14, 1978**
1997-98 WM20 USA 13 1 3 4 12 S

**Simon, Dieter / b. Feb. 20, 1953**
1974-83 WM GDR 40 3 8 11 12 —

**Simond, Gerard / b. May 11, 1903 / d. unknown**
1930-34 WM FRA 11 1 — 1 — —
1928 OG-M FRA 3 2 — 2 — —

**Simons, Mikael / b. Jan. 15, 1978**
1998 WM20 SWE 7 1 1 2 4 —

**Simpson, Harold "Hack" / b. Dec. 7, 1909 / d. Mar. 1978**
1932 OG-M CAN 5 6 1 7 6 G

**Simpson, Sean / b. May 4, 1960**
1980 WM20 CAN 5 0 2 2 0 —

**Sinclair, Alex / b. June 28, 1911 / d. Oct. 2, 2002**
1936 OG-M CAN 6 4 3 7 0 S

**Sinden, Harry / b. Sept. 14, 1932**
1958 WM CAN 7 4 3 7 8 G
1960 OG-M CAN 7 4 5 9 6 S
~IIHF Hall of Fame

**Singewald, Max / b. Feb. 4, 1933**
1956 OG-M AUT 2 0 0 0 0 —

**Sinisalo, Ilkka / b. July 10, 1958**
1978 WM20 FIN 6 1 7 8 4 —
1981-83 WM FIN 19 1 4 5 14 —
1981 CC FIN 5 1 0 1 6 —

**Sinner, Stefan / b. Aug. 14, 1969**
1988-89 WM20 FRG 14 3 1 4 16 —

**Sintschnig, Christian / b. Apr. 21, 1975**
2002 WM AUT 6 0 0 0 2 —

**Siren, Ville / b. Feb. 11, 1964**
1983-84 WM20 FIN 13 1 3 4 10 S
1985-93 WM FIN 21 2 2 4 30 —
1987-91 CC FIN 11 0 1 1 21 —
1984-92 OG-M FIN 14 0 3 3 18 —

**Sirvio, Arto / b. Jan. 6, 1962**
1981-82 WM20 FIN 12 5 4 9 0 S,B
1983 WM FIN 10 1 0 1 2 —
1984 OG-M FIN 6 3 0 3 0 —

**Sitko, Hubert / b. Dec. 26, 1939**
1964 OG-M POL 7 0 3 3 8 —

**Sittler, Darryl / b. Sept. 18, 1950**
1982-83 WM CAN 20 7 4 11 14 2B
1976 CC CAN 7 4 2 6 3 1st

**Sittler, Ryan / b. Jan. 28, 1974**
1992-94 WM20 USA 15 3 3 6 10 B

**Sivec, Leopold / b. Aug. 3, 1958**
1984 OG-M AUT 5 1 1 2 2 —

**Sivek, Michal / b. Jan. 21, 1981**
1999 WM18 CZE 7 2 5 7 12 —
1999-2001 WM20 CZE 20 6 5 11 28 2G

**Sivertsson, Lars-Ake / b. May 8, 1941**
1965-66 WM SWE 12 3 3 6 4 B

**Sivic, Mitja / b. Oct. 1, 1979**
2003-06 WM SLO 16 1 0 1 6 —

**Sjalin, Tommy / b. Jan. 20, 1955**
1982 WM SWE 10 2 1 3 0 —

**Sjoberg, Edmund / b. Feb. 28, 1917 / d. unknown**
1939 WM FIN 5 0 — 0 — —

**Sjoberg, Lars-Erik / b. May 4, 1944**
1969-74 WM SWE 49 7 6 13 6 3S,2B
1976 CC SWE 5 0 3 3 6 —
1968-72 OG-M SWE 12 0 0 0 6 —
~WM IIHF Directorate Best Defenceman (1974), WM All-Star Team/Defence (1974)

**Sjoberg, Mathias / b. Sept. 15, 1988**
2006 WM18 SWE 6 0 0 0 10 —

**Sjoblom, Eerik / b. July 6, 1965**
1985 WM20 FIN 7 2 1 3 0 —

**Sjodin, Tommy / b. Aug. 13, 1965**
1992-96 WM SWE 30 3 5 8 18 G,S,B
1992 OG-M SWE 8 4 1 5 2 —
~WM All-Star Team/Defence (1995)

**Sjodin, Viktor / b. Apr. 21, 1988**
2006 WM18 SWE 6 1 2 3 2 —

**Sjogren, Tomas / b. June 8, 1968**
1987-88 WM20 SWE 13 8 14 22 4 B

**Sjolander, Per / b. Feb. 14, 1959**
1979 WM20 SWE 6 0 0 0 0 B

**Sjoo, Hasse / b. Dec. 17, 1959**
1982 WM SWE 3 0 0 0 0 —

**Sjostrom, Fredrik / b. May 6, 1983**
2001 WM18 SWE 6 3 3 6 4 —
2001-03 WM20 SWE 18 1 3 4 34 —
2004 WM SWE 9 0 0 0 6 S

**Skaare, Bjorn / b. Oct. 29, 1958 / d. June 21, 1989**
1984 OG-M NOR 5 0 3 3 4 —

**Skabelka, Andrei / b. Jan. 20, 1971**
1998-2006 WM BLR 36 4 17 21 16 —
1998-2002 OG-M BLR 9 2 3 5 0 —

**Skadins, Johans / b. Dec. 17, 1905 / d. unknown**
1933 WM LAT 4 0 — 0 0 —

**Skalicky, Pavel / b. Sept. 19, 1958**
1977-78 WM20 TCH 13 2 1 3 4 B

**Skalleberg, Eugen / b. unknown / d. unknown**
1937-38 WM NOR 6 1 0 1 0 —

**Skarczynski, Hilary / b. June 18, 1925 / d. Sept. 30, 1987**
1947 WM POL 5 8 — 8 — —
1948-56 OG-M POL 19 9 0 9 2 —

**Skarda, Randy / b. May 5, 1968**
1988 WM20 USA 6 1 2 3 26 —

**Skjerwen-Olsen, Per / b. Sept. 26, 1939**
1958-62 WM NOR 18 8 8 16 12 —
1964-68 OG-M NOR 11 3 7 10 26 —

**Skime, Larry / b. unknown**
1969 WM USA 7 2 0 2 0 —

**Sklenar, Jaroslav / b. Nov. 22, 1982**
2002 WM20 CZE 6 1 1 2 2 —

**Skoglund, Ulf / b. Jan. 24, 1959**
1978 WM20 SWE 7 1 0 1 4 S

**Skogs, Tomas / b. Feb. 19, 1984**
2002 WM18 SWE 8 0 0 0 4 —

**Skoliak, Michal / b. Apr. 30, 1984**
2002 WM18 SVK 8 0 1 1 8 —

**Skolla, Petter / b. Apr. 6, 1982**
1999 WM18 NOR 6 0 0 0 4 —

**Skoog, Simon / b. Feb. 17, 1983**
2001 WM18 SWE 6 1 1 2 14 —
2003 WM20 SWE 6 0 3 3 4 —

**Skopintsev, Andrei / b. Sept. 28, 1971**
1995-2004 WM RUS 33 6 2 8 10 —

**Skorepa, Zdenek / b. Aug. 10, 1976**
1996 WM20 CZE 6 0 1 1 4 —

**Skorokhod, Olexander / b. Oct. 1, 1983**
1999-2001 WM18 UKR 16 3 8 11 20 —
2000 WM20 UKR 7 0 0 0 2 —

**Skorski, Aug.yn / b. Nov. 6, 1936 / d. Jan. 22, 1981**
1958-59 WM POL 9 0 0 0 2 —
1964 OG-M POL 7 2 0 2 0 —

**Skotnicki, Zbigniew / b. Feb. 3, 1933**
1959 WM POL 8 2 1 3 2 —

**Skouen, Henrik / b. Oct. 25, 1988**
2006 WM18 NOR 6 0 0 0 0 —

**Skovira, Miroslav / b. Nov. 7, 1973**
1992-93 WM20 TCH 10 0 0 0 2 B

**Skrastins, Karlis / b. July 9, 1974 / d. Sept. 7, 2011**
1997-2009 WM LAT 52 11 11 22 49 —
2002-10 OG-M LAT 10 0 1 1 0 —
~perished in Yaroslavl plane crash

**Skrbek, Pavel / b. Aug. 9, 1978**
1998 WM20 CZE 7 2 4 6 8 —
~WM20 IIHF Directorate Best Defenceman (1998)

**Skriko, Petri / b. Mar. 13, 1962**
1981-82 WM20 FIN 12 11 10 21 14 S,B
1983-87 WM FIN 30 7 5 12 8 —
1987-91 CC FIN 11 3 3 6 4 —
1984-92 OG-M FIN 14 7 8 15 12 —
~WM20 IIHF Directorate Best Forward (1982), WM20 All-Star Team/Forward (1982)

**Skrypailov, Andrei / b. June 4, 1982**
2000 WM18 BLR 6 0 0 0 6 —
2001-02 WM20 BLR 12 0 1 1 16 —

**Skugarev, Alexander / b. Mar. 13, 1975**
2004 WM RUS 6 1 1 2 2 —

**Skuhravy, Vaclav / b. Jan. 16, 1979**
2008 WM CZE 2 0 0 0 0 —

**Skurdyuk, Viktor / b. unknown**
1978 WM20 URS 7 10 6 16 0 G

**Skuta, Vyacheslav / b. July 17, 1974**
1994 WM20 CZE 7 1 0 1 16 —

**Skvaridlo, Tomas / b. June 19, 1981**
1999 WM18 SVK 7 0 1 1 8 B
2001 WM20 SVK 7 3 1 4 4 —

**Skvortsov, Alexander / b. Aug. 28, 1954**
1979-85 WM URS 30 13 5 18 6 3G,B
1976-84 CC URS 18 2 4 6 4 —
1980-84 OG-M URS 14 6 8 14 0 G,S

**Skvortsov, Alexander / b. Jan. 26, 1986**
2003 WM18 KAZ 6 0 0 0 0 —

**Slabon, Damian / b. Jan. 28, 1979**
1997 WM20 POL 6 0 1 1 0 —
2002 WM POL 3 0 0 0 0 —

**Sladok, Jozef / b. June 4, 1988**
2006 WM18 SVK 6 0 1 1 10 —

**Slama, Miroslav / b. Feb. 17, 1917 / d. Nov. 30, 2008**
1947 WM TCH 7 3 — 3 — G
1948 OG-M TCH 4 3 — 3 — S

**Slamiar, Peter / b. Feb. 26, 1977**
1997 WM20 SVK 6 2 1 3 10 —

**Slaney, John / b. Feb. 7, 1972**
1991-92 WM20 CAN 14 2 5 7 12 G

**Slanina, Peter / b. Dec. 16, 1959**
1979 WM20 TCH 6 0 1 1 4 S
1986 WM TCH 5 0 0 0 4 —

**Slapke, Peter / b. July 16, 1949**
1970-78 WM GDR 40 4 7 11 35 —

**Slater, Cyril "Sig" / b. Mar. 27, 1897 / d. unknown**
1924 OG-M CAN 5 4 — 4 2 G

**Slater, Jim / b. Dec. 9, 1982**
2002 WM20 USA 7 1 4 5 8 —
2006 WM USA 7 0 1 1 2 —

**Slavetinsky, Lukas / b. June 30, 1981**
1999 WM18 GER 6 0 0 0 2 —

**Slegr, Jiri / b. May 30, 1971**
1990-91 WM20 TCH 14 3 13 16 32 2B
1997-2005 WM CZE 39 3 5 8 103 G,2B
1991-2004 WCH CZE 11 1 1 2 33 —
1992-98 OG-M TCH 14 2 1 3 22 G,B
~Triple Gold Club
~WM20 IIHF Directorate Best Defenceman (1991), WM20 All-Star Team/Defence (1990)

**Slevogt, Marquardt / b. Mar. 22, 1909 / d. unknown**
1930 WM GER 1 0 — 0 — S
1928-32 OG-M GER 7 0 0 0 2 B

**Slezak, Miroslav / b. Apr. 15, 1947**
1977 WM FRG 10 0 0 0 0 —

**Slipchenko, Mikhail / b. June 14, 1957**
1977 WM20 URS 7 1 0 1 0 G

**Slivchenko, Vadym / b. Mar. 28, 1970**
1999-2001 WM UKR 9 4 0 4 0 —
2002 OG-M UKR 4 0 0 0 0 —

**Sloan, Blake / b. July 27, 1975**
1994 WM20 USA 7 0 0 0 2 —
2004 WM USA 9 2 0 2 4 B

**Sloan, Tod / b. Nov. 30, 1927**
1962 WM CAN 6 6 10 16 6 S

**Sloboda, Karol / b. May 16, 1983**
2000-01 WM18 SVK 12 1 1 2 12 —
2002-03 WM20 SVK 13 2 3 5 6 —

**Sloboda, Radovan / b. Nov. 7, 1982**
2000 WM18 SVK 6 0 0 0 0 —
2002 WM20 SVK 7 0 0 0 8 —

**Slovak, Juraj / b. July 18, 1979**
1999 WM20 SVK 6 0 0 0 2 B

**Slovak, Martin / b. Sept. 24, 1984**
2002 WM18 SVK 8 0 2 2 2 —

**Slovak, Tomas / b. Apr. 5, 1983**
2001 WM18 SVK 6 0 1 1 16 —
2001-03 WM20 SVK 13 1 1 2 44 —

**Slowakiewicz, Andrzej / b. Jan. 27, 1951**
1970-79 WM POL 46 0 0 0 38 —
1976 OG-M POL 4 0 0 0 6 —

**Slowakiewicz, Jozef / b. Feb. 7, 1945**
1973-74 WM POL 20 3 3 6 6 —
1972 OG-M POL 5 2 0 2 0 —

**Sluce, Vic / b. unknown**
1954 WM CAN 7 3 3 6 8 S

**Sluczanowski, Alexander / b. unknown / d. unknown**
1928 OG-M POL 1 0 — 0 — —

**Slusarczyk, Artur / b. Nov. 3, 1977**
2002 WM POL 2 0 0 0 0 —

**Sly, Darryl / b. Apr. 3, 1939 / d. Aug. 28, 2007**
1961 WM CAN 7 4 2 6 4 G
1960 OG-M CAN 7 1 1 2 9 S
~WM All-Star Team/Defence (1961)

**Slysh, Maxim / b. Jan. 20, 1979**
1999 WM20 BLR 6 0 2 2 2 —

**Smalhout, Hans / b. Dec. 31, 1920 / d. unknown**
1939 WM NED 2 0 — 0 — —

**Small, Irving / b. July 19, 1891 / d. Dec. 12, 1955**
1924 OG-M USA 5 8 — 8 0 S

**Smazal, Heiko-Michael / b. Jan. 6, 1974**
1992-93 WM20 GER 14 1 2 3 26 —
2001-04 WM GER 8 0 0 0 2 —

**Smefjell, Georg / b. June 9, 1937**
1958-65 WM NOR 24 8 1 9 14 —
1964-68 OG-M NOR 12 6 4 10 4 —

**Smehlik, Richard / b. Jan. 23, 1970**
1990 WM20 TCH 7 0 1 1 4 B
1991-92 WM TCH 16 1 2 3 12 B
1991 CC TCH 5 0 1 1 2 —
1992-2002 OG-M CZE 18 0 2 2 10 G,B

**Smelnitski, Maxim / b. Mar. 24, 1974**
1994 WM20 RUS 7 0 0 0 0 B

**Smerciak, Marian / b. Dec. 24, 1972**
1996 WM SVK 5 0 0 0 6 —
1996 WCH SVK 1 0 0 0 4 —
1994 OG-M SVK 8 0 1 1 12 —

**Smid, Karel / b. May 14, 1968**
1988 WM20 TCH 7 0 0 0 6 —

**Smid, Ladislav / b. Feb. 1, 1986**
2003-04 WM18 CZE 11 0 2 2 2 B
2004-06 WM20 CZE 19 2 5 7 8 B
2007 WM CZE 6 0 0 0 31 —

**Smidt, Michael / b. July 4, 1979**
2004-07 WM DEN 24 1 1 2 6 —

**Smielowski, Krzysztof / b. Apr. 21, 1975**
2002 WM POL 6 1 0 1 4 —

**Smirnov, Alexander / b. Aug. 17, 1964**
1984 WM20 URS 7 3 1 4 2 G
1993-96 WM RUS 27 1 6 7 22 G
1994 OG-M RUS 8 1 0 1 8 —

**Smirnov, Alexei / b. Jan. 28, 1982**
1999-2000 WM18 RUS 12 4 5 9 22 S

**Smirnov, Andrei / b. Mar. 7, 1967**
1987 WM20 URS 6 1 2 3 8 —

**Smirnov, Oleg / b. Apr. 8, 1980**
2000 WM20 RUS 7 2 6 8 2 S

**Smital, Lukas / b. Aug. 15, 1974**
1994 WM20 CZE 6 0 2 2 2 —

**Smith, Art / b. Nov. 29, 1906 / d. unknown**
1934 WM USA 4 0 0 0 — S

**Smith, Bert / b. Sept. 6, 1925**
1950-62 WM GBR 20 5 4 9 4 —
1948 OG-M GBR 3 0 — 0 — —

**Smith, Bobby / b. Feb. 12, 1958**
1978 WM20 CAN 3 1 4 5 0 B
1979-82 WM CAN 18 6 8 14 0 B

**Smith, Dallas / b. Oct. 10, 1941**
1977 WM CAN 10 0 2 2 4 —

**Smith, Derek / b. Apr. 2, 1983**
2001 WM18 USA 6 0 0 0 4 —

**Smith, Geoff / b. Mar. 7, 1969**
1989 WM20 CAN 7 0 1 1 4 —
1993 WM CAN 8 0 0 0 4 —

**Smith, Gord / b. Feb. 14, 1908 / d. unknown**
1931 WM USA 6 4 — 4 — S
1932-36 OG-M USA 9 2 0 2 0 S,B

**Smith, Greg / b. July 8, 1955**
1977-79 WM CAN 15 1 1 2 16 —

**Smith, Harry / b. Sept. 11, 1923 / d. unknown**
1961-63 WM CAN 21 9 10 19 22 G,S
~WM All-Star Team/Defence (1961, 1962, 1963)

**Smith, Jason / b. Nov. 2, 1973**
1993 WM20 CAN 7 1 3 4 10 G
2001 WM CAN 7 1 0 1 4 —

**Smith, Kenny / b. Dec. 31, 1981**
1999 WM18 USA 6 0 0 0 4 —

**Smith, Larry / b. unknown**
1965 WM USA 5 0 0 0 0 —

**Smith, Randy / b. July 7, 1965**
1991-92 WM CAN 16 1 0 1 12 S
1992 OG-M CAN 8 1 7 8 4 S

**Smith, Reginald "Hooley" / b. Jan. 7, 1905 / d. Aug. 24, 1963**
1924 OG-M CAN 5 18 — 18 4 G

**Smith, Richie / b. unknown**
1975 WM USA 8 0 1 1 0 —
**Smith, Sid / b. July 11, 1925**
1958 WM CAN 7 9 5 14 2 G
**Smith, Steve / b. Apr. 4, 1963**
1991 CC CAN 8 0 1 1 30 1st
**Smith, Stuart / b. Mar. 17, 1960**
1980 WM20 CAN 5 0 1 1 10 —
**Smith, Wyatt / b. Feb. 13, 1977**
1996-97 WM20 USA 12 0 3 3 2 S
**Smithurst, Jan Erik / b. June 18, 1969**
1989 WM20 NOR 7 1 1 2 2 —
**Smithurst, Michael / b. Mar. 12, 1971**
1991 WM20 NOR 6 0 2 2 2 —
1996-97 WM NOR 8 1 0 1 0 —
**Smolej, Franc / b. July 18, 1940**
1964-68 OG-M YUG 12 6 3 9 6 —
**Smolej, Roman / b. Sept. 6, 1946**
1968-76 OG-M YUG 13 8 5 13 6 —
**Smolenak, Radek / b. Dec. 3, 1986**
2004 WM18 CZE 5 0 1 1 0 B
**Smolinski, Bryan / b. Dec. 27, 1971**
1990 WM20 USA 7 2 3 5 8 —
1998-99 WM USA 12 6 4 10 18 —
1996-2004 WCH USA 9 1 5 6 0 1st
**Smrke, Lou / b. May 11, 1927**
1959 WM CAN 7 2 2 4 4 G
**Smyl, Stan / b. Jan. 28, 1958**
1978 WM20 CAN 6 1 1 2 6 B
1985 WM CAN 10 1 1 2 6 S
**Sneddon, Bill / b. July 13, 1915 / d. unknown**
1950 WM GBR 6 2 0 2 14 —
**Snell, Chris / b. May 12, 1971**
1991 WM20 CAN 7 0 4 4 0 G
**Snetkov, Nikolai / b. Dec. 12, 1935**
1959-61 WM URS 9 7 2 9 0 S,B
**Snowden, John / b. Jan. 12, 1982**
2000 WM18 USA 6 1 0 1 4 —
**Snowden, Mel / b. 1914 / d. unknown**
1939 WM CAN 8 3 — 3 — G
**Snuggerud, Dave / b. June 20, 1966**
1989 WM USA 10 4 1 5 2 —
1988 OG-M USA 6 3 2 5 4 —
**Sobachkin, Andrei / b. Feb. 23, 1988**
2006 WM18 RUS 6 0 3 3 6 —
**Sobchenko, Danil / b. Apr. 13, 1991 / d. Sept. 7, 2011**
2011 WM20 RUS 7 4 3 7 4 G
~perished in Yaroslavl plane crash
**Sobera, Jerzy / b. Sept. 4, 1970**
1990 WM20 POL 7 0 0 0 2 —
1992 OG-M POL 7 0 0 0 0 —
**Sobye, Ragnar / b. unknown**
1965 WM NOR 7 1 1 2 2 —
**Soccio, Leonard / b. May 28, 1967**
2001-03 WM GER 20 5 8 13 43 —
2002 OG-M GER 7 3 3 6 8 —
**Socha, Daniel / b. Mar. 19, 1976**
1996 WM20 SVK 6 0 1 1 4 —
**Sochor, Jan / b. Jan. 17, 1980**
2000 WM20 CZE 7 0 0 0 0 G
**Sock, Wilfried / b. July 2, 1944**
1965 WM GDR 7 1 0 1 0 —
1968 OG-M GDR 7 0 0 0 6 —
**Soderberg, Anders / b. Oct. 7, 1975**
1994-95 WM20 SWE 14 9 3 12 4 S,B
**Sodergren, Hakan / b. June 14, 1959**
1979 WM20 SWE 6 0 6 6 6 B
1983-89 WM SWE 49 9 18 27 44 G,S
1987 CC SWE 6 0 2 2 2 —
1984-88 OG-M SWE 14 7 6 13 14 2B
**Soderholm, Toni / b. Apr. 14, 1978**
2004-07 WM FIN 19 0 1 1 10 S
**Soderstrom, Dan / b. Apr. 5, 1948**
1973-81 WM SWE 46 19 21 40 23 2S,3B
1980 OG-M SWE 7 2 2 4 2 B
**Sogaard, Kim / b. May 16, 1964**
1983 WM20 NOR 7 0 0 0 6 —
1990-93 WM NOR 21 3 1 4 20 —
1988-92 OG-M NOR 11 0 1 1 12 —
**Soghomonian, Jean-Marc / b. July 24, 1971**
1995-2000 WM FRA 20 2 0 2 12 —
**Soguel, Sergio / b. Nov. 21, 1963**
1982 WM20 SUI 7 0 2 2 0 —

**Soin, Sergei / b. Mar. 31, 1982**
1999-2000 WM18 RUS 13 1 3 4 10 —
2002 WM20 RUS 7 2 0 2 0 G
2003 WM RUS 7 0 2 2 10 —
**Soini, Voitto / b. Feb. 6, 1938**
1957-58 WM FIN 13 4 0 4 0 —
1960 OG-M FIN 4 3 0 3 6 —
**Sokol, Lukasz / b. Sept. 12, 1981**
2002 WM POL 6 0 0 0 0 —
**Sokolov, Andrei / b. Jan. 22, 1968**
1998-2005 WM KAZ 7 0 0 0 12 —
1998 OG-M KAZ 7 1 1 2 4 —
**Sokolov, Anton / b. Apr. 27, 1981**
1999 WM18 RUS 7 1 0 1 0 —
**Sokolowski, Kazimierz / b. Mar. 26, 1908 / d. July 3, 1998**
1930-47 WM POL 34 3 0 3 2 —
1932-36 OG-M POL 9 0 0 0 12 —
**Solaux, Stanislas / b. Dec. 4, 1975**
1998 WM FRA 3 1 0 1 0 —
**Solf, Patrick / b. Dec. 8, 1974**
1994 WM20 GER 6 0 0 0 2 —
**Solheim, Leif / b. July 14, 1932**
1950-54 WM NOR 19 3 1 4 6 —
1952 OG-M NOR 7 3 0 3 — —
**Solheim, Oivind / b. May 28, 1928**
1949-54 WM NOR 19 7 0 7 4 —
1952 OG-M NOR 8 1 1 2 — —
**Solodukhin, Vyacheslav / b. Nov. 11, 1950**
1972 WM URS 8 4 3 7 0 S
1972 SS URS 1 0 0 0 0 2nd
**Sologubov, Nikolai / b. Aug. 8, 1924**
1955-63 WM URS 34 13 6 19 20 G,4S,B
1956-60 OG-M URS 11 2 8 10 4 G,B
~IIHF Hall of Fame
~OG-M IIHF Directorate Best Defenceman (1956, 1960), WM IIHF Directorate Best Defenceman (1957)
**Solyom, Laszlo / b. Nov. 29, 1955**
1977 WM ROM 10 2 0 2 8 —
1980 OG-M ROM 5 0 1 1 6 —
**Somervuori, Eero / b. Feb. 7, 1979**
1997-99 WM20 FIN 19 8 12 20 6 G
~WM20 All-Star Team/Forward (1998)
**Somik, Radovan / b. May 5, 1977**
1996-97 WM20 SVK 12 4 3 7 2 —
2001-08 WM SVK 25 1 4 5 6 G
2004 WCH SVK 1 0 0 0 0 —
**Sommer, Marcel / b. June 19, 1980**
2000 WM20 SUI 7 0 0 0 2 —
**Sommer, Pascal / b. July 16, 1974**
1994 WM20 SUI 7 1 1 2 4 —
**Sommer, Roy / b. Apr. 5, 1957**
1977 WM20 USA 7 3 3 6 8 —
**Sondell, Daniel / b. Mar. 1, 1984**
2002 WM18 SWE 8 3 4 7 2 —
2004 WM20 SWE 6 1 0 1 0 —
**Sopin, Alexei / b. Mar. 4, 1987**
2005 WM18 RUS 6 6 1 7 2 —
**Soracreppa, Martino / b. May 9, 1968**
1992 OG-M ITA 7 0 0 0 0 —
**Sorensen, Bjornar / b. Oct. 13, 1970**
1989-90 WM20 NOR 14 2 0 2 4 —
**Sorensen, Frede / b. unknown**
1949 WM DEN 3 0 — 0 — —
**Sorensen, Roy / b. unknown**
1949-59 WM NOR 6 0 — 0 — —
**Sorlie, Bard / b. Apr. 4, 1977**
1999-2001 WM NOR 12 2 0 2 12 —
**Sormunen, Pasi / b. Mar. 8, 1970**
1994 OG-M FIN 7 0 0 0 10 S
**Sorochan, Lee / b. Sept. 9, 1975**
1995 WM20 CAN 7 0 1 1 6 G
**Sorokin, Sergei / b. Oct. 2, 1969**
1988-89 WM20 URS 14 1 4 5 18 G,S
1993-95 WM RUS 19 2 4 6 16 G
1994 OG-M RUS 8 1 2 3 6 —
**Sorvik, Daniel / b. Mar. 11, 1990**
2006 WM18 NOR 4 0 0 0 2 —
**Sosinski, Wojciech / b. July 31, 1970**
1990 WM20 POL 7 0 1 1 4 —
**Sotlar, Mitja / b. Oct. 17, 1979**
2005-06 WM SLO 12 2 1 3 8 —
**Soucek, Martin / b. May 8, 1983**
2001 WM18 CZE 7 0 0 0 2 —

**Soudek, Karel / b. Oct. 26, 1963**
1982 WM20 TCH 7 3 5 8 8 S
**Souray, Sheldon / b. July 13, 1976**
2005 WM CAN 9 1 1 2 6 S
**Soutokorva, Osmo / b. Oct. 30, 1970**
1990 WM20 SWE 6 0 1 1 2 —
**Sova, Tommi / b. Apr. 8, 1975**
1995 WM20 FIN 7 1 1 2 4 —
**Sozinov, Vadim / b. June 17, 1981**
2000-01 WM20 KAZ 13 6 1 7 57 —
**Spacek, Jaroslav / b. Feb. 11, 1974**
1994 WM20 CZE 7 2 0 2 8 —
1999-2005 WM CZE 52 6 16 22 30 3G
2004 WCH CZE 4 0 0 0 0 —
1998-2006 OG-M CZE 18 0 1 1 6 G,B
**Spain, Frank / b. Feb. 17, 1909 / d. June 23, 1977**
1936 OG-M USA 8 2 0 2 4 B
**Spanhel, Martin / b. July 1, 1977**
1997 WM20 CZE 6 2 0 2 0 —
2000 WM CZE 9 1 1 2 10 G
**Speck, Pascal / b. Apr. 28, 1965**
1984 WM20 SUI 7 0 0 0 6 —
**Spelda, Lukas / b. Jan. 6, 1985**
2003 WM18 CZE 6 0 0 0 16 —
**Spencer, Jim / b. Aug. 11, 1973**
1995 WM USA 6 0 0 0 2 —
**Spevak, Reginald / b. Feb. 21, 1898 / d. unknown**
1928 OG-M AUT 2 0 0 0 2 —
**Spielmann, Fritz / b. Mar. 26, 1933 / d. July 22, 2009**
1956-64 OG-M AUT 12 6 1 7 14 —
**Spina, Dave / b. June 5, 1983**
2001 WM18 USA 6 2 5 7 8 —
**Spirko, Rastislav / b. June 21, 1984**
2002 WM18 SVK 8 1 4 5 0 —
2003-04 WM20 SVK 12 2 7 9 2 —
**Sprecher, Hans-Martin / b. unknown**
1959 WM SUI 8 2 1 3 4 —
**Sprenger, Jim / b. May 28, 1965**
1986 WM USA 8 1 1 2 4 —
**Spring, Don / b. June 16, 1959**
1980 OG-M CAN 6 0 1 1 0 —
**Springer, Gerhard / b. Feb. 6, 1927**
1947-57 WM AUT 7 1 0 1 0 B
1956 OG-M AUT 3 0 0 0 0 —
**Sroka, Rafal / b. Nov. 29, 1970**
1990 WM20 POL 5 0 1 1 2 —
1992 OG-M POL 7 0 1 1 14 —
**Sroubek, Josef / b. Dec. 2, 1891 / d. Aug. 29, 1964**
1920-28 OG-M TCH 8 4 0 4 — B
**Srsen, Tomas / b. Aug. 25, 1966**
1986 WM20 TCH 7 0 2 2 6 —
1994-95 WM CZE 14 2 2 4 8 —
1994 OG-M CZE 8 2 3 5 8 —
**Sryubko, Andri / b. Oct. 21, 1975**
2001-07 WM UKR 34 1 1 2 30 —
2002 OG-M UKR 4 0 1 1 6 —
**Stach, Lubomir / b. May 28, 1986**
2004 WM18 CZE 7 1 2 3 4 B
**Stadele, Michael / b. Jan. 8, 1983**
2001 WM18 GER 6 0 0 0 0 —
**Stadler, Walter / b. Jan. 30, 1952**
1973-77 WM FRG 15 1 2 3 2 —
**Staios, Steve / b. July 28, 1973**
2002-08 WM CAN 33 2 4 6 76 2G,S
**Stajan, Matt / b. Dec. 19, 1983**
2003 WM20 CAN 6 1 1 2 0 S
**Stajduhar, Nick / b. Dec. 6, 1974**
1994 WM20 CAN 7 1 4 5 8 G
**Stammbach, Peter / b. Nov. 27, 1937**
1959-62 WM SUI 15 4 6 10 4 —
1964 OG-M SUI 7 0 3 3 0 —
**Stanek, Willibald / b. Dec. 4, 1913 / d. unknown**
1935-49 WM AUT 18 4 — 4 — B
1936-48 OG-M AUT 14 0 — 0 — —
**Stankovic, Peter / b. July 15, 1962**
1982 WM20 FRG 7 1 2 3 12 —
**Stanley, Don / b. unknown**
1949-50 WM CAN 13 12 5 17 0 G,S
**Stanley, Dylan / b. Jan. 24, 1984**
2002 WM18 CAN 8 3 3 6 6 —
**Stantien, Roman / b. Oct. 16, 1964**
1997-98 WM SVK 14 2 0 2 2 —
1998 OG-M SVK 3 0 0 0 0 —

**Stanton, Paul / b. June 22, 1967**
1995-98 WM USA 18 2 1 3 8 B
**Stapleton, Mike / b. May 5, 1966**
1986 WM20 CAN 7 3 3 6 6 S
**Stapleton, Pat / b. July 4, 1940**
1972 SS CAN 7 0 0 0 6 1st
**Starikov, Sergei / b. Dec. 4, 1958**
1977-78 WM20 URS 14 2 7 9 4 2G
1979-87 WM URS 41 5 13 18 12 3G,S,B
1984 CC URS 6 0 3 3 2 —
1980-88 OG-M URS 19 2 9 11 6 2G,S
**Starkov, Oleg / b. Feb. 7, 1963**
1982-83 WM20 URS 14 9 14 23 8 G
**Starostenko, Dmitri / b. Mar. 18, 1973**
2000-03 WM BLR 15 3 1 4 0 —
**Starovoit, Anton / b. Nov. 1, 1981**
1999 WM18 RUS 7 1 0 1 12 —
**Starshinov, Vyacheslav / b. May 6, 1940**
1961-71 WM URS 63 51 23 74 61 7G,B
1972 SS URS 1 0 0 0 0 2nd
1964-68 OG-M URS 14 13 9 22 8 2G
~WM IIHF Directorate Best Forward (1965) ~IIHF Hall of Fame
**Starsi, Jan / b. Oct. 17, 1933**
1958-63 WM TCH 29 13 6 19 16 S,2B
1960 OG-M TCH 7 4 5 9 6 —
~IIHF Hall of Fame
**Stas, Milan / b. Nov. 26, 1960**
1986 WM TCH 8 0 0 0 4 —
**Stas, Sergei / b. Apr. 28, 1974**
1998-2003 WM BLR 24 5 1 6 24 —
1998-2002 OG-M BLR 16 0 2 2 24 —
**Stasche, Joachim / b. Feb. 2, 1950**
1974-78 WM GDR 30 5 5 10 14 —
**Stashenkov, Ilya / b. Aug. 26, 1974**
1994 WM20 RUS 7 1 1 2 2 B
**Stastny, Anton / b. Aug. 5, 1959**
1978-79 WM20 TCH 12 7 6 13 10 S
1979 WM TCH 8 5 1 6 2 S
1980 OG-M TCH 6 3 4 7 2 —
**Stastny, Bohuslav / b. Apr. 23, 1949**
1971-76 WM TCH 60 31 19 50 28 2G,3S,B
1976 CC TCH 7 1 1 2 10 2nd
1972-76 OG-M TCH 10 3 1 4 0 S,B
**Stastny, Marian / b. Jan. 8, 1953**
1975-79 WM TCH 45 16 19 35 10 2G,3S
1976 CC TCH 7 1 4 5 2 2nd
1980 OG-M TCH 6 5 6 11 4 —
**Stastny, Peter / b. Sept. 18, 1956**
1976-79 WM TCH 38 18 18 36 13 2G,2S
1976 CC TCH 7 0 4 4 2 2nd
1984 CC CAN 8 1 2 3 0 1st
Totals CC 15 1 6 7 2 1st
1980-94 OG-M SVK 14 12 11 23 15 —
~IIHF Hall of Fame
**Staudinger, Konrad / b. July 15, 1927**
1957 WM AUT 7 0 — 0 2 —
1956 OG-M AUT 4 1 0 1 2 —
**Stauffer, Werner / b. unknown**
1954 WM SUI 5 0 — 0 2 —
**Stauner, Gunther / b. Nov. 1, 1959**
1979 WM20 FRG 5 0 1 1 8 —
**Stavjana, Antonin / b. Feb. 10, 1963**
1981-83 WM20 TCH 19 0 9 9 8 2S
1985-96 WM CZE 71 7 15 22 38 2G,4B
1984-87 CC TCH 11 0 1 1 6 —
1988-94 OG-M CZE 16 4 5 9 6 —
**St. Croix, Chris / b. May 2, 1979**
1998-99 WM20 USA 13 0 0 0 12 —
**Steblecki, Roman / b. Mar. 16, 1963**
1986-92 WM POL 26 4 1 5 0 —
1988 OG-M POL 6 1 0 1 2 —
**Stebnicki, Marek / b. Nov. 11, 1965**
1985 WM20 POL 7 0 2 2 8 —
1986-89 WM POL 20 4 4 8 10 —
1988 OG-M POL 6 1 2 3 0 —
**Steckel, David / b. Mar. 15, 1982**
2000 WM18 USA 6 2 5 7 14 —
2001-02 WM20 USA 14 0 2 2 10 —
**Steen, Terje / b. Jan. 13, 1944**
1968-72 OG-M NOR 9 0 0 0 4 —
**Steen, Thomas / b. June 8, 1960**
1978-80 WM20 SWE 18 10 8 18 22 S,2B
1981-89 WM SWE 26 11 10 21 32 2S
1981-91 CC SWE 17 7 4 11 17 —

**Stefan, Leo / b. Feb. 22, 1970**
1994-98 WM GER 29 1 6 7 24 —
1996 WCH GER 4 0 2 2 0 —
1994 OG-M GER 8 3 1 4 4 —
**Stefan, Patrik / b. Sept. 16, 1980**
1998 WM20 CZE 7 1 1 2 4 —
2006 WM CZE 9 1 0 1 4 S
**Stefan, Valentin / b. Oct. 4, 1944**
1968 OG-M ROM 5 1 2 3 0 —
**Stefani, Sune / b. Apr. 2, 1986**
2004 WM18 DEN 6 0 0 0 4 —
**Stefaniak, Jozef / b. Mar. 14, 1941**
1966-76 WM POL 26 1 3 4 47 —
1964 OG-M POL 7 5 2 7 4 —
**Steffen, Franz / b. June 5, 1970**
1998 WM SUI 7 0 0 0 2 —
**Stehlik, Richard / b. June 22, 1984**
2001-02 WM18 SVK 14 4 3 7 14 —
2002-04 WM20 SVK 19 1 5 6 26 —
2006-07 WM SVK 13 0 1 1 4 —
~WM18 All-Star Team/Defence (2002)
**Stehlin, Laurent / b. Mar. 9, 1967**
1987 WM20 SUI 6 1 1 2 2 —
**Steigenhofer, Bohumil / b. Mar. 1, 1905 / d. unknown**
1930-31 WM TCH 8 0 — 0 — —
1928 OG-M TCH 2 0 — 0 2 —
**Steiger, Helmut / b. Jan. 5, 1959**
1978-79 WM20 FRG 11 6 5 11 18 —
1982-90 WM FRG 55 16 19 35 53 —
1984 CC FRG 4 4 0 4 11 —
1984-88 OG-M FRG 13 5 9 14 14 —
**Steiger, Nicolas / b. July 28, 1976**
1996 WM20 SUI 6 0 0 0 6 —
**Stein, Gregor / b. Jan. 29, 1989**
2007 WM18 GER 6 0 0 0 6 —
**Steinbock, Stefan / b. Sept. 27, 1962**
1983 WM GDR 8 1 0 1 2 —
**Steinecker, Stefan / b. Sept. 11, 1967**
1986 WM20 FRG 7 0 0 0 2 —
**Steinegger, Martin / b. Feb. 15, 1972**
1992 WM20 SUI 6 0 0 0 8 —
1993-2007 WM SUI 65 4 4 8 60 —
2002 OG-M SUI 4 0 0 0 6 —
**Steiner, Ondrej / b. Feb. 12, 1974**
1993-94 WM20 CZE 12 1 0 1 2 B
**Steiner, Othmar / b. unknown**
1957 WM AUT 6 0 — 0 — —
**Steingross, Bastian / b. July 16, 1982**
2000 WM18 GER 6 2 0 2 8 —
**Steinsland, William / b. Feb. 25, 1963**
1983 WM20 NOR 5 0 0 0 2 —
**Stelkin, Dmitri / b. May 4, 1986**
2004 WM18 BLR 5 0 2 0 2 —
**Stelnov, Igor / b. Mar. 12, 1963**
1982 WM20 URS 7 3 6 9 9 —
1986-87 WM URS 20 1 3 4 14 G,S
1984-87 CC URS 15 1 5 6 10 2nd
1984-88 OG-M URS 14 1 3 4 13 2G
**Stensberg, Fredrik / b. Jan. 4, 1986**
2004 WM18 NOR 6 1 0 1 8 —
**Stepan, Martin / b. Mar. 18, 1989**
2007 WM18 SVK 6 2 0 2 0 —
**Stepanek, Martin / b. Apr. 2, 1971**
2000 WM CZE 9 2 1 3 10 G
**Stepanyshev, Anatoli / b. Jan. 29, 1961**
1999 WM UKR 3 0 0 0 0 —
**Stephan, Fabian / b. June 21, 1981**
1999 WM18 SUI 7 1 0 1 29 —
2000-01 WM20 SUI 14 1 3 4 24 —
**Stephanson, Ken / b. Nov. 13, 1941**
1969 WM CAN 10 1 1 2 10 —
**Sterflinger, Robert / b. Apr. 7, 1964**
1981-84 WM20 FRG 25 1 4 5 24 —
**Sterling, Brett / b. Apr. 24, 1984**
2002 WM18 USA 8 9 3 12 4 G
2003-04 WM20 USA 13 3 2 5 4 G
**Sterner, Ulf / b. Feb. 11, 1941**
1961-73 WM SWE 74 40 32 72 36 G,5S,B
1960-64 OG-M SWE 12 6 6 12 0 S
~IIHF Hall of Fame
~WM IIHF Directorate Best Forward (1969), WM All-Star Team/Forward (1969), WM All-Star Team/Forward (1962)
**Sternkopf, Rudolf / b. Nov. 4, 1966**
1986 WM20 FRG 7 1 0 1 12 —

**Stertin, Hans / b. Feb. 16, 1909 / d. unknown**
1934-38 WM AUT 5 0 0 0 — —
**Stettler, Martin / b. Jan. 10, 1984**
2002 WM18 SUI 8 0 2 2 12 —
2004 WM20 SUI 6 0 1 1 0 —
**Stetz, Karl-Josef / b. Apr. 4, 1982**
1999 WM18 GER 6 0 1 1 0 —
**Stevens, Kevin / b. Apr. 15, 1965**
1987-96 WM USA 26 10 6 16 40 B
1988 OG-M USA 5 1 3 4 2 —
**Stevens, Scott / b. Apr. 1, 1964**
1983-89 WM CAN 27 3 6 9 18 2S,B
1991-96 WCH CAN 16 1 2 3 6 1st,2nd
1998 OG-M CAN 6 0 0 0 2 —
**Stevenson, Pete / b. 1916 / d. unknown**
1935 WM GBR 7 2 — 2 — B
**Stevenson, Turner / b. May 18, 1972**
1992 WM20 CAN 7 0 2 2 14 —
**Stewart, Bill / b. Oct. 6, 1957**
1992-93 WM ITA 11 0 0 0 10 —
1992-94 OG-M ITA 13 0 3 3 12 —
**Stewart, Mike / b. May 30, 1972**
2005-07 WM AUT 11 1 1 2 10 —
**St. Germain, Ralph / b. Jan. 18, 1904 / d. Aug. 2, 1974**
1936 OG-M CAN 4 5 5 10 0 S
**Stibor, Karel / b. Nov. 5, 1924 / d. Nov. 8, 1948**
1947 WM TCH 5 4 — 4 — G
1948 OG-M TCH 6 6 — 6 — S
**Stiles, Tony / b. Aug. 12, 1959**
1988 OG-M CAN 5 0 0 0 0 —
**Stilling, Robin / b. June 19, 1986**
2004 WM18 DEN 6 0 1 1 16 —
**Stillman, Cory / b. Dec. 20, 1973**
1999 WM CAN 10 4 4 8 14 —
**Stillman, Fredrik / b. Aug. 22, 1966**
1986 WM20 SWE 7 0 1 1 4 —
1991-95 WM SWE 38 6 6 12 6 2G,2S,B
1992-94 OG-M SWE 16 3 2 5 6 G
**Stinchcombe, Archie / b. Nov. 17, 1912 / d. unknown**
1937-38 WM GBR 17 10 2 12 2 2S
1936-48 OG-M GBR 12 1 0 1 0 G
**Stipetic, Zvonko / b. unknown / d. unknown**
1939 WM YUG 1 0 0 0 — —
**St. John, Adelbert / b. Oct. 6, 1931 / d. Dec. 18, 2009**
1964-68 OG-M AUT 12 9 7 16 10 —
**Stockhammer, Gunther / b. Aug. 8, 1962**
1981 WM20 AUT 5 1 2 3 4 —
**Stoffel, Andri / b. Oct. 24, 1984**
2002 WM18 SUI 8 0 0 0 8 —
2004 WM20 SUI 6 0 0 0 6 —
**Stoklasa, Petr / b. Apr. 18, 1989**
2007 WM18 CZE 6 0 1 1 4 —
**Stokvik, Inge / b. Dec. 27, 1981**
1999 WM18 NOR 6 2 2 4 8 —
**Stoltz, Roland / b. Aug. 1, 1931 / d. Feb. 19, 2001**
1957-67 WM SWE 63 11 14 25 38 2G,2S,2B
1960-68 OG-M SWE 18 2 6 8 13 S
~IIHF Hall of Fame
~WM IIHF Directorate Best Defenceman (1963)
**Stoltz, Roland / b. Aug. 15, 1954**
1981 WM SWE 8 1 2 3 6 S
**Stone, Mike / b. Nov. 14, 1959**
1979 WM20 USA 5 0 0 0 8 —
**Stonkus, Alexei / b. May 6, 1984**
2002 WM18 RUS 8 0 1 1 12 S
**Stopczyk, Jan / b. Sept. 28, 1958**
1986-89 WM POL 13 3 0 3 20 —
1984-88 OG-M POL 10 2 1 3 8 —
**Stordahl, Jim / b. Oct. 23, 1942**
1966 WM USA 7 1 1 2 0 —
**Stordahl, Larry / b. Oct. 23, 1942**
1966-69 WM USA 17 5 4 9 16 —
1968 OG-M USA 7 2 0 2 8 —
**Storm, Jim / b. Feb. 5, 1971**
1991 WM20 USA 7 3 4 7 0 —
**Storsteen, Dan / b. unknown**
1965 WM USA 7 1 0 1 8 —
**Stortz, Jurgen / b. June 19, 1965**
1985 WM20 FRG 7 1 0 1 0 —
**Stovik, Vilibald / b. Oct. 9, 1917 / d. Nov. 8, 1948**
1937-47 WM TCH 15 3 0 3 0 G
1948 OG-M TCH 7 0 — 0 — S
**St. Pierre, David / b. Mar. 22, 1972**
1992 WM20 CAN 7 0 0 0 0 —

**Straka, Josef / b. Feb. 11, 1978**
1996-98 WM20 CZE 13 3 3 6 4 —

**Straka, Martin / b. Sept. 3, 1972**
1991-92 WM20 TCH 13 3 11 14 4 B
1994-2005 WM CZE 28 12 7 19 20 G
1996-2004 WCH CZE 6 1 2 3 0 —
1998-2006 OG-M CZE 14 3 8 11 6 G,B

**Strakhov, Alexei / b. Oct. 16, 1975**
2003-07 WM BLR 18 1 0 1 6 —

**Strakhov, Yuri / b. Nov. 6, 1959**
1979 WM20 URS 6 1 2 3 4 G

**Strandem, Roy / b. Apr. 5, 1932**
1952 OG-M NOR 3 0 0 0 — —

**Straube, Christopher / b. May 27, 1974**
1998 WM GER 6 0 0 0 0 —

**Strauss, Wolfgang / b. Sept. 14, 1969**
1994 WM AUT 6 0 0 0 4 —

**Streit, Martin / b. Feb. 2, 1977**
1997 WM20 CZE 7 0 0 0 14 —

**Strelnov, Igor / b. Feb. 12, 1963**
1981 WM20 URS 5 2 0 2 2 B

**Streun, Fredy / b. June 17, 1925**
1950 WM SUI 2 0 0 0 0 B
1952 OG-M SUI 4 0 0 0 — —

**Strida, Martin / b. Aug. 4, 1964**
1984 WM20 TCH 5 0 1 1 0 B

**Striz, Tomas / b. July 4, 1989**
2007 WM18 SVK 6 0 1 1 2 —

**Strobel, Eric / b. June 5, 1958**
1979 WM USA 8 3 4 7 2 —
1980 OG-M USA 7 1 2 3 2 G

**Strobel, Mark / b. Aug. 15, 1973**
1993 WM20 USA 7 0 0 0 6 —

**Strobl, Georg / b. Feb. 9, 1910 / d. unknown**
1933-38 WM GER 27 5 1 6 0 B
1932-36 OG-M GER 9 2 0 2 4 B

**Strodl, Ferdinand / b. Jan. 5, 1961**
1981 WM20 FRG 5 2 2 4 0 —

**Strom, Peter / b. Jan. 14, 1975**
1994-95 WM20 SWE 14 4 7 11 4 S,B

**Stromberg, Mika / b. Feb. 28, 1970**
1989-90 WM20 FIN 14 3 3 6 20 —
1994-97 WM FIN 30 7 8 15 37 G,S
1996 WCH FIN 3 1 2 3 2 —
1994 OG-M FIN 7 2 2 4 10 B

**Stromwall, Johan / b. Jan. 14, 1964**
1989-90 WM SWE 19 2 2 4 10 S

**Strong, Ken / b. May 9, 1963**
1994-95 WM AUT 13 2 1 3 12 —
1994 OG-M AUT 7 3 1 4 12 —

**Strueby, Todd / b. June 15, 1963**
1982 WM20 CAN 7 0 5 5 4 G

**Strzempek, Janusz / b. Feb. 2, 1969**
1988 WM20 POL 7 0 0 0 4 —

**Stuart, Brad / b. Nov. 6, 1979**
1999 WM20 CAN 7 0 1 1 2 S
2001-06 WM CAN 16 1 4 5 20 —

**Stuart, Mike / b. Aug. 31, 1980**
2000 WM20 USA 7 0 0 0 2 —

**Stubbs, Frank / b. July 12, 1909 / d. unknown**
1934 WM USA 4 1 0 1 — S
1936 OG-M USA 8 0 1 1 4 B

**Stuchly, Kurt / b. unknown / d. unknown**
1934 WM AUT 3 0 — 0 — —

**Studstrud, Olle Peter / b. unknown**
1983 WM20 NOR 7 3 0 3 2 —

**Stupnicki, Roman / b. 1915 / d. Jan. 27, 1954**
1935-37 WM POL 13 5 0 5 4 —
1936 OG-M POL 1 1 — 1 — —

**Sturges, A.J. / b. Apr. 6, 1989**
2007 WM18 USA 7 0 1 1 0 S

**Sturm, Soren / b. Dec. 15, 1989**
2007 WM18 GER 6 0 1 1 2 —

**Sturmer, Kurt / b. Feb. 18, 1926**
1957-59 WM GDR 15 5 1 6 6 —

**Stussi, Rene / b. Dec. 13, 1978**
1997-98 WM20 SUI 13 1 4 5 4 B

**Subotin, Dmitri / b. Oct. 20, 1977**
1999 WM RUS 6 0 0 0 0 —

**Suchanek, Rudolf / b. Jan. 27, 1962**
1988 OG-M TCH 8 1 0 1 4 —

**Suchomski, Robert / b. Feb. 6, 1978**
1997 WM20 POL 6 0 0 0 0 —

**Suchy, Jan / b. Oct. 10, 1944**
1965-74 WM TCH 58 18 22 40 41 4S,2B
1968 OG-M TCH 7 2 4 6 8 S
~IIHF Hall of Fame
~WM IIHF Directorate Best Defenceman (1969, 1971), WM All-Star Team/Defence (1969, 1970, 1971), OG-M All-Star Team/Defence (1968)

**Suchy, Radoslav / b. Apr. 7, 1976**
1996 WM20 SVK 6 2 1 3 0 —
2000-05 WM SVK 24 0 8 8 4 S,B
2004 WCH SVK 3 0 0 0 0 —
2006 OG-M SVK 6 1 1 2 0 —

**Suck, Wilhelm / b. Dec. 12, 1915 / d. unknown**
1935-38 WM ROM 12 2 0 2 0 —

**Sugak, Andrei / b. May 15, 1982**
2000 WM18 UKR 6 0 0 0 6 —

**Sugawara, Michio / b. 1930**
1957 WM JPN 3 1 — 1 — —

**Sugawara, Nobuhiro / b. Apr. 9, 1975**
2003-04 WM JPN 12 0 0 0 12 —

**Sugisawa, Akihito / b. July 20, 1967**
1998-99 WM JPN 6 0 0 0 2 —
1998 OG-M JPN 4 2 2 4 4 —

**Suglobov, Alexander / b. Jan. 15, 1982**
2002 WM20 RUS 7 1 0 1 4 G
2003 WM RUS 7 3 0 3 2 —

**Suikkanen, Kai / b. June 29, 1959**
1978-79 WM20 FIN 12 6 5 11 9 —
1986 WM FIN 10 0 3 3 4 —
1988 OG-M FIN 8 1 0 1 4 S

**Sulkovsky, David / b. June 14, 1978**
1998 WM20 GER 6 0 0 0 27 —
2002 WM GER 1 0 0 0 0 —

**Sullivan, Frank / b. July 26, 1898 / d. Jan. 8, 1989**
1928 OG-M CAN 3 2 — 2 — G

**Sullivan, Frank / b. June 7, 1917 / d. Jan. 5, 2007**
1952 OG-M CAN 8 5 7 12 2 G

**Sullivan, Mike / b. Feb. 27, 1968**
1988 WM20 USA 6 0 2 2 14 —
1997 WM USA 8 1 2 3 2 —

**Sullivan, Steve / b. July 6, 1974**
2000-01 WM CAN 16 5 3 8 24 —

**Sulzer, Hans / b. Dec. 22, 1969**
1988 OG-M AUT 4 0 3 3 8 —

**Summanen, Raimo / b. Mar. 2, 1962**
1982 WM20 FIN 7 7 9 16 0 B
1983-95 WM FIN 47 9 8 17 18 G
1987-91 CC FIN 11 1 2 3 0 —
1984-92 OG-M FIN 14 6 7 13 10 —

**Summermatter, Roger / b. Feb. 21, 1987**
2005 WM18 SUI 6 0 0 0 6 —

**Sundblad, Niklas / b. Jan. 3, 1973**
1992-93 WM20 SWE 14 2 6 8 20 2S
1997 WM SWE 11 2 1 3 22 S

**Sundelin, Matti / b. Dec. 4, 1934**
1955-57 WM FIN 13 2 1 3 2 —

**Sundeng, Rune / b. Oct. 28, 1983**
2001 WM18 NOR 6 0 1 1 2 —

**Sundin, Fredrik / b. June 4, 1981**
1999 WM18 SWE 6 0 0 0 2 S
2001 WM20 SWE 7 3 0 3 0 —

**Sundin, Mats / b. Feb. 13, 1971**
1990 WM20 SWE 7 5 2 7 6 —
1990-2003 WM SWE 49 25 31 56 42 3G,2S,2B
1991-2004 WCH SWE 14 7 11 18 20 —
1998-2006 OG-M SWE 16 11 9 20 18 G
~WM MVP (2003), WM IIHF Directorate Best Forward (1992, 2003), WM All-Star Team/Forward (1992, 1998, 2003), OG-M All-Star Team/Forward (2002)

**Sundin, Ronnie / b. Oct. 3, 1970**
1996-2006 WM SWE 54 4 11 15 28 G,3S,B
2006 OG-M SWE 7 0 0 0 6 G

**Sundqvist, Jorgen / b. Sept. 24, 1982**
2000 WM18 SWE 6 0 1 1 2 B
2002 WM20 SWE 7 1 2 3 4 —

**Sundqvist, Karl-Johan / b. Mar. 9, 1949**
1972-75 WM SWE 38 3 3 6 21 S,3B

**Sundstrom, Niklas / b. June 6, 1975**
1993-95 WM20 SWE 21 18 15 33 18 2S,B
1998-99 WM SWE 18 6 7 13 12 G,B
1996 WCH SWE 4 2 2 4 0 —
1998-2002 OG-M SWE 8 2 4 6 2 —
~WM20 IIHF Directorate Best Forward (1994), WM20 All-Star Team/Forward (1994)

**Sundstrom, Patrik / b. Dec. 14, 1961**
1980-81 WM20 SWE 10 7 1 8 12 G,B
1981-82 WM SWE 18 9 2 11 10 S
1981-84 CC SWE 13 1 8 9 10 2nd
~WM20 IIHF Directorate Best Forward (1981), WM20 All-Star Team/Forward (1981)

**Sundstrom, Peter / b. Dec. 14, 1961**
1981 WM20 SWE 5 2 3 5 4 G
1982-87 WM SWE 28 7 5 12 12 G
1984-87 CC SWE 14 3 2 5 10 2nd

**Sundt, Karl Johan / b. Mar. 11, 1982**
1999 WM18 NOR 6 0 0 0 8 —

**Sundt, Robert / b. May 5, 1971**
1991 WM20 NOR 5 0 0 0 2 —

**Sunna, Kim / b. June 14, 1987**
2005 WM18 SWE 7 1 0 1 12 B

**Suokko, Jorma / b. May 27, 1940**
1961-63 WM FIN 17 3 0 3 18 —
1964 OG-M FIN 7 0 0 0 2 —

**Suoraniemi, Kari / b. Sept. 29, 1960**
1980 WM20 FIN 2 0 0 0 10 S
1985-86 WM FIN 16 3 1 4 10 —

**Suoraniemi, Niko / b. Mar. 4, 1984**
2002 WM18 FIN 7 0 1 1 2 —

**Suoraniemi, Seppo / b. Aug. 26, 1951**
1974-81 WM FIN 35 0 2 2 10 —
1980 OG-M FIN 7 1 3 4 6 —

**Sup, Michal / b. Sept. 24, 1973**
2003-04 WM CZE 13 1 0 1 6 —

**Surma, Damian / b. Jan. 22, 1981**
2001 WM20 USA 7 2 2 4 0 —

**Susi, Timo / b. Jan. 25, 1959**
1978-79 WM20 FIN 12 7 5 12 10 —
1983-89 WM FIN 33 5 8 13 6 —
1980-88 OG-M FIN 15 2 6 8 8 S

**Susumago, Taiji / b. Oct. 31, 1973**
1993 WM20 JPN 7 1 0 1 4 —

**Suter, Bob / b. May 16, 1957**
1980 OG-M USA 7 0 0 0 6 G

**Suter, Gary / b. June 24, 1964**
1984 WM20 USA 7 1 1 2 12 —
1985-92 WM USA 16 1 3 4 28 —
1987-96 WCH USA 19 1 8 9 19 1st,2nd
1998-2002 OG-M USA 10 0 1 1 4 S

**Sutherby, Brian / b. Mar. 1, 1982**
2002 WM20 CAN 7 3 3 6 2 S

**Sutherland, Hugh / b. Feb. 2, 1907 / d. Sept. 9, 1990**
1932 OG-M CAN 6 1 4 5 4 G

**Sutinen, Kalevi / b. Jan. 29, 1915 / d. unknown**
1939 WM FIN 1 0 — 0 — —

**Sutinen, Timo / b. Apr. 3, 1949**
1973-77 WM FIN 40 11 13 24 6 —

**Sutter, Brent / b. June 10, 1962**
1986 WM CAN 8 4 7 11 8 B
1984-91 CC CAN 25 6 6 12 22 3/1st

**Sutter, Fabian / b. June 28, 1982**
2000 WM18 SUI 7 0 5 5 4 —
2001-02 WM20 SUI 14 2 2 4 12 —

**Sutter, Patrick / b. July 6, 1970**
1992-2001 WM SUI 43 4 12 16 74 —
2002 OG-M SUI 4 0 2 2 6 —

**Sutter, Ron / b. Dec. 2, 1963**
1990 WM CAN 10 1 1 2 4 —

**Suurbeek, Jan / b. unknown / d. unknown**
1939 WM NED 4 0 — 0 — —

**Suutari, Ari / b. Aug. 8, 1965**
1984-85 WM20 FIN 14 3 0 3 16 S

**Suutarinen, Harri / b. July 16, 1982**
2000 WM18 FIN 7 1 1 2 6 G

**Suvak, Zvone / b. Aug. 29, 1958**
1984 OG-M YUG 5 0 0 0 0 —

**Suvanto, Harri / b. Nov. 30, 1970**
1990 WM20 FIN 7 3 4 7 6 —

**Suzuki, Hideo / b. Oct. 21, 1949**
1972 OG-M JPN 1 0 0 0 0 —

**Suzuki, Takahito / b. Aug. 17, 1975**
1999-2004 WM JPN 33 6 4 10 16 —

**Svanberg, Bo / b. Jan. 5, 1967**
1987 WM20 SWE 7 7 3 10 6 B

**Svanberg, Magnus / b. Mar. 3, 1988**
2006 WM18 SWE 6 0 0 0 4 —

**Svarba, Peter / b. Nov. 2, 1983**
2001 WM18 SVK 6 0 0 0 8 —

**Svartvadet, Per / b. May 17, 1975**
1994-95 WM20 SWE 14 2 9 11 10 S,B
1997 WM SWE 10 0 2 2 0 S

**Svasznek, Bence / b. July 25, 1975**
2009 WM HUN 6 0 0 0 6 —

**Svedberg, Hans / b. Sept. 6, 1931**
1957-61 WM SWE 29 6 2 8 0 G,B
1960 OG-M SWE 7 2 2 4 8 —

**Svedberg, Lennart / b. Feb. 29, 1944 / d. July 29, 1972**
1965-71 WM SWE 43 4 9 13 18 2S,2B
1968 OG-M SWE 7 2 1 3 2 —
~WM IIHF Directorate Best Defenceman (1970), WM All-Star Team/Defence (1969, 1970), OG-M All-Star Team/Defence (1968)

**Svedberg, Mattias / b. Sept. 28, 1969**
1989 WM20 SWE 7 0 4 4 0 S

**Svehla, Robert / b. Jan. 2, 1969**
1992-2003 WM SVK 23 5 8 13 36 2B
1996 WCH SVK 3 0 3 3 4 —
1992-98 OG-M SVK 18 4 6 10 34 B
~WM IIHF Directorate Best Defenceman (1992)

**Svendsberget, Geir / b. May 22, 1974**
1999-2001 WM NOR 18 1 0 1 12 —

**Svendsen, Lars Cato / b. unknown**
1983 WM20 NOR 6 0 1 1 10 —

**Svensson, Einar / b. Sept. 27, 1894 / d. Mar. 20, 1959**
1920 OG-M SWE 5 2 — 2 — —

**Svensson, Jan-Olof / b. Feb. 6, 1949**
1976 WM SWE 10 0 0 0 4 B

**Svensson, Leif / b. July 8, 1951**
1979 WM SWE 8 0 0 0 6 B

**Svensson, Magnus / b. Mar. 1, 1963**
1987-97 WM SWE 30 10 8 18 36 G,2S,B
1994 OG-M SWE 7 4 1 5 6 G
~WM IIHF Directorate Best Defenceman (1994), WM All-Star Team/Defence (1994)

**Svensson, Pelle / b. Feb. 20, 1970**
1990 WM20 SWE 3 0 0 0 0 —

**Sventek, Stanislav / b. Nov. 9, 1930**
1957-63 WM TCH 25 3 5 8 4 S,2B
1964 OG-M TCH 7 1 0 1 0 B

**Sverzhov, Alexander / b. Feb. 5, 1972**
1992 WM20 RUS 6 1 2 3 4 G

**Sverzhov, Sergei / b. Mar. 21, 1965**
1985 WM20 URS 7 4 2 6 8 B

**Svetlov, Sergei / b. Jan. 17, 1961**
1980-81 WM20 URS 10 6 3 9 2 G,B
1985-87 WM URS 30 10 6 16 12 G,S,B
1984-87 CC URS 12 7 5 12 0 —
1988 OG-M URS 8 2 3 5 4 G

**Svihovec, Tomas / b. Jan. 14, 1900 / d. unknown**
1930-34 WM TCH 19 1 1 2 0 B

**Svitek, Vladimir / b. Oct. 19, 1962**
1981-82 WM20 TCH 12 9 6 15 4 S
1986-89 WM TCH 18 7 7 14 4 B

**Svito, Vladimir / b. Aug. 20, 1970**
2005-06 WM BLR 13 0 1 1 6 —

**Svitov, Alexander / b. Nov. 3, 1982**
2000 WM18 RUS 6 3 5 8 8 S
2001-02 WM20 RUS 11 2 2 4 101 G

**Svoboda, Jaroslav / b. June 1, 1980**
2000 WM20 CZE 7 1 2 3 6 G

**Svoboda, Jiri / b. Dec. 3, 1983**
2003 WM20 CZE 6 0 0 0 0 —

**Svoboda, Petr / b. Feb. 14, 1966**
1984 WM20 TCH 7 0 4 4 16 B
1998 OG-M CZE 6 1 1 2 39 G

**Svoboda, Petr / b. June 20, 1980**
1999-2000 WM20 CZE 13 0 2 2 10 G

**Svoboda, Radoslav / b. Dec. 18, 1957**
1982-85 WM TCH 22 2 4 6 10 G,2S
1981-84 CC TCH 7 0 3 3 4 —
1984 OG-M TCH 7 3 2 5 4 S

**Svoboda, Robert / b. July 23, 1967**
1987 WM20 TCH 7 0 2 2 2 S

**Svozil, Ladislav / b. May 8, 1958**
1977-78 WM20 TCH 13 4 3 7 24 B
1979-83 WM TCH 17 3 3 6 6 2S
1984 CC TCH 5 2 2 4 7 —

**Swallow, Kevin / b. May 7, 1986**
2004 WM18 USA 6 0 1 1 12 S

**Swanson, Brian / b. Mar. 24, 1976**
1996 WM20 USA 6 2 1 3 29 —

**Swarbrick, George / b. Feb. 16, 1942**
1964 OG-M CAN 7 3 3 6 2 —

**Sweeney, Don / b. Aug. 17, 1966**
1997 WM CAN 11 1 3 4 6 G

**Sweeney, Tim / b. Apr. 12, 1967**
1994 WM USA 8 3 2 5 0 —
1992 OG-M USA 8 3 4 7 6 —

**Swiatek, Andrzej / b. Jan. 7, 1958**
1977 WM20 POL 7 1 0 1 4 —
1986 WM POL 10 0 1 1 12 —
1988 OG-M POL 6 1 0 1 9 —

**Swicarz, Tadeusz / b. June 5, 1920 / d. June 6, 2002**
1952 OG-M POL 8 0 0 0 — —

**Swistak, Andrzej / b. June 2, 1963**
1992 WM POL 6 0 0 0 0 —
1992 OG-M POL 7 0 1 1 0 —

**Sydor, Darryl / b. May 13, 1972**
1992 WM20 CAN 7 3 1 4 4 —
1994-2002 WM CAN 17 0 2 2 4 G,S

**Sydorenko, Maxim / b. May 15, 1985**
2002 WM18 UKR 8 0 0 0 6 —

**Sydorov, Yevgeni / b. Mar. 13, 1980**
2000 WM20 UKR 7 0 0 0 2 —

**Sykes, Phil / b. Mar. 18, 1959**
1986 WM CAN 9 0 0 0 2 B

**Sykes, Rodger / b. Feb. 28, 1969**
1989 WM20 USA 7 0 5 5 0 —

**Sykko, Tomi / b. Jan. 21, 1983**
2001 WM18 FIN 6 2 1 3 6 B
2003 WM20 FIN 7 1 1 2 4 B

**Sykora, Juraj / b. Sept. 19, 1983**
2003 WM20 SVK 6 2 0 2 0 —

**Sykora, Michal / b. July 5, 1973**
1996-2002 WM CZE 24 6 6 12 34 2G
1996 WCH CZE 2 0 0 0 2 —
2002 OG-M CZE 4 0 0 0 0 —
~WM All-Star Team/Defence (1996, 2000)

**Sykora, Petr / b. Nov. 19, 1976**
1994-95 WM20 CZE 14 6 2 8 6 —
1998-2005 WM CZE 23 3 8 11 20 2G,B
1996-2004 WCH CZE 5 0 2 2 2 —
2002 OG-M CZE 4 1 0 1 0 —

**Sykora, Petr / b. Dec. 21, 1978**
1998 WM20 CZE 7 2 2 4 2 —
2007 WM CZE 7 2 3 5 4 —

**Sylvia, Mike / b. Feb. 5, 1976**
1996 WM20 USA 6 2 5 7 39 —

**Syme, James "Tiny" / b. Oct. 1, 1926**
1950 WM GBR 7 1 1 2 27 —

**Syme, Tom "Tuck" / b. May 15, 1928**
1950 WM GBR 7 1 0 1 6 —
1948 OG-M GBR 7 0 — 0 — —

**Synkov, Oleg / b. Mar. 6, 1965**
1999 WM UKR 3 1 0 1 2 —

**Synott, Frank "Red" / b. Dec. 28, 1890 / d. Oct. 12, 1945**
1920-24 OG-M USA 6 7 — 7 3 2S

**Synowiec, Ludwik / b. Jan. 19, 1958**
1977 WM20 POL 7 0 1 1 4 —
1986 WM POL 7 0 0 0 4 —
1980-84 OG-M POL 11 0 0 0 6 —

**Syomin, Dmitri / b. Aug. 14, 1983**
2001 WM18 RUS 6 1 4 5 0 G

**Syomin, Nikolai / b. Mar. 20, 1973**
1993 WM20 RUS 7 0 1 1 8 —

**Syposz, Janusz / b. Apr. 12, 1966**
1985 WM20 POL 7 0 1 1 4 —
1989 WM POL 10 0 0 0 10 —

**Syversen, Odd / b. Feb. 5, 1945**
1965 WM NOR 7 0 0 0 8 —
1968 OG-M NOR 5 1 1 2 7 —

**Szabo, Geza / b. Dec. 1, 1940 / d. Apr. 14, 1993**
1964-68 OG-M ROM 12 12 6 18 0 —

**Szabo, Gyula / b. Dec. 1, 1940 / d. Mar. 17, 2003**
1964-68 OG-M ROM 12 8 7 15 2 —

**Szabo, Peter / b. Mar. 22, 1981**
1999 WM18 SVK 7 3 3 6 0 B
2001 WM20 SVK 7 1 1 2 4 —

**Szal, Andrzej / b. Jan. 10, 1942**
1966 WM POL 4 0 0 0 4 —
1964 OG-M POL 6 3 2 5 14 —

**Szamosi-Stoics, Ferenc / b. Feb. 15, 1915 / d. unknown**
1933-39 WM HUN 28 3 0 3 0 —
1936 OG-M HUN 6 0 — 0 — —

**Szczepaniec, Andrzej / b. May 10, 1952**
1973-76 WM POL 14 0 1 1 6 —
1972 OG-M POL 5 0 0 0 6 —

**Szeja, Jan / b. Sept. 25, 1949**
1973-79 WM POL 37 7 4 11 16 —

**Szelig, Viktor / b. Sept. 22, 1975**
2009 WM HUN 6 0 0 0 6 —

**Szenajch, Karol / b. Feb. 11, 1907 / d. unknown**
1930-33 WM POL 6 0 — 0 2 —
1928 OG-M POL 2 0 — 0 — —

**Szengel, Gerhard / b. Jan. 18, 1937**
1961 WM GDR 3 1 0 1 0 —

**Szewczyk, Roman / b. May 11, 1965**
1985 WM20 POL 7 0 0 0 4 —

**Szewczyk, Stanislaw / b. Mar. 20, 1947**
1970-76 WM POL 19 0 1 1 0 —

**Szlapa, Piotr / b. Dec. 22, 1941**
1966 WM POL 7 0 0 0 4 —

**Szlapka, Andrzej / b. Mar. 5, 1969**
1988 WM20 POL 5 0 0 0 6 —

**Szlapka, Jacek / b. Jan. 5, 1964**
1990 WM20 POL 7 0 0 0 8 —

**Szoke, Andrei / b. July 5, 1978**
1998 WM20 SVK 6 0 2 2 0 —

**Szopinski, Jacek / b. Jan. 5, 1964**
1989 WM POL 5 0 0 0 0 —
1988 OG-M POL 6 0 1 1 2 —

**Szopinski, Robert / b. Feb. 15, 1961**
1986-89 WM POL 20 1 3 4 10 —
1984-92 OG-M POL 19 1 2 3 8 —

**Szucs, Mark / b. Nov. 4, 1976**
2002-04 WM AUT 18 1 1 2 12 —

**Szybisty, Silvester / b. Jan. 1, 1962**
1988 OG-M AUT 5 1 0 1 4 —

**Szysky, Chris / b. June 8, 1976**
1999 WM CAN 7 0 0 0 4 —

**Tabacek, Peter / b. Jan. 20, 1985**
2003 WM18 SVK 7 1 2 3 2 S

**Taborsky, Pavel / b. Feb. 16, 1968**
1988 WM20 TCH 6 0 0 0 8 —

**Tack, Michael / b. May 11, 1960**
1979 WM20 FRG 5 0 0 0 2 —

**Taconis, Henk "Kappie" / b. Feb. 1, 1918 / d. unknown**
1939-50 WM NED 8 0 0 0 2 —

**Taffe, Jeff / b. Feb. 19, 1981**
1999 WM18 USA 6 3 2 5 29 —
2000-01 WM20 USA 14 7 6 13 8 —

**Taft, John / b. Mar. 8, 1954**
1975 WM USA 10 1 2 3 4 —
1976 OG-M USA 5 1 2 3 8 —

**Taggart, Jack / b. 1925**
1955 WM CAN 3 1 0 1 0 G

**Tahkapaa, Matti / b. Apr. 17, 1983**
2001 WM18 FIN 6 0 1 1 2 B

**Tahtisalo, Petri / b. Jan. 31, 1981**
1999 WM18 FIN 7 0 1 1 8 G

**Taimio, Tomi / b. Oct. 15, 1957**
1977 WM20 FIN 7 0 5 5 10 —

**Taipola, Arto / b. Feb. 24, 1965**
1985 WM20 FIN 7 0 0 0 0 —

**Tait, Victor / b. July 8, 1892 / d. Nov. 27, 1988**
1928 OG-M GBR 3 0 — 0 — —

**Tajcnar, Rudolf / b. Apr. 17, 1948 / d. Aug. 2, 2005**
1971-72 WM TCH 11 5 2 7 4 G,S
1972 OG-M TCH 5 0 1 1 6 B

**Takac, Roman / b. Apr. 12, 1982**
2000 WM18 SVK 6 0 0 0 0 —

**Takagi, Kunio / b. Feb. 8, 1963**
1999 WM JPN 3 0 0 0 0 —

**Takagi, Kunito / b. June 18, 1934**
1960 OG-M JPN 6 0 0 0 4 —

**Takahashi, Junichi / b. Jan. 23, 1978**
2004 WM JPN 6 0 0 0 6 —

**Takala, Teuvo / b. July 24, 1931**
1951-55 WM FIN 16 4 0 4 0 —

**Takashima, Mamoru / b. May 3, 1938**
1960-68 OG-M JPN 18 11 4 15 6 —

**Takko, Karri / b. Jan. 3, 1982**
2000 WM18 FIN 7 1 0 1 4 G

**Talafous, Dean / b. Apr. 25, 1953**
1976-81 CC USA 11 5 4 9 8 —

**Tallackson, Barry / b. Apr. 14, 1983**
2001 WM18 USA 6 2 3 5 2 —
2003 WM20 USA 7 3 0 3 2 —

**Tallarini, Alan / b. May 17, 1984**
2002 WM18 SUI 8 0 0 0 47 —
2003 WM20 SUI 6 0 0 0 20 —

**Talpas, Igor / b. Feb. 18, 1964**
1984 WM20 TCH 7 4 2 6 4 B

**Tambellini, Addie / b. Feb. 4, 1936**
1961-67 WM CAN 19 13 7 20 6 G,B
~WM All-Star Team/Forward (1963)

**Tambellini, Steve / b. May 14, 1958**
1978 WM20 CAN 6 2 2 4 0 B
1981 WM CAN 8 0 3 3 4 —
1988 OG-M CAN 8 1 3 4 2 —

**Tambijevs, Leonids / b. Sept. 26, 1970**
1997-2007 WM LAT 68 15 17 32 42 —
2002-06 OG-M LAT 9 2 2 4 10 —

**Tamer, Chris / b. Nov. 17, 1970**
1999-2002 WM USA 13 1 1 2 10 —

**Tamminen, Juhani / b. May 26, 1950**
1970-82 WM FIN 88 23 23 46 42 —
1976 CC FIN 4 2 1 3 0 —
1972 OG-M FIN 5 1 2 3 6 —

**Tanabe, David / b. July 19, 1980**
1999 WM20 USA 6 0 1 1 4 —
2001 WM USA 9 1 2 3 6 —

**Tanabu, Masami / b. Dec. 7, 1934**
1957 WM JPN 7 0 — 0 — —
1960-64 OG-M JPN 13 1 4 5 20 —

**Tanaka, Yasushin / b. Aug. 18, 1945**
1972-76 OG-M JPN 9 3 4 7 0 —

**Tanase, Radu / b. unknown / d. unknown**
1938-47 WM ROM 6 0 — 0 — —

**Tancill, Chris / b. Feb. 7, 1968**
1996-2000 WM USA 23 8 7 15 14 B

**Tang, Alexander / b. June 27, 1985**
2003 WM18 SWE 6 0 1 1 16 —
2004 WM20 SWE 6 0 3 3 2 —

**Tangen, Joachim / b. Apr. 9, 1983**
2001 WM18 NOR 6 0 1 1 8 —

**Tangnes, Thomas / b. Jan. 9, 1983**
2001 WM18 NOR 6 1 4 5 2 —

**Tanguay, Alex / b. Nov. 21, 1979**
1998 WM20 CAN 7 2 1 3 2 —

**Tanti, Tony / b. Sept. 7, 1963**
1983 WM20 CAN 7 0 4 4 6 B
1985-87 WM CAN 28 16 7 23 40 S,B

**Tanygin, Yevgeni / b. Oct. 3, 1981**
2000-01 WM20 KAZ 13 3 2 5 6 —

**Tarala, Hal / b. Nov. 14, 1927**
1955 WM CAN 8 3 0 3 4 G

**Tarasenko, Andrei / b. Sept. 11, 1968**
1995 WM RUS 6 1 3 4 2 —
1994 OG-M RUS 8 2 0 2 0 —

**Tarasov, Anatoli / b. Jan. 15, 1959**
1978-79 WM20 URS 12 6 7 13 0 2G

**Tarasov, Vladimir / b. Mar. 21, 1968**
1994 OG-M RUS 8 0 0 0 2 —

**Taratukhin, Andrei / b. Feb. 22, 1983**
2001 WM18 RUS 6 2 3 5 10 G
2002-03 WM20 RUS 13 2 8 10 45 2G
2006 OG-M RUS 5 0 0 0 2 —

**Tardif, Jamie / b. Jan. 23, 1985**
2003 WM18 CAN 7 1 4 5 12 G

**Tarvainen, Jussi / b. May 31, 1976**
1994-96 WM20 FIN 18 4 1 5 38 —

**Tatarinov, Alexander / b. Apr. 14, 1982**
2000 WM18 RUS 6 3 2 5 4 S

**Tatarinov, Mikhail / b. July 16, 1966**
1984-86 WM20 URS 19 4 9 13 22 2G,B
1990 WM URS 10 3 8 11 20 G
1991 CC URS 5 0 1 1 17 —
~WM IIHF Directorate Best Defenceman (1990), WM All-Star Team/Defence (1990), WM20 IIHF Directorate Best Defenceman (1986), WM20 All-Star Team/Defence (1985, 1986)

**Taticek, Petr / b. Sept. 22, 1983**
2003 WM20 CZE 6 0 1 1 4 —

**Tatzer, Hans / b. May 25, 1905 / d. Aug. 23, 1944**
1930-38 WM AUT 31 15 — 15 0 B
1936 OG-M AUT 6 2 — 2 — —

**Tavi, Janne / b. Sept. 13, 1989**
2007 WM18 FIN 6 0 3 3 2 —

**Tavzelj, Andrej / b. Mar. 14, 1984**
2008 WM SLO 5 0 0 0 0 —

**Taylor, Dave / b. Dec. 4, 1955**
1983-86 WM CAN 30 7 10 17 20 S,2B

**Taylor, Irving / b. Aug. 13, 1919 / d. Dec. 1991**
1948 OG-M CAN 8 0 — 0 — G

**Taylor, Ross / b. Apr. 26, 1902 / d. 1984**
1928 OG-M CAN 1 2 — 2 — G

**Taylor, Tim / b. unknown**
1965 WM USA 7 1 2 3 4 —

**Teal, Brad / b. unknown**
1966 WM USA 6 0 0 0 6 —

**Tejkl, Petr / b. Apr. 18, 1966**
1994 WM CZE 4 0 0 0 6 —

**Tenisi, Guido / b. July 5, 1953**
1982-83 WM ITA 17 1 1 2 12 —

**Tenkanen, Valtteri / b. Mar. 27, 1985**
2003 WM18 FIN 6 0 3 3 0 —

**Tenkrat, Petr / b. May 31, 1977**
1997 WM20 CZE 7 1 1 2 2 —
2006-07 WM CZE 15 2 0 2 14 S

**Teodorczak, Marek / b. Sept. 6, 1959**
1989 WM POL 7 0 0 0 8 —

**Teodorescu, Alexandru / b. unknown / d. unknown**
1938 WM ROM 1 0 — 0 — —

**Teppert, Anton "Tino" / b. Jan. 9, 1985**
2004 WM20 AUT 2 0 0 0 0 —

**Tergeson, Sven "Joe" / b. Oct. 2, 1927**
1949 WM CAN 7 4 — 4 — S

**Terglav, Edo / b. Jan. 24, 1980**
2002-05 WM SLO 18 1 3 4 37 —

**Terlo, Mykola / b. May 9, 1981**
1999 WM18 UKR 6 0 0 0 8 —

**Ternavski, Artyom / b. June 2, 1983**
2001 WM18 RUS 6 0 1 1 4 G

**Tertyshny, Sergei / b. June 3, 1970**
1990 WM20 URS 7 0 1 1 0 S
1999 WM RUS 6 1 1 2 6 —
1994 OG-M RUS 8 0 0 0 4 —

**Tesarik, Radim / b. June 16, 1974**
1994 WM20 CZE 5 0 0 0 2 —

**Texe, Stefan / b. June 29, 1947**
1968 OG-M ROM 5 1 0 1 2 —

**Tezikov, Alexei / b. June 22, 1978**
1998 WM20 RUS 7 0 3 3 6 S

**Thanner, Rudolf / b. Aug. 20, 1944 / d. Aug. 9, 2007**
1967-76 WM FRG 38 0 4 4 14 —
1968-76 OG-M FRG 14 5 2 7 8 B

**Thayer, Bill / b. Mar. 5, 1956**
1949 WM USA 8 0 — 0 6 B

**Thayer, Richard / b. unknown / d. unknown**
1931 WM USA 4 1 — 1 — S

**Theberge, Gerry / b. Dec. 18, 1930 / d. June 2000**
1956 OG-M CAN 8 9 2 11 8 B

**Thelin, Mats / b. Mar. 30, 1961**
1982-83 WM SWE 15 0 3 3 12 —
1984 CC SWE 8 1 3 4 14 2nd
1984 OG-M SWE 7 0 1 1 4 B

**Thelven, Mikael / b. Jan. 7, 1961**
1981 WM20 SWE 5 2 1 3 4 G
1985 WM SWE 10 0 1 1 10 —
1984-87 CC SWE 14 0 6 6 24 —
1984 OG-M SWE 3 1 3 4 4 B

**Therien, Chris / b. Dec. 14, 1971**
1994 OG-M CAN 4 0 0 0 4 S

**Therrialt, Peter / b. unknown**
1951 WM USA 6 3 — 3 0 —

**Therrien, Henry / b. unknown**
1966 WM USA 5 0 0 0 0 —

**Thiery, Julien / b. Feb. 20, 1982**
2002 WM20 FRA 6 0 0 0 0 —

**Thinn, Sigurd / b. Sept. 23, 1957**
1988 OG-M NOR 6 1 0 1 4 —

**Thoen, Terje / b. Apr. 23, 1944 / d. July 30, 2008**
1965 WM NOR 2 1 0 1 0 —
1968-72 OG-M NOR 9 1 2 3 2 —

**Thoeni, Roger / b. Feb. 8, 1967**
1987 WM20 SUI 7 2 2 4 6 —

**Thomas, Jim / b. unknown**
1964 OG-M USA 1 0 0 0 0 —

**Thomas, John / b. Mar. 11, 1936 / d. Feb. 7, 1995**
1960 OG-M AUS 6 1 0 1 6 —

**Thomas, Ralf / b. Aug. 6, 1949**
1974-76 WM GDR 12 2 1 3 0 —

**Thomas, Steve / b. July 15, 1963**
1991-96 WM CAN 30 10 13 23 45 G,2S

**Thomas, Tim / b. May 28, 1963**
1982-83 WM20 USA 14 4 8 12 14 —
1985 WM USA 10 0 2 2 6 —

**Thommen, Gregor / b. Feb. 16, 1980**
1999 WM20 SUI 6 0 0 0 0 —

**Thompson, Keith / b. 1909 / d. unknown**
1931-34 WM GBR 3 1 — 1 — —

**Thomson, Bill / b. Mar. 23, 1914 / d. Aug. 6, 1993**
1936 OG-M CAN 8 8 0 8 2 S

**Thomson, Greg / b. May 28, 1963**
1993 WM GER 6 0 1 1 29 —

**Thony, Roger / b. Jan. 18, 1967**
1986 WM20 SUI 7 3 1 4 24 —

**Thoresen, Jan Roar / b. Mar. 24, 1940**
1965 WM NOR 7 1 0 1 8 —
1964 OG-M NOR 7 1 0 1 0 —

**Thoresen, Paul / b. unknown**
1983 WM20 NOR 6 1 0 1 14 —

**Thoresen, Petter / b. July 25, 1961**
1979 WM20 NOR 5 0 0 0 6 —
1992-95 WM NOR 22 3 3 6 12 —
1980-94 OG-M NOR 29 3 3 6 15 —

**Thoresen, Steffen / b. June 3, 1985**
2002 WM18 NOR 8 0 1 1 2 —
2007 WM NOR 6 0 0 0 0 —

**Thorndike, Ted / b. Sept. 8, 1952 / d. Jan. 2, 1987**
1976 OG-M USA 5 0 2 2 0 —

**Thornton, Scott / b. Jan. 9, 1971**
1991 WM20 CAN 7 3 1 4 0 G
1999 WM CAN 10 5 1 6 6 —

**Thulin, Kurt / b. Aug. 8, 1939**
1959 WM SWE 8 0 0 0 2 —

**Thunman, Sven / b. Apr. 20, 1920 / d. July 8, 2004**
1949-55 WM SWE 38 4 0 4 20 G,S,B
1948-52 OG-M SWE 8 3 0 3 — B

**Thuresson, Marcus / b. May 31, 1971**
1990-91 WM20 SWE 13 4 4 8 6 —
1997 WM SWE 11 1 6 7 2 S

**Tiala, Harri / b. June 27, 1965**
1985 WM20 SWE 7 0 1 1 6 —

**Tichy, Milan / b. Sept. 22, 1969**
1988-89 WM20 TCH 14 4 4 8 4 B
~WM20 All-Star Team/Defence (1989)

**Tico, Constantin / b. unknown / d. unknown**
1934-38 WM ROM 14 1 — 1 — —

**Tie, Esko / b. Dec. 26, 1928**
1951-55 WM FIN 12 1 0 1 6 —

**Tiilikainen, Jukka / b. Apr. 4, 1974**
1994 WM20 FIN 7 2 2 4 6 —

**Tiinus, Markku / b. Feb. 9, 1963**
1983 WM20 FIN 7 4 2 6 8 —

**Tiitola, Risto / b. Apr. 24, 1915 / d. unknown**
1939 WM FIN 1 0 — 0 — —

**Tikal, Frantisek / b. July 18, 1933 / d. Aug. 10, 2008**
1957-67 WM TCH 48 15 13 28 20 2S,3B
1960-64 OG-M TCH 12 3 5 8 6 B
~IIHF Hall of Fame
~OG-M IIHF Directorate Best Defenceman (1964), WM IIHF Directorate Best Defenceman (1965), WM All-Star Team/Defence (1965)

**Tikal, Zdenek / b. July 18, 1933 / d. Nov. 20, 1991**
1960 OG-M AUS 1 0 0 0 0 —

**Tikkanen, Esa / b. Jan. 25, 1965**
1983-85 WM20 FIN 21 17 18 35 26 S
1985-2000 WM FIN 34 10 10 20 38 B
1987-91 CC FIN 11 2 3 5 12 —
1998 OG-M FIN 6 1 1 2 0 B
~WM20 All-Star Team/Forward (1985)

**Tikkanen, Harri / b. June 2, 1981**
2001 WM20 FIN 7 0 1 1 4 S

**Tillert, Stefan / b. Jan. 26, 1976**
1995 WM20 GER 7 0 0 0 2 —

**Tilley, Tom / b. Mar. 28, 1965**
1995 WM CAN 8 0 0 0 14 B

**Timander, Mattias / b. Apr. 16, 1974**
1994 WM20 SWE 7 0 1 1 0 S
2006 WM SWE 9 0 3 3 6 G

**Timchenko, Oleg / b. Apr. 27, 1978**
2004-05 WM UKR 11 0 0 0 4 —

**Timchenko, Vyacheslav / b. Aug. 16, 1971**
2002-07 WM UKR 23 0 2 2 36 —
2002 OG-M UKR 4 0 0 0 8 —

**Timonen, Jussi / b. June 29, 1983**
2001 WM18 FIN 6 0 2 2 2 B
2003 WM20 FIN 7 1 1 2 6 B

**Timoschuk, Roland / b. July 27, 1970**
1989 WM20 FRG 7 0 2 2 2 —

**Timpone, Christian / b. Mar. 26, 1976**
2002 WM ITA 6 3 1 4 2 —

**Tinordi, Mark / b. May 9, 1966**
1991 CC CAN 3 0 0 0 2 1st

**Tippett, Dave / b. Aug. 25, 1961**
1984-92 OG-M CAN 14 2 3 5 12 S

**Tiriac, Ion / b. May 9, 1939**
1964 OG-M ROM 7 0 0 0 0 —

**Tirkkonen, Paavo / b. Oct. 2, 1947**
1968 OG-M FIN 3 0 0 0 0 —

**Tirkkonen, Pekka / b. July 17, 1969**
1987-88 WM20 FIN 14 10 5 15 2 G,B
1990-91 WM FIN 18 2 3 5 4 —
1991 CC FIN 6 0 1 1 0 —

**Tischer, Gustav / b. Dec. 20, 1932**
1957 WM AUT 5 0 — 0 — —
1964 OG-M AUT 7 1 2 3 0 —

**Tislar, Toni / b. May 9, 1967**
2002 WM SLO 6 1 0 1 0 —

**Tisler, Viktor / b. Nov. 30, 1941**
1964-72 OG-M YUG 16 12 9 21 13 —

**Titov, German / b. Oct. 16, 1965**
1993 WM RUS 8 4 2 6 0 G
1998 OG-M RUS 6 1 0 1 6 S

**Tittus, Nicolai / b. Mar. 4, 1978**
1998 WM20 GER 6 0 0 0 6 —

**Titus, John / b. unknown**
1955 WM USA 8 4 1 5 4 —

**Tjarnqvist, Daniel / b. Oct. 14, 1976**
1995-96 WM20 SWE 12 2 2 4 2 S,B
2000-04 WM SWE 42 6 12 18 8 2S,2B
2004 WCH SWE 3 0 0 0 2 —
2006 OG-M SWE 8 2 1 3 4 G
~WM IIHF Directorate Best Defenceman (2002)

**Tjarnqvist, Mathias / b. Apr. 15, 1979**
1999 WM20 SWE 6 1 4 5 4 —
2003-04 WM SWE 18 1 1 2 8 2S

**Tkachenko, Ivan / b. Nov. 9, 1979 / d. Sept. 7, 2011**
2002 WM RUS 9 3 2 5 2 S
~perished in Yaroslavl plane crash

**Tkachuk, Alexei / b. Sept. 4, 1964**
1992 WM RUS 6 1 1 2 0 —

**Tkachuk, Keith / b. Mar. 28, 1972**
1991-92 WM20 USA 14 9 7 16 18 B
1996-2004 WCH USA 12 10 2 12 57 1st
1992-2006 OG-M USA 23 3 3 6 28 S

**Tkacz, Wojciech / b. May 14, 1969**
1988 WM20 POL 7 0 0 0 8 —
1992 WM POL 6 1 0 1 4 —
1992 OG-M POL 7 0 1 1 2 —

**Tkaczuk, Daniel / b. June 10, 1979**
1998-99 WM20 CAN 14 8 5 13 14 S
~WM20 All-Star Team/Forward (1999)
2005-06 WM18 CZE 14 7 3 10 10 B

**Tobien, Rudolf / b. Feb. 4, 1915 / d. unknown**
1938-39 WM GER 15 0 — 0 — —

**Tocchet, Rick / b. Apr. 9, 1964**
1990 WM CAN 10 4 2 6 14 —
1987-91 CC CAN 15 4 3 7 18 2/1st

**Togni, Stefano / b. Feb. 26, 1974**
1994 WM20 SUI 7 1 1 2 4 —

**Toivola, Tero / b. July 22, 1968**
1988 WM20 FIN 7 3 8 11 4 B

**Tokaji, Viktor / b. Jan. 11, 1977**
2009 WM HUN 6 0 2 2 10 —

**Tokarz, Leszek / b. July 9, 1953**
1973-79 WM POL 37 4 5 9 28 —
1972 OG-M POL 5 3 0 3 6 —

**Tokarz, Wieslaw / b. Aug. 10, 1951**
1973-74 WM POL 16 2 0 2 6 —
1972 OG-M POL 3 0 0 0 0 —

**Tolkunov, Dmitri / b. May 27, 1979**
1996 WM20 UKR 6 0 2 2 10 —
2002-05 WM UKR 18 2 2 4 14 —
2002 OG-M UKR 4 0 0 0 4 —

**Tolochko, Mikhail / b. Aug. 17, 1957**
1977 WM20 URS 7 4 3 7 0 G

**Tolsa, Jari / b. Apr. 20, 1981**
2001 WM20 SWE 7 1 3 4 2 —

**Tomajko, Jan / b. June 19, 1976**
1996 WM20 CZE 6 0 1 1 0 —
2000-01 WM CZE 18 1 2 3 2 2G

**Tomanek, Roman / b. Jan. 28, 1986**
2004 WM18 SVK 6 7 1 8 6 —

**Tomas, Martin / b. May 3, 1978**
1997-98 WM20 SVK 12 0 0 0 10 —

**Tomasek, Martin / b. May 3, 1978**
1998 WM20 CZE 7 3 0 3 4 —

**Tomasik, Miroslaw / b. May 26, 1965**
1985 WM20 POL 7 1 0 1 6 —
1992 OG-M POL 7 1 3 4 2 —

**Tomaszkiewicz, Zbigniew / b. Mar. 10, 1958**
1977 WM20 POL 7 0 1 1 4 —

**Tomassoni, Dave / b. Dec. 5, 1952**
1982-83 WM ITA 17 1 1 2 12 —
1984 OG-M ITA 5 1 1 2 2 —

**Tomei, Bernardo / b. Sept. 10, 1933**
1959 WM ITA 7 4 1 5 2 —
1956 OG-M ITA 6 5 0 5 4 —

**Tomek, Michal / b. Oct. 18, 1965**
1985 WM20 TCH 7 1 2 3 2 S

**Tomic, Jovan / b. unknown / d. unknown**
1939 WM YUG 1 0 0 0 — —

**Tomica, Marek / b. Jan. 1, 1981**
2001 WM20 CZE 6 1 1 2 4 G

**Tomik, Robert / b. Dec. 12, 1976**
1996 WM20 SVK 6 1 0 1 0 —
2002 WM SVK 6 3 0 3 0 G

**Tomilin, Vitali / b. Jan. 15, 1974**
1993 WM20 RUS 7 2 5 7 6 —

**Tommila, Esa / b. Dec. 16, 1962**
1982 WM20 FIN 7 0 0 0 0 B

**Tomovici, Stefan / b. unknown / d. unknown**
1938-47 WM ROM 7 0 — 0 — —

**Tompkins, Dan / b. Jan. 31, 1975**
1995 WM20 USA 7 0 1 1 4 —

**Toms, Martin / b. Dec. 21, 1983**
2001 WM18 CZE 7 1 0 1 4 —
2003 WM20 CZE 6 0 0 0 0 —

**Ton, Andreas / b. Sept. 21, 1962**
1991-95 WM SUI 28 11 11 22 8 —
1992 OG-M SUI 6 0 0 0 2 —

**Ton, Petr / b. Oct. 8, 1973**
1993 WM20 TCH 7 1 5 6 4 B

**Tonelli, John / b. Mar. 23, 1957**
1984 CC CAN 8 3 6 9 2 1st

**Toomey, Dick / b. Apr. 11, 1946**
1971 WM USA 6 0 0 0 0 —

**Tootoo, Jordin / b. Feb. 2, 1983**
2003 WM20 CAN 6 1 1 2 4 S

**Topatigh, Lucio / b. Oct. 19, 1965**
1992-2002 WM ITA 56 15 18 33 42 —
1992-2006 OG-M ITA 23 5 4 9 22 —

**Topoli, Marek / b. Jan. 29, 1978**
1998 WM20 SVK 6 1 1 2 6 —

**Torgayev, Pavel / b. Jan. 25, 1966**
1985-86 WM20 URS 14 4 4 8 16 G,B
1995 WM RUS 6 0 2 2 4 —
1994 OG-M RUS 8 2 1 3 10 —

**Toriyabe, Kenji / b. Feb. 16, 1943**
1968 OG-M JPN 5 2 1 3 0 —

**Torkki, Jari / b. Aug. 11, 1965**
1984-85 WM20 FIN 14 9 6 15 18 S
1987 WM FIN 10 5 2 7 12 —
1988 OG-M FIN 4 1 0 1 2 S

**Tormanen, Antti / b. Sept. 19, 1970**
1995-99 WM FIN 32 3 3 6 20 G,2S
1998 OG-M FIN 5 0 0 0 0 B

**Tornberg, Johan / b. July 12, 1973**
1993 WM20 SWE 7 1 1 2 10 S
1998 WM SWE 9 2 0 2 4 G

**Tornvall, Ilkka / b. Jan. 13, 1983**
2001 WM18 FIN 6 0 0 0 0 B

**Torok, Jaroslav / b. Dec. 1, 1971**
2002 OG-M SVK 4 0 0 0 0 —

**Torp, Tor / b. unknown**
1979 WM20 NOR 5 0 0 0 19 —

**Torquato, Zack / b. June 8, 1989**
2007 WM18 CAN 6 0 3 3 2 —

**Torriani, Conrad / b. Apr. 12, 1910 / d. unknown**
1930-34 WM SUI 17 3 — 3 0 B

**Torriani, Richard "Bibi" / b. Oct. 1, 1911 / d. unknown**
1930-39 WM SUI 49 55 2 57 0 S,3B
1928-48 OG-M SUI 11 3 0 3 0 2B
~IIHF Hall of Fame

**Torstensson, Ulf / b. Aug. 19, 1945**
1966 WM SWE 7 0 0 0 0 —

**Tosse, Jens / b. Mar. 7, 1962**
1981-82 WM20 FRG 12 0 1 1 2 —

**Tottle, Gord / b. Oct. 14, 1924**
1962 WM USA 7 0 6 6 12 B

**Toupal, Radek / b. Aug. 16, 1966**
1986 WM20 TCH 7 5 7 12 4 —
1991-93 WM TCH 18 3 6 9 4 B
1992-94 OG-M TCH 14 2 0 2 10 B

**Tournier, Michel / b. unknown / d. unknown**
1931 WM FRA 5 0 — 0 — —

**Touzimsky, Zdenek / b. June 10, 1973**
1993 WM20 TCH 7 0 1 1 0 B

**Toykkala, Joni / b. Feb. 25, 1984**
2002 WM18 FIN 8 0 3 3 6 —
2004 WM20 FIN 7 2 2 4 2 B

**Tozicka, Jiri / b. Nov. 14, 1901 / d. May 15, 1981**
1930-35 WM TCH 26 11 0 11 0 B
1928-36 OG-M TCH 7 1 0 1 — —

**Trader, Larry / b. July 7, 1963**
1983 WM20 CAN 7 2 3 5 8 B

**Trattner, Jurgen / b. Jan. 13, 1969**
1988 WM20 FRG 7 1 1 2 2 —

**Trauffer, Hans / b. unknown / d. unknown**
1939 WM SUI 8 1 — 1 — B

**Trautmann, Paul / b. Dec. 16, 1916 / d. unknown**
1936 OG-M GER 2 0 — 0 — —

**Trauttenberg, Hans / b. Jan. 6, 1909 / d. unknown**
1930-35 WM AUT 25 4 — 4 0 B
1936 OG-M AUT 6 0 — 0 — —

**Trautwein, Ernst / b. May 8, 1936**
1955-63 WM FRG 33 16 1 17 10 —
1956-64 OG-M FRG 22 4 5 9 2 —

**Traverse, Patrick / b. Mar. 14, 1974**
2000 WM CAN 8 1 0 1 0 —

**Travnicek, Michal / b. Mar. 14, 1980**
1999 WM20 CZE 4 3 2 5 6 —

**Trebil, Dan / b. Apr. 10, 1974**
1998 WM USA 4 0 0 0 0 —

**Treen, Alf / b. Dec. 30, 1931 / d. Jan. 1, 2008**
1958 WM CAN 7 1 1 2 16 G

**Tregubov, Ivan / b. Jan. 19, 1930**
1955-61 WM URS 37 12 11 23 12 4S,B
1956 OG-M URS 7 2 2 4 8 G
~WM IIHF Directorate Best Defenceman (1958, 1961)

**Tregubov, Vitali / b. Jan. 28, 1974**
1998 WM KAZ 3 0 1 1 6 —
1998 OG-M KAZ 7 1 0 1 4 —

**Tremblay, Yannick / b. Nov. 15, 1975**
2000 WM CAN 9 1 1 2 0 —

**Trepp, Hans-Martin / b. Nov. 9, 1922 / d. Aug. 17, 1970**
1947-53 WM SUI 29 32 6 38 8 3B
1948-52 OG-M SUI 14 18 3 21 — B

**Tretowicz, Dave / b. Mar. 15, 1969**
1991 WM USA 10 0 3 3 4 —
1992 OG-M USA 8 0 0 0 0 —

**Tretyakov, Vitali / b. Jan. 24, 1977**
1995 WM20 UKR 7 0 1 1 2 —

**Trevisani, Carter / b. June 15, 1982**
2006-08 WM ITA 17 0 1 1 32 —
2006 OG-M ITA 5 1 0 1 8 —

**Tribuncovs, Atvars / b. Oct. 14, 1976**
1998-2007 WM LAT 61 2 3 5 62 —
2002-06 OG-M LAT 9 2 1 3 18 —

**Triller, Christoph / b. May 2, 1983**
2001 WM18 GER 6 0 0 0 2 —

**Triulzi, Luca / b. Feb. 11, 1983**
2001 WM18 SUI 7 1 0 1 2 S

**Triulzi, Roberto / b. June 3, 1965**
1991-95 WM SUI 32 5 3 8 26 —

**Trnka, Pavel / b. July 27, 1976**
1995 WM20 CZE 7 0 0 0 8 —
2003 WM CZE 5 1 0 1 6 —

**Trofimov, Alexander / b. Sept. 9, 1977**
1997 WM20 RUS 6 1 3 4 2 B

| | | | | | | | | |
|---|---|---|---|---|---|---|---|---|
| **Trojak, Ladislav / b. June 15, 1914 / d. Nov. 8, 1948** | | | | | | | | |
| 1937-47 | WM | TCH | 32 | 17 | 1 | 18 | 4 | G,B |
| 1936-48 | OG-M | TCH | 16 | 5 | — | 5 | — | S |
| ~IIHF Hall of Fame | | | | | | | | |
| **Trojan, Richard / b. Mar. 26, 1966** | | | | | | | | |
| 1985-86 | WM20 | FRG | 14 | 1 | 1 | 2 | 16 | — |
| **Trojanowski, Zdzislaw / b. May 27, 1928 / d. Mar. 20, 2006** | | | | | | | | |
| 1952 | OG-M | POL | 6 | 1 | 0 | 1 | — | — |
| **Troliga, Tomas / b. Apr. 24, 1984** | | | | | | | | |
| 2002 | WM18 | SVK | 8 | 1 | 2 | 3 | 31 | — |
| 2003-04 | WM20 | SVK | 12 | 1 | 2 | 3 | 16 | — |
| **Troshinski, Alexei / b. Oct. 9, 1973** | | | | | | | | |
| 1992 | WM20 | RUS | 7 | 0 | 1 | 1 | 2 | G |
| 1998-2004 | WM | KAZ | 9 | 0 | 5 | 5 | 33 | — |
| 1998 | OG-M | KAZ | 7 | 0 | 1 | 1 | 32 | — |
| **Troshinski, Andrei / b. Feb. 14, 1978** | | | | | | | | |
| 1998 | WM20 | KAZ | 7 | 4 | 2 | 6 | 10 | — |
| 1998-2006 | WM | KAZ | 18 | 0 | 2 | 2 | 4 | — |
| 2006 | OG-M | KAZ | 5 | 0 | 1 | 1 | 6 | — |
| **Trottier, Bryan / b. July 17, 1956** | | | | | | | | |
| 1981 | CC | CAN | 7 | 3 | 8 | 11 | 6 | 2nd |
| 1984 | CC | USA | 6 | 2 | 3 | 5 | 8 | — |
| Totals | CC | | 13 | 5 | 11 | 16 | 14 | — |
| **Trottier, Dave / b. June 25, 1906 / d. Nov. 13, 1956** | | | | | | | | |
| 1928 | OG-M | CAN | 3 | 12 | — | 12 | — | G |
| **Troumbly, Jim / b. unknown** | | | | | | | | |
| 1950 | WM | USA | 7 | 12 | 3 | 15 | 6 | S |
| **Trousilek, Josef / b. Mar. 16, 1918 / d. Oct. 10, 1990** | | | | | | | | |
| 1947-49 | WM | TCH | 13 | 3 | — | 3 | — | 2G |
| 1948 | OG-M | TCH | 4 | 1 | — | 1 | — | S |
| **Trovati, Decio / b. Oct. 16, 1906 / d. unknown** | | | | | | | | |
| 1930-35 | WM | ITA | 13 | 0 | 1 | 1 | 0 | — |
| 1936 | OG-M | ITA | 2 | 0 | 0 | 0 | — | — |
| **Trubachyov, Yuri / b. Mar. 9, 1983** | | | | | | | | |
| 2000-01 | WM18 | RUS | 12 | 4 | 8 | 12 | 10 | G,S |
| 2002-03 | WM20 | RUS | 13 | 5 | 11 | 16 | 6 | 2G |
| ~WM20 All-Star Team/Forward (2003) | | | | | | | | |
| **Trudell, Brett / b. Feb. 15, 1984** | | | | | | | | |
| 2002 | WM18 | CAN | 8 | 0 | 2 | 2 | 16 | — |
| **True, Mads / b. Apr. 17, 1972** | | | | | | | | |
| 2003-05 | WM | DEN | 17 | 0 | 1 | 1 | 4 | — |
| **True, Soren / b. Feb. 9, 1968** | | | | | | | | |
| 2003 | WM | DEN | 6 | 1 | 2 | 3 | 14 | — |
| **Truffer, Herold / b. July 14, 1936** | | | | | | | | |
| 1962 | WM | SUI | 7 | 0 | 2 | 2 | 4 | — |
| 1964 | OG-M | SUI | 7 | 1 | 1 | 2 | 2 | — |
| **Trukhno, Leonid / b. Jan. 6, 1963** | | | | | | | | |
| 1982-83 | WM20 | URS | 14 | 5 | 12 | 17 | 21 | G |
| **Trukhno, Vyacheslav / b. Feb. 22, 1987** | | | | | | | | |
| 2005 | WM18 | RUS | 6 | 0 | 1 | 1 | 6 | — |
| **Trumpler, Andreas / b. June 27, 1960** | | | | | | | | |
| 1980 | WM20 | SUI | 5 | 1 | 0 | 1 | 27 | — |
| **Truntschka, Bernd / b. Aug. 7, 1965** | | | | | | | | |
| 1983-84 | WM20 | FRG | 14 | 1 | 2 | 3 | 8 | — |
| 1990-93 | WM | FRG | 32 | 5 | 7 | 12 | 16 | — |
| 1988-94 | OG-M | FRG | 20 | 3 | 1 | 4 | 10 | — |
| **Truntschka, Gerd / b. Sept. 10, 1958** | | | | | | | | |
| 1977-78 | WM20 | FRG | 13 | 11 | 8 | 19 | 20 | — |
| 1979-93 | WM | FRG | 77 | 21 | 41 | 62 | 88 | — |
| 1980-92 | OG-M | FRG | 26 | 9 | 16 | 25 | 33 | — |
| ~WM All-Star Team/Forward (1987) | | | | | | | | |
| **Trybus, Leszek / b. May 27, 1970** | | | | | | | | |
| 1990 | WM20 | POL | 7 | 1 | 1 | 2 | 2 | — |
| **Trybus, Marek / b. Oct. 3, 1968** | | | | | | | | |
| 1987-88 | WM20 | POL | 14 | 0 | 3 | 3 | 10 | — |
| **Trygg, Marius / b. June 1, 1976** | | | | | | | | |
| 1997-2007 | WM | NOR | 38 | 2 | 5 | 7 | 6 | — |
| **Trzopek, Mariusz / b. Nov. 26, 1977** | | | | | | | | |
| 1997 | WM20 | POL | 6 | 0 | 0 | 0 | 10 | — |
| **Tschida, Marshall / b. unknown** | | | | | | | | |
| 1963-67 | WM | USA | 21 | 7 | 14 | 21 | 34 | — |
| **Tschiemer, Rolf / b. Oct. 23, 1951** | | | | | | | | |
| 1976 | OG-M | SUI | 5 | 3 | 3 | 6 | 2 | — |
| **Tschudy, Marc / b. May 3, 1981** | | | | | | | | |
| 1999 | WM18 | SUI | 7 | 1 | 1 | 2 | 18 | — |
| **Tschumi, Rick / b. Apr. 28, 1963** | | | | | | | | |
| 1991-93 | WM | SUI | 17 | 0 | 0 | 0 | 10 | — |
| **Tschuor, Sandro / b. Jan. 28, 1980** | | | | | | | | |
| 1999 | WM20 | SUI | 6 | 0 | 0 | 0 | 0 | — |
| **Tselios, Nikos / b. Jan. 20, 1979** | | | | | | | | |
| 1998-99 | WM20 | USA | 13 | 1 | 1 | 2 | 14 | — |
| **Tsikhan, Andrei / b. Aug. 15, 1981** | | | | | | | | |
| 2001 | WM20 | BLR | 6 | 1 | 1 | 2 | 2 | — |
| **Tsimikalis, Peter / b. Jan. 10, 1986** | | | | | | | | |
| 2004 | WM18 | CAN | 7 | 0 | 1 | 1 | 4 | — |
| **Tsirkunov, Oleg / b. Mar. 15, 1977** | | | | | | | | |
| 1995 | WM20 | UKR | 7 | 1 | 0 | 1 | 0 | — |
| **Tsuburai, Takeshi / b. Sept. 12, 1951** | | | | | | | | |
| 1972 | OG-M | JPN | 4 | 0 | 1 | 1 | 6 | — |
| **Tsuchida, Hideji / b. Oct. 5, 1973** | | | | | | | | |
| 1993 | WM20 | JPN | 7 | 0 | 1 | 1 | 2 | — |
| 1998-2000 | WM | JPN | 9 | 0 | 0 | 0 | 0 | — |
| **Tsuji, Shinjiro / b. Sept. 14, 1975** | | | | | | | | |
| 1993 | WM20 | JPN | 7 | 0 | 0 | 0 | 2 | — |
| **Tsujiura, Steven / b. Feb. 28, 1962** | | | | | | | | |
| 1998 | OG-M | JPN | 4 | 0 | 0 | 0 | 6 | — |
| **Tsulygin, Nikolai / b. June 29, 1975** | | | | | | | | |
| 1993-94 | WM20 | RUS | 12 | 1 | 2 | 3 | 14 | B |
| **Tsurikov, Yegor / b. Apr. 14, 1980** | | | | | | | | |
| 1999 | WM20 | BLR | 6 | 0 | 0 | 0 | 0 | — |
| **Tsvetkov, Maxim / b. Oct. 13, 1974** | | | | | | | | |
| 1994 | WM20 | RUS | 7 | 0 | 0 | 0 | 8 | B |
| **Tsyareshka, Artur / b. May 31, 1986** | | | | | | | | |
| 2004 | WM18 | BLR | 6 | 0 | 0 | 0 | 0 | — |
| **Tsygankov, Gennadi / b. Aug. 16, 1947 / d. Feb. 16, 2006** | | | | | | | | |
| 1971-79 | WM | URS | 81 | 6 | 19 | 25 | 45 | 6G,2S,B |
| 1972 | SS | URS | 8 | 0 | 2 | 2 | 6 | 2nd |
| 1972-76 | OG-M | URS | 10 | 4 | 4 | 8 | 6 | 2G |
| **Tsygurov, Dmitri / b. Mar. 18, 1967** | | | | | | | | |
| 1987 | WM20 | URS | 6 | 1 | 2 | 3 | 2 | — |
| **Tsyplakov, Viktor / b. Dec. 19, 1937** | | | | | | | | |
| 1961 | WM | URS | 5 | 1 | 0 | 1 | 4 | B |
| **Tsyplakov, Vladimir / b. Apr. 18, 1969** | | | | | | | | |
| 1989 | WM20 | URS | 7 | 1 | 0 | 1 | 8 | G |
| 1999-2005 | WM | BLR | 23 | 8 | 9 | 17 | 10 | — |
| 1998-2002 | OG-M | BLR | 13 | 2 | 4 | 6 | 6 | — |
| **Tsyplakov, Yuri / b. Apr. 4, 1970** | | | | | | | | |
| 1994 | WM | RUS | 6 | 1 | 1 | 2 | 8 | — |
| **Tsyrul, Dmytro / b. Jan. 2, 1979** | | | | | | | | |
| 2002-07 | WM | UKR | 24 | 6 | 2 | 8 | 30 | — |
| **Tsytsynov, Yuri / b. Aug. 24, 1937 / d. 1994** | | | | | | | | |
| 1960 | OG-M | URS | 7 | 5 | 4 | 9 | 4 | B |
| **Tucci, Carmine / b. Dec. 27, 1933** | | | | | | | | |
| 1959 | WM | ITA | 8 | 3 | 0 | 3 | 10 | — |
| 1956 | OG-M | ITA | 6 | 2 | 1 | 3 | 6 | — |
| **Tuck, Leon / b. May 25, 1891 / d. Sept. 2, 1953** | | | | | | | | |
| 1920 | OG-M | USA | 2 | 1 | — | 1 | 0 | S |
| **Tucker, Bobby / b. unknown / d. unknown** | | | | | | | | |
| 1933 | WM | ROM | 2 | 0 | — | 0 | 0 | — |
| **Tucker, Chris / b. Feb. 9, 1972** | | | | | | | | |
| 1992 | WM20 | USA | 7 | 0 | 0 | 0 | 0 | B |
| **Tucker, Darcy / b. Mar. 15, 1975** | | | | | | | | |
| 1995 | WM20 | CAN | 7 | 0 | 4 | 4 | 0 | G |
| **Tudyka, Rainer / b. Jan. 22, 1942** | | | | | | | | |
| 1963-67 | WM | GDR | 27 | 0 | 0 | 0 | 5 | — |
| **Tuiskula, Kari / b. Apr. 18, 1965** | | | | | | | | |
| 1985 | WM20 | FIN | 7 | 0 | 0 | 0 | 4 | — |
| **Tukio, Arto / b. Apr. 4, 1981** | | | | | | | | |
| 1999 | WM18 | FIN | 7 | 0 | 2 | 2 | 0 | G |
| 2000 | WM20 | FIN | 7 | 3 | 3 | 6 | 6 | — |
| **Tukmachev, Sergei / b. Jan. 4, 1958** | | | | | | | | |
| 1978 | WM20 | URS | 7 | 2 | 4 | 6 | 4 | G |
| **Tully, Brent / b. Mar. 26, 1974** | | | | | | | | |
| 1993-94 | WM20 | CAN | 14 | 1 | 3 | 4 | 28 | 2G |
| ~WM20 All-Star Team/Defence (1993) | | | | | | | | |
| **Tulupov, Kirill / b. Apr. 23, 1988** | | | | | | | | |
| 2006 | WM18 | RUS | 6 | 0 | 2 | 2 | 8 | — |
| **Tunik, Yevgeni / b. Nov. 17, 1984** | | | | | | | | |
| 2002 | WM18 | RUS | 8 | 1 | 3 | 4 | 14 | S |
| 2004 | WM20 | RUS | 5 | 0 | 1 | 1 | 4 | — |
| **Tuohimaa, Harri / b. Nov. 2, 1959** | | | | | | | | |
| 1978-79 | WM20 | FIN | 12 | 6 | 2 | 8 | 10 | — |
| 1984 | OG-M | FIN | 6 | 3 | 2 | 5 | 8 | — |
| 1985 | WM | FIN | 9 | 1 | 2 | 3 | 4 | — |
| **Tuohimaa, Juha / b. June 5, 1956** | | | | | | | | |
| 1981 | CC | FIN | 3 | 0 | 0 | 0 | 2 | — |
| **Tuokko, Marco / b. Mar. 27, 1979** | | | | | | | | |
| 1999 | WM20 | FIN | 6 | 0 | 0 | 0 | 8 | — |
| **Tuomainen, Marko / b. Apr. 25, 1972** | | | | | | | | |
| 1992 | WM20 | FIN | 7 | 1 | 4 | 5 | 14 | — |
| 1998-2000 | WM | FIN | 29 | 6 | 6 | 12 | 42 | 2S,B |
| **Tuomainen, Miika / b. May 22, 1986** | | | | | | | | |
| 2004 | WM18 | FIN | 6 | 1 | 0 | 1 | 4 | — |
| **Tuomenoska, Antti / b. Mar. 16, 1967** | | | | | | | | |
| 1986-87 | WM20 | FIN | 14 | 1 | 4 | 5 | 12 | G |
| **Tuomi, Risto / b. Aug. 21, 1960** | | | | | | | | |
| 1980 | WM20 | FIN | 5 | 1 | 0 | 1 | 2 | S |
| **Tuominen, Janne / b. Mar. 6, 1984** | | | | | | | | |
| 2002 | WM18 | FIN | 8 | 0 | 1 | 1 | 2 | — |
| **Tuomisto, Pekka / b. Dec. 29, 1960** | | | | | | | | |
| 1980 | WM20 | FIN | 5 | 0 | 1 | 1 | 2 | S |
| 1991-92 | WM | FIN | 15 | 2 | 0 | 2 | 6 | S |
| 1988-92 | OG-M | FIN | 16 | 5 | 2 | 7 | 10 | S |
| **Tuovinen, Mika / b. June 27, 1969** | | | | | | | | |
| 1988 | WM20 | FIN | 7 | 0 | 0 | 0 | 0 | B |
| **Tupalski, Alexander / b. Oct. 5, 1900 / d. Jan. 9, 1980** | | | | | | | | |
| 1930-31 | WM | POL | 9 | 4 | — | 4 | — | — |
| 1928 | OG-M | POL | 2 | 3 | — | 3 | — | — |
| **Turcotte, Alfie / b. June 5, 1965** | | | | | | | | |
| 1984 | WM20 | USA | 7 | 2 | 9 | 11 | 2 | — |
| 1986 | WM | USA | 9 | 0 | 2 | 2 | 8 | — |
| **Turcotte, Darren / b. Feb. 3, 1968** | | | | | | | | |
| 1987-88 | WM20 | USA | 14 | 8 | 6 | 14 | 14 | — |
| 1993 | WM | USA | 6 | 2 | 1 | 3 | 0 | — |
| **Tureanu, Doru / b. Jan. 11, 1954** | | | | | | | | |
| 1977 | WM | ROM | 10 | 6 | 1 | 7 | 4 | — |
| 1976-80 | OG-M | ROM | 10 | 10 | 7 | 17 | 31 | — |
| ~IIHF Hall of Fame | | | | | | | | |
| **Turgeon, Pierre / b. Aug. 28, 1969** | | | | | | | | |
| 1987 | WM20 | CAN | 6 | 3 | 0 | 3 | 2 | — |
| **Turgeon, Sylvain / b. Jan. 17, 1965** | | | | | | | | |
| 1983 | WM20 | CAN | 7 | 4 | 2 | 6 | 8 | B |
| **Turk, Bob / b. Jan. 21, 1936** | | | | | | | | |
| 1959-61 | WM | USA | 15 | 6 | 5 | 11 | 6 | — |
| **Turkovski, Vasili / b. Sept. 3, 1974** | | | | | | | | |
| 1994 | WM20 | RUS | 7 | 0 | 0 | 0 | 4 | B |
| 2003-04 | WM | RUS | 11 | 0 | 0 | 0 | 6 | — |
| **Turler, Julien / b. Feb. 9, 1982** | | | | | | | | |
| 2000 | WM18 | SUI | 7 | 2 | 2 | 4 | 4 | — |
| **Turler, Michel / b. May 14, 1944 / d. Apr. 8, 2010** | | | | | | | | |
| 1972 | WM | SUI | 8 | 1 | 0 | 1 | 10 | — |
| 1972 | OG-M | SUI | 4 | 4 | 0 | 4 | 6 | — |
| **Turnbull, D.M. / b. unknown / d. unknown** | | | | | | | | |
| 1931 | WM | GBR | — | 0 | — | 0 | — | — |
| **Turon, David / b. Oct. 4, 1983** | | | | | | | | |
| 2001 | WM18 | CZE | 7 | 0 | 1 | 1 | 4 | — |
| 2003 | WM20 | CZE | 6 | 1 | 0 | 1 | 10 | — |
| **Turunen, Antti / b. Apr. 12, 1986** | | | | | | | | |
| 2004 | WM18 | FIN | 6 | 1 | 0 | 1 | 10 | — |
| **Turunen, Mikko / b. Apr. 16, 1974** | | | | | | | | |
| 1994 | WM20 | FIN | 5 | 1 | 0 | 1 | 8 | — |
| **Turunen, Timo / b. Apr. 8, 1948** | | | | | | | | |
| 1972-73 | WM | FIN | 20 | 8 | 3 | 11 | 4 | — |
| 1972 | OG-M | FIN | 4 | 1 | 0 | 1 | 2 | — |
| **Tutt, Brian / b. June 9, 1962** | | | | | | | | |
| 1992-95 | WM | CAN | 12 | 0 | 0 | 0 | 14 | B |
| 1992 | OG-M | CAN | 8 | 0 | 0 | 0 | 4 | S |
| **Tutti, Keijo / b. Jan. 2, 1963** | | | | | | | | |
| 1983 | WM20 | FIN | 7 | 1 | 4 | 5 | 0 | — |
| **Tuulola, Marko / b. Feb. 7, 1971** | | | | | | | | |
| 2002 | WM | FIN | 9 | 1 | 1 | 2 | 0 | — |
| **Tuyembayev, Ivan / b. Apr. 19, 1980** | | | | | | | | |
| 1999-2000 | WM20 | KAZ | 7 | 1 | 0 | 1 | 6 | - |
| **Tuzzolino, Tony / b. Oct. 9, 1975** | | | | | | | | |
| 2006 | OG-M | ITA | 4 | 0 | 1 | 1 | 32 | — |
| **Tveritinov, Olexander / b. Mar. 18, 1984** | | | | | | | | |
| 2001-02 | WM18 | UKR | 14 | 0 | 0 | 0 | 4 | — |
| **Tveten, Erik / b. Aug. 5, 1972** | | | | | | | | |
| 1991 | WM20 | NOR | 6 | 3 | 0 | 3 | 6 | — |
| 1995-97 | WM | NOR | 18 | 1 | 2 | 3 | 4 | — |
| **Tvrdon, Roman / b. Jan. 29, 1981** | | | | | | | | |
| 1999 | WM18 | SVK | 7 | 1 | 4 | 5 | 4 | B |
| 2001 | WM20 | SVK | 7 | 2 | 0 | 2 | 4 | — |
| **Twardy, Rafal / b. Jan. 30, 1978** | | | | | | | | |
| 1997 | WM20 | POL | 6 | 1 | 0 | 1 | 0 | — |
| **Tyrala, Ryszard / b. Jan. 1, 1971** | | | | | | | | |
| 1990 | WM20 | POL | 7 | 0 | 1 | 1 | 6 | — |
| **Tyrvainen, Antti / b. Apr. 3, 1989** | | | | | | | | |
| 2007 | WM18 | FIN | 6 | 0 | 1 | 1 | 4 | — |
| **Tyuluberdinov, Arman / b. Feb. 25, 1985** | | | | | | | | |
| 2003 | WM18 | KAZ | 6 | 0 | 0 | 0 | 0 | — |
| **Tyulyapkin, Mikhail / b. May 4, 1984** | | | | | | | | |
| 2004 | WM20 | RUS | 6 | 0 | 0 | 0 | 2 | — |
| **Tyumenev, Viktor / b. June 1, 1957** | | | | | | | | |
| 1982-90 | WM | URS | 31 | 5 | 9 | 14 | 25 | 3G,B |
| 1984 | OG-M | URS | 6 | 0 | 9 | 9 | 2 | G |
| **Tyurikov, Vladimir / b. July 9, 1963** | | | | | | | | |
| 1981-83 | WM20 | URS | 17 | 1 | 7 | 8 | 10 | G,B |

**Ubersax, Jean-Pierre / b. unknown**
1954 WM SUI 7 0 — 0 2 —

**Uchevatov, Viktor / b. Feb. 10, 1983**
2001 WM18 RUS 6 0 2 2 4 G

**Uchiyama, Tomohiko / b. Oct. 13, 1979**
2001-03 WM JPN 11 0 0 0 6 —

**Uharcek, Marian / b. Mar. 17, 1971**
1990-91 WM20 TCH 6 2 4 6 0 2B

**Ujcik, Viktor / b. May 24, 1972**
1992 WM20 TCH 7 4 1 5 8 —
1996-2002 WM CZE 43 17 9 26 28 3G,B

**Ujwary, Andrzej / b. Aug. 21, 1960**
1986 WM POL 6 1 0 1 2 —
1980-84 OG-M POL 9 0 1 1 4 —

**Ujvary, Lubomir / b. Sept. 24, 1948**
1970 WM TCH 1 0 0 0 2 B

**Ukolov, Dmitri / b. Oct. 23, 1929 / d. Nov. 25, 1992**
1954-59 WM URS 26 8 2 10 14 G,3S
1956 OG-M URS 5 1 1 2 6 G

**Ulander, Mats / b. Aug. 2, 1954**
1982 WM SWE 10 1 1 2 8 —

**Ulanov, Igor / b. Oct. 1, 1969**
1994 WM RUS 6 1 0 1 20 —
1996 WCH RUS 1 0 0 0 4 —

**Ullmann, Christoph / b. May 19, 1983**
2003 WM20 GER 6 4 0 4 4 —

**Ulrich, Diego / b. unknown**
1978 WM20 SUI 6 0 0 0 0 —

**Ulrich, Herbert / b. Sept. 14, 1921 / d. unknown**
1948 OG-M AUT 7 4 — 4 — —

**Ulrich, Martin / b. Dec. 16, 1969**
1993-2007 WM AUT 68 1 10 11 38 —
1994-2002 OG-M AUT 15 1 4 5 4 —

**Ulrich, Walter / b. unknown / d. unknown**
1936 OG-M TCH 1 0 — 0 — —

**Ulseth, Karl Erik / b. unknown**
1983 WM20 NOR 6 1 1 2 2 —

**Ulseth, Steve / b. Feb. 22, 1959**
1978-79 WM20 USA 11 2 6 8 2 —
1981 WM USA 8 2 0 2 0 —

**Umicevic, Dragan / b. Oct. 9, 1984**
2002 WM18 SWE 8 2 1 3 8 —

**Unger, Donald / b. 1894 / d. unknown**
1924 OG-M SUI 2 1 — 1 — —

**Unger, Eric / b. Dec. 29, 1926**
1954 WM CAN 7 8 9 17 0 S

**Unger, Garry / b. Dec. 7, 1947**
1978-79 WM CAN 17 2 1 3 44 B

**Unsinn, Xaver / b. Nov. 29, 1929 / d. Jan. 4, 2012**
1953-59 WM FRG 17 6 1 7 2 S
1952-60 OG-M FRG 14 1 4 5 2 —
~IIHF Hall of Fame

**Unterdorfel, Wolfgang / b. Apr. 28, 1955**
1978 WM GDR 9 0 0 0 0 —

**Upper, Dmitri / b. July 27, 1978**
1998 WM20 KAZ 7 1 0 1 2 —
2004-05 WM KAZ 12 4 2 6 24 —
2006 OG-M KAZ 5 0 1 1 8 —

**Urabe, Hideo / b. Apr. 7, 1951**
1976-80 OG-M JPN 10 5 2 7 6 —

**Uram, Marek / b. Sept. 8, 1974**
2002-07 WM SVK 13 2 3 5 2 G

**Urban, Christian / b. Nov. 10, 1982**
2000 WM18 GER 6 0 1 1 4 —

**Urban, Stefan / b. Dec. 4, 1969**
1989 WM20 FRG 7 0 0 0 4 —

**Urban, Vladimir / b. Aug. 7, 1958**
1977-78 WM20 TCH 13 0 4 4 18 B

**Urban, Vladimir / b. Jan. 15, 1980**
2000 WM20 SVK 6 0 0 0 6 —

**Urson, Herbert / b. Dec. 18, 1917 / d. 1995**
1938-39 WM POL 9 2 — 2 — —

**Urvikko, Jouko / b. Mar. 10, 1958**
1978 WM20 FIN 6 0 1 1 2 —

**Urychev, Yuri / b. Apr. 3, 1991 / d. Sept. 7, 2011**
2011 WM20 RUS 7 1 3 4 4 G
~perished in Yaroslavl plane crash

**Ustorf, Stefan / b. Jan. 3, 1974**
1992-94 WM20 GER 12 3 3 6 6 —
1992-2008 WM GER 29 6 8 14 36 —
1996-2004 WCH GER 8 0 2 2 2 —
1994-2006 OG-M GER 24 3 4 7 4 —

**Ustrnul, Libor / b. Feb. 20, 1982**
2001-02 WM20 CZE 12 0 4 4 28 G

**Uteyev, Inar / b. Oct. 22, 1980**
2000 WM20 KAZ 7 0 2 2 6 —

**Uvarov, Alexander / b. Mar. 7, 1922 / d. Dec. 24, 1994**
1954-57 WM URS 20 6 1 7 2 G,2S
1956 OG-M URS 7 2 2 4 2 G

**Uvira, Eduard / b. July 12, 1961**
1980-81 WM20 TCH 10 0 3 3 4 —
1982-85 WM TCH 30 0 5 5 16 G,2S
1984 CC TCH 5 0 1 1 6 —
1984-88 OG-M TCH 9 1 1 2 4 S

**Vaagensoe, Christian / b. July 12, 1987**
2004-05 WM18 DEN 10 0 0 0 4 —

**Vaal, Frans / b. unknown**
1950 WM NED 4 0 0 0 0 —

**Vaananen, Jani / b. Mar. 20, 1980**
1999-2000 WM20 FIN 12 4 2 6 2 —

**Vaananen, Jarkko / b. July 30, 1977**
1997 WM20 FIN 6 0 0 0 0 —

**Vacatko, Vladimir / b. Sept. 15, 1952**
1976-81 WM FRG 42 10 7 17 8 —
1980 OG-M FRG 4 4 1 5 4 —

**Vacheron, Alexis / b. July 5, 1979**
1999 WM20 SUI 6 0 1 1 14 —

**Vaclav, Vilem / b. Dec. 16, 1925**
1957 WM TCH 7 7 2 9 4 B

**Vaclavicek, Lubomir / b. Feb. 11, 1967**
1987 WM20 TCH 7 1 1 2 4 S

**Vacovsky, Jiri / b. unknown**
1949 WM TCH 2 0 — 0 — G

**Vadnais, Carol / b. Sept. 25, 1945**
1977 WM CAN 10 3 1 4 33 —

**Vaelma, Pertti / b. May 7, 1957**
1977 WM20 FIN 6 0 0 0 2 —

**Vagner, Martin / b. Mar. 16, 1984**
2004 WM20 CZE 7 0 0 0 14 —

**Vaic, Lubomir / b. Mar. 6, 1977**
1996-97 WM20 SVK 12 3 11 14 35 —
2000-06 WM SVK 22 0 4 4 6 S,B

**Vail, Eric / b. Sept. 16, 1953**
1977 WM CAN 9 4 1 5 18 —

**Vainio, Niko / b. Jan. 24, 1985**
2003 WM18 FIN 6 0 0 0 6 —

**Vainio, Seppo / b. Jan. 3, 1937**
1961 WM FIN 6 0 1 1 4 —
1960 OG-M FIN 2 0 0 0 4 —

**Vaive, Justin / b. July 8, 1989**
2007 WM18 USA 7 3 3 6 2 S

**Vaive, Rick / b. May 14, 1959**
1978 WM20 CAN 6 3 0 3 4 B
1982-85 WM CAN 19 9 4 13 30 S,B

**Vajcner, Vlastimil / b. Feb. 22, 1959**
1978-79 WM20 TCH 12 2 3 5 6 S

**Vakar, Lajos / b. Sept. 8, 1910 / d. Sept. 10, 1993**
1933-37 WM ROM 14 2 0 2 0 —

**Vakrushev, Andrei / b. May 17, 1965**
1985 WM20 URS 7 1 1 2 0 B

**Vala, Petr / b. May 20, 1979**
1999 WM20 CZE 6 2 1 3 2 —

**Valach, Stanislav / b. May 19, 1983**
2003 WM20 SVK 6 1 0 1 0 —

**Valchok, Pavel / b. Sept. 4, 1980**
1999 WM20 BLR 6 0 0 0 0 —

**Valdix, Andreas / b. Dec. 6, 1984**
2002 WM18 SWE 8 0 0 0 37 —
2003-04 WM20 SWE 11 2 2 4 0 —

**Valek, Oldrich / b. Mar. 9, 1960**
1980 WM20 TCH 5 3 1 4 14 —
1983-89 WM TCH 27 8 4 12 16 G,S,B
1981 CC TCH 3 0 0 0 4 —

**Valentar, Vinko / b. Mar. 21, 1934**
1964 OG-M YUG 6 1 0 1 0 —

**Valenti, Sven / b. July 20, 1975**
1994-95 WM20 GER 13 4 2 6 4 —

**Valentin, Alexander / b. Apr. 23, 1981**
1999 WM18 SVK 7 1 2 3 2 B
2001 WM20 SVK 7 0 0 0 6 —

**Valila, Mika / b. Feb. 28, 1970**
1989-90 WM20 FIN 12 5 5 10 12 —

**Valkeapaa, Pertti / b. Febraury 13, 1951**
1972-82 WM FIN 16 1 0 1 10 —

**Valko, Pavel / b. Feb. 3, 1968**
1988 WM20 TCH 7 0 2 2 0 —

**Vallin, Ari / b. Mar. 21, 1978**
1998 WM20 FIN 7 1 1 2 8 G

**Valtonen, Tomek / b. Jan. 8, 1980**
1998-2000 WM20 FIN 20 2 1 3 8 —

**Valui, Vitali / b. Apr. 17, 1974**
2000-01 WM BLR 12 1 1 2 2 —

**Van, Al / b. Mar. 30, 1915 / d. Aug. 27, 1995**
1938-50 WM USA 35 9 1 10 2 2S,B
1952 OG-M USA 8 0 1 1 — S

**Vanbiesbrouck, Julian / b. May 17, 1960**
1980 WM20 USA 5 1 1 2 8 —

**van Boxmeer, John / b. Nov. 20, 1952**
1982 WM CAN 8 2 0 2 8 B

**van de Broek, Klaas / b. July 7, 1955**
1980 OG-M NED 5 0 0 0 0 —

**van de Madele, Chris / b. unknown**
1935 WM NED 4 0 0 0 — —

**van de Wouwer, Jean / b. 1910 / d. unknown**
1930-33 WM BEL 3 0 — 0 0 —
1928 OG-M BEL 1 0 — 0 — —

**van den Bussche, Paul / b. unknown**
1939 WM BEL 1 1 — 1 — —

**van den Driessche, Carlos / b. Aug. 31, 1901 / d. May 14, 1972**
1934-35 WM BEL 9 0 — 0 — —
1924-36 OG-M BEL 4 0 — 0 — —

**van der Baumen, Rolf / b. Nov. 20, 1924**
1950 WM NED 1 0 0 0 0 —

**van der Stok, Bob / b. Oct. 13, 1915 / d. unknown**
1935 WM NED 4 0 0 0 — —

**van der Vlugt, Fritz / b. unknown / d. unknown**
1935 WM NED 4 0 0 0 — —

**van Eeckhout, Leon / b. June 14, 1917 / d. unknown**
1939-50 WM BEL 20 6 1 7 0 —

**Vanek, Frantisek / b. Dec. 3, 1931**
1957-63 WM TCH 32 8 9 17 16 S,3B
1956-60 OG-M TCH 12 6 5 11 2 —

**Vanelli, Tom / b. unknown**
1977 WM USA 10 0 0 0 0 —

**van Gog, Rick / b. Apr. 3, 1957**
1981 WM NED 8 0 2 2 8 —
1980 OG-M NED 5 1 3 4 2 —

**van Heeswijk, Piet / b. May 29, 1922 / d. unknown**
1950 WM NED 4 2 0 2 0 —

**van Heumen, Harry / b. Dec. 24, 1959**
1981 WM NED 8 1 2 3 0 —
1980 OG-M NED 5 0 0 0 0 —

**Vaningen, Herb / b. Nov. 17, 1924 / d. Mar. 22, 1976**
1948 OG-M USA 2 0 0 0 2 —

**van Reysschoot, Jacques / b. May 2, 1905 / d. unknown**
1930 WM BEL 1 0 — 0 — —
1928 OG-M BEL 3 1 — 1 — —

**van Reysschoot, Pierre / b. Dec. 9, 1906 / d. 1966**
1933-47 WM BEL 21 6 — 6 0 —
1928-36 OG-M BEL 6 5 — 5 — —

**van Rhede van der Kloot, Johan / b. unknown**
1950 WM NED 3 0 0 0 0 —

**van Riel, Charles / b. unknown / d. unknown**
1933 WM BEL 1 0 — 0 0 —

**van Riel, G. / b. unknown / d. unknown**
1933 WM BEL 1 0 — 0 0 —

**van Rompaey, Willy / b. Mar. 24, 1911 / d. unknown**
1930-33 WM BEL 3 0 — 0 0 —

**Van Ryn, Mike / b. May 14, 1979**
1998-99 WM20 CAN 14 0 1 1 8 S

**van Soldt, Frank / b. July 28, 1953**
1980 OG-M NED 5 0 0 0 0 —

**Vani, Carmine / b. Aug. 7, 1964**
1992 WM ITA 5 0 0 0 2 —

**van Volcksom, Philippe / b. unknown / d. unknown**
1920-24 OG-M BEL 3 1 0 1 — —

**van Volxem, Gaston / b. 1893 / d. unknown**
1920-24 OG-M BEL 4 2 0 2 — —

**van Wieren, Larrie / b. May 3, 1951**
1981 WM NED 8 2 3 5 6 —
1980 OG-M NED 5 1 4 5 2 —

**Varada, Vaclav / b. Apr. 26, 1976**
1995-96 WM20 CZE 13 11 5 16 33 —
2000-05 WM CZE 18 3 4 7 8 2G

**Varakas, Ville / b. Feb. 13, 1984**
2004 WM20 FIN 7 0 4 4 2 B

**Varga, Desideriu / b. May 13, 1939**
1977 WM ROM 10 2 2 4 4 —
1964-76 OG-M ROM 17 2 6 8 6 —

**Varga, John / b. Jan. 31, 1974**
1994 WM20 USA 5 2 0 2 6 —

**Varga, Milan / b. Aug. 1, 1983**
2003 WM20 SVK 6 1 0 1 2 —

**Vargas, Brennan / b. June 15, 1989**
2007 WM18 USA 7 0 4 4 0 S

**Vargas, Ernie / b. Mar. 10, 1964**
1983 WM20 USA 7 2 1 3 0 —

**Varholik, Jan / b. Feb. 28, 1970**
1989-90 WM20 TCH 11 3 3 6 6 2B
1996 WM SVK 5 0 0 0 2 —
1996 WCH SVK 3 0 1 1 2 —
1994-98 OG-M SVK 10 0 0 0 16 —

**Varianov, Nikolai / b. Feb. 3, 1959**
1978-79 WM20 URS 13 7 4 11 16 2G

**Varis, Petri / b. May 13, 1969**
1997 WM FIN 8 2 3 5 2 —
1994 OG-M FIN 5 1 1 2 2 B

**Varitski, Igor / b. Apr. 25, 1971**
1993 WM RUS 8 0 0 0 0 G
1994 OG-M RUS 8 1 1 2 2 —

**Varl, Dejan / b. July 3, 1973**
2005-08 WM SLO 17 0 1 1 24 —

**Varlamov, Sergi / b. July 21, 1978**
2000-05 WM UKR 23 2 7 9 72 —
2002 OG-M UKR 2 1 0 1 14 —

**Varnakov, Mikhail / b. June 25, 1957**
1985-87 WM URS 20 10 6 16 2 G,S,B
1984 CC URS 6 3 1 4 4 —

**Vartovnik, Lukas / b. Mar. 8, 1989**
2006 WM18 SVK 6 0 0 0 2 —

**Varvio, Jarkko / b. Apr. 28, 1972**
1991-91 WM20 FIN 14 13 5 18 12 —
1992-97 WM FIN 22 11 1 12 14 S
~WM All-Star Team/Forward (1992)

**Varyvonchyk, Anatoli / b. Mar. 14, 1983**
2003 WM20 BLR 6 0 0 0 2 —

**Vas, Janos / b. Jan. 29, 1984**
2009 WM HUN 5 0 1 1 29 —

**Vas, Marton / b. Mar. 2, 1980**
2009 WM HUN 6 0 1 1 8 —

**Vasicek, Josef / b. Sept. 12, 1980 / d. Sept. 7, 2011**
2000 WM20 CZE 7 1 3 4 2 G
2003-09 WM CZE 23 2 5 7 12 G
2004 WCH CZE 1 0 0 0 0 —
2010 OG-M CZE 5 0 0 0 2 —
~perished in Yaroslavl plane crash

**Vasilyev, Alexei / b. Sept. 1, 1977**
1996-97 WM20 RUS 13 2 0 2 4 2B

**Vasilyev, Konstantin / b. Apr. 27, 1982**
2001 WM20 KAZ 6 0 0 0 0 —

**Vasilyev, Mikhail / b. June 8, 1962**
1982 WM20 URS 7 5 3 8 13 —
1983-87 WM URS 26 7 10 17 19 G,S,B
1984 CC URS 4 1 1 2 0 —
1984 OG-M URS 7 3 2 5 4 G

**Vasilyev, Valeri / b. Aug. 3, 1949**
1970-82 WM URS 101 15 30 45 50 8G,2S,B
1972 SS URS 6 1 2 3 6 2nd
1976-81 CC URS 11 0 4 4 10 1st
1972-80 OG-M URS 14 3 3 6 4 2G,S
~IIHF Hall of Fame
~WM IIHF Directorate Best Defenceman (1973, 1977, 1979), WM All-Star Team/Defence (1974, 1975, 1977, 1979, 1981)

**Vaske, Dennis / b. Oct. 11, 1967**
1992 WM USA 6 0 0 0 6 —

**Vasyukovich, Nikolai / b. Jan. 12, 1980**
1999 WM20 BLR 6 0 0 0 0 —

**Vasyunov, Alexander / b. Apr. 22, 1988 / d. Sept. 7, 2011**
2006 WM18 RUS 6 2 2 4 6 —
2007 WM20 RUS 6 2 0 2 2 S
~perished in Yaroslavl plane crash

**Vaszjunyin, Artyom / b. Jan. 26, 1984**
2009 WM HUN 6 0 0 0 0 —

**Vauclair, Geoffrey / b. Mar. 8, 1977**
1999 WM SUI 6 0 0 0 2 —

**Vauclair, Tristan / b. Feb. 13, 1984**
2003 WM18 SUI 6 0 1 1 14 —

**Vauhkonen, Jonni / b. Jan. 1, 1975**
1993-94 WM20 FIN 14 2 4 6 47 —

**Vauhkonen, Olavi / b. Jan. 24, 1989**
2007 WM18 FIN 6 2 2 4 4 —

**Vavra, Kamil / b. Jan. 7, 1985**
2003 WM18 CZE 6 0 0 0 2 —

**Vazan, Michal / b. Aug. 9, 1983**
2001 WM18 SVK 6 1 0 1 0 —
2003 WM20 SVK 6 1 2 3 0 —

**Veber, Jiri / b. Nov. 29, 1968**
1996-98 WM CZE 19 0 2 2 14 G,2B
1996 WCH CZE 1 0 0 0 0 —
1994 OG-M CZE 2 0 0 0 2 —

**Veber, Roman / b. Feb. 3, 1969**
1989 WM20 TCH 7 0 1 1 0 B

**Vecchiarelli, John / b. July 24, 1964**
1993 WM ITA 6 2 0 2 6 —
1992 OG-M ITA 7 1 3 4 8 —

**Vedejs, Leonids / b. Oct. 12, 1908 / d. Feb. 4, 1995**
1933-39 WM LAT 19 0 — 0 1 —
1936 OG-M LAT 3 0 — 0 — —

**Vehmanen, Jorma / b. Sept. 18, 1945**
1966-76 WM FIN 58 4 5 9 16 —
1976 CC FIN 4 0 0 0 2 —
1972-76 OG-M FIN 7 3 1 4 2 —

**Veilleux, Keven / b. June 27, 1989**
2007 WM18 CAN 2 0 1 1 0 —

**Veilleux, Steve / b. Mar. 9, 1969**
1989 WM20 CAN 7 0 0 0 8 —

**Veith, Vladimir / b. Aug. 30, 1954**
1974 WM TCH 8 2 2 4 0 S

**Vejvoda, Otakar / b. Nov. 11, 1950**
1995-96 WM CZE 16 6 4 10 10 G
1996 WCH CZE 2 0 0 0 2 —
~WM All-Star Team/Forward (1996)

**Velebny, Lubos / b. Feb. 9, 1982**
1999-2000 WM18 SVK 13 1 2 3 14 —
2001-02 WM20 SVK 14 1 2 3 44 —

**Velich, Jan / b. May 4, 1984**
2002 WM18 CZE 8 0 0 0 4 B

**Velichkin, Igor / b. July 3, 1987**
2005 WM18 RUS 6 0 2 2 4 —

**Venalainen, Sami / b. Oct. 14, 1981**
1999 WM18 FIN 7 0 3 3 2 G
2001 WM20 FIN 7 1 1 2 0 S

**Venkrbec, Miroslav / b. Feb. 11, 1961**
1980 WM20 TCH 5 3 1 4 12 —

**Venosta, Luigi / b. Apr. 28, 1913 / d. unknown**
1930-39 WM ITA 16 3 1 4 0 —

**Venturi, Ontario / b. unknown / d. unknown**
1939 WM ITA 7 1 — 1 — —

**Verbeek, Pat / b. May 24, 1964**
1983 WM20 CAN 7 2 2 4 6 B
1989-94 WM CAN 12 1 3 4 6 G,S
1996 WCH CAN 1 0 0 0 0 2nd

**Verchenko, Vitali / b. June 28, 1985**
2002 WM18 UKR 8 0 0 0 2 —

**Verchota, Phil / b. Dec. 28, 1956**
1979-81 WM USA 16 2 6 8 6 —
1980-84 OG-M USA 13 5 4 9 8 G

**Vercik, Rudolf / b. Mar. 19, 1976**
1996 WM20 SVK 6 1 1 2 32 —

**Verdeil, Andre / b. 1904 / d. unknown**
1924 OG-M SUI 3 1 — 1 — —

**Verenikin, Sergei / b. Sept. 8, 1979**
1999 WM20 RUS 7 3 2 5 4 G

**Verges, Pons / b. unknown / d. unknown**
1947 WM SUI 2 2 — 2 — —

**Vernarsky, Kris / b. Apr. 5, 1982**
2001-02 WM20 USA 14 3 2 5 22 —

**Verocai, Giulio / b. Mar. 31, 1942**
1964 OG-M ITA 7 0 0 0 0 —

**Verrier, Bob / b. Aug. 17, 1925**
1947 WM USA 6 3 — 3 — —

**Verstrepen, Luc / b. Sept. 30, 1923 / d. Feb. 1972**
1950 WM BEL 1 0 0 0 0 —

**Vertala, Timo / b. May 2, 1978**
1997-98 WM20 FIN 13 6 5 11 10 G

**Veselovsky, Peter / b. Nov. 11, 1964**
1992 WM TCH 3 0 0 0 25 B
1992 OG-M TCH 8 1 0 1 2 B

**Vesely, Ivo / b. Apr. 1, 1926 / d. Dec. 4, 2002**
1960 OG-M AUS 2 0 0 0 2 —

**Vestberg, Fredrik / b. Jan. 24, 1983**
2001 WM18 SWE 6 1 1 2 0 —

**Vesterheim, Stig / b. Apr. 10, 1975**
2000-01 WM NOR 11 0 0 0 2 —

**Vestreng, Frank / b. Aug. 19, 1961**
1984 OG-M NOR 5 0 0 0 0 —

**Vidlak, Milan / b. Jan. 29, 1926**
1954-55 WM TCH 8 3 1 4 2 B

**Vidmar, Andrej / b. Mar. 15, 1956**
1984 OG-M YUG 5 0 0 0 0 —

**Vigilante, Mike / b. Aug. 19, 1979**
1999 WM20 USA 6 2 2 4 0 —

**Viinikainen, Juha / b. Sept. 7, 1977**
1997 WM20 FIN 6 1 1 2 0 —

**Viitakoski, Vesa / b. Feb. 13, 1971**
1990-91 WM20 FIN 14 12 6 18 4 —
1992-2002 WM FIN 23 4 4 8 14 S

**Viitala, Jari / b. Dec. 1, 1958**
1978 WM20 FIN 6 2 4 6 2 —

**Viitanen, Mikko / b. Feb. 18, 1982**
2002 WM20 FIN 7 0 0 0 4 B

**Vikstrom, Kjell-Arne / b. Aug. 28, 1951**
1973-75 WM SWE 17 7 5 12 2 S,B
1976 CC SWE 5 0 1 1 0 —

**Viktorsson, Jan / b. July 27, 1964**
1991 WM SWE 10 1 1 2 6 G
1992 OG-M SWE 8 0 2 2 0 —

**Vikulov, Vladimir / b. July 20, 1946**
1966-75 WM URS 63 45 26 71 12 6G,S
1972 SS URS 6 2 1 3 0 2nd
1976 CC URS 4 4 3 7 0 —
1968-72 OG-M URS 12 7 13 20 2 2G
~WM All-Star Team/Forward (1971, 1972)

**Vilander, Jukka / b. Nov. 27, 1962**
1986-90 WM FIN 30 12 5 17 4 —

**Vilgrain, Claude / b. Mar. 1, 1963**
1988 OG-M CAN 6 0 0 0 0 —

**Viljanen, Jaakko / b. Mar. 12, 1984**
2002 WM18 FIN 8 6 1 7 2 —

**Villa, Ismo / b. Nov. 8, 1954**
1980 OG-M FIN 7 1 0 1 0 —

**Villa, Nicolas / b. Mar. 23, 1989**
2007 WM18 SUI 6 0 1 1 2 —

**Ville, Christophe / b. June 15, 1963**
1992-96 WM FRA 24 1 8 9 70 —
1988-94 OG-M FRA 21 5 6 11 28 —

**Vimpari, Ville / b. Mar. 9, 1985**
2002-03 WM18 FIN 14 1 2 3 6 —

**Vindys, Otakar / b. Apr. 9, 1884 / d. Dec. 23, 1949**
1920-24 OG-M TCH 4 0 0 0 — B

**Vinogradov, Alexander / b. Feb. 28, 1918 / d. unknown**
1954 WM URS 6 0 — 0 10 G

**Vinogradov, Alexander / b. June 20, 1970**
1994 OG-M RUS 8 3 2 5 4 —

**Vinokurov, Denis / b. July 14, 1972**
1992 WM20 RUS 7 1 1 2 2 G

**Vins, Miloslav / b. Dec. 3, 1923**
1957 WM TCH 7 6 3 9 — B

**Virkki, Jarno / b. May 12, 1984**
2002 WM18 FIN 8 0 2 2 4 —

**Virkkunen, Teemu / b. Jan. 13, 1979**
1999 WM20 FIN 6 0 2 2 0 —

**Virta, Hannu / b. Mar. 22, 1963**
1982 WM20 FIN 7 1 5 6 4 B
1987-97 WM FIN 54 5 25 30 36 G,S
1987-96 WCH FIN 9 1 1 2 6 —
1994 OG-M FIN 8 2 1 3 2 B

**Virta, Teppo / b. Sept. 2, 1962**
1982 WM20 FIN 7 2 5 7 4 B

**Virta, Tony / b. June 28, 1972**
1992 WM20 FIN 7 0 1 1 10 —
2000-04 WM FIN 27 3 8 11 4 S,B

**Virtanen, Jukka / b. July 15, 1959**
1986-87 WM FIN 17 2 2 4 24 S
1988 OG-M FIN 5 0 1 1 0 —

**Visan, Nicolae / b. Feb. 26, 1953**
1976 OG-M ROM 5 0 0 0 2 —

**Visnak, Bohdan / b. Mar. 2, 1988**
2006 WM18 CZE 7 1 0 1 4 B

**Vitolins, Harijs / b. Oct. 17, 1915 / d. unknown**
1939 WM LAT 2 0 — 0 — —

**Vitolins, Harijs / b. Apr. 30, 1968**
1988 WM20 URS 7 2 0 2 6 S
1997-2002 WM LAT 39 8 13 21 34 —
2002 OG-M LAT 4 2 2 4 0 —

**Vittenberg, Andre / b. unknown**
1995 WM FRA 6 0 0 0 0 —

**Viuhkola, Jari / b. Feb. 27, 1980**
2000 WM20 FIN 7 1 1 2 6 —
2004-07 WM FIN 20 4 1 5 6 S,B

**Viveiros, Emanuel / b. Jan. 8, 1966**
1986 WM20 CAN 7 1 1 2 2 S
2005 WM AUT 5 0 2 2 4 —

**Vlach, Miroslav / b. Oct. 19, 1935**
1957-63 WM TCH 36 31 5 36 16 S,3B
1960-64 OG-M TCH 14 12 5 17 10 B
~WM IIHF Directorate Best Forward (1963), WM All-Star Team/Forward (1963), WM All-Star Team/Forward (1961)

**Vlach, Rostislav / b. July 3, 1962**
1981-82 WM20 TCH 12 5 9 14 11 S
1987-97 WM CZE 22 2 4 6 12 3B
1987 CC TCH 6 0 1 1 0 —
1988 OG-M TCH 8 0 3 3 4 —

**Vladykin, Nikolai / b. Apr. 1, 1982**
2000 WM18 BLR 6 0 0 0 2 —

**Vlaisavljevich, Dan / b. Dec. 10, 1960**
1980 WM20 USA 5 0 0 0 2 —

**Vlasak, Tomas / b. Feb. 1, 1975**
1994 WM20 CZE 7 3 1 4 2 —
1999-2002 WM CZE 37 12 14 26 20 3G
2004 WCH CZE 2 0 1 1 0 —
~WM All-Star Team/Forward (2000)

**Vlasenkov, Dmitri / b. Jan. 1, 1978**
1997-98 WM20 RUS 13 5 0 5 4 S,B

**Vlasov, Sergei / b. Jan. 31, 1982**
2000 WM18 UKR 6 0 0 0 4 —

**Vlassopoulos, Andreas / b. May 15, 1987**
2005 WM18 USA 6 0 0 0 0 G

**Vlcek, Ivan / b. Oct. 20, 1963**
1995 WM CZE 6 0 0 0 4 —

**Vlcek, Ladislav / b. Sept. 26, 1981**
2001 WM20 CZE 6 1 0 1 2 G

**Vlk, Petr / b. Jan. 7, 1964**
1987-91 WM TCH 20 1 3 4 14 B
1987 CC TCH 5 2 0 2 2 —
1988 OG-M TCH 8 1 3 4 12 —

**Vlk, Vladimir / b. Apr. 23, 1968**
1997-99 WM SVK 14 0 2 2 6 —

**Vnuk, Tomaz / b. Apr. 11, 1970**
2002-03 WM SLO 12 3 9 12 0 —

**Vodicka, Tomas / b. Sept. 10, 1983**
2001 WM18 SVK 6 1 0 1 2 —

**Vodila, Jan / b. Mar. 5, 1961**
1980-81 WM20 TCH 10 11 5 16 12 —
1986 WM TCH 7 0 4 4 2 —

**Vogan, Don / b. Aug. 23, 1929**
1951 WM CAN 6 2 — 2 2 G

**Vogel, Gerd / b. Jan. 16, 1960**
1985 WM GDR 9 0 0 0 4 —

**Vogl, Thomas / b. Feb. 9, 1977**
1996 WM20 GER 5 0 0 0 4 —

**Vogler, Rene / b. Dec. 17, 1982**
2000 WM18 SUI 7 0 1 1 2 —

**Vohralik, Karel / b. Feb. 22, 1945**
1973 WM TCH 10 0 2 2 4 B
1972 OG-M TCH 5 0 1 1 6 B

**Voigt, Dieter / b. Feb. 18, 1939**
1961-67 WM GDR 26 0 1 1 20 —
1968 OG-M GDR 7 0 0 0 6 —

**Voigt, Marius / b. Feb. 20, 1962**
1988 OG-M NOR 6 0 0 0 4 —

**Voigt, Per / b. Feb. 12, 1931**
1949-58 WM NOR 30 8 1 9 28 —
1952 OG-M NOR 6 0 1 1 — —

**Voisard, Gaetan / b. Apr. 13, 1973**
1992 WM20 SUI 7 2 2 4 14 —

**Vojta, Rudolf / b. Apr. 15, 1912 / d. unknown**
1938-49 WM AUT 10 0 — 0 — —
1936 OG-M AUT 5 1 — 1 — —

**Volchkov, Alexander / b. Jan. 11, 1952**
1973 WM URS 10 3 3 6 2 G
1972 SS URS 3 0 0 0 0 2nd

**Volchkov, Alexander / b. Sept. 25, 1977**
1997 WM20 RUS 6 0 2 2 4 B

**Volek, David / b. June 18, 1966**
1986 WM20 TCH 7 4 3 7 6 —
1987-91 WM TCH 20 6 3 9 10 B
1987 CC TCH 6 2 2 4 2 —
1988 OG-M TCH 7 1 2 3 2 —

**Volf, Jaroslav / b. Aug. 8, 1933**
1958-59 WM TCH 14 7 5 12 2 B
1960 OG-M TCH 6 1 3 4 0 —

**Volgin, German / b. Mar. 17, 1963**
1983 WM20 URS 7 11 3 14 10 G
~WM20 All-Star Team/Forward (1983)

**Volk, Josef / b. Dec. 3, 1948**
1971-77 WM FRG 46 2 4 6 45 —
1968-76 OG-M FRG 15 3 0 3 4 B

**Volkov, Leonid / b. Dec. 9, 1934**
1965 WM URS 6 4 1 5 4 G
1964 OG-M URS 7 4 2 6 2 G

**Volkov, Mikhail / b. Mar. 9, 1972**
1991-92 WM20 URS 14 5 8 13 2 G,S

**Volkov, Yuri / b. Apr. 18, 1937**
1963-65 WM URS 10 6 3 9 2 2G

**Volland, Andreas / b. Feb. 19, 1966**
1985-86 WM20 FRG 14 2 3 5 6 —
1993 WM GER 6 1 2 3 6 —

**Vollmer, Bruno / b. June 15, 1967**
1986-87 WM20 SUI 14 1 4 5 16 —

**Volmar, Doug / b. Jan. 9, 1945**
1968 OG-M USA 7 5 0 5 4 —

**Volpert, Guy / b. Nov. 10, 1916 / d. unknown**
1935-50 WM FRA 7 0 0 0 2 —
1936 OG-M FRA 1 0 — 0 — —

**Volrab, Daniel / b. Mar. 11, 1983**
2001 WM18 CZE 7 2 0 2 2 —

**Vomela, Lukas / b. Sept. 25, 1985**
2003 WM18 CZE 6 0 1 1 6 —

**von Arx, Jan / b. Feb. 9, 1978**
1997-98 WM20 SUI 8 0 0 0 0 B

**von Arx, Reto / b. Sept. 13, 1976**
1996 WM20 SUI 6 5 2 7 35 —
1998-2000 WM SUI 22 5 6 11 24 —
2002 OG-M SUI 2 0 1 1 0 —

**von Bethmann-Hollweg, Johann Albrecht / b. Dec. 16, 1911 / d. unknown**
1934 WM GER 7 1 — 1 — B
1936 OG-M GER 6 1 — 1 — —

**Vondracek, Roman / b. Sept. 26, 1984**
2002 WM18 CZE 8 2 3 5 39 B
2003-04 WM20 CZE 13 1 1 2 8 —

**Vondrka, Michal / b. May 17, 1982**
2002 WM20 CZE 7 1 1 2 8 —

**Vopat, Jan / b. Mar. 22, 1973**
1992-93 WM20 TCH 14 6 5 11 8 B
1995 WM CZE 8 0 1 1 6 —
1994 OG-M CZE 8 0 1 1 8 —

**Vorel, Marek / b. Aug. 27, 1977**
1996 WM20 CZE 6 0 0 0 4 —

**Vorobel, Slavomir / b. Oct. 26, 1971**
1996 WM SVK 5 0 0 0 0 —

**Vorobyov, Ilya / b. Mar. 16, 1975**
1995 WM20 RUS 7 1 0 1 4 S

**Vorobyov, Pavel / b. May 5, 1982**
2000 WM18 RUS 6 2 6 8 10 S
2001 WM20 RUS 7 2 3 5 6 —

**Vorobyov, Vladimir / b. Oct. 2, 1972**
1995-96 WM RUS 14 0 4 4 8 —

**Voskar, Jozef / b. Sept. 25, 1971**
1998 WM SVK 6 1 0 1 2 —

**Vosta, Ondrej / b. June 4, 1968**
1988 WM20 TCH 5 0 1 1 4 —

**Vostrikov, Sergei / b. Jan. 16, 1964**
1984 WM20 URS 7 0 1 1 4 G

**Vostry, Alexander / b. Apr. 20, 1958**
1977 WM20 TCH 7 1 2 3 7 B

**Voves, Franz / b. Feb. 28, 1953**
1976 OG-M AUT 5 3 2 5 0 —

**Voytsekhivski, Oleksi / b. May 10, 1987**
2004 WM20 UKR 6 0 0 0 4 —

**Voyush, Andri / b. Apr. 28, 1976**
1996 WM20 UKR 6 0 0 0 0 —
2000 WM UKR 6 0 0 0 0 —

**Vozar, Ferenc / b. Apr. 19, 1945**
1976 OG-M FRG 5 0 0 0 2 B

**Vozhakov, Yuri / b. Feb. 5, 1959**
1978-79 WM20 URS 13 2 4 6 10 2G

**Vrabec, Thomas / b. Oct. 22, 1966**
1986 WM20 SUI 7 2 1 3 2 —
1987-93 WM SUI 26 4 4 8 16 —
1988-92 OG-M SUI 13 2 6 8 18 —

**Vujtek, Vladimir / b. Feb. 17, 1972**
1997 WM CZE 8 7 7 14 31 B
~WM All-Star Team/Forward (1997)

**Vuori, Ari / b. June 9, 1962**
1986-90 WM FIN 21 2 2 4 16 —

**Vuorinen, Jouni / b. Feb. 11, 1963**
1983 WM20 FIN 7 0 1 1 6 —

**Vuorinen, Pasi / b. Jan. 11, 1935**
1958 WM FIN 5 0 0 0 4 —

**Vuorivirta, Juha / b. Mar. 5, 1976**
1995-96 WM20 FIN 13 0 1 1 4 —

**Vyazmikin, Igor / b. Jan. 8, 1966**
1984-86 WM20 URS 14 11 10 21 12 2G
~WM20 All-Star Team/Forward (1986)

**Vyborny, David / b. Jan. 22, 1975**
1993-94 WM20 TCH 14 8 14 22 18 —
1996-2007 WM CZE 104 27 36 63 56 5G,S,2B
2004 WCH CZE 5 0 0 0 2 —
2006 OG-M CZE 8 1 3 4 0 B
~WM All-Star Team/Forward (2006), WM20 All-Star Team/Forward (1994)

**Vykoukal, Jiri / b. Mar. 11, 1971**
1989-90 WM20 TCH 14 0 8 8 20 2B
1995-99 WM CZE 45 4 5 9 24 2G,2B
1996 WCH CZE 1 0 0 0 2 —
1994 OG-M CZE 8 1 3 4 4 —

**Vyshedkevich, Sergei / b. Jan. 3, 1975**
1995 WM20 RUS 7 1 6 7 4 S
2002-05 WM RUS 25 1 1 2 16 S,B

**Vytisk, Jan / b. July 20, 1981**
1999 WM18 CZE 7 0 1 1 8 —
2001 WM20 CZE 7 0 0 0 4 G

**Wackerle, Sylvester / b. July 26, 1937**
1963 WM FRG 6 0 1 1 0 —
1964 OG-M FRG 7 2 0 2 4 —

**Waddell, Don / b. Aug. 19, 1958**
1977-78 WM20 USA 13 7 2 9 12 —

**Wager, Roman / b. Feb. 20, 1963**
1982 WM20 SUI 7 1 1 2 10 —
1987-95 WM SUI 22 3 3 6 12 —
1988 OG-M SUI 6 1 0 1 4 —

**Wagner, Bernd / b. July 30, 1964**
1983-84 WM20 FRG 14 1 0 1 12 —
1989-91 WM FRG 15 1 2 3 6 —

**Wagner, Hans / b. Jan. 22, 1923**
1949-57 WM AUT 13 1 — 1 — —
1956 OG-M AUT 6 1 0 1 0 —

**Wagnild, Spencer / b. Oct. 27, 1911 / d. unknown**
1938-39 WM USA 15 1 — 1 — S

**Wahlsten, Jali / b. June 20, 1963**
1983 WM20 FIN 7 7 3 10 0 —

**Wahlsten, Juhani / b. Jan. 13, 1938**
1959-69 WM FIN 37 7 9 16 8 —
1960-68 OG-M FIN 20 7 3 10 8 —
~IIHF Hall of Fame

**Wahlsten, Sami / b. Nov. 25, 1967**
1986-87 WM20 FIN 14 7 10 17 0 G

**Waibel, Jon / b. May 19, 1982**
1999-2000 WM18 USA 12 3 1 4 4 —

**Waidacher, Ludwig / b. Aug. 22, 1960**
1980 WM20 SUI 5 0 0 0 2 —

**Waitl, Leonhard / b. Apr. 5, 1939**
1959-67 WM FRG 27 3 6 9 36 —
1960-68 OG-M FRG 20 3 1 4 34 —

**Wakabayashi, Osamu / b. Dec. 23, 1944**
1972-80 OG-M JPN 10 5 3 8 2 —

**Wakasa, Koji / b. July 12, 1953**
1976-80 OG-M JPN 10 0 0 0 16 —

**Walbye, Knut / b. Jan. 9, 1968**
1990-92 WM NOR 14 0 2 2 4 —

**Walbye, Per Odvar / b. May 15, 1971**
1991 WM20 NOR 8 0 5 5 4 —

**Walbye, Willy / b. unknown**
1958-59 WM NOR 15 5 2 7 4 —

**Walder, Raymond / b. Mar. 7, 1967**
1986-87 WM20 SUI 14 2 4 6 14 —
1991 WM SUI 10 0 1 1 6 —

**Waldschmidt, Andre / b. Dec. 21, 1927**
1950 WM BEL 4 4 0 4 4 —

**Waldschmidt, Robert / b. Dec. 21, 1927**
1950 WM BEL 4 1 0 1 0 —

**Walker, Julian / b. Sept. 10, 1986**
2005-06 WM20 SUI 12 2 3 5 6 —

**Walker, Norm / b. unknown**
1947-49 WM USA 15 2 — 2 4 B

**Walker, Scott / b. July 19, 1973**
1999-2005 WM CAN 26 5 6 11 28 S

**Wallace, Tim / b. Aug. 6, 1984**
2002 WM18 USA 8 2 5 7 6 G

**Wallenberg, Patrik / b. Jan. 4, 1977**
1996-97 WM20 SWE 13 0 2 2 10 S

**Wallgren, Jonas / b. Julu 9, 1988**
2006 WM18 SWE 6 0 0 0 4 —

**Wallin, Anders / b. Sept. 15, 1959**
1978 WM20 SWE 7 1 2 3 0 S

**Wallin, Jesse / b. Mar. 10, 1978**
1997-98 WM20 CAN 11 0 0 0 10 G

**Wallin, Niclas / b. Feb. 20, 1975**
2008 WM SWE 7 2 2 4 33 —

**Wallin, Peter / b. Apr. 30, 1957**
1979 WM SWE 8 1 3 4 2 B

**Wallin, Peter / b. June 21, 1977**
1997 WM20 SWE 6 1 0 1 2 —

**Wallin, Viktor / b. Jan. 17, 1980**
1999-2000 WM20 SWE 13 1 7 8 2 —

**Walter, Fritz / b. Feb. 21, 1924**
1947-49 WM AUT 13 4 — 4 — B
1948 OG-M AUT 8 2 — 2 — —

**Walter, Jaroslav / b. Jan. 6, 1939**
1963 WM TCH 7 3 1 4 8 B
1964 OG-M TCH 7 3 4 7 0 B

**Walter, Martin / b. Oct. 23, 1983**
2003 WM20 GER 6 0 0 0 4 —

**Walter, Ryan / b. Apr. 23, 1958**
1978 WM20 CAN 6 5 3 8 4 B
1979-82 WM CAN 20 5 6 11 6 B

**Waltin, Mats / b. Oct. 7, 1953**
1975-85 WM SWE 72 3 11 14 18 2S,3B
1976-81 CC SWE 10 0 1 1 2 —
1980-84 OG-M SWE 14 3 6 9 6 2B
~WM All-Star Team/Defence (1976)

**Walz, Thorsten / b. Jan. 7, 1977**
1997 WM20 GER 6 0 0 0 16 —

**Walz, Wes / b. May 15, 1970**
1990 WM20 CAN 7 2 3 5 0 G

**Wandell, Tom / b. Jan. 29, 1987**
2004 WM18 SWE 6 0 0 0 4 —

**Warburton, Ralph / b. Feb. 7, 1924**
1948 OG-M USA 8 16 5 21 6 —

**Ward, Jason / b. Jan. 16, 1979**
1998-99 WM20 CAN 14 2 1 3 10 S

**Ware, Jeff / b. May 19, 1977**
1997 WM20 CAN 7 0 0 0 6 G

**Warner, Jim / b. Mar. 26, 1954**
1975-78 WM USA 30 5 11 16 22 —

**Warrener, Rhett / b. Jan. 27, 1976**
1996 WM20 CAN 6 0 0 0 4 G

**Warriner, Todd / b. Jan. 3, 1974**
1994 OG-M CAN 4 1 1 2 0 S

**Warwick, Bill / b. Nov. 17, 1925 / d. Oct. 3, 2007**
1955 WM CAN 8 16 7 23 10 G
~WM IIHF Directorate Best Forward (1955)

**Warwick, Dick / b. Apr. 28, 1928**
1955 WM CAN 8 4 1 5 4 G

**Warwick, Grant / b. Oct. 11, 1921 / d. Sept. 27, 1999**
1955 WM CAN 8 6 7 13 2 G

**Wasama, Jorma / b. Jan. 2, 1943**
1962-65 WM FIN 21 4 4 8 8 —
1964 OG-M FIN 7 0 1 1 4 —

**Wassereck, Joe / b. Sept. 15, 1963**
1982-83 WM20 FRG 10 5 1 6 6 —

**Wassermann, Josef / b. May 15, 1967**
1985-86 WM20 FRG 14 0 1 1 8 —

**Wastlund, Niclas / b. Apr. 18, 1982**
2000 WM18 SWE 6 2 0 2 0 B

**Watanabe, Kazuo / b. unknown**
1957 WM JPN 7 1 — 1 — —

**Watkins, Ray / b. 1906 / d. unknown**
1934 WM CAN 4 0 — 0 — G

**Watson, Blake / b. Oct. 18, 1903 / d. unknown**
1931 WM CAN 6 7 — 7 — G

**Watson, Harry "Moose" / b. July 14, 1898 / d. Sept. 11, 1957**
1924 OG-M CAN 5 36 — 36 2 G
~IIHF Hall of Fame

**Watson, Jim / b. Aug. 19, 1952**
1976 CC CAN 2 0 0 0 2 1st

**Watt, George / b. Sept. 18, 1924**
1951 WM GBR 3 0 — 0 0 —

**Watt, Mike / b. Mar. 31, 1976**
1996 WM20 CAN 6 1 2 3 6 G

**Watt, Robert / b. June 24, 1927**
1950 WM CAN 7 6 3 9 2 G
1952 OG-M CAN 8 3 1 4 2 G

**Watters, Tim / b. July 25, 1959**
1983 WM CAN 10 0 0 0 8 B
1980-88 OG-M CAN 14 1 2 3 2 —

**Watzke, Nils / b. June 3, 1981**
1999 WM18 GER 6 0 1 1 6 —

**Weber, Christian / b. Feb. 19, 1964**
1991-95 WM SUI 32 3 5 8 6 —

**Weber, Marc / b. July 5, 1973**
1992 WM20 SUI 7 3 1 4 4 —

**Weberg, Mats / b. July 17, 1989**
2006 WM18 NOR 6 1 0 1 10 —

**Wechselberger, Fritz / b. Sept. 9, 1938**
1964 OG-M AUT 7 1 0 1 0 —

**Wedgewood, Clarence / b. unknown / d. unknown**
1931 WM GBR — 0 — 0 — —

**Wehrli, Michel / b. 1934**
1953-59 WM SUI 9 1 2 3 0 B

**Weide, Rudolf / b. unknown**
1954-55 WM FRG 8 3 0 3 12 —

**Weide, Erich / b. July 3, 1949**
1973 WM FRG 8 0 0 0 0 —

**Weight, Doug / b. Jan. 21, 1971**
1991 WM20 USA 7 5 14 19 4 —
1993-2005 WM USA 21 1 15 16 28 —
1996-2004 WCH USA 12 4 4 8 16 1st
1998-2006 OG-M USA 16 0 8 8 10 S

**Weigl, Peter / b. Jan. 19, 1963**
1983 WM20 FRG 7 0 0 0 6 —

**Weiner, Bela / b. 1896 / d. unknown**
1931-33 WM HUN 9 4 — 4 1 —
1928 OG-M HUN 3 1 — 1 — —

**Weingartner, Klaus / b. Aug. 29, 1944**
1968 OG-M AUT 5 1 0 1 4 —

**Weingartner, Sepp / b. Apr. 19, 1932**
1959 WM SUI 8 0 0 0 0 —
1956 OG-M SUI 1 0 0 0 0 —

**Weinrich, Eric / b. Dec. 19, 1966**
1985-86 WM20 USA 14 2 1 3 12 B
1991-2004 WM USA 57 3 15 18 48 B
1991-2004 WCH USA 10 0 0 0 2 2nd
1988 OG-M USA 3 0 0 0 0 —

**Weinstock, Ulf / b. Aug. 10, 1952**
1975-79 WM SWE 37 5 3 8 8 S,2B
1980 OG-M SWE 7 1 3 4 0 B

**Weis, Kasper / b. July 8, 1986**
2004 WM18 DEN 6 0 1 1 6 —

**Weisenbach, Heinz / b. Aug. 30, 1945**
1967-71 WM FRG 13 1 0 1 12 —
1968 OG-M FRG 6 0 0 0 4 —

**Weiss, Alfred / b. Jan. 27, 1964**
1983-84 WM20 FRG 14 0 1 1 10 —

**Weiss, Stephen / b. Apr. 3, 1983**
2002 WM20 CAN 6 3 1 4 6 S

**Weissberg, Karol / b. Feb. 5, 1909 / d. Oct. 2, 1974**
1930 WM POL 3 0 — 0 — —

**Weissman, Ondrej / b. Oct. 28, 1959**
1978-79 WM20 TCH 12 3 1 4 12 S

**Weiszdorn, Thomas / b. June 11, 1988**
2006 WM18 GER 6 3 0 3 2 —

**Welch, Dan / b. Feb. 23, 1981**
1999 WM18 USA 6 0 3 3 6 —

**Wellen, Remigius / b. unknown**
1961 WM FRG 4 0 0 0 4 —

**Wellman, Ken / b. June 2, 1930**
1960 OG-M AUS 6 0 0 0 6 —

**Wells, Jay / b. May 18, 1959**
1986 WM CAN 10 0 2 2 16 B

**Wells, Mark / b. Sept. 18, 1957**
1980 OG-M USA 7 2 1 3 0 G

**Wellwood, Kyle / b. May 16, 1983**
2003 WM20 CAN 6 1 4 5 0 S

**Welsh, Ab / b. 1914 / d. unknown**
1934 WM CAN 4 4 — 4 — G

**Wennerberg, Mattias / b. Aug. 6, 1981**
1999 WM18 SWE 7 4 2 6 12 S
2001 WM20 SWE 2 0 1 1 6 —

**Werenka, Brad / b. Feb. 12, 1969**
1994 OG-M CAN 8 2 2 4 8 S

**Werlen, Marc / b. Jan. 12, 1978**
1998 WM20 SUI 7 0 0 0 4 B

**Wernblom, Magnus / b. Feb. 3, 1973**
1993 WM20 SWE 7 2 3 5 24 S

**Werner, Ryszard / b. Feb. 2, 1912 / d. Aug. 31, 1958**
1933-39 WM POL 9 0 — 0 0 —

**Werner, Steve / b. Aug. 8, 1984**
2002 WM18 USA 8 3 4 7 2 G
2004 WM20 USA 6 5 0 5 2 G

**Werner, Thomas / b. Apr. 14, 1966**
1986 WM20 FRG 7 1 0 1 4 —
1991 WM FRG 10 1 0 1 0 —

**Wesley, Glen / b. Oct. 2, 1968**
1987 WM20 CAN 6 2 1 3 6 —
1996 WM CAN 8 0 1 1 4 S

**Wespi, Peter / b. Mar. 22, 1943**
1964 OG-M SUI 7 1 0 1 2 —

**Westby, Jim / b. Mar. 5, 1937**
1959-63 WM USA 16 1 1 2 2 —
1964 OG-M USA 7 2 0 2 4 —

**Westerlund, Gosta / b. Feb. 5, 1936**
1958-59 WM SWE 13 4 4 8 2 B

**Westin, Daniel / b. June 8, 1981**
1999 WM18 SWE 6 0 1 1 4 S

**Westin, Roland / b. Oct. 22, 1964**
1984 WM20 SWE 7 2 1 3 4 —

**Westlund, Andreas / b. Mar. 27, 1978**
1998 WM20 SWE 7 0 0 0 4 —

**Westlund, Tommy / b. Dec. 29, 1974**
1998 WM SWE 1 0 0 0 0 G

**Westrum, Erik / b. July 26, 1979**
2004 WM USA 9 3 2 5 6 B

**Westrum, Patrick / b. Mar. 3, 1948**
1978 WM USA 10 1 1 2 5 —

**Wetzel, Philipp / b. June 5, 1985**
2003 WM18 SUI 6 0 1 1 8 —

**Wharton, Kyle / b. Mar. 3, 1986**
2004 WM18 CAN 7 0 0 0 8 —

**Wheeldon, Simon / b. Aug. 30, 1966**
1998-2001 WM AUT 14 3 5 8 14 —
1998-2002 OG-M AUT 8 1 2 3 12 —

**White, Bill / b. Aug. 26, 1939**
1972 SS CAN 7 1 1 2 8 1st

**White, Bob / b. July 22, 1935**
1956 OG-M CAN 8 1 1 2 2 B

**White, Patrick / b. Jan. 20, 1989**
2007 WM18 USA 7 3 2 5 6 S

**Whitehead, Tony / b. 1936**
1962 WM GBR 5 0 0 0 4 —

**Whitfield, Trent / b. June 17, 1977**
1997 WM20 CAN 7 1 0 1 4 G

**Wichser, Adrian / b. Mar. 18, 1980**
1998-2000 WM20 SUI 20 8 5 13 6 B
2002-2007 WM SUI 31 5 9 14 2 —
2006 OG-M SUI 6 0 0 0 2 —

**Wick, Marcel / b. Mar. 28, 1958**
1978 WM20 SUI 6 0 0 0 2 —

**Wickberg, Anders / b. Jan. 17, 1963**
1983 WM20 SWE 6 2 2 4 8 —

**Wickberg, Hakan / b. Feb. 3, 1943**
1965-74 WM SWE 57 15 15 30 4 2S,4B
1968-72 OG-M SWE 12 5 5 10 0 —

**Wideroe, Paul Ole / b. unknown**
1983 WM20 NOR 5 0 0 0 0 —

**Widing, Daniel / b. Apr. 13, 1982**
2000 WM18 SWE 6 0 2 2 10 B
2001-02 WM20 SWE 14 3 3 6 16 —
2008 WM SWE 3 0 0 0 0 —

**Widing, Juha / b. July 4, 1947**
1976 CC SWE 5 1 1 2 0 —

**Widmer, Daniel / b. Apr. 29, 1953**
1976 OG-M SUI 5 1 2 3 0 —

**Wiecek, Maksymilian / b. Sept. 18, 1920 / d. Dec. 28, 2006**
1948 OG-M POL 3 0 — 0 — —

**Wieck, Doug / b. Mar. 12, 1965**
1985 WM20 USA 7 1 0 1 10 —

**Wiedemann, Anton / b. Dec. 30, 1911 / d. unknown**
1933-38 WM GER 10 0 — 0 — —
1936 OG-M GER 6 1 — 1 — —

**Wiedmer, Thomas / b. Apr. 19, 1966**
1986 WM20 SUI 7 0 2 2 0 —

**Wiegl, Peter / b. Jan. 19, 1963**
1982 WM20 FRG 7 0 0 0 6 —

**Wieland, Markus / b. May 26, 1976**
1994-95 WM20 GER 14 1 0 1 6 —
1995-97 WM GER 19 0 2 2 2 —
1998 OG-M GER 4 0 2 2 6 —

**Wiele, Svend / b. Jan. 21, 1981**
1999 WM18 GER 6 0 1 1 2 —

**Wielgus, Janusz / b. Oct. 30, 1961**
1986 WM POL 4 1 0 1 4 —

**Wieloch, Slawomir / b. Jan. 17, 1969**
1988 WM20 POL 7 0 1 1 4 —
1992 OG-M POL 7 0 0 0 2 —

**Wiemer, Jim / b. Jan. 9, 1961**
1980 WM20 CAN 5 2 2 4 2 —

**Wiitala, Marty / b. Feb. 24, 1964**
1984 WM20 USA 7 2 3 5 4 —

**Wikberg, Anders / b. Jan. 17, 1963**
1982 WM20 SWE 4 1 1 2 0 —

**Wikner, Fred / b. Jan. 1, 1986**
2004 WM18 SWE 6 0 4 4 12 —

**Wikstrom, Mikael / b. Feb. 14, 1964**
1984 WM20 SWE 7 1 2 3 2 —

**Wikstrom, Sami / b. Aug. 9, 1967**
1987 WM20 FIN 3 1 0 1 0 G

**Wilczek, Sylwester / b. Dec. 10, 1936**
1957-66 WM POL 29 0 0 0 4 —
1964 OG-M POL 7 2 4 6 2 —

**Wild, Karl / b. Nov. 23, 1917 / d. unknown**
1937-39 WM GER 13 2 0 2 0 —
1952 OG-M FRG 6 0 0 0 — —

**Wild, Martin / b. Dec. 2, 1952**
1978 WM FRG 10 2 2 4 2 —
1972-80 OG-M FRG 7 0 2 2 0 —

**Wilfan, Franz / b. Oct. 14, 1985**
2004 WM20 AUT 6 0 0 0 2 —

**Wilhelm, Stefan / b. July 12, 1983**
2003 WM20 GER 6 0 1 1 2 —

**Wilkie, David / b. May 30, 1974**
1993-94 WM20 USA 13 2 3 5 2 —

**Wilkins, Dave / b. Apr. 10, 1957**
1977 WM20 USA 7 0 1 1 6 —

**Williams, Bobby / b. Oct. 19, 1985**
2003 WM18 SWE 6 2 0 2 4 —

**Williams, Brian / b. June 27, 1963**
1986 WM USA 8 0 3 3 4 —

**Williams, David / b. Aug. 25, 1967**
1991-92 WM USA 15 0 3 3 16 —

**Williams, Jack / b. unknown**
1961 WM USA 7 2 2 4 2 —

**Williams, Jason / b. Aug. 11, 1980**
2006 WM CAN 9 2 5 7 2 —

**Williams, Martin / b. Oct. 13, 1975**
1995 WM20 GER 7 1 0 1 2 —

**Williams, Nigel / b. Apr. 18, 1988**
2006 WM18 USA 6 0 0 0 18 G

**Williams, Tom / b. Apr. 17, 1940 / d. Nov. 6, 2006**
1959 WM USA 8 7 2 9 0 —
1960 OG-M USA 7 4 6 10 2 G

**Williams, Warren "Butch" / b. Sept. 11, 1952**
1977 WM USA 10 4 6 10 22 —
1976 CC USA 3 0 3 3 2 —

**Williamson, Guy / b. 1906 / d. unknown**
1931 WM CAN 6 2 — 2 — G

**Willis, Shane / b. June 13, 1977**
1997 WM20 CAN 7 0 0 0 0 G

**Willmann, Dieter / b. Jan. 4, 1963**
1990 WM FRG 8 0 2 2 2 —

**Willsie, Brian / b. Mar. 16, 1978**
1998 WM20 CAN 7 0 2 2 4 —

**Wilson, Carey / b. May 11, 1962**
1982 WM20 CAN 7 4 1 5 6 G
1984 OG-M CAN 7 3 2 5 6 —

**Wilson, Doug / b. unknown**
1951 WM GBR 6 0 — 0 12 —

**Wilson, Doug / b. July 5, 1957**
1984 CC CAN 7 2 1 3 4 1st

**Wilson, Gord / b. 1917 / d. unknown**
1937 WM CAN 9 7 2 9 2 G

**Wilson, Harold "Hobb" / b. unknown / d. unknown**
1934 WM CAN 4 0 — 0 — G

**Wilson, Landon / b. Mar. 13, 1975**
1995 WM20 USA 7 3 2 5 37 —
2001 WM USA 9 1 1 2 4 —

**Wilson, Ron / b. May 28, 1955**
1975-87 WM USA 28 5 9 14 18 —

**Wilson, Ronnie / b. unknown / d. unknown**
1938 WM GBR 2 0 — 0 — S

**Winchester, Brad / b. Aug. 1, 1981**
1999 WM18 USA 6 0 3 3 6 —
2000 WM20 USA 7 0 0 0 6 —

**Winger, Helfried / b. Oct. 23, 1921 / d. unknown**
1947 WM AUT 5 2 — 2 — B
1948 OG-M AUT 3 0 — 0 — —

**Winiarski, Wojciech / b. Aug. 31, 1971**
1990 WM20 POL 7 0 1 1 2 —

**Winkler, Benjamin / b. Feb. 22, 1977**
1997 WM20 SUI 5 1 1 2 4 —
1999 WM SUI 6 0 0 0 4 —

**Winkler, Erich / b. Feb. 17, 1935**
1964 OG-M AUT 7 0 2 2 2 —

**Winnes, Chris / b. Feb. 12, 1968**
1992 WM USA 6 3 2 5 4 —

**Wirz, Valentin / b. Sept. 9, 1981**
1999 WM18 SUI 7 1 1 2 2 —
2003-07 WM SUI 24 2 3 5 2 —

**Wise, Alston "Stoney" / b. Oct. 29, 1904 / d. Sept. 23, 1984**
1932 OG-M CAN 5 2 0 2 0 G

**Wishart, Ty / b. May 19, 1988**
2006 WM18 CAN 7 0 0 0 14 —

**Wist, Bernhard / b. Apr. 10, 1961**
1980 WM20 SUI 1 0 0 0 0 —

**Witt, Brendan / b. Feb. 20, 1975**
1994 WM20 CAN 7 0 0 0 6 G

**Wittmann, Matthias / b. Aug. 17, 1984**
2002 WM18 GER 8 1 0 1 10 —

**Wittmann, Theo / b. June 4, 1969**
1995 WM SUI 5 0 0 0 4 —

**Wittwer, Bruno / b. Dec. 15, 1949**
1972 WM SUI 10 3 2 5 2 —

**Wittwer, Otto / b. Dec. 24, 1937**
1964 OG-M SUI 7 0 0 0 2 —

**Wlodarczyk, Zdzislaw / b. Mar. 15, 1950**
1976 WM POL 6 0 0 0 5 —

**Wohlwend, Christian / b. Jan. 4, 1977**
1996 WM20 SUI 6 0 0 0 10 —

**Wolak, Mike / b. Apr. 29, 1968**
1986-87 WM20 USA 14 0 6 6 10 B

**Wolanin, Craig / b. July 27, 1967**
1987-94 WM USA 27 4 3 7 58 —
1991 CC USA 8 0 2 2 2 2nd

**Wold, Ketil / b. Mar. 20, 1972**
1999-2001 WM NOR 18 0 0 0 8 —

**Wolf, Manfred / b. Mar. 26, 1957**
1981-87 WM FRG 44 7 7 14 32 —
1984 CC FRG 5 0 0 0 0 —
1984-88 OG-M FRG 12 3 2 5 0 —

**Wolf, Walter / b. unknown**
1981 WM20 AUT 5 1 0 1 4 —

**Wolkowski, Andrzej / b. Feb. 14, 1913 / d. Mar. 4, 1995**
1933-47 WM POL 37 20 2 22 2 —
1936 OG-M POL 3 3 — 3 — —

**Wood, Dan / b. Oct. 31, 1962**
1984 OG-M CAN 7 0 1 1 2 —

**Wood, Randy / b. Oct. 12, 1963**
1986-89 WM USA 14 1 1 2 10 —
1991 CC USA 3 0 2 2 0 2nd

**Wood, Tom / b. June 13, 1927**
1951 WM CAN 6 1 — 1 2 G

**Woodburn, Steve / b. Oct. 24, 1963**
1992-98 WM FRA 41 1 1 2 30 —
1988-94 OG-M FRA 11 2 2 4 10 —

**Woodman, Allan "Huck" / b. Mar. 11, 1899 / d. Mar. 17, 1963**
1920 OG-M CAN 2 1 — 1 — G

**Woods, Paul / b. Apr. 12, 1955**
1979 WM CAN 8 0 0 0 2 —

**Woog, Doug / b. Jan. 26, 1944**
1967 WM USA 7 1 2 3 4 —

**Woolley, Jason / b. July 27, 1969**
1992 WM CAN 6 1 2 3 2 —
1992 OG-M CAN 8 0 5 5 4 S

**Woozley, Pete / b. unknown / d. unknown**
1938 WM GBR 1 0 — 0 — S

**Worle, Tobias / b. Aug. 1, 1984**
2002 WM18 GER 8 0 1 1 0 —

**Woywitka, Jeff / b. Sept. 1, 1983**
2003 WM20 CAN 6 1 1 2 0 S

**Wretling, Sune / b. Jan. 2, 1939 / d. Apr. 26, 2007**
1960 OG-M SWE 6 0 0 0 2 —

**Wright, Jamie / b. May 13, 1976**
1996 WM20 CAN 6 1 2 3 2 G
2002 WM CAN 7 1 1 2 2 —

**Wright, Pete / b. Jan. 25, 1927**
1950 WM CAN 7 2 2 4 4 G

**Wright, Tyler / b. Apr. 6, 1973**
1992-93 WM20 CAN 14 4 3 7 22 G
2002 WM CAN 7 0 2 2 33 —

**Wrobel, Adolf / b. Oct. 19, 1930**
1955 WM POL 4 0 0 0 0 —
1956 OG-M POL 5 0 0 0 2 —

**Wrobel, Alfred / b. Nov. 29, 1927 / d. Sept. 24, 1993**
1955 WM POL 8 3 0 3 0 —
1952-56 OG-M POL 12 2 0 2 2 —

**Wrobel, Antoni / b. Feb. 11, 1923 / d. unknown**
1952 OG-M POL 6 2 0 2 — —

**Wrobel, Bartolomiej / b. Aug. 12, 1977**
1997 WM20 POL 6 0 1 1 6 —

**Wrobel, Dirk / b. June 18, 1983**
2001 WM18 GER 6 0 1 1 4 —
2003 WM20 GER 6 0 2 2 6 —

**Wroblewski, John / b. May 26, 1981**
1999 WM18 USA 6 0 1 1 2 —

**Wunsch, Josef / b. Oct. 4, 1952**
1973 WM FRG 4 0 0 0 2 —

**Wuolio, Jukka / b. Mar. 5, 1927 / d. June 27, 2001**
1951 WM FIN 6 1 — 1 2 —
1952 OG-M FIN 7 0 2 2 — —

**Wurmbrandt, Rudolf / b. Sept. 20, 1922 / d. unknown**
1947-57 WM AUT 21 14 — 14 2 B
1948 OG-M AUT 5 3 — 3 — —

**Wust, Mathias / b. May 20, 1980**
2000 WM20 SUI 5 0 0 0 6 —

**Wuthrich, Bernhard / b. unknown**
1978 WM20 SUI 6 0 0 0 14 —

**Wuthrich, Markus / b. May 14, 1979**
1998 WM20 SUI 7 1 0 1 2 B

**Wylde, Charles / b. unknown / d. unknown**
1928 OG-M GBR 4 0 — 0 — —

**Wylie, Bill / b. July 15, 1928 / d. Nov. 24, 1983**
1962 WM CAN 7 2 8 10 0 S

**Wyman, Bob / b. Apr. 27, 1909 / d. unknown**
1935-39 WM GBR 19 1 — 1 — S,B
1936 OG-M GBR 1 0 0 0 2 G

**Xandopulo, Georgi / b. unknown**
1998 WM20 KAZ 7 0 1 1 0 —

**Yachmenev, Vitali / b. Jan. 8, 1975**
1995 WM20 RUS 7 3 4 7 2 S

**Yackel, Ken / b. Mar. 5, 1930 / d. July 12, 1991**
1952 OG-M USA 8 6 3 9 — S

**Yahata, Shin / b. May 9, 1974**
1998-2002 WM JPN 18 4 3 7 20 —
1998 OG-M JPN 4 2 3 5 4 —

**Yakhanov, Andrei / b. Feb. 23, 1973**
1993 WM20 RUS 7 0 3 3 10 —
1999 WM RUS 6 0 0 0 8 —

**Yakovenko, Olexander / b. Aug. 15, 1979**
1996 WM20 UKR 6 1 3 4 0 —
2000 WM UKR 6 0 0 0 0 —

**Yakovlev, Pavel / b. Mar. 29, 1980**
1998-2000 WM20 KAZ 20 2 2 4 12 —

**Yakubov, Mikhail / b. Feb. 16, 1982**
2000 WM18 RUS 6 1 5 6 2 S
2001 WM20 RUS 7 0 1 1 6 —

**Yakubov, Ravil / b. July 26, 1970**
1995 WM RUS 6 0 1 1 2 —

**Yakushev, Alexander / b. Jan. 2, 1947**
1967-79 WM URS 83 60 33 93 24 7G,2S,B
1972 SS URS 8 7 4 11 4 2nd
1972-76 OG-M URS 10 3 7 10 6 2G
~IIHF Hall of Fame
~WM IIHF Directorate Best Forward (1975), WM All-Star Team/Forward (1974, 1975)

**Yakushev, Viktor / b. Nov. 16, 1937 / d. July 5, 2001**
1959-67 WM URS 42 21 20 41 14 4G,S,B
1960-64 OG-M URS 14 8 7 15 0 G,B
~OG-M All-Star Team/Forward (1964)

**Yakushyn, Dmitri / b. Jan. 21, 1978**
2000 WM UKR 6 1 1 2 6 —

**Yamada, Toshiniko / b. Apr. 16, 1932**
1957 WM JPN 7 0 — 0 — —
1960 OG-M JPN 6 6 2 8 2 —

**Yamanaka, Takeshi / b. Jan. 30, 1971**
1998-99 WM JPN 6 1 3 4 6 —
1998 OG-M JPN 4 0 2 2 6 —

**Yamazaki, Fumio / b. Aug. 7, 1947**
1972 OG-M JPN 3 0 2 2 2 —

**Yamazaki, Koichi / b. May 1, 1976**
2002-03 WM JPN 9 0 1 1 4 —

**Yanchenko, Olexander / b. June 2, 1981**
1999 WM18 UKR 5 4 0 4 6 —
2000 WM20 UKR 7 1 2 3 4 —

**Yankovich, Igor / b. Apr. 29, 1975**
1995 WM20 UKR 7 3 0 3 12 —

**Yanovski, Sergei / b. June 3, 1987**
2004 WM18 BLR 6 0 1 0 0 —

**Yaprintsev, Nikolai / b. May 20, 1976**
1996 WM20 UKR 6 2 1 3 2 —

**Yarchuk, Artyom / b. May 3, 1990 / d. Sept. 7, 2011**
2008 WM18 RUS 6 2 0 2 6 S
~perished in Yaroslavl plane crash

**Yaremchuk, Ken / b. Jan. 1, 1964**
1988 OG-M CAN 8 3 3 6 2 —

**Yaroslavtsev, Viktor / b. July 16, 1945**
1967 WM URS 5 1 1 2 4 G

**Yashin, Alexei / b. Nov. 5, 1973**
1992-93 WM20 RUS 10 5 2 7 6 G
1993-2005 WM RUS 59 24 16 40 59 G,B
1996-2004 WCH RUS 9 1 4 5 10 —
1998-2006 OG-M RUS 20 5 7 12 4 S,B

**Yashin, Sergei / b. Mar. 6, 1962**
1981-82 WM20 URS 12 10 3 13 6 B
1985-89 WM URS 27 4 3 7 16 2G,B
1984 CC URS 6 0 4 4 0 —
1988 OG-M URS 8 3 1 4 4 G

**Yawney, Trent / b. Sept. 29, 1965**
1991-92 WM CAN 16 2 5 7 8 S
1988 OG-M CAN 8 1 1 2 6 —

**Yderstrom, Dick / b. Aug. 28, 1947**
1969-73 WM SWE 10 0 4 4 6 2S

**Yefremov, Alexei / b. Jan. 13, 1985**
2003 WM18 KAZ 6 0 1 1 6 —

**Yegorov, Igor / b. Jan. 20, 1987**
2002 WM18 UKR 6 0 0 0 0 —

**Yellowhorn, Colton / b. May 5, 1987**
2005 WM18 CAN 6 2 0 2 0 S

**Yellowlees, Norm / b. Mar. 17, 1912 / d. Oct. 14, 1991**
1935 WM CAN 7 10 — 10 — G

**Yelovikov, Vladimir / b. May 21, 1966**
1985 WM20 URS 7 2 3 5 4 B

**Yemeleyev, Igor / b. Mar. 7, 1981**
2006 WM RUS 7 1 2 3 8 —

**Yemelin, Anatoli / b. Oct. 3, 1964**
1994 WM RUS 6 2 0 2 8 —

**Yemelyanenko, Yevgeni / b. Apr. 11, 1981**
1999 WM18 UKR 6 0 1 1 18 —
2000 WM20 UKR 7 0 0 0 2 —

**Yepanchintsev, Vadim / b. Mar. 16, 1976**
1995-96 WM20 RUS 14 2 6 8 36 S,B
1997 WM RUS 9 0 0 0 2 —

**Yerashov, Alexei / b. May 21, 1984**
2002 WM18 BLR 8 1 0 1 4 —
2003 WM20 BLR 6 0 0 0 2 —

**Yerastov, Dmitri / b. Apr. 18, 1960**
1980 WM20 URS 5 1 0 1 2 G

**Yeremeyev, Oleg / b. June 11, 1979**
1999 WM20 KAZ 6 1 0 1 4 —

**Yerkovich, Sergei / b. Sept. 3, 1974**
1998-2007 WM BLR 31 1 5 6 36 —
1998 OG-M BLR 6 2 0 2 16 —

**Yermashkevich, Ilya / b. Mar. 11, 1983**
2002 WM20 BLR 6 0 0 0 6 —

**Yermolin, Yuri / b. July 17, 1984**
2004 WM20 RUS 6 1 0 1 0 —

**Yerofeyev, Dmitri / b. Jan. 28, 1970**
1996-2003 WM RUS 30 4 6 10 18 —

**Yeronov, Alexander / b. May 5, 1989**
2006 WM18 BLR 6 0 0 0 10 —

**Yesaulov, Yevgeni / b. July 1, 1977**
2003-06 WM BLR 11 0 1 1 8 —

**Yesirkenov, Doszhan / b. Sept. 15, 1985**
2003 WM18 KAZ 6 2 1 3 0 —

**Yesirkenov, Rustam / b. June 28, 1980**
1999-2000 WM20 KAZ 13 1 4 5 8 —
2004 WM KAZ 3 0 1 1 0 —

**Yevseyev, Alexander / b. Jan. 15, 1985**
2003 WM18 KAZ 6 0 1 1 4 —

**Yevstafiev, Andrei / b. Aug. 9, 1972**
2001 WM RUS 7 0 2 2 2 —

**Yevstegneyev, Pavel / b. Dec. 5, 1973**
1993 WM20 RUS 7 0 2 2 0 —

**Yevstifeyev, Valeri / b. May 20, 1957**
1977 WM20 URS 7 3 1 4 0 G

**Yevtyukhin, Georgi / b. May 9, 1970**
1994 OG-M RUS 8 0 2 2 10 —

**Yezovski, Pavel / b. Jan. 27, 1958**
1978 WM20 URS 7 2 2 4 12 G

**Yli-Junnila, Juhamatti / b. Jan. 29, 1981**
1999 WM18 FIN 7 1 4 5 8 G

**Yli-Maenpaa, Mika / b. Mar. 26, 1971**
1991 WM20 FIN 4 0 0 0 0 —

**Yli-Torkko, Joni / b. Apr. 14, 1982**
2002 WM20 FIN 7 0 2 2 6 B

**Ylonen, Juha / b. Feb. 13, 1972**
1991-92 WM20 FIN 13 2 6 8 2 —
1993-2003 WM FIN 31 6 14 20 12 G,S
1996 WCH FIN 4 1 3 4 0 —
1998-2002 OG-M FIN 10 0 1 1 10 B

**York, Mike / b. Jan. 3, 1978**
1996-98 WM20 USA 19 9 7 16 10 S
2005 WM USA 7 0 1 1 0 —
2002 OG-M USA 6 0 1 1 0 S
~WM20 All-Star Team/Forward (1997)

**Young, Brian / b. Oct. 2, 1958**
1978 WM20 CAN 6 0 2 2 2 B

**Young, Carl / b. Jan. 1, 1968**
1988 WM20 USA 7 2 1 3 8 —
1992 OG-M USA 8 1 3 4 4 —

**Young, Hassie / b. unknown**
1950 WM CAN 7 11 8 19 5 G

**Young, Hugh / b. unknown / d. unknown**
1938 WM USA 6 1 — 1 — —

**Young, Jerry "B.J." / b. July 23, 1977**
1997 WM20 USA 6 2 2 4 4 S

**Young, Scott / b. Oct. 1, 1967**
1985-87 WM20 USA 21 9 7 16 14 B
1987-94 WM USA 22 3 9 12 12 —
1996 WCH USA 7 2 2 4 4 1st
1988-2002 OG-M USA 20 8 7 15 8 S
~WM20 All-Star Team/Forward (1987)

**Younghans, Tom / b. Jan. 22, 1953**
1976-78 WM USA 30 4 7 11 22 —
1981 CC USA 4 0 0 0 0 —

**Ytfeldt, David / b. Sept. 29, 1979**
1999 WM20 SWE 6 1 3 4 6 —

**Yudashev, Ravil / b. unknown**
1981 WM20 URS 5 4 2 6 0 B

**Yudenko, Dmitriy / b. Apr. 14, 1981**
2000 WM20 UKR 7 0 1 1 4 —

**Yudin, Alexander / b. Feb. 4, 1971**
1989 WM20 URS 7 1 3 4 6 G
2002 WM RUS 9 0 0 0 6 S

**Yudzhin, Alexander / b. Apr. 6, 1983**
2000 WM18 BLR 6 0 0 0 4 —

**Yudzhin, Dmitri / b. Jan. 1, 1984**
2002 WM18 BLR 8 0 1 1 8 —
2003 WM20 BLR 6 0 2 2 12 —

**Yule, Chris / b. Mar. 29, 1975**
1999-2004 WM JPN 30 7 13 20 16 —
1998 OG-M JPN 4 0 0 0 0 —

**Yurkewicz, Al / b. Sept. 8, 1917 / d. unknown**
1949 WM USA 8 5 — 5 — B

**Yurzinov, Vladimir / b. Feb. 20, 1940**
1961-69 WM URS 13 8 10 18 0 2G,B

**Yuryev, Mikhail / b. Mar. 31, 1981**
2000-01 WM20 KAZ 13 4 4 8 6 —

**Yushkevich, Dmitri / b. Nov. 19, 1971**
1989-91 WM20 URS 21 2 11 13 12 G,2S
1992-2004 WM RUS 31 6 11 17 36 G
1996 WCH RUS 5 1 1 2 2 —
1992-98 OG-M RUS 14 1 2 3 6 G,S
~WM20 All-Star Team/Defence (1991)

**Yzerman, Steve / b. May 9, 1965**
1983 WM20 CAN 7 2 3 5 2 B
1985-90 WM CAN 28 17 21 38 16 2S
1984-96 WCH CAN 10 2 1 3 4 1st,2nd
1998-2002 OG-M CAN 12 3 5 8 12 G
~WM IIHF Directorate Best Forward (1990), WM All-Star Team/Forward (1990), WM All-Star Team/Forward (1989)

**Zabawa, Andrzej / b. Nov. 29, 1955**
1975-86 WM POL 32 6 8 14 6 —
1976-84 OG-M POL 15 7 7 14 4 —

**Zabel, Norbert / b. Mar. 8, 1973**
1993 WM20 GER 7 1 0 1 6 —

**Zabludovsky, Denis / b. Mar. 20, 1980**
2000 WM20 UKR 7 1 0 1 0 —

**Zabolotnev, Andrei / b. Jan. 20, 1982**
2000 WM18 RUS 6 0 1 1 14 S
2002 WM20 RUS 7 0 1 1 6 G

**Zabrodsky, Oldrich / b. Feb. 28, 1926**
1948 OG-M TCH 6 0 — 0 — S

**Zabrodsky, Vladimir / b. Mar. 7, 1923**
1947-55 WM TCH 29 50 9 59 2 2G,B
1948-56 OG-M TCH 15 25 3 28 0 S
~IIHF Hall of Fame

**Zach, Dietmar / b. unknown**
1981 WM20 AUT 5 0 0 0 0 —

**Zach, Hans / b. Mar. 30, 1949**
1976-79 WM FRG 18 3 1 4 4 —
1980 OG-M FRG 5 1 1 2 2 —

**Zach, Johann / b. Mar. 30, 1949**
1977-78 WM FRG 20 4 2 6 2 —

**Zach, Martin / b. Jan. 4, 1933 / d. Sept. 27, 2008**
1956 OG-M FRG 7 0 0 0 0 —

**Zachupeyko, Sergei / b. Jan. 5, 1988**
2006 WM18 RUS 6 3 2 5 4 —

**Zadina, Marek / b. Feb. 18, 1972**
1992 WM20 TCH 5 0 0 0 0 —

**Zagar, Luka / b. June 25, 1978**
2002-06 WM SLO 23 0 2 2 4 —

**Zagora, Anton / b. July 18, 1983**
2003 WM20 SVK 6 1 1 2 6 —

**Zagorodny, Anton / b. Aug. 5, 1967**
1987 WM20 URS 6 1 1 2 8 —

**Zainulin, Ruslan / b. Feb. 14, 1982**
2000 WM18 RUS 6 3 4 7 8 S
2002 WM20 RUS 7 0 1 1 2 G

**Zaitsev, Oleg / b. Aug. 4, 1939 / d. Mar. 1, 1993**
1966-67 WM URS 14 4 4 8 12 2G
1964-68 OG-M URS 11 1 3 4 6 2G

**Zajac, Martin / b. Oct. 25, 1981**
1999 WM18 SVK 7 1 1 2 0 B

**Zajac, Travis / b. May 13, 1985**
2009 WM CAN 5 0 0 0 2 S

**Zajc, Bojan / b. Nov. 7, 1965**
2002-05 WM SLO 18 0 0 0 22 —

**Zajgla, Petri / b. Feb. 15, 1981**
1999 WM18 CZE 7 0 1 1 24 —

**Zajic, Josef / b. Sept. 7, 1968**
1988 WM20 TCH 7 1 1 2 0 —

**Zajicek, Jan / b. Jan. 26, 1951**
1978 WM TCH 10 2 2 4 11 S

**Zakharov, Mikhail / b. Jan. 22, 1962**
1981 WM20 URS 5 1 1 2 10 B

**Zalapski, Zarley / b. Apr. 22, 1968**
1987 WM CAN 10 0 3 3 2 —
1988 OG-M CAN 8 1 3 4 2 —

**Zamojski, Jacek / b. Feb. 20, 1968**
1987-88 WM20 POL 9 0 0 0 8 —

**Zamuner, Rob / b. Sept. 17, 1969**
1997-98 WM CAN 16 4 4 8 20 G
1998 OG-M CAN 6 1 0 1 8 —

**Zanatta, Ivano / b. Aug. 3, 1960**
1992-93 WM ITA 11 0 0 0 0 —
1992 OG-M ITA 7 0 2 2 2 —

**Zandegiacomo, Giuseppe / b. Nov. 10, 1936**
1959 WM ITA 8 1 0 1 18 —

**Zanghellini, Helmut / b. Dec. 16, 1939**
1961-63 WM FRG 18 4 3 7 4 —
1964 OG-M FRG 7 0 0 0 0 —

**Zankovets, Eduard / b. Sept. 27, 1969**
1998-2002 OG-M BLR 8 0 0 0 2 —

**Zarrillo, Bruno / b. Sept. 5, 1966**
1992-2001 WM ITA 50 17 18 35 26 —
1992-98 OG-M ITA 18 10 5 15 18 —

**Zaruba, Rudolf / b. June 12, 1967**
1986 WM20 TCH 7 0 1 1 2 —

**Zarzhitski, Nikolai / b. February 18, 1979**
1999 WM20 KAZ 6 3 0 3 16 —
2006 WM KAZ 6 0 1 1 10 —

**Zatonski, Dmitri / b. Mar. 30, 1971**
2002 WM RUS 9 2 3 5 22 S

**Zavalnyuk, Vyacheslav / b. Dec. 10, 1974**
1999-2007 WM UKR 45 2 3 5 107 —
2002 OG-M UKR 4 0 0 0 4 —

**Zavarukhin, Nikolai / b. Mar. 18, 1975**
1994-95 WM20 RUS 14 2 7 9 14 S,B

**Zavoral, Vaclav / b. May 22, 1981**
1999 WM18 CZE 7 1 0 1 4 —

**Zavyalov, Vladimir / b. May 1, 1974**
1998 OG-M KAZ 7 0 3 3 4 —

**Zawada, Marian / b. Aug. 30, 1934**
1958-66 WM POL 14 0 1 1 35 —

**Zawadzki, Janusz / b. Apr. 27, 1931 / d. Jan. 19, 1977**
1957-59 WM POL 14 0 0 0 10 —
1956 OG-M POL 1 0 0 0 4 —

**Zawadzki, Slawomir / b. May 6, 1957**
1977 WM20 POL 6 0 1 1 17 —

**Zbinden, Pascal / b. Jan. 13, 1987**
2005 WM18 SUI 6 0 0 0 0 —

**Zbontar, Franci / b. June 12, 1952**
1972-76 OG-M YUG 9 6 3 9 4 —

**Zdunek, Piotr / b. Feb. 8, 1968**
1987 WM20 POL 7 4 4 8 10 —
1989 WM POL 7 0 0 0 2 —

**Zebrowski, Kazimierz / b. Mar. 4, 1891 / d. unknown**
1928 OG-M POL 1 0 — 0 — —

**Zednik, Richard / b. June 1, 1976**
1996 WM20 SVK 6 5 2 7 10 —
1996-2004 WCH SVK 6 0 0 0 0 —
2001-11 WM SVK 29 9 7 16 32 B
2006-10 OG-M SVK 13 3 4 7 18 —

**Zehetmayer, Franz / b. unknown / d. unknown**
1938-47 WM AUT 4 3 — 3 — B

**Zehnder, Andreas / b. Dec. 11, 1965**
1995 WM SUI 6 1 1 2 4 —

**Zeiter, Michel / b. Apr. 22, 1974**
1994 WM20 SUI 7 2 2 4 14 —
1998-2001 WM SUI 28 2 2 4 26 —

**Zelenka, Jiri / b. Aug. 17, 1972**
1992 WM20 TCH 6 2 0 2 2 —

**Zelepukin, Valeri / b. Sept. 17, 1968**
1987-88 WM20 URS 13 7 3 10 6 S
1991-2004 WM RUS 15 0 6 6 9 B
1996 WCH RUS 3 0 0 0 20 —
1998 OG-M RUS 6 1 2 3 0 S

**Zeliska, Lukas / b. Jan. 8, 1988**
2006 WM18 SVK 6 1 1 2 10 —

**Zemchenko, Igor / b. Jan. 8, 1983**
2001 WM18 UKR 6 2 1 3 35 —

**Zemchenko, Sergei / b. May 31, 1961**
1981 WM20 URS 5 3 2 5 0 B

**Zemko, Andrei / b. May 26, 1961**
1981 WM20 URS 5 0 3 3 8 B

**Zemlicka, Richard / b. Apr. 13, 1964**
1991-97 WM CZE 47 7 9 16 28 3B
1991 CC TCH 5 2 1 3 0 —
1992-94 OG-M CZE 16 4 4 8 12 B

**Zemlyanoy, Igor / b. May 26, 1967**
1998 WM KAZ 3 0 0 0 2 —
1998 OG-M KAZ 7 0 3 3 8 —

**Zenhausern, Aldo / b. unknown / d. Jan. 9, 2012**
1976 OG-M SUI 5 1 0 1 0 —

**Zenhausern, Gerd / b. Apr. 27, 1972**
1992 WM20 SUI 7 0 0 0 2 —

**Zent, Jason / b. Apr. 15, 1971**
1990 WM20 USA 7 1 0 1 4 —

**Zerbetto, Giorgio / b. July 15, 1936**
1959 WM ITA 5 0 0 0 2 —

**Zerwesz, Rainer / b. Jan. 10, 1969**
1998 WM GER 6 0 0 0 4 —

**Zetterberg, Bertz / b. Nov. 23, 1930 / d. Apr. 2, 2011**
1956 OG-M SWE 7 1 0 1 4 —

**Zetterstrom, Lars / b. Nov. 6, 1953**
1977-78 WM SWE 20 1 6 7 20 S

**Zetterstrom, Ulf / b. Apr. 12, 1958**
1978 WM20 SWE 7 0 0 0 2 S

**Zevakhin, Alexander / b. June 4, 1980**
1999-2000 WM20 RUS 12 3 6 9 10 G,S

**Zginca, Florea / b. 1949**
1977 WM ROM 10 4 1 5 8 —

**Zhamnov, Alexei / b. Oct. 1, 1970**
1990 WM20 URS 7 6 1 7 6 S
1991-2000 WM RUS 21 4 6 10 41 B
1991-96 CC RUS 9 3 2 5 8 —
1992-2002 OG-M RUS 20 3 4 7 14 G,S,B

**Zharkov, Vladimir / b. Jan. 10, 1988**
2006 WM18 RUS 6 1 2 3 6 —

**Zharkov, Yegor / b. Jan. 27, 1987**
2005 WM18 RUS 6 0 2 2 2 —

**Zhdan, Alexander / b. Aug. 28, 1971**
2001-03 WM RUS 11 0 3 3 6 —

**Zhiburtovich, Pavel / b. Sept. 4, 1925**
1954-55 WM URS 7 0 0 0 0 G,S

**Zhilinski, Yevgeni / b. May 3, 1986**
2004 WM18 BLR 6 1 3 0 2 —

**Zhitnik, Alexei / b. Oct. 10, 1972**
1991-92 WM20 RUS 14 2 2 4 4 G,S
1992-2002 WM RUS 26 2 4 6 22 —
1991-96 CC RUS 9 1 1 2 6 —
1992-98 OG-M RUS 14 1 2 3 2 G,S
~WM IIHF Directorate Best Defenceman (1996), WM All-Star Team/Defence (1996)

**Zhluktov, Viktor / b. Jan. 29, 1954**
1976-83 WM URS 66 24 27 51 22 5G,S,B
1976-81 CC URS 12 7 4 11 4 1st
1976-80 OG-M URS 12 5 13 18 2 G,S

**Zhubkov, Vladimir / b. unknown**
1978 WM20 URS 6 0 1 1 12 G

**Zhukov, Sergei / b. Nov. 23, 1975**
1998-2006 WM RUS 29 1 4 5 10 S
2006 OG-M RUS 8 0 2 2 6 —

**Zhukov, Valeri / b. Feb. 8, 1988**
2006 WM18 RUS 6 0 0 0 2 —

**Zhydkikh, Alexander / b. Jan. 7, 1984**
2002 WM18 BLR 8 1 3 4 2 —
2003 WM20 BLR 6 0 1 1 2 —

**Ziaja, Ernest / b. Apr. 11, 1919 / d. Aug. 29, 1997**
1947 WM POL 1 0 — 0 — —
1948 OG-M POL 1 0 — 0 — —

**Ziedins, Maris / b. July 3, 1978**
2005 WM LAT 6 1 0 1 0 —
2006 OG-M LAT 5 1 0 1 6 —

**Ziegler, Janos / b. Apr. 6, 1941**
1964 OG-M HUN 7 0 0 0 0 —

**Ziegler, Rolf / b. Sept. 14, 1975**
2000 WM SUI 7 0 0 0 4 —

**Zielinski, Edward / b. Apr. 19, 1909 / d. 1990**
1935-38 WM POL 11 4 — 4 — —
1936 OG-M POL 3 2 — 2 — —

**Ziesche, Joachim / b. July 3, 1939**
1959-70 WM GDR 51 26 11 37 10 —
1968 OG-M GDR 7 0 0 0 6 —
~IIHF Hall of Fame

**Ziesche, Steffen / b. May 2, 1972**
1992 WM20 GER 7 1 0 1 0 —

**Zietara, Walenty / b. Oct. 27, 1948**
1970-79 WM POL 57 13 12 25 40 —
1972-76 OG-M POL 9 0 1 1 6 —

**Zifcak, Ed / b. Jan. 17, 1920 / d. unknown**
1958 WM USA 6 0 1 1 0 —

**Zigomanis, Mike / b. Jan. 17, 1981**
2001 WM20 CAN 7 2 2 4 0 B

**Zilpauss, Karlis / b. 1917 / d. 1944**
1938-39 WM LAT 10 2 — 2 — —

**Zimakov, Sergei / b. Jan. 15, 1978**
1996 WM20 RUS 7 0 1 1 8 B

**Zimin, Yevgeni / b. Aug. 6, 1947**
1969-71 WM URS 14 3 3 6 4 2G
1972 SS URS 2 2 1 3 0 2nd
1968-72 OG-M URS 5 4 2 6 8 2G

**Zimmermann, Jurg / b. Jan. 1, 1943**
1962 WM SUI 5 1 2 3 0 —
1964 OG-M SUI 5 2 0 2 2 —

**Zimmermann, Paul / b. Sept. 27, 1927**
1954-55 WM SUI 14 3 0 3 2 —

**Zinevich, Olexander / b. Mar. 2, 1979**
1996 WM20 UKR 2 2 1 3 0 —
2002-03 WM UKR 11 1 2 3 4 —

**Zini, Peter / b. Oct. 3, 1951**
1976 OG-M AUT 3 1 0 1 4 —

**Zitnik, Ludvik / b. unknown / d. unknown**
1939 WM YUG 5 1 — 1 — —

**Zizka, Tomas / b. Oct. 10, 1979**
1999 WM20 CZE 6 0 3 3 2 —

**Zmolek, Doug / b. Nov. 3, 1970**
1990 WM20 USA 7 0 1 1 2 —

**Zmudzinski, Tomasz / b. May 24, 1969**
1988 WM20 POL 7 0 2 2 4 —

**Znaroks, Olegs / b. July 6, 1963**
1997-99 WM LAT 20 8 11 19 16 —

**Znenahlik, Peter / b. Dec. 9, 1963**
1988 OG-M AUT 6 0 3 3 0 —

**Znenahlik, Walter / b. Jan. 2, 1935**
1957 WM AUT 7 3 0 3 — —
1956-64 OG-M AUT 13 3 0 3 6 —

**Zobel, Tauno / b. Oct. 22, 1964**
1984 WM20 FRG 7 0 0 0 0 —

**Zoller, Lothar / b. Sept. 8, 1931**
1957 WM GDR 5 0 — 0 2 —

**Zollner, Hans / b. Nov. 14, 1929**
1957 WM AUT 2 0 — 0 — —
1956 OG-M AUT 4 0 0 0 4 —

**Zolotov, Sergei / b. Jan. 27, 1971**
1991 WM20 URS 7 3 2 5 4 S

**Zoltoks, Sergejs / b. Nov. 3, 2004**
1991-92 WM20 URS 14 4 6 10 8 G,S
1997-2004 WM LAT 30 15 10 25 18 —
*played under name of Sergei Zholtok in 1991-92 WM20

**Zombo, Rick / b. May 8, 1963**
1983 WM20 USA 7 0 0 0 0 —

**Zsitva, Viktor / b. July 14, 1939**
1964 OG-M HUN 7 2 2 4 0 —

**Zubek, Pavol / b. Feb. 16, 1970**
1989-90 WM20 TCH 14 5 4 9 0 2B

**Zubek, Peter / b. Feb. 16, 1970**
1989-90 WM20 TCH 13 1 3 4 12 2B

**Zubicek, Pavel / b. Oct. 21, 1974**
1994 WM20 CZE 5 0 2 2 2 —

**Zubkov, Vladimir / b. Jan. 14, 1958**
1977 WM20 URS 7 1 3 4 9 G
1982-83 WM URS 12 0 5 5 8 2G
1981-84 CC URS 6 0 3 3 6 1st

**Zubov, Igor / b. July 4, 1988**
2006 WM18 RUS 6 0 2 2 6 —

**Zubov, Sergei / b. July 22, 1970**
1989-90 WM20 URS 14 1 8 9 18 G,S
1992 WM RUS 6 2 2 4 10 —
1996 WCH RUS 3 0 1 1 0 —
1992 OG-M RUS 8 0 1 1 0 G

**Zubrus, Dainius / b. June 16, 1978**
2004 WCH RUS 4 2 1 3 4 —

**Zucchini, Luigi / b. Oct. 22, 1915 / d. unknown**
1936 OG-M ITA 3 0 0 0 — —

**Zucchini, Mario / b. July 5, 1910 / d. unknown**
1935 WM ITA 7 3 — 3 — —
1936 OG-M ITA 3 1 1 2 — —

**Zupancic, Nik / b. Oct. 3, 1968**
2002 WM SLO 6 1 3 4 0 —

**Zupancich, Stelio / b. Apr. 7, 1958**
1980 OG-M CAN 6 1 3 4 0 —

**Zurawski, Andrzej / b. Nov. 6, 1940**
1966 WM POL 7 1 1 2 2 —
1964 OG-M POL 7 1 3 4 6 —

**Zurek, Jan / b. Jan. 21, 1976**
1996 WM20 CZE 6 2 2 4 6 —

**Zurek, Karol / b. Jan. 28, 1949**
1974-76 WM POL 29 1 1 2 6 —
1976 OG-M POL 4 0 0 0 2 —

**Zuzin, Lubor / b. May 22, 1986**
2004 WM18 SVK 6 1 0 1 2 —

**Zuurmond, Jerry / b. Jan. 29, 1975**
1994 WM20 SUI 7 0 0 0 4 —

**Zwolinski, Pawel / b. Aug. 10, 1977**
1997 WM20 POL 6 0 0 0 2 —

**Zybin, Alexander / b. June 10, 1960**
1980 WM20 URS 5 1 1 2 2 G

**Zymankowski, Robert / b. July 31, 1968**
1987 WM20 POL 4 0 0 0 2 —

**Zytynsky, Taras Terrence / b. May 10, 1962**
1995-96 WM FRA 13 0 4 4 10 —

**Zyuzin, Andrei / b. Jan. 21, 1978**
1996-97 WM20 RUS 13 2 5 7 8 2B

**Zyuzin, Dmitri / b. Oct. 21, 1987**
2005 WM18 RUS 6 2 0 2 4 —

**Zywitza, Sven / b. Sept. 30, 1970**
1995 WM GER 5 0 0 0 2 —

*Team Canada celebrates its 40th anniversary in 2012 to commemorate its great victory over the Soviet Union at the 1972 Summit Series. Photo: HHOF–Graphic Artists.*

# Retired Goalies, Men

(career summary for players who have retired from hockey or who have not played recently for their country)

| First-Last<br>Years | Event | NAT | GP | W-T-L | Mins | GA | SO | GAA | A | Pim | Medals |
|---|---|---|---|---|---|---|---|---|---|---|---|
| **Abrahamsson, Christer / b. Apr. 8, 1947** | | | | | | | | | | | |
| 1971-74 | WM | SWE | 21 | 11-4-6 | 1,247:00 | 63 | 1 | 3.03 | 0 | 20 | S,3B |
| 1972 | OG-M | SWE | 2 | 1-1-0 | 120:00 | 6 | 0 | 3.00 | 0 | 0 | — |
| **Abramov, Sergei / b. Sept. 15, 1959** | | | | | | | | | | | |
| 1994 | OG-M | RUS | 3 | 1-0-1 | 140:00 | 5 | 0 | 2.14 | 0 | 0 | — |
| 1995 | WM | RUS | 3 | 3-0-0 | 180:00 | 7 | 0 | 2.33 | 0 | 0 | — |
| **Aebischer, Beat / b. Jan. 18, 1967** | | | | | | | | | | | |
| 1986-87 | WM20 | SUI | 8 | 0-0-8 | 364:43 | 59 | 0 | 9.71 | 0 | 2 | — |
| **Ahl, Boo / b. Oct. 5, 1969** | | | | | | | | | | | |
| 1996 | WM | SWE | 5 | 2-1-2 | 299:50 | 10 | 1 | 2.00 | 0 | 2 | — |
| **Ahonen, Ari / b. Feb. 6, 1981** | | | | | | | | | | | |
| 1999 | WM18 | FIN | 5 | 3-1-0 | 273:24 | 6 | 1 | 1.32 | 0 | 0 | G |
| 2000-01 | WM20 | FIN | 10 | 6-0-3 | 530:54 | 16 | 1 | 1.81 | 1 | 0 | S |
| ~WM20 All-Star Team/Goal (2001) | | | | | | | | | | | |
| **Albreht, Janez / b. Feb. 9, 1940** | | | | | | | | | | | |
| 1976 | OG-M | YUG | 5 | 3-0-2 | 300:00 | 19 | 0 | 3.80 | 0 | 0 | — |
| **Algotsson, Hakan / b. Aug. 5, 1966** | | | | | | | | | | | |
| 1994 | OG-M | SWE | 2 | 1-1-0 | 120:00 | 5 | 0 | 2.50 | 0 | 0 | G |
| **Allman, Steve / b. May 16, 1968** | | | | | | | | | | | |
| 1990-97 | WM | NOR | 10 | 0-0-6 | 441:05 | 38 | 0 | 5.17 | 0 | 0 | — |
| 1992 | OG-M | NOR | 1 | 0-0-1 | 33:14 | 6 | 0 | 10.86 | 0 | 0 | — |
| **Amenth, Otto / b. unknown / d. unknown** | | | | | | | | | | | |
| 1933-34 | WM | AUT | 7 | 3-0-4 | 365:00 | 9 | 3 | 1.48 | 0 | 0 | — |
| **Anderson, William / b. Apr. 1, 1901 / d. Feb. 23, 1983** | | | | | | | | | | | |
| 1924 | OG-M | GBR | 1 | 1-0-0 | 60:00 | 3 | 0 | 3.00 | 0 | 0 | B |
| **Andersson, Andreas / b. Apr. 9, 1979** | | | | | | | | | | | |
| 1998-99 | WM20 | SWE | 5 | 4-0-1 | 300:00 | 14 | 0 | 2.80 | 0 | 0 | — |
| **Andersson, Fredrik / b. Feb. 28, 1968** | | | | | | | | | | | |
| 1988 | WM20 | SWE | 5 | 2-1-2 | 220:00 | 13 | 1 | 3.55 | 0 | 0 | — |
| **Anken, Olivier / b. Feb. 10, 1957** | | | | | | | | | | | |
| 1987 | WM | SUI | 7 | 0-0-6 | 340:00 | 34 | 0 | 6.00 | 0 | 0 | — |
| 1988 | OG-M | SUI | 4 | 2-0-1 | 220:00 | 10 | 1 | 2.73 | 0 | 0 | — |
| **Arnmark, Goran / b. July 27, 1966** | | | | | | | | | | | |
| 1985 | WM20 | SWE | 4 | 3-0-1 | 239:16 | 9 | 1 | 2.26 | 0 | 0 | — |
| **Arystov, Vitali / b. Feb. 9, 1983** | | | | | | | | | | | |
| 1999 | WM20 | BLR | 6 | 0-0-3 | 220:29 | 31 | 0 | 8.44 | 0 | 2 | — |
| 2000 | WM18 | BLR | 5 | 0-0-3 | 119:36 | 28 | 0 | 14.05 | 0 | 0 | — |
| **Askey, Tom / b. Oct. 4, 1974** | | | | | | | | | | | |
| 1997 | WM | USA | 1 | 1-0-0 | 60:00 | 4 | 0 | 4.00 | 0 | 0 | — |
| **Aslin, Peter / b. Sept. 21, 1962 / d. Jan. 19, 2012** | | | | | | | | | | | |
| 1981-82 | WM20 | SWE | 6 | 3-1-2 | 360:00 | 19 | 0 | 3.17 | 0 | 9 | G |
| 1986-93 | WM | SWE | 11 | 4-3-4 | 636:19 | 26 | 2 | 2.45 | 0 | 0 | G,3S |
| 1988 | OG-M | SWE | 2 | 1-0-0 | 79:59 | 5 | 0 | 3.75 | 0 | 4 | B |
| **Asplund, Johan / b. Dec. 15, 1980** | | | | | | | | | | | |
| 1999-2000 | WM20 | SWE | 5 | 3-0-2 | 296:49 | 16 | 0 | 3.23 | 0 | 0 | — |
| **Astrom, Hardy / b. Mar. 29, 1951** | | | | | | | | | | | |
| 1977-78 | WM | SWE | 8 | 3-0-4 | 395:08 | 25 | 1 | 3.80 | 0 | 0 | S |
| 1976 | CC | SWE | 4 | 1-1-2 | 240:00 | 17 | 0 | 4.25 | 0 | 0 | — |
| **Ayer, Jean / b. Jan. 6, 1930 / d. June 15, 2012** | | | | | | | | | | | |
| 1951-59 | WM | SUI | 14 | 3-1-9 | 763:30 | 64 | 0 | 5.03 | 0 | 0 | B |
| **Baba, Tomohiro / b. June 24, 1973** | | | | | | | | | | | |
| 1993 | WM20 | JPN | 4 | 0-0-4 | 243:06 | 43 | 0 | 10.61 | 0 | 0 | — |
| **Baca, Wojciech / b. Dec. 13, 1970** | | | | | | | | | | | |
| 1990 | WM20 | POL | 7 | 0-0-3 | 329:50 | 42 | 0 | 7.64 | 0 | 0 | — |
| **Backman, Gunnar / b. Apr. 23, 1940** | | | | | | | | | | | |
| 1969-70 | WM | SWE | 4 | 3-0-1 | 240:00 | 9 | 1 | 2.25 | 0 | 0 | 2S |
| **Baker, Steve / b. May 6, 1957** | | | | | | | | | | | |
| 1981 | CC | USA | 1 | 0-1-0 | 60:00 | 4 | 0 | 4.00 | 0 | 0 | — |
| **Bannemark, Kjell / b. Oct. 18, 1981** | | | | | | | | | | | |
| 1999 | WM18 | SWE | 6 | 3-2-1 | 360:00 | 9 | 1 | 1.50 | 0 | 0 | S |
| **Banninger, Hans / b. Mar. 17, 1924 / d. Aug. 22, 2007** | | | | | | | | | | | |
| 1947-53 | WM | SUI | 21 | 11-1-5 | 1,038:30 | 72 | 0 | 4.16 | 0 | 0 | 3B |
| 1948-52 | OG-M | SUI | 9 | 6-0-3 | 500:00 | 23 | 3 | 2.76 | 0 | 0 | B |
| **Barek, Martin / b. Feb. 20, 1982** | | | | | | | | | | | |
| 2000 | WM18 | CZE | 5 | 1-0-3 | 264:30 | 15 | 0 | 3.40 | 0 | 0 | — |
| **Barrasso, Tom / b. Mar. 31, 1965** | | | | | | | | | | | |
| 1983 | WM20 | USA | 3 | 0-0-2 | 140:00 | 12 | 0 | 5.14 | 0 | 2 | — |
| 1986 | WM | USA | 5 | 2-3-0 | 260:00 | 18 | 0 | 4.15 | 0 | 8 | — |
| 1984-87 | CC | USA | 6 | 2-1-3 | 311:48 | 18 | 0 | 3.46 | 0 | 2 | — |
| 2002 | OG-M | USA | 1 | 1-0-0 | 60:00 | 1 | 0 | 1.00 | 0 | 0 | S |
| **Bassani, Werner / b. Dec. 14, 1939** | | | | | | | | | | | |
| 1962 | WM | SUI | 3 | 1-0-2 | 180:00 | 17 | 0 | 5.67 | 0 | 0 | — |
| **Batkiewicz, Marek / b. Aug. 14, 1968** | | | | | | | | | | | |
| 1988 | WM20 | POL | 6 | 1-0-5 | 299:49 | 28 | 0 | 5.60 | 0 | 0 | — |
| 1992 | OG-M | POL | 4 | 1-0-1 | 181:12 | 13 | 0 | 4.30 | 0 | 0 | — |
| 1992 | WM | POL | 2 | 0-0-0 | 64:19 | 13 | 0 | 12.15 | 0 | 0 | — |
| **Baudinne, Robert / b. June 10, 1900 / d. unknown** | | | | | | | | | | | |
| 1936 | OG-M | BEL | 3 | 0-0-3 | 155:00 | 20 | 0 | 7.74 | 0 | 0 | — |
| **Bayer, Claudio / b. Sept. 22, 1975** | | | | | | | | | | | |
| 1994 | WM20 | SUI | 1 | 0-0-0 | 30:29 | 2 | 0 | 3.94 | 0 | 0 | — |
| **Behrend, Marc / b. Jan. 11, 1961** | | | | | | | | | | | |
| 1984 | OG-M | USA | 4 | 0-2-1 | 199:59 | 11 | 0 | 3.30 | 0 | 0 | — |
| **Bell, Gordie / b. Mar. 13, 1925 / d. Nov. 3, 1980** | | | | | | | | | | | |
| 1959 | WM | CAN | 6 | 5-0-1 | 360:00 | 9 | 2 | 1.50 | 0 | 0 | G |
| **Belosheikin, Yevgeni / b. Apr. 17, 1966 / d. Nov. 18, 1999** | | | | | | | | | | | |
| 1984-86 | WM20 | URS | 16 | 9-0-2 | 1,054:00 | 40 | 2 | 2.28 | 0 | 2 | 2G,B |
| 1986-87 | WM | URS | 17 | 15-2-0 | 1,020:00 | 26 | 5 | 1.53 | 0 | 2 | G,S |
| 1987 | CC | URS | 3 | 0-1-2 | 210:07 | 14 | 0 | 4.00 | 0 | 0 | 2nd |
| ~WM20 IIHF Directorate Best Goalie (1986), WM20 All-Star Team/Goal (1984, 1986) | | | | | | | | | | | |
| **Beno, Ivan / b. May 13, 1961** | | | | | | | | | | | |
| 1980 | WM20 | TCH | 3 | 2-0-0 | 134:49 | 10 | 0 | 4.45 | 0 | 0 | — |
| **Benyovits, Istvan / b. unknown / d. unknown** | | | | | | | | | | | |
| 1931 | WM | HUN | 1 | 1-0-0 | 45:00 | 1 | 0 | 1.33 | — | — | — |
| **Berge, David / b. Mar. 21, 1977** | | | | | | | | | | | |
| 1997 | WM20 | GER | 3 | 1-0-1 | 158:57 | 8 | 0 | 3.02 | 0 | 0 | — |
| **Bergkvist, Per Ragnar / b. Apr. 11, 1976** | | | | | | | | | | | |
| 1996 | WM20 | SWE | 4 | 2-1-1 | 240:00 | 6 | 2 | 1.50 | 0 | 0 | S |
| **Bergman, Anders / b. Aug. 6, 1963** | | | | | | | | | | | |
| 1983 | WM20 | SWE | 3 | 3-0-0 | 180:00 | 6 | 0 | 2.00 | 0 | 0 | — |
| **Bernhardt, Tim / b. Jan. 17, 1958** | | | | | | | | | | | |
| 1978 | WM20 | CAN | 3 | 3-0-0 | 180:00 | 6 | 1 | 2.00 | 0 | 0 | B |
| **Bester, Allan / b. Mar. 26, 1964** | | | | | | | | | | | |
| 1984 | WM20 | CAN | 2 | 2-0-0 | 120:00 | 2 | 1 | 1.00 | 0 | 0 | — |
| **Bielke, Rene / b. Apr. 9, 1962** | | | | | | | | | | | |
| 1983-92 | WM | GER | 20 | 4-2-13 | 1,100:46 | 88 | 0 | 4.80 | 0 | 0 | — |
| **Billington, Craig / b. Sept. 11, 1966** | | | | | | | | | | | |
| 1985-86 | WM20 | CAN | 10 | 6-2-2 | 600:00 | 27 | 1 | 2.70 | 0 | 0 | G,S |
| 1991 | WM | CAN | 3 | 0-0-0 | 46:01 | 3 | 0 | 3.91 | 0 | 0 | S |
| ~WM20 IIHF Directorate Best Goalie (1985) | | | | | | | | | | | |
| **Birenbaum, Stuart / b. Dec. 17, 1959** | | | | | | | | | | | |
| 1979 | WM20 | USA | 3 | 1-0-2 | 180:00 | 10 | 0 | 3.33 | 0 | 0 | — |
| **Biron, Martin / b. Aug. 15, 1977** | | | | | | | | | | | |
| 1997 | WM20 | CAN | 1 | 0-0-0 | 00:08 | 0 | 0 | 0.00 | 0 | 0 | G |
| **Bittner, Richard / b. Jan. 12, 1922 / d. Mar. 24, 2002** | | | | | | | | | | | |
| 1949 | WM | USA | 8 | 6-0-2 | 479:00 | 22 | 2 | 2.75 | 0 | 0 | B |
| **Bjorkman, Tommy / b. June 16, 1934** | | | | | | | | | | | |
| 1961 | WM | SWE | 2 | 1-0-0 | 100:00 | 5 | 0 | 3.00 | 0 | 0 | — |
| **Blackburn, Joe / b. Jan. 26, 1979** | | | | | | | | | | | |
| 1999 | WM20 | USA | 3 | 2-0-0 | 138:38 | 7 | 0 | 3.03 | 1 | 0 | — |
| **Blackburn, Rod / b. July 29, 1939** | | | | | | | | | | | |
| 1966 | WM | USA | 4 | 2-0-2 | 220:00 | 19 | 1 | 5.18 | 0 | 0 | — |
| **Blom, Lars / b. Jan. 25, 1920 / d. Sept. 13, 1944** | | | | | | | | | | | |
| 1939 | WM | FIN | 3 | 0-0-3 | 135:00 | 18 | 0 | 8.00 | — | — | — |
| **Blomqvist, Alexander / b. Apr. 9, 1984** | | | | | | | | | | | |
| 2002 | WM18 | SWE | 1 | 1-0-0 | 60:00 | 0 | 1 | 0.00 | 0 | 0 | — |
| **Bloomberg, Carl / b. Nov. 9, 1958** | | | | | | | | | | | |
| 1977-78 | WM20 | USA | 5 | 0-1-3 | 182:13 | 17 | 0 | 5.60 | 1 | 0 | — |
| **Blue, John / b. Feb. 19, 1966** | | | | | | | | | | | |
| 1990-97 | WM | USA | 6 | 2-0-1 | 264:40 | 17 | 0 | 3.85 | 0 | 0 | — |
| **Boesch, Marius / b. Mar. 25, 1966** | | | | | | | | | | | |
| 1986 | WM20 | SUI | 6 | 1-0-2 | 262:39 | 26 | 0 | 5.94 | 0 | 0 | — |
| **Bohac, Josef / b. Apr. 20, 1914 / d. unknown** | | | | | | | | | | | |
| 1936 | OG-M | TCH | 1 | 1-0-0 | 45:00 | 0 | 1 | 0.00 | 0 | 0 | — |
| **Bolla, Vittorio / b. Jan. 12, 1931** | | | | | | | | | | | |
| 1959 | WM | ITA | 3 | 0-0-3 | 178:00 | 19 | 0 | 6.40 | 0 | 0 | — |
| 1956-64 | OG-M | ITA | 8 | 2-2-4 | 456:00 | 35 | 0 | 4.61 | 0 | 0 | — |
| **Bonk, Rob / b. Feb. 27, 1981** | | | | | | | | | | | |
| 1999 | WM18 | USA | 2 | 2-0-0 | 120:00 | 2 | 1 | 1.00 | 0 | 0 | — |
| **Bonner, Doug / b. Oct. 15, 1976** | | | | | | | | | | | |
| 1995 | WM20 | USA | 3 | 1-0-1 | 140:31 | 13 | 0 | 5.55 | 0 | 0 | — |
| **Bonney, Ray / b. Apr. 2, 1892 / d. Oct., 1979** | | | | | | | | | | | |
| 1920 | OG-M | USA | 2 | 1-0-1 | 80:00 | 2 | 1 | 1.50 | 0 | 0 | S |
| **Borg, Johan / b. Oct. 5, 1967** | | | | | | | | | | | |
| 1987 | WM20 | SWE | 3 | 2-0-0 | 140:18 | 0 | 2 | 0.00 | 0 | 0 | B |
| **Borgqvist, Robert / b. Feb. 8, 1977** | | | | | | | | | | | |
| 1997 | WM20 | SWE | 4 | 1-1-2 | 240:00 | 12 | 1 | 3.00 | 0 | 0 | — |
| **Borntrager, Thomas / b. June 9, 1962** | | | | | | | | | | | |
| 1982 | WM20 | FRG | 6 | 1-0-2 | 239:57 | 31 | 0 | 7.75 | 1 | 0 | — |
| **Bouchard, Daniel / b. Dec. 12, 1950** | | | | | | | | | | | |
| 1978 | WM | CAN | 6 | 1-0-4 | 344:00 | 24 | 0 | 4.19 | 0 | 10 | B |
| **Boucher, Brian / b. Jan. 2, 1977** | | | | | | | | | | | |
| 1996-97 | WM20 | USA | 10 | 6-1-3 | 576:43 | 22 | 2 | 2.29 | 1 | 0 | S |
| ~WM20 All-Star Team/Goal (1997) | | | | | | | | | | | |

**Bratash, Oleg / b. Jan. 1, 1966**
1985-86 WM20 URS 3 3-0-0 180:00 7 0 2.33 0 0 G,B

**Brathwaite, Fred / b. Nov. 24, 1972**
2000-01 WM CAN 7 2-1-3 394:06 17 1 2.59 0 0 —

**Breuer, Jurgen / b. Apr. 7, 1960**
1980 WM20 FRG 2 0-0-2 83:24 12 0 8.63 0 0 —

**Brikun, Igor / b. June 9, 1986**
2004 WM18 BLR 1 0-0-0 20:00 3 0 9.00 0 0 —

**Briza, Petr / b. Dec. 9, 1964**
1984 WM20 TCH 4 3-0-1 270:00 15 0 3.33 0 0 B
1990-95 WM TCH 31 16-3-12 1,876:55 73 4 2.33 1 0 3B
1996 WCH CZE 2 0-0-1 97:38 7 0 4.30 0 0 —
1992-94 OG-M TCH 14 8-0-5 785:04 33 1 2.52 1 2 B
~WM IIHF Directorate Best Goalie (1993), WM All-Star Team/Goal (1993)

**Broderick, Ken / b. Feb. 16, 1942**
1965-66 WM CAN 8 7-0-1 480:00 13 4 1.63 0 0 B
1964-68 OG-M CAN 11 4-0-3 453:00 25 1 3.31 0 0 B
~OG-M IIHF Directorate Best Goalie (1968), OG-M All-Star Team/Goal (1968)

**Brodeur, Denis / b. Oct. 12, 1930**
1956 OG-M CAN 4 3-0-1 240:00 8 1 2.00 0 0 B

**Brodeur, Hank / b. Feb. 15, 1927 / d. Apr. 15, 1997**
1951 WM USA 6 1-1-4 360:00 42 0 7.00 0 0 —

**Brohee, Georges / b. 1909 / d. unknown**
1935 WM BEL 5 0-0-5 225:00 48 0 12.80 0 0 —

**Brown, Mike / b. Mar. 4, 1985**
2003 WM18 USA 5 1-1-2 241:27 10 1 2.48 0 0 —

**Brunetta, Mario / b. Jan. 25, 1967**
1995-2002 WM ITA 7 0-1-4 327:17 27 0 4.95 0 4 —
1998 OG-M ITA 1 0-0-1 23:36 4 0 10.17 0 0 —

**Buchanan, Buck / b. 1918 / d. Jan. 6, 1942**
1939 WM CAN 4 4-0-0 180:00 1 3 0.33 — — G

**Bucher, Richard / b. Sept. 27, 1955**
1987 WM SUI 5 0-0-2 210:16 26 0 7.42 0 2 —
1988 OG-M SUI 3 1-0-2 140:00 8 0 3.43 0 4 —

**Buk, Henryk / b. Aug. 1, 1953**
1979 WM POL 1 0-0-0 10:03 2 0 11.95 0 0 —

**Burke, Bernie / b. 1925 / d. unknown**
1950 WM USA 2 2-0-0 120:00 11 0 5.50 0 0 S

**Burke, Sean / b. Jan. 29, 1967**
1986 WM20 CAN 2 2-0-0 120:00 7 0 3.50 0 0 S
1987-2003 WM CAN 35 22-6-6 1,991:45 72 5 2.17 0 4 2G,2S
1988-92 OG-M CAN 11 6-1-4 667:20 29 0 2.61 0 16 S
~WM IIHF Directorate Best Goalie (2003), WM All-Star Team/Goal (1991, 2003)

**Byron, Wally / b. Sept. 2, 1884 / d. Dec. 22, 1971**
1920 OG-M CAN 3 3-0-0 120:00 1 2 0.50 0 0 G

**Calcaterra, Enrico / b. Jan. 1, 1905 / d. June 8, 1994**
1930-35 WM ITA 3 0-0-3 130:00 13 0 6.00 0 0 —
~IIHF Hall of Fame

**Callinan, Jeff / b. Jan. 6, 1973**
1993 WM20 USA 3 2-0-1 180:00 9 0 3.00 0 0 —

**Cameron, Jack / b. Dec. 3, 1902 / d. Dec. 29, 1981**
1924 OG-M CAN 3 3-0-0 180:00 1 2 0.33 0 0 G

**Campbell, Ken / b. Apr. 12, 1912 / d. unknown**
1937 WM CAN 9 9-0-0 415:00 4 6 0.58 0 0 G

**Campese, Bruno / b. Aug. 3, 1963**
1993-96 WM ITA 3 1-0-1 167:39 19 0 6.80 0 0 —
1994 OG-M ITA 4 2-0-1 231:02 13 0 3.38 0 0 —

**Capone, Marco / b. Jan. 22, 1959**
1984 OG-M ITA 3 0-0-2 140:00 19 0 8.14 0 0 —

**Caprice, Frank / b. May 12, 1962**
1982 WM20 CAN 3 3-0-0 180:00 7 0 2.33 0 0 G

**Carey, Jim / b. May 31, 1974**
1993 WM20 USA 4 2-0-2 240:00 14 0 3.50 0 0 —

**Caris, Ingemar / b. Nov. 23, 1942**
1966 WM SWE 2 2-0-0 120:00 2 0 1.00 0 0 —

**Carlson, Hermann / b. Sept. 11, 1906 / d. Feb. 18, 1990**
1936 OG-M SWE 3 2-0-1 135:00 1 2 0.44 0 0 —

**Carpano, Andrea / b. Mar. 9, 1976**
1999-2007 WM ITA 13 0-1-7 516:33 51 0 5.92 0 2 —

**Carr-Harris, Lorne / b. Dec. 15, 1899 / d. unknown**
1924 OG-M GBR 4 2-0-2 240:00 35 0 8.75 0 0 B

**Casey, Jon / b. Mar. 29, 1962**
1982 WM20 USA 5 1-0-2 218:49 15 0 4.11 0 0 —
1990 WM USA 6 5-0-1 334:38 15 0 2.69 0 2 —

**Casslind, Yngve / b. June 28, 1932 / d. Sept. 17, 1992**
1956 OG-M SWE 2 0-0-2 120:00 10 0 5.00 0 0 —
1957 WM SWE 3 3-0-0 180:00 6 1 2.00 0 0 G

**Castren, Teuvo / b. Sept. 16, 1918 / d. unknown**
1939 WM FIN 2 0-0-2 90:00 7 0 4.67 — — —

**Cech, Jakub / b. Aug. 13, 1985**
2003 WM18 CZE 2 1-0-0 80:00 6 0 4.50 0 0 —

**Cechmanek, Roman / b. Mar. 2, 1971**
1991 WM20 TCH 3 2-0-1 150:45 5 1 1.99 0 0 B
1995-2007 WM CZE 31 21-0-9 1,801:24 65 2 2.16 0 6 2G,2B
~WM IIHF Directorate Best Goalie (2000), WM All-Star Team/Goal (2000)

**Cerveny, Jiri / b. Mar. 20, 1957**
1977 WM20 TCH 3 0-1-2 155:23 9 0 3.48 0 0 B

**Cherepanov, Yevgeni / b. Aug. 5, 1980**
2000 WM20 KAZ 3 0-0-3 104:50 24 0 13.74 0 0 —

**Chernenko, Valentyn / b. May 30, 1983**
2000-01 WM18 UKR 12 1-1-9 634:48 67 0 6.33 0 0 —

**Cherviakov, Alexei / b. Dec. 5, 1965**
1984 WM20 URS 2 x-x-x 26:00 1 0 2.31 0 0 G
1995 WM RUS 3 2-0-1 180:00 5 1 1.67 0 0 —

**Chiamp, Mark / b. July 27, 1962**
1980 WM20 USA 1 0-0-1 60:00 4 0 4.00 0 0 —

**Chinov, Vladimir / b. Jan. 18, 1940**
1961 WM URS 7 5-0-2 400:00 17 0 2.55 0 0 B

**Chisholm, Ron / b. unknown**
1963 WM USA 2 0-0-1 80:00 12 0 9.00 0 0 —

**Chotteau, Hector / b. unknown / d. unknown**
1930-33 WM BEL 4 0-0-3 149:00 11 0 4.43 0 0 —
1928 OG-M BEL 3 2-0-1 135:00 10 0 4.44 0 0 —

**Chovan, Jan / b. Sept. 7, 1983**
2003 WM20 SVK 3 1-0-1 141:14 7 0 2.97 0 2 —

**Christie, Stan / b. Oct. 15, 1924**
1950-51 WM GBR 10 4-0-5 568:00 58 1 6.13 0 0 —

**Cloutier, Dan / b. Apr. 22, 1976**
1995 WM20 CAN 3 3-0-0 180:00 8 0 2.67 0 0 G

**Cloutier, Jacques / b. Jan. 3, 1960**
1986 WM CAN 5 2-3-0 298:24 15 0 3.02 0 0 B

**Cockburn, Bill / b. Mar. 1, 1902 / d. Mar. 21, 1975**
1932 OG-M CAN 5 4-1-0 265:00 4 2 0.91 0 0 G

**Collett, Ernie / b. Mar. 3, 1895 / d. Dec. 21, 1951**
1924 OG-M CAN 2 2-0-0 120:00 2 1 1.00 0 0 G

**Collins, Don / b. Feb. 12, 1932**
1965 WM CAN 2 0-0-2 120:00 10 0 5.00 0 0 —

**Comstock, Blane / b. Nov. 3, 1949**
1975 WM USA 4 0-0-4 234:08 32 0 8.20 0 0 —

**Conklin, Ty / b. Mar. 30, 1976**
2004-05 WM USA 8 4-3-0 459:39 16 1 2.09 0 2 B

**Conrad, Christian / b. Nov. 17, 1931**
1956 OG-M SUI 3 0-0-2 162:49 18 0 6.63 0 0 —

**Conti, Leonardo / b. Sept. 15, 1978**
1998 WM20 GER 3 0-0-3 152:16 18 0 7.09 0 0 —

**Cooper, Don / b. unknown**
1959 WM USA 3 3-0-0 180:00 5 0 1.67 0 0 —

**Corsi, Jim / b. June 19, 1954**
1982-83 WM ITA 17 2-2-13 958:57 89 0 8.10 0 4 —

**Cosby, Gerry / b. May 15, 1909 / d. Nov. 26, 1996**
1933-38 WM USA 11 8-1-2 505:00 6 6 0.71 0 0 G
~IIHF Hall of Fame

**Coulter, John / b. unknown / d. unknown**
1938 WM CAN 7 6-1-0 325:00 6 3 1.11 — — G

**Craig, Jim / b. May 31, 1957**
1979 WM USA 5 2-1-1 280:00 11 0 2.36 0 2 —
1980 OG-M USA 7 6-1-0 419:36 15 0 2.14 0 2 G
~IIHF Hall of Fame

**Crha, Jiri / b. Apr. 13, 1950**
1973-78 WM TCH 10 7-1-0 515:08 21 1 2.45 0 0 3S,B

**Crisan, Anton / b. Jan. 17, 1942**
1964 OG-M ROM 6 3-1-2 360:00 22 0 3.67 0 0 —

**Cuder, Arno / b. July 10, 1963**
1981 WM20 AUT 4 0-0-2 177:00 39 0 13.22 0 0 —

**Curran, Mike / b. Apr. 14, 1944**
1969-77 WM USA 22 3-1-18 1,280:00 122 1 5.72 0 6 —
1976 CC USA 3 0-1-2 180:00 14 0 4.67 0 2 —
1972 OG-M USA 5 3-0-2 300:00 15 0 3.00 0 0 S
~IIHF Hall of Fame

**Cyr, Claude / b. Mar. 27, 1939**
1961 WM CAN 3 2-0-0 134:00 5 0 2.24 0 0 G

**Dahl, Per / b. Mar. 21, 1916 / d. Feb. 17, 1989**
1949-51 WM NOR 17 4-0-12 1,020:00 100 3 5.88 0 0 —
1952 OG-M NOR 8 0-0-7 425:00 41 0 5.79 0 0 —

**Dahllof, Hans / b. Jan. 25, 1941**
1968 OG-M SWE 1 1-0-0 60:00 2 0 2.00 0 0 —

**Daigneault, Maxime / b. Jan. 23, 1984**
2002 WM18 CAN 5 1-0-4 297:55 26 0 5.24 0 0 —

**Dalpiaz, Claus / b. Oct. 10, 1971**
1993-2003 WM AUT 17 4-1-8 821:25 63 1 4.60 0 0 —
1994-98 OG-M AUT 4 0-2-1 161:13 13 0 4.84 0 0 —

**Danielopol, Dumitru / b. Mar. 18, 1904 / d. unknown**
1931 WM ROM 5 0-0-5 225:00 49 0 13.07 0 0 —

**Daskalakis, Cleon / b. Sept. 29, 1962**
1981 WM20 USA 3 1-0-2 141:00 14 0 5.96 0 0 —
1989 WM USA 1 0-0-0 20:00 1 0 3.00 0 0 —

**De Bruyn, John / b. Feb. 3, 1956**
1980 OG-M NED 2 0-0-1 38:22 13 0 20.33 0 0 —
1981 WM NED 5 0-0-2 192:32 24 0 7.48 0 2 —

**Delaney, Wilbur / b. unknown / d. unknown**
1950 WM CAN 3 3-0-0 180:00 0 3 0.00 0 0 G

**Delfino, David / b. Dec. 29, 1965**
1992-97 WM ITA 10 5-5-8 1,018:42 62 3 3.65 0 2 —
1992-94 OG-M ITA 9 2-0-6 422:35 35 0 4.97 0 0 —

**Della Bella, Paolo / b. Sept. 12, 1977**
1996-97 WM20 SUI 6 1-1-4 359:40 21 0 3.50 0 0 —

**Del Valle, Maurice / b. 1883 / d. unknown**
1924 OG-M FRA 2 0-0-1 100:00 25 0 15.00 0 0 —

**Denis, Marc / b. Aug. 1, 1977**
1996-97 WM20 CAN 9 7-2-0 540:00 15 1 1.67 0 0 2G
2006 WM CAN 5 4-0-1 262:41 11 1 2.51 0 0 —
~WM20 IIHF Directorate Best Goalie (1997)

**De Raaf, Helmut / b. Nov. 5, 1961**
1981 WM20 FRG 2 1-0-1 120:00 13 0 6.50 0 0 —
1985-93 WM FRG 27 7-7-14 1,512:28 110 2 4.36 0 4 —
1988-94 OG-M FRG 8 4-0-4 490:00 22 1 2.69 0 0 —

**DeRouville, Philippe / b. Aug. 7, 1974**
1993 WM20 CAN 1 0-0-1 60:00 7 0 7.00 0 0 G

**Deschamps, Bernard / b. May 29, 1944**
1968 OG-M FRA 3 0-0-3 180:00 15 0 5.00 0 12 —

**Desmond, Dick / b. Mar. 2, 1927 / d. Nov. 1, 1990**
1950 WM USA 5 3-0-2 300:00 18 0 3.60 0 4 S
1952 OG-M USA 4 3-1-0 240:00 10 0 2.50 0 0 S

**Djian, Jean-Marc / b. Mar. 29, 1966**
1988-92 OG-M FRA 2 0-0-2 80:01 15 0 11.25 0 0 —

**Doczi, Ion / b. unknown / d. unknown**
1931 WM ROM 1 0-0-1 45:00 11 0 11.00 0 — —

**Dowey, Murray / b. Jan. 3, 1921**
1948 OG-M CAN 8 7-1-0 480:00 5 5 0.63 0 2 G

**Dragan, Jaromir / b. Sept. 14, 1963**
1996-97 WM SVK 12 3-2-5 609:32 29 0 2.85 0 0 —
1996 WCH SVK 1 0-0-1 60:00 7 0 7.00 0 0 —
1994 OG-M SVK 2 1-0-0 80:00 7 0 5.25 0 0 —

**Driscoll, Charles / b. 1939**
1963 WM USA 6 1-1-4 340:00 52 0 9.18 0 0 —

**Dron, Dorin / b. 1920 / d. unknown**
1947 WM ROM 6 1-0-5 360:00 76 0 12.67 — — —

**Dryden, Ken / b. Aug. 8, 1947**
1969 WM CAN 2 1-0-1 119:00 3 1 1.51 0 0 —
1972 SS CAN 4 2-1-1 240:00 19 0 4.75 0 0 1st

**Duba, Tomas / b. July 2, 1981**
1999 WM18 CZE 2 0-1-1 78:12 3 0 2.30 0 0 —
2001 WM20 CZE 7 7-0-0 420:00 8 2 1.14 0 0 G
~WM20 IIHF Directorate Best Goalie (2001)

**Duffus, Parris / b. Jan. 27, 1970**
1996-99 WM USA 12 8-0-3 683:11 25 1 2.20 0 2 B

**Dumitras, Constantin / b. Jan. 23, 1946**
1968 OG-M ROM 5 2-0-3 266:15 19 0 4.28 0 0 —

**Dunham, Mike / b. June 1, 1972**
1991-92 WM20 USA 9 6-0-3 540:00 25 0 2.78 0 0 B
1992-2004 WM USA 10 1-1-5 444:24 22 0 2.97 0 0 B
1994-2002 OG-M USA 4 1-1-2 240:00 15 1 3.75 0 0 S
~WM20 IIHF Directorate Best Goalie (1992), WM20 All-Star Team/Goal (1992)

**Dupuis, Bob / b. Aug. 26, 1952**
1980 OG-M CAN 3 0-1-2 121:32 7 0 3.46 0 0 —

**Dvoracek, Vladimir / b. Oct. 29, 1934**
1960 OG-M TCH 2 0-0-1 49:00 3 0 3.67 0 0 —

**Dzurilla, Vladimir / b. Aug. 2, 1942 / d. July 27, 1995**
1963-77 WM TCH 48 35-2-8 2,671:55 95 5 2.13 0 5 3G,2S,3B
1976 CC TCH 5 1-1-3 228:24 9 1 2.36 0 0 2nd
1964-72 OG-M TCH 13 8-1-2 612:46 23 0 2.25 0 0 S,2B
~IIHF Hall of Fame
~WM IIHF Directorate Best Goalie (1965), WM All-Star Team/Goal (1965, 1969)

**Eberle, Hansruedi / b. Mar. 12, 1960**
1980 WM20 SUI 2 0-0-2 33:44 8 0 14.23 0 0 —

**Edelmann, Willi / b. Feb. 9, 1931**
1961 WM FRG 5 0-1-3 239:00 29 0 7.28 0 0 —

**Edwards, Don / b. Sept. 28, 1955**
1981 CC CAN 1 1-0-0 60:00 3 0 3.00 0 0 2nd

**Edwards, Marv / b. Aug. 15, 1935**
1959 WM CAN 2 2-0-0 120:00 0 2 0.00 0 0 G

**Edwards, Roy / b. Mar. 12, 1937 / d. Aug. 16, 1999**
1958 WM CAN 7 7-0-0 420:00 6 3 0.86 0 0 G

**Egginger, Wilhelm / b. Apr. 6, 1912 / d. unknown**
1933-39 WM GER 25 11-1-13 1,155:00 54 8 2.81 0 0 —
1936 OG-M GER 6 3-1-2 300:00 9 2 1.80 0 0 —

**Ehelechner, Patrick / b. Sept. 23, 1984**
2002 WM18 GER 7 1-1-4 407:48 26 0 3.83 0 0 —
2003 WM20 GER 3 1-0-0 114:23 3 1 1.57 0 0 —

**Eliot, Darren / b. Nov. 26, 1961**
1984 OG-M CAN 2 0-0-0 39:47 2 0 3.02 0 0 —

**Ellis, Aaron / b. May 13, 1974**
1994 WM20 USA 5 1-1-2 184:10 13 0 4.24 0 2 —

**Elo, Hans Goran / b. June 27, 1966**
1986 WM20 SWE 5 2-0-1 186:07 5 1 1.61 0 0 —

**Engelbrecht, Bernd / b. Feb. 16, 1958**
1977-78 WM20 FRG 12 3-0-9 693:23 57 0 4.93 0 26 —
1978-81 WM FRG 6 2-0-3 337:51 30 0 5.33 0 0 —
1984 CC FRG 1 0-0-1 60:00 8 0 8.00 0 0 —
1980-84 OG-M FRG 4 2-0-1 167:24 15 0 5.38 0 2 —

**Engman, Petri / b. June 9, 1975**
1994 WM20 FIN 4 1-0-3 240:00 13 0 3.25 0 0 —

**Eriksen, Jarl / b. Jan. 15, 1964**
1983 WM20 NOR 3 0-0-3 138:00 28 0 12.17 0 2 —
1988 OG-M NOR 1 0-0-1 60:00 10 0 10.00 0 0 —

**Eriksson, Lars / b. Apr. 16, 1961**
1980-81 WM20 SWE 8 5-1-2 480:00 20 0 2.50 0 0 G,B
~WM20 IIHF Directorate Best Goalie (1981), WM20 All-Star Team/Goal (1981)

**Eskelinen, Henry / b. Jan. 2, 1970**
1989-90 WM20 FIN 9 5-1-3 491:55 30 0 3.66 0 2 —

**Esposito, Tony / b. Apr. 23, 1943**
1977 WM CAN 9 5-2-1 513:00 29 1 3.39 0 0 —
1972 SS CAN 4 2-0-2 240:00 13 0 3.25 0 0 1st
1981 CC USA 5 2-0-3 300:00 19 0 3.80 0 0 —

**Essensa, Bob / b. Jan. 14, 1965**
1990 WM CAN 4 1-0-1 101:29 5 0 2.96 0 0 —

**Fadeyev, Sergei / b. July 16, 1971**
1997 WM RUS 3 2-0-1 180:00 12 0 4.00 0 0 —

**Fagerstrom, Mathias / b. Jan. 28, 1984**
2003 WM20 SWE 2 0-0-2 119:42 13 0 6.52 0 0 —

**Faizov, Radmir / b. Mar. 4, 1977**
1997 WM20 RUS 3 2-0-1 178:29 8 0 2.69 0 0 B

**Falter, Martin / b. Nov. 24, 1983**
2003 WM20 CZE 5 2-1-2 260:25 10 1 2.30 0 2 —

**Farrell, Frank / b. Mar. 23, 1908 / d. July 2, 2003**
1932 OG-M USA 6 4-1-1 310:00 5 3 0.97 0 0 S

**Fasel, Charles / b. May 21, 1898 / d. Jan. 10, 1984**
1928 OG-M SUI 4 2-1-1 155:00 4 1 1.55 0 0 B

**Fatikov, Leonid / b. Apr. 24, 1968**
2000-01 WM BLR 5 2-1-1 194:18 6 1 1.85 0 0 —

**Fernandez, Manny / b. Aug. 27, 1974**
1994 WM20 CAN 3 3-0-0 180:00 10 0 3.33 0 0 G

**Ferraris, Giuliano / b. Feb. 16, 1935**
1956 OG-M ITA 4 3-0-1 240:00 10 0 2.50 0 0 —
1959 WM ITA 5 3-1-1 300:00 20 0 4.00 0 0 —

**Fikrt, Michal / b. Apr. 6, 1982**
2002 WM20 CZE 1 0-0-1 58:54 3 0 3.05 0 0 —

**Filliol, Emil / b. Dec. 16, 1895 / d. unknown**
1924 OG-M SUI 1 0-0-1 59:00 9 0 9.15 0 0 —

**Finley, Brian / b. July 3, 1981**
1999-2000 WM20 CAN 2 1-0-0 80:00 5 0 3.75 0 0 2B

**Fischer, Kai / b. Mar. 25, 1977**
1995-97 WM20 GER 12 1-2-7 591:50 61 1 6.18 0 0 —

**Fischer, Karl / b. Aug. 27, 1929**
1955 WM FRG 2 0-0-2 120:00 15 0 7.50 0 2 —

**Fischer, Wolfgang / b. Nov. 5, 1947**
1974 WM GDR 8 1-4-1 408:26 45 0 6.61 0 0 —

**Fiset, Stephane / b. June 17, 1970**
1989-90 WM20 CAN 13 8-2-3 747:52 36 1 2.89 0 0 G
1994 WM CAN 2 2-0-0 120:00 3 0 1.50 0 0 G
~WM20 IIHF Directorate Best Goalie (1990), WM20 All-Star Team/Goal (1990)

**Fjeld, Hans / b. unknown / d. unknown**
1938 WM NOR 1 0-0-1 45:00 8 0 10.67 — — —

**Flemming, Markus / b. Sept. 16, 1968**
1988 WM20 FRG 2 0-0-2 100:00 16 0 9.60 0 0 —

**Flodqvist, Thord / b. Aug. 5, 1926 / d. Mar. 15, 1988**
1953-58 WM SWE 13 9-1-2 759:36 41 3 3.24 0 0 2G,2B
1952 OG-M SWE 6 4-0-2 340:00 15 0 2.65 0 0 B

**Fluckiger, Michael / b. Feb. 15, 1984**
2002 WM18 SUI 1 0-0-0 40:00 5 0 7.50 0 0 —

**Fluieras, Gheorghe / b. 1910 / d. unknown**
1938-47 WM ROM 4 0-0-4 195:00 19 0 5.85 — — —

**Foliot, Patrick / b. Mar. 1, 1954**
1988 OG-M FRA 5 1-0-3 274:05 33 0 7.22 0 0 —

**Fomichev, Alexander / b. Feb. 19, 1979**
2006 WM RUS 2 0-0-0 21:28 0 0 0.00 0 0 —

**Forsberg, Jonas / b. June 15, 1975**
1995 WM20 SWE 5 3-0-2 299:20 16 0 3.21 0 4 B

**Forys, Ryszard / b. unknown**
1955 WM POL 2 0-0-2 100:00 19 0 11.40 0 0 —

| | | | | | | | | | | | |
|---|---|---|---|---|---|---|---|---|---|---|---|
| **Foster, Jimmy / b. Sept. 13, 1910 / d. Jan. 4, 1969** | | | | | | | | | | | |
| 1937-39 | WM | GBR | 22 | 16-1-5 | 1,010:00 | 19 | 12 | 1.13 | 0 | 0 | 2S |
| 1936 | OG-M | GBR | 7 | 5-2-0 | 375:00 | 3 | 4 | 0.48 | 0 | 0 | G |
| **Foster, Norm / b. Feb. 10, 1965** | | | | | | | | | | | |
| 1985 | WM20 | CAN | 2 | 2-0-0 | 120:00 | 1 | 1 | 0.50 | 0 | 0 | G |
| **Franck, Francois / b. 1904 / d. unknown** | | | | | | | | | | | |
| 1933 | WM | BEL | 1 | 0-0-1 | 11:00 | 3 | 0 | 16.36 | — | 0 | — |
| **Franek, Petr / b. Apr. 6, 1975** | | | | | | | | | | | |
| 1994 | WM20 | CZE | 3 | 1-0-2 | 138:15 | 12 | 0 | 5.21 | 0 | 0 | — |
| **Franke, Peter / b. Mar. 8, 1968** | | | | | | | | | | | |
| 1988 | WM20 | FRG | 6 | 1-0-4 | 320:00 | 31 | 0 | 5.81 | 0 | 0 | — |
| **Fransson, Jonas / b. Feb. 20, 1980** | | | | | | | | | | | |
| 2000 | WM20 | SWE | 4 | 3-0-1 | 237:07 | 7 | 0 | 1.77 | 0 | 0 | — |
| **Frazier, Ed / b. Jan. 21, 1907 / d. Nov. 2, 1971** | | | | | | | | | | | |
| 1931 | WM | USA | 6 | 5-0-1 | 270:00 | 3 | 4 | 0.67 | 0 | 0 | S |
| **Fredriksson, Emanuel / b. Oct. 31, 1977** | | | | | | | | | | | |
| 1997 | WM20 | SWE | 2 | 1-0-1 | 119:10 | 5 | 0 | 2.52 | 0 | 0 | — |
| **Friesen, Karl / b. June 30, 1958** | | | | | | | | | | | |
| 1981-89 | WM | FRG | 39 | 11-7-20 | 2,319:45 | 155 | 2 | 4.01 | 0 | 0 | — |
| 1984 | CC | FRG | 4 | 0-1-3 | 240:00 | 21 | 0 | 5.25 | 0 | 0 | — |
| 1984-92 | OG-M | FRG | 12 | 6-1-4 | 688:00 | 38 | 0 | 3.31 | 0 | 0 | — |
| **Froese, Bob / b. June 30, 1958** | | | | | | | | | | | |
| 1987 | WM | CAN | 5 | 1-1-3 | 300:00 | 18 | 1 | 3.60 | 0 | 0 | — |
| **Frolich, Thomas / b. Apr. 14, 1964** | | | | | | | | | | | |
| 1984 | WM20 | FRG | 2 | 0-0-2 | 71:00 | 11 | 0 | 9.30 | 0 | 2 | — |
| **Frolov, Andrei / b. Mar. 3, 1980** | | | | | | | | | | | |
| 1999 | WM20 | BLR | 6 | 0-1-5 | 318:57 | 33 | 0 | 6.21 | 0 | 0 | — |
| **Fuhr, Grant / b. Sept. 28, 1962** | | | | | | | | | | | |
| 1989 | WM | CAN | 5 | 3-0-2 | 298:18 | 18 | 0 | 3.62 | 0 | 0 | S |
| 1984-87 | CC | CAN | 11 | 7-3-1 | 695:40 | 38 | 0 | 3.28 | 0 | 0 | 1st |
| **Fukufuji, Yutaka / b. Sept. 17, 1982** | | | | | | | | | | | |
| 2004 | WM | JPN | 5 | 0-2-3 | 298:47 | 18 | 0 | 3.61 | 0 | 0 | — |
| **Funk, Franz / b. Oct. 18, 1950** | | | | | | | | | | | |
| 1972 | WM | FRG | 4 | 0-0-3 | 171:00 | 28 | 0 | 9.82 | 0 | 0 | — |
| **Furbacher, Vaclav / b. Feb. 27, 1963** | | | | | | | | | | | |
| 1981-83 | WM20 | TCH | 11 | 4-4-1 | 609:14 | 29 | 1 | 2.86 | 0 | 6 | 2S |
| **Gaittet, Jacques / b. 1893 / d. unknown** | | | | | | | | | | | |
| 1920 | OG-M | FRA | 1 | 0-0-1 | 40:00 | 4 | 0 | 6.00 | 0 | 0 | — |
| **Gale, Anton / b. Mar. 26, 1944** | | | | | | | | | | | |
| 1964-72 | OG-M | YUG | 15 | 7-2-5 | 862:18 | 56 | 1 | 3.90 | 0 | 0 | — |
| **Galyuk, Yevgeni / b. June 22, 1985** | | | | | | | | | | | |
| 2002 | WM18 | UKR | 6 | 1-0-3 | 256:11 | 27 | 0 | 6.32 | 0 | 0 | — |
| 2004 | WM20 | UKR | 4 | 0-0-3 | 113:08 | 16 | 0 | 8.49 | 0 | 0 | — |
| **Gardner, Vic / b. 1902 / d. unknown** | | | | | | | | | | | |
| 1934 | WC | GBR | 6 | 4-0-2 | 270:00 | 7 | 1 | 1.56 | 0 | 0 | — |
| **Garon, Mathieu / b. Jan. 9, 1978** | | | | | | | | | | | |
| 1998 | WM20 | CAN | 5 | 2-0-3 | 273:21 | 9 | 2 | 1.98 | 0 | 0 | — |
| **Garrett, John / b. June 17, 1951** | | | | | | | | | | | |
| 1981 | WM | CAN | 3 | 1-0-2 | 120:00 | 8 | 0 | 4.00 | 0 | 0 | — |
| **Gavrilenok, Alexander / b. Jan. 25, 1965** | | | | | | | | | | | |
| 1998 | WM | BLR | 2 | 0-0-0 | 51:37 | 3 | 0 | 3.49 | 0 | 0 | — |
| **Gavrylyuk, Sergi / b. Mar. 23, 1985** | | | | | | | | | | | |
| 2004 | WM20 | UKR | 2 | 0-0-1 | 81:44 | 10 | 0 | 7.34 | 0 | 0 | — |
| **Geddes, Ron / b. Nov. 1910 / b. unknown** | | | | | | | | | | | |
| 1933 | WM | CAN | 5 | 4-0-1 | 235:00 | 3 | 3 | 0.77 | — | 0 | S |
| **George, Robert / b. unknown / d. unknown** | | | | | | | | | | | |
| 1928 | OG-M | FRA | 1 | 1-0-0 | 45:00 | 0 | 1 | 0.00 | 0 | 0 | — |
| **Gerasimov, Vladimir / b. Mar. 29, 1959** | | | | | | | | | | | |
| 1979 | WM20 | URS | 6 | 5-1-0 | 340:00 | 11 | 1 | 1.94 | 0 | 0 | G |
| **Gerasimov, Yuri / b. Feb. 14, 1979** | | | | | | | | | | | |
| 1999 | WM20 | RUS | 3 | 0-0-0 | 25:19 | 0 | 0 | 0.00 | 0 | 0 | G |
| **Gerber, Roland / b. 1959** | | | | | | | | | | | |
| 1978 | WM20 | SUI | 4 | 0-0-3 | 152:00 | 27 | 0 | 10.66 | 0 | 0 | — |
| **Gerl, Wolfgang / b. unknown** | | | | | | | | | | | |
| 1957 | WM | AUT | 5 | 0-0-5 | 300:00 | 48 | 0 | 9.60 | 0 | 0 | — |
| **Gerosa, Augusto / b. Oct. 1, 1909 / d. unknown** | | | | | | | | | | | |
| 1933-39 | WM | ITA | 24 | 8-8-9 | 1,190:00 | 44 | 6 | 2.22 | 0 | 0 | — |
| 1936 | OG-M | ITA | 3 | 1-0-2 | 155:00 | 5 | 0 | 1.94 | 0 | 0 | — |
| **Gerritsen, Jan / b. May 11, 1906 / d. unknown** | | | | | | | | | | | |
| 1935-39 | WM | NED | 10 | 1-0-9 | 450:00 | 54 | 0 | 7.20 | — | — | — |
| **Glickman, Jason / b. Mar. 25, 1969** | | | | | | | | | | | |
| 1988-89 | WM20 | USA | 9 | 1-0-7 | 451:40 | 36 | 0 | 4.78 | 0 | 4 | — |
| **Goepfert, Robert / b. May 9, 1983** | | | | | | | | | | | |
| 2003 | WM20 | USA | 7 | 4-0-2 | 338:05 | 10 | 0 | 1.77 | 0 | 2 | — |
| **Goldstein, Jorn / b. Mar. 27, 1953** | | | | | | | | | | | |
| 1984 | OG-M | NOR | 5 | 0-1-1 | 213:53 | 26 | 0 | 7.29 | 0 | 0 | — |
| **Goloshumov, Sergei / b. June 8, 1963** | | | | | | | | | | | |
| 1983 | WM20 | URS | 2 | 1-0-0 | 100:00 | 1 | 0 | 0.60 | 0 | 0 | G |
| **Goralczyk, Jozef / b. Nov. 3, 1938 / d. May 18, 1993** | | | | | | | | | | | |
| 1959 | WM | POL | 1 | 0-0-1 | 60:00 | 8 | 0 | 8.00 | 0 | 0 | — |
| **Gordon, Scott / b. Feb. 6, 1963** | | | | | | | | | | | |
| 1991 | WM | USA | 2 | 0-0-0 | 72:10 | 9 | 0 | 7.49 | 1 | 0 | — |
| 1992 | OG-M | USA | 1 | 0-0-0 | 17:21 | 2 | 0 | 6.97 | 0 | 0 | — |
| **Goryelov, Sergei / b. Jan. 3, 1985** | | | | | | | | | | | |
| 2003 | WM18 | RUS | 2 | 0-0-0 | 44:59 | 1 | 0 | 1.33 | 0 | 0 | B |
| **Gosselin, Mario / b. June 15, 1963** | | | | | | | | | | | |
| 1984 | OG-M | CAN | 7 | 4-3-0 | 379:25 | 14 | 0 | 2.21 | 0 | 2 | — |
| **Grahame, John / b. Aug. 31, 1975** | | | | | | | | | | | |
| 1995 | WM20 | USA | 5 | 2-0-3 | 280:00 | 19 | 0 | 4.07 | 0 | 4 | — |
| 1996-2007 | WM | USA | 8 | 4-0-4 | 439:31 | 23 | 1 | 3.14 | 0 | 2 | B |
| 2006 | OG-M | USA | 1 | 0-1-0 | 60:00 | 3 | 0 | 3.00 | 0 | 0 | — |
| **Granlund, Mikael / b. Feb. 27, 1971** | | | | | | | | | | | |
| 1991 | WM20 | FIN | 4 | 1-0-2 | 128:42 | 13 | 0 | 6.06 | 0 | 0 | — |
| **Graovac, Tom / b. Jan. 26, 1961** | | | | | | | | | | | |
| 1981 | WM20 | CAN | 2 | 0-0-1 | 90:00 | 5 | 0 | 3.33 | 0 | 0 | — |
| **Gravel, Francois / b. Oct. 21, 1968** | | | | | | | | | | | |
| 1997-99 | WM | FRA | 12 | 3-0-9 | 591:37 | 47 | 0 | 4.77 | 0 | 0 | — |
| 1998 | OG-M | FRA | 2 | 1-0-1 | 119:34 | 4 | 0 | 2.01 | 0 | 4 | — |
| **Green, Kenneth / b. Jan. 2, 1961** | | | | | | | | | | | |
| 1980 | WM20 | SUI | 5 | 0-0-3 | 266:16 | 39 | 0 | 8.79 | 0 | 0 | — |
| **Gritsenko, Alexei / b. Aug. 2, 1985** | | | | | | | | | | | |
| 2002-03 | WM18 | BLR | 7 | 2-1-2 | 322:29 | 34 | 0 | 6.33 | 0 | 2 | — |
| **Guck, Rainer / b. unknown** | | | | | | | | | | | |
| 1983 | WM20 | FRG | 3 | 0-0-1 | 81:07 | 13 | 0 | 9.62 | 0 | 2 | — |
| **Gustavsson, Jacob / b. Mar. 22, 1964** | | | | | | | | | | | |
| 1983-84 | WM20 | SWE | 8 | 3-0-5 | 480:00 | 31 | 0 | 3.87 | 0 | 0 | — |
| **Haakensen, Mattis / b. Mar. 3, 1970** | | | | | | | | | | | |
| 1989-90 | WM20 | NOR | 9 | 3-0-6 | 527:40 | 53 | 0 | 6.03 | 0 | 0 | — |
| **Haarstad-Evjen, Halvor / b. Dec. 10, 1981** | | | | | | | | | | | |
| 1999 | WM18 | NOR | 6 | 0-0-5 | 265:57 | 29 | 0 | 6.54 | 0 | 0 | — |
| **Hackett, Jeff / b. June 1, 1968** | | | | | | | | | | | |
| 1998 | WM | CAN | 2 | 0-1-1 | 120:00 | 9 | 0 | 4.50 | 0 | 0 | — |
| **Haggroth, Lennart / b. Mar. 2, 1940** | | | | | | | | | | | |
| 1962-63 | WM | SWE | 6 | 6-0-0 | 360:00 | 12 | 0 | 2.00 | 0 | 2 | G,S |
| 1964 | OG-M | SWE | 3 | 1-0-1 | 147:43 | 8 | 0 | 3.25 | 0 | 0 | S |

~WM IIHF Directorate Best Goalie (1962), WM All-Star Team/Goal (1962)

| | | | | | | | | | | | |
|---|---|---|---|---|---|---|---|---|---|---|---|
| **Haider, Reinhard / b. Aug. 14, 1970** | | | | | | | | | | | |
| 1989 | WM20 | FRG | 3 | 0-0-2 | 155:00 | 25 | 0 | 9.68 | 0 | 0 | — |
| **Hamal, Jiri / b. Nov. 1, 1961** | | | | | | | | | | | |
| 1980 | WM20 | TCH | 3 | 0-0-3 | 165:11 | 17 | 0 | 6.18 | 0 | 0 | — |
| **Hamerlik, Peter / b. Jan. 2, 1982** | | | | | | | | | | | |
| 1999-2000 | WM18 | SVK | 9 | 5-0-3 | 500:36 | 20 | 2 | 2.40 | 0 | 0 | |
| 2002 | WM20 | SVK | 4 | 1-1-1 | 207:31 | 8 | 0 | 2.31 | 0 | 10 | — |
| **Hampel, Jan / b. Apr. 25, 1933 / d. Dec. 3, 1962** | | | | | | | | | | | |
| 1948 | OG-M | POL | 3 | 0-0-2 | 70:00 | 15 | 0 | 12.86 | 0 | 0 | — |
| **Hanisz, Andrzej / b. Feb. 3, 1962** | | | | | | | | | | | |
| 1986-92 | WM | POL | 19 | 1-1-10 | 857:55 | 80 | 0 | 5.59 | 0 | 0 | — |
| 1988 | OG-M | POL | 2 | 0-1-1 | 80:02 | 5 | 0 | 3.75 | 0 | 0 | — |
| **Hansch, Ralph / b. May 20, 1924 / d. Feb. 29, 2008** | | | | | | | | | | | |
| 1952 | OG-M | CAN | 3 | 2-1-0 | 180:00 | 7 | 0 | 2.33 | 0 | 0 | G |
| **Hansen, Tommi / b. Jan. 19, 1964** | | | | | | | | | | | |
| 1983 | WM20 | NOR | 6 | 0-0-4 | 282:00 | 41 | 0 | 8.72 | 0 | 0 | — |
| **Hanson, Moray / b. June 21, 1964** | | | | | | | | | | | |
| 1994 | WM | GBR | 3 | 0-0-1 | 137:22 | 17 | 0 | 7.43 | 0 | 0 | — |
| **Hanzl, Jiri / b. July 6, 1920 / d. unknown** | | | | | | | | | | | |
| 1955 | WM | TCH | 5 | 3-1-1 | 300:00 | 13 | 2 | 2.60 | 0 | 0 | B |
| **Harazin, Peter / b. Oct. 17, 1962** | | | | | | | | | | | |
| 1982 | WM20 | TCH | 3 | 2-0-1 | 110:29 | 7 | 0 | 3.80 | 0 | 0 | S |
| **Harding, Goodwin / b. Dec. 11, 1920 / d. May 11, 1951** | | | | | | | | | | | |
| 1948 | OG-M | USA | 8 | 5-0-3 | 480:00 | 33 | 0 | 4.13 | 0 | 0 | — |
| **Harding, Josh / b. June 18, 1984** | | | | | | | | | | | |
| 2002 | WM18 | CAN | 2 | 2-0-0 | 120:00 | 2 | 0 | 1.00 | 0 | 0 | — |
| 2004 | WM20 | CAN | 1 | 1-0-0 | 60:00 | 0 | 1 | 0.00 | 0 | 2 | S |
| **Harnedy, Clem / b. Nov. 22, 1913 / d. unknown** | | | | | | | | | | | |
| 1934 | WM | USA | 4 | 3-0-1 | 240:00 | 2 | 3 | 0.50 | 0 | 0 | S |
| **Hartmann, Eduard / b. June 5, 1965** | | | | | | | | | | | |
| 1985 | WM20 | TCH | 1 | 0-0-0 | 40:00 | 3 | 0 | 4.50 | 0 | 0 | S |
| 1994 | OG-M | SVK | 6 | 2-2-2 | 310:17 | 17 | 0 | 3.29 | 0 | 0 | — |
| **Haruna, Masahito / b. July 16, 1973** | | | | | | | | | | | |
| 2003 | WM | JPN | 2 | 0-0-1 | 67:56 | 10 | 0 | 8.83 | 0 | 0 | — |
| **Hasek, Dominik / b. Jan. 29, 1965** | | | | | | | | | | | |
| 1983-85 | WM20 | TCH | 13 | 9-3-1 | 740:00 | 30 | 1 | 2.43 | 0 | 2 | 2S |
| 1983-90 | WM | TCH | 38 | 20-7-11 | 2,258:40 | 84 | 4 | 2.23 | 1 | 0 | S,3B |
| 1984-91 | CC | TCH | 15 | 3-2-10 | 848:00 | 50 | 0 | 3.54 | 0 | 0 | — |
| 1988-2006 | OG-M | TCH | 16 | 7-1-5 | 835:17 | 32 | 2 | 2.30 | 0 | 4 | G,B |

~OG-M IIHF Directorate Best Goalie (1998), WM IIHF Directorate Best Goalie (1987, 1989), WM All-Star Team/Goal (1987, 1989, 1990), WM20 IIHF Directorate Best Goalie (1983)

| | | | | | | | | | | | |
|---|---|---|---|---|---|---|---|---|---|---|---|
| **Hatinen, Markus / b. Jan. 6, 1974** | | | | | | | | | | | |
| 1993 | WM20 | FIN | 2 | 1-0-0 | 83:42 | 3 | 1 | 2.15 | 0 | 0 | — |
| **Haugh, Tom / b. 1943** | | | | | | | | | | | |
| 1965-67 | WM | USA | 8 | 2-0-5 | 446:38 | 47 | 1 | 6.31 | 0 | 2 | — |
| **Hausler, Oliver / b. Mar. 31, 1975** | | | | | | | | | | | |
| 1995 | WM20 | GER | 7 | 1-0-6 | 376:13 | 44 | 0 | 7.02 | 1 | 2 | — |
| **Head, Don / b. June 30, 1933** | | | | | | | | | | | |
| 1960 | OG-M | CAN | 6 | 5-0-1 | 325:00 | 10 | 2 | 1.85 | 0 | 0 | S |

| | | | | | | | | | | | |
|---|---|---|---|---|---|---|---|---|---|---|---|
| **Hebert, Guy / b. Jan. 7, 1967** | | | | | | | | | | | |
| 1994 | WM | USA | 6 | 4-0-2 | 300:00 | 18 | 0 | 3.60 | 0 | 0 | — |
| 1996 | WCH | USA | 1 | 1-0-0 | 60:00 | 3 | 0 | 3.00 | 0 | 0 | 1st |
| **Hedberg, Johan / b. May 5, 1973** | | | | | | | | | | | |
| 1997-99 | WM | SWE | 3 | 3-0-0 | 120:10 | 3 | 0 | 1.50 | 0 | 0 | G,S,B |
| 2002 | OG-M | SWE | 1 | 1-0-0 | 60:00 | 1 | 0 | 1.00 | 0 | 0 | — |
| **Hegen, Gerhard / b. Dec. 15, 1959** | | | | | | | | | | | |
| 1979 | WM20 | FRG | 4 | 0-0-2 | 142:00 | 16 | 0 | 6.76 | 0 | 0 | — |
| **Heinke, Mike / b. Jan. 11, 1971** | | | | | | | | | | | |
| 1991 | WM20 | USA | 4 | 3-1-0 | 240:00 | 8 | 1 | 2.00 | 0 | 0 | — |
| **Heino-Lindberg, Christopher / b. Jan. 29, 1985** | | | | | | | | | | | |
| 2002-03 | WM18 | SWE | 9 | 3-1-5 | 539:22 | 35 | 0 | 3.89 | 0 | 0 | — |
| 2005 | WM20 | SWE | 4 | 1-0-2 | 162:39 | 12 | 1 | 4.43 | 0 | 2 | — |
| **Heinrich, Tibor / b. Nov. 3, 1898 / d. Nov. 24, 1953** | | | | | | | | | | | |
| 1930 | WM | HUN | 2 | 1-0-1 | 90:00 | 4 | 1 | 2.67 | — | — | — |
| 1928 | OG-M | HUN | 2 | 0-0-2 | 90:00 | 5 | 0 | 3.33 | 0 | 0 | — |
| **Heirman, Henri / b. 1920 / d. unknown** | | | | | | | | | | | |
| 1939-50 | WM | BEL | 16 | 3-1-12 | 862:30 | 143 | 0 | 9.95 | 0 | 0 | — |
| **Heiss, Josef / b. June 13, 1963** | | | | | | | | | | | |
| 1981-83 | WM20 | FRG | 15 | 3-0-10 | 698:56 | 69 | 0 | 5.92 | 0 | 2 | — |
| 1991-98 | WM | FRG | 22 | 7-1-12 | 1,196:18 | 63 | 1 | 3.16 | 0 | 0 | — |
| 1996 | WCH | GER | 2 | 1-0-1 | 120:00 | 5 | 0 | 2.50 | 0 | 0 | — |
| 1992-98 | OG-M | GER | 7 | 3-0-4 | 421:18 | 22 | 0 | 3.13 | 0 | 0 | — |
| **Henriksen, Ernst / b. Feb. 27, 1917 / d. 1975** | | | | | | | | | | | |
| 1937-38 | WM | NOR | 5 | 0-0-5 | 235:00 | 38 | 0 | 9.70 | 0 | 0 | — |
| **Henriksson, Daniel / b. Sept. 4, 1978** | | | | | | | | | | | |
| 2006-07 | WM | SWE | 3 | 2-0-1 | 180:00 | 9 | 0 | 3.00 | 0 | 0 | G |
| **Henriksson, Goran / b. Apr. 4, 1959** | | | | | | | | | | | |
| 1978 | WM20 | SWE | 3 | 1-1-1 | 180:00 | 14 | 0 | 4.67 | 0 | 0 | S |
| **Herron, Dennis / b. June 18, 1952** | | | | | | | | | | | |
| 1978 | WM | CAN | 5 | 4-0-1 | 255:00 | 12 | 0 | 2.82 | 0 | 0 | B |
| **Hertl, Jiri / b. Apr. 24, 1917 / d. 1975** | | | | | | | | | | | |
| 1939 | WM | TCH | 2 | 0-0-1 | 75:00 | 1 | 0 | 0.80 | — | — | — |
| **Herzig, Roland / b. Jan. 12, 1950** | | | | | | | | | | | |
| 1976-78 | WM | GDR | 13 | 0-4-6 | 673:59 | 59 | 1 | 5.25 | 0 | 0 | — |
| **Hetenyi, Zoltan / b. Feb. 18, 1988** | | | | | | | | | | | |
| 2009 | WM | HUN | 3 | 0-0-1 | 96:54 | 6 | 0 | 3.72 | 0 | 0 | — |
| **Hextall, Ron / b. May 3, 1964** | | | | | | | | | | | |
| 1992 | WM | CAN | 5 | 1-1-3 | 273:07 | 13 | 0 | 2.86 | 0 | 0 | — |
| **Heylen, Charel / b. unknown** | | | | | | | | | | | |
| 1950 | WM | BEL | 1 | 0-0-1 | 60:00 | 33 | 0 | 33.00 | 0 | 0 | — |
| **Hilli, Ari / b. Mar. 17, 1968** | | | | | | | | | | | |
| 1988 | WM20 | FIN | 2 | 1-0-1 | 120:00 | 6 | 1 | 3.00 | 0 | 0 | B |
| **Hiraiwa, Kenichi / b. May 31, 1974** | | | | | | | | | | | |
| 1993 | WM20 | JPN | 5 | 0-0-3 | 176:36 | 40 | 0 | 13.59 | 0 | 0 | — |
| **Hirche, Klaus / b. June 7, 1939** | | | | | | | | | | | |
| 1961-70 | WM | GDR | 22 | 2-1-16 | 1,083:33 | 108 | 0 | 5.98 | 0 | 2 | — |
| 1968 | OG-M | GDR | 4 | 0-0-3 | 234:00 | 16 | 0 | 4.10 | 0 | 0 | — |
| **Hircsak, Istvan / b. Feb. 18, 1915 / d. unknown** | | | | | | | | | | | |
| 1933-39 | WM | HUN | 35 | 9-6-20 | 1,695:00 | 73 | 3 | 2.58 | 0 | 0 | — |
| 1936 | OG-M | HUN | 6 | 2-0-4 | 243:00 | 15 | 1 | 3.70 | 0 | 0 | — |
| **Hirsch, Corey / b. July 1, 1972** | | | | | | | | | | | |
| 1995 | WM | CAN | 8 | 4-1-3 | 488:17 | 21 | 0 | 2.58 | 0 | 0 | B |
| 1994 | OG-M | CAN | 8 | 5-1-2 | 495:15 | 17 | 0 | 2.06 | 0 | 2 | S |
| **Hirtz, Arnold / b. Sept. 2, 1910 / d. unknown** | | | | | | | | | | | |
| 1933-38 | WM | SUI | 26 | 16-2-8 | 1,250:00 | 34 | 9 | 1.63 | 0 | 0 | B |
| 1936 | OG-M | SUI | 1 | 1-0-0 | 45:00 | 0 | 1 | 0.00 | 0 | 0 | — |
| **Hnilicka, Milan / b. June 25, 1973** | | | | | | | | | | | |
| 1991-92 | WM20 | TCH | 11 | 5-0-5 | 598:17 | 34 | 0 | 3.41 | 0 | 0 | B |
| 1997-2008 | WM | CZE | 46 | 31-4-9 | 2,737:20 | 91 | 7 | 1.99 | 0 | 2 | 3G,S,2B |
| 2006 | OG-M | CZE | 3 | 1-0-1 | 127:52 | 6 | 0 | 2.82 | 0 | 0 | B |
| ~WM IIHF Directorate Best Goalie (2001), WM All-Star Team/Goal (2001) | | | | | | | | | | | |
| **Hobelsberger, Michael / b. Sept. 25, 1935** | | | | | | | | | | | |
| 1963 | WM | FRG | 5 | 1-1-3 | 300:00 | 38 | 0 | 7.60 | 0 | 0 | — |
| 1960-74 | OG-M | FRG | 8 | 1-0-7 | 480:00 | 64 | 0 | 8.00 | 0 | 0 | — |
| **Hofbauer, Patrik / b. Dec. 14, 1968** | | | | | | | | | | | |
| 1988 | WM20 | SWE | 4 | 1-0-1 | 199:16 | 11 | 0 | 3.31 | 0 | 0 | — |
| **Hoffmann, Alfred / b. Dec. 20, 1914 / d. unknown** | | | | | | | | | | | |
| 1938-39 | WM | GER | 10 | 5-3-2 | 520:00 | 12 | 4 | 1.38 | 0 | 0 | — |
| 1952-56 | OG-M | FRG | 6 | 1-0-4 | 284:42 | 31 | 0 | 6.53 | 0 | 0 | — |
| **Hogosta, Goran / b. Apr. 15, 1954** | | | | | | | | | | | |
| 1975-78 | WM | SWE | 23 | 14-0-9 | 1,384:52 | 63 | 2 | 2.73 | 0 | 2 | S,2B |
| 1976 | CC | SWE | 1 | 1-0-0 | 60:00 | 1 | 0 | 1.00 | 0 | 0 | — |
| ~WM IIHF Directorate Best Goalie (1977), WM All-Star Team/Goal (1977) | | | | | | | | | | | |
| **Holecek, Jiri / b. Mar. 18, 1944** | | | | | | | | | | | |
| 1966-78 | WM | TCH | 66 | 44-8-8 | 3,686:38 | 124 | 12 | 2.02 | 0 | 0 | 3G,5S,B |
| 1976 | CC | TCH | 5 | 2-0-0 | 203:09 | 11 | 1 | 3.25 | 0 | 0 | 2nd |
| 1972-76 | OG-M | TCH | 6 | 3-0-2 | 317:55 | 15 | 1 | 2.83 | 0 | 0 | S,B |
| ~IIHF Hall of Fame | | | | | | | | | | | |
| ~WM IIHF Directorate Best Goalie (1971, 1973, 1975, 1976, 1978), WM All-Star Team/Goal (1971, 1972, 1973, 1976, 1978) | | | | | | | | | | | |
| **Holm, Niklas / b. Jan. 20, 1982** | | | | | | | | | | | |
| 2000 | WM18 | SWE | 2 | 2-0-0 | 120:00 | 1 | 1 | 0.50 | 0 | 0 | B |

| | | | | | | | | | | | |
|---|---|---|---|---|---|---|---|---|---|---|---|
| **Holmqvist, Leif "Honken" / b. Nov. 12, 1942** | | | | | | | | | | | |
| 1965-75 | WM | SWE | 41 | 22-2-14 | 2,359:00 | 103 | 7 | 2.62 | 0 | 0 | 3S,3B |
| 1968-72 | OG-M | SWE | 9 | 4-1-4 | 540:00 | 23 | 0 | 2.56 | 0 | 2 | — |
| ~IIHF Hall of Fame | | | | | | | | | | | |
| ~WM IIHF Directorate Best Goalie (1969) | | | | | | | | | | | |
| **Holt, Chris / b. June 5, 1985** | | | | | | | | | | | |
| 2003 | WM18 | USA | 2 | 2-0-0 | 120:00 | 4 | 0 | 2.00 | 0 | 0 | — |
| **Honma, Teiji / b. Apr. 14, 1911 / d. unknown** | | | | | | | | | | | |
| 1936 | OG-M | JPN | 2 | 0-0-2 | 90:00 | 5 | 0 | 3.33 | — | — | — |
| **Honma, Toshiei / b. Dec. 12, 1935** | | | | | | | | | | | |
| 1960-64 | OG-M | JPN | 12 | 6-1-5 | 675:59 | 73 | 0 | 6.48 | 0 | 0 | — |
| **Hoppe, Matthias / b. Dec. 17, 1958** | | | | | | | | | | | |
| 1977-78 | WM20 | FRG | 2 | 0-0-1 | 86:37 | 9 | 0 | 6.23 | 0 | 0 | — |
| **Horyna, Robert / b. Aug. 10, 1970** | | | | | | | | | | | |
| 1990 | WM20 | TCH | 2 | 1-0-0 | 93:27 | 3 | 0 | 1.93 | 1 | 0 | B |
| **Houba, Antonin / b. May 27, 1909 / d. Oct. 16, 1986** | | | | | | | | | | | |
| 1939 | WM | TCH | 1 | 1-0-0 | 45:00 | 0 | 1 | 0.00 | — | — | — |
| **Howander, Seth / b. Oct. 6, 1892 / d. Sept. 14, 1981** | | | | | | | | | | | |
| 1920 | OG-M | SWE | 5 | 2-0-3 | 200:00 | 20 | 2 | 6.00 | 0 | 0 | — |
| **Hrabak, Jan / b. Jan. 14, 1959** | | | | | | | | | | | |
| 1977-79 | WM20 | TCH | 14 | 8-2-3 | 803:37 | 39 | 1 | 2.91 | 0 | 0 | S,B |
| ~WM20 IIHF Directorate Best Goalie (1977) | | | | | | | | | | | |
| **Hronek, Lukas / b. May 30, 1982** | | | | | | | | | | | |
| 2000 | WM18 | CZE | 2 | 1-0-1 | 105:30 | 4 | 1 | 2.27 | 0 | 0 | — |
| 2002 | WM20 | CZE | 6 | 2-0-4 | 355:22 | 12 | 0 | 2.03 | 0 | 0 | — |
| **Hrudey, Kelly / b. Jan. 13, 1961** | | | | | | | | | | | |
| 1986 | WM | CAN | 5 | 2-3-0 | 299:10 | 22 | 0 | 4.41 | 0 | 0 | B |
| **Huber, Alfred / b. Apr. 15, 1930** | | | | | | | | | | | |
| 1947-49 | WM | AUT | 8 | 2-0-6 | 480:00 | 65 | 0 | 8.13 | 0 | 0 | B |
| 1948 | OG-M | AUT | 6 | 1-0-5 | 340:00 | 57 | 0 | 10.06 | — | — | — |
| **Hughes, Chuck / b. June 13, 1970** | | | | | | | | | | | |
| 1990 | WM20 | USA | 6 | 1-0-4 | 318:58 | 26 | 0 | 4.89 | 0 | 0 | — |
| **Hughes, Mallie / b. unknown / d. unknown** | | | | | | | | | | | |
| 1951 | WM | CAN | 3 | 3-0-0 | 180:00 | 3 | 1 | 1.00 | 0 | 0 | G |
| **Hurbanek, Joachim / b. May 13, 1951** | | | | | | | | | | | |
| 1974 | WM | GDR | 5 | 0-4-0 | 191:34 | 26 | 0 | 8.15 | 0 | 0 | — |
| **Hurley, Harold "Boat" / b. Nov. 16, 1930** | | | | | | | | | | | |
| 1962 | WM | CAN | 5 | 4-0-1 | 299:30 | 8 | 1 | 1.60 | 0 | 0 | S |
| 1960 | OG-M | CAN | 2 | 1-0-0 | 95:00 | 5 | 0 | 3.16 | 0 | 0 | S |
| **Hurme, Jani / b. Jan. 7, 1975** | | | | | | | | | | | |
| 2003 | WM | FIN | 3 | 2-0-0 | 160:00 | 4 | 2 | 1.50 | 0 | 0 | — |
| 2002 | OG-M | FIN | 3 | 1-0-2 | 179:10 | 9 | 0 | 3.01 | 0 | 0 | — |
| **Hutan, Gheorghe / b. Apr. 8, 1954** | | | | | | | | | | | |
| 1977 | WM | ROM | 6 | 0-0-4 | 280:31 | 51 | 0 | 10.91 | 0 | 0 | — |
| 1980 | OG-M | ROM | 4 | 0-1-1 | 161:46 | 17 | 0 | 6.31 | 0 | 0 | — |
| **Ikola, Willard / b. July 28, 1932** | | | | | | | | | | | |
| 1958 | WM | USA | 3 | 2-0-1 | 180:00 | 11 | 0 | 3.67 | 0 | 0 | — |
| 1956 | OG-M | USA | 3 | 1-0-2 | 180:00 | 9 | 0 | 3.00 | 0 | 0 | S |
| ~OG-M IIHF Directorate Best Goalie (1956) | | | | | | | | | | | |
| **Iliev, Atanas / b. Feb. 2, 1943** | | | | | | | | | | | |
| 1976 | OG-M | BUL | 2 | 0-0-1 | 87:13 | 12 | 0 | 8.25 | 0 | 0 | — |
| **Imoo, Dusty / b. July 18, 1970** | | | | | | | | | | | |
| 1998-2000 | WM | JPN | 8 | 0-0-7 | 376:59 | 42 | 0 | 6.68 | 0 | 0 | — |
| 1998 | OG-M | JPN | 3 | 1-1-1 | 189:15 | 8 | 0 | 2.54 | 0 | 0 | — |
| **Innerwinkler, Thomas / b. Jan. 28, 1986** | | | | | | | | | | | |
| 2004 | WM20 | AUT | 4 | 0-1-1 | 170:31 | 10 | 0 | 3.52 | 0 | 0 | — |
| **Irbe, Arturs / b. Feb. 2, 1967** | | | | | | | | | | | |
| 1989-2005 | WM | LAT | 51 | 28-8-13 | 2,931:04 | 104 | 7 | 2.13 | 2 | 22 | 2G |
| 2002-06 | OG-M | LAT | 4 | 0-1-3 | 207:58 | 18 | 0 | 5.19 | 0 | 2 | — |
| ~IIHF Hall of Fame | | | | | | | | | | | |
| ~WM IIHF Directorate Best Goalie (1990) | | | | | | | | | | | |
| **Isaksson, Hans / b. May 28, 1925** | | | | | | | | | | | |
| 1953-54 | WM | SWE | 10 | 8-1-1 | 560:00 | 18 | 1 | 1.93 | 0 | 0 | G,B |
| **Ivannikov, Valeri / b. Jan. 28, 1967** | | | | | | | | | | | |
| 1987 | WM20 | URS | 6 | 2-1-3 | 350:48 | 20 | 0 | 3.42 | 0 | 0 | — |
| 1994 | WM | RUS | 2 | 0-1-0 | 39:32 | 4 | 0 | 6.07 | 0 | 0 | — |
| 1994 | OG-M | RUS | 1 | 0-0-1 | 60:00 | 4 | 0 | 4.00 | 0 | 0 | — |
| **Ivashkin, Alexei / b. May 3, 1969** | | | | | | | | | | | |
| 1988-89 | WM20 | URS | 8 | 5-0-1 | 390:00 | 17 | 0 | 2.62 | 0 | 0 | G,S |
| ~WM20 IIHF Directorate Best Goalie (1989), WM20 All-Star Team/Goal (1989) | | | | | | | | | | | |
| **Iwamoto, Takeshi / b. June 9, 1949** | | | | | | | | | | | |
| 1980 | OG-M | JPN | 3 | 0-1-2 | 150:54 | 18 | 0 | 7.16 | 0 | 0 | — |
| **Iwasaki, Shinichi / b. Aug. 21, 1968** | | | | | | | | | | | |
| 1998-2001 | WM | JPN | 8 | 0-0-6 | 402:30 | 47 | 0 | 7.01 | 0 | 0 | — |
| 1998 | OG-M | JPN | 1 | 0-1-0 | 59:41 | 3 | 0 | 3.02 | 0 | 0 | — |
| **Jaaskelainen, Juha / b. Jan. 17, 1963** | | | | | | | | | | | |
| 1983 | WM20 | FIN | 1 | 1-0-0 | 60:00 | 2 | 0 | 2.00 | 0 | 0 | — |
| **Jablonski, Pat / b. June 20, 1967** | | | | | | | | | | | |
| 1987 | WM20 | USA | 4 | 1-0-2 | 200:00 | 13 | 0 | 3.90 | 0 | 2 | — |
| 1993-95 | WM | USA | 8 | 4-2-1 | 422:23 | 16 | 0 | 2.27 | 0 | 0 | — |
| **Jahn, Milo / b. 1918 / d. unknown** | | | | | | | | | | | |
| 1947 | WM | BEL | 1 | 0-0-1 | 60:00 | 24 | 0 | 24.00 | 0 | 0 | — |

| | | | | | | | | | | | |
|---|---|---|---|---|---|---|---|---|---|---|---|
| **Jaks, Pauli / b. Jan. 25, 1972** | | | | | | | | | | | |
| 1991-92 | WM20 | SUI | 10 | 1-0-9 | 600:00 | 61 | 0 | 6.10 | 0 | 2 | — |
| ~WM20 IIHF Directorate Best Goalie (1991), WM20 All-Star Team/Goal (1991) | | | | | | | | | | | |
| **Janaszak, Steve / b. Jan. 7, 1957** | | | | | | | | | | | |
| 1982 | WM | USA | 3 | 0-1-2 | 180:00 | 17 | 0 | 5.67 | 0 | 0 | — |
| **Jansen, Ulrich / b. June 5, 1931 / d. July 19, 2006** | | | | | | | | | | | |
| 1953-59 | WM | FRG | 23 | 9-2-12 | 1,380:00 | 95 | 2 | 4.13 | 0 | 0 | — |
| 1956-64 | OG-M | FRG | 14 | 3-2-8 | 795:18 | 71 | 1 | 5.36 | 0 | 0 | — |
| **Jansson, Albin / b. Oct. 9, 1897 / d. Mar. 22, 1985** | | | | | | | | | | | |
| 1920 | OG-M | SWE | 1 | 1-0-0 | 40:00 | 0 | 1 | 0.00 | 0 | 0 | — |
| **Jarkovsky, Zdenek / b. Oct. 3, 1918 / d. Nov. 18, 1948** | | | | | | | | | | | |
| 1947 | WM | TCH | 1 | 1-0-0 | 60:00 | 5 | 0 | 5.00 | 0 | 0 | G |
| 1948 | OG-M | TCH | 3 | 3-0-0 | 180:00 | 8 | 0 | 2.67 | 0 | 0 | S |
| **Jaworski, Tomasz / b. July 3, 1971** | | | | | | | | | | | |
| 2002 | WM | POL | 5 | 2-0-3 | 300:00 | 17 | 0 | 3.40 | 0 | 0 | — |
| **Jendek, Jan / b. July 5, 1931** | | | | | | | | | | | |
| 1955 | WM | TCH | 3 | 2-0-1 | 180:00 | 9 | 0 | 3.00 | 0 | 0 | B |
| 1956 | OG-M | TCH | 3 | 1-0-0 | 67:01 | 5 | 0 | 4.46 | 0 | 0 | — |
| **Jensen, Al / b. Nov. 27, 1958** | | | | | | | | | | | |
| 1977-78 | WM20 | CAN | 10 | 6-1-3 | 600:00 | 32 | 1 | 3.20 | 0 | 0 | S,B |
| **Jensen, Flemming / b. Sept. 19, 1914 / d. unknown** | | | | | | | | | | | |
| 1949 | WM | DEN | 3 | 0-0-3 | 180:00 | 80 | 0 | 26.67 | 0 | 0 | — |
| **Jensen, Jan / b. Aug. 19, 1971** | | | | | | | | | | | |
| 2003-04 | WM | DEN | 3 | 0-0-2 | 103:41 | 11 | 0 | 6.37 | 0 | 2 | — |
| **Jetland, Jim / b. Oct. 13, 1959** | | | | | | | | | | | |
| 1979 | WM20 | USA | 2 | 1-0-1 | 120:00 | 13 | 0 | 6.50 | 0 | 2 | — |
| **Jirka, Josef / b. Feb. 3, 1926** | | | | | | | | | | | |
| 1949 | WM | TCH | 1 | 1-0-0 | 60:00 | 2 | 0 | 2.00 | 0 | 0 | G |
| **Johansen, Mats / b. Nov. 2, 1981** | | | | | | | | | | | |
| 1999 | WM18 | NOR | 3 | 0-0-1 | 94:03 | 13 | 0 | 8.29 | 0 | 0 | — |
| **Johansson, Arne / b. Feb. 25, 1915 / d. Oct. 12, 1956** | | | | | | | | | | | |
| 1947-50 | WM | SWE | 19 | 10-2-7 | 1,140:00 | 48 | 1 | 2.53 | 0 | 0 | S |
| 1948 | OG-M | SWE | 6 | 2-0-3 | 330:00 | 19 | 1 | 3.45 | 0 | 0 | — |
| **Johansson, Nils / b. Oct. 3, 1904 / d. Dec. 8, 1936** | | | | | | | | | | | |
| 1928 | OG-M | SWE | 4 | 3-1-0 | 180:00 | 3 | 2 | 1.00 | 0 | 0 | S |
| **Johansson, Yngve / b. Jan. 21, 1929 / d. Dec. 6, 2002** | | | | | | | | | | | |
| 1955-59 | WM | SWE | 4 | 2-0-2 | 240:00 | 12 | 1 | 3.00 | 0 | 0 | — |
| **Jokela, Antti / b. May 7, 1981** | | | | | | | | | | | |
| 1999 | WM18 | FIN | 3 | 2-0-1 | 146:36 | 8 | 0 | 3.27 | 0 | 0 | G |
| **Jopling, Brian / b. June 14, 1964 / d. Aug. 30, 2005** | | | | | | | | | | | |
| 1984 | WM20 | USA | 2 | 0-0-0 | 40:00 | 5 | 0 | 7.50 | 0 | 2 | — |
| **Jorns, Andre / b. Jan. 11, 1951** | | | | | | | | | | | |
| 1976 | OG-M | SUI | 4 | 2-0-2 | 240:00 | 16 | 0 | 4.00 | 0 | 0 | — |
| **Josefsen, Bjorge / b. June 3, 1976** | | | | | | | | | | | |
| 1999-2001 | WM | NOR | 3 | 0-0-3 | 146:48 | 9 | 0 | 3.68 | 0 | 0 | — |
| **Josefsson, Carl / b. Sept. 1, 1895 / d. Nov. 3, 1974** | | | | | | | | | | | |
| 1924 | OG-M | SWE | 1 | 0-0-0 | 10:00 | 5 | 0 | 30.00 | 0 | 0 | — |
| **Joseph, Curtis / b. Apr. 29, 1967** | | | | | | | | | | | |
| 1996 | WM | CAN | 6 | 4-1-2 | 348:48 | 12 | 1 | 2.06 | 1 | 0 | S |
| 1996 | WCH | CAN | 7 | 5-0-2 | 467:54 | 18 | 0 | 2.31 | 0 | 0 | 2nd |
| 2002 | OG-M | CAN | 1 | 0-0-1 | 60:00 | 5 | 0 | 5.00 | 0 | 0 | G |
| **Joswiak, Paul / b. June 12, 1958** | | | | | | | | | | | |
| 1978 | WM20 | USA | 6 | 4-0-1 | 340:00 | 27 | 0 | 4.76 | 0 | 0 | — |
| **Jurt, Andreas / b. Sept. 27, 1964** | | | | | | | | | | | |
| 1984 | WM20 | SUI | 3 | 0-0-3 | 140:00 | 32 | 0 | 13.71 | 0 | 2 | — |
| **Kahane, Bruno / b. unknown / d. unknown** | | | | | | | | | | | |
| 1931 | WM | AUT | 1 | 1-0-0 | 45:00 | 1 | 0 | 1.00 | — | 0 | B |
| **Kaitala, Risto / b. Sept. 11, 1941** | | | | | | | | | | | |
| 1962-66 | WM | FIN | 4 | 0-0-3 | 168:00 | 26 | 0 | 9.29 | 0 | 2 | — |
| **Kames, Jaroslav / b. Aug. 14, 1969** | | | | | | | | | | | |
| 1989 | WM20 | TCH | 1 | 0-0-0 | 30:27 | 3 | 0 | 5.91 | 0 | 0 | B |
| **Kamovich, Dmitri / b. June 6, 1984** | | | | | | | | | | | |
| 2002 | WM18 | BLR | 8 | 3-0-5 | 439:50 | 32 | 0 | 4.37 | 0 | 2 | — |
| 2003 | WM20 | BLR | 5 | 0-0-4 | 285:31 | 30 | 0 | 6.30 | 0 | 2 | — |
| **Kamppuri, Hannu / b. July 1, 1957** | | | | | | | | | | | |
| 1977 | WM20 | FIN | 7 | 4-0-3 | 420:00 | 29 | 0 | 4.14 | 0 | 2 | — |
| 1981-87 | WM | FIN | 22 | 9-4-6 | 1,303:01 | 75 | 0 | 3.45 | 1 | 0 | — |
| **Karamuz, Dariusz / b. May 12, 1970** | | | | | | | | | | | |
| 1990 | WM20 | POL | 4 | 0-0-4 | 90:03 | 23 | 0 | 15.32 | 0 | 0 | — |
| **Karlsson, Jonas / b. Jan. 27, 1969** | | | | | | | | | | | |
| 1989 | WM20 | SWE | 4 | 4-0-0 | 240:00 | 7 | 1 | 1.75 | 1 | 0 | S |
| **Karlstrom, Per Agne / b. Nov. 7, 1931 / d. Nov. 18, 1987** | | | | | | | | | | | |
| 1959 | WM | SWE | 5 | 2-1-2 | 300:00 | 14 | 1 | 2.80 | 0 | 0 | — |
| **Karpenko, Igor / b. July 23, 1976 / d. Nov. 18, 1987** | | | | | | | | | | | |
| 1995-96 | WM20 | UKR | 13 | 2-0-11 | 648:20 | 73 | 0 | 6.76 | 1 | 4 | — |
| 2000-07 | WM | UKR | 20 | 3-0-11 | 984:55 | 78 | 1 | 4.75 | 0 | 12 | — |
| 2002 | OG-M | UKR | 3 | 1-0-1 | 65:29 | 5 | 0 | 4.58 | 0 | 0 | — |
| ~WM20 All-Star Team/Goal (1995) | | | | | | | | | | | |
| **Karpin, Andrei / b. Nov. 26, 1963** | | | | | | | | | | | |
| 1982-83 | WM20 | URS | 8 | 7-0-0 | 400:00 | 18 | 0 | 2.70 | 0 | 2 | G |
| **Katzur, Gunther / b. Nov. 17, 1934** | | | | | | | | | | | |
| 1957-59 | WM | GDR | 6 | 3-0-3 | 340:00 | 23 | 0 | 4.06 | 0 | 0 | — |
| **Kaufmann, Theo / b. Apr. 11, 1912 / d. unknown** | | | | | | | | | | | |
| 1934-37 | WM | GER | 4 | 0-1-3 | 210:00 | 15 | 0 | 4.29 | 0 | 0 | B |

| | | | | | | | | | | | |
|---|---|---|---|---|---|---|---|---|---|---|---|
| **Kauhanen, Ilpo / b. Oct. 21, 1973** | | | | | | | | | | | |
| 1992-93 | WM20 | FIN | 9 | 3-2-4 | 515:30 | 25 | 2 | 2.91 | 0 | 6 | — |
| **Kehle, Toni / b. Nov. 8, 1947 / d. Sept. 24, 1997** | | | | | | | | | | | |
| 1971-77 | WM | FRG | 32 | 5-1-24 | 1,587:44 | 175 | 0 | 6.61 | 0 | 0 | — |
| 1972-76 | OG-M | FRG | 6 | 3-0-2 | 340:00 | 18 | 0 | 3.18 | 0 | 0 | B |
| **Ketterer, Markus / b. Aug. 23, 1967** | | | | | | | | | | | |
| 1987 | WM20 | FIN | 4 | 2-1-1 | 239:27 | 15 | 0 | 3.76 | 0 | 0 | G |
| 1991-96 | WM | FIN | 18 | 10-2-6 | 1,085:04 | 37 | 3 | 2.05 | 1 | 0 | S |
| 1991 | CC | FIN | 5 | 2-1-2 | 280:00 | 15 | 1 | 3.21 | 0 | 0 | 3rd |
| 1992 | OG-M | FIN | 3 | 2-0-1 | 180:00 | 8 | 0 | 2.66 | 0 | 0 | — |
| ~WM IIHF Directorate Best Goalie (1991), WM All-Star Team/Goal (1992), WM20 IIHF Directorate Best Goalie (1987) | | | | | | | | | | | |
| **Khabibulin, Nikolai / b. Jan. 13, 1973** | | | | | | | | | | | |
| 1992-93 | WM20 | RUS | 12 | 6-2-2 | 628:43 | 22 | 3 | 2.10 | 1 | 0 | G |
| 1996 | WCH | RUS | 2 | 0-0-2 | 100:00 | 10 | 0 | 6.00 | 0 | 0 | — |
| 2002 | OG-M | RUS | 6 | 3-1-2 | 359:12 | 14 | 1 | 2.34 | 0 | 0 | B |
| ~OG-M IIHF Directorate Best Goalie (2002) | | | | | | | | | | | |
| **Kidd, Trevor / b. Mar. 29, 1972** | | | | | | | | | | | |
| 1991-92 | WM20 | CAN | 13 | 6-3-4 | 760:00 | 44 | 1 | 3.47 | 0 | 0 | G |
| 1992 | WM | CAN | 1 | 1-0-0 | 60:00 | 3 | 0 | 3.00 | 0 | 0 | — |
| 1992 | OG-M | CAN | 1 | 1-0-0 | 60:00 | 0 | 1 | 0.00 | 0 | 0 | S |
| **Kieca, Mariusz / b. Nov. 5, 1969** | | | | | | | | | | | |
| 1988 | WM20 | POL | 3 | 0-0-1 | 120:00 | 24 | 0 | 12.00 | 0 | 0 | — |
| 1992 | WM | POL | 2 | 0-0-2 | 95:41 | 10 | 0 | 6.29 | 0 | 2 | — |
| 1992 | OG-M | POL | 3 | 0-0-3 | 160:00 | 13 | 0 | 4.87 | 0 | 0 | — |
| **Kiedewicz, Lukasz / b. Apr. 22, 1977** | | | | | | | | | | | |
| 1997 | WM20 | POL | 6 | 0-0-5 | 283:38 | 35 | 0 | 7.40 | 0 | 0 | — |
| **Kiener, Rene / b. May 21, 1938** | | | | | | | | | | | |
| 1959-62 | WM | SUI | 11 | 0-0-11 | 660:00 | 108 | 0 | 9.82 | 0 | 0 | — |
| 1964 | OG-M | SUI | 2 | 0-0-2 | 120:00 | 17 | 0 | 8.50 | 0 | 0 | — |
| **Kilpelainen, Eero / b. May 7, 1985** | | | | | | | | | | | |
| 2003 | WM18 | FIN | 6 | 2-2-2 | 359:38 | 20 | 0 | 3.34 | 0 | 4 | — |
| **Kiili, Lasse / b. Apr. 5, 1946** | | | | | | | | | | | |
| 1969 | WM | FIN | 1 | 0-0-1 | 28:00 | 3 | 0 | 6.43 | 0 | 0 | — |
| **Kikuchi, Naoya / b. Aug. 23, 1975** | | | | | | | | | | | |
| 2002 | WM | JPN | 4 | 0-0-3 | 195:08 | 18 | 0 | 5.53 | 0 | 0 | — |
| **Kindermann, Walter / b. Dec. 12, 1936** | | | | | | | | | | | |
| 1959 | WM | GDR | 6 | 2-0-3 | 320:00 | 27 | 0 | 5.06 | 0 | 0 | — |
| **Kivela, Antero / b. Dec. 26, 1955** | | | | | | | | | | | |
| 1978-79 | WM | FIN | 8 | 2-2-4 | 480:00 | 35 | 0 | 4.38 | 0 | 0 | — |
| 1980 | OG-M | FIN | 3 | 1-1-1 | 180:00 | 10 | 0 | 3.33 | 0 | 2 | — |
| **Klodans, Juris / b. May 25, 1974** | | | | | | | | | | | |
| 1997-98 | WM | LAT | 4 | 0-1-3 | 164:40 | 13 | 0 | 4.74 | 0 | 0 | — |
| **Klyuchnikov, Yuri / b. Sept. 17, 1983** | | | | | | | | | | | |
| 2001 | WM18 | RUS | 2 | 1-0-0 | 72:47 | 2 | 0 | 1.65 | 0 | 0 | G |
| **Knauss, Gunter / b. Feb. 14, 1943** | | | | | | | | | | | |
| 1967 | WM | FRG | 3 | 0-1-3 | 193:22 | 27 | 0 | 8.38 | 0 | 0 | — |
| 1968 | OG-M | FRG | 1 | 0-0-1 | 9:40 | 4 | 0 | 24.82 | 0 | 0 | — |
| **Knez, Rudolf / b. Sept. 12, 1944** | | | | | | | | | | | |
| 1968-72 | OG-M | YUG | 2 | 1-0-1 | 97:42 | 7 | 0 | 4.30 | 0 | 0 | — |
| **Kochan, Dieter / b. May 11, 1974** | | | | | | | | | | | |
| 2002 | WM | USA | 3 | 1-0-2 | 149:26 | 5 | 0 | 2.01 | 0 | 0 | — |
| **Koczab, Edward / b. Aug. 2, 1928 / d. Nov. 17, 2002** | | | | | | | | | | | |
| 1955-58 | WM | POL | 10 | 2-0-8 | 560:00 | 74 | 0 | 7.93 | 0 | 0 | — |
| 1956 | OG-M | POL | 4 | 1-0-3 | 240:00 | 19 | 0 | 4.75 | 0 | 0 | — |
| **Kolbe, Peter / b. June 12, 1939** | | | | | | | | | | | |
| 1961-67 | WM | GDR | 26 | 9-1-11 | 1,328:30 | 101 | 3 | 4.56 | 0 | 0 | — |
| **Kolesnik, Vitali / b. Aug. 20, 1979** | | | | | | | | | | | |
| 1999 | WM20 | KAZ | 6 | 1-1-3 | 306:37 | 27 | 1 | 5.28 | 0 | 0 | — |
| 2004-05 | WM | KAZ | 8 | 2-0-4 | 418:34 | 15 | 0 | 2.15 | 0 | 0 | — |
| 2006 | OG-M | KAZ | 2 | 0-0-2 | 119:51 | 6 | 0 | 3.00 | 0 | 0 | — |
| **Kolouch, Jiri / b. Apr. 26, 1932** | | | | | | | | | | | |
| 1954 | WM | TCH | 5 | 2-0-2 | 280:00 | 13 | 0 | 2.79 | 0 | 0 | — |
| **Kolyuzhny, Alexander / b. July 14, 1981** | | | | | | | | | | | |
| 1999-2001 | WM20 | KAZ | 15 | 1-1-7 | 599:44 | 73 | 0 | 7.30 | 0 | 0 | — |
| **Kolzig, Olaf / b. Apr. 6, 1970** | | | | | | | | | | | |
| 1997-2004 | WM | GER | 9 | 2-1-5 | 497:26 | 24 | 0 | 2.89 | 0 | 0 | — |
| 1996-2004 | WCH | GER | 4 | 0-0-4 | 224:58 | 15 | 0 | 4.00 | 0 | 0 | — |
| 1998-2006 | OG-M | GER | 5 | 2-2-1 | 299:16 | 10 | 1 | 2.00 | 0 | 2 | — |
| **Konovalenko, Viktor / b. Mar. 11, 1938 / d. Feb. 20, 1996** | | | | | | | | | | | |
| 1961-71 | WM | URS | 40 | 34-2-2 | 2,143:00 | 61 | 5 | 1.71 | 0 | 0 | 6G,B |
| 1964-68 | OG-M | URS | 11 | 10-0-1 | 640:00 | 19 | 3 | 1.78 | 0 | 0 | 2G |
| ~IIHF Hall of Fame | | | | | | | | | | | |
| ~WM IIHF Directorate Best Goalie (1970) | | | | | | | | | | | |
| **Konstantinov, Yevgeni / b. Mar. 29, 1981** | | | | | | | | | | | |
| 1999 | WM18 | RUS | 6 | 3-0-3 | 338:52 | 14 | 0 | 2.48 | 0 | 0 | — |
| **Kopf, Bernhard / b. Jan. 20, 1959** | | | | | | | | | | | |
| 1979 | WM20 | FRG | 4 | 1-0-2 | 158:00 | 10 | 1 | 3.80 | 0 | 0 | — |
| **Kopriva, Miroslav / b. Dec. 5, 1983** | | | | | | | | | | | |
| 2001 | WM18 | CZE | 5 | 1-0-3 | 240:29 | 15 | 0 | 3.74 | 0 | 0 | — |
| **Koslow, Patrick / b. Jan. 6, 1985** | | | | | | | | | | | |
| 2002 | WM18 | GER | 2 | 0-0-2 | 72:12 | 13 | 0 | 10.80 | 0 | 0 | — |
| **Kostyukhin, Sergei / b. 1962** | | | | | | | | | | | |
| 1981 | WM20 | URS | 1 | 0-0-0 | 20:00 | 1 | 0 | 3.00 | 0 | 0 | — |

| | | | | | | | | | | | |
|---|---|---|---|---|---|---|---|---|---|---|---|
| **Kosyl, Walery / b. Mar. 17, 1944** | | | | | | | | | | | |
| 1966-74 | WM | POL | 30 | 1-8-19 | 1,668:30 | 166 | 0 | 5.97 | 0 | 6 | — |
| 1972-76 | OG-M | POL | 8 | 0-0-7 | 420:00 | 47 | 0 | 6.71 | 0 | 4 | — |
| **Kovacic, Danijel / b. July 3, 1987** | | | | | | | | | | | |
| 2005 | WM18 | GER | 6 | 2-0-4 | 310:01 | 15 | 1 | 2.90 | 0 | 0 | — |
| **Kowalski, Craig / b. Jan. 15, 1981** | | | | | | | | | | | |
| 2001 | WM20 | USA | 1 | 0-0-1 | 60:00 | 4 | 0 | 4.00 | 0 | 0 | — |
| **Kralik, Jiri / b. Apr. 11, 1952** | | | | | | | | | | | |
| 1979-85 | WM | TCH | 34 | 19-5-6 | 1,933:41 | 70 | 6 | 2.17 | 0 | 0 | G,3S |
| 1981 | CC | TCH | 1 | 0-0-0 | 19:19 | 2 | 0 | 6.21 | 0 | 0 | 3rd |
| 1980-84 | OG-M | TCH | 6 | 4-0-2 | 360:00 | 15 | 2 | 2.50 | 0 | 0 | S |
| ~WM IIHF Directorate Best Goalie (1982, 1985), WM All-Star Team/Goal (1982, 1985) | | | | | | | | | | | |
| **Kraske, Wolfgang / b. Oct. 14, 1952** | | | | | | | | | | | |
| 1976-78 | WM | GDR | 10 | 3-0-7 | 526:01 | 50 | 0 | 5.70 | 0 | 0 | — |
| **Krauzowicz, Wlodzimierz / b. Mar. 8, 1967** | | | | | | | | | | | |
| 1987 | WM20 | POL | 7 | 1-0-6 | 317:00 | 58 | 0 | 10.98 | 0 | 2 | — |
| **Kristiansen, Arthur / b. July 18, 1923 / d. July 7, 2001** | | | | | | | | | | | |
| 1949-54 | WM | NOR | 4 | 1-0-3 | 240:00 | 26 | 0 | 6.50 | 0 | 0 | — |
| 1952 | OG-M | NOR | 1 | 0-0-1 | 55:00 | 4 | 0 | 4.36 | 0 | 0 | — |
| **Kristiansen, Kim / b. Nov. 26, 1971** | | | | | | | | | | | |
| 1991 | WM20 | NOR | 1 | 0-0-1 | 60:00 | 13 | 0 | 13.00 | 0 | 0 | — |
| **Kristiansen, Knut / b. unknown** | | | | | | | | | | | |
| 1954 | WM | NOR | 4 | 1-0-3 | 240:00 | 18 | 0 | 4.50 | 0 | 0 | — |
| **Kristoffersen, Morten / b. June 12, 1972** | | | | | | | | | | | |
| 1991 | WM20 | NOR | 4 | 0-0-4 | 195:52 | 33 | 0 | 10.11 | 0 | 2 | — |
| **Krivolapov, Viktor / b. Mar. 4, 1951** | | | | | | | | | | | |
| 1975 | WM | URS | 3 | 2-0-0 | 151:00 | 5 | 0 | 1.99 | 0 | 0 | G |
| **Krivomazov, Roman / b. Mar. 18, 1978** | | | | | | | | | | | |
| 1998 | WM20 | KAZ | 5 | 1-0-2 | 140:28 | 17 | 0 | 7.26 | 0 | 2 | — |
| 1998 | WM | KAZ | 2 | 0-0-0 | 16:33 | 3 | 0 | 10.88 | 0 | 2 | — |
| **Kucera, Martin / b. May 25, 1978** | | | | | | | | | | | |
| 1998 | WM | SVK | 5 | 2-0-1 | 228:52 | 9 | 1 | 2.36 | 0 | 0 | — |
| **Kudrna, Ladislav / b. Jan. 10, 1977** | | | | | | | | | | | |
| 1996 | WM20 | CZE | 1 | 0-0-0 | 3:59 | 1 | 0 | 15.08 | 0 | 0 | — |
| **Kuivalainen, Pasi / b. July 15, 1972** | | | | | | | | | | | |
| 1991-92 | WM20 | FIN | 10 | 4-1-3 | 530:19 | 30 | 0 | 3.39 | 0 | 2 | — |
| **Kukla, Franciszek / b. July 16, 1953** | | | | | | | | | | | |
| 1986 | WM | POL | 9 | 1-7-0 | 391:04 | 40 | 0 | 6.14 | 0 | 2 | — |
| 1988 | OG-M | POL | 1 | 0-0-1 | 40:01 | 3 | 0 | 4.50 | 0 | 0 | — |
| **Kulicek, Jiri / b. May 17, 1934** | | | | | | | | | | | |
| 1957-59 | WM | TCH | 11 | 7-2-2 | 631:17 | 19 | 3 | 1.81 | 0 | 2 | 2B |
| **Kunast, Christian / b. Mar. 7, 1971** | | | | | | | | | | | |
| 2001 | WM | GER | 4 | 1-1-2 | 239:36 | 10 | 0 | 2.50 | 0 | 0 | — |
| 2002 | OG-M | GER | 2 | 0-0-2 | 39:30 | 7 | 0 | 10.63 | 0 | 0 | — |
| **Kuntar, Les / b. July 28, 1969** | | | | | | | | | | | |
| 1994 | WM | USA | 3 | 0-0-1 | 134:38 | 11 | 0 | 4.90 | 0 | 0 | — |
| **Kunzler, Albert / b. Feb. 9, 1911 / d. unknown** | | | | | | | | | | | |
| 1930-39 | WM | SUI | 15 | 9-2-4 | 690:00 | 24 | 3 | 2.09 | 0 | 0 | S,3B |
| 1936 | OG-M | SUI | 2 | 0-0-2 | 90:00 | 5 | 0 | 3.33 | 0 | 0 | — |
| **Kuokkanen, Juha / b. Jan. 26, 1982** | | | | | | | | | | | |
| 2002 | WM20 | FIN | 1 | 1-0-0 | 60:00 | 1 | 0 | 1.00 | 0 | 0 | B |
| **Kuskis, Herberts / b. Mar. 5, 1913 / d. Dec. 29, 1994** | | | | | | | | | | | |
| 1933-39 | WM | LAT | 10 | 4-0-6 | 450:00 | 33 | 3 | 4.40 | 0 | 0 | — |
| 1936 | OG-M | LAT | 1 | 0-0-1 | 45:00 | 9 | 0 | 12.00 | 0 | 0 | — |
| **Kuzmenko, Denis / b. Jan. 1, 1975** | | | | | | | | | | | |
| 1995 | WM20 | RUS | 3 | 1-0-2 | 177:12 | 14 | 0 | 4.74 | 0 | 0 | S |
| **Kuznetsov, Andrei / b. Apr. 5, 1985** | | | | | | | | | | | |
| 2005 | WM20 | RUS | 2 | 1-0-0 | 96:26 | 5 | 0 | 3.11 | 0 | 0 | S |
| **Kvalevog, Toby / b. Dec. 22, 1974** | | | | | | | | | | | |
| 1994 | WM20 | USA | 5 | 0-0-3 | 235:50 | 20 | 0 | 5.09 | 0 | 0 | — |
| **LaBrosse, Dwight / b. Oct. 6, 1983** | | | | | | | | | | | |
| 2001 | WM18 | USA | 3 | 1-0-2 | 176:54 | 8 | 0 | 2.71 | 0 | 0 | — |
| **Lacky, Miroslav / b. Sept. 4, 1943** | | | | | | | | | | | |
| 1969-70 | WM | TCH | 3 | 2-0-0 | 149:00 | 4 | 0 | 1.61 | 0 | 2 | 2B |
| **LaCroix, Alphonse / b. Oct. 21, 1897 / d. Apr. 12, 1973** | | | | | | | | | | | |
| 1924 | OG-M | USA | 5 | 4-0-1 | 260:00 | 6 | 3 | 1.38 | 0 | 0 | S |
| **Laferriere, Rick / b. Jan. 3, 1961** | | | | | | | | | | | |
| 1980 | WM20 | CAN | 4 | 2-0-2 | 240:00 | 13 | 0 | 3.25 | 0 | 2 | — |
| **Lahn, Stephan / b. May 24, 1975** | | | | | | | | | | | |
| 1995 | WM20 | GER | 1 | 0-0-0 | 14:00 | 3 | 0 | 12.86 | 0 | 2 | — |
| **Lahtinen, Juhani / b. Sept. 28, 1938** | | | | | | | | | | | |
| 1958-67 | WM | FIN | 39 | 8-4-25 | 2,263:00 | 219 | 0 | 5.81 | 0 | 0 | — |
| 1960-64 | OG-M | FIN | 10 | 4-0-6 | 600:00 | 38 | 1 | 3.80 | 0 | 0 | — |
| **Lakosil, Vlastimil / b. July 4, 1979** | | | | | | | | | | | |
| 1998-99 | WM20 | CZE | 10 | 4-0-3 | 503:49 | 26 | 0 | 3.10 | 0 | 0 | — |
| **Laloux, Rene / b. unknown / d. unknown** | | | | | | | | | | | |
| 1934 | WM | BEL | 4 | 1-0-3 | 180:00 | 26 | 1 | 8.67 | 0 | 0 | — |
| **Lambert, Gerard / b. unknown / d. unknown** | | | | | | | | | | | |
| 1937 | WM | FRA | 2 | 0-0-2 | 90:00 | 10 | 0 | 6.67 | 0 | 0 | — |
| **Landsman, Jaroslav / b. May 26, 1966** | | | | | | | | | | | |
| 1986 | WM20 | TCH | 7 | 4-0-2 | 400:00 | 17 | 1 | 2.55 | 0 | 2 | — |
| **Lang, Karel / b. June 9, 1958** | | | | | | | | | | | |
| 1981-82 | WM | TCH | 8 | 4-1-3 | 428:45 | 23 | 0 | 3.22 | 0 | 2 | S,B |
| 1981 | CC | TCH | 6 | 2-2-2 | 340:41 | 15 | 0 | 2.64 | 0 | 4 | 3rd |
| 1980 | OG-M | TCH | 1 | 1-0-0 | 60:00 | 2 | 0 | 2.00 | 0 | 0 | — |
| **Lange, Mathias / b. Apr. 13, 1985** | | | | | | | | | | | |
| 2004 | WM20 | AUT | 5 | 0-0-4 | 189:29 | 22 | 0 | 6.97 | 0 | 0 | — |
| **Langley, Art / b. June 25, 1896 / d. Mar. 5, 1967** | | | | | | | | | | | |
| 1924 | OG-M | USA | 1 | 0-0-0 | 40:00 | 0 | 0 | 0.00 | 0 | 0 | S |
| **Lanicek, Michal / b. July 6, 1981** | | | | | | | | | | | |
| 1999 | WM18 | CZE | 6 | 3-0-2 | 341:48 | 13 | 0 | 2.28 | 0 | 0 | — |
| **Lapainis, Roberts / b. Sept. 10, 1913 / d. Oct. 1947** | | | | | | | | | | | |
| 1935-38 | WM | LAT | 9 | 2-0-7 | 415:00 | 33 | 1 | 4.77 | 0 | 0 | — |
| 1936 | OG-M | LAT | 2 | 0-0-2 | 90:00 | 18 | 0 | 12.00 | 0 | 0 | — |
| **Larson, Mike / b. unknown** | | | | | | | | | | | |
| 1962 | WM | USA | 5 | 3-0-2 | 270:00 | 15 | 0 | 3.33 | 0 | 0 | B |
| **Larsson, Curt / b. Dec. 11, 1944** | | | | | | | | | | | |
| 1972-74 | WM | SWE | 6 | 4-1-0 | 320:00 | 7 | 1 | 1.31 | 0 | 0 | 2B |
| ~WM IIHF Directorate Best Goalie (1974) | | | | | | | | | | | |
| **Larsson, Wilhelm / b. June 23, 1911 / d. Sept. 13, 1971** | | | | | | | | | | | |
| 1935 | WM | SWE | 3 | 1-0-2 | 145:00 | 8 | 0 | 3.31 | 0 | 0 | — |
| 1936 | OG-M | SWE | 2 | 0-0-2 | 90:00 | 6 | 0 | 4.00 | 0 | 0 | — |
| **Laska, Martin / b. Jan. 23, 1983** | | | | | | | | | | | |
| 2001 | WM18 | CZE | 3 | 2-0-1 | 185:43 | 12 | 0 | 3.88 | 1 | 0 | — |
| **Lassila, Hannu / b. Feb. 25, 1954** | | | | | | | | | | | |
| 1981-82 | WM | FIN | 6 | 1-1-4 | 262:18 | 26 | 0 | 5.95 | 0 | 0 | — |
| 1981 | CC | FIN | 3 | 0-1-2 | 180:00 | 16 | 0 | 5.33 | 0 | 0 | — |
| **Laukkanen, Tuomo / b. July 22, 1959** | | | | | | | | | | | |
| 1978 | WM20 | FIN | 2 | 1-0-1 | 100:00 | 4 | 0 | 2.40 | 0 | 0 | — |
| **Lavaivre, Charles / b. Feb. 14, 1905 / d. unknown** | | | | | | | | | | | |
| 1924 | OG-M | FRA | 2 | 1-0-1 | 80:00 | 17 | 0 | 12.75 | 0 | 0 | — |
| **Lebed, Vitaliy / b. Jan. 17, 1980** | | | | | | | | | | | |
| 2000 | WM20 | UKR | 1 | 0-0-1 | 60:00 | 6 | 0 | 6.00 | 0 | 0 | — |
| **LeBlanc, Ray / b. Oct. 24, 1964** | | | | | | | | | | | |
| 1992 | WM | USA | 5 | 2-1-2 | 252:52 | 16 | 2 | 3.80 | 0 | 0 | — |
| 1992 | OG-M | USA | 8 | 5-1-2 | 462:39 | 17 | 2 | 2.20 | 0 | 2 | — |
| ~OG-M All-Star Team/Goal (1992) | | | | | | | | | | | |
| **Lefebure, Philippe / b. unknown / d. unknown** | | | | | | | | | | | |
| 1930-31 | WM | FRA | 7 | 2-0-5 | 390:00 | 18 | 0 | 2.77 | 0 | 0 | — |
| 1928 | OG-M | FRA | 2 | 1-0-1 | 90:00 | 5 | 1 | 3.33 | 0 | 0 | — |
| **Legace, Manny / b. Feb. 4, 1973** | | | | | | | | | | | |
| 1993 | WM20 | CAN | 6 | 6-0-0 | 360:00 | 10 | 1 | 1.67 | 0 | 0 | G |
| ~WM20 IIHF Directorate Best Goalie (1993), WM20 All-Star Team/Goal (1993) | | | | | | | | | | | |
| **Lehkonen, Timo / b. Jan. 8, 1966** | | | | | | | | | | | |
| 1985-86 | WM20 | FIN | 10 | 4-2-4 | 600:00 | 33 | 1 | 3.30 | 1 | 0 | — |
| ~WM20 All-Star Team/Goal (1985) | | | | | | | | | | | |
| **Lehto, Mika / b. Apr. 12, 1979** | | | | | | | | | | | |
| 1999 | WM20 | FIN | 4 | 2-0-1 | 206:52 | 8 | 0 | 2.32 | 0 | 0 | — |
| **Leinweber, Walter / b. Apr. 18, 1907 / d. Mar. 1997** | | | | | | | | | | | |
| 1930-35 | WM | GER | 12 | 9-0-3 | 570:00 | 23 | 1 | 2.42 | 0 | 0 | S,B |
| 1932 | OG-M | GER | 6 | 2-0-4 | 270:00 | 26 | 0 | 5.78 | 0 | 0 | B |
| **Lemelin, Rejean / b. Nov. 19, 1954** | | | | | | | | | | | |
| 1984 | CC | CAN | 3 | 1-0-1 | 138:20 | 7 | 0 | 3.04 | 0 | 0 | 1st |
| **Lemmenmeier, Ludwig / b. Feb. 28, 1962** | | | | | | | | | | | |
| 1982 | WM20 | SUI | 1 | 0-0-1 | 20:00 | 5 | 0 | 15.00 | 0 | 0 | — |
| **LeNeveu, David / b. May 23, 1983** | | | | | | | | | | | |
| 2003 | WM20 | CAN | 2 | 1-0-0 | 91:20 | 4 | 0 | 2.63 | 0 | 0 | S |
| **Lengacher, Cedric / b. Dec. 25, 1963** | | | | | | | | | | | |
| 1982 | WM20 | SUI | 1 | 0-0-1 | 14:43 | 6 | 0 | 24.46 | 0 | 0 | — |
| **Lenssen, Ted / b. May 17, 1952** | | | | | | | | | | | |
| 1981 | WM | NED | 6 | 0-0-6 | 287:28 | 45 | 0 | 9.39 | 0 | 2 | — |
| 1980 | OG-M | NED | 5 | 1-1-2 | 261:38 | 30 | 0 | 6.88 | 0 | 2 | — |
| **Leonhardt, Bjorn / b. Dec. 20, 1978** | | | | | | | | | | | |
| 1998 | WM20 | GER | 4 | 0-0-3 | 207:44 | 23 | 0 | 6.64 | 0 | 2 | — |
| **Leppanen, Antti / b. Nov. 23, 1947** | | | | | | | | | | | |
| 1973-75 | WM | FIN | 17 | 9-2-5 | 989:25 | 38 | 1 | 2.30 | 0 | 0 | — |
| 1976 | CC | FIN | 5 | 1-0-3 | 220:29 | 28 | 0 | 7.62 | 0 | 0 | — |
| 1976 | OG-M | FIN | 2 | 0-0-2 | 120:00 | 7 | 0 | 3.50 | 0 | 0 | — |
| **Leven, Jonas / b. Feb. 23, 1970** | | | | | | | | | | | |
| 1990 | WM20 | SWE | 3 | 1-0-2 | 180:00 | 15 | 0 | 5.00 | 0 | 2 | — |
| **Lichtschein, Fritz / b. unknown / d. unknown** | | | | | | | | | | | |
| 1930 | WM | AUT | 1 | 1-0-0 | 45:00 | 0 | 1 | 0.00 | 0 | 0 | — |
| **Liedstrand, Bengt / b. Oct. 25, 1911 / d. Mar. 26, 2003** | | | | | | | | | | | |
| 1935-37 | WM | SWE | 6 | 3-1-2 | 270:00 | 10 | 2 | 2.22 | 0 | 0 | — |
| **Lilljebjorn, Ake / b. Sept. 23, 1962** | | | | | | | | | | | |
| 1982 | WM20 | SWE | 3 | 2-0-1 | 180:00 | 13 | 1 | 4.33 | 0 | 0 | — |
| 1986-87 | WM | SWE | 7 | 4-0-1 | 332:44 | 14 | 1 | 2.52 | 0 | 0 | G,S |
| **Linc, Jaroslav / b. July 14, 1962** | | | | | | | | | | | |
| 1981 | WM20 | TCH | 1 | 1-0-0 | 60:00 | 4 | 0 | 4.00 | 0 | 0 | — |
| **Lindbergh, Pelle / b. May 24, 1959 / d. Nov. 12, 1985** | | | | | | | | | | | |
| 1977-79 | WM20 | SWE | 17 | 9-2-6 | 1,000:00 | 49 | 2 | 2.94 | 0 | 0 | S,B |
| 1979-83 | WM | SWE | 14 | 5-2-7 | 840:00 | 56 | 0 | 4.00 | 0 | 0 | B |
| 1981 | CC | SWE | 2 | 0-0-1 | 92:23 | 9 | 0 | 5.85 | 0 | 0 | — |
| 1980 | OG-M | SWE | 5 | 2-2-1 | 300:00 | 18 | 0 | 3.60 | 0 | 0 | B |
| ~WM20 IIHF Directorate Best Goalie (1979), WM20 All-Star Team/Goal (1979) | | | | | | | | | | | |

**Lindfors, Sakari / b. Apr. 27, 1966**
1986 WM20 FIN 3 2-0-1 180:00 8 0 2.67 0 0 —
1989-93 WM FIN 13 6-2-4 698:25 23 1 1.98 0 0 S

**Lindmark, Peter / b. Nov. 8, 1956**
1981-91 WM SWE 42 19-8-13 2,330:06 120 1 3.09 0 6 2G,2S
1981-87 CC SWE 17 7-0-9 969:57 51 2 3.15 1 2 2nd
1988 OG-M SWE 7 3-3-1 400:00 16 0 2.40 0 0 B
~WM IIHF Directorate Best Goalie (1981, 1986), WM All-Star Team/Goal (1981, 1986)

**Lindner, Harry / b. unknown**
1961-62 WM FRG 10 2-1-6 541:00 52 1 5.77 0 2 —

**Lindqvist, Bengt / b. Apr. 21, 1934**
1960 OG-M SWE 3 1-0-1 81:00 5 0 3.70 0 0 —

**Lindqvist, Magnus / b. Apr. 26, 1972**
1992 WM20 SWE 2 1-1-0 120:00 8 0 4.00 0 0 S

**Lindsay, Gavin / b. unknown**
1954 WM CAN 1 0-0-0 20:00 0 0 0.00 0 0 S

**Lindstahl, Sam / b. Apr. 23, 1967**
1985-87 WM20 SWE 13 4-1-7 694:19 45 2 3.89 0 0 B
~WM20 All-Star Team/Goal (1987)

**Linkosuo, Juhani / b. June 22, 1923 / d. May 27, 1980**
1949 WM FIN 1 0-0-1 20:00 8 0 24.00 0 0 —

**Little, Herbert / b. Dec. 11, 1907 / d. unknown**
1931 WM GBR 4 2-0-2 240:00 5 1 1.25 0 0 —

**Littman, David / b. June 13, 1967**
1994 WM USA 1 0-0-1 45:22 6 0 7.94 0 0 —

**Liut, Mike / b. Jan. 7, 1956**
1981 CC CAN 6 4-1-1 360:00 19 1 3.17 1 0 2nd

**Liv, Stefan / b. Dec. 21, 1980/ d. Sept. 7, 2011**
2002-09 WM SWE 10 7-0-3 602:47 18 3 1.79 1 2 G,S,2B
2006 OG-M SWE 1 1-0-0 60:00 2 0 2.00 0 0 G
~perished in Yaroslavl plane crash

**Lockhart, Don / b. 1931**
1954 WM CAN 7 6-0-1 400:00 12 2 1.80 0 0 S
~WM IIHF Directorate Best Goalie (1954)

**Lofqvist, William / b. Apr. 12, 1947**
1971-76 WM SWE 12 7-1-3 694:00 28 1 2.42 0 2 S,2B
1980 OG-M SWE 2 2-0-0 120:00 1 1 0.50 0 0 B

**Logue, Jim / b. Mar. 25, 1941**
1962 WM USA 3 2-0-0 150:00 8 0 3.20 0 0 B
1968 OG-M USA 1 0-0-1 40:00 10 0 15.00 0 0 —

**Lopresti, Pete / b. May 23, 1954**
1976-78 WM USA 14 2-3-9 840:00 77 0 5.50 0 0 —
1976 CC USA 2 1-0-1 120:00 6 0 3.00 0 0 —

**Losonczi, Gyorgy / b. Sept. 9, 1940**
1964 OG-M HUN 5 0-0-4 240:00 23 0 5.75 0 0 —

**Lothrop, John / b. unknown**
1969 WM USA 1 0-0-0 20:00 3 0 9.00 0 0 —

**Lukaszka, Pawel / b. Feb. 6, 1962**
1980 OG-M POL 2 0-0-2 66:02 7 0 6.33 0 0 —

**Machreich, Patrick / b. Sept. 29, 1980**
2005 WM AUT 1 0-0-1 60:00 8 0 8.00 0 0 —

**Maciejko, Jan / b. Jan. 2, 1913 / d. Oct. 21, 1993**
1939-47 WM POL 12 5-0-7 615:00 40 3 3.90 0 0 —
1948 OG-M POL 3 0-0-2 140:00 35 0 15.02 0 0 —

**Macius, A. / b. unknown / d. unknown**
1938 WM LTU 4 1-0-3 180:00 33 1 11.00 — — —

**Mack, Hans / b. Sept. 21, 1923 / d. unknown**
1957 WM GDR 4 1-0-3 240:00 40 0 10.00 0 0 —

**Mack, Robert / b. July 1, 1959**
1988 OG-M AUT 1 0-0-1 39:59 5 0 7.50 0 0 —

**Macrez, Landry / b. Apr. 30, 1982**
2002 WM20 FRA 6 1-0-4 288:50 31 0 6.44 0 0 —

**Madden, Chris / b. Mar. 10, 1979**
1999 WM20 USA 4 1-0-3 219:46 15 0 4.10 0 0 —

**Maesciuc, Emil / b. unknown / d. unknown**
1935-38 WM ROM 8 3-0-5 360:00 24 1 4.00 0 0 —

**Magliarditi, Marc / b. July 9, 1976**
1996 WM20 USA 3 1-0-1 143:00 13 0 5.45 0 0 —

**Makatsch, Rainer / b. July 1, 1946**
1972 WM FRG 5 1-0-1 179:00 16 0 5.36 0 0 —
1972 OG-M FRG 1 1-0-0 20:00 0 0 0.00 0 0 —

**Maki, Ed / b. July 25, 1913 / d. unknown**
1939 WM USA 9 7-0-2 425:00 8 6 1.13 — — S

**Makutnyowicz, Mieczyslaw / b. 1917 / d. 1990**
1947 WM POL 2 0-0-2 120:00 19 0 9.50 0 0 —

**Malac, Pavel / b. June 16, 1973**
1993 WM20 TCH 2 0-0-1 39:12 5 0 7.66 0 2 B

**Malek, Roman / b. Sept. 25, 1977**
2003 WM CZE 3 2-0-1 150:21 7 1 2.79 0 0 —

**Mangini, Constanzo / b. June 11, 1918 / d. unknown**
1948 OG-M ITA 3 0-0-3 180:00 49 0 16.33 0 0 —

**Manson, Jack / b. 1914 / d. unknown**
1950 WM CAN 4 4-0-0 240:00 5 0 1.25 0 0 G

**Mansson, Johan / b. Jan. 23, 1973**
1993 WM20 SWE 1 1-0-0 60:00 1 0 1.00 0 0 S

**Maric, Daniel / b. June 11, 1957**
1988 OG-M FRA 2 0-0-1 75:54 13 0 10.28 0 0 —

**Marik, Michal / b. May 18, 1975**
1995 WM20 CZE 4 2-0-1 206:49 14 0 4.06 0 2 —

**Markkanen, Jussi / b. May 8, 1975**
1994-95 WM20 FIN 8 4-1-3 476:00 27 1 3.40 0 20 —
2002-04 WM FIN 8 6-0-2 489:42 11 2 1,.35 1 0 —

**Marthinsen, Jim / b. Apr. 15, 1956**
1990-96 WM NOR 25 5-3-13 1,317:54 87 1 3.96 0 0 —
1980-94 OG-M NOR 17 3-4-9 882:28 74 0 5.03 0 0 —

**Martignoni, Arnold / b. May 19, 1901 / d. unknown**
1928 OG-M SUI 3 0-0-1 70:00 17 0 14.57 0 0 B

**Martin, Seth / b. May 4, 1933**
1961-67 WM CAN 22 13-3-6 1,286:00 50 1 2.33 0 4 G,2B
1964 OG-M CAN 6 4-0-1 247:00 5 0 1.21 0 0 —
~IIHF Hall of Fame
~OG-M IIHF Directorate Best Goalie (1964), WM IIHF Directorate Best Goalie (1961, 1963, 1966), OG-M All-Star Team/Goal (1964), WM All-Star Team/Goal (1961, 1966)

**Martinsen, Remo / b. June 10, 1969**
1989 WM20 NOR 4 0-0-4 240:00 38 0 9.50 0 0 —

**Maryin, Alexei / b. Oct. 29, 1964**
1991 WM URS 4 3-0-0 197:11 7 0 2.13 0 0 B
1991 CC URS 1 0-0-1 60:00 5 0 5.00 0 0 —

**Mason, Bob / b. Apr. 22, 1961**
1984 OG-M USA 3 2-0-1 159:37 10 0 3.76 0 0 —

**Mattsson, Markus / b. July 30, 1957**
1976-81 CC FIN 4 0-0-3 199:31 29 0 8.72 0 0 —

**Mazzoli, Jim / b. Mar. 16, 1970**
1999 WM ITA 1 0-0-1 20:00 4 0 12.00 0 0 —

**McCabe, Robert / b. unknown / d. unknown**
1947 WM USA 3 2-0-1 180:00 11 0 3.67 0 0 —

**McCartan, Jack / b. Aug. 5, 1935**
1959 WM USA 5 2-0-3 300:00 20 0 4.00 0 0 —
1960 OG-M USA 7 7-0-0 413:00 17 0 2.47 0 0 G
~IIHF Hall of Fame
~OG-M IIHF Directorate Best Goalie (1960)

**McCrone, John / b. Feb. 26, 1963**
1994 WM GBR 3 0-0-2 105:22 18 0 10.25 0 0 —

**McKay, Martin / b. Apr. 27, 1968**
1994 WM GBR 3 0-0-3 117:12 14 0 7.17 0 2 —

**McLean, Kirk / b. June 26, 1966**
1990 WM CAN 10 5-1-2 457:26 27 0 3.54 1 0 —

**McLelland, Ivan / b. Mar. 15, 1931**
1955 WM CAN 8 8-0-0 480:00 6 4 0.75 0 0 G

**McLoughlin, Noel / b. Sept. 15, 1929**
1960 OG-M AUS 3 0-0-1 120:00 21 0 10.50 0 0 —

**Medvedev, Andrei / b. Apr. 1, 1983**
2000-01 WM18 RUS 8 7-0-1 465:29 18 0 2.32 0 2 G,S
2001-03 WM20 RUS 17 11-0-4 880:47 31 1 2.11 0 0 2G

**Medvedev, Roman / b. Aug. 31, 1981**
2001 WM20 KAZ 3 0-0-2 127:58 18 0 8.44 0 0 —
2006 WM KAZ 1 0-0-1 29:39 7 0 14.17 0 0 —

**Mega, Roman / b. Oct. 27, 1970**
1996 WCH SVK 2 0-0-2 119:33 12 0 6.02 0 2 —

**Meister, Rupert / b. Mar. 11, 1965**
1984-85 WM20 FRG 11 1-1-7 581:33 62 0 6.40 0 4 —

**Melanson, Rollie / b. June 28, 1960**
1979 WM20 CAN 2 2-0-0 120:00 3 0 1.50 0 0 —

**Mellerud, Oystein / b. July 6, 1938 / d. Nov. 27, 1989**
1962 WM NOR 1 0-0-1 60:00 14 0 14.00 0 0 —
1964 OG-M NOR 6 4-0-2 360:00 18 0 3.00 0 0 —

**Melnikov, Yuri / b. April 9, 1983**
2000 WM18 BLR 6 0-0-3 240:24 35 0 8.74 0 0 —

**Meloche, Gilles / b. July 12, 1950**
1982 WM CAN 5 3-0-2 300:00 16 1 3.20 0 0 B

**Mensator, Lukas / b. Apr. 18, 1984**
2002 WM18 CZE 7 6-0-1 420:00 11 1 1.57 0 0 B
2003 WM20 CZE 3 0-0-1 98:46 3 0 1.82 0 0 —
~WM18 IIHF Directorate Best Goalie (2002), WM18 Al-Star Team/Goal (2002)

**Meoli, John / b. Mar. 22, 1920 / d. unknown**
1947 WM USA 4 2-0-2 240:00 15 0 3.75 0 0 —

**Merk, Klaus / b. Apr. 26, 1967**
1986 WM20 FRG 6 0-0-6 320:00 44 0 8.25 0 0 —
1990-96 WM FRG 20 4-2-13 1,152:15 71 1 3.70 0 6 —
1996 WCH GER 2 0-0-1 74:36 9 0 7.24 0 0 —
1994-98 OG-M GER 3 2-0-1 180:00 13 0 4.33 0 0 —

**Merkle, Robert / b. Jan. 3, 1946**
1973 WM FRG 4 0-0-1 149:00 27 0 10.87 0 2 —

**Metcalfe, Derek / b. 1935**
1962 WM GBR 3 1-0-2 180:00 29 0 9.67 0 0 —

**Micalef, Corrado / b. Apr. 20, 1961**
1981 WM20 CAN 5 1-1-2 207:00 20 0 5.80 0 0 —

| | | | | | | | | | | | |
|---|---|---|---|---|---|---|---|---|---|---|---|
| **Michalek, Miroslav / b. June 30, 1965** | | | | | | | | | | | |
| 1994 | OG-M | SVK | 2 | 1-0-0 | 100:00 | 5 | 0 | 3.00 | 0 | 0 | — |
| **Michaud, Olivier / b. Sept. 14, 1983** | | | | | | | | | | | |
| 2002 | WM20 | CAN | 2 | 1-0-1 | 120:00 | 5 | 0 | 2.50 | 0 | 0 | S |
| **Mikhailovski, Maxim / b. July 24, 1969** | | | | | | | | | | | |
| 1989 | WM20 | URS | 2 | 1-0-0 | 80:00 | 0 | 1 | 0.00 | 1 | 0 | G |
| 1993-97 | WM | RUS | 7 | 3-2-2 | 418:47 | 14 | 0 | 2.01 | 0 | 0 | G |
| **Miklenda, Jaroslav / b. Mar. 7, 1974** | | | | | | | | | | | |
| 1994 | WM20 | CZE | 2 | 0-0-0 | 41:45 | 3 | 0 | 4.31 | 0 | 0 | — |
| **Mikolas, Josef / b. Jan. 23, 1938** | | | | | | | | | | | |
| 1961-63 | WM | TCH | 11 | 8-2-1 | 629:00 | 17 | 2 | 1.62 | 0 | 0 | S,B |
| **Millen, Greg / b. June 25, 1957** | | | | | | | | | | | |
| 1982 | WM | CAN | 5 | 2-2-1 | 300:00 | 14 | 0 | 2.80 | 0 | 10 | B |
| **Milne, Ronnie / b. Jan. 19, 1910 / d. unknown** | | | | | | | | | | | |
| 1935 | WM | GBR | 7 | 4-0-3 | 345:00 | 14 | 1 | 2.43 | 0 | 0 | B |
| **Mindjimba, Antoine / b. Sept. 3, 1968** | | | | | | | | | | | |
| 1995 | WM | FRA | 1 | 0-0-1 | 60:00 | 5 | 0 | 5.00 | 0 | 2 | — |
| **Misawa, Minoru / b. May 1, 1949** | | | | | | | | | | | |
| 1976-80 | OG-M | JPN | 4 | 0-0-2 | 169:06 | 19 | 0 | 6.74 | 0 | 0 | — |
| **Misut, Lubomir / b. Mar. 12, 1983** | | | | | | | | | | | |
| 2001 | WM18 | SVK | 2 | 0-0-0 | 36:51 | 1 | 0 | 1.63 | 0 | 0 | — |
| **Mkrtychan, Grigori / b. Jan. 3, 1925 / d. Feb. 14, 2003** | | | | | | | | | | | |
| 1954-55 | WM | URS | 6 | 5-0-0 | 297:38 | 8 | 0 | 1.61 | 0 | 0 | G,S |
| 1956 | OG-M | URS | 1 | 0-0-0 | 20:00 | 2 | 0 | 6.00 | 0 | 0 | G |
| **Modry, Bohumil / b. Sept. 24, 1916 / d. July 21, 1963** | | | | | | | | | | | |
| 1937-49 | WM | TCH | 35 | 19-5-11 | 1,885:00 | 40 | 12 | 1.27 | 0 | 0 | 2G,B |
| 1948 | OG-M | TCH | 5 | 4-1-0 | 300:00 | 10 | 1 | 2.00 | 0 | 0 | S |
| ~IIHF Hall of Fame | | | | | | | | | | | |
| **Moffat, Mike / b. Feb. 4, 1962** | | | | | | | | | | | |
| 1982 | WM20 | CAN | 4 | 3-1-0 | 240:00 | 7 | 1 | 1.75 | 0 | 0 | G |
| ~WM20 IIHF Directorate Best Goalie (1982), WM20 All-Star Team/Goal (1982) | | | | | | | | | | | |
| **Moffett, Greg / b. Apr. 1, 1959** | | | | | | | | | | | |
| 1981 | WM | USA | 5 | 3-0-2 | 253:45 | 27 | 0 | 6.38 | 0 | 0 | — |
| **Mohoric, Klemen / b. May 25, 1975** | | | | | | | | | | | |
| 2003 | WM | SLO | 1 | 0-0-1 | 32:45 | 7 | 0 | 12.82 | 0 | 0 | — |
| **Molina, Alfio / b. Apr. 20, 1948** | | | | | | | | | | | |
| 1972 | WM | SUI | 6 | 1-0-4 | 327:30 | 42 | 0 | 7.69 | 0 | 0 | — |
| 1972-76 | OG-M | SUI | 3 | 0-2-1 | 177:00 | 11 | 0 | 3.73 | 0 | 0 | — |
| **Monostori-Marx, Ferenc / b. Jan. 26, 1909 / d. unknown** | | | | | | | | | | | |
| 1931-33 | WM | HUN | 4 | 2-1-1 | 180:00 | 6 | 1 | 2.00 | 0 | 0 | — |
| 1936 | OG-M | HUN | 1 | 0-0-0 | 27:00 | 12 | 0 | 26.67 | 0 | 0 | — |
| **Moog, Andy / b. Feb. 18, 1960** | | | | | | | | | | | |
| 1988 | OG-M | CAN | 4 | 4-0-0 | 240:00 | 9 | 1 | 2.25 | 0 | 0 | — |
| **Moone, Tom / b. Nov. 6, 1908 / d. July 27, 1986** | | | | | | | | | | | |
| 1936 | OG-M | USA | 8 | 5-1-2 | 410:00 | 4 | 5 | 0.59 | 0 | 0 | B |
| **Moore, Francis "Dinty" / b. Oct. 29, 1900 / d. Jan. 21, 1976** | | | | | | | | | | | |
| 1936 | OG-M | CAN | 5 | 4-0-1 | 225:00 | 5 | 2 | 1.33 | 0 | 0 | S |
| **Morar, Vasile / b. June 23, 1952** | | | | | | | | | | | |
| 1976 | OG-M | ROM | 1 | 1-0-0 | 60:00 | 4 | 0 | 4.00 | 0 | 0 | — |
| **Morishima, Katsuyi / b. Oct. 22, 1942** | | | | | | | | | | | |
| 1968 | OG-M | JPN | 5 | 4-0-1 | 267:35 | 9 | 1 | 2.02 | 0 | 2 | — |
| **Morisson, Jacques / b. Mar. 28, 1907 / d. unknown** | | | | | | | | | | | |
| 1935 | WM | FRA | 6 | 2-1-3 | 270:00 | 15 | 0 | 3.33 | 0 | 0 | — |
| 1936 | OG-M | FRA | 1 | 1-0-0 | 65:00 | 2 | 0 | 1.85 | 0 | 0 | — |
| **Morschauser, Gus / b. Mar. 26, 1969** | | | | | | | | | | | |
| 1989 | WM20 | CAN | 2 | 1-0-0 | 91:08 | 5 | 0 | 3.29 | 0 | 0 | — |
| **Mott, Vernon / b. Mar. 26, 1957** | | | | | | | | | | | |
| 1988 | OG-M | NOR | 5 | 0-1-4 | 302:14 | 29 | 0 | 5.76 | 0 | 0 | — |
| **Mueller, Norbert "Stuffy" / b. Feb. 14, 1906 / d. July 6, 1956** | | | | | | | | | | | |
| 1928 | OG-M | CAN | 1 | 1-0-0 | 45:00 | 0 | 1 | 0.00 | 0 | 0 | G |
| **Mukhometov, Ildar / b. Sept. 21, 1972** | | | | | | | | | | | |
| 1992 | WM20 | RUS | 3 | 2-0-1 | 131:17 | 5 | 0 | 2.29 | 0 | 0 | G |
| **Muller, Hugo / b. unknown / d. unknown** | | | | | | | | | | | |
| 1939 | WM | SUI | 9 | 6-1-1 | 405:00 | 5 | 6 | 0.74 | 0 | 0 | B |
| **Muller, Robert / b. June 25, 1980 / d. May 21, 2009** | | | | | | | | | | | |
| 2001-08 | WM | GER | 17 | 3-3-10 | 996:34 | 55 | 0 | 3.31 | 1 | 0 | — |
| 2004 | WCH | GER | 1 | 0-0-1 | 30:17 | 3 | 0 | 5.94 | 0 | 0 | — |
| 2002-06 | OG-M | GER | 3 | 0-0-0 | 138:15 | 6 | 0 | 2.60 | 0 | 0 | — |
| **Munce, Ryan / b. Apr. 16, 1985** | | | | | | | | | | | |
| 2003 | WM18 | CAN | 6 | 4-1-1 | 363:22 | 10 | 2 | 1.65 | 0 | 0 | G |
| **Murin, Igor / b. Mar. 1, 1973** | | | | | | | | | | | |
| 1992-93 | WM20 | TCH | 9 | 5-1-1 | 471:46 | 26 | 0 | 3.31 | 0 | 0 | B |
| 1996-99 | WM | SVK | 3 | 0-1-0 | 115:10 | 6 | 0 | 3.13 | 0 | 0 | — |
| 1998 | OG-M | SVK | 4 | 1-1-2 | 240:00 | 13 | 0 | 3.25 | 0 | 0 | — |
| **Musil, Lukas / b. May 9, 1984** | | | | | | | | | | | |
| 2002 | WM18 | CZE | 1 | 1-0-0 | 60:00 | 4 | 0 | 4.00 | 0 | 0 | B |
| **Muzzatti, Jason / b. Feb. 3, 1970** | | | | | | | | | | | |
| 2006-07 | WM | ITA | 7 | 1-0-5 | 364:02 | 21 | 0 | 3.46 | 0 | 0 | — |
| 2006 | OG-M | ITA | 4 | 0-2-1 | 212:10 | 14 | 0 | 3.96 | 0 | 0 | — |
| **Myllyla, Pekka / b. July 7, 1932** | | | | | | | | | | | |
| 1952 | OG-M | FIN | 4 | 0-0-4 | 240:00 | 36 | 0 | 9.00 | 0 | 0 | — |
| **Myllys, Jarmo / b. May 29, 1965** | | | | | | | | | | | |
| 1984-85 | WM20 | FIN | 5 | 4-0-1 | 300:00 | 15 | 0 | 3.00 | 1 | 0 | S |
| 1987-98 | WM | FIN | 34 | 18-6-10 | 2,006:14 | 74 | 6 | 2.21 | 1 | 10 | G,2S |
| 1987-96 | WCH | FIN | 3 | 1-0-1 | 140:00 | 9 | 0 | 3.86 | 0 | 2 | — |
| 1988-98 | OG-M | FIN | 15 | 10-1-4 | 897:33 | 28 | 3 | 1.87 | 0 | 0 | S,2B |
| ~WM IIHF Directorate Best Goalie (1995), WM All-Star Team/Goal (1995) | | | | | | | | | | | |
| **Mylnikov, Dmitri / b. June 30, 1978** | | | | | | | | | | | |
| 1998 | WM20 | RUS | 1 | 0-0-0 | 20:00 | 1 | 0 | 3.00 | 0 | 0 | S |
| **Mylnikov, Sergei / b. Oct. 6, 1958** | | | | | | | | | | | |
| 1977-78 | WM20 | URS | 5 | 2-0-0 | 190:00 | 7 | 0 | 2.21 | 0 | 0 | 2G |
| 1985-90 | WM | URS | 16 | 14-0-1 | 904:07 | 26 | 1 | 1.73 | 1 | 0 | 3G,B |
| 1987 | CC | URS | 6 | 5-0-1 | 365:33 | 18 | 1 | 2.96 | 0 | 0 | 2nd |
| 1988 | OG-M | URS | 8 | 7-0-1 | 479:30 | 13 | 2 | 1.63 | 0 | 0 | G |
| **Mylnikov, Sergei / b. June 18, 1982** | | | | | | | | | | | |
| 2000 | WM18 | RUS | 3 | 2-0-1 | 180:00 | 4 | 0 | 1.33 | 0 | 0 | S |
| 2002 | WM20 | RUS | 3 | 2-0-0 | 117:50 | 2 | 1 | 1.02 | 0 | 0 | G |
| **Myre, Phil / b. Nov. 1, 1948** | | | | | | | | | | | |
| 1981 | WM | CAN | 7 | 1-1-3 | 360:00 | 26 | 0 | 4.33 | 0 | 0 | — |
| **Myshkin, Vladimir / b. June 19, 1955** | | | | | | | | | | | |
| 1979-91 | WM | URS | 22 | 13-2-2 | 1,040:20 | 23 | 3 | 1.33 | 0 | 0 | 6G,2B |
| 1981-84 | CC | URS | 5 | 3-0-2 | 312:29 | 13 | 1 | 2.50 | 0 | 0 | 1st |
| 1980-84 | OG-M | URS | 5 | 3-0-1 | 260:01 | 9 | 0 | 2.08 | 0 | 0 | G,S |
| **Naapuri, Matti / b. Jan. 10, 1926** | | | | | | | | | | | |
| 1951 | WM | FIN | 2 | 0-0-2 | 120:00 | 15 | 0 | 7.50 | 0 | 0 | — |
| **Nadrchal, Vladimir / b. Mar. 4, 1938** | | | | | | | | | | | |
| 1958-67 | WM | TCH | 13 | 5-1-6 | 617:02 | 40 | 0 | 3.89 | 0 | 14 | S,B |
| 1960-68 | OG-M | TCH | 15 | 8-1-5 | 820:19 | 47 | 1 | 3.44 | 0 | 0 | S,B |
| ~WM IIHF Directorate Best Goalie (1958) | | | | | | | | | | | |
| **Nagel, Hans-Jorg / b. unknown** | | | | | | | | | | | |
| 1963 | WM | FRG | 1 | 0-0-1 | 60:00 | 8 | 0 | 8.00 | 0 | 0 | — |
| **Naipak, Olexander / b. Sept. 3, 1983** | | | | | | | | | | | |
| 2001 | WM18 | UKR | 3 | 0-0-1 | 85:12 | 14 | 0 | 9.86 | 0 | 0 | — |
| **Nash, Arthur "Jakie" / b. Sept. 5, 1914 / d. Dec. 2000** | | | | | | | | | | | |
| 1936 | OG-M | CAN | 3 | 3-0-0 | 135:00 | 2 | 2 | 0.89 | 0 | 0 | S |
| **Naumenko, Gregg / b. Mar. 30, 1977** | | | | | | | | | | | |
| 2002 | WM | USA | 1 | 0-0-0 | 29:15 | 4 | 0 | 8.21 | 0 | 0 | — |
| **Naumovs, Sergejs / b. Apr. 4, 1969** | | | | | | | | | | | |
| 2002-08 | WM | LAT | 20 | 4-1-13 | 1,093:33 | 56 | 1 | 3.07 | 0 | 2 | — |
| 2002-06 | OG-M | LAT | 5 | 2-1-2 | 300:00 | 21 | 0 | 4.20 | 0 | 0 | — |
| **Nestak, Pavel / b. Mar. 12, 1975** | | | | | | | | | | | |
| 1995 | WM20 | CZE | 4 | 1-0-3 | 212:46 | 11 | 1 | 3.10 | 0 | 0 | — |
| **Netedu, Valerian / b. Jan. 26, 1953** | | | | | | | | | | | |
| 1977 | WM | ROM | 9 | 1-0-4 | 319:29 | 35 | 0 | 6.57 | 0 | 0 | — |
| 1976-80 | OG-M | ROM | 8 | 4-0-3 | 378:14 | 23 | 3 | 3.65 | 0 | 2 | — |
| **Nielsen, Simon / b. Oct. 27, 1986** | | | | | | | | | | | |
| 2004 | WM18 | DEN | 2 | 0-0-2 | 120:00 | 6 | 0 | 3.00 | 0 | 0 | — |
| **Nielsen, Thure / b. unknown** | | | | | | | | | | | |
| 1965 | WM | NOR | 1 | 0-0-1 | 60:00 | 14 | 0 | 14.00 | 0 | 0 | — |
| **Niemi, Esko / b. June 11, 1934** | | | | | | | | | | | |
| 1954-59 | WM | FIN | 13 | 2-1-10 | 780:00 | 76 | 0 | 5.85 | 0 | 0 | — |
| 1960 | OG-M | FIN | 3 | 1-1-1 | 180:00 | 16 | 0 | 5.33 | 0 | 0 | — |
| **Nihei, Jiro / b. Mar. 9, 1971** | | | | | | | | | | | |
| 1998-2004 | WM | JPN | 15 | 0-2-12 | 814:14 | 69 | 0 | 5.08 | 0 | 0 | — |
| **Nikitin, Yuri / b. Sept. 1, 1961** | | | | | | | | | | | |
| 1980-81 | WM20 | URS | 6 | 3-0-2 | 286:51 | 13 | 0 | 2.72 | 0 | 0 | G,B |
| **Nilsson, Magnus / b. Sept. 21, 1976** | | | | | | | | | | | |
| 1996 | WM20 | SWE | 3 | 2-0-1 | 180:00 | 7 | 1 | 2.33 | 0 | 0 | S |
| **Nilsson, Ulf / b. Feb. 7, 1965** | | | | | | | | | | | |
| 1984 | WM20 | SWE | 3 | 1-0-2 | 180:00 | 14 | 0 | 4.67 | 0 | 0 | — |
| **Nissinen, Tuomas / b. July 17, 1983** | | | | | | | | | | | |
| 2001 | WM18 | FIN | 2 | 2-0-0 | 120:00 | 1 | 1 | 0.50 | 0 | 0 | B |
| 2003 | WM20 | FIN | 1 | 1-0-0 | 60:00 | 2 | 0 | 2.00 | 0 | 0 | B |
| **Nordstrom, Roger / b. Apr. 27, 1966** | | | | | | | | | | | |
| 1994-95 | WM | SWE | 7 | 5-0-2 | 420:00 | 17 | 2 | 2.43 | 0 | 0 | S,B |
| 1992 | OG-M | SWE | 3 | 2-1-0 | 178:54 | 6 | 0 | 2.01 | 0 | 2 | — |
| **Norgren, Jonas / b. Nov. 10, 1972** | | | | | | | | | | | |
| 2001 | WM | NOR | 2 | 0-1-1 | 118:52 | 8 | 0 | 4.04 | 0 | 0 | — |
| **Noronen, Mika / b. June 17, 1979** | | | | | | | | | | | |
| 1997-99 | WM20 | FIN | 10 | 8-0-2 | 593:03 | 23 | 1 | 2.33 | 0 | 0 | G |
| 2004 | WM | FIN | 5 | 2-1-2 | 309:06 | 12 | 1 | 2.33 | 0 | 2 | — |
| **Norovsky, Pavol / b. Apr. 8, 1959** | | | | | | | | | | | |
| 1979 | WM20 | TCH | 1 | 0-0-1 | 60:00 | 9 | 0 | 9.00 | 0 | 0 | S |
| **Norrena, Fredrik / b. Nov. 29, 1973** | | | | | | | | | | | |
| 2002-07 | WM | FIN | 14 | 9-0-4 | 506:19 | 21 | 7 | 2.49 | 1 | 4 | S,B |
| 2006 | OG-M | FIN | 2 | 2-0-0 | 120:00 | 0 | 2 | 0.00 | 0 | 0 | S |
| **Norrild, Casper / b. Aug. 20, 1987** | | | | | | | | | | | |
| 2005 | WM18 | DEN | 1 | 0-0-0 | 23:40 | 8 | 0 | 20.28 | 0 | 0 | — |
| **Nurminen, Pasi / b. Dec. 7, 1975** | | | | | | | | | | | |
| 2000-03 | WM | FIN | 13 | 7-1-4 | 728:10 | 23 | 0 | 1.90 | 0 | 2 | S,B |
| 2002 | OG-M | FIN | 1 | 1-0-0 | 60:00 | 1 | 0 | 1.00 | 0 | 0 | — |
| **Nusser, Robert / b. Apr. 15, 1931** | | | | | | | | | | | |
| 1957 | WM | AUT | 2 | 0-1-1 | 120:00 | 13 | 0 | 6.50 | 0 | 0 | — |
| 1956 | OG-M | AUT | 2 | 0-0-0 | 64:38 | 10 | 0 | 9.29 | 0 | 0 | — |

**Nygaard, Knut / b. unknown**
1959-62 WM NOR 11 5-0-6 640:00 75 0 7.03 0 0 —

**Obermann, Hans / b. Feb. 13, 1935**
1959 WM FRG 1 1-0-0 60:00 4 0 4.00 0 0 —

**O'Connor, Bob / b. unknown**
1981 WM20 USA 3 1-0-1 159:00 11 0 4.15 0 0 —

**Odling, Sune / b. June 10, 1948**
1979 WM SWE 3 2-0-1 180:00 17 0 5.67 0 0 B

**Oerdoegh, Karl / b. unknown / d. unknown**
1934-35 WM AUT 11 4-2-3 475:00 15 0 1.89 0 0 —

**Ogoreshnikov, Sergei / b. Apr. 4, 1977**
2005-06 WM KAZ 7 1-0-6 365:52 21 2 3.44 0 0 —

**Ohlberg, Heinz / b. unknown**
1963 WM FRG 1 0-0-1 60:00 10 0 10.00 0 0 —

**Ohtsubo, Toshimitsu / b. Apr. 4, 1945**
1968-76 OG-M JPN 10 5-1-3 552:25 36 0 3.91 0 0 —

**Olsen, Per / b. Jan. 9, 1983**
2001 WM18 NOR 6 1-2-2 317:47 21 0 3.96 0 0 —

**Olsson, Einar / b. July 9, 1896 / d. Dec. 20, 1974**
1924 OG-M SWE 5 2-0-3 290:00 44 1 9.10 0 0 —

**Olsson, Kristoffer / b. Apr. 18, 1983**
2001 WM18 SWE 4 2-0-2 238:34 11 0 2.77 0 0 —

**Olsson, Peter / b. Aug. 3, 1974**
1994 WM20 SWE 7 6-0-1 420:00 15 1 2.14 0 2 S

**Olszewski, Wlodzimierz / b. Jan. 12, 1956**
1984 OG-M POL 6 1-4-0 280:01 32 0 6.86 0 0 —

**Ordody, Bela / b. Jan. 13, 1880 / d. unknown**
1928 OG-M HUN 1 0-0-1 45:00 1 0 1.33 0 0 —

**Ostensen, Kare / b. Dec. 5, 1943**
1965 WM NOR 6 0-0-6 360:00 42 0 7.00 0 0 —
1964-72 OG-M NOR 10 7-0-3 600:00 30 0 3.00 0 0 —

**Ostlund, Thomas / b. Sept. 9, 1965**
1995-96 WM SWE 7 4-2-1 428:17 14 2 1.96 0 0 S

**Ouellet, Maxime / b. June 17, 1981**
2000-01 WM20 CAN 13 7-3-3 759:01 21 1 1.66 0 0 2B

**Paavola, Jari / b. Mar. 18, 1960**
1979-80 WM20 FIN 6 4-0-2 320:00 13 0 2.44 1 0 S
~WM20 IIHF Directorate Best Goalie (1980), WM20 All-Star Team/Goal (1980)

**Pabisz, Wladyslaw / b. Jan. 5, 1931 / d. Mar. 11, 2007**
1957-59 WM POL 10 2-0-8 580:00 60 0 6.21 0 0 —
1956-64 OG-M POL 6 5-0-1 360:00 17 1 2.83 0 0 —

**Paccard, Michel / b. Nov. 1, 1908 / d. unknown**
1934-37 WM FRA 12 2-0-10 540:00 60 0 6.67 0 0 —
1936 OG-M FRA 2 0-0-2 90:00 5 0 3.33 0 0 —

**Pageau, Paul / b. Oct. 2, 1951**
1980 OG-M CAN 4 2-0-1 236:50 11 1 2.79 0 0 —

**Palmer, Larry / b. Jan. 7, 1938**
1961 WM USA 3 1-1-1 180:00 12 0 4.00 0 0 —
1960 OG-M USA 1 0-0-0 7:00 0 0 0.00 0 0 G

**Pannoni, Nick / b. Nov. 6, 1982**
2000 WM18 USA 4 0-0-4 209:21 14 0 4.01 0 2 —

**Parker, Mike / b. June 7, 1958**
1977 WM20 USA 5 1-0-3 257:47 31 0 7.22 0 2 —

**Partridge, Ray / b. unknown**
1962 WM GBR 4 0-0-4 240:00 44 0 11.00 0 0 —

**Pashelyuk, Dmitri / b. Oct. 3, 1981**
2001 WM20 BLR 4 1-1-2 240:00 19 0 4.75 0 0 —

**Pashkov, Alexander / b. Aug. 28, 1944**
1978 WM URS 2 2-0-0 120:00 5 0 2.50 0 0 G
1972 OG-M URS 1 1-0-0 60:00 3 0 3.00 0 0 G

**Paterson, Eric / b. Sept. 11, 1929**
1952 OG-M CAN 5 5-0-0 300:00 7 1 1.40 0 0 G

**Paulgaard, Lars Simen / b. Jan. 25, 1987**
2004 WM18 NOR 5 0-0-4 188:10 24 0 7.65 0 0 —

**Pavoni, Reto / b. Jan. 24, 1968**
1987 WM20 SUI 4 0-0-3 212:38 31 0 8.75 0 0 —
1991-2000 WM SUI 25 6-2-15 1,426:16 77 0 3.24 0 0 —
1992 OG-M SUI 1 0-0-1 60:00 8 0 8.00 0 0 —

**Peeters, Pete / b. Aug. 17, 1957**
1984 CC CAN 4 3-0-1 234:09 13 0 3.33 2 2 1st

**Pejchar, Rudolf / b. Mar. 23, 1968**
1987-88 WM20 TCH 7 2-1-2 331:36 23 0 4.16 0 0 S

**Peka, Jan / b. July 27, 1894 / d. Jan. 21, 1985**
1931-35 WM TCH 27 16-1-10 1,460:00 35 8 1.44 0 0 B
1920-36 OG-M TCH 11 5-0-6 485:00 52 2 6.43 0 0 B

**Pelletier, Jean-Marc / b. Mar. 4, 1978**
1998 WM20 USA 3 2-0-1 179:37 5 1 1.67 0 4 —

**Pelletier, Pier-Olivier / b. Apr. 8, 1987**
2005 WM18 CAN 2 2-0-0 120:00 2 0 1.00 0 0 S

**Perl, Reto / b. Nov. 23, 1923**
1947-49 WM SUI 14 5-2-3 578:00 33 1 3.43 0 0 —
1948 OG-M SUI 4 3-0-1 240:00 15 0 3.75 0 0 B

**Perry, Alan / b. Aug. 30, 1966**
1984-86 WM20 USA 18 5-0-11 968:40 78 0 4.83 0 0 B
~WM20 IIHF Directorate Best Goalie (1984)

**Persson, Joakim / b. May 4, 1970**
1990 WM20 SWE 4 3-1-0 240:00 14 1 3.50 0 2 —

**Pesat, Ivo / b. Nov. 11, 1965**
1984 WM20 TCH 3 2-0-1 150:00 9 0 3.60 0 0 B

**Pethke, Marc / b. Nov. 30, 1973**
1993 WM20 GER 3 0-0-2 122:30 10 0 4.90 0 0 —

**Petrik, Stanislav / b. Aug. 4, 1977**
1996-97 WM20 SVK 12 4-3-4 675:34 47 0 4.17 0 6 —

**Petrov, Alexei / b. Apr. 13, 1981**
1999 WM18 RUS 2 0-0-1 80:00 5 0 3.75 0 0 —
2001 WM20 RUS 3 0-1-1 147:26 7 0 2.85 0 0 —

**Philipp, Andreas / b. unknown**
1981 WM20 AUT 3 0-0-3 123:00 28 0 13.66 0 0 —

**Picard, Al / b. Mar. 17, 1923 / d. unknown**
1949 WM CAN 7 4-2-1 419:00 10 2 1.43 0 0 S

**Pisar, Lubomir / b. Feb. 4, 1981**
2001 WM20 SVK 3 1-0-2 179:40 8 1 2.67 0 0 —

**Plumejeau, Jerome / b. Aug. 5, 1983**
2002 WM20 FRA 3 0-0-1 71:04 11 0 9.29 0 0 —

**Podoinikov, Andrei / b. June 3, 1985**
2003 WM18 KAZ 6 0-0-6 318:48 37 0 6.96 0 2 —

**Podomatski, Yegor / b. Nov. 22, 1976**
1998-2004 WM RUS 23 10-4-6 1,224:15 53 0 2.60 0 2 S

**Poliakov, Alexei / b. July 31, 1973**
1993 WM20 RUS 2 0-0-1 80:00 5 0 3.75 0 0 —

**Poliakov, Sergei / b. June 20, 1970**
1990 WM20 URS 1 0-0-0 20:00 1 0 3.00 0 0 S

**Polski, Sergei / b. Oct. 13, 1985**
2003 WM18 KAZ 1 0-0-0 40:50 6 0 8.82 0 0 —

**Popperle, Tomas / b. Oct. 10, 1984**
2004 WM20 CZE 2 0-0-0 30:31 7 0 13.76 0 0 —

**Pospisil, Jaroslav / b. unknown / d. unknown**
1930 WM TCH 1 0-0-1 45:00 3 0 4.00 0 0 —

**Potvin, Felix / b. June 23, 1971**
1991 WM20 CAN 2 1-0-0 80:00 3 0 2.25 0 0 G
1998 WM CAN 4 3-1-0 240:00 8 0 2.00 0 0 —

**Pregl, Karl / b. May 7, 1944**
1968 OG-M AUT 5 1-0-4 280:00 23 0 4.93 0 0 —

**Pretnar, Cveto / b. Jan. 27, 1957**
1984 OG-M YUG 5 1-4-0 299:55 37 0 7.40 0 0 —

**Privalov, Vadim / b. June 22, 1967**
1987 WM20 URS 1 0-0-0 8:37 0 0 0.00 0 0 —

**Prohaska, Gert / b. Mar. 31, 1976**
2002-03 WM AUT 3 0-0-3 160:00 19 0 7.13 0 0 —

**Przezdziecki, Henryk / b. Feb. 20, 1909 / d. Nov. 1, 1977**
1937 WM POL 2 0-0-2 90:00 19 0 12.67 0 0 —
1936-48 OG-M POL 6 3-0-3 325:00 42 0 7.75 0 0 —

**Puchkov, Nikolai / b. Jan. 30, 1930 / d. Aug. 8, 2005**
1954-59 WM URS 28 21-3-3 1,574:22 44 5 1.68 0 0 G,4S
1956-60 OG-M URS 12 9-1-2 679:30 26 3 2.30 0 0 G,B
~WM IIHF Directorate Best Goalie (1959)

**Puchkov, Viktor / b. Mar. 10, 1944**
1969 WM URS 1 0-0-0 30:00 2 0 4.00 0 0 G

**Puls, Alfred / b. Aug. 1, 1933**
1956-64 OG-M AUT 12 3-2-7 655:22 61 1 5.58 0 0 —

**Purschel, Dieter / b. Feb. 7, 1941**
1970 WM GDR 4 0-0-2 167:57 18 0 6.43 0 0 —
1968 OG-M GDR 5 0-0-4 186:00 31 0 10.00 0 0 —

**Puschacher, Michael / b. Sept. 15, 1968**
1994-96 WM AUT 14 2-1-11 769:39 48 1 3.74 0 2 —
1994 OG-M AUT 4 1-0-3 226:29 21 0 5.56 0 0 —

**Puttee, Art / b. Oct. 14, 1904 / d. Oct. 18, 1966**
1931 WM CAN 6 5-1-0 270:00 0 6 0.00 0 0 G

**Puurula, Joni / b. Aug. 4, 1982**
2000 WM18 FIN 2 1-0-0 112:49 2 0 1.06 0 0 G

**Pye, Billy / b. Apr. 9, 1969**
1990 WM USA 2 0-0-2 60:42 12 0 11.86 0 0 —

**Radev, Petar / b. July 6, 1948**
1976 OG-M BUL 4 0-0-4 212:47 26 0 7.33 0 2 —

**Rakovski, Sergei / b. July 2, 1983**
2002-03 WM20 BLR 7 1-0-6 372:50 29 0 4.67 0 0 —

**Ranford, Bill / b. Dec. 14, 1966**
1993-94 WM CAN 12 11-0-1 724:33 18 3 1.49 0 0 G
1991 CC CAN 8 6-2-0 480:00 14 1 1.75 0 0 1st
~WM IIHF Directorate Best Goalie (1994), WM All-Star Team/Goal (1994)

**Ranzoni, Bruno / b. Jan. 26, 1927**
1950 WM FRA 1 0-0-1 60:00 7 0 7.00 0 0 —

**Ratiu, Mircea / b. unknown / d. unknown**
1933 WM ROM 5 2-0-3 225:00 19 1 5.07 0 0 —

| | | | | | | | | | | | |
|---|---|---|---|---|---|---|---|---|---|---|---|
| **Raty, Pasi / b. Feb. 1, 1970** | | | | | | | | | | | |
| 1990 | WM20 | FIN | 1 | 0-0-0 | 48:05 | 3 | 0 | 3.74 | 0 | 0 | — |
| **Rautiainen, Matti / b. May 25, 1963** | | | | | | | | | | | |
| 1983 | WM20 | FIN | 6 | 2-0-4 | 360:00 | 27 | 0 | 4.50 | 0 | 0 | — |
| ~WM20 All-Star Team/Goal (1983) | | | | | | | | | | | |
| **Rautio, Mika / b. Mar. 27, 1968** | | | | | | | | | | | |
| 1988 | WM20 | FIN | 5 | 4-1-0 | 300:00 | 14 | 0 | 2.80 | 0 | 0 | B |
| **Reddick, Stan / b. Dec. 6, 1969** | | | | | | | | | | | |
| 2002 | WM | SLO | 2 | 0-0-2 | 118:55 | 13 | 0 | 6.56 | 0 | 2 | — |
| **Reece, Dave / b. Sept. 13, 1948** | | | | | | | | | | | |
| 1977 | WM | USA | 5 | 3-0-2 | 300:00 | 16 | 0 | 3.20 | 0 | 0 | — |
| **Reichel, Jorg / b. July 20, 1922 / d. unknown** | | | | | | | | | | | |
| 1948 | OG-M | AUT | 3 | 0-0-2 | 140:00 | 20 | 0 | 8.57 | 0 | 0 | — |
| **Reid, Robert / b. Dec. 21, 1932** | | | | | | | | | | | |
| 1960 | OG-M | AUS | 5 | 0-0-5 | 240:00 | 66 | 0 | 16.50 | 0 | 0 | — |
| **Resch, Glenn "Chico" / b. July 10, 1948** | | | | | | | | | | | |
| 1982 | WM | USA | 4 | 0-0-4 | 240:00 | 21 | 0 | 5.25 | 0 | 0 | — |
| 1984 | CC | USA | 2 | 1-0-0 | 108:12 | 9 | 0 | 5.00 | 0 | 0 | — |
| **Rexe, Steve / b. Feb. 26, 1947** | | | | | | | | | | | |
| 1969 | WM | CAN | 1 | 0-0-0 | 32:00 | 2 | 0 | 3.75 | 0 | 0 | — |
| **Rhodes, Damian / b. May 28, 1969** | | | | | | | | | | | |
| 1988 | WM20 | USA | 5 | 1-0-2 | 205:25 | 22 | 0 | 6.43 | 0 | 0 | — |
| 2000-03 | WM | USA | 6 | 3-1-1 | 311:58 | 12 | 1 | 2.31 | 0 | 0 | — |
| **Rice-Jones, Art / b. Dec. 12, 1912 / d. Nov. 12, 1989** | | | | | | | | | | | |
| 1935 | WM | CAN | 7 | 7-0-0 | 315:00 | 7 | 3 | 1.33 | 0 | 0 | G |
| **Richards, Mark / b. July 24, 1969** | | | | | | | | | | | |
| 1989 | WM20 | USA | 4 | 2-1-0 | 180:00 | 11 | 0 | 3.67 | 0 | 0 | — |
| **Richter, Jan / b. Mar. 29, 1923 / d. 1999** | | | | | | | | | | | |
| 1954 | WM | TCH | 3 | 2-0-1 | 140:00 | 8 | 0 | 3.43 | 0 | 0 | — |
| 1952 | OG-M | TCH | 8 | 5-0-3 | 480:00 | 21 | 2 | 2.63 | 0 | 0 | — |
| **Richter, Mike / b. Sept. 22, 1966** | | | | | | | | | | | |
| 1985-86 | WM20 | USA | 7 | 3-0-2 | 251:20 | 15 | 0 | 3.58 | 0 | 0 | B |
| 1986-93 | WM | USA | 8 | 1-1-3 | 371:00 | 26 | 0 | 4.20 | 0 | 0 | — |
| 1991-96 | WCH | USA | 13 | 9-0-4 | 789:37 | 37 | 0 | 2.81 | 0 | 0 | 1st,2nd |
| 1988-2002 | OG-M | USA | 12 | 4-1-7 | 707:10 | 38 | 1 | 3.22 | 0 | 0 | S |
| ~OG-M All-Star Team/Goal (2002) | | | | | | | | | | | |
| **Ridderwall, Rolf / b. Nov. 20, 1958** | | | | | | | | | | | |
| 1985-91 | WM | SWE | 23 | 14-5-3 | 1,348:30 | 63 | 2 | 2.80 | 0 | 2 | G,S |
| 1991 | CC | SWE | 2 | 0-0-2 | 120:00 | 9 | 0 | 4.50 | 0 | 0 | — |
| 1984 | OG-M | SWE | 6 | 3-1-0 | 311:51 | 9 | 2 | 1.73 | 0 | 0 | B |
| **Riesen, Martin / b. July 8, 1926** | | | | | | | | | | | |
| 1950-55 | WM | SUI | 12 | 1-1-8 | 620:00 | 72 | 0 | 6.97 | 0 | 0 | 2B |
| 1956 | OG-M | SUI | 3 | 1-0-2 | 137:11 | 16 | 0 | 7.00 | 0 | 0 | — |
| **Rigazio, Don / b. July 3, 1934** | | | | | | | | | | | |
| 1955-58 | WM | USA | 12 | 5-3-4 | 720:00 | 51 | 0 | 4.25 | 0 | 0 | — |
| 1956 | OG-M | USA | 4 | 4-0-0 | 240:00 | 7 | 1 | 1.75 | 0 | 0 | S |
| ~WM IIHF Directorate Best Goalie (1955) | | | | | | | | | | | |
| **Riggin, Pat / b. May 26, 1959** | | | | | | | | | | | |
| 1985 | WM | CAN | 4 | 2-0-1 | 212:25 | 11 | 0 | 3.11 | 0 | 0 | S |
| **Rigolet, Gerald / b. Mar. 26, 1941** | | | | | | | | | | | |
| 1972 | WM | SUI | 6 | 0-0-5 | 272:30 | 54 | 0 | 11.89 | 0 | 0 | — |
| 1964-72 | OG-M | SUI | 8 | 0-0-7 | 422:00 | 49 | 0 | 6.97 | 0 | 0 | — |
| **Rihar, Ivan / b. unknown / d. unknown** | | | | | | | | | | | |
| 1939 | WM | YUG | 5 | 0-1-4 | 225:00 | 60 | 0 | 16.00 | — | — | — |
| **Rogers, John / b. unknown / d. unknown** | | | | | | | | | | | |
| 1930 | WM | GBR | 1 | 0 | 0 | 0 | 0 | — | | | |
| 1928 | OG-M | GBR | 2 | 1-0-0 | 60:00 | 4 | 0 | 4.00 | 0 | 0 | — |
| **Rogles, Chris / b. Jan. 22, 1969** | | | | | | | | | | | |
| 2003 | WM | USA | 3 | 1-0-1 | 153:03 | 6 | 0 | 2.35 | 0 | 0 | — |
| **Rolland, Patrick / b. June 7, 1979** | | | | | | | | | | | |
| 2000 | WM | FRA | 1 | 0-0-1 | 25:11 | 5 | 0 | 11.91 | 0 | 0 | — |
| 2002 | OG-M | FRA | 1 | 0-0-1 | 60:00 | 7 | 0 | 7.00 | 0 | 0 | — |
| **Roloson, Dwayne / b. Oct. 12, 1969** | | | | | | | | | | | |
| 2007-09 | WM | CAN | 9 | 7-0-2 | 544:15 | 21 | 0 | 2.32 | 0 | 2 | G,S |
| **Romano, Roberto / b. Oct. 10, 1962** | | | | | | | | | | | |
| 1992 | WM | ITA | 3 | 0-0-3 | 150:52 | 11 | 0 | 4.38 | 0 | 0 | — |
| **Ronnqvist, Petter / b. Feb. 7, 1973** | | | | | | | | | | | |
| 1993 | WM20 | SWE | 6 | 5-0-1 | 360:00 | 14 | 0 | 2.33 | 0 | 0 | S |
| 1999 | WM | SWE | 3 | 1-0-0 | 119:56 | 3 | 0 | 1.50 | 0 | 2 | B |
| **Rosati, Mike / b. Jan. 7, 1968** | | | | | | | | | | | |
| 1994-2002 | WM | ITA | 32 | 12-3-14 | 1,700:55 | 97 | 2 | 3.42 | 1 | 4 | — |
| 1994-98 | OG-M | ITA | 6 | 1-0-2 | 246:01 | 17 | 0 | 4.15 | 0 | 0 | — |
| **Rosenberg, Kari / b. Dec. 20, 1967** | | | | | | | | | | | |
| 1987 | WM20 | FIN | 4 | 3-0-0 | 180:33 | 8 | 0 | 2.66 | 0 | 2 | G |
| **Rosset, Stephane / b. Jan. 4, 1976** | | | | | | | | | | | |
| 1996 | WM20 | SUI | 1 | 0-0-1 | 60:00 | 7 | 0 | 7.00 | 0 | 0 | — |
| **Roth, Tim / b. Mar. 29, 1984** | | | | | | | | | | | |
| 2002 | WM18 | USA | 2 | 2-0-0 | 120:00 | 2 | 1 | 1.00 | 0 | 0 | G |
| **Roy, Patrick / b. Oct. 5, 1965** | | | | | | | | | | | |
| 1998 | OG-M | CAN | 6 | 4-0-2 | 369:07 | 9 | 1 | 1.46 | 1 | 0 | — |
| **Roznik, Marek / b. Mar. 25, 1985** | | | | | | | | | | | |
| 2002 | WM18 | SVK | 2 | 0-0-2 | 63:46 | 7 | 0 | 6.59 | 0 | 0 | — |
| **Rudman, Michael / b. Oct. 11, 1954** | | | | | | | | | | | |
| 1984 | OG-M | AUT | 5 | 1-4-0 | 300:00 | 37 | 0 | 7.40 | 0 | 0 | — |
| **Rugdal, Joakim / b. Jan. 9, 1985** | | | | | | | | | | | |
| 2002 | WM18 | NOR | 5 | 1-1-3 | 280:00 | 23 | 0 | 4.93 | 0 | 0 | — |
| **Rupp, Pat / b. Aug. 12, 1942 / d. Feb. 2, 2006** | | | | | | | | | | | |
| 1964-68 | OG-M | USA | 13 | 4-1-6 | 708:35 | 40 | 0 | 3.39 | 0 | 0 | — |
| **Rutherford, Jim / b. Feb. 17, 1949** | | | | | | | | | | | |
| 1977-79 | WM | CAN | 8 | 4-0-3 | 406:51 | 30 | 0 | 4.42 | 0 | 0 | — |
| **Ryabchikov, Yevgeni / b. Jan. 16, 1974** | | | | | | | | | | | |
| 1994 | WM20 | RUS | 7 | 5-1-1 | 420:00 | 17 | 1 | 2.43 | 0 | 2 | B |
| ~WM20 All-Star Team/Goal (1994) | | | | | | | | | | | |
| **Rybar, Pavol / b. Oct. 12, 1971** | | | | | | | | | | | |
| 1997-2003 | WM | SVK | 14 | 8-1-5 | 300:18 | 33 | 2 | 6.59 | 0 | 2 | S,B |
| 2002 | OG-M | SVK | 2 | 0-0-1 | 84:46 | 5 | 0 | 3.54 | 0 | 0 | — |
| **Sachs, Tadeusz / b. June 12, 1899 / d. Aug. 3, 1942** | | | | | | | | | | | |
| 1930-31 | WM | POL | 3 | 1-0-1 | 103:00 | 4 | 0 | 2.33 | 0 | 0 | — |
| **Sagbakken, Vegard / b. Apr. 6, 1984** | | | | | | | | | | | |
| 2001-02 | WM18 | NOR | 6 | 0-0-4 | 238:13 | 22 | 0 | 5.54 | 0 | 0 | — |
| **Sakac, Marcel / b. Sept. 23, 1947** | | | | | | | | | | | |
| 1971-79 | WM | TCH | 6 | 3-0-1 | 308:05 | 21 | 1 | 4.09 | 0 | 0 | 2S |
| **Salat, Andreas / b. June 5, 1964** | | | | | | | | | | | |
| 1988 | OG-M | AUT | 1 | 0-0-0 | 20:01 | 3 | 0 | 8.99 | 0 | 0 | — |
| **Salficky, Dusan / b. Mar. 28, 1972** | | | | | | | | | | | |
| 2000-01 | WM | CZE | 2 | 1-0-0 | 80:00 | 3 | 0 | 2.25 | 0 | 0 | 2G |
| **Salo, Tommy / b. Feb. 1, 1971** | | | | | | | | | | | |
| 1991 | WM20 | SWE | 6 | 3-0-3 | 342:54 | 19 | 1 | 3.32 | 0 | 0 | — |
| 1994-2003 | WM | SWE | 54 | 34-4-13 | 3,166:51 | 100 | 8 | 1.89 | 1 | 8 | 1G,2S,4B |
| 1996-2004 | WCH | SWE | 3 | 2-0-1 | 219:47 | 6 | 0 | 1.64 | 0 | 0 | — |
| 1994-2002 | OG-M | SWE | 13 | 9-2-3 | 787:26 | 29 | 1 | 2.21 | 0 | 4 | G |
| ~WM IIHF Directorate Best Goalie (1997, 1999), WM All-Star Team/Goal (1997, 1998, 1999) | | | | | | | | | | | |
| **Samoilov, Vitali / b. Apr. 17, 1962** | | | | | | | | | | | |
| 1982 | WM20 | URS | 6 | 3-0-3 | 339:29 | 19 | 1 | 3.36 | 0 | 0 | — |
| **Samolej, Gabriel / b. June 1, 1960** | | | | | | | | | | | |
| 1989 | WM | POL | 3 | 0-0-3 | 122:21 | 28 | 0 | 13.73 | 0 | 0 | — |
| 1984-92 | OG-M | POL | 10 | 1-1-4 | 397:48 | 32 | 0 | 4.83 | 0 | 0 | — |
| **Sands, Mike / b. Apr. 6, 1963** | | | | | | | | | | | |
| 1983 | WM20 | CAN | 5 | 2-1-2 | 240:00 | 14 | 1 | 3.50 | 0 | 0 | B |
| **Sanza, Nicola / b. Feb. 6, 1955** | | | | | | | | | | | |
| 1983 | WM | ITA | 1 | 0-0-0 | 32:08 | 6 | 0 | 11.21 | 0 | 0 | — |
| **Saprykin, Dmitri / b. June 5, 1960** | | | | | | | | | | | |
| 1979-80 | WM20 | URS | 6 | 5-0-0 | 312:09 | 9 | 0 | 1.73 | 0 | 0 | 2G |
| **Sato, Toshio / b. 1929** | | | | | | | | | | | |
| 1957 | WM | JPN | 2 | 0-0-1 | 94:00 | 20 | 0 | 12.77 | 0 | 0 | — |
| **Saurdiff, Corwin / b. Oct. 17, 1972** | | | | | | | | | | | |
| 1992 | WM20 | USA | 1 | 0-0-1 | 60:00 | 8 | 0 | 8.00 | 0 | 0 | B |
| **Sauve, Phillipe / b. Feb. 27, 1980** | | | | | | | | | | | |
| 2000 | WM20 | USA | 2 | 0-1-1 | 119:43 | 5 | 0 | 2.51 | 0 | 0 | — |
| **Savoie, Rene / b. Feb. 9, 1896 / d. unknown** | | | | | | | | | | | |
| 1920-24 | OG-M | SUI | 5 | 0-0-4 | 201:00 | 77 | 0 | 22.99 | 0 | 0 | — |
| **Scheibli, Roland / b. 1958** | | | | | | | | | | | |
| 1978 | WM20 | SUI | 5 | 0-0-3 | 208:00 | 43 | 0 | 12.40 | 0 | 0 | — |
| **Schilcher, Frans / b. Aug. 19, 1943** | | | | | | | | | | | |
| 1968-76 | OG-M | AUT | 6 | 3-0-2 | 320:00 | 18 | 0 | 3.38 | 0 | 0 | — |
| **Schistad, Robert / b. Oct. 28, 1966** | | | | | | | | | | | |
| 1992-2000 | WM | NOR | 26 | 3-4-17 | 1,392:18 | 83 | 0 | 3.58 | 0 | 0 | — |
| 1992-94 | OG-M | NOR | 3 | 0-0-3 | 178:41 | 18 | 0 | 6.04 | 0 | 0 | — |
| **Schlickenrieder, Josef / b. May 7, 1958** | | | | | | | | | | | |
| 1989 | WM | FRG | 2 | 0-0-2 | 119:20 | 10 | 0 | 5.03 | 0 | 0 | — |
| 1988 | OG-M | FRG | 2 | 0-0-2 | 91:20 | 11 | 0 | 7.23 | 0 | 0 | — |
| **Schmeisser, Egon / b. Jan. 1, 1957** | | | | | | | | | | | |
| 1985 | WM | GDR | 5 | 0-0-1 | 135:46 | 13 | 0 | 5.75 | 0 | 0 | — |
| **Schmengler, Heinz / b. unknown** | | | | | | | | | | | |
| 1967 | WM | FRG | 4 | 0-0-3 | 226:38 | 29 | 0 | 7.68 | 0 | 0 | — |
| **Schmidt, Michael / b. Mar. 11, 1966** | | | | | | | | | | | |
| 1986 | WM20 | FRG | 2 | 0-0-1 | 100:00 | 21 | 0 | 12.60 | 0 | 0 | — |
| **Schmitt, Torsten / b. June 17, 1981** | | | | | | | | | | | |
| 1999 | WM18 | GER | 4 | 1-0-3 | 205:09 | 12 | 0 | 3.51 | 0 | 0 | — |
| **Schoder, Matthias / b. July 20, 1982** | | | | | | | | | | | |
| 2000 | WM18 | SUI | 6 | 4-0-2 | 321:22 | 13 | 1 | 2.43 | 0 | 0 | — |
| 2002 | WM20 | SUI | 1 | 1-0-0 | 60:00 | 0 | 1 | 0.00 | 0 | 0 | — |
| **Schramm, Josef / b. June 5, 1938** | | | | | | | | | | | |
| 1971 | WM | FRG | 4 | 0-0-2 | 179:44 | 23 | 0 | 7.68 | 0 | 0 | — |
| 1968 | OG-M | FRG | 7 | 1-0-5 | 410:20 | 35 | 0 | 5.12 | 0 | 0 | — |
| **Scodellaro, Duke / b. May 23, 1914 / d. Dec. 17, 1983** | | | | | | | | | | | |
| 1939 | WM | CAN | 4 | 4-0-0 | 180:00 | 0 | 4 | 0.00 | — | — | G |
| **Seliger, Marc / b. May 1, 1974** | | | | | | | | | | | |
| 1992-94 | WM20 | GER | 17 | 3-0-14 | 1,017:30 | 75 | 0 | 4.42 | 0 | 4 | — |
| 1995-2002 | WM | GER | 11 | 3-2-5 | 619:43 | 37 | 1 | 3.58 | 0 | 0 | — |
| 2002 | OG-M | GER | 6 | 3-0-2 | 302:11 | 15 | 1 | 2.98 | 0 | 0 | — |
| **Seliverstov, Vadym / b. Feb. 18, 1981** | | | | | | | | | | | |
| 1999 | WM18 | UKR | 6 | 2-0-4 | 360:00 | 26 | 2 | 4.33 | 0 | 0 | — |
| 2000 | WM20 | UKR | 6 | 1-0-4 | 310:00 | 22 | 0 | 4.26 | 0 | 0 | — |
| 2007 | WM | UKR | 5 | 1-0-3 | 215:01 | 14 | 0 | 3.91 | 0 | 2 | — |
| **Semenchuk, Tom / b. Sept. 13, 1959** | | | | | | | | | | | |
| 1979 | WM20 | CAN | 3 | 1-0-2 | 180:00 | 7 | 0 | 2.33 | 0 | 0 | — |

| Year | Event | Team | GP | W-L-T | Mins | GA | SO | GAA | A | PIM | Medals |
|---|---|---|---|---|---|---|---|---|---|---|---|
| **Seredenko, Valeriy / b. Dec. 27, 1977** | | | | | | | | | | | |
| 1996 | WM20 | UKR | 1 | 0-0-0 | 31:40 | 0 | 0 | 0.00 | 0 | 0 | — |
| **Sevela, Peter / b. Oct. 16, 1983** | | | | | | | | | | | |
| 2003 | WM20 | SVK | 5 | 2-0-2 | 218:46 | 7 | 2 | 1.92 | 1 | 0 | — |
| **Sheblanov, Alexei / b. Jan. 24, 1968** | | | | | | | | | | | |
| 1988 | WM20 | URS | 7 | 6-0-1 | 368:18 | 14 | 0 | 2.28 | 0 | 0 | S |
| **Shepovalov, Vladimir / b. Feb. 15, 1948** | | | | | | | | | | | |
| 1972 | WM | URS | 4 | 3-0-0 | 190:00 | 2 | 2 | 0.63 | 0 | 0 | S |
| **Shevtsov, Oleg / b. Nov. 29, 1971** | | | | | | | | | | | |
| 1998 | WM | RUS | 4 | 2-1-1 | 240:00 | 9 | 0 | 2.25 | 0 | 2 | — |
| **Shimin, Alexander / b. Jan. 2, 1970** | | | | | | | | | | | |
| 1998 | WM | KAZ | 1 | 0-0-1 | 20:00 | 5 | 0 | 15.00 | 0 | 0 | — |
| 1998 | OG-M | KAZ | 5 | 1-0-0 | 128:18 | 12 | 0 | 5.61 | 0 | 0 | — |
| **Shirgaziev, Albert / b. Jan. 3, 1965** | | | | | | | | | | | |
| 1994 | WM | RUS | 2 | 0-0-0 | 22:32 | 0 | 0 | 0.00 | 0 | 0 | — |
| **Shtalenkov, Mikhail / b. Oct. 20, 1965** | | | | | | | | | | | |
| 1992-2001 | WM | RUS | 16 | 9-1-4 | 878:16 | 31 | 3 | 2.12 | 0 | 0 | — |
| 1991 | CC | URS | 4 | 1-1-2 | 235:49 | 9 | 0 | 2.29 | 0 | 2 | — |
| 1992-98 | OG-M | RUS | 13 | 11-0-2 | 730:57 | 20 | 0 | 1.64 | 0 | 2 | G,S |
| **Shumidub, Alexander / b. Mar. 17, 1964** | | | | | | | | | | | |
| 1998 | OG-M | BLR | 2 | 0-1-0 | 64:14 | 2 | 0 | 1.87 | 0 | 0 | — |
| **Shundrov, Yuriy / b. June 6, 1956** | | | | | | | | | | | |
| 1999 | WM | UKR | 2 | 0-0-1 | 57:26 | 5 | 0 | 5.22 | 0 | 0 | — |
| **Sidelnikov, Alexander / b. Aug. 12, 1950** | | | | | | | | | | | |
| 1973-77 | WM | URS | 12 | 7-0-0 | 543:00 | 21 | 2 | 2.32 | 0 | 0 | 2G,S,B |
| 1976 | OG-M | URS | 1 | 1-0-0 | 60:00 | 1 | 0 | 1.00 | 0 | 0 | G |
| **Sidikov, Rustam / b. May 7, 1985** | | | | | | | | | | | |
| 2003 | WM18 | RUS | 6 | 5-0-1 | 324:47 | 12 | 0 | 2.22 | 0 | 0 | B |
| **Sidorkiewicz, Peter / b. June 29, 1963** | | | | | | | | | | | |
| 1989 | WM | CAN | 1 | 0-0-0 | 24:56 | 0 | 0 | 0.00 | 0 | 0 | S |
| **Sievert, Pasqual / b. June 10, 1981** | | | | | | | | | | | |
| 1999 | WM18 | SUI | 3 | 3-0-0 | 180:00 | 4 | 0 | 1.33 | 0 | 0 | — |
| 2000-01 | WM20 | SUI | 6 | 2-0-3 | 329:35 | 26 | 0 | 4.73 | 0 | 0 | — |
| **Simchuk, Kostyantyn / b. Feb. 12, 1974** | | | | | | | | | | | |
| 2001-06 | WM | UKR | 29 | 7-4-18 | 1,588:35 | 89 | 2 | 3.36 | 0 | 10 | — |
| 2002 | OG-M | UKR | 3 | 1-0-1 | 174:00 | 9 | 0 | 3.10 | 0 | 0 | — |
| **Simon, Stan / b. July 9, 1920 / d. Feb. 1993** | | | | | | | | | | | |
| 1948 | OG-M | GBR | 8 | 3-5-0 | 480:00 | 47 | 0 | 5.88 | 0 | 0 | — |
| **Simonovic, Miroslav / b. Aug. 10, 1974** | | | | | | | | | | | |
| 1998-99 | WM | SVK | 11 | 4-2-5 | 623:18 | 27 | 0 | 2.60 | 0 | 2 | — |
| **Simpson, Shawn / b. Aug. 10, 1968** | | | | | | | | | | | |
| 1987 | WM20 | CAN | 3 | 1-1-1 | 140:00 | 11 | 0 | 4.71 | 0 | 0 | — |
| **Sindel, Jaromir / b. Nov. 30, 1959** | | | | | | | | | | | |
| 1978 | WM20 | TCH | 2 | 1-0-1 | 120:00 | 14 | 0 | 7.00 | 0 | 0 | — |
| 1981-87 | WM | TCH | 6 | 1-2-1 | 269:10 | 18 | 0 | 4.01 | 0 | 0 | G,2B |
| 1984 | CC | TCH | 3 | 0-0-1 | 112:00 | 9 | 0 | 4.82 | 0 | 0 | — |
| 1984-88 | OG-M | TCH | 11 | 8-1-2 | 621:02 | 18 | 3 | 1.74 | 0 | 2 | S |
| **Skaarberg, Tommy / b. Oct. 6, 1960** | | | | | | | | | | | |
| 1979 | WM20 | NOR | 4 | 0-0-4 | 197:00 | 25 | 0 | 7.61 | 0 | 0 | — |
| 1988 | OG-M | NOR | 1 | 0-0-0 | 6:53 | 1 | 0 | 8.72 | 0 | 0 | — |
| **Skudra, Peter / b. Apr. 24, 1973** | | | | | | | | | | | |
| 1997 | WM | LAT | 1 | 0-0-0 | 25:08 | 3 | 0 | 7.16 | 0 | 0 | — |
| **Skuja, Peteris / b. 1904 / d. 1998** | | | | | | | | | | | |
| 1933 | WM | LAT | 1 | 0-0-0 | 3:00 | 0 | 0 | 0.00 | 0 | 0 | — |
| **Slavik, Robert / b. May 29, 1974** | | | | | | | | | | | |
| 1994 | WM20 | CZE | 4 | 2-0-2 | 240:00 | 13 | 1 | 3.25 | 0 | 0 | — |
| **Slowakiewicz, Tadeusz / b. Jan. 1, 1953 / d. May 30, 1989** | | | | | | | | | | | |
| 1975 | WM | POL | 5 | 0-0-1 | 188:34 | 29 | 0 | 9.23 | 1 | 0 | — |
| **Smangs, Henrik / b. Jan. 19, 1976** | | | | | | | | | | | |
| 1995 | WM20 | SWE | 2 | 1-1-0 | 120:00 | 4 | 0 | 2.00 | 0 | 0 | B |
| **Smid, Zdenek / b. Feb. 3, 1980** | | | | | | | | | | | |
| 2000 | WM20 | CZE | 7 | 5-2-0 | 420:00 | 11 | 1 | 1.57 | 0 | 0 | G |
| **Smith, Harold / b. unknown / d. unknown** | | | | | | | | | | | |
| 1950-51 | WM | GBR | 4 | 1-1-2 | 212:00 | 16 | 1 | 4.53 | 0 | 0 | — |
| **Snow, Garth / b. July 28, 1969** | | | | | | | | | | | |
| 1998 | WM | USA | 5 | 1-1-2 | 259:44 | 12 | 0 | 2.77 | 0 | 2 | — |
| 1994 | OG-M | USA | 5 | 1-2-2 | 299:21 | 17 | 0 | 3.41 | 0 | 2 | — |
| **Soderstrom, Tommy / b. July 17, 1969** | | | | | | | | | | | |
| 1989 | WM20 | SWE | 3 | 2-0-1 | 180:00 | 7 | 0 | 2.33 | 0 | 0 | S |
| 1991-93 | WM | SWE | 13 | 7-1-4 | 745:39 | 30 | 2 | 2.41 | 0 | 0 | 2G,S |
| 1991-96 | WCH | SWE | 6 | 4-0-2 | 360:00 | 14 | 1 | 2.33 | 0 | 0 | — |
| 1992 | OG-M | SWE | 5 | 3-1-1 | 298:20 | 13 | 0 | 2.61 | 1 | 0 | — |
| ~WM IIHF Directorate Best Goalie (1992) | | | | | | | | | | | |
| **Sofiak, John / b. Nov. 29, 1927 / d. Mar. 24, 2003** | | | | | | | | | | | |
| 1962 | WM | CAN | 2 | 2-0-0 | 120:00 | 3 | 0 | 1.50 | 0 | 0 | S |
| **Sofian, Iosif / b. 1939** | | | | | | | | | | | |
| 1964 | OG-M | ROM | 1 | 0-0-1 | 60:00 | 6 | 0 | 6.00 | 0 | 0 | — |
| **Sohlman, Rauli / b. Mar. 23, 1959** | | | | | | | | | | | |
| 1978-79 | WM20 | FIN | 10 | 4-1-4 | 560:00 | 34 | 0 | 3.64 | 0 | 2 | — |
| **Sokolov, Maxim / b. May 27, 1972** | | | | | | | | | | | |
| 2001-06 | WM | RUS | 28 | 13-2-12 | 1,566:19 | 61 | 2 | 2.34 | 0 | 2 | S,B |
| 2004 | WCH | RUS | 1 | 0-0-1 | 59:54 | 3 | 0 | 3.01 | 0 | 0 | — |
| 2006 | OG-M | RUS | 2 | 1-0-0 | 60:00 | 4 | 0 | 4.00 | 0 | 0 | — |
| ~WM IIHF Directorate Best Goalie (2002), WM All-Star Team/Goal (2002) | | | | | | | | | | | |
| **Sorli, Oyvind / b. Oct. 10, 1972** | | | | | | | | | | | |
| 1991 | WM20 | NOR | 3 | 0-0-2 | 164:08 | 29 | 0 | 10.60 | 0 | 0 | — |
| 1999 | WM | NOR | 1 | 0-0-0 | 32:17 | 2 | 0 | 3.72 | 0 | 0 | — |
| **Sorokoski, Carl / b. Mar. 17, 1921 / d. June 7, 1977** | | | | | | | | | | | |
| 1951 | WM | CAN | 3 | 3-0-0 | 180:00 | 3 | 0 | 1.00 | 0 | 0 | G |
| **Sozzi, Jean-Claude / b. Oct. 31, 1943** | | | | | | | | | | | |
| 1968 | OG-M | FRA | 2 | 0-0-2 | 120:00 | 17 | 0 | 8.50 | 0 | 0 | — |
| **Spantig, Ingolf / b. June 29, 1960** | | | | | | | | | | | |
| 1983 | WM | GDR | 1 | 0-0-0 | 23:28 | 4 | 0 | 10.23 | 0 | 0 | — |
| **Speechley, William / b. July 5, 1906 / d. unknown** | | | | | | | | | | | |
| 1930 | WM | GBR | 1 | 0-0-1 | 45:00 | 4 | 0 | 5.33 | — | — | — |
| 1928 | OG-M | GBR | 5 | 1-0-4 | 210:00 | 23 | 1 | 6.57 | 0 | 0 | — |
| **Spillar, Martin / b. Apr. 21, 1978** | | | | | | | | | | | |
| 1997-98 | WM20 | SVK | 4 | 1-0-3 | 175:01 | 11 | 0 | 3.77 | 0 | 0 | — |
| **Sprencz, Pal / b. unknown / d. unknown** | | | | | | | | | | | |
| 1937 | WM | ROM | 2 | 0-0-2 | 90:00 | 15 | 0 | 10.00 | 0 | 0 | — |
| **Staniowski, Ed / b. July 7, 1955** | | | | | | | | | | | |
| 1979 | WM | CAN | 3 | 0-0-3 | 160:00 | 19 | 0 | 7.13 | 0 | 0 | — |
| **Stankiewicz, Brian / b. June 20, 1956** | | | | | | | | | | | |
| 1993 | WM | AUT | 4 | 1-1-2 | 239:01 | 8 | 0 | 2.01 | 0 | 2 | — |
| 1988-94 | OG-M | AUT | 8 | 1-1-6 | 489:25 | 33 | 0 | 4.05 | 0 | 0 | — |
| **Stauber, Robb / b. Nov. 25, 1967** | | | | | | | | | | | |
| 1987 | WM20 | USA | 4 | 3-0-1 | 220:00 | 17 | 0 | 4.64 | 0 | 0 | — |
| 1989 | WM | USA | 6 | 3-0-3 | 313:17 | 19 | 0 | 3.64 | 0 | 2 | — |
| **Stecher, Dino / b. May 4, 1964** | | | | | | | | | | | |
| 1984 | WM20 | SUI | 5 | 0-0-4 | 280:00 | 40 | 0 | 8.57 | 0 | 0 | — |
| **Steinbo, Frank / b. unknown** | | | | | | | | | | | |
| 1958 | WM | NOR | 1 | 0-0-1 | 41:00 | 9 | 0 | 13.17 | 0 | 2 | — |
| **Steinke, Alfred / b. June 6, 1881 / d. May 1945** | | | | | | | | | | | |
| 1928 | OG-M | GER | 2 | 0-1-1 | 90:00 | 1 | 1 | 0.67 | 0 | 0 | — |
| **Stephenson, Wayne / b. Jan. 29, 1945 / d. June 22, 2010** | | | | | | | | | | | |
| 1967-69 | WM | CAN | 10 | 4-0-5 | 528:00 | 27 | 1 | 3.07 | 0 | 2 | B |
| 1968 | OG-M | CAN | 3 | 2-0-0 | 140:00 | 2 | 1 | 0.86 | 0 | 0 | B |
| **Stogowski, Jozef / b. Nov. 27, 1899 / d. May 14, 1940** | | | | | | | | | | | |
| 1930-38 | WM | POL | 31 | 11-4-14 | 1,427:00 | 45 | 7 | 1.89 | 0 | 0 | — |
| 1928-36 | OG-M | POL | 10 | 0-1-9 | 450:00 | 49 | 0 | 6.53 | 0 | 0 | — |
| **Stoiculescu, Mihai / b. Apr. 25, 1948** | | | | | | | | | | | |
| 1968 | OG-M | ROM | 2 | 0-0-0 | 33:45 | 4 | 0 | 7.11 | 0 | 0 | — |
| **Stolp, Jeff / b. June 20, 1970** | | | | | | | | | | | |
| 1990 | WM20 | USA | 2 | 0-0-2 | 99:32 | 10 | 0 | 6.03 | 0 | 0 | — |
| **Stolzner, Scott / b. Nov. 8, 1960** | | | | | | | | | | | |
| 1980 | WM20 | USA | 4 | 1-1-2 | 240:00 | 22 | 0 | 5.50 | 0 | 0 | — |
| **Storr, Jamie / b. Dec. 28, 1975** | | | | | | | | | | | |
| 1994-95 | WM20 | CAN | 8 | 7-1-0 | 480:00 | 24 | 0 | 3.00 | 0 | 2 | 2G |
| ~WM20 IIHF Directorate Best Goalie (1994) | | | | | | | | | | | |
| **Straka, Karel / b. Aug. 8, 1931** | | | | | | | | | | | |
| 1957 | WM | TCH | 6 | 4-1-1 | 360:00 | 9 | 1 | 1.50 | 0 | 0 | B |
| ~WM IIHF Directorate Best Goalie (1957) | | | | | | | | | | | |
| **Stransky, Jaroslav / b. June 6, 1899 / d. unknown** | | | | | | | | | | | |
| 1924 | OG-M | TCH | 3 | 1-0-2 | 180:00 | 41 | 0 | 13.67 | 0 | 0 | — |
| **Stromsnes, Frank / b. 1959** | | | | | | | | | | | |
| 1979 | WM20 | NOR | 2 | 0-0-1 | 103:00 | 21 | 0 | 12.23 | 0 | 2 | — |
| **Sucksdorff, Curt / b. May 10, 1904 / d. Jan. 1, 1960** | | | | | | | | | | | |
| 1931 | WM | SWE | 5 | 1-1-3 | 300:00 | 6 | 2 | 1.20 | 0 | 0 | — |
| 1928 | OG-M | SWE | 1 | 0-0-1 | 45:00 | 11 | 0 | 14.67 | 0 | 0 | S |
| **Sulander, Ari / b. Jan. 6, 1969** | | | | | | | | | | | |
| 1995-2000 | WM | FIN | 23 | 12-3-6 | 1,359:47 | 42 | 4 | 1.85 | 0 | 6 | G,2S,B |
| 1998 | OG-M | FIN | 2 | 2-0-0 | 120:00 | 4 | 0 | 2.00 | 0 | 0 | B |
| ~WM IIHF Directorate Best Goalie (1998) | | | | | | | | | | | |
| **Sullivan, Joe / b. Jan. 8, 1901 / d. unknown** | | | | | | | | | | | |
| 1928 | OG-M | CAN | 2 | 2-0-0 | 90:00 | 0 | 2 | 0.00 | 0 | 0 | G |
| **Sundberg, Reino / b. Feb. 27, 1957** | | | | | | | | | | | |
| 1977 | WM20 | SWE | 1 | 0-0-0 | 20:00 | 3 | 0 | 9.00 | 0 | 0 | — |
| 1981 | WM | SWE | 1 | 0-0-0 | 20:00 | 7 | 0 | 21.00 | 0 | 0 | S |
| **Suttner, Sigmund / b. Feb. 7, 1953** | | | | | | | | | | | |
| 1977-79 | WM | FRG | 13 | 4-1-5 | 639:13 | 47 | 0 | 4.41 | 0 | 2 | — |
| 1980 | OG-M | FRG | 4 | 0-0-3 | 192:36 | 20 | 0 | 6.23 | 0 | 0 | — |
| **Suttnig, Michael / b. Nov. 8, 1973** | | | | | | | | | | | |
| 1994-2003 | WM | AUT | 7 | 0-0-4 | 256:46 | 27 | 0 | 6.31 | 0 | 0 | — |
| **Svacina, Roman / b. May 26, 1969** | | | | | | | | | | | |
| 1988 | WM20 | TCH | 2 | 1-0-1 | 119:57 | 3 | 0 | 1.50 | 0 | 2 | — |
| **Svanberg, Kurt / b. Sept. 26, 1913 / d. Oct. 7, 2001** | | | | | | | | | | | |
| 1937-38 | WM | SWE | 8 | 2-2-4 | 390:00 | 19 | 3 | 2.92 | 0 | 0 | — |
| 1948 | OG-M | SWE | 3 | 1-0-1 | 90:00 | 4 | 0 | 2.67 | 0 | 0 | — |
| **Svensson, Kjell / b. Sept. 10, 1938** | | | | | | | | | | | |
| 1961-67 | WM | SWE | 23 | 15-2-5 | 1,300:00 | 54 | 4 | 2.49 | 0 | 0 | G,2S,B |
| 1960-64 | OG-M | SWE | 11 | 5-1-4 | 611:17 | 27 | 3 | 2.65 | 0 | 0 | S |
| ~WM IIHF Directorate Best Goalie (1963) | | | | | | | | | | | |
| **Svensson, Lars / b. June 30, 1926 / d. June 25, 1999** | | | | | | | | | | | |
| 1950-55 | WM | SWE | 15 | 9-2-4 | 899:00 | 31 | 4 | 2.97 | 0 | 0 | S |
| 1952-56 | OG-M | SWE | 9 | 5-1-2 | 500:00 | 24 | 1 | 2.88 | 0 | 0 | B |
| **Svoboda, Adam / b. Jan. 26, 1978** | | | | | | | | | | | |
| 1997-98 | WM20 | CZE | 13 | 4-3-6 | 713:33 | 33 | 0 | 2.77 | 1 | 0 | — |

| | | | | | | | | | | | |
|---|---|---|---|---|---|---|---|---|---|---|---|
| **Svoboda, Oldrich / b. Jan. 28, 1967** | | | | | | | | | | | |
| 1986-87 | WM20 | TCH | 8 | 5-0-3 | 408:24 | 23 | 0 | 3.38 | 0 | 0 | S |
| 1991 | WM | TCH | 2 | 1-0-1 | 118:41 | 4 | 0 | 2.03 | 0 | 0 | — |
| 1992 | OG-M | TCH | 1 | 1-0-0 | 60:00 | 2 | 0 | 2.00 | 0 | 0 | B |
| **Syversen, Lasse / b. July 18, 1970** | | | | | | | | | | | |
| 1990 | WM20 | NOR | 2 | 0-0-1 | 72:20 | 16 | 0 | 13.27 | 0 | 0 | — |
| **Szlendak, Stanislav / b. May 21, 1920 / d. Jan. 24, 1998** | | | | | | | | | | | |
| 1952 | OG-M | POL | 8 | 2-1-3 | 410:00 | 41 | 0 | 6.00 | 0 | 0 | — |
| **Sznajder, Jozef / b. July 21, 1909 / d. Mar. 3, 1994** | | | | | | | | | | | |
| 1933 | WM | POL | 1 | 0-0-1 | 15:00 | 3 | 0 | 12.00 | — | 0 | — |
| **Szuper, Levente / b. June 11, 1980** | | | | | | | | | | | |
| 2009 | WM | HUN | 5 | 0-0-5 | 262:43 | 22 | 0 | 5.02 | 0 | 0 | — |
| **Tabaracci, Rick / b. Jan. 2, 1969** | | | | | | | | | | | |
| 1992-99 | WM | CAN | 8 | 2-0-2 | 294:46 | 15 | 0 | 3.05 | 0 | 2 | G |
| **Takahashi, Toshio / b. unknown / d. unknown** | | | | | | | | | | | |
| 1930 | WM | JPN | 1 | 0-0-1 | 45:00 | 5 | 0 | 6.67 | 0 | 0 | — |
| **Takko, Kari / b. June 23, 1962** | | | | | | | | | | | |
| 1981-82 | WM20 | FIN | 11 | 7-1-3 | 659:49 | 41 | 0 | 3.73 | 0 | 0 | S,B |
| 1983-91 | WM | FIN | 16 | 6-2-8 | 958:26 | 57 | 1 | 3.57 | 0 | 0 | — |
| 1987-96 | WCH | FIN | 7 | 1-0-6 | 399:05 | 29 | 0 | 4.36 | 0 | 0 | — |
| 1984 | OG-M | FIN | 5 | 1-3-1 | 254:58 | 19 | 0 | 4.47 | 0 | 2 | — |
| **Tambulov, Sergei / b. July 2, 1974** | | | | | | | | | | | |
| 2006 | WM | KAZ | 2 | 0-0-0 | 44:08 | 4 | 0 | 5.44 | 0 | 0 | — |
| **Tammi, Jukka / b. Apr. 10, 1962** | | | | | | | | | | | |
| 1982 | WM20 | FIN | 1 | 0-0-0 | 0:11 | 0 | 0 | 0.00 | 0 | 0 | B |
| 1985-94 | WM | FIN | 23 | 9-3-10 | 820:05 | 69 | 2 | 5.04 | 0 | 0 | S |
| 1991 | CC | FIN | 2 | 0-0-1 | 80:00 | 5 | 0 | 3.75 | 0 | 0 | 3rd |
| 1988-94 | OG-M | FIN | 10 | 5-1-4 | 597:46 | 23 | 1 | 2.31 | 0 | 0 | S,B |
| **Tancon, Adriano / b. Nov. 18, 1958** | | | | | | | | | | | |
| 1984 | OG-M | ITA | 4 | 1-0-2 | 180:00 | 12 | 0 | 4.00 | 0 | 0 | — |
| **Tarankov, Ilia / b. Oct. 29, 1985** | | | | | | | | | | | |
| 2004 | WM20 | UKR | 3 | 0-1-1 | 165:08 | 23 | 0 | 8.36 | 0 | 0 | — |
| **Tarasov, Yevgeni / b. Nov. 2, 1975** | | | | | | | | | | | |
| 1995 | WM20 | RUS | 5 | 4-0-0 | 243:48 | 10 | 0 | 2.46 | 0 | 0 | S |
| ~WM20 IIHF Directorate Best Goalie (1995) | | | | | | | | | | | |
| **Tarlowski, Kazimierz / b. Feb. 25, 1915 / d. 1943** | | | | | | | | | | | |
| 1938 | WM | POL | 1 | 0-0-1 | 45:00 | 7 | 0 | 9.33 | 0 | 0 | — |
| **Terreri, Chris / b. Nov. 15, 1964** | | | | | | | | | | | |
| 1985-97 | WM | USA | 17 | 4-5-5 | 854:57 | 60 | 1 | 4.21 | 0 | 2 | — |
| 1988 | OG-M | USA | 3 | 1-0-1 | 127:39 | 14 | 0 | 6.58 | 0 | 0 | — |
| **Tervo, Tommi / b. Feb. 13, 1984** | | | | | | | | | | | |
| 2002 | WM18 | FIN | 4 | 3-0-1 | 237:37 | 7 | 1 | 1.77 | 0 | 0 | — |
| **Timosaari, Ari / b. Sept. 29, 1960** | | | | | | | | | | | |
| 1980 | WM20 | FIN | 1 | 0-0-0 | 40:00 | 1 | 0 | 1.50 | 0 | 0 | S |
| **Timpson, Percy / b. unknown / d. unknown** | | | | | | | | | | | |
| 1930 | WM | CAN | 1 | 1-0-0 | 45:00 | 1 | 0 | 1.33 | 0 | 0 | G |
| **Tkachenko, Sergei / b. June 6, 1971** | | | | | | | | | | | |
| 1990 | WM20 | URS | 7 | 5-1-1 | 400:00 | 22 | 1 | 3.30 | 0 | 0 | S |
| **Tkacz, Andrzej / b. Sept. 20, 1946** | | | | | | | | | | | |
| 1970-76 | WM | POL | 27 | 5-4-15 | 1,238:39 | 138 | 0 | 6.68 | 0 | 0 | — |
| 1972-76 | OG-M | POL | 3 | 0-0-2 | 120:00 | 29 | 0 | 14.50 | 0 | 0 | — |
| **Tomasoni, Dick / b. unknown** | | | | | | | | | | | |
| 1971 | WM | USA | 2 | 1-0-1 | 100:00 | 6 | 0 | 3.60 | 0 | 0 | — |
| **Tomita, Shoichi / b. Jan. 1, 1936** | | | | | | | | | | | |
| 1960 | OG-M | JPN | 2 | 0-0-0 | 44:00 | 12 | 0 | 16.36 | 0 | 0 | — |
| ~IIHF Hall of Fame | | | | | | | | | | | |
| **Tosio, Renato / b. Nov. 16, 1964** | | | | | | | | | | | |
| 1982 | WM20 | SUI | 7 | 0-0-5 | 384:37 | 69 | 0 | 10.76 | 0 | 0 | — |
| 1987-95 | WM | SUI | 23 | 4-3-14 | 1,189:34 | 80 | 0 | 4.04 | 0 | 2 | — |
| 1992 | OG-M | SUI | 6 | 2-0-4 | 359:00 | 24 | 0 | 4.01 | 0 | 2 | — |
| **Toskala, Vesa / b. May 20, 1977** | | | | | | | | | | | |
| 1996-97 | WM20 | FIN | 8 | 3-0-4 | 453:39 | 27 | 0 | 3.57 | 0 | 0 | — |
| 2000 | WM | FIN | 5 | 3-1-1 | 298:50 | 15 | 0 | 3.01 | 0 | 2 | B |
| **Trefilov, Andrei / b. Aug. 31, 1969** | | | | | | | | | | | |
| 1991-96 | WM | URS | 22 | 13-2-4 | 1,136:41 | 41 | 3 | 2.16 | 0 | 8 | G,B |
| 1991-96 | WCH | RUS | 5 | 2-0-1 | 204:04 | 9 | 1 | 2.65 | 1 | 2 | |
| 1992-98 | OG-M | RUS | 6 | 1-0-0 | 108:12 | 6 | 0 | 3.33 | 0 | 2 | G,S |
| **Tregubov, Vyacheslav / b. Oct. 20, 1978** | | | | | | | | | | | |
| 1998 | WM20 | KAZ | 6 | 1-0-3 | 277:07 | 34 | 0 | 7.36 | 0 | 0 | — |
| **Tretiak, Vladislav / b. Apr. 25, 1952** | | | | | | | | | | | |
| 1970-83 | WM | URS | 96 | 76-6-10 | 5,344:37 | 174 | 9 | 1.95 | 2 | 6 | 10G,2S,B |
| 1972 | SS | URS | 8 | 3-1-4 | 480:00 | 31 | 0 | 3.87 | 0 | 0 | 2nd |
| 1976-81 | CC | URS | 11 | 7-2-2 | 660:00 | 22 | 1 | 2.00 | 0 | 2 | 1st |
| 1972-84 | OG-M | URS | 19 | 17-1-0 | 1,059:41 | 33 | 2 | 1.87 | 0 | 0 | 3G,S |
| ~IIHF Hall of Fame | | | | | | | | | | | |
| ~WM IIHF Directorate Best Goalie (1974, 1979, 1983), WM All-Star Team/Goal (1975, 1979, 1983) | | | | | | | | | | | |
| **Trvaj, Jiri / b. Apr. 13, 1974** | | | | | | | | | | | |
| 2002 | WM | CZE | 2 | 2-0-0 | 120:00 | 8 | 0 | 4.00 | 0 | 0 | — |
| **Tsarev, Andrei / b. Aug. 30, 1975** | | | | | | | | | | | |
| 1999 | WM | RUS | 1 | 0-0-0 | 36:57 | 0 | 0 | 0.00 | 0 | 0 | — |
| **Tugnutt, Ron / b. Oct. 22, 1967** | | | | | | | | | | | |
| 1993-99 | WM | CAN | 9 | 5-0-2 | 453:40 | 17 | 0 | 2.25 | 1 | 0 | — |
| **Turco, Marty / b. Aug. 13, 1975** | | | | | | | | | | | |
| 2002 | WM | CAN | 3 | 2-0-1 | 165:31 | 5 | 1 | 1.81 | 0 | 0 | — |
| **Turek, Friedrich / b. July 24, 1940** | | | | | | | | | | | |
| 1964 | OG-M | AUT | 1 | 0-0-1 | 60:00 | 8 | 0 | 8.00 | 0 | 0 | — |
| **Turek, Roman / b. May 21, 1970** | | | | | | | | | | | |
| 1989-90 | WM20 | TCH | 13 | 8-1-4 | 715:36 | 30 | 0 | 2.52 | 1 | 0 | 2B |
| 1994-96 | WM | CZE | 16 | 11-2-3 | 959:03 | 28 | 3 | 1.75 | 2 | 0 | G |
| 1996 | WCH | CZE | 3 | 0-0-2 | 82:22 | 10 | 0 | 7.29 | 0 | 0 | — |
| 1994 | OG-M | CZE | 2 | 2-0-0 | 120:00 | 4 | 0 | 2.00 | 0 | 0 | — |
| ~WM IIHF Directorate Best Goalie (1996), WM All-Star Team/Goal (1996) | | | | | | | | | | | |
| **Tyzhnykh, Alexander / b. May 26, 1958** | | | | | | | | | | | |
| 1977-78 | WM20 | URS | 12 | 11-0-1 | 650:00 | 28 | 2 | 2.58 | 0 | 0 | 2G |
| 1984 | CC | URS | 2 | 2-0-0 | 120:00 | 4 | 0 | 2.00 | 0 | 0 | 3rd |
| ~WM20 IIHF Directorate Best Goalie (1978), WM20 All-Star Team/Goal (1977, 1978) | | | | | | | | | | | |
| **Uotila, Ilmo / b. Apr. 14, 1961** | | | | | | | | | | | |
| 1981 | WM20 | FIN | 1 | 1-0-0 | 60:00 | 6 | 0 | 6.00 | 0 | 0 | S |
| **Uronen, Jarmo / b. Mar. 18, 1964** | | | | | | | | | | | |
| 1984 | WM20 | FIN | 3 | 3-0-0 | 180:00 | 8 | 0 | 2.67 | 0 | 0 | S |
| **Vachon, Rogie / b. Sept. 8, 1945** | | | | | | | | | | | |
| 1976 | CC | CAN | 7 | 6-0-1 | 431:33 | 10 | 2 | 1.39 | 0 | 0 | 1st |
| **Valliere, Michel / b. Mar. 20, 1962** | | | | | | | | | | | |
| 1992-96 | WM | FRA | 11 | 2-0-8 | 557:13 | 46 | 0 | 4.95 | 0 | 2 | — |
| 1994 | OG-M | FRA | 2 | 0-0-2 | 120:00 | 13 | 0 | 6.50 | 0 | 0 | — |
| **Valtonen, Jorma / b. Dec. 22, 1946** | | | | | | | | | | | |
| 1970-79 | WM | FIN | 53 | 18-8-25 | 3,120:41 | 228 | 1 | 4.38 | 0 | 4 | — |
| 1972-84 | OG-M | FIN | 11 | 5-0-5 | 644:41 | 45 | 0 | 4.19 | 0 | 2 | — |
| ~IIHF Hall of Fame | | | | | | | | | | | |
| ~WM IIHF Directorate Best Goalie (1972) | | | | | | | | | | | |
| **Vanbiesbrouck, John / b. Sept. 4, 1963** | | | | | | | | | | | |
| 1982-83 | WM20 | USA | 10 | 4-0-5 | 479:36 | 36 | 0 | 4.50 | 0 | 0 | — |
| 1985-91 | WM | USA | 31 | 12-3-15 | 1,700:40 | 135 | 0 | 4.76 | 0 | 8 | — |
| 1987-91 | CC | USA | 5 | 3-0-2 | 300:00 | 12 | 0 | 2.40 | 0 | 0 | 2nd |
| 1998 | OG-M | USA | 1 | 0-0-0 | 0:46 | 0 | 0 | 0.00 | 0 | 0 | — |
| **van den Broeck, Paul / b. Sept. 18, 1904 / d. unknown** | | | | | | | | | | | |
| 1924 | OG-M | BEL | 1 | 0-0-1 | 60:00 | 19 | 0 | 19.00 | 0 | 0 | — |
| **van der Heyden, Bob / b. unknown / d. unknown** | | | | | | | | | | | |
| 1947 | WM | BEL | 3 | 0-0-3 | 217:30 | 49 | 0 | 13.52 | 0 | 0 | — |
| **van der Heyden, Jan / b. Apr. 26, 1916 / d. unknown** | | | | | | | | | | | |
| 1950 | WM | NED | 3 | 1-0-2 | 180:00 | 16 | 0 | 5.33 | 0 | 0 | — |
| **van Os, Joost / b. unknown** | | | | | | | | | | | |
| 1950 | WM | NED | 1 | 0-0-1 | 60:00 | 17 | 0 | 17.00 | 0 | 0 | — |
| **van Rompaey, Willy / b. Mar. 24, 1911 / d. unknown** | | | | | | | | | | | |
| 1933 | WM | BEL | 1 | 0-0-0 | 20:00 | 0 | 0 | 0.00 | 0 | 0 | — |
| **Vedres, Matyas / b. 1943 / d. May 23, 2009** | | | | | | | | | | | |
| 1964 | OG-M | HUN | 5 | 0-0-3 | 180:00 | 16 | 0 | 5.33 | 0 | 0 | — |
| **Vergult, Francois / b. unknown / d. unknown** | | | | | | | | | | | |
| 1920 | OG-M | BEL | 1 | 0-0-1 | 40:00 | 8 | 0 | 12.00 | 0 | 0 | — |
| **Vernon, Mike / b. Feb. 24, 1963** | | | | | | | | | | | |
| 1983 | WM20 | CAN | 4 | 2-0-0 | 180:00 | 10 | 1 | 3.33 | 1 | 0 | B |
| 1991 | WM | CAN | 2 | 0-0-2 | 73:35 | 6 | 0 | 4.91 | 0 | 0 | S |
| **Verscheuren, Victor / b. Apr. 19, 1893 / d. unknown** | | | | | | | | | | | |
| 1924 | OG-M | BEL | 2 | 0-0-2 | 120:00 | 26 | 0 | 13.00 | 0 | 0 | — |
| **Viitala, Unto ~see Wiitala, Unto** | | | | | | | | | | | |
| **Virenius, Juha / b. Nov. 7, 1969** | | | | | | | | | | | |
| 1989 | WM20 | FIN | 5 | 1-1-3 | 300:00 | 25 | 0 | 5.00 | 1 | 0 | — |
| **Vodicka, Jan / b. Apr. 13, 1932** | | | | | | | | | | | |
| 1956 | OG-M | TCH | 7 | 2-0-4 | 352:59 | 31 | 0 | 5.27 | 0 | 2 | — |
| **Vogel, Arthur / b. unknown / d. unknown** | | | | | | | | | | | |
| 1934 | WC | ROM | 6 | 1-0-5 | 270:00 | 21 | 0 | 4.67 | 0 | 0 | — |
| **Volkov, Alexei / b. Mar. 15, 1980** | | | | | | | | | | | |
| 1999-2000 | WM20 | RUS | 12 | 9-0-1 | 592:38 | 14 | 0 | 1.42 | 0 | 0 | G,S |
| **Voroshnov, Mykola / b. Mar. 24, 1985** | | | | | | | | | | | |
| 2002 | WM18 | UKR | 5 | 0-0-4 | 223:49 | 19 | 0 | 5.09 | 0 | 0 | — |
| **Vuorio, Mikael / b. Jan. 4, 1984** | | | | | | | | | | | |
| 2004 | WM20 | FIN | 1 | 1-0-0 | 60:00 | 1 | 0 | 1.00 | 0 | 2 | B |
| **Vyukhin, Olexander / b. Jan. 9, 1973 / d. Sept. 7, 2011** | | | | | | | | | | | |
| 1999 | WM | UKR | 3 | 0-0-2 | 122:34 | 8 | 0 | 3.92 | 0 | 0 | — |
| ~perished in Yaroslavl plane crash | | | | | | | | | | | |
| **Wackers, Hans / b. Sept. 20, 1925** | | | | | | | | | | | |
| 1952 | OG-M | FRG | 4 | 0-1-3 | 240:00 | 31 | 0 | 7.75 | 0 | 0 | — |
| **Waclaw, Jozef / b. July 20, 1932** | | | | | | | | | | | |
| 1957-58 | WM | POL | 9 | 1-1-6 | 500:00 | 58 | 0 | 6.96 | 0 | 0 | — |
| **Wadas, Stefan / b. Nov. 4, 1958** | | | | | | | | | | | |
| 1977 | WM20 | POL | 7 | 0-1-6 | 420:00 | 58 | 0 | 8.29 | 0 | 0 | — |
| **Wagner, Ulysses "Stanley" / b. Mar. 2, 1908 / d. Oct. 11, 2002** | | | | | | | | | | | |
| 1932 | OG-M | CAN | 1 | 1-0-0 | 45:00 | 0 | 1 | 0.00 | 0 | 0 | G |
| **Waite, Jimmy / b. Apr. 15, 1969** | | | | | | | | | | | |
| 1987-88 | WM20 | CAN | 11 | 9-1-0 | 639:56 | 28 | 0 | 2.63 | 0 | 2 | G |
| ~WM20 IIHF Directorate Best Goalie (1988), WM20 All-Star Team/Goal (1988) | | | | | | | | | | | |
| **Wajda, Jaroslaw / b. Sept. 10, 1966** | | | | | | | | | | | |
| 1985 | WM20 | POL | 4 | 0-0-4 | 218:22 | 34 | 0 | 9.34 | 0 | 2 | — |
| **Walberg, Tore / b. Aug. 19, 1953** | | | | | | | | | | | |
| 1980 | OG-M | NOR | 3 | 0-0-2 | 129:33 | 22 | 0 | 10.19 | 0 | 0 | — |
| **Walczewski, Robert / b. Sept. 30, 1965** | | | | | | | | | | | |
| 1985 | WM20 | POL | 5 | 0-0-3 | 201:38 | 25 | 0 | 7.44 | 0 | 0 | — |

| | | | | | | | | | | | |
|---|---|---|---|---|---|---|---|---|---|---|---|
| **Walitalo, Gote / b. July 18, 1956** | | | | | | | | | | | |
| 1982-83 | WM | SWE | 5 | 0-1-4 | 284:26 | 20 | 0 | 4.22 | 0 | 0 | — |
| 1984 | CC | SWE | 2 | 1-0-1 | 76:44 | 7 | 0 | 5.37 | 0 | 0 | 2nd |
| 1984 | OG-M | SWE | 3 | 1-1-1 | 107:33 | 7 | 0 | 3.91 | 0 | 0 | B |
| **Walsh, Ed / b. Aug. 18, 1951** | | | | | | | | | | | |
| 1981 | WM | USA | 4 | 1-1-1 | 226:15 | 16 | 0 | 4.24 | 0 | 0 | — |
| **Walzer, Karel / b. Aug. 28, 1888 / d. unknown** | | | | | | | | | | | |
| 1920 | OG-M | TCH | 1 | 1-0-0 | 40:00 | 0 | 1 | 0.00 | 0 | 0 | B |
| **Wamsley, Rick / b. May 25, 1959** | | | | | | | | | | | |
| 1983-85 | WM | CAN | 12 | 7-0-5 | 720:00 | 41 | 1 | 3.42 | 0 | 0 | S,B |
| **Wanhainen, Rolf / b. Feb. 9, 1972** | | | | | | | | | | | |
| 1991-92 | WM20 | SWE | 7 | 4-0-2 | 377:06 | 26 | 0 | 4.14 | 0 | 0 | S |
| **Warden, Jim / b. June 22, 1954** | | | | | | | | | | | |
| 1975-79 | WM | USA | 12 | 0-1-10 | 625:52 | 77 | 0 | 7.38 | 0 | 0 | — |
| 1976 | OG-M | USA | 5 | 2-0-3 | 300:00 | 21 | 0 | 4.20 | 0 | 4 | — |
| **Wawrzkiewicz, Tomasz / b. June 14, 1977** | | | | | | | | | | | |
| 1997 | WM20 | POL | 2 | 0-0-1 | 76:22 | 11 | 0 | 8.64 | 0 | 0 | — |
| 2002 | WM | POL | 1 | 0-0-1 | 60:00 | 8 | 0 | 8.00 | 0 | 2 | — |
| **Weber, Travis / b. May 26, 1983** | | | | | | | | | | | |
| 2000-01 | WM18 | USA | 6 | 4-0-1 | 340:39 | 8 | 2 | 1.41 | 0 | 0 | — |
| **Weeks, Steve / b. June 30, 1958** | | | | | | | | | | | |
| 1985 | WM | CAN | 5 | 3-1-1 | 265:05 | 9 | 1 | 2.04 | 0 | 0 | S |
| **Wegmuller, Marco / b. Sept. 9, 1982** | | | | | | | | | | | |
| 2000 | WM18 | SUI | 2 | 0-0-1 | 98:38 | 10 | 0 | 6.08 | 0 | 0 | — |
| **Weibel, Lars / b. May 20, 1974** | | | | | | | | | | | |
| 1992-94 | WM20 | SUI | 9 | 1-1-7 | 509:31 | 36 | 0 | 4.24 | 0 | 2 | — |
| 2002-03 | WM | SUI | 4 | 1-0-3 | 239:22 | 17 | 0 | 4.26 | 0 | 0 | — |
| **Weidenborner, Cy / b. Mar. 30, 1895 / d. Nov. 26, 1983** | | | | | | | | | | | |
| 1920 | OG-M | USA | 2 | 2-0-0 | 80:00 | 0 | 2 | 0.00 | 0 | 0 | S |
| **Weiman, Tyler / b. June 5, 1984** | | | | | | | | | | | |
| 2002 | WM18 | CAN | 2 | 0-0-1 | 62:05 | 7 | 0 | 6.77 | 0 | 0 | — |
| **Weishaupt, Erich / b. May 16, 1952** | | | | | | | | | | | |
| 1976-86 | WM | FRG | 28 | 10-8-10 | 1,569:58 | 91 | 2 | 3.48 | 0 | 6 | — |
| 1976 | OG-M | FRG | 3 | 1-0-2 | 180:00 | 16 | 0 | 5.33 | 0 | 0 | B |
| **Weiss, Hermann / b. Mar. 17, 1909 / d. unknown** | | | | | | | | | | | |
| 1930-35 | WM | AUT | 17 | 9-0-8 | 857:00 | 33 | 3 | 2.31 | 0 | 0 | B |
| 1928-36 | OG-M | AUT | 8 | 2-2-4 | 360:00 | 15 | 1 | 2.50 | 0 | 0 | — |
| **Weissenberger, Oliver / b. July 30, 1966** | | | | | | | | | | | |
| 1985 | WM20 | FRG | 5 | 0-0-3 | 187:27 | 25 | 0 | 8.00 | 0 | 0 | — |
| **Wesslau, Gustaf / b. Feb. 5, 1985** | | | | | | | | | | | |
| 2003 | WM18 | SWE | 1 | 1-0-0 | 68:20 | 2 | 0 | 1.76 | 0 | 0 | — |
| **Westlund, Alex / b. Dec. 28, 1975** | | | | | | | | | | | |
| 2004 | WM | USA | 1 | 1-0-0 | 40:00 | 0 | 0 | 0.00 | 0 | 0 | B |
| **Wetzel, Carl / b. Dec. 12, 1938** | | | | | | | | | | | |
| 1967-71 | WM | USA | 15 | 4-1-8 | 793:22 | 58 | 2 | 4.39 | 0 | 0 | — |
| ~WM IIHF Directorate Best Goalie (1967), WM All-Star Team/Goal (1967) | | | | | | | | | | | |
| **Wetzell, Stig / b. Oct. 7, 1945** | | | | | | | | | | | |
| 1972-74 | WM | FIN | 3 | 1-0-2 | 150:35 | 7 | 0 | 2.79 | 0 | 0 | — |
| **Whiston, Don / b. June 19, 1927** | | | | | | | | | | | |
| 1952 | OG-M | USA | 4 | 3-0-1 | 240:00 | 11 | 0 | 2.75 | 0 | 0 | S |
| **Wieczorek, Dariusz / b. Jan. 14, 1962** | | | | | | | | | | | |
| 1989 | WM | POL | 1 | 0-0-1 | 26:29 | 10 | 0 | 22.82 | 0 | 0 | — |
| **Wieser, Nando / b. Sept. 22, 1971** | | | | | | | | | | | |
| 1991 | WM20 | SUI | 2 | 0-0-2 | 120:00 | 18 | 0 | 9.00 | 0 | 0 | — |
| **Wifladt, Lorang / b. June 24, 1926 / d. Dec. 11, 2008** | | | | | | | | | | | |
| 1958-59 | WM | NOR | 11 | 3-1-5 | 579:00 | 46 | 0 | 4.77 | 0 | 0 | — |
| **Wiitala, Unto / b. July 5, 1925** | | | | | | | | | | | |
| 1949-57 | WM | FIN | 27 | 9-1-16 | 1,180:00 | 176 | 2 | 8.95 | 0 | 0 | — |
| 1952 | OG-M | FIN | 4 | 2-0-2 | 240:00 | 24 | 0 | 6.00 | 0 | 0 | — |
| ~IIHF Hall of Fame | | | | | | | | | | | |
| **Wilhelm, Thomas / b. July 5, 1973** | | | | | | | | | | | |
| 1992 | WM20 | GER | 2 | 0-0-2 | 120:00 | 17 | 0 | 8.50 | 0 | 0 | — |
| **Willaume, Rolland / b. unknown** | | | | | | | | | | | |
| 1950 | WM | FRA | 3 | 0-0-3 | 180:00 | 24 | 0 | 8.00 | 0 | 0 | — |
| **Wisniewski, Jozef / b. Nov. 1, 1940 / d. Jan. 9, 1996** | | | | | | | | | | | |
| 1966 | WM | POL | 5 | 0-0-2 | 232:51 | 19 | 0 | 4.90 | 0 | 0 | — |
| 1964 | OG-M | POL | 2 | 2-0-0 | 120:00 | 3 | 0 | 1.50 | 0 | 0 | — |
| **Wojakiewicz, Grzegorz / b. Feb. 22, 1968** | | | | | | | | | | | |
| 1987 | WM20 | POL | 4 | 0-0-0 | 103:00 | 22 | 0 | 12.82 | 0 | 0 | — |
| **Wojtynek, Henryk / b. Mar. 23, 1950** | | | | | | | | | | | |
| 1973-79 | WM | POL | 11 | 0-2-6 | 554:14 | 66 | 0 | 7.15 | 0 | 0 | — |
| 1980 | OG-M | POL | 5 | 2-0-1 | 233:58 | 16 | 0 | 4.10 | 0 | 0 | — |
| **Wold, Vidar / b. Mar. 7, 1974** | | | | | | | | | | | |
| 2000-01 | WM | NOR | 7 | 2-1-4 | 391:31 | 28 | 1 | 4.29 | 0 | 0 | — |
| **Woodall, Keith / b. Apr. 8, 1926** | | | | | | | | | | | |
| 1956 | OG-M | CAN | 4 | 3-0-1 | 240:00 | 4 | 2 | 1.00 | 0 | 0 | B |
| **Woods, Ralph "Cooney" / b. Oct. 15, 1898 / d. unknown** | | | | | | | | | | | |
| 1934 | WM | CAN | 4 | 4-0-0 | 190:00 | 2 | 2 | 0.63 | 0 | 0 | G |
| **Worschhauser, Richard / b. Mar. 19, 1930** | | | | | | | | | | | |
| 1954 | WM | FRG | 1 | 0-0-1 | 60:00 | 9 | 0 | 9.00 | 0 | 0 | — |
| **Wregget, Ken / b. Mar. 25, 1964** | | | | | | | | | | | |
| 1984 | WM20 | CAN | 5 | 2-1-2 | 300:00 | 14 | 1 | 2.80 | 0 | 0 | — |
| 1990 | WM | CAN | 1 | 0-0-0 | 40:00 | 0 | 0 | 0.00 | 0 | 0 | — |
| **Wright, Terry / b. June 19, 1960** | | | | | | | | | | | |
| 1980 | WM20 | CAN | 1 | 1-0-0 | 60:00 | 5 | 0 | 5.00 | 0 | 0 | — |
| **Wurm, Josef / b. unknown / d. unknown** | | | | | | | | | | | |
| 1938-47 | WM | AUT | 9 | 4-1-4 | 495:00 | 32 | 0 | 3.88 | 0 | 0 | B |
| **Wyss, Paul / b. July 7, 1928** | | | | | | | | | | | |
| 1952 | OG-M | SUI | 4 | 1-0-2 | 220:00 | 23 | 0 | 6.27 | 0 | 0 | — |
| **Yasumoto, Takagi / b. 1926** | | | | | | | | | | | |
| 1957 | WM | JPN | 5 | 0-1-4 | 266:00 | 46 | 0 | 10.38 | 0 | 0 | — |
| **Yegorov, Alexei / b. Oct. 22, 1976** | | | | | | | | | | | |
| 1996 | WM20 | RUS | 7 | 4-1-2 | 418:54 | 18 | 0 | 2.58 | 1 | 4 | B |
| **Yerkin, Yevgeni / b. Aug. 23, 1932** | | | | | | | | | | | |
| 1957-59 | WM | URS | 6 | 4-1-0 | 347:00 | 10 | 1 | 1.73 | 0 | 2 | 3S |
| 1960 | OG-M | URS | 3 | 2-0-0 | 140:00 | 4 | 1 | 1.71 | 0 | 0 | B |
| **Ylonen, Petri / b. Oct. 2, 1962** | | | | | | | | | | | |
| 1992-96 | WM | FRA | 21 | 6-1-12 | 1,177:11 | 63 | 1 | 3.21 | 0 | 2 | — |
| 1992-94 | OG-M | FRA | 12 | 3-1-8 | 725:24 | 47 | 0 | 3.89 | 0 | 0 | — |
| **Ylonen, Urpo / b. May 25, 1943** | | | | | | | | | | | |
| 1963-78 | WM | FIN | 37 | 13-1-20 | 2,101:00 | 154 | 1 | 4.40 | 0 | 0 | — |
| 1968-76 | OG-M | FIN | 10 | 5-1-4 | 600:00 | 34 | 0 | 3.40 | 0 | 0 | — |
| ~IIHF Hall of Fame | | | | | | | | | | | |
| ~WM IIHF Directorate Best Goalie (1970) | | | | | | | | | | | |
| **Yurkovich, Tom / b. Sept. 29, 1935** | | | | | | | | | | | |
| 1961-66 | WM | USA | 8 | 0-0-7 | 440:00 | 51 | 0 | 6.95 | 0 | 0 | — |
| 1964 | OG-M | USA | 2 | 0-0-2 | 91:25 | 11 | 0 | 7.22 | 0 | 0 | — |
| **Zahorsky, Josef / b. Jan. 6, 1929** | | | | | | | | | | | |
| 1952 | OG-M | TCH | 1 | 1-0-0 | 60:00 | 0 | 1 | 0.00 | 0 | 0 | — |
| **Zaitsev, Boris / b. Mar. 23, 1937** | | | | | | | | | | | |
| 1963 | WM | URS | 1 | 0-0-0 | 20:00 | 1 | 0 | 3.00 | 0 | 0 | G |
| 1964 | OG-M | URS | 2 | 1-0-0 | 80:00 | 0 | 1 | 0.00 | 0 | 0 | G |
| **Zajkowski, Michal / b. July 11, 1983** | | | | | | | | | | | |
| 2001 | WM18 | SWE | 2 | 2-0-0 | 120:00 | 4 | 0 | 2.00 | 0 | 0 | — |
| 2003 | WM20 | SWE | 4 | 2-0-2 | 239:54 | 12 | 0 | 3.00 | 0 | 0 | — |
| **Zanier, Mike / b. Aug. 22, 1962** | | | | | | | | | | | |
| 1992 | OG-M | ITA | 3 | 0-0-3 | 154:43 | 14 | 0 | 5.43 | 0 | 0 | — |
| **Zankl, Peter / b. May 24, 1961** | | | | | | | | | | | |
| 1980 | WM20 | FRG | 4 | 2-0-1 | 216:36 | 16 | 0 | 4.43 | 0 | 0 | — |
| **Zerzuben, Martin / b. Feb. 2, 1981** | | | | | | | | | | | |
| 1999 | WM18 | SUI | 4 | 2-0-2 | 239:23 | 9 | 1 | 2.26 | 0 | 0 | — |
| 2001 | WM20 | SUI | 5 | 1-1-3 | 299:43 | 16 | 0 | 3.20 | 0 | 0 | — |
| **Zimmer, Bernd / b. Sept. 30, 1970** | | | | | | | | | | | |
| 1989 | WM20 | FRG | 5 | 0-0-5 | 265:00 | 41 | 0 | 9.28 | 0 | 0 | — |
| **Zinger, Viktor / b. Oct. 29, 1941** | | | | | | | | | | | |
| 1965-69 | WM | URS | 16 | 12-0-2 | 850:00 | 25 | 2 | 1.76 | 0 | 0 | 4G |
| 1968 | OG-M | URS | 2 | 2-0-0 | 120:00 | 1 | 1 | 0.50 | 0 | 0 | G |
| **Zinkovs, Andrejs / b. Jan. 24, 1968** | | | | | | | | | | | |
| 1999 | WM | LAT | 2 | 0-0-1 | 109:29 | 7 | 0 | 3.84 | 0 | 2 | — |
| **Zirath, Magnus / b. Feb. 16, 1981** | | | | | | | | | | | |
| 1999 | WM18 | SWE | 1 | 1-0-0 | 60:00 | 2 | 0 | 2.00 | 0 | 0 | S |
| **Zopegni, Gianantonio / b. Mar. 8, 1915 / d. unknown** | | | | | | | | | | | |
| 1948 | OG | ITA | 3 | 0-0-3 | 180:00 | 53 | 0 | 17.67 | 0 | 0 | — |
| **Zuger, Simon / b. June 4, 1981** | | | | | | | | | | | |
| 2000 | WM20 | SUI | 4 | 2-0-2 | 210:25 | 14 | 1 | 3.99 | 0 | 2 | — |
| **Zuyev, Andrei / b. May 18, 1964** | | | | | | | | | | | |
| 1993 | WM | RUS | 1 | 0-1-0 | 60:00 | 2 | 0 | 2.00 | 0 | 0 | G |
| 1994 | OG-M | RUS | 5 | 3-0-2 | 287:49 | 15 | 0 | 3.13 | 0 | 4 | — |
| **Zvyagin, Sergei / b. Feb. 17, 1971** | | | | | | | | | | | |
| 1991 | WM20 | URS | 7 | 5-1-1 | 419:02 | 15 | 1 | 2.15 | 1 | 0 | S |
| 2005-06 | WM | RUS | 7 | 6-1-0 | 398:32 | 12 | 1 | 1.81 | 0 | 0 | B |

# PLAYERS' REGISTER, WOMEN

## Active Skaters, Women

(event-by-event summary for recently-active skaters internationally who play in the top level)

| Year Event | #-Pos | NAT | GP | G | A | P | Pim | Finish |
|---|---|---|---|---|---|---|---|---|
| Totals | | | GP | G | A | P | Pim | Medals |

**Abe, Nodoka** — b. Hokkaido, Japan, May 19, 1994

| Year Event | #-Pos | NAT | GP | G | A | P | Pim | Finish |
|---|---|---|---|---|---|---|---|---|
| 2010 WW18 | 15-F | JPN | 5 | 2 | 0 | 2 | 4 | 6th |
| 2011 WW18 | 13-F | JPN | 6 | 2 | 0 | 2 | 2 | 8th |
| **Totals WW18** | | | **11** | **4** | **0** | **4** | **6** | **—** |

**Abgottspon, Celine** — b. Staldenried, Switzerland, November 24, 1995

| Year Event | #-Pos | NAT | GP | G | A | P | Pim | Finish |
|---|---|---|---|---|---|---|---|---|
| 2011 WW18 | 6-D | SUI | 6 | 0 | 0 | 0 | 0 | 7th |
| 2012 WW18 | 6-D | SUI | 2 | 0 | 0 | 0 | 0 | 8th |
| **Totals WW18** | | | **8** | **0** | **0** | **0** | **0** | **—** |

**Adachi, Yurie** — b. Hokkaido, Japan, April 26, 1985

| Year Event | #-Pos | NAT | GP | G | A | P | Pim | Finish |
|---|---|---|---|---|---|---|---|---|
| 2008 WW | 11-F | JPN | 4 | 2 | 1 | 3 | 0 | 7th |
| 2009 WW | 11-F | JPN | 4 | 0 | 2 | 2 | 2 | 8th |
| **Totals WW** | | | **8** | **2** | **3** | **5** | **2** | **—** |

**Afonina, Oxana** — b. Sverdlovsk (Yekaterinburg), Soviet Union (Russia), November 10, 1989

| Year Event | #-Pos | NAT | GP | G | A | P | Pim | Finish |
|---|---|---|---|---|---|---|---|---|
| 2008 WW | 29-F | RUS | 4 | 0 | 0 | 0 | 0 | 6th |

**Agosta, Meghan** — b. Windsor, Ontario, Canada, February 12, 1987

| Year Event | #-Pos | NAT | GP | G | A | P | Pim | Finish |
|---|---|---|---|---|---|---|---|---|
| 2006 OG-W | 2-F | CAN | 5 | 3 | 1 | 4 | 2 | G |
| 2007 WW | 2-F | CAN | 5 | 0 | 4 | 4 | 4 | G |
| 2008 WW | 2-F | CAN | 5 | 3 | 0 | 3 | 8 | S |
| 2009 WW | 2-F | CAN | 5 | 2 | 2 | 4 | 2 | S |
| 2010 OG-W | 2-F | CAN | 5 | 9 | 6 | 15 | 2 | G |
| 2011 WW | 2-F | CAN | 5 | 0 | 5 | 5 | 2 | S |
| 2012 WW | 2-F | CAN | 5 | 4 | 4 | 8 | 8 | G |
| **Totals WW** | | | **25** | **9** | **15** | **24** | **24** | **2G,3S** |
| **Totals OG-W** | | | **10** | **12** | **7** | **19** | **4** | **2G** |

~OG-W MVP (2010), OG-W IIHF Directorate Best Forward (2010), OG-W All-Star Team/Forward (2010)

**Ajchlerova, Denisa** — b. Decin, Czechoslovakia (Czech Republic), August 7, 1991

| Year Event | #-Pos | NAT | GP | G | A | P | Pim | Finish |
|---|---|---|---|---|---|---|---|---|
| 2008 WW18 | 9-F | CZE | 5 | 0 | 0 | 0 | 0 | B |
| 2009 WW18 | 19-F | CZE | 5 | 0 | 0 | 0 | 2 | 4th |
| **Totals WW18** | | | **10** | **0** | **0** | **0** | **2** | **B** |

**Akesson, Fanny** — b. Olofstrom, Sweden, October 16, 1992

| Year Event | #-Pos | NAT | GP | G | A | P | Pim | Finish |
|---|---|---|---|---|---|---|---|---|
| 2010 WW18 | 9-D | SWE | 6 | 0 | 0 | 0 | 4 | B |

**Akmanayeva, Tatyana** — b. Tyumen, Russia, January 17, 1995

| Year Event | #-Pos | NAT | GP | G | A | P | Pim | Finish |
|---|---|---|---|---|---|---|---|---|
| 2010 WW18 | 20-F | RUS | 5 | 0 | 0 | 0 | 2 | 8th |
| 2012 WW18 | 14-F | RUS | 6 | 0 | 0 | 0 | 0 | 7th |
| **Totals WW18** | | | **11** | **0** | **0** | **0** | **2** | **—** |

**Alanko, Christa** — b. Vaasa, Finland, June 20, 1994

| Year Event | #-Pos | NAT | GP | G | A | P | Pim | Finish |
|---|---|---|---|---|---|---|---|---|
| 2011 WW18 | 20-F | FIN | 6 | 0 | 0 | 0 | 4 | B |
| 2012 WW18 | 20-F | FIN | 5 | 0 | 3 | 3 | 2 | 5th |
| **Totals WW18** | | | **11** | **0** | **3** | **3** | **6** | **B** |

**Alasalmi, Emmy** — b. Stockholm, Sweden, January 17, 1994

| Year Event | #-Pos | NAT | GP | G | A | P | Pim | Finish |
|---|---|---|---|---|---|---|---|---|
| 2010 WW18 | 21-D | SWE | 5 | 0 | 0 | 0 | 0 | B |
| 2012 WW18 | 21-D | SWE | 6 | 0 | 0 | 0 | 0 | B |
| **Totals WW18** | | | **11** | **0** | **0** | **0** | **0** | **2B** |

**~Alexeyeva, Lyubov ~see Ibragimova (Alexeyeva), Lyubov**

**Altmann, Livia** — b. Engi, Switzerland, December 13, 1994

| Year Event | #-Pos | NAT | GP | G | A | P | Pim | Finish |
|---|---|---|---|---|---|---|---|---|
| 2011 WW18 | 10-D | SUI | 6 | 0 | 1 | 1 | 2 | 7th |
| 2012 WW18 | 10-D | SUI | 6 | 0 | 0 | 0 | 0 | 8th |
| **Totals WW18** | | | **12** | **0** | **1** | **1** | **2** | **—** |

**Ambrose, Erin** — b. Keswick, Ontario, Canada, April 30, 1994

| Year Event | #-Pos | NAT | GP | G | A | P | Pim | Finish |
|---|---|---|---|---|---|---|---|---|
| 2010 WW18 | 13-D | CAN | 5 | 0 | 9 | 9 | 0 | G |
| 2011 WW18 | 13-D | CAN | 5 | 0 | 2 | 2 | 4 | S |
| 2012 WW18 | 13-D | CAN | 5 | 2 | 3 | 5 | 0 | G |
| **Totals WW18** | | | **15** | **2** | **14** | **16** | **4** | **2G,S** |

~IIHF Directorate WW18 Best Defenceman (2012)

**Ammerman, Brittany** — b. River Vale, New Jersey, United States, June 19, 1992

| Year Event | #-Pos | NAT | GP | G | A | P | Pim | Finish |
|---|---|---|---|---|---|---|---|---|
| 2009 WW18 | 10-F | USA | 5 | 5 | 5 | 10 | 2 | G |
| 2010 WW18 | 10-F | USA | 5 | 5 | 3 | 8 | 4 | S |
| **Totals WW18** | | | **10** | **10** | **8** | **18** | **6** | **G,S** |

**Ammerman, Brooke** — b. River Vale, New Jersey, United States, July 13, 1990

| Year Event | #-Pos | NAT | GP | G | A | P | Pim | Finish |
|---|---|---|---|---|---|---|---|---|
| 2008 WW18 | 12-F | USA | 5 | 6 | 4 | 10 | 4 | G |

**Ananina, Yekaterina** — b. Sverdlovsk (Yekaterinburg), Soviet Union (Russia), June 13, 1991

| Year Event | #-Pos | NAT | GP | G | A | P | Pim | Finish |
|---|---|---|---|---|---|---|---|---|
| 2008 WW18 | 13-F | RUS | 5 | 1 | 0 | 1 | 2 | 8th |
| 2009 WW18 | 13-F | RUS | 5 | 3 | 0 | 3 | 0 | 7th |
| 2009 WW | 14-F | RUS | 4 | 1 | 1 | 2 | 2 | 5th |
| 2010 OG-W | 91-F | RUS | 5 | 0 | 0 | 0 | 0 | 6th |
| 2012 WW | 19-F | RUS | 5 | 0 | 0 | 0 | 4 | 6th |
| **Totals WW18** | | | **10** | **4** | **0** | **4** | **2** | **—** |
| **Totals WW** | | | **9** | **1** | **1** | **2** | **6** | **—** |

**Anderson, Stephanie** — b. North St. Paul, Minnesota, United States, November 27, 1992

| Year Event | #-Pos | NAT | GP | G | A | P | Pim | Finish |
|---|---|---|---|---|---|---|---|---|
| 2010 WW18 | 24-F | USA | 1 | 0 | 0 | 0 | 0 | S |

**Andersson, Emilia** — b. Stockholm, Sweden, August 31, 1988

| Year Event | #-Pos | NAT | GP | G | A | P | Pim | Finish |
|---|---|---|---|---|---|---|---|---|
| 2007 WW | 10-D | SWE | 5 | 0 | 0 | 0 | 2 | B |
| 2008 WW | 10-D | SWE | 4 | 0 | 0 | 0 | 4 | 5th |
| 2009 WW | 10-D | SWE | 5 | 0 | 0 | 0 | 2 | 4th |
| 2010 OG-W | 10-D | SWE | 5 | 0 | 1 | 1 | 4 | 4th |
| 2012 WW | 10-D | SWE | 5 | 0 | 0 | 0 | 0 | 5th |
| **Totals WW** | | | **19** | **0** | **0** | **0** | **8** | **B** |

**Andersson, Gunilla** — b. Skutskar, Sweden, April 26, 1975

| Year Event | #-Pos | NAT | GP | G | A | P | Pim | Finish |
|---|---|---|---|---|---|---|---|---|
| 1992 WW | 23-D | SWE | 5 | 2 | 2 | 4 | 4 | 4th |
| 1994 WW | 23-D | SWE | 5 | 0 | 2 | 2 | 6 | 5th |
| 1997 WW | 23-D | SWE | 5 | 3 | 2 | 5 | 8 | 5th |
| 1998 OG-W | 23-D | SWE | 5 | 1 | 1 | 2 | 20 | 5th |
| 1999 WW | 23-D | SWE | 5 | 2 | 1 | 3 | 2 | 4th |
| 2000 WW | 23-D | SWE | 5 | 1 | 2 | 3 | 6 | 4th |
| 2001 WW | 23-D | SWE | 5 | 2 | 1 | 3 | 6 | 5th |
| 2002 OG-W | 23-D | SWE | 5 | 1 | 1 | 2 | 12 | B |
| 2004 WW | 23-D | SWE | 4 | 0 | 2 | 2 | 0 | 4th |
| 2005 WW | 23-D | SWE | 5 | 1 | 2 | 3 | 2 | B |
| 2006 OG-W | 23-D | SWE | 5 | 3 | 3 | 6 | 4 | S |
| 2007 WW | 23-D | SWE | 5 | 2 | 2 | 4 | 4 | B |
| 2009 WW | 23-D | SWE | 5 | 0 | 3 | 3 | 2 | 4th |
| 2010 OG-W | 23-D | SWE | 5 | 0 | 2 | 2 | 4 | 4th |
| 2011 WW | 23-D | SWE | 5 | 0 | 3 | 3 | 8 | 5th |
| **Totals WW** | | | **54** | **13** | **22** | **35** | **48** | **2B** |
| **Totals OG-W** | | | **20** | **5** | **7** | **12** | **40** | **S,B** |

~WW All-Star Team/Defence (2004)

**Andersson, Matilda** — b. Norrkoping, Sweden, March 20, 1994

| Year Event | #-Pos | NAT | GP | G | A | P | Pim | Finish |
|---|---|---|---|---|---|---|---|---|
| 2012 WW18 | 11-F | SWE | 6 | 3 | 0 | 3 | 2 | B |

**Anselm, Vanessa** — b. Mannheim, Germany, October 27, 1991

| Year Event | #-Pos | NAT | GP | G | A | P | Pim | Finish |
|---|---|---|---|---|---|---|---|---|
| 2008 WW18 | 13-D | GER | 5 | 2 | 0 | 2 | 0 | 5th |
| 2009 WW18 | 27-D | GER | 5 | 0 | 0 | 0 | 2 | 6th |
| **Totals WW18** | | | **10** | **2** | **0** | **2** | **2** | **—** |

**Anwander, Manuela** — b. Grafelfing, Germany, January 9, 1992

| Year Event | #-Pos | NAT | GP | G | A | P | Pim | Finish |
|---|---|---|---|---|---|---|---|---|
| 2008 WW18 | 21-F | GER | 5 | 4 | 3 | 7 | 0 | 5th |
| 2008 WW | 5-F | GER | 4 | 2 | 0 | 2 | 0 | 9th |
| 2009 WW18 | 21-F | GER | 5 | 1 | 0 | 1 | 4 | 6th |
| 2010 WW18 | 21-F | GER | 6 | 4 | 0 | 4 | 12 | 4th |
| 2012 WW | 5-F | GER | 5 | 2 | 0 | 2 | 2 | 7th |
| **Totals WW18** | | | **16** | **9** | **3** | **12** | **16** | **—** |
| **Totals WW** | | | **9** | **4** | **0** | **4** | **2** | **—** |

**Apps, Gillian** — b. North York (Toronto), Ontario, Canada, November 2, 1983

| Year Event | #-Pos | NAT | GP | G | A | P | Pim | Finish |
|---|---|---|---|---|---|---|---|---|
| 2004 WW | 10-F | CAN | 5 | 4 | 0 | 4 | 10 | G |
| 2005 WW | 10-F | CAN | 5 | 4 | 2 | 6 | 8 | S |
| 2006 OG-W | 10-F | CAN | 5 | 7 | 7 | 14 | 14 | G |
| 2007 WW | 10-F | CAN | 5 | 1 | 3 | 4 | 6 | G |
| 2008 WW | 10-F | CAN | 5 | 1 | 0 | 1 | 8 | S |
| 2009 WW | 10-F | CAN | 5 | 2 | 1 | 3 | 4 | S |
| 2010 OG-W | 10-F | CAN | 5 | 3 | 4 | 7 | 2 | G |
| 2011 WW | 10-F | CAN | 5 | 2 | 1 | 3 | 0 | S |
| 2012 WW | 10-F | CAN | 5 | 2 | 2 | 4 | 10 | G |
| **Totals WW** | | | **25** | **12** | **6** | **18** | **36** | **2G, 3S** |
| **Totals OG-W** | | | **20** | **14** | **14** | **28** | **26** | **3G,1S** |

~OG-W All-Star Team/Forward (2006)

**Aralinna, Reetta** — b. Seinajoki, Finland, August 11, 1991

| Year Event | #-Pos | NAT | GP | G | A | P | Pim | Finish |
|---|---|---|---|---|---|---|---|---|
| 2009 WW18 | 22-F | FIN | 5 | 0 | 0 | 0 | 0 | 5th |

**Armstrong, Hannah** — b. Sharon, Ontario, Canada, April 19, 1992

| Year Event | #-Pos | NAT | GP | G | A | P | Pim | Finish |
|---|---|---|---|---|---|---|---|---|
| 2010 WW18 | 20-F | CAN | 5 | 3 | 0 | 3 | 4 | G |

| **Ashikhina (Babushkina), Alexandra** | | | | | | | | **b. Almaty, Soviet Union (Kazakhstan), February 19, 1986** |
|---|---|---|---|---|---|---|---|---|
| 2005 WW* | 3-F | KAZ | 5 | 0 | 0 | 0 | 0 | 7th |
| 2007 WW* | 29-F | KAZ | 4 | 0 | 0 | 0 | 0 | 9th |
| 2011 WW | 3-F | KAZ | 5 | 0 | 0 | 0 | 0 | 8th |
| **Totals WW** | | | **14** | **0** | **0** | **0** | **0** | **—** |

*played under maiden name Alexandra Babushkina

| **Asserholt, Jenni** | | | | | | | | **b. Orebro, Sweden, April 8, 1988** |
|---|---|---|---|---|---|---|---|---|
| 2004 WW | 4-D | SWE | 5 | 1 | 0 | 1 | 12 | 4th |
| 2005 WW | 4-D | SWE | 5 | 0 | 1 | 1 | 6 | B |
| 2006 OG-W | 4-D | SWE | 5 | 0 | 2 | 2 | 12 | S |
| 2007 WW | 4-D | SWE | 5 | 0 | 2 | 2 | 4 | B |
| 2008 WW | 4-D | SWE | 4 | 1 | 0 | 1 | 4 | 5th |
| 2009 WW | 4-D | SWE | 5 | 0 | 0 | 0 | 0 | 4th |
| 2010 OG-W | 4-D | SWE | 5 | 1 | 0 | 1 | 4 | 4th |
| 2011 WW | 4-F | SWE | 5 | 0 | 1 | 1 | 8 | 5th |
| 2012 WW | 4-F | SWE | 5 | 2 | 5 | 7 | 10 | 5th |
| **Totals WW** | | | **34** | **4** | **9** | **13** | **44** | **2B** |
| **Totals OG-W** | | | **10** | **1** | **2** | **3** | **16** | **S** |

| **Astrom, Hanna** | | | | | | | | **b. Ornskoldsvik, Sweden, August 12, 1992** |
|---|---|---|---|---|---|---|---|---|
| 2010 WW18 | 20-F | SWE | 6 | 1 | 2 | 3 | 4 | B |

| **Aunio, Erika** | | | | | | | | **b. Turku, Finland, July 25, 1990** |
|---|---|---|---|---|---|---|---|---|
| 2008 WW18 | 12-F | FIN | 5 | 0 | 1 | 1 | 2 | 6th |

| **Baba, Itsuki** | | | | | | | | **b. Tokyo, Japan, July 13, 1992** |
|---|---|---|---|---|---|---|---|---|
| 2010 WW18 | 4-D | JPN | 5 | 0 | 0 | 0 | 2 | 6th |

| **Babiakova, Petra** | | | | | | | | **b. Zvolen, Czechoslovakia (Slovakia), July 27, 1977** |
|---|---|---|---|---|---|---|---|---|
| 2010 OG-W | 9-D | SVK | 5 | 0 | 0 | 0 | 2 | 8th |

| **Babonyova, Natalie** | | | | | | | | **b. Oshawa, Ontario, Canada, October 22, 1983** |
|---|---|---|---|---|---|---|---|---|
| 2010 OG-W | 8-F | SVK | 5 | 0 | 1 | 1 | 4 | 8th |

**~Babushkina, Alexandra** ~see Ashikhina (Babushkina), Alexandra

| **Bachmann, Fabiola** | | | | | | | | **b. Amsoldingen, Switzerland, July 21, 1992** |
|---|---|---|---|---|---|---|---|---|
| 2008 WW18 | 4-D | SUI | 5 | 2 | 0 | 2 | 4 | 7th |
| 2009 WW18 | 4-D | SUI | 5 | 2 | 1 | 3 | 10 | 8th |
| **Totals WW18** | | | **10** | **4** | **1** | **5** | **14** | **—** |

| **Backlin, Lina** | | | | | | | | **b. Gavle, Sweden, October 3, 1994** |
|---|---|---|---|---|---|---|---|---|
| 2010 WW18 | 6-D | SWE | 6 | 0 | 0 | 0 | 14 | B |
| 2011 WW18 | 6-D | SWE | 5 | 2 | 1 | 3 | 4 | 5th |
| 2012 WW18 | 6-D | SWE | 6 | 1 | 0 | 1 | 6 | B |
| **Totals WW18** | | | **17** | **3** | **1** | **4** | **24** | **2B** |

| **Backman, Linnea** | | | | | | | | **b. Stockholm, Sweden, April 18, 1991** |
|---|---|---|---|---|---|---|---|---|
| 2008 WW18 | 10-D | SWE | 5 | 0 | 0 | 0 | 0 | 4th |
| 2009 WW18 | 3-D | SWE | 5 | 1 | 0 | 1 | 4 | B |
| 2011 WW | 17-D | SWE | 5 | 0 | 1 | 1 | 6 | 5th |
| 2012 WW | 17-D | SWE | 5 | 0 | 2 | 2 | 0 | 5th |
| **Totals WW18** | | | **10** | **1** | **0** | **1** | **4** | **B** |
| **Totals WW** | | | **10** | **0** | **3** | **3** | **6** | **—** |

| **Bacon, Kate** | | | | | | | | **b. Chanhassen, Minnesota, United States, April 25, 1990** |
|---|---|---|---|---|---|---|---|---|
| 2008 WW18 | 9-F | USA | 5 | 3 | 0 | 3 | 0 | G |

| **Baibakova, Xenia** | | | | | | | | **b. Tyumen Region, Russia, June 22, 1994** |
|---|---|---|---|---|---|---|---|---|
| 2010 WW18 | 15-F | RUS | 5 | 0 | 0 | 0 | 2 | 8th |
| 2012 WW18 | 15-F | RUS | 6 | 1 | 0 | 1 | 0 | 7th |
| **Totals WW18** | | | **11** | **1** | **0** | **1** | **2** | **—** |

| **Balanche, Camille** | | | | | | | | **b. Le Locle, Switzerland, March 1, 1990** |
|---|---|---|---|---|---|---|---|---|
| 2008 WW18 | 14-F | SUI | 5 | 1 | 1 | 2 | 8 | 7th |
| 2008 WW | 49-F | SUI | 5 | 0 | 0 | 0 | 0 | 4th |

| **Bartsch, Anne** | | | | | | | | **b. Zittau, Germany, September 22, 1995** |
|---|---|---|---|---|---|---|---|---|
| 2012 WW18 | 2-D | GER | 6 | 0 | 0 | 0 | 2 | 4th |

| **Bashurova, Olga** | | | | | | | | **b. Yakutia, Soviet Union (Russia), January 5, 1990** |
|---|---|---|---|---|---|---|---|---|
| 2008 WW18 | 4-D | RUS | 2 | 0 | 0 | 0 | 0 | 8th |

| **Batalova, Maria** | | | | | | | | **b. May 3, 1996** |
|---|---|---|---|---|---|---|---|---|
| 2012 WW18 | 8-D | RUS | 6 | 0 | 1 | 1 | 8 | 7th |

| **Bauer, Leonie** | | | | | | | | **b. Bayreuth, Germany, April 21, 1995** |
|---|---|---|---|---|---|---|---|---|
| 2012 WW18 | 8-F | GER | 6 | 0 | 0 | 0 | 0 | 4th |

| **Bellamy, Kacey** | | | | | | | | **b. Westfield, Massachusetts, United States, April 22, 1987** |
|---|---|---|---|---|---|---|---|---|
| 2008 WW | 22-D | USA | 4 | 0 | 2 | 2 | 6 | G |
| 2009 WW | 22-D | USA | 5 | 0 | 2 | 2 | 4 | G |
| 2010 OG-W | 22-D | USA | 5 | 0 | 1 | 1 | 4 | S |
| 2011 WW | 22-D | USA | 5 | 1 | 1 | 2 | 2 | G |
| 2012 WW | 22-D | USA | 5 | 0 | 1 | 1 | 6 | S |
| **Totals WW** | | | **19** | **1** | **6** | **7** | **18** | **3G,S** |

| **Belyakova, Lyudmila** | | | | | | | | **b. Moscow, Russia, August 12, 1994** |
|---|---|---|---|---|---|---|---|---|
| 2010 WW18 | 10-F | RUS | 5 | 1 | 2 | 3 | 6 | 8th |
| 2012 WW18 | 12-F | RUS | 6 | 6 | 1 | 7 | 6 | 7th |
| 2012 WW | 10-F | RUS | 5 | 0 | 0 | 0 | 12 | 6th |
| **Totals WW18** | | | **11** | **7** | **3** | **10** | **12** | **—** |

| **Bendus, Vicki** | | | | | | | | **b. Wasaga Beach, Ontario, Canada, April 17, 1989** |
|---|---|---|---|---|---|---|---|---|
| 2012 WW | 28-F | CAN | 5 | 0 | 1 | 1 | 0 | G |

| **Benz, Laura** | | | | | | | | **b. Kloten, Switzerland, August 25, 1992** |
|---|---|---|---|---|---|---|---|---|
| 2008 WW18 | 6-D | SUI | 5 | 0 | 1 | 1 | 18 | 7th |
| 2009 WW18 | 6-D | SUI | 4 | 0 | 1 | 1 | 4 | 8th |
| 2009 WW | 17-D | SUI | 4 | 1 | 0 | 1 | 4 | 7th |
| 2010 OG-W | 21-D | SUI | 5 | 0 | 2 | 2 | 2 | 5th |
| **Totals WW18** | | | **9** | **0** | **2** | **2** | **22** | **—** |

| **Benz, Sara** | | | | | | | | **b. Kloten, Switzerland, August 25, 1992** |
|---|---|---|---|---|---|---|---|---|
| 2008 WW18 | 13-F | SUI | 5 | 4 | 2 | 6 | 2 | 7th |
| 2009 WW18 | 13-F | SUI | 2 | 0 | 2 | 2 | 2 | 8th |
| 2009 WW | 12-F | SUI | 4 | 0 | 2 | 2 | 0 | 7th |
| 2010 OG-W | 13-F | SUI | 5 | 1 | 0 | 1 | 2 | 5th |
| 2011 WW | 13-F | SUI | 5 | 3 | 2 | 5 | 2 | 6th |
| 2012 WW | 13-F | SUI | 5 | 2 | 2 | 4 | 2 | B |
| **Totals WW18** | | | **7** | **4** | **4** | **8** | **4** | **—** |
| **Totals WW** | | | **14** | **5** | **6** | **11** | **4** | **B** |

| **Bergius, Emilia** | | | | | | | | **b. Ornskoldsvik, Sweden, May 4, 1991** |
|---|---|---|---|---|---|---|---|---|
| 2009 WW18 | 2-D | SWE | 5 | 0 | 1 | 1 | 10 | B |

| **Bestland, Christine** | | | | | | | | **b. Brunkild, Manitoba, Canada, April 28, 1992** |
|---|---|---|---|---|---|---|---|---|
| 2009 WW18 | 7-F | CAN | 5 | 0 | 1 | 1 | 0 | S |
| 2010 WW18 | 11-F | CAN | 5 | 3 | 5 | 8 | 8 | G |
| **Totals WW18** | | | **10** | **3** | **6** | **9** | **8** | **G,S** |

| **Bigler, Jana** | | | | | | | | **b. Worb, Switzerland, January 20, 1994** |
|---|---|---|---|---|---|---|---|---|
| 2011 WW18 | 12-F | SUI | 6 | 1 | 1 | 2 | 0 | 7th |
| 2012 WW18 | 12-F | SUI | 6 | 0 | 0 | 0 | 0 | 8th |
| **Totals WW18** | | | **12** | **1** | **1** | **2** | **0** | **—** |

| **Birchard, Courtney** | | | | | | | | **b. Etobicoke (Toronto), Ontario, Canada, July 14, 1989** |
|---|---|---|---|---|---|---|---|---|
| 2012 WW | 11-D | CAN | 5 | 1 | 0 | 1 | 2 | G |

| **Bittner, Monika** | | | | | | | | **b. Peissenberg, West Germany (Germany), January 29, 1988** |
|---|---|---|---|---|---|---|---|---|
| 2007 WW | 26-F | GER | 4 | 0 | 0 | 0 | 0 | 8th |
| 2008 WW | 26-F | GER | 4 | 0 | 0 | 0 | 0 | 9th |
| 2012 WW | 26-F | GER | 5 | 1 | 0 | 1 | 0 | 7th |
| **Totals WW** | | | **13** | **1** | **0** | **1** | **0** | **—** |

| **Bizzari, Melissa** | | | | | | | | **b. Stowe, Vermont, United States, March 27, 1992** |
|---|---|---|---|---|---|---|---|---|
| 2010 WW18 | 6-F | USA | 5 | 1 | 5 | 6 | 0 | S |

| **Blom, Gizela** | | | | | | | | **b. Norrtalje, Sweden, August 13, 1985** |
|---|---|---|---|---|---|---|---|---|
| 2012 WW | 29-F | SWE | 5 | 0 | 0 | 0 | 2 | 5th |

| **Bolden, Blake** | | | | | | | | **b. Stow, Ohio, United States, March 10, 1991** |
|---|---|---|---|---|---|---|---|---|
| 2008 WW18 | 2-D | USA | 5 | 0 | 0 | 0 | 4 | G |
| 2009 WW18 | 4-D | USA | 5 | 1 | 5 | 6 | 6 | G |
| **Totals WW18** | | | **10** | **1** | **5** | **6** | **10** | **2G** |

| **Bona, Rachael** | | | | | | | | **b. Coon Rapids, Minnesota, United States, October 25, 1992** |
|---|---|---|---|---|---|---|---|---|
| 2010 WW18 | 26-F | USA | 5 | 2 | 0 | 2 | 4 | S |

| **Bonhomme, Tessa** | | | | | | | | **b. Sudbury, Ontario, Canada, July 23, 1985** |
|---|---|---|---|---|---|---|---|---|
| 2007 WW | 25-D | CAN | 5 | 1 | 1 | 2 | 6 | G |
| 2009 WW | 25-D | CAN | 5 | 0 | 3 | 3 | 0 | S |
| 2010 OG-W | 25-D | CAN | 5 | 2 | 2 | 4 | 0 | G |
| 2011 WW | 25-D | CAN | 5 | 1 | 3 | 4 | 0 | S |
| 2012 WW | 25-D | CAN | 5 | 0 | 1 | 1 | 2 | G |
| **Totals WW** | | | **20** | **2** | **8** | **10** | **8** | **2G,2S** |

| **Borgfeldt, Anna** | | | | | | | | **b. Kristianstad, Sweden, March 26, 1993** |
|---|---|---|---|---|---|---|---|---|
| 2009 WW18 | 10-F | SWE | 5 | 0 | 0 | 0 | 2 | B |
| 2010 WW18 | 10-F | SWE | 6 | 2 | 2 | 4 | 6 | B |
| 2011 WW18 | 10-F | SWE | 4 | 0 | 3 | 3 | 2 | 5th |
| **Totals WW18** | | | **15** | **2** | **5** | **7** | **10** | **2B** |

| Borgqvist, Anna | | | | | | | | b. Vaxjo, Sweden, June 11, 1992 |
|---|---|---|---|---|---|---|---|---|
| 2008 WW18 | 16-F | SWE | 5 | 2 | 2 | 4 | 8 | 4th |
| 2009 WW18 | 16-F | SWE | 4 | 3 | 1 | 4 | 2 | B |
| 2011 WW | 18-F | SWE | 5 | 1 | 0 | 1 | 0 | 5th |
| **Totals WW18** | | | **9** | **5** | **3** | **8** | **10** | **B** |

| Boucher, Kasey | | | | | | | | b. Lewiston, Maine, United States, October 25, 1990 |
|---|---|---|---|---|---|---|---|---|
| 2008 WW18 | 3-D | USA | 5 | 0 | 1 | 1 | 0 | G |

| Boulier, Amanda | | | | | | | | b. Watertown, Connecticut, United States, March 30, 1993 |
|---|---|---|---|---|---|---|---|---|
| 2011 WW18 | 11-D | USA | 5 | 1 | 3 | 4 | 0 | G |

| Bozek, Megan | | | | | | | | b. Buffalo Grove, Illinois, United States, March 27, 1991 |
|---|---|---|---|---|---|---|---|---|
| 2009 WW18 | 3-D | USA | 5 | 1 | 5 | 6 | 0 | G |
| 2012 WW | 25-D | USA | 5 | 2 | 3 | 5 | 0 | S |

| Bram, Bailey | | | | | | | | b. Ste. Anne, Manitoba, Canada, September 5, 1990 |
|---|---|---|---|---|---|---|---|---|
| 2008 WW18 | 15-F | CAN | 5 | 3 | 4 | 7 | 6 | S |
| 2012 WW | 17-F | CAN | 5 | 0 | 1 | 1 | 4 | G |

| Bram, Shelby | | | | | | | | b. Ste. Anne, Manitoba, Canada, August 20, 1993 |
|---|---|---|---|---|---|---|---|---|
| 2011 WW18 | 12-F | CAN | 5 | 2 | 1 | 3 | 8 | S |

| Brandt, Hannah | | | | | | | | b. Vadnais Heights, Minnesota, United States, November 27, 1993 |
|---|---|---|---|---|---|---|---|---|
| 2011 WW18 | 8-F | USA | 5 | 5 | 5 | 10 | 2 | G |
| 2012 WW | 20-F | USA | 5 | 0 | 0 | 0 | 0 | S |

| Bremova, Barbora | | | | | | | | b. Kosice, Czechoslovakia (Slovakia), August 24, 1991 |
|---|---|---|---|---|---|---|---|---|
| 2010 OG-W | 7-D | SVK | 5 | 0 | 0 | 0 | 4 | 8th |
| 2011 WW | 7-D | SVK | 5 | 0 | 0 | 0 | 2 | 7th |
| 2012 WW | 7-D | SVK | 5 | 0 | 0 | 0 | 0 | 8th |
| **Totals WW** | | | **10** | **0** | **0** | **0** | **2** | **—** |

| Brock, Kate | | | | | | | | b. Marblehead, Massachusetts, United States, October 30, 1991 |
|---|---|---|---|---|---|---|---|---|
| 2009 WW18 | 2-D | USA | 5 | 0 | 1 | 1 | 4 | G |

| Browne, Hailey | | | | | | | | b. Oakville, Ontario, Canada, May 13, 1993 |
|---|---|---|---|---|---|---|---|---|
| 2011 WW18 | 24-F | CAN | 5 | 0 | 0 | 0 | 8 | S |

| Bruckl, Isabell | | | | | | | | b. Garmisch-Partenkirchen, Germany, March 26, 1990 |
|---|---|---|---|---|---|---|---|---|
| 2008 WW18 | 18-F | GER | 5 | 1 | 0 | 1 | 4 | 5th |

| Brugger, Luisa | | | | | | | | b. Kempten, Germany, June 25, 1995 |
|---|---|---|---|---|---|---|---|---|
| 2011 WW18 | 7-F | GER | 5 | 0 | 0 | 0 | 0 | 6th |

| Brykaliuk, Ashleigh | | | | | | | | b. Brandon, Manitoba, June 15, 1995 |
|---|---|---|---|---|---|---|---|---|
| 2012 WW18 | 5-F | CAN | 5 | 0 | 1 | 1 | 0 | G |

| Bukshevannaya, Maria | | | | | | | | b. Moscow, Russia, July 1, 1994 |
|---|---|---|---|---|---|---|---|---|
| 2010 WW18 | 16-D | RUS | 5 | 0 | 0 | 0 | 4 | 8th |
| 2012 WW18 | 5-D | RUS | 6 | 0 | 0 | 0 | 8 | 7th |
| **Totals WW18** | | | **11** | **0** | **0** | **0** | **12** | **—** |

| Bulatova, Diana | | | | | | | | b. April 7, 1995 |
|---|---|---|---|---|---|---|---|---|
| 2012 WW18 | 10-F | RUS | 5 | 0 | 0 | 0 | 4 | 7th |

| Bullo, Nicole | | | | | | | | b. Bellinzona, Switzerland, July 18, 1987 |
|---|---|---|---|---|---|---|---|---|
| 2004 WW | 10-D | SUI | 4 | 1 | 0 | 1 | 2 | 8th |
| 2006 OG-W | 10-D | SUI | 5 | 0 | 1 | 1 | 6 | 7th |
| 2007 WW | 10-D | SUI | 4 | 0 | 0 | 0 | 8 | 5th |
| 2008 WW | 10-D | SUI | 5 | 0 | 0 | 0 | 4 | 4th |
| 2009 WW | 10-F | SUI | 4 | 2 | 1 | 3 | 2 | 7th |
| 2010 OG-W | 10-F | SUI | 5 | 0 | 0 | 0 | 6 | 5th |
| 2011 WW | 10-F | SUI | 5 | 2 | 0 | 2 | 0 | 6th |
| 2012 WW | 10-D | SUI | 6 | 1 | 2 | 3 | 4 | B |
| **Totals WW** | | | **28** | **6** | **3** | **9** | **20** | **B** |
| **Totals OG-W** | | | **10** | **1** | **1** | **1** | **12** | **—** |

| Burina, Tatyana | | | | | | | | b. Novosibirsk, Soviet Union (Russia), March 20, 1980 |
|---|---|---|---|---|---|---|---|---|
| 1999 WW | 24-F | RUS | 5 | 1 | 0 | 1 | 16 | 6th |
| 2000 WW | 24-F | RUS | 5 | 0 | 1 | 1 | 2 | 5th |
| 2001 WW | 23-F | RUS | 5 | 1 | 1 | 2 | 6 | B |
| 2002 OG-W | 23-F | RUS | 5 | 4 | 0 | 4 | 0 | 5th |
| 2005 WW | 23-F | RUS | 5 | 1 | 0 | 1 | 0 | 8th |
| 2006 OG-W | 23-F | RUS | 5 | 1 | 0 | 1 | 14 | 6th |
| 2007 WW | 23-F | RUS | 4 | 2 | 0 | 2 | 4 | 7th |
| 2008 WW | 23-F | RUS | 4 | 0 | 1 | 1 | 2 | 6th |
| 2009 WW | 23-F | RUS | 4 | 3 | 0 | 3 | 12 | 5th |
| 2010 OG-W | 23-F | RUS | 5 | 1 | 2 | 3 | 4 | 6th |
| 2011 WW | 23-F | RUS | 6 | 3 | 0 | 3 | 8 | 4th |
| 2012 WW | 23-F | RUS | 5 | 3 | 1 | 4 | 6 | 6th |
| **Totals WW** | | | **43** | **14** | **4** | **18** | **56** | **B** |
| **Totals OG-W** | | | **15** | **6** | **2** | **8** | **18** | **—** |

| Burke, Courtney | | | | | | | | b. Albany, New York, United States, September 2, 1994 |
|---|---|---|---|---|---|---|---|---|
| 2011 WW18 | 6-D | USA | 5 | 0 | 4 | 4 | 2 | G |
| 2012 WW18 | 6-D | USA | 5 | 1 | 5 | 6 | 4 | S |
| **Totals WW18** | | | **10** | **1** | **9** | **10** | **6** | **G,S** |

| Busch, Franziska | | | | | | | | b. Seesen, West Germany (Germany), October 20, 1985 |
|---|---|---|---|---|---|---|---|---|
| 2004 WW | 25-F | GER | 4 | 0 | 0 | 0 | 0 | 6th |
| 2005 WW | 25-F | GER | 5 | 0 | 1 | 1 | 2 | 5th |
| 2006 OG-W | 25-F | GER | 5 | 0 | 0 | 0 | 0 | 5th |
| 2007 WW | 25-F | GER | 4 | 1 | 0 | 1 | 0 | 8th |
| 2008 WW | 25-F | GER | 3 | 0 | 0 | 0 | 0 | 9th |
| 2012 WW | 25-F | GER | 5 | 0 | 2 | 2 | 2 | 7th |
| **Totals WW** | | | **21** | **1** | **3** | **4** | **4** | **—** |

| Byszio, Eva | | | | | | | | b. Ingolstadt, Germany, May 25, 1993 |
|---|---|---|---|---|---|---|---|---|
| 2011 WW18 | 17-F | GER | 5 | 1 | 0 | 1 | 0 | 6th |

| Cahow, Caitlin | | | | | | | | b. New Haven, Connecticut, United States, May 20, 1985 |
|---|---|---|---|---|---|---|---|---|
| 2006 OG-W | 8-D | USA | 5 | 0 | 0 | 0 | 2 | B |
| 2007 WW | 8-D | USA | 5 | 2 | 2 | 4 | 2 | S |
| 2008 WW | 8-D | USA | 5 | 2 | 3 | 5 | 0 | G |
| 2009 WW | 8-D | USA | 5 | 2 | 4 | 6 | 0 | G |
| 2010 OG-W | 8-D | USA | 5 | 2 | 2 | 4 | 10 | S |
| 2011 WW | 8-D | USA | 5 | 1 | 4 | 5 | 4 | G |
| **Totals WW** | | | **20** | **7** | **13** | **20** | **6** | **3G,S** |
| **Totals OG-W** | | | **10** | **2** | **2** | **4** | **12** | **S,B** |

~WW All-Star Team/Defence (2011)

| Cameranesi, Dani | | | | | | | | b. Plymouth, Minnesota, United States, June 30, 1995 |
|---|---|---|---|---|---|---|---|---|
| 2012 WW18 | 18-F | USA | 5 | 0 | 2 | 2 | 2 | S |

| Campbell, Caroline | | | | | | | | b. Fordland, Montana, United States, August 22, 1991 |
|---|---|---|---|---|---|---|---|---|
| 2009 WW18 | 5-D | USA | 5 | 1 | 1 | 2 | 4 | G |

| Campbell, Jessica | | | | | | | | b. Melville, Saskatchewan, Canada, June 24, 1992 |
|---|---|---|---|---|---|---|---|---|
| 2009 WW18 | 14-F | CAN | 5 | 2 | 7 | 9 | 0 | S |
| 2010 WW18 | 8-F | CAN | 5 | 7 | 8 | 15 | 4 | G |
| **Totals WW18** | | | **10** | **9** | **15** | **24** | **4** | **G,S** |

~WW18 MVP (2010), WW18 IIHF Directorate Best Forward (2010)

| Capizzano, Kristyn | | | | | | | | b. Oakville, Ontario, January 3, 1995 |
|---|---|---|---|---|---|---|---|---|
| 2012 WW18 | 12-F | CAN | 5 | 1 | 1 | 2 | 2 | G |

| Carlsson, Olivia | | | | | | | | b. Karlstad, Sweden, March 2, 1995 |
|---|---|---|---|---|---|---|---|---|
| 2012 WW18 | 20-F | SWE | 6 | 0 | 2 | 2 | 4 | B |

| Carpenter, Alex | | | | | | | | b. North Reading, Massachusetts, United States, April 13, 1994 |
|---|---|---|---|---|---|---|---|---|
| 2010 WW18 | 5-F | USA | 5 | 8 | 1 | 9 | 0 | S |
| 2011 WW18 | 5-F | USA | 5 | 6 | 4 | 10 | 0 | G |
| 2012 WW18 | 5-F | USA | 5 | 4 | 5 | 9 | 2 | S |
| **Totals WW18** | | | **15** | **18** | **10** | **28** | **0** | **G,2S** |

~IIHF Directorate WW18 Best Forward (2011, 2012)

| Celarova, Nikoleta | | | | | | | | b. Kezmarok, Czechoslovakia (Slovakia), February 27, 1983 |
|---|---|---|---|---|---|---|---|---|
| 2010 OG-W | 21-F | SVK | 5 | 0 | 0 | 0 | 0 | 8th |

| Chernukhina, Yulia | | | | | | | | b. Ust-Kamenogorsk, Soviet Union (Kazakhstan), July 21, 1991 |
|---|---|---|---|---|---|---|---|---|
| 2009 WW | 31-D | KAZ | 4 | 0 | 0 | 0 | 0 | 6th |

| Chesson, Lisa | | | | | | | | b. Plainfield, Illinois, United States, August 18, 1986 |
|---|---|---|---|---|---|---|---|---|
| 2009 WW | 11-D | USA | 5 | 1 | 2 | 3 | 4 | G |
| 2010 OG-W | 11-D | USA | 5 | 2 | 3 | 5 | 2 | S |
| 2012 WW | 11-D | USA | 5 | 0 | 3 | 3 | 0 | S |
| **Totals WW** | | | **10** | **1** | **5** | **6** | **4** | **G,S** |

| Chmelova, Klara | | | | | | | | b. Kadan, Czech Republic, August 15, 1995 |
|---|---|---|---|---|---|---|---|---|
| 2011 WW18 | 22-F | CZE | 6 | 1 | 2 | 3 | 0 | 4th |
| 2012 WW18 | 22-F | CZE | 5 | 3 | 0 | 3 | 4 | 6th |
| **Totals WW18** | | | **11** | **4** | **2** | **6** | **4** | **—** |

| Chu, Julie | | | | | | | | b. Fairfield, Connecticut, United States, March 13, 1982 |
|---|---|---|---|---|---|---|---|---|
| 2001 WW | 13-F | USA | 5 | 1 | 7 | 8 | 2 | S |
| 2002 OG-W | 13-F | USA | 5 | 2 | 2 | 4 | 2 | S |
| 2004 WW | 13-F | USA | 4 | 1 | 1 | 2 | 2 | S |
| 2005 WW | 13-F | USA | 5 | 2 | 4 | 6 | 2 | G |
| 2006 OG-W | 13-F | USA | 5 | 0 | 5 | 5 | 0 | B |
| 2007 WW | 13-F | USA | 5 | 0 | 3 | 3 | 0 | S |
| 2008 WW | 13-D | USA | 5 | 0 | 7 | 7 | 2 | G |
| 2009 WW | 13-F | USA | 5 | 5 | 5 | 10 | 0 | G |

| | | | | | | | | |
|---|---|---|---|---|---|---|---|---|
| 2010 OG-W | 13-F | USA | 5 | 2 | 4 | 6 | 0 | S |
| 2011 WW | 13-F | USA | 5 | 1 | 6 | 7 | 0 | G |
| 2012 WW | 13-F | USA | 5 | 2 | 1 | 3 | 2 | S |
| **Totals WW** | | | **39** | **12** | **34** | **46** | **10** | **4G,4S** |
| **Totals OG-W** | | | **15** | **4** | **11** | **15** | **2** | **2S,B** |

~WW All-Star Team/Defence (2008), WW All-Star Team/Forward (2009)

**Cipriani, Tiziana** b. Trimmis, Switzerland, November 30, 1995

| | | | | | | | | |
|---|---|---|---|---|---|---|---|---|
| 2011 WW18 | 25-F | SUI | 6 | 0 | 0 | 0 | 0 | 7th |
| 2012 WW18 | 25-F | SUI | 6 | 0 | 0 | 0 | 0 | 8th |
| **Totals WW18** | | | **12** | **0** | **0** | **0** | **0** | **—** |

**Clark, Emily** b. Saskatoon, Saskatchewan, November 28, 1995

| | | | | | | | | |
|---|---|---|---|---|---|---|---|---|
| 2012 WW18 | 3-F | CAN | 5 | 2 | 2 | 4 | 2 | G |

**Connery, Nicole** b. Newmarket, Ontario, January 27, 1994

| | | | | | | | | |
|---|---|---|---|---|---|---|---|---|
| 2012 WW18 | 24-F | CAN | 5 | 2 | 4 | 6 | 6 | G |

**Cottrell, Ashley** b. Sterling Heights, Michigan, United States, April 4, 1990

| | | | | | | | | |
|---|---|---|---|---|---|---|---|---|
| 2008 WW18 | 10-F | USA | 5 | 5 | 5 | 10 | 0 | G |

**Cournoyer, Audrey** b. Montreal, Quebec, Canada, September 10, 1990

| | | | | | | | | |
|---|---|---|---|---|---|---|---|---|
| 2008 WW18 | 21-F | CAN | 4 | 2 | 3 | 5 | 0 | S |

**Coyne, Kendall** b. Palos Heights, Illinois, United States, May 25, 1992

| | | | | | | | | |
|---|---|---|---|---|---|---|---|---|
| 2008 WW18 | 11-F | USA | 5 | 4 | 2 | 6 | 4 | G |
| 2009 WW18 | 19-F | USA | 5 | 8 | 7 | 15 | 2 | G |
| 2010 WW18 | 19-F | USA | 5 | 10 | 2 | 12 | 2 | S |
| 2011 WW | 26-F | USA | 5 | 4 | 2 | 6 | 0 | G |
| 2012 WW | 26-F | USA | 5 | 4 | 5 | 9 | 0 | S |
| **Totals WW18** | | | **15** | **22** | **11** | **33** | **8** | **2G,S** |
| **Totals WW** | | | **10** | **8** | **7** | **15** | **0** | **G,S** |

~WW18 IIHF Directorate Best Forward (2010)

**Crossley, Alexis** b. Cole Harbour, Nova Scotia, April 7, 1994

| | | | | | | | | |
|---|---|---|---|---|---|---|---|---|
| 2012 WW18 | 10-D | CAN | 5 | 2 | 3 | 5 | 4 | G |

**Crossman, Demi** b. Livonia, Michigan, United States, December 14, 1994

| | | | | | | | | |
|---|---|---|---|---|---|---|---|---|
| 2012 WW18 | 10-F | USA | 5 | 0 | 1 | 1 | 2 | S |

**Cruickshank, Rayna** b. Cumberland, British Columbia, Canada, August 28, 1991

| | | | | | | | | |
|---|---|---|---|---|---|---|---|---|
| 2009 WW18 | 4-D | CAN | 5 | 0 | 0 | 0 | 0 | S |

**Cudmore, Hayleigh** b. Oakville, Ontario, Canada, May 25, 1992

| | | | | | | | | |
|---|---|---|---|---|---|---|---|---|
| 2010 WW18 | 24-D | CAN | 5 | 2 | 2 | 4 | 2 | G |

**Cui, Shanshan** b. Heilongjiang, China, May 8, 1987

| | | | | | | | | |
|---|---|---|---|---|---|---|---|---|
| 2007 WW | 17-F | CHN | 4 | 0 | 0 | 0 | 0 | 6th |
| 2008 WW | 17-F | CHN | 4 | 0 | 0 | 0 | 0 | 8th |
| 2009 WW | 17-F | CHN | 4 | 0 | 0 | 0 | 0 | 9th |
| 2010 OG-W | 17-F | CHN | 5 | 0 | 0 | 0 | 2 | 7th |
| **Totals WW** | | | **12** | **0** | **0** | **0** | **0** | **—** |

**Culikova, Janka** b. Martin, Czechoslovakia (Slovakia), June 30, 1987

| | | | | | | | | |
|---|---|---|---|---|---|---|---|---|
| 2010 OG-W | 18-F | SVK | 5 | 2 | 1 | 3 | 6 | 8th |
| 2011 WW | 18-F | SVK | 5 | 0 | 0 | 0 | 2 | 7th |
| 2012 WW | 18-F | SVK | 5 | 0 | 0 | 0 | 4 | 8th |
| **Totals WW** | | | **10** | **0** | **0** | **0** | **6** | **—** |

**Cupkova, Nicol** b. Kosice, Czechoslovakia (Slovakia), November 4, 1992

| | | | | | | | | |
|---|---|---|---|---|---|---|---|---|
| 2010 OG-W | 3-F | SVK | 5 | 1 | 2 | 3 | 0 | 8th |
| 2011 WW | 28-F | SVK | 5 | 0 | 0 | 0 | 0 | 7th |
| 2012 WW | 28-F | SVK | 5 | 3 | 3 | 6 | 2 | 8th |
| **Totals WW** | | | **10** | **3** | **3** | **6** | **2** | **—** |

**Dale, Mariko** b. Grindelwald, Switzerland, July 9, 1994

| | | | | | | | | |
|---|---|---|---|---|---|---|---|---|
| 2011 WW18 | 19-F | SUI | 6 | 0 | 0 | 0 | 2 | 7th |
| 2012 WW18 | 19-F | SUI | 6 | 0 | 3 | 3 | 4 | 8th |
| **Totals WW18** | | | **12** | **0** | **3** | **3** | **6** | **—** |

**Daniels, Anna** b. Falun, Sweden, March 27, 1993

| | | | | | | | | |
|---|---|---|---|---|---|---|---|---|
| 2011 WW18 | 11-F | SWE | 5 | 0 | 0 | 0 | 2 | 5th |

**Daniels, Sydney** b. Southwick, Massachusetts, United States, April 19, 1995

| | | | | | | | | |
|---|---|---|---|---|---|---|---|---|
| 2011 WW18 | 25-F | USA | 5 | 4 | 2 | 6 | 4 | G |
| 2012 WW18 | 25-F | USA | 5 | 1 | 4 | 5 | 2 | S |
| **Totals WW18** | | | **10** | **5** | **6** | **11** | **6** | **G,S** |

**Daoust, Melodie** b. Valleyfield, Quebec, Canada, January 7, 1992

| | | | | | | | | |
|---|---|---|---|---|---|---|---|---|
| 2009 WW18 | 15-F | CAN | 5 | 6 | 6 | 12 | 4 | S |
| 2010 WW18 | 17-F | CAN | 5 | 4 | 4 | 8 | 4 | G |
| **Totals WW18** | | | **10** | **10** | **10** | **20** | **8** | **G,S** |

**Darkangelo, Shiann** b. Brighton, Michigan, United States, November 28, 1993

| | | | | | | | | |
|---|---|---|---|---|---|---|---|---|
| 2011 WW18 | 9-F | USA | 5 | 2 | 1 | 3 | 0 | G |

**Darwitz, Natalie** b. Eagan, Minnesota, United States, October 13, 1983

| | | | | | | | | |
|---|---|---|---|---|---|---|---|---|
| 1999 WW | 22-F | USA | 5 | 2 | 1 | 3 | 2 | S |
| 2000 WW | 22-F | USA | 5 | 2 | 6 | 8 | 18 | S |
| 2001 WW | 22-F | USA | 5 | 3 | 1 | 4 | 4 | S |
| 2002 OG-W | 22-F | USA | 5 | 7 | 1 | 8 | 2 | S |
| 2004 WW | 22-F | USA | 5 | 7 | 3 | 10 | 2 | S |
| 2005 WW | 22-F | USA | 5 | 2 | 2 | 4 | 8 | G |
| 2006 OG-W | 22-F | USA | 5 | 3 | 3 | 6 | 8 | B |
| 2007 WW | 20-F | USA | 5 | 4 | 5 | 9 | 6 | S |
| 2008 WW | 20-F | USA | 5 | 6 | 4 | 10 | 2 | G |
| 2009 WW | 20-F | USA | 5 | 3 | 7 | 10 | 2 | G |
| 2010 OG-W | 20-F | USA | 5 | 4 | 7 | 11 | 0 | S |
| **Totals WW** | | | **40** | **29** | **29** | **58** | **44** | **3G,5S** |
| **Totals OG-W** | | | **15** | **14** | **11** | **25** | **10** | **2S,B** |

~OG-W All-Star Team/Forward (2002), WW IIHF Directorate Best Forward (2008), WW All-Star Team/Forward (2004, 2007, 2008, 2009)

**Davidson, Gabrielle** b. Pointe Claire, Quebec, Canada, February 25, 1993

| | | | | | | | | |
|---|---|---|---|---|---|---|---|---|
| 2011 WW18 | 11-F | CAN | 5 | 1 | 2 | 3 | 0 | S |

**Davis, Sarah** b. Paradise, Newfoundland, Canada, June 23, 1992

| | | | | | | | | |
|---|---|---|---|---|---|---|---|---|
| 2010 WW18 | 21-F | CAN | 5 | 3 | 1 | 4 | 0 | G |

**Decker, Brianna** b. Dousman, Wisconsin, United States, May 13, 1991

| | | | | | | | | |
|---|---|---|---|---|---|---|---|---|
| 2008 WW18 | 14-F | USA | 5 | 3 | 4 | 7 | 2 | G |
| 2009 WW18 | 11-F | USA | 5 | 8 | 1 | 9 | 4 | G |
| 2011 WW | 14-F | USA | 5 | 4 | 7 | 11 | 8 | G |
| 2012 WW | 14-F | USA | 5 | 4 | 6 | 10 | 6 | S |
| **Totals WW18** | | | **10** | **11** | **5** | **16** | **6** | **2G** |
| **Totals WW** | | | **10** | **8** | **13** | **21** | **14** | **G,S** |

**Delarbre, Marie** b. Aalen, Germany, January 22, 1994

| | | | | | | | | |
|---|---|---|---|---|---|---|---|---|
| 2010 WW18 | 19-F | GER | 6 | 1 | 0 | 1 | 4 | 4th |
| 2011 WW18 | 19-F | GER | 5 | 0 | 0 | 0 | 8 | 6th |
| 2012 WW18 | 19-F | GER | 6 | 2 | 6 | 8 | 10 | 4th |
| **Totals WW18** | | | **17** | **3** | **6** | **9** | **22** | **—** |

**Dempsey, Jillian** b. Winthrop, Massachusetts, United States, January 19, 1991

| | | | | | | | | |
|---|---|---|---|---|---|---|---|---|
| 2009 WW18 | 12-F | USA | 5 | 0 | 1 | 1 | 0 | G |
| 2012 WW | 6-F | USA | 4 | 0 | 0 | 0 | 0 | S |

**Dergacheva, Yelena** b. November 8, 1995

| | | | | | | | | |
|---|---|---|---|---|---|---|---|---|
| 2012 WW18 | 9-F | RUS | 6 | 0 | 3 | 3 | 0 | 7th |

**Desboeufs, Laura** b. September 2, 1996

| | | | | | | | | |
|---|---|---|---|---|---|---|---|---|
| 2012 WW18 | 13-F | SUI | 5 | 0 | 0 | 0 | 2 | 8th |

**Deulina, Yulia** b. Moscow Region, Soviet Union (Russia), April 14, 1984

| | | | | | | | | |
|---|---|---|---|---|---|---|---|---|
| 2010 OG-W | 22-F | RUS | 5 | 0 | 0 | 0 | 0 | 6th |

**Dinges, Gesa** b. Bergisch Gladbach, Germany, May 19, 1992

| | | | | | | | | |
|---|---|---|---|---|---|---|---|---|
| 2010 WW18 | 20-F | GER | 6 | 0 | 0 | 0 | 0 | 4th |

**D'Oench, Miye** b. New York, New York, United States, January 26, 1994

| | | | | | | | | |
|---|---|---|---|---|---|---|---|---|
| 2012 WW18 | 14-F | USA | 5 | 2 | 0 | 2 | 0 | S |

**Doyle, Shannon** b. Baldwin, Ontario, Canada, March 6, 1992

| | | | | | | | | |
|---|---|---|---|---|---|---|---|---|
| 2010 WW18 | 2-D | CAN | 5 | 2 | 2 | 4 | 6 | G |

**Dubois, Catherine** b. Quebec City, Quebec, July 29, 1995

| | | | | | | | | |
|---|---|---|---|---|---|---|---|---|
| 2012 WW18 | 28-F | CAN | 5 | 4 | 1 | 5 | 6 | G |

**Dufault, Meghan** b. Winnipeg, Manitoba, Canada, April 17, 1994

| | | | | | | | | |
|---|---|---|---|---|---|---|---|---|
| 2011 WW18 | 15-F | CAN | 5 | 2 | 6 | 8 | 2 | S |
| 2012 WW18 | 15-F | CAN | 5 | 1 | 4 | 5 | 4 | G |
| **Totals WW18** | | | **10** | **3** | **10** | **13** | **6** | **G,S** |

**Duggan, Meghan** b. Danvers, Massachusetts, United States, September 3, 1987

| | | | | | | | | |
|---|---|---|---|---|---|---|---|---|
| 2007 WW | 10-F | USA | 5 | 0 | 1 | 1 | 4 | S |
| 2008 WW | 10-F | USA | 5 | 4 | 1 | 5 | 2 | G |
| 2009 WW | 10-F | USA | 5 | 2 | 0 | 2 | 2 | G |
| 2010 OG-W | 10-F | USA | 5 | 4 | 0 | 4 | 2 | S |
| 2011 WW | 10-F | USA | 5 | 4 | 3 | 7 | 2 | G |
| **Totals WW** | | | **20** | **10** | **5** | **15** | **10** | **3G,S** |

**Dumais, Camille** b. Beaconsfield, Quebec, Canada, August 15, 1990

| | | | | | | | | |
|---|---|---|---|---|---|---|---|---|
| 2008 WW18 | 18-F | CAN | 5 | 5 | 9 | 14 | 0 | S |

**Dvorakova, Nikola** b. Jindrichuv Hradec, Czechoslovakia (Czech Republic), June 26, 1990

| | | | | | | | | |
|---|---|---|---|---|---|---|---|---|
| 2008 WW18 | 11-D | CZE | 5 | 0 | 2 | 2 | 16 | B |

| **Dyubanok, Inna** | | | | | | | | **b. Moscow, Soviet Union (Russia), February 20, 1990** |
|---|---|---|---|---|---|---|---|---|
| 2008 WW18 | 22-F | RUS | 5 | 0 | 2 | 2 | 26 | 8th |
| 2008 WW | 27-D | RUS | 4 | 0 | 0 | 0 | 4 | 6th |
| 2009 WW | 27-D | RUS | 4 | 1 | 0 | 1 | 2 | 5th |
| 2010 OG-W | 95-D | RUS | 5 | 0 | 1 | 1 | 4 | 6th |
| 2011 WW | 27-D | RUS | 6 | 1 | 0 | 1 | 14 | 4th |
| 2012 WW | 27-D | RUS | 5 | 1 | 2 | 3 | 8 | 6th |
| **Totals WW** | | | **19** | **3** | **2** | **5** | **28** | **—** |

| **Dyupina, Yevgenia** | | | | | | | | **b. Udmurtiya, Russia, June 30, 1994** |
|---|---|---|---|---|---|---|---|---|
| 2010 WW18 | 12-F | RUS | 5 | 0 | 0 | 0 | 4 | 8th |
| 2012 WW18 | 7-F | RUS | 6 | 2 | 2 | 4 | 2 | 7th |
| 2012 WW | 24-F | RUS | 5 | 0 | 1 | 1 | 2 | 6th |
| **Totals WW18** | | | **11** | **2** | **2** | **4** | **6** | **—** |

| **Dzurnakova, Anna** | | | | | | | | **b. Kezmarok, Czechoslovakia (Slovakia), January 24, 1983** |
|---|---|---|---|---|---|---|---|---|
| 2010 OG-W | 14-F | SVK | 5 | 1 | 0 | 1 | 2 | 8th |
| 2011 WW | 14-F | SVK | 5 | 1 | 0 | 1 | 2 | 7th |
| 2012 WW | 14-F | SVK | 5 | 0 | 0 | 0 | 0 | 8th |
| **Totals WW** | | | **10** | **1** | **0** | **1** | **2** | **—** |

| **Eckefjord, Deborah** | | | | | | | | **b. Uppsala, Sweden, May 10, 1990** |
|---|---|---|---|---|---|---|---|---|
| 2008 WW18 | 14-F | SWE | 5 | 0 | 0 | 0 | 0 | 4th |

| **Edney, Sarah** | | | | | | | | **b. Mississauga, Ontario, Canada, September 2, 1993** |
|---|---|---|---|---|---|---|---|---|
| 2011 WW18 | 3-D | CAN | 5 | 1 | 2 | 3 | 2 | S |

| **Eggimann, Romy** | | | | | | | | **b. Sumiswald, Switzerland, September 29, 1995** |
|---|---|---|---|---|---|---|---|---|
| 2011 WW18 | 16-F | SUI | 6 | 0 | 0 | 0 | 2 | 7th |
| 2012 WW18 | 16-F | SUI | 6 | 2 | 2 | 4 | 2 | 8th |
| **Totals WW18** | | | **12** | **2** | **2** | **4** | **4** | **—** |

| **Eibinova, Stepanka** | | | | | | | | **b. Kadan, Czech Republic, July 26, 1994** |
|---|---|---|---|---|---|---|---|---|
| 2010 WW18 | 4-F | CZE | 5 | 0 | 0 | 0 | 0 | 7th |
| 2011 WW18 | 5-F | CZE | 6 | 0 | 0 | 0 | 0 | 4th |
| **Totals WW18** | | | **11** | **0** | **0** | **0** | **0** | **—** |

| **Eidensten, Johanna** | | | | | | | | **b. Stockholm, Sweden, January 18, 1994** |
|---|---|---|---|---|---|---|---|---|
| 2012 WW18 | 22-F | SWE | 6 | 0 | 0 | 0 | 0 | B |

| **Eisenschmid, Tanja** | | | | | | | | **b. Marktoberdorf, Germany, April 20, 1993** |
|---|---|---|---|---|---|---|---|---|
| 2009 WW18 | 13-D | GER | 5 | 0 | 0 | 0 | 4 | 6th |
| 2010 WW18 | 13-D | GER | 6 | 1 | 2 | 3 | 18 | 4th |
| 2011 WW18 | 13-D | GER | 5 | 0 | 0 | 0 | 31 | 6th |
| 2012 WW | 23-D | GER | 5 | 1 | 0 | 1 | 6 | 7th |
| **Totals WW18** | | | **16** | **1** | **2** | **3** | **53** | **—** |

| **Ekstrom, Wilma** | | | | | | | | **b. Karlskoga, Sweden, October 20, 1994** |
|---|---|---|---|---|---|---|---|---|
| 2012 WW18 | 3-D | SWE | 6 | 0 | 0 | 0 | 4 | B |

| **Eliasson, Emma** | | | | | | | | **b. Kiruna, Sweden, June 12, 1989** |
|---|---|---|---|---|---|---|---|---|
| 2005 WW | 22-D | SWE | 5 | 0 | 0 | 0 | 4 | B |
| 2006 OG-W | 22-D | SWE | 5 | 0 | 1 | 1 | 6 | S |
| 2007 WW | 22-D | SWE | 5 | 0 | 1 | 1 | 8 | B |
| 2008 WW | 22-D | SWE | 4 | 1 | 2 | 3 | 6 | 5th |
| 2009 WW | 22-D | SWE | 5 | 0 | 2 | 2 | 2 | 4th |
| 2010 OG-W | 22-D | SWE | 5 | 0 | 2 | 2 | 6 | 4th |
| 2011 WW | 22-F | SWE | 5 | 1 | 1 | 2 | 6 | 5th |
| **Totals WW** | | | **24** | **2** | **6** | **8** | **26** | **2B** |
| **Totals OG-W** | | | **10** | **0** | **3** | **3** | **12** | **S** |

| **Engel, Katja-Lisa** | | | | | | | | **b. Munich, Germany, June 18, 1995** |
|---|---|---|---|---|---|---|---|---|
| 2011 WW18 | 16-F | GER | 5 | 0 | 2 | 2 | 0 | 6th |
| 2012 WW18 | 16-F | GER | 6 | 0 | 0 | 0 | 2 | 4th |
| **Totals WW18** | | | **11** | **0** | **2** | **2** | **2** | **—** |

| **Engstrom, Molly** | | | | | | | | **b. Siren, Wisconsin, United States, March 1, 1983** |
|---|---|---|---|---|---|---|---|---|
| 2004 WW | 3-D | USA | 5 | 0 | 3 | 3 | 0 | S |
| 2005 WW | 9-D | USA | 5 | 1 | 1 | 2 | 4 | G |
| 2006 OG-W | 9-D | USA | 4 | 0 | 0 | 0 | 6 | B |
| 2007 WW | 9-D | USA | 5 | 2 | 3 | 5 | 4 | S |
| 2008 WW | 9-D | USA | 4 | 1 | 1 | 2 | 2 | G |
| 2009 WW | 9-D | USA | 5 | 0 | 1 | 1 | 8 | G |
| 2010 OG-W | 9-D | USA | 5 | 3 | 4 | 7 | 6 | S |
| 2011 WW | 9-D | USA | 5 | 0 | 2 | 2 | 4 | G |
| **Totals WW** | | | **29** | **4** | **11** | **15** | **22** | **4G,2S** |
| **Totals OG-W** | | | **9** | **3** | **4** | **7** | **12** | **S,B** |

~OG-W IIHF Directorate Best Defenceman (2010), OG-W All-Star Team/Defence (2010), WW IIHF Directorate Best Defenceman (2007)

| **Enstrom, Tina** | | | | | | | | **b. Ornskoldsvik, Sweden, February 23, 1991** |
|---|---|---|---|---|---|---|---|---|
| 2007 WW | 9-F | SWE | 5 | 1 | 0 | 1 | 0 | B |
| 2008 WW18 | 9-F | SWE | 5 | 1 | 5 | 6 | 4 | 4th |
| 2008 WW | 9-F | SWE | 4 | 1 | 4 | 5 | 4 | 5th |
| 2009 WW18 | 9-F | SWE | 5 | 2 | 7 | 9 | 2 | B |
| 2009 WW | 9-F | SWE | 5 | 2 | 2 | 4 | 2 | 4th |
| 2010 OG-W | 9-F | SWE | 5 | 1 | 0 | 1 | 2 | 4th |
| 2011 WW | 9-F | SWE | 5 | 2 | 1 | 3 | 6 | 5th |
| 2012 WW | 9-F | SWE | 4 | 0 | 0 | 0 | 0 | 5th |
| **Totals WW18** | | | **10** | **3** | **12** | **15** | **6** | **B** |
| **Totals WW** | | | **23** | **6** | **7** | **13** | **12** | **B** |

| **Erb, Alea** | | | | | | | | **b. Winterthur, Switzerland, September 27, 1992** |
|---|---|---|---|---|---|---|---|---|
| 2009 WW18 | 23-F | SUI | 5 | 0 | 0 | 0 | 0 | 8th |

| **Erickson, Sarah** | | | | | | | | **b. LaPorte, Minnesota, United States, March 28, 1990** |
|---|---|---|---|---|---|---|---|---|
| 2008 WW18 | 16-F | USA | 5 | 5 | 4 | 9 | 2 | G |

| **Evers, Bettina** | | | | | | | | **b. Hanover, West Germany (Germany), August 17, 1981** |
|---|---|---|---|---|---|---|---|---|
| 1999 WW | 66-F | GER | 5 | 1 | 1 | 2 | 2 | 7th |
| 2000 WW | 66-F | GER | 5 | 0 | 1 | 1 | 0 | 7th |
| 2001 WW | 66-F | GER | 5 | 0 | 2 | 2 | 0 | 6th |
| 2002 OG-W | 66-F | GER | 5 | 0 | 0 | 0 | 0 | 6th |
| 2004 WW | 66-F | GER | 4 | 0 | 0 | 0 | 4 | 6th |
| 2005 WW | 66-F | GER | 5 | 0 | 0 | 0 | 4 | 5th |
| 2006 OG-W | 66-F | GER | 5 | 0 | 0 | 0 | 0 | 5th |
| 2007 WW | 66-F | GER | 4 | 1 | 0 | 1 | 2 | 8th |
| 2008 WW | 66-F | GER | 4 | 1 | 0 | 1 | 4 | 9th |
| 2012 WW | 6-F | GER | 5 | 1 | 0 | 1 | 0 | 7th |
| **Totals WW** | | | **37** | **4** | **4** | **8** | **16** | **—** |
| **Totals OG-W** | | | **10** | **0** | **0** | **0** | **0** | **—** |

| **Falkeborn, Teddie** | | | | | | | | **b. Nykoping, Sweden, February 12, 1993** |
|---|---|---|---|---|---|---|---|---|
| 2011 WW18 | 24-F | SWE | 5 | 0 | 1 | 1 | 2 | 5th |

| **Fallman, Johanna** | | | | | | | | **b. Lulea, Sweden, June 21, 1990** |
|---|---|---|---|---|---|---|---|---|
| 2008 WW18 | 2-D | SWE | 5 | 1 | 0 | 1 | 6 | 4th |
| 2011 WW | 5-D | SWE | 5 | 0 | 0 | 0 | 2 | 5th |
| 2012 WW | 5-D | SWE | 4 | 0 | 1 | 1 | 0 | 5th |
| **Totals WW** | | | **9** | **0** | **1** | **1** | **2** | **—** |

| **Fellner, Susanne** | | | | | | | | **b. Ravensburg, West Germany (Germany), February 26, 1985** |
|---|---|---|---|---|---|---|---|---|
| 2005 WW | 18-D | GER | 5 | 1 | 0 | 1 | 0 | 5th |
| 2006 OG-W | 18-D | GER | 5 | 0 | 0 | 0 | 0 | 5th |
| 2007 WW | 18-D | GER | 4 | 0 | 1 | 1 | 4 | 8th |
| 2008 WW | 18-D | GER | 4 | 0 | 1 | 1 | 2 | 9th |
| 2012 WW | 18-D | GER | 5 | 0 | 2 | 2 | 2 | 7th |
| **Totals WW** | | | **14** | **1** | **3** | **4** | **6** | **—** |

| **Fialova, Jana** | | | | | | | | **b. Karvina, Czech Republic, March 2, 1993** |
|---|---|---|---|---|---|---|---|---|
| 2009 WW18 | 25-D | CZE | 5 | 0 | 2 | 2 | 8 | 4th |
| 2010 WW18 | 25-D | CZE | 5 | 2 | 0 | 2 | 4 | 7th |
| 2011 WW18 | 4-D | CZE | 6 | 0 | 1 | 1 | 2 | 4th |
| **Totals WW18** | | | **16** | **2** | **3** | **5** | **14** | **—** |

| **Fiegert, Anna-Maria** | | | | | | | | **b. Landshut, Germany, April 3, 1994** |
|---|---|---|---|---|---|---|---|---|
| 2010 WW18 | 12-D | GER | 6 | 0 | 1 | 1 | 2 | 4th |
| 2011 WW18 | 12-D | GER | 5 | 0 | 0 | 0 | 0 | 6th |
| 2012 WW18 | 12-D | GER | 6 | 0 | 1 | 1 | 2 | 4th |
| **Totals WW18** | | | **17** | **0** | **2** | **2** | **4** | **—** |

| **Field, Emily** | | | | | | | | **b. Littleton, Massachusetts, United States, April 6, 1993** |
|---|---|---|---|---|---|---|---|---|
| 2011 WW18 | 17-F | USA | 5 | 4 | 5 | 9 | 0 | G |

| **Figueroa, Gabie** | | | | | | | | **b. Branchburg, New Jersey, United States, February 21, 1992** |
|---|---|---|---|---|---|---|---|---|
| 2010 WW18 | 3-D | USA | 5 | 0 | 3 | 3 | 6 | S |

| **Fischer, Andrea** | | | | | | | | **b. Berne, Switzerland, July 11, 1990** |
|---|---|---|---|---|---|---|---|---|
| 2008 WW18 | 24-F | SUI | 5 | 1 | 0 | 1 | 2 | 7th |
| 2012 WW | 8-F | SUI | 6 | 0 | 0 | 0 | 0 | B |

| **Flug, Kate** | | | | | | | | **b. Roseville, Minnesota, United States, February 15, 1995** |
|---|---|---|---|---|---|---|---|---|
| 2012 WW18 | 11-F | USA | 2 | 2 | 0 | 2 | 0 | S |

| **Forster, Sarah** | | | | | | | | **b. Berneck, Switzerland, May 19, 1993** |
|---|---|---|---|---|---|---|---|---|
| 2009 WW18 | 3-D | SUI | 5 | 1 | 1 | 2 | 24 | 8th |
| 2011 WW18 | 3-D | SUI | 6 | 1 | 3 | 4 | 2 | 7th |
| 2012 WW | 17-D | SUI | 4 | 0 | 0 | 0 | 0 | B |
| **Totals WW18** | | | **11** | **2** | **4** | **6** | **26** | **—** |

| **Fortino, Laura** | | | | | | | | **b. Hamilton, Ontario, Canada, January 30, 1991** |
|---|---|---|---|---|---|---|---|---|
| 2008 WW18 | 23-D | CAN | 4 | 1 | 4 | 5 | 0 | S |
| 2009 WW18 | 23-D | CAN | 5 | 0 | 4 | 4 | 0 | S |
| 2012 WW | 8-D | CAN | 5 | 2 | 2 | 4 | 6 | G |
| **Totals WW18** | | | **9** | **1** | **8** | **9** | **0** | **2S** |

~WW All-Star Team/Defence (2012)

| Fratkin, Kaleigh | | | | | | | | b. Burnaby, British Columbia, Canada, March 24, 1992 |
|---|---|---|---|---|---|---|---|---|
| 2009 WW18 | 13-D | CAN | 5 | 1 | 3 | 4 | 8 | S |

| Frautschi, Angela | | | | | | | | b. Interlaken, Switzerland, June 5, 1987 |
|---|---|---|---|---|---|---|---|---|
| 2006 OG-W | 11-D | SUI | 5 | 0 | 0 | 0 | 2 | 7th |
| 2008 WW | 11-D | SUI | 5 | 0 | 0 | 0 | 6 | 4th |
| 2009 WW | 11-D | SUI | 4 | 0 | 1 | 1 | 6 | 7th |
| 2010 OG-W | 11-D | SUI | 5 | 0 | 0 | 0 | 8 | 5th |
| 2011 WW | 11-D | SUI | 5 | 0 | 0 | 0 | 2 | 6th |
| 2012 WW | 11-D | SUI | 5 | 0 | 2 | 2 | 8 | B |
| **Totals WW** | | | **19** | **0** | **3** | **3** | **22** | **B** |
| **Totals OG-W** | | | **10** | **0** | **0** | **0** | **10** | **—** |

| Frautschi, Seraina | | | | | | | | b. Saanen, Switzerland, June 18, 1993 |
|---|---|---|---|---|---|---|---|---|
| 2009 WW18 | 12-F | SUI | 5 | 1 | 0 | 1 | 10 | 8th |

| Frazer, Abbey | | | | | | | | b. Hudson, Quebec, July 25, 1994 |
|---|---|---|---|---|---|---|---|---|
| 2012 WW18 | 23-D | CAN | 5 | 0 | 0 | 0 | 2 | G |

| Fridh, Emily | | | | | | | | b. Stockholm, Sweden, July 1, 1995 |
|---|---|---|---|---|---|---|---|---|
| 2012 WW18 | 25-D | SWE | 6 | 0 | 0 | 0 | 6 | B |

| Fritz, Theresa | | | | | | | | b. Schongau, Germany, October 27, 1994 |
|---|---|---|---|---|---|---|---|---|
| 2011 WW18 | 21-D | GER | 5 | 0 | 1 | 1 | 2 | 6th |
| 2012 WW18 | 21-D | GER | 6 | 0 | 0 | 0 | 0 | 4th |
| **Totals WW18** | | | **11** | **0** | **1** | **1** | **2** | **—** |

| Frolova, Katya | | | | | | | | b. Moscow, Soviet Union (Russia), October 17, 1990 |
|---|---|---|---|---|---|---|---|---|
| 2008 WW18 | 5-D | RUS | 5 | 0 | 0 | 0 | 6 | 8th |

| Fry, Lyndsey | | | | | | | | b. Chandler, Arizona, United States, October 30, 1992 |
|---|---|---|---|---|---|---|---|---|
| 2009 WW18 | 13-F | USA | 5 | 4 | 1 | 5 | 0 | G |
| 2010 WW18 | 13-F | USA | 5 | 3 | 1 | 4 | 4 | S |
| **Totals WW18** | | | **10** | **7** | **2** | **9** | **4** | **G,S** |

| Frykas, Breann | | | | | | | | b. East St. Paul, Manitoba, Canada, January 5, 1991 |
|---|---|---|---|---|---|---|---|---|
| 2009 WW18 | 9-F | CAN | 5 | 1 | 2 | 3 | 8 | S |

| Fujii (Tsuchida), Aki | | | | | | | | b. Hokkaido, Japan, May 29, 1979 |
|---|---|---|---|---|---|---|---|---|
| 1998 OG-W* | 18-F | JPN | 5 | 0 | 0 | 0 | 6 | 6th |
| 2000 WW* | 18-F | JPN | 5 | 1 | 2 | 3 | 4 | 8th |
| 2004 WW* | 18-F | JPN | 4 | 0 | 0 | 0 | 0 | 9th |
| 2008 WW | 12-F | JPN | 4 | 1 | 2 | 3 | 2 | 7th |
| 2009 WW | 12-F | JPN | 4 | 0 | 0 | 0 | 2 | 8th |
| **Totals WW** | | | **17** | **2** | **4** | **6** | **8** | **—** |

*played under maiden name Aki Tsuchida

| Fujimoto, Moeko | | | | | | | | b. Hokkaido, Japan, August 5, 1992 |
|---|---|---|---|---|---|---|---|---|
| 2010 WW18 | 14-F | JPN | 5 | 1 | 1 | 2 | 0 | 6th |

| Fujimoto, Nachi | | | | | | | | b. Hokkaido, Japan, May 7, 1991 |
|---|---|---|---|---|---|---|---|---|
| 2008 WW | 26-D | JPN | 4 | 0 | 0 | 0 | 0 | 7th |
| 2009 WW | 26-D | JPN | 4 | 1 | 0 | 1 | 2 | 8th |
| **Totals WW** | | | **8** | **1** | **0** | **1** | **2** | **—** |

| Fulton, Emily | | | | | | | | b. Stratford, Ontario, Canada, February 11, 1993 |
|---|---|---|---|---|---|---|---|---|
| 2010 WW18 | 12-F | CAN | 5 | 0 | 4 | 4 | 0 | G |
| 2011 WW18 | 7-F | CAN | 5 | 3 | 2 | 5 | 0 | S |
| **Totals WW18** | | | **10** | **3** | **6** | **9** | **0** | **G,S** |

| Fux, Alyona | | | | | | | | b. Ust-Kamenogorsk, Soviet Union (Kazakhstan), May 1, 1987 |
|---|---|---|---|---|---|---|---|---|
| 2007 WW | 28-D | KAZ | 4 | 0 | 0 | 0 | 0 | 9th |
| 2009 WW | 28-F | KAZ | 4 | 1 | 2 | 3 | 4 | 6th |
| 2011 WW | 28-F | KAZ | 5 | 0 | 0 | 0 | 0 | 8th |
| **Totals WW** | | | **13** | **1** | **2** | **3** | **4** | **—** |

| Gajdosova, Maria | | | | | | | | b. Zittau, Germany, November 8, 1987 |
|---|---|---|---|---|---|---|---|---|
| 2011 WW | 25-D | SVK | 5 | 0 | 0 | 0 | 0 | 7th |

| Gao, Fujin | | | | | | | | b. Heilongjiang, China, July 15, 1984 |
|---|---|---|---|---|---|---|---|---|
| 2005 WW | 29-F | CHN | 5 | 0 | 0 | 0 | 0 | 6th |
| 2007 WW | 29-F | CHN | 4 | 0 | 1 | 1 | 2 | 6th |
| 2008 WW | 29-F | CHN | 4 | 0 | 0 | 0 | 0 | 8th |
| 2009 WW | 29-F | CHN | 4 | 0 | 0 | 0 | 0 | 9th |
| 2010 OG-W | 29-F | CHN | 5 | 0 | 0 | 0 | 0 | 7th |
| **Totals WW** | | | **17** | **0** | **1** | **1** | **2** | **—** |

| Gapova, Nikola | | | | | | | | b. Poprad, Czechoslovakia (Slovakia), June 19, 1989 |
|---|---|---|---|---|---|---|---|---|
| 2010 OG-W | 22-F | SVK | 5 | 0 | 0 | 0 | 0 | 8th |
| 2011 WW | 22-F | SVK | 5 | 0 | 1 | 1 | 0 | 7th |
| 2012 WW | 22-F | SVK | 5 | 0 | 0 | 0 | 0 | 8th |
| **Totals WW** | | | **10** | **0** | **1** | **1** | **0** | **—** |

| Gasde, Vanessa | | | | | | | | b. Berlin, Germany, February 11, 1995 |
|---|---|---|---|---|---|---|---|---|
| 2012 WW18 | 6 | 0 | 0 | 0 | 2 | 4th | | |

| Gavrilova, Iya | | | | | | | | b. Krasnoyarsk, Soviet Union (Russia), September 3, 1987 |
|---|---|---|---|---|---|---|---|---|
| 2004 WW | 24-F | RUS | 4 | 1 | 1 | 2 | 2 | 5th |
| 2005 WW | 24-F | RUS | 5 | 1 | 0 | 1 | 0 | 8th |
| 2006 OG-W | 24-F | RUS | 5 | 2 | 0 | 2 | 14 | 6th |
| 2007 WW | 8-F | RUS | 4 | 4 | 1 | 5 | 2 | 7th |
| 2008 WW | 8-F | RUS | 4 | 2 | 4 | 6 | 4 | 6th |
| 2009 WW | 8-F | RUS | 4 | 1 | 2 | 3 | 4 | 5th |
| 2010 OG-W | 8-F | RUS | 5 | 2 | 0 | 2 | 6 | 6th |
| 2011 WW | 8-F | RUS | 6 | 1 | 3 | 4 | 10 | 4th |
| 2012 WW | 8-F | RUS | 5 | 0 | 3 | 3 | 2 | 6th |
| **Totals WW** | | | **32** | **10** | **14** | **24** | **24** | **—** |
| **Totals OG-W** | | | **10** | **4** | **0** | **4** | **20** | **—** |

| Gedman, Marissa | | | | | | | | b. Framingham, Massachusetts, United States, March 12, 1992 |
|---|---|---|---|---|---|---|---|---|
| 2010 WW18 | 7-D | USA | 5 | 1 | 3 | 4 | 8 | S |

| Geml, Jessica | | | | | | | | b. Peissenberg, Germany, October 30, 1991 |
|---|---|---|---|---|---|---|---|---|
| 2008 WW18 | 23-F | GER | 5 | 2 | 0 | 2 | 2 | 5th |
| 2009 WW18 | 23-F | GER | 5 | 1 | 1 | 2 | 2 | 6th |
| **Totals WW18** | | | **10** | **3** | **1** | **4** | **4** | **—** |

| Genilloud, Elodie | | | | | | | | b. Cressier, Switzerland, June 24, 1992 |
|---|---|---|---|---|---|---|---|---|
| 2009 WW18 | 22-F | SUI | 5 | 0 | 0 | 0 | 0 | 8th |

| Gerstmeir, Katharina | | | | | | | | b. Garmisch-Partenkirchen, Germany, November 24, 1993 |
|---|---|---|---|---|---|---|---|---|
| 2009 WW18 | 20-F | GER | 5 | 0 | 0 | 0 | 0 | 6th |
| 2010 WW18 | 5-F | GER | 6 | 0 | 0 | 0 | 2 | 4th |
| **Totals WW18** | | | **11** | **0** | **0** | **0** | **2** | **—** |

| Gillberg, Cornelia | | | | | | | | b. Norrkoping, Sweden, October 11, 1993 |
|---|---|---|---|---|---|---|---|---|
| 2011 WW18 | 16-F | SWE | 5 | 0 | 2 | 2 | 2 | 5th |

| Gleissner, Daria | | | | | | | | b. Kaufbeuren, Germany, June 30, 1993 |
|---|---|---|---|---|---|---|---|---|
| 2009 WW18 | 25-D | GER | 5 | 0 | 0 | 0 | 6 | 6th |
| 2010 WW18 | 22-D | GER | 6 | 0 | 1 | 1 | 8 | 4th |
| 2011 WW18 | 22-D | GER | 5 | 0 | 1 | 1 | 6 | 6th |
| 2012 WW | 20-D | GER | 5 | 0 | 0 | 0 | 4 | 7th |
| **Totals WW18** | | | **16** | **0** | **2** | **2** | **20** | **—** |

| Golebiowski, Tanja | | | | | | | | b. Mannheim, Germany, October 20, 1991 |
|---|---|---|---|---|---|---|---|---|
| 2008 WW18 | 12-F | GER | 5 | 0 | 5 | 5 | 4 | 5th |
| 2009 WW18 | 16-F | GER | 5 | 0 | 1 | 1 | 4 | 6th |
| **Totals WW18** | | | **10** | **0** | **6** | **6** | **8** | **—** |

| Goncharenko, Angelina | | | | | | | | b. Moscow Region, Russia, May 23, 1994 |
|---|---|---|---|---|---|---|---|---|
| 2010 WW18 | 22-D | RUS | 5 | 0 | 0 | 0 | 6 | 8th |
| 2012 WW18 | 22-D | RUS | 6 | 0 | 1 | 1 | 0 | 7th |
| 2012 WW | 2-D | RUS | 5 | 1 | 0 | 1 | 6 | 6th |
| **Totals WW18** | | | **11** | **0** | **1** | **1** | **6** | **—** |

| Gotz, Susann | | | | | | | | b. Bad Muskau, East Germany (Germany), December 14, 1982 |
|---|---|---|---|---|---|---|---|---|
| 2004 WW | 12-F | GER | 4 | 0 | 0 | 0 | 6 | 6th |
| 2005 WW | 12-F | GER | 5 | 1 | 0 | 1 | 2 | 5th |
| 2006 OG-W | 12-F | GER | 5 | 0 | 0 | 0 | 6 | 5th |
| 2007 WW | 12-F | GER | 4 | 0 | 0 | 0 | 2 | 8th |
| 2008 WW | 12-F | GER | 4 | 1 | 0 | 1 | 2 | 9th |
| 2012 WW | 12-F | GER | 5 | 0 | 3 | 3 | 4 | 7th |
| **Totals WW** | | | **22** | **2** | **3** | **5** | **16** | **—** |

| Graeve, Rebecca | | | | | | | | b. Iserlohn, Germany, April 28, 1993 |
|---|---|---|---|---|---|---|---|---|
| 2009 WW18 | 28-D | GER | 5 | 0 | 0 | 0 | 6 | 6th |
| 2010 WW18 | 9-F | GER | 6 | 0 | 0 | 0 | 4 | 4th |
| 2011 WW18 | 9-D | GER | 5 | 0 | 2 | 2 | 10 | 6th |
| 2012 WW | 16-D | GER | 5 | 0 | 0 | 0 | 0 | 7th |
| **Totals WW18** | | | **16** | **0** | **2** | **2** | **20** | **—** |

| Grahm, Erika | | | | | | | | b. Kramfors, Sweden, January 26, 1991 |
|---|---|---|---|---|---|---|---|---|
| 2008 WW18 | 15-F | SWE | 5 | 2 | 1 | 3 | 2 | 4th |
| 2009 WW18 | 15-F | SWE | 5 | 2 | 0 | 2 | 4 | B |
| 2011 WW | 24-F | SWE | 5 | 3 | 3 | 6 | 0 | 5th |
| 2012 WW | 24-F | SWE | 5 | 0 | 1 | 1 | 0 | 5th |
| **Totals WW18** | | | **10** | **4** | **1** | **5** | **6** | **B** |
| **Totals WW** | | | **10** | **3** | **4** | **7** | **0** | **—** |

| Gritl, Michaela | | | | | | | | b. Grafelfing, Germany, April 16, 1991 |
|---|---|---|---|---|---|---|---|---|
| 2009 WW18 | 2-F | GER | 5 | 0 | 0 | 0 | 4 | 6th |

| Grunewald, Michelle | | | | | | | | b. Frankfurt, Germany, August 13, 1991 |
|---|---|---|---|---|---|---|---|---|
| 2008 WW18 | 5-F | GER | 5 | 0 | 0 | 0 | 0 | 5th |

| **Gubler, Nicole** | | | | | | | | **b. May 31, 1996** |
|---|---|---|---|---|---|---|---|---|
| 2012 WW18 | 3-D | SUI | 6 | 0 | 0 | 0 | 0 | 8th |

| **Guslistaya, Yelena** | | | | | | | | **b. Magadan Region, Soviet Union (Russia), July 19, 1990** |
|---|---|---|---|---|---|---|---|---|
| 2008 WW18 | 24-F | RUS | 5 | 0 | 0 | 0 | 2 | 8th |

| **Haarala, Lotta** | | | | | | | | **b. Uurainen, Finland, October 17, 1991** |
|---|---|---|---|---|---|---|---|---|
| 2008 WW18 | 9-D | FIN | 2 | 0 | 0 | 0 | 0 | 6th |
| 2009 WW18 | 9-D | FIN | 5 | 0 | 0 | 0 | 2 | 5th |
| **Totals WW18** | | | **7** | **0** | **0** | **0** | **2** | **—** |

| **Hablutzel, Seraina** | | | | | | | | **b. Trullikon, Switzerland, August 11, 1990** |
|---|---|---|---|---|---|---|---|---|
| 2008 WW18 | 8-D | SUI | 5 | 0 | 0 | 0 | 4 | 7th |

| **Hafliger, Melanie** | | | | | | | | **b. Schenkon, Switzerland, September 29, 1982** |
|---|---|---|---|---|---|---|---|---|
| 2004 WW | 3-F | SUI | 4 | 0 | 0 | 0 | 2 | 8th |
| 2007 WW | 29-F | SUI | 4 | 0 | 0 | 0 | 8 | 5th |
| 2008 WW | 29-F | SUI | 5 | 1 | 1 | 2 | 10 | 4th |
| 2010 OG-W | 29-F | SUI | 5 | 0 | 1 | 1 | 2 | 5th |
| 2011 WW | 29-F | SUI | 5 | 0 | 1 | 1 | 2 | 6th |
| **Totals WW** | | | **18** | **1** | **2** | **3** | **22** | **—** |

| **Hajdova, Sabina** | | | | | | | | **b. Karlovy Vary, Czechoslovakia (Czech Republic), January 18, 1991** |
|---|---|---|---|---|---|---|---|---|
| 2008 WW18 | 8-F | CZE | 5 | 0 | 0 | 0 | 0 | B |

| **Hallikainen, Heidi** | | | | | | | | **b. Nivala, Finland, September 21, 1992** |
|---|---|---|---|---|---|---|---|---|
| 2009 WW18 | 15-F | FIN | 5 | 0 | 1 | 1 | 2 | 5th |
| 2010 WW18 | 15-F | FIN | 5 | 1 | 0 | 1 | 2 | 5th |
| **Totals WW18** | | | **10** | **1** | **1** | **2** | **4** | **—** |

| **Hallvar, Essi** | | | | | | | | **b. Oulu, Finland, April 2, 1983** |
|---|---|---|---|---|---|---|---|---|
| 2011 WW | 10-D | FIN | 6 | 0 | 1 | 1 | 0 | B |
| 2012 WW | 10-D | FIN | 6 | 0 | 0 | 0 | 0 | 4th |
| **Totals WW** | | | **12** | **0** | **1** | **1** | **0** | **B** |

| **Hammerl, Jessica** | | | | | | | | **b. Landshut, West Germany (Germany), July 10, 1988** |
|---|---|---|---|---|---|---|---|---|
| 2012 WW | 4-D | GER | 5 | 0 | 0 | 0 | 6 | 7th |

| **Hampton, Jordan** | | | | | | | | **b. Exeter, New Hampshire, United States, February 17, 1994** |
|---|---|---|---|---|---|---|---|---|
| 2012 WW18 | 17-D | USA | 5 | 0 | 1 | 1 | 0 | S |

| **Hanggi, Carmen** | | | | | | | | **b. Grindel, Switzerland, June 28, 1995** |
|---|---|---|---|---|---|---|---|---|
| 2011 WW18 | 21-F | SUI | 6 | 0 | 0 | 0 | 0 | 7th |

| **Hanke, Maike** | | | | | | | | **b. Wesel, Germany, January 14, 1992** |
|---|---|---|---|---|---|---|---|---|
| 2008 WW18 | 17-F | GER | 5 | 1 | 3 | 4 | 33 | 5th |
| 2009 WW18 | 7-F | GER | 4 | 1 | 0 | 1 | 4 | 6th |
| **Totals WW18** | | | **9** | **2** | **3** | **5** | **37** | **—** |

| **Haringer, Melanie** | | | | | | | | **b. Starnberg, Germany, March 21, 1994** |
|---|---|---|---|---|---|---|---|---|
| 2012 WW18 | 6-F | GER | 6 | 0 | 0 | 0 | 6 | 4th |

| **Haverstock, Brittany** | | | | | | | | **b. Hammonds Plains, Nova Scotia, Canada, May 3, 1990** |
|---|---|---|---|---|---|---|---|---|
| 2008 WW18 | 5-D | CAN | 5 | 0 | 2 | 2 | 0 | S |

| **Hedengren, Lisa** | | | | | | | | **b. Stockholm, Sweden, February 14, 1992** |
|---|---|---|---|---|---|---|---|---|
| 2010 WW18 | 27-F | SWE | 6 | 3 | 3 | 6 | 8 | B |

| **Hedin, Linnea** | | | | | | | | **b. Stockholm, Sweden, January 24, 1995** |
|---|---|---|---|---|---|---|---|---|
| 2010 WW18 | 12-D | SWE | 6 | 0 | 0 | 0 | 6 | B |
| 2011 WW18 | 12-D | SWE | 5 | 0 | 2 | 2 | 10 | 5th |
| 2012 WW18 | 12-D | SWE | 6 | 0 | 2 | 2 | 4 | B |
| 2012 WW | 12-D | SWE | 5 | 0 | 0 | 0 | 0 | 5th |
| **Totals WW18** | | | **17** | **0** | **4** | **4** | **20** | **2B** |

| **Hefford, Jayna** | | | | | | | | **b. Trenton, Ontario, Canada, May 14, 1977** |
|---|---|---|---|---|---|---|---|---|
| 1997 WW | 16-F | CAN | 5 | 1 | 3 | 4 | 2 | G |
| 1998 OG-W | 16-F | CAN | 6 | 1 | 0 | 1 | 6 | S |
| 1999 WW | 16-F | CAN | 5 | 5 | 6 | 11 | 0 | G |
| 2000 WW | 16-F | CAN | 5 | 5 | 3 | 8 | 4 | G |
| 2001 WW | 16-F | CAN | 5 | 2 | 2 | 4 | 6 | G |
| 2002 OG-W | 16-F | CAN | 5 | 3 | 4 | 7 | 2 | G |
| 2004 WW | 16-F | CAN | 5 | 7 | 3 | 10 | 2 | G |
| 2005 WW | 16-F | CAN | 5 | 6 | 2 | 8 | 0 | S |
| 2006 OG-W | 16-F | CAN | 5 | 3 | 4 | 7 | 0 | G |
| 2007 WW | 16-F | CAN | 5 | 2 | 1 | 3 | 2 | G |
| 2008 WW | 16-F | CAN | 5 | 3 | 5 | 8 | 8 | S |
| 2009 WW | 16-F | CAN | 5 | 1 | 6 | 7 | 2 | S |
| 2010 OG-W | 16-F | CAN | 5 | 5 | 7 | 12 | 8 | G |
| 2011 WW | 16-F | CAN | 5 | 3 | 2 | 5 | 2 | S |
| 2012 WW | 16-F | CAN | 5 | 3 | 6 | 9 | 4 | G |
| **Totals WW** | | | **55** | **38** | **39** | **77** | **32** | **7G,4S** |
| **Totals OG-W** | | | **21** | **12** | **15** | **27** | **16** | **3G,S** |

~WW IIHF Directorate Best Forward (2004, 2005), WW All-Star Team/Forward (1999, 2004, 2008)

**~Heikkila, Venla** ~see Hovi (Heikkila), Venla

| **Heikkinen, Milla** | | | | | | | | **b. Kiiminki, Finland, July 7, 1993** |
|---|---|---|---|---|---|---|---|---|
| 2009 WW18 | 12-F | FIN | 5 | 0 | 1 | 1 | 4 | 5th |
| 2010 WW18 | 12-F | FIN | 5 | 0 | 0 | 0 | 2 | 5th |
| 2011 WW18 | 12-F | FIN | 6 | 0 | 2 | 2 | 2 | B |
| **Totals WW18** | | | **16** | **0** | **3** | **3** | **8** | **B** |

| **Heiz, Aline** | | | | | | | | **b. Menziken, Switzerland, February 3, 1990** |
|---|---|---|---|---|---|---|---|---|
| 2008 WW18 | 22-F | SUI | 5 | 1 | 1 | 2 | 4 | 7th |

| **Helin, Anne** | | | | | | | | **b. Helsinki, Finland, January 28, 1987** |
|---|---|---|---|---|---|---|---|---|
| 2008 WW | 26-F | FIN | 5 | 3 | 1 | 4 | 4 | B |
| 2009 WW | 27-F | FIN | 5 | 1 | 2 | 3 | 4 | B |
| 2010 OG-W | 27-F | FIN | 5 | 0 | 0 | 0 | 0 | B |
| 2011 WW | 27-F | FIN | 6 | 0 | 2 | 2 | 4 | B |
| 2012 WW | 27-F | FIN | 6 | 1 | 1 | 2 | 10 | 4th |
| **Totals WW** | | | **22** | **5** | **6** | **11** | **22** | **3B** |

| **Herichova, Maria** | | | | | | | | **b. Poprad, Czechoslovakia (Slovakia), June 12, 1990** |
|---|---|---|---|---|---|---|---|---|
| 2010 OG-W | 12-F | SVK | 5 | 0 | 1 | 1 | 0 | 8th |
| 2011 WW | 12-F | SVK | 5 | 0 | 0 | 0 | 2 | 7th |
| 2012 WW | 12-F | SVK | 5 | 0 | 2 | 2 | 2 | 8th |
| **Totals WW** | | | **10** | **0** | **2** | **2** | **4** | **—** |

| **Heuscher, Jana** | | | | | | | | **b. Herisau, Switzerland, December 17, 1992** |
|---|---|---|---|---|---|---|---|---|
| 2009 WW18 | 5-D | SUI | 5 | 0 | 0 | 0 | 0 | 8th |

| **Hewett, Rebecca** | | | | | | | | **b. Oak Bluff, Manitoba, Canada, September 19, 1990** |
|---|---|---|---|---|---|---|---|---|
| 2008 WW18 | 8-D | CAN | 5 | 0 | 2 | 2 | 4 | S |

| **Hickel, Zoe** | | | | | | | | **b. Anchorage, Alaska, United States, July 10, 1992** |
|---|---|---|---|---|---|---|---|---|
| 2010 WW18 | 17-F | USA | 5 | 2 | 2 | 4 | 8 | S |

| **Hiirikoski, Jenni** | | | | | | | | **b. Lempaala, Finland, March 30, 1987** |
|---|---|---|---|---|---|---|---|---|
| 2004 WW | 6-D | FIN | 5 | 0 | 0 | 0 | 0 | B |
| 2005 WW | 6-D | FIN | 5 | 1 | 0 | 1 | 4 | 4th |
| 2007 WW | 6-D | FIN | 5 | 0 | 1 | 1 | 8 | 4th |
| 2008 WW | 6-D | FIN | 5 | 1 | 2 | 3 | 4 | B |
| 2009 WW | 6-D | FIN | 5 | 1 | 2 | 3 | 2 | B |
| 2010 OG-W | 6-D | FIN | 5 | 0 | 2 | 2 | 4 | B |
| 2011 WW | 6-D | FIN | 6 | 0 | 2 | 2 | 2 | B |
| 2012 WW | 6-D | FIN | 6 | 0 | 5 | 5 | 2 | 4th |
| **Totals WW** | | | **37** | **3** | **12** | **15** | **22** | **4B** |

~WW IIHF Directorate Best Defenceman (2009, 2012)

| **Hirano, Yuka** | | | | | | | | **b. Yokkaichi, Japan, January 26, 1987** |
|---|---|---|---|---|---|---|---|---|
| 2004 WW | 19-F | JPN | 4 | 0 | 0 | 0 | 0 | 9th |
| 2008 WW | 17-F | JPN | 4 | 1 | 0 | 1 | 2 | 7th |
| 2009 WW | 17-F | JPN | 4 | 0 | 4 | 4 | 0 | 8th |
| **Totals WW** | | | **12** | **1** | **4** | **5** | **2** | **—** |

| **Hochuli, Nadja** | | | | | | | | **b. Zurich, Switzerland, June 24, 1990** |
|---|---|---|---|---|---|---|---|---|
| 2008 WW18 | 3-D | SUI | 5 | 0 | 0 | 0 | 4 | 7th |

| **Hoffmann, Carina** | | | | | | | | **b. Regensburg, Germany, October 12, 1990** |
|---|---|---|---|---|---|---|---|---|
| 2008 WW18 | 7-D | GER | 5 | 0 | 0 | 0 | 10 | 5th |

| **Hofstetter, Nadine** | | | | | | | | **b. Romoos, Switzerland, October 21, 1994** |
|---|---|---|---|---|---|---|---|---|
| 2011 WW18 | 4-D | SUI | 6 | 0 | 0 | 0 | 0 | 7th |
| 2012 WW18 | 4-D | SUI | 3 | 0 | 0 | 0 | 0 | 8th |
| **Totals WW18** | | | **9** | **0** | **0** | **0** | **0** | **—** |

| **Holmbom, Emma** | | | | | | | | **b. Sundsvall, Sweden, April 10, 1990** |
|---|---|---|---|---|---|---|---|---|
| 2008 WW18 | 3-D | SWE | 5 | 2 | 1 | 3 | 6 | 4th |

| **Holmgren, Josefine** | | | | | | | | **b. Uppsala, Sweden, April 11, 1993** |
|---|---|---|---|---|---|---|---|---|
| 2009 WW18 | 4-D | SWE | 5 | 1 | 0 | 1 | 4 | B |
| 2010 WW18 | 4-D | SWE | 6 | 1 | 3 | 4 | 4 | B |
| 2011 WW18 | 4-D | SWE | 5 | 0 | 0 | 0 | 2 | 5th |
| **Totals WW18** | | | **16** | **2** | **3** | **5** | **10** | **2B** |

**Holmlov, Elin** b. Knivsta, Sweden, August 5, 1987

| | | | | | | | | |
|---|---|---|---|---|---|---|---|---|
| 2004 WW | 2-F | SWE | 5 | 2 | 4 | 6 | 8 | 4th |
| 2005 WW | 2-F | SWE | 5 | 0 | 3 | 3 | 4 | B |
| 2007 WW | 2-F | SWE | 5 | 0 | 2 | 2 | 8 | B |
| 2008 WW | 2-F | SWE | 4 | 0 | 2 | 2 | 2 | 5th |
| 2009 WW | 2-F | SWE | 5 | 6 | 2 | 8 | 2 | 4th |
| 2010 OG-W | 2-F | SWE | 5 | 1 | 3 | 4 | 2 | 4th |
| 2011 WW | 2-F | SWE | 5 | 2 | 4 | 6 | 4 | 5th |
| 2012 WW | 2-F | SWE | 5 | 4 | 3 | 7 | 6 | 5th |
| **Totals WW** | | | **34** | **14** | **20** | **34** | **34** | **2B** |

**Holst, Erika** b. Varo, Sweden, April 8, 1979

| | | | | | | | | |
|---|---|---|---|---|---|---|---|---|
| 1997 WW | 8-F | SWE | 5 | 2 | 2 | 4 | 4 | 5th |
| 1998 OG-W | 8-F | SWE | 5 | 2 | 3 | 5 | 8 | 5th |
| 1999 WW | 8-F | SWE | 5 | 3 | 2 | 5 | 4 | 4th |
| 2000 WW | 8-F | SWE | 3 | 1 | 1 | 2 | 4 | 4th |
| 2001 WW | 8-F | SWE | 4 | 0 | 1 | 1 | 4 | 5th |
| 2002 OG-W | 8-F | SWE | 5 | 2 | 3 | 5 | 10 | B |
| 2004 WW | 8-F | SWE | 5 | 4 | 1 | 5 | 2 | 4th |
| 2005 WW | 8-F | SWE | 5 | 1 | 1 | 2 | 2 | B |
| 2006 OG-W | 8-F | SWE | 5 | 1 | 4 | 5 | 2 | S |
| 2007 WW | 8-F | SWE | 5 | 1 | 4 | 5 | 6 | B |
| 2008 WW | 8-F | SWE | 3 | 0 | 0 | 0 | 4 | 5th |
| 2009 WW | 8-F | SWE | 5 | 4 | 5 | 9 | 4 | 4th |
| 2010 OG-W | 8-F | SWE | 5 | 0 | 2 | 2 | 4 | 4th |
| 2011 WW | 8-F | SWE | 5 | 2 | 6 | 8 | 2 | 5th |
| 2012 WW | 8-F | SWE | 4 | 2 | 2 | 4 | 2 | 5th |
| **Totals WW** | | | **49** | **20** | **25** | **45** | **38** | **2B** |
| **Totals OG-W** | | | **20** | **5** | **12** | **17** | **24** | **S,B** |

**Horakova, Nikola** b. Usti nad Labem, Czechoslovakia (Czech Republic), September 24, 1992

| | | | | | | | | |
|---|---|---|---|---|---|---|---|---|
| 2008 WW18 | 10-D | CZE | 5 | 0 | 2 | 2 | 0 | B |
| 2010 WW18 | 16-D | CZE | 5 | 1 | 2 | 3 | 4 | 7th |
| **Totals WW18** | | | **10** | **1** | **4** | **5** | **4** | **B** |

**Horalkova, Pavlina** b. Benesov, Czechoslovakia (Czech Republic), May 24, 1991

| | | | | | | | | |
|---|---|---|---|---|---|---|---|---|
| 2008 WW18 | 13-D | CZE | 5 | 0 | 0 | 0 | 10 | B |
| 2009 WW18 | 6-D | CZE | 4 | 0 | 0 | 0 | 25 | 4th |
| **Totals WW18** | | | **9** | **0** | **0** | **0** | **35** | **B** |

**Hori, Mika** b. Tokkaido, Japan, February 17, 1992

| | | | | | | | | |
|---|---|---|---|---|---|---|---|---|
| 2010 WW18 | 13-D | JPN | 5 | 0 | 0 | 0 | 10 | 6th |

**Hovi (Heikkila), Venla** b. Tampere, Finland, October 28, 1987

| | | | | | | | | |
|---|---|---|---|---|---|---|---|---|
| 2007 WW* | 9-F | FIN | 5 | 0 | 0 | 0 | 0 | 4th |
| 2008 WW* | 9-F | FIN | 4 | 0 | 0 | 0 | 0 | B |
| 2009 WW* | 9-F | FIN | 5 | 1 | 2 | 3 | 2 | B |
| 2010 OG-W | 9-F | FIN | 5 | 2 | 0 | 2 | 2 | B |
| 2012 WW | 9-F | FIN | 6 | 1 | 1 | 2 | 4 | 4th |
| **Totals WW** | | | **20** | **2** | **3** | **5** | **6** | **2B** |

*played under maiden name Venla Heikkila

**Huang, Haijing** b. Harbin, China, July 2, 1988

| | | | | | | | | |
|---|---|---|---|---|---|---|---|---|
| 2008 WW | 11-F | CHN | 4 | 0 | 0 | 0 | 4 | 8th |
| 2009 WW | 11-F | CHN | 4 | 0 | 0 | 0 | 0 | 9th |
| 2010 OG-W | 11-F | CHN | 5 | 0 | 0 | 0 | 4 | 7th |
| **Totals WW** | | | **8** | **0** | **0** | **0** | **4** | **—** |

**Hudeckova, Klara** b. Havirov, Czech Republic, November 15, 1994

| | | | | | | | | |
|---|---|---|---|---|---|---|---|---|
| 2010 WW18 | 19-D | CZE | 5 | 0 | 0 | 0 | 0 | 7th |
| 2011 WW18 | 19-D | CZE | 6 | 0 | 0 | 0 | 2 | 4th |
| 2012 WW18 | 19-D | CZE | 5 | 0 | 0 | 0 | 0 | 6th |
| **Totals WW18** | | | **16** | **0** | **0** | **0** | **2** | **—** |

**Huhta, Mira** b. Helsinki, Finland, October 28, 1987

| | | | | | | | | |
|---|---|---|---|---|---|---|---|---|
| 2011 WW | 2-F | FIN | 6 | 0 | 0 | 0 | 0 | B |

**Huo, Cui** b. Harbin, China, September 13, 1988

| | | | | | | | | |
|---|---|---|---|---|---|---|---|---|
| 2008 WW | 22-F | CHN | 4 | 0 | 1 | 1 | 2 | 8th |
| 2009 WW | 22-F | CHN | 4 | 0 | 0 | 0 | 2 | 9th |
| 2010 OG-W | 22-F | CHN | 5 | 0 | 0 | 0 | 0 | 7th |
| **Totals WW** | | | **8** | **0** | **1** | **1** | **4** | **—** |

**Ibragimova (Alexeyeva), Lyubov** b. Almaty, Soviet Union (Kazakhstan), May 5, 1984

| | | | | | | | | |
|---|---|---|---|---|---|---|---|---|
| 2001 WW* | 7-F | KAZ | 5 | 0 | 0 | 0 | 0 | 8th |
| 2002 OG-W* | 7-F | KAZ | 5 | 0 | 0 | 0 | 0 | 8th |
| 2005 WW* | 8-F | KAZ | 5 | 0 | 0 | 0 | 2 | 7th |
| 2007 WW | 7-F | KAZ | 4 | 0 | 0 | 0 | 2 | 9th |
| 2009 WW | 7-F | KAZ | 4 | 1 | 0 | 1 | 2 | 6th |
| 2011 WW | 7-F | KAZ | 5 | 0 | 0 | 0 | 4 | 8th |
| **Totals WW** | | | **23** | **1** | **0** | **1** | **10** | **—** |

*played under maiden name Lyubov Alexeyeva

**Ihnatova, Viktoria** b. June 15, 1993

| | | | | | | | | |
|---|---|---|---|---|---|---|---|---|
| 2012 WW | 27-F | SVK | 4 | 0 | 0 | 0 | 2 | 8th |

**Illikainen, Molly** b. Grand Rapids, Minnesota, United States, April 10, 1994

| | | | | | | | | |
|---|---|---|---|---|---|---|---|---|
| 2012 WW18 | 23-F | USA | 5 | 1 | 3 | 4 | 2 | S |

**Irwin, Haley** b. Thunder Bay, Ontario, Canada, June 6, 1988

| | | | | | | | | |
|---|---|---|---|---|---|---|---|---|
| 2009 WW | 21-F | CAN | 5 | 2 | 3 | 5 | 2 | S |
| 2010 OG-W | 21-F | CAN | 5 | 4 | 1 | 5 | 4 | G |
| 2011 WW | 21-F | CAN | 5 | 2 | 2 | 4 | 4 | S |
| 2012 WW | 21-F | CAN | 1 | 0 | 0 | 0 | 0 | G |
| **Totals WW** | | | **11** | **4** | **5** | **9** | **6** | **G,2S** |

**Isanbayeva, Renata** b. August 24, 1995

| | | | | | | | | |
|---|---|---|---|---|---|---|---|---|
| 2012 WW18 | 16-F | RUS | 6 | 1 | 0 | 1 | 0 | 7th |

**Ishiura, Fuka** b. Hokkaido, Japan, May 6, 1993

| | | | | | | | | |
|---|---|---|---|---|---|---|---|---|
| 2010 WW18 | 21-F | JPN | 5 | 0 | 1 | 1 | 0 | 6th |
| 2011 WW18 | 19-F | JPN | 6 | 0 | 3 | 3 | 6 | 8th |
| **Totals WW18** | | | **11** | **0** | **4** | **4** | **6** | **—** |

**Iwahara, Tomomi** b. Hokkaido, Japan, December 19, 1987

| | | | | | | | | |
|---|---|---|---|---|---|---|---|---|
| 2008 WW | 28-F | JPN | 4 | 0 | 0 | 0 | 0 | 7th |
| 2009 WW | 28-F | JPN | 4 | 0 | 0 | 0 | 2 | 8th |
| **Totals WW** | | | **8** | **0** | **0** | **0** | **2** | **—** |

**Jaakkola, Noora** b. Toijala, Finland, May 14, 1991

| | | | | | | | | |
|---|---|---|---|---|---|---|---|---|
| 2008 WW18 | 6-D | FIN | 3 | 0 | 1 | 1 | 0 | 6th |
| 2009 WW18 | 6-D | FIN | 5 | 1 | 1 | 2 | 4 | 5th |
| **Totals WW18** | | | **8** | **1** | **2** | **3** | **4** | **—** |

**Jackova, Michaela** b. Pardubice, Czech Republic, July 22, 1992

| | | | | | | | | |
|---|---|---|---|---|---|---|---|---|
| 2009 WW18 | 5-D | CZE | 5 | 0 | 0 | 0 | 0 | 4th |
| 2010 WW18 | 27-D | CZE | 5 | 0 | 0 | 0 | 0 | 7th |
| **Totals WW18** | | | **10** | **0** | **0** | **0** | **0** | **—** |

**Jacobs, Tami** b. Stockholm, Sweden, February 29, 1992

| | | | | | | | | |
|---|---|---|---|---|---|---|---|---|
| 2010 WW18 | 3-D | SWE | 6 | 0 | 0 | 0 | 2 | B |

**Jalosuo, Mira** b. Joensuu, Finland, February 3, 1989

| | | | | | | | | |
|---|---|---|---|---|---|---|---|---|
| 2007 WW | 7-D | FIN | 5 | 0 | 0 | 0 | 2 | 4th |
| 2008 WW | 7-D | FIN | 5 | 0 | 0 | 0 | 4 | B |
| 2009 WW | 7-D | FIN | 5 | 0 | 0 | 0 | 2 | B |
| 2011 WW | 7-D | FIN | 6 | 0 | 0 | 0 | 2 | B |
| 2012 WW | 7-D | FIN | 5 | 0 | 1 | 1 | 4 | 4th |
| **Totals WW** | | | **26** | **0** | **1** | **1** | **14** | **3B** |

**Janzen, Jacqueline** b. Villingen-Schwenningen, Germany, November 29, 1993

| | | | | | | | | |
|---|---|---|---|---|---|---|---|---|
| 2009 WW18 | 8-F | GER | 5 | 1 | 0 | 1 | 2 | 6th |
| 2010 WW18 | 8-F | GER | 5 | 1 | 4 | 5 | 0 | 4th |
| 2011 WW18 | 8-F | GER | 5 | 4 | 0 | 4 | 2 | 6th |
| **Totals WW18** | | | **15** | **6** | **4** | **10** | **4** | **—** |

**Jenner, Brianne** b. Oakville, Ontario, Canada, May 4, 1991

| | | | | | | | | |
|---|---|---|---|---|---|---|---|---|
| 2008 WW18 | 11-F | CAN | 5 | 6 | 3 | 9 | 2 | S |
| 2009 WW18 | 11-F | CAN | 5 | 5 | 1 | 6 | 2 | S |
| 2012 WW | 19-F | CAN | 5 | 0 | 1 | 1 | 0 | G |
| **Totals WW18** | | | **10** | **11** | **4** | **15** | **4** | **2S** |

**Jiang, Na** b. Harbin, China, October 18, 1988

| | | | | | | | | |
|---|---|---|---|---|---|---|---|---|
| 2008 WW | 21-D | CHN | 4 | 0 | 0 | 0 | 0 | 8th |
| 2009 WW | 21-D | CHN | 4 | 1 | 0 | 1 | 8 | 9th |
| 2010 OG-W | 21-D | CHN | 5 | 0 | 1 | 1 | 4 | 7th |
| **Totals WW** | | | **8** | **1** | **0** | **1** | **8** | **—** |

**Jin, Fengling** b. Heilongjiang, China, November 20, 1982

| | | | | | | | | |
|---|---|---|---|---|---|---|---|---|
| 2000 WW | 12-F | CHN | 5 | 0 | 0 | 0 | 4 | 6th |
| 2001 WW | 12-F | CHN | 5 | 0 | 0 | 0 | 4 | 7th |
| 2002 OG-W | 12-F | CHN | 5 | 0 | 1 | 1 | 4 | 7th |
| 2004 WW | 12-F | CHN | 4 | 1 | 2 | 3 | 12 | 7th |
| 2005 WW | 12-F | CHN | 5 | 3 | 0 | 3 | 4 | 6th |
| 2007 WW | 12-F | CHN | 4 | 1 | 2 | 3 | 6 | 6th |
| 2008 WW | 12-F | CHN | 4 | 1 | 3 | 4 | 8 | 8th |
| 2009 WW | 12-F | CHN | 4 | 0 | 1 | 1 | 2 | 9th |
| 2010 OG-W | 12-F | CHN | 5 | 2 | 1 | 3 | 4 | 7th |
| **Totals WW** | | | **31** | **6** | **8** | **14** | **40** | **—** |
| **Totals OG-W** | | | **10** | **2** | **2** | **4** | **8** | **—** |

**Jirsova, Veronika** b. Opocno, Czech Republic, February 17, 1994

| | | | | | | | | |
|---|---|---|---|---|---|---|---|---|
| 2011 WW18 | 18-F | CZE | 6 | 0 | 0 | 0 | 4 | 4th |

**Johansson, Anna** b. Angelholm, Sweden, August 4, 1994

| | | | | | | | | |
|---|---|---|---|---|---|---|---|---|
| 2011 WW18 | 27-F | SWE | 5 | 0 | 1 | 1 | 2 | 5th |

| **Johansson, Elin** | | | | | | | | **b. Hudiksvall, Sweden, February 21, 1995** |
|---|---|---|---|---|---|---|---|---|
| 2011 WW18 | 15-F | SWE | 5 | 0 | 0 | 0 | 6 | 5th |
| 2012 WW18 | 15-F | SWE | 6 | 1 | 2 | 3 | 2 | B |
| **Totals WW18** | | | **11** | **1** | **2** | **3** | **8** | **B** |

| **Johansson, Emelie** | | | | | | | | **b. Sunne, Sweden, July 9, 1992** |
|---|---|---|---|---|---|---|---|---|
| 2010 WW18 | 14-F | SWE | 6 | 1 | 0 | 1 | 2 | B |

| **Johansson, Lisa** | | | | | | | | **b. Nybro, Sweden, April 11, 1992** |
|---|---|---|---|---|---|---|---|---|
| 2008 WW18 | 17-F | SWE | 5 | 2 | 0 | 2 | 4 | 4th |
| 2009 WW18 | 17-F | SWE | 5 | 0 | 0 | 0 | 0 | B |
| 2010 WW18 | 17-F | SWE | 6 | 3 | 0 | 3 | 2 | B |
| **Totals WW18** | | | **16** | **5** | **0** | **5** | **6** | **2B** |

| **Johnson, Kaliya** | | | | | | | | **b. Chandler, Arizona, United States, December 2, 1994** |
|---|---|---|---|---|---|---|---|---|
| 2012 WW18 | 27-D | USA | 5 | 0 | 0 | 0 | 0 | S |

| **Johnston, Rebecca** | | | | | | | | **b. Sudbury, Ontario, Canada, September 24, 1989** |
|---|---|---|---|---|---|---|---|---|
| 2008 WW | 6-F | CAN | 5 | 0 | 0 | 0 | 0 | S |
| 2009 WW | 6-F | CAN | 5 | 3 | 2 | 5 | 0 | S |
| 2010 OG-W | 6-F | CAN | 5 | 1 | 5 | 6 | 2 | G |
| 2011 WW | 6-F | CAN | 5 | 4 | 2 | 6 | 0 | S |
| 2012 WW | 6-F | CAN | 5 | 1 | 6 | 7 | 0 | G |
| **Totals WW** | | | **20** | **8** | **10** | **18** | **0** | **G,3S** |

| **Jokinen, Janna** | | | | | | | | **b. Loppi, Finland, June 2, 1992** |
|---|---|---|---|---|---|---|---|---|
| 2010 WW18 | 28-D | FIN | 5 | 0 | 1 | 1 | 0 | 5th |

| **Jones, Jessica** | | | | | | | | **b. Belleville, Ontario, Canada, August 30, 1990** |
|---|---|---|---|---|---|---|---|---|
| 2008 WW18 | 6-F | CAN | 5 | 2 | 4 | 6 | 4 | S |

| **Jordansson, Isabelle** | | | | | | | | **b. Stockholm, Sweden, March 8, 1991** |
|---|---|---|---|---|---|---|---|---|
| 2008 WW18 | 12-F | SWE | 5 | 1 | 3 | 4 | 6 | 4th |
| 2008 WW | 12-F | SWE | 4 | 2 | 2 | 4 | 0 | 5th |
| 2009 WW18 | 12-F | SWE | 5 | 2 | 2 | 4 | 2 | B |
| 2009 WW | 12-F | SWE | 5 | 0 | 2 | 2 | 2 | 4th |
| 2010 OG-W | 12-F | SWE | 5 | 0 | 3 | 3 | 0 | 4th |
| **Totals WW18** | | | **10** | **3** | **5** | **8** | **8** | **B** |
| **Totals WW** | | | **9** | **2** | **4** | **6** | **2** | **—** |

| **Josephs, Katy** | | | | | | | | **b. Calgary, Alberta, Canada, March 15, 1993** |
|---|---|---|---|---|---|---|---|---|
| 2011 WW18 | 14-F | CAN | 5 | 2 | 2 | 4 | 2 | S |

| **Jurcova, Petra** | | | | | | | | **b. Kosice, Czechoslovakia (Slovakia), June 22, 1987** |
|---|---|---|---|---|---|---|---|---|
| 2010 OG-W | 13-F | SVK | 5 | 0 | 1 | 1 | 0 | 8th |
| 2011 WW | 13-F | SVK | 5 | 0 | 0 | 0 | 4 | 7th |
| 2012 WW | 13-F | SVK | 5 | 0 | 0 | 0 | 4 | 8th |
| **Totals WW** | | | **10** | **0** | **0** | **0** | **8** | **—** |

| **Juutilainen, Johanna** | | | | | | | | **b. Varkaus, Finland, March 8, 1990** |
|---|---|---|---|---|---|---|---|---|
| 2008 WW18 | 22-F | FIN | 5 | 0 | 5 | 5 | 4 | 6th |

| **Kamber, Stephanie** | | | | | | | | **b. Hauenstein-Ifenthal, Switzerland, February 21, 1995** |
|---|---|---|---|---|---|---|---|---|
| 2011 WW18 | 26-F | SUI | 6 | 1 | 1 | 2 | 0 | 7th |

| **Kamenik, Nina** | | | | | | | | **b. Berlin, West Germany (Germany), April 27, 1987** |
|---|---|---|---|---|---|---|---|---|
| 2008 WW | 21-F | GER | 4 | 0 | 0 | 0 | 2 | 9th |
| 2012 WW | 7-F | GER | 5 | 0 | 1 | 1 | 2 | 7th |
| **Totals** | | | **9** | **0** | **1** | **1** | **4** | **—** |

| **Kanders, Kira** | | | | | | | | **b. Essen, Germany, December 1, 1992** |
|---|---|---|---|---|---|---|---|---|
| 2010 WW18 | 16-D | GER | 6 | 0 | 0 | 0 | 4 | 4th |

| **Kaplanova, Katerina** | | | | | | | | **b. Sternberk, Czech Republic, October 14, 1993** |
|---|---|---|---|---|---|---|---|---|
| 2010 WW18 | 21-F | CZE | 5 | 2 | 0 | 2 | 0 | 7th |
| 2011 WW18 | 21-F | CZE | 6 | 2 | 2 | 4 | 0 | 4th |
| **Totals WW18** | | | **11** | **4** | **2** | **6** | **0** | **—** |

| **Kapustina, Alexandra** | | | | | | | | **b. Sverdlovsk (Yekaterinburg), Soviet Union (Russia), April 7, 1984** |
|---|---|---|---|---|---|---|---|---|
| 2004 WW | 16-D | RUS | 4 | 0 | 0 | 0 | 6 | 5th |
| 2006 OG-W | 16-D | RUS | 5 | 1 | 0 | 1 | 8 | 6th |
| 2007 WW | 44-D | RUS | 4 | 0 | 0 | 0 | 6 | 7th |
| 2008 WW | 44-D | RUS | 4 | 1 | 0 | 1 | 4 | 6th |
| 2009 WW | 44-D | RUS | 4 | 1 | 0 | 1 | 2 | 5th |
| 2010 OG-W | 44-D | RUS | 5 | 0 | 2 | 2 | 2 | 6th |
| 2011 WW | 44-D | RUS | 6 | 1 | 2 | 3 | 4 | 4th |
| 2012 WW | 44-D | RUS | 5 | 0 | 0 | 0 | 6 | 6th |
| **Totals WW** | | | **27** | **3** | **2** | **5** | **28** | **—** |
| **Totals OG-W** | | | **10** | **1** | **2** | **3** | **10** | **—** |

| **Kapustova, Jana** | | | | | | | | **b. Zilina, Czechoslovakia (Slovakia), August 11, 1983** |
|---|---|---|---|---|---|---|---|---|
| 2010 OG-W | 6-F | SVK | 4 | 1 | 2 | 3 | 4 | 8th |
| 2011 WW | 6-F | SVK | 5 | 1 | 0 | 1 | 0 | 7th |
| 2012 WW | 6-F | SVK | 5 | 2 | 3 | 5 | 4 | 8th |
| **Totals WW** | | | **10** | **3** | **3** | **6** | **4** | **—** |

| **Karafiatova, Iveta** | | | | | | | | **b. Bratislava, Czechoslovakia (Slovakia), May 14, 1988** |
|---|---|---|---|---|---|---|---|---|
| 2010 OG-W | 19-D | SVK | 5 | 0 | 0 | 0 | 6 | 8th |
| 2011 WW | 19-D | SVK | 5 | 1 | 0 | 1 | 0 | 7th |
| 2012 WW | 19-D | SVK | 5 | 1 | 1 | 2 | 8 | 8th |
| **Totals WW** | | | **10** | **2** | **1** | **3** | **8** | **—** |

| **Karlsson, Felicia** | | | | | | | | **b. Hallefors, Sweden, March 28, 1993** |
|---|---|---|---|---|---|---|---|---|
| 2011 WW18 | 13-F | SWE | 5 | 0 | 0 | 0 | 0 | 5th |

| **Karoyan, Lilit** | | | | | | | | **b. Ashtarak, Armenia, February 16, 1993** |
|---|---|---|---|---|---|---|---|---|
| 2010 WW18 | 23-F | RUS | 5 | 0 | 0 | 0 | 2 | 8th |

| **Karpenko, Chelsea** | | | | | | | | **b. Winnipeg, Manitoba, Canada, April 27, 1990** |
|---|---|---|---|---|---|---|---|---|
| 2008 WW18 | 16-F | CAN | 5 | 1 | 2 | 3 | 6 | S |

| **Karpeyeva, Natalya** | | | | | | | | **b. Almaty, Kazakhstan, March 25, 1993** |
|---|---|---|---|---|---|---|---|---|
| 2011 WW | 26-D | KAZ | 5 | 0 | 0 | 0 | 0 | 8th |

| **Karpf, Bernadette** | | | | | | | | **b. Landshut, Germany, July 3, 1996** |
|---|---|---|---|---|---|---|---|---|
| 2012 WW18 | 17-F | GER | 6 | 0 | 0 | 0 | 0 | 4th |

| **Karvinen, Michelle** | | | | | | | | **b. Rodovre, Denmark, March 27, 1990** |
|---|---|---|---|---|---|---|---|---|
| 2009 WW | 21-F | FIN | 5 | 5 | 2 | 7 | 6 | B |
| 2010 OG-W | 21-F | FIN | 5 | 1 | 2 | 3 | 4 | B |
| 2011 WW | 21-F | FIN | 6 | 4 | 4 | 8 | 8 | B |
| 2012 WW | 21-F | FIN | 6 | 0 | 5 | 5 | 4 | 4th |
| **Totals WW** | | | **17** | **9** | **11** | **20** | **18** | **2B** |

~WW All-Star Team/Forward (2009, 2011)

| **Kato, Moe** | | | | | | | | **b. Hokkaido, Japan, May 31, 1994** |
|---|---|---|---|---|---|---|---|---|
| 2011 WW18 | 8-D | JPN | 6 | 0 | 0 | 0 | 2 | 8th |

| **Kawashima, Yae** | | | | | | | | **b. Saitama, Japan, August 6, 1983** |
|---|---|---|---|---|---|---|---|---|
| 2004 WW | 14-F | JPN | 4 | 0 | 0 | 0 | 4 | 9th |
| 2008 WW | 14-F | JPN | 4 | 0 | 0 | 0 | 4 | 7th |
| **Totals WW** | | | **8** | **0** | **0** | **0** | **8** | **—** |

| **Kelter, Alev** | | | | | | | | **b. Eagle River, Alaska, United States, March 21, 1991** |
|---|---|---|---|---|---|---|---|---|
| 2008 WW18 | 5-D | USA | 5 | 0 | 6 | 6 | 2 | G |
| 2009 WW18 | 6-D | USA | 5 | 5 | 3 | 8 | 16 | G |
| **Totals WW18** | | | **10** | **5** | **9** | **14** | **18** | **2G** |

~WW18 IIHF Directorate Best Defenceman (2009)

| **Kennedy-Menefee, Maryanne** | | | | | | | | **b. Lansing, Michigan, United States, January 30, 1994** |
|---|---|---|---|---|---|---|---|---|
| 2012 WW18 | 21-F | USA | 5 | 2 | 7 | 9 | 2 | S |

| **Kenyon, Jamie** | | | | | | | | **b. Sparta, Wisconsin, United States, September 23, 1991** |
|---|---|---|---|---|---|---|---|---|
| 2009 WW18 | 16-F | USA | 5 | 1 | 3 | 4 | 4 | G |

| **Kessel, Amanda** | | | | | | | | **b. Madison, Wisconsin, United States, August 28, 1991** |
|---|---|---|---|---|---|---|---|---|
| 2008 WW18 | 18-F | USA | 5 | 4 | 7 | 11 | 2 | G |
| 2009 WW18 | 18-F | USA | 5 | 6 | 13 | 19 | 2 | G |
| 2012 WW | 28-F | USA | 5 | 3 | 7 | 10 | 0 | S |
| **Totals WW18** | | | **10** | **10** | **20** | **30** | **4** | **2G** |

~WW18 IIHF Directorate Best Forward (2009)

| **Kettunen, Anni** | | | | | | | | **b. Joensuu, Finland, January 22, 1993** |
|---|---|---|---|---|---|---|---|---|
| 2010 WW18 | 14-F | FIN | 5 | 0 | 1 | 1 | 0 | 5th |
| 2011 WW18 | 14-F | FIN | 5 | 0 | 0 | 0 | 6 | B |
| **Totals WW18** | | | **10** | **0** | **1** | **1** | **6** | **B** |

| **Kezmarska, Barbora** | | | | | | | | **b. Levoca, Czechoslovakia (Slovakia), September 28, 1988** |
|---|---|---|---|---|---|---|---|---|
| 2011 WW | 23-D | SVK | 5 | 0 | 0 | 0 | 2 | 7th |
| 2012 WW | 23-D | SVK | 5 | 0 | 0 | 0 | 2 | 8th |
| **Totals WW** | | | **10** | **0** | **0** | **0** | **4** | **—** |

| **Khomich, Alyona** | | | | | | | | **b. Pervouralsk, Soviet Union (Russia), February 26, 1981** |
|---|---|---|---|---|---|---|---|---|
| 1999 WW | 4-D | RUS | 5 | 0 | 0 | 0 | 6 | 6th |
| 2000 WW | 4-D | RUS | 5 | 0 | 1 | 1 | 6 | 5th |
| 2001 WW | 4-D | RUS | 5 | 0 | 0 | 0 | 2 | B |
| 2002 OG-W | 4-D | RUS | 5 | 0 | 0 | 0 | 0 | 5th |
| 2004 WW | 4-D | RUS | 4 | 0 | 0 | 0 | 0 | 5th |
| 2005 WW | 4-D | RUS | 5 | 0 | 0 | 0 | 6 | 8th |
| 2006 OG-W | 4-D | RUS | 5 | 0 | 1 | 1 | 4 | 6th |
| 2007 WW | 4-D | RUS | 4 | 0 | 1 | 1 | 2 | 7th |
| 2008 WW | 4-D | RUS | 4 | 0 | 1 | 1 | 2 | 6th |
| 2009 WW | 4-D | RUS | 4 | 0 | 1 | 1 | 2 | 5th |
| 2010 OG-W | 4-D | RUS | 5 | 0 | 1 | 1 | 0 | 6th |
| 2011 WW | 4-D | RUS | 6 | 0 | 1 | 1 | 8 | 4th |
| **Totals WW** | | | **42** | **0** | **5** | **5** | **34** | **B** |
| **Totals OG-W** | | | **15** | **0** | **2** | **2** | **4** | **—** |

| **Kilponen, Anna** | | | | | | | | **b. Orivesi, Finland, May 16, 1995** |
|---|---|---|---|---|---|---|---|---|
| 2011 WW18 | 3-D | FIN | 6 | 0 | 1 | 1 | 4 | B |
| 2012 WW18 | 3-D | FIN | 5 | 1 | 2 | 3 | 4 | 5th |
| 2012 WW | 2-D | FIN | 6 | 0 | 0 | 0 | 0 | 4th |
| **Totals WW18** | | | **11** | **1** | **3** | **4** | **8** | **B** |

| **Kingsbury, Laurie** | | | | | | | | **b. Valleyfield, Quebec, Canada, May 18, 1992** |
|---|---|---|---|---|---|---|---|---|
| 2009 WW18 | 18-F | CAN | 5 | 5 | 4 | 9 | 8 | S |
| 2010 WW18 | 18-F | CAN | 3 | 2 | 2 | 4 | 4 | G |
| **Totals WW18** | | | **8** | **7** | **6** | **13** | **12** | **G,S** |

| **Kinisjarvi, Annukka** | | | | | | | | **b. Oulu, Finland, July 8, 1991** |
|---|---|---|---|---|---|---|---|---|
| 2009 WW18 | 21-F | FIN | 5 | 1 | 0 | 1 | 0 | 5th |

| **Kirilenko, Maria** | | | | | | | | **b. Yakutia, Soviet Union (Russia), October 6, 1990** |
|---|---|---|---|---|---|---|---|---|
| 2008 WW18 | 19-F | RUS | 5 | 0 | 0 | 0 | 2 | 8th |

| **Kitayeva, Tatiana** | | | | | | | | **b. January 5, 1995** |
|---|---|---|---|---|---|---|---|---|
| 2012 WW18 | 13-F | RUS | 6 | 0 | 0 | 0 | 0 | 7th |

| **Kjellbin, Anna** | | | | | | | | **b. Gothenburg, Sweden, March 16, 1994** |
|---|---|---|---|---|---|---|---|---|
| 2011 WW18 | 5-D | SWE | 5 | 0 | 2 | 2 | 4 | 5th |
| 2012 WW18 | 5-D | SWE | 6 | 3 | 1 | 4 | 0 | B |
| **Totals WW18** | | | **11** | **3** | **3** | **6** | **4** | **B** |

| **Kluge, Laura** | | | | | | | | **b. Berlin, Germany, November 6, 1996** |
|---|---|---|---|---|---|---|---|---|
| 2012 WW18 | 25-F | GER | 6 | 0 | 2 | 2 | 6 | 4th |

| **Knight, Hilary** | | | | | | | | **b. Hannover, New Hampshire, United States, July 12, 1989** |
|---|---|---|---|---|---|---|---|---|
| 2007 WW | 16-F | USA | 5 | 0 | 0 | 0 | 4 | S |
| 2008 WW | 21-F | USA | 5 | 0 | 1 | 1 | 0 | G |
| 2009 WW | 21-F | USA | 5 | 7 | 2 | 9 | 4 | G |
| 2010 OG-W | 21-F | USA | 5 | 1 | 7 | 8 | 0 | S |
| 2011 WW | 21-F | USA | 5 | 5 | 9 | 14 | 2 | G |
| 2012 WW | 21-F | USA | 5 | 5 | 2 | 7 | 0 | S |
| **Totals WW** | | | **25** | **17** | **14** | **31** | **10** | **3G,2S** |

~WW All-Star Team/Forward (2011)

| **Kohler, Rebecca** | | | | | | | | **b. St. Thomas, Ontario, Canada, September 3, 1994** |
|---|---|---|---|---|---|---|---|---|
| 2011 WW18 | 25-F | CAN | 5 | 2 | 3 | 5 | 4 | S |
| 2012 WW18 | 25-F | CAN | 5 | 3 | 2 | 5 | 4 | G |
| **Totals WW18** | | | **10** | **5** | **5** | **10** | **8** | **G,S** |

| **Kohnle, Angela** | | | | | | | | **b. Sonthofen, Germany, October 29, 1990** |
|---|---|---|---|---|---|---|---|---|
| 2008 WW18 | 22-F | GER | 5 | 0 | 0 | 0 | 0 | 5th |

| **Koike, Shiori** | | | | | | | | **b. Tochigi, Japan, March 21, 1993** |
|---|---|---|---|---|---|---|---|---|
| 2010 WW18 | 7-D | JPN | 5 | 1 | 1 | 2 | 2 | 6th |
| 2011 WW18 | 2-D | JPN | 6 | 0 | 0 | 0 | 4 | 8th |
| **Totals WW18** | | | **11** | **1** | **1** | **2** | **6** | **—** |

| **Koivisto, Johanna** | | | | | | | | **b. Oulu, Finland, July 24, 1994** |
|---|---|---|---|---|---|---|---|---|
| 2010 WW18 | 2-D | FIN | 5 | 0 | 0 | 0 | 27 | 5th |
| 2011 WW18 | 2-D | FIN | 6 | 0 | 0 | 0 | 2 | B |
| 2012 WW18 | 2-D | FIN | 5 | 0 | 2 | 2 | 8 | 5th |
| **Totals WW18** | | | **16** | **0** | **2** | **2** | **37** | **B** |

| **Kolowratova, Samantha** | | | | | | | | **b. July 12, 1996** |
|---|---|---|---|---|---|---|---|---|
| 2012 WW18 | 4-D | CZE | 5 | 1 | 0 | 1 | 2 | 6th |

| **Kondo, Yoko** | | | | | | | | **b. Aomori, Japan, February 13, 1979** |
|---|---|---|---|---|---|---|---|---|
| 1998 OG-W | 2-D | JPN | 5 | 0 | 0 | 0 | 0 | 6th |
| 2000 WW | 10-D | JPN | 5 | 0 | 0 | 0 | 2 | 8th |
| 2004 WW | 10-D | JPN | 4 | 0 | 1 | 1 | 2 | 9th |
| 2008 WW | 3-D | JPN | 4 | 0 | 1 | 1 | 4 | 7th |
| 2009 WW | 3-D | JPN | 4 | 0 | 0 | 0 | 6 | 8th |
| **Totals WW** | | | **17** | **0** | **2** | **2** | **14** | **—** |

| **Konysheva, Olga** | | | | | | | | **b. Omsk, Soviet Union (Russia), May 29, 1972** |
|---|---|---|---|---|---|---|---|---|
| 2001 WW | 16-F | KAZ | 5 | 0 | 0 | 0 | 0 | 8th |
| 2002 OG-W | 16-D | KAZ | 5 | 0 | 0 | 0 | 0 | 8th |
| 2005 WW | 16-D | KAZ | 5 | 0 | 0 | 0 | 6 | 7th |
| 2009 WW | 16-D | KAZ | 4 | 0 | 0 | 0 | 2 | 6th |
| 2011 WW | 16-D | KAZ | 5 | 0 | 2 | 2 | 4 | 8th |
| **Totals WW** | | | **19** | **0** | **2** | **2** | **12** | **—** |

| **Korolyova, Tatyana** | | | | | | | | **b. Almaty, Soviet Union (Kazakhstan), March 29, 1986** |
|---|---|---|---|---|---|---|---|---|
| 2005 WW | 23-D | KAZ | 5 | 0 | 0 | 0 | 0 | 7th |
| 2007 WW | 23-F | KAZ | 4 | 0 | 0 | 0 | 0 | 9th |
| 2009 WW | 23-F | KAZ | 4 | 0 | 1 | 1 | 0 | 6th |
| 2011 WW | 22-F | KAZ | 5 | 0 | 0 | 0 | 6 | 8th |
| **Totals WW** | | | **18** | **0** | **1** | **1** | **6** | **—** |

| **Kosta, Nicole** | | | | | | | | **b. Mississauga, Ontario, Canada, February 27, 1993** |
|---|---|---|---|---|---|---|---|---|
| 2011 WW18 | 19-F | CAN | 5 | 5 | 3 | 8 | 6 | S |

| **Kotkaslahti, Venla** | | | | | | | | **b. Tampere, Finland, January 25, 1995** |
|---|---|---|---|---|---|---|---|---|
| 2011 WW18 | 15-F | FIN | 6 | 1 | 0 | 1 | 6 | B |
| 2012 WW18 | 15-F | FIN | 5 | 2 | 1 | 3 | 4 | 5th |
| 2012 WW | 18-F | FIN | 6 | 0 | 0 | 0 | 0 | 4th |
| **Totals WW18** | | | **11** | **3** | **4** | **4** | **10** | **B** |

| **Kovarova, Karolina** | | | | | | | | **b. Valasske Mezirici, Czech Republic, July 7, 1993** |
|---|---|---|---|---|---|---|---|---|
| 2009 WW18 | 24-D | CZE | 5 | 1 | 0 | 1 | 0 | 4th |
| 2010 WW18 | 24-F | CZE | 5 | 0 | 0 | 0 | 0 | 7th |
| 2011 WW18 | 27-D | CZE | 6 | 0 | 0 | 0 | 2 | 4th |
| **Totals WW18** | | | **16** | **1** | **0** | **1** | **2** | **—** |

| **Kozlovskikh, Anna** | | | | | | | | **b. Sverdlovsk Region, Soviet Union (Russia), October 4, 1990** |
|---|---|---|---|---|---|---|---|---|
| 2008 WW18 | 16-D | RUS | 5 | 0 | 0 | 0 | 2 | 8th |

| **Krause, Jordan** | | | | | | | | **b. Kelowna, British Columbia, September 30, 1994** |
|---|---|---|---|---|---|---|---|---|
| 2012 WW18 | 14-D | CAN | 5 | 0 | 0 | 0 | 0 | G |

| **Kresse, Miriam** | | | | | | | | **b. Berlin, West Germany (Germany), May 19, 1987** |
|---|---|---|---|---|---|---|---|---|
| 2007 WW | 6-F | GER | 4 | 0 | 0 | 0 | 8 | 8th |
| 2008 WW | 6-D | GER | 4 | 0 | 0 | 0 | 2 | 9th |
| **Totals WW** | | | **8** | **0** | **0** | **0** | **10** | **—** |

| **Krizova, Denisa** | | | | | | | | **b. Pelhrimov, Czech Republic, November 3, 1994** |
|---|---|---|---|---|---|---|---|---|
| 2010 WW18 | 14-F | CZE | 5 | 5 | 1 | 6 | 6 | 7th |
| 2011 WW18 | 14-F | CZE | 6 | 1 | 2 | 3 | 2 | 4th |
| 2012 WW18 | 14-F | CZE | 5 | 0 | 3 | 3 | 6 | 6th |
| **Totals WW18** | | | **16** | **6** | **6** | **12** | **14** | **—** |

| **Krupkova, Martina** | | | | | | | | **b. Olomouc, Czech Republic, November 21, 1991** |
|---|---|---|---|---|---|---|---|---|
| 2008 WW18 | 16-F | CZE | 5 | 0 | 0 | 0 | 0 | B |
| 2009 WW18 | 21-F | CZE | 5 | 0 | 0 | 0 | 8 | 4th |
| **Totals WW18** | | | **10** | **0** | **0** | **0** | **8** | **B** |

| **Krzyzaniak, Halli** | | | | | | | | **b. Neepawa, Manitoba, February 4, 1995** |
|---|---|---|---|---|---|---|---|---|
| 2012 WW18 | 18-D | CAN | 5 | 0 | 1 | 1 | 8 | G |

| **Kubatova, Adela** | | | | | | | | **b. Tabor, Czech Republic, November 3, 1994** |
|---|---|---|---|---|---|---|---|---|
| 2010 WW18 | 18-D | CZE | 5 | 0 | 0 | 0 | 4 | 7th |
| 2011 WW18 | 8-D | CZE | 6 | 0 | 1 | 1 | 4 | 4th |
| 2012 WW18 | 8-D | CZE | 5 | 0 | 0 | 0 | 4 | 6th |
| **Totals WW18** | | | **16** | **0** | **1** | **1** | **8** | **—** |

| **Kuhn, Alexandra** | | | | | | | | **b. Mannheim, Germany, November 6, 1991** |
|---|---|---|---|---|---|---|---|---|
| 2008 WW18 | 6-F | GER | 5 | 0 | 0 | 0 | 0 | 5th |
| 2009 WW18 | 6-F | GER | 5 | 1 | 0 | 1 | 4 | 6th |
| **Totals WW18** | | | **10** | **1** | **0** | **1** | **4** | **—** |

| **Kujala, Roosa** | | | | | | | | **b. Ruovesi, Finland, March 27, 1991** |
|---|---|---|---|---|---|---|---|---|
| 2009 WW18 | 14-F | FIN | 5 | 0 | 0 | 0 | 0 | 5th |

| **Kuller, Sabina** | | | | | | | | **b. September 22, 1994** |
|---|---|---|---|---|---|---|---|---|
| 2012 WW18 | 26-F | SWE | 6 | 1 | 0 | 1 | 0 | B |

| **Kumano, Haruna** | | | | | | | | **b. Kushiro, Japan, January 5, 1986** |
|---|---|---|---|---|---|---|---|---|
| 2004 WW | 2-D | JPN | 4 | 0 | 0 | 0 | 0 | 9th |
| 2008 WW | 2-D | JPN | 4 | 0 | 0 | 0 | 0 | 7th |
| 2009 WW | 2-D | JPN | 4 | 0 | 0 | 0 | 6 | 8th |
| **Totals WW** | | | **12** | **0** | **0** | **0** | **6** | **—** |

| **Kuzelova, Veronika** | | | | | | | | **b. Prague, Czech Republic, April 1, 1994** |
|---|---|---|---|---|---|---|---|---|
| 2010 WW18 | 15-F | CZE | 5 | 0 | 0 | 0 | 2 | 7th |
| 2011 WW18 | 15-F | CZE | 6 | 0 | 0 | 0 | 0 | 4th |
| 2012 WW18 | 15-F | CZE | 5 | 0 | 0 | 0 | 0 | 6th |
| **Totals WW18** | | | **16** | **0** | **0** | **0** | **2** | **—** |

| **Lacquette, Brigette** | | | | | | | | **b. Waterhen, Manitoba, Canada, November 10, 1992** |
|---|---|---|---|---|---|---|---|---|
| 2009 WW18 | 2-D | CAN | 5 | 1 | 4 | 5 | 4 | S |
| 2010 WW18 | 22-D | CAN | 5 | 2 | 11 | 13 | 6 | G |
| **Totals WW18** | | | **10** | **3** | **15** | **18** | **10** | **G,S** |

~WW18 IIHF Directorate Best Defenceman (2010)

| **Laggerbauer, Bianca** | | | | | | | | **b. Rosenheim, Germany, September 19, 1993** |
|---|---|---|---|---|---|---|---|---|
| 2011 WW18 | 14-F | GER | 5 | 0 | 0 | 0 | 8 | 6th |

| **Laitila, Katariina** | | | | | | | | **b. Haapavesi, Finland, September 22, 1993** |
|---|---|---|---|---|---|---|---|---|
| 2010 WW18 | 19-F | FIN | 5 | 0 | 1 | 1 | 4 | 5th |

| **Lalikova, Denisa** | | | | | | | | **b. August 28, 1995** |
|---|---|---|---|---|---|---|---|---|
| 2012 WW | 9-D | SVK | 5 | 0 | 0 | 0 | 0 | 8th |

| **Lamoureux, Jocelyne** | | | | | | | | **b. Grand Forks, North Dakota, United States, July 3, 1989** |
|---|---|---|---|---|---|---|---|---|
| 2009 WW | 17-F | USA | 5 | 0 | 2 | 2 | 2 | G |
| 2010 OG-W | 17-F | USA | 5 | 2 | 4 | 6 | 0 | S |
| 2011 WW | 17-F | USA | 5 | 3 | 3 | 6 | 4 | G |
| 2012 WW | 17-F | USA | 5 | 4 | 5 | 9 | 8 | S |
| **Totals WW** | | | **15** | **7** | **10** | **17** | **14** | **2G,S** |

**~Lamoureux, Monique** ~see Lamoureux-Kolls, Monique

| **Lamoureux-Kolls, Monique** | | | | | | | | **b. Grand Forks, North Dakota, United States, July 3, 1989** |
|---|---|---|---|---|---|---|---|---|
| 2009 WW* | 27-F | USA | 5 | 2 | 3 | 5 | 10 | G |
| 2010 OG-W* | 7-F | USA | 5 | 4 | 6 | 10 | 2 | S |
| 2011 WW | 7-F | USA | 3 | 2 | 5 | 7 | 6 | G |
| 2012 WW | 7-F | USA | 5 | 7 | 7 | 14 | 6 | S |
| **Totals WW** | | | **13** | **11** | **15** | **26** | **22** | **2G,S** |

*played under maiden name Monique Lamoureux
~WW IIHF Directorate Best Forward (2011), WW All-Star Team/Forward (2012)

| **Landis, Bianca** | | | | | | | | **b. Hirzel, Switzerland, March 9, 1991** |
|---|---|---|---|---|---|---|---|---|
| 2008 WW18 | 21-F | SUI | 5 | 0 | 0 | 0 | 0 | 7th |

| **Langan, Casandra** | | | | | | | | **b. Chatham, Ontario, Canada, June 3, 1991** |
|---|---|---|---|---|---|---|---|---|
| 2009 WW18 | 5-F | CAN | 5 | 4 | 0 | 4 | 2 | S |

| **Lanzl, Andrea** | | | | | | | | **b. Starnberg, West Germany (Germany), October 8, 1987** |
|---|---|---|---|---|---|---|---|---|
| 2005 WW | 28-F | GER | 5 | 0 | 0 | 0 | 2 | 5th |
| 2006 OG-W | 28-F | GER | 5 | 0 | 0 | 0 | 4 | 5th |
| 2007 WW | 28-F | GER | 4 | 1 | 0 | 1 | 4 | 8th |
| 2008 WW | 28-F | GER | 4 | 0 | 2 | 2 | 4 | 9th |
| 2012 WW | 15-F | GER | 5 | 0 | 1 | 1 | 2 | 7th |
| **Totals WW** | | | **18** | **1** | **3** | **4** | **12** | **—** |

| **Larocque, Jocelyne** | | | | | | | | **b. Ste. Anne, Manitoba, Canada, May 19, 1988** |
|---|---|---|---|---|---|---|---|---|
| 2011 WW | 3-D | CAN | 5 | 0 | 2 | 2 | 6 | S |
| 2012 WW | 3-D | CAN | 5 | 0 | 1 | 1 | 6 | G |
| **Totals WW** | | | **10** | **0** | **3** | **3** | **12** | **G,S** |

| **LaShomb, Samantha** | | | | | | | | **b. Inver Grove Heights, Minnesota, United States, July 3, 1994** |
|---|---|---|---|---|---|---|---|---|
| 2012 WW18 | 8-D | USA | 5 | 0 | 0 | 0 | 6 | S |

| **Laskova, Dominika** | | | | | | | | **b. December 20, 1996** |
|---|---|---|---|---|---|---|---|---|
| 2012 WW18 | 5-F | CZE | 5 | 0 | 0 | 0 | 10 | 6th |

| **Lavelina, Yulia** | | | | | | | | **b. Chelyabinsk Region, Russia, March 17, 1993** |
|---|---|---|---|---|---|---|---|---|
| 2010 WW18 | 8-D | RUS | 5 | 0 | 0 | 0 | 4 | 8th |

| **Lawler, Erika** | | | | | | | | **b. Fitchburg, Massachusetts, February 5, 1987** |
|---|---|---|---|---|---|---|---|---|
| 2007 WW | 2-F | USA | 5 | 2 | 4 | 6 | 2 | S |
| 2008 WW | 2-F | USA | 5 | 0 | 2 | 2 | 6 | G |
| 2009 WW | 2-F | USA | 5 | 0 | 4 | 4 | 2 | G |
| 2010 OG-W | 2-F | USA | 4 | 0 | 2 | 2 | 0 | S |
| 2012 WW | 2-F | USA | 5 | 1 | 0 | 1 | 0 | S |
| **Totals WW** | | | **20** | **3** | **10** | **13** | **10** | **2G,2S** |

| **Lebedeva, Yekaterina** | | | | | | | | **b. Sverdlovsk (Yekaterinburg), Soviet Union (Russia), September 14, 1989** |
|---|---|---|---|---|---|---|---|---|
| 2007 WW | 25-F | RUS | 4 | 0 | 0 | 0 | 0 | 7th |
| 2008 WW | 25-F | RUS | 4 | 0 | 0 | 0 | 2 | 6th |
| 2009 WW | 25-F | RUS | 4 | 0 | 1 | 1 | 4 | 5th |
| 2010 OG-W | 25-F | RUS | 5 | 0 | 1 | 1 | 2 | 6th |
| 2011 WW | 25-F | RUS | 6 | 1 | 0 | 1 | 0 | 4th |
| 2012 WW | 25-F | RUS | 5 | 1 | 0 | 1 | 2 | 6th |
| **Totals WW** | | | **23** | **2** | **1** | **3** | **8** | **—** |

| **Ledlova, Aneta** | | | | | | | | **b. Kadan, Czech Republic, December 31, 1996** |
|---|---|---|---|---|---|---|---|---|
| 2012 WW18 | 11-F | CZE | 5 | 0 | 2 | 2 | 2 | 6th |

| **Lefort, Sarah** | | | | | | | | **b. Ormstown, Quebec, February 9, 1994** |
|---|---|---|---|---|---|---|---|---|
| 2012 WW18 | 16-F | CAN | 5 | 3 | 4 | 7 | 4 | G |

| **Lehmann, Kathrin** | | | | | | | | **b. Kusnacht, Switzerland, February 27, 1980** |
|---|---|---|---|---|---|---|---|---|
| 1997 WW | 20-F | SUI | 5 | 1 | 0 | 1 | 8 | 7th |
| 1999 WW | 20-F | SUI | 5 | 1 | 0 | 1 | 2 | 8th |
| 2004 WW | 20-F | SUI | 4 | 0 | 0 | 0 | 0 | 8th |
| 2006 OG-W | 20-F | SUI | 5 | 3 | 2 | 5 | 29 | 7th |
| 2007 WW | 20-F | SUI | 4 | 1 | 1 | 2 | 6 | 5th |
| 2008 WW | 20-F | SUI | 5 | 4 | 2 | 6 | 8 | 4th |
| 2009 WW | 20-F | SUI | 4 | 2 | 2 | 4 | 4 | 7th |
| 2010 OG-W | 20-F | SUI | 5 | 2 | 4 | 6 | 0 | 5th |
| 2011 WW | 20-F | SUI | 5 | 0 | 1 | 1 | 2 | 6th |
| 2012 WW | 20-F | SUI | 6 | 2 | 3 | 5 | 4 | B |
| **Totals WW** | | | **38** | **11** | **9** | **20** | **34** | **B** |
| **Totals OG-W** | | | **10** | **5** | **6** | **11** | **29** | **—** |

| **Lehner, Stephanie** | | | | | | | | **b. Rorschacherberg, Switzerland, December 31, 1995** |
|---|---|---|---|---|---|---|---|---|
| 2011 WW18 | 18-F | SUI | 6 | 1 | 0 | 1 | 8 | 7th |
| 2012 WW18 | 18-F | SUI | 6 | 0 | 0 | 0 | 6 | 8th |
| **Totals WW18** | | | **12** | **1** | **0** | **1** | **14** | **—** |

| **Leimgruber, Darcia** | | | | | | | | **b. Basel, Switzerland, May 19, 1989** |
|---|---|---|---|---|---|---|---|---|
| 2008 WW | 7-F | SUI | 5 | 0 | 1 | 1 | 6 | 4th |
| 2009 WW | 7-F | SUI | 4 | 3 | 1 | 4 | 12 | 7th |
| 2010 OG-W | 7-F | SUI | 5 | 1 | 3 | 4 | 8 | 5th |
| 2011 WW | 7-F | SUI | 5 | 3 | 0 | 3 | 12 | 6th |
| 2012 WW | 7-F | SUI | 6 | 1 | 3 | 4 | 6 | B |
| **Totals WW** | | | **20** | **7** | **5** | **12** | **36** | **B** |

| **Lennartsson, Julia** | | | | | | | | **b. Vaxjo, Sweden, November 26, 1995** |
|---|---|---|---|---|---|---|---|---|
| 2012 WW18 | 24-F | SWE | 6 | 1 | 1 | 2 | 0 | B |

| **Leppo, Maijaliisa** | | | | | | | | **b. Espoo, Finland, February 16, 1995** |
|---|---|---|---|---|---|---|---|---|
| 2010 WW18 | 27-F | FIN | 5 | 0 | 0 | 0 | 0 | 5th |

| **Leushina, Tatyana** | | | | | | | | **b. Kirov, Russia, January 25, 1992** |
|---|---|---|---|---|---|---|---|---|
| 2009 WW18 | 14-D | RUS | 5 | 0 | 0 | 0 | 4 | 7th |

| **Lilja, Astrid** | | | | | | | | **b. Gothenburg, Sweden, July 28, 1992** |
|---|---|---|---|---|---|---|---|---|
| 2010 WW18 | 15-F | SWE | 6 | 1 | 4 | 5 | 0 | B |

| **Lillback, Cajsa** | | | | | | | | **b. Stockholm, Sweden, July 13, 1994** |
|---|---|---|---|---|---|---|---|---|
| 2010 WW18 | 2-D | SWE | 6 | 0 | 1 | 1 | 0 | B |
| 2011 WW18 | 2-D | SWE | 5 | 0 | 1 | 1 | 2 | 5th |
| 2012 WW18 | 2-D | SWE | 6 | 0 | 0 | 0 | 2 | B |
| **Totals WW18** | | | **17** | **0** | **2** | **2** | **4** | **2B** |

| **Lind, Maria** | | | | | | | | **b. Stockholm, Sweden, September 29, 1993** |
|---|---|---|---|---|---|---|---|---|
| 2011 WW18 | 17-F | SWE | 5 | 0 | 2 | 2 | 0 | 5th |

| **Lindberg, Amanda** | | | | | | | | **b. February 3, 1994** |
|---|---|---|---|---|---|---|---|---|
| 2012 WW18 | 18-F | SWE | 6 | 0 | 1 | 1 | 6 | B |

| **Lindholm, Reetta** | | | | | | | | **b. April 3, 1996** |
|---|---|---|---|---|---|---|---|---|
| 2012 WW18 | 5-D | FIN | 5 | 0 | 1 | 1 | 0 | 5th |

| **Lindstedt, Rosa** | | | | | | | | **b. Ylojarvi, Finland, January 24, 1988** |
|---|---|---|---|---|---|---|---|---|
| 2010 OG-W | 4-D | FIN | 5 | 0 | 1 | 1 | 10 | B |
| 2011 WW | 4-D | FIN | 6 | 0 | 1 | 1 | 22 | B |
| 2012 WW | 4-D | FIN | 6 | 1 | 0 | 1 | 6 | 4th |
| **Totals WW** | | | **12** | **1** | **1** | **2** | **28** | **B** |

| **Lintula, Tytti** | | | | | | | | **b. Sodankyla, Finland, May 19, 1992** |
|---|---|---|---|---|---|---|---|---|
| 2009 WW18 | 23-F | FIN | 5 | 0 | 0 | 0 | 6 | 5th |
| 2010 WW18 | 23-F | FIN | 5 | 0 | 2 | 2 | 8 | 5th |
| **Totals WW18** | | | **10** | **0** | **2** | **2** | **14** | **—** |

| **Liu, Zhixin** | | | | | | | | **b. Harbin, China, April 25, 1993** |
|---|---|---|---|---|---|---|---|---|
| 2010 OG-W | 6-D | CHN | 5 | 0 | 0 | 0 | 4 | 7th |

| **Lorence, Meghan** | | | | | | | | **b. Mounds View, Minnesota, United States, June 25, 1992** |
|---|---|---|---|---|---|---|---|---|
| 2010 WW18 | 11-F | USA | 5 | 1 | 3 | 4 | 2 | S |

| **Lorsell, Angelica** | | | | | | | | **b. Lidingo, Sweden, January 31, 1986** |
|---|---|---|---|---|---|---|---|---|
| 2004 WW | 14-F | SWE | 5 | 0 | 1 | 1 | 2 | 4th |
| 2007 WW | 14-F | SWE | 5 | 0 | 0 | 0 | 6 | B |
| 2008 WW | 14-F | SWE | 4 | 1 | 0 | 1 | 0 | 5th |
| **Totals WW** | | | **14** | **1** | **1** | **2** | **8** | **B** |

| **Lou, Yue** | | | | | | | | **b. Harbin, China, April 22, 1987** |
|---|---|---|---|---|---|---|---|---|
| 2009 WW | 5-D | CHN | 4 | 0 | 0 | 0 | 0 | 9th |
| 2010 OG-W | 5-D | CHN | 5 | 0 | 0 | 0 | 2 | 7th |

| **Lowenhielm, Michelle** | | | | | | | | **b. Stockholm, Sweden, March 22, 1995** |
|---|---|---|---|---|---|---|---|---|
| 2010 WW18 | 19-F | SWE | 6 | 0 | 1 | 1 | 6 | B |
| 2011 WW18 | 19-F | SWE | 5 | 3 | 0 | 3 | 6 | 5th |
| 2012 WW18 | 19-F | SWE | 6 | 2 | 3 | 5 | 2 | B |
| 2012 WW | 27-F | SWE | 5 | 0 | 1 | 1 | 2 | 5th |
| **Totals WW18** | | | **17** | **5** | **4** | **9** | **14** | **2B** |

| **Lubbert, Michelle** | | | | | | | | **b. Werne, Germany, November 20, 1996** |
|---|---|---|---|---|---|---|---|---|
| 2012 WW18 | 3-F | GER | 6 | 0 | 0 | 0 | 4 | 4th |

| **Lucova, Livia** | | | | | | | | **b. January 16, 1993** |
|---|---|---|---|---|---|---|---|---|
| 2012 WW | 71-F | SVK | 5 | 0 | 0 | 0 | 0 | 8th |

| **Lund, Pia** | | | | | | | | **b. Nurmijarvi, Finland, July 19, 1990** |
|---|---|---|---|---|---|---|---|---|
| 2008 WW18 | 23-F | FIN | 5 | 3 | 1 | 4 | 4 | 6th |
| 2011 WW | 25-F | FIN | 6 | 1 | 0 | 1 | 4 | B |

| **Ma, Rui** | | | | | | | | **b. Harbin, China, March 29, 1989** |
|---|---|---|---|---|---|---|---|---|
| 2007 WW | 16-F | CHN | 4 | 1 | 0 | 1 | 0 | 6th |
| 2008 WW | 16-F | CHN | 4 | 0 | 0 | 0 | 6 | 8th |
| 2009 WW | 16-F | CHN | 4 | 0 | 0 | 0 | 4 | 9th |
| 2010 OG-W | 16-F | CHN | 5 | 0 | 1 | 1 | 4 | 7th |
| **Totals WW** | | | **12** | **1** | **0** | **1** | **10** | **—** |

| **Maamaki, Jenni** | | | | | | | | **b. August 28, 1996** |
|---|---|---|---|---|---|---|---|---|
| 2012 WW18 | 29-F | FIN | 5 | 0 | 0 | 0 | 0 | 5th |

| **MacAulay, Shannon** | | | | | | | | **b. Mt. Herbert, Prince Edward Island, June 22, 1994** |
|---|---|---|---|---|---|---|---|---|
| 2012 WW18 | 26-F | CAN | 5 | 0 | 3 | 3 | 0 | G |

| **MacDonald, Caitlin** | | | | | | | | **b. Prince George, British Columbia, Canada, May 8, 1992** |
|---|---|---|---|---|---|---|---|---|
| 2010 WW18 | 5-D | CAN | 5 | 1 | 3 | 4 | 2 | G |

| **MacDonnell, Sarah** | | | | | | | | **b. Quispamsis, New Brunswick, Canada, February 24, 1993** |
|---|---|---|---|---|---|---|---|---|
| 2011 WW18 | 26-F | CAN | 5 | 3 | 2 | 5 | 2 | S |

| **Maenpanen, Karoliina** | | | | | | | | **b. Kauhava, Finland, April 11, 1992** |
|---|---|---|---|---|---|---|---|---|
| 2008 WW18 | 5-D | FIN | 5 | 1 | 0 | 1 | 12 | 6th |
| 2009 WW18 | 4-D | FIN | 5 | 0 | 0 | 0 | 6 | 5th |
| 2010 WW18 | 4-D | FIN | 5 | 0 | 1 | 1 | 14 | 5th |
| **Totals WW18** | | | **15** | **1** | **1** | **2** | **32** | **—** |

| **Makinen, Niina** | | | | | | | | **b. Hankasalmi, Finland, April 18, 1992** |
|---|---|---|---|---|---|---|---|---|
| 2008 WW18 | 18-F | FIN | 5 | 0 | 0 | 0 | 8 | 6th |
| 2009 WW18 | 18-F | FIN | 5 | 0 | 0 | 0 | 6 | 5th |
| 2010 WW18 | 18-F | FIN | 5 | 1 | 4 | 5 | 12 | 5th |
| 2011 WW | 14-F | FIN | 6 | 0 | 0 | 0 | 0 | B |
| **Totals WW18** | | | **15** | **1** | **4** | **5** | **26** | **—** |

| **Malmstrom, Johanna** | | | | | | | | **b. Gavle, Sweden, April 10, 1986** |
|---|---|---|---|---|---|---|---|---|
| 2011 WW | 6-D | SWE | 5 | 0 | 0 | 0 | 16 | 5th |

| **Mangene, Meagan** | | | | | | | | **b. Manorville, New York, United States, August 21, 1992** |
|---|---|---|---|---|---|---|---|---|
| 2008 WW18 | 19-F | USA | 5 | 2 | 1 | 3 | 0 | G |
| 2009 WW18 | 25-D | USA | 4 | 1 | 2 | 3 | 2 | G |
| 2010 WW18 | 25-D | USA | 5 | 2 | 5 | 7 | 4 | S |
| **Totals WW18** | | | **14** | **5** | **8** | **13** | **6** | **2G,S** |

| **Manhartova, Lucie** | | | | | | | | **b. Prague, Czechoslovakia (Czech Republic), May 14, 1991** |
|---|---|---|---|---|---|---|---|---|
| 2008 WW18 | 22-F | CZE | 5 | 3 | 1 | 4 | 8 | B |
| 2009 WW18 | 22-F | CZE | 5 | 1 | 1 | 2 | 6 | 4th |
| **Totals WW18** | | | **10** | **4** | **2** | **6** | **14** | **B** |

| **Maresova, Adela** | | | | | | | | **b. Trebic, Czech Republic, April 6, 1994** |
|---|---|---|---|---|---|---|---|---|
| 2010 WW18 | 17-F | CZE | 5 | 0 | 0 | 0 | 0 | 7th |

| **Markova, Elvira** | | | | | | | | **b. Kirov, Russia, February 1, 1992** |
|---|---|---|---|---|---|---|---|---|
| 2010 WW18 | 2-D | RUS | 5 | 0 | 0 | 0 | 0 | 8th |

| **Markstrom, Caroline** | | | | | | | | **b. Sundsvall, Sweden, May 29, 1994** |
|---|---|---|---|---|---|---|---|---|
| 2011 WW18 | 9-D | SWE | 5 | 0 | 0 | 0 | 2 | 5th |
| 2012 WW18 | 4-D | SWE | 6 | 0 | 0 | 0 | 6 | B |
| **Totals WW18** | | | **11** | **0** | **0** | **0** | **8** | **B** |

| **Martinsson, Emma** | | | | | | | | **b. Gothenburg, Sweden, July 29, 1993** |
|---|---|---|---|---|---|---|---|---|
| 2011 WW18 | 8-F | SWE | 5 | 2 | 0 | 2 | 4 | 5th |

| **Marty, Julia** | | | | | | | | **b. Zurich, Switzerland, April 16, 1988** |
|---|---|---|---|---|---|---|---|---|
| 2004 WW | 6-D | SUI | 4 | 2 | 0 | 2 | 0 | 8th |
| 2006 OG-W | 6-D | SUI | 5 | 2 | 1 | 3 | 4 | 7th |
| 2007 WW | 6-D | SUI | 4 | 0 | 1 | 1 | 6 | 5th |
| 2008 WW | 6-D | SUI | 5 | 0 | 2 | 2 | 12 | 4th |
| 2009 WW | 6-D | SUI | 4 | 0 | 0 | 0 | 0 | 7th |
| 2010 OG-W | 6-D | SUI | 5 | 0 | 1 | 1 | 2 | 5th |
| 2011 WW | 6-D | SUI | 5 | 1 | 2 | 3 | 6 | 6th |
| 2012 WW | 6-D | SUI | 6 | 5 | 2 | 7 | 6 | B |
| **Totals WW** | | | **28** | **8** | **7** | **15** | **30** | **B** |
| **Totals OG-W** | | | **10** | **2** | **2** | **4** | **6** | **—** |

| **Marty, Stefanie** | | | | | | | | **b. Zurich, Switzerland, April 16, 1988** |
|---|---|---|---|---|---|---|---|---|
| 2004 WW | 18-F | SUI | 4 | 1 | 0 | 1 | 0 | 8th |
| 2006 OG-W | 69-F | SUI | 5 | 2 | 1 | 3 | 2 | 7th |
| 2007 WW | 69-F | SUI | 4 | 1 | 0 | 1 | 6 | 5th |
| 2008 WW | 9-F | SUI | 5 | 4 | 2 | 6 | 10 | 4th |
| 2009 WW | 9-F | SUI | 4 | 0 | 0 | 0 | 0 | 7th |
| 2010 OG-W | 9-F | SUI | 5 | 9 | 2 | 11 | 6 | 5th |
| 2011 WW | 9-F | SUI | 5 | 2 | 1 | 3 | 4 | 6th |
| 2012 WW | 9-F | SUI | 6 | 2 | 4 | 6 | 10 | B |
| **Totals WW** | | | **28** | **10** | **7** | **17** | **30** | **B** |
| **Totals OG-W** | | | **10** | **11** | **3** | **14** | **8** | **—** |

| **Marvin, Gisele "Gigi"** | | | | | | | | **b. Warroad, Minnesota, United States, March 7, 1987** |
|---|---|---|---|---|---|---|---|---|
| 2007 WW | 18-F | USA | 5 | 2 | 1 | 3 | 8 | S |
| 2008 WW | 18-F | USA | 5 | 1 | 2 | 3 | 12 | G |
| 2009 WW | 19-F | USA | 5 | 2 | 1 | 3 | 4 | G |
| 2010 OG-W | 19-F | USA | 5 | 0 | 3 | 3 | 2 | S |
| 2011 WW | 19-F | USA | 5 | 0 | 3 | 3 | 0 | G |
| 2012 WW | 19-D | USA | 5 | 3 | 6 | 9 | 2 | S |
| **Totals WW** | | | **25** | **8** | **13** | **21** | **26** | **3G,2S** |

~WW All-Star Team/Defence (2012)

| **Marvin, Layla** | | | | | | | | **b. Warroad, Minnesota, United States, March 8, 1993** |
|---|---|---|---|---|---|---|---|---|
| 2011 WW18 | 3-F | USA | 5 | 6 | 1 | 7 | 2 | G |

| **Marx, Nadine** | | | | | | | | **b. Munich, Germany, November 2, 1992** |
|---|---|---|---|---|---|---|---|---|
| 2010 WW18 | 23-F | GER | 6 | 0 | 1 | 1 | 2 | 4th |

| **Mastel, Briana** | | | | | | | | **b. Wallingford, Connecticut, United States, November 8, 1994** |
|---|---|---|---|---|---|---|---|---|
| 2012 WW18 | 7-D | USA | 5 | 1 | 1 | 2 | 0 | S |

| **Matejova, Michaela** | | | | | | | | **b. Martin, Czechoslovakia (Slovakia), March 2, 1986** |
|---|---|---|---|---|---|---|---|---|
| 2010 OG-W | 15-D | SVK | 4 | 0 | 0 | 0 | 0 | 8th |
| 2011 WW | 20-D | SVK | 5 | 0 | 1 | 1 | 4 | 7th |

| **Mazankova, Klara** | | | | | | | | **b. Brno, Czech Republic, September 10, 1995** |
|---|---|---|---|---|---|---|---|---|
| 2012 WW18 | 17-F | CZE | 5 | 1 | 0 | 1 | 29 | 6th |

| **McIntosh, Laura** | | | | | | | | **b. Waterloo, Ontario, Canada, January 21, 1990** |
|---|---|---|---|---|---|---|---|---|
| 2008 WW18 | 17-F | CAN | 5 | 0 | 4 | 4 | 2 | S |

| **McKeough, Stefanie** | | | | | | | | **b. Carlsbad Springs, Ontario, Canada, January 27, 1991** |
|---|---|---|---|---|---|---|---|---|
| 2009 WW18 | 3-D | CAN | 5 | 0 | 5 | 5 | 6 | S |

| **McMillen, Milica** | | | | | | | | **b. St. Paul, Minnesota, United States, July 13, 1993** |
|---|---|---|---|---|---|---|---|---|
| 2011 WW18 | 10-D | USA | 5 | 4 | 2 | 6 | 4 | G |

~WW18 IIHF Directorate Best Defenceman (2011)

| **McParland, Jenna** | | | | | | | | **b. Schreiber, Ontario, Canada, May 12, 1992** |
|---|---|---|---|---|---|---|---|---|
| 2010 WW18 | 15-F | CAN | 5 | 4 | 3 | 7 | 2 | G |

| **Meier, Christine** | | | | | | | | **b. Bulach, Switzerland, May 24, 1986** |
|---|---|---|---|---|---|---|---|---|
| 2004 WW | 16-D | SUI | 4 | 0 | 0 | 0 | 0 | 8th |
| 2006 OG-W | 66-F | SUI | 5 | 1 | 0 | 1 | 2 | 7th |
| 2007 WW | 66-F | SUI | 4 | 1 | 2 | 3 | 4 | 5th |
| 2008 WW | 66-F | SUI | 5 | 0 | 2 | 2 | 2 | 4th |
| 2009 WW | 16-F | SUI | 4 | 2 | 3 | 5 | 4 | 7th |
| 2010 OG-W | 16-F | SUI | 5 | 0 | 3 | 3 | 6 | 5th |
| 2011 WW | 16-D | SUI | 5 | 1 | 1 | 2 | 2 | 6th |
| **Totals WW** | | | **22** | **4** | **8** | **12** | **12** | **—** |
| **Totals OG-W** | | | **10** | **1** | **3** | **4** | **8** | **—** |

| **Mercer, Carly** | | | | | | | | **b. Exeter, Ontario, Canada, February 17, 1992** |
|---|---|---|---|---|---|---|---|---|
| 2010 WW18 | 10-F | CAN | 5 | 1 | 2 | 3 | 2 | G |

| **Mercer, Cayley** | | | | | | | | **b. Exeter, Ontario, Canada, January 18, 1994** |
|---|---|---|---|---|---|---|---|---|
| 2011 WW18 | 20-F | CAN | 5 | 2 | 3 | 5 | 0 | S |
| 2012 WW18 | 20-F | CAN | 5 | 4 | 3 | 7 | 0 | G |
| **Totals WW18** | | | **10** | **6** | **6** | **12** | **0** | **G,S** |

| **Merilainen, Kristiina** | | | | | | | | **b. January 20, 1995** |
|---|---|---|---|---|---|---|---|---|
| 2012 WW18 | 6-D | FIN | 5 | 0 | 0 | 0 | 2 | 5th |

| **Mertanen, Terhi** | | | | | | | | **b. Joensuu, Finland, April 4, 1981** |
|---|---|---|---|---|---|---|---|---|
| 2001 WW | 6-D | FIN | 5 | 0 | 2 | 2 | 6 | 4th |
| 2002 OG-W | 9-D | FIN | 5 | 0 | 1 | 1 | 2 | 4th |
| 2004 WW | 9-D | FIN | 5 | 2 | 1 | 3 | 2 | B |
| 2005 WW | 9-D | FIN | 5 | 1 | 1 | 2 | 2 | 4th |
| 2006 OG-W | 9-D | FIN | 5 | 0 | 0 | 0 | 6 | 4th |
| 2010 OG-W | 19-D | FIN | 5 | 0 | 0 | 0 | 6 | B |
| 2011 WW | 19-D | FIN | 6 | 0 | 0 | 0 | 4 | B |
| 2012 WW | 19-D | FIN | 6 | 0 | 3 | 3 | 0 | 4th |
| **Totals WW** | | | **27** | **3** | **7** | **10** | **14** | **2B** |
| **Totals OG-W** | | | **15** | **0** | **1** | **1** | **14** | **B** |

| **Michielin, Rahel** | | | | | | | | **b. Frauenfeld, Switzerland, October 11, 1990** |
|---|---|---|---|---|---|---|---|---|
| 2008 WW18 | 19-F | SUI | 5 | 0 | 1 | 1 | 6 | 7th |
| 2008 WW | 21-F | SUI | 5 | 0 | 0 | 0 | 4 | 4th |
| 2009 WW | 19-F | SUI | 4 | 0 | 0 | 0 | 0 | 7th |
| 2010 OG-W | 19-F | SUI | 5 | 0 | 0 | 0 | 2 | 5th |
| 2011 WW | 19-F | SUI | 5 | 0 | 0 | 0 | 0 | 6th |
| 2012 WW | 19-D | SUI | 6 | 0 | 0 | 0 | 2 | B |
| **Totals WW** | | | **20** | **0** | **0** | **0** | **6** | **B** |

| Mihalicova, Alica | | | | | | | | b. Topolcany, Slovakia, May 27, 1993 |
|---|---|---|---|---|---|---|---|---|
| 2011 WW | 29-F | SVK | 5 | 0 | 0 | 0 | 0 | 7th |
| 2012 WW | 29-F | SVK | 5 | 0 | 0 | 0 | 2 | 8th |
| **Totals WW** | | | **10** | **0** | **0** | **0** | **2** | **—** |

| Mikeskova, Miriam | | | | | | | | b. May 19, 1995 |
|---|---|---|---|---|---|---|---|---|
| 2012 WW | 16-F | SVK | 5 | 0 | 0 | 0 | 0 | 8th |

| Mikkelson, Meaghan | | | | | | | | b. St. Albert, Alberta, Canada, January 4, 1985 |
|---|---|---|---|---|---|---|---|---|
| 2008 WW | 12-D | CAN | 5 | 0 | 0 | 0 | 2 | S |
| 2009 WW | 12-D | CAN | 5 | 0 | 3 | 3 | 6 | S |
| 2010 OG-W | 12-D | CAN | 5 | 0 | 0 | 0 | 2 | G |
| 2011 WW | 12-D | CAN | 5 | 3 | 0 | 3 | 0 | S |
| 2012 WW | 12-D | CAN | 5 | 0 | 5 | 5 | 2 | G |
| **Totals WW** | | | **20** | **3** | **8** | **11** | **10** | **G,3S** |

~WW IIHF Directorate Best Defenceman (2011), WW All-Star Team/Defence (2011)

| Mishlanova, Anastasia | | | | | | | | b. Saha Yakutia, Russia, November 24, 1993 |
|---|---|---|---|---|---|---|---|---|
| 2009 WW18 | 4-F | RUS | 5 | 0 | 0 | 0 | 4 | 7th |

| Mitrofanova, Elina | | | | | | | | b. Sverdlovsk Region, Russia, January 28, 1992 |
|---|---|---|---|---|---|---|---|---|
| 2008 WW18 | 8-D | RUS | 5 | 0 | 0 | 0 | 12 | 8th |
| 2009 WW18 | 9-D | RUS | 5 | 0 | 2 | 2 | 29 | 7th |
| 2010 WW18 | 9-F | RUS | 5 | 1 | 0 | 1 | 8 | 8th |
| **Totals WW18** | | | **15** | **1** | **2** | **3** | **49** | **—** |

| Moldabai, Daria | | | | | | | | b. Uzyn-Agash, Kazakhstan, January 23, 1993 |
|---|---|---|---|---|---|---|---|---|
| 2009 WW | 33-D | KAZ | 4 | 0 | 0 | 0 | 0 | 6th |
| 2011 WW | 25-D | KAZ | 5 | 0 | 0 | 0 | 0 | 8th |
| **Totals WW** | | | **9** | **0** | **0** | **0** | **0** | **—** |

| Monakhova, Elizaveta | | | | | | | | b. Moscow, Russia, June 24, 1992 |
|---|---|---|---|---|---|---|---|---|
| 2008 WW18 | 3-F | RUS | 5 | 0 | 0 | 0 | 2 | 8th |
| 2009 WW18 | 5-F | RUS | 5 | 0 | 0 | 0 | 2 | 7th |
| **Totals WW18** | | | **10** | **0** | **0** | **0** | **4** | **—** |

| Moravcikova, Zuzana | | | | | | | | b. Ruzomberok, Czechoslovakia (Slovakia), October 23, 1980 |
|---|---|---|---|---|---|---|---|---|
| 2010 OG-W | 10-F | SVK | 5 | 0 | 0 | 0 | 0 | 8th |

| Morii, Mai | | | | | | | | b. Toyama, Japan, December 28, 1993 |
|---|---|---|---|---|---|---|---|---|
| 2010 WW18 | 11-F | JPN | 5 | 1 | 1 | 2 | 0 | 6th |
| 2011 WW18 | 12-F | JPN | 6 | 1 | 2 | 3 | 6 | 8th |
| **Totals WW18** | | | **11** | **2** | **3** | **5** | **6** | **—** |

| Moritake, Runa | | | | | | | | b. Hokkaido, Japan, March 9, 1993 |
|---|---|---|---|---|---|---|---|---|
| 2010 WW18 | 12-F | JPN | 5 | 1 | 0 | 1 | 0 | 6th |
| 2011 WW18 | 26-F | JPN | 6 | 2 | 1 | 3 | 0 | 8th |
| **Totals WW18** | | | **11** | **3** | **1** | **4** | **0** | **—** |

| Mrazova, Katerina | | | | | | | | b. Prague, Czechoslovakia (Czech Republic), October 19, 1992 |
|---|---|---|---|---|---|---|---|---|
| 2008 WW18 | 12-F | CZE | 5 | 1 | 2 | 3 | 6 | B |
| 2009 WW18 | 23-F | CZE | 5 | 2 | 2 | 4 | 4 | 4th |
| 2010 WW18 | 23-F | CZE | 5 | 0 | 5 | 5 | 2 | 7th |
| **Totals WW18** | | | **15** | **3** | **9** | **12** | **12** | **B** |

| Muller, Laura | | | | | | | | b. Runenberg, Switzerland, June 2, 1992 |
|---|---|---|---|---|---|---|---|---|
| 2008 WW18 | 17-F | SUI | 5 | 0 | 0 | 0 | 0 | 7th |
| 2009 WW18 | 17-F | SUI | 5 | 0 | 0 | 0 | 0 | 8th |
| **Totals WW18** | | | **10** | **0** | **0** | **0** | **0** | **—** |

| Mussatayeva, Viktoria | | | | | | | | b. Uch-Aral, Soviet Union (Kazakhstan), April 25, 1981 |
|---|---|---|---|---|---|---|---|---|
| 2009 WW | 12-D | KAZ | 4 | 0 | 0 | 0 | 6 | 6th |
| 2011 WW | 12-D | KAZ | 5 | 0 | 0 | 0 | 0 | 8th |
| **Totals WW** | | | **9** | **0** | **0** | **0** | **6** | **—** |

| Myren, Klara | | | | | | | | b. Borlange, Sweden, May 25, 1991 |
|---|---|---|---|---|---|---|---|---|
| 2008 WW18 | 19-F | SWE | 5 | 3 | 3 | 6 | 12 | 4th |
| 2008 WW | 19-F | SWE | 4 | 3 | 0 | 3 | 4 | 5th |
| 2009 WW18 | 19-F | SWE | 5 | 2 | 8 | 10 | 14 | B |
| 2009 WW | 19-F | SWE | 5 | 1 | 0 | 1 | 2 | 4th |
| 2010 OG-W | 19-F | SWE | 5 | 0 | 2 | 2 | 0 | 4th |
| 2012 WW | 19-F | SWE | 5 | 0 | 1 | 1 | 0 | 5th |
| **Totals WW18** | | | **10** | **5** | **11** | **16** | **26** | **B** |
| **Totals WW** | | | **14** | **4** | **1** | **5** | **6** | **—** |

| Nabholz, Katrin | | | | | | | | b. Basel, Switzerland, April 3, 1986 |
|---|---|---|---|---|---|---|---|---|
| 2007 WW | 2-F | SUI | 4 | 0 | 1 | 1 | 0 | 5th |
| 2008 WW | 2-F | SUI | 5 | 0 | 0 | 0 | 2 | 4th |
| 2009 WW | 2-F | SUI | 4 | 0 | 1 | 1 | 2 | 7th |
| 2010 OG-W | 2-F | SUI | 5 | 0 | 0 | 0 | 0 | 5th |
| 2011 WW | 2-F | SUI | 5 | 0 | 0 | 0 | 2 | 6th |
| 2012 WW | 2-F | SUI | 6 | 1 | 1 | 2 | 0 | B |
| **Totals WW** | | | **24** | **1** | **3** | **4** | **6** | **B** |

| Nakagawa, Mizuho | | | | | | | | b. Hokkaido, Japan, June 18, 1993 |
|---|---|---|---|---|---|---|---|---|
| 2011 WW18 | 23-F | JPN | 6 | 0 | 0 | 0 | 4 | 8th |

| Nakamura, Ami | | | | | | | | b. Hokkaido, Japan, November 15, 1987 |
|---|---|---|---|---|---|---|---|---|
| 2008 WW | 23-F | JPN | 4 | 0 | 0 | 0 | 2 | 7th |

| Navratilova, Dominika | | | | | | | | b. Karvina, Czechoslovakia (Czech Republic), July 25, 1991 |
|---|---|---|---|---|---|---|---|---|
| 2008 WW18 | 17-D | CZE | 5 | 0 | 0 | 0 | 0 | B |
| 2009 WW18 | 17-D | CZE | 5 | 0 | 0 | 0 | 6 | 4th |
| **Totals WW18** | | | **10** | **0** | **0** | **0** | **6** | **B** |

| Nelson, Alex | | | | | | | | b. Andover, Minnesota, United States, January 17, 1991 |
|---|---|---|---|---|---|---|---|---|
| 2009 WW18 | 23-F | USA | 5 | 1 | 2 | 3 | 0 | G |

| Ness, Abby | | | | | | | | b. Roseau, Minnesota, United States, April 8, 1993 |
|---|---|---|---|---|---|---|---|---|
| 2011 WW18 | 23-F | USA | 5 | 3 | 2 | 5 | 0 | G |

| Nesutova, Denisa | | | | | | | | b. October 18, 1996 |
|---|---|---|---|---|---|---|---|---|
| 2012 WW18 | 10-F | CZE | 5 | 0 | 0 | 0 | 0 | 6th |

| Nevalainen, Frida | | | | | | | | b. Umea, Sweden, January 27, 1987 |
|---|---|---|---|---|---|---|---|---|
| 2004 WW | 3-D | SWE | 5 | 0 | 1 | 1 | 12 | 4th |
| 2005 WW | 3-D | SWE | 5 | 1 | 0 | 1 | 2 | B |
| 2006 OG-W | 3-D | SWE | 5 | 0 | 2 | 2 | 6 | S |
| 2007 WW | 3-D | SWE | 5 | 0 | 1 | 1 | 2 | B |
| 2008 WW | 3-D | SWE | 4 | 0 | 0 | 0 | 4 | 5th |
| 2009 WW | 3-D | SWE | 5 | 1 | 3 | 4 | 4 | 4th |
| 2010 OG-W | 3-D | SWE | 5 | 0 | 1 | 1 | 6 | 4th |
| 2011 WW | 3-D | SWE | 5 | 2 | 0 | 2 | 8 | 5th |
| 2012 WW | 3-D | SWE | 5 | 0 | 2 | 2 | 2 | 5th |
| **Totals WW** | | | **34** | **4** | **7** | **11** | **34** | **2B** |
| **Totals OG-W** | | | **10** | **0** | **3** | **3** | **12** | **S** |

| Nihonyanagi, Shoko | | | | | | | | b. Asahikawa, Japan, September 5, 1981 |
|---|---|---|---|---|---|---|---|---|
| 2004 WW | 13-F | JPN | 4 | 1 | 2 | 3 | 4 | 9th |
| 2008 WW | 13-F | JPN | 4 | 0 | 0 | 0 | 2 | 7th |
| **Totals WW** | | | **8** | **1** | **2** | **3** | **6** | **—** |

| Nikolayeva, Yekaterina | | | | | | | | b. October 5, 1995 |
|---|---|---|---|---|---|---|---|---|
| 2012 WW18 | 18-D | RUS | 6 | 0 | 0 | 0 | 6 | 7th |

| Niskanen, Tanja | | | | | | | | b. Juankoski, Finland, September 11, 1992 |
|---|---|---|---|---|---|---|---|---|
| 2008 WW18 | 16-F | FIN | 5 | 2 | 0 | 2 | 14 | 6th |
| 2009 WW18 | 16-F | FIN | 5 | 0 | 1 | 1 | 2 | 5th |
| 2010 WW18 | 16-F | FIN | 5 | 3 | 2 | 5 | 4 | 5th |
| 2011 WW | 24-F | FIN | 6 | 1 | 3 | 4 | 2 | B |
| **Totals WW18** | | | **15** | **5** | **3** | **8** | **20** | **—** |

| Nonaka, Emi | | | | | | | | b. Tomakomai, Japan, August 21, 1984 |
|---|---|---|---|---|---|---|---|---|
| 2000 WW | 5-D | JPN | 5 | 0 | 0 | 0 | 2 | 8th |
| 2004 WW | 8-D | JPN | 4 | 0 | 0 | 0 | 6 | 9th |
| 2009 WW | 4-D | JPN | 4 | 0 | 1 | 1 | 4 | 8th |
| **Totals WW** | | | **13** | **0** | **1** | **1** | **12** | **—** |

| Nordin, Emma | | | | | | | | b. Ornskoldsvik, Sweden, March 22, 1991 |
|---|---|---|---|---|---|---|---|---|
| 2008 WW18 | 5-D | SWE | 5 | 1 | 0 | 1 | 2 | 4th |
| 2008 WW | 27-D | SWE | 4 | 0 | 2 | 2 | 0 | 5th |
| 2009 WW18 | 5-D | SWE | 5 | 2 | 1 | 3 | 8 | B |
| 2009 WW | 17-D | SWE | 5 | 0 | 1 | 1 | 0 | 4th |
| 2010 OG-W | 27-D | SWE | 5 | 0 | 1 | 1 | 2 | 4th |
| 2011 WW | 27-D | SWE | 5 | 0 | 1 | 1 | 0 | 5th |
| **Totals WW18** | | | **10** | **3** | **1** | **4** | **10** | **B** |
| **Totals WW** | | | **14** | **0** | **4** | **4** | **0** | **—** |

| Novakova, Lucie | | | | | | | | b. Kladno, Czechoslovakia (Czech Republic), May 29, 1991 |
|---|---|---|---|---|---|---|---|---|
| 2008 WW18 | 7-F | CZE | 5 | 0 | 0 | 0 | 0 | B |
| 2009 WW18 | 7-F | CZE | 5 | 2 | 0 | 2 | 6 | 4th |
| **Totals WW18** | | | **10** | **2** | **0** | **2** | **6** | **B** |

| Novakova, Mikaela | | | | | | | | b. Prague, Czech Republic, December 2, 1994 |
|---|---|---|---|---|---|---|---|---|
| 2010 WW18 | 13-D | CZE | 5 | 0 | 0 | 0 | 2 | 7th |
| 2011 WW18 | 28-D | CZE | 6 | 0 | 0 | 0 | 2 | 4th |
| 2012 WW18 | 28-D | CZE | 5 | 0 | 0 | 0 | 10 | 6th |
| **Totals WW18** | | | **16** | **0** | **0** | **0** | **14** | **—** |

| Novotny, Miriam | | | | | | | | b. Fritzlar, Germany, October 22, 1992 |
|---|---|---|---|---|---|---|---|---|
| 2008 WW18 | 4-D | GER | 5 | 0 | 1 | 1 | 4 | 5th |
| 2009 WW18 | 4-D | GER | 5 | 0 | 0 | 0 | 10 | 6th |
| 2010 WW18 | 4-D | GER | 6 | 0 | 0 | 0 | 2 | 4th |
| **Totals WW18** | | | **16** | **0** | **1** | **1** | **16** | **—** |

| **Nurgalieva, Galia** | **b. Kyzyl-Orda, Kazakhstan, January 27, 1992** | | | | | | | |
|---|---|---|---|---|---|---|---|---|
| 2009 WW | 15-F | KAZ | 4 | 0 | 0 | 0 | 0 | 6th |
| 2011 WW | 15-F | KAZ | 5 | 0 | 0 | 0 | 0 | 8th |
| **Totals WW** | | | **9** | **0** | **0** | **0** | **0** | **—** |

| **Nurmesniemi, Katja** | **b. Espoo, Finland, April 29, 1993** | | | | | | | |
|---|---|---|---|---|---|---|---|---|
| 2010 WW18 | 6-D | FIN | 4 | 0 | 0 | 0 | 0 | 5th |
| 2011 WW18 | 6-D | FIN | 5 | 0 | 0 | 0 | 12 | B |
| **Totals WW18** | | | **9** | **0** | **0** | **0** | **12** | **B** |

| **Nussbaum, Lucrece** | **b. Worb, Switzerland, October 7, 1986** | | | | | | | |
|---|---|---|---|---|---|---|---|---|
| 2007 WW | 18-D | SUI | 4 | 0 | 0 | 0 | 4 | 5th |
| 2008 WW | 18-D | SUI | 5 | 1 | 3 | 4 | 14 | 4th |
| 2009 WW | 18-D | SUI | 4 | 1 | 0 | 1 | 6 | 7th |
| 2010 OG-W | 18-D | SUI | 5 | 1 | 2 | 3 | 4 | 5th |
| **Totals WW** | | | **13** | **2** | **3** | **5** | **24** | **—** |

| **Nuutinen, Emma** | **b. December 7, 1996** | | | | | | | |
|---|---|---|---|---|---|---|---|---|
| 2012 WW18 | 24-F | FIN | 5 | 1 | 1 | 2 | 4 | 5th |

| **Nystrom, Olivia** | **b. Vaxholm, Sweden, May 5, 1993** | | | | | | | |
|---|---|---|---|---|---|---|---|---|
| 2011 WW18 | 23-F | SWE | 5 | 0 | 0 | 0 | 4 | 5th |

| **Odaira, Momoka** | **b. Tochigi, Japan, June 3, 1993** | | | | | | | |
|---|---|---|---|---|---|---|---|---|
| 2011 WW18 | 28-F | JPN | 6 | 1 | 0 | 1 | 0 | 8th |

| **Offermann, Valerie** | **b. Cologne, Germany, December 16, 1994** | | | | | | | |
|---|---|---|---|---|---|---|---|---|
| 2010 WW18 | 26-F | GER | 6 | 0 | 0 | 0 | 2 | 4th |
| 2011 WW18 | 26-F | GER | 5 | 0 | 0 | 0 | 2 | 6th |
| **Totals WW18** | | | **11** | **0** | **0** | **0** | **4** | **—** |

| **Ohtani (Tamada), Yoko** | **b. Hokkaido, Japan, August 2, 1980** | | | | | | | |
|---|---|---|---|---|---|---|---|---|
| 2000 WW* | 20-F | JPN | 5 | 0 | 0 | 0 | 2 | 8th |
| 2008 WW | 19-F | JPN | 4 | 0 | 0 | 0 | 0 | 7th |
| **Totals WW** | | | **9** | **0** | **0** | **0** | **2** | **—** |

*played under maiden name Yoko Tamada

| **Oinonen, Jenni** | **b. Joensuu, Finland, June 4, 1993** | | | | | | | |
|---|---|---|---|---|---|---|---|---|
| 2010 WW18 | 9-D | FIN | 5 | 0 | 1 | 1 | 2 | 5th |
| 2011 WW18 | 9-D | FIN | 6 | 1 | 0 | 1 | 4 | B |
| **Totals WW18** | | | **11** | **1** | **1** | **2** | **6** | **B** |

| **Oles, Leslie** | **b. Beaconsfield, Quebec, Canada, November 18, 1990** | | | | | | | |
|---|---|---|---|---|---|---|---|---|
| 2008 WW18 | 7-F | CAN | 4 | 2 | 1 | 3 | 4 | S |

| **Ollikainen, Suvi** | **b. Kristiinankaupunki, Finland, March 6, 1995** | | | | | | | |
|---|---|---|---|---|---|---|---|---|
| 2011 WW18 | 16-F | FIN | 6 | 0 | 1 | 1 | 0 | B |
| 2012 WW18 | 16-F | FIN | 5 | 1 | 2 | 3 | 2 | 5th |
| **Totals WW18** | | | **11** | **1** | **3** | **4** | **2** | **B** |

| **Olofsson, Johanna** | **b. Stensele, Sweden, July 13, 1991** | | | | | | | |
|---|---|---|---|---|---|---|---|---|
| 2009 WW18 | 23-D | SWE | 5 | 0 | 0 | 0 | 0 | B |
| 2012 WW | 7-D | SWE | 5 | 1 | 0 | 1 | 4 | 5th |

| **Olsson, Melinda** | **b. Overkalix, Sweden, September 9, 1992** | | | | | | | |
|---|---|---|---|---|---|---|---|---|
| 2009 WW18 | 18-F | SWE | 5 | 1 | 0 | 1 | 2 | B |
| 2010 WW18 | 18-F | SWE | 6 | 1 | 1 | 2 | 4 | B |
| **Totals WW18** | | | **11** | **2** | **1** | **3** | **6** | **2B** |

| **Orlova, Anastasia** | **b. Kazakhstanskaya, Kazakhstan, October 29, 1992** | | | | | | | |
|---|---|---|---|---|---|---|---|---|
| 2011 WW | 23-F | KAZ | 5 | 0 | 0 | 0 | 0 | 8th |

| **Orszaghova, Petra** | **b. Banska Bystrica, Czechoslovakia (Slovakia), April 7, 1981** | | | | | | | |
|---|---|---|---|---|---|---|---|---|
| 2010 OG-W | 4-D | SVK | 5 | 0 | 0 | 0 | 2 | 8th |
| 2011 WW | 4-D | SVK | 5 | 0 | 0 | 0 | 2 | 7th |
| 2012 WW | 4-D | SVK | 5 | 0 | 0 | 0 | 4 | 8th |
| **Totals WW** | | | **10** | **0** | **0** | **0** | **6** | **—** |

| **Osawa, Chiho** | **b. Hokkaido, Japan, February 10, 1992** | | | | | | | |
|---|---|---|---|---|---|---|---|---|
| 2009 WW | 9-F | JPN | 4 | 0 | 0 | 0 | 0 | 8th |
| 2010 WW18 | 9-F | JPN | 5 | 1 | 0 | 1 | 2 | 6th |

| **Ostberg, Cecilia** | **b. Leksand, Sweden, January 15, 1991** | | | | | | | |
|---|---|---|---|---|---|---|---|---|
| 2008 WW18 | 11-F | SWE | 5 | 5 | 4 | 9 | 0 | 4th |
| 2008 WW | 11-F | SWE | 4 | 0 | 3 | 3 | 2 | 5th |
| 2009 WW18 | 11-F | SWE | 5 | 6 | 6 | 12 | 4 | B |
| 2009 WW | 11-F | SWE | 5 | 0 | 2 | 2 | 2 | 4th |
| 2010 OG-W | 11-F | SWE | 5 | 0 | 2 | 2 | 0 | 4th |
| **Totals WW18** | | | **10** | **11** | **10** | **21** | **4** | **B** |
| **Totals WW** | | | **9** | **0** | **5** | **5** | **4** | **—** |

| **Ostling, Madeleine** | **b. Valbo, Sweden, February 2, 1990** | | | | | | | |
|---|---|---|---|---|---|---|---|---|
| 2008 WW18 | 8-D | SWE | 5 | 1 | 3 | 4 | 6 | 4th |

| **Ostlund, Angelica** | **b. Gavle, Sweden, July 5, 1991** | | | | | | | |
|---|---|---|---|---|---|---|---|---|
| 2008 WW18 | 22-F | SWE | 5 | 1 | 1 | 2 | 4 | 4th |
| 2009 WW18 | 22-F | SWE | 5 | 1 | 0 | 1 | 2 | B |
| **Totals WW18** | | | **10** | **2** | **1** | **3** | **6** | **B** |

| **Ota, Yukina** | **b. Hokkaido, Japan, February 13, 1992** | | | | | | | |
|---|---|---|---|---|---|---|---|---|
| 2010 WW18 | 18-F | JPN | 5 | 0 | 0 | 0 | 0 | 6th |

| **Ouellette, Caroline** | **b. Montreal, Quebec, Canada, May 25, 1979** | | | | | | | |
|---|---|---|---|---|---|---|---|---|
| 1999 WW | 13-F | CAN | 5 | 2 | 5 | 7 | 4 | G |
| 2000 WW | 13-F | CAN | 5 | 0 | 2 | 2 | 2 | G |
| 2001 WW | 13-F | CAN | 5 | 2 | 3 | 5 | 4 | G |
| 2002 OG-W | 13-F | CAN | 5 | 2 | 4 | 6 | 6 | G |
| 2004 WW | 13-F | CAN | 5 | 3 | 6 | 9 | 0 | G |
| 2005 WW | 13-F | CAN | 5 | 2 | 6 | 8 | 0 | S |
| 2006 OG-W | 13-F | CAN | 5 | 5 | 4 | 9 | 4 | G |
| 2007 WW | 13-F | CAN | 5 | 1 | 3 | 4 | 2 | G |
| 2008 WW | 13-F | CAN | 5 | 2 | 4 | 6 | 4 | S |
| 2009 WW | 13-F | CAN | 5 | 3 | 5 | 8 | 6 | S |
| 2010 OG-W | 13-F | CAN | 5 | 2 | 9 | 11 | 2 | G |
| 2011 WW | 13-F | CAN | 5 | 1 | 2 | 3 | 2 | S |
| 2012 WW | 13-F | CAN | 5 | 4 | 5 | 9 | 6 | G |
| **Totals WW** | | | **50** | **20** | **41** | **61** | **30** | **6G,4S** |
| **Totals OG-W** | | | **15** | **9** | **17** | **26** | **12** | **3G** |

| **Pacholok, Saige** | **b. Edmonton, Alberta, Canada, April 5, 1991** | | | | | | | |
|---|---|---|---|---|---|---|---|---|
| 2009 WW18 | 6-D | CAN | 5 | 0 | 8 | 8 | 2 | S |

| **Packer, Madison** | **b. Birmingham, Michigan, United States, June 25, 1991** | | | | | | | |
|---|---|---|---|---|---|---|---|---|
| 2008 WW18 | 21-F | USA | 5 | 5 | 4 | 9 | 6 | G |
| 2009 WW18 | 24-F | USA | 5 | 6 | 5 | 11 | 14 | G |
| **Totals WW18** | | | **10** | **11** | **9** | **20** | **20** | **2G** |

| **Padyanova, Anna** | **b. Sverdlovsk Region, Soviet Union (Russia), August 5, 1991** | | | | | | | |
|---|---|---|---|---|---|---|---|---|
| 2008 WW18 | 10-D | RUS | 5 | 0 | 0 | 0 | 10 | 8th |
| 2009 WW18 | 10-D | RUS | 5 | 0 | 2 | 2 | 6 | 7th |
| **Totals WW18** | | | **10** | **0** | **2** | **2** | **16** | **—** |

| **Palm, Isabell** | **b. Skelleftea, Sweden, October 13, 1995** | | | | | | | |
|---|---|---|---|---|---|---|---|---|
| 2012 WW18 | 23-F | SWE | 6 | 1 | 0 | 1 | 12 | B |

| **Pankowski, Anne** | **b. Laguna Hills, California, United States, November 4, 1994** | | | | | | | |
|---|---|---|---|---|---|---|---|---|
| 2012 WW18 | 15-F | USA | 5 | 4 | 6 | 10 | 2 | S |

| **Parsons, Sarah** | **b. Dover, Massachusetts, United States, July 27, 1987** | | | | | | | |
|---|---|---|---|---|---|---|---|---|
| 2005 WW | 27-F | USA | 5 | 2 | 2 | 4 | 0 | G |
| 2006 OG-W | 27-F | USA | 5 | 4 | 3 | 7 | 0 | B |
| 2007 WW | 27-F | USA | 5 | 3 | 3 | 6 | 2 | S |
| 2008 WW | 27-F | USA | 5 | 1 | 3 | 4 | 10 | G |
| **Totals WW** | | | **15** | **6** | **8** | **14** | **12** | **2G,S** |

| **Pavlova, Valeria** | **b. April 15, 1995** | | | | | | | |
|---|---|---|---|---|---|---|---|---|
| 2012 WW18 | 23-F | RUS | 6 | 2 | 1 | 3 | 0 | 7th |
| 2012 WW | 17-F | RUS | 5 | 0 | 1 | 1 | 0 | 6th |

| **Pechnikova, Maria** | **b. Izhevsk, Russia, June 8, 1992** | | | | | | | |
|---|---|---|---|---|---|---|---|---|
| 2009 WW18 | 24-F | RUS | 5 | 0 | 1 | 1 | 6 | 7th |
| 2010 WW18 | 24-D | RUS | 5 | 0 | 2 | 2 | 2 | 8th |
| 2012 WW | 4-D | RUS | 5 | 0 | 0 | 0 | 2 | 6th |
| **Totals WW18** | | | **10** | **0** | **3** | **3** | **8** | **—** |

| **Pecinova, Adriena** | **b. Marianska Lazne, Czech Republic, November 8, 1995** | | | | | | | |
|---|---|---|---|---|---|---|---|---|
| 2011 WW18 | 23-F | CZE | 6 | 0 | 0 | 0 | 2 | 4th |
| 2012 WW18 | 23-F | CZE | 5 | 0 | 0 | 0 | 4 | 6th |
| **Totals WW18** | | | **11** | **0** | **0** | **0** | **6** | **—** |

| **Pehkonen, Mari** | **b. Tampere, Finland, February 6, 1985** | | | | | | | |
|---|---|---|---|---|---|---|---|---|
| 2006 OG-W | 25-F | FIN | 5 | 3 | 0 | 3 | 2 | 4th |
| 2007 WW | 25-F | FIN | 5 | 1 | 1 | 2 | 10 | 4th |
| 2008 WW | 25-F | FIN | 5 | 3 | 3 | 6 | 4 | B |
| 2009 WW | 25-F | FIN | 5 | 3 | 2 | 5 | 4 | B |
| **Totals WW** | | | **15** | **7** | **6** | **13** | **18** | **2B** |

| **Pekarkova, Barbora** | **b. Melnik, Czechoslovakia (Czech Republic), September 15, 1992** | | | | | | | |
|---|---|---|---|---|---|---|---|---|
| 2008 WW18 | 4-D | CZE | 5 | 0 | 0 | 0 | 0 | B |
| 2009 WW18 | 26-D | CZE | 5 | 0 | 0 | 0 | 0 | 4th |
| 2010 WW18 | 26-D | CZE | 5 | 0 | 1 | 1 | 4 | 7th |
| **Totals WW18** | | | **15** | **0** | **1** | **1** | **4** | **B** |

| **Pelikanova, Dana** | **b. September 14, 1996** | | | | | | | |
|---|---|---|---|---|---|---|---|---|
| 2012 WW18 | 21-D | CZE | 5 | 0 | 0 | 0 | 2 | 6th |

| Pelkey, Amanda | | | | | | | | b. Montpelier, Vermont, United States, May 29, 1993 |
|---|---|---|---|---|---|---|---|---|
| 2009 WW18 | 14-F | USA | 5 | 3 | 3 | 6 | 4 | G |
| 2010 WW18 | 14-F | USA | 5 | 0 | 7 | 7 | 4 | S |
| 2011 WW18 | 14-F | USA | 5 | 4 | 6 | 10 | 2 | G |
| **Totals WW18** | | | **15** | **7** | **16** | **23** | **10** | **2G,S** |

| Pelttari, Heidi | | | | | | | | b. Tampere, Finland, August 2, 1985 |
|---|---|---|---|---|---|---|---|---|
| 2005 WW | 4-D | FIN | 5 | 0 | 0 | 0 | 4 | 4th |
| 2006 OG-W | 4-D | FIN | 5 | 1 | 2 | 3 | 6 | 4th |
| 2007 WW | 4-D | FIN | 5 | 0 | 0 | 0 | 4 | 4th |
| 2008 WW | 4-D | FIN | 5 | 2 | 3 | 5 | 2 | B |
| 2009 WW | 26-D | FIN | 5 | 1 | 1 | 2 | 2 | B |
| 2010 OG-W | 26-D | FIN | 5 | 1 | 2 | 3 | 4 | B |
| **Totals WW** | | | **20** | **3** | **4** | **7** | **12** | **2B** |
| **Totals OG-W** | | | **10** | **2** | **4** | **6** | **10** | **B** |

| Permyakova, Olga | | | | | | | | b. Chelyabinsk, Soviet Union (Russia), April 12, 1982 |
|---|---|---|---|---|---|---|---|---|
| 2002 OG-W | 15-D | RUS | 5 | 0 | 1 | 1 | 6 | 5th |
| 2004 WW | 15-D | RUS | 4 | 1 | 0 | 1 | 6 | 5th |
| 2005 WW | 15-D | RUS | 5 | 0 | 2 | 2 | 4 | 8th |
| 2006 OG-W | 15-D | RUS | 3 | 0 | 0 | 0 | 0 | 6th |
| 2007 WW | 15-D | RUS | 4 | 0 | 1 | 1 | 4 | 7th |
| 2008 WW | 15-D | RUS | 4 | 0 | 0 | 0 | 2 | 6th |
| 2009 WW | 15-D | RUS | 4 | 0 | 2 | 2 | 0 | 5th |
| 2010 OG-W | 15-D | RUS | 4 | 0 | 2 | 2 | 10 | 6th |
| 2011 WW | 15-D | RUS | 4 | 1 | 2 | 3 | 0 | 4th |
| 2012 WW | 15-D | RUS | 5 | 0 | 0 | 0 | 4 | 6th |
| **Totals WW** | | | **30** | **2** | **7** | **9** | **20** | **—** |
| **Totals OG-W** | | | **12** | **0** | **3** | **3** | **16** | **—** |

| Peskova, Laura | | | | | | | | b. Prague, Czechoslovakia (Czech Republic), February 8, 1991 |
|---|---|---|---|---|---|---|---|---|
| 2008 WW18 | 2-D | CZE | 5 | 0 | 0 | 0 | 0 | B |
| 2009 WW18 | 4-F | CZE | 5 | 0 | 0 | 0 | 0 | 4th |
| **Totals WW18** | | | **10** | **0** | **0** | **0** | **0** | **B** |

| Peterson, Linn | | | | | | | | b. Mariestad, Sweden, January 8, 1994 |
|---|---|---|---|---|---|---|---|---|
| 2011 WW18 | 14-F | SWE | 5 | 2 | 0 | 2 | 2 | 5th |
| 2012 WW18 | 14-F | SWE | 6 | 3 | 1 | 4 | 2 | B |
| **Totals WW18** | | | **11** | **5** | **1** | **6** | **4** | **B** |

| Petrovskaya, Kristina | | | | | | | | b. Moscow, Soviet Union (Russia), June 3, 1980 |
|---|---|---|---|---|---|---|---|---|
| 1997 WW | 3-F | RUS | 5 | 0 | 0 | 0 | 0 | 6th |
| 1999 WW | 3-D | RUS | 4 | 0 | 0 | 0 | 16 | 6th |
| 2000 WW | 3-D | RUS | 5 | 1 | 1 | 2 | 4 | 5th |
| 2001 WW | 3-F | RUS | 5 | 0 | 2 | 2 | 10 | B |
| 2002 OG-W | 3-D | RUS | 5 | 0 | 0 | 0 | 0 | 5th |
| 2006 OG-W | 14-D | RUS | 2 | 0 | 0 | 0 | 6 | 6th |
| 2007 WW | 13-D | RUS | 4 | 0 | 1 | 1 | 2 | 7th |
| 2009 WW | 19-D | RUS | 4 | 0 | 1 | 1 | 10 | 5th |
| 2010 OG-W | 13-D | RUS | 5 | 0 | 0 | 0 | 4 | 6th |
| **Totals WW** | | | **27** | **1** | **5** | **6** | **42** | **B** |
| **Totals OG-W** | | | **12** | **0** | **0** | **0** | **10** | **—** |

| Pfalzer, Emily | | | | | | | | b. Getzville, New York, United States, June 14, 1993 |
|---|---|---|---|---|---|---|---|---|
| 2010 WW18 | 2-D | USA | 5 | 0 | 6 | 6 | 0 | S |
| 2011 WW18 | 2-D | USA | 5 | 2 | 2 | 4 | 0 | G |
| **Totals WW18** | | | **10** | **2** | **8** | **10** | **0** | **G,S** |

| Phillips, Brittany | | | | | | | | b. Lauder, Manitoba, Canada, January 21, 1991 |
|---|---|---|---|---|---|---|---|---|
| 2009 WW18 | 12-F | CAN | 5 | 4 | 0 | 4 | 0 | S |

| Picard, Michelle | | | | | | | | b. Taunton, Massachusetts, United States, May 27, 1993 |
|---|---|---|---|---|---|---|---|---|
| 2010 WW18 | 12-D | USA | 5 | 0 | 3 | 3 | 4 | S |
| 2011 WW18 | 12-D | USA | 5 | 0 | 4 | 4 | 0 | G |
| 2012 WW | 23-D | USA | 4 | 0 | 1 | 1 | 0 | S |
| **Totals WW18** | | | **10** | **0** | **7** | **7** | **4** | **G,S** |

| Pietikainen, Ella | | | | | | | | b. Jarvenpaa, Finland, May 7, 1994 |
|---|---|---|---|---|---|---|---|---|
| 2011 WW18 | 8-D | FIN | 6 | 0 | 1 | 1 | 2 | B |

| Piper, Cherie | | | | | | | | b. Toronto, Ontario, Canada, June 29, 1981 |
|---|---|---|---|---|---|---|---|---|
| 2002 OG-W | 7-F | CAN | 5 | 3 | 2 | 5 | 0 | G |
| 2004 WW | 7-F | CAN | 5 | 1 | 6 | 7 | 4 | G |
| 2005 WW | 7-F | CAN | 5 | 3 | 1 | 4 | 2 | S |
| 2006 OG-W | 7-F | CAN | 5 | 7 | 8 | 15 | 0 | G |
| 2008 WW | 7-F | CAN | 5 | 2 | 6 | 8 | 0 | S |
| 2010 OG-W | 7-F | CAN | 5 | 5 | 5 | 10 | 0 | G |
| 2011 WW | 7-F | CAN | 5 | 3 | 1 | 4 | 2 | S |
| **Totals WW** | | | **20** | **9** | **14** | **23** | **8** | **G,3S** |
| **Totals OG-W** | | | **15** | **15** | **15** | **30** | **0** | **3G** |

| Pipkova, Katerina | | | | | | | | b. Kutna Hora, Czech Republic (Czech Republic), April 24, 1991 |
|---|---|---|---|---|---|---|---|---|
| 2009 WW18 | 12-D | CZE | 5 | 0 | 0 | 0 | 4 | 4th |

| Pokopec, Miriam | | | | | | | | b. Augsburg, Germany, April 7, 1992 |
|---|---|---|---|---|---|---|---|---|
| 2008 WW18 | 15-F | GER | 5 | 0 | 0 | 0 | 6 | 5th |
| 2009 WW18 | 15-F | GER | 5 | 0 | 0 | 0 | 8 | 6th |
| 2010 WW18 | 15-F | GER | 6 | 0 | 0 | 0 | 2 | 4th |
| **Totals WW18** | | | **16** | **0** | **0** | **0** | **16** | **—** |

| Polenska, Alena | | | | | | | | b. Caslav, Czechoslovakia (Czech Republic), June 9, 1990 |
|---|---|---|---|---|---|---|---|---|
| 2008 WW18 | 5-F | CZE | 5 | 6 | 3 | 9 | 0 | B |

| Polunina, Zoya | | | | | | | | b. Tula Region, Russia, June 12, 1991 |
|---|---|---|---|---|---|---|---|---|
| 2008 WW18 | 6-D | RUS | 5 | 0 | 0 | 0 | 4 | 8th |
| 2009 WW | 26-D | RUS | 4 | 0 | 0 | 0 | 0 | 5th |
| 2010 OG-W | 26-D | RUS | 5 | 0 | 0 | 0 | 0 | 6th |
| 2011 WW | 26-D | RUS | 6 | 0 | 0 | 0 | 2 | 4th |
| 2012 WW | 22-D | RUS | 5 | 0 | 0 | 0 | 0 | 6th |
| **Totals WW** | | | **15** | **0** | **0** | **0** | **2** | **—** |

| Popova, Alexandra | | | | | | | | b. Yakutia, Soviet Union (Russia), June 19, 1990 |
|---|---|---|---|---|---|---|---|---|
| 2008 WW18 | 2-D | RUS | 5 | 0 | 0 | 0 | 0 | 8th |

| Port, Karina | | | | | | | | b. Weingarten, Germany, August 10, 1995 |
|---|---|---|---|---|---|---|---|---|
| 2011 WW18 | 10-F | GER | 5 | 1 | 0 | 1 | 4 | 6th |

| Posa, Mariia | | | | | | | | b. Hyvinkaa, Finland, February 21, 1988 |
|---|---|---|---|---|---|---|---|---|
| 2009 WW | 5-D | FIN | 5 | 0 | 0 | 0 | 0 | B |
| 2010 OG-W | 5-D | FIN | 5 | 0 | 0 | 0 | 2 | B |

| Poschung, Valeska | | | | | | | | b. November 2, 1994 |
|---|---|---|---|---|---|---|---|---|
| 2012 WW18 | 15-F | SUI | 6 | 0 | 0 | 0 | 0 | 8th |

| Potapova, Olga | | | | | | | | b. Almaty, Soviet Union (Kazakhstan), December 16, 1976 |
|---|---|---|---|---|---|---|---|---|
| 2001 WW | 9-D | KAZ | 5 | 0 | 0 | 0 | 6 | 8th |
| 2002 OG-W | 9-D | KAZ | 5 | 0 | 1 | 1 | 4 | 8th |
| 2005 WW | 9-F | KAZ | 5 | 2 | 0 | 2 | 2 | 7th |
| 2007 WW | 9-F | KAZ | 4 | 0 | 0 | 0 | 0 | 9th |
| 2009 WW | 9-F | KAZ | 4 | 0 | 0 | 0 | 2 | 6th |
| 2011 WW | 9-F | KAZ | 5 | 0 | 0 | 0 | 4 | 8th |
| **Totals WW** | | | **23** | **2** | **0** | **2** | **14** | **—** |

| Potter (Schmidgall), Jenny | | | | | | | | b. Edina, Minnesota, United States, January 12, 1979 |
|---|---|---|---|---|---|---|---|---|
| 1998 OG-W* | 12-F | USA | 6 | 2 | 3 | 5 | 4 | G |
| 1999 WW* | 12-F | USA | 5 | 5 | 7 | 12 | 0 | S |
| 2000 WW* | 12-F | USA | 5 | 0 | 3 | 3 | 0 | S |
| 2001 WW* | 12-F | USA | 5 | 3 | 7 | 10 | 4 | S |
| 2002 OG-W | 12-F | USA | 5 | 1 | 6 | 7 | 2 | S |
| 2004 WW | 12-F | USA | 5 | 3 | 3 | 6 | 4 | S |
| 2005 WW | 12-F | USA | 5 | 2 | 4 | 6 | 0 | G |
| 2006 OG-W | 12-F | USA | 5 | 2 | 7 | 9 | 4 | B |
| 2007 WW | 12-F | USA | 5 | 2 | 2 | 4 | 8 | S |
| 2008 WW | 12-F | USA | 5 | 5 | 2 | 7 | 2 | G |
| 2009 WW | 12-F | USA | 5 | 1 | 4 | 5 | 2 | G |
| 2010 OG-W | 12-F | USA | 5 | 6 | 5 | 11 | 2 | S |
| 2011 WW | 12-F | USA | 5 | 2 | 3 | 5 | 4 | G |
| 2012 WW | 12-F | USA | 5 | 0 | 3 | 3 | 0 | S |
| **Totals WW** | | | **50** | **23** | **38** | **61** | **24** | **4G,6S** |
| **Totals OG-W** | | | **21** | **11** | **21** | **32** | **12** | **G,2S,B** |

*played under maiden name Jenny Schmidgall
~OG-W All-Star Team/Forward (2010), WW IIHF Directorate Best Forward (1999), WW All-Star Team/Forward (1999)

| Poudrier, Cassandra | | | | | | | | b. Lachenaie, Quebec, Canada, December 5, 1992 |
|---|---|---|---|---|---|---|---|---|
| 2010 WW18 | 6-D | CAN | 5 | 0 | 4 | 4 | 4 | G |

| Poulin, Marie-Philip | | | | | | | | b. Beauceville, Quebec, Canada, March 28, 1991 |
|---|---|---|---|---|---|---|---|---|
| 2008 WW18 | 10-F | CAN | 5 | 8 | 6 | 14 | 4 | S |
| 2009 WW18 | 10-F | CAN | 5 | 5 | 7 | 12 | 2 | S |
| 2009 WW | 29-F | CAN | 5 | 2 | 3 | 5 | 0 | S |
| 2010 OG-W | 29-F | CAN | 5 | 5 | 2 | 7 | 2 | G |
| 2011 WW | 29-F* | CAN | 5 | 3 | 1 | 4 | 4 | S |
| 2012 WW | 29-F | CAN | 5 | 3 | 4 | 7 | 6 | G |
| **Totals WW18** | | | **15** | **16** | **14** | **30** | **10** | **3S** |
| **Totals WW** | | | **15** | **8** | **8** | **16** | **10** | **G,2S** |

*played as Marie-Philip Poulin-Nadeau
~OG-W All-Star Team/Forward (2010), WW18 IIHF Directorate Best Forward (2008)

| Povova, Lucie | | | | | | | | b. Roudnice nad Laben, Czechoslovakia (Czech Republic), September 16, 1992 |
|---|---|---|---|---|---|---|---|---|
| 2008 WW18 | 9-F | CZE | 5 | 3 | 3 | 6 | 10 | B |
| 2009 WW18 | 10-F | CZE | 5 | 1 | 1 | 2 | 4 | 4th |
| 2010 WW18 | 10-F | CZE | 5 | 2 | 2 | 4 | 6 | 7th |
| **Totals WW18** | | | **15** | **6** | **6** | **12** | **20** | **B** |

| **Pravlikova, Petra** | | | | | | | | **b. Levoca, Czechoslovakia (Slovakia), June 4, 1985** |
|---|---|---|---|---|---|---|---|---|
| 2010 OG-W | 24-F | SVK | 5 | 2 | 0 | 2 | 10 | 8th |
| 2011 WW | 24-F | SVK | 5 | 0 | 0 | 0 | 2 | 7th |

| **Prevost, Carolyne** | | | | | | | | **b. Sarnia, Ontario, Canada, January 6, 1990** |
|---|---|---|---|---|---|---|---|---|
| 2008 WW18 | 14-F | CAN | 5 | 6 | 3 | 9 | 0 | S |

| **Pribylova, Vendula** | | | | | | | | **b. March 23, 1996** |
|---|---|---|---|---|---|---|---|---|
| 2012 WW18 | 26-F | CZE | 5 | 0 | 0 | 0 | 0 | 6th |

| **Pucci, Josephine** | | | | | | | | **b. Pearl River, New York, United States, December 27, 1990** |
|---|---|---|---|---|---|---|---|---|
| 2011 WW | 24-D | USA | 5 | 1 | 0 | 1 | 12 | G |
| 2012 WW | 24-D | USA | 5 | 3 | 3 | 6 | 4 | S |
| **Totals WW** | | | **10** | **4** | **3** | **7** | **16** | **G,S** |

| **Qi, Xueting** | | | | | | | | **b. Heilongjiang, China, November 11, 1986** |
|---|---|---|---|---|---|---|---|---|
| 2004 WW | 55-D | CHN | 4 | 0 | 0 | 0 | 2 | 7th |
| 2005 WW | 55-D | CHN | 5 | 0 | 0 | 0 | 10 | 6th |
| 2007 WW | 55-D | CHN | 4 | 0 | 0 | 0 | 2 | 6th |
| 2008 WW | 55-D | CHN | 4 | 0 | 2 | 2 | 6 | 8th |
| 2009 WW | 55-D | CHN | 4 | 1 | 0 | 1 | 35 | 9th |
| 2010 OG-W | 55-D | CHN | 5 | 0 | 0 | 0 | 6 | 7th |
| **Totals WW** | | | **21** | **1** | **2** | **3** | **55** | **—** |

| **Rachlin, Natasha** | | | | | | | | **b. Brookline, Massachusetts, United States, April 4, 1995** |
|---|---|---|---|---|---|---|---|---|
| 2012 WW18 | 3-D | USA | 5 | 0 | 0 | 0 | 0 | S |

| **Rahunen, Isa** | | | | | | | | **b. Kuopio, Finland, April 16, 1993** |
|---|---|---|---|---|---|---|---|---|
| 2009 WW18 | 5-D | FIN | 5 | 0 | 1 | 1 | 6 | 5th |
| 2010 WW18 | 5-D | FIN | 5 | 0 | 2 | 2 | 12 | 5th |
| 2011 WW18 | 5-D | FIN | 6 | 0 | 0 | 0 | 10 | B |
| **Totals WW18** | | | **16** | **0** | **3** | **3** | **28** | **B** |

| **Raitala, Salla-Maaria** | | | | | | | | **b. Hyvinkaa, Finland, July 25, 1993** |
|---|---|---|---|---|---|---|---|---|
| 2011 WW18 | 25-D | FIN | 6 | 0 | 0 | 0 | 2 | B |

| **Rajahuhta, Annina** | | | | | | | | **b. Helsinki, Finland, March 8, 1989** |
|---|---|---|---|---|---|---|---|---|
| 2010 OG-W | 11-F | FIN | 5 | 0 | 0 | 0 | 0 | B |
| 2011 WW | 11-F | FIN | 6 | 2 | 1 | 3 | 2 | B |
| 2012 WW | 11-F | FIN | 6 | 1 | 0 | 1 | 2 | 4th |
| **Totals WW** | | | **12** | **3** | **1** | **4** | **4** | **B** |

| **Rakova, Edita** | | | | | | | | **b. Humenne, Czechoslovakia (Slovakia), May 18, 1978** |
|---|---|---|---|---|---|---|---|---|
| 2010 OG-W | 11-D | SVK | 5 | 0 | 0 | 0 | 8 | 8th |
| 2012 WW | 11-D | SVK | 3 | 0 | 0 | 0 | 0 | 8th |

| **Rantamaki, Karoliina** | | | | | | | | **b. Espoo, Finland, February 23, 1978** |
|---|---|---|---|---|---|---|---|---|
| 1997 WW | 29-F | FIN | 5 | 1 | 2 | 3 | 2 | B |
| 1998 OG-W | 29-F | FIN | 6 | 2 | 1 | 3 | 0 | B |
| 1999 WW | 29-F | FIN | 5 | 3 | 3 | 6 | 2 | B |
| 2000 WW | 29-F | FIN | 5 | 1 | 3 | 4 | 0 | B |
| 2001 WW | 29-F | FIN | 5 | 1 | 2 | 3 | 0 | 4th |
| 2002 OG-W | 29-F | FIN | 5 | 1 | 0 | 1 | 0 | 4th |
| 2004 WW | 29-F | FIN | 5 | 0 | 0 | 0 | 4 | B |
| 2005 WW | 29-F | FIN | 5 | 2 | 3 | 5 | 4 | 4th |
| 2006 OG-W | 29-F | FIN | 5 | 1 | 2 | 3 | 2 | 4th |
| 2007 WW | 29-F | FIN | 5 | 0 | 1 | 1 | 0 | 4th |
| 2008 WW | 29-F | FIN | 5 | 0 | 4 | 4 | 6 | B |
| 2009 WW | 29-F | FIN | 5 | 0 | 5 | 5 | 4 | B |
| 2010 OG-W | 29-F | FIN | 5 | 2 | 1 | 3 | 4 | B |
| 2011 WW | 29-F | FIN | 6 | 4 | 2 | 6 | 4 | B |
| 2012 WW | 29-F | FIN | 6 | 5 | 0 | 5 | 2 | 4th |
| **Totals WW** | | | **57** | **17** | **25** | **42** | **28** | **7B** |
| **Totals OG-W** | | | **21** | **6** | **4** | **10** | **6** | **2B** |

| **Rantanen, Anni** | | | | | | | | **b. Lempaala, Finland, November 22, 1995** |
|---|---|---|---|---|---|---|---|---|
| 2011 WW18 | 18-F | FIN | 6 | 1 | 2 | 3 | 2 | B |
| 2012 WW18 | 18-F | FIN | 5 | 1 | 2 | 3 | 2 | 5th |
| 2012 WW | 5-F | FIN | 6 | 0 | 0 | 0 | 0 | 4th |
| **Totals WW18** | | | **11** | **2** | **4** | **6** | **4** | **B** |

| **Rantanen, Salla** | | | | | | | | **b. Riihimaki, Finland, July 12, 1992** |
|---|---|---|---|---|---|---|---|---|
| 2009 WW18 | 10-F | FIN | 5 | 1 | 0 | 1 | 2 | 5th |
| 2010 WW18 | 10-F | FIN | 5 | 4 | 0 | 4 | 4 | 5th |
| **Totals WW18** | | | **10** | **5** | **0** | **5** | **6** | **—** |

| **Raselli, Evelina** | | | | | | | | **b. Poschiavo, Switzerland, May 3, 1992** |
|---|---|---|---|---|---|---|---|---|
| 2008 WW18 | 18-F | SUI | 5 | 0 | 0 | 0 | 2 | 7th |
| 2009 WW18 | 18-F | SUI | 5 | 3 | 3 | 6 | 6 | 8th |
| 2011 WW | 18-F | SUI | 5 | 0 | 1 | 1 | 0 | 6th |
| 2012 WW | 18-F | SUI | 6 | 2 | 0 | 2 | 6 | B |
| **Totals WW18** | | | **10** | **3** | **3** | **6** | **8** | **—** |
| **Totals WW** | | | **11** | **2** | **1** | **3** | **6** | **B** |

| **Rask, Fanny** | | | | | | | | **b. Leksand, Sweden, May 21, 1991** |
|---|---|---|---|---|---|---|---|---|
| 2008 WW18 | 13-F | SWE | 5 | 0 | 1 | 1 | 0 | 4th |
| 2009 WW18 | 13-F | SWE | 5 | 1 | 2 | 3 | 2 | B |
| **Totals WW18** | | | **10** | **1** | **3** | **4** | **2** | **B** |

| **Ratinen, Susanna** | | | | | | | | **b. Pernaja, Finland, September 14, 1990** |
|---|---|---|---|---|---|---|---|---|
| 2008 WW18 | 19-F | FIN | 5 | 0 | 1 | 1 | 6 | 6th |

| **Rattray, Jamie Lee** | | | | | | | | **b. Kanata, Ontario, Canada, September 30, 1992** |
|---|---|---|---|---|---|---|---|---|
| 2009 WW18 | 16-F | CAN | 5 | 5 | 0 | 5 | 4 | S |
| 2010 WW18 | 16-F | CAN | 5 | 2 | 6 | 8 | 6 | G |
| **Totals WW18** | | | **10** | **7** | **6** | **13** | **10** | **G,S** |

| **Rau, Jennifer** | | | | | | | | **b. Velbert, Germany, December 14, 1994** |
|---|---|---|---|---|---|---|---|---|
| 2011 WW18 | 23-F | GER | 5 | 0 | 0 | 0 | 0 | 6th |

| **Reimann, Dana** | | | | | | | | **b. Rodewisch, Germany, May 17, 1996** |
|---|---|---|---|---|---|---|---|---|
| 2012 WW18 | 22-D | GER | 6 | 0 | 0 | 0 | 2 | 4th |

| **Repaci, Gina** | | | | | | | | **b. Etobicoke (Toronto), Ontario, Canada, May 13, 1993** |
|---|---|---|---|---|---|---|---|---|
| 2011 WW18 | 23-D | CAN | 5 | 1 | 1 | 2 | 2 | S |

| **Resor, Helen** | | | | | | | | **b. Greenwich, Connecticut, United States, October 18, 1985** |
|---|---|---|---|---|---|---|---|---|
| 2005 WW | 6-D | USA | 5 | 0 | 1 | 1 | 2 | G |
| 2006 OG-W | 6-D | USA | 5 | 0 | 2 | 2 | 10 | B |
| 2007 WW | 6-D | USA | 5 | 0 | 2 | 2 | 4 | S |
| 2009 WW | 6-D | USA | 5 | 0 | 0 | 0 | 2 | G |
| **Totals WW** | | | **15** | **0** | **3** | **3** | **8** | **2G,S** |

| **Richardson, Morgan** | | | | | | | | **b. Ottawa, Ontario, Canada, June 17, 1994** |
|---|---|---|---|---|---|---|---|---|
| 2012 WW18 | 2-D | CAN | 5 | 0 | 1 | 1 | 2 | G |

| **Richter, Ronja** | | | | | | | | **b. Hamburg, West Germany (Germany), December 28, 1989** |
|---|---|---|---|---|---|---|---|---|
| 2012 WW | 21-D | GER | 5 | 0 | 0 | 0 | 4 | 7th |

| **Riechsteiner, Claudia** | | | | | | | | **b. Schotz, Switzerland, January 3, 1986** |
|---|---|---|---|---|---|---|---|---|
| 2010 OG-W | 86-D | SUI | 5 | 0 | 0 | 0 | 0 | 5th |

| **Riedi, Nicole** | | | | | | | | **b. Niederhasli, Switzerland, April 2, 1991** |
|---|---|---|---|---|---|---|---|---|
| 2009 WW18 | 7-D | SUI | 5 | 0 | 0 | 0 | 0 | 8th |

| **Rigoli, Sandy** | | | | | | | | **b. Montreux, Switzerland, December 1, 1990** |
|---|---|---|---|---|---|---|---|---|
| 2008 WW18 | 5-D | SUI | 5 | 0 | 0 | 0 | 4 | 7th |

| **Ritari, Emma** | | | | | | | | **b. Joensuu, Finland, May 3, 1994** |
|---|---|---|---|---|---|---|---|---|
| 2010 WW18 | 13-F | FIN | 5 | 0 | 0 | 0 | 14 | 5th |
| 2012 WW18 | 13-F | FIN | 5 | 1 | 0 | 1 | 2 | 5th |
| **Totals WW18** | | | **10** | **1** | **0** | **1** | **16** | **—** |

| **Robson, Sarah** | | | | | | | | **b. Mississauga, Ontario, Canada, September 2, 1993** |
|---|---|---|---|---|---|---|---|---|
| 2011 WW18 | 16-F | CAN | 5 | 2 | 0 | 2 | 0 | S |

| **Roesler, Cydney** | | | | | | | | **b. Stittsville, Ontario, Canada, February 21, 1994** |
|---|---|---|---|---|---|---|---|---|
| 2011 WW18 | 21-D | CAN | 5 | 1 | 3 | 4 | 0 | S |
| 2012 WW18 | 21-D | CAN | 5 | 4 | 1 | 5 | 4 | G |
| **Totals WW18** | | | **10** | **5** | **4** | **9** | **4** | **G,S** |

| **Roth, Nathalie** | | | | | | | | **b. Hemberg, Switzerland, October 31, 1993** |
|---|---|---|---|---|---|---|---|---|
| 2009 WW18 | 9-D | SUI | 5 | 0 | 0 | 0 | 0 | 8th |

| **Rothemund, Yvonne** | | | | | | | | **b. Kulmbach, Germany, September 23, 1992** |
|---|---|---|---|---|---|---|---|---|
| 2008 WW18 | 10-D | GER | 5 | 0 | 1 | 1 | 4 | 5th |
| 2009 WW18 | 10-D | GER | 5 | 0 | 2 | 2 | 4 | 6th |
| 2010 WW18 | 10-D | GER | 6 | 1 | 0 | 1 | 6 | 4th |
| **Totals WW18** | | | **16** | **1** | **3** | **4** | **14** | **—** |

| **Rougeau, Lauriane** | | | | | | | | **b. Beaconsfield, Quebec, Canada, April 12, 1990** |
|---|---|---|---|---|---|---|---|---|
| 2008 WW18 | 4-D | CAN | 5 | 0 | 4 | 4 | 2 | S |
| 2012 WW | 5-D | CAN | 5 | 1 | 1 | 2 | 2 | G |

~WW18 IIHF Directorate Best Defenceman (2008)

| **Rouru, Julia** | | | | | | | | **b. Seinajoki, Finland, March 10, 1993** |
|---|---|---|---|---|---|---|---|---|
| 2010 WW18 | 24-F | FIN | 5 | 0 | 0 | 0 | 0 | 5th |

| **Ruegg, Dominique** | | | | | | | | **b. February 5, 1996** |
|---|---|---|---|---|---|---|---|---|
| 2012 WW18 | 11-F | SUI | 6 | 0 | 1 | 1 | 0 | 8th |

| **Ruhnke, Laura** | | | | | | | | **b. Biel, Switzerland, December 25, 1983** |
|---|---|---|---|---|---|---|---|---|
| 2006 OG-W | 27-F | SUI | 5 | 2 | 1 | 3 | 8 | 7th |
| 2007 WW | 27-F | SUI | 4 | 2 | 0 | 2 | 0 | 5th |
| 2008 WW | 27-F | SUI | 5 | 1 | 0 | 1 | 6 | 4th |
| 2009 WW | 27-F | SUI | 4 | 1 | 0 | 1 | 10 | 7th |
| **Totals WW** | | | **13** | **4** | **0** | **4** | **16** | **—** |

| **Rundqvist, Danijela** | | | | | | | | **b. Stockholm, Sweden, September 26, 1984** |
|---|---|---|---|---|---|---|---|---|
| 2002 OG-W | 28-F | SWE | 5 | 0 | 0 | 0 | 2 | B |
| 2004 WW | 28-F | SWE | 5 | 0 | 0 | 0 | 8 | 4th |
| 2005 WW | 28-F | SWE | 5 | 1 | 0 | 1 | 10 | B |
| 2006 OG-W | 28-F | SWE | 5 | 0 | 0 | 0 | 10 | S |
| 2007 WW | 28-F | SWE | 5 | 1 | 1 | 2 | 0 | B |
| 2008 WW | 28-F | SWE | 4 | 0 | 2 | 2 | 2 | 5th |
| 2009 WW | 28-F | SWE | 5 | 4 | 1 | 5 | 6 | 4th |
| 2010 OG-W | 28-F | SWE | 5 | 2 | 0 | 2 | 2 | 4th |
| 2011 WW | 28-F | SWE | 5 | 0 | 2 | 2 | 4 | 5th |
| 2012 WW | 28-F | SWE | 5 | 0 | 0 | 0 | 0 | 5th |
| **Totals WW** | | | **34** | **6** | **6** | **12** | **30** | **2B** |
| **Totals OG-W** | | | **15** | **2** | **0** | **2** | **14** | **S,B** |

| **Rytkonen, Elisa** | | | | | | | | **b. Vantaa, Finland, January 5, 1991** |
|---|---|---|---|---|---|---|---|---|
| 2008 WW18 | 26-F | FIN | 5 | 0 | 0 | 0 | 2 | 6th |
| 2009 WW18 | 26-F | FIN | 5 | 1 | 1 | 2 | 2 | 5th |
| **Totals WW18** | | | **10** | **1** | **1** | **2** | **4** | **—** |

| **Saarimaki, Tiina** | | | | | | | | **b. Salo, Finland, June 10, 1991** |
|---|---|---|---|---|---|---|---|---|
| 2008 WW18 | 7-D | FIN | 5 | 0 | 0 | 0 | 4 | 6th |
| 2009 WW18 | 7-F | FIN | 5 | 2 | 0 | 2 | 12 | 5th |
| 2011 WW | 26-F | FIN | 5 | 0 | 1 | 1 | 4 | B |
| **Totals WW18** | | | **10** | **2** | **0** | **2** | **16** | **—** |

| **Saarinen, Mari** | | | | | | | | **b. Kangasala, Finland, July 30, 1981** |
|---|---|---|---|---|---|---|---|---|
| 2001 WW | 13-F | FIN | 5 | 0 | 1 | 1 | 4 | 4th |
| 2004 WW | 17-F | FIN | 5 | 2 | 1 | 3 | 4 | B |
| 2005 WW | 12-F | FIN | 5 | 0 | 0 | 0 | 4 | 4th |
| 2006 OG-W | 12-F | FIN | 5 | 1 | 1 | 2 | 4 | 4th |
| 2007 WW | 12-F | FIN | 5 | 0 | 2 | 2 | 6 | 4th |
| 2008 WW | 12-F | FIN | 5 | 3 | 2 | 5 | 6 | B |
| 2009 WW | 12-F | FIN | 5 | 1 | 1 | 2 | 4 | B |
| 2010 OG-W | 12-F | FIN | 5 | 0 | 1 | 1 | 2 | B |
| **Totals WW** | | | **30** | **6** | **7** | **13** | **28** | **3B** |
| **Totals OG-W** | | | **10** | **1** | **2** | **3** | **6** | **B** |

| **Sadilkova, Sara** | | | | | | | | **b. Valtice, Czech Republic, November 16, 1995** |
|---|---|---|---|---|---|---|---|---|
| 2011 WW18 | 7-F | CZE | 6 | 0 | 0 | 0 | 0 | 4th |
| 2012 WW18 | 7-F | CZE | 5 | 0 | 0 | 0 | 0 | 6th |
| **Totals WW18** | | | **11** | **0** | **0** | **0** | **0** | **—** |

| **Saeki, Rina** | | | | | | | | **b. Hokkaido, Japan, May 17, 1994** |
|---|---|---|---|---|---|---|---|---|
| 2011 WW18 | 25-F | JPN | 6 | 0 | 0 | 0 | 0 | 8th |

| **Sakagami, Tomoko** | | | | | | | | **b. Hokkaido, Japan, October 18, 1983** |
|---|---|---|---|---|---|---|---|---|
| 2008 WW | 18-D | JPN | 4 | 0 | 1 | 1 | 6 | 7th |
| 2009 WW | 18-F | JPN | 4 | 3 | 0 | 3 | 2 | 8th |
| **Totals WW** | | | **8** | **3** | **1** | **4** | **8** | **—** |

| **Sauer, Caroline** | | | | | | | | **b. Dortmund, Germany, June 27, 1990** |
|---|---|---|---|---|---|---|---|---|
| 2008 WW18 | 8-F | GER | 5 | 0 | 0 | 0 | 0 | 5th |

| **Saulnier, Jillian** | | | | | | | | **b. Halifax, Nova Scotia, Canada, March 7, 1992** |
|---|---|---|---|---|---|---|---|---|
| 2009 WW18 | 19-F | CAN | 5 | 0 | 3 | 3 | 4 | S |
| 2010 WW18 | 19-F | CAN | 5 | 4 | 6 | 10 | 2 | G |
| **Totals WW18** | | | **10** | **4** | **9** | **13** | **6** | **G,S** |

| **Savage, Paige** | | | | | | | | **b. Carrollton, Texas, United States, July 25, 1994** |
|---|---|---|---|---|---|---|---|---|
| 2011 WW18 | 19-F | USA | 5 | 2 | 4 | 6 | 2 | G |
| 2012 WW18 | 19-F | USA | 5 | 2 | 6 | 8 | 2 | S |
| **Totals WW18** | | | **10** | **4** | **10** | **14** | **4** | **G,S** |

| **Savikuja, Henna** | | | | | | | | **b. Kalix, Sweden, March 28, 1978** |
|---|---|---|---|---|---|---|---|---|
| 2000 WW | 26-F | FIN | 5 | 1 | 0 | 1 | 6 | 4th |
| 2002 OG-W | 26-F | FIN | 5 | 0 | 0 | 0 | 4 | 4th |
| 2004 WW | 26-F | FIN | 5 | 1 | 1 | 2 | 2 | B |
| 2012 WW | 26-F | FIN | 6 | 0 | 0 | 0 | 0 | 4th |
| **Totals WW** | | | **16** | **2** | **1** | **3** | **8** | **B** |

| **Sawade, Yui** | | | | | | | | **b. Hokkaido, Japan, August 23, 1994** |
|---|---|---|---|---|---|---|---|---|
| 2011 WW18 | 20-F | JPN | 6 | 0 | 0 | 0 | 2 | 8th |

| **Sazonova, Viktoria** | | | | | | | | **b. Eberswalde, East Germany (Germany), August 30, 1983** |
|---|---|---|---|---|---|---|---|---|
| 2001 WW | 21-D | KAZ | 5 | 0 | 0 | 0 | 0 | 8th |
| 2002 OG-W | 21-D | KAZ | 5 | 0 | 1 | 1 | 0 | 8th |
| 2005 WW | 21-D | KAZ | 5 | 0 | 0 | 0 | 4 | 7th |
| 2007 WW | 21-D | KAZ | 4 | 0 | 0 | 0 | 2 | 9th |
| 2009 WW | 21-D | KAZ | 4 | 0 | 0 | 0 | 2 | 6th |
| 2011 WW | 21-D | KAZ | 5 | 0 | 0 | 0 | 2 | 8th |
| **Totals WW** | | | **18** | **0** | **0** | **0** | **8** | **—** |

| **Scheurer, Dominique** | | | | | | | | **b. June 21, 1995** |
|---|---|---|---|---|---|---|---|---|
| 2012 WW18 | 9-D | SUI | 6 | 0 | 2 | 2 | 6 | 8th |

| **Scheuerlein, Muriel** | | | | | | | | **b. Berlin, Germany, March 9, 1996** |
|---|---|---|---|---|---|---|---|---|
| 2012 WW18 | 27-D | GER | 6 | 0 | 0 | 0 | 2 | 4th |

| **Schipper, Kate** | | | | | | | | **b. Brooklyn Park, Minnesota, United States, June 28, 1995** |
|---|---|---|---|---|---|---|---|---|
| 2012 WW18 | 12-F | USA | 5 | 1 | 0 | 1 | 4 | S |

| **Schleper, Anne** | | | | | | | | **b. St. Cloud, Minnesota, United States, January 30, 1990** |
|---|---|---|---|---|---|---|---|---|
| 2008 WW18 | 7-D | USA | 5 | 1 | 2 | 3 | 4 | G |
| 2011 WW | 15-D | USA | 5 | 1 | 1 | 2 | 2 | G |
| 2012 WW | 15-D | USA | 5 | 0 | 2 | 2 | 0 | S |
| **Totals WW** | | | **10** | **1** | **3** | **4** | **2** | **G,S** |

| **Schmid, Lea** | | | | | | | | **b. Meggen, Switzerland, April 18, 1991** |
|---|---|---|---|---|---|---|---|---|
| 2008 WW18 | 12-D | SUI | 5 | 0 | 0 | 0 | 0 | 7th |

| **Schmid, Kristin** | | | | | | | | **b. Garmisch-Partenkirchen, Germany, December 15, 1996** |
|---|---|---|---|---|---|---|---|---|
| 2012 WW18 | 20-F | GER | 6 | 0 | 0 | 0 | 0 | 4th |

**~Schmidgall, Jenny** ~see Potter (Schmidgall), Jenny

| **Schneider, Nicole** | | | | | | | | **b. Uetendorf, Switzerland, July 13, 1993** |
|---|---|---|---|---|---|---|---|---|
| 2009 WW18 | 14-F | SUI | 5 | 2 | 0 | 2 | 14 | 8th |
| 2011 WW18 | 14-F | SUI | 6 | 0 | 0 | 0 | 4 | 7th |
| **Totals WW18** | | | **11** | **2** | **0** | **2** | **18** | **—** |

| **Schoullis, Jen** | | | | | | | | **b. Erie, Pennsylvania, United States, March 7, 1989** |
|---|---|---|---|---|---|---|---|---|
| 2011 WW | 3-F | USA | 5 | 2 | 0 | 2 | 2 | G |

| **Schroder, Britta** | | | | | | | | **b. St. Tonis, West Germany (Germany), September 18, 1987** |
|---|---|---|---|---|---|---|---|---|
| 2008 WW | 16-D | GER | 4 | 0 | 0 | 0 | 0 | 9th |
| 2012 WW | 11-D | GER | 5 | 0 | 0 | 0 | 0 | 7th |
| **Totals WW** | | | **9** | **0** | **0** | **0** | **0** | **—** |

| **Schuster, Lisa** | | | | | | | | **b. May 28, 1987** |
|---|---|---|---|---|---|---|---|---|
| 2008 WW | 24-F | GER | 4 | 0 | 0 | 0 | 2 | — |
| 2012 WW | 24-F | GER | 5 | 1 | 0 | 1 | 2 | 7th |
| **Totals WW** | | | **9** | **1** | **0** | **1** | **4** | **—** |

| **Seiler, Sara** | | | | | | | | **b. Hausham, West Germany (Germany), January 25, 1983** |
|---|---|---|---|---|---|---|---|---|
| 2004 WW | 17-F | GER | 4 | 1 | 0 | 1 | 2 | 6th |
| 2005 WW | 17-F | GER | 5 | 0 | 1 | 1 | 0 | 5th |
| 2006 OG-W | 17-F | GER | 5 | 1 | 0 | 1 | 8 | 5th |
| 2007 WW | 17-F | GER | 4 | 0 | 0 | 0 | 0 | 8th |
| 2008 WW | 17-F | GER | 4 | 0 | 1 | 1 | 2 | 9th |
| 2012 WW | 17-F | GER | 5 | 0 | 1 | 1 | 0 | 7th |
| **Totals WW** | | | **22** | **1** | **3** | **4** | **4** | **—** |

| **Seitz, Julia** | | | | | | | | **b. Kaufbeuren, Germany, February 14, 1994** |
|---|---|---|---|---|---|---|---|---|
| 2010 WW18 | 11-F | GER | 3 | 0 | 0 | 0 | 0 | 4th |
| 2011 WW18 | 11-F | GER | 5 | 0 | 0 | 0 | 0 | 6th |
| 2012 WW18 | 11-F | GER | 6 | 0 | 0 | 0 | 0 | 4th |
| **Totals WW18** | | | **14** | **0** | **0** | **0** | **0** | **—** |

| **Selzer, Saskia** | | | | | | | | **b. Kaufbeuren, Germany, November 1, 1994** |
|---|---|---|---|---|---|---|---|---|
| 2011 WW18 | 18-F | GER | 5 | 0 | 0 | 0 | 0 | 6th |

| **Semenets, Olga** | | | | | | | | **b. Chelyabinsk, Soviet Union (Russia), August 12, 1987** |
|---|---|---|---|---|---|---|---|---|
| 2007 WW | 19-F | RUS | 4 | 1 | 0 | 1 | 2 | 7th |
| 2008 WW | 19-F | RUS | 4 | 0 | 0 | 0 | 2 | 6th |
| 2011 WW | 22-F | RUS | 6 | 0 | 0 | 0 | 0 | 4th |
| **Totals WW** | | | **14** | **1** | **0** | **1** | **4** | **—** |

| **Sergina, Marina** | | | | | | | | **b. Murmansk, Soviet Union (Russia), March 2, 1986** |
|---|---|---|---|---|---|---|---|---|
| 2008 WW | 10-F | RUS | 4 | 0 | 1 | 1 | 6 | 6th |
| 2009 WW | 11-F | RUS | 4 | 0 | 1 | 1 | 6 | 5th |
| 2010 OG-W | 11-F | RUS | 5 | 1 | 2 | 3 | 8 | 6th |
| 2011 WW | 11-F | RUS | 6 | 1 | 5 | 6 | 12 | 4th |
| 2012 WW | 11-F | RUS | 5 | 1 | 1 | 2 | 8 | 6th |
| **Totals WW** | | | **19** | **2** | **8** | **10** | **32** | **—** |

| **Shegebayeva, Arai** | | | | | | | | **b. Taldy-Kurgan, Soviet Union (Kazakhstan), December 27, 1991** |
|---|---|---|---|---|---|---|---|---|
| 2009 WW | 55-F | KAZ | 4 | 0 | 0 | 0 | 0 | 6th |

| **Shepelinskaya, Maria** | | | | | | | | **b. April 23, 1995** |
|---|---|---|---|---|---|---|---|---|
| 2012 WW18 | 19-F | RUS | 6 | 0 | 0 | 0 | 2 | 7th |

| **Sherry, Sasha** | | | | | | | | **b. Lehighton, Pennsylvania, United States, April 5, 1990** |
|---|---|---|---|---|---|---|---|---|
| 2008 WW18 | 15-D | USA | 5 | 1 | 2 | 3 | 4 | G |

| **Sherstyuk, Kristina** | | | | | | | | **b. Sakha Yakutia, Soviet Union (Russia), April 18, 1991** |
|---|---|---|---|---|---|---|---|---|
| 2009 WW18 | 11-F | RUS | 5 | 0 | 0 | 0 | 2 | 7th |

| Shibanova, Anna | | | | | | | | b. Omsk, Russia, November 10, 1994 |
|---|---|---|---|---|---|---|---|---|
| 2010 WW18 | 26-F | RUS | 5 | 1 | 0 | 1 | 6 | 8th |
| 2012 WW18 | 24-D | RUS | 6 | 0 | 0 | 0 | 8 | 7th |
| **Totals WW18** | | | **11** | **1** | **0** | **1** | **14** | **—** |

| Shibanova, Tatyana | | | | | | | | b. Omsk, Russia, November 10, 1994 |
|---|---|---|---|---|---|---|---|---|
| 2010 WW18 | 6-F | RUS | 5 | 0 | 1 | 1 | 6 | 8th |
| 2012 WW18 | 11-F | RUS | 6 | 0 | 0 | 0 | 6 | — |
| **Totals WW18** | | | **11** | **0** | **1** | **1** | **12** | **—** |

| Shields, Jennifer | | | | | | | | b. Ingersoll, Ontario, Canada, February 20, 1993 |
|---|---|---|---|---|---|---|---|---|
| 2011 WW18 | 2-D | CAN | 5 | 0 | 2 | 2 | 0 | S |

| Shimozawa, Saki | | | | | | | | b. Hokkaido, Japan, June 5, 1988 |
|---|---|---|---|---|---|---|---|---|
| 2009 WW | 14-F | JPN | 4 | 0 | 0 | 0 | 0 | 8th |

| Shishiuchi, Miho | | | | | | | | b. Hokkaido, Japan, August 21, 1992 |
|---|---|---|---|---|---|---|---|---|
| 2010 WW18 | 5-F | JPN | 5 | 0 | 1 | 1 | 0 | 6th |

| Shondra, Anastasia | | | | | | | | b. Chelyabinsk Region, Russia, September 7, 1992 |
|---|---|---|---|---|---|---|---|---|
| 2009 WW18 | 6-D | RUS | 5 | 0 | 0 | 0 | 0 | 7th |

| Shtelmaister, Yelena | | | | | | | | b. Karagadinsk, Soviet Union (Kazakhstan), September 15, 1977 |
|---|---|---|---|---|---|---|---|---|
| 2001 WW | 10-F | KAZ | 5 | 1 | 1 | 2 | 6 | 8th |
| 2002 OG-W | 10-F | KAZ | 5 | 0 | 0 | 0 | 2 | 8th |
| 2005 WW | 10-D | KAZ | 5 | 0 | 0 | 0 | 6 | 7th |
| 2007 WW | 10-D | KAZ | 4 | 0 | 0 | 0 | 6 | 9th |
| 2009 WW | 10-F | KAZ | 4 | 0 | 0 | 0 | 4 | 6th |
| 2011 WW | 10-D | KAZ | 5 | 0 | 1 | 1 | 6 | 8th |
| **Totals WW** | | | **23** | **1** | **2** | **3** | **28** | **—** |

| Shu (Zyatkova), Galina | | | | | | | | b. Almaty, Soviet Union (Kazakhstan), November 27, 1986 |
|---|---|---|---|---|---|---|---|---|
| 2005 WW* | 5-D | KAZ | 5 | 0 | 1 | 1 | 0 | 7th |
| 2007 WW | 5-D | KAZ | 4 | 0 | 0 | 0 | 12 | 9th |
| 2009 WW | 5-D | KAZ | 4 | 0 | 1 | 1 | 6 | 6th |
| 2011 WW | 5-D | KAZ | 5 | 1 | 1 | 2 | 4 | 8th |
| **Totals WW** | | | **18** | **1** | **3** | **4** | **22** | **—** |

*played under maiden name of Galina Zyatkova

| Shukina, Anna | | | | | | | | b. Vladimir Region, Soviet Union (Russia), November 5, 1987 |
|---|---|---|---|---|---|---|---|---|
| 2008 WW | 18-D | RUS | 4 | 0 | 0 | 0 | 2 | 6th |
| 2009 WW | 21-D | RUS | 4 | 1 | 0 | 1 | 4 | 5th |
| 2011 WW | 21-D | RUS | 6 | 0 | 0 | 0 | 4 | 4th |
| 2012 WW | 21-D | RUS | 5 | 0 | 1 | 1 | 2 | 6th |
| **Totals WW** | | | **19** | **1** | **1** | **2** | **12** | **—** |

| Siggelin-Alstermark, Madeleine | | | | | | | | b. Stockholm, Sweden, September 14, 1992 |
|---|---|---|---|---|---|---|---|---|
| 2009 WW18 | 7-D | SWE | 5 | 0 | 1 | 1 | 2 | B |
| 2010 WW18 | 7-D | SWE | 6 | 0 | 0 | 0 | 0 | B |
| **Totals WW18** | | | **11** | **0** | **1** | **1** | **2** | **2B** |

| Sirvio, Noora | | | | | | | | b. Kaarina, Finland, February 15, 1991 |
|---|---|---|---|---|---|---|---|---|
| 2008 WW18 | 24-F | FIN | 5 | 0 | 0 | 0 | 4 | 6th |

| Skarupa, Haley | | | | | | | | b. Rockville, Maryland, United States, January 3, 1994 |
|---|---|---|---|---|---|---|---|---|
| 2010 WW18 | 16-F | USA | 5 | 3 | 6 | 9 | 0 | S |
| 2011 WW18 | 16-F | USA | 5 | 3 | 5 | 8 | 0 | G |
| 2012 WW18 | 16-F | USA | 5 | 11 | 0 | 11 | 0 | S |
| **Totals WW18** | | | **15** | **17** | **11** | **28** | **0** | **G,2S** |

| Skiba, Galina | | | | | | | | b. Kharkov, Soviet Union (Russia), May 9, 1984 |
|---|---|---|---|---|---|---|---|---|
| 2005 WW | 5-F | RUS | 5 | 0 | 0 | 0 | 2 | 8th |
| 2006 OG-W | 5-F | RUS | 5 | 0 | 0 | 0 | 2 | 6th |
| 2007 WW | 55-F | RUS | 4 | 0 | 1 | 1 | 2 | 7th |
| 2008 WW | 55-F | RUS | 4 | 0 | 0 | 0 | 2 | 6th |
| 2011 WW | 55-F | RUS | 6 | 0 | 1 | 1 | 2 | 4th |
| 2012 WW | 55-F | RUS | 5 | 1 | 1 | 2 | 2 | 6th |
| **Totals WW** | | | **24** | **1** | **2** | **3** | **10** | **—** |

| Skorodumova, Yekaterina | | | | | | | | b. Chelyabinsk, Russia, March 24, 1993 |
|---|---|---|---|---|---|---|---|---|
| 2009 WW18 | 19-F | RUS | 5 | 0 | 2 | 2 | 4 | 7th |
| 2010 WW18 | 19-F | RUS | 5 | 0 | 0 | 0 | 4 | 8th |
| **Totals WW18** | | | **10** | **0** | **2** | **2** | **8** | **—** |

| Slavin, Jordan | | | | | | | | b. Erie, Colorado, United States, February 5, 1992 |
|---|---|---|---|---|---|---|---|---|
| 2010 WW18 | 28-D | USA | 5 | 0 | 2 | 2 | 2 | S |

| Slusar, Bobbi Jo | | | | | | | | b. Swift Current, Saskatchewan, Canada, June 6, 1985 |
|---|---|---|---|---|---|---|---|---|
| 2011 WW | 14-D | CAN | 5 | 0 | 2 | 2 | 2 | S |

| Smolentseva, Yekaterina | | | | | | | | b. Pervouralsk, Soviet Union (Russia), September 15, 1981 |
|---|---|---|---|---|---|---|---|---|
| 1997 WW | 27-F | RUS | 5 | 0 | 2 | 2 | 6 | 6th |
| 1999 WW | 27-F | RUS | 5 | 0 | 2 | 2 | 12 | 6th |
| 2000 WW | 17-F | RUS | 5 | 4 | 3 | 7 | 0 | 5th |
| 2001 WW | 17-F | RUS | 5 | 0 | 1 | 1 | 2 | B |
| 2002 OG-W | 17-F | RUS | 5 | 1 | 3 | 4 | 6 | 5th |
| 2006 OG-W | 17-F | RUS | 5 | 0 | 2 | 2 | 0 | 6th |
| 2007 WW | 17-F | RUS | 4 | 4 | 1 | 5 | 0 | 7th |
| 2008 WW | 17-F | RUS | 4 | 4 | 2 | 6 | 33 | 6th |
| 2009 WW | 17-F | RUS | 3 | 2 | 4 | 6 | 2 | 5th |
| 2010 OG-W | 17-F | RUS | 5 | 1 | 1 | 2 | 10 | 6th |
| 2011 WW | 17-F | RUS | 6 | 2 | 1 | 3 | 6 | 4th |
| **Totals WW** | | | **37** | **16** | **16** | **32** | **61** | **B** |
| **Totals OG-W** | | | **15** | **2** | **6** | **8** | **16** | **—** |

| Smolina, Yekaterina | | | | | | | | b. Ust-Kamenogorsk, Soviet Union (Kazakhstan), October 8, 1988 |
|---|---|---|---|---|---|---|---|---|
| 2006 OG-W | 7-F | RUS | 5 | 0 | 0 | 0 | 12 | 6th |
| 2007 WW | 71-F | RUS | 4 | 0 | 1 | 1 | 0 | 7th |
| 2008 WW | 71-F | RUS | 4 | 0 | 0 | 0 | 2 | 6th |
| 2009 WW | 18-F | RUS | 4 | 0 | 0 | 0 | 0 | 5th |
| 2012 WW | 28-F | RUS | 5 | 0 | 0 | 0 | 2 | 6th |
| **Totals WW** | | | **17** | **0** | **1** | **1** | **14** | **—** |

| Solnickova, Katerina | | | | | | | | b. Prague, Czech Republic, March 25, 1993 |
|---|---|---|---|---|---|---|---|---|
| 2009 WW18 | 11-F | CZE | 1 | 0 | 0 | 0 | 4 | 4th |
| 2010 WW18 | 7-F | CZE | 5 | 2 | 2 | 4 | 16 | 7th |
| 2011 WW18 | 13-F | CZE | 6 | 3 | 1 | 4 | 6 | 4th |
| **Totals WW18** | | | **12** | **5** | **3** | **8** | **26** | **—** |

| Solovyova, Yekaterina | | | | | | | | b. Sverdlovsk Region, Soviet Union (Russia), June 20, 1991 |
|---|---|---|---|---|---|---|---|---|
| 2008 WW18 | 7-F | RUS | 5 | 1 | 0 | 1 | 10 | 8th |
| 2009 WW18 | 7-F | RUS | 5 | 0 | 2 | 2 | 16 | 7th |
| 2011 WW | 29-F | RUS | 6 | 0 | 0 | 0 | 0 | 4th |
| **Totals WW18** | | | **10** | **1** | **3** | **3** | **26** | **—** |

| Sosina, Olga | | | | | | | | b. Almetyevsk, Russia, July 27, 1992 |
|---|---|---|---|---|---|---|---|---|
| 2008 WW18 | 17-F | RUS | 5 | 2 | 0 | 2 | 4 | 8th |
| 2009 WW18 | 17-F | RUS | 5 | 5 | 1 | 6 | 10 | 7th |
| 2009 WW | 7-F | RUS | 3 | 1 | 0 | 1 | 0 | 5th |
| 2010 WW18 | 17-F | RUS | 5 | 3 | 1 | 4 | 4 | 8th |
| 2010 OG-W | 7-F | RUS | 5 | 0 | 0 | 0 | 2 | 6th |
| 2011 WW | 7-F | RUS | 6 | 1 | 2 | 3 | 0 | 4th |
| 2012 WW | 7-F | RUS | 4 | 0 | 0 | 0 | 2 | 6th |
| **Totals WW18** | | | **15** | **10** | **2** | **12** | **18** | **—** |
| **Totals WW** | | | **13** | **2** | **2** | **4** | **2** | **—** |

| Sotnikova, Tatyana | | | | | | | | b. Moscow, Soviet Union (Russia), January 20, 1981 |
|---|---|---|---|---|---|---|---|---|
| 1999 WW | 21-F | RUS | 5 | 0 | 0 | 0 | 0 | 6th |
| 2000 WW | 21-F | RUS | 5 | 0 | 0 | 0 | 2 | 5th |
| 2001 WW | 11-F | RUS | 5 | 0 | 0 | 0 | 4 | B |
| 2002 OG-W | 11-F | RUS | 5 | 0 | 0 | 0 | 0 | 5th |
| 2004 WW | 11-F | RUS | 4 | 2 | 1 | 3 | 0 | 5th |
| 2005 WW | 11-F | RUS | 5 | 1 | 0 | 1 | 2 | 8th |
| 2006 OG-W | 11-F | RUS | 5 | 0 | 1 | 1 | 4 | 6th |
| 2009 WW | 29-F | RUS | 4 | 0 | 2 | 2 | 0 | 5th |
| 2010 OG-W | 29-F | RUS | 5 | 1 | 0 | 1 | 2 | 6th |
| **Totals WW** | | | **28** | **3** | **3** | **6** | **8** | **B** |
| **Totals OG-W** | | | **15** | **1** | **1** | **2** | **6** | **—** |

| Sowchuk, Erika | | | | | | | | b. Fernie, British Columbia, February 19, 1994 |
|---|---|---|---|---|---|---|---|---|
| 2012 WW18 | 19-F | CAN | 5 | 1 | 1 | 2 | 0 | G |

| Spasich, Edit | | | | | | | | b. Leningrad (St. Petersburg), Soviet Union (Russia), August 31, 1991 |
|---|---|---|---|---|---|---|---|---|
| 2008 WW18 | 15-F | RUS | 2 | 0 | 0 | 0 | 0 | 8th |
| 2009 WW18 | 23-F | RUS | 5 | 0 | 0 | 0 | 4 | 7th |
| **Totals WW18** | | | **7** | **0** | **0** | **0** | **4** | **—** |

| Spielberger, Kerstin | | | | | | | | b. Burghausen, Germany, December 14, 1995 |
|---|---|---|---|---|---|---|---|---|
| 2011 WW18 | 28-F | GER | 5 | 1 | 0 | 1 | 4 | 6th |
| 2012 WW18 | 28-F | GER | 6 | 8 | 0 | 8 | 4 | 4th |
| 2012 WW | 2-F | GER | 5 | 0 | 0 | 0 | 4 | 7th |
| **Totals WW18** | | | **11** | **9** | **0** | **9** | **8** | **—** |

| Spooner, Natalie | | | | | | | | b. Scarborough (Toronto), Ontario, Canada, October 17, 1990 |
|---|---|---|---|---|---|---|---|---|
| 2008 WW18 | 22-F | CAN | 5 | 3 | 8 | 11 | 0 | S |
| 2011 WW | 24-F | CAN | 5 | 1 | 2 | 3 | 0 | S |
| 2012 WW | 24-F | CAN | 5 | 4 | 2 | 6 | 4 | G |
| **Totals WW** | | | **10** | **5** | **4** | **9** | **4** | **G,S** |

| Spuhler, Carina | | | | | | | | b. Bad Tolz, West Germany (Germany), September 3, 1990 |
|---|---|---|---|---|---|---|---|---|
| 2007 WW | 3-D | GER | 4 | 1 | 0 | 1 | 0 | 8th |
| 2008 WW18 | 3-D | GER | 5 | 0 | 1 | 1 | 2 | 5th |

| Sramkova, Marketa | | | | | | | | b. Most, Czechoslovakia (Czech Republic), February 10, 1991 |
|---|---|---|---|---|---|---|---|---|
| 2009 WW18 | 14-F | CZE | 5 | 2 | 1 | 3 | 0 | 4th |

| Srokova, Lenka | | | | | | | | b. Levoca, Czechoslovakia (Slovakia), May 11, 1991 |
|---|---|---|---|---|---|---|---|---|
| 2011 WW | 30-F | SVK | 5 | 0 | 0 | 0 | 2 | 7th |
| 2012 WW | 30-F | SVK | 5 | 0 | 0 | 0 | 0 | 8th |
| **Totals WW** | | | **10** | **0** | **0** | **0** | **2** | **—** |

| Stacey, Laura | | | | | | | | b. Kleinburg, Ontario, Canada, May 5, 1994 |
|---|---|---|---|---|---|---|---|---|
| 2011 WW18 | 27-F | CAN | 5 | 3 | 4 | 7 | 2 | S |
| 2012 WW18 | 7-F | CAN | 5 | 4 | 3 | 7 | 4 | G |
| **Totals WW18** | | | **10** | **7** | **7** | **14** | **6** | **G,S** |

| Stack, Kelli | | | | | | | | b. Brooklyn Heights, Ohio, United States, January 13, 1988 |
|---|---|---|---|---|---|---|---|---|
| 2008 WW | 25-F | USA | 5 | 1 | 0 | 1 | 2 | G |
| 2009 WW | 16-F | USA | 5 | 2 | 3 | 5 | 4 | G |
| 2010 OG-W | 16-F | USA | 5 | 3 | 5 | 8 | 2 | S |
| 2011 WW | 16-F | USA | 5 | 2 | 2 | 4 | 4 | G |
| 2012 WW | 16-F | USA | 5 | 5 | 8 | 13 | 2 | S |
| **Totals WW** | | | **20** | **10** | **13** | **23** | **12** | **3G,S** |

~WW IIHF Directorate Award Best Forward (2012), WW All-Star Team/Forward (2012)

| Staiger, Reica | | | | | | | | b. November 8, 1996 |
|---|---|---|---|---|---|---|---|---|
| 2012 WW18 | 8-D | SUI | 5 | 0 | 0 | 0 | 6 | 8th |

| Stalder, Lara | | | | | | | | b. Lucerne, Switzerland, May 15, 1994 |
|---|---|---|---|---|---|---|---|---|
| 2011 WW18 | 7-D | SUI | 6 | 3 | 4 | 7 | 6 | 7th |
| 2011 WW | 17-D | SUI | 5 | 0 | 2 | 2 | 10 | 6th |
| 2012 WW18 | 7-D | SUI | 6 | 4 | 2 | 6 | 12 | 8th |
| **Totals WW18** | | | **12** | **7** | **6** | **13** | **18** | **—** |

| Stanz, Phoebe | | | | | | | | b. Zetzwil, Switzerland, January 7, 1994 |
|---|---|---|---|---|---|---|---|---|
| 2011 WW18 | 22-F | SUI | 6 | 3 | 4 | 7 | 14 | 7th |
| 2011 WW | 94-F | SUI | 5 | 0 | 1 | 1 | 12 | 6th |
| 2012 WW18 | 22-F | SUI | 6 | 6 | 3 | 9 | 12 | 8th |
| 2012 WW | 88-F | SUI | 6 | 1 | 1 | 2 | 6 | B |
| **Totals WW18** | | | **12** | **9** | **7** | **16** | **26** | **—** |
| **Totals WW** | | | **11** | **1** | **2** | **3** | **18** | **B** |

| Stastna, Tereza | | | | | | | | b. Pisek, Czechoslovakia (Czech Republic), October 1, 1990 |
|---|---|---|---|---|---|---|---|---|
| 2008 WW18 | 15-F | CZE | 5 | 0 | 1 | 1 | 2 | B |

| Steadman, Kelley | | | | | | | | b. Plattsburgh, New York, United States, July 17, 1990 |
|---|---|---|---|---|---|---|---|---|
| 2008 WW18 | 17-F | USA | 5 | 0 | 5 | 5 | 2 | G |
| 2011 WW | 27-F | USA | 5 | 0 | 2 | 2 | 0 | G |

| Stearns, Corey | | | | | | | | b. Falmouth, Massachusetts, United States, December 27, 1990 |
|---|---|---|---|---|---|---|---|---|
| 2008 WW18 | 22-F | USA | 5 | 2 | 4 | 6 | 0 | G |

| Steck, Martina | | | | | | | | b. January 22, 1990 |
|---|---|---|---|---|---|---|---|---|
| 2012 WW | 96-F | SUI | 6 | 0 | 1 | 1 | 0 | B |

| Stecklein, Lee | | | | | | | | b. Roseville, Minnesota, United States, April 23, 1994 |
|---|---|---|---|---|---|---|---|---|
| 2011 WW18 | 4-D | USA | 5 | 0 | 1 | 1 | 2 | G |
| 2012 WW18 | 4-D | USA | 5 | 0 | 3 | 3 | 0 | S |
| **Totals WW18** | | | **10** | **0** | **4** | **4** | **2** | **G,S** |

| Stenberg, Rebecca | | | | | | | | b. Pitea, Sweden, September 18, 1992 |
|---|---|---|---|---|---|---|---|---|
| 2010 WW18 | 13-F | SWE | 6 | 4 | 1 | 5 | 4 | B |
| 2011 WW | 21-F | SWE | 5 | 1 | 0 | 1 | 0 | 5th |
| 2012 WW | 21-F | SWE | 5 | 0 | 0 | 0 | 0 | 5th |
| **Totals WW** | | | **10** | **1** | **0** | **1** | **0** | **—** |

| Stiefel, Anja | | | | | | | | b. Wil, Switzerland, August 9, 1990 |
|---|---|---|---|---|---|---|---|---|
| 2008 WW18 | 9-F | SUI | 5 | 1 | 3 | 4 | 8 | 7th |
| 2008 WW | 63-F | SUI | 5 | 0 | 0 | 0 | 0 | 4th |
| 2009 WW | 69-F | SUI | 4 | 0 | 1 | 1 | 2 | 7th |
| 2010 OG-W | 63-F | SUI | 5 | 0 | 0 | 0 | 0 | 5th |
| 2011 WW | 63-F | SUI | 5 | 1 | 2 | 3 | 0 | 6th |
| 2012 WW | 63-F | SUI | 6 | 1 | 2 | 3 | 2 | B |
| **Totals WW** | | | **20** | **2** | **5** | **7** | **4** | **B** |

| Stoltenberg, Jutta | | | | | | | | b. Hamburg, Germany, September 7, 1991 |
|---|---|---|---|---|---|---|---|---|
| 2008 WW18 | 13-D | FIN | 5 | 0 | 0 | 0 | 0 | 6th |
| 2009 WW18 | 13-D | FIN | 5 | 0 | 0 | 0 | 6 | 5th |
| **Totals WW18** | | | **10** | **0** | **0** | **0** | **6** | **—** |

| Strohmaier, Ines | | | | | | | | b. Munich, Germany, April 17, 1992 |
|---|---|---|---|---|---|---|---|---|
| 2009 WW18 | 18-D | GER | 5 | 0 | 0 | 0 | 6 | 6th |
| 2010 WW18 | 18-D | GER | 6 | 4 | 3 | 7 | 4 | 4th |
| **Totals WW18** | | | **11** | **4** | **3** | **7** | **10** | **—** |

| Sugawara, Risa | | | | | | | | b. Hokkaido, Japan, May 26, 1993 |
|---|---|---|---|---|---|---|---|---|
| 2011 WW18 | 6-D | JPN | 6 | 0 | 0 | 0 | 0 | 8th |

| Sugisawa, Nene | | | | | | | | b. Hokkaido, Japan, August 17, 1994 |
|---|---|---|---|---|---|---|---|---|
| 2010 WW18 | 10-F | JPN | 5 | 1 | 0 | 1 | 0 | 6th |
| 2011 WW18 | 16-F | JPN | 6 | 0 | 0 | 0 | 0 | 8th |
| **Totals WW18** | | | **11** | **1** | **0** | **1** | **0** | **—** |

| Sun, Rui | | | | | | | | b. Heilongjiang, China, May 14, 1982 |
|---|---|---|---|---|---|---|---|---|
| 1999 WW | 14-F | CHN | 5 | 1 | 0 | 1 | 2 | 5th |
| 2000 WW | 14-F | CHN | 5 | 1 | 3 | 4 | 6 | 6th |
| 2001 WW | 14-F | CHN | 5 | 1 | 2 | 3 | 4 | 7th |
| 2002 OG-W | 14-F | CHN | 5 | 2 | 2 | 4 | 2 | 7th |
| 2004 WW | 14-F | CHN | 4 | 4 | 0 | 4 | 0 | 7th |
| 2005 WW | 14-F | CHN | 5 | 4 | 0 | 4 | 6 | 6th |
| 2007 WW | 14-F | CHN | 4 | 3 | 1 | 4 | 2 | 6th |
| 2008 WW | 14-F | CHN | 4 | 3 | 3 | 6 | 2 | 8th |
| 2009 WW | 14-F | CHN | 4 | 5 | 1 | 6 | 8 | 9th |
| 2010 OG-W | 14-F | CHN | 5 | 1 | 2 | 3 | 0 | 7th |
| **Totals WW** | | | **36** | **22** | **10** | **32** | **30** | **—** |
| **Totals OG-W** | | | **10** | **3** | **4** | **7** | **2** | **—** |

| Suokko, Jenna | | | | | | | | b. Tampere, Finland, June 14, 1995 |
|---|---|---|---|---|---|---|---|---|
| 2011 WW18 | 28-F | FIN | 6 | 0 | 0 | 0 | 8 | B |
| 2012 WW18 | 28-F | FIN | 5 | 2 | 2 | 4 | 8 | 5th |
| **Totals WW18** | | | **11** | **2** | **2** | **4** | **16** | **B** |

| Suprun, Albina | | | | | | | | b. Almaty, Soviet Union (Kazakhstan), March 28, 1988 |
|---|---|---|---|---|---|---|---|---|
| 2005 WW | 22-D | KAZ | 5 | 0 | 0 | 0 | 0 | 7th |
| 2007 WW | 24-D | KAZ | 4 | 0 | 0 | 0 | 2 | 9th |
| 2009 WW | 24-D | KAZ | 4 | 0 | 0 | 0 | 0 | 6th |
| 2011 WW | 24-D | KAZ | 5 | 0 | 0 | 0 | 2 | 8th |
| **Totals WW** | | | **18** | **0** | **0** | **0** | **4** | **—** |

| Suzuki, Ami | | | | | | | | b. Hokkaido, Japan, January 30, 1992 |
|---|---|---|---|---|---|---|---|---|
| 2010 WW18 | 17-F | JPN | 5 | 0 | 0 | 0 | 0 | 6th |

| Suzuki, Sena | | | | | | | | b. Hokkaido, Japan, August 4, 1991 |
|---|---|---|---|---|---|---|---|---|
| 2009 WW | 6-D | JPN | 4 | 0 | 0 | 0 | 2 | 8th |

| Svedin, Annie | | | | | | | | b. Sundsvall, Sweden, October 12, 1991 |
|---|---|---|---|---|---|---|---|---|
| 2008 WW18 | 6-D | SWE | 5 | 1 | 0 | 1 | 4 | 4th |
| 2009 WW18 | 8-D | SWE | 5 | 2 | 1 | 3 | 2 | B |
| 2011 WW | 20-D | SWE | 5 | 0 | 0 | 0 | 4 | 5th |
| 2012 WW | 20-D | SWE | 5 | 1 | 0 | 1 | 2 | 5th |
| **Totals WW18** | | | **10** | **3** | **1** | **4** | **6** | **B** |
| **Totals WW** | | | **10** | **1** | **0** | **1** | **6** | **—** |

| Svedin-Thunstrom, Frida | | | | | | | | b. Sundsvall, Sweden, November 4, 1989 |
|---|---|---|---|---|---|---|---|---|
| 2009 WW | 25-F | SWE | 5 | 1 | 2 | 3 | 2 | 4th |
| 2010 OG-W | 25-F | SWE | 5 | 0 | 1 | 1 | 6 | 4th |

| Sviridova, Larisa | | | | | | | | b. Almaty, Soviet Union (Kazakhstan), September 23, 1985 |
|---|---|---|---|---|---|---|---|---|
| 2005 WW | 14-F | KAZ | 5 | 0 | 0 | 0 | 0 | 7th |
| 2007 WW | 19-F | KAZ | 4 | 0 | 0 | 0 | 0 | 9th |
| 2009 WW | 14-F | KAZ | 4 | 0 | 0 | 0 | 4 | 6th |
| 2011 WW | 14-F | KAZ | 5 | 0 | 1 | 1 | 6 | 8th |
| **Totals WW** | | | **18** | **0** | **1** | **1** | **10** | **—** |

| Swikull, Larissa | | | | | | | | b. October 5, 1996 |
|---|---|---|---|---|---|---|---|---|
| 2012 WW18 | 15-F | GER | 4 | 0 | 0 | 0 | 0 | 4th |

| Sylvester, Karley | | | | | | | | b. Warroad, Minnesota, United States, January 30, 1993 |
|---|---|---|---|---|---|---|---|---|
| 2011 WW18 | 21-F | USA | 5 | 1 | 5 | 6 | 4 | G |

| Takahashi, Mai | | | | | | | | b. Hokkaido, Japan, December 9, 1988 |
|---|---|---|---|---|---|---|---|---|
| 2008 WW | 20-F | JPN | 4 | 0 | 0 | 0 | 0 | 7th |
| 2009 WW | 20-F | JPN | 4 | 0 | 0 | 0 | 0 | 8th |
| **Totals WW** | | | **8** | **0** | **0** | **0** | **0** | **—** |

| Takahashi, Sawako | | | | | | | | b. Hokkaido, Japan, December 5, 1992 |
|---|---|---|---|---|---|---|---|---|
| 2010 WW18 | 19-D | JPN | 5 | 0 | 0 | 0 | 0 | 6th |

| Takashima, Haruka | | | | | | | | b. Tomakomai, Japan, January 30, 1988 |
|---|---|---|---|---|---|---|---|---|
| 2004 WW | 77-F | JPN | 4 | 0 | 0 | 0 | 2 | 9th |
| 2008 WW | 21-F | JPN | 4 | 0 | 0 | 0 | 6 | 7th |
| 2009 WW | 21-F | JPN | 4 | 0 | 0 | 0 | 0 | 8th |
| **Totals WW** | | | **12** | **0** | **0** | **0** | **8** | **—** |

| Takeda, Rina | | | | | | | | b. Hokkaido, Japan, January 16, 1993 |
|---|---|---|---|---|---|---|---|---|
| 2010 WW18 | 2-D | JPN | 5 | 0 | 0 | 0 | 2 | 6th |
| 2011 WW18 | 4-D | JPN | 6 | 1 | 0 | 1 | 10 | 8th |
| **Totals WW18** | | | **11** | **1** | **0** | **1** | **12** | **—** |

**Tamada, Yoko** ~see Ohtani (Tamada), Yoko

| **Tamas, Jenny** | | | | | | | | **b. Herford, West Germany (Germany), January 18, 1990** |
|---|---|---|---|---|---|---|---|---|
| 2006 OG-W | 2-D | GER | 5 | 0 | 1 | 1 | 4 | 5th |
| 2007 WW | 2-D | GER | 4 | 0 | 0 | 0 | 2 | 8th |
| 2008 WW18 | 2-D | GER | 5 | 2 | 0 | 2 | 8 | 5th |
| 2008 WW | 2-D | GER | 4 | 0 | 2 | 2 | 2 | 9th |
| **Totals WW** | | | **8** | **0** | **2** | **2** | **4** | **—** |

| **Tan, Anqi** | | | | | | | | **b. Heilongjiang, China, June 10, 1986** |
|---|---|---|---|---|---|---|---|---|
| 2005 WW | 26-D | CHN | 5 | 0 | 0 | 0 | 6 | 6th |
| 2007 WW | 26-D | CHN | 4 | 0 | 1 | 1 | 6 | 6th |
| 2008 WW | 26-D | CHN | 4 | 0 | 0 | 0 | 6 | 8th |
| 2009 WW | 26-D | CHN | 4 | 0 | 0 | 0 | 4 | 9th |
| 2010 OG-W | 26-D | CHN | 5 | 0 | 0 | 0 | 4 | 7th |
| **Totals WW** | | | **17** | **0** | **1** | **1** | **22** | **—** |

| **Tang, Liang** | | | | | | | | **b. Heilongjiang, China, August 26, 1985** |
|---|---|---|---|---|---|---|---|---|
| 2004 WW | 24-F | CHN | 4 | 0 | 0 | 0 | 0 | 7th |
| 2005 WW | 24-F | CHN | 5 | 0 | 0 | 0 | 2 | 6th |
| 2007 WW | 24-F | CHN | 4 | 1 | 0 | 1 | 0 | 6th |
| 2009 WW | 24-F | CHN | 3 | 0 | 0 | 0 | 0 | 9th |
| 2010 OG-W | 24-F | CHN | 5 | 0 | 0 | 0 | 0 | 7th |
| **Totals WW** | | | **16** | **1** | **0** | **1** | **2** | **—** |

| **Tanninen, Marianne** | | | | | | | | **b. Leppavirta, Finland, October 2, 1993** |
|---|---|---|---|---|---|---|---|---|
| 2011 WW18 | 22-F | FIN | 4 | 0 | 0 | 0 | 2 | B |

| **Tanskanen, Vilma** | | | | | | | | **b. April 14, 1995** |
|---|---|---|---|---|---|---|---|---|
| 2012 WW18 | 21-F | FIN | 5 | 1 | 0 | 1 | 0 | 5th |

| **Tapani, Susanna** | | | | | | | | **b. Laitila, Finland, March 2, 1993** |
|---|---|---|---|---|---|---|---|---|
| 2009 WW18 | 11-F | FIN | 5 | 3 | 0 | 3 | 0 | 5th |
| 2010 WW18 | 11-F | FIN | 5 | 2 | 1 | 3 | 4 | 5th |
| 2011 WW18 | 11-F | FIN | 6 | 4 | 2 | 6 | 33 | B |
| 2011 WW | 12-F | FIN | 6 | 1 | 2 | 3 | 4 | B |
| 2012 WW | 12-F | FIN | 6 | 1 | 0 | 1 | 2 | 4th |
| **Totals WW18** | | | **16** | **9** | **3** | **12** | **37** | **B** |
| **Totals WW** | | | **12** | **2** | **2** | **4** | **6** | **B** |

| **Tarkki (-Sirvio), Saija** | | | | | | | | **b. Oulu, Finland, December 29, 1982** |
|---|---|---|---|---|---|---|---|---|
| 2001 WW* | 26-D | FIN | 5 | 0 | 0 | 0 | 8 | 4th |
| 2002 OG-W* | 6-D | FIN | 5 | 1 | 1 | 2 | 10 | 4th |
| 2004 WW* | 20-D | FIN | 5 | 2 | 1 | 3 | 2 | B |
| 2005 WW* | 20-D | FIN | 5 | 1 | 4 | 5 | 6 | 4th |
| 2006 OG-W* | 20-D | FIN | 5 | 0 | 0 | 0 | 10 | 4th |
| 2007 WW* | 20-D | FIN | 5 | 1 | 0 | 1 | 2 | 4th |
| 2008 WW* | 20-D | FIN | 5 | 0 | 0 | 0 | 6 | B |
| 2009 WW* | 20-D | FIN | 5 | 0 | 3 | 3 | 4 | B |
| 2010 OG-W* | 20-D | FIN | 5 | 1 | 0 | 1 | 4 | B |
| 2012 WW | 20-D | FIN | 6 | 0 | 1 | 1 | 4 | 4th |
| **Totals WW** | | | **36** | **4** | **9** | **13** | **32** | **3B** |
| **Totals OG-W** | | | **15** | **2** | **1** | **3** | **24** | **B** |

*played as Saija Sirvio

| **Teggi, Simona** | | | | | | | | **b. Turbenthal, Switzerland, January 29, 1992** |
|---|---|---|---|---|---|---|---|---|
| 2009 WW18 | 15-F | SUI | 5 | 0 | 3 | 3 | 2 | 8th |

| **Tejralova, Aneta** | | | | | | | | **b. Prague, Czech Republic, January 4, 1996** |
|---|---|---|---|---|---|---|---|---|
| 2011 WW18 | 2-D | CZE | 6 | 1 | 0 | 1 | 14 | 4th |
| 2012 WW18 | 2-D | CZE | 5 | 0 | 0 | 0 | 10 | 6th |
| **Totals WW18** | | | **11** | **1** | **0** | **1** | **24** | **—** |

| **Terashima, Naho** | | | | | | | | **b. Hokkaido, Japan, May 2, 1993** |
|---|---|---|---|---|---|---|---|---|
| 2010 WW18 | 16-F | JPN | 5 | 1 | 1 | 2 | 6 | 6th |
| 2011 WW18 | 17-F | JPN | 1 | 0 | 0 | 0 | 0 | 8th |
| **Totals WW18** | | | **6** | **1** | **1** | **2** | **6** | **—** |

| **Terentieva, Svetlana** | | | | | | | | **b. Sverdlovsk (Yekaterinburg), Soviet Union (Russia), September 25, 1983** |
|---|---|---|---|---|---|---|---|---|
| 1999 WW | 23-F | RUS | 5 | 1 | 1 | 2 | 0 | 6th |
| 2000 WW | 23-F | RUS | 5 | 2 | 3 | 5 | 0 | 5th |
| 2001 WW | 22-F | RUS | 5 | 0 | 0 | 0 | 2 | B |
| 2002 OG-W | 22-F | RUS | 5 | 1 | 0 | 1 | 2 | 5th |
| 2004 WW | 22-F | RUS | 4 | 0 | 1 | 1 | 0 | 5th |
| 2005 WW | 22-F | RUS | 5 | 0 | 0 | 0 | 0 | 8th |
| 2007 WW | 22-F | RUS | 4 | 1 | 3 | 4 | 2 | 7th |
| 2008 WW | 22-F | RUS | 4 | 1 | 4 | 5 | 2 | 6th |
| 2009 WW | 22-F | RUS | 4 | 1 | 0 | 1 | 2 | 5th |
| 2010 OG-W | 28-F | RUS | 5 | 1 | 0 | 1 | 2 | 6th |
| 2011 WW | 28-F | RUS | 6 | 0 | 1 | 1 | 0 | 4th |
| **Totals WW** | | | **42** | **6** | **13** | **19** | **8** | **B** |
| **Totals OG-W** | | | **10** | **2** | **0** | **2** | **4** | **—** |

| **Terho (Laaksonen), Emma** | | | | | | | | **b. Washington D.C., United States, December 17, 1981** |
|---|---|---|---|---|---|---|---|---|
| 1998 OG-W* | 3-D | FIN | 4 | 0 | 0 | 0 | 2 | B |
| 2000 WW* | 3-D | FIN | 5 | 0 | 0 | 0 | 2 | B |
| 2001 WW* | 3-D | FIN | 5 | 0 | 1 | 1 | 4 | 4th |
| 2002 OG-W* | 3-D | FIN | 5 | 1 | 1 | 2 | 2 | 4th |
| 2004 WW* | 3-D | FIN | 5 | 0 | 1 | 1 | 2 | B |
| 2005 WW* | 3-D | FIN | 5 | 0 | 1 | 1 | 2 | 4th |
| 2006 OG-W* | 3-D | FIN | 5 | 1 | 0 | 1 | 8 | 4th |
| 2007 WW* | 3-D | FIN | 5 | 0 | 0 | 0 | 10 | 4th |
| 2008 WW* | 3-D | FIN | 5 | 1 | 3 | 4 | 0 | B |
| 2009 WW* | 3-D | FIN | 5 | 0 | 2 | 2 | 4 | B |
| 2010 OG-W* | 3-D | FIN | 5 | 0 | 0 | 0 | 2 | B |
| **Totals WW** | | | **39** | **1** | **8** | **9** | **26** | **4B** |
| **Totals OG-W** | | | **15** | **2** | **1** | **3** | **12** | **B** |

~played under maiden name Emma Laaksonen
~WW All-Star Team/Defence (2008)

| **Terry, Kelly** | | | | | | | | **b. Whitby, Ontario, Canada, June 6, 1992** |
|---|---|---|---|---|---|---|---|---|
| 2010 WW18 | 14-F | CAN | 5 | 4 | 3 | 7 | 4 | G |

| **Thalmann, Sandra** | | | | | | | | **b. Basel, Switzerland, December 18, 1992** |
|---|---|---|---|---|---|---|---|---|
| 2008 WW18 | 2-D | SUI | 5 | 1 | 0 | 1 | 12 | 7th |
| 2009 WW18 | 2-D | SUI | 5 | 1 | 2 | 3 | 36 | 8th |
| 2009 WW | 35-D | SUI | 4 | 0 | 0 | 0 | 8 | 7th |
| 2010 OG-W | 92-D | SUI | 5 | 0 | 0 | 0 | 4 | 5th |
| 2011 WW | 92-F | SUI | 5 | 1 | 1 | 2 | 8 | 6th |
| 2012 WW | 92-D | SUI | 5 | 0 | 0 | 0 | 8 | B |
| **Totals WW18** | | | **10** | **2** | **2** | **4** | **48** | **—** |
| **Totals WW** | | | **14** | **1** | **1** | **2** | **24** | **B** |

| **Thatcher, Karen** | | | | | | | | **b. Douglas, Massachusetts, United States, February 29, 1984** |
|---|---|---|---|---|---|---|---|---|
| 2008 WW | 5-F | USA | 5 | 2 | 0 | 2 | 2 | G |
| 2009 WW | 5-F | USA | 5 | 0 | 1 | 1 | 0 | G |
| 2010 OG-W | 5-F | USA | 5 | 3 | 3 | 6 | 2 | S |
| **Totals WW** | | | **10** | **2** | **1** | **3** | **2** | **2G** |

| **Tikkinen, Nina** | | | | | | | | **b. Salo, Finland, February 6, 1987** |
|---|---|---|---|---|---|---|---|---|
| 2007 WW | 23-F | FIN | 5 | 0 | 0 | 0 | 0 | 4th |
| 2008 WW | 23-F | FIN | 5 | 1 | 0 | 1 | 2 | B |
| 2009 WW | 23-F | FIN | 5 | 3 | 1 | 4 | 0 | B |
| 2010 OG-W | 23-F | FIN | 5 | 2 | 0 | 2 | 0 | B |
| 2012 WW | 23-F | FIN | 6 | 2 | 0 | 2 | 6 | 4th |
| **Totals WW** | | | **21** | **6** | **1** | **7** | **8** | **2B** |

| **Timglas, Katarina** | | | | | | | | **b. Malmo, Sweden, November 24, 1985** |
|---|---|---|---|---|---|---|---|---|
| 2005 WW | 15-F | SWE | 4 | 0 | 0 | 0 | 0 | B |
| 2006 OG-W | 15-F | SWE | 5 | 1 | 0 | 1 | 0 | S |
| 2007 WW | 15-F | SWE | 5 | 2 | 1 | 3 | 2 | B |
| 2008 WW | 15-F | SWE | 4 | 2 | 0 | 2 | 2 | 5th |
| 2009 WW | 15-F | SWE | 5 | 1 | 1 | 2 | 12 | 4th |
| 2010 OG-W | 15-F | SWE | 5 | 1 | 0 | 1 | 12 | 4th |
| **Totals WW** | | | **18** | **5** | **2** | **7** | **16** | **2B** |
| **Totals OG-W** | | | **10** | **2** | **0** | **2** | **12** | **S** |

| **Timofeyeva, Kristina** | | | | | | | | **b. March 20, 1995** |
|---|---|---|---|---|---|---|---|---|
| 2012 WW18 | 3-D | RUS | 6 | 0 | 0 | 0 | 0 | 7th |

| **Tjarnstrom, Miranda** | | | | | | | | **b. Skelleftea, Sweden, January 14, 1990** |
|---|---|---|---|---|---|---|---|---|
| 2008 WW18 | 7-D | SWE | 5 | 0 | 0 | 0 | 10 | 4th |

| **Tkachyova, Svetlana** | | | | | | | | **b. Moscow, Soviet Union (Russia), November 3, 1984** |
|---|---|---|---|---|---|---|---|---|
| 2010 OG-W | 34-D | RUS | 5 | 0 | 0 | 0 | 2 | 6th |
| 2011 WW | 34-D | RUS | 6 | 0 | 0 | 0 | 2 | 4th |
| 2012 WW | 34-D | RUS | 5 | 0 | 0 | 0 | 2 | 6th |
| **Totals WW** | | | **11** | **0** | **0** | **0** | **4** | **—** |

| **Togawa, Yuki** | | | | | | | | **b. Kushiro, Japan, February 28, 1978** |
|---|---|---|---|---|---|---|---|---|
| 1998 OG-W | 10-F | JPN | 5 | 0 | 0 | 0 | 16 | 6th |
| 2000 WW | 17-F | JPN | 5 | 0 | 0 | 0 | 4 | 8th |
| 2004 WW | 17-F | JPN | 4 | 0 | 0 | 0 | 2 | 9th |
| 2008 WW | 10-F | JPN | 4 | 0 | 0 | 0 | 2 | 7th |
| **Totals WW** | | | **13** | **0** | **0** | **0** | **8** | **—** |

| **Toko, Ayaka** | | | | | | | | **b. Hokkaido, Japan, August 22, 1994** |
|---|---|---|---|---|---|---|---|---|
| 2010 WW18 | 8-D | JPN | 5 | 0 | 3 | 3 | 0 | 6th |
| 2011 WW18 | 7-D | JPN | 6 | 1 | 0 | 1 | 6 | 8th |
| **Totals WW18** | | | **11** | **1** | **3** | **4** | **6** | **—** |

| **Tomigova, Nikola** | | | | | | | | **b. Prostejov, Czechoslovakia (Czech Republic), May 18, 1991** |
|---|---|---|---|---|---|---|---|---|
| 2008 WW18 | 23-F | CZE | 5 | 1 | 4 | 5 | 4 | B |
| 2009 WW18 | 15-F | CZE | 5 | 0 | 1 | 1 | 4 | 4th |
| **Totals WW18** | | | **10** | **1** | **5** | **6** | **8** | **B** |

| **Trager, Stephanie** | | | | | | | | **b. Dresden, Germany, June 15, 1990** |
|---|---|---|---|---|---|---|---|---|
| 2008 WW18 | 11-F | GER | 5 | 0 | 0 | 0 | 6 | 5th |

| **Trivigno, Dana** | | | | | | | | **b. Setauket, New York, United States, January 7, 1994** |
|---|---|---|---|---|---|---|---|---|
| 2011 WW18 | 24-F | USA | 5 | 0 | 1 | 1 | 4 | G |
| 2012 WW18 | 24-F | USA | 5 | 3 | 3 | 6 | 0 | S |
| **Totals WW18** | | | **10** | **3** | **4** | **7** | **4** | **G,S** |

| **Tsirkunova, Alexandra** | | | | | | | | **b. Moscow Region, Russia, January 26, 1994** |
|---|---|---|---|---|---|---|---|---|
| 2010 WW18 | 4-D | RUS | 5 | 0 | 1 | 1 | 0 | 8th |

**Tsuchida, Aki** ~see Fujii (Tsuchida), Aki

| **Tukhtieva, Zarina** | | | | | | | | **b. Almaty, Soviet Union (Kazakhstan), June 18, 1987** |
|---|---|---|---|---|---|---|---|---|
| 2005 WW | 11-F | KAZ | 5 | 0 | 0 | 0 | 2 | 7th |
| 2007 WW | 11-F | KAZ | 4 | 0 | 0 | 0 | 4 | 9th |
| 2011 WW | 11-F | KAZ | 5 | 1 | 0 | 1 | 0 | 8th |
| **Totals WW** | | | **14** | **1** | **0** | **1** | **6** | **—** |

| **Tulus, Noora** | | | | | | | | **b. Vantaa, Finland, August 15, 1995** |
|---|---|---|---|---|---|---|---|---|
| 2011 WW18 | 23-F | FIN | 6 | 1 | 0 | 1 | 2 | B |
| 2012 WW18 | 23-F | FIN | 5 | 1 | 1 | 2 | 2 | 5th |
| **Totals WW18** | | | **11** | **2** | **1** | **3** | **4** | **B** |

| **Tuomanen, Anne** | | | | | | | | **b. Jyvaskyla, Finland, April 15, 1987** |
|---|---|---|---|---|---|---|---|---|
| 2011 WW | 28-F | FIN | 6 | 0 | 0 | 0 | 2 | B |

| **Tuominen, Minnamari** | | | | | | | | **b. Helsinki, Finland, June 26, 1990** |
|---|---|---|---|---|---|---|---|---|
| 2008 WW18 | 15-F | FIN | 5 | 0 | 2 | 2 | 4 | 6th |
| 2010 OG-W | 15-F | FIN | 5 | 0 | 0 | 0 | 0 | B |
| 2011 WW | 15-F | FIN | 6 | 2 | 2 | 4 | 10 | B |
| 2012 WW | 15-F | FIN | 6 | 0 | 0 | 0 | 4 | 4th |
| **Totals WW** | | | **12** | **2** | **2** | **4** | **14** | **B** |

| **Tuominen, Saara** | | | | | | | | **b. Ylojarvi, Finland, January 1, 1986** |
|---|---|---|---|---|---|---|---|---|
| 2004 WW | 22-F | FIN | 5 | 0 | 1 | 1 | 4 | B |
| 2005 WW | 22-F | FIN | 5 | 1 | 4 | 5 | 2 | 4th |
| 2006 OG-W | 22-F | FIN | 5 | 1 | 2 | 3 | 2 | 4th |
| 2007 WW | 22-F | FIN | 5 | 0 | 0 | 0 | 0 | 4th |
| 2008 WW | 22-F | FIN | 2 | 0 | 0 | 0 | 0 | B |
| 2009 WW | 22-F | FIN | 5 | 0 | 5 | 5 | 4 | B |
| 2010 OG-W | 22-F | FIN | 5 | 0 | 2 | 2 | 2 | B |
| **Totals WW** | | | **22** | **1** | **10** | **11** | **10** | **3B** |
| **Totals OG-W** | | | **10** | **1** | **4** | **5** | **4** | **B** |

| **Tuominen, Satu** | | | | | | | | **b. Vantaa, Finland, November 19, 1985** |
|---|---|---|---|---|---|---|---|---|
| 2004 WW | 8-F | FIN | 5 | 0 | 0 | 0 | 0 | B |
| 2006 OG-W | 8-F | FIN | 5 | 0 | 0 | 0 | 2 | 4th |
| 2007 WW | 8-F | FIN | 5 | 0 | 0 | 0 | 2 | 4th |
| 2009 WW | 15-F | FIN | 5 | 0 | 1 | 1 | 2 | B |
| **Totals WW** | | | **15** | **0** | **1** | **1** | **4** | **2B** |

| **Tuovinen, Jenna** | | | | | | | | **b. July 25, 1994** |
|---|---|---|---|---|---|---|---|---|
| 2012 WW18 | 4-D | FIN | 5 | 0 | 0 | 0 | 2 | 5th |

| **Turgeon, Elizabeth** | | | | | | | | **b. Cherry Hills Village, Colorado, United States, July 24, 1992** |
|---|---|---|---|---|---|---|---|---|
| 2008 WW18 | 23-F | USA | 5 | 0 | 1 | 1 | 2 | G |

| **Turpeinen, Hanna-Riikka** | | | | | | | | **b. Lieksa, Finland, July 4, 1990** |
|---|---|---|---|---|---|---|---|---|
| 2008 WW18 | 11-D | FIN | 5 | 0 | 0 | 0 | 6 | 6th |

| **Uden-Johansson, Erica** | | | | | | | | **b. Sundsvall, Sweden, July 20, 1989** |
|---|---|---|---|---|---|---|---|---|
| 2009 WW | 13-F | SWE | 5 | 1 | 2 | 3 | 0 | 4th |
| 2010 OG-W | 13-F | SWE | 5 | 1 | 1 | 2 | 2 | 4th |
| 2012 WW | 11-F | SWE | 5 | 1 | 0 | 1 | 0 | 5th |
| **Totals WW** | | | **10** | **2** | **2** | **4** | **0** | **—** |

| **Ujcik, Jessica** | | | | | | | | **b. Prien am Chiemsee, Germany, April 20, 1996** |
|---|---|---|---|---|---|---|---|---|
| 2012 WW18 | 9-D | GER | 6 | 0 | 2 | 2 | 6 | 4th |

| **Ukita, Risa** | | | | | | | | **b. Hokkaido, Japan, March 26, 1993** |
|---|---|---|---|---|---|---|---|---|
| 2010 WW18 | 6-F | JPN | 5 | 0 | 0 | 0 | 2 | 6th |
| 2011 WW18 | 15-F | JPN | 6 | 1 | 0 | 1 | 0 | 8th |
| **Totals WW18** | | | **11** | **1** | **0** | **1** | **2** | **—** |

| **Uppgard, Susanne** | | | | | | | | **b. February 26, 1994** |
|---|---|---|---|---|---|---|---|---|
| 2012 WW18 | 11-D | FIN | 5 | 0 | 0 | 0 | 0 | 5th |

| **Uusitalo, Elin** | | | | | | | | **b. Pajala, Sweden, January 30, 1990** |
|---|---|---|---|---|---|---|---|---|
| 2008 WW18 | 18-F | SWE | 5 | 0 | 3 | 3 | 8 | 4th |

| **Vafina, Alexandra** | | | | | | | | **b. Almaty, Soviet Union (Kazakhstan), July 28, 1990** |
|---|---|---|---|---|---|---|---|---|
| 2008 WW18 | 9-F | RUS | 5 | 0 | 1 | 1 | 4 | 8th |
| 2008 WW | 5-F | RUS | 4 | 0 | 0 | 0 | 2 | 6th |
| 2009 WW | 9-F | RUS | 4 | 0 | 1 | 1 | 2 | 5th |
| 2010 OG-W | 9-F | RUS | 5 | 1 | 0 | 1 | 2 | 6th |
| 2011 WW | 9-F | RUS | 6 | 2 | 1 | 3 | 4 | 4th |
| 2012 WW | 9-F | RUS | 5 | 0 | 0 | 0 | 2 | 6th |
| **Totals WW** | | | **19** | **2** | **2** | **4** | **10** | **—** |

| **Vaillancourt, Sarah** | | | | | | | | **b. Fleurimont, Quebec, Canada, May 8, 1985** |
|---|---|---|---|---|---|---|---|---|
| 2005 WW | 26-F | CAN | 5 | 3 | 5 | 8 | 2 | S |
| 2006 OG-W | 26-F | CAN | 5 | 2 | 4 | 6 | 2 | G |
| 2007 WW | 26-F | CAN | 5 | 2 | 4 | 6 | 4 | G |
| 2008 WW | 26-F | CAN | 5 | 4 | 2 | 6 | 8 | S |
| 2009 WW | 26-F | CAN | 5 | 3 | 4 | 7 | 8 | S |
| 2010 OG-W | 26-F | CAN | 5 | 3 | 5 | 8 | 6 | G |
| 2011 WW | 26-F | CAN | 5 | 0 | 3 | 3 | 4 | S |
| **Totals WW** | | | **25** | **12** | **18** | **30** | **26** | **G,4S** |
| **Totals OG-W** | | | **10** | **5** | **9** | **14** | **8** | **2G** |

| **Vainionpaa, Laura** | | | | | | | | **b. April 11, 1994** |
|---|---|---|---|---|---|---|---|---|
| 2012 WW18 | 5 | 0 | 0 | 0 | 4 | 5th | | |

| **Valimaki, Linda** | | | | | | | | **b. Ylojarvi, Finland, May 31, 1990** |
|---|---|---|---|---|---|---|---|---|
| 2008 WW18 | 10-F | FIN | 5 | 5 | 2 | 7 | 8 | 6th |
| 2010 OG-W | 13-F | FIN | 5 | 0 | 2 | 2 | 4 | B |

| **Valkama, Saana** | | | | | | | | **b. Pirkkala, Finland, June 27, 1994** |
|---|---|---|---|---|---|---|---|---|
| 2011 WW18 | 26-F | FIN | 6 | 3 | 1 | 4 | 6 | B |
| 2012 WW18 | 26-F | FIN | 4 | 1 | 0 | 1 | 2 | 5th |
| 2012 WW | 28-F | FIN | 6 | 0 | 0 | 0 | 2 | 4th |
| **Totals WW18** | | | **10** | **4** | **1** | **5** | **8** | **B** |

| **Valkjarvi, Reetta** | | | | | | | | **b. July 3, 1996** |
|---|---|---|---|---|---|---|---|---|
| 2012 WW18 | 7-D | FIN | 5 | 0 | 1 | 1 | 4 | 5th |

| **Vanisova, Tereza** | | | | | | | | **b. January 30, 1996** |
|---|---|---|---|---|---|---|---|---|
| 2012 WW18 | 16-F | CZE | 5 | 3 | 0 | 3 | 2 | 6th |

| **Vanouckova, Katerina** | | | | | | | | **b. Jilemnice, Czech Republic, May 27, 1995** |
|---|---|---|---|---|---|---|---|---|
| 2011 WW18 | 6-D | CZE | 6 | 0 | 1 | 1 | 4 | 4th |
| 2012 WW18 | 6-D | CZE | 5 | 0 | 0 | 0 | 2 | 6th |
| **Totals WW18** | | | **11** | **0** | **1** | **1** | **6** | **—** |

| **Vargova, Romana** | | | | | | | | **b. Levice, Czechoslovakia (Slovakia), September 23, 1988** |
|---|---|---|---|---|---|---|---|---|
| 2011 WW | 10-D | SVK | 5 | 0 | 0 | 0 | 2 | 7th |

| **Vasilieva, Maria** | | | | | | | | **b. Moscow, Soviet Union (Russia), August 4, 1991** |
|---|---|---|---|---|---|---|---|---|
| 2009 WW18 | 8-F | RUS | 5 | 2 | 1 | 3 | 8 | 7th |

| **Vasyukova, Yulia** | | | | | | | | **b. Sverdlovsk Region, Soviet Union (Russia), April 15, 1990** |
|---|---|---|---|---|---|---|---|---|
| 2008 WW18 | 14-F | RUS | 5 | 0 | 2 | 2 | 4 | 8th |

| **Velickova, Martina** | | | | | | | | **b. Presov, Czechoslovakia (Slovakia), February 17, 1989** |
|---|---|---|---|---|---|---|---|---|
| 2010 OG-W | 17-F | SVK | 5 | 0 | 3 | 3 | 2 | 8th |
| 2011 WW | 17-F | SVK | 5 | 1 | 0 | 1 | 0 | 7th |
| 2012 WW | 17-F | SVK | 5 | 2 | 0 | 2 | 4 | 8th |
| **Totals WW** | | | **10** | **3** | **0** | **3** | **4** | **—** |

| **Vershinina, Yana** | | | | | | | | **b. Yekaterinburg, Russia, August 20, 1992** |
|---|---|---|---|---|---|---|---|---|
| 2009 WW18 | 18-D | RUS | 5 | 0 | 0 | 0 | 6 | 7th |
| 2010 WW18 | 18-D | RUS | 5 | 0 | 0 | 0 | 6 | 8th |
| **Totals WW18** | | | **10** | **0** | **0** | **0** | **12** | **—** |

| **Viitasuo, Ella** | | | | | | | | **b. May 27, 1996** |
|---|---|---|---|---|---|---|---|---|
| 2012 WW18 | 9-D | FIN | 5 | 0 | 0 | 0 | 4 | 5th |

| **Villila, Tea** | | | | | | | | **b. Hyvinkaa, Finland, April 16, 1991** |
|---|---|---|---|---|---|---|---|---|
| 2008 WW18 | 8-D | FIN | 5 | 0 | 3 | 3 | 12 | 6th |
| 2009 WW18 | 8-D | FIN | 5 | 0 | 0 | 0 | 16 | 5th |
| 2011 WW | 8-D | FIN | 6 | 0 | 1 | 1 | 4 | B |
| 2012 WW | 8-D | FIN | 6 | 0 | 1 | 1 | 6 | 4th |
| **Totals WW** | | | **12** | **0** | **2** | **2** | **10** | **B** |
| **Totals WW18** | | | **10** | **0** | **3** | **3** | **28** | **—** |

| **Voigt, Tatjana** | | | | | | | | **b. Ulm, Germany, February 20, 1992** |
|---|---|---|---|---|---|---|---|---|
| 2010 WW18 | 28-D | GER | 6 | 0 | 1 | 1 | 8 | 4th |

| **Vojtechova, Petra** | | | | | | | | **b. Brno, Czechoslovakia (Czech Republic), November 22, 1992** |
|---|---|---|---|---|---|---|---|---|
| 2008 WW18 | 14-D | CZE | 5 | 0 | 0 | 0 | 0 | B |
| 2009 WW18 | 18-D | CZE | 5 | 0 | 1 | 1 | 2 | 4th |
| **Totals WW18** | | | **10** | **0** | **1** | **1** | **2** | **B** |

| **Vonkova, Martina** | | | | | | | | **b. Ceske Budejovice, Czech Republic, May 25, 1993** |
|---|---|---|---|---|---|---|---|---|
| 2010 WW18 | 22-F | CZE | 5 | 0 | 0 | 0 | 2 | 7th |
| 2011 WW18 | 24-F | CZE | 6 | 0 | 3 | 3 | 2 | 4th |
| **Totals WW18** | | | **11** | **0** | **3** | **3** | **4** | **—** |

| **Voog, Ann-Kathrin** | **b. Garmisch-Partenkirchen, Germany, June 3, 1995** | | | | | | | |
|---|---|---|---|---|---|---|---|---|
| 2012 WW18 | 13-D | GER | 6 | 0 | 0 | 0 | 2 | 4th |

| **Vopravilova, Dominika** | **b. Rakovnik, Czech Republic, July 7, 1996** | | | | | | | |
|---|---|---|---|---|---|---|---|---|
| 2012 WW18 | 20-F | CZE | 5 | 0 | 0 | 0 | 0 | 6th |

| **Vosykova, Andrea** | **b. Pardubice, Czechoslovakia (Czech Republic), November 21, 1990** | | | | | | | |
|---|---|---|---|---|---|---|---|---|
| 2008 WW18 | 6-F | CZE | 5 | 0 | 0 | 0 | 0 | B |

| **Voutilainen, Marjo** | **b. Kuopio, Finland, March 22, 1981** | | | | | | | |
|---|---|---|---|---|---|---|---|---|
| 2001 WW | 8-F | FIN | 5 | 0 | 1 | 1 | 2 | 4th |
| 2002 OG-W | 8-F | FIN | 5 | 0 | 1 | 1 | 2 | 4th |
| 2008 WW | 8-F | FIN | 5 | 1 | 2 | 3 | 4 | B |
| 2009 WW | 8-F | FIN | 5 | 1 | 1 | 2 | 4 | B |
| 2010 OG-W | 8-F | FIN | 5 | 1 | 0 | 1 | 4 | B |
| **Totals WW** | | | **15** | **2** | **4** | **6** | **10** | **2B** |
| **Totals OG-W** | | | **10** | **1** | **1** | **2** | **6** | **B** |

| **Vovrushko, Alexandra** | **b. Khabarovsk, Russia, February 3, 1992** | | | | | | | |
|---|---|---|---|---|---|---|---|---|
| 2008 WW18 | 21-F | RUS | 5 | 0 | 0 | 0 | 0 | 8th |
| 2009 WW18 | 3-F | RUS | 4 | 0 | 1 | 1 | 0 | 7th |
| 2010 WW18 | 3-F | RUS | 5 | 0 | 1 | 1 | 0 | 8th |
| **Totals WW18** | | | **14** | **0** | **2** | **2** | **0** | **—** |

| **Vuille-dit-Bille, Johanna** | **b. June 22, 1989** | | | | | | | |
|---|---|---|---|---|---|---|---|---|
| 2012 WW | 22-D | SUI | 6 | 0 | 0 | 0 | 0 | B |

| **Vytiskova, Marketa** | **b. Havirov, Czech Republic, April 25, 1994** | | | | | | | |
|---|---|---|---|---|---|---|---|---|
| 2010 WW18 | 3-D | CZE | 5 | 0 | 2 | 2 | 8 | 7th |
| 2011 WW18 | 3-D | CZE | 6 | 2 | 0 | 2 | 14 | 4th |
| 2012 WW18 | 3-D | CZE | 5 | 0 | 0 | 0 | 0 | 6th |
| **Totals WW18** | | | **16** | **2** | **2** | **4** | **22** | **—** |

| **Wada, Etsuko** | **b. Kushiro, Japan, June 13, 1979** | | | | | | | |
|---|---|---|---|---|---|---|---|---|
| 2000 WW | 22-D | JPN | 5 | 1 | 2 | 3 | 2 | 8th |
| 2004 WW | 9-D | JPN | 4 | 1 | 0 | 1 | 6 | 9th |
| 2008 WW | 7-D | JPN | 4 | 1 | 2 | 3 | 14 | 7th |
| 2009 WW | 7-D | JPN | 4 | 0 | 0 | 0 | 4 | 8th |
| **Totals WW** | | | **17** | **3** | **4** | **7** | **26** | **—** |

| **Wagner, Theresa** | **b. Muhldorf am Inn, Germany, May 5, 1995** | | | | | | | |
|---|---|---|---|---|---|---|---|---|
| 2011 WW18 | 4-D | GER | 5 | 0 | 0 | 0 | 2 | 6th |
| 2012 WW18 | 4-D | GER | 6 | 0 | 0 | 0 | 2 | 4th |
| **Totals WW18** | | | **11** | **0** | **0** | **0** | **4** | **—** |

| **Waidacher, Isabel** | **b. Arosa, Switzerland, July 25, 1994** | | | | | | | |
|---|---|---|---|---|---|---|---|---|
| 2011 WW18 | 24-F | SUI | 6 | 0 | 1 | 1 | 6 | 7th |
| 2012 WW18 | 24-F | SUI | 6 | 3 | 6 | 9 | 4 | 8th |
| **Totals WW18** | | | **12** | **3** | **7** | **10** | **10** | **—** |

| **Waidacher, Monika** | **b. Zurich, Switzerland, July 9, 1990** | | | | | | | |
|---|---|---|---|---|---|---|---|---|
| 2008 WW18 | 15-F | SUI | 5 | 0 | 1 | 1 | 2 | 7th |
| 2009 WW | 15-F | SUI | 4 | 0 | 0 | 0 | 0 | 7th |
| 2012 WW | 15-F | SUI | 6 | 0 | 0 | 0 | 2 | B |
| **Totals WW** | | | **10** | **0** | **0** | **0** | **2** | **B** |

| **Waidacher, Nina** | **b. Zurich, Switzerland, August 23, 1992** | | | | | | | |
|---|---|---|---|---|---|---|---|---|
| 2008 WW18 | 16-F | SUI | 5 | 2 | 1 | 3 | 4 | 7th |
| 2009 WW18 | 16-F | SUI | 5 | 1 | 2 | 3 | 6 | 8th |
| 2012 WW | 16-F | SUI | 6 | 0 | 0 | 0 | 0 | B |
| **Totals WW18** | | | **10** | **3** | **3** | **6** | **10** | **—** |

| **Wakefield, Jennifer** | **b. Pickering, Ontario, Canada, June 15, 1989** | | | | | | | |
|---|---|---|---|---|---|---|---|---|
| 2011 WW | 20-F | CAN | 5 | 1 | 2 | 3 | 4 | S |
| 2012 WW | 20-F | CAN | 5 | 1 | 0 | 1 | 8 | G |
| **Totals WW** | | | **10** | **2** | **2** | **4** | **12** | **G,S** |

| **Wang, Linuo** | **b. Heilongjiang, China, August 28, 1979** | | | | | | | |
|---|---|---|---|---|---|---|---|---|
| 1999 WW | 19-F | CHN | 5 | 0 | 0 | 0 | 2 | 5th |
| 2000 WW | 19-F | CHN | 5 | 0 | 0 | 0 | 4 | 6th |
| 2001 WW | 19-F | CHN | 5 | 2 | 0 | 2 | 4 | 7th |
| 2002 OG-W | 19-F | CHN | 5 | 0 | 2 | 2 | 4 | 7th |
| 2004 WW | 19-F | CHN | 4 | 1 | 1 | 2 | 0 | 7th |
| 2005 WW | 19-D | CHN | 5 | 0 | 1 | 1 | 4 | 6th |
| 2007 WW | 19-F | CHN | 4 | 0 | 1 | 1 | 6 | 6th |
| 2008 WW | 19-F | CHN | 4 | 1 | 2 | 3 | 6 | 8th |
| 2009 WW | 19-F | CHN | 4 | 0 | 1 | 1 | 2 | 9th |
| 2010 OG-W | 19-F | CHN | 5 | 3 | 0 | 3 | 4 | 7th |
| **Totals WW** | | | **36** | **4** | **6** | **10** | **28** | **—** |
| **Totals OG-W** | | | **10** | **3** | **2** | **5** | **8** | **—** |

| **Wang, Nan** | **b. Harbin, China, April 22, 1988** | | | | | | | |
|---|---|---|---|---|---|---|---|---|
| 2009 WW | 28-D | CHN | 4 | 0 | 0 | 0 | 0 | 9th |

| **Ward, Catherine** | **b. Montreal, Quebec, Canada, February 27, 1987** | | | | | | | |
|---|---|---|---|---|---|---|---|---|
| 2009 WW | 18-D | CAN | 5 | 0 | 4 | 4 | 2 | S |
| 2010 OG-W | 18-D | CAN | 5 | 2 | 2 | 4 | 4 | G |
| 2011 WW | 18-D | CAN | 5 | 0 | 2 | 2 | 2 | S |
| 2012 WW | 18-D | CAN | 5 | 0 | 2 | 2 | 4 | G |
| **Totals WW** | | | **15** | **0** | **8** | **8** | **8** | **G,2S** |

| **Wasylk, Taylor** | **b. Port Huron, Michigan, United States, February 21, 1992** | | | | | | | |
|---|---|---|---|---|---|---|---|---|
| 2009 WW18 | 9-F | USA | 5 | 6 | 1 | 7 | 27 | G |
| 2010 WW18 | 9-F | USA | 5 | 2 | 1 | 3 | 0 | S |
| 2012 WW | 27-F | USA | 2 | 0 | 0 | 0 | 0 | S |
| **Totals WW18** | | | **10** | **8** | **2** | **10** | **27** | **G,S** |

| **Watchorn, Tara** | **b. Newcastle, Ontario, Canada, May 30, 1990** | | | | | | | |
|---|---|---|---|---|---|---|---|---|
| 2008 WW18 | 3-D | CAN | 5 | 4 | 6 | 10 | 0 | S |
| 2011 WW | 15-D | CAN | 5 | 0 | 2 | 2 | 4 | S |

| **Watt, Samantha** | **b. Calgary, Alberta, Canada, January 24, 1990** | | | | | | | |
|---|---|---|---|---|---|---|---|---|
| 2008 WW18 | 2-D | CAN | 5 | 0 | 1 | 1 | 6 | S |

| **Weatherston, Katie** | **b. Thunder Bay, Ontario, Canada, April 6, 1983** | | | | | | | |
|---|---|---|---|---|---|---|---|---|
| 2006 OG-W | 8-F | CAN | 5 | 4 | 1 | 5 | 2 | G |
| 2007 WW | 8-F | CAN | 5 | 3 | 1 | 4 | 0 | G |
| 2008 WW | 8-F | CAN | 5 | 2 | 0 | 2 | 2 | S |
| **Totals WW** | | | **10** | **5** | **1** | **6** | **2** | **G,S** |

| **Weiland, Kerry** | **b. Palmer, Alaska, United States, October 18, 1980** | | | | | | | |
|---|---|---|---|---|---|---|---|---|
| 2004 WW | 8-D | USA | 5 | 0 | 0 | 0 | 2 | S |
| 2007 WW | 23-D | USA | 5 | 0 | 1 | 1 | 2 | S |
| 2008 WW | 23-D | USA | 5 | 0 | 0 | 0 | 6 | G |
| 2009 WW | 23-D | USA | 5 | 0 | 0 | 0 | 2 | G |
| 2010 OG-W | 23-D | USA | 5 | 1 | 1 | 2 | 4 | S |
| **Totals WW** | | | **20** | **0** | **1** | **1** | **12** | **2G,2S** |

| **Weisser, Anja** | **b. Marktoberdorf, Germany, October 2, 1991** | | | | | | | |
|---|---|---|---|---|---|---|---|---|
| 2008 WW18 | 14-D | GER | 5 | 1 | 0 | 1 | 4 | 5th |
| 2009 WW18 | 14-D | GER | 5 | 0 | 2 | 2 | 10 | 6th |
| 2012 WW | 10-D | GER | 5 | 0 | 0 | 0 | 2 | 7th |
| **Totals WW18** | | | **10** | **1** | **2** | **3** | **14** | **—** |

| **Wester, Lina** | **b. Boda Kyrkby, Sweden, November 7, 1992** | | | | | | | |
|---|---|---|---|---|---|---|---|---|
| 2010 WW18 | 24-F | SWE | 6 | 1 | 3 | 4 | 4 | B |
| 2011 WW | 13-F | SWE | 5 | 0 | 0 | 0 | 0 | 5th |
| 2012 WW | 13-F | SWE | 5 | 0 | 1 | 1 | 14 | 5th |
| **Totals WW** | | | **10** | **0** | **1** | **1** | **14** | **—** |

| **Weyand, Sarah** | **b. Duisburg, West Germany (Germany), December 20, 1988** | | | | | | | |
|---|---|---|---|---|---|---|---|---|
| 2008 WW | 4-D | GER | 4 | 0 | 0 | 0 | 0 | 9th |
| 2012 WW | 28-D | GER | 5 | 1 | 0 | 1 | 0 | 7th |
| **Totals WW** | | | **9** | **1** | **0** | **1** | **0** | **—** |

| **White, Catherine** | **b. Brampton, Ontario, Canada, February 5, 1990** | | | | | | | |
|---|---|---|---|---|---|---|---|---|
| 2008 WW18 | 19-F | CAN | 5 | 4 | 2 | 6 | 4 | S |

| **Wickenheiser, Hayley** | **b. Shaunavon, Saskatchewan, Canada, August 12, 1978** | | | | | | | |
|---|---|---|---|---|---|---|---|---|
| 1994 WW | 22-F | CAN | 3 | 0 | 1 | 1 | 4 | G |
| 1997 WW | 22-F | CAN | 5 | 4 | 5 | 9 | 12 | G |
| 1998 OG-W | 22-F | CAN | 6 | 2 | 6 | 8 | 4 | S |
| 1999 WW | 22-F | CAN | 5 | 3 | 5 | 8 | 8 | G |
| 2000 WW | 22-F | CAN | 5 | 1 | 7 | 8 | 4 | G |
| 2002 OG-W | 22-F | CAN | 5 | 7 | 3 | 10 | 2 | G |
| 2004 WW | 22-F | CAN | 5 | 3 | 2 | 5 | 2 | G |
| 2005 WW | 22-F | CAN | 5 | 5 | 3 | 8 | 6 | S |
| 2006 OG-W | 22-F | CAN | 5 | 5 | 12 | 17 | 6 | G |
| 2007 WW | 22-F | CAN | 5 | 8 | 6 | 14 | 0 | G |
| 2008 WW | 22-F | CAN | 5 | 3 | 6 | 9 | 6 | S |
| 2009 WW | 22-F | CAN | 5 | 4 | 4 | 8 | 4 | S |
| 2010 OG-W | 22-F | CAN | 5 | 2 | 9 | 11 | 0 | G |
| 2011 WW | 22-F | CAN | 5 | 3 | 2 | 5 | 4 | S |
| 2012 WW | 22-F | CAN | 5 | 3 | 7 | 10 | 4 | G |
| **Totals WW** | | | **53** | **37** | **48** | **85** | **54** | **7G,4S** |
| **Totals OG-W** | | | **21** | **16** | **30** | **46** | **12** | **3G,S** |

~OG-W MVP (2002, 2006), OG-W IIHF Directorate Best Forward (2002, 2006), OG-W All-Star Team/Forward (2002, 2006), WW MVP (2007), WW IIHF Directorate Best Forward (2007, 2009), WW All-Star Team/Forward (1997, 1999, 2005, 2007, 2008, 2011, 2012)

| **Wild, Kelly** | **b. Mendota Heights, Minnesota, United States, March 8, 1990** | | | | | | | |
|---|---|---|---|---|---|---|---|---|
| 2008 WW18 | 8-D | USA | 5 | 0 | 2 | 2 | 2 | G |

| **Williner, Karin** | **b. Embd, Switzerland, February 4, 1995** | | | | | | | |
|---|---|---|---|---|---|---|---|---|
| 2011 WW18 | 5-D | SUI | 6 | 0 | 0 | 0 | 6 | 7th |
| 2012 WW18 | 5-D | SUI | 6 | 0 | 0 | 0 | 4 | 8th |
| **Totals WW18** | | | **12** | **0** | **0** | **0** | **10** | **—** |

| Winberg, Pernilla | | | | | | | | b. Limhamn, Sweden, February 24, 1989 |
|---|---|---|---|---|---|---|---|---|
| 2004 WW | 16-F | SWE | 5 | 0 | 0 | 0 | 2 | 4th |
| 2005 WW | 16-F | SWE | 4 | 0 | 3 | 3 | 0 | B |
| 2006 OG-W | 16-F | SWE | 5 | 1 | 3 | 4 | 2 | S |
| 2007 WW | 16-F | SWE | 5 | 5 | 3 | 8 | 8 | B |
| 2008 WW | 16-F | SWE | 4 | 1 | 1 | 2 | 2 | 5th |
| 2009 WW | 16-F | SWE | 5 | 1 | 6 | 7 | 0 | 4th |
| 2010 OG-W | 16-F | SWE | 5 | 5 | 0 | 5 | 4 | 4th |
| 2011 WW | 16-F | SWE | 4 | 1 | 1 | 2 | 4 | 5th |
| 2012 WW | 16-F | SWE | 4 | 1 | 3 | 4 | 6 | 5th |
| **Totals WW** | | | **31** | **9** | **17** | **26** | **22** | **2B** |
| **Totals OG-W** | | | **10** | **6** | **3** | **9** | **6** | **S** |

| Wolfgruber, Stefanie | | | | | | | | b. Trostberg, Germany, August 15, 1992 |
|---|---|---|---|---|---|---|---|---|
| 2009 WW18 | 17-F | GER | 5 | 1 | 0 | 1 | 2 | 6th |

| Wong, Jessica | | | | | | | | b. Baddeck, Nova Scotia, Canada, March 29, 1991 |
|---|---|---|---|---|---|---|---|---|
| 2009 WW18 | 24-F | CAN | 5 | 4 | 8 | 12 | 0 | S |

| Wong, Malin | | | | | | | | b. September 3, 1994 |
|---|---|---|---|---|---|---|---|---|
| 2012 WW18 | 27-F | SWE | 6 | 0 | 1 | 1 | 2 | B |

| Woods, Taylor | | | | | | | | b. Morden, Manitoba, September 26, 1994 |
|---|---|---|---|---|---|---|---|---|
| 2012 WW18 | 11-F | CAN | 5 | 3 | 3 | 6 | 0 | G |

| Wuffli, Sarina | | | | | | | | b. Rothrist, Switzerland, May 19, 1993 |
|---|---|---|---|---|---|---|---|---|
| 2009 WW18 | 8-D | SUI | 5 | 0 | 0 | 0 | 2 | 8th |

| Wuttke, Selina | | | | | | | | b. Schlossrued, Switzerland, December 13, 1994 |
|---|---|---|---|---|---|---|---|---|
| 2011 WW18 | 2-D | SUI | 5 | 0 | 1 | 1 | 0 | 7th |
| 2012 WW18 | 2-D | SUI | 6 | 1 | 0 | 1 | 12 | 8th |
| **Totals WW18** | | | **11** | **1** | **1** | **2** | **12** | **—** |

| Wyss, Stefanie | | | | | | | | b. Berne, Switzerland, October 19, 1985 |
|---|---|---|---|---|---|---|---|---|
| 2007 WW | 85-F | SUI | 4 | 0 | 0 | 0 | 0 | 5th |
| 2008 WW | 85-F | SUI | 5 | 0 | 0 | 0 | 2 | 4th |
| 2010 OG-W | 85-D | SUI | 5 | 0 | 0 | 0 | 0 | 5th |
| 2011 WW | 85-D | SUI | 5 | 0 | 0 | 0 | 0 | 6th |
| **Totals WW** | | | **14** | **0** | **0** | **0** | **2** | **—** |

| Yakovchuk, Natalya | | | | | | | | b. Vladivostok, Soviet Union (Russia), July 29, 1975 |
|---|---|---|---|---|---|---|---|---|
| 2001 WW | 19-F | KAZ | 5 | 1 | 0 | 1 | 6 | 8th |
| 2002 OG-W | 19-F | KAZ | 5 | 1 | 0 | 1 | 0 | 8th |
| 2005 WW | 19-F | KAZ | 5 | 1 | 0 | 1 | 2 | 7th |
| 2009 WW | 19-F | KAZ | 4 | 2 | 0 | 2 | 0 | 6th |
| 2011 WW | 19-F | KAZ | 5 | 3 | 0 | 3 | 0 | 8th |
| **Totals WW** | | | **19** | **7** | **0** | **7** | **8** | **—** |

| Yamanaka, Chiaki | | | | | | | | b. Tomakomai, Japan, May 20, 1983 |
|---|---|---|---|---|---|---|---|---|
| 2004 WW | 21-F | JPN | 4 | 0 | 0 | 0 | 2 | 9th |
| 2008 WW | 22-F | JPN | 4 | 0 | 1 | 1 | 0 | 7th |
| 2009 WW | 22-F | JPN | 4 | 1 | 0 | 1 | 0 | 8th |
| **Totals WW** | | | **12** | **1** | **1** | **2** | **2** | **—** |

| Yamane, Tomoe | | | | | | | | b. Kushiro, Japan, March 24, 1986 |
|---|---|---|---|---|---|---|---|---|
| 2004 WW | 4-D | JPN | 4 | 0 | 0 | 0 | 2 | 9th |
| 2008 WW | 8-D | JPN | 4 | 0 | 1 | 1 | 2 | 7th |
| 2009 WW | 8-D | JPN | 4 | 0 | 0 | 0 | 4 | 8th |
| **Totals WW** | | | **12** | **0** | **1** | **1** | **8** | **—** |

| Yamaya, Riko | | | | | | | | b. Hokkaido, Japan, November 27, 1995 |
|---|---|---|---|---|---|---|---|---|
| 2011 WW18 | 5-D | JPN | 6 | 0 | 1 | 1 | 2 | 8th |

| Yegorova, Viktoriya | | | | | | | | b. November 17, 1994 |
|---|---|---|---|---|---|---|---|---|
| 2012 WW18 | 6-D | RUS | 6 | 0 | 0 | 0 | 4 | 7th |

| Yelfimova, Xenia | | | | | | | | b. Almaty, Soviet Union (Kazakhstan), June 20, 1990 |
|---|---|---|---|---|---|---|---|---|
| 2007 WW | 42-F | KAZ | 4 | 0 | 0 | 0 | 2 | 9th |

| Yliniemi, Maiju | | | | | | | | b. Haukipudas, Finland, February 22, 1990 |
|---|---|---|---|---|---|---|---|---|
| 2008 WW18 | 21-F | FIN | 5 | 2 | 2 | 4 | 0 | 6th |

| Yoneyama, Haruna | | | | | | | | b. Hokkaido, Japan, November 7, 1991 |
|---|---|---|---|---|---|---|---|---|
| 2009 WW | 10-F | JPN | 4 | 0 | 0 | 0 | 0 | 8th |

| Young, Jacqueline | | | | | | | | b. Medford, Massachsuetts, United States, January 10, 1991 |
|---|---|---|---|---|---|---|---|---|
| 2009 WW18 | 7-D | USA | 5 | 1 | 2 | 3 | 4 | G |

| Yu, Baiwei | | | | | | | | b. Harbin, China, July 17, 1988 |
|---|---|---|---|---|---|---|---|---|
| 2007 WW | 2-D | CHN | 4 | 0 | 0 | 0 | 0 | 6th |
| 2008 WW | 2-D | CHN | 4 | 0 | 0 | 0 | 2 | 8th |
| 2009 WW | 2-D | CHN | 4 | 0 | 0 | 0 | 4 | 9th |
| 2010 OG-W | 2-D | CHN | 5 | 0 | 1 | 1 | 2 | 7th |
| **Totals WW** | | | **12** | **0** | **0** | **0** | **6** | **—** |

| Yucel, Michelle | | | | | | | | b. Stockholm, Sweden, December 15, 1995 |
|---|---|---|---|---|---|---|---|---|
| 2012 WW18 | 28-F | SWE | 6 | 0 | 0 | 0 | 0 | B |

| Yudina, Anastasia | | | | | | | | b. Sverdlovsk Region, Soviet Union (Russia), May 19, 1991 |
|---|---|---|---|---|---|---|---|---|
| 2009 WW18 | 2-F | RUS | 5 | 0 | 0 | 0 | 0 | 7th |

| Yuyama, Seika | | | | | | | | b. Tokyo, Japan, March 7, 1994 |
|---|---|---|---|---|---|---|---|---|
| 2011 WW18 | 22-F | JPN | 6 | 0 | 0 | 0 | 0 | 8th |

| Zakharova, Yekaterina | | | | | | | | b. September 8, 1994 |
|---|---|---|---|---|---|---|---|---|
| 2012 WW18 | 21-F | RUS | 6 | 0 | 0 | 0 | 0 | 7th |

| Zgraja, Katarina | | | | | | | | b. Waterloo, Ontario, Canada, July 19, 1993 |
|---|---|---|---|---|---|---|---|---|
| 2011 WW18 | 5-D | CAN | 4 | 1 | 1 | 2 | 2 | S |

| Zhang, Ben | | | | | | | | b. Heilongjiang, China, July 22, 1985 |
|---|---|---|---|---|---|---|---|---|
| 2004 WW | 10-F | CHN | 4 | 1 | 0 | 1 | 2 | 7th |
| 2005 WW | 10-F | CHN | 5 | 2 | 0 | 2 | 2 | 6th |
| 2007 WW | 10-F | CHN | 4 | 2 | 0 | 2 | 0 | 6th |
| 2008 WW | 10-F | CHN | 4 | 0 | 1 | 1 | 0 | 8th |
| 2009 WW | 10-F | CHN | 4 | 0 | 0 | 0 | 0 | 9th |
| 2010 OG-W | 10-F | CHN | 5 | 0 | 1 | 1 | 2 | 7th |
| **Totals WW** | | | **21** | **5** | **1** | **6** | **4** | **—** |

| Zhang, Lu | | | | | | | | b. Harbin, China, March 15, 1987 |
|---|---|---|---|---|---|---|---|---|
| 2008 WW | 27-F | CHN | 4 | 0 | 0 | 0 | 0 | 8th |

| Zhang, Mengying | | | | | | | | b. Qiqihar, China, December 22, 1993 |
|---|---|---|---|---|---|---|---|---|
| 2010 OG-W | 7-F | CHN | 5 | 0 | 0 | 0 | 0 | 7th |

| Zhang, Shuang | | | | | | | | b. Heilongjiang, China, March 7, 1977 |
|---|---|---|---|---|---|---|---|---|
| 2005 WW | 66-D | CHN | 5 | 0 | 0 | 0 | 2 | 6th |
| 2007 WW | 66-D | CHN | 4 | 0 | 1 | 1 | 0 | 6th |
| 2008 WW | 66-D | CHN | 4 | 1 | 0 | 1 | 4 | 8th |
| 2009 WW | 66-D | CHN | 4 | 0 | 1 | 1 | 4 | 9th |
| 2010 OG-W | 66-D | CHN | 5 | 0 | 1 | 1 | 4 | 7th |
| **Totals WW** | | | **17** | **1** | **2** | **3** | **10** | **—** |

| Zitnanska, Gabriela | | | | | | | | b. September 7, 1996 |
|---|---|---|---|---|---|---|---|---|
| 2012 WW | 25-D | SVK | 5 | 0 | 0 | 0 | 0 | 8th |

| Zollinger, Sabrina | | | | | | | | b. Maur, Switzerland, March 27, 1993 |
|---|---|---|---|---|---|---|---|---|
| 2009 WW18 | 11-F | SUI | 5 | 0 | 0 | 0 | 8 | 8th |
| 2009 WW | 26-F | SUI | 4 | 0 | 0 | 0 | 0 | 7th |
| 2010 OG-W | 93-F | SUI | 5 | 0 | 0 | 0 | 0 | 5th |
| 2011 WW18 | 11-F | SUI | 6 | 4 | 2 | 6 | 12 | 7th |
| 2011 WW | 93-F | SUI | 5 | 0 | 1 | 1 | 10 | 6th |
| 2012 WW | 24-D | SUI | 6 | 0 | 1 | 1 | 2 | B |
| **Totals WW18** | | | **11** | **4** | **2** | **6** | **20** | **—** |
| **Totals WW** | | | **15** | **0** | **2** | **2** | **12** | **B** |

| Zorn, Julia | | | | | | | | b. Grafeling, West Germany (Germany), February 6, 1990 |
|---|---|---|---|---|---|---|---|---|
| 2012 WW | 8-F | GER | 5 | 4 | 0 | 4 | 2 | 7th |

~also see Active Goalies

| Zvezdina, Arina | | | | | | | | b. Kareliya, Soviet Union (Russia), May 22, 1991 |
|---|---|---|---|---|---|---|---|---|
| 2009 WW18 | 15-F | RUS | 5 | 0 | 0 | 0 | 0 | 7th |

**Zyatkova, Galina** ~see Shu (Zyatkova), Galina

*She started in 1994 as the youngest player in women's hockey, but now, 18 years later, Hayley Wickenheiser is a veteran with three Olympic and seven World Championship gold medals and is the all-time leading scorer in women's hockey history. Photo: Dave Sandford / HHOF-IIHF Images.*

# Active Goalies, Women

(event-by-event summary for recently-active goalies internationally who play in the top level)

| Year Event | #-Pos | NAT | GP | W-T-L | Mins | GA | SO | GAA | A | Pim | Finish |
|---|---|---|---|---|---|---|---|---|---|---|---|
| Totals | | | GP | W-T-L | Mins | GA | SO | GAA | A | Pim | Medals |
| **Albl, Franziska** | b. Fussen, Germany, April 29, 1995 | | | | | | | | | | |
| 2011 WW18 | 1-G | GER | 1 | 0-0-1 | 60:00 | 8 | 0 | 8.00 | 0 | 0 | 6th |
| 2012 WW18 | 1-G | GER | 4 | 2-0-2 | 238:41 | 11 | 0 | 2.77 | 0 | 0 | 4th |
| **Totals WW18** | | | **5** | **2-0-3** | **298:41** | **19** | **0** | **3.82** | **0** | **0** | **—** |
| ~WW18 IIHF Directorate Best Goalie (2012) | | | | | | | | | | | |
| **Airaksinen, Susanna** | b. Hirvilahti, Finland, March 4, 1992 | | | | | | | | | | |
| 2009 WW18 | 1-G | FIN | 5 | 3-0-2 | 307:12 | 13 | 0 | 2.54 | 0 | 0 | 5th |
| 2010 WW18 | 1-G | FIN | 3 | 2-0-1 | 180:00 | 5 | 0 | 1.67 | 0 | 0 | 5th |
| **Totals WW18** | | | **8** | **5-0-3** | **487:12** | **18** | **0** | **2.22** | **0** | **0** | **—** |
| **Alder, Janine** | b. July 5, 1995 | | | | | | | | | | |
| 2012 WW18 | 30-G | SUI | 6 | 2-0-4 | 341:20 | 25 | 0 | 4.39 | 0 | 0 | 8th |
| **Alexandrova, Nadezhda** | b. Moscow, Soviet Union (Russia), January 3, 1986 | | | | | | | | | | |
| 2006 OG-W | 33-G | RUS | 1 | 0-0-0 | 43:35 | 7 | 0 | 9.64 | 0 | 0 | 6th |
| 2009 WW | 33-G | RUS | 3 | 0-0-2 | 91:10 | 11 | 0 | 7.24 | 0 | 0 | 5th |
| **Anthamatten, Sophie** | b. Saas-Grund, Switzerland, July 26, 1991 | | | | | | | | | | |
| 2008 WW18 | 20-G | SUI | 5 | 2-0-3 | 299:30 | 24 | 0 | 4.81 | 0 | 0 | 7th |
| 2009 WW18 | 29-G | SUI | 5 | 1-0-3 | 290:00 | 27 | 0 | 5.59 | 0 | 2 | 8th |
| 2010 OG-W | | SUI | 3RD GK—DID NOT PLAY | | | | | | | | |
| 2011 WW | 26-G | SUI | 1 | 0-0-0 | 25:58 | 6 | 0 | 13.86 | 0 | 0 | 6th |
| 2012 WW | 28-G | SUI | 2 | 0-0-1 | 70:58 | 4 | 0 | 3.38 | 0 | 0 | B |
| **Totals WW18** | | | **10** | **3-0-6** | **589:30** | **51** | **0** | **5.19** | **0** | **2** | **—** |
| **Totals WW** | | | **3** | **0-0-1** | **96:56** | **10** | **0** | **6.19** | **0** | **0** | **B** |
| **Becevova, Katerina** | b. Chrudim, Czechoslovakia (Czech Republic), July 30, 1990 | | | | | | | | | | |
| 2008 WW18 | 1-G | CZE | 5 | 3-0-2 | 300:00 | 26 | 0 | 5.20 | 0 | 2 | B |
| **Besseling, Sara** | b. Vaxholm, Sweden, April 1, 1994 | | | | | | | | | | |
| 2012 WW18 | 30-G | SWE | 3 | 2-0-1 | 187:27 | 9 | 0 | 2.88 | 0 | 0 | B |
| **Boyles, Corinne** | b. Wheaton, Illinois, United States, January 3, 1991 | | | | | | | | | | |
| 2009 WW18 | 1-G | USA | 2 | 2-0-0 | 120:00 | 0 | 2 | 0.00 | 0 | 0 | G |
| **Brian, Delayne** | b. Winnipeg, Manitoba, Canada, July 24, 1990 | | | | | | | | | | |
| 2008 WW18 | 1-G | CAN | 4 | 3-0-1 | 210:05 | 8 | 0 | 2.28 | 0 | 0 | S |
| **Budajova, Jana** | b. Liptovsky Mikulas, Slovakia, November 16, 1992 | | | | | | | | | | |
| 2010 OG-W | | SVK | 3RD GK—DID NOT PLAY | | | | | | | | |
| 2011 WW | | SVK | 3RD GK—DID NOT PLAY | | | | | | | | |
| 2012 WW | | SVK | 3RD GK—DID NOT PLAY | | | | | | | | |
| **Carlstrom, Sofia** | b. Stockholm, Sweden, February 9, 1993 | | | | | | | | | | |
| 2010 WW18 | 1-G | SWE | 4 | 3-0-1 | 240:00 | 10 | 0 | 2.50 | 0 | 0 | B |
| 2011 WW18 | 1-G | SWE | 4 | 2-0-2 | 220:06 | 13 | 0 | 3.54 | 0 | 0 | 5th |
| **Totals WW18** | | | **8** | **5-0-3** | **460:06** | **23** | **0** | **3.00** | **0** | **0** | **B** |
| **Chuli, Elaine** | b. Simcoe, Ontario, May 16, 1994 | | | | | | | | | | |
| 2012 WW18 | 29-G | CAN | 2 | 2-0-0 | 120:00 | 0 | 2 | 0.00 | 0 | 0 | G |
| **Craigova, Lenka** | b. Litomysl, Czech Republic, February 24, 1994 | | | | | | | | | | |
| 2010 WW18 | 30-G | CZE | 2 | 1-0-1 | 80:37 | 9 | 0 | 6.70 | 0 | 0 | 7th |
| 2011 WW18 | 30-G | CZE | 2 | 0-0-1 | 89:18 | 19 | 0 | 12.77 | 0 | 0 | 4th |
| 2012 WW18 | 30-G | CZE | 1 | 0-0-0 | 36:06 | 8 | 0 | 13.30 | 0 | 0 | 6th |
| **Totals WW18** | | | **5** | **1-0-2** | **206:01** | **36** | **0** | **10.48** | **0** | **0** | **—** |
| **Desbiens, Ann-Renee** | b. La Malbaie, Quebec, Canada, April 10, 1994 | | | | | | | | | | |
| 2011 WW18 | 30-G | CAN | 3 | 2-0-1 | 179:24 | 5 | 1 | 1.67 | 0 | 0 | S |
| **Douville, Roxanne** | b. Beloiel, Quebec, Canada, May 23, 1991 | | | | | | | | | | |
| 2009 WW18 | 30-G | CAN | 3 | 2-0-1 | 186:47 | 4 | 1 | 1.28 | 0 | 0 | S |
| **Emanuelsson, Hanna** | b. Karlstad, Sweden, January 4, 1990 | | | | | | | | | | |
| 2008 WW18 | 20-G | SWE | 2 | 0-0-2 | 119:20 | 9 | 0 | 4.53 | 0 | 0 | 4th |
| **Ferngren, Annika** | b. Stockholm, Sweden, November 2, 1992 | | | | | | | | | | |
| 2010 WW18 | 30-G | SWE | 2 | 1-0-1 | 120:00 | 12 | 0 | 6.00 | 0 | 2 | B |
| **Flotgen, Jule** | b. Dinslaken, Germany, December 24, 1991 | | | | | | | | | | |
| 2009 WW18 | 30-G | GER | 5 | 1-0-3 | 266:31 | 21 | 0 | 4.73 | 0 | 0 | 6th |
| **Fujimoto, Nana** | b. Hokkaido, Japan, March 3, 1989 | | | | | | | | | | |
| 2008 WW | 30-G | JPN | 1 | 0-0-1 | 60:00 | 6 | 0 | 6.00 | 0 | 0 | 7th |
| **Fuchs, Janina** | b. Dachau, Germany, September 1, 1995 | | | | | | | | | | |
| 2012 WW18 | 29-G | GER | 2 | 0-0-2 | 120:00 | 10 | 0 | 5.00 | 0 | 0 | 4th |
| **Gashennikova, Irina** | b. Moscow, Soviet Union (Russia), May 11, 1975 | | | | | | | | | | |
| 1997 WW | 20-G | RUS | 5 | 1-1-3 | 240:00 | 22 | 0 | 5.50 | 0 | 0 | 6th |
| 1999 WW | 20-G | RUS | 3 | 0-0-3 | 158:51 | 15 | 0 | 5.67 | 0 | 0 | 6th |
| 2000 WW | 20-G | RUS | 3 | 2-0-1 | 220:00 | 13 | 0 | 3.55 | 0 | 0 | 5th |
| 2001 WW | 20-G | RUS | 5 | 3-0-2 | 286:07 | 13 | 1 | 2.73 | 0 | 0 | B |
| 2002 OG-W | 20-G | RUS | 5 | 3-0-2 | 300:00 | 12 | 1 | 2.40 | 0 | 0 | 5th |
| 2004 WW | 20-G | RUS | 4 | 2-0-2 | 240:00 | 13 | 0 | 3.25 | 0 | 0 | 5th |
| 2006 OG-W | 20-G | RUS | 5 | 2-0-3 | 266:25 | 12 | 1 | 2.70 | 0 | 0 | 6th |
| 2007 WW | 20-G | RUS | 4 | 2-0-2 | 220:00 | 8 | 0 | 2.18 | 0 | 0 | 7th |
| 2009 WW | 30-G | RUS | 4 | 2-0-0 | 148:50 | 8 | 0 | 3.23 | 0 | 0 | 5th |
| 2010 OG-W | 20-G | RUS | 4 | 2-0-2 | 250:00 | 10 | 0 | 2.40 | 0 | 0 | 6th |
| **Totals WW** | | | **28** | **12-1-13** | **1,513:48** | **92** | **1** | **3.65** | **0** | **0** | **B** |
| **Totals OG-W** | | | **14** | **7-0-7** | **816:25** | **34** | **2** | **2.50** | **0** | **0** | **—** |
| **Grahn, Sara** | b. Orebro, Sweden, September 25, 1988 | | | | | | | | | | |
| 2007 WW | 1-G | SWE | 3 | 2-0-0 | 126:30 | 2 | 1 | 0.95 | 0 | 0 | B |
| 2008 WW | 1-G | SWE | 1 | 1-0-0 | 60:00 | 0 | 1 | 0.00 | 0 | 0 | 5th |
| 2009 WW | 1-G | SWE | 1 | 0-0-1 | 60:00 | 7 | 0 | 7.00 | 0 | 0 | 4th |
| 2010 OG-W | 1-G | SWE | 3 | 1-0-1 | 153:46 | 8 | 0 | 3.13 | 0 | 0 | 4th |
| 2011 WW | 1-G | SWE | 3 | 1-0-2 | 101:32 | 11 | 0 | 6.50 | 0 | 0 | 5th |
| 2012 WW | 1-G | SWE | 2 | 1-0-1 | 120:01 | 3 | 0 | 1.50 | 0 | 0 | 5th |
| **Totals WW** | | | **10** | **5-0-4** | **468:03** | **23** | **2** | **2.95** | **0** | **0** | **B** |
| **Grogan, Alyssa** | b. Eagan, Minnesota, United States, May 15, 1990 | | | | | | | | | | |
| 2008 WW18 | 1-G | USA | 5 | 5-0-0 | 240:17 | 4 | 1 | 1.00 | 0 | 2 | G |
| ~WW18 IIHF Directorate Best Goalie (2008) | | | | | | | | | | | |
| **Gruber, Nadja** | b. Landshut, Germany, April 30, 1993 | | | | | | | | | | |
| 2010 WW18 | 29-G | GER | 5 | 2-0-2 | 230:17 | 18 | 0 | 4.69 | 0 | 0 | 4th |
| 2011 WW18 | 29-G | GER | 4 | 2-0-2 | 239:27 | 7 | 1 | 1.75 | 0 | 0 | 6th |
| **Totals WW18** | | | **9** | **4-0-4** | **469:44** | **25** | **1** | **3.19** | **0** | **0** | **—** |
| **Han, Danni** | b. Harbin, China, January 9, 1991 | | | | | | | | | | |
| 2010 OG-W | | CHN | 3RD GK—DID NOT PLAY | | | | | | | | |
| **Harrer, Viona** | b. Rosenheim, West Germany (Germany), November 5, 1986 | | | | | | | | | | |
| 2004 WW | 31-G | GER | 2 | 0-0-2 | 73:28 | 8 | 0 | 6.53 | 0 | 0 | 6th |
| 2005 WW | 31-G | GER | 1 | 0-0-1 | 33:31 | 6 | 0 | 10.74 | 0 | 0 | 5th |
| 2007 WW | 31-G | GER | 2 | 0-0-2 | 113:41 | 10 | 0 | 5.28 | 0 | 0 | 8th |
| 2008 WW | 31-G | GER | 2 | 1-0-1 | 120:00 | 9 | 0 | 4.50 | 0 | 0 | 9th |
| 2012 WW | 29-G | GER | 3 | 1-0-1 | 185:00 | 7 | 0 | 2.27 | 0 | 0 | 7th |
| **Totals WW** | | | **10** | **2-0-7** | **525:40** | **40** | **0** | **4.57** | **0** | **0** | **—** |
| **Harss, Jennifer** | b. Fussen, West Germany (Germany), July 14, 1987 | | | | | | | | | | |
| 2005 WW | 22-G | GER | 1 | 0-0-0 | 0:35 | 0 | 0 | 0.00 | 0 | 0 | 5th |
| 2006 OG-W | 30-G | GER | 3 | 2-0-1 | 190:00 | 6 | 1 | 1.89 | 0 | 0 | 5th |
| 2007 WW | 30-G | GER | 3 | 1-0-1 | 123:55 | 2 | 1 | 0.97 | 0 | 0 | 8th |
| 2008 WW | 30-G | GER | 2 | 0-0-2 | 120:00 | 7 | 0 | 3.50 | 0 | 0 | 9th |
| 2012 WW | 30-G | GER | 2 | 1-0-1 | 120:24 | 3 | 0 | 1.50 | 0 | 0 | 7th |
| **Totals WW** | | | **8** | **2-0-4** | **364:54** | **12** | **1** | **1.97** | **0** | **0** | **—** |
| **Hassinen, Maija** | b. Hameenlinna, Finland, January 2, 1984 | | | | | | | | | | |
| 2006 OG-W | 30-G | FIN | 4 | 1-0-2 | 195:17 | 11 | 1 | 3.38 | 0 | 0 | 4th |
| 2008 WW | 30-G | FIN | 1 | 1-0-0 | 63:00 | 2 | 0 | 1.90 | 0 | 0 | B |
| 2009 WW | 30-G | FIN | 3 | 1-0-1 | 129:12 | 9 | 1 | 4.18 | 0 | 0 | B |
| 2011 WW | 31-G | FIN | 1 | 1-0-0 | 60:00 | 3 | 0 | 3.00 | 0 | 0 | B |
| **Totals WW** | | | **5** | **3-0-1** | **252:12** | **14** | **1** | **3.33** | **0** | **0** | **3B** |
| **Heim, Sandra** | b. Wilderswil, Switzerland, June 25, 1995 | | | | | | | | | | |
| 2011 WW18 | 29-G | SUI | 3 | 0-0-3 | 122:15 | 14 | 0 | 6.87 | 0 | 0 | 7th |
| 2012 WW18 | 29-G | SUI | 1 | 0-0-0 | 20:00 | 6 | 0 | 18.00 | 0 | 0 | 8th |
| **Totals WW18** | | | **4** | **0-0-3** | **142:15** | **20** | **0** | **8.44** | **0** | **0** | **—** |
| **Hjorth, Jessica** | b. Trelleborg, Sweden, November 4, 1994 | | | | | | | | | | |
| 2012 WW18 | 1-G | SWE | 3 | 2-0-1 | 180:00 | 10 | 0 | 3.33 | 0 | 0 | B |
| **Hladikova, Veronika** | b. Vysoke Myto, Czech Republic, February 25, 1994 | | | | | | | | | | |
| 2010 WW18 | 1-G | CZE | 5 | 2-0-1 | 219:23 | 15 | 1 | 4.10 | 0 | 0 | 7th |
| 2011 WW18 | 1-G | CZE | 5 | 2-0-3 | 270:31 | 14 | 0 | 3.11 | 0 | 0 | 4th |
| 2012 WW18 | 1-G | CZE | 5 | 1-0-4 | 261:37 | 16 | 1 | 3.67 | 0 | 0 | 6th |
| **Totals WW18** | | | **15** | **5-0-8** | **751:31** | **45** | **2** | **3.59** | **0** | **0** | **—** |
| **Howe, Erica** | b. Orleans, Ontario, Canada, July 17, 1992 | | | | | | | | | | |
| 2010 WW18 | 1-G | CAN | 2 | 1-0-0 | 90:08 | 3 | 0 | 2.00 | 0 | 0 | G |
| **Hruby, Stefanie** | b. Novosibirsk, Russia, April 22, 1992 | | | | | | | | | | |
| 2010 WW18 | 1-G | GER | 3 | 0-0-2 | 134:52 | 21 | 0 | 9.34 | 0 | 0 | 4th |

| **Jia, Dandan** | | | | | | | | | | | **b. Harbin, China, May 5, 1982** |
|---|---|---|---|---|---|---|---|---|---|---|---|
| 2008 WW | 88-G | CHN | 1 | 0-0-0 | 12:38 | 2 | 0 | 9.50 | 0 | 0 | 8th |
| 2009 WW | 88-G | CHN | 2 | 0-0-0 | 47:34 | 6 | 0 | 7.57 | 0 | 0 | 9th |
| 2010 OG-W | 88-G | CHN | 1 | 0-0-0 | 52:07 | 4 | 0 | 4.61 | 0 | 0 | 7th |
| **Totals WW** | | | **3** | **0-0-0** | **60:12** | **8** | **0** | **7.98** | **0** | **0** | **—** |

| **Juutilainen, Jenna** | | | | | | | | | | | **b. Varkaus, Finland, March 8, 1990** |
|---|---|---|---|---|---|---|---|---|---|---|---|
| 2008 WW18 | 1-G | FIN | 2 | 0-0-1 | 72:44 | 18 | 0 | 14.85 | 0 | 0 | 6th |

| **Kiapesova, Romana** | | | **b. Liptovsky Mikulas, Slovakia, September 26, 1994** |
|---|---|---|---|
| 2011 WW | | SVK | 3RD GK—DID NOT PLAY |

| **Kiribuchi, Eri** | | | | | | | | | | | **b. Hokkaido, Japan, November 22, 1988** |
|---|---|---|---|---|---|---|---|---|---|---|---|
| 2009 WW | 29-G | JPN | 1 | 0-0-0 | 29:27 | 4 | 0 | 8.15 | 0 | 0 | 8th |

| **Klossner, Tamara** | | | | | | | | | | | **b. Diemtigen, Switzerland, February 22, 1994** |
|---|---|---|---|---|---|---|---|---|---|---|---|
| 2011 WW18 | 1-G | SUI | 4 | 2-0-1 | 237:34 | 8 | 1 | 2.02 | 0 | 0 | 7th |

| **Kossenko, Anna** | | | **b. Almaty, Soviet Union (Kazakhstan), April 27, 1989** |
|---|---|---|---|
| 2009 WW | | KAZ | 3RD GK—DID NOT PLAY |
| 2011 WW | | KAZ | 3RD GK—DID NOT PLAY |

| **Kuisma, Mira** | | | **b. Kuopio, Finland, May 6, 1987** |
|---|---|---|---|
| 2009 WW | | FIN | 3RD GK—DID NOT PLAY |
| 2010 OG-W | | FIN | 3RD GK—DID NOT PLAY |

| **Kung, Sarah** | | | | | | | | | | | **b. Muhlehorn, Switzerland, November 1, 1993** |
|---|---|---|---|---|---|---|---|---|---|---|---|
| 2009 WW18 | 30-G | SUI | 1 | 0-0-1 | 20:00 | 4 | 0 | 12.00 | 0 | 0 | 8th |

| **Kvakova, Monika** | | | **b.Ziar nad Hronon, Czechoslovakia (Slovakia), December 15, 1988** |
|---|---|---|---|
| 2010 OG-W | | SVK | 3RD GK—DID NOT PLAY |
| 2012 WW | | SVK | 3RD GK—DID NOT PLAY |

| **Labonte, Charline** | | | | | | | | | | | **b. Greenfield Park, Quebec, Canada, October 15, 1982** |
|---|---|---|---|---|---|---|---|---|---|---|---|
| 2005 WW | 32-G | CAN | 2 | 2-0-0 | 120:00 | 0 | 2 | 0.00 | 1 | 0 | S |
| 2006 OG-W | 32-G | CAN | 3 | 3-0-0 | 180:00 | 1 | 2 | 0.33 | 0 | 0 | G |
| 2007 WW | 32-G | CAN | 2 | 2-0-0 | 130:00 | 4 | 1 | 1.85 | 0 | 0 | G |
| 2008 WW | 32-G | CAN | 3 | 1-0-1 | 138:29 | 3 | 1 | 1.30 | 0 | 0 | S |
| 2009 WW | 32-G | CAN | 3 | 2-0-1 | 179:04 | 5 | 0 | 1.68 | 0 | 0 | S |
| 2010 OG-W | 32-G | CAN | 1 | 0-0-0 | 20:00 | 1 | 0 | 3.00 | 0 | 0 | G |
| 2011 WW | 32-G | CAN | 2 | 2-0-0 | 120:00 | 1 | 1 | 0.50 | 0 | 0 | S |
| 2012 WW | 32-G | CAN | 2 | 1-0-1 | 103:32 | 8 | 0 | 4.64 | 0 | 0 | G |
| **Totals WW** | | | **14** | **10-0-3** | **791:05** | **21** | **5** | **1.59** | **1** | **0** | **2G,4S** |
| **Totals OG-W** | | | **4** | **3-0-0** | **200:00** | **2** | **2** | **0.60** | **0** | **0** | **2G** |

~WW IIHF Directorate Best Goalie (2009)

| **Lacasse, Genevieve** | | | **b. Kingston, Ontario, May 5, 1989** |
|---|---|---|---|
| 2012 WW | | CAN | 3RD GK—DID NOT PLAY |

| **Laing, Brianna** | | | | | | | | | | | **b. Marblehead, Massachusetts, December 27, 1994** |
|---|---|---|---|---|---|---|---|---|---|---|---|
| 2012 WW18 | 1-G | USA | 4 | 2-0-1 | 207:39 | 4 | 1 | 1.16 | 0 | 0 | S |

| **Lennstrom, Josephin** | | | | | | | | | | | **b. Stockholm, Sweden, August 23, 1992** |
|---|---|---|---|---|---|---|---|---|---|---|---|
| 2009 WW18 | 1-G | SWE | 5 | 3-0-2 | 253:40 | 17 | 0 | 4.02 | 0 | 0 | B |

| **Leskina, Yulia** | | | | | | | | | | | **b. Sverdlovsk Region, Soviet Union (Russia), February 9, 1991** |
|---|---|---|---|---|---|---|---|---|---|---|---|
| 2008 WW18 | 20-G | RUS | 3 | 0-0-0 | 86:33 | 15 | 0 | 10.40 | 0 | 0 | 8th |
| 2009 WW18 | 1-G | RUS | 2 | 0-0-1 | 53:15 | 12 | 0 | 13.52 | 0 | 0 | 7th |
| **Totals WW18** | | | **5** | **0-0-1** | **139:48** | **27** | **0** | **11.59** | **0** | **0** | **—** |

| **Lizana, Valentina** | | | | | | | | | | | **b. Stockholm, Sweden, March 30, 1990** |
|---|---|---|---|---|---|---|---|---|---|---|---|
| 2008 WW18 | 1-G | SWE | 4 | 2-0-1 | 180:15 | 8 | 1 | 2.66 | 0 | 0 | 4th |
| 2009 WW | 35-G | SWE | 4 | 3-0-1 | 240:00 | 5 | 2 | 1.25 | 0 | 0 | 4th |
| 2010 OG-W | | SWE | 3RD GK—DID NOT PLAY | | | | | | | | |
| 2011 WW | | SWE | 3RD GK—DID NOT PLAY | | | | | | | | |
| 2012 WW | | SWE | 3RD GK—DID NOT PLAY | | | | | | | | |

| **Lundberg, Shenae** | | | | | | | | | | | **b. Peterborough, New Hampshire, United States, March 14, 1993** |
|---|---|---|---|---|---|---|---|---|---|---|---|
| 2011 WW18 | 1-G | USA | 1 | 1-0-0 | 60:00 | 1 | 0 | 1.00 | 0 | 0 | G |

| **MacDonald, Carmen** | | | | | | | | | | | **b. Pictou, Nova Scotia, Canada, December 4, 1992** |
|---|---|---|---|---|---|---|---|---|---|---|---|
| 2010 WW18 | 30-G | CAN | 4 | 4-0-0 | 213:02 | 4 | 2 | 1.13 | 0 | 0 | G |

| **Makela, Amanda** | | | | | | | | | | | **b. Thunder Bay, Ontario, Canada, December 20, 1993** |
|---|---|---|---|---|---|---|---|---|---|---|---|
| 2011 WW18 | 1-G | CAN | 2 | 2-0-0 | 120:00 | 2 | 0 | 1.00 | 0 | 0 | S |

| **Martin, Kim** | | | | | | | | | | | **b. Stockholm, Sweden, February 28, 1986** |
|---|---|---|---|---|---|---|---|---|---|---|---|
| 2001 WW | 30-G | SWE | 2 | 1-0-0 | 84:36 | 4 | 0 | 2.84 | 0 | 0 | 5th |
| 2002 OG-W | 30-G | SWE | 3 | 2-0-1 | 180:00 | 5 | 1 | 1.67 | 0 | 0 | B |
| 2004 WW | 30-G | SWE | 5 | 1-1-3 | 279:34 | 18 | 0 | 3.86 | 0 | 0 | 4th |
| 2005 WW | 30-G | SWE | 4 | 2-0-2 | 209:12 | 13 | 0 | 3.73 | 0 | 0 | B |
| 2006 OG-W | 30-G | SWE | 3 | 2-0-1 | 190:00 | 7 | 0 | 2.21 | 0 | 0 | S |
| 2007 WW | 30-G | SWE | 3 | 2-0-1 | 175:02 | 3 | 0 | 1.03 | 0 | 0 | B |
| 2008 WW | 30-G | SWE | 3 | 1-0-2 | 188:00 | 8 | 0 | 2.55 | 0 | 0 | 5th |
| 2009 WW | | SWE | 3RD GK—DID NOT PLAY | | | | | | | | |
| 2010 OG-W | 30-G | SWE | 3 | 1-0-2 | 148:47 | 19 | 1 | 7.66 | 0 | 0 | 4th |
| 2011 WW | 30-G | SWE | 4 | 2-0-0 | 208:28 | 6 | 1 | 1.73 | 0 | 0 | 5th |
| 2012 WW | 30-G | SWE | 3 | 2-0-1 | 179:48 | 5 | 0 | 1.67 | 0 | 0 | 5th |
| **Totals WW** | | | **24** | **11-1-11** | **1,324:40** | **57** | **0** | **2.58** | **0** | **0** | **2B** |
| **Totals OG-W** | | | **9** | **5-0-4** | **518:47** | **31** | **2** | **3.59** | **0** | **0** | **S,B** |

~OG-W IIHF Directorate Best Goalie (2006), OG-W All-Star Team/Goal (2006)

| **Maschmeyer, Emerance** | | | | | | | | | | | **b. Fort Saskatchewan, Alberta, Canada, October 5, 1994** |
|---|---|---|---|---|---|---|---|---|---|---|---|
| 2012 WW18 | 30-G | CAN | 3 | 3-0-0 | 180:00 | 1 | 2 | 0.33 | 0 | 0 | G |

| **Mazzotta, Amanda** | | | | | | | | | | | **b. London, Ontario, Canada, March 20, 1990** |
|---|---|---|---|---|---|---|---|---|---|---|---|
| 2008 WW18 | 25-G | CAN | 2 | 1-0-0 | 89:55 | 1 | 0 | 0.67 | 0 | 0 | S |

| **McLaughlin, Brianne** | | | | | | | | | | | **b. Elyria, Ohio, United States, June 20, 1987** |
|---|---|---|---|---|---|---|---|---|---|---|---|
| 2010 OG-W | 29-G | USA | 1 | 0-0-0 | 8:00 | 1 | 0 | 7.50 | 0 | 0 | S |
| 2011 WW | 29-G | USA | 1 | 1-0-0 | 60:00 | 0 | 1 | 0.00 | 0 | 0 | G |
| 2012 WW | 29-G | USA | 1 | 1-0-0 | 60:00 | 0 | 1 | 0.00 | 1 | 0 | S |
| **Totals WW** | | | **2** | **2-0-0** | **120:00** | **0** | **2** | **0.00** | **1** | **0** | **G,S** |

| **Miller, Megan** | | | | | | | | | | | **b. Long Grove, Illinois, United States, May 2, 1994** |
|---|---|---|---|---|---|---|---|---|---|---|---|
| 2011 WW18 | 30-G | USA | 4 | 4-0-0 | 240:00 | 3 | 2 | 0.75 | 0 | 0 | G |

| **Moberg, Elin** | | | | | | | | | | | **b. Stockholm, Sweden, March 24, 1993** |
|---|---|---|---|---|---|---|---|---|---|---|---|
| 2011 WW18 | 30-G | SWE | 2 | 1-0-0 | 81:40 | 3 | 1 | 2.20 | 0 | 0 | 5th |

| **Monakhova, Margarita** | | | | | | | | | | | **b. Moscow, Russia, April 26, 1994** |
|---|---|---|---|---|---|---|---|---|---|---|---|
| 2010 WW18 | 1-G | RUS | 1 | 0-0-0 | 22:27 | 1 | 0 | 2.67 | 0 | 0 | 8th |
| 2011 WW | | RUS | 3RD GK—DID NOT PLAY | | | | | | | | |
| 2012 WW18 | 20-G | RUS | 6 | 2-0-4 | 341:45 | 24 | 0 | 4.21 | 0 | 2 | 7th |
| 2012 WW | 33-G | RUS | 1 | 0-0-0 | 45:04 | 9 | 0 | 11.98 | 0 | 0 | 6th |
| **Totals WW18** | | | **7** | **2-0-4** | **364:12** | **25** | **0** | **4.12** | **0** | **2** | **—** |

| **Moore, Aubree** | | | | | | | | | | | **b. Bowie, Maryland, United States, October 13, 1992** |
|---|---|---|---|---|---|---|---|---|---|---|---|
| 2010 WW18 | 1-G | USA | 2 | 2-0-0 | 120:00 | 1 | 1 | 0.50 | 0 | 0 | S |

| **Morozova, Nadezhda** | | | | | | | | | | | **b. November 29, 1996** |
|---|---|---|---|---|---|---|---|---|---|---|---|
| 2012 WW18 | 1-G | RUS | 1 | 0-0-0 | 19:59 | 1 | 0 | 3.00 | 0 | 0 | 7th |

| **Nakaoku, Azusa** | | | | | | | | | | | **b. Hokkaido, Japan, May 17, 1985** |
|---|---|---|---|---|---|---|---|---|---|---|---|
| 2008 WW | 1-G | JPN | 3 | 1-0-2 | 179:31 | 8 | 0 | 2.67 | 0 | 0 | 7th |
| 2009 WW | 1-G | JPN | 4 | 1-0-3 | 208:10 | 11 | 0 | 3.17 | 0 | 0 | 8th |
| **Totals WW** | | | **7** | **2-0-5** | **387:41** | **19** | **0** | **2.94** | **0** | **0** | **—** |

| **Obydennova, Daria** | | | | | | | | | | | **b. Kazakhstanskaya, Soviet Union (Kazakhstan), November 18, 1990** |
|---|---|---|---|---|---|---|---|---|---|---|---|
| 2007 WW | 1-G | KAZ | 2 | 0-0-1 | 88:45 | 12 | 0 | 8.11 | 0 | 0 | 9th |
| 2009 WW | 20-G | KAZ | 4 | 1-0-3 | 205:47 | 20 | 0 | 5.83 | 0 | 0 | 6th |
| 2011 WW | 20-G | KAZ | 5 | 0-0-5 | 304:23 | 21 | 0 | 4.14 | 0 | 0 | 8th |
| **Totals WW** | | | **11** | **1-0-9** | **598:55** | **53** | **0** | **5.31** | **0** | **0** | **—** |

| **Okada, Kumiko** | | | **b. Hokkaido, Japan, December 1, 1988** |
|---|---|---|---|
| 2009 WW | | JPN | 3RD GK—DID NOT PLAY |

| **Onolbayeva, Maria** | | | | | | | | | | | **b. Murmansk, Soviet Union (Russia), December 25, 1978** |
|---|---|---|---|---|---|---|---|---|---|---|---|
| 2005 WW | 30-G | RUS | 5 | 0-1-4 | 281:56 | 13 | 0 | 2.77 | 0 | 0 | 8th |
| 2007 WW | 30-G | RUS | 1 | 0-0-0 | 20:00 | 0 | 0 | 0.00 | 0 | 0 | 7th |
| 2008 WW | 30-G | RUS | 4 | 1-0-3 | 220:00 | 12 | 0 | 3.27 | 0 | 0 | 6th |
| 2009 WW | | RUS | 3RD GK—DID NOT PLAY | | | | | | | | |
| 2010 OG-W | 30-G | RUS | 1 | 0-0-0 | 29:00 | 3 | 0 | 6.21 | 0 | 0 | 6th |
| **Totals WW** | | | **10** | **1-1-7** | **521:56** | **25** | **0** | **2.87** | **0** | **0** | **—** |

| **Ostrovlyanchik, Valentina** | | | | | | | | | | | **b. Khabarovsk, Soviet Union (Russia), June 3, 1988** |
|---|---|---|---|---|---|---|---|---|---|---|---|
| 2008 WW | 20-G | RUS | 1 | 0-0-0 | 20:00 | 4 | 0 | 12.00 | 0 | 0 | 6th |
| 2009 WW | 20-G | RUS | 2 | 0-0-1 | 74:07 | 14 | 0 | 11.33 | 0 | 0 | 4th |
| 2012 WW | 20-G | RUS | 2 | 0-0-1 | 34:56 | 10 | 0 | 17.18 | 0 | 0 | 6th |
| **Totals WW** | | | **5** | **0-0-2** | **129:03** | **28** | **0** | **13.02** | **0** | **0** | **—** |

| **Pencikova, Monika** | | | | | | | | | | | **b. Ostrava, Czechoslovakia (Czech Republic), April 9, 1992** |
|---|---|---|---|---|---|---|---|---|---|---|---|
| 2009 WW18 | 29-G | CZE | 5 | 1-0-4 | 260:42 | 34 | 0 | 7.83 | 0 | 2 | 4th |

| **Peters, Sidney** | | | | | | | | | | | **b. Geneva, Illinois, February 26, 1995** |
|---|---|---|---|---|---|---|---|---|---|---|---|
| 2012 WW18 | 29-G | USA | 2 | 2-0-0 | 91:36 | 1 | 1 | 0.66 | 0 | 0 | S |

| **Portnoj, Isabella** | | | | | | | | | | | **b. Turku, Finland, February 15, 1994** |
|---|---|---|---|---|---|---|---|---|---|---|---|
| 2010 WW18 | 30-G | FIN | 2 | 0-0-2 | 126:21 | 7 | 0 | 3.32 | 0 | 0 | 5th |
| 2011 WW18 | 1-G | FIN | 6 | 3-0-3 | 341:46 | 15 | 1 | 2.63 | 0 | 0 | B |
| 2012 WW18 | 1-G | FIN | 4 | 2-0-2 | 247:27 | 10 | 1 | 2.42 | 0 | 0 | 5th |
| 2012 WW | 31-G | FIN | 1 | 0-0-1 | 25:50 | 6 | 0 | 13.94 | 0 | 0 | 4th |
| **Totals WW18** | | | **12** | **5-0-7** | **715:34** | **32** | **2** | **2.68** | **0** | **0** | **B** |

~WW18 IIHF Directorate Best Goalie (2011)

| Prugova, Anna | | | | | | | | | | | b. Khabarovsk Region, Russia, November 20, 1993 |
|---|---|---|---|---|---|---|---|---|---|---|---|
| 2009 WW18 | 30-G | RUS | 5 | 2-0-2 | 255:25 | 17 | 0 | 3.99 | 0 | 0 | 7th |
| 2010 WW18 | 30-G | RUS | 5 | 0-0-5 | 277:33 | 20 | 0 | 4.32 | 0 | 0 | 8th |
| 2010 OG-W | 1-G | RUS | 1 | 0-0-1 | 31:00 | 10 | 0 | 19.35 | 0 | 0 | 6th |
| 2011 WW | 1-G | RUS | 5 | 2-0-3 | 291:40 | 19 | 0 | 3.91 | 0 | 0 | 4th |
| 2012 WW | 1-G | RUS | 4 | 0-0-4 | 219:56 | 16 | 0 | 4.36 | 0 | 0 | 6th |
| **Totals WW18** | | | **10** | **2-0-7** | **532:58** | **37** | **0** | **4.17** | **0** | **0** | **—** |
| **Totals WW** | | | **9** | **2-0-7** | **511:36** | **35** | **0** | **4.10** | **0** | **0** | **—** |

| Ramajzl, Janna | | | | | | | | | | | b. Hamburg, Germany, November 26, 1991 |
|---|---|---|---|---|---|---|---|---|---|---|---|
| 2009 WW18 | 1-G | GER | 2 | 0-0-1 | 37:57 | 6 | 0 | 9.49 | 0 | 0 | 6th |

| Raisanen, Meeri | | | | | | | | | | | b. |
|---|---|---|---|---|---|---|---|---|---|---|---|
| 2012 WW | 30-G | FIN | 3 | 1-0-0 | 98:42 | 9 | 0 | 5.47 | 0 | 0 | 4th |

| Ranne, Tina | | | | | | | | | | | b. Harjavalta, Finland, December 6, 1994 |
|---|---|---|---|---|---|---|---|---|---|---|---|
| 2011 WW18 | 30-G | FIN | 1 | 0-0-0 | 20:00 | 1 | 0 | 3.00 | 0 | 0 | B |
| 2012 WW18 | 30-G | FIN | 1 | 0-0-1 | 60:00 | 7 | 0 | 7.00 | 0 | 0 | 5th |
| **Totals WW18** | | | **2** | **0-0-1** | **80:00** | **8** | **0** | **6.00** | **0** | **0** | **B** |

| Raty, Noora | | | | | | | | | | | b. Espoo, Finland, May 29, 1989 |
|---|---|---|---|---|---|---|---|---|---|---|---|
| 2005 WW | 1-G | FIN | 1 | 0-0-1 | 29:27 | 4 | 0 | 8.15 | 0 | 0 | 4th |
| 2006 OG-W | 1-G | FIN | 3 | 1-0-1 | 104:43 | 6 | 1 | 3.44 | 0 | 0 | 4th |
| 2007 WW | 1-G | FIN | 5 | 2-0-3 | 301:32 | 10 | 2 | 1.99 | 0 | 0 | 4th |
| 2008 WW | 1-G | FIN | 4 | 3-0-1 | 243:42 | 6 | 1 | 1.48 | 0 | 0 | 8th |
| 2009 WW | 31-G | FIN | 3 | 2-0-1 | 170:48 | 10 | 0 | 3.51 | 0 | 4 | B |
| 2010 OG-W | 31-G | FIN | 5 | 3-0-2 | 302:33 | 15 | 0 | 2.97 | 0 | 0 | B |
| 2011 WW | 41-G | FIN | 5 | 2-0-3 | 304:05 | 10 | 0 | 1.97 | 0 | 0 | B |
| 2012 WW | 41-G | FIN | 4 | 1-0-3 | 234:48 | 15 | 0 | 3.83 | 0 | 2 | 4th |
| **Totals WW** | | | **22** | **10-0-12** | **1,284:22** | **55** | **3** | **2.57** | **0** | **6** | **2B** |
| **Totals OG-W** | | | **8** | **4-0-3** | **407:16** | **21** | **1** | **3.09** | **0** | **0** | **B** |

~WW MVP (2008), WW IIHF Directorate Best Goalie (2007, 2008, 2011), WW All-Star Team/Goal (2008)

| Raty, Pia | | | | | | | | | | | b. Kuopio, Finland, February 22, 1990 |
|---|---|---|---|---|---|---|---|---|---|---|---|
| 2008 WW18 | 25-G | FIN | 4 | 1-0-3 | 224:01 | 13 | 0 | 3.48 | 0 | 0 | 6th |

| Raushanova, Aizhan | | | | | | | | | | | b.Almaty, Soviet Union (Kazakhstan), January 16, 1988 |
|---|---|---|---|---|---|---|---|---|---|---|---|
| 2011 WW | | KAZ | 3RD GK—DID NOT PLAY | | | | | | | | |

| Rigsby, Alex | | | | | | | | | | | b. Delafield, Wisconsin, United States, January 3, 1992 |
|---|---|---|---|---|---|---|---|---|---|---|---|
| 2009 WW18 | 30-G | USA | 3 | 3-0-0 | 186:47 | 4 | 1 | 1.28 | 0 | 0 | G |
| 2010 WW18 | 30-G | USA | 3 | 2-0-1 | 183:10 | 5 | 2 | 1.64 | 0 | 0 | S |
| **Totals WW18** | | | **6** | **5-0-1** | **369:57** | **9** | **3** | **1.46** | **0** | **0** | **G,S** |

~WW18 IIHF Directorate Best Goalie (2009, 2010)

| Ruegsegger, Rebecca | | | | | | | | | | | b. Lakewood, Colorado, United States, September 21, 1990 |
|---|---|---|---|---|---|---|---|---|---|---|---|
| 2008 WW18 | 20-G | USA | 2 | 0-0-0 | 59:43 | 0 | 0 | 0.00 | 0 | 0 | G |

| Ryzhova, Yekaterina | | | | | | | | | | | b. Novosibirsk, Soviet Union (Russia), July 14, 1989 |
|---|---|---|---|---|---|---|---|---|---|---|---|
| 2005 WW | 20-G | KAZ | 2 | 0-0-0 | 30:33 | 5 | 0 | 9.82 | 0 | 0 | 7th |
| 2007 WW | 20-G | KAZ | 4 | 0-0-3 | 151:15 | 14 | 0 | 5.55 | 0 | 0 | 9th |
| **Totals WW** | | | **6** | **0-0-3** | **181:48** | **19** | **0** | **6.27** | **0** | **0** | **—** |

| Schaus, Molly | | | | | | | | | | | b. Natick, Massachusetts, United States, July 29, 1988 |
|---|---|---|---|---|---|---|---|---|---|---|---|
| 2008 WW | 1-G | USA | 1 | 1-0-0 | 60:00 | 1 | 0 | 1.00 | 0 | 0 | G |
| 2009 WW | 1-G | USA | 2 | 1-0-1 | 119:22 | 2 | 1 | 1.01 | 1 | 0 | G |
| 2010 OG-W | 1-G | USA | 1 | 1-0-0 | 52:00 | 0 | 0 | 0.00 | 0 | 0 | S |
| 2011 WW | 1-G | USA | 1 | 1-0-0 | 60:00 | 1 | 0 | 1.00 | 0 | 0 | G |
| 2012 WW | 1-G | USA | 3 | 2-0-1 | 181:50 | 7 | 1 | 2.31 | 0 | 0 | S |
| **Totals WW** | | | | **5-0-2** | **421:12** | **11** | **2** | **1.57** | **1** | **0** | **3G,S** |

| Schelander, Madeleine | | | | | | | | | | | b. Stockholm, Sweden, July 10, 1991 |
|---|---|---|---|---|---|---|---|---|---|---|---|
| 2009 WW18 | 30-G | SWE | 2 | 0-0-0 | 46:20 | 1 | 0 | 1.29 | 0 | 0 | B |

| Schelling, Florence | | | | | | | | | | | b. Zurich, Switzerland, March 9, 1989 |
|---|---|---|---|---|---|---|---|---|---|---|---|
| 2004 WW | 30-G | SUI | 3 | 1-0-2 | 166:21 | 5 | 1 | 1.80 | 0 | 0 | 8th |
| 2006 OG-W | 41-G | SUI | 3 | 1-0-1 | 150:00 | 6 | 1 | 2.40 | 0 | 0 | 7th |
| 2007 WW | 41-G | SUI | 4 | 2-0-2 | 230:55 | 13 | 1 | 3.38 | 0 | 2 | 5th |
| 2008 WW | 41-G | SUI | 5 | 3-0-2 | 305:00 | 15 | 1 | 2.95 | 1 | 2 | 4th |
| 2009 WW | 41-G | SUI | 3 | 0-0-2 | 153:13 | 12 | 0 | 4.70 | 0 | 0 | 7th |
| 2010 OG-W | 41-G | SUI | 5 | 3-0-2 | 301:55 | 16 | 1 | 3.18 | 1 | 0 | 5th |
| 2011 WW | 41-G | SUI | 5 | 2-0-3 | 288:50 | 16 | 0 | 3.32 | 1 | 0 | 6th |
| 2012 WW | 41-G | SUI | 5 | 4-0-1 | 288:23 | 16 | 0 | 3.33 | 0 | 0 | B |
| **Totals WW** | | | **25** | **12-0-12** | **1,432:42** | **77** | **3** | **3.22** | **2** | **4** | **B** |
| **Totals OG-W** | | | **8** | **4-0-3** | **451:55** | **22** | **2** | **2.92** | **1** | **0** | **—** |

~WW IIHF Directorate Best Goalie (2012), WW All-Star Team/Goal (2012)

| Schroder, Ivonne | | | | | | | | | | | b. Bad Muskau, East Germany (Germany), July 25, 1988 |
|---|---|---|---|---|---|---|---|---|---|---|---|
| 2012 WW | | GER | 3RD GK—DID NOT PLAY | | | | | | | | |

| Seguin, Cassie | | | | | | | | | | | b. Ingleside, Ontario, Canada, October 30, 1991 |
|---|---|---|---|---|---|---|---|---|---|---|---|
| 2009 WW18 | 29-G | CAN | 2 | 2-0-0 | 120:00 | 1 | 1 | 0.50 | 0 | 0 | S |

| Shi, Yao | | | | | | | | | | | b. Heilongjiang, China, January 13, 1987 |
|---|---|---|---|---|---|---|---|---|---|---|---|
| 2007 WW | 30-G | CHN | 4 | 1-0-3 | 240:00 | 26 | 1 | 6.50 | 0 | 0 | 6th |
| 2008 WW | 30-G | CHN | 4 | 1-0-3 | 226:09 | 18 | 0 | 4.78 | 0 | 0 | 8th |
| 2009 WW | 30-G | CHN | 4 | 0-0-4 | 195:58 | 20 | 0 | 6.12 | 0 | 0 | 9th |
| 2010 OG-W | 30-G | CHN | 5 | 1-0-4 | 247:53 | 19 | 0 | 4.60 | 0 | 0 | 7th |
| **Totals WW** | | | **12** | **2-0-10** | **662:07** | **64** | **1** | **5.80** | **0** | **0** | **—** |

| Simunkova, Karolina | | | | | | | | | | | b. Plzen, Czech Republic, June 12, 1993 |
|---|---|---|---|---|---|---|---|---|---|---|---|
| 2009 WW18 | 1-G | CZE | 2 | 0-0-0 | 44:18 | 11 | 0 | 14.90 | 0 | 0 | 4th |

| Slongo, Dominique | | | | | | | | | | | b. Berne, Switzerland, October 13, 1988 |
|---|---|---|---|---|---|---|---|---|---|---|---|
| 2007 WW | 30-G | SUI | 1 | 0-0-0 | 9:05 | 1 | 0 | 6.61 | 0 | 0 | 5th |
| 2008 WW | | SUI | 3RD GK—DID NOT PLAY | | | | | | | | |
| 2009 WW | 33-G | SUI | 2 | 2-0-0 | 96:47 | 2 | 0 | 1.24 | 0 | 0 | 7th |
| 2010 OG-W | 33-G | SUI | 1 | 0-0-0 | 8:05 | 0 | 0 | 0.00 | 0 | 0 | 5th |
| 2011 WW | | SUI | 3RD GK—DID NOT PLAY | | | | | | | | |
| 2012 WW | | SUI | 3RD GK—DID NOT PLAY | | | | | | | | |
| **Totals WW** | | | **3** | **2-0-0** | **105:52** | **3** | **0** | **1.70** | **0** | **0** | **—** |

| Steeger, Janine | | | | | | | | | | | b. Bayreuth, Germany, April 21, 1990 |
|---|---|---|---|---|---|---|---|---|---|---|---|
| 2008 WW18 | 20-G | GER | 1 | 0-0-0 | 24:29 | 5 | 0 | 12.25 | 0 | 0 | 5th |

| St. Pierre, Kim | | | | | | | | | | | b. LaSalle, Quebec, Canada, December 14, 1978 |
|---|---|---|---|---|---|---|---|---|---|---|---|
| 1999 WW | 33-G | CAN | 2 | 2-0-0 | 120:00 | 1 | 1 | 0.50 | 0 | 0 | G |
| 2000 WW | 35-G | CAN | 2 | 2-0-0 | 149:58 | 3 | 0 | 1.20 | 0 | 0 | G |
| 2001 WW | 33-G | CAN | 3 | 3-0-0 | 180:00 | 2 | 2 | 0.67 | 0 | 0 | G |
| 2002 OG-W | 33-G | CAN | 4 | 4-0-0 | 240:00 | 5 | 2 | 1.25 | 1 | 0 | G |
| 2004 WW | 33-G | CAN | 4 | 2-0-1 | 179:44 | 3 | 2 | 1.00 | 0 | 0 | G |
| 2005 WW | 33-G | CAN | 3 | 2-0-1 | 200:00 | 1 | 3 | 0.30 | 0 | 0 | S |
| 2006 OG-W | 33-G | CAN | 2 | 2-0-0 | 120:00 | 1 | 1 | 0.50 | 0 | 0 | G |
| 2007 WW | 33-G | CAN | 3 | 3-0-0 | 180:00 | 1 | 2 | 0.33 | 0 | 0 | G |
| 2008 WW | 33-G | CAN | 3 | 2-0-1 | 160:00 | 7 | 0 | 2.63 | 0 | 0 | S |
| 2009 WW | 33-G | CAN | 2 | 2-0-0 | 120:00 | 0 | 2 | 0.00 | 0 | 0 | S |
| 2010 OG-W | 33-G | CAN | 2 | 2-0-0 | 100:00 | 0 | 1 | 0.00 | 0 | 0 | G |
| 2011 WW | 33-G | CAN | 1 | 1-0-0 | 60:00 | 0 | 1 | 0.00 | 0 | 0 | S |
| **Totals WW** | | | **23** | **19-0-3** | **1,349:42** | **18** | **13** | **0.80** | **0** | **0** | **5G,4S** |
| **Totals OG-W** | | | **8** | **8-0-0** | **460:00** | **6** | **4** | **0.78** | **1** | **0** | **3G** |

~OG-W IIHF Directorate Best Goalie (2002), OG-W All-Star Team/Goal (2002), WW IIHF Directorate Best Goalie (2001, 2004), WW All-Star Team/Goal (2007)

| Szabados, Shannon | | | | | | | | | | | b. Edmonton, Alberta, Canada, August 6, 1986 |
|---|---|---|---|---|---|---|---|---|---|---|---|
| 2009 WW | | CAN | 3RD GK—DID NOT PLAY | | | | | | | | |
| 2010 OG-W | 1-G | CAN | 3 | 3-0-0 | 180:00 | 1 | 2 | 0.33 | 0 | 0 | G |
| 2011 WW | 1-G | CAN | 2 | 1-0-1 | 127:48 | 3 | 1 | 1.41 | 0 | 0 | S |
| 2012 WW | 1-G | CAN | 4 | 2-0-0 | 198:18 | 9 | 0 | 2.72 | 0 | 0 | G |
| **Totals WW** | | | **6** | **3-0-1** | **326:06** | **12** | **1** | **2.21** | **0** | **0** | **G,S** |

~OG-W IIHF Directorate Best Goalie (2010), OG-W All-Star Team/Goal (2010)

| Takahashi, Shizuka | | | | | | | | | | | b. Hokkaido, Japan, June 8, 1994 |
|---|---|---|---|---|---|---|---|---|---|---|---|
| 2010 WW18 | 25-G | JPN | 5 | 1-0-2 | 236:38 | 10 | 0 | 2.54 | 0 | 0 | 6th |
| 2011 WW18 | 1-G | JPN | 5 | 0-0-4 | 259:36 | 17 | 0 | 3.93 | 0 | 0 | 8th |
| **Totals WW18** | | | **10** | **1-0-6** | **496:14** | **27** | **0** | **3.26** | **0** | **0** | **—** |

| Tokoro, Ai | | | | | | | | | | | b. Kokkaido, Japan, October 24, 1993 |
|---|---|---|---|---|---|---|---|---|---|---|---|
| 2010 WW18 | 20-G | JPN | 2 | 0-0-2 | 60:00 | 11 | 0 | 11.00 | 0 | 0 | 6th |
| 2011 WW18 | 29-G | JPN | 3 | 1-0-1 | 99:59 | 5 | 0 | 3.00 | 0 | 0 | 8th |
| **Totals WW18** | | | **5** | **1-0-3** | **159:59** | **16** | **0** | **6.00** | **0** | **0** | **—** |

| Tomcikova, Zuzana | | | | | | | | | | | b. Zvolen, Czechoslovakia (Slovakia), April 23, 1988 |
|---|---|---|---|---|---|---|---|---|---|---|---|
| 2010 OG-W | 1-G | SVK | 5 | 0-0-5 | 300:00 | 36 | 0 | 7.20 | 0 | 0 | 8th |
| 2011 WW | 1-G | SVK | 5 | 2-0-3 | 305:00 | 13 | 1 | 2.56 | 0 | 2 | 7th |
| 2012 WW | 1-G | SVK | 5 | 1-0-4 | 304:43 | 14 | 0 | 2.76 | 0 | 0 | 8th |
| **Totals WW** | | | **10** | **3-0-7** | **609:43** | **27** | **1** | **2.66** | **0** | **0** | **—** |

~WW MVP (2011), WW All-Star Team/Goal (2011)

| Vanhatalo, Anna | | | | | | | | | | | b. Helsinki, Finland, Febnruary 29, 1984 |
|---|---|---|---|---|---|---|---|---|---|---|---|
| 2011 WW | | FIN | 3RD GK—DID NOT PLAY | | | | | | | | |

| Vetter, Jessie | | | | | | | | | | | b. Cottage Grove, Wisconsin, United States, December 19, 1985 |
|---|---|---|---|---|---|---|---|---|---|---|---|
| 2007 WW | 31-G | USA | 2 | 1-0-1 | 130:00 | 5 | 1 | 2.31 | 0 | 0 | S |
| 2008 WW | 31-G | USA | 4 | 3-0-1 | 243:42 | 7 | 0 | 1.72 | 0 | 0 | G |
| 2009 WW | 31-G | USA | 2 | 2-0-0 | 120:00 | 1 | 1 | 0.50 | 0 | 0 | G |
| 2010 OG-W | 31-G | USA | 4 | 3-0-1 | 239:50 | 3 | 2 | 0.75 | 0 | 0 | S |
| 2011 WW | 31-G | USA | 3 | 3-0-0 | 187:48 | 4 | 0 | 1.28 | 0 | 0 | G |
| 2012 WW | 31-G | USA | 1 | 1-0-0 | 60:00 | 0 | 1 | 0.00 | 0 | 0 | S |
| **Totals WW** | | | **12** | **10-0-2** | **741:30** | **17** | **3** | **1.38** | **0** | **0** | **3G,2S** |

~WW All-Star Team/Goal (2009)

| Vinogradova, Anna | | | | | | | | | | | b. Tyumen Region, Soviet Union (Russia), April 6, 1991 |
|---|---|---|---|---|---|---|---|---|---|---|---|
| 2008 WW18 | 1-G | RUS | 5 | 0-0-5 | 212:57 | 21 | 0 | 5.92 | 0 | 0 | 8th |

| **Zanetti, Anja** | | | | | | | | | | | **b. February 10, 1996** |
|---|---|---|---|---|---|---|---|---|---|---|---|
| 2012 WW18 | | SUI | 3 | RD GK—DID NOT PLAY | | | | | | | |

| **Zorn, Julia** | | | | **b. Grafeling, West Germany (Germany), February 6, 1990** | | | | | | | |
|---|---|---|---|---|---|---|---|---|---|---|---|
| 2008 WW18 | 1-G | GER | 5 | 3-0-2 | 275:31 | 12 | 0 | 2.61 | 0 | 0 | 5th |

~see also Active Skaters

*Goalie Florence Schelling (middle) was the key reason Switzerland won its first ever medal in women's hockey, a bronze at the 2012 Women's World Championship. Photo: Dave Sandford / HHOF-IIHF Images.*

# Retired Skaters, Women

(career summary for players who have retired from hockey or who have not played recently for their country)

| First-Last Years | Event | NAT | GP | G | A | P | Pim | Medals |
|---|---|---|---|---|---|---|---|---|
| **Adyeva, Viktoria / b. Apr. 25, 1981** | | | | | | | | |
| 2001-07 | WW | KAZ | 9 | 0 | 0 | 0 | 10 | — |
| 2002 | OG-W | KAZ | 5 | 0 | 0 | 0 | 6 | — |
| **Ahonen (-Blomqvist), Pirjo / b. Nov. 5, 1970** | | | | | | | | |
| 1999 | WW | FIN | 5 | 0 | 1 | 1 | 4 | B |
| 2002 | OG-W | FIN | 5 | 0 | 0 | 0 | 2 | — |
| **Akama, Masami / b. Dec. 2, 1985** | | | | | | | | |
| 2004 | WW | JPN | 4 | 0 | 0 | 0 | B | — |
| **Almblad, Charlotte / b. Apr. 28, 1972** | | | | | | | | |
| 1992-2000 | WW | SWE | 25 | 10 | 3 | 13 | 4 | — |
| 1998-2002 | OG-W | SWE | 9 | 2 | 2 | 4 | 4 | B |
| **Amhof, Brigitte / b. Mar. 4, 1971** | | | | | | | | |
| 1992-1994 | WW | SUI | 10 | 0 | 0 | 0 | 2 | — |
| **Amidon, Michele / b. June 7, 1972** | | | | | | | | |
| 1992 | WW | USA | 4 | 0 | 1 | 1 | 4 | S |
| **Andermatt, Nicole / b. Aug. 7, 1971** | | | | | | | | |
| 1990-1994 | WW | SUI | 10 | 0 | 1 | 1 | 2 | — |
| **Andersson, Anna / b. Jan. 28, 1982** | | | | | | | | |
| 2000-2001 | WW | SWE | 10 | 0 | 2 | 2 | 16 | — |
| 2002 | OG-W | SWE | 5 | 0 | 1 | 1 | 8 | B |
| **Andersson, Karin / b. Apr. 10, 1963** | | | | | | | | |
| 1990-1992 | WW | SWE | 9 | 0 | 1 | 1 | 14 | — |
| **Angeloni, Michela / b. Sept. 25, 1984** | | | | | | | | |
| 2006 | OG-W | ITA | 5 | 0 | 0 | 0 | 4 | — |
| **Ansnes, May Olaug / b. Nov. 1, 1962** | | | | | | | | |
| 1990 | WW | NOR | 1 | 0 | 0 | 0 | 0 | — |
| **Antal, Dana / b. Apr. 19, 1977** | | | | | | | | |
| 2001-2004 | WW | CAN | 10 | 5 | 7 | 12 | 0 | 2G |
| 2002 | OG-W | CAN | 5 | 2 | 1 | 3 | 2 | G |
| **Aoki, Kanae / b. Feb. 20, 1985** | | | | | | | | |
| 2004 | WW | JPN | 4 | 0 | 0 | 0 | 2 | — |
| **Apollo, Lauren / b. June 17, 1963** | | | | | | | | |
| 1990-1992 | WW | USA | 10 | 1 | 4 | 5 | 16 | 2S |
| **Araki, Miharu / b. July 20, 1971** | | | | | | | | |
| 1998 | OG-W | JPN | 5 | 0 | 0 | 0 | 0 | — |
| **Arnet, Sabrina / b. Jan. 2, 1985** | | | | | | | | |
| 2004 | WW | SUI | 4 | 1 | 0 | 1 | 0 | — |
| **Ask, Hege / b. Dec. 25, 1975** | | | | | | | | |
| 1994-1997 | WW | NOR | 10 | 0 | 1 | 1 | 0 | — |
| **Asonova, Antonida / b. Aug. 24, 1979** | | | | | | | | |
| 2001 | WW | KAZ | 5 | 0 | 0 | 0 | 0 | — |
| 2002 | OG-W | KAZ | 5 | 0 | 0 | 0 | 4 | — |
| **Atarskaya, Maria / b. Aug. 10, 1980** | | | | | | | | |
| 2005 | WW | KAZ | 5 | 1 | 1 | 2 | 8 | — |
| **Baechler, Mirjam / b. Dec. 16, 1972** | | | | | | | | |
| 1990-2004 | WW | SUI | 26 | 1 | 4 | 5 | 12 | — |
| **Baert, Beate / b. Nov. 15, 1968** | | | | | | | | |
| 1990 | WW | FRG | 5 | 2 | 1 | 3 | 4 | — |
| **Bailey, Chris / b. Feb. 5, 1972** | | | | | | | | |
| 1994-2001 | WW | USA | 25 | 5 | 9 | 14 | 14 | 5S |
| 1998-2002 | OG-W | USA | 11 | 1 | 3 | 4 | 4 | G,S |
| **Baker, Laurie / b. Nov. 6, 1976** | | | | | | | | |
| 1997-2000 | WW | USA | 10 | 2 | 8 | 10 | 16 | 2S |
| 1998-2002 | OG-W | USA | 11 | 7 | 5 | 12 | 10 | G,S |
| **Bandelow, Birgit / b. July 3, 1972** | | | | | | | | |
| 1994 | WW | GER | 5 | 0 | 0 | 0 | 2 | — |
| **Barykina (-Misropian), Maria / b. Dec. 9, 1973** | | | | | | | | |
| 1997-2007 | WW | RUS | 24 | 2 | 4 | 6 | 30 | B |
| 2002-2006 | OG-W | RUS | 5 | 0 | 1 | 1 | 8 | — |
| **Bazzanella, Evelyn / b. June 15, 1976** | | | | | | | | |
| 2006 | OG-W | ITA | 5 | 0 | 1 | 1 | 4 | — |
| **Beagan, Beth / b. Oct. 20, 1970** | | | | | | | | |
| 1990-1994 | WW | USA | 15 | 10 | 16 | 26 | 11 | 3S |
| **Bechard, Kelly / b. Jan. 22, 1978** | | | | | | | | |
| 2000-08 | WW | CAN | 30 | 8 | 17 | 25 | 30 | 4G,2S |
| 2002 | OG-W | CAN | 5 | 0 | 1 | 1 | 2 | G |
| **Becker, Maritta / b. Mar. 11, 1981** | | | | | | | | |
| 1999-2007 | WW | GER | 28 | 5 | 8 | 13 | 30 | — |
| 2002-2006 | OG-W | GER | 10 | 6 | 4 | 10 | 18 | — |
| **Benoit, Amanda / b. Jan. 22, 1976** | | | | | | | | |
| 1999-2000 | WW | CAN | 10 | 2 | 4 | 6 | 4 | 2G |
| **Berger, Kira / b. July 30, 1962** | | | | | | | | |
| 1990 | WW | FRG | 5 | 0 | 0 | 0 | 0 | — |
| **Bergersen, Lena / b. Oct. 17, 1965** | | | | | | | | |
| 1990-1994 | WW | NOR | 8 | 0 | 1 | 1 | 0 | — |
| **Bergesen, Janne / b. Sept. 2, 1971** | | | | | | | | |
| 1997 | WW | NOR | 5 | 0 | 0 | 0 | 2 | — |
| **Berggren, Emelie / b. Sep. 15, 1982** | | | | | | | | |
| 2008 | WW | SWE | 4 | 0 | 0 | 0 | 0 | — |
| 2002 | OG-W | SWE | 5 | 0 | 0 | 0 | 2 | B |
| **Bergstrand, Kristina / b. Oct. 4, 1963** | | | | | | | | |
| 1990-2001 | WW | SWE | 30 | 11 | 9 | 20 | 24 | — |
| 1998-2002 | OG-W | SWE | 9 | 2 | 1 | 3 | 4 | B |
| **Berndaner, Christine / b. Mar. 8, 1984** | | | | | | | | |
| 2001 | WW | GER | 5 | 0 | 0 | 0 | 2 | — |
| **Bettarini, Valentina / b. June 29, 1990** | | | | | | | | |
| 2006 | OG-W | ITA | 5 | 0 | 1 | 1 | 4 | — |
| **Bissardella, Celeste / b. Oct. 17, 1988** | | | | | | | | |
| 2006 | OG-W | ITA | 5 | 0 | 0 | 0 | 2 | — |
| **Bjork, Tina / b. Oct. 1963** | | | | | | | | |
| 1990 | WW | SWE | 3 | 1 | 0 | 1 | 4 | — |
| **Blahoski, Alana / b. Apr. 29, 1974** | | | | | | | | |
| 1997-2001 | WW | USA | 20 | 8 | 7 | 15 | 6 | 4S |
| 1998 | OG-W | USA | 6 | 0 | 2 | 2 | 0 | G |
| **Blattler, Claudia / b. Nov. 19, 1966** | | | | | | | | |
| 1990-1992 | WW | SUI | 10 | 0 | 0 | 0 | 10 | — |
| **~Blomqvist, Pirjo** ~see Ahonen (-Blomqvist), Pirjo | | | | | | | | |
| **Bobrova (-Rodikova), Yelena / b. Aug. 23, 1974** | | | | | | | | |
| 1997-2007 | WW | RUS | 19 | 1 | 1 | 2 | 16 | B |
| 2002 | OG-W | RUS | 5 | 0 | 2 | 2 | 4 | — |
| **Boldt, Lisbeth / b. Nov. 17, 1962** | | | | | | | | |
| 1992 | WW | DEN | 5 | 0 | 0 | 0 | 2 | — |
| **Borisova, Marina / b. Nov. 16, 1978** | | | | | | | | |
| 2004-2005 | WW | RUS | 9 | 1 | 2 | 3 | 0 | — |
| **Botterill, Jennifer / b. May 1, 1979** | | | | | | | | |
| 1999-2009 | WW | CAN | 40 | 26 | 33 | 59 | 20 | 5G,3S |
| 1998-2010 | OG-W | CAN | 21 | 4 | 11 | 15 | 12 | 3G,S |
| ~WW MVP (2001, 2004), WW IIHF Directorate Best Forward (2001), WW All-Star Team/Forward (2004) | | | | | | | | |
| **Boyd, Stephanie / b. Dec. 11, 1972** | | | | | | | | |
| 1994 | WW | USA | 5 | 3 | 3 | 6 | 6 | S |
| **Brandshaug, Guro / b. Oct. 6, 1980** | | | | | | | | |
| 1997 | WW | NOR | 5 | 0 | 1 | 1 | 6 | — |
| **Brask, Helle / b. July 6, 1966** | | | | | | | | |
| 1992 | WW | DEN | 3 | 0 | 0 | 0 | 0 | — |
| **Bredin, Correne / b. Feb. 11, 1980** | | | | | | | | |
| 2001-2005 | WW | CAN | 10 | 4 | 3 | 7 | 6 | G,S |
| **Brisson, Therese / b. Oct. 5, 1966** | | | | | | | | |
| 1994-2004 | WW | CAN | 30 | 3 | 16 | 19 | 20 | 6G |
| 1998-2002 | OG-W | CAN | 11 | 7 | 5 | 12 | 12 | G,S |
| ~WW All-Star Team/Defence (1994) | | | | | | | | |
| **Brodt (-Brown), Winny / b. Feb. 18, 1978** | | | | | | | | |
| 2000-2001 | WW | USA | 10 | 0 | 5 | 5 | 0 | 2S |
| **Brown (-Miller), Lisa / b. Nov. 16, 1966** | | | | | | | | |
| 1990-1997 | WW | USA | 20 | 8 | 18 | 26 | 24 | 4S |
| 1998 | OG-W | USA | 6 | 1 | 2 | 3 | 2 | G |
| **~Brown, Winny** ~see Brodt (-Brown), Winny | | | | | | | | |
| **Bruggmann, Silvia / b. Feb. 20, 1978** | | | | | | | | |
| 2004-08 | WW | SUI | 13 | 0 | 1 | 1 | 4 | — |
| 2006 | OG-W | SUI | 5 | 0 | 0 | 0 | 0 | — |
| **Bruun, Merita / b. Nov. 7, 1977** | | | | | | | | |
| 2004 | WW | FIN | 5 | 0 | 1 | 1 | 0 | B |
| **Bruvik, Sissel / b. Sept. 27, 1973** | | | | | | | | |
| 1997 | WW | NOR | 5 | 0 | 0 | 0 | 2 | — |
| **Burholm, Pernilla / b. Feb. 16, 1974** | | | | | | | | |
| 1992-2001 | WW | SWE | 29 | 0 | 7 | 7 | 38 | — |
| 1998 | OG-W | SWE | 4 | 1 | 0 | 1 | 4 | — |
| **Byalkovskaya, Yelena / b. Mar. 22, 1977** | | | | | | | | |
| 1997-2007 | WW | RUS | 17 | 2 | 4 | 6 | 2 | — |
| 2002-06 | OG-W | RUS | 10 | 0 | 2 | 2 | 2 | — |
| **Bye (-Dietz), Karyn / b. May 18, 1971** | | | | | | | | |
| 1992-2001 | WW | USA | 30 | 27 | 24 | 51 | 18 | 6S |
| 1998-2002 | OG-W | USA | 11 | 8 | 6 | 14 | 4 | G,S |
| ~IIHF Hall of Fame | | | | | | | | |
| ~WW IIHF Directorate Best Defenceman (2001), WW All-Star Team/Forward (1994) | | | | | | | | |
| **Caldart, Heidi / b. Oct. 19, 1983** | | | | | | | | |
| 2006 | OG-W | ITA | 5 | 0 | 0 | 0 | 2 | — |
| **Cameron, Shirley / b. Aug. 12, 1952** | | | | | | | | |
| 1990 | WW | CAN | 5 | 5 | 6 | 11 | 0 | G |
| **Campbell (-Pascall), Cassie / b. Nov. 22, 1973** | | | | | | | | |
| 1994-2005 | WW | CAN | 35 | 11 | 20 | 31 | 12 | 6G,S |
| 1998-2006 | OG-W | CAN | 16 | 3 | 8 | 11 | 12 | 2G,S |
| ~WW All-Star Team/Defence (1997) | | | | | | | | |
| **Cardinale, Tina / b. Oct. 20, 1966** | | | | | | | | |
| 1990-1992 | WW | USA | 9 | 5 | 12 | 17 | 2 | 2S |
| **Carignano, Silvia / b. Aug. 11, 1987** | | | | | | | | |
| 2006 | OG-W | ITA | 5 | 0 | 0 | 0 | 2 | — |
| **Cattaneo, Sandra / b. Jan. 25, 1975** | | | | | | | | |
| 1992-2004 | WW | SUI | 24 | 3 | 4 | 7 | 2 | — |
| 2006 | OG-W | SUI | 5 | 0 | 1 | 1 | 2 | — |
| **Ceder, Susanne / b. June 30, 1967** | | | | | | | | |
| 1990-2000 | WW | SWE | 23 | 4 | 10 | 14 | 14 | — |
| 1998 | OG-W | SWE | 4 | 0 | 0 | 0 | 2 | — |
| **Chalupnik, Heidi / b. Sept. 21, 1968** | | | | | | | | |
| 1990 | WW | USA | 5 | 2 | 1 | 3 | 0 | S |
| **Chartrand, Isabelle / b. Apr. 20, 1978** | | | | | | | | |
| 2001 | WW | CAN | 5 | 0 | 3 | 3 | 2 | G |
| 2002 | OG-W | CAN | 5 | 2 | 1 | 3 | 2 | G |
| **Chen, Jing / b. Apr. 22, 1971** | | | | | | | | |
| 1992-2001 | WW | CHN | 26 | 0 | 5 | 5 | 16 | — |
| 1998-2002 | OG-W | CHN | 11 | 0 | 1 | 1 | 6 | — |
| **Chen, Yuzhi / b. Oct. 9, 1967** | | | | | | | | |
| 1992 | WW | CHN | 5 | 0 | 0 | 0 | 4 | — |
| **Chiavi, Patrizia / b. May 29, 1974** | | | | | | | | |
| 1999 | WW | SUI | 5 | 0 | 0 | 0 | 6 | — |
| **Christensen, Lene / b. June 22, 1967** | | | | | | | | |
| 1992 | WW | DEN | 3 | 0 | 0 | 0 | 0 | — |
| **Christoffersen, Tina / b. Sept. 26, 1965** | | | | | | | | |
| 1992 | WW | DEN | 5 | 1 | 1 | 2 | 8 | — |
| **Coelho, Amy / b. May 24, 1975** | | | | | | | | |
| 1999 | WW | USA | 5 | 0 | 1 | 1 | 2 | S |
| **Collins, Delaney / b. May 2, 1977** | | | | | | | | |
| 2000-08 | WW | CAN | 25 | 4 | 11 | 15 | 12 | 3G,2S |
| ~WW All-Star Team/Defence (2007) | | | | | | | | |
| **Coyne, Colleen / b. Sept. 19, 1971** | | | | | | | | |
| 1992-1997 | WW | USA | 15 | 3 | 9 | 12 | 6 | 3S |
| 1998 | OG-W | USA | 6 | 0 | 0 | 0 | 4 | G |
| **Curley, Cindy / b. Nov. 12, 1963** | | | | | | | | |
| 1990-1994 | WW | USA | 15 | 15 | 19 | 34 | 2 | 3S |
| **Dahlstrom, Marianne / b. Sept. 29, 1966** | | | | | | | | |
| 1992-1997 | WW | NOR | 15 | 1 | 4 | 5 | 16 | — |
| **Dai, Qiuwa / b. Aug. 11, 1982** | | | | | | | | |
| 2001-2004 | WW | CHN | 9 | 0 | 0 | 0 | 0 | — |
| 2002 | OG-W | CHN | 5 | 0 | 0 | 0 | 0 | — |
| **Dang, Hong / b. Jan. 28, 1969** | | | | | | | | |
| 1992-1997 | WW | CHN | 15 | 7 | 8 | 15 | 2 | — |
| 1998 | OG-W | CHN | 6 | 0 | 0 | 0 | 0 | — |
| **Danielsen, Line Baun / b. Dec. 8, 1961** | | | | | | | | |
| 1992 | WW | DEN | 5 | 0 | 0 | 0 | 4 | — |
| **da Rugna, Diana / b. Oct. 16, 1989** | | | | | | | | |
| 2006 | OG-W | ITA | 5 | 0 | 0 | 0 | 4 | — |
| **Davidson, Shawna / b. June 23, 1970** | | | | | | | | |
| 1990-1994 | WW | USA | 15 | 3 | 8 | 11 | 12 | 3S |
| **de la Forest, Anna / b. June 24, 1988** | | | | | | | | |
| 2006 | OG-W | ITA | 5 | 0 | 0 | 0 | 2 | — |
| **de Nardin, Nadia / b. Nov. 14, 1975** | | | | | | | | |
| 2006 | OG-W | ITA | 5 | 0 | 0 | 0 | 10 | — |
| **Dennis Maria / b. Feb. 8, 1966** | | | | | | | | |
| 1990 | WW | USA | 5 | 1 | 0 | 1 | 2 | S |
| **de Rocco, Linda / b. Jan. 3, 1986** | | | | | | | | |
| 2006 | OG-W | ITA | 5 | 0 | 0 | 0 | 34 | — |
| **Diao, Ying / b. Nov. 24, 1974** | | | | | | | | |
| 1994-1999 | WW | CHN | 15 | 0 | 0 | 0 | 8 | — |
| 1998 | OG-W | CHN | 3 | 0 | 0 | 0 | 0 | — |
| **Diaz, Daniela / b. June 16, 1982** | | | | | | | | |
| 1997-2007 | WW | SUI | 18 | 4 | 3 | 7 | 6 | — |
| 2006 | OG-W | SUI | 5 | 2 | 1 | 3 | 4 | — |
| **Diduck, Judy / b. Apr. 21, 1966** | | | | | | | | |
| 1990-1997 | WW | CAN | 20 | 1 | 10 | 11 | 12 | 4G |
| 1998 | OG-W | CAN | 6 | 1 | 2 | 3 | 10 | S |
| **DiFronzo, Shelly / b. Feb. 17, 1967** | | | | | | | | |
| 1994 | WW | USA | 5 | 0 | 0 | 0 | 6 | S |
| **Dikambayeva, Dinara / b. May 11, 1982** | | | | | | | | |
| 2001 | WW | KAZ | 5 | 2 | 1 | 3 | 4 | — |
| 2002 | OG-W | KAZ | 5 | 0 | 0 | 0 | 6 | — |
| **Dil, Yekaterina / b. Oct. 31, 1979** | | | | | | | | |
| 1999-2005 | WW | RUS | 10 | 0 | 1 | 1 | 0 | — |
| **Ding, Xiaolin / b. Aug. 7, 1988** | | | | | | | | |
| 2007 | WW | CHN | 4 | 0 | 0 | 0 | 0 | — |
| **Drazan, Rachael / b. Jan. 11, 1986** | | | | | | | | |
| 2008 | WW | USA | 5 | 0 | 3 | 3 | 4 | G |
| **Drolet, Nancy / b. Aug. 2, 1973** | | | | | | | | |
| 1992-2001 | WW | CAN | 30 | 18 | 23 | 41 | 6 | 6G |
| 1998 | OG-W | CAN | 6 | 1 | 2 | 3 | 10 | S |
| **Dunder, Minna / b. June 11, 1966** | | | | | | | | |
| 1992-1997 | WW | SWE | 10 | 0 | 1 | 1 | 8 | — |

**Dunn (-Luoma), Tricia / b. Apr. 25, 1974**
1997-2004 WW USA 25 16 4 20 8 5S
1998-2006 OG-W USA 16 2 0 2 49 G,S,B

**Dupuis, Lori / b. Nov. 14, 1972**
1997-2000 WW CAN 15 4 7 11 14 3G
1998-200 OG-W CAN 11 3 2 5 10 G,S

**Edstrand, Ann-Louise / b. Apr. 25, 1975**
1994-2008 WW SWE 41 7 7 14 24 2B
1998-2006 OG-W SWE 15 3 0 3 8 S,B

**Ehrbar, Nadine / b. Sept. 11, 1988**
2008 WW SUI 5 0 1 1 0 —

**Eisenreid, Kim / b. Nov. 14, 1966**
1990 WW USA 5 5 5 10 2 S

**Elfsberg, Joa / b. July 30, 1979**
1997-2007 WW SWE 23 3 4 7 53 B
1998-2006 OG-W SWE 15 0 1 1 22 S,B

**Elfving, Asa / b. Feb. 1, 1970**
1990-1997 WW SWE 20 5 5 10 6 —
1998 OG-W SWE 4 0 1 1 2 —

**Enzler, Edith / b. Oct. 24, 1975**
1992-1994 WW SUI 10 3 5 8 8 —

**Eriksen-Moseby, Anne / b. June 11, 1971**
1990 WW NOR 1 0 0 0 0 —

**Erikson, Ann-Sofie / b. Mar. 23, 1959**
1990 WW SWE 4 1 1 2 4 —

**Eriksson, Annika / b. Sept. 3, 1971**
1992-1994 WW SWE 10 1 3 4 19 —

**Faber, Sam / b. May 8, 1987**
2008 WW USA 4 0 0 0 4 G

**Fagernes, Inger Lise / b. June 6, 1971**
1990-1997 WW NOR 20 11 6 17 36 —

**Fahey, Rebecca / b. Jan. 31, 1975**
1997 WW CAN 5 1 0 1 2 G

**~Fellner, Christina** ~see Oswald (-Fellner), Christina

**Feng, Chun / b. July 23, 1982**
2000 WW CHN 5 0 0 0 0 —

**Feng, Ruolan / b. Nov. 1, 1969**
1992 WW CHN 5 0 0 0 4 —

**Ferm, Anne / b. Aug. 26, 1969**
1992-1997 WW SWE 15 1 4 5 2 —
1998 OG-W SWE 5 0 0 0 0 —

**Ferrari, Gillian / b. June 23, 1980**
2004-09 WW CAN 20 0 3 3 12 2G,2S
2006 OG-W CAN 5 0 0 0 0 G

**Fiorese, Rebecca / b. Sept. 4, 1980**
2006 OG-W ITA 5 0 0 0 6 —

**Fisher, Brandy / b. Oct. 28, 1975**
1999-2000 WW USA 10 5 7 12 0 2S

**Fisk, Sari / b. Dec. 17, 1971**
1992-2005 WW FIN 40 9 14 23 14 6B
1998-2006 OG-W FIN 16 2 7 9 8 B

**Flolo, Heidi / b. Feb. 4, 1975**
1992-1994 WW NOR 10 0 0 0 0 —

**Florian, Sabina / b. May 28, 1983**
2006 OG-W ITA 5 1 0 1 2 —

**Friz, Manuela / b. Aug. 16, 1978**
2006 OG-W ITA 5 0 0 0 2 —

**Fruhwirt, Stephanie / b. July 22, 1980**
1999-2008 WW GER 28 4 3 7 24 —
2002-06 OG-W GER 10 0 1 1 14 —

**Fu, Yue / b. Mar. 11, 1986**
2005-08 WW CHN 13 0 0 0 6 —

**Fuhrer, Ramona / b. Apr. 13, 1979**
1994-2004 WW SUI 19 3 3 6 4 —
2006 OG-W SUI 5 0 0 0 8 —

**Fujiwara, Shiho / b. Nov. 16, 1971**
1990 WW JPN 5 0 2 2 4 —
1998 OG-W JPN 5 0 1 1 4 —

**Gall, Nina / b. Apr. 20, 1983**
2000-2004 WW GER 14 0 0 0 2 —

**Gao, Guofeng / b. Sept. 12, 1969**
1992 WW CHN 5 1 4 5 0 —

**Gavrilova, Svetlana / b. Oct. 29, 1970**
1997 WW RUS 5 0 0 0 6 —

**Ginzel, Heather / b. Aug. 14, 1962**
1990-1992 WW CAN 10 10 7 17 0 2G

**Giortz, Jeanette / b. May 11, 1975**
1992-1997 WW NOR 15 0 0 0 14 —

**Gladysheva, Yulia / b. Dec. 4, 1981**
2001-2005 WW RUS 13 0 1 1 4 B
2002-2006 OG-W RUS 10 1 0 1 4 —

**Gomsrud, Marianne / b. Jan. 25, 1965**
1990 WW NOR 5 0 1 1 0 —

**Gong, Ming / b. Feb. 15, 1973**
1992-1997 WW CHN 15 2 1 3 16 —
1998 OG-W CHN 6 0 1 1 10 —

**Goyette, Danielle / b. Jan. 30, 1966**
1992-2007 WW CAN 45 37 31 68 16 8G,S
1998-2006 OG-W CAN 16 15 10 25 16 2G,S
~WW All-Star Team/Forward (1994)

**Granato, Catherine "Cammi" / b. Mar. 25, 1971**
1990-2005 WW USA 43 44 34 78 18 G,8S
1998-2002 OG-W USA 11 10 8 18 0 G,S
~IIHF Hall of Fame
~WW IIHF Directorate Best Forward (1992), OG-W All-Star Team/Forward (2002), WW All-Star Team/Forward (1992, 1997)

**Gregersen, Susan / b. May 23, 1967**
1992 WW DEN 5 0 1 1 4 —

**Grnak, Marianne / b. Sept. 1, 1967**
1994 WW CAN 5 2 3 5 2 G

**Grundmann, Claudia / b. Apr. 22, 1976**
1999-2007 WW GER 22 0 3 3 12 —
2002-2006 OG-W GER 10 1 0 1 8 —

**Grutter, Sandra / b. Mar. 28, 1968**
1990 WW SUI 5 0 0 0 4 —

**Guan, Weinan / b. Oct. 10, 1981**
2000-2004 WW CHN 14 0 0 0 2 —
2002 OG-W CHN 5 0 0 0 0 —

**Guo, Lili / b. May 5, 1976**
1997-1999 WW CHN 10 0 0 0 0 —
1998 OG-W CHN 1 0 0 0 0 —

**Guo, Wei / b. Nov. 7, 1969**
1992-1997 WW CHN 15 5 9 14 8 —
1998 OG-W CHN 6 3 1 4 6 —

**Gustafsson, Ann Sofie / b. May 20, 1974**
1994-1997 WW SWE 10 0 1 1 8 —

**Gustafsson, Linda / b. Feb. 20, 1974**
1990-1992 WW SWE 10 1 3 4 2 —
1998 OG-W SWE 4 0 0 0 2 —

**Gustafsson, Malin / b. Jan. 24, 1980**
1997 WW SWE 4 0 1 1 4 —
1998 OG-W SWE 4 2 0 2 16 —

**Gyseler, Stephanie / b. Oct. 24, 1986**
2007 WW SUI 4 0 0 0 0 —

**Haaf, Claudia / b. Dec. 12, 1969**
1990 WW FRG 5 0 0 0 4 —

**Haanpaa, Anne / b. May 25, 1959**
1990-1997 WW FIN 20 8 6 14 14 4B

**Hagerman, Jamie / b. May 7, 1981**
2005 WW USA 5 0 1 1 4 G
2006 OG-W USA 5 0 0 0 6 B

**Hagge, Tiffany / b. May 3, 1984**
2007 WW USA 5 0 0 0 0 S

**Halcisak, Kelli / b. Jan. 26, 1982**
2004-2007 WW USA 10 0 0 0 2 2S

**Hallengren, Pernilla / b. July 7, 1974**
1990-1992 WW SWE 10 0 1 1 2 —

**Halonen, Paivi / b. Aug. 3, 1964**
1990-2000 WW FIN 24 1 14 15 14 5B

**Haman, Kim / b. June 28, 1973**
1992 WW USA 4 2 1 3 4 S

**Hanninen, Kirsi / b. Oct. 3, 1976**
1994-2000 WW FIN 20 8 10 18 14 4B
1998-2002 OG-W FIN 11 4 6 10 6 B
~WW IIHF Directorate Best Forward (1999), WW All-Star Team/Defence (1999)

**Hansen, Jeanette / b. Dec. 16, 1974**
1990-1994 WW NOR 15 0 1 1 9 —

**Hansen, Sussi / b. Mar. 13, 1967**
1992 WW DEN 5 0 1 1 0 —

**Hanson, Catherine / b. June 6, 1976**
1999 WW USA 5 0 2 2 0 S

**Hasegawa, Rika / b. Apr. 27, 1964**
1990 WW JPN 5 1 0 1 4 —

**Hatakeyama, Michiko / b. Dec. 4, 1960**
1990 WW JPN 5 0 1 1 0 —

**Hatanaka, Akiko / b. Apr. 23, 1975**
2000 WW JPN 5 1 1 2 4 —
1998 OG-W JPN 5 1 0 1 4 —

**Haugen, Hege / b. Jan. 16, 1975**
1992-1997 WW NOR 15 0 4 4 8 —

**Haugen, Unn / b. Dec. 17, 1978**
1994-1997 WW NOR 10 0 3 3 10 —

**Heaney, Geraldine / b. Oct. 1, 1967**
1990-2001 WW CAN 35 8 28 36 22 7G
1998-2002 OG-W CAN 11 2 6 8 2 G,S
~IIHF Hall of Fame
~WW IIHF Directorate Best Defenceman (1992, 1994), WW All-Star Team/Defence (1992)

**Hedlund, Maria / b. Feb. 26, 1968**
1992 WW SWE 5 0 0 0 0 —

**Heussen, Iris / b. Nov. 24, 1977**
1994 WW GER 5 0 0 0 2 —

**Hille, Camilla / b. Apr. 26, 1974**
1990-1997 WW NOR 20 1 3 4 12 —

**Hinrichs, Jette / b. June 13, 1961**
1992 WW DEN 4 2 1 3 0 —

**Hirvonen, Kirsi / b. June 29, 1969**
1990-1994 WW FIN 14 2 3 5 2 3B

**Hockauf, Silvia / b. Jan. 8, 1969**
1994 WW GER 5 0 0 0 2 —

**Hoikkala, Satu / b. Jan. 14, 1980**
2004-2007 WW FIN 15 4 5 9 10 B
2002-2006 OG-W FIN 10 0 2 2 6 —

**Holliday, Ilona / b. Jan. 19, 1966**
1994 WW GER 5 0 0 0 6 —

**Holmes, Annamarie / b. May 16, 1979**
2001 WW USA 5 1 2 3 2 S

**Holmes, Nikola / b. Feb. 18, 1981**
2007 WW GER 4 0 0 0 2 —
2006 OG-W GER 5 1 0 1 0 —

**Holzer, Iris / b. Mar. 4, 1976**
1990-1997 WW SUI 20 2 3 5 28 —

**Honda, Sairi / b. Dec. 8, 1967**
1990 WW JPN 5 0 0 0 4 —

**Honkanen, Minna / b. Mar. 29, 1965**
1990 WW FIN 5 1 2 3 0 B

**Hood, Sarah / b. Feb. 1, 1976**
1999 WW USA 5 0 0 0 0 S

**Hougaard, Susanne / b. Feb. 13, 1973**
1992 WW DEN 5 0 1 1 0 —

**Hove, Aina / b. Apr. 30, 1975**
1992-1997 WW NOR 15 0 0 0 6 —

**Hu, Chunrong / b. May 11, 1979**
1999-2001 WW CHN 10 0 1 1 0 —
2002 OG-W CHN 5 0 3 3 4 —

**Huang, Jingzi / b. Dec. 27, 1969**
1992 WW CHN 5 0 0 0 4 —

**Hunter, Andria / b. Dec. 22, 1967**
1992-1994 WW CAN 9 5 6 11 0 2G

**Huotari, Satu / b. Mar. 13, 1967**
1992-1999 WW FIN 15 2 6 8 6 3B
1998 OG-W FIN 6 0 1 1 4 B

**Hutchinson, Theresa / b. Oct. 21, 1966**
1990 WW CAN 5 0 3 3 18 G

**Ibe, Michiko / b. June 16, 1983**
2004 WW JPN 4 0 0 0 4 —

**Igarashi, Mitsuko / b. Aug. 21, 1977**
2000 WW JPN 5 0 0 0 2 —
1998 OG-W JPN 5 0 0 0 2 —

**Ihalainen, Marianne / b. Feb. 22, 1967**
1990-2000 WW FIN 25 15 11 26 6 5B
1998 OG-W FIN 5 0 0 0 0 B

**Ikonen, Johanna / b. Jan. 9, 1969**
1990-1997 WW FIN 20 9 7 16 10 4B
1998 OG-W FIN 6 4 1 5 6 B

**Insalaco, Kim / b. Nov. 4, 1980**
2004-2005 WW USA 10 0 2 2 10 G,S
2006 OG-W USA 5 0 0 0 4 B

**Ishii, Chihomi / b. Jan. 21, 1965**
1990 WW JPN 5 0 0 0 2 —

**Issel, Kathy / b. Oct. 5, 1973**
1992 WW USA 5 1 3 4 0 S

**Itoh, Yumiko / b. July 20, 1973**
1990 WW JPN 5 0 0 0 0 —

**Ivchenko, Yevgenia / b. July 10, 1987**
2007 WW KAZ 4 0 0 0 0 —

**Iwase, Akiko / b. Dec. 11, 1978**
2000 WW JPN 5 0 0 0 2 —

**James, Angela / b. Dec. 22, 1964**
1990-1997 WW CAN 20 22 12 34 16 4G
~IIHF Hall of Fame
~WW All-Star Team/Forward (1992)

**Jansson, Nanna / b. July 7, 1983**
2001-2007 WW SWE 20 4 1 5 22 2B
2002-2006 OG-W SWE 10 2 1 3 6 S,B

**Jarvi, Anette / b. Aug. 1, 1968**
1990 WW SWE 5 0 1 1 2 —
**Javanainen, Katri / b. Mar. 4, 1969**
1990 WW FIN 3 0 1 1 0 B
**Jeannottat, Gillian / b. Oct. 25, 1973**
1994-1999 WW SUI 14 0 0 0 14 —
**Jensen, Linda / b. July 3, 1967**
1992 WW DEN 5 0 0 0 2 —
**Jensen, Susanne / b. Aug. 27, 1966**
1992 WW DEN 3 0 0 0 0 —
**Johansen, Hilde / b. Dec. 23, 1964**
1990 WW NOR 5 1 3 4 2 —
**Johansen, Jeanette / b. Sept. 3, 1966**
1992 WW DEN 4 0 0 0 4 —
**Johansen, Nina / b. Mar. 26, 1965**
1990-1997 WW NOR 19 7 7 14 32 —
**Kanerva, Sanna / b. June 24, 1974**
1999 WW FIN 5 0 3 3 0 B
**Karikoski, Liisa / b. Aug. 11, 1956**
1990-1992 WW FIN 10 2 11 13 6 2B
**Kaser, Waltraud / b. July 3, 1980**
2006 OG-W ITA 5 0 1 1 8 —
**Kauth, Kathleen / b. Mar. 28, 1979**
2004-2005 WW USA 10 3 4 7 0 G,S
2006 OG-W USA 5 0 0 0 4 B
**Kazakova (-Nikolayva), Svetlana / b. Nov. 9, 1975**
1997-2004 WW RUS 14 0 2 2 4 —
**Kellar, Becky / b. Jan. 1, 1975**
1999-2009 WW CAN 40 6 12 18 18 4G,3S
1998-2010 OG-W CAN 15 0 6 6 14 3G
**Kempe, Camilla / b. Feb. 12, 1972**
1990-1997 WW SWE 20 14 2 16 8 —
**Kennedy, Courtney / b. Mar. 29, 1979**
2005 WW USA 5 1 0 1 4 G
2002-2006 OG-W USA 10 0 2 2 16 S,B
**Khlyzova, Tatyana / b. Mar. 10, 1981**
2001 WW KAZ 5 0 0 0 0 —
2002 OG-W KAZ 5 0 0 0 2 —
**Kienle, Gina / b. Jan. 28, 1974**
1997 WW SUI 5 0 0 0 0 —
**Kiipeli, Satu / b. Dec. 24, 1980**
2001-2005 WW FIN 10 1 0 1 2 —
2006 OG-W FIN 5 0 0 0 2 —
**Kilbourne, Andrea / b. Apr. 19, 1980**
2004 WW USA 5 2 2 4 4 S
2002 OG-W USA 5 1 1 2 2 S
**Kiljunen, Taina / b. Feb. 6, 1966**
1992 WW FIN 5 0 0 0 0 B
**King, Katie / b. May 24, 1975**
1997-2005 WW USA 30 19 17 36 18 G,5S
1998-2006 OG-W USA 16 14 9 23 8 G,S,B
**King, Kristin / b. July 21, 1979**
2004-2007 WW USA 15 3 4 7 8 G,2S
2006 OG-W USA 5 1 1 2 4 B
**Kingsbury, Gina / b. Nov. 26, 1981**
2001-09 WW CAN 29 9 8 17 10 3G,3S
2006-10 OG-W CAN 10 2 4 6 8 2G
**Kinza, Sandra / b. Aug. 1, 1969**
1990-2001 WW GER 20 2 5 7 18 —
2002 OG-W GER 5 0 0 0 2 —
**Kirschner, Bettina / b. Apr. 13, 1967**
1990 WW FRG 5 0 0 0 0 —
**Koizumi, Jessica / b. Apr. 15, 1985**
2008 WW USA 5 0 0 0 0 G
**Korn, Karin / b. Sept. 29, 1963**
1990 WW FRG 5 1 0 1 2 —
**Kovalainen, Kati / b. Jan. 24, 1975**
1997-2009 WW FIN 44 8 6 14 12 6B
2006 OG-W FIN 5 1 0 1 6 —
**Krooks, Sari / b. Feb. 2, 1968**
1990-1999 WW FIN 24 16 12 28 30 5B
1998 OG-W FIN 6 2 2 4 12 B
**Kruck, Sabrina / b. Nov. 3, 1981**
1999-2008 WW GER 27 1 4 5 20 —
2002-10 OG-W GER 10 0 0 0 8 —
**Kryukova, Olga / b. Nov. 27, 1974**
2001-09 WW KAZ 18 0 2 2 54 —
2002 OG-W KAZ 5 0 0 0 14 —
**Kubo, Hanae / b. Dec. 10, 1982**
2000-2004 WW JPN 9 4 2 6 8 —
**Kuisle, Sonja / b. Jan. 27, 1978**
1994-2001 WW GER 20 1 0 1 16 —

**Kunzle, Ruth / b. Mar. 29, 1972**
1992-2007 WW SUI 28 3 6 9 28 —
2006 OG-W SUI 5 0 1 1 6 —
**Kuoppala, Hanna / b. Sept. 12, 1975**
2001-2004 WW FIN 10 0 0 0 22 B
2006 OG-W FIN 5 0 0 0 4 —
**Kurihashi, Yuko / b. Feb. 20, 1966**
1990 WW JPN 5 0 2 2 0 —
**~Kurten, Sabina** ~see Ruckauer (-Kurten), Sabine
**Kurten, Sandra / b. Aug. 25, 1980**
1999 WW GER 5 0 0 0 0 —
**Laederach, Carole / b. Sept. 10, 1973**
1994 WW SUI 5 0 0 0 0 —
**Laerum, Vibeke / b. Nov. 18, 1974**
1992-1994 WW NOR 10 0 0 0 2 —
**Lallukka (-Kotikumpu), Piia / b. June 11, 1985**
2008-09 WW FIN 10 0 0 0 0 2B
**Lankosaari, Sanna / b. Aug. 20, 1978**
1997-2000 WW FIN 15 3 7 10 10 3B
1998 OG-W FIN 5 2 1 3 6 B
**Lanzl, Michaela / b. Feb. 21, 1983**
1999-2007 WW GER 22 8 4 12 18 —
2002-06 OG-W GER 10 4 4 8 8 —
**Larsen, Tonje / b. Apr. 26, 1974**
1990-1997 WW NOR 20 2 1 3 14 —
**Larssen, Marit / b. May 26, 1965**
1990-1994 WW NOR 15 0 4 4 2 —
**Larsson, Maria / b. Feb. 18, 1979**
1999-2004 WW SWE 15 0 1 1 2 —
2002 OG-W SWE 5 0 0 0 0 B
**Lavonius, Katja / b. Apr. 6, 1965**
1990-1994 WW FIN 10 5 0 5 2 2B
**Le, Mai-Lan / b. July 31, 1971**
1999 WW CAN 5 0 2 2 0 G
**Lehtimaki, Marika / b. Feb. 7, 1975**
1990-1994 WW FIN 15 5 10 15 2 3B
1998 OG-W FIN 5 2 3 5 0 B
**Lehtinen, Eini / b. Mar. 14, 1979**
2007-08 WW FIN 10 0 0 0 6 B
**Lehto, Katja / b. Aug. 14, 1972**
1997-2000 WW FIN 14 1 11 12 2 3B
1998 OG-W FIN 6 1 3 4 0 B
**Leitner, Maria Michaela / b. Dec. 30, 1981**
2006 OG-W ITA 5 2 1 3 0 —
**Lersbryggen, Birgitte / b. Feb. 21, 1975**
1992-1997 WW NOR 15 11 3 14 8 —
**Leslie, Laura / b. May 17, 1969**
1994 WW CAN 5 1 2 3 0 G
**Letendre, Luce / b. Apr. 19, 1971**
1997 WW CAN 5 1 0 1 4 G
**Leuenberger, Monika / b. Apr. 11, 1973**
1990-2009 WW SUI 37 2 0 2 54 —
2006 OG-W SUI 5 0 0 0 14 —
**Li, Xiuli / b. Aug. 14, 1984**
2004-2005 WW CHN 9 0 0 0 6 —
**Li, Xuan / b. Feb. 29, 1972**
1992-2004 WW CHN 34 2 9 11 52 —
1998-2002 OG-W CHN 11 0 1 1 8 —
**Li, Xuefei / b. May 23, 1983**
2004-2005 WW CHN 9 0 0 0 4 —
**Li, Yanan / b. July 15, 1978**
1999 WW CHN 5 0 0 0 0 —
**Liang, Yan / b. Mar. 23, 1970**
1992 WW CHN 5 0 0 0 12 —
**Lidstrom, Asa / b. Aug. 15, 1968**
1992-1997 WW SWE 15 1 6 7 10 —
1998 OG-W SWE 5 0 0 0 2 —
**Lindberg, Ylva / b. June 29, 1976**
1994-2005 WW SWE 30 3 5 8 20 B
1998-2006 OG-W SWE 13 1 3 4 8 S,B
**Linde, Nina / b. June 10, 1980**
1999-2005 WW GER 20 0 0 0 14 —
2002 OG-W GER 5 0 1 1 0 —
**Lindqvist, Jenny / b. July 21, 1978**
1999-2004 WW SWE 20 0 0 0 2 —
2006 OG-W SWE 5 0 0 0 2 S
**Lindstrom, Ulrica / b. Mar. 30, 1979**
1999-2001 WW SWE 15 0 3 3 8 —
2002 OG-W SWE 5 0 0 0 4 B
**Lipsonen, Vilja / b. Oct. 15, 1978**
2000-2005 WW FIN 20 1 4 5 24 B
**Lisewski, Birgit / b. Dec. 19, 1965**
1990 WW FRG 5 2 2 4 0 —

**Liu, Chunhua / b. May 6, 1974**
1998 OG-W CHN 5 0 0 0 4 —
**Liu, Hongjiao / b. July 18, 1975**
1994 WW CHN 5 0 0 0 0 —
**Liu, Hongmei / b. Dec. 27, 1973**
1992-2001 WW CHN 30 23 13 36 16 —
1998-2002 OG-W CHN 11 5 4 9 8 —
**Liu, Yanhui / b. June 20, 1982**
2000-2005 WW CHN 19 0 0 0 0 —
2002 OG-W CHN 5 0 0 0 6 —
**Looney, Shelley / b. Jan. 21, 1972**
1992-2005 WW USA 35 17 19 36 6 G,7S
1998-2002 OG-W USA 11 5 3 8 4 G,S
**Losyeva, Nadezhda / b. Dec. 24, 1974**
2001 WW KAZ 5 1 1 2 0 —
2002 OG-W KAZ 5 1 0 1 2 —
**Lu, Yan / b. July 25, 1972**
1992-2004 WW CHN 34 3 10 13 40 —
1998-2002 OG-W CHN 11 0 1 1 10 —
**Lundberg, Kristina / b. June 10, 1985**
2004-2005 WW SWE 10 1 1 2 8 B
2006 OG-W SWE 5 0 0 0 4 S
**~Lundmark, Emilie** ~see O'Konor (-Lundmark), Emilie
**~Luoma, Tricia** ~see Dunn (-Luoma), Tricia
**Luomajoki, Katri-Helena / b. Apr. 10, 1965**
1990-2000 WW FIN 30 2 7 9 16 6B
**Luongo, Nicki / b. Feb. 9, 1976**
2000-2001 WW USA 10 0 2 2 2 2S
**Lyskova, Oxana / b. Jan. 28, 1980**
2004-2005 WW RUS 9 0 0 0 0 —
**Ma, Jinping / b. Jan. 1, 1972**
1992-2005 WW CHN 24 2 0 2 12 —
1998 OG-W CHN 6 0 0 0 6 —
**Ma, Xiaojuan / b. Feb. 9, 1967**
1992 WW CHN 5 0 0 0 0 —
**Ma, Xiaojun / b. July 12, 1978**
1997-2005 WW CHN 29 2 4 6 20 —
1998-2002 OG-W CHN 6 1 0 1 2 —
**Maag, Daniela / b. July 11, 1973**
1990-1992 WW SUI 10 0 2 2 20 —
**Mabuchi, Hiroko / b. Jan. 15, 1962**
1990 WW JPN 5 0 0 0 2 —
**MacLeod, Carla / b. June 16, 1982**
2005-09 WW CAN 20 4 12 16 8 G,3S
2006-10 OG-W CAN 10 4 5 9 4 2G
~WW IIHF Directorate Best Forward (2009), OG-W All-Star Team/Defence (2006), WW All-Star Team/Defence (2009)
**Madsen, Jannie / b. Aug. 23, 1974**
1992 WW DEN 5 2 0 2 18 —
**Majaranta, Leena / b. Nov. 14, 1958**
1990 WW FIN 5 3 2 5 0 B
**Maltseva, Svetlana / b. Oct. 29, 1970**
2005 WW KAZ 5 1 1 2 0 —
2002 OG-W KAZ 5 0 0 0 0 —
**Maltseva, Yekaterina / b. Mar. 31, 1985**
2002 OG-W KAZ 5 0 0 0 0 —
**Mansson, Tina / b. Apr. 22, 1968**
1990-1999 WW SWE 24 6 4 10 14 —
1998 OG-W SWE 5 1 0 1 2 —
**Marano, Christina / b. Jan. 6, 1976**
1997-1999 WW SUI 9 0 0 0 2 —
**Marty, Jeanette / b. Aug. 11, 1975**
1992-2004 WW SUI 19 1 2 3 20 —
2006 OG-W SUI 5 0 0 0 6 —
**Masuda, Yasuko / b. Nov. 24, 1963**
1990 WW JPN 5 0 0 0 10 —
**Matilainen, Rose / b. Aug. 11, 1966**
1994 WW FIN 4 1 0 1 0 B
**Maurer, Karin / b. Apr. 17, 1966**
1992 WW SUI 5 0 0 0 0 —
**McCormack, Kathy / b. Feb. 16, 1974**
1998 OG-W CAN 6 0 0 0 0 S
**McGuire, Dawn / b. Mar. 26, 1960**
1990-1992 WW CAN 10 2 6 8 6 2G
**Meisingset, Anne / b. Jan. 15, 1972**
1992-1994 WW NOR 10 0 0 0 2 —
**Merkel, Anja / b. May 29, 1970**
1999 WW GER 5 0 0 0 4 —
**Merz, Sue / b. Apr. 10, 1972**
1990-2001 WW USA 28 8 14 22 27 6S
1998-2002 OG-W USA 10 2 5 7 2 G,S
~WW All-Star Team/Defence (1999)

**Michaud, Diane / b. Mar. 1, 1962**
1990-1992 WW CAN 10 2 7 9 6 2G

**Micheli, Anita / b. Dec. 17, 1970**
1992 WW SUI 5 0 0 0 0 —

**~Miller, Lisa** ~see Brown (-Miller), Lisa

**Mishina, Larisa / b. Sept. 10, 1975**
1997-2004 WW RUS 24 3 2 5 8 B
2002-2006 OG-W RUS 10 5 1 6 2 —

**~Misropian, Maria** ~see Barykina (-Misropian), Maria

**Miura, Kayoko / b. Oct. 1, 1962**
1990 WW JPN 5 0 0 0 0 —

**Mleczko (-Griswold), Allison "A.J." / b. June 14, 1975**
1997-2001 WW USA 15 2 11 13 10 3S
1998-2002 OG-W USA 11 3 5 8 10 G,S

**Moe, Gine Marie / b. Dec. 18, 1967**
1990 WW NOR 5 5 1 6 0 —

**Moesgaard, Katja / b. July 14, 1967**
1992 WW DEN 5 0 1 1 0 —

**Molitor, Ines / b. Jan. 19, 1973**
1990-1994 WW GER 10 0 2 2 4 —

**Monteiro, Yasmina / b. May 19, 1987**
2007 WW SUI 4 0 0 0 4 —

**Montour, France / b. Dec. 17, 1965**
1990-1992 WW CAN 10 10 5 15 16 2G

**Morelius, Pia / b. Mar. 31, 1966**
1990-1997 WW SWE 18 0 6 6 20 —
1998 OG-W SWE 4 0 0 0 14 —

**Mosimann, Prisca / b. Mar. 19, 1975**
1994-1999 WW SUI 15 0 1 1 10 —
2006 OG-W SUI 5 0 2 2 4 —

**Mounsey, Tara / b. Mar. 12, 1978**
1997-1999 WW USA 10 2 5 7 12 2S
1998-2002 OG-W USA 11 2 11 13 16 G,S
~OG-W All-Star Team/Defence (2002)

**Movsessian, Vicki / b. Nov. 6, 1972**
1994-1997 WW USA 10 0 4 5 6 2S
1998 OG-W USA 6 1 0 1 10 G

**Muller, Regula / b. Dec. 29, 1975**
1994-1999 WW SUI 15 0 0 0 33 —

**Myhrvold, Trude / b. Mar. 7, 1976**
1997 WW NOR 5 0 0 0 0 —

**Naka, Akiko / b. June 5, 1980**
2000 WW JPN 5 0 0 0 4 —
1998 OG-W JPN 5 0 0 0 0 —

**Nazyrova, Vera / b. Dec. 23, 1986**
2005-07 WW KAZ 9 0 0 0 12 —

**Nedergaard, Anne Mette / b. July 4, 1962**
1992 WW DEN 5 0 1 1 4 —

**Niederhauser, Edith / b. Dec. 7, 1968**
1990-1997 WW SUI 20 4 8 12 6 —

**Niemela, Katri / b. Jan. 4, 1972**
1992 WW FIN 2 0 0 0 0 B

**Nieminen (-Valila), Riikka / b. June 12, 1973**
1990-1997 WW FIN 20 23 18 41 8 4B
1998-2002 OG-W FIN 11 7 8 15 6 B
~IIHF Hall of Fame
~WW IIHF Directorate Best Forward (1994), WW All-Star Team/Forward (1992, 1994, 1997)

**~Nikolayva, Svetlana** ~see Kazakova (-Nikolayva), Svetlana

**Nilsson, Lena / b. Jan. 23, 1969**
1994 WW SWE 5 1 1 2 2 —

**Nishida, Tamami / b. Aug. 23, 1959**
1990 WW JPN 4 0 0 0 6 —

**Nordgren, Marie / b. Aug. 25, 1975**
1994 WW SWE 5 0 0 0 0 —

**Noshita, Chiemi / b. Oct. 11, 1984**
2004 WW JPN 4 0 0 0 0 —

**Nothiger, Mireille / b. May 3, 1973**
1990-1999 WW SUI 25 2 2 4 16 —

**Nurmi, Anne / b. Oct. 14, 1958**
1992 WW FIN 4 2 3 5 2 B

**Nyberg, Helena / b. Feb. 16, 1967**
1990 WW SWE 4 0 0 0 2 —

**Nystrom, Karen / b. June 17, 1969**
1992-1997 WW CAN 14 5 5 10 14 3G
1998 OG-W CAN 5 1 0 1 2 S

**Obermaier, Karin / b. June 4, 1965**
1990 WW FRG 5 0 1 1 2 —

**Obikawa, Maiko / b. Mar. 13, 1973**
1998 OG-W JPN 5 0 1 1 4 —

**Ochsner, Cornelia / b. Sept. 28, 1968**
1990 WW SUI 5 0 3 3 6 —

**Ohno, Yukari / b. Aug. 10, 1975**
1998 OG-W JPN 5 0 0 0 8 —

**Okada, Ayako / b. July 25, 1967**
1990 WW JPN 5 1 3 4 2 —

**O'Konor (-Lundmark), Emilie / b. Feb. 21, 1983**
1999-2005 WW SWE 10 2 1 3 4 B
2006 OG-W SWE 5 0 2 2 2 S

**O'Leary, Kelly / b. Jan. 19, 1968**
1990-1997 WW USA 20 11 9 20 34 4S
~WW All-Star Team/Defence (1994, 1997)

**Olofsson, Elisabet / b. Jan. 16, 1983**
2000 WW SWE 5 0 1 1 0 —

**Ono, Satomi / b. Nov. 18, 1975**
1998 OG-W JPN 5 0 0 0 8 —

**Oppegard, Tone / b. Mar. 3, 1962**
1990 WW NOR 5 0 0 0 0 —

**Osanai, Yuko / b. July 25, 1979**
2000 WW JPN 5 0 0 0 2 —

**Ossipova, Yelena / b. Nov. 14, 1966**
1997 WW RUS 5 0 0 0 2 —

**Ostrowski, Cornelia / b. July 16, 1963**
1990 WW FRG 5 0 0 0 4 —

**O'Sullivan, Stephanie / b. July 30, 1971**
1994-2000 WW USA 20 12 20 32 6 4S

**Oswald (-Fellner), Christina / b. July 26, 1973**
1990-2007 WW GER 38 14 1 15 52 —
2002-2006 OG-W GER 10 2 2 4 14 —

**Oversveen, Ingvild / b. Apr. 27, 1979**
1997 WW NOR 5 0 0 0 2 —

**Owen, Kelley / b. May 19, 1962**
1990 WW USA 5 1 1 2 4 S

**Paananen, Tiina / b.July 5, 1972**
1997-1999 WW FIN 10 2 1 3 0 2B

**Page (-Verlaan), Margot / b. June 27, 1964**
1990-1994 WW CAN 15 6 13 19 4 3G

**Pajunen, Leena / b. Dec. 3, 1967**
1990-1992 WW FIN 10 1 2 3 10 2B

**Palsmar, Christina / b. Feb. 10, 1974**
1992 WW DEN 5 0 0 0 12 —

**Palvila, Marja-Helena / b. Mar. 4, 1970**
1997-2001 WW FIN 15 5 5 10 6 2B
1998-2006 OG-W FIN 16 1 0 1 4 B

**Parish, Judy / b. Feb. 24, 1969**
1990 WW USA 5 0 4 4 6 S

**Parviainen, Oona / b. Sept. 5, 1977**
2005 WW FIN 5 0 0 0 2 —
2002-2006 OG-W FIN 10 1 0 1 2 —

**Pashkevich, Yekaterina / b. Dec. 19, 1972**
1997-2001 WW RUS 20 19 4 23 46 B
2002-2006 OG-W RUS 10 3 3 6 10 —

**Patzold, Claudia / b. Dec. 11, 1964**
1990 WW FRG 5 0 0 0 6 —

**Pedersen, Louise / b. Feb. 18, 1973**
1992 WW DEN 4 0 0 0 0 —

**Percy, Yvonne / b. May 23, 1964**
1990 WW USA 5 0 1 1 2 S

**Perova, Yulia / b. Aug. 3, 1970**
1997 WW RUS 4 0 0 0 0 —

**Persson, Annika / b. June 11, 1964**
1990 WW SWE 4 4 0 4 2 —

**Persson, Malin / b. Aug. 26, 1969**
1990-1997 WW SWE 10 2 0 2 8 —

**Petersen, Anne Therese / b. Aug. 29, 1966**
1990 WW NOR 5 0 0 0 6 —

**Pettersson, Josefin / b. Jan. 13, 1984**
2001 WW SWE 5 1 1 2 4 —
2002 OG-W SWE 5 0 1 1 2 B

**Peura, Sanna / b. Jan. 13, 1981**
2000-2001 WW FIN 10 2 1 3 0 —

**Pfau, Antje / b. June 30, 1967**
1994 WW GER 5 0 0 0 0 —

**Picard, Nathalie / b. Sept. 12, 1964**
1992-1994 WW CAN 10 1 5 6 4 2G

**Pihala, Tiina / b. Mar. 13, 1967**
1990 WW FIN 5 3 2 5 10 B

**Plahn, Lisa / b. Nov. 14, 1964**
1990-1994 WW SWE 15 8 4 12 2 —

**~Pohl, Krissy**
~see Wendell (-Pohl), Krissy

**Pounder, Cheryl / b. June 21, 1976**
1994-2007 WW CAN 35 3 13 16 14 6G,S
2002-2006 OG-W CAN 10 2 2 4 6 2G
~WW All-Star Team/Defence (2005)

**Prokopyeva, Maria / b. Dec. 4, 1981**
2001-2005 WW KAZ 10 0 1 1 2 —

**Putz, Stefanie / b. Oct. 9, 1969**
1990-1994 WW GER 10 2 4 6 14 —

**Puzikova, Natalya / b. Jan. 6, 1981**
2007-08 WW RUS 8 0 0 0 12 —

**Ratushny, Kim / b. June 24, 1969**
1990 WW CAN 5 1 4 5 0 G

**Rautavuoma, Jaana / b. Mar. 28, 1961**
1990 WW FIN 5 0 1 1 8 B

**Ray, Sandrine / b. May 11, 1983**
1999-2004 WW SUI 9 1 0 1 2 —
2006 OG-W SUI 5 0 0 0 2 —

**Reima, Susan / b. June 7, 1966**
1992-1994 WW FIN 10 1 4 5 0 2B

**Reima, Tiia / b. Feb. 1, 1973**
1990-2005 WW FIN 30 14 20 34 36 5B
1998-2002 OG-W FIN 9 4 2 6 2 B

**Reindl, Franziska / b. Sept. 16, 1982**
2002 OG-W GER 5 0 0 0 2 —

**Richard, Brenda / b. May 10,1968 / d. 1995**
1990 WW CAN 5 1 5 6 6 G

**Richaud, Anna / b. Apr. 11, 1973**
2001 WW SWE 5 0 0 0 0 —

**Riipi, Katja / b. Oct. 26, 1975**
1997-2007 WW FIN 35 14 7 21 18 4B
1998-2002 OG-W FIN 11 4 5 9 10 B
~WW IIHF Directorate Best Forward (2000)

**Ritter, Nina / b. Jan. 26, 1981**
2000-08 WW GER 23 1 1 2 30 —
2002-06 OG-W GER 10 2 2 4 2 —

**Rivard, Nathalie / b. Jan. 21, 1972**
1992-2000 WW CAN 15 1 3 4 27 3G

**Robinson, Jane / b. July 29, 1963**
1994 WW CAN 5 4 4 8 0 G

**Rochat, Rachel / b. Sept. 10, 1972**
1999-2007 WW SUI 8 4 0 4 0 —
2006 OG-W SUI 5 1 2 3 0 —

**~Rodikova, Yelena** ~see Bobrova (-Rodikova), Yelena

**Rooth, Maria / b. Nov. 2, 1979**
1997-2009 WW SWE 44 21 14 35 42 2B
1998-2010 OG-W SWE 20 9 9 18 12 S,B
~OG-W All-Star Team/Forward (2006), WW All-Star Team/Forward (2005)

**Ruckauer (-Kurten), Sabine / b. Apr. 13, 1977**
1994-1999 WW GER 10 0 1 1 6 —
2002 OG-W GER 5 0 2 2 2 —

**Rudberg, Josefin / b. Apr. 14, 1981**
1999-2004 WW SWE 20 2 0 2 14 —

**Ruggiero, Angela / b. Jan. 3, 1980**
1997-2011 WW USA 50 13 30 43 56 4G,6S
1998-2010 OG-W USA 21 6 9 15 38 G,2S,B
~OG-W IIHF Directorate Best Defenceman (2002, 2006), OG-W All-Star Team/Defence (2002, 2006, 2010), WW IIHF Directorate Best Defenceman (2000, 2004, 2005, 2008), WW All-Star Team/Defence (2004, 2005, 2007, 2009)

**Rumswinkel, Sandra / b. Aug. 13, 1977**
1999-2004 WW GER 14 0 2 2 0 —

**Saager, Elvira / b. Mar. 29, 1963**
1990 WW FRG 5 2 0 2 0 —

**Sado, Sayaka / b. Dec. 1, 1982**
2000 WW JPN 5 0 0 0 0 —

**Sainio, Sanna / b. Oct. 2, 1972**
2001 WW FIN 5 0 1 1 0 —

**Sakuma, Chie / b. Mar. 1, 1972**
1998 OG-W JPN 5 0 0 0 6 —

**Salo, Paivi / b. Jan. 31, 1974**
1997-2001 WW FIN 10 2 1 3 10 B
1998-2002 OG-W FIN 11 0 0 0 16 B

**Samuelsson, Evelina / b. Mar. 14, 1984**
2000-2005 WW SWE 14 2 3 5 4 B
2002 OG-W SWE 5 2 0 2 0 B

**Sang, Hong / b. Apr. 29, 1974**
2007-08 WW CHN 8 4 0 4 10 —

**Sang, Hong / b. Feb. 9, 1975**
1994-2001 WW CHN 25 9 2 11 12 —
1998-2002 OG-W CHN 11 1 0 1 8 —

**Sasner, Julie / b. Jan. 3, 1966**
1990 WW USA 4 0 1 1 0 S

**Sato, Ayumi / b. July 16, 1977**
2000 WW JPN 5 0 0 0 0 —
1998 OG-W JPN 5 0 0 0 0 —

**Sato, Masako / b. June 9, 1973**
1990-2004 WW JPN 14 5 1 6 12 —
1998 OG-W JPN 5 1 0 1 6 —

**Sato, Rie / b. Jan. 31, 1972**
1990-2000 WW JPN 10 4 0 4 4 —
1998 OG-W JPN 5 0 0 0 2 —

**Satomi, Yuiko / b. Oct. 22, 1975**
1998 OG-W JPN 5 0 0 0 0 —

**~Savenkova, Olga** ~see Volkova (-Savenkova), Olga

**Schaeffer, Dorthe / b. Aug. 12, 1974**
1992 WW DEN 5 0 1 1 2 —

**Schaffrik, Natascha / b. May 6, 1975**
1990-2001 WW GER 25 3 4 7 10 —

**Scherer, Sue / b. Aug. 29, 1956**
1990-1992 WW CAN 10 2 7 9 2 2G

**Scheytt, Anja / b. Dec. 5, 1980**
1999-2008 WW GER 32 3 3 6 20 —
2002-06 OG-W GER 10 0 1 1 8 —

**Schmitten, Nicole / b. Dec. 21, 1977**
1994 WW GER 5 0 1 1 0 —

**Schnabel, Simone / b. Nov. 28, 1973**
1994 WW GER 5 0 0 0 2 —

**Schneegans, Silvia / b. July 21, 1967**
1990-1994 WW GER 10 0 2 2 10 —

**Schneiter, Helga / b. Aug. 30, 1980**
2007 WW SUI 4 0 0 0 2 —

**Schou-Nielsen, Charlotte / b. June 6, 1963**
1992 WW DEN 5 0 0 0 6 —

**Schreckenbach, Jana / b. July 8, 1982**
2001-2004 WW GER 9 0 0 0 2 —
2002 OG-W GER 5 0 0 0 8 —

**Schuler, Laura / b. Dec. 3, 1970**
1990-1997 WW CAN 15 7 6 13 20 3G
1998 OG-W CAN 6 0 0 0 4 S

**Schumacher, Nicole / b. Jan. 1, 1971**
1990 WW SUI 5 0 0 0 4 —

**Schumacher, Tina / b. Mar. 20, 1978**
2004 WW SUI 4 0 0 0 0 —
2006 OG-W SUI 5 1 0 1 4 —

**Schweizer, Andrea / b. Dec. 20, 1961**
1990 WW SUI 5 2 0 2 4 —

**Selin, Maria / b. Sept. 8, 1977**
1999-2000 WW FIN 10 0 1 1 4 2B
1998 OG-W FIN 5 0 1 1 2 B

**Seppala, Suvi / b. June 10, 1979**
2001 WW FIN 5 0 0 0 2 —

**Shelchkova, Zhanna / b. Feb. 10, 1969**
1997-2005 WW RUS 29 3 7 10 10 B
2002-2006 OG-W RUS 10 0 5 5 4 —

**Shen, Tiantian / b. June 12, 1982**
2004 WW CHN 4 0 0 0 2 —
2002 OG-W CHN 5 0 0 0 0 —

**Shewchuk, Tammy / b. Dec. 31, 1977**
2000-2001 WW CAN 10 7 4 11 2 2G
2002 OG-W CAN 5 1 1 2 0 G

**Shibata, Misayo / b. Mar. 16, 1967**
1990 WW JPN 5 0 0 0 2 —

**Sikio, Hanne / b. Mar. 19, 1978**
1999-2001 WW FIN 15 6 3 9 8 2B
2002 OG-W FIN 5 2 0 2 2 —

**Silyeva, Yulia / b. Apr. 14, 1984**
2004-2005 WW RUS 9 0 0 0 6 —

**Simanova, Violetta / b. June 24, 1973**
1997-2001 WW RUS 20 1 5 6 2 B

**Simila, Eveliina / b. Apr. 10, 1978**
2004-2005 WW FIN 10 0 2 2 2 B
2006 OG-W FIN 5 0 0 0 0 —

**Sjolander, Therese / b. May 4, 1981**
1999-2005 WW SWE 23 5 3 8 10 B
1998-2006 OG-W SWE 15 4 3 7 12 S,B

**Smerud, Christin / b. Oct. 3, 1967**
1990-1997 WW NOR 15 3 2 5 16 —

**Smith, Fiona / b. Oct. 31, 1973**
1997-1999 WW CAN 7 0 3 3 6 2G
1998 OG-W CAN 5 1 1 2 2 S

**Sobek, Jeanine / b. Feb. 22, 1972**
1990-1994 WW USA 14 6 10 16 6 3S

**Soderstrom, Kristina / b. May 13, 1975**
1990-1997 WW NOR 14 0 0 0 4 —

**Soesilo, Denise / b. May 10, 1987**
2004-07 WW GER 10 0 1 1 4 —
2006 OG-W GER 5 0 1 1 0 —

**Soikkanen, Katariina / b. Apr. 7, 1987**
2007 WW FIN 5 0 0 0 2 —

**Sokolova, Oxana / b. Jan. 4, 1967**
2001 WW KAZ 5 0 0 0 0 —

**Solovyeva, Yulia / b. Jan. 4, 1967**
2002 OG-W KAZ 5 0 0 0 4 —

**Sostorics, Colleen / b. Dec. 17, 1979**
2001-09 WW CAN 30 4 8 12 22 3G,3S
2002-10 OG-W CAN 15 1 8 9 12 3G

**Sparer, Katharina / b. Feb. 22, 1990**
2006 OG-W ITA 5 0 0 0 4 —

**Spring, Monika / b. Sept. 16, 1969**
1990-1994 WW GER 7 2 2 4 6 —

**Stebler, Regula / b. Mar. 24, 1969**
1990-1992 WW SUI 10 2 3 5 14 —

**Steinmann, Anita / b. Apr. 8, 1980**
2004 WW SUI 4 0 0 0 0 —

**Stephens, Kelly / b. June 4, 1983**
2004-2005 WW USA 10 4 6 10 24 G,S
2006 OG-W USA 5 2 2 4 12 B

**Stidsen, Sharon / b. Jan. 30, 1964**
1990 WW USA 5 0 3 3 6 S

**St. Louis, France / b. Oct. 17, 1958**
1990-1999 WW CAN 25 14 14 28 14 5G
1998 OG-W CAN 6 1 2 3 0 S

**Stromsborg, Eva / b. Mar. 14, 1964**
1990-1992 WW NOR 10 0 0 0 10 —

**Su, Ziwei / b. Dec. 9, 1984**
2005-09 WW CHN 17 1 2 3 2 —

**Sudo, Aki / b. Jan. 20, 1975**
2000 WW JPN 5 0 0 0 2 —
1998 OG-W JPN 5 0 0 0 20 —

**Sun, Lu / b. May 28, 1983**
2000 WW CHN 5 0 0 0 0 —

**Sunohara, Vicky / b. May 18, 1970**
1990-2007 WW CAN 40 19 22 41 20 7G,S
1998-2006 OG-W CAN 16 6 7 13 8 2G,S

**Suzuki, Yoko / b. May 5, 1962**
1990 WW JPN 5 0 0 0 6 —

**Svendsen, Maibrit / b. Jan. 7, 1974**
1992 WW DEN 4 2 0 2 2 —

**Svensson, Chanette / b. June 8, 1987**
2007 WW SWE 5 0 0 0 2 B

**Tageson, Helena / b. Apr. 8, 1983**
2007 WW SWE 5 0 0 0 2 B

**Taikevich, Oxana / b. July 26, 1974**
2001 WW KAZ 5 0 1 1 14 —
2002 OG-W KAZ 5 0 0 0 16 —

**Tallus, Nora / b. Feb. 9, 1981**
2004-08 WW FIN 20 2 5 7 22 2B
2006 OG-W FIN 5 0 1 1 4 —

**Tanaka, Chieko / b. Apr. 25, 1959**
1990 WW JPN 5 1 2 3 2 —

**Tanner, Cornelia / b. July 5, 1970**
1990 WW SUI 5 0 0 0 2 —

**Tarvainen, Vilma / b. May 2, 1986**
2008 WW FIN 5 0 0 0 0 B

**Tatarouns, Wendy / b. Nov. 20, 1972**
1992 WW USA 3 0 0 0 0 S

**Teerijoki, Hanna / b. July 15, 1963**
1992-1994 WW FIN 9 8 9 17 2 2B

**Timofeyeva, Yelena / b. Nov. 14, 1982**
2008 WW RUS 4 0 0 0 8 —

**Toffano, Silvia / b. Jan. 5, 1985**
2006 OG-W ITA 5 0 0 0 2 —

**Tornstrom, Caroline / b. June 4, 1980**
1999 WW SWE 5 0 0 0 2 —

**Trefilova, Svetlana / b. May 20, 1973**
1997-2007 WW RUS 33 9 7 16 38 B
2002-2006 OG-W RUS 10 5 2 7 8 —

**Tretiakova, Oxana / b. Mar. 10, 1979**
1997-2007 WW RUS 30 5 6 11 8 B
2002-2006 OG-W RUS 10 0 0 0 6 —

**Tsareva, Tatyana / b. Dec. 30, 1977**
1997-2001 WW RUS 19 4 6 10 18 —
2002 OG-W RUS 5 3 0 3 18 —

**Tsukamoto, Yumiko / b. June 28, 1963**
1990 WW JPN 5 0 0 0 0 —

**Ulion, Gretchen / b. May 4, 1972**
1994-1997 WW USA 10 7 8 15 0 2S
1998 OG-W USA 6 3 5 8 4 G

**Urech, Kim / b. Oct. 5, 1960**
1990 WW SUI 5 8 6 14 2 —

**Vaarakallio, Petra / b. June 17, 1975**
1994-2000 WW FIN 20 9 17 26 6 4B
1998-2002 OG-W FIN 11 2 2 4 18 B

**Vafina, Lyubov / b. Nov. 25, 1967**
2001 WW KAZ 5 0 0 0 2 —
2002 OG-W KAZ 5 0 0 0 2 —

**Valenti, Maren / b. Oct. 25, 1976**
1990-2001 WW GER 25 6 9 15 20 —
2002 OG-W GER 5 0 1 1 2 —

**Vasichek, Julianne / b. Feb. 9, 1983**
2004 WW USA 5 0 0 0 10 S

**Vassina, Svetlana / b. Nov. 19, 1971**
2001-07 WW KAZ 14 0 0 0 6 —
2002 OG-W KAZ 5 0 1 1 6 —

**~Verlaan, Margot** ~see Page (-Verlaan), Margot

**Viel, Sabrina / b. Feb. 17, 1973**
2006 OG-W ITA 5 0 0 0 0 —

**Vikman, Anna / b. Jan. 13, 1981**
1999-2005 WW SWE 20 3 3 6 18 B
2002-2006 OG-W SWE 9 1 0 1 0 S,B

**Volkova (-Savenkova), Olga / b. July 2, 1982**
1999-2005 WW RUS 24 1 0 1 22 B
2002 OG-W RUS 5 0 0 0 12 —

**Volobuyeva, Viktoria / b. Sept. 24, 1980**
1999-2004 WW RUS 14 0 0 0 0 —

**Voronina, Yulia / b. Jan. 4, 1967**
1997 WW RUS 5 0 1 1 4 —

**Walder, Nicole / b. Nov. 21, 1975**
1990-1999 WW SUI 14 1 3 4 10 —

**Wall, Lyndsay / b. May 12, 1985**
2005 WW USA 5 1 1 2 0 G
2002-2006 OG-W USA 10 0 3 3 10 S,B

**Walther, Ursula / b. May 26, 1968**
1992-1994 WW SUI 10 2 0 2 20 —

**Wang, Wei / b. Feb. 15, 1977**
1994-2001 WW CHN 25 2 8 10 30 —
1998 OG-W CHN 6 0 2 2 2 —

**Wang, Ying / b. Oct. 8, 1981**
2000-2005 WW CHN 19 0 0 0 0 —
2002 OG-W CHN 5 0 0 0 2 —

**Waters, Vibeke / b. July 4, 1968**
1992-1994 WW NOR 10 0 0 0 14 —

**Weber, Petra / b. Dec. 17, 1966**
1994 WW GER 5 0 0 0 4 —

**Weinberg, Ellen / b. July 8, 1968**
1992 WW USA 5 0 3 3 2 S
~WW All-Star Team/Defence (1992)

**Weissbach, Andrea / b. Mar. 19, 1970**
1994 WW GER 5 0 0 0 2 —

**Wendell (-Pohl), Krissy / b. Sept. 12, 1981**
1999-2007 WW USA 29 21 38 59 22 G,5S
2002-2006 OG-W USA 10 4 6 10 10 S,B
~WW IIHF Directorate Best Forward (2005), WW All-Star Team/Forward (2005, 2007)

**Wennerberg, Christine / b. Sept. 24, 1959**
1990 WW NOR 4 0 0 0 0 —

**Whyte, Sandra / b. Aug. 24, 1970**
1992-1997 WW USA 15 4 8 12 4 3S
1998 OG-W USA 6 2 2 4 0 G

**Wierscher, Julia / b. May 10, 1971**
1999-2004 WW GER 19 0 3 3 2 —
2002 OG-W GER 5 1 0 1 0 —

**Wikstrom, Petra / b. May 11, 1969**
1990 WW SWE 5 0 0 0 18 —

**Wild, Rachel / b. June 12, 1977**
1997 WW SUI 5 0 0 0 0 —

**Wilson, Stacy / b. May 12, 1965**
1990-1997 WW CAN 20 9 17 26 10 4G
1998 OG-W CAN 6 1 5 6 0 S

**Wolf, Barbara / b. July 15, 1969**
1990-1992 WW SUI 10 3 5 8 6 —

**Wolf, Raffaela / b. June 20, 1978**
2000-2005 WW GER 19 2 0 2 4 —
2002-2006 OG-W GER 10 0 1 1 4 —

**Wyss, Doris / b. Feb. 3, 1972**
1990-1999 WW SUI 18 4 4 8 20 —

**Xia, Zhenglai / b. Nov. 3, 1986**
2007 WW CHN 4 0 0 0 0 —

| Years | Event | Team | GP | G | A | P | Pim | Medal |
|---|---|---|---|---|---|---|---|---|
| **Xin, Xiuyan / b. May 19, 1968** | | | | | | | | |
| 1992-1994 | WW | CHN | 10 | 1 | 1 | 2 | 8 | — |
| **Xu, Lei / b. Jan. 26, 1977** | | | | | | | | |
| 1994-2001 | WW | CHN | 25 | 2 | 5 | 7 | 14 | — |
| 1998-2002 | OG-W | CHN | 11 | 0 | 1 | 1 | 10 | — |
| **Yang, Xiuqing / b. Feb. 9, 1975** | | | | | | | | |
| 1997-2001 | WW | CHN | 20 | 2 | 3 | 5 | 26 | — |
| 1998-2002 | OG-W | CHN | 11 | 6 | 3 | 9 | 26 | — |
| **Yeshenko, Svetlana / b. Jan. 31, 1974** | | | | | | | | |
| 2001 | WW | KAZ | 5 | 0 | 0 | 0 | 0 | — |
| **Yoshimi, Naho / b. Jan. 31, 1972** | | | | | | | | |
| 2000 | WW | JPN | 5 | 0 | 0 | 0 | 4 | — |
| 1998 | OG-W | JPN | 5 | 0 | 1 | 1 | 4 | — |
| **Yuen, Susie / b. Aug. 2, 1966** | | | | | | | | |
| 1990 | WW | CAN | 5 | 5 | 7 | 12 | 0 | G |
| **Yurlova, Lyudmila / b. Apr. 1, 1972** | | | | | | | | |
| 1997-2001 | WW | RUS | 20 | 0 | 2 | 2 | 14 | B |
| **Zaban, Carisa / b. Sept. 12, 1977** | | | | | | | | |
| 2001 | WW | USA | 5 | 3 | 1 | 4 | 4 | S |
| **Zach, Leila / b. Nov. 18, 1974** | | | | | | | | |
| 1990 | WW | SUI | 5 | 1 | 0 | 1 | 0 | — |
| **Zaugg (-Siergiej), Ginelle / b. Mar. 27, 1986** | | | | | | | | |
| 2007 | WW | USA | 5 | 2 | 1 | 3 | 0 | S |
| 2010 | OG-W | USA | 5 | 0 | 0 | 0 | 4 | S |
| **Zhang, Caili / b. Sept. 11, 1970** | | | | | | | | |
| 1992-1994 | WW | CHN | 10 | 0 | 1 | 1 | 15 | — |
| **Zhang, Haiyan / b. Aug. 8, 1978** | | | | | | | | |
| 1997-1999 | WW | CHN | 10 | 0 | 0 | 0 | 2 | — |
| **Zhang, Jing / b. Mar. 18, 1977** | | | | | | | | |
| 1997-2007 | WW | CHN | 33 | 6 | 5 | 11 | 18 | — |
| 1998-2002 | OG-W | CHN | 11 | 0 | 0 | 0 | 2 | — |
| **Zhang, Lan / b. Sept. 18, 1968** | | | | | | | | |
| 1992-1999 | WW | CHN | 20 | 7 | 9 | 16 | 18 | — |
| 1998 | OG-W | CHN | 6 | 2 | 1 | 3 | 0 | — |
| **Zheng, Jianhua / b. Nov. 28, 1976** | | | | | | | | |
| 1994 | WW | CHN | 5 | 0 | 0 | 0 | 0 | — |
| **Ziegenhals, Nina / b. May 23, 1982** | | | | | | | | |
| 2000-2005 | WW | GER | 19 | 0 | 1 | 1 | 2 | — |
| 2002 | OG-W | GER | 5 | 0 | 2 | 2 | 2 | — |

*Angela Ruggiero retired in 2011 after a distinguished international career for Team USA, climaxing with a gold medal at the 1998 Olympics. Photo: Matthew Manor / HHOF-IIHF Images.*

# Retired Goalies, Women

(career summary for players who have retired from hockey or who have not played recently for their country)

| First-Last Years | Event | NAT | GP | W-T-L | Mins | GA | SO | GAA | A | Pim | Medals |
|---|---|---|---|---|---|---|---|---|---|---|---|
| **Ahlen, Annica / b. Jan. 17, 1975** | | | | | | | | | | | |
| 1990-2001 | WW | SWE | 16 | 7-1-8 | 904:10 | 64 | 0 | 4.25 | 0 | 0 | — |
| 1998-2002 | OG-W | SWE | 5 | 1-0-4 | 299:10 | 29 | 0 | 5.82 | 0 | 2 | B |
| ~WW IIHF Directorate Best Goalie (1992) | | | | | | | | | | | |
| **Ahola, Ritva / b. Mar. 21, 1956** | | | | | | | | | | | |
| 1990 | WW | FIN | 1 | 1-0-0 | 60:00 | 0 | 1 | 0.00 | 0 | 0 | B |
| **Ahonen, Katariina / b. Nov. 7, 1966** | | | | | | | | | | | |
| 1992-1994 | WW | FIN | 5 | 3-0-0 | 229:37 | 6 | 1 | 1.57 | 0 | 2 | 2B |
| **Akimbetyeva, Anna / b. Aug. 20, 1976** | | | | | | | | | | | |
| 2001 | WW | KAZ | 1 | 0-0-0 | 32:44 | 1 | 0 | 1.83 | 0 | 0 | — |
| **Andersson, Cecilia / b. Oct. 4, 1982** | | | | | | | | | | | |
| 2005 | WW | SWE | 3 | 1-0-0 | 90:45 | 5 | 0 | 3.31 | 0 | 0 | B |
| 2006 | OG-W | SWE | 2 | 1-0-1 | 120:00 | 8 | 1 | 4.00 | 0 | 0 | S |
| **Belliveau (-Rousseau), Laurie / b. Sept. 17, 1976** | | | | | | | | | | | |
| 1999 | WW | USA | 2 | 2-0-0 | 120:00 | 2 | 1 | 1.00 | 0 | 0 | S |
| **Berg, Kari / b. Apr. 28, 1965** | | | | | | | | | | | |
| 1990 | WW | NOR | 2 | 0-0-0 | 45:00 | 6 | 0 | 8.00 | 0 | 0 | — |
| **Berlinghof, Karin / b. May 6, 1962** | | | | | | | | | | | |
| 1990 | WW | FRG | 2 | 0-0-2 | 120:00 | 23 | 0 | 11.50 | 0 | 0 | — |
| **Bischofberger, Christiane / b. Jan. 1, 1966** | | | | | | | | | | | |
| 1990 | WW | SUI | 3 | 1-0-1 | 153:00 | 24 | 0 | 9.40 | 0 | 0 | — |
| **Caron, Denise / b. Dec. 31, 1960** | | | | | | | | | | | |
| 1990 | WW | CAN | 3 | 2-1-0 | 144:00 | 5 | 1 | 2.08 | 0 | 0 | G |
| **DeCosta, Sara / b. May 13, 1977** | | | | | | | | | | | |
| 2000-2001 | WW | USA | 5 | 4-0-1 | 300:00 | 8 | 1 | 1.60 | 0 | 0 | 2S |
| 1998-2002 | OG-W | USA | 6 | 5-0-1 | 329:36 | 7 | 3 | 1.27 | 1 | 0 | G,S |
| **Dreyer, Pam / b. Aug. 9, 1981** | | | | | | | | | | | |
| 2004 | WW | USA | 3 | 2-0-1 | 158:39 | 4 | 0 | 1.51 | 0 | 0 | S |
| 2006 | OG-W | USA | 1 | 1-0-0 | 60:00 | 0 | 1 | 0.00 | 0 | 0 | B |
| ~WW All-Star Team/Goal (2004) | | | | | | | | | | | |
| **Dube, Danielle / b. Mar. 10, 1976** | | | | | | | | | | | |
| 1997 | WW | CAN | 2 | 2-0-0 | 120:00 | 1 | 1 | 0.50 | 0 | 0 | G |
| **Dyer, Kelly / b. Mar. 1, 1966** | | | | | | | | | | | |
| 1990-1994 | WW | USA | 7 | 5-0-1 | 349:32 | 15 | 2 | 2.58 | 0 | 0 | 3S |
| **Elsmore (-Sautter), Patricia / b. Feb. 28, 1979** | | | | | | | | | | | |
| 1994-2004 | WW | SUI | 15 | 3-1-9 | 758:19 | 73 | 1 | 5.78 | 0 | 0 | — |
| 2006 | OG-W | SUI | 3 | 0-0-3 | 149:40 | 12 | 0 | 4.81 | 0 | 0 | — |
| ~WW All-Star Team/Goal (1992, 1997) | | | | | | | | | | | |
| **Fjellhammer, Kari / b. Apr. 15, 1963** | | | | | | | | | | | |
| 1990-1994 | WW | NOR | 14 | 4-0-10 | 780:55 | 84 | 1 | 6.45 | 0 | 4 | — |
| **Frasnelli, Luana / b. July 25, 1975** | | | | | | | | | | | |
| 2006 | OG-W | ITA | 3 | 0-0-0 | 80:00 | 17 | 0 | 12.75 | 0 | 0 | — |
| **Frenzel, Claudia / b. Nov. 27, 1966** | | | | | | | | | | | |
| 1992 | WW | SUI | 5 | 0-0-4 | 259:07 | 26 | 0 | 6.02 | 0 | 0 | — |
| **Fujimoto, Tomoko / b. June 30, 1979** | | | | | | | | | | | |
| 2000-2004 | WW | JPN | 7 | 0-1-5 | 365:36 | 24 | 0 | 3.93 | 0 | 0 | — |
| **Glavhammar, Frida / b. July 22, 1985** | | | | | | | | | | | |
| 2004 | WW | SWE | 1 | 0-0-0 | 20:00 | 5 | 0 | 15.00 | 0 | 0 | — |
| **Gothesson, Lotta / b. Apr. 6, 1974** | | | | | | | | | | | |
| 1997-2000 | WW | SWE | 14 | 5-2-6 | 811:11 | 51 | 1 | 3.77 | 0 | 0 | — |
| 1998 | OG-W | SWE | 2 | 1-0-1 | 120:00 | 5 | 1 | 2.50 | 0 | 0 | — |
| **Gunn, Chanda / b. Jan. 27, 1980** | | | | | | | | | | | |
| 2004-2007 | WW | USA | 11 | 8-0-1 | 549:19 | 10 | 3 | 1.09 | 0 | 0 | G,2S |
| 2006 | OG-W | USA | 4 | 3-0-1 | 249:58 | 6 | 2 | 1.44 | 0 | 2 | B |
| ~WW IIHF Directorate Best Goalie (2005) | | | | | | | | | | | |
| **Guo, Hong / b. May 1, 1973** | | | | | | | | | | | |
| 1992-2004 | WW | CHN | 31 | 14-4-11 | 1,655:10 | 107 | 3 | 3.88 | 0 | 8 | — |
| 1998-2002 | OG-W | CHN | 11 | 3-1-5 | 651:08 | 42 | 0 | 3.87 | 0 | 4 | — |
| **Halonen, Minna / b. Oct. 11, 1975** | | | | | | | | | | | |
| 2001-2004 | WW | FIN | 3 | 2-0-1 | 149:41 | 8 | 0 | 3.20 | 0 | 0 | B |
| **Hanley, Jennifer / b. Mar. 10, 1973** | | | | | | | | | | | |
| 1992 | WW | USA | 2 | 2-0-0 | 41:49 | 2 | 0 | 2.86 | 0 | 0 | S |
| **Hayashi, Risa / b. Dec. 23, 1981** | | | | | | | | | | | |
| 2000 | WW | JPN | 2 | 0-0-2 | 89:41 | 14 | 0 | 9.37 | 0 | 0 | — |
| **Hirschbeck, Manuela / b. May 28, 1979** | | | | | | | | | | | |
| 2000 | WW | GER | 4 | 0-1-3 | 218:34 | 13 | 0 | 3.57 | 0 | 0 | — |
| **Hirvinen, Johanna / b. June 17, 1976** | | | | | | | | | | | |
| 2000 | WW | FIN | 1 | 1-0-0 | 60:00 | 1 | 0 | 1.00 | 0 | 0 | B |
| **Holmberg, Hanna / b. Feb. 7, 1981** | | | | | | | | | | | |
| 1999 | WW | SWE | 1 | 0-0-0 | 5:27 | 0 | 0 | 0.00 | 0 | 0 | — |
| **Huo, Lina / b. Mar. 30, 1973** | | | | | | | | | | | |
| 1994-2005 | WW | CHN | 14 | 1-0-9 | 694:53 | 53 | 1 | 4.58 | 1 | 0 | — |
| 1998 | OG-W | CHN | 1 | 0-0-1 | 9:56 | 2 | 0 | 12.08 | 0 | 0 | — |
| **Hurskainen, Minna-Riikka / b. May 7, 1978** | | | | | | | | | | | |
| 1999 | WW | FIN | 1 | 1-0-0 | 60:00 | 0 | 1 | 0.00 | 0 | 0 | B |
| **Johansson, Helen / b. Feb. 19, 1973** | | | | | | | | | | | |
| 1992 | WW | SWE | 2 | 0-0-2 | 119:28 | 12 | 0 | 6.05 | 0 | 0 | — |
| **Jones, Mary / b. Mar. 14, 1960** | | | | | | | | | | | |
| 1990 | WW | USA | 2 | 2-0-0 | 100:00 | 3 | 1 | 1.80 | 0 | 0 | S |
| **Keller, Nadine / b. Dec. 2, 1976** | | | | | | | | | | | |
| 1992-1994 | WW | SUI | 3 | 0-0-3 | 149:09 | 29 | 0 | 11.68 | 0 | 0 | — |
| **Moe, Hege / b. Sept. 17, 1972** | | | | | | | | | | | |
| 1994-1997 | WW | NOR | 7 | 0-1-4 | 312:35 | 26 | 0 | 4.98 | 0 | 0 | — |
| **Montanari, Debora / b. Oct. 17, 1980** | | | | | | | | | | | |
| 2006 | OG-W | ITA | 5 | 0-0-5 | 220:00 | 31 | 0 | 8.45 | 0 | 0 | — |
| **Muller, Tanja / b. Oct. 22, 1967** | | | | | | | | | | | |
| 1990 | WW | SUI | 3 | 2-0-1 | 147:00 | 15 | 0 | 6.10 | 0 | 0 | — |
| **Nilsson, Agneta / b. Oct. 28, 1968** | | | | | | | | | | | |
| 1990 | WW | SWE | 3 | 1-0-2 | 180:00 | 25 | 1 | 8.33 | 0 | 0 | — |
| **Oda, Yuka / b. Mar. 15, 1973** | | | | | | | | | | | |
| 2004 | WW | JPN | 2 | 0-0-1 | 82:55 | 10 | 0 | 7.24 | 0 | 0 | — |
| 1998 | OG-W | JPN | 5 | 0-0-3 | 225:35 | 30 | 0 | 7.98 | 0 | 0 | — |
| **Pfreundschuh, Nadine / b. Nov. 10, 1975** | | | | | | | | | | | |
| 2001 | WW | GER | 1 | 0-0-0 | 33:15 | 4 | 0 | 7.22 | 0 | 0 | — |
| **Phillips, Cathy / b. Aug. 7, 1960** | | | | | | | | | | | |
| 1990 | WW | CAN | 4 | 3-1-0 | 156:00 | 3 | 0 | 1.15 | 0 | 0 | G |
| **Piiroinen, Annakaisa / b. Dec. 12, 1984** | | | | | | | | | | | |
| 2005 | WW | FIN | 5 | 2-0-2 | 269:38 | 13 | 0 | 2.89 | 0 | 0 | — |
| **Puputti, Tuula / b. Nov. 5, 1977** | | | | | | | | | | | |
| 1997-2001 | WW | FIN | 14 | 5-1-7 | 803:03 | 39 | 1 | 2.91 | 2 | 0 | 3B |
| 1998-2002 | OG-W | FIN | 10 | 5-0-4 | 570:04 | 22 | 2 | 2.32 | 0 | 0 | B |
| **Rasmussen, Lene / b. Aug. 27, 1964** | | | | | | | | | | | |
| 1992 | WW | DEN | 5 | 1-0-4 | 305:56 | 24 | 0 | 4.71 | 0 | 0 | — |
| **Reddon, Lesley / b. Nov. 15, 1970** | | | | | | | | | | | |
| 1994-1997 | WW | CAN | 5 | 5-0-0 | 283:59 | 6 | 1 | 1.27 | 0 | 0 | 2G |
| 1998 | OG-W | CAN | 3 | 2-0-1 | 150:56 | 9 | 0 | 3.58 | 0 | 0 | S |
| **Rheaume, Manon / b. Feb. 24, 1972** | | | | | | | | | | | |
| 1992-1994 | WW | CAN | 7 | 6-0-0 | 389:00 | 8 | 2 | 1.23 | 0 | 0 | 2G |
| 1998 | OG-W | CAN | 4 | 2-0-1 | 207:59 | 4 | 1 | 1.15 | 0 | 0 | S |
| ~WW All-Star Team/Goal (1992, 1994) | | | | | | | | | | | |
| **Roy, Marie-Claude / b. Apr. 3, 1970** | | | | | | | | | | | |
| 1992 | WW | CAN | 2 | 2-0-0 | 120:00 | 1 | 1 | 0.50 | 0 | 0 | G |
| **Satsu, Tamae / b. June 12, 1966** | | | | | | | | | | | |
| 1990 | WW | JPN | 4 | 0-0-2 | 151:00 | 17 | 0 | 6.70 | 0 | 0 | — |
| **~Sautter, Patricia** ~see Elsmore (-Sautter), Patricia | | | | | | | | | | | |
| **Small, Sami Jo / b. Mar. 25, 1976** | | | | | | | | | | | |
| 1999-2004 | WW | CAN | 10 | 10-0-0 | 570:01 | 5 | 5 | 0.53 | 0 | 0 | 4G |
| 2002 | OG-W | CAN | 1 | 1-0-0 | 60:00 | 0 | 1 | 0.00 | 0 | 0 | G |
| ~WW IIHF Directorate Best Goalie (1999, 2000), WW All-Star Team/Goal (1999) | | | | | | | | | | | |
| **Sneck, Liisa-Maria / b. Nov. 10, 1968** | | | | | | | | | | | |
| 1990-1997 | WW | FIN | 14 | 8-0-6 | 797:50 | 36 | 3 | 2.71 | 0 | 0 | 4B |
| 1998 | OG-W | FIN | 2 | 1-0-1 | 88:53 | 4 | 0 | 2.70 | 0 | 0 | B |
| **Takahashi, Kaori / b. Nov. 2, 1962** | | | | | | | | | | | |
| 1990 | WW | JPN | 4 | 0-0-3 | 149:00 | 30 | 0 | 12.00 | 0 | 0 | — |
| **Thyssen, Esther / b. July 31, 1979** | | | | | | | | | | | |
| 1999 | WW | GER | 2 | 0-0-0 | 52:07 | 11 | 0 | 12.66 | 0 | 0 | — |
| 2002 | OG-W | GER | 2 | 0-0-0 | 71:07 | 9 | 0 | 7.59 | 0 | 0 | — |
| **Trunova, Natalya / b. Jan. 20, 1982** | | | | | | | | | | | |
| 2001-09 | WW | KAZ | 12 | 1-1-8 | 585:56 | 53 | 0 | 5.43 | 0 | 6 | — |
| 2002 | OG-W | KAZ | 5 | 0-0-5 | 301:39 | 24 | 0 | 4.77 | 0 | 0 | 8th |
| ~WW All-Star Team/Goal (2005) | | | | | | | | | | | |
| **Tueting, Sarah / b. Apr. 26, 1976** | | | | | | | | | | | |
| 1997-2001 | WW | USA | 6 | 4-0-1 | 315:02 | 8 | 4 | 1.52 | 0 | 2 | 3S |
| 1998-2002 | OG-W | USA | 6 | 5-0-0 | 329:21 | 5 | 2 | 0.91 | 0 | 0 | G,S |
| **Van Beusekom (-Sweerin), Megan / b. Dec. 14, 1981** | | | | | | | | | | | |
| 2005-09 | WW | USA | 4 | 2-0-0 | 149:59 | 2 | 2 | 0.80 | 0 | 0 | 2G |
| **Vetsch, Monika / b. Apr. 13, 1966** | | | | | | | | | | | |
| 1992 | WW | SUI | 1 | 0-0-0 | 27:49 | 5 | 0 | 10.79 | 0 | 0 | — |
| **von Allmen, Michelle / b. June 17, 1982** | | | | | | | | | | | |
| 1999 | WW | SUI | 1 | 1-0-0 | 32:27 | 2 | 0 | 3.70 | 0 | 0 | — |
| **Vonderstrass, Aurelia / b. Mar. 18, 1968** | | | | | | | | | | | |
| 1990-1994 | WW | GER | 4 | 2-0-2 | 240:00 | 26 | 0 | 6.50 | 0 | 0 | — |
| **Votintseva, Irina / b. Sept. 19, 1970** | | | | | | | | | | | |
| 1999-2001 | WW | RUS | 7 | 2-0-2 | 297:33 | 27 | 1 | 5.45 | 0 | 0 | B |
| **Wagner, Erika / b. Mar. 31, 1979** | | | | | | | | | | | |
| 1997 | WW | NOR | 1 | 0-0-1 | 60:00 | 7 | 0 | 7.00 | 0 | 0 | — |
| **Wartosch-Kurten, Stephanie / b. Nov. 12, 1978** | | | | | | | | | | | |
| 1994-2005 | WW | GER | 24 | 6-3-12 | 1,266:39 | 110 | 4 | 5.21 | 1 | 8 | — |
| 2002-2006 | OG-W | GER | 7 | 2-1-4 | 348:53 | 19 | 1 | 3.27 | 1 | 0 | — |
| **Watanabe, Haruka / b. Dec. 13, 1972** | | | | | | | | | | | |
| 1998 | OG-W | JPN | 3 | 0-0-2 | 74:09 | 15 | 0 | 12.14 | 0 | 0 | — |
| **Whitten, Erin / b. Oct. 26, 1971** | | | | | | | | | | | |
| 1992-1999 | WW | USA | 15 | 10-1-4 | 884:26 | 29 | 5 | 1.97 | 0 | 0 | 4S |
| ~WW IIHF Directorate Best Goalie (1994) | | | | | | | | | | | |
| **Wiik, Heidi / b. Jan. 6, 1980** | | | | | | | | | | | |
| 2004 | WW | FIN | 4 | 3-1-0 | 240:00 | 5 | 1 | 1.25 | 0 | 0 | B |
| **Yudina, Marina / b. July 18, 1980** | | | | | | | | | | | |
| 2005 | WW | RUS | 1 | 0-0-0 | 26:55 | 8 | 0 | 17:83 | 0 | 0 | — |

*Goalie Sami Jo Small (far right) allowed only five goals and recoded five shutouts in 10 career Women's World Championship games. Photo: Matthew Manor / HHOF-IIHF Images.*

# COACHES' REGISTER

1920-2006:
Year Event NAT GP W T L Finish

2007-present:
Year Event NAT GP W OTW OTL L Finish

**Abrahamsson, Carl**
1935 WM SWE* 8 4 1 3 5th
1937 WM SWE 3 0 0 3 9th
*co-coach with Viking Harbom

**Achtzener, John**
1937 WM CAN 9 9 0 0 G

**Adamowski, Tadeusz**
1928 OG-M POL 2 0 1 1 9th
1930 WM POL 3 1 0 2 5th

**Ahearne, Bunny**
1935 WM GBR 7 4 0 3 B
~IIHF Hall of Fame

**Ahlberg, Lennart**
1988 OG-M NOR 6 0 1 5 12th

**Ahner, Sten**
1947 WM SWE 7 5 1 1 S

**Ahola, Harri**
2004 WM18 FIN 6 3 2 1 7th

**Aitken, Joe**
1952 OG-M FRG 8 1 1 6 8th

**Alain, Pierre**
2012 WW18 CAN 5 5 0 0 0 G

**Alexandrov, Boris**
1998 OG-M KAZ 7 2 1 4 8th
1998 WM KAZ 3 0 0 3 16th

**Allain, Keith**
2001 WM20 USA 7 5 0 2 5th
2002 WM20 USA 7 4 2 1 5th
2011 WM20 USA 6 4 1 0 1 B

**Allen, Les**
1930 WM CAN 1 1 0 0 G

**Altorfer, Rolf**
1986 WM20 SUI 7 1 0 6 7th
1987 WM20 SUI 7 0 0 7 6th

**Amend, Hanspeter**
1994 WW GER 5 0 0 5 8th

**Andreola, Andy**
1950 WM NED 4 1 0 3 8th

**Andreossi, Mezzi**
1933 WM SUI 6 3 1 2 5th

**Andrst, Jiri**
1961 WM TCH* 7 6 1 0 S
*co-coach with Vladimir Kostka

**Annala, Jukka-Pekka**
2002 WM18 FIN 8 5 0 3 4th
2008 WM18 FIN 6 2 0 0 4 6th

**Anton, Jiri**
1954 WM TCH* 7 4 0 3 4th
1963 WM TCH 7 5 1 1 B
1964 OG-M TCH 7 5 0 2 B
*co-coach with Vladimir Bouzek

**Aravirta, Hannu**
1994 OG-M FIN* 8 7 0 1 B
1998 OG-M FIN 6 3 0 3 B
1998 WM FIN 10 4 3 3 S
1999 WM FIN 9 6 1 2 S
2000 WM FIN 9 5 2 2 B
2001 WM FIN 9 7 0 2 S
2002 OG-M FIN 4 2 0 2 6th
2002 WM FIN 9 6 0 3 4th
2003 WM FIN 7 3 1 3 5th
2004 WM20 FIN 7 5 0 2 B
2006 WM20 FIN 7 4 0 3 B
*co-coach with Curt Lindstrom

**Augusta, Josef**
2000 WM CZE 9 8 0 1 G
2001 WM CZE 9 8 1 0 G
2002 OG-M CZE 4 1 1 2 7th
2002 WM CZE 7 6 0 1 5th

**Babcock, Mike**
1997 WM20 CAN 7 5 2 0 G
2004 WM CAN 9 7 1 1 G
2010 OG-M CAN 7 4 2 0 1 G
~only Triple Gold Club coach

**Babey, Ken**
2008 WM20 DEN 6 0 0 0 6 10th

**Backman, Per**
2009 WM DEN 6 3 0 1 2 13th
2010 WM DEN 7 2 1 0 4 8th
2011 WM DEN 6 0 2 0 4 11th
2012 WM DEN 7 1 0 1 5 13th

**Bader, Roger**
2002 WM18 SUI 8 5 0 3 7th
2003 WM18 SUI 6 1 1 4 9th

**Ballard, Harold**
1933 WM CAN 5 4 0 1 S

**Baroni, Giogrio**
1934 WM ITA 7 2 2 3 9th

**Barto, Jackie**
2008 WW USA 5 4 0 1 0 G

**Barton, Slavomir**
1964 OG-M ITA 7 2 0 5 15th
1979 WM POL 8 0 2 6 8th

**Bates, Lou**
1950 WM GBR 7 4 0 3 4th

**Bauer, Bobby**
1956 OG-M CAN 8 6 0 2 B
1960 OG-M CAN 7 6 0 1 S

**Bauer, Father David**
1964 OG-M CAN 7 5 0 2 4th
1965 WM CAN 7 4 0 3 4th
~IIHF Hall of Fame

**Baulin, Yuri**
1976 OG-M AUT 5 3 0 2 8th

**Becker, Maritta**
2012 WW18 GER 6 2 0 0 4 4th

**Bednar, Vladimir**
2007 WM20 CZE 6 3 0 0 3 5th

**Bell, Bobby**
1928 OG-M SUI 5 2 1 2 B
1930 WM SUI 3 2 0 1 B
1937 WM GER 9 3 1 5 4th
1938 WM GER 8 3 0 5 4th
1939 WM GER 8 4 2 2 5th

**Belyayev, Vladimir**
1998 WM20 KAZ 7 2 0 5 7th
2003 WM18 KAZ 6 0 0 6 10th

**Bendelin, Torgny**
2004 WM20 SWE 6 3 0 3 7th
2005 WM20 SWE 6 2 0 4 6th
2006 WM20 SWE 6 4 0 2 5th
2007 WM20 SWE 7 3 0 1 3 4th

**Beresnevs, Leonids**
1997 WM LAT 8 4 2 2 7th
1998 WM LAT 6 3 1 2 9th
1999 WM LAT 6 2 0 4 11th
2005 WM LAT 6 2 1 3 9th
2006 OG-M LAT 5 0 1 4 12th
2010 WM18 LAT 6 0 1 0 5 9th

**Berger, Stanislav**
2000 WM18 CZE 6 2 0 4 6th

**Bergman, Sune**
1999 WM SWE* 9 7 0 2 B
*co-coach with Stephan Lundh

**Bergqvist, Sven**
1948 OG-M SWE 8 4 0 4 5th
1949 WM SWE 7 4 1 2 4th

**Bergstrom, Lars**
2009 WM AUT 6 2 0 0 4 14th

**Billkvam, Arne**
2004 WM18 NOR 6 0 0 6 10th

**Bilyaletdinov, Zinetula**
2004 WCH RUS 4 2 0 2 6th
2012 WM RUS 10 10 0 0 0 G

**Biryukov, Alexander**
2008 WM18 RUS 6 5 0 0 1 S

**Bjerklund, Egil**
1968 OG-M NOR 5 3 0 2 11th
1979 WM20 NOR 5 0 0 5 8th

**Bjorkstrand, Todd**
2012 WM20 DEN 6 0 0 2 4 10th

**Blais, Dean**
1994 WM20 USA 7 1 1 5 6th
2010 WM20 USA 7 5 1 1 0 G
2012 WM20 USA 6 3 0 0 3 7th

**Bobrov, Vsevolod**
1972 WM URS 10 7 2 1 S
1972 SS URS 8 3 1 4 2nd
1973 WM URS 10 10 0 0 G
1974 WM URS 10 9 0 1 G

**Bogdanov, Anatoli**
1999 WM UKR 3 0 0 3 14th
2000 WM UKR 6 2 0 4 14th
2001 WM UKR 6 2 0 4 10th
2002 OG-M UKR 4 2 0 2 10th
2002 WM UKR 6 2 1 3 9th
2003 WM UKR 6 1 0 5 12th

**Bohren, Alfred**
1999 WM18 SUI 7 5 0 2 4th
2005 WM18 SUI 7 1 0 6 9th
2008 WM18 SUI 6 2 0 0 4 8th
2012 WM18 SUI 6 2 0 0 4 7th

**Bohunicky, Peter**
2009 WM18 SVK 6 2 0 1 3 7th

**Boller, Heinrich**
1954 WM SUI 7 0 2 5 7th
1955 WM SUI 8 1 0 7 8th
1956 OG-M SUI 5 1 0 4 9th

**Bokros, Ernest**

| | | | | | | | |
|---|---|---|---|---|---|---|---|
| 2012 WM20 | SVK | 6 | 2 | 0 | 0 | 4 | 6th |

**Bolyakin, Oleg**

| | | | | | | | |
|---|---|---|---|---|---|---|---|
| 2008 WM20 | KAZ | 6 | 2 | 0 | 0 | 4 | 8th |
| 2009 WM20 | KAZ | 6 | 0 | 0 | 0 | 6 | 10th |

**Boni, Jim**

| | | | | | | | |
|---|---|---|---|---|---|---|---|
| 2007 WM | AUT | 6 | 1 | 0 | 1 | 4 | 15th |

**Boork, Leif**

| | | | | | | | |
|---|---|---|---|---|---|---|---|
| 1984 CC | SWE | 8 | 4 | 0 | | 4 | 2nd |
| 1985 WM | SWE | 10 | 4 | 0 | | 6 | 6th |
| 1999 WM | NOR | 6 | 1 | 0 | | 5 | 12th |
| 2000 WM | NOR | 6 | 2 | 1 | | 3 | 10th |
| 2001 WM | NOR | 6 | 0 | 2 | | 4 | 15th |

**Borowicz, Czeslaw**

| | | | | | | | |
|---|---|---|---|---|---|---|---|
| 1980 OG-M | POL | 5 | 2 | 0 | | 3 | 7th |

**Boucher, Frank**

| | | | | | | | |
|---|---|---|---|---|---|---|---|
| 1948 OG-M | CAN | 8 | 7 | 1 | | 0 | G |

**Bourdereau, Louis**

| | | | | | | | |
|---|---|---|---|---|---|---|---|
| 1950 WM | FRA | 4 | 0 | 0 | | 4 | 9th |

**Bouzek, Vladimir**

| | | | | | | | |
|---|---|---|---|---|---|---|---|
| 1954 WM | TCH* | 7 | 4 | 0 | | 3 | 4th |
| 1955 WM | TCH | 8 | 5 | 1 | | 2 | B |
| 1956 OG-M | TCH | 7 | 3 | 0 | | 4 | 5th |
| 1965 WM | TCH** | 7 | 6 | 0 | | 1 | S |
| 1966 WM | TCH* | 7 | 6 | 0 | | 1 | S |

*co-coach with Jiri Anton
**co-coach with Vladimir Kostka

**Bowman, Scotty**

| | | | | | | | |
|---|---|---|---|---|---|---|---|
| 1976 CC | CAN | 7 | 6 | 0 | | 1 | 1st |
| 1981 CC | CAN | 7 | 5 | 1 | | 1 | 2nd |

**Bragin, Valeri**

| | | | | | | | |
|---|---|---|---|---|---|---|---|
| 2004 WM18 | RUS | 6 | 4 | 2 | | 0 | G |
| 2005 WM20 | RUS | 6 | 4 | 0 | | 2 | S |
| 2011 WM20 | RUS | 7 | 3 | 2 | 0 | 2 | G |
| 2012 WM20 | RUS | 7 | 4 | 1 | 2 | 0 | S |

**Brambilla, Camillo Erba**

| | | | | | | | |
|---|---|---|---|---|---|---|---|
| 1930 WM | ITA | 1 | 0 | 0 | | 1 | 10th |

**Brask, Ake**

| | | | | | | | |
|---|---|---|---|---|---|---|---|
| 1965 WM | NOR* | 7 | 0 | 0 | | 7 | 8th |
| 1972 OG-M | NOR | 4 | 3 | 0 | | 1 | 8th |

*co-coach with Gunnar Kroge

**Brooks, Herb**

| | | | | | | | |
|---|---|---|---|---|---|---|---|
| 1979 WM | USA | 8 | 2 | 3 | | 3 | 7th |
| 1980 OG-M | USA | 7 | 6 | 1 | | 0 | G |
| 1998 OG-M | FRA | 4 | 2 | 0 | | 2 | 11th |
| 1998 WM | FRA | 3 | 1 | 0 | | 2 | 13th |
| 2002 OG-M | USA | 6 | 4 | 1 | | 1 | S |

~IIHF Hall of Fame

**Brown, Walter**

| | | | | | | | |
|---|---|---|---|---|---|---|---|
| 1931 WM | USA | 6 | 5 | 0 | | 1 | S |
| 1933 WM | USA | 5 | 5 | 0 | | 0 | G |
| 1934 WM | USA | 4 | 3 | 0 | | 1 | S |

~IIHF Hall of Fame

**Brunclik, Bedrich**

| | | | | | | | |
|---|---|---|---|---|---|---|---|
| 1992 WM20 | TCH | 7 | 3 | 0 | | 4 | 5th |

**Bubnik, Gustav**

| | | | | | | | |
|---|---|---|---|---|---|---|---|
| 1967 WM | FIN | 7 | 2 | 1 | | 4 | 6th |
| 1968 OG-M | FIN | 7 | 3 | 1 | | 3 | 5th |
| 1969 WM | FIN* | 10 | 2 | 0 | | 8 | 5th |
| 1981 WM | NED | 8 | 0 | 0 | | 8 | 8th |

*co-coach with Seppo Liitsola

**Bubnik, Vaclav**

| | | | | | | | |
|---|---|---|---|---|---|---|---|
| 1964 OG-M | YUG | 7 | 3 | 1 | | 3 | 14th |

**Buckna, Mike**

| | | | | | | | |
|---|---|---|---|---|---|---|---|
| 1938 WM | TCH | 7 | 4 | 1 | | 2 | B |
| 1939 WM | TCH | 10 | 3 | 2 | | 5 | 4th |
| 1947 WM | TCH | 7 | 6 | 0 | | 1 | G |
| 1948 OG-M | TCH | 8 | 7 | 1 | | 0 | S |

~IIHF Hall of Fame

**Bujar, Tadeusz**

| | | | | | | | |
|---|---|---|---|---|---|---|---|
| 1985 WM20 | POL | 7 | 0 | 1 | | 6 | 8th |

**Bukac, Ludek**

| | | | | | | | |
|---|---|---|---|---|---|---|---|
| 1980 OG-M | TCH* | 6 | 4 | 0 | | 2 | 5th |
| 1981 WM | TCH | 8 | 4 | 2 | | 2 | B |
| 1981 CC | TCH | 6 | 2 | 2 | | 2 | 3rd |
| 1982 WM | TCH | 10 | 5 | 2 | | 3 | S |
| 1983 WM | TCH | 10 | 6 | 2 | | 2 | S |
| 1984 CC | TCH | 5 | 0 | 1 | | 4 | 6th |
| 1985 WM | TCH | 10 | 7 | 1 | | 2 | G |
| 1988 OG-M | AUT | 6 | 1 | 1 | | 4 | 9th |
| 1992 OG-M | GER | 8 | 3 | 0 | | 5 | 6th |
| 1992 WM | GER | 6 | 4 | 0 | | 2 | 6th |
| 1994 OG-M | GER** | 8 | 4 | 0 | | 4 | 7th |
| 1994 WM | GER | 5 | 1 | 1 | | 3 | 9th |
| 1995 WM | CZE | 8 | 4 | 0 | | 4 | 4th |
| 1996 WM | CZE | 8 | 7 | 1 | | 0 | G |
| 1996 WCH | CZE | 3 | 0 | 0 | | 3 | 8th |

*co-coach with Karel Gut
**co-coach with Franz Reindl
~IIHF Hall of Fame

**Butler, Stan**

| | | | | | | | |
|---|---|---|---|---|---|---|---|
| 2001 WM20 | CAN | 7 | 4 | 1 | | 2 | B |
| 2002 WM20 | CAN | 7 | 5 | 0 | | 2 | S |

**Bykov, Vyacheslav**

| | | | | | | | |
|---|---|---|---|---|---|---|---|
| 2007 WM | RUS | 9 | 8 | 0 | 1 | 0 | B |
| 2008 WM | RUS | 9 | 6 | 3 | 0 | 0 | G |
| 2009 WM | RUS | 9 | 8 | 1 | 0 | 0 | G |
| 2010 OG-M | RUS | 4 | 2 | 0 | 1 | 1 | 6th |
| 2010 WM | RUS | 9 | 8 | 0 | 0 | 1 | S |
| 2011 WM | RUS | 9 | 4 | 0 | 1 | 4 | 4th |

**Camp, Shawn**

| | | | | | | | |
|---|---|---|---|---|---|---|---|
| 2005 WM18 | CAN | 6 | 4 | 0 | | 2 | S |

**Cameron, Dave**

| | | | | | | | |
|---|---|---|---|---|---|---|---|
| 2011 WM20 | CAN | 7 | 5 | 0 | 1 | 1 | S |

**Canale, Jos**

| | | | | | | | |
|---|---|---|---|---|---|---|---|
| 1994 WM20 | CAN | 7 | 6 | 1 | | 0 | G |

**Carbonneau, Guy**

| | | | | | | | |
|---|---|---|---|---|---|---|---|
| 2010 WM18 | CAN | 6 | 3 | 0 | 0 | 3 | 7th |

**Carlsson, Herman**

| | | | | | | | |
|---|---|---|---|---|---|---|---|
| 1951 WM | SWE* | 6 | 4 | 1 | | 1 | S |
| 1952 OG-M | SWE* | 9 | 7 | 0 | | 2 | B |
| 1954 WM | SWE* | 7 | 5 | 1 | | 1 | B |
| 1955 WM | SWE | 8 | 4 | 1 | | 3 | 5th |

*co-coach with Folke Jansson

**Carlsson, Ingvar**

| | | | | | | | |
|---|---|---|---|---|---|---|---|
| 1986 WM20 | SWE | 7 | 4 | 0 | | 3 | 5th |

**Carlyle, Steve**

| | | | | | | | |
|---|---|---|---|---|---|---|---|
| 2008 WW | CHN | 4 | 1 | 0 | 0 | 3 | 8th |

**Carpenter, Doug**

| | | | | | | | |
|---|---|---|---|---|---|---|---|
| 1985 WM | CAN | 10 | 6 | 1 | | 3 | S |

**Cedergren, Henrik**

| | | | | | | | |
|---|---|---|---|---|---|---|---|
| 2011 WW18 | SWE | 5 | 3 | 0 | 1 | 1 | 5th |
| 2012 WW18 | SWE | 6 | 3 | 1 | 0 | 2 | B |

**Cedorchuk, Steve**

| | | | | | | | |
|---|---|---|---|---|---|---|---|
| 1989 WM20 | USA | 7 | 3 | 1 | | 3 | 5th |
| 1990 WM20 | USA | 7 | 1 | 0 | | 6 | 7th |

**Celio, Manuele**

| | | | | | | | |
|---|---|---|---|---|---|---|---|
| 2009 WM18 | SUI | 6 | 2 | 0 | 0 | 4 | 8th |
| 2010 WM18 | SUI | 6 | 3 | 0 | 0 | 3 | 5th |
| 2011 WM18 | SUI | 6 | 3 | 0 | 0 | 3 | 7th |
| 2012 WM20 | SUI | 6 | 1 | 1 | 1 | 3 | 8th |

**Cepan, Jozef**

| | | | | | | | |
|---|---|---|---|---|---|---|---|
| 2005 WM18 | SVK | 5 | 2 | 0 | | 3 | 6th |
| 2008 WM18 | SVK | 6 | 3 | 0 | 1 | 2 | 7th |

**Ceretti, Francois**

| | | | | | | | |
|---|---|---|---|---|---|---|---|
| 1994 WW | SUI | 5 | 2 | 0 | | 3 | 7th |

**Cernicky, Julius**

| | | | | | | | |
|---|---|---|---|---|---|---|---|
| 1986 WM20 | TCH | 7 | 4 | 0 | | 3 | 4th* |

*co-coach with Jiri Justra

**Chambers, Dave**

| | | | | | | | |
|---|---|---|---|---|---|---|---|
| 1982 WM | ITA | 7 | 1 | 1 | | 5 | 7th |
| 1983 WM | ITA | 10 | 1 | 1 | | 8 | 8th |
| 1988 WM20 | CAN | 7 | 6 | 1 | | 0 | G |

**Charest, Larry**

| | | | | | | | |
|---|---|---|---|---|---|---|---|
| 1951 WM | USA | 6 | 1 | 1 | | 4 | 6th |

**Charron, Guy**

| | | | | | | | |
|---|---|---|---|---|---|---|---|
| 1990 WM20 | CAN | 7 | 5 | 1 | | 1 | G |

**Cherenkov, Robert**

| | | | | | | | |
|---|---|---|---|---|---|---|---|
| 1989 WM20 | URS | 7 | 6 | 0 | | 1 | G |
| 1990 WM20 | URS | 7 | 5 | 1 | | 1 | S |
| 1991 WM20 | URS | 7 | 5 | 1 | | 1 | S |

**Chernyshev, Arkadi**

| | | | | | | | |
|---|---|---|---|---|---|---|---|
| 1954 WM | URS | 7 | 6 | 1 | | 0 | G |
| 1955 WM | URS | 8 | 7 | 0 | | 1 | S |
| 1956 OG-M | URS | 7 | 7 | 0 | | 0 | G |
| 1957 WM | URS | 7 | 5 | 2 | | 0 | S |
| 1961 WM | URS | 7 | 5 | 0 | | 2 | B |
| 1963 WM | URS* | 7 | 6 | 0 | | 1 | G |
| 1964 OG-M | URS* | 7 | 7 | 0 | | 0 | G |
| 1965 WM | URS* | 7 | 7 | 0 | | 0 | G |
| 1966 WM | URS* | 7 | 6 | 1 | | 0 | G |
| 1967 WM | URS* | 7 | 7 | 0 | | 0 | G |
| 1968 OG-M | URS* | 7 | 6 | 0 | | 1 | G |
| 1969 WM | URS* | 10 | 8 | 0 | | 2 | G |
| 1970 WM | URS* | 10 | 9 | 0 | | 1 | G |
| 1971 WM | URS* | 10 | 8 | 1 | | 1 | G |
| 1972 OG-M | URS* | 5 | 4 | 1 | | 0 | G |

*co-coach with Anatoli Tarasov
~IIHF Hall of Fame

**Cherry, Don**

| | | | | | | | |
|---|---|---|---|---|---|---|---|
| 1981 WM | CAN | 8 | 2 | 1 | | 5 | 4th |

**Chibirev, Viktor**

| | | | | | | | |
|---|---|---|---|---|---|---|---|
| 1995 WM20 | UKR | 7 | 1 | 0 | | 6 | 8th |
| 1996 WM20 | UKR | 6 | 1 | 0 | | 5 | 10th |

**Chmura, Mieczyslaw**

| | | | | | | | |
|---|---|---|---|---|---|---|---|
| 1972 OG-M | POL* | 5 | 0 | 0 | | 5 | 6th |

*co-coach with Anatoli Yegorov

**Christensen, Carsten**

| | | | | | | | |
|---|---|---|---|---|---|---|---|
| 1954 WM | NOR | 7 | 1 | 0 | | 6 | 8th |

**Christensen, Terry**

| | | | | | | | |
|---|---|---|---|---|---|---|---|
| 1988 WM20 | USA | 7 | 1 | 0 | | 6 | 6th |

**Christiansen, Dion**

| | | | | | | | |
|---|---|---|---|---|---|---|---|
| 1992 WW | DEN | 5 | 1 | 0 | | 4 | 7th |

**Church, Dan**

| | | | | | | | |
|---|---|---|---|---|---|---|---|
| 2010 WW18 | CAN | 5 | 4 | 1 | 0 | 0 | G |
| 2012 WW | CAN | 5 | 3 | 1 | 0 | 1 | G |

**Chynoweth, Dean**

| | | | | | | | |
|---|---|---|---|---|---|---|---|
| 2004 WM18 | CAN | 7 | 4 | 0 | | 3 | 4th |

**Cleverly, Harry**

| | | | | | | | |
|---|---|---|---|---|---|---|---|
| 1963 WM | USA | 7 | 1 | 1 | | 5 | 8th |

**Cole, Danton**

| | | | | | | | |
|---|---|---|---|---|---|---|---|
| 2012 WM18 | USA | 6 | 6 | 0 | 0 | 0 | G |

**Comeau, Marcel**

| | | | | | | | |
|---|---|---|---|---|---|---|---|
| 1996 WM20 | CAN | 6 | 6 | 0 | | 0 | G |

**Constantine, Kevin**

| | | | | | | | |
|---|---|---|---|---|---|---|---|
| 1991 WM20 | USA | 7 | 4 | 1 | | 2 | 4th |

**Contzen, Jacques**
1950 WM BEL 4 2 0 2 7th

**Cook, Wyn**
1948 OG-M SUI 8 6 0 2 B

**Cornacchia, Rick**
1992 WM20 CAN 7 2 2 3 6th
2010 WM ITA 6 1 0 1 4 15th
2012 WM ITA 7 0 1 0 6 15th

**Cortina, Pat**
2001 WM ITA 6 1 1 4 12th
2002 WM ITA 6 1 0 5 15th
2009 WM HUN 6 0 0 0 6 16th

**Crawford, Marc**
1998 OG-M CAN 6 4 0 2 4th

**Crivelli, Giuseppe**
1935 WM ITA 7 1 3 3 8th

**Cupolo, Bill**
1959 WM ITA 8 3 1 4 10th

**Currie, Greg**
1954 WM CAN 7 6 0 1 S

**Damberg, Kjell**
1981 WM20 SWE 5 4 1 0 G

**Dampier, Alex**
1994 WM GBR 6 0 0 6 12th

**Danielopol, Dumitru**
1935 WM ROU 6 3 0 3 11th

**Danis, Tibor**
2007 WM18 SVK 6 3 0 1 2 5th

**Davidson, Mel**
2000 WW CAN 5 5 0 0 G
2005 WW CAN 5 4 0 1 S
2006 OG-W CAN 5 5 0 0 G
2007 WW CAN 5 4 1 0 0 G
2008 WW18 CAN 5 4 0 0 1 S
2010 OG-W CAN 5 5 0 0 0 G

**Davis, Lorne**
1980 OG-M CAN* 6 3 0 3 6th
*co-coach with Clare Drake & Tom Watt

**Davydov, Vitali**
1977 WM20 URS 7 7 0 0 G
1978 WM20 URS 7 6 0 1 G
1979 WM20 URS 6 5 1 0 G

**de Backer, Gusty**
1949 WM BEL 6 1 0 5 9th

**de Craene, Jean**
1928 OG-M BEL 3 2 0 1 7th

**del Curto, Arno**
1994 WM20 SUI 7 0 1 6 8th
1996 WM20 SUI 6 1 1 4 9th

**Delisle, Pierre**
1990 WW GER 5 2 0 3 7th

**Delnon, Othmar**
1948 OG-M ITA 8 0 0 8 9th

**Desjardins, Willie**
2010 WM20 CAN 6 4 1 1 0 S

**Dewar, John**
1934 WM HUN 6 1 1 4 6th

**De Weerdt, Paul**
1939 WM BEL 4 0 1 3 11th

**Dietrichstein, Edgar**
1928 OG-M AUT 2 0 2 0 7th

**Dmitriev, Igor**
1984 WM20 URS 7 6 1 0 G
1995 WM20 RUS 7 5 0 2 S
1996 WM20 RUS 7 4 1 2 B
1997 WM RUS 10 5 2 3 4th
~IIHF Hall of Fame

**Dolgushin, Vyacheslav**
2001 WW RUS 5 3 0 2 B
2002 OG-W RUS 5 3 0 2 5th

**Donika, Anatoli**
2002 WM18 UKR 8 1 0 7 12th

**Drake, Clare**
1980 OG-M CAN* 6 3 0 3 6th
*co-coach with Lorne Davis & Tom Watt

**Dube, Dany**
1997 WM FRA 8 2 0 6 10th

**Dufva, Risto**
2005 WM20 FIN 5 2 0 3 5th

**Durocher, Mario**
2004 WM20 CAN 6 5 0 1 S

**Dusek, Adolf**
1920 OG-M TCH 3 1 0 2 B

**Eaves, Mike**
2001 WM18 USA 6 3 0 3 6th
2002 WM18 USA 8 7 0 1 G
2004 WM20 USA 6 6 0 0 G
2006 WM USA 7 4 0 3 7th

**Egen, Markus**
1961 WM FRG 7 0 2 5 8th
1964 OG-M FRG* 7 2 0 5 7th
*co-coach with Xaver Unsinn & Engelbert Holdereid

**Egli, Hansjorg**
1990 WW SUI 5 3 0 2 5th

**Elander, Peter**
2004 WW SWE 5 1 1 3 4th
2005 WW SWE 5 3 0 2 B
2006 OG-W SWE 5 3 0 2 S
2007 WW SWE 5 4 0 1 0 B
2008 WW SWE 4 2 0 2 0 5th
2009 WW SWE 5 3 0 0 2 4th
2010 OG-W SWE 5 2 0 1 2 4th

**Elliott, George**
1924 OG-M GBR 5 3 0 2 B

**Erhardt, Carl**
1948 OG-M GBR 8 3 0 5 6th

**Evensson, Conny**
1983 WM20 SWE 7 4 0 3 4th
1984 WM20 SWE 7 3 0 4 5th
1991 WM SWE 10 5 5 0 G
1991 CC SWE 6 2 0 4 4th
1992 OG-M SWE 8 5 2 1 5th
1992 WM SWE 8 4 2 2 G

**Fakhrutdinov, Miskhat**
2007 WM18 RUS 7 5 1 0 1 G

**Farda, Eduard**
1960 OG-M TCH 7 3 0 4 4th

**Farlow, Harold**
1931 WM POL 7 2 1 4 4th

**Fasel, Charles**
1934 WM SUI 7 5 0 2 4th
1935 WM SUI 8 5 2 1 S

**Fellowes, Cornelius**
1920 OG-M USA 4 3 0 1 S

**Fetisov, Vyacheslav**
2002 OG-M RUS 6 3 1 2 B

**Filc, Jan**
1999 WM20 SVK 6 4 1 1 B
2000 WM SVK 9 5 1 3 S
2001 WM SVK 7 3 0 4 7th
2002 OG-M SVK 4 1 1 2 13th
2002 WM SVK 9 8 0 1 G
2004 WCH SVK 4 0 0 4 7th
2009 WM SVK 6 1 1 2 2 10th
2010 OG-M SVK 7 3 1 0 3 4th

**Flamaropol, Mihai**
1964 OG-M ROM 7 3 1 3 12th
1968 OG-M ROM* 5 2 0 3 12th
*co-coach with Constantin Tico

**Fleming, Wayne**
2001 WM CAN 7 4 1 2 5th
2002 WM CAN 7 5 0 2 6th

**Forsberg, Kent**
1996 WM SWE 6 2 2 2 6th
1996 WCH SWE 4 3 0 1 3rd
1997 WM SWE 11 7 1 3 S
1998 OG-M SWE 4 2 0 2 5th
1998 WM SWE 10 9 1 0 G

**Forsyth, Bert**
1936 OG-M BEL 3 0 0 3 13th

**Fraser, Curt**
2007 WM BLR 6 1 0 0 5 11th
2008 WM BLR 6 1 0 3 2 9th

**Fritzmeier, Franz**
1999 WM18 GER 6 1 0 5 9th

**Fruhauf, Jozef**
2004 WM20 SVK 6 2 1 3 6th
2006 WM18 SVK 6 2 0 4 7th
2011 WM18 SVK 6 1 0 0 5 10th

**Fukada, Norio**
1990 WW JPN 5 0 0 5 8th

**Galiamin, Oleg**
2000 WW RUS 5 3 0 2 5th

**Gansiniec, Alfred**
1959 WM POL 8 1 0 7 11th

**Garon, Joseph**
1920 OG-M FRA 1 0 0 1 6th

**Garrison, John**
1948 OG-M USA 8 5 0 3 4th

**Gilbert, Greg**
2006 WM18 CAN 7 3 1 3 4th

**Gilligan, Bill**
1992 WM SUI 8 3 2 3 4th
1993 WM SUI 7 2 0 5 12th
1998 WM20 SUI 7 4 1 2 B
2011 WM AUT 6 1 0 0 5 15th

**Girard, Andre**
1959 WM SUI 8 1 1 6 12th

**Golonka, Jozef**
1980 WM20 TCH 5 2 0 3 4th
1981 WM20 TCH 5 1 3 1 4th
1996 WCH SVK 3 0 0 3 7th
1997 WM SVK 8 3 1 4 9th

**Gordon, Scott**
2010 WM USA 6 2 1 2 1 13th
2011 WM USA 7 3 0 1 3 8th
2012 WM USA 8 4 2 0 2 7th

**Gostick, Glen**
1976 WM USA* 10 3 1 6 4th
*co-coach with John Mariucci

**Goulet, Michel**
2006 OG-M ITA 5 0 2 3 11th
2006 WM ITA 6 1 1 4 14th
2007 WM ITA 6 0 1 0 5 12th
2008 WM ITA 5 0 0 0 5 16th

**Graham, Jimmy**
1950 WM CAN 7 7 0 0 G

**Grant, Howie**
1934 WM TCH 6 3 0 3 5th

**Gray, Dick**
1951 WM CAN 6 6 0 0 G

**Green, Flemming**
2008 WM18 DEN 6 0 0 0 6 10th

**Gregor, Dusan**
2005 WM20 SVK 6 4 0 2 7th

**Gronborg, Rikard**
2011 WM18 SWE 6 4 0 1 1 S
2012 WM18 SWE 6 5 0 0 1 S

**Grubauer, Edi**
1999 WW SUI 5 0 0 5 8th

**Guocheng, Wang**
1992 WW CHN 5 3 0 2 5th

**Gureyev, Valentin**
1999 WM18 RUS 7 3 0 4 6th
2009 WW RUS 4 2 0 0 2 5th
2010 OG-W RUS 5 2 0 1 2 6th
2011 WW RUS 6 1 1 1 3 4th
2012 WW RUS 5 0 0 1 4 6th

**Gustafsson, Bengt-Ake**
2005 WM SWE 9 6 0 3 4th
2006 OG-M SWE 8 6 0 2 G
2006 WM SWE 9 6 2 1 G
2007 WM SWE 9 6 0 0 3 4th
2008 WM SWE 9 4 1 0 4 4th
2009 WM SWE 9 5 1 2 1 B
2010 OG-M SWE 4 3 0 0 1 5th
2010 WM SWE 9 7 0 1 1 B

**Gustafsson, Erik**
1924 OG-M SWE* 5 2 0 3 4th
*co-coach with Ruben Rundqvist

**Gut, Karel**
1974 WM TCH* 10 7 0 3 S
1975 WM TCH* 10 8 0 2 S
1976 OG-M TCH* 5 3 0 2 S
1976 WM TCH* 10 9 1 0 G
1976 CC TCH* 7 3 1 3 2nd
1977 WM TCH* 10 7 1 2 G
1978 WM TCH 10 9 0 1 S
1979 WM TCH* 8 4 2 2 S
1980 OG-M TCH** 6 4 0 2 5th
*co-coach with Jan Starsi
**co-coach with Ludek Bukac

**Habscheid, Marc**
2003 WM20 CAN 6 5 0 1 S
2005 WM CAN 9 6 1 2 S
2006 WM CAN 9 6 0 3 4th

**Hadamczik, Alois**
2004 WM20 CZE 7 3 0 4 4th
2005 WM20 CZE 7 5 0 2 B
2006 OG-M CZE 8 4 0 4 B
2006 WM CZE 9 5 2 2 S
2007 WM CZE 7 3 0 1 3 7th
2008 WM CZE 7 3 1 2 1 5th
2011 WM CZE 9 8 0 0 1 B
2012 WM CZE 10 6 1 0 3 B

**Haddock, William**
1924 OG-M USA 5 4 0 1 S

**Haga, Tor Johan**
1989 WM20 NOR 7 1 0 6 7th

**Hagen, Morten**
2012 WM18 DEN 6 0 1 0 5 10th

**Hajny, Premsyl**
1976 OG-M YUG 5 3 0 2 10th

**Hallin, Mats**
1999 WM20 SWE 6 4 0 2 4th

**Hamalainen, Pekka**
2001 WM18 FIN 6 5 0 1 B
2009 WW18 FIN 5 1 2 0 2 5
2010 OG-W FIN 5 2 1 0 2 B
2011 WW FIN 6 2 1 1 2 B
2012 WW FIN 6 2 0 0 4 4th

**Hanlon, Glen**
2005 WM BLR 6 2 0 4 10th
2006 WM BLR 7 4 0 3 6th
2009 WM BLR 7 1 3 0 3 8th
2010 WM SVK 6 2 0 0 4 12th
2011 WM SVK 6 2 0 0 4 10th

**Hanzl, Jiri**
1968 OG-M AUT 5 1 0 4 13th

**Harbom, Viking**
1928 OG-M SWE* 5 3 1 1 S
1931 WM SWE 6 2 1 3 6th
1935 WM SWE** 8 4 1 3 5th
1938 WM SWE 6 2 2 2 5th
*co-coach with Sten Mellgren
**co-coach with Carl Abrahamsson

**Harris, Billy**
1972 OG-M SWE 5 2 1 2 4th
1972 WM SWE 10 5 1 4 B

**Hartsburg, Craig**
2007 WM20 CAN 6 5 1 0 0 G
2008 WM20 CAN 7 5 1 0 1 G

**Hasler, Bill**
1983 WM20 USA 7 3 0 4 5th

**Hattanda, Takayuki**
2000 WW JPN 5 0 0 5 8th

**Haugen, Harald**
1990 WW NOR 5 1 0 4 6th
1992 WW NOR 5 2 0 3 6th
1994 WW NOR 5 1 0 4 6th

**Haukvic, Antonin**
1957 WM POL 7 2 0 5 6th

**Hay, Don**
1995 WM20 CAN 7 7 0 0 G
2012 WM20 CAN 6 5 0 0 1 B

**Heikkila, Kari**
2012 WM BLR 7 1 0 0 6 14th

**Heikkila, Lasse**
1976 WM FIN* 10 2 4 4 5th
1976 CC FIN 5 1 0 4 6th
1977 WM FIN 10 5 0 5 5th
*co-coach with Seppo Liitsola

**Helminen, Raimo**
2012 WM20 FIN 7 4 0 1 2 4th

**Henderson, Dave**
2002 WM20 FRA 6 1 0 5 10th
2008 WM FRA 5 2 0 0 3 14th
2009 WM FRA 6 1 0 0 5 12th
2010 WM FRA 6 2 0 0 4 14th
2011 WM FRA 6 0 1 1 4 12th
2012 WM FRA 7 3 0 0 4 9th

**Herman, Josef**
1952 OG-M TCH* 9 6 0 3 4th
*co-coach with Jiri Tozicka

**Heyliger, Vic**
1962 WM FRG 7 2 0 5 6th
1963 WM FRG 7 1 1 5 7th
1966 WM USA 7 2 0 5 6th

**Hietanen, Olli**
1980 WM20 FIN* 5 4 0 1 S
1981 WM20 FIN 5 3 1 1 S
*co-coach with Rauno Korpio

**Hildebrand, Ike**
1959 WM CAN 8 7 0 1 G

**Hirche, Klaus**
1974 WM GDR 10 1 1 8 6th
1976 WM GDR* 10 2 1 7 8th
*co-coach with Joachim Ziesche

**Hitchcock, Ken**
2008 WM CAN 9 8 0 1 0 S
2011 WM CAN 7 4 2 0 1 5th

**Hlinka, Ivan**
1992 OG-M TCH* 8 6 0 2 B
1992 WM CZE 8 6 0 2 B
1993 WM CZE 8 6 1 1 B
1994 OG-M CZE 8 5 0 3 5th
1997 WM CZE 9 6 0 3 B
1998 OG-M CZE** 6 5 0 1 G
1998 WM CZE 9 6 2 1 B
1999 WM CZE 10 7 0 3 G
*co-coach with Jaroslav Walter
**co-coach with Slavomir Lener

**Hodges, Sarah**
2011 WW18 CAN 5 4 0 0 1 S

**Hoff, Geir**
2011 WM20 NOR 6 1 0 0 5 9th

**Hoffinger, Val**
1935 WM GER 7 4 0 3 9th
1936 OG-M GER 6 3 1 2 5th

**Hofner, Ernst**
2003 WM20 GER 6 1 0 5 9th
2005 WM20 GER 6 1 0 5 9th
2007 WM20 GER 7 2 1 0 4 9th
2009 WM20 GER 6 1 0 0 5 9th
2011 WM20 GER 6 0 0 1 4 10th

**Hogberg, Niklas**
2008 WW18 SWE 5 2 0 0 3 4
2009 WW18 SWE 5 3 0 0 2 B
2010 WW18 SWE 6 4 0 0 2 B
2011 WW SWE 5 2 1 0 2 5th
2012 WW SWE 5 1 2 0 2 5th

**Hohlfeld, Udo**
1956 OG-M AUT 6 0 1 5 10th
1957 WM AUT 7 0 1 6 7th

**Holdereid, Engelbert**
1964 OG-M FRG* 7 2 0 5 7th
*co-coach with Xaver Unsinn & Markus Egen

**Holik, Jaroslav**
2000 WM20 CZE 7 5 2 0 G
2001 WM20 CZE 7 7 0 0 G
2002 WM20 CZE 7 2 0 5 7th
2003 WM20 CZE 6 2 1 3 6th

**Hollenstein, Felix**
2007 WM18 SUI 6 2 0 1 3 6th

**Holmes, Derek**
1961 WM FIN 7 1 1 5 7th
1972 OG-M SUI* 4 0 2 2 10th
*co-coach with Gaston Pelletier
~IIHF Hall of Fame

**Holmes, Jack**
1982 WM20 SUI 7 0 0 7 8th

**Holmes, Lou**
1952 OG-M CAN 8 7 1 0 G

**Holter, Trygve**
1949 WM NOR 6 3 0 3 8th

**Honkavaara, Aarne**
1955 WM FIN 8 1 0 7 9th
1957 WM FIN 7 4 0 3 4th
1958 WM FIN 7 1 1 5 6th
1959 WM FIN 8 1 1 6 6th
1960 OG-M FIN* 6 3 1 2 7th
1963 WM FIN* 7 1 1 5 5th
1964 OG-M FIN* 7 2 0 5 6th
1965 WM FIN* 7 1 1 5 7th
1966 WM FIN* 7 2 0 5 7th
*co-coach with Joe Wirkkunen

**Horava, Miloslav**
2008 WM20 CZE 6 3 0 0 3 5th

**Horsky, Ladislav**
1977 WM20 TCH 7 4 1 2 B
1978 WM20 TCH 6 2 0 4 4th
1979 WM20 TCH 6 3 2 1 S
~IIHF Hall of Fame

**Hoshino, Nijuro**
1964 OG-M JPN 7 4 1 2 11th

**Hossa, Frantisek**
1997 WM20 SVK 6 2 0 4 6th
1998 OG-M SVK 4 1 1 2 10th
2003 WM SVK 9 7 1 1 B
2004 WM SVK 9 5 2 2 4th
2005 WM SVK 7 4 1 2 5th
2006 OG-M SVK 6 5 0 1 5th
2006 WM SVK 7 3 1 3 8th

**Howell, Harry**
1978 WM CAN 10 5 0 5 B

**Hughes, Gary**
1964 OG-M POL 7 6 0 1 9th

**Hughes, Jack**
1932 OG-M CAN 6 5 1 0 G

**Hughes, Karen**
2004 WW CAN 5 4 0 1 G

**Hutchinson, John**
1938 WM USA 6 3 1 2 7th
1939 WM USA 9 7 0 2 S

**Hynes, John**
2004 WM18 USA 6 5 0 1 S
2006 WM18 USA 6 6 0 0 G
2008 WM18 USA 7 5 0 0 2 B
2008 WM20 USA 6 4 0 0 2 4th

**Iizuka, Yuji**
2009 WW18 JPN 4 1 0 0 3 8th
2010 WW18 JPN 5 1 0 0 4 6th
2011 WW18 JPN 6 1 0 0 5 8th

**Insam, Adolf**
1998 OG-M ITA 4 1 0 3 12th
1998 WM ITA 6 2 2 2 10th
1999 WM ITA 3 0 0 3 13th
2000 WM ITA 6 1 1 4 12th

**Ionescu, Stefan**
1976 OG-M ROM* 5 4 0 1 7th
1977 WM ROM 10 1 0 9 8th
1980 OG-M ROM* 5 1 1 3 8th
*co-coach with Ion Tiron

**Ishmatov, Rafael**
2003 WM20 RUS 6 6 0 0 G
2004 WM20 RUS 6 3 1 2 5th

**Iskhakov, Ravil**
2002 WM18 RUS 8 7 0 1 S

**Itabashi, Toru**
1998 OG-W JPN 5 0 0 5 6th

**Ivany, Ron**
1984 OG-M ITA 5 2 0 3 9th

**Jackson, Jeff**
1995 WM20 USA 7 3 0 4 5th
1997 WM20 USA 6 4 1 1 S
1997 WM USA 8 4 1 3 6th
1998 WM20 USA 7 4 0 3 5th
1998 WM USA 6 1 1 4 12th
1999 WM18 USA 6 3 0 3 7th
1999 WM20 USA 6 3 0 3 8th
2000 WM18 USA 6 2 0 4 8th
2000 WM20 USA 7 2 2 3 4th

**Jagr, Jaroslav**
1995 WM20 CZE 7 3 0 4 6th

**Jalonen, Jukka**
2009 WM FIN 7 3 2 1 1 5th
2010 OG-M FIN 6 4 0 0 2 B
2010 WM FIN 7 4 0 1 2 6th
2011 WM FIN 9 5 3 0 1 G
2012 WM FIN 10 6 0 0 4 4th

**Jalonen, Kari**
2001 WM20 FIN 7 5 1 1 S

**Jansson, Folke**
1951 WM SWE* 6 4 1 1 S
1952 OG-M SWE* 9 7 0 2 B
1953 WM SWE 4 4 0 0 G
1954 WM SWE* 7 5 1 1 B
1956 OG-M SWE 7 2 1 4 4th
1957 WM SWE 7 6 1 0 G
*co-coach with Herman Carlsson

**Jansson, Lars-Gunnar**
1987 WM20 SWE 7 4 1 2 B

**Jasko, Jan**
2007 WM20 SVK 7 1 0 0 6 8th

**Jeremiah, Ed**
1964 OG-M USA 7 2 0 5 5th

**Johansen, Roy**
2006 WM NOR 6 1 0 5 11th
2007 WM NOR 6 1 1 0 4 14th
2008 WM NOR 7 1 0 1 5 8th
2009 WM NOR 6 0 1 2 3 11th
2010 OG-M NOR 4 0 0 1 3 10th
2010 WM NOR 6 3 0 0 3 9th
2011 WM NOR 7 3 1 0 3 6th
2012 WM NOR 8 4 0 1 3 8th

**Johnson, Bob**
1975 WM USA 10 0 0 10 6th
1976 OG-M USA 5 2 0 3 5th
1981 WM USA 8 4 1 3 5th
1981 CC USA 6 2 1 3 4th
1984 CC USA 6 3 1 2 4th
1987 CC USA 5 2 0 3 5th
1991 CC USA 8 5 0 3 2nd

**Johnson, Mark**
2007 WW USA 5 3 0 1 1 S
2009 WW18 USA 5 4 1 0 0 G
2009 WW USA 5 4 0 0 1 G
2010 OG-W USA 5 4 0 0 1 S

**Johansson, Lennart**
1977 WM20 SWE 7 3 0 4 5th

**Johansson, Peter**
2003 WM18 SWE 6 2 1 3 5th

**Johnston, Marshall**
1977 WM20 USA 7 1 1 5 7th
1979 WM CAN 8 3 0 5 4th
1982 WM CAN 10 5 2 3 B

**Johnston, Mike**
1999 WM CAN 9 6 0 3 4th
2009 WM18 CAN 6 3 1 1 1 4th

**Jortikka, Hannu**
1986 WM20 FIN 7 3 0 4 6th
1987 WM20 FIN 7 5 1 1 G
1988 WM20 FIN 7 5 1 1 B
1988 OG-M FIN* 8 5 1 2 S
1990 WM20 FIN 7 4 1 2 4th
1997 WM20 FIN 6 4 0 2 5th
2010 WM20 FIN 6 3 0 0 3 5th
*co-coach with Pentti Matikiainen

**Jost, Richard**
2011 WM20 SUI 6 2 1 0 3 5th

**Julien, Claude**
2000 WM20 CAN 7 4 2 1 B

**Justra, Jiri**
1986 WM20 TCH* 7 4 0 3 4th
1987 WM20 TCH 7 5 0 2 S
*co-coach with Julius Cernicky

**Kalintsev, Alexei**
2006 OG-W RUS 5 2 0 3 6th

**Kalous, Jiri**
2001 WM18 CZE 7 3 0 4 4th

**Kamenetski, Jakov**
1999 WW RUS 5 1 0 4 6th

**Kammerer, Rene**
2006 OG-W SUI 5 1 0 4 7th
2007 WW SUI 4 2 0 0 2 5th
2008 WW SUI 5 2 1 0 2 4th
2009 WW SUI 4 1 1 1 1 7th
2010 OG-W SUI 5 2 1 0 2 5th
2011 WW SUI 5 1 1 2 1 6th
2012 WW SUI 6 4 0 0 2 B

**Kanareykin, Fedor**
2006 WM18 RUS 5 3 0 2 5th

**Kaneda, Yuji**
1968 OG-M JPN* 5 4 0 1 10th
*co-coach with Tadao Nakajima

**Kapanen, Hannu**
1998 WM20 FIN 7 6 1 0 G
2000 WM20 FIN 7 2 1 4 7th

**Karafiat, Miroslav**
2010 OG-W SVK 5 0 0 0 5 8th
2011 WW SVK 5 1 1 0 3 7th
2012 WW SVK 5 1 0 1 3 8th

**Karjalainen, Seppo**
2008 WW18 FIN 5 1 0 0 4 6th

**Kasprzak, Zbigniew**
1948 OG-M POL 8 2 0 6 6th

**Kasprzycki, Mieczyslaw**
1952 OG-M POL 8 2 1 5 6th

**Kathan, Peter**
2004 WW GER 4 1 0 3 6th
2005 WW GER 5 2 1 2 5th
2006 OG-W GER 5 3 0 2 5th
2007 WW GER 4 1 0 0 3 8th
2008 WW GER 4 1 0 0 3 9th
2008 WW18 GER 5 3 0 0 2 5th
2010 WW18 GER 6 1 1 0 4 4th
2012 WW GER 5 2 1 1 1 7th

**Kay, Karen**
1994 WW USA 5 4 0 1 S

**Keenan, Mike**
1980 WM20 CAN 5 3 0 2 5th
1987 CC CAN 8 5 2 1 1st
1991 CC CAN 8 6 2 0 1st
1993 WM CAN 8 6 0 2 4th

**Kelly, Mike**
2003 WM18 CAN 7 5 1 1 G

**Kennedy, Ron**
1994 WM AUT 6 1 1 4 8th
1998 OG-M AUT 4 0 2 2 14th
1998 WM AUT 3 0 0 3 15th
1999 WM AUT 6 3 0 3 10th
2000 WM AUT 6 2 2 2 13th
2001 WM AUT 6 2 0 4 11th
2002 OG-M AUT 4 1 0 3 12th
2002 WM AUT 6 1 0 5 12th

**Kiessling, Gerhard**
1957 WM GDR 7 3 0 4 5th
1959 WM FRG 8 5 1 2 9th
1971 WM FRG 10 2 0 8 5th
1972 OG-M FRG 4 3 0 1 7th
1972 WM FRG 10 2 0 8 5th
1973 WM FRG 10 1 0 9 6th

**Kilger, Bob**
1981 WM20 CAN 5 1 1 3 7th

**Killias, Rudolf**
1976 OG-M SUI 5 2 0 3 11th
1984 OG-M AUT 5 1 0 4 11th

**Kilrea, Brian**
1984 WM20 CAN 7 4 1 2 4th

**Kimijan, Miroslav**
1999 WM18 SVK 7 5 0 2 B
2000 WM18 SVK 6 3 0 3 5th

**Kinding, Bjorn**
1998 OG-M JPN 4 1 1 2 13th

**King, Dave**
1982 WM20 CAN 7 6 1 0 G
1983 WM20 CAN 7 4 1 2 B
1983 WM CAN 10 6 0 4 B
1984 OG-M CAN 7 4 0 3 4th
1987 WM CAN 10 3 2 5 4th
1988 OG-M CAN 8 5 1 2 4th
1989 WM CAN 10 7 0 3 S
1990 WM CAN 10 6 1 3 4th
1991 WM CAN 10 5 3 2 S
1992 OG-M CAN 8 6 0 2 S
1992 WM CAN 6 2 1 3 8th
~IIHF Hall of Fame

**King, Katie**
2010 WW18 USA 5 4 0 1 0 S

**Kingston, George**
1990 WM20 NOR 7 2 0 5 6th
1990 WM NOR 10 1 1 8 8th
1991 WM20 NOR 7 0 0 7 8th
1994 WM CAN 8 8 0 0 G
1995 WM GER 5 1 0 4 9th
1996 WM GER 6 2 0 4 8th
1996 WCH GER 4 1 0 3 6th
1997 WM GER 8 2 0 6 11th
1998 OG-M GER 4 3 0 1 9th
1998 WM GER 6 1 2 3 11th

**Kirkvaag, Rolf**
1964 OG-M NOR 7 5 0 2 10th

**Kiselev, Vladimir**
1985 WM20 URS 7 5 0 2 B

**Kleinendorst, Kurt**
2010 WM18 USA 7 6 0 0 1 G

**Klinisovs, Aleksandrs**
2007 WM18 LAT 6 0 0 0 6 10th

**Kluc, Vladimir**
1972 OG-M YUG 4 0 1 3 11th

**Knoll, Hermann**
1981 WM20 AUT 5 0 0 5 8th

**Kolliker, Jakob**
2000 WM20 SUI 7 3 0 4 6th
2001 WM20 SUI 7 2 1 4 6th
2002 WM20 SUI 7 3 0 4 4th
2003 WM20 SUI 6 3 0 3 7th
2004 WM20 SUI 6 2 0 4 8th
2005 WM20 SUI 6 2 0 4 8th
2006 WM20 SUI 6 2 2 2 7th
2007 WM20 SUI 7 4 0 0 3 7th
2008 WM20 SUI 6 1 0 1 4 9th
2010 WM20 SUI 7 2 1 0 4 4th
2012 WM GER 7 2 0 0 5 12th

**Kominek, Vladimir**
1964 OG-M HUN 7 0 0 7 16th

**Kopecky, Jiri**
2010 WM18 CZE 6 2 0 1 3 6th

**Kopitar, Matjaz**
2011 WM SLO 6 1 0 1 4 16th

**Kopriva, Bretislav**
2002 WM18 CZE 8 7 0 1 B
2005 WM18 CZE 7 4 0 3 4th

**Korpio, Rauno**
1980 WM20 FIN* 5 4 0 1 S
1986 WM FIN 10 4 3 3 4th
1987 WM FIN 10 5 1 4 5th
1987 CC FIN 5 0 0 5 6th
1997 WW FIN 5 3 1 1 B
1998 OG-W FIN 6 4 0 2 B
*co-coach with Olli Hietanen

**Kosarev, Barys**
2000 WM18 BLR 6 0 0 6 10th

**Kostka, Vladimir**
1957 WM TCH^ 7 5 1 1 B
1961 WM TCH** 7 6 1 0 S
1965 WM TCH+ 7 6 0 1 S
1966 WM TCH+ 7 6 0 1 S
1967 WM TCH* 7 3 2 2 4th
1968 OG-M TCH* 7 5 1 1 S
1969 WM TCH* 10 8 0 2 B
1970 WM TCH* 10 5 1 4 B
1971 WM TCH* 10 7 1 2 S
1972 OG-M TCH* 5 3 0 2 B
1972 WM TCH* 10 9 1 0 G
1973 WM TCH* 10 6 1 3 B
1984 OG-M TCH 7 6 0 1 S
^co-coach with Bohumil Rejda
**co-coach with Jiri Andrst
+co-coach with Vladimir Bouzek
*co-coach with Jaroslav Pitner
~IIHF Hall of Fame

**Kostriukov, Anatoli**
1983 WM20 URS 7 7 0 0 G
1988 WM20 URS 7 6 0 1 S

**Krikunov, Vladimir**
2002 OG-M BLR 9 3 0 6 4th
2003 WM BLR 6 2 0 4 14th
2005 WM RUS 9 6 2 1 B
2006 OG-M RUS 8 5 0 3 4th
2006 WM RUS 7 5 1 1 5th

**Kroge, Gunnar**
1965 WM NOR* 7 0 0 7 8th
*co-coach with Ake Brask

**Kromm, Bobby**
1961 WM CAN 7 6 1 0 G
1963 WM CAN 7 4 1 2 4th

**Krueger, Ralph**
1998 WM SUI 9 2 1 6 4th
1999 WM SUI 6 2 0 4 8th
2000 WM SUI 7 2 2 3 6th
2001 WM SUI 6 2 0 4 9th
2002 WM SUI 6 2 0 4 10th
2003 WM SUI 7 3 0 4 8th
2002 OG-M SUI 4 2 1 1 11th
2004 WM SUI 7 2 2 3 8th
2005 WM SUI 7 3 1 3 8th
2006 OG-M SUI 6 2 2 2 6th
2006 WM SUI 6 2 2 2 9th
2007 WM SUI 7 3 0 0 4 8th
2008 WM SUI 7 4 0 0 3 7th
2009 WM SUI 6 1 2 0 3 9th
2010 OG-M SUI 5 1 1 1 2 8th

**Krupp, Uwe**
2006 OG-M GER 5 0 2 3 10th
2007 WM GER 6 3 0 0 3 9th
2008 WM GER 6 2 0 0 4 10th
2009 WM GER 6 1 0 1 4 15th
2010 OG-M GER 4 0 0 0 4 11th
2010 WM GER 9 3 1 1 4 4th
2011 WM GER 7 2 1 2 2 7th

**Krutov, Viktor**
2004 WW RUS 4 2 0 2 5th
2005 WW RUS 5 0 1 4 8th

**Kryuchkov, Vladimir**
2003 WM18 RUS 6 5 0 1 B

**Kuchar, Waclaw**
1947 WM POL 7 2 0 5 6th

**Kucherenko, Vladimir**
2007 WW RUS 4 2 0 0 2 7th
2008 WW RUS 4 1 0 0 3 6th

**Kuhnhackl, Erich**
1989 WM FRG* 10 1 2 7 7th
1993 WM20 GER 7 1 0 6 7th
1994 WM20 GER 7 1 0 6 7th
1995 WM20 GER 7 1 0 6 7th
1996 WM20 GER 6 1 2 3 8th
1997 WM20 GER 6 1 0 5 9th
*co-coach with Xaver Unsinn

**Kuitunen, Samu**
1991 WM20 FIN 7 3 1 3 5th

**Kulagin, Boris**
1975 WM URS 10 10 0 0 G
1976 OG-M URS 5 5 0 0 G
1976 WM URS 10 6 1 3 S
1977 WM URS 10 7 0 3 B

**Kulej, Lucjan**
1936 OG-M POL* 3 1 0 2 9th
*co-coach with Alexander Tupalski

**Kulikov, Olexander**
2000 WM20 UKR 6 1 0 5 10th

**Kunzi, Res**
1984 WM20 SUI 7 0 0 7 8th

**Kurek, Jozef**
1976 OG-M POL 5 1 0 4 6th

**Kvist, Henry**
1949 WM FIN 2 0 0 2 7th

**Kyle, Walt**
1992 WM20 USA 7 5 0 2 B
1993 WM20 USA 7 4 0 3 4th
2006 WM20 USA 7 3 1 3 4th

**Lacroix, Robert**
1924 OG-M FRA 3 1 0 2 5th

**LaLiberte, Pete**
1968 OG-M FRA 5 0 0 5 14th

**Lalonde, Herve**
1964 OG-M SUI 7 0 0 7 8th

**Larntvedt, Johnny**
1958 WM NOR 7 1 0 6 7th
1959 WM NOR 8 4 1 3 8th

**Larsson, Kjell**
1982 WM20 SWE 7 4 0 3 5th
1985 WM20 SWE 7 3 0 4 5th
1988 OG-M FRA 6 2 0 4 11th
1992 OG-M FRA 8 2 0 6 8th
1992 WM FRA 5 1 0 4 10th
1994 OG-M FRA 7 1 1 5 10th
1994 WM FRA 5 1 0 4 10th

**Larsson, Peo**
2003 WM20 SWE 6 2 0 4 8th

**Lator, Geza**
1935 WM HUN 5 2 2 1 11th
1936 OG-M HUN 6 2 0 4 7th
1937 WM HUN 9 3 2 4 5th
1938 WM HUN 6 2 1 3 7th

**Laurila, Harri**
2007 WM18 FIN 6 3 0 1 2 7th
2010 WW18 FIN 5 2 0 1 2 5

**Lautenschlager, Beat**
2000 WM18 SUI 7 4 0 3 4th

**Laviolette, Peter**
2004 WM USA 9 5 1 3 B
2005 WM USA 7 3 2 2 6th
2006 OG-M USA 6 1 1 4 8th

**Lawton, Les**
1994 WW CAN 5 5 0 0 G

**Lefley, Bryan**
1992 WM ITA 5 1 1 3 9th
1993 WM ITA 6 1 2 3 8th
1994 OG-M ITA 7 3 0 4 9th
1994 WM ITA 6 3 0 3 6th
1995 WM ITA 6 3 1 2 7th
1996 WM ITA 6 2 1 3 7th
1997 WM ITA 8 3 1 4 8th

**Leime, Heikki**
2002 OG-M FRA 4 0 1 3 14th
2004 WM FRA 6 0 1 5 16th

**Leinweber, Bruno**
1953 WM FRG 4 1 0 3 S
1954 WM FRG 7 2 1 4 5th

**Lejczyk, Leszek**
1986 WM POL 10 1 1 8 8th
1988 OG-M POL 6 0 1 5 10th
1989 WM POL 10 1 0 9 8th
1990 WM20 POL 7 0 0 7 8th
1992 OG-M POL 7 1 0 6 11th
1992 WM POL 6 0 0 6 12th

**Le Mat, Raoul**
1920 OG-M SWE 6 3 0 3 4th

**Lener, Slavomir**
1996 WM20 CZE 6 2 2 2 4th
1997 WM CZE* 9 6 0 3 B
1998 OG-M CZE* 6 5 0 1 G
1998 WM CZE* 9 6 2 1 B
2003 WM CZE 9 6 1 2 4th
2004 WM CZE 7 6 0 1 5th
*co-coach with Ivan Hlinka

**Lennartsson, Bo**
2001 WM20 SWE 7 3 0 4 4th
2002 WM20 SWE 7 3 2 2 6th

**Liitsola, Seppo**
1969 WM FIN** 10 2 0 8 5th
1970 WM FIN 10 5 0 5 4th
1971 WM FIN* 10 4 1 5 4th
1972 OG-M FIN* 5 2 0 3 5th
1972 WM FIN* 10 4 0 6 4th
1975 WM FIN 10 5 0 5 4th
1976 OG-M FIN 5 2 0 3 4th
1976 WM FIN+ 10 2 4 4 5th
*co-coach with Rauli Virtanen
**co-coach with Gustav Bubnik
+co-coach with Lasse Heikkila

**Lilyholm, Len**
1978 WM20 USA 6 4 0 2 5th

**Lindberg, Hans "Virus"**
1976 WM SWE 10 6 0 4 B
1976 CC SWE 5 2 1 2 4th
1977 WM SWE 10 7 0 3 S
1978 WM SWE 10 4 0 6 4th
1991 WM SUI 10 2 1 7 7th

**Lindgren, Lars**
2007 WM18 SWE 6 3 1 0 2 B

**Lindquist, Vic**
1936 OG-M SWE 5 2 0 3 5th

**Lindroos, Risto**
1951 WM FIN 6 1 0 5 7th
1952 OG-M FIN 8 2 0 6 7th
1954 WM FIN 7 1 1 5 6th

**Lindstrom, Curt**
1986 WM SWE 10 6 2 2 S
1994 OG-M FIN 8 7 0 1 B*
1994 WM FIN 8 6 1 1 S
1995 WM FIN 8 6 1 1 G
1996 WM FIN 6 2 2 2 5th
1996 WCH FIN 4 2 0 2 5th
1997 WM FIN 8 5 0 3 5th
2002 OG-M LAT 4 2 1 1 9th
2002 WM LAT 6 1 0 5 11th
2003 WM LAT 6 3 0 3 9th
2004 WM LAT 6 2 2 2 7th
*co-coach with Hannu Aravirta

**Linstad, Heather**
2012 WW18 USA 5 4 0 0 1 S

**Lisspers, Lars**
2000 WM18 SWE 6 5 0 1 B

**Loicq, Paul**
1920 OG-M BEL 1 0 0 1 7th
~IIHF Hall of Fame

**Lorenz, Frantisek**
1928 OG-M TCH 2 1 0 1 6th

**Lovdal, Orjan**
2001 WM18 NOR 6 1 2 3 9th
2006 WM18 NOR 6 0 2 4 10th
2009 WM18 NOR 6 1 0 0 5 9th
2011 WM18 NOR 6 1 0 0 5 9th

**Lubnin, Sergei**
1999 WM18 UKR 6 2 0 4 8th
2000 WM18 UKR 6 1 1 4 9th
2001 WM18 UKR 7 0 0 7 10th
2004 WM20 UKR 6 0 1 5 10th

**Luckner, Harald**
1996 WM20 SWE 7 4 1 2 S
1997 WM20 SWE 6 2 1 3 8th
1998 WM20 SWE 7 3 0 4 6th

**Ludwiczak, Witalis**
1955 WM POL* 8 2 0 6 7th
*co-coach with Kazimierz Osmanski

**Lukkarila, Jouko**
1999 WM18 FIN 7 5 1 1 G
2001 WW FIN 5 2 0 3 4th
2002 OG-W FIN 5 2 0 3 4th

**Lunde, Len**
1973 WM FIN 10 3 1 6 4th

**Lundh, Stephan**
1999 WM SWE* 9 7 0 2 B
2000 WM SWE** 7 3 1 3 7th
2008 WM18 SWE 6 4 0 0 2 4th
2009 WM18 SWE 6 4 0 0 2 5th
2010 WM18 SWE 6 5 0 0 1 S
*co-coach with Sune Bergman
**co-coach with Hardy Nilsson

**Lundmark, Curt**
1990 WM20 SWE 7 4 1 2 5th
1993 WM SWE 8 5 0 3 S
1994 OG-M SWE 8 6 1 1 G
1994 WM SWE 8 5 1 2 B
1995 WM SWE 8 5 1 2 S

**Lundstrom, Lars-Erik**
1999 WM18 SWE 7 4 2 1 S

**Lundstrom, Mikael**
1999 WM FRA 3 0 0 3 15th
2003 WM DEN 6 1 1 4 11th
2004 WM DEN 6 1 0 5 12th
2005 WM DEN 6 2 0 4 14th
2006 WM DEN 6 2 1 3 13th

**Lynch, Bernie**
1983 WM20 NOR 7 0 0 7 8th

**Lytkis, Ivar**
1937 WM NOR 2 0 0 2 9th

**Maattanen, Raimo**
1974 WM FIN 10 4 2 4 4th
*co-coach with Kalevi Numminen

**MacLeod, Don**
1990 WW USA 5 4 0 1 S

**MacTavish, Craig**
2010 WM CAN 7 3 0 0 4 7th

**Magwood, John**
1934 WM GBR 6 4 0 2 8th

**Mahon, Mark**
2004 WM JPN 6 0 2 4 15th

**Maier, Roger**
1992 WW SUI 5 0 0 5 8th

**Malez, Jerzy**
1987 WM20 POL 7 1 0 6 5th

**Maltsev, Alexander**
2001 WW KAZ 5 0 0 5 8th
2002 OG-W KAZ 5 0 0 5 8th
2005 WW KAZ 5 1 1 3 7th
2009 WW KAZ 4 0 1 0 3 6th
2011 WW KAZ 5 0 0 1 4 8th

**Manners, Rem**
1936 OG-M AUT 6 2 0 4 7th

**Mantha, Moe**
2003 WM18 USA 6 3 1 2 4th

**Mariucci, John**
1956 OG-M USA 7 5 0 2 S
1976 WM USA* 10 3 1 6 4th
1977 WM USA 10 3 1 6 6th
1978 WM USA 10 2 2 6 6th
*co-coach with Glen Gostick

**Marjamaki, Lauri**
2011 WM20 FIN 6 3 0 3 0 6th

**Marsh, Larry**
1939 WM LAT 6 3 0 3 10th

**Martinec, Vladimir**
1997 WM20 CZE 7 2 2 3 4th
1998 WM20 CZE 7 3 1 3 4th
1999 WM20 CZE 6 3 0 3 7th

**Marts, Par**
2008 WM20 SWE 6 4 1 1 0 S
2009 WM20 SWE 6 5 0 0 1 S
2010 WM20 SWE 6 5 0 0 1 B
2011 WM SWE 9 6 0 1 2 S
2012 WM SWE 8 6 0 0 2 6th

**Marttila, Mika**
2009 WM18 FIN 6 3 1 0 2 B

**Marvin, Cal**
1958 WM USA 7 3 1 3 5th

**Maselko, Zdzislaw**
1966 WM POL 7 0 0 7 8th

**Maticins, Andrejs**
2009 WM20 LAT 6 2 0 0 4 8th
2010 WM20 LAT 6 1 0 0 5 9th

**Matikainen, Pentti**
1984 WM20 FIN 7 6 0 1 S
1985 WM20 FIN 7 4 2 1 4th
1988 OG-M FIN* 8 5 1 2 S
1989 WM FIN 10 5 1 4 5th
1990 WM FIN 10 2 2 7 6th
1991 WM FIN 10 6 1 3 5th
1991 CC FIN 6 2 1 3 3rd
1992 OG-M FIN 8 4 1 3 7th
1992 WM FIN 8 7 0 1 S
1993 WM FIN 6 2 1 3 7th
*co-coach with Hannu Jortikka

**Maxwell, Fred "Steamer"**
1920 OG-M CAN 3 3 0 0 G

**Mayasich, John**
1969 WM USA 10 0 0 10 6th

**McCurdy, Russ**
1992 WW USA 5 4 0 1 S

**McEachern, Bud**
1951 WM NOR 6 2 0 4 4th
1952 OG-M NOR 8 0 0 8 9th
1960 OG-M AUS 6 0 0 6 9th

**McEwen, Brent**
1997 WM NOR 8 0 1 7 12th

**McKenna, Jodi**
2011 WW18 USA 5 5 0 0 0 G

**McLean, Ernie**
1978 WM20 CAN 6 4 0 2 B
1979 WM20 CAN 5 3 0 2 5th

**McLeod, Jackie**
1966 WM CAN 7 5 0 2 B
1967 WM CAN 7 4 1 2 B
1968 OG-M CAN 7 5 0 2 B
1969 WM CAN 10 4 0 6 4th

**McMaster, Dave**
1990 WW CAN 5 5 0 0 G

**Medri, Giampiero**
1936 OG-M ITA 3 1 0 2 9th

**Melenchuk, Vladimir**
2001 WM20 BLR 6 1 1 4 9th
2002 WM20 BLR 6 1 0 5 9th
2003 WM20 BLR 6 0 0 6 10th

**Mellgren, Sten**
1928 OG-M SWE* 5 3 1 1 S
*co-coach with Viking Harbom

**Michaud, Diane**
2004 WW SUI 4 1 0 3 8th

**Mikes, Stefan**
2008 WM20 SVK 6 3 0 0 3 7th
2009 WM20 SVK 7 2 1 0 4 4th
2010 WM20 SVK 6 2 0 0 4 8th
2011 WM20 SVK 6 1 1 0 4 8th

**Mikhailov, Boris**
1993 WM RUS 8 5 1 2 G
1994 WM RUS 6 4 0 2 5th
1995 WM RUS 6 5 0 1 5th
1996 WCH RUS 5 2 0 3 4th
2001 WM RUS 7 4 0 3 6th
2002 WM RUS 9 4 1 4 S

**Mikhalev, Sergei**
2006 WM20 RUS 6 5 0 1 S

**Miller, Shannon**
1997 WW CAN 5 5 0 0 G
1998 OG-W CAN 6 4 0 2 S

**Milton, Kjell-Rune**
2001 WM18 SWE 7 5 0 2 7th

**Miluns, Eriks**
2012 WM20 LAT 6 0 1 0 5 9th

**Minder, Frigyes**
1930 WM HUN 2 1 0 1 6th
1931 WM HUN 4 3 0 1 7th
1933 WM HUN 6 1 1 4 7th

**Misek, Petr**
1999 WM18 CZE 7 3 1 3 5th

**Miyazaki, Yoshihiro**
1976 OG-M JPN 5 3 0 2 9th

**Mlcoh, Oldrich**
1968 OG-M YUG 5 5 0 0 9th

**Moiseyev, Yuri**
1993 WM20 RUS 7 2 2 3 6th

**Molin, Lars**
2000 WM20 SWE 7 5 0 2 5th

**Montour, France**
1997 WW SUI 5 1 1 3 7th

**Morozov, Yuri**
1980 WM20 URS 5 5 0 0 G
1981 WM20 URS 5 3 0 2 B

**Mowat, J.B.**
1951 WM GBR 6 1 1 4 5th

**Muller, Paul**
1924 OG-M SUI 3 0 0 3 7th

**Murray, Andy**
1997 WM CAN 11 7 1 3 G
1998 WM CAN 6 3 2 1 6th
2003 WM CAN 9 8 1 0 G
2007 WM CAN 9 8 1 0 0 G
~IIHF Hall of Fame

**Murray, John**
1962 WM GBR 7 1 0 6 8th

**Murray, Terry**
1999 WM USA 6 3 0 3 6th

**Myhre, Geir**
1995 WM NOR 5 1 0 4 10th
1996 WM NOR 5 1 2 2 9th

**Myshagin, Nikolai**
2004 WM KAZ 6 2 1 3 13th
2005 WM KAZ 6 1 0 5 12th
2006 OG-M KAZ 5 1 0 4 9th
2006 WM KAZ 6 1 0 5 15th

**Najman, Karel**
2003 WM18 CZE 6 2 1 3 6th

**Nakajima, Tadao**
1968 OG-M JPN* 5 4 0 1 10th
*co-coach with Yuji Kaneda

**Narvestad, Johan**
1950 WM NOR 7 1 0 6 6th
1962 WM NOR 7 3 0 4 5th

**Nemchinov, Sergei**
2008 WM20 RUS 7 5 0 1 1 B
2009 WM20 RUS 7 5 0 1 1 B

**Nevesely, Stanislav**
1991 WM TCH 10 4 0 6 6th
1991 CC TCH 5 1 0 4 6th
1994 WM CZE 6 1 2 3 7th

**Nicklin, Percy**
1936 OG-M GBR 7 5 2 0 G
1937 WM GBR 9 8 0 1 S
1938 WM GBR 8 6 1 1 S
1939 WM GBR 5 2 0 3 8th

**Nikodemowicz, Emil**
1984 OG-M POL 6 1 0 5 8th

**Nilsson, Hardy**
2000 WM SWE* 7 3 1 3 7th
2001 WM SWE 9 6 1 2 B
2002 OG-M SWE 4 3 0 1 5th
2002 WM SWE 9 7 0 2 B
2003 WM SWE 9 7 0 2 S
2004 WM SWE 9 6 2 1 S
2004 WCH SWE 4 2 1 1 5th
*co-coach with Stephan Lundh

**Nishiura, Kiyoteru**
1957 WM JPN 7 0 1 6 8th

**Nittel, Rainer**
1999 WW GER 5 2 0 3 7th
2000 WW GER 5 1 0 4 7th
2001 WW GER 5 2 1 2 6th
2002 OG-W GER 5 1 1 3 6th

**Nobuta. Kenji**
2004 WW JPN 4 0 0 4 9th

**Nokelainen, Esko**
1994 WM20 FIN 7 4 0 3 4th

**Nolan, Ted**
2012 WM LAT 7 2 0 0 5 10th

**Novotny, Jindrich**
2003 WM18 SVK 7 5 0 2 S
2004 WM18 SVK 6 1 3 2 6th

**Numminen, Kalevi**
1974 WM FIN* 10 4 2 4 4th
1978 WM FIN 10 2 2 6 7th
1979 WM FIN 8 4 1 3 5th
1980 OG-M FIN 7 3 1 3 4th
1981 WM FIN 8 3 2 3 6th
1981 CC FIN 5 0 1 4 6th
1982 WM FIN 7 3 1 3 5th
*co-coach with Raimo Maattanen
~IIHF Hall of Fame

**Ohlson, Bengt "Fisken"**
1978 WM20 SWE 7 4 1 2 S
1979 WM20 SWE 6 4 1 1 B
1980 WM20 SWE 5 2 1 2 B
1981 WM SWE 8 5 1 2 S
1991 WM20 SWE 7 3 0 4 6th
1992 OG-M NOR 7 2 0 5 9th
1992 WM NOR 5 1 0 4 10th
1993 WM NOR 7 2 0 5 11th
1994 OG-M NOR 7 1 0 6 11th
1994 WM NOR 6 1 2 3 11th
1997 WW SWE 5 2 1 2 5th
1998 OG-W SWE 5 1 0 4 5th

**Olejnik, Ladislav**
1979 WM20 FRG 5 1 0 4 7th
1980 WM20 FRG 5 2 0 3 6th
1991 WM GER 10 0 2 8 8th

**Oliver, Scotty**
1935 WM CAN 7 7 0 0 G

**Onikura, Hiroki**
1960 OG-M JPN 6 2 1 3 8th

**Oppliger, Charly**
2001 WM18 SUI 7 4 0 3 S

**Orskaug, Torbjorn**
1997 WW NOR 5 0 1 4 8th

**Osmanski, Kazimierz**
1955 WM POL* 8 2 0 6 7th
*co-coach with Witalis Ludwiczak

**Oystila, Jouko**
1990 WW FIN 5 3 0 2 B
1992 WW FIN 5 3 0 2 B

**Paiement, Real**
1998 WM20 CAN 7 2 0 5 8th

**Pajouja, Juha**
2005 WM18 FIN 7 4 0 3 7th

**Palus, Mieczyslaw**
1956 OG-M POL* 5 2 0 3 8th
*co-coach with Wladyslaw Wiro-Kiro

**Pankov, Vasili**
2006 WM18 BLR 6 1 1 4 9th

**Pantev, Pantelei**
1976 OG-M BUL 5 0 0 5 13th

**Parfyonov, Andrei**
2012 WM18 RUS 6 3 0 0 3 5th

**Parker, Jack**
1996 WM20 USA 6 3 0 3 5th

**Parmstrom, Anders**
1981 CC SWE 5 1 0 4 5th
1982 WM SWE 10 3 3 4 4th
1983 WM SWE 10 4 1 5 4th
1984 OG-M SWE 7 3 1 3 B

**Paruszewski, Zenon**
1939 WM POL 7 3 0 4 6th

**Pearn, Perry**
1993 WM20 CAN 7 6 0 1 G

**Pelino, Mike**
2002 WM18 CAN 8 3 0 5 6th

**Pelletier, Gaston**
1972 OG-M SUI* 4 0 2 2 10th
1972 WM SUI 10 1 0 9 6th
*co-coach with Derek Holmes

**Perkuhn, Helmut**
1978 WM20 FRG 6 1 0 5 7th
1981 WM20 FRG 5 3 0 2 5th

**Perpich, John**
1984 WM20 USA 7 2 0 5 6th

**Pesout, Martin**
2006 WM18 CZE 7 4 0 3 B
2007 WM18 CZE 6 2 1 0 3 9th

**Peterson, Dave**
1985 WM USA 10 4 1 5 4th
1986 WM20 USA 7 4 0 3 B
1986 WM USA 10 4 0 6 6th
1987 WM20 USA 7 4 0 3 4th
1987 WM USA 10 4 0 6 7th
1988 OG-M USA 6 3 0 3 7th
1992 OG-M USA 8 5 1 2 4th

**Pettersson, Ronald**
1975 WM SWE 10 5 0 5 B
1980 OG-M NOR 5 0 1 4 11th

**Piatanov, Andrei**
2000 WM18 RUS 6 5 0 1 S

**Pietila, Sakari**
2010 WM18 FIN 6 4 1 0 1 B

**Piper, Elmer**
1939 WM CAN 8 8 0 0 G

**Pitner, Jaroslav**
1967 WM TCH* 7 3 2 2 4th
1968 OG-M TCH* 7 5 1 1 S
1969 WM TCH* 10 8 0 2 4th
1970 WM TCH* 10 5 1 4 B
1971 WM TCH* 10 7 1 2 S
1972 OG-M TCH* 5 3 0 2 B
1972 WM TCH* 10 9 1 0 G
1973 WM TCH* 10 6 1 3 B
*co-coach with Vladimir Kostka

**Pleban, John**
1950 WM USA 7 5 0 2 S
1952 OG-M USA 8 6 1 1 S
1961 WM USA 7 1 1 5 6th
1962 WM USA 7 5 0 2 B

**Plyushev, Vladimir**
2001 WM18 RUS 6 5 0 1 G
2002 WM20 RUS 7 5 0 2 G
2003 WM RUS 7 3 0 4 7th
2009 WM18 RUS 7 5 0 0 2 S
2010 WM20 RUS 6 3 0 1 2 6th

**Pock, Herbert**
2003 WM AUT 6 2 0 4 10th
2004 WM AUT 6 1 2 3 11th
2005 WM AUT 6 0 1 5 16th

**Polutnik, Rick**
1992 WW CAN 5 5 0 0 G

**Popikhin, Yevgeni**
2007 WM20 RUS 6 5 0 0 1 S

**Poplimont, Andre**
1924 OG-M BEL 3 0 0 3 7th

**Porges, Antonin**
1936 OG-M TCH 8 5 0 3 4th

**Pospisil, Frantisek**
1982 WM20 TCH 7 5 1 1 S
1983 WM20 TCH 7 5 1 1 S
1984 WM20 TCH 7 5 0 2 B
1985 WM20 TCH 7 5 2 0 S
1988 OG-M TCH 8 4 0 4 6th*
*co-coach with Jan Starsi

**Poss, Greg**
2005 WM GER 6 1 1 4 15th

**Prerost, Miroslav**
2011 WM20 CZE 6 3 0 0 3 7th
2012 WM20 CZE 6 3 0 1 2 5th

**Prettyman, Bert**
1936 OG-M USA 8 5 1 2 B

**Pudas, Al**
1936 OG-M CAN 8 7 0 1 S

**Pulford, Bob**
1976 CC USA 5 1 1 3 5th

**Pysz, Wiktor**
2002 WM POL 6 2 0 4 14th

**Quinn, Francis**
1937 WM ROM 3 0 0 3 9th

**Quinn, Pat**
1986 WM CAN 10 4 0 6 B
2002 OG-M CAN 6 4 1 1 G
2004 WCH CAN 6 6 0 0 1st
2006 OG-M CAN 6 3 0 3 7th
2008 WM18 CAN 7 6 0 0 1 G
2009 WM20 CAN 6 5 1 0 0 G

**Ralby, Herb**
1947 WM USA 7 4 0 3 5th

**Rampf, Hans**
1977 WM20 FRG 7 2 0 5 6th
1977 WM FRG 10 2 1 7 7th
1978 WM FRG 10 3 3 4 5th
1979 WM FRG 8 3 1 4 6th
1980 OG-M FRG 5 1 0 4 10th
1981 WM FRG 8 3 1 4 7th
1982 WM20 FRG 7 1 0 6 7th
1983 WM20 FRG 7 1 0 6 7th
1984 WM20 FRG 7 1 0 6 7th
1985 WM20 FRG 7 0 1 6 7th
1986 WM20 FRG 7 0 0 7 8th
1988 WM20 FRG 7 1 0 6 7th
1989 WM20 FRG 7 0 0 7 8th
1992 WM20 GER 7 1 0 6 7th

**Rankin, Frank**
1924 OG-M CAN 5 5 0 0 G

**Rautakorpi, Jukka**
1999 WM20 FIN 6 3 0 3 5th
2008 WM20 FIN 6 1 1 0 4 6th
2009 WM20 FIN 6 3 0 1 2 7th
2011 WM18 FIN 6 3 0 0 3 5th

**Reigle, Ed**
1958 WM SWE 7 5 0 2 B
1959 WM SWE 8 3 1 4 5th
1960 OG-M SWE 7 2 1 4 5th
1967 WM FRG 7 0 1 6 8th
1968 OG-M FRG 7 1 0 6 7th

**Reindl, Franz**
1993 WM GER 6 4 0 2 5th
1994 OG-M GER* 8 4 0 4 7th
2004 WCH GER 4 0 0 4 8th
*co-coach with Ludek Bukac

**Rejda, Bohumil**
1957 WM TCH* 7 5 1 1 B
1958 WM TCH 7 3 2 2 4th
*co-coach with Vladimir Kostka

**Renney, Tom**
1994 OG-M CAN 8 5 1 2 S
1995 WM CAN 8 4 1 3 B
1996 WM CAN 8 4 1 3 S
1999 WM20 CAN 7 4 1 2 S
2000 WM CAN 9 5 0 4 4th

**Reunamaki, Matti**
1979 WM20 FIN 6 2 0 4 4th

**Rezac, Jaroslav**
1924 OG-M TCH 3 1 0 2 5th

**Riley, Jack**
1949 WM USA 8 6 0 2 B
1960 OG-M USA 7 7 0 0 G
~IIHF Hall of Fame

**Rindell, Harri**
1995 WM20 FIN 7 3 1 3 4th
1996 WM20 FIN 6 2 0 4 6th

**Rochat, Georges**
1980 WM20 SUI 5 0 0 5 8th

**Rolston, Ron**
2005 WM18 USA 6 6 0 0 G
2007 WM18 USA 7 3 1 1 2 S
2007 WM20 USA 7 3 1 2 1 B
2009 WM18 USA 7 6 0 0 1 G
2009 WM20 USA 6 3 1 0 2 5th
2011 WM18 USA 6 4 2 0 0 G

**Romer, Erich**
1928 OG-M GER 2 0 1 1 10th
1930 WM GER 5 4 0 1 S
1932 OG-M GER 6 2 0 4 B
1933 WM GER 6 3 1 2 5th
1934 WM GER 8 5 0 3 B

**Ronnberg, Roger**
2011 WM20 SWE 6 3 1 1 1 4th
2012 WM20 SWE 6 2 4 0 0 G

**Roubell, Lloyd**
1962 WM CAN 7 6 0 1 S

**Ruedi, Beat**
1962 WM SUI 7 1 0 6 7th

**Ruff, Lindy**
2009 WM CAN 9 7 0 1 1 S

**Rulik, Radim**
2006 WM20 CZE 6 2 0 4 6th

**Rumyantsev, Yuri**
2011 WM18 RUS 7 4 1 0 2 B

**Rundqvist, Ruben**
1924 OG-M SWE* 5 2 0 3 4th
*co-coach with Erik Gustafsson

**Ruotsalainen, Reino**
1984 OG-M FIN* 6 2 1 3 6th
*co-coach with Alpo Suhonen

**Ruzicka, Vladimir**
2004 WCH CZE 5 2 0 3 3rd
2005 WM CZE 9 8 0 1 G
2009 WM CZE 7 4 0 0 3 6th
2010 OG-M CZE 5 2 1 0 2 7th
2010 WM CZE 9 5 2 0 2 G

**Rychkov, Yuri**
2009 WW18 RUS 5 1 1 1 2 7th
2010 WW18 RUS 5 0 0 0 5 8th

**Ryman, Marsh**
1959 WM USA 8 5 0 3 4th

**Saarinen, Erkki**
1939 WM FIN 5 0 0 5 13th

**Saarinen, Mika**
2003 WM18 FIN 6 2 2 2 7th

**Sabourin, Stephane**
2000 WM FRA 6 2 1 3 15th

**Sachs, Tadeusz**
1932 OG-M POL 6 0 0 6 4th
1933 WM POL 6 1 1 4 7th
1935 WM POL 6 2 2 2 10th
1937 WM POL 9 3 0 6 8th

**Safonov, Vladimir**
1997 WM20 POL 6 0 0 6 10th
2010 WM18 BLR 6 0 0 1 5 10th

**Saintula, Hannu**
2000 WW FIN 5 3 0 2 B
2004 WW FIN 5 4 1 0 B
2005 WW FIN 5 2 0 3 4th
2006 OG-W FIN 5 2 0 3 4th
2007 WW FIN 5 1 1 0 3 4th
2008 WW FIN 5 2 2 0 1 B
2009 WW FIN 5 3 0 0 2 B
2010 OG-W CHN 5 1 0 0 4 7th

**Sajban, Branislav**
2006 WM20 SVK 6 2 1 3 8th

**Sandelin, Scott**
2005 WM20 USA 7 3 0 4 4th

**Sandlin, Tommy**
1979 WM SWE 8 3 1 4 B
1980 OG-M SWE 7 4 2 1 B
1987 WM SWE 10 5 2 3 G
1987 CC SWE 5 3 0 2 3rd
1988 OG-M SWE 8 4 3 1 B
1989 WM SWE 10 4 2 4 4th
1990 WM SWE 10 7 1 2 S

**Sather, Glen**
1984 CC CAN 8 5 1 2 1st
1996 WCH CAN 8 5 0 3 2nd

**Sauer, Jeff**
1995 WM USA 6 3 2 1 6th

**Sauvageau, Danielle**
1999 WW CAN 5 5 0 0 G
2001 WW CAN 5 5 0 0 G
2002 OG-W CAN 5 5 0 0 G

**Savolainen, Kari**
1999 WW FIN 5 3 0 2 B
2005 WM SLO 6 2 0 4 13th

**Schar, Dominik**
2011 WW18 SUI 6 2 0 0 4 7th

**Schenk, Simon**
1987 WM SUI 10 0 0 10 8th
1988 OG-M SUI 6 3 0 3 8th

**Schillgard, Johan**
2002 WM18 SWE 8 4 0 4 9th

**Schischefski, Gunther**
1978 WM GDR 10 1 3 6 8th

**Schmieder, Rudi**
1959 WM GDR 8 3 0 5 9th
1961 WM GDR 7 2 0 5 5th
1963 WM GDR 7 1 1 5 6th
1965 WM GDR 7 3 0 4 5th
1966 WM GDR 7 3 0 4 5th
1967 WM GDR 7 1 1 5 7th
1968 OG-M GDR 7 0 0 7 8th
1970 WM GDR 10 2 1 7 5th

**Schneider, Werner**
2009 WW18 GER 5 0 1 0 4 6
2011 WW18 GER 5 2 0 0 3 6th

**Schramm, Peter**
2004 WM20 AUT 6 0 1 5 9th

**Schwarz, Ueli**
1997 WM20 SUI 6 3 1 2 7th

**Seino, Masaru**
1993 WM20 JPN 7 0 0 7 8th
1998 WM JPN 3 0 0 3 14th

**Sekelj, Matjaz**
2002 WM SLO 6 3 0 3 13th
2003 WM SLO 6 0 1 5 15th

**Sell, Walter**
1933 WM ROM 5 2 0 3 9th

**Selman, Bill**
1982 WM USA* 7 0 1 6 8th
*co-coach with Mike Smith

**Selvek, Jan**
2001 WM20 SVK 7 1 0 6 8th

**Seme, Stefan**
1984 OG-M YUG 5 1 0 4 11th

**Sethereng, Morten**
1999 WM18 NOR 6 0 0 6 10th
2002 WM18 NOR 8 1 1 6 11th

**Setters, Jim**
1998 WM20 GER 6 0 0 6 10th
2000 WM18 GER 6 2 1 3 7th
2001 WM18 GER 6 3 1 2 5th
2002 WM18 GER 8 1 1 6 10th
2005 WM18 GER 7 3 0 4 8th
2006 WM18 GER 6 1 1 4 8th
2007 WM18 GER 6 2 0 0 4 8th
2008 WM18 GER 6 2 1 0 3 5th
2009 WM18 GER 6 1 1 0 4 10th
2011 WM18 GER 6 1 0 1 4 6th
2012 WM18 GER 6 2 0 0 4 6th

**Seukand, Olexander**
2004 WM UKR 6 1 2 3 14th
2005 WM UKR 6 1 1 4 11th
2006 WM UKR 6 1 0 5 12th
2007 WM UKR 6 1 0 0 5 16th

**Shayanov, Andrei**
2010 WM KAZ 6 0 0 0 6 16th
2012 WM KAZ 7 0 0 1 6 16th

**Shedden, Doug**
2008 WM FIN 9 5 2 0 2 B

**Siitarinen, Jorma**
2007 WW CHN 4 1 0 0 3 6th

**Sillig, Max**
1920 OG-M SUI 2 0 0 2 5th

**Silverman, Max**
1938 WM CAN 7 6 1 0 G
1949 WM CAN 7 4 2 1 S

**Simcik, Jan**
2001 WM18 SVK 7 2 1 4 8th

**Simpson, Sean**
2010 WM SUI 7 4 0 0 3 5th
2011 WM SUI 6 2 1 1 2 9th
2012 WM SUI 7 2 0 0 5 11th

**Simpson, Terry**
1985 WM20 CAN 7 5 2 0 G
1986 WM20 CAN 7 5 0 2 S

**Sindel, Jaromir**
2004 WM18 CZE 7 3 3 1 B
2010 WM20 CZE 6 3 0 0 3 7th

**Sinden, Harry**
1972 SS CAN 8 4 1 3 1st

**Sinitsyn, Vladimir**
2004 WM18 BLR 6 1 0 5 9th

**Sirant, Mike**
2007 WM DEN 6 2 0 0 4 10th
2008 WM DEN 6 1 1 0 4 12th

**Skobelkina, Natalya**
2007 WW KAZ 4 0 0 0 4 9th

**Skorski, Augustyn**
1977 WM20 POL* 7 0 1 6 8th
*co-coach with Sylwester Wilczek

**Slettvoll, John**
1999 WM20 SUI 6 1 0 5 9th

**Slipchenko, Mikhail**
2005 WM18 RUS 6 4 0 2 5th

**Smith, Ben**
1997 WW USA 5 3 1 1 S
1998 OG-W USA 6 6 0 0 G
1999 WW USA 5 4 0 1 S
2000 WW USA 5 4 0 1 S
2001 WW USA 5 4 0 1 S
2002 OG-W USA 5 4 0 1 S
2004 WW USA 5 4 0 1 S
2005 WW USA 5 5 0 0 G
2006 OG-W USA 5 4 0 1 B

**Smith, Mike**
1982 WM USA* 7 0 1 6 8th
*co-coach with Bill Selman

**Smith, Peter**
2008 WW CAN 5 3 0 0 2 S

**Smith, Sid**
1958 WM CAN 7 7 0 0 G

**Smythe, Conn**
1928 OG-M CAN 3 3 0 0 G

**Solc, Jiri**
2011 WM18 CZE 6 3 0 0 3 8th

**Sozzi, Jean-Claude**
1993 WM FRA 6 1 0 5 10th

**Sparer, Markus**
2006 OG-W ITA 5 0 0 5 8th

**Spisak, Robert**
2003 WM20 SVK 6 3 0 3 5th

**Starsi, Jan**
1974 WM TCH* 10 7 0 3 S
1975 WM TCH* 10 8 0 2 S
1976 OG-M TCH* 5 3 0 2 S
1976 WM TCH* 10 9 1 0 G
1976 CC TCH* 7 3 1 3 2nd
1977 WM TCH* 10 7 1 2 G
1979 WM TCH* 8 4 2 2 S
1986 WM TCH 10 5 1 4 5th
1987 WM TCH 10 6 2 2 B
1987 CC TCH 5 2 1 2 4th
1988 OG-M TCH** 8 4 0 4 6th
*co-coach with Karel Gut
**co-coach with Frantisek Pospisil
~IIHF Hall of Fame

**Starygin, Sergei**
2001 WM20 KAZ 6 0 1 5 10th

**Stephen, Robert**
1978 WM20 SUI 6 0 0 6 8th

**Sterbak, Jan**
1993 WM20 TCH+ 7 4 1 2 B
1998 WM SVK 6 2 2 2 7th
1999 WM SVK 6 2 1 3 7th
+played as Czech/Slovak Republics

**Stone, Katey**
2008 WW18 USA 5 5 0 0 0 G
2011 WW USA 5 4 1 0 0 G
2012 WW USA 5 4 0 1 0 S

**Stromberg, Arne**
1961 WM SWE 7 4 0 3 4th
1962 WM SWE 7 7 0 0 G
1963 WM SWE 7 6 0 1 S
1964 OG-M SWE 7 5 0 2 S
1965 WM SWE 7 4 1 2 B
1966 WM SWE 7 3 1 3 4th
1967 WM SWE 7 4 1 2 S
1968 OG-M SWE 7 4 1 2 4th
1969 WM SWE 10 8 0 2 S
1970 WM SWE 10 7 1 2 S
1971 WM SWE 10 5 1 4 B
~IIHF Hall of Fame

**Strople, Paul**
2005 WW CHN 5 1 1 3 6th
2009 WW CHN 4 0 0 1 3 9th

**Suhonen, Alpo**
1982 WM20 FIN* 7 5 0 2 B
1983 WM FIN 10 2 2 6 7th
1984 OG-M FIN^ 6 2 1 3 6th
1985 WM FIN 10 4 2 4 5th
*co-coach with Jorma Thusberg
^co-coach with Reino Ruotsalainen

**Sullivan, Frank**
1953 WM SUI 4 1 0 3 B

**Sullivan, Mike**
2007 WM USA 7 4 0 1 2 5th

**Summanen, Raimo**
2004 WM FIN 7 4 1 2 6th
2004 WCH FIN 6 4 1 1 2nd

**Supler, Julius**
1994 OG-M SVK 8 4 2 2 6th
1996 WM20 SVK 6 2 3 1 7th
1996 WM SVK 5 1 1 3 10th
2002 WM20 SVK 7 2 2 3 8th
2007 WM SVK 7 4 0 0 3 6th
2008 WM SVK 5 2 1 0 2 13th

**Sutter, Brent**
2005 WM20 CAN 6 6 0 0 G
2006 WM20 CAN 6 6 0 0 G
2012 WM CAN 8 6 0 1 1 5th

**Svensson, Kjell**
1973 WM SWE 10 7 1 2 S
1974 WM SWE 10 5 1 4 B

**Sykora, Marek**
2009 WM18 CZE 6 1 0 1 4 6th
2009 WM20 CZE 6 2 0 1 3 6th

**Sykora, Vlastimil**
1959 WM TCH 8 5 0 3 B

**Szczepaniec, Andrzej**
1988 WM20 POL 7 1 0 6 8th

**Tambijevs, Leonids**
2012 WM18 LAT 6 2 0 1 3 9th

**Tamminen, Juhani**
1992 WM20 SUI 7 1 0 6 8th
1992 OG-M SUI 7 2 0 5 10th
1995 WM FRA 6 3 0 3 8th
1996 WM FRA 7 2 0 5 11th

**Tanabu, Masami**
1972 OG-M JPN 4 2 1 1 9th

**Tapola, Jussi**
2012 WM18 FIN 7 4 0 1 2 4th

**Tarasov, Anatoli**
1958 WM URS 7 5 1 1 S
1959 WM URS 8 7 0 1 S
1960 OG-M URS 7 4 1 2 B
1963 WM URS* 7 6 0 1 G
1964 OG-M URS* 7 7 0 0 G
1965 WM URS* 7 7 0 0 G
1966 WM URS* 7 6 1 0 G
1967 WM URS* 7 7 0 0 G
1968 OG-M URS* 7 6 0 1 G
1969 WM URS* 10 8 0 2 G
1970 WM URS* 10 9 0 1 G
1971 WM URS* 10 8 1 1 G
1972 OG-M URS* 5 4 1 0 G
*co-coach with Arkadi Chernyshev
~IIHF Hall of Fame

**Taylor, Phil**
1928 OG-M HUN 3 0 0 3 11th

**Taylor, Tim**
1989 WM USA 10 4 1 5 6th
1990 WM USA 10 6 0 4 5th
1991 WM USA 10 3 2 5 4th
1992 WM USA 6 2 1 3 7th
1993 WM USA 6 2 2 2 6th
1994 OG-M USA 8 1 3 4 8th

**Templeton, Bert**
1977 WM20 CAN 7 5 1 1 S
1987 WM20 CAN 6 4 1 1 DQ

**Tezuka, Shunichi**
1936 OG-M JPN 2 0 0 2 9th

**Thelin, Tomas**
2004 WM18 SWE 6 3 0 3 5th

**Thomsen, Leif**
2004 WM18 DEN 6 2 0 4 8th
2005 WM18 DEN 6 0 0 6 10th

**Thoresen, Petter**
2006 WM20 NOR 6 0 0 6 10th

**Thusberg, Jorma**
1982 WM20 FIN* 7 5 0 2 B
*co-coach with Alpo Suhonen

**Tico, Constantin**
1968 OG-M ROM* 5 2 0 3 12th
*co-coach with Mihai Flamaropol

**Tikhonov, Viktor**
1976 CC URS 5 2 1 2 3rd
1978 WM URS 10 9 0 1 G
1979 WM URS 8 8 0 0 G
1980 OG-M URS 7 6 0 1 S
1981 WM URS 8 6 2 0 G
1981 CC URS 7 5 1 1 1st
1982 WM URS 10 9 1 0 G
1983 WM URS 10 9 1 0 G
1984 OG-M URS 7 7 0 0 G
1984 CC URS 6 5 0 1 3rd
1985 WM URS 10 8 0 2 B
1986 WM URS 10 10 0 0 G
1987 WM URS 10 8 2 0 S
1987 CC URS 8 4 1 3 2nd
1988 OG-M URS 8 7 0 1 G
1989 WM URS 10 10 0 0 G
1990 WM URS 10 8 1 1 G
1991 WM URS 10 7 2 1 B
1991 CC URS 5 1 1 3 5th
1992 OG-M RUS 8 7 0 1 G
1992 WM RUS 6 4 1 1 5th
1994 OG-M RUS 8 4 0 4 4th
2004 WM RUS 6 2 0 4 10th
~IIHF Hall of Fame

**Tiron, Ion**
1976 OG-M ROM* 5 4 0 1 7th
1980 OG-M* ROM 5 1 1 3 8th
*co-coach with Stefan Ionescu

**Tisell, Mikael**
2005 WM18 SWE 7 5 0 2 B
2006 WM18 SWE 5 3 0 2 6th

**Todd, Dick**
1991 WM20 CAN 7 5 1 1 G

**Toggwiler, Jorg**
2008 WW18 SUI 5 2 0 0 3 7th
2009 WW18 SUI 5 1 0 2 2 8th

**Toivola, Juuso**
2011 WW18 FIN 6 2 1 0 3 B
2012 WW18 FIN 5 2 0 1 2 5th

**Tolvanen, Jarmo**
1992 WM20 FIN 7 3 1 3 4th
1993 WM20 FIN 7 3 1 3 5th
2007 WM20 FIN 6 2 0 0 4 6th

**Tomth, Tommy**
1992 WM20 SWE 7 5 1 1 S
1993 WM20 SWE 7 6 0 1 S
1994 WM20 SWE 7 6 0 1 S
1995 WM20 SWE 7 4 1 2 B

**Torriani, Richard "Bibi"**
1947 WM SUI 7 4 1 2 4th
1949 WM SUI 8 4 1 3 5th
1950 WM SUI 7 4 0 3 B
1951 WM SUI 6 4 1 1 B
1952 OG-M SUI 8 4 0 4 5th
1956 OG-M ITA 6 3 2 1 7th

**Tortorella, John**
2008 WM USA 7 4 0 1 2 6th

**Toth, Igor**
2002 WM18 SVK 8 3 0 5 8th

**Tozicka, Jiri**
1952 OG-M TCH* 9 6 0 3 4th
*co-coach with Josef Herman

**Trottier, Edward**
1939 WM HUN 7 1 0 6 7th

**Trottier, Frank**
1950 WM SWE 7 3 0 4 5th
1955 WM FRG 8 2 0 6 6th
1956 OG-M FRG 8 1 2 5 6th

**Tsujiura, Steve**
1999 WM JPN 3 0 0 3 16th
2000 WM JPN 6 0 0 6 16th
2001 WM JPN 6 0 1 5 16th
2002 WM JPN 6 0 0 6 16th

**Tsygurov, Gennadi**
1994 WM20 RUS 7 5 1 1 B
1999 WM20 RUS 7 6 0 1 G

**Tsyplakov, Vladimir**
2008 WM18 BLR 6 1 0 0 5 9th

**Tuomi, Timo**
2000 WM18 FIN 7 6 0 1 G
2003 WM JPN 6 0 1 5 16th

**Tupalski, Alexander**
1936 OG-M POL* 3 1 0 2 9th
*co-coach with Lucjan Kulej

**Tuzik, Igor**
1982 WM20 URS 7 4 0 3 4th

**Tyler, Ken**
1993 WM AUT 6 1 1 4 9th
1994 OG-M AUT 7 1 0 6 12th
1995 WM AUT 7 1 1 5 11th
1996 WM AUT 7 1 0 6 12th

**Ubriaco, Gene**
1992 OG-M ITA 7 1 0 6 12th

**Uher, Zdenek**
1988 WM20 TCH 7 3 1 3 4th

**Ujcik, Zdenek**
1964 OG-M AUT 7 3 1 3 13th

**Ulyankin, Alexander**
2012 WW18 RUS 6 1 1 0 4 7th

**Unsinn, Xaver**
1964 OG-M FRG* 7 2 0 5 7th
1976 OG-M FRG 5 2 0 3 B
1976 WM FRG 10 3 2 5 6th
1982 WM FRG 7 2 1 4 6th
1983 WM FRG 10 3 0 7 6th
1984 OG-M FRG 6 4 1 1 5th
1984 CC FRG 5 0 1 4 5th
1985 WM FRG 10 3 1 6 7th
1986 WM FRG 10 2 1 7 7th
1987 WM FRG 10 4 1 5 6th
1988 OG-M FRG 8 4 0 4 5th
1989 WM FRG** 10 1 2 7 7th
1990 WM FRG 10 1 1 8 7th
*co-coach with Markus Egen & Engelbert Holdereid
**co-coach with Erich Kuhnhackl
~IIHF Hall of Fame

**Urama, Rauli**
2006 WM18 FIN 6 4 1 1 S

**Vairo, Lou**
1979 WM20 USA 5 2 0 3 6th
1980 WM20 USA 5 1 1 3 7th
1981 WM20 USA 5 2 0 3 6th
1982 WM20 USA 7 2 0 5 6th
1984 OG-M USA 6 2 2 2 7th
2000 WM USA 7 4 2 1 5th
2001 WM USA 9 4 1 4 4th
2002 WM USA 7 3 1 3 7th
2003 WM20 USA 7 4 0 3 4th
2003 WM USA 6 3 0 3 13th
~IIHF Hall of Fame

**Vaisanen, Matti**
1977 WM20 FIN 7 4 0 3 4th
1978 WM20 FIN 6 3 1 2 6th

**Valtonen, Jorma**
1994 WW FIN 5 3 0 2 B

**van den Driessche, Carlos**
1947 WM BEL 7 0 0 7 8th

**Van Reysschoot, Pierre**
1930 WM BEL 1 0 0 1 10th
1933 WM BEL 3 0 0 3 12th
1934 WM BEL 4 1 0 3 12th
1935 WM BEL 5 0 0 5 14th

**Varivonchik, Anatoli**
1998 OG-M BLR 7 2 1 4 7th
1998 WM BLR 6 2 0 4 8th
1999 WM BLR 6 4 1 1 9th
2000 WM BLR 6 3 0 3 9th
2001 WM BLR 6 3 1 2 14th

**Vasilchenko, Vasili**
1999 WM20 KAZ 6 1 1 4 6th
2000 WM20 KAZ 7 1 0 6 8th

**Vasiliev, Mikhail**
2010 WM18 RUS 7 4 0 0 3 4th

**Vasiliev, Vladimir**
1986 WM20 URS 7 7 0 0 G
1987 WM20 URS 6 2 1 3 DQ
1996 WM RUS 8 6 0 2 4th

**Vasiljevs, Haralds**
2000 WM LAT 6 3 1 2 8th
2001 WM LAT 6 3 1 2 13th

**Veber, Jiri**
2012 WM18 CZE 6 2 0 0 4 8th

**Vimmer, Josef**
1989 WM20 TCH 7 4 1 2 B
1990 WM20 TCH 7 5 0 2 B
1991 WM20 TCH 7 5 0 2 B

**Virtanen, Rauli**
1971 WM FIN* 10 4 1 5 4th
1972 OG-M FIN* 5 2 0 3 5th
1972 WM FIN* 10 4 0 6 4th
*co-coach with Seppo Liitsola

**Viryasov, Alexander**
2008 WW18 RUS 5 0 0 0 5 8th

**Vodicka, Antonin**
1949 WM TCH 7 5 0 2 G

**Vodisek, Viktor**
1939 WM YUG 5 0 1 4 13th

**von Sury, Ulrich**
1936 OG-M SUI 3 1 0 2 13th
1937 WM SUI 8 4 1 3 B
1938 WM SUI 7 5 0 2 6th
1939 WM SUI 9 6 1 2 B

**Vorobyov, Pyotr**
1992 WM20 RUS 7 6 0 1 G
1997 WM20 RUS 6 4 1 1 B
1998 WM20 RUS 7 5 1 1 S
2000 WM20 RUS 7 6 0 1 S
2001 WM20 RUS 7 3 1 3 7th
2006 WM LAT 6 2 1 3 10th

**Votruba, Jan**
2004 WW CHN 4 2 0 2 7th

**Vujtek, Vladimir**
1994 WM20 CZE 7 3 0 4 5th
2012 WM SVK 10 7 0 0 3 S

**Vyboh, Andrej**
2010 WM18 SVK 6 2 0 0 4 8th

**Vyborny, Frantisek**
2006 WM SLO 6 0 2 4 16th

**Vytisk, Tomas**
2008 WW18 CZE 5 3 0 0 2 B
2009 WW18 CZE 5 1 0 1 3 4th
2010 WW18 CZE 5 3 0 0 2 7th
2011 WW18 CZE 6 2 0 0 4 4th
2012 WW18 CZE 5 1 0 0 4 6th

**Wahlsten, Juhani**
1983 WM20 FIN 7 3 0 4 6th

**Wakabayashi, Hitoshi**
1980 OG-M JPN 5 0 1 4 12th

**Walker, Johnny**
1934 WM CAN 4 4 0 0 G

**Wallin, Clas-Goran**
1988 WM20 SWE 7 3 1 3 5th
1989 WM20 SWE 7 6 0 1 S

**Wallin, Jesse**
2012 WM18 CAN 7 3 1 0 3 B

**Walter, Jaroslav**
1992 OG-M TCH* 8 6 0 2 B
*co-coach with Ivan Hlinka

**Walter, Ryan**
2011 WW CAN 5 4 0 1 0 S

**Waltin, Mats**
1995 WM SUI 7 0 1 6 12th
2008 WM SLO 5 0 0 1 4 15th

**Warminski, Przemyslaw**
1938 WM POL 6 3 0 3 7th

**Warwick, Grant**
1955 WM CAN 8 8 0 0 G

**Watson, Blake**
1930 WM AUT 3 2 0 1 4th
1931 WM CAN 6 5 1 0 G

**Watt, Tom**
1980 OG-M CAN* 6 3 0 3 6th
*co-coach with Lorne Davis & Clare Drake

**Webster, Tom**
1989 WM20 CAN 7 4 1 2 4th

**Weinberg, Hans**
1935 WM NED 6 0 0 6 14th

**Weinberger, Hans**

| | | | | | | |
|---|---|---|---|---|---|---|
| 1931 WM | AUT | 8 | 4 | 0 | 4 | B |
| 1933 WM | AUT | 8 | 4 | 0 | 4 | 4th |
| 1934 WM | AUT | 7 | 3 | 1 | 3 | 7th |
| 1935 WM | AUT | 8 | 4 | 1 | 3 | 6th |
| 1938 WM | AUT | 3 | 0 | 1 | 2 | 10th |

**Werfring, Dieter**

| | | | | | | |
|---|---|---|---|---|---|---|
| 2010 WM20 | AUT | 6 | 0 | 0 0 | 6 | 10th |

**Westberg, Hans**

| | | | | | | |
|---|---|---|---|---|---|---|
| 1980 OG-M | NED | 5 | 1 | 1 | 3 | 9th |
| 1984 OG-M | NOR | 5 | 0 | 1 | 4 | 10th |

**Westerlund, Erkka**

| | | | | | | |
|---|---|---|---|---|---|---|
| 1989 WM20 | FIN | 7 | 2 | 1 | 4 | 6th |
| 2002 WM20 | FIN | 7 | 5 | 0 | 2 | B |
| 2003 WM20 | FIN | 7 | 4 | 1 | 2 | B |
| 2005 WM | FIN | 7 | 2 | 3 | 2 | 7th |
| 2006 OG-M | FIN | 8 | 7 | 0 | 1 | S |
| 2006 WM | FIN | 9 | 6 | 1 | 2 | B |
| 2007 WM | FIN | 9 | 4 | 2 0 | 3 | S |

**White, Stephanie**

| | | | | | | |
|---|---|---|---|---|---|---|
| 2009 WW18 | CAN | 5 | 4 | 0 1 | 0 | S |

**Wilczek, Sylwester**

| | | | | | | |
|---|---|---|---|---|---|---|
| 1977 WM20 | POL* | 7 | 0 | 1 | 6 | 8th |

*co-coach with Augustyn Skorski

**Wild, Karl**

| | | | | | | |
|---|---|---|---|---|---|---|
| 1960 OG-M | FRG | 7 | 1 | 0 | 6 | 6th |

**Williamson, Mike**

| | | | | | | |
|---|---|---|---|---|---|---|
| 2011 WM18 | CAN | 7 | 4 | 0 1 | 2 | 4th |

**Williamson, Murray**

| | | | | | | |
|---|---|---|---|---|---|---|
| 1967 WM | USA | 7 | 3 | 1 | 3 | 5th |
| 1968 OG-M | USA | 7 | 2 | 1 | 4 | 6th |
| 1971 WM | USA | 10 | 2 | 0 | 8 | 6th |
| 1972 OG-M | USA | 5 | 3 | 0 | 2 | S |

**Wilson, Johnny**

| | | | | | | |
|---|---|---|---|---|---|---|
| 1977 WM | CAN | 10 | 6 | 1 | 3 | 4th |

**Wilson, Ron**

| | | | | | | |
|---|---|---|---|---|---|---|
| 1994 WM | USA | 8 | 4 | 0 | 4 | 4th |
| 1996 WM | USA | 8 | 5 | 0 | 3 | B |
| 1996 WCH | USA | 7 | 6 | 0 | 1 | 1st |
| 1998 OG-M | USA | 4 | 1 | 0 | 3 | 6th |
| 2004 WCH | USA | 5 | 2 | 0 | 3 | 4th |
| 2009 WM | USA | 9 | 4 | 0 2 | 3 | 4th |
| 2010 OG-M | USA | 6 | 5 | 0 1 | 0 | S |

**Winsor, Alfred**

| | | | | | | |
|---|---|---|---|---|---|---|
| 1932 OG-M | USA | 6 | 4 | 1 | 1 | S |

**Wirkkunen, Joe**

| | | | | | | |
|---|---|---|---|---|---|---|
| 1960 OG-M | FIN* | 6 | 3 | 1 | 2 | 7th |
| 1962 WM | FIN | 7 | 3 | 0 | 4 | 4th |
| 1963 WM | FIN* | 7 | 1 | 1 | 5 | 5th |
| 1964 OG-M | FIN* | 7 | 2 | 0 | 5 | 6th |
| 1965 WM | FIN* | 7 | 1 | 1 | 5 | 7th |
| 1966 WM | FIN* | 7 | 2 | 0 | 5 | 7th |

*co-coach with Arne Honkavaara

**Wiro-Kiro, Wladyslaw**

| | | | | | | |
|---|---|---|---|---|---|---|
| 1956 OG-M | POL* | 5 | 2 | 0 | 3 | 8th |
| 1958 WM | POL** | 7 | 0 | 1 | 6 | 8th |

*co-coach with Mieczyslaw Palus
**co-coach with Andrzej Wolkowski

**Wohl, Pavel**

| | | | | | | |
|---|---|---|---|---|---|---|
| 1989 WM | TCH | 10 | 4 | 2 | 2 | B |
| 1990 WM | TCH | 10 | 5 | 1 | 4 | B |

**Wolkowski, Andrzej**

| | | | | | | |
|---|---|---|---|---|---|---|
| 1958 WM | POL* | 7 | 0 | 1 | 6 | 8th |

*co-coach with Wladyslaw Wiro-Kiro

**Woog, Doug**

| | | | | | | |
|---|---|---|---|---|---|---|
| 1985 WM20 | USA | 7 | 2 | 0 | 5 | 6th |

**Yackel, Ken**

| | | | | | | |
|---|---|---|---|---|---|---|
| 1965 WM | USA | 7 | 2 | 0 | 5 | 6th |

**Yakushev, Alexander**

| | | | | | | |
|---|---|---|---|---|---|---|
| 1999 WM | RUS | 6 | 2 | 3 | 1 | 5th |
| 2000 WM | RUS | 6 | 2 | 0 | 4 | 11th |

**Yamaguchi, Seiji**

| | | | | | | |
|---|---|---|---|---|---|---|
| 1930 WM | JPN | 1 | 0 | 0 | 1 | 6th |

**Yao, Naifeng**

| | | | | | | |
|---|---|---|---|---|---|---|
| 2001 WW | CHN | 5 | 1 | 1 | 3 | 7th |
| 2002 OG-W | CHN | 5 | 1 | 1 | 3 | 7th |

**Yawney, Trent**

| | | | | | | |
|---|---|---|---|---|---|---|
| 2007 WM18 | CAN | 6 | 3 | 1 1 | 1 | 4th |

**Yegorov, Anatoli**

| | | | | | | |
|---|---|---|---|---|---|---|
| 1970 WM | POL | 10 | 0 | 1 | 9 | 6th |
| 1972 OG-M | POL* | 5 | 0 | 0 | 5 | 6th |
| 1973 WM | POL | 10 | 1 | 1 | 8 | 5th |
| 1974 WM | POL | 10 | 1 | 2 | 7 | 5th |
| 1975 WM | POL | 10 | 2 | 0 | 8 | 5th |

*co-coach with Mieczyslaw Chmura

**Yegorov, Valentin**

| | | | | | | |
|---|---|---|---|---|---|---|
| 1997 WW | RUS | 5 | 1 | 1 | 3 | 6th |

**Yngve, Christian**

| | | | | | | |
|---|---|---|---|---|---|---|
| 1990 WW | SWE | 5 | 2 | 0 | 3 | 4th |
| 1992 WW | SWE | 5 | 2 | 0 | 3 | 4th |
| 1994 WW | SWE | 5 | 3 | 1 | 1 | 5th |
| 1999 WW | SWE | 5 | 2 | 0 | 3 | 4th |
| 2000 WW | SWE | 5 | 1 | 1 | 3 | 4th |
| 2001 WW | SWE | 5 | 2 | 0 | 3 | 5th |
| 2002 OG-W | SWE | 5 | 3 | 0 | 2 | B |

**Yurkewicz, Al**

| | | | | | | |
|---|---|---|---|---|---|---|
| 1955 WM | USA | 8 | 4 | 2 | 2 | 4th |

**Yurzinov, Vladimir**

| | | | | | | |
|---|---|---|---|---|---|---|
| 1998 OG-M | RUS | 6 | 5 | 0 | 1 | S |
| 1998 WM | RUS | 6 | 4 | 1 | 1 | 5th |

~IIHF Hall of Fame

**Zach, Hans**

| | | | | | | |
|---|---|---|---|---|---|---|
| 2001 WM | GER | 6 | 1 | 2 | 3 | 8th |
| 2002 OG-M | GER | 7 | 3 | 0 | 4 | 8th |
| 2002 WM | GER | 7 | 3 | 1 | 3 | 8th |
| 2003 WM | GER | 7 | 3 | 1 | 3 | 6th |
| 2004 WM | GER | 6 | 2 | 1 | 3 | 9th |

**Zakharov, Mikhail**

| | | | | | | |
|---|---|---|---|---|---|---|
| 1999 WM20 | BLR | 6 | 0 | 1 | 5 | 10th |
| 2002 WM18 | BLR | 8 | 3 | 0 | 5 | 5th |
| 2003 WM18 | BLR | 6 | 2 | 1 | 3 | 8th |
| 2005 WM20 | BLR | 6 | 1 | 0 | 5 | 10th |
| 2010 OG-M | BLR | 4 | 1 | 0 0 | 3 | 9th |

**Zankovets, Eduard**

| | | | | | | |
|---|---|---|---|---|---|---|
| 2007 WM20 | BLR | 6 | 2 | 0 0 | 4 | 10th |
| 2010 WM | BLR | 6 | 2 | 1 0 | 3 | 10th |
| 2011 WM | BLR | 6 | 2 | 0 1 | 3 | 14th |

**Zenhausern, Bruno**

| | | | | | | |
|---|---|---|---|---|---|---|
| 1991 WM20 | SUI | 7 | 1 | 0 | 6 | 7th |

**Zhang, Zhinan**

| | | | | | | |
|---|---|---|---|---|---|---|
| 1994 WW | CHN | 5 | 1 | 1 | 3 | 4th |
| 1997 WW | CHN | 5 | 2 | 0 | 3 | 4th |
| 1998 OG-W | CHN | 6 | 2 | 0 | 4 | 4th |
| 1999 WW | CHN | 5 | 3 | 0 | 2 | 5th |
| 2000 WW | CHN | 5 | 2 | 1 | 2 | 6th |

**Ziesche, Joachim**

| | | | | | | |
|---|---|---|---|---|---|---|
| 1974 WM | GDR* | 10 | 1 | 1 | 8 | 6th |
| 1976 WM | GDR* | 10 | 2 | 1 | 7 | 8th |
| 1983 WM | GDR | 10 | 5 | 1 | 4 | 5th |
| 1985 WM | GDR | 10 | 0 | 2 | 8 | 8th |

*co-coach with Klaus Hirche

**Ziska, Dusan**

| | | | | | | |
|---|---|---|---|---|---|---|
| 1998 WM20 | SVK | 6 | 3 | 0 | 3 | 9th |
| 2000 WM20 | SVK | 6 | 1 | 1 | 4 | 9th |

**Znaroks, Olegs**

| | | | | | | |
|---|---|---|---|---|---|---|
| 2006 WM20 | LAT | 6 | 1 | 0 | 5 | 9th |
| 2007 WM | LAT | 6 | 2 | 0 1 | 3 | 13th |
| 2008 WM | LAT | 6 | 2 | 0 0 | 4 | 11th |
| 2009 WM | LAT | 7 | 3 | 1 0 | 3 | 7th |
| 2010 OG-M | LAT | 4 | 0 | 0 1 | 3 | 12th |
| 2010 WM | LAT | 6 | 2 | 0 0 | 4 | 11th |
| 2011 WM | LAT | 6 | 2 | 0 2 | 2 | 13th |

*The Class of 2012 IIHF Hall of Fame inductees: (l-r) Andy Murray, Pavel Bure, Milan Novy, Raimo Helminen, Kent Angus, and Phil Housley. Photo: Jeff Vinnick / HHOF-IIHF Images.*

*Andy Murray was inducted into the IIHF Hall of Fame in 2012 in recognition of his leading Canada to World Championship gold on three occasions. Photo: Jeff Vinnick / HHOF-IIHF Images.*

# OFFICIALS' REGISTER

## Officials' History

**OG-M**

| | |
|---|---|
| 1920-28 | One referee |
| 1932-76 | Two referees |
| 1980-2006 | One referee, two linesmen |
| 1998 | NHL officials introduced |
| 2010-present | Two referees, two linesmen |

**WM**

| | |
|---|---|
| 1930-33 | One referee |
| 1934-76 | Two referees |
| 1977-2007 | One referee, two linesmen |
| 2008-present | Two referees, two linesmen |

**WM20**

| | |
|---|---|
| 1977-2007 | One referee, two linesmen |
| 2008-present | Two referees, two linesmen |

**WM18**

| | |
|---|---|
| 1999-2007 | One referee, two linesmen |
| 2008-present | Two referees, two linesmen |

**OG-W**

| | |
|---|---|
| 1998-present | One referee, two linesmen |

**WW**

| | |
|---|---|
| 1990-1994 | One referee, two linesmen |
| 1997-present | One referee, two linesmen (women only) |

**WW18**

| | |
|---|---|
| 2008-present | One referee, two linesmen |

**(includes top-level events for OG-M, OG-W, WM, WW, WM20, WM18, WW18)**

Year Event NAT POS # games

**Aberg, Kim**
2001 WM18 FIN L 6 games

**Abrahamsson, Carl**
1935 WM SWE R 2 games

**Acheson, Kevin**
1998 WM CAN R 7 games
2000 WM CAN R 10 games
2002 OG-M CAN R 3 games
~1998 WM gold-medal game 2
~2000 WM gold-medal game

**Adam, Don**
1991 WM USA R 6 games
1992 OG-M USA R 7 games
1996 WM20 USA R 4 games
1997 WM USA R 8 games
1998 OG-M USA R 5 games
~1997 WM gold-medal games 1 and 3

**Adamec, Quido**
1955 WM TCH R 3 games
1956 OG-M TCH R 4 games
1957 WM TCH R 4 games
1958 WM TCH R 4 games
1959 WM TCH R 6 games
1961 WM TCH R 2 games
1965 WM TCH R 3 games
~IIHF Hall of Fame

**Adler, Judith**
2011 WW GER L 4 games
2012 WW GER L 4 games

**Ahlin, Gosta**
1948 OG-M SWE R 6 games
1949 WM SWE R 6 games
1951 WM SWE R 5 games
1952 OG-M SWE R 10 games
1953 WM SWE R 2 games
1954 WM SWE R 5 games
1955 WM SWE R 4 games
1956 OG-M SWE R 8 games
1957 WM SWE R 5 games
1958 WM SWE R 7 games
1959 WM SWE R 7 games

**Alajmo, Gustavo**
1982 WM ITA L 3 games
1983 WM ITA L 6 games
1984 OG-M ITA L 2 games

**Alander, Stig**
1954 WM FIN R 2 games

**Aleshin, Petr**
2003 WM18 RUS L 6 games

**Alexiou, Fotis**
1996 WM CAN L 5 games

**Alis, Natan**
1937 WM TCH R 5 games
1938 WM TCH R 3 games

**Allen, Dina**
2012 WW18 USA R 4 games
2012 WW USA R 4 games
~2012 WW bronze-medal game

**Amell, Derek**
2004 WCH CAN L 4 games

**Ammian, Harry**
1992 WM USA R 5 games
1994 WM20 USA R 1 game

**Ancel, Arthur**
1950 WM BEL R 3 games

**Andersen, Alf**
1995 WM NOR L 4 games
1996 WM NOR L 5 games

**Andersson, Bengt**
1998 OG-M SWE R 2 games

**Andersson, Peter**
1996 WM20 SWE R 4 games
1997 WM20 SWE R 4 games
1997 WM SWE R 7 games
2000 WM SWE R 2 games
~1996 WM20 bronze-medal game

**Andersson, Thomas**
1996 WM SWE R 2 games
1998 WM SWE R 5 games
1999 WM20 SWE R 5 games
2001 WM SWE R 4 games
2003 WM SWE R 7 games
2004 WM20 SWE R 5 games
2005 WM SWE R 5 games
2006 OG-M SWE R 4 games
~2004 WM20 gold-medal game
~2005 WM gold-medal game
~2006 OG-M bronze-medal game

**Andreossi, Gianni**
1933 WM SUI R 1 game
1935 WM SUI R 4 games
1936 OG-M SUI R 1 game

**Angus, Blaine**
1991 WM20 CAN R 5 games

**Anisimov, Alexei**
2007 WM20 RUS L 5 games

**Arazimova, Zuzana**
2009 WW CZE L 4 games
2010 OG-W CZE L 4 games
2011 WW CZE L 5 games
2012 WW CZE L 6 games
~2009 WW bronze-medal game
~2011 WW gold-medal game
~2012 WW bronze-medal game

**Arcon, Beat**
1978 WM20 SUI L 4 games

**Arm, Roger**
2007 WM18 SUI L 6 games
2008 WM18 SUI L 6 games
2009 WM20 SUI L 6 games
2010 WM SUI L 8 games
2011 WM SUI L 8 games
2012 WM SUI L 9 games
~2012 WM gold-medal game

**Armstrong, Howard**
1930 WM CAN R 3 games

**Auger, Stephane**
1998 WM20 CAN R 6 games
1999 WM CAN R 6 games

**Awizus, Frank**
2005 WM18 GER R 4 games
2006 WM20 GER R 4 games

**Axberg, Alf**
1949 WM SWE R 4 games
1950 WM SWE R 5 games
1954 WM SWE R 6 games
1955 WM SWE R 4 games
1956 OG-M SWE R 7 games

**Axelsson, Malin**
2011 WW18 SWE R 3 games
2012 WW18 SWE R 3 games

**Badal, Milos**
2001 WM18 CZE L 7 games
~2001 WM18 bronze-medal game

**Bader, Franz**
1971 WM FRG R 4 games
1972 OG-M GER R 6 games
1972 SS FRG R 1 game
1973 WM FRG R 6 games

**Baker, Hans**
1997 WM20 USA L 6 games

**Baker, Joanne**
1990 WW CAN L 4 games

**Balaberda, Kelly**
2006 WM18 CAN L 6 games
2007 WM20 CAN L 6 games
~2006 WM18 gold-medal game

**Balej, Jiri**
1999 WM18 CZE R 4 games

**Ball, Rudi**
1935 WM GER R 1 game

**Baluska, Vladimir**
2007 WM18 SVK R 5 games
2009 WM SVK R 6 games
2010 WM20 SVK R 5 games
2010 WM SVK R 8 games
2011 WM SVK R 6 games
2012 WM SVK R 7 games
~2007 WM18 bronze-medal game
~2010 WM gold-medal game

**Bandlofsky, Katja**
1999 WW GER L 5 games
2001 WW GER L 4 games
~1999 WW gold-medal game

**Banfield, Charlie**
1986 WM CAN R 6 games
1987 WM CAN R 7 games
1988 OG-M CAN R 7 games

**Bardin, Anatoli**
1996 WM20 RUS R 3 games
1997 WM20 RUS R 5 games

**Baril, Maurice**
1978 WM20 CAN L 4 games

**Barinov, Anatoli**
1979 WM URS L 9 games
1983 WM20 URS L 7 games
1983 WM URS L 12 games
1984 WM20 URS R 3 games

**Baroni, Georgio**
1934 WM ITA R 4 games

**Barry, Robert**
1960 OG-M USA R 9 games
1961 WM USA R 3 games
1962 WM USA R 10 games
1963 WM USA R 10 games

**Barton, Lucjan**
1988 WM20 POL L 6 games

**Barvir, Stanislav**
1998 WM20 CZE L 7 games
1999 WM20 CZE L 4 games
2002 WM CZE L 7 games
2004 WM20 CZE L 6 games

**Bata, Rudolf**
1967 WM TCH R 6 games
1969 WM TCH R 7 games
1970 WM TCH R 6 games
1971 WM TCH R 7 games
1972 OG-M TCH R 5 games
1972 SS TCH R 3 games
1973 WM TCH R 5 games
1975 WM TCH R 6 games
1976 OG-M TCH R 6 games
~1972 SS Game 8 with Jozef Kompalla

**Bauer, Stephan**
2010 WM18 GER R 5 games
2011 WM20 GER R 4 games
~2010 WM18 gold-medal game

**Baumgartner, Geo**
1996 WM SUI L 4 games

**Bechard, Daniel**
2008 WM18 CAN L 6 games
2009 WM20 CAN L 6 games
2010 WM CAN L 7 games

**Bednarova, Barbora**
2012 WW18 CZE L 4 games

**Bell, Bob**
1990 WM CAN L 8 games

**Bell, Bobby**
1928 OG-M CAN R 1 game

**Benek, Milos**
1992 OG-M TCH L 8 games
1993 WM20 CZE L 5 games
1994 OG-M TCH L 5 games

**Benedetto, Tim**
1990 WM USA L 8 games

**Benoist, Jean-Christophe**
1992 OG-M FRA L 7 games
1994 WM FRA L 3 games

**Beranek, Vaclav**
1952 OG-M TCH R 5 games
1954 WM TCH R 2 games

**Berg, Hans Petter**
1990 WW NOR L 4 games

**Berkmiller, Hans**
1979 WM GDR L 3 games
1981 WM20 FRG L 5 games

**Bernhard, Willy**
1952 OG-M SUI R 9 games
1953 WM SUI R 1 game
1956 OG-M SUI R 5 games

**Bertolotti, Reto**
1992 WM20 SUI R 4 games
1995 WM SUI R 3 games
1997 WM20 SUI R 4 games
1997 WM SUI R 5 games
1998 WM SUI R 2 games

**Best, Bobby**
1990 WW CAN R 2 games+
+information incomplete
~1990 WW gold-medal game

**Bezshaposhnikova, Yelena**
1997 WW RUS R 2 games

**Bibeau, Sylvain**
1994 WM20 CAN R 4 games
1995 WM CAN R 5 games
~1995 WM bronze-medal game

**Biehn, Charlie**
1986 WM20 CAN L 7 games

**Birin, Viktor**
2011 WM18 RUS L 6 games

**Biryukov, Andrei**
2002 WM RUS L 5 games

**Bischof, Robert**
1936 OG-M GER R 2 games

**Bissonette, Julie**
2000 WW CAN L 4 games
2001 WW CAN L 4 games
2002 OG-W CAN L 5 games
~2000 WW bronze-medal game

**Bjorkman, Hakan**
1984 WM20 SWE L 6 games
1989 WM20 SWE R 5 games
1991 WM20 SWE R 3 games
1992 WM SWE R 7 games

**Bjorkman, Therese**
2008 WW18 SWE L 5 games
2010 WW18 SWE L 6 games
2011 WW18 SWE L 5 games
2011 WW SWE L 5 games
2012 WW SWE L 5 games
~2010 WW18 gold-medal game
~2011 WW18 gold-medal game
~2011 WW gold-medal game
~2012 WW bronze-medal game

**Blaha, Jaromir**
2000 WM18 CZE L 6 games
2003 WM18 CZE L 6 games
2004 WM18 CZE L 6 games
2008 WM20 CZE L 6 games
2009 WM18 CZE L 6 games
2011 WM20 CZE L 6 games

**Blair, Erin**
2009 WW18 USA R 4 games
2011 WW USA R 3 games
~2009 WW18 gold-medal game

**Blumel, Petr**
2000 WM20 CZE L 7 games
2001 WM20 CZE L 6 games
2001 WM CZE L 8 games
2002 OG-M CZE L 6 games
2003 WM CZE L 9 games
2004 WM CZE L 10 games
2005 WM CZE L 7 games
2006 OG-M CZE L 4 games
2007 WM20 CZE L 7 games
2008 WM20 CZE L 7 games
2009 WM CZE L 8 games
2010 OG-M CZE L 5 games
2012 WM CZE L 9 games
~2000 WM20 bronze-medal game
~2003 WM gold-medal game
~2004 WM gold-medal game
~2007 WM20 bronze-medal game
~2009 WM gold-medal game
~2010 OG-M bronze-medal game
~2012 WM gold-medal game

**Blumel, Rainer**
1977 WM20 FRG L 7 games

**Bohm, Helmut**
1977 WM20 FRG R 2 games

**Bohm, K.**
1931 WM TCH R 1 game

**Boikov, Valeri**
1988 WM20 URS L 7 games

**Bokal, Scott**
2010 WM18 USA R 5 games

**Bokarev, Valeri**
1992 WM RUS R 3 games
1993 WM RUS R 6 games
1994 OG-M RUS R 5 games
1998 WM RUS R 3 games
~1993 WM bronze-medal game

**Bolina, Petr**
1993 WM20 CZE R 3 games
1994 OG-M CZE R 3 games
1996 WM20 CZE R 3 games
1997 WM CZE R 5 games
1998 WM20 CZE R 5 games

**Boman, Antti**
2010 WM18 FIN R 5 games
2011 WM20 FIN R 5 games
2012 WM FIN R 5 games

**Boniface, Anne-Sophie**
2006 WW FRA L 3 games
2007 WW FRA L 4 games
2008 WW FRA L 4 games
2009 WW FRA L 4 games
2011 WW FRA L 5 games
2012 WW FRA L 4 games
~2007 WW bronze-medal game
~2009 WW gold-medal game

**Bonney, Wayne**
1996 WCH CAN L 4 games

**Bordeleau, Melanie**
2009 WW18 CAN R 4 games
2010 WW18 CAN R 4 games
2011 WW CAN R 4 games
2012 WW CAN R 4 games
~2011 WW bronze-medal game
~2012 WW gold-medal game

**Borden, Daryl**
1992 WM20 CAN R 3 games

**Borman, Jay**
1989 WM20 USA L 6 games
1992 WM USA L 8 games
1993 WM USA L 8 games
1994 OG-M USA L 8 games
~1993 WM gold-medal game
~1994 OG-M gold-medal game

**Bostrom, Finar**
1970 WM SWE R 8 games

**Botez, Alexandru**
1935 WM ROU R 1 game
1937 WM ROU R 1 game

**Bouguin, Eric**
2009 WM FRA L 6 games

**Bowles, Cory**
1993 WM20 USA L 5 games

**Bradley, Jeff**
1998 WM20 CAN L 6 games

**Brazdil, Jaromir**
1992 WM20 TCH L 6 games
1994 WM CZE L 4 games

**Braun, Hans-Rudolf**
1961 WM SUI R 3 games
1965 WM SUI R 5 games
1967 WM SUI R 4 games

**Breitenstein, Max**
1961 WM SUI R 5 games

**Brewster, Earl**
1992 WM20 USA L 5 games

**Brodnicki, Gregor**
2002 WM GER L 6 games
2003 WM GER L 5 games
2005 WM GER L 5 games

**Broseker, Gord**
1984 CC USA L 4 games
1987 CC USA L 5 games
1996 WCH USA L 6 games
1998 OG-M USA L 5 games
~1996 WCH games 2 & 3 finals
~1998 OG-M bronze-medal game

**Brousseau, Doug**
1986 WM20 CAN L 7 games
1988 OG-M CAN L 9 games

**Brown, David**
2008 WM18 USA L 7 games
2009 WM20 USA L 6 games
2010 WM USA L 8 games
2011 WM20 USA L 6 games
~2008WM18 gold-medal game
~2010 WM gold-medal game

**Brown, Sjoukje**
1994 WW USA L 4 games

**Brown, Tom**
1975 WM CAN R 9 games

**Brown, Walter**
1933 WM USA R 4 games
1934 WM USA R 17 games
1936 OG-M USA R 12 games
1947 WM USA R 4 games
1948 OG-M USA R 4 games
1949 WM USA R 3 games
~1933 WM bronze-medal game
~1934 WM bronze-medal game

**Bruck, Walter**
1933 WM AUT R 7 games
~1933 WM gold-medal game

**Bruggemann, Lars**
2011 WM18 GER R 5 games
2012 WM GER R 10 games

**Brunclik, Jiri**
1985 WM20 TCH L 4 games
1987 WM20 TCH L 6 games

**Bruun, Panu**
1997 WM20 FIN L 6 games
1997 WM FIN L 9 games
1998 WM FIN L 9 games
1999 WM FIN L 10 games
2000 WM FIN L 10 games
2002 OG-M FIN L 3 games
~1997 WM gold-medal game 3
~1998 WM bronze-medal game
~1999 WM bronze-medal game

**Bucala, Michal**
1968 OG-M TCH R 7 games
1972 WM TCH R 1 game

**Bucala, Roman**
1988 WM20 TCH L 6 games

**Bulanov, Vyacheslav**
1996 WM20 RUS L 5 games
1998 WM20 RUS L 7 games
1999 WM RUS L 6 games
2003 WM18 RUS R 4 games
2005 WM20 RUS R 4 games
2005 WM RUS R 5 games
2006 OG-M RUS R 3 games
2007 WM RUS R 5 games
2008 WM20 RUS R 6 games
2008 WM RUS R 7 games
2009 WM20 RUS R 5 games
2009 WM RUS R 7 games
2010 OG-M RUS R 3 games
2011 WM RUS R 6 games
2012 WM20 RUS R 6 games
2012 WM RUS R 10 games
~2008 WM20 gold-medal game
~2009 WM20 gold-medal game
~2012 WM20 bronze-medal game
~2012 WM bronze-medal game

**Burchell, Darcy**
2009 WM18 CAN R 6 games
2010 WM20 CAN R 6 games
2011 WM CAN R 9 games
~2009 WM18 gold-medal game
~2011 WM gold-medal game

**Burlew, Jim**
1985 WM20 USA R 5 games

**Burt, Gerry**
1994 WM USA L 7 games
1995 WM USA L 8 games
~1994 WM gold-medal game
~1995 WM gold-medal game

**Burton, Mike**
1992 WM20 CAN L 7 games

**Caban, Slavomir**
1984 WM20 TCH L 6 games
1985 WM TCH L 8 games

**Calamoneri, Thierry**
1996 WM FRA L 4 games

**Calcaterra, Enrico**
1935 WM ITA R 2 games
1939 WM ITA R 3 games

**Cameron, Lonnie**
1994 OG-M CAN L 7 games

**Caprnka, Jan**
2001 WM18 SVK R 4 games

**Carlman, Fredrik**
2007 WM18 SWE L 7 games
2008 WM20 SWE L 6 games
~2007 WM18 gold-medal game

**Carlson, Chris**
2010 WM18 CAN L 7 games
2011 WM CAN L 8 games
2012 WM20 CAN L 7 games
~2010 WM18 gold-medal game
~2011 WM gold-medal game
~2012 WM20 gold-medal game

**Carlsson, Christer**
1979 WM SWE L 7 games

**Carman, Jim**
1992 OG-M CAN L 9 games

**Carnathan, Paul**
2009 WM18 USA L 6 games
2010 WM20 USA L 6 games
2011 WM USA L 6 games
~2009 WM18 bronze-medal game
~2010 WM20 bronze-medal game

**Carpentier, Serge**
1996 WM20 CAN L 5 games
2000 WM CAN L 11 games
2002 WM CAN L 9 games
~1996 WM20 bronze-medal game
~2000 WM gold-medal game
~2002 WM bronze-medal game

**Casagrande, Dino**
1998 WM20 FIN L 7 games
~1998 WM20 bronze-medal game

**Cassidy, Sue**
1997 WW CAN L 5 games
2000 WW CAN L 5 games
2002 OG-W CAN L 5 games
~1997 WW bronze-medal game
~2000 WW gold-medal game
~2002 OG-W bronze-medal game

**Caughey, Denise**
2008 WW18 CAN L 4 games
2009 WW18 CAN L 4 games
2012 WW CAN L 5 games
~2009 WW18 bronze-medal game

**Castle, Roger**
1993 WM CAN L 7 games

**Cebulj, Boris**
1965 WM YUG R 1 game
1966 WM YUG R 3 games
1968 OG-M YUG R 2 games

**Cech, Michal**
2005 WM18 CZE L 6 games

**Cemazar, Matevz**
1984 OG-M YUG L 5 games

**Cerbo, Jim**
1977 WM20 USA R 2 games

**Cerhitova, Magdalena**
2011 WW18 SVK L 4 games
2012 WW18 SVK L 5 games
~2012 WW18 bronze-medal game

**Cerny, Otto**
1964 OG-M TCH R 7 games

**Cerwall, Orwar**
1977 WM20 SWE R 4 games

**Cesky, Vaclav**
1994 OG-M CZE L 7 games
1995 WM CZE L 7 games
1996 WM20 CZE L 7 games
1997 WM CZE L 10 games
1998 OG-M CZE L 7 games
1999 WM CZE L 7 games
2000 WM CZE L 8 games
~1994 OG-M gold-medal game
~1997 WM gold-medal game 1

**Chadzinski, Jacek**
1997 WM POL L 6 games

**Champagne, Chantal**
2001 WW CAN R 4 games
2007 WW CAN R 2 games
~2001 WW gold-medal game

**Champagne, Manon**
1990 WW CAN L 5 games
~1990 WW gold-medal game

**Chappell, Jimmy**
1950 WM GBR R 4 games

**Charbonneau, Jacques**
1978 WM20 CAN L 1 game

**Charron, Francis**
2005 WM18 CAN R 5 games
2007 WM20 CAN R 6 games
2008 WM20 CAN R 3 games
~2007 WM20 bronze-medal game

**Chojnacki, Zbigniew**
1966 WM POL R 2 games

**Christensen, Carsten**
1952 OG-M NOR R 2 games

**Claesson, Per**
2000 WM18 SWE L 7 games
2010 WM18 SWE R 6 games
2011 WM20 SWE R 5 games
~2010 WM18 bronze-medal game

**Clancy, R**
1958 WM GBR R 6 games

**Clarkson, George**
1924 OG-M GBR R 1 game

**Clemencon, Michel**
1990 WM SUI L 7 games

**Cloutier, Sylvain**
1995 WM20 CAN L 7 games
1999 WM CAN L 10 games

**Coenen, Marco**
2001 WM NED L 5 games
2002 WM NED L 7 games
2003 WM NED L 5 games
2004 WM NED L 6 games
2005 WM18 NED L 6 games
~2005 WM18 bronze-medal game

**Collins, Kevin**
1981 CC USA L 6 games
1984 CC USA L 5 games
1987 CC USA L 6 games
1991 CC USA L 5 games
1996 WCH USA L 5 games
1998 OG-M USA L 5 games
~1987 CC game 1 finals
~1991 CC game 1 finals
~1996 WCH game 1 finals

**Connolly, Kate**
2012 WW18 USA L 5 games

**Cormier, Michel**
2003 WM20 CAN L 7 games
~2003 WM20 bronze-medal game

**Costello, John**
1996 WM20 USA L 6 games
2000 WM USA L 11 games
2003 WM20 USA L 6 games
~2000 WM gold-medal game

**Cournoyer, Dan**
1982 WM20 CAN R 4 games

**Creed, Jimmy**
1950 WM GBR R 2 games

**Croft, Ian**
2012 WM20 USA R 6 games
~2012 WM20 bronze-medal game

**Curry, Michael**
1993 WM20 GBR R 3 games

**Cvik, Mike**
2002 OG-M CAN L 5 games
~2002 OG-M gold-medal game

**Czerny, Otto**
1966 WM TCH R 2 games

**Dahl, Jorgen**
1992 WW SWE R 3 games

**Dahlberg, Ove**
1965 WM SWE R 6 games
1966 WM SWE R 5 games
1967 WM SWE R 5 games
1968 OG-M SWE R 6 games
1969 WM SWE R 9 games
1970 WM SWE R 6 games
1971 WM SWE R 6 games
1972 SS SWE R 2 games
1973 WM SWE R 7 games
1974 WM SWE R 7 games
1976 CC SWE R 3 games
~IIHF Hall of Fame

**Dahle, Heiko**
1992 WM GER L 6 games
1993 WM GER L 4 games

**Dahmen, Jimmy**
2011 WM18 SWE L 7 games
2012 WM SWE L 7 games
~2011 WM18 bronze-medal game

**Daily, —**
1967 WM USA R 6 games

**Dalgleish, Scott**
2012 WM18 GBR L 6 games

**Dalton, Andrew**
2011 WM18 GBR L 6 games

**D'Amico, John**
1981 CC CAN L 5 games
1984 CC CAN L 7 games
1987 CC CAN L 8 games
~1987 CC games 2 & 3 finals

**Dammrich, Hans**
1970 WM GDR R 4 games
1971 WM GDR R 4 games
1972 WM GDR R 6 games

**Danielopol, Dumitru**
1934 WM ROU R 1 game
1935 WM ROU R 8 games

**Danielsson, Stefan**
1997 WM20 SWE L 7 games
1998 WM SWE L 9 games
~1997 WM20 gold-medal game
~1998 WM bronze-medal game

**Danko, Anton**
1992 WM TCH R 4 games
1993 WM SVK R 4 games
1994 WM SVK R 7 games
1995 WM20 SVK R 4 games
1995 WM SVK R 5 games
1996 WM SVK R 5 games
~1994 WM gold-medal game

**Dapuzzo, Pat**
1991 CC USA L 6 games
~1991 CC game 2 finals

**Davey, Gerry**
1950 WM GBR R 1 game

**Davison, Dallas**
2000 WM20 CAN L 6 games

**de Backer, Gusty**
1949 WM BEL R 1 game

**Dedyulya, Ivan**
2005 WM18 BLR L 6 games
2006 WM20 BLR L 7 games
2007 WM BLR L 8 games
2008 WM BLR L 7 games
2009 WM BLR L 6 games
2010 WM BLR L 8 games
2011 WM BLR L 8 games
2012 WM BLR L 7 games
~2008 WM gold-medal game
~2011 WM bronze-medal game

**de Haan, Chris**
2004 WM18 CAN L 7 games
2005 WM20 CAN L 7 games
2008 WM CAN L 7 games
2009 WM CAN L 7 games
~2004 WM18 gold-medal game
~2005 WM20 bronze-medal game

**Dehaen, Pierre**
2010 WM18 FRA L 6 games
2012 WM FRA L 7 games

**Dell, Alex**
1997 WM20 USA R 5 games
1998 WM USA R 9 games
1999 WM USA R 6 games
2001 WM USA R 5 games
~1997 WM20 bronze-medal game
~1998 WM gold-medal game 1

**de Marwicz, Frank**
1934 WM GBR R 6 games
1937 WM GBR R 15 games
1948 OG-M GBR R 7 games
1950 WM GBR R 3 games

**Demers, Marty**
1980 OG-M USA L 6 games

**Demetz, Giulio**
1956 OG-M ITA R 3 games
1964 OG-M ITA R 4 games

**de Rauch, Alfred**
- 1920 OG-M FRA R 1 game
- 1924 OG-M FRA R 3 games

**Devorski, Greg**
- 2004 WCH CAN L 6 games
- ~2004 WCH finals

**Devorski, Paul**
- 2004 WCH CAN R 6 games
- 2006 OG-M CAN R 5 games
- 2010 OG-M CAN R 5 games
- ~2004 WCH finals
- ~2006 OG-M gold-medal game
- ~2010 OG-M bronze-medal game

**Dewar, Tommy**
- 1934 WM CAN R 9 games

**Dietrichstein, Edgar**
- 1928 OG-M AUT R 1 game

**Dimmers, Ralph**
- 1989 WM20 FRG L 6 games
- 1990 WM FRG L 7 games

**Dombrovski, Viktor**
- 1972 WM URS R 6 games
- 1974 WM URS R 5 games
- 1975 WM URS R 7 games
- 1976 OG-M URS R 6 games
- 1976 WM URS R 9 games
- 1977 WM URS R 5 games
- 1978 WM URS R 5 games
- 1979 WM URS R 5 games
- 1980 OG-M URS R 5 games
- 1981 WM URS R 2 games

**Dombrowski, Sandra**
- 1992 WW SUI R 3 games
- 1994 WW SUI R 3 games
- 1997 WW SUI R 4 games
- 1998 OG-W SUI R 3 games
- 1998 WW SUI L 1 game
- ~1992 WW gold-medal game
- ~1994 WW gold-medal game
- ~1997 WW gold-medal game

**Dominguez, Luis**
- 1981 WM20 ESP L 4 games

**Door, Andras**
- 1990 WW HUN R 1 game+
- +information incomplete

**Doucette, Derek**
- 2003 WM20 CAN L 7 games
- 2004 WM20 CAN L 6 games
- 2005 WM CAN L 7 games
- 2006 OG-M CAN L 5 games
- ~2003 WM20 bronze-medal game
- ~2004 WM20 bronze-medal game

**Dowling, Steve**
- 1972 SS USA R 1 game

**Doyle, Jim**
- 1980 OG-M USA L 6 games
- 1982 WM USA R 7 games

**Dremelj, Igor**
- 2012 WM18 SLO R 4 games

**Driscoll, Scott**
- 1996 WCH CAN L 4 games

**Drukarenko, Alexei**
- 1992 WM20 RUS R 4 games

**Drury, Herb**
- 1924 OG-M USA R 1 game

**Dumas, Harry**
- 2012 WM18 USA R 5 games
- ~2012 WM18 bronze-medal game

**Dunne, Matt**
- 1986 WM20 USA L 7 games
- 1992 WW USA R 4 games

**Durante, Lodovico**
- 1996 WM ITA L 3 games

**Dussureault, Francois**
- 2011 WM18 CAN L 7 games
- 2012 WM CAN L 9 games
- ~2011 WM18 gold-medal game

**Dutil, Nicolas**
- 2003 WM CAN R 5 games
- 2004 WM CAN R 7 games

**Dvorsky, Jaroslav**
- 1947 WM TCH R 2 games

**Dwars, Wim**
- 1950 WM NED R 5 games
- 1951 WM NED R 6 games
- 1952 OG-M NED R 10 games
- 1953 WM NED R 3 games
- 1955 WM NED R 6 games
- 1956 OG-M NED R 5 games

**Dzieciolowski, Grzegorz**
- 1993 WM20 POL L 4 games
- 1994 WM20 POL L 4 games
- 1996 WM POL L 6 games
- 1997 WM20 POL L 5 games

**Earle, Brewster**
- 1993 WM USA L 6 games
- ~1993 WM gold-medal game

**Edelmann, Willy**
- 1979 WM FRG R 3 games

**Edgley, Jeff**
- 2001 WM20 CAN L 6 games

**Egginger, Wilhelm**
- 1959 WM FRG R 6 games

**Eglitis, Ansis**
- 2006 WM LAT L 7 games
- 2007 WM LAT L 6 games
- 2008 WM LAT L 5 games
- 2010 WM LAT L 6 games

**Ehrensperger, Heini**
- 1968 OG-M SUI R 1 game
- 1971 WM SUI R 10 games
- 1972 OG-M SUI R 4 games
- 1972 WM SUI R 4 games
- 1973 WM SUI R 10 games
- 1976 OG-M SUI R 5 games

**Eichmann, Stefan**
- 2002 WM18 SUI L 8 games

**Ekhagen, Anders**
- 1984 WM20 SWE L 6 games
- 1987 WM20 SWE L 7 games
- 1988 OG-M SWE L 8 games
- 1989 WM SWE L 10 games
- 1990 WM SWF I 9 games

**Elvy, John**
- 1994 WM USA L 6 games

**Emerson, Dan**
- 1986 WM20 CAN L 7 games

**Enciu, Stefan**
- 1980 OG-M ROU L 5 games

**Enestedt, Johan**
- 1989 WM SWE L 9 games
- 1990 WM SWE L 8 games
- 1991 WM SWE L 9 games
- 1992 OG-M SWE L 11 games
- 1995 WM SWE L 7 games
- ~1992 OG-M gold- and bronze-medal games
- ~1995 WM gold-medal game

**Erhard, Martin**
- 1976 WM FRG R 5 games
- 1977 WM FRG L 11 games
- 1978 WM20 FRG L 4 games

**Erhardt, Carl**
- 1935 WM GBR R 1 game
- 1936 OG-M GBR R 7 games
- 1937 WM GBR R 6 games
- 1939 WM GBR R 1 game
- 1947 WM GBR R 4 games
- 1948 OG-M GBR R 2 games
- 1950 WM GBR R 4 games
- ~1939 WM bronze-medal game

**Eriksson, Gary**
- 1981 WM20 SWE R 3 games
- 1981 WM20 SWE L 1 games
- 1984 WM20 SWE R 4 games
- 1986 WM SWE R 6 games
- ~was both referee and linesman at 1981 WM20

**Eriksson, Stephan**
- 1993 WM20 SWE L 7 games
- 1993 WM SWE L 7 games
- 1994 OG-M SWE L 7 games
- ~1993 WM bronze-medal game
- ~1994 OG-M bronze-medal game

**Erzen, Mirko**
- 1984 OG-M YUG L 3 games

**Erzinova, Eva**
- 1997 WW SVK L 3 games
- 1999 WW SVK L 5 games

**Espedal, Olav**
- 2006 WM18 NOR L 6 games

**Exner, Ludek**
- 1977 WM20 TCH L 7 games
- 1978 WM TCH L 10 games
- 1979 WM TCH L 9 games

**Eymard, Pierre**
- 1968 OG-M FRA R 1 game

**Fasakhudinov, Rais**
- 1983 WM20 URS L 4 games

**Fasel, Charles**
- 1935 WM SUI R 7 games

**Fasel, René**
- 1980 WM20 SUI L 5 games
- ~IIHF President 1994-present

**Faucette, Marc**
- 1980 OG-M USA R 1 game
- 1983 WM USA R 6 games
- 1985 WM USA R 5 games
- 1996 WCH USA R 5 games
- 1998 OG-M USA R 4 games
- ~1996 WCH game 1 finals

**Favorin, Jukka**
- 2001 WM18 FIN L 8 games
- ~2001 WM18 gold-medal game

**Favorin, Timo**
- 1999 WM18 FIN R 4 games
- 2000 WM18 FIN R 5 games
- 2003 WM20 FIN R 2 games
- 2003 WM FIN R 4 games
- 2006 OG-M FIN R 3 games

**Fedorocko, Alexander**
- 1994 WM20 CZE L 5 games

**Fedoseyev, Alexander**
- 1983 WM20 URS L 6 games
- 1994 WM20 RUS R 3 games

**Fedotov, Alexander**
- 1980 WM20 URS R 4 games
- 1981 CC URS L 3 games
- 1982 WM URS R 3 games
- 1991 WM20 URS R 4 games

**Feofanov, Sergei**
- 1991 WM URS L 8 games
- 1992 WM RUS L 7 games
- 1993 WM RUS L 8 games
- 1994 OG-M RUS L 8 games
- 1999 WM18 RUS R 4 games
- ~1992 WM gold-medal game

**Feola, Peter**
- 2003 WM20 USA L 7 games
- 2004 WM USA L 8 games
- 2005 WM USA L 8 games
- 2006 WM18 USA L 7 games
- 2007 WM USA L 8 games
- 2008 WM20 USA L 6 games
- 2008 WM USA L 8 games
- 2009 WM USA L 8 games
- 2010 OG-M USA L 4 games
- ~2003 WM20 gold-medal game
- ~2006 WM18 bronze-medal game
- ~2008 WM20 gold-medal game
- ~2008 WM gold-medal game
- ~2009 WM gold-medal game

**Ferber, Bjorn**
- 1978 WM SWE L 11 games

**Filip, Ivo**
- 1976 WM CZE R 7 games
- 1977 WM CZE R 5 games

**Finegold, Hal**
- 1962 WM USA R 1 game

**Finn, Ron**
- 1981 CC CAN L 3 games
- 1984 CC CAN L 4 games
- 1987 CC CAN L 6 games

**Fiquet, Andre**
- 1968 OG-M FRA R 1 game

**Fischer, Alfred**
- 1980 OG-M NOR L 4 games

**Fisher, Dave**
- 1981 WM USA R 6 games

**Fisher, Frank**
- 1928 OG-M CAN R 1 game

**Flaherty, Paul**
- 1978 WM20 USA L 7 games

**Fleischlinger, Josef**
- 1947 WM TCH R 2 games
- 1948 OG-M TCH R 4 games

**Floden, Annika**
- 2005 WW SWE L 4 games
- 2006 OG-W SWE L 3 games
- 2007 WW SWE L 4 games
- 2008 WW SWE L 4 games
- 2009 WW18 SWE L 4 games
- 2010 OG-W SWE L 4 games
- ~2009 WW18 gold-medal game

**Fluri, Nicolas**
2010 WM18 SUI L 6 games
2012 WM20 SUI L 6 games

**Folka, Matthew**
2004 WM GBR L 4 games

**Fonselius, Stefan**
2002 WM18 FIN L 8 games
2003 WM20 FIN L 5 games
2004 WM20 FIN L 7 games
2005 WM FIN L 7 games
2006 OG-M FIN L 6 games
2007 WM FIN L 8 games
2008 WM FIN L 9 games
2010 OG-M FIN L 5 games
~2004 WM20 gold-medal game
~2007 WM bronze-medal game
~2008 WM gold-medal game
~2010 OG-M gold-medal game

**Forbes, Darwin**
1999 WM18 CAN R 4 games

**Fournier, Ron**
1983 WM CAN R 11 games

**Frano, Martin**
2009 WM18 CZE R 5 games
2010 WM18 CZE R 6 games
2011 WM20 CZE R 6 games
2012 WM CZE R 8 games
~2010 WM18 bronze-medal game
~2011 WM20 gold-medal game

**Fraser, Kerry**
1996 WCH CAN R 5 games
1998 OG-M CAN R 6 games
~1996 WCH game 2 finals
~1998 OG-M bronze-medal game

**Fredrickson, Frank**
1920 OG-M CAN R 2 games
~1920 OG-M bronze-medal game

**Fredriksson, Billy**
1988 WM20 SWE R 4 games

**Frei, Egon**
1981 WM20 SUI L 5 games

**Frey, Christian**
1992 OG-M SUI R 4 games

**Frey, Walter**
1983 WM FRG L 6 games

**Friday, Bill**
1976 CC CAN R 2 games

**Frizzell, Brent**
1995 WM CAN L 6 games
~1995 WM bronze-medal game

**Frohlich, Vilem**
1938 WM TCH R 8 games
1939 WM TCH R 10 games

**Fuchsel, Maria-Raabye**
2012 WW18 DEN L 4 games

**Fukuda, Norio**
1980 OG-M JPN L 4 games

**Furakawa, Hiromi**
1993 WM20 JPN L 4 games

**Furmanek, Josef**
1987 WM20 TCH L 6 games
1991 WM TCH L 5 games

**Gage, Mary Anne**
2008 WW18 CAN R 3 games
2009 WW CAN R 3 games
2010 OG-W CAN R 3 games
2012 WW18 CAN R 5 games
~2008 WW18 bronze-medal game
~2012 WW18 bronze-medal game

**Gagnon, Len**
1971 WM USA R 7 games
1972 OG-M USA R 5 games
1972 SS USA R 3 games

**Gagnon, Nelson**
1978 WM20 CAN L 4 games

**Gagnon, Stephanie**
2012 WW18 CAN L 5 games

**Galetti, Gherardino**
1956 OG-M ITA R 3 games

**Galinovski, Mikhail**
1983 WM20 URS L 7 games
1986 WM URS L 10 games
1987 WM20 URS L 7 games
1987 CC URS L 6 games
1988 WM20 URS L 6 games
1989 WM URS L 7 games
1994 WM RUS R 3 games
~1987 CC games 1 & 3 finals

**Galloway, Ryan**
1997 WM20 CAN L 7 games

**Gambucci, Andy**
1962 WM USA R 4 games

**Gardiner, Jeff**
1991 WM20 CAN L 6 games

**Garofalo, Jim**
1990 WW USA L 5 games
1998 WM USA L 9 games
1999 WM USA L 11 games
2001 WM USA L 8 games
2002 OG-M USA L 4 games
~1990 WW gold-medal game
~1998 WM gold-medal game 2
~1999 WM gold-medal game 2

**Garon, Joseph**
1920 OG-M CAN R 1 game

**Garsjo, Pal**
1999 WM NOR L 7 games
2000 WM NOR L 8 games
2006 WM NOR L 6 games

**Gashilov, Viktor**
2004 WM18 RUS L 6 games
2010 WM18 RUS R 5 games

**Gasser, Thomas**
1992 OG-M ITA L 7 games
1994 WM ITA L 5 games
1995 WM ITA L 4 games

**Gaudet, Don**
1990 WM CAN R 5 games

**Gauthier, Gerard**
1984 CC CAN L 4 games
1991 CC CAN L 6 games
1998 OG-M CAN L 5 games
~1991 CC game 2 finals

**Gawlik, Brent**
2003 WM18 USA L 6 games

**Gebauer, Jiri**
2006 WM18 CZE L 6 games
2010 WM18 CZE L 6 games
2011 WM CZE L 6 games
2012 WM20 CZE L 6 games
~2010 WM18 gold-medal game

**Gebei, Peter**
2012 WM18 HUN R 4 games

**Gemeinhardt, Thomas**
2003 WM18 GER L 4 games
2004 WM GER L 4 games
2006 OG-M GER L 4 games
2007 WM GER L 7 games
2009 WM20 GER L 6 games
2010 WM GER L 6 games
~2003 WM18 gold-medal game

**George, Tommy**
2012 WM18 USA L 7 games
~2012 WM18 bronze-medal game

**Gerasimov, Kirill**
1985 WM20 BUL L 6 games
1986 WM BUL L 8 games
1987 WM BUL L 8 games

**Gerber, Hans-Rudolf**
1971 WM SUI R 4 games

**Geromini, Albert**
1935 WM SUI 9 games
1938 WM SUI 5 games

**Gerstberger, Holger**
1992 WW GER L 5 games
~1992 WW bronze-medal game

**Gibbs, Darren**
1995 WM20 CAN L 6 games
1997 WM CAN L 9 games
~1997 WM bronze-medal game

**Gienke, Thomas**
2004 WM20 NOR L 6 games
2008 WM NOR L 5 games

**Giguere, Isabelle**
1997 WW CAN L 5 games
1998 OG-W CAN L 6 games
2000 WW CAN R 4 games
~1997 WW bronze-medal game
~1998 OG-W gold-medal game
~2000 WW bronze-medal game

**Girard, Serge**
1978 WM20 CAN L 4 games

**Glines, Steve**
2005 WM18 USA L 6 games
2006 WM20 USA L 6 games

**Gobbi, Candido**
1992 WM SUI L 4 games

**Gobetzky, Aladar**
1973 WM AUT R 3 games

**Goel, Emile**
1948 OG-M SUI R 2 games

**Gofman, Roman**
2008 WM18 RUS L 6 games
2012 WM18 RUS R 7 games
~2012 WM18 gold-medal game

**Golyak, Dmitri**
2010 WM18 BLR L 6 games

**Gonchar, Yevgeni**
1988 WM20 URS L 6 games

**Gorbunov, Mikhail**
1957 WM URS R 4 games

**Gordenko, Konstantin**
2003 WM18 RUS L 7 games
2004 WM20 RUS L 6 games
2006 WM20 RUS L 7 games
2007 WM RUS L 6 games
2008 WM20 RUS L 6 games
2009 WM RUS L 6 games
2010 WM RUS L 6 games

**Gorski, Julian**
1987 WM20 POL L 5 games
1988 OG-M POL L 9 games
1989 WM POL L 6 games
1990 WM20 POL L 6 games

**Gotsulya, Valeri**
2003 WM BLR L 7 games
2004 WM18 BLR L 6 games

**Graff, Roger**
1990 WW USA L 5 games
1991 WM20 USA L 7 games
1992 WW USA L 5 games

**Graham, Blair**
1977 WM20 CAN R 5 games

**Grandin, Kjell**
1980 WM20 SWE R 4 games

**Grant, Petre**
1934 WM ROM R 6 games

**Gregson, Terry**
1982 WM CAN R 6 games
1996 WCH CAN R 5 games
~1996 WCH game 3 finals

**Grillmayer, Eberhard**
1964 OG-M AUT R 5 games

**Groger, Manuela**
1994 WW GER L 4 games
1997 WW GER R 3 games
1998 OG-W GER R 3 games
1998 OG-W GER L 1 game
1999 WW GER R 5 games
~1994 WW gold-medal game

**Gross, Fritz**
1961 WM GDR R 3 games
1963 WM GDR R 1 game
1965 WM GDR R 1 game
1966 WM GDR R 2 games
1967 WM GDR R 1 game
1968 OG-M DDR R 2 games

**Grumsen, Jacob**
2011 WM18 DEN R 4 games

**Grun, Milos**
1987 WM20 TCH L 6 games

**Grundstrom, Jorgen**
1992 WM20 SWE R 3 games
1994 WM SWE R 4 games

**Gubernatorov, Viktor**
1988 WM20 URS R 4 games
1989 WM20 URS R 4 games
1990 WM20 URS R 4 games
1993 WM20 RUS R 3 games

**Guijie, Meng**
2000 WW CHN L 3 games

**Guldner, Josef**
1947 WM AUT R 1 game
1957 WM AUT R 4 games

**Gustavson, Andy**
1959 WM USA R 7 games

**Gustavsson, Tommy**
1985 WM20 SWE L 7 games

**Guynn, Dan**
1974 WM USA R 8 games
1976 WM USA R 8 games

**Haajanen, Pekka**
1996 WM20 FIN R 4 games
1997 WM20 FIN R 4 games
1998 OG-M FIN R 3 games
2000 WM FIN R 7 games
~1996 WM20 gold-medal game

**Haanpaa, Anne**
2000 WW FIN R 3 games
2001 WW FIN R 3 games
2002 OG-W FIN R 3 games

**Haapalahti, Sanna**
2008 WW FIN L 4 games
~2008 WW gold-medal game

**Haapanen, Eeva**
2004 WW FIN L 5 games
2009 WW18 FIN L 4 games

**Haidinger, Karl**
1976 OG-M AUT R 3 games

**Halas, Pavel**
1994 WM20 CZE L 6 games
1996 WM CZE L 6 games
1997 WM20 CZE L 7 games
1998 WM CZE L 9 games
~1996 WM bronze-medal game
~1997 WM20 gold-medal game
~1998 WM gold-medal game 1

**Halecky, Miroslav**
2000 WM18 SVK L 6 games
2002 WM18 SVK L 8 games
2003 WM20 SVK L 6 games
2004 WM20 SVK L 6 games
2005 WM SVK L 9 games
2006 OG-M SVK L 5 games
~2004 WM20 bronze-medal game
~2005 WM bronze-medal game

**Haley, Bernie**
1972 WM CAN R 7 games
1980 OG-M CAN R 5 games
1981 WM CAN R 4 games

**Halin, Harry**
1992 WM20 NED L 6 games

**Hamalainen, Antti**
2000 WM20 FIN L 7 games
2001 WM20 FIN L 6 games
2001 WM FIN L 8 games
2002 OG-M FIN L 6 games
2003 WM FIN L 9 games
2005 WM FIN L 7 games
2006 OG-M FIN L 5 games
~2001 WM20 bronze-medal game
~2001 WM bronze-medal game
~2002 OG-M gold-medal game
~2003 WM gold-medal game
~2005 WM gold-medal game

**Hands, Deb**
1990 WW CAN L 5 games

**Hanqvist, Ake**
1972 OG-M SWE R 4 games
1975 WM SWE R 8 games
1976 OG-M SWE R 6 games

**Hanrahan, Alicia**
2010 WW18 USA L 4 games
2011 WW USA L 5 games
2012 WW USA L 5 games
~2011 WW bronze-medal game
~2012 WW gold-medal game

**Hansen, Dave**
2004 WM18 USA R 5 games
2005 WM20 USA R 5 games
2006 WM USA R 5 games
~2005 WM20 gold-medal game

**Hansen, Ole**
2004 WM NOR R 4 games
2006 WM20 NOR R 3 games
2007 WM NOR R 4 games
2008 WM18 NOR R 5 games
2009 WM NOR R 6 games
2010 WM NOR R 6 games
~2008 WM18 bronze-medal game

**Hansen, Scott**
1998 WM20 USA R 5 games
1999 WM20 USA R 5 games
2000 WM USA R 6 games
2001 WM20 USA R 5 games
2002 OG-M USA R 2 games
~1998 WM20 bronze-medal game
~1999 WM20 gold-medal game
~2000 WM20 gold-medal game

**Hansen, Tommy**
1996 WM NOR R 2 games

**Hansen, Tor**
1990 WM NOR R 3 games
1991 WM NOR R 4 games
1992 WM NOR R 2 games
1994 OG-M NOR R 4 games

**Hansen-Fnug, Joe**
1992 WW DEN L 4 games

**Hanson, Moray**
2004 WM GBR R 4 games

**Haraldsen, Jon**
1972 OG-M NOR R 2 games

**Hart, Brian**
1982 WM20 USA R 4 games
1983 WM20 USA R 5 games
1987 WM USA R 5 games

**Hascher, Alfred**
1998 WM20 GER L 6 games
1999 WM18 GER L 7 games
2001 WM GER L 7 games

**Hasenfratz, Mike**
1991 WM20 CAN L 5 games

**Hauchart, Alexandre**
2000 WM18 FRA L 7 games

**Hauser, Kurt**
1948 OG-M SUI R 8 games
1949 WM SUI R 7 games
1950 WM SUI R 7 games
1951 WM SUI R 5 games
1952 OG-M SUI R 3 games
1955 WM SUI R 6 games
1956 OG-M SUI R 7 games
1958 WM SUI R 5 games
1959 WM SUI R 8 games
1960 OG-M SUI R 6 games

**Hausner, Michael**
1987 WM AUT L 7 games

**Havlik, Jaroslav**
2003 WM18 CZE R 4 games

**Hayashi, Kan**
1957 WM JPN R 4 games
1960 OG-M JPN R 2 games

**Hearn, Rob**
1988 WM20 USA R 4 games
1989 WM USA R 6 games
1993 WM USA R 8 games
1994 OG-M USA R 7 games
1995 WM USA R 5 games
~1993 WM gold-medal game
~1994 OG-M gold-medal game
~1995 WM gold-medal game

**Hebert, Karen**
1990 WW CAN L 4 games
1992 WW CAN R 3 games
~1992 WW bronze-medal game

**Heinecke, Werner**
1952 OG-M GER R 1 game

**Henderson, Sarah**
2004 WW USA R 3 games

**Hengst, Debby**
2011 WW18 NED R 4 games
~2011 WW18 gold-medal game

**Henriksson, Hannu**
2003 WM18 FIN R 5 games
2004 WM FIN R 7 games
2005 WM FIN R 6 games
~2003 WM18 gold-medal game
~2004 WM gold-medal game

**Henriksson, Lars**
1987 WM20 SWE R 4 games

**Henry, Bob**
1981 CC USA R 4 games

**Herman, Derek**
2004 WM20 CAN R 5 games

**Hermann, Josef**
1938 WM TCH R 1 game
1947 WM TCH R 4 games
1948 OG-M TCH R 5 games
1949 WM TCH R 6 games

**Hertrich, Nicole**
2008 WW GER R 4 games
2009 WW GER R 3 games
2010 OG-W GER R 4 games
2011 WW GER R 4 games
2012 WW GER R 3 games
~2008 WW gold-medal game
~2010 OG-W bronze-medal game
~2011 WW gold-medal game

**Hewitt, William**
1920 OG-M CAN R 1 game
1924 OG-M CAN R 2 games
~IIHF Hall of Fame

**Heximer, Fan**
1950 WM GBR R 6 games
1951 WM GBR R 7 games

**Heyer, Shane**
1996 WCH USA L 4 games
2010 OG-M USA L 5 games

**Hilker, Greg**
1982 WM20 CAN L 7 games

**Hirter, Fritz**
1987 WM20 SUI L 6 games

**Hirtz, Arnold**
1939 WM SUI R 10 games

**Hirvi, Ilkka**
1996 WM20 FIN L 7 games
~1996 WM20 gold-medal game

**Hirvonen, Anu**
1999 WW FIN R 3 games
2000 WW FIN R 4 games
2002 OG-W FIN R 3 games
2004 WW FIN R 4 games
2005 WW FIN R 3 games
2006 OG-W FIN R 3 games
2007 WW FIN R 3 games
2008 WW18 FIN R 3 games
2012 WW18 FIN R 3 games
~2004 WW gold-medal game
~2005 WW gold-medal game
~2006 OG-W gold-medal game

**Hirzel, Niklaus**
2000 WM18 SUI L 7 games
~2000 WM18 gold-medal game

**Hishmeh, Meghan**
2007 WW USA L 4 games
2008 WW USA L 4 games
2009 WW USA L 4 games
2010 OG-W USA L 4 games
~2008 WW bronze-medal game

**Hobor, Terry**
2004 WM18 CAN R 4 games

**Hollenstein, Manuel**
2011 WM AUT L 6 games

**Hollett, Gary**
1980 OG-M CAN L 6 games

**Holmroos, Mauri**
1985 WM20 FIN L 6 games

**Holsboer, Max**
1936 OG-M SUI R 2 games

**Homola, Martin**
2001 WM20 CZE R 5 games

**Honkanen, Eino**
1977 WM20 FIN R 4 games

**Hood, Bruce**
1976 CC CAN R 3 games
1981 CC CAN R 4 games
1985 WM CAN R 6 games

**Horinek, Martin**
2011 WM18 SVK L 6 games

**Horne, Ed**
1988 OG-M USA L 8 games

**Hove, Aina**
2007 WW NOR R 3 games
2008 WW NOR R 3 games
2009 WW NOR R 3 games
2010 OG-W NOR R 4 games
2011 WW NOR R 3 games
2012 WW NOR R 3 games
~2009 WW gold-medal game
~2010 OG-W gold-medal game

**Hove, Marta**
2006 OG-W NOR L 3 games

**Hoviseppa, Ilkka**
1982 WM FIN L 6 games

**Howard, Danyel**
2005 WW USA R 3 games
2006 OG-W USA R 4 games
2008 WW18 USA R 3 games
~2006 WW bronze-medal game

**Hribar, Matjaz**
2011 WM SLO L 6 games

**Hribik, Jan**
2012 WM18 CZE R 6 games
~2012 WM18 bronze-medal game

**Huber, Steve**
1980 OG-M USA L 5 games

**Hugli, Erhard**
1939 WM SUI R 9 games

**Huguenin, Frederique**
2005 WW CAN L 4 games
~2005 WW bronze-medal game

**Hujdusova, Henrieta**
2000 WW SVK L 4 games
2001 WW SVK L 5 games
2002 OG-W SVK L 4 games
~2001 WW bronze-medal game
~2002 OG-W gold-medal game

**Hull, Justin**
2012 WM18 CAN L 7 games
~2012 WM18 gold-medal game

**Hutchinson, Scott**
2002 WM CAN R 7 games

**Huvos, Istvan**
1947 WM HUN R 1 game
1948 OG-M HUN R 1 game

**Idenstedt, Borje**
1963 WM SWE R 1 game

**Ingman, Jyrki**
1990 WM20 FIN L 6 games
1991 WM FIN L 7 games
1994 WM20 FIN R 5 games
1995 WM20 FIN R 4 games

**Inoue, Chieko**
2012 WW18 JPN R 6 games
~2012 WW18 gold-medal game

**Isotalo, Pentti**
1963 WM FIN R 2 games
1964 OG-M FIN R 5 games
1965 WM FIN R 3 games
1966 WM FIN R 1 game
1972 WM FIN R 5 games
1973 WM FIN R 6 games

**Ivanova, Yelena**
2009 WW18 RUS L 3 games
2011 WW18 RUS L 4 games

**Ivicicova, Katerina**
2004 WW CZE R 3 games
2005 WW CZE R 4 games
2006 OG-W CZE R 3 games
2007 WW CZE R 3 games
2008 WW18 CZE R 3 games

**Izumisawa, Kenichi**
1973 WM JPN R 2 games

**Jaala, Lennart**
1966 WM FIN R 1 game

**Jablukov, Georgij**
2006 WM20 GER L 6 games
2009 WM18 GER R 5 games
2011 WM20 GER R 6 games
2012 WM GER R 8 games
~2011 WM20 bronze-medal game

**Jacobs, Jay**
1994 WM20 USA L 6 games
1995 WM20 USA L 2 games

**Jacquet, Emile**
1936 OG-M SUI R 1 game

**Jakobsen, Ronni**
2003 WM DEN L 6 games
2006 WM DEN L 7 games
2007 WM DEN L 6 games

**Jakonin, Ivan**
1957 WM URS R 4 games
1958 WM URS R 4 games

**Jalarvo, Jarmo**
1985 WM20 FIN R 3 games
1985 WM20 FIN L 1 game
1986 WM FIN R 6 games
1987 WM FIN R 5 games

**Janezic, Milka**
1972 OG-M YUG R 2 games

**Janicek, Boris**
1991 CC TCH L 3 games
1992 WM TCH L 6 games
1993 WM CZE L 5 games
~1992 WM gold-medal game

**Janovsky, Jaroslav**
1947 WM TCH R 1 game

**Jarvela, Arto**
1989 WM FIN L 8 games
1990 WM FIN L 9 games
1998 WM FIN R 3 games

**Jarvi, Harri**
1976 WM FIN R 6 games
1987 WM20 FIN R 5 games

**Jay, Jeff**
1982 WM20 USA L 5 games

**Jensen, Ingvar**
1997 WM NOR L 8 games

**Jerabek, Antonin**
2010 WM20 CZE R 4 games
2011 WM CZE R 6 games
2012 WM CZE R 10 games
~2012 WM gold-medal game

**Jirka, Milan**
1983 WM20 TCH R 3 games
1984 WM20 TCH R 4 games
1988 OG-M TCH R 4 games

**Joannette, Marc**
1996 WM20 CAN R 3 games
1997 WM CAN R 6 games
2004 WCH CAN R 5 games
2010 OG-M CAN R 4 games

**Jobson, Jeff**
2008 WM20 CAN L 8 games
2010 WM20 CAN L 5 games
~2008 WM20 bronze-medal game

**Johannesson, Borje**
1965 WM NOR R 1 game
1968 OG-M NOR R 1 game

**Johannesson, Tore**
1951 WM SWE R 1 game
1954 WM SWE R 4 games
1955 WM SWE R 5 games
1956 OG-M SWE R 4 games
1959 WM SWE R 6 games

**Johansson, Borje**
1990 WM20 SWE R 4 games
1991 WM SWE R 5 games
1991 CC SWE R 2 games
1994 OG-M SWE R 5 games
1995 WM SWE R 4 games
~1994 OG-M bronze-medal game

**Johansson, Morgan**
2010 WM20 SWE R 5 games
2011 WM18 SWE R 6 games
2012 WM SWE R 7 games
~2011 WM18 bronze-medal game

**Johnsen, Tor-Olav**
1990 WM20 NOR R 3 games
1991 WM20 NOR R 4 games
1998 WM NOR R 4 games
1999 WM NOR R 3 games
2000 WM NOR R 5 games
2001 WM20 NOR R 5 games
2002 WM NOR R 5 games
2003 WM20 NOR R 4 games

**Johnson, Laura**
2011 WW18 USA L 5 games
2012 WW USA L 4 games
~2011 WW18 bronze-medal game

**Jokela, Juhani**
1982 WM FIN L 6 games
1989 WM20 FIN R 4 games
1992 WM FIN R 3 games

**Jonak, Peter**
1996 WM20 SVK R 2 games
1998 WM20 SVK R 5 games
2000 WM18 SVK R 4 games
2003 WM SVK R 4 games
2006 WM SVK R 5 games
2007 WM SVK R 5 games
2008 WM18 SVK R 5 games
~2006 WM bronze-medal game

**Jonchev, Joncho**
1990 WW BUL R 2 games+
+information incomplete

**Jones, Robert**
1998 WM CAN L 9 games
~1998 WM gold-medal game 2

**Josek, Gustav**
1938 WM TCH R 1 game
1947 WM TCH R 3 games

**Joyal, Lou**
1969 WM CAN R 6 games

**Juhala, Pertti**
1981 WM20 FIN R 2 games

**Juhola, Pertti**
1983 WM FIN R 6 games
1984 OG-M FIN R 4 games
1985 WM FIN R 7 games
1990 WM20 FIN R 5 games
1991 WM20 FIN R 3 games

**Jurgens, A**
1939 WM LAT R 1 game

**Jursa, Libor**
1977 WM20 TCH L 7 games

**Kack, Johannes**
2012 WM20 SWE L 6 games

**Kadyrov, Rafail**
2005 WM18 RUS R 4 games
2006 WM20 RUS R 3 games
2008 WM18 RUS R 5 games
2009 WM RUS R 7 games
2010 WM RUS R 6 games
2011 WM20 RUS R 5 games
~2005 WM18 gold-medal game
~2009 WM bronze-medal game

**Kahlert, Ulrike**
1997 WW GER L 4 games

**Kaisla, Karl-Gustav**
1977 WM FIN L 13 games
1978 WM20 FIN R 6 games
1979 WM FIN R 4 games
1980 OG-M FIN R 6 games
1981 WM FIN R 5 games
1984 WM20 FIN R 4 games
1986 WM20 FIN R 3 games
1987 CC FIN R 3 games
~1978 WM20 gold-medal game
~1980 OG-M URS-USA game

**Kale, Vicki**
1997 WW USA R 3 games
1998 OG-W USA R 3 games*
1999 WW USA R 5 games
*officiated under married name Renfer-Kale

**Kalivoda, Frantisek**
2005 WM18 CZE L 7 games
2006 WM20 CZE L 7 games
2007 WM18 CZE L 7 games
2008 WM CZE L 6 games
2009 WM20 CZE L 6 games
2010 WM CZE L 7 games
~2005 WM18 gold-medal game
~2006 WM20 gold-medal game
~2007 WM18 bronze-medal game

**Kanunikov, Nikolai**
1954 WM URS R 5 games
1956 OG-M URS R 3 games
1957 WM URS R 4 games
1959 WM URS R 5 games

**Kapolka, Andrzej**
1980 OG-M POL L 5 games

**Karabanov, Sergei**
1993 WM RUS L 7 games
1994 WM RUS L 8 games
1998 WM20 RUS R 3 games
1999 WM20 RUS R 3 games
1999 WM RUS R 3 games
2000 WM RUS R 5 games
2001 WM20 RUS R 4 games
2002 WM RUS R 6 games
2004 WM20 RUS R 5 games
~1994 WM gold-medal game
~2001 WM20 bronze-medal game
~2004 WM20 bronze-medal game

**Karandin, Yuri**
1970 WM URS R 7 games
1971 WM URS R 5 games
1972 OG-M URS R 4 games
1973 WM URS R 3 games
1978 WM20 URS R 4 games
1976 CC URS R 2 games
1983 WM20 URS R 4 games
1983 WM URS R 7 games
1984 OG-M URS R 7 games
1984 CC URS R 4 games
1985 WM URS R 6 games
1986 WM URS R 8 games
1987 WM20 URS R 4 games
1987 WM URS R 1 game
~IIHF Hall of Fame

**Karlberg, Anders**
2004 WM18 SWE L 6 games
2005 WM20 SWE L 6 games
2006 WM18 SWE L 7 games
2007 WM SWE L 9 games
~2006 WM18 gold-medal game
~2007 WM gold-medal game

**Karlsson, Joacim**
2000 WM20 SWE L 6 games
2001 WM18 SWE L 7 games
2002 WM SWE L 9 games
2003 WM SWE L 10 games
2005 WM SWE L 7 games
2006 OG-M SWE L 6 games
~2000 WM20 gold-medal game
~2003 WM bronze-medal game
~2005 WM gold-medal game
~2006 OG-M bronze-medal game

**Karlsson, Kjell**
1984 WM20 SWE L 6 games
1985 WM SWE L 8 games

**Karlsson, Stig**
1976 WM SWE R 10 games
1977 WM SWE R 5 games
1978 WM SWE R 5 games

**Kaspar, Christian**
2008 WM AUT L 5 games
2009 WM AUT L 6 games
2010 WM AUT L 6 games
2011 WM20 AUT L 5 games

**Kaufmann, Theo**
1937 WM GER R 6 games

**Kaukonen, Teemu**
1992 WW FIN R 4 games
1994 WW FIN R 3 games

**Kautto, Juha**
2003 WM FIN L 7 games
2004 WM FIN L 9 games
2005 WM20 FIN L 6 games
2006 WM20 FIN L 6 games
~2004 WM gold-medal game
~2005 WM20 gold-medal game
~2006 WM20 gold-medal game

**Kaval, Keith**
2009 WM18 USA R 5 games
2010 WM20 USA R 6 games
2011 WM20 USA R 6 games
2012 WM USA R 6 games
~2009 WM18 bronze-medal game
~2010 WM20 bronze-medal game
~2011 WM20 gold-medal game

**Kekalainen, Mikko**
2004 WM18 FIN L 6 games
2005 WM18 FIN L 6 games
2006 WM FIN L 7 games
2007 WM20 FIN L 7 games
2008 WM20 FIN L 5 games
2011 WM20 FIN L 8 games
~2007 WM20 bronze-medal game
~2011 WM20 bronze-medal game

**Keller, Max**
1939 WM SUI R 1 game

**Keller, Rene**
1966 WM FRG R 3 games

**Kelly, John**
1999 WM18 USA R 5 games
2000 WM18 USA R 4 games

**Keronen, Tuula**
1990 WW FIN L 4 games
1992 WW FIN L 4 games

**Kerkos, Albert**
1964 OG-M YUG R 5 games
1965 WM YUG R 2 games
1966 WM YUG R 2 games

**Kerr, Gordon**
1976 OG-M CAN R 5 games

**Kerr, Richard**
1982 WM20 CAN L 5 games

**Kessler, Charlie**
1948 OG-M SUI R 4 games
1949 WM SUI R 6 games

**Kicha, Andri**
2007 WM UKR L 7 games
2008 WM UKR L 7 games
2009 WM UKR L 8 games
2010 OG-M UKR L 3 games
2010 WM UKR L 6 games
2011 WM20 UKR L 5 games
~2009 WM bronze-medal game

**Kiefer, Daniela**
2008 WW GER L 4 games
2009 WW18 GER L 5 games

**Kiefer, Michaela**
2005 WW GER L 5 games
2006 OG-W GER L 3 games
2009 WW18 GER R 3 games
2010 WW18 GER R 3 games

**Kilian, Jon**
2012 WM NOR L 7 games

**Kirk, Matt**
2011 WM20 CAN R 5 games
~2011 WM20 bronze-medal game

**Kirschner, Tina**
2002 OG-W GER L 3 games

**Kiselyov, Vladislav**
2002 WM18 RUS L 8 games

**Kiviano, Kari**
1988 WM20 FIN L 6 games

**Kladrubsky, Jaroslav**
1938 WM TCH R 4 games
1939 WM TCH R 9 games

**Klein, Devin**
2011 WM18 CAN R 6 games
2012 WM20 CAN R 5 games
~2011 WM18 gold-medal game

**Klein, Robert**
1950 WM GBR R 2 games

**Kluge, Rainer**
1985 WM GDR L 8 games
1994 WW GER R 3 games

**Knight, Krista**
1999 WW USA R 4 games
2000 WW USA R 3 games
2001 WW USA R 4 games
2002 OG-W USA R 3 games
~1999 WW bronze-medal game

**Knox, Swede**
1987 CC CAN L 2 games

**Koch, Andreas**
2012 WM18 SUI R 5 games

**Koharski, Don**
1987 CC CAN R 6 games
1991 CC CAN R 5 games
2004 WCH CAN R 5 games
~1987 CC games 1 & 3 finals
~1991 CC game 1 finals

**Kohler, Andreas**
2012 WM18 SUI L 7 games
~2012 WM18 bronze-medal game

**Kolar, Karel**
1938 WM TCH R 1 game
1939 WM TCH R 7 games

**Kolisek, Milan**
2000 WM18 CZE R 4 games

**Komissarov, Konstantin**
1989 WM20 URS L 7 games
1990 WM20 URS L 6 games
1991 WM20 URS L 6 games
1992 WM RUS L 6 games
~1992 WM bronze-medal game

**Kompalla, Josef**
1972 WM FRG R 10 games
1972 SS FRG R 2 games
1974 WM FRG R 8 games
1975 WM FRG R 9 games
1976 OG-M GER R 6 games
1977 WM FRG R 5 games
1978 WM FRG R 4 games
1980 OG-M FRG R 5 games
1981 WM20 FRG R 1 game
1981 WM FRG R 3 games
1982 WM FRG R 2 games
1984 OG-M FRG R 6 games
1985 WM FRG R 4 games
1986 WM FRG R 3 games
~1972 SS Game 8 with Rudolf Bata
~IIHF Hall of Fame

**Kompalla-Doucet, Nicole**
1990 WW GER L 4 games

**Konc, Daniel**
2005 WM18 SVK R 7 games
2008 WM20 SVK R 5 games
2010 WM SVK R 6 games
2011 WM20 SVK R 5 games
2012 WM18 SVK R 6 games

**Konc, Juraj**
2006 WM18 SVK R 4 games
2007 WM20 SVK R 3 games
2009 WM18 SVK R 5 games
~2009 WM18 gold-medal game

**Konstantinova, Marina**
1999 WW RUS L 4 games
2000 WW RUS L 3 games
2001 WW RUS L 4 games
2002 OG-W RUS L 4 games
2004 WW RUS L 5 games
2005 WW RUS L 4 games
2006 OG-W RUS L 3 games
2007 WW RUS L 4 games
2008 WW18 RUS L 4 games
~1999 WW bronze-medal game
~2005 WW bronze-medal game
~2008 WW18 gold-medal game

**Korentschnig, Karl**
1981 WM20 AUT L 5 games
1982 WM AUT L 6 games
1983 WM20 AUT L 6 games
1984 OG-M AUT L 6 games
1985 WM20 AUT L 6 games
1987 WM AUT L 7 games
1988 OG-M AUT L 8 games
1994 OG-M AUT R 3 games
1996 WM AUT R 2 games

**Korinek, Zdenek**
1966 WM TCH R 4 games
1967 WM TCH R 5 games
1968 OG-M TCH R 7 games
1970 WM TCH R 8 games
1972 WM TCH R 1 game

**Koskela, Harri**
1992 WW FIN L 4 games

**Koskinen, Antti**
1980 WM20 FIN R 4 games
1988 OG-M FIN R 4 games

**Koskinen, Kari**
1985 WM20 FIN L 6 games

**Kost, Karen**
1992 WW CAN L 4 games
1994 WW CAN R 2 games
~1992 WW bronze-medal game

**Kotyra, Tim**
1995 WM20 USA L 8 games
1996 WM USA L 5 games
1997 WM USA L 9 games
1998 OG-M USA L 4 games
~1997 WM bronze-medal game

**Kovacik, Brad**
2004 WCH CAN L 4 games

**Kovalchuk, Vladimir**
1995 WM20 UKR L 4 games
1999 WM18 UKR L 7 games

**Kowal, Tom**
1997 WM20 CAN R 4 games

**Kowert, Andreas**
2006 WM18 GER L 6 games
2008 WM18 GER L 6 games
2009 WM18 GER L 6 games
2010 WM GER L 6 games
2011 WM18 GER L 6 games
~2008 WM18 bronze-medal game

**Kozlov, Sergei**
1997 WM20 RUS L 5 games

**Kraatz, Fritz**
1935 WM SUI R 1 game
1936 OG-M SUI R 1 game
1938 WM SUI R 6 games

**Krasl, Jean**
1938 WM TCH R 3 games
1947 WM TCH R 3 games
1955 WM TCH R 5 games

**Kreisel, Franz**
1935 WM GER R 8 games
1936 OG-M GER R 9 games
1938 WM GER R 1 game
1939 WM GER R 1 game
~1935 WM gold-medal game
~1939 WM bronze-medal game

**Kriska, Josef**
1985 WM TCH L 8 games
1987 WM20 TCH L 7 games

**Kronborg, Lars**
2000 WM20 NOR L 7 games
2001 WM18 NOR L 6 games
2002 WM NOR L 7 games
2003 WM20 NOR L 6 games
2004 WM NOR L 9 games

**Kronenberg, Dave**
1991 WM20 USA L 4 games
1999 WM20 USA L 5 games

**Kruus, Markku**
2000 WM20 FIN R 4 games
2001 WM18 FIN R 3 games

**Krystufek, Karel**
1947 WM TCH R 1 game

**Kuba, Ivo**
1994 WM20 CZE R 4 games

**Kubinec, John**
1968 OG-M CAN R 6 games

**Kubiszewski, Leszek**
1992 WM POL L 4 games

**Kubus, Jozef**
2009 WM18 SVK R 5 games
2010 WM18 SVK R 5 games
2011 WM18 SVK R 5 games

**Kuchar, Waclaw**
1931 WM POL R 1 game

**Kudelova, Michaela**
2009 WW18 SVK L 5 games
2010 WW18 SVK L 4 games
2012 WW SVK L 4 games
~2009 WW18 gold-medal game

**Kuhnert, Adolf**
1964 OG-M AUT R 3 games

**Kuisma, Johanna**
1997 WW FIN L 5 games
1998 OG-W FIN L 6 games
1999 WW FIN L 5 games
~1997 WW gold-medal game
~1998 OG-W bronze-medal game
~1999 WW gold-medal game

**Kulakov, Sergei**
1999 WM20 RUS L 6 games
2000 WM RUS L 10 games
2001 WM RUS L 8 games
2002 OG-M RUS L 6 games
2008 WM18 RUS R 5 games
2009 WM20 RUS R 5 games
~2000 WM bronze-medal game

**Kulej, Lucjan**
1931 WM POL R 1 game
1936 OG-M POL R 1 game

**Kummetz, Gunther**
1935 WM GER R 6 games

**Kung, Peter**
2007 WM20 SUI L 5 games

**Kunz, Bernhard**
1987 WM SUI L 10 games
1988 WM20 SUI L 7 games
1989 WM SUI L 8 games
1990 WM20 SUI L 4 games

**Kurmann, Danny**
1999 WM20 SUI R 4 games
1999 WM SUI R 6 games
2000 WM20 SUI R 6 games
2000 WM SUI R 4 games
2001 WM SUI R 7 games
2002 OG-M SUI R 3 games
2003 WM20 SUI R 4 games
2003 WM SUI R 5 games
2004 WM SUI R 4 games
2006 OG-M SUI R 3 games
2007 WM20 SUI R 4 games
2007 WM SUI R 7 games
2008 WM20 SUI R 7 games
2008 WM SUI R 7 games
2009 WM20 SUI R 5 games
2009 WM SUI R 8 games
2010 OG-M SUI R 3 games
2011 WM SUI R 8 games
2012 WM SUI R 9 games
~1999 WM gold-medal games 1 and 2
~2000 WM20 gold-medal game
~2001 WM bronze-medal game
~2003 WM20 bronze-medal game
~2007 WM20 gold-medal game
~2008 WM20 bronze-medal game
~2009 WM20 gold-medal game
~2011 WM bronze-medal game
~2012 WM bronze-medal game

**Kurokowa, Hideki**
1983 WM20 JPN R 2 games

**Kuryk, Don**
1980 WM20 CAN R 3 games

**Kuznetsov, Vladimir**
1964 OG-M URS R 6 games

**Laaksonen, Tom**
2004 WM18 FIN R 4 games
2008 WM18 FIN R 5 games
2009 WM20 FIN R 4 games
2010 WM20 FIN R 6 games
2010 WM FIN R 7 games
2012 WM20 FIN R 5 games
~2008WM18 gold-medal game
~2010 WM20 gold-medal game

**Lacarriere, Jacques**
1947 WM FRA R 4 games
1948 OG-M FRA R 3 games

**Lacroix, Alphonse "Frenchy"**
1924 OG-M FRA R 2 games

**Lagasse, Mike**
1976 WM CAN R 13 games

**Lahti, Robert**
1994 WW SWE R 3 games
~1994 WW bronze-medal game (last women's game refereed by a man)

**Laitanen, Henna**
2001 WW FIN R 3 games

**Langer, Michael**
1994 WM20 GER L 6 games
1995 WM GER L 7 games
1996 WM20 GER L 5 games

**Langley, Kristine**
2011 WW18 USA R 4 games
~2011 WW18 bronze-medal game

**Lapointe, Benoit**
1993 WM20 CAN R 3 games

**Lapratte, France**
2008 WW CAN R 3 games

**Larking, Christer**
1988 WM20 SWE L 6 games
1989 WM SWE L 8 games
1990 WM20 SWE L 7 games
1991 WM SWE L 8 games
1992 WM SWE L 6 games
1999 WM18 SWE R 4 games
2000 WM20 SWE R 6 games
2001 WM20 SWE R 5 games
2002 WM SWE R 6 games
2003 WM18 SWE R 4 games
2004 WM SWE R 7 games
2006 OG-M SWE R 3 games
2008 WM20 SWE R 6 games
2008 WM SWE R 8 games
2009 WM20 SWE R 5 games
2010 WM20 SWE R 5 games
2010 WM SWE R 7 games
2011 WM SWE R 9 games
2012 WM SWE R 7 games
~2000 WM20 bronze-medal game
~2004 WM bronze-medal game
~2008 WM gold-medal game
~2010 WM20 gold-medal game
~2011 WM bronze-medal game

**Larochelle, Francois**
1980 OG-M CAN L 6 games

**Larsen, Frank**
1972 SS USA R 1 game
1974 WM USA R 10 games

**Larssen, Erik**
1989 WM20 NOR L 6 games
1990 WM20 NOR L 5 games
1992 OG-M NOR L 7 games
1993 WM NOR L 4 games
1994 OG-M NOR L 6 games

**Larsson, Gert**
1984 WM20 SWE L 7 games

**LaRue, Dennis**
1986 WM20 USA R 3 games
1986 WM USA R 3 games
1988 OG-M USA R 7 games
1991 CC USA R 3 games
2002 OG-M USA R 4 games
2006 OG-M USA R 4 games
2010 OG-M USA R 5 games

**Laschowski, Dean**
2003 WM CAN L 8 games
2004 WM CAN L 9 games
2005 WM CAN L 9 games
2006 WM CAN L 7 games
~2004 WM bronze-medal game
~2005 WM bronze-medal game

**Lator, Geza**
1936 OG-M HUN R 3 games
1937 WM HUN R 2 games
1938 WM HUN R 2 games
1939 WM HUN R 1 game

**Lauff, Rudolf**
1996 WM SVK L 8 games
1997 WM SVK L 10 games
1998 OG-M SVK L 4 games
1999 WM SVK L 7 games
2000 WM SVK L 8 games
2001 WM SVK L 8 games
2002 OG-M SVK L 7 games
2005 WM SVK R 5 games
~1996 WM bronze-medal game
~1997 WM gold-medal game 2
~2001 WM bronze-medal game

**Laurla, Paivi**
2010 WW18 FIN R 4 games
2010 WW18 FIN L 1 game
~worked as both R & L at 2010 WW18
~2010 WW18 bronze-medal game

**Lazarowich, Brad**
1996 WCH CAN L 4 games
2004 WCH CAN L 6 games
~2004 WCH finals

**Leacock, Ernest**
1950 WM GBR R 7 games
1951 WM GBR R 9 games
1952 OG-M GBR R 10 games

**LeClair, Dennis**
1996 WM20 USA L 6 games

**Lecompte, Louis**
1955 WM CAN R 5 games
1956 OG-M CAN R 5 games

**Lederer, Ulrich**
1934 WM AUT R 3 games
1947 WM AUT R 3 games

**Lederer, Vit**
2010 WM20 CZE L 6 games
2012 WM18 CZE L 7 games
~2010 WM20 bronze-medal game
~2012 WM18 gold-medal game

**Ledermann, Martin**
2002 WM18 GER L 8 games

**Lee, Chris**
1999 WM20 CAN R 7 games
~1999 WM20 bronze-medal game

**Lee, Gord**
1972 WM USA R 12 games
1972 SS USA R 3 games
1973 WM USA R 10 games
1975 WM USA R 9 games
1976 OG-M USA R 6 games
1976 CC USA R 4 games

**Leet, Kaire**
2011 WW18 EST L 4 games

**Lefebure, Philippe**
1935 WM FRA R 4 games
1936 OG-M FRA R 3 games
~1935 WM gold-medal game

**Legasse, Andy**
1976 CC CAN R 2 games

**Leighton, Tara**
2010 WW18 USA R 4 games
~2010 WW18 gold-medal game

**Leinweber, Walter**
1936 OG-M GER R 1 game

**LeMat, Raoul**
1920 OG-M SWE R 1 game

**Lepaus, Marko**
1994 OG-M FIN R 4 games
1995 WM FIN R 5 games
1996 WM FIN R 4 games
2002 WM FIN R 5 games

**Lesnjak, Ales**
2003 WM SLO L 6 games
2004 WM SLO L 6 games
2005 WM SLO L 6 games
2006 WM SLO L 8 games
2008 WM20 SLO L 4 games

**Lever, Jim**
1981 WM20 CAN R 4 games
1984 OG-M CAN R 6 games

**Levonen, Jari**
2005 WM18 FIN R 4 games
2006 WM FIN R 5 games
2008 WM18 FIN R 5 games
2009 WM20 FIN R 4 games
2010 WM FIN R 9 games
2011 WM20 FIN R 5 games
2012 WM FIN R 9 games
~2010 WM gold-medal game

**Lewis, Bryan**
1984 CC CAN R 6 games

**Lewis, David**
2012 WM CAN R 7 games

**Lichtnecker, Gerhard**
1992 WM GER R 4 games
1994 WM GER R 3 games
2001 WM18 GER R 4 games
2002 WM GER R 4 games
~1992 WM bronze-medal game

**Lind, Kjell**
1985 WM SWE R 7 games
1988 OG-M SWE R 5 games
1989 WM SWE R 6 games

**Linde, Indrek**
2001 WM20 EST L 6 games
2002 WM18 EST L 8 games
2003 WM18 EST L 6 games

**Lindgren, Jorgen**
2001 WM20 SWE L 6 games

**Lindgren, Ulf**
1978 WM20 SWE R 4 games
1979 WM SWE R 4 games
1980 OG-M SWE R 4 games
1985 WM20 SWE R 5 games
1987 WM SWE R 5 games

**Lindholm, Juha**
1990 WM20 FIN L 4 games
1994 WW FIN L 5 games

**Lindquist, Vic**
1962 WM CAN R 9 games
1963 WM CAN R 11 games

**Lindroos, Risto**
1949 WM FIN R 3 games
1955 WM FIN R 2 games
1957 WM FIN R 3 games
1958 WM FIN R 2 games

**Lindroos, Seppo**
2004 WM20 FIN L 7 games
~2004 WM20 gold-medal game

**Lindroos, Tuomo**
1955 WM FIN R 2 games

**Linke, Michael**
2000 WM18 SUI L 7 games
2002 WM SUI L 6 games
2003 WM SUI L 6 games
~2000 WM18 gold-medal game

**Lipa, Jiri**
1985 WM20 TCH R 3 games
1987 WM20 TCH R 4 games
1988 WM20 TCH R 4 games
1989 WM TCH R 5 games
1990 WM TCH R 5 games
1991 WM TCH R 3 games
1992 OG-M TCH R 6 games

**Lipina, Miroslav**
1985 WM TCH L 11 games
1986 WM TCH L 10 games
1987 WM TCH L 9 games

**Lischetti, Sandra**
2000 WW SUI L 4 games
2001 WW SUI L 4 games
2002 OG-W SUI L 3 games

**Liu, Chunhua**
2008 WW CHN L 4 games
2009 WW18 CHN L 3 games

**Livingston, Stacey**
2001 WW USA R 4 games
2002 OG-W USA R 4 games
~2002 OG-W gold-medal game

**Ljungqvist, Mikael**
2003 WM18 SWE L 6 games
2004 WM20 SWE L 6 games
2005 WM18 SWE L 6 games
~2003 WM18 bronze-medal game
~2005 WM18 gold-medal game

**Loicq, Paul**
1920 OG-M BEL R 1 game
1924 OG-M BEL R 3 games
1928 OG-M BEL R 4 games
1930 WM BEL R 4 games
1931 WM BEL R 5 games
1933 WM BEL R 3 games
1934 WM BEL R 8 games
1935 WM BEL R 3 games
1936 OG-M BEL R 5 games
1937 WM BEL R 1 game
~IIHF President 1922-1947
~1920 OG-M silver-medal game
~1930 WM gold-medal game
~1935 WM bronze-medal game
~IIHF Hall of Fame

**Lojander, Jouni**
1991 WM20 FIN L 7 games
1992 WM FIN L 7 games
1993 WM20 FIN L 6 games
1994 OG-M FIN L 7 games

**Loksik, Peter**
2001 WM18 SVK L 7 games
~2001 WM18 bronze-medal game

**Lonardi, Fabrizio**
1994 WM ITA L 5 games

**Looker, Rick**
2003 WM20 USA R 4 games
2003 WM USA R 7 games
2004 WM USA R 7 games
2005 WM USA R 5 games
2006 WM USA R 4 games
2008 WM USA R 7 games
2009 WM USA R 7 games
2010 WM USA R 7 games

**Loraas, Darren**
1993 WM CAN R 5 games

**Loretan, Evelyn**
2009 WW18 SUI L 4 games
2010 WW18 SUI L 3 games

**Losier, Sylvain**
2006 WM20 CAN L 6 games
2007 WM CAN L 9 games
2008 WM CAN L 9 games
2009 WM20 CAN L 6 games
2010 OG-M CAN L 3 games
~2006 WM20 bronze-medal game
~2007 WM bronze-medal game
~2008 WM bronze-medal game
~2009 WM20 bronze-medal game

**Lovecchio, Phil**
1980 WM20 USA R 2 games

**Lowell, Dick**
1992 WM CAN L 7 games
~1992 WM bronze-medal game

**Lundberg, Pertti**
1995 WM20 FIN L 5 games

**Lundby, Bjorn**
1988 OG-M NOR L 6 games

**Lundstrom, Bert-Olof**
1984 WM20 SWE L 7 games

**Lundstrom, Sven-Olof**
1986 WM SWE L 10 games
1987 WM SWE L 10 games
1987 CC SWE L 5 games
1989 WM SWE L 10 games
~1987 CC game 2 finals

**Luthcke, Owe**
1999 WM18 NOR L 8 games
2000 WM20 NOR L 5 games
2002 WM18 NOR L 8 games
2009 WM18 NOR R 5 games

**Luther, Bob**
1979 WM USA L 8 games
1981 CC USA L 6 games

**Lutta, Jack**
1947 WM SUI R 4 games
1948 OG-M SUI R 3 games
1951 WM SUI R 6 games
1955 WM SUI R 6 games

**Lynch, Dave**
1988 WM20 CAN R 4 games
1991 WM CAN R 6 games

**MacDonald, Geoff**
2006 WM20 CAN L 6 games

**MacDonnell, Mike**
2002 WM18 CAN L 8 games

**MacKenzie, Megan**
2000 WW USA L 6 games
2001 WW USA L 4 games
2002 OG-W USA L 4 games
~2000 WW bronze-medal game
~2001 WW bronze-medal game

**MacLean, Hugh**
1961 WM CAN R 4 games

**MacMillan, Bob**
1978 WM20 CAN L 4 games
~1978 WM20 gold-medal game

**MacPherson, Matt**
2009 WM18 CAN L 6 games

**Madill, Greg**
1979 WM CAN R 6 games

**Magwood, John**
1931 WM GBR R 2 games
1933 WM GBR R 1 game
1934 WM GBR R 6 games
1935 WM GBR R 11 games
~1934 WM gold-medal game

**Maheux, Jean**
1978 WM20 CAN L 2 games

**Mai, Carletto**
1939 WM SUI R 1 game

**Mair, Helmuth**
1994 OG-M GER L 6 games

**Majapuro, Anna**
1999 WW FIN L 5 games
2009 WW FIN L 4 games
2010 OG-W FIN L 4 games
2012 WW18 FIN L 5 games
~2012 WW18 gold-medal game

**Makarov, Pavel**
1999 WM18 RUS L 8 games
2000 WM20 RUS L 6 games
2001 WM20 RUS L 6 games
2002 WM RUS L 8 games
2003 WM20 RUS L 5 games
2003 WM RUS L 7 games
2004 WM RUS L 6 games
~2001 WM20 gold-medal game
~2002 WM gold-medal game

**Makela, Miika**
1990 WM20 FIN L 4 games

**Makela, Seppo**
1988 WM20 FIN R 4 games
1989 WM FIN R 5 games
1990 WM FIN R 6 games
1991 WM FIN R 7 games
1992 OG-M FIN R 5 games
1993 WM20 FIN R 4 games
1994 WM FIN R 4 games
1997 WM FIN R 7 games
~1997 WM bronze-medal game

**Malecek, Josef**
1934 WM TCH R 1 game
~1934 WM gold-medal game

**Malinovski, John**
1989 WM20 USA L 8 games
1992 OG-M USA L 10 games

**Malletroit, Eric**
1992 OG-M FRA R 2 games
1993 WM FRA R 2 games

**Malliet, Jean-Yves**
1994 WM20 CAN L 6 games

**Mandioni, Nadir**
1998 WM20 SUI L 7 games
1999 WM20 SUI L 6 games
1999 WM SUI L 9 games
2000 WM SUI L 9 games
2006 WM18 SUI R 5 games
2008 WM18 SUI R 6 games
~1998 WM20 gold-medal game
~1999 WM gold-medal game 1
~2006 WM18 gold-medal game
~2008 WM18 bronze-medal game

**Manoshkov, Yakov**
2008 WM18 RUS L 6 games

**Mariconda, Paul**
2000 WM20 USA R 5 games
2001 WM18 USA R 6 games
2002 WM USA R 5 games
2003 WM18 USA R 5 games
~2001 WM18 gold-medal game

**Marouelli, Dan**
1996 WCH CAN R 4 games
2004 WCH CAN R 4 games
2006 OG-M CAN R 6 games

**Marsh, Lou**
1932 OG-M CAN R 12 games
~called all games 1932 OG-M with Don Sands

**Martin, Derek**
1990 WM20 USA R 3 games

**Martin, Paul**
1938 WM GER R 6 games
1939 WM GER R 5 games

**Maschio, Lou**
1962 WM CAN R 9 games
1964 OG-M CAN R 10 games

**Masik, Milan**
1997 WM20 SVK L 5 games
1998 WM SVK L 9 games
1999 WM20 SVK L 4 games
1999 WM18 SVK L 7 games
2001 WM20 SVK L 7 games
2003 WM18 SVK L 7 games
2004 WM SVK L 7 games
2006 OG-M SVK L 7 games
2007 WM SVK L 9 games
2008 WM20 SVK L 6 games
~1998 WM gold-medal game 1
~2001 WM20 gold-medal game
~2003 WM18 bronze-medal game
~2006 OG-M gold-medal game
~2008 WM20 gold-medal game

**Matsuoka, Rob**
2001 WM18 CAN R 5 games
2003 WM20 CAN R 4 games
2003 WM CAN R 7 games
2005 WM CAN R 6 games
2006 WM20 CAN R 3 games
~2001 WM18 bronze-medal game
~2003 WM bronze-medal game

**Mattila, Sanna**
2005 WW FIN L 4 games
2006 OG-W FIN L 4 games
2007 WW FIN L 4 games
~2005 WW gold-medal game
~2007 WW gold-medal game

**Maybury, Deb**
1990 WW CAN R 2 games+
+information incomplete

**McAvoy, George**
1968 OG-M CAN R 7 games

**McCormack, Pat**
1978 WM CAN R 8 games

**McCormick, Joe**
1920 OG-M USA R 1 game
~1920 OG-M gold-medal game

**McCorry, George**
1989 WM20 CAN R 5 games
1992 OG-M CAN R 7 games
~1992 OG-M bronze-medal game

**McCreary, Bill**
1991 CC CAN R 3 games
1998 OG-M CAN R 6 games
2002 OG-M CAN R 7 games
2010 OG-M CAN R 5 games
~1998 OG-M gold-medal game
~2002 OG-M gold-medal game
~2010 OG-M gold-medal game

**McElman, Andy**
1986 WM20 USA R 4 games

**McGaughey, Pat**
1984 WM20 USA R 4 games

**McKenzie, Bill**
1960 OG-M CAN R 8 games

**McLean, Hugh**
1960 OG-M CAN R 9 games

**McTague, Chuck**
1994 WM CAN L 7 games
~1994 WM bronze-medal game

**Medvedev, Alexei**
2009 WM18 RUS L 6 games

**Medzihradsky, Mikulas**
1957 WM TCH R 4 games

**Meier, Brad**
1995 WM20 USA R 4 games
1996 WM USA R 5 games
1998 OG-M USA R 3 games

**Melbye, Bjorn**
1992 WW NOR R 3 games

**Mendlowitcz, Marc**
1998 WM FRA L 7 games

**Meszynski, Pawel**
2002 WM18 POL L 8 games
2003 WM POL L 5 games
2004 WM POL L 6 games

**Michalik, Wladislaw**
1948 OG-M POL R 2 games
1949 WM POL R 4 games

**Michaud, Diane**
1994 WW CAN L 5 games

**Mihalik, Vladimir**
1991 WM20 TCH L 6 games
1992 WM SVK L 4 games
1998 WM SVK R 6 games
1999 WM20 SVK R 4 games
1999 WM SVK R 5 games
2000 WM SVK R 7 games
2001 WM SVK R 6 games
2002 OG-M SVK R 3 games
2002 WM SVK R 5 games
~2000 WM bronze-medal game

**Mikhel, Alexei**
2009 WM20 RUS L 6 games

**Mikula, Pavel**
2007 WM18 CZE R 3 games
2008 WM18 CZE R 5 games

**Miller, Steve**
1999 WM20 CAN L 7 games
2006 OG-M CAN L 6 games
~1999 WM20 bronze-medal game
~2006 OG-M bronze-medal game

**Minakovska, Sandra**
2009 WW18 LAT L 4 games
~2009 WW18 bronze-medal game

**Minar, Milan**
2002 WM18 CZE R 6 games
2004 WM18 CZE R 5 games
2005 WM20 CZE R 4 games
2005 WM CZE R 6 games
2006 WM20 CZE R 3 games
2006 WM CZE R 6 games
2007 WM CZE R 5 games
2008 WM CZE R 5 games
2009 WM18 CZE R 6 games
2010 WM CZE R 6 games
~2004 WM18 gold-medal game
~2009 WM18 bronze-medal game

**Minder, Frigyes**
1938 WM HUN R 1 game
1939 WM HUN R 2 games

**Minder, Sandor**
1928 OG-M HUN R 1 game
1931 WM HUN R 1 game
1935 WM HUN R 1 game
1937 WM HUN R 5 games
1938 WM HUN R 2 games
1939 WM HUN R 2 games
~1938 WM bronze-medal game

**Minyailo, Alexander**
1994 WM20 RUS L 5 games

**Mitton, Randy**
1987 CC CAN L 2 games

**Mondalek, Mike**
2002 WM18 USA R 6 games

**Moor, Rudolf**
1994 WM SUI R 3 games

**Moore, Dinty**
1949 WM CAN R 6 games

**Moreno, Vincent**
1991 WM20 SUI R 2 games
1992 WM SUI R 3 games
1993 WM SUI R 4 games
1994 WM20 SUI R 3 games
1999 WM18 SUI R 4 games

**Morin, Jean**
2002 OG-M CAN L 5 games
2004 WCH CAN L 5 games
2010 OG-M CAN L 5 games
~2010OG-M gold-medal game

**Moriya, Hidaki**
1994 WW JPN L 4 games

**Morley, Bob**
1989 WM CAN R 5 games

**Morozov, Nikolai**
1985 WM20 URS R 3 games
1987 WM URS R 6 games
1988 OG-M URS R 5 games
1989 WM URS R 5 games
1990 WM URS R 4 games
1991 WM URS R 6 games
1992 OG-M RUS R 6 games

**Morrison, John**
1981 WM20 USA L 5 games
1982 WM20 USA R 4 games

**Morrison, Johnathan**
2009 WM18 USA L 6 games
2011 WM20 USA L 7 games
2012 WM USA L 9 games
~2011 WM20 gold-medal game

**Morrissey, Pat**
1980 OG-M USA L 6 games

**Moser, Franz**
1964 OG-M AUT R 4 games

**Mostrom, Tomas**
1983 WM20 SWE L 6 games
1984 OG-M SWE L 6 games

**Mousseaux, Oliver**
2007 WM18 USA L 6 games

**Muench, Kevin**
1990 WM20 CAN R 5 games
1992 WM CAN R 6 games
1994 OG-M CAN R 6 games
~1992 WM gold-medal game

**Muller, Gerhard**
1994 WM20 GER R 5 games
1995 WM20 GER R 4 games
1996 WM GER R 8 games
1997 WM GER R 8 games
1998 OG-M GER R 6 games
1999 WM GER R 5 games
~1996 WM gold-medal game
~1996 WM bronze-medal game
~1997 WM gold-medal game 2

**Muller, Joris**
2011 WM18 SUI L 7 games
~2011 WM18 bronze-medal game

**Muller, Karl**
1961 WM SUI R 5 games

**Muller, Peter**
1928 OG-M SUI R 1 game
1935 WM SUI R 5 games
1947 WM SUI R 4 games
1955 WM SUI R 6 games

**Munro, Dunc**
1924 OG-M CAN R 1 game

**Murchison, Kiel**
2011 WM CAN L 8 games
2012 WM20 CAN L 6 games
~2011 WM gold-medal game
~2012 WM20 gold-medal game

**Murphy, Brian**
2004 WCH USA L 4 games
2010 OG-M USA L 4 games

**Murphy, Dan**
1994 WM USA R 4 games

**Murphy, John**
1994 WW USA R 3 games

**Murray, Simon**
1994 WM GBR L 4 games

**Mutsaers, Sylena**
2011 WW18 CAN R 4 games

**Muylaert, Marc**
2003 WM18 CAN R 4 games
2008 WM20 CAN R 5 games
2009 WM20 CAN R 6 games
2010 WM CAN R 6 games
~2009 WM20 bronze-medal game

**Muzalewski, Henryk**
1977 WM20 POL L 6 games

**Mykkanen, Ari**
1992 WM20 FIN R 4 games

**Nadin, Bob**
1972 OG-M CAN R 7 games

**Nakano, Minoru**
1972 OG-M JPN R 2 games

**Nakaoka, Hidenori**
1986 WM20 JPN L 7 games

**Nakayama, Miyuki**
2008 WW JPN L 5 games
2009 WW JPN L 4 games
2010 OG-W JPN L 5 games
~2008 WW gold-medal game
~2010 OG-W bronze-medal game

**Nansen, Derek**
2001 WM CAN L 8 games
2002 OG-M CAN L 5 games
~2001 WM gold-medal game

**Narvestad, Johan**
1948 OG-M NOR R 1 game
1949 WM NOR R 1 game
1952 OG-M NOR R 3 games
1958 WM NOR R 4 games
1959 WM NOR R 5 games

**Nater, Daniel**
1996 WM20 SUI L 6 games
1997 WM20 SUI L 7 games
1998 WM SUI L 7 games
~1996 WM20 gold-medal game
~1997 WM20 bronze-medal game

**Neagles, Jim**
1976 CC USA R 2 games
1977 WM USA R 7 games
1979 WM USA R 6 games
1980 OG-M USA R 5 games

**Nelibova, Ludmila**
2009 WW18 CZE R 3 games
2012 WW18 CZE R 3 games

**Nelson, Thor**
2006 OG-M USA L 6 games
2010 OG-M USA L 5 games
~2006 OG-M gold-medal game

**Neubert, Christian**
2004 WM20 GER L 6 games

**Neumaier, Toni**
1954 WM FRG R 3 games
1957 WM FRG R 4 games
1958 WM FRG R 6 games

**Neuwirth, Kurt**
1999 WM18 AUT L 7 games
2001 WM AUT L 6 games

**Nieminen, Kari**
1993 WM FIN R 3 games

**Noeth, Mike**
1984 CC USA R 3 games
1987 CC USA R 4 games

**Nonas, Sigrid-Lise**
1992 WW NOR L 4 games
1994 WW NOR L 4 games
1997 WW NOR L 5 games
1998 OG-W NOR L 5 games
1999 WW NOR L 4 games
~1994 WW bronze-medal game
~1997 WW gold-medal game

**Nord, Mikael**
SWE R 5 games

**Nordlie, Henry**
1961 WM NOR R 1 game
1963 WM NOR R 1 game
1966 WM NOR R 2 games

**Normand, Stephanie**
2004 WW CAN R 4 games
2005 WW CAN R 4 games
2006 OG-W CAN R 3 games
~2004 WW bronze-medal game

**Norrman, Johan**
1991 WM20 SWE L 6 games
1992 WM20 SWE L 6 games
1993 WM20 SWE L 7 games
1993 WM SWE L 7 games
1994 OG-M SWE L 7 games
1995 WM SWE L 7 games
1999 WM20 SWE L 8 games
2000 WM SWE L 10 games
2001 WM SWE L 8 games
2002 OG-M SWE L 6 games
~1993 WM bronze-medal game
~1999 WM20 gold-medal game
~2001 WM gold-medal game
~2002 OG-M bronze-medal game

**Norrman, Patrick**
1994 WM SWE L 7 games

**Nosov, Valeri**
1994 WM RUS L 5 games

**Novak, Milan**
2002 WM18 SVK L 8 games
2006 WM SVK L 8 games
2007 WM20 SVK L 7 games
2008 WM SVK L 7 games
2009 WM20 SVK L 7 games
2010 OG-M SVK L 4 games
2011 WM SVK L 6 games
2012 WM20 SVK L 6 games
~2006 WM gold-medal game
~2007 WM20 gold-medal game
~2009 WM20 gold-medal game

**Novotna, Ilona**
2010 WW18 CZE L 4 games
2011 WW18 CZE L 6 games

**Nowak, Tim**
2002 OG-M USA L 5 games
2004 WCH USA L 4 games
2010 OG-M USA L 4 games

**Oberg, Roger**
1994 WM20 SWE R 3 games
2000 WM18 SWE R 4 games

**O'Brian, Kelli**
2004 WW USA L 5 games
2005 WW USA L 5 games
2007 WW USA L 4 games
2008 WW18 USA L 4 games
2009 WW18 USA L 4 games
~2004 WW bronze-medal game
~2008 WW18 bronze-medal game

**Odins, Eduards**
1997 WM LAT L 6 games
1999 WM LAT L 6 games
2001 WM LAT L 7 games
2002 OG-M LAT L 4 games
2010 WM18 LAT R 5 games
2011 WM LAT R 6 games

**O'Halloran, Dan**
2010 OG-M CAN R 6 games
~2010 OG-M gold-medal game

**Okolicany, Juraj**
1977 WM20 TCH L 7 games
1978 WM20 TCH R 3 games
1980 WM20 TCH R 3 games
1981 WM20 TCH R 4 games

**Okolicany, Vojtech**
1947 WM TCH R 3 games
1948 OG-M TCH R 6 games
1959 WM TCH R 4 games

**Olenin, Konstantin**
2005 WM18 RUS L 6 games
2006 WM18 RUS L 6 games
2010 WM20 RUS R 4 games
2010 WM RUS R 6 games
2011 WM RUS R 6 games
2012 WM RUS R 8 games
~2006 WM18 bronze-medal game

**Olivieri, Gennaro**
1954 WM SUI R 8 games
1961 WM SUI R 7 games
1962 WM SUI R 8 games
1963 WM SUI R 7 games
1964 OG-M SUI R 6 games
1965 WM SUI R 5 games
1966 WM SUI R 4 games

**Ollier, Jean-Philippe**
1992 OG-M FRA L 6 games
1995 WM FRA L 4 games

**Ollier, Lionel**
1992 WM FRA L 5 games
1994 OG-M FRA L 5 games

**Olsson, Dag**
1981 WM SWE R 7 games
1981 CC SWE R 4 games
1982 WM SWE R 5 games
1983 WM SWE R 5 games
1984 OG-M SWE R 7 games
1984 CC SWE R 2 games
1986 WM20 SWE R 4 games
1990 WM SWE R 6 games

**Orelma, Antti**
2006 WM18 FIN L 6 games
2007 WM18 FIN L 7 games
2008 WM18 FIN L 7 games
2009 WM FIN L 8 games
2010 WM18 FIN L 6 games
~2007 WM18 gold-medal game
~2008 WM18 bronze-medal game
~2009 WM bronze-medal game

**Orolin, Tomas**
2010 WM18 SVK L 6 games

**Orszag, Peter**
2002 WM18 SVK R 6 games
2003 WM18 SVK R 5 games
2004 WM20 SVK R 4 games
2008 WM SVK R 7 games
2009 WM20 SVK R 5 games
2009 WM SVK R 8 games
2010 OG-M SVK R 4 games
2011 WM SVK R 7 games
~2003 WM18 bronze-medal game
~2009 WM gold-medal game

**Osiecimski-Czapski, Andrzej**
1931 WM POL R 2 games

**Oskirko, Yuri**
2005 WM20 RUS L 6 games
2005 WM RUS L 6 games
2006 WM RUS L 8 games
2007 WM RUS L 7 games
2008 WM RUS L 7 games
2009 WM RUS L 7 games
2010 OG-M RUS L 5 games
~2005 WM20 bronze-medal game
~2006 WM gold-medal game
~2008 WM bronze-medal game
~2010 OG-M bronze-medal game

**Oswald, Christian**
1997 WM20 GER L 7 games
1998 WM GER L 7 games
2000 WM GER L 7 games
~1997 WM20 bronze-medal game

**Pakaslahti, Jukka**
2001 WM20 FIN R 5 games
2002 WM FIN R 7 games
~2002 WM gold-medal game

**Palm, Jacquei**
2000 WW CAN R 3 games
2002 OG-W CAN R 3 games

**Pammer, Werner**
1996 WM AUT L 4 games

**Parece, Debora**
1997 WW USA L 5 games
1998 OG-W USA L 6 games
~1998 OG-W gold-medal game

**Parson, Brett**
1993 WM20 USA R 4 games

**Partanen, Jonna**
2008 WW18 FIN L 4 games
2011 WW18 FIN L 6 games
~2011 WW18 gold-medal game

**Partanen, Sami**
2006 WM18 FIN R 6 games
2007 WM20 FIN R 3 games
2008 WM20 FIN R 3 games
2008 WM FIN R 6 games
2009 WM FIN R 6 games
2010 WM18 FIN R 5 games
2011 WM FIN R 6 games
~2006 WM18 bronze-medal game
~2010 WM18 gold-medal game

**Patafie, Steve**
2012 WM USA R 7 games

**Paulsberg, Karelius**
1958 WM NOR R 1 game

**Pavlovic, Alexander**
2005 WM18 SVK L 6 games
2007 WM18 SVK L 6 games
2008 WM18 SVK L 6 games
~2007 WM18 bronze-medal game

**Pavlovsky, Alexander**
1986 WM URS L 8 games

**Pellerin, Christine**
2004 WW CAN L 5 games
~2004 WW bronze-medal game

**Pellerin, Guy**
2006 WM20 CAN R 4 games
2007 WM CAN R 7 games
2008 WM CAN R 8 games
2009 WM20 CAN R 6 games
2010 OG-M CAN R 3 games
~2007 WM bronze-medal game
~2008 WM bronze-medal game
~2009 WM20 bronze-medal game

**Peltonen, Riku**
1998 WM20 FIN L 8 games
1999 WM20 FIN L 6 games
2001 WM FIN L 8 games
2002 WM FIN L 6 games
~1998 WM20 bronze-medal game
~1999 WM20 gold-medal game

**Perkins, Sarah**
2000 WW USA R 3 games
~2000 WW gold-medal game

**Perkuhn, Helmut**
1955 WM FRG R 5 games
1968 OG-M FRG R 2 games

**Perreault, Denis**
1978 WM20 CAN L 2 games

**Persson, Soren**
2006 WM18 SWE R 4 games
2008 WM18 SWE R 5 games
2009 WM SWE R 6 games
2011 WM SWE R 7 games
2012 WM20 SWE R 4 games

**Pesek, Tomas**
2011 WM18 CZE L 4 games
2012 WM18 CZE L 5 games

**Petschenig, Jim**
1982 WM20 CAN L 6 games

**Pettersson, Torbjorn**
1992 WW SWE L 5 games
~1992 WW gold-medal game

**Pfaler, Wolfgang**
1990 WM20 FRG L 6 games

**Pfister, Markus**
1993 WM SUI L 4 games

**Piacentini, Julie**
2000 WW USA L 6 games
2001 WW USA L 5 games
2002 OG-W USA L 4 games
2006 OG-W USA L 4 games
~2001 WW gold-medal game
~2002 OG-W bronze-medal game
~2006 OG-W bronze-medal game

**Pianfetti, Calixte**
1968 OG-M FRA R 1 game

**Picavet, Marie**
2008 WW18 FRA R 3 games
2009 WW18 FRA R 3 games
2010 WW18 FRA R 3 games
2012 WW FRA R 4 games
~2009 WW18 bronze-medal game

**Piechaczek, Daniel**
2008 WM20 GER R 5 games
2008 WM GER R 8 games
2009 WM GER R 7 games
2010 WM20 GER R 6 games
2010 WM GER R 7 games
2011 WM GER R 7 games
2012 WM20 GER R 4 games
~2008 WM bronze-medal game

**Pierce, Ken**
1978 WM USA R 6 games
~refereed both games on final day of 1978 WM

**Pihl, Kim**
1991 CC FIN L 4 games

**Piotrowski, Steve**
1989 WM20 USA R 5 games
1990 WM USA R 5 games

**Plas, Jarik**
1984 WM20 NED L 6 games

**Plaxton, Bert**
1928 OG-M CAN R 1 game

**Pokorny, Jaroslav**
1947 WM TCH R 1 game
1958 WM TCH R 5 games

**Pokorny, Miloslav**
1959 WM TCH R 7 games
1961 WM TCH R 5 games
1963 WM TCH R 6 games
1964 OG-M TCH R 7 games
1965 WM TCH R 3 games

**Pollock, Kevin**
2004 WCH CAN R 4 games

**Poloni, Michal**
1947 WM TCH R 1 game
1948 OG-M TCH R 3 games

**Polyakov, Alexander**
1995 WM20 RUS L 5 games
1996 WM RUS L 8 games
1997 WM RUS L 10 games
1998 OG-M RUS L 7 games
2000 WM18 RUS R 5 games
2001 WM18 RUS R 5 games
2003 WM20 RUS R 3 games
2004 WM RUS R 5 games
2006 WM RUS R 6 games
2007 WM20 RUS R 3 games
2008 WM RUS R 8 games
~1997 WM gold-medal game 2
~1998 OG-M bronze-medal game
~2001 WM18 bronze-medal game

**Pomol, Peter**
1982 WM FIN L 10 games
1983 WM20 FIN L 6 games
1984 WM20 FIN L 6 games
1985 WM20 FIN L 7 games
1987 WM20 FIN L 6 games

**Ponomarjow, Nikolaj**
2012 WM18 GER L 5 games

**Poplimont, Andre**
1928 OG-M BEL R 5 games
1931 WM BEL R 9 games
1933 WM BEL R 2 games
1934 WM BEL R 1 game
1935 WM BEL R 6 games
1936 OG-M BEL R 3 games
1937 WM BEL R 14 games
1938 WM BEL R 12 games
1939 WM BEL R 11 games
1947 WM BEL R 2 games
~1935 WM bronze-medal game
~1938 WM gold-medal game

**Popovic, Karol**
2001 WM SUI L 6 games
2002 WM SUI L 8 games
2003 WM SUI L 7 games
2004 WM SUI L 7 games
2005 WM SUI L 6 games
~2002 WM bronze-medal game

**Popovic, Marko**
2000 WM20 SVK L 7 games
2002 WM SVK L 1 game

**Porter, Bob**
1988 OG-M CAN L 9 games

**Porter, Red**
1928 OG-M CAN R 2 games

**Postinghel, Renato**
1977 WM20 ITA L 6 games

**Pottage, Dennis**
1986 WM20 CAN R 5 games

**Pouzar, Roman**
2001 WM CZE L 6 games
2002 WM18 CZE L 8 games
2004 WM CZE L 7 games
2005 WM CZE L 6 games
2006 WM CZE L 9 games
2007 WM CZE L 8 games
~2006 WM bronze-medal game

**Prazak, Alec**
1972 WM TCH R 3 games
1974 WM TCH R 4 games

**Prescott, Joe**
1982 WM20 USA L 6 games
1987 WM20 USA R 4 games

**Presneanu, Mihai**
1976 OG-M ROU R 3 games
1977 WM ROU L 6 games

**Prevost, Patrice**
1968 OG-M FRA R 2 games

**Proctor, Sandy**
1983 WM20 CAN R 6 games

**Proskurov, Vladimir**
2007 WM18 BLR R 2 games

**Prusov, Igor**
1983 WM20 URS L 7 games
1984 OG-M URS L 7 games
1986 WM URS L 9 games
1987 WM URS L 9 games
1988 WM20 URS L 6 games
1988 OG-M URS L 9 games

**Pudas, Al**
1936 OG-M CAN R 3 games

**Puolakka, Masi**
2012 WM FIN L 6 games

**Purks, Mark**
1982 WM20 USA L 5 games

**Puttee, Art**
1933 WM CAN R 5 games

**Quagliato, Klara**
2006 OG-W CZE L 4 games
~2006 OG-W gold-medal game

**Racicot, Pierre**
2004 WCH CAN L 5 games
2006 OG-M CAN L 6 games

**Radbjer, Ulf**
1998 WM20 SWE R 5 games
1999 WM SWE R 5 games
2001 WM SWE R 6 games
2002 OG-M SWE R 4 games
2003 WM20 SWE R 5 games
~1998 WM20 gold-medal game
~2001 WM gold-medal game
~2002 OG-M bronze-medal game
~2003 WM20 gold-medal game

**Radke, Fred**
1930 WM CAN R 4 games

**Radosei, Peter**
1981 WM20 FRG L 5 games

**Ramsay, Beattie**
1924 OG-M CAN R 2 games

**Ramus, Ernie**
1950 WM GBR R 4 games

**Rantala, Aleksi**
2007 WM18 FIN R 3 games
2009 WM18 FIN R 5 games

**Rautavuori, Janne**
1989 WM20 FIN L 6 games
1990 WM20 FIN L 5 games
1991 WM FIN L 8 games
1992 OG-M FIN L 10 games
1993 WM FIN L 7 games
1994 WM FIN L 7 games
1995 WM FIN L 7 games
1996 WM FIN L 9 games
1997 WM FIN L 9 games
1998 OG-M FIN L 8 games
~1992 OG-M gold- and bronze-medal games
~1996 WM gold-medal game
~1997 WM gold-medal game 3

**Ravodin, Alexei**
2006 WM18 RUS R 4 games
2009 WM18 RUS R 5 games
2010 WM20 RUS R 4 games

**Redding, Kevin**
2000 WM20 USA L 6 games
2001 WM20 USA L 6 games
2002 WM USA L 9 games
2003 WM USA L 9 games
2005 WM20 USA L 7 games
2006 OG-M USA L 5 games
~2002 WM gold-medal game
~2003 WM bronze-medal game
~2005 WM20 gold-medal game

**Reddy, Janet**
2004 WW CAN R 3 games

**Reeners, Marty**
1980 OG-M USA L 6 games

**Rehman, Kyle**
2007 WM18 CAN R 6 games
~2007 WM18 gold-medal game

**Reiber, Brent**
2005 WM SUI R 7 games
2006 WM SUI R 6 games
2007 WM SUI R 5 games
2008 WM SUI R 8 games
2009 WM20 SUI R 6 games
2009 WM SUI R 9 games
2010 OG-M SUI R 3 games
2011 WM SUI R 9 games
2012 WM20 SUI R 7 games
2012 WM SUI R 10 games
~2005 WM bronze-medal game
~2009 WM bronze-medal game
~2011 WM gold-medal game
~2012 WM20 gold-medal game
~2012 WM gold-medal game

**Reichert, Martin**
2000 WM18 GER L 7 games
2001 WM GER L 5 games

**Reissenzahn, Georg**
1933 WM TCH R 1 game
1938 WM TCH R 2 games
1939 WM TCH R 3 games
1947 WM TCH R 1 game

**Rejthar, Frantisek**
1991 WM20 TCH R 3 games
1994 WM CZE R 4 games
1995 WM20 CZE R 3 games
1995 WM CZE R 5 games
1996 WM CZE R 3 games
1997 WM20 CZE R 5 games
1998 WM CZE R 3 games
~1994 WM bronze-medal game
~1997 WM20 gold-medal game

**Rektorik, Zdenek**
1936 OG-M TCH R 1 game

**Rennberg, Ron**
1982 WM20 CAN R 5 games

**Reppa, Francis**
1991 WM CAN L 7 games

**Rezac, Jaroslav**
1931 WM TCH R 2 games
1933 WM TCH R 2 games

**Reznikov, Alexei**
1981 WM20 URS R 3 games

**Richardson, Heather**
2007 WW CAN L 4 games
2008 WW CAN L 4 games
2009 WW CAN L 4 games
2010 OG-W CAN L 5 games
~2007 WW gold-medal game
~2008 WW bronze-medal game
~2009 WW bronze-medal game
~2010 OG-W gold-medal game

**Riley, Bill**
1960 OG-M USA R 12 games

**Riley, Everett**
1960 OG-M USA R 2 games
1962 WM USA R 4 games

**Rindell, Pekka**
1985 WM20 FIN L 6 games

**Ringbom, Reijo**
1992 WM20 FIN L 6 games
1994 WM20 FIN L 7 games
1995 WM FIN L 4 games
2002 WM18 FIN R 5 games

**Ritchie, Rob**
2006 WM18 USA R 5 games
2007 WM20 USA R 4 games
2008 WM18 USA R 6 games
2009 WM20 USA R 6 games
~2008 WM18 gold-medal game

**Robb, Doug**
1978 WM20 CAN R 5 games

**Robben, Ilse**
2002 OG-W NED L 3 games
2004 WW NED L 5 games
2005 WW NED L 4 games
2006 OG-W NED L 3 games
2007 WW NED L 4 games
~2004 WW gold-medal game
~2006 OG-W bronze-medal game

**Robichaud, Kim**
2001 WW CAN L 5 games
2004 WW CAN L 5 games
2005 WW CAN L 5 games
2006 OG-W CAN L 3 games

**Rody, Vaughan**
1999 WM20 CAN L 5 games
~1999 WM20 bronze-medal game

**Rolstad, Kelli**
2010 OG-W USA L 5 games
~2010 OG-W gold-medal game

**Romer, Erich**
1935 WM GER R 1 game

**Rommerskirchen, Josef**
1966 WM FRG R 3 games

**Roncarelli, Francesco**
1933 WM ITA R 5 games
1934 WM ITA R 1 game
~1933 WM gold-medal game
~1934 WM bronze-medal game

**Ronn, Jyri**
1999 WM18 FIN L 8 games
2000 WM18 FIN L 8 games
2001 WM20 FIN L 6 games
2004 WM20 FIN L 4 games
2005 WM20 FIN R 4 games
2006 WM20 FIN R 3 games
2007 WM FIN R 6 games
2008 WM20 FIN R 6 games
2008 WM FIN R 8 games
2009 WM FIN R 8 games
2010 OG-M FIN R 5 games
2011 WM FIN R 7 games
2012 WM20 FIN R 5 games
~2000 WM18 bronze-medal game
~2008 WM20 bronze-medal game
~2009 WM gold-medal game

**Ronning, Hans**
1984 OG-M NOR L 6 games
1986 WM20 NOR R 2 games
1987 WM20 NOR R 3 games

**Ronnmark, Ulf**
1995 WM20 SWE L 8 games
1996 WM SWE L 9 games
1997 WM SWE L 8 games
1998 OG-M SWE L 7 games
2005 WM20 SWE R 5 games
2007 WM20 SWE R 4 games
2008 WM20 SWE R 5 games
~1996 WM gold-medal game
~1998 OG-M gold-medal game

**Rooney, Chris**
2010 OG-M USA R 4 games

**Ross, Joe**
2004 WM18 USA L 6 games
2005 WM20 USA L 6 games
2006 WM USA L 9 games
2007 WM20 USA L 6 games

**Rost, Ron**
1986 WM20 CAN L 7 games

**Rouspetr, Ladislav**
1989 WM20 TCH L 7 games
1990 WM TCH L 8 games

**Roy, Helene**
2010 WW18 CAN L 5 games
~2010 WW18 gold-medal game

**Rumble, Kerri**
2007 WW CAN L 4 games
2008 WW18 CAN L 5 games
2010 OG-W CAN L 4 games
2011 WW CAN L 5 games
~2007 WW bronze-medal game
~2008 WW18 bronze-medal game
~2011 WW bronze-medal game

**Ruzickova, Radka**
2010 WW18 CZE R 3 games
2011 WW18 CZE R 4 games

**Ryhed, Lars-Johan**
2001 WM18 SWE R 4 games
2002 WM18 SWE R 6 games

**Ryman, Marsh**
1960 OG-M USA R 6 games

**Saarnio, Torkel**
2003 WM18 FIN L 8 games
~2003 WM18 gold-medal game

**Sabelstrom, Peter**
2008 WM18 SWE L 7 games
2009 WM SWE L 7 games
2010 WM SWE L 7 games
~2008 WM18 gold-medal game

**Sable, Adriana**
2008 WW18 USA L 3 games

**Sachs, Tadeusz**
1931 WM POL R 2 games
1935 WM POL R 6 games
1937 WM POL R 4 games
1938 WM POL R 16 games
1939 WM POL R 11 games
~1938 WM gold-medal game
~1938 WM bronze-medal game

**Salminen, Teemu**
2011 WM18 FIN R 6 games
~2011 WM18 gold-medal game

**Salonen, Anssi**
2012 WM18 FIN R 4 games

**Samoilov, Sergei**
1985 WM20 URS L 7 games

**Samwald, Theodor**
1949 WM AUT R 4 games
1956 OG-M AUT R 1 game

**Sando, Axel**
1947 WM SWE R 4 games
1949 WM SWE R 5 games
1951 WM SWE R 3 games
1952 OG-M SWE R 5 games
1953 WM SWE R 1 game

**Sandor, Zsuzsana**
2011 WW18 HUN L 4 games

**Sands, Don**
1932 OG-M USA R 12 games
~called all games 1932 OG-M with Lou Marsh

**Sandsund, Per**
1952 OG-M FIN R 3 games

**Sartison, Ken**
1995 WM CAN L 6 games
1998 OG-M CAN L 7 games
~1995 WM bronze-medal game

**Saue, Raoul**
1938 WM EST R 4 games

**Savage, Chris**
2002 WM18 CAN R 6 games
2005 WM20 CAN R 5 games
2006 WM CAN R 6 games
2008 WM CAN R 5 games
2010 WM CAN R 9 games
~2005 WM20 bronze-medal game
~2010 WM bronze-medal game

**Savaris, Ruggero**
1992 WM ITA R 2 games
1993 WM ITA R 2 games
1994 OG-M ITA R 3 games

**Savelkouls, Jan**
1977 WM20 NED L 7 games

**Savin, Sergei**
1954 WM URS R 5 games
1955 WM URS R 4 games

**Savolainen, Rami**
1998 WM20 FIN R 5 games
1999 WM FIN R 6 games
2001 WM FIN R 5 games
2002 OG-M FIN R 4 games
~1999 WM bronze-medal game

**Scapinello, Ray**
1981 CC CAN L 5 games
1991 CC CAN L 6 games
1996 WCH CAN L 7 games
1998 OG-M CAN L 5 games
~1991 CC game 1 finals
~1996 WCH games 1, 2, 3 finals
~1998 OG-M gold-medal game

**Schachte, Dan**
1991 CC USA L 4 games
1996 WCH USA L 4 games
2002 OG-M USA L 5 games
~2002 OG-M bronze-medal game

**Schafer, Ingo**
1999 WM18 GER L 7 games

**Schell, Laszlo**
1977 WM HUN L 10 games
1978 WM HUN L 10 games
1979 WM HUN L 8 games
1982 WM HUN L 10 games
~IIHF Hall of Fame

**Schimki, Bernd**
1981 WM20 FRG R 3 games
1988 WM20 FRG R 4 games

**Schimm, Wilhelm**
1992 WM20 GER L 7 games
1993 WM GER L 4 games
1994 OG-M GER L 7 games
1999 WM18 GER R 4 games
2000 WM GER R 5 games
2001 WM GER R 4 games
2003 WM GER R 5 games
2004 WM20 GER R 4 games
~1994 OG-M bronze-medal game

**Schipper-Poeteray, Bianca**
2008 WW18* NED L 5 games
2011 WW NED L 4 games
2012 WW18 NED L 5 games
*officiated as Bianca Schipper

**Schmid, Helmut**
1959 WM SUI R 5 games
1964 OG-M SUI R 5 games

**Schmid, Helmut**
1983 WM FRG L 5 games

**Schmidt, Hans**
1936 OG-M GER R 5 games

**Schmitt, Mike**
1992 WM20 USA R 3 games
1995 WM20 USA R 5 games
1996 WM USA R 5 games

**Schneider, Bernd**
1981 WM20 FRG L 5 games
1983 WM FRG R 9 games
1984 OG-M FRG L 8 games
1984 CC FRG L 3 games
1985 WM20 FRG R 4 games
1991 WM GER R 3 games
1992 OG-M GER R 3 games

**Schrader, Andre**
2011 WM GER L 6 games
2012 WM20 GER L 7 games
2012 WM GER L 8 games
~2012 WM20 bronze-medal game

**Schreiber, Christine**
2005 WW GER R 3 games

**Schroeter, Lars**
2005 WM20 GER L 6 games
2006 WM GER L 8 games
2007 WM20 GER L 6 games
2008 WM GER L 7 games

**Schulz, Sirko**
2010 WM20 GER L 6 games
2011 WM GER L 7 games
2012 WM GER L 9 games
~2010 WM20 gold-medal game

**Schurr, Tom**
1995 WM20 GER L 5 games
1996 WM GER L 4 games
1997 WM GER L 10 games
1998 OG-M GER L 3 games
2004 WM18 GER R 4 games
2005 WM20 GER R 4 games
~1997 WM gold-medal game 1

**Schuster, Heinz**
1957 WM GDR R 4 games

**Schutz, Richard**
1989 WM FRG L 6 games
1990 WM FRG L 9 games
1991 WM FRG L 8 games
1992 OG-M GER L 7 games
2002 WM18 GER R 7 games
2004 WM GER R 6 games
2005 WM GER R 5 games
2006 WM GER R 7 games
2007 WM GER R 4 games
2008 WM GER R 3 games
2010 WM18 GER R 5 games
2011 WM GER L 7 games
~2006 WM gold-medal game

**Schweiger, Berthold**
1974 WM GDR R 2 games
1976 WM GDR R 2 games
1978 WM GDR L 9 games

**Seglin, Anatoli**
1965 WM URS R 4 games
1966 WM URS R 4 games
1967 WM URS R 4 games
1968 OG-M URS R 8 games
1969 WM URS R 7 games
1970 WM URS R 3 games

**Semjonov, Anton**
2001 WM18 EST L 6 games
2003 WM EST L 6 games
2004 WM EST L 6 games
2005 WM20 EST L 6 games
2008 WM EST L 6 games
2009 WM EST L 7 games
2010 WM EST L 7 games
2011 WM EST L 8 games
2012 WM EST L 7 games

**Seppanen, Raimo**
1974 WM FIN R 6 games
1975 WM FIN R 7 games
1976 OG-M FIN R 6 games
1977 WM FIN R 6 games
1978 WM FIN R 6 games
1982 WM FIN R 5 games

**Serdyuk, Sergei**
1998 WM KAZ L 8 games

**Sericolo, Anthony**
2006 OG-M USA L 6 games

**Shabunevich, Dmitri**
2008 WM18 BLR L 5 games

**Shakirov, Shamil**
1990 WM URS L 7 games
1991 WM URS L 8 games
1992 OG-M RUS L 10 games

**Sharrers, Jay**
1989 WM20 CAN L 5 games
2010 OG-M CAN L 4 games

**Shelchkov, Vitali**
1959 WM URS R 5 games

**Shell, Jeff**
1986 WM20 USA L 7 games

**Shelyanin, Sergei**
2000 WM RUS L 10 games
2001 WM20 RUS L 6 games
2002 OG-M RUS L 3 games
2005 WM RUS L 7 games
2006 OG-M RUS L 5 games
2011 WM RUS L 8 games
2012 WM RUS L 9 games
~2000 WM bronze-medal game
~2001 WM20 bronze-medal game
~2012 WM bronze-medal game

**Shewan, Cam**
1935 WM CAN R 6 games

**Shikhanov, Roman**
2007 WM18 RUS L 6 games
2010 WM20 RUS L 6 games
2012 WM18 RUS L 6 games

**Sidorenko, Maxim**
2010 WM18 BLR R 5 games
2011 WM18 BLR R 5 games
2012 WM18 BLR R 5 games

**Sillankorva, Sakari**
1968 OG-M FIN R 6 games
1969 WM FIN R 7 games
1970 WM FIN R 6 games
1971 WM FIN R 6 games

**Sillig, Max**
1920 OG-M SUI R 1 game

**Simonds, Bob**
1994 WM CAN R 5 games

**Sindler, Vladimir**
1999 WM20 CZE R 2 games
1999 WM CZE R 4 games
2000 WM20 CZE R 4 games
2000 WM CZE R 5 games
2001 WM CZE R 5 games
2002 WM CZE R 6 games
2003 WM20 CZE R 4 games
2003 WM CZE R 8 games
2004 WM20 CZE R 4 games
2004 WM CZE R 5 games
2005 WM CZE R 4 games
2006 OG-M CZE R 2 games
2007 WM20 CZE R 4 games
2008 WM20 CZE R 6 games
2009 WM CZE R 6 games
2010 WM20 CZE R 4 games
2010 WM CZE R 8 games
2011 WM CZE R 7 games
2012 WM20 CZE R 4 games
~2002 WM bronze-medal game
~2003 WM gold-medal game
~2008 WM20 gold-medal game
~2010 WM bronze-medal game

**Sinkkonen, Timo**
1982 WM FIN L 7 games

**Sipila, Ulla**
2008 WW FIN R 3 games
2009 WW FIN R 3 games
2010 OG-W FIN R 3 games
2011 WW FIN R 3 games

**Sir, Robin**
2011 WM18 CZE R 5 games

**Sivov, Dmitri**
2012 WM20 RUS L 6 games

**Sjoberg, Patrik**
2007 WM18 SWE R 4 games
2008 WM18 SWE R 5 games
2009 WM20 SWE R 5 games
2010 WM SWE R 7 games
2011 WM20 SWE R 5 games

**Sjoqvist, Mikael**
2012 WM18 SWE R 7 games

**Skingle, Ken**
1982 WM20 CAN L 6 games

**Skoglund, Thomas**
1994 WM20 SWE L 6 games

**Skovbakke, Malene**
2008 WW DEN L 3 games
2009 WW DEN L 4 games
2010 OG-W DEN L 5 games
2011 WW DEN L 4 games
~2009 WW gold-medal game
~2010 OG-W bronze-medal game

**Sladacek, Karel**
1977 WM20 TCH L 7 games
1978 WM TCH L 9 games

**Slapke, Peter**
1993 WM20 GER R 4 games
1993 WM GER R 2 games
1994 OG-M GER R 6 games
1995 WM GER R 4 games
1996 WM20 GER R 3 games
1998 WM GER R 7 games
~1998 WM bronze-medal game

**Slivkova, Petra**
2008 WW SVK L 4 games

**Smirnov, Yuri**
1978 WM URS L 10 games
1979 WM URS L 8 games
1983 WM20 URS L 5 games
1984 WM20 URS L 6 games

**Smith, Alan**
2001 WM20 CAN R 5 games

**Smith, Pat**
2010 WM18 CAN R 5 games
2011 WM20 CAN R 5 games

**Smith, Ron**
1978 WM20 USA R 3 games

**Smith, Travis**
2007 WM18 USA R 6 games
2009 WM18 USA R 5 games

**Snetkov, Nikolai**
1967 WM URS R 6 games
1968 OG-M URS R 6 games

**Sold, Svein-Erik**
1992 OG-M SWE R 6 games
1993 WM20 SWE R 4 games
1993 WM SWE R 5 games
1995 WM20 SWE R 4 games
~1992 OG-M gold-medal game

**Solem, Per Gustav**
2011 WM18 NOR R 4 games

**Soltys, Stefan**
1947 WM TCH R 1 game

**Sommerschuh, Peter**
1983 WM GDR L 5 games

**Sormunen, Hannu**
2012 WM20 FIN L 6 games

**Sorokin, Viktor**
1977 WM20 URS R 4 games

**Sotiroff, Jim**
1990 WW USA R 2 games+
1991 WM20 USA R 4 games
+information incomplete

**Spengler, Carl**
1935 WM SUI R 2 games
~Founder of Spengler Cup 1923

**Stadler, Bernhard**
1993 WM AUT L 4 games

**Stalder, Roland**
1991 WM SUI L 5 games

**Stangle, Frank**
1950 WM GBR R 1 game

**Staniforth, Paul**
2001 WM GBR L 6 games
2002 WM GBR L 6 games

**Stanley, Alice**
2007 WW GBR L 4 games
2008 WW18 GBR L 5 games
2008 WW GBR L 4 games
~2008 WW18 gold-medal game

**Starovoitov, Andrei**
1955 WM URS R 4 games
1956 OG-M URS R 4 games
1957 WM URS R 4 games
1958 WM URS R 5 games
1961 WM URS R 3 games
1963 WM URS R 4 games
1964 OG-M URS R 7 games
1965 WM URS R 5 games
1966 WM URS R 5 games
~IIHF Hall of Fame

**Stebin, Michel**
1978 WM20 CAN L 3 games
~1978 WM20 gold-medal game

**Stefkova, Michaela**
2012 WW18 CZE L 5 games
~2012 WW18 bronze-medal game

**Steigenhofer, Karel**
1938 WM TCH R 1 game

**Steinke, Alfred**
1936 OG-M GER R 1 game
1937 WM GER R 2 games

**Stenico, Renzo**
1994 WM ITA R 2 games

**Stensland, Al**
1998 WM20 USA L 7 games
1999 WM20 USA L 4 games
2004 WM20 USA L 6 games

**Stenzel, Veronika**
2009 WW GER L 4 games
2010 WW18 GER L 6 games
~2010 WW18 bronze-medal game

**Sterns, Tom**
2008 WM20 USA R 5 games
2008 WM USA R 5 games
2009 WM USA R 7 games
2010 WM USA R 7 games
2011 WM USA R 6 games
2012 WM20 USA R 4 games

**Stewart, Paul**
1987 CC USA R 4 games
1991 CC USA R 4 games
~1987 CC game 2 finals
~1991 CC game 2 finals

**Stickle, Leon**
1981 CC CAN L 5 games
1984 CC CAN L 5 games

**St. Jacques, Pascal**
2012 WM18 CAN R 5 games
~2012 WM18 gold-medal game

**Strasil, Erich**
1994 WM AUT L 4 games
1995 WM AUT L 4 games

**Stricker, Daniel**
2002 WM SUI L 7 games
2003 WM20 SUI L 4 games
2009 WM18 SUI R 5 games
2011 WM18 SUI R 6 games
~2011 WM18 bronze-medal game

**Striganov, Igor**
1993 WM20 RUS L 6 games

**Stuart, Kent**
1980 OG-M CAN L 5 games

**Suban, Johanna**
2000 WW FIN L 5 games
2001 WW FIN L 5 games
2002 OG-W FIN L 5 games
2004 WW FIN L 5 games
2006 OG-W FIN L 4 games
~2000 WW gold-medal game
~2001 WW gold-medal game
~2002 OG-W gold-medal game
~2004 WW gold-medal game
~2006 OG-W gold-medal game

**Subrt, Miroslav**
1979 WM TCH R 4 games
1980 OG-M TCH R 5 games
1984 OG-M TCH R 5 games
1985 WM TCH R 5 games
~IIHF Hall of Fame

**Subrt, Vladimir**
1977 WM20 TCH R 6 games
1978 WM TCH R 6 games
1981 WM TCH R 5 games
1981 CC TCH R 2 games
1982 WM TCH R 6 games
1983 WM TCH R 5 games
1986 WM TCH R 5 games
1987 WM TCH R 8 games
1987 CC TCH R 3 games
1989 WM20 TCH R 5 games
1990 WM20 TCH R 4 games

**Sudol, Dariusz**
1998 WM20 POL L 6 games

**Suominen, Sakari**
2009 WM18 FIN L 7 games
2010 WM20 FIN L 6 games
2011 WM18 FIN L 7 games
2012 WM FIN L 8 games
~2009 WM18 gold-medal game
~2011 WM18 gold-medal game

**Sutherland, Kelly**
2000 WM20 CAN R 5 games

**Svarstad, John**
1992 WM SWE L 4 games
1994 OG-M SWE L 6 games

**Svensson, Bengt**
1990 WW SWE R 2 games+
+information incomplete

**Svensson, Per**
1994 WW SWE L 5 games
1999 WM18 SWE L 7 games
2000 WM20 SWE L 6 games
2001 WM18 SWE L 8 games
2002 WM SWE L 6 games
2006 WM18 SWE L 6 games
~1994 WW gold-medal game (last women's game with a male linesman)
~2001 WM18 gold-medal game

**Synott, Frank**
1924 OG-M USA R 1 game

**Szczepek, Wojciech**
1973 WM POL R 4 games
1974 WM POL R 4 games
1975 WM POL R 5 games
1976 WM POL R 7 games

**Takagi, Kunio**
1972 OG-M JPN R 2 games

**Takahashi, Hirokazu**
1994 OG-M JPN L 3 games
1999 WM JPN L 8 games
2000 WM JPN L 10 games
~1999 WM bronze-medal game

**Takizawa, Shinichi**
2009 WM18 JPN L 6 games

**Takula, Leo**
2002 WM18 SWE L 8 games
2003 WM20 SWE L 7 games
2004 WM SWE L 8 games
2005 WM SWE L 9 games
2006 WM SWE L 7 games
2007 WM20 SWE L 6 games
2009 WM20 SWE L 7 games
~2003 WM20 gold-medal game
~2004 WM bronze-medal game
~2009 WM20 bronze-medal game

**Tarko, Kari-Pekka**
2000 WM20 FIN L 5 games

**Taticek, Jan**
1983 WM TCH L 8 games
1984 OG-M TCH L 6 games
1984 CC TCH L 6 games
1985 WM TCH L 10 games
1988 OG-M TCH L 10 games
1989 WM TCH L 8 games
1990 WM20 TCH L 7 games

**Tauriainen, Johanna**
2009 WW FIN L 4 games
2010 WW18 FIN L 4 games
2011 WW FIN L 5 games
2012 WW FIN L 5 games
~2012 WW gold-medal game

**Taveroff, Dave**
1993 WM20 CAN L 6 games

**Taylor-Bolton, Laurie**
1994 WW CAN L 5 games*
1997 WW CAN R 4 games
1998 OG-W CAN R 4 games
1998 OG-W CAN L 2 games
*officiated under maiden name Laurie Taylor
~1994 WW bronze-medal game
~1997 WW bronze-medal game
~1998 OG-W bronze-medal game

**Tegner, Lars**
1972 WM SWE R 5 games

**Tencza, Ladislav**
1949 WM TCH R 4 games
1952 OG-M TCH R 8 games
1953 WM TCH R 5 games
1954 WM TCH R 4 games
1956 OG-M TCH R 4 games
1959 WM TCH R 5 games

**Terho, Jussi**
2007 WM18 FIN L 6 games
2009 WM20 FIN L 6 games
2010 WM FIN L 8 games
2011 WM FIN L 8 games
~2009 WM20 gold-medal game
~2010 WM bronze-medal game

**Therien, Louis**
1978 WM20 CAN L 4 games

**Thomander, Todd**
1996 WM20 CAN L 4 games

**Thuden, Kent**
1996 WM20 SWE L 6 games
1998 WM20 SWE L 7 games
1999 WM SWE L 11 games
~1996 WM20 bronze-medal game
~1998 WM20 gold-medal game
~1999 WM gold-medal games 1 & 2

**Thul, Brian**
2005 WM18 USA R 8 games
2006 WM20 USA R 4 games
~2005 WM18 bronze-medal game
~2006 WM20 gold-medal game

**Tillerqvist-Jonsson, Christian**
2010 WM20 SWE L 7 games
2011 WM SWE L 6 games
~2010 WM20 gold-medal game

**Toeman, Niko**
1977 WM NED L 13 games
1980 OG-M NED L 6 games
1982 WM20 NED R 5 games
1983 WM20 NED R 5 games
1984 WM20 NED R 6 games
1986 WM20 NED R 4 games

**Toffel, Marcel**
1954 WM SUI R 8 games

**Tomilov, Viktor**
2010 WM18 RUS L 6 games

**Tonsberg, Knud**
1948 OG-M DEN R 2 games
1949 WM DEN R 2 games

**Tottman, Joy**
2005 WW GBR R 3 games
2006 OG-W GBR R 3 games
2007 WW GBR R 3 games
2008 WW18 GBR R 3 games
2009 WW GBR R 3 games
2010 OG-W GBR R 3 games
2011 WW GBR R 4 games
2012 WW GBR R 3 games
~2005 WW bronze-medal game
~2007 gold-medal game
~2008 WW18 gold-medal game

**Trainer, Stefan**
1992 WM20 GER L 7 games
1993 WM20 GER L 6 games
1994 WM GER L 6 games

**Traub, Matt**
2010 WM20 CAN L 7 games

**Trauttenberg, Hans**
1935 WM AUT R 1 game
1936 OG-M AUT R 3 games
1937 WM AUT R 13 games

**Tremblay, Pierre**
1994 OG-M CAN L 6 games

**Trottier, Richard**
1985 WM20 CAN R 5 games
1987 WM20 CAN R 4 games

**Trovati, Decio**
1931 WM ITA R 3 games

**Trumble, Hal**
1962 WM USA R 1 game
1965 WM USA R 5 games
1968 OG-M USA R 8 games
1969 WM USA R 8 games
~IIHF Hall of Fame

**Trumble, Skip**
1978 WM20 USA L 7 games

**Tschappeler, Hans-Kurt**
1948 OG-M SUI R 4 games

**Tupalski, Alexander**
1936 OG-M POL R 7 games

**Turcan, Tomas**
2005 WM18 CZE R 8 games

**Tvrdon, Jozef**
2006 WM18 SVK L 6 games
2010 WM20 SVK L 6 games
2011 WM20 SVK L 6 games

**Tyszkiewicz, Bogdan**
1983 WM20 POL R 3 games
1984 OG-M POL L 7 games
1986 WM POL R 3 games
1987 WM POL R 3 games

**Ugajin, Kyoko**
2012 WW18 JPN R 4 games
~2012 WW18 gold-medal game

**Ulriksson, Fredrik**
2006 WM20 SWE L 6 games
2007 WM20 SWE L 7 games
2008 WM SWE L 7 games
2009 WM18 SWE L 7 games
~2006 WM20 bronze-medal game
~2007 WM20 gold-medal game
~2009 WM18 bronze-medal game

**Unger, Hans**
1954 WM FRG R 4 games
1956 OG-M GER R 2 games

**Ustinova, Arina**
2006 OG-W RUS R 2 games
2007 WW RUS R 3 games
2009 WW RUS R 2 games
2011 WW18 RUS R 3 games

**Utgard, Stein**
1994 WW NOR R 3 games

**Utsumi, Mamiko**
2008 WW18 JPN R 3 games
2009 WW18 JPN R 3 games

**Vaillancourt, Marcel**
1969 WM CAN R 9 games
1977 WM CAN R 7 games

**Vaisfeld, Leonid**
1995 WM RUS R 4 games
1996 WM RUS R 4 games
1997 WM RUS R 6 games
1998 OG-M RUS R 1 game
2001 WM RUS R 7 games

**Valach, Miroslav**
2004 WM18 SVK L 7 games
2005 WM20 SVK L 6 games
2006 WM20 SVK L 5 games
2009 WM18 SVK L 6 games
2009 WM SVK L 7 games
2010 WM SVK L 8 games
2011 WM SVK L 7 games
2012 WM SVK L 8 games
~2004 WM18 gold-medal game
~2009 WM18 gold-medal game
~2010 WM bronze-medal game
~2011 WM bronze-medal game
~2012 WM bronze-medal game

**Valentin, Willy**
1964 OG-M AUT R 4 games
1966 WM AUT R 1 game
1967 WM AUT R 1 game
1968 OG-M AUT R 3 games
1976 OG-M AUT R 3 games

**van Deelen, Dutch**
1967 WM CAN R 9 games

**van de Fenn, Uwe**
1985 WM FRG L 6 games
1986 WM FRG L 8 games
1987 WM FRG L 10 games

**Vanderhorst, Laura**
1999 WW CAN L 6 games
2001 WW CAN R 3 games
2002 OG-W CAN R 4 games
~1999 WW bronze-medal game
~2001 WW bronze-medal game
~2002 OG-W bronze-medal game

**Vanhanen, Lasse**
1978 WM FIN L 10 games
1979 WM FIN L 7 games
1981 CC FIN L 3 games
1982 WM FIN L 10 games
1983 WM FIN L 14 games
1984 OG-M FIN L 8 games
1985 WM FIN L 11 games
1986 WM FIN L 10 games
1987 WM FIN L 10 games
1988 OG-M FIN L 8 games

**van Hellemond, Andy**
1981 CC CAN R 4 games

**van Massenhoven, Don**
2004 WCH CAN R 4 games
2006 OG-M CAN R 5 games

**van Reysschoot, Pierre**
1948 OG-M BEL R 4 games

**Vasilyev, Alexei**
2000 WM18 RUS L 7 games
2011 WM18 RUS R 5 games
~2000 WM18 bronze-medal game

**Vasko, Andrei**
1998 WM BLR L 7 games
1999 WM BLR L 6 games
2001 WM20 BLR L 6 games
2002 WM BLR L 5 games
2003 WM18 BLR L 6 games
2004 WM18 BLR L 6 games
2005 WM BLR L 6 games
2006 WM BLR L 6 games
2007 WM18 BLR L 5 games
~2004 WM18 bronze-medal game

**Vaughan, Roday**
1999 WM20 CAN L 2 games

**Vidic, Nikola**
1984 OG-M YUG L 3 games

**Vikman, Kristian**
2012 WM18 FIN L 6 games

**Vines, Mark**
1991 CC CAN L 4 games

**Vinnerborg, Marcus**
2004 WM18 SWE R 4 games
2006 WM20 SWE R 4 games
2006 WM SWE R 6 games
2007 WM SWE R 8 games
2008 WM SWE R 8 games
2009 WM SWE R 7 games
2010 OG-M SWE R 5 games
~2006 WM20 bronze-medal game
~2007 WM gold-medal game
~2008 WM gold-medal game
**~first European referee in NHL, 2010**

**Vister, Ciril**
1984 OG-M YUG L 5 games

**Vogt, Herbert**
1983 WM FRG L 9 games
1988 OG-M FRG R 2 games
1989 WM FRG R 3 games

**Vogtlin, Willi**
1988 OG-M SUI R 8 games
1989 WM SUI R 5 games
1990 WM SUI R 6 games

**Volker, Didier**
1994 WM20 SUI L 5 games

**von de Fenn, Uwe**
1992 WM20 GER R 3 games

**Voracek, Annette**
2004 WW USA R 3 games

**Vores, Eszter**
1997 WW HUN L 3 games
1999 WW HUN L 3 games

**Vrabel, Jozef**
1992 WM20 TCH R 4 games

**Vuillemin, Andre**
1966 WM SUI R 3 games

**Wagner, Richard**
1955 WM FRG R 5 games
1959 WM FRG R 4 games
1960 OG-M GER R 6 games
1961 WM FRG R 2 games

**Wahl, Derek**
2010 WM18 USA L 6 games
2011 WM18 USA L 6 games
~2010 WM18 bronze-medal game

**Walkom, Stephen**
2002 OG-M CAN R 5 games
2004 WCH CAN R 6 games
~2004 WCH finals

**Walter, Bianca**
2006 OG-W GER R 2 games

**Warschaw, Shane**
2011 WM18 USA R 5 games

**Watson, Harry**
1933 WM CAN R 5 games

**Watson, Brad**
1989 WM20 CAN L 5 games
2004 WCH CAN R 4 games
2010 OG-M CAN R 5 games
~2010OG-M bronze-medal game

**Wehrli, Tobias**
2004 WM18 SUI L 6 games
2005 WM20 SUI L 6 games
2006 WM SUI L 8 games
2007 WM SUI L 7 games
2008 WM SUI L 6 games
2009 WM SUI L 6 games
2010 WM SUI L 8 games
~2004 WM18 bronze-medal game
~2006 WM bronze-medal game
~2010 WM gold-medal game

**Weidmann, Werner**
1976 WM SUI R 7 games

**Weinburger, Hans**
1928 OG-M AUT R 1 game
1934 WM AUT R 2 games
1935 WM AUT R 3 games
1936 OG-M AUT R 3 games

**Weissman, Andrea**
2010 WW18 USA L 5 games
~2010 WW18 bronze-medal game

**Welting, Frank**
1991 WM20 FRG L 5 games

**Westreicher, Harry**
1977 WM AUT L 11 games
1978 WM AUT L 11 games
1982 WM20 AUT R 4 games
1984 WM20 AUT R 3 games

**Wicks, Ron**
1984 CC CAN R 4 games

**Wieland, Alwin**
1952 OG-M SUI R 2 games

**Wieler, Haley**
2008 WW18 CAN L 1 game
2011 WW18 CAN L 6 games
~2011 WW18 bronze-medal game

**Wieler, Nate**
2005 WM18 CAN L 7 games
~2005 WM18 bronze-medal game

**Wieser, Walter**
1977 WM AUT L 8 games

**Wiitala, Unto**
1964 OG-M FIN R 6 games
1965 WM FIN R 2 games
1972 OG-M FIN R 4 games
1974 WM FIN R 7 games
~IIHF Hall of Fame

**Wiking, Jan**
1982 WM SWE L 10 games

**Wiking, Olle**
1958 WM SWE R 6 games
1959 WM SWE R 7 games
1961 WM SWE R 4 games
1962 WM SWE R 10 games
1963 WM SWE R 5 games
1964 OG-M SWE R 8 games
1965 WM SWE R 5 games
1966 WM SWE R 4 games
1967 WM SWE R 8 games
1968 OG-M SWE R 4 games
1969 WM SWE R 7 games
1970 WM SWE R 4 games

**Wilkert, Ernst**
1963 WM SWE R 6 games

**Wilkert, Olle**
1957 WM SWE R 4 games
1961 WM SWE R 4 games
1964 OG-M SWE R 7 games

**Willsie, John**
1986 WM20 CAN R 3 games

**Wilmot, Jesse**
2011 WM20 CAN L 7 games
2012 WM CAN L 9 games
~2011 WM20 bronze-medal game

**Winge, Daniel**
2010 WM18 SWE L 7 games
2011 WM20 SWE L 6 games
~2010 WM18 bronze-medal game

**Winkler, Ferdinand**
1947 WM TCH R 1 game

**Winnekens, Felix**
2007 WM18 GER L 6 games
2008 WM20 GER L 8 games
2009 WM GER L 8 games
2010 OG-M GER L 4 games
2011 WM20 GER L 6 games
~2008 WM20 bronze-medal game
~2011 WM20 gold-medal game

**Wirth, Daniel**
2009 WM SUI L 7 games
2010 WM20 SUI L 7 games

**Wirtz, —**
1939 WM USA R 8 games

**Wogerer, Oscar**
1977 WM AUT L 8 games

**Wollinger, Kurt**
1948 OG-M AUT R 1 game

**Woodworth, Chris**
2012 WM20 USA L 6 games
~2012 WM20 bronze-medal game

**Worthy, Rich**
1986 WM20 CAN L 7 games

**Wrazidlo, Leah**
2007 WW USA R 3 games
2008 WW USA R 4 games
2009 WW USA R 3 games
2010 OG-W USA R 3 games
~2007 WW bronze-medal game
~2008 WW bronze-medal game
~2009 WW bronze-medal game

**Wright, Dave**
2000 WM18 CAN R 5 games
2001 WM CAN R 7 games
~2000 WM18 gold-medal game

**Wujek, Edward**
1959 WM POL R 3 games

**Wurth, Werner**
1981 WM20 FRG L 5 games
1983 WM FRG L 6 games

**Wycisk, Jan**
1958 WM POL R 2 games
1959 WM POL R 6 games
1961 WM POL R 3 games
1963 WM POL R 2 games
1964 OG-M POL R 7 games
1965 WM POL R 5 games
1966 WM POL R 5 games
1967 WM POL R 1 game
1968 OG-M POL R 4 games
1970 WM POL R 8 games
1971 WM POL R 7 games
1972 OG-M POL R 3 games

**Yackel, Kym "Chic"**
1982 WM20 USA L 7 games

**Yakushev, Viktor**
1991 CC URS R 2 games

**Yegorov, Anatoli**
1986 WM URS L 7 games

**Yletyinen, Emil**
2012 WM18 SWE L 6 games

**Young, Evonne**
1994 WW USA L 4 games
1997 WW USA L 5 games
1998 OG-W USA L 6 games
~1998 OG-W bronze-medal game

**Zagorski, Alexander**
1976 OG-M POL R 5 games
1976 WM POL R 6 games
1979 WM POL L 5 games

**Zainutdinov, Rafik**
1992 WM20 RUS L 6 games
1995 WM RUS L 5 games

**Zaitsev, Alexander**
1992 WW RUS L 5 games
~1992 WW gold-medal game

**Zaitsev, Alexei**
2001 WM18 RUS L 7 games

**Zakharov, Anatoli**
1998 WM RUS L 8 games
2000 WM20 RUS R 4 games
2002 WM18 RUS R 6 games
2003 WM RUS R 4 games
2004 WM18 RUS R 5 games
2007 WM18 RUS R 2 games
~2004 WM18 bronze-medal game

**Zakharov, Andrei**
1973 WM URS R 5 games

**Zalaski, Derek**
2006 WM18 CAN R 4 games
2008 WM18 CAN R 5 games
2009 WM CAN R 7 games
2010 WM20 CAN R 7 games
2012 WM20 CAN R 7 games
~2010 WM20 bronze-medal game
~2012 WM20 gold-medal game

**Zarzycki, Jerzy**
1952 OG-M POL R 3 games
1956 OG-M POL R 1 game

**Zatta, Luca**
2006 WM ITA L 7 games
2007 WM ITA L 7 games

**Zehetleitner, Florian**
2012 WM18 GER R 4 games

**Zelkin, Scott**
1991 WM USA L 7 games

**Zeller, Georg**
1964 OG-M GER R 4 games

**Zemskov, Vladimir**
1996 WM20 UKR R 1 game

**Zenisek, Josef**
1938 WM TCH R 1 game
1947 WM TCH R 1 game

**Zenk, Marina**

| | | | |
|---|---|---|---|
| 1997 WW | CAN | R | 4 games |
| 1998 OG-W | CAN | R | 4 games |
| 1998 OG-W | CAN | L | 1 game |
| 1999 WW | CAN | R | 3 games |

~1998 OG-W gold-medal game
~1999 WW gold-medal game

**Zerbi, Gianfranco**

| | | | |
|---|---|---|---|
| 1992 WM | ITA | L | 4 games |

**Zhang, Yuenan**

| | | | |
|---|---|---|---|
| 1999 WW | CHN | L | 3 games |

**Zitkova, Jana**

| | | | |
|---|---|---|---|
| 2004 WW | CZE | L | 5 games |
| 2005 WW | CZE | L | 5 games |
| 2006 OG-W | CZE | L | 3 games |
| 2008 WW | CZE | R | 3 games |

~2005 WW gold-medal game

*IIHF president René Fasel poses with the all-Canadian crew at the 2011 gold-medal game of the World Championship: (l-r) Darcy Burchell, Brent Reiber, Chris Carlson, Kiel Murchison. Photo: Matthew Manor / HHOF-IIHF.*

*Hockey executives from across the world met in June 2012 in Barcelona for the first Hockey Forum to discuss the future of the game both in Europe and across the international stage. Photo: Martin Merk.*